GB Rail Timetable

Sunday 23 May to Saturday 11 Dec

Britain's national railway network and stations are owned by Network F
included in this timetable, who work together closely to provide a c
opportunities. Details and identification codes are shown on the Trair

This timetable contains rail services operated over the National Ra ... shipping connections with Ireland, the Isle of Man, the Isle of Wight and the Channel Islands. Network Rail operates managed stations but the remainder are operated on their behalf by the Train Operating Companies. Details are shown in the station index. The Timetable Network map shows the number of the individual table for each route.

Contents

Services on Public Holidays

An amended service will operate on many parts of the rail network during public holidays and you are strongly advised to confirm your journey details if travelling around a holiday period. For more information, visit nationalrail.co.uk/holidays

Engineering Work

It is sometimes necessary to carry out essential engineering work which means that services may be changed, particularly late at night ar at weekend to allow this work to be carried out. Engineering Work is usually planned many weeks in advance and details of changes to train times can be obtained from the National Rail Enquiries website – www.nationalrail.co.uk/engineering

National Rail Conditions of Carriage

Details of the conditions against which all National Rail tickets are issued, including the conditions which apply to the carriage of luggage and cycles can be obtained from the National Rail Enquiries website – www.nationalrail.co.uk/nrcc.

What's New

Welcome to the GB Rail Timetable valid from Sunday 23 May to Saturday 11 December 2010.

Chiltern Railways

From May 2010 we will once again be introducing a regular summer Sunday service between London Marylebone and Stratford-upon-Avon. We have no other major timetable changes in May 2010. However, the major Evergreen 3 investment being made this year will result in a much improved Chiltern Mainline timetable with reduced journey times to London to be introduced in December 2010 and May 2011. As part of this work our late night and weekend services will be subject to major disruption in 2010, so please check before you travel.

East Coast

Our timetable is broadly similar to that which operated in December 2009. A few minor alterations have been made to calling points, however, these are limited to weekday afternoons and Sunday mornings. On weekends from 17 July to 5 September there is engineering work taking place in the Stevenage area meaning services are timed to depart London Kings Cross earlier than normal.

East Midlands Trains

The London to Corby services and vice versa will have a reduced journey time as the long layovers at Kettering have been removed. Additional stops at Chesterfield have been added to the majority of the southbound xx.47 Sheffield to St Pancras services on weekdays and Saturdays. The SO St Pancras to York and return service has been extended to Scarborough until 4 September.

Grand Central

Brand new intercity services introduced between London Kings Cross and Bradford, calling at Halifax, Brighouse, Wakefield, Pontefract and Doncaster. Initially three services per day operate in each direction - full timetabled details are shown on Table 26. Catering and First Class accommodation are available on all these new services.

London Overground

The London Overground network is being extended with three new routes introduced. Services will run 7 days a week, up to 4 trains per hour:

- Between Dalston Junction and New Cross
- Between Dalston Junction and Crystal Palace
- Between Dalston Junction and West Croydon

The above three routes will provide a service of up to 12 trains per hour between Dalston Junction and Surrey Quays

Services between Gospel Oak and Barking will be enhanced, up to 4 trains per hour Mondays to Saturdays.

ScotRail

We will be commencing a service of three trains per day on Mondays to Fridays from Edinburgh to Dunbar, with two in the opposite direction.

Southern

To accommodate the new London Overground train service of 8 trains per hour between the East London Line and Crystal Palace and West Croydon stopping at all stations via Forest Hill, the Southern Metro train service is extensively revised with many consequential alterations to Main Line trains. These are the most significant alterations.

- Peak trains between London Bridge, Wallington, Sutton, and the Epsom Line run fast between Norwood Junction and London Bridge
- Off Peak trains between London Bridge, Wallington and Sutton replaced by a connection at Norwood Junction with fast London Bridge trains
- Off Peak and evening peak Victoria, Norwood Junction, West Croydon trains extended to Sutton
- Off Peak additional fast journeys between London Bridge and Norwood Junction provided by an additional stop for Tattenham Corner trains
- New morning peak trains between the Forest Hill Line and London Victoria
- Morning peak Beckenham Junction to London Victoria trains diverted via Tulse Hill to London Bridge
- Additional morning peak trains to London Bridge via Norbury and Tulse Hill route
- Additional morning peak trains between East or South Croydon and West London Line via Norbury
- Caterham, Tattenham Corner and East Grinstead peak trains become half hourly to both London Bridge and Victoria

Plus many alterations on other routes, please check the new times before travelling.

How to use this Timetable

Some tables are self-contained (such as Table 1 London–Shoeburyness) showing every train running between any two stations on the route. Train journey-lengths vary from the under-three-quarters-of-a-mile Stourbridge Town – Stourbridge Junction shuttle to the 703 mile Penzance–Dundee service. To show details of longer-distance services in a single table, short-distance services are omitted, these appearing in separate 'composite' tables.

WHICH TABLE?

General Layout of the Timetable

There are several ways of finding the correct table(s) for a journey. Tables start with the north bank of the Thames and radiate anti-clockwise around London as far as the south bank (Table 212, London-Faversham-Margate) with non-London tables (like the Cardiff Valleys) placed close to the appropriate London route. Internal Scottish routes follow from Table 216. Tables numbered 400-406 cover domestic Sleeper services. Once used to this geographic layout, required tables can usually be found with relative ease, but there are more precise methods:

Using the Index

Look up your destination. If it appears in up to five tables, those tables are listed (for example Hilsea appears in Tables 156, 157, 158, 165 and 188). If it appears in six or more then there may be sub-divisions. If your destination is sub-divided in this way and your origin is NOT shown (for example Shipley is not shown under Lancaster) then look up the origin instead as it probably has fewer tables. Alongside the station name is shown a two character code indicating which operator is responsible for operating the facilities at that station (see also Train Operator pages).

Using the Timetable Network map

If your journey is more complicated and involves several changes between tables, the Timetable Network map will be very useful. For example, to plan a journey from North Berwick to Pontypridd one would not expect to find both in the same table. The map makes it clear that one has to change at Edinburgh and Cardiff and, as there is no through service between North Berwick and Pontypridd, allows one to look up possible routes, for example, via Crewe and Shrewsbury (Tables 65 and 131), Crewe and Birmingham (Tables 57 and 65) or York and Birmingham (Tables 51 and 57).

Using Route/Network Diagrams

For many tables a Route or Network Diagram is also provided. Route Diagrams are generally used for longer distance tables (for example Table 26) and show the route and stations served in diagrammatic form as well as the principal connecting links. Network Diagrams (for example Tables 152–154) are generally used where there is a dense network of shorter distance routes and show *all* stations and routes in the area concerned in diagrammatic form.

Using the Table

Having found the table you require make sure you look at the correct set of pages: Mondays to Fridays, Mondays to Saturdays, Saturdays, Sundays plus any relevant dates. Look for the station from which you will leave, read across until you find a suitable train, then read down to see when you will arrive at your destination.

↪ indicates the train is continued in a later column.

↩ indicates the train is continued from an earlier column.

Bold times denote through trains whilst light, *italic*, times are connections (PLEASE READ CAREFULLY THE SECTION ON THE CONNECTIONS PAGE). Check if there is a column-heading and if there is, refer to the foot of the table for an explanation.

Because of the large number of services that 'cross' midnight, a railway timetable needs to be precise in the meaning of 'a day'. Trains starting their journeys before midnight are shown towards the end of a table – but if you are looking for the 'last' train don't stop there, as there may be later ones at the start of the table!

A train crossing midnight will be shown in full at the END of a table and any column heading denoting the day of the week applies to the day the train STARTS. For example a 2350 train headed 'SO' (see the general notes on inside front cover) commences 2350 Saturday and runs into Sunday. The train will also be shown at the front of the Sunday table with the times prior to midnight shown with note 'p', e.g. 23p50, to indicate that they refer to the previous night.

Don't worry about the ambiguity as to which day midnight itself belongs, for, to avoid this problem, all times skip from 2359 to 0001 and neither 0000 nor 2400 is ever used!

A two character code is shown at the head of each train column indicating which operator is providing the train service (see also Train Operator pages).

How to use this Timetable

Mileages between stations served (but not those shown for connecting purposes) are shown on the first page of each timetable.

Unique Timetable Number (as shown on the Insert Map and in the Index to Stations).

Stations served.

Catering Information.

Indicates the Operating Company of the train concerned

Indicates the days of the week (and in some cases dates) on which the timetable operates

Principal stations on the route are shown in **bold**.

For non-connecting stations only - indicates that additional services between these stations are included on other timetables (see also below under Route Diagrams).

Indicates the minimum interchange time (in minutes) that should be allowed when connecting between trains. Where no figure is shown, a minimum of 5 minutes should be allowed.

Train runs on Saturdays Only

Seat Reservations symbols.

Train time in ***italics*** indicate connecting times. The letter '**a**' alongside a connecting station indicates the arrival time at that station. Conversely, the letter '**d**' indicates the departure time.

Table 97
Colne, Burnley, Accrington and Blackburn—Preston—Blackpool

Mondays to Saturdays

Miles	Miles		NT ◇ H	NT ◇ H	NT	NT	NT J		NT	NT ◇ H	NT ◇ H	NT	NT	NT ◇ H	NT ◇ H	NT SO ◇ K
0	—	**Colne** d			09 25							10 16				
2	—	Nelson d			09 31							10 22				
3½	—	Briefield d			09 34							10 25				
5½	—	**Burnley Central** 98 d			09 39							10 30				
6	—	Burnley Barracks 98 d										10 32				
—	—	Leeds 39 d	08 18							09 18				10 18		
—	—	Burnley Manchester Road 39 d	09 21							10 21				11 21		
7	—	Rose Grove d			09 44						10 36					
8½	—	Hapton d										10 39				
10	—	Huncoat d										10 42				
11½	—	Accrington d	09 31		09 51					10 31		10 46		11 31		
12½	—	Church & Oswaldtwistle d			09 54							10 49				
14½	—	Rishton d			09 58							10 52				
18	—	**Blackburn** a	09 39		10 03					10 39		10 57		11 39		
—	—	Manchester Victoria 94 a	*10 39*		*11 06*							*12 06*				
—	—	Clitheroe 94 d								*09 58*				*10 58*		
—	—	**Blackburn** d	09 39		10 03					10 39		10 59		11 39		
19½	—	Mill Hill (Lancashire) d			10 06							11 02				
20	—	Cherry Tree d			10 08							11 04				
21	—	Pleasington d										11 06				
26	—	Bamber Bridge d			10 16							11 13				
27½	—	Lostock Hall d			10 19							11 15				
30	—	**Preston** 10 a	09 56		10 26					10 56		11 24		11 56		
—	—	London Euston 65 a	*12c 55*							*14c 75*				*14g 49*		
—	—	London Euston 65 d							*07f 40*			*08f 40*				
—	0	**Preston** 10 d	09 58	10 02	10 27	10 32	10 38		10 50	10 58	11 02	11 26	11 45	11 58	12 02	12 21
35½	5½	Salwick d														
37½	7½	Kirkham & Wesham d			10 36				10 59			11 35	11 54			
41	—	Moss Side d										11 40				
43½	—	Lytham d			10 44							11 44				
44½	—	Ansdell & Fairhaven d			10 47							11 47				
46½	—	St Annes-on-the-Sea d			10 51							11 51				
48½	—	Squires Gate d			10 54							11 54				
49½	—	Blackpool Pleasure Beach d			10 57							11 57				
50	—	**Blackpool South** a			11 02							12 02				
—	14½	Poulton-le-Fylde d	10 14	10 18					11 07	11 14	11 18		12 02	12 14	12 18	
—	16½	Layton d							11 10				12 06			
—	17½	Blackpool North a	10 24	10 28		10 57	11 04		11 18	11 24	11 28		12 13	12 24	12 28	12 50

For general notes see front of timetable

J Mondays to Fridays until 1 November and from 31 March, also Saturdays until 2 November and from 1 March
K Until 2 November
c Saturdays arr. 10 minutes later
f Saturdays dep. 10 minutes earlier
g Saturdays arr. 1500.

Intra-time letter indicating note at foot of page.

For connecting stations only - indicates the timetables on which the full service to and from the connecting station can be found (see also below under Route Diagrams).

A wavy line indicates that the train does not run on all dates included in the timetable. In all such cases an additional headnote (in this case '**J**') will be used to provide full details.

Train times in bold indicate that the train stops at the station concerned. Arrival times are denoted by '**a**' against the station name and departure times by '**d**'. Where there is no time shown against a station then the train concerned does not serve that station.

Route/Network Diagrams (see previous page): For many tables a Route/Network Diagram is also provided to show the routes and stations served in diagrammatic form. Where this is the case, a reference to the Route/Network Diagram will be provided at the top of each page of the timetable concerned. Timetable numbers for connecting or alternative services will not be included within the Table itself but will instead be indicated on the accompanying Route/Network Diagram.

General Information

Smoking Policy

Smoking is not permitted on any National Rail service or in any station. In England and Wales, this includes all covered and uncovered concourses, ticket halls, platforms, footbridges and subways at station premises.

Left Luggage Facilities

Details of Left Luggage facilities at individual stations are available at nationalrail.co.uk/stations.

Penalty Fares

Penalty Fares are charged by Train Companies at some stations and on some trains. Where this is the case, warning notices will be displayed. Those stations at which Penalty Fares are in operation are indicated in the Station Index and Table numbers section (see also Train Operator pages). Please be aware that at some stations where Penalty Fare Schemes are in place not all Train Operator services calling at that station are included in the scheme.

If you can not produce a valid ticket for your entire journey when asked to do so you may be charged a Penalty Fare. This will be either twice the full single fare to the next station at which the train is due to stop, or £20 (£50 on Transport for London services and stations, reducing to £25 if paid within 21 days), whichever is the greater. Any travel beyond the next station will be charged at the full single fare.

To avoid paying a Penalty Fare, you must purchase a valid ticket to your destination, before starting your journey. If the ticket office is closed and you can not buy the ticket you want from a self service ticket machine, you must buy a Permit to Travel paying as much of your fare as possible. This permit must be exchanged for a valid ticket at the first opportunity.

More information is available at nationalrail.co.uk/penaltyfares.

Timetable Accuracy, Contents, Presentation

Every effort is made to ensure that the information contained in the timetable is correct, but errors can still occur. If you have any questions or queries about the train services shown in this timetable, please contact the appropriate operator shown in the Directory of Train Operators.

General comments about this publication should be addressed to:–

TSO,
PO Box 29,
Norwich,
NR3 1GN.

Additional Amendments

A facility is available whereby details of any train service alterations introduced subsequent to the production of the GB Rail Timetable may be accessed through the Network Rail website (see http:networkrail.co.uk). Follow the link to the "Electronic National Rail Timetable" in the "For Passengers" section. Additional amendments can be found under "Supporting Documentation".

From time to time, further alterations may apply at short notice and details of these may be found at nationalrail.co.uk/engineering.

Other National Rail Timetables

Regional and route specific timetables are available from individual train companies. Please contact the relevant train company to request the latest version of the timetable you require.

National Rail Enquiries offers an online 'Pocket Timetable' service which gives you the flexibility to create a customised timetable based around your origin and destination, your own time requirements and the days of the week that you intend to travel. Visit www.nationalrail.co.uk/pockettimetables for more details.

Connections

Bold type times in vertical columns in the timetable show direct trains. In a few cases, where one train overtakes another, the times appear in more than one column and arrow symbols indicate where the train continues in the timetable.

Many more journey opportunities are possible by changing trains. To help plan such journeys, times in light italic type are shown in some of the timetables for departures (if the time is earlier than the bold type times for the station below in the column at which you should change trains) or arrivals (if they are later than the bold type times for the station above in the column at which you should change trains).

Where light type italic times are not shown you may have to refer to other tables in the book to work out your connecting services. In order to find the right table to reference, first look at the Route/Network Diagram that covers the table you are working from. This will show the principal connecting links and their table references, which may include the destination you are searching for. If your journey is not covered, follow the advice given on 'How to use this Timetable' under the headings 'Using the Timetable Network map' and 'Using the Index'.

Connections between trains cannot be guaranteed. The nature of the integrated operation of railway passenger services means that to delay one train to await customers from a late running train arriving at a station may cause significant disruption to many other customers when they make connections at other stations along the route. Every endeavour is made to minimise the total disruption and particular attention is given to services operating infrequently and the last train services each day.

The aim of all Train Operating Companies is to run punctually, but inevitably some disruption occurs from time to time. When planning a journey you may wish to consider the effects which any disruption could have and to allow some contingency margin when planning connections.

Minimum Interchange Times at Stations

Unless a connection is shown by times printed in light type, you should generally allow a minimum of five minutes between arrival and departure.

The exceptions to this rule are indicated by minimum interchange times (e.g. 15) alongside the station name in the tables. In certain cases the minimum interchange time is different according to the Train Operators involved.

These are detailed below:-

STATION AND 'STANDARD' MINIMUM CONNECTIONAL ALLOWANCE (Minutes)		***EXCEPTIONS*** ***Showing the Train Operator(s) and minimum connectional allowance applicable***	
Barnham	5	*SN*	2
Bournemouth	5	*SW*	3
Brighton	10	*SN*	4
Cardiff Central	7	*AW*	3*
Clapham Junction	10	*SN*	5
Gatwick Airport	10	*SN*	5

STATION AND 'STANDARD' MINIMUM CONNECTIONAL ALLOWANCE (Minutes)		***EXCEPTIONS*** ***Showing the Train Operator(s) and minimum connectional allowance applicable***	
Guildford	5	*GW*	4
Leatherhead	5	*SN*	3
London Blackfriars	3	SE	5
London Victoria	15	*SE, SN*	10
Luton	10	*FC*	4
Luton Airport Parkway	7	*FC*	4

STATION AND 'STANDARD' MINIMUM CONNECTIONAL ALLOWANCE (Minutes)		***EXCEPTIONS*** ***Showing the Train Operator(s) and minimum connectional allowance applicable***	
Redhill	5	*SN*	3
St. Denys	5	*SW*	3
Southampton Central	5	*SN, SW*	4
Tulse Hill	3	FC	4
Wimbledon	6	*SN, FC*	5

Example

At Barnham a different minimum connectional allowance applies for Train Operator SN. This means that if your journey involves changing between two trains *both of which* are operated by SN, you need only allow 2 minutes. If, however, one or both trains are provided by any other Operator then the minimum of 5 minutes (as shown after the station name) applies.

* Applicable to Valley Lines services only (table 130).

Train Information

National Rail Enquiries

Timetable and fares are available 24 hours a day at www.nationalrail.co.uk or, if you are on the move, at mobile.nationalrail.co.uk.

National Rail Enquiries provides up-to-the-minute advice on all aspects of journey planning, fares and buying tickets, live train running updates and other useful information.

08457 48 49 50 — 24 Hours Daily

(calls may be recorded for training purposes)

0845 60 40 500 — Welsh Language

0845 60 50 600 — Textphone – 06.00 - 21.00 Daily

TrainTracker

For live train times for today and train timetables for the next three months call TrainTracker™ on:

0871 200 49 50

Average calls to TrainTracker cost 10p a minute from a BT land line. Charges from other operators may vary. Calls may be recorded for training purposes.

TrainTracker Text

For live departure and arrival times direct to your mobile text station name to TrainTracker™ on:

8 49 50

TrainTracker texts cost 25p for each successful response (plus usual text costs)

Train company numbers for disabled passengers requiring assistance:–

Company	Telephone	Textphone
Arriva Trains Wales	08453 003 005	08457 585 469
c2c	01702 357640	08457 125 988
Chiltern Railways	08456 005 165	08457 078051
CrossCountry	0844 811 0125	0844 811 0126
East Coast	08457 225 225	08451 202 067
East Midlands Trains	08457 125 678	08457 078 051
Eurostar	08705 186 186	Not available
First Capital Connect	0800 058 2844	0800 975 1052
First Great Western	0800 197 1329/0845 600 5604	0800 294 9209
First Hull Trains	08450 710 222	08456 786 967
First TransPennine Express	0800 107 2149	0800 107 2061
Gatwick Express	0800 138 0225	0800 138 1018
Grand Central	0844 811 0071	0845 305 6815
Heathrow Connect	0800 197 1329	0800 294 9209
Heathrow Express	0845 600 1515	Not available
Island Line	0845 6000 650	0800 692 0792
London Midland	0800 0924260	0844 811 0134
London Overground	0845 601 4867	Not available
Merseyrail	0151 702 2071	0870 0552 681
National Express East Anglia	0800 028 28 78	0845 606 7245
Northern	0808 1561606	08456 045 608
ScotRail	0800 912 2 901	18001 0800 912 2 901
South West Trains	0800 52 82 100	0800 692 0792
Southeastern	0800 783 4524	0800 783 4548
Southern	0800 138 1016	0800 138 1018
Virgin Trains	08457 443366	08457 443367
Wrexham & Shropshire	0845 260 5200	Not available

Train Information

London Travel Information

020 7222 1234 — 24 hours (Daily) — www.tfl.gov.uk

Services to Europe on Eurostar via the Channel Tunnel

08432 186 186 — 0800-1900 (Daily) — www.eurostar.com

Ireland

NI Railways 028 90 66 6630 — 0700-2000 (Daily) — www.translink.co.uk.
Iarnrod Eireann (IE) (Irish Rail) 00 353 183 66 222 — www.irishrail.ie

Transport Direct

Plan journeys by car, bus, train, tube, coach, plane at www.transportdirect.info. Transport Direct is the first door-to-door on-line journey planner for Great Britain.

It's free to use; simply enter your departure point, destination and time of travel and Transport Direct will offer a number of options by different modes of transport - both public and private. Journey plans are presented as step-by-step instructions supported by detailed maps including bus stops and other points of interest to travellers. Tickets for rail and coach journeys can be booked via retail web sites without the need to re-enter journey details. Transport Direct includes live travel news for rail and car users. The car journey planner gives route information that takes account of historical traffic level data, offering the user the choice to travel at a different time, or choose public transport. When travelling by public transport, users can adjust their expected walking speed to plan rail, coach and bus connections more efficiently. You can also access Transport Direct via mobile phone and PDA to find out when your next train is due or to check road conditions.

Bus Information in Great Britain

For details of buses within Greater London ring the Transport for London line: 020 7222 1234 (24-hours).

Bus information for the rest of Great Britain is available nationally from 'Traveline' which is run by local authorities and bus operators. There are regional call centres all of which share the same telephone number and any centre will switch calls pertaining to another part of the country through to the relevant centre. Alternatively codes for reaching the appropriate centre direct can be obtained from www.traveline.info/powercodes.htm.

The number is 0871 200 22 33 (calls from landlines cost 10p per minute) and centres are open at least between the hours of 0800 and 2000 daily (except Christmas Day and Boxing Day). Website: www.traveline.info.

PlusBus

PlusBus is an easy-to-use add-on to your train ticket which gives unlimited bus travel on most bus services around the whole urban area of your origin or destination town or city. ***PlusBus*** is available to over 270 towns and cities across Great Britain with season tickets also available for most ***PlusBus*** destinations. For more information visit www.plusbus.info.

Traintaxi

Taxi symbols on the Station index pages

Where [TAXI] appears against any station that has sub-entries, there will be a taxi rank outside the station from which taxis should usually be available. This also applies to Basingstoke, Bournemouth, Chelmsford, Cheltenham, Colchester, Lincoln, Middlesbrough, Milton Keynes, Northampton, Sunderland and Swindon.

Where [TAXI] appears against any other station, there will be a taxi rank or a cab office within 100 metres of the station. However, you are advised to check availability before travelling, and to pre-book if necessary. Indication of a rank or office is no guarantee of cabs being available.

Visit **www.traintaxi.co.uk** for information on cab firms serving **all** train, tram, metro and underground stations in Great Britain, and all bus and ferry destinations listed in this *GB Rail Timetable*.

Rail Travel for Disabled Passengers

All train operators are able to carry disabled passengers and can provide additional assistance for boarding and alighting rail services and during train journeys.

If using a wheelchair, it is recommended that passengers book assistance in advance as space on trains for wheelchair users is limited.

National Rail produce a booklet called 'Rail Travel Made Easy' which details the provisions Train Companies make for disabled people. The booklet is available from major stations or can be obtained by writing to: Disability & Inclusion Section, ATOC, 3rd Floor, 40 Bernard Street, London WC1N 1BY. Alternatively, you can download a copy by visiting www.nationalrail.co.uk/passenger_services/disabled_passengers/RTME.pdf

Seat Reservations, Luggage, Cycles and Animals

Seat Reservations

You can reserve seats on any train marked 🄁, 🄁, ◇ or ◇ at the top of the column in the timetable pages. Further detailed information is shown in the Directory of Train Operators.

Reservations can normally be made from about 12 weeks in advance of the day of travel, up to about 2 hours before the train departs from its start point, or, for early morning trains, up to 1600 hours the previous evening.

Where and How to reserve

You can reserve either by visiting a station identified in the Index pages by ◇, or a rail appointed travel agent or by calling one of the telephone booking facilities listed on each Train Operator's page. Telephone reservations are only available when made in conjunction with purchasing a ticket. When reserving you will need to tell your station or agent:

1. Starting and finishing point of your journey.
2. Date of travel (Take care if your departure is soon after midnight – see How to use this Timetable).
3. Departure time of train.
4. Number of seats required.
5. You may be able to specify other preferences such as facing or back to direction of travel*, window seat, seat in Restaurant Car where available, seats round a table or airline style with fold down table where available.

   *Customers should note that some trains reverse their direction of travel during the journey.
6. First Class or Standard accommodation (if you do not specify class of travel it will be assumed that you require Standard accommodation).

Names on seats

Your name can be included in your seat reservation label or on the electronic display above your seat, if you wish, when travelling First Class on some East Coast, East Midlands Trains and National Express East Anglia services or First and Standard Class on CrossCountry, First Great Western, First TransPennine Express, ScotRail and Virgin Trains services.

Connecting reservations

If your journey involves changing between trains on which seats are reservable (including journeys crossing London or other major cities), through reservations on both services are available.

Children

Seats may be reserved for children, but for a child under 5 years of age a seat may be reserved only if an appropriate child rail ticket is held.

Reservations Recommended

Trains shown 🄁 at the head of a column in the timetable pages are expected to be very busy. Seat reservations are therefore recommended for a comfortable journey and will consequently be provided free of charge to holders of valid travel tickets.

Seat Reservations, Luggage, Cycles and Animals

Reservations Compulsory
On trains shown 🅁 at the head of a column, seat reservations are compulsory and are available free of charge. Passengers may not be able to board the train if they do not have a reservation.

Trains For Weekends Away
Most long distance services after 1400 on Fridays and on Saturday mornings, also trains arriving in London on Sunday evenings and Monday mornings can be extremely busy.

Customers are advised to reserve seats in advance if planning to travel at these times.

Travelling at Peak Holiday Periods
Trains are usually extremely busy immediately before and after Bank Holidays and in some cases access to trains is only by reservation and/or boarding pass. Customers are advised to reserve seats as early as possible.

Cycles by Train
You can take your cycle on many National Rail services, however reservations may be required and restrictions may apply for peak services. Folded cycles can be carried on most train services. More information is shown in the Directory of Train Operators, the National Rail 'Cycling by Train' leaflet and online at www.nationalrail.co.uk/cycling. Cycle storage is also available at many stations.

Weekend First

Weekend First is available on many CrossCountry, East Coast*, East Midlands Trains, First Great Western, First TransPennine Express*, Grand Central, National Express East Anglia, ScotRail*, South West Trains*, Virgin Trains and Wrexham & Shropshire* services on Saturdays, Sundays and Bank Holidays. If you hold a ticket for travel in Standard Class, you may be able to upgrade to the added comfort of First Class accommodation on payment of an additional fare. On some services a 'Weekend First' ticket allows you to upgrade to First Class at weekends and Bank Holidays. Holders of Annual Gold Cards may also be able to upgrade on off peak services for a small amount. Costs vary depending on the journey you are making.
*may only be purchased on trains at time of travel
More information can be found at nationalrail.co.uk/firstclass.

Customers' Luggage and Animals

Customers may take up to 3 items of personal luggage free of charge, this includes 2 large items (such as suitcases or rucksacks) and 1 item of smaller hand luggage (such as a briefcase). Folded prams, non-folding prams and carrycots are also able to be carried. Full details of the free allowances are available at stations. Excess luggage and certain more bulky items (such as skis) may be carried, subject to available space, at an extra charge. On Gatwick Express services, bulky items such as skis are conveyed free in the luggage van. There is plenty of space on board for other luggage.
Passengers may take dogs, cats and other small animals (maximum two per passenger), free of charge and subject to certain conditions, provided they do not endanger or inconvenience other passengers or staff.
ScotRail allows dogs to accompany able-bodied passengers in Sleeper services subject to a charge for cleaning of the compartment. The booking must be First Class, Standard Class with two people travelling together, or a Solo supplement is payable for exclusive use of a twin-berth cabin. First Great Western do not allow animals (except Guide Dogs) to travel in Sleeper accommodation. There is no charge for guide dogs.
More information can be found at nationalrail.co.uk/luggageandanimals

Directory of Train Operators

The following pages contain details of the Train Operating Companies who operate trains included in this timetable and indicate the services they provide.

Each operator is identified by a two character code listed below. The codes are displayed in the index alongside the station name indicating which operator is responsible for operating the facilities at that station. The code is also shown at the head of each train column in the timetable pages indicating which operator is providing the train service.

18 stations are the operating responsibility of Network Rail and are shown in the index by the code NR and information about Network Rail is shown at the end of the Train Operating Company pages.

Page No	Train Company Name	Code
12	Arriva Trains Wales	AW
13	c2c	CC
14	CrossCountry	XC
15	Chiltern Railways	CH
16	Devon & Cornwall Railway	DC
17	East Coast	GR
18	East Midlands Trains	EM
19	First Capital Connect	FC
20	First Great Western	GW
21	First Hull Trains	HT
22	First TransPennine Express	TP
23	Gatwick Express	GX
24	Grand Central	GC
25	Heathrow Connect	HC
26	Heathrow Express	HX
27	Island Line	IL
28	London Midland	LM
29	London Overground	LO
30	Merseyrail	ME
31	National Express East Anglia	LE
32	North Yorkshire Moors Railway	NY
33	Northern	NT
34	ScotRail	SR
35	South West Trains	SW
36	Southeastern	SE
37	Southern	SN
38	Virgin Trains	VT
39	West Coast Railway Co.	WR
40	Wrexham & Shropshire	WS

Arriva Trains Wales

AW

ADDRESS	St Mary's House, 47 Penarth Road, Cardiff CF10 5DJ Telephone: 08456 061 660 Website: www.arrivatrainswales.co.uk Email: customer.relations@arrivatrainswales.co.uk
MANAGING DIRECTOR	Tim Bell
RESERVATIONS AND TICKETS BY TELEPHONE AND ONLINE	Tickets may be booked in advance and seats reserved, by telephone, from the following numbers (0800–2000 daily): 0870 9000 773 for Great Britain, tickets and reservations. 0870 9000 767 for Group and 0845 300 3005 for Disabled travel arrangements. Textphone 0845 300 6105 Please allow 5 days for delivery.
RESERVATION DETAILS	All seat reservations are free to ticket holders.
CATERING ON TRAINS	At-seat catering service of cold snacks, sandwiches and hot and cold drinks on all services marked ⚲, for all or part of the journey. Complimentary meal service for first class and a counter service of hot and cold snacks for standard class on trains with ⊠. Train catering on Arriva Trains Wales services is provided by: At Seat Catering (2003) Ltd, Arriva Trains Wales 1st Floor St Mary's House 47 Penarth Road Cardiff CF10 5DJ
CYCLES	See Cycling by Train leaflet, a guide to Arriva Trains Wales services for full details.
LOST PROPERTY	Contact Arriva Trains Wales Customer Relations on 0845 6061 660.
TRAIN SERVICE UPDATE	Please consult our website at www.arrivatrainswales.co.uk for real time service updates.
PENALTY FARES	Penalty Fares are not in force on Arriva Trains Wales services. Customers are reminded that they must have a valid ticket when boarding at a staffed station, if not it will be necessary to charge you the full single/return fare for the journey.
DISABLED PERSON'S PROTECTION POLICY	Address as above.
CODE OF PRACTICE FOR COMMENTS, COMPLAINTS AND SUGGESTIONS	Address as above.

ALCOHOL POLICY

Arriva Trains Wales have prohibited the consumption of alcohol on all services and stations between Caerphilly - Rhymney, and Pontypridd - Treherbert/Merthr Tydfil/Aberdare

c2c

CC

A member of the National Express Group plc

ADDRESS	207 Old Street, London EC1V 9NR Telephone: 0845 601 4873 Fax: 01603 214517 Website: www.c2c-online.co.uk
MANAGING DIRECTOR	Julian Drury
RESERVATIONS AND TICKETS BY TELEPHONE AND ONLINE	Tickets may be booked in advance by telephoning 08457 44 44 22 - 0800 to 2000 daily.
RESERVATION DETAILS	Reservations are not available.
CATERING ON TRAINS	Not available.
CYCLES	Cycles can be taken on off-peak trains free-of-charge when accompanied by a fare-paying passenger, subject to space availability. Bicycles are not permitted, Mondays to Fridays on services that arrive in London between 0715 and 0945, or those which leave London between 1630 and 1840. To comply with safety regulations, all cycles, with the exception of folding cycles which are completely enclosed in a container or case throughout the journey, must be conveyed in the designated area on trains. During engineering work, cycles cannot be accommodated on replacement bus services.
LOST PROPERTY	Telephone: 01702 357 699
TRAIN SERVICE UPDATE	Up to date train running information is available on the c2c website www.c2c-online.co.uk, the National Rail Enquiries website at nationalrail.co.uk or on ceefax page 433.
PENALTY FARES	If you travel without a valid ticket you may be charged a penalty fare of £20 or twice the full single fare, whichever is the greater.
DISABLED PERSON'S PROTECTION POLICY	Available from:- Customer Relations, c2c, FREEPOST ADM3968, Southend SS1 1ZS Telephone: 0845 601 4873 - 0830 to 1700 Monday to Friday
CODE OF PRACTICE FOR COMMENTS, COMPLAINTS AND SUGGESTIONS	Available from Customer Relations at above address or telephone 0845 601 4873.

CrossCountry

XC

ADDRESS

CrossCountry
5th Floor, Cannon House,
18 Priory Queensway, Birmingham B4 6BS
Telephone: 08447 369 123
Textphone: 0121 200 6420
Fax: 0121 200 6005
Website: www.crosscountrytrains.co.uk
Email: customer.relations@crosscountrytrains.co.uk

MANAGING DIRECTOR

Andy Cooper

RESERVATIONS AND TICKETS BY TELEPHONE AND ONLINE

On-line at crosscountrytrains.co.uk is the easiest way to purchase your tickets. If you prefer, you can also make telephone bookings on 0844 811 0124 between 0800 and 2200 daily. Parties of 10 or more should contact Group Travel on 0871 244 2388 between 0800 and 1800 weekdays

RESERVATION DETAILS

You are strongly advised to make a seat reservation in advance; especially when travelling on trains shown with the R symbol in timetables. Seat reservations are free of charge.

CATERING ON TRAINS

Catering is available on most CrossCountry trains.
In First Class, on weekdays between 0630 and 1830 customers can enjoy complimentary light refreshments including hot and soft drinks, served at seat. In Standard Class we offer a range of quality snacks, sandwiches and hot drinks plus soft and alcoholic beverages between 0600 and 2000. For more information on the Nottingham - Cardiff and Birmingham - Stansted Airport routes please refer to our timetables.

CYCLES

We do not charge to carry your cycle. However, as space is very limited you will need to reserve in advance on nearly all our services. Please enquire before travelling. We are unable to accept powered cycles, tricycles, tandems or trailers on any of our services.

LOST PROPERTY

Contact Customer Relations on 08447 369 123 between 0800 and 2000 Monday to Saturday; or email lost.property@crosscountrytrains.co.uk

TRAIN SERVICE UPDATE

Details of major disruption to services and weekend engineering work are summarised on BBC Ceefax and BBCi on digital TV. Live travel updates are available on-line at crosscountrytrains.co.uk and details of all service disruptions can be found at nationalrail.co.uk/disruption/

PENALTY FARES

A Penalty Fares scheme is not currently in operation on CrossCountry trains. Visit crosscountrytrains.co.uk for the most up to date information. Should you board one of our trains without a valid ticket you will be charged the full Single or Return fare for your journey unless the ticket office is closed and a self-service ticket machine is not available.

DISABLED PERSON'S PROTECTION POLICY

We provide a Journey Care service for the disabled, elderly and infirm. By phoning our team on 0844 811 0125, textphone 0844 811 0126, beforehand we will, where possible, arrange help for your journey. Our Disabled Persons Protection Policy is available on-line at crosscountrytrains.co.uk

CODE OF PRACTICE FOR COMMENTS, COMPLAINTS AND SUGGESTIONS

Copies of our Complaints Handling Procedure and Passenger's Charter are available on-line at crosscountrytrains.co.uk

Chiltern Railways

CH

ADDRESS

Customer Services, Banbury ICC, Merton Street
Banbury, Oxfordshire OX16 4RN
Telephone: 08456 005 165 (Mondays to Fridays 0830-1730)
Fax: 01926 729 914
Website: www.chilternrailways.co.uk

MANAGING DIRECTOR

Adrian Shooter (Acting)

RESERVATIONS AND TICKETS BY TELEPHONE AND ONLINE

Telephone 08456 005 165 (0700-2000, 7 days a week)

RESERVATION DETAILS

Reservations are not available.

CATERING ON TRAINS

We aim to provide an at-seat trolley catering service on many of our most popular longer distance trains. The trains providing this service change from time to time depending on circumstances and expected demand. If your train does not have a trolley don't forget that our main stations offer excellent catering facilities. For more details check our website. Please allow enough time to purchase your refreshments before boarding your train.

CYCLES

On Mondays to Fridays we're unable to convey cycles on our busiest trains. These are trains arriving at London Marylebone or Birmingham Snow Hill between 0745 and 1000 and trains departing London Marylebone or Birmingham Snow Hill between 1630 and 1930. These restrictions apply even if you're only travelling for part of the journey. Tandems are not carried at any time on Chiltern Railways. There are no restrictions on folding bikes. Bikes are not allowed on rail replacement buses.

LOST PROPERTY

If we find any item of lost property, we'll always do our best to contact the owner if they can be identified. Items can be collected from London Marylebone up to 3 months after they've been handed in - we charge a collection fee to cover our administration costs.

If you lose something on one of our trains or stations you can report it by:

* Using the online form on our website

* Using a Lost Property form available at any Chiltern Railways ticket office, and returning it to a member of Chiltern Railways Staff.

* By phone, fax or post using the contact details below

Phone: 08456 005 165
Fax: 020 7333 3002
Write to: Chiltern Railways Lost Property, Marylebone Station,
London NW1 6JJ.

Lost Property Office Operating Hours: Mondays to Fridays 1200 to 2000. Please allow up to 2 weeks for processing lost items. If you do not hear from us in that period, you should assume the item has not been found.

TRAIN SERVICE UPDATE

Visit our website www.chilternrailways.co.uk for current train running information and details of changes to train times because of engineering work or other special events.

PENALTY FARES

If you do not have a valid rail ticket for the journey you are making, you will have to pay a Penalty Fare of £20 or twice the single fare, whichever is the greater, for the journey you are making on Chiltern Railways services. For full details write to the above address, or see our website.

DISABLED PERSON'S PROTECTION POLICY

Copies of the Disabled Person's Protection Policy can be obtained from the above address, or from our website.

CODE OF PRACTICE FOR COMMENTS, COMPLAINTS AND SUGGESTIONS

If you have any comments, complaints or suggestions regarding Chiltern Railways services, please write to the address shown above or telephone 08456 005 165 (0830-1730 Mondays to Fridays), Fax 01926 729 914. Alternatively you can use the 'Contact Us' option on our website.

Devon & Cornwall Railway

ADDRESS

MANAGING DIRECTOR

RESERVATIONS AND TICKETS BY TELEPHONE AND ONLINE

New operator due to commence operation during this timetable – for full details see National Rail website nearer the time

RESERVATION DETAILS

CATERING ON TRAINS

CYCLES

LOST PROPERTY

TRAIN SERVICE UPDATE

PENALTY FARES

DISABLED PERSON'S PROTECTION POLICY

CODE OF PRACTICE FOR COMMENTS, COMPLAINTS AND SUGGESTIONS

East Coast

ADDRESS	Freepost RRZG-ZZZX-LKXK, Newcastle upon Tyne NE1 5DN Telephone: 08457 225 225 Open 0830-1700 Monday-Friday Fax: 0191 227 5986 Website: www.eastcoast.co.uk Email: customers@eastcoast.co.uk
MANAGING DIRECTOR	Karen Boswell
RESERVATIONS AND TICKETS BY TELEPHONE AND ONLINE	Internet Purchase tickets via the internet 24 hours a day at www.eastcoast.co.uk Self service ticket machines are available at all East Coast stations. Purchase tickets for today or collect pre-booked tickets. Telephone 08457 225 225 Telesales Open 0800-2000 Monday-Saturday, 1000-2000 Sunday Business Travel Open 0800-1800 Monday-Friday For corporate credit card and account holder bookings. Group Travel Open 0900-1800 Monday-Friday Discounts may be available for groups of 10 or more people. Assisted Travel Open 0800-2000 Monday-Saturday, 1000-2000 Sunday The minimum transaction is £10. Please allow 7 days from the time of booking for tickets to reach you through the post.
RESERVATION DETAILS	Seat reservations can usually be made on any East Coast train up to ten weeks in advance. They are available to any ticket holder upon request, and are compulsory with some ticket types. Only one reservation can be made per single journey.
CATERING ON TRAINS	We aim to offer excellent food with plenty of choice. Through our talented team of top chefs, we bring you the best of British cuisine in our Restaurant*, Café Bar and from our At Seat Dining*. * Available on selected services. Further details are available on our website.
CYCLES	Bicycles are welcome on East Coast trains. A reservation must be made and bookings are subject to space being available. Reservations can be made by calling 08457 225 225 or at any East Coast ticket office.
LOST PROPERTY	If you lose something on a East Coast train or at a station please speak to a member of staff or contact us on 08457 225 333. Please note that charges are normally made for returning items of lost property and that we are unable to forward items of lost property on train services.
TRAIN SERVICE UPDATE	Visit www.eastcoast.co.uk or call National Rail Enquiries on 08457 48 49 50 (calls may be recorded for training purposes).
PENALTY FARES	East Coast does not operate Penalty Fares scheme. However, you should always purchase a ticket valid for travel before you board any East Coast service as only full fare tickets are sold on our trains. The only exception being Disabled Railcard holders who will be sold appropriate discounted tickets on-board.
DISABLED PERSON'S PROTECTION POLICY	A copy of our DPPP can be obtained free of charge from the address at the top of this page. Our Assisted Travel team can help you plan your journey and organise tickets, assistance and seat reservations. To ensure the best possible levels of assistance we recommend that you contact us no later than 1800 the day before you intend to travel. Telephone 08457 225 225 or textphone 08457 202 067* (open 0800-2000 Monday-Saturday, 1000-2000 Sunday). * Please note that this number should only be used to contact the Assisted Travel team. For all other enquiries please telephone 08457 225 225.
CODE OF PRACTICE FOR COMMENTS, COMPLAINTS AND SUGGESTIONS	Our Passenger's Charter is available from all East Coast stations or from our website www.eastcoast.co.uk. All correspondence should be sent using the address at the top of this page.

East Midlands Trains

EM

ADDRESS	Customer Relations East Midlands Trains FREEPOST RSAK-GETK-BSJX Nottingham NG2 3DQ Telephone: 08457 125 678 Website: eastmidlandstrains.co.uk Email: getintouch@eastmidlandstrains.co.uk
MANAGING DIRECTOR	Tim Shoveller
RESERVATIONS AND TICKETS BY TELEPHONE AND ONLINE	Buy your tickets online at eastmidlandstrains.co.uk. You can buy tickets for all rail journeys (within Great Britain) with us. Alternatively call 08457 125 678 between 0800-2000 (7 days a week).
RESERVATION DETAILS	Seat reservations on East Midlands Trains services are free. Just book in advance when you buy your ticket. We advise that you always make a reservation, as seats cannot be guaranteed without one. On our Local services reservations are available on the Liverpool to Norwich services.
CATERING ON TRAINS	On our East Midlands London services (to/from St Pancras International), we offer a range of delicious food options, plus snacks and hot and cold drinks. A trolley service is available on selected East Midlands Local services (denoted by a symbol within the timetable).
CYCLES	Two bicycles per train are accepted for free on all East Midlands Trains services; however reservations must be made in advance on reservable services subject to availability.
LOST PROPERTY	Please allow a minimum of 24 hours for the items to be received at a lost property office. If your item is located you may be charged for the return of it and will be advised of this cost. To enquire about lost property, please call our Lost Property office, ideally between the hours of 1000 and 1600 Monday to Saturday on 0115 9576525.
TRAIN SERVICE UPDATE	Details of services and real time running information, including travel alerts by email are available through our website. Visit eastmidlandstrains.co.uk. Alternatively, call National Rail Enquiries on 08457 48 49 50 (calls may be recorded for training purposes).
PENALTY FARES	You should always buy a ticket in advance of boarding your train. Penalty fares may be in operation on your service.
DISABLED PERSON'S PROTECTION POLICY	We aim to make travelling with us accessible to all our customers. If you require assistance in travelling, have special needs or mobility problems please call our team on 08457 125 678 to arrange help for your journey. A text direct service is also available on 18001 08457 125 678 (for people with hearing problems).
CODE OF PRACTICE FOR COMMENTS, COMPLAINTS AND SUGGESTIONS	Our Customer Relations team is available to receive your comments, complaints or suggestions. Please write to Customer Relations at the above address, or email getintouch@eastmidlandstrains.co.uk

FC First Capital Connect FC

A member of the First Rail Division

ADDRESS

Freepost, RRBR-REEJ-KTKY, First Capital Connect, Customer Relations Department, PO Box 443, Plymouth PL4 6WP
Telephone: 0845 026 4700 (open 7 days a week 0700-2200 with the exception of Christmas Day)
Fax: 0845 676 9904
Website: www.firstcapitalconnect.co.uk
Email: customer.relations.fcc@firstgroup.com

CHIEF EXECUTIVE

Moir Lockhead

MANAGING DIRECTOR

Neal Lawson

RESERVATIONS AND TICKETS BY TELEPHONE AND ONLINE

First Capital Connect does not offer telesales, however tickets can be booked at www.firstcapitalconnect.co.uk

RESERVATION DETAILS

Reservations are not available.

CATERING ON TRAINS

None.

CYCLES

We welcome passengers with bicycles on services where they can be safely accommodated, however restrictions apply, bicycles cannot be carried on:

- trains that are scheduled to arrive at a London terminal between 07:00 and 10:00;
- trains that are scheduled to depart from a London terminal between 16:00 and 19:00;
- trains running between Drayton Park and Moorgate;
- services between Royston and Ely that depart or arrive at Cambridge between 07:45 and 08:45, with the exception of the 07:15 and 07:45 departures from King's Cross;
- replacement bus services unless stated otherwise in any associated publicity; and
- any train where a member of our staff asks you to remove your bicycle.
- Bicycles cannot be conveyed within Travelcard zone 1 in any direction between the hours of 0700-1000 and 1600-1900 Monday to Friday

Compact, folding bicycles can be carried on any service at any time.

LOST PROPERTY

In order to trace lost property please contact our Customer Relations department on 0845 026 4700, between 07:00 - 22:00 Monday to Sunday.

TRAIN SERVICE UPDATE

For current train information call National Rail enquiries on 08457 48 49 50 (calls may be recorded for training purposes) or check our website at: www.firstcapitalconnect.co.uk/live-info

PENALTY FARES

First Capital Connect operates a Penalty Fares System. If you do not have a valid ticket or permit to travel, you will be liable to pay a penalty fare. This is £20 or twice the appropriate single fare to the next station stop, whichever is greater. This does not apply for travel from Crews Hill.

If you do not buy a ticket, you could also be prosecuted and this can lead to a criminal conviction.

DISABLED PERSON'S PROTECTION POLICY

Our Disabled Person's Protection Policy is available from Customer Relations, and is also available on our website and available at all staffed sations. First Capital Connect operates a dedicated telephone and textphone service for disabled or mobility impaired customers, the contact details are:
Telephone: 0800 058 2844
Textphone: 0800 975 1052
These are available 07:00 - 22:00, Monday to Sunday, with the exception of Christmas Day.

CODE OF PRACTICE FOR COMMENTS, COMPLAINTS AND SUGGESTIONS

Our Passenger's Charter details our code of practice and is available from all staffed stations and from our Customer Relations department. The Customer Relations department will be happy to assist with any comments, complaints or suggestions and can be contacted using the contact details above.

GW First Great Western GW

A member of the First Rail Division

ADDRESS
Milford House, 1 Milford Street, Swindon SN1 1HL
Telephone: 01793 499400
Fax: 01793 499460
Website: www.firstgreatwestern.co.uk. On our website you can create and print your own personalised timetables, download complete timetable booklets, find departure and arrival times for specific journeys, buy tickets, obtain live timetable updates specific to individual stations, check any late alterations to our services, view promotions and contact us with your comments.

MANAGING DIRECTOR
Mark Hopwood

RESERVATIONS AND TICKETS BY TELEPHONE AND ONLINE
Tickets may be booked in advance using credit and debit cards and seats reserved by ringing **08457 000 125** (open 0700-2200 Mondays to Fridays and 0700-2100 Saturdays and Sundays). Allow at least 5 working days for postal delivery. A next day delivery can be arranged at £5 per transaction. Arrangements can be made for tickets to be collected from Fast Ticket machines (the credit or debit card used for purchase will be needed at many stations). For Group Travel call **08457 000 125**.

RESERVATION DETAILS
One seat reservation per single journey when purchasing a ticket, additional reservations, including those made by season ticket holders, will be subject to a £5 fee.

CATERING ON TRAINS
Most First Great Western high speed services offer an Express Cafe service with a wide range of hot and cold drinks and snacks, beers, wines, sandwiches, crisps and confectionary.

A Travelling Chef is available on 32 weekday services, preparing meals and snacks to order for both First and Standard Class customers. On 4 weekday services, a Pullman restaurant provides a la carte dining to First and Standard Class customers, subject to availability.

First Class customers also enjoy additional complimentary services:

- An at-seat trolley service offering light refreshments (available on most Monday to Friday services between 0700-1900), including hot and cold drinks and light snacks appropriate to the time of day.
- At the weekend and on weekdays after 1900, complimentary refreshments are available from the Express Cafe on production of valid travel tickets.

CYCLES
First Great Western welcomes customers with bicycles on services where they can be safely accommodated. However it is not possible to carry bicycles on some services particularly during peak periods. For full details of when bicycles cannot be carried or when reservations are required, please visit our website or pick up a leaflet at any of our staffed stations.

LOST PROPERTY
Customers who have left property on First Great Western services should contact our Customer Services team on **08457 000 125**.

TRAIN SERVICE UPDATE
For current train information including details of engineering work please visit our website: www.firstgreatwestern.co.uk

PENALTY FARES
These operate on most of our services. A penalty fare of £20 or twice the appropriate single fare to the next station stop (whichever is the greater) will be charged to anybody who is unable to produce a valid ticket or other authority when required to do so. For further information, pick up a leaflet about penalty fares from any staffed station.

DISABLED PERSON'S PROTECTION POLICY
Available from Customer Services Team
First Great Western
PO Box 313
Plymouth PL4 6YD
Tel: 08457 000 125
Email: fgwfeedback@firstgroup.com
Opening hours 0700-2200, daily.

Customers requiring assistance should contact 0800 197 1329 (18001 0800 197 1329 textphone service), if possible giving 24 hours notice of travel plans.

CODE OF PRACTICE FOR COMMENTS, COMPLAINTS AND SUGGESTIONS
Your views leaflets and copies of the Passenger's Charter are available to download from our website www.firstgreatwestern.co.uk, at all staffed First Great Western stations or alternatively from the Customer Services Team at the address above.

First Hull Trains

HT

ADDRESS	First Hull Trains Customer Services, Freepost RLYY-XSTG-YXCK, 4th Floor, Europa House, 184 Ferensway, Hull HU1 3UT. Telephone: 08456 76 99 05 Website: www.hulltrains.co.uk Email: customer.services@hulltrains.co.uk
GENERAL MANAGER	James Adeshiyan
RESERVATIONS AND TICKETS BY TELEPHONE AND ONLINE	First Hull Trains tickets can be booked in advance and seats reserved by ringing 08450 710 222 (0700 to 2200 Monday to Friday and 0800 to 1900 Saturday and Sunday). Please allow five working days for delivery. Tickets on departure are available.
RESERVATION DETAILS	Seat reservations are free for First and Standard Class ticket holders. Season Ticket holders may reserve seats at a cost of £2 for First class and £1 for Standard class.
CATERING ON TRAINS	First Hull Trains provides a buffet on all services, and a comprehensive catering package for First Class passengers. Catering is subject to availability and may be limited when services are disrupted by engineering works or Bank Holidays.
CYCLES	Cycles and tandems are carried free of charge, however, a reservation is compulsory. Please telephone 08450 710 222
LOST PROPERTY	Please contact Customer Services.
TRAIN SERVICE UPDATE	Available at www.hulltrains.co.uk, or by telephone on 08450 710222.
PENALTY FARES	Penalty fares are not in force on any Hull Trains Service
DISABLED PERSON'S PROTECTION POLICY	Available at: www.hulltrains.co.uk. Alternatively, a copy can be requested from Customer Services.
CODE OF PRACTICE FOR COMMENTS, COMPLAINTS AND SUGGESTIONS	First Hull Trains' Passenger's Charter is available at www.hulltrains.co.uk. Alternatively, any comments, complaints or suggestions can be sent to Customer Services

First TransPennine Express

A joint venture between First and Keolis

ADDRESS	7th Floor, Bridgewater House, 60 Whitworth Street, Manchester M1 6LT Telephone: 08700 005151 Website: www.tpexpress.co.uk
MANAGING DIRECTOR	Vernon Barker
RESERVATIONS AND TICKETS BY TELEPHONE AND ONLINE	Reservations and tickets are available from all local staffed stations.
RESERVATION DETAILS	Seat reservations are available at staffed stations. Seat reservations for travel on First TransPennine Express services can be booked up until the day before travel. There is no charge for making a seat reservation if you have a rail ticket, or buy one at the same time.
CATERING ON TRAINS	Catering trolley services are available between 0700 and 1900 Monday to Friday on First TransPennine Express trains between Manchester Piccadilly and York, Manchester Piccadilly and Doncaster and Manchester Piccadilly and Preston. In addition to the above, all services between Manchester Airport, Manchester Piccadilly, Carlisle, Glasgow Central and Edinburgh convey a trolley service for the whole journey. This facility is also provided at weekends.
CYCLES	Customers may take their bicycle with them on First TransPennine Express trains at no extra cost. As space is limited reservations for cycle space should be made at least 24 hours before the journey.
LOST PROPERTY	Customers who have left their property on First TransPennine Express trains or stations should contact 0845 600 1672.
TRAIN SERVICE UPDATE	Call TrainTracker on 0871 200 4950 for updated information on train departures and arrivals.
PENALTY FARES	Penalty Fares are not applicable on First TransPennine Express services. Customers are reminded that they must have a valid ticket when they travel. If not it will be necessary to charge the full Open Single or Return fare for the journey.
DISABLED PERSON'S PROTECTION POLICY	Available from: Customer Relations, First TransPennine Express, ADMAIL 3878, Freepost, Manchester M1 9YB Customers who have special needs and require customer assistance should contact us on 0800 107 2149. A textphone service is available on 0800 107 2061.
CODE OF PRACTICE FOR COMMENTS, COMPLAINTS AND SUGGESTIONS	Feedback leaflets and copies of the Passenger's Charter are available from all stations served by First TransPennine Express services or alternatively contact: Customer Relations, First TransPennine Express, ADMAIL 3878, Freepost, Manchester M1 9YB. Telephone: 0845 600 1671 Email: tpecustomer.relations@firstgroup.com

Gatwick Express

GX

ADDRESS	P.O. Box 227, Tonbridge, Kent TN9 2ZP Telephone: 0845 850 1530 Fax: 020 8929 8687 (Overseas: +44 208 9298687) Website: www.gatwickexpress.com Email: queries.gex@airexp.co.uk
MANAGING DIRECTOR	Chris Burchell
RESERVATIONS AND TICKETS BY TELEPHONE AND ONLINE	Reservations are not necessary on Gatwick Express services. For information and telesales please call 0845 850 1530. Tickets can also be purchased through our website at www.gatwickexpress.com
RESERVATION DETAILS	Reservations are not available.
CATERING ON TRAINS	An at-seat trolley service of drinks and light refreshments is available throughout the day.
CYCLES	Cycles and other bulky items such as skis are conveyed free in the luggage van of the Gatwick Expresss trains that do not run to/from Brighton. However, the following trains, cycles are not permitted unless they are standard size folding cycles provided they are folded, Brighton depart 0632, 0640, 0656, 0715, 0730, 0744, Gatwick Airport depart 0705, 0720, 0735, 0750, 0805, 0820, London Victoria depart 1730, 1745, 1800, 1815, 1830, 1845.
LOST PROPERTY	Please call our Lost Property Office on 0845 850 15 30, select option 3.
TRAIN SERVICE UPDATE	Journey time is 30 minutes (35 minutes on Sundays). First Class and Express Class accommodation is available. From London Victoria at 0330, 0430, 0500 then every 15 minutes (15, 30, 45, 00 minutes past each hour) until 0001, 0030. From Gatwick Airport at 0435, 0520, 0550 then every 15 minutes (05, 20, 35, 50 minutes past each hour) until 0050, 0135. For current train information call 0845 850 15 30.
PENALTY FARES	Penalty Fares will be applied for passengers without the correct ticket between Brighton and Gatwick Airport. The only passengers permitted to buy a ticket on the train are those travelling between Gatwick Airport and London Victoria in either direction.
DISABLED PERSON'S PROTECTION POLICY	Customers requiring assistance can book this prior to travel. Arrangements can be made by calling 0845 850 15 30, textphone available. It is advisable to give 24 hours notice of travel plans, although customers will be given assistance if they arrive at the stations without notice but please allow a little extra time.
CODE OF PRACTICE FOR COMMENTS, COMPLAINTS AND SUGGESTIONS	Initially comments or issues requiring immediate attention should be addressed to any member of Gatwick Express staff on the train or platforms. Additionally Customer Comments forms and our Passenger's Charter are available at Gatwick Express ticket offices. Alternatively you may write to the Listening Company, P.O. Box 277, Tonbridge, Kent TN9 2ZP.

Grand Central

ADDRESS	Grand Central Railway Company Ltd River House 17 Museum Street York YO1 7DJ Telephone: 0845 603 4852 Fax: 01904 466066 Website: www.grandcentralrail.com Email: info@grandcentralrail.com
MANAGING DIRECTOR	Tom Clift
RESERVATIONS AND TICKETS BY TELEPHONE AND ONLINE	Reservations are strongly advised at weekends and bank holidays. Tickets and seat reservations are available in advance on our website www.grandcentral.com or over the phone by calling 0844 811 0071 (0800-2200 7 days a week) or 0845 603 4852 (Mon-Fri 0900-1700). You can book tickets for all rail journeys within Great Britain with us. Tickets booked in advance can be sent by post (allow 3 working days), collected from self service ticket machines at certain station or sent electronically by text message or e-mail to print at home. Tickets can be purchased from the staff on the train at no extra cost. For group bookings, business travel and Carnet tickets please call 0845 603 4852 (Mon-Fri 0900-1700)
RESERVATION DETAILS	Complimentary seat reservations are available; these must be booked at least 24 hours in advance. To guarantee a seat we advise that you always make a reservation. Reservations are strongly advised at weekends and bank holidays.
CATERING ON TRAINS	A buffet service is available on all services. In First Class customers can enjoy complimentary light refreshments including hot and cold drinks, served at seat. A complimentary light breakfast is served between York and London before 1000. Daily and weekend newspapers are provided. In Standard Class a buffet is available offering a selection of fair trade and locally sourced products, including hot, soft and alcoholic drinks, sandwiches, crisps and a large selection of other snacks. A complimentary tea or coffee is provided to standard class customers travelling to or from London. Please present your ticket at the buffet counter to claim your complimentary drink. A standard class trolley service is provided on selected trains.
CYCLES	Normal sized cycles are conveyed free of charge subject to room being available, cycle reservations can be made by calling 0845 603 4852 or at any station ticket office. Passengers wishing to travel with larger sized cycles (Tandems etc) should call 0845 603 4852 (Mon-Fri 0900-1700) in advance of travelling. During engineering work cycles cannot be accommodated on replacement bus services.
LOST PROPERTY	For trains travelling towards Sunderland or Bradford, please contact Northern Rail's Lost Property office on 0845 00 00 125. For trains travelling towards London, please contact King's Cross Lost Property Office on 0207 837 4334.
TRAIN SERVICE UPDATE	For live travel updates contact National Rail Enquiries on 08457 48 49 50, visit www.nationalrail.co.uk or call Train Tracker on 0871 200 4950. You can also text your station to 8 49 50 for live departures. Details of weekend engineering work will be available on our website www.grandcentralrail.com or by calling 0845 603 4852.
PENALTY FARES	Grand Central does not operate a penalty fares system. Passengers can purchase tickets on the train at the same price as if purchased in advance or at stations.
DISABLED PERSON'S PROTECTION POLICY	Assisted travel can be booked by calling 0844 811 0071 (0800-2200 7 days a week) or using our text phone service on 0845 305 6815 please call at least 48 hours in advance. Our full Disabled Person's Protection Policy is available on our website, by calling 0845 603 4852 or by writing to us at the address above. Copies are also available at staffed stations on our route.
CODE OF PRACTICE FOR COMMENTS, COMPLAINTS AND SUGGESTIONS	Copies of our Passenger's Charter and comments forms are available from the above address or on our website. Customer Services can be contacted on 0845 603 4852 (Mon-Fri 0900-1700). Copies of comments forms available at staffed stations on our route and from any member of Grand Central staff.

Heathrow Connect

A joint venture between First Rail Division and BAA (Heathrow Express)

ADDRESS	Freepost RLRZ-TZXE-BYKY Heathrow Connect 6th Floor, 50 Eastbourne Terrace London W2 6LG Telephone: 0845 678 6975 Fax: 020 8750 6615 Website: www.heathrowconnect.com Email: web_customer_correspondence@baa.com
MANAGING DIRECTORS	*Heathrow Connect is a joint venture between First Great Western and BAA (Heathrow Express).* Mark Hopwood (First Great Western) Richard Robinson (Heathrow Express)
RESERVATIONS AND TICKETS BY TELEPHONE AND ONLINE	Reservations are not necessary. Tickets can be booked by telephone on 0845 700 0125. Open 0700-2200 (0800-1900 Saturdays and Sundays). Allow 3 working days for delivery. A next day delivery can be arranged at £5 per transaction. Tickets may also be purchased through our website www.heathrowconnect.com
RESERVATION DETAILS	Reservations are not available.
CATERING ON TRAINS	Catering on trains is not available.
CYCLES	Cycles are carried free of charge, but are not allowed on trains timed to arrive at London Paddington between 0745-0945, or depart London Paddington between 1630-1830 Mondays to Fridays. In the interest of safety and customer comfort, we reserve the right to limit the number of cycles at other times.
LOST PROPERTY	For property lost on a Heathrow Connect train or at London Paddington, call the Lost Property Office at Paddington on 0207 313 1514. For property left at Heathrow call the BAA Lost Property Office at Heathrow Central Station on 0208 745 7727. For property left at one of the intermediate stations contact the FGW Lost Property helpline on 0845 602 4304.
TRAIN SERVICE UPDATE	For current train information call 0845 678 6975. Website: www.heathrowconnect.com
PENALTY FARES	Penalty Fares apply at stations between Hayes & Harlington and Paddington (incl). Customers are liable to a Penalty Fare of £20 to the next station stop.
DISABLED PERSON'S PROTECTION POLICY	This is available from Customer Relations at the above address and telephone number.
CODE OF PRACTICE FOR COMMENTS, COMPLAINTS AND SUGGESTIONS	This is available from Customer Relations at the above address and telephone number.

Heathrow Express

HX

ADDRESS

Freepost RLXY-ETJG-XKZS
Heathrow Express,
6th Floor, 50 Eastbourne Terrace,
London W2 6LG
Telephone: 0845 600 1515
(call centre)
Fax: 020 8750 6615
Website: www.heathrowexpress.com
Email: web_customer_correspondence@baa.com

MANAGING DIRECTOR

Richard Robinson

RESERVATIONS AND TICKETS BY TELEPHONE AND ONLINE

Reservations are not necessary on Heathrow Express services. Tickets may be purchased online and from www.heathrowexpress.com as well as our ticket offices at Heathrow Airport, Paddington station and travel other appointed outlets. For details call our Customer Services team on 0845 600 1515 (24 hour service - local rate call) or visit www.heathrowexpress.com.

RESERVATION DETAILS

Reservations are not available.

CATERING ON TRAINS

As the overall journey time is only 15 minutes, or 21 minutes to Terminal 5, there is currently no catering on Heathrow Express services.

CYCLES

Limited accommodation is available for cycles on Heathrow Express services, for passengers flying with their cycles from the airport. Heathrow Express reserve the right to limit the number of cycles conveyed on each train to no more than three at busy times. Cyclists not travelling onwards by air may use the service to and from Heathrow Terminals, subject to space being available for airline passengers.

LOST PROPERTY

Property lost at Paddington station is collected by Network Rail, who can be contacted on 020 7313 1514. For items lost at Heathrow Airport call 020 8745 7727. For items lost on Heathrow Express trains, please ask our Customer Service Representatives, or alternatively write to: Excess Baggage Co., Heathrow Airport, Middlesex UB3 5AP or Email to heathrow.lostproperty@excess-baggage.com.

TRAIN SERVICE UPDATE

For current information on train services please contact our customer care line on 0845 600 15 15, or through our website www.heathrowexpress.com.

PENALTY FARES

Penalty Fares do not apply on Heathrow Express services, therefore customers may join the train without having first purchased a ticket or authority to travel. Customer Service Representatives on every train will accept cash, debit and credit cards, for ticket purchase. Please note however for tickets purchased on board there is a £5.00 premium to pay. Only full fare tickets are available to purchase on board the train. (However Disabled Railcard is accepted on board).

DISABLED PERSON'S PROTECTION POLICY

Heathrow Express trains have been specially designed with the needs of the disabled in mind. Platforms at all our stations give level access into the trains and there is space for wheelchairs on all trains.

For further information on facilities for the disabled, call the Customer Care Line on 0845 600 15 15, or write to the Managing Director at the address at the top of this page.

CODE OF PRACTICE FOR COMMENTS, COMPLAINTS AND SUGGESTIONS

It is our aim to try and resolve any issues or grievances on the spot. All our Customer Service Representatives have a supply of comment forms and our Customer Care Line on 0845 600 15 15 can deal with any issues over the telephone or submit any comments at queries.hex@airexp.co.uk. If you wish to write with a suggestion or complaint, please write to the Managing Director at the address at the top of this page, or through our website www.heathrowexpress.com.

Island Line

ADDRESS	Friars Bridge Court, 41–45 Blackfriars Road, London SE1 8NZ Telephone: 08700 005151 Fax: 020 7620 5177 Website: www.southwesttrains.co.uk Email: customerrelations@swtrains.co.uk
MANAGING DIRECTOR	Andy Pitt
RESERVATIONS AND TICKETS BY TELEPHONE AND ONLINE	Reservations are not required on Island Line Trains services. Group travel information can be obtained by calling 023 8072 8162.
RESERVATION DETAILS	Reservations are not available.
CATERING ON TRAINS	There are no catering facilities on trains.
CYCLES	A maximum of 4 cycles may be carried in the Shanklin end of all trains at no extra charge. For the safety and comfort of our passengers, the guard may refuse to carry any further cycles on the train.
LOST PROPERTY	All items of lost property are retained at Ryde Esplanade Ticket Office. If you have lost an item please telephone the Ticket Office on 01983 562492 (0900-1700 Daily). A charge may be applicable on collection.
TRAIN SERVICE UPDATE	For current train information, please call our helpline on 0845 6000 650 or visit www.island-line.com.
PENALTY FARES	Penalty Fares are not in force on any Island Line Trains services.
DISABLED PERSON'S PROTECTION POLICY	Island Line Trains is committed to making travel easier for customers with disabilities including wheelchair users. For travel on the mainland, please call our Assisted Travel line on 0800 5282 100 (textphone 0800 692 0792), giving 24 hours notice before travelling. For journeys wholly within Island Line Trains, please telephone 01983 812591 giving 24 hours notice if assistance is required.
CODE OF PRACTICE FOR COMMENTS, COMPLAINTS AND SUGGESTIONS	Feedback leaflets are available at Ryde Esplanade or Shanklin Ticket Offices. Copies of Island Line Trains' and South West Trains' Passenger's Charters are available from any staffed station or by writing to: Customer Service Centre, South West Trains, Overline House, Southampton SO15 1GW Telephone 0845 6000 650. Fax 023 8072 8187 Email: customerrelations@swtrains.co.uk The Passenger's Charter is also featured on the website www.island-line.com and www.southwesttrains.co.uk.

London Midland

LM

ADDRESS
PO Box 4323
Birmingham B2 4JB
Telephone: 0844 811 0133
Website: www.londonmidland.com
Email: comments@londonmidland.com

MANAGING DIRECTOR
Mike Hodson

RESERVATIONS AND TICKETS BY TELEPHONE AND ONLINE
Tickets can be booked in advance on-line at www.londonmidland.com or by ringing 0844 811 0133, 0800-2000 Monday to Sunday, please allow 5 days for delivery.

RESERVATION DETAILS
Reservations are not available. Group travel enquiries and bookings can also be made on 0844 811 0133.

CATERING ON TRAINS
A trolley service of drinks and light refreshments is available on a number of our Birmingham–Liverpool and Crewe–London trains, as indicated by a trolley symbol in the timetable pages.

CYCLES
Cycles are carried free of charge on most off-peak services, however, advance reservations are required for our Birmingham–Liverpool and Crewe–London services. Cycles cannot be conveyed on trains arriving into London Euston between 0700 and 0959 and departing London Euston between 1600 and 1859 on Mondays to Fridays (excluding Bank Holidays). Folding cycles, completely folded down, are regarded as accompanied luggage and carried free.

LOST PROPERTY
Enquiries can be made at your nearest staffed station or by ringing Customer Relations on 0844 811 0133.

TRAIN SERVICE UPDATE
Available from National Rail Enquiries on 08457 48 49 50 (calls may be recorded for training purposes).

PENALTY FARES
A Penalty Fares system is in place across most of the London Midland network. If you board a service from a staffed station without a valid ticket or permit to travel, you will be liable to a £20 penalty fare or twice the standard single fare to the next station whichever is the greater. You can only purchase a ticket on-train when travelling from an unstaffed station. Details of the scheme are available at www.londonmidland.com or by writing to Customer Relations at the address below.

DISABLED PERSON'S PROTECTION POLICY
Available from Customer Relations,
London Midland
PO Box 4323
Birmingham B2 4JB
Telephone: 0844 811 0133

CODE OF PRACTICE FOR COMMENTS, COMPLAINTS AND SUGGESTIONS
Available from Customer Relations at the above address.

London Overground

Operated by London Overground Rail Operations Ltd. (LOROL)
on behalf of Rail for London Ltd., a subsidiary of TfL

ADDRESS	125 Finchley Road London NW3 6HY Telephone: 0845 601 4867 Website: www.tfl.gov/overground Email: overgroundinfo@tfl.gov.uk
MANAGING DIRECTOR	Steve Murphy
RESERVATIONS AND TICKETS BY TELEPHONE AND ONLINE	Tickets may be booked in advance and seats reserved on many long distance national rail services from most London Overground ticket offices. Oyster tickets may be purchased online from https://oyster.tfl.gov.uk
RESERVATION DETAILS	Reservations are not available.
CATERING ON TRAINS	Catering is not provided on London Overground services.
CYCLES	London Overground allows cycles on its trains and conveys them free of charge provided it is safe to do so. Due to space constraints, cycles are not permitted on services between Willesden Junction High Level and Gospel Oak and between Gospel Oak and Blackhorse Road in either direction between 0800–1000 and 1630–1830. On the Euston to Watford Junction Line cycles are not permitted on London Overground services timed to arrive at London Euston between 0700–1000 or depart London Euston between 1630 and 1900. These restrictions apply on Mondays to Fridays only. There are no restrictions on Saturdays, Sundays and Bank Holidays. Folding bicycles can be carried on any London Overground Service at any time. Only one cycle is allowed per customer and this must be folded and within a limit of one cycle per vestibule area. Tandems and three-wheeled vehicles cannot be accommodated on any London Overground service. Cycles are not carried on buses that replace trains due to engineering work.
LOST PROPERTY	Please contact the TfL Lost Property Office at Baker Street on 0845 330 9882 or our Customer Services Team on 0845 601 4867.
TRAIN SERVICE UPDATE	Information about London Overground services and fares can be obtained by telephoning either: • London Travel Information on 020 7222 1234 (Textphone 020 7918 3015) • National Rail Enquiries 08457 48 49 50 (calls may be recorded for training purposes). (Textphone 08456 050 600, 0800-2000 daily) A wide range of information about London Overground is also available from our website: www.tfl.gov/overground
PENALTY FARES	London Overground operates a Penalty Fares scheme. If you cannot produce, on request, a valid ticket for your entire journey or, when using Oyster to Pay as You Go, your Oyster card containing a record of the start of your Pay as You Go journey, you will be liable to pay a Penalty Fare.
DISABLED PERSON'S PROTECTION POLICY	This can be obtained at any London Overground Station or from our Customer Services Team at the above address.
CODE OF PRACTICE FOR COMMENTS, COMPLAINTS AND SUGGESTIONS	For a copy of the London Overground Customer Charter leaflet please ask at any London Overground Station or contact our Customer Services Team at the above address.

Merseyrail

A Serco/Abellio company

ADDRESS	Rail House, Lord Nelson Street, Liverpool L1 1JF Telephone: 0151 702 2534 Fax: 0151 702 3074
MANAGING DIRECTOR	Bart Schmeink
RESERVATIONS AND TICKETS BY TELEPHONE AND ONLINE	Tickets may be booked in advance and seats reserved from most Merseyrail stations for National Rail Services.
RESERVATION DETAILS	Reservations are not available.
CATERING ON TRAINS	Catering is not available.
CYCLES	Cycles carried free of charge at any time, subject to sufficient space being available.
LOST PROPERTY	Please contact:- Station Supervisor James Street Station James Street Liverpool L2 7PQ Phone: 0151 702 2951
TRAIN SERVICE UPDATE	For current train information please call 08457 48 49 50 (calls may be recorded for training purposes). ***For details of Bank Holiday services see also the boxed note immediately preceding Table 103.***
PENALTY FARES	Please refer to notices displayed at stations for details of the penalty fare scheme in operation.
DISABLED PERSON'S PROTECTION POLICY	Available from:– Customer Relations Merseyrail Rail House, Lord Nelson Street, Liverpool L1 1JF Phone : 0151 702 2071 (Textphone 0870 0552 681) Fax : 0151 702 2413
CODE OF PRACTICE FOR COMMENTS, COMPLAINTS AND SUGGESTIONS	Available from above address

National Express East Anglia (NXEA)

LE

ADDRESS

Customer Relations, National Express East Anglia, Norwich station,
Station Approach, Norwich, NR1 1EF
Telephone: 0845 600 7245
Fax: 01603 214567
Website: www.nationalexpresseastanglia.com
Email: nxea.customerrelations@nationalexpress.com

MANAGING DIRECTOR

Andrew Chivers

RESERVATIONS AND TICKETS BY TELEPHONE AND ONLINE

Tickets may be booked in advance by telephoning 0845 600 7245 between 0800 and 2200 (Mondays to Fridays) and 0900 and 1800 (weekends and Bank Holidays). For Business Travel, please telephone 0845 850 9080

RESERVATION DETAILS

NXEA offers seat reservations on services between London Liverpool Street and Norwich, Lowestoft & Peterborough (via Ipswich) at a charge of £2.50 per seat (£1 for season ticket holders).

CATERING ON TRAINS

Hot and cold drinks, sandwiches and light snacks are generally available on main line services between Norwich and London Liverpool Street and on Stansted Express services.

CYCLES

Accompanied bicycles are conveyed free of charge on most NXEA services, but are not permitted on Stansted Express services at any time or on weekday peak services to and from London. A similar restriction also applies at Cambridge. On main line and rural services, the number of bicycles per train is limited, so a free reservation is recommended. For further details, please call NXEA customer services on 0845 600 7245.

LOST PROPERTY

If you have lost an item of property on one of our trains or stations, please contact NXEA customer services on 0845 600 7245 or email us at nxea.lostproperty@nationalexpress.com

TRAIN SERVICE UPDATE

For current train service information, please contact NXEA customer services on 0845 600 7245 or call our recorded information line on 020 7247 5488.

PENALTY FARES

NXEA operates a Penalty Fares System on most of its network, except on designated 'paytrain' routes and from certain specified stations without ticket issuing facilities. Stations within the Penalty Fares area are identified by warning notices at each entrance. When travelling from these stations, you must have a valid ticket for your journey. For journeys where Oyster Pay as you Go (PAYG) is accepted, you must hold a valid Oyster card which has been touched in at the start of your journey.Oyster PAYG is not valid for travel outside the area where PAYG is accepted. If you cannot present a valid ticket for the journey you are making, you may be liable for a Penalty Fare (minimum £20).

DISABLED PERSON'S PROTECTION POLICY

Available from: Customer Relations, National Express East Anglia, Norwich Station, Station Approach, Norwich NR1 1EF.
Customers who require assistance are recommended to book at least 24 hours in advance on 0800 028 28 78 or Textphone 0845 606 7245.

CODE OF PRACTICE FOR COMMENTS, COMPLAINTS AND SUGGESTIONS

Available from: Customer Relations, National Express East Anglia, Norwich Station, Station Approach, Norwich NR1 1EF.
The NXEA Passenger's Charter is also available from the same address.

North Yorkshire Moors Railway

NY

(Operators of the steam and heritage services between Whitby, Grosmont, Goathland and Pickering)

ADDRESS

Pickering Station, Pickering, North Yorkshire, YO18 7AJ
Telephone: 01751-472508 (Customer Services and Information)
Fax: 01751-476048
Website: www.nymr.co.uk
Email: info@nymr.co.uk

GENERAL MANAGER

Philip Benham

RESERVATIONS AND TICKETS BY TELEPHONE AND ONLINE

Telephone: 01751-472508
Hours of operation: 27 March to 31 October and other operating dates: 09:30-16:30 (Monday - Friday), 10:00-14:30 (Saturday and Sunday); All other times: 10:00-14:30 (Monday - Friday).

At least 7 days should be allowed for receipt of tickets purchased by telephone. National Rail tickets can be booked in advance from our office in Whitby – telephone 01947 605872.

RESERVATION DETAILS

Reservations are not available on normal services. They can be made for groups of 20 or more passengers and are required on North Yorkshire Moors Railways dining train services (between Pickering and Grosmont).

CATERING ON TRAINS

An at seat trolley service of drinks and snacks is provided on most trains.

CYCLES

Cycles and dogs are carried for a charge of £2 (subject to space being available).

LOST PROPERTY

Enquiries about lost property should be made to Pickering Station at the above, or by telephone (01751-472508).

TRAIN SERVICE UPDATE

Updated train service information on all North Yorkshire Moors Railway is available on the website (see address above). A 'talking timetable' is also available giving current details of all North Yorkshire Moors Railway services by telephoning 01751-473535.

PENALTY FARES

Penalty fares are not in force on any North Yorkshire Moors Railway service.

DISABLED PERSON'S PROTECTION POLICY

Available from the address above, or Pickering and Grosmont Stations.

CODE OF PRACTICE FOR COMMENTS, COMPLAINTS AND SUGGESTIONS

North Yorkshire Moors Railway welcomes comments from passengers. Comments/suggestion cards are available from stations and on-board staff, or alternatively please write to the General Manager. Details of the company's policy are available from the above address, or Pickering and Grosmont Stations.

NT **Northern** NT

Northern

A joint venture between Serco and Abellio (formerly NedRailways)

ADDRESS

Northern Rail Ltd.,
Northern House
9 Rougier Street
York
YO1 6HZ
Telephone: 08700 005151
Website: www.northernrail.org

MANAGING DIRECTOR

Ian Bevan (Interim)

RESERVATIONS AND TICKETS BY TELEPHONE AND ONLINE

Reservations and tickets are available from all local staffed stations.

RESERVATION DETAILS

Reservations are not available.

For groups of 10 or more travelling together, telephone 01132 479 659.

For groups of 10 or more travelling on the Leeds-Settle-Carlisle line, blocks of seats will be reserved wherever possible. Telephone 0800 9800 766, between 0900 and 1700 on Mondays to Fridays to make a booking.

All accommodation on Northern trains is standard class.

CATERING ON TRAINS

On most Leeds-Settle-Carlisle services, food and drink can be purchased from the trolley which will pass through the train.

CYCLES

Up to two cycles can be carried on each service. This is subject to space being available, however, and cannot be booked in advance. For further details telephone 0845 000 0125.

LOST PROPERTY

Call 0870 602 3322, contact your nearest staffed station or write to Northern at the address below.

TRAIN SERVICE UPDATE

Information about Northern services and fares can be obtained by telephoning: **08457 48 49 50** (calls may be recorded for training purposes) or access the website on www.nationalrail.co.uk.

For more information on our services, please visit our website on www.northernrail.org

The latest information on train running is available by phoning TrainTracker™ from National Rail Enquiries on 0871 200 4915 or by texting TrainTracker™. Text to 84950.

PENALTY FARES

Penalty fares are not in force on any Northern service.

DISABLED PERSON'S PROTECTION POLICY

If you would like a copy of Northern's Policy or wish to arrange assistance for your journey, please phone: 0808 1561606. (Textphone 0845 604 5608) or by writing to Customer Relations, Northern, Freepost (RLSL-ABEC-BGUU), Leeds LS1 4DY, or email: assistance@northernrail.org.

CODE OF PRACTICE FOR COMMENTS, COMPLAINTS AND SUGGESTIONS

Please contact our Customer Helpline on 0845 000 0125, a textphone is available on 0845 604 5608. Alternatively you can write to us at: Customer Relations, Northern, Freepost (RLSL-ABEC-BGUU), Leeds LS1 4DY.

If you would like a copy of the Northern Passenger's Charter, or Northern's Guide for Customers with Disabilities please contact our Customer Relations team.

SR ScotRail SR

A member of the First Rail Division

ADDRESS

1st Floor, Atrium Court, 50 Waterloo Street, Glasgow G2 6HQ
Telephone: 08700 00 51 51
Fax: 0141 335 4592
Website: www.scotrail.co.uk
Email: scotrailcustomer.relations@firstgroup.com

MANAGING DIRECTOR

Steve Montgomery

RESERVATIONS AND TICKETS BY TELEPHONE AND ONLINE

Tickets may be purchased in advance and Sleepers or seats reserved, by telephone, using a debit/credit card from the following number:
08457 550033 (opening hours 0700-2200)

Please allow 3 days for tickets by post, tickets on departure arrangements available at selected stations. Tickets can also be purchased through the website - scotrail.co.uk

ScotRail customers can buy selected Caledonian Sleeper tickets online - and have the ticket confirmation sent to their mobile phone. Passengers simply turn up for their train, show the text message to train staff and hop on board. A confirmatory email is sent as a back-up. This free SMS service is available for 'Bargain Berth' tickets on the Caledonian Sleeper, which connects Scottish cities to Central London. Tickets can be booked up to 12 weeks in advance of travel - and right up until midday on the day of travel, subject to availability. The berths start from just £19.

RESERVATION DETAILS

Seat Reservations are free and can be made from 12 weeks in advance up to approximately two hours prior to the departure of the train.

CATERING ON TRAINS

A Lounge Car is provided on all Caledonian Sleeper services offering a wide range of drinks, snacks and hot meals. A trolley service is available on many longer distance services as indicated in the timetable. Any comments about our daytime catering services should be made to Garry Clark, Hospitality and Sleeper Manager tel: 0141 335 2685.

CYCLES

Cycles are carried free on all ScotRail services subject to availability. Reservations are required on Caledonian Sleeper services and on longer distance routes. Tandems, tricycles, cycle trailers, motorcycles, mopeds or motorised cycles are not carried on any ScotRail service.

LOST PROPERTY

Please phone 0141 335 3276 (0700-1900 Mon-Sat)

TRAIN SERVICE UPDATE

Register with JourneyCheck/JourneyAlert on our website: www.scotrail.co.uk

PENALTY FARES

Penalty Fares are not in force on any ScotRail services.

DISABLED PERSON'S PROTECTION POLICY

Available from the ScotRail Customer Relations, PO Box 7031, Fort William PH33 6WW. Tel: 0800 912 2 901 or Typetalk 18001 0800 912 2 901 Fax: 0141 335 4611

Travel arrangements may be made for disabled people by calling 0800 912 2 901*. A light travel scooter, length 104cm, width 56cm with a turning radius of 99cm and combined weight of 300kg can be conveyed. Customers who are unable to hear or speak on the phone can contact us through the BT TextDirect system, Typetalk on 18001 0800 912 2 901. This advanced technology provides a text-to-voice translation at no additional cost to your phone providers standard rate. Details of station facilities and information on accessibility are available at www.nationalrail.co.uk or www.scotrail.co.uk.

*For assisted travel, an advance notice of up to 24 hours notice is appreciated.

CODE OF PRACTICE FOR COMMENTS, COMPLAINTS AND SUGGESTIONS

ScotRail welcomes comments on the services we provide. A leaflet is available at all staffed ScotRail stations explaining the procedures and is also available from the Customer Relations Manager at the address above.
Tel: 0845 601 5929

South West Trains

SW

ADDRESS

Friars Bridge Court, 41–45 Blackfriars Road, London SE1 8NZ
Telephone: 08700 005151 Fax: 020 7620 5177
Website: www.southwesttrains.co.uk
Email: customerrelations@swtrains.co.uk

MANAGING DIRECTOR

Andy Pitt

RESERVATIONS AND TICKETS BY TELEPHONE AND ONLINE

Tickets may be booked in advance by telephone, on the following number: 0845 6000 650.

Tickets may also be purchased via the South West Trains' website (see above). When ordering, please allow 5 working days for ticket delivery.

RESERVATION DETAILS

Reservations are not available.

CATERING ON TRAINS

Catering on South West Trains is provided on those services marked with the symbol ☕ for all or part of the journey. Catering may be provided from a buffet area, at seat trolley service or a combination of both according to the route and time of day. Comments on the service should be sent to the Customer Service Centre at the address below.

CYCLES

A limited number of cycles can be carried on most of our services except during the Monday to Friday peak periods. Restrictions apply on certain routes into and out of London Waterloo between 0715 and 1000 and between 1645 and 1900. At all times some services require advance reservations, as space is limited.

To obtain full details of South West Trains Cycling Policy and full details of routes and times when cycles are not carried visit www.southwesttrains.co.uk, pick up a leaflet from stations served by South West Trains or contact our Customer Service Centre at the address shown.

Cycles that can be folded to a size which allows them to be carried safely in the luggage racks on our services may be carried folded at all times.

For reasons of safety and comfort of our passengers, if the available identified cycle spaces on the train are already taken, the guard has the right to refuse to carry any further cycles on that train.

LOST PROPERTY

A lost property helpline is available between 0730-1900 Mondays to Fridays by calling 020 7401 7861

TRAIN SERVICE UPDATE

For current train information, please call our helpline on 0845 6000 650 or visit www.southwesttrains.co.uk

PENALTY FARES

South West Trains has a duty to its fare paying passengers to ensure no-one travels for free. To this end South West Trains operates a penalty fares scheme across its network, with the only exceptions being Dean, Mottisfont & Dunbridge and Romsey and Chandlers Ford.

Passengers travelling to and from stations within the penalty fares area without a valid ticket may be liable to a penalty of £20 or twice the single fare to the next station at which their train stops (whichever is the greater).

DISABLED PERSON'S PROTECTION POLICY

For a copy of this publication, please contact the Customer Service Centre at the address below.

Assistance for mobility impaired passengers can be arranged by telephoning 0800 5282 100 between 0600 - 2200 daily. Please give at least 24 hours notice.

A textphone facility is available on 0800 6920 792 (calls are charged at local rates).

CODE OF PRACTICE FOR COMMENTS, COMPLAINTS AND SUGGESTIONS

Copies of South West Trains' Passenger's Charter are available from any staffed station or by writing to:
Customer Service Centre, South West Trains, Overline House, Blechynden Terrace, Southampton SO15 1GW
Telephone 0845 6000 650. Fax 023 8072 8187
Email: customerrelations@swtrains.co.uk

The Passenger's Charter is also available on our website www.southwesttrains.co.uk

Southeastern

SE

ADDRESS

Southeastern Customer Services, PO Box 63428, London SE1P 5FD
Telephone: 0845 000 2222
Assisted Travel: 0800 783 4524 (Textphone 0800 783 4548)
Fax: 0845 678 6976
Textphone: 0800 783 4548

Website: southeasternrailway.co.uk

Southeastern Customer Services is staffed 24 hours a day, seven days a week (closed Christmas Day). Comments and complaints are dealt with here by post, fax, and web as well as on the telephone.

MANAGING DIRECTOR

Charles Horton

RESERVATIONS AND TICKETS BY TELEPHONE AND ONLINE

Group travel (parties of 10 persons or more) on Southeastern services must be booked at least seven days in advance so that space can be allocated. To order, go to www.southeasternrailway.co.uk, select tickets, then group tickets then complete the online form.

Customers can renew their Season Tickets for one month or longer by completing the Season Ticket application form at their local ticket office or online at southeasternrailway.co.uk (photocard required). Payment may be made by debit card and by most major credit and charge cards.

For new monthly season ticket purchases, please complete an application form available at local stations or online at southeasternrailway.co.uk.

Southeastern's Network Business Travel Service (NBTS) at London Wall provides a comprehensive season ticket and rail travel service dedicated to the corporate traveller. Tickets can be issued and delivered to your office, beating the queues at stations. NBTS also welcome employers who operate season ticket loan schemes for employees. Customers can discuss the benefits of this free service in one of the following ways:-

Phone: 020 7904 0500

e-mail: nbts.sales@southeasternrailway.co.uk

website: southeasternrailway.co.uk/nbts

RESERVATIONS

Reservations are not available. Reservations are only needed on Southeastern services for Group Travel and mobility impaired customers who require assistance.

CATERING ON TRAINS

A light refreshment trolley is available on trains marked with ᴨ in the timetable.

CYCLES

Cycles are not permitted on peak time services, which are those timed to arrive in London terminals between 0700 and 0959, and those timed to leave between 1600 and 1859. Folding cycles are permitted provided they are folded.

LOST PROPERTY

Customers who have lost property on a train or at a station should contact Southeastern Customer Services on 0845 000 2222.

TRAIN SERVICE UPDATE

For current train running information contact Southeastern Customer Services on 0845 000 2222

Information is also available from national and local radio station travel updates on Ceefax page 433, and from our website: southeasternrailway.co.uk, select plan my journey.

PENALTY FARES

Please check notices displayed at stations for details of any penalty fares or other revenue protection systems in operation on Southeastern services.

DISABLED PERSON'S PROTECTION POLICY

Copies of the Disabled Person's Protection Policy are available from Southeastern Customer Services.
If you have any special needs and would like help with planning your journey anywhere in Great Britain please call 0800 783 4524 or use the Textphone 0800 783 4548 - open 24 hours a day.

The Southeastern Assisted Travel team will offer advice and make any special arrangements you need. If at least 24 hours' notice can be given, this will be very much appreciated.

CODE OF PRACTICE FOR COMMENTS, COMPLAINTS AND SUGGESTIONS

Southeastern Passengers' Charter leaflets are available at any Southeastern sales point or Southeastern Customer Services at the address shown above.

Southern

SN

ADDRESS	Southern Customer Services, PO Box 277, Tonbridge TN9 2ZP Telephone: 08451 27 29 20 (Customer Services) Fax: 08451 27 29 30 (Customer Services) Website: www.southernrailway.com
MANAGING DIRECTOR	Chris Burchell
RESERVATIONS AND TICKETS BY TELEPHONE AND ONLINE	Discounted Advance Tickets are available from the Southern website.
RESERVATION DETAILS	Reservations are only required for Advance tickets. These reservations authorise the holder to travel on the specified train but do not identify individual seats.
CATERING ON TRAINS	A light refreshment of food and drinks is available on trains marked with ☕ in the timetable.
CYCLES	Standard size folding cycles are welcome on all Southern trains (as long as they are folded) Non-folding cycles are not permitted on Monday – Friday trains scheduled to arrive between 0700 and 1000 to, or depart between 1600 and 1900 from London Bridge, London Victoria, Kensington Olympia or Brighton.
LOST PROPERTY	Please call Southern Customer Services on 08451 27 29 20.
TRAIN SERVICE UPDATE	For current train information call Customer Services on 08451 27 29 20 or check our website at www.southernrailway.com
PENALTY FARES	Southern operate a Penalty Fares Scheme on all routes. You must buy a valid ticket (or permit to travel) for your journey before boarding a train. If you do not have a valid ticket or permit to travel, you may have to pay a Penalty Fare of £20.00 or twice the single fare, whichever is the greater. Please pick up a Penalty Fare leaflet from a staffed station for your information.
DISABLED PERSON'S PROTECTION POLICY	Available from Southern Customer Services at P.O. Box 277, Tonbridge TN9 2ZP. Disabled and Special needs assistance on 0800 138 1016; minicom/textphone - 0800 138 1018; Fax - 0800 138 1017.
CODE OF PRACTICE FOR COMMENTS, COMPLAINTS AND SUGGESTIONS	Write to Southern Customer Services at the above address. Copies of Southern Passenger's charter are available from any staffed stations. You can also obtain a copy by contacting Customer Services or from Southern's website.

Virgin Trains

VT

The trading name of West Coast Trains Ltd

ADDRESS Virgin Trains, 85 Smallbrook Queensway, Birmingham B5 4HA
Telephone: 0845 000 8000 Textphone: 0121 654 7528
Website: www.virgintrains.com
Email: customer.relations@virgintrains.co.uk

CHIEF EXECUTIVE Tony Collins

MANAGING DIRECTOR Chris Gibb

RESERVATIONS AND TICKETS BY TELEPHONE AND ONLINE Buy tickets for Virgin Trains and any other train company in Great Britain on the internet at www.virgintrains.com or by calling 08457 222 333 - between 0800 and 2200 7 days a week.

If you have a disability or have specific needs and wish to arrange assistance on your journey call the Virgin Trains JourneyCare service on 08457 44 33 66 (Textphone 08457 44 33 67) between 0800 and 2200 every day except Christmas Day or Boxing Day.

RESERVATION DETAILS You are strongly advised to make a seat reservation in advance. Reservations can be made for the Quiet Zone carriage, where customers should refrain from using mobile phones or creating unnecessary noise. On routes to and from London, Standard Class Quiet Zone is in coach A and in coach H for First Class. On other routes, Quiet Zone is located in Standard Class, coach F. Seat reservations are free of charge.

CATERING ON TRAINS In First Class on a Pendolino from Monday to Friday customers can enjoy a selection of snacks throughout the day, including a cooked breakfast on many morning peak services. In addition, Fairtrade tea, Fairtrade coffee, soft drinks and alcoholic drinks (alcohol is not offered with breakfast services) are served at seat throughout the day. A complimentary newspaper is also available.

In First Class on Super Voyager from Monday to Friday customers can enjoy complimentary light refreshments, including Fairtrade tea, Fairtrade coffee, soft drinks and a newspaper with an at-seat service available, on most services.

In Standard, we have a wide range of snacks and sandwiches, Fairtrade teas, fresh ground Fairtrade coffee, soft and alcoholic drinks and a selection of non-food items available at our onboard shop. The shop is generally open throughout. Pendolinos offer an at-seat trolley service to standard customers on Mondays to Fridays. For more information about our onboard service pick up a copy of Travelling with Virgin Trains.

CYCLES Subject to availability of space cycles can be carried on all trains. Most trains can carry 3 cycles, and on journeys to and from London Euston, Pendolinos can carry tandems (however, tandems are not carried on Voyager services). An advance reservation is required for all journeys.

LOST PROPERTY Call Customer Relations on 0845 000 8000 – 0830 to 1800 Mondays to Fridays, 0900 to 1600 Saturdays, answerphone available at all other times.

TRAIN SERVICE UPDATE Details of any disruption to services or weekend engineering work are summarised on BBC Ceefax and on BBCi on digital TV. Details of Engineering work can also be found at www.virgintrains.com.

PENALTY FARES Penalty Fares are not applicable on any Virgin Trains service.

DISABLED PERSON'S PROTECTION POLICY Our Customer Relations Manager (at the address above) will be pleased to supply a free copy of the Disabled Person's Protection Policy. It can also be downloaded at www.virgintrains.com. For information on station accessibility and to arrange special help please contact Virgin Trains JourneyCare (details above).

CODE OF PRACTICE FOR COMMENTS, COMPLAINTS AND SUGGESTIONS We want you to tell us what you think of our service, good or bad.

A copy of our Code of Practice for handling comments, complaints and suggestions together with Virgin Trains Passenger's Charter is available free on request from our Customer Relations Manager at the above address.

WR West Coast Railway Company WR

(Operators of the 'Jacobite' and 'Cambrian' Steam Services)

ADDRESS	Jesson Way, Carnforth, Lancashire LA5 9UR Telephone: 01524 737751/737753 Fax: 01524 735518 Website: www.westcoastrailways.co.uk Email: jacobite@wcrc.co.uk
GENERAL MANAGER	Mrs Pat Marshall
COMMERCIAL MANAGER	James Shuttleworth
RESERVATIONS AND TICKETS BY TELEPHONE AND ONLINE	Advance bookings are recommended and can be made on line, at www.westcoastrailways.co.uk, by post (enclose SAE) to the Carnforth Office (address above) or by telephone, on 01524 737751/737753, during normal office hours. Credit cards accepted. Tickets can also be purchased from the WCR Guard/Train Manager, on the train, on the day of travel (subject to availablility).
RESERVATION DETAILS	Phone 01524 737751/737753
CATERING ON TRAINS	A buffet service, serving hot and cold drinks and cold snacks, is available on all trains.
CYCLES	Cycles carried free-of-charge, subject to space.
LOST PROPERTY	Telephone: 01524 737751/737753
PENALTY FARES	Penalty fares are not in force on any West Coast Railway Co. service.
TRAIN SERVICE UPDATE	For current train information please phone 08457 48 49 50 (calls may be recorded for training purposes).
DISABLED PERSON'S PROTECTION POLICY	Available from the above address.
CODE OF PRACTICE FOR COMMENTS, COMPLAINTS AND SUGGESTIONS	West Coast Railway Co. welcomes comments on services provided. Write to Carnforth office (address above).

Wrexham & Shropshire

WS

ADDRESS	The Pump House, Coton Hill, Shrewsbury SY1 2DP Telephone: 0845 260 5233 Website: www.wrexhamandshropshire.co.uk Email: info@wrexhamandshropshire.co.uk
MANAGING DIRECTOR	Andy Hamilton
RESERVATIONS AND TICKETS BY TELEPHONE AND ONLINE	Wrexham & Shropshire tickets can be bought in advance and seats reserved by calling 0845 260 5900.
RESERVATION DETAILS	All First and Standard Class seats are reservable at no charge.
CATERING ON TRAINS	Wrexham & Shropshire provides a comprehensive range of catering on all services, seven days a week.
CYCLES	Cycles are carried free of charge.
LOST PROPERTY	Please contact the above address, or call 0845 260 5200.
TRAIN SERVICE UPDATE	Available at www.wrexhamandshropshire.co.uk
PENALTY FARES	Wrexham & Shropshire does not operate a penalty fares policy.
DISABLED PERSON'S PROTECTION POLICY	Please call Customer Services on 0845 260 5200.
CODE OF PRACTICE FOR COMMENTS, COMPLAINTS AND SUGGESTIONS	Please call Customer Services on 0845 260 5200.

Network Rail

ADDRESS	King's Place, Yorkway, London N1 9AG Telephone: 020 7557 8000 Fax: 020 7557 9000 Website: www.networkrail.co.uk
CHIEF EXECUTIVE	Iain Coucher

Network Rail is responsible for operating 18 managed stations, indicated in the index by the code **NR**. Details of facilities provided, including the Disabled Peoples Protection Policy, are obtainable from the Network Rail Station Manager at the following station addresses:–

London Bridge	Network Rail Offices, Platform 14, London Bridge Station, Station Approach, London SE1 9SP.
London Cannon Street	Cannon Street Station, Cannon Street, London EC4N 6AP.
London Charing Cross	Network Rail Offices, Charing Cross Station, The Strand, London WC2 5HS.
London Euston	Room 430, Stephenson Room, East Colonnade, Euston, London NW1 2RT.
London Fenchurch Street	Network Rail Office, Fenchurch Place, London EC3M 4AJ.
London Kings Cross	Room 304, West Side Offices, Kings Cross Station, London N1 9AP.
London Liverpool Street	Network Rail Station Reception, Platform 10, Liverpool Street Station, London EC2M 7PY.
London Paddington	Room B115, Tournament House, Paddington Station, London W2 1FT.
London Victoria	3rd Floor, Kent Side Offices, Victoria Station, London SW1V 1JU.
London Waterloo	CP2-4-G General Offices, Waterloo Station, London SE1 8SW.
Birmingham New Street	Reception, Network Rail Offices, Station Forecourt, Birmingham New Street Station, Birmingham B2 4ND.
Edinburgh Waverley	Room 255, North Block, Waverley Station, Edinburgh EH1 1BB.
Gatwick Airport	Gatwick Airport Station, Gatwick Airport, Sussex RH6 0RD.
Glasgow Central	Glasgow Central Station, Gordon Street, Glasgow G1 3SL.
Leeds City	Room 405, Administration Block, Leeds City Station, Leeds LS1 4DY.
Manchester Piccadilly	9th Floor, Piccadilly Tower, Piccadilly Station, Manchester M60 7RA.
Liverpool Lime Street	Station Manager, The Barrier Line Building, Liverpool Lime Street Station, Liverpool L1 1JF.
St Pancras	Station Reception, St Pancras International Station, Pancras Road, London NW1 2QP.

Staffed Left Luggage facilities, offering maximum security, are available at all Network Rail Stations.

If you wish to raise any issue concerning the rail infrastructure or the 18 managed stations operated by Network Rail (excluding matters concerning the running of trains or ticket purchase) please call the national 24 hour Helpline:- **08457 11 41 41**

Other Addresses

Department for Transport

Great Minster House, 76 Marsham Street, London SW1P 4DR

Telephone: 0300 330 3000

Email: rail@dft.gsi.gov.uk

Office of Rail Regulation

One Kemble Street, London WC2B 4AN
Telephone: 020 7282 2000 Fax: 020 7282 2040

Chair of the Board: Anna Walker
Chief Executive: Bill Emery

The main areas of the Regulator's statutory functions are:

- the issue, modification and enforcement of licences to operate trains, networks, stations and light maintenance depots;
- the approval of agreements for access by operators of railway assets to track, stations and light maintenance depots;
- the enforcement of domestic competition law; and consumer protection including a duty under the Railways Act 1993 in relation to the protection of the interests of users of railway services, including the disabled.

Publications are available from:

Sue MacSwan, The Library, ORR, 1 Waterhouse Square, 138–142 Holborn, London EC1N 2TQ (Telephone: 020 7282 2001). Email: rail.library@orr.gsi.gov.uk

Association of Train Operating Companies (ATOC)

3rd Floor, 40 Bernard Street, London WC1N 1BY. Telephone: 020 7841 8000

Chief Executive: Michael Roberts

ATOC represents the interests of most of the national and international passenger Train Operating Companies whose services are shown in this timetable. It manages a range of network services, products and responsibilities on behalf of these train operators including:

- the National Rail Conditions of Carriage (the passenger's contract with the train operators)
- the National Rail Enquiry Service
- the licensing of rail appointed travel agents
- national Railcards, the London Travelcard and Network Railcard.

London Underground Limited

55 Broadway, London SW1H 0BD Telephone: 020 7222 5600

Responsible for the operation of stations indicated in the index by the code **LT**

How to Cross London

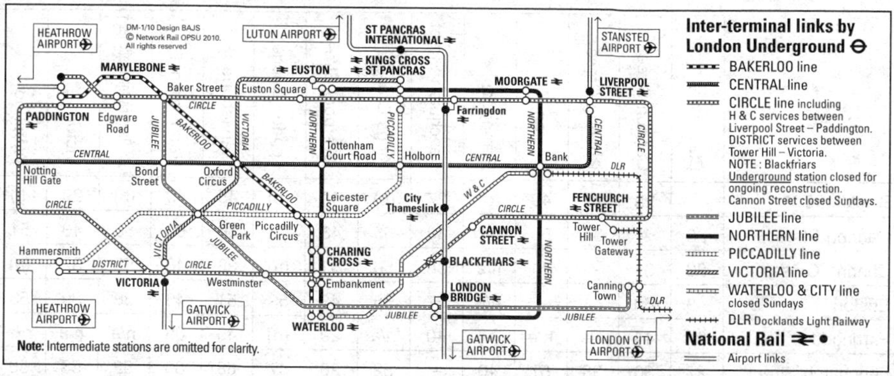

Introduction

The time taken to travel between London's stations will vary from journey to journey dependent on distance, mode of transport, time of day and the need to change en route. The quickest way to cross London is usually by the Underground network with frequent services operating between the following hours*:

- 0530 to 0015 on Monday to Friday
- 0630 to 0115 on Saturday
- 0700 to 0001 on Sunday

(* Times shown are approximate)

Buses also link many of London's main terminal stations including an extensive network of Night Bus services.

Ticket & Fares

Rail tickets for journeys routed via London are valid for transfer by London Underground or First Capital Connect services between London terminal stations, and other designated interchange stations* appropriate to the route of the through journey being made, at no extra cost. For example a Brighton to Leeds ticket is valid on London Underground services from Victoria to Kings Cross (Victoria Line), or alternatively on First Capital Connect services to St Pancras International. A Chelmsford to Southampton ticket is valid on London Underground services to Waterloo via either Liverpool Street (Circle Line) or Stratford (Jubilee Line).

(*NB. check which cross London routes your ticket is valid before you travel. A break of journey is permitted at an intermediate Underground station, but a further ticket must be purchased in order to continue the journey)

London's Fare Zones – National Rail, Underground and Docklands Light Railway (DLR) stations within the Greater London area are in one of nine Fare Zones. Single and return tickets are available for through journeys to and from all Underground and DLR stations with prices determined by the number of zones crossed or travelled through.

A range of day and longer period Travelcards are also available and provide unlimited travel on National Rail, London Underground, Docklands Light Railway and Croydon Tramlink services within the Fare Zones for which they are valid. All Travelcards, irrespective of the zones for which they are issued, can also be used on any London bus displaying this sign ⊖.

For information on ticket prices and availability contact your local staffed station, call National Rail Enquiries anytime on **08457 48 49 50*** (Textphone **0845 60 50 600**), or visit www.nationalrail.co.uk. * Calls may be recorded for training purposes.

More detailed information about London's Underground and Bus services, also Docklands Light Railway and Croydon Tramlink is available anytime from London Travel Information on **020 7222 1234** (textphone **020 7918 3015**) or visit **www.tfl.gov.uk**.

First Capital Connect and Southeastern

First Capital Connect operates fast, direct services from Bedford, Luton and St Albans via Central London to East Croydon, Gatwick Airport and Brighton and stopping trains between Luton, St Albans, North London, the City, Streatham, Wimbledon and Sutton. There are nine Central London First Capital Connect stations with Underground connections. First Capital Connect connects with East Midlands Trains at Luton, Luton Airport Parkway and Bedford – see Tables 52 and 53.

Southeastern, in partnership with First Capital Connect also operate trains between Kentish Town, the City and Sevenoaks and at peak times between Bedford, Luton, the City and various destinations in Kent.

London Overground

Trains run daily between Willesden Junction, Shepherd's Bush, Kensington (Olympia), West Brompton, Imperial Wharf and Clapham Junction on Mondays to Sundays – see Table 186.

Southern Services

Direct trains are provided between East Croydon, South London, Clapham Junction and stations to Watford Junction and Milton Keynes Central. These trains also stop at Imperial Wharf, West Brompton, Kensington (Olympia) and Shepherd's Bush.

These trains provide connections to most of the Southern network at Clapham Junction.

Passengers requiring step free interchange for Southern main line trains to Gatwick Airport and the Sussex Coast should change at East Croydon, and step free interchange for Southern Metro trains is usually available at Balham.

Interchange for the West Midlands and North West is available at either Watford Junction or Milton Keynes.

Cross London Transfer Times (in minutes)

	Blackfriars **	Cannon Street	Charing Cross	Euston	Farringdon	Fenchurch Street*	Kings Cross	Liverpool Street	London Bridge	Marylebone	Paddington	St. Pancras International †	Victoria	Waterloo
Blackfriars **	–	23	23	49	(b)	27	(b)	40	(b)	45	49	(b)	29	40
Cannon Street	23	–	34	60	44	30	55	43	(a)	56	60	58	40	51
Charing Cross	23	34	–	44	n/a	38	50	51	(a)	38	43	52	32	(a)
Euston	49	60	44	–	n/a	57	35	43	52	51	43	38	39	53
Farringdon	(b)	44	n/a	n/a	–	40	n/a	29	(b)	45	39	n/a	n/a	n/a
Fenchurch Street*	27	30	38	57	40	–	52	26	47	68	60	52	53	56
Kings Cross	(b)	55	50	35	n/a	52	–	41	50	50	45	30	41	55
Liverpool Street	40	43	51	43	29	26	41	–	49	56	55	41	57	62
London Bridge	(b)	(a)	(a)	52	(b)	47	50	49	–	58	62	60	n/a	(a)
Marylebone	45	56	38	51	45	68	50	56	58	–	32	53	43	47
Paddington	49	60	43	43	39	60	45	55	62	32	–	45	47	51
St. Pancras International †	(b)	58	52	38	n/a	52	30	41	60	53	45	–	41	61
Victoria	29	40	32	39	n/a	53	41	57	n/a	43	47	41	–	47
Waterloo	40	51	(a)	53	n/a	56	55	62	(a)	47	51	61	47	–

All times are based on use of London Underground services and are shown as a guide only – extra time should be allowed during the early morning/late evening and on Sundays.

* Tower Hill Underground station

† An additional 35 minutes should be allowed for Eurostar Connections

(a) Direct train services available (operated by Southeastern)

(b) Direct train services available (operated by First Capital Connect)

n/a Transfer not likely to be required as part of a through rail journey.

** Blackfriars Underground station is closed until 2011 to allow for major reconstruction work as part of the Thameslink improvement programme. During the period of closure, passengers are advised to use St Pancras, Farringdon or Elephant and Castle to connect with the Underground network. You should allow extra time for these connections.

Some other useful transfers

If your journey requires a transfer between any of the following pairs of stations, you should allow a margin of at least the number of minutes shown when planning connections. All transfers are assumed to be by foot unless otherwise stated.

Ash Vale – North Camp	19
Bicester North – Town	30
Burnley Central – Manchester Rd	25
Burscough Bridge – Junction	20
Canterbury East – West	25
Catford – Bridge	10
Clock House – Kent House	15
Dorchester South – West	15
Dorking – Deepdene	9
East Croydon – West Croydon	25
Edenbridge – Town	20
Enfield Chase – Town	29
Falkirk High – Grahamston	44
Farnborough Main – North	24
Forest Gate – Wanstead Park	13
Gainsborough Central – Lea Rd	33
Hackney Central – Downs	14
Harringay – Green Lanes	14
Heath High Level – Low Level	10
Hertford North – East	34
Maidstone Barracks – East	16
New Mills Central – Newtown	25
Penge East – West	19
Purley Oaks – Sanderstead	10
Seven Sisters – South Tottenham	14
Southend Central – Victoria	17
Upper Warlingham – Whyteleafe	10
Walthamstow Central – Queen's Rd	14
West Hampstead – Thameslink	11
Windsor & Eton Central – Riverside	14
Yeovil Junction – Pen Mill	60*

* There are no direct links by public transport between Yeovil Junction and Yeovil Pen Mill stations. Passengers are advised to seek alternative arrangements and should allow 60 minutes to make this connection.

Airport Links

Aberdeen Airport

Dyce station is situated close to Aberdeen Airport and is served by trains between Aberdeen and Inverness (see Table 240). A new shuttle bus service has been introduced between Dyce station and the airport - these run approx. 0645 and 1940 Monday to Friday. Taxis are also available. In addition, there are several through trains daily to and from Glasgow and Edinburgh (see Table 229). Journey time by taxi is approx. 20 minutes from Aberdeen station. For full bus timetable information call Traveline Scotland on **0871 200 22 33.**

Birmingham International Airport

Birmingham Airport is alongside Birmingham International station. The free Air-Rail Link transit system operates to the passenger terminals about every 2 minutes with a journey time of less than 2 minutes. Birmingham International station is served by direct trains from London Euston, Derby, Edinburgh, Glasgow, Manchester, Newcastle, Oxford, Sheffield, Southampton, York and other principal towns and cities. In addition a frequent service operates between Birmingham New Street and Birmingham International providing connections at Birmingham New Street to and from all parts of the country. (See Tables 65, 66, 68, 71, 74 and 116). Regular buses operated by Travel West Midlands (966) also run from Solihull station (see Tables 71 and 115) and through fares are available by purchasing a PlusBus ticket. The journey time is approximately 20 minutes and through ticketing is available. Solihull is served by Chiltern Railways services from London Marylebone, Gerrards Cross, Beaconsfield, High Wycombe, Princes Risborough, Haddenham & Thame Parkway, Bicester North, Banbury, Leamington Spa and Warwick and by London Midland local services.

Bristol International Airport

First runs a frequent coach service from directly outside Bristol Temple Meads station. It departs every 10 minutes Monday to Friday between 0600 and 1900, every 10 minutes on Saturdays between 0600 and 1500 and at a reduced frequency at other times. The journey time is approximately 25 minutes depending on traffic and further information is available from Traveline on **0871 200 22 33** or visit **www.traveline.info.**

Cardiff International Airport

The airport is served by a free bus link from Rhoose Cardiff International Rail Station to/from the airport operated by Veolia Transport Cymru. Full details of the timetable and further information can be obtained from Traveline on **0871 200 22 33** or visit **www.traveline.info.**

The airport is served by bus service X45 and is operated by Veolia Transport Cymru on Mon-Sat and First on Sundays. This operates on an hourly daytime frequency to/from Barry station, Monday to Saturday. Journey time is 7 minutes. Cardiff bus service (X91) runs every 2 hours during the day from Cardiff Central Bus Station (stop E1) direct to Cardiff International Airport. Services run every hour Monday to Saturday daytimes and every 2 hours on Sundays. Journey time is 30 minutes and through ticketing is available from any rail station.

Coventry Airport

Coventry Airport is accessible from Coventry rail station by a scheduled bus service (No. 737). A combined discounted bus and rail ticket can be purchased for travel to the airport.

For bus times call **0871 200 22 33** or visit **www.traveline.info.**

Durham Tees Valley Airport

Darlington Railway station is situated just 5 miles away. Passengers should use the Arriva service 12 between Darlington and the airport. Visit **www.durhamteesvalleyairport.com.**

East Midlands Airport

The most convenient way to get to East Midlands Airport is via East Midlands Parkway station, served by East Midlands Trains. Railink buses operates every 30 minutes from 0700 to 2330.

Other connections include:

To and from the North and West

If you're travelling via Sheffield, Leeds, Manchester, Birmingham and York, you can make a connection at Derby railway station using the Derby Airline Shuttle bus.

To and from the South

If you travel via Kettering, Luton and London for destinations in the south, you can make a connection at Loughborough railway station using the Loughborough Airline Shuttle bus.

To and from the East

If you're travelling to or from easterly destinations you can connect via Grantham, Lincoln, Newark, Peterborough and Mansfield to Nottingham railway station where you'll find the Nottingham Skylink bus.

For details of bus times call **Traveline on 0871 200 22 33**

Edinburgh Airport

A frequent bus service (No. 100) links Edinburgh Waverley and Haymarket stations with Edinburgh Airport. Journey time is approx. 25 minutes. Stagecoach operate a 747 service half hourly during the day, hourly evenings and Sundays between Inverkeithing and Edinburgh Airport. Through ticketing is available. For full bus timetable information call Traveline Scotland on **0871 200 22 33.**

Exeter International Airport

Stagecoach operates an hourly daytime service (56 Monday - Saturday, 379 Sundays) from Exeter St. Davids station forecourt direct to Exeter Airport. For more information call Traveline on **0871 200 22 33** or visit **www.traveline.info.**

Airport Links

Glasgow Airport

Regular direct bus services are available to and from Glasgow Airport from the city centre (Central/Queen Street), Paisley Gilmour Street and Partick stations from early morning to late evening daily. Through bus/rail tickets are available between any station and Glasgow Airport via the Paisley Gilmour Street bus link, city centre bus link and First Glasgow bus service via Partick.

For further information on these services please contact the Strathclyde Partnership for Transport Travel Centre at Glasgow Airport, on **0141 887 1111** or **0141 848 4330.**

For full bus timetable information call Traveline Scotland on **0871 200 22 33**.

Leeds Bradford International Airport

Leeds Bradford International Airport is located to the north of the cities of Bradford and Leeds, to the south of the spa town of Harrogate and to the west of the historic city of York. For more information on Leeds Bradford International Airport visit **www.lbia.co.uk**

From Leeds a direct bus service, MetroConnect 757, operates half hourly throughout the day Mondays to Saturdays (hourly early mornings, evenings and Sundays) every day from Stand S8 from outside Leeds Rail Station (Leeds Station Interchange). The journey time is approximately 40 minutes. Through ticketing is available.

From Bradford a half hourly direct bus service, MetroConnect 747, operates throughout the day Mondays to Saturdays (hourly evenings and Sundays) from Bradford Interchange and Forster Square rail stations. The journey time from Bradford is approximately 40 minutes. Through ticketing is available with a PlusBus ticket.

From Harrogate a direct bus service, Bus2Jet 767, operates daily from Harrogate, from Stand 11 in the Bus Station, to the airport. The journey time from Harrogate is approximately 35 minutes. Through ticketing is available with a PlusBus ticket.

For further information on the above services please telephone MetroLine **0113 245 7676** or visit **www.wymetro.com**.

Liverpool John Lennon Airport

Regular bus services operate between Liverpool John Lennon Airport and the Liverpool South Parkway station; journey time is 10 minutes. Liverpool South Parkway is served by direct services from North, South and East Liverpool, Manchester, Warrington, Southport, Crewe, Stafford, Wolverhampton and Birmingham.

The airport is located to the south of the city centre. A direct bus service operates between Lime Street, Moorfields and James Street stations to the airport seven days a week. Buses run every 30 minutes between 0600 & 0100 hours from the Liverpool City Centre Stations to the Airport, and between 0515 and 0015 from the Airport to the Liverpool City Centre Stations. Journey time is approximately 45 minutes.

For further information please contact **0871 200 22 33,** or visit **www.traveline.info**.

London City Airport

London City Airport is located in London's Docklands, to the east of the capital. There are no National Rail services direct to the airport.

Access to the airport is available via the Docklands Light Railway to and from London City Airport Station which is located next to the terminal building. Between Central London and the airport, passengers can travel on the London Underground Jubilee Line and change at Canning Town for the Docklands Light Railway. Connections between National Rail and the Docklands Light Railway are available at Greenwich, Lewisham, Limehouse, Stratford and Woolwich Arsenal.

For further information on London City Airport telephone **020 7646 0088** or visit **www.londoncityairport.com**.

London Gatwick Airport

Gatwick has its own railway station underneath the South Terminal. Access to the North Terminal is via a free transit.

Airport to/from London

Gatwick Express operate a dedicated non-stop service every 15 minutes throughout most of the day between London Victoria and Gatwick Airport (See Table 186).

Southern provides frequent trains throughout the day and hourly throughout the night between London Victoria and Gatwick Airport (See Table 186).

First Capital Connect operate direct services throughout the day between St Pancras International, Farringdon, City Thameslink, London Blackfriars, London Bridge and Gatwick Airport (generally every 15 mins, See Table 52), a reduced frequency operates throughout the night. Overnight and at weekends it may be necessary to use London bus or Tube services to travel to/from stations north of London Bridge. Your rail ticket will be valid.

Airport to/from Reading

First Great Western operate a direct rail service between Reading and Gatwick – (See Table 148). Customers using this route should allow at least 7 minutes at Reading to make a connection.

Other direct services to/from Airport

Southern also operates direct services to/from Hastings, Southampton, Portsmouth and intermediate stations on the South Coast (See Tables 186, 187, 188, 189) Clapham Jn and East Croydon (SeeTable 186).

First Great Western operate services from Wokingham, North Camp and Guildford (See Table 148).

First Capital Connect provide regular direct services from Gatwick Airport to St. Albans, Luton, Bedford, East Croydon, Haywards Heath and Brighton (See Table 52). At Luton Airport Parkway, Luton and Bedford, they also offer convenient connections with East Midlands Trains to Leicester, Derby, Nottingham and Sheffield (See Table 53).

Airport Links

London Heathrow Airport

Express dedicated coaches link Reading and Woking with all four terminals at Heathrow Airport. Other services link Watford, Luton, Stevenage, Feltham and Central London with the airport. For full details see the individual route information below.

Airport to/from Central London

Heathrow Express operates a direct rail service from the airport to London Paddington. Stations are located at Terminal 4, Terminal 5 and in the Central Terminal Area, serving Terminals 1, 2 and 3. Minimum journey time is 15 minutes between Paddington and Terminals 1, 2 and 3, 23 minutes to Terminal 5. Trains run every 15 minutes. (Terminal 4 is served by a connecting 'shuttle' service to/ from Heathrow Terminals 1, 2 and 3, taking a minimum of 8 minutes extra.)

- 0510 to 2325 from Paddington
- 0507 to 2342 from Heathrow Terminal 5 (0503 to 2348 on Sundays)
- 0512 to 2348 from Heathrow Terminal 1, 2 and 3 (0508 to 2353 on Sundays)

For further details see Table 118.

Through tickets can be purchased from any National Rail or London Underground Station to the airport via Heathrow Express. For further information visit **www.heathrowexpress.com**.

Heathrow Connect operates a local rail service every 30 minutes between Heathrow Terminal 4 and London Paddington, calling at Heathrow Terminals 1, 2, 3, Hayes & Harlington, Southall, Hanwell, West Ealing and Ealing Broadway. For details see Table 117. Through tickets are available from most stations.

The London Underground Piccadilly Line connects central London with all five terminals (Terminal 1/2/3, Terminal 4 and Terminal 5). Through single and return tickets can be issued to customers travelling via a Rail terminus in Zone 1.

Sample journey time from Piccadilly Circus to the Airport is approximately one hour.

Airport to/from Reading

RailAir coaches leave from Reading railway station every 20 minutes during the daytime on Mondays to Fridays (every 30 minutes early weekday mornings and evenings, on weekends and public holidays). The luxury, air-conditioned coaches run non-stop to Terminals 1, 2 and 3 in 40-50 minutes. On the return journey from Heathrow Airport they only pick up passengers at Heathrow Central Bus Station (stands one and two) and not the terminals. Customers travelling to/from Terminal 4 should use Heathrow Connect from Terminal 1.

Follow the RailAir signs from your platform at Reading station. You can buy your ticket in the RailAir lounge, or combined rail and coach tickets are also available from many stations. You should allow 15 minutes at Reading to transfer between train and coach.

For further information telephone **0118 957 9425** or visit **www.RailAir.com.**

Airport to/from Woking

Coaches leave at half-hourly intervals throughout most of the day to/from Terminal 5 and Heathrow Central Bus Station (for Terminals 1, 2 and 3) (see Table 158A).

Customers travelling to Heathrow should exit on platform 5 and the coach leaves from outside the station.

On arrival at Woking customers should allow at least 10 minutes to transfer to your train after the arrival of the coach at the station. Combined rail and coach tickets are available from most National Rail stations and from the Railair sales points at the airport. Tickets may also be booked at **www.nationalexpress.com** or by calling **08717 818 181**. For through trains and coach times, telephone **08457 48 49 50.** (calls may be recorded for training purposes)

Airport to/from Feltham

London Buses operates frequent bus services from Feltham Station to Heathrow Airport. Route 285 operates to Hatton Cross and Heathrow Central Bus Station for Terminals 1, 2 and 3. Buses operate every 10 minutes during the day, 15 minutes in the evenings and on Sundays and 30 minutes throughout the night.

Route 490 operates to Hatton Cross and Terminals 4 and 5. Buses operate every 12 minutes during the day, 20 minutes in the evenings and on Sundays.

Customers should allow 10 minutes at Feltham to transfer between train and bus from the station forecourt adjoining platform 1.

Other direct services to/from Airport

A coach service, Green Line 724, runs throughout the day between Heathrow, West Drayton, Uxbridge, Rickmansworth, Watford, St. Albans, Hatfield, Welwyn Garden City, Hertford and Harlow. Tickets can only be purchased on the coach. A frequent bus service (route 140) runs 24 hours between Hayes & Harlington and Heathrow Airport (Central Bus Station).

For further information telephone **0870 608 7261** (Green Line Travel Information)

London Luton Airport

A frequent dedicated shuttle bus links Luton Airport with Luton Airport Parkway station – journey time 5 minutes. Luton Airport Parkway is served by frequent First Capital Connect services direct to Bedford, Central London, South London, Gatwick Airport and Brighton – see Table 52 for details. East Midlands Trains services link Luton Airport Parkway with St Pancras International and Leicester, Derby, Nottingham and Sheffield – see Table 53 for details. In addition a dedicated coach link operates between the Airport, Luton railway station and town centre and Milton Keynes Central railway station and town centre (see Table 65B for details).

Airport Links

London Stansted Airport

Stansted Airport has its own railway station right in the heart of the airport terminal building.

The Stansted Express is a dedicated rail service operating between London Liverpool Street and Stansted Airport station (See Table 22). Trains run every 15 minutes throughout the day, seven days per week.

Typical journey time is 46 minutes including an intermediate stop at Tottenham Hale to enable transfer onto the Victoria Line (London Underground) for the West End.

CrossCountry operates an hourly express service seven days a week between Birmingham and Stansted Airport calling at Leicester, Peterborough and Cambridge – see Table 49 – offering connections with services to Yorkshire and the North East. Customers should be advised to arrive at the airport 1 hour 45 minutes prior to their latest check-in time.

The airport is also served by the Stansted Coachlink (Service X22) – a limited stop coach service from Colchester station – which also calls intermediately at Braintree station. Coaches run hourly throughout the day, seven days per week.

For further information telephone **0871 200 22 33** or visit **www.traveline.info**

Manchester Airport

The airport railway station is right in the heart of the airport complex, linked by covered travellators. The station is served by up to 8 trains per hour from Manchester Piccadilly and direct services operate between Middlesbrough, Newcastle, York, Leeds, Huddersfield, Cleethorpes, Doncaster, Sheffield, Edinburgh, Glasgow, Carlisle, Barrow-in-Furness, Windermere, Lancaster, Preston, Liverpool and the Airport. Additional regular services operate during the day, to/from many stations which can be found under the entry for Manchester Airport in the index in this timetable.

Newcastle Airport

A frequent Tyne and Wear Metro service runs between Newcastle Central Station and Newcastle Airport providing links with Northern, East Coast, First TransPennine Express and CrossCountry services. Inclusive 'Train and Metro' tickets are available at discount prices.

Metro journey time approximately 20 minutes.

Metro frequency up to 6 trains each way each hour. Service operates between approx. 0600 and 2300.

Prestwick International Airport

Prestwick International Airport Station is situated directly opposite the main airport terminal buildings. A covered walkway links the station with the airport terminal. The station is served by direct trains from Glasgow Central and Ayr, with a half hourly frequency operating between the hours of 0600 and 0015 approximately. (See Table 221). Journey time is approx. 45 minutes. Some services operate direct from Kilmarnock and Stranraer. For further information telephone **01292 678000**.

Robin Hood Airport

Robin Hood Airport, the UK's newest purpose built international airport, is built on the site of the former RAF Finningley airbase. It is situated 7 miles south of Doncaster. For more information on Robin Hood Airport visit **www.robinhoodairport.com**

From Doncaster a dedicated bus service, The Airport Arrow 707, operates hourly throughout the day from the Frenchgate Interchange (Stand A1) adjacent to Doncaster Rail Station from 0535 to 2235. The journey takes under 25 minutes.

The Airport Arrow 707 service runs alongside other local bus services which link to Robin Hood Airport, including service X19 from Barnsley.

For further information on the above services please telephone Travel South Yorkshire **01709 515151** or visit **www.travelsouthyorkshire.com**

Southampton Airport

Southampton Airport (Parkway) station is adjacent to Southampton Airport.

South West Trains operate up to 3 trains per hour between London Waterloo, Winchester and Southampton Airport with up to 2 direct services to Bournemouth, Poole, Wareham and Weymouth and most intermediate stations (See Table 158).

CrossCountry services link Southampton Airport Parkway with Bournemath, Reading, Oxford and Manchester (see Table 51).

Station index and table numbers

■10 Connection time
Ⓟ Station Car Park
🚲 Bicycle storage facility
◇ Seat reservations can be made at this station
⚠ Penalty Fare Schemes in operation on some or all services from this station
🚕 Taxi rank or cab office at station, or signposted and within 100 metres
Ⓤ Unstaffed station
[ ] Station Operator Code

A

Abbey Wood [SE] Ⓟ 🚲 ◇ ⚠ 🚕 200
Aber [AW] Ⓟ 130
Abercynon [AW] Ⓤ 130
Aberdare [AW] ■3 Ⓟ ◇ 130
Aberdeen [SR] Ⓟ 🚲 ◇ 🚕
- Birmingham 51, 65
- Blackpool 65
- Bournemouth 51
- Bristol 51
- Cambridge 26
- Cardiff 51
- Carlisle 65
- Crewe 65, *Sleepers* 402
- Darlington 26
- Derby 51
- Doncaster 26
- Dundee 229
- Dyce 240
- Edinburgh 229
- Elgin 240
- Exeter 51
- Glasgow 229
- Grantham 26
- Inverkeithing 229
- Inverness 240
- Inverurie 240
- Kirkcaldy 229
- Leeds 26
- Liverpool 65
- London 26, *Sleepers* 402
- Manchester 65
- Newcastle 26
- Newport (South Wales) 51
- Norwich 26
- Oxenholme Lake District 65
- Oxford 51
- Paignton 51
- Penzance 51
- Perth 229
- Peterborough 26
- Plymouth 51
- Preston 65, *Sleepers* 402
- Reading 51
- Sheffield 26
- Southampton 51
- Stirling 229
- Torquay 51
- Watford 65
- York 26

Aberdour [SR] Ⓟ 🚲 242
Aberdovey [AW] 🚲 Ⓤ 75
Abererch [AW] Ⓤ 75
Abergavenny [AW] Ⓟ 🚲 ◇ 🚕 131
Abergele & Pensarn [AW] Ⓟ Ⓤ 81
Aberystwyth [AW] Ⓟ ◇ 🚕 75
Abingdon Stratton Way *Bus* 116B
Accrington [NT] Ⓟ ◇ 🚕 41, 97
Achanalt [SR] Ⓟ 🚲 Ⓤ 239
Achnasheen [SR] Ⓟ 🚲 Ⓤ 239
Achnashellach [SR] Ⓟ 🚲 Ⓤ 239
Acklington [NT] Ⓟ 🚲 Ⓤ 48
Acle [LE] Ⓟ 🚲 Ⓤ 15
Acocks Green [LM] Ⓟ ⚠ 71
Acton Bridge [LM] Ⓟ Ⓤ 91
Acton Central [LO] 🚲 ⚠ 59
Acton Main Line [GW] ⚠ 117
Acton, South [LO] (see South Acton)
Adderley Park [LM] ◇ ⚠ 68
Addiewell [SR] Ⓟ 🚲 Ⓤ 225
Addlestone [SW] ⚠ 🚕 149
Adisham [SE] Ⓟ ⚠ Ⓤ 212
Adlington (Cheshire) [NT] Ⓟ Ⓤ 84
Adlington (Lancashire) [NT] Ⓟ 82
Adwick [NT] Ⓟ 🚲 Ⓤ 29, 31
Agbrigg [NT] (See Sandal & Agbrigg)
Aigburth [ME] Ⓟ ⚠ 103
Ainsdale [ME] Ⓟ ⚠ 103
Aintree [ME] Ⓟ ⚠ 103
Airbles [SR] Ⓟ 🚲 Ⓤ 226
Airdrie [SR] Ⓟ 🚲 🚕 226
Albany Park [SE] ◇ ⚠ 200
Albrighton [LM] Ⓟ Ⓤ 74
Alderley Edge [NT] Ⓟ 🚲 84
Aldermaston [GW] Ⓟ Ⓤ 116
Aldershot [SW] Ⓟ 🚲 ◇ ⚠ 🚕 149, 155
Aldrington [SN] ⚠ Ⓤ 188
Alexandra Palace [FC] 🚲 ⚠ 🚕 24
Alexandra Parade [SR] 🚲 Ⓤ 226
Alexandria [SR] Ⓟ 🚲 226
Alfreton [EM] Ⓟ ◇ 🚕 34, 49, 53
Allens West [NT] 🚲 Ⓤ 44
Alloa [SR] Ⓟ 🚲 Ⓤ 230
Alness [SR] Ⓟ 🚲 Ⓤ 239
Alnmouth for Alnwick [NT] Ⓟ 🚲 ◇ 26, 48, 51
Alresford [LE] 🚲 ⚠ 11
Alsager [EM] Ⓤ 50, 67
Althorne [LE] Ⓟ 🚲 Ⓤ 5
Althorpe [NT] Ⓤ 29
Altnabreac [SR] 🚲 Ⓤ 239
Alton [SW] Ⓟ 🚲 ◇ ⚠ 🚕 155
Altrincham [NT] Ⓟ 🚲 ◇ 🚕 88
Alvechurch [LM] Ⓟ ⚠ Ⓤ 69
Ambergate [EM] Ⓟ Ⓤ 56
Amberley [SN] 🚲 ⚠ Ⓤ 188
Amersham [LT] Ⓟ 🚲 ⚠ 🚕 114
Ammanford [AW] Ⓤ 129
Ancaster [EM] Ⓟ Ⓤ 19
Anderston [SR] 🚲 226
Andover [SW] Ⓟ 🚲 ⚠ ◇ 🚕 160
Anerley [LO] 🚲 ⚠ 178
Angel Road [LE] ⚠ Ⓤ 22
Angmering [SN] ■3 Ⓟ 🚲 ◇ ⚠ 🚕 188
Annan [SR] Ⓟ 🚲 Ⓤ 216
Anniesland [SR] 🚲 🚕 226, 232
Ansdell & Fairhaven [NT] Ⓤ 97
Appleby [NT] Ⓟ ◇ 36
Appledore (Kent) [SN] Ⓤ 189
Appleford [GW] Ⓤ 116
Appley Bridge [NT] Ⓟ Ⓤ 82
Apsley [LM] Ⓟ 66
Arbroath [SR] Ⓟ 🚲 ◇ 🚕 26, 51, 229, *Sleepers* 402
Ardgay [SR] Ⓟ 🚲 Ⓤ 239
Ardlui [SR] 🚲 Ⓤ 227, *Sleepers* 404
Ardrossan Harbour [SR] Ⓟ 🚲 Ⓤ 221, *Ship* 221A
Ardrossan South Beach [SR] Ⓟ 🚲 221
Ardrossan Town [SR] 🚲 Ⓤ 221
Ardwick [NT] Ⓤ 78, 79
Argyle Street [SR] 226
Arisaig [SR] Ⓟ 🚲 Ⓤ 227
Arlesey [FC] Ⓟ 🚲 ⚠ 25
Armadale *Ship* 227A
Armathwaite [NT] Ⓟ Ⓤ 36
Arnside [TP] Ⓤ 82
Arram [NT] Ⓤ 43
Arrochar & Tarbet [SR] Ⓟ 🚲 Ⓤ 227, *Sleepers* 404
Arundel [SN] Ⓟ 🚲 ◇ ⚠ 🚕 188
Ascot [SW] ■3 Ⓟ 🚲 ◇ ⚠ 🚕 149
Ascott-under-Wychwood [GW] Ⓤ 126
Ash [SW] Ⓟ 🚲 ◇ ⚠ 148, 149
Ash Vale [SW] 🚲 ◇ ⚠ 149, 155
Ashburys [NT] Ⓤ 78, 79
Ashchurch for Tewkesbury [GW] Ⓟ 🚲 Ⓤ 57
Ashfield [SR] 🚲 Ⓤ 232
Ashford International [SE] Ⓟ 🚲 ◇ ⚠ 🚕 189, 194, 196, 207
Ashford (Surrey) [SW] Ⓟ 🚲 ◇ ⚠ 149
Ashley [NT] Ⓟ Ⓤ 88
Ashtead [SN] Ⓟ 🚲 ◇ ⚠ 152, 182
Ashton-under-Lyne [NT] Ⓟ 🚲 39
Ashurst [SN] Ⓟ ⚠ Ⓤ 184
Ashurst New Forest [SW] Ⓟ 🚲 ⚠ Ⓤ 158
Ashwell & Morden [FC] Ⓟ 🚲 ⚠ 25
Askam [NT] Ⓟ Ⓤ 100
Aslockton [EM] Ⓟ Ⓤ 19
Aspatria [NT] Ⓟ Ⓤ 100
Aspley Guise [LM] Ⓤ 64
Aston [LM] ⚠ 69, 70
Atherstone [LM] Ⓟ Ⓤ 67
Atherton [NT] Ⓟ 🚲 82
Attadale [SR] 🚲 Ⓤ 239
Attenborough [EM] Ⓤ 56, 57
Attleborough [LE] Ⓟ Ⓤ 17
Auchinleck [SR] Ⓟ 🚲 Ⓤ 216

Station index and table numbers

[10] Connection time
Ⓟ Station Car Park
🚲 Bicycle storage facility
◇ Seat reservations can be made at this station
⚠ Penalty Fare Schemes in operation on some or all services from this station
🚕 Taxi rank or cab office at station, or signposted and within 100 metres
Ⓤ Unstaffed station
[ ] Station Operator Code

Audley End [LE] Ⓟ 🚲 ⚠ 🚕 22, 49
Aughton Park [ME] ⚠ 103
Aviemore [SR] Ⓟ 🚲 ◇ 🚕 229, *Sleepers* 403
Avoncliff [GW] Ⓤ 123
Avonmouth [GW] [2] Ⓟ 🚲 Ⓤ 133
Axminster [SW] Ⓟ 🚲 ◇ 🚕 160
Aylesbury [CH] Ⓟ 🚲 ◇ ⚠ 🚕 114, 115
Aylesbury Vale Parkway [CH] Ⓟ 🚲 ◇ ⚠ 114
Aylesford [SE] ⚠ Ⓤ 208
Aylesham [SE] Ⓟ ◇ ⚠ 212
Ayr [SR] Ⓟ 🚲 ◇ 🚕 218, 221

B

Bache [ME] Ⓤ 106
Backwell [GW] (see Nailsea)
Baglan [AW] Ⓟ 🚲 Ⓤ 128
Bagshot [SW] Ⓟ 🚲 ◇ ⚠ 149
Baildon [NT] Ⓟ Ⓤ 38
Baillieston [SR] 🚲 Ⓤ 220
Balcombe [SN] ◇ ⚠ 52, 186
Baldock [FC] Ⓟ ⚠ 25
Balham [SN] [4] ◇ ⚠ 🚕 176, 177, 178, 182
Balloch [SR] 🚲 🚕 226
Balmossie [SR] 🚲 Ⓤ 229
Bamber Bridge [NT] Ⓟ Ⓤ 97
Bamford [NT] Ⓟ Ⓤ 78
Banavie [SR] Ⓟ 🚲 Ⓤ 227
Banbury [CH] Ⓟ 🚲 ◇ ⚠ 🚕 51, 71, 75, 115, 116
Bangor (Gwynedd) [AW] Ⓟ ◇ 🚕 65, 81, 131
Bank Hall [ME] ⚠ 103
Banstead [SN] ⚠ Ⓤ 182
Barassie [SR] Ⓟ 🚲 Ⓤ 221
Bardon Mill [NT] Ⓟ Ⓤ 48
Bare Lane [NT] Ⓟ Ⓤ 36, 98
Bargeddie [SR] Ⓟ 🚲 Ⓤ 220
Bargoed [AW] 🚕 130
Barking [CC] ◇ ⚠ 🚕 1, 62
Barlaston Orchard Place *Bus* 67
Barming [SE] Ⓟ ◇ ⚠ 196
Barmouth [AW] 🚲 75
Barnehurst [SE] [4] Ⓟ ◇ ⚠ 🚕 200
Barnes [SW] 🚲 ◇ ⚠ 149
Barnes Bridge [SW] 🚲 ◇ ⚠ Ⓤ 149
Barnetby [TP] Ⓟ Ⓤ 27, 29, 30
Barnham [SN] Ⓟ 🚲 ◇ ⚠ 🚕 123, 188
Barnhill [SR] 🚲 Ⓤ 226
Barnsbury [LO] (see Caledonian Road)
Barnsley [NT] Ⓟ 🚲 ◇ 🚕 30, 34
Barnstaple [GW] Ⓟ 🚲 ◇ 🚕 136
Barnt Green [LM] Ⓟ ⚠ Ⓤ 69, 71
Barrhead [SR] Ⓟ 🚲 🚕 222
Barrhill [SR] Ⓟ 🚲 218
Barrow Haven [NT] Ⓤ 29
Barrow-in-Furness [TP] Ⓟ ◇ 🚕 65, 82, 100
Barrow Upon Soar [EM] Ⓤ 53
Barry [AW] [3] Ⓟ ◇ 🚕 130
Barry Docks [AW] Ⓤ 130
Barry Island [AW] Ⓤ 130
Barry Links [SR] 🚲 Ⓤ 229
Barton-on-Humber [NT] Ⓟ Ⓤ 29
Basildon [CC] 🚲 ◇ ⚠ 🚕 1
Basingstoke [SW] Ⓟ 🚲 ◇ ⚠ 🚕
Aberdeen 51
Bath 160
Birmingham 51
Bournemouth 158
Bristol 160
Brockenhurst 158
Clapham Junction 155
Coventry 51
Crewe 51
Derby 51
Dorchester 158
Dundee 51
Eastleigh 158
Edinburgh 51
Exeter 160
Fareham 158
Farnborough 158
Glasgow 51
Leeds 51
London 155
Lymington 158
Manchester 51
Newcastle 51
Oxford 51
Poole 158
Portsmouth 158
Preston 51
Reading 122
Salisbury 160
Sheffield 51
Southampton 158
Southampton Airport 158
Stoke-on-Trent 51
Surbiton 155
Weymouth 158
Weybridge 155
Wimbledon 155
Winchester 158
Woking 155
Wolverhampton 51
Yeovil 160
York 51
Bat & Ball [SE] Ⓟ ⚠ Ⓤ 52, 195
Bath Spa [GW] [7] Ⓟ 🚲 ◇ ⚠ 🚕 123, 125, 132, 135, 160
Bathgate [SR] Ⓟ 🚲 🚕 Ⓤ 237
Batley [NT] Ⓟ 🚲 Ⓤ 39
Battersby [NT] Ⓤ 45
Battersea Park [SN] [4] ◇ ⚠ 177, 178
Battle [SE] Ⓟ ◇ ⚠ 🚕 206
Battlesbridge [LE] Ⓟ 🚲 Ⓤ 5
Bayford [FC] Ⓟ ⚠ Ⓤ 24
Beaconsfield [CH] Ⓟ 🚲 ◇ ⚠ 🚕 115
Bearley [LM] Ⓟ ⚠ Ⓤ 115
Bearsden [SR] Ⓟ 🚲 🚕 226
Bearsted [SE] Ⓟ 🚲 ◇ ⚠ 196
Beasdale [SR] 🚲 Ⓤ 227
Beaulieu Road [SW] 🚲 ⚠ Ⓤ 158
Beauly [SR] Ⓟ 🚲 Ⓤ 239
Bebington [ME] Ⓟ ⚠ 🚕 106
Beccles [LE] Ⓟ 🚲 Ⓤ 13
Beckenham Hill [SE] 🚲 ◇ ⚠ 52, 195
Beckenham Junction [SE] [4] Ⓟ 🚲 ◇ ⚠ 🚕 177, 195
Bedford [FC] [7] Ⓟ 🚲 ◇ ⚠ 🚕
Barnsley 53
Bletchley 64
Brighton 52, 186
Chesterfield 53
Derby 53
Doncaster 53
East Croydon 52
Gatwick Airport 52, 186
Haywards Heath 52, 186
Herne Hill 52
Hove 186
Kettering 53
Leeds 53
Leicester 53
London 52
Luton 52
Luton Airport Parkway 52
Meadowhall 53
Milton Keynes Central *Bus* 65C
Nottingham 53
Redhill 52, 186
St Albans 52
Sheffield 53
Sutton (Surrey) 52
Wakefield 53
Wellingborough 53
Wimbledon 52
York 53
Bedford Bus Station 🚕 *Bus* 65C
Bedford St Johns [LM] Ⓤ 64
Bedhampton [SW] 🚲 ◇ ⚠ 156, 157, 188
Bedminster [GW] Ⓤ 134
Bedworth [LM] Ⓟ Ⓤ 67
Bedwyn [GW] Ⓟ 🚲 Ⓤ 116
Beeston [EM] Ⓟ 🚲 ◇ 53, 56, 57
Bekesbourne [SE] Ⓟ ⚠ Ⓤ 212
Belfast
Port *Catamaran/Ship* (via Stranraer Harbour) 218
Belle Vue [NT] Ⓤ 78
Bellgrove [SR] 🚲 Ⓤ 226
Bellingham [SE] 🚲 ◇ ⚠ 52, 195
Bellshill [SR] Ⓟ 🚲 225, 226
Belmont [SN] ⚠ Ⓤ 182

Station index and table numbers

[10] Connection time
Ⓟ Station Car Park
🚲 Bicycle storage facility
◇ Seat reservations can be made at this station
⚠ Penalty Fare Schemes in operation on some or all services from this station
🚕 Taxi rank or cab office at station, or signposted and within 100 metres
Ⓤ Unstaffed station
[ ] Station Operator Code

Belper [EM] Ⓤ 56
Beltring [SE] ⚠ Ⓤ 208
Belvedere [SE] ◇ ⚠ 200
Bempton [NT] Ⓤ 43
Ben Rhydding [NT] Ⓟ Ⓤ 38
Benfleet [CC] Ⓟ 🚲 ◇ ⚠ 🚕 1
Bentham [NT] Ⓟ Ⓤ 36
Bentley [SW] Ⓟ 🚲 ◇ ⚠ 155
Bentley (S. Yorks.) [NT] Ⓟ 🚲 Ⓤ 29, 31
Bere Alston [GW] Ⓟ Ⓤ 139
Bere Ferrers [GW] Ⓟ 🚲 Ⓤ 139
Berkhamsted [LM] Ⓟ 🚲 ◇ ⚠ 🚕 66, 176
Berkswell [LM] Ⓟ 🚲 ⚠ 68
Berney Arms [LE] 🚲 Ⓤ 15
Berry Brow [NT] Ⓤ 34
Berrylands [SW] Ⓟ 🚲 ◇ ⚠ 152
Berwick [SN] Ⓟ 🚲 ◇ ⚠ 189
Berwick-upon-Tweed [GR] Ⓟ 🚲 ◇ 🚕 26, 26K, 51
Bescar Lane [NT] Ⓤ 82
Bescot Stadium [LM] Ⓟ ◇ ⚠ 70
Betchworth [GW] Ⓤ 148
Bethnal Green [LE] 🚲 ⚠ Ⓤ 20, 21, 22
Betws-y-Coed [AW] Ⓤ 102
Beverley [NT] Ⓟ ◇ 🚕 43
Bexhill [SN] [4] ◇ ⚠ 🚕 189
Bexley [SE] Ⓟ ◇ ⚠ 🚕 200
Bexleyheath [SE] Ⓟ 🚲 ◇ ⚠ 🚕 200
Bicester (Bure Place) *Bus* 65A
Bicester North [CH] [3] Ⓟ 🚲 ◇ ⚠ 🚕 115
Bicester Town [GW] Ⓟ 🚲 Ⓤ 116
Bickley [SE] [4] Ⓟ ◇ ⚠ 52, 195
Bidston [ME] Ⓟ ⚠ 101, 106
Biggleswade [FC] Ⓟ 🚲 ⚠ 25
Bilbrook [LM] Ⓤ 74
Billericay [LE] Ⓟ 🚲 ⚠ 🚕 5
Billingham [NT] 🚲 🚕 Ⓤ 44
Billingshurst [SN] Ⓟ 🚲 ◇ ⚠ 🚕 188
Bingham [EM] Ⓟ Ⓤ 19
Bingley [NT] Ⓟ 🚲 ◇ 36
Birchgrove [AW] Ⓤ 130
Birchington-on-Sea [SE] Ⓟ 🚲 ◇ ⚠ 🚕 194, 212
Birchwood [TP] Ⓟ 🚲 🚕 39, 89
Birkbeck [SN] ⚠ Ⓤ 177
Birkdale [ME] Ⓟ ⚠ 103
Birkenhead Central [ME] ⚠ 106
Birkenhead North [ME] ⚠ 106
Birkenhead Park [ME] ⚠ 106
Birmingham International [VT] (for National Exhibition Centre and Airport) Ⓟ 🚲 ◇ ⚠ 🚕
Aberdeen 65
Aberystwyth 75
Banbury 71
Bangor (Gwynedd) 65, 81
Basingstoke 51
Birmingham 68
Blackpool 65
Bournemouth 51
Carlisle 65
Chester 65, 75, 81
Clapham Junction 66
Coventry 68
Crewe 65, 81
Derby 51
Dundee 65
East Croydon 66
Edinburgh 51, 65
Glasgow 51, 65
Holyhead 65, 75, 81
Inverness 65
Leamington Spa 71
Leeds 51
Liverpool 65
London 66, 116
Manchester 65
Manchester Airport 65
Milton Keynes Central 66
Newcastle 51
Northampton 66
Nottingham 51
Oxenholme Lake District 65
Oxford 51
Preston 65
Pwllheli 75
Reading 51
Rugby 66
Sheffield 51
Shrewsbury 75
Southampton 51
Stafford 68
Stoke-on-Trent 65
Watford 66
Wolverhampton 68
Wrexham 75
York 51
Birmingham
Moor Street [CH] ◇ ⚠ 🚕
New Street [NR] [12] 🚲 ◇ ⚠ 🚕
Snow Hill [LM] Ⓟ ◇ ⚠
Aberdeen 51, 65
Aberystwyth 75
Banbury 71
Bangor (Gwynedd) 65, 81
Barmouth 75
Barrow-in-Furness 65
Basingstoke 51
Birmingham International 68
Blackpool 65
Bournemouth 51
Bristol 57
Bromsgrove 71
Burton-on-Trent 57
Cambridge 49
Cardiff 57
Carlisle 65
Cheltenham Spa 57
Chester 75, 81
Clapham Junction 66
Coventry 68
Crewe 65
Darlington 51
Derby 57
Douglas (IOM) 98A
Dundee 51, 65
East Croydon 66
Edinburgh 51, 65
Ely 49
Exeter 51
Glasgow 51, 65
Gloucester 57
Hereford 71
Holyhead 65, 81
Inverness 65
Kidderminster 71
Leamington Spa 71
Leeds 51
Leicester 57
Lichfield 69
Liverpool 65, 91
Llandudno 81
London 66, 115, 116
Longbridge 69
Manchester 65, 84
Manchester Airport 65, 84
Milton Keynes Central 66
Newcastle 51
Newport (South Wales) 57
Northampton 66
Norwich 49
Nottingham 57
Nuneaton 57
Oxenholme Lake District 65
Oxford 116
Paignton 135
Penzance 135
Peterborough 49
Plymouth 135
Preston 65
Reading 116
Redditch 69
Rugby 66
Rugeley 70
Sheffield 51
Shrewsbury 74
Solihull 71
Southampton 51
Stafford 68
Stansted Airport 49
Stockport 65
Stoke-on-Trent 65
Stourbridge 71
Stratford-upon-Avon 71
Telford 74
Torquay 135
Walsall 70
Warrington 65
Warwick 71
Watford 66
Wigan 65
Wolverhampton 68
Worcester 71
Wrexham 75
York 51
Birnam [SR] (see Dunkeld)

Station index and table numbers

- **10** Connection time
- Ⓟ Station Car Park
- 🚲 Bicycle storage facility
- ◇ Seat reservations can be made at this station
- ⚠ Penalty Fare Schemes in operation on some or all services from this station
- 🚕 Taxi rank or cab office at station, or signposted and within 100 metres
- Ⓤ Unstaffed station
- [ ] Station Operator Code

Bishop Auckland [NT] Ⓟ 🚕 Ⓤ 44
Bishopbriggs [SR] 🚲 228, 230
Bishops Lydeard Hithermead *Bus* 135E
Bishops Stortford [LE] Ⓟ 🚲 ◇ ⚠ 🚕 22
Bishopstone [SN] Ⓤ 189
Bishopton [SR] Ⓟ 🚲 219
Bitterne [SW] Ⓟ 🚲 ⚠ Ⓤ 165
Blackburn [NT] Ⓟ ◇ 🚕 41, 94, 97
Blackfriars [FC] (see London)
Blackheath [SE] **4** ◇ ⚠ 🚕 200
Blackhorse Road [LT] ⚠ 62
Blackpool
  North [NT] Ⓟ ◇ 🚕
  Pleasure Beach [NT] Ⓤ
  South [NT] 🚕 Ⓤ
 Birmingham 65
 Birmingham International 65
 Blackburn 97
 Bolton 82
 Bradford 41
 Burnley 97
 Colne 97
 Coventry 65
 Crewe 65
 Lancaster 65
 Leeds 41
 Liverpool 65, 90
 London 65
 Manchester 82
 Manchester Airport 82
 Milton Keynes Central 65
 Preston 97
 Rugby 65
 St Helens 90
 Stafford 65
 Stockport 82
 Warrington 65
 Watford 65
 Wigan 65
 Wolverhampton 65
 York 41
Blackrod [NT] Ⓤ 82
Blackwater [GW] Ⓟ Ⓤ 148
Blaenau Ffestiniog [AW] Ⓤ 102
Blair Atholl [SR] Ⓟ 🚲 229, *Sleepers* 403
Blairhill [SR] Ⓟ 🚲 🚕 226
Blake Street [LM] Ⓟ ⚠ 69
Blakedown [LM] Ⓟ ⚠ Ⓤ 71
Blantyre [SR] Ⓟ 🚲 226
Blaydon [NT] Ⓤ 48
Bleasby [EM] Ⓤ 27
Bledlow, Village Hall *Bus* 115A
Bletchley [LM] Ⓟ 🚲 ◇ ⚠ 🚕 64, 66, 176
Bloxwich [LM] ⚠ Ⓤ 70
Bloxwich North [LM] ⚠ Ⓤ 70
Bluewater [SE] (see Greenhithe for Bluewater)
Blundellsands & Crosby [ME] Ⓟ ⚠ 103
Blythe Bridge [EM] Ⓟ Ⓤ 50
Bodmin Mount Folly *Bus* 135C
Bodmin Parkway [GW] Ⓟ 🚲 ◇ 🚕 51, 135, *Bus* 135C, *Sleepers* 406
Bodorgan [AW] Ⓟ Ⓤ 81
Bognor Regis [SN] Ⓟ 🚲 ◇ ⚠ 🚕 188
Bogston [SR] 🚲 Ⓤ 219
Bolton [NT] 🚲 ◇ 🚕 65, 82, 94
Bolton-upon-Dearne [NT] Ⓟ Ⓤ 31
Bookham [SW] Ⓟ 🚲 ◇ ⚠ 🚕 152, 182
Bootle [NT] Ⓤ 100
Bootle New Strand [ME] ⚠ 🚕 103
Bootle Oriel Road [ME] Ⓟ ⚠ 103
Bordesley [LM] ⚠ Ⓤ 71
Borehamwood [FC] (see Elstree)
Borough Green & Wrotham [SE] Ⓟ ◇ ⚠ 🚕 196
Borth [AW] Ⓟ Ⓤ 75
Bosham [SN] 🚲 ⚠ 188
Boston [EM] Ⓟ 🚲 ◇ 🚕 19
Botley [SW] Ⓟ 🚲 ⚠ Ⓤ 158
Bottesford [EM] Ⓟ Ⓤ 19
Bourne End [GW] **3** Ⓟ 🚲 ⚠ 120
Bournemouth [SW] Ⓟ 🚲 ◇ ⚠ 🚕 51, 158
Bournville [LM] ⚠ 69
Bow Brickhill [LM] Ⓤ 64
Bowes Park [FC] ⚠ 24
Bowling [SR] Ⓟ 🚲 Ⓤ 226
Boxhill & Westhumble [SN] Ⓟ ⚠ Ⓤ 152, 182
Bracknell [SW] Ⓟ 🚲 ◇ ⚠ 🚕 149
Bradford
  Forster Square [NT] Ⓟ 🚲 ◇ 🚕
  Interchange [NT] 🚲 ◇ 🚕
 Blackpool 41
 Blackburn 41
 Brighouse 41
 Cambridge 26
 Carlisle 36
 Grantham 26
 Halifax 41
 Huddersfield 41
 Ilkley 38
 Lancaster 36
 Leeds 37
 London 26
 Manchester 41
 Morecambe 36
 Newark 26
 Norwich 26
 Peterborough 26
 Preston 41
 Retford 26
 Rochdale 41
 Selby 40
 Settle 36
 Shipley 37
 Skipton 36
 York 40
Bradford-on-Avon [GW] Ⓟ 🚲 ◇ 🚕 123, 160
Brading [IL] Ⓟ Ⓤ 167
Braintree [LE] Ⓟ 🚲 ⚠ 🚕 11
Braintree Freeport [LE] 🚲 ⚠ Ⓤ 11
Bramhall [NT] 84
Bramley (Hants) [GW] ⚠ 122
Bramley [NT] Ⓟ Ⓤ 37, 41
Brampton (Cumbria) [NT] Ⓟ Ⓤ 48
Brampton (Suffolk) [LE] Ⓤ 13
Branchton [SR] Ⓟ 🚲 Ⓤ 219
Brandon [LE] Ⓟ Ⓤ 17
Branksome [SW] Ⓟ 🚲 ◇ ⚠ 158
Braystones [NT] Ⓤ 100
Bredbury [NT] Ⓟ 🚲 78
Breich [SR] 🚲 Ⓤ 225
Brentford [SW] Ⓟ 🚲 ◇ 🚕 149
Brentwood [LE] Ⓟ 🚲 ⚠ 🚕 5
Bricket Wood [LM] Ⓤ 61
Bridge of Allan [SR] Ⓟ 🚲 Ⓤ 230
Bridge of Orchy [SR] Ⓟ 🚲 Ⓤ 227, *Sleepers* 404
Bridgend [AW] Ⓟ 🚲 ◇ 🚕 125, 128, 130
Bridgeton [SR] 🚲 🚕 226
Bridgwater [GW] Ⓟ ◇ 134, 135
Bridlington [NT] Ⓟ 🚲 ◇ 🚕 43
Brierfield [NT] Ⓟ Ⓤ 97
Brigg [NT] Ⓟ Ⓤ 30
Brighouse [NT] Ⓟ Ⓤ 41
Brighton [SN] **10** Ⓟ 🚲 ◇ ⚠ 🚕
 Ashford International 189
 Bath Spa 123
 Bedford 52
 Bognor Regis 188
 Bristol 123
 Cardiff 123
 Chichester 188
 Eastbourne 189
 East Croydon 176, 186
 Elstree & Borehamwood 52
 Gatwick Airport 176, 186
 Hastings 189
 Haywards Heath 186
 Hove 188
 Isle of Wight 167
 Kensington (Olympia) 176
 Lewes 189
 Littlehampton 188
 London 186
 Luton 52
 Luton Airport Parkway 52
 Mill Hill Broadway 52
 Milton Keynes Central 176
 Portsmouth 188
 Radlett 52
 Redhill 186
 St Albans 52
 Salisbury 123
 Seaford 189

Station index and table numbers

10 Connection time
Ⓟ Station Car Park
🚲 Bicycle storage facility
◇ Seat reservations can be made at this station
⚠ Penalty Fare Schemes in operation on some or all services from this station
🚕 Taxi rank or cab office at station, or signposted and within 100 metres
⊛ Unstaffed station
[ ] Station Operator Code

Southampton Central 188
Watford Junction 176
West Hampstead Thameslink 52
Worthing 188
Brimsdown [LE] ⚠ 22
Brinnington [NT] 78
Bristol International Airport *Bus* 🚕 125B
Bristol
Parkway [GW] **7** Ⓟ 🚲 ◇ ⚠ 🚕
Temple Meads [GW] **10** Ⓟ 🚲 ◇ ⚠ 🚕
Aberdeen 51
Bath Spa 132
Birmingham 57
Brighton 123
Bristol International Airport *Bus* 125B
Cardiff 132
Carlisle 51
Cheltenham Spa 57
Crewe 51
Darlington 51
Derby 57
Dundee 51
Edinburgh 51
Exeter 135
Glasgow 51
Gloucester 134
Leeds 51
London 125, 160
Manchester 51
Newcastle 51
Newport (South Wales) 132
Nottingham 57
Paignton 135
Penzance 135
Plymouth 135
Portsmouth 123
Preston 51
Reading 125
Salisbury 123
Severn Beach 133
Sheffield 51
Slough 125
Southampton Central 123
Stoke-on-Trent 51
Swindon 125
Taunton 134
Temple Meads/Parkway 134
Torquay 135
Westbury 123
Weston-super-Mare 134
Weymouth 123
Wolverhampton 51
Worcester 57
York 51
Brithdir [AW] ⊛ 130
British Steel Redcar [NT] ⊛ 44
Briton Ferry [AW] Ⓟ ⊛ 128
Brixton [SE] ◇ ⚠ 195
Broad Green [NT] 90
Broadbottom [NT] Ⓟ 79
Broadstairs [SE] Ⓟ 🚲 ◇ 🚕 194, 207, 212
Brockenhurst [SW] **3** Ⓟ 🚲 ◇ ⚠ 🚕 51, 158
Brockholes [NT] ⊛ 34
Brockley [LO] 🚲 ⚠ 178
Brodick *Ship* 221A
Bromborough [ME] Ⓟ 🚲 ⚠ 106
Bromborough Rake [ME] ⚠ 106
Bromley Cross [NT] Ⓟ 🚲 94
Bromley North [SE] Ⓟ ◇ ⚠ 🚕 204
Bromley South [SE] **4** ◇ ⚠ 🚕 52, 195, 196, 212
Bromsgrove [LM] Ⓟ ⊛ 69, 71
Brondesbury [LO] 🚲 ⚠ 59
Brondesbury Park [LO] 🚲 ⚠ 59
Brookmans Park [FC] Ⓟ 🚲 ⚠ 24
Brookwood [SW] **3** Ⓟ 🚲 ◇ ⚠ 🚕 155
Broome [AW] ⊛ 129
Broomfleet [NT] Ⓟ ⊛ 29
Brora [SR] Ⓟ 🚲 ⊛ 239
Brough [TP] Ⓟ 🚲 ◇ 🚕 29, 39
Broughty Ferry [SR] 🚲 ⊛ 229
Broxbourne [LE] **3** Ⓟ 🚲 ⚠ 🚕 22
Bruce Grove [LE] ⚠ 21
Brundall [LE] Ⓟ 🚲 15
Brundall Gardens [LE] 🚲 ⊛ 15
Brunstane [SR] 🚲 ⊛ 242
Brunswick [ME] Ⓟ 🚲 103
Bruton [GW] Ⓟ ⊛ 123
Bryn [NT] ⊛ 90
Buckenham [LE] 🚲 ⊛ 15
Buckingham (Tesco) *Bus* 65A
Buckley [AW] Ⓟ ⊛ 101
Bucknell [AW] ⊛ 129
Bude Strand *Bus* 135D
Bugle [GW] 🚲 ⊛ 142
Builth Road [AW] ⊛ 129
Bulwell [EM] Ⓟ ⊛ 55
Bures [LE] 🚲 ⊛ 10
Burgess Hill [SN] **4** Ⓟ 🚲 ◇ ⚠ 🚕 52, 186, 188
Burley Park [NT] Ⓟ ⊛ 35
Burley-in-Wharfedale [NT] Ⓟ 🚲 ⊛ 38
Burnage [NT] 85
Burneside [TP] ⊛ 83
Burnham [GW] Ⓟ 🚲 ⚠ 🚕 117
Burnham-on-Crouch [LE] Ⓟ 🚲 5
Burnham-on-Sea [GW] (see Highbridge)
Burnley Barracks [NT] ⊛ 97
Burnley Central [NT] Ⓟ ◇ 97
Burnley Manchester Road [NT] Ⓟ ⊛ 41, 97
Burnside [SR] 🚲 223
Burntisland [SR] Ⓟ 🚲 242
Burry Port [AW] (see Pembrey)
Burscough Bridge [NT] Ⓟ 82
Burscough Junction [NT] Ⓟ ⊛ 99
Bursledon [SW] Ⓟ 🚲 ⚠ ⊛ 165
Burton Joyce [EM] ⊛ 27
Burton-on-Trent [EM] Ⓟ ◇ 🚕 51, 57
Bury St Edmunds [LE] Ⓟ 🚲 ◇ 🚕 14
Busby [SR] Ⓟ 🚲 ⊛ 222
Bushey [LO] Ⓟ 🚲 ⚠ 🚕 60, 66
Bush Hill Park [LE] Ⓟ ⚠ 🚕 21
Butlers Lane [LM] ⚠ 69
Buxted [SN] Ⓟ ⚠ 184
Buxton [NT] Ⓟ ◇ 82, 86
Byfleet & New Haw [SW] 🚲 ◇ ⚠ 🚕 149, 155
Bynea [AW] ⊛ 129

C

Cadoxton [AW] Ⓟ ◇ 130
Caerau Park *Bus* 128A
Caerau (Square) *Bus* 128A
Caergwrle [AW] ⊛ 101
Caerphilly [AW] **3** Ⓟ 🚲 ◇ 🚕 130
Caersws [AW] Ⓟ ⊛ 75
Caldicot [AW] ⊛ 132
Caledonian Rd & Barnsbury [LO] ⚠ 59
Calstock [GW] Ⓟ 🚲 ⊛ 139
Cam & Dursley [GW] Ⓟ 🚲 ⊛ 134
Camberley [SW] Ⓟ 🚲 ◇ ⚠ 🚕 149
Camborne [GW] Ⓟ 🚲 ◇ 🚕 51, 135, *Sleepers* 406
Cambridge [LE] Ⓟ 🚲 ◇ ⚠ 🚕
Birmingham 49
Bishops Stortford 22
Broxbourne 22
Doncaster 26
Edinburgh 26
Ely 17
Finsbury Park 25
Grantham 26
Harlow 22
Harwich International 14
Hitchin 25
Ipswich 14
Kings Lynn 17
Leeds 26
Leicester 49
Liverpool 49
London
Kings Cross 17, 25
Liverpool St. 17, 22
Manchester 49
Newark 26
Newcastle 26
Norwich 17
Nottingham 49

Station index and table numbers

■10 Connection time
Ⓟ Station Car Park
🚲 Bicycle storage facility
◇ Seat reservations can be made at this station
⚠ Penalty Fare Schemes in operation on some or all services from this station
🚕 Taxi rank or cab office at station, or signposted and within 100 metres
🚶 Unstaffed station
[ ] Station Operator Code

Peterborough 17
Retford 26
Royston 25
Sheffield 49
Stansted Airport 22
Stevenage 25
Stockport 49
Tottenham Hale 22
Welwyn Garden City 25
York 26
Cambridge Bus Station 🚕 *Bus* 65C
Cambridge Heath [LE] ⚠ 🚶 21
Cambuslang [SR] 🚲 🚕 225, 226
Camden Road [LO] 🚲 ⚠ 59
Camelon [SR] Ⓟ 🚲 🚶 224, 230
Canada Water [LT] 178
Canley [LM] Ⓟ 🚲 ⚠ 68
Canna *Ship* 227A
Cannock [LM] Ⓟ ⚠ 🚶 70
Cannon Street [NR] (see London)
Canonbury [LO] ⚠ 59
Canterbury East [SE] ■4 Ⓟ 🚲 ◇ ⚠ 🚕 212
Canterbury West [SE] ■4 Ⓟ 🚲 ◇ ⚠ 🚕 194, 196, 207
Cantley [LE] Ⓟ 🚲 🚶 15
Capenhurst [ME] Ⓟ 🚶 106
Carbis Bay [GW] Ⓟ 🚶 144
Cardenden [SR] Ⓟ 🚲 🚶 242
Cardiff
Bay [AW] 🚶
Central [AW] ■7 Ⓟ 🚲 ◇ 🚕
Queen Street [AW] ■3 ◇
Aberdeen 51
Aberystwyth 75
Bangor (Gwynedd) 81, 131
Barry Island 130
Bath Spa 132
Birmingham 57
Bridgend 128, 130
Brighton 123
Bristol 132
Cardiff International Airport *Bus* 125C (also see Rhoose)
Cheltenham Spa 57
Chester 75, 81, 131
Coryton 130
Crewe 131
Darlington 51
Derby 57
Dundee 51
Durham 51
Ebbw Vale Parkway 127
Edinburgh 51
Exeter 135
Fishguard Harbour 128
Gloucester 132
Hereford 131
Holyhead 81, 131
Leeds 51
Llandudno Junction 81, 131
London 125
Maesteg 128
Manchester 131
Merthyr Tydfil 130
Milford Haven 128
Newcastle 51
Newport (South Wales) 132
Nottingham 57
Paignton 135
Penzance 135
Plymouth 135
Pontypridd 130
Portsmouth 123
Reading 125
Rhoose 130
Rhymney 130
Rosslare Harbour 128
Sheffield 51
Shrewsbury 131
Slough 125
Southampton Central 123
Swansea 128
Swindon 125
Taunton 132, 134
Torquay 135
Treherbert 130
Weymouth 123
Worcester 57
Wrexham 75
York 51
Cardiff International Airport *Bus* 🚕 125C
Cardiff International Airport [AW] (see Rhoose)
Cardonald [SR] 🚲 219
Cardross [SR] Ⓟ 🚲 226
Carfin [SR] Ⓟ 🚲 🚶 225
Cark [NT] Ⓟ 🚶 82
Carlisle [VT] ■8 Ⓟ 🚲 ◇ 🚕
Aberdeen 65
Barrow-in-Furness 100
Birmingham 65
Blackpool 36, 65
Bolton 65
Bournemouth 51
Bradford 36
Bristol 51
Coventry 65
Crewe 65
Dumfries 216
Dundee 65
Exeter 51
Edinburgh 65
Galashiels *Bus* 65G
Glasgow 65, 216
Hawick *Bus* 65G
Haymarket 65
Hexham 48
Inverness 65
Kilmarnock 216
Lancaster 65
Langholm *Bus* 65G
Leeds 36
Liverpool 65
London 65, *Sleepers* 400, 401
Manchester 65
Manchester Airport 65
Milton Keynes Central 65
Motherwell 65
Newcastle 48
Oxenholme Lake District 65
Oxford 51
Penzance 51
Perth 65
Plymouth 51
Preston 65
Reading 51
Rugby 65
Selkirk *Bus* 65G
Settle 36
Skipton 36
Southampton 51
Stafford 65
Warrington 65
Watford 65, *Sleepers* 400, 401
Whitehaven 100
Wigan 65
Wolverhampton 65
Workington 100
Carlton [EM] Ⓟ 🚶 27
Carluke [SR] Ⓟ 🚲 226
Carmarthen [AW] Ⓟ 🚲 ◇ ⚠ 🚕 128
Carmyle [SR] 🚲 🚶 220
Carnforth [TP] Ⓟ 🚶 36, 82
Carnoustie [SR] Ⓟ 🚲 🚕 🚶 229, *Sleepers* 402
Carntyne [SR] 🚲 🚶 226
Carpenders Park [LO] 🚲 ⚠ 🚕 60
Carrbridge [SR] Ⓟ 🚲 🚶 229
Carshalton [SN] Ⓟ ◇ ⚠ 52, 179, 182
Carshalton Beeches [SN] ◇ ⚠ 182
Carstairs [SR] 🚲 65, 225, *Sleepers* 401
Cartsdyke [SR] 🚲 219
Castle Bar Park [GW] 117
Castle Cary [GW] Ⓟ ◇ 🚕 123, 135
Castlebay *Ship* 227C
Castleford [NT] Ⓟ 🚕 🚶 32, 34
Castleton (Greater Manchester) **[NT]** Ⓟ 🚶 41
Castleton Moor [NT] Ⓟ 🚶 45
Caterham [SN] 🚲 ◇ ⚠ 🚕 181
Catford [SE] 🚲 ◇ ⚠ 52, 195
Catford Bridge [SE] 🚲 ◇ ⚠ 203
Cathays [AW] 🚶 130
Cathcart [SR] 🚲 223
Cattal [NT] 🚲 🚶 35
Catterick Camp Centre *Bus* 26H
Catterick Garrison Kemmel *Bus* 26H
Catterick Garrison Tesco *Bus* 26H
Causeland [GW] 🚶 140
Cefn-y-Bedd [AW] Ⓟ 101
Chadwell Heath [LE] 🚲 ⚠ 5
Chafford Hundred [CC] Ⓟ 🚲 ◇ ⚠ 1

Station index and table numbers

[10] Connection time
Ⓟ Station Car Park
🚲 Bicycle storage facility
◇ Seat reservations can be made at this station
⚠ Penalty Fare Schemes in operation on some or all services from this station
🚕 Taxi rank or cab office at station, or signposted and within 100 metres
Ⓤ Unstaffed station
[ ] Station Operator Code

Chalfont & Latimer [LT] Ⓟ 🚲 ⚠ 🚕 114
Chalkwell [CC] 🚲 ◇ ⚠ 🚕 1
Chandlers Ford [SW] Ⓟ 🚲 ◇ 158
Chapel-en-le-Frith [NT] Ⓟ Ⓤ 86
Chapelton [GW] Ⓟ Ⓤ 136
Chapeltown [NT] Ⓤ 34
Chappel & Wakes Colne [LE] 🚲 Ⓤ 10
Charing [SE] Ⓟ ◇ ⚠ 196
Charing Cross (Glasgow) **[SR]** 🚲 226
Charing Cross [NR] (see London)
Charlbury [GW] Ⓟ 🚲 126
Charlton [SE] [4] ◇ ⚠ 200
Chartham [SE] ⚠ Ⓤ 207
Chassen Road [NT] 89
Chatelherault [SR] 🚲 Ⓤ 226
Chatham [SE] [4] Ⓟ ◇ ⚠ 🚕 194, 200, 212
Chathill [NT] Ⓟ Ⓤ 48
Cheadle Hulme [NT] Ⓟ 🚲 84
Cheam [SN] Ⓟ 🚲 ◇ ⚠ 🚕 182
Cheddington [LM] Ⓟ 66
Chelford [NT] Ⓟ 🚲 Ⓤ 84
Chelmsford [LE] [3] Ⓟ 🚲 ◇ ⚠ 🚕 11, 13, 14
Chelsfield [SE] [3] Ⓟ ◇ ⚠ 🚕 204
Cheltenham Spa [GW] Ⓟ 🚲 ◇ 🚕 51, 57, 125
Chepstow [AW] Ⓟ Ⓤ 132
Cherry Tree [NT] Ⓟ Ⓤ 97
Chertsey [SW] Ⓟ 🚲 ◇ ⚠ 149
Cheshunt [LE] Ⓟ 🚲 ⚠ 🚕 21, 22
Chessington North [SW] Ⓟ 🚲 ◇ ⚠ 🚕 152
Chessington South [SW] Ⓟ 🚲 ◇ ⚠ 152
Chester [AW] Ⓟ ◇ 🚕
Altrincham 88
Bangor (Gwynedd) 81
Birmingham 75, 81
Cardiff 75, 81, 131
Crewe 81
Hereford 131
Holyhead 81
Liverpool 106
Llandudno 81
Llandudno Junction 81
London 65
Manchester 81, 88
Newport (South Wales) 131
Northwich 88
Rhyl 81
Runcorn East 81
Shrewsbury 75, 131
Stafford 65
Stockport 88
Warrington 81
Wolverhampton 65, 75
Wrexham 75
Chester Road [LM] Ⓟ ⚠ 69
Chesterfield [EM] Ⓟ 🚲 ◇ 🚕 34, 49, 51, 53
Chester-le-Street [NT] Ⓟ 🚲 ◇ 🚕 Ⓤ 26, 39, 44, 51
Chestfield & Swalecliffe [SE] ◇ ⚠ 212
Chetnole [GW] Ⓤ 123
Chichester [SN] [4] Ⓟ 🚲 ◇ ⚠ 🚕 123, 165, 188
Chilham [SE] Ⓟ ⚠ Ⓤ 207
Chilworth [GW] Ⓤ 148
Chingford [LE] Ⓟ 🚲 ⚠ 🚕 20
Chinley [NT] Ⓟ Ⓤ 78
Chinnor, Estover Way *Bus* 115A
Chinnor, Lower Road *Bus* 115A
Chinnor, The Red Lion *Bus* 115A
Chinnor, The Wheatsheaf *Bus* 115A
Chippenham [GW] Ⓟ 🚲 ◇ ⚠ 🚕 123, 125
Chipping Norton West Street *Bus* 126A
Chipstead [SN] Ⓟ ⚠ 181
Chirk [AW] Ⓟ Ⓤ 75
Chislehurst [SE] Ⓟ ◇ ⚠ 🚕 204
Chiswick [SW] Ⓟ 🚲 Ⓤ 149
Cholsey [GW] Ⓟ 🚲 116
Chorley [NT] Ⓟ ◇ 82
Chorleywood [LT] Ⓟ 🚲 ⚠ 🚕 114
Christchurch [SW] Ⓟ 🚲 ◇ ⚠ 🚕 158
Christs Hospital [SN] Ⓟ 🚲 ◇ ⚠ 188
Church Fenton [NT] Ⓟ 🚲 Ⓤ 33, 40
Church & Oswaldtwistle [NT] Ⓤ 97
Church Stretton [AW] Ⓟ Ⓤ 129, 131
Cilmeri [AW] Ⓤ 129
City Thameslink [FC] (see London)
Clacton-on-Sea [LE] Ⓟ 🚲 ◇ ⚠ 🚕 11
Clandon [SW] Ⓟ 🚲 ◇ ⚠ 152
Clapham High Street [SN] 🚲 ⚠ Ⓤ 178
Clapham Junction [SW] [10] ◇ ⚠
Alton 155
Andover 160
Ascot 149
Basingstoke 155, 158
Bexhill 189
Birmingham 66
Birmingham International 66
Bognor Regis 188
Bournemouth 158
Brighton 186
Bristol 160
Chertsey 149
Chessington 152
Chichester 188
Coventry 66
Crystal Palace 177, 178
Dorking 152, 182
Eastbourne 189
East Croydon 175, 176
East Grinstead 184
Effingham Junction 152
Epsom 152, 182
Epsom Downs 182
Exeter 160
Gatwick Airport 186
Guildford 152, 156
Hampton Court 152
Hastings 189
Haywards Heath 186
Horsham 186
Hounslow 149
Hove 186
Kensington (Olympia) 66, 176, 186
Kingston 149, 152
Lewes 189
London
Victoria 175, 177
Waterloo 149, 152
Milton Keynes Central 66, 176
Northampton 66
Oxted 184
Portsmouth 156, 158, 188
Purley 175
Reading 149
Redhill 186
Rugby 66
Salisbury 160
Shepperton 152
Southampton 158, 188
Staines 149
Surbiton 152
Sutton (Surrey) 182
Tattenham Corner 181
Twickenham 149
Uckfield 184
Watford Junction 66, 176, 186
West Croydon 177
Weybridge 155
Willesden Junction 176, 186
Wimbledon 152
Windsor 149
Woking 155
Worthing 188
Yeovil Junction 160
Clapham (Nth Yorkshire) [NT] Ⓟ Ⓤ 36
Clapton [LE] ⚠ 20, 22
Clarbeston Road [AW] Ⓤ 128
Clarkston [SR] 🚲 222
Claverdon [LM] ⚠ Ⓤ 115
Claygate [SW] Ⓟ 🚲 ◇ ⚠ 🚕 152
Cleethorpes [TP] Ⓟ 🚲 ◇ 🚕 27, 29, 30
Cleland [SR] Ⓟ 🚲 Ⓤ 225
Clifton [NT] Ⓤ 82
Clifton Down [GW] Ⓟ Ⓤ 133
Clitheroe [NT] Ⓟ 94
Clock House [SE] 🚲 ◇ ⚠ 🚕 203

Station index and table numbers

■10 Connection time
℗ Station Car Park
🚲 Bicycle storage facility
◇ Seat reservations can be made at this station
⚠ Penalty Fare Schemes in operation on some or all services from this station
🚕 Taxi rank or cab office at station, or signposted and within 100 metres
Ⓤ Unstaffed station
[ ] Station Operator Code

Clunderwen [AW] ℗ Ⓤ 128
Clydebank [SR] 🚲 🚕 226
Coatbridge Central [SR] ℗ 🚲 🚕 Ⓤ 224, 226
Coatbridge Sunnyside [SR] ℗ 🚲 226
Coatdyke [SR] ℗ 🚲 Ⓤ 226
Cobham & Stoke d'Abernon [SW] ℗ 🚲 ◇ ⚠ 🚕 152
Cockermouth (Main Street) *Bus* 65F
Codsall [LM] ℗ Ⓤ 74
Cogan [AW] ℗ Ⓤ 130
Colchester [LE] ■4 ℗ 🚲 ◇ ⚠ 🚕 10, 11, 13, 14
Colchester Town [LE] ℗ 🚲 ⚠ 11
Coleshill Parkway [LM] ℗ 🚲 ◇ 🚕 49, 57
Coll *Ship* 227B
Collingham [EM] Ⓤ 27
Collington [SN] ⚠ Ⓤ 189
Colne [NT] ℗ Ⓤ 97
Colonsay *Ship* 227B
Colwall [LM] ℗ ⚠ Ⓤ 71, 126
Colwyn Bay [AW] ℗ ◇ 🚕 81
Combe [GW] Ⓤ 126
Commondale [NT] Ⓤ 45
Congleton [NT] ℗ ◇ 51, 65, 84
Conisbrough [NT] ℗ Ⓤ 29
Connel Ferry [SR] ℗ 🚲 Ⓤ 227
Cononley [NT] ℗ Ⓤ 36
Conway Park [ME] 106
Conwy [AW] Ⓤ 81
Cooden Beach [SN] ℗ 🚲 ◇ ⚠ 189
Cookham [GW] ℗ 120
Cooksbridge [SN] ℗ ⚠ Ⓤ 189
Coombe Junction Halt [GW] Ⓤ 140
Copplestone [GW] ℗ Ⓤ 136
Corbridge [NT] ℗ Ⓤ 48
Corby [EM] 53
Corby George Street *Bus* 26B
Corkerhill [SR] 🚲 Ⓤ 217
Corkickle [NT] Ⓤ 100
Corpach [SR] ℗ 🚲 Ⓤ 227
Corrour [SR] 🚲 Ⓤ 227, *Sleepers* 404
Coryton [AW] Ⓤ 130
Coseley [LM] ℗ ⚠ 68
Cosford [LM] ℗ Ⓤ 74, 75
Cosham [SW] ℗ 🚲 ◇ ⚠ 🚕 123, 158, 165, 188
Cottingham [NT] ℗ 🚕 Ⓤ 43
Cottingley [NT] Ⓤ 39
Coulsdon South [SN] ℗ ⚠ 🚕 186
Coventry [VT] ℗ 🚲 ◇ ⚠ 🚕
Aberdeen 65
Barrow-in-Furness 65
Banbury 71
Basingstoke 51
Birmingham 68
Birmingham International 68
Blackpool 65
Bournemouth 51
Brighton 66
Carlisle 65
Clapham Junction 66
Crewe 65
Derby 51
Dundee 65
East Croydon 66
Edinburgh 51, 65
Gatwick Airport 66
Glasgow 51, 65
Holyhead 65
Inverness 65
Leamington Spa 71
Leeds 51
Liverpool 65
London 66
Manchester 65
Manchester Airport 65
Milton Keynes Central 66
Newcastle 51
Northampton 66
Nuneaton 67
Oxenholme Lake District 65
Oxford 51
Preston 65
Reading 51
Rugby 66
Sheffield 51
Southampton 51
Stafford 67, 68
Stoke-on-Trent 65
Watford 66
Wolverhampton 68
York 51
Cowden [SN] ℗ ⚠ Ⓤ 184
Cowdenbeath [SR] 🚲 ◇ 242
Cradley Heath [LM] ℗ 🚲 ◇ ⚠ 71, 115
Craigendoran [SR] ℗ 🚲 Ⓤ 226
Craignure *Ship* 227B
Cramlington [NT] ℗ 🚲 Ⓤ 48
Craven Arms [AW] ℗ Ⓤ 129, 131
Crawley [SN] ℗ 🚲 ◇ ⚠ 🚕 186, 188
Crayford [SE] ℗ ◇ ⚠ 200
Crediton [GW] ℗ 🚲 Ⓤ 136
Cressing [LE] 🚲 ⚠ Ⓤ 11
Cressington [ME] ℗ ⚠ 103
Creswell [EM] Ⓤ 55
Crewe [VT] ■10 ℗ 🚲 ◇ 🚕
Aberdeen 65, *Sleepers* 402
Bangor (Gwynedd) 81
Barrow-in-Furness 65
Birmingham 65
Birmingham International 65
Blackpool 65
Bournemouth 51
Bristol 51
Cardiff 131
Carlisle 65
Cheltenham Spa 51
Chester 81
Coventry 65, 67
Derby 50
Douglas (IOM) 98A
Dundee 65, *Sleepers* 402
Edinburgh 65
Exeter 51
Fort William *Sleepers* 404
Glasgow 65
Hartford 91
Hereford 131
Holyhead 81
Inverkeithing *Sleepers* 402
Inverness 65, *Sleepers* 403
Kirkcaldy *Sleepers* 402
Lancaster 65
Liverpool 91
Liverpool South Parkway 91
Llandudno 81
London 65, 67
Manchester 84
Manchester Airport 84
Milton Keynes Central 65, 67
Newport (South Wales) 131
Northampton 67
Oxenholme Lake District 65
Oxford 51
Paignton 51
Penzance 51
Perth 65, *Sleepers* 403
Plymouth 51
Preston 65
Reading 51
Rugby 65, 67
Runcorn 91
Shrewsbury 131
Southampton 51
Stafford 65, 67
Stirling *Sleepers* 403
Stockport 84
Stoke-on-Trent 50
Torquay 51
Watford 65
Wilmslow 84
Wolverhampton 65
Crewkerne [SW] ℗ 🚲 ◇ 160
Crews Hill [FC] ⚠ Ⓤ 24
Crianlarich [SR] ℗ 🚲 Ⓤ 227, *Sleepers* 404
Criccieth [AW] ℗ 🚲 Ⓤ 75
Cricklewood [FC] 🚲 ◇ ⚠ 52
Croftfoot [SR] 🚲 223
Crofton Park [SE] ◇ ⚠ 52, 195
Cromer [LE] ℗ 🚲 Ⓤ 16
Cromford [EM] ℗ Ⓤ 54, 56
Crompton [NT] (see Shaw)
Crookston [SR] 🚲 Ⓤ 217
Crosby [ME] (see Blundellsands)
Crossflatts [NT] ℗ 🚲 Ⓤ 36
Cross Gates [NT] ℗ 40
Cross Keys [AW] Ⓤ 127
Crosshill [SR] 223
Crossmyloof [SR] 🚲 Ⓤ 222
Croston [NT] ℗ Ⓤ 99
Crouch Hill [LO] ⚠ 62
Crowborough [SN] ℗ ◇ ⚠ 184
Crowhurst [SE] ℗ ⚠ 206

Station index and table numbers

❿ Connection time
Ⓟ Station Car Park
🚲 Bicycle storage facility
◇ Seat reservations can be made at this station
⚠ Penalty Fare Schemes in operation on some or all services from this station
🚕 Taxi rank or cab office at station, or signposted and within 100 metres
Ⓤ Unstaffed station
[ ] Station Operator Code

Station index and table numbers

[10] Connection time
Ⓟ Station Car Park
🚲 Bicycle storage facility
◇ Seat reservations can be made at this station
⚠ Penalty Fare Schemes in operation on some or all services from this station
🚕 Taxi rank or cab office at station, or signposted and within 100 metres
Ⓤ Unstaffed station
[ ] Station Operator Code

Dundee 26
Durham 26
Edinburgh 26
Exeter 51
Gainsborough 18
Glasgow 26
Goole 29
Grantham 26
Grimsby 29
Hull 29
Leeds 31
Leicester 53
Lincoln 18
London 26
Luton 53
Manchester 29
Manchester Airport 29
Middlesbrough 26
Newark 26
Newcastle 26
Norwich 26
Nottingham 53
Oxford 51
Paignton 51
Penzance 51
Peterborough 18, 26
Plymouth 51
Reading 51
Retford 26
Robin Hood Airport *Bus* 26F
Rotherham 29
Scunthorpe 29
Selby 29
Sheffield 29
Sleaford 18
Southampton 51
Spalding 18
Stansted Airport 26
Stevenage 26
Stockport 29
Sunderland 26
Torquay 51
Wakefield 31
York 26

Doncaster Interchange *Bus* 🚕 26F
Dorchester South [SW] Ⓟ 🚲 ◇ ⚠ 🚕 158
Dorchester West [GW] Ⓤ 123, 158
Dore & Totley [NT] Ⓟ Ⓤ 78
Dorking [SN] [4] Ⓟ 🚲 ◇ ⚠ 🚕 152, 182
Dorking Deepdene [GW] Ⓤ 148
Dorking West [GW] Ⓤ 148
Dormans [SN] ◇ ⚠ 184
Dorridge [LM] Ⓟ 🚲 ◇ ⚠ 71, 115
Douglas (IOM) *Ship* 98A
Dove Holes [NT] Ⓟ Ⓤ 86
Dovercourt [LE] Ⓟ 🚲 11
Dover Priory [SE] [4] Ⓟ 🚲 ◇ ⚠ 🚕 194, 207, 212
Dovey Junction [AW] [4] Ⓤ 75
Downham Market [FC] Ⓟ 🚲 ⚠ 🚕 17
Drayton Green [GW] Ⓤ 117
Drayton Park [FC] 🚲 ⚠ 24
Drem [SR] Ⓟ 🚲 Ⓤ 238
Driffield [NT] Ⓟ 🚲 🚕 43
Drigg [NT] Ⓤ 100
Droitwich Spa [LM] Ⓟ ◇ ⚠ 71
Dronfield [NT] Ⓟ Ⓤ 34
Drumchapel [SR] Ⓟ 🚲 🚕 226
Drumfrochar [SR] 🚲 Ⓤ 219
Drumgelloch [SR] 🚲 Ⓤ 226
Drumry [SR] Ⓟ 🚲 226
Dublin Ferryport *Ship* 81A
Duddeston [LM] ⚠ 69, 70
Dudley Port [LM] Ⓟ ⚠ 68
Duffield [EM] Ⓟ Ⓤ 56
Duirinish [SR] Ⓟ 🚲 Ⓤ 239
Duke Street [SR] 🚲 Ⓤ 226
Dullingham [LE] Ⓟ 🚲 Ⓤ 14
Dumbarton Central [SR] 🚲 ◇ 🚕 226, 227
Dumbarton East [SR] 🚲 Ⓤ 226
Dumbreck [SR] 🚲 Ⓤ 217
Dumfries [SR] Ⓟ 🚲 ◇ 🚕 218
Dumpton Park [SE] ⚠ Ⓤ 212
Dun Laoghaire *Ship* 81A
Dunbar [GR] Ⓟ 🚲 ◇ 26, 51, 238
Dunblane [SR] Ⓟ 🚲 ◇ 229, 230, *Sleepers* 403
Duncraig [SR] 🚲 Ⓤ 239
Dundee [SR] Ⓟ 🚲 ◇ 🚕 26, 51, 65, 229, *Sleepers* 402
Dunfermline Queen Margaret [SR] Ⓟ 🚲 Ⓤ 242
Dunfermline Town [SR] Ⓟ 🚲 ◇ 🚕 242
Dunkeld & Birnam [SR] Ⓟ 🚲 Ⓤ 229, *Sleepers* 403
Dunlop [SR] 🚲 Ⓤ 222
Dunoon *Ship* 219A
Dunrobin Castle [SR] Ⓤ *Summer only* 239
Duns *Bus* 26K
Dunstable *Bus* 52A
Dunster Steep *Bus* 135E
Dunston [NT] Ⓤ 48
Dunton Green [SE] Ⓟ ⚠ Ⓤ 204
Durham [GR] Ⓟ 🚲 ◇ 🚕 26, 39, 44, 51
Durrington-on-Sea [SN] 🚲 ⚠ 188
Dursley [GW] (see Cam & Dursley)
Dyce [SR] Ⓟ 🚲 🚕 Ⓤ 229, 240
Dyffryn Ardudwy [AW] Ⓤ 75

E

Eaglescliffe [NT] Ⓟ 🚲 🚕 Ⓤ 26, 44
Ealing Broadway [GW] [3] ◇ ⚠ 🚕 116, 117
Earlestown [NT] [8] 81, 90
Earley [SW] Ⓟ 🚲 ⚠ 149
Earlsfield [SW] 🚲 ◇ ⚠ 152, 155
Earlston *Bus* 26K
Earlswood (Surrey) [SN] 🚲 ◇ ⚠ 186
Earlswood (West Midlands) [LM] Ⓟ ⚠ Ⓤ 71
East Croydon [SN] 🚲 ◇ ⚠ 🚕
Bedford 52
Bexhill 189
Birmingham 66
Birmingham International 66
Bognor Regis 188
Brighton 186
Caterham 181
Chichester 188
Clapham Junction 175, 176
Coventry 66
Eastbourne 189
East Grinstead 184
Gatwick Airport 186
Hastings 189
Haywards Heath 186
Horsham 186
Hove 186
Kensington (Olympia) 66, 176, 186
Lewes 189
Littlehampton 188
London 175
Luton 52
Luton Airport Parkway 52
Milton Keynes Central 66, 176
Northampton 66
Norwood Junction 177, 178
Oxted 184
Portsmouth 188
Purley 175
Redhill 186
Rugby 66
St Albans 52
St Pancras International 52
Seaford 189
Southampton Central 188
Tattenham Corner 181
Tonbridge 186
Uckfield 184
Watford Junction 66, 176, 186
West Hampstead Thameslink 52
Wolverhampton 66
Worthing 188
East Didsbury [NT] Ⓟ 85
East Dulwich [SN] ⚠ 177, 179
East Farleigh [SE] Ⓟ ⚠ Ⓤ 208
East Garforth [NT] Ⓤ 40
East Grinstead [SN] Ⓟ 🚲 ◇ ⚠ 🚕 184
East Kilbride [SR] Ⓟ 🚲 ◇ 🚕 222
East Malling [SE] ⚠ Ⓤ 196
East Midlands Parkway [EM] 53
East Tilbury [CC] ◇ ⚠ 1
East Worthing [SN] ⚠ Ⓤ 188

Station index and table numbers

❿ Connection time
Ⓟ Station Car Park
🚲 Bicycle storage facility
◇ Seat reservations can be made at this station
⚠ Penalty Fare Schemes in operation on some or all services from this station
🚕 Taxi rank or cab office at station, or signposted and within 100 metres
Ⓤ Unstaffed station
[ ] Station Operator Code

Eastbourne [SN] ❹ Ⓟ 🚲 ◇ ⚠ 🚕 189
Eastbrook [AW] Ⓟ Ⓤ 130
Easterhouse [SR] Ⓟ 🚲 226
Eastham Rake [ME] Ⓟ 🚲 ⚠ 106
Eastleigh [SW] ❸ Ⓟ 🚲 ◇ ⚠ 🚕 158
Eastrington [NT] Ⓤ 29
Ebbsfleet International [SE] ◇ ⚠ 🚕 194, 196, 200, 207, 212
Ebbw Vale Parkway [AW] Ⓟ Ⓤ 127
Eccles [NT] Ⓟ 90
Eccles Road [LE] Ⓟ Ⓤ 17
Eccleston Park [NT] 90
Edale [NT] Ⓟ Ⓤ 78
Eden Camp *Bus* 26G
Eden Park [SE] ◇ ⚠ 203
Eden Project *Bus* 135B
Edenbridge [SN] Ⓟ ⚠ Ⓤ 186
Edenbridge Town [SN] ◇ ⚠ 🚕 184
Edge Hill [NT] Ⓟ 89, 90, 91
Edinburgh [NR] ❿ Ⓟ 🚲 ◇ 🚕
Aberdeen 229
Bathgate 237
Birmingham New Street 51, 65
Birmingham International 51, 65
Blackpool 65
Bournemouth 51
Bristol 51
Cambridge 26
Cardiff 51
Carlisle 65
Carstairs 225
Cowdenbeath 242
Crewe 65
Croy 228
Darlington 26
Derby 51
Doncaster 26
Dunbar 238
Dunblane 230
Dundee 229
Dunfermline 242
Dyce 229
Edinburgh Park 230, 237
Exeter 51
Falkirk 228, 230
Fort William 227
Glasgow 225, 228
Glenrothes with Thornton 242
Grantham 26
Inverkeithing 242
Inverness 229
Inverurie 229
Kirkcaldy 242
Lancaster 65
Larbert 230
Leeds 26
Linlithgow 230
Liverpool 65
Livingston 225, 237
London 26, *Sleepers* 400
Mallaig 227
Manchester 65
Manchester Airport 65
Markinch 229
Motherwell 225
Newcastle 26
Newcraighall 242
Newport (South Wales) 51
North Berwick 238
Oban 227
Oxenholme Lake District 65
Oxford 51
Paignton 51
Penzance 51
Perth 229
Peterborough 26
Plymouth 51
Polmont 230
Preston 65
Reading 51
Sheffield 26
Shotts 225
Southampton 51
Stafford 65
Stirling 230
Thurso 239
Torquay 51
Warrington 65
Watford 65, *Sleepers* 400
West Calder 225
Western Isles *Ship* 239B
Wigan 65
York 26
Edinburgh Park [SR] 🚲 Ⓤ 230, 237
Edmonton Green [LE] ⚠ 21
Effingham Junction [SW] ❻ Ⓟ 🚲 ◇ ⚠ 152, 182
Eggesford [GW] Ⓟ Ⓤ 136
Egham [SW] Ⓟ 🚲 ◇ ⚠ 🚕 149
Egton [NT] Ⓤ 45
Eigg *Ship* 227A
Elephant & Castle [FC] 🚲 ◇ ⚠
Ashford 196
Bromley South 195
Canterbury 212
Catford 195
Chatham 212
Dover 212
East Croydon 177
Faversham 212
London 52, 177
Luton 52
Maidstone 196
Margate 212
Ramsgate 212
Rochester 212
St Albans 52
St Pancras International 52, 177
Sevenoaks 195
Streatham 177
Sutton (Surrey) 179
Swanley 195
Wimbledon 179
Elgin [SR] Ⓟ 🚲 ◇ 🚕 240
Ellesmere Port [ME] 🚕 106, 109
Elmers End [SE] ❹ Ⓟ 🚲 ◇ ⚠ 203
Elmstead Woods [SE] Ⓟ ◇ ⚠ 🚕 204
Elmswell [LE] 🚲 Ⓤ 14
Elsecar [NT] Ⓤ 34
Elsenham [LE] 🚲 ⚠ 22
Elstree & Borehamwood [FC] Ⓟ 🚲 ◇ ⚠ 🚕 52
Eltham [SE] Ⓟ 🚲 ◇ ⚠ 🚕 200
Elton (Ches.) **[NT]** (see Ince & Elton)
Elton & Orston [EM] Ⓟ Ⓤ 19
Ely [LE] ❻ Ⓟ 🚲 ◇ ⚠ 🚕 14, 17, 49
Emerson Park [LE] 🚲 ⚠ Ⓤ 4
Emsworth [SN] Ⓟ 🚲 ◇ ⚠ 188
Enfield Chase [FC] Ⓟ 🚲 ⚠ 24
Enfield Lock [LE] 🚲 ⚠ 22
Enfield Town [LE] ⚠ 🚕 21
Entwistle [NT] Ⓤ 94
Epsom [SN] ❸ Ⓟ 🚲 ◇ ⚠ 🚕 152, 182
Epsom Downs [SN] ⚠ Ⓤ 182
Erdington [LM] ⚠ 69
Eridge [SN] ⚠ 184
Erith [SE] ◇ ⚠ 🚕 200
Esher [SW] Ⓟ 🚲 ◇ ⚠ 🚕 155
Eskdale [NT] (see Ravenglass)
Essex Road [FC] 🚲 ⚠ 24
Etchingham [SE] Ⓟ 🚲 ◇ ⚠ 206
Eton (see Windsor)
Euston [NR] (see London)
Euxton Balshaw Lane [NT] Ⓟ Ⓤ 90
Evesham [GW] Ⓟ 🚲 🚕 126
Ewell East [SN] Ⓟ ◇ ⚠ 182
Ewell West [SW] Ⓟ 🚲 ◇ ⚠ 152
Exeter
Central [GW] Ⓟ 🚲 ◇
St Davids [GW] ❻ Ⓟ 🚲 ◇ ⚠ 🚕
St Thomas [GW] Ⓤ
Aberdeen 51
Andover 160
Barnstaple 136
Basingstoke 160
Birmingham 51
Bristol 135
Bude Strand *Bus* 135D
Cardiff 135
Carlisle 51
Clapham Junction 160
Crewe 51
Derby 51
Dundee 51
Edinburgh 51
Exmouth 136
Glasgow 51
Holsworthy *Bus* 135D
Leeds 51
London 135, 160, *Sleepers* 406
Manchester 51
Newcastle 51
Newport (South Wales) 135

[10] Connection time
Ⓟ Station Car Park
🚲 Bicycle storage facility
◇ Seat reservations can be made at this station
⚠ Penalty Fare Schemes in operation on some or all services from this station
🚕 Taxi rank or cab office at station, or signposted and within 100 metres
ⓤ Unstaffed station
[ ] Station Operator Code

Station index and table numbers

Newquay 135
Newton Abbot 135
Nottingham 51
Okehampton *Summer only* 136
Okehampton West Street *Bus* 135D
Paignton 135
Penzance 135
Plymouth 135
Preston 51
Reading 135, *Sleepers* 406
Salisbury 160
Sheffield 51
Taunton 135
Torquay 135
Truro 135
Weston-super-Mare 135
Wolverhampton 51
York 51
Exhibition Centre [SR] 🚲 226
Exmouth [GW] Ⓟ 🚲 ◇ 135, 136
Exton [GW] Ⓟ 🚲 ⓤ 136
Eynsford [SE] Ⓟ ◇ ⚠ 52, 195
Eynsham Church *Bus* 116C

F

Fairbourne [AW] Ⓟ ⓤ 75
Fairfield [NT] ⓤ 78
Fairhaven [NT] (see Ansdell)
Fairlie [SR] Ⓟ 🚲 ⓤ 221
Fairwater [AW] ⓤ 130
Falconwood [SE] ◇ ⚠ 🚕 200
Falkirk Grahamston [SR] Ⓟ 🚲 ◇ 🚕 224, 230, *Sleepers* 403
Falkirk High [SR] Ⓟ 🚲 ◇ 🚕 228
Falls of Cruachan [SR] ⓤ *Summer only* 227
Falmer [SN] Ⓟ 🚲 ⚠ 189
Falmouth Docks [GW] Ⓟ ⓤ 143
Falmouth Town [GW] ⓤ 143
Fambridge [LE] (North Fambridge)
Fareham [SW] Ⓟ 🚲 ◇ ⚠ 🚕 123, 158, 165, 188
Farnborough (Main) [SW] Ⓟ 🚲 ◇ ⚠ 🚕 155,158
Farnborough North [GW] Ⓟ ⓤ 148
Farncombe [SW] Ⓟ 🚲 ◇ ⚠ 156
Farnham [SW] Ⓟ 🚲 ◇ ⚠ 🚕 155
Farningham Road [SE] Ⓟ ◇ ⚠ 212
Farnworth [NT] 82
Farringdon [LT] (see London)
Fauldhouse [SR] Ⓟ 🚲 ⓤ 225
Faversham [SE] [2] Ⓟ 🚲 ◇ ⚠ 🚕 194, 212
Faygate [SN] ⚠ ⓤ 186
Fazakerley [ME] ⚠ 103
Fearn [SR] Ⓟ 🚲 ⓤ 239
Featherstone [NT] ⓤ 32
Felixstowe [LE] 🚲 🚕 ⓤ 13
Feltham [SW] Ⓟ 🚲 ◇ ⚠ 149
Fenchurch Street [NR] (see London)
Feniton [SW] Ⓟ 🚲 ◇ 160
Fenny Stratford [LM] ⓤ 64
Fernhill [AW] ⓤ 130
Ferriby [NT] Ⓟ 🚲 ⓤ 29
Ferryside [AW] ⓤ 128
Ffairfach [AW] ⓤ 129
Filey [NT] Ⓟ 🚕 ⓤ 43
Filton Abbey Wood [GW] Ⓟ 🚲 123, 132, 134, 135
Finchley Road & Frognal [LO] ⚠ 59
Finsbury Park [FC] ⚠ 🚕 24, 25
Finstock [GW] ⓤ 126
Fishbourne (Sussex) [SN] ⚠ ⓤ 188
Fishersgate [SN] ⚠ ⓤ 188
Fishguard Harbour [AW] ⓤ 128
Fiskerton [EM] Ⓟ ⓤ 27
Fitzwilliam [NT] Ⓟ ⓤ 31
Five Ways [LM] ⚠ 69
Flamingo Land *Bus* 26G
Fleet [SW] Ⓟ 🚲 ◇ ⚠ 🚕 155, 158
Flimby [NT] ⓤ 100
Flint [AW] Ⓟ ◇ 81
Flitwick [FC] Ⓟ 🚲 ◇ ⚠ 🚕 52
Flixton [NT] 🚲 89
Flowery Field [NT] ⓤ 79
Folkestone Central [SE] Ⓟ 🚲 ◇ ⚠ 🚕 194, 207
Folkestone West [SE] Ⓟ ◇ ⚠ 194, 207
Ford [SN] [4] 🚲 ◇ ⚠ 188
Forest Gate [LE] 🚲 ⚠ 5
Forest Hill [LO] [4] Ⓟ 🚲 ◇ ⚠ 🚕 178
Formby [ME] Ⓟ 🚲 ⚠ 103
Forres [SR] Ⓟ 🚲 ◇ 🚕 240
Forsinard [SR] Ⓟ 🚲 ⓤ 239
Fort Matilda [SR] Ⓟ 🚲 ⓤ 219
Fort William [SR] Ⓟ 🚲 ◇ 🚕 227, *Ship* 227A, *Sleepers* 404
Four Oaks [LM] Ⓟ ⚠ 69
Foxfield [NT] ⓤ 100
Foxton [FC] ⚠ ⓤ 25
Frant [SE] Ⓟ ◇ ⚠ 206
Fratton [SW] Ⓟ 🚲 ◇ ⚠ 🚕 123, 156, 157, 158, 165, 188
Freshfield [ME] Ⓟ 🚲 ⚠ 103
Freshford [GW] Ⓟ ⓤ 123
Frimley [SW] Ⓟ 🚲 ◇ ⚠ 149
Frinton-on-Sea [LE] Ⓟ 🚲 ⚠ 11
Frizinghall [NT] Ⓟ ⓤ 36, 37, 38
Frodsham [AW] Ⓟ ⓤ 81
Frognal [LO] (see Finchley Road)
Frome [GW] Ⓟ 🚲 🚕 123
Fulwell [SW] 🚲 ◇ ⚠ 149, 152
Furness Vale [NT] ⓤ 86
Furze Platt [GW] 120

G

Gainsborough Central [NT] Ⓟ ⓤ 30
Gainsborough Lea Road [EM] Ⓟ 🚲 ⓤ 18, 30
Galashiels 🚕 *Bus* 26K, 65G
Galton Bridge (Smethwick) [LM] (see Smethwick Galton Bridge)
Garelochhead [SR] Ⓟ 🚲 ⓤ 227, *Sleepers* 404
Garforth [NT] Ⓟ 🚲 39, 40
Gargrave [NT] ⓤ 36
Garrowhill [SR] 🚲 226
Garscadden [SR] 🚲 226
Garsdale [NT] Ⓟ ⓤ 36
Garston (Hertfordshire) [LM] ⓤ 61
Garswood [NT] Ⓟ 90
Gartcosh [SR] Ⓟ 🚲 ⓤ 224
Garth (Powys) [AW] ⓤ 129
Garth (Mid Glamorgan) [AW] ⓤ 128
Garve [SR] Ⓟ 🚲 ⓤ 239
Gateshead [NT] (see Metrocentre)
Gathurst [NT] Ⓟ 🚲 ⓤ 82
Gatley [NT] Ⓟ 85
Gatwick Airport [NR] [10] ◇ ⚠ 🚕
Bedford 52
Bognor Regis 188
Brighton 176, 186
Chichester 188
City Thameslink 52, 186
Clapham Junction 176, 186
Eastbourne 189
East Croydon 176, 186
Elstree & Borehamwood 52
Guildford 148
Hastings 189
Haywards Heath 186
Hove 186
Kensington (Olympia) 176
Lewes 189
London 186
Luton 52, 186
Luton Airport Parkway 52
Mill Hill Broadway 52
Milton Keynes Central 176
Portsmouth 188
Radlett 52
Reading 148
St Albans 52
St Pancras International 52
Southampton Central 188
Watford Junction 176
West Hampstead Thameslink 52
Worthing 188
York 53
Georgemas Junction [SR] [1] Ⓟ 🚲 ⓤ 239

Station index and table numbers

■10 Connection time
Ⓟ Station Car Park
🚲 Bicycle storage facility
◇ Seat reservations can be made at this station
⚠ Penalty Fare Schemes in operation on some or all services from this station
🚕 Taxi rank or cab office at station, or signposted and within 100 metres
Ⓤ Unstaffed station
[ ] Station Operator Code

Gerrards Cross [CH] ■1 Ⓟ 🚲 ◇ ⚠ 🚕 115
Gidea Park [LE] ■2 Ⓟ 🚲 ⚠ 🚕 5
Giffnock [SR] Ⓟ 🚲 Ⓤ 222
Giggleswick [NT] Ⓟ Ⓤ 36
Gilberdyke [NT] Ⓟ Ⓤ 29
Gilfach Fargoed [AW] Ⓤ 130
Gillingham (Dorset) [SW] Ⓟ 🚲 ◇ 🚕 160
Gillingham (Kent) [SE] ■4 Ⓟ ◇ ⚠ 🚕 194, 200, 212
Gilshochill [SR] 🚲 Ⓤ 232
Gipsy Hill [SN] ◇ ⚠ 177, 178
Girvan [SR] Ⓟ 🚲 218
Glaisdale [NT] Ⓟ Ⓤ 45
Glan Conwy [AW] Ⓤ 102
Glasgow
- **Central [NR]** ■15 Ⓟ 🚲 ◇ 🚕
- **Queen Street [SR]** ■10 Ⓟ 🚲 ◇ 🚕
  - Aberdeen 229
  - Airdrie 226
  - Alloa 230
  - Anniesland 226, 232
  - Ardrossan 221
  - Ayr 221
  - Balloch 226
  - Barrhead 222
  - Belfast *Catamaran/Ship* 218
  - Birmingham New Street 51, 65
  - Birmingham International 51, 65
  - Blackpool 65
  - Bournemouth 51
  - Bristol 51
  - Cambridge 26
  - Carlisle 65
  - Carstairs 225
  - Cathcart 223
  - Clyde Coast *Ship* 219A, 219B, 221A
  - Crewe 65
  - Croy 230
  - Cumbernauld 224
  - Dalmuir 226
  - Darlington 26
  - Doncaster 26
  - Drumgelloch 226
  - Dumfries 216
  - Dunblane 230
  - Dundee 229
  - Dyce 229
  - East Kilbride 222
  - Edinburgh 225, 228
  - Exeter 51
  - Falkirk 224, 228
  - Fort William 227
  - Girvan 218
  - Gourock 219
  - Greenock 219
  - Hamilton 226
  - Helensburgh 226, 227
  - Inverness 229
  - Inverurie 229
  - Kilmarnock 222
  - Kyle of Lochalsh 239
  - Lanark 226
  - Lancaster 65
  - Largs 221
  - Larkhall 226
  - Leeds 26
  - Lenzie 230
  - Liverpool 65
  - Livingston South 225
  - London 26, 65, *Sleepers* 401
  - Mallaig 227
  - Manchester 65
  - Manchester Airport 65
  - Maryhill 232
  - Milngavie 226
  - Milton Keynes Central 65
  - Motherwell 225, 226
  - Neilston 223
  - Newcastle 26, 216
  - Newton 223, 226
  - Norwich 26
  - Oban 227
  - Oxenholme Lake District 65
  - Oxford 51
  - Paignton 51
  - Paisley 217, 219, 221
  - Penzance 51
  - Perth 229
  - Peterborough 26
  - Plymouth 51
  - Preston 65
  - Prestwick International Airport 221
  - Reading 51
  - Sheffield 26
  - Shotts 225
  - Southampton 51
  - Springburn 224, 226
  - Stafford 65
  - Stirling 230
  - Stranraer 218
  - Thurso 239
  - Torquay 51
  - Warrington 65
  - Watford 65, *Sleepers* 401
  - Wemyss Bay 219
  - Western Isles *Ship*
    - via Inverness 239B
    - via Mallaig 227A
    - via Oban 227B, 227C
  - Whifflet 220
  - Wigan 65
  - York 26

Glasshoughton [NT] Ⓟ 🚲 Ⓤ 32
Glazebrook [NT] Ⓟ 89
Gleneagles [SR] Ⓟ 🚲 Ⓤ 229, *Sleepers* 403
Glenfinnan [SR] Ⓟ 🚲 Ⓤ 227
Glengarnock [SR] Ⓟ 🚲 221
Glenrothes With Thornton [SR] Ⓟ 🚲 Ⓤ 242
Glossop [NT] Ⓟ 🚲 79
Gloucester [GW] ■7 Ⓟ 🚲 ◇ 🚕
- Birmingham 57
- Bristol 134
- Cardiff 132
- Carmarthen 128
- Cheltenham 57
- Chepstow 132
- Derby 57
- Didcot 125
- Kemble 125
- London 125
- Lydney 132
- Maesteg 128
- Newcastle 51
- Newport (South Wales) 132
- Nottingham 57
- Reading 125
- Sheffield 51
- Stroud 125
- Swansea 128
- Swindon 125
- Taunton 134
- Weston-super-Mare 134
- Worcester 57
- York 51

Glynde [SN] Ⓟ ⚠ Ⓤ 189
Goathland [NY] Ⓟ 45
Gobowen [AW] Ⓟ 75
Godalming [SW] Ⓟ 🚲 ◇ ⚠ 🚕 156
Godley [NT] Ⓤ 79
Godstone [SN] ⚠ Ⓤ 186
Goldthorpe [NT] Ⓟ Ⓤ 31
Golf Street [SR] Ⓤ 229
Golspie [SR] Ⓟ 🚲 Ⓤ 239
Gomshall [GW] Ⓟ Ⓤ 148
Goodmayes [LE] 🚲 ⚠ 5
Goole [NT] Ⓟ 🚲 ◇ 🚕 29, 32
Goostrey [NT] Ⓟ Ⓤ 84
Gordon Hill [FC] Ⓟ 🚲 ⚠ 24
Goring & Streatley [GW] Ⓟ 🚲 116
Goring-by-Sea [SN] Ⓟ 🚲 ◇ ⚠ 188
Gorton [NT] 78, 79
Gospel Oak [LO] 🚲 ⚠ 59, 62, 176
Gourock [SR] Ⓟ 🚲 ◇ 🚕 219, *Ship* 219A
Gowerton [AW] Ⓟ Ⓤ 128, 129
Goxhill [NT] Ⓤ 29
Grange Park [FC] Ⓟ ⚠ 24
Grange-over-Sands [TP] ◇ 82
Grangetown [AW] Ⓤ 130
Grantham [GR] ■7 Ⓟ 🚲 ◇ 🚕 19, 26, 49
Grateley [SW] Ⓟ 🚲 ⚠ Ⓤ 160
Gravelly Hill [LM] ⚠ 69
Gravesend [SE] ■4 Ⓟ ◇ ⚠ 🚕 194, 200, 212
Grays [CC] Ⓟ 🚲 ◇ ⚠ 🚕 1
Great Ayton [NT] Ⓟ 🚲 Ⓤ 45
Great Bentley [LE] 🚲 ⚠ 11
Great Chesterford [LE] ⚠ 22
Great Coates [NT] Ⓤ 29
Great Malvern [LM] Ⓟ ◇ ⚠ 🚕 71, 126
Great Missenden [CH] Ⓟ 🚲 ◇ ⚠ 🚕 114

Station index and table numbers

[10] Connection time
Ⓟ Station Car Park
🚲 Bicycle storage facility
◇ Seat reservations can be made at this station
⚠ Penalty Fare Schemes in operation on some or all services from this station
🚕 Taxi rank or cab office at station, or signposted and within 100 metres
Ⓤ Unstaffed station
[ ] Station Operator Code

Great Yarmouth [LE] Ⓟ 🚲 ◇ 🚕 15
Green Lane [ME] ⚠ 106
Green Road [NT] Ⓟ Ⓤ 100
Greenbank [NT] Ⓟ Ⓤ 88
Greenfaulds [SR] Ⓟ 🚲 Ⓤ 224
Greenfield [NT] 🚲 39
Greenford [LT] Ⓟ ⚠ 🚕 117
Greenhithe for Bluewater [SE] ◇ ⚠ 200, 212
Greenock Central [SR] Ⓟ 🚲 219
Greenock West [SR] 🚕 219
Greenwich [SE] **[4]** ◇ ⚠ 200
Gretna Green [SR] Ⓟ 🚲 Ⓤ 216
Grimsby Docks [NT] Ⓤ 29
Grimsby Town [TP] Ⓟ 🚲 ◇ 🚕 26, 27, 29, 30
Grindleford [NT] Ⓤ 78
Grosmont [NT] [NY] Ⓟ Ⓤ 45
Grove Park [SE] **[4]** ◇ ⚠ 🚕 204
Guide Bridge [NT] Ⓟ 78, 79
Guildford [SW] Ⓟ 🚲 ◇ ⚠ 🚕
Ascot 149
Birmingham 51
Clapham Junction 152, 155, 156
Gatwick Airport 148
London 152, 155, 156
Portsmouth 156
Reading 148
Surbiton 152
West Croydon 182
Guiseley [NT] Ⓟ 🚲 ◇ 38
Gunnersbury [LT] 59
Gunnislake [GW] Ⓟ 🚲 Ⓤ 139
Gunton [LE] Ⓟ 🚲 Ⓤ 16
Gwersyllt [AW] Ⓟ Ⓤ 101
Gypsy Lane [NT] 🚲 Ⓤ 45

H

Habrough [NT] Ⓟ Ⓤ 27, 29, 30
Hackbridge [SN] Ⓟ ◇ ⚠ 52, 179, 182
Hackney Central [LO] 🚲 ⚠ 🚕 59
Hackney Downs [LE] 🚲 ⚠ 20, 21, 22
Hackney Wick [LO] ⚠ 59
Haddenham & Thame Parkway [CH] Ⓟ 🚲 ◇ ⚠ 🚕 115
Haddiscoe [LE] Ⓟ 🚲 Ⓤ 15
Hadfield [NT] Ⓟ 🚲 79
Hadley Wood [FC] ⚠ 24
Hag Fold [NT] 82
Haggerston [LO] ⚠ 178
Hagley [LM] Ⓟ ⚠ 71
Hairmyres [SR] Ⓟ 🚲 Ⓤ 222
Hale [NT] Ⓟ 88
Halesworth [LE] Ⓟ 🚲 Ⓤ 13
Halewood [NT] 89
Halifax [NT] Ⓟ 🚲 ◇ 🚕 41
Hall Green [LM] Ⓟ ⚠ 71
Hall I' Th' Wood [NT] Ⓤ 94
Hall Road [ME] 🚲 ⚠ 103
Halling [SE] ⚠ Ⓤ 208
Haltwhistle [NT] Ⓟ 🚲 Ⓤ 48
Ham Street [SN] Ⓟ ◇ ⚠ 189
Hamble [SW] 🚲 ⚠ Ⓤ 165
Hamilton Central [SR] Ⓟ 🚲 ◇ 🚕 226
Hamilton Square [ME] ◇ ⚠ 🚕 106
Hamilton West [SR] Ⓟ 🚲 🚕 226
Hammerton [NT] Ⓟ Ⓤ 35
Hampden Park [SN] **[4]** ◇ ⚠ 189
Hampstead Heath [LO] 🚲 ⚠ 59
Hampstead (South) [LO] (see South Hampstead)
Hampstead (West)
(see West Hampstead)
(see West Hampstead Thameslink)
Hampton [SW] 🚲 ⚠ 152
Hampton-in-Arden [LM] Ⓟ ⚠ 68
Hampton Court [SW] Ⓟ 🚲 ◇ ⚠ 152
Hampton Wick [SW] 🚲 ⚠ 149, 152
Hamstead [LM] ⚠ 70
Hamworthy [SW] 🚲 ◇ ⚠ 158
Hanborough [GW] Ⓟ 🚲 Ⓤ 126
Handforth [NT] 🚲 84
Hanley Bus Station *Bus* 67
Hanwell [GW] 🚲 ⚠ 117
Hapton [NT] Ⓤ 97
Harlech [AW] Ⓟ 🚲 Ⓤ 75
Harlesden [LT] 60
Harling Road [LE] Ⓟ 🚲 Ⓤ 17
Harlington (Beds.) **[FC]** Ⓟ 🚲 ◇ ⚠ 🚕 52
Harlington (Middx.) **[GW]** (see Hayes & Harlington)
Harlow Mill [LE] Ⓟ 🚲 ⚠ 22
Harlow Town [LE] Ⓟ 🚲 ◇ ⚠ 🚕 22
Harold Wood [LE] Ⓟ 🚲 ⚠ 🚕 5
Harpenden [FC] Ⓟ 🚲 ◇ ⚠ 🚕 52
Harrietsham [SE] Ⓟ ◇ ⚠ 196
Harringay [FC] ⚠ 24
Harringay Green Lanes [LO] ⚠ 62
Harrington [NT] Ⓟ Ⓤ 100
Harrogate [NT] Ⓟ 🚲 ◇ 🚕 26, 35
Harrow & Wealdstone [LT] Ⓟ ⚠ 🚕 60, 66, 176, 177
Harrow Road [CH] (see Sudbury & Harrow Road)
Harrow Sudbury Hill [CH] (see Sudbury Hill Harrow)
Harrow-on-the-Hill [LT] **[3]** Ⓟ 🚲 ⚠ 🚕 114
Hartford [LM] Ⓟ ◇ 65, 91
Hartlebury [LM] Ⓟ ⚠ Ⓤ 71
Hartlepool [NT] Ⓟ 🚲 ◇ 🚕 26, 44
Hartwood [SR] Ⓟ 🚲 Ⓤ 225
Harwich International [LE] 🚲 ◇ 11, 14
Harwich Town [LE] 🚲 Ⓤ 11
Haslemere [SW] **[4]** Ⓟ 🚲 ◇ ⚠ 🚕 156
Hassocks [SN] **[4]** Ⓟ 🚲 ◇ ⚠ 🚕 52, 186
Hastings [SE] **[4]** Ⓟ ◇ ⚠ 🚕 189, 206
Hatch End [LO] Ⓟ 🚲 ⚠ 🚕 60
Hatfield [FC] Ⓟ 🚲 ⚠ 🚕 24, 25
Hatfield & Stainforth [NT] Ⓟ 🚕 Ⓤ 29
Hatfield Peverel [LE] Ⓟ 🚲 ⚠ 11
Hathersage [NT] Ⓟ Ⓤ 78
Hattersley [NT] Ⓤ9
Hatton (Derbyshire) **[EM]** (see Tutbury & Hatton)
Hatton (Warwickshire) **[CH]** Ⓟ ⚠ Ⓤ 71, 115
Havant [SW] Ⓟ 🚲 ◇ ⚠ 🚕 123, 156, 157, 165, 188
Havenhouse [EM] Ⓤ 19
Haverfordwest [AW] Ⓟ ◇ 🚕 128
Hawarden [AW] Ⓟ Ⓤ 101
Hawarden Bridge [AW] Ⓤ 101
Hawick *Bus* 65G
Hawkhead [SR] 🚲 Ⓤ 217
Haydon Bridge [NT] Ⓟ 🚲 Ⓤ 48
Haydons Road [FC] Ⓟ ⚠ 52, 179
Hayes & Harlington [GW] **[3]** Ⓟ 🚲 ◇ ⚠ 🚕 117
Hayes (Kent) [SE] Ⓟ 🚲 ◇ ⚠ 🚕 203
Hayle [GW] Ⓟ Ⓤ 51, 135, *Sleepers* 406
Haymarket (Edinburgh) **[SR]** Ⓟ 🚲 ◇ 🚕
Aberdeen 229
Bathgate 237
Birmingham 51, 65
Birmingham International 51, 65
Blackpool 65
Bournemouth 51
Bristol 51
Cambridge 26
Carlisle 65
Carstairs 225
Cowdenbeath 242
Crewe 65
Croy 228
Darlington 26
Derby 51
Doncaster 26
Dunblane 230
Dundee 229
Dunfermline 242
Edinburgh Park 237
Exeter 51
Glasgow 225, 228
Inverness 229
Lancaster 65

Station index and table numbers

[10] Connection time
Ⓟ Station Car Park
🚲 Bicycle storage facility
◇ Seat reservations can be made at this station
⚠ Penalty Fare Schemes in operation on some or all services from this station
🚕 Taxi rank or cab office at station, or signposted and within 100 metres
Ⓤ Unstaffed station
[ ] Station Operator Code

Larbert 230
Leeds 26
Liverpool 65
Livingston 225, 237
London 26, 65
Manchester 65
Manchester Airport 65
Motherwell 225
Newcastle 26
Newcraighall 242
North Berwick 238
Oxenholme Lake District 65
Oxford 51
Paignton 51
Penzance 51
Perth 229
Peterborough 26
Plymouth 51
Preston 65
Reading 51
Sheffield 26
Southampton 51
Stirling 230
Torquay 51
York 26

Haywards Heath [SN] [3] Ⓟ 🚲 ◇ ⚠ 🚕
Bedford 52
Brighton 186
Clapham Junction 186
Eastbourne 189
East Croydon 186
Gatwick Airport 186
Hastings 189
Hove 188
Lewes 189
London 186
Littlehampton 188
Luton 52, 186
Portsmouth 188
St Albans 52
Seaford 189
Southampton Central 188
West Hampstead Thameslink 52
Worthing 188

Hazel Grove [NT] Ⓟ 🚲 78, 82, 86
Headcorn [SE] Ⓟ ◇ ⚠ 🚕 207
Headingley [NT] Ⓟ Ⓤ 35
Headstone Lane [LO] ⚠ 60
Heald Green [NT] Ⓟ 🚲 82, 85
Healing [NT] Ⓤ 29
Heath High Level [AW] Ⓤ 130
Heath Low Level [AW] Ⓤ 130
Heathrow London Airport [HX] ◇ 🚕 117, 118, *Bus* 125A, *Bus* 158A
Heaton Chapel [NT] 🚲 84, 86
Hebden Bridge [NT] Ⓟ 🚲 ◇ 41
Heckington [EM] Ⓟ 🚲 Ⓤ 19
Hedge End [SW] Ⓟ 🚲 ◇ ⚠ 158
Hednesford [LM] Ⓟ ⚠ Ⓤ 70
Heighington [NT] Ⓟ Ⓤ 44
Helensburgh Central [SR] Ⓟ 🚲 ◇ 🚕 226
Helensburgh Pier *Ship* 219A
Helensburgh Upper [SR] 🚲 Ⓤ 227, *Sleepers* 404
Hellifield [NT] Ⓟ Ⓤ 36
Helmsdale [SR] Ⓟ 🚲 Ⓤ 239
Helsby [AW] Ⓟ Ⓤ 81, 109
Helston Coinagehall Street *Bus* 135A
Hemel Hempstead [LM] Ⓟ ◇ ⚠ 🚕 66, 176
Hendon [FC] Ⓟ 🚲 ◇ ⚠ 52
Hengoed [AW] Ⓟ Ⓤ 130
Henley-in-Arden [LM] Ⓟ ⚠ Ⓤ 71
Henley-on-Thames [GW] Ⓟ 🚲 🚕 121
Hensall [NT] Ⓤ 32
Hereford [AW] [7] Ⓟ 🚲 ◇ 🚕 71, 126, 131
Herne Bay [SE] Ⓟ 🚲 ◇ ⚠ 194, 212
Herne Hill [SE] [4] 🚲 ◇ ⚠ 52, 177, 179, 195
Hersham [SW] 🚲 ◇ ⚠ 155
Hertford East [LE] Ⓟ 🚲 ⚠ 🚕 22
Hertford North [FC] Ⓟ 🚲 ⚠ 🚕 24, 25
Hessle [NT] Ⓤ 29
Heswall [AW] Ⓟ Ⓤ 101
Hever [SN] Ⓟ ⚠ Ⓤ 184
Heworth [NT] Ⓟ 🚲 🚕 Ⓤ 44
Hexham [NT] Ⓟ 🚲 ◇ 🚕 44, 48
Heyford [GW] Ⓟ Ⓤ 116
Heysham Port [NT] Ⓤ 98, 98A
High Brooms [SE] Ⓟ ◇ ⚠ 207
High Street (Glasgow) **[SR]** 226
High Wycombe [CH] [1] Ⓟ 🚲 ◇ ⚠ 🚕 115
Higham [SE] Ⓟ ◇ ⚠ 200
Highams Park [LE] Ⓟ 🚲 ⚠ 20
Highbridge & Burnham [GW] Ⓟ 🚲 Ⓤ 134
Highbury & Islington [LT] ⚠ 24, 59, 176
Hightown [ME] 🚲 ⚠ 103
Hildenborough [SE] Ⓟ 🚲 ◇ ⚠ 204
Hillfoot [SR] Ⓟ 🚲 🚕 Ⓤ 226
Hillington East [SR] 🚲 219
Hillington West [SR] 🚲 219
Hillside [ME] ⚠ 103
Hilsea [SW] ⚠ 156, 157, 158, 165, 188
Hinchley Wood [SW] 🚲 ◇ ⚠ 152
Hinckley [EM] Ⓟ ◇ 🚕 57
Hindley [NT] Ⓟ 82
Hinton Admiral [SW] Ⓟ 🚲 ◇ ⚠ 158
Hitchin [FC] [4] Ⓟ 🚲 ◇ ⚠ 🚕 24, 25
Hither Green [SE] [4] ◇ ⚠ 199, 200, 204
Hockley [LE] Ⓟ 🚲 ⚠ 🚕 5
Hollingbourne [SE] Ⓟ ⚠ Ⓤ 196
Holmes Chapel [NT] Ⓟ 🚲 84
Holmwood [SN] ⚠ Ⓤ 182
Holsworthy *Bus* 135D
Holton Heath [SW] Ⓟ 🚲 ⚠ Ⓤ 158
Holyhead [AW] ◇ 🚕 65, 81, 81A, 131
Holytown [SR] Ⓟ 🚲 Ⓤ 225, 226
Homerton [LO] 🚲 ⚠ 59
Honeybourne [GW] Ⓟ Ⓤ 126
Honiton [SW] Ⓟ 🚲 ◇ 🚕 160
Honley [NT] Ⓤ 34
Honor Oak Park [LO] 🚲 ⚠ 178
Hook [SW] Ⓟ 🚲 🚕 155
Hooton [ME] Ⓟ 🚲 ⚠ 106
Hope (Derbyshire) [NT] Ⓟ Ⓤ 78
Hope (Flintshire) [AW] Ⓤ 101
Hopton Heath [AW] Ⓤ 129
Horley [SN] [4] 🚲 ◇ ⚠ 186, 188
Hornbeam Park [NT] Ⓟ Ⓤ 35
Hornsey [FC] 🚲 ⚠ 24
Horsforth [NT] Ⓟ 🚲 ◇ 35
Horsham [SN] [4] Ⓟ 🚲 ◇ ⚠ 🚕 182, 186, 188
Horsley [SW] Ⓟ 🚲 ◇ ⚠ 🚕 152
Horton-in-Ribblesdale [NT] Ⓟ Ⓤ 36
Horwich Parkway [NT] Ⓟ 🚲 82
Hoscar [NT] Ⓤ 82
Hough Green [NT] Ⓟ 89
Hounslow [SW] Ⓟ 🚲 ◇ ⚠ 🚕 149
Hove [SN] [2] Ⓟ 🚲 ◇ ⚠ 🚕 123, 186, 188
Hoveton & Wroxham [LE] Ⓟ 🚲 🚕 Ⓤ 16
Howden [NT] Ⓟ 🚲 Ⓤ 29, 39
How Wood (Herts) **[LM]** Ⓤ 61
Howwood (Renfrewshire) **[SR]** Ⓟ 🚲 Ⓤ 221
Hoxton [LO] ⚠ 178
Hoylake [ME] Ⓟ 🚲 ⚠ 106
Hubberts Bridge [EM] Ⓤ 19
Hucknall [EM] Ⓟ Ⓤ 55
Huddersfield [TP] Ⓟ 🚲 ◇ 🚕
Barnsley 34
Bradford 41
Brighouse 41
Darlington 39
Durham 39
Halifax 41
Hull 39
Leeds 39
Liverpool 39
London 26
Manchester 39
Manchester Airport 39
Meadowhall 34
Middlesbrough 39
Newcastle 39
Peterborough 26
Scarborough 39
Selby 39, 41
Sheffield 34
Wakefield 39

[10] Connection time
Ⓟ Station Car Park
🚲 Bicycle storage facility
◇ Seat reservations can be made at this station
⚠ Penalty Fare Schemes in operation on some or all services from this station
🚕 Taxi rank or cab office at station, or signposted and within 100 metres
⊛ Unstaffed station
[ ] Station Operator Code

Station index and table numbers

York 39
Hull [TP] Ⓟ 🚲 ◇ 🚕
Aberdeen 26
Beverley 43
Bridlington 43
Cambridge 26
Darlington 26
Doncaster 29
Durham 26
Edinburgh 26
Filey 43
Glasgow 26
Goole 29
Grantham 26
Huddersfield 39
Leeds 39
Liverpool 39
London 26, 29
Manchester 29, 39
Manchester Airport 29, 39
Newark 26
Newcastle 26
Norwich 26
Peterborough 26
Retford 26
Scarborough 43
Selby 29
Sheffield 29
Stockport 29
York 33
Hull Paragon Interchange 🚕
Bus 29
Humphrey Park [NT] ⊛ 89
Huncoat [NT] ⊛ 97
Hungerford [GW] Ⓟ 🚲 🚕 ⊛ 116, 135
Hunmanby [NT] ⊛ 43
Hunstanton Bus Station *Bus* 17A
Hunts Cross [ME] ⚠ 89, 103
Huntingdon [FC] Ⓟ 🚲 ◇ ⚠ 🚕 25
Huntly [SR] Ⓟ 🚲 ◇ 240
Hurst Green [SN] Ⓟ ◇ ⚠ 184
Hutton Cranswick [NT] Ⓟ ⊛ 43
Huyton [NT] Ⓟ 90
Hyde [NT] (see Newton for Hyde)
Hyde Central [NT] Ⓟ ⊛ 78
Hyde North [NT] Ⓟ ⊛ 78
Hykeham [EM] Ⓟ ⊛ 27
Hyndland [SR] 🚲 226
Hythe (Essex) **[LE]** 🚲 ⚠ ⊛ 11

I

IBM [SR] 🚲 ⊛ 219
Ifield [SN] 🚲 ◇ ⚠ 186
Ilford [LE] [2] 🚲 ◇ ⚠ 5
Ilkley [NT] Ⓟ 🚲 ◇ 38
Imperial Wharf [LO] 🚲 ⚠ 66, 176
Ince [NT] ⊛ 82
Ince & Elton [NT] Ⓟ ⊛ 109
Ingatestone [LE] Ⓟ 🚲 ⚠ 11
Insch [SR] Ⓟ 🚲 ⊛ 240
Invergordon [SR] Ⓟ 🚲 ⊛ 239
Invergowrie [SR] 🚲 ⊛ 229
Inverkeithing [SR] Ⓟ 🚲 ◇ 🚕
Aberdeen 229
Birmingham 51
Bournemouth 51
Bristol 51
Carlisle 51
Crewe *Sleepers* 402
Derby 51
Dundee 229
Edinburgh 242
Inverness 229
London 26, *Sleepers* 402
Newcastle 26
Oxford 51
Penzance 51
Perth 229
Plymouth 51
Preston 51, *Sleepers* 402
Reading 51
Sheffield 51
Southampton 51
York 26
Inverkip [SR] Ⓟ 🚲 ⊛ 219
Inverness [SR] Ⓟ 🚲 ◇ 🚕
Aberdeen 240
Birmingham 65
Cambridge 26
Carlisle 65
Crewe 65, *Sleepers* 403
Dingwall 239
Edinburgh 229
Elgin 240
Glasgow 229
Inverkeithing 229
Kingussie 229
Kirkcaldy 229
Kyle of Lochalsh 239
Leeds 26
Liverpool 65
London 26, 65, *Sleepers* 403
Manchester 65
Newcastle 26
Norwich 26
Orkney Isles *Ship* 239A
Perth 229
Preston 65, *Sleepers* 403
Stirling 229
Thurso 239
Western Isles *Ship* 239B
Wick 239
York 26
Inverness Bus Station 🚕 *Bus* 239B
Invershin [SR] Ⓟ 🚲 ⊛ 239
Inverurie [SR] Ⓟ 🚲 ◇ 🚕 229, 240
Ipswich [LE] Ⓟ 🚲 ◇ 🚕 11, 13, 14, 17
Irlam [NT] Ⓟ ⊛ 89
Irvine [SR] Ⓟ 🚲 🚕 221
Isle of Man *Ship* 98A
Isle of Wight [IL] 158, 167
Isleworth [SW] Ⓟ 🚲 ⚠ 🚕 ⊛ 149
Islington (see Highbury & Islington)
Islip [GW] Ⓟ 🚲 ⊛ 116
Iver [GW] 🚲 ⚠ 117
Ivybridge [GW] Ⓟ 🚲 ⊛ 135

J

James Street [ME] (see Liverpool)
Jewellery Quarter [LM] ⚠ 71
Johnston [AW] ⊛ 128
Johnstone [SR] Ⓟ 🚲 🚕 221
Jordanhill [SR] 🚲 ⊛ 226

K

Kearsley [NT] ⊛ 82
Kearsney [SE] Ⓟ ⚠ 212
Keighley [NT] Ⓟ 🚲 ◇ 🚕 26, 36
Keith [SR] Ⓟ 🚲 ◇ 240
Kelvedon [LE] Ⓟ 🚲 ⚠ 11
Kelvindale [SR] Ⓟ 🚲 ⊛ 232
Kemble [GW] Ⓟ ◇ 🚕 125
Kempston Hardwick [LM] ⊛ 64
Kempton Park [SW] ⚠ 152
Kemsing [SE] Ⓟ ⚠ ⊛ 196
Kemsley [SE] ⚠ ⊛ 212
Kendal [TP] Ⓟ 🚕 ⊛ 83
Kenley [SN] Ⓟ ◇ ⚠ 181
Kennett [LE] Ⓟ 🚲 ⊛ 14
Kennishead [SR] 🚲 ⊛ 222
Kensal Green [LT] 60
Kensal Rise [LO] 🚲 ⚠ 59
Kensington (Olympia) [LO] Ⓟ 🚲 ◇ ⚠ 66, 176, 177
Kent House [SE] [4] 🚲 ◇ ⚠ 195
Kentish Town [LT] ⚠ 🚕 52, 195
Kentish Town West [LO] 🚲 ⚠ 59
Kenton [LT] 60
Kenton (South) [LT] (see South Kenton)
Kents Bank [NT] ⊛ 82
Keswick (Bus Station) 🚕 *Bus* 65F
Kettering [EM] [4] Ⓟ 🚲 ◇ 🚕 53
Kettering Library *Bus* 26B
Kew Bridge [SW] 🚲 ⊛ 149
Kew Gardens [LT] 59
Keyham [GW] ⊛ 135, 139
Keynsham [GW] Ⓟ 🚲 123, 132
Kidbrooke [SE] Ⓟ 🚲 ◇ ⚠ 200
Kidderminster [LM] Ⓟ ◇ ⚠ 🚕 71, 115
Kidsgrove [EM] Ⓟ ◇ 50, 67, 84
Kidwelly [AW] ⊛ 128
Kilburn High Road [LO] ⚠ 60

Station index and table numbers

⟦10⟧ Connection time
Ⓟ Station Car Park
🚲 Bicycle storage facility
◇ Seat reservations can be made at this station
⚠ Penalty Fare Schemes in operation on some or all services from this station
🚕 Taxi rank or cab office at station, or signposted and within 100 metres
Ⓤ Unstaffed station
[ ] Station Operator Code

Kilcreggan *Ship* 219A
Kildale [NT] Ⓟ Ⓤ 45
Kildonan [SR] Ⓟ 🚲 Ⓤ 239
Kilgetty [AW] Ⓤ 128
Kilmarnock [SR] ⟦3⟧ Ⓟ 🚲 ◇ 🚕 216, 218, 222
Kilmaurs [SR] Ⓟ 🚲 Ⓤ 222
Kilpatrick [SR] Ⓟ 🚲 Ⓤ 226
Kilwinning [SR] Ⓟ 🚲 🚕 218, 221
Kinbrace [SR] Ⓟ 🚲 Ⓤ 239
Kingham [GW] Ⓟ 🚲 126, *Bus* 126A
Kinghorn [SR] 🚲 242
Kings Cross [NR] (see London)
Kings Langley [LM] Ⓟ 🚲 🚕 66
Kings Lynn [FC] Ⓟ 🚲 ◇ ⚠ 🚕 17, *Bus* 17A
Kings Lynn Bus Station 🚕 *Bus* 26A
Kings Norton [LM] Ⓟ ◇ ⚠ 69
Kings Nympton [GW] Ⓟ Ⓤ 136
Kings Park [SR] 🚲 223
Kings Sutton [CH] ⚠ Ⓤ 115, 116
Kingsknowe [SR] 🚲 Ⓤ 225
Kingston [SW] ◇ ⚠ 🚕 149, 152
Kingswood [SN] Ⓟ ◇ ⚠ 181
Kingussie [SR] Ⓟ 🚲 229, *Sleepers* 403
Kintbury [GW] Ⓟ 🚲 Ⓤ 116
Kirby Cross [LE] 🚲 ⚠ Ⓤ 11
Kirkby [ME] Ⓟ ⚠ 🚕 82, 103
Kirkby in Ashfield [EM] Ⓟ Ⓤ 55
Kirkby-in-Furness [NT] Ⓤ 100
Kirkby Stephen [NT] Ⓟ Ⓤ 36
Kirkcaldy [SR] Ⓟ 🚲 ◇ 🚕
  Aberdeen 229
  Birmingham 51
  Bournemouth 51
  Bristol 51
  Carlisle 51
  Crewe *Sleepers* 402
  Derby 51
  Dundee 229
  Edinburgh 242
  Inverness 229
  London 26, *Sleepers* 402
  Newcastle 26
  Oxford 51
  Penzance 51
  Perth 229
  Plymouth 51
  Preston 51, *Sleepers* 402
  Reading 51
  Sheffield 51
  Southampton 51
  York 26
Kirkconnel [SR] Ⓟ 🚲 Ⓤ 216
Kirkdale [ME] ⚠ 103
Kirkham & Wesham [NT] Ⓟ ◇ 82, 97
Kirk Sandall [NT] Ⓟ Ⓤ 29
Kirkhill [SR] Ⓟ 🚲 Ⓤ 223
Kirknewton [SR] Ⓟ 🚲 Ⓤ 225
Kirkoswald [NT] (see Lazonby)
Kirkwood [SR] Ⓤ 220
Kirton Lindsey [NT] Ⓟ Ⓤ 30
Kiveton Bridge [NT] Ⓤ 30
Kiveton Park [NT] Ⓟ 🚲 Ⓤ 30
Knaresborough [NT] Ⓟ Ⓤ 35
Knebworth [FC] Ⓟ 🚲 ⚠ 24, 25
Knighton [AW] Ⓤ 129
Knockholt [SE] Ⓟ ◇ ⚠ 204
Knottingley [NT] Ⓟ Ⓤ 32
Knucklas [AW] Ⓤ 129
Knutsford [NT] Ⓟ 88
Kyle of Lochalsh [SR] Ⓟ 🚲 ◇ 239, *Ship* 239B

L

Ladybank [SR] Ⓟ 🚲 51, 229
Ladywell [SE] 🚲 ◇ ⚠ 203
Laindon [CC] Ⓟ 🚲 ◇ ⚠ 🚕 1
Lairg [SR] Ⓟ 🚲 Ⓤ 239
Lake [IL] (IOW) Ⓤ 167
Lake District [VT] (see Oxenholme)
Lakenheath [LE] Ⓤ 17
Lamphey [AW] Ⓤ 128
Lanark [SR] Ⓟ 🚲 🚕 226
Lancaster [VT] ⟦6⟧ Ⓟ 🚲 ◇ 🚕
  Aberdeen 65
  Barrow-in-Furness 82
  Birmingham 65
  Blackpool 65
  Bolton 82
  Bournemouth 51
  Bradford 36
  Bristol 51
  Carlisle 65
  Chorley 82
  Crewe 65
  Douglas (IOM) 98A
  Edinburgh 65
  Exeter 51
  Glasgow 65
  Heysham Port 98
  Leeds 36
  Liverpool 65
  London 65
  Manchester 82
  Manchester Airport 82
  Millom 100
  Milton Keynes Central 65
  Morecambe 98
  Oxenholme Lake District 65
  Oxford 51
  Paignton 51
  Penzance 51
  Plymouth 51
  Preston 65
  Reading 51
  Skipton 36
  Southampton 51
  Stafford 65
  Torquay 51
  Warrington 65
  Whitehaven 100
  Wigan 65
  Windermere 65
  Workington 100
Lancing [SN] Ⓟ 🚲 ◇ ⚠ 🚕 188
Landywood [LM] Ⓟ ⚠ Ⓤ 70
Langbank [SR] Ⓟ 🚲 Ⓤ 219
Langho [NT] Ⓟ Ⓤ 94
Langholm *Bus* 65G
Langley [GW] Ⓟ 🚲 ⚠ 🚕 117
Langley Green [LM] Ⓟ ⚠ 71
Langley Mill [EM] Ⓤ 34, 49, 53
Langside [SR] 🚲 Ⓤ 223
Langwathby [NT] Ⓤ 36
Langwith - Whaley Thorns [EM] Ⓤ 55
Lapford [GW] Ⓤ 136
Lapworth [CH] Ⓟ ⚠ Ⓤ 71, 115
Larbert [SR] Ⓟ 🚲 ◇ 🚕 229, 230
Largs [SR] Ⓟ 🚲 🚕 221
Larkhall [SR] 🚲 Ⓤ 226
Latimer [LT] (see Chalfont & Latimer)
Laurencekirk [SR] Ⓟ 🚲 Ⓤ 229
Lawrence Hill [GW] Ⓤ 133, 134
Layton [NT] Ⓟ Ⓤ 82, 97
Lazonby & Kirkoswald [NT] Ⓤ 36
Lea Green [NT] Ⓟ 🚲 90
Lea Hall [LM] Ⓟ ⚠ 68
Leagrave [FC] Ⓟ 🚲 ◇ ⚠ 🚕 52
Lealholm [NT] Ⓤ 45
Leamington Spa [CH] ⟦8⟧ Ⓟ 🚲 ◇ ⚠ 🚕 51, 71, 75, 115, 116
Leasowe [ME] Ⓟ ⚠ 106
Leatherhead [SN] Ⓟ 🚲 ◇ ⚠ 🚕 152, 182
Ledbury [LM] Ⓟ ⚠ Ⓤ 71, 126
Lee [SE] Ⓟ ◇ ⚠ 200
Leeds [NR] ⟦10⟧ Ⓟ 🚲 ◇ 🚕
  Barnsley 34
  Bedford 53
  Birmingham 51
  Birmingham International 51
  Blackburn 41
  Blackpool 41
  Bournemouth 51
  Bradford 37
  Brighouse 41
  Bristol 51
  Burnley 41
  Cambridge 26
  Cardiff 51
  Carlisle 36
  Carnforth 36
  Chesterfield 53
  Darlington 26
  Derby 53
  Dewsbury 39
  Doncaster 31
  Edinburgh 26
  Exeter 51
  Glasgow 26

■10 Connection time
Ⓟ Station Car Park
🚲 Bicycle storage facility
◇ Seat reservations can be made at this station
⚠ Penalty Fare Schemes in operation on some or all services from this station
🚕 Taxi rank or cab office at station, or signposted and within 100 metres
Ⓤ Unstaffed station
[ ] Station Operator Code

Station index and table numbers

- Goole 32
- Grantham 26
- Halifax 41
- Harrogate 35
- Huddersfield 39, 41
- Hull 39
- Ilkley 38
- Keighley 36
- Knaresborough 35
- Lancaster 36
- Leicester 53
- Liverpool 39, 41
- London 26, 53
- Luton 53
- Manchester 39, 41
- Manchester Airport 39
- Meadowhall 31
- Morecambe 36
- Newark 26
- Newcastle 26
- Newport (South Wales) 51
- Norwich 26
- Nottingham 53
- Oxford 51
- Paignton 51
- Penzance 51
- Peterborough 26
- Plymouth 51
- Preston 41
- Reading 51
- Retford 26
- Rochdale 41
- Scarborough 39
- Selby 40
- Settle 36
- Sheffield 31
- Shipley 37
- Skipton 36
- Stansted Airport 26
- Southampton 51
- Torquay 51
- Wakefield 31
- Warrington 39
- York 35, 40

Leicester [EM] Ⓟ 🚲 ◇ 🚕 49, 53, 57
Leigh (Kent) [SN] ⚠ Ⓤ 186
Leigh-on-Sea [CC] Ⓟ 🚲 ◇ ⚠ 🚕 1
Leighton Buzzard [LM] Ⓟ 🚲 ◇ ⚠ 🚕 66, 176
Lelant [GW] Ⓟ Ⓤ 144
Lelant Saltings [GW] Ⓟ Ⓤ 144
Lenham [SE] Ⓟ ◇ ⚠ 196
Lenzie [SR] ■3 Ⓟ 🚲 🚕 228, 230
Leominster [AW] Ⓟ 131
Letchworth Garden City [FC] 🚲 ⚠ 🚕 24, 25
Leuchars [SR] ■3 Ⓟ 🚲 ◇ 🚕 26, 51, 229, *Sleepers* 402
Levenshulme [NT] 84, 86
Levisham [NY] 🚲 45
Lewes [SN] ■4 Ⓟ 🚲 ◇ ⚠ 🚕 186, 189
Lewisham [SE] ■4 Ⓟ 🚲 ◇ ⚠ 🚕
- Bexleyheath 200
- Dartford 200
- Gillingham (Kent) 200
- Gravesend 200
- Hayes (Kent) 203
- London 195, 199
- Orpington 199, 204
- Sidcup 200
- Woolwich Arsenal 200

Leyland [NT] Ⓟ ◇ 🚕 82, 90
Leyton Midland Road [LO] 🚲 ⚠ 62
Leytonstone High Road [LO] 🚲 ⚠ 62
Lichfield City [LM] Ⓟ ◇ ⚠ 🚕 69
Lichfield Trent Valley [LM] Ⓟ ◇ ⚠ 65, 67, 69
Lidlington [LM] Ⓤ 64
Limehouse [CC] ⚠ 1
Lincoln [EM] Ⓟ 🚲 ◇ 🚕 18, 26, 27, 30, 53
Lingfield [SN] Ⓟ 🚲 ◇ ⚠ 🚕 184
Lingwood [LE] Ⓟ 🚲 Ⓤ 15
Linlithgow [SR] Ⓟ 🚲 ◇ 228, 230
Liphook [SW] Ⓟ 🚲 ◇ ⚠ 🚕 156
Liskeard [GW] ■6 Ⓟ 🚲 ◇ 51, 135, 140, *Sleepers* 406
Lismore *Ship* 227B
Liss [SW] Ⓟ 🚲 ◇ ⚠ 156
Lisvane & Thornhill [AW] Ⓟ Ⓤ 130
Litherland [ME] (see Seaforth & Litherland)
Little Kimble [CH] ⚠ Ⓤ 115
Little Sutton [ME] Ⓤ 106
Littleborough [NT] Ⓟ 41
Littlehampton [SN] ■4 Ⓟ 🚲 ◇ ⚠ 🚕 188
Littlehaven [SN] ◇ ⚠ 186
Littleport [FC] 🚲 ⚠ Ⓤ 17
Liverpool
- **Central [ME]** ■10 ⚠ 🚕
- **James Street [ME]** ◇ ⚠
- **Lime Street** (Main Line) **[NR]** ■10 Ⓟ 🚲 ◇ 🚕
- **Lime Street** (Low Level) **[ME]** ■10 ◇ ⚠ 🚕
- **Moorfields [ME]** ■10 ⚠
- Aberdeen 65
- Barrow-in-Furness 65
- Birkenhead 106
- Birmingham 65
- Birmingham International 65
- Blackpool 65, 90
- Bolton 82
- Cambridge 49
- Carlisle 65
- Chester 106
- Coventry 65
- Crewe 91
- Darlington 39
- Douglas (IOM) 98A
- Dundee 65
- Durham 39
- Edinburgh 65
- Ellesmere Port 106
- Ely 49
- Gatwick Airport 65
- Glasgow 65
- Hartford 91
- Hooton 106
- Huddersfield 39
- Hull 39
- Hunts Cross 89, 103
- Inverness 65
- Kirkby 103
- Lancaster 65
- Leeds 39
- Liverpool South Parkway 91
- London 65
- Manchester 89, 90
- Manchester Airport 89
- Middlesbrough 39
- Milton Keynes Central 65
- Mossley Hill 91
- Motherwell 65
- New Brighton 106
- Newcastle 39
- Norwich 49
- Nottingham 49
- Nuneaton 65
- Ormskirk 103
- Oxenholme Lake District 65
- Peterborough 49
- Preston 90
- Rhyl 81
- Rochdale 95
- Rock Ferry 106
- Rugby 65
- Runcorn 91
- St Helens 90
- Scarborough 39
- Sheffield 89
- Southport 103
- Stafford 65
- Stansted Airport 49
- Stockport 89
- Wakefield 39
- Warrington 89, 90
- Watford 65
- West Kirby 106
- Wigan 82, 90
- Windermere 65
- Wolverhampton 65
- York 39

Liverpool Landing Stage *Ship* 98A
Liverpool South Parkway [ME] ■7 Ⓟ 🚲 ⚠ 🚕 49, 65, 89, 91, 103
Liverpool Street [NR] (see London)
Livingston North [SR] Ⓟ 🚲 Ⓤ 237
Livingston South [SR] Ⓟ 🚲 Ⓤ 225
Llanaber [AW] Ⓤ 75
Llanbedr [AW] Ⓤ 75
Llanbister Road [AW] Ⓤ 129

Station index and table numbers

■10 Connection time
Ⓟ Station Car Park
🚲 Bicycle storage facility
◇ Seat reservations can be made at this station
⚠ Penalty Fare Schemes in operation on some or all services from this station
🚕 Taxi rank or cab office at station, or signposted and within 100 metres
Ⓤ Unstaffed station
[ ] Station Operator Code

- **10** Connection time
- ℗ Station Car Park
- Bicycle storage facility
- ◇ Seat reservations can be made at this station
- ⚠ Penalty Fare Schemes in operation on some or all services from this station
- Taxi rank or cab office at station, or signposted and within 100 metres
- Unstaffed station
- [ ] Station Operator Code

Station index and table numbers

Station index and table numbers

[10] Connection time
Ⓟ Station Car Park
🚲 Bicycle storage facility
◇ Seat reservations can be made at this station
⚠ Penalty Fare Schemes in operation on some or all services from this station
🚕 Taxi rank or cab office at station, or signposted and within 100 metres
ⓤ Unstaffed station
[ ] Station Operator Code

London Stansted Airport [LE] (see Stansted Airport)
Long Buckby [LM] Ⓟ 68
Long Eaton [EM] Ⓟ 🚲 ◇ 53, 56, 57
Long Preston [NT] Ⓟ ⓤ 36
Longbeck [NT] 🚲 ⓤ 44
Longbridge [LM] ◇ ⚠ 69
Longcross [SW] ⚠ ⓤ 149
Longfield [SE] Ⓟ ◇ ⚠ 🚕 212
Longniddry [SR] Ⓟ 🚲 ⓤ 238
Longport [EM] Ⓟ ⓤ 50, 84
Longton [EM] Ⓟ ⓤ 50
Looe [GW] Ⓟ 🚲 ⓤ 140
Lostock [NT] Ⓟ 82
Lostock Gralam [NT] Ⓟ ⓤ 88
Lostock Hall [NT] Ⓟ ⓤ 97
Lostwithiel [GW] Ⓟ ⓤ 51,135, *Sleepers* 406
Loughborough [EM] Ⓟ 🚲 ◇ 🚕 53
Loughborough Junction [FC] 🚲 ◇ ⚠ 52, 177, 179, 195
Lowdham [EM] Ⓟ ⓤ 27
Lower Sydenham [SE] 🚲 ◇ ⚠ 203
Lowestoft [LE] Ⓟ 🚲 ◇ 🚕 11, 13, 15
Ludlow [AW] Ⓟ ◇ 131
Luton [FC] [10] Ⓟ 🚲 ◇ ⚠ 🚕 52, *Bus* 52A, 53, *Bus* 65B
Luton Airport (see London Luton Airport)
Luton Airport Parkway [FC] [7] Ⓟ 🚲 ◇ ⚠ 🚕 52, 53, 177, 179, 186
Luxulyan [GW] Ⓟ ⓤ 142
Lydney [AW] Ⓟ ⓤ 132
Lye [LM] Ⓟ ⚠ 71
Lymington Pier [SW] 🚲 ⚠ ⓤ 158
Lymington Town [SW] Ⓟ 🚲 ◇ ⚠ 158
Lympstone Commando [GW] ⓤ 136
Lympstone Village [GW] Ⓟ 🚲 ⓤ 136
Lytham [NT] ⓤ 97

M

Macclesfield [VT] Ⓟ 🚲 ◇ 🚕 51, 65, 84
Machynlleth [AW] [4] Ⓟ ◇ 75
Maesteg [AW] Ⓟ ⓤ 128, *Bus* 128A
Maesteg (Ewenny Road) [AW] ⓤ 128
Maghull [ME] Ⓟ 🚲 ⚠ 🚕 103
Maidenhead [GW] [3] Ⓟ 🚲 ◇ ⚠ 🚕 116, 117, 120
Maiden Newton [GW] Ⓟ ⓤ 123
Maidstone Barracks [SE] ⚠ ⓤ 208
Maidstone East [SE] [4] Ⓟ ◇ ⚠ 🚕 196
Maidstone West [SE] [4] Ⓟ ◇ ⚠ 🚕 207, 208
Malden Manor [SW] Ⓟ 🚲 ◇ ⚠ 152
Mallaig [SR] 🚲 ◇ 227, *Ship* 227A
Malton [TP] Ⓟ 🚲 ◇ 🚕 39
Malvern Link [LM] Ⓟ ◇ ⚠ 71, 126
Manchester
  Oxford Road [NT] ◇ 🚕
  Piccadilly [NR] [10] Ⓟ 🚲 ◇ 🚕
  Victoria [NT] ◇ 🚕
 Aberdeen 65
 Altrincham 88
 Bangor (Gwynedd) 81
 Barrow-in-Furness 82
 Birmingham 65
 Birmingham International 65
 Blackpool 82
 Bolton 82
 Bournemouth 51
 Bradford 41
 Bristol 51
 Burnley 97
 Buxton 86
 Cambridge 49
 Cardiff 131
 Carlisle 65
 Carmarthen 128
 Cheadle Hulme 84
 Chester 81, 88
 Chinley 78
 Cleethorpes 29
 Clitheroe 94
 Coventry 65
 Crewe 84
 Darlington 39
 Doncaster 29
 Douglas (IOM) 98A
 Dundee 65
 Durham 39
 Edinburgh 65
 Exeter 51
 Glasgow 65
 Glossop 79
 Grimsby 29
 Guide Bridge 78
 Hadfield 79
 Heysham Port 98A
 Holyhead 81
 Huddersfield 39
 Hull 29, 39
 Inverness 65
 Kirkby 82
 Lancaster 82
 Leeds 39, 41
 Liverpool 89, 90
 Liverpool South Parkway 89
 Llandudno 81
 London 65
 Macclesfield 84
 Manchester Airport 85
 Marple 78
 Middlesbrough 39
 Milford Haven 128
 Milton Keynes Central 65
 Motherwell 65
 Newcastle 39
 New Mills 78, 86
 Newport (South Wales) 131
 Northwich 88
 Nottingham 49
 Oxenholme Lake District 65
 Oxford 51
 Paignton 51
 Penzance 51
 Peterborough 49
 Plymouth 51
 Preston 82
 Reading 51
 Rhyl 81
 Rochdale 41
 Rose Hill Marple 78
 Rugby 65
 St Helens 90
 Salford 82
 Scarborough 39
 Sheffield 78
 Shrewsbury 131
 Southampton 51
 Southport 82
 Stafford 84
 Stalybridge 39
 Stansted Airport 49
 Stockport 84
 Stoke-on-Trent 84
 Swansea 131
 Tenby 128
 Torquay 51
 Wakefield 39
 Warrington 89, 90
 Watford 65
 Wigan 82
 Wilmslow 84
 Windermere 82
 Wolverhampton 65
 York 39
Manchester Airport [TP] ◇
 Bangor (Gwynedd) 81
 Barrow-in-Furness 82
 Birmingham 65
 Birmingham International 65
 Blackburn 94
 Blackpool 82
 Bolton 82
 Carlisle 65
 Coventry 65
 Crewe 84
 Darlington 39
 Doncaster 29
 Durham 39
 Edinburgh 65
 Glasgow 65
 Huddersfield 39
 Hull 29, 39

[10] Connection time
Ⓟ Station Car Park
🚲 Bicycle storage facility
◇ Seat reservations can be made at this station
⚠ Penalty Fare Schemes in operation on some or all services from this station
🚕 Taxi rank or cab office at station, or signposted and within 100 metres
Ⓤ Unstaffed station
[ ] Station Operator Code

Station index and table numbers

Holyhead 81
Lancaster 82
Leeds 39
Liverpool 89
London 65
Manchester 85
Middlesbrough 39
Motherwell 65
Newcastle 39
Oxenholme Lake District 82
Penrith North Lakes 65
Preston 82
St Helens 90
Salford 82
Scarborough 39
Sheffield 78
Southport 82
Stafford 65, 84
Wakefield 39
Warrington 89
Watford 65
Wigan 82
Wilmslow 84
Windermere 82
Wolverhampton 65
York 39

Manea [LE] Ⓤ 14, 17
Manningtree [LE] [2] Ⓟ 🚲 ⚠ 🚕 11, 13, 14
Manor Park [LE] 🚲 ⚠ 5
Manor Road [ME] 🚲 ⚠ 106
Manorbier [AW] Ⓤ 128
Manors [NT] Ⓤ 48
Mansfield [EM] Ⓟ 🚲 🚕 55
Mansfield Woodhouse [EM] Ⓟ Ⓤ 55
March [LE] Ⓟ ◇ 🚕 14, 17, 49
Marden [SE] Ⓟ ◇ ⚠ 207
Margate [SE] [4] Ⓟ 🚲 ◇ ⚠ 🚕 194, 207, 212
Market Harborough [EM] Ⓟ 🚲 ◇ 🚕 53
Market Rasen [EM] Ⓟ 🚲 Ⓤ 27
Markinch [SR] Ⓟ 🚲 🚕 51, 229
Marks Tey [LE] [2] Ⓟ 🚲 ⚠ 10, 11, 13, 14
Marlow [GW] 🚲 Ⓤ 120
Marple [NT] Ⓟ 🚲 78
Marsden [NT] Ⓟ Ⓤ 39
Marske [NT] 🚲 Ⓤ 44
Marston Green [LM] Ⓟ ◇ ⚠ 68
Martin Mill [SE] Ⓟ ⚠ 207
Martins Heron [SW] Ⓟ 🚲 ◇ ⚠ 149
Marton [NT] Ⓟ 🚲 Ⓤ 45
Maryhill [SR] 🚲 Ⓤ 232
Maryland [LE] 🚲 ⚠ 🚕 5
Marylebone [CH] (see London)
Maryport [NT] Ⓟ Ⓤ 100
Matlock [EM] Ⓟ Ⓤ 56
Matlock Bath [EM] Ⓟ Ⓤ 56
Mauldeth Road [NT] 85
Maxwell Park [SR] 🚲 Ⓤ 223
Maybole [SR] Ⓟ 🚲 Ⓤ 218
Maze Hill [SE] ◇ ⚠ 200
Meadowhall [NT] Ⓟ 🚲 ◇
Barnsley 34
Castleford 34
Cleethorpes 29
Doncaster 29
Gainsborough 30
Grimsby 29
Huddersfield 34
Hull 29
Leeds 31
Lincoln 30
Manchester 29
Manchester Airport 29
Penistone 34
Pontefract 33
Retford 30
Rotherham 29
Scunthorpe 29
Sheffield 29
Wakefield 31
Worksop 30
York 29, 33
Meldreth [FC] Ⓟ 🚲 ⚠ 25
Melksham [GW] Ⓟ Ⓤ 123
Melrose *Bus* 26K
Melton [LE] Ⓟ 🚲 🚕 Ⓤ 13
Melton Mowbray [EM] Ⓟ 🚲 ◇ 🚕 49
Menheniot [GW] Ⓟ Ⓤ 135
Menston [NT] Ⓟ 🚲 ◇ 38
Meols [ME] Ⓟ 🚲 ⚠ 🚕 106
Meols Cop [NT] Ⓤ 82
Meopham [SE] Ⓟ ◇ ⚠ 🚕 212
Merryton [SR] 🚲 Ⓤ 226
Merstham [SN] Ⓟ 🚲 ◇ ⚠ 🚕 186
Merthyr Tydfil [AW] Ⓟ ◇ 130
Merthyr Vale [AW] Ⓤ 130
Metheringham [EM] Ⓟ 🚲 Ⓤ 18
Metrocentre [NT] Ⓤ 44, 48
Mexborough [NT] Ⓟ 🚲 ◇ 29
Micheldever [SW] Ⓟ 🚲 ◇ ⚠ 158
Micklefield [NT] Ⓟ 🚲 Ⓤ 40
Middlesbrough [TP] Ⓟ 🚲 ◇ 🚕 26, 39, 44, 45
Middlewood [NT] Ⓤ 86
Midgham [GW] Ⓟ Ⓤ 116
Milford Haven [AW] Ⓟ 🚕 Ⓤ 128
Milford (Surrey) [SW] Ⓟ 🚲 ⚠ 156
Millbrook (Bedfordshire) [LM] Ⓤ 64
Millbrook (Hants.) [SW] 🚲 ⚠ Ⓤ 158
Mill Hill Broadway [FC] Ⓟ 🚲 ◇ ⚠ 52
Mill Hill (Lancashire) [NT] Ⓤ 97
Milliken Park [SR] 🚲 Ⓤ 221
Millom [NT] Ⓟ Ⓤ 100
Mills Hill [NT] Ⓟ Ⓤ 41
Milngavie [SR] Ⓟ 🚲 226
Milton Keynes Central [LM] Ⓟ 🚲 ◇ ⚠ 🚕
Bedford *Bus* 65C
Bicester *Bus* 65A
Birmingham International 66
Birmingham New Street 66
Blackpool 65
Bletchley 66
Brighton 66
Buckingham *Bus* 65A
Cambridge *Bus* 65C
Coventry 66, 67
Crewe 65, 67
Edinburgh 65
Gatwick Airport 66
Glasgow 65
Lancaster 65
Liverpool 65
London 67
Luton *Bus* 65B
Luton Airport *Bus* 65B
Manchester 65
Northampton 66, 67
Oxenholme Lake District 65
Preston 65
Rugby 66, 67
St Neots *Bus* 65C
Stafford 65, 67
Stockport 65
Stoke-on-Trent 65, 67
Tring 66
Warrington 65
Watford Junction 66, 176, 177
Wembley Central 66, 176, 177
Wigan 65
Wolverhampton 66
Milton Keynes City Centre *Bus* 65B
Minehead Bancks Street *Bus* 135E
Minehead Butlins *Bus* 135E
Minehead Parade *Bus* 135E
Minffordd [AW] Ⓤ 75
Minster [SE] [4] Ⓟ ⚠ Ⓤ 207
Mirfield [NT] Ⓟ 🚲 Ⓤ 39, 41
Mistley [LE] 🚲 Ⓤ 11
Mitcham Eastfields [SN] ◇ ⚠ 52, 179, 182
Mitcham Junction [SN] Ⓟ 🚲 ◇ ⚠ 52, 179, 182
Mobberley [NT] Ⓤ 88
Monifieth [SR] 🚲 Ⓤ 229
Monks Risborough [CH] ⚠ Ⓤ 115
Montpelier [GW] 🚲 Ⓤ 133
Montrose [SR] Ⓟ 🚲 ◇ 🚕 26, 51, 229, *Sleepers* 402
Moorfields [ME] (see Liverpool)
Moorgate [LT] ⚠ 24
Moorside [NT] 82
Moorthorpe [NT] Ⓟ Ⓤ 31, 33
Morar [SR] Ⓟ 🚲 Ⓤ 227
Morchard Road [GW] Ⓟ Ⓤ 136
Morden (Herts) **[FC]** (see Ashwell & Morden)
Morden South [FC] ⚠ Ⓤ 52, 179
Morecambe [NT] Ⓟ 🚲 ◇ 36, 98, 98A

Station index and table numbers

■10 Connection time
Ⓟ Station Car Park
🚲 Bicycle storage facility
◇ Seat reservations can be made at this station
⚠ Penalty Fare Schemes in operation on some or all services from this station
🚕 Taxi rank or cab office at station, or signposted and within 100 metres
Ⓤ Unstaffed station
[ ] Station Operator Code

Station index and table numbers

[10] Connection time
Ⓟ Station Car Park
🚲 Bicycle storage facility
◇ Seat reservations can be made at this station
⚠ Penalty Fare Schemes in operation on some or all services from this station
🚕 Taxi rank or cab office at station, or signposted and within 100 metres
ⓤ Unstaffed station
[ ] Station Operator Code

Darlington 51
Derby 57
Dundee 51
Durham 51
Edinburgh 51
Exeter 135
Gloucester 132
Hereford 131
Holyhead 131
Leeds 51
Llandudno Junction 131
London 125
Maesteg 128
Manchester 131
Milford Haven 128
Newcastle 51
Nottingham 57
Paignton 135
Penzance 135
Plymouth 135
Portsmouth 123
Reading 125
Sheffield 51
Shrewsbury 131
Slough 125
Swansea 128
Swindon 125
Torquay 135
Weymouth 123
Worcester 57
York 51

Newquay [GW] Ⓟ 🚲 🚕 ⓤ 51, 135, 142
Newstead [EM] Ⓟ ⓤ 55
Newton (Lanarks.) **[SR]** 🚲 223, 226
Newton Abbot [GW] Ⓟ 🚲 ◇ ⚠ 🚕 51, 135, *Sleepers* 406
Newton Aycliffe [NT] Ⓟ ⓤ 44
Newton for Hyde [NT] Ⓟ ◇ 79
Newton St Cyres [GW] ⓤ 136
Newton-le-Willows [NT] Ⓟ 81, 90
Newtonmore [SR] Ⓟ 🚲 ⓤ 229, *Sleepers* 403
Newton-on-Ayr [SR] 🚲 ⓤ 221
Newtown (Powys) [AW] 🚕 75
Ninian Park [AW] ⓤ 130
Nitshill [SR] 🚲 ⓤ 222
Norbiton [SW] Ⓟ 🚲 ◇ ⚠ 152
Norbury [SN] Ⓟ 🚲 ◇ ⚠ 176, 177
Normans Bay [SN] ⓤ 189
Normanton [NT] Ⓟ ⓤ 34
North Berwick [SR] Ⓟ 🚲 ⓤ 238
North Camp [GW] Ⓟ 🚲 148
North Dulwich [SN] 🚲 ⚠ 177, 179
North Fambridge [LE] Ⓟ 🚲 ⓤ 5
North Llanrwst [AW] Ⓟ ⓤ 102
North Queensferry [SR] Ⓟ 🚲 ⓤ 242
North Road [NT] 🚲 ⓤ 44
North Sheen [SW] ◇ ⚠ 149
North Walsham [LE] Ⓟ 🚲 🚕 16
North Wembley [LT] 60
Northallerton [TP] Ⓟ 🚲 ◇ 🚕 26, 39
Northampton [LM] Ⓟ 🚲 ◇ 🚕 65, 66, 67, 68
Northfield [LM] Ⓟ ◇ ⚠ 69
Northfleet [SE] ◇ ⚠ 200
Northolt Park [CH] ⚠ 115
Northumberland Park [LE] ⚠ 22
Northwich [NT] Ⓟ ◇ 88
Norton Bridge Station Drive *Bus* 67A
Norwich [LE] Ⓟ 🚲 ◇ 🚕

Birmingham 49
Cambridge 17
Colchester 11
Cromer 16
Darlington 26
Doncaster 26
Edinburgh 26
Ely 17
Great Yarmouth 15
Harwich 11
Ipswich 11
Leeds 26
Leicester 49
Liverpool 49
London 11
Lowestoft 15
Manchester 49
Newcastle 26
Nottingham 49
Peterborough 17
Retford 26
Sheffield 49
Sheringham 16
Stockport 49
Stratford 11
York 26

Norwood Junction [LO] [2] 🚲 ⚠ 🚕

Balham 177
Brighton 186
Caterham 181
Clapham Junction 177
Crystal Palace 177
Dorking 182
East Croydon 177
East Grinstead 184
Epsom 182
Gatwick Airport 186
Guildford 182
Haywards Heath 186
Horsham 182, 186
Leatherhead 182
London 175
New Cross Gate 178
Oxted 184
Peckham Rye 177
Penge West 178
Purley 175
Redhill 186
Sutton (Surrey) 182
Tattenham Corner 181
Tonbridge 186
Tulse Hill 177
Uckfield 184
Wandsworth Common 177
West Croydon 177

Nottingham [EM] [8] Ⓟ 🚲 ◇ 🚕

Barnsley 34
Bedford 53
Birmingham 57
Birmingham International 51
Bournemouth 51
Bristol 57
Cambridge 49
Cardiff 57
Cheltenham Spa 57
Cleethorpes 27
Coventry 51
Derby 56
Doncaster 53
Exeter 51
Gloucester 57
Grantham 19
Grimsby Town 27
Kettering 53
Leeds 34, 53
Leicester 53
Lincoln 27
Liverpool 49
London 53
Loughborough 53
Luton 53
Manchester 49
Mansfield 55
Market Harborough 53
Matlock 56
Meadowhall 34, 53
Newark 27
Newport (South Wales) 57
Nuneaton 57
Oxford 51
Paignton 51
Penzance 51
Peterborough 49
Plymouth 51
Reading 51
Sheffield 34, 53
Skegness 19
Southampton 51
Stockport 49
Wakefield 34, 53
Wellingborough 53
Worksop 55
York 53

Nuneaton [LM] Ⓟ ◇ 🚕 49, 57, 65, 66, 67
Nunhead [SE] [4] ◇ ⚠ 52, 195, 200
Nunthorpe [NT] Ⓟ 🚲 ⓤ 45
Nutbourne [SN] ⚠ ⓤ 188
Nutfield [SN] ⚠ ⓤ 186

O

Oakengates [LM] Ⓟ ⓤ 74

Station index and table numbers

10 Connection time
Ⓟ Station Car Park
🚲 Bicycle storage facility
◇ Seat reservations can be made at this station
⚠ Penalty Fare Schemes in operation on some or all services from this station
🚕 Taxi rank or cab office at station, or signposted and within 100 metres
Ⓤ Unstaffed station
[ ] Station Operator Code

P

■10 Connection time
Ⓟ Station Car Park
🚲 Bicycle storage facility
◇ Seat reservations can be made at this station
⚠ Penalty Fare Schemes in operation on some or all services from this station
🚕 Taxi rank or cab office at station, or signposted and within 100 metres
⊛ Unstaffed station
[ ] Station Operator Code

Station index and table numbers

Plumstead [SE] ◇ ⚠ 200
Plymouth [GW] Ⓟ 🚲 ◇ ⚠ 🚕
Aberdeen 51
Birmingham 51, 135
Bristol 135
Cardiff 135
Carlisle 51
Crewe 51
Derby 51
Dundee 51
Edinburgh 51
Exeter 135
Glasgow 51
Gunnislake 139
Leeds 51
London 135, *Sleepers* 406
Manchester 51
Newcastle 51
Newton Abbot 135
Nottingham 51
Paignton 135
Penzance 135
Preston 51
Reading 135, *Sleepers* 406
Sheffield 51
Taunton 135
Torquay 135
Wolverhampton 51
York 51
Pokesdown [SW] 🚲 ◇ ⚠ 158
Polegate [SN] Ⓟ 🚲 ◇ ⚠ 🚕 189
Polesworth [LM] Ⓟ ⊛ 67
Pollokshaws East [SR] 🚲 ⊛ 223
Pollokshaws West [SR] 🚲 ⊛ 222
Pollokshields East [SR] 🚲 223
Pollokshields West [SR] 🚲 ⊛ 223
Polmont [SR] ■3 Ⓟ 🚲 ◇ 🚕 228, 230
Polsloe Bridge [GW] ⊛ 136
Ponders End [LE] ⚠ 22
Pontarddulais [AW] Ⓟ ⊛ 129
Pontefract Baghill [NT] Ⓟ ⊛ 33
Pontefract Monkhill [NT] Ⓟ ⊛ 32
Pontefract Tanshelf [NT] Ⓟ ⊛ 32
Pontlottyn [AW] Ⓟ ⊛ 130
Pont-y-Pant [AW] ⊛ 102
Pontyclun [AW] Ⓟ ⊛ 128
Pontypool & New Inn [AW] Ⓟ ⊛ 131
Pontypridd [AW] ■3 🚲 ◇ 🚕 130
Poole [SW] ■4 Ⓟ 🚲 ◇ ⚠ 🚕 158
Poppleton [NT] Ⓟ 🚲 ⊛ 35
Portchester [SW] 🚲 ⚠ 158, 165, 188
Port Glasgow [SR] 🚲 🚕 219
Porth [AW] Ⓟ ◇ 130
Porthmadog [AW] ⊛ 75
Portlethen [SR] Ⓟ 🚲 ⊛ 229
Portslade [SN] Ⓟ 🚲 ◇ ⚠ 188
Portsmouth Arms [GW] Ⓟ ⊛ 136
Portsmouth
Harbour [SW] 🚲 ◇ ⚠ 🚕
& Southsea [SW] Ⓟ 🚲 ◇ ⚠ 🚕
Bognor Regis 188
Brighton 188
Bristol 123
Cardiff 123
Chichester 188
Crawley 188
East Croydon 188
Exeter 160
Fareham 165
Gatwick Airport 188
Guildford 156
Haslemere 156
Havant 157
Horsham 188
Littlehampton 188
London 156, 158, 188
Reading
via Eastleigh 158
via Guildford 156
Redhill 188
Ryde 167
Salisbury 123
Sandown 167
Shanklin 167
Southampton Central 165
Winchester 158
Worthing 188
Port Sunlight [ME] 🚲 ⚠ 106
Port Talbot Parkway [AW] Ⓟ 🚲 ◇ 🚕 125, 128
Possilpark & Parkhouse [SR] 🚲 ⊛ 232
Potters Bar [FC] Ⓟ ◇ ⚠ 🚕 24, 25
Poulton-le-Fylde [NT] Ⓟ ◇ 🚕 41, 82, 97
Poynton [NT] Ⓟ 84
Prees [AW] ⊛ 131
Prescot [NT] Ⓟ 90
Prestatyn [AW] ◇ 🚕 ⊛ 81
Prestbury [NT] Ⓟ ⊛ 84
Preston [VT] ■8 Ⓟ 🚲 ◇ 🚕
Aberdeen 65, *Sleepers* 402
Barrow-in-Furness 82
Birmingham 65
Birmingham International 65
Blackburn 97
Blackpool 97
Bolton 82
Bournemouth 51
Bradford 41
Bristol 51
Burnley 97
Carlisle 65
Chorley 82
Clitheroe 94, 97
Colne 97
Coventry 65
Crewe 65
Douglas (IOM) 98A
Dundee 65, *Sleepers* 402
Edinburgh 65
Exeter 51
Fort William *Sleepers* 404
Glasgow 65
Inverkeithing *Sleepers* 402
Inverness 65, *Sleepers* 403
Kirkcaldy *Sleepers* 402
Lancaster 65
Leeds 41
Liverpool 90
London 65
Manchester 82
Manchester Airport 82
Milton Keynes Central 65
Ormskirk 99
Oxenholme Lake District 65
Oxford 51
Paignton 51
Penzance 51
Perth 65, *Sleepers* 403
Plymouth 51
Reading 51
Rugby 65
Southampton 51
Stafford 65
Stirling *Sleepers* 403
Stockport 82
Torquay 51
Warrington 65
Watford 65
Wigan 65
Windermere 65
Wolverhampton 65
York 41
Preston Park [SN] ◇ ⚠ 52, 186
Preston (Fishergate) *Bus* 65E
Prestonpans [SR] Ⓟ 🚲 ⊛ 238
Prestwick International Airport 🚕 ⊛ 218, 221
Prestwick Town [SR] Ⓟ 🚲 🚕 218, 221
Priesthill & Darnley [SR] 🚲 ⊛ 222
Princes Risborough [CH] ■2 Ⓟ 🚲 ◇ ⚠ 🚕 115, 115A
Prittlewell [LE] Ⓟ 🚲 ⚠ 5
Prudhoe [NT] Ⓟ 🚲 ⊛ 48
Pulborough [SN] Ⓟ 🚲 ◇ ⚠ 🚕 188
Purfleet [CC] Ⓟ 🚲 ◇ ⚠ 1
Purley [SN] ■4 Ⓟ ◇ ⚠ 🚕 175, 181, 186
Purley Oaks [SN] Ⓟ ⚠ 175, 181
Putney [SW] 🚲 ◇ ⚠ 149
Pwllheli [AW] 🚲 🚕 75
Pyle [AW] Ⓟ 🚲 ⊛ 128

Q

Quakers Yard [AW] ⊛ 130
Queenborough [SE] Ⓟ ◇ ⚠ 212

Station index and table numbers

[10] Connection time
Ⓟ Station Car Park
🚲 Bicycle storage facility
◇ Seat reservations can be made at this station
⚠ Penalty Fare Schemes in operation on some or all services from this station
🚕 Taxi rank or cab office at station, or signposted and within 100 metres
Ⓤ Unstaffed station
[ ] Station Operator Code

Queens Park (Glasgow) **[SR]** 🚲 223
Queen's Park (London) **[LT]** 60
Queens Road, Peckham [SN] 🚲 ◇ ⚠ 177, 178, 179
Queen's Road, Walthamstow [LO] (see Walthamstow Queen's Road)
Queenstown Road (Battersea) [SW] ⚠ Ⓤ 149
Quintrell Downs [GW] Ⓤ 142

R

Radcliffe (Notts.) **[EM]** Ⓟ Ⓤ 19
Radlett [FC] Ⓟ 🚲 ◇ ⚠ 🚕 52
Radley [GW] Ⓟ Ⓤ 116
Radyr [AW] [3] Ⓟ 🚲 ◇ 130
Rainford [NT] Ⓟ Ⓤ 82
Rainham (Essex) **[CC]** Ⓟ 🚲 ◇ ⚠ 1
Rainham (Kent) [SE] Ⓟ ◇ ⚠ 🚕 194, 212
Rainhill [NT] 90
Ramsgate [SE] [4] Ⓟ 🚲 ◇ ⚠ 🚕 194, 207, 212
Ramsgreave & Wilpshire [NT] Ⓟ Ⓤ 94
Rannoch [SR] Ⓟ 🚲 Ⓤ 227, *Sleepers* 404
Rauceby [EM] Ⓤ 19
Ravenglass for Eskdale [NT] Ⓤ 100
Ravensbourne [SE] ◇ ⚠ 52, 195
Ravensthorpe [NT] Ⓤ 39
Rawcliffe [NT] Ⓤ 32
Rayleigh [LE] Ⓟ 🚲 ⚠ 🚕 5
Raynes Park [SW] [6] 🚲 ◇ ⚠ 🚕 152
Reading [GW] [7] Ⓟ 🚲 ◇ ⚠ 🚕
- Aberdeen 51
- Ascot 149
- Banbury 116
- Basingstoke 122
- Bath Spa 125
- Birmingham 116
- Bodmin Parkway 135, *Sleepers* 406
- Bournemouth 158
- Bristol 125
- Camborne 135, *Sleepers* 406
- Cardiff 125
- Carlisle 51
- Cheltenham Spa 125
- Clapham Junction 149
- Coventry 51
- Crewe 51
- Derby 51
- Didcot 116
- Dundee 51
- Edinburgh 51
- Exeter 135, *Sleepers* 406
- Gatwick Airport 148
- Glasgow 51
- Gloucester 125
- Guildford 148
- Hayle 135, *Sleepers* 406
- Heathrow Airport *Bus* 125A
- Henley-on-Thames 121
- Hereford 126
- Leamington Spa 116
- Leeds 51
- Liskeard 135, *Sleepers* 406
- London 116, 117, 149
- Lostwithiel 135, *Sleepers* 406
- Manchester 51
- Milford Haven 128
- Moreton-in-Marsh 126
- Newbury 116
- Newcastle 51
- Newport (South Wales) 125
- Newton Abbot 135, *Sleepers* 406
- Oxford 116
- Paignton 135
- Par 135, *Sleepers* 406
- Penzance 135, *Sleepers* 406
- Plymouth 135, *Sleepers* 406
- Poole 158
- Portsmouth
  - via Basingstoke 158
  - via Guildford 156
- Preston 51
- Redhill 148
- Redruth 135, *Sleepers* 406
- Rosslare Harbour 128
- Sheffield 51
- Slough 117
- Southampton 158
- St Austell 135, *Sleepers* 406
- St Erth 135, *Sleepers* 406
- Staines 149
- Swansea 125
- Swindon 125
- Taunton 135
- Torquay 135
- Truro 135, *Sleepers* 406
- Wallingford *Bus* 116A
- Weston-super-Mare 125
- Weymouth 158
- Winchester 158
- Wolverhampton 51
- Worcester 126
- York 51

Reading West [GW] [3] 116, 122
Rectory Road [LE] ⚠ 21
Redbridge [SW] Ⓟ ⚠ Ⓤ 158
Redcar British Steel [NT] Ⓤ 44
Redcar Central [NT] Ⓟ 🚲 ◇ 🚕 44
Redcar East [NT] 🚲 Ⓤ 44
Reddish North [NT] Ⓟ 🚲 78
Reddish South [NT] Ⓤ 78
Redditch [LM] Ⓟ ◇ ⚠ 69
Redhill [SN] Ⓟ 🚲 ◇ ⚠ 🚕 148, 186, 188
Redland [GW] 🚲 Ⓤ 133
Redruth [GW] Ⓟ 🚲 ◇ 🚕 51, 135, *Sleepers* 406
Reedham (Norfolk) [LE] Ⓟ 🚲 Ⓤ 15
Reedham (Surrey) **[SN]** ⚠ 181
Reigate [SN] Ⓟ 🚲 ◇ ⚠ 148, 186
Renton [SR] 🚲 Ⓤ 226
Retford [GR] [10] Ⓟ 🚲 ◇ 🚕 26, 30
Rhiwbina [AW] Ⓤ 130
Rhoose Cardiff Int. Airport [AW] Ⓟ 🚲 Ⓤ 130
Rhosneigr [AW] Ⓤ 81
Rhyl [AW] ◇ 🚕 81
Rhymney [AW] [3] Ⓟ 🚕 Ⓤ 130
Ribblehead [NT] Ⓟ Ⓤ 36
Rice Lane [ME] ⚠ 103
Richmond (Greater London) **[SW]** Ⓟ 🚲 ◇ ⚠ 🚕 59, 149
Richmond (Market) 🚕 *Bus* 26H
Rickmansworth [LT] Ⓟ 🚲 ⚠ 114
Riddlesdown [SN] ◇ ⚠ 184
Ridgmont [LM] Ⓤ 64
Riding Mill [NT] Ⓟ 🚲 Ⓤ 48
Risca & Pontymister [AW] Ⓟ Ⓤ 127
Rishton [NT] Ⓟ 🚲 Ⓤ 97
Robin Hood Airport 🚕 *Bus* 26F
Robertsbridge [SE] Ⓟ ◇ ⚠ 206
Roby [NT] 90
Rochdale [NT] Ⓟ ◇ 🚕 41, 82
Roche [GW] Ⓤ 142
Rochester [SE] [4] Ⓟ ◇ ⚠ 🚕 194, 200, 212
Rochford [LE] Ⓟ 🚲 ⚠ 🚕 5
Rock Ferry [ME] Ⓟ 🚲 ◇ ⚠ 🚕 106
Rogart [SR] Ⓟ 🚲 Ⓤ 239
Rogerstone [AW] Ⓟ Ⓤ 127
Rolleston [EM] Ⓤ 27
Roman Bridge [AW] Ⓤ 102
Romford [LE] 🚲 ◇ ⚠ 🚕 4, 5, 11
Romiley [NT] Ⓟ 🚲 78
Romsey [GW] Ⓟ 🚲 123, 158
Roose [NT] Ⓟ Ⓤ 82
Rose Grove [NT] Ⓤ 97
Rose Hill Marple [NT] Ⓟ 🚲 ◇ 78
Rosslare Harbour *Ship* 128
Rosyth [SR] Ⓟ Ⓤ 242
Rotherham Central [NT] Ⓟ ◇ 🚕 29, 31, 33
Rotherhithe [LO] ⚠ 178
Rothesay *Ship* 219B
Roughton Road [LE] 🚲 Ⓤ 16
Rowlands Castle [SW] Ⓟ 🚲 ◇ ⚠ 156
Rowley Regis [LM] Ⓟ ◇ ⚠ 71, 115
Roy Bridge [SR] 🚲 Ⓤ 227, *Sleepers* 404
Roydon [LE] Ⓟ ⚠ 22
Royston [FC] Ⓟ 🚲 ◇ ⚠ 🚕 25
Ruabon [AW] Ⓟ Ⓤ 75

Station index and table numbers

[10] Connection time
℗ Station Car Park
🚲 Bicycle storage facility
◇ Seat reservations can be made at this station
⚠ Penalty Fare Schemes in operation on some or all services from this station
🚕 Taxi rank or cab office at station, or signposted and within 100 metres
ⓤ Unstaffed station
[ ] Station Operator Code

Rufford [NT] ℗ ⓤ 99
Rugby [VT] ℗ 🚲 ◇ 🚕 65, 66, 67, 68
Rugeley Town [LM] ℗ ⓤ 70
Rugeley Trent Valley [LM] ⓤ 67, 70
Ruislip [CH] (see South and West Ruislip)
Rum *Ship* 227A
Runcorn [VT] ℗ 🚲 ◇ 🚕 65, 91
Runcorn East [AW] ℗ 81
Ruskington [EM] ℗ 🚲 ⓤ 18
Ruswarp [NT] ⓤ 45
Rutherglen [SR] 🚲 226
Ryde Esplanade [IL] ◇ 🚕 167
Ryde Pier Head [IL] ℗ 🚲 ◇ 167
Ryde St. Johns Road [IL] ℗ 🚲 ⓤ 167
Ryder Brow [NT] ⓤ 78
Rye [SN] ℗ ⚠ 🚕 189
Rye House [LE] ⚠ 22

S

St Albans [FC] ℗ 🚲 ◇ ⚠ 🚕 52, 186
St Albans Abbey [LM] ℗ ⓤ 61
St Andrews Bus Station *Bus* 229
St Andrews Road [GW] ℗ 🚲 ⓤ 133
St Annes-on-the-Sea [NT] ℗ ◇ 🚕 97
St Austell [GW] ℗ 🚲 ◇ 🚕 51, 135, *Bus* 135B, *Sleepers* 406
St Bees [NT] ℗ ⓤ 100
St Budeaux Ferry Road [GW] ⓤ 135, 139
St Budeaux Victoria Road [GW] ⓤ 139
St Columb Road [GW] ℗ ⓤ 142
St Denys [SW] ℗ 🚲 ◇ ⚠ 158, 165
St Erth [GW] ℗ ◇ 51, 135, 144, *Sleepers* 406
St Germans [GW] ⓤ 135
St Helens Central [NT] ℗ ◇ 🚕 90
St Helens Junction [NT] ℗ 90
St Helier (Surrey) **[FC]** 🚲 ⚠ ⓤ 52, 179
St Ives [GW] ℗ ⓤ 144
St James' Park [GW] ⓤ 136
St James Street [LE] 🚲 ⚠ 20
St Johns [SE] ◇ ⚠ 199, 200, 203, 204
St Keyne Wishing Well Halt [GW] ⓤ 140
St Leonards Warrior Square [SE] [4] ℗ ◇ ⚠ 🚕 189, 206
St Margarets (Herts.) [LE] ℗ ⚠ 🚕 22
St Margarets (Greater London) **[SW]** 🚲 ◇ ⚠ 🚕 149
St Mary Cray [SE] ℗ ◇ ⚠ 52, 195, 196, 212
St Michaels [ME] ℗ ⚠ 103
St Neots [FC] ℗ 🚲 ⚠ 🚕 25
St Neots Cross Keys Mall *Bus* 65C
St Neots Square *Bus* 65C
St Pancras International (see London)
Salford Central [NT] 82, 94
Salford Crescent [NT] 82, 94
Salfords [SN] ◇ ⚠ 186
Salhouse [LE] ℗ 🚲 ⓤ 16
Salisbury [SW] ℗ 🚲 ◇ ⚠ 🚕 123, 158, 160
Saltaire [NT] ⓤ 36
Saltash [GW] ℗ 🚲 ⓤ 135
Saltburn [NT] ⓤ 44
Saltcoats [SR] ℗ 🚲 🚕 221
Saltmarshe [NT] ℗ ⓤ 29
Salwick [NT] ⓤ 97
Sampford Courtenay ⓤ 136
Sandal & Agbrigg [NT] ℗ 🚲 ⓤ 31
Sandbach [NT] ℗ 🚲 84
Sanderstead [SN] ℗ ◇ ⚠ 184
Sandhills [ME] ⚠ 103
Sandhurst [GW] ⓤ 148
Sandling [SE] ℗ ◇ ⚠ 207
Sandown [IL] ℗ 🚲 ⓤ 167
Sandplace [GW] ⓤ 140
Sandringham Norwich Gates *Bus* 17A
Sandringham Visitor Centre *Bus* 17A
Sandwell & Dudley [LM] ℗ 🚲 ◇ ⚠ 🚕 66, 68, 74
Sandwich [SE] ℗ ◇ ⚠ 207
Sandy [FC] ℗ 🚲 ⚠ 25
Sankey for Penketh [NT] ℗ 89
Sanquhar [SR] ℗ 🚲 ⓤ 216
Sarn [AW] ℗ ⓤ 128
Saundersfoot [AW] ⓤ 128
Saunderton [CH] ℗ 🚲 ⚠ ⓤ 115
Sawbridgeworth [LE] ℗ ⚠ 22
Saxilby [EM] ℗ 🚲 ⓤ 18, 30
Saxmundham [LE] ℗ 🚲 ⓤ 13
Scarborough [TP] ℗ 🚲 ◇ 🚕 26, 39, 43
Scotscalder [SR] ℗ 🚲 ⓤ 239
Scotstounhill [SR] ℗ 🚲 226
Scrabster *Ship* 239A
Scunthorpe [TP] ℗ ◇ 🚕 29
Sea Mills [GW] 🚲 ⓤ 133
Seaford [SN] ℗ 🚲 ◇ ⚠ 🚕 189
Seaforth & Litherland [ME] ⚠ 🚕 103
Seaham [NT] ℗ ⓤ 44
Seamer [TP] ℗ ⓤ 39, 43
Seascale [NT] ℗ ⓤ 100
Seaton Carew [NT] ℗ 🚲 ⓤ 44
Seer Green [CH] ℗ 🚲 ⚠ 115
Selby [TP] ℗ 🚲 ◇ 🚕 26, 29, 39, 40, 41
Selhurst [SN] [4] 🚲 ◇ ⚠ 176, 177
Selkirk *Bus* 65G
Sellafield [NT] ℗ ⓤ 100
Selling [SE] ℗ ⚠ ⓤ 212
Selly Oak [LM] ℗ 🚲 ◇ ⚠ 69
Settle [NT] ℗ ◇ 36
Seven Kings [LE] 🚲 ⚠ 5
Seven Sisters [LE] ⚠ 21, 22
Sevenoaks [SE] [4] ℗ ◇ ⚠ 🚕 52, 195, 204, 206, 207
Severn Beach [GW] 🚲 ⓤ 133
Severn Tunnel Junction [AW] ℗ 🚲 ◇ 123, 132
Shadwell [LO] ⚠ 178
Shalford [GW] ℗ ⓤ 148
Shanklin [IL] ℗ 🚲 ◇ 🚕 167
Shawford [SW] ℗ 🚲 ⓤ 158
Shawlands [SR] 🚲 ⓤ 223
Sheerness-on-Sea [SE] 🚲 ◇ ⚠ 🚕 212
Sheffield [EM] [7] ℗ 🚲 ◇ 🚕
- Barnsley 34
- Birmingham 51
- Bournemouth 51
- Bristol 51
- Cambridge 49
- Cardiff 51
- Chesterfield 53
- Cleethorpes 29
- Darlington 26
- Derby 53
- Doncaster 29
- Edinburgh 26
- Exeter 51
- Glasgow 26
- Goole 29
- Grimsby 29
- Huddersfield 34
- Hull 29
- Leeds 31
- Leicester 53
- Lincoln 30
- Liverpool 89
- London 53
- Luton 53
- Manchester 78
- Manchester Airport 78
- Meadowhall 29, 35
- Newcastle 26
- New Mills 78
- Newport (South Wales) 51
- Norwich 49
- Nottingham 53
- Oxford 51
- Paignton 51
- Penistone 34
- Penzance 51
- Peterborough 49
- Plymouth 51
- Reading 51
- Retford 30
- Rotherham 29

Station index and table numbers

■10 Connection time
Ⓟ Station Car Park
🚲 Bicycle storage facility
◇ Seat reservations can be made at this station
⚠ Penalty Fare Schemes in operation on some or all services from this station
🚕 Taxi rank or cab office at station, or signposted and within 100 metres
Ⓤ Unstaffed station
[ ] Station Operator Code

Scunthorpe 29
Southampton 51
Stockport 78
Torquay 51
Wakefield 31
Warrington 89
York 29

Shelford [LE] ⚠ 22
Shenfield [LE] ■3 Ⓟ 🚲 ◇ ⚠ 🚕 5, 11, 13, 14
Shenstone [LM] Ⓟ ⚠ 69
Shepherd's Bush [LO] ⚠ 66, 176, 177
Shepherds Well [SE] Ⓟ ⚠ 212
Shepley [NT] Ⓤ 34
Shepperton [SW] Ⓟ 🚲 ◇ ⚠ 🚕 152
Shepreth [FC] Ⓟ 🚲 ⚠ Ⓤ 25
Sherborne [SW] Ⓟ 🚲 ◇ 🚕 160
Sherburn-in-Elmet [NT] Ⓤ 33
Sheringham [LE] Ⓟ 🚲 Ⓤ 16
Shettleston [SR] Ⓟ 🚲 🚕 226
Shieldmuir [SR] 🚲 Ⓤ 226
Shifnal [LM] Ⓟ Ⓤ 74
Shildon [NT] Ⓤ 44
Shiplake [GW] Ⓟ Ⓤ 121
Shipley [NT] Ⓟ 🚲 ◇ 26, 36, 37, 38
Shippea Hill [LE] Ⓟ Ⓤ 17
Shipton [GW] Ⓤ 126
Shirebrook [EM] Ⓤ 55
Shirehampton [GW] Ⓟ 🚲 Ⓤ 133
Shireoaks [NT] Ⓤ 30
Shirley [LM] Ⓟ 🚲 ◇ ⚠ 71
Shoeburyness [CC] Ⓟ 🚲 ◇ ⚠ 🚕 1
Sholing [SW] 🚲 ⚠ Ⓤ 165
Shoreditch High Street [LO] ⚠ 178
Shoreham (Kent) [SE] Ⓟ ⚠ Ⓤ 52, 195
Shoreham-by-Sea (Sussex) **[SN]** Ⓟ 🚲 ◇ ⚠ 🚕 188
Shortlands [SE] ■4 Ⓟ 🚲 ◇ ⚠ 52, 195
Shotton [AW] Ⓟ 🚕 81
Shotton High Level [AW] Ⓟ 🚕 101
Shotts [SR] Ⓟ 🚲 225
Shrewsbury [AW] Ⓟ ◇ 🚕
Aberystwyth 75
Bangor (Gwynedd) 131
Barmouth 75
Birmingham 74
Cardiff 131
Chester 75, 131
Crewe 131
Hereford 131
Holyhead 131
Llandudno Junction 131
Llandrindod 129
Llanelli 129
Machynlleth 75
Manchester 131
Newport (South Wales) 131
Pwllheli 75
Swansea 129
Telford Central 74
Whitchurch (Salop) 131
Wrexham 75
Wolverhampton 74

Sidcup [SE] ■4 Ⓟ ◇ ⚠ 🚕 200
Sileby [EM] Ⓤ 53
Silecroft [NT] Ⓤ 100
Silsden [NT] (see Steeton & Silsden)
Silkstone Common [NT] Ⓟ Ⓤ 34
Silverdale [NT] Ⓤ 82
Silver Street [LE] ⚠ 21
Singer [SR] 🚲 🚕 226
Sittingbourne [SE] ■4 Ⓟ ◇ ⚠ 🚕 194, 212
Skegness [EM] 🚲 ◇ 🚕 19
Skewen [AW] Ⓟ Ⓤ 128
Skipton [NT] Ⓟ 🚲 ◇ 🚕 26, 36
Slade Green [SE] ■4 Ⓟ ◇ ⚠ 200
Slaithwaite [NT] Ⓟ Ⓤ 39
Slateford [SR] 🚲 Ⓤ 225
Sleaford [EM] Ⓟ 🚲 ◇ 🚕 18, 19
Sleights [NT] Ⓟ Ⓤ 45
Slough [GW] ■3 Ⓟ 🚲 ◇ ⚠ 🚕 116, 117, 119, 125, 135
Small Heath [LM] ⚠ 71
Smallbrook Junction [IL] Ⓤ 167
Smethwick Galton Bridge [LM] ■7 ◇ ⚠ 68, 71, 74, 75
Smethwick Rolfe Street [LM] ⚠ 68
Smitham (for Coulsdon) **[SN]** Ⓟ ⚠ 181
Smithy Bridge [NT] Ⓟ Ⓤ 41
Snaith [NT] Ⓟ Ⓤ 32
Snodland [SE] Ⓟ ⚠ 🚕 Ⓤ 208
Snowdown [SE] ⚠ Ⓤ 212
Sole Street [SE] Ⓟ ◇ ⚠ 212
Solihull [LM] Ⓟ 🚲 ◇ ⚠ 71, 115
Somerleyton [LE] Ⓟ 🚲 Ⓤ 15
South Acton [LO] 🚲 ⚠ 59
South Bank [NT] 🚲 Ⓤ 44
South Bermondsey [SN] ◇ ⚠ 177, 178, 179
South Croydon [SN] ■4 Ⓟ ◇ ⚠ 175, 181, 184
South Elmsall [NT] Ⓟ 🚲 Ⓤ 31
South Greenford [GW] Ⓤ 117
South Gyle [SR] Ⓟ 🚲 Ⓤ 242
South Hampstead [LO] ⚠ 60
South Kenton [LT] 60
South Merton [FC] ⚠ Ⓤ 52, 179
South Milford [NT] Ⓟ Ⓤ 39, 40
South Ruislip [CH] Ⓟ 🚲 ⚠ 🚕 115
South Tottenham [LO] ⚠ 62
South Wigston [EM] Ⓤ 57
South Woodham Ferrers [LE] Ⓟ 🚲 🚕 5
Southall [GW] ⚠ 117
Southampton Airport Parkway [SW] Ⓟ 🚲 ◇ ⚠ 🚕 51, 158
Southampton Central [SW] Ⓟ 🚲 ◇ ⚠ 🚕
Aberdeen 51
Basingstoke 158
Bath Spa 123
Birmingham 51
Bognor Regis 188
Bournemouth 158
Brighton 188
Bristol 123
Brockenhurst 158
Cardiff 123
Carlisle 51
Chichester 188
Clapham Junction 158, 188
Crawley 188
Crewe 51
Derby 51
Dorchester 158
Dundee 51
East Croydon 188
Eastleigh 158
Edinburgh 51
Exeter 160
Fareham 165, 188
Gatwick Airport 188
Glasgow 51
Havant 165, 188
Horsham 188
Leeds 51
Littlehampton 188
London 158, 188
Lymington Pier 158
Manchester 51
Newcastle 51
Newport (South Wales) 123
Oxford 51
Poole 158
Portsmouth 165
Preston 51
Reading 158
Redhill 188
Romsey 123
Ryde 167
Salisbury 123
Shanklin 167
Sheffield 51
Swindon 123
Westbury (Wilts.) 123
Weymouth 158
Winchester 158
Woking 158
Wolverhampton 51
Worthing 188
Yarmouth (IOW) 158
Yeovil 160
York 51

Southbourne [SN] ◇ ⚠ 188
Southbury [LE] ⚠ 21
Southease [SN] Ⓤ 189
Southend Central [CC] Ⓟ 🚲 ◇ ⚠ 🚕 1
Southend East [CC] Ⓟ 🚲 ◇ ⚠ 1
Southend Victoria [LE] 🚲 ◇ ⚠ 🚕 5

Station index and table numbers

10 Connection time
Ⓟ Station Car Park
🚲 Bicycle storage facility
◇ Seat reservations can be made at this station
⚠ Penalty Fare Schemes in operation on some or all services from this station
🚕 Taxi rank or cab office at station, or signposted and within 100 metres
⊛ Unstaffed station
[ ] Station Operator Code

Southminster [LE] Ⓟ 🚲 ⊛ 5
Southport [ME] 🚲 ◇ ⚠ 🚕 82, 103
Southport (Lord Street) *Bus* 65E
Southsea [SW] (see Portsmouth & Southsea)
Southwick [SN] 🚲 ◇ ⚠ 188
Sowerby Bridge [NT] Ⓟ 🚲 ⊛ 41
Sowton [GW] (see Digby & Sowton)
Spalding [EM] Ⓟ 🚲 🚕 18
Spean Bridge [SR] Ⓟ 🚲 ⊛ 227, *Sleepers* 404
Spital [ME] 🚲 ⚠ 106
Spondon [EM] ⊛ 56
Spooner Row [LE] ⊛ 17
Spring Road [LM] ⚠ 71
Springburn [SR] 🚲 224, 226
Springfield [SR] 🚲 ⊛ 229
Squires Gate [NT] ⊛ 97
Stafford [VT] Ⓟ 🚲 ◇ 🚕
- Bangor (Gwynedd) 65
- Birmingham 68
- Blackpool 65
- Bournemouth 51
- Bristol 51
- Carlisle 65
- Chester 65
- Coventry 67, 68
- Crewe 65
- Edinburgh 65
- Exeter 51
- Glasgow 65
- Holyhead 65
- Lichfield 67
- Liverpool 65
- London 65
- Manchester 84
- Manchester Airport 84
- Nuneaton 67
- Oxenholme Lake District 65
- Oxford 51
- Paignton 51
- Penzance 51
- Plymouth 51
- Preston 65
- Reading 51
- Rugby 65
- Southampton 51
- Stockport 84
- Stoke-on-Trent 65, 68A
- Tamworth 67
- Torquay 51
- Watford 65
- Wolverhampton 68

Staines [SW] Ⓟ 🚲 ◇ ⚠ 🚕 149
Stainforth [NT] (see Hatfield & Stainforth)
Stallingborough [NT] ⊛ 29
Stalybridge [TP] Ⓟ 🚲 ◇ 39
Stamford [EM] Ⓟ ◇ 49
Stamford Hill [LE] ⚠ 21
Stanford-le-Hope [CC] Ⓟ 🚲 ◇ ⚠ 1
Stanlow & Thornton [NT] ⊛ 109
Stansted Airport [LE] 🚲 ◇ ⚠ 🚕 22, 26, 49
Stansted Mountfitchet [LE] Ⓟ 🚲 ⚠ 🚕 22
Staplehurst [SE] Ⓟ 🚲 ◇ ⚠ 🚕 207
Stapleton Road [GW] 🚲 ⊛ 133, 134
Starbeck [NT] 🚲 ⊛ 35
Starcross [GW] 🚲 ⊛ 135
Staveley [TP] ⊛ 83
Stechford [LM] ⚠ 68
Steeton & Silsden [NT] Ⓟ 🚲 ⊛ 36
Stepps [SR] Ⓟ 🚲 ⊛ 224
Stevenage [FC] **4** Ⓟ 🚲 ◇ ⚠ 🚕 24, 25, 26
Stevenston [SR] 🚲 ⊛ 221
Stewartby [LM] ⊛ 64
Stewarton [SR] Ⓟ 🚲 ⊛ 222
Stirling [SR] Ⓟ 🚲 ◇ 🚕 26, 229, 230, *Sleepers* 403
Stockport [VT] Ⓟ 🚲 ◇ 🚕
- Altrincham 88
- Birmingham 65
- Birmingham International 65
- Blackpool 82
- Bolton 82
- Bournemouth 51
- Bristol 51
- Buxton 86
- Cambridge 49
- Cardiff 131
- Chester 88
- Coventry 65
- Crewe 84
- Doncaster 29
- Ely 49
- Exeter 51
- Hazel Grove 86
- Hull 29
- Liverpool 89
- London 65
- Macclesfield 84
- Manchester 84
- Newport (South Wales) 131
- Northwich 88
- Norwich 49
- Nottingham 49
- Oxford 51
- Paignton 51
- Penzance 51
- Peterborough 49
- Plymouth 51
- Preston 82
- Reading 51
- Rugby 65
- Salford Crescent 82
- Sheffield 78
- Southampton 51
- Stafford 84
- Stoke-on-Trent 84
- Torquay 51
- Watford 65
- Wigan 82
- Wolverhampton 65

Stocksfield [NT] Ⓟ 🚲 ⊛ 48
Stocksmoor [NT] Ⓟ 🚲 ⊛ 34
Stockton [NT] 🚲 🚕 ⊛ 44
Stoke d'Abernon [SW] (see Cobham)
Stoke Mandeville [CH] Ⓟ 🚲 ⚠ 114
Stoke Newington [LE] ⚠ 21
Stoke-on-Trent [VT] Ⓟ 🚲 ◇ 🚕 50, 51, 65, 67, 84
Stone [LM] 67
Stone Crown Street *Bus* 67
Stone Granville Square *Bus* 67
Stone Crossing [SE] ◇ ⚠ 200
Stonebridge Park [LT] 60
Stonegate [SE] Ⓟ 🚲 ◇ ⚠ 206
Stonehaven [SR] Ⓟ 🚲 ◇ 26, 51, 229, *Sleepers* 402
Stonehouse [GW] Ⓟ 125
Stoneleigh [SW] 🚲 ◇ ⚠ 152
Stornoway *Ship* 239B
Stourbridge Junction [LM] **2** Ⓟ ◇ ⚠ 71, 72, 115
Stourbridge Town [LM] ⚠ 72
Stowmarket [LE] Ⓟ 🚲 ◇ 🚕 11, 14
Stranraer [SR] 🚲 ◇ 218
Stranraer Harbour *Ship and Catamaran* 218
Stratford (London) **[LE]** **7** ⚠ 🚕
- Barking 1
- Basildon 1
- Bishops Stortford 22
- Braintree 11
- Broxbourne 22
- Bury St. Edmunds 14
- Cambridge 14
- Chelmsford 11
- Cheshunt 22
- Clacton-on-Sea 11
- Colchester 11
- Ely 14
- Gospel Oak 59, 176
- Hackney 59
- Harlow 22
- Harwich 11
- Hertford East 22
- Highbury & Islington 59, 176
- Ilford 5
- Ipswich 11
- London 5
- Manningtree 11
- Norwich 11
- Peterborough 14
- Richmond 59
- Romford 5
- Shenfield 5
- Shoeburyness 1
- Southend 1, 5
- Southminster 5
- Stansted Airport 22
- Stowmarket 11
- Tottenham Hale 22
- Upminster 1

Station index and table numbers

■10 Connection time
Ⓟ Station Car Park
🚲 Bicycle storage facility
◇ Seat reservations can be made at this station
⚠ Penalty Fare Schemes in operation on some or all services from this station
🚕 Taxi rank or cab office at station, or signposted and within 100 metres
ⓤ Unstaffed station
[ ] Station Operator Code

Walton-on-the-Naze 11
West Hampstead 59, 176
Wickford 5
Willesden Junction 59
Witham 11
Stratford International [SE] ⚠ 194, 196, 200, 207, 212
Stratford-upon-Avon [LM] Ⓟ 🚲 ◇ ⚠ 🚕 71, 115
Strathcarron [SR] Ⓟ 🚲 ⓤ 239
Strawberry Hill [SW] 🚲 ◇ ⚠ 149, 152
Streatham [SN] ■4 ◇ ⚠ 52, 177, 179
Streatham Common [SN] ■4 Ⓟ 🚲 ◇ ⚠ 176, 177
Streatham Hill [SN] ◇ ⚠ 🚕 177, 178
Streatley [GW] (see Goring & Streatley)
Streethouse [NT] Ⓟ ⓤ 32
Strines [NT] Ⓟ ⓤ 78
Stromeferry [SR] Ⓟ 🚲 ⓤ 239
Stromness 🚕 *Ship* 239A
Strood [SE] ■4 Ⓟ 🚲 ◇ ⚠ 🚕 194, 200, 208, 212
Stroud [GW] Ⓟ 🚲 ◇ 🚕 125
Sturry [SE] ⚠ 207
Styal [NT] Ⓟ ⓤ 84
Sudbury (Suffolk) **[LE]** 🚲 ⓤ 10
Sudbury & Harrow Road [CH] ⚠ ⓤ 115
Sudbury Hill Harrow [CH] ⚠ ⓤ 115
Sugar Loaf [AW] ⓤ 129
Summerston [SR] ⓤ 232
Sunbury [SW] Ⓟ 🚲 ◇ ⚠ 152
Sunderland [NT] ◇ 🚕 26, 44, 48
Sundridge Park [SE] Ⓟ ◇ ⚠ 204
Sunningdale [SW] Ⓟ 🚲 ◇ ⚠ 🚕 149
Sunnymeads [SW] ⚠ ⓤ 149
Surbiton [SW] ■6 Ⓟ 🚲 ◇ ⚠ 🚕 152, 155
Surrey Quays [LO] ⚠ 178
Sutton Coldfield [LM] Ⓟ 🚲 ◇ ⚠ 69
Sutton Common [FC] ⚠ ⓤ 52, 179
Sutton Parkway [EM] Ⓟ ⓤ 55
Sutton (Surrey) [SN] ■4 Ⓟ 🚲 ◇ ⚠ 🚕 52, 179, 182
Swaffham *Bus* 26A
Swale [SE] ⚠ ⓤ 212
Swalecliffe [SE] (see Chestfield & Swalecliffe)
Swanley [SE] ■4 Ⓟ ◇ ⚠ 🚕 52, 195, 196, 212
Swanscombe [SE] ◇ ⚠ 200
Swansea [AW] Ⓟ 🚲 ◇ 🚕
Bristol 128
Cardiff 128
Camarthen 128
Crewe 131
Derby 57
Fishguard Harbour 128
Gloucester 57
Hereford 131
Llandrindod 129
London 125, 128
Manchester 128, 131
Pembroke Dock 128
Portsmouth 128
Reading 125, 128
Rosslare Harbour 128
Shrewsbury 129
Slough 125
Tenby 128
Swanwick [SW] Ⓟ 🚲 ◇ ⚠ 🚕 165, 188
Sway [SW] Ⓟ 🚲 ◇ ⚠ 158
Swaythling [SW] Ⓟ 🚲 ◇ ⚠ 158
Swinderby [EM] ⓤ 27
Swindon [GW] Ⓟ 🚲 ◇ ⚠ 🚕 123, 125
Swineshead [EM] ⓤ 19
Swinton (Gtr. Manchester) **[NT]** 82
Swinton (S. Yorks.) [NT] Ⓟ 🚲 ◇ 29, 31, 33
Sydenham [LO] Ⓟ ◇ ⚠ 178
Sydenham Hill [SE] Ⓟ ⚠ 195
Syon Lane [SW] 🚲 ⚠ ⓤ 149
Syston [EM] Ⓟ ⓤ 53

T

Tackley [GW] ⓤ 116
Tadworth [SN] ◇ ⚠ 181
Taffs Well [AW] ■3 Ⓟ ⓤ 130
Tain [SR] Ⓟ ⓤ 239
Talsarnau [AW] ⓤ 75
Talybont [AW] ⓤ 75
Tal-y-Cafn [AW] ⓤ 102
Tame Bridge Parkway [LM] Ⓟ 🚲 ◇ ⚠ 70, 75
Tamworth [LM] Ⓟ ◇ 🚕 51, 57, 65, 67
Taplow [GW] Ⓟ 🚲 ⚠ 🚕 117
Tarbert *Ship* 239B
Tattenham Corner [SN] Ⓟ ◇ ⚠ 181
Taunton [GW] Ⓟ 🚲 ◇ ⚠ 🚕 51, 134, 135, *Bus* 135E
Taynuilt [SR] Ⓟ 🚲 ⓤ 227
Teddington [SW] 🚲 ◇ ⚠ 149, 152
Tees-side Airport [NT] ⓤ 44
Teignmouth [GW] Ⓟ 🚲 ◇ 🚕 51, 135
Telford Central [LM] Ⓟ ◇ 🚕 74, 75
Templecombe [SW] Ⓟ 🚲 ◇ 160
Tenby [AW] Ⓟ ⓤ 128
Tewkesbury [GW] (see Ashchurch)
Teynham [SE] Ⓟ ◇ ⚠ 212
Thame [CH] (see Haddenham & Thame Parkway)
Thames Ditton [SW] 🚲 ⚠ 152
Thatcham [GW] Ⓟ 🚲 116, 135
Thatto Heath [NT] Ⓟ 90
The Hawthorns [LM] Ⓟ ⚠ 71
The Lakes (Warwickshire) **[LM]** ⚠ ⓤ 71
Theale [GW] Ⓟ 🚲 116, 135
Theobalds Grove [LE] ⚠ 21
Thetford [LE] Ⓟ ◇ 🚕 17, 49
Thirsk [TP] Ⓟ ◇ 26, 39
Thornaby [TP] Ⓟ 🚲 ◇ 🚕 39, 44
Thorne North [NT] Ⓟ 🚲 29
Thorne South [NT] Ⓟ ⓤ 29
Thornford [GW] ⓤ 123
Thornhill [AW] (see Lisvane)
Thornliebank [SR] 🚲 ⓤ 222
Thornton (Ches.) **[NT]** (see Stanlow & Thornton)
Thornton (Fife) **[SR]** (see Glenrothes With Thornton)
Thornton Abbey [NT] ⓤ 29
Thorntonhall [SR] 🚲 ⓤ 222
Thornton Heath [SN] 🚲 ◇ ⚠ 🚕 176, 177
Thorpe Bay [CC] Ⓟ 🚲 ◇ ⚠ 🚕 1
Thorpe Culvert [EM] Ⓟ ⓤ 19
Thorpe-le-Soken [LE] ■1 Ⓟ 🚲 ⚠ 11
Three Bridges [SN] ■4 Ⓟ 🚲 ◇ ⚠ 🚕 52, 186, 188
Three Oaks [SN] ⓤ 189
Thurgarton [EM] ⓤ 27
Thurnscoe [NT] Ⓟ ⓤ 31
Thurso [SR] Ⓟ 🚲 ◇ 🚕 239, *Ship* 239A
Thurston [LE] Ⓟ 🚲 ⓤ 14
Tilbury Riverside [CC] ⓤ *Bus* 1A
Tilbury Town [CC] ■3 🚲 ◇ ⚠ 1, *Bus* 1A
Tile Hill [LM] Ⓟ ⚠ 68
Tilehurst [GW] Ⓟ 🚲 116
Tipton [LM] Ⓟ ⚠ 68
Tiree *Ship* 227B
Tir-phil [AW] Ⓟ ⓤ 130
Tisbury [SW] Ⓟ 🚲 ◇ 160
Tiverton Parkway [GW] Ⓟ 🚲 ◇ ⚠ 🚕 51, 135
Todmorden [NT] Ⓟ 🚲 🚕 41
Tolworth [SW] Ⓟ 🚲 ◇ ⚠ 🚕 152
Tonbridge [SE] ■4 Ⓟ 🚲 ◇ ⚠ 🚕 186, 204, 206, 207, 208
Ton Pentre [AW] ⓤ 130
Tondu [AW] Ⓟ ⓤ 128
Tonfanau [AW] ⓤ 75
Tonypandy [AW] ⓤ 130
Tooting [FC] ◇ ⚠ 52, 179
Topsham [GW] Ⓟ 🚲 ⓤ 136
Torquay [GW] Ⓟ 🚲 ◇ 🚕 51, 135
Torre [GW] Ⓟ ⓤ 135

Station index and table numbers

10 Connection time
Ⓟ Station Car Park
🚲 Bicycle storage facility
◇ Seat reservations can be made at this station
⚠ Penalty Fare Schemes in operation on some or all services from this station
🚕 Taxi rank or cab office at station, or signposted and within 100 metres
Ⓤ Unstaffed station
[ ] Station Operator Code

Totley [NT] (see Dore & Totley)
Totnes [GW] Ⓟ 🚲 ◇ ⚠ 🚕 51, 135, *Sleepers* 406
Tottenham Hale [LE] ⚠ 🚕 22
Tottenham South [LO] (see South Tottenham)
Totton [SW] Ⓟ 🚲 ◇ ⚠ 158
Town Green [ME] Ⓟ ⚠ 103
Trafford Park [NT] 🚕 Ⓤ 89
Treforest [AW] Ⓟ ◇ 130
Treforest Estate [AW] Ⓤ 130
Trehafod [AW] Ⓟ Ⓤ 130
Treherbert [AW] Ⓤ 130
Treorchy [AW] Ⓟ Ⓤ 130
Trimley [LE] Ⓟ 🚲 Ⓤ 13
Tring [LM] Ⓟ 🚲 ⚠ 🚕 66, 176
Troed-y-rhiw [AW] Ⓤ 130
Troon [SR] Ⓟ 🚲 🚕 218, 221
Trowbridge [GW] Ⓟ 🚲 ◇ 🚕 123, 160
Truro [GW] Ⓟ 🚲 ◇ 🚕 51, 135, 143, *Sleepers* 406
Tulloch [SR] Ⓟ 🚲 Ⓤ 227, *Sleepers* 404
Tulse Hill [SN] **3** ◇ ⚠ 52, 177, 179, 182
Tunbridge Wells [SE] **4** Ⓟ 🚲 ◇ ⚠ 🚕 206
Turkey Street [LE] ⚠ 21
Tutbury & Hatton [EM] Ⓤ 50
Twickenham [SW] Ⓟ 🚲 ◇ ⚠ 149
Twyford [GW] **3** Ⓟ 🚲 ⚠ 🚕 116, 117, 121
Ty Croes [AW] Ⓤ 81
Ty Glas [AW] Ⓤ 130
Tygwyn [AW] Ⓟ Ⓤ 75
Tyndrum Lower [SR] Ⓟ 🚲 Ⓤ 227
Tyndrum Upper [SR] (see Upper Tyndrum)
Tyseley [LM] ⚠ 71
Tywyn [AW] 🚲 Ⓤ 75

U

Uckfield [SN] Ⓟ ◇ ⚠ 184
Uddingston [SR] Ⓟ 🚲 🚕 225, 226
Uig *Ship* 239B
Ulceby [NT] Ⓤ 29
Ullapool *Ship* 239B
Ulleskelf [NT] Ⓤ 33, 40
Ulverston [TP] ◇ 82
Umberleigh [GW] Ⓟ Ⓤ 136
University [LM] ◇ ⚠ 69, 71
Uphall [SR] Ⓟ 🚲 Ⓤ 237
Upholland [NT] Ⓤ 82
Upminster [CC] Ⓟ 🚲 ◇ ⚠ 🚕 1, 4
Upper Halliford [SW] ◇ ⚠ 152
Upper Holloway [LO] ⚠ 62
Upper Tyndrum [SR] Ⓟ 🚲 Ⓤ 227, *Sleepers* 404
Upper Warlingham [SN] Ⓟ 🚲 ◇ ⚠ 🚕 184
Upton [AW] Ⓤ 101
Upwey [SW] Ⓟ 🚲 ⚠ Ⓤ 123, 158
Urmston [NT] Ⓟ 🚲 89
Uttoxeter [EM] Ⓟ Ⓤ 50

V

Valley [AW] Ⓟ Ⓤ 81
Vauxhall (London) **[SW]** ◇ ⚠ 149, 152, 155
Victoria [NR] (see London)
Virginia Water [SW] Ⓟ 🚲 ◇ ⚠ 🚕 149

W

Waddon [SN] ◇ ⚠ 182
Wadebridge Bus Station *Bus* 135C
Wadhurst [SE] Ⓟ ◇ ⚠ 206
Wainfleet [EM] Ⓟ 🚲 Ⓤ 19
Wakefield
Kirkgate [NT] **4** Ⓟ 🚲 Ⓤ
Westgate [GR] **7** Ⓟ 🚲 ◇ 🚕
Barnsley 34
Bedford 53
Birmingham 51
Bournemouth 51
Bristol 51
Cambridge 26
Derby 53
Doncaster 31
Exeter 51
Huddersfield 39
Knottingley 32
Leeds 31
Leicester 53
Liverpool 39
London 26, 53
Luton 53
Manchester 39
Manchester Airport 39
Meadowhall 31
Newquay 51
Norwich 26
Nottingham 53
Paignton 51
Penzance 51
Plymouth 51
Pontefract 32
Sheffield 31
Southampton 51
Torquay 51
Wakes Colne [LE] (see Chappel & Wakes Colne)
Walkden [NT] 82
Wallasey Grove Road [ME] Ⓟ ⚠ 106
Wallasey Village [ME] ⚠ 106
Wallingford Market Place *Bus* 116A
Wallingford Town Hall *Bus* 116A
Wallington [SN] Ⓟ ◇ ⚠ 🚕 182
Wallyford [SR] Ⓟ 🚲 Ⓤ 238
Walmer [SE] Ⓟ ◇ ⚠ 🚕 207
Walsall [LM] ◇ ⚠ 70
Walsden [NT] Ⓤ 41
Waltham Cross [LE] Ⓟ ⚠ 🚕 22
Walthamstow Central [LE] Ⓟ 🚲 ⚠ 🚕 20
Walthamstow Queen's Road [LO] 🚲 ⚠ 62
Walton (Merseyside) [ME] ⚠ 103
Walton-on-the-Naze [LE] 🚲 ⚠ 11
Walton-on-Thames [SW] Ⓟ 🚲 ◇ ⚠ 🚕 155
Wanborough [SW] ⚠ Ⓤ 148, 149
Wandsworth Common [SN] Ⓟ 🚲 ◇ ⚠ 🚕 176, 177, 178
Wandsworth Road [SN] ⚠ Ⓤ 176, 178
Wandsworth Town [SW] 🚲 ◇ ⚠ 149
Wanstead Park [LO] 🚲 ⚠ 62
Wapping [LO] ⚠ 178
Warblington [SN] ⚠ Ⓤ 188
Ware [LE] Ⓟ 🚲 ⚠ 🚕 22
Wareham [SW] Ⓟ 🚲 ◇ ⚠ 🚕 158
Wargrave [GW] Ⓟ 🚲 Ⓤ 121
Warminster [GW] Ⓟ 🚲 ◇ 🚕 123, 160
Warnham [SN] ⚠ Ⓤ 182
Warrington
Bank Quay [VT] Ⓟ ◇ 🚕
Central [TP] Ⓟ 🚲 ◇ 🚕
Aberdeen 65
Bangor (Gwynedd) 81
Birmingham 65
Bournemouth 51
Bristol 51
Cambridge 49
Carlisle 65
Chester 81
Crewe 65
Dundee 65
Edinburgh 65
Ellesmere Port 109
Exeter 51
Glasgow 65
Holyhead 81
Huddersfield 39
Hull 39
Inverness 65
Lancaster 65
Leeds 39
Liverpool 89, 90
Llandudno 81

Station index and table numbers

■10 Connection time
Ⓟ Station Car Park
🚲 Bicycle storage facility
◇ Seat reservations can be made at this station
⚠ Penalty Fare Schemes in operation on some or all services from this station
🚕 Taxi rank or cab office at station, or signposted and within 100 metres
Ⓤ Unstaffed station
[ ] Station Operator Code

Station index and table numbers

[10] Connection time
Ⓟ Station Car Park
🚲 Bicycle storage facility
◇ Seat reservations can be made at this station
⚠ Penalty Fare Schemes in operation on some or all services from this station
🚕 Taxi rank or cab office at station, or signposted and within 100 metres
Ⓤ Unstaffed station
[ ] Station Operator Code

Whitchurch (Cardiff) [AW] Ⓤ 130
Whitchurch (Hants.) [SW] Ⓟ 🚲 ◇ ⚠ 160
Whitchurch (Shrops) [AW] Ⓟ Ⓤ 131
White Hart Lane [LE] ⚠ 21
White Notley [LE] 🚲 ⚠ Ⓤ 11
Whitechapel [LT] 178
Whitecraigs [SR] Ⓟ 🚲 223
Whitehaven [NT] Ⓟ ◇ 100
Whitland [AW] Ⓟ Ⓤ 128
Whitley Bridge [NT] Ⓟ Ⓤ 32
Whitlock's End [LM] ⚠ Ⓤ 71
Whitstable [SE] Ⓟ ◇ ⚠ 🚕 194, 212
Whittlesea [LE] Ⓟ Ⓤ 14, 17
Whittlesford Parkway [LE] Ⓟ 🚲 ⚠ 22
Whitton [SW] 🚲 ◇ ⚠ 149
Whitwell [EM] Ⓤ 55
Whyteleafe [SN] Ⓟ 🚲 ◇ ⚠ 181
Whyteleafe South [SN] Ⓟ 🚲 ◇ ⚠ 181
Wick [SR] Ⓟ 🚲 ◇ 🚕 239
Wickford [LE] [2] Ⓟ 🚲 ⚠ 🚕 5
Wickham Market [LE] Ⓟ 🚲 Ⓤ 13
Widdrington [NT] Ⓟ 🚲 Ⓤ 48
Widnes [NT] Ⓟ 🚕 49, 89
Widney Manor [LM] Ⓟ ⚠ 71
Wigan
North Western [VT] Ⓟ ◇ 🚕
Wallgate [NT] 🚲 🚕
Barrow-in-Furness 65
Birmingham 65
Blackpool 90
Bolton 82
Bournemouth 51
Bristol 51
Carlisle 65
Crewe 65
Edinburgh 65
Exeter 51
Glasgow 65
Kirkby 82
Lancaster 65
Liverpool 82, 90
London 65
Manchester 82
Milton Keynes Central 65
Manchester Airport 82
Paignton 51
Penzance 51
Plymouth 51
Preston 65
Oxenholme Lake District 65
Oxford 51
Reading 51
St Helens 90
Southampton 51
Southport 82
Stafford 65
Stockport 82
Torquay 51
Warrington 65
Wolverhampton 65
Windermere 65
Wigton [NT] Ⓟ 🚕 Ⓤ 100
Wildmill [AW] Ⓤ 128
Willesden Junction [LO] 🚲 ⚠ 59, 60, 176
Williamwood [SR] 🚲 223
Willington [EM] Ⓤ 57
Wilmcote [LM] ⚠ Ⓤ 71, 115
Wilmslow [NT] Ⓟ 🚲 ◇ 🚕 51, 65, 84, 85, 131
Wilnecote [LM] Ⓤ 57
Wilpshire [NT] (see Ramsgreave and Wilpshire)
Wimbledon [SW] [6] Ⓟ 🚲 ◇ ⚠ 🚕 52, 152, 155, 179, 182
Wimbledon Chase [FC] ⚠ Ⓤ 52, 179
Winchelsea [SN] Ⓤ 189
Winchester [SW] Ⓟ 🚲 ◇ ⚠ 🚕 51, 158
Winchfield [SW] Ⓟ 🚲 ◇ ⚠ 155
Winchmore Hill [FC] ⚠ 24
Windermere [TP] Ⓟ ◇ 🚕 65, 82, 83
Windsor & Eton Central [GW] ⚠ 🚕 119
Windsor & Eton Riverside [SW] Ⓟ 🚲 ◇ ⚠ 🚕 149
Winnersh [SW] 🚲 ◇ ⚠ 149
Winnersh Triangle [SW] ◇ ⚠ 149
Winsford [LM] Ⓟ ◇ 91
Wisbech *Bus* 🚕 26A
Wishaw [SR] Ⓟ 🚲 226
Witham [LE] [2] Ⓟ 🚲 ◇ ⚠ 🚕 11, 13, 14
Witley [SW] Ⓟ 🚲 ⚠ 156
Witney Market Place *Bus* 116C
Witton [LM] ⚠ 70
Wivelsfield [SN] [4] 🚲 ◇ ⚠ 52, 186, 189
Wivenhoe [LE] [3] Ⓟ 🚲 ⚠ 🚕 11
Woburn Sands [LM] Ⓤ 64
Woking [SW] Ⓟ 🚲 ◇ ⚠ 🚕
Aldershot 155
Basingstoke 155
Bournemouth 158
Bristol 160
Exeter 160
Fareham 158
Guildford 156
Heathrow Airport *Bus* 158A
London 149, 155, 156
Portsmouth 156
Salisbury 160
Southampton 158
Surbiton 155
Weymouth 158
Wokingham [SW] Ⓟ 🚲 ◇ ⚠ 🚕 148, 149
Woldingham [SN] Ⓟ 🚲 ◇ ⚠ 🚕 184
Wolverhampton [VT] [7] Ⓟ 🚲 ◇ ⚠ 🚕
Bangor (Gwynedd) 65
Birmingham 68
Birmingham International 68
Bournemouth 51
Bristol 51
Carlisle 65
Chester 65, 75
Coventry 68
Crewe 65
Edinburgh 65
Exeter 51
Glasgow 65
Holyhead 65
Liverpool 65
London 66
Macclesfield 84
Manchester 65
Manchester Airport 65
Oxenholme Lake District 65
Oxford 51
Paignton 51
Penzance 51
Plymouth 51
Preston 65
Reading 51
Rugby 66
Shrewsbury 74
Southampton 51
Stafford 68
Stockport 65
Stoke-on-Trent 65
Torquay 51
Walsall 70
Watford 66
Wrexham 75
Wolverton [LM] Ⓟ 🚲 66
Wombwell [NT] Ⓟ Ⓤ 34
Wood End [LM] ⚠ Ⓤ 71
Wood Street [LE] ⚠ 20
Woodbridge [LE] Ⓟ 🚲 🚕 Ⓤ 13
Woodgrange Park [LO] 🚲 ⚠ 62
Woodhall [SR] 🚲 219
Woodham Ferrers [LE] (South Woodham Ferrers)
Woodhouse [NT] Ⓟ Ⓤ 30
Woodlesford [NT] Ⓟ 🚲 Ⓤ 32, 34
Woodley [NT] Ⓟ Ⓤ 78
Woodmansterne [SN] ⚠ 181
Woodsmoor [NT] 86
Wool [SW] Ⓟ 🚲 ◇ ⚠ 🚕 158
Woolston [SW] Ⓟ 🚲 ◇ ⚠ 165
Woolwich Arsenal [SE] [4] Ⓟ ◇ ⚠ 🚕 200
Woolwich Dockyard [SE] ◇ ⚠ 200
Wootton Wawen [LM] ⚠ Ⓤ 71
Worcester Foregate Street [LM] [7] ◇ ⚠ 🚕 71, 126
Worcester Shrub Hill [LM] [7] Ⓟ ◇ ⚠ 🚕 57, 71, 126

Station index and table numbers

[10] Connection time
Ⓟ Station Car Park
🚲 Bicycle storage facility
◇ Seat reservations can be made at this station
⚠ Penalty Fare Schemes in operation on some or all services from this station
🚕 Taxi rank or cab office at station, or signposted and within 100 metres
Ⓤ Unstaffed station
[ ] Station Operator Code

Worcester Park [SW] Ⓟ 🚲 ◇ ⚠ 🚕 152
Workington [NT] Ⓟ ◇ 100
Workington (Bus Station) *Bus* 65F
Worksop [NT] Ⓟ ◇ 30, 55
Worle [GW] Ⓟ 🚲 Ⓤ 134
Worplesdon [SW] Ⓟ 🚲 ◇ ⚠ 155, 156
Worstead [LE] Ⓟ 🚲 Ⓤ 16
Worthing [SN] [4] Ⓟ 🚲 ◇ ⚠ 🚕 123, 188
Wrabness [LE] Ⓟ 🚲 Ⓤ 11
Wraysbury [SW] Ⓟ ⚠ Ⓤ 149
Wrenbury [AW] Ⓟ Ⓤ 131
Wressle [NT] Ⓤ 29
Wrexham Central [AW] Ⓤ 101
Wrexham General [AW] Ⓟ ◇ 🚕 65, 75, 101
Wrotham [SE] (see Borough Green & Wrotham)
Wroxham [LE] (see Hoveton & Wroxham)
Wye [SE] Ⓟ ◇ ⚠ 207
Wylam [NT] Ⓟ 🚲 Ⓤ 48
Wylde Green [LM] Ⓟ ⚠ 69
Wymondham [LE] Ⓟ 🚕 17
Wythall [LM] ⚠ 71

Y

Yalding [SE] Ⓟ ⚠ Ⓤ 208
Yardley Wood [LM] Ⓟ ⚠ 71
Yarm [TP] Ⓟ Ⓤ 39
Yarmouth (IOW) *Ship* 🚕 158
Yate [GW] Ⓟ 🚲 134
Yatton [GW] Ⓟ 🚲 134
Yeoford [GW] Ⓤ 136
Yeovil Junction [SW] Ⓟ 🚲 ◇ 🚕 160
Yeovil Pen Mill [GW] Ⓟ ◇ 123
Yetminster [GW] Ⓟ Ⓤ 123
Ynyswen [AW] Ⓤ 130
Yoker [SR] 🚲 Ⓤ 226
York [GR] [8] Ⓟ 🚲 ◇ 🚕
Aberdeen 26
Bedford 53
Birmingham 51
Birmingham International 51
Blackpool 41
Bournemouth 51
Bradford 40
Bristol 51
Cambridge 26
Cardiff 51
Darlington 26
Derby 53
Doncaster 26
Dundee 26
Eden Camp *Bus* 26G
Edinburgh 26
Exeter 51
Flamingo Land *Bus* 26G
Glasgow 26
Grantham 26
Halifax 41
Harrogate 35
Hartlepool 26
Huddersfield 39
Hull 33
Knaresborough 35
Leeds 35, 40
Leicester 53
Liverpool 39
London 26
Luton 53
Manchester 39
Manchester Airport 39
Middlesbrough 26
Newark 26
Newcastle 26
Newport (South Wales) 51
Newton Abbot 51
Norwich 26
Nottingham 53
Oxford 51
Paignton 51
Penzance 51
Peterborough 26
Pickering Eastgate *Bus* 26G
Plymouth 51
Preston 41
Reading 51
Retford 26
Scarborough 39
Selby 33
Sheffield 29
Stansted Airport 26
Southampton 51
Sunderland 26
Torquay 51
Whitby *Bus* 26G
Yorton [AW] Ⓟ Ⓤ 131
Ystrad Mynach [AW] [3] Ⓟ ◇ 130
Ystrad Rhondda [AW] Ⓟ Ⓤ 130

Network Diagram for Tables 1, 4

DM-1/06
Design BAJS

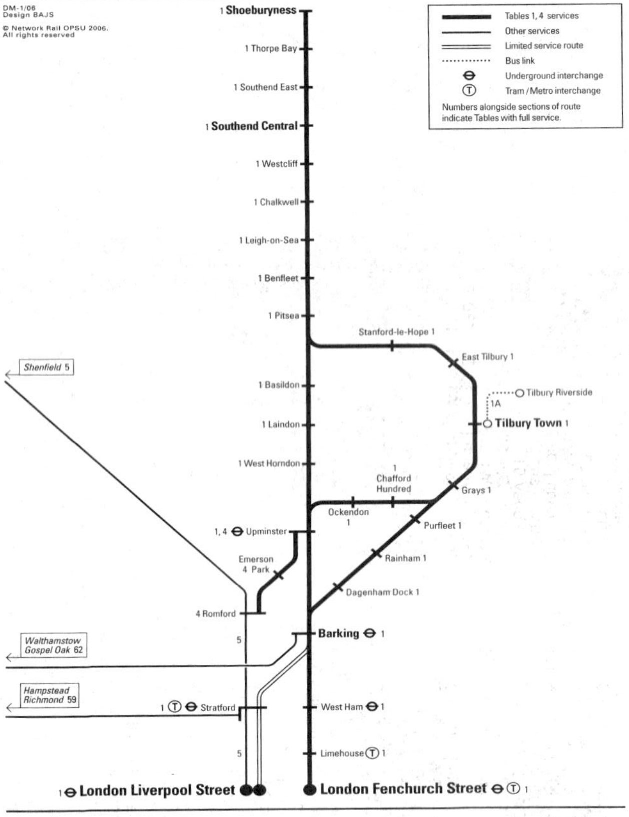

London - Southend Central and Shoeburyness

		CC MO	CC MX	CC MX	CC MO	CC MX	CC MX	CC MX	CC MX	CC MO		CC MX	CC MX	CC MX	CC MO	CC MX	CC MX	CC	CC	CC	CC	CC	CC	CC	CC
London Fenchurch Street ⊖	d	22p50	22p50	23p00	23p10	23p10	23p05	23p20	23p35	23p40		23p40	23p50	00 01	00 10	00 15	00 25	05 10		05 40				06 10	
Limehouse	d	22p54	22p54		23p14	23p14	23p09	23p24	23p39	23p44		23p44	23p54		00 14	00 19	00 29	05 14		05 44				06 14	
West Ham ⊖	d	22p59	22p59	23p08	23p19	23p19	23p14	23p29	23p44	23p49		23p49	23p59	00 09	00 19	00 24	00 34	05 19		05 49				06 19	
London Liverpool Street ⊖	d																								
Stratford ⊖	d																								
Barking ⊖	d	23p04	23p05	23p14	23p24	23p25	23p20	23p35	23p50	23p54		23p55	00 05	00 15	00 24	00 30	00 40	05 25		05 55	05 45	06 05		06 25	
Upminster ⊖	d	23p12	23p14	23p23	23p32	23p34		23p44		00 02		00 04	00 14	00 24	00 32		00 49	05 34	05 32	06 04			06 10	06 34	06 32
Ockendon	d	23p18	23p19					23p49					00 19						05 37				06a15		06 37
Chafford Hundred	d	23p21	23p23					23p53					00 23						05 41						06 41
West Horndon	d				23p37	23p39				00 07		00 09			00 37		00 54	05 39		06 09				06 39	
Laindon	d			23p31	23p42	23p44				00 12		00 16		00 32	00 42		00 59	05 44		06 14				06 44	
Basildon	d			23p34	23p45	23p47				00 15		00 19		00 35	00 45		01 02	05 47		06 17				06 47	
Dagenham Dock	d						23p25		23p55							00 35					05 50	06 10			
Rainham	d						23p29		23p59							00 39					05 54	06 14			
Purfleet	d						23p34		00 04							00 44					05 59	06 19			
Grays	d	23p25	23p27				23p42	23p57	00a10				00 27			00a50			05a45		06 05	06 25			06a46
Tilbury Town	d	23p28	23p30				23p45	00 01					00 30								06 08	06 28			
East Tilbury	d	23p34	23p36				23p51	00 06					00 36								06 14	06 34			
Stanford-le-Hope	d	23p37	23p40				23p55	00 10					00 40								06 18	06 38			
Pitsea	d	23p45	23p48		23p49	23p52	00 06	00 18		00 19		00 22	00 48		00 49		01 06	05 51		06 21	06 27	06a46		06 51	
Benfleet	d	23p49	23p52	23p41	23p52	23p56	00 10	00 22		00 22		00 26	00 52	00 42	00 52		01 10	05 55		06 25	06 32			06 55	
Leigh-on-Sea	d	23p53	23p56	23p45	23p57	23p59	00 15	00 27		00 27		00 31	00 56	00 46	00 57		01 14	06 00		06 30	06 36			07 00	
Chalkwell	d	23p56	23p59	23p48	23p59	00 03	00 18	00 30		00 29		00 34	00 59	00 49	00 59		01 17	06 03		06 33	06 39			07 03	
Westcliff	d	23p58	00 02	23p51	00 02	00 06	00 20	00 32		00 32		00 36	01 02	00 52	01 02		01 20	06 05		06 35	06 42			07 05	
Southend Central	a	00 01	00 05	23p54	00 05	00 09	00 23	00 35		00 35		00 39	01 05	00 55	01 05		01 23	06 08		06 38	06 44			07 08	
	d	00 01	00 05	23p54	00 06	00 09	00 23	00 35		00 36		00 40	01 05	00 55	01 06		01 23	06 08		06 38	06 44			07 08	
Southend East	d	00 03	00 07	23p56	00 08	00 11	00 26	00 38		00 38		00 42	01 07	00 57	01 08		01 25	06 10		06 40	06 46			07 10	
Thorpe Bay	d	00 06	00 11	23p59	00 10	00 15	00 29	00 41		00 40		00 46	01 11	01 01	01 10		01 29	06 14		06 44	06 50			07 14	
Shoeburyness	a	00 13	00 17	00 06	00 18	00 21	00 36	00 48		00 48		00 52	01 17	01 07	01 18		01 35	06 18		06 48	06 54			07 18	

		CC	CC	CC	CC	CC		CC	CC	CC	CC	CC	CC	CC	CC	CC		CC	CC	CC	CC	CC	CC	CC	CC
London Fenchurch Street ⊖	d	06 20	06 40		06 44	06 50		07 00	07 09	07 13	07 17	07 30	07 40	07 52	08 00	07 42		07 48	08 10	08 05	08 15	08 30	08 20	08 40	08 50
Limehouse	d	06 24	06 44		06 48	06 54			07 13				07 44	07 56					08 14	08 09			08 24	08 44	08 54
West Ham ⊖	d	06 29	06 49		06 53	06 59		07 08	07 18		07 25	07 38	07 49	08 01	08 08	07 52			08 19			08 38	08 29	08 49	08 59
London Liverpool Street ⊖	d																								
Stratford ⊖	d																								
Barking ⊖	d	06 35	06 55	06 52	07 00	07 05		07 14	07 24	07 26	07 31	07 44	07 55	08 07	08 14	07 57			08 25	08 18	08 29	08 45	08 37	08 55	09 07
Upminster ⊖	d		07 04		07 12			07 23	07 33		07 41	07 53	08 04	08 16	08 23			08 10	08 34		08 41	08 54		09 04	
Ockendon	d				07 17						07 47							08 19			08 46				
Chafford Hundred	d				07 21						07 51							08 23			08 50				
West Horndon	d		07 09						07 38				08 09	08 21					08 39					09 09	
Laindon	d		07 14						07 43				08 14	08a27	08 31				08 44			09 03		09 14	
Basildon	d		07 17					07 33	07 46			08 03	08 17		08 34				08 47			09 06		09 17	
Dagenham Dock	d	06 40		06 57		07 10				07 31						08 02				08 23			08 42		09 12
Rainham	d	06 44		07 01		07 14				07 35						08 06				08 27			08 46		09 16
Purfleet	d	06 49		07 06		07 19				07 40						08 12				08 33			08 52		09 21
Grays	d	06 55		07 12	07a25	07 28				07 46	07 55					08 17		08 27		08 38	08a54		08 57		09 27
Tilbury Town	d	06 58		07 15		07 31					07 59					08 21				08 42			09 01		09 30
East Tilbury	d	07 04		07 21		07 37					08 05					08 27				08 48			09 07		09 36
Stanford-le-Hope	d	07 08		07 25		07 41				07 56	08 09					08 31		08 37		08 52			09 11		09 40
Pitsea	d	07 16	07 21	07a33		07a48			07 50	08a03	08a16		08 21		08 38	08 41		08a45	08 51	08a59		09 09	09 18	09 21	09 48
Benfleet	d	07 20	07 25					07 39	07 54			08 09	08 25		08 42	08 45			08 55			09 13	09 22	09 26	09 52
Leigh-on-Sea	d	07 24	07 29					07 44	07 58			08 14	08 30		08 46	08 50			09 00			09 18	09 27	09 30	09 57
Chalkwell	d	07 27	07 32					07 47	08 01			08 17	08 33		08 49	08 53			09 03			09 21	09 30	09 33	10 00
Westcliff	d	07 30	07 35					07 49	08 04			08 19	08 35		08 52	08 55			09 05			09 23	09 32	09 36	10 02
Southend Central	a	07 32	07 37					07 52	08 07			08 22	08 38		08 54	08 58			09 08			09 26	09 35	09 38	10 05
	d	07 33	07 37					07 52	08 07			08 22	08 38		08 55				09 08			09 26		09 38	
Southend East	d	07 35	07 39					07 54	08 09			08 24	08 40		08 57				09 10			09 28		09 40	
Thorpe Bay	d	07 38	07 43					07 58	08 12			08 28	08 44		09 00				09 14			09 32		09 44	
Shoeburyness	a	07 43	07 47					08 02	08 19			08 32	08 48		09 05				09 18			09 36		09 48	

		CC		CC	CC	CC	CC	CC	CC	CC	CC	CC		CC	CC	CC	CC	CC	CC	CC	CC	CC		CC	CC
London Fenchurch Street ⊖	d	08 54		09 00	09 10	09 16	09 20	09 30	09 35	09 40	09 50	10 00		10 05	10 10	10 20	10 30	10 35	10 40	10 50	11 00	11 05		11 10	11 20
Limehouse	d				09 14	09 20	09 24		09 39	09 44	09 54			10 09	10 14	10 24		10 39	10 44	10 54		11 09		11 14	11 24
West Ham ⊖	d			09 08	09 19	09 25	09 29	09 38	09 44	09 49	09 59	10 08		10 14	10 19	10 29	10 38	10 44	10 49	10 59	11 08	11 14		11 19	11 29
London Liverpool Street ⊖	d																								
Stratford ⊖	d																								
Barking ⊖	d	09 09		09 16	09 25	09 31	09 35	09 44	09 50	09 55	10 05	10 14		10 20	10 25	10 35	10 44	10 50	10 55	11 05	11 14	11 20		11 25	11 35
Upminster ⊖	d	09 18		09 25	09 34		09 45	09 53		10 04	10 14	10 23			10 34	10 44	10 53		11 04	11 14	11 23			11 34	11 44
Ockendon	d	09 23					09 50				10 19					10 49				11 19					11 49
Chafford Hundred	d	09 27					09 54				10 23					10 53				11 23					11 53
West Horndon	d				09 39					10 09					10 39				11 09					11 39	
Laindon	d			09 34	09 44			10 01		10 14		10 31			10 44		11 01		11 14		11 31			11 44	
Basildon	d			09 37	09 47			10 04		10 17		10 34			10 47		11 04		11 17		11 34			11 47	
Dagenham Dock	d					09 36			09 55					10 25				10 55				11 25			
Rainham	d					09 40			09 59					10 29				10 59				11 29			
Purfleet	d					09 45			10 04					10 34				11 04				11 34			
Grays	d	09a31				09 51	09 58		10a10		10 27			10a40		10 57		11a10		11 27		11a40			11 57
Tilbury Town	d					09 54	10 02				10 30					11 00				11 30					12 00
East Tilbury	d					10 00	10 08				10 36					11 06				11 36					12 06
Stanford-le-Hope	d					10 04	10 12				10 40					11 10				11 40					12 10
Pitsea	d				09 51	10 12	10b25			10 21	10 48				10 51	11 18			11 21	11 48				11 51	12 18
Benfleet	d			09 43	09 55	10 16	10 29	10 10		10 25	10 52	10 40			10 55	11 22	11 10		11 25	11 52	11 40			11 55	12 22
Leigh-on-Sea	d			09 48	10 00	10 20	10 34	10 15		10 30	10 56	10 45			11 00	11 26	11 15		11 30	11 56	11 45			12 00	12 26
Chalkwell	d			09 51	10 03	10 23	10 37	10 18		10 33	10 59	10 48			11 03	11 29	11 18		11 33	11 59	11 48			12 03	12 29
Westcliff	d			09 53	10 05	10 26	10 39	10 20		10 35	11 02	10 50			11 05	11 32	11 20		11 35	12 02	11 50			12 05	12 32
Southend Central	a			09 56	10 08	10 29	10 42	10 23		10 38	11 05	10 53			11 08	11 35	11 23		11 38	12 05	11 53			12 08	12 35
	d			09 56	10 08			10 23		10 38		10 53			11 08		11 23		11 38		11 53			12 08	
Southend East	d			09 58	10 10			10 25		10 40		10 55			11 10		11 25		11 40		11 55			12 10	
Thorpe Bay	d			10 02	10 14			10 29		10 44		10 59			11 14		11 29		11 44		11 59			12 14	
Shoeburyness	a			10 06	10 18			10 33		10 48		11 03			11 18		11 33		11 48		12 03			12 18	

b arr. 1019

Table I

Mondays to Fridays

London - Southend Central and Shoeburyness

		CC	CC	CC	CC	CC	CC	CC	CC	CC	CC	CC	CC	CC	CC	CC	CC	CC	CC	CC	CC	CC	CC
London Fenchurch Street [7] ⊖	d	11 30	11 35	11 40	11 50	12 00	12 05	12 10	12 20	12 30	12 35	12 40	12 50	13 00	13 05	13 10	13 20	13 30	13 35	13 40	13 50	14 00	14 05
Limehouse	d		11 39	11 44	11 54		12 09	12 14	12 24		12 39	12 44	12 54		13 09	13 14	13 24		13 39	13 44	13 54		14 09
West Ham ⊖	d	11 38	11 44	11 49	11 59	12 08	12 14	12 19	12 29	12 38	12 44	12 49	12 59	13 08	13 14	13 19	13 29	13 38	13 44	13 49	13 59	14 08	14 14
London Liverpool Street [15] ⊖	d																						
Stratford [7] ⊖	d																						
Barking ⊖	d	11 44	11 50	11 55	12 05	12 14	12 20	12 25	12 35	12 44	12 50	12 55	13 05	13 14	13 20	13 25	13 35	13 44	13 50	13 55	14 05	14 14	14 20
Upminster ⊖	d	11 53		12 04	12 14	12 23		12 34	12 44	12 53		13 04	13 14	13 23		13 34	13 44	13 53		14 04	14 14	14 23	
Ockendon	d				12 19				12 49				13 19				13 49				14 19		
Chafford Hundred	d				12 23				12 53				13 23				13 53				14 23		
West Horndon	d			12 09				12 39				13 09				13 39				14 09			
Laindon	d	12 01		12 14		12 31		12 44		13 01		13 14		13 31		13 44		14 01		14 14		14 31	
Basildon	d	12 04		12 17		12 34		12 47		13 04		13 17		13 34		13 47		14 04		14 17		14 34	
Dagenham Dock	d		11 55				12 25				12 55				13 25				13 55				14 25
Rainham	d		11 59				12 29				12 59				13 29				13 59				14 29
Purfleet	d		12 04				12 34				13 04				13 34				14 04				14 34
Grays	d		12a10		12 27		12a40		12 57		13a10		13 27		13a40		13 57		14a10		14 27		14a40
Tilbury Town [3]	d				12 30				13 00				13 30				14 00				14 30		
East Tilbury	d				12 36				13 06				13 36				14 06				14 36		
Stanford-le-Hope	d				12 40				13 10				13 40				14 10				14 40		
Pitsea	d			12 21	12 48			12 51	13 18			13 21	13 48			13 51	14 18			14 21	14 48		
Benfleet	d	12 10		12 25	12 52	12 40		12 55	13 22	13 10		13 25	13 52	13 40		13 55	14 22	14 10		14 25	14 52	14 40	
Leigh-on-Sea	d	12 15		12 30	12 56	12 45		13 00	13 26	13 15		13 30	13 56	13 45		14 00	14 26	14 15		14 30	14 56	14 45	
Chalkwell	d	12 18		12 33	12 59	12 48		13 03	13 29	13 18		13 33	13 59	13 48		14 03	14 29	14 18		14 33	14 59	14 48	
Westcliff	d	12 20		12 35	13 02	12 50		13 05	13 32	13 20		13 35	14 02	13 50		14 05	14 32	14 20		14 35	15 02	14 50	
Southend Central	a	12 23		12 38	13 05	12 53		13 08	13 35	13 23		13 38	14 05	13 53		14 08	14 35	14 23		14 38	15 05	14 53	
	d	12 23		12 38		12 53		13 08		13 23		13 38		13 53		14 08		14 23		14 38		14 53	
Southend East	d	12 25		12 40		12 55		13 10		13 25		13 40		13 55		14 10		14 25		14 40		14 55	
Thorpe Bay	d	12 29		12 44		12 59		13 14		13 29		13 44		13 59		14 14		14 29		14 44		14 59	
Shoeburyness	a	12 33		12 48		13 03		13 18		13 33		13 48		14 03		14 18		14 33		14 48		15 03	

		CC	CC	CC	CC	CC	CC	CC	CC	CC	CC	CC	CC	CC	CC	CC	CC	CC	CC	CC	CC	CC
London Fenchurch Street [7] ⊖	d	14 10	14 20	14 30	14 35	14 40	14 50	15 00	15 05	15 10	15 25	15 20	15 30	15 35	15 40	15 50	15 55	16 00	16 10	16 13	16 20	16 28
Limehouse	d	14 14	14 24		14 39	14 44	14 54		15 09	15 14		15 24		15 39	15 44	15 54	15 59		16 14	16 17	16 24	
West Ham ⊖	d	14 19	14 29	14 38	14 44	14 49	14 59	15 08	15 14	15 19	15 33	15 29	15 38	15 44	15 49	15 59	16 04	16 08	16 19	16 22	16 29	16 36
London Liverpool Street [15] ⊖	d																					
Stratford [7] ⊖	d																					
Barking ⊖	d	14 25	14 35	14 44	14 50	14 55	15 05	15 14	15 20	15 25	15 39	15 35	15 44	15 50	15 54	16 05	16 10	16 14	16 25	16 28	16 35	
Upminster ⊖	d	14 34	14 44	14 53		15 04	15 14	15 23		15 34	15 48	15 44	15 53		16 02	16 14		16 23	16 34		16 45	
Ockendon	d		14 49				15 19					15 49				16 19					16 50	
Chafford Hundred	d		14 53				15 23					15 53				16 23					16 54	
West Horndon	d	14 39				15 09				15 39					16 07				16 39			
Laindon	d	14 44		15 01		15 14		15 31		15 44	15 56		16 01		16 12				16 44			16 56
Basildon	d	14 47		15 04		15 17		15 34		15 47	15 59		16 04		16 15			16 33	16 47			16 59
Dagenham Dock	d				14 55				15 25					15 55			16 15			16 33		
Rainham	d				14 59				15 29					15 59			16 19			16 37		
Purfleet	d				15 04				15 34					16 04			16 25			16 43		
Grays	d		14 57		15a10		15 27		15a40			15 57		16a10		16 27	16a33			16 49	16 59	
Tilbury Town [3]	d		15 00				15 30					16 00				16 30				16 52	17 02	
East Tilbury	d		15 06				15 36					16 06				16 36				16 58	17 08	
Stanford-le-Hope	d		15 10				15 40					16 10				16 40				17 02	17a15	
Pitsea	d	14 51	15 18			15 21	15 48			15 51	16 03	16 22			16 19	16a48			16 51	17a12		
Benfleet	d	14 55	15 22	15 10		15 25	15 52	15 40		15 55	16 07	16 26	16 10		16 22			16 40	16 55			17 06
Leigh-on-Sea	d	15 00	15 26	15 15		15 30	15 56	15 45		16 00	16a12	16 30	16 15		16 27			16 45	17 00			17 11
Chalkwell	d	15 03	15 29	15 18		15 33	15 59	15 48		16 03		16 33	16 18		16 29			16 48	17 03			17 14
Westcliff	d	15 05	15 32	15 20		15 35	16 02	15 50		16 05		16 36	16 20		16 32			16 50	17 05			17 16
Southend Central	a	15 08	15 35	15 23		15 38	16 05	15 53		16 08		16 41	16 23		16 34			16 53	17 08			17 19
	d	15 08		15 23		15 38		15 53		16 08			16 23		16 35			16 53	17 08			17 19
Southend East	d	15 10		15 25		15 40		15 55		16 10			16 25		16 37			16 55	17 10			17 21
Thorpe Bay	d	15 14		15 29		15 44		15 59		16 14			16 29		16 39			16 59	17 14			17 24
Shoeburyness	a	15 18		15 33		15 48		16 03		16 20			16 33		16 44			17 05	17 20			17 31

		CC	CC	CC	CC	CC	CC	CC	CC	CC	CC	CC	CC	CC	CC	CC	CC	CC	CC	CC	CC	CC	CC
London Fenchurch Street [7] ⊖	d	16 30	16 45	16 33	16 37	16 48	17 00	17 05	16 54	17 02	17 07	17 15	17 18	17 20	17 11	17 22	17 30	17 35	17 26	17 32	17 37	17 45	17 50
Limehouse	d	16 34	16 49	16 37	16 41	16 52		17 09	16 58		17 12	17 19		17 24	17 16	17 27		17 39	17 30		17 42	17 49	
West Ham ⊖	d	16 39		16 42	16 46	16 57			17 03		17 17					17 32					17 47		17 58
London Liverpool Street [15] ⊖	d																						
Stratford [7] ⊖	d																						
Barking ⊖	d	16 45	16 59	16 48	16 52	17 03		17 19	17 09	17 15	17 22			17 34	17 25	17 37		17 49	17 40	17 45	17 52		
Upminster ⊖	d	16 55	17 08		17 02	17 13				17 24	17 31	17 36	17 39			17 46				17 54	18 01		18 12
Ockendon	d				17 08					17 29										18 00			
Chafford Hundred	d				17 12					17 34										18 04			
West Horndon	d	17 00				17 18					17 36					17 51					18 06		
Laindon	d	17a08	17 17			17a26		17 35			17a43			17 50		17a58		18 05			18a13		
Basildon	d		17 20					17 38					17 50	17 54				18 08					18 23
Dagenham Dock	d			16 53					17 14						17 30				17 45				
Rainham	d			16 57					17 18						17 34				17 49				
Purfleet	d			17 03					17 24						17 39				17 54				
Grays	d			17 09	17a18				17 30	17a40					17 48				18 00	18a10			
Tilbury Town [3]	d			17 12					17 33						17 51				18 04				
East Tilbury	d			17 18					17 39						17 57				18 10				
Stanford-le-Hope	d			17 22					17 43						18 01				18 14				
Pitsea	d		17 24	17a32				17 42	17a53				17 53	17 57	18a11			18 12	18a23				18 26
Benfleet	d		17 28				17 33	17 46				17 52	17 58	18 02			18 07	18 16				18 22	18 31
Leigh-on-Sea	d		17 33				17 38	17 51				17 56	18 02	18 06			18 11	18 21				18 26	18 35
Chalkwell	d		17 36				17 41	17 54				17 59	18 05	18 09			18 14	18 24				18 29	18 38
Westcliff	d		17 38				17 43	17 56				18 02	18 08	18 12			18 17	18 26				18 32	18 41
Southend Central	a		17 41				17 46	17 59				18 04	18 13	18 14			18 19	18 29				18 34	18 43
	d		17 41				17 46	17 59				18 04		18 15			18 19	18 29				18 34	18 43
Southend East	d		17 43				17 48	18 01				18 06		18 17			18 21	18 31				18 36	18 45
Thorpe Bay	d		17 46				17 50	18 04				18 10		18 20			18 25	18 34				18 40	18 49
Shoeburyness	a		17 53				17 57	18 11				18 16		18 28			18 31	18 41				18 49	18 55

Table I

Mondays to Fridays

London - Southend Central and Shoeburyness

		CC	CC	CC	CC	CC	CC	CC	CC	CC	CC	CC	CC	CC	CC	CC	CC	CC	CC	CC	CC	CC	CC
London Fenchurch Street [7] ⊖	d	17 53	18 00	17 41	17 47	18 06	18 09	17 56	18 02	18 20	18 25	18 12	18 22	18 40	18 45	18 30	18 33	19 00	19 05	18 51	19 08	19 10	19 02
Limehouse	d	17 57		17 45	17 52	18 10	18 13	18 00	18 06		18 29	18 16	18 26		18 50	18 34	18 37		19 09	18 55	19 12	19 14	
West Ham ⊖	d		18 08				18 18				18 34	18 21		18 48	18 55					19 00	19 17	19 19	19 10
London Liverpool Street [15] ⊖	d																						
Stratford [7] ⊖	d																						
Barking ⊖	d	18 07		17 55		18 20	18 24	18 10	18 16		18 40	18 28			19 00	18 45	18 47		19 19	19 06	19 23	19 25	19 16
Upminster ⊖	d				18 09		18 33		18 26		18 50		18 43		19 09		18 56		19 30			19 34	19 26
Ockendon	d				18 14				18 32				18 48				19 03						19 33
Chafford Hundred	d				18 18				18 36				18 52				19 08						19 39
West Horndon	d	18 19					18 38				18 55				19 14							19 39	
Laindon	d	18 25				18 36	18 42			18 46	19 00				19 19			19 26				19 44	
Basildon	d	18 28	18 33			18 40	18 46			18 50	19 04			19 12	19 22				19 40			19 47	
Dagenham Dock	d			18 00				18 15				18 33				18 50				19 11	19 28		
Rainham	d			18 04				18 19				18 37				18 54				19 15	19 32		
Purfleet	d			18 09				18 24				18 42				18 59				19 21	19 37		
Grays	d			18 18	18a24			18 32	18 41			18 48	18 57			19 05	19a14			19 27	19a43		19 46
Tilbury Town [3]	d			18 21				18 35	18 44			18 52	19 00			19 09				19 30			19 50
East Tilbury	d			18 27				18 41	18 50			18 58	19 06			19 15				19 36			19 56
Stanford-le-Hope	d			18 31				18 46	18 54			19 02	19 10			19 19				19 40			20 00
Pitsea	d	18 32	18 37	18a41		18 43	18 49	18 56	19a04		19 08	19a11	19a22		19 26	19a28			19 44	19 48		19 51	20a07
Benfleet	d	18 36	18 40			18 48	18 53	19 01		18 57	19 12			19 19	19 30			19 32	19 48	19 52		19 55	
Leigh-on-Sea	d	18 41	18 46			18 52	18 58	19 05		19 02	19 16			19 24	19 34			19 36	19 52	19 56		20 00	
Chalkwell	d	18 44	18 49			18 55	19 00	19 08		19 05	19 19			19 27	19 37			19 39	19 55	19 59		20 03	
Westcliff	d	18 47	18 51			18 58	19 03	19 11		19 07	19 22			19 29	19 39			19 42	19 58	20 02		20 05	
Southend Central	a	18 49	18 54			19 00	19 05	19 16		19 10	19 24			19 32	19 42			19 44	20 00	20 07		20 08	
	d	18 49	18 54			19 00	19 06			19 10	19 24			19 32	19 42			19 44	20 00			20 08	
Southend East	d	18 51	18 56			19 02	19 08			19 12	19 26			19 34	19 44			19 47	20 02			20 10	
Thorpe Bay	d	18 55	18 59			19 06	19 10			19 15	19 30			19 37	19 46			19 51	20a06			20 14	
Shoeburyness	a	19 01	19 06			19 12	19 17			19 24	19 36			19 44	19 53			19 58				20 18	

		CC	CC	CC	CC	CC	CC	CC	CC	CC	CC	CC	CC	CC	CC	CC	CC	CC	CC	CC	CC	CC
London Fenchurch Street [7] ⊖	d	19 20	19 30	19 32	19 35	19 40	19 50	20 00	20 05	20 10	20 20	20 30		20 40	20 50	21 00	21 05	21 10	21 20	21 30		21 40
Limehouse	d	19 24			19 39	19 44	19 54		20 09	20 14	20 24	20 34		20 44	20 54		21 09	21 14	21 24	21 34		21 44
West Ham ⊖	d	19 29		19 40	19 44	19 49	19 59	20 08	20 14	20 19	20 29	20 39		20 49	20 59	21 08	21 14	21 19	21 29	21 39		21 49
London Liverpool Street [15] ⊖	d												20 35								21 35	
Stratford [7] ⊖	d												20 42								21 42	
Barking ⊖	d	19 35		19 46	19 50	19 55	20 05	20 14	20 20	20 25	20 35	20 45	20 50	20 55	21 05	21 14	21 20	21 25	21 35	21 45	21 50	21 55
Upminster ⊖	d	19 44	19 50	19 55		20 04	20 14	20 23		20 34	20 44	20 54		21 04	21 14	21 23		21 34	21 44	21 54		22 04
Ockendon	d	19 49					20 19				20 49				21 19				21 49			
Chafford Hundred	d	19 53					20 23				20 53				21 23				21 53			
West Horndon	d			20 00		20 09				20 39				21 09				21 39				22 09
Laindon	d			20a06		20 14		20 31		20 44		21 02		21 14		21 31		21 44		22 02		22 14
Basildon	d		20 00			20 17		20 34		20 47		21 05		21 17		21 34		21 47		22 05		22 17
Dagenham Dock	d				19 55				20 25				20 55				21 25				21 55	
Rainham	d				19 59				20 29				20 59				21 29				21 59	
Purfleet	d				20 04				20 34				21 04				21 34				22 04	
Grays	d	19 57			20a10		20 27		20a40		20 57		21a12		21 27		21a40		21 57		22a12	
Tilbury Town [3]	d	20 00					20 30				21 00				21 30				22 00			
East Tilbury	d	20 06					20 36				21 06				21 36				22 06			
Stanford-le-Hope	d	20 10					20 40				21 10				21 40				22 10			
Pitsea	d	20 18				20 21	20 48			20 51	21 18			21 21	21 48			21 51	22 18			22 21
Benfleet	d	20 22	20 06			20 26	20 52	20 40		20 55	21 22	21 12		21 25	21 52	21 40		21 55	22 22	22 12		22 25
Leigh-on-Sea	d	20 27	20 11			20 30	20 56	20 45		21 00	21 26	21 16		21 30	21 56	21 45		22 00	22 26	22 16		22 30
Chalkwell	d	20 30	20 14			20 33	20 59	20 48		21 03	21 29	21 19		21 33	21 59	21 48		22 03	22 29	22 19		22 33
Westcliff	d	20 32	20 16			20 36	21 02	20 50		21 05	21 32	21 22		21 35	22 02	21 50		22 05	22 32	22 22		22 35
Southend Central	a	20 35	20 19			20 38	21 05	20 53		21 08	21 35	21 24		21 38	22 05	21 53		22 08	22 35	22 24		22 38
	d		20 19			20 38		20 53		21 08		21 24		21 38		21 53		22 08		22 24		22 38
Southend East	d		20 21			20 40		20 55		21 10		21 26		21 40		21 55		22 10		22 26		22 40
Thorpe Bay	d		20 25			20 44		20 59		21 14		21 30		21 44		21 59		22 14		22 30		22 44
Shoeburyness	a		20 29			20 48		21 03		21 18		21 34		21 48		22 03		22 18		22 34		22 48

		CC	CC	CC	CC	CC	CC	CC	CC	CC	CC	CC	CC	CC	CC	CC
London Fenchurch Street [7] ⊖	d	21 50	22 00	22 05	22 10	22 20	22 35	22 40	22 50	23 00	23 10	23 05	23 20	23 35	23 40	23 50
Limehouse	d	21 54		22 09	22 14	22 24	22 39	22 44	22 54		23 14	23 09	23 24	23 39	23 44	23 54
West Ham ⊖	d	21 59	22 08	22 14	22 19	22 29	22 44	22 49	22 59	23 08	23 19	23 14	23 29	23 44	23 49	23 59
London Liverpool Street [15] ⊖	d															
Stratford [7] ⊖	d															
Barking ⊖	d	22 05	22 14	22 20	22 25	22 35	22 50	22 55	23 05	23 14	23 25	23 20	23 35	23 50	23 55	00 05
Upminster ⊖	d	22 14	22 23		22 34	22 44		23 04	23 14	23 23	23 34		23 44		00 04	00 14
Ockendon	d	22 19				22 49			23 19				23 49			00 19
Chafford Hundred	d	22 23				22 53			23 23				23 53			00 23
West Horndon	d				22 39			23 09			23 39				00 09	
Laindon	d		22 31		22 44			23 14		23 31	23 44				00 16	
Basildon	d		22 34		22 47			23 17		23 34	23 47				00 19	
Dagenham Dock	d			22 25			22 55					23 25		23 55		
Rainham	d			22 29			22 59					23 29		23 59		
Purfleet	d			22 34			23 04					23 34		00 04		
Grays	d	22 27		22a40		22 57	23a10		23 27			23 42	23 57	00a10		00 27
Tilbury Town [3]	d	22 30				23 00			23 30			23 45	00 01			00 30
East Tilbury	d	22 36				23 06			23 36			23 51	00 06			00 36
Stanford-le-Hope	d	22 40				23 10			23 40			23 55	00 10			00 40
Pitsea	d	22 48			22 51	23 18		23 22	23 48		23 52	00 06	00 18		00 22	00 48
Benfleet	d	22 52	22 40		22 55	23 22		23 26	23 52	23 41	23 56	00 10	00 22		00 26	00 52
Leigh-on-Sea	d	22 56	22 45		23 00	23 26		23 30	23 56	23 45	23 59	00 15	00 27		00 31	00 56
Chalkwell	d	22 59	22 48		23 03	23 29		23 33	23 59	23 48	00 03	00 18	00 30		00 34	00 59
Westcliff	d	23 02	22 50		23 05	23 32		23 36	00 02	23 51	00 06	00 20	00 32		00 36	01 02
Southend Central	a	23 05	22 53		23 08	23 35		23 39	00 05	23 54	00 09	00 23	00 35		00 39	01 05
	d	23 05	22 53		23 08	23 35		23 39	00 05	23 54	00 09	00 23	00 35		00 40	01 05
Southend East	d	23 07	22 55		23 10	23 37		23 41	00 07	23 56	00 11	00 26	00 38		00 42	01 07
Thorpe Bay	d	23 10	22 59		23 14	23 41		23 45	00 11	23 59	00 15	00 29	00 41		00 46	01 11
Shoeburyness	a	23 15	23 03		23 18	23 47		23 51	00 17	00 06	00 21	00 36	00 48		00 52	01 17

London - Southend Central and Shoeburyness

	CC	CC	CC	CC	CC	CC	CC	CC	CC	CC		CC	CC	CC	CC	CC	CC	CC	CC	CC	CC	CC	CC	CC
London Fenchurch Street ⊖ d	22p50	23p00	23p10	23p05	23p20	23p35	23p40	23p50	00 01	00 15		00 25		05 10		05 35	05 50	06 05	06 10	06 20	06 35	06 40	06 50	07 05
Limehouse d	22p54		23p14	23p09	23p24	23p39	23p44	23p54		00 19		00 29		05 14		05 39	05 54	06 09	06 14	06 24	06 39	06 44	06 54	07 09
West Ham ⊖ d	22p59	23p08	23p19	23p14	23p29	23p44	23p49	23p59	00 09	00 24		00 34		05 19		05 44	05 59	06 14	06 19	06 29	06 44	06 49	06 59	07 14
London Liverpool Street ⊖ d																								
Stratford ⊖ d																								
Barking ⊖ d	23p05	23p14	23p25	23p20	23p35	23p50	23p55	00 05	00 15	00 30		00 40		05 24		05 49	06 04	06 19	06 24	06 34	06 49	06 54	07 04	07 19
Upminster ⊖ d	23p14	23p23	23p34		23p44		00 04	00 14	00 24			00 49	05 05	05 32	05 27		06 12		06 32	06 42		07 02	07 12	
Ockendon d	23p19				23p49			00 19					05a12		05 32		06 18			06 48			07 18	
Chafford Hundred d	23p23				23p53			00 23							05 36		06 21			06 51			07 21	
West Horndon d			23p39				00 09					00 54		05 37					06 37			07 07		
Laindon d		23p31	23p44				00 16		00 32			00 59		05 42					06 42			07 12		
Basildon d		23p34	23p47				00 19		00 35			01 02		05 45					06 45			07 15		
Dagenham Dock d				23p25		23p55				00 35						05 54		06 24			06 54			07 24
Rainham d				23p29		23p59				00 39						05 57		06 27			06 57			07 27
Purfleet d				23p34		00 04				00 44						06 03		06 33			07 03			07 33
Grays d	23p27			23p42	23p57	00a10		00 27		00a50					05a42	06a12	06 25	06a42		06 55	07a12		07 25	07a42
Tilbury Town d	23p30			23p45	00 01			00 30									06 28			06 58			07 28	
East Tilbury d	23p36			23p51	00 06			00 36									06 34			07 04			07 34	
Stanford-le-Hope d	23p40			23p55	00 10			00 40									06 37			07 07			07 37	
Pitsea d	23p48		23p52	00 06	00 18		00 22	00 48				01 06		05 50			06 45		06 49	07 15		07 19	07 45	
Benfleet d	23p52	23p41	23p56	00 10	00 22		00 26	00 52	00 42			01 10		05 54			06 49		06 52	07 19		07 22	07 49	
Leigh-on-Sea d	23p56	23p45	23p59	00 15	00 27		00 31	00 56	00 46			01 14		05 58			06 53		06 57	07 23		07 27	07 53	
Chalkwell d	23p59	23p48	00 03	00 18	00 30		00 34	00 59	00 49			01 17		06 01			06 56		06 59	07 26		07 29	07 56	
Westcliff d	00 02	23p51	00 06	00 20	00 32		00 36	01 02	00 52			01 20		06 03			06 58		07 02	07 28		07 32	07 58	
Southend Central a	00 05	23p54	00 09	00 23	00 35		00 39	01 05	00 55			01 23		06 06			07 04		07 05	07 34		07 35	08 04	
d	00 05	23p54	00 09	00 23	00 35		00 40	01 05	00 55			01 23		06 07					07 06			07 36		
Southend East d	00 07	23p56	00 11	00 26	00 38		00 42	01 07	00 57			01 25		06 09					07 08			07 38		
Thorpe Bay d	00 11	23p59	00 15	00 29	00 41		00 46	01 11	01 01			01 29		06 12					07 10			07 40		
Shoeburyness a	00 17	00 06	00 21	00 36	00 48		00 52	01 17	01 07			01 35		06 19					07 18			07 48		

	CC	CC	CC	CC	CC		CC	CC	CC	CC	CC	CC	CC	CC	CC		CC	CC	CC	CC	CC	CC	CC	CC
London Fenchurch Street ⊖ d	07 10	07 20	07 35	07 40	07 50		08 05	08 10	08 20	08 35	08 40	08 50	09 00	09 05	09 10		09 20	09 30	09 35	09 40	09 50	10 00	10 05	10 10
Limehouse d	07 14	07 24	07 39	07 44	07 54		08 09	08 14	08 24	08 39	08 44	08 54		09 09	09 14		09 24		09 39	09 44	09 54		10 09	10 14
West Ham ⊖ d	07 19	07 29	07 44	07 49	07 59		08 14	08 19	08 29	08 44	08 49	08 59	09 08	09 14	09 19		09 29	09 38	09 44	09 49	09 59	10 08	10 14	10 19
London Liverpool Street ⊖ d																								
Stratford ⊖ d																								
Barking ⊖ d	07 24	07 34	07 49	07 54	08 04		08 19	08 24	08 34	08 49	08 54	09 04	09 13	09 19	09 24		09 34	09 43	09 49	09 54	10 04	10 13	10 19	10 24
Upminster ⊖ d	07 32	07 42		08 02	08 12			08 32	08 42		09 02	09 12	09 21		09 32		09 42	09 51		10 02	10 12	10 21		10 32
Ockendon d		07 48			08 18				08 48			09 18					09 48				10 18			
Chafford Hundred d		07 51			08 21				08 51			09 21					09 51				10 21			
West Horndon d	07 37			08 07				08 37			09 07				09 37					10 07				10 37
Laindon d	07 42			08 12				08 42			09 12		09 29		09 42			09 59		10 12		10 29		10 42
Basildon d	07 45			08 15				08 45			09 15		09 32		09 45			10 02		10 15		10 32		10 45
Dagenham Dock d			07 54				08 24			08 54				09 24					09 54				10 24	
Rainham d			07 57				08 27			08 57				09 27					09 57				10 27	
Purfleet d			08 03				08 33			09 03				09 33					10 03				10 33	
Grays d		07 55	08a12		08 25		08a42		08 55	09a12		09 25		09a42			09 55		10a12		10 25		10a42	
Tilbury Town d		07 58			08 28				08 58			09 28					09 58				10 28			
East Tilbury d		08 04			08 34				09 04			09 34					10 04				10 34			
Stanford-le-Hope d		08 07			08 37				09 07			09 37					10 07				10 37			
Pitsea d	07 49	08 15		08 19	08 45			08 49	09 15		09 19	09 45			09 49		10 15			10 19	10 45			10 49
Benfleet d	07 52	08 19		08 22	08 49			08 52	09 19		09 22	09 49	09 38		09 52		10 19	10 08		10 22	10 49	10 38		10 52
Leigh-on-Sea d	07 57	08 23		08 27	08 53			08 57	09 23		09 27	09 53	09 42		09 57		10 23	10 12		10 27	10 53	10 42		10 57
Chalkwell d	07 59	08 26		08 29	08 56			08 59	09 26		09 29	09 56	09 45		09 59		10 26	10 15		10 29	10 56	10 45		10 59
Westcliff d	08 02	08 28		08 32	08 58			09 02	09 28		09 32	09 58	09 47		10 02		10 28	10 17		10 32	10 58	10 47		11 02
Southend Central a	08 05	08 34		08 35	09 04			09 05	09 34		09 35	10 04	09 50		10 05		10 34	10 20		10 35	11 04	10 50		11 05
d	08 06			08 36				09 06			09 36		09 50		10 06			10 20		10 36		10 50		11 06
Southend East d	08 08			08 38				09 08			09 38		09 52		10 08			10 22		10 38		10 52		11 08
Thorpe Bay d	08 10			08 40				09 10			09 40		09 55		10 10			10 25		10 40		10 55		11 10
Shoeburyness a	08 18			08 48				09 18			09 48		10 02		10 18			10 32		10 48		11 02		11 18

	CC		CC	CC	CC	CC	CC	CC	CC	CC	CC		CC	CC	CC	CC	CC	CC	CC	CC	CC		CC	CC
London Fenchurch Street ⊖ d	10 20		10 30	10 35	10 40	10 50	11 00	11 05	11 10	11 20	11 30		11 35	11 40	11 50	12 00	12 05	12 10	12 20	12 30	12 35		12 40	12 50
Limehouse d	10 24			10 39	10 44	10 54		11 09	11 14	11 24			11 39	11 44	11 54		12 09	12 14	12 24		12 39		12 44	12 54
West Ham ⊖ d	10 29		10 38	10 44	10 49	10 59	11 08	11 14	11 19	11 29	11 38		11 44	11 49	11 59	12 08	12 14	12 19	12 29	12 38	12 44		12 49	12 59
London Liverpool Street ⊖ d																								
Stratford ⊖ d																								
Barking ⊖ d	10 34		10 43	10 49	10 54	11 04	11 13	11 19	11 24	11 34	11 43		11 49	11 54	12 04	12 13	12 19	12 24	12 34	12 43	12 49		12 54	13 04
Upminster ⊖ d	10 42		10 51		11 02	11 12	11 21		11 32	11 42	11 51			12 02	12 12	12 21		12 32	12 42	12 51			13 02	13 12
Ockendon d	10 48					11 18				11 48					12 18				12 48					13 18
Chafford Hundred d	10 51					11 21				11 51					12 21				12 51					13 21
West Horndon d					11 07				11 37					12 07				12 37					13 07	
Laindon d			10 59		11 12		11 29		11 42		11 59			12 12		12 29		12 42		12 59			13 12	
Basildon d			11 02		11 15		11 32		11 45		12 02			12 15		12 32		12 45		13 02			13 15	
Dagenham Dock d				10 54				11 24					11 54				12 24				12 54			
Rainham d				10 57				11 27					11 57				12 27				12 57			
Purfleet d				11 03				11 33					12 03				12 33				13 03			
Grays d	10 55			11a12		11 25		11a42		11 55			12a12		12 25		12a42		12 55		13a12			13 25
Tilbury Town d	10 58					11 28				11 58					12 28				12 58					13 28
East Tilbury d	11 04					11 34				12 04					12 34				13 04					13 34
Stanford-le-Hope d	11 07					11 37				12 07					12 37				13 07					13 37
Pitsea d	11 15				11 19	11 45			11 49	12 15				12 19	12 45			12 49	13 15				13 19	13 45
Benfleet d	11 19		11 08		11 22	11 49	11 38		11 52	12 19	12 08			12 22	12 49	12 38		12 52	13 19	13 08			13 22	13 49
Leigh-on-Sea d	11 23		11 12		11 27	11 53	11 42		11 57	12 23	12 12			12 27	12 53	12 42		12 57	13 23	13 12			13 27	13 53
Chalkwell d	11 26		11 15		11 29	11 56	11 45		11 59	12 26	12 15			12 29	12 56	12 45		12 59	13 26	13 15			13 29	13 56
Westcliff d	11 28		11 17		11 32	11 58	11 47		12 02	12 28	12 17			12 32	12 58	12 47		13 02	13 28	13 17			13 32	13 58
Southend Central a	11 34		11 20		11 35	12 04	11 50		12 05	12 34	12 20			12 35	13 04	12 50		13 05	13 34	13 20			13 35	14 04
d			11 20		11 36		11 50		12 06		12 20			12 36		12 50		13 06		13 20			13 36	
Southend East d			11 22		11 38		11 52		12 08		12 22			12 38		12 52		13 08		13 22			13 38	
Thorpe Bay d			11 25		11 40		11 55		12 10		12 25			12 40		12 55		13 10		13 25			13 40	
Shoeburyness a			11 32		11 48		12 02		12 18		12 32			12 48		13 02		13 18		13 32			13 48	

London - Southend Central and Shoeburyness

	CC	CC	CC	CC	CC	CC	CC		CC	CC	CC	CC	CC	CC	CC	CC	CC		CC	CC	CC	CC	CC	CC
London Fenchurch Street ⊖ d	13 00	13 05	13 10	13 20	13 30	13 35	13 40		13 50	14 00	14 05	14 10	14 20	14 30	14 35	14 40	14 50		15 00	15 05	15 10	15 20	15 30	15 35
Limehouse d		13 09	13 14	13 24		13 39	13 44		13 54		14 09	14 14	14 24		14 39	14 44	14 54			15 09	15 14	15 24		15 39
West Ham ⊖ d	13 08	13 14	13 19	13 29	13 38	13 44	13 49		13 59	14 08	14 14	14 19	14 29	14 38	14 44	14 49	14 59		15 08	15 14	15 19	15 29	15 38	15 44
London Liverpool Street ⊖ d																								
Stratford ⊖ d																								
Barking ⊖ d	13 13	13 19	13 24	13 34	13 43	13 49	13 54		14 04	14 13	14 19	14 24	14 34	14 43	14 49	14 54	15 04		15 13	15 19	15 24	15 34	15 43	15 49
Upminster ⊖ d	13 21		13 32	13 42	13 51		14 02		14 12	14 21		14 32	14 42	14 51		15 02	15 12		15 21		15 32	15 42	15 51	
Ockendon d				13 48					14 18				14 48				15 18					15 48		
Chafford Hundred d				13 51					14 21				14 51				15 21					15 51		
West Horndon d			13 37				14 07					14 37				15 07					15 37			
Laindon d	13 29		13 42		13 59		14 12			14 29		14 42		14 59		15 12			15 29		15 42		15 59	
Basildon d	13 32		13 45		14 02		14 15			14 32		14 45		15 02		15 15			15 32		15 45		16 02	
Dagenham Dock d		13 24				13 54					14 24				14 54					15 24				15 54
Rainham d		13 27				13 57					14 27				14 57					15 27				15 57
Purfleet d		13 33				14 03					14 33				15 03					15 33				16 03
Grays d		13a42		13 55		14a12			14 25		14a42		14 55		15a12		15 25			15a42		15 55		16a12
Tilbury Town d				13 58					14 28				14 58				15 28					15 58		
East Tilbury d				14 04					14 34				15 04				15 34					16 04		
Stanford-le-Hope d				14 07					14 37				15 07				15 37					16 07		
Pitsea d			13 49	14 15			14 19		14 45			14 49	15 15			15 19	15 45				15 49	16 15		
Benfleet d	13 38		13 52	14 19	14 08		14 22		14 49	14 38		14 52	15 19	15 08		15 22	15 49		15 38		15 52	16 19	16 08	
Leigh-on-Sea d	13 42		13 57	14 23	14 12		14 27		14 53	14 42		14 57	15 23	15 12		15 27	15 53		15 42		15 57	16 23	16 12	
Chalkwell d	13 45		13 59	14 26	14 15		14 29		14 56	14 45		14 59	15 26	15 15		15 29	15 56		15 45		15 59	16 26	16 15	
Westcliff d	13 47		14 02	14 28	14 17		14 32		14 58	14 47		15 02	15 28	15 17		15 32	15 58		15 47		16 02	16 28	16 17	
Southend Central a	13 50		14 05	14 34	14 20		14 35		15 04	14 50		15 05	15 34	15 20		15 35	16 04		15 50		16 05	16 34	16 20	
d	13 50		14 06		14 20		14 36			14 50		15 06		15 20		15 36			15 50		16 06		16 20	
Southend East d	13 52		14 08		14 22		14 38			14 52		15 08		15 22		15 38			15 52		16 08		16 22	
Thorpe Bay d	13 55		14 10		14 25		14 40			14 55		15 10		15 25		15 40			15 55		16 10		16 25	
Shoeburyness a	14 02		14 18		14 32		14 48			15 02		15 18		15 32		15 48			16 02		16 18		16 32	

	CC	CC	CC		CC	CC	CC	CC	CC	CC	CC	CC	CC		CC	CC	CC	CC	CC	CC	CC	CC	CC
London Fenchurch Street ⊖ d	15 40	15 50	16 00		16 05	16 10	16 20	16 30	16 35	16 40	16 50	17 00	17 05		17 10	17 20	17 30	17 35	17 40	17 50	18 00	18 05	18 10
Limehouse d	15 44	15 54			16 09	16 14	16 24		16 39	16 44	16 54		17 09		17 14	17 24		17 39	17 44	17 54		18 09	18 14
West Ham ⊖ d	15 49	15 59	16 08		16 14	16 19	16 29	16 38	16 44	16 49	16 59	17 08	17 14		17 19	17 29	17 38	17 44	17 49	17 59	18 08	18 14	18 19
London Liverpool Street ⊖ d																							
Stratford ⊖ d																							
Barking ⊖ d	15 54	16 04	16 13		16 19	16 24	16 34	16 43	16 49	16 54	17 04	17 13	17 19		17 24	17 34	17 43	17 49	17 54	18 04	18 13	18 19	18 24
Upminster ⊖ d	16 02	16 12	16 21			16 32	16 42	16 51		17 02	17 12	17 21			17 32	17 42	17 51		18 02	18 12	18 21		18 32
Ockendon d		16 18					16 48				17 18					17 48				18 18			
Chafford Hundred d		16 21					16 51				17 21					17 51				18 21			
West Horndon d	16 07					16 37				17 07					17 37				18 07				18 37
Laindon d	16 12		16 29			16 42		16 59		17 12		17 29			17 42		17 59		18 12		18 29		18 42
Basildon d	16 15		16 32			16 45		17 02		17 15		17 32			17 45		18 02		18 15		18 32		18 45
Dagenham Dock d					16 24				16 54				17 24					17 54				18 24	
Rainham d					16 27				16 57				17 27					17 57				18 27	
Purfleet d					16 33				17 03				17 33					18 03				18 33	
Grays d		16 25			16a42		16 55		17a12		17 25		17a42			17 55		18a12		18 25		18a42	
Tilbury Town d		16 28					16 58				17 28					17 58				18 28			
East Tilbury d		16 34					17 04				17 34					18 04				18 34			
Stanford-le-Hope d		16 37					17 07				17 37					18 07				18 37			
Pitsea d	16 19	16 45				16 49	17 15			17 19	17 45				17 49	18 15			18 19	18 45			18 49
Benfleet d	16 22	16 49	16 38			16 52	17 19	17 08		17 22	17 49	17 38			17 52	18 19	18 08		18 22	18 49	18 38		18 52
Leigh-on-Sea d	16 27	16 53	16 42			16 57	17 23	17 12		17 27	17 53	17 42			17 57	18 23	18 12		18 27	18 53	18 42		18 57
Chalkwell d	16 29	16 56	16 45			16 59	17 26	17 15		17 29	17 56	17 45			17 59	18 26	18 15		18 29	18 56	18 45		18 59
Westcliff d	16 32	16 58	16 47			17 02	17 28	17 17		17 32	17 58	17 47			18 02	18 28	18 17		18 32	18 58	18 47		19 02
Southend Central a	16 35	17 04	16 50			17 05	17 34	17 20		17 35	18 04	17 50			18 05	18 34	18 20		18 35	19 04	18 50		19 05
d	16 36		16 50			17 06		17 20		17 36		17 50			18 06		18 20		18 36		18 50		19 06
Southend East d	16 38		16 52			17 08		17 22		17 38		17 52			18 08		18 22		18 38		18 52		19 08
Thorpe Bay d	16 40		16 55			17 10		17 25		17 40		17 55			18 10		18 25		18 40		18 55		19 10
Shoeburyness a	16 48		17 02			17 18		17 32		17 48		18 02			18 18		18 32		18 48		19 02		19 18

	CC	CC	CC	CC	CC	CC	CC	CC	CC		CC	CC	CC	CC	CC	CC	CC	CC	CC		CC	CC	CC	CC
London Fenchurch Street ⊖ d	18 20	18 30	18 35	18 40	18 50	19 00	19 05	19 10	19 20		19 30	19 35	19 40	19 50	20 00	20 05	20 10	20 20	20 35		20 40	20 50	21 00	21 05
Limehouse d	18 24		18 39	18 44	18 54		19 09	19 14	19 24			19 39	19 44	19 54		20 09	20 14	20 24	20 39		20 44	20 54		21 09
West Ham ⊖ d	18 29	18 38	18 44	18 49	18 59	19 08	19 14	19 19	19 29		19 38	19 44	19 49	19 59	20 08	20 14	20 19	20 29	20 44		20 49	20 59	21 08	21 14
London Liverpool Street ⊖ d																								
Stratford ⊖ d																								
Barking ⊖ d	18 34	18 43	18 49	18 54	19 04	19 13	19 19	19 24	19 34		19 43	19 49	19 54	20 04	20 13	20 19	20 24	20 34	20 49		20 54	21 04	21 13	21 19
Upminster ⊖ d	18 42	18 51		19 02	19 12	19 21		19 32	19 42		19 51		20 02	20 12	20 21		20 32	20 42			21 02	21 12	21 21	
Ockendon d	18 48				19 18				19 48					20 18				20 48				21 18		
Chafford Hundred d	18 51				19 21				19 51					20 21				20 51				21 21		
West Horndon d				19 07				19 37					20 07				20 37				21 07			
Laindon d		18 59		19 12		19 29		19 42			19 59		20 12		20 29		20 42				21 12		21 29	
Basildon d		19 02		19 15		19 32		19 45			20 02		20 15		20 32		20 45				21 15		21 32	
Dagenham Dock d			18 54				19 24					19 54				20 24			20 54					21 24
Rainham d			18 57				19 27					19 57				20 27			20 57					21 27
Purfleet d			19 03				19 33					20 03				20 33			21 03					21 33
Grays d	18 55		19a12		19 25		19a42		19 55			20a12		20 25		20a42		20 55	21a12			21 25		21a42
Tilbury Town d	18 58				19 28				19 58					20 28				20 58				21 28		
East Tilbury d	19 04				19 34				20 04					20 34				21 04				21 34		
Stanford-le-Hope d	19 07				19 37				20 07					20 37				21 07				21 37		
Pitsea d	19 15			19 19	19 45			19 49	20 15				20 19	20 45			20 49	21 15			21 19	21 45		
Benfleet d	19 19	19 08		19 22	19 49	19 38		19 52	20 19		20 08		20 22	20 49	20 38		20 52	21 19			21 22	21 49	21 38	
Leigh-on-Sea d	19 23	19 12		19 27	19 53	19 42		19 57	20 23		20 12		20 27	20 53	20 42		20 57	21 23			21 27	21 53	21 42	
Chalkwell d	19 26	19 15		19 29	19 56	19 45		19 59	20 26		20 15		20 29	20 56	20 45		20 59	21 26			21 29	21 56	21 45	
Westcliff d	19 28	19 17		19 32	19 58	19 47		20 02	20 28		20 17		20 32	20 58	20 47		21 02	21 28			21 32	21 58	21 47	
Southend Central a	19 34	19 20		19 35	20 04	19 50		20 05	20 34		20 20		20 35	21 04	20 50		21 05	21 34			21 35	22 04	21 50	
d		19 20		19 36		19 50		20 06			20 20		20 36		20 50		21 06				21 36		21 50	
Southend East d		19 22		19 38		19 52		20 08			20 22		20 38		20 52		21 08				21 38		21 52	
Thorpe Bay d		19 25		19 40		19 55		20 10			20 25		20 40		20 55		21 10				21 40		21 55	
Shoeburyness a		19 32		19 48		20 02		20 18			20 32		20 48		21 02		21 18				21 48		22 02	

Table I

London - Southend Central and Shoeburyness

Saturdays

		CC	CC	CC	CC	CC	CC	CC	CC	CC	CC	CC	CC	CC	CC	CC	CC	CC	CC
London Fenchurch Street 7 ⊖	d	21 10	21 20	21 35	21 40	21 50	22 00	22 05	22 10	22 20	22 35	22 40	22 50	23 10	23 05	23 20	23 40	23 35	23 50
Limehouse	d	21 14	21 24	21 39	21 44	21 54		22 09	22 14	22 24	22 39	22 44	22 54	23 14	23 09	23 24	23 44	23 39	23 54
West Ham ⊖	d	21 19	21 29	21 44	21 49	21 59	22 08	22 14	22 19	22 29	22 44	22 49	22 59	23 19	23 14	23 29	23 49	23 44	23 59
London Liverpool Street 15 ⊖	d																		
Stratford 7 ⊖	d																		
Barking ⊖	d	21 24	21 34	21 49	21 54	22 04	22 13	22 19	22 24	22 34	22 49	22 54	23 04	23 24	23 19	23 34	23 54	23 49	00 04
Upminster ⊖	d	21 32	21 42		22 02	22 12	22 21		22 32	22 42		23 02	23 12	23 32		23 42	00 02		00 12
Ockendon	d		21 48			22 18				22 48			23 18			23 48			00 18
Chafford Hundred	d		21 51			22 21				22 51			23 21			23 51			00 21
West Horndon	d	21 37			22 07				22 37			23 07		23 37			00 07		
Laindon	d	21 42			22 12		22 29		22 42			23 12		23 42			00 12		
Basildon	d	21 45			22 15		22 32		22 45			23 15		23 45			00 15		
Dagenham Dock	d			21 54				22 24			22 54				23 24			23 54	
Rainham	d			21 57				22 27			22 57				23 27			23 57	
Purfleet	d			22 03				22 33			23 03				23 33			00 03	
Grays	d		21 55	22a12		22 25		22a42		22 55	23a12		23 25		23 38	23 55		00 08	00 25
Tilbury Town 3	d		21 58			22 28				22 58			23 28		23 41	23 58		00 11	00 28
East Tilbury	d		22 04			22 34				23 04			23 34		23 47	00 04		00 17	00 34
Stanford-le-Hope	d		22 07			22 37				23 07			23 37		23 50	00 07		00 20	00 37
Pitsea	d	21 49	22 15		22 19	22 45			22 49	23 15		23 19	23 45	23 49	23 58	00 15	00 19	00 28	00 45
Benfleet	d	21 52	22 19		22 22	22 49	22 38		22 52	23 19		23 22	23 49	23 52	00 01	00 19	00 22	00 31	00 49
Leigh-on-Sea	d	21 57	22 23		22 27	22 53	22 42		22 57	23 23		23 27	23 53	23 57	00 06	00 23	00 27	00 36	00 53
Chalkwell	d	21 59	22 26		22 29	22 56	22 45		22 59	23 26		23 29	23 56	23 59	00 08	00 26	00 29	00 38	00 56
Westcliff	d	22 02	22 28		22 32	22 58	22 47		23 02	23 28		23 32	23 58	00 02	00 11	00 28	00 32	00 41	00 58
Southend Central	a	22 05	22 34		22 35	23 04	22 50		23 05	23 31		23 35	00 01	00 05	00 14	00 31	00 35	00 44	01 01
	d	22 06			22 36		22 50		23 06	23 31		23 36	00 01	00 06	00 14	00 31	00 36	00 44	01 01
Southend East	d	22 08			22 38		22 52		23 08	23 34		23 38	00 04	00 08	00 16	00 34	00 38	00 46	01 04
Thorpe Bay	d	22 10			22 40		22 55		23 10	23 36		23 41	00 06	00 11	00 19	00 36	00 41	00 49	01 06
Shoeburyness	a	22 18			22 48		23 02		23 18	23 43		23 48	00 13	00 18	00 26	00 43	00 48	00 56	01 13

Sundays

		CC	CC	CC	CC	CC	CC	CC	CC	CC	CC	CC	CC	CC	CC	CC	CC	CC	CC	CC	CC	CC	CC
London Fenchurch Street 7 ⊖	d	22p50	23p10	23p05	23p20	23p40	23p35	23p50	00 10	00 40	06 40		07 10	07 40	07 50	08 10			08 40	08 50	09 10		
Limehouse	d	22p54	23p14	23p09	23p24	23p44	23p39	23p54	00 14	00 44	06 44		07 14	07 44	07 54	08 14			08 44	08 54	09 14		
West Ham ⊖	d	22p59	23p19	23p14	23p29	23p49	23p44	23p59	00 19	00 49	06 49		07 19	07 49	07 59	08 19			08 49	08 59	09 19		
London Liverpool Street 15 ⊖	d																						
Stratford 7 ⊖	d																						
Barking ⊖	d	23p04	23p24	23p19	23p34	23p54	23p49	00 04	00 24	00 54	06 54	07 04	07 24	07 54	08 04	08 24	08 29	08 34	08 54	09 04	09 24	09 29	09 34
Upminster ⊖	d	23p12	23p32		23p42	00 02		00 12	00 32	01 02	07 02	07 12	07 32	08 02	08 12	08 32		08 42	09 02	09 12	09 32		09 42
Ockendon	d	23p18			23p48			00 18				07 18			08 18			08 48		09 18			09 48
Chafford Hundred	d	23p21			23p51			00 21				07 21			08 21			08 51		09 21			09 51
West Horndon	d		23p37			00 07			00 37	01 07	07 07		07 37	08 07		08 37			09 07		09 37		
Laindon	d		23p42			00 12			00 42	01 12	07 12		07 42	08 12		08 42			09 12		09 42		
Basildon	d		23p45			00 15			00 45	01 15	07 15		07 45	08 15		08 45			09 15		09 45		
Dagenham Dock	d			23p24			23p54										08 33					09 33	
Rainham	d			23p27			23p57										08 37					09 37	
Purfleet	d			23p33			00 03										08 42					09 42	
Grays	d	23p25		23p38	23p55		00 08	00 25				07 25			08 25		08a50	08 55		09 25		09a50	09 55
Tilbury Town 3	d	23p28		23p41	23p58		00 11	00 28				07 28			08 28			08 58		09 28			09 58
East Tilbury	d	23p34		23p47	00 04		00 17	00 34				07 34			08 34			09 04		09 34			10 04
Stanford-le-Hope	d	23p37		23p50	00 07		00 20	00 37				07 37			08 37			09 07		09 37			10 07
Pitsea	d	23p45	23p49	23p58	00 15	00 19	00 28	00 45	00 49	01 19	07 19	07 45	07 49	08 19	08 45	08 49		09 15	09 19	09 45	09 49		10 15
Benfleet	d	23p49	23p52	00 01	00 19	00 22	00 31	00 49	00 52	01 22	07 22	07 49	07 52	08 22	08 49	08 52		09 19	09 22	09 49	09 52		10 19
Leigh-on-Sea	d	23p53	23p57	00 06	00 23	00 27	00 36	00 53	00 57	01 27	07 27	07 53	07 57	08 27	08 53	08 57		09 23	09 27	09 53	09 57		10 23
Chalkwell	d	23p56	23p59	00 08	00 26	00 29	00 38	00 56	00 59	01 29	07 29	07 56	07 59	08 29	08 56	08 59		09 26	09 29	09 56	09 59		10 26
Westcliff	d	23p58	00 02	00 11	00 28	00 32	00 41	00 58	01 02	01 32	07 32	07 58	08 02	08 32	08 58	09 02		09 28	09 32	09 58	10 02		10 28
Southend Central	a	00 01	00 05	00 14	00 31	00 35	00 44	01 01	01 05	01 35	07 34	08 04	08 05	08 34	09 04	09 05		09 34	09 35	10 04	10 05		10 34
	d	00 01	00 06	00 14	00 31	00 36	00 44	01 01	01 06	01 36	07 36		08 06	08 36		09 06			09 36		10 06		
Southend East	d	00 04	00 08	00 16	00 34	00 38	00 46	01 04	01 08	01 38	07 38		08 08	08 38		09 08			09 38		10 08		
Thorpe Bay	d	00 06	00 11	00 19	00 36	00 41	00 49	01 06	01 11	01 41	07 40		08 10	08 40		09 10			09 40		10 10		
Shoeburyness	a	00 13	00 18	00 26	00 43	00 48	00 56	01 13	01 18	01 48	07 48		08 18	08 48		09 18			09 48		10 18		

Table I

London - Southend Central and Shoeburyness

Sundays

		CC	CC	CC	CC	CC	CC	CC	CC	CC	CC	CC	CC	CC	CC	CC	CC	CC	CC	CC	CC	CC	CC
London Fenchurch Street 7 ⊖	d	09 40	09 50	10 10		10 20	10 40	10 50	11 10		11 20	11 40	11 50	12 10		12 20	12 40	12 50	13 10		13 20	13 40	13 50
Limehouse	d	09 44	09 54	10 14		10 24	10 44	10 54	11 14		11 24	11 44	11 54	12 14		12 24	12 44	12 54	13 14		13 24	13 44	13 54
West Ham ⊖	d	09 49	09 59	10 19		10 29	10 49	10 59	11 19		11 29	11 49	11 59	12 19		12 29	12 49	12 59	13 19		13 29	13 49	13 59
London Liverpool Street 15 ⊖	d																						
Stratford 7 ⊖	d																						
Barking ⊖	d	09 54	10 04	10 24	10 29	10 34	10 54	11 04	11 24	11 29	11 34	11 54	12 04	12 24	12 29	12 34	12 54	13 04	13 24	13 29	13 34	13 54	14 04
Upminster ⊖	d	10 02	10 12	10 32		10 42	11 02	11 12	11 32		11 42	12 02	12 12	12 32		12 42	13 02	13 12	13 32		13 42	14 02	14 12
Ockendon	d		10 18			10 48		11 18			11 48		12 18			12 48		13 18			13 48		14 18
Chafford Hundred	d		10 21			10 51		11 21			11 51		12 21			12 51		13 21			13 51		14 21
West Horndon	d	10 07		10 37			11 07		11 37			12 07		12 37			13 07		13 37			14 07	
Laindon	d	10 12		10 42			11 12		11 42			12 12		12 42			13 12		13 42			14 12	
Basildon	d	10 15		10 45			11 15		11 45			12 15		12 45			13 15		13 45			14 15	
Dagenham Dock	d				10 33					11 33					12 33					13 33			
Rainham	d				10 37					11 37					12 37					13 37			
Purfleet	d				10 42					11 42					12 42					13 42			
Grays	d		10 25		10a50	10 55		11 25		11a50	11 55		12 25		12a50	12 55		13 25		13a50	13 55		14 25
Tilbury Town 3	d		10 28			10 58		11 28			11 58		12 28			12 58		13 28			13 58		14 28
East Tilbury	d		10 34			11 04		11 34			12 04		12 34			13 04		13 34			14 04		14 34
Stanford-le-Hope	d		10 37			11 07		11 37			12 07		12 37			13 07		13 37			14 07		14 37
Pitsea	d	10 19	10 45	10 49		11 15	11 19	11 45	11 49		12 15	12 19	12 45	12 49		13 15	13 19	13 45	13 49		14 15	14 19	14 45
Benfleet	d	10 22	10 49	10 52		11 19	11 22	11 49	11 52		12 19	12 22	12 49	12 52		13 19	13 22	13 49	13 52		14 19	14 22	14 49
Leigh-on-Sea	d	10 27	10 53	10 57		11 23	11 27	11 53	11 57		12 23	12 27	12 53	12 57		13 23	13 27	13 53	13 57		14 23	14 27	14 53
Chalkwell	d	10 29	10 56	10 59		11 26	11 29	11 56	11 59		12 26	12 29	12 56	12 59		13 26	13 29	13 56	13 59		14 26	14 29	14 56
Westcliff	d	10 32	10 58	11 02		11 28	11 32	11 58	12 02		12 28	12 32	12 58	13 02		13 28	13 32	13 58	14 02		14 28	14 32	14 58
Southend Central	a	10 35	11 04	11 05		11 34	11 35	12 04	12 05		12 34	12 35	13 04	13 05		13 34	13 35	14 04	14 05		14 34	14 35	15 04
	d	10 36		11 06			11 36		12 06			12 36		13 06			13 36		14 06			14 36	
Southend East	d	10 38		11 08			11 38		12 08			12 38		13 08			13 38		14 08			14 38	
Thorpe Bay	d	10 40		11 10			11 40		12 10			12 40		13 10			13 40		14 10			14 40	
Shoeburyness	a	10 48		11 18			11 48		12 18			12 48		13 18			13 48		14 18			14 48	

		CC	CC	CC	CC	CC	CC	CC	CC	CC	CC	CC	CC	CC	CC	CC	CC	CC	CC	CC	CC	CC
London Fenchurch Street 7 ⊖	d	14 10		14 20	14 40	14 50	15 10		15 20	15 40	15 50	16 10		16 20	16 40	16 50	17 10		17 20	17 40	17 50	18 10
Limehouse	d	14 14		14 24	14 44	14 54	15 14		15 24	15 44	15 54	16 14		16 24	16 44	16 54	17 14		17 24	17 44	17 54	18 14
West Ham ⊖	d	14 19		14 29	14 49	14 59	15 19		15 29	15 49	15 59	16 19		16 29	16 49	16 59	17 19		17 29	17 49	17 59	18 19
London Liverpool Street 15 ⊖	d																					
Stratford 7 ⊖	d																					
Barking ⊖	d	14 24	14 29	14 34	14 54	15 04	15 24	15 29	15 34	15 54	16 04	16 24	16 29	16 34	16 54	17 04	17 24	17 29	17 34	17 54	18 04	18 24
Upminster ⊖	d	14 32		14 42	15 02	15 12	15 32		15 42	16 02	16 12	16 32		16 42	17 02	17 12	17 32		17 42	18 02	18 12	18 32
Ockendon	d			14 48		15 18			15 48		16 18			16 48		17 18			17 48		18 18	
Chafford Hundred	d			14 51		15 21			15 51		16 21			16 51		17 21			17 51		18 21	
West Horndon	d	14 37			15 07		15 37			16 07		16 37			17 07		17 37			18 07		18 37
Laindon	d	14 42			15 12		15 42			16 12		16 42			17 12		17 42			18 12		18 42
Basildon	d	14 45			15 15		15 45			16 15		16 45			17 15		17 45			18 15		18 45
Dagenham Dock	d		14 33					15 33					16 33					17 33				
Rainham	d		14 37					15 37					16 37					17 37				
Purfleet	d		14 42					15 42					16 42					17 42				
Grays	d		14a50	14 55		15 25		15a50	15 55		16 25		16a50	16 55		17 25		17a50	17 55		18 25	
Tilbury Town 3	d			14 58		15 28			15 58		16 28			16 58		17 28			17 58		18 28	
East Tilbury	d			15 04		15 34			16 04		16 34			17 04		17 34			18 04		18 34	
Stanford-le-Hope	d			15 07		15 37			16 07		16 37			17 07		17 37			18 07		18 37	
Pitsea	d	14 49		15 15	15 19	15 45	15 49		16 15	16 19	16 45	16 49		17 15	17 19	17 45	17 49		18 15	18 19	18 45	18 49
Benfleet	d	14 52		15 19	15 22	15 49	15 52		16 19	16 22	16 49	16 52		17 19	17 22	17 49	17 52		18 19	18 22	18 49	18 52
Leigh-on-Sea	d	14 57		15 23	15 27	15 53	15 57		16 23	16 27	16 53	16 57		17 23	17 27	17 53	17 57		18 23	18 27	18 53	18 57
Chalkwell	d	14 59		15 26	15 29	15 56	15 59		16 26	16 29	16 56	16 59		17 26	17 29	17 56	17 59		18 26	18 29	18 56	18 59
Westcliff	d	15 02		15 28	15 32	15 58	16 02		16 28	16 32	16 58	17 02		17 28	17 32	17 58	18 02		18 28	18 32	18 58	19 02
Southend Central	a	15 05		15 34	15 35	16 04	16 05		16 34	16 35	17 04	17 05		17 34	17 35	18 04	18 05		18 34	18 35	19 04	19 05
	d	15 06			15 36		16 06			16 36		17 06			17 36		18 06			18 36		19 06
Southend East	d	15 08			15 38		16 08			16 38		17 08			17 38		18 08			18 38		19 08
Thorpe Bay	d	15 10			15 40		16 10			16 40		17 10			17 40		18 10			18 40		19 10
Shoeburyness	a	15 18			15 48		16 18			16 48		17 18			17 48		18 18			18 48		19 18

		CC	CC	CC	CC	CC	CC	CC	CC	CC	CC	CC	CC	CC	CC	CC	CC	CC	CC	CC	CC	CC	CC
London Fenchurch Street 7 ⊖	d		18 20	18 40	18 50	19 10		19 20	19 40	19 50	20 10		20 20	20 40	20 50	21 10		21 20	21 40	21 50	22 10	22 40	22 50
Limehouse	d		18 24	18 44	18 54	19 14		19 24	19 44	19 54	20 14		20 24	20 44	20 54	21 14		21 24	21 44	21 54	22 14	22 44	22 54
West Ham ⊖	d		18 29	18 49	18 59	19 19		19 29	19 49	19 59	20 19		20 29	20 49	20 59	21 19		21 29	21 49	21 59	22 19	22 49	22 59
London Liverpool Street 15 ⊖	d																						
Stratford 7 ⊖	d																						
Barking ⊖	d	18 29	18 34	18 54	19 04	19 24	19 29	19 34	19 54	20 04	20 24	20 29	20 34	20 54	21 04	21 24	21 29	21 34	21 54	22 04	22 24	22 54	23 04
Upminster ⊖	d		18 42	19 02	19 12	19 32		19 42	20 02	20 12	20 32		20 42	21 02	21 12	21 32		21 42	22 02	22 12	22 32	23 02	23 12
Ockendon	d		18 48		19 18			19 48		20 18			20 48		21 18			21 48		22 18			23 18
Chafford Hundred	d		18 51		19 21			19 51		20 21			20 51		21 21			21 51		22 21			23 21
West Horndon	d			19 07		19 37			20 07		20 37			21 07		21 37			22 07		22 37	23 07	
Laindon	d			19 12		19 42			20 12		20 42			21 12		21 42			22 12		22 42	23 12	
Basildon	d			19 15		19 45			20 15		20 45			21 15		21 45			22 15		22 45	23 15	
Dagenham Dock	d	18 33					19 33					20 33					21 33						
Rainham	d	18 37					19 37					20 37					21 37						
Purfleet	d	18 42					19 42					20 42					21 42						
Grays	d	18a50	18 55		19 25		19a50	19 55		20 25		20a50	20 55		21 25		21a50	21 55		22 25			23 25
Tilbury Town 3	d		18 58		19 28			19 58		20 28			20 58		21 28			21 58		22 28			23 28
East Tilbury	d		19 04		19 34			20 04		20 34			21 04		21 34			22 04		22 34			23 34
Stanford-le-Hope	d		19 07		19 37			20 07		20 37			21 07		21 37			22 07		22 37			23 37
Pitsea	d		19 15	19 19	19 45	19 49		20 15	20 19	20 45	20 49		21 15	21 19	21 45	21 49		22 15	22 19	22 45	22 49	23 19	23 45
Benfleet	d		19 19	19 22	19 49	19 52		20 19	20 22	20 49	20 52		21 19	21 22	21 49	21 52		22 19	22 22	22 49	22 52	23 22	23 49
Leigh-on-Sea	d		19 23	19 27	19 53	19 57		20 23	20 27	20 53	20 57		21 23	21 27	21 53	21 57		22 23	22 27	22 53	22 57	23 27	23 53
Chalkwell	d		19 26	19 29	19 56	19 59		20 26	20 29	20 56	20 59		21 26	21 29	21 56	21 59		22 26	22 29	22 56	22 59	23 29	23 56
Westcliff	d		19 28	19 32	19 58	20 02		20 28	20 32	20 58	21 02		21 28	21 32	21 58	22 02		22 28	22 32	22 58	23 02	23 32	23 58
Southend Central	a		19 34	19 35	20 04	20 05		20 34	20 35	21 04	21 05		21 34	21 35	22 04	22 05		22 31	22 35	23 01	23 05	23 35	00 01
	d			19 36		20 06			20 36		21 06			21 36		22 06		22 31	22 36	23 01	23 06	23 36	00 01
Southend East	d			19 38		20 08			20 38		21 08			21 38		22 08		22 33	22 38	23 03	23 08	23 38	00 03
Thorpe Bay	d			19 40		20 10			20 40		21 10			21 40		22 10		22 36	22 40	23 06	23 10	23 40	00 06
Shoeburyness	a			19 48		20 18			20 48		21 18			21 48		22 18		22 43	22 48	23 13	23 18	23 48	00 13

Table 1

Sundays

London - Southend Central and Shoeburyness

		CC	CC
London Fenchurch Street 7 ⊖	d	23 10	23 40
Limehouse	d	23 14	23 44
West Ham ⊖	d	23 19	23 49
London Liverpool Street 15 ⊖	d		
Stratford 7 ⊖	d		
Barking ⊖	d	23 24	23 54
Upminster ⊖	d	23 32	00 02
Ockendon	d		
Chafford Hundred	d		
West Horndon	d	23 37	00 07
Laindon	d	23 42	00 12
Basildon	d	23 45	00 15
Dagenham Dock	d		
Rainham	d		
Purfleet	d		
Grays	d		
Tilbury Town 3	d		
East Tilbury	d		
Stanford-le-Hope	d		
Pitsea	d	23 49	00 19
Benfleet	d	23 52	00 22
Leigh-on-Sea	d	23 57	00 27
Chalkwell	d	23 59	00 29
Westcliff	d	00 02	00 32
Southend Central	a	00 05	00 35
	d	00 06	00 36
Southend East	d	00 08	00 38
Thorpe Bay	d	00 10	00 40
Shoeburyness	a	00 18	00 48

Table 1

Mondays to Fridays

Shoeburyness and Southend Central - London

		CC MX	CC MX	CC MX	CC	CC	CC	CC	CC	CC		CC	CC	CC	CC	CC	CC	CC	CC	CC		CC	CC	CC	CC
Shoeburyness	d		23p05		04 20		04 59		04 40	05 24		05 45		05 13	05 28		05 58	06 04	06 13	06 17			06 28		
Thorpe Bay	d		23p09		04 24		05 03		04 44	05 28		05 49		05 17	05 32		06 02	06 08	06 17	06 21			06 32		05 58
Southend East	d		23p12		04 27		05 06		04 47	05 31		05 52		05 20	05 35		06 05	06 11	06 20	06 24			06 35		06 01
Southend Central	a		23p14		04 29		05 08		04 49	05 33		05 54		05 22	05 37		06 07	06 13	06 22	06 26			06 37		06 03
	d	22p50	23p15		04 29		05 09		04 50	05 34		05 55		05 23	05 38	05 47	06 08	06 14	06 23	06 27			06 38		06 04
Westcliff	d	22p53	23p17		04 31		05 11		04 52	05 36		05 57		05 25	05 40	05 49	06 10	06 16	06 25	06 29			06 40		06 06
Chalkwell	d	22p55	23p19		04 34		05 13		04 54	05 38		05 59		05 27	05 42	05 51	06 12	06 18	06 27	06 31			06 42		06 08
Leigh-on-Sea	d	22p58	23p22		04 37		05 16		04 57	05 41		06 02		05 30	05 45	05 54	06 15	06 21	06 30	06 34			06 45		06 11
Benfleet	d	23p03	23p27		04 41		05 21		05 02	05 46		06 07		05 35	05 50	05 59	06 20	06 26	06 35	06 39			06 50		06 16
Pitsea	d	23p07	23p32		04 45		05 25		05 06	05 50		06 11		05 39	05 54	06 04		06 30		06 43					06 24
Stanford-le-Hope	d	23p14				04 29			05 14					05 46	06 01	06 11									06 31
East Tilbury	d	23p18				04 33			05 18					05 50	06 05	06 15									06 35
Tilbury Town 3	d	23p24				04 39			05 24					05 56	06 11	06 21									06 41
Grays	d	23p27		23p31		04 42		05 12	05 27				05 50	06 00	06 15	06 25								06 29	06 45
Purfleet	d			23p36					05 33					06 05	06 20									06 34	06 51
Rainham	d			23p41					05 38					06 10	06 25									06 40	06 56
Dagenham Dock	d			23p45					05 41					06 14	06 29									06 43	07 00
Basildon	d		23p36		04 50		05 29			05 54		06 16					06 27	06 35	06 42	06 48			06 57		
Laindon	d		23p39		04 53		05 32			05 57		06 19					06 31	06 38		06 51					
West Horndon	d		23p44		04 58		05 37			06 02		06 24						06 43		06 56					
Chafford Hundred	d	23p31				04 46		05 16					05 54			06 30									
Ockendon	d	23p35				04 50		05 20					05 58			06 37						06 20			
Upminster ⊖	d	23p42	23p50		05 04	04 57	05 42	05a25		06 08		06 30	06 03			06 44	06 40	06 49		07 02		06a25	07 10		
Barking ⊖	d	23p50	23p59	23p51	05 13	05 06	05 51		05 47	06 16		06 38	06 12	06 20	06 35			06 58	07 01	07 11				06 50	07 06
Stratford 7 ⊖	a			23p57		05 14																			
London Liverpool Street 15 ⊖	a			00 11		05 27																			
West Ham ⊖	d	23p56	00 04		05 18		05 57		05 53	06 22		06 44	06 17	06 26	06 41	06 59		07 03	07 07				07 23	06 56	07 12
Limehouse	d	00 01	00 09		05 23		06 02		05 58	06 27		06 49	06 22	06 31	06 46	07 04	06 57			07 20				07 01	07 17
London Fenchurch Street 7 ⊖	a	00 05	00 14		05 30		06 08		06 04	06 31		06 53	06 29	06 37	06 52	07 10	07 03	07 14	07 17	07 26			07 34	07 07	07 23

		CC	CC	CC	CC	CC		CC	CC	CC	CC	CC	CC	CC	CC	CC		CC	CC	CC	CC	CC	CC	CC	CC
Shoeburyness	d	06 32	06 46			06 53				07 05		07 20		07 24					07 35						07 50
Thorpe Bay	d	06 36	06 50		06 13	06 57				07 09	07 14	07 24		07 28					07 39		07 43				07 54
Southend East	d	06 39	06 53		06 16	07 00				07 12	07 17	07 27		07 31					07 42		07 46				07 57
Southend Central	a	06 41	06 55		06 18	07 02				07 14	07 19	07 29		07 33					07 44		07 48				07 59
	d	06 42	06 56		06 19	07 03				07 15	07 20	07 30		07 34				07 10	07 45		07 49				08 00
Westcliff	d	06 44	06 58		06 21	07 05				07 17	07 22	07 32		07 36				07 12	07 47		07 51				08 02
Chalkwell	d	06 46	07 00		06 23	07 07				07 19	07 24	07 34		07 38				07 14	07 49		07 53				08 04
Leigh-on-Sea	d	06 49	07 03		06 26	07 10				07 22	07 27	07 37		07 41				07 18	07 52		07 56				08 07
Benfleet	d	06 54	07 08		06 31	07 15				07 27	07 32	07 42		07 46				07 22	07 57		08 01				08 12
Pitsea	d	06 58			06 39	07 19		06 55	07 02		07 36			07 50		07 15		07 27			08 05		07 42	07 49	
Stanford-le-Hope	d				06 46			07 02	07 09							07 22		07 34				07 44	07 49	07 56	
East Tilbury	d				06 50			07 06	07 13							07 26		07 38					07 53		
Tilbury Town 3	d				06 56			07 12	07 20							07 32		07 44					07 59		
Grays	d			06 51	07 00			07 16	07 24						07 32	07 36		07 48				07 54	08 03	08 07	
Purfleet	d				07 05			07 21							07 37			07 53					08 08		
Rainham	d				07 11			07 27							07 43			07 59					08 14		
Dagenham Dock	d				07 14			07 30							07 46			08 02					08 17		
Basildon	d	07 03	07 15			07 24				07 34	07 41			07 55							08 10				
Laindon	d	07 06				07 27					07 44		07 22	07 58						07 39	08 13				
West Horndon	d	07 11											07 27							07 44					
Chafford Hundred	d			06 55					07 28							07 40						07 59		08 11	
Ockendon	d			07 00					07 32							07 48						08 03		08 18	
Upminster ⊖	d	07 17		07 06					07 39				07 32			07 56			08 14	07 49		08 10		08 25	08 29
Barking ⊖	d	07 27		07 15	07 21	07 45		07 37	07 48		08 01		07 41	08 15	07 54			08 09		07 58	08 30	08 19	08 24		
Stratford 7 ⊖	a																								
London Liverpool Street 15 ⊖	a																								
West Ham ⊖	d			07 20	07 26								07 46							08 03					
Limehouse	d	07 36		07 25	07 32	07 54		07 46		08 00	08 10	08 16	07 51	08 25	08 03			08 19	08 31	08 08	08 39		08 34		08 48
London Fenchurch Street 7 ⊖	a	07 42	07 46	07 32	07 38	08 00		07 52	08 03	08 07	08 17	08 22	07 58	08 32	08 10	08 19		08 25	08 37	08 14	08 46	08 34	08 40	08 48	08 55

		CC		CC	CC	CC	CC	CC	CC	CC	CC	CC		CC	CC	CC	CC	CC	CC	CC	CC	CC		CC	CC
Shoeburyness	d				07 54	08 05		08 10				08 25					08 40				09 05				
Thorpe Bay	d				07 58	08 09		08 14				08 29					08 44				09 09				
Southend East	d				08 01	08 12		08 17				08 32					08 47				09 12				
Southend Central	a				08 03	08 14		08 19				08 34					08 49				09 14				
	d				08 04	08 15		08 20				08 34					08 50				09 15	09 06			
Westcliff	d				08 06	08 17		08 22				08 36					08 52				09 17	09 08			
Chalkwell	d				08 08	08 19		08 24				08 39					08 54				09 19	09 11			
Leigh-on-Sea	d				08 11	08 22		08 27				08 42					08 57				09 22	09 14			
Benfleet	d				08 16	08 27		08 32				08 47					09 02				09 27	09 19			
Pitsea	d			07 54	08 20			08 36		08 13		08 51			08 34		09 06		08 54		09 32			09 08	
Stanford-le-Hope	d			08 02					08 12	08 20				08 32	08 41				09 01					09 16	
East Tilbury	d			08 06					08 16	08 24				08 36	08 45				09 05					09 20	
Tilbury Town 3	d			08 12					08 22	08 30				08 42	08 51				09 11					09 26	
Grays	d			08 16					08 26	08 34				08 46	08 56			09 03	09 15					09 29	
Purfleet	d			08 21						08 40				08 51				09 08	09 20						
Rainham	d			08 27						08 45				08 57				09 13	09 26						
Dagenham Dock	d			08 30						08 49				09 00				09 17	09 29						
Basildon	d				08 25			08 41				08 55					09 11				09 36	09 26			
Laindon	d	07 52			08 28		08 08	08 44			08 23					08 38	09 14			09 04	09 39	09 29			09 17
West Horndon	d	07 57					08 13				08 28					08 43				09 10	09 44				09 22
Chafford Hundred	d								08 30						09 01									09 34	
Ockendon	d								08 34						09 05									09 38	
Upminster ⊖	d	08 03					08 18	08 54	08 41		08 33	09 06			09 11	08 49				09 16	09 50	09 38		09 45	09 28
Barking ⊖	d	08 12		08 37	08 47		08 27	09 03	08 51	08 55	08 43			09 07	09 20	08 58	09 30	09 23	09 35	09 25	09 58	09 47		09 54	09 37
Stratford 7 ⊖	a																								
London Liverpool Street 15 ⊖	a																								
West Ham ⊖	d	08 17					08 32	09 08		09 01	08 48				09 25	09 04		09 29		09 31	10 04	09 52		09 59	09 43
Limehouse	d	08 22		08 46	08 56		08 37	09 14		09 06	08 53	09 23		09 17	09 30	09 09		09 34	09 44	09 36	10 09	09 57		10 04	
London Fenchurch Street 7 ⊖	a	08 28		08 52	09 02	09 08	08 43	09 20	09 06	09 12	08 59	09 29		09 26	09 38	09 15	09 45	09 40	09 51	09 43	10 13	10 04		10 09	09 53

Table I

Mondays to Fridays

Shoeburyness and Southend Central - London

		CC	CC	CC	CC	CC	CC	CC		CC	CC	CC	CC	CC	CC	CC	CC	CC		CC	CC	CC	CC	CC	CC
Shoeburyness	d	09 20	09 35			09 50	10 05				10 20	10 35			10 50	11 05				11 20	11 35			11 50	12 05
Thorpe Bay	d	09 24	09 39			09 54	10 09				10 24	10 39			10 54	11 09				11 24	11 39			11 54	12 09
Southend East	d	09 27	09 42			09 57	10 12				10 27	10 42			10 57	11 12				11 27	11 42			11 57	12 12
Southend Central	a	09 29	09 44			09 59	10 14				10 29	10 44			10 59	11 14				11 29	11 44			11 59	12 14
	d	09 30	09 45		09 20	10 00	10 15			09 50	10 30	10 45		10 20	11 00	11 15		10 50		11 30	11 45		11 20	12 00	12 15
Westcliff	d	09 32	09 47		09 23	10 02	10 17			09 53	10 32	10 47		10 23	11 02	11 17		10 53		11 32	11 47		11 23	12 02	12 17
Chalkwell	d	09 34	09 49		09 25	10 04	10 19			09 55	10 34	10 49		10 25	11 04	11 19		10 55		11 34	11 49		11 25	12 04	12 19
Leigh-on-Sea	d	09 37	09 52		09 28	10 07	10 22			09 58	10 37	10 52		10 28	11 07	11 22		10 58		11 37	11 52		11 28	12 07	12 22
Benfleet	d	09 42	09 57		09 33	10 12	10 27			10 03	10 42	10 57		10 33	11 12	11 27		11 03		11 42	11 57		11 33	12 12	12 27
Pitsea	d		10 02		09 37		10 32			10 07		11 02		10 37		11 32		11 07			12 02		11 37		12 32
Stanford-le-Hope	d				09 44					10 14				10 44				11 14					11 44		
East Tilbury	d				09 48					10 18				10 48				11 18					11 48		
Tilbury Town 3	d				09 54					10 24				10 54				11 24					11 54		
Grays	d			09 46	09 57			10 16		10 27			10 46	10 57			11 16	11 27				11 46	11 57		
Purfleet	d			09 51				10 21					10 51				11 21					11 51			
Rainham	d			09 56				10 26					10 56				11 26					11 56			
Dagenham Dock	d			10 00				10 30					11 00				11 30					12 00			
Basildon	d	09 49	10 06			10 19	10 36				10 49	11 06			11 19	11 36				11 49	12 06			12 19	12 36
Laindon	d	09 52	10 09			10 22	10 39				10 52	11 09			11 22	11 39				11 52	12 09			12 22	12 39
West Horndon	d		10 14				10 44					11 14				11 44					12 14				12 44
Chafford Hundred	d				10 01					10 31				11 01				11 31					12 01		
Ockendon	d				10 05					10 35				11 05				11 35					12 05		
Upminster ⊖	d	10 02	10 20		10 12	10 32	10 50			10 42	11 02	11 20		11 12	11 32	11 50		11 42		12 02	12 20		12 12	12 32	12 50
Barking ⊖	d	10 10	10 28	10 06	10 20	10 40	10 58	10 36		10 50	11 10	11 28	11 06	11 20	11 40	11 58	11 36	11 50		12 10	12 28	12 06	12 20	12 40	12 58
Stratford 7 ⊖	a																								
London Liverpool Street 15 ⊖	a																								
West Ham ⊖	d	10 16	10 34	10 11	10 26	10 46	11 04	10 41		10 56	11 16	11 34	11 11	11 26	11 46	12 04	11 41	11 56		12 16	12 34	12 11	12 26	12 46	13 04
Limehouse	d		10 39	10 16	10 31		11 09	10 46		11 01		11 39	11 16	11 31		12 09	11 46	12 01			12 39	12 16	12 31		13 09
London Fenchurch Street 7 ⊖	a	10 24	10 43	10 21	10 35	10 54	11 13	10 51		11 05	11 24	11 43	11 21	11 35	11 54	12 13	11 51	12 05		12 24	12 43	12 21	12 35	12 54	13 13

		CC	CC	CC		CC	CC	CC	CC	CC	CC	CC	CC	CC		CC	CC	CC	CC	CC	CC	CC	CC	CC	
Shoeburyness	d			12 20		12 35			12 50	13 05			13 20	13 35				13 50	14 05			14 20	14 35		
Thorpe Bay	d			12 24		12 39			12 54	13 09			13 24	13 39				13 54	14 09			14 24	14 39		
Southend East	d			12 27		12 42			12 57	13 12			13 27	13 42				13 57	14 12			14 27	14 42		
Southend Central	a			12 29		12 44			12 59	13 14			13 29	13 44				13 59	14 14			14 29	14 44		
	d		11 50	12 30		12 45		12 20	13 00	13 15		12 50	13 30	13 45			13 20	14 00	14 15		13 50	14 30	14 45		
Westcliff	d		11 53	12 32		12 47		12 23	13 02	13 17		12 53	13 32	13 47			13 23	14 02	14 17		13 53	14 32	14 47		
Chalkwell	d		11 55	12 34		12 49		12 25	13 04	13 19		12 55	13 34	13 49			13 25	14 04	14 19		13 55	14 34	14 49		
Leigh-on-Sea	d		11 58	12 37		12 52		12 28	13 07	13 22		12 58	13 37	13 52			13 28	14 07	14 22		13 58	14 37	14 52		
Benfleet	d		12 03	12 42		12 57		12 33	13 12	13 27		13 03	13 42	13 57			13 33	14 12	14 27		14 03	14 42	14 57		
Pitsea	d		12 07			13 02		12 37		13 32		13 07		14 02			13 37		14 32		14 07		15 02		
Stanford-le-Hope	d		12 14					12 44				13 14					13 44				14 14				
East Tilbury	d		12 18					12 48				13 18					13 48				14 18				
Tilbury Town 3	d		12 24					12 54				13 24					13 54				14 24				
Grays	d	12 16	12 27				12 46	12 57			13 16	13 27				13 46	13 57			14 16	14 27			14 46	
Purfleet	d	12 21					12 51				13 21					13 51				14 21				14 51	
Rainham	d	12 26					12 56				13 26					13 56				14 26				14 56	
Dagenham Dock	d	12 30					13 00				13 30					14 00				14 30				15 00	
Basildon	d			12 49		13 06			13 19	13 36			13 49	14 06				14 19	14 36			14 49	15 06		
Laindon	d			12 52		13 09			13 22	13 39			13 52	14 09				14 22	14 39			14 52	15 09		
West Horndon	d					13 14				13 44				14 14					14 44				15 14		
Chafford Hundred	d		12 31					13 01				13 31					14 01				14 31				
Ockendon	d		12 35					13 05				13 35					14 05				14 35				
Upminster ⊖	d		12 42	13 02		13 20		13 12	13 32	13 50		13 42	14 02	14 20			14 12	14 32	14 50		14 42	15 02	15 20		
Barking ⊖	d	12 36	12 50	13 10		13 28	13 06	13 20	13 40	13 58	13 36	13 50	14 10	14 28		14 06	14 20	14 40	14 58	14 36	14 50	15 10	15 28	15 06	
Stratford 7 ⊖	a																								
London Liverpool Street 15 ⊖	a																								
West Ham ⊖	d	12 41	12 56	13 16		13 34	13 11	13 26	13 46	14 04	13 41	13 56	14 16	14 34		14 11	14 26	14 46	15 04	14 41	14 56	15 16	15 34	15 11	
Limehouse	d	12 46	13 01			13 39	13 16	13 31		14 09	13 46	14 01		14 39		14 16	14 31		15 09	14 46	15 01		15 39	15 16	
London Fenchurch Street 7 ⊖	a	12 51	13 05	13 24		13 43	13 21	13 35	13 54	14 13	13 51	14 05	14 24	14 43		14 21	14 35	14 54	15 13	14 51	15 05	15 24	15 43	15 21	

		CC	CC	CC	CC	CC	CC	CC	CC	CC		CC	CC	CC	CC	CC	CC	CC	CC	CC		CC	CC	CC	CC
Shoeburyness	d		14 50	15 05			15 20	15 35				15 50	16 05	16 15			16 28			16 49					16 56
Thorpe Bay	d		14 54	15 09			15 24	15 39				15 54	16 09	16 19			16 32			16 53					17 00
Southend East	d		14 57	15 12			15 27	15 42				15 57	16 12	16 22			16 35			16 56					17 03
Southend Central	a		14 59	15 14			15 29	15 44				15 59	16 14	16 24			16 37			16 58					17 05
	d	14 20	15 00	15 15		14 50	15 30	15 45		15 20		16 00	16 15	16 25		15 48	16 38	16 31		16 59			16 19	16 54	17 06
Westcliff	d	14 23	15 02	15 17		14 53	15 32	15 47		15 23		16 02	16 17	16 27		15 50	16 40	16 33		17 01			16 21	16 56	17 08
Chalkwell	d	14 25	15 04	15 19		14 55	15 34	15 49		15 25		16 04	16 19	16 29		15 53	16 42	16 35		17 03			16 23	16 59	17 10
Leigh-on-Sea	d	14 28	15 07	15 22		14 58	15 37	15 52		15 28		16 07	16 22	16 32		15 56	16 45	16 38		17 06			16 26	17 02	17 13
Benfleet	d	14 33	15 12	15 27		15 03	15 42	15 57		15 33		16 12	16 27	16 37		16 00	16 50	16 43		17 11			16 31	17 06	17 18
Pitsea	d	14 37		15 32		15 07		16 02		15 37			16 31			16 04	16 54	16 47		17 15			16 35	17 10	17 22
Stanford-le-Hope	d	14 44				15 14				15 44						16 11							16 42		
East Tilbury	d	14 48				15 18				15 48						16 15							16 46		
Tilbury Town 3	d	14 54				15 24				15 54						16 21							16 52		
Grays	d	14 57			15 16	15 27			15 46	15 57					16 16	16 26			16 39			16 52	16 57		
Purfleet	d				15 21				15 51						16 21				16 44			16 57			
Rainham	d				15 26				15 56						16 26				16 49			17 02			
Dagenham Dock	d				15 30				16 00						16 30				16 53			17 06			
Basildon	d		15 19	15 36			15 49	16 06				16 19	16 35	16 43			16 58	16 51		17 19				17 14	17 26
Laindon	d		15 22	15 39			15 52	16 09					16 38				17 01							17 17	
West Horndon	d			15 44				16 14					16 43				17 06							17 22	
Chafford Hundred	d	15 01				15 31				16 01						16 30							17 01		
Ockendon	d	15 05				15 35				16 05						16 34							17 07		
Upminster ⊖	d	15 12	15 32	15 50		15 42	16 02	16 20		16 12		16 30	16 48	16 54		16 41	17 11			17 31			17 15	17 28	
Barking ⊖	d	15 20	15 40	15 58	15 36	15 50	16 10	16 28	16 06	16 20		16 38	16 57	17 03	16 36	16 49	17 20		17 00	17 40		17 16	17 25	17 36	
Stratford 7 ⊖	a																								
London Liverpool Street 15 ⊖	a																								
West Ham ⊖	d	15 26	15 46	16 04	15 41	15 56	16 17	16 34	16 11	16 26		16 44	17 02	17 09								17 22	17 31		17 49
Limehouse	d	15 31		16 09	15 46	16 01		16 39	16 16	16 31			17 08	17 14			17 29		17 10						
London Fenchurch Street 7 ⊖	a	15 35	15 54	16 13	15 51	16 05	16 26	16 43	16 21	16 36		16 52	17 12	17 18	16 48	17 03	17 33	17 24	17 15	17 52		17 30	17 39	17 49	17 58

Table I

Mondays to Fridays

Shoeburyness and Southend Central - London

		CC	CC	CC	CC	CC		CC	CC	CC	CC	CC	CC	CC	CC	CC		CC	CC	CC	CC	CC	CC	CC	CC
Shoeburyness	d		17 10			17 30					17 45			18 05	18 20					18 35	18 50	19 05			19 20
Thorpe Bay	d		17 14			17 34					17 49			18 09	18 24					18 39	18 54	19 09			19 24
Southend East	d		17 17			17 37					17 52			18 12	18 27					18 42	18 57	19 12			19 27
Southend Central	a		17 19			17 39					17 54			18 14	18 29					18 44	18 59	19 15			19 29
	d		17 19			17 40					17 55			18 15	18 30				18 20	18 45	19 00	19 15		18 49	19 30
Westcliff	d		17 21			17 42					17 57			18 17	18 32				18 23	18 47	19 02	19 17		18 51	19 32
Chalkwell	d		17 24			17 44					17 59			18 19	18 34				18 25	18 49	19 04	19 19		18 53	19 34
Leigh-on-Sea	d		17 27			17 47					18 02			18 22	18 37				18 28	18 52	19 07	19 22		18 56	19 37
Benfleet	d		17 32			17 52					18 07			18 27	18 42				18 33	18 57	19 12	19 27		19 01	19 42
Pitsea	d	16 57	17 36			17 56			17 24	17 43	18 11		17 59	18 32				18 31	18 37	19 02		19 32		19 05	
Stanford-le-Hope	d	17 04			17 19				17 32	17 50			18 06					18 38	18 44					19 12	
East Tilbury	d	17 08			17 23				17 36	17 54			18 10					18 42	18 48					19 16	
Tilbury Town 3	d	17 14			17 29				17 42	18 00			18 16					18 48	18 54					19 22	
Grays	d	17 19		17 22	17 32			17 44	17 50	18 04			18 20			18 28		18 54	18 57				19 18	19 25	
Purfleet	d			17 27	17 38			17 49		18 09						18 33			19 04				19 23		
Rainham	d			17 32	17 43			17 54		18 14						18 38			19 09				19 28		
Dagenham Dock	d			17 36	17 46			17 58		18 18						18 42			19 12				19 32		
Basildon	d		17 40			18 00					18 15			18 36	18 49					19 06	19 19	19 36			19 49
Laindon	d		17 44			18 05					18 18	17 47		18 39	18 52					19 09	19 22	19 39			19 52
West Horndon	d					18 10					18 23	17 52		18 44						19 14		19 44			
Chafford Hundred	d	17 23							17 54				18 25					18 59						19 29	
Ockendon	d	17 30							17 59				18 31					19 04						19 34	
Upminster ⊖	d	17 39				18 15			18 06		18 30	17 58	18 38	18 50	19 02			19 10		19 20	19 32	19 50		19 40	20 02
Barking ⊖	d	17 47		17 42	17 52	18 24		18 04	18 14	18 26	18 38	18 06		18 58	19 10	18 48		19 20	19 18	19 28	19 40	19 58	19 37	19 50	20 10
Stratford 7 ⊖	a																								
London Liverpool Street 15 ⊖	a																								
West Ham ⊖	d				17 58	18 29		18 09		18 32	18 44	18 12		19 04	19 16	18 53		19 26		19 34	19 46	20 04	19 43	19 56	20 16
Limehouse	d				18 03					18 37	18 49	18 17		19 09		18 58			19 27	19 39		20 09	19 48	20 01	
London Fenchurch Street 7 ⊖	a	18 00	18 11	17 54	18 09	18 38		18 18	18 27	18 41	18 53	18 21	19 00	19 13	19 24	19 03		19 36	19 32	19 43	19 55	20 13	19 53	20 05	20 25

		CC		CC	CC	CC	CC	CC	CC	CC	CC	CC		CC	CC	CC	CC	CC	CC	CC	CC	CC		CC	CC
Shoeburyness	d	19 35				19 50	20 05			20 20	20 35					21 05			21 20	21 35				22 05	
Thorpe Bay	d	19 39				19 54	20 09			20 24	20 39					21 09			21 24	21 39				22 09	
Southend East	d	19 42				19 57	20 12			20 27	20 42					21 12			21 27	21 42				22 12	
Southend Central	a	19 44				19 59	20 14			20 29	20 44					21 14			21 29	21 45				22 14	
	d	19 45			19 20	20 00	20 15		19 50	20 30	20 45			20 20		21 15		20 50	21 30	21 45		21 20		22 15	
Westcliff	d	19 47			19 23	20 02	20 17		19 53	20 32	20 47			20 23		21 17		20 53	21 32	21 47		21 23		22 17	
Chalkwell	d	19 49			19 25	20 04	20 19		19 55	20 34	20 49			20 25		21 19		20 55	21 34	21 49		21 25		22 19	
Leigh-on-Sea	d	19 52			19 28	20 07	20 22		19 58	20 37	20 52			20 28		21 22		20 58	21 37	21 52		21 28		22 22	
Benfleet	d	19 57			19 33	20 12	20 27		20 03	20 42	20 57			20 33		21 27		21 03	21 42	21 57		21 33		22 27	
Pitsea	d	20 02			19 37		20 32		20 07		21 02			20 37		21 32		21 07		22 02		21 37		22 32	
Stanford-le-Hope	d				19 44				20 14					20 44				21 14				21 44			
East Tilbury	d				19 48				20 18					20 48				21 18				21 48			
Tilbury Town 3	d				19 54				20 24					20 54				21 24				21 54			
Grays	d			19 48	19 57			20 16	20 27			20 46		20 57			21 16	21 27			21 46	21 57			22 16
Purfleet	d			19 53				20 21				20 51					21 21				21 51				22 21
Rainham	d			19 58				20 26				20 56					21 26				21 56				22 26
Dagenham Dock	d			20 02				20 30				21 00					21 30				22 00				22 30
Basildon	d	20 06				20 19	20 36			20 49	21 06					21 36			21 49	22 06				22 36	
Laindon	d	20 09				20 22	20 39			20 52	21 09					21 39			21 52	22 09				22 39	
West Horndon	d	20 14					20 44				21 14					21 44				22 14				22 44	
Chafford Hundred	d				20 01				20 31					21 01				21 31				22 01			
Ockendon	d				20 05				20 35					21 05				21 35				22 05			
Upminster ⊖	d	20 20			20 12	20 32	20 50		20 42	21 02	21 20			21 12		21 50		21 42	22 02	22 20		22 12		22 50	
Barking ⊖	d	20 28		20 11	20 20	20 40	20 58	20 36	20 50	21 10	21 28	21 06		21 20	20 51	21 58	21 36	21 50	22 10	22 28	22 06	22 20		22 58	22 36
Stratford 7 ⊖	a			20 20								21 14			21 00										
London Liverpool Street 15 ⊖	a			20 33								21 26			21 12										
West Ham ⊖	d	20 34			20 26	20 46	21 04	20 41	20 56	21 16	21 34			21 26		22 04	21 41	21 56	22 16	22 34	22 11	22 26		23 04	22 41
Limehouse	d	20 39			20 31		21 09	20 46	21 01		21 39			21 31		22 09	21 46	22 01		22 39	22 16	22 31		23 09	22 46
London Fenchurch Street 7 ⊖	a	20 43			20 35	20 54	21 13	20 51	21 05	21 24	21 43			21 35		22 13	21 52	22 05	22 24	22 43	22 21	22 35		23 13	22 52

		CC	CC	CC	CC	CC	CC	CC
Shoeburyness	d		22 35				23 05	
Thorpe Bay	d		22 39				23 09	
Southend East	d		22 42				23 12	
Southend Central	a		22 44				23 14	
	d	21 50	22 45		22 20	22 50	23 15	
Westcliff	d	21 53	22 47		22 23	22 53	23 17	
Chalkwell	d	21 55	22 49		22 25	22 55	23 19	
Leigh-on-Sea	d	21 58	22 52		22 28	22 58	23 22	
Benfleet	d	22 03	22 57		22 33	23 03	23 27	
Pitsea	d	22 07	23 02		22 37	23 07	23 32	
Stanford-le-Hope	d	22 14			22 44	23 14		
East Tilbury	d	22 18			22 48	23 18		
Tilbury Town 3	d	22 24			22 54	23 24		
Grays	d	22 27		22 46	22 57	23 27		23 31
Purfleet	d			22 51				23 36
Rainham	d			22 56				23 41
Dagenham Dock	d			23 00				23 45
Basildon	d		23 06				23 36	
Laindon	d		23 09				23 39	
West Horndon	d		23 14				23 44	
Chafford Hundred	d	22 31			23 01	23 31		
Ockendon	d	22 35			23 05	23 35		
Upminster ⊖	d	22 42	23 20		23 12	23 42	23 50	
Barking ⊖	d	22 50	23 28	23 06	23 20	23 50	23 59	23 51
Stratford 7 ⊖	a							23 57
London Liverpool Street 15 ⊖	a							00 11
West Ham ⊖	d	22 56	23 34	23 11	23 26	23 56	00 04	
Limehouse	d	23 01	23 39	23 16	23 31	00 01	00 09	
London Fenchurch Street 7 ⊖	a	23 05	23 43	23 21	23 35	00 05	00 14	

Table I

Shoeburyness and Southend Central - London

	CC	CC	CC	CC	CC	CC	CC	CC	CC		CC	CC	CC	CC	CC	CC	CC	CC	CC		CC	CC	CC	CC
Shoeburyness d		23p05		04 20		05 05		05 35				06 05			06 35			07 05				07 35		
Thorpe Bay d		23p09		04 23		05 08		05 38				06 08			06 38			07 08				07 38		
Southend East d		23p12		04 26		05 11		05 41				06 11			06 41			07 11				07 41		
Southend Central a		23p14		04 28		05 13		05 43				06 13			06 43			07 13				07 43		
Southend Central d	22p50	23p15		04 29		05 14		05 44			05 20	06 14		05 50	06 44		06 20	07 14			06 50	07 44		07 20
Westcliff d	22p53	23p17		04 31		05 16		05 46			05 23	06 16		05 53	06 46		06 23	07 16			06 53	07 46		07 23
Chalkwell d	22p55	23p19		04 33		05 18		05 48			05 25	06 18		05 55	06 48		06 25	07 18			06 55	07 48		07 25
Leigh-on-Sea d	22p58	23p22		04 36		05 21		05 51			05 28	06 21		05 58	06 51		06 28	07 21			06 58	07 51		07 28
Benfleet d	23p03	23p27		04 40		05 25		05 55			05 32	06 25		06 02	06 55		06 32	07 25			07 02	07 55		07 32
Pitsea d	23p07	23p32		04 44		05 29		05 59			05 36	06 29		06 06	06 59		06 36	07 29			07 06	07 59		07 36
Stanford-le-Hope d	23p14				04 29						05 42			06 12			06 42				07 12			07 42
East Tilbury d	23p18				04 32						05 45			06 15			06 45				07 15			07 45
Tilbury Town d	23p24				04 38						05 51			06 21			06 51				07 21			07 51
Grays d	23p27		23p31		04 41				05 48		05 54		06 18	06 24		06 48	06 54		07 18		07 24		07 48	07 54
Purfleet d			23p36						05 53				06 23			06 53			07 23				07 53	
Rainham d			23p41						05 58				06 28			06 58			07 28				07 58	
Dagenham Dock d			23p45						06 02				06 32			07 02			07 32				08 02	
Basildon d		23p36		04 47		05 32		06 02				06 32			07 02			07 32				08 02		
Laindon d		23p39		04 50		05 35		06 05				06 35			07 05			07 35				08 05		
West Horndon d		23p44		04 55		05 40		06 10				06 40			07 10			07 40				08 10		
Chafford Hundred d	23p31				04 45						05 59			06 29			06 59				07 29			07 59
Ockendon d	23p35				04 49		05 16				06 02			06 32			07 02				07 32			08 02
Upminster ⊖ d	23p42	23p50		05 02	04a57	05 46	05a23	06 16			06 09	06 46		06 39	07 16		07 09	07 46			07 39	08 16		08 09
Barking ⊖ d	23p50	23p59	23p51	05 10		05 54		06 24	06 08		06 17	06 54	06 38	06 47	07 24	07 08	07 17	07 54	07 38		07 47	08 24	08 08	08 17
Stratford ⊖ a			23p57																					
London Liverpool Street ⊖ a			00 11																					
West Ham ⊖ d	23p56	00 04		05 16		06 00		06 30	06 14		06 23	07 00	06 44	06 53	07 30	07 14	07 23	08 00	07 44		07 53	08 30	08 14	08 23
Limehouse d	00 01	00 09		05 21		06 05		06 35	06 19		06 28	07 05	06 49	06 58	07 35	07 19	07 28	08 05	07 49		07 58	08 35	08 19	08 28
London Fenchurch Street ⊖ a	00 05	00 14		05 27		06 12		06 42	06 26		06 34	07 12	06 56	07 04	07 42	07 26	07 34	08 12	07 56		08 04	08 42	08 26	08 34

	CC	CC	CC	CC	CC		CC	CC	CC	CC	CC	CC	CC	CC	CC		CC	CC	CC	CC	CC	CC	CC	CC
Shoeburyness d	07 50	08 05			08 20		08 35			08 50	09 05			09 20	09 35				09 50	10 05			10 20	10 35
Thorpe Bay d	07 53	08 08			08 23		08 38			08 53	09 08			09 23	09 38				09 53	10 08			10 23	10 38
Southend East d	07 56	08 11			08 26		08 41			08 56	09 11			09 26	09 41				09 56	10 11			10 26	10 41
Southend Central a	07 58	08 13			08 28		08 43			08 58	09 13			09 28	09 43				09 58	10 13			10 28	10 43
Southend Central d	07 59	08 14		07 50	08 29		08 44		08 20	08 59	09 14		08 50	09 29	09 44			09 20	09 59	10 14		09 50	10 29	10 44
Westcliff d	08 01	08 16		07 53	08 31		08 46		08 23	09 01	09 16		08 53	09 31	09 46			09 23	10 01	10 16		09 53	10 31	10 46
Chalkwell d	08 03	08 18		07 55	08 33		08 48		08 25	09 03	09 18		08 55	09 33	09 48			09 25	10 03	10 18		09 55	10 33	10 48
Leigh-on-Sea d	08 06	08 21		07 58	08 36		08 51		08 28	09 06	09 21		08 58	09 36	09 51			09 28	10 06	10 21		09 58	10 36	10 51
Benfleet d	08 10	08 25		08 02	08 40		08 55		08 32	09 10	09 25		09 02	09 40	09 55			09 32	10 10	10 25		10 02	10 40	10 55
Pitsea d		08 29		08 06			08 59		08 36		09 29		09 06		09 59			09 36		10 29		10 06		10 59
Stanford-le-Hope d				08 12					08 42				09 12					09 42				10 12		
East Tilbury d				08 15					08 45				09 15					09 45				10 15		
Tilbury Town d				08 21					08 51				09 21					09 51				10 21		
Grays d			08 18	08 24				08 48	08 54			09 18	09 24				09 48	09 54			10 18	10 24		
Purfleet d			08 23					08 53				09 23					09 53				10 23			
Rainham d			08 28					08 58				09 28					09 58				10 28			
Dagenham Dock d			08 32					09 02				09 32					10 02				10 32			
Basildon d	08 16	08 32			08 46		09 02			09 16	09 32			09 46	10 02				10 16	10 32			10 46	11 02
Laindon d	08 19	08 35			08 49		09 05			09 19	09 35			09 49	10 05				10 19	10 35			10 49	11 05
West Horndon d		08 40					09 10				09 40				10 10					10 40				11 10
Chafford Hundred d				08 29					08 59				09 29					09 59				10 29		
Ockendon d				08 32					09 02				09 32					10 02				10 32		
Upminster ⊖ d	08 28	08 46		08 39	08 58		09 16		09 09	09 28	09 46		09 39	09 58	10 16			10 09	10 28	10 46		10 39	10 58	11 16
Barking ⊖ d	08 36	08 54	08 38	08 47	09 06		09 24	09 08	09 17	09 36	09 54	09 38	09 47	10 06	10 24		10 08	10 17	10 36	10 54	10 38	10 47	11 06	11 24
Stratford ⊖ a																								
London Liverpool Street ⊖ a																								
West Ham ⊖ d	08 42	09 00	08 44	08 53	09 12		09 30	09 14	09 23	09 42	10 00	09 44	09 53	10 12	10 30		10 14	10 23	10 42	11 00	10 44	10 53	11 12	11 30
Limehouse d		09 05	08 49	08 58			09 35	09 19	09 28		10 05	09 49	09 58		10 35		10 19	10 28		11 05	10 49	10 58		11 35
London Fenchurch Street ⊖ a	08 53	09 12	08 56	09 04	09 23		09 42	09 26	09 34	09 53	10 12	09 56	10 04	10 23	10 42		10 26	10 34	10 53	11 12	10 56	11 04	11 23	11 42

	CC		CC	CC	CC	CC	CC	CC	CC	CC	CC		CC	CC	CC	CC	CC	CC	CC	CC	CC		CC	CC
Shoeburyness d				10 50	11 05			11 20	11 35				11 50	12 05			12 20	12 35			12 50		13 05	
Thorpe Bay d				10 53	11 08			11 23	11 38				11 53	12 08			12 23	12 38			12 53		13 08	
Southend East d				10 56	11 11			11 26	11 41				11 56	12 11			12 26	12 41			12 56		13 11	
Southend Central a				10 58	11 13			11 28	11 43				11 58	12 13			12 28	12 43			12 58		13 13	
Southend Central d			10 20	10 59	11 14		10 50	11 29	11 44		11 20		11 59	12 14		11 50	12 29	12 44		12 20	12 59		13 14	
Westcliff d			10 23	11 01	11 16		10 53	11 31	11 46		11 23		12 01	12 16		11 53	12 31	12 46		12 23	13 01		13 16	
Chalkwell d			10 25	11 03	11 18		10 55	11 33	11 48		11 25		12 03	12 18		11 55	12 33	12 48		12 25	13 03		13 18	
Leigh-on-Sea d			10 28	11 06	11 21		10 58	11 36	11 51		11 28		12 06	12 21		11 58	12 36	12 51		12 28	13 06		13 21	
Benfleet d			10 32	11 10	11 25		11 02	11 40	11 55		11 32		12 10	12 25		12 02	12 40	12 55		12 32	13 10		13 25	
Pitsea d			10 36		11 29		11 06		11 59		11 36			12 29		12 06		12 59		12 36			13 29	
Stanford-le-Hope d			10 42				11 12				11 42					12 12				12 42				
East Tilbury d			10 45				11 15				11 45					12 15				12 45				
Tilbury Town d			10 51				11 21				11 51					12 21				12 51				
Grays d	10 48		10 54			11 18	11 24			11 48	11 54				12 18	12 24			12 48	12 54				13 18
Purfleet d	10 53					11 23				11 53					12 23				12 53					13 23
Rainham d	10 58					11 28				11 58					12 28				12 58					13 28
Dagenham Dock d	11 02					11 32				12 02					12 32				13 02					13 32
Basildon d				11 16	11 32			11 46	12 02				12 16	12 32			12 46	13 02			13 16		13 32	
Laindon d				11 19	11 35			11 49	12 05				12 19	12 35			12 49	13 05			13 19		13 35	
West Horndon d					11 40				12 10					12 40				13 10					13 40	
Chafford Hundred d			10 59				11 29				11 59					12 29				12 59				
Ockendon d			11 02				11 32				12 02					12 32				13 02				
Upminster ⊖ d			11 09	11 28	11 46		11 39	11 58	12 16		12 09		12 28	12 46		12 39	12 58	13 16		13 09	13 28		13 46	
Barking ⊖ d	11 08		11 17	11 36	11 54	11 38	11 47	12 06	12 24	12 08	12 17		12 36	12 54	12 38	12 47	13 06	13 24	13 08	13 17	13 36		13 54	13 38
Stratford ⊖ a																								
London Liverpool Street ⊖ a																								
West Ham ⊖ d	11 14		11 23	11 42	12 00	11 44	11 53	12 12	12 30	12 14	12 23		12 42	13 00	12 44	12 53	13 12	13 30	13 14	13 23	13 42		14 00	13 44
Limehouse d	11 19		11 28		12 05	11 49	11 58		12 35	12 19	12 28			13 05	12 49	12 58		13 35	13 19	13 28			14 05	13 49
London Fenchurch Street ⊖ a	11 26		11 34	11 53	12 12	11 56	12 04	12 23	12 42	12 26	12 34		12 53	13 12	12 56	13 04	13 23	13 42	13 26	13 34	13 53		14 12	13 56

Table I

Shoeburyness and Southend Central - London

	CC	CC	CC	CC	CC	CC	CC		CC	CC	CC	CC	CC	CC	CC	CC	CC		CC	CC	CC	CC	CC	CC
Shoeburyness d		13 20	13 35			13 50	14 05				14 20	14 35			14 50	15 05				15 20	15 35			15 50
Thorpe Bay d		13 23	13 38			13 53	14 08				14 23	14 38			14 53	15 08				15 23	15 38			15 53
Southend East d		13 26	13 41			13 56	14 11				14 26	14 41			14 56	15 11				15 26	15 41			15 56
Southend Central a		13 28	13 43			13 58	14 13				14 28	14 43			14 58	15 13				15 28	15 43			15 58
Southend Central d	12 50	13 29	13 44		13 20	13 59	14 14			13 50	14 29	14 44		14 20	14 59	15 14			14 50	15 29	15 44		15 20	15 59
Westcliff d	12 53	13 31	13 46		13 23	14 01	14 16			13 53	14 31	14 46		14 23	15 01	15 16			14 53	15 31	15 46		15 23	16 01
Chalkwell d	12 55	13 33	13 48		13 25	14 03	14 18			13 55	14 33	14 48		14 25	15 03	15 18			14 55	15 33	15 48		15 25	16 03
Leigh-on-Sea d	12 58	13 36	13 51		13 28	14 06	14 21			13 58	14 36	14 51		14 28	15 06	15 21			14 58	15 36	15 51		15 28	16 06
Benfleet d	13 02	13 40	13 55		13 32	14 10	14 25			14 02	14 40	14 55		14 32	15 10	15 25			15 02	15 40	15 55		15 32	16 10
Pitsea d	13 06		13 59		13 36		14 29			14 06		14 59		14 36		15 29			15 06		15 59		15 36	
Stanford-le-Hope d	13 12				13 42					14 12				14 42					15 12				15 42	
East Tilbury d	13 15				13 45					14 15				14 45					15 15				15 45	
Tilbury Town d	13 21				13 51					14 21				14 51					15 21				15 51	
Grays d	13 24			13 48	13 54				14 18	14 24			14 48	14 54			15 18		15 24			15 48	15 54	
Purfleet d				13 53					14 23				14 53				15 23					15 53		
Rainham d				13 58					14 28				14 58				15 28					15 58		
Dagenham Dock d				14 02					14 32				15 02				15 32					16 02		
Basildon d		13 46	14 02			14 16	14 32				14 46	15 02			15 16	15 32				15 46	16 02			16 16
Laindon d		13 49	14 05			14 19	14 35				14 49	15 05			15 19	15 35				15 49	16 05			16 19
West Horndon d			14 10				14 40					15 10				15 40					16 10			
Chafford Hundred d	13 29				13 59					14 29				14 59					15 29				15 59	
Ockendon d	13 32				14 02					14 32				15 02					15 32				16 02	
Upminster ⊖ d	13 39	13 58	14 16		14 09	14 28	14 46			14 39	14 58	15 16		15 09	15 28	15 46			15 39	15 58	16 16		16 09	16 28
Barking ⊖ d	13 47	14 06	14 24	14 08	14 17	14 36	14 54		14 38	14 47	15 06	15 24	15 08	15 17	15 36	15 54	15 38		15 47	16 06	16 24	16 08	16 17	16 36
Stratford ⊖ a																								
London Liverpool Street ⊖ a																								
West Ham ⊖ d	13 53	14 12	14 30	14 14	14 23	14 42	15 00		14 44	14 53	15 12	15 30	15 14	15 23	15 42	16 00	15 44		15 53	16 12	16 30	16 14	16 23	16 42
Limehouse d	13 58		14 35	14 19	14 28		15 05		14 49	14 58		15 35	15 19	15 28		16 05	15 49		15 58		16 35	16 19	16 28	
London Fenchurch Street ⊖ a	14 04	14 23	14 42	14 26	14 34	14 53	15 12		14 56	15 04	15 23	15 42	15 26	15 34	15 53	16 12	15 56		16 04	16 23	16 42	16 26	16 34	16 53

	CC	CC	CC		CC	CC	CC	CC	CC	CC	CC	CC	CC		CC	CC	CC	CC	CC	CC	CC	CC	CC	
Shoeburyness d	16 05				16 20	16 35			16 50	17 05			17 20		17 35			17 50	18 05			18 20	18 35	
Thorpe Bay d	16 08				16 23	16 38			16 53	17 08			17 23		17 38			17 53	18 08			18 23	18 38	
Southend East d	16 11				16 26	16 41			16 56	17 11			17 26		17 41			17 56	18 11			18 26	18 41	
Southend Central a	16 13				16 28	16 43			16 58	17 13			17 28		17 43			17 58	18 13			18 28	18 43	
Southend Central d	16 14		15 50		16 29	16 44		16 20	16 59	17 14		16 50	17 29		17 44		17 20	17 59	18 14		17 50	18 29	18 44	
Westcliff d	16 16		15 53		16 31	16 46		16 23	17 01	17 16		16 53	17 31		17 46		17 23	18 01	18 16		17 53	18 31	18 46	
Chalkwell d	16 18		15 55		16 33	16 48		16 25	17 03	17 18		16 55	17 33		17 48		17 25	18 03	18 18		17 55	18 33	18 48	
Leigh-on-Sea d	16 21		15 58		16 36	16 51		16 28	17 06	17 21		16 58	17 36		17 51		17 28	18 06	18 21		17 58	18 36	18 51	
Benfleet d	16 25		16 02		16 40	16 55		16 32	17 10	17 25		17 02	17 40		17 55		17 32	18 10	18 25		18 02	18 40	18 55	
Pitsea d	16 29		16 06			16 59		16 36		17 29		17 06			17 59		17 36		18 29		18 06		18 59	
Stanford-le-Hope d			16 12					16 42				17 12					17 42				18 12			
East Tilbury d			16 15					16 45				17 15					17 45				18 15			
Tilbury Town d			16 21					16 51				17 21					17 51				18 21			
Grays d		16 18	16 24				16 48	16 54			17 18	17 24				17 48	17 54			18 18	18 24			
Purfleet d		16 23					16 53				17 23					17 53				18 23				
Rainham d		16 28					16 58				17 28					17 58				18 28				
Dagenham Dock d		16 32					17 02				17 32					18 02				18 32				
Basildon d	16 32				16 46	17 02			17 16	17 32			17 46		18 02			18 16	18 32			18 46	19 02	
Laindon d	16 35				16 49	17 05			17 19	17 35			17 49		18 05			18 19	18 35			18 49	19 05	
West Horndon d	16 40					17 10				17 40					18 10				18 40				19 10	
Chafford Hundred d			16 29					16 59				17 29					17 59				18 29			
Ockendon d			16 32					17 02				17 32					18 02				18 32			
Upminster ⊖ d	16 46		16 39		16 58	17 16		17 09	17 28	17 46		17 39	17 58		18 16		18 09	18 28	18 46		18 39	18 58	19 16	
Barking ⊖ d	16 54	16 38	16 47		17 06	17 24	17 08	17 17	17 36	17 54	17 38	17 47	18 06		18 24	18 08	18 17	18 36	18 54	18 38	18 47	19 06	19 24	
Stratford ⊖ a																								
London Liverpool Street ⊖ a																								
West Ham ⊖ d	17 00	16 44	16 53		17 12	17 30	17 14	17 23	17 42	18 00	17 44	17 53	18 12		18 30	18 14	18 23	18 42	19 00	18 44	18 53	19 12	19 30	
Limehouse d	17 05	16 49	16 58			17 35	17 19	17 28		18 05	17 49	17 58			18 35	18 19	18 28		19 05	18 49	18 58		19 35	
London Fenchurch Street ⊖ a	17 12	16 56	17 04		17 23	17 42	17 26	17 34	17 53	18 12	17 56	18 04	18 23		18 42	18 26	18 34	18 53	19 12	18 56	19 04	19 23	19 42	

	CC	CC	CC	CC	CC	CC	CC	CC	CC		CC	CC	CC	CC	CC	CC	CC	CC	CC		CC	CC	CC	CC
Shoeburyness d			18 50	19 05			19 20	19 35				19 50	20 05			20 35			20 50		21 05			21 35
Thorpe Bay d			18 53	19 08			19 23	19 38				19 53	20 08			20 38			20 53		21 08			21 38
Southend East d			18 56	19 11			19 26	19 41				19 56	20 11			20 41			20 56		21 11			21 41
Southend Central a			18 58	19 13			19 28	19 43				19 58	20 13			20 43			20 58		21 13			21 43
Southend Central d		18 20	18 59	19 14		18 50	19 29	19 44			19 20	19 59	20 14		19 50	20 44		20 20	20 59		21 14		20 50	21 44
Westcliff d		18 23	19 01	19 16		18 53	19 31	19 46			19 23	20 01	20 16		19 53	20 46		20 23	21 01		21 16		20 53	21 46
Chalkwell d		18 25	19 03	19 18		18 55	19 33	19 48			19 25	20 03	20 18		19 55	20 48		20 25	21 03		21 18		20 55	21 48
Leigh-on-Sea d		18 28	19 06	19 21		18 58	19 36	19 51			19 28	20 06	20 21		19 58	20 51		20 28	21 06		21 21		20 58	21 51
Benfleet d		18 32	19 10	19 25		19 02	19 40	19 55			19 32	20 10	20 25		20 02	20 55		20 32	21 10		21 25		21 02	21 55
Pitsea d		18 36		19 29		19 06		19 59			19 36		20 29		20 06	20 59		20 36			21 29		21 06	21 59
Stanford-le-Hope d		18 42				19 12					19 42				20 12			20 42					21 12	
East Tilbury d		18 45				19 15					19 45				20 15			20 45					21 15	
Tilbury Town d		18 51				19 21					19 51				20 21			20 51					21 21	
Grays d	18 48	18 54			19 18	19 24			19 48		19 54			20 18	20 24		20 48	20 54				21 18	21 24	
Purfleet d	18 53				19 23				19 53					20 23			20 53					21 23		
Rainham d	18 58				19 28				19 58					20 28			20 58					21 28		
Dagenham Dock d	19 02				19 32				20 02					20 32			21 02					21 32		
Basildon d			19 16	19 32			19 46	20 02				20 16	20 32			21 02			21 16		21 32			22 02
Laindon d			19 19	19 35			19 49	20 05				20 19	20 35			21 05			21 19		21 35			22 05
West Horndon d				19 40				20 10					20 40			21 10					21 40			22 10
Chafford Hundred d		18 59				19 29					19 59				20 29			20 59					21 29	
Ockendon d		19 02				19 32					20 02				20 32			21 02					21 32	
Upminster ⊖ d		19 09	19 28	19 46		19 39	19 58	20 16			20 09	20 28	20 46		20 39	21 16		21 09	21 28		21 46		21 39	22 16
Barking ⊖ d	19 08	19 17	19 36	19 54	19 38	19 47	20 06	20 24	20 08		20 17	20 36	20 54	20 38	20 47	21 24	21 08	21 17	21 36		21 54	21 38	21 47	22 24
Stratford ⊖ a																								
London Liverpool Street ⊖ a																								
West Ham ⊖ d	19 14	19 23	19 42	20 00	19 44	19 53	20 12	20 30	20 14		20 23	20 42	21 00	20 44	20 53	21 30	21 14	21 23	21 42		22 00	21 44	21 53	22 30
Limehouse d	19 19	19 28		20 05	19 49	19 58		20 35	20 19		20 28		21 05	20 49	20 58	21 35	21 19	21 28			22 05	21 49	21 58	22 35
London Fenchurch Street ⊖ a	19 26	19 34	19 53	20 12	19 56	20 04	20 23	20 42	20 26		20 34	20 53	21 12	20 56	21 04	21 42	21 26	21 34	21 53		22 12	21 56	22 04	22 42

Table I

Shoeburyness and Southend Central - London

Saturdays

		CC	CC	CC	CC	CC		CC	CC	CC	CC	CC	CC	CC
Shoeburyness	d			22 05				22 35			23 05			
Thorpe Bay	d			22 08				22 38			23 08			
Southend East	d			22 11				22 41			23 11			
Southend Central	a			22 13				22 43			23 13			
	d		21 20	22 14		21 50		22 44		22 20	23 14		22 50	23 20
Westcliff	d		21 23	22 16		21 53		22 46		22 23	23 16		22 53	23 23
Chalkwell	d		21 25	22 18		21 55		22 48		22 25	23 18		22 55	23 25
Leigh-on-Sea	d		21 28	22 21		21 58		22 51		22 28	23 21		22 58	23 28
Benfleet	d		21 32	22 25		22 02		22 55		22 32	23 25		23 02	23 32
Pitsea	d		21 36	22 29		22 06		22 59		22 36	23 29		23 06	23 36
Stanford-le-Hope	d		21 42			22 12				22 42			23 12	23 42
East Tilbury	d		21 45			22 15				22 45			23 15	23 45
Tilbury Town 3	d		21 51			22 21				22 51			23 21	23 51
Grays	d	21 48	21 54		22 18	22 24			22 48	22 54		23 18	23 24	23 54
Purfleet	d	21 53			22 23				22 53			23 23		
Rainham	d	21 58			22 28				22 58			23 28		
Dagenham Dock	d	22 02			22 32				23 02			23 32		
Basildon	d			22 32				23 02			23 32			
Laindon	d			22 35				23 05			23 35			
West Horndon	d			22 40				23 10			23 40			
Chafford Hundred	d		21 59			22 29				22 59			23 29	23 59
Ockendon	d		22 02			22 32				23 02			23 32	00 02
Upminster ⊖	d		22 09	22 46		22 39		23 16		23 09	23 46		23 39	00 08
Barking ⊖	d	22 08	22 17	22 54	22 38	22 47		23 24	23 08	23 17	23 55	23a39	23 47	00a18
Stratford 7 ⊖	a													
London Liverpool Street 15 ⊖	a													
West Ham ⊖	d	22 14	22 23	23 00	22 44	22 53		23 30	23 14	23 23	00 01		23 53	
Limehouse	d	22 19	22 28	23 05	22 49	22 58		23 35	23 19	23 28	00 06		23 58	
London Fenchurch Street 7 ⊖	a	22 26	22 34	23 12	22 56	23 04		23 42	23 26	23 34	00 12		00 04	

Sundays

		CC	CC	CC	CC	CC	CC	CC	CC	CC		CC	CC	CC	CC	CC	CC	CC	CC	CC		CC	CC	CC	CC
Shoeburyness	d		23p05		05 35	06 05	06 11	06 35	07 05	07 11		07 35	08 05		08 35			09 05		09 35				10 05	
Thorpe Bay	d		23p08		05 38	06 08	06 14	06 38	07 08	07 14		07 38	08 08		08 38			09 08		09 38				10 08	
Southend East	d		23p11		05 41	06 11	06 17	06 41	07 11	07 17		07 41	08 11		08 41			09 11		09 41				10 11	
Southend Central	a		23p13		05 43	06 13	06 19	06 43	07 13	07 19		07 43	08 13		08 43			09 13		09 43				10 13	
	d	22p50	23p14	23p20	05 44	06 14	06 20	06 44	07 14	07 20		07 44	08 14	08 20	08 44		08 50	09 14	09 20	09 44			09 50	10 14	10 20
Westcliff	d	22p53	23p16	23p23	05 46	06 16	06 23	06 46	07 16	07 23		07 46	08 16	08 23	08 46		08 53	09 16	09 23	09 46			09 53	10 16	10 23
Chalkwell	d	22p55	23p18	23p25	05 48	06 18	06 25	06 48	07 18	07 25		07 48	08 18	08 25	08 48		08 55	09 18	09 25	09 48			09 55	10 18	10 25
Leigh-on-Sea	d	22p58	23p21	23p28	05 51	06 21	06 28	06 51	07 21	07 28		07 51	08 21	08 28	08 51		08 58	09 21	09 28	09 51			09 58	10 21	10 28
Benfleet	d	23p02	23p25	23p32	05 55	06 25	06 32	06 55	07 25	07 32		07 55	08 25	08 32	08 55		09 02	09 25	09 32	09 55			10 02	10 25	10 32
Pitsea	d	23p06	23p29	23p36	05 59	06 29	06 36	06 59	07 29	07 36		07 59	08 29	08 36	08 59		09 06	09 29	09 36	09 59			10 06	10 29	10 36
Stanford-le-Hope	d	23p12		23p42			06 42			07 42				08 42			09 12		09 42				10 12		10 42
East Tilbury	d	23p15		23p45			06 45			07 45				08 45			09 15		09 45				10 15		10 45
Tilbury Town 3	d	23p21		23p51			06 51			07 51				08 51			09 21		09 51				10 21		10 51
Grays	d	23p24		23p54			06 54			07 54				08 54		08 59	09 24		09 54			09 59	10 24		10 54
Purfleet	d															09 04						10 04			
Rainham	d															09 09						10 09			
Dagenham Dock	d															09 13						10 13			
Basildon	d		23p32		06 02	06 32		07 02	07 32			08 02	08 32		09 02			09 32		10 02				10 32	
Laindon	d		23p35		06 05	06 35		07 05	07 35			08 05	08 35		09 05			09 35		10 05				10 35	
West Horndon	d		23p40		06 10	06 40		07 10	07 40			08 10	08 40		09 10			09 40		10 10				10 40	
Chafford Hundred	d	23p29		23p59			06 59			07 59				08 59			09 29		09 59				10 29		10 59
Ockendon	d	23p32		00 02			07 02			08 02				09 02			09 32		10 02				10 32		11 02
Upminster ⊖	d	23p39	23p46	00 08	06 16	06 46	07 09	07 16	07 46	08 09		08 16	08 46	09 09	09 16		09 39	09 46	10 09	10 16			10 39	10 46	11 09
Barking ⊖	d	23p47	23p55	00a18	06 25	06 55	07 17	07 25	07 55	08 17		08 25	08 55	09 17	09 25	09a20	09 47	09 55	10 17	10 25		10a20	10 47	10 55	11 17
Stratford 7 ⊖	a																								
London Liverpool Street 15 ⊖	a																								
West Ham ⊖	d	23p53	00 01		06 31	07 01	07 23	07 31	08 01	08 23		08 31	09 01	09 23	09 31		09 53	10 01	10 23	10 31			10 53	11 01	11 23
Limehouse	d	23p58	00 06		06 36	07 06	07 28	07 36	08 06	08 28		08 36	09 06	09 28	09 36		09 58	10 06	10 28	10 36			10 58	11 06	11 28
London Fenchurch Street 7 ⊖	a	00 04	00 12		06 42	07 12	07 34	07 42	08 12	08 34		08 42	09 12	09 34	09 42		10 04	10 12	10 34	10 42			11 04	11 12	11 34

Table I

Shoeburyness and Southend Central - London

Sundays

		CC	CC	CC	CC	CC		CC	CC	CC	CC	CC	CC	CC	CC	CC		CC	CC	CC	CC	CC	CC	CC	CC
Shoeburyness	d	10 35			11 05			11 35			12 05		12 35			13 05			13 35			14 05		14 35	
Thorpe Bay	d	10 38			11 08			11 38			12 08		12 38			13 08			13 38			14 08		14 38	
Southend East	d	10 41			11 11			11 41			12 11		12 41			13 11			13 41			14 11		14 41	
Southend Central	a	10 43			11 13			11 43			12 13		12 43			13 13			13 43			14 13		14 43	
	d	10 44		10 50	11 14	11 20		11 44		11 50	12 14	12 20	12 44		12 50	13 14		13 20	13 44		13 50	14 14	14 20	14 44	
Westcliff	d	10 46		10 53	11 16	11 23		11 46		11 53	12 16	12 23	12 46		12 53	13 16		13 23	13 46		13 53	14 16	14 23	14 46	
Chalkwell	d	10 48		10 55	11 18	11 25		11 48		11 55	12 18	12 25	12 48		12 55	13 18		13 25	13 48		13 55	14 18	14 25	14 48	
Leigh-on-Sea	d	10 51		10 58	11 21	11 28		11 51		11 58	12 21	12 28	12 51		12 58	13 21		13 28	13 51		13 58	14 21	14 28	14 51	
Benfleet	d	10 55		11 02	11 25	11 32		11 55		12 02	12 25	12 32	12 55		13 02	13 25		13 32	13 55		14 02	14 25	14 32	14 55	
Pitsea	d	10 59		11 06	11 29	11 36		11 59		12 06	12 29	12 36	12 59		13 06	13 29		13 36	13 59		14 06	14 29	14 36	14 59	
Stanford-le-Hope	d			11 12		11 42				12 12		12 42			13 12			13 42			14 12		14 42		
East Tilbury	d			11 15		11 45				12 15		12 45			13 15			13 45			14 15		14 45		
Tilbury Town 3	d			11 21		11 51				12 21		12 51			13 21			13 51			14 21		14 51		
Grays	d		10 59	11 24		11 54			11 59	12 24		12 54		12 59	13 24			13 54		13 59	14 24		14 54		14 59
Purfleet	d		11 04						12 04					13 04						14 04					15 04
Rainham	d		11 09						12 09					13 09						14 09					15 09
Dagenham Dock	d		11 13						12 13					13 13						14 13					15 13
Basildon	d	11 02			11 32			12 02			12 32		13 02			13 32			14 02			14 32		15 02	
Laindon	d	11 05			11 35			12 05			12 35		13 05			13 35			14 05			14 35		15 05	
West Horndon	d	11 10			11 40			12 10			12 40		13 10			13 40			14 10			14 40		15 10	
Chafford Hundred	d			11 29		11 59				12 29		12 59			13 29			13 59			14 29		14 59		
Ockendon	d			11 32		12 02				12 32		13 02			13 32			14 02			14 32		15 02		
Upminster ⊖	d	11 16		11 39	11 46	12 09		12 16		12 39	12 46	13 09	13 16		13 39	13 46		14 09	14 16		14 39	14 46	15 09	15 16	
Barking ⊖	d	11 25	11a20	11 47	11 55	12 17		12 25	12a20	12 47	12 55	13 17	13 25	13a20	13 47	13 55		14 17	14 25	14a20	14 47	14 55	15 17	15 25	15a20
Stratford 7 ⊖	a																								
London Liverpool Street 15 ⊖	a																								
West Ham ⊖	d	11 31		11 53	12 01	12 23		12 31		12 53	13 01	13 23	13 31		13 53	14 01		14 23	14 31		14 53	15 01	15 23	15 31	
Limehouse	d	11 36		11 58	12 06	12 28		12 36		12 58	13 06	13 28	13 36		13 58	14 06		14 28	14 36		14 58	15 06	15 28	15 36	
London Fenchurch Street 7 ⊖	a	11 42		12 04	12 12	12 34		12 42		13 04	13 12	13 34	13 42		14 04	14 12		14 34	14 42		15 04	15 12	15 34	15 42	

		CC		CC	CC	CC	CC	CC	CC	CC	CC	CC		CC	CC	CC	CC	CC	CC	CC	CC	CC		CC	CC
Shoeburyness	d			15 05		15 35			16 05		16 35				17 05		17 35			18 05		18 35			
Thorpe Bay	d			15 08		15 38			16 08		16 38				17 08		17 38			18 08		18 38			
Southend East	d			15 11		15 41			16 11		16 41				17 11		17 41			18 11		18 41			
Southend Central	a			15 13		15 43			16 13		16 43				17 13		17 43			18 13		18 43			
	d	14 50		15 14	15 20	15 44		15 50	16 14	16 20	16 44			16 50	17 14	17 20	17 44		17 50	18 14	18 20	18 44			18 50
Westcliff	d	14 53		15 16	15 23	15 46		15 53	16 16	16 23	16 46			16 53	17 16	17 23	17 46		17 53	18 16	18 23	18 46			18 53
Chalkwell	d	14 55		15 18	15 25	15 48		15 55	16 18	16 25	16 48			16 55	17 18	17 25	17 48		17 55	18 18	18 25	18 48			18 55
Leigh-on-Sea	d	14 58		15 21	15 28	15 51		15 58	16 21	16 28	16 51			16 58	17 21	17 28	17 51		17 58	18 21	18 28	18 51			18 58
Benfleet	d	15 02		15 25	15 32	15 55		16 02	16 25	16 32	16 55			17 02	17 25	17 32	17 55		18 02	18 25	18 32	18 55			19 02
Pitsea	d	15 06		15 29	15 36	15 59		16 06	16 29	16 36	16 59			17 06	17 29	17 36	17 59		18 06	18 29	18 36	18 59			19 06
Stanford-le-Hope	d	15 12			15 42			16 12		16 42				17 12		17 42			18 12		18 42				19 12
East Tilbury	d	15 15			15 45			16 15		16 45				17 15		17 45			18 15		18 45				19 15
Tilbury Town 3	d	15 21			15 51			16 21		16 51				17 21		17 51			18 21		18 51				19 21
Grays	d	15 24			15 54		15 59	16 24		16 54		16 59		17 24		17 54		17 59	18 24		18 54			18 59	19 24
Purfleet	d						16 04					17 04						18 04						19 04	
Rainham	d						16 09					17 09						18 09						19 09	
Dagenham Dock	d						16 13					17 13						18 13						19 13	
Basildon	d			15 32		16 02			16 32		17 02				17 32		18 02			18 32		19 02			
Laindon	d			15 35		16 05			16 35		17 05				17 35		18 05			18 35		19 05			
West Horndon	d			15 40		16 10			16 40		17 10				17 40		18 10			18 40		19 10			
Chafford Hundred	d	15 29			15 59			16 29		16 59				17 29		17 59			18 29		18 59				19 29
Ockendon	d	15 32			16 02			16 32		17 02				17 32		18 02			18 32		19 02				19 32
Upminster ⊖	d	15 39		15 46	16 09	16 16		16 39	16 46	17 09	17 16			17 39	17 46	18 09	18 16		18 39	18 46	19 09	19 16			19 39
Barking ⊖	d	15 47		15 55	16 17	16 25	16a20	16 47	16 55	17 17	17 25	17a20		17 47	17 55	18 17	18 25	18a20	18 47	18 55	19 17	19 25		19a20	19 47
Stratford 7 ⊖	a																								
London Liverpool Street 15 ⊖	a																								
West Ham ⊖	d	15 53		16 01	16 23	16 31		16 53	17 01	17 23	17 31			17 53	18 01	18 23	18 31		18 53	19 01	19 23	19 31			19 53
Limehouse	d	15 58		16 06	16 28	16 36		16 58	17 06	17 28	17 36			17 58	18 06	18 28	18 36		18 58	19 06	19 28	19 36			19 58
London Fenchurch Street 7 ⊖	a	16 04		16 12	16 34	16 42		17 04	17 12	17 34	17 42			18 04	18 12	18 34	18 42		19 04	19 12	19 34	19 42			20 04

		CC	CC	CC	CC	CC	CC	CC		CC	CC	CC	CC	CC	CC	CC	CC	CC		CC
Shoeburyness	d	19 05		19 35			20 05			20 35			21 05		21 35		22 05			22 35
Thorpe Bay	d	19 08		19 38			20 08			20 38			21 08		21 38		22 08			22 38
Southend East	d	19 11		19 41			20 11			20 41			21 11		21 41		22 11			22 41
Southend Central	a	19 13		19 43			20 13			20 43			21 13		21 43		22 13			22 43
	d	19 14	19 20	19 44		19 50	20 14	20 20		20 44		20 50	21 14	21 20	21 44		22 14	22 20		22 44
Westcliff	d	19 16	19 23	19 46		19 53	20 16	20 23		20 46		20 53	21 16	21 23	21 46		22 16	22 23		22 46
Chalkwell	d	19 18	19 25	19 48		19 55	20 18	20 25		20 48		20 55	21 18	21 25	21 48		22 18	22 25		22 48
Leigh-on-Sea	d	19 21	19 28	19 51		19 58	20 21	20 28		20 51		20 58	21 21	21 28	21 51		22 21	22 28		22 51
Benfleet	d	19 25	19 32	19 55		20 02	20 25	20 32		20 55		21 02	21 25	21 32	21 55		22 25	22 32		22 55
Pitsea	d	19 29	19 36	19 59		20 06	20 29	20 36		20 59		21 06	21 29	21 36	21 59		22 29	22 36		22 59
Stanford-le-Hope	d		19 42			20 12		20 42				21 12		21 42				22 42		
East Tilbury	d		19 45			20 15		20 45				21 15		21 45				22 45		
Tilbury Town 3	d		19 51			20 21		20 51				21 21		21 51				22 51		
Grays	d		19 54		19 59	20 24		20 54			20 59	21 24		21 54		21 59		22 54		
Purfleet	d				20 04						21 04					22 04				
Rainham	d				20 09						21 09					22 09				
Dagenham Dock	d				20 13						21 13					22 13				
Basildon	d	19 32		20 02			20 32			21 02			21 32		22 02		22 32			23 02
Laindon	d	19 35		20 05			20 35			21 05			21 35		22 05		22 35			23 05
West Horndon	d	19 40		20 10			20 40			21 10			21 40		22 10		22 40			23 10
Chafford Hundred	d		19 59			20 29		20 59				21 29		21 59				22 59		
Ockendon	d		20 02			20 32		21 02				21 32		22 02				23 02		
Upminster ⊖	d	19 46	20 09	20 16		20 39	20 46	21 09		21 16		21 39	21 46	22 09	22 16		22 46	23 09		23 16
Barking ⊖	d	19 55	20 17	20 25	20a20	20 47	20 55	21 17		21 25	21a20	21 47	21 55	22 17	22 25	22a20	22 55	23 17		23 25
Stratford 7 ⊖	a																			
London Liverpool Street 15 ⊖	a																			
West Ham ⊖	d	20 01	20 23	20 31		20 53	21 01	21 23		21 31		21 53	22 01	22 23	22 31		23 01	23 23		23 31
Limehouse	d	20 06	20 28	20 36		20 58	21 06	21 28		21 36		21 58	22 06	22 28	22 36		23 06	23 28		23 36
London Fenchurch Street 7 ⊖	a	20 12	20 34	20 42		21 04	21 12	21 34		21 42		22 04	22 12	22 34	22 42		23 12	23 34		23 42

Tilbury Town - Tilbury Riverside

Bus Service

		CC	CC	CC	CC	CC	CC	CC	CC	CC		CC	CC	CC	CC	CC	CC	CC	CC	CC		CC	CC	CC	CC
Tilbury Town ■	d	05 40	06 18	06 50	07 18	07 45	08 13	08 38	09 03	09 33		10 03	10 33	11 03	11 33	12 03	12 33	13 03	13 33	14 03		14 33	15 03	15 33	16 03
Tilbury Riverside	a	05 47	06 25	06 57	07 25	07 52	08 20	08 45	09 10	09 40		10 10	10 40	11 10	11 40	12 10	12 40	13 10	13 40	14 10		14 40	15 10	15 40	16 10

		CC	CC	CC	CC	CC		CC
Tilbury Town ■	d	16 33	17 03	17 33	18 00	18 30		19 00
Tilbury Riverside	a	16 40	17 10	17 40	18 07	18 37		19 07

Saturdays

		CC	CC	CC	CC	CC	CC	CC	CC	CC		CC	CC	CC	CC	CC	CC	CC	CC	CC		CC	CC	CC	CC
Tilbury Town ■	d	05 40	06 15	07 01	07 31	08 01	08 31	09 01	09 31	10 01		10 31	11 01	11 31	12 01	12 31	13 01	13 31	14 01	14 31		15 01	15 31	16 01	16 31
Tilbury Riverside	a	05 47	06 22	07 08	07 38	08 08	08 38	09 08	09 38	10 08		10 38	11 08	11 38	12 08	12 38	13 08	13 38	14 08	14 38		15 08	15 38	16 08	16 38

		CC	CC	CC	CC	CC
Tilbury Town ■	d	17 01	17 31	18 01	18 31	19 01
Tilbury Riverside	a	17 08	17 38	18 08	18 38	19 08

No Sunday Service

Tilbury Riverside - Tilbury Town

Bus Service

		CC	CC	CC	CC	CC	CC	CC	CC	CC		CC	CC	CC	CC	CC	CC	CC	CC	CC		CC	CC	CC	CC
Tilbury Riverside	d	05 50	06 30	07 00	07 30	07 55	08 23	08 50	09 12	09 42		10 12	10 42	11 12	11 42	12 12	12 42	13 12	13 42	14 12		14 42	15 12	15 42	16 12
Tilbury Town ■	a	05 57	06 37	07 07	07 37	08 02	08 30	08 57	09 19	09 49		10 19	10 49	11 19	11 49	12 19	12 49	13 19	13 49	14 19		14 49	15 19	15 49	16 19

		CC	CC	CC	CC	CC		CC
Tilbury Riverside	d	16 40	17 15	17 45	18 15	18 40		19 10
Tilbury Town ■	a	16 47	17 22	17 52	18 22	18 47		19 17

Saturdays

		CC	CC	CC	CC	CC	CC	CC	CC	CC		CC	CC	CC	CC	CC	CC	CC	CC	CC		CC	CC	CC	CC
Tilbury Riverside	d	05 50	06 30	07 10	07 50	08 09	08 39	09 09	09 39	10 09		10 39	11 09	11 39	12 09	12 39	13 09	13 39	14 09	14 39		15 09	15 39	16 09	16 39
Tilbury Town ■	a	05 57	06 37	07 17	07 57	08 16	08 46	09 16	09 46	10 16		10 46	11 16	11 46	12 16	12 46	13 16	13 46	14 16	14 46		15 16	15 46	16 16	16 46

		CC	CC	CC	CC	CC
Tilbury Riverside	d	17 09	17 39	18 09	18 39	19 09
Tilbury Town ■	a	17 16	17 46	18 16	18 46	19 16

Table 4

Mondays to Fridays

Romford - Upminster

		LE	LE	LE	LE	LE	LE	LE	LE	LE	LE	LE	LE	LE	LE	LE	LE	LE	LE	LE	LE	LE	LE
Romford	d	06 12	06 42	07 06	07 30	07 54	08 18	08 42	09 12	09 42	10 12	10 42	11 12	11 42	12 12	12 42	13 12	13 42	14 12	14 42	15 12	15 42	16 12
Emerson Park	d	06 16	06 46	07 10	07 34	07 58	08 22	08 46	09 16	09 46	10 16	10 46	11 16	11 46	12 16	12 46	13 16	13 46	14 16	14 46	15 16	15 46	16 16
UPMINSTER ⊖	a	06 20	06 50	07 14	07 38	08 02	08 26	08 50	09 20	09 50	10 20	10 50	11 20	11 50	12 20	12 50	13 20	13 50	14 20	14 50	15 20	15 50	16 20

		LE	LE	LE	LE	LE		LE	LE
Romford	d	16 42	17 12	17 42	18 12	18 42		19 12	19 42
Emerson Park	d	16 46	17 16	17 46	18 16	18 46		19 16	19 46
UPMINSTER ⊖	a	16 50	17 20	17 50	18 20	18 50		19 20	19 50

Saturdays

		LE	LE	LE	LE	LE	LE	LE	LE	LE	LE	LE	LE	LE	LE	LE	LE	LE	LE	LE	LE	LE	LE
Romford	d	06 12	06 42	07 12	07 42	08 12	08 42	09 12	09 42	10 12	10 42	11 12	11 42	12 12	12 42	13 12	13 42	14 12	14 42	15 12	15 42	16 12	16 42
Emerson Park	d	06 16	06 46	07 16	07 46	08 16	08 46	09 16	09 46	10 16	10 46	11 16	11 46	12 16	12 46	13 16	13 46	14 16	14 46	15 16	15 46	16 16	16 46
UPMINSTER ⊖	a	06 20	06 50	07 20	07 50	08 20	08 50	09 20	09 50	10 20	10 50	11 20	11 50	12 20	12 50	13 20	13 50	14 20	14 50	15 20	15 50	16 20	16 50

		LE	LE	LE	LE	LE		LE
Romford	d	17 12	17 42	18 12	18 42	19 12		19 42
Emerson Park	d	17 16	17 46	18 16	18 46	19 16		19 46
UPMINSTER ⊖	a	17 20	17 50	18 20	18 50	19 20		19 50

No Sunday Service

Table 4

Mondays to Fridays

Upminster - Romford

		LE	LE	LE	LE	LE	LE	LE	LE	LE	LE	LE	LE	LE	LE	LE	LE	LE	LE	LE	LE	LE	LE
UPMINSTER ⊖	d	06 24	06 54	07 18	07 42	08 06	08 30	08 54	09 24	09 54	10 24	10 54	11 24	11 54	12 24	12 54	13 24	13 54	14 24	14 54	15 24	15 54	16 24
Emerson Park	d	06 28	06 58	07 22	07 46	08 10	08 34	08 58	09 28	09 58	10 28	10 58	11 28	11 58	12 28	12 58	13 28	13 58	14 28	14 58	15 28	15 58	16 28
Romford	a	06 32	07 02	07 26	07 50	08 14	08 38	09 02	09 32	10 02	10 32	11 02	11 32	12 02	12 32	13 02	13 32	14 02	14 32	15 02	15 32	16 02	16 32

		LE	LE	LE	LE	LE		LE	LE
UPMINSTER ⊖	d	16 54	17 24	17 54	18 24	18 54		19 24	19 54
Emerson Park	d	16 58	17 28	17 58	18 28	18 58		19 28	19 58
Romford	a	17 02	17 32	18 02	18 32	19 02		19 32	20 02

Saturdays

		LE	LE	LE	LE	LE	LE	LE	LE	LE	LE	LE	LE	LE	LE	LE	LE	LE	LE	LE	LE	LE	LE
UPMINSTER ⊖	d	06 24	06 54	07 24	07 54	08 24	08 54	09 24	09 54	10 24	10 54	11 24	11 54	12 24	12 54	13 24	13 54	14 24	14 54	15 24	15 54	16 24	16 54
Emerson Park	d	06 28	06 58	07 28	07 58	08 28	08 58	09 28	09 58	10 28	10 58	11 28	11 58	12 28	12 58	13 28	13 58	14 28	14 58	15 28	15 58	16 28	16 58
Romford	a	06 32	07 02	07 32	08 02	08 32	09 02	09 32	10 02	10 32	11 02	11 32	12 02	12 32	13 02	13 32	14 02	14 32	15 02	15 32	16 02	16 32	17 02

		LE	LE	LE	LE	LE		LE
UPMINSTER ⊖	d	17 24	17 54	18 24	18 54	19 24		19 54
Emerson Park	d	17 28	17 58	18 28	18 58	19 28		19 58
Romford	a	17 32	18 02	18 32	19 02	19 32		20 02

No Sunday Service

Network Diagram for Tables 5, 10, 11

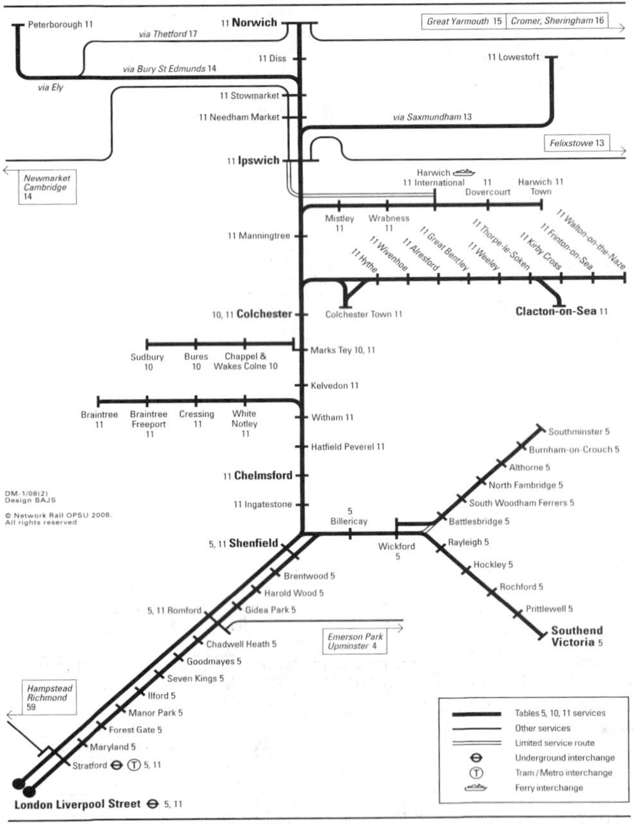

London - Shenfield, Southminster and Southend Victoria

Station		LE MX ■	LE MO ■	LE MX	LE MO ■	LE MO	LE MX	LE MX ■	LE MO ■	LE MX ■	LE MX	LE MO ■	LE MO	LE MX ■	LE MO ■	LE MX ■	LE MX	LE MX	LE MO	LE MO ■	LE MX ■	LE MX ■	LE	LE ■	LE ■
London Liverpool Street ■ ⊖	d	23p15	23p15	23p20	23p32	23p35	23p35	23p45	23p45	23p48	23p50	00 02	00 05	00 15	00 15	00 18	00 20	00 32	00 35	00 45	00 46	00 50	00 55		05 23
Stratford ■ ⊖	d	23p22	23p22	23p27	23p39	23p42	23p42	23p52	23p52	23p55	23p57	00 09	00 12	00 22	00 22	00 25	00 27	00 39	00 42	00 52	00 55	00 57	01 02		05 30
Maryland	d			23p29		23p43	23p44				23p59		00 13				00 29	00 41	00 43				01 04		
Forest Gate	d			23p31		23p45	23p46				00 01		00 15				00 31	00 43	00 45				01 06		
Manor Park	d			23p33		23p47	23p48				00 03		00 17				00 33	00 45	00 47				01 08		
Ilford ■	d			23p36		23p50	23p51				00 06		00 20				00 36	00 48	00 50				01 11		
Seven Kings	d			23p38		23p53	23p53				00 08		00 23				00 38	00 50	00 53				01 13		
Goodmayes	d			23p40		23p55	23p55				00 10		00 25				00 40	00 52	00 55				01 15		
Chadwell Heath	d			23p42		23p57	23p57				00 12		00 27				00 42	00 54	00 57				01 17		
Romford	d		23p33	23p46		23p59	00 01		00 03		00 16		00 30	00 32	00 33		00 46	00 58	01 00	01 03		01 08	01 21		05 38
Gidea Park ■	d		23p37	23p50		00 04	00 05		00 07		00 20		00a36		00 37		00 50	01a02	01a06	01 07	01 07		01 25		
Harold Wood	d		23p40	23p53		00 07	00 08		00 10		00 23				00 40		00 53			01 10			01 28		
Brentwood	d		23p44	23p57		00 11	00 12		00 14		00 27				00 44		00 57			01 14			01 32		
Shenfield ■	a	23p40	23p50	00 03	00 01	00 18	00 18	00 10	00 20	00 12	00 33	00 30		00 44	00 50	00 47	01 03			01 20	01 17	01 20	01 38		05 48
	d	23p40	23p50		00 01			00 10	00 20	00 12		00 31		00 45	00 50	00 47				01 20	01 17	01 20			05 49
Billericay	d	23p46	23p56					00 16	00 26					00 51	00 56					01 26		01 26			
Wickford ■	d	23p52	00 01					00 22	00 31					00 56	01 01					01 31		01 31		05 20	
Battlesbridge	d																							05 24	
South Woodham Ferrers	d																							05 28	
North Fambridge	d																							05b45	
Althorne	d																							05 50	
Burnham-on-Crouch	d																							05 55	
Southminster	a																							06 00	
Rayleigh	d	23p57	00 06					00 27	00 36					01 01	01 06					01 36		01 36			
Hockley	d	00 02	00 11					00 31	00 41					01 06	01 11					01 41		01 41			
Rochford	d	00 05	00 14					00 35	00 44					01 09	01 14					01 44		01 44			
Prittlewell	d	00 08						00 38						01 13								01 48			
Southend Victoria	a	00 16	00 24					00 46	00 54					01 20	01 24					01 54		01 55			

Station		LE ■	LE	LE	LE ■		LE ■	LE	LE ■	LE ■	LE	LE ■	LE ■	LE	LE	LE ■	LE	LE ■	LE	LE	LE ■	LE	LE ■	LE ■	LE ■
London Liverpool Street ■ ⊖	d		05 28	05 37	05 52		05 55	06 00	06 02		06 10	06 12	06 15	06 20	06 30	06 34	06 40	06 48	06 50		07 08	07 10		07 15	07 18
Stratford ■ ⊖	d		05 35	05 44	06 03		06 02	06 07	06 09		06 17	06 19	06 22	06 27	06 37	06 41	06 47	06 55	06 57	07 00	07 15	07 17		07 22	07 25
Maryland	d			05 46				06 09			06 19			06 29	06 39		06 49		06 59	07 07		07 19			
Forest Gate	d			05 48				06 11			06 21			06 31	06 41		06 51		07 01	07 09		07 21			
Manor Park	d			05 50				06 13			06 23			06 33	06 43		06 53		07 03	07 11		07 23			
Ilford ■	d		05 40	05 53				06 16			06 26			06 36	06 46		06 56		07 06	07 13		07 26			
Seven Kings	d		05 42	05 55				06 18			06 28			06 38	06 48		06 58		07 08	07 16		07 28			
Goodmayes	d			05 57				06 20			06 30			06 40	06 50		07 00		07 10	07 18		07 30			
Chadwell Heath	d			05 59				06 22			06 32			06 42	06 52		07 02		07 12	07 20		07 32			
Romford	d		05 48	06 03				06 26	06 17		06 36			06 46	06 56	06 49	07 06		07 16	07 22	07 23	07 36			
Gidea Park ■	d		05 51	06 07				06 30			06 40			06 50	07 00		07 10		07 20	07 26		07 40			
Harold Wood	d		05 54	06 10				06 33			06 43			06 53	07 03		07 13		07 23	07 30		07 43			
Brentwood	d		05 59	06 14				06 37			06 47			06 57	07 07		07 17		07 27	07 33		07 47			
Shenfield ■	a		06 04	06 20			06 19	06 43	06 27		06 53	06 36	06 40	07 03	07 13	07 00	07 23	07 12	07 33	07 37	07 33	07 53		07 40	07 41
	d	05 58	06 04				06 20		06 28	06 35		06 37	06 40			07 00		07 12		07 43	07 34			07 41	07 42
Billericay	d	06 04	06 10				06 26			06 41			06 46			07 06								07 47	
Wickford ■	d	06 10	06 15				06 31			06 47			06 51			07 11							07 35	07 52	
Battlesbridge	d	06 14								06 51													07 39		
South Woodham Ferrers	d	06 18								06 55													07 43		
North Fambridge	d	06 25								07c07													07 51		
Althorne	d	06 30								07 12													07 56		
Burnham-on-Crouch	d	06 35								07 17													08 01		
Southminster	a	06 40								07 22													08 06		
Rayleigh	d		06 21				06 36						06 56			07 16								07 57	
Hockley	d		06 25				06 41						07 01			07 21								08 02	
Rochford	d		06 29				06 44						07 04			07 24								08 05	
Prittlewell	d		06 32				06 48						07 08			07 28								08 09	
Southend Victoria	a		06 36				06 51						07 11			07 31								08 14	

b arr. 0534

c arr. 0701

London - Shenfield, Southminster and Southend Victoria

		LE	LE 1	LE	LE 1	LE 1	LE	LE 1	LE	LE 1	LE	LE 1	LE 1	LE	LE 1	LE 1	LE	LE	LE 1	LE 1	LE 1	LE	LE 1	LE	LE 1
London Liverpool Street 15 ⊖	d	07 20	07 27	07 30	07 34	07 40	07 40	07 48	07 50	07 55	08 00	08 02	08 08	08 10	08 14	08 18	08 20	08 30	08 35	08 38		08 40	08 48	08 50	08 55
Stratford 7 ⊖	d	07 27		07 37	07 41	07 47	07 47	07 55	07 57	08 02	08 07		08 15	08 17	08 21	08 25	08 27	08 37	08 42			08 47	08 55	08 57	09 02
Maryland	d	07 29		07 39			07 49		07 59		08 09			08 19			08 29	08 39				08 49		08 59	
Forest Gate	d	07 31		07 41			07 51		08 01		08 11			08 21			08 31	08 41				08 51		09 01	
Manor Park	d	07 33		07 43			07 53		08 03		08 13			08 23			08 33	08 43				08 53		09 03	
Ilford 2	d	07 36		07 46			07 56		08 06		08 16			08 26			08 36	08 46				08 56		09 06	
Seven Kings	d	07 38		07 48			07 58		08 08		08 18			08 28			08 38	08 48				08 58		09 08	
Goodmayes	d	07 40		07 50			08 00		08 10		08 20			08 30			08 40	08 50				09 00		09 10	
Chadwell Heath	d	07 42		07 52			08 02		08 12		08 22			08 32			08 42	08 52				09 02		09 12	
Romford	d	07 46		07 56	07 49		08 06		08 16		08 26	08 16		08 36	08 29		08 46	08 56				09 06		09 16	
Gidea Park 2	d	07 50		08 00			08 10		08 20		08 30			08 40			08 50	09 00				09 10		09 20	
Harold Wood	d	07 53		08 03			08 13		08 23		08 33			08 43			08 53	09 03				09 13		09 23	
Brentwood	d	07 57		08 07			08 17		08 27		08 37			08 47			08 57	09 07				09 17		09 27	
Shenfield 3	a	08 03	07 50	08 13	08 00	08 06	08 23	08 12	08 33	08 19	08 43	08 26	08 31	08 53	08 40	08 41	09 03	09 13	08 59	09 02		09 23	09 12	09 33	09 19
	d		07 51		08 00	08 08		08 12		08 20		08 26	08 32		08 40	08 42			09 00	09 02	09 08		09 12		09 20
Billericay	d				08 06	08 14				08 26					08 46				09 06		09 14				09 26
Wickford 2	d				08 11	08 20				08 31					08 51				09 11		09 20				09 31
Battlesbridge	d					08 24															09 24				
South Woodham Ferrers	d					08 28															09 28				
North Fambridge	d					08 34															09 34				
Althorne	d					08 39															09 39				
Burnham-on-Crouch	d					08 44															09 44				
Southminster	a					08 49															09 49				
Rayleigh	d				08 16					08 36					08 56				09 16						09 36
Hockley	d				08 21					08 41					09 01				09 21						09 41
Rochford	d				08 24					08 44					09 04				09 24						09 44
Prittlewell	d				08 28					08 48					09 08				09 28						09 48
Southend Victoria	a				08 31					08 51					09 11				09 31						09 51

		LE	LE 1	LE	LE 1	LE 1	LE	LE	LE 1	LE	LE 1	LE 1	LE	LE 1	LE	LE 1	LE	LE 1	LE 1	LE	LE	LE 1	LE 1	LE	LE 1
London Liverpool Street 15 ⊖	d	09 00	09 08	09 10	09 15	09 18	09 20	09 30	09 34	09 40	09 40	09 48	09 50	09 55	10 00	10 08	10 10	10 15	10 18	10 20	10 30	10 34		10 40	10 48
Stratford 7 ⊖	d	09 07	09 15	09 17	09 22	09 25	09 27	09 37	09 41	09 47	09 47	09 55	09 57	10 02	10 07	10 15	10 17	10 22	10 25	10 27	10 37	10 41		10 47	10 55
Maryland	d	09 09		09 19			09 29	09 39		09 49			09 59		10 09		10 19			10 29	10 39			10 49	
Forest Gate	d	09 11		09 21			09 31	09 41		09 51			10 01		10 11		10 21			10 31	10 41			10 51	
Manor Park	d	09 13		09 23			09 33	09 43		09 53			10 03		10 13		10 23			10 33	10 43			10 53	
Ilford 2	d	09 16		09 26			09 36	09 46		09 56			10 06		10 16		10 26			10 36	10 46			10 56	
Seven Kings	d	09 18		09 28			09 38	09 48		09 58			10 08		10 18		10 28			10 38	10 48			10 58	
Goodmayes	d	09 20		09 30			09 40	09 50		10 00			10 10		10 20		10 30			10 40	10 50			11 00	
Chadwell Heath	d	09 22		09 32			09 42	09 52		10 02			10 12		10 22		10 32			10 42	10 52			11 02	
Romford	d	09 26	09 23	09 36			09 46	09 56	09 49	10 06			10 16		10 26	10 23	10 36			10 46	10 56	10 49		11 06	
Gidea Park 2	d	09 30		09 40			09 50	10 00		10 10			10 20		10 30		10 40			10 50	11 00			11 10	
Harold Wood	d	09 33		09 43			09 53	10 03		10 13			10 23		10 33		10 43			10 53	11 03			11 13	
Brentwood	d	09 37		09 47			09 57	10 07		10 17			10 27		10 37		10 47			10 57	11 07			11 17	
Shenfield 3	a	09 43	09 33	09 53	09 39	09 41	10 03	10 13	10 00	10 23	10 05	10 12	10 33	10 19	10 43	10 33	10 53	10 39	10 41	11 03	11 13	11 00		11 23	11 12
	d		09 34		09 40	09 42			10 00		10 08	10 12		10 20		10 34		10 40	10 42			11 00	11 08		11 12
Billericay	d				09 46				10 06		10 14			10 26				10 46				11 06	11 14		
Wickford 2	d				09 51				10 11		10 20			10 31				10 51				11 11	11 20		
Battlesbridge	d										10 24												11 24		
South Woodham Ferrers	d										10 28												11 28		
North Fambridge	d										10 34												11 34		
Althorne	d										10 39												11 39		
Burnham-on-Crouch	d										10 44												11 44		
Southminster	a										10 49												11 49		
Rayleigh	d				09 56				10 16					10 36				10 56				11 16			
Hockley	d				10 01				10 21					10 41				11 01				11 21			
Rochford	d				10 04				10 24					10 44				11 04				11 24			
Prittlewell	d				10 08				10 28					10 48				11 08				11 28			
Southend Victoria	a				10 11				10 31					10 51				11 11				11 31			

		LE	LE 1	LE	LE 1	LE	LE 1	LE 1	LE	LE	LE 1	LE 1	LE	LE 1	LE	LE 1	LE	LE 1	LE	LE 1	LE 1	LE	LE	LE 1	LE 1
London Liverpool Street 15 ⊖	d	10 50	10 55	11 00	11 08	11 10	11 15	11 18	11 20	11 30	11 34		11 40	11 48	11 50	11 55	12 00	12 08	12 10	12 15	12 18	12 20	12 30	12 34	
Stratford 7 ⊖	d	10 57	11 02	11 07	11 15	11 17	11 22	11 25	11 27	11 37	11 41		11 47	11 55	11 57	12 02	12 07	12 15	12 17	12 22	12 25	12 27	12 37	12 41	
Maryland	d	10 59		11 09		11 19			11 29	11 39			11 49		11 59		12 09		12 19			12 29	12 39		
Forest Gate	d	11 01		11 11		11 21			11 31	11 41			11 51		12 01		12 11		12 21			12 31	12 41		
Manor Park	d	11 03		11 13		11 23			11 33	11 43			11 53		12 03		12 13		12 23			12 33	12 43		
Ilford 2	d	11 06		11 16		11 26			11 36	11 46			11 56		12 06		12 16		12 26			12 36	12 46		
Seven Kings	d	11 08		11 18		11 28			11 38	11 48			11 58		12 08		12 18		12 28			12 38	12 48		
Goodmayes	d	11 10		11 20		11 30			11 40	11 50			12 00		12 10		12 20		12 30			12 40	12 50		
Chadwell Heath	d	11 12		11 22		11 32			11 42	11 52			12 02		12 12		12 22		12 32			12 42	12 52		
Romford	d	11 16		11 26	11 23	11 36			11 46	11 56	11 49		12 06		12 16		12 26	12 23	12 36			12 46	12 56	12 49	
Gidea Park 2	d	11 20		11 30		11 40			11 50	12 00			12 10		12 20		12 30		12 40			12 50	13 00		
Harold Wood	d	11 23		11 33		11 43			11 53	12 03			12 13		12 23		12 33		12 43			12 53	13 03		
Brentwood	d	11 27		11 37		11 47			11 57	12 07			12 17		12 27		12 37		12 47			12 57	13 07		
Shenfield 3	a	11 33	11 19	11 43	11 33	11 53	11 39	11 41	12 03	12 13	12 00		12 23	12 12	12 33	12 19	12 43	12 33	12 53	12 39	12 41	13 03	13 13	13 00	
	d		11 20		11 34		11 40	11 42			12 00	12 08		12 12		12 20		12 34		12 40	12 42			13 00	13 08
Billericay	d		11 26				11 46				12 06	12 14				12 26				12 46				13 06	13 14
Wickford 2	d		11 31				11 51				12 11	12 20				12 31				12 51				13 11	13 20
Battlesbridge	d											12 24													13 24
South Woodham Ferrers	d											12 28													13 28
North Fambridge	d											12 34													13 34
Althorne	d											12 39													13 39
Burnham-on-Crouch	d											12 44													13 44
Southminster	a											12 49													13 49
Rayleigh	d		11 36				11 56				12 16					12 36				12 56				13 16	
Hockley	d		11 41				12 01				12 21					12 41				13 01				13 21	
Rochford	d		11 44				12 04				12 24					12 44				13 04				13 24	
Prittlewell	d		11 48				12 08				12 28					12 48				13 08				13 28	
Southend Victoria	a		11 51				12 11				12 31					12 51				13 11				13 31	

London - Shenfield, Southminster and Southend Victoria

		LE	LE 1	LE	LE 1	LE	LE 1	LE	LE 1	LE 1	LE	LE	LE 1	LE 1	LE	LE 1	LE	LE 1	LE	LE 1	LE	LE 1	LE 1	LE	LE
London Liverpool Street 15 ⊖	d	12 40	12 48	12 50	12 55	13 00	13 08	13 10	13 15	13 18	13 20	13 30	13 34		13 40	13 48	13 50	13 55	14 00	14 08	14 10	14 15	14 18	14 20	14 30
Stratford 7 ⊖	d	12 47	12 55	12 57	13 02	13 07	13 15	13 17	13 22	13 25	13 27	13 37	13 41		13 47	13 55	13 57	14 02	14 07	14 15	14 17	14 22	14 25	14 27	14 37
Maryland	d	12 49		12 59		13 09		13 19			13 29	13 39			13 49		13 59		14 09		14 19			14 29	14 39
Forest Gate	d	12 51		13 01		13 11		13 21			13 31	13 41			13 51		14 01		14 11		14 21			14 31	14 41
Manor Park	d	12 53		13 03		13 13		13 23			13 33	13 43			13 53		14 03		14 13		14 23			14 33	14 43
Ilford 2	d	12 56		13 06		13 16		13 26			13 36	13 46			13 56		14 06		14 16		14 26			14 36	14 46
Seven Kings	d	12 58		13 08		13 18		13 28			13 38	13 48			13 58		14 08		14 18		14 28			14 38	14 48
Goodmayes	d	13 00		13 10		13 20		13 30			13 40	13 50			14 00		14 10		14 20		14 30			14 40	14 50
Chadwell Heath	d	13 02		13 12		13 22		13 32			13 42	13 52			14 02		14 12		14 22		14 32			14 42	14 52
Romford	d	13 06		13 16		13 26	13 23	13 36			13 46	13 56	13 49		14 06		14 16		14 26	14 23	14 36			14 46	14 56
Gidea Park 2	d	13 10		13 20		13 30		13 40			13 50	14 00			14 10		14 20		14 30		14 40			14 50	15 00
Harold Wood	d	13 13		13 23		13 33		13 43			13 53	14 03			14 13		14 23		14 33		14 43			14 53	15 03
Brentwood	d	13 17		13 27		13 37		13 47			13 57	14 07			14 17		14 27		14 37		14 47			14 57	15 07
Shenfield 3	a	13 23	13 12	13 33	13 19	13 43	13 33	13 53	13 39	13 41	14 03	14 13	14 00		14 23	14 12	14 33	14 19	14 43	14 33	14 53	14 39	14 41	15 03	15 13
	d		13 12		13 20		13 34		13 40	13 42			14 00	14 08		14 12		14 20		14 34		14 40	14 42		
Billericay	d				13 26				13 46				14 06	14 14				14 26				14 46			
Wickford 2	d				13 31				13 51				14 11	14 20				14 31				14 51			
Battlesbridge	d													14 24											
South Woodham Ferrers	d													14 28											
North Fambridge	d													14 34											
Althorne	d													14 39											
Burnham-on-Crouch	d													14 44											
Southminster	a													14 49											
Rayleigh	d				13 36				13 56				14 16					14 36				14 56			
Hockley	d				13 41				14 01				14 21					14 41				15 01			
Rochford	d				13 44				14 04				14 24					14 44				15 04			
Prittlewell	d				13 48				14 08				14 28					14 48				15 08			
Southend Victoria	a				13 51				14 11				14 31					14 51				15 11			

		LE 1	LE 1	LE	LE 1	LE	LE 1	LE	LE 1	LE	LE 1	LE 1	LE	LE	LE 1	LE 1	LE 1	LE	LE 1	LE	LE 1	LE	LE 1	LE	LE
London Liverpool Street 15 ⊖	d	14 34		14 40	14 48	14 50	14 55	15 00	15 08	15 10	15 15	15 18	15 20	15 30	15 32	15 34		15 40	15 48	15 50	15 55	16 00	16 02	16 10	16 38
Stratford 7 ⊖	d	14 41		14 47	14 55	14 57	15 02	15 07	15 15	15 17	15 22	15 25	15 27	15 37		15 41		15 47	15 55	15 57	16 02	16 07	16 10	16 17	16 45
Maryland	d			14 49		14 59		15 09		15 19			15 29	15 39				15 49		15 59		16 09		16 19	16 47
Forest Gate	d			14 51		15 01		15 11		15 21			15 31	15 41				15 51		16 01		16 11		16 21	16 49
Manor Park	d			14 53		15 03		15 13		15 23			15 33	15 43				15 53		16 03		16 13		16 23	16 51
Ilford 2	d			14 56		15 06		15 16		15 26			15 36	15 46				15 56		16 06		16 16		16 26	16 54
Seven Kings	d			14 58		15 08		15 18		15 28			15 38	15 48				15 58		16 08		16 18		16 28	16 57
Goodmayes	d			15 00		15 10		15 20		15 30			15 40	15 50				16 00		16 10		16 20		16 30	16 59
Chadwell Heath	d			15 02		15 12		15 22		15 32			15 42	15 52				16 02		16 12		16 22		16 32	17 01
Romford	d	14 49		15 06		15 16		15 26	15 23	15 36			15 46	15 56		15 49		16 06		16 16		16 26		16 36	17 05
Gidea Park 2	d			15 10		15 20		15 30		15 40			15 50	16 00				16 10		16 20		16 30		16 40	17a10
Harold Wood	d			15 13		15 23		15 33		15 43			15 53	16 03				16 13		16 23		16 33		16 43	
Brentwood	d			15 17		15 27		15 37		15 47			15 57	16 07				16 17		16 27		16 37		16 47	
Shenfield 3	a	15 00		15 23	15 12	15 33	15 19	15 43	15 33	15 53	15 39	15 41	16 03	16 13	15 54	16 00		16 23	16 12	16 33	16 19	16 43	16 25	16 53	
	d	15 00	15 08		15 12		15 20		15 34		15 40	15 42			15 55	16 00	16 08		16 12		16 20		16 25		
Billericay	d	15 06	15 14				15 26				15 46					16 06	16 14				16 26				
Wickford 2	d	15 11	15 20				15 31				15 51					16 11	16 20				16 31				
Battlesbridge	d		15 24														16 24								
South Woodham Ferrers	d		15 28														16 28								
North Fambridge	d		15 34														16 34								
Althorne	d		15 39														16 39								
Burnham-on-Crouch	d		15 44														16 44								
Southminster	a		15 49														16 49								
Rayleigh	d	15 16					15 36				15 56					16 16					16 36				
Hockley	d	15 21					15 41				16 01					16 21					16 41				
Rochford	d	15 24					15 44				16 04					16 24					16 44				
Prittlewell	d	15 28					15 48				16 08					16 28					16 48				
Southend Victoria	a	15 31					15 51				16 11					16 31					16 51				

		LE 1	LE 1	LE 1	LE	LE 1	LE 1	LE	LE 1	LE	LE 1	LE 1	LE	LE	LE 1	LE 1	LE	LE 1	LE	LE	LE 1	LE 1	LE	LE	LE
London Liverpool Street 15 ⊖	d	16 40	16 10	16 17	16 20	16 25	17 15	17 17	17 17	17 20	17 22	17 25	17 27	17 30	17 32	17 34	17 36	17 38	17 39	17 42	17 42	17 45	17 46	17 49	17 52
Stratford 7 ⊖	d	16 48	16 18	16 25	16 27	16 33		17 24		17 27		17 33	17 34	17 37		17 42	17 43	17 46	17 46	17 49	17 50	17 53	17 53	17 56	17 59
Maryland	d				16 29					17 29				17 39			17 45						17 55		
Forest Gate	d				16 31					17 31				17 41						17 52					18 02
Manor Park	d				16 33					17 33				17 43					17 50					18 00	
Ilford 2	d				16 36			17 30		17 36			17 40	17 46			17 50		17 53	17 56			18 00	18 03	18 06
Seven Kings	d				16 38			17 32					17 42				17 52		17 56	17 59			18 02	18 06	18 09
Goodmayes	d				16 40			17 34					17 44				17 54		17 58	18 01			18 04	18 08	18 11
Chadwell Heath	d				16 42			17 36		17 40			17 46	17 50			17 56		18 00	18 03			18 06	18 10	18 13
Romford	d				16 46			17 40		17 44			17 50	17 54			18 00		18 04	18 07			18 10	18 14	18 17
Gidea Park 2	d				16 50			17 44		17a50			17 54	18a00			18 04		18a08	18a11			18 14	18 18	18a22
Harold Wood	d				16 53			17 47					17 57				18 07						18 17	18 21	
Brentwood	d				16 57			17 51					18 01				18 11						18 21	18 25	
Shenfield 3	a	17 04	16 34	16 40	17 03	16 50		17 59	17 41		17 43	17 51	18 09		17 54	17 59	18 19					18 10	18 29	18 31	
	d	17 05	16 35	16 40		16 50			17 42		17 44	17 52			17 54	17 59						18 11		18 35	
Billericay	d	17 11	16 41			16 56			17 48			17 58				18 06						18 17		18 41	
Wickford 2	d	17 16	16 46			17 01	17 49		17 54			18 04				18 12						18 23		18 47	
Battlesbridge	d																								
South Woodham Ferrers	d						17 56																		
North Fambridge	d						18 02																		
Althorne	d						18 07																		
Burnham-on-Crouch	d						18 12																		
Southminster	a						18 19																		
Rayleigh	d	17 21	16 51			17 06			17 59			18 09				18 17						18 28		18 53	
Hockley	d	17 26	16 56			17 11			18 04			18 14				18 22						18 33		18 57	
Rochford	d	17 29	16 59			17 14			18 07			18 17				18 25						18 36		19 01	
Prittlewell	d	17 33	17 03			17 18			18 11			18 21				18 29						18 40		19 04	
Southend Victoria	a	17 39	17 09			17 24			18 16			18 26				18 34						18 45		19 10	

London - Shenfield, Southminster and Southend Victoria

		LE ■	LE ■	LE ■	LE	LE	LE ■	LE ■	LE	LE ■	LE	LE ■	LE ■	LE	LE	LE ■	LE ■	LE	LE	LE ■	LE ■	LE	LE ■	LE	LE ■
London Liverpool Street ⊖	d	17 52	17 54	17 56	17 57	18 00	18 02	18 04	18 07	18 08	18 10	18 12	18 15	18 17	18 20	18 22	18 25	18 27	18 30	18 32	18 35	18 37	18 38	18 40	18 42
Stratford ⊖	d				18 04	18 07	18 10	18 13	18 14	18 16	18 17	18 20	18 23	18 24	18 27		18 33	18 34	18 37	18 40	18 43	18 44	18 46	18 47	18 50
Maryland	d					18 09					18 19				18 29				18 39					18 49	
Forest Gate	d					18 11					18 21				18 31				18 41					18 51	
Manor Park	d					18 13					18 23				18 33				18 43					18 53	
Ilford	d				18 10	18 16			18 20		18 26			18 30	18 36			18 40	18 46			18 50		18 56	
Seven Kings	d				18 12				18 22					18 32				18 42				18 52			
Goodmayes	d				18 14				18 24					18 34				18 44				18 54			
Chadwell Heath	d				18 16	18 20			18 26		18 30			18 36	18 40			18 46	18 50			18 56		19 00	
Romford	d				18 20	18 24			18 30		18 34			18 40	18 44			18 50	18 54			19 00		19 04	
Gidea Park	d				18 24	18a30			18 34		18a40			18 44	18a50			18 54	19a00			19 04		19 08	
Harold Wood	d				18 27				18 37					18 47				18 57				19 07		19 11	
Brentwood	d				18 31				18 41					18 51				19 01				19 11		19 15	
Shenfield	a	18 14		18 21	18 39			18 29	18 49				18 40	18 59		18 44	18 50	19 09			19 00	19 19	19 01	19 23	
	d	18 14		18 22				18 29					18 41			18 44	18 51				19 01		19 01		
Billericay	d			18 28				18 36					18 47				18 57				19 07				
Wickford	d		18 29	18 34				18 42					18 53				19 03				19 13				19 17
Battlesbridge	d		18 33																						19 22
South Woodham Ferrers	d		18 37																						19 26
North Fambridge	d		18 43																						19 32
Althorne	d		18 48																						19 37
Burnham-on-Crouch	d		18 53																						19 42
Southminster	a		19 00																						19 49
Rayleigh	d			18 39				18 47					18 58				19 08				19 18				
Hockley	d			18 44				18 52					19 03				19 13				19 23				
Rochford	d			18 47				18 55					19 06				19 16				19 26				
Prittlewell	d			18 51				18 59					19 10				19 20				19 30				
Southend Victoria	a			18 56				19 04					19 15				19 25				19 35				

		LE ■	LE	LE ■	LE	LE ■	LE	LE	LE ■	LE ■	LE	LE ■	LE ■	LE	LE	LE ■	LE ■	LE	LE ■	LE	LE ■	LE ■	LE	LE ■	LE
London Liverpool Street ⊖	d	18 45	18 47	18 48	18 50	18 55	18 57	19 00	19 02	19 08	19 10	19 15	19 18	19 20	19 30	19 35	19 38	19 40	19 48	19 50		19 55	20 00	20 08	20 10
Stratford ⊖	d	18 53	18 54		18 57	19 03	19 04	19 07	19 09	19 15	19 17	19 22	19 25	19 27	19 37	19 42	19 45	19 47	19 55	19 57		20 03	20 07	20 15	20 17
Maryland	d				18 59			19 09			19 19			19 29	19 39			19 49		19 59			20 09		20 19
Forest Gate	d				19 01			19 11			19 21			19 31	19 41			19 51		20 01			20 11		20 21
Manor Park	d				19 03			19 13			19 23			19 33	19 43			19 53		20 03			20 13		20 23
Ilford	d		19 00		19 06		19 10	19 16			19 26			19 36	19 46			19 56		20 06			20 16		20 26
Seven Kings	d		19 02				19 12	19 18			19 28			19 38	19 48			19 58		20 08			20 18		20 28
Goodmayes	d		19 04				19 14	19 20			19 30			19 40	19 50			20 00		20 10			20 20		20 30
Chadwell Heath	d		19 06		19 10		19 16	19 22			19 32			19 42	19 52			20 02		20 12			20 22		20 32
Romford	d		19 10		19 14		19 20	19 26			19 36			19 46	19 56			20 06		20 16			20 26		20 36
Gidea Park	d		19 14		19a20		19 24	19 30			19 40			19 50	20 00			20 10		20 20			20 30		20 40
Harold Wood	d		19 17				19 27	19 33			19 43			19 53	20 03			20 13		20 23			20 33		20 43
Brentwood	d		19 21				19 31	19 37			19 47			19 57	20 07			20 17		20 27			20 37		20 47
Shenfield	a	19 10	19 29	19 11		19 20	19 39	19 43	19 25		19 53	19 39	19 41	20 03	20 13	19 59	20 01	20 23	20 12	20 33		20 20	20 43	20 31	20 53
	d	19 11		19 11		19 21			19 26			19 40	19 42			20 00	20 02		20 12			20 20		20 32	
Billericay	d	19 17				19 27						19 46				20 06						20 26			
Wickford	d	19 23				19 33						19 51				20 11					20 20	20 31			
Battlesbridge	d																				20 24				
South Woodham Ferrers	d																				20 28				
North Fambridge	d																				20 34				
Althorne	d																				20 39				
Burnham-on-Crouch	d																				20 44				
Southminster	a																				20 49				
Rayleigh	d	19 28				19 38						19 57				20 16						20 36			
Hockley	d	19 33				19 43						20 02				20 21						20 41			
Rochford	d	19 36				19 46						20 05				20 24						20 44			
Prittlewell	d	19 40				19 50						20 09				20 28						20 48			
Southend Victoria	a	19 45				19 55						20 12				20 31						20 51			

		LE ■	LE ■	LE	LE	LE ■	CC	LE ■	LE ■	LE	LE ■	LE	LE ■	LE	LE ■	LE	LE ■	LE ■	LE	LE	LE ■	CC	LE ■	LE	LE ■
London Liverpool Street ⊖	d	20 15	20 18	20 20	20 30	20 34	20 35	20 38		20 40	20 48	20 50	20 55	21 00	21 08	21 10	21 15	21 18	21 20	21 30	21 34	21 35		21 40	21 48
Stratford ⊖	d	20 22	20 25	20 27	20 37	20 41	20 42	20 45		20 47	20 55	20 57	21 02	21 07	21 15	21 17	21 22	21 25	21 27	21 37	21 41	21 42		21 47	21 55
Maryland	d			20 29	20 39					20 49		20 59		21 09		21 19			21 29	21 39				21 49	
Forest Gate	d			20 31	20 41					20 51		21 01		21 11		21 21			21 31	21 41				21 51	
Manor Park	d			20 33	20 43					20 53		21 03		21 13		21 23			21 33	21 43				21 53	
Ilford	d			20 36	20 46					20 56		21 06		21 16		21 26			21 36	21 46				21 56	
Seven Kings	d			20 38	20 48					20 58		21 08		21 18		21 28			21 38	21 48				21 58	
Goodmayes	d			20 40	20 50					21 00		21 10		21 20		21 30			21 40	21 50				22 00	
Chadwell Heath	d			20 42	20 52					21 02		21 12		21 22		21 32			21 42	21 52				22 02	
Romford	d			20 46	20 56	20 49				21 06		21 16		21 26	21 23	21 36			21 46	21 56	21 49			22 06	
Gidea Park	d			20 50	21 00					21 10		21 20		21 30		21 40			21 50	22 00				22 10	
Harold Wood	d			20 53	21 03					21 13		21 23		21 33		21 43			21 53	22 03				22 13	
Brentwood	d			20 57	21 07					21 17		21 27		21 37		21 47			21 57	22 07				22 17	
Shenfield	a	20 39	20 41	21 03	21 13	21 00		21 01		21 23	21 12	21 33	21 19	21 43	21 33	21 53	21 39	21 41	22 03	22 13	22 00			22 23	22 12
	d	20 40	20 42			21 00		21 02	21 08		21 12		21 20		21 34		21 40	21 42			22 00		22 08		22 12
Billericay	d	20 46				21 06			21 14				21 26				21 46				22 06		22 14		
Wickford	d	20 51				21 11			21 20				21 31				21 51				22 11		22 20		
Battlesbridge	d								21 24														22 24		
South Woodham Ferrers	d								21 28														22 28		
North Fambridge	d								21 34														22 34		
Althorne	d								21 39														22 39		
Burnham-on-Crouch	d								21 44														22 44		
Southminster	a								21 49														22 49		
Rayleigh	d	20 56				21 16							21 36				21 56				22 16				
Hockley	d	21 01				21 21							21 41				22 01				22 21				
Rochford	d	21 04				21 24							21 44				22 04				22 24				
Prittlewell	d	21 08				21 28							21 48				22 08				22 28				
Southend Victoria	a	21 11				21 31							21 51				22 11				22 31				

London - Shenfield, Southminster and Southend Victoria

		LE	LE ■	LE ■	LE	LE ■	LE ■	LE ■	LE	LE	LE ■	LE ■	LE	LE ■	LE	LE ■	LE ■	LE	LE	LE ■	LE ■	LE
London Liverpool Street ⊖	d	21 50	21 55	22 00	22 05	22 15		22 18	22 20	22 35	22 45	22 48	22 50	23 00	23 05	23 15	23 18	23 20	23 35	23 45	23 48	23 50
Stratford ⊖	d	21 57	22 02		22 12	22 22		22 25	22 27	22 42	22 52	22 55	22 57	23 07	23 12	23 22	23 25	23 27	23 42	23 52	23 55	23 57
Maryland	d	21 59			22 14				22 29	22 44			22 59		23 14			23 29	23 44			23 59
Forest Gate	d	22 01			22 16				22 31	22 46			23 01		23 16			23 31	23 46			00 01
Manor Park	d	22 03			22 18				22 33	22 48			23 03		23 18			23 33	23 48			00 03
Ilford	d	22 06			22 21				22 36	22 51			23 06		23 21			23 36	23 51			00 06
Seven Kings	d	22 08			22 23				22 38	22 53			23 08		23 23			23 38	23 53			00 08
Goodmayes	d	22 10			22 25				22 40	22 55			23 10		23 25			23 40	23 55			00 10
Chadwell Heath	d	22 12			22 27				22 42	22 57			23 12		23 27			23 42	23 57			00 12
Romford	d	22 16			22 31				22 46	23 01			23 16		23 31			23 46	00 01			00 16
Gidea Park	d	22 20			22 35				22 50	23 05			23 20		23 35			23 50	00 05			00 20
Harold Wood	d	22 23			22 38				22 53	23 08			23 23		23 38			23 53	00 08			00 23
Brentwood	d	22 27			22 42				22 57	23 12			23 27		23 42			23 57	00 12			00 27
Shenfield	a	22 33	22 19	22 22	22 48	22 39		22 41	23 03	23 18	23 09	23 12	23 33	23 23	23 48	23 39	23 41	00 03	00 18	00 09	00 12	00 33
	d		22 20	22 22		22 40		22 42			23 10	23 12		23 24		23 40	23 42			00 10	00 12	
Billericay	d		22 26			22 46					23 16					23 46				00 16		
Wickford	d		22 31			22 51	22 58				23 21					23 51				00 21		
Battlesbridge	d						23 02															
South Woodham Ferrers	d						23 06															
North Fambridge	d						23 12															
Althorne	d						23 17															
Burnham-on-Crouch	d						23 22															
Southminster	a						23 27															
Rayleigh	d		22 36			22 56					23 26					23 56				00 26		
Hockley	d		22 41			23 01					23 31					00 01				00 31		
Rochford	d		22 44			23 04					23 34					00 04				00 34		
Prittlewell	d		22 48			23 08					23 38					00 08				00 38		
Southend Victoria	a		22 51			23 11					23 45					00 15				00 45		

Table 5 — Saturdays

London - Shenfield, Southminster and Southend Victoria

		LE ■	LE	LE	LE ■	LE ■	LE	LE	LE ■	LE ■	LE	LE	LE ■	LE ■	LE	LE ■	LE	LE ■	LE	LE ■	LE ■	LE	LE ■	LE	LE
London Liverpool Street ⊖	d	23p15	23p20	23p35	23p45	23p48	23p50	00 01	00 15	00 18	00 20	00 32	00 46	00 50	00 55	05 23	05 28		05 28	05 30		05 40	06 00	06 04	06 10
Stratford ⊖	d	23p22	23p27	23p42	23p52	23p55	23p57	00 08	00 22	00 25	00 27	00 39	00 55	00 57	01 02	05 33	05 37		05 35	05 37		05 47	06 07	06 11	06 17
Maryland	d		23p29	23p44			23p59	00 10			00 29	00 41			01 04							05 49			06 19
Forest Gate	d		23p31	23p46			00 01	00 12			00 31	00 43			01 06							05 51			06 21
Manor Park	d		23p33	23p48			00 03	00 14			00 33	00 45			01 08							05 53			06 23
Ilford	d		23p36	23p51			00 06	00 17			00 36	00 48			01 11				05 40			05 56			06 26
Seven Kings	d		23p38	23p53			00 08	00 19			00 38	00 50			01 13				05 42			05 58			06 28
Goodmayes	d		23p40	23p55			00 10	00 21			00 40	00 52			01 15							06 00			06 30
Chadwell Heath	d		23p42	23p57			00 12	00 23			00 42	00 54			01 17							06 02			06 32
Romford	d		23p46	00 01			00 16	00 27	00 32		00 46	00 58		01 08	01 21				05 48	05 45		06 06	06 15		06 36
Gidea Park	d		23p50	00 05			00 20	00a31			00 50	01a02	01 07		01 25				05 51			06 10			06 40
Harold Wood	d		23p53	00 08			00 23				00 53				01 28				05 54			06 13			06 43
Brentwood	d		23p57	00 12			00 27				00 57				01 32				05 59			06 17			06 47
Shenfield	a	23p40	00 03	00 18	00 10	00 12	00 33		00 44	00 47	01 03		01 17	01 20	01 38				06 04	05 55		06 23	06 25	06 30	06 53
	d	23p40			00 10	00 12			00 45	00 47			01 17	01 20					06 04	05 56	06 08		06 26	06 30	
Billericay	d	23p46			00 16				00 51					01 26					06 10		06 14			06 36	
Wickford	d	23p52			00 22				00 56					01 31				05 39	06 15		06 20			06 41	
Battlesbridge	d																	05 43			06 24				
South Woodham Ferrers	d																	05 47			06 28				
North Fambridge	d																	05 53			06 34				
Althorne	d																	05 58			06 39				
Burnham-on-Crouch	d																	06 03			06 44				
Southminster	a																	06 08			06 49				
Rayleigh	d	23p57			00 27				01 01					01 36					06 21					06 46	
Hockley	d	00 02			00 31				01 06					01 41					06 25					06 51	
Rochford	d	00 05			00 35				01 09					01 44					06 29					06 54	
Prittlewell	d	00 08			00 38				01 13					01 48					06 32					06 58	
Southend Victoria	a	00 16			00 46				01 20					01 55					06 36					07 02	

Table 5

Saturdays

London - Shenfield, Southminster and Southend Victoria

		LE 1	LE 1	LE 1	LE 1	LE	LE 1	LE 1	LE	LE 1	LE	LE 1	LE 1	LE	LE	LE 1	LE 1	LE	LE 1	LE	LE 1	LE	LE 1	LE	LE 1
London Liverpool Street 15 ⊖	d	06 18	06 23	06 34		06 40	06 48	06 55	07 00	07 08	07 10	07 15	07 18	07 20	07 30	07 34		07 40	07 48	07 50	07 55	08 00	08 08	08 10	08 15
Stratford 7 ⊖	d	06 25	06 33	06 41		06 47	06 55	07 02	07 07	07 15	07 17	07 22	07 25	07 27	07 37	07 41		07 47	07 55	07 57	08 02	08 07	08 15	08 17	08 22
Maryland	d					06 49			07 09		07 19			07 29	07 39			07 49		07 59		08 09		08 19	
Forest Gate	d					06 51			07 11		07 21			07 31	07 41			07 51		08 01		08 11		08 21	
Manor Park	d					06 53			07 13		07 23			07 33	07 43			07 53		08 03		08 13		08 23	
Ilford 2	d					06 56			07 16		07 26			07 36	07 46			07 56		08 06		08 16		08 26	
Seven Kings	d					06 58			07 18		07 28			07 38	07 48			07 58		08 08		08 18		08 28	
Goodmayes	d					07 00			07 20		07 30			07 40	07 50			08 00		08 10		08 20		08 30	
Chadwell Heath	d					07 02			07 22		07 32			07 42	07 52			08 02		08 12		08 22		08 32	
Romford	d			06 49		07 06			07 26	07 23	07 36			07 46	07 56	07 49		08 06		08 16		08 26	08 23	08 36	
Gidea Park 2	d					07 10			07 30		07 40			07 50	08 00			08 10		08 20		08 30		08 40	
Harold Wood	d					07 13			07 33		07 43			07 53	08 03			08 13		08 23		08 33		08 43	
Brentwood	d					07 17			07 37		07 47			07 57	08 07			08 17		08 27		08 37		08 47	
Shenfield 3	a	06 41		07 00		07 23	07 12	07 19	07 43	07 33	07 53	07 39	07 41	08 03	08 13	08 00		08 23	08 12	08 33	08 19	08 43	08 33	08 53	08 39
	d	06 42		07 00	07 08		07 12	07 20		07 34		07 40	07 42			08 00	08 08		08 12		08 20		08 34		08 40
Billericay	d			07 06	07 14			07 26				07 46				08 06	08 14				08 26				08 46
Wickford 2	d			07 11	07 20			07 31				07 51				08 11	08 20				08 31				08 51
Battlesbridge	d				07 24												08 24								
South Woodham Ferrers	d				07 28												08 28								
North Fambridge	d				07 34												08 34								
Althorne	d				07 39												08 39								
Burnham-on-Crouch	d				07 44												08 44								
Southminster	a				07 49												08 49								
Rayleigh	d			07 16				07 36				07 57				08 16					08 36				08 56
Hockley	d			07 21				07 41				08 01				08 21					08 41				09 01
Rochford	d			07 24				07 44				08 05				08 24					08 44				09 04
Prittlewell	d			07 28				07 48				08 08				08 28					08 48				09 08
Southend Victoria	a			07 31				07 51				08 12				08 31					08 51				09 11

		LE 1	LE	LE	LE 1	LE 1	LE	LE 1	LE	LE 1	LE	LE 1	LE	LE 1	LE 1	LE	LE	LE 1	LE 1	LE	LE 1	LE	LE 1	LE	LE 1
London Liverpool Street 15 ⊖	d	08 18	08 20	08 30	08 34		08 40	08 48	08 50	08 55	09 00	09 08	09 10	09 15	09 18	09 20	09 30	09 34		09 40	09 48	09 50	09 55	10 00	10 08
Stratford 7 ⊖	d	08 25	08 27	08 37	08 41		08 47	08 55	08 57	09 02	09 07	09 15	09 17	09 22	09 25	09 27	09 37	09 41		09 47	09 55	09 57	10 02	10 07	10 15
Maryland	d		08 29	08 39			08 49		08 59		09 09		09 19			09 29	09 39			09 49		09 59		10 09	
Forest Gate	d		08 31	08 41			08 51		09 01		09 11		09 21			09 31	09 41			09 51		10 01		10 11	
Manor Park	d		08 33	08 43			08 53		09 03		09 13		09 23			09 33	09 43			09 53		10 03		10 13	
Ilford 2	d		08 36	08 46			08 56		09 06		09 16		09 26			09 36	09 46			09 56		10 06		10 16	
Seven Kings	d		08 38	08 48			08 58		09 08		09 18		09 28			09 38	09 48			09 58		10 08		10 18	
Goodmayes	d		08 40	08 50			09 00		09 10		09 20		09 30			09 40	09 50			10 00		10 10		10 20	
Chadwell Heath	d		08 42	08 52			09 02		09 12		09 22		09 32			09 42	09 52			10 02		10 12		10 22	
Romford	d		08 46	08 56	08 49		09 06		09 16		09 26	09 23	09 36			09 46	09 56	09 49		10 06		10 16		10 26	10 23
Gidea Park 2	d		08 50	09 00			09 10		09 20		09 30		09 40			09 50	10 00			10 10		10 20		10 30	
Harold Wood	d		08 53	09 03			09 13		09 23		09 33		09 43			09 53	10 03			10 13		10 23		10 33	
Brentwood	d		08 57	09 07			09 17		09 27		09 37		09 47			09 57	10 07			10 17		10 27		10 37	
Shenfield 3	a	08 41	09 03	09 13	09 00		09 23	09 12	09 33	09 19	09 43	09 33	09 53	09 39	09 41	10 03	10 13	10 00		10 23	10 12	10 33	10 19	10 43	10 33
	d	08 42			09 00	09 08		09 12		09 20		09 34		09 40	09 42			10 00	10 08		10 12		10 20		10 34
Billericay	d				09 06	09 14				09 26				09 46				10 06	10 14				10 26		
Wickford 2	d				09 11	09 20				09 32				09 51				10 11	10 20				10 31		
Battlesbridge	d					09 24													10 24						
South Woodham Ferrers	d					09 28													10 28						
North Fambridge	d					09 34													10 34						
Althorne	d					09 39													10 39						
Burnham-on-Crouch	d					09 44													10 44						
Southminster	a					09 49													10 49						
Rayleigh	d				09 16					09 36				09 56				10 16					10 36		
Hockley	d				09 21					09 41				10 01				10 21					10 41		
Rochford	d				09 24					09 44				10 04				10 24					10 44		
Prittlewell	d				09 28					09 48				10 08				10 28					10 48		
Southend Victoria	a				09 31					09 51				10 11				10 31					10 51		

		LE	LE	LE	LE 1	LE 1	LE	LE 1	LE	LE 1	LE	LE 1	LE	LE 1	LE 1	LE 1	LE 1	LE	LE	LE 1	LE 1	LE	LE 1	LE	LE 1
London Liverpool Street 15 ⊖	d	10 10	10 20	10 30	10 34		10 40	10 48	10 50	10 55	11 00	11 08	11 10	11 15	10 15	10 18	11 18	11 20	11 30	11 34		11 40	11 48	11 50	11 55
Stratford 7 ⊖	d	10 17	10 27	10 37	10 41		10 47	10 55	10 57	11 02	11 07	11 15	11 17	11 22	10 22	10 25	11 25	11 27	11 37	11 41		11 47	11 55	11 57	12 02
Maryland	d	10 19	10 29	10 39			10 49		10 59		11 09		11 19					11 29	11 39			11 49		11 59	
Forest Gate	d	10 21	10 31	10 41			10 51		11 01		11 11		11 21					11 31	11 41			11 51		12 01	
Manor Park	d	10 23	10 33	10 43			10 53		11 03		11 13		11 23					11 33	11 43			11 53		12 03	
Ilford 2	d	10 26	10 36	10 46			10 56		11 06		11 16		11 26					11 36	11 46			11 56		12 06	
Seven Kings	d	10 28	10 38	10 48			10 58		11 08		11 18		11 28					11 38	11 48			11 58		12 08	
Goodmayes	d	10 30	10 40	10 50			11 00		11 10		11 20		11 30					11 40	11 50			12 00		12 10	
Chadwell Heath	d	10 32	10 42	10 52			11 02		11 12		11 22		11 32					11 42	11 52			12 02		12 12	
Romford	d	10 36	10 46	10 56	10 49		11 06		11 16		11 26	11 23	11 36					11 46	11 56	11 49		12 06		12 16	
Gidea Park 2	d	10 40	10 50	11 00			11 10		11 20		11 30		11 40					11 50	12 00			12 10		12 20	
Harold Wood	d	10 43	10 53	11 03			11 13		11 23		11 33		11 43					11 53	12 03			12 13		12 23	
Brentwood	d	10 47	10 57	11 07			11 17		11 27		11 37		11 47					11 57	12 07			12 17		12 27	
Shenfield 3	a	10 53	11 03	11 13	11 00		11 23	11 12	11 33	11 19	11 43	11 33	11 53	11 39	10 39	10 41	11 41	12 03	12 13	12 00		12 23	12 12	12 33	12 19
	d				11 00	11 08		11 12		11 20		11 34		11 40	10 40	10 42	11 42			12 00	12 08		12 12		12 20
Billericay	d				11 06	11 14				11 26				11 46	10 46					12 06	12 14				12 26
Wickford 2	d				11 11	11 20				11 31				11 51	10 51					12 11	12 20				12 31
Battlesbridge	d					11 24															12 24				
South Woodham Ferrers	d					11 28															12 28				
North Fambridge	d					11 34															12 34				
Althorne	d					11 39															12 39				
Burnham-on-Crouch	d					11 44															12 44				
Southminster	a					11 49															12 49				
Rayleigh	d				11 16					11 36				11 56	10 56					12 16					12 36
Hockley	d				11 21					11 41				12 01	11 01					12 21					12 41
Rochford	d				11 24					11 44				12 04	11 04					12 24					12 44
Prittlewell	d				11 28					11 48				12 08	11 08					12 28					12 48
Southend Victoria	a				11 31					11 51				12 11	11 11					12 31					12 51

Table 5

Saturdays

London - Shenfield, Southminster and Southend Victoria

		LE	LE 1	LE	LE 1	LE 1	LE	LE	LE 1	LE 1	LE	LE 1	LE	LE 1	LE	LE 1	LE	LE 1	LE 1	LE	LE	LE 1	LE 1	LE	LE 1
London Liverpool Street 15 ⊖	d	12 00	12 08	12 10	12 15	12 18	12 20	12 30	12 34		12 40	12 48	12 50	12 55	13 00	13 08	13 10	13 15	13 18	13 20	13 30	13 34		13 40	13 48
Stratford 7 ⊖	d	12 07	12 15	12 17	12 22	12 25	12 27	12 37	12 41		12 47	12 55	12 57	13 02	13 07	13 15	13 17	13 22	13 25	13 27	13 37	13 41		13 47	13 55
Maryland	d	12 09		12 19			12 29	12 39			12 49		12 59		13 09		13 19			13 29	13 39			13 49	
Forest Gate	d	12 11		12 21			12 31	12 41			12 51		13 01		13 11		13 21			13 31	13 41			13 51	
Manor Park	d	12 13		12 23			12 33	12 43			12 53		13 03		13 13		13 23			13 33	13 43			13 53	
Ilford 2	d	12 16		12 26			12 36	12 46			12 56		13 06		13 16		13 26			13 36	13 46			13 56	
Seven Kings	d	12 18		12 28			12 38	12 48			12 58		13 08		13 18		13 28			13 38	13 48			13 58	
Goodmayes	d	12 20		12 30			12 40	12 50			13 00		13 10		13 20		13 30			13 40	13 50			14 00	
Chadwell Heath	d	12 22		12 32			12 42	12 52			13 02		13 12		13 22		13 32			13 42	13 52			14 02	
Romford	d	12 26	12 23	12 36			12 46	12 56	12 49		13 06		13 16		13 26	13 23	13 36			13 46	13 56	13 49		14 06	
Gidea Park 2	d	12 30		12 40			12 50	13 00			13 10		13 20		13 30		13 40			13 50	14 00			14 10	
Harold Wood	d	12 33		12 43			12 53	13 03			13 13		13 23		13 33		13 43			13 53	14 03			14 13	
Brentwood	d	12 37		12 47			12 57	13 07			13 17		13 27		13 37		13 47			13 57	14 07			14 17	
Shenfield 3	a	12 43	12 33	12 53	12 39	12 41	13 03	13 13	13 00		13 23	13 12	13 33	13 19	13 43	13 33	13 53	13 39	13 41	14 03	14 13	14 00		14 23	14 12
	d		12 34		12 40	12 42			13 00	13 08		13 12		13 20		13 34		13 40	13 42			14 00	14 08		14 12
Billericay	d				12 46				13 06	13 14				13 26				13 46				14 06	14 14		
Wickford 2	d				12 51				13 11	13 20				13 31				13 51				14 11	14 20		
Battlesbridge	d									13 24													14 24		
South Woodham Ferrers	d									13 28													14 28		
North Fambridge	d									13 34													14 34		
Althorne	d									13 39													14 39		
Burnham-on-Crouch	d									13 44													14 44		
Southminster	a									13 49													14 49		
Rayleigh	d				12 56				13 16					13 36				13 56				14 16			
Hockley	d				13 01				13 21					13 41				14 01				14 21			
Rochford	d				13 04				13 24					13 45				14 04				14 24			
Prittlewell	d				13 08				13 28					13 48				14 08				14 28			
Southend Victoria	a				13 11				13 31					13 51				14 11				14 31			

		LE	LE 1	LE	LE 1	LE	LE 1	LE 1	LE	LE	LE 1	LE 1	LE	LE 1	LE	LE 1	LE	LE 1	LE	LE 1	LE 1	LE	LE	LE 1	LE 1
London Liverpool Street 15 ⊖	d	13 50	13 55	14 00	14 08	14 10	14 15	14 18	14 20	14 30	14 34		14 40	14 48	14 50	14 55	15 00	15 08	15 10	15 15	15 18	15 20	15 30	15 34	
Stratford 7 ⊖	d	13 57	14 02	14 07	14 15	14 17	14 22	14 25	14 27	14 37	14 41		14 47	14 55	14 57	15 02	15 07	15 15	15 17	15 22	15 25	15 27	15 37	15 41	
Maryland	d	13 59		14 09		14 19			14 29	14 39			14 49		14 59		15 09		15 19			15 29	15 39		
Forest Gate	d	14 01		14 11		14 21			14 31	14 41			14 51		15 01		15 11		15 21			15 31	15 41		
Manor Park	d	14 03		14 13		14 23			14 33	14 43			14 53		15 03		15 13		15 23			15 33	15 43		
Ilford 2	d	14 06		14 16		14 26			14 36	14 46			14 56		15 06		15 16		15 26			15 36	15 46		
Seven Kings	d	14 08		14 18		14 28			14 38	14 48			14 58		15 08		15 18		15 28			15 38	15 48		
Goodmayes	d	14 10		14 20		14 30			14 40	14 50			15 00		15 10		15 20		15 30			15 40	15 50		
Chadwell Heath	d	14 12		14 22		14 32			14 42	14 52			15 02		15 12		15 22		15 32			15 42	15 52		
Romford	d	14 16		14 26	14 23	14 36			14 46	14 56	14 49		15 06		15 16		15 26	15 23	15 36			15 46	15 56	15 49	
Gidea Park 2	d	14 20		14 30		14 40			14 50	15 00			15 10		15 20		15 30		15 40			15 50	16 00		
Harold Wood	d	14 23		14 33		14 43			14 53	15 03			15 13		15 23		15 33		15 43			15 53	16 03		
Brentwood	d	14 27		14 37		14 47			14 57	15 07			15 17		15 27		15 37		15 47			15 57	16 07		
Shenfield 3	a	14 33	14 19	14 43	14 33	14 53	14 39	14 41	15 03	15 13	15 00		15 23	15 12	15 33	15 19	15 43	15 33	15 53	15 39	15 41	16 03	16 13	16 00	
	d		14 20		14 34		14 40	14 42			15 00	15 08		15 12		15 20		15 34		15 40	15 42			16 00	16 08
Billericay	d		14 26				14 46				15 06	15 14				15 26				15 46				16 06	16 14
Wickford 2	d		14 31				14 51				15 11	15 20				15 31				15 51				16 11	16 20
Battlesbridge	d											15 24													16 24
South Woodham Ferrers	d											15 28													16 28
North Fambridge	d											15 34													16 34
Althorne	d											15 39													16 39
Burnham-on-Crouch	d											15 44													16 44
Southminster	a											15 49													16 49
Rayleigh	d		14 36				14 56				15 16					15 36				15 56				16 16	
Hockley	d		14 41				15 01				15 21					15 41				16 01				16 21	
Rochford	d		14 44				15 04				15 24					15 45				16 04				16 24	
Prittlewell	d		14 48				15 08				15 28					15 48				16 08				16 28	
Southend Victoria	a		14 51				15 11				15 31					15 51				16 11				16 31	

A from 2 October

B until 25 September

Table 5

London - Shenfield, Southminster and Southend Victoria

		LE	LE ■	LE	LE ■	LE	LE ■	LE	LE ■	LE ■	LE	LE	LE ■
London Liverpool Street 15 ⊖	d	15 40	15 48	15 50	15 55	16 00	16 08	16 10	16 15	16 18	16 20	16 30	16 34
Stratford 7 ⊖	d	15 47	15 55	15 57	16 02	16 07	16 15	16 17	16 22	16 25	16 27	16 37	16 41
Maryland	d	15 49		15 59		16 09		16 19			16 29	16 39	
Forest Gate	d	15 51		16 01		16 11		16 21			16 31	16 41	
Manor Park	d	15 53		16 03		16 13		16 23			16 33	16 43	
Ilford 2	d	15 56		16 06		16 16		16 26			16 36	16 46	
Seven Kings	d	15 58		16 08		16 18		16 28			16 38	16 48	
Goodmayes	d	16 00		16 10		16 20		16 30			16 40	16 50	
Chadwell Heath	d	16 02		16 12		16 22		16 32			16 42	16 52	
Romford	d	16 06		16 16		16 26	16 23	16 36			16 46	16 56	16 49
Gidea Park 2	d	16 10		16 20		16 30		16 40			16 50	17 00	
Harold Wood	d	16 13		16 23		16 33		16 43			16 53	17 03	
Brentwood	d	16 17		16 27		16 37		16 47			16 57	17 07	
Shenfield 3	a	16 23	16 12	16 33	16 19	16 43	16 33	16 53	16 39	16 41	17 03	17 13	17 00
	d		16 12		16 20		16 34		16 40	16 42			17 00
Billericay	d				16 26				16 46				17 06
Wickford 2	d				16 31				16 51				17 11
Battlesbridge	d												
South Woodham Ferrers	d												
North Fambridge	d												
Althorne	d												
Burnham-on-Crouch	d												
Southminster	a												
Rayleigh	d				16 36				16 56				17 16
Hockley	d				16 41				17 01				17 21
Rochford	d				16 45				17 04				17 24
Prittlewell	d				16 48				17 08				17 28
Southend Victoria	a				16 51				17 11				17 31

		LE ■	LE	LE ■	LE	LE ■	LE	LE ■	LE	LE ■	LE ■	LE	LE
London Liverpool Street 15 ⊖	d		16 40	16 48	16 50	16 55	17 00	17 08	17 10	17 15	17 18	17 20	17 30
Stratford 7 ⊖	d		16 47	16 55	16 57	17 02	17 07	17 15	17 17	17 22	17 25	17 27	17 37
Maryland	d		16 49		16 59		17 09		17 19			17 29	17 39
Forest Gate	d		16 51		17 01		17 11		17 21			17 31	17 41
Manor Park	d		16 53		17 03		17 13		17 23			17 33	17 43
Ilford 2	d		16 56		17 06		17 16		17 26			17 36	17 46
Seven Kings	d		16 58		17 08		17 18		17 28			17 38	17 48
Goodmayes	d		17 00		17 10		17 20		17 30			17 40	17 50
Chadwell Heath	d		17 02		17 12		17 22		17 32			17 42	17 52
Romford	d		17 06		17 16		17 26	17 23	17 36			17 46	17 56
Gidea Park 2	d		17 10		17 20		17 30		17 40			17 50	18 00
Harold Wood	d		17 13		17 23		17 33		17 43			17 53	18 03
Brentwood	d		17 17		17 27		17 37		17 47			17 57	18 07
Shenfield 3	a		17 23	17 12	17 33	17 19	17 43	17 33	17 53	17 39	17 41	18 03	18 13
	d	17 08		17 12		17 20		17 34		17 40	17 42		
Billericay	d	17 14				17 26				17 46			
Wickford 2	d	17 20				17 19				17 51			
Battlesbridge	d	17 24											
South Woodham Ferrers	d	17 28											
North Fambridge	d	17 34											
Althorne	d	17 39											
Burnham-on-Crouch	d	17 44											
Southminster	a	17 49											
Rayleigh	d					17 36				17 56			
Hockley	d					17 41				18 01			
Rochford	d					17 44				18 04			
Prittlewell	d					17 48				18 08			
Southend Victoria	a					17 51				18 11			

		LE ■	LE ■	LE	LE ■	LE	LE ■	LE	LE ■	LE	LE ■	LE ■	LE
London Liverpool Street 15 ⊖	d	17 34		17 40	17 48	17 50	17 55	18 00	18 08	18 10	18 15	18 18	18 20
Stratford 7 ⊖	d	17 41		17 47	17 55	17 57	18 02	18 07	18 15	18 17	18 22	18 25	18 27
Maryland	d			17 49		17 59		18 09		18 19			18 29
Forest Gate	d			17 51		18 01		18 11		18 21			18 31
Manor Park	d			17 53		18 03		18 13		18 23			18 33
Ilford 2	d			17 56		18 06		18 16		18 26			18 36
Seven Kings	d			17 58		18 08		18 18		18 28			18 38
Goodmayes	d			18 00		18 10		18 20		18 30			18 40
Chadwell Heath	d			18 02		18 12		18 22		18 32			18 42
Romford	d	17 49		18 06		18 16		18 26	18 23	18 36			18 46
Gidea Park 2	d			18 10		18 20		18 30		18 40			18 50
Harold Wood	d			18 13		18 23		18 33		18 43			18 53
Brentwood	d			18 17		18 27		18 37		18 47			18 57
Shenfield 3	a	18 00		18 23	18 12	18 33	18 19	18 43	18 33	18 53	18 39	18 41	19 03
	d	18 00	18 08		18 12		18 20		18 34		18 40	18 42	
Billericay	d	18 06	18 14				18 26				18 46		
Wickford 2	d	18 11	18 20				18 31				18 51		
Battlesbridge	d		18 24										
South Woodham Ferrers	d		18 28										
North Fambridge	d		18 34										
Althorne	d		18 39										
Burnham-on-Crouch	d		18 44										
Southminster	a		18 49										
Rayleigh	d	18 16					18 36				18 56		
Hockley	d	18 21					18 41				19 01		
Rochford	d	18 24					18 45				19 04		
Prittlewell	d	18 28					18 48				19 08		
Southend Victoria	a	18 31					18 51				19 11		

		LE	LE ■	LE ■	LE	LE ■	LE	LE ■	LE	LE ■	LE	LE ■	LE ■
London Liverpool Street 15 ⊖	d	18 30	18 34		18 40	18 48	18 50	18 55	19 00	19 08	19 10	19 15	19 18
Stratford 7 ⊖	d	18 37	18 41		18 47	18 55	18 57	19 02	19 07	19 15	19 17	19 22	19 25
Maryland	d	18 39			18 49		18 59		19 09		19 19		
Forest Gate	d	18 41			18 51		19 01		19 11		19 21		
Manor Park	d	18 43			18 53		19 03		19 13		19 23		
Ilford 2	d	18 46			18 56		19 06		19 16		19 26		
Seven Kings	d	18 48			18 58		19 08		19 18		19 28		
Goodmayes	d	18 50			19 00		19 10		19 20		19 30		
Chadwell Heath	d	18 52			19 02		19 12		19 22		19 32		
Romford	d	18 56	18 49		19 06		19 16		19 26	19 23	19 36		
Gidea Park 2	d	19 00			19 10		19 20		19 30		19 40		
Harold Wood	d	19 03			19 13		19 23		19 33		19 43		
Brentwood	d	19 07			19 17		19 27		19 37		19 47		
Shenfield 3	a	19 13	19 00		19 23	19 12	19 33	19 19	19 43	19 33	19 53	19 39	19 41
	d		19 00	19 08		19 12		19 20		19 34		19 40	19 42
Billericay	d		19 06	19 14				19 26				19 46	
Wickford 2	d		19 11	19 20				19 31				19 51	
Battlesbridge	d			19 24									
South Woodham Ferrers	d			19 28									
North Fambridge	d			19 34									
Althorne	d			19 39									
Burnham-on-Crouch	d			19 44									
Southminster	a			19 49									
Rayleigh	d		19 16					19 36				19 56	
Hockley	d		19 21					19 41				20 01	
Rochford	d		19 24					19 45				20 04	
Prittlewell	d		19 28					19 48				20 08	
Southend Victoria	a		19 31					19 51				20 11	

		LE	LE	LE ■	LE ■	LE	LE ■	LE	LE ■	LE	LE ■	LE	LE ■
London Liverpool Street 15 ⊖	d	19 20	19 30	19 34		19 40	19 48	19 50	19 55	20 00	20 08	20 10	20 15
Stratford 7 ⊖	d	19 27	19 37	19 41		19 47	19 55	19 57	20 02	20 07	20 15	20 17	20 22
Maryland	d	19 29	19 39			19 49		19 59		20 09		20 19	
Forest Gate	d	19 31	19 41			19 51		20 01		20 11		20 21	
Manor Park	d	19 33	19 43			19 53		20 03		20 13		20 23	
Ilford 2	d	19 36	19 46			19 56		20 06		20 16		20 26	
Seven Kings	d	19 38	19 48			19 58		20 08		20 18		20 28	
Goodmayes	d	19 40	19 50			20 00		20 10		20 20		20 30	
Chadwell Heath	d	19 42	19 52			20 02		20 12		20 22		20 32	
Romford	d	19 46	19 56	19 49		20 06		20 16		20 26	20 23	20 36	
Gidea Park 2	d	19 50	20 00			20 10		20 20		20 30		20 40	
Harold Wood	d	19 53	20 03			20 13		20 23		20 33		20 43	
Brentwood	d	19 57	20 07			20 17		20 27		20 37		20 47	
Shenfield 3	a	20 03	20 13	20 00		20 23	20 12	20 33	20 19	20 43	20 33	20 53	20 39
	d			20 00	20 08		20 12		20 20		20 34		20 40
Billericay	d			20 06	20 14				20 26				20 46
Wickford 2	d			20 11	20 20				20 31				20 51
Battlesbridge	d				20 24								
South Woodham Ferrers	d				20 28								
North Fambridge	d				20 34								
Althorne	d				20 39								
Burnham-on-Crouch	d				20 44								
Southminster	a				20 49								
Rayleigh	d			20 16					20 36				20 56
Hockley	d			20 21					20 41				21 01
Rochford	d			20 24					20 45				21 04
Prittlewell	d			20 28					20 48				21 08
Southend Victoria	a			20 31					20 51				21 11

		LE ■	LE	LE	LE ■	LE ■	LE ■	LE	LE ■	LE	LE ■	LE	LE ■
London Liverpool Street 15 ⊖	d	20 18	20 20	20 30	20 34	20 38		20 40	20 48	20 50	20 55	21 05	21 08
Stratford 7 ⊖	d	20 25	20 27	20 37	20 41	20 45		20 47	20 55	20 57	21 02	21 12	21 15
Maryland	d		20 29	20 39				20 49		20 59		21 14	
Forest Gate	d		20 31	20 41				20 51		21 01		21 16	
Manor Park	d		20 33	20 43				20 53		21 03		21 18	
Ilford 2	d		20 36	20 46				20 56		21 06		21 21	
Seven Kings	d		20 38	20 48				20 58		21 08		21 23	
Goodmayes	d		20 40	20 50				21 00		21 10		21 25	
Chadwell Heath	d		20 42	20 52				21 02		21 12		21 27	
Romford	d		20 46	20 56	20 49			21 06		21 16		21 31	21 23
Gidea Park 2	d		20 50	21 00				21 10		21 20		21 35	
Harold Wood	d		20 53	21 03				21 13		21 23		21 38	
Brentwood	d		20 57	21 07				21 17		21 27		21 42	
Shenfield 3	a	20 41	21 03	21 13	20 59	21 02		21 23	21 12	21 33	21 19	21 48	21 33
	d	20 42			21 00	21 02	21 08		21 12		21 20		21 34
Billericay	d				21 06		21 14				21 26		
Wickford 2	d				21 11		21 20				21 31		
Battlesbridge	d						21 24						
South Woodham Ferrers	d						21 28						
North Fambridge	d						21 34						
Althorne	d						21 39						
Burnham-on-Crouch	d						21 44						
Southminster	a						21 49						
Rayleigh	d				21 16						21 36		
Hockley	d				21 21						21 41		
Rochford	d				21 24						21 45		
Prittlewell	d				21 28						21 48		
Southend Victoria	a				21 31						21 51		

Table 5

London - Shenfield, Southminster and Southend Victoria

		LE ■	LE ■	LE	LE	LE ■	LE ■	LE ■	LE	LE ■	LE	LE ■	LE ■
London Liverpool Street 15 ⊖	d	21 15	21 18	21 20	21 35	21 45	21 48		21 50	22 00	22 05	22 15	22 18
Stratford 7 ⊖	d	21 22	21 25	21 27	21 42	21 52	21 55		21 57	22 07	22 12	22 22	22 25
Maryland	d			21 29	21 44				21 59		22 14		
Forest Gate	d			21 31	21 46				22 01		22 16		
Manor Park	d			21 33	21 48				22 03		22 18		
Ilford 2	d			21 36	21 51				22 06		22 21		
Seven Kings	d			21 38	21 53				22 08		22 23		
Goodmayes	d			21 40	21 55				22 10		22 25		
Chadwell Heath	d			21 42	21 57				22 12		22 27		
Romford	d			21 46	22 01				22 16		22 31		
Gidea Park 2	d			21 50	22 05				22 20		22 35		
Harold Wood	d			21 53	22 08				22 23		22 38		
Brentwood	d			21 57	22 12				22 27		22 42		
Shenfield 3	a	21 39	21 41	22 03	22 18	22 09	22 12		22 33	22 23	22 48	22 39	22 41
	d	21 40	21 42			22 10	22 12	22 22		22 24		22 40	22 42
Billericay	d	21 46				22 16		22 28				22 46	
Wickford 2	d	21 51				22 21		22 34				22 51	
Battlesbridge	d							22 38					
South Woodham Ferrers	d							22 42					
North Fambridge	d							22 48					
Althorne	d							22 53					
Burnham-on-Crouch	d							22 58					
Southminster	a							23 03					
Rayleigh	d	21 56				22 26						22 56	
Hockley	d	22 01				22 31						23 01	
Rochford	d	22 05				22 35						23 04	
Prittlewell	d	22 08				22 38						23 08	
Southend Victoria	a	22 11				22 41						23 11	

		LE	LE	LE ■	LE ■	LE	LE ■	LE	LE ■	LE ■	LE	LE	LE ■
London Liverpool Street 15 ⊖	d	22 20	22 35	22 45	22 48	22 50	23 00	23 05	23 15	23 18	23 20	23 35	23 45
Stratford 7 ⊖	d	22 27	22 42	22 52	22 55	22 57	23 07	23 12	23 22	23 25	23 27	23 42	23 52
Maryland	d	22 29	22 44			22 59		23 14			23 29	23 44	
Forest Gate	d	22 31	22 46			23 01		23 16			23 31	23 46	
Manor Park	d	22 33	22 48			23 03		23 18			23 33	23 48	
Ilford 2	d	22 36	22 51			23 06		23 21			23 36	23 51	
Seven Kings	d	22 38	22 53			23 08		23 23			23 38	23 53	
Goodmayes	d	22 40	22 55			23 10		23 25			23 40	23 55	
Chadwell Heath	d	22 42	22 57			23 12		23 27			23 42	23 57	
Romford	d	22 46	23 01			23 16		23 31			23 46	00 01	
Gidea Park 2	d	22 50	23 05			23 20		23 35			23 50	00 05	
Harold Wood	d	22 53	23 08			23 23		23 38			23 53	00 08	
Brentwood	d	22 57	23 12			23 27		23 42			23 57	00 12	
Shenfield 3	a	23 03	23 18	23 09	23 11	23 33	23 23	23 48	23 39	23 41	00 03	00 18	00 09
	d			23 10	23 12		23 24		23 40	23 42			00 10
Billericay	d			23 16					23 46				00 16
Wickford 2	d			23 21					23 51				00 21
Battlesbridge	d												
South Woodham Ferrers	d												
North Fambridge	d												
Althorne	d												
Burnham-on-Crouch	d												
Southminster	a												
Rayleigh	d			23 26					23 56				00 26
Hockley	d			23 31					00 01				00 31
Rochford	d			23 34					00 04				00 34
Prittlewell	d			23 38					00 08				00 38
Southend Victoria	a			23 45					00 15				00 45

		LE ■	LE
London Liverpool Street 15 ⊖	d	23 48	23 50
Stratford 7 ⊖	d	23 55	23 57
Maryland	d		23 59
Forest Gate	d		00 01
Manor Park	d		00 03
Ilford 2	d		00 06
Seven Kings	d		00 08
Goodmayes	d		00 10
Chadwell Heath	d		00 12
Romford	d		00 16
Gidea Park 2	d		00 20
Harold Wood	d		00 23
Brentwood	d		00 27
Shenfield 3	a	00 11	00 33
	d	00 12	
Billericay	d		
Wickford 2	d		
Battlesbridge	d		
South Woodham Ferrers	d		
North Fambridge	d		
Althorne	d		
Burnham-on-Crouch	d		
Southminster	a		
Rayleigh	d		
Hockley	d		
Rochford	d		
Prittlewell	d		
Southend Victoria	a		

Table 5

Sundays

London - Shenfield, Southminster and Southend Victoria

	LE ■	LE	LE	LE ■	LE ■	LE	LE	LE ■	LE ■	LE	LE	LE ■	LE	LE	LE	LE ■	LE ■	LE	LE ■	LE ■	LE ■	LE	LE ■
London Liverpool Street ⊖ d	23p15	23p20	23p35	23p45	23p48	23p50	00 01	00 15	00 18	00 20	00 32	00 50	00 55	06 35	07 05		07 15	07 35		07 45	08 02	08 05	08 15
Stratford ⊖ d	23p22	23p27	23p42	23p52	23p55	23p57	00 08	00 22	00 25	00 27	00 39	00 57	01 02	06 42	07 12		07 22	07 42		07 52	08 09	08 12	08 22
Maryland d		23p29	23p44			23p59	00 10			00 29	00 41		01 04	06 43	07 13			07 43				08 13	
Forest Gate d		23p31	23p46			00 01	00 12			00 31	00 43		01 06	06 45	07 15			07 45				08 15	
Manor Park d		23p33	23p48			00 03	00 14			00 33	00 45		01 08	06 47	07 17			07 47				08 17	
Ilford d		23p36	23p51			00 06	00 17			00 36	00 48		01 11	06 50	07 20			07 50				08 20	
Seven Kings d		23p38	23p53			00 08	00 19			00 38	00 50		01 13	06 53	07 23			07 53				08 23	
Goodmayes d		23p40	23p55			00 10	00 21			00 40	00 52		01 15	06 55	07 25			07 55				08 25	
Chadwell Heath d		23p42	23p57			00 12	00 23			00 42	00 54		01 17	06 57	07 27			07 57				08 27	
Romford d		23p46	00 01			00 16	00 27	00 32		00 46	00 58	01 08	01 21	07 00	07 30		07 33	08 00		08 03		08 30	08 33
Gidea Park d		23p50	00 05			00 20	00a31			00 50	01a02		01 25	07 04	07 34		07 37	08 04		08 07		08 34	08 37
Harold Wood d		23p53	00 08			00 23				00 53			01 28	07 07	07 37		07 40	08 07		08 10		08 37	08 40
Brentwood d		23p57	00 12			00 27				00 57			01 32	07 11	07 41		07 44	08 11		08 14		08 41	08 44
Shenfield a	23p40	00 03	00 18	00 09	00 11	00 33		00 44	00 47	01 03		01 20	01 38	07 18	07 48		07 50	08 18		08 20	08 30	08 48	08 50
d	23p40			00 10	00 2			00 45	00 47			01 20					07 50			08 20	08 31		08 50
Billericay d	23p46			00 16				00 51				01 26					07 56			08 26			08 56
Wickford d	23p52			00 21				00 56				01 31				07 30	08 01		08 05	08 31			09 01
Battlesbridge d																07 34			08 09				
South Woodham Ferrers d																07 38			08 13				
North Fambridge d																07 44			08 20				
Althorne d																07 49			08 25				
Burnham-on-Crouch d																07 54			08 30				
Southminster a																07 59			08 35				
Rayleigh d	23p57			00 26				01 01				01 36					08 06			08 36			09 06
Hockley d	00 02			00 31				01 06				01 41					08 11			08 41			09 11
Rochford d	00 05			00 34				01 09				01 44					08 14			08 44			09 14
Prittlewell d	00 08			00 38				01 13				01 48											
Southend Victoria a	00 16			00 45				01 20				01 55					08 22			08 52			09 22

	LE ■	LE	LE ■	LE ■	LE	LE ■	LE	LE ■	LE	LE ■	LE	LE ■	LE ■	LE	LE ■	LE	LE ■	LE	LE ■	LE	LE ■	LE ■	LE
London Liverpool Street ⊖ d	08 32	08 35		08 45	08 47	09 02	09 05	09 15	09 17	09 32	09 35		09 45	09 47	10 02	10 05	10 15	10 17	10 32	10 35		10 45	10 47
Stratford ⊖ d	08 39	08 42		08 52	08 54	09 09	09 12	09 22	09 24	09 39	09 42		09 52	09 54	10 09	10 12	10 22	10 24	10 39	10 42		10 52	10 54
Maryland d		08 43					09 13				09 43					10 13				10 43			
Forest Gate d		08 45			08 57		09 15		09 27		09 45			09 57		10 15		10 27		10 45			10 57
Manor Park d		08 47			08 59		09 17		09 29		09 47			09 59		10 17		10 29		10 47			10 59
Ilford d		08 50			09 02		09 20		09 32		09 50			10 02		10 20		10 32		10 50			11 02
Seven Kings d		08 53			09 04		09 23		09 34		09 53			10 04		10 23		10 34		10 53			11 04
Goodmayes d		08 55			09 06		09 25		09 36		09 55			10 06		10 25		10 36		10 55			11 06
Chadwell Heath d		08 57			09 08		09 27		09 38		09 57			10 08		10 27		10 38		10 57			11 08
Romford d		09 00		09 03	09 12		09 30	09 33	09 42		10 00		10 03	10 12		10 30	10 33	10 42		11 00		11 03	11 12
Gidea Park d		09 04		09 07	09a17		09 34	09 37	09a47		10 04		10 07	10a17		10 34	10 37	10a47		11 04		11 07	11a17
Harold Wood d		09 07		09 10			09 37	09 40			10 07		10 10			10 37	10 40			11 07		11 10	
Brentwood d		09 11		09 14			09 41	09 44			10 11		10 14			10 41	10 44			11 11		11 14	
Shenfield a	09 00	09 18		09 20		09 30	09 48	09 50		10 00	10 18		10 20		10 30	10 48	10 50		11 00	11 18		11 20	
d	09 01			09 20		09 31		09 50		10 01			10 20		10 31		10 50		11 01			11 20	
Billericay d				09 26				09 56					10 26				10 56					11 26	
Wickford d			09 05	09 31				10 01				10 05	10 31				11 01				11 05	11 31	
Battlesbridge d			09 09									10 09									11 09		
South Woodham Ferrers d			09 13									10 13									11 13		
North Fambridge d			09 20									10 20									11 20		
Althorne d			09 25									10 25									11 25		
Burnham-on-Crouch d			09 30									10 30									11 30		
Southminster a			09 35									10 35									11 35		
Rayleigh d				09 36				10 06					10 36				11 06					11 36	
Hockley d				09 41				10 11					10 41				11 11					11 41	
Rochford d				09 44				10 14					10 44				11 14					11 44	
Prittlewell d																							
Southend Victoria a				09 52				10 22					10 52				11 22					11 52	

	LE ■	LE	LE ■	LE	LE ■	LE	LE ■	LE ■	LE	LE ■	LE	LE ■	LE	LE ■	LE	LE ■	LE ■	LE	LE ■	LE	LE ■	LE	LE ■
London Liverpool Street ⊖ d	11 02	11 05	11 15	11 17	11 32	11 35		11 45	11 47	12 02	12 05	12 15	12 17	12 32	12 35		12 45	12 47	13 02	13 05	13 15	13 17	13 32
Stratford ⊖ d	11 09	11 12	11 22	11 24	11 39	11 42		11 52	11 54	12 09	12 12	12 22	12 24	12 39	12 42		12 52	12 54	13 09	13 12	13 22	13 24	13 39
Maryland d		11 13				11 43					12 13				12 43					13 13			
Forest Gate d		11 15		11 27		11 45			11 57		12 15		12 27		12 45			12 57		13 15		13 27	
Manor Park d		11 17		11 29		11 47			11 59		12 17		12 29		12 47			12 59		13 17		13 29	
Ilford d		11 20		11 32		11 50			12 02		12 20		12 32		12 50			13 02		13 20		13 32	
Seven Kings d		11 23		11 34		11 53			12 04		12 23		12 34		12 53			13 04		13 23		13 34	
Goodmayes d		11 25		11 36		11 55			12 06		12 25		12 36		12 55			13 06		13 25		13 36	
Chadwell Heath d		11 27		11 38		11 57			12 08		12 27		12 38		12 57			13 08		13 27		13 38	
Romford d		11 30	11 33	11 42		12 00		12 03	12 12		12 30	12 33	12 42		13 00		13 03	13 12		13 30	13 33	13 42	
Gidea Park d		11 34	11 37	11a47		12 04		12 07	12a17		12 34	12 37	12a47		13 04		13 07	13a17		13 34	13 37	13a47	
Harold Wood d		11 37	11 40			12 07		12 10			12 37	12 40			13 07		13 10			13 37	13 40		
Brentwood d		11 41	11 44			12 11		12 14			12 41	12 44			13 11		13 14			13 41	13 44		
Shenfield a	11 30	11 48	11 50		12 00	12 18		12 20		12 30	12 48	12 50		13 00	13 18		13 20		13 30	13 48	13 50		14 00
d	11 31		11 50		12 01			12 20		12 31		12 50		13 01			13 20		13 31		13 50		14 01
Billericay d			11 56					12 26				12 56					13 26				13 56		
Wickford d			12 01				12 05	12 31				13 01				13 05	13 31				14 01		
Battlesbridge d							12 09									13 09							
South Woodham Ferrers d							12 13									13 13							
North Fambridge d							12 20									13 20							
Althorne d							12 25									13 25							
Burnham-on-Crouch d							12 30									13 30							
Southminster a							12 35									13 35							
Rayleigh d			12 06					12 36				13 06					13 36				14 06		
Hockley d			12 11					12 41				13 11					13 41				14 11		
Rochford d			12 14					12 44				13 14					13 44				14 14		
Prittlewell d																							
Southend Victoria a			12 22					12 52				13 22					13 52				14 22		

Table 5

Sundays

London - Shenfield, Southminster and Southend Victoria

	LE	LE ■	LE ■	LE	LE ■	LE	LE ■	LE	LE ■	LE	LE ■	LE ■	LE	LE ■	LE	LE ■	LE	LE ■	LE	LE ■	LE ■	LE	LE ■	LE
London Liverpool Street ⊖ d	13 35		13 45	13 47	14 02	14 05	14 15	14 17	14 32	14 35		14 45	14 47	15 02	15 05	15 15	15 17	15 32	15 35		15 45	15 47	16 02	16 05
Stratford ⊖ d	13 42		13 52	13 54	14 09	14 12	14 22	14 24	14 39	14 42		14 52	14 54	15 09	15 12	15 22	15 24	15 39	15 42		15 52	15 54	16 09	16 12
Maryland d	13 43					14 13				14 43					15 13				15 43					16 13
Forest Gate d	13 45			13 57		14 15		14 27		14 45			14 57		15 15		15 27		15 45			15 57		16 15
Manor Park d	13 47			13 59		14 17		14 29		14 47			14 59		15 17		15 29		15 47			15 59		16 17
Ilford d	13 50			14 02		14 20		14 32		14 50			15 02		15 20		15 32		15 50			16 02		16 20
Seven Kings d	13 53			14 04		14 23		14 34		14 53			15 04		15 23		15 34		15 53			16 04		16 23
Goodmayes d	13 55			14 06		14 25		14 36		14 55			15 06		15 25		15 36		15 55			16 06		16 25
Chadwell Heath d	13 57			14 08		14 27		14 38		14 57			15 08		15 27		15 38		15 57			16 08		16 27
Romford d	14 00		14 03	14 12		14 30	14 33	14 42		15 00		15 03	15 12		15 30	15 33	15 42		16 00		16 03	16 12		16 30
Gidea Park d	14 04		14 07	14a17		14 34	14 37	14a47		15 04		15 07	15a17		15 34	15 37	15a47		16 04		16 07	16a17		16 34
Harold Wood d	14 07		14 10			14 37	14 40			15 07		15 10			15 37	15 40			16 07		16 10			16 37
Brentwood d	14 11		14 14			14 41	14 44			15 11		15 14			15 41	15 44			16 11		16 14			16 41
Shenfield a	14 18		14 20		14 30	14 48	14 50		15 00	15 18		15 20		15 30	15 48	15 50		16 00	16 18		16 20		16 30	16 48
d			14 20		14 31		14 50		15 01			15 20		15 31		15 50		16 01			16 20		16 31	
Billericay d			14 26				14 56					15 26				15 56					16 26			
Wickford d		14 05	14 31				15 01				15 05	15 31				16 01				16 05	16 31			
Battlesbridge d		14 09									15 09									16 09				
South Woodham Ferrers d		14 13									15 13									16 13				
North Fambridge d		14 20									15 20									16 20				
Althorne d		14 25									15 25									16 25				
Burnham-on-Crouch d		14 30									15 30									16 30				
Southminster a		14 35									15 35									16 35				
Rayleigh d			14 36				15 06					15 36				16 06					16 36			
Hockley d			14 41				15 11					15 41				16 11					16 41			
Rochford d			14 44				15 14					15 44				16 14					16 44			
Prittlewell d																								
Southend Victoria a			14 52				15 22					15 52				16 22					16 52			

	LE ■	LE	LE ■	LE	LE ■	LE ■	LE	LE ■	LE	LE ■	LE	LE ■	LE	LE ■	LE ■	LE	LE ■	LE	LE ■	LE	LE ■	LE	LE ■	LE ■
London Liverpool Street ⊖ d	16 15	16 17	16 32	16 35		16 45	16 47	17 02	17 05	17 15	17 17	17 32	17 35		17 45	17 47	18 02	18 05	18 15	18 17	18 32	18 35		18 45
Stratford ⊖ d	16 22	16 24	16 39	16 42		16 52	16 54	17 09	17 12	17 22	17 24	17 39	17 42		17 52	17 54	18 09	18 12	18 22	18 24	18 39	18 42		18 52
Maryland d				16 43					17 13				17 43					18 13				18 43		
Forest Gate d		16 27		16 45			16 57		17 15		17 27		17 45			17 57		18 15		18 27		18 45		
Manor Park d		16 29		16 47			16 59		17 17		17 29		17 47			17 59		18 17		18 29		18 47		
Ilford d		16 32		16 50			17 02		17 20		17 32		17 50			18 02		18 20		18 32		18 50		
Seven Kings d		16 34		16 53			17 04		17 23		17 34		17 53			18 04		18 23		18 34		18 53		
Goodmayes d		16 36		16 55			17 06		17 25		17 36		17 55			18 06		18 25		18 36		18 55		
Chadwell Heath d		16 38		16 57			17 08		17 27		17 38		17 57			18 08		18 27		18 38		18 57		
Romford d	16 33	16 42		17 00		17 03	17 12		17 30	17 33	17 42		18 00		18 03	18 12		18 30	18 33	18 42		19 00		19 03
Gidea Park d	16 37	16a47		17 04		17 07	17a17		17 34	17 37	17a47		18 04		18 07	18a17		18 34	18 37	18a47		19 04		19 07
Harold Wood d	16 40			17 07		17 10			17 37	17 40			18 07		18 10			18 37	18 40			19 07		19 10
Brentwood d	16 44			17 11		17 14			17 41	17 44			18 11		18 14			18 41	18 44			19 11		19 14
Shenfield a	16 50		17 00	17 18		17 20		17 30	17 48	17 50		18 00	18 18		18 20		18 30	18 48	18 50		19 00	19 18		19 20
d	16 50		17 01			17 20		17 31		17 50		18 01			18 20		18 31		18 50		19 01			19 20
Billericay d	16 56					17 26				17 56					18 26				18 56					19 26
Wickford d	17 01				17 05	17 31				18 01				18 05	18 31				19 01				19 05	19 31
Battlesbridge d					17 09									18 09									19 09	
South Woodham Ferrers d					17 13									18 13									19 13	
North Fambridge d					17 20									18 20									19 20	
Althorne d					17 25									18 25									19 25	
Burnham-on-Crouch d					17 30									18 30									19 30	
Southminster a					17 35									18 35									19 35	
Rayleigh d	17 06					17 36				18 06					18 36				19 06					19 36
Hockley d	17 11					17 41				18 11					18 41				19 11					19 41
Rochford d	17 14					17 44				18 14					18 44				19 14					19 44
Prittlewell d																								
Southend Victoria a	17 22					17 52				18 22					18 52				19 22					19 52

	LE	LE ■	LE	LE ■	LE	LE ■	LE	LE ■	LE ■	LE	LE ■	LE ■	LE	LE ■	LE	LE ■	LE	LE ■	LE ■	LE	LE ■	LE	LE ■	LE
London Liverpool Street ⊖ d	18 47	19 02	19 05	19 15	19 17	19 32	19 35		19 45	19 47	20 00	20 02	20 05	20 15	20 17	20 32	20 35		20 45	20 47	21 02	21 05	21 15	21 17
Stratford ⊖ d	18 54	19 09	19 12	19 22	19 24	19 39	19 42		19 52	19 54		20 09	20 12	20 22	20 24	20 39	20 42		20 52	20 54	21 09	21 12	21 22	21 24
Maryland d			19 13				19 43						20 13				20 43					21 13		
Forest Gate d	18 57		19 15		19 27		19 45			19 57			20 15		20 27		20 45			20 57		21 15		21 27
Manor Park d	18 59		19 17		19 29		19 47			19 59			20 17		20 29		20 47			20 59		21 17		21 29
Ilford d	19 02		19 20		19 32		19 50			20 02			20 20		20 32		20 50			21 02		21 20		21 32
Seven Kings d	19 04		19 23		19 34		19 53			20 04			20 23		20 34		20 53			21 04		21 23		21 34
Goodmayes d	19 06		19 25		19 36		19 55			20 06			20 25		20 36		20 55			21 06		21 25		21 36
Chadwell Heath d	19 08		19 27		19 38		19 57			20 08			20 27		20 38		20 57			21 08		21 27		21 38
Romford d	19 12		19 30	19 33	19 42		20 00		20 03	20 12			20 30	20 33	20 42		21 00		21 03	21 12		21 30	21 33	21 42
Gidea Park d	19a17		19 34	19 37	19a47		20 04		20 07	20a17			20 34	20 37	20a47		21 04		21 07	21a17		21 34	21 37	21a47
Harold Wood d			19 37	19 40			20 07		20 10				20 37	20 40			21 07		21 10			21 37	21 40	
Brentwood d			19 41	19 44			20 11		20 14				20 41	20 44			21 11		21 14			21 41	21 44	
Shenfield a		19 30	19 48	19 50		20 00	20 18		20 20		20 27	20 30	20 48	20 50		21 00	21 18		21 20		21 30	21 48	21 50	
d		19 31		19 50		20 01			20 20		20 27	20 31		20 50		21 01			21 20		21 31		21 50	
Billericay d				19 56					20 26					20 56					21 26				21 56	
Wickford d				20 01				20 05	20 31					21 01				21 05	21 31				22 01	
Battlesbridge d								20 09										21 09						
South Woodham Ferrers d								20 13										21 13						
North Fambridge d								20 20										21 20						
Althorne d								20 25										21 25						
Burnham-on-Crouch d								20 30										21 30						
Southminster a								20 35										21 35						
Rayleigh d				20 06					20 36					21 06					21 36				22 06	
Hockley d				20 11					20 41					21 11					21 41				22 11	
Rochford d				20 14					20 44					21 14					21 44				22 14	
Prittlewell d																								
Southend Victoria a				20 22					20 52					21 22					21 52				22 22	

Table 5

Sundays

London - Shenfield, Southminster and Southend Victoria

		LE ■	LE	LE ■	LE ■	LE	LE ■	LE	LE ■	LE	LE ■	LE	LE ■	LE ■	LE	LE ■	LE ■	LE	LE ■
London Liverpool Street ■ ⊖	d	21 32	21 35		21 45	21 47	22 02	22 05	22 15	22 17	22 32	22 35	22 45	23 02	23 05	23 15	23 32	23 35	23 45
Stratford ■ ⊖	d	21 39	21 42		21 52	21 54	22 09	22 12	22 22	22 24	22 39	22 42	22 52	23 09	23 12	23 22	23 39	23 42	23 52
Maryland	d		21 43					22 13				22 43			23 13			23 43	
Forest Gate	d		21 45			21 57		22 15		22 27		22 45			23 15			23 45	
Manor Park	d		21 47			21 59		22 17		22 29		22 47			23 17			23 47	
Ilford ■	d		21 50			22 02		22 20		22 32		22 50			23 20			23 50	
Seven Kings	d		21 53			22 04		22 23		22 34		22 53			23 23			23 53	
Goodmayes	d		21 55			22 06		22 25		22 36		22 55			23 25			23 55	
Chadwell Heath	d		21 57			22 08		22 27		22 38		22 57			23 27			23 57	
Romford	d		22 00		22 03	22 12		22 30	22 33	22 42		23 00	23 03		23 30	23 33		23 59	00 03
Gidea Park ■	d		22 04		22 07	22a17		22 34	22 37	22a47		23 04	23 07		23 34	23 37		00 04	00 07
Harold Wood	d		22 07		22 10			22 37	22 40			23 07	23 10		23 37	23 40		00 07	00 10
Brentwood	d		22 11		22 14			22 41	22 44			23 11	23 14		23 41	23 44		00 11	00 14
Shenfield ■	a	22 00	22 18		22 20		22 30	22 48	22 50		23 00	23 18	23 20	23 30	23 48	23 50	00 01	00 18	00 20
	d	22 01			22 20		22 31		22 50		23 01		23 20	23 31		23 50	00 01		00 20
Billericay	d				22 26				22 56				23 26			23 56			00 26
Wickford ■	d			22 05	22 31				23 01				23 31			00 01			00 31
Battlesbridge	d			22 09															
South Woodham Ferrers	d			22 13															
North Fambridge	d			22 20															
Althorne	d			22 25															
Burnham-on-Crouch	d			22 30															
Southminster	a			22 35															
Rayleigh	d				22 36				23 06				23 36			00 06			00 36
Hockley	d				22 41				23 11				23 41			00 11			00 41
Rochford	d				22 44				23 14				23 44			00 14			00 44
Prittlewell	d																		
Southend Victoria	a				22 52				23 24				23 54			00 24			00 54

Table 5

Mondays to Fridays

Southend Victoria, Southminster and Shenfield - London

		LE MX	LE MX ◇■	LE MO ◇■	LE MX ■	LE MX ■	LE MO	LE MX	CC MX	LE	LE	LE	CC	LE ■	LE	LE	LE ■	LE	LE ■	LE ■	LE ■	LE	LE	LE	LE ■
Southend Victoria	d				23p06					04 02		04 32					05 06		05 26						05 46
Prittlewell	d				23p08					04 04		04 34					05 08		05 28						05 48
Rochford	d				23p12					04 08		04 38					05 12		05 32						05 52
Hockley	d				23p16					04 12		04 42					05 16		05 36						05 56
Rayleigh	d				23p20					04 16		04 46					05 20		05 40						06 00
Southminster	d					22p56														05 30					
Burnham-on-Crouch	d					23p00														05 34					
Althorne	d					23p05														05 39					
North Fambridge	d					23p12														05 45					
South Woodham Ferrers	d					23p17														05 50					
Battlesbridge	d					23p21														05 54					
Wickford ■	d				23p25	23p29				04 21		04 51					05 25		05 45	06a00					06 05
Billericay	d				23p31	23p35				04 28		04 58					05 31		05 51						06 11
Shenfield ■	a		23b36	23b36	23p38	23p42				04 39		05 09		05 25			05 38		05 58		06 01				06 18
	d	23p29	23b37	23b37	23p38	23p42	23p43	23p44		04 39		05 09		05 26		05 29	05 38	05 44	05 58		06 02		06 04	06 14	06 18
Brentwood	d	23p32					23p46	23p47		04 42		05 12				05 32		05 47					06 07	06 17	
Harold Wood	d	23p37					23p51	23p52		04 47		05 17				05 37		05 52					06 12	06 22	
Gidea Park ■	d	23p41					23p55	23p56		04 51		05 21		05 33		05 41		05 56				06 06	06 16	06 26	
Romford	d	23p43				23p50	23p57	23p58		04 53		05 23				05 43		05 58				06 08	06 18	06 28	
Chadwell Heath	d	23p47					00 01	00 02		04 57		05 27				05 47		06 02				06 12	06 22	06 32	
Goodmayes	d	23p49					00 03	00 04		04 59		05 29				05 49		06 04				06 14	06 24	06 34	
Seven Kings	d	23p51					00 05	00 06		05 01		05 31		05 38		05 51		06 06				06 16	06 26	06 36	
Ilford ■	d	23p54					00 08	00 09		05 04	05 09	05 34			05 39	05 54		06 09				06 19	06 29	06 39	
Manor Park	d	23p57					00 10	00 12			05 11				05 41	05 57		06 12				06 22	06 32	06 42	
Forest Gate	d	23p59					00 12	00 14			05 14				05 44	05 59		06 14				06 24	06 34	06 44	
Maryland	d	00 01					00 14	00 16			05 16				05 46	06 01		06 16				06 26	06 36	06 46	
Stratford ■ ⊖	d	00 03	23p52	23b57	23p54	23p58	00 16	00 18	23p57	05 10	05 18	05 40	05 14	05 44	05 48	06 03	05 53	06 18	06 15		06 18	06 28	06 38	06 48	06 32
London Liverpool Street ■ ⊖	a	00 12	00 03	00 07	00 03	00 07	00 26	00 27	00 11	05 18	05 26	05 48	05 27	05 57	05 56	06 12	06 01	06 27	06 24		06 27	06 37	06 47	06 57	06 41

		LE	LE ■	LE ■	LE	LE ■	LE	LE	LE ■	LE ■	LE	LE	LE	LE	LE	LE ■	LE ■	LE	LE	LE ■	LE ■	LE	LE	LE ■	LE ■
Southend Victoria	d			06 01					06 16				06 29				06 40							06 56	
Prittlewell	d			06 03					06 18				06 31				06 42							06 58	
Rochford	d			06 07					06 22				06 35				06 46							07 02	
Hockley	d			06 11					06 26				06 39				06 50							07 06	
Rayleigh	d			06 15					06 30				06 43				06 54							07 10	
Southminster	d									06 10															06 52
Burnham-on-Crouch	d									06 14															06 56
Althorne	d									06 19															07 01
North Fambridge	d									06 26															07 08
South Woodham Ferrers	d									06 32															07 14
Battlesbridge	d									06 36															07 18
Wickford ■	d			06 20					06 35	06 41			06 48				06 59							07 15	07 23
Billericay	d			06 26					06 42	06 48			06 55				07 05							07 22	07 30
Shenfield ■	a		06 25	06 33		06 39			06 48	06 54			07 01			07 06	07 12			07 16	07 20			07 28	
	d	06 24	06 26	06 33	06 34	06 39		06 44	06 48	06 54		06 54	07 01		07 04	07 06	07 12		07 14	07 16	07 20		07 27	07 28	
Brentwood	d	06 27			06 37			06 47				06 57			07 07				07 17				07 30		
Harold Wood	d	06 32			06 42			06 52				07 02			07 12				07 22				07 35		
Gidea Park ■	d	06 36			06 46		06 49	06 56			06 59	07 06		07 09	07 16			07 19	07 26			07 32	07 39		
Romford	d	06 38			06 48		06 51	06 58			07 01	07 08		07 11	07 18			07 21	07 28			07 34	07 41		
Chadwell Heath	d	06 42			06 52		06 55	07 02			07 05	07 12		07 15	07 22			07 25	07 32			07 38	07 45		
Goodmayes	d	06 44					06 57				07 07			07 17				07 27	07 34			07 40	07 47		
Seven Kings	d	06 46					06 59				07 09			07 19				07 29	07 36			07 42	07 49		
Ilford ■	d	06 49			06 57		07 02	07 07			07 12	07 17		07 22	07 27			07 32	07 39			07 45	07 52		
Manor Park	d	06 52					07 05				07 15			07 25				07 35				07 48			
Forest Gate	d	06 54					07 07				07 17			07 27				07 37				07 50			
Maryland	d	06 56					07 09				07 19			07 29				07 39				07 52			
Stratford ■ ⊖	d	06 58	06 41	06 47	07 03	06s56	07 11	07 14	07s06	07s12	07 21	07 24	07s18	07 31	07 34		07s29	07 41	07 45	07s33	07s37	07 54	07 58	07s46	
London Liverpool Street ■ ⊖	a	07 07	06 49	06 56	07 13	07 07	07 22	07 25	07 16	07 24	07 32	07 35	07 29	07 42	07 45	07 33	07 40	07 52	07 55	07 44	07 48	08 05	08 08	07 57	08 01

b previous night, stops to set down only

Table 5

Mondays to Fridays

Southend Victoria, Southminster and Shenfield - London

		LE ■	LE	LE ■	LE ■	LE ■	LE	LE	LE ■	LE	LE	LE	LE ■	LE ■	LE ■	LE ■	LE ■	LE ■	LE	LE	LE	LE ■	LE ■	LE ■	LE
Southend Victoria	d				07 09	07 17							07 21	07 25			07 33					07 40			
Prittlewell	d				07 11	07 19							07 23	07 27			07 35					07 42			
Rochford	d				07 15	07 23							07 27	07 31			07 39					07 46			
Hockley	d				07 19	07 27							07 31	07 35			07 43					07 50			
Rayleigh	d				07 23	07 31							07 35	07 39			07 47					07 54			
Southminster	d																						07 35		
Burnham-on-Crouch	d																						07 39		
Althorne	d																						07 44		
North Fambridge	d																						07 50		
South Woodham Ferrers	d																						07 58		
Battlesbridge	d																								
Wickford ■	d				07 28	07 36							07 40	07 44			07 52					07 59	08 06		
Billericay	d				07 35	07 43							07 47	07 51			07 59					08 06	08 13		
Shenfield ■	a	07 32		07 38	07 42				07 50				07 55	07 58		08 02	08 06	08 08				08 13		08 20	
	d	07 32	07 34	07 38	07 42			07 44	07 50		07 50		07 56	07 58	08 00	08 02	08 06	08 08			08 10	08 13		08 20	
Brentwood	d		07 37					07 47			07 53		07 59		08 03						08 13				
Harold Wood	d		07 42					07 52			07 58		08 04		08 08						08 18				
Gidea Park ■	d		07 46				07 49	07 56		07 59	08 02	08 05	08 09		08 12				08 15	08 19	08 22				08 29
Romford	d		07 48				07 51	07 58		08 01	08 04	08 07	08 11		08 14				08 17	08 21	08 24				08 31
Chadwell Heath	d		07 52				07 55	08 02		08 05	08 08	08 11	08 15		08 18				08 21	08 25	08 28				08 35
Goodmayes	d		07 54				07 57	08 04		08 07	08 10	08 13	08 17		08 20				08 23	08 27	08 30				08 37
Seven Kings	d		07 56				07 59	08 06		08 09	08 12	08 15	08 19		08 22				08 25	08 29	08 32				08 39
Ilford ■	d		07 59				08 02	08 09		08 12	08 15	08 18	08 22		08 25				08 28	08 32	08 35				08 42
Manor Park	d						08 05					08 21							08 31						
Forest Gate	d						08 07					08 23							08 33						
Maryland	d						08 09					08 25							08 35						
Stratford ■ ⊖	d		08 05	07s55	08s01		08 11	08 15		08 18	08 21	08 27	08 31	08s15	08 33			08s25	08 37	08 40	08 43	08s31			08 50
London Liverpool Street ■ ⊖	a	07 59	08 15	08 06	08 12	08 14	08 22	08 25	08 16	08 28	08 31	08 38	08 39	08 26	08 43	08 28	08 32	08 36	08 48	08 51	08 53	08 44	08 46	08 48	09 01

		LE	LE	LE ■	LE ■	LE	LE	LE	LE ■	LE ■	LE ■	LE	LE	LE ■	LE	LE ■	LE ■	LE ■	LE	LE	LE ■	LE ■	LE	LE ■	LE
Southend Victoria	d			07 53					08 03		08 11						08 26				08 46				
Prittlewell	d			07 55					08 05		08 13						08 28				08 48				
Rochford	d			07 59					08 09		08 17						08 32				08 52				
Hockley	d			08 03					08 13		08 21						08 36				08 56				
Rayleigh	d			08 07					08 17		08 25						08 40				09 00				
Southminster	d																	08 17							
Burnham-on-Crouch	d																	08 21							
Althorne	d																	08 26							
North Fambridge	d																	08 34							
South Woodham Ferrers	d																	08 40							
Battlesbridge	d																	08 44							
Wickford ■	d			08 12					08 22		08 30						08 45	08 49			09 05				
Billericay	d			08 19					08 29		08 37						08 52	08 56			09 12				
Shenfield ■	a			08 26	08 32				08 36	08 40	08 43			08 52		08 55	08 59	09 03			09 19	09 22		09 25	
	d		08 20	08 26	08 32			08 34	08 36	08 40	08 44		08 44	08 52	08 54	08 55	08 59	09 03	09 04	09 14	09 19	09 22	09 24	09 25	09 34
Brentwood	d		08 23					08 37					08 47		08 57				09 07	09 17			09 27		09 37
Harold Wood	d		08 28					08 42					08 52		09 02				09 12	09 22			09 32		09 42
Gidea Park ■	d		08 32				08 39	08 46					08 56		09 06				09 16	09 26			09 36		09 46
Romford	d		08 34				08 41	08 48			08 52		08 58		09 08				09 18	09 28			09 38		09 48
Chadwell Heath	d		08 38				08 45	08 52					09 02		09 12				09 22	09 32			09 42		09 52
Goodmayes	d		08 40				08 47	08 54					09 04		09 14				09 24	09 34			09 44		09 54
Seven Kings	d		08 42				08 49	08 56					09 06		09 16				09 26	09 36			09 46		09 56
Ilford ■	d	08 38	08 45			08 48	08 52	08 59				09 02	09 09		09 19				09 29	09 39			09 49		09 59
Manor Park	d	08 41				08 51						09 05	09 12		09 22				09 32	09 42			09 52		10 02
Forest Gate	d	08 43				08 53						09 07	09 14		09 24				09 34	09 44			09 54		10 04
Maryland	d	08 45				08 55						09 09	09 16		09 26				09 36	09 46			09 56		10 06
Stratford ■ ⊖	d	08 47	08 53	08s45	08s49	08 57	09 00	09 05	08s53		09s03	09 11	09 18	09s09	09 28		09s17	09s20	09 38	09 48	09s36	09s39	09 58		10 08
London Liverpool Street ■ ⊖	a	08 58	09 03	08 56	09 01	09 08	09 11	09 15	09 04	09 06	09 14	09 22	09 27	09 20	09 37	09 22	09 28	09 31	09 47	09 57	09 47	09 50	10 07	09 52	10 17

		LE ■	LE ■	LE	LE ■	LE	LE ■	LE ■	LE	LE ■	LE	LE ■	LE	LE	LE ■	LE ■	LE	LE ■	LE	LE ■	LE ■	LE	LE ■	LE	LE ■
Southend Victoria	d	09 06					09 26					09 46			10 06					10 26					10 46
Prittlewell	d	09 08					09 28					09 48			10 08					10 28					10 48
Rochford	d	09 12					09 32					09 52			10 12					10 32					10 52
Hockley	d	09 16					09 36					09 56			10 16					10 36					10 56
Rayleigh	d	09 20					09 40					10 00			10 20					10 40					11 00
Southminster	d							09 17													10 17				
Burnham-on-Crouch	d							09 21													10 21				
Althorne	d							09 26													10 26				
North Fambridge	d							09 34													10 34				
South Woodham Ferrers	d							09 39													10 39				
Battlesbridge	d							09 43													10 43				
Wickford ■	d	09 25					09 45	09 49				10 05			10 25					10 45	10 49				11 05
Billericay	d	09 31					09 51	09 55				10 11			10 31					10 51	10 55				11 11
Shenfield ■	a	09 38	09 40		09 54		09 58	10 02		10 09		10 18			10 38	10 40		10 51		10 58	11 02		11 09		11 18
	d	09 38	09 40	09 44	09 54	09 54	09 58	10 02	10 04	10 10	10 14	10 18	10 24	10 34	10 38	10 40	10 44	10 51	10 54	10 58		11 04	11 10	11 14	11 18
Brentwood	d			09 47		09 57			10 07		10 17		10 27	10 37			10 47		10 57			11 07		11 17	
Harold Wood	d			09 52		10 02			10 12		10 22		10 32	10 42			10 52		11 02			11 12		11 22	
Gidea Park ■	d			09 56		10 06			10 16		10 26		10 36	10 46			10 56		11 06			11 16		11 26	
Romford	d	09 46		09 58		10 08			10 18		10 28	10 26	10 38	10 48			10 58	10 59	11 08			11 18		11 28	11 26
Chadwell Heath	d			10 02		10 12			10 22		10 32		10 42	10 52			11 02		11 12			11 22		11 32	
Goodmayes	d			10 04		10 14			10 24		10 34		10 44	10 54			11 04		11 14			11 24		11 34	
Seven Kings	d			10 06		10 16			10 26		10 36		10 46	10 56			11 06		11 16			11 26		11 36	
Ilford ■	d			10 09		10 19			10 29		10 39		10 49	10 59			11 09		11 19			11 29		11 39	
Manor Park	d			10 12		10 22			10 32		10 42		10 52	11 02			11 12		11 22			11 32		11 42	
Forest Gate	d			10 14		10 24			10 34		10 44		10 54	11 04			11 14		11 24			11 34		11 44	
Maryland	d			10 16		10 26			10 36		10 46		10 56	11 06			11 16		11 26			11 36		11 46	
Stratford ■ ⊖	d	09s52	09 57	10 18	10 08	10 28	10 13	10 16	10 38	10 24	10 48	10 34	10 58	11 08	10 52	10 55	11 18	11 07	11 28	11 14		11 38	11 24	11 48	11 34
London Liverpool Street ■ ⊖	a	10 03	10 05	10 27	10 17	10 37	10 23	10 25	10 47	10 33	10 57	10 44	11 07	11 17	11 01	11 03	11 27	11 18	11 37	11 23		11 47	11 33	11 57	11 43

Table 5

Mondays to Fridays

Southend Victoria, Southminster and Shenfield - London

		LE	LE	LE ■	LE ■	LE	LE ■	LE	LE ■	LE ■	LE	LE ■	LE	LE ■	LE	LE	LE ■	LE ■	LE	LE ■	LE	LE ■	LE ■	LE	LE ■
Southend Victoria	d			11 06					11 26					11 46			12 06					12 26			
Prittlewell	d			11 08					11 28					11 48			12 08					12 28			
Rochford	d			11 12					11 32					11 52			12 12					12 32			
Hockley	d			11 16					11 36					11 56			12 16					12 36			
Rayleigh	d			11 20					11 40					12 00			12 20					12 40			
Southminster	d									11 17													12 17		
Burnham-on-Crouch	d									11 21													12 21		
Althorne	d									11 26													12 26		
North Fambridge	d									11 34													12 34		
South Woodham Ferrers	d									11 39													12 39		
Battlesbridge	d									11 43													12 43		
Wickford ■	d			11 25					11 45	11 49				12 05			12 25					12 45	12 49		
Billericay	d			11 31					11 51	11 55				12 11			12 31					12 51	12 55		
Shenfield ■	a			11 38	11 40		11 51		11 58	12 02		12 09		12 18			12 38	12 40		12 51		12 58	13 02		13 09
	d	11 24	11 34	11 38	11 40	11 44	11 51	11 54	11 58		12 04	12 10	12 14	12 18	12 24	12 34	12 38	12 40	12 44	12 51	12 54	12 58		13 04	13 10
Brentwood	d	11 27	11 37			11 47		11 57			12 07		12 17		12 27	12 37			12 47		12 57			13 07	
Harold Wood	d	11 32	11 42			11 52		12 02			12 12		12 22		12 32	12 42			12 52		13 02			13 12	
Gidea Park ■	d	11 36	11 46			11 56		12 06			12 16		12 26		12 36	12 46			12 56		13 06			13 16	
Romford	d	11 38	11 48			11 58	11 59	12 08			12 18		12 28	12 26	12 38	12 48			12 58	12 59	13 08			13 18	
Chadwell Heath	d	11 42	11 52			12 02		12 12			12 22		12 32		12 42	12 52			13 02		13 12			13 22	
Goodmayes	d	11 44	11 54			12 04		12 14			12 24		12 34		12 44	12 54			13 04		13 14			13 24	
Seven Kings	d	11 46	11 56			12 06		12 16			12 26		12 36		12 46	12 56			13 06		13 16			13 26	
Ilford ■	d	11 49	11 59			12 09		12 19			12 29		12 39		12 49	12 59			13 09		13 19			13 29	
Manor Park	d	11 52	12 02			12 12		12 22			12 32		12 42		12 52	13 02			13 12		13 22			13 32	
Forest Gate	d	11 54	12 04			12 14		12 24			12 34		12 44		12 54	13 04			13 14		13 24			13 34	
Maryland	d	11 56	12 06			12 16		12 26			12 36		12 46		12 56	13 06			13 16		13 26			13 36	
Stratford ■ ⊖	d	11 58	12 08	11 52	11 55	12 18	12 07	12 28	12 12		12 38	12 24	12 48	12 34	12 58	13 08	12 52	12 55	13 18	13s07	13 28	13 12		13 38	13 24
London Liverpool Street ■ ⊖	a	12 07	12 17	12 01	12 03	12 27	12 16	12 37	12 23		12 47	12 33	12 57	12 43	13 07	13 17	13 01	13 03	13 27	13 16	13 37	13 23		13 47	13 33

		LE	LE ■	LE	LE	LE ■	LE ■	LE	LE ■	LE	LE ■	LE ■	LE	LE ■	LE	LE ■	LE	LE	LE ■	LE ■	LE	LE ■	LE	LE ■	LE ■
Southend Victoria	d		12 46			13 06					13 26					13 46			14 06					14 26	
Prittlewell	d		12 48			13 08					13 28					13 48			14 08					14 28	
Rochford	d		12 52			13 12					13 32					13 52			14 12					14 32	
Hockley	d		12 56			13 16					13 36					13 56			14 16					14 36	
Rayleigh	d		13 00			13 20					13 40					14 00			14 20					14 40	
Southminster	d											13 17													14 17
Burnham-on-Crouch	d											13 21													14 21
Althorne	d											13 26													14 26
North Fambridge	d											13 34													14 34
South Woodham Ferrers	d											13 39													14 39
Battlesbridge	d											13 43													14 43
Wickford ■	d		13 05			13 25					13 45	13 49				14 05			14 25					14 45	14 49
Billericay	d		13 11			13 31					13 51	13 55				14 11			14 31					14 51	14 55
Shenfield ■	a		13 18			13 38	13 40		13 51		13 58	14 02		14 09		14 18			14 38	14 40		14 51		14 58	15 02
	d	13 14	13 18	13 24	13 34	13 38	13 40	13 44	13 51	13 54	13 58		14 04	14 10	14 14	14 18	14 24	14 34	14 38	14 40	14 44	14 51	14 54	14 58	
Brentwood	d	13 17		13 27	13 37			13 47		13 57			14 07		14 17		14 27	14 37			14 47		14 57		
Harold Wood	d	13 22		13 32	13 42			13 52		14 02			14 12		14 22		14 32	14 42			14 52		15 02		
Gidea Park ■	d	13 26		13 36	13 46			13 56		14 06			14 16		14 26		14 36	14 46			14 56		15 06		
Romford	d	13 28	13 26	13 38	13 48			13 58	13 59	14 08			14 18		14 28	14 26	14 38	14 48			14 58	14 59	15 08		
Chadwell Heath	d	13 32		13 42	13 52			14 02		14 12			14 22		14 32		14 42	14 52			15 02		15 12		
Goodmayes	d	13 34		13 44	13 54			14 04		14 14			14 24		14 34		14 44	14 54			15 04		15 14		
Seven Kings	d	13 36		13 46	13 56			14 06		14 16			14 26		14 36		14 46	14 56			15 06		15 16		
Ilford ■	d	13 39		13 49	13 59			14 09		14 19			14 29		14 39		14 49	14 59			15 09		15 19		
Manor Park	d	13 42		13 52	14 02			14 12		14 22			14 32		14 42		14 52	15 02			15 12		15 22		
Forest Gate	d	13 44		13 54	14 04			14 14		14 24			14 34		14 44		14 54	15 04			15 14		15 24		
Maryland	d	13 46		13 56	14 06			14 16		14 26			14 36		14 46		14 56	15 06			15 16		15 26		
Stratford ■ ⊖	d	13 48	13 34	13 58	14 08	13 52	13 55	14 18	14 07	14 28	14 12		14 38	14 24	14 48	14 34	14 58	15 08	14 52	14 55	15 18	15 07	15 28	15 13	
London Liverpool Street ■ ⊖	a	13 57	13 43	14 07	14 17	14 03	14 03	14 27	14 16	14 37	14 23		14 47	14 33	14 57	14 43	15 07	15 17	15 01	15 03	15 27	15 16	15 37	15 24	

		LE	LE ■		LE	LE ■	LE	LE	LE ■	LE ■	LE	LE ■	LE	LE ■	LE ■	LE	LE ■	LE	LE ■	LE	LE ■	LE	LE ■	LE ■	LE
Southend Victoria	d					14 46			15 06					15 26					15 46				16 06		
Prittlewell	d					14 48			15 08					15 28					15 48				16 08		
Rochford	d					14 52			15 12					15 32					15 52				16 12		
Hockley	d					14 56			15 16					15 36					15 56				16 16		
Rayleigh	d					15 00			15 20					15 40					16 00				16 20		
Southminster	d														15 17										
Burnham-on-Crouch	d														15 21										
Althorne	d														15 26										
North Fambridge	d														15 34										
South Woodham Ferrers	d														15 39										
Battlesbridge	d														15 43										
Wickford ■	d					15 05			15 25					15 45	15 49				16 05				16 25		
Billericay	d					15 11			15 31					15 51	15 55				16 11				16 31		
Shenfield ■	a		15 09			15 18			15 38	15 40		15 51		15 58	16 02		16 11		16 18		16 25		16 38	16 40	
	d	15 04	15 10		15 14	15 18	15 24	15 34	15 38	15 40	15 44	15 51	15 54	15 58		16 04	16 12	16 14	16 18	16 24	16 25	16 34	16 38	16 40	16 44
Brentwood	d	15 07			15 17		15 27	15 37			15 47		15 57			16 07		16 17		16 27		16 37			16 47
Harold Wood	d	15 12			15 22		15 32	15 42			15 52		16 02			16 12		16 22		16 32		16 42			16 52
Gidea Park ■	d	15 16			15 26		15 36	15 46			15 56		16 06			16 16		16 26		16 36		16 46			16 56
Romford	d	15 18			15 28	15 26	15 38	15 48			15 58	15 59	16 08			16 18		16 28	16 26	16 38		16 48			16 58
Chadwell Heath	d	15 22			15 32		15 42	15 52			16 02		16 12			16 22		16 32		16 42		16 52			17 02
Goodmayes	d	15 24			15 34		15 44	15 54			16 04		16 14			16 24		16 34		16 44		16 54			17 04
Seven Kings	d	15 26			15 36		15 46	15 56			16 06		16 16			16 26		16 36		16 46		16 56			17 06
Ilford ■	d	15 29			15 39		15 49	15 59			16 09		16 19			16 29		16 39		16 49		16 59			17 09
Manor Park	d	15 32			15 42		15 52	16 02			16 12		16 22			16 32		16 42		16 52		17 02			17 12
Forest Gate	d	15 34			15 44		15 54	16 04			16 14		16 24			16 34		16 44		16 54		17 04			17 14
Maryland	d	15 36			15 46		15 56	16 06			16 16		16 26			16 36		16 46		16 56		17 06			17 16
Stratford ■ ⊖	d	15 38	15 24		15 48	15 34	15 58	16 08	15 52	15 55	16 18	16 07	16 28	16 13		16 38	16 26	16 48	16 34	16 58	16 40	17 08	16 52	16 55	17 18
London Liverpool Street ■ ⊖	a	15 47	15 34		15 57	15 43	16 07	16 17	16 01	16 03	16 27	16 16	16 37	16 22		16 47	16 35	16 57	16 43	17 07	16 49	17 17	17 03	17 05	17 27

Southend Victoria, Southminster and Shenfield - London

Station		LE [1]	LE [1]	LE [1]	LE	LE	LE [1]	LE [1]	LE	LE	LE [1]	LE	LE
Southend Victoria	d		16 21				16 35				16 51		
Prittlewell	d		16 23				16 37				16 53		
Rochford	d		16 27				16 41				16 57		
Hockley	d		16 31				16 45				17 01		
Rayleigh	d		16 35				16 49				17 05		
Southminster	d			16 17									
Burnham-on-Crouch	d			16 21									
Althorne	d			16 26									
North Fambridge	d			16 34									
South Woodham Ferrers	d			16 39									
Battlesbridge	d			16 43									
Wickford [2]	d		16 40	16a50			16 54				17 10		
Billericay	d		16 46				17 00				17 16		
Shenfield [3]	a	16 51	16 53				17 07	17 11			17 23		
	d	16 51	16 53		16 54	17 04	17 07	17 12		17 14	17 23		17 24
Brentwood	d				16 57	17 07				17 17			17 27
Harold Wood	d				17 02	17 12				17 22			17 32
Gidea Park [2]	d				17 06	17 16			17 22	17 26		17 32	17 36
Romford	d				17 08	17 18			17 24	17 28		17 34	17 38
Chadwell Heath	d				17 12	17 22				17 32			17 42
Goodmayes	d				17 14	17 24				17 34			17 44
Seven Kings	d				17 16	17 26				17 36			17 46
Ilford [2]	d				17 19	17 29			17 32	17 39		17 42	17 49
Manor Park	d				17 22				17 35			17 45	
Forest Gate	d				17 24				17 37			17 47	
Maryland	d				17 26				17 39			17 49	
Stratford [7] ⊖	d	17 05	17 08		17 28	17 35		17 26	17 41	17 45	17 37	17 51	17 55
London Liverpool Street [15] ⊖	a	17 15	17 18		17 37	17 43	17 29	17 38	17 50	17 53	17 46	18 00	18 03

Station		LE [1]	LE	LE	LE [1]	LE [1]	LE	LE	LE [1]	LE [1]	LE [1]	LE [1]	LE
Southend Victoria	d					17 06						17 21	
Prittlewell	d					17 08						17 23	
Rochford	d					17 12						17 27	
Hockley	d					17 16						17 31	
Rayleigh	d					17 20						17 35	
Southminster	d									17 05			
Burnham-on-Crouch	d									17 09			
Althorne	d									17 14			
North Fambridge	d									17 21			
South Woodham Ferrers	d									17 26			
Battlesbridge	d									17 30			
Wickford [2]	d					17 25				17 36		17 40	
Billericay	d					17 31				17 42		17 46	
Shenfield [3]	a	17 27			17 36	17 38			17 45	17 49	17 51	17 53	
	d	17 27		17 34	17 36	17 38		17 44	17 46	17 49	17 51	17 53	
Brentwood	d			17 37				17 47					
Harold Wood	d			17 42				17 52					
Gidea Park [2]	d		17 42	17 46			17 52	17 56					18 02
Romford	d		17 44	17 48			17 54	17 58			17 59		18 04
Chadwell Heath	d			17 52				18 02					
Goodmayes	d			17 54				18 04					
Seven Kings	d			17 56				18 06					
Ilford [2]	d		17 52	17 59			18 02	18 09					18 12
Manor Park	d		17 55				18 05						18 15
Forest Gate	d		17 57				18 07						18 17
Maryland	d		17 59				18 09						18 19
Stratford [7] ⊖	d		18 01	18 05	17 50	17 53	18 11	18 15	18 00	18 08	18 07	18 10	18 21
London Liverpool Street [15] ⊖	a	17 49	18 10	18 13	18 00	18 02	18 20	18 23	18 14	18 17	18 19	18 21	18 30

Station		LE	LE	LE	LE [1]	LE	LE	LE [1]	LE [1]	LE	LE	LE [1]	LE
Southend Victoria	d				17 36				17 51				
Prittlewell	d				17 38				17 53				
Rochford	d				17 42				17 57				
Hockley	d				17 46				18 01				
Rayleigh	d				17 50				18 05				
Southminster	d											17 46	
Burnham-on-Crouch	d											17 50	
Althorne	d											17 55	
North Fambridge	d											18 03	
South Woodham Ferrers	d											18 08	
Battlesbridge	d											18 12	
Wickford [2]	d				17 55				18 10			18 18	
Billericay	d				18 01				18 16			18 24	
Shenfield [3]	a				18 08			18 14	18 23			18 31	
	d	17 54		18 04	18 08		18 14	18 15	18 23		18 24	18 31	18 34
Brentwood	d	17 57		18 07			18 17				18 27		18 37
Harold Wood	d	18 02		18 12			18 22				18 32		18 42
Gidea Park [2]	d	18 06	18 12	18 16		18 22	18 26			18 32	18 36		18 46
Romford	d	18 08	18 14	18 18		18 24	18 28			18 34	18 38		18 48
Chadwell Heath	d	18 12		18 22			18 32				18 42		18 52
Goodmayes	d	18 14		18 24			18 34				18 44		18 54
Seven Kings	d	18 16		18 26			18 36				18 46		18 56
Ilford [2]	d	18 19	18 22	18 29		18 32	18 39			18 42	18 49		18 59
Manor Park	d		18 25			18 35				18 45	18 52		19 02
Forest Gate	d		18 27			18 37				18 47	18 54		19 04
Maryland	d		18 29			18 39				18 49	18 56		19 06
Stratford [7] ⊖	d	18 25	18 31	18 35	18 22	18 41	18 45	18 29	18 37	18 51	18 58	18 46	19 08
London Liverpool Street [15] ⊖	a	18 33	18 40	18 43	18 31	18 50	18 53	18 38	18 48	19 00	19 07	18 55	19 17

Station		LE [1]	LE [1]	LE	LE [1]	LE	LE [1]	LE	LE [1]	LE [1]	LE	LE [1]	LE [1]
Southend Victoria	d	18 06					18 26						18 46
Prittlewell	d	18 08					18 28						18 48
Rochford	d	18 12					18 32						18 52
Hockley	d	18 16					18 36						18 56
Rayleigh	d	18 20					18 40						19 00
Southminster	d									18 27			
Burnham-on-Crouch	d									18 31			
Althorne	d									18 36			
North Fambridge	d									18 43			
South Woodham Ferrers	d									18 48			
Battlesbridge	d									18 52			
Wickford [2]	d	18 25					18 45			18 58			19 05
Billericay	d	18 31					18 51			19 04			19 11
Shenfield [3]	a	18 38	18 40		18 51		18 58		19 09	19 11		19 15	19 18
	d	18 38	18 40	18 44	18 51	18 54	18 58	19 04	19 10		19 14	19 16	19 18
Brentwood	d			18 47		18 57		19 07			19 17		
Harold Wood	d			18 52		19 02		19 12			19 22		
Gidea Park [2]	d			18 56		19 06		19 16			19 26		
Romford	d			18 58	18 59	19 08		19 18			19 28		19 26
Chadwell Heath	d			19 02		19 12		19 22			19 32		
Goodmayes	d			19 04		19 14		19 24			19 34		
Seven Kings	d			19 06		19 16		19 26			19 36		
Ilford [2]	d			19 09		19 19		19 29			19 39		
Manor Park	d			19 12		19 22		19 32			19 42		
Forest Gate	d			19 14		19 24		19 34			19 44		
Maryland	d			19 16		19 26		19 36			19 46		
Stratford [7] ⊖	d	18 52	18 55	19 18	19 07	19 28	19 12	19 38	19 26		19 48		19 35
London Liverpool Street [15] ⊖	a	19 01	19 05	19 27	19 16	19 37	19 23	19 47	19 35		19 57	19 40	19 44

Station		LE	LE	LE [1]	LE [1]	LE	LE [1]	LE	LE [1]	LE [1]	LE	LE [1]	LE
Southend Victoria	d			19 06					19 26				
Prittlewell	d			19 08					19 28				
Rochford	d			19 12					19 32				
Hockley	d			19 16					19 36				
Rayleigh	d			19 20					19 40				
Southminster	d									19 17			
Burnham-on-Crouch	d									19 21			
Althorne	d									19 26			
North Fambridge	d									19 34			
South Woodham Ferrers	d									19 39			
Battlesbridge	d									19 43			
Wickford [2]	d			19 25					19 45	19 49			
Billericay	d			19 31					19 51	19 55			
Shenfield [3]	a			19 38	19 40		19 51		19 58	20 03		20 09	
	d	19 24	19 34	19 38	19 40	19 44	19 51	19 54	19 58		20 04	20 10	20 14
Brentwood	d	19 27	19 37			19 47		19 57			20 07		20 17
Harold Wood	d	19 32	19 42			19 52		20 02			20 12		20 22
Gidea Park [2]	d	19 36	19 46			19 56		20 06			20 16		20 26
Romford	d	19 38	19 48			19 58	19 59	20 08			20 18		20 28
Chadwell Heath	d	19 42	19 52			20 02		20 12			20 22		20 32
Goodmayes	d	19 44	19 54			20 04		20 14			20 24		20 34
Seven Kings	d	19 46	19 56			20 06		20 16			20 26		20 36
Ilford [2]	d	19 49	19 59			20 09		20 19			20 29		20 39
Manor Park	d	19 52	20 02			20 12		20 22			20 32		20 42
Forest Gate	d	19 54	20 04			20 14		20 24			20 34		20 44
Maryland	d	19 56	20 06			20 16		20 26			20 36		20 46
Stratford [7] ⊖	d	19 58	20 08	19 52	19 55	20 18	20 07	20 28	20 12		20 38	20 24	20 48
London Liverpool Street [15] ⊖	a	20 07	20 17	20 03	20 04	20 27	20 16	20 37	20 21		20 47	20 33	20 57

Station		LE [1]	CC	LE	LE	LE [1]	LE [1]	LE	LE [1]	LE	LE [1]	LE [1]	CC
Southend Victoria	d	19 46				20 06					20 26		
Prittlewell	d	19 48				20 08					20 28		
Rochford	d	19 52				20 12					20 32		
Hockley	d	19 56				20 16					20 36		
Rayleigh	d	20 00				20 20					20 40		
Southminster	d											20 17	
Burnham-on-Crouch	d											20 21	
Althorne	d											20 26	
North Fambridge	d											20 34	
South Woodham Ferrers	d											20 39	
Battlesbridge	d											20 43	
Wickford [2]	d	20 05				20 25					20 45	20 49	
Billericay	d	20 11				20 31					20 51	20 55	
Shenfield [3]	a	20 18				20 38	20 40		20 51		20 58	21 02	
	d	20 18		20 24	20 34	20 38	20 40	20 44	20 51	20 54	20 58		
Brentwood	d			20 27	20 37			20 47		20 57			
Harold Wood	d			20 32	20 42			20 52		21 02			
Gidea Park [2]	d			20 36	20 46			20 56		21 06			
Romford	d	20 26		20 38	20 48			20 58	20 59	21 08			
Chadwell Heath	d			20 42	20 52			21 02		21 12			
Goodmayes	d			20 44	20 54			21 04		21 14			
Seven Kings	d			20 46	20 56			21 06		21 16			
Ilford [2]	d			20 49	20 59			21 09		21 19			
Manor Park	d			20 52	21 02			21 12		21 22			
Forest Gate	d			20 54	21 04			21 14		21 24			
Maryland	d			20 56	21 06			21 16		21 26			
Stratford [7] ⊖	d	20 34	20 20	20 58	21 08	20 52	20 55	21 18	21 07	21 28	21 13		21 00
London Liverpool Street [15] ⊖	a	20 43	20 33	21 07	21 17	21 01	21 04	21 27	21 16	21 37	21 22		21 12

Table 5 — Mondays to Fridays

Southend Victoria, Southminster and Shenfield - London

Station		LE	LE [1]	CC	LE	LE [1]	LE	LE	LE [1]	LE [1]	LE	LE [1]	LE [1]
Southend Victoria	d					20 46			21 06				
Prittlewell	d					20 48			21 08				
Rochford	d					20 52			21 12				
Hockley	d					20 56			21 16				
Rayleigh	d					21 00			21 20				
Southminster	d												
Burnham-on-Crouch	d												
Althorne	d												
North Fambridge	d												
South Woodham Ferrers	d												
Battlesbridge	d												
Wickford [2]	d					21 05			21 25				
Billericay	d					21 11			21 31				
Shenfield [3]	a		21 09			21 18			21 38	21 40		21 51	21 58
	d	21 04	21 10		21 14	21 18	21 24	21 34	21 38	21 40	21 44	21 51	21 58
Brentwood	d	21 07			21 17		21 27	21 37			21 47		
Harold Wood	d	21 12			21 22		21 32	21 42			21 52		
Gidea Park [2]	d	21 16			21 26		21 36	21 46			21 56		
Romford	d	21 18			21 28	21 26	21 38	21 48			21 58	21 59	
Chadwell Heath	d	21 22			21 32		21 42	21 52			22 02		
Goodmayes	d	21 24			21 34		21 44	21 54			22 04		
Seven Kings	d	21 26			21 36		21 46	21 56			22 06		
Ilford [2]	d	21 29			21 39		21 49	21 59			22 09		
Manor Park	d	21 32			21 42		21 52	22 02			22 12		
Forest Gate	d	21 34			21 44		21 54	22 04			22 14		
Maryland	d	21 36			21 46		21 56	22 06			22 16		
Stratford [7] ⊖	d	21 38	21 24	21 14	21 48	21 34	21 58	22 08	21 52	21 55	22 18	22 07	22 12
London Liverpool Street [15] ⊖	a	21 47	21 33	21 26	21 57	21 43	22 07	22 17	22 01	22 03	22 27	22 16	22 23

Station		LE	LE [1]	LE [1]	LE [1]	LE	LE	LE [1]	LE [1]	LE [1]	LE	LE [1]	LE
Southend Victoria	d			21 36				22 06					
Prittlewell	d			21 38				22 08					
Rochford	d			21 42				22 12					
Hockley	d			21 46				22 16					
Rayleigh	d			21 50				22 20					
Southminster	d		21 17						22 17				
Burnham-on-Crouch	d		21 21						22 21				
Althorne	d		21 26						22 26				
North Fambridge	d		21 34						22 34				
South Woodham Ferrers	d		21 39						22 39				
Battlesbridge	d		21 43						22 43				
Wickford [2]	d		21 49	21 55				22 25	22a49				
Billericay	d		21 55	22 01				22 31					
Shenfield [3]	a		22 02	22 08	22 10			22 38		22 40		22 51	
	d	21 59		22 08	22 11	22 14	22 29	22 38		22 40	22 44	22 51	22 59
Brentwood	d	22 02				22 17	22 32				22 47		23 02
Harold Wood	d	22 07				22 22	22 37				22 52		23 07
Gidea Park [2]	d	22 11				22 26	22 41				22 56		23 11
Romford	d	22 13				22 28	22 43				22 58	22 59	23 13
Chadwell Heath	d	22 17				22 32	22 47				23 02		23 17
Goodmayes	d	22 19				22 34	22 49				23 04		23 19
Seven Kings	d	22 21				22 36	22 51				23 06		23 21
Ilford [2]	d	22 24				22 39	22 54				23 09		23 24
Manor Park	d	22 27				22 42	22 57				23 12		23 27
Forest Gate	d	22 29				22 44	22 59				23 14		23 29
Maryland	d	22 31				22 46	23 01				23 16		23 31
Stratford [7] ⊖	d	22 33		22 22	22 27	22 48	23 03	22 52		22 55	23 18	23 07	23 33
London Liverpool Street [15] ⊖	a	22 42		22 31	22 36	22 57	23 12	23 01		23 03	23 27	23 16	23 42

Station		LE [1]	LE [1]	LE	LE	LE [1]	LE [1]	LE	LE	LE ◇[1]	LE [1]	LE [1]	LE
Southend Victoria	d	22 36				23 06					23p06		
Prittlewell	d	22 38				23 08					23p08		
Rochford	d	22 42				23 12					23p12		
Hockley	d	22 46				23 16					23p16		
Rayleigh	d	22 50				23 20					23p20		
Southminster	d						22 56					22p56	
Burnham-on-Crouch	d						23 00					23p00	
Althorne	d						23 05					23p05	
North Fambridge	d						23 12					23p12	
South Woodham Ferrers	d						23 17					23p17	
Battlesbridge	d						23 21					23p21	
Wickford [2]	d	22 55				23 25	23 29				23p25	23p29	
Billericay	d	23 01				23 31	23 35				23p31	23p35	
Shenfield [3]	a	23 08	23 09			23 38	23 42			23b36	23p38	23p42	
	d	23 08	23 10	23 14	23 29	23 38	23 42	23 44	23p29	23b37	23p38	23p42	23p44
Brentwood	d			23 17	23 32			23 47	23p32				23p47
Harold Wood	d			23 22	23 37			23 52	23p37				23p52
Gidea Park [2]	d			23 26	23 41			23 56	23p41				23p56
Romford	d			23 28	23 43		23 50	23 58	23p43			23p50	23p58
Chadwell Heath	d			23 32	23 47			00 02	23p47				00 02
Goodmayes	d			23 34	23 49			00 04	23p49				00 04
Seven Kings	d			23 36	23 51			00 06	23p51				00 06
Ilford [2]	d			23 39	23 54			00 09	23p54				00 09
Manor Park	d			23 42	23 57			00 12	23p57				00 12
Forest Gate	d			23 44	23 59			00 14	23p59				00 14
Maryland	d			23 46	00 01			00 16	00 01				00 16
Stratford [7] ⊖	d	23 22	23 25	23 48	00 03	23 54	23 58	00 18	00 03	23p52	23p54	23p58	00 18
London Liverpool Street [15] ⊖	a	23 31	23 34	23 57	00 12	00 03	00 07	00 27	00 12	00 03	00 03	00 07	00 27

Station		CC	LE	LE	LE	LE [1]	LE [1]	LE	LE	CC	LE [1]	LE [1]	LE [1]
Southend Victoria	d		04 02		04 32		05 06				05 36		
Prittlewell	d		04 04		04 34		05 08				05 38		
Rochford	d		04 08		04 38		05 12				05 42		
Hockley	d		04 12		04 42		05 16				05 46		
Rayleigh	d		04 16		04 46		05 20				05 50		
Southminster	d												
Burnham-on-Crouch	d												
Althorne	d												
North Fambridge	d												
South Woodham Ferrers	d												
Battlesbridge	d												
Wickford [2]	d		04 21		04 51		05 25				05 55		
Billericay	d		04 28		04 58		05 31				06 01		
Shenfield [3]	a		04 39		05 09	05 25	05 38				06 08		06 10
	d		04 39		05 09	05 26	05 38		05 44		06 08		06 11
Brentwood	d		04 42		05 12				05 47				
Harold Wood	d		04 47		05 17				05 52				
Gidea Park [2]	d		04 51		05 21	05 33			05 56				
Romford	d		04 53		05 23		05 46		05 58		06 16		06 19
Chadwell Heath	d		04 57		05 27				06 02				
Goodmayes	d		04 59		05 29				06 04				
Seven Kings	d		05 01		05 31	05 38			06 06				
Ilford [2]	d		05 04	05 09	05 34			05 39	06 09				
Manor Park	d			05 11				05 41	06 12				
Forest Gate	d			05 14				05 44	06 14				
Maryland	d			05 16				05 46	06 16				
Stratford [7] ⊖	d	23p57	05 10	05 18	05 40	05 44	05 54	05 48	06 18	23 57	06 24	06 05	06 27
London Liverpool Street [15] ⊖	a	00 11	05 18	05 26	05 48	05 57	06 03	05 56	06 27	00 11	06 33	06 14	06 36

Station		LE	LE	LE ◇[1]	LE [1]	LE	LE	LE
Southend Victoria	d				06 06			
Prittlewell	d				06 08			
Rochford	d				06 12			
Hockley	d				06 16			
Rayleigh	d				06 20			
Southminster	d							
Burnham-on-Crouch	d							
Althorne	d							
North Fambridge	d							
South Woodham Ferrers	d							
Battlesbridge	d							
Wickford [2]	d				06 25			
Billericay	d				06 31			
Shenfield [3]	a			06s29	06 38			
	d		06 14	06s29	06 38			06 44
Brentwood	d		06 17					06 47
Harold Wood	d		06 22					06 52
Gidea Park [2]	d	06 16	06 26			06 36	06 46	06 56
Romford	d	06 18	06 28			06 38	06 48	06 58
Chadwell Heath	d	06 22	06 32			06 42	06 52	07 02
Goodmayes	d	06 24	06 34			06 44	06 54	07 04
Seven Kings	d	06 26	06 36			06 46	06 56	07 06
Ilford [2]	d	06 29	06 39			06 49	06 59	07 09
Manor Park	d	06 32	06 42			06 52	07 02	07 12
Forest Gate	d	06 34	06 44			06 54	07 04	07 14
Maryland	d	06 36	06 46			06 56	07 06	07 16
Stratford [7] ⊖	d	06 38	06 48		06 52	06 58	07 08	07 18
London Liverpool Street [15] ⊖	a	06 47	06 57	06 54	07 01	07 07	07 17	07 27

Table 5

Southend Victoria, Southminster and Shenfield - London

		LE 1	LE 1	LE 1	LE 1	LE	LE	LE 1	LE 1	LE	LE	LE	LE 1	LE 1	LE	LE 1	LE	LE 1	LE 1	LE	LE 1	LE 1	LE	LE 1	LE
Southend Victoria	d			06 26					06 46				07 06					07 26						07 46	
Prittlewell	d			06 28					06 48				07 08					07 28						07 48	
Rochford	d			06 32					06 52				07 12					07 32						07 52	
Hockley	d			06 36					06 56				07 16					07 36						07 56	
Rayleigh	d			06 40					07 00				07 20					07 40						08 00	
Southminster	d				06 17														07 17						
Burnham-on-Crouch	d				06 21														07 21						
Althorne	d				06 26														07 26						
North Fambridge	d				06 34														07 34						
South Woodham Ferrers	d				06 39														07 39						
Battlesbridge	d				06 43														07 43						
Wickford 2	d			06 45	06 49				07 05				07 25					07 45	07 49					08 05	
Billericay	d			06 51	06 55				07 11				07 31					07 51	07 55					08 11	
Shenfield 3	a	06 46	06 51	06 58	07 02			07 09	07 18				07 38	07 40		07 51		07 58	08 02		08 09	08 13		08 18	
	d	06 46	06 51	06 58			07 04	07 10	07 18		07 24	07 34	07 38	07 40	07 44	07 51	07 54	07 58		08 04	08 10	08 14	08 14	08 18	08 24
Brentwood	d						07 07				07 27	07 37			07 47		07 57			08 07			08 17		08 27
Harold Wood	d						07 12				07 32	07 42			07 52		08 02			08 12			08 22		08 32
Gidea Park 2	d					07 06	07 16			07 26	07 36	07 46			07 56		08 06			08 16			08 26		08 36
Romford	d		06 59			07 08	07 18		07 26	07 28	07 38	07 48			07 58	07 59	08 08			08 18			08 28	08 26	08 38
Chadwell Heath	d					07 12	07 22			07 32	07 42	07 52			08 02		08 12			08 22			08 32		08 42
Goodmayes	d					07 14	07 24			07 34	07 44	07 54			08 04		08 14			08 24			08 34		08 44
Seven Kings	d					07 16	07 26			07 36	07 46	07 56			08 06		08 16			08 26			08 36		08 46
Ilford 2	d					07 19	07 29			07 39	07 49	07 59			08 09		08 19			08 29			08 39		08 49
Manor Park	d					07 22	07 32			07 42	07 52	08 02			08 12		08 22			08 32			08 42		08 52
Forest Gate	d					07 24	07 34			07 44	07 54	08 04			08 14		08 24			08 34			08 44		08 54
Maryland	d					07 26	07 36			07 46	07 56	08 06			08 16		08 26			08 36			08 46		08 56
Stratford 7 ⊖	d	07 01	07 07	07 12		07 28	07 38	07 24	07 34	07 48	07 58	08 08	07 52	07 55	08 18	08 07	08 28	08 12		08 38	08 24	08 28	08 48	08 34	08 58
London Liverpool Street 15 ⊖	a	07 10	07 16	07 23		07 37	07 47	07 33	07 43	07 57	08 07	08 17	08 01	08 03	08 27	08 16	08 37	08 23		08 47	08 33	08 39	08 57	08 43	09 07

b previous night, stops to set down only

		LE	LE 1	LE 1	LE	LE 1	LE	LE 1	LE 1	LE	LE 1	LE	LE 1	LE	LE	LE 1	LE 1	LE	LE 1	LE	LE 1	LE 1	LE	LE 1	LE
Southend Victoria	d		08 06					08 26					08 46			09 06					09 26				
Prittlewell	d		08 08					08 28					08 48			09 08					09 28				
Rochford	d		08 12					08 32					08 52			09 12					09 32				
Hockley	d		08 16					08 36					08 56			09 16					09 36				
Rayleigh	d		08 20					08 40					09 00			09 20					09 40				
Southminster	d								08 17													09 17			
Burnham-on-Crouch	d								08 21													09 21			
Althorne	d								08 26													09 26			
North Fambridge	d								08 34													09 34			
South Woodham Ferrers	d								08 39													09 39			
Battlesbridge	d								08 43													09 43			
Wickford 2	d		08 25					08 45	08 49				09 05			09 25					09 45	09 49			
Billericay	d		08 31					08 51	08 55				09 11			09 31					09 51	09 55			
Shenfield 3	a		08 38	08 40		08 51		08 58	09 02		09 09		09 18			09 38	09 40		09 51		09 58	10 02		10 09	
	d	08 34	08 38	08 40	08 44	08 51	08 54	08 58		09 04	09 10	09 14	09 18	09 24	09 34	09 38	09 40	09 44	09 51	09 54	09 58		10 04	10 10	10 14
Brentwood	d	08 37			08 47		08 57			09 07		09 17		09 27	09 37			09 47		09 57			10 07		10 17
Harold Wood	d	08 42			08 52		09 02			09 12		09 22		09 32	09 42			09 52		10 02			10 12		10 22
Gidea Park 2	d	08 46			08 56		09 06			09 16		09 26		09 36	09 46			09 56		10 06			10 16		10 26
Romford	d	08 48			08 58	08 59	09 08			09 18		09 28	09 26	09 38	09 48			09 58	09 59	10 08			10 18		10 28
Chadwell Heath	d	08 52			09 02		09 12			09 22		09 32		09 42	09 52			10 02		10 12			10 22		10 32
Goodmayes	d	08 54			09 04		09 14			09 24		09 34		09 44	09 54			10 04		10 14			10 24		10 34
Seven Kings	d	08 56			09 06		09 16			09 26		09 36		09 46	09 56			10 06		10 16			10 26		10 36
Ilford 2	d	08 59			09 09		09 19			09 29		09 39		09 49	09 59			10 09		10 19			10 29		10 39
Manor Park	d	09 02			09 12		09 22			09 32		09 42		09 52	10 02			10 12		10 22			10 32		10 42
Forest Gate	d	09 04			09 14		09 24			09 34		09 44		09 54	10 04			10 14		10 24			10 34		10 44
Maryland	d	09 06			09 16		09 26			09 36		09 46		09 56	10 06			10 16		10 26			10 36		10 46
Stratford 7 ⊖	d	09 08	08 52	08 55	09 18	09 07	09 28	09 12		09 38	09 24	09 48	09 34	09 58	10 08	09 52	09 55	10 18	10 07	10 28	10 12		10 38	10 24	10 48
London Liverpool Street 15 ⊖	a	09 17	09 01	09 03	09 27	09 16	09 37	09 23		09 47	09 33	09 57	09 43	10 07	10 17	10 01	10 03	10 27	10 16	10 37	10 23		10 47	10 33	10 57

Table 5

Southend Victoria, Southminster and Shenfield - London

		LE 1	LE	LE	LE 1	LE 1	LE	LE 1	LE	LE 1	LE 1	LE	LE 1	LE	LE 1	LE	LE	LE 1	LE 1	LE	LE 1	LE	LE 1	LE 1	LE
Southend Victoria	d	09 46			10 06					10 26					10 46			11 06					11 26		
Prittlewell	d	09 48			10 08					10 28					10 48			11 08					11 28		
Rochford	d	09 52			10 12					10 32					10 52			11 12					11 32		
Hockley	d	09 56			10 16					10 36					10 56			11 16					11 36		
Rayleigh	d	10 00			10 20					10 40					11 00			11 20					11 40		
Southminster	d										10 17													11 17	
Burnham-on-Crouch	d										10 21													11 21	
Althorne	d										10 26													11 26	
North Fambridge	d										10 34													11 34	
South Woodham Ferrers	d										10 39													11 39	
Battlesbridge	d										10 43													11 43	
Wickford 2	d	10 05			10 25					10 45	10 49				11 05			11 25					11 45	11 49	
Billericay	d	10 11			10 31					10 51	10 55				11 11			11 31					11 51	11 55	
Shenfield 3	a	10 18			10 38	10 40		10 51		10 58	11 02		11 09		11 18			11 38	11 40		11 51		11 58	12 02	
	d	10 18	10 24	10 34	10 38	10 40	10 44	10 51	10 54	10 58		11 04	11 10	11 14	11 18	11 24	11 34	11 38	11 40	11 44	11 51	11 54	11 58		12 04
Brentwood	d		10 27	10 37			10 47		10 57			11 07		11 17		11 27	11 37			11 47		11 57			12 07
Harold Wood	d		10 32	10 42			10 52		11 02			11 12		11 22		11 32	11 42			11 52		12 02			12 12
Gidea Park 2	d		10 36	10 46			10 56		11 06			11 16		11 26		11 36	11 46			11 56		12 06			12 16
Romford	d	10 26	10 38	10 48			10 58	10 59	11 08			11 18		11 28	11 26	11 38	11 48			11 58	11 59	12 08			12 18
Chadwell Heath	d		10 42	10 52			11 02		11 12			11 22		11 32		11 42	11 52			12 02		12 12			12 22
Goodmayes	d		10 44	10 54			11 04		11 14			11 24		11 34		11 44	11 54			12 04		12 14			12 24
Seven Kings	d		10 46	10 56			11 06		11 16			11 26		11 36		11 46	11 56			12 06		12 16			12 26
Ilford 2	d		10 49	10 59			11 09		11 19			11 29		11 39		11 49	11 59			12 09		12 19			12 29
Manor Park	d		10 52	11 02			11 12		11 22			11 32		11 42		11 52	12 02			12 12		12 22			12 32
Forest Gate	d		10 54	11 04			11 14		11 24			11 34		11 44		11 54	12 04			12 14		12 24			12 34
Maryland	d		10 56	11 06			11 16		11 26			11 36		11 46		11 56	12 06			12 16		12 26			12 36
Stratford 7 ⊖	d	10 34	10 58	11 08	10 52	10 55	11 18	11 07	11 28	11 12		11 38	11 24	11 48	11 36	11 58	12 08	11 52	11 55	12 18	12 07	12 28	12 12		12 38
London Liverpool Street 15 ⊖	a	10 43	11 07	11 17	11 01	11 03	11 27	11 16	11 37	11 23		11 47	11 33	11 57	11 45	12 07	12 17	12 01	12 03	12 27	12 16	12 37	12 23		12 47

		LE 1	LE	LE 1	LE	LE	LE 1	LE 1	LE	LE 1	LE	LE 1	LE 1	LE	LE 1	LE	LE 1	LE	LE	LE 1	LE 1	LE	LE 1	LE	LE 1
Southend Victoria	d			11 46			12 06					12 26					12 46			13 06					13 26
Prittlewell	d			11 48			12 08					12 28					12 48			13 08					13 28
Rochford	d			11 52			12 12					12 32					12 52			13 12					13 32
Hockley	d			11 56			12 16					12 36					12 56			13 16					13 36
Rayleigh	d			12 00			12 20					12 40					13 00			13 20					13 40
Southminster	d												12 17												
Burnham-on-Crouch	d												12 21												
Althorne	d												12 26												
North Fambridge	d												12 34												
South Woodham Ferrers	d												12 39												
Battlesbridge	d												12 43												
Wickford 2	d			12 05			12 25					12 45	12 49				13 05			13 25					13 45
Billericay	d			12 11			12 31					12 51	12 55				13 11			13 31					13 51
Shenfield 3	a	12 09		12 18			12 38	12 40		12 51		12 58	13 02		13 09		13 18			13 38	13 40		13 51		13 58
	d	12 10	12 14	12 18	12 24	12 34	12 38	12 40	12 44	12 51	12 54	12 58		13 04	13 10	13 14	13 18	13 24	13 34	13 38	13 40	13 44	13 51	13 54	13 58
Brentwood	d		12 17		12 27	12 37			12 47		12 57			13 07		13 17		13 27	13 37			13 47		13 57	
Harold Wood	d		12 22		12 32	12 42			12 52		13 02			13 12		13 22		13 32	13 42			13 52		14 02	
Gidea Park 2	d		12 26		12 36	12 46			12 56		13 06			13 16		13 26		13 36	13 46			13 56		14 06	
Romford	d		12 28	12 26	12 38	12 48			12 58	12 59	13 08			13 18		13 28	13 26	13 38	13 48			13 58	13 59	14 08	
Chadwell Heath	d		12 32		12 42	12 52			13 02		13 12			13 22		13 32		13 42	13 52			14 02		14 12	
Goodmayes	d		12 34		12 44	12 54			13 04		13 14			13 24		13 34		13 44	13 54			14 04		14 14	
Seven Kings	d		12 36		12 46	12 56			13 06		13 16			13 26		13 36		13 46	13 56			14 06		14 16	
Ilford 2	d		12 39		12 49	12 59			13 09		13 19			13 29		13 39		13 49	13 59			14 09		14 19	
Manor Park	d		12 42		12 52	13 02			13 12		13 22			13 32		13 42		13 52	14 02			14 12		14 22	
Forest Gate	d		12 44		12 54	13 04			13 14		13 24			13 34		13 44		13 54	14 04			14 14		14 24	
Maryland	d		12 46		12 56	13 06			13 16		13 26			13 36		13 46		13 56	14 06			14 16		14 26	
Stratford 7 ⊖	d	12 24	12 48	12 34	12 58	13 08	12 52	12 55	13 18	13 07	13 28	13 12		13 38	13 24	13 48	13 34	13 58	14 08	13 52	13 55	14 18	14 07	14 28	14 12
London Liverpool Street 15 ⊖	a	12 33	12 57	12 43	13 07	13 17	13 01	13 03	13 27	13 16	13 37	13 23		13 47	13 33	13 57	13 43	14 07	14 17	14 01	14 03	14 27	14 16	14 37	14 23

A until 25 September

B from 2 October

Southend Victoria, Southminster and Shenfield - London

Station		LE ■	LE	LE ■	LE	LE ■	LE	LE	LE ■	LE ■	LE	LE ■	LE	LE ■	LE ■	LE	LE ■	LE	LE ■	LE	LE	LE ■	LE ■	LE	LE ■
Southend Victoria	d					13 46			14 06					14 26					14 46			15 06			
Prittlewell	d					13 48			14 08					14 28					14 48			15 08			
Rochford	d					13 52			14 12					14 32					14 52			15 12			
Hockley	d					13 56			14 16					14 36					14 56			15 16			
Rayleigh	d					14 00			14 20					14 40					15 00			15 20			
Southminster	d	13 17													14 17										
Burnham-on-Crouch	d	13 21													14 21										
Althorne	d	13 26													14 26										
North Fambridge	d	13 34													14 34										
South Woodham Ferrers	d	13 39													14 39										
Battlesbridge	d	13 43													14 43										
Wickford ■	d	13 49				14 05			14 25					14 45	14 49				15 05			15 25			
Billericay	d	13 55				14 11			14 31					14 51	14 55				15 11			15 31			
Shenfield ■	a	14 02		14 09		14 18			14 38	14 40		14 51		14 58	15 02		15 09		15 18			15 38	15 40		15 51
	d		14 04	14 10	14 14	14 18	14 24	14 34	14 38	14 40	14 44	14 51	14 54	14 58		15 04	15 10	15 14	15 18	15 24	15 34	15 38	15 40	15 44	15 51
Brentwood	d		14 07		14 17		14 27	14 37			14 47		14 57			15 07		15 17		15 27	15 37			15 47	
Harold Wood	d		14 12		14 22		14 32	14 42			14 52		15 02			15 12		15 22		15 32	15 42			15 52	
Gidea Park ■	d		14 16		14 26		14 36	14 46			14 56		15 06			15 16		15 26		15 36	15 46			15 56	
Romford	d		14 18		14 28	14 26	14 38	14 48			14 58	14 59	15 08			15 18		15 28	15 26	15 38	15 48			15 58	15 59
Chadwell Heath	d		14 22		14 32		14 42	14 52			15 02		15 12			15 22		15 32		15 42	15 52			16 02	
Goodmayes	d		14 24		14 34		14 44	14 54			15 04		15 14			15 24		15 34		15 44	15 54			16 04	
Seven Kings	d		14 26		14 36		14 46	14 56			15 06		15 16			15 26		15 36		15 46	15 56			16 06	
Ilford ■	d		14 29		14 39		14 49	14 59			15 09		15 19			15 29		15 39		15 49	15 59			16 09	
Manor Park	d		14 32		14 42		14 52	15 02			15 12		15 22			15 32		15 42		15 52	16 02			16 12	
Forest Gate	d		14 34		14 44		14 54	15 04			15 14		15 24			15 34		15 44		15 54	16 04			16 14	
Maryland	d		14 36		14 46		14 56	15 06			15 16		15 26			15 36		15 46		15 56	16 06			16 16	
Stratford ■ ⊖	d		14 38	14 24	14 48	14 34	14 58	15 08	14 52	14 55	15 18	15 07	15 28	15 12		15 38	15 24	15 48	15 34	15 58	16 08	15 52	15 55	16 18	16 07
London Liverpool Street ■ ⊖	a		14 47	14 33	14 57	14 43	15 07	15 17	15 01	15 03	15 27	15 16	15 37	15 23		15 47	15 33	15 57	15 43	16 07	16 17	16 01	16 03	16 27	16 16

Station		LE	LE ■	LE ■	LE	LE ■	LE	LE ■	LE	LE	LE ■	LE ■	LE	LE ■	LE	LE ■	LE ■	LE	LE ■	LE	LE ■	LE	LE	LE ■	LE ■
Southend Victoria	d		15 26					15 46			16 06					16 26					16 46			17 06	
Prittlewell	d		15 28					15 48			16 08					16 28					16 48			17 08	
Rochford	d		15 32					15 52			16 12					16 32					16 52			17 12	
Hockley	d		15 36					15 56			16 16					16 36					16 56			17 16	
Rayleigh	d		15 40					16 00			16 20					16 40					17 00			17 20	
Southminster	d			15 17													16 17								
Burnham-on-Crouch	d			15 21													16 21								
Althorne	d			15 26													16 26								
North Fambridge	d			15 34													16 34								
South Woodham Ferrers	d			15 39													16 39								
Battlesbridge	d			15 43													16 43								
Wickford ■	d		15 45	15 49				16 05			16 25					16 45	16 49				17 05			17 25	
Billericay	d		15 51	15 55				16 11			16 31					16 51	16 55				17 11			17 31	
Shenfield ■	a		15 58	16 02		16 09		16 18			16 38	16 40		16 51		16 58	17 02		17 09		17 18			17 38	17 40
	d	15 54	15 58		16 04	16 10	16 14	16 18	16 24	16 34	16 38	16 40	16 44	16 51	16 54	16 58		17 04	17 10	17 14	17 18	17 24	17 34	17 38	17 40
Brentwood	d	15 57			16 07		16 17		16 27	16 37			16 47		16 57			17 07		17 17		17 27	17 37		
Harold Wood	d	16 02			16 12		16 22		16 32	16 42			16 52		17 02			17 12		17 22		17 32	17 42		
Gidea Park ■	d	16 06			16 16		16 26		16 36	16 46			16 56		17 06			17 16		17 26		17 36	17 46		
Romford	d	16 08			16 18		16 28	16 26	16 38	16 48			16 58	16 59	17 08			17 18		17 28	17 26	17 38	17 48		
Chadwell Heath	d	16 12			16 22		16 32		16 42	16 52			17 02		17 12			17 22		17 32		17 42	17 52		
Goodmayes	d	16 14			16 24		16 34		16 44	16 54			17 04		17 14			17 24		17 34		17 44	17 54		
Seven Kings	d	16 16			16 26		16 36		16 46	16 56			17 06		17 16			17 26		17 36		17 46	17 56		
Ilford ■	d	16 19			16 29		16 39		16 49	16 59			17 09		17 19			17 29		17 39		17 49	17 59		
Manor Park	d	16 22			16 32		16 42		16 52	17 02			17 12		17 22			17 32		17 42		17 52	18 02		
Forest Gate	d	16 24			16 34		16 44		16 54	17 04			17 14		17 24			17 34		17 44		17 54	18 04		
Maryland	d	16 26			16 36		16 46		16 56	17 06			17 16		17 26			17 36		17 46		17 56	18 06		
Stratford ■ ⊖	d	16 28	16 12		16 38	16 24	16 48	16 34	16 58	17 08	16 52	16 55	17 18	17 07	17 28	17 12		17 38	17 24	17 48	17 34	17 58	18 08	17 52	17 55
London Liverpool Street ■ ⊖	a	16 37	16 23		16 47	16 33	16 57	16 43	17 07	17 17	17 01	17 03	17 27	17 16	17 37	17 23		17 47	17 33	17 57	17 43	18 07	18 17	18 01	18 03

Table 5 Saturdays

Southend Victoria, Southminster and Shenfield - London

Station		LE	LE ■	LE	LE ■	LE ■	LE	LE ■	LE	LE ■	LE	LE	LE ■	LE ■	LE	LE ■	LE	LE ■	LE ■	LE	LE ■	LE	LE ■	LE	LE
Southend Victoria	d				17 26					17 46			18 06					18 26					18 46		
Prittlewell	d				17 28					17 48			18 08					18 28					18 48		
Rochford	d				17 32					17 52			18 12					18 32					18 52		
Hockley	d				17 36					17 56			18 16					18 36					18 56		
Rayleigh	d				17 40					18 00			18 20					18 40					19 00		
Southminster	d					17 17													18 17						
Burnham-on-Crouch	d					17 21													18 21						
Althorne	d					17 26													18 26						
North Fambridge	d					17 34													18 34						
South Woodham Ferrers	d					17 39													18 39						
Battlesbridge	d					17 43													18 43						
Wickford ■	d				17 45	17 49				18 05			18 25					18 45	18 49				19 05		
Billericay	d				17 51	17 55				18 11			18 31					18 51	18 55				19 11		
Shenfield ■	a		17 51		17 58	18 02		18 09		18 18			18 38	18 40		18 51		18 58	19 02		19 12		19 18		
	d	17 44	17 51	17 54	17 58		18 04	18 10	18 14	18 18	18 24	18 34	18 38	18 40	18 44	18 51	18 54	18 58		19 04	19 13	19 14	19 18	19 24	19 34
Brentwood	d	17 47		17 57			18 07		18 17		18 27	18 37			18 47		18 57			19 07		19 17		19 27	19 37
Harold Wood	d	17 52		18 02			18 12		18 22		18 32	18 42			18 52		19 02			19 12		19 22		19 32	19 42
Gidea Park ■	d	17 56		18 06			18 16		18 26		18 36	18 46			18 56		19 06			19 16		19 26		19 36	19 46
Romford	d	17 58	17 59	18 08			18 18		18 28	18 26	18 38	18 48			18 58	18 59	19 08			19 18		19 28	19 26	19 38	19 48
Chadwell Heath	d	18 02		18 12			18 22		18 32		18 42	18 52			19 02		19 12			19 22		19 32		19 42	19 52
Goodmayes	d	18 04		18 14			18 24		18 34		18 44	18 54			19 04		19 14			19 24		19 34		19 44	19 54
Seven Kings	d	18 06		18 16			18 26		18 36		18 46	18 56			19 06		19 16			19 26		19 36		19 46	19 56
Ilford ■	d	18 09		18 19			18 29		18 39		18 49	18 59			19 09		19 19			19 29		19 39		19 49	19 59
Manor Park	d	18 12		18 22			18 32		18 42		18 52	19 02			19 12		19 22			19 32		19 42		19 52	20 02
Forest Gate	d	18 14		18 24			18 34		18 44		18 54	19 04			19 14		19 24			19 34		19 44		19 54	20 04
Maryland	d	18 16		18 26			18 36		18 46		18 56	19 06			19 16		19 26			19 36		19 46		19 56	20 06
Stratford ■ ⊖	d	18 18	18 07	18 28	18 12		18 38	18 24	18 48	18 34	18 58	19 08	18 52	18 55	19 18	19 07	19 28	19 12		19 38	19 27	19 48	19 34	19 58	20 08
London Liverpool Street ■ ⊖	a	18 27	18 16	18 37	18 23		18 47	18 33	18 57	18 43	19 07	19 17	19 01	19 03	19 27	19 16	19 37	19 23		19 47	19 37	19 57	19 43	20 07	20 17

Station		LE ■	LE ■	LE	LE ■	LE	LE ■	LE ■	LE	LE ■	LE	LE ■	LE	LE	LE ■	LE ■	LE	LE ■	LE	LE ■	LE ■	LE ■	LE	LE	LE ■
Southend Victoria	d	19 06					19 26					19 46			20 06						20 36				21 06
Prittlewell	d	19 08					19 28					19 48			20 08						20 38				21 08
Rochford	d	19 12					19 32					19 52			20 12						20 42				21 12
Hockley	d	19 16					19 36					19 56			20 16						20 46				21 16
Rayleigh	d	19 20					19 40					20 00			20 20						20 50				21 20
Southminster	d							19 17												20 17					
Burnham-on-Crouch	d							19 21												20 21					
Althorne	d							19 26												20 26					
North Fambridge	d							19 34												20 34					
South Woodham Ferrers	d							19 39												20 39					
Battlesbridge	d							19 43												20 43					
Wickford ■	d	19 25					19 45	19 49				20 05			20 25					20 49	20 55				21 25
Billericay	d	19 31					19 51	19 55				20 11			20 31					20 55	21 01				21 31
Shenfield ■	a	19 38	19 40		19 51		19 58	20 02		20 09		20 18			20 38	20 40		20 51		21 02	21 08	21 10			21 38
	d	19 38	19 40	19 44	19 51	19 54	19 58		20 04	20 10	20 14	20 18	20 24	20 34	20 38	20 40	20 44	20 51	20 59		21 08	21 11	21 14	21 29	21 38
Brentwood	d			19 47		19 57			20 07		20 17		20 27	20 37			20 47		21 02				21 17	21 32	
Harold Wood	d			19 52		20 02			20 12		20 22		20 32	20 42			20 52		21 07				21 22	21 37	
Gidea Park ■	d			19 56		20 06			20 16		20 26		20 36	20 46			20 56		21 11				21 26	21 41	
Romford	d			19 58	19 59	20 08			20 18		20 28	20 26	20 38	20 48			20 58	20 59	21 13				21 28	21 43	
Chadwell Heath	d			20 02		20 12			20 22		20 32		20 42	20 52			21 02		21 17				21 32	21 47	
Goodmayes	d			20 04		20 14			20 24		20 34		20 44	20 54			21 04		21 19				21 34	21 49	
Seven Kings	d			20 06		20 16			20 26		20 36		20 46	20 56			21 06		21 21				21 36	21 51	
Ilford ■	d			20 09		20 19			20 29		20 39		20 49	20 59			21 09		21 24				21 39	21 54	
Manor Park	d			20 12		20 22			20 32		20 42		20 52	21 02			21 12		21 27				21 42	21 57	
Forest Gate	d			20 14		20 24			20 34		20 44		20 54	21 04			21 14		21 29				21 44	21 59	
Maryland	d			20 16		20 26			20 36		20 46		20 56	21 06			21 16		21 31				21 46	22 01	
Stratford ■ ⊖	d	19 52	19 55	20 18	20 07	20 28	20 12		20 38	20 24	20 48	20 34	20 58	21 08	20 52	20 55	21 18	21 07	21 33		21 22	21 25	21 48	22 03	21 52
London Liverpool Street ■ ⊖	a	20 01	20 03	20 27	20 16	20 37	20 21		20 47	20 33	20 57	20 43	21 07	21 17	21 01	21 03	21 27	21 16	21 42		21 31	21 34	21 57	22 12	22 01

Station		LE ■	LE	LE ■	LE ■	LE	LE ■	LE ■	LE ■	LE	LE	LE ■	LE ■	LE ■	LE	LE ■	LE	LE ■	LE ■	LE ■	LE	LE	LE ■	LE ■	LE
Southend Victoria	d							21 36				22 06						22 36					23 06		
Prittlewell	d							21 38				22 08						22 38					23 08		
Rochford	d							21 42				22 12						22 42					23 12		
Hockley	d							21 46				22 16						22 46					23 16		
Rayleigh	d							21 50				22 20						22 50					23 20		
Southminster	d						21 17							21 59										23 07	
Burnham-on-Crouch	d						21 21							22 03										23 11	
Althorne	d						21 26							22 08										23 16	
North Fambridge	d						21 34							22 14										23 22	
South Woodham Ferrers	d						21 39							22 19										23 27	
Battlesbridge	d						21 43							22 23										23 31	
Wickford ■	d						21 49	21 55				22 25		22 29				22 55					23 25	23a37	
Billericay	d						21 55	22 01				22 31		22 35				23 01					23 31		
Shenfield ■	a	21 40		21 51	21 58		22 02	22 08	22 10			22 38	22 40	22 42		22 51		23 08		23 09			23 38		
	d	21 40	21 44	21 51	21 58	21 59		22 08	22 11	22 14	22 29	22 38	22 40		22 44	22 51	22 59	23 08		23 10	23 14	23 29	23 38		23 44
Brentwood	d		21 47			22 02				22 17	22 32				22 47		23 02				23 17	23 32			23 47
Harold Wood	d		21 52			22 07				22 22	22 37				22 52		23 07				23 22	23 37			23 52
Gidea Park ■	d		21 56			22 11				22 26	22 41				22 56		23 11				23 26	23 41			23 56
Romford	d		21 58	21 59		22 13				22 28	22 43				22 58	22 59	23 13				23 28	23 43			23 58
Chadwell Heath	d		22 02			22 17				22 32	22 47				23 02		23 17				23 32	23 47			00 02
Goodmayes	d		22 04			22 19				22 34	22 49				23 04		23 19				23 34	23 49			00 04
Seven Kings	d		22 06			22 21				22 36	22 51				23 06		23 21				23 36	23 51			00 06
Ilford ■	d		22 09			22 24				22 39	22 54				23 09		23 24				23 39	23 54			00 09
Manor Park	d		22 12			22 27				22 42	22 57				23 12		23 27				23 42	23 57			00 12
Forest Gate	d		22 14			22 29				22 44	22 59				23 14		23 29				23 44	23 59			00 14
Maryland	d		22 16			22 31				22 46	23 01				23 16		23 31				23 46	00 01			00 16
Stratford ■ ⊖	d	21 55	22 18	22 07	22 12	22 33		22 22	22 25	22 48	23 03	22 52	22 55		23 18	23 07	23 33	23 22	23 05	23 25	23 48	00 03	23 55		00 18
London Liverpool Street ■ ⊖	a	22 03	22 27	22 16	22 21	22 42		22 31	22 34	22 57	23 12	23 01	23 03		23 27	23 16	23 42	23 31	23 14	23 34	23 57	00 12	00 04		00 27

Table 5

Sundays

Southend Victoria, Southminster and Shenfield - London

	LE	LE ◇1	LE 1	LE 1	LE	LE	LE	LE	LE 1	LE 1	LE	LE
Southend Victoria d			23p06						06 18			
Prittlewell d			23p08									
Rochford d			23p12						06 22			
Hockley d			23p16						06 26			
Rayleigh d			23p20						06 30			
Southminster d												
Burnham-on-Crouch d												
Althorne d												
North Fambridge d												
South Woodham Ferrers d												
Battlesbridge d												
Wickford 2 d			23p25						06 35			
Billericay d			23p31						06 41			
Shenfield 3 a		23b36	23p38						06 52	07 06		
d	23p29	23b37	23p38		23p44			06 43	06 53	07 07		07 13
Brentwood d	23p32				23p47			06 46	06 56			07 16
Harold Wood d	23p37				23p52			06 51	07 01			07 21
Gidea Park 2 d	23p41				23p56	05 55	06 25	06 55	07 05		07 11	07 25
Romford d	23p43				23p58	05 57	06 27	06 57	07 07		07 13	07 27
Chadwell Heath d	23p47				00 02	06 01	06 31	07 01			07 17	07 31
Goodmayes d	23p49				00 04	06 03	06 33	07 03			07 19	07 33
Seven Kings d	23p51				00 06	06 05	06 35	07 05			07 21	07 35
Ilford 2 d	23p54				00 09	06 08	06 38	07 08			07 24	07 38
Manor Park d	23p57				00 12	06 10	06 40	07 10			07 26	07 40
Forest Gate d	23p59				00 14	06 12	06 42	07 12			07 28	07 42
Maryland d	00 01				00 16	06 14	06 44	07 14				07 44
Stratford 7 ⊖ d	00 03	23p52	23p55	00 05	00 18	06 16	06 46	07 16	07 19	07s34	07 31	07 46
London Liverpool Street 15 ⊖ a	00 12	00 03	00 04	00 14	00 27	06 26	06 56	07 26	07 27	07 42	07 41	07 56

	LE 1	LE 1	LE	LE	LE 1	LE 1	LE	LE	LE 1	LE 1	LE 1	LE 1
Southend Victoria d	06 48				07 18					07 52		
Prittlewell d												
Rochford d	06 52				07 22					07 56		
Hockley d	06 56				07 26					08 00		
Rayleigh d	07 00				07 30					08 04		
Southminster d											08 05	
Burnham-on-Crouch d											08 09	
Althorne d											08 14	
North Fambridge d											08 20	
South Woodham Ferrers d											08 25	
Battlesbridge d											08 29	
Wickford 2 d	07 05				07 35					08 09	08a35	
Billericay d	07 11				07 41					08 15		
Shenfield 3 a	07 22	07 36			07 52	08 06			08 18	08 22		08 40
d	07 23	07 37		07 43	07 53	08 07		08 13	08 18	08 23		08 41
Brentwood d	07 26			07 46	07 56			08 16		08 26		
Harold Wood d	07 31			07 51	08 01			08 21		08 31		
Gidea Park 2 d	07 35		07 41	07 55	08 05		08 11	08 25		08 35		
Romford d	07 37		07 43	07 57	08 07		08 13	08 27		08 37		
Chadwell Heath d			07 47	08 01			08 17	08 31				
Goodmayes d			07 49	08 03			08 19	08 33				
Seven Kings d			07 51	08 05			08 21	08 35				
Ilford 2 d			07 54	08 08			08 24	08 38				
Manor Park d			07 56	08 10			08 26	08 40				
Forest Gate d			07 58	08 12			08 28	08 42				
Maryland d				08 14				08 44				
Stratford 7 ⊖ d	07 49	08s04	08 01	08 16	08 19	08s34	08 31	08 46	08s49	08 49		09s04
London Liverpool Street 15 ⊖ a	07 57	08 12	08 11	08 26	08 27	08 42	08 41	08 56	08 59	08 59		09 12

	LE	LE	LE 1	LE 1	LE	LE	LE 1	LE 1	LE 1	LE	LE	LE 1
Southend Victoria d			08 22				08 52					09 22
Prittlewell d												
Rochford d			08 26				08 56					09 26
Hockley d			08 30				09 00					09 30
Rayleigh d			08 34				09 04					09 34
Southminster d								09 05				
Burnham-on-Crouch d								09 09				
Althorne d								09 14				
North Fambridge d								09 20				
South Woodham Ferrers d								09 25				
Battlesbridge d								09 29				
Wickford 2 d			08 39				09 09	09a35				09 39
Billericay d			08 45				09 15					09 45
Shenfield 3 a			08 52	09 10			09 22		09 40			09 52
d		08 43	08 53	09 11		09 13	09 23		09 41		09 43	09 53
Brentwood d		08 46	08 56			09 16	09 26				09 46	09 56
Harold Wood d		08 51	09 01			09 21	09 31				09 51	10 01
Gidea Park 2 d	08 41	08 55	09 05		09 11	09 25	09 35			09 41	09 55	10 05
Romford d	08 43	08 57	09 07		09 13	09 27	09 37			09 43	09 57	10 07
Chadwell Heath d	08 47	09 01			09 17	09 31				09 47	10 01	
Goodmayes d	08 49	09 03			09 19	09 33				09 49	10 03	
Seven Kings d	08 51	09 05			09 21	09 35				09 51	10 05	
Ilford 2 d	08 54	09 08			09 24	09 38				09 54	10 08	
Manor Park d	08 56	09 10			09 26	09 40				09 56	10 10	
Forest Gate d	08 58	09 12			09 28	09 42				09 58	10 12	
Maryland d		09 14				09 44					10 14	
Stratford 7 ⊖ d	09 01	09 16	09 19	09s34	09 31	09 46	09 49		10s04	10 01	10 16	10 21
London Liverpool Street 15 ⊖ a	09 11	09 26	09 29	09 42	09 41	09 56	09 59		10 12	10 11	10 26	10 31

	LE 1	LE	LE	LE 1	LE 1	LE 1	LE	LE	LE 1	LE 1	LE	LE
Southend Victoria d				09 52					10 22			
Prittlewell d												
Rochford d				09 56					10 26			
Hockley d				10 00					10 30			
Rayleigh d				10 04					10 34			
Southminster d					10 05							
Burnham-on-Crouch d					10 09							
Althorne d					10 14							
North Fambridge d					10 20							
South Woodham Ferrers d					10 25							
Battlesbridge d					10 29							
Wickford 2 d				10 09	10a35				10 39			
Billericay d				10 15					10 45			
Shenfield 3 a	10 10			10 22		10 40			10 52	11 10		
d	10 11		10 13	10 23		10 41		10 43	10 53	11 11		11 13
Brentwood d			10 16	10 26				10 46	10 56			11 16
Harold Wood d			10 21	10 31				10 51	11 01			11 21
Gidea Park 2 d		10 11	10 25	10 35			10 41	10 55	11 05		11 11	11 25
Romford d		10 13	10 27	10 37			10 43	10 57	11 07		11 13	11 27
Chadwell Heath d		10 17	10 31				10 47	11 01			11 17	11 31
Goodmayes d		10 19	10 33				10 49	11 03			11 19	11 33
Seven Kings d		10 21	10 35				10 51	11 05			11 21	11 35
Ilford 2 d		10 24	10 38				10 54	11 08			11 24	11 38
Manor Park d		10 26	10 40				10 56	11 10			11 26	11 40
Forest Gate d		10 28	10 42				10 58	11 12			11 28	11 42
Maryland d			10 44					11 14				11 44
Stratford 7 ⊖ d	10s34	10 31	10 46	10 49		11s04	11 01	11 16	11 19	11s34	11 31	11 46
London Liverpool Street 15 ⊖ a	10 42	10 41	10 56	10 59		11 12	11 11	11 26	11 29	11 42	11 41	11 56

A not 23 May

b previous night, stops to set down only

Table 5

Sundays

Southend Victoria, Southminster and Shenfield - London

	LE 1	LE 1	LE 1	LE	LE	LE 1	LE 1	LE	LE	LE 1	LE 1	LE 1
Southend Victoria d	10 52					11 22				11 52		
Prittlewell d												
Rochford d	10 56					11 26				11 56		
Hockley d	11 00					11 30				12 00		
Rayleigh d	11 04					11 34				12 04		
Southminster d		11 05									12 05	
Burnham-on-Crouch d		11 09									12 09	
Althorne d		11 14									12 14	
North Fambridge d		11 20									12 20	
South Woodham Ferrers d		11 25									12 25	
Battlesbridge d		11 29									12 29	
Wickford 2 d	11 09	11a35				11 39				12 09	12a35	
Billericay d	11 15					11 45				12 15		
Shenfield 3 a	11 22		11 40			11 52	12 10			12 22		12 40
d	11 23		11 41		11 43	11 53	12 11		12 13	12 23		12 41
Brentwood d	11 26				11 46	11 56			12 16	12 26		
Harold Wood d	11 31				11 51	12 01			12 21	12 31		
Gidea Park 2 d	11 35			11 41	11 55	12 05		12 11	12 25	12 35		
Romford d	11 37			11 43	11 57	12 07		12 13	12 27	12 37		
Chadwell Heath d				11 47	12 01			12 17	12 31			
Goodmayes d				11 49	12 03			12 19	12 33			
Seven Kings d				11 51	12 05			12 21	12 35			
Ilford 2 d				11 54	12 08			12 24	12 38			
Manor Park d				11 56	12 10			12 26	12 40			
Forest Gate d				11 58	12 12			12 28	12 42			
Maryland d					12 14				12 44			
Stratford 7 ⊖ d	11 49		12s04	12 01	12 16	12 19	12s34	12 31	12 46	12 49		13s04
London Liverpool Street 15 ⊖ a	11 59		12 12	12 11	12 26	12 29	12 42	12 41	12 56	12 59		13 12

	LE	LE	LE 1	LE 1	LE	LE	LE 1	LE 1	LE 1	LE	LE	LE 1
Southend Victoria d			12 22				12 52					13 22
Prittlewell d												
Rochford d			12 26				12 56					13 26
Hockley d			12 30				13 00					13 30
Rayleigh d			12 34				13 04					13 34
Southminster d								13 05				
Burnham-on-Crouch d								13 09				
Althorne d								13 14				
North Fambridge d								13 20				
South Woodham Ferrers d								13 25				
Battlesbridge d								13 29				
Wickford 2 d			12 39				13 09	13a35				13 39
Billericay d			12 45				13 15					13 45
Shenfield 3 a			12 52	13 10			13 22		13 40			13 52
d		12 43	12 53	13 11		13 13	13 23		13 41		13 43	13 53
Brentwood d		12 46	12 56			13 16	13 26				13 46	13 56
Harold Wood d		12 51	13 01			13 21	13 31				13 51	14 01
Gidea Park 2 d	12 41	12 55	13 05		13 11	13 25	13 35			13 41	13 55	14 05
Romford d	12 43	12 57	13 07		13 13	13 27	13 37			13 43	13 57	14 07
Chadwell Heath d	12 47	13 01			13 17	13 31				13 47	14 01	
Goodmayes d	12 49	13 03			13 19	13 33				13 49	14 03	
Seven Kings d	12 51	13 05			13 21	13 35				13 51	14 05	
Ilford 2 d	12 54	13 08			13 24	13 38				13 54	14 08	
Manor Park d	12 56	13 10			13 26	13 40				13 56	14 10	
Forest Gate d	12 58	13 12			13 28	13 42				13 58	14 12	
Maryland d		13 14				13 44					14 14	
Stratford 7 ⊖ d	13 01	13 16	13 19	13s34	13 31	13 46	13 49		14s04	14 01	14 16	14 19
London Liverpool Street 15 ⊖ a	13 11	13 26	13 29	13 42	13 41	13 56	13 59		14 12	14 11	14 26	14 29

	LE 1	LE	LE	LE 1	LE 1	LE 1	LE	LE	LE 1	LE 1	LE	LE
Southend Victoria d				13 52					14 22			
Prittlewell d												
Rochford d				13 56					14 26			
Hockley d				14 00					14 30			
Rayleigh d				14 04					14 34			
Southminster d					14 05							
Burnham-on-Crouch d					14 09							
Althorne d					14 14							
North Fambridge d					14 20							
South Woodham Ferrers d					14 25							
Battlesbridge d					14 29							
Wickford 2 d				14 09	14a35				14 39			
Billericay d				14 15					14 45			
Shenfield 3 a	14 10			14 22		14 40			14 52	15 10		
d	14 11		14 13	14 23		14 41		14 43	14 53	15 11		15 13
Brentwood d			14 16	14 26				14 46	14 56			15 16
Harold Wood d			14 21	14 31				14 51	15 01			15 21
Gidea Park 2 d		14 11	14 25	14 35			14 41	14 55	15 05		15 11	15 25
Romford d		14 13	14 27	14 37			14 43	14 57	15 07		15 13	15 27
Chadwell Heath d		14 17	14 31				14 47	15 01			15 17	15 31
Goodmayes d		14 19	14 33				14 49	15 03			15 19	15 33
Seven Kings d		14 21	14 35				14 51	15 05			15 21	15 35
Ilford 2 d		14 24	14 38				14 54	15 08			15 24	15 38
Manor Park d		14 26	14 40				14 56	15 10			15 26	15 40
Forest Gate d		14 28	14 42				14 58	15 12			15 28	15 42
Maryland d			14 44					15 14				15 44
Stratford 7 ⊖ d	14s34	14 31	14 46	14 49		15s04	15 01	15 16	15 19	15s34	15 31	15 46
London Liverpool Street 15 ⊖ a	14 42	14 41	14 56	14 59		15 12	15 11	15 26	15 29	15 42	15 41	15 56

	LE 1	LE 1	LE 1	LE	LE	LE 1	LE 1	LE	LE	LE 1	LE 1	LE 1
Southend Victoria d	14 52					15 22				15 52		
Prittlewell d												
Rochford d	14 56					15 26				15 56		
Hockley d	15 00					15 30				16 00		
Rayleigh d	15 04					15 34				16 04		
Southminster d		15 05									16 05	
Burnham-on-Crouch d		15 09									16 09	
Althorne d		15 14									16 14	
North Fambridge d		15 20									16 20	
South Woodham Ferrers d		15 25									16 25	
Battlesbridge d		15 29									16 29	
Wickford 2 d	15 09	15a35				15 39				16 09	16a35	
Billericay d	15 15					15 45				16 15		
Shenfield 3 a	15 22		15 40			15 52	16 10			16 22		16 40
d	15 23		15 41		15 43	15 53	16 11		16 13	16 23		16 41
Brentwood d	15 26				15 46	15 56			16 16	16 26		
Harold Wood d	15 31				15 51	16 01			16 21	16 31		
Gidea Park 2 d	15 35			15 41	15 55	16 05		16 11	16 25	16 35		
Romford d	15 37			15 43	15 57	16 07		16 13	16 27	16 37		
Chadwell Heath d				15 47	16 01			16 17	16 31			
Goodmayes d				15 49	16 03			16 19	16 33			
Seven Kings d				15 51	16 05			16 21	16 35			
Ilford 2 d				15 54	16 08			16 24	16 38			
Manor Park d				15 56	16 10			16 26	16 40			
Forest Gate d				15 58	16 12			16 28	16 42			
Maryland d					16 14				16 44			
Stratford 7 ⊖ d	15 49		16s04	16 01	16 16	16 19	16s34	16 31	16 46	16 49		17s04
London Liverpool Street 15 ⊖ a	15 59		16 12	16 11	16 26	16 29	16 42	16 41	16 56	16 59		17 12

	LE	LE	LE 1	LE 1	LE	LE	LE 1	LE 1	LE 1	LE	LE	LE 1
Southend Victoria d			16 22				16 52					17 22
Prittlewell d												
Rochford d			16 26				16 56					17 26
Hockley d			16 30				17 00					17 30
Rayleigh d			16 34				17 04					17 34
Southminster d								17 05				
Burnham-on-Crouch d								17 09				
Althorne d								17 14				
North Fambridge d								17 20				
South Woodham Ferrers d								17 25				
Battlesbridge d								17 29				
Wickford 2 d			16 39				17 09	17a35				17 39
Billericay d			16 45				17 15					17 45
Shenfield 3 a			16 52	17 10			17 22		17 40			17 52
d		16 43	16 53	17 11		17 13	17 23		17 41		17 43	17 53
Brentwood d		16 46	16 56			17 16	17 26				17 46	17 56
Harold Wood d		16 51	17 01			17 21	17 31				17 51	18 01
Gidea Park 2 d	16 41	16 55	17 05		17 11	17 25	17 35			17 41	17 55	18 05
Romford d	16 43	16 57	17 07		17 13	17 27	17 37			17 43	17 57	18 07
Chadwell Heath d	16 47	17 01			17 17	17 31				17 47	18 01	
Goodmayes d	16 49	17 03			17 19	17 33				17 49	18 03	
Seven Kings d	16 51	17 05			17 21	17 35				17 51	18 05	
Ilford 2 d	16 54	17 08			17 24	17 38				17 54	18 08	
Manor Park d	16 56	17 10			17 26	17 40				17 56	18 10	
Forest Gate d	16 58	17 12			17 28	17 42				17 58	18 12	
Maryland d		17 14				17 44					18 14	
Stratford 7 ⊖ d	17 01	17 16	17 19	17s34	17 31	17 46	17 49		18s04	18 01	18 16	18 19

	LE 1	LE	LE	LE 1	LE 1	LE 1	LE	LE	LE 1	LE 1	LE	LE
Southend Victoria d				17 52					18 22			
Prittlewell d												
Rochford d				17 56					18 26			
Hockley d				18 00					18 30			
Rayleigh d				18 04					18 34			
Southminster d					18 05							
Burnham-on-Crouch d					18 09							
Althorne d					18 14							
North Fambridge d					18 20							
South Woodham Ferrers d					18 25							
Battlesbridge d					18 29							
Wickford 2 d				18 09	18a35				18 39			
Billericay d				18 15					18 45			
Shenfield 3 a	18 10			18 22		18 40			18 52	19 10		
d	18 11		18 13	18 23		18 41		18 43	18 53	19 11		19 13
Brentwood d			18 16	18 26				18 46	18 56			19 16
Harold Wood d			18 21	18 31				18 51	19 01			19 21
Gidea Park 2 d		18 11	18 25	18 35			18 41	18 55	19 05		19 11	19 25
Romford d		18 13	18 27	18 37			18 43	18 57	19 07		19 13	19 27
Chadwell Heath d		18 17	18 31				18 47	19 01			19 17	19 31
Goodmayes d		18 19	18 33				18 49	19 03			19 19	19 33
Seven Kings d		18 21	18 35				18 51	19 05			19 21	19 35
Ilford 2 d		18 24	18 38				18 54	19 08			19 24	19 38
Manor Park d		18 26	18 40				18 56	19 10			19 26	19 40
Forest Gate d		18 28	18 42				18 58	19 12			19 28	19 42
Maryland d			18 44					19 14				19 44
Stratford 7 ⊖ d	18s34	18 31	18 46	18 49		19s04	19 01	19 16	19 19	19s34	19 31	19 46

Table 5

Sundays

Southend Victoria, Southminster and Shenfield - London

		LE 1	LE 1	LE 1	LE	LE	LE 1	LE 1	LE	LE	LE 1	LE 1	LE 1	LE	LE	LE 1	LE 1	LE	LE	LE 1	LE 1	LE 1	LE	LE 1	LE 1
Southend Victoria	d	18 52					19 22				19 52					20 22				20 52				21 22	
Prittlewell	d																								
Rochford	d	18 56					19 26				19 56					20 26				20 56				21 26	
Hockley	d	19 00					19 30				20 00					20 30				21 00				21 30	
Rayleigh	d	19 04					19 34				20 04					20 34				21 04				21 34	
Southminster	d		19 05									20 05									21 05				
Burnham-on-Crouch	d		19 09									20 09									21 09				
Althorne	d		19 14									20 14									21 14				
North Fambridge	d		19 20									20 20									21 20				
South Woodham Ferrers	d		19 25									20 25									21 25				
Battlesbridge	d		19 29									20 29									21 29				
Wickford [2]	d	19 09	19a35				19 39				20 09	20a35				20 39				21 09	21a35			21 39	
Billericay	d	19 15					19 45				20 15					20 45				21 15				21 45	
Shenfield [3]	a	19 22		19 40			19 52	20 10			20 22		20 40			20 52	21 10			21 22		21 40		21 52	22 10
	d	19 23		19 41		19 43	19 53	20 11		20 13	20 23		20 41		20 43	20 53	21 11		21 13	21 23		21 41	21 43	21 53	22 11
Brentwood	d	19 26				19 46	19 56			20 16	20 26				20 46	20 56			21 16	21 26			21 46	21 56	
Harold Wood	d	19 31				19 51	20 01			20 21	20 31				20 51	21 01			21 21	21 31			21 51	22 01	
Gidea Park [2]	d	19 35			19 41	19 55	20 05		20 11	20 25	20 35			20 41	20 55	21 05		21 11	21 25	21 35			21 55	22 05	
Romford	d	19 37			19 43	19 57	20 07		20 13	20 27	20 37			20 43	20 57	21 07		21 13	21 27	21 37			21 57	22 07	
Chadwell Heath	d				19 47	20 01			20 17	20 31				20 47	21 01			21 17	21 31				22 01		
Goodmayes	d				19 49	20 03			20 19	20 33				20 49	21 03			21 19	21 33				22 03		
Seven Kings	d				19 51	20 05			20 21	20 35				20 51	21 05			21 21	21 35				22 05		
Ilford [2]	d				19 54	20 08			20 24	20 38				20 54	21 08			21 24	21 38				22 08		
Manor Park	d				19 56	20 10			20 26	20 40				20 56	21 10			21 26	21 40				22 10		
Forest Gate	d				19 58	20 12			20 28	20 42				20 58	21 12			21 28	21 42				22 12		
Maryland	d					20 14				20 44					21 14				21 44				22 14		
Stratford [7] ⊖	d	19 49		20s04	20 01	20 16	20 19	20s34	20 31	20 46	20 49		21s04	21 01	21 16	21 19	21s34	21 31	21 46	21 49		22s04	22 16	22 19	22s34
London Liverpool Street [15] ⊖	a	19 59		20 12	20 11	20 26	20 29	20 42	20 41	20 56	20 59		21 12	21 11	21 26	21 29	21 42	21 41	21 56	21 59		22 12	22 26	22 29	22 42

		LE	LE 1	LE 1	LE 1	LE	LE 1	LE 1	LE	LE 1	LE 1	LE 1	LE
Southend Victoria	d		21 52				22 22			22 52			
Prittlewell	d												
Rochford	d		21 56				22 26			22 56			
Hockley	d		22 00				22 30			23 00			
Rayleigh	d		22 04				22 34			23 04			
Southminster	d			22 05							22 45		
Burnham-on-Crouch	d			22 09							22 49		
Althorne	d			22 14							22 54		
North Fambridge	d			22 20							23 00		
South Woodham Ferrers	d			22 25							23 05		
Battlesbridge	d			22 29							23 09		
Wickford [2]	d		22 09	22a35			22 39			23 09	23 15		
Billericay	d		22 15				22 45			23 15			
Shenfield [3]	a		22 22		22 40		22 52	23 10		23 22	23 26		
	d	22 13	22 23		22 41	22 43	22 53	23 11	23 13	23 23			23 43
Brentwood	d	22 16	22 26			22 46	22 56		23 16	23 26			23 46
Harold Wood	d	22 21	22 31			22 51	23 01		23 21	23 31			23 51
Gidea Park [2]	d	22 25	22 35			22 55	23 05		23 25	23 35			23 55
Romford	d	22 27	22 37			22 57	23 07		23 27	23 37			23 57
Chadwell Heath	d	22 31				23 01			23 31				00 01
Goodmayes	d	22 33				23 03			23 33				00 03
Seven Kings	d	22 35				23 05			23 35				00 05
Ilford [2]	d	22 38				23 08			23 38				00 08
Manor Park	d	22 40				23 10			23 40				00 10
Forest Gate	d	22 42				23 12			23 42				00 12
Maryland	d	22 44				23 14			23 44				00 14
Stratford [7] ⊖	d	22 46	22 49		23s04	23 16	23 19	23s34	23 46	23 49		23 22	00 16
London Liverpool Street [15] ⊖	a	22 56	22 59		23 12	23 26	23 31	23 42	23 56	23 59		23 36	00 26

Table 10

Mondays to Fridays

Marks Tey - Sudbury

		LE	LE	LE	LE	LE	LE	LE	LE	LE	LE	LE	LE	LE	LE	LE	LE	LE	LE
Colchester [4]	d																		
Marks Tey [2]	d	05 57	06 53	07 40	08 33	09 33	10 33	11 33	12 33	13 33	14 33	15 31	16 17	17 07	18 05	18 59	19 45	20 33	21 33
Chappel & Wakes Colne	d	06 03	06 59		08 39	09 39	10 39	11 39	12 39	13 39	14 39	15 37	16 23	17 13	18 11	19 05	19 51	20 39	21 39
Bures	d	06 09	07 05		08 45	09 45	10 45	11 45	12 45	13 45	14 45	15 43	16 29	17 19	18 17	19 11	19 57	20 45	21 45
Sudbury	a	06 16	07 12	07 56	08 52	09 52	10 52	11 52	12 52	13 52	14 52	15 52	16 36	17 26	18 24	19 20	20 06	20 52	21 52

Saturdays

		LE	LE	LE	LE	LE	LE	LE	LE	LE	LE	LE	LE	LE	LE	LE	LE
Colchester [4]	d																
Marks Tey [2]	d	06 33	07 33	08 33	09 33	10 33	11 33	12 33	13 33	14 33	15 33	16 33	17 33	18 33	19 33	20 33	21 33
Chappel & Wakes Colne	d	06 39	07 39	08 39	09 39	10 39	11 39	12 39	13 39	14 39	15 39	16 39	17 39	18 39	19 39	20 39	21 39
Bures	d	06 45	07 45	08 45	09 45	10 45	11 45	12 45	13 45	14 45	15 45	16 45	17 45	18 45	19 45	20 45	21 45
Sudbury	a	06 52	07 52	08 52	09 52	10 52	11 52	12 52	13 52	14 52	15 52	16 52	17 52	18 52	19 52	20 52	21 52

Sundays

		LE	LE	LE	LE	LE	LE	LE	LE	LE	LE	LE	LE	LE	LE	LE
Colchester [4]	d	07 07														
Marks Tey [2]	d	07 15	08 15	09 15	10 15	11 15	12 15	13 15	14 15	15 15	16 15	17 15	18 15	19 15	20 15	21 15
Chappel & Wakes Colne	d	07 21	08 21	09 21	10 21	11 21	12 21	13 21	14 21	15 21	16 21	17 21	18 21	19 21	20 21	21 21
Bures	d	07 27	08 27	09 27	10 27	11 27	12 27	13 27	14 27	15 27	16 27	17 27	18 27	19 27	20 27	21 27
Sudbury	a	07 34	08 34	09 34	10 34	11 34	12 34	13 34	14 34	15 34	16 34	17 34	18 34	19 34	20 34	21 34

Table 10

Sudbury - Marks Tey

		LE	LE	LE	LE	LE	LE	LE	LE	LE		LE	LE	LE	LE	LE	LE	LE	LE	LE		LE
Sudbury	d	05 30	06 30	07 17	08 00	09 00	10 00	11 00	12 00	13 00		14 00	15 00	15 54	16 40	17 31	18 31	19 22	20 08	21 00		22 00
Bures	d	05 37	06 37	07 24	08 07	09 07	10 07	11 07	12 07	13 07		14 07	15 07	16 01		17 38	18 38	19x29	20x15	21 07		22 07
Chappel & Wakes Colne	d	05 43	06 43	07 30	08 13	09 13	10 13	11 13	12 13	13 13		14 13	15 13	16 07		17 44	18 44	19x35	20x21	21 13		22 13
Marks Tey ■	a	05 49	06 49	07 36	08 19	09 19	10 19	11 19	12 19	13 19		14 19	15 19	16 13	16 56	17 50	18 50	19 41	20 27	21 19		22 19
Colchester ■	a																					22 30

Saturdays

		LE	LE	LE	LE	LE	LE	LE	LE	LE		LE	LE	LE	LE	LE	LE	LE
Sudbury	d	07 00	08 00	09 00	10 00	11 00	12 00	13 00	14 00	15 00		16 00	17 00	18 00	19 00	20 00	21 00	22 00
Bures	d	07 07	08 07	09 07	10 07	11 07	12 07	13 07	14 07	15 07		16 07	17 07	18 07	19 07	20 07	21 07	22 07
Chappel & Wakes Colne	d	07 13	08 13	09 13	10 13	11 13	12 13	13 13	14 13	15 13		16 13	17 13	18 13	19 13	20 13	21 13	22 13
Marks Tey ■	a	07 19	08 19	09 19	10 19	11 19	12 19	13 19	14 19	15 19		16 19	17 19	18 19	19 19	20 19	21 19	22 19
Colchester ■	a																	22 30

Sundays

		LE	LE	LE	LE	LE	LE	LE	LE	LE		LE	LE	LE	LE	LE	LE
Sudbury	d	07 40	08 40	09 40	10 40	11 40	12 40	13 40	14 40	15 40		16 40	17 40	18 40	19 40	20 40	21 40
Bures	d	07 47	08 47	09 47	10 47	11 47	12 47	13 47	14 47	15 47		16 47	17 47	18 47	19 47	20 47	21 47
Chappel & Wakes Colne	d	07 53	08 53	09 53	10 53	11 53	12 53	13 53	14 53	15 53		16 53	17 53	18 53	19 53	20 53	21 53
Marks Tey ■	a	07 59	08 59	09 59	10 59	11 59	12 59	13 59	14 59	15 59		16 59	17 59	18 59	19 59	20 59	21 59
Colchester ■	a																22 09

Table 11

London - Chelmsford, Colchester, Walton-on-Naze, Clacton, Harwich, Ipswich and Norwich

		LE MX	LE MO	LE MO	LE MX	LE MO	LE FO	LE	LE MX	LE MO		LE MO	LE MX	LE MO	LE MX	LE MX	LE	LE	LE	LE	LE	LE	LE	LE	LE
		◇■	◇■	■	■	■	■	■	◇■	◇■		■	■	■	■	■		■	■	■		■	■	■	■
								A																	
		⊏⊐	⊏⊐						⊏⊐																
London Liverpool Street ■ ⊖	d	22p30	22p30	22p32	23p00	23p02	23p18	23p18	23p30	23p30		23p32	23p48	00 02	00 18	00 46									
Stratford ■ ⊖	d	22b38		22p39	23p07	23p09	23p25	23p25	23b38			23p39	23p55	00 09	00 25	00 55									
Romford	d																								
Shenfield ■	d		22b57	23p01	23p24	23p31	23p42	23p42		23b57		00 01	00 12	00 31	00 47	01 17									
Ingatestone	d					23p36	23p47	23p47					00 17	00 35	00 51	01 21									
Chelmsford ■	d	23p03		23p10	23p33	23p43	23p54	23p54	00 03			00 10	00 24	00 42	00 58	01 28									
Hatfield Peverel	d					23p49							00 30	00 49	01 05										
Witham ■	d			23p19	23p43	23p55	00 03	00 03				00 19	00 36	00 54	01 10	01 38		05 21							
White Notley	d																	05 28							
Cressing	d																	05 30							
Braintree Freeport	d																	05 33							
Braintree	a																	05 37							
Kelvedon	d					23p59							00 40	00 59	01 15										
Marks Tey ■	d			23p27		00 05						00 27	00 46	01 04	01 20										
Colchester ■	a	23p23	23p23	23p35	23p54	00 12	00 17	00 22	00 23	00 27		00 40	00 58	01 18	01 32	02 03									
	d	23p23	23p24	23p35	23p55	00 13	00 18		00 25	00 28									05 30	05 35		06 06			
Colchester Town	a																								
	d																								
Hythe	d																								
Wivenhoe ■	d			23p43			00 25																		
Alresford (Essex)	d			23p46			00 28																		
Great Bentley	d			23p50			00 32																		
Weeley	d																								
Thorpe-le-Soken ■	a			23p55			00 38																		
	d			23p55			00 38																		
Clacton-on-Sea	a			00 05			00 52															06 26			06 41
Kirby Cross	d																					06 30			06 49
Frinton-on-Sea	d																					06 33			06 52
Walton-on-the-Naze	a																					06 38			06 57
Manningtree ■	d	23p32	23p33		00 05	00 21			00 32	00 37									05 38	05 44		06 14		06 36	
Mistley	d																		05 42					06 40	
Wrabness	d																		05 47					06 45	
Harwich International	d																		05 56					06 52	
Dovercourt	d																		05 59					06 55	
Harwich Town	a																		06 01					06 57	
Ipswich	a	23p42	23p44		00 21	00 37			00 44	00 46										05 55		06 26			
	d	23p43	23p44						00 46	00 48							05 10			06 01	06 13				
Lowestoft	a																								
Needham Market	d																05 20				06 23				
Stowmarket	d	23p54	23p55						00 55	00 59							05 26			06 12	06 29				
Peterborough ■	a																			07 38					
Diss	d	00 07	00 07						01 08	01 11															
Norwich	a	00 47	00 39						01 45	01 43															

		LE	LE	LE	LE	LE		LE	LE	LE	LE	LE	LE	LE	LE	LE	LE	LE		LE	LE	LE	LE	LE	LE
		■	■	■	■			◇■	■	■	■	■	◇■	■	■	◇■	■	■		◇■	■	■	■		◇■
																									⊏⊐
London Liverpool Street ■ ⊖	d	05 23						06 00		06 02	06 12		06 25			06 38		06 48		07 00	07 04	07 08	07 18		07 30
Stratford ■ ⊖	d	05 30								06 09	06 19		06u33					06 55			07 11	07 15	07 25		07u38
Romford	d	05 38								06 17												07 23			
Shenfield ■	d	05 49						06u23		06 28	06 37					07u02		07 12		07u23	07 28	07 34	07 42		
Ingatestone	d	05 53									06 41							07 16					07 46		
Chelmsford ■	d	06 00								06 37	06 49		06 57			07 12		07 23			07 37	07 43	07 53		08 04
Hatfield Peverel	d	06 07									06 55							07 30							
Witham ■	d	06 12	06 14							06 46	07 03		07 07			07 21		07 36			07 47	07 52	08 03		
White Notley	d		06 21								07 10										07 54				
Cressing	d		06 23								07 12										07 56				
Braintree Freeport	d		06 26								07 15										07 59				
Braintree	a		06 30								07 20										08 04				
Kelvedon	d	06 17								06 51						07 27							08 07		
Marks Tey ■	d	06 22								06 56						07 33		07 47					08 13		
Colchester ■	a	06 30						06 50		07 04			07 22			07 41		07 56		07 49		08 06	08 20		08 23
	d	06 31			06 45			06 50		07 04		07 18	07 22		07 26	07 41	07 48			07 50		08 07	08 21		08 24
Colchester Town	a				06 52										07 33		07 55								
	d														07 37										
Hythe	d									07 09					07 41							08 11			
Wivenhoe ■	d	06 38								07 13		07 25			07 45							08 15			
Alresford (Essex)	d									07 16		07 29			07 49							08 18			
Great Bentley	d									07 20		07 33			07 53							08 22			
Weeley	d									07 23					07 56										
Thorpe-le-Soken ■	a	06 48								07 27		07 39			08 00							08 28			
	d	06 48							07 20	07 27		07 39			08 00							08 28			
Clacton-on-Sea	a	06 58								07 36					08 10							08 37			
Kirby Cross	d								07 24			07 46													
Frinton-on-Sea	d								07 27			07 49													
Walton-on-the-Naze	a								07 32			07 55													
Manningtree ■	d							06 59					07 32	07 35		07 50				07 59			08 29		08 34
Mistley	d													07 39									08 33	07 59	
Wrabness	d													07 44									08 38		
Harwich International	d													07 51									08 46		
Dovercourt	d													07 54									08 49		
Harwich Town	a													07 56									08 51		
Ipswich	a							07 08					07 42			07 59				08 08				08 15	08 43
	d			06 42		06 52		07 09					07 42			08 02				08 09				08 16	08 44
Lowestoft	a																								
Needham Market	d					07 02																		08 26	
Stowmarket	d			06 53		07 08		07 20					07 53			08 13				08 20				08 32	08 55
Peterborough ■	a															09 37									
Diss	d			07 06				07 33					08 06							08 33					09 07
Norwich	a			07 27				07 54					08 27							08 54					09 27

A TWThO

b previous night, stops to pick up only

London - Chelmsford, Colchester, Walton-on-Naze, Clacton, Harwich, Ipswich and Norwich

		LE ■	LE ◇■	LE ■	LE ■	LE ■	LE ◇■ ☕	LE	LE ■	LE ■	LE ■	LE ■	LE ■	LE ◇■ ☕	LE ■	LE ■	LE ■	LE ■	LE ■	LE ◇■ ☕	LE ■	LE ■	LE ■
London Liverpool Street ■ ⊖	d	07 27	07 38	07 48			08 00		08 02			08 08	08 18	08 30		08 38	08 48			09 00		09 08	09 18
Stratford ■ ⊖	d			07 55								08 15	08 25	08u38			08 55					09 15	09 25
Romford	d								08 16													09 23	
Shenfield ■	d	07 51	08u02	08 12			08u23		08 26			08 32	08 42			09 02	09 12			09u23		09 34	09 42
Ingatestone	d			08 16								08 36	08 46				09 16						
Chelmsford ■	d	08 00	08 12	08 23					08 35			08 43	08 53	09 02		09 12	09 23					09 43	09 51
Hatfield Peverel	d			08 30													09 30						
Witham ■	d	08 12	08 22	08 38					08 44			08 52	09 03			09 21	09 37					09 52	10 00
White Notley	d			08 44													09 43						
Cressing	d			08 47													09 46						
Braintree Freeport	d			08 49													09 48						
Braintree	a			08 53													09 53						
Kelvedon	d	08 19							08 49				09 07										10 05
Marks Tey ■	d	08 24	08 30										09 13			09 29							10 10
Colchester ■	a	08 32	08 38				08 49		09 00			09 06	09 20	09 23		09 37				09 49		10 06	10 18
	d	08 32	08 38			08 46	08 50		09 04	09 06	09 14	09 07		09 24	09 30	09 38		09 46		09 50	10 00	10 07	10 21
Colchester Town	a	08 40				08 53			09 11						09 37			09 53			10 07		
	d					08 57												09 57					
Hythe	d					09 00												10 00					
Wivenhoe ■	d					09 04						09 15						10 04				10 14	
Alresford (Essex)	d					09 08												10 08					
Great Bentley	d					09 12												10 12					
Weeley	d					09 16												10 16					
Thorpe-le-Soken ■	a					09 19						09 25						10 19				10 24	
	d				08 30	09 26						09 25						10 26				10 24	
Clacton-on-Sea	a											09 34										10 34	
Kirby Cross	d				08 34	09 31												10 30					
Frinton-on-Sea	d				08 37	09 34												10 33					
Walton-on-the-Naze	a				08 41	09 39												10 39					
Manningtree ■	d						08 59			09 14	09 22			09 34		09 46				09 59			10 29
Mistley	d										09 26												10 33
Wrabness	d										09 31												10 38
Harwich International	d										09 39												10 47
Dovercourt	d										09 42												10 50
Harwich Town	a										09 44												10 52
Ipswich	a		08 56				09 08			09 25				09 44		09 58				10 09			
	d		09 02				09 09	09 16						09 44					10 02	10 09			
Lowestoft	a		10 32																				
Needham Market	d							09 26															
Stowmarket	d							09 32						09 55					10 13				
Peterborough ■	a																		11 37				
Diss	d						09 30							10 07						10 30			
Norwich	a						09 52							10 27						10 52			

		LE	LE ◇■ ☕	LE ■	LE ◇■	LE ■	LE ■		LE ◇■ ☕	LE ■	LE ■	LE ■	LE	LE ◇■ ☕	LE ■	LE ◇■	LE ■		LE ■	LE ◇■ ☕	LE ■	LE ■	LE ■
London Liverpool Street ■ ⊖	d		09 30		09 38	09 48			10 00		10 08	10 18		10 30		10 38	10 48			11 00		11 08	11 18
Stratford ■ ⊖	d		09u38			09 55					10 15	10 25		10u38			10 55					11 15	11 25
Romford	d										10 23											11 23	
Shenfield ■	d				10u02	10 12			10u23		10 34	10 42				11u02	11 12			11u23		11 34	11 42
Ingatestone	d					10 16											11 16						
Chelmsford ■	d		10 02		10 12	10 23					10 43	10 51		11 02		11 12	11 23					11 43	11 51
Hatfield Peverel	d					10 30											11 30						
Witham ■	d				10 21	10 36					10 52	11 00				11 21	11 36					11 52	12 00
White Notley	d					10 43											11 43						
Cressing	d					10 45											11 45						
Braintree Freeport	d					10 48											11 48						
Braintree	a					10 53											11 53						
Kelvedon	d											11 05											12 05
Marks Tey ■	d				10 29							11 10				11 29							12 10
Colchester ■	a		10 21		10 37				10 49		11 06	11 18		11 21		11 37				11 49		12 06	12 18
	d		10 24	10 30	10 38		10 46		10 50	11 00	11 07	11 18		11 22	11 30	11 38			11 46	11 50	12 00	12 07	12 18
Colchester Town	a			10 37			10 53			11 07					11 37				11 53		12 07		
	d						10 57												11 57				
Hythe	d						11 00												12 00				
Wivenhoe ■	d						11 04				11 14								12 04			12 14	
Alresford (Essex)	d						11 08												12 08				
Great Bentley	d						11 12												12 12				
Weeley	d						11 16												12 16				
Thorpe-le-Soken ■	a						11 19				11 24								12 19			12 24	
	d						11 26				11 24								12 26			12 24	
Clacton-on-Sea	a										11 34											12 34	
Kirby Cross	d						11 30												12 30				
Frinton-on-Sea	d						11 33												12 33				
Walton-on-the-Naze	a						11 39												12 39				
Manningtree ■	d		10 34						10 59			11 26		11 31						11 59			12 26
Mistley	d											11 30											12 30
Wrabness	d											11 35											12 35
Harwich International	d											11 44											12 44
Dovercourt	d											11 47											12 47
Harwich Town	a											11 49											12 49
Ipswich	a		10 44		10 56				11 09					11 42		11 56				12 09			
	d	10 16	10 44		11 02				11 09				11 16	11 42		12 02				12 09			
Lowestoft	a				12 32																		
Needham Market	d	10 26											11 26										
Stowmarket	d	10 32	10 55										11 32	11 53		12 13							
Peterborough ■	a															13 37							
Diss	d		11 07						11 30					12 05						12 30			
Norwich	a		11 27						11 52					12 27						12 52			

		LE	LE ◇■ ☕	LE ■		LE ◇■	LE ■	LE ■	LE ◇■ ☕	LE ■	LE ■	LE ■	LE	LE ◇■ ☕		LE ■	LE ◇■	LE ■	LE ■	LE ◇■ ☕	LE ■	LE ■	LE ■	LE
London Liverpool Street ■ ⊖	d		11 30			11 38	11 48		12 00		12 08	12 18		12 30			12 38	12 48		13 00		13 08	13 18	
Stratford ■ ⊖	d		11u38				11 55				12 15	12 25		12u38				12 55				13 15	13 25	
Romford	d										12 23											13 23		
Shenfield ■	d					12u02	12 12		12u23		12 34	12 42					13u02	13 12		13u23		13 34	13 42	
Ingatestone	d						12 16											13 16						
Chelmsford ■	d		12 02			12 12	12 23				12 43	12 51		13 02			13 12	13 23				13 43	13 51	
Hatfield Peverel	d						12 30											13 30						
Witham ■	d					12 21	12 36				12 52	13 00					13 21	13 36				13 52	14 00	
White Notley	d						12 43											13 43						
Cressing	d						12 45											13 45						
Braintree Freeport	d						12 48											13 48						
Braintree	a						12 53											13 53						
Kelvedon	d											13 05											14 05	
Marks Tey ■	d					12 29						13 10					13 29						14 10	
Colchester ■	a		12 21			12 37			12 49		13 06	13 18		13 21			13 37			13 49		14 06	14 18	
	d		12 22	12 30		12 38		12 46	12 50	13 00	13 07	13 18		13 22		13 30	13 38		13 46	13 50	14 00	14 07	14 18	
Colchester Town	a			12 37				12 53		13 07						13 37			13 53		14 07			
	d							12 57											13 57					
Hythe	d							13 00											14 00					
Wivenhoe ■	d							13 04			13 14								14 04			14 14		
Alresford (Essex)	d							13 08											14 08					
Great Bentley	d							13 12											14 12					
Weeley	d							13 16											14 16					
Thorpe-le-Soken ■	a							13 19			13 24								14 19			14 24		
	d							13 26			13 24								14 26			14 24		
Clacton-on-Sea	a										13 34											14 34		
Kirby Cross	d							13 30											14 30					
Frinton-on-Sea	d							13 33											14 33					
Walton-on-the-Naze	a							13 39											14 39					
Manningtree ■	d		12 31						12 59			13 26		13 31						13 59			14 26	
Mistley	d											13 30											14 30	
Wrabness	d											13 35											14 35	
Harwich International	d											13 44											14 44	
Dovercourt	d											13 47											14 47	
Harwich Town	a											13 49											14 49	
Ipswich	a		12 42			12 56			13 09					13 42			13 56			14 09				
	d	12 16	12 42			13 02			13 09				13 16	13 42			14 02			14 09				14 16
Lowestoft	a					14 32																		
Needham Market	d	12 26											13 26											14 26
Stowmarket	d	12 32	12 53										13 32	13 53			14 13							14 32
Peterborough ■	a																15 37							
Diss	d		13 05						13 30					14 05						14 30				
Norwich	a		13 27						13 52					14 27						14 52				

		LE ◇■ ☕	LE ■	LE ◇■	LE ■	LE ■	LE ◇■ ☕	LE ■	LE ■	LE ■		LE	LE ◇■ ☕	LE ■	LE ◇■	LE ■	LE ■	LE ◇■ ☕	LE ■	LE ■	LE ■	LE	LE ■ ■ ☕	LE ■	LE ■
London Liverpool Street ■ ⊖	d	13 30		13 38	13 48		14 00		14 08	14 18			14 30		14 38	14 48		15 00		15 08	15 18		15 30	15 32	
Stratford ■ ⊖	d	13u38			13 55				14 15	14 25			14u38			14 55				15 15	15 25				
Romford	d								14 23											15 23					
Shenfield ■	d			14u02	14 12		14u23		14 34	14 42					15u02	15 12		15u23		15 34	15 42			15 55	
Ingatestone	d				14 16											15 16								15 59	
Chelmsford ■	d	14 02		14 12	14 23				14 43	14 51			15 02		15 12	15 23				15 43	15 51		15 59	16 06	
Hatfield Peverel	d				14 30											15 30								16 13	
Witham ■	d			14 21	14 36				14 52	15 00					15 21	15 36				15 52	16 00			16 19	
White Notley	d				14 43											15 43									
Cressing	d				14 45											15 45									
Braintree Freeport	d				14 48											15 48									
Braintree	a				14 53											15 53									
Kelvedon	d									15 05											16 05			16 24	
Marks Tey ■	d			14 29						15 10					15 29						16 10				
Colchester ■	a	14 21		14 37			14 49		15 06	15 18			15 21		15 37			15 49		16 06	16 18		16 21	16 37	
	d	14 22	14 30	14 38		14 46	14 50	15 00	15 07	15 18			15 22	15 30	15 38		15 46	15 50	16 00	16 07	16 18		16 22		16 41
Colchester Town	a		14 37			14 53		15 07						15 37			15 53		16 07						16 48
	d					14 57											15 57								16 52
Hythe	d					15 00											16 00								16 55
Wivenhoe ■	d					15 04			15 14								16 04			16 14					16 59
Alresford (Essex)	d					15 08											16 08								17 03
Great Bentley	d					15 12											16 12								17 07
Weeley	d					15 16											16 16								17 11
Thorpe-le-Soken ■	a					15 19			15 24								16 19			16 24					17 14
	d					15 26			15 24								16 26			16 24					17 22
Clacton-on-Sea	a								15 34											16 34					
Kirby Cross	d					15 30											16 30								17 26
Frinton-on-Sea	d					15 33											16 33								17 29
Walton-on-the-Naze	a					15 39											16 39								17 35
Manningtree ■	d	14 31					14 59			15 26			15 31					15 59			16 26		16 31		
Mistley	d									15 30											16 30				
Wrabness	d									15 35											16 35				
Harwich International	d									15 44											16 44				
Dovercourt	d									15 47											16 47				
Harwich Town	a									15 49											16 49				
Ipswich	a	14 42		14 56			15 09						15 42		15 56			16 09					16 42		
	d	14 42		15 02			15 09					15 16	15 42		16 02			16 09				16 16	16 42		
Lowestoft	a			16 32																					
Needham Market	d											15 26										16 26			
Stowmarket	d	14 53										15 32	15 53		16 13							16 32	16 53		
Peterborough ■	a														17 37										
Diss	d	15 05					15 30						16 05					16 30					17 05		
Norwich	a	15 27					15 52						16 27					16 52					17 27		

London - Chelmsford, Colchester, Walton-on-Naze, Clacton, Harwich, Ipswich and Norwich

		LE ■ 1	LE 1	LE ■ 1 ⊡	LE	LE 1	LE 1	LE 1	LE 1	LE ■ 1 ⊡	LE 1	LE ◇1	LE 1	LE 1	LE 1	LE 1	LE ■ 1 ⊡	LE 1	LE 1	LE 1	LE 1
London Liverpool Street [15] ⊖	d	15 38	15 48	16 00			16 02	16 15	16 17	16 30		16 32	16 34	16 45		16 47	17 00			17 02	17 08
Stratford [7] ⊖	d		15 55				16 10		16 25				16 42			16 55					17 16
Romford	d																				
Shenfield [3]	d	16u02	16 12				16 25		16 40			16u54	16 57			17 10				17 24	
Ingatestone	d		16 16						16 44							17 14					
Chelmsford [3]	d	16u12	16 23	16 31			16 36	16 45	16 53				17 08	17 15		17 23				17 35	
Hatfield Peverel	d		16 30										17 15								
Witham [2]	d	16 23	16 36				16 45		17a06			17 13	17 21			17a36				17 45	17 50
White Notley	d		16 43										17 28								
Cressing	d		16 45										17 30								
Braintree Freeport	d		16 48										17 33								
Braintree	a		16 53										17 40								
Kelvedon	d						16 50	16 56						17 26						17 50	17 54
Marks Tey [2]	d	16 32						17 01						17 31						17 55	18 00
Colchester [4]	a	16 41		16 49			17 01	17 09		17 17		17 26		17 39	>					18 03	18 08
	d	16 41		16 50		16 54	17 02	17 13		17 18	17 24	17 26		17 43	17 47			17 51	17 52	18 03	18 12
Colchester Town	a					17 01					17 31								17 59		
	d										17 35								18 03		
Hythe	d						17 06				17 38			17 47					18 06		18 17
Wivenhoe [3]	d						17 10				17 42			17 51					18 10		18 21
Alresford (Essex)	d										17 46								18 14		18 24
Great Bentley	d										17 50								18 18		18 28
Weeley	d										17 54								18 22		
Thorpe-le-Soken [1]	a						17 20				17 57			18 02					18 25		18 33
	d						17 20				18 04			18 02					18 35		18 33
Clacton-on-Sea	a						17 32							18 13							18 45
Kirby Cross	d										18 08								18 39		
Frinton-on-Sea	d										18 11								18 42		
Walton-on-the-Naze	a										18 17								18 48		
Manningtree [2]	d			16 59				17 21				17 35			17 55			17 59		18 11	
Mistley	d							17 25							17 59						
Wrabness	d							17 30							18 04						
Harwich International	d							17 38							18 12					18a29	
Dovercourt	d							17 41							18 15						
Harwich Town	a							17 45							18 19						
Ipswich	a	16 58		17 09						17 35		17 47					17 59	18 10			
	d	17 02		17 09	17 16					17 35		17 49					17 59				
Lowestoft	a	18 33																			
Needham Market	d				17 26							17 58									
Stowmarket	d			17 20	17 32					17 46		18 03									
Peterborough [8]	a											19 42									
Diss	d			17 33						17 59							18 20				
Norwich	a			17 55						18 22							18 43				

		LE 1	LE	LE 1	LE 1	LE 1	LE ■ 1 ⊡	LE 1	LE 1	LE 1	LE 1	LE 1	LE ■ 1 ⊡	LE 1	LE 1	LE ■ 1 ⊡	LE 1	LE	LE 1	LE 1	LE 1	LE ■ 1 ⊡
London Liverpool Street [15] ⊖	d	17 12		17 20	17 22		17 30	17 32	17 38			17 42	17 50		17 52	18 00			18 02	18 08	18 12	18 20
Stratford [7] ⊖	d	17 20							17 46			17 50							18 10	18 16	18 20	
Romford	d																					
Shenfield [3]	d				17 44			17 54							18 14							
Ingatestone	d				17 48										18 18							
Chelmsford [3]	d	17 44		17 51	17 58			18 05				18 14			18 28				18 35	18 40	18 44	
Hatfield Peverel	d	17 51										18 21									18 51	
Witham [2]	d	17a59			18 09			18 15	18 20			18 30			18a41				18 45	18 50	18 57	
White Notley	d				18 16																19 04	
Cressing	d				18 18																19 06	
Braintree Freeport	d				18 21																19 09	
Braintree	a				18 28																19 16	
Kelvedon	d							18 20	18 24			18 36							18 50	18 54		
Marks Tey [2]	d								18 30										18 55	19 00		
Colchester [4]	a			18 11				18 31	18 38			18 48	18 43			18 51			19 03	19 08		19 12
	d			18 11				18 34	18 38	18 42		18 52	18 43			18 53	18 56		19 03	19 09		19 12
Colchester Town	a							18 42									19 03					
	d							18 48														
Hythe	d								18 43											19 13		
Wivenhoe [3]	d							18 55	18 47	18 51		18 59								19 17		
Alresford (Essex)	d							18 59		18 54		19 03										
Great Bentley	d							19 03		18 58		19 07										
Weeley	d							19 07			←											
Thorpe-le-Soken [1]	a							19 11	18 57	19 03	19 11	19 15								19 27		
	d							19 11	18 57	19 04	19 11	19 15								19 27		
Clacton-on-Sea	a							→	19 08		19 22	19 26								19 38		
Kirby Cross	d									19 08												
Frinton-on-Sea	d									19 11												
Walton-on-the-Naze	a									19 16												
Manningtree [2]	d			18 19		18 23	18 27						18 53	18 57		19 02			19 11			19 22
Mistley	d					18 27								19 01								
Wrabness	d					18 32								19 06								
Harwich International	d					18 39								19 13								
Dovercourt	d					18 42								19 16								
Harwich Town	a					18 46								19 18								
Ipswich	a			18 33			18 39						19 03			19 11			19 24			19 31
	d		18 16				18 39						19 03			19 13		19 16				19 32
Lowestoft	a																					
Needham Market	d		18 26															19 26				
Stowmarket	d		18 32				18 51									19 24		19 32				
Peterborough [8]	a																					
Diss	d						19 04									19 37						
Norwich	a						19 25						19 44			19 59						20 14

Table 11

Mondays to Fridays

London - Chelmsford, Colchester, Walton-on-Naze, Clacton, Harwich, Ipswich and Norwich

		LE 1	LE 1	LE 1	LE ■ 1 ⊡	LE 1	LE 1	LE 1	LE 1	LE 1	LE ■ 1 ⊡	LE 1	LE 1	LE 1	LE 1	LE 1	LE ■ 1 ⊡	LE ■ 1	LE 1	LE 1	LE 1	LE ◇1 ⊡	LE 1
London Liverpool Street [15] ⊖	d			18 22	18 30	18 32	18 38			18 48	19 00		19 02	19 08	19 18		19 30	19 32	19 38	19 48		20 00	20 08
Stratford [7] ⊖	d					18 40	18 46						19 09	19 15	19 25				19 45	19 55			20 15
Romford	d																						
Shenfield [3]	d			18 44			19 01			19 11			19 26		19 42			19u55	20 02	20 12			20 32
Ingatestone	d			18 48						19 15					19 46					20 16			
Chelmsford [3]	d			18 58		19 05	19 13			19 24			19 35	19 39	19 53		20 00		20 11	20 23			20 41
Hatfield Peverel	d					19 12							19 41							20 30			
Witham [2]	d			19 11		19 18	19 23			19 34			19 47	19 50	20 03			20 12	20 20	20 36			20 50
White Notley	d												19 54							20 43			
Cressing	d												19 56							20 45			
Braintree Freeport	d												19 59							20 48			
Braintree	a												20 04							20 53			
Kelvedon	d			19 17		19 23	19 27							19 54					20 25				20 55
Marks Tey [2]	d			19 23			19 33							20 00					20 30				21 00
Colchester [4]	a			19 31	19 23	19 34	19 41			19 50	19 53			20 08	20 16		20 21	20 25	20 38			20 49	21 08
	d			19 31	19 23	19 34	19 41		19 46		19 53			20 08	20 17		20 21	20 26	20 38		20 46	20 50	21 09
Colchester Town	a								19 53												20 53		
	d								19 57												20 57		
Hythe	d						19 46		20 00												21 00		
Wivenhoe [3]	d			19 39			19 50		20 04					20 16							21 04		21 16
Alresford (Essex)	d			19 42					20 08												21 08		
Great Bentley	d			19 46					20 12												21 12		
Weeley	d			19 49					20 16												21 16		
Thorpe-le-Soken [1]	a			19 53			20 00		20 19					20 26							21 19		21 26
	d		19 29	19 53			20 00	20 04	20 28					20 26							21 28		21 26
Clacton-on-Sea	a			20 04			20 11							20 35									21 36
Kirby Cross	d		19 33					20 08	20 32												21 32		
Frinton-on-Sea	d		19 36					20 11	20 35												21 35		
Walton-on-the-Naze	a		19 41					20 16	20 41												21 41		
Manningtree [2]	d	19 27				19 42					20 02	20 07			20 25		20 30					20 59	
Mistley	d	19 31										20 11			20 29								
Wrabness	d	19 36										20 16			20 34								
Harwich International	d	19 43										20 23			20 42								
Dovercourt	d	19 46										20 26			20 45								
Harwich Town	a	19 48										20 28			20 47								
Ipswich	a				19 41	19 56					20 11						20 41	20 44	20 57			21 09	
	d				19 41						20 13					20 16	20 41	20 52				21 09	
Lowestoft	a																	22 22					
Needham Market	d															20 25							
Stowmarket	d				19 53						20 24					20 30	20 52					21 20	
Peterborough [8]	a															21 58							
Diss	d				20 06						20 37						21 04					21 32	
Norwich	a				20 28						20 59						21 26					21 54	

		LE 1	LE	LE ◇1 ⊡	LE 1	LE 1	LE	LE 1	LE ◇1	LE 1	LE 1	LE	LE ◇1 ⊡	LE 1	LE	LE 1	LE 1	LE 1	LE 1	LE 1	LE ◇1 ⊡	LE 1
London Liverpool Street [15] ⊖	d	20 18		20 30	20 38	20 48			21 00	21 08	21 18		21 30			21 38	21 48	22 00		22 18	22 30	22 48
Stratford [7] ⊖	d	20 25		20u38	20 45	20 55				21 15	21 25		21u38				21 55			22 25	22u38	22 55
Romford	d									21 23												
Shenfield [3]	d	20 42			21 02	21 12			21u23	21 34	21 42					22u02	22 12	22 22		22 42		23 12
Ingatestone	d	20 46				21 16											22 16					23 16
Chelmsford [3]	d	20 53		21 03	21 11	21 23				21 43	21 51		22 03			22u12	22 23	22 31		22 51	23 03	23 23
Hatfield Peverel	d					21 30											22 30					23 30
Witham [2]	d	21 03			21 20	21 36				21 52	22 00					22 21	22 36	22 40		23 00		23 35
White Notley	d					21 43											22 43					
Cressing	d					21 45											22 45					
Braintree Freeport	d					21 48											22 48					
Braintree	a					21 53											22 53					
Kelvedon	d				21 25						22 05									23 05		23 40
Marks Tey [2]	d				21 30						22 10				22 21	22 29				23 10		23 45
Colchester [4]	a	21 16		21 23	21 38				21 49	22 06	22 18		22 23		22 30	22 37		22 54		23 18	23 23	23 57
	d	21 17		21 23	21 38			21 46	21 50	22 07	22 26		22 23			22 38		22 54	22 58	23 19	23 23	
Colchester Town	a							21 53											23 05			
	d							21 57											23 09			
Hythe	d							22 00											23 12			
Wivenhoe [3]	d							22 04		22 14	22 33								23 16	23 26		
Alresford (Essex)	d							22 08			22 36								23 20	23 29		
Great Bentley	d							22 12			22 40								23 24	23 33		
Weeley	d							22 16											23 28			
Thorpe-le-Soken [1]	a							22 19		22 24	22 46								23 31	23 39		
	d							22 26		22 24	22 46								23 31	23 39		
Clacton-on-Sea	a									22 34									23 41	23 48		
Kirby Cross	d							22 30			22 51											
Frinton-on-Sea	d							22 33			22 54											
Walton-on-the-Naze	a							22 39			23 00											
Manningtree [2]	d	21 25		21 32	21 46				21 58				22 32	22 38				23 02			23 32	
Mistley	d	21 29												22 42								
Wrabness	d	21 34												22 47								
Harwich International	d	21 42			22a02		21 34							22 54								
Dovercourt	d	21 45												22 57								
Harwich Town	a	21 47												22 59								
Ipswich	a			21 43			22 00		22 07				22 43			22 56		23 14			23 43	
	d		21 16	21 43					22 15			22 16	22 43								23 43	
Lowestoft	a								23 45													
Needham Market	d		21 26									22 26										
Stowmarket	d		21 32	21 54								22 32	22 54								23 54	
Peterborough [8]	a																					
Diss	d			22 06									23 07								00 07	
Norwich	a			22 28									23 29								00 47	

London - Chelmsford, Colchester, Walton-on-Naze, Clacton, Harwich, Ipswich and Norwich

		LE ■	LE ■	LE ■	LE ■ A	LE ■ B	LE ◇■	LE ■
London Liverpool Street ■ ⊖	d		23 00		23 18	23 18	23 30	23 48
Stratford ■ ⊖	d		23 07		23 25	23 25	23u38	23 55
Romford	d							
Shenfield ■	d		23 24		23 42	23 42		00 12
Ingatestone	d				23 46	23 46		00 16
Chelmsford ■	d		23 33		23 53	23 53	00 03	00 23
Hatfield Peverel	d							00 30
Witham ■	d		23 42	23 44	00 03	00 03		00 35
White Notley	d			23 50				
Cressing	d			23 53				
Braintree Freeport	d			23 55				
Braintree	a			23 59				
Kelvedon	d							00 40
Marks Tey ■	d							00 45
Colchester ■	a		23 56		00 17	00 21	00 23	00 57
	d		23 57		00 17		00 23	
Colchester Town	a							
	d							
Hythe	d							
Wivenhoe ■	d				00 25			
Alresford (Essex)	d				00 28			
Great Bentley	d				00 32			
Weeley	d							
Thorpe-le-Soken ■	a				00 37			
	d				00 37			
Clacton-on-Sea	a				00 51			
Kirby Cross	d							
Frinton-on-Sea	d							
Walton-on-the-Naze	a							
Manningtree ■	d	23 38	00 04				00 32	
Mistley	d	23 42						
Wrabness	d	23 47						
Harwich International	d	23 54						
Dovercourt	d	23 57						
Harwich Town	a	23 59						
Ipswich	a		00 20				00 44	
	d						00 44	
Lowestoft	a							
Needham Market	d							
Stowmarket	d						00 55	
Peterborough ■	a							
Diss	d						01 08	
Norwich	a						01 45	

A ThFO   B MTWO

London - Chelmsford, Colchester, Walton-on-Naze, Clacton, Harwich, Ipswich and Norwich

		LE ◇■	LE ■	LE ■	LE ◇■	LE ■	LE ■	LE ■	LE	LE ■	LE ■		LE ■
London Liverpool Street ■ ⊖	d	22p30	23p00	23p18	23p30	23p48	00 18	00 46					
Stratford ■ ⊖	d	22b38	23p07	23p25	23b38	23p55	00 25	00 55					
Romford	d												
Shenfield ■	d		23p24	23p42		00 12	00 47	01 17					
Ingatestone	d			23p47		00 17	00 51	01 21					
Chelmsford ■	d	23p03	23p33	23p54	00 03	00 24	00 58	01 28					
Hatfield Peverel	d					00 30	01 05						
Witham ■	d		23p43	00 03		00 36	01 10	01 38			05 36		
White Notley	d										05 43		
Cressing	d										05 45		
Braintree Freeport	d										05 48		
Braintree	a										05 52		
Kelvedon	d					00 40	01 15						
Marks Tey ■	d					00 46	01 20						
Colchester ■	a	23p23	23p54	00 17	00 23	00 58	01 32	02 03					
	d	23p23	23p55	00 18	00 25					05 18			05 38
Colchester Town	a												
	d												
Hythe	d												
Wivenhoe ■	d			00 25									
Alresford (Essex)	d			00 28									
Great Bentley	d			00 32									
Weeley	d												
Thorpe-le-Soken ■	a			00 38									
	d			00 38									
Clacton-on-Sea	a			00 52									
Kirby Cross	d												
Frinton-on-Sea	d												
Walton-on-the-Naze	a												
Manningtree ■	d	23p32	00 05		00 32					05 26			05 46
Mistley	d									05 30			
Wrabness	d									05 35			
Harwich International	d									05 44			
Dovercourt	d									05 47			
Harwich Town	a									05 49			
Ipswich	a	23p42	00 21		00 44								05 58
	d	23p43			00 46				05 10				06 00
Lowestoft	a												
Needham Market	d								05 20				
Stowmarket	d	23p54			00 55				05 26				06 11
Peterborough ■	a												07 37
Diss	d	00 07			01 08								
Norwich	a	00 47			01 45								

		LE	LE ■	LE ■	LE ■	LE ■	LE ■	LE ■		LE ■	LE ■	LE	LE ◇■
London Liverpool Street ■ ⊖	d				05 30			06 00		06 18			06 30
Stratford ■ ⊖	d				05 37			06 07		06 25			06u38
Romford	d				05 45			06 15					
Shenfield ■	d				05 56			06 26		06 42			
Ingatestone	d				06 00			06 30					
Chelmsford ■	d				06 07			06 37		06 51			07 02
Hatfield Peverel	d				06 14			06 44					
Witham ■	d				06 19	06 25		06 49		07 00			
White Notley	d					06 32							
Cressing	d					06 34							
Braintree Freeport	d					06 37							
Braintree	a					06 41							
Kelvedon	d				06 24					07 05			
Marks Tey ■	d				06 29					07 10			
Colchester ■	a				06 37			07 03		07 18			07 22
	d		06 18		06 37		06 46	07 07		07 18			07 22
Colchester Town	a						06 53						
	d						06 57						
Hythe	d						07 00						
Wivenhoe ■	d						07 04	07 14					
Alresford (Essex)	d						07 08						
Great Bentley	d						07 12						
Weeley	d						07 16						
Thorpe-le-Soken ■	a						07 19	07 24					
	d			06 26			07 26	07 24					
Clacton-on-Sea	a							07 34					
Kirby Cross	d			06 30			07 30						
Frinton-on-Sea	d			06 33			07 33						
Walton-on-the-Naze	a			06 38			07 39						
Manningtree ■	d		06 26		06 45					07 26			07 31
Mistley	d		06 30							07 30			
Wrabness	d		06 35							07 35			
Harwich International	d		06 44							07 44			
Dovercourt	d		06 47							07 47			
Harwich Town	a		06 49							07 49			
Ipswich	a				06 56								07 42
	d	06 14									07 09	07 16	07 42
Lowestoft	a												
Needham Market	d	06 24										07 26	
Stowmarket	d	06 30									07 20	07 32	07 53
Peterborough ■	a												
Diss	d										07 33		08 05
Norwich	a										07 52		08 27

b previous night, stops to pick up only

Table 11

Saturdays

London - Chelmsford, Colchester, Walton-on-Naze, Clacton, Harwich, Ipswich and Norwich

		LE	LE	LE	LE	LE	LE	LE	LE	LE	LE	LE	LE	LE	LE	LE	LE	LE	LE	LE	LE	LE	LE
		◇1	1	1	◇1		1	1	1	◇1	1	◇1	1	1	◇1	1	1	1		◇1	◇1	1	◇1
																				A	B		
										☕					☕					☕	☕		
London Liverpool Street 15 ⊖	d	06 38	06 48		07 00			07 08	07 18	07 30		07 38	07 48		08 00		08 08	08 18		08 30	08 30		08 38
Stratford 7 ⊖	d		06 55					07 15	07 25	07u38			07 55				08 15	08 25		08u38	08u38		
Romford	d							07 23									08 23						
Shenfield 3	d	07u02	07 12		07u23			07 34	07 42			08u02	08 12		08u23		08 34	08 42					09u02
Ingatestone	d		07 16										08 16										
Chelmsford 3	d	07 12	07 23					07 43	07 51	08 02		08 12	08 23				08 43	08 51		09 02	09 02		09 12
Hatfield Peverel	d		07 30										08 30										
Witham 2	d	07 21	07 36					07 52	08 00			08 21	08 36				08 52	09 00					09 21
White Notley	d		07 43										08 43										
Cressing	d		07 45										08 45										
Braintree Freeport	d		07 48										08 48										
Braintree	a		07 53										08 53										
Kelvedon	d								08 05									09 05					
Marks Tey 2	d	07 29							08 10			08 29						09 10					09 29
Colchester 4	a	07 37			07 49			08 06	08 18	08 21		08 37			08 49		09 06	09 18		09 21	09 21		09 37
	d	07 38		07 46	07 50		08 00	08 07	08 18	08 22	08 30	08 38		08 46	08 50	09 00	09 07	09 18		09 22	09 22	09 30	09 38
Colchester Town	a			07 53			08 07				08 37			08 53		09 07						09 37	
	d			07 57										08 57									
Hythe	d			08 00										09 00									
Wivenhoe 3	d			08 04				08 14						09 04			09 14						
Alresford (Essex)	d			08 08										09 08									
Great Bentley	d			08 12										09 12									
Weeley	d			08 16										09 16									
Thorpe-le-Soken 1	a			08 19				08 24						09 19			09 24						
	d			08 26				08 24						09 26			09 24						
Clacton-on-Sea	a							08 34									09 34						
Kirby Cross	d			08 30										09 30									
Frinton-on-Sea	d			08 33										09 33									
Walton-on-the-Naze	a			08 39										09 39									
Manningtree 2	d	07 46			07 59				08 26	08 31					08 59			09 26		09 31	09 31		09 46
Mistley	d					07 59			08 30									09 30					
Wrabness	d								08 35									09 35					
Harwich International	d								08 44									09 44					
Dovercourt	d								08 47									09 47					
Harwich Town	a								08 49									09 49					
Ipswich	a	07 58			08 08	08 15				08 42		08 56			09 08					09 42	09 42		09 58
	d	08 02			08 09	08 16				08 42		09 02			09 09				09 16	09 42	09 42		10 02
Lowestoft	a											10 32											
Needham Market	d					08 26													09 26				
Stowmarket	d	08 13				08 32				08 53									09 32	09 53	09 53		10 13
Peterborough 8	a	09 38																					11 37
Diss	d				08 30					09 05					09 30					10 05	10 05		
Norwich	a				08 52					09 27					09 52					10 27	10 29		

A from 2 October

B until 25 September

Table 11

Saturdays

London - Chelmsford, Colchester, Walton-on-Naze, Clacton, Harwich, Ipswich and Norwich

		LE	LE	LE	LE	LE	LE	LE	LE	LE	LE	LE	LE	LE	LE	LE	LE	LE	LE	LE	LE
		1	1	◇1	1	1	1		◇1	1	1	1	1	◇1	1	1	1	1		◇1	1
														A	B						
				☕					☕					☕	☕					☕	
London Liverpool Street 15 ⊖	d	08 48		09 00		09 08	09 18		09 30		09 38	09 48		10 00	10 00		10 08	10 18		10 30	
Stratford 7 ⊖	d	08 55				09 15	09 25					09 55					10 15	10 25		10u38	
Romford	d					09 23											10 23				
Shenfield 3	d	09 12		09u23		09 34	09 42		09u38		10u02	10 12		10u23	10u23		10 34	10 42			
Ingatestone	d	09 16										10 16									
Chelmsford 3	d	09 23				09 43	09 51		10 02		10 12	10 23					10 43	10 51		11 02	
Hatfield Peverel	d	09 30										10 30									
Witham 2	d	09 36				09 52	10 00				10 21	10 36					10 52	11 00			
White Notley	d	09 43										10 43									
Cressing	d	09 45										10 45									
Braintree Freeport	d	09 48										10 48									
Braintree	a	09 53										10 53									
Kelvedon	d						10 05											11 05			
Marks Tey 2	d						10 10				10 29							11 10			
Colchester 4	a			09 49		10 06	10 18		10 21		10 37			10 49	10 49		11 06	11 18		11 21	
	d		09 46	09 50	10 00	10 07	10 18		10 22	10 30	10 38		10 46	10 50	10 50	11 00	11 07	11 18		11 22	11 30
Colchester Town	a		09 53		10 07					10 37			10 53			11 07					11 37
	d		09 57										10 57								
Hythe	d		10 00										11 00								
Wivenhoe 3	d		10 04			10 14							11 04				11 14				
Alresford (Essex)	d		10 08										11 08								
Great Bentley	d		10 12										11 12								
Weeley	d		10 16										11 16								
Thorpe-le-Soken 1	a		10 19			10 24							11 19				11 24				
	d		10 26			10 24							11 26				11 24				
Clacton-on-Sea	a					10 34											11 34				
Kirby Cross	d		10 30										11 30								
Frinton-on-Sea	d		10 33										11 33								
Walton-on-the-Naze	a		10 39										11 39								
Manningtree 2	d			09 59			10 26		10 31					10 59	10 59			11 26		11 31	
Mistley	d						10 30											11 30			
Wrabness	d						10 35											11 35			
Harwich International	d						10 44											11 44			
Dovercourt	d						10 47											11 47			
Harwich Town	a						10 49											11 49			
Ipswich	a			10 09					10 42		10 56			11 09	11 09					11 42	
	d			10 09				10 16	10 42		11 02			11 09	11 09				11 16	11 42	
Lowestoft	a										12 32										
Needham Market	d							10 26											11 26		
Stowmarket	d							10 32	10 53										11 32	11 53	
Peterborough 8	a																				
Diss	d			10 30					11 05					11 30	11 30					12 05	
Norwich	a			10 52					11 27					11 52	11 52					12 27	

A from 2 October

B until 25 September

Table 11 — Saturdays

London - Chelmsford, Colchester, Walton-on-Naze, Clacton, Harwich, Ipswich and Norwich

		LE	LE	LE	LE	LE	LE	LE	LE	LE	LE	LE	LE	LE	LE	LE	LE	LE	LE	LE	LE	LE
		■ ■	■	■	◇■ ☕	■	■	■		◇■ A ☕	◇■ B ☕	■	■ ■	■	■	◇■ A ☕	■ ■ B ☕	■	■	■		◇■ ☕
London Liverpool Street ■ ⊖	d	10 38	10 48		11 00		11 08	11 18		11 30	11 30		11 38	11 48		12 00	12 00		12 08	12 18		12 30
Stratford ■ ⊖	d		10 55				11 15	11 25		11u38	11u38			11 55					12 15	12 25		12u38
Romford	d						11 23												12 23			
Shenfield ■	d	11u02	11 12		11u23		11 34	11 42					12u02	12 12		12u23	12u23		12 34	12 42		
Ingatestone	d		11 16											12 16								
Chelmsford ■	d	11 12	11 23				11 43	11 51		12 02	12 02		12 12	12 23					12 43	12 51		13 02
Hatfield Peverel	d		11 30											12 30								
Witham ■	d	11 21	11 36				11 52	12 00					12 21	12 36					12 52	13 00		
White Notley	d		11 43											12 43								
Cressing	d		11 45											12 45								
Braintree Freeport	d		11 48											12 48								
Braintree	a		11 53											12 53								
Kelvedon	d							12 05												13 05		
Marks Tey ■	d	11 29						12 10					12 29							13 10		
Colchester ■	a	11 37			11 49		12 06	12 18		12 21	12 21		12 37			12 49	12 49		13 06	13 18		13 21
	d	11 38		11 46	11 50	12 00	12 07	12 18		12 22	12 22	12 30	12 38		12 46	12 50	12 50	13 00	13 07	13 18		13 22
Colchester Town	a			11 53		12 07						12 37			12 53			13 07				
	d			11 57											12 57							
Hythe	d			12 00											13 00							
Wivenhoe ■	d			12 04			12 14								13 04				13 14			
Alresford (Essex)	d			12 08											13 08							
Great Bentley	d			12 12											13 12							
Weeley	d			12 16											13 16							
Thorpe-le-Soken ■	a			12 19			12 24								13 19				13 24			
	d			12 26			12 24								13 26				13 24			
Clacton-on-Sea	a						12 34												13 34			
Kirby Cross	d			12 30											13 30							
Frinton-on-Sea	d			12 33											13 33							
Walton-on-the-Naze	a			12 39											13 39							
Manningtree ■	d				11 59			12 26		12 31	12 31					12 59	12 59			13 26		13 31
Mistley	d							12 30												13 30		
Wrabness	d							12 35												13 35		
Harwich International	d							12 44												13 44		
Dovercourt	d							12 47												13 47		
Harwich Town	a							12 49												13 49		
Ipswich	a	11 56			12 09					12 42	12 42		12 56			13 09	13 09					13 42
	d	12 02			12 09				12 16	12 42	12 42		13 02			13 09	13 09				13 16	13 42
Lowestoft	a												14 32									
Needham Market	d								12 26												13 26	
Stowmarket	d	12 13							12 32	12 53	12 53										13 32	13 53
Peterborough ■	a	13 37																				
Diss	d				12 30					13 05	13 05					13 30	13 30					14 05
Norwich	a				12 52					13 27	13 30					13 52	13 52					14 27

A from 2 October
B until 25 September

Table 11 — Saturdays

London - Chelmsford, Colchester, Walton-on-Naze, Clacton, Harwich, Ipswich and Norwich

		LE	LE	LE	LE	LE	LE	LE	LE	LE	LE	LE	LE	LE	LE	LE	LE	LE	LE	LE	LE	LE
		■	■ ■	■	■	◇■ ☕	■	■	■		◇■ ☕	■	■ ■	■	■	◇■ ☕	■	■	■		◇■ ☕	■
London Liverpool Street ■ ⊖	d		12 38	12 48		13 00		13 08	13 18		13 30		13 38	13 48		14 00		14 08	14 18		14 30	
Stratford ■ ⊖	d			12 55				13 15	13 25		13u38			13 55				14 15	14 25		14u38	
Romford	d							13 23										14 23				
Shenfield ■	d		13u02	13 12		13u23		13 34	13 42				14u02	14 12		14u23		14 34	14 42			
Ingatestone	d			13 16										14 16								
Chelmsford ■	d		13 12	13 23				13 43	13 51		14 02		14 12	14 23				14 43	14 51		15 02	
Hatfield Peverel	d			13 30										14 30								
Witham ■	d		13 21	13 36				13 52	14 00				14 21	14 36				14 52	15 00			
White Notley	d			13 43										14 43								
Cressing	d			13 45										14 45								
Braintree Freeport	d			13 48										14 48								
Braintree	a			13 53										14 53								
Kelvedon	d								14 05										15 05			
Marks Tey ■	d		13 29						14 10				14 29						15 10			
Colchester ■	a		13 37			13 49		14 06	14 18		14 21		14 37			14 49		15 06	15 18		15 21	
	d	13 30	13 38		13 46	13 50	14 00	14 07	14 18		14 22	14 30	14 38		14 46	14 50	15 00	15 07	15 18		15 22	15 30
Colchester Town	a	13 37			13 53		14 07					14 37			14 53		15 07					15 37
	d				13 57										14 57							
Hythe	d				14 00										15 00							
Wivenhoe ■	d				14 04			14 14							15 04			15 14				
Alresford (Essex)	d				14 08										15 08							
Great Bentley	d				14 12										15 12							
Weeley	d				14 16										15 16							
Thorpe-le-Soken ■	a				14 19			14 24							15 19			15 24				
	d				14 26			14 24							15 26			15 24				
Clacton-on-Sea	a							14 34										15 34				
Kirby Cross	d				14 30										15 30							
Frinton-on-Sea	d				14 33										15 33							
Walton-on-the-Naze	a				14 39										15 39							
Manningtree ■	d					13 59			14 26		14 31					14 59			15 26		15 31	
Mistley	d								14 30										15 30			
Wrabness	d								14 35										15 35			
Harwich International	d								14 44										15 44			
Dovercourt	d								14 47										15 47			
Harwich Town	a								14 49										15 49			
Ipswich	a		13 56			14 09					14 42		14 56			15 09					15 42	
	d		14 02			14 09				14 16	14 42		15 02			15 09				15 16	15 42	
Lowestoft	a												16 32									
Needham Market	d									14 26										15 26		
Stowmarket	d		14 13							14 32	14 53									15 32	15 53	
Peterborough ■	a		15 37																			
Diss	d					14 30					15 05					15 30					16 05	
Norwich	a					14 52					15 27					15 52					16 27	

Table 11

Saturdays

London - Chelmsford, Colchester, Walton-on-Naze, Clacton, Harwich, Ipswich and Norwich

		LE	LE	LE	LE	LE	LE	LE	LE	LE	LE	LE	LE	LE	LE	LE	LE	LE	LE	LE	LE	LE	LE
		◇1	1	1	◇1	1	1	1		◇1	1	▪1	1	1	◇1	1	1	1		◇1	1	▪1	1
London Liverpool Street ⊖	d	14 38	14 48		15 00		15 08	15 18		15 30		15 38	15 48		16 00		16 08	16 18		16 30		16 38	16 48
Stratford ⊖	d		14 55				15 15	15 25		15u38			15 55				16 15	16 25		16u38			16 55
Romford	d						15 23										16 23						
Shenfield	d	15u02	15 12		15u23		15 34	15 42				16u02	16 12		16u23		16 34	16 42				17u02	17 12
Ingatestone	d		15 16										16 16										17 16
Chelmsford	d	15 12	15 23				15 43	15 51		16 02		16 12	16 23				16 43	16 51		17 02		17 12	17 23
Hatfield Peverel	d		15 30										16 30										17 30
Witham	d	15 21	15 36				15 52	16 00				16 21	16 36				16 52	17 00				17 21	17 36
White Notley	d		15 43										16 43										17 43
Cressing	d		15 45										16 45										17 45
Braintree Freeport	d		15 48										16 48										17 48
Braintree	a		15 53										16 53										17 53
Kelvedon	d							16 05										17 05					
Marks Tey	d	15 29						16 10				16 29						17 10				17 29	
Colchester	a	15 37			15 49		16 06	16 18		16 21		16 37			16 49		17 06	17 18		17 21		17 37	
	d	15 38		15 46	15 50	16 00	16 07	16 18		16 22	16 30	16 38		16 46	16 50	17 00	17 07	17 18		17 22	17 30	17 38	
Colchester Town	a			15 53		16 07					16 37			16 53		17 07					17 37		
	d			15 57										16 57									
Hythe	d			16 00										17 00									
Wivenhoe	d			16 04			16 14							17 04			17 14						
Alresford (Essex)	d			16 08										17 08									
Great Bentley	d			16 12										17 12									
Weeley	d			16 16										17 16									
Thorpe-le-Soken	a			16 19			16 24							17 19			17 24						
	d			16 26			16 24							17 26			17 24						
Clacton-on-Sea	a						16 34										17 34						
Kirby Cross	d			16 30										17 30									
Frinton-on-Sea	d			16 33										17 33									
Walton-on-the-Naze	a			16 39										17 39									
Manningtree	d				15 59			16 26		16 31					16 59			17 26		17 31			
Mistley	d							16 30										17 30					
Wrabness	d							16 35										17 35					
Harwich International	d							16 44										17 44					
Dovercourt	d							16 47										17 47					
Harwich Town	a							16 49										17 49					
Ipswich	a	15 56			16 09					16 42		16 56			17 09					17 42		17 56	
	d	16 02			16 09				16 16	16 42		17 02			17 09				17 16	17 42		18 02	
Lowestoft	a											18 32											
Needham Market	d								16 26										17 26				
Stowmarket	d	16 13							16 32	16 53					17 20				17 32	17 53		18 13	
Peterborough	a	17 37																				19 38	
Diss	d				16 30					17 05					17 32					18 05			
Norwich	a				16 52					17 27					17 52					18 27			

Table 11

Saturdays

London - Chelmsford, Colchester, Walton-on-Naze, Clacton, Harwich, Ipswich and Norwich

		LE	LE	LE	LE	LE	LE	LE	LE	LE	LE	LE	LE	LE	LE	LE	LE	LE	LE	LE	LE	LE	LE
		1	◇1	1	1	1		◇1	1	1	▪1	1	1	◇1	1	1	1		◇1	1	1	▪1	1
London Liverpool Street ⊖	d		17 00		17 08	17 18		17 30		17 38	17 46	17 48		18 00		18 08	18 18		18 30		18 38	18 46	18 48
Stratford ⊖	d				17 15	17 25		17u38				17 55				18 15	18 25		18u38				18 55
Romford	d				17 23											18 23							
Shenfield	d		17u23		17 34	17 42				18u02		18 12		18u23		18 34	18 42				19u02		19 12
Ingatestone	d											18 16											19 16
Chelmsford	d				17 43	17 51		18 02		18 11	18u16	18 23				18 43	18 51		19 02		19 11	19u16	19 23
Hatfield Peverel	d											18 30											19 30
Witham	d				17 52	18 00				18 21		18 36				18 52	19 00				19 21		19 36
White Notley	d											18 43											19 43
Cressing	d											18 45											19 45
Braintree Freeport	d											18 48											19 48
Braintree	a											18 53											19 53
Kelvedon	d					18 05											19 05						
Marks Tey	d					18 10				18 28							19 10				19 28		
Colchester	a		17 49		18 06	18 18		18 21		18 36	18 39			18 49		19 06	19 18		19 21		19 36	19 39	
	d	17 46	17 50	18 00	18 07	18 18		18 22	18 30		18 40		18 46	18 50	19 00	19 07	19 18		19 22	19 30		19 40	
Colchester Town	a	17 53		18 07					18 37				18 53		19 07					19 37			
	d	17 57											18 57										
Hythe	d	18 00											19 00										
Wivenhoe	d	18 04			18 14								19 04			19 14							
Alresford (Essex)	d	18 08											19 08										
Great Bentley	d	18 12											19 12										
Weeley	d	18 16											19 16										
Thorpe-le-Soken	a	18 19			18 24								19 19			19 24							
	d	18 26			18 24								19 26			19 24							
Clacton-on-Sea	a				18 34											19 34							
Kirby Cross	d	18 30											19 30										
Frinton-on-Sea	d	18 33											19 33										
Walton-on-the-Naze	a	18 39											19 39										
Manningtree	d		17 59			18 26		18 31						18 59			19 26		19 31				
Mistley	d					18 30											19 30						
Wrabness	d					18 35											19 35						
Harwich International	d					18 44											19 44						
Dovercourt	d					18 47											19 47						
Harwich Town	a					18 49											19 49						
Ipswich	a		18 09					18 42			18 56			19 09					19 42			19 56	
	d		18 09				18 16	18 42			19 02			19 09				19 16	19 42			20 02	
Lowestoft	a										20 32												
Needham Market	d						18 26											19 26					
Stowmarket	d						18 32	18 53										19 32	19 53			20 13	
Peterborough	a																					21 37	
Diss	d		18 30					19 05						19 30					20 05				
Norwich	a		18 52					19 27						19 52					20 27				

		LE	LE	LE	LE	LE	LE	LE	LE	LE	LE	LE	LE	LE	LE	LE	LE	LE	LE	LE	LE	LE
		1	◇1	1	1		◇1	▪1	1	1	◇1	1	1	◇1	1	1		1	◇1	1	1	
London Liverpool Street ⊖	d		19 00	19 08	19 18		19 30	19 38	19 48		20 00	20 08	20 18	20 30	20 38	20 48			21 00	21 08	21 18	
Stratford ⊖	d			19 15	19 25		19u38		19 55			20 15	20 25	20u38	20 45	20 55				21 15	21 25	
Romford	d			19 23								20 23								21 23		
Shenfield	d		19u23	19 34	19 42			20u02	20 12		20u23	20 34	20 42		21 02	21 12			21u23	21 34	21 42	
Ingatestone	d								20 16							21 16						
Chelmsford	d			19 43	19 51		20 03	20 12	20 23			20 43	20 51	21 03	21 12	21 23				21 43	21 51	
Hatfield Peverel	d								20 30							21 30						
Witham	d			19 52	20 00			20 21	20 36			20 52	21 00		21 21	21 36				21 52	22 00	
White Notley	d								20 43							21 43						
Cressing	d								20 45							21 45						
Braintree Freeport	d								20 48							21 48						
Braintree	a								20 53							21 53						
Kelvedon	d				20 05								21 05								22 05	
Marks Tey	d				20 10			20 29					21 10		21 29						22 10	
Colchester	a		19 49	20 06	20 18		20 23	20 37			20 49	21 06	21 18	21 23	21 37				21 49	22 06	22 18	
	d	19 46	19 50	20 07	20 18		20 23	20 38		20 46	20 50	21 07	21 18	21 23	21 38			21 46	21 50	22 07		
Colchester Town	a	19 53								20 53								21 53				
	d	19 57								20 57								21 57				
Hythe	d	20 00								21 00								22 00				
Wivenhoe	d	20 04		20 14						21 04		21 14						22 04		22 14		
Alresford (Essex)	d	20 08								21 08								22 08				
Great Bentley	d	20 12								21 12								22 12				
Weeley	d	20 16								21 16								22 16				
Thorpe-le-Soken	a	20 19		20 24						21 19		21 24						22 19		22 24		
	d	20 26		20 24						21 26		21 24						22 26		22 24		
Clacton-on-Sea	a			20 34								21 34								22 34		
Kirby Cross	d	20 30								21 30								22 30				
Frinton-on-Sea	d	20 33								21 33								22 33				
Walton-on-the-Naze	a	20 39								21 39								22 39				
Manningtree	d		19 59		20 26		20 32				20 59		21 26	21 32	21 46				21 58			
Mistley	d				20 30								21 30									
Wrabness	d				20 35								21 35									
Harwich International	d				20 44								21 44		22a02		21 34					
Dovercourt	d				20 47								21 47									
Harwich Town	a				20 49								21 49									
Ipswich	a		20 09				20 43	20 56			21 09			21 43			22 00		22 09			
	d		20 09			20 16	20 43	21 02			21 09			21 43					22 15			22 17
Lowestoft	a							22 32											23 45			
Needham Market	d					20 26																22 27
Stowmarket	d					20 32	20 54							21 54								22 33
Peterborough	a																					
Diss	d		20 30				21 06				21 30			22 06								
Norwich	a		20 52				21 28				21 52			22 28								

London - Chelmsford, Colchester, Walton-on-Naze, Clacton, Harwich, Ipswich and Norwich

		LE	LE	LE	LE	LE	LE	LE	LE	LE	LE	LE	LE	LE	LE	LE	LE
		◇1 ⊡		1	1	1	1	1	1	◇1 ⊡	1	1	1	1	1	◇1 ⊡	1
London Liverpool Street 15 ⊖	d	21 30		21 38	21 48			22 00	22 18	22 30	22 48	23 00			23 18	23 30	23 48
Stratford 7 ⊖	d	21u38			21 55			22 07	22 25	22u38	22 55	23 07			23 25	23u38	23 55
Romford	d																
Shenfield 3	d			22u02	22 12			22 24	22 42		23 12	23 24			23 42		00 12
Ingatestone	d				22 16						23 16				23 46		00 16
Chelmsford 3	d	22 03		22 12	22 23			22 33	22 51	23 03	23 23	23 33			23 53	00 03	00 23
Hatfield Peverel	d				22 30						23 30						00 30
Witham 2	d			22 21	22 36			22 42	23 00		23 35	23 42		23 44	00 03		00 35
White Notley	d				22 43									23 50			
Cressing	d				22 45									23 53			
Braintree Freeport	d				22 48									23 55			
Braintree	a				22 53									23 59			
Kelvedon	d								23 05		23 40						00 40
Marks Tey 2	d		22 21	22 29					23 10		23 45						00 45
Colchester 4	a	22 23	22 30	22 37				22 56	23 18	23 23	23 57	23 56			00 21	00 23	00 57
	d	22 23		22 38			22 46	22 56	23 19	23 23		23 57				00 23	
Colchester Town	a						22 53										
	d						22 57										
Hythe	d						23 00										
Wivenhoe 3	d						23 04		23 26								
Alresford (Essex)	d						23 08		23 29								
Great Bentley	d						23 12		23 33								
Weeley	d						23 16										
Thorpe-le-Soken 1	a						23 19		23 39								
	d						23 19		23 39								
Clacton-on-Sea	a						23 29		23 48								
Kirby Cross	d																
Frinton-on-Sea	d																
Walton-on-the-Naze	a																
Manningtree 2	d	22 32				22 38		23 04		23 32		00 04	23 38			00 32	
Mistley	d					22 42							23 42				
Wrabness	d					22 47							23 47				
Harwich International	d					22 54							23 54				
Dovercourt	d					22 57							23 57				
Harwich Town	a					22 59							23 59				
Ipswich	a	22 43		22 56				23 16		23 43		00 20				00 44	
	d	22 43								23 43						00 44	
Lowestoft	a																
Needham Market	d																
Stowmarket	d	22 54								23 54						00 55	
Peterborough 8	a																
Diss	d	23 07								00 07						01 08	
Norwich	a	23 29								00 29						01 34	

London - Chelmsford, Colchester, Walton-on-Naze, Clacton, Harwich, Ipswich and Norwich

		LE	LE	LE	LE	LE	LE	LE	LE	LE	LE	LE	LE	LE	LE	LE	LE	LE	LE	LE	LE	LE	LE
		◇1 ⊡	1	1	◇1 ⊡	1	1	1	B	1	1	1	1	1			1	1	◇1	1	1	1	1
London Liverpool Street 15 ⊖	d	22p30	23p00	23p18	23p30	23p48	00 18										08 02		08 30		08 32		
Stratford 7 ⊖	d	22b38	23p07	23p25	23b38	23p55	00 25										08 09				08 39		
Romford	d																						
Shenfield 3	d		23p24	23p42		00 12	00 47										08 31		08u57		09 01		
Ingatestone	d			23p46		00 16	00 51										08 35						
Chelmsford 3	d	23p03	23p33	23p53	00 03	00 23	00 58										08 42				09 10		
Hatfield Peverel	d					00 30	01 05										08 49						
Witham 2	d		23p43	00⌇03		00 35	01 10	07 33					08 23				08 54				09 19	09 23	
White Notley	d							07 39					08 29									09 29	
Cressing	d							07 42					08 32									09 32	
Braintree Freeport	d							07 44					08 34									09 34	
Braintree	a							07 48					08 38									09 38	
Kelvedon	d					00 40	01 15										08 59						
Marks Tey 2	d					00 45	01 20										09 04				09 27		
Colchester 4	a	23p22	23p54	00⌇21	00 23	00 57	01 32										09 12		09 23		09 35		
	d	23p23	23p55		00 25					07 40	08 12	08 18		08 35			09 12		09 24		09 35		
Colchester Town	a																						
	d																						
Hythe	d																						
Wivenhoe 3	d													08 43							09 43		
Alresford (Essex)	d													08 46							09 46		
Great Bentley	d													08 50							09 50		
Weeley	d																						
Thorpe-le-Soken 1	a													08 55							09 55		
	d													08 55						08 57	09 55		
Clacton-on-Sea	a													09 07							10 05		
Kirby Cross	d																			09 01			
Frinton-on-Sea	d																			09 04			
Walton-on-the-Naze	a																			09 09			
Manningtree 2	d	23p32	00⌇05		00 32					07 48	08 20	08 26					09 20	09 26	09 33				
Mistley	d											08 30						09 30					
Wrabness	d											08 35						09 35					
Harwich International	d											08 42				08 30		09 42					
Dovercourt	d											08 45						09 45					
Harwich Town	a											08 47						09 47					
Ipswich	a	23p42	00⌇21		00 44					08 00	08 32					08 55	09 32		09 44				
	d	23p43			00 46				07⌇55						08 45	09 02			09 44				09 55
Lowestoft	a																						
Needham Market	d															09 12							
Stowmarket	d	23p54			00 55				08⌇07						08 59	09 18			09 55				10 07
Peterborough 8	a								09⌇36														11 36
Diss	d	00 07			01 08														10 07				
Norwich	a	00 29			01 34														10 29				

B until 5 September

b previous night, stops to pick up only

Table 11

Sundays

London - Chelmsford, Colchester, Walton-on-Naze, Clacton, Harwich, Ipswich and Norwich

		LE ■	LE ■	LE ■	LE ◇■ ☕	LE ■	LE ■	LE ■	LE	LE ■	LE ■	LE ◇■ ☕	LE ■	LE ■	LE ■	LE ■	LE ■	LE ■	LE ◇■ ☕	LE ■	LE ■
London Liverpool Street ■ ⊖	d		09 02		09 30	09 32				10 02		10 30	10 32				11 02		11 30	11 32	
Stratford ■ ⊖	d		09 09			09 39				10 09			10 39				11 09			11 39	
Romford	d																				
Shenfield ■	d		09 31		09u57	10 01				10 31		10u57	11 01				11 31		11u57	12 01	
Ingatestone	d		09 35							10 35							11 35				
Chelmsford ■	d		09 42			10 10				10 42			11 10				11 42			12 10	
Hatfield Peverel	d		09 49							10 49							11 49				
Witham ■	d		09 54			10 19	10 23			10 54			11 19	11 23			11 54			12 19	12 23
White Notley	d						10 29							11 29							12 29
Cressing	d						10 32							11 32							12 32
Braintree Freeport	d						10 34							11 34							12 34
Braintree	a						10 38							11 38							12 38
Kelvedon	d		09 59							10 59							11 59				
Marks Tey ■	d		10 04			10 27				11 04			11 27				12 04			12 27	
Colchester ■	a		10 12		10 23	10 35				11 12		11 23	11 35				12 12		12 23	12 35	
	d		10 12		10 24	10 35				11 12		11 24	11 35				12 12		12 24	12 35	
Colchester Town	a																				
	d																				
Hythe	d																				
Wivenhoe ■	d					10 43							11 43							12 43	
Alresford (Essex)	d					10 46							11 46							12 46	
Great Bentley	d					10 50							11 50							12 50	
Weeley	d																				
Thorpe-le-Soken ■	a					10 55							11 55							12 55	
	d	09 57				10 55		10 57					11 55			11 57				12 55	
Clacton-on-Sea	a					11 05							12 05							13 05	
Kirby Cross	d	10 01						11 01								12 01					
Frinton-on-Sea	d	10 04						11 04								12 04					
Walton-on-the-Naze	a	10 09						11 09								12 09					
Manningtree ■	d		10 20	10 26	10 33					11 20	11 26	11 33					12 20	12 26	12 33		
Mistley	d			10 30							11 30							12 30			
Wrabness	d			10 35							11 35							12 35			
Harwich International	d			10 42							11 42							12 42			
Dovercourt	d			10 45							11 45							12 45			
Harwich Town	a			10 47							11 47							12 47			
Ipswich	a		10 32		10 44					11 32		11 44					12 32		12 44		
	d				10 44				11 02			11 44			11 55				12 44		
Lowestoft	a																				
Needham Market	d								11 12												
Stowmarket	d				10 55				11 18			11 55			12 07				12 55		
Peterborough ■	a														13 31						
Diss	d				11 07							12 07							13 07		
Norwich	a				11 29							12 29							13 29		

		LE ■	LE	LE ■	LE ■	LE ◇■ ☕	LE ■	LE ■	LE ■	LE ■	LE ■	LE ■	LE ◇■ ☕	LE ■	LE ■	LE ■	LE	LE ■	LE ■	LE ◇■ ☕	LE ■
London Liverpool Street ■ ⊖	d			12 02		12 30	12 32				13 02		13 30	13 32				14 02		14 30	14 32
Stratford ■ ⊖	d			12 09			12 39				13 09			13 39				14 09			14 39
Romford	d																				
Shenfield ■	d			12 31		12u57	13 01				13 31		13u57	14 01				14 31		14u57	15 01
Ingatestone	d			12 35							13 35							14 35			
Chelmsford ■	d			12 42			13 10				13 42			14 10				14 42			15 10
Hatfield Peverel	d			12 49							13 49							14 49			
Witham ■	d			12 54			13 19	13 23			13 54			14 19	14 23			14 54			15 19
White Notley	d							13 29							14 29						
Cressing	d							13 32							14 32						
Braintree Freeport	d							13 34							14 34						
Braintree	a							13 38							14 38						
Kelvedon	d			12 59							13 59							14 59			
Marks Tey ■	d			13 04			13 27				14 04			14 27				15 04			15 27
Colchester ■	a			13 12		13 23	13 35				14 12		14 23	14 35				15 12		15 23	15 35
	d			13 12		13 24	13 35				14 12		14 24	14 35				15 12		15 24	15 35
Colchester Town	a																				
	d																				
Hythe	d																				
Wivenhoe ■	d						13 43							14 43							15 43
Alresford (Essex)	d						13 46							14 46							15 46
Great Bentley	d						13 50							14 50							15 50
Weeley	d																				
Thorpe-le-Soken ■	a						13 55							14 55							15 55
	d	12 57					13 55			13 57				14 55		14 57					15 55
Clacton-on-Sea	a						14 05							15 05							16 05
Kirby Cross	d	13 01								14 01						15 01					
Frinton-on-Sea	d	13 04								14 04						15 04					
Walton-on-the-Naze	a	13 09								14 09						15 09					
Manningtree ■	d			13 20	13 26	13 33					14 20	14 26	14 33					15 20	15 26	15 33	
Mistley	d				13 30							14 30							15 30		
Wrabness	d				13 35							14 35							15 35		
Harwich International	d				13 42							14 42							15 42		
Dovercourt	d				13 45							14 45							15 45		
Harwich Town	a				13 47							14 47							15 47		
Ipswich	a			13 32		13 44					14 32		14 44					15 32		15 44	
	d		13 02			13 44			13 55				14 44				15 02			15 44	
Lowestoft	a																				
Needham Market	d		13 12														15 12				
Stowmarket	d		13 18			13 55			14 07				14 55				15 18			15 55	
Peterborough ■	a								15 31												
Diss	d					14 07							15 07							16 07	
Norwich	a					14 29							15 29							16 29	

Table 11

Sundays

London - Chelmsford, Colchester, Walton-on-Naze, Clacton, Harwich, Ipswich and Norwich

		LE ■	LE ■	LE ■	LE ■	LE ■	LE ◇■ ☕	LE ■	LE ■	LE ■	LE	LE ■	LE ■	LE ◇■ ☕	LE ■	LE ■	LE ■	LE ■	LE ■	LE ■	LE ◇■ ☕
London Liverpool Street ■ ⊖	d				15 02		15 30	15 32				16 02		16 30	16 32				17 02		17 30
Stratford ■ ⊖	d				15 09			15 39				16 09			16 39				17 09		
Romford	d																				
Shenfield ■	d				15 31		15u57	16 01				16 31		16u57	17 01				17 31		17u57
Ingatestone	d				15 35							16 35							17 35		
Chelmsford ■	d				15 42			16 10				16 42			17 10				17 42		
Hatfield Peverel	d				15 49							16 49							17 49		
Witham ■	d	15 23			15 54			16 19	16 23			16 54			17 19	17 23			17 54		
White Notley	d	15 29							16 29							17 29					
Cressing	d	15 32							16 32							17 32					
Braintree Freeport	d	15 34							16 34							17 34					
Braintree	a	15 38							16 38							17 38					
Kelvedon	d				15 59							16 59							17 59		
Marks Tey ■	d				16 04			16 27				17 04			17 27				18 04		
Colchester ■	a				16 12		16 23	16 35				17 12		17 23	17 35				18 12		18 23
	d				16 12		16 24	16 35				17 12		17 24	17 35				18 12		18 24
Colchester Town	a																				
	d																				
Hythe	d																				
Wivenhoe ■	d							16 43							17 43						
Alresford (Essex)	d							16 46							17 46						
Great Bentley	d							16 50							17 50						
Weeley	d																				
Thorpe-le-Soken ■	a							16 55							17 55						
	d			15 57				16 55		16 57					17 55			17 57			
Clacton-on-Sea	a							17 05							18 05						
Kirby Cross	d			16 01						17 01								18 01			
Frinton-on-Sea	d			16 04						17 04								18 04			
Walton-on-the-Naze	a			16 09						17 09								18 09			
Manningtree ■	d				16 20	16 26	16 33					17 20	17 26	17 33					18 20	18 26	18 33
Mistley	d					16 30							17 30							18 30	
Wrabness	d					16 35							17 35							18 35	
Harwich International	d					16 42							17 42							18 42	
Dovercourt	d					16 45							17 45							18 45	
Harwich Town	a					16 47							17 47							18 47	
Ipswich	a				16 32		16 44					17 32		17 44					18 32		18 44
	d		15 55				16 44				17 02			17 44			17 55				18 44
Lowestoft	a																				
Needham Market	d										17 12										
Stowmarket	d		16 07				16 55				17 18			17 55			18 07				18 55
Peterborough ■	a		17 31														19 32				
Diss	d						17 07							18 07							19 07
Norwich	a						17 29							18 29							19 29

		LE ■	LE ■	LE ■	LE	LE ■	LE ■	LE ◇■ ☕	LE ■	LE ■	LE ■	LE ◇■ ☕	LE ■	LE ■	LE ◇■ ☕	LE ■	LE ■	LE ■	LE ■	LE
London Liverpool Street ■ ⊖	d	17 32				18 02		18 30	18 32			19 00	19 02		19 30	19 32	20 00			
Stratford ■ ⊖	d	17 39				18 09			18 39				19 09			19 39				
Romford	d																			
Shenfield ■	d	18 01				18 31		18u57	19 01				19 31		19u57	20 01	20 27			
Ingatestone	d					18 35							19 35							
Chelmsford ■	d	18 10				18 42			19 10			19 37	19 42			20 10	20 37			
Hatfield Peverel	d					18 49							19 49							
Witham ■	d	18 19	18 23			18 54			19 19	19 23			19 54			20 19		20 23		
White Notley	d		18 29							19 29								20 29		
Cressing	d		18 32							19 32								20 32		
Braintree Freeport	d		18 34							19 34								20 34		
Braintree	a		18 38							19 38								20 38		
Kelvedon	d					18 59							19 59							
Marks Tey ■	d	18 27				19 04			19 27				20 04			20 27				
Colchester ■	a	18 35				19 12		19 23	19 35			19 55	20 12		20 23	20 35	20 55			
	d	18 35				19 12		19 24	19 35			19 56	20 12		20 24	20 35	20 56			
Colchester Town	a																			
	d																			
Hythe	d																			
Wivenhoe ■	d	18 43							19 43							20 43				
Alresford (Essex)	d	18 46							19 46							20 46				
Great Bentley	d	18 50							19 50							20 50				
Weeley	d																			
Thorpe-le-Soken ■	a	18 55							19 55							20 55				
	d	18 55		18 57					19 55		19 57					20 55			20 57	
Clacton-on-Sea	a	19 05							20 05							21 05				
Kirby Cross	d			19 01							20 01								21 01	
Frinton-on-Sea	d			19 04							20 04								21 04	
Walton-on-the-Naze	a			19 09							20 09								21 09	
Manningtree ■	d					19 20	19 26	19 33				20 04	20 20	20 26	20 33		21 04			
Mistley	d						19 30							20 30						
Wrabness	d						19 35							20 35						
Harwich International	d						19 42							20 42			21a22			
Dovercourt	d						19 45							20 45						
Harwich Town	a						19 47							20 47						
Ipswich	a					19 32		19 44				20 17	20 32		20 44					
	d				19 02			19 44				20 17			20 44					21 02
Lowestoft	a																			
Needham Market	d				19 12															21 12
Stowmarket	d				19 18			19 55				20 28			20 55					21 18
Peterborough ■	a																			
Diss	d							20 07				20 41			21 07					
Norwich	a							20 29				21 02			21 29					

Table 11 — Sundays

London - Chelmsford, Colchester, Walton-on-Naze, Clacton, Harwich, Ipswich and Norwich

		LE [1]	LE [1]	LE	LE ◇[1] ☕	LE [1]	LE [1]	LE [1]	LE	LE [1]	LE [1]	LE ◇[1] ☕	LE [1]	LE [1]	LE [1]	LE ◇[1] ☕	LE [1]	LE [1]	LE [1]	LE [1]	LE ◇[1]	LE [1]
London Liverpool Street [15] ⊖	d	20 02			20 30	20 32				21 02		21 30	21 32		22 02	22 30		22 32		23 02	23 30	23 32
Stratford [7] ⊖	d	20 09				20 39				21 09			21 39		22 09			22 39		23 09		23 39
Romford	d																					
Shenfield [3]	d	20 31			20u57	21 01				21 31		21u57	22 01		22 31	22u57		23 01		23 31	23u57	00 01
Ingatestone	d	20 35								21 35					22 35					23 35		
Chelmsford [3]	d	20 42				21 10				21 42			22 10		22 42			23 10		23 42		00 10
Hatfield Peverel	d	20 49								21 49					22 49					23 49		
Witham [2]	d	20 54				21 19	21 23			21 54			22 19	22 23	22 54			23 19	23 23	23 54		00 19
White Notley	d						21 29							22 29					23 29			
Cressing	d						21 32							22 32					23 32			
Braintree Freeport	d						21 34							22 34					23 34			
Braintree	a						21 38							22 38					23 38			
Kelvedon	d	20 59								21 59					22 59					23 59		
Marks Tey [2]	d	21 04				21 27			22 00	22 04			22 27		23 04			23 27		00 04		00 27
Colchester [4]	a	21 12			21 23	21 35			22 09	22 12		22 23	22 35		23 12	23 23		23 35		00 12	00 27	00 40
	d	21 12			21 24	21 35				22 12		22 24	22 35		23 12	23 24		23 35		00 12	00 28	
Colchester Town	a																					
	d																					
Hythe	d																					
Wivenhoe [3]	d					21 43							22 43					23 43				
Alresford (Essex)	d					21 46							22 46					23 46				
Great Bentley	d					21 50							22 50					23 50				
Weeley	d																					
Thorpe-le-Soken [1]	a					21 55							22 55					23 55				
	d					21 55		21 57					22 55				22 57	23 55				
Clacton-on-Sea	a					22 05							23 05					00 05				
Kirby Cross	d							22 01									23 01					
Frinton-on-Sea	d							22 04									23 04					
Walton-on-the-Naze	a							22 09									23 09					
Manningtree [2]	d	21 20	21 26		21 33					22 20	22 26	22 33			23 20	23 33				00 20	00 37	
Mistley	d		21 30								22 30											
Wrabness	d		21 35								22 35											
Harwich International	d		21 42	21 10							22 42											
Dovercourt	d		21 45								22 45											
Harwich Town	a		21 47								22 47											
Ipswich	a	21 32		21 37	21 44					22 32		22 44			23 32	23 44				00 36	00 46	
	d				21 44							22 44				23 44					00 48	
Lowestoft	a																					
Needham Market	d																					
Stowmarket	d				21 55							22 55				23 55					00 59	
Peterborough [8]	a																					
Diss	d				22 07							23 07				00 07					01 11	
Norwich	a				22 29							23 29				00 39					01 43	

Table 11 — Mondays to Fridays

Norwich, Ipswich, Harwich, Clacton, Walton-on-Naze, Colchester and Chelmsford - London

		LE MX ◇[1]	LE MO ◇[1]	LE MX	LE MX [1]	LE MO	LE [1]	LE [1]	LE ◇[1]	LE [1]	LE [1]	LE [1]	LE [1]	LE [1]	LE [1] ☕	LE [1]	LE	LE [1]	LE [1]	LE [1] ☕	LE [1]	LE [1]	LE [1]	LE [1]
Norwich	d	22p00	22p00												05 10					05 40				
Diss	d	22p17	22p17												05 28					05 58				
Peterborough [8]	d																							
Stowmarket	d	22p29	22p29	23p46		00 04									05 40		05 57			06 10				
Needham Market	d			23p52		00 09											06 03							
Lowestoft	d																							
Ipswich	a	22p42	22p42	00 03		00 21									05 51		06 15			06 23				
	d	22p42	22p42						05 23						05 53					06 23				
Harwich Town	d									05 37														06 22
Dovercourt	d									05 39														06 24
Harwich International	d									05 42														06 27
Wrabness	d									05 48														06 33
Mistley	d									05 53														06 38
Manningtree [2]	d	22p52	22p52						05 33	05a58					06 03					06 33				06 43
Walton-on-the-Naze	d												05 38					06 10						
Frinton-on-Sea	d												05 41					06 13						
Kirby Cross	d												05 44					06 16						
Clacton-on-Sea	d											05 20				05 44							06 17	
Thorpe-le-Soken [1]	a											05 27	05 50			05 51		06 22					06 25	
	d											05 27				05 51							06 25	
Weeley	d															05 55								
Great Bentley	d															05 59								
Alresford (Essex)	d															06 03								
Wivenhoe [3]	d											05 38				06 06							06 36	
Hythe	d															06 10							06 40	
Colchester Town	a																							
	d																		06 21					
Colchester [4]	a	23p01	23p01						05 43			05 47			06 13	06 17			06 28	06 43			06 47	06 53
	d	23p03	23p03				04 45	05 21	05 43			05 48			06 15	06 18			06 29	06 45			06 48	
Marks Tey [2]	d						04 51	05 27				05 54							06 35				06 54	
Kelvedon	d						04 56	05 32				06 00				06 28			06 41				07 00	
Braintree	d				00 03						05 45											06 42		
Braintree Freeport	d				00 05						05 47											06 44		
Cressing	d				00 08						05 50											06 47		
White Notley	d				00 11						05 53											06 50		
Witham [2]	d	23p15	23p15		00a18		05 01	05 37	05 56		06a01	06 05		06 15	06 27	06 33			06 46			06 58	07 05	
Hatfield Peverel	d						05 05	05 41						06 19								07 02		
Chelmsford [3]	d	23p24	23p24				05 12	05 48	06 05			06 14		06 26		06 42			06 55		07 03	07 09	07 14	
Ingatestone	d						05 19	05 55						06 33		06 48					07 10			
Shenfield [3]	a	23b36	23b36				05 26	06 01				06 25		06 39					07 06		07 16	07 20		
Romford	a																							
Stratford [7] ⊖	a	23p52	23b57				05 43	06 18	06s29			06 41		06s56	06s59	07s08				07s26	07s33	07s37	07s40	
London Liverpool Street [15] ⊖	a	00 03	00 07				05 57	06 27	06 41			06 49		07 07	07 10	07 20			07 33	07 37	07 44	07 48	07 51	

b previous night, stops to set down only

Table 11

Norwich, Ipswich, Harwich, Clacton, Walton-on-Naze, Colchester and Chelmsford - London

Mondays to Fridays

		LE 1	LE 1	LE 1	LE 1	LE ■ 1 ⊡	LE	LE 1	LE 1	LE ■ 1 ⊡	LE 1	LE 1	LE 1	LE 1	LE 1	LE 1	LE ■ 1 ⊡	LE 1	LE ■ 1 ⊡	LE	LE 1	LE 1	LE ■ 1 ⊡
Norwich	d					06 10				06 25							06 40		06 55				07 10
Diss	d					06 28				06 43							06 58		07 13				07 28
Peterborough 8	d																						
Stowmarket	d					06 40	06 44			06 55							07 10		07 25				07 40
Needham Market	d																						
Lowestoft	d																						
Ipswich	a					06 53	07 00			07 08							07 23		07 38				07 53
	d	06 38				06 53	07 00			07 08							07 23		07 38				07 53
Harwich Town	d															07 08							
Dovercourt	d															07 10							
Harwich International	d						07a25								07 10	07 13				07 47			
Wrabness	d															07 19				07 53			
Mistley	d															07 24				07 59			
Manningtree 2	d	06 48				07 03				07 18					07 25	07a29	07 33		07 48				08 03
Walton-on-the-Naze	d								06 43					07 04									
Frinton-on-Sea	d								06 46					07 07									
Kirby Cross	d								06 49					07 10									
Clacton-on-Sea	d		06 34	06 38				06 47					07 04					07 09					
Thorpe-le-Soken 1	a		06 42	06 46				06 55	06 54				07 12	07 16				07 17					
	d		06 42	06 46				06 55	07 01				07 12					07 17					
Weeley	d			06 50					07 05									07 21					
Great Bentley	d			06 53					07 08									07 24					
Alresford (Essex)	d			06 58					07 13									07 28					
Wivenhoe 3	d		06 53	07 01				07 06	07 16				07 23					07 32					
Hythe	d			07 05				07 10	07 20									07 36					
Colchester Town	a			07 09					07 24														
	d			07 13	06 59				07 28														
Colchester 4	a	06 58	07 02	07 22	07 06	07 13		07 17	07 37	07 28			07 32		07 37		07 43	07 44	07 58				08 13
	d	06 59	07 03		07 07	07 15		07 18		07 30			07 33		07 37		07 45	07 49	08 00			08 03	08 15
Marks Tey 2	d				07 13			07 24							07 43							08 09	
Kelvedon	d		07 13					07 30					07 43					07 59				08 15	
Braintree	d											07 27											
Braintree Freeport	d											07 29											
Cressing	d											07 32											
White Notley	d											07 35											
Witham 2	d	07 11	07 18		07b28			07 35				07 43	07 48		07c58			08 04				08 20	
Hatfield Peverel	d				07 32										08 02								
Chelmsford 3	d	07 20	07 27		07 39						07 49	07 53	07 57		08 09			08 13			08 19	08 29	
Ingatestone	d	07 26									07 56										08 26		
Shenfield 3	a	07 32	07 38		07 50						08 02		08 08		08 20						08 32	08 40	
Romford	a																						
Stratford 7 ⊖	a		07s55					08s09					08s25					08s39			08s49		08s59
London Liverpool Street 15 ⊖	a	07 59	08 06		08 16	08 09		08 20		08 23	08 28	08 30	08 36		08 48		08 39	08 50	08 55		09 01	09 06	09 10

b arr. 0722 c arr. 0752

Table 11

Norwich, Ipswich, Harwich, Clacton, Walton-on-Naze, Colchester and Chelmsford - London

Mondays to Fridays

		LE	LE ■ 1	LE ■ 1	LE 1	LE 1	LE 1	LE 1	LE 1	LE ◇1 ⊡	LE 1	LE 1	LE 1	LE 1	LE ◇1 ⊡	LE	LE 1	LE 1	LE 1	LE ■ 1 ⊡	LE 1
Norwich	d			07b30						07 40					08 00					08 30	
Diss	d									07 58					08 17					08 47	
Peterborough 8	d																				
Stowmarket	d	07 45								08 10					08 29	08 45					
Needham Market	d	07 50														08 51					
Lowestoft	d		06 44																		
Ipswich	a	08 02	08 12	08 07						08 23					08 42	09 03				09 08	
	d		<	08 18						08 23					08 42					09 08	
Harwich Town	d								08 00												09 00
Dovercourt	d								08 02												09 02
Harwich International	d								08 06												09 06
Wrabness	d								08 12												09 12
Mistley	d								08 17												09 17
Manningtree 2	d								08 22	08 33					08 52					09 18	09 22
Walton-on-the-Naze	d							07 40			08 09										
Frinton-on-Sea	d							07 43			08 12										
Kirby Cross	d							07 46			08 15										
Clacton-on-Sea	d						07 45						08 15					08 50			
Thorpe-le-Soken 1	a						07 52	07 51			08 21		08 22					08 57			
	d						07 52	07 56					08 22					08 57			
Weeley	d							08 00													
Great Bentley	d							08 03					08 28								
Alresford (Essex)	d							08 08					08 32								
Wivenhoe 3	d						08 03	08 11					08 35					09 07			
Hythe	d							08 15													
Colchester Town	a					<		08 19													
	d					08 02		08 23						08 45					09 16		
Colchester 4	a					08 09	08 16	08 32	08 32	08 43			08 44	08 52	09 01			09 17	09 23	09 27	09 32
	d					08 18			08 37	08 45			08 48		09 03			09 17		09 29	09 33
Marks Tey 2	d					08 24							08 54					09 23			09 39
Kelvedon	d					08 30							09 00					09 29			09 44
Braintree	d				08 12												09 00				
Braintree Freeport	d				08 14												09 02				
Cressing	d				08 17												09 05				
White Notley	d				08 20												09 08				
Witham 2	d				08 28	08 35			08 49			08 58	09 05				09 15	09 34			09 49
Hatfield Peverel	d				08 32							09 02					09 20				
Chelmsford 3	d				08 39	08 44			08 58	09 02		09 09	09 14				09 27	09 43		09 47	09 58
Ingatestone	d				08 46							09 16					09 33				
Shenfield 3	a				08 52	08 55						09 22	09 25		09s29		09 40	09 54			10 09
Romford	a																				
Stratford 7 ⊖	a				09s09				09s23	09s28		09s39					09 57	10 08		10s11	10 24
London Liverpool Street 15 ⊖	a			09 25	09 20	09 22			09 35	09 40		09 50	09 52		09 56		10 05	10 17		10 24	10 33

b arr. 0714

Norwich, Ipswich, Harwich, Clacton, Walton-on-Naze, Colchester and Chelmsford - London

		LE	LE	LE	LE	LE	LE	LE	LE	LE	LE	LE	LE	LE	LE	LE	LE	LE	LE	LE	LE	LE	LE
		1	1	■ 1	1	■ 1 ⊡		1	1	1	◇1 ⊡	1	1	■ 1	1	◇1 ⊡		1	1	1	◇1 ⊡	1	1
Norwich	d					09 00					09 30					10 00					10 30		
Diss	d					09 17					09 47					10 17					10 47		
Peterborough 8	d			07 46																			
Stowmarket	d			09 12		09 29	09 45									10 29	10 45						
Needham Market	d						09 50										10 50						
Lowestoft	d													08 58									
Ipswich	a			09 26		09 42	10 03				10 08			10 26		10 42	11 03				11 08		
	d			09 30		09 42					10 08			10 30		10 42					11 08		
Harwich Town	d											10 00										11 00	
Dovercourt	d											10 02										11 02	
Harwich International	d											10 06										11 06	
Wrabness	d											10 12										11 12	
Mistley	d											10 17										11 17	
Manningtree 2	d					09 52					10 18	10 22				10 52					11 18	11 22	
Walton-on-the-Naze	d	08 45											09 45										10 45
Frinton-on-Sea	d	08 48											09 48										10 48
Kirby Cross	d	08 51											09 51										10 51
Clacton-on-Sea	d								09 50										10 50				
Thorpe-le-Soken 1	a	08 56							09 57				09 56						10 57				10 56
	d	09 01							09 57				10 01						10 57				11 01
Weeley	d	09 05											10 05										11 05
Great Bentley	d	09 08											10 08										11 08
Alresford (Essex)	d	09 13											10 13										11 13
Wivenhoe 3	d	09 16							10 07				10 16						11 07				11 16
Hythe	d	09 20											10 20										11 20
Colchester Town	a	09 24											10 24										11 24
	d	09 28			09 45					10 15			10 28		10 45					11 15			11 28
Colchester 4	a	09 37		09 48	09 52	10 01			10 17	10 22	10 27	10 32	10 37	10 48	10 52	11 01			11 17	11 22	11 27	11 32	11 37
	d		09 44	09 49		10 03			10 17		10 29	10 33		10 49		11 03			11 17		11 29	11 33	
Marks Tey 2	d								10 23			10 39							11 23			11 39	
Kelvedon	d											10 44										11 44	
Braintree	d							10 00										11 00					
Braintree Freeport	d							10 02										11 02					
Cressing	d							10 05										11 05					
White Notley	d							10 08										11 08					
Witham 2	d		09 56	10 02				10 15	10 31			10 49		11 02				11 15	11 31			11 49	
Hatfield Peverel	d							10 20										11 20					
Chelmsford 3	d		10 05	10s11				10 27	10 40		10 46	10 58		11 11				11 27	11 40		11 46	11 58	
Ingatestone	d		10 12					10 33										11 33					
Shenfield 3	a			10s22		10s29		10 40	10 51			11 09		11s22		11s29		11 40	11 51			12 09	
Romford	a								10 59										11 59				
Stratford 7 ⊖	a		10s32					10 55	11 07		11s10	11 24						11 55	12 07		12s10	12 24	
London Liverpool Street 15 ⊖	a		10 41	10 46		10 54		11 03	11 18		11 24	11 33		11 45		11 54		12 03	12 16		12 24	12 33	

		LE	LE	LE	LE	LE	LE	LE	LE	LE	LE	LE	LE	LE	LE	LE	LE	LE	LE	LE	LE	LE
		◇1	1	◇1 ⊡		1	1	1	◇1 ⊡	1	1	◇1	1	◇1 ⊡		1	1	1	◇1 ⊡	1	1	◇1
Norwich	d			11 00					11 30					12 00					12 30			
Diss	d			11 17					11 47					12 17					12 47			
Peterborough 8	d	09 45																				11 45
Stowmarket	d	11 12		11 29	11 45									12 29	12 45							13 12
Needham Market	d				11 50										12 50							
Lowestoft	d											10 58										
Ipswich	a	11 25		11 42	12 03				12 08			12 26		12 42	13 03				13 08			13 25
	d	11 30		11 42					12 08			12 30		12 42					13 08			13 30
Harwich Town	d									12 00										13 00		
Dovercourt	d									12 02										13 02		
Harwich International	d									12 06										13 06		
Wrabness	d									12 12										13 12		
Mistley	d									12 17										13 17		
Manningtree 2	d			11 52					12 18	12 22				12 52					13 18	13 22		
Walton-on-the-Naze	d										11 45										12 45	
Frinton-on-Sea	d										11 48										12 48	
Kirby Cross	d										11 51										12 51	
Clacton-on-Sea	d						11 50										12 50					
Thorpe-le-Soken 1	a						11 57				11 56						12 57				12 56	
	d						11 57				12 01						12 57				13 01	
Weeley	d										12 05										13 05	
Great Bentley	d										12 08										13 08	
Alresford (Essex)	d										12 13										13 13	
Wivenhoe 3	d						12 07				12 16						13 07				13 16	
Hythe	d										12 20										13 20	
Colchester Town	a										12 24										13 24	
	d		11 45					12 15			12 28		12 45					13 15			13 28	
Colchester 4	a	11 48	11 52	12 01			12 17	12 22	12 27	12 32	12 37	12 48	12 52	13 01			13 17	13 22	13 27	13 32	13 37	13 48
	d	11 49		12 03			12 17		12 29	12 33		12 49		13 03			13 17		13 29	13 33		13 49
Marks Tey 2	d						12 23			12 39							13 23			13 39		
Kelvedon	d									12 44										13 44		
Braintree	d					12 00										13 00						
Braintree Freeport	d					12 02										13 02						
Cressing	d					12 05										13 05						
White Notley	d					12 08										13 08						
Witham 2	d	12 02				12 15	12 31			12 49		13 02				13 15	13 31			13 49		14 02
Hatfield Peverel	d					12 20										13 20						
Chelmsford 3	d	12 11				12 27	12 40		12 46	12 58		13 11				13 27	13 40		13 46	13 58		14 11
Ingatestone	d					12 33										13 33						
Shenfield 3	a	12s22		12s29		12 40	12 51			13 09		13s22		13s29		13 40	13 51			14 09		14s22
Romford	a						12 59										13 59					
Stratford 7 ⊖	a					12 55	13s07		13s10	13 24						13 55	14 07		14s10	14 24		
London Liverpool Street 15 ⊖	a	12 45		12 54		13 03	13 16		13 24	13 33		13 45		13 54		14 03	14 16		14 24	14 33		14 45

Norwich, Ipswich, Harwich, Clacton, Walton-on-Naze, Colchester and Chelmsford - London

		LE	LE	LE	LE	LE	LE	LE	LE	LE	LE	LE	LE	LE	LE	LE	LE	LE	LE	LE	LE	LE	LE
		1	◇1 ⊡		1	1	1	◇1 ⊡	1	1	◇1	1	◇1 ⊡		1	1	1	◇1 ⊡	1	1	1	1	1
Norwich	d		13 00					13 30					14 00					14 30					
Diss	d		13 17					13 47					14 17					14 47					
Peterborough 8	d																				13 45		
Stowmarket	d		13 29	13 45									14 29	14 45							15 12		
Needham Market	d			13 50										14 50									
Lowestoft	d										12 58												
Ipswich	a		13 42	14 03				14 08			14 26		14 42	15 03				15 08			15 25		
	d		13 42					14 08			14 30		14 42					15 08			15 26		
Harwich Town	d								14 00										15 00				
Dovercourt	d								14 02										15 02				
Harwich International	d								14 06										15 06				
Wrabness	d								14 12										15 12				
Mistley	d								14 17										15 17				
Manningtree 2	d		13 52					14 18	14 22				14 52					15 18	15 22				
Walton-on-the-Naze	d									13 45										14 45			
Frinton-on-Sea	d									13 48										14 48			
Kirby Cross	d									13 51										14 51			
Clacton-on-Sea	d					13 50										14 50							
Thorpe-le-Soken 1	a					13 57				13 56						14 57				14 56			
	d					13 57				14 01						14 57				15 01			
Weeley	d									14 05										15 05			
Great Bentley	d									14 08										15 08			
Alresford (Essex)	d									14 13										15 13			
Wivenhoe 3	d					14 07				14 16						15 07				15 16			
Hythe	d									14 20										15 20			
Colchester Town	a									14 24										15 24			
	d	13 45					14 15			14 28		14 45					15 15			15 28			15 45
Colchester 4	a	13 52	14 01			14 17	14 22	14 27	14 32	14 37	14 48	14 52	15 01			15 17	15 22	15 27	15 32	15 37	15 43		15 52
	d		14 03			14 17		14 29	14 33		14 49		15 03			15 17		15 29	15 36			15 47	
Marks Tey 2	d					14 23			14 39							15 23						15 54	
Kelvedon	d								14 44										15 45			16 00	
Braintree	d				14 00										15 00								
Braintree Freeport	d				14 02										15 02								
Cressing	d				14 05										15 05								
White Notley	d				14 08										15 08								
Witham 2	d				14 15	14 31			14 49		15 02				15 15	15 31			15 49			16 05	
Hatfield Peverel	d				14 20										15 20								
Chelmsford 3	d				14 27	14 40		14 46	14 58		15 11				15 27	15 40		15 46	15 58			16 14	
Ingatestone	d				14 33										15 33				16 05				
Shenfield 3	a		14s29		14 40	14 51			15 09		15s22		15s29		15 40	15 51			16 11			16 25	
Romford	a					14 59										15 59							
Stratford 7 ⊖	a				14 55	15 07		15s10	15 24						15 55	16 07		16s10	16 26			16 40	
London Liverpool Street 15 ⊖	a		14 54		15 03	15 16		15 24	15 34		15 45		15 54		16 03	16 16		16 24	16 35			16 49	

		LE	LE	LE	LE	LE	LE	LE	LE	LE	LE	LE	LE	LE	LE	LE	LE	LE	LE	LE	LE	LE
		◇1 ⊡		1	1	1	◇1 ⊡	1	1	1	1	◇1 ⊡		1	1	1	1	◇1 ⊡	1	1	1	◇1
Norwich	d	15 00					15 30					16 00						16 30				
Diss	d	15 17					15 47					16 18						16 48				
Peterborough 8	d																					15 45
Stowmarket	d	15 29	15 45									16 30	16 45									17 12
Needham Market	d		15 50										16 50									
Lowestoft	d																					
Ipswich	a	15 42	16 03				16 08					16 42	17 03					17 08				17 27
	d	15 42					16 08				16 32	16 42						17 08				17 30
Harwich Town	d									16 05									17 00			
Dovercourt	d									16 07									17 02			
Harwich International	d									16 11									17 06			
Wrabness	d									16 17									17 12			
Mistley	d									16 22									17 17			
Manningtree 2	d	15 52					16 18			16 27	16 41	16 52						17 18	17 22			
Walton-on-the-Naze	d								15 45											16 43		
Frinton-on-Sea	d								15 48											16 46		
Kirby Cross	d								15 51											16 49		
Clacton-on-Sea	d				15 50												16 48					
Thorpe-le-Soken 1	a				15 57				15 56								16 55			16 54		
	d				15 57				16 01								16 55			17 01		
Weeley	d								16 05											17 05		
Great Bentley	d								16 08											17 08		
Alresford (Essex)	d								16 13											17 13		
Wivenhoe 3	d				16 07				16 16								17 05			17 16		
Hythe	d								16 20								17 09			17 20		
Colchester Town	a								16 24											17 24		
	d					16 15			16 28						17 05					17 28		
Colchester 4	a	16 01			16 17	16 22	16 27		16 38	16 40	16 51	17 01			17 12		17 17	17 27	17 32	17 37		17 48
	d	16 03			16 17		16 29	16 33			16 53	17 03					17 17	17 29	17 36			17 49
Marks Tey 2	d				16 23			16 39			16 59						17 23		17 42			17 55
Kelvedon	d							16 44											17 47			
Braintree	d			16 00										17 00							17 44	
Braintree Freeport	d			16 02										17 02							17 46	
Cressing	d			16 05										17 05							17 49	
White Notley	d			16 08										17 08							17 52	
Witham 2	d			16 15	16 31			16 49			17 07			17 15		17 21	17 31		17 52		18 00	18 04
Hatfield Peverel	d			16 20												17 25						
Chelmsford 3	d			16 27	16 40		16 46	16 58			17 16			17 25		17 32	17 40	17 46	18 01		18 09	18 13
Ingatestone	d			16 33				17 05								17 39			18 08			
Shenfield 3	a	16s29		16 40	16 51			17 11			17 27	17s30		17 36		17 45	17 51		18 14			18s25
Romford	a																17 59					
Stratford 7 ⊖	a			16 55	17 05		17s10	17 26						17 50		18 00	18 07	18s14	18 29			
London Liverpool Street 15 ⊖	a	16 54		17 05	17 15		17 24	17 38			17 49	17 54		18 00		18 14	18 19	18 24	18 38		18 41	18 51

Table 11

Mondays to Fridays

Norwich, Ipswich, Harwich, Clacton, Walton-on-Naze, Colchester and Chelmsford - London

		LE		LE	LE	LE	LE	LE	LE	LE	LE	LE		LE	LE	LE	LE	LE	LE	LE	LE	LE	LE	LE
		◇1 🍴			1	1	1	◇1 🍴	1	1	1	1		◇1	◇1 🍴	1	1	1		1	◇1 🍴	1	1	1
Norwich	d	17 00						17 30							18 00						18 30			
Diss	d	17 18						17 48							18 17						18 47			
Peterborough 8	d																							
Stowmarket	d	17 30		17 46				18 00							18 29				18 46					
Needham Market	d			17 52															18 52					
Lowestoft	d													16 58										
Ipswich	a	17 42		18 03				18 11						18 26	18 42				19 03		19 08			
	d	17 42						18 11						18 30	18 42			18 56			19 08			
Harwich Town	d				17 53					18 25										18 53				
Dovercourt	d				17 55					18 27										18 55				
Harwich International	d				17 58					18 30										18 58				
Wrabness	d				18 04					18 36										19 04				
Mistley	d				18 09					18 41										19 09				
Manningtree 2	d	17 52			18a14			18 21		18a46					18 52			19 06		19a14	19 18			
Walton-on-the-Naze	d								17 39		18 31													18 52
Frinton-on-Sea	d								17 42		18 34													18 55
Kirby Cross	d								17 45		18 40													18 58
Clacton-on-Sea	d						17 45										18 45							
Thorpe-le-Soken 1	a						17 52		17 50		18 46						18 52							19 03
	d						17 52		17 56								18 52							19 04
Weeley	d								18 00															19 08
Great Bentley	d						17 58		18 03								18 58							19 11
Alresford (Essex)	d						18 02		18 08								19 02							19 16
Wivenhoe 3	d						18 05		18 11								19 05							19 19
Hythe	d								18 15															19 23
Colchester Town	a								18 19															19 27
	d								18 23														19 15	19 31
Colchester 4	a	18 01					18 14	18 30	18 32					18 48	19 01		19 14	19 17			19 27		19 24	19 40
	d	18 03					18 15	18 32	18 35					18 49	19 03		19 15				19 29		19 33	
Marks Tey 2	d						18 21							18 55			19 21						19 39	
Kelvedon	d						18 26		18 44								19 26						19 44	
Braintree	d											18 36										19 25		
Braintree Freeport	d											18 38										19 27		
Cressing	d											18 41										19 30		
White Notley	d											18 44										19 33		
Witham 2	d					18 15	18 31		18 49			18 52		19 04		19 15	19 31					19 41	19 49	
Hatfield Peverel	d					18 20										19 20								
Chelmsford 3	d					18 27	18 40	18 49	18 58			19 02		19 13		19 27	19 40				19 46	19 50	19 58	
Ingatestone	d					18 33						19 09				19 33								
Shenfield 3	a	18s29				18 40	18 51		19 09			19 15		19s24	19s29	19 40	19 51						20 09	
Romford	a						18 59										19 59							
Stratford 7 ⊖	a					18 55	19 07	19s15	19 26							19 55	20 07				20s10		20 24	
London Liverpool Street 15 ⊖	a	18 54				19 05	19 16	19 27	19 35			19 40		19 47	19 54	20 04	20 16				20 24	20 23	20 33	

		LE	LE	LE	LE	LE	LE	LE		LE	LE	LE	LE	LE	LE	LE	LE	LE	LE	LE	LE	LE	LE	LE
		◇1	1	1	1	◇1 🍴		1		1	1	1	1	1	◇1	◇1 🍴	1	1		1	1	1	1	1
Norwich	d					19 00										20 00								
Diss	d					19 17										20 17								
Peterborough 8	d	17 45																						
Stowmarket	d	19 12				19 29	19 45									20 29			20 45					
Needham Market	d						19 50												20 50					
Lowestoft	d														18 43									
Ipswich	a	19 25				19 42	20 03								20 16	20 42			21 03					
	d	19 27		19 35		19 42						20 08			20 30	20 42			21 04			21 08		
Harwich Town	d				19 28								20 00					20 33					21 00	
Dovercourt	d				19 30								20 02					20 35					21 02	
Harwich International	d				19 33								20 06					20 38	21a28				21 06	
Wrabness	d				19 39								20 12					20 44					21 12	
Mistley	d				19 44								20 17					20 49					21 17	
Manningtree 2	d	19 37		19 46	19a49	19 52						20 18	20 22			20 52		20 56				21 18	21 22	
Walton-on-the-Naze	d		19 25											19 52			20 24							20 45
Frinton-on-Sea	d		19 28											19 55			20 27							20 48
Kirby Cross	d		19 34											19 58			20 33							20 51
Clacton-on-Sea	d										19 45										20 50			
Thorpe-le-Soken 1	a		19 40								19 52			20 03			20 39				20 57			20 56
	d										19 52			20 04							20 57			21 01
Weeley	d													20 08										21 05
Great Bentley	d										19 58			20 11										21 08
Alresford (Essex)	d										20 02			20 16										21 13
Wivenhoe 3	d										20 05			20 19							21 07			21 16
Hythe	d													20 23										21 20
Colchester Town	a													20 27										21 24
	d													20 31										21 28
Colchester 4	a	19 47		19 57		20 01					20 14	20 28	20 32	20 40	20 48	21 01		21 06			21 17	21 28	21 29	21 37
	d	19 48				20 03					20 15	20 29	20 33		20 49	21 03					21 17	21 29	21 33	
Marks Tey 2	d	19 54									20 21		20 39								21 23		21 39	
Kelvedon	d										20 26		20 44										21 44	
Braintree	d									20 10										21 00				
Braintree Freeport	d									20 12										21 02				
Cressing	d									20 15										21 05				
White Notley	d									20 18										21 08				
Witham 2	d	20 02						20 15		20a25	20 31		20 49		21 02					21 15	21 31		21 49	
Hatfield Peverel	d							20 20												21 20				
Chelmsford 3	d	20 11						20 27			20 40	20 46	20 58		21 11					21 27	21 40	21 46	21 58	
Ingatestone	d							20 33												21 33				
Shenfield 3	a	20s23				20s29		20 40			20 51		21 09		21s23	21s29				21 40	21 51	21 58	22 10	
Romford	a										20 59										21 59			
Stratford 7 ⊖	a							20 55			21 07	21s10	21 24							21 55	22 07	22 12	22 27	
London Liverpool Street 15 ⊖	a	20 46				20 54		21 04			21 16	21 21	21 33		21 46	21 54				22 03	22 16	22 23	22 36	

Table 11

Mondays to Fridays

Norwich, Ipswich, Harwich, Clacton, Walton-on-Naze, Colchester and Chelmsford - London

		LE	LE	LE		LE	LE	LE	LE	LE	LE	LE	LE	LE		LE	LE	LE	LE	LE	LE
		◇1	◇1 🍴			1	1	1	1		1	1	1	1		◇1	1	1	1	1	
Norwich	d		21 00													22 00				23 05	
Diss	d		21 17													22 17				23 22	
Peterborough 8	d	19 46																	22 05		
Stowmarket	d	21 08	21 29	21 46												22 29			23 24	23 34	23 46
Needham Market	d			21 52																	23 52
Lowestoft	d									20 58											
Ipswich	a	21 25	21 42	22 03						22 26						22 42			23 37	23 48	00 03
	d	21 27	21 42						22 08							22 42		23 22	23 38		
Harwich Town	d					21 54											23 05				
Dovercourt	d					21 56											23 07				
Harwich International	d					21 59											23 10				
Wrabness	d					22 05											23 16				
Mistley	d					22 10											23 21				
Manningtree 2	d	21 37	21 52			22a15			22 18							22 52	23a26	23 31	23 48		
Walton-on-the-Naze	d										21 45		22 43								
Frinton-on-Sea	d										21 48		22 46								
Kirby Cross	d										21 51		22 52								
Clacton-on-Sea	d							21 50				22 24									
Thorpe-le-Soken 1	a							21 57			21 56	22 31	22 58								
	d							21 57			22 01	22 31									
Weeley	d										22 05	22 35									
Great Bentley	d										22 08	22 39									
Alresford (Essex)	d										22 13	22 43									
Wivenhoe 3	d							22 07			22 16	22 46									
Hythe	d										22 20	22 50									
Colchester Town	a										22 24										
	d										22 28										
Colchester 4	a	21 48	22 01					22 17	22 28		22 37	22 57				23 01		23 41	23 58		
	d	21 49	22 03					22 17	22 29							23 03					
Marks Tey 2	d							22 23	22 35												
Kelvedon	d								22 40												
Braintree	d						22 00							22 57							
Braintree Freeport	d						22 02							22 59							
Cressing	d						22 05							23 02							
White Notley	d						22 08							23 05							
Witham 2	d	22 02					22 15	22 31	22 45					23a12		23 15					
Hatfield Peverel	d						22 20		22 49												
Chelmsford 3	d	22 11					22 27	22 40	22 56							23 24					
Ingatestone	d						22 33		23 03												
Shenfield 3	a	22s22	22s29				22 40	22 51	23 09							23s36					
Romford	a							22 59													
Stratford 7 ⊖	a						22 55	23 07	23 25							23 52					
London Liverpool Street 15 ⊖	a	22 46	22 54				23 03	23 16	23 34							00 03					

Norwich, Ipswich, Harwich, Clacton, Walton-on-Naze, Colchester and Chelmsford - London

Station		LE	LE	LE	LE	LE	LE	LE	LE	LE	LE	LE	LE	LE	LE	LE	LE	LE	LE	LE	LE	LE	LE	LE	LE
		◇1		1	1	1	◇1 ☕	1	1	1	◇1 ☕	1	1	1	◇1 ☕			1	1	◇1 ☕	1	1	1	▣ 1	◇1 ☕
Norwich	d	22p00					05 00				05 30				06 00					06 30					07 00
Diss	d	22p17					05 17				05 47				06 17					06 47					07 17
Peterborough 8	d																								
Stowmarket	d	22p29	23p46				05 29								06 29	06 45									07 29
Needham Market	d		23p52													06 50									
Lowestoft	d																							05 58	
Ipswich	a	22p42	00 03				05 42				06 08				06 42	07 03				07 08				07 26	07 42
	d	22p42					05 42				06 08			06 30	06 42		07 00			07 08				07 30	07 42
Harwich Town	d											06 00									07 00				
Dovercourt	d											06 02									07 02				
Harwich International	d											06 06					07a25				07 06		07 15		
Wrabness	d											06 12									07 12				
Mistley	d											06 17									07 17				
Manningtree 2	d	22p52					05 52				06 18	06 22			06 52					07 18	07 22		07 28		07 52
Walton-on-the-Naze	d												05 45									06 45			
Frinton-on-Sea	d												05 48									06 48			
Kirby Cross	d												05 51									06 51			
Clacton-on-Sea	d									05 50									06 50						
Thorpe-le-Soken 1	a									05 57			05 56						06 57			06 56			
	d									05 57			06 01						06 57			07 01			
Weeley	d												06 05									07 05			
Great Bentley	d												06 08									07 08			
Alresford (Essex)	d												06 13									07 13			
Wivenhoe 3	d									06 07			06 16						07 07			07 16			
Hythe	d												06 20									07 20			
Colchester Town	a												06 24									07 24			
	d												06 28									07 28			
Colchester 4	a	23p01					06 01			06 17	06 27	06 32	06 37	06 48	07 01				07 17	07 27	07 32	07 37	07 38	07 48	08 01
	d	23p03			04 45	05 30	06 03		06 06	06 17	06 29	06 33		06 49	07 03				07 17	07 29	07 33		07 41	07 49	08 03
Marks Tey 2	d				04 51	05 36			06 12	06 23		06 39							07 23		07 39				
Kelvedon	d				04 56	05 41			06 17			06 44									07 44				
Braintree	d			00 03				06 00										07 00							
Braintree Freeport	d			00 05				06 02										07 02							
Cressing	d			00 08				06 05										07 05							
White Notley	d			00 11				06 08										07 08							
Witham 2	d	23p15		00a18	05 01	05 46		06a15	06 22	06 31		06 49		07 02				07 15	07 31		07 49			08 02	
Hatfield Peverel	d				05 05	05 50			06 26									07 20							
Chelmsford 3	d	23p24			05 12	05 57			06 33	06 40	06 46	06 58		07 11				07 27	07 40	07 46	07 58		08 02	08 11	
Ingatestone	d				05 19	06 04			06 40									07 33							
Shenfield 3	a	23b36			05 26	06 10	06s29		06 46	06 51		07 09		07s22	07s29			07 40	07 51		08 09		08 13	08s22	08s29
Romford	a					06 19				06 59									07 59						
Stratford 7 ⊖	a	23p52			05 43	06 27			07 01	07 07	07s10	07 24						07 55	08 07	08s10	08 24		08 28		
London Liverpool Street 15 ⊖	a	00 03			05 57	06 36	06 54		07 10	07 16	07 24	07 33		07 45	07 54			08 03	08 16	08 24	08 33		08 39	08 45	08 54

b previous night, stops to set down only

Norwich, Ipswich, Harwich, Clacton, Walton-on-Naze, Colchester and Chelmsford - London

Station		LE	LE	LE	LE	LE	LE		LE	LE	LE	LE	LE	LE	LE	LE		LE	LE	LE	LE	LE	LE	LE
			1		1	1	◇1 ☕		1	1	▣ 1	1	1	◇1 ☕		1		1	1	◇1 ☕	1	1	▣ 1	1
Norwich	d						07 30							08 00						08 30				
Diss	d						07 47							08 17						08 47				
Peterborough 8	d																						07 45	
Stowmarket	d	07 45												08 29	08 45								09 12	
Needham Market	d	07 50													08 50									
Lowestoft	d										06 58													
Ipswich	a	08 03					08 08				08 26			08 42	09 03					09 08			09 25	
	d						08 08				08 30			08 42						09 08			09 30	
Harwich Town	d								08 00												09 00			
Dovercourt	d								08 02												09 02			
Harwich International	d			07 47					08 06												09 06			
Wrabness	d			07 53					08 12												09 12			
Mistley	d			07a59					08 17												09 17			
Manningtree 2	d						08 18		08 22					08 52						09 18	09 22			
Walton-on-the-Naze	d									07 45												08 45		
Frinton-on-Sea	d									07 48												08 48		
Kirby Cross	d									07 51												08 51		
Clacton-on-Sea	d				07 50													08 50						
Thorpe-le-Soken 1	a				07 57					07 56								08 57				08 56		
	d				07 57					08 01								08 57				09 01		
Weeley	d									08 05												09 05		
Great Bentley	d									08 08												09 08		
Alresford (Essex)	d									08 13												09 13		
Wivenhoe 3	d				08 07					08 16								09 07				09 16		
Hythe	d									08 20												09 20		
Colchester Town	a									08 24												09 24		
	d					08 15				08 28			08 45						09 15			09 28		
Colchester 4	a				08 17	08 22	08 27		08 32	08 37	08 48		08 52	09 01				09 17	09 22	09 27	09 32	09 37	09 48	
	d				08 17		08 29		08 33		08 49	08 52		09 03				09 17		09 29	09 33		09 49	09 52
Marks Tey 2	d				08 23				08 39									09 23			09 39			
Kelvedon	d								08 44												09 44			
Braintree	d		08 00													09 00								
Braintree Freeport	d		08 02													09 02								
Cressing	d		08 05													09 05								
White Notley	d		08 08													09 08								
Witham 2	d		08 15		08 31				08 49			09 04				09 15		09 31			09 49			10 04
Hatfield Peverel	d		08 20													09 20								
Chelmsford 3	d		08 27		08 40		08 46		08 58		09s07	09 13				09 27		09 40		09 46	09 58		10s07	10 13
Ingatestone	d		08 33													09 33								
Shenfield 3	a		08 40		08 51				09 09			09s24		09s29		09 40		09 51			10 09			10s24
Romford	a				08 59													09 59						
Stratford 7 ⊖	a		08 55		09 07		09s10		09 24							09 55		10 07		10s10	10 24			
London Liverpool Street 15 ⊖	a		09 03		09 16		09 24		09 33		09 38	09 47		09 54		10 03		10 16		10 24	10 33		10 38	10 47

Station		LE	LE		LE	LE	LE	LE	LE	LE	LE	LE		LE	LE	LE	LE	LE	LE	LE	LE	LE	LE	LE	LE
		1	◇1 ☕			1	1	1	◇1 ☕	1	1	▣ 1		1	1	◇1 ☕		1	1	1	◇1 ☕	1	1	▣ 1	1
Norwich	d		09 00						09 30							10 00					10 30				
Diss	d		09 17						09 47							10 17					10 47				
Peterborough 8	d																							09 55	
Stowmarket	d		09 29		09 45											10 29	10 45							11 14	
Needham Market	d				09 50												10 50								
Lowestoft	d											08 58													
Ipswich	a		09 42		10 03				10 08			10 26				10 42	11 03				11 08			11 27	
	d		09 42						10 08			10 30				10 42					11 08			11 30	
Harwich Town	d									10 00												11 00			
Dovercourt	d									10 02												11 02			
Harwich International	d									10 06												11 06			
Wrabness	d									10 12												11 12			
Mistley	d									10 17												11 17			
Manningtree 2	d		09 52						10 18	10 22						10 52					11 18	11 22			
Walton-on-the-Naze	d										09 45												10 45		
Frinton-on-Sea	d										09 48												10 48		
Kirby Cross	d										09 51												10 51		
Clacton-on-Sea	d						09 50												10 50						
Thorpe-le-Soken 1	a						09 57				09 56								10 57				10 56		
	d						09 57				10 01								10 57				11 01		
Weeley	d										10 05												11 05		
Great Bentley	d										10 08												11 08		
Alresford (Essex)	d										10 13												11 13		
Wivenhoe 3	d						10 07				10 16								11 07				11 16		
Hythe	d										10 20												11 20		
Colchester Town	a										10 24												11 24		
	d	09 45						10 15			10 28				10 45					11 15			11 28		11 45
Colchester 4	a	09 52	10 01				10 17	10 22	10 27	10 32	10 37	10 48			10 52	11 01			11 17	11 22	11 27	11 32	11 37	11 48	11 52
	d		10 03				10 17		10 29	10 33		10 49		10 52		11 03			11 17		11 29	11 33		11 49	
Marks Tey 2	d						10 23			10 39									11 23			11 39			
Kelvedon	d									10 44												11 44			
Braintree	d					10 00												11 00							
Braintree Freeport	d					10 02												11 02							
Cressing	d					10 05												11 05							
White Notley	d					10 08												11 08							
Witham 2	d					10 15	10 31			10 49				11 04				11 15	11 31			11 49		12 02	
Hatfield Peverel	d					10 20												11 20							
Chelmsford 3	d					10 27	10 40		10 46	10 58		11s07		11 13				11 27	11 40		11 46	11 58		12 11	
Ingatestone	d					10 33												11 33							
Shenfield 3	a		10s29			10 40	10 51			11 09				11s24		11s29		11 40	11 51			12 09		12s22	
Romford	a						10 59												11 59						
Stratford 7 ⊖	a					10 55	11 07		11s10	11 24								11 55	12 07		12s10	12 24			
London Liverpool Street 15 ⊖	a		10 54			11 03	11 16		11 24	11 33		11 42		11 47		11 54		12 03	12 16		12 24	12 33		12 45	

Table 11

Norwich, Ipswich, Harwich, Clacton, Walton-on-Naze, Colchester and Chelmsford - London

		LE	LE	LE	LE	LE	LE	LE	LE	LE	LE	LE	LE	LE	LE	LE	LE	LE	LE	LE	LE	LE	LE
		■ ■	◇■		■	■	■	◇■	■	■	■ ■	■	◇■		■	■	■	◇■	■	■	◇■	■	◇■
		A	B																				
		⊏⊐	⊏⊐					⊏⊐					⊏⊐					⊏⊐					⊏⊐
Norwich	d	11b00	11 00					11 30					12 00					12 30					13 00
Diss	d	11 17	11 17					11 47					12 17					12 47					13 17
Peterborough ■	d																				11 45		
Stowmarket	d	11 29	11 29	11 45									12 29	12 45							13 12		13 29
Needham Market	d			11 50										12 50									
Lowestoft	d										10 58												
Ipswich	a	11 42	11 42	12 03				12 08			12 26		12 42	13 03				13 08			13 27		13 42
	d	11 42	11 42					12 08			12 30		12 42					13 08			13 30		13 42
Harwich Town	d								12 00										13 00				
Dovercourt	d								12 02										13 02				
Harwich International	d								12 06										13 06				
Wrabness	d								12 12										13 12				
Mistley	d								12 17										13 17				
Manningtree ■	d	11 52	11 52					12 18	12 22				12 52					13 18	13 22				13 52
Walton-on-the-Naze	d									11 45										12 45			
Frinton-on-Sea	d									11 48										12 48			
Kirby Cross	d									11 51										12 51			
Clacton-on-Sea	d					11 50										12 50							
Thorpe-le-Soken ■	a					11 57				11 56						12 57				12 56			
	d					11 57				12 01						12 57				13 01			
Weeley	d									12 05										13 05			
Great Bentley	d									12 08										13 08			
Alresford (Essex)	d									12 13										13 13			
Wivenhoe ■	d					12 07				12 16						13 07				13 16			
Hythe	d									12 20										13 20			
Colchester Town	a									12 24										13 24			
	d						12 15			12 28		12 45					13 15			13 28		13 45	
Colchester ■	a	12 01	12 01			12 17	12 22	12 27	12 32	12 37	12 48	12 52	13 01			13 17	13 22	13 27	13 32	13 37	13 48	13 52	14 01
	d	12 03	12 03			12 17		12 29	12 33		12 49		13 03			13 17		13 29	13 33		13 49		14 03
Marks Tey ■	d					12 23			12 39							13 23			13 39				
Kelvedon	d								12 44										13 44				
Braintree	d				12 00										13 00								
Braintree Freeport	d				12 02										13 02								
Cressing	d				12 05										13 05								
White Notley	d				12 08										13 08								
Witham ■	d				12 15	12 31			12 49		13 02				13 15	13 31			13 49		14 02		
Hatfield Peverel	d				12 20										13 20								
Chelmsford ■	d				12 27	12 40		12 46	12 58		13 11				13 27	13 40		13 46	13 58		14 11		
Ingatestone	d				12 33										13 33								
Shenfield ■	a	12s29	12s29		12 40	12 51			13 09		13s21		13s29		13 40	13 51			14 09		14s22		14s29
Romford	a					12 59										13 59							
Stratford ■ ⊖	a				12 55	13 07		13s10	13 24						13 55	14 07		14s10	14 24				
London Liverpool Street ■ ⊖	a	12 54	12 54		13 03	13 16		13 24	13 33		13 45		13 54		14 03	14 16		14 24	14 33		14 45		14 54

A until 25 September

B from 2 October

b arr. 1044

Table 11

Norwich, Ipswich, Harwich, Clacton, Walton-on-Naze, Colchester and Chelmsford - London

		LE	LE	LE	LE	LE	LE	LE	LE	LE	LE	LE	LE	LE	LE	LE	LE	LE	LE	LE	LE	LE
			■	■	■	◇■	■	■	◇■	■	■ ■	◇■		■	■	■	◇■	■	■	◇■	■	◇■
											A	B										
						⊏⊐					⊏⊐	⊏⊐					⊏⊐					⊏⊐
Norwich	d					13 30					14b00	14 00					14 30					15 00
Diss	d					13 47					14 17	14 17					14 47					15 17
Peterborough ■	d																			13 45		
Stowmarket	d	13 45									14 29	14 29	14 45							15 12		15 29
Needham Market	d	13 50											14 50									
Lowestoft	d								12 58													
Ipswich	a	14 03				14 08			14 26		14 42	14 42	15 03				15 08			15 25		15 42
	d					14 08			14 30		14 42	14 42					15 08			15 30		15 42
Harwich Town	d						14 00											15 00				
Dovercourt	d						14 02											15 02				
Harwich International	d						14 06											15 06				
Wrabness	d						14 12											15 12				
Mistley	d						14 17											15 17				
Manningtree ■	d					14 18	14 22				14 52	14 52					15 18	15 22				15 52
Walton-on-the-Naze	d							13 45											14 45			
Frinton-on-Sea	d							13 48											14 48			
Kirby Cross	d							13 51											14 51			
Clacton-on-Sea	d			13 50											14 50							
Thorpe-le-Soken ■	a			13 57				13 56							14 57				14 56			
	d			13 57				14 01							14 57				15 01			
Weeley	d							14 05											15 05			
Great Bentley	d							14 08											15 08			
Alresford (Essex)	d							14 13											15 13			
Wivenhoe ■	d			14 07				14 16							15 07				15 16			
Hythe	d							14 20											15 20			
Colchester Town	a							14 24											15 24			
	d				14 15			14 28		14 45						15 15			15 28		15 45	
Colchester ■	a			14 17	14 22	14 27	14 32	14 37	14 48	14 52	15 01	15 01			15 17	15 22	15 27	15 32	15 37	15 48	15 52	16 01
	d			14 17		14 29	14 33		14 49		15 03	15 03			15 17		15 29	15 33		15 49		16 03
Marks Tey ■	d			14 23			14 39								15 23			15 39				
Kelvedon	d						14 44											15 44				
Braintree	d		14 00											15 00								
Braintree Freeport	d		14 02											15 02								
Cressing	d		14 05											15 05								
White Notley	d		14 08											15 08								
Witham ■	d		14 15	14 31			14 49		15 02					15 15	15 31			15 49		16 02		
Hatfield Peverel	d		14 20											15 20								
Chelmsford ■	d		14 27	14 40		14 46	14 58		15 11					15 27	15 40		15 46	15 58		16 11		
Ingatestone	d		14 33											15 33								
Shenfield ■	a		14 40	14 51			15 09		15s22		15s29	15s29		15 40	15 51			16 09		16s22		16s29
Romford	a			14 59											15 59							
Stratford ■ ⊖	a		14 55	15 07		15s10	15 24							15 55	16 07		16s10	16 24				
London Liverpool Street ■ ⊖	a		15 03	15 16		15 24	15 33		15 45		15 54	15 54		16 03	16 16		16 24	16 33		16 45		16 54

A until 25 September

B from 2 October

b arr. 1344

Norwich, Ipswich, Harwich, Clacton, Walton-on-Naze, Colchester and Chelmsford - London

	LE	LE 1	LE 1	LE 1	LE ◇1 ☕	LE 1	LE 1	LE ◇1	LE 1	LE ◇1 ☕	LE	LE 1	LE 1	LE 1	LE ◇1 ☕	LE 1	LE 1	LE ◇1	LE 1	LE ◇1 ☕	LE	LE 1
Norwich d					15 30					16 00					16 30					17 00		
Diss d					15 47					16 17					16 47					17 17		
Peterborough 8 d																		15 45				
Stowmarket d	15 45									16 29	16 45							17 12		17 29	17 46	
Needham Market d	15 50										16 50										17 52	
Lowestoft d								14 58														
Ipswich a	16 03				16 08			16 26		16 42	17 03				17 08			17 27		17 42	18 03	
d					16 08			16 30		16 42					17 08			17 30		17 42		
Harwich Town d						16 00										17 00						
Dovercourt d						16 02										17 02						
Harwich International d						16 06										17 06						
Wrabness d						16 12										17 12						
Mistley d						16 17										17 17						
Manningtree 2 d					16 18	16 22				16 52					17 18	17 22				17 52		
Walton-on-the-Naze d							15 45										16 45					
Frinton-on-Sea d							15 48										16 48					
Kirby Cross d							15 51										16 51					
Clacton-on-Sea d			15 50										16 50									
Thorpe-le-Soken 1 a			15 57				15 56						16 57				16 56					
d			15 57				16 01						16 57				17 01					
Weeley d							16 05										17 05					
Great Bentley d							16 08										17 08					
Alresford (Essex) d							16 13										17 13					
Wivenhoe 3 d			16 07				16 16						17 07				17 16					
Hythe d							16 20										17 20					
Colchester Town a							16 24										17 24					
d				16 15			16 28		16 45					17 15			17 28		17 45			
Colchester 4 a			16 17	16 22	16 27	16 32	16 37	16 48	16 52	17 01			17 17	17 22	17 27	17 32	17 37	17 48	17 52	18 01		
d			16 17		16 29	16 33		16 49		17 03			17 17		17 29	17 33		17 49		18 03		
Marks Tey 2 d			16 23			16 39							17 23			17 39						
Kelvedon d						16 44										17 44						
Braintree d		16 00										17 00										18 00
Braintree Freeport d		16 02										17 02										18 02
Cressing d		16 05										17 05										18 05
White Notley d		16 08										17 08										18 08
Witham 2 d		16 15	16 31			16 49		17 02				17 15	17 31			17 49		18 02				18 15
Hatfield Peverel d		16 20										17 20										18 20
Chelmsford 3 d		16 27	16 40		16 46	16 58		17 11				17 27	17 40		17 46	17 58		18 11				18 27
Ingatestone d		16 33										17 33										18 33
Shenfield 3 a		16 40	16 51			17 09		17s22		17s29		17 40	17 51			18 09		18s22		18s29		18 40
Romford a			16 59										17 59									
Stratford 7 ⊖ a		16 55	17 07		17s10	17 24						17 55	18 07		18s10	18 24						18 55
London Liverpool Street 15 ⊖ a		17 03	17 16		17 24	17 33		17 45		17 54		18 03	18 16		18 24	18 33		18 45		18 54		19 03

	LE 1	LE 1	LE ◇1 ☕	LE 1	LE 1	LE ◇1	LE 1	LE ◇1 ☕	LE	LE 1	LE 1	LE 1	LE ◇1 ☕	LE 1	LE 1	LE ◇1	LE 1	LE ◇1 ☕	LE	LE 1	LE 1	LE 1
Norwich d			17 30					18 00					18 30					19 00				
Diss d			17 47					18 17					18 47					19 17				
Peterborough 8 d																17 45						
Stowmarket d			17 59					18 29	18 46							19 12		19 29	19 45			
Needham Market d									18 52										19 50			
Lowestoft d						16 58																
Ipswich a			18 11			18 26		18 42	19 03				19 08			19 25		19 42	20 03			
d			18 11			18 30		18 42					19 08			19 27		19 42				20 08
Harwich Town d				18 03										19 00								
Dovercourt d				18 05										19 02								
Harwich International d				18 09										19 06								
Wrabness d				18 15										19 12								
Mistley d				18 20										19 17								
Manningtree 2 d			18 21	18 25				18 52					19 18	19 22		19 37		19 52				20 18
Walton-on-the-Naze d					17 45										18 45							
Frinton-on-Sea d					17 48										18 48							
Kirby Cross d					17 51										18 51							
Clacton-on-Sea d	17 50										18 50										19 50	
Thorpe-le-Soken 1 a	17 57				17 56						18 57				18 56						19 57	
d	17 57				18 01						18 57				19 01						19 57	
Weeley d					18 05										19 05							
Great Bentley d					18 08										19 08							
Alresford (Essex) d					18 13										19 13							
Wivenhoe 3 d	18 07				18 16						19 07				19 16						20 07	
Hythe d					18 20										19 20							
Colchester Town a					18 24										19 24							
d		18 15			18 28		18 45					19 15			19 28		19 45					
Colchester 4 a	18 17	18 22	18 30	18 35	18 37	18 48	18 52	19 01			19 17	19 22	19 27	19 32	19 37	19 48	19 52	20 01			20 17	20 28
d	18 17		18 32	18 36		18 49		19 03			19 17		19 29	19 33		19 49		20 03			20 17	20 29
Marks Tey 2 d	18 23			18 42							19 23			19 39							20 23	
Kelvedon d				18 47										19 44								
Braintree d										19 00										20 00		
Braintree Freeport d										19 02										20 02		
Cressing d										19 05										20 05		
White Notley d										19 08										20 08		
Witham 2 d	18 31			18 52		19 02				19 15	19 31			19 49		20 02				20 15	20 31	
Hatfield Peverel d										19 20										20 20		
Chelmsford 3 d	18 40		18 49	19 01		19 11				19 27	19 40		19 46	19 58		20 11				20 27	20 40	20 46
Ingatestone d										19 33										20 33		
Shenfield 3 a	18 51			19 12		19s22		19s29		19 40	19 51			20 09		20s22		20s29		20 40	20 51	
Romford a	18 59										19 59										20 59	
Stratford 7 ⊖ a	19 07		19s15	19 27						19 55	20 07		20s10	20 24						20 55	21 07	21s10
London Liverpool Street 15 ⊖ a	19 16		19 26	19 37		19 45		19 54		20 03	20 16		20 24	20 33		20 45		20 54		21 03	21 16	21 19

Norwich, Ipswich, Harwich, Clacton, Walton-on-Naze, Colchester and Chelmsford - London

	LE 1	LE 1	LE ◇1	LE ◇1 ☕	LE	LE 1	LE 1	LE 1	LE 1	LE 1	LE ◇1	LE ◇1 ☕	LE	LE 1	LE 1	LE 1	LE 1	LE 1	LE 1	LE 1
Norwich d				20 00								21 00								
Diss d				20 17								21 17								
Peterborough 8 d											19 45									
Stowmarket d				20 29	20 45						21 12	21 29	21 45							
Needham Market d					20 50								21 50							
Lowestoft d			18 58																	
Ipswich a			20 26	20 42	21 03						21 27	21 42	22 03							
d			20 30	20 42	21 04			21 08			21 27	21 42					22 08			
Harwich Town d	20 00								21 00					21 54						
Dovercourt d	20 02								21 02					21 56						
Harwich International d	20 06				21a28				21 06					21 59						
Wrabness d	20 12								21 12					22 05						
Mistley d	20 17								21 17					22 10						
Manningtree 2 d	20 22			20 52				21 18	21 22		21 37	21 52		22a15			22 18			
Walton-on-the-Naze d		19 45								20 45								21 45		22 45
Frinton-on-Sea d		19 48								20 48								21 48		22 48
Kirby Cross d		19 51								20 51								21 51		22 51
Clacton-on-Sea d						20 50										21 50			22 25	
Thorpe-le-Soken 1 a		19 56				20 57				20 56						21 57		21 56	22 32	22 57
d		20 01				20 57				21 01						21 57		22 01	22 32	
Weeley d		20 05								21 05								22 05	22 36	
Great Bentley d		20 08								21 08								22 08	22 40	
Alresford (Essex) d		20 13								21 13								22 13	22 44	
Wivenhoe 3 d		20 16				21 07				21 16						22 07		22 16	22 47	
Hythe d		20 20								21 20								22 20	22 51	
Colchester Town a		20 24								21 24								22 24		
d		20 28								21 28								22 28		
Colchester 4 a	20 32	20 37	20 48	21 01			21 17	21 28	21 32	21 37	21 48	22 01				22 17	22 28	22 37	22 58	
d	20 33		20 49	21 03			21 17	21 29	21 33		21 49	22 03				22 17	22 29			
Marks Tey 2 d	20 39						21 23		21 39							22 23	22 35			
Kelvedon d	20 44								21 44								22 40			
Braintree d						21 00									22 00					
Braintree Freeport d						21 02									22 02					
Cressing d						21 05									22 05					
White Notley d						21 08									22 08					
Witham 2 d	20 49		21 02			21 15	21 31		21 49		22 02				22 15	22 31	22 45			
Hatfield Peverel d						21 20									22 20		22 49			
Chelmsford 3 d	20 58		21 11			21 27	21 40	21 46	21 58		22 11				22 27	22 40	22 56			
Ingatestone d						21 33									22 33		23 03			
Shenfield 3 a	21 10		21s22	21s29		21 40	21 51	21 58	22 10		22s22	22s29			22 40	22 51	23 09			
Romford a							21 59									22 59				
Stratford 7 ⊖ a	21 25					21 55	22 07	22 12	22 25						22 55	23 07	23 25			
London Liverpool Street 15 ⊖ a	21 34		21 45	21 54		22 03	22 16	22 21	22 34		22 45	22 54			23 03	23 16	23 34			

	LE 1	LE ◇1	LE	LE 1	LE 1	LE 1	LE 1
Norwich d		22 00					23 05
Diss d		22 17					23 22
Peterborough 8 d						21 45	
Stowmarket d		22 29	22 46			23 17	23 34
Needham Market d			22 52			23 22	
Lowestoft d							
Ipswich a		22 42	23 03			23 32	23 50
d		22 42			23 22	23 35	
Harwich Town d				23 05			
Dovercourt d				23 07			
Harwich International d				23 10			
Wrabness d				23 16			
Mistley d				23 21			
Manningtree 2 d		22 52		23a26	23 31	23 45	
Walton-on-the-Naze d							
Frinton-on-Sea d							
Kirby Cross d							
Clacton-on-Sea d							
Thorpe-le-Soken 1 a							
d							
Weeley d							
Great Bentley d							
Alresford (Essex) d							
Wivenhoe 3 d							
Hythe d							
Colchester Town a							
d							
Colchester 4 a		23 01			23 41	23 56	
d		23 03					
Marks Tey 2 d							
Kelvedon d							
Braintree d	22 57						
Braintree Freeport d	22 59						
Cressing d	23 02						
White Notley d	23 05						
Witham 2 d	23a12	23 15					
Hatfield Peverel d							
Chelmsford 3 d		23 24					
Ingatestone d							
Shenfield 3 a		23s36					
Romford a							
Stratford 7 ⊖ a		23 52					
London Liverpool Street 15 ⊖ a		00 03					

Table 11

Sundays

Norwich, Ipswich, Harwich, Clacton, Walton-on-Naze, Colchester and Chelmsford - London

		LE ◇1	LE 1	LE 1	LE 1	LE	LE 1	LE 1	LE ◇1 🍴	LE 1	LE	LE 1	LE 1	LE ◇1 🍴	LE 1	LE 1	LE 1	LE 1	LE 1	LE 1		LE 1	LE ◇1 🍴	LE 1	LE 1
Norwich	d	22p00							07 00					08 00									09 00		
Diss	d	22p17							07 17					08 17									09 17		
Peterborough 8	d																								
Stowmarket	d	22p29							07 29					08 29									09 29		
Needham Market	d																								
Lowestoft	d																					08 05			
Ipswich	a	22p42							07 40		07 45			08 40								09 33	09 42		
	d	22p42							07 42				08 08	08 42						09 08			09 42		
Harwich Town	d																08 53								09 53
Dovercourt	d																08 55								09 55
Harwich International	d							07 25			08a10					08 50	08 58								09 58
Wrabness	d																09 04								10 04
Mistley	d																09 09								10 09
Manningtree 2	d	22p52						07 38	07 52				08 18	08 52			09a14			09 18			09 52		10a14
Walton-on-the-Naze	d														08 30									09 30	
Frinton-on-Sea	d														08 33									09 33	
Kirby Cross	d														08 36									09 36	
Clacton-on-Sea	d											07 36							08 36						
Thorpe-le-Soken 1	a											07 43			08 42				08 43					09 42	
	d											07 43							08 43						
Weeley	d																								
Great Bentley	d											07 49							08 49						
Alresford (Essex)	d											07 53							08 53						
Wivenhoe 3	d											07 56							08 56						
Hythe	d																								
Colchester Town	a																								
	d																								
Colchester 4	a	23p01						07 48	08 01			08 06	08 29	09 01					09 06	09 29			10 01		
	d	23p03			06 56	07 07	07 26	07 49	08 03			08 06	08 30	09 03					09 06	09 30			10 03		
Marks Tey 2	d				07 02	07 15	07 32					08 12	08 36						09 12	09 36					
Kelvedon	d				07 07		07 37						08 41							09 41					
Braintree	d		00 03							08 00								09 00							
Braintree Freeport	d		00 05							08 02								09 02							
Cressing	d		00 08							08 05								09 05							
White Notley	d		00 11							08 08								09 08							
Witham 2	d	23p15	00a18		07 12		07 42			08a16		08 20	08 46					09a16	09 20	09 46					
Hatfield Peverel	d				07 16		07 46						08 50							09 50					
Chelmsford 3	d	23p24		06 53	07 23		07 53	08 07				08 29	08 57						09 29	09 57					
Ingatestone	d			07 00	07 30		08 00						09 04							10 04					
Shenfield 3	a	23b36		07 06	07 36		08 06	08 18	08s29			08 40	09 10	09s29					09 40	10 10			10s29		
Romford	a																								
Stratford 7 ⊖	a	23p52		07s34	08s04		08s34	08s49				09s04	09s34						10s04	10s34					
London Liverpool Street 15 ⊖	a	00 03		07 42	08 12		08 42	08 59	09 03			09 12	09 42	10 01		10 28			10 12	10 42			11 01		

b previous night, stops to set down only

Table 11

Sundays

Norwich, Ipswich, Harwich, Clacton, Walton-on-Naze, Colchester and Chelmsford - London

		LE 1	LE 1	LE 1	LE	LE ◇1 🍴		LE 1	LE 1	LE 1	LE 1	LE 1	LE 1 A	LE ◇1 🍴	LE 1		LE 1	LE 1	LE 1	LE 1	LE	LE ◇1 🍴	LE 1	LE 1
Norwich	d					10 00								11 00								12 00		
Diss	d					10 17								11 17								12 17		
Peterborough 8	d												09 46											
Stowmarket	d				10 17	10 29							11 12	11 29							12 17	12 29		
Needham Market	d				10 22																12 22			
Lowestoft	d																							
Ipswich	a				10 34	10 42							11 25	11 42							12 34	12 42		
	d			10 08		10 42						11 08		11 42						12 08		12 42		
Harwich Town	d								10 53								11 53							12 53
Dovercourt	d								10 55								11 55							12 55
Harwich International	d								10 58								11 58							12 58
Wrabness	d								11 04								12 04							13 04
Mistley	d								11 09								12 09							13 09
Manningtree 2	d			10 18		10 52			11a14			11 18		11 52			12a14			12 18		12 52		13a14
Walton-on-the-Naze	d							10 30							11 30								12 30	
Frinton-on-Sea	d							10 33							11 33								12 33	
Kirby Cross	d							10 36							11 36								12 36	
Clacton-on-Sea	d		09 36								10 36								11 36					
Thorpe-le-Soken 1	a		09 43					10 42			10 43				11 42				11 43				12 42	
	d		09 43								10 43								11 43					
Weeley	d																							
Great Bentley	d		09 49								10 49								11 49					
Alresford (Essex)	d		09 53								10 53								11 53					
Wivenhoe 3	d		09 56								10 56								11 56					
Hythe	d																							
Colchester Town	a																							
	d																							
Colchester 4	a		10 06	10 29		11 01					11 06	11 29		12 01					12 06	12 29		13 01		
	d		10 06	10 30		11 03					11 06	11 30		12 03					12 06	12 30		13 03		
Marks Tey 2	d		10 12	10 36							11 12	11 36							12 12	12 36				
Kelvedon	d			10 41								11 41								12 41				
Braintree	d	10 00								11 00								12 00						
Braintree Freeport	d	10 02								11 02								12 02						
Cressing	d	10 05								11 05								12 05						
White Notley	d	10 08								11 08								12 08						
Witham 2	d	10a16	10 20	10 46						11a16	11 20	11 46						12a16	12 20	12 46				
Hatfield Peverel	d			10 50								11 50								12 50				
Chelmsford 3	d		10 29	10 57							11 29	11 57							12 29	12 57				
Ingatestone	d			11 04								12 04								13 04				
Shenfield 3	a		10 40	11 10		11s29					11 40	12 10		12s29					12 40	13 10		13s29		
Romford	a																							
Stratford 7 ⊖	a		11s04	11s34							12s04	12s34							13s04	13s34				
London Liverpool Street 15 ⊖	a		11 12	11 42		12 01					12 12	12 42		13 01					13 12	13 42		14 01		

		LE 1		LE 1	LE 1	LE 1	LE ◇1 🍴	LE 1	LE 1	LE 1	LE 1		LE 1	LE	LE ◇1 🍴	LE 1	LE 1	LE 1	LE 1	LE 1	LE 1		LE	LE ◇1 🍴
Norwich	d						13 00								14 00									15 00
Diss	d						13 17								14 17									15 17
Peterborough 8	d					11 46															13 46			
Stowmarket	d					13 12	13 29							14 17	14 29						15 12			15 29
Needham Market	d													14 22										
Lowestoft	d																						14 05	
Ipswich	a					13 25	13 42							14 34	14 42						15 25		15 33	15 42
	d				13 08		13 42						14 08		14 42					15 08				15 42
Harwich Town	d								13 53								14 53							
Dovercourt	d								13 55								14 55							
Harwich International	d								13 58								14 58							
Wrabness	d								14 04								15 04							
Mistley	d								14 09								15 09							
Manningtree 2	d				13 18		13 52		14a14				14 18		14 52		15a14			15 18				15 52
Walton-on-the-Naze	d							13 30								14 30								
Frinton-on-Sea	d							13 33								14 33								
Kirby Cross	d							13 36								14 36								
Clacton-on-Sea	d			12 36							13 36								14 36					
Thorpe-le-Soken 1	a			12 43				13 42			13 43					14 42			14 43					
	d			12 43							13 43								14 43					
Weeley	d																							
Great Bentley	d			12 49							13 49								14 49					
Alresford (Essex)	d			12 53							13 53								14 53					
Wivenhoe 3	d			12 56							13 56								14 56					
Hythe	d																							
Colchester Town	a																							
	d																							
Colchester 4	a			13 06	13 29		14 01				14 06		14 29		15 01				15 06	15 29				16 01
	d			13 06	13 30		14 03				14 06		14 30		15 03				15 06	15 30				16 03
Marks Tey 2	d			13 12	13 36						14 12		14 36						15 12	15 36				
Kelvedon	d				13 41								14 41							15 41				
Braintree	d	13 00								14 00								15 00						
Braintree Freeport	d	13 02								14 02								15 02						
Cressing	d	13 05								14 05								15 05						
White Notley	d	13 08								14 08								15 08						
Witham 2	d	13a16		13 20	13 46					14a16	14 20		14 46					15a16	15 20	15 46				
Hatfield Peverel	d				13 50								14 50							15 50				
Chelmsford 3	d			13 29	13 57						14 29		14 57						15 29	15 57				
Ingatestone	d				14 04								15 04							16 04				
Shenfield 3	a			13 40	14 10		14s29				14 40		15 10		15s29				15 40	16 10				16s29
Romford	a																							
Stratford 7 ⊖	a			14s04	14s34						15s04		15s34						16s04	16s34				
London Liverpool Street 15 ⊖	a			14 12	14 42		15 01				15 12		15 42		16 01				16 12	16 42				17 01

A until 5 September

Norwich, Ipswich, Harwich, Clacton, Walton-on-Naze, Colchester and Chelmsford - London

		LE 1	LE 1	LE 1	LE 1	LE 1	LE	LE 1 ⊐		LE 1	LE 1	LE 1	LE 1	LE ◇1 ⊐	LE 1	LE 1	LE ◇1 ⊐		LE 1	LE 1	LE 1	LE 1	LE 1	LE
Norwich	d							16 00						16 20			17 00							
Diss	d							16 17						16 37			17 17							
Peterborough	d															15 46								
Stowmarket	d						16 17	16 29						16 49		17 12	17 29							18 17
Needham Market	d						16 22																	18 22
Lowestoft	d																							
Ipswich	a						16 34	16 42						17 00		17 25	17 42							18 34
	d					16 08		16 42						17 03	17 08		17 42						18 08	
Harwich Town	d		15 53								16 53									17 53				
Dovercourt	d		15 55								16 55									17 55				
Harwich International	d		15 58								16 58									17 58				
Wrabness	d		16 04								17 04									18 04				
Mistley	d		16 09								17 09									18 09				
Manningtree	d		16a14			16 18		16 52			17a14				17 18		17 52			18a14			18 18	
Walton-on-the-Naze	d	15 30								16 30									17 30					
Frinton-on-Sea	d	15 33								16 33									17 33					
Kirby Cross	d	15 36								16 36									17 36					
Clacton-on-Sea	d				15 36								16 36									17 36		
Thorpe-le-Soken	a	15 42			15 43					16 42			16 43						17 42			17 43		
	d				15 43								16 43									17 43		
Weeley	d																							
Great Bentley	d				15 49								16 49									17 49		
Alresford (Essex)	d				15 53								16 53									17 53		
Wivenhoe	d				15 56								16 56									17 56		
Hythe	d																							
Colchester Town	a																							
	d																							
Colchester	a				16 06	16 29		17 01					17 06	17 19	17 29		18 01					18 06	18 29	
	d				16 06	16 30		17 03					17 06	17 21	17 30		18 03					18 06	18 30	
Marks Tey	d				16 12	16 36							17 12		17 36							18 12	18 36	
Kelvedon	d					16 41									17 41								18 41	
Braintree	d			16 00								17 00									18 00			
Braintree Freeport	d			16 02								17 02									18 02			
Cressing	d			16 05								17 05									18 05			
White Notley	d			16 08								17 08									18 08			
Witham	d			16a16	16 20	16 46						17a16	17 20		17 46						18a16	18 20	18 46	
Hatfield Peverel	d					16 50									17 50								18 50	
Chelmsford	d				16 29	16 57							17 29		17 57							18 29	18 57	
Ingatestone	d					17 04									18 04								19 04	
Shenfield	a				16 40	17 10		17s29					17 40		18 10		18s29					18 40	19 10	
Romford	a																							
Stratford ⊖	a				17s04	17s34							18s04		18s34							19s04	19s34	
London Liverpool Street ⊖	a				17 12	17 42		18 01					18 12	18 28	18 42		19 01					19 12	19 42	

		LE ◇1 ⊐	LE 1	LE 1		LE 1	LE 1	LE 1	LE 1	LE ◇1 ⊐	LE 1	LE 1	LE 1		LE 1	LE 1	LE	LE ◇1 ⊐	LE 1	LE 1	LE 1	LE 1	LE 1
Norwich	d	18 00								19 00								20 00					
Diss	d	18 17								19 17								20 17					
Peterborough	d								17 46														
Stowmarket	d	18 29							19 12	19 29							20 17	20 29					
Needham Market	d																20 22						
Lowestoft	d																						
Ipswich	a	18 42							19 27	19 42							20 34	20 42					
	d	18 42						19 08		19 42						20 08	20 35	20 42					21 08
Harwich Town	d			18 53								19 53								20 53			
Dovercourt	d			18 55								19 55								20 55			
Harwich International	d			18 58								19 58					21a00			20 58			
Wrabness	d			19 04								20 04								21 04			
Mistley	d			19 09								20 09								21 09			
Manningtree	d	18 52		19a14				19 18		19 52		20a14				20 18		20 52		21a14			21 18
Walton-on-the-Naze	d		18 30								19 30								20 30				
Frinton-on-Sea	d		18 33								19 33								20 33				
Kirby Cross	d		18 36								19 36								20 36				
Clacton-on-Sea	d						18 36								19 36							20 36	
Thorpe-le-Soken	a		18 42				18 43				19 42				19 43				20 42			20 43	
	d						18 43								19 43							20 43	
Weeley	d																						
Great Bentley	d						18 49								19 49							20 49	
Alresford (Essex)	d						18 53								19 53							20 53	
Wivenhoe	d						18 56								19 56							20 56	
Hythe	d																						
Colchester Town	a																						
	d																						
Colchester	a	19 01					19 06	19 29		20 01					20 06	20 29		21 01				21 06	21 29
	d	19 03					19 06	19 30		20 03					20 06	20 30		21 03				21 06	21 30
Marks Tey	d						19 12	19 36							20 12	20 36						21 12	21 36
Kelvedon	d							19 41								20 41							21 41
Braintree	d					19 00							20 00								21 00		
Braintree Freeport	d					19 02							20 02								21 02		
Cressing	d					19 05							20 05								21 05		
White Notley	d					19 08							20 08								21 08		
Witham	d					19a16	19 20	19 46					20a16		20 20	20 46					21a16	21 20	21 46
Hatfield Peverel	d							19 50								20 50							21 50
Chelmsford	d						19 29	19 57							20 29	20 57						21 29	21 57
Ingatestone	d							20 04								21 04							22 04
Shenfield	a	19s29					19 40	20 10		20s29					20 40	21 10		21s29				21 40	22 10
Romford	a																						
Stratford ⊖	a						20s04	20s34							21s04	21s34						22s04	22s34
London Liverpool Street ⊖	a	20 01					20 12	20 42		21 01					21 12	21 42		22 01				22 12	22 42

Norwich, Ipswich, Harwich, Clacton, Walton-on-Naze, Colchester and Chelmsford - London

		LE 1	LE	LE ◇1	LE 1	LE 1	LE 1	LE 1	LE 1	LE 1		LE	LE 1	LE 1	LE ◇1	LE 1	LE 1
Norwich	d			21 00											22 00		23 05
Diss	d			21 17											22 17		23 22
Peterborough	d	19 44															
Stowmarket	d	21 05		21 29								22 17			22 29		23 34
Needham Market	d											22 22					
Lowestoft	d		20 05														
Ipswich	a	21 18	21 33	21 42								22 34			22 42		23 48
	d	21 19		21 42					22 08						22 42		
Harwich Town	d					21 53										22 53	
Dovercourt	d					21 55										22 55	
Harwich International	d					21 58										22 58	
Wrabness	d					22 04										23 04	
Mistley	d					22 09										23 09	
Manningtree	d	21 29		21 52		22a14			22 18						22 52	23 14	
Walton-on-the-Naze	d				21 30					22 13							
Frinton-on-Sea	d				21 33					22 16							
Kirby Cross	d				21 36					22 19							
Clacton-on-Sea	d							21 36					22 20				
Thorpe-le-Soken	a				21 42			21 43		22 25			22 27				
	d							21 43					22 27				
Weeley	d																
Great Bentley	d							21 49									
Alresford (Essex)	d							21 53									
Wivenhoe	d							21 56					22 37				
Hythe	d																
Colchester Town	a																
	d																
Colchester	a	21 40		22 01				22 06	22 29				22 47		23 01	23 24	
	d			22 03				22 06	22 30						23 03		
Marks Tey	d							22 12	22 36								
Kelvedon	d								22 41								
Braintree	d						22 00							22 56			
Braintree Freeport	d						22 02							22 58			
Cressing	d						22 05							23 01			
White Notley	d						22 08							23 04			
Witham	d						22a16	22 20	22 46					23a12	23 15		
Hatfield Peverel	d								22 50								
Chelmsford	d							22 29	22 57						23 24		
Ingatestone	d								23 04								
Shenfield	a			22s29				22 40	23 10						23s36		
Romford	a																
Stratford ⊖	a							23s04	23s34						23s57		
London Liverpool Street ⊖	a			23 01				23 12	23 42						00 07		

Network Diagram for Tables 13, 14, 15, 16, 17

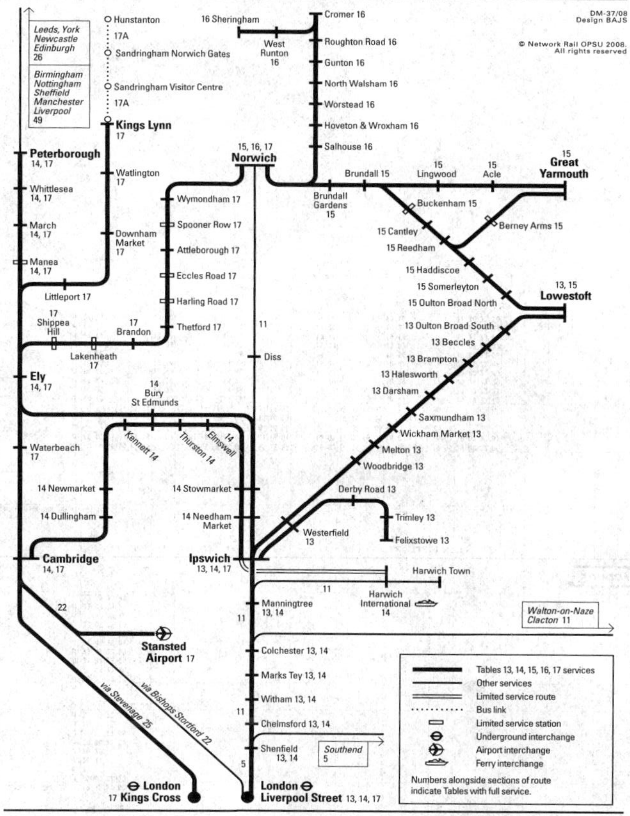

Ipswich - Felixstowe and Lowestoft

		LE	LE	LE	LE	LE	LE	LE	LE	LE
				[1]				◇[1]		
London Liverpool Street [15] ⊖	d							07 38		
Shenfield [3]	d							08u02		
Chelmsford [3]	d							08 12		
Witham [2]	d							08 22		
Marks Tey [2]	d							08 30		
Colchester [4]	d							08 38		
Manningtree [2]	d									
Ipswich	d	05 04	06 04	06 47	07 13	07 32	08 27	09c02	09 27	10 27
Westerfield	d	05 10	06 10	06 54	07 19	07 39	08 33	09 09	09 33	10 33
Derby Road	d	05 15	06 15		07 24		08 38		09 38	10 38
Trimley	d	05 24	06 24		07 33		08 47		09 47	10 47
Felixstowe	a	05 30	06 30		07 39		08 53		09 53	10 53
Woodbridge	d			07 06		07b55		09 21		
Melton	d			07 10		07 59		09 25		
Wickham Market	d			07 16		08 05		09 31		
Saxmundham	d			07 27		08a17		09 42		
Darsham	d			07 33				09 48		
Halesworth	d			07 43				09 58		
Brampton (Suffolk)	d			07 50				10 05		
Beccles	d			07 58				10 13		
Oulton Broad South	d			08 08				10 23		
Lowestoft	a			08 17				10 32		

		LE	LE	LE	LE	LE	LE	LE	LE	LE	LE	LE	LE	LE
		◇[1]			◇[1]			◇[1]			[2] [1]			
London Liverpool Street [15] ⊖	d	09 38			11 38			13 38			15 38			
Shenfield [3]	d	10u02			12u02			14u02			16u02			
Chelmsford [3]	d	10 12			12 12			14 12			16u12			
Witham [2]	d	10 21			12 21			14 21			16 23			
Marks Tey [2]	d	10 29			12 29			14 29			16 32			
Colchester [4]	d	10 38			12 38			14 38			16 41			
Manningtree [2]	d													
Ipswich	d	11e02	11 27	12 27	13f02	13 27	14 27	15g02	15 27	16 27	17 02	17 27	18 13	18 27
Westerfield	d	11 09	11 33	12 33	13 09	13 33	14 33	15 09	15 33	16 33	17 09	17 33	18 20	18 33
Derby Road	d		11 38	12 38		13 38	14 38		15 38	16 38		17 38		18 38
Trimley	d		11 47	12 47		13 47	14 47		15 47	16 47		17 47		18 47
Felixstowe	a		11 53	12 53		13 53	14 53		15 53	16 53		17 53		18 53
Woodbridge	d	11 21			13 21			15 21			17 22		18 32	
Melton	d	11 25			13 25			15 25			17 26		18 36	
Wickham Market	d	11 31			13 31			15 31			17 32		18 42	
Saxmundham	d	11 42			13 42			15 42			17 43		18 53	
Darsham	d	11 48			13 48			15 48			17 49		18 59	
Halesworth	d	11 58			13 58			15 58			17 59		19h16	
Brampton (Suffolk)	d	12 05			14 05			16 05			18 06		19 23	
Beccles	d	12 13			14 13			16 13			18 14		19 31	
Oulton Broad South	d	12 23			14 23			16 23			18 24		19 41	
Lowestoft	a	12 32			14 32			16 32			18 33		19 50	

		LE	LE	LE	LE	LE	LE
					[2] [1]	◇[1]	
London Liverpool Street [15] ⊖	d				19 32	21 00	
Shenfield [3]	d				19u55	21u23	
Chelmsford [3]	d						
Witham [2]	d				20 12		
Marks Tey [2]	d						
Colchester [4]	d				20 26	21 50	
Manningtree [2]	d					21 58	
Ipswich	d	18 55	19 27	20 27	20i52	22j15	22 27
Westerfield	d	19 02	19 33	20 33	20 59	22 22	22 33
Derby Road	d		19 38	20 38			22 38
Trimley	d		19 47	20 47			22 47
Felixstowe	a		19 53	20 53			22 53
Woodbridge	d	19 14			21 11	22 34	
Melton	d	19 18			21 15	22 38	
Wickham Market	d	19 24			21 21	22 44	
Saxmundham	d	19 35			21 32	22 55	
Darsham	d	19 41			21 38	23 01	
Halesworth	d	19 51			21 48	23 11	
Brampton (Suffolk)	d	19 58			21 55	23 18	
Beccles	d	20 06			22 03	23 26	
Oulton Broad South	d	20 16			22 13	23 36	
Lowestoft	a	20 25			22 22	23 45	

Saturdays

		LE	LE	LE	LE	LE	LE	LE	LE	LE
			[1]			◇[1]			[2] [1]	
London Liverpool Street [15] ⊖	d					07 38			09 38	
Shenfield [3]	d					08u02			10u02	
Chelmsford [3]	d					08 12			10 12	
Witham [2]	d					08 21			10 21	
Marks Tey [2]	d					08 29			10 29	
Colchester [4]	d					08 38			10 38	
Manningtree [2]	d									
Ipswich	d	06 27	06 50	07 27	08 27	09c02	09 27	10 27	11e02	11 27
Westerfield	d	06 33	06 57	07 33	08 33	09 09	09 33	10 33	11 09	11 33
Derby Road	d	06 38		07 38	08 38		09 38	10 38		11 38
Trimley	d	06 47		07 47	08 47		09 47	10 47		11 47
Felixstowe	a	06 53		07 53	08 53		09 53	10 53		11 53
Woodbridge	d		07 09			09 21			11 21	
Melton	d		07 13			09 25			11 25	
Wickham Market	d		07 19			09 31			11 31	
Saxmundham	d		07 30			09 42			11 42	
Darsham	d		07 36			09 48			11 48	
Halesworth	d		07 46			09 58			11 58	
Brampton (Suffolk)	d		07 53			10 05			12 05	
Beccles	d		08 01			10 13			12 13	
Oulton Broad South	d		08 11			10 23			12 23	
Lowestoft	a		08 20			10 32			12 32	

		LE	LE	LE	LE	LE	LE	LE	LE	LE	LE	LE	LE	LE
			[2] [1]			[2] [1]			[2] [1]			[2] [1]		
London Liverpool Street [15] ⊖	d		11 38			13 38			15 38			17 46		
Shenfield [3]	d		12u02			14u02			16u02					
Chelmsford [3]	d		12 12			14 12			16 12			18u16		
Witham [2]	d		12 21			14 21			16 21					
Marks Tey [2]	d		12 29			14 29			16 29					
Colchester [4]	d		12 38			14 38			16 38			18 40		
Manningtree [2]	d													
Ipswich	d	12 27	13f02	13 27	14 27	15g02	15 27	16 27	17k02	17 27	18 27	19l02	19 27	20 27
Westerfield	d	12 33	13 09	13 33	14 33	15 09	15 33	16 33	17 09	17 33	18 33	19 09	19 33	20 33
Derby Road	d	12 38		13 38	14 38		15 38	16 38		17 38	18 38		19 38	20 38
Trimley	d	12 47		13 47	14 47		15 47	16 47		17 47	18 47		19 47	20 47
Felixstowe	a	12 53		13 53	14 53		15 53	16 53		17 53	18 53		19 53	20 53
Woodbridge	d		13 21			15 21			17 21			19 21		
Melton	d		13 25			15 25			17 25			19 25		
Wickham Market	d		13 31			15 31			17 31			19 31		
Saxmundham	d		13 42			15 42			17 42			19 42		
Darsham	d		13 48			15 48			17 48			19 48		
Halesworth	d		13 58			15 58			17 58			19 58		
Brampton (Suffolk)	d		14 05			16 05			18 05			20 05		
Beccles	d		14 13			16 13			18 13			20 13		
Oulton Broad South	d		14 23			16 23			18 23			20 23		
Lowestoft	a		14 32			16 32			18 32			20 32		

b arr. 0749
c arr. 0856
e arr. 1056
f arr. 1256
g arr. 1456
h arr. 1908
i arr. 2044
j arr. 2207
k arr. 1656
l arr. 1856

Ipswich - Felixstowe and Lowestoft

		LE	LE	LE
		■ [1]	◇ [1]	
London Liverpool Street [15] ⊖	d	19 38	21 00	
Shenfield [3]	d	20u02	21u23	
Chelmsford [3]	d	20 12		
Witham [2]	d	20 21		
Marks Tey [2]	d	20 29		
Colchester [4]	d	20 38	21 50	
Manningtree [2]	d		21 58	
Ipswich	d	21b02	22c15	22 27
Westerfield	d	21 09	22 22	22 33
Derby Road	d			22 38
Trimley	d			22 47
Felixstowe	a			22 53
Woodbridge	d	21 21	22 34	
Melton	d	21 25	22 38	
Wickham Market	d	21 31	22 44	
Saxmundham	d	21 42	22 55	
Darsham	d	21 48	23 01	
Halesworth	d	21 58	23 11	
Brampton (Suffolk)	d	22 05	23 18	
Beccles	d	22 13	23 26	
Oulton Broad South	d	22 23	23 36	
Lowestoft	a	22 32	23 45	

Sundays

		LE	LE	LE	LE	LE	LE	LE	LE	LE
		[1]	A					[1]		
London Liverpool Street [15] ⊖	d									
Shenfield [3]	d									
Chelmsford [3]	d									
Witham [2]	d									
Marks Tey [2]	d									
Colchester [4]	d									
Manningtree [2]	d									
Ipswich	d	10 00	10 55	11 55	12 00	12 55	13 55	14 00	14 55	15 55
Westerfield	d	10 07	11 01	12 01	12 07	13 01	14 01	14 07	15 01	16 01
Derby Road	d		11 06	12 06		13 06	14 06		15 06	16 06
Trimley	d		11 15	12 15		13 15	14 15		15 15	16 15
Felixstowe	a		11 21	12 21		13 21	14 21		15 21	16 21
Woodbridge	d	10 19			12 19			14 19		
Melton	d	10 23			12 23			14 23		
Wickham Market	d	10 29			12 29			14 29		
Saxmundham	d	10 40			12 40			14 40		
Darsham	d	10 46			12 46			14 46		
Halesworth	d	10 56			12 56			14 56		
Brampton (Suffolk)	d	11 03			13 03			15 03		
Beccles	d	11 11			13 11			15 11		
Oulton Broad South	d	11 21			13 21			15 21		
Lowestoft	a	11 30			13 30			15 30		

		LE	LE	LE	LE	LE	LE	LE	LE
					[1]			[1]	
London Liverpool Street [15] ⊖	d								
Shenfield [3]	d								
Chelmsford [3]	d								
Witham [2]	d								
Marks Tey [2]	d								
Colchester [4]	d								
Manningtree [2]	d								
Ipswich	d	16 00	16 55	17 55	18 00	18 55	19 55	20 00	22 00
Westerfield	d	16 07	17 01	18 01	18 07	19 01	20 01	20 07	22 07
Derby Road	d		17 06	18 06		19 06	20 06		
Trimley	d		17 15	18 15		19 15	20 15		
Felixstowe	a		17 21	18 21		19 21	20 21		
Woodbridge	d	16 19			18 19			20 19	22 19
Melton	d	16 23			18 23			20 23	22 23
Wickham Market	d	16 29			18 29			20 29	22 29
Saxmundham	d	16 40			18 40			20 40	22 40
Darsham	d	16 46			18 46			20 46	22 46
Halesworth	d	16 56			18 56			20 56	22 56
Brampton (Suffolk)	d	17 03			19 03			21 03	23 03
Beccles	d	17 11			19 11			21 11	23 11
Oulton Broad South	d	17 21			19 21			21 21	23 21
Lowestoft	a	17 30			19 30			21 30	23 30

A until 5 September   b arr. 2056   c arr. 2209

Lowestoft and Felixstowe - Ipswich

		LE	LE	LE	LE	LE	LE	LE	LE	LE	LE	LE
					■ [1]					■ [1]		
Lowestoft	d		05 31		06 44					08 58		
Oulton Broad South	d		05 38		06 51					09 05		
Beccles	d		05 47		07 00					09 14		
Brampton (Suffolk)	d		05 55		07 08					09 22		
Halesworth	d		06 03		07 16					09 30		
Darsham	d		06 11		07 24					09 38		
Saxmundham	d		06 19		07 32		08 21			09 46		
Wickham Market	d		06 28		07 41		08 30			09 55		
Melton	d		06 35		07 48		08 37			10 02		
Woodbridge	d		06 40		07 53		08 42			10 07		
Felixstowe	d	05 34		06 38		07 50		08 56	09 56		10 56	11 56
Trimley	d	05 37		06 41		07 53		08 59	09 59		10 59	11 59
Derby Road	d	05 47		06 51		08 03		09 09	10 09		11 09	12 09
Westerfield	d	05 52	06 51	06 56	08 04	08 08	08 53	09 14	10 14	10 18	11 14	12 14
Ipswich	a	06 00	06 59	07 03	08 12	08 16	09 01	09 22	10 22	10 26	11 22	12 22
Manningtree [2]	a											
Colchester [4]	a									10 48		
Marks Tey [2]	a											
Witham [2]	a									11 02		
Chelmsford [3]	a									11 10		
Shenfield [3]	a									11s22		
London Liverpool Street [15] ⊖	a				09 25					11 45		

		LE	LE	LE	LE	LE	LE	LE	LE	LE	LE	LE
		◇ [1]			◇ [1]						◇ [1]	
Lowestoft	d	10 58			12 58			14 58			16 58	
Oulton Broad South	d	11 05			13 05			15 05			17 05	
Beccles	d	11 14			13 14			15 14			17 14	
Brampton (Suffolk)	d	11 22			13 22			15 22			17 22	
Halesworth	d	11 30			13 30			15 30			17 30	
Darsham	d	11 38			13 38			15 38			17 38	
Saxmundham	d	11 46			13 46			15 46			17 46	
Wickham Market	d	11 55			13 55			15 55			17 55	
Melton	d	12 02			14 02			16 02			18 02	
Woodbridge	d	12 07			14 07			16 07			18 07	
Felixstowe	d		12 56	13 56		14 56	15 56		16 56	17 56		18 56
Trimley	d		12 59	13 59		14 59	15 59		16 59	17 59		18 59
Derby Road	d		13 09	14 09		15 09	16 09		17 09	18 09		19 09
Westerfield	d	12 18	13 14	14 14	14 18	15 14	16 14	16 18	17 14	18 14	18 18	19 14
Ipswich	a	12 26	13 22	14 22	14 26	15 22	16 22	16 26	17 22	18 22	18 26	19 22
Manningtree [2]	a											
Colchester [4]	a	12 48			14 48						18 48	
Marks Tey [2]	a										18 55	
Witham [2]	a	13 02			15 02						19 03	
Chelmsford [3]	a	13 10			15 10						19 12	
Shenfield [3]	a	13s22			15s22						19s24	
London Liverpool Street [15] ⊖	a	13 45			15 45						19 47	

		LE	LE	LE	LE	LE
		◇ [1]				
Lowestoft	d	18 43			20 58	
Oulton Broad South	d	18 50			21 05	
Beccles	d	18 59			21 14	
Brampton (Suffolk)	d	19 07			21 22	
Halesworth	d	19 15			21 30	
Darsham	d	19 23			21 38	
Saxmundham	d	19b36			21 46	
Wickham Market	d	19 45			21 55	
Melton	d	19 52			22 02	
Woodbridge	d	19 57			22 07	
Felixstowe	d		19 56	20 56		22 56
Trimley	d		19 59	20 59		22 59
Derby Road	d		20 09	21 09		23 09
Westerfield	d	20 08	20 14	21 14	22 18	23 14
Ipswich	a	20 16	20 22	21 22	22 26	23 22
Manningtree [2]	a					
Colchester [4]	a	20 48				
Marks Tey [2]	a					
Witham [2]	a	21 02				
Chelmsford [3]	a	21 10				
Shenfield [3]	a	21s23				
London Liverpool Street [15] ⊖	a	21 46				

Saturdays

		LE	LE	LE	LE	LE	LE	LE	LE	LE	LE	LE
			■ [1]		■ [1]			■ [1]			■ [1]	
Lowestoft	d		05 58		06 58			08 58			10 58	
Oulton Broad South	d		06 05		07 05			09 05			11 05	
Beccles	d		06 14		07 14			09 14			11 14	
Brampton (Suffolk)	d		06 22		07 22			09 22			11 22	
Halesworth	d		06 30		07 30			09 30			11 30	
Darsham	d		06 38		07 38			09 38			11 38	
Saxmundham	d		06 46		07 46			09 46			11 46	
Wickham Market	d		06 55		07 55			09 55			11 55	
Melton	d		07 02		08 02			10 02			12 02	
Woodbridge	d		07 07		08 07			10 07			12 07	
Felixstowe	d	06 56		07 56		08 56	09 56		10 56	11 56		12 56
Trimley	d	06 59		07 59		08 59	09 59		10 59	11 59		12 59
Derby Road	d	07 09		08 09		09 09	10 09		11 09	12 09		13 09
Westerfield	d	07 14	07 18	08 14	08 18	09 14	10 14	10 18	11 14	12 14	12 18	13 14
Ipswich	a	07 22	07 26	08 22	08 26	09 22	10 22	10 26	11 22	12 22	12 26	13 22
Manningtree [2]	a											
Colchester [4]	a		07 48		08 48			10 48			12 48	
Marks Tey [2]	a											
Witham [2]	a		08 02								13 02	
Chelmsford [3]	a		08 10		09s06			11s06			13 10	
Shenfield [3]	a		08s22								13s21	
London Liverpool Street [15] ⊖	a		08 45		09 38			11 42			13 45	

		LE	LE	LE	LE	LE	LE	LE	LE	LE	LE	LE
			◇ [1]			◇ [1]			◇ [1]			◇ [1]
Lowestoft	d		12 58			14 58			16 58			18 58
Oulton Broad South	d		13 05			15 05			17 05			19 05
Beccles	d		13 14			15 14			17 14			19 14
Brampton (Suffolk)	d		13 22			15 22			17 22			19 22
Halesworth	d		13 30			15 30			17 30			19 30
Darsham	d		13 38			15 38			17 38			19 38
Saxmundham	d		13 46			15 46			17 46			19 46
Wickham Market	d		13 55			15 55			17 55			19 55
Melton	d		14 02			16 02			18 02			20 02
Woodbridge	d		14 07			16 07			18 07			20 07
Felixstowe	d	13 56		14 56	15 56		16 56	17 56		18 56	19 56	
Trimley	d	13 59		14 59	15 59		16 59	17 59		18 59	19 59	
Derby Road	d	14 09		15 09	16 09		17 09	18 09		19 09	20 09	
Westerfield	d	14 14	14 18	15 14	16 14	16 18	17 14	18 14	18 18	19 14	20 14	20 18
Ipswich	a	14 22	14 26	15 22	16 22	16 26	17 22	18 22	18 26	19 22	20 22	20 26
Manningtree [2]	a											
Colchester [4]	a		14 48			16 48			18 48			20 48
Marks Tey [2]	a											
Witham [2]	a		15 02			17 02			19 02			21 02
Chelmsford [3]	a		15 10			17 10			19 10			21 10
Shenfield [3]	a		15s22			17s22			19s22			21s22
London Liverpool Street [15] ⊖	a		15 45			17 45			19 45			21 45

b arr. 1930

Table 13

Lowestoft and Felixstowe - Ipswich

Saturdays

		LE	LE	LE
Lowestoft	d		20 58	
Oulton Broad South	d		21 05	
Beccles	d		21 14	
Brampton (Suffolk)	d		21 22	
Halesworth	d		21 30	
Darsham	d		21 38	
Saxmundham	d		21 46	
Wickham Market	d		21 55	
Melton	d		22 02	
Woodbridge	d		22 07	
Felixstowe	d	20 56		22 56
Trimley	d	20 59		22 59
Derby Road	d	21 09		23 09
Westerfield	d	21 14	22 18	23 14
Ipswich	a	21 22	22 26	23 22
Manningtree ■2	a			
Colchester ■4	a			
Marks Tey ■2	a			
Witham ■2	a			
Chelmsford ■3	a			
Shenfield ■3	a			
London Liverpool Street ■15 ⊖	a			

Sundays

		LE ■1	LE	LE A	LE	LE ■1	LE	LE	LE	LE	LE	LE ■1	LE	LE	LE ■1	LE	LE	LE
Lowestoft	d	08 05	10 05			12 05			14 05			16 05			18 05			20 05
Oulton Broad South	d	08 12	10 12			12 12			14 12			16 12			18 12			20 12
Beccles	d	08 21	10 21			12 21			14 21			16 21			18 21			20 21
Brampton (Suffolk)	d	08 29	10 29			12 29			14 29			16 29			18 29			20 29
Halesworth	d	08 37	10 37			12 37			14 37			16 37			18 37			20 37
Darsham	d	08 45	10 45			12 45			14 45			16 45			18 45			20 45
Saxmundham	d	08 53	10 53			12 53			14 53			16 53			18 53			20 53
Wickham Market	d	09 02	11 02			13 02			15 02			17 02			19 02			21 02
Melton	d	09 09	11 09			13 09			15 09			17 09			19 09			21 09
Woodbridge	d	09 14	11 14			13 14			15 14			17 14			19 14			21 14
Felixstowe	d			11 25	12 25		13 25	14 25		15 25	16 25		17 25	18 25		19 25	20 25	
Trimley	d			11 28	12 28		13 28	14 28		15 28	16 28		17 28	18 28		19 28	20 28	
Derby Road	d			11 38	12 38		13 38	14 38		15 38	16 38		17 38	18 38		19 38	20 38	
Westerfield	d	09 25	11 25	11 43	12 43	13 25	13 43	14 43	15 25	15 43	16 43	17 25	17 43	18 43	19 25	19 43	20 43	21 25
Ipswich	a	09 33	11 33	11 50	12 50	13 33	13 50	14 50	15 33	15 50	16 50	17 33	17 50	18 50	19 33	19 50	20 50	21 33
Manningtree ■2	a																	
Colchester ■4	a																	
Marks Tey ■2	a																	
Witham ■2	a																	
Chelmsford ■3	a																	
Shenfield ■3	a																	
London Liverpool Street ■15 ⊖	a																	

A until 5 September

Table 14

Ipswich - Bury St Edmunds, Cambridge, Ely and Peterborough

Mondays to Fridays

		LE	LE ■1	LE	LE	LE ◇■1	LE	LE	LE ■1	LE	LE	LE ◇■1	LE	LE	LE ◇■1	LE	LE	LE ◇■1	LE	LE	LE ◇■1	LE	LE
London Liverpool Street ■15 ⊖	d					06 38						10 38			12 38			14 38			16 32		
Shenfield	d					07u02						11u02			13u02			15u02			16u54		
Chelmsford	d					07 12						11 12			13 12			15 12					
Witham	d					07 21						11 21			13 21			15 21			17 13		
Marks Tey	d					07 33						11 29			13 29			15 29					
Colchester	d		05 35			07 41						11 38			13 38			15 38			17 26		
Manningtree	d		05 44			07 50															17 35		
Harwich International	d						07 47																
Ipswich	d	05 10	06b01	06 13	06 52	08 02	08 16	09 16	10 02	10 16	11 16	12c02	12 16	13 16	14e02	14 16	15 16	16f02	16 16	17 16	17 49	18 16	19 16
Needham Market	d	05 20		06 23	07 02		08 26	09 26		10 26	11 26		12 26	13 26		14 26	15 26		16 26	17 26	17 58	18 26	19 26
Stowmarket	d	05 26	06 12	06 29	07 08	08 13	08 32	09 32	10 13	10 32	11 32	12 13	12 32	13 32	14 13	14 32	15 32	16 13	16 32	17 32	18 03	18 32	19 32
Elmswell	d	05 35		06 38	07 18		08 41	09 41		10 41	11 41		12 41	13 41		14 41	15 41		16 41	17 41	18 12	18 41	19 41
Thurston	d	05 41		06 44	07 24		08 47	09 47		10 47	11 47		12 47	13 47		14 47	15 47		16 47	17 47	18 17	18 47	19 47
Bury St Edmunds	a	05 47	06 28	06 50	07 30	08 29	08 53	09 53	10 29	10 53	11 53	12 29	12 53	13 53	14 29	14 53	15 53	16 29	16 53	17 53	18 23	18 53	19 53
	d	05 49	06 28	06 51	07 30	08 29	08 55	09 55	10 29	10 55	11 55	12 29	12 55	13 55	14 29	14 55	15 55	16 29	16 55	17 55	18 23	18 55	19 55
Kennett	d	06 00		07 02	07 42			10 06			12 06			14 06			16 06			18 06			20 06
Newmarket	d	06 10		07 13	07 51		09 15	10 17		11 15	12 17		13 15	14 17		15 15	16 17		17 17	18 17		19 15	20 17
Dullingham	d	06 15		07 18	08 00		09 20			11 20			13 20			15 20						19 20	
Cambridge	a	06 33		07 37	08 19		09 39	10 39		11 39	12 39		13 39	14 39		15 39	16 39		17 39	18 39		19 39	20 39
Ely ■6	d		07 00			08 58			10 58			12 58			14 58			16 58			19 01		
Manea	d																						
March	d		07 16			09 15			11 15			13 15			15 15			17 15			19 17		
Whittlesea	d		07 27			09 26			11 26			13 26			15 26			17 26			19 29		
Peterborough ■8	a		07 38			09 37			11 37			13 37			15 37			17 37			19 42		

		LE ■1	LE	LE
London Liverpool Street ■15 ⊖	d			
Shenfield	d			
Chelmsford	d			
Witham	d			
Marks Tey	d			
Colchester	d			
Manningtree	d			
Harwich International	d			
Ipswich	d	20 16	21 16	22 16
Needham Market	d	20 25	21 26	22 26
Stowmarket	d	20 30	21 32	22 32
Elmswell	d	20 39	21 41	22 41
Thurston	d	20 44	21 47	22 47
Bury St Edmunds	a	20 50	21 53	22 54
	d	20 50	21 55	
Kennett	d		22 06	
Newmarket	d		22 15	
Dullingham	d		22 20	
Cambridge	a		22 39	
Ely ■6	d	21 19		
Manea	d			
March	d	21 36		
Whittlesea	d	21 47		
Peterborough ■8	a	21 58		

Saturdays

		LE	LE ■1	LE	LE	LE ◇■1	LE	LE	LE ◇■1	LE	LE	LE ■ ■1	LE	LE	LE ■ ■1	LE	LE	LE ◇■1	LE	LE	LE ■ ■1	LE
London Liverpool Street ■15 ⊖	d					06 38			08 38			10 38			12 38			14 38			16 38	
Shenfield	d					07u02			09u02			11u02			13u02			15u02			17u02	
Chelmsford	d					07 12			09 12			11 12			13 12			15 12			17 12	
Witham	d					07 21			09 21			11 21			13 21			15 21			17 21	
Marks Tey	d					07 29			09 29			11 29			13 29			15 29			17 29	
Colchester	d		05 38			07 38			09 38			11 38			13 38			15 38			17 38	
Manningtree	d		05 46			07 46			09 46													
Harwich International	d						07 47															
Ipswich	d	05 10	06 00	06 14	07 16	08 02	08 16	09 16	10 02	10 16	11 16	12c02	12 16	13 16	14e02	14 16	15 16	16f02	16 16	17 16	18g02	18 16
Needham Market	d	05 20		06 24	07 26		08 26	09 26		10 26	11 26		12 26	13 26		14 26	15 26		16 26	17 26		18 26
Stowmarket	d	05 26	06 11	06 30	07 32	08 13	08 32	09 32	10 13	10 32	11 32	12 13	12 32	13 32	14 13	14 32	15 32	16 13	16 32	17 32	18 13	18 32
Elmswell	d	05 35		06 39	07 41		08 41	09 41		10 41	11 41		12 41	13 41		14 41	15 41		16 41	17 41		18 41
Thurston	d	05 41		06 45	07 47		08 47	09 47		10 47	11 47		12 47	13 47		14 47	15 47		16 47	17 47		18 47
Bury St Edmunds	a	05 47	06 27	06 51	07 53	08 29	08 53	09 53	10 29	10 53	11 53	12 29	12 53	13 53	14 29	14 53	15 53	16 29	16 53	17 53	18 29	18 53
	d	05 49	06 27	06 53	07 55	08 29	08 55	09 55	10 29	10 55	11 55	12 29	12 55	13 55	14 29	14 55	15 55	16 29	16 55	17 55	18 29	18 55
Kennett	d	06 00		07 04	08 06			10 06			12 06			14 06			16 06			18 06		
Newmarket	d	06 10		07 15	08 17		09 15	10 17		11 15	12 17		13 15	14 17		15 15	16 17		17 17	18 17		19 15
Dullingham	d	06 15		07 20	08 22		09 20			11 20			13 20			15 20						19 20
Cambridge	a	06 36		07 39	08 39		09 39	10 39		11 39	12 39		13 39	14 39		15 39	16 39		17 39	18 39		19 39
Ely ■6	d		06 57			08 58			10 58			12 58			14 58			16 58			19 00	
Manea	d																					
March	d		07 14			09 16			11 15			13 15			15 15			17 15			19 16	
Whittlesea	d		07 25			09 27			11 26			13 26			15 26			17 26			19 28	
Peterborough ■8	a		07 37			09 38			11 37			13 37			15 37			17 37			19 38	

b arr. 0555
c arr. 1156
e arr. 1356
f arr. 1556
g arr. 1756

Table 14

Saturdays

Ipswich - Bury St Edmunds, Cambridge, Ely and Peterborough

		LE	LE	LE	LE
			■ ■1		
London Liverpool Street ■ ⊖	d		18 46		
Shenfield	d				
Chelmsford	d		19u16		
Witham	d				
Marks Tey	d				
Colchester	d		19 40		
Manningtree	d				
Harwich International	d				
Ipswich	d	19 16	20b02	20 16	22 17
Needham Market	d	19 26		20 26	22 27
Stowmarket	d	19 32	20 13	20 32	22 33
Elmswell	d	19 41		20 41	22 42
Thurston	d	19 47		20 47	22 48
Bury St Edmunds	a	19 53	20 29	20 53	22 55
	d	19 55	20 29	20 55	
Kennett	d	20 06		21 06	
Newmarket	d	20 17		21 15	
Dullingham	d			21 20	
Cambridge	a	20 39		21 39	
Ely ■	d		20 58		
Manea	d				
March	d		21 15		
Whittlesea	d		21 26		
Peterborough ■	a		21 37		

Sundays

		LE	LE	LE	LE	LE	LE	LE	LE	LE	LE	LE	LE	LE	LE
		A			■1		■1		■1		■1		■1		
London Liverpool Street ■ ⊖	d														
Shenfield	d														
Chelmsford	d														
Witham	d														
Marks Tey	d														
Colchester	d														
Manningtree	d														
Harwich International	d			08 30											
Ipswich	d	07 55	08 45	09c02	09 55	11 02	11 55	13 02	13 55	15 02	15 55	17 02	17 55	19 02	21 02
Needham Market	d			09 12		11 12		13 12		15 12		17 12		19 12	21 12
Stowmarket	d	08 07	08 59	09 18	10 07	11 18	12 07	13 18	14 07	15 18	16 07	17 18	18 07	19 18	21 18
Elmswell	d			09 27		11 27		13 27		15 27		17 27		19 27	21 27
Thurston	d			09 33		11 33		13 33		15 33		17 33		19 33	21 33
Bury St Edmunds	a	08 22	09 17	09 39	10 22	11 39	12 22	13 39	14 22	15 39	16 22	17 39	18 22	19 39	21 39
	d	08 23		09 40	10 23	11 40	12 23	13 40	14 23	15 40	16 23	17 40	18 23	19 40	21 40
Kennett	d			09 51		11 51		13 51		15 51		17 51		19 51	21 51
Newmarket	d			10 00		12 00		14 00		16 00		18 00		20 00	22 00
Dullingham	d			10 05		12 05		14 05		16 05		18 05		20 05	22 05
Cambridge	a			10 24		12 24		14 24		16 24		18 24		20 24	22 24
Ely ■	d	08 52			10 52		12 52		14 52		16 52		18 52		
Manea	d														
March	d	09 09			11 09		13 09		15 09		17 09		19 09		
Whittlesea	d	09 20			11 20		13 20		15 20		17 20		19 20		
Peterborough ■	a	09 36			11 36		13 31		15 31		17 31		19 32		

A until 5 September

b arr. 1956

c arr. 0855

Table 14

Mondays to Fridays

Peterborough, Ely, Cambridge and Bury St Edmunds - Ipswich

		LE MX	LE MO	LE	LE	LE	LE	LE	LE	LE	LE	LE	LE	LE	LE	LE
								■ ■1			◇■1			◇■1		
Peterborough ■	d							07 46			09 45			11 45		
Whittlesea	d							07 54			09 53			11 53		
March	d							08 05			10 04			12 04		
Manea	d															
Ely ■	d							08 30			10 26			12b30		
Cambridge	d	22p43	23p00			06 41	07 43		08 43	09 43		10 43	11 43		12 43	13 43
Dullingham	d	22p59	23p16				08 00			09 59			11 59			13 59
Newmarket	d	23p04	23p21			07 01	08 04		09 03	10 04		11 03	12 04		13 03	14 04
Kennett	d	23p12	23p29			07 09			09 11			11 11			13 11	
Bury St Edmunds	a	23p24	23p41			07 21	08 23	08 55	09 23	10 23	10 51	11 23	12 23	12 55	13 23	14 23
	d	23p25	23p42	05 36	06 22	07 23	08 24	08 56	09 23	10 23	10 56	11 23	12 23	12 56	13 23	14 23
Thurston	d	23p31	23p48	05 42	06 28	07 30	08 30		09 30	10 30		11 30	12 30		13 30	14 30
Elmswell	d	23p38	23p55	05 49	06 35	07 36	08 37		09 36	10 36		11 36	12 36		13 36	14 36
Stowmarket	d	23p46	00 04	05 57	06 44	07 45	08 45	09 12	09 45	10 45	11 12	11 45	12 45	13 12	13 45	14 45
Needham Market	d	23p52	00 09	06 03		07 50	08 51		09 50	10 50		11 50	12 50		13 50	14 50
Ipswich	a	00 03	00 21	06 15	07 00	08 02	09 03	09 26	10 03	11 03	11 25	12 03	13 03	13 25	14 03	15 03
Harwich International	a				07 25											
Manningtree	a															
Colchester	a							09 48			11 48			13 48		
Marks Tey	a															
Witham	a							10 02			12 02			14 02		
Chelmsford	a							10s10			12 10			14 10		
Shenfield	a							10s22			12s22			14s22		
London Liverpool Street ■ ⊖	a							10 46			12 45			14 45		

		LE	LE	LE	LE	LE	LE	LE	LE	LE	LE	LE	LE	LE
		■1			◇■1			◇■1			◇■1		■1	
Peterborough ■	d	13 45			15 45			17 45			19 46		22 05	
Whittlesea	d	13 53			15 53			17 53			19 54		22 13	
March	d	14 04			16 04			18 04			20 05		22 24	
Manea	d													
Ely ■	d	14 30			16c30			18e30			20 27		22 42	
Cambridge	d		14 43	15 43		16 43	17 43		18 43	19 43		20 43		22 43
Dullingham	d			15 59		16 59	17 59			19 59		20 59		22 59
Newmarket	d		15 03	16 04		17 04	18 04		19 03	20 04		21 04		23 04
Kennett	d		15 11			17 12	18 12		19 11			21 12		23 12
Bury St Edmunds	a	14 55	15 23	16 23	16 55	17 24	18 24	18 55	19 23	20 23	20 52	21 24	23 07	23 24
	d	14 56	15 23	16 23	16 56	17 25	18 25	18 56	19 23	20 23	20 52	21 25	23 08	23 25
Thurston	d		15 30	16 30		17 31	18 31		19 30	20 30		21 31		23 31
Elmswell	d		15 36	16 36		17 38	18 38		19 36	20 36		21 38		23 38
Stowmarket	d	15 12	15 45	16 45	17 12	17 46	18 46	19 12	19 45	20 45	21 08	21 46	23 24	23 46
Needham Market	d		15 50	16 50		17 52	18 52		19 50	20 50		21 52		23 52
Ipswich	a	15 25	16 03	17 03	17 27	18 03	19 03	19 25	20 03	21 03	21 25	22 03	23 37	00 03
Harwich International	a									21 28				
Manningtree	a							19 36			21 36		23 47	
Colchester	a	15 43			17 48			19 47			21 48		23 58	
Marks Tey	a				17 55			19 54						
Witham	a				18 03			20 02			22 02			
Chelmsford	a				18 13			20 11			22 10			
Shenfield	a				18s25			20s23			22s22			
London Liverpool Street ■ ⊖	a				18 51			20 46			22 46			

Saturdays

		LE	LE	LE	LE	LE	LE	LE	LE	LE	LE	LE	LE	LE	LE
						■ ■1			■ ■1			◇■1			◇■1
Peterborough ■	d					07 45			09 55			11 45			13 45
Whittlesea	d					07 53			10 03			11 53			13 53
March	d					08 04			10 14			12 04			14 04
Manea	d														
Ely ■	d					08f30			10 32			12b30			14g30
Cambridge	d	22p43		06 43	07 43		08 43	09 43		10 43	11 43		12 43	13 43	
Dullingham	d	22p59			07 59			09 59			11 59			13 59	
Newmarket	d	23p04		07 03	08 04		09 03	10 04		11 03	12 04		13 03	14 04	
Kennett	d	23p12		07 11			09 11			11 11			13 11		
Bury St Edmunds	a	23p24		07 23	08 23	08 55	09 23	10 23	10 57	11 23	12 23	12 55	13 23	14 23	14 55
	d	23p25	06 23	07 23	08 23	08 56	09 23	10 23	10 58	11 23	12 23	12 56	13 23	14 23	14 56
Thurston	d	23p31	06 30	07 30	08 30		09 30	10 30		11 30	12 30		13 30	14 30	
Elmswell	d	23p38	06 36	07 36	08 36		09 36	10 36		11 36	12 36		13 36	14 36	
Stowmarket	d	23p46	06 45	07 45	08 45	09 12	09 45	10 45	11 14	11 45	12 45	13 12	13 45	14 45	15 12
Needham Market	d	23p52	06 50	07 50	08 50		09 50	10 50		11 50	12 50		13 50	14 50	
Ipswich	a	00 03	07 03	08 03	09 03	09 25	10 03	11 03	11 27	12 03	13 03	13 27	14 03	15 03	15 25
Harwich International	a														
Manningtree	a														
Colchester	a					09 48			11 48			13 48			15 48
Marks Tey	a														
Witham	a								12 02			14 02			16 02
Chelmsford	a					10s06			12 10			14 10			16 10
Shenfield	a								12s22			14s22			16s22
London Liverpool Street ■ ⊖	a					10 38			12 45			14 45			16 45

b arr. 1222

c arr. 1622

e arr. 1822

f arr. 0822

g arr. 1422

Table 14

Saturdays

Peterborough, Ely, Cambridge and Bury St Edmunds - Ipswich

		LE	LE	LE ◇[1]	LE	LE	LE ◇[1]	LE	LE	LE ◇[1]	LE	LE	LE [1]
Peterborough ■	d			15 45			17 45			19 45			21 45
Whittlesea	d			15 53			17 53			19 53			21 53
March	d			16 04			18 04			20 04			22 04
Manea	d												
Ely ■	d			16b30			18c30			20 30			22e30
Cambridge	d	14 43	15 43		16 43	17 43		18 43	19 43		20 43	21 43	
Dullingham	d		15 59		16 59	17 59			19 59			21 59	
Newmarket	d	15 03	16 04		17 04	18 04		19 03	20 04		21 03	22 04	
Kennett	d	15 11			17 12	18 12		19 11			21 11	22 12	22 47
Bury St Edmunds	a	15 23	16 23	16 55	17 24	18 24	18 55	19 23	20 23	20 55	21 23	22 24	22 57
	d	15 23	16 23	16 56	17 25	18 25	18 56	19 23	20 23	20 56	21 23	22 25	22 58
Thurston	d	15 30	16 30		17 31	18 31		19 30	20 30		21 30	22 31	23 03
Elmswell	d	15 36	16 36		17 38	18 38		19 36	20 36		21 36	22 38	23 09
Stowmarket	d	15 45	16 45	17 12	17 46	18 46	19 12	19 45	20 45	21 12	21 45	22 46	23 17
Needham Market	d	15 50	16 50		17 52	18 52		19 50	20 50		21 50	22 52	23 22
Ipswich	a	16 03	17 03	17 27	18 03	19 03	19 25	20 03	21 03	21 27	22 03	23 03	23 32
Harwich International	a								21 28				
Manningtree	a						19 36			21 37			23 44
Colchester	a			17 48			19 48			21 48			23 56
Marks Tey	a												
Witham	a			18 02			20 02			22 02			
Chelmsford	a			18 10			20 10			22 10			
Shenfield	a			18s22			20s22			22s22			
London Liverpool Street [15] ⊖	a			18 45			20 45			22 45			

Sundays

		LE	LE [1] A	LE	LE [1]	LE	LE [1]	LE	LE [1]	LE	LE [1]	LE	LE [1]	LE
Peterborough ■	d		09 46		11 46		13 46		15 46		17 46		19 44	
Whittlesea	d		09 54		11 54		13 54		15 54		17 54		19 52	
March	d		10 05		12 05		14 05		16 05		18 05		20 03	
Manea	d													
Ely ■	d		10 30		12 30		14 30		16 30		18 30		20 22	
Cambridge	d			11 12		13 12		15 12		17 12		19 12		21 12
Dullingham	d			11 28		13 28		15 28		17 28		19 28		21 28
Newmarket	d			11 34		13 34		15 34		17 34		19 34		21 34
Kennett	d			11 42		13 42		15 42		17 42		19 42		21 42
Bury St Edmunds	a		10 55	11 54	12 55	13 54	14 55	15 54	16 55	17 54	18 55	19 54	20 47	21 54
	d	09 55	10 56	11 55	12 56	13 55	14 56	15 55	16 56	17 55	18 56	19 55	20 47	21 55
Thurston	d	10 01		12 01		14 01		16 01		18 01		20 01		22 01
Elmswell	d	10 08		12 08		14 08		16 08		18 08		20 08		22 08
Stowmarket	d	10 17	11 12	12 17	13 12	14 17	15 12	16 17	17 12	18 17	19 12	20 17	21 05	22 17
Needham Market	d	10 22		12 22		14 22		16 22		18 22		20 22		22 22
Ipswich	a	10 34	11 25	12 34	13 25	14 34	15 25	16 34	17 25	18 34	19 27	20 34	21 18	22 34
Harwich International	a											21 00		
Manningtree	a												21 28	
Colchester	a												21 40	
Marks Tey	a													
Witham	a													
Chelmsford	a													
Shenfield	a													
London Liverpool Street [15] ⊖	a													

		LE
Peterborough ■	d	
Whittlesea	d	
March	d	
Manea	d	
Ely ■	d	
Cambridge	d	23 00
Dullingham	d	23 16
Newmarket	d	23 21
Kennett	d	23 29
Bury St Edmunds	a	23 41
	d	23 42
Thurston	d	23 48
Elmswell	d	23 55
Stowmarket	d	00 04
Needham Market	d	00 09
Ipswich	a	00 21
Harwich International	a	
Manningtree	a	
Colchester	a	
Marks Tey	a	
Witham	a	
Chelmsford	a	
Shenfield	a	
London Liverpool Street [15] ⊖	a	

A until 5 September
b arr. 1622
c arr. 1822
e arr. 2222

Table 15

Mondays to Fridays

Norwich-Great Yarmouth and Lowestoft

		LE [1]	LE	LE [1]	LE	LE	LE	LE [1]	LE	LE	LE	LE	LE	LE	LE	LE	LE	LE	LE	LE [1]	LE	LE	LE [1]
London Liverpool Street [15] ⊖	d																						
Norwich	d	05 15	05 45	06 24	06 34	06 57	07 05	07 36	07 54	08 36	08 57	09 36	09 57	10 36	10 57	11 36	11 57	12 36	12 57	13 36	13 57	14 36	14 57
Brundall Gardens	d		05 52		06 41		07 12		08 01	08 43		09 43		10 43		11 43		12 43		13 43		14 43	
Brundall	d	05 24	05 55	06 32	06 44	07 05	07 15	07 44	08 04	08 46		09 46	10 05	10 46		11 46	12 05	12 46		13 46	14 05	14 46	
Lingwood	d				06 49		07 20			08 51		09 51				11 51		12 51		13 51		14 51	
Acle	d				06 54		07 27			08 55		09 55				11 55		12 55		13 55		14 55	
Buckenham	d																						
Cantley	d		06 01			07 11		07 50	08 10				10 11	10 52			12 11				14 11		15 09
Reedham (Norfolk)	d		06 06	06 41		07 16		07 55	08 15				10 16	10 57			12 16				14 16		15 14
Berney Arms	d							08x01						11x03									
Great Yarmouth	a	05 46			07 07		07 40	08 12		09 08		10 08		11 13		12 08		13 08		14 08		15 08	
Haddiscoe	d		06 14			07 24			08 23				10 24				12 24				14 24		
Somerleyton	d		06 18			07 28			08 27				10 28				12 28				14 28		
Oulton Broad North	d		06 24	06 56		07 34			08 33		09 26		10 34		11 26		12 34		13 26		14 34		15 29
Lowestoft	a		06 30	07 03		07 41			08 38		09 36		10 41		11 33		12 41		13 33		14 41		15 36

		LE [1]	LE	LE	LE [1]	LE	LE	LE	LE [1]	LE [1]	LE	LE	LE [1]	LE	LE	LE [1]	LE [1]	LE
London Liverpool Street [15] ⊖	d																	
Norwich	d	15 36	15 57	16 40	16 57	17 05	17 36	17 57	18 40	18 57	19 36	19 57	20 40	20 57	21 40	21 57	22 40	23 00
Brundall Gardens	d	15 43		16 47		17 12	17 43		18 47		19 43		20 47		21 47			
Brundall	d	15 46	16 05	16 50	17 05	17 15	17 46	18 05	18 50	19 05	19 46	20 05	20 50	21 05	21 50	22 05	22 48	23 08
Lingwood	d	15 51		16 55		17 20	17 51		18 55		19 51		20 55		21 55			23 13
Acle	d	15 55		16 59		17 27	17 55		18 59		19 55		20 59		21 59			23 17
Buckenham	d																	
Cantley	d		16 11		17 11			18 11		19 11		20 11		21 11		22 11	22 54	
Reedham (Norfolk)	d		16 16		17 16			18 16		19 16		20 16		21 16		22 16	22 59	
Berney Arms	d																	
Great Yarmouth	a	16 08		17 12		17 40	18 08		19 12		20 08		21 12		22 12			23 30
Haddiscoe	d		16 24		17 24			18 24		19 24		20 24				22 24	23 07	
Somerleyton	d		16 28		17 28			18 28		19 28		20 28				22 28	23 11	
Oulton Broad North	d		16 34		17 34			18 34		19 34		20 34		21 31		22 34	23 17	
Lowestoft	a		16 41		17 41			18 41		19 41		20 41		21 38		22 41	23 24	

Saturdays

		LE	LE	LE	LE	LE	LE	LE	LE	LE	LE	LE	LE A	LE	LE	LE A	LE	LE	LE ■ [1] A	LE	LE	LE A
London Liverpool Street [15] ⊖	d																		10 00			
Norwich	d	05 36	05 49	06 36	06 55	07 05	07 36	07 54	08 36	08 57	09 36	09 57	10 06	10 36	10 57	11 13	11 36	11 57	12b05	12 36	12 57	13 18
Brundall Gardens	d		05 56	06 43		07 12		08 01	08 43		09 43			10 43			11 43			12 43		
Brundall	d	05 44	05 59	06 46	07 03	07 15	07 44	08 04	08 46		09 46	10 05		10 46			11 46	12 05		12 46		
Lingwood	d			06 51		07 20			08 51		09 51						11 51			12 51		
Acle	d			06 55		07 27			08 55		09 55						11 55			12 55		
Buckenham	d											10x09										
Cantley	d		06 05		07 09		07 50	08 10				10 13		10 52				12 11				
Reedham (Norfolk)	d	05 52	06 10		07 14		07 55	08 15				10 17	10 23	10 57				12 16				
Berney Arms	d						08x01							11x03								
Great Yarmouth	a	06 08		07 08		07 40	08 12		09 08		10 08		10 38	11 13		11 43	12 08		12 39	13 08		13 48
Haddiscoe	d		06 18		07 22			08 23				10 26						12 24				
Somerleyton	d		06 22		07 26			08 27				10 29						12 28				
Oulton Broad North	d		06 28		07 32			08 33		09 26		10 35			11 26			12 34			13 26	
Lowestoft	a		06 34		07 38			08 38		09 33		10 41			11 33			12 41			13 33	

		LE	LE	LE A	LE	LE	LE A	LE	LE	LE	LE	LE	LE	LE	LE	LE	LE	LE	LE	LE	LE	LE	LE [1]	LE
London Liverpool Street [15] ⊖	d			12 00																				
Norwich	d	13 36	13 57	14c17	14 36	14 57	15 18	15 36	15 57	16 40	16 57	17 05	17 36	17 57	18 40	18 57	19 36	19 57	20 40	20 57	21 40	21 57	22 40	23 00
Brundall Gardens	d	13 43			14 43			15 43		16 47		17 12	17 43		18 47		19 43		20 47		21 47			
Brundall	d	13 46	14 05		14 46			15 46	16 05	16 50	17 05	17 15	17 46	18 05	18 50	19 05	19 46	20 05	20 50	21 05	21 50	22 05	22 48	23 08
Lingwood	d	13 51			14 51			15 51		16 55		17 20	17 51		18 55		19 51		20 55		21 55			23 13
Acle	d	13 55			14 55			15 55		16 59		17 27	17 55		18 59		19 55		20 59		21 59			23 17
Buckenham	d																							
Cantley	d		14 11			15 09			16 11		17 11			18 11		19 11		20 11		21 11		22 11	22 54	
Reedham (Norfolk)	d		14 16			15 14			16 16		17 16			18 16		19 16		20 16		21 16		22 16	22 59	
Berney Arms	d																							
Great Yarmouth	a	14 08		14 51	15 08		15 48	16 08		17 12		17 40	18 08		19 12		20 08		21 12		22 12			23 30
Haddiscoe	d		14 24						16 24		17 24			18 24		19 24		20 24				22 24	23 07	
Somerleyton	d		14 28						16 28		17 28			18 28		19 28		20 28				22 28	23 11	
Oulton Broad North	d		14 34			15 29			16 34		17 34			18 34		19 34		20 34		21 31		22 34	23 17	
Lowestoft	a		14 41			15 36			16 41		17 41			18 41		19 41		20 41		21 38		22 41	23 24	

A until 25 September
b arr. 1151
c arr. 1351

Norwich-Great Yarmouth and Lowestoft

		LE 1	LE	LE	LE 1	LE	LE	LE 1	LE	LE	LE	LE	LE	LE 1	LE A	LE B	LE	LE 1 A	LE 1 B	LE	LE	LE	LE
London Liverpool Street 15 ⊖	d																						
Norwich	d	07 25	07 36	08 45	08 57	09 36	10 45	10 57	11 36	12 45	12 57	13 36	14 45	14 57	15 36	15 36	16 45	16 57	16 57	17 36	18 45	18 57	19 36
Brundall Gardens	d			08 52			10 52			12 52			14 52				16 52				18 52		
Brundall	d		07 44	08 55	09 05	09 44	10 55	11 05	11 44	12 55	13 05	13 44	14 55	15 05	15 44	15 44	16 55	17 05	17 05	17 44	18 55	19 05	19 44
Lingwood	d			09 00			11 00			13 00			15 00				17 00				19 00		
Acle	d			09 04			11 04			13 04			15 04				17 04				19 04		
Buckenham	d					09x48			11x48						15x48	15x48		17x09					
Cantley	d		07 50		09 11	09 52		11 11	11 52		13 11	13 50		15 11	15 52	15 52		17 13	17 13	17 50		19 11	19 50
Reedham (Norfolk)	d		07 55		09 16	09 56		11 16	11 56		13 16	13 55		15 16	15 56	15 56		17 17	17 17	17 55		19 16	19 55
Berney Arms	d		08x01			10x03			12x03			14x01			16x03								
Great Yarmouth	a		08 12	09 17		10 13	11 17		12 13	13 17		14 12	15 17		16 13	16 13	17 17			18 10	19 17		20 10
Haddiscoe	d				09 24			11 24			13 24			15 24				17 26	17 26			19 24	
Somerleyton	d				09 28			11 28			13 28			15 28				17 29	17 29			19 28	
Oulton Broad North	d	07 53			09 34			11 34			13 34			15 34				17 35	17 35			19 34	
Lowestoft	a	07 59			09 40			11 40			13 40			15 40				17 41	17 41			19 40	

		LE	LE 1	LE	LE
London Liverpool Street 15 ⊖	d				
Norwich	d	20 45	20 57	21 36	22 36
Brundall Gardens	d	20 52			22 43
Brundall	d	20 55	21 05	21 44	22 46
Lingwood	d	21 00			22 51
Acle	d	21 04			22 55
Buckenham	d				
Cantley	d		21 11	21 50	
Reedham (Norfolk)	d		21 16	21 55	
Berney Arms	d				
Great Yarmouth	a	21 17		22 10	23 08
Haddiscoe	d		21 24		
Somerleyton	d		21 28		
Oulton Broad North	d		21 34		
Lowestoft	a		21 40		

A until 5 September

B from 12 September

Lowestoft and Great Yarmouth-Norwich

		LE MX 1	LE MX	LE MO	LE	LE 1	LE 1	LE	LE	LE	LE 1	LE	LE 1	LE	LE	LE	LE	LE	LE	LE	LE	LE	LE
Lowestoft	d	23p30		23p35	05 36			06 38			07 40	07 55		08 42		09 42		10 50		11 42		12 50	
Oulton Broad North	d	23p34		23p39	05 40			06 42			07 44	07 59		08 46		09 46		10 54		11 46		12 54	
Somerleyton	d				05 46			06 48			07 50			08 52		09 52				11 52			
Haddiscoe	d				05 49			06 51			07 54			08 55		09 55				11 55			
Great Yarmouth	d		23p33			05 55	06 40		07 17	07 44			08 17		09 17		10 17		11 17		12 17		13 17
Berney Arms	d																						
Reedham (Norfolk)	d	23p51	23p46	23p54	05 58			07 00			08 03	08 14		09 04		10 04				12 04			
Cantley	d	23p55			06 02			07 04			08 07	08 19		09 08		10 08				12 08			
Buckenham	d																						
Acle	d					06 06	06 54		07 27	07 54			08 27		09 27		10 27		11 27		12 27		13 27
Lingwood	d					06 11	06 59		07 32	07 59			08 32		09 32		10 32		11 32		12 32		13 32
Brundall	d	00 01	23p54	00 03	06 08	06 15	07 03	07 10	07 36	08 03	08 13		08 36	09 14	09 36	10 14	10 36		11 36	12 14	12 36		13 36
Brundall Gardens	d					06 18		07 13	07 39	08 06			08 39		09 39		10 39		11 39		12 39		13 39
Norwich	a	00 12	00 05	00 13	06 19	06 28	07 14	07 23	07 50	08 19	08 25	08 38	08 50	09 25	09 50	10 25	10 50	11 25	11 50	12 25	12 50	13 25	13 50
London Liverpool Street 15 ⊖	a						09 25																

		LE	LE 1	LE 1	LE	LE 1	LE 1	LE	LE	LE A	LE B	LE 1	LE	LE	LE 1	LE 1	LE	LE	LE 1	LE	LE	LE 1	LE 1	LE 1
Lowestoft	d	13 42		14 50		15 42		16 47				17 47		18 47		19 47		20 50		21 42		22 45		23 30
Oulton Broad North	d	13 46		14 54		15 46		16 51				17 51		18 51		19 51		20 54		21 46		22 49		23 34
Somerleyton	d	13 52				15 52		16 57				17 57		18 57		19 57				21 52		22 55		
Haddiscoe	d	13 55				15 55		17 00				18 00		19 00		20 00				21 55		22 58		
Great Yarmouth	d		14 12		15 17		16 17		17 17	17 47	17 47		18 17		19 17		20 17		21 17		22 17		23 33	
Berney Arms	d		14x19								17x54													
Reedham (Norfolk)	d	14 04	14 26			16 04		17 09		18 01	18 01	18 09		19 09		20 09				22 04		23 07	23 46	23 51
Cantley	d	14 08	14 30			16 08		17 13		18 05	18 05	18 13		19 13		20 13				22 08		23 11		23 55
Buckenham	d																							
Acle	d				15 27		16 27		17 27				18 27		19 27		20 27		21 27		22 27			
Lingwood	d				15 32		16 32		17 32				18 32		19 32		20 32		21 32		22 32			
Brundall	d	14 14	14 36		15 36	16 14	16 36	17 19	17 36	18 12	18 12	18 19	18 36	19 19	19 36	20 19	20 36		21 36	22 14	22 36	23 17	23 54	00 01
Brundall Gardens	d		14 39		15 39		16 39		17 39				18 39		19 39		20 39		21 39		22 39			
Norwich	a	14 25	14 49	15 25	15 50	16 25	16 50	17 30	17 50	18 23	18 23	18 30	18 52	19 30	19 50	20 30	20 50	21 25	21 50	22 25	22 50	23 28	00 05	00 12
London Liverpool Street 15 ⊖	a																							

Saturdays

		LE 1	LE	LE	LE	LE	LE	LE	LE	LE	LE	LE	LE 1 C	LE	LE D	LE	LE	LE D	LE	LE	LE	LE 1 C	LE
Lowestoft	d	23p30			06 40			07 42		08 42		09 42				10 50			11 42		12 50		
Oulton Broad North	d	23p34			06 44			07 46		08 46		09 46				10 54			11 46		12 54		
Somerleyton	d				06 50			07 52		08 52		09 52							11 52				
Haddiscoe	d				06 53			07 55		08 55		09 55							11 55				
Great Yarmouth	d		23p33	06 17		07 17	07 44		08 17		09 17		10 08	10 17	10 42		11 17	11 47		12 17		13 10	13 17
Berney Arms	d																						
Reedham (Norfolk)	d	23p51	23p46		07 02			08 04		09 04		10 04							12 04				
Cantley	d	23p55			07 06			08 08		09 08		10 08							12 08				
Buckenham	d																						
Acle	d			06 27		07 27	07 54		08 27		09 27			10 27			11 27			12 27			13 27
Lingwood	d			06 32		07 32	07 59		08 32		09 32			10 32			11 32			12 32			13 32
Brundall	d	00 01	23p54	06 36	07 12	07 36	08 03	08 14	08 36	09 14	09 36	10 14		10 36			11 36		12 14	12 36			13 36
Brundall Gardens	d			06 39	07 15	07 39	08 06		08 39		09 39			10 39			11 39			12 39			13 39
Norwich	a	00 12	00 05	06 50	07 25	07 50	08 19	08 25	08 50	09 25	09 50	10 25	10 44	10 53	11 08	11 25	11 50	12 16	12 25	12 50	13 25	13 44	13 53
London Liverpool Street 15 ⊖	a												12 54									15 54	

A from 27 September

B until 24 September

C until 25 September. ⊡ from Norwich

D until 25 September

Table 15

Saturdays

Lowestoft and Great Yarmouth-Norwich

		LE	LE A	LE	LE	LE	LE	LE A	LE	LE	LE	LE A	LE B	LE	LE	LE	LE	LE	LE	LE 1	LE	LE	LE
Lowestoft	d	13 42			14 50		15 42			16 47				17 47		18 47		19 47		20 50		21 42	
Oulton Broad North	d	13 46			14 54		15 46			16 51				17 51		18 51		19 51		20 54		21 46	
Somerleyton	d	13 52					15 52			16 57				17 57		18 57		19 57				21 52	
Haddiscoe	d	13 55					15 55			17 00				18 00		19 00		20 00				21 55	
Great Yarmouth	d		13 58	14 12		15 17		16 02	16 17		17 17	17 47	17 47		18 17		19 17		20 17		21 17		22 17
Berney Arms	d			14x19								17x54											
Reedham (Norfolk)	d	14 04		14 26			16 04			17 09		18 01	18 01	18 09		19 09		20 09				22 04	
Cantley	d	14 08		14 30			16 08			17 13		18 05	18 05	18 13		19 13		20 13				22 08	
Buckenham	d						16x11																
Acle	d					15 27			16 27		17 27				18 27		19 27		20 27		21 27		22 27
Lingwood	d					15 32			16 32		17 32				18 32		19 32		20 32		21 32		22 32
Brundall	d	14 14		14 36		15 36	16 14		16 36	17 19	17 36	18 12	18 12	18 19	18 36	19 19	19 36	20 19	20 36		21 36	22 14	22 36
Brundall Gardens	d			14 39		15 39			16 39		17 39				18 39		19 39		20 39		21 39		22 39
Norwich	a	14 25	14 35	14 49	15 25	15 50	16 25	16 34	16 50	17 30	17 50	18 23	18 23	18 30	18 52	19 30	19 50	20 30	20 50	21 25	21 50	22 25	22 50
London Liverpool Street 15 ⊖	a																						

		LE		LE	LE 1
Lowestoft	d	22 45			23 30
Oulton Broad North	d	22 49			23 34
Somerleyton	d	22 55			
Haddiscoe	d	22 58			
Great Yarmouth	d			23 33	
Berney Arms	d				
Reedham (Norfolk)	d	23 07		23 46	23 51
Cantley	d	23 11			23 55
Buckenham	d				
Acle	d				
Lingwood	d				
Brundall	d	23 17		23 54	00 01
Brundall Gardens	d				
Norwich	a	23 28		00 05	00 12
London Liverpool Street 15 ⊖	a				

Sundays

		LE 1	LE	LE	LE	LE 1	LE	LE	LE 1	LE	LE	LE	LE	LE	LE 1	LE D	LE E	LE	LE	LE	LE	LE 1	LE
Lowestoft	d	23p30				09 50			11 50			13 50			15 50				17 50			19 50	
Oulton Broad North	d	23p34				09 54			11 54			13 54			15 54				17 54			19 54	
Somerleyton	d					10 00			12 00			14 00			16 00				18 00			20 00	
Haddiscoe	d					10 03			12 03			14 03			16 03				18 03			20 03	
Great Yarmouth	d		23p33	08 20	09 22		10 18	11 22		12 18	13 22		14 20	15 22		16 18	16 18	17 22		18 18	19 22		20 22
Berney Arms	d			08x27			10x25			12x25			14x27			16x25							
Reedham (Norfolk)	d	23p51	23p46	08 34		10 12	10 32		12 12	12 32		14 12	14 34		16 12	16 32	16 32		18 12	18 30		20 12	20 34
Cantley	d	23p55		08 38		10 16	10 36		12 16	12 36		14 16	14 38		16 16	16 36	16 36		18 16	18 34		20 16	20 38
Buckenham	d					10x20	10x40			12x40						16x40							
Acle	d				09 32			11 32			13 32			15 32				17 32			19 32		
Lingwood	d				09 37			11 37			13 37			15 37				17 37			19 37		
Brundall	d	00 01	23p54	08 45	09 41	10 24	10 44	11 41	12 22	12 44	13 41	14 22	14 45	15 41	16 22	16 44	16 44	17 41	18 22	18 41	19 41	20 22	20 45
Brundall Gardens	d				09 44			11 44			13 44			15 44				17 44			19 44		
Norwich	a	00 12	00 05	08 55	09 55	10 34	10 55	11 55	12 33	12 55	13 55	14 33	14 55	15 55	16 33	16 55	16 55	17 55	18 33	18 52	19 55	20 33	20 55
London Liverpool Street 15 ⊖	a																						

		LE	LE 1	LE	LE	LE
Lowestoft	d		21 50			23 35
Oulton Broad North	d		21 54			23 39
Somerleyton	d		22 00			
Haddiscoe	d		22 03			
Great Yarmouth	d	21 22		22 22	23 20	
Berney Arms	d					
Reedham (Norfolk)	d		22 12	22 34	23 32	23 54
Cantley	d		22 16	22 38	23 36	
Buckenham	d					
Acle	d	21 32				
Lingwood	d	21 37				
Brundall	d	21 41	22 22	22 45	23 43	00 03
Brundall Gardens	d	21 44			23 45	
Norwich	a	21 55	22 33	22 55	23 55	00 13
London Liverpool Street 15 ⊖	a					

A until 25 September
B from 2 October
C not 23 May
D until 5 September
E from 12 September

Table 16

Mondays to Saturdays

Norwich-Cromer and Sheringham

		LE SX	LE SO	LE SO	LE SX	LE	LE	LE	LE	LE	LE	LE	LE	LE	LE	LE	LE	LE	LE	LE
Norwich	d	05 20	05 20	05 45	05 50	07 15	08 23	09 45	10 45	11 45	12 45	13 45	14 45	15 45	16 45	17 45	18 47	19 45	21 15	22 45
Salhouse	d		05 30	05 55	06 00	07 25	08 33	09 55		11 55		13 55		15 55	16 55	17 55		19 55	21 25	22 55
Hoveton & Wroxham	d	05 34	05 35	06 00	06 05	07 30	08 38	10 00	10 59	12 00	12 59	14 00	14 59	16 00	17 00	18 00	19 00	20 00	21 30	23 00
Worstead	d		05 42	06 07	06 12	07 37	08 45		11 06		13 06		15 06	16 07	17 07	18 07	19 07	20 07	21 37	23 07
North Walsham	a	05 44	05 48	06 13	06 18	07 43	08 51	10 10	11 11	12 10	13 11	14 10	15 11	16 13	17 13	18 13	19 13	20 13	21 43	23 13
	d	05 44	05 48	06 13	06 21	07 46	08 53	10 13	11 14	12 13	13 14	14 13	15 14	16 15	17 15	18 16	19 15	20 16	21 43	23 13
Gunton	d		05 54	06 19	06 27	07 52	08 59	10 19		12 19		14 19		16 21	17 21	18 22	19 21	20 22	21 49	23 19
Roughton Road	d		06 01	06 26	06 34	07 59	09 06		11 25		13 25		15 25	16 28	17 28	18 29	19 28	20 29	21 56	23 26
Cromer	a	05 59	06 06	06 31	06 39	08 04	09 11	10 29	11 30	12 29	13 30	14 29	15 30	16 33	17 33	18 34	19 33	20 34	22 01	23 31
	d	06 06	06 10	06 36	06 46	08 07	09 15	10 33	11 33	12 33	13 33	14 33	15 33	16 36	17 36	18 37	19 36	20 37	22 04	23 34
West Runton	d	06 10	06 14	06 40	06 50	08 11	09 19	10 37	11 37	12 37	13 37	14 37	15 37	16 40	17 40	18 41	19 40	20 41	22 08	23 38
Sheringham	a	06 15	06 19	06 45	06 55	08 15	09 23	10 42	11 42	12 42	13 42	14 42	15 42	16 45	17 45	18 45	19 45	20 45	22 13	23 43

Sundays

		LE	LE A	LE	LE A	LE	LE A	LE	LE A	LE	LE A	LE	LE A	LE
Norwich	d	08 36	09 45	10 36	11 45	12 36	13 45	14 36	15 45	16 36	17 45	18 36	19 45	20 36
Salhouse	d	08 46		10 46		12 46		14 46		16 46		18 46		20 46
Hoveton & Wroxham	d	08 51	09 59	10 51	11 59	12 51	13 59	14 51	15 59	16 51	17 59	18 51	19 59	20 51
Worstead	d	08 58		10 58		12 58		14 58		16 58		18 58		20 58
North Walsham	a	09 04	10 09	11 04	12 09	13 04	14 09	15 04	16 09	17 04	18 09	19 04	20 09	21 04
	d	09 04	10 11	11 07	12 11	13 07	14 11	15 07	16 11	17 07	18 11	19 07	20 11	21 07
Gunton	d	09 10		11 13		13 13		15 13		17 13		19 13		21 13
Roughton Road	d	09 17		11 20		13 20		15 20		17 20		19 20		21 20
Cromer	a	09 22	10 26	11 25	12 26	13 25	14 26	15 25	16 26	17 25	18 26	19 25	20 26	21 25
	d	09 26	10 30	11 29	12 30	13 29	14 30	15 29	16 30	17 29	18 30	19 29	20 30	21 29
West Runton	d	09 30		11 33		13 33		15 33		17 33		19 33		21 33
Sheringham	a	09 35	10 38	11 38	12 38	13 38	14 38	15 38	16 38	17 38	18 38	19 38	20 38	21 38

A until 5 September

Table 16

Mondays to Saturdays

Sheringham and Cromer-Norwich

		LE MX	LE SX	LE SO	LE SX	LE	LE	LE	LE	LE	LE	LE	LE	LE	LE	LE	LE	LE	LE	LE	LE
Sheringham	d	23p46		06 22	06 32	07 17	08 25	09 46	10 46	11 46	12 46	13 46	14 46	15 46	16 49	17 48	18 49	19 48	20 49	22 16	23 46
West Runton	d	23p50		06 26	06 36	07 21	08 29	09 50	10 50	11 50	12 50	13 50	14 50	15 50	16 53	17 52	18 53	19 52	20 53	22 20	23 50
Cromer	a	23p54		06 30	06 40	07 25	08 33	09 54	10 54	11 54	12 54	13 54	14 54	15 54	16 57	17 56	18 57	19 56	20 57	22 24	23 54
	d	23p57	06 03	06 33	06 43	07 28	08 36	09 57	10 57	11 57	12 57	13 57	14 57	15 57	17 00	17 59	19 00	19 59	21 00	22 27	23 57
Roughton Road	d		06 08	06 38	06 48	07 33	08 41	10 02		12 02		14 02	15 02	16 02		18 04		20 04	21 05	22 32	
Gunton	d		06 15	06 45	06 55	07 40	08 48		11 08		13 08			16 09		18 11		20 11	21 12	22 39	
North Walsham	a	00 12	06 20	06 50	07 00	07 45	08 53	10 12	11 13	12 12	13 13	14 12	15 13	16 15	17 15	18 16	19 15	20 16	21 17	22 44	00 12
	d	00 12	06 21	06 51	07 01	07 46	08 54	10 13	11 14	12 13	13 14	14 13	15 14	16 15	17 15	18 17	19 15	20 17	21 18	22 45	00 12
Worstead	d		06 25	06 55	07 05	07 50	08 58	10 17		12 17		14 17		16 20		18 21		20 21	21 22	22 49	
Hoveton & Wroxham	d	00 22	06 33	07 03	07 13	07 58	09 06	10 25	11 24	12 25	13 24	14 25	15 24	16 27	17 26	18 29	19 26	20 29	21 30	22 57	00 22
Salhouse	d		06 38	07 08	07 18	08 03	09 11		11 29		13 29		15 29	16 32		18 34		20 34	21 35	23 02	
Norwich	a	00 37	06 49	07 19	07 30	08 14	09 22	10 41	11 41	12 41	13 41	14 41	15 41	16 44	17 41	18 45	19 41	20 45	21 46	23 13	00 37

Sundays

		LE A	LE	LE B	LE	LE B	LE	LE B	LE	LE B	LE	LE B	LE	LE B	LE
Sheringham	d	23p46	09 43	10 43	11 43	12 43	13 43	14 43	15 43	16 43	17 43	18 43	19 43	20 43	21 43
West Runton	d	23p50	09 47		11 47		13 47		15 47		17 47		19 47		21 47
Cromer	a	23p54	09 51	10 49	11 51	12 49	13 51	14 49	15 51	16 49	17 51	18 49	19 51	20 49	21 51
	d	23p57	09 54	10 53	11 54	12 53	13 54	14 53	15 54	16 53	17 54	18 53	19 54	20 53	21 54
Roughton Road	d		09 59		11 59		13 59		15 59		17 59		19 59		21 59
Gunton	d		10 06		12 06		14 06		16 06		18 06		20 06		22 06
North Walsham	a	00 12	10 11	11 07	12 11	13 07	14 11	15 07	16 11	17 07	18 11	19 07	20 11	21 07	22 11
	d	00 12	10 12	11 08	12 12	13 08	14 12	15 08	16 12	17 08	18 12	19 08	20 12	21 08	22 12
Worstead	d		10 16		12 16		14 16		16 16		18 16		20 16		22 16
Hoveton & Wroxham	d	00 22	10 24	11 18	12 24	13 18	14 24	15 18	16 24	17 18	18 24	19 18	20 24	21 18	22 24
Salhouse	d		10 29		12 29		14 29		16 29		18 29		20 29		22 29
Norwich	a	00 37	10 40	11 33	12 40	13 33	14 40	15 33	16 40	17 33	18 40	19 33	20 40	21 33	22 40

A not 23 May

B until 5 September

Table 17

Mondays to Fridays

London, Norwich and Cambridge - Ely, Kings Lynn and Peterborough

		FC ■ A	LE MX ■	FC ■ B	FC MX ■	FC ■ A	XC ◇■ ⊼	XC ◇■ ⊼	LE ■	FC ■	EM ◇	LE ■	XC ◇■ ⊼	FC ■	LE ■	LE ■	EM ◇	FC ■	XC ◇■ ⊼	FC ■	LE ■	EM ◇
London Liverpool Street	d																					
London Kings Cross	d	22p04		23p15	23p15	23p02								05 45				06 45		07 15		
Ipswich	d											06b01										
Stansted Airport	d							05 15					06 06						07 21			
Norwich	d		22p40						05 33		05 50				06 33		06 52				07 37	07 57
Wymondham	d		22p52						05 45		06 02				06 45						07 49	
Spooner Row	d																					
Attleborough	d		22p59						05 52		06 09				06 52						07 56	
Eccles Road	d																					
Harling Road	d																					
Thetford	d		23p12						06 05		06 23				07 05		07 20				08 09	08 24
Brandon	d		23p20						06 13						07 13						08 17	
Lakenheath	d																					
Shippea Hill	d																					
Cambridge	d	23p16		00 13	00 13	00 15		05 55		06 18			06c52	06 58		07 22		07 35	08 00	08 04		
Waterbeach	d	23p22		00 19	00 19	00 21				06 24				07 04				07 41		08 10		
Ely ■	a	23p31	23p38	00 29	00 29	00 31		06 09	06 30	06 33	06 45	06 59	07 06	07 13	07 30	07 38	07 41	07 51	08 14	08 19	08 37	08 46
Cambridge	a		00 02				05d15		06 51						07 51						08 55	
Ely ■	d	23p31					05 30	06 10		06 33	06 51	07 00	07 08	07 13			07 45	07 51	08 15	08 21		08 50
Littleport	d	23p38								06 43				07 20				07 58		08 28		
Downham Market	d	23p47								06 54				07 29				08 07		08 37		
Watlington	d	23p52								07 00				07 35				08 13		08 43		
Kings Lynn	a	00 01								07 10				07 45				08 23		08 53		
Manea	d							06x20														
March	d						05 46	06 28			07 07	07 16	07 26				08 01		08 31			09 07
Whittlesea	d						05 58	06 39				07 27	07 39				08 13					
Peterborough ■	a						06 08	06 50			07 25	07 38	07 50				08 24		08 50			09 25

		FC ■	LE ◇■	XC ◇■ ⊼	LE ■	EM ◇	FC ■	XC ◇■ ⊼	LE ■	EM ◇	FC ■	LE ■	XC ◇■ ⊼	LE ■	EM ◇	FC ■	XC ◇■ ⊼	LE ■	EM ◇	FC ■	LE ◇■	XC ◇■ ⊼	LE ■
London Liverpool Street	d		06 38																		10 38		
London Kings Cross	d	07 45					08 45				09 45					10 45				11 45			
Ipswich	d		08 02									10 02									12f02		
Stansted Airport	d			08 21				09 21					10 21				11 25					12 25	
Norwich	d				08 40	08 57			09 40	09 57				10 40	10 57			11 40	11 57				12 40
Wymondham	d				08 52				09 52					10 52				11 52					12 52
Spooner Row	d																						
Attleborough	d				08 59				09 59					10 59				11 59					12 59
Eccles Road	d																						
Harling Road	d																						
Thetford	d				09 12	09 24			10 12	10 24				11 12	11 24			12 12	12 24				13 12
Brandon	d				09 20				10 20					11 20				12 20					13 20
Lakenheath	d																						
Shippea Hill	d																						
Cambridge	d	08 38		09 00			09 35	10e00			10 35		11 00			11 33	12 00			12 33		13 00	
Waterbeach	d	08 44					09 41				10 41					11 39				12 39			
Ely ■	a	08 53	08 58	09 14	09 38	09 45	09 50	10 14	10 37	10 48	10 50	10 58	11 14	11 37	11 46	11 48	12 14	12 37	12 45	12 48	12 58	13 14	13 38
Cambridge	a				09 58				10 58					11 58				12 58					13 58
Ely ■	d	08 54	08 58	09 15		09 52	09 50	10 15		10 52	10 50	10 58	11 15		11 52	11 48	12 15		12 52	12 48	12 58	13 15	
Littleport	d	09 01					09 57				10 57					11 55				12 55			
Downham Market	d	09 10					10 06				11 06					12 04				13 04			
Watlington	d	09 16					10 12				11 12					12 10				13 10			
Kings Lynn	a	09 25					10 21				11 21					12 20				13 20			
Manea	d																						
March	d		09 15	09 31				10 31				11 15	11 31				12 31				13 15	13 31	
Whittlesea	d		09 26									11 26									13 26		
Peterborough ■	a		09 37	09 50		10 26		10 50		11 25		11 37	11 50		12 24		12 50		13 25		13 37	13 50	

A MO from 19 July until 6 September

B MO until 12 July, MO from 13 September

b arr. 0555

c arr. 0638

e arr. 0954

f arr. 1156

Table 17

London, Norwich and Cambridge - Ely, Kings Lynn and Peterborough

Mondays to Fridays

		FC ■		EM ◇	XC ◇■	LE ■	EM ◇	FC ■	LE ◇■	XC ◇■	LE ■	FC ■		EM ◇	FC ■	XC ◇■	LE ■	FC ■	EM ◇	FC ■	LE ◇■	XC ◇■		LE ■	LE ■
London Liverpool Street	d								12 38												14 38				15 58
London Kings Cross	d	12 45						13 45							14 45					15 45					
Ipswich	d								14b02												16c02				
Stansted Airport	d				13 25					14 25						15 20						16 25			
Norwich	d			12 57		13 40	13 57				14 40			14 57			15 40		15 52					16 38	
Wymondham	d					13 52					14 52						15 52							16 50	
Spooner Row	d																							16x54	
Attleborough	d					13 59					14 59						15 59		16 09					16 59	
Eccles Road	d																		16 14						
Harling Road	d																		16 18						
Thetford	d			13 24		14 12	14 24				15 12			15 24			16 12		16 27					17 12	
Brandon	d					14 20					15 20						16 20							17 20	
Lakenheath	d																								
Shippea Hill	d																								
Cambridge	d	13 33			14 00			14 33		15 00		15 24			15 35	16 00		16 24		16 35		17 00			17 22
Waterbeach	d	13 39						14 39				15 30			15 41			16 30		16 41					17 28
Ely ■	a	13 48		13 47	14 14	14 40	14 45	14 48	14 58	15 14	15 37	15 40		15 45	15 50	16 14	16 37	16 40	16 48	16 50	16 58	17 14		17 37	17 38
Cambridge	a					14 58					15 58						16 58							17 58	
Ely ■	d	13 48		13 52	14 15		14 52	14 49	14 58	15 15				15 52	15 50	16 15			16 52	16 50	16 58	17 15			
Littleport	d	13 55						14 57							15 57					16 57					
Downham Market	d	14 04						15 06							16 06					17 06					
Watlington	d	14 10						15 12							16 12					17 12					
Kings Lynn	a	14 20						15 21							16 21					17 21					
Manea	d																								
March	d				14 31				15 15	15 31						16 31					17 15	17 31			
Whittlesea	d								15 26												17 26				
Peterborough ■	a			14 25	14 50		15 25		15 37	15 50				16 25		16 50			17 26		17 37	17 50			

		EM ◇	FC ■	XC ◇■	FC ■	LE ■	LE ■	LE ■	EM ◇	FC ■	LE ■	XC ◇■	FC ■	LE ■	LE ■	EM ◇	FC ■	XC ◇■		LE ■	LE ■	FC ■	XC ◇■	LE ■	FC ■
London Liverpool Street	d					16 58					16 32			17 58						18 58					
London Kings Cross	d		16 44		17 14					17 44			18 14				18 44					19 45			20 15
Ipswich	d										17 49													20 16	
Stansted Airport	d			17 18								18 21						19 21					20 21		
Norwich	d	16 57					17 35		17 54						18 40	18 57					19 45				
Wymondham	d	17 09					17 47		18 06						18 52						19 57				
Spooner Row	d																								
Attleborough	d						17 54		18 13						18 59						20 04				
Eccles Road	d						17 59																		
Harling Road	d						18 03																		
Thetford	d	17 27					18 12		18 27						19 12	19 24					20 17				
Brandon	d						18 20								19 20						20 25				
Lakenheath	d																								
Shippea Hill	d																								
Cambridge	d		17 39	17 51	18 05	18 14		18 24		18e39		19 00	19 05	19 19			19f39	20 00		20 15		20 40	21 00		21 10
Waterbeach	d		17 45			18 20		18 30		18 45				19 25			19 45			20 21		20 46			21 16
Ely ■	a	17 48	17 55	18 06	18 20	18 30	18 39	18 40	18 48	18 55	18 52	19 14	19 18	19 34	19 37	19 48	19 55	20 14		20 30	20 44	20 55	21 14	21 19	21 25
Cambridge	a						18 58								19 58						21 04				
Ely ■	d	17 52	17 56	18 06		18 30			18 52	18 56	19 01	19 15	19 22	19 35		19 52	19 56	20 15		20 31		20 55	21 15	21 19	21 25
Littleport	d		18 03			18 37				19 03				19 42			20 03			20 38		21 02			21 32
Downham Market	d		18 12			18 47				19 12			19 38	19 52			20 12			20 47		21 11			21 41
Watlington	d		18 18			18 53				19 18				19 58			20 18			20 53		21 17			21 47
Kings Lynn	a		18 28			19 05				19 28			19 53	20 10			20 28			21 05		21 26			21 56
Manea	d			18x17																					
March	d			18 25					19 08		19 17	19 31						20 31					21 31	21 36	
Whittlesea	d										19 29													21 47	
Peterborough ■	a	18 25		18 50					19 31		19 42	19 50				20 26		20 50					21 50	21 58	

		FC FO ■	FC FX ■	LE ■		FC ■	FC ■	LE ■	FC FO ■	FC FX ■
London Liverpool Street	d									
London Kings Cross	d	20 45	20 45			21 15	22 15		23 15	23 15
Ipswich	d									
Stansted Airport	d									
Norwich	d			21 15				22 40		
Wymondham	d			21 27				22 52		
Spooner Row	d									
Attleborough	d			21 34				22 59		
Eccles Road	d									
Harling Road	d									
Thetford	d			21 47				23 12		
Brandon	d			21 55				23 20		
Lakenheath	d									
Shippea Hill	d									
Cambridge	d	21 35	21 35			22 08	23 08		00 13	00 13
Waterbeach	d	21 41	21 41			22 14	23 14		00 19	00 19
Ely ■	a	21 52	21 54	22 14		22 23	23 23	23 38	00 28	00 29
Cambridge	a			22 33				00 02		
Ely ■	d	21 53				22 23	23 23		00 29	
Littleport	d	22 00				22 30	23 30		00 36	
Downham Market	d	22 09				22 39	23 39		00 45	
Watlington	d	22 15				22 45	23 45		00 50	
Kings Lynn	a	22 24				22 54	23 54		01 00	
Manea	d									
March	d									
Whittlesea	d									
Peterborough ■	a									

b arr. 1356
c arr. 1556
e arr. 1831
f arr. 1933

Table 17

London, Norwich and Cambridge - Ely, Kings Lynn and Peterborough

Saturdays

		LE ■	FC ■	XC ◇■	XC ◇■	LE ■	EM ◇	FC ■	LE ■	XC ◇■		LE ■	EM ◇	FC ■	XC ◇■	LE ■	LE ■	EM ◇	FC ■	LE ◇■		XC ◇■	LE ■	EM ◇	FC ■
London Liverpool Street	d															06 58				06 38					
London Kings Cross	d		23p15											06 45					07 45						08 45
Ipswich	d								06 00											08 02					
Stansted Airport	d				05 25					06 25					07 25							08 25			
Norwich	d	22p40				05 38	05 52					06 40	06 52				07 40	07 57					08 40	08 57	
Wymondham	d	22p52				05 50	06 04					06 52					07 52						08 52		
Spooner Row	d																								
Attleborough	d	22p59				05 57	06 11					06 59					07 59						08 59		
Eccles Road	d																								
Harling Road	d																								
Thetford	d	23p12				06 10	06 25					07 12	07 20				08 12	08 24					09 12	09 24	
Brandon	d	23p20				06 18						07 20					08 20						09 20		
Lakenheath	d																								
Shippea Hill	d																								
Cambridge	d		00 13		05 55			06 32		06 56				07 35	08 00	08 20			08 35			09 00			09 35
Waterbeach	d		00 19					06 38						07 41		08 26			08 41						09 41
Ely ■	a	23p38	00 28		06 09	06 35	06 46	06 47	06 56	07 10		07 37	07 41	07 50	08 14	08 36	08 37	08 47	08 50	08 58		09 14	09 38	09 45	09 50
Cambridge	a	00 02		05d15		06 55						07 58					08 58						09 58		
Ely ■	d		00 29	05 30	06 10		06 51	06 47	06 57	07 11			07 44	07 50	08 15			08 54	08 50	08 58		09 15		09 51	09 50
Littleport	d		00 36					06 54						07 57					08 57						09 57
Downham Market	d		00 45					07 03						08 06					09 06						10 06
Watlington	d		00 50					07 09						08 11					09 11						10 11
Kings Lynn	a		01 00					07 20						08 21					09 21						10 21
Manea	d				06x20																				
March	d			05 46	06 28		07 07		07 14	07 29			08 01		08 31			09 11		09 16		09 31			
Whittlesea	d			05 58	06 39				07 25	07 40			08 12							09 27					
Peterborough ■	a			06 08	06 50		07 25		07 37	07 50			08 26		08 50			09 28		09 38		09 50		10 25	

		XC ◇■	LE ■	EM ◇	FC ■	LE ◇■		XC ◇■	LE ■	EM ◇	FC ■	XC ◇■	LE ■	EM ◇	FC ■	LE ■			XC ◇■	LE ■	EM ◇	FC ■	XC ◇■	LE ■	EM ◇
London Liverpool Street	d					08 38										10 38									
London Kings Cross	d				09 45						10 45				11 45							12 45			
Ipswich	d					10 02										12b02									
Stansted Airport	d	09 25						10 25				11 25							12 25				13 25		
Norwich	d		09 40	09 57					10 40	10 57			11 40	11 57						12 40	12 57			13 40	13 57
Wymondham	d		09 52						10 52				11 52							12 52				13 52	
Spooner Row	d																								
Attleborough	d		09 59						10 59				11 59							12 59				13 59	
Eccles Road	d																								
Harling Road	d																								
Thetford	d		10 12	10 24					11 12	11 24			12 12	12 24						13 12	13 24			14 12	14 24
Brandon	d		10 20						11 20				12 20							13 20				14 20	
Lakenheath	d		10x25																						
Shippea Hill	d																								
Cambridge	d	10 00			10 35			11 00			11 35	12 00			12 35				13 00			13 35	14 00		
Waterbeach	d				10 41						11 41				12 41							13 41			
Ely ■	a	10 14	10 38	10 46	10 50	10 58		11 14	11 38	11 46	11 50	12 14	12 37	12 45	12 50	12 58			13 14	13 37	13 46	13 50	14 14	14 37	14 45
Cambridge	a		10 58						11 58				12 58							13 58				14 58	
Ely ■	d	10 15		10 53	10 50	10 58		11 15		11 53	11 50	12 15		12 54	12 50	12 58			13 15		13 53	13 50	14 15		14 53
Littleport	d				10 57						11 57				12 57							13 57			
Downham Market	d				11 06						12 06				13 06							14 06			
Watlington	d				11 11						12 11				13 11							14 11			
Kings Lynn	a				11 21						12 21				13 21							14 21			
Manea	d																								
March	d	10 31				11 15		11 31				12 31				13 15			13 31				14 31		
Whittlesea	d					11 26										13 26									
Peterborough ■	a	10 50		11 24		11 37		11 50		12 24		12 50		13 26		13 37			13 50		14 25		14 50		15 25

b arr. 1156

Table 17

London, Norwich and Cambridge - Ely, Kings Lynn and Peterborough

		FC ■	LE ■	XC ◇■ ✠	LE ■	EM ◇	FC ■	XC ◇■ ✠	LE ■	EM ◇	FC ■ A	LE ◇■	FC ■ B	XC ◇■ ✠	LE ■	EM ◇	FC ■ A	FC ■ B	XC ◇■ ✠	LE ■	EM ◇	FC ■ A
London Liverpool Street	d		12 38									14 38										
London Kings Cross	d	13 45					14 45				15 45		15 38				16 45	16 38				17 45
Ipswich	d		14b02									16c02										
Stansted Airport	d			14 25				15 25						16 25					17 25			
Norwich	d				14 40	14 57			15 35	15 52					16 38	16 57				17 35	17 54	
Wymondham	d				14 52				15 47						16 50	17 09				17 47	18 06	
Spooner Row	d														16x54							
Attleborough	d				14 59				15 54	16 09					16 59					17 54	18 13	
Eccles Road	d								15 59											17 59		
Harling Road	d								16 03											18 03		
Thetford	d				15 12	15 24			16 12	16 23					17 12	17 27				18 12	18 27	
Brandon	d				15 20				16 20						17 20					18 20		
Lakenheath	d																					
Shippea Hill	d																					
Cambridge	d	14 35		15 00			15 35	16 00			16 35		16 50	17 00			17 35	17 50	18 00			18 40
Waterbeach	d	14 41					15 41				16 41		16 56				17 41	17 56				18 46
Ely ■	a	14 50	14 58	15 14	15 37	15 48	15 50	16 14	16 37	16 47	16 50	16 58	17 05	17 14	17 37	17 48	17 50	18 05	18 14	18 37	18 48	18 55
Cambridge	a				15 58				16 58						17 58					18 58		
Ely ■	d	14 50	14 58	15 15		15 52	15 50	16 15		16 52	16 50	16 58	17 05	17 15		17 52	17 50	18 05	18 15		18 53	18 55
Littleport	d	14 57					15 57				16 57		17 12				17 57	18 12				19 02
Downham Market	d	15 06					16 06				17 06		17 21				18 06	18 21				19 11
Watlington	d	15 11					16 11				17 11		17 26				18 11	18 26				19 17
Kings Lynn	a	15 21					16 21				17 21		17 35				18 21	18 35				19 27
Manea	d																		18x25			
March	d		15 15	15 31				16 31				17 15		17 31					18 33		19 09	
Whittlesea	d		15 26									17 26										
Peterborough ■	a		15 37	15 50		16 25		16 50		17 26		17 37		17 50		18 25			18 50		19 29	

		LE ■	FC ■ B	XC ◇■ ✠	FC ■ A	LE ■	EM ◇	FC ■ A	FC ■ B	XC ◇■ ✠	LE ■	FC ■ A	LE ■	FC ■ B	LE ■	FC ■ A	FC ■ B	FC ■ A	FC ■ B	LE ■	FC ■ A	FC ■ B
London Liverpool Street	d	16 38											18 46									
London Kings Cross	d		17 38		18 15			18 45	18 38			19 45		19 38		20 45	20 38	22 15	22 04		23 15	23 04
Ipswich	d	18e02											20f02									
Stansted Airport	d			18 25						19 25												
Norwich	d					18 40	18 57				19 40				20 40					22 40		
Wymondham	d					18 52					19 52				20 52					22 52		
Spooner Row	d																					
Attleborough	d					18 59					19 59				20 59					22 59		
Eccles Road	d																					
Harling Road	d																					
Thetford	d					19 12	19 24				20 12				21 12					23 12		
Brandon	d					19 20					20 20				21 20					23 20		
Lakenheath	d																					
Shippea Hill	d					19x28																
Cambridge	d		18 50	19 00	19 04			19 40	19 50	20 00		20 40		20 50		21 40	21 50	23g11	23g16		00 13	00 16
Waterbeach	d		18 56					19 46	19 56			20 46		20 56		21 46	21 56	23 17	23 21		00 19	00 21
Ely ■	a	18 58	19 05	19 14	19 18	19 37	19 47	19 55	20 05	20 14	20 37	20 55	20 58	21 05	21 37	21 55	22 05	23 26	23 30	23 37	00 28	00 30
Cambridge	a					19 58					20 58				21 58					23 58		
Ely ■	d	19 00	19 05	19 15			19 53	19 55	20 05	20 15		20 55	20 58	21 05		21 55	22 05	23 26	23 30		00 29	00 30
Littleport	d		19 12					20 02	20 12			21 02		21 12		22 02	22 12	23 33	23 37		00 36	00 37
Downham Market	d		19 21					20 11	20 21			21 11		21 21		22 11	22 21	23 43	23 46		00 45	00 46
Watlington	d		19 26					20 17	20 26			21 17		21 26		22 17	22 26	23 48	23 51		00 50	00 51
Kings Lynn	a		19 35					20 27	20 35			21 27		21 35		22 27	22 35	23 58	00 01		00 59	01 01
Manea	d																					
March	d	19 16		19 31						20 31			21 15									
Whittlesea	d	19 28											21 26									
Peterborough ■	a	19 38		19 50			20 25			20 50			21 37									

A until 10 July, from 11 September
B from 17 July until 4 September
b arr. 1356
c arr. 1556
e arr. 1756
f arr. 1956
g arr. 2305

Table 17

London, Norwich and Cambridge - Ely, Kings Lynn and Peterborough

		FC ■ A	LE B	FC ■ C	FC ■ D	FC ■ E	FC ■ C	LE ■	FC ■ F	EM ◇ B	LE ■	FC ■ C	XC ◇■ ✠	FC ■ F	EM ◇	FC ■ C	XC ◇■ ✠	LE ■	FC ■ F	LE ■	FC ■ C	LE ■	XC ◇■ ✠	FC ■ F
London Liverpool Street	d																							
London Kings Cross	d	23p15		07 38	07 52		08 38		09 15			09 38		10 15		10 38			11 15		11 38			12 15
Ipswich	d		07 55								09 55									11 55				
Stansted Airport	d												10 25				11 25						12 25	
Norwich	d							09 15		09 33					10 47			11 15				12 15		
Wymondham	d							09 27										11 27				12 27		
Spooner Row	d																							
Attleborough	d							09 34										11 34				12 34		
Eccles Road	d																							
Harling Road	d																							
Thetford	d							09 47		10 00					11 14			11 47				12 47		
Brandon	d							09 55										11 55				12 55		
Lakenheath	d							10x00										12x00						
Shippea Hill	d																							
Cambridge	d	00 13		08 50	09 07	09 07	09 50		10 05			10 50	10 56	11 05		11 50	11 57		12 05		12 50		12 57	13 05
Waterbeach	d	00 19		08 56	09 13	09 13	09 56		10 10			10 56		11 10		11 56			12 10		12 56			13 10
Ely ■	a	00 28	08 51	09 05	09 22	09 22	10 04	10 19	10 19	10 25	10 51	11 05	11 10	11 19	11 35	12 05	12 12	12 19	12 19	12 51	13 05	13 12	13 12	13 19
Cambridge	a							10 36										12 36				13 32		
Ely ■	d	00 29	08 52	09 05	09 22	09 22	10 05		10 19	10 32	10 52	11 05	11 11	11 19	11 39	12 05	12 15		12 19	12 52	13 05		13 15	13 19
Littleport	d	00 36		09 12	09 29	09 29	10 12		10 26			11 12		11 26		12 12			12 26		13 12			13 26
Downham Market	d	00 45		09 21	09 38	09 38	10 21		10 35			11 21		11 35		12 21			12 35		13 21			13 35
Watlington	d	00 50		09 26	09 43	09 44	10 26		10 40			11 26		11 40		12 26			12 40		13 26			13 40
Kings Lynn	a	00 59		09 35	09 52	09 52	10 35		10 50			11 35		11 50		12 35			12 50		13 35			13 50
Manea	d																							
March	d		09 09								11 09		11 27				12 31			13 09			13 31	
Whittlesea	d		09 20								11 20									13 20				
Peterborough ■	a		09 36							11 09	11 36		11 50		12 16		12 50			13 31			13 50	

		FC ■ C	LE ■	XC ◇■ ✠	FC ■ F	EM ◇ B	EM ◇ E	LE ■	FC ■ C	LE ■	XC ◇■ ✠	FC ■ F	EM ◇ B	EM ◇ E	FC ■ C	XC ◇■ ✠	LE ■	FC ■ F	LE ■	FC ■ C	LE ■	XC ◇■ ✠	FC ■ F
London Liverpool Street	d																						
London Kings Cross	d	12 38			13 15				13 38			14 15			14 38			15 15		15 38			16 15
Ipswich	d							13 55											15 55				
Stansted Airport	d			13 25							14 25					15 25						16 25	
Norwich	d		13 15			13 49	13 49			14 15			14 47	14 49			15 15				16 15		
Wymondham	d		13 27							14 27							15 27				16 27		
Spooner Row	d																						
Attleborough	d		13 34							14 34							15 34				16 34		
Eccles Road	d																						
Harling Road	d																						
Thetford	d		13 47			14 16	14 16			14 47			15 14	15 16			15 47				16 47		
Brandon	d		13 55							14 55							15 55				16 55		
Lakenheath	d																16x00						
Shippea Hill	d																						
Cambridge	d	13 50		13 57	14 05				14 50		14 57	15 05			15 50	15 57		16 05		16 50		16 56	17 05
Waterbeach	d	13 56			14 10				14 56			15 10			15 56			16 10		16 56			17 10
Ely ■	a	14 05	14 12	14 11	14 19	14 42	14 42	14 51	15 05	15 12	15 11	15 19	15 40	15 42	16 05	16 12	16 14	16 19	16 51	17 05	17 12	17 12	17 19
Cambridge	a		14 32							15 32							16 32				17 32		
Ely ■	d	14 05		14 15	14 19	14 45	14 45	14 52	15 05		15 15	15 19	15 48	15 48	16 05	16 15		16 19	16 52	17 05		17 15	17 19
Littleport	d	14 12			14 26				15 12			15 26			16 12			16 26		17 12			17 26
Downham Market	d	14 21			14 35				15 21			15 35			16 21			16 35		17 21			17 35
Watlington	d	14 26			14 40				15 26			15 40			16 26			16 40		17 26			17 40
Kings Lynn	a	14 35			14 50				15 35			15 50			16 35			16 50		17 35			17 50
Manea	d																						
March	d			14 31				15 09			15 31					16 31			17 09			17 31	
Whittlesea	d							15 20											17 20				
Peterborough ■	a			14 50		15 24	15 24	15 31			15 50		16 22	16 22		16 50			17 31			17 50	

A from 23 May until 11 July, from 12 September
B until 5 September
C from 18 July until 5 September
D until 11 July
E from 12 September
F until 11 July, from 12 September

Table 17

Sundays

London, Norwich and Cambridge - Ely, Kings Lynn and Peterborough

		EM ◇ A	EM ◇ B	FC 1 C	LE 1	XC ◇1	FC 1 D	EM ◇	LE 1	FC 1 C	LE 1	XC ◇1	FC 1 D	EM ◇ E	EM ◇ F	FC 1 C	XC ◇1	FC 1 D	FC 1 C	LE 1	FC 1 D	EM ◇
London Liverpool Street	d																					
London Kings Cross	d			16 38			17 15			17 38			18 15			18 38		19 15	19 38		20 15	
Ipswich	d								17 55													
Stansted Airport	d					17 25						18 25					19 25					
Norwich	d	16 57	16 57		17 15			17 56			18 15			18 57	18 57					20 15		20 52
Wymondham	d				17 27						18 27									20 27		
Spooner Row	d																					
Attleborough	d				17 34						18 34									20 34		
Eccles Road	d																					
Harling Road	d																					
Thetford	d	17 24	17 24		17 47			18 23			18 47			19 24	19 24					20 47		21 19
Brandon	d				17 55						18 55									20 55		
Lakenheath	d																					
Shippea Hill	d																					
Cambridge	d			17 50		17 57	18 04			18 50		18 57	19 05			19 50	19 57	20 05	20 50		21 05	
Waterbeach	d			17 56			18 10			18 56			19 10			19 56		20 10	20 56		21 10	
Ely 6	a	17 45	17 46	18 05	18 12	18 12	18 19	18 44	18 51	19 05	19 12	19 12	19 19	19 45	19 45	20 05	20 12	20 19	21 05	21 12	21 19	21 40
Cambridge	a				18 32						19 32									21 32		
Ely 6	d	17 48	17 50	18 05		18 15	18 19	18 48	18 52	19 05		19 15	19 19	19 49	19 49	20 05	20 15	20 19	21 05		21 19	21 44
Littleport	d			18 12			18 26			19 12			19 26			20 12		20 26	21 12		21 26	
Downham Market	d			18 21			18 35			19 21			19 35			20 21		20 35	21 21		21 35	
Watlington	d			18 26			18 40			19 26			19 40			20 26		20 40	21 26		21 40	
Kings Lynn	a			18 35			18 50			19 35			19 50			20 35		20 50	21 35		21 50	
Manea	d																					
March	d					18 31			19 09			19 31					20 31					
Whittlesea	d								19 20													
Peterborough 8	a	18 25	18 25			18 50		19 24	19 32			19 50		20 29	20 28		20 50					22 20

		FC 1 C	FC 1 D	FC 1 D	FC 1 C	FC 1 D	FC 1 C
London Liverpool Street	d						
London Kings Cross	d	20 38	21 15	22 15	22 04	23 15	23 02
Ipswich	d						
Stansted Airport	d						
Norwich	d						
Wymondham	d						
Spooner Row	d						
Attleborough	d						
Eccles Road	d						
Harling Road	d						
Thetford	d						
Brandon	d						
Lakenheath	d						
Shippea Hill	d						
Cambridge	d	21 50	22 05	23 05	23 16	00 13	00 15
Waterbeach	d	21 56	22 10	23 10	23 22	00 19	00 21
Ely 6	a	22 05	22 19	23 19	23 31	00 29	00 31
Cambridge	a						
Ely 6	d	22 05	22 19	23 19	23 31		
Littleport	d	22 12	22 26	23 26	23 38		
Downham Market	d	22 21	22 35	23 35	23 47		
Watlington	d	22 26	22 40	23 40	23 52		
Kings Lynn	a	22 35	22 50	23 50	00 01		
Manea	d						
March	d						
Whittlesea	d						
Peterborough 8	a						

A until 5 September, from 24 October
B from 12 September until 17 October
C from 18 July until 5 September
D until 11 July, from 12 September
E from 12 September
F until 5 September

Table 17

Mondays to Fridays

Peterborough, Kings Lynn and Ely - Cambridge, Norwich and London

		FC MX 1	LE MX 1	FC 1	LE 1	LE 1	FC 1	LE 1	FC 1	EM ◇	LE 1	FC 1	XC ◇1	LE 1	FC 1	LE 1	EM ◇	FC 1	LE 1	LE 1	XC ◇1	FC 1	LE 1
Peterborough 8	d									06b27			07 09				07 35			07 46	08 18		
Whittlesea	d												07 18							07 54			
March	d									06 43			07 29				07 51			08 05	08 34		
Manea	d												07x37										
Kings Lynn	d	22p28			05 19		05 52	06 18				06 52			07 23			07 55				08 27	
Watlington	d	22p35			05 26		05 59	06 25				06 59			07 30			08 02				08 34	
Downham Market	d	22p41			05 33		06 05	06 32				07 05			07 36			08 08				08 40	
Littleport	d	22p50			05 42		06 14	06 41				07 14			07 45			08 17				08 49	
Ely 6	a	22p58			05 51		06 22	06 49		07 01		07 22	07 51		07 54		08 11	08 25		08 30	08 50	08 57	
Cambridge	d		22p55			06 05					07 04		08 09						08 12		09 10		09 12
Ely 6	d	22p58	23p10	05 26	05 52	06 20	06 22	06 50	06 54	07 05	07 19	07 22		07 30	07 54	08 03	08 15	08 25	08 28	08 30		08 57	09 27
Waterbeach	d	23p07		05 35	06 01		06 32	06 59				07 32			08 04	08 12		08 35				09 07	
Cambridge	a	23p14		05 44	06 10		06 40	07 08	07 11			07 40	08 08	07 47	08 14	08 20		08 43			09 08	09 16	
Shippea Hill	d										07x28												
Lakenheath	d																						
Brandon	d		23p26			06 36				07 20	07 38								08 44				09 43
Thetford	d		23p34			06 45				07 29	07 47						08 37		08 53				09 52
Harling Road	d					06 53					07 55												
Eccles Road	d					06 57					07 59												
Attleborough	d		23p48			07 03				07 43	08 05						08 51		09 07				10 06
Spooner Row	d										08x10												10x11
Wymondham	d		23p55			07 10				07 50	08 14						08 58		09 14				10 15
Norwich	a		00 12			07 30				08 13	08 30						09 13		09 30				10 30
Stansted Airport	a												08 38								09 38		
Ipswich	a																			09 26			
London Kings Cross	a	00 42		06 38			07 39		08 06			08 39			09 12			09 41				10 13	
London Liverpool Street	a				07 34			08 34						09 19		09 49				10 46			

		FC 1	EM ◇	XC ◇1	EM ◇	LE ◇1	LE 1	FC 1	XC ◇1	EM ◇	FC 1	LE 1	XC ◇1	EM ◇	LE ◇1	FC 1	LE 1	XC ◇1	EM ◇	FC 1	LE 1	XC ◇1	EM ◇
Peterborough 8	d		08 59	09 18	09 40	09 45			10 18	10 44			11 18	11 38	11 45			12 18	12 43			13 16	13 40
Whittlesea	d					09 53									11 53								
March	d			09 34		10 04			10 34				11 34		12 04			12 34				13 34	
Manea	d																						
Kings Lynn	d	08 59						09 59			10 56					11 56				12 56			
Watlington	d	09 06						10 06			11 03					12 03				13 03			
Downham Market	d	09 12						10 12			11 09					12 09				13 09			
Littleport	d	09 21						10 21			11 18					12 18				13 18			
Ely 6	a	09 29	09 41	09 52	10 13	10 23		10 29	10 52	11 16	11 26		11 52	12 11	12 22	12 26		12 52	13 16	13 26		13 52	14 13
Cambridge	d			10 08			10 12		11 10			11 12	12 10				12 12	13 10			13 12	14 10	
Ely 6	d	09 29	09 44		10 16	10 26	10 27	10 29		11 19	11 26	11 28		12 15	12 30	12 26	12 27		13 20	13 26	13 29		14 16
Waterbeach	d	09 38						10 38			11 35					12 35				13 35			
Cambridge	a	09 47		10 08				10 47	11 08		11 44		12 08			12 44		13 08		13 44		14 08	
Shippea Hill	d																						
Lakenheath	d																						
Brandon	d						10 43					11 44					12 43				13 45		
Thetford	d		10 05		10 39		10 52			11 41		11 53		12 36			12 52		13 41		13 54		14 37
Harling Road	d																						
Eccles Road	d																						
Attleborough	d						11 06					12 07					13 06				14 08		
Spooner Row	d																						
Wymondham	d						11 13					12 14					13 13				14 15		
Norwich	a		10 43		11 13		11 30			12 13		12 30		13 13			13 30		14 13		14 30		15 13
Stansted Airport	a			10 45					11 45				12 45					13 45				14 45	
Ipswich	a					11 25									13 25								
London Kings Cross	a	10 46						11 40			12 32					13 33				14 33			
London Liverpool Street	a					12 45									14 45								

b arr. 0617

Table 17

Peterborough, Kings Lynn and Ely - Cambridge, Norwich and London

		FC	LE	LE	XC	EM	FC	LE	XC	FC	EM	LE	FC	LE	XC	EM	FC	LE	XC	FC	LE	LE
		■	■	■	◇■ ⊥	◇	■	■	◇■ ⊥	■	◇	◇■	■	■	◇■ ⊥	◇	■	■	◇■ ⊥	■	■	◇■
Peterborough ■	d			13 45	14 18	14 40			15 16		15 35	15 45			16 18	16 36			17 18			17 45
Whittlesea	d			13 53								15 53							17 26			17 53
March	d			14 04	14 34				15 34			16 04			16 34				17 37			18 04
Manea	d																		17x44			
Kings Lynn	d	13 56					14 56						15 56				16 54			17 36		
Watlington	d	14 03					15 03						16 03				17 01			17 43		
Downham Market	d	14 09					15 09						16 09				17 07			17 49		
Littleport	d	14 18					15 18						16 18				17 16			17 58		
Ely ■	a	14 26		14 29	14 52	15 13	15 26		15 52		16 08	16 22	16 26		16 52	17 09	17 24		17 58	18 06		18 22
Cambridge	d		14 12		15 10			15 12	16 10					16 12	17 10			17 12	18 18		18 10	
Ely ■	d	14 26	14 27	14 30		15 16	15 26	15 27		16 02	16 12	16 30	16 26	16 27		17 13	17 24	17 27		18 06	18 25	18 30
Waterbeach	d	14 35					15 35			16 11			16 35				17 33			18 15		
Cambridge	a	14 44			15 08		15 44		16 08	16 19			16 44		17 08		17 43		18 16	18 22		
Shippea Hill	d																					
Lakenheath	d																					
Brandon	d		14 43					15 43						16 43				17 43			18 41	
Thetford	d		14 52			15 37		15 52			16 33			16 52		17 34		17 52			18 50	
Harling Road	d																					
Eccles Road	d																					
Attleborough	d		15 06					16 06						17 06				18 06			19 04	
Spooner Row	d																					
Wymondham	d		15 13					16 13						17 13				18 13			19 11	
Norwich	a		15 30			16 13		16 30			17 13			17 30		18 13		18 30			19 28	
Stansted Airport	a				15 45				16 45						17 39				18 45			
Ipswich	a			15 25								17 27										19 25
London Kings Cross	a	15 33					16 33						17 39				18 37			19 34		
London Liverpool Street	a											18 51										20 46

		XC	FC	FC	EM	XC	LE	FC	EM	LE	LE	FC	LE	XC	FC	EM	LE	XC	FC	LE
		◇■ ⊥	■ A	■ B	◇	◇■ ⊥	■	■	◇	◇■	■	■	■	◇■ ⊥	■	◇	■	◇■ ⊥	■	■
Peterborough ■	d	18 18			18 42	19 18			19 37	19 46				21 16		21 37	22 05	22 18		
Whittlesea	d									19 54							22 13			
March	d	18 34			18 58	19 34				20 05				21 34			22 24	22 35		
Manea	d																			
Kings Lynn	d		18 35	18 36				19 36				20 36			21 36				22 28	
Watlington	d		18 42	18 43				19 43				20 43			21 43				22 35	
Downham Market	d		18 48	18 49				19 49				20 49			21 49				22 41	
Littleport	d		18 57	18 58				19 58				20 58			21 58				22 50	
Ely ■	a	18 52	19 05	19 06	19 24	19 52		20 08	20 13	20 26		21 08		21 52	22 08	22 10	22 42	22 54	22 58	
Cambridge	d	19 10				20 10	19 25				20 20		21 13	22 10				23a11		22 55
Ely ■	d		19 05	19 06	19 27		19 40	20 08	20 16	20 27	20 36	21 08	21 31		22 08	22 14	22 42		22 58	23 10
Waterbeach	d		19 15	19 15				20 17				21 17			22 17				23 07	
Cambridge	a	19 08	19 21	19 22		20 08		20 26				21 26		22 08	22 24				23 14	
Shippea Hill	d																			
Lakenheath	d																			
Brandon	d						19 56				20 52		21 47							23 26
Thetford	d				19 49		20 04		20 37		21 00		21 56			22 35				23 34
Harling Road	d																			
Eccles Road	d																			
Attleborough	d						20 18				21 15		22 10			22 49				23 48
Spooner Row	d																			
Wymondham	d						20 25				21 23		22 17			22 56				23 55
Norwich	a				20 22		20 42		21 13		21 38		22 31			23 18				00 12
Stansted Airport	a	19 42				20 45								22 53						
Ipswich	a									21 25							23 37			
London Kings Cross	a		20 30	20 33				21 29				22 30			23 30				00 42	
London Liverpool Street	a									22 46										

A 31 May B not 31 May

Table 17

Peterborough, Kings Lynn and Ely - Cambridge, Norwich and London

		FC	LE	FC	LE	FC	EM	LE	FC	XC	EM	LE	FC	LE	XC	LE	EM	FC	LE	XC	FC	EM	FC
		■	■	■	■	■	◇	■	■	◇■ ⊥	◇	■ ■	■	■	◇■ ⊥	■	◇	■	■	◇■ ⊥	■	◇	■
Peterborough ■	d						06b27			07 13	07 35	07 45			08 18		08 46			09 18		09 46	
Whittlesea	d									07 21		07 53											
March	d						06 43			07 32	07 51	08 04			08 34					09 34			
Manea	d									07x39													
Kings Lynn	d	22p28				05 56			06 56				07 56					08 56			09 30		09 56
Watlington	d	22p35				06 03			07 03				08 03					09 03					10 03
Downham Market	d	22p41				06 09			07 09				08 09					09 09			09 41		10 09
Littleport	d	22p50				06 18			07 18				08 18					09 18					10 18
Ely ■	a	22p58				06 26	07 01		07 26	07 52	08 11	08 22	08 26		08 52		09 19	09 26		09 52	09 58	10 19	10 26
Cambridge	d		22p55		06 08			07 00		08 10				08 12	09 10				09 12	10 10	10 15		
Ely ■	d	22p58	23p10	05 26	06 23	06 26	07 06	07 15	07 26		08 14	08 30	08 26	08 27		09 11	09 22	09 26	09 29			10 22	10 26
Waterbeach	d	23p07		05 35		06 35			07 35				08 35			09 20		09 35					10 35
Cambridge	a	23p14		05 44		06 44			07 44	08 08			08 44		09 08	09 28		09 44		10 08	10 13		10 44
Shippea Hill	d							07x23															
Lakenheath	d																						
Brandon	d		23p26		06 39		07 22	07 33						08 43					09 45				
Thetford	d		23p34		06 48		07 30	07 42			08 36			08 52			09 44		09 54			10 44	
Harling Road	d				06 56			07 50															
Eccles Road	d				07 00			07 54															
Attleborough	d		23p48		07 06		07 44	08 00			08 50			09 06					10 08				
Spooner Row	d							08x05															
Wymondham	d		23p55		07 13		07 51	08 09			08 57			09 13					10 15				
Norwich	a		00 12		07 29		08 13	08 24			09 15			09 30			10 19		10 32			11 18	
Stansted Airport	a									08 45					09 45					10 45			
Ipswich	a											09 25											
London Kings Cross	a	00 42		06 38		07 34			08 34				09 34					10 34			11 03		11 34
London Liverpool Street	a											10 38				10 43							

		LE	LE	XC	EM	FC	LE	XC	EM	LE	FC	LE	XC	EM	FC	LE	XC	EM	LE	FC	LE	FC	XC
		■	■ ■	◇■ ⊥	◇	■	■	◇■ ⊥	◇	◇■	■	■	◇■ ⊥	◇	■	■	◇■ ⊥	◇	◇■	■ A	■	■ B	◇■ ⊥
Peterborough ■	d		09 55	10 18	10c44			11 16	11 38	11 45			12 18	12 40			13 18	13 38	13 45				14 18
Whittlesea	d		10 03							11 53									13 53				
March	d		10 14	10 34				11 34		12 04			12 34				13 34		14 04				14 34
Manea	d																						
Kings Lynn	d					10 56					11 56				12 56					13 56		14 12	
Watlington	d					11 03					12 03				13 03					14 03		14 19	
Downham Market	d					11 09					12 09				13 09					14 09		14 25	
Littleport	d					11 18					12 18				13 18					14 18		14 34	
Ely ■	a		10 32	10 52	11 17	11 26		11 52	12 11	12 22	12 26		12 52	13 13	13 26		13 52	14 11	14 22	14 26		14 42	14 52
Cambridge	d	10 12		11 10			11 12	12 10				12 12	13 10			13 12	14 10				14 12		15 10
Ely ■	d	10 29	10 32		11 22	11 26	11 29		12 15	12 30	12 26	12 27		13 17	13 26	13 28		14 15	14 30	14 26	14 27	14 42	
Waterbeach	d					11 35					12 35				13 35					14 35		14 51	
Cambridge	a			11 08		11 44		12 08			12 44		13 08		13 44		14 08			14 44		15 00	15 08
Shippea Hill	d																						
Lakenheath	d																						
Brandon	d	10 45					11 45					12 43				13 45					14 43		
Thetford	d	10 54			11 44		11 54		12 36			12 52		13 39		13 54		14 36			14 52		
Harling Road	d																						
Eccles Road	d																						
Attleborough	d	11 08					12 08					13 06				14 08					15 06		
Spooner Row	d																						
Wymondham	d	11 15					12 15					13 13				14 15					15 13		
Norwich	a	11 30			12 18		12 30		13 13			13 33		14 13		14 30		15 13			15 30		
Stansted Airport	a			11 45				12 45					13 45				14 45						15 45
Ipswich	a		11 27							13 27									15 25				
London Kings Cross	a					12 34					13 34				14 34					15 34		16 21	
London Liverpool Street	a		12 45							14 45									16 45				

A until 10 July, from 11 September
B from 17 July until 4 September
b arr. 0619
c arr. 1037

Table 17

Saturdays

Peterborough, Kings Lynn and Ely - Cambridge, Norwich and London

		EM ◇	FC 1 A	LE 1	FC 1 B	XC ◇1	EM ◇	LE ◇1	FC 1 A	LE 1	FC 1 B	XC ◇1	EM ◇	FC 1 A	LE 1	FC 1 B	XC ◇1	LE ◇1	FC 1 A	LE 1	FC 1 B	XC ◇1
Peterborough	d	14 41				15 18	15 36	15 45				16 18	16 39				17 18	17 45				18 18
Whittlesea	d							15 53									17 27	17 53				
March	d					15 34		16 04				16 34					17 38	18 04				18 34
Manea	d																17x45					
Kings Lynn	d		14 56		15 12				15 56		16 12			16 56		17 12			17 56		18 12	
Watlington	d		15 03		15 19				16 03		16 19			17 03		17 19			18 03		18 19	
Downham Market	d		15 09		15 25				16 09		16 25			17 09		17 25			18 09		18 25	
Littleport	d		15 18		15 34				16 18		16 34			17 18		17 34			18 18		18 34	
Ely	a	15 14	15 26		15 42	15 52	16 09	16 22	16 26		16 42	16 52	17 13	17 26		17 42	17 59	18 22	18 26		18 42	18 52
Cambridge	d			15 12		16 10				16 12		17 10			17 12		18 20			18 12		19 10
Ely	d	15 17	15 26	15 27	15 42		16 13	16 30	16 26	16 27	16 42		17 17	17 26	17 27	17 42		18 30	18 26	18 27	18 42	
Waterbeach	d		15 35		15 51				16 35		16 51			17 35		17 51			18 35		18 51	
Cambridge	a		15 44		16 00	16 08			16 44		17 00	17 08		17 44		18 00	18 16		18 44		19 00	19 08
Shippea Hill	d																					
Lakenheath	d			15x40																		
Brandon	d			15 45						16 43					17 43					18 43		
Thetford	d	15 38		15 54			16 34			16 52			17 38		17 52					18 52		
Harling Road	d																					
Eccles Road	d																					
Attleborough	d			16 08						17 06					18 06					19 06		
Spooner Row	d																					
Wymondham	d			16 15						17 13					18 13					19 13		
Norwich	a	16 13		16 30			17 13			17 30			18 18		18 30					19 30		
Stansted Airport	a					16 45						17 45					18 53					19 45
Ipswich	a							17 27										19 25				
London Kings Cross	a		16 35		17 19				17 35		18 15			18 34		19 14			19 34		20 13	
London Liverpool Street	a							18 45										20 45				

		FC 1 A	EM ◇	LE 1	FC 1 B	XC ◇1	FC 1 A	EM ◇	LE 1	LE ◇1	FC 1 B	XC ◇1	FC 1 A	LE 1	FC 1 B	XC ◇1	FC 1 A	EM ◇	FC 1 B	LE 1	XC ◇1	LE 1	FC 1
Peterborough	d		18 42			19 18		19 37		19 45		20 18				21 18		21 36		21 45	22 18		
Whittlesea	d									19 53										21 53			
March	d		19 01			19 34				20 04		20 34				21 34				22 04	22 34		
Manea	d																						
Kings Lynn	d	18 35			19 12		19 35				20 12		20 35		21 12		21 35		21 45				23 10
Watlington	d	18 42			19 19		19 42				20 19		20 42		21 19		21 42		21 52				23 17
Downham Market	d	18 48			19 25		19 48				20 25		20 48		21 25		21 48		21 58				23 23
Littleport	d	18 57			19 34		19 57				20 34		20 57		21 34		21 57		22 07				23 32
Ely	a	19 05	19 19		19 42	19 52	20 05	20 12		20 26	20 42	20 52	21 05		21 42	21 52	22 05	22 10	22 15	22 22	22 53		23 41
Cambridge	d			19 12		20 10			20 12			21 10		21 12		22 10					23a10	22 30	
Ely	d	19 05	19 23	19 29	19 42		20 05	20 16	20 27	20 30	20 42		21 05	21 27	21 42		22 05	22 14	22 15	22 30		22 45	23 43
Waterbeach	d	19 15			19 51		20 15				20 51		21 15		21 51		22 15		22 25				23 52
Cambridge	a	19 21			20 00	20 08	20 21				21 00	21 08	21 21		22 00	22 08	22 21		22 31				23 59
Shippea Hill	d																						
Lakenheath	d																						
Brandon	d			19 45					20 43					21 43								23 01	
Thetford	d		19 44	19 54				20 36	20 52					21 52				22 35				23 09	
Harling Road	d																						
Eccles Road	d																						
Attleborough	d			20 08					21 06					22 06				22 49				23 23	
Spooner Row	d																						
Wymondham	d			20 15					21 13					22 13				22 56				23 30	
Norwich	a		20 18	20 30				21 13	21 30					22 30				23 18				23 45	
Stansted Airport	a					20 45						21 45				22 45							
Ipswich	a									21 27										23 32			
London Kings Cross	a	20 31			21 15		21 31				22 14		22 31		23 14		23 31		23 45				
London Liverpool Street	a									22 45													

A until 10 July, from 11 September

B from 17 July until 4 September

Table 17

Sundays

Peterborough, Kings Lynn and Ely - Cambridge, Norwich and London

		FC 1 A	FC 1 B	FC 1 C	FC 1 A	FC 1 B	FC 1 C	LE 1 D	FC 1 A	FC 1 E	LE 1	FC 1 A	EM ◇ D	FC 1 E	LE 1	FC 1 A	FC 1 E	LE 1	EM ◇ D	FC 1 A	XC ◇1	FC 1 E	LE 1
Peterborough	d							09 46					11 09		11 46				12 53		13 18		
Whittlesea	d							09 54							11 54								
March	d							10 05					11 25		12 05						13 34		
Manea	d																						
Kings Lynn	d	08 12	08 28	08 28	09 12	09 28	09 28		10 12	10 28		11 12		11 28		12 12	12 28			13 12		13 28	
Watlington	d	08 19	08 35	08 35	09 19	09 35	09 35		10 19	10 35		11 19		11 35		12 19	12 35			13 19		13 35	
Downham Market	d	08 25	08 41	08 41	09 25	09 41	09 41		10 25	10 41		11 25		11 41		12 25	12 41			13 25		13 41	
Littleport	d	08 34	08 50	08 50	09 34	09 50	09 50		10 34	10 50		11 34		11 50		12 34	12 50			13 34		13 50	
Ely	a	08 42	08 58	08 58	09 42	09 58	09 58	10 28	10 42	10 58		11 42	11 48	11 58	12 28	12 42	12 58		13 32	13 42	13 52	13 58	
Cambridge	d										10 46							12 46			14 10		13 46
Ely	d	08 42	08 58	08 58	09 42	09 58	09 58	10 30	10 42	10 58	11 02	11 42	11 59	11 58	12 30	12 42	12 58	13 02	13 36	13 42		13 58	14 02
Waterbeach	d	08 51	09 07	09 07	09 51	10 07	10 07		10 51	11 07		11 51		12 07		12 51	13 07			13 51		14 07	
Cambridge	a	09 00	09 16	09 16	10 00	10 16	10 16		11 00	11 16		12 00		12 16		13 00	13 16			14 00	14 08	14 18	
Shippea Hill	d																						
Lakenheath	d										11x15							13x15					
Brandon	d										11 20		12 15					13 20					14 18
Thetford	d										11 29		12 23					13 29	13 57				14 26
Harling Road	d																						
Eccles Road	d																						
Attleborough	d										11 43		12 37					13 43					14 40
Spooner Row	d																						
Wymondham	d										11 50		12 44					13 50					14 47
Norwich	a										12 09		13 11					14 09	14 35				15 09
Stansted Airport	a																				14 43		
Ipswich	a							11 25							13 25								
London Kings Cross	a	10 13	10 08	10 15	11 18	11 08	11 14		12 19	12 08		13 16		13 08		14 16	14 09			15 18		15 08	
London Liverpool Street	a																						

		EM ◇ B	EM ◇ D	LE 1	FC 1 A	XC ◇1	FC 1 E	LE 1	EM ◇ D	EM ◇ B	FC 1 A	XC ◇1	FC 1 E	LE 1	LE 1	EM ◇ B	EM ◇ D	FC 1 A	XC ◇1	FC 1 E	LE 1	EM ◇ F	EM ◇ G
Peterborough	d	13 43	13 43	13 46		14 18			14 42	14 53		15 18			15 46	16 03	16 05		16 18			16 58	17 00
Whittlesea	d			13 54											15 54								
March	d			14 05		14 34						15 34			16 05				16 34				
Manea	d																						
Kings Lynn	d				14 12		14 28				15 12		15 28					16 12		16 28			
Watlington	d				14 19		14 35				15 19		15 35					16 19		16 35			
Downham Market	d				14 25		14 41				15 25		15 41					16 25		16 41			
Littleport	d				14 34		14 50				15 34		15 50					16 34		16 50			
Ely	a	14 16	14 21	14 29	14 42	14 52	14 58		15 21	15 29	15 42	15 52	15 58		16 28	16 38	16 38	16 42	16 52	16 58		17 31	17 33
Cambridge	d					15 10		14 46				16 10		15 46					17 10		16 46		
Ely	d	14 24	14 28	14 30	14 42		14 58	15 02	15 28	15 33	15 42		15 58	16 02	16 30	16 41	16 41	16 42		16 58	17 02	17 35	17 38
Waterbeach	d				14 51		15 07				15 51		16 07					16 51		17 07			
Cambridge	a				15 00	15 08	15 18				16 00	16 08	16 18					17 00	17 07	17 16			
Shippea Hill	d																						
Lakenheath	d													16x15									
Brandon	d	14 42						15 18						16 20							17 18		
Thetford	d	14 50	14 49					15 26	15 49	15 54				16 29		17 02	17 02				17 26	17 56	17 59
Harling Road	d																						
Eccles Road	d																						
Attleborough	d	15 04						15 40						16 43							17 40		
Spooner Row	d																						
Wymondham	d	15 11						15 47						16 50							17 47		
Norwich	a	15 31	15 28					16 09	16 35	16 35				17 09		17 35	17 35				18 09	18 29	18 32
Stansted Airport	a					15 43						16 37							17 43				
Ipswich	a			15 25											17 25								
London Kings Cross	a				16 19		16 09				17 18		17 11					18 19		18 08			
London Liverpool Street	a																						

A from 18 July until 5 September

B from 12 September

C until 11 July

D until 5 September

E until 11 July, from 12 September

F until 5 September, from 24 October

G from 12 September until 17 October

Peterborough, Kings Lynn and Ely - Cambridge, Norwich and London

		FC ■1 A	XC ◇■1	FC ■1 B	LE ■1	LE ■1	EM ◇ C	EM ◇ D	FC ■1 A	XC ◇■1	FC ■1 B	LE ■1	EM ◇ B	EM ◇ A	FC ■1 A	XC ◇■1	FC ■1 B	LE ■1	LE ■1	EM ◇	FC ■1 A	XC ◇■1
Peterborough ■	d		17 18			17 46	17 53	17 56		18 18			18 47	18 51		19 18			19 44	19 58		20 18
Whittlesea	d					17 54													19 52			
March	d		17 34			18 05	18 12	18 12		18 34						19 34			20 03			20 34
Manea	d																					
Kings Lynn	d	17 12		17 28					18 12		18 28				19 12		19 28				20 12	
Watlington	d	17 19		17 35					18 19		18 35				19 19		19 35				20 19	
Downham Market	d	17 25		17 41					18 25		18 41				19 25		19 41				20 25	
Littleport	d	17 34		17 50					18 34		18 50				19 34		19 50				20 34	
Ely ■	a	17 42	17 52	17 58		18 27	18 31	18 31	18 42	18 52	18 58		19 20	19 24	19 42	19 52	19 58		20 21	20 31	20 42	20 52
Cambridge	d		18 10		17 46					19 10		18 46				20 10		19 48				21 10
Ely ■	d	17 42		17 58	18 02	18 30	18 35	18 35	18 42		18 58	19 02	19 25	19 29	19 42		19 58	20 03	20 22	20 35	20 42	
Waterbeach	d	17 51		18 07					18 51		19 07				19 51		20 07				20 51	
Cambridge	a	18 00	18 07	18 16					19 00	19 07	19 16				20 00	20 07	20 16				21 00	21 07
Shippea Hill	d																					
Lakenheath	d																					
Brandon	d				18 18							19 18						20 19				
Thetford	d				18 26		18 56	18 56				19 26	19 49	19 53				20 27		20 56		
Harling Road	d																					
Eccles Road	d																					
Attleborough	d				18 40							19 40						20 41		21 10		
Spooner Row	d																					
Wymondham	d				18 47							19 47						20 48		21 17		
Norwich	a				19 09		19 29	19 29				20 09	20 28	20 32				21 09		21 35		
Stansted Airport	a		18 43							19 43						20 43						21 43
Ipswich	a					19 27													21 18			
London Kings Cross	a	19 15		19 08					20 21		20 08				21 19		21 08				22 18	
London Liverpool Street	a																					

		FC ■1 B	FC ■1 A	XC ◇■1	FC ■1 B	LE ■1	EM ◇	XC ◇■1
Peterborough ■	d			21 18			21 48	22 18
Whittlesea	d							
March	d			21 34				22 34
Manea	d							
Kings Lynn	d	20 28	21 12		21 28			
Watlington	d	20 35	21 19		21 35			
Downham Market	d	20 41	21 25		21 41			
Littleport	d	20 50	21 34		21 50			
Ely ■	a	20 58	21 42	21 52	21 58		22 21	22 52
Cambridge	d			22 10		21 48		23a07
Ely ■	d	20 58	21 42		21 58	22 03	22 24	
Waterbeach	d	21 07	21 51		22 07			
Cambridge	a	21 16	22 00	22 07	22 16			
Shippea Hill	d							
Lakenheath	d							
Brandon	d					22 19		
Thetford	d					22 27	22 45	
Harling Road	d							
Eccles Road	d							
Attleborough	d					22 41	22 59	
Spooner Row	d							
Wymondham	d					22 48	23 06	
Norwich	a					23 05	23 25	
Stansted Airport	a			22 43				
Ipswich	a							
London Kings Cross	a	22 08	23 18		23 08			
London Liverpool Street	a							

A from 18 July until 5 September
B until 11 July, from 12 September
C until 5 September
D from 12 September

Kings Lynn - Sandringham and Hunstanton

Bus Service

		FC	FC	FC	FC	FC	FC	FC	FC	FC	FC	FC	FC	FC	FC	FC	FC	FC	FC	FC	FC	FC	FC
Kings Lynn	d	06 25	06 55	07 28	08 35	08 50	09 05	09 20	09 35	09 50	10 05	10 20	10 35	10 50	11 05	11 20	11 35	11 50	12 05	12 20	12 35	12 50	13 05
Sandringham Visitor Centre	a					09 12		09 42		10 12		10 42		11 12		11 42		12 12		12 42		13 12	
Sandringham Norwich Gates	a			07 51		09 14		09 44		10 14		10 44		11 14		11 44		12 14		12 44		13 14	
Hunstanton Bus Station	a	07 14	07 44	08 21	09 25	09 44	09 55	10 14	10 25	10 44	10 55	11 14	11 25	11 44	11 55	12 14	12 25	12 44	12 55	13 14	13 25	13 44	13 55

		FC	FC	FC	FC	FC	FC	FC	FC	FC	FC	FC	FC	FC	FC	FC	FC	FC	FC	FC	FC	FC	FC
Kings Lynn	d	13 20	13 35	13 50	14 05	14 20	14 30	15 05	15 35	15 50	16 05	16 20	16 35	16 50	17 05	17 20	17 35	17 50	18 20	19 00	20 00	21 30	23 00
Sandringham Visitor Centre	a	13 42		14 12		14 42		15 27		16 12		16 42		17 12		17 42		18 12					
Sandringham Norwich Gates	a	13 44		14 14		14 44		15 29		16 14		16 44		17 14		17 44		18 14					
Hunstanton Bus Station	a	14 14	14 25	14 44	14 55	15 14	15 20	15 59	16 25	16 44	16 55	17 14	17 25	17 44	17 55	18 14	18 25	18 41	19 03	19 40	20 40	22 10	23 40

Saturdays

		FC	FC	FC	FC	FC	FC	FC	FC	FC	FC	FC	FC	FC	FC	FC	FC	FC	FC	FC	FC	FC	FC
Kings Lynn	d	06 35	07 35	08 35	08 50	09 05	09 20	09 35	09 50	10 05	10 20	10 35	10 50	11 05	11 20	11 35	11 50	12 05	12 20	12 35	12 50	13 05	13 20
Sandringham Visitor Centre	a				09 12		09 42		10 12		10 42		11 12		11 42		12 12		12 42		13 12		13 42
Sandringham Norwich Gates	a				09 14		09 44		10 14		10 44		11 14		11 44		12 14		12 44		13 14		13 44
Hunstanton Bus Station	a	07 25	08 25	09 25	09 44	09 55	10 14	10 25	10 44	10 55	11 14	11 25	11 44	11 55	12 14	12 25	12 44	12 55	13 14	13 25	13 44	13 55	14 14

		FC	FC	FC	FC	FC	FC	FC	FC	FC	FC	FC	FC	FC	FC	FC	FC	FC	FC	FC	FC	FC	FC
Kings Lynn	d	13 35	13 50	14 05	14 20	14 35	14 50	15 05	15 20	15 35	15 50	16 05	16 20	16 35	16 50	17 05	17 20	17 35	17 50	18 20	19 00	20 00	21 30
Sandringham Visitor Centre	a		14 12		14 42		15 12	15 27	15 42		16 12		16 42		17 12		17 42		18 12				
Sandringham Norwich Gates	a		14 14		14 44		15 14	15 29	15 44		16 14		16 44		17 14		17 44		18 14				
Hunstanton Bus Station	a	14 25	14 44	14 55	15 14	15 25	15 44	15 59	16 14	16 25	16 44	16 55	17 14	17 25	17 44	17 55	18 14	18 25	18 41	19 03	19 40	20 40	22 10

		FC
Kings Lynn	d	23 00
Sandringham Visitor Centre	a	
Sandringham Norwich Gates	a	
Hunstanton Bus Station	a	23 40

Sundays

		FC	FC	FC	FC	FC	FC	FC	FC	FC	FC	FC	FC	FC
Kings Lynn	d	08 50	09 50	10 50	11 50	12 50	13 50	14 50	15 50	16 50	17 50	20 00	21 30	23 00
Sandringham Visitor Centre	a	09 12	10 12	11 12	12 12	13 12	14 12	15 12	16 12	17 12	18 12			
Sandringham Norwich Gates	a	09 14	10 14	11 14	12 14	13 14	14 14	15 14	16 14	17 14	18 14			
Hunstanton Bus Station	a	09 42	10 42	11 42	12 42	13 42	14 42	15 42	16 42	17 42	18 42	20 40	22 10	23 40

Table 17A

Mondays to Fridays

Hunstanton and Sandringham - Kings Lynn

Bus Service

		FC	FC	FC	FC	FC	FC	FC	FC	FC		FC	FC	FC	FC	FC	FC	FC	FC	FC		FC	FC	FC	FC
Hunstanton Bus Station	d	23p44	06 30	07 16	07 48	08 33	08 48	09 03	09 18	09 33		09 48	10 03	10 18	10 33	10 48	11 03	11 18	11 33	11 48		12 03	12 18	12 33	12 48
Sandringham Norwich Gates	d		06 55	07 43			09 15		09 45			10 15		10 45		11 15		11 45		12 15			12 45		13 15
Sandringham Visitor Centre	d						09 17		09 47			10 17		10 47		11 17		11 47		12 17			12 47		13 17
Kings Lynn	a	00 22	07 20	08 10	08 40	09 25	09 44	09 55	10 14	10 25		10 44	10 55	11 14	11 25	11 44	11 55	12 14	12 25	12 44		12 55	13 14	13 25	13 44

		FC	FC	FC	FC	FC		FC	FC	FC	FC	FC	FC	FC	FC	FC		FC	FC	FC	FC	FC	FC	FC	FC
Hunstanton Bus Station	d	13 03	13 18	13 33	13 48	14 03		14 18	14 33	14 48	15 18	15 25	16 03	16 18	16 33	16 48		17 08	17 18	17 33	17 48	18 03	18 44	19 14	19 44
Sandringham Norwich Gates	d		13 45		14 15			14 45		15 15	15 45	15 56		16 45		17 15			17 45		18 15				
Sandringham Visitor Centre	d		13 47		14 17			14 47		15 17	15 47	15 58		16 47		17 17			17 47		18 17				
Kings Lynn	a	13 55	14 14	14 25	14 44	14 55		15 14	15 25	15 44	16 14	16 25	16 55	17 14	17 25	17 44		18 00	18 14	18 25	18 44	18 55	19 22	19 52	20 22

		FC		FC	FC
Hunstanton Bus Station	d	20 44		22 14	23 44
Sandringham Norwich Gates	d				
Sandringham Visitor Centre	d				
Kings Lynn	a	21 22		22 52	00 22

Saturdays

		FC	FC	FC	FC	FC	FC	FC	FC	FC		FC	FC	FC	FC	FC	FC	FC	FC	FC		FC	FC	FC	FC
Hunstanton Bus Station	d	23p44	06 30	07 30	08 33	08 48	09 03	09 18	09 33	09 48		10 03	10 18	10 33	10 48	11 03	11 18	11 33	11 48	12 03		12 18	12 33	12 48	13 03
Sandringham Norwich Gates	d		06 55	07 55		09 15		09 45		10 15			10 45		11 15		11 45		12 15			12 45		13 15	
Sandringham Visitor Centre	d					09 17		09 47		10 17			10 47		11 17		11 47		12 17			12 47		13 17	
Kings Lynn	a	00 22	07 20	08 20	09 25	09 44	09 55	10 14	10 25	10 44		10 55	11 14	11 25	11 44	11 55	12 14	12 25	12 44	12 55		13 14	13 25	13 44	13 55

		FC	FC	FC	FC	FC		FC	FC	FC	FC	FC	FC	FC	FC	FC		FC	FC	FC	FC	FC	FC	FC	FC
Hunstanton Bus Station	d	13 18	13 33	13 48	14 03	14 18		14 33	14 48	15 03	15 18	15 33	15 48	16 03	16 18	16 33		16 48	17 03	17 18	17 33	17 48	18 03	18 44	19 14
Sandringham Norwich Gates	d	13 45		14 15		14 45			15 15		15 45		16 15		16 45			17 15		17 45		18 15			
Sandringham Visitor Centre	d	13 47		14 17		14 47			15 17		15 47		16 17		16 47			17 17		17 47		18 17			
Kings Lynn	a	14 14	14 25	14 44	14 55	15 14		15 25	15 44	15 55	16 14	16 25	16 44	16 55	17 14	17 25		17 44	17 55	18 14	18 25	18 44	18 55	19 22	19 52

		FC		FC	FC	FC
Hunstanton Bus Station	d	19 44		20 44	22 14	23 44
Sandringham Norwich Gates	d					
Sandringham Visitor Centre	d					
Kings Lynn	a	20 22		21 22	22 52	00 22

Sundays

		FC A	FC	FC	FC	FC	FC	FC	FC	FC		FC	FC	FC	FC	FC
Hunstanton Bus Station	d	23p44	09 47	10 47	11 47	12 47	13 47	14 47	15 47	16 47		17 47	18 47	20 44	22 14	23 44
Sandringham Norwich Gates	d		10 14	11 14	12 14	13 14	14 14	15 14	16 14	17 14		18 14	19 14			
Sandringham Visitor Centre	d		10 16	11 16	12 16	13 16	14 16	15 16	16 16	17 16		18 16				
Kings Lynn	a	00 22	10 40	11 40	12 40	13 40	14 40	15 40	16 40	17 40		18 40	19 38	21 22	22 52	00 22

A not 23 May

Network Diagram for Tables 18, 19, 27, 29, 30

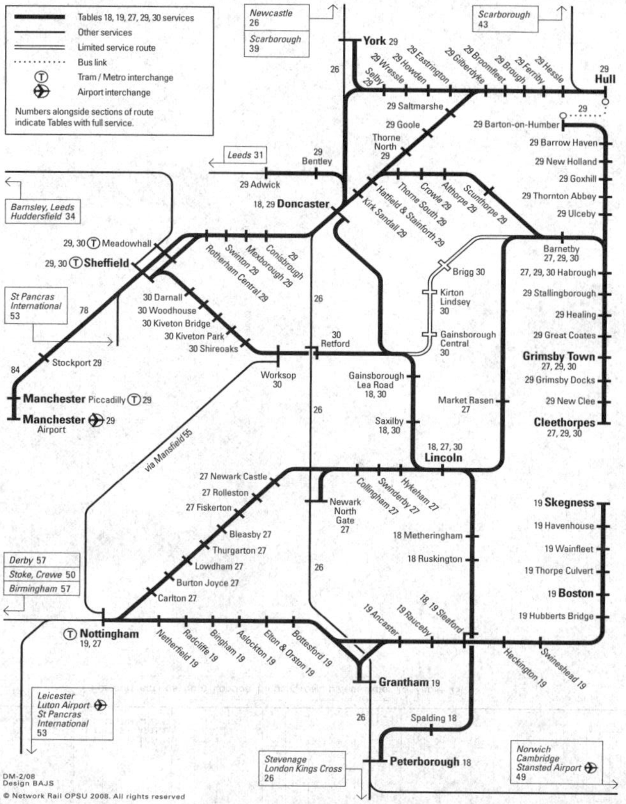

DM-2/08
Design BAJS

Table 18

Peterborough - Sleaford, Lincoln and Doncaster

Mondays to Fridays

		EM	NT	EM	EM	EM	NT	EM	NT	EM		NT	EM	NT	EM	EM	NT	EM	NT	EM		NT	EM	NT	NT
Peterborough 8	d	06 30			07 30					08 33			09 35			10 38		11 48		12 41			13 40		
Spalding	d	06a56			07a56					08 57			09 57			11 01		12 10		13 03			14 02		
Sleaford	a									09 25			10 25			11 29		12 38		13 31			14 30		
	d			06 50		07 42		08 40		09 25			10 25			11 30		12 42		13 32			14 32		
Ruskington	d			06 58		07 50		08 48		09 33			10 33			11 38		12 50		13 39			14 39		
Metheringham	d			07 08		08 00		08 58		09 43			10 43			11 48		12 59		13 49			14 49		
Lincoln	a			07 21		08 13		09 11		09 59			10 59			12 04		13 14		14 05			15 05		
	d		07 04	07 26			08 27	09 15	09 27			10 27		11 27	11 54		12 27	13 15	13 27	14 05		14 27		15 27	16 27
Saxilby	d		07 14				08 36	09 24	09 36			10 36		11 36	12 04		12 36	13 24	13 36			14 36		15 36	16 36
Gainsborough Lea Road	d		07 26				08 49	09 37	09 49			10 49		11 49	12 17		12 49	13 37	13 49			14 49		15 49	16 49
Doncaster 7	a						10 36	10 05	11 35			12 35		13 35	12 47		14 35	14 13	15 36			16 35		17 35	18 38

		EM	NT	EM	EM	NT		EM	EM	EM	NT	NT	EM	EM	NT
Peterborough 8	d	15 10		16 25	17 32				18 36					20 28	
Spalding	d	15 32		16 48	17a58				19a02					20a54	
Sleaford	a	16 00		17 16											
	d	16 14		17 17				17 54		19 00			20 07		
Ruskington	d	16 22		17 25				18 01		19 07			20 14		
Metheringham	d	16 32		17 35				18 11		19 17			20 24		
Lincoln	a	16 48		17 51				18 27		19 32			20 41		
	d		17 22			18 24		18 29		19 32	19 43	20 27			21 27
Saxilby	d		17 31			18 33		18 41		19 41	19 52	20 36			21 36
Gainsborough Lea Road	d		17 44			18 46		18 57		19 53	20 05	20 49			21 49
Doncaster 7	a							19 25		20 23					

Saturdays

		EM	NT	EM	EM	EM	NT	EM	NT	EM		NT	EM	NT	EM	NT	EM	NT	EM	EM		NT	EM	NT	NT
Peterborough 8	d	06 30			07 30					08 33			09 33				11 48		12 41						
Spalding	d	06a56			07a56					08 57			09 57				12 10		13 03						
Sleaford	a									09 25			10 25				12 38		13 31						
	d			06 50		07 42				09 25			10 25				12 42		13 32						
Ruskington	d			06 58		07 50				09 33			10 33				12 50		13 39						
Metheringham	d			07 08		08 00				09 43			10 43				12 59		13 49						
Lincoln	a			07 21		08 13				09 59			10 59				13 14		14 05						
	d		07 04	07 26			08 27	09 15	09 27			10 27		11 27	11 54	12 27		13 27	14 05	14 10		14 27	15 10	15 27	16 27
Saxilby	d		07 14				08 36	09 24	09 36			10 36		11 36	12 04	12 36		13 36		14 19		14 36	15 20	15 36	16 36
Gainsborough Lea Road	d		07 26				08 49	09 37	09 49			10 49		11 49	12 17	12 49		13 49		14 32		14 49	15 32	15 49	16 49
Doncaster 7	a						10 36	10 07	11 35			12 35		13 35	12 47	14 35		15 36		15 01		16 35	16 02	17 35	18 38

		EM	NT	EM	EM	NT		EM	EM	EM	NT	NT	EM	EM	NT
Peterborough 8	d	15 11		16 25	17 30				18 36					20 28	
Spalding	d	15 33		16 48	17a56				19a02					20a54	
Sleaford	a	16 02		17 16											
	d	16 14		17 17				17 54		19 00			20 07		
Ruskington	d	16 22		17 25				18 01		19 07			20 14		
Metheringham	d	16 32		17 35				18 11		19 17			20 24		
Lincoln	a	16 48		17 51				18 27		19 32			20 37		
	d		17 22			18 24				19 32	19 43	20 27			21 24
Saxilby	d		17 31			18 33				19 41	19 52	20 36			21 33
Gainsborough Lea Road	d		17 44			18 46				19 53	20 05	20 49			21 46
Doncaster 7	a									20 23					

Sundays
until 11 July

		NT	NT	NT	NT
Peterborough 8	d				
Spalding	d				
Sleaford	a				
	d				
Ruskington	d				
Metheringham	d				
Lincoln	a				
	d	15 15	17 35	19 35	21 15
Saxilby	d	15 25	17 45	19 45	21 25
Gainsborough Lea Road	d	15 37	17 57	19 57	21 37
Doncaster 7	a				

Sundays
18 July to 05 September

		NT (bus)	NT (bus)	NT (bus)	NT (bus)	NT (bus)
Peterborough 8	d					
Spalding	d					
Sleaford	a					
	d					
Ruskington	d					
Metheringham	d					
Lincoln	a					
	d	14 41	17 01	19 01	20 40	21 15
Saxilby	d	15 01	17 21	19 21	21 00	21 35
Gainsborough Lea Road	d	15 20	17 40	19 40	21 19	21 54
Doncaster 7	a					

For connections from London Kings Cross please refer to Table 25

Table 18

Peterborough - Sleaford, Lincoln and Doncaster

Sundays
from 12 September

		NT	NT	NT	NT
Peterborough 8	d				
Spalding	d				
Sleaford	a				
	d				
Ruskington	d				
Metheringham	d				
Lincoln	a				
	d	15 15	17 35	19 35	21 15
Saxilby	d	15 25	17 45	19 45	21 25
Gainsborough Lea Road	d	15 37	17 57	19 57	21 37
Doncaster 7	a				

For connections from London Kings Cross please refer to Table 25

Table 18

Mondays to Fridays

Doncaster, Lincoln and Sleaford - Peterborough

Station		NT	EM	EM	EM	EM	NT	NT	EM	NT	EM	NT	EM	EM	NT	EM	NT	EM	EM	NT	EM	NT	EM
Doncaster 7	d											09 01		10 26	10 02		11 02		13 04	11 59		12 59	
Gainsborough Lea Road	d	06 25					07 38	08 24		09 38		10 38		10 52	11 38		12 38		13 30	13 41		14 38	
Saxilby	d	06 37					07 51	08 37		09 51		10 51		11 05	11 51		12 51		13 43	13 53		14 51	
Lincoln	a	06 53				07 58	08 06	08 52		10 06		11 06		11 16	12 06		13 06	13 30	13 54	14 09		15 06	
	d			07 05		08 00			09 10		10 15		11 10			12 10		13 30			14 41		15 12
Metheringham	d			07 17		08 12			09 22		10 27		11 23			12 22		13 43			14 53		15 24
Ruskington	d			07 27		08 22			09 32		10 37		11 33			12 32		13 53			15 03		15 34
Sleaford	a			07 36		08 31			09 41		10 50		11 42			12 41		14 02			15 13		15 43
	d					08 34			09 42		10 50		11 42			12 42		14 03			15 16		
Spalding	d		07 00		08 00	09 02			10 07		11 15		12 07			13 07		14 28			15 41		
Peterborough 8	a		07 25		08 25	09 27			10 31		11 41		12 34			13 32		14 53			16 09		

Station		EM	EM	NT	NT	EM A	EM B	NT	EM	EM	EM	NT	EM	EM	EM	NT	EM	EM
Doncaster 7	d	14 27		14 01	15 02			16 02					19 34				20 33	
Gainsborough Lea Road	d	14 54		15 38	16 38			17 38				19 39	20 00			20 42	21 00	
Saxilby	d	15 07		15 51	16 51			17 51				19 52	20 13			20 55	21 14	
Lincoln	a	15 18	16 03	16 06	17 06	17 14	17 15	18 06				20 06	20 26			21 10	21 26	
	d		16 03			17 15	17 15			18 10	19 10				20 48			
Metheringham	d		16 15			17 28	17 28			18 23	19 22				21 01			
Ruskington	d		16 25			17 38	17 38			18 33	19 32				21 10			
Sleaford	a		16 34			17 47	17 47			18 42	19 41				21 19			
	d		16 34												21 20			
Spalding	d		16 59						18 02					19 56				21 00
Peterborough 8	a		17 24						18 27					20 21				21 26

Saturdays

Station		NT	EM	EM	EM	EM	NT	NT	NT	EM	NT	EM	EM	NT	NT	EM	EM	NT	EM	EM	EM	NT	NT
Doncaster 7	d										09b01		10 26	10 02	11 02		13 04	12 02		15 07		14 01	15 02
Gainsborough Lea Road	d	06 25					07 38	08 24	09 38		10 38		10 52	11 38	12 38		13 30	13 38		15 33		15 45	16 38
Saxilby	d	06 37					07 51	08 37	09 51		10 51		11 05	11 51	12 51		13 43	13 51		15 46		15 58	16 51
Lincoln	a	06 53				07 58	08 06	08 52	10 06		11 06		11 16	12 06	13 06	13 30	13 54	14 06		15 57	16 03	16 09	17 06
	d			07 05		08 00				10 15		11 10				13 30			14 41		16 03		
Metheringham	d			07 17		08 12				10 27		11 23				13 43			14 53		16 15		
Ruskington	d			07 27		08 22				10 37		11 33				13 53			15 03		16 25		
Sleaford	a			07 36		08 31				10 50		11 42				14 02			15 13		16 34		
	d					08 34				10 50		11 42				14 03			15 16		16 34		
Spalding	d		07 00		08 00	09 02				11 15		12 07				14 28			15 41		16 59		
Peterborough 8	a		07 25		08 25	09 27				11 41		12 33				14 53			16 07		17 24		

Station		EM	EM	NT	EM	EM	NT	EM	NT	EM	EM	NT	EM	EM
Doncaster 7	d		16 27	16 00			17 01		18 02				20 33	
Gainsborough Lea Road	d		16 56	17 38			18 38		19 39			20 42	21 00	
Saxilby	d		17 09	17 51			18 51		19 52			20 55	21 14	
Lincoln	a		17 20	18 06			19 07		20 06			21 10	21 26	
	d	17 15				18 10		19 10			20 48			
Metheringham	d	17 28				18 23		19 22			21 01			
Ruskington	d	17 38				18 33		19 32			21 10			
Sleaford	a	17 47				18 42		19 41			21 19			
	d										21 20			
Spalding	d				18 02					19 56				20 58
Peterborough 8	a				18 27					20 21				21 23

Sundays
until 11 July

Station		NT	NT	NT	NT
Doncaster 7	d				
Gainsborough Lea Road	d	14 26	16 54	18 54	20 18
Saxilby	d	14 39	17 07	19 07	20 31
Lincoln	a	14 54	17 21	19 22	20 45
	d				
Metheringham	d				
Ruskington	d				
Sleaford	a				
	d				
Spalding	d				
Peterborough 8	a				

Sundays
18 July to 05 September

Station		NT 🚌	NT 🚌	NT 🚌	NT 🚌
Doncaster 7	d				
Gainsborough Lea Road	d	14 40	17 10	19 10	20 30
Saxilby	d	14 55	17 25	19 25	20 45
Lincoln	a	15 20	17 50	19 50	21 10
	d				
Metheringham	d				
Ruskington	d				
Sleaford	a				
	d				
Spalding	d				
Peterborough 8	a				

A until 24 September B from 27 September

For connections to London Kings Cross please refer to Table 25

Table 18

Sundays
from 12 September

Doncaster, Lincoln and Sleaford - Peterborough

Station		NT	NT	NT	NT
Doncaster 7	d				
Gainsborough Lea Road	d	14 26	16 54	18 54	20 18
Saxilby	d	14 39	17 07	19 07	20 31
Lincoln	a	14 54	17 21	19 22	20 45
	d				
Metheringham	d				
Ruskington	d				
Sleaford	a				
	d				
Spalding	d				
Peterborough 8	a				

Skegness - Grantham and Nottingham

Mondays to Fridays

		EM	EM	EM	EM	EM	EM	EM	EM	EM	EM	EM	EM	EM	EM	EM	EM	EM	EM	EM	EM	EM	EM
						◇		◇		◇		◇		◇		◇		◇		◇		◇	
				A	B																		
Skegness	d						07 08		08 10		09 06		10 15		11 15		12 15		13 15		14 15		15 09
Havenhouse	d						07 14																
Wainfleet	d						07 18		08 18		09 14		10 23		11 23		12 23		13 23		14 23		15 17
Thorpe Culvert	d						07 22																
Boston	d		06 14				07 45		08 45		09 41		10 50		11 50		12 50		13 50		14 50		15 44
Hubberts Bridge	d						07 51																15 50
Swineshead	d						07 56																15 55
Heckington	d		06 28				08 02		08 59		09 55		11 04		12 04		13 04		14 04		15 04		16 01
Sleaford	d		06 36	06 50	06 50		08 11		09 07		10 03		11 12		12 12		13 12		14 13		15 12		16 10
Rauceby	d						08 15																16 14
Ancaster	d		06 45				08 21						11 21										16 20
Grantham	a		07 04				08 42		09 35		10 31		11 41		12 41		13 41		14 42		15 41		16 41
	d	06 10	07 10			07 58	08 45	08 58	09 40	09 58	10 36	11 13	11 45	11 56	12 45	12 58	13 45	13 58	14 45	14 58	15 45	15 58	16 45
Bottesford	d	06 21	07 21			08 11			09 52				11 56				13 56				15 56		
Elton & Orston	d	06 25																					
Aslockton	d	06 29	07 27			08 17	09 00				10 52				13 00				15 00				
Bingham	d	06 33	07 31			08 21	09 05		10 00		10 57		12 04		13 04		14 04		15 05		16 04		17 02
Radcliffe (Notts)	d	06 39	07 37			08 27							12 09										
Netherfield	d		07 41			08 31																	
Nottingham	a	06 54	07 53	08 32	08 30	08 38	09 23	09 36	10 18	10 36	11 14	11 43	12 23	12 36	13 23	13 36	14 22	14 36	15 23	15 36	16 22	16 36	17 22

		EM	EM	EM	EM	EM	EM	EM	EM	EM	EM	EM
		◇			◇	◇		◇		◇		
Skegness	d		16 10	17 30			18 14		19 14		20 15	21 02
Havenhouse	d		16 16									
Wainfleet	d		16 20	17 38			18 22		19 22		20 23	21 10
Thorpe Culvert	d		16 24									
Boston	d		16 48	18 05			18 49		19 49		20 50	21 37
Hubberts Bridge	d											
Swineshead	d											
Heckington	d		17 04	18 19			19 04		20 04		21 04	21 51
Sleaford	d		17 13	18 27			19 13		20 13		21 12	22 00
Rauceby	d											
Ancaster	d											
Grantham	a		17 42				19 41		20 40		21 43	
	d	16 58	17 45		17 58	18 58	19 45	20 03	20 44	20 58	21 47	
Bottesford	d		17 56				19 56				21 58	
Elton & Orston	d											
Aslockton	d		18 02				20 02				22 04	
Bingham	d		18 07	19 03			20 06		21 01		22 08	22 35
Radcliffe (Notts)	d						20 12					
Netherfield	d						20 16					
Nottingham	a	17 36	18 25	19 22	18 36	19 36	20 28	20 37	21 21	21 35	22 25	22 54

Saturdays

		EM	EM	EM	EM	EM	EM	EM	EM	EM	EM	EM	EM	EM	EM	EM	EM	EM	EM	EM	EM	EM	EM
						◇		◇		◇			◇		◇			◇		◇		◇	
				C	D						E	F					E						
Skegness	d						07 08		08 15		09 10	09 15		10 15		11 15	11 26		12 15		13 15		14 15
Havenhouse	d						07 14																
Wainfleet	d						07 18		08 23		09 18	09 23		10 23		11 23			12 23		13 23		14 23
Thorpe Culvert	d						07 22																
Boston	d		06 14				07 45		08 50		09 50	09 50		10 50		11 50	12 25		12 50		13 50		14 50
Hubberts Bridge	d						07 51																
Swineshead	d						07 56																
Heckington	d		06 28				08 02		09 04		10 05	10 05		11 04		12 04			13 04		14 04		15 04
Sleaford	d		06 36	06 50	06 50		08 11		09 12		10 14	10 14		11 12		12 12	12 47		13 12		14 13		15 12
Rauceby	d						08 15																
Ancaster	d		06 45				08 21							11 21									
Grantham	a		07 06				08 42		09 41		10 43	10 43		11 41		12 41			13 41		14 42		15 41
	d	06 10	07 10			07 58	08 45	08 58	09 45	09 58	10 45	10 45	10 58	11 45	11 58	12 45		12 58	13 45	13 58	14 45	14 58	15 45
Bottesford	d	06 21	07 21			08 11			09 56					11 56					13 56				15 56
Elton & Orston	d	06 25																					
Aslockton	d	06 29	07 27			08 17	09 00				11 01	11 01				13 00					15 00		
Bingham	d	06 33	07 31			08 21	09 05		10 04		11 06	11 06		12 04		13 04			14 04		15 05		16 04
Radcliffe (Notts)	d	06 39	07 37			08 27								12 09									
Netherfield	d		07 41			08 31																	
Nottingham	a	06 54	07 53	08 32	08 30	08 39	09 23	09 36	10 22	10 36	11 24	11 24	11 35	12 23	12 36	13 23	13 44	13 36	14 22	14 36	15 23	15 36	16 22

A from 27 September
B until 24 September
C from 2 October
D until 25 September
E from 17 July until 4 September
F until 10 July, from 11 September

For connections to London Kings Cross please refer to Table 26

Skegness - Grantham and Nottingham

Saturdays

		EM	EM	EM	EM	EM	EM	EM	EM	EM	EM	EM	EM	EM	EM
		◇		◇			◇	◇		◇		◇			
Skegness	d		15 09		16 10	17 30			18 14		19 19		20 15	21 02	
Havenhouse	d				16 16										
Wainfleet	d		15 17		16 20	17 38			18 22		19 27		20 23	21 10	
Thorpe Culvert	d				16 24										
Boston	d		15 44		16 48	18 05			18 49		19 54		20 50	21 37	
Hubberts Bridge	d		15 50												
Swineshead	d		15 55												
Heckington	d		16 01		17 04	18 19			19 04		20 10		21 04	21 51	
Sleaford	d		16 10		17 13	18 27			19 13		20 18		21 12	22 00	
Rauceby	d		16 14												
Ancaster	d		16 20												
Grantham	a		16 41		17 42				19 41		20 45		21 43		
	d	15 58	16 45	16 58	17 45		18 03	18 58	19 45	20 03	20 48	20 58	21 47		22 02
Bottesford	d				17 56				19 56				21 58		
Elton & Orston	d														
Aslockton	d				18 02				20 02				22 04		
Bingham	d		17 02		18 07	19 03			20 06		21 05		22 08	22 35	
Radcliffe (Notts)	d								20 12						
Netherfield	d								20 16						
Nottingham	a	16 36	17 22	17 36	18 25	19 22	18 36	19 36	20 28	20 37	21 24	21 32	22 25	22 54	22 32

Sundays

until 05 September

		EM	EM	EM	EM	EM	EM	EM	EM	EM	EM	EM	EM	EM	EM	EM	EM	EM	EM	EM	EM
				◇			◇	◇		◇			◇	◇	◇		◇		◇		◇
							A	B													
Skegness	d		10 14		11 08	12 27			14 10		15 04	16 22				18 07		19 15		20 43	
Havenhouse	d																				
Wainfleet	d		10 22		11 16	12 35			14 18		15 12	16 30				18 15		19 23		20 51	
Thorpe Culvert	d																				
Boston	d	09 06	10 49		11 43	13 02			14 45		15 42	16 57				18 42		19 50		21 18	
Hubberts Bridge	d																				
Swineshead	d																				
Heckington	d	09 20	11 03		11 57	13 16			14 59		15 56	17 11				18 56		20 04		21 32	
Sleaford	d	09 28	11 11		12 05	13 24			15 07		16 04	17 19				19 04		20 12		21 41	
Rauceby	d																				
Ancaster	d																				
Grantham	a	09 57	11 40		12 34				15 35		16 33					19 33		20 41		22 10	
	d	10 01	11 45	11 56	12 39		12 47	12 50	15 40	15 59	16 37		16 56	17 55	19 01	19 37	19 57	20 45	21 03	22 13	22 51
Bottesford	d		11 56				12 58	13 01													
Elton & Orston	d																				
Aslockton	d		12 02				13 04	13 07													
Bingham	d	10 18	12 06		12 56	14 00	13 09	13 11	15 57		16 54			18 14		19 54		21 02		22 30	
Radcliffe (Notts)	d		12 12				13 14	13 17													
Netherfield	d		12 16				13 18	13 21													
Nottingham	a	10 37	12 27	12 33	13 15	14 19	13 26	13 28	16 17	16 28	17 13	18 11	17 25	18 29	19 30	20 14	20 31	21 21	21 35	22 49	23 26

Sundays

12 September to 17 October

		EM	EM	EM	EM	EM	EM
Skegness	d		14 10	16 05	18 05	19 28	
Havenhouse	d						
Wainfleet	d		14 18	16 13	18 13	19 36	
Thorpe Culvert	d						
Boston	d	12 13	14 45	16 41	18 41	20 03	
Hubberts Bridge	d						
Swineshead	d						
Heckington	d	12 27	14 59	16 55	18 55	20 18	
Sleaford	d	12 35	15 07	17 03	19 03	20 26	21 41
Rauceby	d						
Ancaster	d						
Grantham	a	13 07	15 36	17 32	19 33	20 55	22 10
	d						
Bottesford	d						
Elton & Orston	d						
Aslockton	d						
Bingham	d						
Radcliffe (Notts)	d						
Netherfield	d						
Nottingham	a						

A from 18 July until 5 September
B until 11 July

For connections to London Kings Cross please refer to Table 26

Skegness - Grantham and Nottingham

Sundays from 24 October

		EM ◇	EM	EM	EM ◇	EM ◇	EM	EM ◇	EM ◇	EM	EM ◇	EM	EM ◇	EM	EM ◇
Skegness	d			14 10			16 17			18 07		19 15			
Havenhouse	d														
Wainfleet	d			14 18			16 25			18 15		19 23			
Thorpe Culvert	d														
Boston	d		12 13	14 45			16 52			18 42		19 50			
Hubberts Bridge	d														
Swineshead	d														
Heckington	d		12 27	14 59			17 06			18 56		20 04			
Sleaford	d		12 35	15 07			17 14			19 04		20 12		21 41	
Rauceby	d														
Ancaster	d														
Grantham 7	a		13 07	15 35			17 43			19 33		20 41		22 10	
	d	12 50		15 40	15 59	16 56	17 47	17 55	19 01	19 37	19 57	20 45	21 03	22 13	22 51
Bottesford	d	13 01													
Elton & Orston	d														
Aslockton	d	13 07													
Bingham	d	13 11		15 57			18 04	18 14		19 54		21 02		22 30	
Radcliffe (Notts)	d	13 17													
Netherfield	d	13 21													
Nottingham 8	a	13 28		16 17	16 28	17 25	18 23	18 29	19 30	20 14	20 31	21 21	21 35	22 49	23 26

For connections to London Kings Cross please refer to Table 26

Nottingham and Grantham - Skegness

Mondays to Fridays

		EM	EM	EM	EM	EM A	EM B	EM	EM ◇	EM ◇	EM	EM ◇	EM	EM ◇	EM	EM ◇	EM	EM ◇	EM	EM ◇	EM	EM ◇	EM
Nottingham 8	d	05 10		05 50	06 45	06 53	06 55	07 34	07 52	08 34	08 45	09 34	09 55	10 34	10 45	11 34	11 45	12 34	12 45	13 34	13 45	14 34	14 45
Netherfield	d										08 51												
Radcliffe (Notts)	d										08 56								12 55				
Bingham	d	05 24		06 04	06 59			07 48			09 02		10 09		10 59		11 59		13 01		13 59		14 59
Aslockton	d	05 28						07 52			09 06				11 03						14 03		
Elton & Orston	d																						
Bottesford	d	05 35		06 13	07 08			07 59			09 12				11 10				13 09				15 08
Grantham 7	a	05 49		06 27	07 22			08 12	08 23	09 07	09 26	10 06		11 05	11 23	12 05	12 19	13 07	13 23	14 05	14 21	15 05	15 22
	d			06 31	07 26			08 16			09 36				11 27		12 23		13 27		14 25		15 26
Ancaster	d							08 34											13 45				
Rauceby	d							08 40															
Sleaford	d			06 57	07 52	08 34	08 34	08 45			10 04		10 44		11 53		12 49		13 55		14 51		15 52
Heckington	d			07 04	07 59			08 52			10 11		10 51		12 00		12 56		14 02		14 58		15 59
Swineshead	d				08 05																		16 05
Hubberts Bridge	d				08 10																		16 10
Boston	d		06 25	07 24	08 20			09 12			10 29		11 11		12 19		13 15		14 21		15 17		16 20
Thorpe Culvert	d			07 46																			
Wainfleet	d		06 49	07 51	08 45			09 36			10 53		11 35		12 44		13 40		14 46		15 42		16 45
Havenhouse	d			07 54																			
Skegness	a		07 03	08 06	08 59			09 51			11 08		11 50		12 58		13 54		15 00		15 56		16 59

		EM ◇	EM	EM A	EM B	EM	EM ◇	EM	EM ◇	EM	EM ◇	EM	EM
Nottingham 8	d	15 34	15 45	16 13	16 14	16 45	17 34	17 45	18 35	18 45	20 34		20 51
Netherfield	d		15 51			16 51							
Radcliffe (Notts)	d		15 56			16 56		17 55					21 01
Bingham	d		16 02			17 02	17 48	18 01		18 59			21 07
Aslockton	d		16 06			17 06	17 52	18 05		19 03			21 11
Elton & Orston	d					17 10							
Bottesford	d		16 12			17 14		18 12		19 10			21 17
Grantham 7	a	16 05	16 25			17 28	18 09	18 25	19 06	19 23	21 05		21 32
	d		16 29			17 32		18 29		19 26			21 36
Ancaster	d					17 50				19 44			
Rauceby	d					17 56				19 50			
Sleaford	d		16 55	17a47	17a47	18 01		18 55		19 55		21 20	22 01
Heckington	d		17 02			18 08		19 02		20 02			22 08
Swineshead	d												
Hubberts Bridge	d											21 43	
Boston	d		17 21			18 26		19 21		20 19		21a53	22a29
Thorpe Culvert	d		17 43										
Wainfleet	d		17 48			18 51		19 46		20 43			
Havenhouse	d		17 51										
Skegness	a		18 03			19 05		20 00		20 57			

Saturdays

		EM	EM	EM	EM	EM C	EM D	EM	EM ◇	EM E	EM ◇	EM	EM ◇	EM	EM ◇	EM F	EM E	EM ◇	EM	EM ◇	EM	EM ◇	EM
Nottingham 8	d	05 10		05 50	06 45	06 53	06 55	07 28	07 45	08 24	08 34	08 45	09 34	09 55	10 34	10 45	10 45	11 34	11 45	12 34	12 45	13 34	13 45
Netherfield	d											08 51											
Radcliffe (Notts)	d											08 56									12 55		
Bingham	d	05 24		06 04	06 59			07 42				09 02		10 09		10 59	10 59		11 59		13 01		13 59
Aslockton	d	05 28						07 46				09 06				11 03	11 03						14 03
Elton & Orston	d																						
Bottesford	d	05 35		06 13	07 08			07 53				09 12				11 10	11 10				13 09		
Grantham 7	a	05 49		06 27	07 22			08 07	08 15		09 07	09 26	10 07		11 06	11 23	11 23	12 06	12 19	13 07	13 25	14 05	14 21
	d			06 31	07 26			08 16				09 30				11 27	11 27		12 23		13 29		14 25
Ancaster	d							08 34															
Rauceby	d							08 40															
Sleaford	d			06 57	07 52	08 34	08 34	08 45		09 14		09 56		10 44		11 53	11 53		12 49		13 55		14 51
Heckington	d			07 04	07 59			08 52				10 03		10 51		12 00	12 00		12 56		14 02		14 58
Swineshead	d				08 05																		
Hubberts Bridge	d				08 10																		
Boston	d		06 25	07 24	08 20			09 12		09 44		10 22		11 11		12 19	12 22		13 15		14 21		15 17
Thorpe Culvert	d			07 46																			
Wainfleet	d		06 49	07 51	08 45			09 36				10 47		11 35		12 44	12 47		13 40		14 46		15 42
Havenhouse	d			07 54																			
Skegness	a		07 03	08 06	08 59			09 51		10 47		11 01		11 50		12 58	13 01		13 54		15 00		15 56

A from 27 September
B until 24 September
C from 2 October
D until 25 September
E from 17 July until 4 September
F until 10 July, from 11 September

For connections from London Kings Cross please refer to Table 26

Table 19

Saturdays

Nottingham and Grantham - Skegness

		EM ◇	EM	EM ◇	EM	EM	EM ◇	EM	EM ◇	EM	EM ◇	EM	EM
Nottingham ■	d	14 34	14 45	15 34	15 45	16 45	17 34	17 45	18 34	18 45	20 34		20 51
Netherfield	d				15 51	16 51							
Radcliffe (Notts)	d				15 56	16 56		17 55					21 01
Bingham	d		14 59		16 02	17 02	17 48	18 01		18 59			21 07
Aslockton	d				16 06	17 06	17 52	18 05		19 03			21 11
Elton & Orston	d					17 10							
Bottesford	d		15 08		16 12	17 14		18 12		19 10			21 17
Grantham ■	a	15 06	15 22	16 05	16 25	17 28	18 10	18 25	19 05	19 23	21 05		21 31
	d		15 26		16 29	17 32		18 29		19 26			21 36
Ancaster	d					17 50				19 44			
Rauceby	d					17 56				19 50			
Sleaford	d		15 52		16 55	18 01		18 55		19 55		21 20	22 01
Heckington	d		15 59		17 02	18 08		19 02		20 02			22 08
Swineshead	d		16 05										
Hubberts Bridge	d		16 10									21 43	
Boston	d		16 20		17 21	18 26		19 21		20 19		21a53	22a29
Thorpe Culvert	d				17 43								
Wainfleet	d		16 45		17 48	18 51		19 46		20 43			
Havenhouse	d				17 51								
Skegness	a		16 59		18 03	19 05		20 00		20 57			

Sundays

until 05 September

		EM	EM	EM	EM ◇	EM	EM ◇ 🚌	EM	EM ◇	EM ◇	EM	EM	EM ◇	EM	EM ◇	EM ◇	EM	EM ◇	EM	EM ◇
Nottingham ■	d		09 00	09 40	09 52	11 09	11 45	11 55	12 39	13 41	14 03	14 56	15 52	16 21	16 45	17 36	18 17	18 47	19 48	2044
Netherfield	d													16 27		17 42				
Radcliffe (Notts)	d													16 32		17 46				
Bingham	d		09 14	09 54		11 23		12 11	12 53		14 17	15 10		16 38		17 52	18 31	19 01	20 02	20 58
Aslockton	d													16 42		17 56				
Elton & Orston	d																			
Bottesford	d													16 48		18 03				
Grantham ■	a			10 14	10 25	11 44	12 16	12 29	13 13	14 12	14 37	15 31	16 23	17 03	17 15	18 16	18 51	19 21	20 22	21 18
	d			10 18		11 49		12 35			14 41	15 36		17 07			18 55		20 26	
Ancaster	d																			
Rauceby	d																			
Sleaford	d		09 49	10 44		12 15		13 01			15 09	16 04		17 36			19 21		20 52	
Heckington	d		09 56	10 51		12 22		13 08			15 16	16 11		17 43			19 28		20 59	
Swineshead	d																			
Hubberts Bridge	d																			
Boston	d	09 31	10 16	11 10		12 41		13 27			15 39	16 31		18 02			19 50		21a20	
Thorpe Culvert	d																			
Wainfleet	d	09 55	10 40	11 35		13 06		13 52			16 03	16 55		18 27			20 14			
Havenhouse	d																			
Skegness	a	10 07	10 55	11 49		13 20		14 06			16 18	17 10		18 41			20 29			

Sundays

12 September to 17 October

		EM	EM	EM	EM	EM	EM
Nottingham ■	d						
Netherfield	d						
Radcliffe (Notts)	d						
Bingham	d						
Aslockton	d						
Elton & Orston	d						
Bottesford	d						
Grantham ■	a						
	d		13 50	15 46	17 45	19 43	21 02
Ancaster	d						
Rauceby	d						
Sleaford	d		14 16	16 11	18 13	20 08	21a30
Heckington	d		14 23	16 18	18 20	20 16	
Swineshead	d						
Hubberts Bridge	d						
Boston	d	13 27	14 45	16 40	18 40	20a37	
Thorpe Culvert	d						
Wainfleet	d	13 52	15 09	17 04	19 05		
Havenhouse	d						
Skegness	a	14 06	15 24	17 19	19 19		

For connections from London Kings Cross please refer to Table 26

Table 19

Sundays

from 24 October

Nottingham and Grantham - Skegness

		EM	EM ◇	EM	EM ◇	EM	EM ◇	EM	EM ◇	EM ◇	EM	EM ◇	EM	EM ◇
Nottingham ■	d	11 55	12 39		13 49	14 56	15 52	16 21	16 45	17 36	18 31	18 47	19 48	20 44
Netherfield	d							16 27		17 42				
Radcliffe (Notts)	d							16 32		17 46				
Bingham	d	12 11	12 53			15 10		16 38		17 52	18 45	19 01	20 02	20 58
Aslockton	d							16 42		17 56				
Elton & Orston	d													
Bottesford	d							16 48		18 03				
Grantham ■	a	12 29	13 13		14 20	15 31	16 23	17 03	17 15	18 16	19 08	19 21	20 22	21 18
	d	12 35		13 50		15 36		17 07			19 13		20 26	
Ancaster	d													
Rauceby	d													
Sleaford	d	13 01		14 16		16 04		17 36			19 41		20a54	
Heckington	d	13 08		14 23		16 11		17 43			19 48			
Swineshead	d													
Hubberts Bridge	d													
Boston	d	13 27		14 45		16 31		18 02			20a10			
Thorpe Culvert	d													
Wainfleet	d	13 52		15 09		16 55		18 27						
Havenhouse	d													
Skegness	a	14 06		15 24		17 10		18 41						

Network Diagram for Tables 20, 21, 22

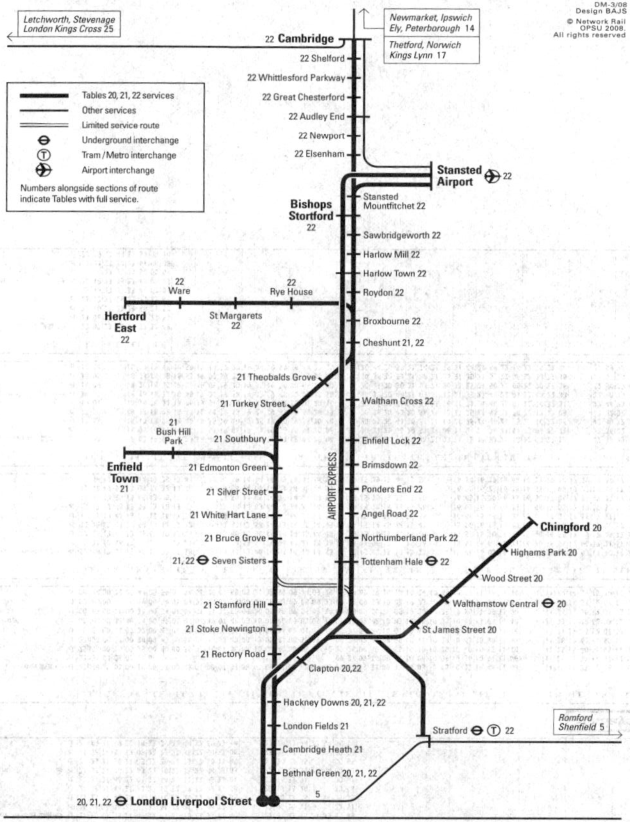

Table 20

Mondays to Fridays

London - Chingford

		LE	LE	LE	LE	LE MX	LE	LE	LE	LE	LE	LE	LE	LE	LE	LE	LE	LE	LE	LE		LE	LE	LE	LE
London Liverpool Street 15 ⊖	d	23p48	00 03	00 18	00 33	00 48	01 03	06 03	06 33	07 03	07 30	07 48	08 00	08 18	08 33	08 48	09 03	09 18	09 33	09 48		10 03	10 18	10 33	10 48
Bethnal Green	d	23p51	00 06	00 21	00 36			06 06	06 36	07 06	07 33	07 51	08 03	08 21	08 36	08 51	09 06	09 21	09 36	09 51		10 06	10 21	10 36	10 51
Hackney Downs	d	23p55	00 10	00 25	00 40	00 55	01 10	06 10	06 40	07 10	07 37	07 55	08 07	08 25	08 40	08 55	09 10	09 25	09 40	09 55		10 10	10 25	10 40	10 55
Clapton	d	23p58	00 13	00 28	00 43	00 58	01 13	06 13	06 43	07 13	07 40	07 58	08 10	08 28	08 43	08 58	09 13	09 28	09 43	09 58		10 13	10 28	10 43	10 58
St James Street	d	00 01	00 16	00 32	00 47	01 02	01 17	06 16	06 46	07 16	07 44	08 01	08 14	08 31	08 46	09 01	09 16	09 31	09 46	10 01		10 16	10 31	10 46	11 01
Walthamstow Central ⊖	d	00 03	00 18	00 34	00 49	01 04	01 19	06 18	06 48	07 18	07 46	08 03	08 16	08 33	08 48	09 03	09 18	09 33	09 48	10 03		10 18	10 33	10 48	11 03
Wood Street	d	00 05	00 20	00 36	00 51	01 06	01 21	06 20	06 50	07 20	07 48	08 05	08 18	08 35	08 50	09 05	09 20	09 35	09 50	10 05		10 20	10 35	10 50	11 05
Highams Park	d	00 08	00 23	00 39	00 54	01 09	01 24	06 23	06 53	07 23	07 51	08 08	08 21	08 38	08 53	09 08	09 23	09 38	09 53	10 08		10 23	10 38	10 53	11 08
Chingford	a	00 14	00 29	00 44	00 59	01 14	01 29	06 29	06 59	07 29	07 56	08 14	08 26	08 44	08 59	09 15	09 30	09 44	10 00	10 14		10 29	10 44	10 59	11 14

		LE	LE	LE	LE	LE		LE	LE	LE	LE	LE	LE	LE	LE	LE		LE	LE	LE	LE	LE	LE	LE	LE
London Liverpool Street 15 ⊖	d	11 03	11 18	11 33	11 48	12 03		12 18	12 33	12 48	13 03	13 18	13 33	13 48	14 03	14 18		14 33	14 48	15 03	15 18	15 33	15 48	16 03	16 18
Bethnal Green	d	11 06	11 21	11 36	11 51	12 06		12 21	12 36	12 51	13 06	13 21	13 36	13 51	14 06	14 21		14 36	14 51	15 06	15 21	15 36	15 51	16 06	
Hackney Downs	d	11 10	11 25	11 40	11 55	12 10		12 25	12 40	12 55	13 10	13 25	13 40	13 55	14 10	14 25		14 40	14 55	15 10	15 25	15 40	15 55	16 10	16 25
Clapton	d	11 13	11 28	11 43	11 58	12 13		12 28	12 43	12 58	13 13	13 28	13 43	13 58	14 13	14 28		14 43	14 58	15 13	15 28	15 43	15 58	16 13	16 28
St James Street	d	11 16	11 31	11 46	12 01	12 16		12 31	12 46	13 01	13 16	13 31	13 46	14 01	14 16	14 31		14 46	15 01	15 16	15 31	15 46	16 01	16 16	16 31
Walthamstow Central ⊖	d	11 18	11 33	11 48	12 03	12 18		12 33	12 48	13 03	13 18	13 33	13 48	14 03	14 18	14 33		14 48	15 03	15 18	15 33	15 48	16 03	16 19	16 34
Wood Street	d	11 20	11 35	11 50	12 05	12 20		12 35	12 50	13 05	13 20	13 35	13 50	14 05	14 20	14 35		14 50	15 05	15 20	15 35	15 50	16 05	16 21	16 36
Highams Park	d	11 23	11 38	11 53	12 08	12 23		12 38	12 53	13 08	13 23	13 38	13 53	14 08	14 23	14 38		14 53	15 08	15 23	15 38	15 53	16 08	16 24	16 39
Chingford	a	11 29	11 44	11 59	12 14	12 29		12 44	12 59	13 14	13 29	13 44	13 59	14 14	14 29	14 44		14 59	15 14	15 29	15 44	15 59	16 14	16 31	16 46

		LE		LE	LE	LE	LE	LE	LE	LE	LE	LE		LE	LE	LE	LE	LE	LE	LE	LE	LE		LE	LE
London Liverpool Street 15 ⊖	d	16 33		16 48	17 03	17 18	17 33	17 48	18 03	18 18	18 33	18 48		19 03	19 18	19 33	19 48	20 03	20 18	20 33	20 48	21 03		21 18	21 33
Bethnal Green	d	16 36			17 06		17 36		18 06		18 36			19 06		19 36	19 51	20 06	20 21	20 36	20 51	21 06		21 21	21 36
Hackney Downs	d	16 40		16 55	17 10	17 25	17 40	17 55	18 10	18 25	18 40	18 55		19 10	19 25	19 40	19 55	20 10	20 25	20 40	20 55	21 10		21 25	21 40
Clapton	d	16 43		16 58	17 13	17 28	17 43	17 58	18 13	18 28	18 43	18 58		19 13	19 28	19 43	19 58	20 13	20 28	20 43	20 58	21 13		21 28	21 43
St James Street	d	16 46		17 01	17 16	17 31	17 46	18 01	18 16	18 31	18 46	19 01		19 16	19 31	19 46	20 01	20 16	20 31	20 46	21 01	21 16		21 31	21 46
Walthamstow Central ⊖	d	16 49		17 04	17 19	17 34	17 49	18 04	18 19	18 34	18 49	19 04		19 18	19 33	19 48	20 03	20 18	20 33	20 48	21 03	21 18		21 33	21 48
Wood Street	d	16 51		17 06	17 21	17 36	17 51	18 06	18 21	18 36	18 51	19 06		19 20	19 35	19 50	20 05	20 20	20 35	20 50	21 05	21 20		21 35	21 50
Highams Park	d	16 54		17 09	17 24	17 39	17 54	18 09	18 24	18 39	18 54	19 09		19 23	19 38	19 53	20 08	20 23	20 38	20 53	21 08	21 23		21 38	21 53
Chingford	a	17 01		17 16	17 31	17 46	18 01	18 16	18 31	18 46	19 01	19 16		19 29	19 44	19 59	20 14	20 29	20 44	20 59	21 14	21 29		21 44	21 59

		LE	LE	LE	LE	LE	LE	LE		LE	LE
London Liverpool Street 15 ⊖	d	21 48	22 03	22 18	22 33	22 48	23 03	23 18		23 33	23 48
Bethnal Green	d	21 51	22 06	22 21	22 36	22 51	23 06	23 21			23 51
Hackney Downs	d	21 55	22 10	22 25	22 40	22 55	23 10	23 25			23 55
Clapton	d	21 58	22 13	22 28	22 43	22 58	23 13	23 28			23 58
St James Street	d	22 01	22 16	22 31	22 46	23 01	23 16	23 31			00 01
Walthamstow Central ⊖	d	22 03	22 18	22 33	22 48	23 03	23 18	23 33		23 44	00 03
Wood Street	d	22 05	22 20	22 35	22 50	23 05	23 20	23 35			00 05
Highams Park	d	22 08	22 23	22 38	22 53	23 08	23 23	23 38			00 08
Chingford	a	22 14	22 29	22 44	22 59	23 13	23 29	23 44		23 54	00 14

Saturdays

		LE	LE	LE	LE	LE	LE	LE	LE	LE	LE	LE	LE	LE	LE	LE	LE	LE	LE	LE		LE	LE	LE	LE
London Liverpool Street 15 ⊖	d	23p48	00 03	00 18	00 33	00 48	01 03	06 03	06 33	06 48	07 03	07 18	07 33	07 48	08 03	08 18	08 33	08 48	09 03	09 18		09 33	09 48	10 03	10 18
Bethnal Green	d	23p51	00 06	00 21	00 36			06 06	06 36	06 51	07 06	07 21	07 36	07 51	08 06	08 21	08 36	08 51	09 06	09 21		09 36	09 51	10 06	10 21
Hackney Downs	d	23p55	00 10	00 25	00 40	00 55	01 10	06 10	06 40	06 55	07 10	07 25	07 40	07 55	08 10	08 25	08 40	08 55	09 10	09 25		09 40	09 55	10 10	10 25
Clapton	d	23p58	00 13	00 28	00 43	00 58	01 13	06 13	06 43	06 58	07 13	07 28	07 43	07 58	08 13	08 28	08 43	08 58	09 13	09 28		09 43	09 58	10 13	10 28
St James Street	d	00 01	00 16	00 32	00 47	01 02	01 17	06 16	06 46	07 01	07 16	07 31	07 46	08 01	08 16	08 31	08 46	09 01	09 16	09 31		09 46	10 01	10 16	10 31
Walthamstow Central ⊖	d	00 03	00 18	00 34	00 49	01 04	01 19	06 18	06 48	07 03	07 18	07 33	07 48	08 03	08 18	08 33	08 48	09 03	09 18	09 33		09 48	10 03	10 18	10 33
Wood Street	d	00 05	00 20	00 36	00 51	01 06	01 21	06 20	06 50	07 05	07 20	07 35	07 50	08 05	08 20	08 35	08 50	09 05	09 20	09 35		09 50	10 05	10 20	10 35
Highams Park	d	00 08	00 23	00 39	00 54	01 09	01 24	06 23	06 53	07 08	07 23	07 38	07 53	08 08	08 23	08 38	08 53	09 08	09 23	09 38		09 53	10 08	10 23	10 38
Chingford	a	00 14	00 29	00 44	00 59	01 14	01 29	06 29	06 59	07 14	07 29	07 44	07 59	08 14	08 29	08 44	08 59	09 14	09 29	09 44		09 59	10 14	10 29	10 44

		LE	LE	LE	LE	LE		LE	LE	LE	LE	LE	LE	LE	LE	LE		LE	LE	LE	LE	LE	LE	LE	LE
London Liverpool Street 15 ⊖	d	10 33	10 48	11 03	11 18	11 33		11 48	12 03	12 18	12 33	12 48	13 03	13 18	13 33	13 48		14 03	14 18	14 33	14 48	15 03	15 18	15 33	15 48
Bethnal Green	d	10 36	10 51	11 06	11 21	11 36		11 51	12 06	12 21	12 36	12 51	13 06	13 21	13 36	13 51		14 06	14 21	14 36	14 51	15 06	15 21	15 36	15 51
Hackney Downs	d	10 40	10 55	11 10	11 25	11 40		11 55	12 10	12 25	12 40	12 55	13 10	13 25	13 40	13 55		14 10	14 25	14 40	14 55	15 10	15 25	15 40	15 55
Clapton	d	10 43	10 58	11 13	11 28	11 43		11 58	12 13	12 28	12 43	12 58	13 13	13 28	13 43	13 58		14 13	14 28	14 43	14 58	15 13	15 28	15 43	15 58
St James Street	d	10 46	11 01	11 16	11 31	11 46		12 01	12 16	12 31	12 46	13 01	13 16	13 31	13 46	14 01		14 16	14 31	14 46	15 01	15 16	15 31	15 46	16 01
Walthamstow Central ⊖	d	10 48	11 03	11 18	11 33	11 48		12 03	12 18	12 33	12 48	13 03	13 18	13 33	13 48	14 03		14 18	14 33	14 48	15 03	15 18	15 33	15 48	16 03
Wood Street	d	10 50	11 05	11 20	11 35	11 50		12 05	12 20	12 35	12 50	13 05	13 20	13 35	13 50	14 05		14 20	14 35	14 50	15 05	15 20	15 35	15 50	16 05
Highams Park	d	10 53	11 08	11 23	11 38	11 53		12 08	12 23	12 38	12 53	13 08	13 23	13 38	13 53	14 08		14 23	14 38	14 53	15 08	15 23	15 38	15 53	16 08
Chingford	a	10 59	11 14	11 29	11 44	11 59		12 14	12 29	12 44	12 59	13 14	13 29	13 44	13 59	14 14		14 29	14 44	14 59	15 14	15 29	15 44	15 59	16 14

		LE		LE	LE	LE	LE	LE	LE	LE	LE	LE		LE	LE	LE	LE	LE	LE	LE	LE	LE		LE	LE
London Liverpool Street 15 ⊖	d	16 03		16 18	16 33	16 48	17 03	17 18	17 33	17 48	18 03	18 18		18 33	18 48	19 03	19 18	19 33	19 48	20 03	20 18	20 33		20 48	21 03
Bethnal Green	d	16 06		16 21	16 36	16 51	17 06	17 21	17 36	17 51	18 06	18 21		18 36	18 51	19 06	19 21	19 36	19 51	20 06	20 21	20 36		20 51	21 06
Hackney Downs	d	16 10		16 25	16 40	16 55	17 10	17 25	17 40	17 55	18 10	18 25		18 40	18 55	19 10	19 25	19 40	19 55	20 10	20 25	20 40		20 55	21 10
Clapton	d	16 13		16 28	16 43	16 58	17 13	17 28	17 43	17 58	18 13	18 28		18 43	18 58	19 13	19 28	19 43	19 58	20 13	20 28	20 43		20 58	21 13
St James Street	d	16 16		16 31	16 46	17 01	17 16	17 31	17 46	18 01	18 16	18 31		18 46	19 01	19 16	19 31	19 46	20 01	20 16	20 31	20 46		21 01	21 16
Walthamstow Central ⊖	d	16 18		16 33	16 48	17 03	17 18	17 33	17 48	18 03	18 18	18 33		18 48	19 03	19 18	19 33	19 48	20 03	20 18	20 33	20 48		21 03	21 18
Wood Street	d	16 20		16 35	16 50	17 05	17 20	17 35	17 50	18 05	18 20	18 35		18 50	19 05	19 20	19 35	19 50	20 05	20 20	20 35	20 50		21 05	21 20
Highams Park	d	16 23		16 38	16 53	17 08	17 23	17 38	17 53	18 08	18 23	18 38		18 53	19 08	19 23	19 38	19 53	20 08	20 23	20 38	20 53		21 08	21 23
Chingford	a	16 29		16 44	16 59	17 14	17 29	17 44	17 59	18 14	18 29	18 44		18 59	19 14	19 29	19 44	19 59	20 14	20 29	20 44	20 59		21 14	21 29

Table 20

Saturdays

London - Chingford

		LE	LE	LE	LE	LE	LE	LE	LE	LE	LE	LE
London Liverpool Street [15] ⊖	d	21 18	21 33	21 48	22 03	22 18	22 33	22 48	23 03	23 18	23 33	23 48
Bethnal Green	d	21 21	21 36	21 51	22 06	22 21	22 36	22 51	23 06	23 21		23 51
Hackney Downs	d	21 25	21 40	21 55	22 10	22 25	22 40	22 55	23 10	23 25		23 55
Clapton	d	21 28	21 43	21 58	22 13	22 28	22 43	22 58	23 13	23 28		23 58
St James Street	d	21 31	21 46	22 01	22 16	22 31	22 46	23 01	23 16	23 31		00 01
Walthamstow Central ⊖	d	21 33	21 48	22 03	22 18	22 33	22 48	23 03	23 18	23 33	23 44	00 03
Wood Street	d	21 35	21 50	22 05	22 20	22 35	22 50	23 05	23 20	23 35		00 05
Highams Park	d	21 38	21 53	22 08	22 23	22 38	22 53	23 08	23 23	23 38		00 08
Chingford	a	21 44	21 59	22 14	22 29	22 44	22 59	23 14	23 29	23 44	23 54	00 14

Sundays

		LE	LE	LE	LE	LE	LE	LE	LE	LE	LE	LE	LE	LE	LE	LE	LE	LE	LE	LE	LE	LE	LE	LE
London Liverpool Street [15] ⊖	d	23p48	00 03	00 18	00 33	00 48	01 03	07 33	08 03	08 33	08 48	09 03	09 18	09 33	09 48	10 03	10 18	10 33	10 48	11 03	11 18	11 33	11 48	12 03
Bethnal Green	d	23p51	00 06	00 21	00 36								09 21	09 36	09 51	10 06	10 21	10 36	10 51	11 06	11 21	11 36	11 51	12 06
Hackney Downs	d	23p55	00 10	00 25	00 40	00 55	01 10	07 40	08 10	08 40	08 55	09 10	09 25	09 40	09 55	10 10	10 25	10 40	10 55	11 10	11 25	11 40	11 55	12 10
Clapton	d	23p58	00 13	00 28	00 43	00 58	01 13	07 43	08 13	08 43	08 58	09 13	09 28	09 43	09 58	10 13	10 28	10 43	10 58	11 13	11 28	11 43	11 58	12 13
St James Street	d	00 01	00 16	00 32	00 47	01 02	01 17	07 46	08 16	08 46	09 01	09 16	09 31	09 46	10 01	10 16	10 31	10 46	11 01	11 16	11 31	11 46	12 01	12 16
Walthamstow Central ⊖	d	00 03	00 18	00 34	00 49	01 04	01 19	07 48	08 18	08 48	09 03	09 18	09 33	09 48	10 03	10 18	10 33	10 48	11 03	11 18	11 33	11 48	12 03	12 18
Wood Street	d	00 05	00 20	00 36	00 51	01 06	01 21	07 50	08 20	08 50	09 05	09 20	09 35	09 50	10 05	10 20	10 35	10 50	11 05	11 20	11 35	11 50	12 05	12 20
Highams Park	d	00 08	00 23	00 39	00 54	01 09	01 24	07 53	08 23	08 53	09 08	09 23	09 38	09 53	10 08	10 23	10 38	10 53	11 08	11 23	11 38	11 53	12 08	12 23
Chingford	a	00 14	00 29	00 44	00 59	01 14	01 29	07 59	08 29	08 59	09 14	09 29	09 44	09 59	10 14	10 29	10 44	10 59	11 14	11 29	11 44	11 59	12 14	12 29

		LE	LE	LE	LE	LE	LE	LE	LE	LE	LE	LE	LE	LE	LE	LE	LE	LE	LE	LE	LE	LE	LE
London Liverpool Street [15] ⊖	d	12 18	12 33	12 48	13 03	13 18	13 33	13 48	14 03	14 18	14 33	14 48	15 03	15 18	15 33	15 48	16 03	16 18	16 33	16 48	17 03	17 18	17 33
Bethnal Green	d	12 21	12 36	12 51	13 06	13 21	13 36	13 51	14 06	14 21	14 36	14 51	15 06	15 21	15 36	15 51	16 06	16 21	16 36	16 51	17 06	17 21	17 36
Hackney Downs	d	12 25	12 40	12 55	13 10	13 25	13 40	13 55	14 10	14 25	14 40	14 55	15 10	15 25	15 40	15 55	16 10	16 25	16 40	16 55	17 10	17 25	17 40
Clapton	d	12 28	12 43	12 58	13 13	13 28	13 43	13 58	14 13	14 28	14 43	14 58	15 13	15 28	15 43	15 58	16 13	16 28	16 43	16 58	17 13	17 28	17 43
St James Street	d	12 31	12 46	13 01	13 16	13 31	13 46	14 01	14 16	14 31	14 46	15 01	15 16	15 31	15 46	16 01	16 16	16 31	16 46	17 01	17 16	17 31	17 46
Walthamstow Central ⊖	d	12 33	12 48	13 03	13 18	13 33	13 48	14 03	14 18	14 33	14 48	15 03	15 18	15 33	15 48	16 03	16 18	16 33	16 48	17 03	17 18	17 33	17 48
Wood Street	d	12 35	12 50	13 05	13 20	13 35	13 50	14 05	14 20	14 35	14 50	15 05	15 20	15 35	15 50	16 05	16 20	16 35	16 50	17 05	17 20	17 35	17 50
Highams Park	d	12 38	12 53	13 08	13 23	13 38	13 53	14 08	14 23	14 38	14 53	15 08	15 23	15 38	15 53	16 08	16 23	16 38	16 53	17 08	17 23	17 38	17 53
Chingford	a	12 44	12 59	13 14	13 29	13 44	13 59	14 14	14 29	14 44	14 59	15 14	15 29	15 44	15 59	16 14	16 29	16 44	16 59	17 14	17 29	17 44	17 59

		LE	LE	LE	LE	LE	LE	LE	LE	LE	LE	LE	LE	LE	LE	LE	LE	LE	LE	LE	LE	LE
London Liverpool Street [15] ⊖	d	17 48	18 03	18 18	18 33	18 48	19 03	19 18	19 33	19 48	20 03	20 18	20 33	20 48	21 03	21 18	21 33	21 48	22 03	22 18	22 33	22 48
Bethnal Green	d	17 51	18 06	18 21	18 36	18 51	19 06	19 21	19 36	19 51	20 06	20 21	20 36	20 51	21 06	21 21	21 36	21 51	22 06	22 21	22 36	22 51
Hackney Downs	d	17 55	18 10	18 25	18 40	18 55	19 10	19 25	19 40	19 55	20 10	20 25	20 40	20 55	21 10	21 25	21 40	21 55	22 10	22 25	22 40	22 55
Clapton	d	17 58	18 13	18 28	18 43	18 58	19 13	19 28	19 43	19 58	20 13	20 28	20 43	20 58	21 13	21 28	21 43	21 58	22 13	22 28	22 43	22 58
St James Street	d	18 01	18 16	18 31	18 46	19 01	19 16	19 31	19 46	20 01	20 16	20 31	20 46	21 01	21 16	21 31	21 46	22 01	22 16	22 31	22 46	23 01
Walthamstow Central ⊖	d	18 03	18 18	18 33	18 48	19 03	19 18	19 33	19 48	20 03	20 18	20 33	20 48	21 03	21 18	21 33	21 48	22 03	22 18	22 33	22 48	23 03
Wood Street	d	18 05	18 20	18 35	18 50	19 05	19 20	19 35	19 50	20 05	20 20	20 35	20 50	21 05	21 20	21 35	21 50	22 05	22 20	22 35	22 50	23 05
Highams Park	d	18 08	18 23	18 38	18 53	19 08	19 23	19 38	19 53	20 08	20 23	20 38	20 53	21 08	21 23	21 38	21 53	22 08	22 23	22 38	22 53	23 08
Chingford	a	18 14	18 29	18 44	18 59	19 14	19 29	19 44	19 59	20 14	20 29	20 44	20 59	21 14	21 29	21 44	21 59	22 14	22 29	22 44	22 59	23 14

		LE	LE	LE	LE
London Liverpool Street [15] ⊖	d	23 03	23 18	23 33	23 48
Bethnal Green	d	23 06	23 21	23 36	23 51
Hackney Downs	d	23 10	23 25	23 40	23 55
Clapton	d	23 13	23 28	23 43	23 58
St James Street	d	23 16	23 31	23 46	00 01
Walthamstow Central ⊖	d	23 18	23 33	23 48	00 03
Wood Street	d	23 20	23 35	23 50	00 05
Highams Park	d	23 23	23 38	23 53	00 08
Chingford	a	23 29	23 44	23 59	00 14

A not 23 May

Table 20

Mondays to Fridays

Chingford - London

		LE	LE	LE	LE	LE	LE	LE	LE	LE	LE	LE	LE	LE	LE	LE	LE	LE	LE	LE	LE	LE	LE
Chingford	d	05 10	05 25	05 40	05 55	06 10	06 25	06 42	06 57	07 12	07 27	07 42	07 54	08 12	08 27	08 32	08 42	08 57	09 12	09 27	09 40	09 55	10 10
Highams Park	d	05 14	05 29	05 44	05 59	06 14	06 29	06 46	07 01	07 16	07 31	07 46	07 58	08 16	08 31	08 36	08 46	09 01	09 16	09 31	09 44	09 59	10 14
Wood Street	d	05 17	05 32	05 47	06 02	06 17	06 33	06 50	07 05	07 20	07 35	07 50	08 02	08 20	08 35	08 40	08 50	09 05	09 20	09 35	09 47	10 02	10 17
Walthamstow Central ⊖	d	05 19	05 34	05 49	06 04	06 19	06 35	06 52	07 07	07 22	07 37	07 52	08 04	08 22	08 37	08 42	08 52	09 07	09 22	09 37	09 49	10 04	10 19
St James Street	d	05 21	05 36	05 51	06 06	06 21	06 38	06 55	07 10	07 25	07 40	07 55	08 07	08 25	08 40		08 55	09 10	09 25	09 40	09 51	10 06	10 21
Clapton	d	05 24	05 39	05 54	06 09	06 24	06 41	06 58	07 13	07 28	07 43	07 58	08 10	08 28	08 43		08 58	09 13	09 28	09 43	09 54	10 09	10 24
Hackney Downs	d	05 28	05 43	05 58	06 13	06 28	06 45	07 02	07 17	07 32	07 47	08 02	08 14	08 32	08 47		09 02	09 17	09 32	09 47	09 58	10 13	10 28
Bethnal Green	d	05 32	05 47	06 02	06 17	06 32	06 49		07 21		07 51		08 18		08 51			09 21		09 51	10 02	10 17	10 32
London Liverpool Street [15] ⊖	a	05 36	05 51	06 07	06 21	06 36	06 53	07 12	07 27	07 42	07 57	08 12	08 24	08 42	08 57	09 00	09 12	09 27	09 42	09 57	10 07	10 21	10 36

		LE	LE	LE	LE	LE	LE	LE	LE	LE	LE	LE	LE	LE	LE	LE	LE	LE	LE	LE	LE	LE	LE
Chingford	d	10 25	10 40	10 55	11 10	11 25	11 40	11 55	12 10	12 25	12 40	12 55	13 10	13 25	13 40	13 55	14 10	14 25	14 40	14 55	15 10	15 25	15 40
Highams Park	d	10 29	10 44	10 59	11 14	11 29	11 44	11 59	12 14	12 29	12 44	12 59	13 14	13 29	13 44	13 59	14 14	14 29	14 44	14 59	15 14	15 29	15 44
Wood Street	d	10 32	10 47	11 02	11 17	11 32	11 47	12 02	12 17	12 32	12 47	13 02	13 17	13 32	13 47	14 02	14 17	14 32	14 47	15 02	15 17	15 32	15 47
Walthamstow Central ⊖	d	10 34	10 49	11 04	11 19	11 34	11 49	12 04	12 19	12 34	12 49	13 04	13 19	13 34	13 49	14 04	14 19	14 34	14 49	15 04	15 19	15 34	15 49
St James Street	d	10 36	10 51	11 06	11 21	11 36	11 51	12 06	12 21	12 36	12 51	13 06	13 21	13 36	13 51	14 06	14 21	14 36	14 51	15 06	15 21	15 36	15 51
Clapton	d	10 39	10 54	11 09	11 24	11 39	11 54	12 09	12 24	12 39	12 54	13 09	13 24	13 39	13 54	14 09	14 24	14 39	14 54	15 09	15 24	15 39	15 54
Hackney Downs	d	10 43	10 58	11 13	11 28	11 43	11 58	12 13	12 28	12 43	12 58	13 13	13 28	13 43	13 58	14 13	14 28	14 43	14 58	15 13	15 28	15 43	15 58
Bethnal Green	d	10 47	11 02	11 17	11 32	11 47	12 02	12 17	12 32	12 47	13 02	13 17	13 32	13 47	14 02	14 17	14 32	14 47	15 02	15 17	15 32	15 47	16 02
London Liverpool Street [15] ⊖	a	10 51	11 06	11 21	11 36	11 51	12 06	12 21	12 36	12 51	13 06	13 21	13 36	13 51	14 06	14 21	14 36	14 51	15 06	15 21	15 36	15 51	16 06

		LE	LE	LE	LE	LE	LE	LE	LE	LE	LE	LE	LE	LE	LE	LE	LE	LE	LE	LE	LE	LE
Chingford	d	15 55	16 10	16 25	16 40	16 55	17 10	17 25	17 40	17 55	18 10	18 25	18 40	18 55	19 10	19 25	19 40	19 55	20 10	20 25	20 40	20 55
Highams Park	d	15 59	16 14	16 29	16 44	16 59	17 14	17 29	17 44	17 59	18 14	18 29	18 44	18 59	19 14	19 29	19 44	19 59	20 14	20 29	20 44	20 59
Wood Street	d	16 02	16 17	16 32	16 47	17 02	17 17	17 32	17 47	18 02	18 17	18 32	18 47	19 02	19 17	19 32	19 47	20 02	20 17	20 32	20 47	21 02
Walthamstow Central ⊖	d	16 04	16 19	16 34	16 49	17 04	17 19	17 34	17 49	18 04	18 19	18 34	18 49	19 04	19 19	19 34	19 49	20 04	20 19	20 34	20 49	21 04
St James Street	d	16 06	16 21	16 36	16 51	17 06	17 21	17 36	17 51	18 06	18 21	18 36	18 51	19 06	19 21	19 36	19 51	20 06	20 21	20 36	20 51	21 06
Clapton	d	16 09	16 24	16 39	16 54	17 09	17 24	17 39	17 54	18 09	18 24	18 39	18 54	19 09	19 24	19 39	19 56	20 09	20 24	20 39	20 54	21 09
Hackney Downs	d	16 13	16 28	16 43	16 58	17 13	17 28	17 43	17 58	18 13	18 28	18 43	18 58	19 13	19 28	19 43	19 59	20 13	20 28	20 43	20 58	21 13
Bethnal Green	d	16 17	16 32	16 47	17 02	17 17	17 32	17 47	18 02	18 17	18 32	18 47	19 02	19 17	19 32	19 47	20 03	20 17	20 32	20 47	21 02	21 17
London Liverpool Street [15] ⊖	a	16 21	16 36	16 51	17 06	17 21	17 36	17 51	18 07	18 21	18 36	18 51	19 07	19 21	19 37	19 51	20 07	20 21	20 37	20 51	21 06	21 21

		LE	LE	LE	LE	LE	LE	LE	LE	LE	LE
Chingford	d	21 10	21 25	21 40	21 55	22 10	22 25	22 40	22 55	23 10	23 25
Highams Park	d	21 14	21 29	21 44	21 59	22 14	22 29	22 44	22 59	23 14	23 29
Wood Street	d	21 17	21 32	21 47	22 02	22 17	22 32	22 47	23 02	23 17	23 32
Walthamstow Central ⊖	d	21 19	21 34	21 49	22 04	22 19	22 34	22 49	23 04	23 19	23 34
St James Street	d	21 21	21 36	21 51	22 06	22 21	22 36	22 51	23 06	23 21	23 36
Clapton	d	21 24	21 39	21 54	22 09	22 24	22 39	22 54	23 09	23 24	23 39
Hackney Downs	d	21 28	21 43	21 58	22 13	22 28	22 43	22 58	23 13	23 28	23 43
Bethnal Green	d	21 32	21 47	22 02	22 17	22 32	22 47	23 02	23 17	23 32	23 47
London Liverpool Street [15] ⊖	a	21 36	21 51	22 06	22 21	22 36	22 51	23 06	23 21	23 36	23 51

Saturdays

		LE	LE	LE	LE	LE	LE	LE	LE	LE	LE	LE	LE	LE	LE	LE	LE	LE	LE	LE	LE	LE	LE
Chingford	d	05 10	05 25	05 40	05 55	06 10	06 25	06 40	06 55	07 10	07 25	07 40	07 55	08 10	08 25	08 40	08 55	09 10	09 25	09 40	09 55	10 10	10 25
Highams Park	d	05 14	05 29	05 44	05 59	06 14	06 29	06 44	06 59	07 14	07 29	07 44	07 59	08 14	08 29	08 44	08 59	09 14	09 29	09 44	09 59	10 14	10 29
Wood Street	d	05 17	05 32	05 47	06 02	06 17	06 32	06 47	07 02	07 17	07 32	07 47	08 02	08 17	08 32	08 47	09 02	09 17	09 32	09 47	10 02	10 17	10 32
Walthamstow Central ⊖	d	05 19	05 34	05 49	06 04	06 19	06 34	06 49	07 04	07 19	07 34	07 49	08 04	08 19	08 34	08 49	09 04	09 19	09 34	09 49	10 04	10 19	10 34
St James Street	d	05 21	05 36	05 51	06 06	06 21	06 36	06 51	07 06	07 21	07 36	07 51	08 06	08 21	08 36	08 51	09 06	09 21	09 36	09 51	10 06	10 21	10 36
Clapton	d	05 24	05 39	05 54	06 09	06 24	06 39	06 54	07 09	07 24	07 39	07 54	08 09	08 24	08 39	08 54	09 09	09 24	09 39	09 54	10 09	10 24	10 39
Hackney Downs	d	05 28	05 43	05 58	06 13	06 28	06 43	06 58	07 13	07 28	07 43	07 58	08 13	08 28	08 43	08 58	09 13	09 28	09 43	09 58	10 13	10 28	10 43
Bethnal Green	d	05 32	05 47	06 02	06 17	06 32	06 47	07 02	07 17	07 32	07 47	08 02	08 17	08 32	08 47	09 02	09 17	09 32	09 47	10 02	10 17	10 32	10 47
London Liverpool Street [15] ⊖	a	05 36	05 51	06 06	06 21	06 36	06 51	07 06	07 21	07 36	07 51	08 06	08 21	08 36	08 51	09 06	09 21	09 36	09 51	10 06	10 21	10 36	10 51

		LE	LE	LE	LE	LE	LE	LE	LE	LE	LE	LE	LE	LE	LE	LE	LE	LE	LE	LE	LE	LE	LE
Chingford	d	10 40	10 55	11 10	11 25	11 40	11 55	12 10	12 25	12 40	12 55	13 10	13 25	13 40	13 55	14 10	14 25	14 40	14 55	15 10	15 25	15 40	15 55
Highams Park	d	10 44	10 59	11 14	11 29	11 44	11 59	12 14	12 29	12 44	12 59	13 14	13 29	13 44	13 59	14 14	14 29	14 44	14 59	15 14	15 29	15 44	15 59
Wood Street	d	10 47	11 02	11 17	11 32	11 47	12 02	12 17	12 32	12 47	13 02	13 17	13 32	13 47	14 02	14 17	14 32	14 47	15 02	15 17	15 32	15 47	16 02
Walthamstow Central ⊖	d	10 49	11 04	11 19	11 34	11 49	12 04	12 19	12 34	12 49	13 04	13 19	13 34	13 49	14 04	14 19	14 34	14 49	15 04	15 19	15 34	15 49	16 04
St James Street	d	10 51	11 06	11 21	11 36	11 51	12 06	12 21	12 36	12 51	13 06	13 21	13 36	13 51	14 06	14 21	14 36	14 51	15 06	15 21	15 36	15 51	16 06
Clapton	d	10 54	11 09	11 24	11 39	11 54	12 09	12 24	12 39	12 54	13 09	13 24	13 39	13 54	14 09	14 24	14 39	14 54	15 09	15 24	15 39	15 54	16 09
Hackney Downs	d	10 58	11 13	11 28	11 43	11 58	12 13	12 28	12 43	12 58	13 13	13 28	13 43	13 58	14 13	14 28	14 43	14 58	15 13	15 28	15 43	15 58	16 13
Bethnal Green	d	11 02	11 17	11 32	11 47	12 02	12 17	12 32	12 47	13 02	13 17	13 32	13 47	14 02	14 17	14 32	14 47	15 02	15 17	15 32	15 47	16 02	16 17
London Liverpool Street [15] ⊖	a	11 06	11 21	11 36	11 51	12 06	12 21	12 36	12 51	13 06	13 21	13 36	13 51	14 06	14 21	14 36	14 51	15 06	15 21	15 36	15 51	16 06	16 21

		LE	LE	LE	LE	LE	LE	LE	LE	LE	LE	LE	LE	LE	LE	LE	LE	LE	LE	LE	LE	LE
Chingford	d	16 10	16 25	16 40	16 55	17 10	17 25	17 40	17 55	18 10	18 25	18 40	18 55	19 10	19 25	19 40	19 55	20 10	20 25	20 40	20 55	21 10
Highams Park	d	16 14	16 29	16 44	16 59	17 14	17 29	17 44	17 59	18 14	18 29	18 44	18 59	19 14	19 29	19 44	19 59	20 14	20 29	20 44	20 59	21 14
Wood Street	d	16 17	16 32	16 47	17 02	17 17	17 32	17 47	18 02	18 17	18 32	18 47	19 02	19 17	19 32	19 47	20 02	20 17	20 32	20 47	21 02	21 17
Walthamstow Central ⊖	d	16 19	16 34	16 49	17 04	17 19	17 34	17 49	18 04	18 19	18 34	18 49	19 04	19 19	19 34	19 49	20 04	20 19	20 34	20 49	21 04	21 19
St James Street	d	16 21	16 36	16 51	17 06	17 21	17 36	17 51	18 06	18 21	18 36	18 51	19 06	19 21	19 36	19 51	20 06	20 21	20 36	20 51	21 06	21 21
Clapton	d	16 24	16 39	16 54	17 09	17 24	17 39	17 54	18 09	18 24	18 39	18 54	19 09	19 24	19 39	19 54	20 09	20 24	20 39	20 54	21 09	21 24
Hackney Downs	d	16 28	16 43	16 58	17 13	17 28	17 43	17 58	18 13	18 28	18 43	18 58	19 13	19 28	19 43	19 58	20 13	20 28	20 43	20 58	21 13	21 28
Bethnal Green	d	16 32	16 47	17 02	17 17	17 32	17 47	18 02	18 17	18 32	18 47	19 02	19 17	19 32	19 47	20 02	20 17	20 32	20 47	21 02	21 17	21 32
London Liverpool Street [15] ⊖	a	16 36	16 51	17 06	17 21	17 36	17 51	18 06	18 21	18 36	18 51	19 06	19 21	19 36	19 51	20 06	20 21	20 36	20 51	21 06	21 21	21 36

		LE	LE	LE	LE	LE	LE	LE	LE	LE
Chingford	d	21 25	21 40	21 55	22 10	22 25	22 40	22 55	23 10	23 25
Highams Park	d	21 29	21 44	21 59	22 14	22 29	22 44	22 59	23 14	23 29
Wood Street	d	21 32	21 47	22 02	22 17	22 32	22 47	23 02	23 17	23 32
Walthamstow Central ⊖	d	21 34	21 49	22 04	22 19	22 34	22 49	23 04	23 19	23 34
St James Street	d	21 36	21 51	22 06	22 21	22 36	22 51	23 06	23 21	23 36
Clapton	d	21 39	21 54	22 09	22 24	22 39	22 54	23 09	23 24	23 39
Hackney Downs	d	21 43	21 58	22 13	22 28	22 43	22 58	23 13	23 28	23 43
Bethnal Green	d	21 47	22 02	22 17	22 32	22 47	23 02	23 17	23 32	23 47
London Liverpool Street [15] ⊖	a	21 51	22 06	22 21	22 36	22 51	23 06	23 22	23 36	23 51

Table 20

Sundays

Chingford - London

		LE	LE	LE	LE	LE	LE	LE	LE	LE	LE	LE	LE	LE	LE	LE	LE	LE	LE	LE	LE	LE	LE
Chingford	d	06 40	06 55	07 10	07 25	07 40	07 55	08 10	08 25	08 40	08 55	09 10	09 25	09 40	09 55	10 10	10 25	10 40	10 55	11 10	11 25	11 40	11 55
Highams Park	d	06 44	06 59	07 14	07 29	07 44	07 59	08 14	08 29	08 44	08 59	09 14	09 29	09 44	09 59	10 14	10 29	10 44	10 59	11 14	11 29	11 44	11 59
Wood Street	d	06 47	07 02	07 17	07 32	07 47	08 02	08 17	08 32	08 47	09 02	09 17	09 32	09 47	10 02	10 17	10 32	10 47	11 02	11 17	11 32	11 47	12 02
Walthamstow Central ⊖	d	06 49	07 04	07 19	07 34	07 49	08 04	08 19	08 34	08 49	09 04	09 19	09 34	09 49	10 04	10 19	10 34	10 49	11 04	11 19	11 34	11 49	12 04
St James Street	d	06 51	07 06	07 21	07 36	07 51	08 06	08 21	08 36	08 51	09 06	09 21	09 36	09 51	10 06	10 21	10 36	10 51	11 06	11 21	11 36	11 51	12 06
Clapton	d	06 54	07 09	07 24	07 39	07 54	08 09	08 24	08 39	08 54	09 09	09 24	09 39	09 54	10 09	10 24	10 39	10 54	11 09	11 24	11 39	11 54	12 09
Hackney Downs	d	06 58	07 13	07 28	07 43	07 58	08 13	08 28	08 43	08 58	09 13	09 28	09 43	09 58	10 13	10 28	10 43	10 58	11 13	11 28	11 43	11 58	12 13
Bethnal Green	d										09 17	09 32	09 47	10 02	10 17	10 32	10 47	11 02	11 17	11 32	11 47	12 02	12 17
London Liverpool Street ⊖	a	07 06	07 21	07 37	07 52	08 06	08 21	08 38	08 51	09 06	09 21	09 36	09 51	10 06	10 21	10 36	10 51	11 06	11 21	11 36	11 51	12 06	12 21

		LE	LE	LE	LE	LE	LE	LE	LE	LE	LE	LE	LE	LE	LE	LE	LE	LE	LE	LE	LE	LE	LE
Chingford	d	12 10	12 25	12 40	12 55	13 10	13 25	13 40	13 55	14 10	14 25	14 40	14 55	15 10	15 25	15 40	15 55	16 10	16 25	16 40	16 55	17 10	17 25
Highams Park	d	12 14	12 29	12 44	12 59	13 14	13 29	13 44	13 59	14 14	14 29	14 44	14 59	15 14	15 29	15 44	15 59	16 14	16 29	16 44	16 59	17 14	17 29
Wood Street	d	12 17	12 32	12 47	13 02	13 17	13 32	13 47	14 02	14 17	14 32	14 47	15 02	15 17	15 32	15 47	16 02	16 17	16 32	16 47	17 02	17 17	17 32
Walthamstow Central ⊖	d	12 19	12 34	12 49	13 04	13 19	13 34	13 49	14 04	14 19	14 34	14 49	15 04	15 19	15 34	15 49	16 04	16 19	16 34	16 49	17 04	17 19	17 34
St James Street	d	12 21	12 36	12 51	13 06	13 21	13 36	13 51	14 06	14 21	14 36	14 51	15 06	15 21	15 36	15 51	16 06	16 21	16 36	16 51	17 06	17 21	17 36
Clapton	d	12 24	12 39	12 54	13 09	13 24	13 39	13 54	14 09	14 24	14 39	14 54	15 09	15 24	15 39	15 54	16 09	16 24	16 39	16 54	17 09	17 24	17 39
Hackney Downs	d	12 28	12 43	12 58	13 13	13 28	13 43	13 58	14 13	14 28	14 43	14 58	15 13	15 28	15 43	15 58	16 13	16 28	16 43	16 58	17 13	17 28	17 43
Bethnal Green	d	12 32	12 47	13 02	13 17	13 32	13 47	14 02	14 17	14 32	14 47	15 02	15 17	15 32	15 47	16 02	16 17	16 32	16 47	17 02	17 17	17 32	17 47
London Liverpool Street ⊖	a	12 36	12 51	13 06	13 21	13 36	13 51	14 06	14 21	14 36	14 51	15 06	15 21	15 36	15 51	16 06	16 21	16 36	16 51	17 06	17 21	17 36	17 51

		LE	LE	LE	LE	LE	LE	LE	LE	LE	LE	LE	LE	LE	LE	LE	LE	LE	LE	LE	LE	LE
Chingford	d	17 40	17 55	18 10	18 25	18 40	18 55	19 10	19 25	19 40	19 55	20 10	20 25	20 40	20 55	21 10	21 25	21 40	21 55	22 10	22 25	22 40
Highams Park	d	17 44	17 59	18 14	18 29	18 44	18 59	19 14	19 29	19 44	19 59	20 14	20 29	20 44	20 59	21 14	21 29	21 44	21 59	22 14	22 29	22 44
Wood Street	d	17 47	18 02	18 17	18 32	18 47	19 02	19 17	19 32	19 47	20 02	20 17	20 32	20 47	21 02	21 17	21 32	21 47	22 02	22 17	22 32	22 47
Walthamstow Central ⊖	d	17 49	18 04	18 19	18 34	18 49	19 04	19 19	19 34	19 49	20 04	20 19	20 34	20 49	21 04	21 19	21 34	21 49	22 04	22 19	22 34	22 49
St James Street	d	17 51	18 06	18 21	18 36	18 51	19 06	19 21	19 36	19 51	20 06	20 21	20 36	20 51	21 06	21 21	21 36	21 51	22 06	22 21	22 36	22 51
Clapton	d	17 54	18 09	18 24	18 39	18 54	19 09	19 24	19 39	19 54	20 09	20 24	20 39	20 54	21 09	21 24	21 39	21 54	22 09	22 24	22 39	22 54
Hackney Downs	d	17 58	18 13	18 28	18 43	18 58	19 13	19 28	19 43	19 58	20 13	20 28	20 43	20 58	21 13	21 28	21 43	21 58	22 13	22 28	22 43	22 58
Bethnal Green	d	18 02	18 17	18 32	18 47	19 02	19 17	19 32	19 47	20 02	20 17	20 32	20 47	21 02	21 17	21 32	21 47	22 02	22 17	22 32	22 47	23 02
London Liverpool Street ⊖	a	18 06	18 21	18 36	18 51	19 06	19 21	19 36	19 51	20 06	20 21	20 36	20 51	21 06	21 21	21 36	21 51	22 06	22 21	22 36	22 51	23 06

		LE	LE
Chingford	d	22 55	23 10
Highams Park	d	22 59	23 14
Wood Street	d	23 02	23 17
Walthamstow Central ⊖	d	23 04	23 19
St James Street	d	23 06	23 21
Clapton	d	23 09	23 24
Hackney Downs	d	23 13	23 28
Bethnal Green	d	23 17	23 32
London Liverpool Street ⊖	a	23 21	23 36

Table 21

Mondays to Fridays

London - Cheshunt (via Seven Sisters) and Enfield Town

		LE	LE MX	LE	LE	LE	LE	LE	LE	LE	LE	LE	LE	LE	LE	LE	LE	LE	LE	LE	LE	LE	LE	LE
London Liverpool Street ⊖	d	23p30	23p45	00 01	05 45	06 00	06 14	06 21	06 30	06 44	06 51	07 00	07 18	07 21	07 33	07 44	07 51	08 03	08 14	08 21	08 30	08 44	08 51	09 00
Bethnal Green	d	23p33	23p48	00 03	05 48	06 03		06 24	06 33		06 54	07 03		07 24	07 36		07 54	08 06		08 24	08 33		08 54	09 03
Cambridge Heath	d	23p35	23p50	00 05	05 50	06 05		06 26	06 35		06 56	07 05		07 26	07 38		07 56	08 08		08 26	08 35		08 56	09 05
London Fields	d	23p37	23p52	00 07	05 52	06 07		06 28	06 37		06 58	07 07		07 28	07 40		07 58	08 10		08 28	08 37		08 58	09 07
Hackney Downs	d	23p39	23p54	00 09	05 54	06 09	06 22	06 30	06 39	06 52	07 00	07 09	07 25	07 30	07 42	07 52	08 00	08 12	08 22	08 30	08 39	08 52	09 00	09 09
Rectory Road	d	23p42	23p57	00 12	05 57	06 12	06 24	06 33	06 42	06 54	07 03	07 12		07 33	07 45	07 54	08 03	08 15	08 24	08 33	08 42	08 54	09 03	09 12
Stoke Newington	d	23p43	23p58	00 13	05 58	06 13	06 26	06 34	06 43	06 56	07 04	07 13		07 34	07 46	07 56	08 04	08 16	08 26	08 34	08 43	08 56	09 04	09 13
Stamford Hill	d	23p45	23p59	00 15	06 00	06 15	06 28	06 36	06 45	06 58	07 06	07 15		07 36	07 48	07 58	08 06	08 18	08 28	08 36	08 45	08 58	09 06	09 15
Seven Sisters ⊖	d	23p47	00 02	00 17	06 02	06 17	06 30	06 38	06 47	07 00	07 08	07 17	07 30	07 38	07 50	08 00	08 08	08 20	08 30	08 38	08 47	09 00	09 08	09 17
Bruce Grove	d	23p49	00 04	00 19	06 04	06 19	06 32	06 40	06 49	07 02	07 10	07 19	07 32	07 40	07 52	08 02	08 10	08 22	08 32	08 40	08 49	09 02	09 10	09 19
White Hart Lane	d	23p51	00 06	00 21	06 06	06 21	06 34	06 42	06 51	07 04	07 12	07 21	07 34	07 42	07 54	08 04	08 12	08 24	08 34	08 42	08 51	09 04	09 12	09 21
Silver Street	d	23p53	00 08	00 23	06 08	06 23	06 36	06 44	06 53	07 06	07 14	07 23	07 36	07 44	07 56	08 06	08 14	08 26	08 36	08 44	08 53	09 06	09 14	09 23
Edmonton Green	d	23p55	00 10	00 25	06 10	06 25	06 38	06 46	06 55	07 08	07 16	07 25	07 38	07 46	07 58	08 08	08 16	08 28	08 38	08 46	08 55	09 08	09 16	09 25
Bush Hill Park	d	23p58		00 28		06 28		06 49	06 58		07 19	07 28		07 49	08 01		08 19	08 31		08 49	08 58		09 19	09 28
Enfield Town	a	00 03		00 33		06 33		06 54	07 03		07 24	07 33		07 54	08 06		08 24	08 36		08 54	09 03		09 24	09 33
Southbury	d		00 14		06 14		06 41			07 11			07 41			08 11			08 41			09 11		
Turkey Street	d		00 17		06 17		06 44			07 14			07 44			08 14			08 44			09 14		
Theobalds Grove	d		00 19		06 19		06 47			07 17			07 47			08 17			08 47			09 17		
Cheshunt	a		00 22		06 24		06 51			07 21			07 51			08 21			08 51			09 21		

		LE	LE	LE	LE	LE	LE	LE	LE	LE	LE	LE	LE	LE	LE	LE	LE	LE	LE	LE	LE	LE	LE
London Liverpool Street ⊖	d	09 15	09 30	09 45	10 00	10 15	10 30	10 45	11 00	11 15	11 30	11 45	12 00	12 15	12 30	12 45	13 00	13 15	13 30	13 45	14 00	14 15	14 30
Bethnal Green	d	09 18	09 33	09 48	10 03	10 18	10 33	10 48	11 03	11 18	11 33	11 48	12 03	12 18	12 33	12 48	13 03	13 18	13 33	13 48	14 03	14 18	14 33
Cambridge Heath	d	09 20	09 35	09 50	10 05	10 20	10 35	10 50	11 05	11 20	11 35	11 50	12 05	12 20	12 35	12 50	13 05	13 20	13 35	13 50	14 05	14 20	14 35
London Fields	d	09 22	09 37	09 52	10 07	10 22	10 37	10 52	11 07	11 22	11 37	11 52	12 07	12 22	12 37	12 52	13 07	13 22	13 37	13 52	14 07	14 22	14 37
Hackney Downs	d	09 24	09 39	09 54	10 09	10 24	10 39	10 54	11 09	11 24	11 39	11 54	12 09	12 24	12 39	12 54	13 09	13 24	13 39	13 54	14 09	14 24	14 39
Rectory Road	d	09 27	09 42	09 57	10 12	10 27	10 42	10 57	11 12	11 27	11 42	11 57	12 12	12 27	12 42	12 57	13 12	13 27	13 42	13 57	14 12	14 27	14 42
Stoke Newington	d	09 28	09 43	09 58	10 13	10 28	10 43	10 58	11 13	11 28	11 43	11 58	12 13	12 28	12 43	12 58	13 13	13 28	13 43	13 58	14 13	14 28	14 43
Stamford Hill	d	09 30	09 45	10 00	10 15	10 30	10 45	11 00	11 15	11 30	11 45	12 00	12 15	12 30	12 45	13 00	13 15	13 30	13 45	14 00	14 15	14 30	14 45
Seven Sisters ⊖	d	09 32	09 47	10 02	10 17	10 32	10 47	11 02	11 17	11 32	11 47	12 02	12 17	12 32	12 47	13 02	13 17	13 32	13 47	14 02	14 17	14 32	14 47
Bruce Grove	d	09 34	09 49	10 04	10 19	10 34	10 49	11 04	11 19	11 34	11 49	12 04	12 19	12 34	12 49	13 04	13 19	13 34	13 49	14 04	14 19	14 34	14 49
White Hart Lane	d	09 36	09 51	10 06	10 21	10 36	10 51	11 06	11 21	11 36	11 51	12 06	12 21	12 36	12 51	13 06	13 21	13 36	13 51	14 06	14 21	14 36	14 51
Silver Street	d	09 38	09 53	10 08	10 23	10 38	10 53	11 08	11 23	11 38	11 53	12 08	12 23	12 38	12 53	13 08	13 23	13 38	13 53	14 08	14 23	14 38	14 53
Edmonton Green	d	09 40	09 55	10 10	10 25	10 40	10 55	11 10	11 25	11 40	11 55	12 10	12 25	12 40	12 55	13 10	13 25	13 40	13 55	14 10	14 25	14 40	14 55
Bush Hill Park	d		09 58		10 28		10 58		11 28		11 58		12 28		12 58		13 28		13 58		14 28		14 58
Enfield Town	a		10 03		10 33		11 03		11 33		12 03		12 33		13 03		13 33		14 03		14 33		15 03
Southbury	d	09 44		10 14		10 44		11 14		11 44		12 14		12 44		13 14		13 44		14 14		14 44	
Turkey Street	d	09 47		10 17		10 47		11 17		11 47		12 17		12 47		13 17		13 47		14 17		14 47	
Theobalds Grove	d	09 49		10 19		10 49		11 19		11 49		12 19		12 49		13 19		13 49		14 19		14 49	
Cheshunt	a	09 54		10 24		10 54		11 24		11 54		12 24		12 54		13 24		13 54		14 24		14 54	

		LE	LE	LE	LE	LE	LE	LE	LE	LE	LE	LE	LE	LE	LE	LE	LE	LE	LE	LE	LE	LE
London Liverpool Street ⊖	d	14 45	15 00	15 15	15 30	15 45	16 00	16 15	16 20	16 30	16 38	16 50	17 00	17 08	17 20	17 30	17 38	17 50	18 00	18 08	18 20	18 30
Bethnal Green	d	14 48	15 03	15 18	15 33	15 48	16 03	16 18	16 23	16 33		16 53	17 03		17 23	17 33		17 53	18 03		18 23	18 33
Cambridge Heath	d	14 50	15 05	15 20	15 35	15 50	16 05	16 20	16 25	16 35	16 43	16 55	17 05	17 13	17 25	17 35	17 43	17 55	18 05	18 13	18 25	18 35
London Fields	d	14 52	15 07	15 22	15 37	15 52	16 07	16 22	16 27	16 37	16 45	16 57	17 07	17 15	17 27	17 37	17 45	17 57	18 07	18 15	18 27	18 37
Hackney Downs	d	14 54	15 09	15 24	15 39	15 54	16 09	16 24	16 29	16 39	16 47	16 59	17 09	17 17	17 29	17 39	17 47	17 59	18 09	18 17	18 29	18 39
Rectory Road	d	14 57	15 12	15 27	15 42	15 57	16 12	16 27	16 32	16 42	16 49	17 02	17 12	17 19	17 32	17 42	17 49	18 02	18 12	18 19	18 32	18 42
Stoke Newington	d	14 58	15 13	15 28	15 43	15 58	16 13	16 28	16 33	16 43	16 51	17 03	17 13	17 21	17 33	17 43	17 51	18 03	18 13	18 21	18 33	18 43
Stamford Hill	d	15 00	15 15	15 30	15 45	16 00	16 15	16 30	16 35	16 45	16 53	17 05	17 15	17 23	17 35	17 45	17 53	18 05	18 15	18 23	18 35	18 45
Seven Sisters ⊖	d	15 02	15 17	15 32	15 47	16 02	16 17	16 33	16 38	16 48	16 56	17 08	17 18	17 26	17 38	17 48	17 56	18 08	18 18	18 26	18 38	18 48
Bruce Grove	d	15 04	15 19	15 34	15 49	16 04	16 19	16 35	16 40	16 50	16 58	17 10	17 20	17 28	17 40	17 50	17 58	18 10	18 20	18 28	18 40	18 50
White Hart Lane	d	15 06	15 21	15 36	15 51	16 06	16 21	16 37	16 42	16 52	17 00	17 12	17 22	17 30	17 42	17 52	18 00	18 12	18 22	18 30	18 42	18 52
Silver Street	d	15 08	15 23	15 38	15 53	16 08	16 23	16 39	16 44	16 54	17 02	17 14	17 24	17 32	17 44	17 54	18 02	18 14	18 24	18 32	18 44	18 54
Edmonton Green	d	15 10	15 25	15 40	15 55	16 10	16 25	16 41	16 46	16 56	17 04	17 16	17 26	17 34	17 46	17 56	18 04	18 16	18 26	18 34	18 46	18 56
Bush Hill Park	d		15 28		15 58		16 28		16 49	16 59		17 19	17 29		17 49	17 59		18 19	18 29		18 49	18 59
Enfield Town	a		15 33		16 03		16 34		16 55	17 06		17 25	17 36		17 55	18 06		18 25	18 36		18 55	19 06
Southbury	d	15 14		15 44		16 14		16 45			17 08			17 38			18 08			18 38		
Turkey Street	d	15 17		15 47		16 17		16 48			17 11			17 41			18 11			18 41		
Theobalds Grove	d	15 19		15 49		16 19		16 50			17 14			17 44			18 14			18 44		
Cheshunt	a	15 24		15 54		16 24		16 56			17 19			17 49			18 19			18 49		

		LE	LE	LE	LE	LE	LE	LE	LE	LE	LE	LE	LE	LE	LE	LE	LE	LE	LE	LE	LE	LE	LE
London Liverpool Street ⊖	d	18 38	18 50	19 00	19 08	19 20	19 30	19 45	20 00	20 15	20 30	20 45	21 00	21 15	21 30	21 45	22 00	22 15	22 30	22 45	23 00	23 15	23 30
Bethnal Green	d		18 53	19 03		19 23	19 33	19 48	20 03	20 18	20 33	20 48	21 03	21 18	21 33	21 48	22 03	22 18	22 33	22 48	23 03	23 18	23 33
Cambridge Heath	d	18 43	18 55	19 05	19 13	19 25	19 35	19 50	20 05	20 20	20 35	20 50	21 05	21 20	21 35	21 50	22 05	22 20	22 35	22 50	23 05	23 20	23 35
London Fields	d	18 45	18 57	19 07	19 15	19 27	19 37	19 52	20 07	20 22	20 37	20 52	21 07	21 22	21 37	21 52	22 07	22 22	22 37	22 52	23 07	23 22	23 37
Hackney Downs	d	18 47	18 59	19 09	19 17	19 29	19 39	19 54	20 09	20 24	20 39	20 54	21 09	21 24	21 39	21 54	22 09	22 24	22 39	22 54	23 09	23 24	23 39
Rectory Road	d	18 49	19 02	19 12	19 19	19 32	19 42	19 57	20 12	20 27	20 42	20 57	21 12	21 27	21 42	21 57	22 12	22 27	22 42	22 57	23 12	23 27	23 42
Stoke Newington	d	18 51	19 03	19 13	19 21	19 33	19 43	19 58	20 13	20 28	20 43	20 58	21 13	21 28	21 43	21 58	22 13	22 28	22 43	22 58	23 13	23 28	23 43
Stamford Hill	d	18 53	19 05	19 15	19 23	19 35	19 45	20 00	20 15	20 30	20 45	21 00	21 15	21 30	21 45	22 00	22 15	22 30	22 45	23 00	23 15	23 30	23 45
Seven Sisters ⊖	d	18 56	19 08	19 18	19 26	19 38	19 47	20 02	20 17	20 32	20 47	21 02	21 17	21 32	21 47	22 02	22 17	22 32	22 47	23 02	23 17	23 32	23 47
Bruce Grove	d	18 58	19 10	19 20	19 28	19 40	19 49	20 04	20 19	20 34	20 49	21 04	21 19	21 34	21 49	22 04	22 19	22 34	22 49	23 04	23 19	23 34	23 49
White Hart Lane	d	19 00	19 12	19 22	19 30	19 42	19 51	20 06	20 21	20 36	20 51	21 06	21 21	21 36	21 51	22 06	22 21	22 36	22 51	23 06	23 21	23 36	23 51
Silver Street	d	19 02	19 14	19 24	19 32	19 44	19 53	20 08	20 23	20 38	20 53	21 08	21 23	21 38	21 53	22 08	22 23	22 38	22 53	23 08	23 23	23 38	23 53
Edmonton Green	d	19 04	19 16	19 26	19 34	19 46	19 55	20 10	20 25	20 40	20 55	21 10	21 25	21 40	21 55	22 10	22 25	22 40	22 55	23 10	23 25	23 40	23 55
Bush Hill Park	d		19 19	19 29		19 49	19 58		20 28		20 58		21 28		21 58		22 28		22 58		23 28		23 58
Enfield Town	a		19 25	19 35		19 54	20 03		20 33		21 03		21 33		22 03		22 33		23 03		23 33		00 03
Southbury	d	19 08			19 38			20 14		20 44		21 14		21 44		22 14		22 44		23 14		23 44	
Turkey Street	d	19 11			19 41			20 17		20 47		21 17		21 47		22 17		22 47		23 17		23 47	
Theobalds Grove	d	19 14			19 44			20 19		20 49		21 19		21 49		22 19		22 49		23 19		23 49	
Cheshunt	a	19 19			19 48			20 24		20 54		21 24		21 54		22 24		22 54		23 24		23 54	

London - Cheshunt (via Seven Sisters) and Enfield Town

		LE
London Liverpool Street ⊖	d	23 45
Bethnal Green	d	23 48
Cambridge Heath	d	23 50
London Fields	d	23 52
Hackney Downs	d	23 54
Rectory Road	d	23 57
Stoke Newington	d	23 58
Stamford Hill	d	23 59
Seven Sisters ⊖	d	00 02
Bruce Grove	d	00 04
White Hart Lane	d	00 06
Silver Street	d	00 08
Edmonton Green	d	00 10
Bush Hill Park	d	
Enfield Town	a	
Southbury	d	00 14
Turkey Street	d	00 17
Theobalds Grove	d	00 19
Cheshunt	a	00 22

Saturdays

		LE	LE	LE	LE	LE	LE	LE	LE	LE	LE	LE	LE	LE	LE	LE	LE	LE	LE	LE	LE	LE	LE	LE
London Liverpool Street ⊖	d	23p30	23p45	00 01	05 15	05 28	05 45	06 00	06 15	06 30	06 45	07 00	07 15	07 30	07 45	08 00	08 15	08 30	08 45	09 00	09 15	09 30	09 45	10 00
Bethnal Green	d	23p33	23p48	00 03	05 18		05 48	06 03	06 18	06 33	06 48	07 03	07 18	07 33	07 48	08 03	08 18	08 33	08 48	09 03	09 18	09 33	09 48	10 03
Cambridge Heath	d	23p35	23p50	00 05	05 20		05 50	06 05	06 20	06 35	06 50	07 05	07 20	07 35	07 50	08 05	08 20	08 35	08 50	09 05	09 20	09 35	09 50	10 05
London Fields	d	23p37	23p52	00 07	05 22		05 52	06 07	06 22	06 37	06 52	07 07	07 22	07 37	07 52	08 07	08 22	08 37	08 52	09 07	09 22	09 37	09 52	10 07
Hackney Downs	d	23p39	23p54	00 09	05 24		05 54	06 09	06 24	06 39	06 54	07 09	07 24	07 39	07 54	08 09	08 24	08 39	08 54	09 09	09 24	09 39	09 54	10 09
Rectory Road	d	23p42	23p57	00 12	05 27		05 57	06 12	06 27	06 42	06 57	07 12	07 27	07 42	07 57	08 12	08 27	08 42	08 57	09 12	09 27	09 42	09 57	10 12
Stoke Newington	d	23p43	23p58	00 13	05 28		05 58	06 13	06 28	06 43	06 58	07 13	07 28	07 43	07 58	08 13	08 28	08 43	08 58	09 13	09 28	09 43	09 58	10 13
Stamford Hill	d	23p45	23p59	00 15	05 30		06 00	06 15	06 30	06 45	07 00	07 15	07 30	07 45	08 00	08 15	08 30	08 45	09 00	09 15	09 30	09 45	10 00	10 15
Seven Sisters ⊖	d	23p47	00 02	00 17	05 32	05 51	06 02	06 17	06 32	06 47	07 02	07 17	07 32	07 47	08 02	08 17	08 32	08 47	09 02	09 17	09 32	09 47	10 02	10 17
Bruce Grove	d	23p49	00 04	00 19	05 34	05 53	06 04	06 19	06 34	06 49	07 04	07 19	07 34	07 49	08 04	08 19	08 34	08 49	09 04	09 19	09 34	09 49	10 04	10 19
White Hart Lane	d	23p51	00 06	00 21	05 36	05 55	06 06	06 21	06 36	06 51	07 06	07 21	07 36	07 51	08 06	08 21	08 36	08 51	09 06	09 21	09 36	09 51	10 06	10 21
Silver Street	d	23p53	00 08	00 23	05 38	05 57	06 08	06 23	06 38	06 53	07 08	07 23	07 38	07 53	08 08	08 23	08 38	08 53	09 08	09 23	09 38	09 53	10 08	10 23
Edmonton Green	d	23p55	00 10	00 25	05 40	05 59	06 10	06 25	06 40	06 55	07 10	07 25	07 40	07 55	08 10	08 25	08 40	08 55	09 10	09 25	09 40	09 55	10 10	10 25
Bush Hill Park	d	23p58		00 28		06 02		06 28		06 58		07 28		07 58		08 28		08 58		09 28		09 58		10 28
Enfield Town	a	00 03		00 33		06 06		06 33		07 03		07 33		08 03		08 33		09 03		09 33		10 03		10 33
Southbury	d		00 14		05 44		06 14		06 44		07 14		07 44		08 14		08 44		09 14		09 44		10 14	
Turkey Street	d		00 17		05 47		06 17		06 47		07 17		07 47		08 17		08 47		09 17		09 47		10 17	
Theobalds Grove	d		00 19		05 49		06 19		06 49		07 19		07 49		08 19		08 49		09 19		09 49		10 19	
Cheshunt	a		00 22		05 54		06 24		06 54		07 24		07 54		08 24		08 54		09 24		09 54		10 24	

		LE	LE	LE	LE	LE	LE	LE	LE	LE	LE	LE	LE	LE	LE	LE	LE	LE	LE	LE	LE	LE	LE
London Liverpool Street ⊖	d	10 15	10 30	10 45	11 00	11 15	11 30	11 45	12 00	12 15	12 30	12 45	13 00	13 15	13 30	13 45	14 00	14 15	14 30	14 45	15 00	15 15	15 30
Bethnal Green	d	10 18	10 33	10 48	11 03	11 18	11 33	11 48	12 03	12 18	12 33	12 48	13 03	13 18	13 33	13 48	14 03	14 18	14 33	14 48	15 03	15 18	15 33
Cambridge Heath	d	10 20	10 35	10 50	11 05	11 20	11 35	11 50	12 05	12 20	12 35	12 50	13 05	13 20	13 35	13 50	14 05	14 20	14 35	14 50	15 05	15 20	15 35
London Fields	d	10 22	10 37	10 52	11 07	11 22	11 37	11 52	12 07	12 22	12 37	12 52	13 07	13 22	13 37	13 52	14 07	14 22	14 37	14 52	15 07	15 22	15 37
Hackney Downs	d	10 24	10 39	10 54	11 09	11 24	11 39	11 54	12 09	12 24	12 39	12 54	13 09	13 24	13 39	13 54	14 09	14 24	14 39	14 54	15 09	15 24	15 39
Rectory Road	d	10 27	10 42	10 57	11 12	11 27	11 42	11 57	12 12	12 27	12 42	12 57	13 12	13 27	13 42	13 57	14 12	14 27	14 42	14 57	15 12	15 27	15 42
Stoke Newington	d	10 28	10 43	10 58	11 13	11 28	11 43	11 58	12 13	12 28	12 43	12 58	13 13	13 28	13 43	13 58	14 13	14 28	14 43	14 58	15 13	15 28	15 43
Stamford Hill	d	10 30	10 45	11 00	11 15	11 30	11 45	12 00	12 15	12 30	12 45	13 00	13 15	13 30	13 45	14 00	14 15	14 30	14 45	15 00	15 15	15 30	15 45
Seven Sisters ⊖	d	10 32	10 47	11 02	11 17	11 32	11 47	12 02	12 17	12 32	12 47	13 02	13 17	13 32	13 47	14 02	14 17	14 32	14 47	15 02	15 17	15 32	15 47
Bruce Grove	d	10 34	10 49	11 04	11 19	11 34	11 49	12 04	12 19	12 34	12 49	13 04	13 19	13 34	13 49	14 04	14 19	14 34	14 49	15 04	15 19	15 34	15 49
White Hart Lane	d	10 36	10 51	11 06	11 21	11 36	11 51	12 06	12 21	12 36	12 51	13 06	13 21	13 36	13 51	14 06	14 21	14 36	14 51	15 06	15 21	15 36	15 51
Silver Street	d	10 38	10 53	11 08	11 23	11 38	11 53	12 08	12 23	12 38	12 53	13 08	13 23	13 38	13 53	14 08	14 23	14 38	14 53	15 08	15 23	15 38	15 53
Edmonton Green	d	10 40	10 55	11 10	11 25	11 40	11 55	12 10	12 25	12 40	12 55	13 10	13 25	13 40	13 55	14 10	14 25	14 40	14 55	15 10	15 25	15 40	15 55
Bush Hill Park	d		10 58		11 28		11 58		12 28		12 58		13 28		13 58		14 28		14 58		15 28		15 58
Enfield Town	a		11 03		11 33		12 03		12 33		13 03		13 33		14 03		14 33		15 03		15 33		16 03
Southbury	d	10 44		11 14		11 44		12 14		12 44		13 14		13 44		14 14		14 44		15 14		15 44	
Turkey Street	d	10 47		11 17		11 47		12 17		12 47		13 17		13 47		14 17		14 47		15 17		15 47	
Theobalds Grove	d	10 49		11 19		11 49		12 19		12 49		13 19		13 49		14 19		14 49		15 19		15 49	
Cheshunt	a	10 54		11 24		11 54		12 24		12 54		13 24		13 54		14 24		14 54		15 24		15 54	

		LE	LE	LE	LE	LE	LE	LE	LE	LE	LE	LE	LE	LE	LE	LE	LE	LE	LE	LE	LE	LE
London Liverpool Street ⊖	d	15 45	16 00	16 15	16 30	16 45	17 00	17 15	17 30	17 45	18 00	18 15	18 30	18 45	19 00	19 15	19 30	19 45	20 00	20 15	20 30	20 45
Bethnal Green	d	15 48	16 03	16 18	16 33	16 48	17 03	17 18	17 33	17 48	18 03	18 18	18 33	18 48	19 03	19 18	19 33	19 48	20 03	20 18	20 33	20 48
Cambridge Heath	d	15 50	16 05	16 20	16 35	16 50	17 05	17 20	17 35	17 50	18 05	18 20	18 35	18 50	19 05	19 20	19 35	19 50	20 05	20 20	20 35	20 50
London Fields	d	15 52	16 07	16 22	16 37	16 52	17 07	17 22	17 37	17 52	18 07	18 22	18 37	18 52	19 07	19 22	19 37	19 52	20 07	20 22	20 37	20 52
Hackney Downs	d	15 54	16 09	16 24	16 39	16 54	17 09	17 24	17 39	17 54	18 09	18 24	18 39	18 54	19 09	19 24	19 39	19 54	20 09	20 24	20 39	20 54
Rectory Road	d	15 57	16 12	16 27	16 42	16 57	17 12	17 27	17 42	17 57	18 12	18 27	18 42	18 57	19 12	19 27	19 42	19 57	20 12	20 27	20 42	20 57
Stoke Newington	d	15 58	16 13	16 28	16 43	16 58	17 13	17 28	17 43	17 58	18 13	18 28	18 43	18 58	19 13	19 28	19 43	19 58	20 13	20 28	20 43	20 58
Stamford Hill	d	16 00	16 15	16 30	16 45	17 00	17 15	17 30	17 45	18 00	18 15	18 30	18 45	19 00	19 15	19 30	19 45	20 00	20 15	20 30	20 45	21 00
Seven Sisters ⊖	d	16 02	16 17	16 32	16 47	17 02	17 17	17 32	17 47	18 02	18 17	18 32	18 47	19 02	19 17	19 32	19 47	20 02	20 17	20 32	20 47	21 02
Bruce Grove	d	16 04	16 19	16 34	16 49	17 04	17 19	17 34	17 49	18 04	18 19	18 34	18 49	19 04	19 19	19 34	19 49	20 04	20 19	20 34	20 49	21 04
White Hart Lane	d	16 06	16 21	16 36	16 51	17 06	17 21	17 36	17 51	18 06	18 21	18 36	18 51	19 06	19 21	19 36	19 51	20 06	20 21	20 36	20 51	21 06
Silver Street	d	16 08	16 23	16 38	16 53	17 08	17 23	17 38	17 53	18 08	18 23	18 38	18 53	19 08	19 23	19 38	19 53	20 08	20 23	20 38	20 53	21 08
Edmonton Green	d	16 10	16 25	16 40	16 55	17 10	17 25	17 40	17 55	18 10	18 25	18 40	18 55	19 10	19 25	19 40	19 55	20 10	20 25	20 40	20 55	21 10
Bush Hill Park	d		16 28		16 58		17 28		17 58		18 28		18 58		19 28		19 58		20 28		20 58	
Enfield Town	a		16 33		17 03		17 33		18 03		18 33		19 03		19 33		20 03		20 33		21 03	
Southbury	d	16 14		16 44		17 14		17 44		18 14		18 44		19 14		19 44		20 14		20 44		21 14
Turkey Street	d	16 17		16 47		17 17		17 47		18 17		18 47		19 17		19 47		20 17		20 47		21 17
Theobalds Grove	d	16 19		16 49		17 19		17 49		18 19		18 49		19 19		19 49		20 19		20 49		21 19
Cheshunt	a	16 24		16 54		17 24		17 54		18 24		18 54		19 24		19 54		20 24		20 54		21 24

London - Cheshunt (via Seven Sisters) and Enfield Town

		LE	LE	LE	LE	LE	LE	LE	LE	LE	LE	LE	LE
London Liverpool Street ⊖	d	21 00	21 15	21 30	21 45	22 00	22 15	22 30	22 45	23 00	23 15	23 30	23 45
Bethnal Green	d	21 03	21 18	21 33	21 48	22 03	22 18	22 33	22 48	23 03	23 18	23 33	23 48
Cambridge Heath	d	21 05	21 20	21 35	21 50	22 05	22 20	22 35	22 50	23 05	23 20	23 35	23 50
London Fields	d	21 07	21 22	21 37	21 52	22 07	22 22	22 37	22 52	23 07	23 22	23 37	23 52
Hackney Downs	d	21 09	21 24	21 39	21 54	22 09	22 24	22 39	22 54	23 09	23 24	23 39	23 54
Rectory Road	d	21 12	21 27	21 42	21 57	22 12	22 27	22 42	22 57	23 12	23 27	23 42	23 57
Stoke Newington	d	21 13	21 28	21 43	21 58	22 13	22 28	22 43	22 58	23 13	23 28	23 43	23 58
Stamford Hill	d	21 15	21 30	21 45	22 00	22 15	22 30	22 45	23 00	23 15	23 30	23 45	23 59
Seven Sisters ⊖	d	21 17	21 32	21 47	22 02	22 17	22 32	22 47	23 02	23 17	23 32	23 47	00 02
Bruce Grove	d	21 19	21 34	21 49	22 04	22 19	22 34	22 49	23 04	23 19	23 34	23 49	00 04
White Hart Lane	d	21 21	21 36	21 51	22 06	22 21	22 36	22 51	23 06	23 21	23 36	23 51	00 06
Silver Street	d	21 23	21 38	21 53	22 08	22 23	22 38	22 53	23 08	23 23	23 38	23 53	00 08
Edmonton Green	d	21 25	21 40	21 55	22 10	22 25	22 40	22 55	23 10	23 25	23 40	23 55	00 10
Bush Hill Park	d	21 28		21 58		22 28		22 58		23 28		23 58	
Enfield Town	a	21 33		22 03		22 33		23 03		23 33		00 03	
Southbury	d		21 44		22 14		22 44		23 14		23 44		00 14
Turkey Street	d		21 47		22 17		22 47		23 17		23 47		00 17
Theobalds Grove	d		21 49		22 19		22 49		23 19		23 49		00 19
Cheshunt	a		21 54		22 24		22 54		23 24		23 54		00 24

Sundays

		LE	LE	LE	LE	LE	LE	LE	LE	LE	LE	LE	LE	LE	LE	LE	LE	LE	LE	LE	LE	LE	LE	LE
London Liverpool Street ⊖	d	23p30	23p45	00 01	07 30	07 52	08 00	08 22	08 30	08 52	09 00	09 22	09 30	09 52	10 00	10 22	10 30	10 52	11 00	11 22	11 30	11 52	12 00	12 22
Bethnal Green	d	23p33	23p48	00 03									09 33		10 03		10 33		11 03		11 33		12 03	
Cambridge Heath	d	23p35	23p50	00 05									09 35		10 05		10 35		11 05		11 35		12 05	
London Fields	d	23p37	23p52	00 07									09 37		10 07		10 37		11 07		11 37		12 07	
Hackney Downs	d	23p39	23p54	00 09	07 39	07 59	08 09	08 29	08 39	08 59	09 09	09 29	09 39	09 59	10 09	10 29	10 39	10 59	11 09	11 29	11 39	11 59	12 09	12 29
Rectory Road	d	23p42	23p57	00 12	07 42		08 12		08 42		09 12		09 42		10 12		10 42		11 12		11 42		12 12	
Stoke Newington	d	23p43	23p58	00 13	07 43		08 13		08 43		09 13		09 43		10 13		10 43		11 13		11 43		12 13	
Stamford Hill	d	23p45	23p59	00 15	07 45		08 15		08 45		09 15		09 45		10 15		10 45		11 15		11 45		12 15	
Seven Sisters ⊖	d	23p47	00 02	00 17	07 47	08 04	08 17	08 34	08 47	09 04	09 17	09 34	09 47	10 04	10 17	10 34	10 47	11 04	11 17	11 34	11 47	12 04	12 17	12 34
Bruce Grove	d	23p49	00 04	00 19	07 49		08 19		08 49		09 19		09 49		10 19		10 49		11 19		11 49		12 19	
White Hart Lane	d	23p51	00 06	00 21	07 51		08 21		08 51		09 21		09 51		10 21		10 51		11 21		11 51		12 21	
Silver Street	d	23p53	00 08	00 23	07 53		08 23		08 53		09 23		09 53		10 23		10 53		11 23		11 53		12 23	
Edmonton Green	d	23p55	00 10	00 25	07 55	08 08	08 25	08 38	08 55	09 08	09 25	09 38	09 55	10 08	10 25	10 38	10 55	11 08	11 25	11 38	11 55	12 08	12 25	12 38
Bush Hill Park	d	23p58		00 28	07 58		08 28		08 58		09 28		09 58		10 28		10 58		11 28		11 58		12 28	
Enfield Town	a	00 03		00 33	08 03		08 33		09 03		09 33		10 03		10 33		11 03		11 33		12 03		12 33	
Southbury	d		00 14			08 12		08 42		09 12		09 42		10 12		10 42		11 12		11 42		12 12		12 42
Turkey Street	d		00 17			08 15		08 45		09 15		09 45		10 15		10 45		11 15		11 45		12 15		12 45
Theobalds Grove	d		00 19			08 17		08 47		09 17		09 47		10 17		10 47		11 17		11 47		12 17		12 47
Cheshunt	a		00 24			08 20		08 52		09 20		09 52		10 20		10 52		11 20		11 52		12 20		12 52

		LE	LE	LE	LE	LE	LE	LE	LE	LE	LE	LE	LE	LE	LE	LE	LE	LE	LE	LE	LE	LE	LE
London Liverpool Street ⊖	d	12 30	12 52	13 00	13 22	13 30	13 52	14 00	14 22	14 30	14 52	15 00	15 22	15 30	15 52	16 00	16 22	16 30	16 52	17 00	17 22	17 30	17 52
Bethnal Green	d	12 33		13 03		13 33		14 03		14 33		15 03		15 33		16 03		16 33		17 03		17 33	
Cambridge Heath	d	12 35		13 05		13 35		14 05		14 35		15 05		15 35		16 05		16 35		17 05		17 35	
London Fields	d	12 37		13 07		13 37		14 07		14 37		15 07		15 37		16 07		16 37		17 07		17 37	
Hackney Downs	d	12 39	12 59	13 09	13 29	13 39	13 59	14 09	14 29	14 39	14 59	15 09	15 29	15 39	15 59	16 09	16 29	16 39	16 59	17 09	17 29	17 39	17 59
Rectory Road	d	12 42		13 12		13 42		14 12		14 42		15 12		15 42		16 12		16 42		17 12		17 42	
Stoke Newington	d	12 43		13 13		13 43		14 13		14 43		15 13		15 43		16 13		16 43		17 13		17 43	
Stamford Hill	d	12 45		13 15		13 45		14 15		14 45		15 15		15 45		16 15		16 45		17 15		17 45	
Seven Sisters ⊖	d	12 47	13 04	13 17	13 34	13 47	14 04	14 17	14 34	14 47	15 04	15 17	15 34	15 47	16 04	16 17	16 34	16 47	17 04	17 17	17 34	17 47	18 04
Bruce Grove	d	12 49		13 19		13 49		14 19		14 49		15 19		15 49		16 19		16 49		17 19		17 49	
White Hart Lane	d	12 51		13 21		13 51		14 21		14 51		15 21		15 51		16 21		16 51		17 21		17 51	
Silver Street	d	12 53		13 23		13 53		14 23		14 53		15 23		15 53		16 23		16 53		17 23		17 53	
Edmonton Green	d	12 55	13 08	13 25	13 38	13 55	14 08	14 25	14 38	14 55	15 08	15 25	15 38	15 55	16 08	16 25	16 38	16 55	17 08	17 25	17 38	17 55	18 08
Bush Hill Park	d	12 58		13 28		13 58		14 28		14 58		15 28		15 58		16 28		16 58		17 28		17 58	
Enfield Town	a	13 03		13 33		14 03		14 33		15 03		15 33		16 03		16 33		17 03		17 33		18 03	
Southbury	d		13 12		13 42		14 12		14 42		15 12		15 42		16 12		16 42		17 12		17 42		18 12
Turkey Street	d		13 15		13 45		14 15		14 45		15 15		15 45		16 15		16 45		17 15		17 45		18 15
Theobalds Grove	d		13 17		13 47		14 17		14 47		15 17		15 47		16 17		16 47		17 17		17 47		18 17
Cheshunt	a		13 20		13 52		14 20		14 52		15 20		15 52		16 20		16 52		17 20		17 52		18 20

		LE	LE	LE	LE	LE	LE	LE	LE	LE	LE	LE	LE	LE	LE	LE	LE	LE	LE	LE	LE	LE
London Liverpool Street ⊖	d	18 00	18 22	18 30	18 52	19 00	19 22	19 30	19 52	20 00	20 22	20 30	20 52	21 00	21 22	21 30	21 52	22 00	22 22	22 30	22 52	23 00
Bethnal Green	d	18 03		18 33		19 03		19 33		20 03		20 33		21 03		21 33		22 03		22 33		23 03
Cambridge Heath	d	18 05		18 35		19 05		19 35		20 05		20 35		21 05		21 35		22 05		22 35		23 05
London Fields	d	18 07		18 37		19 07		19 37		20 07		20 37		21 07		21 37		22 07		22 37		23 07
Hackney Downs	d	18 09	18 29	18 39	18 59	19 09	19 29	19 39	19 59	20 09	20 29	20 39	20 59	21 09	21 29	21 39	21 59	22 09	22 29	22 39	22 59	23 09
Rectory Road	d	18 12		18 42		19 12		19 42		20 12		20 42		21 12		21 42		22 12		22 42		23 12
Stoke Newington	d	18 13		18 43		19 13		19 43		20 13		20 43		21 13		21 43		22 13		22 43		23 13
Stamford Hill	d	18 15		18 45		19 15		19 45		20 15		20 45		21 15		21 45		22 15		22 45		23 15
Seven Sisters ⊖	d	18 17	18 34	18 47	19 04	19 17	19 34	19 47	20 04	20 17	20 34	20 47	21 04	21 17	21 34	21 47	22 04	22 17	22 34	22 47	23 04	23 17
Bruce Grove	d	18 19		18 49		19 19		19 49		20 19		20 49		21 19		21 49		22 19		22 49		23 19
White Hart Lane	d	18 21		18 51		19 21		19 51		20 21		20 51		21 21		21 51		22 21		22 51		23 21
Silver Street	d	18 23		18 53		19 23		19 53		20 23		20 53		21 23		21 53		22 23		22 53		23 23
Edmonton Green	d	18 25	18 38	18 55	19 08	19 25	19 38	19 55	20 08	20 25	20 38	20 55	21 08	21 25	21 38	21 55	22 08	22 25	22 38	22 55	23 08	23 25
Bush Hill Park	d	18 28		18 58		19 28		19 58		20 28		20 58		21 28		21 58		22 28		22 58		23 28
Enfield Town	a	18 33		19 03		19 33		20 03		20 33		21 03		21 33		22 03		22 33		23 03		23 33
Southbury	d		18 42		19 12		19 42		20 12		20 42		21 12		21 42		22 12		22 42		23 12	
Turkey Street	d		18 45		19 15		19 45		20 15		20 45		21 15		21 45		22 15		22 45		23 15	
Theobalds Grove	d		18 47		19 17		19 47		20 17		20 47		21 17		21 47		22 17		22 47		23 17	
Cheshunt	a		18 52		19 20		19 52		20 20		20 52		21 20		21 52		22 20		22 52		23 20	

Table 21

London - Cheshunt (via Seven Sisters) and Enfield Town

	LE	LE
London Liverpool Street 15 ⊖ d	23 22	23 30
Bethnal Green d		23 33
Cambridge Heath d		23 35
London Fields d		23 37
Hackney Downs d	23 29	23 39
Rectory Road d		23 42
Stoke Newington d		23 43
Stamford Hill d		23 45
Seven Sisters ⊖ d	23 34	23 47
Bruce Grove d		23 49
White Hart Lane d		23 51
Silver Street d		23 53
Edmonton Green d	23 38	23 55
Bush Hill Park d		23 58
Enfield Town a		00 03
Southbury d	23 42	
Turkey Street d	23 45	
Theobalds Grove d	23 47	
Cheshunt a	23 50	

Table 21

Cheshunt (via Seven Sisters) and Enfield Town - London

	LE MX	LE MX 1	LE	LE MX 1	LE	LE	LE	LE	LE	LE	LE	LE	LE	LE	LE	LE	LE	LE	LE	LE	LE	LE	LE	LE
Cheshunt d	23p31	23p51		23p58		05 16		06 01			06 33			07 03			07 33			08 03			08 33	
Theobalds Grove d	23p34					05 19		06 04			06 36			07 06			07 36			08 06			08 36	
Turkey Street d	23p36					05 21		06 06			06 38			07 08			07 38			08 08			08 38	
Southbury d	23p39					05 24		06 09			06 41			07 11			07 41			08 11			08 41	
Enfield Town d							05 52		06 20	06 32		06 48	07 02		07 18	07 32		07 50	08 02		08 18	08 33		08 48
Bush Hill Park d							05 55		06 23	06 35		06 51	07 05		07 21	07 35		07 53	08 05		08 21	08 36		08 51
Edmonton Green d	23p43					05 28	05 58	06 13	06 26	06 38	06 45	06 54	07 08	07 15	07 26	07 38	07 45	07 56	08 08	08 15	08 25	08 39	08 45	08 54
Silver Street d	23p45					05 30	06 00	06 15	06 28	06 40	06 47	06 56	07 10	07 17	07 28	07 40	07 47	07 58	08 10	08 17	08 27	08 41	08 47	08 56
White Hart Lane d	23p47					05 32	06 02	06 17	06 30	06 42	06 49	06 58	07 12	07 19	07 30	07 42	07 49	08 00	08 12	08 19	08 29	08 43	08 49	08 58
Bruce Grove d	23p49					05 34	06 04	06 19	06 32	06 44	06 51	07 00	07 14	07 21	07 32	07 44	07 51	08 02	08 14	08 21	08 31	08 45	08 51	09 00
Seven Sisters ⊖ d	23p51	00 04	00 07	00 11	00 21	05 36	06 06	06 21	06 35	06 47	06 55	07 03	07 17	07 25	07 34	07 47	07 55	08 05	08 17	08 25	08 33	08 48	08 55	09 03
Stamford Hill d	23p53					05 38	06 08	06 23	06 37	06 49	06 57	07 05	07 19	07 27	07 36	07 49	07 57	08 07	08 19	08 27	08 35	08 50	08 57	09 05
Stoke Newington d	23p55					05 40	06 10	06 25	06 39	06 51	06 59	07 07	07 21	07 29	07 38	07 51	07 59	08 09	08 21	08 29	08 37	08 52	08 59	09 07
Rectory Road d	23p56					05 41	06 11	06 26	06 41	06 53	07 00	07 09	07 23	07 30	07 40	07 53	08 00	08 10	08 23	08 30	08 39	08 54	09 00	09 09
Hackney Downs d	23p59			00 16		05 44	06 14	06 29	06 45	06 58	07 04	07 13	07 28	07 34	07 43	07 58	08 04	08 14	08 28	08 34	08 43	08 58	09 04	09 13
London Fields d	00 01					05 46	06 16	06 31	06 47	07 00	07 06	07 15	07 30	07 36	07 45	08 00	08 06	08 16	08 30	08 36	08 45	09 00	09 06	09 15
Cambridge Heath d	00 03					05 48	06 18	06 33	06 49	07 02	07 08	07 17	07 32	07 38	07 47	08 02	08 08	08 18	08 32	08 38	08 47	09 02	09 08	09 17
Bethnal Green d	00 05					05 50	06 21	06 35	06 51		07 10	07 19		07 40	07 49		08 10	08 20		08 40	08 49		09 11	09 19
London Liverpool Street 15 ⊖ a	00 10	00 18	00 22	00 24	00 35	05 55	06 25	06 40	06 55	07 10	07 16	07 25	07 40	07 46	07 55	08 10	08 16	08 26	08 40	08 46	08 55	09 10	09 16	09 25

	LE	LE	LE	LE	LE		LE	LE	LE	LE	LE	LE	LE	LE	LE		LE	LE	LE	LE	LE	LE	LE	LE
Cheshunt d		09 03			09 31			10 01		10 31		11 01		11 31			12 01		12 31		13 01		13 31	
Theobalds Grove d		09 06			09 34			10 04		10 34		11 04		11 34			12 04		12 34		13 04		13 34	
Turkey Street d		09 08			09 36			10 06		10 36		11 06		11 36			12 06		12 36		13 06		13 36	
Southbury d		09 11			09 39			10 09		10 39		11 09		11 39			12 09		12 39		13 09		13 39	
Enfield Town d	09 02		09 18	09 29			09 52		10 22		10 52		11 22		11 52			12 22		12 52		13 22		13 52
Bush Hill Park d	09 05		09 21	09 32			09 55		10 25		10 55		11 25		11 55			12 25		12 55		13 25		13 55
Edmonton Green d	09 08	09 15	09 24	09 35	09 43		09 58	10 13	10 28	10 43	10 58	11 13	11 28	11 43	11 58		12 13	12 28	12 43	12 58	13 13	13 28	13 43	13 58
Silver Street d	09 10	09 17	09 26	09 37	09 45		10 00	10 15	10 30	10 45	11 00	11 15	11 30	11 45	12 00		12 15	12 30	12 45	13 00	13 15	13 30	13 45	14 00
White Hart Lane d	09 12	09 19	09 28	09 39	09 47		10 02	10 17	10 32	10 47	11 02	11 17	11 32	11 47	12 02		12 17	12 32	12 47	13 02	13 17	13 32	13 47	14 02
Bruce Grove d	09 14	09 21	09 30	09 41	09 49		10 04	10 19	10 34	10 49	11 04	11 19	11 34	11 49	12 04		12 19	12 34	12 49	13 04	13 19	13 34	13 49	14 04
Seven Sisters ⊖ d	09 17	09 25	09 33	09 43	09 51		10 06	10 21	10 36	10 51	11 06	11 21	11 36	11 51	12 06		12 21	12 36	12 51	13 06	13 21	13 36	13 51	14 06
Stamford Hill d	09 19	09 27	09 35	09 45	09 53		10 08	10 23	10 38	10 53	11 08	11 23	11 38	11 53	12 08		12 23	12 38	12 53	13 08	13 23	13 38	13 53	14 08
Stoke Newington d	09 21	09 29	09 37	09 47	09 55		10 10	10 25	10 40	10 55	11 10	11 25	11 40	11 55	12 10		12 25	12 40	12 55	13 10	13 25	13 40	13 55	14 10
Rectory Road d	09 23	09 30	09 39	09 49	09 56		10 11	10 26	10 41	10 56	11 11	11 26	11 41	11 56	12 11		12 26	12 41	12 56	13 11	13 26	13 41	13 56	14 11
Hackney Downs d	09 28	09 34	09 43	09 52	09 59		10 14	10 29	10 44	10 59	11 14	11 29	11 44	11 59	12 14		12 29	12 44	12 59	13 14	13 29	13 44	13 59	14 14
London Fields d	09 30	09 36	09 45	09 54	10 01		10 16	10 31	10 46	11 01	11 16	11 31	11 46	12 01	12 16		12 31	12 46	13 01	13 16	13 31	13 46	14 01	14 16
Cambridge Heath d	09 32	09 38	09 47	09 56	10 03		10 18	10 33	10 48	11 03	11 18	11 33	11 48	12 03	12 18		12 33	12 48	13 03	13 18	13 33	13 48	14 03	14 18
Bethnal Green d		09 41	09 49		10 05		10 20	10 35	10 50	11 05	11 20	11 35	11 50	12 05	12 20		12 35	12 50	13 05	13 20	13 35	13 50	14 05	14 20
London Liverpool Street 15 ⊖ a	09 40	09 46	09 55	10 03	10 10		10 25	10 40	10 55	11 10	11 25	11 40	11 55	12 10	12 25		12 40	12 55	13 10	13 25	13 40	13 55	14 10	14 25

	LE		LE	LE	LE	LE	LE	LE	LE	LE	LE		LE	LE	LE	LE	LE	LE	LE	LE	LE		LE	LE
Cheshunt d	14 01			14 31		15 01		15 31		16 01			16 31			17 01			17 31				18 01	
Theobalds Grove d	14 04			14 34		15 04		15 34		16 04			16 34			17 04			17 34				18 04	
Turkey Street d	14 06			14 36		15 06		15 36		16 06			16 36			17 06			17 36				18 06	
Southbury d	14 09			14 39		15 09		15 39		16 09			16 39			17 09			17 39				18 09	
Enfield Town d			14 22		14 52		15 22		15 52		16 22			16 52	17 00		17 22	17 30		17 52	18 00			18 22
Bush Hill Park d			14 25		14 55		15 25		15 55		16 25			16 55	17 03		17 25	17 33		17 55	18 03			18 25
Edmonton Green d	14 13		14 28	14 43	14 58	15 13	15 28	15 43	15 58	16 13	16 28		16 43	16 58	17 06	17 13	17 28	17 36	17 43	17 58	18 06		18 13	18 28
Silver Street d	14 15		14 30	14 45	15 00	15 15	15 30	15 45	16 00	16 15	16 30		16 45	17 00	17 08	17 15	17 30	17 38	17 45	18 00	18 08		18 15	18 30
White Hart Lane d	14 17		14 32	14 47	15 02	15 17	15 32	15 47	16 02	16 17	16 32		16 47	17 02	17 10	17 17	17 32	17 40	17 47	18 02	18 10		18 17	18 32
Bruce Grove d	14 19		14 34	14 49	15 04	15 19	15 34	15 49	16 04	16 19	16 34		16 49	17 04	17 12	17 19	17 34	17 42	17 49	18 04	18 12		18 19	18 34
Seven Sisters ⊖ d	14 21		14 36	14 51	15 06	15 21	15 36	15 51	16 06	16 21	16 36		16 51	17 06	17 14	17 21	17 36	17 44	17 51	18 06	18 14		18 21	18 36
Stamford Hill d	14 23		14 38	14 53	15 08	15 23	15 38	15 53	16 08	16 23	16 38		16 53	17 08		17 23	17 38		17 53	18 08			18 23	18 38
Stoke Newington d	14 25		14 40	14 55	15 10	15 25	15 40	15 55	16 10	16 25	16 40		16 55	17 10	17 17	17 25	17 40	17 47	17 55	18 10	18 17		18 25	18 40
Rectory Road d	14 26		14 41	14 56	15 11	15 26	15 41	15 56	16 11	16 26	16 41		16 56	17 11		17 26	17 41		17 56	18 11			18 26	18 41
Hackney Downs d	14 29		14 44	14 59	15 14	15 29	15 44	15 59	16 14	16 29	16 44		16 59	17 14	17 20	17 29	17 44	17 50	17 59	18 14	18 20		18 29	18 44
London Fields d	14 31		14 46	15 01	15 16	15 31	15 46	16 01	16 16	16 31	16 46		17 01	17 16		17 31	17 46		18 01	18 16			18 31	18 46
Cambridge Heath d	14 33		14 48	15 03	15 18	15 33	15 48	16 03	16 18	16 33	16 48		17 03	17 18		17 33	17 48		18 03	18 18			18 33	18 48
Bethnal Green d	14 35		14 50	15 05	15 20	15 35	15 50	16 06	16 20	16 35	16 51		17 05	17 21		17 35	17 51		18 06	18 21			18 35	18 51
London Liverpool Street 15 ⊖ a	14 40		14 55	15 10	15 25	15 40	15 55	16 11	16 25	16 40	16 56		17 10	17 26	17 29	17 40	17 56	17 59	18 11	18 26	18 29		18 40	18 56

	LE	LE	LE	LE	LE	LE	LE		LE	LE	LE	LE	LE	LE	LE	LE	LE		LE	LE	LE	LE	LE	LE
Cheshunt d		18 31			19 01				19 31		20 01		20 31		21 01		21 31			22 01		22 31		23 01
Theobalds Grove d		18 34			19 04				19 34		20 04		20 34		21 04		21 34			22 04		22 34		23 04
Turkey Street d		18 36			19 06				19 36		20 06		20 36		21 06		21 36			22 06		22 36		23 06
Southbury d		18 39			19 09				19 39		20 09		20 39		21 09		21 39			22 09		22 39		23 09
Enfield Town d	18 30		18 52	19 00		19 22	19 30			19 52		20 22		20 52		21 22			21 52		22 22		22 52	
Bush Hill Park d	18 33		18 55	19 03		19 25	19 33			19 55		20 25		20 55		21 25			21 55		22 25		22 55	
Edmonton Green d	18 36	18 43	18 58	19 06	19 13	19 28	19 36		19 43	19 58	20 13	20 28	20 43	20 58	21 13	21 28	21 43		21 58	22 13	22 28	22 43	22 58	23 13
Silver Street d	18 38	18 45	19 00	19 08	19 15	19 30	19 38		19 45	20 00	20 15	20 30	20 45	21 00	21 15	21 30	21 45		22 00	22 15	22 30	22 45	23 00	23 15
White Hart Lane d	18 40	18 47	19 02	19 10	19 17	19 32	19 40		19 47	20 02	20 17	20 32	20 47	21 02	21 17	21 32	21 47		22 02	22 17	22 32	22 47	23 02	23 17
Bruce Grove d	18 42	18 49	19 04	19 12	19 19	19 34	19 42		19 49	20 04	20 19	20 34	20 49	21 04	21 19	21 34	21 49		22 04	22 19	22 34	22 49	23 04	23 19
Seven Sisters ⊖ d	18 44	18 51	19 06	19 14	19 21	19 36	19 44		19 51	20 06	20 21	20 36	20 51	21 06	21 21	21 36	21 51		22 06	22 21	22 36	22 51	23 06	23 21
Stamford Hill d		18 53	19 08		19 23	19 38			19 53	20 08	20 23	20 38	20 53	21 08	21 23	21 38	21 53		22 08	22 23	22 38	22 53	23 08	23 23
Stoke Newington d	18 47	18 55	19 10	19 17	19 25	19 40	19 47		19 55	20 10	20 25	20 40	20 55	21 10	21 25	21 40	21 55		22 10	22 25	22 40	22 55	23 10	23 25
Rectory Road d		18 56	19 11		19 26	19 41			19 56	20 11	20 26	20 41	20 56	21 11	21 26	21 41	21 56		22 11	22 26	22 41	22 56	23 11	23 26
Hackney Downs d	18 50	18 59	19 14	19 20	19 29	19 44	19 50		19 59	20 14	20 29	20 44	20 59	21 14	21 29	21 44	21 59		22 14	22 29	22 44	22 59	23 14	23 29
London Fields d		19 01	19 16		19 31	19 46			20 01	20 16	20 31	20 46	21 01	21 16	21 31	21 46	22 01		22 16	22 31	22 46	23 01	23 16	23 31
Cambridge Heath d		19 03	19 18		19 33	19 48			20 03	20 18	20 33	20 48	21 03	21 18	21 33	21 48	22 03		22 18	22 33	22 48	23 03	23 18	23 33
Bethnal Green d		19 06	19 21		19 36	19 50			20 06	20 20	20 35	20 50	21 05	21 20	21 35	21 50	22 05		22 20	22 35	22 50	23 05	23 20	23 35
London Liverpool Street 15 ⊖ a	18 59	19 11	19 26	19 29	19 41	19 55	19 59		20 11	20 25	20 40	20 55	21 10	21 25	21 40	21 55	22 10		22 25	22 40	22 55	23 10	23 25	23 40

Table 21

Cheshunt (via Seven Sisters) and Enfield Town - London

		LE	LE	LE [1]	LE [1]
Cheshunt	d		23 31	23 51	23 58
Theobalds Grove	d		23 34		
Turkey Street	d		23 36		
Southbury	d		23 39		
Enfield Town	d	23 22			
Bush Hill Park	d	23 25			
Edmonton Green	d	23 28	23 43		
Silver Street	d	23 30	23 45		
White Hart Lane	d	23 32	23 47		
Bruce Grove	d	23 34	23 49		
Seven Sisters ⊖	d	23 36	23 51	00 04	00 11
Stamford Hill	d	23 38	23 53		
Stoke Newington	d	23 40	23 55		
Rectory Road	d	23 41	23 56		
Hackney Downs	d	23 44	23 59		00 16
London Fields	d	23 46	00 01		
Cambridge Heath	d	23 48	00 03		
Bethnal Green	d	23 50	00 05		
London Liverpool Street 15 ⊖	a	23 55	00 10	00 18	00 24

Saturdays

		LE	LE [1]	LE	LE [1]	LE	LE [1]	LE	LE	LE	LE	LE	LE	LE	LE	LE	LE	LE	LE	LE	LE	LE	LE	LE	LE
Cheshunt	d	23p31	23p51		23p58		05 16	06 01		06 31		07 01		07 31		08 01		08 31		09 01		09 31		10 01	
Theobalds Grove	d	23p34					05 19	06 04		06 34		07 04		07 34		08 04		08 34		09 04		09 34		10 04	
Turkey Street	d	23p36					05 21	06 06		06 36		07 06		07 36		08 06		08 36		09 06		09 36		10 06	
Southbury	d	23p39					05 24	06 09		06 39		07 09		07 39		08 09		08 39		09 09		09 39		10 09	
Enfield Town	d								06 22		06 52		07 22		07 52		08 22		08 52		09 22		09 52		10 22
Bush Hill Park	d								06 25		06 55		07 25		07 55		08 25		08 55		09 25		09 55		10 25
Edmonton Green	d	23p43					05 28	06 13	06 28	06 43	06 58	07 13	07 28	07 43	07 58	08 13	08 28	08 43	08 58	09 13	09 28	09 43	09 58	10 13	10 28
Silver Street	d	23p45					05 30	06 15	06 30	06 45	07 00	07 15	07 30	07 45	08 00	08 15	08 30	08 45	09 00	09 15	09 30	09 45	10 00	10 15	10 30
White Hart Lane	d	23p47					05 32	06 17	06 32	06 47	07 02	07 17	07 32	07 47	08 02	08 17	08 32	08 47	09 02	09 17	09 32	09 47	10 02	10 17	10 32
Bruce Grove	d	23p49					05 34	06 19	06 34	06 49	07 04	07 19	07 34	07 49	08 04	08 19	08 34	08 49	09 04	09 19	09 34	09 49	10 04	10 19	10 34
Seven Sisters ⊖	d	23p51	00 04	00 07	00 11	00 21	05 36	06 21	06 36	06 51	07 06	07 21	07 36	07 51	08 06	08 21	08 36	08 51	09 06	09 21	09 36	09 51	10 06	10 21	10 36
Stamford Hill	d	23p53					05 38	06 23	06 38	06 53	07 08	07 23	07 38	07 53	08 08	08 23	08 38	08 53	09 08	09 23	09 38	09 53	10 08	10 23	10 38
Stoke Newington	d	23p55					05 40	06 25	06 40	06 55	07 10	07 25	07 40	07 55	08 10	08 25	08 40	08 55	09 10	09 25	09 40	09 55	10 10	10 25	10 40
Rectory Road	d	23p56					05 41	06 26	06 41	06 56	07 11	07 26	07 41	07 56	08 11	08 26	08 41	08 56	09 11	09 26	09 41	09 56	10 11	10 26	10 41
Hackney Downs	d	23p59			00 16		05 45	06 29	06 44	06 59	07 14	07 29	07 44	07 59	08 14	08 29	08 44	08 59	09 14	09 29	09 44	09 59	10 14	10 29	10 44
London Fields	d	00 01						06 31	06 46	07 01	07 16	07 31	07 46	08 01	08 16	08 31	08 46	09 01	09 16	09 31	09 46	10 01	10 16	10 31	10 46
Cambridge Heath	d	00 03						06 33	06 48	07 03	07 18	07 33	07 48	08 03	08 18	08 33	08 48	09 03	09 18	09 33	09 48	10 03	10 18	10 33	10 48
Bethnal Green	d	00 05					05 49	06 35	06 50	07 05	07 20	07 35	07 50	08 05	08 20	08 35	08 50	09 05	09 20	09 35	09 50	10 05	10 20	10 35	10 50
London Liverpool Street 15 ⊖	a	00 10	00 18	00 22	00 24	00 36	05 54	06 40	06 55	07 10	07 25	07 40	07 55	08 10	08 25	08 40	08 55	09 10	09 25	09 40	09 55	10 10	10 25	10 40	10 55

		LE	LE	LE	LE	LE	LE	LE	LE	LE	LE	LE	LE	LE	LE	LE	LE	LE	LE	LE	LE	LE	LE
Cheshunt	d	10 31		11 01		11 31		12 01		12 31		13 01		13 31		14 01		14 31		15 01		15 31	
Theobalds Grove	d	10 34		11 04		11 34		12 04		12 34		13 04		13 34		14 04		14 34		15 04		15 34	
Turkey Street	d	10 36		11 06		11 36		12 06		12 36		13 06		13 36		14 06		14 36		15 06		15 36	
Southbury	d	10 39		11 09		11 39		12 09		12 39		13 09		13 39		14 09		14 39		15 09		15 39	
Enfield Town	d		10 52		11 22		11 52		12 22		12 52		13 22		13 52		14 22		14 52		15 22		15 52
Bush Hill Park	d		10 55		11 25		11 55		12 25		12 55		13 25		13 55		14 25		14 55		15 25		15 55
Edmonton Green	d	10 43	10 58	11 13	11 28	11 43	11 58	12 13	12 28	12 43	12 58	13 13	13 28	13 43	13 58	14 13	14 28	14 43	14 58	15 13	15 28	15 43	15 58
Silver Street	d	10 45	11 00	11 15	11 30	11 45	12 00	12 15	12 30	12 45	13 00	13 15	13 30	13 45	14 00	14 15	14 30	14 45	15 00	15 15	15 30	15 45	16 00
White Hart Lane	d	10 47	11 02	11 17	11 32	11 47	12 02	12 17	12 32	12 47	13 02	13 17	13 32	13 47	14 02	14 17	14 32	14 47	15 02	15 17	15 32	15 47	16 02
Bruce Grove	d	10 49	11 04	11 19	11 34	11 49	12 04	12 19	12 34	12 49	13 04	13 19	13 34	13 49	14 04	14 19	14 34	14 49	15 04	15 19	15 34	15 49	16 04
Seven Sisters ⊖	d	10 51	11 06	11 21	11 36	11 51	12 06	12 21	12 36	12 51	13 06	13 21	13 36	13 51	14 06	14 21	14 36	14 51	15 06	15 21	15 36	15 51	16 06
Stamford Hill	d	10 53	11 08	11 23	11 38	11 53	12 08	12 23	12 38	12 53	13 08	13 23	13 38	13 53	14 08	14 23	14 38	14 53	15 08	15 23	15 38	15 53	16 08
Stoke Newington	d	10 55	11 10	11 25	11 40	11 55	12 10	12 25	12 40	12 55	13 10	13 25	13 40	13 55	14 10	14 25	14 40	14 55	15 10	15 25	15 40	15 55	16 10
Rectory Road	d	10 56	11 11	11 26	11 41	11 56	12 11	12 26	12 41	12 56	13 11	13 26	13 41	13 56	14 11	14 26	14 41	14 56	15 11	15 26	15 41	15 56	16 11
Hackney Downs	d	10 59	11 14	11 29	11 44	11 59	12 14	12 29	12 44	12 59	13 14	13 29	13 44	13 59	14 14	14 29	14 44	14 59	15 14	15 29	15 44	15 59	16 14
London Fields	d	11 01	11 16	11 31	11 46	12 01	12 16	12 31	12 46	13 01	13 16	13 31	13 46	14 01	14 16	14 31	14 46	15 01	15 16	15 31	15 46	16 01	16 16
Cambridge Heath	d	11 03	11 18	11 33	11 48	12 03	12 18	12 33	12 48	13 03	13 18	13 33	13 48	14 03	14 18	14 33	14 48	15 03	15 18	15 33	15 48	16 03	16 18
Bethnal Green	d	11 05	11 20	11 35	11 50	12 05	12 20	12 35	12 50	13 05	13 20	13 35	13 50	14 05	14 20	14 35	14 50	15 05	15 20	15 35	15 50	16 05	16 20
London Liverpool Street 15 ⊖	a	11 10	11 25	11 40	11 55	12 10	12 25	12 40	12 55	13 10	13 25	13 40	13 55	14 10	14 25	14 40	14 55	15 10	15 25	15 40	15 55	16 10	16 25

		LE	LE	LE	LE	LE	LE	LE	LE	LE	LE	LE	LE	LE	LE	LE	LE	LE	LE	LE	LE	LE
Cheshunt	d	16 01		16 31		17 01		17 31		18 01		18 31		19 01		19 31		20 01		20 31		21 01
Theobalds Grove	d	16 04		16 34		17 04		17 34		18 04		18 34		19 04		19 34		20 04		20 34		21 04
Turkey Street	d	16 06		16 36		17 06		17 36		18 06		18 36		19 06		19 36		20 06		20 36		21 06
Southbury	d	16 09		16 39		17 09		17 39		18 09		18 39		19 09		19 39		20 09		20 39		21 09
Enfield Town	d		16 22		16 52		17 22		17 52		18 22		18 52		19 22		19 52		20 22		20 52	
Bush Hill Park	d		16 25		16 55		17 25		17 55		18 25		18 55		19 25		19 55		20 25		20 55	
Edmonton Green	d	16 13	16 28	16 43	16 58	17 13	17 28	17 43	17 58	18 13	18 28	18 43	18 58	19 13	19 28	19 43	19 58	20 13	20 28	20 43	20 58	21 13
Silver Street	d	16 15	16 30	16 45	17 00	17 15	17 30	17 45	18 00	18 15	18 30	18 45	19 00	19 15	19 30	19 45	20 00	20 15	20 30	20 45	21 00	21 15
White Hart Lane	d	16 17	16 32	16 47	17 02	17 17	17 32	17 47	18 02	18 17	18 32	18 47	19 02	19 17	19 32	19 47	20 02	20 17	20 32	20 47	21 02	21 17
Bruce Grove	d	16 19	16 34	16 49	17 04	17 19	17 34	17 49	18 04	18 19	18 34	18 49	19 04	19 19	19 34	19 49	20 04	20 19	20 34	20 49	21 04	21 19
Seven Sisters ⊖	d	16 21	16 36	16 51	17 06	17 21	17 36	17 51	18 06	18 21	18 36	18 51	19 06	19 21	19 36	19 51	20 06	20 21	20 36	20 51	21 06	21 21
Stamford Hill	d	16 23	16 38	16 53	17 08	17 23	17 38	17 53	18 08	18 23	18 38	18 53	19 08	19 23	19 38	19 53	20 08	20 23	20 38	20 53	21 08	21 23
Stoke Newington	d	16 25	16 40	16 55	17 10	17 25	17 40	17 55	18 10	18 25	18 40	18 55	19 10	19 25	19 40	19 55	20 10	20 25	20 40	20 55	21 10	21 25
Rectory Road	d	16 26	16 41	16 56	17 11	17 26	17 41	17 56	18 11	18 26	18 41	18 56	19 11	19 26	19 41	19 56	20 11	20 26	20 41	20 56	21 11	21 26
Hackney Downs	d	16 29	16 44	16 59	17 14	17 29	17 44	17 59	18 14	18 29	18 44	18 59	19 14	19 29	19 44	19 59	20 14	20 29	20 44	20 59	21 14	21 29
London Fields	d	16 31	16 46	17 01	17 16	17 31	17 46	18 01	18 16	18 31	18 46	19 01	19 16	19 31	19 46	20 01	20 16	20 31	20 46	21 01	21 16	21 31
Cambridge Heath	d	16 33	16 48	17 03	17 18	17 33	17 48	18 03	18 18	18 33	18 48	19 03	19 18	19 33	19 48	20 03	20 18	20 33	20 48	21 03	21 18	21 33
Bethnal Green	d	16 35	16 50	17 05	17 20	17 35	17 50	18 05	18 20	18 35	18 50	19 05	19 20	19 35	19 50	20 05	20 20	20 35	20 50	21 05	21 20	21 35
London Liverpool Street 15 ⊖	a	16 40	16 55	17 10	17 25	17 40	17 55	18 10	18 25	18 40	18 55	19 10	19 25	19 40	19 55	20 10	20 25	20 40	20 55	21 10	21 25	21 40

Table 21

Cheshunt (via Seven Sisters) and Enfield Town - London

		LE	LE	LE	LE	LE	LE	LE	LE	LE	LE	LE
Cheshunt	d		21 31		22 01		22 31		23 01		23 31	
Theobalds Grove	d		21 34		22 04		22 34		23 04		23 34	
Turkey Street	d		21 36		22 06		22 36		23 06		23 36	
Southbury	d		21 39		22 09		22 39		23 09		23 39	
Enfield Town	d	21 22		21 52		22 22		22 52		23 22		23 52
Bush Hill Park	d	21 25		21 55		22 25		22 55		23 25		23 55
Edmonton Green	d	21 28	21 43	21 58	22 13	22 28	22 43	22 58	23 13	23 28	23 43	23 58
Silver Street	d	21 30	21 45	22 00	22 15	22 30	22 45	23 00	23 15	23 30	23 45	23 59
White Hart Lane	d	21 32	21 47	22 02	22 17	22 32	22 47	23 02	23 17	23 32	23 47	00 02
Bruce Grove	d	21 34	21 49	22 04	22 19	22 34	22 49	23 04	23 19	23 34	23 49	00 04
Seven Sisters ⊖	d	21 36	21 51	22 06	22 21	22 36	22 51	23 06	23 21	23 36	23 51	00 06
Stamford Hill	d	21 38	21 53	22 08	22 23	22 38	22 53	23 08	23 23	23 38	23 53	00 08
Stoke Newington	d	21 40	21 55	22 10	22 25	22 40	22 55	23 10	23 25	23 40	23 55	00 10
Rectory Road	d	21 41	21 56	22 11	22 26	22 41	22 56	23 11	23 26	23 41	23 56	00 11
Hackney Downs	d	21 44	21 59	22 14	22 29	22 44	22 59	23 14	23 29	23 44	23 59	00 14
London Fields	d	21 46	22 01	22 16	22 31	22 46	23 01	23 16	23 31	23 46	00 01	00 16
Cambridge Heath	d	21 48	22 03	22 18	22 33	22 48	23 03	23 18	23 33	23 48	00 03	00 18
Bethnal Green	d	21 50	22 05	22 20	22 35	22 50	23 05	23 20	23 35	23 50	00 05	00 20
London Liverpool Street 15 ⊖	a	21 55	22 10	22 25	22 40	22 55	23 10	23 25	23 40	23 55	00 10	00 25

Sundays

		LE	LE	LE	LE	LE	LE	LE	LE	LE	LE	LE	LE	LE	LE	LE	LE	LE	LE	LE	LE	LE	LE
Cheshunt	d	23p31			08 15		08 45		09 15		09 45		10 15		10 45		11 15		11 45		12 15		12 45
Theobalds Grove	d	23p34			08 18		08 48		09 18		09 48		10 18		10 48		11 18		11 48		12 18		12 48
Turkey Street	d	23p36			08 21		08 51		09 21		09 51		10 21		10 51		11 21		11 51		12 21		12 51
Southbury	d	23p39			08 24		08 54		09 24		09 54		10 24		10 54		11 24		11 54		12 24		12 54
Enfield Town	d		23p52	07 57		08 27		08 57		09 27		09 57		10 27		10 57		11 27		11 57		12 27	
Bush Hill Park	d		23p55	08 00		08 30		09 00		09 30		10 00		10 30		11 00		11 30		12 00		12 30	
Edmonton Green	d	23p43	23p58	08 03	08 27	08 33	08 57	09 03	09 27	09 33	09 57	10 03	10 27	10 33	10 57	11 03	11 27	11 33	11 57	12 03	12 27	12 33	12 57
Silver Street	d	23p45	23p59	08 05		08 35		09 05		09 35		10 05		10 35		11 05		11 35		12 05		12 35	
White Hart Lane	d	23p47	00 02	08 07		08 37		09 07		09 37		10 07		10 37		11 07		11 37		12 07		12 37	
Bruce Grove	d	23p49	00 04	08 09		08 39		09 09		09 39		10 09		10 39		11 09		11 39		12 09		12 39	
Seven Sisters ⊖	d	23p51	00 06	08 11	08 33	08 41	09 03	09 11	09 33	09 41	10 03	10 11	10 33	10 41	11 03	11 11	11 33	11 41	12 03	12 11	12 33	12 41	13 03
Stamford Hill	d	23p53	00 08	08 13		08 43		09 13		09 43		10 13		10 43		11 13		11 43		12 13		12 43	
Stoke Newington	d	23p55	00 10	08 15		08 45		09 15		09 45		10 15		10 45		11 15		11 45		12 15		12 45	
Rectory Road	d	23p56	00 11	08 16		08 46		09 16		09 46		10 16		10 46		11 16		11 46		12 16		12 46	
Hackney Downs	d	23p59	00 14	08 19	08 39	08 49	09 09	09 19	09 39	09 49	10 09	10 19	10 39	10 49	11 09	11 19	11 39	11 49	12 09	12 19	12 39	12 49	13 09
London Fields	d	00 01	00 16					09 21		09 51		10 21		10 51		11 21		11 51		12 21		12 51	
Cambridge Heath	d	00 03	00 18					09 23		09 53		10 23		10 53		11 23		11 53		12 23		12 53	
Bethnal Green	d	00 05	00 20					09 25		09 55		10 25		10 55		11 25		11 55		12 25		12 55	
London Liverpool Street 15 ⊖	a	00 10	00 25	08 30	08 48	09 00	09 18	09 30	09 48	10 00	10 18	10 30	10 48	11 00	11 18	11 30	11 48	12 00	12 18	12 30	12 48	13 00	13 18

		LE	LE	LE	LE	LE	LE	LE	LE	LE	LE	LE	LE	LE	LE	LE	LE	LE	LE	LE	LE	LE	LE
Cheshunt	d		13 15		13 45		14 15		14 45		15 15		15 45		16 15		16 45		17 15		17 45		18 15
Theobalds Grove	d		13 18		13 48		14 18		14 48		15 18		15 48		16 18		16 48		17 18		17 48		18 18
Turkey Street	d		13 21		13 51		14 21		14 51		15 21		15 51		16 21		16 51		17 21		17 51		18 21
Southbury	d		13 24		13 54		14 24		14 54		15 24		15 54		16 24		16 54		17 24		17 54		18 24
Enfield Town	d	12 57		13 27		13 57		14 27		14 57		15 27		15 57		16 27		16 57		17 27		17 57	
Bush Hill Park	d	13 00		13 30		14 00		14 30		15 00		15 30		16 00		16 30		17 00		17 30		18 00	
Edmonton Green	d	13 03	13 27	13 33	13 57	14 03	14 27	14 33	14 57	15 03	15 27	15 33	15 57	16 03	16 27	16 33	16 57	17 03	17 27	17 33	17 57	18 03	18 27
Silver Street	d	13 05		13 35		14 05		14 35		15 05		15 35		16 05		16 35		17 05		17 35		18 05	
White Hart Lane	d	13 07		13 37		14 07		14 37		15 07		15 37		16 07		16 37		17 07		17 37		18 07	
Bruce Grove	d	13 09		13 39		14 09		14 39		15 09		15 39		16 09		16 39		17 09		17 39		18 09	
Seven Sisters ⊖	d	13 11	13 33	13 41	14 03	14 11	14 33	14 41	15 03	15 11	15 33	15 41	16 03	16 11	16 33	16 41	17 03	17 11	17 33	17 41	18 03	18 11	18 33
Stamford Hill	d	13 13		13 43		14 13		14 43		15 13		15 43		16 13		16 43		17 13		17 43		18 13	
Stoke Newington	d	13 15		13 45		14 15		14 45		15 15		15 45		16 15		16 45		17 15		17 45		18 15	
Rectory Road	d	13 16		13 46		14 16		14 46		15 16		15 46		16 16		16 46		17 16		17 46		18 16	
Hackney Downs	d	13 19	13 39	13 49	14 09	14 19	14 39	14 49	15 09	15 19	15 39	15 49	16 09	16 19	16 39	16 49	17 09	17 19	17 39	17 49	18 09	18 19	18 39
London Fields	d	13 21		13 51		14 21		14 51		15 21		15 51		16 21		16 51		17 21		17 51		18 21	
Cambridge Heath	d	13 23		13 53		14 23		14 53		15 23		15 53		16 23		16 53		17 23		17 53		18 23	
Bethnal Green	d	13 25		13 55		14 25		14 55		15 25		15 55		16 25		16 55		17 25		17 55		18 25	
London Liverpool Street 15 ⊖	a	13 30	13 48	14 00	14 18	14 30	14 48	15 00	15 18	15 30	15 48	16 00	16 18	16 30	16 48	17 00	17 18	17 30	17 48	18 00	18 18	18 30	18 48

		LE	LE	LE	LE	LE	LE	LE	LE	LE	LE	LE	LE	LE	LE	LE	LE	LE	LE	LE	LE	LE
Cheshunt	d		18 45		19 15		19 45		20 15		20 45		21 15		21 45		22 15		22 45		23 16	
Theobalds Grove	d		18 48		19 18		19 48		20 18		20 48		21 18		21 48		22 18		22 48		23 18	
Turkey Street	d		18 51		19 21		19 51		20 21		20 51		21 21		21 51		22 21		22 51		23 21	
Southbury	d		18 54		19 24		19 54		20 24		20 54		21 24		21 54		22 24		22 54		23 24	
Enfield Town	d	18 27		18 57		19 27		19 57		20 27		20 57		21 27		21 57		22 27		22 57		23 27
Bush Hill Park	d	18 30		19 00		19 30		20 00		20 30		21 00		21 30		22 00		22 30		23 00		23 30
Edmonton Green	d	18 33	18 57	19 03	19 27	19 33	19 57	20 03	20 27	20 33	20 57	21 03	21 27	21 33	21 57	22 03	22 27	22 33	22 57	23 03	23 27	23 33
Silver Street	d	18 35		19 05		19 35		20 05		20 35		21 05		21 35		22 05		22 35		23 05		23 35
White Hart Lane	d	18 37		19 07		19 37		20 07		20 37		21 07		21 37		22 07		22 37		23 07		23 37
Bruce Grove	d	18 39		19 09		19 39		20 09		20 39		21 09		21 39		22 09		22 39		23 09		23 39
Seven Sisters ⊖	d	18 41	19 03	19 11	19 33	19 41	20 03	20 11	20 33	20 41	21 03	21 11	21 33	21 41	22 03	22 11	22 33	22 41	23 03	23 11	23 33	23 41
Stamford Hill	d	18 43		19 13		19 43		20 13		20 43		21 13		21 43		22 13		22 43		23 13		23 43
Stoke Newington	d	18 45		19 15		19 45		20 15		20 45		21 15		21 45		22 15		22 45		23 15		23 45
Rectory Road	d	18 46		19 16		19 46		20 16		20 46		21 16		21 46		22 16		22 46		23 16		23 46
Hackney Downs	d	18 49	19 09	19 19	19 39	19 49	20 09	20 19	20 39	20 49	21 09	21 19	21 39	21 49	22 09	22 19	22 39	22 49	23 09	23 19	23 39	23 49
London Fields	d	18 51		19 21		19 51		20 21		20 51		21 21		21 51		22 21		22 51		23 21		23 51
Cambridge Heath	d	18 53		19 23		19 53		20 23		20 53		21 23		21 53		22 23		22 53		23 23		23 53
Bethnal Green	d	18 55		19 25		19 55		20 25		20 55		21 25		21 55		22 25		22 55		23 25		23 55
London Liverpool Street 15 ⊖	a	19 00	19 18	19 30	19 48	20 00	20 18	20 30	20 48	21 00	21 18	21 30	21 48	22 00	22 18	22 30	22 48	23 00	23 18	23 30	23 48	23 59

London - Broxbourne, Hertford East, Bishops Stortford, Stansted Airport and Cambridge

		LE MO ■	LE MX ■	LE MX ■	LE MO	LE MO ■	LE MX ■	LE MX ■	LE MO	LE MO ■		LE MX ■	LE ■	LE MO ■	LE MFO ■	LE ■	LE TWO ■	LE ■	XC ◇■	LE	LE ■	XC ◇■	LE ■		LE ■
																A			✠			✠			
London Liverpool Street 15 ⊖	d		22p58	23p12	23p22	23p25	23p25	23p28		23p28		23p40	23p58	03 40	04 10	04 40	04 40	05 10					05 25		05 28
Bethnal Green	d																								
Hackney Downs	d			23p18	23p29							23p46													
Stratford 7 ⊖	d	22p45																							
Clapton	d											23p49													
Seven Sisters ⊖	d				23p34																				
Tottenham Hale ⊖	d	22p55	23p10	23p25		23p37	23b37	23p40		23p40		23p53	00 10			04u52	04u59	05u22					05u37		05 40
Northumberland Park	d											23p55													
Angel Road	d																								
Ponders End	d	22p59		23p29						23p44		23p59													
Brimsdown	d	23p02		23p32						23p47		00 02													
Enfield Lock	d	23p04		23p34						23p49		00 04													
Waltham Cross	d	23p07		23p37					←	23p52		00 07													
Cheshunt	d	23p09	23p18	23p39	23p50			23p48	23p50	23p54		00 09	00 18			05 00	05 07						05 45		05 48
Broxbourne 3	a	23p14	23p22	23p44	→			23p52	23p55	23p59		00 14	00 22			05 04	05 11						05 49		05 53
	d	23p19	23p22	23p44				23p52	00 02	23p59		00 14	00 22			05 04	05 11			05 40			05 49		05 53
Rye House	d			23p47					00 06			00 17								05 43					
St Margarets (Herts)	d			23p50					00 09			00 20								05 46					
Ware	d			23p54					00 13			00 24								05 50					
Hertford East	a			00 01					00 19			00 31								05 56					
Roydon	d	23p24	23p26										00 26												05 57
Harlow Town	d	23p28	23p30			23p52	23p54	23p58		00 05			00 30			05 10	05 17	05 37					05 55		06 01
Harlow Mill	d	23p31	23p33										00 33												06 04
Sawbridgeworth	d	23p34	23p37					00 03		00 10			00 37					05 42							06 07
Bishops Stortford	a	23p41	23p44			00 02	00 04	00 10		00 17			00 44			05 20	05 27	05 49					06 05		06 14
	d	23p42	23p44			00 03	00 04	00 11								05 20	05 27	05 50			05 55		06 05		06 14
Stansted Mountfitchet	d	23p46	23p48					00 15								05 24	05 31		05c27		05 59				06 19
Stansted Airport	a					00 12	00 13							04 30	05 00	05 39	05 39	05 59					06 15		
	d																					06 06			
Elsenham	d	23p50	23p52					00 19													06 03				06 22
Newport (Essex)	d	23p55	23p57					00 24													06 08				06 28
Audley End	d	23p58	23p59					00 27											05 36		06 11	06 23			06 31
Great Chesterford	d	00 03	00 05					00 32													06 16				06 36
Whittlesford Parkway	d	00 08	00 10					00 37													06 21				06 40
Shelford	d	00 12	00 14					00 41													06 25				06 45
Cambridge	a	00 19	00 21					00 48											05 53		06 32	06 38			06 58

		LE ■	LE	LE ■	LE ■	LE ■		LE ■	LE ■	LE ■	LE ■	XC ◇■	LE ■	LE ■	LE	LE ■	LE ■	LE ■	LE ■	LE	LE ■	LE ■	LE ■	XC ◇■	LE ■
												✠												✠	
London Liverpool Street 15 ⊖	d	05 40	05 42	05 52	05 55	05 58			06 10	06 12	06 25		06 28	06 40	06 42	06 55	06 58		07 10	07 12	07 25	07 28			07 40
Bethnal Green	d																								
Hackney Downs	d		05 49							06 18					06 49					07 19					
Stratford 7 ⊖	d			06 03														07 02					07 33		
Clapton	d																								
Seven Sisters ⊖	d																								
Tottenham Hale ⊖	d	05u52	05 55	06 15	06u07	06 10			06u22	06 25	06u37		06 40	06u52	06 55	07u07	07 10	07 13	07u22	07 25	07u37	07 40	07 43		07u52
Northumberland Park	d			06 17														07 15					07 45		
Angel Road	d			06 19														07 17					07 47		
Ponders End	d		05 59							06 29					06 59					07 29					
Brimsdown	d		06 02							06 32					07 02					07 32					
Enfield Lock	d		06 04	06 24						06 34					07 04			07 22		07 34			07 52		
Waltham Cross	d		06 07					←		06 37					07 07					07 37					
Cheshunt	d		06 09	06 28		06 18		06 28		06 39			06 48		07 09		07 18	07 26		07 39		07 48	07 56		
Broxbourne 3	a		06 14	→		06 22		06 32		06 44			06 52		07 14		07 22	07 30		07 44		07 52	08 00		
	d		06 14			06 24		06 36		06 44			06 54		07 14		07 22	07 34		07 44		07 52			
Rye House	d							06 39		06 47					07 17					07 47					
St Margarets (Herts)	d							06 42		06 50					07 20					07 50					
Ware	d							06 46		06 54					07 24					07 54					
Hertford East	a		06 27					06 53		07 01					07 31					08 01					
Roydon	d					06 28							06 58				07 26					07 56			
Harlow Town	d				06 25	06 32					06 55		07e08			07 24	07 30	07 40			07 54	08 00			
Harlow Mill	d					06 35							07 11				07 33					08 03			
Sawbridgeworth	d					06 38							07 14				07 37					08 07			
Bishops Stortford	a	06 18				06 45			06 49				07 21	07 15			07 44	07 51	07 47			08 14			08 18
	d	06 18				06 45			06 49				07 26	07 18			07 44		07 48			08 14			08 18
Stansted Mountfitchet	d	06 23				06 50							07 30	07 23			07 48					08 18			08 23
Stansted Airport	a	06 29			06 43				06 59		07 13			07 30		07 42			07 59		08 13				08 30
	d											07 21												08 21	
Elsenham	d					06 53							07 34				07 52					08 22			
Newport (Essex)	d					06 59							07 39				07 57					08 27			
Audley End	d					07 02						07 37	07 42				08 00					08 30		08 37	
Great Chesterford	d					07 07							07 47				08 05					08 35			
Whittlesford Parkway	d					07 11							07 52				08 10					08 40			
Shelford	d					07 16							07 56				08 14					08 44			
Cambridge	a					07 25						07 58	08 06				08 23					08 55		08 58	

A MThFO
b previous night, stops to pick up only
c arr. 0521
e arr. 0702

Table 22

Mondays to Fridays

London - Broxbourne, Hertford East, Bishops Stortford, Stansted Airport and Cambridge

		LE ■		LE ■		LE ■	LE ■	LE ■	LE ■	LE ■	LE ■	LE ■	XC ◇■	LE ■	LE	LE ■		LE ■	LE ■	LE ■	LE	LE ■	LE ■	XC ◇■	LE ■
													✠											✠	
London Liverpool Street 15 ⊖	d	07 42		07 55		07 58		08 10	08 12		08 25	08 28		08 40	08 42	08 55		08 58		09 10	09 12	09 25	09 28		09 40
Bethnal Green	d																								
Hackney Downs	d	07 48							08 18						08 49						09 19				
Stratford 7 ⊖	d						08 03			08 20									08 58						
Clapton	d																								
Seven Sisters ⊖	d																								
Tottenham Hale ⊖	d	07 55		08u07		08 10	08 13	08u22	08 25	08 29	08u37	08 40		08u52	08 55	09u07		09 10	09 14	09u22	09 25	09u37	09 40		09u52
Northumberland Park	d						08 15			08 32									09 16						
Angel Road	d						08 17			08 34									09 18						
Ponders End	d	07 59							08 29						08 59						09 29				
Brimsdown	d	08 02							08 32						09 02						09 32				
Enfield Lock	d	08 04					08 22		08 34	08 39					09 04				09 23		09 34				
Waltham Cross	d	08 07							08 37						09 07						09 37				
Cheshunt	d	08 09				08 18	08 26		08 39	08 42		08 48			09 09			09 18	09 27		09 39		09 48		
Broxbourne 3	a	08 14				08 22	08 30		08 44	08 47		08 52			09 14			09 22	09 31		09 44		09 52		
	d	08 14				08 22	08 34		08 44			08 52			09 14			09 22	09 35		09 44		09 52		
Rye House	d	08 17							08 47						09 17						09 47				
St Margarets (Herts)	d	08 20							08 50						09 20						09 50				
Ware	d	08 24							08 54						09 24						09 54				
Hertford East	a	08 31							09 01						09 31						10 01				
Roydon	d					08 26												09 26							
Harlow Town	d			08 24		08 30	08 40				08 54	08 58				09 24		09 30	09 41			09 54	09 58		
Harlow Mill	d					08 33												09 33							
Sawbridgeworth	d					08 37						09 03						09 37					10 03		
Bishops Stortford	a					08 44	08 52	08 47				09 10		09 16				09 44	09 52	09 47			10 10		10 14
	d					08 44		08 48				09 11		09 18				09 44		09 48			10 11		10 15
Stansted Mountfitchet	d					08 48								09 23				09 48							
Stansted Airport	a			08 42				09 00			09 12			09 30		09 42				09 57		10 12			10 30
	d												09 21											10 21	
Elsenham	d					08 52												09 52							
Newport (Essex)	d					08 57												09 57							
Audley End	d					09 00						09 23	09 37					10 00					10 23	10 37	
Great Chesterford	d					09 05												10 05							
Whittlesford Parkway	d					09 10						09 30						10 10					10 30		
Shelford	d					09 14												10 14							
Cambridge	a					09 24						09 42	09 54					10 24					10 41	10 58	

		LE ■	LE ■	LE ■	LE ■	LE ■	LE ■		LE ■	LE ■	LE ■	XC ◇■	LE ■	LE ■	LE ■	LE ■	LE ■		LE ■	LE ■	LE ■	LE ■	XC ◇■	LE ■	LE ■
												✠											✠		
London Liverpool Street 15 ⊖	d		09 42	09 55	09 58		10 10		10 12	10 25	10 28		10 40		10 42	10 55	10 58		11 10	11 12	11 25	11 28		11 40	
Bethnal Green	d																								
Hackney Downs	d		09 48						10 18						10 48					11 18					
Stratford 7 ⊖	d	09 25				09 55								10 33											11 33
Clapton	d																								
Seven Sisters ⊖	d																								
Tottenham Hale ⊖	d	09 44	09 55	10u07	10 10	10 13	10u22		10 25	10u37	10 40		10u52	10 43	10 55	11u07	11 10		11u22	11 25	11u37	11 40		11u52	11 43
Northumberland Park	d	09 46				10 15								10 45											11 45
Angel Road	d	09 48																							
Ponders End	d		09 59						10 29						10 59					11 29					
Brimsdown	d		10 02						10 32						11 02					11 32					
Enfield Lock	d	09 53	10 04			10 21			10 34					10 51	11 04					11 34					11 51
Waltham Cross	d		10 07						10 37						11 07					11 37					
Cheshunt	d	09 57	10 09		10 18	10 25			10 39		10 48			10 55	11 09		11 18			11 39		11 48			11 55
Broxbourne 3	a	10 01	10 14		10 22	10 29			10 44		10 52			10 59	11 14		11 22			11 44		11 52			11 59
	d	10 05	10 14		10 22	10 33			10 44		10 52			11 03	11 14		11 22			11 44		11 52			12 03
Rye House	d		10 17						10 47						11 17					11 47					
St Margarets (Herts)	d		10 20						10 50						11 20					11 50					
Ware	d		10 24						10 54						11 24					11 54					
Hertford East	a		10 31						11 01						11 31					12 01					
Roydon	d	10 09			10 26									11 08			11 26								12 08
Harlow Town	d	10 13		10 24	10 30	10 40				10 54	10 58			11 12		11 24	11 30				11 54	11 58			12 12
Harlow Mill	d	10 16			10 33									11 15			11 33								12 15
Sawbridgeworth	d	10 20			10 37						11 03			11 18			11 37					12 03			12 18
Bishops Stortford	a	10 27			10 44	10 51	10 47				11 10		11 15	11 25			11 44		11 47			12 10		12 15	12 25
	d	10 27			10 44		10 48				11 11		11 15	11 26			11 44		11 48			12 11		12 15	12 26
Stansted Mountfitchet	d	10 31			10 48									11 30			11 48								12 30
Stansted Airport	a	10 39		10 42			10 57			11 12			11 25	11 39		11 42			11 57		12 12			12 25	12 39
	d											11 25											12 25		
Elsenham	d				10 52												11 52								
Newport (Essex)	d				10 57												11 57								
Audley End	d				11 00						11 23	11 37					12 00					12 23	12 37		
Great Chesterford	d				11 05												12 05								
Whittlesford Parkway	d				11 10						11 30						12 10					12 30			
Shelford	d				11 14												12 14								
Cambridge	a				11 21						11 40	11 58					12 21					12 40	12 58		

Table 22

London - Broxbourne, Hertford East, Bishops Stortford, Stansted Airport and Cambridge

		LE 1	LE 1	LE 1	LE 1	LE 1	LE 1	LE 1	XC ◇1	LE 1	LE 1	LE 1	LE 1	LE 1	LE 1	LE 1	LE 1	LE 1	XC ◇1	LE 1	LE 1	LE 1
London Liverpool Street 15 ⊖	d	11 42	11 55	11 58	12 10	12 12	12 25	12 28		12 40		12 42	12 55	12 58	13 10	13 12	13 25	13 28		13 40		13 42
Bethnal Green	d																					
Hackney Downs	d	11 47				12 18						12 48				13 18						13 48
Stratford 7 ⊖	d										12 33										13 33	
Clapton	d																					
Seven Sisters ⊖	d																					
Tottenham Hale ⊖	d	11 55	12u07	12 10	12u22	12 25	12u37	12 40		12u52	12 43	12 55	13u07	13 10	13u22	13 25	13u37	13 40		13u52	13 43	13 55
Northumberland Park	d										12 45										13 45	
Angel Road	d																					
Ponders End	d	11 58				12 29						12 59				13 29						13 59
Brimsdown	d	12 02				12 32						13 02				13 32						14 02
Enfield Lock	d	12 03				12 34					12 51	13 04				13 34					13 51	14 04
Waltham Cross	d	12 07				12 37						13 07				13 37						14 07
Cheshunt	d	12 08		12 18		12 39		12 48			12 55	13 09		13 18		13 39		13 48			13 55	14 09
Broxbourne 3	a	12 14		12 22		12 44		12 52			12 59	13 14		13 22		13 44		13 52			13 59	14 14
	d	12 14		12 22		12 44		12 52			13 03	13 14		13 22		13 44		13 52			14 03	14 14
Rye House	d	12 17				12 47						13 17				13 47						14 17
St Margarets (Herts)	d	12 20				12 50						13 20				13 50						14 20
Ware	d	12 24				12 54						13 24				13 54						14 24
Hertford East	a	12 31				13 01						13 31				14 01						14 31
Roydon	d			12 26							13 08			13 26							14 08	
Harlow Town	d		12 24	12 30			12 54	12 58			13 12		13 24	13 30			13 54	13 58			14 12	
Harlow Mill	d			12 33							13 15			13 33							14 15	
Sawbridgeworth	d			12 37				13 03			13 18			13 37				14 03			14 18	
Bishops Stortford	a			12 44	12 47			13 10		13 15	13 25			13 44	13 47			14 10		14 15	14 25	
	d			12 44	12 48			13 11		13 15	13 26			13 44	13 48			14 11		14 15	14 26	
Stansted Mountfitchet	d			12 48							13 30			13 48							14 30	
Stansted Airport	a		12 42		12 57		13 12			13 25	13 39		13 42		13 57		14 12			14 25	14 39	
	d								13 25										14 25			
Elsenham	d			12 52										13 52								
Newport (Essex)	d			12 57										13 57								
Audley End	d			13 00				13 23	13 37					14 00				14 23	14 37			
Great Chesterford	d			13 05										14 05								
Whittlesford Parkway	d			13 10				13 30						14 10				14 30				
Shelford	d			13 14										14 14								
Cambridge	a			13 21				13 40	13 58					14 21				14 40	14 58			

		LE 1	LE 1	LE 1	LE 1	LE 1	LE 1	XC ◇1	LE 1	LE 1	LE 1	LE 1	LE 1	LE 1	LE 1	LE 1	LE 1	XC ◇1	LE 1	LE 1	LE 1	LE 1
London Liverpool Street 15 ⊖	d	13 55	13 58	14 10	14 12	14 25	14 28		14 40		14 42	14 55	14 58	15 10	15 12	15 25	15 28		15 40		15 42	15 55
Bethnal Green	d																					
Hackney Downs	d				14 18						14 48				15 18						15 48	
Stratford 7 ⊖	d									14 33										15 33		
Clapton	d																					
Seven Sisters ⊖	d																					
Tottenham Hale ⊖	d	14u07	14 10	14u22	14 25	14u37	14 40		14u52	14 43	14 55	15u07	15 10	15u22	15 25	15u37	15 40		15u52	15 43	15 55	16u07
Northumberland Park	d									14 45										15 45		
Angel Road	d																			15 47		
Ponders End	d				14 29						14 59				15 29						15 59	
Brimsdown	d				14 32						15 02				15 32						16 02	
Enfield Lock	d				14 34					14 51	15 04				15 34					15 52	16 04	
Waltham Cross	d				14 37						15 07				15 37						16 07	
Cheshunt	d		14 18		14 39		14 48			14 55	15 09		15 18		15 39		15 48			15 56	16 09	
Broxbourne 3	a		14 22		14 44		14 52			14 59	15 14		15 22		15 44		15 52			16 00	16 14	
	d		14 22		14 44		14 52			15 03	15 14		15 22		15 44		15 52			16 04	16 14	
Rye House	d				14 47						15 17				15 47						16 17	
St Margarets (Herts)	d				14 50						15 20				15 50						16 20	
Ware	d				14 54						15 24				15 54						16 24	
Hertford East	a				15 01						15 31				16 01						16 31	
Roydon	d		14 26							15 08			15 26							16 08		
Harlow Town	d	14 24	14 30			14 54	14 58			15 12		15 24	15 30			15 54	15 58			16 12		16 24
Harlow Mill	d		14 33							15 15			15 33							16 15		
Sawbridgeworth	d		14 37				15 03			15 18			15 37				16 03			16 19		
Bishops Stortford	a		14 44	14 47			15 10		15 15	15 25			15 44	15 47			16 10		16 15	16 26		
	d		14 44	14 48			15 11		15 15	15 26			15 44	15 48			16 11		16 15	16 26		
Stansted Mountfitchet	d		14 48							15 30			15 48				16 15			16 30		
Stansted Airport	a	14 42		14 57		15 12			15 29	15 39		15 42		15 59		16 12			16 25	16 39		16 42
	d							15 20										16 25				
Elsenham	d		14 52										15 52				16 19					
Newport (Essex)	d		14 57										15 58				16 24					
Audley End	d		15 00				15 23	15 37					16 02				16 27	16 37				
Great Chesterford	d		15 05										16 07				16 32					
Whittlesford Parkway	d		15 10				15 30						16 12				16 37					
Shelford	d		15 14										16 16				16 41					
Cambridge	a		15 21				15 40	15 58					16 28				16 49	16 58				

Table 22

London - Broxbourne, Hertford East, Bishops Stortford, Stansted Airport and Cambridge

		LE 1	LE 1	LE	LE 1	LE 1	LE	XC ◇1	LE 1	LE 1	LE	LE 1	LE 1	LE	LE 1	LE 1	LE	LE 1	LE 1	LE	XC ◇1	LE 1	LE 1
London Liverpool Street 15 ⊖	d	15 58	16 10	16 12	16 25	16 28			16 40	16 43	16 45	16 55	16 58		17 10	17 13	17 15	17 25	17 28			17 40	17 43
Bethnal Green	d																						
Hackney Downs	d			16 18							16 51						17 21						
Stratford 7 ⊖	d						16 32							17 02						17 32			
Clapton	d																						
Seven Sisters ⊖	d																						
Tottenham Hale ⊖	d	16 10	16u22	16 25	16u37	16 40	16 43		16u52	16 55	16 58	17u07	17 10	17 13	17u22	17 25	17 28	17u37	17 40	17 43		17u52	17 55
Northumberland Park	d						16 45							17 15						17 45			
Angel Road	d						16 47							17 17						17 47			
Ponders End	d			16 29							17 02						17 32						
Brimsdown	d			16 32							17 05						17 35						
Enfield Lock	d			16 34			16 52				17 07			17 22			17 37			17 52			
Waltham Cross	d			16 37			16 55				17 10			17 25			17 40			17 55			
Cheshunt	d	16 18		16 39			16 57			17 04	17 12			17 27		17 34	17 42			17 57			18 04
Broxbourne 3	a	16 22		16 44		16 51	17 04			17 08	17 17		17 24	17 32		17 39	17 47		17 54	18 04			18 08
	d	16 22		16 44		16 52				17 09	17 17		17 25	17 35		17 39	17 50		17 54				18 09
Rye House	d			16 48							17 21			17 39			17 54						
St Margarets (Herts)	d			16 51							17 24			17 42			17 57						
Ware	d			16 55							17 28			17 48			18 01						
Hertford East	a			17 03							17 36			17 56			18 09						
Roydon	d	16 26								17 13						17 43							18 13
Harlow Town	d	16 30			16 54	16 59				17 18		17 27	17 32			17 48		17 54				18 10	18 18
Harlow Mill	d	16 33								17 21						17 51							18 21
Sawbridgeworth	d	16 37				17 04				17 24						17 54			18 04				18 24
Bishops Stortford	a	16 44	16 47			17 11			17 17	17 31			17 42		17 47	18 01		18 05	18 11			18 20	18 31
	d	16 44	16 48			17 11			17 18	17 32			17 42		17 48	18 02		18 06	18 11			18 20	18 32
Stansted Mountfitchet	d	16 48				17 15				17 36					17 52	18 06							18 36
Stansted Airport	a		17 01		17 14				17 32			17 47			18 01			18 17				18 32	
	d							17 18													18 21		
Elsenham	d	16 52								17 40						18 10							18 40
Newport (Essex)	d	16 57								17 45						18 15							18 45
Audley End	d	17 00				17 25		17 33		17 49			17 55			18 19			18 24		18 37		18 49
Great Chesterford	d	17 05								17 54						18 24							18 54
Whittlesford Parkway	d	17 10				17 33				17 58			18 03			18 28			18 32				18 58
Shelford	d	17 14								18 03						18 33							19 03
Cambridge	a	17 21				17 44		17 49		18 12			18 13			18 42			18 45		18 58		19 12

		LE	LE 1	LE 1	LE	LE 1	LE 1	LE	LE 1	LE 1	XC ◇1	LE 1	LE	LE 1	LE	LE 1	LE 1	LE	LE 1	LE 1	LE 1	LE 1
London Liverpool Street 15 ⊖	d	17 45	17 55	17 58		18 10	18 13	18 15	18 25	18 28		18 40		18 43	18 45	18 55	18 58		19 10	19 13	19 15	19 25
Bethnal Green	d																					
Hackney Downs	d	17 51						18 21							18 51						19 21	
Stratford 7 ⊖	d				18 02								18 32					19 02				
Clapton	d																					
Seven Sisters ⊖	d																					
Tottenham Hale ⊖	d	17 58	18u07	18 10	18 13	18u22	18 25	18 28	18u37	18 40		18u52	18 43	18 55	18 58	19u07	19 10	19 13	19u22	19 25	19 28	19u37
Northumberland Park	d				18 15								18 45					19 15				
Angel Road	d				18 17								18 47					19 17				
Ponders End	d	18 02						18 32							19 02						19 32	
Brimsdown	d	18 05						18 35							19 05						19 35	
Enfield Lock	d	18 07			18 22			18 37					18 52		19 07			19 22			19 37	
Waltham Cross	d	18 10			18 25			18 40					18 55		19 10			19 25			19 40	
Cheshunt	d	18 12			18 27		18 34	18 42					18 57	19 04	19 12			19 27		19 34	19 42	
Broxbourne 3	a	18 17		18 24	18 32		18 39	18 47		18 54			19 02	19 09	19 17		19 24	19 32		19 39	19 47	
	d	18 17		18 25	18 35		18 39	18 47		18 55			19 05	19 09	19 17		19 25	19 35		19 39	19 47	
Rye House	d	18 21			18 39			18 51							19 21						19 50	
St Margarets (Herts)	d	18 24			18 42			18 54							19 24						19 53	
Ware	d	18 28			18 48			18 58							19 28						19 57	
Hertford East	a	18 36			18 56			19 06							19 36						20 04	
Roydon	d						18 43						19 10	19 13						19 43		
Harlow Town	d		18 27				18 48		18 57	19 02			19 14	19 18		19 27	19 32	19 42		19 48		19 57
Harlow Mill	d						18 51						19 17	19 21						19 51		
Sawbridgeworth	d			18 35			18 54			19 07			19 20	19 24				19 47		19 54		
Bishops Stortford	a		18 35	18 42		18 47	19 01			19 14		19 18	19 27	19 31			19 42	19 56	19 47	20 01		
	d		18 36	18 42		18 48	19 02			19 14		19 18	19 28	19 32			19 42		19 47	20 02		
Stansted Mountfitchet	d					18 52	19 06					19 23	19 32	19 36						20 06		
Stansted Airport	a		18 56			19 01			19 17			19 32	19 41			19 47			19 57			20 15
	d										19 21											
Elsenham	d						19 10							19 40						20 10		
Newport (Essex)	d						19 15							19 45						20 15		
Audley End	d			18 55			19 19			19 27	19 37			19 49			19 55			20 19		
Great Chesterford	d						19 24							19 54						20 24		
Whittlesford Parkway	d			19 03			19 28			19 35				19 58			20 03			20 28		
Shelford	d						19 33							20 03						20 33		
Cambridge	a			19 16			19 42			19 46	19 58			20 13			20 14			20 40		

Table 22

London - Broxbourne, Hertford East, Bishops Stortford, Stansted Airport and Cambridge

		XC ◇1	LE 1		LE 1	LE 1	LE 1	LE 1	LE 1	LE 1	LE 1	LE 1	XC ◇1	LE 1	LE 1	LE 1	LE 1	LE 1	LE 1	LE 1	LE 1		LE 1	XC ◇1	LE 1
London Liverpool Street [15] ⊖	d		08 40			08 42	08 55	08 58	09 10	09 12	09 25	09 28		09 40		09 42	09 55	09 58	10 10	10 12	10 25		10 28		10 40
Bethnal Green	d																								
Hackney Downs	d					08 48				09 18						09 48				10 18					
Stratford [7] ⊖	d				08 33										09 33										
Clapton	d																								
Seven Sisters ⊖	d																								
Tottenham Hale ⊖	d		08u52		08 43	08 55	09u07	09 10	09u22	09 25	09u37	09 40		09u52	09 43	09 55	10u07	10 10	10u22	10 25	10u37		10 40		10u52
Northumberland Park	d				08 45										09 45										
Angel Road	d																								
Ponders End	d					08 59				09 29						09 59				10 29					
Brimsdown	d					09 02				09 32						10 02				10 32					
Enfield Lock	d				08 51	09 04				09 34					09 51	10 04				10 34					
Waltham Cross	d					09 07				09 37						10 07				10 37					
Cheshunt	d				08 55	09 09		09 18		09 39		09 48			09 55	10 09		10 18		10 39			10 48		
Broxbourne [3]	a				08 59	09 14		09 22		09 44		09 52			09 59	10 14		10 22		10 44			10 52		
	d				09 03	09 14		09 22		09 44		09 52			10 03	10 14		10 22		10 44			10 52		
Rye House	d					09 17				09 47						10 17				10 47					
St Margarets (Herts)	d					09 20				09 50						10 20				10 50					
Ware	d					09 24				09 54						10 24				10 54					
Hertford East	a					09 31				10 01						10 31				11 01					
Roydon	d				09 08			09 26							10 08			10 26							
Harlow Town	d				09 12		09 24	09 30			09 54	09 58			10 12		10 24	10 30			10 54		10 58		
Harlow Mill	d				09 15			09 33							10 15			10 33							
Sawbridgeworth	d				09 18			09 37				10 03			10 18			10 37					11 03		
Bishops Stortford	a		09 15		09 25			09 44	09 47			10 10		10 15	10 25			10 44	10 47				11 10		11 15
	d		09 15		09 26			09 44	09 48			10 11		10 15	10 26			10 44	10 48				11 11		11 15
Stansted Mountfitchet	d				09 30			09 48			10 05				10 30			10 48			11 05				
Stansted Airport	a		09 25		09 39		09 42		09 57		10 13			10 25	10 39		10 42		10 57		11 13				11 25
	d	09 25											10 25											11 25	
Elsenham	d							09 52										10 52							
Newport (Essex)	d							09 57										10 57							
Audley End	d	09 37						10 00				10 23	10 37					11 00					11 23	11 37	
Great Chesterford	d							10 05										11 05							
Whittlesford Parkway	d							10 10				10 30						11 10					11 30		
Shelford	d							10 14										11 14							
Cambridge	a	09 58						10 21				10 40	10 58					11 21					11 40	11 58	

		LE 1	LE 1	LE 1	LE 1	LE 1	LE 1		LE 1	LE 1	XC ◇1	LE 1	LE 1	LE 1	LE 1	LE 1	LE 1		LE 1	LE 1	LE 1	XC ◇1	LE 1	LE 1	LE 1
London Liverpool Street [15] ⊖	d		10 42	10 55	10 58	11 10	11 12		11 25	11 28		11 40		11 42	11 55	11 58	12 10		12 12	12 25	12 28		12 40		12 42
Bethnal Green	d																								
Hackney Downs	d		10 48				11 18							11 47					12 18						12 48
Stratford [7] ⊖	d	10 33											11 33											12 33	
Clapton	d																								
Seven Sisters ⊖	d																								
Tottenham Hale ⊖	d	10 43	10 55	11u07	11 10	11u22	11 25		11u37	11 40		11u52	11 43	11 55	12u07	12 10	12u22		12 25	12u37	12 40		12u52	12 43	12 55
Northumberland Park	d	10 45											11 45											12 45	
Angel Road	d																								
Ponders End	d		10 59				11 29							11 59					12 29						12 59
Brimsdown	d		11 02				11 32							12 02					12 32						13 02
Enfield Lock	d	10 51	11 04				11 34						11 51	12 04					12 34					12 51	13 04
Waltham Cross	d		11 07				11 37							12 07					12 37						13 07
Cheshunt	d	10 55	11 09		11 18		11 39			11 48			11 55	12 09		12 18			12 39		12 48			12 55	13 09
Broxbourne [3]	a	10 59	11 14		11 22		11 44			11 52			11 59	12 14		12 22			12 44		12 52			12 59	13 14
	d	11 03	11 14		11 22		11 44			11 52			12 03	12 14		12 22			12 44		12 52			13 03	13 14
Rye House	d		11 17				11 47							12 17					12 47						13 17
St Margarets (Herts)	d		11 20				11 50							12 20					12 50						13 20
Ware	d		11 24				11 54							12 24					12 54						13 24
Hertford East	a		11 31				12 01							12 31					13 01						13 31
Roydon	d	11 08			11 26								12 08			12 26								13 08	
Harlow Town	d	11 12		11 24	11 30				11 54	11 58			12 12		12 24	12 30				12 54	12 58			13 12	
Harlow Mill	d	11 15			11 33								12 15			12 33								13 15	
Sawbridgeworth	d	11 18			11 37					12 03			12 18			12 37					13 03			13 18	
Bishops Stortford	a	11 25			11 44	11 47				12 10		12 15	12 25			12 44	12 47				13 10		13 15	13 25	
	d	11 26			11 44	11 48				12 11		12 15	12 26			12 44	12 48				13 11		13 15	13 26	
Stansted Mountfitchet	d	11 30			11 48				12 05				12 30			12 48				13 05				13 30	
Stansted Airport	a	11 39		11 42		11 57			12 13			12 25	12 39		12 42		12 57			13 13			13 25	13 39	
	d										12 25											13 25			
Elsenham	d				11 52											12 52									
Newport (Essex)	d				11 57											12 57									
Audley End	d				12 00					12 23	12 37					13 00					13 23	13 37			
Great Chesterford	d				12 05											13 05									
Whittlesford Parkway	d				12 10					12 30						13 10					13 30				
Shelford	d				12 14											13 14									
Cambridge	a				12 21					12 40	12 58					13 21					13 40	13 58			

Table 22

London - Broxbourne, Hertford East, Bishops Stortford, Stansted Airport and Cambridge

		LE 1	LE 1		LE 1	LE 1	LE 1	LE 1	XC ◇1	LE 1	LE 1	LE 1	LE 1			LE 1	LE 1	LE 1	LE 1	LE 1	LE 1	LE 1	LE 1	LE 1	
London Liverpool Street [15] ⊖	d	12 55	12 58		13 10	13 12	13 25	13 28		13 40		13 42	13 55			13 58	14 10	14 12	14 25	14 28	14 40		14 42	14 55	
Bethnal Green	d																								
Hackney Downs	d					13 18						13 48						14 18					14 48		
Stratford [7] ⊖	d										13 33											14 33			
Clapton	d																								
Seven Sisters ⊖	d																								
Tottenham Hale ⊖	d	13u07	13 10		13u22	13 25	13u37	13 40		13u52	13 43	13 55	14u07			14 10	14u22	14 25	14u37	14 40	14u52	14 43	14 55	15u07	
Northumberland Park	d										13 45											14 45			
Angel Road	d																								
Ponders End	d					13 29						13 59						14 29					14 59		
Brimsdown	d					13 32						14 02						14 32					15 02		
Enfield Lock	d					13 34					13 51	14 04						14 34				14 51	15 04		
Waltham Cross	d					13 37						14 07						14 37					15 07		
Cheshunt	d		13 18			13 39		13 48			13 55	14 09				14 18		14 39		14 48		14 55	15 09		
Broxbourne [3]	a		13 22			13 44		13 52			13 59	14 14				14 22		14 44		14 52		14 59	15 14		
	d		13 22			13 44		13 52			14 03	14 14				14 22		14 44		14 52		15 03	15 14		
Rye House	d					13 47						14 17						14 47					15 17		
St Margarets (Herts)	d					13 50						14 20						14 50					15 20		
Ware	d					13 54						14 24						14 54					15 24		
Hertford East	a					14 01						14 31						15 01					15 31		
Roydon	d		13 26								14 08					14 26						15 08			
Harlow Town	d	13 24	13 30				13 54	13 58			14 12		14 24			14 30			14 54	14 58		15 12		15 24	
Harlow Mill	d		13 33								14 15					14 33						15 15			
Sawbridgeworth	d		13 37					14 03			14 18					14 37				15 03		15 18			
Bishops Stortford	a		13 44		13 47			14 10		14 15	14 25					14 44	14 47			15 10	15 15	15 25			
	d		13 44		13 48			14 11		14 15	14 26					14 44	14 48			15 11	15 15	15 26			
Stansted Mountfitchet	d		13 48				14 05				14 30					14 48			15 05			15 30			
Stansted Airport	a	13 42			13 57		14 13			14 25	14 39		14 42				14 57		15 13		15 25	15 39		15 42	
	d								14 25																
Elsenham	d		13 52													14 52									
Newport (Essex)	d		13 57													14 57									
Audley End	d		14 00					14 23	14 37							15 00				15 23					
Great Chesterford	d		14 05													15 05									
Whittlesford Parkway	d		14 10					14 30								15 10				15 30					
Shelford	d		14 14													15 14									
Cambridge	a		14 21					14 40	14 58							15 21				15 40					

		XC ◇1	LE 1	LE 1	LE 1	LE 1	LE 1	XC ◇1	LE 1	LE 1	LE 1		LE 1	LE 1	LE 1	LE 1	LE 1	LE 1	XC ◇1	LE 1	LE 1		LE 1	LE 1	LE 1
London Liverpool Street [15] ⊖	d		14 58	15 10	15 12	15 25	15 28		15 40		15 42		15 55	15 58	16 10	16 12	16 25	16 28		16 40			16 42	16 55	16 58
Bethnal Green	d																								
Hackney Downs	d				15 18						15 48					16 18							16 48		
Stratford [7] ⊖	d									15 33											16 33				
Clapton	d																								
Seven Sisters ⊖	d																								
Tottenham Hale ⊖	d		15 10	15u22	15 25	15u37	15 40		15u52	15 43	15 55		16u07	16 10	16u22	16 25	16u37	16 40		16u52	16 43		16 55	17u07	17 10
Northumberland Park	d									15 45											16 45				
Angel Road	d																								
Ponders End	d				15 29						15 59					16 29							16 59		
Brimsdown	d				15 32						16 02					16 32							17 02		
Enfield Lock	d				15 34					15 51	16 04					16 34					16 51		17 04		
Waltham Cross	d				15 37						16 07					16 37							17 07		
Cheshunt	d		15 18		15 39		15 48			15 55	16 09			16 18		16 39		16 48			16 55		17 09		17 18
Broxbourne [3]	a		15 22		15 44		15 52			15 59	16 14			16 22		16 44		16 52			16 59		17 14		17 22
	d		15 22		15 44		15 52			16 03	16 14			16 22		16 44		16 52			17 03		17 14		17 22
Rye House	d				15 47						16 17					16 47							17 17		
St Margarets (Herts)	d				15 50						16 20					16 50							17 20		
Ware	d				15 54						16 24					16 54							17 24		
Hertford East	a				16 01						16 31					17 01							17 3		
Roydon	d		15 26							16 08				16 26							17 08				17 26
Harlow Town	d		15 30			15 54	15 58			16 12			16 24	16 30			16 54	16 58			17 12			17 24	17 30
Harlow Mill	d		15 33							16 15				16 33							17 15				17 33
Sawbridgeworth	d		15 37				16 03			16 18				16 37				17 03			17 18				17 37
Bishops Stortford	a		15 44	15 47			16 10		16 15	16 25				16 44	16 47			17 10		17 15	17 25				17 44
	d		15 44	15 48			16 11		16 15	16 26				16 44	16 48			17 11		17 15	17 26				17 44
Stansted Mountfitchet	d		15 48			16 05				16 30				16 48			17 05				17 30				17 48
Stansted Airport	a			15 57		16 13			16 25	16 39			16 42		16 57		17 13			17 25	17 39			17 42	
	d	15 25						16 25											17 25						
Elsenham	d		15 52											16 52											17 52
Newport (Essex)	d		15 57											16 57											17 57
Audley End	d	15 37	16 00				16 23	16 37						17 00				17 23	17 37						18 00
Great Chesterford	d		16 05											17 05											18 05
Whittlesford Parkway	d		16 10				16 30							17 10				17 30							18 10
Shelford	d		16 14											17 14											18 14
Cambridge	a	15 58	16 21				16 40	16 58						17 21				17 40	17 58						18 21

Table 22

London - Broxbourne, Hertford East, Bishops Stortford, Stansted Airport and Cambridge

		LE	XC	LE	LE	LE	LE	LE	LE	LE	LE	LE	XC	LE	LE	LE	LE	LE	LE	LE	LE	LE	XC	LE
London Liverpool Street	d	19 28		19 40		19 42	19 55	19 58	20 10	20 12	20 25	20 28		20 40		20 42	20 55	20 58	21 10	21 12	21 25	21 28		21 40
Bethnal Green	d																							
Hackney Downs	d					19 48				20 18						20 48				21 18				
Stratford	d				19 33										20 33									
Clapton	d																							
Seven Sisters	d																							
Tottenham Hale	d	19 40		19u52	19 43	19 55	20u07	20 10	20u22	20 25	20u37	20 40		20u52	20 43	20 55	21u07	21 10	21u22	21 25	21u37	21 40		21u52
Northumberland Park	d				19 45										20 45									
Angel Road	d																							
Ponders End	d					19 59				20 29						20 59				21 29				
Brimsdown	d					20 02				20 32						21 02				21 32				
Enfield Lock	d				19 51	20 04				20 34					20 51	21 04				21 34				
Waltham Cross	d					20 07				20 37						21 07				21 37				
Cheshunt	d	19 49			19 55	20 09		20 18		20 39		20 48			20 55	21 09		21 18		21 39		21 48		
Broxbourne	a	19 54			19 59	20 14		20 22		20 44		20 52			20 59	21 14		21 22		21 44		21 52		
	d	19 54			20 03	20 14		20 22		20 44		20 52			21 03	21 14		21 22		21 44		21 52		
Rye House	d					20 17				20 47						21 17				21 47				
St Margarets (Herts)	d					20 20				20 50						21 20				21 50				
Ware	d					20 24				20 54						21 24				21 54				
Hertford East	a					20 31				21 01						21 31				22 01				
Roydon	d	19 59			20 08			20 26							21 08			21 26						
Harlow Town	d	20 03			20 12		20 24	20 30			20 54	20 58			21 12		21 24	21 30			21 54	21 58		
Harlow Mill	d	20 06			20 15			20 33							21 15			21 33						
Sawbridgeworth	d	20 09			20 18			20 37				21 03			21 18			21 37				22 03		
Bishops Stortford	a	20 16		20 20	20 25			20 44	20 48			21 10		21 15	21 25			21 44	21 47			22 10		22 15
	d	20 17		20 21	20 26			20 44	20 48			21 11		21 15	21 26			21 44	21 48			22 11		22 15
Stansted Mountfitchet	d	20 21			20 30			20 48			21 05				21 30			21 48			22 05			
Stansted Airport	a			20 30	20 39		20 42		20 58		21 13			21 25	21 39		21 42		21 57		22 13			22 25
	d		20 21										21 25										22 25	
Elsenham	d	20 25						20 52										21 52						
Newport (Essex)	d	20 30						20 57										21 57						
Audley End	d	20 33	20 37					21 00				21 23	21 37					22 00				22 23	22 37	
Great Chesterford	d	20 38						21 05										22 05						
Whittlesford Parkway	d	20 43						21 10				21 30						22 10				22 30		
Shelford	d	20 47						21 14										22 14						
Cambridge	a	20 56	20 59					21 22				21 40	21 58					22 21				22 40	22 55	

		LE	LE	LE	LE	XC	LE	LE	LE	LE	LE	LE	LE	LE	LE	LE	LE	LE	LE	LE FX	LE FO
London Liverpool Street	d		21 42	21 55	21 58		22 10	22 12	22 25	22 28		22 40	22 42	22 55	22 58	23 12	23 25	23 28	23 40	23 58	23 58
Bethnal Green	d																				
Hackney Downs	d		21 48					22 18					22 48			23 18			23 46		
Stratford	d	21 33									22 33										
Clapton	d																				
Seven Sisters	d																		23 49		
Tottenham Hale	d	21 43	21 55	22u07	22 10		22u22	22 25	22u37	22 40	22 43	22u52	22 55	23u07	23 10	23 25	23u37	23 40	23 53	00 10	00 10
Northumberland Park	d	21 45									22 45								23 55		
Angel Road	d																				
Ponders End	d		21 59					22 29					22 59			23 29			23 59		
Brimsdown	d		22 02					22 32					23 02			23 32			00 02		
Enfield Lock	d	21 51	22 04					22 34			22 51		23 04			23 34			00 04		
Waltham Cross	d		22 07					22 37					23 07			23 37			00 07		
Cheshunt	d	21 55	22 09		22 18			22 39		22 48	22 55		23 09		23 18	23 39		23 48	00 09	00 18	00 18
Broxbourne	a	21 59	22 14		22 22			22 44		22 52	22 59		23 14		23 22	23 44		23 52	00 14	00 22	00 22
	d	22 03	22 14		22 22			22 44		22 52	23 03		23 14		23 22	23 44		23 52	00 14	00 22	00 22
Rye House	d		22 17					22 47					23 17			23 47			00 17		
St Margarets (Herts)	d		22 20					22 50					23 20			23 50			00 20		
Ware	d		22 24					22 54					23 24			23 54			00 24		
Hertford East	a		22 31					23 01					23 31			00 01			00 31		
Roydon	d	22 08			22 26						23 08				23 26					00 26	00 26
Harlow Town	d	22 12		22 24	22 30				22 54	22 58	23 12			23 24	23 30		23 54	23 58		00 30	00 30
Harlow Mill	d	22 15			22 33						23 15				23 33					00 33	00 33
Sawbridgeworth	d	22 18			22 37					23 03	23 18				23 37			00 03		00 37	00 37
Bishops Stortford	a	22 25			22 44		22 47			23 10	23 26	23 15			23 44		00 04	00 10		00 44	00 44
	d	22 26			22 44		22 48			23 11		23 15			23 44		00 04	00 11			00 44
Stansted Mountfitchet	d	22 30			22 48				23 05					23 35	23 48			00 15			00 48
Stansted Airport	a	22 39		22 42			22 57		23 13			23 25		23 43			00 13				
	d					22 57															
Elsenham	d				22 52										23 52			00 19			00 52
Newport (Essex)	d				22 57										23 57			00 24			00 57
Audley End	d				23 00	23 09				23 23					23 59			00 27			01 00
Great Chesterford	d				23 05										00 05			00 32			01 05
Whittlesford Parkway	d				23 10					23 30					00 10			00 37			01 10
Shelford	d				23 14										00 14			00 41			
Cambridge	a				23 22	23 31				23 40					00 21			00 48			01 19

Table 22

London - Broxbourne, Hertford East, Bishops Stortford, Stansted Airport and Cambridge

		LE	LE	LE	LE	LE	LE	LE	XC	LE	LE	LE	LE	LE	LE	XC	LE	LE	LE	LE	LE	LE	LE	LE
London Liverpool Street	d	22p58	23p12	23p25	23p28	23p40	23p58	04 10		04 40		05 10	05 23	05 25	05 28		05 40		05 42	05 55	05 58	06 10	06 12	06 23
Bethnal Green	d																							
Hackney Downs	d		23p18			23p46													05 48				06 18	
Stratford	d												05 33		05 37									06 33
Clapton	d					23p49																		
Seven Sisters	d														05a50									
Tottenham Hale	d	23p10	23p25	23b37	23p40	23p53	00 10			04u52		05u22	05 43	05u37			05u52		05 55	06u07	06 10	06u22	06 25	06 43
Northumberland Park	d					23p55							05 45											06 45
Angel Road	d																							
Ponders End	d		23p29			23p59													05 59				06 29	
Brimsdown	d		23p32			00 02													06 02				06 32	
Enfield Lock	d		23p34			00 04							05 51						06 04				06 34	06 51
Waltham Cross	d		23p37			00 07												←	06 07				06 37	
Cheshunt	d	23p18	23p39		23p48	00 09	00 18						05 55	05 45				05 55	06 09		06 18		06 39	06 55
Broxbourne	a	23p22	23p44		23p52	00 14	00 22						→	05 49				05 59	06 14		06 22		06 44	→
	d	23p22	23p44		23p52	00 14	00 22							05 49				06 03	06 14		06 22		06 44	
Rye House	d		23p47			00 17													06 17				06 47	
St Margarets (Herts)	d		23p50			00 20													06 20				06 50	
Ware	d		23p54			00 24													06 24				06 54	
Hertford East	a		00 01			00 31													06 31				07 01	
Roydon	d	23p26					00 26											06 08			06 26			
Harlow Town	d	23p30		23p54	23p58		00 30			05 10		05 37		05 55				06 12		06 24	06 30			
Harlow Mill	d	23p33					00 33											06 15			06 33			
Sawbridgeworth	d	23p37			00 03		00 37					05 42						06 18			06 37			
Bishops Stortford	a	23p44		00 04	00 10		00 44			05 20		05 49		06 05			06 15	06 25			06 44	06 47		
	d	23p44		00 04	00 11		00 44			05 20	05 42	05 50		06 06			06 15	06 26			06 44	06 48		
Stansted Mountfitchet	d	23p48			00 15		00 48			05 24	05 46							06 30			06 48			
Stansted Airport	a			00 13				05 00		05 39	05 53	05 59		06 15			06 25	06 39		06 42		06 57		
	d								05 25							06 25								
Elsenham	d	23p52			00 19		00 52														06 52			
Newport (Essex)	d	23p57			00 24		00 57														06 57			
Audley End	d	23p59			00 27		01 00		05 37							06 37					07 00			
Great Chesterford	d	00 05			00 32		01 05														07 05			
Whittlesford Parkway	d	00 10			00 37		01 10														07 10			
Shelford	d	00 14			00 41																07 14			
Cambridge	a	00 21			00 48		01 19		05 54							06 55					07 21			

		LE	LE	XC	LE	LE	LE	LE	LE	LE	LE	LE	LE	XC	LE	LE	LE	LE	LE	LE	LE	LE	LE
London Liverpool Street	d	06 25	06 28		06 40		06 42	06 55	06 58	07 10	07 12	07 25	07 28		07 40		07 42	07 55	07 58	08 10	08 12	08 25	08 28
Bethnal Green	d																						
Hackney Downs	d						06 48				07 18						07 48				08 18		
Stratford	d															07 33							
Clapton	d																						
Seven Sisters	d																						
Tottenham Hale	d	06u37	06 40		06u52		06 55	07u07	07 10	07u22	07 25	07u37	07 40		07u52	07 43	07 55	08u07	08 10	08u22	08 25	08u37	08 40
Northumberland Park	d															07 45							
Angel Road	d																						
Ponders End	d						06 59				07 29						07 59				08 29		
Brimsdown	d						07 02				07 32						08 02				08 32		
Enfield Lock	d						07 04				07 34					07 51	08 04				08 34		
Waltham Cross	d					←	07 07				07 37						08 07				08 37		
Cheshunt	d		06 48			06 55	07 09		07 18		07 39		07 48			07 55	08 09		08 18		08 39		08 48
Broxbourne	a		06 52			06 59	07 14		07 22		07 44		07 52			07 59	08 14		08 22		08 44		08 52
	d		06 52			07 03	07 14		07 22		07 44		07 52			08 03	08 14		08 22		08 44		08 52
Rye House	d						07 17				07 47						08 17				08 47		
St Margarets (Herts)	d						07 20				07 50						08 20				08 50		
Ware	d						07 24				07 54						08 24				08 54		
Hertford East	a						07 31				08 01						08 31				09 01		
Roydon	d					07 08			07 26							08 08			08 26				
Harlow Town	d	06 54	06 58			07 12		07 24	07 30			07 54	07 58			08 12		08 24	08 30			08 54	08 58
Harlow Mill	d					07 15			07 33							08 15			08 33				
Sawbridgeworth	d		07 03			07 18			07 37				08 03			08 18			08 37				09 03
Bishops Stortford	a		07 10		07 15	07 25			07 44	07 47			08 10		08 15	08 25			08 44	08 47			09 10
	d		07 11		07 15	07 26			07 44	07 48			08 11		08 15	08 26			08 44	08 48			09 11
Stansted Mountfitchet	d	07 05				07 30			07 48			08 05				08 30			08 48			09 05	
Stansted Airport	a	07 13			07 25	07 39		07 42		07 57		08 13			08 25	08 39		08 42		08 57		09 13	
	d			07 25										08 25									
Elsenham	d								07 52										08 52				
Newport (Essex)	d								07 57										08 57				
Audley End	d		07 23	07 37					08 00				08 23	08 37					09 00				09 23
Great Chesterford	d								08 05										09 05				
Whittlesford Parkway	d		07 30						08 10				08 30						09 10				09 30
Shelford	d		07 35										08 35										09 35
Cambridge	a		07 42	07 55					08 19				08 42	08 58					09 19				09 42

b previous night, stops to pick up only

Table 22

Saturdays

London - Broxbourne, Hertford East, Bishops Stortford, Stansted Airport and Cambridge

		LE 1	LE 1	LE 1	LE 1	XC ◇1	LE 1	LE 1	LE 1	LE 1	LE 1	LE 1	LE 1	LE 1	LE 1	XC ◇1	LE 1	LE 1	LE 1	LE 1	LE 1	LE 1	LE 1
London Liverpool Street 15 ⊖	d	17 10	17 12	17 25	17 28		17 40		17 42	17 55	17 58	18 10	18 12	18 25	18 28		18 40		18 42	18 55	18 58	19 10	19 12
Bethnal Green	d																						
Hackney Downs	d		17 18						17 48				18 18						18 48				19 18
Stratford 7 ⊖	d							17 33										18 33					
Clapton	d																						
Seven Sisters ⊖	d																						
Tottenham Hale ⊖	d	17u22	17 25	17u37	17 40		17u52	17 43	17 55	18u07	18 10	18u22	18 25	18u37	18 40		18u52	18 43	18 55	19u07	19 10	19u22	19 25
Northumberland Park	d							17 45										18 45					
Angel Road	d																						
Ponders End	d		17 29						17 59				18 29						18 59				19 29
Brimsdown	d		17 32						18 02				18 32						19 02				19 32
Enfield Lock	d		17 34					17 51	18 04				18 34					18 51	19 04				19 34
Waltham Cross	d		17 37						18 07				18 37						19 07				19 37
Cheshunt	d		17 39		17 48			17 55	18 09		18 18		18 39		18 48			18 55	19 09		19 18		19 39
Broxbourne 3	a		17 44		17 52			17 59	18 14		18 22		18 44		18 52			18 59	19 14		19 22		19 44
	d		17 44		17 52			18 03	18 14		18 22		18 44		18 52			19 03	19 14		19 22		19 44
Rye House	d		17 47						18 17				18 47						19 17				19 47
St Margarets (Herts)	d		17 50						18 20				18 50						19 20				19 50
Ware	d		17 54						18 24				18 54						19 24				19 54
Hertford East	a		18 01						18 31				19 01						19 31				20 01
Roydon	d							18 08			18 26							19 08			19 26		
Harlow Town	d			17 54	17 58			18 12		18 24	18 30			18 54	18 58			19 12		19 24	19 30		
Harlow Mill	d							18 15			18 33							19 15			19 33		
Sawbridgeworth	d				18 03			18 18			18 37				19 03			19 18			19 37		
Bishops Stortford	a	17 47			18 10		18 15	18 25			18 44	18 47			19 10		19 15	19 25			19 44	19 47	
	d	17 48			18 11		18 15	18 26			18 44	18 48			19 11		19 15	19 26			19 44	19 48	
Stansted Mountfitchet	d			18 05				18 30			18 48			19 05				19 30			19 48		
Stansted Airport	a	17 57		18 13			18 25	18 39		18 42		18 57		19 13			19 25	19 39		19 42		19 57	
	d					18 25										19 25							
Elsenham	d										18 52										19 52		
Newport (Essex)	d										18 57										19 57		
Audley End	d				18 23	18 37					19 00				19 23	19 37					20 00		
Great Chesterford	d										19 05										20 05		
Whittlesford Parkway	d				18 30						19 10				19 30						20 10		
Shelford	d										19 14										20 14		
Cambridge	a				18 40	18 58					19 21				19 40	19 58					20 21		

		LE 1	LE 1	XC ◇1	LE 1	LE 1	LE 1	LE 1	LE 1	LE 1	LE 1	LE 1	LE 1	XC ◇1	LE 1	LE 1	LE 1	LE 1	LE 1	LE 1	LE 1	LE 1
London Liverpool Street 15 ⊖	d	19 25	19 28		19 40		19 42	19 55	19 58	20 10	20 12	20 25	20 28		20 40		20 42	20 55	20 58	21 10	21 12	21 25
Bethnal Green	d																					
Hackney Downs	d						19 48				20 18						20 48				21 18	
Stratford 7 ⊖	d					19 33										20 33						
Clapton	d																					
Seven Sisters ⊖	d																					
Tottenham Hale ⊖	d	19u37	19 40		19u52	19 43	19 55	20u07	20 10	20u22	20 25	20u37	20 40		20u52	20 43	20 55	21u07	21 10	21u22	21 25	21u37
Northumberland Park	d					19 45										20 45						
Angel Road	d																					
Ponders End	d						19 59				20 29						20 59				21 29	
Brimsdown	d						20 02				20 32						21 02				21 32	
Enfield Lock	d					19 51	20 04				20 34					20 51	21 04				21 34	
Waltham Cross	d						20 07				20 37						21 07				21 37	
Cheshunt	d		19 48			19 55	20 09		20 18		20 39		20 48			20 55	21 09		21 18		21 39	
Broxbourne 3	a		19 52			19 59	20 14		20 22		20 44		20 52			20 59	21 14		21 22		21 44	
	d		19 52			20 03	20 14		20 22		20 44		20 52			21 03	21 14		21 22		21 44	
Rye House	d						20 17				20 47						21 17				21 47	
St Margarets (Herts)	d						20 20				20 50						21 20				21 50	
Ware	d						20 24				20 54						21 24				21 54	
Hertford East	a						20 31				21 01						21 31				22 01	
Roydon	d					20 08			20 26							21 08			21 26			
Harlow Town	d	19 54	19 58			20 12		20 24	20 30			20 54	20 58			21 12		21 24	21 30			21 54
Harlow Mill	d					20 15			20 33							21 15			21 33			
Sawbridgeworth	d		20 03			20 18			20 37				21 03			21 18			21 37			
Bishops Stortford	a		20 10		20 15	20 25			20 44	20 47			21 10		21 15	21 25			21 44	21 47		
	d		20 11		20 15	20 26			20 44	20 48			21 11		21 15	21 26			21 44	21 48		
Stansted Mountfitchet	d	20 05				20 30			20 48			21 05				21 30			21 48			22 05
Stansted Airport	a	20 13			20 25	20 39		20 42		20 57		21 13			21 25	21 39		21 42		21 57		22 13
	d			20 25										21 25								
Elsenham	d								20 52										21 52			
Newport (Essex)	d								20 57										21 57			
Audley End	d		20 23	20 38					21 00				21 23	21 38					22 00			
Great Chesterford	d								21 05										22 05			
Whittlesford Parkway	d		20 30						21 10				21 30						22 10			
Shelford	d								21 14										22 14			
Cambridge	a		20 40	20 57					21 21				21 40	22 01					22 21			

Table 22

Saturdays

London - Broxbourne, Hertford East, Bishops Stortford, Stansted Airport and Cambridge

		LE 1	XC ◇1	LE 1	LE 1	LE 1	LE 1	LE 1	LE 1	LE 1	LE 1	LE 1	LE 1	XC ◇1	LE 1	LE 1	LE 1	LE 1	LE 1	LE 1	LE 1	LE 1	LE 1
London Liverpool Street 15 ⊖	d	21 28		21 40		21 42	21 55	21 58	22 10	22 12	22 25	22 28			22 40	22 42	22 55	22 58	23 10	23 25	23 28	23 40	23 58
Bethnal Green	d																						
Hackney Downs	d					21 48				22 18						22 48			23 16			23 46	
Stratford 7 ⊖	d				21 33								22 33										
Clapton	d																					23 49	
Seven Sisters ⊖	d																						
Tottenham Hale ⊖	d	21 40		21u52	21 43	21 55	22u07	22 10	22u22	22 25	22u37	22 40	22 43		22u52	22 55	23u07	23 10	23 23	23u37	23 40	23 53	00 10
Northumberland Park	d				21 45								22 45						23 25			23 55	
Angel Road	d																						
Ponders End	d					21 59				22 29						22 59			23 29			23 59	
Brimsdown	d					22 02				22 32						23 02			23 32			00 02	
Enfield Lock	d				21 51	22 04				22 34			22 51			23 04			23 34			00 04	
Waltham Cross	d					22 07				22 37						23 07			23 37			00 07	
Cheshunt	d	21 48			21 55	22 09		22 18		22 39		22 48	22 55			23 09		23 18	23 39		23 48	00 09	00 18
Broxbourne 3	a	21 52			21 59	22 14		22 22		22 44		22 52	22 59			23 14		23 22	23 44		23 52	00 14	00 22
	d	21 52			22 03	22 14		22 22		22 44		22 52	23 03			23 14		23 22	23 44		23 52	00 14	00 22
Rye House	d					22 17				22 47						23 17			23 47			00 17	
St Margarets (Herts)	d					22 20				22 50						23 20			23 50			00 20	
Ware	d					22 24				22 54						23 24			23 54			00 24	
Hertford East	a					22 31				23 01						23 31			00 01			00 31	
Roydon	d				22 08			22 26					23 08					23 26					00 26
Harlow Town	d	21 58			22 12		22 24	22 30			22 54	22 58	23 12				23 24	23 30		23 54	23 58		00 30
Harlow Mill	d				22 15			22 33					23 15					23 33					00 33
Sawbridgeworth	d	22 03			22 18			22 37				23 03	23 18					23 37			00 03		00 37
Bishops Stortford	a	22 10		22 15	22 25			22 44	22 47			23 10	23 26		23 15			23 44		00 04	00 10		00 44
	d	22 11		22 15	22 26			22 44	22 48			23 11			23 15			23 44		00 04	00 11		00 44
Stansted Mountfitchet	d				22 30			22 48			23 05							23 48					00 48
Stansted Airport	a			22 25	22 39		22 42		22 57		23 13				23 25		23 42			00 13			
	d		22 25											23 25									
Elsenham	d							22 52										23 52					00 52
Newport (Essex)	d							22 57										23 57					00 57
Audley End	d	22 23	22 38					23 00				23 23		23 38				23 59			00 23		01 00
Great Chesterford	d							23 05										00 05					01 05
Whittlesford Parkway	d	22 30						23 10				23 30						00 10			00 30		01 10
Shelford	d							23 14										00 14					
Cambridge	a	22 40	23 01					23 21				23 40		23 53				00 21			00 40		01 19

Sundays

		LE 1	LE 1	LE 1	LE 1	LE 1	LE 1	LE 1	LE 1	LE 1	LE 1	LE 1	LE 1	LE 1	LE 1	LE 1	LE 1	LE	LE 1	LE 1	LE	LE 1	LE 1
London Liverpool Street 15 ⊖	d	22p58	23p10	23p25	23p28	23p40	23p58	04 10	04 40	05 10	05 40	06 10	06 25	06 40	06 55	07 10	07 25		07 40	07 43	07 52	07 55	08 10
Bethnal Green	d																						
Hackney Downs	d		23p16			23p46															07 59		
Stratford 7 ⊖	d																						
Clapton	d					23p49																	
Seven Sisters ⊖	d																				08 04		
Tottenham Hale ⊖	d	23p10	23p23	23b37	23p40	23p53	00 10		04u52	05u22	05u52	06u22	06u37	06u52	07 07	07 22	07 37		07 52	07 55		08 07	08 22
Northumberland Park	d		23p25			23p55																	
Angel Road	d																						
Ponders End	d		23p29			23p59														07 59			
Brimsdown	d		23p32			00 02														08 02			
Enfield Lock	d		23p34			00 04														08 04			
Waltham Cross	d		23p37			00 07														08 07			
Cheshunt	d	23p18	23p39		23p48	00 09	00 18													08 09	08 20		
Broxbourne 3	a	23p22	23p44		23p52	00 14	00 22													08 14	08 25		
	d	23p22	23p44		23p52	00 14	00 22											07 57		08 19	08 25		
Rye House	d		23p47			00 17												08 00			08 28		
St Margarets (Herts)	d		23p50			00 20												08 03			08 31		
Ware	d		23p54			00 24												08 07			08 35		
Hertford East	a		00 01			00 31												08 14			08 42		
Roydon	d	23p26					00 26													08 24			
Harlow Town	d	23p30		23p54	23p58		00 30		05 07	05 37	06 10		06 52		07 22		07 52			08 28		08 22	
Harlow Mill	d	23p33					00 33													08 31			
Sawbridgeworth	d	23p37			00 03		00 37													08 34			
Bishops Stortford	a	23p44		00 04	00 10		00 44		05 17	05 47	06 20	06 45		07 15		07 45			08 15	08 41			08 45
	d	23p44		00 04	00 11		00 44		05 18	05 48	06 21	06 46		07 16		07 46			08 16	08 42			08 46
Stansted Mountfitchet	d	23p48					00 48		05 22				07 03				08 03			08 46			
Stansted Airport	a			00 13				04 58	05 29	05 57	06 30	06 55	07 12	07 25	07 40	07 55	08 13		08 25			08 40	08 55
	d																						
Elsenham	d	23p52					00 52													08 50			
Newport (Essex)	d	23p57					00 57													08 55			
Audley End	d	23p59			00 23		01 00													08 58			
Great Chesterford	d	00 05					01 05													09 03			
Whittlesford Parkway	d	00 10			00 30		01 10													09 08			
Shelford	d	00 14																		09 12			
Cambridge	a	00 21			00 40		01 19													09 19			

b previous night, stops to pick up only

London - Broxbourne, Hertford East, Bishops Stortford, Stansted Airport and Cambridge

		LE	LE ■	LE ■	LE	LE ■	LE ■	LE	LE ■	LE ■	LE	LE ■	LE ■	LE	LE ■	XC ◇■ 🍴	LE ■	LE	LE ■	LE ■	LE	LE ■	LE ■
London Liverpool Street 15 ⊖	d	08 22	08 25	08 28		08 40		08 52	08 55	09 10	09 22	09 25	09 28		09 40			09 52	09 55	10 10	10 22	10 25	10 28
Bethnal Green	d																						
Hackney Downs	d	08 29						08 59			09 29							09 59			10 29		
Stratford 7 ⊖	d						08 45										09 45						
Clapton	d																						
Seven Sisters ⊖	d	08 34						09 04			09 34							10 04			10 34		
Tottenham Hale ⊖	d		08 37	08 40		08 52	08 55		09 07	09 22		09 37	09 40		09 52		09 55		10 07	10 22		10 37	10 40
Northumberland Park	d																						
Angel Road	d																						
Ponders End	d						08 59										09 59						
Brimsdown	d						09 02										10 02						
Enfield Lock	d						09 04										10 04						
Waltham Cross	d				←		09 07							←			10 07						
Cheshunt	d	08 52		08 49	08 52		09 09	09 20			09 52		09 49	09 52			10 09	10 20			10 52		10 49
Broxbourne 3	a	→		08 53	08 57		09 14	09 25			→		09 53	09 57			10 14	10 25			→		10 53
	d			08 53	08 57		09 19	09 25					09 53	09 57			10 19	10 25					10 53
Rye House	d				09 00			09 28						10 00				10 28					
St Margarets (Herts)	d				09 03			09 31						10 03				10 31					
Ware	d				09 07			09 35						10 07				10 35					
Hertford East	a				09 14			09 42						10 14				10 42					
Roydon	d						09 24										10 24						
Harlow Town	d		08 52	08 59			09 28		09 22			09 52	09 59				10 28		10 22			10 52	10 59
Harlow Mill	d						09 31										10 31						
Sawbridgeworth	d			09 04			09 34						10 04				10 34						11 04
Bishops Stortford	a			09 11		09 15	09 41			09 45			10 11		10 15		10 41			10 45			11 11
	d			09 12		09 16	09 42			09 46			10 12		10 16		10 42			10 46			11 12
Stansted Mountfitchet	d		09 03				09 46					10 03					10 46					11 03	
Stansted Airport	a		09 12			09 25			09 40	09 55		10 12			10 25				10 40	10 55		11 12	
	d															10 25							
Elsenham	d						09 50										10 50						
Newport (Essex)	d						09 55										10 55						
Audley End	d			09 24			09 58						10 24			10 39	10 58						11 24
Great Chesterford	d						10 03										11 03						
Whittlesford Parkway	d			09 31			10 08						10 31				11 08						11 31
Shelford	d						10 12										11 12						
Cambridge	a			09 41			10 19						10 41			10 54	11 19						11 41

		LE	LE ■	XC ◇■ 🍴	LE ■	LE	LE ■	LE ■	LE	LE ■	LE ■	LE	LE ■	XC ◇■ 🍴	LE ■	LE	LE ■	LE ■	LE	LE ■	LE ■	LE
London Liverpool Street 15 ⊖	d		10 40			10 52	10 55	11 10	11 22	11 25	11 28		11 40			11 52	11 55	12 10	12 22	12 25	12 28	
Bethnal Green	d																					
Hackney Downs	d					10 59			11 29							11 59			12 29			
Stratford 7 ⊖	d				10 45										11 45							
Clapton	d																					
Seven Sisters ⊖	d					11 04			11 34							12 04			12 34			
Tottenham Hale ⊖	d		10 52		10 55		11 07	11 22		11 37	11 40		11 52		11 55		12 07	12 22		12 37	12 40	
Northumberland Park	d																					
Angel Road	d																					
Ponders End	d				10 59										11 59							
Brimsdown	d				11 02										12 02							
Enfield Lock	d				11 04										12 04							
Waltham Cross	d	←			11 07							←			12 07							←
Cheshunt	d	10 52			11 09	11 20			11 52		11 49	11 52			12 09	12 20			12 52		12 49	12 52
Broxbourne 3	a	10 57			11 14	11 25			→		11 53	11 57			12 14	12 25			→		12 53	12 57
	d	10 57			11 19	11 25					11 53	11 57			12 19	12 25					12 53	12 57
Rye House	d	11 00				11 28						12 00				12 28						13 00
St Margarets (Herts)	d	11 03				11 31						12 03				12 31						13 03
Ware	d	11 07				11 35						12 07				12 35						13 07
Hertford East	a	11 14				11 42						12 14				12 42						13 14
Roydon	d				11 24										12 24							
Harlow Town	d				11 28		11 22			11 52	11 59				12 28		12 22			12 52	12 59	
Harlow Mill	d				11 31										12 31							
Sawbridgeworth	d				11 34						12 04				12 34						13 04	
Bishops Stortford	a		11 15		11 41			11 45			12 11		12 15		12 41			12 45			13 11	
	d		11 16		11 42			11 46			12 12		12 16		12 42			12 46			13 12	
Stansted Mountfitchet	d				11 46					12 03					12 46					13 03		
Stansted Airport	a		11 25				11 40	11 55		12 12			12 25				12 40	12 55		13 12		
	d			11 25										12 25								
Elsenham	d				11 50										12 50							
Newport (Essex)	d				11 55										12 55							
Audley End	d			11 39	11 58						12 24			12 39	12 58						13 24	
Great Chesterford	d				12 03										13 03							
Whittlesford Parkway	d				12 08						12 31				13 08						13 31	
Shelford	d				12 12										13 12							
Cambridge	a			11 54	12 19						12 41			12 54	13 19						13 41	

London - Broxbourne, Hertford East, Bishops Stortford, Stansted Airport and Cambridge

		LE ■	XC ◇■ 🍴	LE ■	LE	LE ■	LE ■	LE	LE ■	LE ■	LE	LE ■	XC ◇■ 🍴	LE ■	LE	LE ■	LE ■	LE	LE ■	LE ■	LE	LE ■	XC ◇■ 🍴
London Liverpool Street 15 ⊖	d	12 40			12 52	12 55	13 10	13 22	13 25	13 28		13 40			13 52	13 55	14 10	14 22	14 25	14 28		14 40	
Bethnal Green	d																						
Hackney Downs	d				12 59			13 29							13 59			14 29					
Stratford 7 ⊖	d			12 45										13 45									
Clapton	d																						
Seven Sisters ⊖	d				13 04			13 34							14 04			14 34					
Tottenham Hale ⊖	d	12 52		12 55		13 07	13 22		13 37	13 40		13 52		13 55		14 07	14 22		14 37	14 40		14 52	
Northumberland Park	d																						
Angel Road	d																						
Ponders End	d			12 59										13 59									
Brimsdown	d			13 02										14 02									
Enfield Lock	d			13 04										14 04									
Waltham Cross	d			13 07							←			14 07							←		
Cheshunt	d			13 09	13 20			13 52		13 49	13 52			14 09	14 20			14 52		14 49	14 52		
Broxbourne 3	a			13 14	13 25			→		13 53	13 57			14 14	14 25			→		14 53	14 57		
	d			13 19	13 25					13 53	13 57			14 19	14 25					14 53	14 57		
Rye House	d				13 28						14 00				14 28						15 00		
St Margarets (Herts)	d				13 31						14 03				14 31						15 03		
Ware	d				13 35						14 07				14 35						15 07		
Hertford East	a				13 42						14 14				14 42						15 14		
Roydon	d			13 24										14 24									
Harlow Town	d			13 28		13 22			13 52	13 59				14 28		14 22			14 52	14 59			
Harlow Mill	d			13 31										14 31									
Sawbridgeworth	d			13 34						14 04				14 34						15 04			
Bishops Stortford	a	13 15		13 41			13 45			14 11		14 15		14 41			14 45			15 11		15 15	
	d	13 16		13 42			13 46			14 12		14 16		14 42			14 46			15 12		15 16	
Stansted Mountfitchet	d			13 46					14 03					14 46					15 03				
Stansted Airport	a	13 25				13 40	13 55		14 12			14 25				14 40	14 55		15 12			15 25	
	d		13 25										14 25										15 25
Elsenham	d			13 50										14 50									
Newport (Essex)	d			13 55										14 55									
Audley End	d		13 39	13 58						14 24			14 39	14 58						15 24			15 39
Great Chesterford	d			14 03										15 03									
Whittlesford Parkway	d			14 08						14 31				15 08						15 31			
Shelford	d			14 12										15 12									
Cambridge	a		13 54	14 19						14 41			14 54	15 19						15 41			15 54

		LE ■	LE	LE ■	LE ■	LE	LE ■	LE ■	LE	LE ■	XC ◇■ 🍴	LE ■	LE	LE ■	LE ■	LE	LE ■	LE ■	LE	LE ■	XC ◇■ 🍴	LE ■
London Liverpool Street 15 ⊖	d		14 52	14 55	15 10	15 22	15 25	15 28		15 40			15 52	15 55	16 10	16 22	16 25	16 28		16 40		
Bethnal Green	d																					
Hackney Downs	d		14 59			15 29							15 59			16 29						
Stratford 7 ⊖	d	14 45										15 45										16 45
Clapton	d																					
Seven Sisters ⊖	d		15 04			15 34							16 04			16 34						
Tottenham Hale ⊖	d	14 55		15 07	15 22		15 37	15 40		15 52		15 55		16 07	16 22		16 37	16 40		16 52		16 55
Northumberland Park	d																					
Angel Road	d																					
Ponders End	d	14 59										15 59										16 59
Brimsdown	d	15 02										16 02										17 02
Enfield Lock	d	15 04										16 04										17 04
Waltham Cross	d	15 07							←			16 07							←			17 07
Cheshunt	d	15 09	15 20			15 52		15 49	15 52			16 09	16 20			16 52		16 49	16 52			17 09
Broxbourne 3	a	15 14	15 25			→		15 53	15 57			16 14	16 25			→		16 53	16 57			17 14
	d	15 19	15 25					15 53	15 57			16 19	16 25					16 53	16 57			17 19
Rye House	d		15 28						16 00				16 28						17 00			
St Margarets (Herts)	d		15 31						16 03				16 31						17 03			
Ware	d		15 35						16 07				16 35						17 07			
Hertford East	a		15 42						16 14				16 42						17 14			
Roydon	d	15 24										16 24										17 24
Harlow Town	d	15 28		15 22			15 52	15 59				16 28		16 22			16 52	16 59				17 28
Harlow Mill	d	15 31										16 31										17 31
Sawbridgeworth	d	15 34						16 04				16 34						17 04				17 34
Bishops Stortford	a	15 41			15 45			16 11		16 15		16 41			16 45			17 11		17 15		17 41
	d	15 42			15 46			16 12		16 16		16 42			16 46			17 12		17 16		17 42
Stansted Mountfitchet	d	15 46					16 03					16 46					17 03					17 46
Stansted Airport	a			15 40	15 55		16 12			16 25				16 40	16 55		17 12			17 25		
	d										16 25										17 25	
Elsenham	d	15 50										16 50										17 50
Newport (Essex)	d	15 55										16 55										17 55
Audley End	d	15 58						16 24			16 39	16 58						17 24			17 39	17 58
Great Chesterford	d	16 03										17 03										18 03
Whittlesford Parkway	d	16 08						16 31				17 08						17 31				18 08
Shelford	d	16 12										17 12										18 12
Cambridge	a	16 19						16 41			16 54	17 19						17 41			17 54	18 19

Table 22

London - Broxbourne, Hertford East, Bishops Stortford, Stansted Airport and Cambridge

		LE	LE 1	LE 1	LE	LE 1	LE 1	LE	LE 1	XC ◇1		LE 1	LE	LE 1	LE 1	LE	LE 1	LE 1	LE	LE 1		XC ◇1	LE 1	LE	LE 1
London Liverpool Street 15 ⊖	d	16 52	16 55	17 10	17 22	17 25	17 28		17 40				17 52	17 55	18 10	18 22	18 25	18 28		18 40				18 52	18 55
Bethnal Green	d																								
Hackney Downs	d	16 59			17 29								17 59			18 29								18 59	
Stratford 7 ⊖	d											17 45											18 45		
Clapton	d																								
Seven Sisters ⊖	d	17 04			17 34								18 04			18 34								19 04	
Tottenham Hale ⊖	d		17 07	17 22		17 37	17 40		17 52			17 55		18 07	18 22		18 37	18 40		18 52			18 55		19 07
Northumberland Park	d																								
Angel Road	d																								
Ponders End	d											17 59											18 59		
Brimsdown	d											18 02											19 02		
Enfield Lock	d											18 04											19 04		
Waltham Cross	d							←				18 07							←				19 07		
Cheshunt	d	17 20			17 52		17 49	17 52				18 09	18 20			18 52		18 49	18 52				19 09	19 20	
Broxbourne 3	a	17 25			→		17 53	17 57				18 14	18 25			→		18 53	18 57				19 14	19 25	
	d	17 25					17 53	17 57				18 19	18 25					18 53	18 57				19 19	19 25	
Rye House	d	17 28						18 00					18 28						19 00					19 28	
St Margarets (Herts)	d	17 31						18 03					18 31						19 03					19 31	
Ware	d	17 35						18 07					18 35						19 07					19 35	
Hertford East	a	17 42						18 14					18 42						19 14					19 42	
Roydon	d											18 24											19 24		
Harlow Town	d		17 22			17 52	17 59					18 28		18 22			18 52	18 59					19 28		19 22
Harlow Mill	d											18 31											19 31		
Sawbridgeworth	d						18 04					18 34						19 04					19 34		
Bishops Stortford	a			17 45			18 11		18 15			18 41			18 45			19 11		19 15			19 41		
	d			17 46			18 12		18 16			18 42			18 46			19 12		19 16			19 42		
Stansted Mountfitchet	d					18 03						18 46					19 03						19 46		
Stansted Airport	a		17 40	17 55		18 12			18 25					18 40	18 55		19 12			19 25					19 40
	d									18 25												19 25			
Elsenham	d											18 50											19 50		
Newport (Essex)	d											18 55											19 55		
Audley End	d						18 24			18 39		18 58						19 24				19 39	19 58		
Great Chesterford	d											19 03											20 03		
Whittlesford Parkway	d						18 31					19 08						19 31					20 08		
Shelford	d											19 12											20 12		
Cambridge	a						18 41			18 55		19 19						19 41				19 54	20 19		

		LE 1	LE	LE 1	LE 1	LE		LE 1	XC ◇1	LE 1	LE	LE 1	LE 1	LE	LE 1	LE 1		LE	XC ◇1	LE 1	LE 1	LE	LE 1	LE 1	LE
London Liverpool Street 15 ⊖	d	19 10	19 22	19 25	19 28			19 40			19 52	19 55	20 10	20 22	20 25	20 28				20 40		20 52	20 55	21 10	21 22
Bethnal Green	d																								
Hackney Downs	d		19 29								19 59			20 29								20 59			21 29
Stratford 7 ⊖	d									19 45											20 45				
Clapton	d																								
Seven Sisters ⊖	d		19 34								20 04			20 34								21 04			21 34
Tottenham Hale ⊖	d	19 22		19 37	19 40			19 52		19 55		20 07	20 22		20 37	20 40				20 52	20 55		21 07	21 22	
Northumberland Park	d																								
Angel Road	d																								
Ponders End	d									19 59											20 59				
Brimsdown	d									20 02											21 02				
Enfield Lock	d									20 04											21 04				
Waltham Cross	d					←				20 07								←			21 07				
Cheshunt	d		19 52		19 48	19 52				20 09	20 20			20 52		20 48		20 52			21 09	21 20			21 52
Broxbourne 3	a		→		19 52	19 57				20 14	20 25			→		20 52		20 57			21 14	21 25			→
	d				19 52	19 57				20 19	20 25					20 52		20 57			21 19	21 25			
Rye House	d					20 00					20 28							21 00				21 28			
St Margarets (Herts)	d					20 03					20 31							21 03				21 31			
Ware	d					20 07					20 35							21 07				21 35			
Hertford East	a					20 14					20 42							21 14				21 42			
Roydon	d									20 24											21 24				
Harlow Town	d			19 52	19 58					20 28		20 22			20 52	20 58					21 28		21 22		
Harlow Mill	d									20 31											21 31				
Sawbridgeworth	d				20 03					20 34						21 03					21 34				
Bishops Stortford	a	19 45			20 10			20 15		20 41			20 45			21 10				21 15	21 41			21 45	
	d	19 46			20 11			20 16		20 42			20 46			21 11				21 16	21 42			21 46	
Stansted Mountfitchet	d			20 03						20 46					21 03						21 46				
Stansted Airport	a	19 55		20 12				20 25				20 40	20 55		21 12					21 26			21 40	21 55	
	d								20 25										21 18						
Elsenham	d									20 50											21 50				
Newport (Essex)	d									20 55											21 55				
Audley End	d				20 23				20 38	20 58						21 23			21 33		21 58				
Great Chesterford	d									21 03											22 03				
Whittlesford Parkway	d				20 30					21 08						21 30					22 08				
Shelford	d									21 12											22 12				
Cambridge	a				20 40				20 55	21 19						21 40			21 47		22 19				

Table 22

London - Broxbourne, Hertford East, Bishops Stortford, Stansted Airport and Cambridge

		LE 1		LE 1	LE	LE 1	XC ◇1	LE 1	LE	LE 1	LE 1	LE	XC ◇1	LE 1	LE 1	LE	LE 1	LE 1	LE	LE 1	LE			LE 1	LE 1
London Liverpool Street 15 ⊖	d	21 25		21 28		21 40			21 52	21 55	22 10	22 22		22 25	22 28		22 40		22 52	22 55	23 22			23 25	23 28
Bethnal Green	d																								
Hackney Downs	d								21 59			22 29							22 59		23 29				
Stratford 7 ⊖	d							21 45										22 45							
Clapton	d																								
Seven Sisters ⊖	d								22 04			22 34							23 04		23 34				
Tottenham Hale ⊖	d	21 37		21 40		21 52		21 55		22 07	22 22			22 37	22 40		22 52	22 55		23 07				23 37	23 40
Northumberland Park	d																								
Angel Road	d																								
Ponders End	d							21 59										22 59							23 44
Brimsdown	d							22 02										23 02							23 47
Enfield Lock	d							22 04										23 04							23 49
Waltham Cross	d				←			22 07								←		23 07							23 52
Cheshunt	d			21 48	21 52			22 09	22 20			22 52			22 48	22 52		23 09	23 20		23 50				23 54
Broxbourne 3	a			21 52	21 57			22 14	22 25			→			22 52	22 57		23 14	23 25		23 55				23 59
	d			21 52	21 57			22 19	22 25						22 52	22 57		23 19	23 25		00 02				23 59
Rye House	d				22 00				22 28							23 00					00 06				
St Margarets (Herts)	d				22 03				22 31							23 03					00 09				
Ware	d				22 07				22 35							23 07					00 13				
Hertford East	a				22 14				22 42							23 14					00 19				
Roydon	d							22 24										23 24							
Harlow Town	d	21 52		21 58				22 28		22 22				22 52	22 58			23 28	23 32	23 22				23 52	00 05
Harlow Mill	d							22 31										23 31							
Sawbridgeworth	d			22 03				22 34							23 03			23 34							00 10
Bishops Stortford	a			22 10		22 15		22 41			22 45				23 10		23 15	23 41	23 45					00 02	00 17
	d			22 11		22 16		22 42			22 46				23 11		23 16	23 42						00 03	
Stansted Mountfitchet	d	22 03						22 46						23 03				23 46							
Stansted Airport	a	22 12				22 25				22 40	22 55			23 11			23 25			23 40				00 12	
	d						22 25						23 02												
Elsenham	d							22 50										23 50							
Newport (Essex)	d							22 55										23 55							
Audley End	d			22 23			22 40	22 58					23 20		23 23			23 58							
Great Chesterford	d							23 03										00 03							
Whittlesford Parkway	d			22 30				23 08							23 30			00 08							
Shelford	d							23 12										00 12							
Cambridge	a			22 40			22 57	23 19					23 35		23 40			00 19							

		LE 1
London Liverpool Street 15 ⊖	d	23 58
Bethnal Green	d	
Hackney Downs	d	
Stratford 7 ⊖	d	
Clapton	d	
Seven Sisters ⊖	d	
Tottenham Hale ⊖	d	00 10
Northumberland Park	d	
Angel Road	d	
Ponders End	d	
Brimsdown	d	
Enfield Lock	d	
Waltham Cross	d	
Cheshunt	d	00 18
Broxbourne 3	a	00 22
	d	00 22
Rye House	d	
St Margarets (Herts)	d	
Ware	d	
Hertford East	a	
Roydon	d	00 26
Harlow Town	d	00 30
Harlow Mill	d	00 33
Sawbridgeworth	d	00 37
Bishops Stortford	a	00 44
	d	
Stansted Mountfitchet	d	
Stansted Airport	a	
	d	
Elsenham	d	
Newport (Essex)	d	
Audley End	d	
Great Chesterford	d	
Whittlesford Parkway	d	
Shelford	d	
Cambridge	a	

Cambridge, Stansted Airport, Bishops Stortford, Hertford East and Broxbourne - London

Station		LE MO 1	LE MX 1	LE MX 1	LE MO 1	LE MX 1	LE MX 1	LE MO 1	LE MX 1	LE MX 1	LE 1	LE 1	LE MFO 1	LE MFO 1	XC ◇1	LE 1	LE 1	LE MFO 1	XC ◇1	LE 1 A	LE 1	LE 1	LE 1
Cambridge	d			22p51											04 44	04 48			05 17			05 21	
Shelford	d			22p56																		05 26	
Whittlesford Parkway	d			23p00												04 55						05 30	
Great Chesterford	d			23p04																		05 34	
Audley End	d			23p10											04 58	05 03			05 35			05 40	
Newport (Essex)	d			23p13																		05 43	
Elsenham	d			23p19																		05 49	
Stansted Airport	a														05 11				05 50				
	d	23p15	23p15		23p30	23p30		23p45	23p45		23p59	00 30	01 00	01 30				05 30					06 00
Stansted Mountfitchet	d			23p22																		05 52	06 06
Bishops Stortford	a			23p28	23p39	23p39					00 08	00 39				05 16		05 39				05 58	06 10
	d			23p28	23p39	23p39					00 08	00 39				05 16		05 39		05 39	05 45	05 58	06 10
Sawbridgeworth	d			23p32												05 21					05 49	06 03	
Harlow Mill	d			23p36												05 24					05 53	06 06	
Harlow Town	d	23p30	23p30	23p39	23p47			23p59	23p59		00 16	00 47				05 27		05 47		05 47	05 56	06 10	06 18
Roydon	d			23p43												05 31					06 00	06 14	
Hertford East	d						23p39			00 07							05 25						
Ware	d						23p43										05 29						
St Margarets (Herts)	d						23p47										05 33						
Rye House	d						23p50										05 36						
Broxbourne 3	a			23p47			23p54			00 19						05 36	05 40	05 53		05 53	06 04	06 18	
	d			23p47			23p54			00 19						05 36	05 40	05 53		05 53	06 04	06 18	
Cheshunt	d			23p51			23p58									05 41	05 44	05 57		05 57	06 08	06 23	
Waltham Cross	d																05 47				06 10		
Enfield Lock	d																05 49				06 13		
Brimsdown	d																05 52				06 15		
Ponders End	d																05 54				06 17		
Angel Road	d																05 57				06 21		
Northumberland Park	d																05 59				06 23		
Tottenham Hale ⊖	d	23p46	23p47													05 49	06 03	06 07		06 07	06 26	06 31	06 34
Seven Sisters ⊖	d			00 04	00 08	00 07	00 11	00 21	00 21														
Clapton	d																						
Stratford 7 ⊖	a																				06 39		
Hackney Downs	d						00 16										06 08						
Bethnal Green	d																						
London Liverpool Street 15 ⊖	a	00 01	00 01	00 18	00 22	00 22	00 24	00 35	00 36	00 49	00 51	01 21	01 50	02 20		06 03	06 17	06 23		06 23		06 47	06 49

Station		LE	LE 1	LE 1	LE 1	LE 1	LE 1	LE	LE 1	LE 1	LE 1	LE 1	LE 1	LE 1	XC ◇1	LE	LE 1	LE 1	LE	LE 1	LE 1	LE	LE 1
Cambridge	d			05 41		05 51				06b18			06 21		06 32		06 48			06 51			07c18
Shelford	d			05 46		05 56							06 26							06 56			
Whittlesford Parkway	d			05 50		06 00				06 25			06 30				06 55			07 00			07 25
Great Chesterford	d			05 54		06 04							06 34							07 04			
Audley End	d			06 00		06 10				06 34			06 40		06 46		07 04			07 10			07 34
Newport (Essex)	d			06 03		06 13							06 43							07 13			
Elsenham	d			06 09		06 19							06 49							07 19			
Stansted Airport	a														07 08								
	d				06 15		06 30				06 43			07 00				07 15			07 30		
Stansted Mountfitchet	d			06 12		06 22					06 49		06 52							07 22			
Bishops Stortford	a			06 18	06 24	06 28	06 39			06 47	06 53		06 58	07 09			07 17	07 24		07 28	07 39		07 47
	d		06 14	06 18	06 24	06 28	06 39		06 42	06 48	06 54		06 58	07 09			07 17	07 24		07 28	07 39		07 48
Sawbridgeworth	d		06 18			06 33			06 46				07 03				07 22			07 33			
Harlow Mill	d					06 36			06 50				07 06							07 36			
Harlow Town	d		06 23	06 27		06 40	06 47		06 53	06 57	07 02		07 10				07 27	07 32		07 40			07 57
Roydon	d					06 44			06 57				07 14							07 44			
Hertford East	d	06 05						06 35								07 09			07 15			07 39	
Ware	d	06 09						06 39								07 13			07 19			07 43	
St Margarets (Herts)	d	06 13						06 43								07 17			07 23			07 47	
Rye House	d	06 16						06 46								07 20			07 26			07 50	
Broxbourne 3	a	06 21	06 30	06 33		06 48		06 51	07 02	07 04		←	07 18	07 22		07 25	07 33		07 30	07 48	07 52	07 55	08 03
	d	06 25	06 39	06 34		06 48		06 55	07 11	07 05			07 18	07 22		07 25	07 34		07 40	07 48	07 52	07 55	08 04
Cheshunt	d	06 30	06 43			06 53		07 00	07 15		07 12	07 15		07 27		07 30			07 44	07 53		08 00	
Waltham Cross	d	06 32	06 46					07 02	→			07 18				07 32			07 47		07 58	08 02	
Enfield Lock	d	06 35	06 48					07 05				07 20				07 35			07 49			08 05	
Brimsdown	d	06 37						07 07						07 31		07 37			07 52		08 02	08 07	
Ponders End	d	06 39						07 09						07 33		07 39					08 04	08 09	
Angel Road	d		06 53									07 25											
Northumberland Park	d		06 55									07 27							07 57				
Tottenham Hale ⊖	d	06 45	06 58	06 48	06 51	07 01	07 04	07 15		07 18	07 21	07 30	07 33	07 38		07 45	07 48	07 51	08 00	08 03	08 10	08 15	08 18
Seven Sisters ⊖	d																						
Clapton	d																						
Stratford 7 ⊖	a		07 12									07 44							08 13				
Hackney Downs	d	06 51						07 21								07 51						08 21	
Bethnal Green	d																						
London Liverpool Street 15 ⊖	a	07 02		07 04	07 07	07 18	07 21	07 32		07 34	07 37		07 49	07 59		08 02	08 04	08 07		08 19	08 28	08 32	08 34

A TWThO

b arr. 0610

c arr. 0708

Cambridge, Stansted Airport, Bishops Stortford, Hertford East and Broxbourne - London

Station		LE 1	LE	LE 1	LE 1	XC ◇1	LE	LE	LE 1	LE 1	LE 1	XC ◇1	LE 1	LE	LE 1	LE 1	LE	LE 1	LE 1	LE 1	LE 1	LE 1
Cambridge	d			07 21		07 29			07 48		07 51	08 09			08 18			08 21				
Shelford	d			07 26							07 56							08 26				
Whittlesford Parkway	d			07 30					07 55		08 00				08 25			08 30				
Great Chesterford	d			07 34							08 04							08 34				
Audley End	d			07 40		07 44			08 04		08 10	08 24			08 34			08 40				
Newport (Essex)	d			07 43							08 13							08 43				
Elsenham	d			07 49							08 19							08 49				
Stansted Airport	a					08 09						08 38										
	d	07 43			08 00					08 15			08 30			08 45			09 00			09 15
Stansted Mountfitchet	d	07 49		07 52							08 22					08 51		08 52				
Bishops Stortford	a	07 54		07 58	08 09				08 17		08 28		08 39		08 48			08 58	09 09			
	d	07 54		07 58	08 09			08 12	08 17		08 28		08 39		08 48			08 58	09 09		09 14	
Sawbridgeworth	d			08 03				08 16	08 22		08 33							09 03			09 18	
Harlow Mill	d			08 06				08 20			08 36							09 06			09 22	
Harlow Town	d	08 02		08 10				08 23	08 27	08 31	08 40				08 57	09 02		09 10			09 25	09 30
Roydon	d			08 14				08 27			08 44							09 14			09 29	
Hertford East	d						08 09							08 39						09 09		
Ware	d						08 13							08 43						09 13		
St Margarets (Herts)	d						08 17							08 47						09 17		
Rye House	d						08 20							08 50						09 20		
Broxbourne 3	a			08 18			08 25	08 32	08 34		08 48			08 55	09 03			09 18		09 25	09 34	
	d		08 10	08 18			08 25	08 40	08 35		08 48			08 55	09 04		09 10	09 18		09 25	09 37	
Cheshunt	d		08 14	08 23			08 30	08 44			08 53			09 00			09 14	09 23		09 30	09 42	
Waltham Cross	d		08 17				08 32	08 47						09 02			09 17			09 32		
Enfield Lock	d		08 19				08 35	08 49						09 05			09 19			09 35	09 45	
Brimsdown	d						08 37							09 07						09 37		
Ponders End	d						08 39							09 09						09 39		
Angel Road	d		08 24					08 54									09 24				09 50	
Northumberland Park	d		08 26					08 56									09 26				09 52	
Tottenham Hale ⊖	d	08 21	08 29	08 32	08 35		08 45	08 59	08 48	08 51	09 02		09 05	09 15	09 18	09 21	09 29	09 32	09 35	09 45	09 56	09 48
Seven Sisters ⊖	d																					
Clapton	d																					
Stratford 7 ⊖	a		08 43					09 13									09 43				10 08	
Hackney Downs	d						08 51							09 21						09 51		
Bethnal Green	d																					
London Liverpool Street 15 ⊖	a	08 37		08 49	08 52		09 02		09 04	09 07	09 19		09 22	09 32	09 34	09 37		09 49	09 52	10 00		10 05

Station		LE 1	LE 1	XC ◇1	LE	LE 1	LE 1	LE 1	LE	LE 1	LE 1	LE 1	LE 1	LE 1	LE 1	XC ◇1	LE 1	LE 1	LE 1	LE 1	LE 1	LE 1	XC ◇1
Cambridge	d	08 51		09 10			09 32					09 48				10 08	10 32					10 48	11 10
Shelford	d	08 56										09 53										10 53	
Whittlesford Parkway	d	09 00					09 39					10 00					10 39					11 00	
Great Chesterford	d	09 04										10 04										11 04	
Audley End	d	09 10		09 24			09 47					10 10				10 24	10 47					11 10	11 24
Newport (Essex)	d	09 13										10 13										11 13	
Elsenham	d	09 19										10 19										11 19	
Stansted Airport	a			09 38												10 45							11 45
	d		09 30			09 45		10 00			10 15		10 30		10 45			11 00		11 03	11 15		
Stansted Mountfitchet	d	09 22				09 51						10 22								11 09		11 22	
Bishops Stortford	a	09 28	09 39				10 00	10 09				10 28	10 39				11 00	11 09		11 13		11 28	
	d	09 28	09 39				10 00	10 09		10 14		10 28	10 39				11 00	11 09		11 14		11 28	
Sawbridgeworth	d	09 32					10 05			10 18		10 32					11 05			11 18		11 32	
Harlow Mill	d	09 36								10 22		10 36								11 22		11 36	
Harlow Town	d	09 39				10 02	10 10			10 25	10 30	10 39			11 00		11 10			11 25	11 30	11 39	
Roydon	d	09 43								10 29		10 43								11 29		11 43	
Hertford East	d				09 39				10 09					10 39					11 09				
Ware	d				09 43				10 13					10 43					11 13				
St Margarets (Herts)	d				09 47				10 17					10 47					11 17				
Rye House	d				09 50				10 20					10 50					11 20				
Broxbourne 3	a	09 47			09 54		10 16		10 24	10 34		10 47		10 54			11 16		11 24	11 34		11 47	
	d	09 47			09 54		10 16		10 24	10 37		10 47		10 54			11 16		11 24	11 37		11 47	
Cheshunt	d	09 51			09 58		10 20		10 28	10 42		10 51		10 58			11 20		11 28	11 42		11 51	
Waltham Cross	d				10 01				10 31					11 01					11 31				
Enfield Lock	d				10 03				10 33	10 45				11 03					11 33	11 45			
Brimsdown	d				10 06				10 36					11 06					11 36				
Ponders End	d				10 08				10 38					11 08					11 38				
Angel Road	d																						
Northumberland Park	d									10 51										11 51			
Tottenham Hale ⊖	d	10 00	10 03		10 14	10 17	10 29	10 32	10 44	10 55	10 47	11 00	11 03	11 14	11 17		11 29	11 32	11 44	11 55	11 47	12 00	
Seven Sisters ⊖	d																						
Clapton	d																						
Stratford 7 ⊖	a									11 05										12 05			
Hackney Downs	d				10 20				10 50					11 20					11 50				
Bethnal Green	d																						
London Liverpool Street 15 ⊖	a	10 13	10 18		10 28	10 31	10 43	10 46	10 58		11 01	11 13	11 17	11 28	11 31		11 43	11 46	11 58		12 01	12 13	

Table 22

Cambridge, Stansted Airport, Bishops Stortford, Hertford East and Broxbourne - London

		LE	LE	LE	LE	LE	LE	LE	LE	LE	LE	XC	LE	LE	LE	LE	LE	LE	LE	LE	LE
Cambridge	d				11 32					11 51		12 10			12 32					12 51	
Shelford	d									11 56										12 56	
Whittlesford Parkway	d				11 39					12 00					12 39					13 00	
Great Chesterford	d									12 04										13 04	
Audley End	d				11 47					12 10		12 24			12 47					13 10	
Newport (Essex)	d									12 13										13 13	
Elsenham	d									12 19										13 19	
Stansted Airport	a											12 45									
	d	11 30		11 45		12 00		12 03	12 15		12 30			12 45		13 00		13 03	13 15		13 30
Stansted Mountfitchet	d							12 09		12 22								13 09		13 22	
Bishops Stortford	a	11 39			12 00	12 09		12 13		12 28	12 39				13 00	13 09		13 13		13 28	13 39
	d	11 39			12 00	12 09		12 14		12 28	12 39				13 00	13 09		13 14		13 28	13 39
Sawbridgeworth	d				12 05			12 18		12 32					13 05			13 18		13 32	
Harlow Mill	d							12 22		12 36								13 22		13 36	
Harlow Town	d			12 00	12 10			12 25	12 30	12 39				13 00	13 10			13 25	13 30	13 39	
Roydon	d							12 29		12 43								13 29		13 43	
Hertford East	d		11 39				12 09						12 39				13 09				
Ware	d		11 43				12 13						12 43				13 13				
St Margarets (Herts)	d		11 47				12 17						12 47				13 17				
Rye House	d		11 50				12 20						12 50				13 20				
Broxbourne	a		11 54		12 16		12 24	12 34		12 47			12 54		13 16		13 24	13 34		13 47	
	d		11 54		12 16		12 24	12 37		12 47			12 54		13 16		13 24	13 37		13 47	
Cheshunt	d		11 58		12 20		12 28	12 42		12 51			12 58		13 20		13 28	13 42		13 51	
Waltham Cross	d		12 01				12 31						13 01				13 31				
Enfield Lock	d		12 03				12 33	12 45					13 03				13 33	13 45			
Brimsdown	d		12 06				12 36						13 06				13 36				
Ponders End	d		12 08				12 38						13 08				13 38				
Angel Road	d																				
Northumberland Park	d							12 51										13 51			
Tottenham Hale ⊖	d	12 03	12 14	12 17	12 29	12 32	12 44	12 55	12 47	13 00	13 03		13 14	13 17	13 29	13 32	13 44	13 55	13 47	14 00	14 03
Seven Sisters ⊖	d																				
Clapton	d																				
Stratford ⊖	a							13 05										14 05			
Hackney Downs	d		12 20				12 50						13 20				13 50				
Bethnal Green	d																				
London Liverpool Street ⊖	a	12 17	12 28	12 31	12 43	12 46	12 58		13 01	13 13	13 17		13 28	13 31	13 43	13 46	13 58		14 01	14 13	14 17

		LE	LE	XC	LE	LE FO	LE FX	LE	LE	LE	LE FO	LE FX	LE	LE	LE	XC	LE	LE	LE	LE	LE	LE	LE
Cambridge	d			13 10	13 32						13 51	13 51				14 10	14 32					14 51	
Shelford	d										13 56	13 56										14 56	
Whittlesford Parkway	d				13 39						14 00	14 00					14 39					15 00	
Great Chesterford	d										14 04	14 04										15 04	
Audley End	d			13 24	13 47						14 10	14 10				14 24	14 47					15 10	
Newport (Essex)	d										14 13	14 13										15 13	
Elsenham	d										14 19	14 19										15 19	
Stansted Airport	a			13 45												14 45							
	d		13 45			14 00	14 00		14 03	14 15			14 30		14 45			15 00		15 03	15 15		15 30
Stansted Mountfitchet	d								14 09		14 22	14 22								15 09		15 22	
Bishops Stortford	a				14 00	14 09	14 09		14 13		14 28	14 28	14 39				15 00	15 09		15 13		15 28	15 39
	d				14 00	14 09	14 09		14 14		14 28	14 28	14 39				15 00	15 09		15 14		15 28	15 39
Sawbridgeworth	d				14 05				14 18		14 32	14 32					15 05			15 18		15 32	
Harlow Mill	d								14 22		14 36	14 36								15 22		15 36	
Harlow Town	d		14 00		14 10				14 25	14 30	14 39	14 39			15 00		15 10			15 25	15 30	15 39	
Roydon	d								14 29		14 43	14 43								15 29		15 43	
Hertford East	d	13 39						14 09						14 39					15 09				
Ware	d	13 43						14 13						14 43					15 13				
St Margarets (Herts)	d	13 47						14 17						14 47					15 17				
Rye House	d	13 50						14 20						14 50					15 20				
Broxbourne	a	13 54			14 16			14 24	14 34		14 47	14 47		14 54			15 16		15 24	15 34		15 47	
	d	13 54			14 16			14 24	14 37		14 47	14 47		14 54			15 16		15 24	15 37		15 47	
Cheshunt	d	13 58			14 20			14 28	14 42		14 51	14 51		14 58			15 20		15 28	15 42		15 51	
Waltham Cross	d	14 01						14 31						15 01					15 31				
Enfield Lock	d	14 03						14 33	14 45					15 03					15 33	15 45			
Brimsdown	d	14 06						14 36						15 06					15 36				
Ponders End	d	14 08						14 38						15 08					15 38				
Angel Road	d																			15 50			
Northumberland Park	d								14 51											15 52			
Tottenham Hale ⊖	d	14 14	14 17		14 29	14 32	14 32	14 44	14 55	14 47	15 00	15 00	15 03	15 14	15 17		15 29	15 32	15 44	15 56	15 47	16 00	16 03
Seven Sisters ⊖	d																						
Clapton	d																						
Stratford ⊖	a								15 05											16 06			
Hackney Downs	d	14 20						14 50						15 20					15 50				
Bethnal Green	d																						
London Liverpool Street ⊖	a	14 28	14 31		14 43	14 46	14 48	14 58		15 01	15 13	15 15	15 17	15 28	15 31		15 45	15 47	15 58		16 01	16 13	16 17

Table 22

Cambridge, Stansted Airport, Bishops Stortford, Hertford East and Broxbourne - London

		LE	LE	XC	LE	LE	LE	LE	LE	LE	LE	LE	LE	LE	XC	LE	LE	LE	LE	LE	LE	LE	LE	XC
Cambridge	d			15 10		15 21					15 51				16 10		16 21					16 51		17 10
Shelford	d					15 26					15 56						16 26					16 56		
Whittlesford Parkway	d					15 30					16 00						16 30					17 00		
Great Chesterford	d					15 34					16 04						16 34					17 04		
Audley End	d			15 24		15 40					16 10				16 24		16 40					17 10		17 24
Newport (Essex)	d					15 43					16 13						16 43					17 13		
Elsenham	d					15 49					16 19						16 49					17 19		
Stansted Airport	a			15 45											16 45									17 39
	d		15 45				16 00		16 03	16 15		16 30		16 45				17 00		17 03	17 15		17 30	
Stansted Mountfitchet	d					15 52			16 09		16 22						16 52			17 09		17 22		
Bishops Stortford	a					15 58	16 09		16 13		16 28	16 39					16 58	17 09		17 13		17 28	17 39	
	d				15 48	15 58	16 09		16 14		16 28	16 39					16 58	17 09		17 14		17 28	17 39	
Sawbridgeworth	d					16 02			16 18		16 32						17 02			17 18		17 32		
Harlow Mill	d					16 06			16 22		16 36						17 06			17 22		17 36		
Harlow Town	d		16 00		15 56	16 09			16 25	16 30	16 39			17 00			17 09			17 25	17 30	17 39		
Roydon	d					16 13			16 29		16 43						17 13			17 29		17 43		
Hertford East	d	15 39						16 09					16 39						17 12					
Ware	d	15 43						16 13					16 43						17 16					
St Margarets (Herts)	d	15 47						16 17					16 47						17 20					
Rye House	d	15 50						16 20					16 50						17 23					
Broxbourne	a	15 54			16 03	16 17		16 24	16 34		16 47		16 54				17 17		17 27	17 34		17 47		
	d	15 54			16 07	16 17		16 24	16 37		16 47		16 54			17 09	17 17		17 27	17 37		17 47		
Cheshunt	d	15 58			16 12	16 21		16 28	16 42		16 51		16 58			17 13	17 21		17 31	17 42		17 51		
Waltham Cross	d	16 01						16 31					17 01						17 34					
Enfield Lock	d	16 03			16 15			16 33	16 45				17 03			17 17			17 36	17 45				
Brimsdown	d	16 06						16 36					17 06						17 39					
Ponders End	d	16 08						16 38					17 08						17 41					
Angel Road	d				16 20				16 50							17 22				17 50				
Northumberland Park	d				16 22				16 52							17 24				17 52				
Tottenham Hale ⊖	d	16 14	16 17		16 26	16 30	16 33	16 44	16 56	16 47	17 00	17 03	17 14	17 17		17 27	17 30	17 33	17 46	17 56	17 49	18 00	18 03	
Seven Sisters ⊖	d																							
Clapton	d																							
Stratford ⊖	a				16 39				17 10							17 40				18 10				
Hackney Downs	d	16 20						16 50					17 20						17 52					
Bethnal Green	d																							
London Liverpool Street ⊖	a	16 29	16 31			16 43	16 48	16 58		17 03	17 13	17 17	17 30	17 32			17 44	17 48	18 01		18 03	18 13	18 17	

		LE	LE	LE	LE	LE	LE	LE	LE	LE	LE	LE	LE	XC	LE	LE	LE	LE	LE	LE	LE
Cambridge	d				17 21					17 51				18 18	18 21					18 51	
Shelford	d				17 26					17 56					18 26					18 56	
Whittlesford Parkway	d				17 30					18 00					18 30					19 00	
Great Chesterford	d				17 34					18 04					18 34					19 04	
Audley End	d				17 40					18 10				18 32	18 40					19 10	
Newport (Essex)	d				17 43					18 13					18 43					19 13	
Elsenham	d				17 49					18 19					18 49					19 19	
Stansted Airport	a													18 45							
	d		17 45			18 00		18 15			18 30		18 45			19 00		19 15			19 30
Stansted Mountfitchet	d				17 52	18 06				18 22					18 52	19 06				19 22	
Bishops Stortford	a				17 58	18 10				18 28	18 39				18 58	19 10				19 28	19 39
	d				17 58	18 11				18 28	18 39				19 00	19 11				19 28	19 39
Sawbridgeworth	d				18 02					18 32					19 05					19 32	
Harlow Mill	d				18 06					18 36										19 36	
Harlow Town	d		18 00		18 09			18 30		18 39			19 00		19 10			19 30		19 39	
Roydon	d				18 13					18 43										19 43	
Hertford East	d	17 40					18 13		18 18			18 40					19 12		19 18		
Ware	d	17 44							18 22			18 44					19 16		19 22		
St Margarets (Herts)	d	17 48							18 26			18 48					19 20		19 26		
Rye House	d	17 51							18 29			18 51					19 23		19 29		
Broxbourne	a	17 55			18 17		18 27		18 33	18 47		18 57			19 16		19 27		19 33	19 47	
	d	17 55		18 09	18 17		18 27		18 37	18 47		18 57			19 16		19 27		19 37	19 47	
Cheshunt	d	17 59		18 13	18 21		18 31		18 42	18 51		19 01			19 20		19 31		19 42	19 51	
Waltham Cross	d	18 02					18 34					19 04					19 34				
Enfield Lock	d	18 04		18 17			18 36		18 45			19 06					19 36		19 45		
Brimsdown	d	18 07					18 39					19 09					19 39				
Ponders End	d	18 09					18 41					19 11					19 41				
Angel Road	d			18 22					18 50										19 50		
Northumberland Park	d			18 24					18 52										19 52		
Tottenham Hale ⊖	d	18 14	18 18	18 27	18 30	18 33	18 46	18 49	18 56	19 00	19 03	19 16	19 19		19 29	19 32	19 46	19 49	19 56	20 00	20 03
Seven Sisters ⊖	d																				
Clapton	d																				
Stratford ⊖	a			18 40					19 10										20 06		
Hackney Downs	d	18 20					18 52					19 22					19 52				
Bethnal Green	d																				
London Liverpool Street ⊖	a	18 31	18 33		18 44	18 48	19 01	19 03		19 13	19 17	19 31	19 33		19 43	19 46	20 01	20 03		20 13	20 17

Cambridge, Stansted Airport, Bishops Stortford, Hertford East and Broxbourne - London

	LE	LE	XC	LE	LE	LE	LE	LE	LE	LE	LE	LE	XC	LE	LE	LE	LE	LE	LE	LE	LE	LE	LE
Cambridge d			19 10	19 21					19 51				20 10	20 32					20 51				21 32
Shelford d				19 26					19 56										20 56				
Whittlesford Parkway d				19 30					20 00					20 39					21 00				21 39
Great Chesterford d				19 34					20 04										21 04				
Audley End d			19 24	19 40					20 10				20 24	20 47					21 10				21 47
Newport (Essex) d				19 43					20 13										21 13				
Elsenham d				19 49					20 19										21 19				
Stansted Airport a			19 42										20 45										
d		19 45			20 00		20 03	20 15		20 30		20 45			21 00		21 03	21 15		21 30		21 45	
Stansted Mountfitchet d				19 53			20 09		20 22								21 09		21 22				
Bishops Stortford a				20 00	20 09		20 13		20 28	20 39				21 00	21 09		21 13		21 28	21 39			22 00
d				20 00	20 09		20 14		20 28	20 39				21 00	21 09		21 14		21 28	21 39			22 00
Sawbridgeworth d				20 05			20 18		20 32					21 05			21 18		21 32				22 05
Harlow Mill d							20 22		20 36								21 22		21 36				
Harlow Town d		20 00		20 10			20 25	20 30	20 39			21 00		21 10			21 25	21 30	21 39			22 00	22 10
Roydon d							20 29		20 43								21 29		21 43				
Hertford East d	19 40					20 10					20 39					21 09					21 39		
Ware d	19 44					20 14					20 43					21 13					21 43		
St Margarets (Herts) d	19 48					20 18					20 47					21 17					21 47		
Rye House d	19 51					20 21					20 50					21 20					21 50		
Broxbourne a	19 57			20 16		20 25	20 34		20 47		20 54			21 16		21 24	21 34		21 47		21 54		22 16
d	19 57			20 16		20 25	20 40		20 47		20 54			21 16		21 24	21 37		21 47		21 54		22 16
Cheshunt d	20 01			20 20		20 29	20 45		20 51		20 58			21 20		21 28	21 42		21 51		21 58		22 20
Waltham Cross d	20 03					20 32					21 01					21 31					22 01		
Enfield Lock d	20 06					20 34	20 48				21 03					21 33	21 45				22 03		
Brimsdown d	20 08					20 37					21 06					21 36					22 06		
Ponders End d	20 10					20 39					21 08					21 38					22 08		
Angel Road d																							
Northumberland Park d							20 54										21 51						
Tottenham Hale ⊖ d	20 15	20 18		20 29	20 32	20 45	20 57	20 48	21 00	21 03	21 14	21 17		21 29	21 32	21 44	21 55	21 47	22 00	22 03	22 14	22 17	22 29
Seven Sisters ⊖ d																							
Clapton d																							
Stratford ⊖ a							21 08										22 05						
Hackney Downs d	20 22					20 50					21 20					21 50					22 20		
Bethnal Green d																							
London Liverpool Street ⊖ a	20 31	20 33		20 45	20 47	21 01		21 03	21 14	21 17	21 28	21 31		21 43	21 46	21 58		22 01	22 13	22 17	22 28	22 31	22 43

	LE	LE	LE	LE	LE	LE	LE	XC	LE	LE	LE	LE	LE	LE	LE	LE	LE	LE
Cambridge d				21 51				22 10	22 32					22 51				
Shelford d				21 56										22 56				
Whittlesford Parkway d				22 00					22 39					23 00				
Great Chesterford d				22 04										23 04				
Audley End d				22 10				22 24	22 47					23 10				
Newport (Essex) d				22 13										23 13				
Elsenham d				22 19										23 19				
Stansted Airport a								22 55										
d	22 00		22 15		22 30		22 45			23 00	23 03		23 15		23 30		23 45	23 59
Stansted Mountfitchet d				22 22							23 09			23 22				
Bishops Stortford a	22 09			22 28	22 39				23 00	23 09	23 13			23 28	23 39			00 08
d	22 09			22 28	22 39				23 00	23 09				23 28	23 39			00 08
Sawbridgeworth d				22 32					23 05					23 32				
Harlow Mill d				22 36										23 36				
Harlow Town d			22 30	22 39			23 00		23 10				23 30	23 39			23 59	00 16
Roydon d				22 43										23 43				
Hertford East d		22 09				22 39						23 09				23 39		
Ware d		22 13				22 43						23 13				23 43		
St Margarets (Herts) d		22 17				22 47						23 17				23 47		
Rye House d		22 20				22 50						23 20				23 50		
Broxbourne a		22 24		22 47		22 54			23 16			23 24		23 47		23 54		
d		22 24		22 47		22 54			23 16			23 24		23 47		23 54		
Cheshunt d		22 28		22 51		22 58			23 20			23 28		23 51		23 58		
Waltham Cross d		22 31				23 01						23 31						
Enfield Lock d		22 33				23 03						23 33						
Brimsdown d		22 36				23 06						23 36						
Ponders End d		22 38				23 08						23 38						
Angel Road d																		
Northumberland Park d																		
Tottenham Hale ⊖ d	22 32	22 44	22 47	23 00	23 03	23 14	23 17		23 29	23 32		23 44	23 47					
Seven Sisters ⊖ d														00 04	00 07	00 11	00 21	
Clapton d																		
Stratford ⊖ a																		
Hackney Downs d		22 50				23 20						23 50				00 16		
Bethnal Green d																		
London Liverpool Street ⊖ a	22 46	22 58	23 01	23 13	23 17	23 28	23 31		23 43	23 46		23 58	00 01	00 18	00 22	00 24	00 36	00 51

Cambridge, Stansted Airport, Bishops Stortford, Hertford East and Broxbourne - London

	LE	LE	LE	LE	LE	LE	LE	LE	LE	LE	XC	LE	LE	LE	LE	LE	LE	LE	XC	LE	LE
Cambridge d		22p51									04 56				05 21				05 42		05 51
Shelford d		22p56													05 26						05 56
Whittlesford Parkway d		23p00													05 30						06 00
Great Chesterford d		23p04													05 34						06 04
Audley End d		23p10													05 40				05 56		06 10
Newport (Essex) d		23p13													05 43						06 13
Elsenham d		23p19													05 49						06 19
Stansted Airport a											05 20								06 11		
d	23p15		23p30		23p45		23p59	00 30	01 00	01 30			05 30			06 00		06 03		06 15	
Stansted Mountfitchet d		23p22													05 52			06 09			06 22
Bishops Stortford a		23p28	23p39				00 08	00 39					05 39		05 58	06 09		06 13			06 28
d		23p28	23p39				00 08	00 39				05 15	05 39		05 58	06 09		06 14			06 28
Sawbridgeworth d		23p32										05 19			06 02			06 18			06 32
Harlow Mill d		23p36										05 23			06 06			06 22			06 36
Harlow Town d	23p30	23p39			23p59		00 16	00 47				05 26			06 09			06 25		06 30	06 39
Roydon d		23p43										05 30			06 13			06 29			06 43
Hertford East d				23p39		00 07											06 09				
Ware d				23p43													06 13				
St Margarets (Herts) d				23p47													06 17				
Rye House d				23p50													06 20				
Broxbourne a		23p47		23p54		00 19						05 34			06 17		06 24	06 34			06 47
d		23p47		23p54		00 19						05 34		05 54	06 17		06 24	06 37			06 47
Cheshunt d		23p51		23p58								05 38		05 58	06 21		06 28	06 42			06 51
Waltham Cross d												05 40		06 01			06 31				
Enfield Lock d												05 43		06 03			06 33	06 45			
Brimsdown d												05 45		06 06			06 36				
Ponders End d												05 47		06 08			06 38				
Angel Road d																					
Northumberland Park d												05 51						06 51			
Tottenham Hale ⊖ d	23p47											05 55	06 01	06 14	06 30	06 33	06 44	06 55		06 47	07 00
Seven Sisters ⊖ d		00 04	00 07	00 11	00 21																
Clapton d																					
Stratford ⊖ a												06 04						07 05			
Hackney Downs d				00 16										06 20			06 50				
Bethnal Green d																					
London Liverpool Street ⊖ a	00 01	00 18	00 22	00 24	00 36	00 49	00 51	01 21	01 50	02 20		06 14	06 15	06 28	06 43	06 47	06 58			07 01	07 13

	LE	LE	LE	XC	LE	LE	LE	LE	LE	LE	LE	LE	LE	XC	LE	LE	LE	LE	LE	LE	LE
Cambridge d				06 25	06 32					06 51				07 25	07 32					07 51	
Shelford d										06 56										07 56	
Whittlesford Parkway d					06 39					07 00					07 39					08 00	
Great Chesterford d										07 04										08 04	
Audley End d				06 39	06 47					07 10				07 39	07 47					08 10	
Newport (Essex) d										07 13										08 13	
Elsenham d										07 19										08 19	
Stansted Airport a				06 53										07 53							
d	06 30		06 45			07 00		07 03	07 15		07 30		07 45			08 00		08 03	08 15		08 30
Stansted Mountfitchet d			06 51					07 09		07 22			07 51					08 09		08 22	
Bishops Stortford a	06 39				07 00	07 09		07 13		07 28	07 39				08 00	08 09		08 13		08 28	08 39
d	06 39				07 00	07 09		07 14		07 28	07 39				08 00	08 09		08 14		08 28	08 39
Sawbridgeworth d					07 05			07 18		07 32					08 05			08 18		08 32	
Harlow Mill d								07 22		07 36								08 22		08 36	
Harlow Town d			07 02		07 10			07 25	07 30	07 39			08 02		08 10			08 25	08 30	08 39	
Roydon d								07 29		07 43								08 29		08 43	
Hertford East d		06 39					07 09					07 39					08 09				
Ware d		06 43					07 13					07 43					08 13				
St Margarets (Herts) d		06 47					07 17					07 47					08 17				
Rye House d		06 50					07 20					07 50					08 20				
Broxbourne a		06 54			07 16		07 24	07 34		07 47		07 54			08 16		08 24	08 34		08 47	
d		06 54			07 16		07 24	07 37		07 47		07 54			08 16		08 24	08 37		08 47	
Cheshunt d		06 58			07 20		07 28	07 42		07 51		07 58			08 20		08 28	08 42		08 51	
Waltham Cross d		07 01					07 31					08 01					08 31				
Enfield Lock d		07 03					07 33	07 45				08 03					08 33	08 45			
Brimsdown d		07 06					07 36					08 06					08 36				
Ponders End d		07 08					07 38					08 08					08 38				
Angel Road d																					
Northumberland Park d								07 51										08 51			
Tottenham Hale ⊖ d	07 03	07 14	07 17		07 29	07 32	07 44	07 55	07 47	08 00	08 03	08 14	08 17		08 29	08 32	08 44	08 55	08 47	09 00	09 03
Seven Sisters ⊖ d																					
Clapton d																					
Stratford ⊖ a								08 05										09 05			
Hackney Downs d		07 20					07 50					08 20					08 50				
Bethnal Green d																					
London Liverpool Street ⊖ a	07 17	07 28	07 31		07 43	07 46	07 58		08 01	08 13	08 17	08 28	08 31		08 43	08 46	08 58		09 01	09 13	09 17

Table 22

Cambridge, Stansted Airport, Bishops Stortford, Hertford East and Broxbourne - London

Station		LE		LE	XC	LE	LE	LE	LE	LE	LE	LE		LE	LE	XC	LE	LE	LE	LE	LE	LE		LE	LE
Cambridge	d				08 10	08 32					08 51					09 10	09 32					09 51			
Shelford	d										08 56											09 56			
Whittlesford Parkway	d					08 39					09 00						09 39					10 00			
Great Chesterford	d										09 04											10 04			
Audley End	d				08 24	08 47					09 10					09 24	09 47					10 10			
Newport (Essex)	d										09 13											10 13			
Elsenham	d										09 19											10 19			
Stansted Airport	a				08 45											09 45									
	d			08 45			09 00		09 03	09 15		09 30			09 45			10 00		10 03	10 15			10 30	
Stansted Mountfitchet	d			08 51					09 09		09 22				09 51					10 09		10 22			
Bishops Stortford	a					09 00	09 09		09 13		09 28	09 39					10 00	10 09		10 13		10 28		10 39	
	d					09 00	09 09		09 14		09 28	09 39					10 00	10 09		10 14		10 28		10 39	
Sawbridgeworth	d					09 05			09 18		09 32						10 05			10 18		10 32			
Harlow Mill	d								09 22		09 36									10 22		10 36			
Harlow Town	d			09 02		09 10			09 25	09 30	09 39				10 02		10 10			10 25	10 30	10 39			
Roydon	d								09 29		09 43									10 29		10 43			
Hertford East	d	08 39						09 09						09 39					10 09						10 39
Ware	d	08 43						09 13						09 43					10 13						10 43
St Margarets (Herts)	d	08 47						09 17						09 47					10 17						10 47
Rye House	d	08 50						09 20						09 50					10 20						10 50
Broxbourne ■	a	08 54				09 16		09 24	09 34		09 47			09 54			10 16		10 24	10 34		10 47			10 54
	d	08 54				09 16		09 24	09 37		09 47			09 54			10 16		10 24	10 37		10 47			10 54
Cheshunt	d	08 58				09 20		09 28	09 42		09 51			09 58			10 20		10 28	10 42		10 51			10 58
Waltham Cross	d	09 01						09 31						10 01					10 31						11 01
Enfield Lock	d	09 03						09 33	09 45					10 03					10 33	10 45					11 03
Brimsdown	d	09 06						09 36						10 06					10 36						11 06
Ponders End	d	09 08						09 38						10 08					10 38						11 08
Angel Road	d																								
Northumberland Park	d								09 51											10 51					
Tottenham Hale ⊖	d	09 14		09 17		09 29	09 32	09 44	09 55	09 47	10 00	10 03		10 14	10 17		10 29	10 32	10 44	10 55	10 47	11 00		11 03	11 14
Seven Sisters ⊖	d																								
Clapton	d																								
Stratford ■ ⊖	a								10 05											11 05					
Hackney Downs	d	09 20						09 50						10 20					10 50						11 20
Bethnal Green	d																								
London Liverpool Street ■ ⊖	a	09 28		09 31		09 43	09 46	09 58		10 01	10 13	10 17		10 28	10 31		10 43	10 46	10 58		11 01	11 13		11 17	11 28

Station		LE	XC	LE	LE	LE	LE	LE	LE	LE	LE	LE	XC	LE	LE	LE	LE	LE		LE	LE	LE	LE	XC	LE
Cambridge	d		10 10	10 32					10 51				11 10	11 32						11 51				12 10	12 32
Shelford	d								10 56											11 56					
Whittlesford Parkway	d			10 39					11 00					11 39						12 00					12 39
Great Chesterford	d								11 04											12 04					
Audley End	d		10 24	10 47					11 10				11 24	11 47						12 10				12 24	12 47
Newport (Essex)	d								11 13											12 13					
Elsenham	d								11 19											12 19					
Stansted Airport	a		10 45										11 45											12 45	
	d	10 45			11 00		11 03	11 15		11 30		11 45			12 00		12 03	12 15			12 30		12 45		
Stansted Mountfitchet	d	10 51					11 09		11 22			11 51					12 09			12 22			12 51		
Bishops Stortford	a			11 00	11 09		11 13		11 28	11 39				12 00	12 09		12 13			12 28	12 39				13 00
	d			11 00	11 09		11 14		11 28	11 39				12 00	12 09		12 14			12 28	12 39				13 00
Sawbridgeworth	d			11 05			11 18		11 32					12 05			12 18			12 32					13 05
Harlow Mill	d						11 22		11 36								12 22			12 36					
Harlow Town	d	11 02		11 10			11 25	11 30	11 39			12 02		12 10			12 25	12 30		12 39			13 02		13 10
Roydon	d						11 29		11 43								12 29			12 43					
Hertford East	d					11 09					11 39					12 09						12 39			
Ware	d					11 13					11 43					12 13						12 43			
St Margarets (Herts)	d					11 17					11 47					12 17						12 47			
Rye House	d					11 20					11 50					12 20						12 50			
Broxbourne ■	a			11 16		11 24	11 34		11 47		11 54			12 16		12 24	12 34			12 47		12 54			13 16
	d			11 16		11 24	11 37		11 47		11 54			12 16		12 24	12 37			12 47		12 54			13 16
Cheshunt	d			11 20		11 28	11 42		11 51		11 58			12 20		12 28	12 42			12 51		12 58			13 20
Waltham Cross	d					11 31					12 01					12 31						13 01			
Enfield Lock	d					11 33	11 45				12 03					12 33	12 45					13 03			
Brimsdown	d					11 36					12 06					12 36						13 06			
Ponders End	d					11 38					12 08					12 38						13 08			
Angel Road	d																								
Northumberland Park	d						11 51										12 51								
Tottenham Hale ⊖	d	11 17		11 29	11 32	11 44	11 55	11 47	12 00	12 03	12 14	12 17		12 29	12 32	12 44	12 55	12 47		13 00	13 03	13 14	13 17		13 29
Seven Sisters ⊖	d																								
Clapton	d																								
Stratford ■ ⊖	a						12 05										13 05								
Hackney Downs	d					11 50					12 20					12 50						13 20			
Bethnal Green	d																								
London Liverpool Street ■ ⊖	a	11 31		11 43	11 46	11 58		12 01	12 13	12 17	12 28	12 31		12 43	12 46	12 58		13 01		13 13	13 17	13 28	13 31		13 43

Table 22

Cambridge, Stansted Airport, Bishops Stortford, Hertford East and Broxbourne - London

Station		LE	LE	LE		LE	LE	LE	LE	LE	XC	LE	LE	LE		LE	LE	LE	LE	LE	LE	XC	LE	LE	
Cambridge	d						12 51				13 10	13 32						13 51				14 10	14 32		
Shelford	d						12 56											13 56							
Whittlesford Parkway	d						13 00					13 39						14 00					14 39		
Great Chesterford	d						13 04											14 04							
Audley End	d						13 10				13 24	13 47						14 10				14 24	14 47		
Newport (Essex)	d						13 13											14 13							
Elsenham	d						13 19											14 19							
Stansted Airport	a										13 45											14 45			
	d	13 00		13 03		13 15		13 30		13 45			14 00			14 03	14 15		14 30		14 45			15 00	
Stansted Mountfitchet	d			13 09			13 22			13 51						14 09		14 22			14 51				
Bishops Stortford	a	13 09		13 13			13 28	13 39				14 00	14 09			14 13		14 28	14 39				15 00	15 09	
	d	13 09		13 14			13 28	13 39				14 00	14 09			14 14		14 28	14 39				15 00	15 09	
Sawbridgeworth	d			13 18			13 32					14 05				14 18		14 32					15 05		
Harlow Mill	d			13 22			13 36									14 22		14 36							
Harlow Town	d			13 25		13 30	13 39			14 02		14 10				14 25	14 30	14 39			15 02		15 10		
Roydon	d			13 29			13 43									14 29		14 43							
Hertford East	d		13 09						13 39					14 09						14 39					
Ware	d		13 13						13 43					14 13						14 43					
St Margarets (Herts)	d		13 17						13 47					14 17						14 47					
Rye House	d		13 20						13 50					14 20						14 50					
Broxbourne ■	a		13 24	13 34			13 47		13 54			14 16		14 24		14 34		14 47		14 54			15 16		
	d		13 24	13 37			13 47		13 54			14 16		14 24		14 37		14 47		14 54			15 16		
Cheshunt	d		13 28	13 42			13 51		13 58			14 20		14 28		14 42		14 51		14 58			15 20		
Waltham Cross	d		13 31						14 01					14 31						15 01					
Enfield Lock	d		13 33	13 45					14 03					14 33		14 45				15 03					
Brimsdown	d		13 36						14 06					14 36						15 06					
Ponders End	d		13 38						14 08					14 38						15 08					
Angel Road	d																								
Northumberland Park	d			13 51												14 51									
Tottenham Hale ⊖	d	13 32	13 44	13 55		13 47	14 00	14 03	14 14	14 17		14 29	14 32	14 44		14 55	14 47	15 00	15 03	15 14	15 17		15 29	15 32	
Seven Sisters ⊖	d																								
Clapton	d																								
Stratford ■ ⊖	a			14 05												15 05									
Hackney Downs	d		13 50						14 20					14 50						15 20					
Bethnal Green	d																								
London Liverpool Street ■ ⊖	a	13 46	13 58			14 01	14 13	14 17	14 28	14 31		14 43	14 46	14 58			15 01	15 13	15 17	15 28	15 31		15 43	15 46	

Station		LE	LE	LE	LE	LE	LE	LE	XC	LE			LE	LE	LE	LE	LE	LE	LE	LE	XC	LE	LE	LE	LE
Cambridge	d				14 51				15 10	15 32							15 51				16 10	16 32			
Shelford	d				14 56												15 56								
Whittlesford Parkway	d				15 00					15 39							16 00					16 39			
Great Chesterford	d				15 04												16 04								
Audley End	d				15 10				15 24	15 47							16 10				16 24	16 47			
Newport (Essex)	d				15 13												16 13								
Elsenham	d				15 19												16 19								
Stansted Airport	a								15 45												16 45				
	d		15 03	15 15		15 30		15 45					16 00		16 03	16 15		16 30		16 45			17 00		17 03
Stansted Mountfitchet	d		15 09		15 22			15 51							16 09		16 22			16 51					17 09
Bishops Stortford	a		15 13		15 28	15 39				16 00			16 09		16 13		16 28	16 39				17 00	17 09		17 13
	d		15 14		15 28	15 39				16 00			16 09		16 14		16 28	16 39				17 00	17 09		17 14
Sawbridgeworth	d		15 18		15 32					16 05					16 18		16 32					17 05			17 18
Harlow Mill	d		15 22		15 36										16 22		16 36								17 22
Harlow Town	d		15 25	15 30	15 39			16 02		16 10					16 25	16 30	16 39			17 02		17 10			17 25
Roydon	d		15 29		15 43										16 29		16 43								17 29
Hertford East	d	15 09					15 39							16 09					16 39					17 09	
Ware	d	15 13					15 43							16 13					16 43					17 13	
St Margarets (Herts)	d	15 17					15 47							16 17					16 47					17 17	
Rye House	d	15 20					15 50							16 20					16 50					17 20	
Broxbourne ■	a	15 24	15 34		15 47		15 54			16 16				16 24	16 34		16 47		16 54			17 16		17 24	17 34
	d	15 24	15 37		15 47		15 54			16 16				16 24	16 37		16 47		16 54			17 16		17 24	17 37
Cheshunt	d	15 28	15 42		15 51		15 58			16 20				16 28	16 42		16 51		16 58			17 20		17 28	17 42
Waltham Cross	d	15 31					16 01							16 31					17 01					17 31	
Enfield Lock	d	15 33	15 45				16 03							16 33	16 45				17 03					17 33	17 45
Brimsdown	d	15 36					16 06							16 36					17 06					17 36	
Ponders End	d	15 38					16 08							16 38					17 08					17 38	
Angel Road	d																								
Northumberland Park	d		15 51												16 51										17 51
Tottenham Hale ⊖	d	15 44	15 55	15 47	16 00	16 03	16 14	16 17		16 29			16 32	16 44	16 55	16 47	17 00	17 03	17 14	17 17		17 29	17 32	17 44	17 55
Seven Sisters ⊖	d																								
Clapton	d																								
Stratford ■ ⊖	a		16 05												17 05										18 05
Hackney Downs	d	15 50					16 20							16 50					17 20					17 50	
Bethnal Green	d																								
London Liverpool Street ■ ⊖	a	15 58		16 01	16 13	16 17	16 28	16 31		16 43			16 46	16 58		17 01	17 13	17 17	17 28	17 31		17 43	17 46	17 58	

Table 22

Cambridge, Stansted Airport, Bishops Stortford, Hertford East and Broxbourne - London

		LE	LE	LE	LE	LE	XC	LE	LE	LE	LE	LE	LE	LE	LE	LE	XC	LE	LE	LE	LE	LE	LE
Cambridge	d		16 51				17 10	17 32					17 51				18 20	18 32					18 51
Shelford	d		16 56										17 56										18 56
Whittlesford Parkway	d		17 00					17 39					18 00					18 39					19 00
Great Chesterford	d		17 04										18 04										19 04
Audley End	d		17 10				17 24	17 47					18 10				18 34	18 47					19 10
Newport (Essex)	d		17 13										18 13										19 13
Elsenham	d		17 19										18 19										19 19
Stansted Airport	a						17 45										18 53						
	d	17 15		17 30		17 45			18 00		18 03	18 15		18 30		18 45			19 00		19 03	19 15	
Stansted Mountfitchet	d		17 22			17 51					18 09		18 22			18 51					19 09		19 22
Bishops Stortford	a		17 28	17 39				18 00	18 09		18 13		18 28	18 39				19 00	19 09		19 13		19 28
	d		17 28	17 39				18 00	18 09		18 14		18 28	18 39				19 00	19 09		19 14		19 28
Sawbridgeworth	d		17 32					18 05			18 18		18 32					19 05			19 18		19 32
Harlow Mill	d		17 36								18 22		18 36								19 22		19 36
Harlow Town	d	17 30	17 39			18 02		18 10			18 25	18 30	18 39			19 02		19 10			19 25	19 30	19 39
Roydon	d		17 43								18 29		18 43								19 29		19 43
Hertford East	d				17 39					18 09					18 39					19 09			
Ware	d				17 43					18 13					18 43					19 13			
St Margarets (Herts)	d				17 47					18 17					18 47					19 17			
Rye House	d				17 50					18 20					18 50					19 20			
Broxbourne 3	a		17 47		17 54			18 16		18 24	18 34		18 47		18 54			19 16		19 24	19 34		19 47
	d		17 47		17 54			18 16		18 24	18 37		18 47		18 54			19 16		19 24	19 37		19 47
Cheshunt	d		17 51		17 58			18 20		18 28	18 42		18 51		18 58			19 20		19 28	19 42		19 51
Waltham Cross	d				18 01					18 31					19 01					19 31			
Enfield Lock	d				18 03					18 33	18 45				19 03					19 33	19 45		
Brimsdown	d				18 06					18 36					19 06					19 36			
Ponders End	d				18 08					18 38					19 08					19 38			
Angel Road	d																						
Northumberland Park	d										18 51										19 51		
Tottenham Hale ⊖	d	17 47	18 00	18 03	18 14	18 17		18 29	18 32	18 44	18 55	18 47	19 00	19 03	19 14	19 17		19 29	19 32	19 44	19 55	19 47	20 00
Seven Sisters ⊖	d																						
Clapton	d																						
Stratford 7 ⊖	a										19 05										20 05		
Hackney Downs	d				18 20					18 50					19 20					19 50			
Bethnal Green	d																						
London Liverpool Street 15 ⊖	a	18 01	18 13	18 17	18 28	18 31		18 43	18 46	18 58		19 01	19 13	19 17	19 28	19 31		19 43	19 46	19 58		20 01	20 13

		LE	LE	LE	XC	LE	LE	LE	LE	LE	LE	LE	LE	LE	XC	LE	LE	LE	LE	LE	LE
Cambridge	d				19 10	19 32					19 51				20 10	20 32					20 51
Shelford	d										19 56										20 56
Whittlesford Parkway	d					19 39					20 00					20 39					21 00
Great Chesterford	d										20 04										21 04
Audley End	d				19 24	19 47					20 10				20 24	20 47					21 10
Newport (Essex)	d										20 13										21 13
Elsenham	d										20 19										21 19
Stansted Airport	a				19 45										20 45						
	d	19 30		19 45			20 00		20 03	20 15		20 30		20 45			21 00		21 03	21 15	
Stansted Mountfitchet	d			19 51					20 09		20 22			20 51					21 09		21 22
Bishops Stortford	a	19 39				20 00	20 09		20 13		20 28	20 39				21 00	21 09		21 13		21 28
	d	19 39				20 00	20 09		20 14		20 28	20 39				21 00	21 09		21 14		21 28
Sawbridgeworth	d					20 05			20 18		20 32					21 05			21 18		21 32
Harlow Mill	d								20 22		20 36								21 22		21 36
Harlow Town	d			20 02		20 10			20 25	20 30	20 39			21 02		21 10			21 25	21 30	21 39
Roydon	d								20 29		20 43								21 29		21 43
Hertford East	d		19 39					20 09					20 39					21 09			
Ware	d		19 43					20 13					20 43					21 13			
St Margarets (Herts)	d		19 47					20 17					20 47					21 17			
Rye House	d		19 50					20 20					20 50					21 20			
Broxbourne 3	a		19 54			20 16		20 24	20 34		20 47		20 54			21 16		21 24	21 34		21 47
	d		19 54			20 16		20 24	20 37		20 47		20 54			21 16		21 24	21 37		21 47
Cheshunt	d		19 58			20 20		20 28	20 42		20 51		20 58			21 20		21 28	21 42		21 51
Waltham Cross	d		20 01					20 31					21 01					21 31			
Enfield Lock	d		20 03					20 33	20 45				21 03					21 33	21 45		
Brimsdown	d		20 06					20 36					21 06					21 36			
Ponders End	d		20 08					20 38					21 08					21 38			
Angel Road	d																				
Northumberland Park	d								20 51										21 51		
Tottenham Hale ⊖	d	20 03	20 14	20 17		20 29	20 32	20 44	20 55	20 47	21 00	21 03	21 14	21 17		21 29	21 32	21 44	21 55	21 47	22 00
Seven Sisters ⊖	d																				
Clapton	d																				
Stratford 7 ⊖	a								21 05										22 05		
Hackney Downs	d		20 20					20 50					21 20					21 50			
Bethnal Green	d																				
London Liverpool Street 15 ⊖	a	20 17	20 28	20 31		20 43	20 46	20 58		21 01	21 13	21 17	21 28	21 31		21 43	21 46	21 58		22 01	22 13

Table 22

Cambridge, Stansted Airport, Bishops Stortford, Hertford East and Broxbourne - London

		LE	LE	LE	XC	LE	LE	LE	LE	LE	LE	LE	LE	LE	XC	LE	LE	LE	LE	LE	LE	LE	LE	LE
Cambridge	d				21 10	21 32					21 51				22 10	22 32					22 51			
Shelford	d										21 56										22 56			
Whittlesford Parkway	d					21 39					22 00					22 39					23 00			
Great Chesterford	d										22 04										23 04			
Audley End	d				21 24	21 47					22 10				22 24	22 47					23 10			
Newport (Essex)	d										22 13										23 13			
Elsenham	d										22 19										23 19			
Stansted Airport	a				21 45										22 45									
	d	21 30		21 45			22 00		22 15	22 03		22 30		22 45			23 00	23 03		23 15		23 30		23 45
Stansted Mountfitchet	d			21 51						22 09	22 22			22 51				23 09			23 22			
Bishops Stortford	a	21 39				22 00	22 09			22 13	22 28	22 39				23 00	23 09	23 13			23 28	23 39		
	d	21 39				22 00	22 09			22 14	22 28	22 39				23 00	23 09				23 28	23 39		
Sawbridgeworth	d					22 05				22 18	22 32					23 05					23 32			
Harlow Mill	d									22 22	22 36										23 36			
Harlow Town	d			22 02		22 10			22 30	22 25	22 39			23 02		23 10				23 30	23 39			23 59
Roydon	d									22 29	22 43										23 43			
Hertford East	d		21 39					22 09					22 39						23 09				23 39	
Ware	d		21 43					22 13					22 43						23 13				23 43	
St Margarets (Herts)	d		21 47					22 17					22 47						23 17				23 47	
Rye House	d		21 50					22 20					22 50						23 20				23 50	
Broxbourne 3	a		21 54			22 16		22 24		22 34	22 47		22 54			23 16			23 24		23 47		23 54	
	d		21 54			22 16		22 24		22 37	22 47		22 54			23 16			23 24		23 47		23 54	
Cheshunt	d		21 58			22 20		22 28		22 42	22 51		22 58			23 20			23 28		23 51		23 58	
Waltham Cross	d		22 01					22 31					23 01						23 31				00 01	
Enfield Lock	d		22 03					22 33		22 45			23 03						23 33				00 03	
Brimsdown	d		22 06					22 36					23 06						23 36				00 06	
Ponders End	d		22 08					22 38					23 08						23 38				00 08	
Angel Road	d																							
Northumberland Park	d									22 51	22 58													
Tottenham Hale ⊖	d	22 03	22 14	22 17		22 29	22 32	22 44	22 47	22 55	23 01	23 03	23 14	23 17		23 29	23 32		23 44	23 47	23 59	00 03	00 14	00 17
Seven Sisters ⊖	d																							
Clapton	d																							
Stratford 7 ⊖	a									23 04														
Hackney Downs	d		22 20					22 50					23 20						23 50				00 20	
Bethnal Green	d																							
London Liverpool Street 15 ⊖	a	22 17	22 28	22 31		22 43	22 46	22 58	23 01	23 14	23 15	23 18	23 28	23 31		23 43	23 46		23 58	00 01	00 13	00 17	00 28	00 31

		LE
Cambridge	d	
Shelford	d	
Whittlesford Parkway	d	
Great Chesterford	d	
Audley End	d	
Newport (Essex)	d	
Elsenham	d	
Stansted Airport	a	
	d	23 59
Stansted Mountfitchet	d	
Bishops Stortford	a	00 08
	d	00 08
Sawbridgeworth	d	
Harlow Mill	d	
Harlow Town	d	00 16
Roydon	d	
Hertford East	d	
Ware	d	
St Margarets (Herts)	d	
Rye House	d	
Broxbourne 3	a	
	d	
Cheshunt	d	
Waltham Cross	d	
Enfield Lock	d	
Brimsdown	d	
Ponders End	d	
Angel Road	d	
Northumberland Park	d	
Tottenham Hale ⊖	d	
Seven Sisters ⊖	d	
Clapton	d	
Stratford 7 ⊖	a	
Hackney Downs	d	
Bethnal Green	d	
London Liverpool Street 15 ⊖	a	00 51

Table 22

Sundays

Cambridge, Stansted Airport, Bishops Stortford, Hertford East and Broxbourne - London

		LE 1	LE 1	LE 1	LE 1	LE 1	LE 1	LE 1	LE 1	LE 1	LE 1	LE 1	LE 1	LE 1	LE 1	LE 1	LE 1	LE 1	LE	LE 1	LE 1	LE 1	LE
Cambridge	d		22p51																	07 32			
Shelford	d		22p56																				
Whittlesford Parkway	d		23p00																	07 39			
Great Chesterford	d		23p04																				
Audley End	d		23p10																	07 47			
Newport (Essex)	d		23p13																				
Elsenham	d		23p19																				
Stansted Airport	a																						
	d	23p15		23p30		23p45	23p59		00 30	05 30	06 00	06 30		07 00	07 15		07 30	07 45			08 00	08 15	
Stansted Mountfitchet	d		23p22															07 51					
Bishops Stortford	a		23p28	23p39			00 08		00 39	05 39	06 09	06 39		07 09			07 39			08 00	08 09		
	d		23p28	23p39			00 08		00 39	05 39	06 09	06 39	06 42	07 09		07 28	07 39			08 00	08 09		
Sawbridgeworth	d		23p32										06 46			07 32				08 05			
Harlow Mill	d		23p36													07 36							
Harlow Town	d	23p30	23p39			23p59	00 16		00 47	05 47	06 17	06 47	06 51	07 17	07 30	07 39		08 02		08 10		08 30	
Roydon	d		23p43													07 43							
Hertford East	d				23p39			00 07											07 55				08 25
Ware	d				23p43														07 59				08 29
St Margarets (Herts)	d				23p47														08 03				08 33
Rye House	d				23p50														08 06				08 36
Broxbourne 3	a		23p47		23p54			00 19					06 57			07 48			08 11	08 16			08 41
	d		23p47		23p54								06 57			07 52			08 11	08 16			08 41
Cheshunt	d		23p51		23p58								07 01			07 57			08 15	08 20			08 45
Waltham Cross	d				00 01								07 04			07 59							
Enfield Lock	d				00 03								07 06			08 02							
Brimsdown	d				00 06								07 09			08 04							
Ponders End	d				00 08								07 11			08 06							
Angel Road	d																						
Northumberland Park	d																						
Tottenham Hale ⊖	d	23p47	23p59	00 03	00 14	00 17				06 04	06 33	07 03	07 17	07 33	07 46	08 12	08 01	08 17		08 29	08 32	08 46	
Seven Sisters ⊖	d																		08 33				09 03
Clapton	d																						
Stratford 7 ⊖	a															08 23							
Hackney Downs	d				00 20														08 39				09 09
Bethnal Green	d																						
London Liverpool Street 15 ⊖	a	00 01	00 13	00 17	00 28	00 31	00 51		01 21	06 17	06 46	07 16	07 30	07 46	08 01		08 15	08 31	08 48	08 43	08 46	09 03	09 18

		LE 1	LE 1	LE 1	LE	LE 1	LE 1	LE 1	LE	LE 1	LE 1	XC ◇1	LE 1	LE	LE 1	LE 1	LE 1	LE	LE 1	LE 1	XC ◇1	LE 1	LE
Cambridge	d	07 51				08 32				08 51		09 15			09 32				09 51		10 15		
Shelford	d	07 56								08 56									09 56				
Whittlesford Parkway	d	08 00				08 39				09 00					09 39				10 00				
Great Chesterford	d	08 04								09 04									10 04				
Audley End	d	08 10				08 47				09 10		09 28			09 47				10 10		10 28		
Newport (Essex)	d	08 13								09 13									10 13				
Elsenham	d	08 19								09 19									10 19				
Stansted Airport	a											09 43									10 43		
	d		08 30	08 45			09 00	09 15			09 30		09 45			10 00	10 15			10 30		10 45	
Stansted Mountfitchet	d	08 22		08 51						09 22			09 51						10 22			10 51	
Bishops Stortford	a	08 28	08 39			09 00	09 09			09 28	09 39				10 00	10 09			10 28	10 39			
	d	08 28	08 39			09 00	09 09			09 28	09 39				10 00	10 09			10 28	10 39			
Sawbridgeworth	d	08 32				09 05				09 32					10 05				10 32				
Harlow Mill	d	08 36								09 36									10 36				
Harlow Town	d	08 39		09 02		09 10		09 30		09 39			10 02		10 10		10 30		10 39			11 02	
Roydon	d	08 43								09 43									10 43				
Hertford East	d				08 55				09 25					09 55				10 25					10 55
Ware	d				08 59				09 29					09 59				10 29					10 59
St Margarets (Herts)	d				09 03				09 33					10 03				10 33					11 03
Rye House	d				09 06				09 36					10 06				10 36					11 06
Broxbourne 3	a	08 48			09 11	09 16			09 41	09 48				10 11	10 16			10 41	10 48				11 11
	d	08 52			09 11	09 16			09 41	09 52				10 11	10 16			10 41	10 52				11 11
Cheshunt	d	08 57			09 15	09 20			09 45	09 57				10 15	10 20			10 45	10 57				11 15
Waltham Cross	d	08 59								09 59									10 59				
Enfield Lock	d	09 02								10 02									11 02				
Brimsdown	d	09 04								10 04									11 04				
Ponders End	d	09 06								10 06									11 06				
Angel Road	d																						
Northumberland Park	d																						
Tottenham Hale ⊖	d	09 12	09 01	09 17		09 29	09 32	09 46		10 12	10 01		10 17		10 29	10 32	10 46		11 12	11 01		11 17	
Seven Sisters ⊖	d				09 33				10 03					10 33				11 03					11 33
Clapton	d																						
Stratford 7 ⊖	a	09 23								10 23									11 23				
Hackney Downs	d				09 39				10 09					10 39				11 09					11 39
Bethnal Green	d																						
London Liverpool Street 15 ⊖	a		09 15	09 31	09 48	09 43	09 46	10 01	10 18		10 15		10 31	10 48	10 43	10 46	11 01	11 18		11 15		11 31	11 48

Table 22

Sundays

Cambridge, Stansted Airport, Bishops Stortford, Hertford East and Broxbourne - London

		LE 1	LE 1	LE 1	LE	LE 1	LE 1	XC ◇1	LE 1	LE	LE 1	LE 1	LE 1	LE	LE 1	LE 1	XC ◇1	LE 1	LE	LE 1	LE 1	LE 1
Cambridge	d	10 32				10 51		11 15			11 32				11 51		12 15			12 32		
Shelford	d					10 56									11 56							
Whittlesford Parkway	d	10 39				11 00					11 39				12 00					12 39		
Great Chesterford	d					11 04									12 04							
Audley End	d	10 47				11 10		11 28			11 47				12 10		12 28			12 47		
Newport (Essex)	d					11 13									12 13							
Elsenham	d					11 19									12 19							
Stansted Airport	a							11 43									12 43					
	d		11 00	11 15			11 30		11 45			12 00	12 15			12 30		12 45			13 00	13 15
Stansted Mountfitchet	d					11 22			11 51						12 22			12 51				
Bishops Stortford	a	11 00	11 09			11 28	11 39				12 00	12 09			12 28	12 39				13 00	13 09	
	d	11 00	11 09			11 28	11 39				12 00	12 09			12 28	12 39				13 00	13 09	
Sawbridgeworth	d	11 05				11 32					12 05				12 32					13 05		
Harlow Mill	d					11 36									12 36							
Harlow Town	d	11 10		11 30		11 39			12 02		12 10		12 30		12 39			13 02		13 10		13 30
Roydon	d					11 43									12 43							
Hertford East	d				11 25					11 55				12 25					12 55			
Ware	d				11 29					11 59				12 29					12 59			
St Margarets (Herts)	d				11 33					12 03				12 33					13 03			
Rye House	d				11 36					12 06				12 36					13 06			
Broxbourne 3	a	11 16			11 41	11 48				12 11	12 16			12 41	12 48				13 11	13 16		
	d	11 16			11 41	11 52				12 11	12 16			12 41	12 52				13 11	13 16		
Cheshunt	d	11 20			11 45	11 57				12 15	12 20			12 45	12 57				13 15	13 20		
Waltham Cross	d					11 59									12 59							
Enfield Lock	d					12 02									13 02							
Brimsdown	d					12 04									13 04							
Ponders End	d					12 06									13 06							
Angel Road	d																					
Northumberland Park	d																					
Tottenham Hale ⊖	d	11 29	11 32	11 46		12 12	12 01		12 17		12 29	12 32	12 46		13 12	13 01		13 17		13 29	13 32	13 46
Seven Sisters ⊖	d				12 03					12 33				13 03					13 33			
Clapton	d																					
Stratford 7 ⊖	a					12 23									13 23							
Hackney Downs	d				12 09					12 39				13 09					13 39			
Bethnal Green	d																					
London Liverpool Street 15 ⊖	a	11 43	11 46	12 01	12 18		12 15		12 31	12 48	12 43	12 46	13 01	13 18		13 15		13 31	13 48	13 43	13 46	14 01

		LE	LE 1	LE 1	XC ◇1	LE 1	LE	LE 1	LE 1	LE 1	LE	LE 1	LE 1	XC ◇1	LE 1	LE	LE 1	LE 1	LE 1	LE	LE 1	LE 1	XC ◇1
Cambridge	d		12 51		13 15			13 32				13 51		14 10			14 32				14 51		15 10
Shelford	d		12 56									13 56									14 56		
Whittlesford Parkway	d		13 00					13 39				14 00					14 39				15 00		
Great Chesterford	d		13 04									14 04									15 04		
Audley End	d		13 10		13 28			13 47				14 10		14 24			14 47				15 10		15 24
Newport (Essex)	d		13 13									14 13									15 13		
Elsenham	d		13 19									14 19									15 19		
Stansted Airport	a				13 43									14 43									15 43
	d			13 30		13 45			14 00	14 15			14 30		14 45			15 00	15 15			15 30	
Stansted Mountfitchet	d		13 22			13 51						14 22			14 51						15 22		
Bishops Stortford	a		13 28	13 39				14 00	14 09			14 28	14 39				15 00	15 09			15 28	15 39	
	d		13 28	13 39				14 00	14 09			14 28	14 39				15 00	15 09			15 28	15 39	
Sawbridgeworth	d		13 32					14 05				14 32					15 05				15 32		
Harlow Mill	d		13 36									14 36									15 36		
Harlow Town	d		13 39			14 02		14 10		14 30		14 39			15 02		15 10		15 30		15 39		
Roydon	d		13 43									14 43									15 43		
Hertford East	d	13 25					13 55				14 25					14 55				15 25			
Ware	d	13 29					13 59				14 29					14 59				15 29			
St Margarets (Herts)	d	13 33					14 03				14 33					15 03				15 33			
Rye House	d	13 36					14 06				14 36					15 06				15 36			
Broxbourne 3	a	13 41	13 48				14 11	14 16			14 41	14 48				15 11	15 16			15 41	15 48		
	d	13 41	13 52				14 11	14 16			14 41	14 52				15 11	15 16			15 41	15 52		
Cheshunt	d	13 45	13 57				14 15	14 20			14 45	14 57				15 15	15 20			15 45	15 57		
Waltham Cross	d		13 59									14 59									15 59		
Enfield Lock	d		14 02									15 02									16 02		
Brimsdown	d		14 04									15 04									16 04		
Ponders End	d		14 06									15 06									16 06		
Angel Road	d																						
Northumberland Park	d																						
Tottenham Hale ⊖	d		14 12	14 01		14 17		14 29	14 32	14 46		15 12	15 01		15 17		15 29	15 32	15 46		16 12	16 01	
Seven Sisters ⊖	d	14 03					14 33				15 03					15 33				16 03			
Clapton	d																						
Stratford 7 ⊖	a		14 23									15 23									16 23		
Hackney Downs	d	14 09					14 39				15 09					15 39				16 09			
Bethnal Green	d																						
London Liverpool Street 15 ⊖	a	14 18		14 15		14 31	14 48	14 43	14 46	15 01	15 18		15 15		15 31	15 48	15 43	15 46	16 01	16 18		16 15	

Table 22

Sundays

Cambridge, Stansted Airport, Bishops Stortford, Hertford East and Broxbourne - London

		LE 1	LE	LE 1	LE 1	LE 1	LE	LE 1	LE 1	XC ◇1	LE 1	LE	LE 1	LE 1	LE 1	LE	LE 1	LE 1	XC ◇1	LE 1	LE	LE 1
Cambridge	d			15 32				15 51		16 10			16 32				16 51		17 10			17 32
Shelford	d							15 56									16 56					
Whittlesford Parkway	d			15 39				16 00					16 39				17 00					17 39
Great Chesterford	d							16 04									17 04					
Audley End	d			15 47				16 10		16 23			16 47				17 10		17 24			17 47
Newport (Essex)	d							16 13									17 13					
Elsenham	d							16 19									17 19					
Stansted Airport	a									16 37									17 43			
	d	15 45			16 00	16 15			16 30		16 45			17 00	17 15			17 30		17 45		
Stansted Mountfitchet	d	15 51						16 22			16 51						17 22			17 51		
Bishops Stortford	a			16 00	16 09			16 28	16 39				17 00	17 09			17 28	17 39				18 00
	d			16 00	16 09			16 28	16 39				17 00	17 09			17 28	17 39				18 00
Sawbridgeworth	d			16 05				16 32					17 05				17 32					18 05
Harlow Mill	d							16 36									17 36					
Harlow Town	d	16 02		16 10		16 30		16 39			17 02		17 10		17 30		17 39			18 02		18 10
Roydon	d							16 43									17 43					
Hertford East	d		15 55				16 25					16 55				17 25					17 55	
Ware	d		15 59				16 29					16 59				17 29					17 59	
St Margarets (Herts)	d		16 03				16 33					17 03				17 33					18 03	
Rye House	d		16 06				16 36					17 06				17 36					18 06	
Broxbourne 3	a		16 11	16 16			16 41	16 48				17 11	17 16			17 41	17 48				18 11	18 16
	d		16 11	16 16			16 41	16 52				17 11	17 16			17 41	17 52				18 11	18 16
Cheshunt	d		16 15	16 20			16 45	16 57				17 15	17 20			17 45	17 57				18 15	18 20
Waltham Cross	d							16 59									17 59					
Enfield Lock	d							17 02									18 02					
Brimsdown	d							17 04									18 04					
Ponders End	d							17 06									18 06					
Angel Road	d																					
Northumberland Park	d																					
Tottenham Hale ⊖	d	16 17		16 29	16 32	16 46		17 12	17 01		17 17		17 29	17 32	17 46		18 12	18 01		18 17		18 29
Seven Sisters ⊖	d		16 33				17 03					17 33				18 03					18 33	
Clapton	d																					
Stratford 7 ⊖	a							17 23									18 23					
Hackney Downs	d		16 39				17 09					17 39				18 09					18 39	
Bethnal Green	d																					
London Liverpool Street 15 ⊖	a	16 31	16 48	16 43	16 46	17 01	17 18		17 15		17 31	17 48	17 43	17 46	18 01	18 18		18 15		18 31	18 48	18 43

		LE 1	LE 1	LE	LE 1	LE 1	XC ◇1	LE 1	LE	LE 1	LE 1	LE 1	LE	LE 1	LE 1	XC ◇1	LE 1	LE	LE 1	LE 1	LE 1	LE	LE 1
Cambridge	d				17 51		18 10			18 32				18 51		19 10			19 32				19 51
Shelford	d				17 56									18 56									19 56
Whittlesford Parkway	d				18 00					18 39				19 00					19 39				20 00
Great Chesterford	d				18 04									19 04									20 04
Audley End	d				18 10		18 24			18 47				19 10		19 24			19 47				20 10
Newport (Essex)	d				18 13									19 13									20 13
Elsenham	d				18 19									19 19									20 19
Stansted Airport	a						18 43									19 43							
	d	18 00	18 15			18 30		18 45			19 00	19 15			19 30		19 45			20 00	20 15		
Stansted Mountfitchet	d				18 22			18 51						19 22			19 51						20 22
Bishops Stortford	a	18 09			18 28	18 39				19 00	19 09			19 28	19 39				20 00	20 09			20 28
	d	18 09			18 28	18 39				19 00	19 09			19 28	19 39				20 00	20 09			20 28
Sawbridgeworth	d				18 32					19 05				19 32					20 05				20 32
Harlow Mill	d				18 36									19 36									20 36
Harlow Town	d		18 30		18 39			19 02		19 10		19 30		19 39			20 02		20 10		20 30		20 39
Roydon	d				18 43									19 43									20 43
Hertford East	d			18 25					18 55				19 25					19 55				20 25	
Ware	d			18 29					18 59				19 29					19 59				20 29	
St Margarets (Herts)	d			18 33					19 03				19 33					20 03				20 33	
Rye House	d			18 36					19 06				19 36					20 06				20 36	
Broxbourne 3	a			18 41	18 48				19 11	19 16			19 41	19 48				20 11	20 16			20 41	20 48
	d			18 41	18 52				19 11	19 16			19 41	19 52				20 11	20 16			20 41	20 52
Cheshunt	d			18 45	18 57				19 15	19 20			19 45	19 57				20 15	20 20			20 45	20 57
Waltham Cross	d				18 59									19 59									20 59
Enfield Lock	d				19 02									20 02									21 02
Brimsdown	d				19 04									20 04									21 04
Ponders End	d				19 06									20 06									21 06
Angel Road	d																						
Northumberland Park	d																						
Tottenham Hale ⊖	d	18 32	18 46		19 12	19 01		19 17		19 29	19 32	19 46		20 12	20 01		20 17		20 29	20 32	20 46		21 12
Seven Sisters ⊖	d			19 03					19 33				20 03					20 33				21 03	
Clapton	d																						
Stratford 7 ⊖	a				19 23									20 23									21 23
Hackney Downs	d			19 09					19 39				20 09					20 39				21 09	
Bethnal Green	d																						
London Liverpool Street 15 ⊖	a	18 46	19 01	19 18		19 15		19 31	19 48	19 43	19 46	20 01	20 18		20 15		20 31	20 48	20 43	20 46	21 01	21 18	

Table 22

Sundays

Cambridge, Stansted Airport, Bishops Stortford, Hertford East and Broxbourne - London

		LE 1	XC ◇1	LE 1	LE	LE 1	LE 1	LE 1	LE	LE 1	LE 1	XC ◇1	LE 1	LE	LE 1	LE 1	LE 1	LE	LE 1	LE 1	XC ◇1	LE 1	LE
Cambridge	d		20 10			20 32				20 51		21 10			21 32				21 51		22 10		
Shelford	d									20 56									21 56				
Whittlesford Parkway	d					20 39				21 00					21 39				22 00				
Great Chesterford	d									21 04									22 04				
Audley End	d		20 24			20 47				21 10		21 24			21 47				22 10		22 24		
Newport (Essex)	d									21 13									22 13				
Elsenham	d									21 19									22 19				
Stansted Airport	a		20 43									21 43									22 43		
	d	20 30		20 45			21 00	21 15			21 30		21 45			22 00	22 15			22 30		22 45	
Stansted Mountfitchet	d			20 51						21 22			21 51						22 22			22 51	
Bishops Stortford	a	20 39				21 00	21 09			21 28	21 39				22 00	22 09			22 28	22 39			
	d	20 39				21 00	21 09			21 28	21 39				22 00	22 09			22 28	22 39			
Sawbridgeworth	d					21 05				21 32					22 05				22 32				
Harlow Mill	d									21 36									22 36				
Harlow Town	d			21 02		21 10		21 30		21 39			22 02		22 10		22 30		22 39			23 02	
Roydon	d									21 43									22 43				
Hertford East	d				20 55				21 25					21 55				22 25					22 55
Ware	d				20 59				21 29					21 59				22 29					22 59
St Margarets (Herts)	d				21 03				21 33					22 03				22 33					23 03
Rye House	d				21 06				21 36					22 06				22 36					23 06
Broxbourne 3	a				21 11	21 16			21 41	21 48				22 11	22 16			22 41	22 48				23 11
	d				21 11	21 16			21 41	21 52				22 11	22 16			22 41	22 52				23 11
Cheshunt	d				21 15	21 20			21 45	21 57				22 15	22 20			22 45	22 57				23 16
Waltham Cross	d									21 59									22 59				
Enfield Lock	d									22 02									23 02				
Brimsdown	d									22 04									23 04				
Ponders End	d									22 06									23 06				
Angel Road	d																						
Northumberland Park	d																						
Tottenham Hale ⊖	d	21 01		21 17		21 29	21 32	21 46		22 12	22 01		22 17		22 29	22 32	22 46		23 12	23 01		23 17	
Seven Sisters ⊖	d				21 33				22 03					22 33				23 03					23 33
Clapton	d																						
Stratford 7 ⊖	a									22 23									23 22				
Hackney Downs	d				21 39				22 09					22 39				23 09					23 39
Bethnal Green	d																						
London Liverpool Street 15 ⊖	a	21 15		21 31	21 48	21 43	21 46	22 01	22 18		22 15		22 31	22 48	22 43	22 46	23 01	23 18	23 36	23 15		23 31	23 48

		LE 1	LE 1	LE 1	LE 1	LE 1	LE 1	LE 1
Cambridge	d	22 32			22 51			
Shelford	d				22 56			
Whittlesford Parkway	d	22 39			23 00			
Great Chesterford	d				23 04			
Audley End	d	22 47			23 10			
Newport (Essex)	d				23 13			
Elsenham	d				23 19			
Stansted Airport	a							
	d		23 00	23 15		23 30	23 45	23 59
Stansted Mountfitchet	d				23 22			
Bishops Stortford	a	23 00	23 09		23 28	23 39		00 08
	d	23 00	23 09			23 39		00 08
Sawbridgeworth	d	23 05						
Harlow Mill	d							
Harlow Town	d	23 10		23 30		23 47	23 59	00 16
Roydon	d							
Hertford East	d							
Ware	d							
St Margarets (Herts)	d							
Rye House	d							
Broxbourne 3	a	23 16						
	d	23 16						
Cheshunt	d	23 20						
Waltham Cross	d							
Enfield Lock	d							
Brimsdown	d							
Ponders End	d							
Angel Road	d							
Northumberland Park	d							
Tottenham Hale ⊖	d	23 29	23 32	23 46				
Seven Sisters ⊖	d					00 08	00 21	
Clapton	d							
Stratford 7 ⊖	a							
Hackney Downs	d							
Bethnal Green	d							
London Liverpool Street 15 ⊖	a	23 43	23 46	00 01		00 22	00 35	00 51

Network Diagram for Tables 24, 25

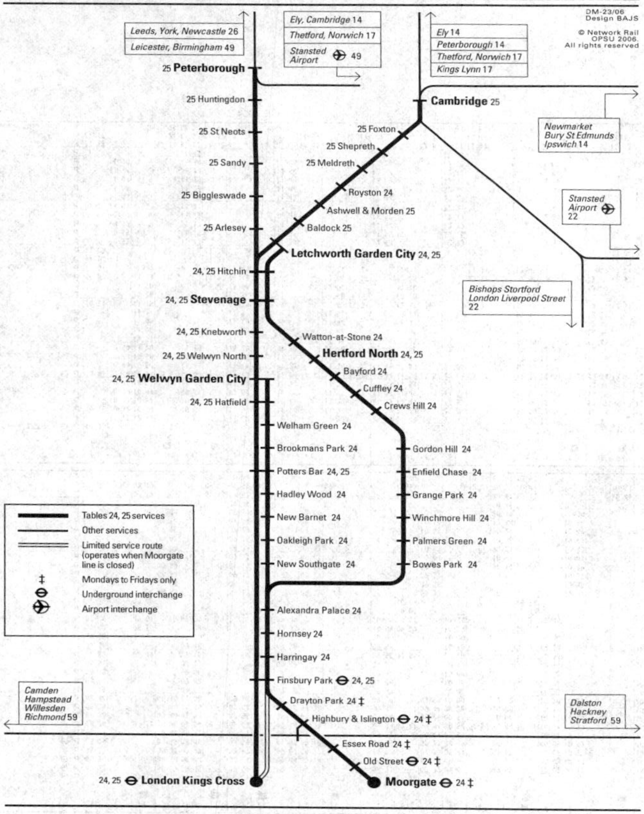

Table 24

London - Welwyn Garden City, Hertford North and Letchworth Garden City

		FC A	FC B	FC MX	FC MX ■1	FC F	FC MX	FC MX ■1	FC ■1 A	FC ■1 C	FC A	FC MO ■1 E	FC MX
London Kings Cross ■15 ⊖	d		23p26	23p26	23p36	23p41	23p41	00 04	00 07	00 07		00 14	00 06
Moorgate ⊖	d												
Old Street ⊖	d												
Essex Road	d												
Highbury & Islington ⊖	d												
Drayton Park	d												
Finsbury Park ⊖	d		23p31	23p32	23p41	23p47	23p47	00 09	00 12	00 12		00 20	00 12
Harringay	d		23p33	23p34		23p49	23p49					00 22	00 14
Hornsey	d		23p35	23p36		23p51	23p51					00 24	00 16
Alexandra Palace	d		23p38	23p38		23p53	23p53		00 17	00 17		00 26	00 18
New Southgate	d					23p56	23p56						
Oakleigh Park	d					23p59	23p59						
New Barnet	d					00 01	00 01						
Hadley Wood	d					00 04	00 04						
Potters Bar	d				23p51	00 08	00 08						
Brookmans Park	d					00 11	00 11						
Welham Green	d					00 13	00 13						
Hatfield	d				23p57	00 16	00 16						
Welwyn Garden City ■4	d				00 01	00 20	00a24						
Welwyn North	d				00 04	00 23							
Knebworth	d				00 08	00 28							
Bowes Park	d		23p40	23p41								00 29	00 21
Palmers Green	d		23p42	23p43						00 20		00 31	00 23
Winchmore Hill	d		23p45	23p45						00 22		00 33	00 25
Grange Park	d		23p47	23p47								00 35	00 27
Enfield Chase	d		23p49	23p49						00 25		00 37	00 29
Gordon Hill	d		23p51	23p51						00 27		00 39	00 31
Crews Hill	d		23p54	23p54								00 42	00 34
Cuffley	d	23p56	23p57	23p57						00 31	00 33	00 45	00 37
Bayford	d	00 02	00 02	00 02							00 38	00 50	00 42
Hertford North	d	00 07	00 07	00 07						00 39	00a45	00a59	00 47
Watton-at-Stone	d	00 12	00 12	00 13									00 53
Stevenage ■4	d	00a20	00a20	00 20	00 12	00 31		00 31	00 48	00 48			01 00
Hitchin ■4	d			00 26	00 20	00 37		00 39	00 56	00 56			01 06
Letchworth Garden City	a			00 36	00 29	00 52		00 42	01 00	01 00			01 16

		FC D	FC A (bus)	FC ■1 D	FC ■1 E	FC MX ■1	FC ■1 A	FC ■1 C	FC ■1 D	FC ■1 E	FC A (bus)	FC ■1	FC
London Kings Cross ■15 ⊖	d	00 11		00 36	00 36	01 06	01 06	01 06	01 36	01 36		05 22	
Moorgate ⊖	d												
Old Street ⊖	d												
Essex Road	d												
Highbury & Islington ⊖	d												
Drayton Park	d												
Finsbury Park ⊖	d	00 17		00 41	00 41	01 11	01 11	01 11	01 41	01 41		05 27	
Harringay	d	00 19											
Hornsey	d	00 21											
Alexandra Palace	d	00 23	00 23			01 16	01 16	01 16	01 45	01 47	01 23		
New Southgate	d	00 26											
Oakleigh Park	d	00 29							01 50				
New Barnet	d	00 31							01 52				
Hadley Wood	d	00 34							01 54				
Potters Bar	d	00 38		00 51					01 58			05 37	
Brookmans Park	d	00 41											
Welham Green	d	00 43											
Hatfield	d	00 46		00 57					02 04			05 43	
Welwyn Garden City ■4	d	00a54		01 01					02 08			05 47	
Welwyn North	d			01s04					02s11			05 50	
Knebworth	d			01s08					02s15			05 54	
Bowes Park	d												
Palmers Green	d		00 34			01 19		01 18			01 34		
Winchmore Hill	d		00 42			01 21		01 21			01 42		
Grange Park	d												
Enfield Chase	d		00 52			01 24		01 24			01 52		
Gordon Hill	d		00 58			01 26		01 26			01 58		
Crews Hill	d												
Cuffley	d		01 13			01 30		01 30			02 13		
Bayford	d												
Hertford North	d		01 38			01 38		01 38			02 38		05 50
Watton-at-Stone	d												05 55
Stevenage ■4	d		02a00	01 12	01 12	01 47	01 47	01 49	02 18	02b18	03a00	05 58	06a05
Hitchin ■4	d			01 17	01 17	01 52	01 52	01 52	02 23	02 23		06a06	
Letchworth Garden City	a					02 06	02 06	02 06					

		FC	FC ■1	FC	FC ■1	FC	FC ■1		FC	FC ■1	FC	FC ■1	FC
London Kings Cross ■15 ⊖	d	05 26	05 45	05 56	06 06	06 11	06 22		06 26	06 36		06 52	
Moorgate ⊖	d										06 35		06 50
Old Street ⊖	d										06 37		06 52
Essex Road	d										06 40		06 55
Highbury & Islington ⊖	d										06 42		06 57
Drayton Park	d										06 44		06 59
Finsbury Park ⊖	d	05 32	05 50	06 02	06 11	06 17	06 27		06 32	06 41	06 47	06 57	07 02
Harringay	d	05 34		06 04		06 19			06 34		06 49		07 04
Hornsey	d	05 36		06 06		06 21			06 36		06 51		07 06
Alexandra Palace	d	05 38		06 08		06 23			06 38		06 53		07 08
New Southgate	d					06 26					06 56		
Oakleigh Park	d					06 29					06 59		
New Barnet	d					06 31					07 01		
Hadley Wood	d					06 34					07 04		
Potters Bar	d				06 21	06 38				06 51	07 08		
Brookmans Park	d					06 41					07 11		
Welham Green	d					06 43					07 13		
Hatfield	d				06 27	06 46				06 57	07 16		
Welwyn Garden City ■4	d				06 31	06a53				07 01	07a21		
Welwyn North	d				06 34					07 04			
Knebworth	d				06 38					07 08			
Bowes Park	d	05 41		06 11					06 41				07 11
Palmers Green	d	05 43		06 13					06 43				07 13
Winchmore Hill	d	05 45		06 15					06 45				07 15
Grange Park	d	05 47		06 17					06 47				07 17
Enfield Chase	d	05 49		06 19					06 49				07 19
Gordon Hill	d	05 51		06 21					06 51				07 21
Crews Hill	d	05 54		06 24					06 54				07 24
Cuffley	d	05 57		06 27					06 57				07 27
Bayford	d	06 02		06 32					07 02				07 32
Hertford North	d	06a10		06 40					07 10				07 40
Watton-at-Stone	d			06 45					07 15				07 45
Stevenage ■4	d		06 08	06a55	06 42		06 46		07a25	07 12		07 17	07a55
Hitchin ■4	d		06 13		06 47		06a51			07a17		07 22	
Letchworth Garden City	a		06 17		06 51							07 26	

		FC ■1	FC	FC ■1	FC	FC ■1	FC	FC ■1	FC	FC ■1	FC	FC	FC ■1
London Kings Cross ■15 ⊖	d	07 06		07 22		07 36		07 52		08 03			08 22
Moorgate ⊖	d		07 05		07 20		07 35		07 50		08 05	08 12	
Old Street ⊖	d		07 07		07 22		07 37		07 52		08 07	08 14	
Essex Road	d		07 10		07 25		07 40		07 55		08 10	08 17	
Highbury & Islington ⊖	d		07 12		07 27		07 42		07 57		08 12	08 19	
Drayton Park	d		07 14		07 29		07 44		07 59		08 14	08 21	
Finsbury Park ⊖	d	07 11	07 17	07 27	07 32	07 41	07 47	07 57	08 02	08 08	08 17	08 24	08 27
Harringay	d		07 19		07 34		07 49		08 04		08 19	08 26	
Hornsey	d		07 21		07 36		07 51		08 06		08 21	08 28	
Alexandra Palace	d		07 23		07 38		07 53		08 08		08 23	08 30	
New Southgate	d		07 26				07 56				08 26		
Oakleigh Park	d		07 29				07 59				08 29		
New Barnet	d		07 31				08 01				08 31		
Hadley Wood	d		07 34				08 04				08 34		
Potters Bar	d	07 21	07 38			07 51	08 08			08 19	08 38		
Brookmans Park	d		07 41				08 11				08 41		
Welham Green	d		07 43				08 13				08 43		
Hatfield	d	07 27	07 46			07 57	08 16			08 25	08 46		
Welwyn Garden City ■4	d	07 31	07a51			08 01	08a22			08 31	08a51		
Welwyn North	d	07 34				08 04				08 34			
Knebworth	d	07 38				08 08				08 38			
Bowes Park	d				07 41				08 11			08 33	
Palmers Green	d				07 43				08 13			08 35	
Winchmore Hill	d				07 45				08 15			08 37	
Grange Park	d				07 47				08 17			08 39	
Enfield Chase	d				07 49				08 19			08 41	
Gordon Hill	d				07 51				08 21			08 43	
Crews Hill	d				07 54				08 24			08 46	
Cuffley	d				07 57				08 27			08 49	
Bayford	d				08 02				08 32			08 54	
Hertford North	d				08 10				08 37			09c07	
Watton-at-Stone	d				08 15				08 43			09 13	
Stevenage ■4	d	07 42		07 46	08a25	08 12		08 17	08 50	08 42		09a22	08 46
Hitchin ■4	d	07 47		07a51		08a17		08 22	08 55	08 47			08a51
Letchworth Garden City	a	07 51						08 26	09 03	08 51			

A MO until 12 July
B MO from 13 September
C MO from 19 July
D until 16 July, MX from 20 July until 3 September, from 7 September
E MO from 19 July until 6 September
F MO until 12 July, from 13 September
b arr. 0210
c arr. 0859

London - Welwyn Garden City, Hertford North and Letchworth Garden City

		FC	FC ■	FC	FC	FC ■	FC	FC ■	FC	FC	FC ■	FC	FC ■	FC	FC	FC ■	FC	FC ■	FC	FC	FC ■	FC
London Kings Cross ■	⊖ d		08 33			08 52		09 06			09 22		09 36			09 52		10 06			10 22	
Moorgate	⊖ d	08 22		08 32	08 42		08 52		09 02	09 12		09 22		09 32	09 42		09 52		10 02	10 12		10 22
Old Street	⊖ d	08 24		08 34	08 44		08 54		09 04	09 14		09 24		09 34	09 44		09 54		10 04	10 14		10 24
Essex Road	d	08 27		08 37	08 47		08 57		09 07	09 17		09 27		09 37	09 47		09 57		10 07	10 17		10 27
Highbury & Islington	⊖ d	08 29		08 39	08 49		08 59		09 09	09 19		09 29		09 39	09 49		09 59		10 09	10 19		10 29
Drayton Park	d	08 31		08 41	08 51		09 01		09 11	09 21		09 31		09 41	09 51		10 01		10 11	10 21		10 31
Finsbury Park	⊖ d	08 34	08 38	08 44	08 54	08 57	09 04	09 11	09 14	09 24	09 27	09 34	09 41	09 44	09 54	09 57	10 04	10 11	10 14	10 24	10 27	10 34
Harringay	d	08 36		08 46	08 56		09 06		09 16	09 26		09 36		09 46	09 56		10 06		10 16	10 26		10 36
Hornsey	d	08 38		08 48	08 58		09 08		09 18	09 28		09 38		09 48	09 58		10 08		10 18	10 28		10 38
Alexandra Palace	d	08 40		08 50	09 00		09 10		09 20	09 30		09 40		09 50	10 00		10 10		10 20	10 30		10 40
New Southgate	d	08 43			09 03				09 23			09 43			10 03				10 23			10 43
Oakleigh Park	d	08 46			09 06				09 26			09 46			10 06				10 26			10 46
New Barnet	d	08 48			09 08				09 28			09 48			10 08				10 28			10 48
Hadley Wood	d	08 51			09 11				09 31			09 51			10 11				10 31			10 51
Potters Bar	d	08 55	08 49		09 15			09 21	09 35			09 55	09 51		10 15			10 21	10 35			10 55
Brookmans Park	d	08 58			09 18				09 38			09 58			10 18				10 38			10 58
Welham Green	d	09 00			09 20				09 40			10 00			10 20				10 40			11 00
Hatfield	d	09 03	08 55		09 23			09 27	09 43			10 03	09 57		10 23			10 27	10 43			11 03
Welwyn Garden City ■	d	09a09	09 01		09a29			09 31	09a49			10a09	10 01		10a29			10 31	10a49			11a09
Welwyn North	d		09 04					09 34					10 04					10 34				
Knebworth	d		09 08					09 38					10 08					10 38				
Bowes Park	d			08 53			09 13			09 33				09 53			10 13			10 33		
Palmers Green	d			08 55			09 15			09 35				09 55			10 15			10 35		
Winchmore Hill	d			08 57			09 17			09 37				09 57			10 17			10 37		
Grange Park	d			08 59			09 19			09 39				09 59			10 19			10 39		
Enfield Chase	d			09 01			09 21			09 41				10 01			10 21			10 41		
Gordon Hill	d			09 03			09 23			09 43				10 03			10 23			10 43		
Crews Hill	d			09 06			09 26			09 46				10 06			10 26			10 46		
Cuffley	d			09 09			09 29			09 49				10 09			10 29			10 49		
Bayford	d			09 14			09 34			09 54				10 14			10 34			10 54		
Hertford North	d			09a20			09 39			10a00				10a20			10 39			11a00		
Watton-at-Stone	d						09 45										10 45					
Stevenage ■	d		09 12			09 16	09 51	09 42			09 46		10 12			10 16	10 51	10 42			10 46	
Hitchin ■	d		09a17			09 21	09 57	09 47			09a51		10a17			10 21	10 57	10 47			10a51	
Letchworth Garden City	a					09 25	10 04	09 51								10 25	11 04	10 51				

		FC ■	FC	FC	FC ■	FC	FC ■	FC	FC	FC ■	FC	FC ■	FC	FC	FC ■	FC	FC ■	FC	FC	FC ■	FC	FC ■	FC
London Kings Cross ■	⊖ d	10 36			10 52		11 06			11 22		11 36			11 52		12 06			12 22		12 36	
Moorgate	⊖ d		10 32	10 42		10 52		11 02	11 12		11 22		11 32	11 42		11 52		12 02	12 12		12 22		12 32
Old Street	⊖ d		10 34	10 44		10 54		11 04	11 14		11 24		11 34	11 44		11 54		12 04	12 14		12 24		12 34
Essex Road	d		10 37	10 47		10 57		11 07	11 17		11 27		11 37	11 47		11 57		12 07	12 17		12 27		12 37
Highbury & Islington	⊖ d		10 39	10 49		10 59		11 09	11 19		11 29		11 39	11 49		11 59		12 09	12 19		12 29		12 39
Drayton Park	d		10 41	10 51		11 01		11 11	11 21		11 31		11 41	11 51		12 01		12 11	12 21		12 31		12 41
Finsbury Park	⊖ d	10 41	10 44	10 54	10 57	11 04	11 11	11 14	11 24	11 27	11 34	11 41	11 44	11 54	11 57	12 04	12 11	12 14	12 24	12 27	12 34	12 41	12 44
Harringay	d		10 46	10 56		11 06		11 16	11 26		11 36		11 46	11 56		12 06		12 16	12 26		12 36		12 46
Hornsey	d		10 48	10 58		11 08		11 18	11 28		11 38		11 48	11 58		12 08		12 18	12 28		12 38		12 48
Alexandra Palace	d		10 50	11 00		11 10		11 20	11 30		11 40		11 50	12 00		12 10		12 20	12 30		12 40		12 50
New Southgate	d			11 03				11 23			11 43			12 03				12 23			12 43		
Oakleigh Park	d			11 06				11 26			11 46			12 06				12 26			12 46		
New Barnet	d			11 08				11 28			11 48			12 08				12 28			12 48		
Hadley Wood	d			11 11				11 31			11 51			12 11				12 31			12 51		
Potters Bar	d	10 51		11 15			11 21	11 35			11 55	11 51		12 15			12 21	12 35			12 55	12 51	
Brookmans Park	d			11 18				11 38			11 58			12 18				12 38			12 58		
Welham Green	d			11 20				11 40			12 00			12 20				12 40			13 00		
Hatfield	d	10 57		11 23			11 27	11 43			12 03	11 57		12 23			12 27	12 43			13 03	12 57	
Welwyn Garden City ■	d	11 01		11a29			11 31	11a49			12a09	12 01		12a29			12 31	12a49			13a09	13 01	
Welwyn North	d	11 04					11 34					12 04					12 34					13 04	
Knebworth	d	11 08					11 38					12 08					12 38					13 08	
Bowes Park	d		10 53			11 13			11 33				11 53			12 13			12 33				12 53
Palmers Green	d		10 55			11 15			11 35				11 55			12 15			12 35				12 55
Winchmore Hill	d		10 57			11 17			11 37				11 57			12 17			12 37				12 57
Grange Park	d		10 59			11 19			11 39				11 59			12 19			12 39				12 59
Enfield Chase	d		11 01			11 21			11 41				12 01			12 21			12 41				13 01
Gordon Hill	d		11 03			11 23			11 43				12 03			12 23			12 43				13 03
Crews Hill	d		11 06			11 26			11 46				12 06			12 26			12 46				13 06
Cuffley	d		11 09			11 29			11 49				12 09			12 29			12 49				13 09
Bayford	d		11 14			11 34			11 54				12 14			12 34			12 54				13 14
Hertford North	d		11a20			11 39			12a00				12a20			12 39			13a00				13a20
Watton-at-Stone	d					11 45										12 45							
Stevenage ■	d	11 12			11 16	11 51	11 42			11 46		12 12			12 16	12 51	12 42			12 46		13 12	
Hitchin ■	d	11a17			11 21	11 57	11 47			11a51		12a17			12 21	12 57	12 47			12a51		13a17	
Letchworth Garden City	a				11 25	12 04	11 51								12 25	13 04	12 51						

Table 24 — Mondays to Fridays

London - Welwyn Garden City, Hertford North and Letchworth Garden City

		FC	FC ■	FC	FC ■	FC	FC	FC ■	FC	FC ■	FC	FC	FC ■	FC	FC ■	FC	FC	FC ■	FC	FC ■	FC	FC
London Kings Cross ■	⊖ d		12 52		13 06			13 22		13 36			13 52		14 06			14 22		14 36		
Moorgate	⊖ d	12 42		12 52		13 02	13 12		13 22		13 32	13 42		13 52		14 02	14 12		14 22		14 32	14 42
Old Street	⊖ d	12 44		12 54		13 04	13 14		13 24		13 34	13 44		13 54		14 04	14 14		14 24		14 34	14 44
Essex Road	d	12 47		12 57		13 07	13 17		13 27		13 37	13 47		13 57		14 07	14 17		14 27		14 37	14 47
Highbury & Islington	⊖ d	12 49		12 59		13 09	13 19		13 29		13 39	13 49		13 59		14 09	14 19		14 29		14 39	14 49
Drayton Park	d	12 51		13 01		13 11	13 21		13 31		13 41	13 51		14 01		14 11	14 21		14 31		14 41	14 51
Finsbury Park	⊖ d	12 54	12 57	13 04	13 11	13 14	13 24	13 27	13 34	13 41	13 44	13 54	13 57	14 04	14 11	14 14	14 24	14 27	14 34	14 41	14 44	14 54
Harringay	d	12 56		13 06		13 16	13 26		13 36		13 46	13 56		14 06		14 16	14 26		14 36		14 46	14 56
Hornsey	d	12 58		13 08		13 18	13 28		13 38		13 48	13 58		14 08		14 18	14 28		14 38		14 48	14 58
Alexandra Palace	d	13 00		13 10		13 20	13 30		13 40		13 50	14 00		14 10		14 20	14 30		14 40		14 50	15 00
New Southgate	d	13 03				13 23			13 43			14 03				14 23			14 43			15 03
Oakleigh Park	d	13 06				13 26			13 46			14 06				14 26			14 46			15 06
New Barnet	d	13 08				13 28			13 48			14 08				14 28			14 48			15 08
Hadley Wood	d	13 11				13 31			13 51			14 11				14 31			14 51			15 11
Potters Bar	d	13 15			13 21	13 35			13 55	13 51		14 15			14 21	14 35			14 55	14 51		15 15
Brookmans Park	d	13 18				13 38			13 58			14 18				14 38			14 58			15 18
Welham Green	d	13 20				13 40			14 00			14 20				14 40			15 00			15 20
Hatfield	d	13 23			13 27	13 43			14 03	13 57		14 23			14 27	14 43			15 03	14 57		15 23
Welwyn Garden City ■	d	13a29			13 31	13a49			14a10	14 01		14a29			14 31	14a49			15a09	15 01		15a29
Welwyn North	d				13 34					14 04					14 34					15 04		
Knebworth	d				13 38					14 08					14 38					15 08		
Bowes Park	d			13 13			13 33				13 53			14 13			14 33				14 53	
Palmers Green	d			13 15			13 35				13 55			14 15			14 35				14 55	
Winchmore Hill	d			13 17			13 37				13 57			14 17			14 37				14 57	
Grange Park	d			13 19			13 39				13 59			14 19			14 39				14 59	
Enfield Chase	d			13 21			13 41				14 01			14 21			14 41				15 01	
Gordon Hill	d			13 23			13 43				14 03			14 23			14 43				15 03	
Crews Hill	d			13 26			13 46				14 06			14 26			14 46				15 06	
Cuffley	d			13 29			13 49				14 09			14 29			14 49				15 09	
Bayford	d			13 34			13 54				14 14			14 34			14 54				15 14	
Hertford North	d			13 39			14a00				14a20			14 39			15a00				15a20	
Watton-at-Stone	d			13 45										14 45								
Stevenage ■	d		13 16	13 51	13 42			13 46		14 12			14 16	14 51	14 42			14 46		15 12		
Hitchin ■	d		13 21	13 57	13 47			13a51		14a17			14 21	14 57	14 47			14a51		15a17		
Letchworth Garden City	a		13 25	14 04	13 51								14 25	15 04	14 51							

		FC ■	FC	FC ■	FC	FC	FC ■	FC	FC ■	FC	FC	FC ■	FC	FC ■	FC	FC	FC ■	FC	FC	FC ■	FC	FC	FC ■
London Kings Cross ■	⊖ d	14 52		15 06			15 22		15 36			15 52		16 06			16 22			16 32			16 50
Moorgate	⊖ d		14 52		15 02	15 12		15 22		15 32	15 42		15 52		16 02	16 08		16 18	16 23		16 28	16 38	
Old Street	⊖ d		14 54		15 04	15 14		15 24		15 34	15 44		15 54		16 04	16 10		16 20	16 25		16 30	16 40	
Essex Road	d		14 57		15 07	15 17		15 27		15 37	15 47		15 57		16 07	16 13		16 23	16 28		16 33	16 43	
Highbury & Islington	⊖ d		14 59		15 09	15 19		15 29		15 39	15 49		15 59		16 09	16 16		16 26	16 31		16 36	16 46	
Drayton Park	d		15 01		15 11	15 21		15 31		15 41	15 51		16 01		16 11	16 17		16 27	16 32		16 37	16 47	
Finsbury Park	⊖ d	14 57	15 04	15 11	15 14	15 24	15 27	15 34	15 41	15 44	15 54	15 57	16 04	16 11	16 14	16 20	16 27	16 30	16 35	16 37	16 40	16 50	16 55
Harringay	d		15 06		15 16	15 26		15 36		15 46	15 56		16 06		16 16	16 23		16 33			16 43	16 53	
Hornsey	d		15 08		15 18	15 28		15 38		15 48	15 58		16 08		16 18	16 25		16 35			16 45	16 55	
Alexandra Palace	d		15 10		15 20	15 30		15 40		15 50	16 00		16 10		16 20	16 28		16 38	16 41		16 47	16 58	
New Southgate	d				15 23			15 43			16 03				16 23						16 50		
Oakleigh Park	d				15 26			15 46			16 06				16 26						16 54		
New Barnet	d				15 28			15 48			16 08				16 28						16 56		
Hadley Wood	d				15 31			15 51			16 11				16 31						16 59		
Potters Bar	d			15 21	15 35			15 55	15 51		16 15			16 21	16 35					16 48	17 03		
Brookmans Park	d				15 38			15 58			16 18				16 38						17 06		
Welham Green	d				15 40			16 00			16 20				16 40						17 08		
Hatfield	d			15 27	15 43			16 03	15 57		16 23			16 27	16 43					16 54	17 11		
Welwyn Garden City ■	d			15 31	15a49			16a09	16 01		16a29			16 32	16a49					16 59	17a16		
Welwyn North	d			15 34					16 04					16 35						17 03			17 11
Knebworth	d			15 38					16 08					16 39						17 07			
Bowes Park	d		15 13			15 33				15 53			16 13			16 30			16 44			17 00	
Palmers Green	d		15 15			15 35				15 55			16 15			16 32		16 41	16 46			17 02	
Winchmore Hill	d		15 17			15 37				15 57			16 17			16 35		16 44	16 49			17 05	
Grange Park	d		15 19			15 39				15 59			16 19			16 37			16 51			17 07	
Enfield Chase	d		15 21			15 41				16 01			16 21			16 39		16 47	16 53			17 09	
Gordon Hill	d		15 23			15 43				16 03			16 23			16 41		16a51	16 55			17 11	
Crews Hill	d		15 26			15 46				16 06			16 26			16 44						17 14	
Cuffley	d		15 29			15 49				16 09			16 29			16 47			17 00			17 17	
Bayford	d		15 34			15 54				16 14			16 34			16 52						17 22	
Hertford North	d		15 39			16b09				16a20			16 39			16a58			17 09			17a28	
Watton-at-Stone	d		15 45			16 15							16 45						17 15				
Stevenage ■	d	15 16	15 51	15 42		16a23	15 46		16 12			16 16	16a53	16 43			16 47		17a23	17 11			17 17
Hitchin ■	d	15 21	15 57	15 47			15a51		16a17			16 21		16 49			16a53			17 17			17a23
Letchworth Garden City	a	15 25	16 04	15 51								16 25		16 53						17 21			

b arr. 1559

London - Welwyn Garden City, Hertford North and Letchworth Garden City

		FC 1	FC	FC	FC	FC		FC	FC 1	FC	FC 1	FC	FC	FC	FC	FC		FC 1	FC	FC 1	FC	FC	FC	FC	FC
London Kings Cross 15 ⊖	d	16 54		16 57					17 14		17 22		17 27					17 44		17 52		17 57			
Moorgate ⊖	d		16 48		16 53	16 58		17 03		17 08		17 18		17 23	17 28	17 33			17 38		17 48		17 53	17 58	18 03
Old Street ⊖	d		16 50		16 55	17 00		17 05		17 10		17 20		17 25	17 30	17 35			17 40		17 50		17 55	18 00	18 05
Essex Road	d		16 53		16 58	17 03		17 08		17 13		17 23		17 28	17 33	17 38			17 43		17 53		17 58	18 03	18 08
Highbury & Islington ⊖	d		16 56		17 01	17 06		17 11		17 16		17 26		17 31	17 36	17 41			17 46		17 56		18 01	18 06	18 11
Drayton Park	d		16 57		17 02	17 07		17 12		17 17		17 27		17 32	17 37	17 42			17 47		17 57		18 02	18 07	18 12
Finsbury Park ⊖	d	16 59	17 00	17 03	17 05	17 10		17 15	17 19	17 20	17 28	17 30	17 33	17 35	17 40	17 45		17 49	17 50	17 58	18 00	18 03	18 05	18 10	18 15
Harringay	d				17 08			17 18		17 23				17 38		17 48			17 53				18 08		18 18
Hornsey	d				17 10			17 20		17 25				17 40		17 50			17 55				18 10		18 20
Alexandra Palace	d				17 12	17 16		17 23		17 27				17 42	17 46	17 53			17 57				18 12	18 16	18 23
New Southgate	d			17 08	17 15					17 30			17 38	17 45					18 00			18 08	18 15		
Oakleigh Park	d			17 11	17 19					17 34			17 41	17 49					18 04			18 11	18 19		
New Barnet	d			17 13	17 21					17 36			17 43	17 51					18 06			18 13	18 21		
Hadley Wood	d				17 24					17 39				17 54					18 09				18 24		
Potters Bar	d			17 19	17 28					17 43			17 49	17 58					18 13			18 19	18 28		
Brookmans Park	d				17 31					17 46				18 01					18 16				18 31		
Welham Green	d				17 33					17 48				18 03					18 18				18 33		
Hatfield	d	17 15		17 25	17 36					17 51			17 55	18 06					18 21			18 25	18 36		
Welwyn Garden City 4	d	17 19		17a30	17a41					17a56	17 47		18a00	18a11					18a26	18 17		18a30	18a41		
Welwyn North	d	17 22									17 51									18 21					
Knebworth	d	17 26							17 35		17 55									18 25					
Bowes Park	d		17 07					17 25				17 37				17 55					18 07				18 25
Palmers Green	d		17 09			17 19		17 27				17 39			17 49	17 57					18 09			18 19	18 27
Winchmore Hill	d		17 12			17 22		17 30				17 42			17 52	18 00					18 12			18 22	18 30
Grange Park	d		17 14					17 32				17 44				18 02					18 14				18 32
Enfield Chase	d		17 16			17 26		17 34				17 46			17 56	18 04					18 16			18 26	18 34
Gordon Hill	d		17 18			17a31		17 37				17 49			17 58	18 07					18 19			18 28	18 37
Crews Hill	d							17 40								18 10									18 40
Cuffley	d		17 23					17 43				17 53			18 03	18 13					18 23			18 33	18 43
Bayford	d							17 48								18 18									18 48
Hertford North	d		17 33					17a53				18 03			18a12	18a23					18 33			18a42	18a53
Watton-at-Stone	d		17 38									18 08									18 38				
Stevenage 4	d	17 36	17a46						17 40		18 04	18a16						18 09		18 34	18a46				
Hitchin 4	d	17 42							17a46		18 10							18a16		18 40					
Letchworth Garden City	a	17 47									18 16									18 46					

		FC 1		FC	FC 1	FC	FC	FC	FC	FC	FC 1	FC		FC 1	FC	FC	FC	FC	FC 1	FC	FC 1	FC		FC 1	FC
London Kings Cross 15 ⊖	d	18 14			18 22		18 27				18 44			18 52		18 57			19 18		19 22			19 34	
Moorgate ⊖	d			18 08		18 18		18 23	18 28	18 35		18 40			18 50		18 55	19 02		19 12		19 22			19 32
Old Street ⊖	d			18 10		18 20		18 25	18 30	18 37		18 42			18 52		18 57	19 04		19 14		19 24			19 34
Essex Road	d			18 13		18 23		18 28	18 33	18 40		18 45			18 55		19 00	19 07		19 17		19 27			19 37
Highbury & Islington ⊖	d			18 16		18 26		18 31	18 36	18 43		18 48			18 58		19 03	19 10		19 20		19 30			19 40
Drayton Park	d			18 17		18 27		18 32	18 37	18 44		18 49			18 59		19 04	19 11		19 21		19 31			19 41
Finsbury Park ⊖	d	18 19		18 20	18 28	18 30	18 33	18 35	18 40	18 47	18 49	18 52		18 58	19 02	19 03	19 07	19 14	19 23	19 24	19 27	19 34		19 39	19 44
Harringay	d			18 23				18 38		18 50		18 55					19 10	19 17		19 27		19 37			
Hornsey	d			18 25				18 40		18 52		18 57					19 12	19 19		19 29		19 39			
Alexandra Palace	d			18 27				18 42	18 46	18 55		18 59					19 14	19 22		19 31		19 42			
New Southgate	d			18 30			18 38	18 45				19 02				19 08	19 17			19 34					
Oakleigh Park	d			18 34			18 41	18 49				19 06				19 11	19 21			19 38					
New Barnet	d			18 36			18 43	18 51				19 08				19 13	19 23			19 40					
Hadley Wood	d			18 39				18 54				19 11				19 16	19 26			19 43					
Potters Bar	d			18 43			18 49	18 58				19 15				19 20	19 30		19 34	19 47					
Brookmans Park	d			18 46				19 01				19 18					19 33			19 50					
Welham Green	d			18 48				19 03				19 20					19 35			19 52					
Hatfield	d			18 51			18 55	19 06				19 23		19 14		19 27	19 38		19 42	19 55				19 53	
Welwyn Garden City 4	d			18a56	18 47		19a00	19a11				19a28		19 18		19a32	19a43		19 48	20a00				20 00	
Welwyn North	d				18 51									19 22					19 52					20 04	
Knebworth	d				18 55						19 05			19 26					19 56					20 08	
Bowes Park	d					18 37				18 57					19 09			19 24				19 44			19 51
Palmers Green	d					18 39			18 49	18 59					19 11			19 26				19 46			19 53
Winchmore Hill	d					18 42			18 52	19 02					19 14			19 29				19 49			19 56
Grange Park	d					18 44				19 04					19 16			19 31				19 51			19 58
Enfield Chase	d					18 46			18 56	19 06					19 18			19 33				19 53			20 00
Gordon Hill	d					18 49			18 58	19 09					19 21			19 36				19 56			20 03
Crews Hill	d									19 12								19 39							20 06
Cuffley	d					18 53			19 03	19 15					19 25			19 42				20 00			20 09
Bayford	d									19 20								19 47							20 14
Hertford North	d					19 03			19a12	19a25					19 35			19a52				20 10			20a19
Watton-at-Stone	d					19 08									19 40							20 15			
Stevenage 4	d	18 39			19 04	19 16					19 10			19b36	19a52				20 04		19 47	20 23		20 12	
Hitchin 4	d	18a46			19 10	19 22					19a16			19 42					20 10		19a53	20 28		20 17	
Letchworth Garden City	a				19 16	19 27								19 47					20 15			20 35		20 23	

b arr. 1930

Table 24

Mondays to Fridays

London - Welwyn Garden City, Hertford North and Letchworth Garden City

		FC	FC	FC	FC 1	FC	FC 1	FC		FC	FC 1	FC 1	FC	FC	FC 1	FC	FC 1	FC		FC	FC 1	FC 1	FC	FC	FC 1
London Kings Cross 15 ⊖	d	19 40			19 52		20 06				20 22	20 36			20 52		21 06				21 22	21 36			21 52
Moorgate ⊖	d		19 37	19 42		19 52		20 07		20 12			20 32	20 37		20 52		21 07		21 12			21 32	21 37	
Old Street ⊖	d		19 39	19 44		19 54		20 09		20 14			20 34	20 39		20 54		21 09		21 14			21 34	21 39	
Essex Road	d		19 42	19 47		19 57		20 12		20 17			20 37	20 42		20 57		21 12		21 17			21 37	21 42	
Highbury & Islington ⊖	d		19 45	19 50		19 59		20 14		20 19			20 39	20 44		20 59		21 14		21 19			21 39	21 44	
Drayton Park	d		19 46	19 51		20 01		20 16		20 21			20 41	20 46		21 01		21 16		21 21			21 41	21 46	
Finsbury Park ⊖	d	19 45	19 49	19 54	19 57	20 04	20 11	20 19		20 24	20 27	20 41	20 44	20 49	20 57	21 04	21 11	21 19		21 24	21 27	21 41	21 44	21 49	21 57
Harringay	d		19 52	19 57		20 06		20 21		20 26			20 46	20 51		21 06		21 21		21 26			21 46	21 51	
Hornsey	d		19 54	19 59		20 08		20 23		20 28			20 48	20 53		21 08		21 23		21 28			21 48	21 53	
Alexandra Palace	d		19 56	20 02		20 10		20 25		20 30			20 50	20 55		21 10		21 25		21 30			21 50	21 55	
New Southgate	d	19 50	19 59					20 28						20 58				21 28						21 58	
Oakleigh Park	d	19 54	20 03					20 31						21 01				21 31						22 01	
New Barnet	d	19 56	20 05					20 33						21 03				21 33						22 03	
Hadley Wood	d		20 08					20 36						21 06				21 36						22 06	
Potters Bar	d	20 01	20 12				20 21	20 40				20 51		21 10			21 21	21 40				21 51		22 10	
Brookmans Park	d		20 15					20 43						21 13				21 43						22 13	
Welham Green	d		20 17					20 45						21 15				21 45						22 15	
Hatfield	d	20 07	20 20				20 27	20 48				20 57		21 18			21 27	21 48				21 57		22 18	
Welwyn Garden City 4	d	20a13	20a25				20 31	20a54				21 01		21a24			21 31	21a54				22 01		22a24	
Welwyn North	d						20 34					21 04					21 34					22 04			
Knebworth	d						20 38					21 08					21 38					22 08			
Bowes Park	d			20 04		20 13				20 33			20 53			21 13				21 33			21 53		
Palmers Green	d			20 06		20 15				20 35			20 55			21 15				21 35			21 55		
Winchmore Hill	d			20 09		20 17				20 37			20 57			21 17				21 37			21 57		
Grange Park	d			20 11		20 19				20 39			20 59			21 19				21 39			21 59		
Enfield Chase	d			20 13		20 21				20 41			21 01			21 21				21 41			22 01		
Gordon Hill	d			20 16		20 23				20 43			21 03			21 23				21 43			22 03		
Crews Hill	d					20 26				20 46			21 06			21 26				21 46			22 06		
Cuffley	d			20 20		20 29				20 49			21 09			21 29				21 49			22 09		
Bayford	d					20 34				20 54			21 14			21 34				21 54			22 14		
Hertford North	d			20a30		20 40				21b10			21a20			21a40				22c07			22a20		
Watton-at-Stone	d					20 45				21 15										22 13					
Stevenage 4	d				20 17	20a53	20 42			21 23	20 47	21 12			21 16		21 42			22 20	21 47	22 12			22 16
Hitchin 4	d				20a23		20 47			21 28	20a53	21 17			21 21		21 47			22 25	21a53	22 17			22 21
Letchworth Garden City	a						20 51			21 34		21 23			21 28		21 51			22 33		22 23			22 28

		FC	FC 1	FC		FC 1	FC	FC 1	FC	FC 1	FC	FC 1	FC	FC 1		FC	FC 1	FC
London Kings Cross 15 ⊖	d		22 06	22 11		22 22	22 26	22 36	22 41	22 52	22 56	23 06	23 11	23 22		23 26	23 36	23 41
Moorgate ⊖	d	21 52																
Old Street ⊖	d	21 54																
Essex Road	d	21 57																
Highbury & Islington ⊖	d	21 59																
Drayton Park	d	22 01																
Finsbury Park ⊖	d	22 04	22 11	22 17		22 27	22 32	22 41	22 47	22 57	23 02	23 11	23 17	23 27		23 32	23 41	23 47
Harringay	d	22 06		22 19			22 34		22 49		23 04		23 19			23 34		23 49
Hornsey	d	22 08		22 21			22 36		22 51		23 06		23 21			23 36		23 51
Alexandra Palace	d	22 10		22 23			22 38		22 53		23 08		23 23			23 38		23 53
New Southgate	d			22 26					22 56				23 26					23 56
Oakleigh Park	d			22 29					22 59				23 29					23 59
New Barnet	d			22 31					23 01				23 31					00 01
Hadley Wood	d			22 34					23 04				23 34					00 04
Potters Bar	d		22 21	22 38				22 51	23 08			23 21	23 38				23 51	00 08
Brookmans Park	d			22 41					23 11				23 41					00 11
Welham Green	d			22 43					23 13				23 43					00 13
Hatfield	d		22 27	22 46				22 57	23 16			23 27	23 46				23 57	00 16
Welwyn Garden City 4	d		22 31	22a51				23 01	23a24			23 31	23a54				00 01	00a24
Welwyn North	d		22 34					23 04				23 34					00 04	
Knebworth	d		22 38					23 08				23 38					00 08	
Bowes Park	d	22 13					22 41				23 11					23 41		
Palmers Green	d	22 15					22 43				23 13					23 43		
Winchmore Hill	d	22 17					22 45				23 15					23 45		
Grange Park	d	22 19					22 47				23 17					23 47		
Enfield Chase	d	22 21					22 49				23 19					23 49		
Gordon Hill	d	22 23					22 51				23 21					23 51		
Crews Hill	d	22 26					22 54				23 24					23 54		
Cuffley	d	22 29					22 57				23 27					23 57		
Bayford	d	22 34					23 02				23 32					00 02		
Hertford North	d	22a40					23 07				23a38					00 07		
Watton-at-Stone	d						23 13									00 13		
Stevenage 4	d		22 42			22 48	23 20	23 12		23 16		23 42		23 46		00 20	00 12	
Hitchin 4	d		22 47			22a53	23 28	23 17		23 24		23 50		23a54		00 26	00 20	
Letchworth Garden City	a		22 51				23 36	23 26		23 31		23 54				00 36	00 29	

b arr. 2059

c arr. 2159

Table 24

Saturdays until 10 July

London - Welwyn Garden City, Hertford North and Letchworth Garden City

	FC	FC 1	FC	FC 1	FC	FC	FC 1	FC 1	FC	FC 1	FC 1	FC	FC 1	FC	FC 1	FC	FC 1	FC	FC 1	FC	FC 1	FC
London Kings Cross ⊖ d	23p26	23p36	23p41	00 04	00 06	00 11	00 36	01 06	01 11	01 36	05 22	05 26	05 45	05 56	06 06	06 11	06 22	06 26	06 36	06 41	06 52	06 56
Moorgate ⊖ d																						
Old Street ⊖ d																						
Essex Road d																						
Highbury & Islington ⊖ d																						
Drayton Park d																						
Finsbury Park ⊖ d	23p32	23p41	23p47	00 09	00 12	00 17	00 41	01 11	01 17	01 41	05 27	05 32	05 50	06 02	06 11	06 17	06 27	06 32	06 41	06 47	06 57	07 02
Harringay d	23p34		23p49		00 14	00 19			01 19			05 34		06 04		06 19		06 34		06 49		07 04
Hornsey d	23p36		23p51		00 16	00 21			01 21			05 36		06 06		06 21		06 36		06 51		07 06
Alexandra Palace d	23p38		23p53		00 18	00 23		01 16	01 23	01 45		05 38		06 08		06 23		06 38		06 53		07 08
New Southgate d			23p56			00 26			01 26							06 26				06 56		
Oakleigh Park d			23p59			00 29			01 29	01 50						06 29				06 59		
New Barnet d			00 01			00 31			01 31	01 52						06 31				07 01		
Hadley Wood d			00 04			00 34			01 34	01 54						06 34				07 04		
Potters Bar d		23p51	00 08			00 38	00 51		01 38	01 58	05 37				06 21	06 38			06 51	07 08		
Brookmans Park d			00 11			00 41			01 41							06 41				07 11		
Welham Green d			00 13			00 43			01 43							06 43				07 13		
Hatfield d		23p57	00 16			00 46	00 57		01 46	02 04	05 43				06 27	06 46			06 57	07 16		
Welwyn Garden City d		00 01	00a24			00a54	01 01		01a54	02 08	05 47				06 31	06a51			07 01	07a21		
Welwyn North d		00 04					01s04			02s11	05 50				06 34				07 04			
Knebworth d		00 08					01s08			02s15	05 54				06 38				07 08			
Bowes Park d	23p41				00 21							05 41		06 11				06 41				07 11
Palmers Green d	23p43				00 23			01 19				05 43		06 13				06 43				07 13
Winchmore Hill d	23p45				00 25			01 21				05 45		06 15				06 45				07 15
Grange Park d	23p47				00 27							05 47		06 17				06 47				07 17
Enfield Chase d	23p49				00 29			01 24				05 49		06 19				06 49				07 19
Gordon Hill d	23p51				00 31			01 26				05 51		06 21				06 51				07 21
Crews Hill d	23p54				00 34							05 54		06 24				06 54				07 24
Cuffley d	23p57				00 37			01 30				05 57		06 27				06 57				07 27
Bayford d	00 02				00 42							06 02		06 32				07 02				07 32
Hertford North d	00 07				00 47			01 38				06a08		06a38				07 07				07a38
Watton-at-Stone d	00 13				00 53													07 13				
Stevenage d	00 20	00 12		00 31	01 00		01 12	01 47		02 18	05 58		06 08		06 42		06 46	07a20	07 12		07 16	
Hitchin d	00 28	00 20		00 39	01 06		01a17	01 52		02a23	06a06		06 13		06 47		06a51		07a17		07 21	
Letchworth Garden City a	00 36	00 29		00 42	01 16			02 06					06 16		06 51						07 25	

	FC 1	FC	FC 1	FC	FC 1	FC	FC 1	FC	FC 1	FC	FC 1	FC	FC 1	FC	FC 1	FC	FC 1	FC	FC 1	FC	FC 1	FC
London Kings Cross ⊖ d	07 06	07 11	07 22	07 26	07 36	07 41	07 52	07 56	08 06	08 11	08 22	08 26	08 36	08 41	08 52	08 56	09 06	09 11	09 22	09 26	09 36	09 41
Moorgate ⊖ d																						
Old Street ⊖ d																						
Essex Road d																						
Highbury & Islington ⊖ d																						
Drayton Park d																						
Finsbury Park ⊖ d	07 11	07 17	07 27	07 32	07 41	07 47	07 57	08 02	08 11	08 17	08 27	08 32	08 41	08 47	08 57	09 02	09 11	09 17	09 27	09 32	09 41	09 47
Harringay d		07 19		07 34		07 49		08 04		08 19		08 34		08 49		09 04		09 19		09 34		09 49
Hornsey d		07 21		07 36		07 51		08 06		08 21		08 36		08 51		09 06		09 21		09 36		09 51
Alexandra Palace d		07 23		07 38		07 53		08 08		08 23		08 38		08 53		09 08		09 23		09 38		09 53
New Southgate d		07 26				07 56				08 26				08 56				09 26				09 56
Oakleigh Park d		07 29				07 59				08 29				08 59				09 29				09 59
New Barnet d		07 31				08 01				08 31				09 01				09 31				10 01
Hadley Wood d		07 34				08 04				08 34				09 04				09 34				10 04
Potters Bar d	07 21	07 38			07 51	08 08			08 21	08 38			08 51	09 08			09 21	09 38			09 51	10 08
Brookmans Park d		07 41				08 11				08 41				09 11				09 41				10 11
Welham Green d		07 43				08 13				08 43				09 13				09 43				10 13
Hatfield d	07 27	07 46			07 57	08 16			08 27	08 46			08 57	09 16			09 27	09 46			09 57	10 16
Welwyn Garden City d	07 31	07a51			08 01	08a21			08 31	08a51			09 01	09a21			09 31	09a51			10 01	10a21
Welwyn North d	07 34				08 04				08 34				09 04				09 34				10 04	
Knebworth d	07 38				08 08				08 38				09 08				09 38				10 08	
Bowes Park d				07 41				08 11				08 41				09 11				09 41		
Palmers Green d				07 43				08 13				08 43				09 13				09 43		
Winchmore Hill d				07 45				08 15				08 45				09 15				09 45		
Grange Park d				07 47				08 17				08 47				09 17				09 47		
Enfield Chase d				07 49				08 19				08 49				09 19				09 49		
Gordon Hill d				07 51				08 21				08 51				09 21				09 51		
Crews Hill d				07 54				08 24				08 54				09 24				09 54		
Cuffley d				07 57				08 27				08 57				09 27				09 57		
Bayford d				08 02				08 32				09 02				09 32				10 02		
Hertford North d				08 07				08a38				09 07				09a38				10 07		
Watton-at-Stone d				08 13								09 13								10 13		
Stevenage d	07 42		07 46	08a20	08 12		08 16		08 42		08 46	09a20	09 12		09 16		09 42		09 46	10a20	10 12	
Hitchin d	07 47		07a51		08a17		08 21		08 47		08a51		09a17		09 21		09 47		09a51		10a17	
Letchworth Garden City a	07 51						08 25		08 51						09 25		09 51					

Table 24

Saturdays until 10 July

London - Welwyn Garden City, Hertford North and Letchworth Garden City

	FC 1	FC	FC 1	FC	FC 1	FC	FC 1	FC	FC 1	FC	FC 1	FC	FC 1	FC	FC 1	FC	FC 1	FC	FC 1	FC	FC 1
London Kings Cross ⊖ d	09 52	09 56	10 06	10 11	10 22	10 26	10 36	10 41	10 52	10 56	11 06	11 11	11 22	11 26	11 36	11 41	11 52	11 56	12 06	12 11	12 22
Moorgate ⊖ d																					
Old Street ⊖ d																					
Essex Road d																					
Highbury & Islington ⊖ d																					
Drayton Park d																					
Finsbury Park ⊖ d	09 57	10 02	10 11	10 17	10 27	10 32	10 41	10 47	10 57	11 02	11 11	11 17	11 27	11 32	11 41	11 47	11 57	12 02	12 11	12 17	12 27
Harringay d		10 04		10 19		10 34		10 49		11 04		11 19		11 34		11 49		12 04		12 19	
Hornsey d		10 06		10 21		10 36		10 51		11 06		11 21		11 36		11 51		12 06		12 21	
Alexandra Palace d		10 08		10 23		10 39		10 53		11 08		11 23		11 38		11 53		12 08		12 23	
New Southgate d				10 26				10 56				11 26				11 56				12 26	
Oakleigh Park d				10 29				10 59				11 29				12 00				12 29	
New Barnet d				10 31				11 01				11 31				12 02				12 31	
Hadley Wood d				10 34				11 04				11 34				12 04				12 34	
Potters Bar d			10 21	10 38			10 51	11 08			11 21	11 38			11 51	12 08			12 21	12 38	
Brookmans Park d				10 41				11 11				11 41				12 11				12 41	
Welham Green d				10 43				11 13				11 43				12 13				12 43	
Hatfield d			10 27	10 46			10 57	11 16			11 27	11 46			11 57	12 17			12 27	12 46	
Welwyn Garden City d			10 31	10a51			11 01	11a21			11 31	11a51			12 01	12a22			12 31	12a51	
Welwyn North d			10 34				11 04				11 34				12 04				12 34		
Knebworth d			10 38				11 08				11 38				12 08				12 38		
Bowes Park d		10 11				10 41				11 11				11 41				12 11			
Palmers Green d		10 13				10 43				11 13				11 43				12 13			
Winchmore Hill d		10 15				10 46				11 15				11 45				12 15			
Grange Park d		10 17				10 48				11 17				11 47				12 17			
Enfield Chase d		10 19				10 50				11 19				11 49				12 19			
Gordon Hill d		10 21				10 52				11 21				11 51				12 21			
Crews Hill d		10 24				10 55				11 24				11 54				12 24			
Cuffley d		10 27				10 58				11 27				11 57				12 27			
Bayford d		10 32				11 03				11 32				12 02				12 32			
Hertford North d		10a38				11 08				11a38				12 07				12a38			
Watton-at-Stone d						11 13								12 13							
Stevenage d	10 16		10 42		10 46	11a21	11 12		11 16		11 42		11 46	12a20	12 12		12 16		12 42		12 46
Hitchin d	10 21		10 47		10a51		11a17		11 21		11 47		11a51		12a17		12 21		12 47		12a51
Letchworth Garden City a	10 25		10 51						11 25		11 51						12 25		12 51		

	FC	FC 1	FC	FC 1	FC	FC 1	FC	FC 1	FC	FC 1	FC	FC 1	FC	FC 1	FC	FC 1	FC	FC 1	FC	FC 1	FC	FC 1
London Kings Cross ⊖ d	12 26	12 36	12 41	12 52	12 56	13 06	13 11	13 22	13 26	13 36	13 41	13 52	13 56	14 06	14 11	14 22	14 26	14 36	14 41	14 52	14 56	15 06
Moorgate ⊖ d																						
Old Street ⊖ d																						
Essex Road d																						
Highbury & Islington ⊖ d																						
Drayton Park d																						
Finsbury Park ⊖ d	12 32	12 41	12 47	12 57	13 02	13 11	13 17	13 27	13 32	13 42	13 47	13 57	14 02	14 11	14 17	14 27	14 32	14 41	14 47	14 56	15 02	15 11
Harringay d	12 34		12 49		13 04		13 19		13 34		13 49		14 04		14 19		14 34		14 49		15 04	
Hornsey d	12 36		12 51		13 06		13 21		13 36		13 51		14 06		14 21		14 36		14 51		15 06	
Alexandra Palace d	12 38		12 53		13 08		13 23		13 38		13 53		14 08		14 23		14 38		14 53		15 08	
New Southgate d			12 56				13 26				13 56				14 26				14 56			
Oakleigh Park d			12 59				13 29				13 59				14 30				14 59			
New Barnet d			13 01				13 31				14 01				14 32				15 01			
Hadley Wood d			13 04				13 34				14 04				14 34				15 04			
Potters Bar d		12 51	13 08			13 21	13 38			13 52	14 08			14 21	14 38			14 51	15 08			15 21
Brookmans Park d			13 11				13 41				14 11				14 41				15 11			
Welham Green d			13 13				13 43				14 13				14 43				15 13			
Hatfield d		12 57	13 16			13 27	13 46			13 58	14 16			14 27	14 47			14 57	15 16			15 27
Welwyn Garden City d		13 01	13a21			13 31	13a51			14 02	14a21			14 31	14a52			15 01	15a21			15 31
Welwyn North d		13 04				13 34				14 05				14 34				15 04				15 34
Knebworth d		13 08				13 38				14 09				14 38				15 08				15 38
Bowes Park d	12 41				13 11				13 41				14 11				14 41				15 11	
Palmers Green d	12 43				13 13				13 43				14 13				14 43				15 13	
Winchmore Hill d	12 45				13 15				13 45				14 15				14 45				15 15	
Grange Park d	12 47				13 17				13 47				14 17				14 47				15 17	
Enfield Chase d	12 49				13 19				13 49				14 19				14 49				15 19	
Gordon Hill d	12 51				13 21				13 51				14 21				14 51				15 21	
Crews Hill d	12 54				13 24				13 54				14 24				14 54				15 24	
Cuffley d	12 57				13 27				13 57				14 27				14 57				15 27	
Bayford d	13 02				13 32				14 02				14 32				15 02				15 32	
Hertford North d	13 07				13a38				14 07				14a38				15 07				15a38	
Watton-at-Stone d	13 13								14 13								15 13					
Stevenage d	13a20	13 12		13 16		13 42		13 46	14a20	14 12		14 16		14 42		14 46	15a20	15 12		15 16		15 42
Hitchin d		13a17		13 21		13 47		13a51		14a17		14 21		14 47		14a51		15a17		15 21		15 47
Letchworth Garden City a				13 25		13 51						14 25		14 51						15 25		15 51

Table 24

Saturdays
until 10 July

London - Welwyn Garden City, Hertford North and Letchworth Garden City

		FC	FC ■	FC	FC ■	FC	FC ■	FC	FC ■	FC	FC ■	FC	FC ■	FC	FC ■	FC	FC ■	FC	FC ■	FC	FC ■	FC
London Kings Cross ■15 ⊖	d	15 11	15 22	15 26	15 36	15 41	15 52	15 56	16 06	16 11	16 22	16 26	16 36	16 41	16 52	16 56	17 06	17 11	17 22	17 26	17 36	17 41
Moorgate ⊖	d																					
Old Street ⊖	d																					
Essex Road	d																					
Highbury & Islington ⊖	d																					
Drayton Park	d																					
Finsbury Park ⊖	d	15 17	15 27	15 32	15 41	15 47	15 57	16 02	16 11	16 17	16 27	16 32	16 41	16 47	16 57	17 02	17 11	17 17	17 27	17 32	17 41	17 47
Harringay	d	15 19		15 34		15 49		16 04		16 19		16 34		16 49		17 04		17 19		17 34		17 49
Hornsey	d	15 21		15 36		15 51		16 06		16 21		16 36		16 51		17 06		17 21		17 36		17 51
Alexandra Palace	d	15 23		15 38		15 53		16 08		16 23		16 38		16 53		17 08		17 23		17 38		17 53
New Southgate	d	15 26				15 56				16 26				16 56				17 26				17 56
Oakleigh Park	d	15 29				15 59				16 29				16 59				17 29				17 59
New Barnet	d	15 31				16 01				16 31				17 01				17 31				18 01
Hadley Wood	d	15 34				16 04				16 34				17 04				17 34				18 04
Potters Bar	d	15 38			15 51	16 08			16 21	16 38			16 51	17 08			17 21	17 38			17 51	18 08
Brookmans Park	d	15 41				16 11				16 41				17 11				17 41				18 11
Welham Green	d	15 43				16 13				16 43				17 13				17 43				18 13
Hatfield	d	15 46			15 57	16 16			16 27	16 46			16 57	17 16			17 27	17 46			17 57	18 16
Welwyn Garden City ■4	d	15a51			16 01	16a21			16 31	16a51			17 01	17a21			17 31	17a51			18 01	18a21
Welwyn North	d				16 04				16 34				17 04				17 34				18 04	
Knebworth	d				16 08				16 38				17 08				17 38				18 08	
Bowes Park	d			15 41				16 11				16 41				17 11				17 41		
Palmers Green	d			15 43				16 13				16 43				17 13				17 43		
Winchmore Hill	d			15 45				16 15				16 45				17 15				17 45		
Grange Park	d			15 47				16 17				16 47				17 17				17 47		
Enfield Chase	d			15 49				16 19				16 49				17 19				17 49		
Gordon Hill	d			15 51				16 21				16 51				17 21				17 51		
Crews Hill	d			15 54				16 24				16 54				17 24				17 54		
Cuffley	d			15 57				16 27				16 57				17 27				17 57		
Bayford	d			16 02				16 32				17 02				17 32				18 02		
Hertford North	d			16 07				16a38				17 07				17a38				18 07		
Watton-at-Stone	d			16 13								17 13								18 13		
Stevenage ■4	d		15 46	16a20	16 12		16 16		16 42		16 46	17a20	17 12		17 16		17 42		17 46	18a20	18 12	
Hitchin ■4	d		15a51		16a17		16 22		16 47		16a51		17a17		17 21		17 47		17a51		18a17	
Letchworth Garden City	a						16 25		16 51						17 25		17 51					

		FC ■	FC	FC ■	FC	FC ■	FC	FC ■	FC	FC ■	FC	FC ■	FC	FC ■	FC	FC ■	FC	FC ■	FC	FC ■	FC	FC ■	FC
London Kings Cross ■15 ⊖	d	17 52	17 56	18 06	18 11	18 22	18 26	18 36	18 41	18 52	18 56	19 06	19 11	19 22	19 26	19 36	19 41	19 52	19 56	20 06	20 11	20 22	20 26
Moorgate ⊖	d																						
Old Street ⊖	d																						
Essex Road	d																						
Highbury & Islington ⊖	d																						
Drayton Park	d																						
Finsbury Park ⊖	d	17 57	18 02	18 11	18 17	18 27	18 32	18 41	18 47	18 57	19 02	19 11	19 17	19 27	19 32	19 41	19 47	19 57	20 02	20 11	20 17	20 27	20 32
Harringay	d		18 04		18 19		18 34		18 49		19 04		19 19		19 34		19 49		20 04		20 19		20 34
Hornsey	d		18 06		18 21		18 36		18 51		19 06		19 21		19 36		19 51		20 06		20 21		20 36
Alexandra Palace	d		18 08		18 23		18 38		18 53		19 08		19 23		19 38		19 53		20 08		20 23		20 38
New Southgate	d				18 26				18 56				19 26				19 56				20 26		
Oakleigh Park	d				18 29				18 59				19 29				19 59				20 29		
New Barnet	d				18 31				19 01				19 31				20 01				20 31		
Hadley Wood	d				18 34				19 04				19 34				20 04				20 34		
Potters Bar	d			18 21	18 38			18 51	19 08			19 21	19 38			19 51	20 08			20 21	20 38		
Brookmans Park	d				18 41				19 11				19 41				20 11				20 41		
Welham Green	d				18 43				19 13				19 43				20 13				20 43		
Hatfield	d			18 27	18 46			18 57	19 16			19 27	19 46			19 57	20 16			20 27	20 46		
Welwyn Garden City ■4	d			18 31	18a51			19 01	19a21			19 31	19a51			20 01	20a21			20 31	20a51		
Welwyn North	d			18 34				19 04				19 34				20 04				20 34			
Knebworth	d			18 38				19 08				19 38				20 08				20 38			
Bowes Park	d		18 11				18 41				19 11				19 41				20 11				20 41
Palmers Green	d		18 13				18 43				19 13				19 43				20 13				20 43
Winchmore Hill	d		18 15				18 45				19 15				19 45				20 15				20 45
Grange Park	d		18 17				18 47				19 17				19 47				20 17				20 47
Enfield Chase	d		18 19				18 49				19 19				19 49				20 19				20 49
Gordon Hill	d		18 21				18 51				19 21				19 51				20 21				20 51
Crews Hill	d		18 24				18 54				19 24				19 54				20 24				20 54
Cuffley	d		18 27				18 57				19 27				19 57				20 27				20 57
Bayford	d		18 32				19 02				19 32				20 02				20 32				21 02
Hertford North	d		18a38				19 07				19a38				20 07				20a38				21 07
Watton-at-Stone	d						19 13								20 13								21 13
Stevenage ■4	d	18 15		18 42		18 46	19a20	19 12		19 16		19 42		19 46	20a20	20 12		20 16		20 42		20 46	21a20
Hitchin ■4	d	18 21		18 47		18a51		19a17		19 21		19 47		19a51		20a17		20 21		20 47		20a51	
Letchworth Garden City	a	18 25		18 51						19 25		19 51						20 25		20 51			

Table 24

Saturdays
until 10 July

London - Welwyn Garden City, Hertford North and Letchworth Garden City

		FC ■	FC	FC ■	FC	FC ■	FC	FC ■	FC	FC ■	FC	FC ■	FC	FC ■	FC	FC ■	FC	FC ■	FC	FC ■	FC	FC ■	FC
London Kings Cross ■15 ⊖	d	20 36	20 41	20 52	20 56	21 06	21 11	21 22	21 26	21 36	21 41	21 52	21 56	22 06	22 11	22 22	22 26	22 36	22 41	22 52	22 56	23 06	23 11
Moorgate ⊖	d																						
Old Street ⊖	d																						
Essex Road	d																						
Highbury & Islington ⊖	d																						
Drayton Park	d																						
Finsbury Park ⊖	d	20 41	20 47	20 57	21 02	21 11	21 17	21 27	21 32	21 41	21 47	21 57	22 02	22 11	22 17	22 27	22 32	22 41	22 47	22 57	23 02	23 11	23 17
Harringay	d		20 49		21 04		21 19		21 34		21 49		22 04		22 19		22 34		22 49		23 04		23 19
Hornsey	d		20 51		21 06		21 21		21 36		21 51		22 06		22 21		22 36		22 51		23 06		23 21
Alexandra Palace	d		20 53		21 08		21 23		21 38		21 53		22 08		22 23		22 38		22 53		23 08		23 23
New Southgate	d		20 56				21 26				21 56				22 26				22 56				23 26
Oakleigh Park	d		20 59				21 29				21 59				22 29				22 59				23 29
New Barnet	d		21 01				21 31				22 01				22 31				23 01				23 31
Hadley Wood	d		21 04				21 34				22 04				22 34				23 04				23 34
Potters Bar	d	20 51	21 08			21 21	21 38			21 51	22 08			22 21	22 38			22 51	23 08			23 21	23 38
Brookmans Park	d		21 11				21 41				22 11				22 41				23 11				23 41
Welham Green	d		21 13				21 43				22 13				22 43				23 13				23 43
Hatfield	d	20 57	21 16			21 27	21 46			21 57	22 16			22 27	22 46			22 57	23 16			23 27	23 46
Welwyn Garden City ■4	d	21 01	21a21			21 31	21a51			22 01	22a21			22 31	22a51			23 01	23a21			23 31	23a53
Welwyn North	d	21 04				21 34				22 04				22 34				23 04				23 34	
Knebworth	d	21 08				21 38				22 08				22 38				23 08				23 38	
Bowes Park	d				21 11				21 41				22 11				22 41				23 11		
Palmers Green	d				21 13				21 43				22 13				22 43				23 13		
Winchmore Hill	d				21 15				21 45				22 15				22 45				23 15		
Grange Park	d				21 17				21 47				22 17				22 47				23 17		
Enfield Chase	d				21 19				21 49				22 19				22 49				23 19		
Gordon Hill	d				21 21				21 51				22 21				22 51				23 21		
Crews Hill	d				21 24				21 54				22 24				22 54				23 24		
Cuffley	d				21 27				21 57				22 27				22 57				23 27		
Bayford	d				21 32				22 02				22 32				23 02				23 32		
Hertford North	d				21a38				22 07				22a38				23 07				23a38		
Watton-at-Stone	d								22 13								23 13						
Stevenage ■4	d	21 12		21 16		21 42		21 46	22a20	22 12		22 16		22 42		22 46	23a20	23 12		23 16		23 42	
Hitchin ■4	d	21a17		21 21		21 47		21a51		22a17		22 21		22 47		22a54		23 20		23a24		23 50	
Letchworth Garden City	a			21 25		21 51						22 25		22 51				23 26				23 54	

		FC ■	FC	FC	FC ■
London Kings Cross ■15 ⊖	d	23 22	23 26	23 41	23 52
Moorgate ⊖	d				
Old Street ⊖	d				
Essex Road	d				
Highbury & Islington ⊖	d				
Drayton Park	d				
Finsbury Park ⊖	d	23 27	23 32	23 47	23 57
Harringay	d		23 34	23 49	
Hornsey	d		23 36	23 51	
Alexandra Palace	d		23 38	23 53	
New Southgate	d			23 56	
Oakleigh Park	d			23 59	
New Barnet	d			00 01	
Hadley Wood	d			00 04	
Potters Bar	d			00 08	
Brookmans Park	d			00 11	
Welham Green	d			00 13	
Hatfield	d			00 16	
Welwyn Garden City ■4	d			00b31	
Welwyn North	d			00 34	
Knebworth	d			00 38	
Bowes Park	d		23 41		
Palmers Green	d		23 43		
Winchmore Hill	d		23 45		
Grange Park	d		23 47		
Enfield Chase	d		23 49		
Gordon Hill	d		23 51		
Crews Hill	d		23 54		
Cuffley	d		23 57		
Bayford	d		00 02		
Hertford North	d		00 07		
Watton-at-Stone	d		00 13		
Stevenage ■4	d	23 56	00 20	00 42	00 26
Hitchin ■4	d	00a04	00 28	00 50	00s34
Letchworth Garden City	a		00 35	00 59	

b arr. 0024

London - Welwyn Garden City, Hertford North and Letchworth Garden City

		FC	FC ■	FC	FC ■	FC	FC	FC ■	FC ■	FC		FC ■	FC ■	FC	FC ■	FC	FC ■	FC	FC ■	FC		FC ■	FC	FC ■	FC
London Kings Cross ■15 ⊖	d	23p26	23p36	23p41	00 04	00 06	00 11	00 36	01 06	01 11		01 36	05 22	05 26	05 45	05 56	06 06	06 11	06 22	06 26		06 36	06 41	06 52	06 56
Moorgate ⊖	d																								
Old Street ⊖	d																								
Essex Road	d																								
Highbury & Islington ⊖	d																								
Drayton Park	d																								
Finsbury Park ⊖	d	23p32	23p41	23p47	00 09	00 12	00 17	00 41	01 11	01 17		01 41	05 27	05 32	05 50	06 02	06 11	06 17	06 27	06 32		06 41	06 47	06 57	07 02
Harringay	d	23p34		23p49		00 14	00 19			01 19				05 34		06 04		06 19		06 34			06 49		07 04
Hornsey	d	23p36		23p51		00 16	00 21			01 21				05 36		06 06		06 21		06 36			06 51		07 06
Alexandra Palace	d	23p38		23p53		00 18	00 23		01 16	01 23		01 45		05 38		06 08		06 23		06 38			06 53		07 08
New Southgate	d			23p56			00 26			01 26								06 26					06 56		
Oakleigh Park	d			23p59			00 29			01 29		01 50						06 29					06 59		
New Barnet	d			00 01			00 31			01 31		01 52						06 31					07 01		
Hadley Wood	d			00 04			00 34			01 34		01 54						06 34					07 04		
Potters Bar	d		23p51	00 08			00 38	00 51		01 38		01 58	05 37				06 21	06 38				06 51	07 08		
Brookmans Park	d			00 11			00 41			01 41								06 41					07 11		
Welham Green	d			00 13			00 43			01 43								06 43					07 13		
Hatfield	d		23p57	00 16			00 46	00 57		01 46		02 04	05 43				06 27	06 46				06 57	07 16		
Welwyn Garden City ■4	d		00 01	00a24			00a54	01 01		01a54		02 08	05 47				06 31	06a51				07 01	07a21		
Welwyn North	d		00 04					01s04				02s11	05 50				06 34					07 04			
Knebworth	d		00 08					01s08				02s15	05 54				06 38					07 08			
Bowes Park	d	23p41				00 21								05 41		06 11				06 41					07 11
Palmers Green	d	23p43				00 23			01 19					05 43		06 13				06 43					07 13
Winchmore Hill	d	23p45				00 25			01 21					05 45		06 15				06 45					07 15
Grange Park	d	23p47				00 27								05 47		06 17				06 47					07 17
Enfield Chase	d	23p49				00 29			01 24					05 49		06 19				06 49					07 19
Gordon Hill	d	23p51				00 31			01 26					05 51		06 21				06 51					07 21
Crews Hill	d	23p54				00 34								05 54		06 24				06 54					07 24
Cuffley	d	23p57				00 37			01 30					05 57		06 27				06 57					07 27
Bayford	d	00 02				00 42								06 02		06 32				07 02					07 32
Hertford North	d	00 07				00 47			01 38					06a08		06a38				07 07					07a38
Watton-at-Stone	d	00 13				00 53														07 13					
Stevenage ■4	d	00 20	00 12		00 31	01 00		01 12	01 47			02 18	05 58		06 08		06 42		06 46	07a20		07 12		07 16	
Hitchin ■4	d	00 26	00 20		00 39	01 06		01a17	01 52			02a23	06a06		06 13		06 47		06a51			07a17		07 21	
Letchworth Garden City	a	00 36	00 29		00 42	01 16			02 06						06 16		06 51							07 25	

		FC ■	FC	FC ■	FC	FC ■		FC	FC ■	FC	FC ■	FC	FC ■	FC	FC ■	FC		FC ■	FC	FC ■	FC	FC ■	FC	FC ■	FC
London Kings Cross ■15 ⊖	d	07 06	07 11	07 22	07 26	07 36		07 41	07 52	07 56	08 06	08 11	08 22	08 26	08 36	08 41		08 52	08 56	09 06	09 11	09 22	09 26	09 36	09 41
Moorgate ⊖	d																								
Old Street ⊖	d																								
Essex Road	d																								
Highbury & Islington ⊖	d																								
Drayton Park	d																								
Finsbury Park ⊖	d	07 11	07 17	07 27	07 32	07 41		07 47	07 57	08 02	08 11	08 17	08 27	08 32	08 41	08 47		08 57	09 02	09 11	09 17	09 27	09 32	09 41	09 47
Harringay	d		07 19		07 34			07 49		08 04		08 19		08 34		08 49			09 04		09 19		09 34		09 49
Hornsey	d		07 21		07 36			07 51		08 06		08 21		08 36		08 51			09 06		09 21		09 36		09 51
Alexandra Palace	d		07 23		07 38			07 53		08 08		08 23		08 38		08 53			09 08		09 23		09 38		09 53
New Southgate	d		07 26					07 56				08 26				08 56					09 26				09 56
Oakleigh Park	d		07 29					07 59				08 29				08 59					09 29				09 59
New Barnet	d		07 31					08 01				08 31				09 01					09 31				10 01
Hadley Wood	d		07 34					08 04				08 34				09 04					09 34				10 04
Potters Bar	d	07 21	07 38			07 51		08 08			08 21	08 38			08 51	09 08				09 21	09 38			09 51	10 08
Brookmans Park	d		07 41					08 11				08 41				09 11					09 41				10 11
Welham Green	d		07 43					08 13				08 43				09 13					09 43				10 13
Hatfield	d	07 27	07 46			07 57		08 16			08 27	08 46			08 57	09 16				09 27	09 46			09 57	10 16
Welwyn Garden City ■4	d	07 31	07a51			08 01		08a21			08 31	08a51			09 01	09a21				09 31	09a51			10 01	10a21
Welwyn North	d	07 34				08 04					08 34				09 04					09 34				10 04	
Knebworth	d	07 38				08 08					08 38				09 08					09 38				10 08	
Bowes Park	d				07 41					08 11				08 41					09 11				09 41		
Palmers Green	d				07 43					08 13				08 43					09 13				09 43		
Winchmore Hill	d				07 45					08 15				08 45					09 15				09 45		
Grange Park	d				07 47					08 17				08 47					09 17				09 47		
Enfield Chase	d				07 49					08 19				08 49					09 19				09 49		
Gordon Hill	d				07 51					08 21				08 51					09 21				09 51		
Crews Hill	d				07 54					08 24				08 54					09 24				09 54		
Cuffley	d				07 57					08 27				08 57					09 27				09 57		
Bayford	d				08 02					08 32				09 02					09 32				10 02		
Hertford North	d				08 07					08a38				09 07					09a38				10 07		
Watton-at-Stone	d				08 13									09 13									10 13		
Stevenage ■4	d	07 42		07 46	08a20	08 12			08 16		08 42		08 46	09a20	09 12			09 16		09 42		09 46	10a20	10 12	
Hitchin ■4	d	07 47		07a51		08a17			08 21		08 47		08a51		09a17			09 21		09 47		09a51		10a17	
Letchworth Garden City	a	07 51							08 25		08 51							09 25		09 51					

Table 24

Saturdays

17 July to 04 September

London - Welwyn Garden City, Hertford North and Letchworth Garden City

		FC ■		FC	FC ■	FC	FC ■	FC	FC ■	FC	FC ■	FC		FC ■	FC	FC ■	FC	FC ■	FC	FC ■	FC	FC ■		FC	FC ■
London Kings Cross ■15 ⊖	d	09 52		09 56	10 06	10 11	10 22	10 26	10 36	10 41	10 52	10 56		11 06	11 11	11 22	11 26	11 36	11 41	11 52	11 56	12 06		12 11	12 22
Moorgate ⊖	d																								
Old Street ⊖	d																								
Essex Road	d																								
Highbury & Islington ⊖	d																								
Drayton Park	d																								
Finsbury Park ⊖	d	09 57		10 02	10 11	10 17	10 27	10 32	10 41	10 47	10 57	11 02		11 11	11 17	11 27	11 32	11 41	11 47	11 57	12 02	12 11		12 17	12 27
Harringay	d			10 04		10 19		10 34		10 49		11 04			11 19		11 34		11 49		12 04			12 19	
Hornsey	d			10 06		10 21		10 36		10 51		11 06			11 21		11 36		11 51		12 06			12 21	
Alexandra Palace	d			10 08		10 23		10 39		10 53		11 08			11 23		11 38		11 53		12 08			12 23	
New Southgate	d					10 26				10 56					11 26				11 56					12 26	
Oakleigh Park	d					10 29				10 59					11 29				12 00					12 29	
New Barnet	d					10 31				11 01					11 31				12 02					12 31	
Hadley Wood	d					10 34				11 04					11 34				12 04					12 34	
Potters Bar	d				10 21	10 38			10 51	11 08				11 21	11 38			11 51	12 08			12 21		12 38	
Brookmans Park	d					10 41				11 11					11 41				12 11					12 41	
Welham Green	d					10 43				11 13					11 43				12 13					12 43	
Hatfield	d				10 27	10 46			10 57	11 16				11 27	11 46			11 57	12 17			12 27		12 46	
Welwyn Garden City ■4	d				10 31	10a51			11 01	11a21				11 31	11a51			12 01	12a22			12 31		12a51	
Welwyn North	d				10 34				11 04					11 34				12 04				12 34			
Knebworth	d				10 38				11 08					11 38				12 08				12 38			
Bowes Park	d			10 11				10 41				11 11					11 41				12 11				
Palmers Green	d			10 13				10 43				11 13					11 43				12 13				
Winchmore Hill	d			10 15				10 46				11 15					11 45				12 15				
Grange Park	d			10 17				10 48				11 17					11 47				12 17				
Enfield Chase	d			10 19				10 50				11 19					11 49				12 19				
Gordon Hill	d			10 21				10 52				11 21					11 51				12 21				
Crews Hill	d			10 24				10 55				11 24					11 54				12 24				
Cuffley	d			10 27				10 58				11 27					11 57				12 27				
Bayford	d			10 32				11 03				11 32					12 02				12 32				
Hertford North	d			10a38				11 08				11a38					12 07				12a38				
Watton-at-Stone	d							11 13									12 13								
Stevenage ■4	d	10 16			10 42		10 46	11a21	11 12		11 16			11 42		11 46	12a20	12 12		12 16		12 42			12 46
Hitchin ■4	d	10 21			10 47		10a51		11a17		11 21			11 47		11a51		12a17		12 21		12 47			12a51
Letchworth Garden City	a	10 25			10 51						11 25			11 51						12 25		12 51			

		FC	FC ■	FC	FC ■	FC	FC ■	FC		FC ■	FC	FC ■	FC	FC ■	FC	FC ■	FC	FC ■		FC	FC ■	FC	FC ■	FC ■	FC
London Kings Cross ■15 ⊖	d	12 26	12 36	12 41	12 52	12 56	13 06	13 11		13 22	13 26	13 36	13 41	13 52	13 56	14 06	14 11	14 22		14 26	14 36	14 41	14 52	15 09	15 14
Moorgate ⊖	d																								
Old Street ⊖	d																								
Essex Road	d																								
Highbury & Islington ⊖	d																								
Drayton Park	d																								
Finsbury Park ⊖	d	12 32	12 41	12 47	12 57	13 02	13 11	13 17		13 27	13 32	13 42	13 47	13 57	14 02	14 11	14 17	14 28		14 32	14 41	14 47	14 56	15 14	15 20
Harringay	d	12 34		12 49		13 04		13 19			13 34		13 49		14 04		14 19			14 34		14 49			15 22
Hornsey	d	12 36		12 51		13 06		13 21			13 36		13 51		14 06		14 21			14 36		14 51			15 24
Alexandra Palace	d	12 38		12 53		13 08		13 23			13 38		13 53		14 08		14 23			14 38		14 53			15 26
New Southgate	d			12 56				13 26					13 56				14 26					14 56			
Oakleigh Park	d			12 59				13 29					13 59				14 29					14 59			
New Barnet	d			13 01				13 31					14 01				14 31					15 01			
Hadley Wood	d			13 04				13 34					14 04				14 34					15 04			
Potters Bar	d		12 51	13 08			13 21	13 38				13 52	14 08			14 21	14 38				14 51	15 08			
Brookmans Park	d			13 11				13 41					14 11				14 41					15 11			
Welham Green	d			13 13				13 43					14 13				14 43					15 13			
Hatfield	d		12 57	13 16			13 27	13 46				13 58	14 16			14 27	14 46				14 57	15 16			
Welwyn Garden City ■4	d		13 01	13a21			13 31	13a51				14 02	14a21			14 31	14a51				15 01	15a21			
Welwyn North	d		13 04				13 34					14 05				14 34					15 04				
Knebworth	d		13 08				13 38					14 09				14 38					15 08				
Bowes Park	d	12 41				13 11					13 41				14 11					14 41					15 29
Palmers Green	d	12 43				13 13					13 43				14 13					14 43					15 31
Winchmore Hill	d	12 45				13 15					13 45				14 15					14 45					15 33
Grange Park	d	12 47				13 17					13 47				14 17					14 47					15 35
Enfield Chase	d	12 49				13 19					13 49				14 19					14 49					15 37
Gordon Hill	d	12 51				13 21					13 51				14 21					14 51					15 39
Crews Hill	d	12 54				13 24					13 54				14 24					14 54					15 42
Cuffley	d	12 57				13 27					13 57				14 27					14 57					15 45
Bayford	d	13 02				13 32					14 02				14 32					15 02					15 50
Hertford North	d	13 07				13a38					14 07				14a38					15 07					15a56
Watton-at-Stone	d	13 13									14 13									15 13					
Stevenage ■4	d	13a20	13 12		13 16		13 42			13 46	14a20	14 12		14 16		14 42		14 46		15 21	15 12		15 16	15 40	
Hitchin ■4	d		13a17		13 21		13 47			13a51		14a17		14 21		14 47		14a51		15 28	15a17		15 21	15a45	
Letchworth Garden City	a				13 25		13 51							14 25		14 51				15 33			15 25		

Table 24

Saturdays

17 July to 04 September

London - Welwyn Garden City, Hertford North and Letchworth Garden City

Station		FC ■	FC ■	FC	FC ■	FC ■	FC	FC ■	FC ■	FC	FC ■	FC ■	FC	FC ■	FC ■	FC	FC ■	FC ■	FC ■	FC	FC ■	FC ■
London Kings Cross 15 ⊖	d	15 38	16 09	16 14	16 38	17 09	17 14	17 38	18 09	18 14	18 38	19 09	19 14	19 38	20 09	20 14	20 38	20 54	21 09	21 14	21 38	21 54
Moorgate ⊖	d																					
Old Street ⊖	d																					
Essex Road	d																					
Highbury & Islington ⊖	d																					
Drayton Park	d																					
Finsbury Park ⊖	d	15 43	16 14	16 20	16 43	17 14	17 20	17 43	18 14	18 20	18 43	19 14	19 20	19 43	20 14	20 20	20 43	20 59	21 14	21 20	21 43	21 59
Harringay	d			16 22			17 22			18 22			19 22			20 22				21 22		
Hornsey	d			16 24			17 24			18 24			19 24			20 24				21 24		
Alexandra Palace	d			16 26			17 26			18 26			19 26			20 26				21 26		
New Southgate	d																					
Oakleigh Park	d																					
New Barnet	d																					
Hadley Wood	d																					
Potters Bar	d																					
Brookmans Park	d																					
Welham Green	d																					
Hatfield	d																					
Welwyn Garden City 4	d																					
Welwyn North	d																					
Knebworth	d																					
Bowes Park	d			16 29			17 29			18 29			19 29			20 29				21 29		
Palmers Green	d			16 31			17 31			18 31			19 31			20 31				21 31		
Winchmore Hill	d			16 33			17 33			18 33			19 33			20 33				21 33		
Grange Park	d			16 35			17 35			18 35			19 35			20 35				21 35		
Enfield Chase	d			16 37			17 37			18 37			19 37			20 37				21 37		
Gordon Hill	d			16 39			17 39			18 39			19 39			20 39				21 39		
Crews Hill	d			16 42			17 42			18 42			19 42			20 42				21 42		
Cuffley	d			16 45			17 45			18 45			19 45			20 45				21 45		
Bayford	d			16 50			17 50			18 50			19 50			20 50				21 50		
Hertford North	d			16a56			17a56			18a56			19a56			20a56				21a56		
Watton-at-Stone	d																					
Stevenage 4	d	16 09	16 40		17 09	17 42		18 09	18 40		19 09	19 40		20 09	20 40		21 09	21 25	21 40		22 09	22 25
Hitchin 4	d	16 14	16a45		17 14	17a47		18 14	18a45		19 14	19a45		20 14	20a45		21 14	21a30	21a45		22 14	22a30
Letchworth Garden City	a	16 18			17 18			18 18			19 18			20 18			21 18				22 18	

Station		FC ■	FC	FC ■	FC ■	FC	FC ■	FC ■
London Kings Cross 15 ⊖	d	22 09	22 14	22 38	23 09	23 14	23 38	23 52
Moorgate ⊖	d							
Old Street ⊖	d							
Essex Road	d							
Highbury & Islington ⊖	d							
Drayton Park	d							
Finsbury Park ⊖	d	22 14	22 20	22 43	23 14	23 20	23 43	23 57
Harringay	d		22 22			23 22		
Hornsey	d		22 24			23 24		
Alexandra Palace	d		22 26			23 26		
New Southgate	d							
Oakleigh Park	d							
New Barnet	d							
Hadley Wood	d							
Potters Bar	d							
Brookmans Park	d							
Welham Green	d							
Hatfield	d							
Welwyn Garden City 4	d							
Welwyn North	d							
Knebworth	d							
Bowes Park	d		22 29			23 29		
Palmers Green	d		22 31			23 31		
Winchmore Hill	d		22 33			23 33		
Grange Park	d		22 35			23 35		
Enfield Chase	d		22 37			23 37		
Gordon Hill	d		22 39			23 39		
Crews Hill	d		22 42			23 42		
Cuffley	d		22 45			23 45		
Bayford	d		22 50			23 50		
Hertford North	d		22a56			23a56		
Watton-at-Stone	d							
Stevenage 4	d	22 40		23 09	23 40		00 08	00 26
Hitchin 4	d	22a45		23 14	23a45		00 11	00a34
Letchworth Garden City	a			23 18			00 16	

Table 24

Saturdays

from 11 September

London - Welwyn Garden City, Hertford North and Letchworth Garden City

Station		FC	FC ■	FC	FC ■	FC	FC	FC ■	FC ■	FC	FC ■	FC ■	FC	FC ■	FC	FC ■	FC	FC ■	FC	FC ■	FC	FC ■	FC
London Kings Cross 15 ⊖	d	23p26	23p36	23p41	00 04	00 06	00 11	00 36	01 06	01 11	01 36	05 22	05 26	05 45	05 56	06 06	06 11	06 22	06 26	06 36	06 41	06 52	06 56
Moorgate ⊖	d																						
Old Street ⊖	d																						
Essex Road	d																						
Highbury & Islington ⊖	d																						
Drayton Park	d																						
Finsbury Park ⊖	d	23p32	23p41	23p47	00 09	00 12	00 17	00 41	01 11	01 17	01 41	05 27	05 32	05 50	06 02	06 11	06 17	06 27	06 32	06 41	06 47	06 57	07 02
Harringay	d	23p34		23p49		00 14	00 19			01 19			05 34		06 04		06 19		06 34		06 49		07 04
Hornsey	d	23p36		23p51		00 16	00 21			01 21			05 36		06 06		06 21		06 36		06 51		07 06
Alexandra Palace	d	23p38		23p53		00 18	00 23		01 16	01 23	01 45		05 38		06 08		06 23		06 38		06 53		07 08
New Southgate	d			23p56			00 26			01 26							06 26				06 56		
Oakleigh Park	d			23p59			00 29			01 29	01 50						06 29				06 59		
New Barnet	d			00 01			00 31			01 31	01 52						06 31				07 01		
Hadley Wood	d			00 04			00 34			01 34	01 54						06 34				07 04		
Potters Bar	d		23p51	00 08			00 38	00 51		01 38	01 58	05 37				06 21	06 38			06 51	07 08		
Brookmans Park	d			00 11			00 41			01 41							06 41				07 11		
Welham Green	d			00 13			00 43			01 43							06 43				07 13		
Hatfield	d		23p57	00 16			00 46	00 57		01 46	02 04	05 43				06 27	06 46			06 57	07 16		
Welwyn Garden City 4	d		00 01	00a24			00a54	01 01		01a54	02 08	05 47				06 31	06a51			07 01	07a21		
Welwyn North	d		00 04					01s04			02s11	05 50				06 34				07 04			
Knebworth	d		00 08					01s08			02s15	05 54				06 38				07 08			
Bowes Park	d	23p41				00 21							05 41		06 11				06 41				07 11
Palmers Green	d	23p43				00 23			01 19				05 43		06 13				06 43				07 13
Winchmore Hill	d	23p45				00 25			01 21				05 45		06 15				06 45				07 15
Grange Park	d	23p47				00 27							05 47		06 17				06 47				07 17
Enfield Chase	d	23p49				00 29			01 24				05 49		06 19				06 49				07 19
Gordon Hill	d	23p51				00 31			01 26				05 51		06 21				06 51				07 21
Crews Hill	d	23p54				00 34							05 54		06 24				06 54				07 24
Cuffley	d	23p57				00 37			01 30				05 57		06 27				06 57				07 27
Bayford	d	00 02				00 42							06 02		06 32				07 02				07 32
Hertford North	d	00 07				00 47			01 38				06a08		06a38				07 07				07a38
Watton-at-Stone	d	00 13				00 53													07 13				
Stevenage 4	d	00 20	00 12		00 31	01 00		01 12	01 47		02 18	05 58		06 08		06 42		06 46	07a20	07 12		07 16	
Hitchin 4	d	00 26	00 20		00 39	01 06		01a17	01 52		02a23	06a06		06 13		06 47		06a51		07a17		07 21	
Letchworth Garden City	a	00 36	00 29		00 42	01 16			02 06					06 16		06 51						07 25	

Station		FC ■	FC	FC ■	FC	FC ■	FC	FC ■	FC	FC ■	FC	FC ■	FC	FC ■	FC	FC ■	FC	FC ■	FC	FC ■	FC	FC ■	FC
London Kings Cross 15 ⊖	d	07 06	07 11	07 22	07 26	07 36	07 41	07 52	07 56	08 06	08 11	08 22	08 26	08 36	08 41	08 52	08 56	09 06	09 11	09 22	09 26	09 36	09 41
Moorgate ⊖	d																						
Old Street ⊖	d																						
Essex Road	d																						
Highbury & Islington ⊖	d																						
Drayton Park	d																						
Finsbury Park ⊖	d	07 11	07 17	07 27	07 32	07 41	07 47	07 57	08 02	08 11	08 17	08 27	08 32	08 41	08 47	08 57	09 02	09 11	09 17	09 27	09 32	09 41	09 47
Harringay	d		07 19		07 34		07 49		08 04		08 19		08 34		08 49		09 04		09 19		09 34		09 49
Hornsey	d		07 21		07 36		07 51		08 06		08 21		08 36		08 51		09 06		09 21		09 36		09 51
Alexandra Palace	d		07 23		07 38		07 53		08 08		08 23		08 38		08 53		09 08		09 23		09 38		09 53
New Southgate	d		07 26				07 56				08 26				08 56				09 26				09 56
Oakleigh Park	d		07 29				07 59				08 29				08 59				09 29				09 59
New Barnet	d		07 31				08 01				08 31				09 01				09 31				10 01
Hadley Wood	d		07 34				08 04				08 34				09 04				09 34				10 04
Potters Bar	d	07 21	07 38			07 51	08 08			08 21	08 38			08 51	09 08			09 21	09 38			09 51	10 08
Brookmans Park	d		07 41				08 11				08 41				09 11				09 41				10 11
Welham Green	d		07 43				08 13				08 43				09 13				09 43				10 13
Hatfield	d	07 27	07 46			07 57	08 16			08 27	08 46			08 57	09 16			09 27	09 46			09 57	10 16
Welwyn Garden City 4	d	07 31	07a51			08 01	08a21			08 31	08a51			09 01	09a21			09 31	09a51			10 01	10a21
Welwyn North	d	07 34				08 04				08 34				09 04				09 34				10 04	
Knebworth	d	07 38				08 08				08 38				09 08				09 38				10 08	
Bowes Park	d				07 41				08 11				08 41				09 11				09 41		
Palmers Green	d				07 43				08 13				08 43				09 13				09 43		
Winchmore Hill	d				07 45				08 15				08 45				09 15				09 45		
Grange Park	d				07 47				08 17				08 47				09 17				09 47		
Enfield Chase	d				07 49				08 19				08 49				09 19				09 49		
Gordon Hill	d				07 51				08 21				08 51				09 21				09 51		
Crews Hill	d				07 54				08 24				08 54				09 24				09 54		
Cuffley	d				07 57				08 27				08 57				09 27				09 57		
Bayford	d				08 02				08 32				09 02				09 32				10 02		
Hertford North	d				08 07				08a38				09 07				09a38				10 07		
Watton-at-Stone	d				08 13								09 13								10 13		
Stevenage 4	d	07 42		07 46	08a20	08 12		08 16		08 42		08 46	09a20	09 12		09 16		09 42		09 46	10a20	10 12	
Hitchin 4	d	07 47		07a51		08a17		08 21		08 47		08a51		09a17		09 21		09 47		09a51		10a17	
Letchworth Garden City	a	07 51						08 25		08 51						09 25		09 51					

Table 24

London - Welwyn Garden City, Hertford North and Letchworth Garden City

		FC ■	FC	FC ■	FC	FC ■	FC	FC ■	FC	FC ■	FC	FC ■	FC	FC ■	FC	FC ■	FC	FC ■	FC	FC ■	FC	FC ■
London Kings Cross ■ ⊖	d	09 52	09 56	10 06	10 11	10 22	10 26	10 36	10 41	10 52	10 56	11 06	11 11	11 22	11 26	11 36	11 41	11 52	11 56	12 06	12 11	12 22
Moorgate ⊖	d																					
Old Street ⊖	d																					
Essex Road	d																					
Highbury & Islington ⊖	d																					
Drayton Park	d																					
Finsbury Park ⊖	d	09 57	10 02	10 11	10 17	10 27	10 32	10 41	10 47	10 57	11 02	11 11	11 17	11 27	11 32	11 41	11 47	11 57	12 02	12 11	12 17	12 27
Harringay	d		10 04		10 19		10 34		10 49		11 04		11 19		11 34		11 49		12 04		12 19	
Hornsey	d		10 06		10 21		10 36		10 51		11 06		11 21		11 36		11 51		12 06		12 21	
Alexandra Palace	d		10 08		10 23		10 39		10 53		11 08		11 23		11 38		11 53		12 08		12 23	
New Southgate	d				10 26				10 56				11 26				11 56				12 26	
Oakleigh Park	d				10 29				10 59				11 29				12 00				12 29	
New Barnet	d				10 31				11 01				11 31				12 02				12 31	
Hadley Wood	d				10 34				11 04				11 34				12 04				12 34	
Potters Bar	d			10 21	10 38			10 51	11 08			11 21	11 38			11 51	12 08			12 21	12 38	
Brookmans Park	d				10 41				11 11				11 41				12 11				12 41	
Welham Green	d				10 43				11 13				11 43				12 13				12 43	
Hatfield	d			10 27	10 46			10 57	11 16			11 27	11 46			11 57	12 17			12 27	12 46	
Welwyn Garden City ■	d			10 31	10a51			11 01	11a21			11 31	11a51			12 01	12a22			12 31	12a51	
Welwyn North	d			10 34				11 04				11 34				12 04				12 34		
Knebworth	d			10 38				11 08				11 38				12 08				12 38		
Bowes Park	d		10 11				10 41				11 11				11 41				12 11			
Palmers Green	d		10 13				10 43				11 13				11 43				12 13			
Winchmore Hill	d		10 15				10 46				11 15				11 45				12 15			
Grange Park	d		10 17				10 48				11 17				11 47				12 17			
Enfield Chase	d		10 19				10 50				11 19				11 49				12 19			
Gordon Hill	d		10 21				10 52				11 21				11 51				12 21			
Crews Hill	d		10 24				10 55				11 24				11 54				12 24			
Cuffley	d		10 27				10 58				11 27				11 57				12 27			
Bayford	d		10 32				11 03				11 32				12 02				12 32			
Hertford North	d		10a38				11 08				11a38				12 07				12a38			
Watton-at-Stone	d						11 13								12 13							
Stevenage ■	d	10 16		10 42		10 46	11a21	11 12		11 16		11 42		11 46	12a20	12 12		12 16		12 42		12 46
Hitchin ■	d	10 21		10 47		10a51		11a17		11 21		11 47		11a51		12a17		12 21		12 47		12a51
Letchworth Garden City	a	10 25		10 51						11 25		11 51						12 25		12 51		

		FC	FC ■	FC	FC ■	FC	FC ■	FC	FC ■	FC	FC ■	FC	FC ■	FC	FC ■	FC	FC ■	FC	FC ■	FC	FC ■	FC	FC ■
London Kings Cross ■ ⊖	d	12 26	12 36	12 41	12 52	12 56	13 06	13 11	13 22	13 26	13 36	13 41	13 52	13 56	14 06	14 11	14 22	14 26	14 36	14 41	14 52	14 56	15 06
Moorgate ⊖	d																						
Old Street ⊖	d																						
Essex Road	d																						
Highbury & Islington ⊖	d																						
Drayton Park	d																						
Finsbury Park ⊖	d	12 32	12 41	12 47	12 57	13 02	13 11	13 17	13 27	13 32	13 42	13 47	13 57	14 02	14 11	14 17	14 27	14 32	14 41	14 47	14 56	15 02	15 11
Harringay	d	12 34		12 49		13 04		13 19		13 34		13 49		14 04		14 19		14 34		14 49		15 04	
Hornsey	d	12 36		12 51		13 06		13 21		13 36		13 51		14 06		14 21		14 36		14 51		15 06	
Alexandra Palace	d	12 38		12 53		13 08		13 23		13 38		13 53		14 08		14 23		14 38		14 53		15 08	
New Southgate	d			12 56				13 26				13 56				14 26				14 56			
Oakleigh Park	d			12 59				13 29				13 59				14 30				14 59			
New Barnet	d			13 01				13 31				14 01				14 32				15 01			
Hadley Wood	d			13 04				13 34				14 04				14 34				15 04			
Potters Bar	d		12 51	13 08			13 21	13 38			13 52	14 08			14 21	14 38			14 51	15 08			15 21
Brookmans Park	d			13 11				13 41				14 11				14 41				15 11			
Welham Green	d			13 13				13 43				14 13				14 43				15 13			
Hatfield	d		12 57	13 16			13 27	13 46			13 58	14 16			14 27	14 47			14 57	15 16			15 27
Welwyn Garden City ■	d		13 01	13a21			13 31	13a51			14 02	14a21			14 31	14a52			15 01	15a21			15 31
Welwyn North	d		13 04				13 34				14 05				14 34				15 04				15 34
Knebworth	d		13 08				13 38				14 09				14 38				15 08				15 38
Bowes Park	d	12 41				13 11				13 41				14 11				14 41				15 11	
Palmers Green	d	12 43				13 13				13 43				14 13				14 43				15 13	
Winchmore Hill	d	12 45				13 15				13 45				14 15				14 45				15 15	
Grange Park	d	12 47				13 17				13 47				14 17				14 47				15 17	
Enfield Chase	d	12 49				13 19				13 49				14 19				14 49				15 19	
Gordon Hill	d	12 51				13 21				13 51				14 21				14 51				15 21	
Crews Hill	d	12 54				13 24				13 54				14 24				14 54				15 24	
Cuffley	d	12 57				13 27				13 57				14 27				14 57				15 27	
Bayford	d	13 02				13 32				14 02				14 32				15 02				15 32	
Hertford North	d	13 07				13a38				14 07				14a38				15 07				15a38	
Watton-at-Stone	d	13 13								14 13								15 13					
Stevenage ■	d	13a20	13 12		13 16		13 42		13 46	14a20	14 12		14 16		14 42		14 46	15a20	15 12		15 16		15 42
Hitchin ■	d		13a17		13 21		13 47		13a51		14a17		14 21		14 47		14a51		15a17		15 21		15 47
Letchworth Garden City	a				13 25		13 51						14 25		14 51						15 25		15 51

Table 24

London - Welwyn Garden City, Hertford North and Letchworth Garden City

		FC	FC ■	FC	FC ■	FC	FC ■	FC	FC ■	FC	FC ■	FC	FC ■	FC	FC ■	FC	FC ■	FC	FC ■	FC	FC ■	FC
London Kings Cross ■ ⊖	d	15 11	15 22	15 26	15 36	15 41	15 52	15 56	16 06	16 11	16 22	16 26	16 36	16 41	16 52	16 56	17 06	17 11	17 22	17 26	17 36	17 41
Moorgate ⊖	d																					
Old Street ⊖	d																					
Essex Road	d																					
Highbury & Islington ⊖	d																					
Drayton Park	d																					
Finsbury Park ⊖	d	15 17	15 27	15 32	15 41	15 47	15 57	16 02	16 11	16 17	16 27	16 32	16 41	16 47	16 57	17 02	17 11	17 17	17 27	17 32	17 41	17 47
Harringay	d	15 19		15 34		15 49		16 04		16 19		16 34		16 49		17 04		17 19		17 34		17 49
Hornsey	d	15 21		15 36		15 51		16 06		16 21		16 36		16 51		17 06		17 21		17 36		17 51
Alexandra Palace	d	15 23		15 38		15 53		16 08		16 23		16 38		16 53		17 08		17 23		17 38		17 53
New Southgate	d	15 26				15 56				16 26				16 56				17 26				17 56
Oakleigh Park	d	15 29				15 59				16 29				16 59				17 29				17 59
New Barnet	d	15 31				16 01				16 31				17 01				17 31				18 01
Hadley Wood	d	15 34				16 04				16 34				17 04				17 34				18 04
Potters Bar	d	15 38			15 51	16 08			16 21	16 38			16 51	17 08			17 21	17 38			17 51	18 08
Brookmans Park	d	15 41				16 11				16 41				17 11				17 41				18 11
Welham Green	d	15 43				16 13				16 43				17 13				17 43				18 13
Hatfield	d	15 46			15 57	16 16			16 27	16 46			16 57	17 16			17 27	17 46			17 57	18 16
Welwyn Garden City ■	d	15a51			16 01	16a21			16 31	16a51			17 01	17a21			17 31	17a51			18 01	18a21
Welwyn North	d				16 04				16 34				17 04				17 34				18 04	
Knebworth	d				16 08				16 38				17 08				17 38				18 08	
Bowes Park	d			15 41				16 11				16 41				17 11				17 41		
Palmers Green	d			15 43				16 13				16 43				17 13				17 43		
Winchmore Hill	d			15 45				16 15				16 45				17 15				17 45		
Grange Park	d			15 47				16 17				16 47				17 17				17 47		
Enfield Chase	d			15 49				16 19				16 49				17 19				17 49		
Gordon Hill	d			15 51				16 21				16 51				17 21				17 51		
Crews Hill	d			15 54				16 24				16 54				17 24				17 54		
Cuffley	d			15 57				16 27				16 57				17 27				17 57		
Bayford	d			16 02				16 32				17 02				17 32				18 02		
Hertford North	d			16 07				16a38				17 07				17a38				18 07		
Watton-at-Stone	d			16 13								17 13								18 13		
Stevenage ■	d		15 46	16a20	16 12		16 16		16 42		16 46	17a20	17 12		17 16		17 42		17 46	18a20	18 12	
Hitchin ■	d		15a51		16a17		16 22		16 47		16a51		17a17		17 21		17 47		17a51		18a17	
Letchworth Garden City	a						16 25		16 51						17 25		17 51					

		FC ■	FC	FC ■	FC	FC ■	FC	FC ■	FC	FC ■	FC	FC ■	FC	FC ■	FC	FC ■	FC	FC ■	FC	FC ■	FC	FC ■	FC
London Kings Cross ■ ⊖	d	17 52	17 56	18 06	18 11	18 22	18 26	18 36	18 41	18 52	18 56	19 06	19 11	19 22	19 26	19 36	19 41	19 52	19 56	20 06	20 11	20 22	20 26
Moorgate ⊖	d																						
Old Street ⊖	d																						
Essex Road	d																						
Highbury & Islington ⊖	d																						
Drayton Park	d																						
Finsbury Park ⊖	d	17 57	18 02	18 11	18 17	18 27	18 32	18 41	18 47	18 57	19 02	19 11	19 17	19 27	19 32	19 41	19 47	19 57	20 02	20 11	20 17	20 27	20 32
Harringay	d		18 04		18 19		18 34		18 49		19 04		19 19		19 34		19 49		20 04		20 19		20 34
Hornsey	d		18 06		18 21		18 36		18 51		19 06		19 21		19 36		19 51		20 06		20 21		20 36
Alexandra Palace	d		18 08		18 23		18 38		18 53		19 08		19 23		19 38		19 53		20 08		20 23		20 38
New Southgate	d				18 26				18 56				19 26				19 56				20 26		
Oakleigh Park	d				18 29				18 59				19 29				19 59				20 29		
New Barnet	d				18 31				19 01				19 31				20 01				20 31		
Hadley Wood	d				18 34				19 04				19 34				20 04				20 34		
Potters Bar	d			18 21	18 38			18 51	19 08			19 21	19 38			19 51	20 08			20 21	20 38		
Brookmans Park	d				18 41				19 11				19 41				20 11				20 41		
Welham Green	d				18 43				19 13				19 43				20 13				20 43		
Hatfield	d			18 27	18 46			18 57	19 16			19 27	19 46			19 57	20 16			20 27	20 46		
Welwyn Garden City ■	d			18 31	18a51			19 01	19a21			19 31	19a51			20 01	20a21			20 31	20a51		
Welwyn North	d			18 34				19 04				19 34				20 04				20 34			
Knebworth	d			18 38				19 08				19 38				20 08				20 38			
Bowes Park	d		18 11				18 41				19 11				19 41				20 11				20 41
Palmers Green	d		18 13				18 43				19 13				19 43				20 13				20 43
Winchmore Hill	d		18 15				18 45				19 15				19 45				20 15				20 45
Grange Park	d		18 17				18 47				19 17				19 47				20 17				20 47
Enfield Chase	d		18 19				18 49				19 19				19 49				20 19				20 49
Gordon Hill	d		18 21				18 51				19 21				19 51				20 21				20 51
Crews Hill	d		18 24				18 54				19 24				19 54				20 24				20 54
Cuffley	d		18 27				18 57				19 27				19 57				20 27				20 57
Bayford	d		18 32				19 02				19 32				20 02				20 32				21 02
Hertford North	d		18a38				19 07				19a38				20 07				20a38				21 07
Watton-at-Stone	d						19 13								20 13								21 13
Stevenage ■	d	18 15		18 42		18 46	19a20	19 12		19 16		19 42		19 46	20a20	20 12		20 16		20 42		20 46	21a20
Hitchin ■	d	18 21		18 47		18a51		19a17		19 21		19 47		19a51		20a17		20 21		20a47		20a51	
Letchworth Garden City	a	18 25		18 51						19 25		19 51						20 25		20 51			

Table 24

Saturdays from 11 September

London - Welwyn Garden City, Hertford North and Letchworth Garden City

	FC ■	FC	FC ■	FC	FC ■	FC	FC ■	FC	FC ■	FC	FC ■
London Kings Cross ⊖ d	20 36	20 41	20 52	20 56	21 06	21 11	21 22	21 26	21 36	21 41	21 52
Moorgate ⊖ d											
Old Street ⊖ d											
Essex Road d											
Highbury & Islington ⊖ d											
Drayton Park d											
Finsbury Park ⊖ d	20 41	20 47	20 57	21 02	21 11	21 17	21 27	21 32	21 41	21 47	21 57
Harringay d		20 49		21 04		21 19		21 34		21 49	
Hornsey d		20 51		21 06		21 21		21 36		21 51	
Alexandra Palace d		20 53		21 08		21 23		21 38		21 53	
New Southgate d		20 56				21 26				21 56	
Oakleigh Park d		20 59				21 29				21 59	
New Barnet d		21 01				21 31				22 01	
Hadley Wood d		21 04				21 34				22 04	
Potters Bar d	20 51	21 08			21 21	21 38			21 51	22 08	
Brookmans Park d		21 11				21 41				22 11	
Welham Green d		21 13				21 43				22 13	
Hatfield d	20 57	21 16			21 27	21 46			21 57	22 16	
Welwyn Garden City ■ d	21 01	21a21			21 31	21a51			22 01	22a21	
Welwyn North d	21 04				21 34				22 04		
Knebworth d	21 08				21 38				22 08		
Bowes Park d				21 11				21 41			
Palmers Green d				21 13				21 43			
Winchmore Hill d				21 15				21 45			
Grange Park d				21 17				21 47			
Enfield Chase d				21 19				21 49			
Gordon Hill d				21 21				21 51			
Crews Hill d				21 24				21 54			
Cuffley d				21 27				21 57			
Bayford d				21 32				22 02			
Hertford North d				21a38				22 07			
Watton-at-Stone d								22 13			
Stevenage ■ d	21 12		21 16		21 42		21 46	22a20	22 12		22 16
Hitchin ■ d	21a17		21 21		21a47		21a51		22a17		22 21
Letchworth Garden City a			21 25		21 51						22 25

	FC	FC ■	FC	FC ■	FC	FC ■	FC	FC ■	FC	FC ■	FC
London Kings Cross ⊖ d	21 56	22 06	22 11	22 22	22 26	22 36	22 41	22 52	22 56	23 06	23 11
Moorgate ⊖ d											
Old Street ⊖ d											
Essex Road d											
Highbury & Islington ⊖ d											
Drayton Park d											
Finsbury Park ⊖ d	22 02	22 11	22 17	22 27	22 32	22 41	22 47	22 57	23 02	23 11	23 17
Harringay d	22 04		22 19		22 34		22 49		23 04		23 19
Hornsey d	22 06		22 21		22 36		22 51		23 06		23 21
Alexandra Palace d	22 08		22 23		22 38		22 53		23 08		23 23
New Southgate d			22 26				22 56				23 26
Oakleigh Park d			22 29				22 59				23 29
New Barnet d			22 31				23 01				23 31
Hadley Wood d			22 34				23 04				23 34
Potters Bar d		22 21	22 38			22 51	23 08			23 21	23 38
Brookmans Park d			22 41				23 11				23 41
Welham Green d			22 43				23 13				23 43
Hatfield d		22 27	22 46			22 57	23 16			23 27	23 46
Welwyn Garden City ■ d		22 31	22a51			23 01	23a21			23 31	23a53
Welwyn North d		22 34				23 04				23 34	
Knebworth d		22 38				23 08				23 38	
Bowes Park d	22 11				22 41				23 11		
Palmers Green d	22 13				22 43				23 13		
Winchmore Hill d	22 15				22 45				23 15		
Grange Park d	22 17				22 47				23 17		
Enfield Chase d	22 19				22 49				23 19		
Gordon Hill d	22 21				22 51				23 21		
Crews Hill d	22 24				22 54				23 24		
Cuffley d	22 27				22 57				23 27		
Bayford d	22 32				23 02				23 32		
Hertford North d	22a38				23 07				23a38		
Watton-at-Stone d					23 13						
Stevenage ■ d		22 42		22 46	23a20	23 12		23 16		23 42	
Hitchin ■ d		22 47		22a54		23 20		23a24		23 50	
Letchworth Garden City a		22 51				23 26				23 54	

	FC ■	FC	FC	FC ■
London Kings Cross ⊖ d	23 22	23 26	23 41	23 52
Moorgate ⊖ d				
Old Street ⊖ d				
Essex Road d				
Highbury & Islington ⊖ d				
Drayton Park d				
Finsbury Park ⊖ d	23 27	23 32	23 47	23 57
Harringay d		23 34	23 49	
Hornsey d		23 36	23 51	
Alexandra Palace d		23 38	23 53	
New Southgate d			23 56	
Oakleigh Park d			23 59	
New Barnet d			00 01	
Hadley Wood d			00 04	
Potters Bar d			00 08	
Brookmans Park d			00 11	
Welham Green d			00 13	
Hatfield d			00 16	
Welwyn Garden City ■ d			00b31	
Welwyn North d			00 34	
Knebworth d			00 38	
Bowes Park d		23 41		
Palmers Green d		23 43		
Winchmore Hill d		23 45		
Grange Park d		23 47		
Enfield Chase d		23 49		
Gordon Hill d		23 51		
Crews Hill d		23 54		
Cuffley d		23 57		
Bayford d		00 02		
Hertford North d		00 07		
Watton-at-Stone d		00 13		
Stevenage ■ d	23 56	00 20	00 42	
Hitchin ■ d	00a04	00 28	00 50	00s36
Letchworth Garden City a		00 35	00 59	

b arr. 0024

Table 24

Sundays until 11 July

London - Welwyn Garden City, Hertford North and Letchworth Garden City

	FC	FC	FC ■	FC ■	FC	FC	FC	FC	FC	FC	FC ■	FC
London Kings Cross ⊖ d	23p26	23p41	00 04	00 07	00 11	00 26	00 41	06 11		06 41	06 52	
Moorgate ⊖ d												
Old Street ⊖ d												
Essex Road d												
Highbury & Islington ⊖ d												
Drayton Park d												
Finsbury Park ⊖ d	23p32	23p47	00 09	00 12	00 17	00 32	00 47	06 17		06 47	06 57	
Harringay d	23p34	23p49			00 19	00 34	00 49	06 19		06 49		
Hornsey d	23p36	23p51			00 21	00 36	00 51	06 21		06 51		
Alexandra Palace d	23p38	23p53		00 17	00 23	00 38	00 53	06 23		06 53		
New Southgate d		23p56			00 26		00 56	06 26		06 56		
Oakleigh Park d		23p59			00 29		00 59	06 29		06 59		
New Barnet d		00 01			00 31		01 01	06 31		07 01		
Hadley Wood d		00 04			00 34		01 04	06 34		07 04		
Potters Bar d		00 08			00 38		01 08	06 38		07 08		
Brookmans Park d		00 11			00 41		01 11	06 41		07 11		
Welham Green d		00 13			00 43		01 13	06 43		07 13		
Hatfield d		00 16			00 46		01 16	06 46		07 16		
Welwyn Garden City ■ d		00b31	00 27		00a58		01a26	06a55		07a25		
Welwyn North d		00 34										
Knebworth d		00 38										
Bowes Park d	23p41					00 41						
Palmers Green d	23p43			00 20		00 43						
Winchmore Hill d	23p45			00 22		00 45						
Grange Park d	23p47					00 47						
Enfield Chase d	23p49			00 25		00 49						
Gordon Hill d	23p51			00 27		00 51						
Crews Hill d	23p54					00 54						
Cuffley d	23p57			00 31		00 57			06 33			06 57
Bayford d	00 02					01 02			06 38			07 02
Hertford North d	00 10			00 39		01a10			06a45			07 07
Watton-at-Stone d	00 13											07 12
Stevenage ■ d	00 20	00 42	00 33	00 48							07 17	07a22
Hitchin ■ d	00 28	00 50	00 41	00 56							07 26	
Letchworth Garden City a	00 35	00 59	00 44	01 01							07 34	

	FC ■	FC	FC ■	FC	FC	FC ■	FC	FC ■	FC	FC ■	FC	FC
London Kings Cross ⊖ d	07 06	07 11	07 22		07 41	07 52		08 06	08 11	08 22		08 41
Moorgate ⊖ d												
Old Street ⊖ d												
Essex Road d												
Highbury & Islington ⊖ d												
Drayton Park d												
Finsbury Park ⊖ d	07 11	07 17	07 27		07 47	07 58		08 11	08 17	08 27		08 47
Harringay d		07 19			07 49				08 19			08 49
Hornsey d		07 21			07 51				08 21			08 51
Alexandra Palace d		07 23			07 53				08 23			08 53
New Southgate d		07 26			07 56				08 26			08 56
Oakleigh Park d		07 29			07 59				08 29			08 59
New Barnet d		07 31			08 01				08 31			09 01
Hadley Wood d		07 34			08 04				08 34			09 04
Potters Bar d	07 21	07 38			08 08			08 21	08 38			09 08
Brookmans Park d		07 41			08 11				08 41			09 11
Welham Green d		07 43			08 13				08 43			09 13
Hatfield d	07 27	07 46			08 16			08 27	08 46			09 16
Welwyn Garden City ■ d	07 33	07a55			08a25			08 31	08a55			09a21
Welwyn North d	07 36							08 34				
Knebworth d	07 40							08 38				
Bowes Park d												
Palmers Green d												
Winchmore Hill d												
Grange Park d												
Enfield Chase d												
Gordon Hill d												
Crews Hill d												
Cuffley d				07 33			08 05				08 33	
Bayford d				07 38			08 10				08 38	
Hertford North d				07a45			08 15				08a45	
Watton-at-Stone d							08 21					
Stevenage ■ d	07 45		07 50			08 16	08a28	08 42		08 46		
Hitchin ■ d	07 52		08a00			08 30		08 47		08a51		
Letchworth Garden City a	07 56					08 33		08 54				

	FC ■	FC	FC ■	FC	FC ■	FC	FC	FC ■	FC	FC ■	FC	FC ■
London Kings Cross ⊖ d	08 52		09 06	09 11	09 22		09 41	09 52		10 06	10 11	10 22
Moorgate ⊖ d												
Old Street ⊖ d												
Essex Road d												
Highbury & Islington ⊖ d												
Drayton Park d												
Finsbury Park ⊖ d	08 57		09 11	09 17	09 27		09 47	09 57		10 11	10 17	10 27
Harringay d				09 19			09 49				10 19	
Hornsey d				09 21			09 51				10 21	
Alexandra Palace d				09 23			09 53				10 23	
New Southgate d				09 26			09 56				10 26	
Oakleigh Park d				09 29			09 59				10 29	
New Barnet d				09 31			10 01				10 31	
Hadley Wood d				09 34			10 04				10 34	
Potters Bar d			09 21	09 38			10 08			10 21	10 38	
Brookmans Park d				09 41			10 11				10 41	
Welham Green d				09 43			10 13				10 43	
Hatfield d			09 27	09 46			10 16			10 27	10 46	
Welwyn Garden City ■ d			09 31	09a51			10a21			10 31	10a51	
Welwyn North d			09 34							10 34		
Knebworth d			09 38							10 38		
Bowes Park d												
Palmers Green d												
Winchmore Hill d												
Grange Park d												
Enfield Chase d												
Gordon Hill d												
Crews Hill d												
Cuffley d		09 05				09 33			10 05			
Bayford d		09 10				09 38			10 10			
Hertford North d		09 15				09a45			10 15			
Watton-at-Stone d		09 21							10 21			
Stevenage ■ d	09 16	09a28	09 42		09 46			10 16	10a28	10 42		10 46
Hitchin ■ d	09 21		09 47		09a51			10 21		10 47		10a51
Letchworth Garden City a	09 25		09 51					10 25		10 51		

	FC	FC	FC ■	FC	FC ■	FC	FC ■	FC	FC	FC ■	FC
London Kings Cross ⊖ d		10 41	10 52		11 06	11 11	11 22		11 41	11 52	
Moorgate ⊖ d											
Old Street ⊖ d											
Essex Road d											
Highbury & Islington ⊖ d											
Drayton Park d											
Finsbury Park ⊖ d		10 47	10 57		11 11	11 17	11 27		11 47	11 57	
Harringay d		10 49				11 19			11 49		
Hornsey d		10 51				11 21			11 51		
Alexandra Palace d		10 53				11 23			11 53		
New Southgate d		10 56				11 26			11 56		
Oakleigh Park d		10 59				11 29			11 59		
New Barnet d		11 01				11 31			12 01		
Hadley Wood d		11 04				11 34			12 04		
Potters Bar d		11 08			11 21	11 38			12 08		
Brookmans Park d		11 11				11 41			12 11		
Welham Green d		11 13				11 43			12 13		
Hatfield d		11 16			11 27	11 46			12 16		
Welwyn Garden City ■ d		11a21			11 31	11a51			12a21		
Welwyn North d					11 34						
Knebworth d					11 38						
Bowes Park d											
Palmers Green d											
Winchmore Hill d											
Grange Park d											
Enfield Chase d											
Gordon Hill d											
Crews Hill d											
Cuffley d	10 33			11 05				11 33			12 05
Bayford d	10 38			11 10				11 38			12 10
Hertford North d	10a45			11 15				11a45			12 15
Watton-at-Stone d				11 21							12 21
Stevenage ■ d			11 16	11a28	11 42		11 46			12 16	12a28
Hitchin ■ d			11 21		11a47		11a51			12 21	
Letchworth Garden City a			11 25		11 51					12 25	

A not 23 May

b arr. 0024

Table 24

Sundays until 11 July

London - Welwyn Garden City, Hertford North and Letchworth Garden City

		FC 1		FC	FC 1	FC	FC	FC 1	FC	FC 1	FC	FC 1		FC	FC	FC 1	FC	FC 1	FC	FC 1	FC	FC		FC 1	FC
London Kings Cross 15 ⊖	d	12 06		12 11	12 22		12 41	12 52		13 06	13 11	13 22			13 41	13 52		14 06	14 11	14 22		14 41		14 52	
Moorgate ⊖	d																								
Old Street ⊖	d																								
Essex Road	d																								
Highbury & Islington ⊖	d																								
Drayton Park	d																								
Finsbury Park ⊖	d	12 11		12 17	12 27		12 47	12 57		13 11	13 17	13 27			13 46	13 57		14 11	14 17	14 27		14 47		14 57	
Harringay	d			12 19			12 49				13 19				13 48				14 19			14 49			
Hornsey	d			12 21			12 51				13 21				13 50				14 21			14 51			
Alexandra Palace	d			12 23			12 53				13 23				13 52				14 23			14 53			
New Southgate	d			12 26			12 56				13 26				13 55				14 26			14 56			
Oakleigh Park	d			12 29			12 59				13 29				13 59				14 29			14 59			
New Barnet	d			12 31			13 01				13 31				14 01				14 31			15 01			
Hadley Wood	d			12 34			13 04				13 34				14 03				14 34			15 04			
Potters Bar	d	12 21		12 38			13 08			13 21	13 38				14 07			14 21	14 38			15 08			
Brookmans Park	d			12 41			13 11				13 41				14 10				14 41			15 11			
Welham Green	d			12 43			13 13				13 43				14 12				14 43			15 13			
Hatfield	d	12 27		12 46			13 16			13 27	13 46				14 16			14 27	14 46			15 16			
Welwyn Garden City 4	d	12 31		12a51			13a21			13 31	13a51				14a21			14 31	14a51			15a21			
Welwyn North	d	12 34								13 34								14 34							
Knebworth	d	12 38								13 38								14 38							
Bowes Park	d																								
Palmers Green	d																								
Winchmore Hill	d																								
Grange Park	d																								
Enfield Chase	d																								
Gordon Hill	d																								
Crews Hill	d																								
Cuffley	d					12 33			13 05					13 33			14 05				14 33				15 05
Bayford	d					12 38			13 10					13 38			14 10				14 38				15 10
Hertford North	d					12a45			13 15					13a45			14 15				14a45				15 15
Watton-at-Stone	d								13 21								14 21								15 21
Stevenage 4	d	12 42			12 46			13 16	13a28	13 42		13 46				14 16	14a28	14 42		14 46				15 16	15a28
Hitchin 4	d	12 47			12a51			13 21		13 47		13a51				14 21		14 47		14a51				15 21	
Letchworth Garden City	a	12 51						13 25		13 51						14 25		14 51						15 25	

		FC 1	FC	FC 1	FC	FC	FC 1	FC		FC 1	FC	FC 1	FC	FC 1	FC	FC 1	FC	FC 1		FC	FC 1	FC	FC 1	FC	FC 1
London Kings Cross 15 ⊖	d	15 06	15 11	15 22		15 41	15 52			16 06	16 11	16 22		16 36	16 41	16 52		17 06		17 11	17 22		17 36	17 41	17 52
Moorgate ⊖	d																								
Old Street ⊖	d																								
Essex Road	d																								
Highbury & Islington ⊖	d																								
Drayton Park	d																								
Finsbury Park ⊖	d	15 11	15 17	15 27		15 47	15 57			16 11	16 17	16 27		16 41	16 47	16 57		17 11		17 17	17 27		17 41	17 47	17 57
Harringay	d		15 19			15 49					16 19				16 49					17 19				17 49	
Hornsey	d		15 21			15 51					16 21				16 51					17 21				17 51	
Alexandra Palace	d		15 23			15 53					16 23				16 53					17 23				17 53	
New Southgate	d		15 26			15 56					16 26				16 56					17 26				17 56	
Oakleigh Park	d		15 29			15 59					16 29				16 59					17 29				17 59	
New Barnet	d		15 31			16 01					16 31				17 01					17 31				18 01	
Hadley Wood	d		15 34			16 04					16 34				17 04					17 34				18 04	
Potters Bar	d	15 21	15 38			16 08				16 21	16 38			16 51	17 08			17 21		17 38			17 51	18 08	
Brookmans Park	d		15 41			16 11					16 41				17 11					17 41				18 11	
Welham Green	d		15 43			16 13					16 43				17 13					17 43				18 13	
Hatfield	d	15 27	15 46			16 16				16 27	16 46			16 57	17 16			17 27		17 46			17 57	18 16	
Welwyn Garden City 4	d	15 31	15a51			16a21				16 31	16a51			17 01	17a21			17 31		17a51			18 01	18a21	
Welwyn North	d	15 34								16 34				17 04				17 34					18 04		
Knebworth	d	15 38								16 38				17 08				17 38					18 08		
Bowes Park	d																								
Palmers Green	d																								
Winchmore Hill	d																								
Grange Park	d																								
Enfield Chase	d																								
Gordon Hill	d																								
Crews Hill	d																								
Cuffley	d				15 33			16 05					16 33				17 05					17 33			
Bayford	d				15 38			16 10					16 38				17 10					17 38			
Hertford North	d				15a45			16 15					16a45				17 15					17a45			
Watton-at-Stone	d							16 21									17 21								
Stevenage 4	d	15 42		15 46			16 16	16a28		16 42		16 46		17 12		17 16	17a28	17 42			17 46		18 12		18 16
Hitchin 4	d	15 47		15a51			16 21			16 47		16a51		17a17		17 21		17 47			17a51		18a17		18 21
Letchworth Garden City	a	15 51					16 25			16 51						17 25		17 51							18 25

Table 24

Sundays until 11 July

London - Welwyn Garden City, Hertford North and Letchworth Garden City

		FC	FC 1	FC		FC 1	FC	FC	FC 1	FC	FC 1	FC	FC 1	FC		FC	FC 1	FC	FC 1	FC	FC 1	FC	FC	FC 1	
London Kings Cross 15 ⊖	d		18 06	18 11		18 22		18 41	18 52		19 06	19 11	19 22			19 41	19 52		20 06	20 11	20 22		20 41	20 52	
Moorgate ⊖	d																								
Old Street ⊖	d																								
Essex Road	d																								
Highbury & Islington ⊖	d																								
Drayton Park	d																								
Finsbury Park ⊖	d		18 11	18 17		18 27		18 47	18 57		19 11	19 17	19 27			19 47	19 57		20 11	20 17	20 27		20 47	20 57	
Harringay	d			18 19				18 49				19 19				19 49				20 19			20 49		
Hornsey	d			18 21				18 51				19 21				19 51				20 21			20 51		
Alexandra Palace	d			18 23				18 53				19 23				19 53				20 23			20 53		
New Southgate	d			18 26				18 56				19 26				19 56				20 26			20 56		
Oakleigh Park	d			18 29				18 59				19 29				19 59				20 29			20 59		
New Barnet	d			18 31				19 01				19 31				20 01				20 31			21 01		
Hadley Wood	d			18 34				19 04				19 34				20 04				20 34			21 04		
Potters Bar	d		18 21	18 38				19 08			19 21	19 38				20 08			20 21	20 38			21 08		
Brookmans Park	d			18 41				19 11				19 41				20 11				20 41			21 11		
Welham Green	d			18 43				19 13				19 43				20 13				20 43			21 13		
Hatfield	d		18 27	18 46				19 16			19 27	19 46				20 16			20 27	20 46			21 16		
Welwyn Garden City 4	d		18 31	18a51				19a21			19 31	19a51				20a21			20 31	20a51			21a21		
Welwyn North	d		18 34								19 34								20 34						
Knebworth	d		18 38								19 38								20 38						
Bowes Park	d																								
Palmers Green	d																								
Winchmore Hill	d																								
Grange Park	d																								
Enfield Chase	d																								
Gordon Hill	d																								
Crews Hill	d																								
Cuffley	d	18 05					18 33			19 05				19 33				20 05				20 33			
Bayford	d	18 10					18 38			19 10				19 38				20 10				20 38			
Hertford North	d	18 15					18a45			19 15				19a45				20 15				20a45			
Watton-at-Stone	d	18 21								19 21								20 21							
Stevenage 4	d	18a28	18 42			18 46			19 16	19a28	19 42		19 46				20 16	20a28	20 42		20 46			21 16	
Hitchin 4	d		18 47			18a51			19 21		19 47		19a51				20 21		20 47		20a51			21 21	
Letchworth Garden City	a		18 51						19 25		19 51						20 25		20 51					21 25	

		FC	FC 1	FC	FC 1	FC	FC	FC 1	FC	FC 1		FC	FC 1	FC	FC	FC 1	FC	FC 1	FC	FC 1		FC	FC	FC	
London Kings Cross 15 ⊖	d		21 06	21 11	21 22		21 41	21 52		22 06		22 11	22 22		22 41	22 52		23 06	23 11	23 22				23 41	
Moorgate ⊖	d																								
Old Street ⊖	d																								
Essex Road	d																								
Highbury & Islington ⊖	d																								
Drayton Park	d																								
Finsbury Park ⊖	d		21 11	21 17	21 27		21 47	21 57		22 11		22 17	22 27		22 47	22 57		23 11	23 17	23 27				23 47	
Harringay	d			21 19			21 49					22 19			22 49				23 19					23 49	
Hornsey	d			21 21			21 51					22 21			22 51				23 21					23 51	
Alexandra Palace	d			21 23			21 53					22 23			22 53				23 23					23 53	
New Southgate	d			21 26			21 56					22 26			22 56				23 26					23 56	
Oakleigh Park	d			21 29			21 59					22 29			22 59				23 30					23 59	
New Barnet	d			21 31			22 01					22 31			23 01				23 32					00 01	
Hadley Wood	d			21 34			22 04					22 34			23 04				23 34					00 04	
Potters Bar	d		21 21	21 38			22 08			22 21		22 38			23 08			23 21	23 38					00 08	
Brookmans Park	d			21 41			22 11					22 41			23 11				23 41					00 11	
Welham Green	d			21 43			22 13					22 43			23 13				23 43					00 13	
Hatfield	d		21 27	21 46			22 16			22 27		22 46			23 16			23 27	23 47					00 16	
Welwyn Garden City 4	d		21 31	21a51			22a21			22 31		22a51			23a21			23 31	23a52					00 20	
Welwyn North	d		21 34							22 34								23 34						00 23	
Knebworth	d		21 38							22 38								23 38						00 28	
Bowes Park	d																								
Palmers Green	d																								
Winchmore Hill	d																								
Grange Park	d																								
Enfield Chase	d																								
Gordon Hill	d																								
Crews Hill	d																								
Cuffley	d	21 05				21 33			22 05					22 33			23 05					23 33	23 56		
Bayford	d	21 10				21 38			22 10					22 38			23 10					23 38	00 02		
Hertford North	d	21 15				21a45			22 15					22a45			23 15					23a45	00 07		
Watton-at-Stone	d	21 21							22 21								23 21						00 12		
Stevenage 4	d	21a28	21 42		21 46			22 16	22a28	22 42			22 46			23 16	23a28	23 42		23 46			00a20	00 31	
Hitchin 4	d		21 47		21a51			22 21		22 47			22a51			23 21		23 50		23a54				00 37	
Letchworth Garden City	a		21 51					22 25		22 51						23 25		23 54						00 52	

Table 24

Sundays
18 July to 05 September

London - Welwyn Garden City, Hertford North and Letchworth Garden City

	FC 1	FC 1	FC 1	FC 1	FC	FC 1	FC	FC 1	FC 1	FC	FC 1	FC 1	FC	FC 1	FC 1	FC	FC 1	FC 1	FC		FC 1	FC 1	FC	FC 1
London Kings Cross ⊖ d	23p38	00 01	00 04	00 07	00 14	00 36	06 14	06 38	07 09	07 14	07 38	08 09	08 14	08 38	09 09	09 14	09 38	10 09	10 14		10 38	11 09	11 14	11 38
Moorgate ⊖ d																								
Old Street ⊖ d																								
Essex Road d																								
Highbury & Islington ⊖ d																								
Drayton Park d																								
Finsbury Park ⊖ d	23p43	00 06	00 10	00 12	00 20	00 41	06 20	06 43	07 14	07 20	07 43	08 14	08 20	08 43	09 14	09 20	09 43	10 14	10 20		10 43	11 14	11 20	11 43
Harringay d					00 22		06 22			07 22			08 22			09 22			10 22				11 22	
Hornsey d					00 24		06 24			07 24			08 24			09 24			10 24				11 24	
Alexandra Palace d				00 17	00 26		06 26			07 26			08 26			09 26			10 26				11 26	
New Southgate d																								
Oakleigh Park d																								
New Barnet d																								
Hadley Wood d																								
Potters Bar d																								
Brookmans Park d																								
Welham Green d																								
Hatfield d																								
Welwyn Garden City 4 d																								
Welwyn North d																								
Knebworth d																								
Bowes Park d					00 29		06 29			07 29			08 29			09 29			10 29				11 29	
Palmers Green d				00 20	00 31		06 31			07 31			08 31			09 31			10 31				11 31	
Winchmore Hill d				00 22	00 33		06 33			07 33			08 33			09 33			10 33				11 33	
Grange Park d					00 35		06 35			07 35			08 35			09 35			10 35				11 35	
Enfield Chase d				00 25	00 37		06 37			07 37			08 37			09 37			10 37				11 37	
Gordon Hill d				00 27	00 39		06 39			07 39			08 39			09 39			10 39				11 39	
Crews Hill d					00 42		06 42			07 42			08 42			09 42			10 42				11 42	
Cuffley d				00 31	00 45		06 45			07 45			08 45			09 45			10 45				11 45	
Bayford d					00 50		06 50			07 50			08 50			09 50			10 50				11 50	
Hertford North d				00 39	00a58		06a58			07a58			08a58			09a56			10a56				11a56	
Watton-at-Stone d																								
Stevenage 4 d	00 08		00 40	00 48		01 16		07 11	07 42		08 11	08 41		09 09	09 41		10 09	10 40			11 09	11 41		12 09
Hitchin 4 d	00 11	00a39	00 41	00 56		01a23		07 16	07a51		08 16	08a46		09 12	09a46		10 14	10a45			11 14	11a46		12 14
Letchworth Garden City a	00 16		00 45	01 01				07 20			08 20			09 17			10 18				11 18			12 18

	FC 1	FC	FC 1	FC 1	FC		FC 1	FC 1	FC	FC 1	FC 1	FC	FC 1	FC 1	FC		FC 1	FC 1	FC	FC 1	FC 1	FC	FC 1	FC 1
London Kings Cross ⊖ d	12 09	12 14	12 38	13 09	13 14		13 38	14 09	14 14	14 38	15 09	15 14	15 38	16 09	16 14		16 38	17 09	17 14	17 38	18 09	18 14	18 38	19 09
Moorgate ⊖ d																								
Old Street ⊖ d																								
Essex Road d																								
Highbury & Islington ⊖ d																								
Drayton Park d																								
Finsbury Park ⊖ d	12 14	12 20	12 43	13 14	13 20		13 43	14 14	14 20	14 43	15 14	15 20	15 43	16 14	16 20		15 43	17 14	17 20	17 43	18 14	18 20	18 43	19 14
Harringay d		12 22			13 22				14 22			15 22			16 22				17 22			18 22		
Hornsey d		12 24			13 24				14 24			15 24			16 24				17 24			18 24		
Alexandra Palace d		12 26			13 26				14 26			15 26			16 26				17 26			18 26		
New Southgate d																								
Oakleigh Park d																								
New Barnet d																								
Hadley Wood d																								
Potters Bar d																								
Brookmans Park d																								
Welham Green d																								
Hatfield d																								
Welwyn Garden City 4 d																								
Welwyn North d																								
Knebworth d																								
Bowes Park d		12 29			13 29				14 29			15 29			16 29				17 29			18 29		
Palmers Green d		12 31			13 31				14 31			15 31			16 31				17 31			18 31		
Winchmore Hill d		12 33			13 33				14 33			15 33			16 33				17 33			18 33		
Grange Park d		12 35			13 35				14 35			15 35			16 35				17 35			18 35		
Enfield Chase d		12 37			13 37				14 37			15 37			16 37				17 37			18 37		
Gordon Hill d		12 39			13 39				14 39			15 39			16 39				17 39			18 39		
Crews Hill d		12 42			13 42				14 42			15 42			16 42				17 42			18 42		
Cuffley d		12 45			13 45				14 45			15 45			16 45				17 45			18 45		
Bayford d		12 50			13 50				14 50			15 50			16 50				17 50			18 50		
Hertford North d		12a56			13a56				14a56			15a56			16a56				17a56			18a56		
Watton-at-Stone d																								
Stevenage 4 d	12 40		13 09	13 40			14 09	14 41		15 09	15 40		16 09	16 40			17 09	17 40		18 09	18 40		19 09	19 40
Hitchin 4 d	12a45		13 14	13a45			14 14	14a46		15 14	15a45		16 14	16a45			17 14	17a45		18 14	18a45		19 14	19a45
Letchworth Garden City a			13 18				14 18			15 18			16 18				17 18			18 18			19 18	

Table 24

Sundays
18 July to 05 September

London - Welwyn Garden City, Hertford North and Letchworth Garden City

	FC		FC 1	FC 1	FC	FC 1	FC 1	FC	FC 1	FC 1	FC		FC 1	FC 1	FC
London Kings Cross ⊖ d	19 14		19 38	20 09	20 14	20 38	21 09	21 14	21 38	22 09	22 14		22 38	23 05	23 08
Moorgate ⊖ d															
Old Street ⊖ d															
Essex Road d															
Highbury & Islington ⊖ d															
Drayton Park d															
Finsbury Park ⊖ d	19 20		19 43	20 14	20 20	20 43	21 14	21 20	21 43	22 14	22 20		22 43	23 10	23 14
Harringay d	19 22				20 22			21 22			22 22				23 16
Hornsey d	19 24				20 24			21 24			22 24				23 18
Alexandra Palace d	19 26				20 26			21 26			22 26				23 20
New Southgate d															
Oakleigh Park d															
New Barnet d															
Hadley Wood d															
Potters Bar d															
Brookmans Park d															
Welham Green d															
Hatfield d															
Welwyn Garden City 4 d															
Welwyn North d															
Knebworth d															
Bowes Park d	19 29				20 29			21 29			22 29				23 23
Palmers Green d	19 31				20 31			21 31			22 31				23 25
Winchmore Hill d	19 33				20 33			21 33			22 33				23 27
Grange Park d	19 35				20 35			21 35			22 35				23 29
Enfield Chase d	19 37				20 37			21 37			22 37				23 31
Gordon Hill d	19 39				20 39			21 39			22 39				23 33
Crews Hill d	19 42				20 42			21 42			22 42				23 36
Cuffley d	19 45				20 45			21 45			22 45				23 39
Bayford d	19 50				20 50			21 50			22 50				23 44
Hertford North d	19a56				20a56			21a56			22a56				23a50
Watton-at-Stone d															
Stevenage 4 d			20 09	20 40		21 09	21 40		22 09	22 40			23 09	23 40	
Hitchin 4 d			20 14	20a45		21 14	21a45		22 14	22a45			23 14	23a45	
Letchworth Garden City a			20 18			21 18			22 18				23 18		

Sundays
from 12 September

	FC	FC	FC 1	FC 1	FC	FC	FC 1	FC	FC	FC 1	FC	FC	FC 1	FC	FC	FC 1	FC	FC	FC	FC	FC 1	FC	FC	FC 1
London Kings Cross ⊖ d	23p26	23p41	00 04	00 07	00 11	00 26	00 36	00 41	05 56	06 06	06 11	06 26	06 36	06 41	06 56	07 06	07 11	07 26	07 41	07 56	08 06	08 11	08 26	08 30
Moorgate ⊖ d																								
Old Street ⊖ d																								
Essex Road d																								
Highbury & Islington ⊖ d																								
Drayton Park d																								
Finsbury Park ⊖ d	23p32	23p47	00 09	00 12	00 17	00 32	00 41	00 47	06 02	06 11	06 17	06 32	06 41	06 47	07 02	07 11	07 17	07 32	07 47	08 02	08 11	08 17	08 32	08 35
Harringay d	23p34	23p49			00 19	00 34		00 49	06 04		06 19	06 34		06 49	07 04		07 19	07 34	07 49	08 04		08 19	08 34	
Hornsey d	23p36	23p51			00 21	00 36		00 51	06 06		06 21	06 36		06 51	07 06		07 21	07 36	07 51	08 06		08 21	08 36	
Alexandra Palace d	23p38	23p53		00 17	00 23	00 38		00 53	06 08		06 23	06 38		06 53	07 08		07 23	07 38	07 53	08 08		08 23	08 38	
New Southgate d		23p56			00 26			00 56			06 26			06 56			07 26		07 56			08 26		
Oakleigh Park d		23p59			00 29			00 59			06 29			06 59			07 29		07 59			08 29		
New Barnet d		00 01			00 31			01 01			06 31			07 01			07 31		08 01			08 31		
Hadley Wood d		00 04			00 34			01 04			06 34			07 04			07 34		08 04			08 34		
Potters Bar d		00 08			00 38		00 51	01 08		06 21	06 38		06 51	07 08		07 21	07 38		08 08		08 21	08 38		08 44
Brookmans Park d		00 11			00 41			01 11			06 41			07 11			07 41		08 11			08 41		
Welham Green d		00 13			00 43			01 13			06 43			07 13			07 43		08 13			08 43		
Hatfield d		00 16			00 46		00 57	01 16		06 27	06 46		06 57	07 16		07 27	07 46		08 16		08 27	08 46		08 49
Welwyn Garden City 4 d		00b31	00 27		00a58		01 03	01a26		06 31	06a55		07 01	07a25		07 31	07a55		08a25		08 31	08a55		08 53
Welwyn North d		00 34					01s06			06 37			07 07			07 37					08 34			08 56
Knebworth d		00 38					01s10			06 41			07 11			07 41					08 38			09 00
Bowes Park d	23p41					00 41			06 11			06 41			07 11			07 41		08 11			08 41	
Palmers Green d	23p43			00 20		00 43			06 13			06 43			07 13			07 43		08 13			08 43	
Winchmore Hill d	23p45			00 22		00 45			06 15			06 45			07 15			07 45		08 15			08 45	
Grange Park d	23p47					00 47			06 17			06 47			07 17			07 47		08 17			08 47	
Enfield Chase d	23p49			00 25		00 49			06 19			06 49			07 19			07 49		08 19			08 49	
Gordon Hill d	23p51			00 27		00 51			06 21			06 51			07 21			07 51		08 21			08 51	
Crews Hill d	23p54					00 54			06 24			06 54			07 24			07 54		08 24			08 54	
Cuffley d	23p57			00 31		00 57			06 27			06 57			07 27			07 57		08 27			08 57	
Bayford d	00 02					01 02			06 32			07 02			07 32			08 02		08 32			09 02	
Hertford North d	00 10			00 39		01a10			06a40			07 07			07a40			08 07		08a40			09 07	
Watton-at-Stone d	00 13											07 13						08 13					09 13	
Stevenage 4 d	00 20	00 42	00 33	00 48			01a18			06a49		07a22	07a19			07a49		08a23			08a46		09a20	09a06
Hitchin 4 d	00 28	00 50	00 41	00 56																				
Letchworth Garden City a	00 35	00 59	00 44	01 01																				

b arr. 0024

Table 24

Sundays from 12 September

London - Welwyn Garden City, Hertford North and Letchworth Garden City

		FC	FC 1	FC	FC 1	FC	FC 1	FC	FC	FC 1	FC	FC 1	FC	FC 1	FC	FC	FC 1	FC	FC 1	FC	FC 1	FC	FC	FC 1	FC
London Kings Cross 15 ⊖	d	08 41	08 52	08 56	09 06	09 11	09 22	09 26	09 41	09 52	09 56	10 06	10 11	10 22	10 26	10 41	10 52	10 56	11 06	11 11	11 22	11 26	11 41	11 52	11 56
Moorgate ⊖	d																								
Old Street ⊖	d																								
Essex Road	d																								
Highbury & Islington ⊖	d																								
Drayton Park	d																								
Finsbury Park ⊖	d	08 47	08 57	09 02	09 11	09 17	09 27	09 32	09 47	09 57	10 02	10 11	10 17	10 27	10 32	10 47	10 57	11 02	11 11	11 17	11 27	11 32	11 47	11 57	12 02
Harringay	d	08 49		09 04		09 19		09 34	09 49		10 04		10 19		10 34	10 49		11 04		11 19		11 34	11 49		12 04
Hornsey	d	08 51		09 06		09 21		09 36	09 51		10 06		10 21		10 36	10 51		11 06		11 21		11 36	11 51		12 06
Alexandra Palace	d	08 53		09 08		09 23		09 38	09 53		10 08		10 23		10 38	10 53		11 08		11 23		11 38	11 53		12 08
New Southgate	d	08 56				09 26			09 56				10 26			10 56				11 26			11 56		
Oakleigh Park	d	08 59				09 29			09 59				10 29			10 59				11 29			11 59		
New Barnet	d	09 01				09 31			10 01				10 31			11 01				11 31			12 01		
Hadley Wood	d	09 04				09 34			10 04				10 34			11 04				11 34			12 04		
Potters Bar	d	09 08			09 21	09 38			10 08			10 21	10 38			11 08			11 21	11 38			12 08		
Brookmans Park	d	09 11				09 41			10 11				10 41			11 11				11 41			12 11		
Welham Green	d	09 13				09 43			10 13				10 43			11 13				11 43			12 13		
Hatfield	d	09 16			09 27	09 46			10 16			10 27	10 46			11 16			11 27	11 46			12 16		
Welwyn Garden City 4	d	09a21			09 31	09a51			10a21			10 31	10a51			11a21			11 31	11a51			12a21		
Welwyn North	d				09 34							10 34							11 34						
Knebworth	d				09 38							10 38							11 38						
Bowes Park	d			09 11				09 41			10 11				10 41			11 11				11 41			12 11
Palmers Green	d			09 13				09 43			10 13				10 43			11 13				11 43			12 13
Winchmore Hill	d			09 15				09 45			10 15				10 45			11 15				11 45			12 15
Grange Park	d			09 17				09 47			10 17				10 47			11 17				11 47			12 17
Enfield Chase	d			09 19				09 49			10 19				10 49			11 19				11 49			12 19
Gordon Hill	d			09 21				09 51			10 21				10 51			11 21				11 51			12 21
Crews Hill	d			09 24				09 54			10 24				10 54			11 24				11 54			12 24
Cuffley	d			09 27				09 57			10 27				10 57			11 27				11 57			12 27
Bayford	d			09 32				10 02			10 32				11 02			11 32				12 02			12 32
Hertford North	d			09a38				10 07			10a38				11 07			11a38				12 07			12a38
Watton-at-Stone	d							10 13							11 13							12 13			
Stevenage 4	d		09 16		09 42		09 46	10a20		10 16		10 42		10 46	11a20		11 16		11 42		11 46	12a20		12 16	
Hitchin 4	d		09 21		09 47		09a51			10 21		10 47		10a51			11 21		11 47		11a51			12 21	
Letchworth Garden City	a		09 25		09 51					10 25		10 51					11 25		11 51					12 25	

		FC 1	FC	FC 1	FC	FC	FC 1	FC	FC 1	FC	FC 1	FC	FC	FC 1	FC	FC 1	FC	FC 1	FC	FC	FC 1	FC		FC 1	FC
London Kings Cross 15 ⊖	d	12 06	12 11	12 22	12 26	12 41	12 52	12 56	13 06	13 11	13 22	13 26	13 41	13 52	13 56	14 06	14 11	14 22	14 26	14 41	14 52	14 56		15 06	15 11
Moorgate ⊖	d																								
Old Street ⊖	d																								
Essex Road	d																								
Highbury & Islington ⊖	d																								
Drayton Park	d																								
Finsbury Park ⊖	d	12 11	12 17	12 27	12 32	12 47	12 57	13 02	13 11	13 17	13 27	13 32	13 46	13 57	14 02	14 11	14 17	14 27	14 32	14 47	14 57	15 02		15 11	15 17
Harringay	d		12 19		12 34	12 49		13 04		13 19		13 34	13 48		14 04		14 19		14 34	14 49		15 04			15 19
Hornsey	d		12 21		12 36	12 51		13 06		13 21		13 36	13 50		14 06		14 21		14 36	14 51		15 06			15 21
Alexandra Palace	d		12 23		12 38	12 53		13 08		13 23		13 38	13 52		14 08		14 23		14 38	14 53		15 08			15 23
New Southgate	d		12 26			12 56				13 26			13 55				14 26			14 56					15 26
Oakleigh Park	d		12 29			12 59				13 29			13 59				14 29			14 59					15 29
New Barnet	d		12 31			13 01				13 31			14 01				14 31			15 01					15 31
Hadley Wood	d		12 34			13 04				13 34			14 03				14 34			15 04					15 34
Potters Bar	d	12 21	12 38			13 08			13 21	13 38			14 07			14 21	14 38			15 08				15 21	15 38
Brookmans Park	d		12 41			13 11				13 41			14 10				14 41			15 11					15 41
Welham Green	d		12 43			13 13				13 43			14 12				14 43			15 13					15 43
Hatfield	d	12 27	12 46			13 16			13 27	13 46			14 16			14 27	14 46			15 16				15 27	15 46
Welwyn Garden City 4	d	12 31	12a51			13a21			13 31	13a51			14a21			14 31	14a51			15a21				15 31	15a51
Welwyn North	d	12 34							13 34							14 34								15 34	
Knebworth	d	12 38							13 38							14 38								15 38	
Bowes Park	d				12 41			13 11				13 41			14 11				14 41			15 11			
Palmers Green	d				12 43			13 13				13 43			14 13				14 43			15 13			
Winchmore Hill	d				12 45			13 15				13 45			14 15				14 45			15 15			
Grange Park	d				12 47			13 17				13 47			14 17				14 47			15 17			
Enfield Chase	d				12 49			13 19				13 49			14 19				14 49			15 19			
Gordon Hill	d				12 51			13 21				13 51			14 21				14 51			15 21			
Crews Hill	d				12 54			13 24				13 54			14 24				14 54			15 24			
Cuffley	d				12 57			13 27				13 57			14 27				14 57			15 27			
Bayford	d				13 02			13 32				14 02			14 32				15 02			15 32			
Hertford North	d				13 07			13a38				14 07			14a38				15 07			15a38			
Watton-at-Stone	d				13 13							14 13							15 13						
Stevenage 4	d	12 42		12 46	13a20		13 16		13 42		13 46	14a20		14 16		14 42		14 46	15a20		15 16			15 42	
Hitchin 4	d	12 47		12a51			13 21		13 47		13a51			14 21		14 47		14a51			15 21			15 47	
Letchworth Garden City	a	12 51					13 25		13 51					14 25		14 51					15 25			15 51	

Table 24

Sundays from 12 September

London - Welwyn Garden City, Hertford North and Letchworth Garden City

		FC 1	FC	FC	FC 1	FC	FC 1	FC		FC 1	FC	FC 1	FC	FC 1	FC	FC 1	FC	FC 1		FC	FC 1	FC	FC 1	FC	FC 1
London Kings Cross 15 ⊖	d	15 22	15 26	15 41	15 52	15 56	16 06	16 11		16 22	16 26	16 36	16 41	16 52	16 56	17 06	17 11	17 22		17 26	17 36	17 41	17 52	17 56	18 06
Moorgate ⊖	d																								
Old Street ⊖	d																								
Essex Road	d																								
Highbury & Islington ⊖	d																								
Drayton Park	d																								
Finsbury Park ⊖	d	15 27	15 32	15 47	15 57	16 02	16 11	16 17		16 27	16 32	16 41	16 47	16 57	17 02	17 11	17 17	17 27		17 32	17 41	17 47	17 57	18 02	18 11
Harringay	d		15 34	15 49		16 04		16 19			16 34		16 49		17 04		17 19			17 34		17 49		18 04	
Hornsey	d		15 36	15 51		16 06		16 21			16 36		16 51		17 06		17 21			17 36		17 51		18 06	
Alexandra Palace	d		15 38	15 53		16 08		16 23			16 38		16 53		17 08		17 23			17 38		17 53		18 08	
New Southgate	d			15 56				16 26					16 56				17 26					17 56			
Oakleigh Park	d			15 59				16 29					16 59				17 29					17 59			
New Barnet	d			16 01				16 31					17 01				17 31					18 01			
Hadley Wood	d			16 04				16 34					17 04				17 34					18 04			
Potters Bar	d			16 08			16 21	16 38				16 51	17 08			17 21	17 38				17 51	18 08			18 21
Brookmans Park	d			16 11				16 41					17 11				17 41					18 11			
Welham Green	d			16 13				16 43					17 13				17 43					18 13			
Hatfield	d			16 16			16 27	16 46				16 57	17 16			17 27	17 46				17 57	18 16			18 27
Welwyn Garden City 4	d			16a21			16 31	16a51				17 01	17a21			17 31	17a51				18 01	18a21			18 31
Welwyn North	d						16 34					17 04				17 34					18 04				18 34
Knebworth	d						16 38					17 08				17 38					18 08				18 38
Bowes Park	d		15 41			16 11					16 41				17 11					17 41				18 11	
Palmers Green	d		15 43			16 13					16 43				17 13					17 43				18 13	
Winchmore Hill	d		15 45			16 15					16 45				17 15					17 45				18 15	
Grange Park	d		15 47			16 17					16 47				17 17					17 47				18 17	
Enfield Chase	d		15 49			16 19					16 49				17 19					17 49				18 19	
Gordon Hill	d		15 51			16 21					16 51				17 21					17 51				18 21	
Crews Hill	d		15 54			16 24					16 54				17 24					17 54				18 24	
Cuffley	d		15 57			16 27					16 57				17 27					17 57				18 27	
Bayford	d		16 02			16 32					17 02				17 32					18 02				18 32	
Hertford North	d		16 07			16a38					17 07				17a38					18 07				18a38	
Watton-at-Stone	d		16 13								17 13									18 13					
Stevenage 4	d	15 46	16a20		16 16		16 42			16 46	17a20	17 12		17 16		17 42		17 46		18a20	18 12		18 16		18 42
Hitchin 4	d	15a51			16 21		16 47			16a51		17a17		17 21		17 47		17a51			18a17		18 21		18 47
Letchworth Garden City	a				16 25		16 51							17 25		17 51							18 25		18 51

		FC	FC 1	FC		FC	FC 1	FC	FC 1	FC	FC 1	FC	FC	FC 1		FC	FC 1	FC	FC 1	FC	FC	FC 1	FC	FC 1	
London Kings Cross 15 ⊖	d	18 11	18 22	18 26		18 41	18 52	18 56	19 06	19 11	19 22	19 26	19 41	19 52		19 56	20 06	20 11	20 22	20 26	20 41	20 52	20 56	21 06	
Moorgate ⊖	d																								
Old Street ⊖	d																								
Essex Road	d																								
Highbury & Islington ⊖	d																								
Drayton Park	d																								
Finsbury Park ⊖	d	18 17	18 27	18 32		18 47	18 57	19 02	19 11	19 17	19 27	19 32	19 47	19 57		20 02	20 11	20 17	20 27	20 32	20 47	20 57	21 02	21 11	
Harringay	d	18 19		18 34		18 49		19 04		19 19		19 34	19 49			20 04		20 19		20 34	20 49		21 04		
Hornsey	d	18 21		18 36		18 51		19 06		19 21		19 36	19 51			20 06		20 21		20 36	20 51		21 06		
Alexandra Palace	d	18 23		18 38		18 53		19 08		19 23		19 38	19 53			20 08		20 23		20 38	20 53		21 08		
New Southgate	d	18 26				18 56				19 26			19 56					20 26			20 56				
Oakleigh Park	d	18 29				18 59				19 29			19 59					20 29			20 59				
New Barnet	d	18 31				19 01				19 31			20 01					20 31			21 01				
Hadley Wood	d	18 34				19 04				19 34			20 04					20 34			21 04				
Potters Bar	d	18 38				19 08			19 21	19 38			20 08				20 21	20 38			21 08			21 21	
Brookmans Park	d	18 41				19 11				19 41			20 11					20 41			21 11				
Welham Green	d	18 43				19 13				19 43			20 13					20 43			21 13				
Hatfield	d	18 46				19 16			19 27	19 46			20 16				20 27	20 46			21 16			21 27	
Welwyn Garden City 4	d	18a51				19a21			19 31	19a51			20a21				20 31	20a51			21a21			21 31	
Welwyn North	d								19 34								20 34							21 34	
Knebworth	d								19 38								20 38							21 38	
Bowes Park	d			18 41				19 11				19 41				20 11				20 41			21 11		
Palmers Green	d			18 43				19 13				19 43				20 13				20 43			21 13		
Winchmore Hill	d			18 45				19 15				19 45				20 15				20 45			21 15		
Grange Park	d			18 47				19 17				19 47				20 17				20 47			21 17		
Enfield Chase	d			18 49				19 19				19 49				20 19				20 49			21 19		
Gordon Hill	d			18 51				19 21				19 51				20 21				20 51			21 21		
Crews Hill	d			18 54				19 24				19 54				20 24				20 54			21 24		
Cuffley	d			18 57				19 27				19 57				20 27				20 57			21 27		
Bayford	d			19 02				19 32				20 02				20 32				21 02			21 32		
Hertford North	d			19 07				19a38				20 07				20a38				21 07			21a38		
Watton-at-Stone	d			19 13								20 13								21 13					
Stevenage 4	d		18 46	19a20			19 16		19 42		19 46	20a20		20 16			20 42		20 46	21a20		21 16		21 42	
Hitchin 4	d		18a51				19 21		19 47		19a51			20 21			20 47		20a51			21 21		21 47	
Letchworth Garden City	a						19 25		19 51					20 25			20 51					21 25		21 51	

Table 24

London - Welwyn Garden City, Hertford North and Letchworth Garden City

Sundays from 12 September

	FC	FC ■	FC	FC	FC ■	FC	FC ■	FC	FC ■	FC	FC	FC ■	FC	FC ■	FC	FC ■	FC	FC
London Kings Cross ⊖ d	21 11	21 22	21 26	21 41	21 52	21 56	22 06	22 11	22 22	22 26	22 41	22 52	22 56	23 06	23 11	23 22	23 26	23 41
Moorgate ⊖ d																		
Old Street ⊖ d																		
Essex Road d																		
Highbury & Islington ⊖ d																		
Drayton Park d																		
Finsbury Park ⊖ d	21 17	21 27	21 32	21 47	21 57	22 02	22 11	22 17	22 27	22 32	22 47	22 57	23 02	23 11	23 17	23 27	23 31	23 47
Harringay d	21 19		21 34	21 49		22 04		22 19		22 34	22 49		23 04		23 19		23 33	23 49
Hornsey d	21 21		21 36	21 51		22 06		22 21		22 36	22 51		23 06		23 21		23 35	23 51
Alexandra Palace d	21 23		21 38	21 53		22 08		22 23		22 38	22 53		23 08		23 23		23 38	23 53
New Southgate d	21 26			21 56				22 26			22 56				23 26			23 56
Oakleigh Park d	21 29			21 59				22 29			22 59				23 30			23 59
New Barnet d	21 31			22 01				22 31			23 01				23 32			00 01
Hadley Wood d	21 34			22 04				22 34			23 04				23 34			00 04
Potters Bar d	21 38			22 08			22 21	22 38			23 08			23 21	23 38			00 08
Brookmans Park d	21 41			22 11				22 41			23 11				23 41			00 11
Welham Green d	21 43			22 13				22 43			23 13				23 43			00 13
Hatfield d	21 46			22 16			22 27	22 46			23 16			23 27	23 47			00 16
Welwyn Garden City ■ d	21a51			22a21			22 31	22a51			23a21			23 31	23a52			00 20
Welwyn North d							22 34							23 34				00 23
Knebworth d							22 38							23 38				00 28
Bowes Park d			21 41			22 11				22 41			23 11				23 40	
Palmers Green d			21 43			22 13				22 43			23 13				23 42	
Winchmore Hill d			21 45			22 15				22 45			23 15				23 45	
Grange Park d			21 47			22 17				22 47			23 17				23 47	
Enfield Chase d			21 49			22 19				22 49			23 19				23 49	
Gordon Hill d			21 51			22 21				22 51			23 21				23 51	
Crews Hill d			21 54			22 24				22 54			23 24				23 54	
Cuffley d			21 57			22 27				22 57			23 27				23 57	
Bayford d			22 02			22 32				23 02			23 32				00 02	
Hertford North d			22 07			22a38				23 07			23a38				00 07	
Watton-at-Stone d			22 13							23 13							00 12	
Stevenage ■ d		21 46	22a20		22 16		22 42		[illegible]	23a20		23 16		23 42		23 46	00a20	00 31
Hitchin ■ d		21a51			22 21		[illegible]		22a51			23 21		23 50		23a54		00 37
Letchworth Garden City a					22 25		22 51					23 25		23 54				00 52

Table 24

Mondays to Fridays

Letchworth Garden City, Hertford North and Welwyn Garden City - London

	FC MX	FC B	FC ■ C	FC ■ A	FC C	FC MX ■	FC ■ A	FC	FC ■	FC	FC	FC ■	FC	FC ■	FC	FC ■	FC	FC ■	FC	FC ■	FC ■	FC	FC
Letchworth Garden City d	23p18				23p39	23p47	23p54				04 50		05 20	05 29	05 48			05 59			06 19		
Hitchin ■ d	23p22		23p34	23p34	23p43	23p54	23p58		04 08		04 54	04 58	05 24	05 33	05 52	05 58		06 03		06 19	06 23		
Stevenage ■ d	23p27	23p29	23p39	23p40	23p48	23p59	00 03		04 13		04 59	05 04	05 29	05 39	05 57	06 03		06 09	06 10	06 25	06 29		
Watton-at-Stone d	23p34	23p36					00 08				05 06		05 36		06 04				06 17				
Hertford North d	23p40	23p42					00 14		04 23	00 20	05 12		05 42		06 10				06 25				06 34
Bayford d	23p44	23p46								00 24	05 16		05 46		06 14								06 38
Cuffley d	23p49	23p51							04 30	00 29	05 21		05 51		06 19				06 32				06 43
Crews Hill d	23p52	23p54								00 32	05 24		05 54		06 22								06 46
Gordon Hill d	23p55	23p57							04 34	00 35	05 27		05 57		06 25				06 37				06 49
Enfield Chase d	23p57	23p59							04 36	00 37	05 29		05 59		06 27				06 39				06 52
Grange Park d	23p59	00 01								00 39	05 31		06 01		06 29								06 54
Winchmore Hill d	00 01	00 03								00 41	05 33		06 03		06 31				06 41				06 56
Palmers Green d	00 03	00 05								00 43	05 35		06 05		06 33				06 44				06 58
Bowes Park d	00 06	00 08								0046	05 38		06 08		06 36								07 01
Knebworth d					23p51	00 02						05 07		05 43				06 13			06 33		
Welwyn North d					23p55	00 06						05 11		05 47				06 17			06 37		
Welwyn Garden City ■ d					23p58	00 09		04 10				05 15		05 50			05 58	06 20			06 40	06 25	
Hatfield d					00 01	00 12		04 14				05 19		05 53			06 02	06 23			06 44	06 29	
Welham Green d																	06 06					06 33	
Brookmans Park d								04 19									06 08					06 35	
Potters Bar d					00 07	00 18		04 22				05 25		05 59			06 11	06 29			06 49	06 38	
Hadley Wood d																	06 15					06 42	
New Barnet d								04 27				05 29					06 17					06 44	
Oakleigh Park d								04 29				05 31					06 19					06 46	
New Southgate d								04 32				05 34					06 22					06 49	
Alexandra Palace d	00 08	00 10						04 35		00 48	05 40	05 37	06 10		06 38		06 25					06 52	07 03
Hornsey d	00 10	00 12						04 37	04 43	00 50	05 42		06 12		06 40		06 27					06 54	07 05
Harringay d	00 12	00 14						04 39		00 52	05 44		06 14		06 42		06 29					06 56	07 07
Finsbury Park ⊖ d	00 15	00 17	00 05	00 09	00 20	00 29	00 30	04 42	04s46	00 55	05 47	05 41	06 17	06 08	06 45	06 21	06 32	06 38	06 51	06 44	06 58	06 59	07 10
Drayton Park d													06 19		06 47		06 34		06 53			07 01	07 12
Highbury & Islington ⊖ d													06 20		06 49		06 35		06 55			07 03	07 14
Essex Road d													06 22		06 51		06 37		06 57			07 05	07 16
Old Street ⊖ d													06 25		06 54		06 40		07 00			07 08	07 19
Moorgate ⊖ a													06 30		07 00		06 45		07 05			07 13	07 24
London Kings Cross ■ ⊖ a	00 26	00 27	00 14	00 17	00 32	00 42	00 42	04 51	04 59	01 05	05 58	05 55		06 18		06 30		06 48		06 52	07 07		

	FC	FC	FC ■	FC ■	FC	FC	FC	FC	FC ■	FC ■	FC	FC ■	FC	FC	FC	FC	FC	FC	FC ■	FC	FC ■	FC ■
Letchworth Garden City d	06 24		06 39			06 48			06 57	07 04				07 20					07 27		07 32	07 47
Hitchin ■ d	06 28		06 43	06 46		06 52			07 01	07 08		07 18		07 24					07 31		07 36	07 51
Stevenage ■ d	06 34		06 48	06 52		06 58		07 04	07 07	07 14		07 24		07 30				07 35	07 37		07 42	
Watton-at-Stone d	06 40							07 11										07 42				
Hertford North d	06 48						07 04	07 18							07 25	07 33	07 38	07 50				
Bayford d							07 08										07 42					
Cuffley d	06 55						07 13	07 25							07 32	07 40	07 47	07 57				
Crews Hill d							07 16										07 50					
Gordon Hill d	07 00						07 19	07 30			07 09				07 37	07 45	07 53	08 02				
Enfield Chase d	07 02						07 22	07 32			07 12				07 39	07 47	07 56	08 04				
Grange Park d							07 24				07 14				07 41	07 49	07 58					
Winchmore Hill d	07 04						07 26	07 34			07 16				07 43	07 51	08 00					
Palmers Green d	07 07						07 28	07 37			07 18				07 45	07 53	08 02					
Bowes Park d							07 31				07 21				07 48	07 56	08 05	08 08				
Knebworth d				06 55					07 11	07 18											07 46	
Welwyn North d				06 59						07 22											07 50	07 59
Welwyn Garden City ■ d		06 35		07 03	06 48	07 08				07 26			07 16	07 42						07 30	07 54	
Hatfield d		06 39			06 52	07 12				07 30			07 20	07 46						07 34		
Welham Green d					06 56								07 24							07 38		
Brookmans Park d					06 58								07 26							07 40		
Potters Bar d		06 46			07 01	07 18							07 29	07 52						07 43		
Hadley Wood d		06 49			07 05								07 33							07 47		
New Barnet d		06 52			07 07	07 23							07 36	07 57						07 49		
Oakleigh Park d		06 54			07 09	07 25							07 38	07 59						07 51		
New Southgate d		06 57			07 12	07 28							07 41	08 02						07 54		
Alexandra Palace d					07 15		07 33				07 23		07 44		07 50	07 58	08 07	08 11				
Hornsey d					07 17		07 35				07 25		07 46		07 52	08 00		08 13				
Harringay d					07 19		07 37				07 27		07 48		07 54	08 02		08 15				
Finsbury Park ⊖ d	07 15	07 03	07 06	07 17	07 22	07 34	07 40	07 45	07 27	07 46	07 30	07 41	07 51	08 09	07 57	08 06	08 12	08 18	07 56	08 01	08 09	
Drayton Park d	07 17				07 24		07 42	07 47			07 32		07 53		07 59	08 08	08 14	08 20		08 03		
Highbury & Islington ⊖ d	07 19				07 26		07 44	07 49			07 34		07 55		08 01	08 10	08 16	08 22		08 05		
Essex Road d	07 21				07 28		07 46	07 51			07 36		07 57		08 03	08 12	08 18	08 24		08 07		
Old Street ⊖ d	07 24				07 31		07 49	07 54			07 39		08 00		08 06	08 15	08 21	08 27		08 10		
Moorgate ⊖ a	07 29				07 36		07 54	07 59			07 44		08 05		08 11	08 20	08 27	08 32		08 16		
London Kings Cross ■ ⊖ a		07 10	07 15	07 25		07 42			07 35	07 56		07 50		08 17					08 04		08 18	08 19

A MO from 19 July until 6 September
B MO from 13 September
C MO until 12 July, MO from 13 September
b previous night, stops to set down only

Letchworth Garden City, Hertford North and Welwyn Garden City - London

		FC [1]	FC	FC	FC	FC	FC	FC	FC [1]	FC [1]	FC
Letchworth Garden City	d								07 57	08 02	
Hitchin [4]	d	07 55							08 01	08 06	
Stevenage [4]	d	08 01						08 05	08 07	08 12	
Watton-at-Stone	d							08 12			
Hertford North	d			07 55			08 05	08 20			
Bayford	d						08 09				
Cuffley	d			08 02			08 14	08 27			
Crews Hill	d						08 17				
Gordon Hill	d			08 07		08 15	08 20	08 32			
Enfield Chase	d			08 09		08 17	08 22	08 34			
Grange Park	d			08 11		08 19	08 24				
Winchmore Hill	d			08 13		08 21	08 26				
Palmers Green	d			08 15		08 23	08 28				
Bowes Park	d			08 18		08 26	08 31	08 38			
Knebworth	d								08 11	08 16	
Welwyn North	d									08 20	
Welwyn Garden City [4]	d		07 47		07 58					08 24	08 14
Hatfield	d		07 51		08 02						08 18
Welham Green	d		07 55		08 06						
Brookmans Park	d		07 57		08 08						
Potters Bar	d		08 00		08 11						08 25
Hadley Wood	d		08 04		08 15						
New Barnet	d		08 06		08 18						08 29
Oakleigh Park	d		08 08		08 20						08 31
New Southgate	d		08 11		08 23						08 34
Alexandra Palace	d		08 14	08 20		08 28	08 33	08 41			08 37
Hornsey	d		08 16	08 22	08 26	08 30		08 43			
Harringay	d		08 18	08 24	08 28	08 32		08 45			
Finsbury Park ⊖	d	08 19	08 22	08 27	08 31	08 35	08 39	08 48		08 39	08 42
Drayton Park	d		08 24	08 29	08 33	08 37	08 41	08 50			
Highbury & Islington ⊖	d		08 26	08 31	08 35	08 39	08 43	08 52			
Essex Road	d		08 28	08 33	08 37	08 41	08 45	08 54			
Old Street ⊖	d		08 31	08 36	08 40	08 44	08 48	08 57			
Moorgate ⊖	a		08 36	08 41	08 46	08 50	08 55	09 02			
London Kings Cross [15] ⊖	a	08 28							08 36	08 49	08 50

		FC [1]	FC	FC [1]	FC	FC	FC	FC	FC	FC [1]	FC	FC
Letchworth Garden City	d			08 27						08 47		
Hitchin [4]	d	08 21		08 31				08 39		08 51		
Stevenage [4]	d	08 27					08 34	08 45		08 57		09 04
Watton-at-Stone	d						08 41					09 11
Hertford North	d				08 27		08 48					09 17
Bayford	d						08 52					09 21
Cuffley	d				08 34		08 57					09 26
Crews Hill	d						09 00					09 29
Gordon Hill	d				08 39		09 03				08 55	09 32
Enfield Chase	d				08 41		09 05				08 57	09 34
Grange Park	d				08 43		09 07				08 59	09 36
Winchmore Hill	d				08 45		09 09				09 01	09 38
Palmers Green	d				08 47		09 12				09 03	09 41
Bowes Park	d				08 50		09 14				09 06	09 43
Knebworth	d							08 49				
Welwyn North	d							08 53				
Welwyn Garden City [4]	d		08 18			08 30		08 58	08 42			
Hatfield	d		08 22			08 34		09 02	08 46			
Welham Green	d		08 26			08 38						
Brookmans Park	d		08 28			08 40						
Potters Bar	d		08 31			08 44			08 53			
Hadley Wood	d		08 35			08 47						
New Barnet	d		08 37			08 50			08 57			
Oakleigh Park	d		08 39			08 52			08 59			
New Southgate	d		08 42			08 55			09 02			
Alexandra Palace	d		08 45		08 52	08 58	09 17		09 05		09 08	09 46
Hornsey	d		08 47		08 54	09 00	09 19				09 10	09 48
Harringay	d		08 49		08 56	09 02	09 21				09 12	09 50
Finsbury Park ⊖	d	08 46	08 52		08 59	09 05	09 24	09 19	09 10	09 15	09 15	09 53
Drayton Park	d		08 54		09 01	09 07	09 26				09 17	09 55
Highbury & Islington ⊖	d		08 56		09 03	09 09	09 28				09 19	09 56
Essex Road	d		08 58		09 05	09 11	09 30				09 21	09 58
Old Street ⊖	d		09 01		09 08	09 14	09 33				09 24	10 01
Moorgate ⊖	a		09 06		09 13	09 20	09 38				09 29	10 06
London Kings Cross [15] ⊖	a	08 56		09 00				09 27	09 18	09 23		

		FC [1]	FC	FC	FC [1]	FC [1]	FC	FC	FC	FC	FC [1]	FC
Letchworth Garden City	d				09 00						09 29	
Hitchin [4]	d	09 00			09 04	09 29					09 33	
Stevenage [4]	d	09 05			09 10	09 34				09 34	09 39	
Watton-at-Stone	d									09 41		
Hertford North	d								09 32	09 52		
Bayford	d								09 36	09 56		
Cuffley	d								09 41	10 01		
Crews Hill	d								09 44	10 04		
Gordon Hill	d		09 12						09 47	10 07		
Enfield Chase	d		09 14						09 49	10 09		
Grange Park	d		09 16						09 51	10 11		
Winchmore Hill	d		09 18						09 53	10 13		
Palmers Green	d		09 21						09 55	10 15		
Bowes Park	d		09 23						[illegible]	[illegible]		
Knebworth	d				09 13						09 43	
Welwyn North	d				09 17						09 47	
Welwyn Garden City [4]	d			09 03	09 20		09 23	09 40			09 50	09 43
Hatfield	d			09 07	09 24		09 27	09 43			09 54	09 47
Welham Green	d			09 11			09 31					09 51
Brookmans Park	d			09 13			09 33					09 53
Potters Bar	d			09 16	09 30		09 36	09 49			10 00	09 56
Hadley Wood	d			09 20			09 40					10 00
New Barnet	d			09 22			09 42					10 02
Oakleigh Park	d			09 24			09 44					10 04
New Southgate	d			09 27			09 47					10 07
Alexandra Palace	d		09 26	09 30			09 50		10 00	10 20		10 10
Hornsey	d		09 28	09 32			09 52		10 02	10 22		10 12
Harringay	d		09 30	09 34			09 54		10 04	10 24		10 14
Finsbury Park ⊖	d	09 23	09 33	09 37	09 41	09 52	09 57	10 01	10 07	10 27	10 09	10 17
Drayton Park	d		09 35	09 39			09 59		10 09	10 29		10 19
Highbury & Islington ⊖	d		09 36	09 40			10 00		10 10	10 30		10 20
Essex Road	d		09 38	09 42			10 02		10 12	10 32		10 22
Old Street ⊖	d		09 41	09 45			10 05		10 15	10 35		10 25
Moorgate ⊖	a		09 46	09 50			10 10		10 20	10 40		10 30
London Kings Cross [15] ⊖	a	09 32			09 50	10 02		10 08			10 18	

		FC	FC [1]	FC	FC [1]	FC [1]	FC [1]	FC	FC	FC [1]	FC	FC
Letchworth Garden City	d	09 50	09 54		09 59					10 29		
Hitchin [4]	d	09 54	09 58		10 03	10 12	10 28			10 33		
Stevenage [4]	d	09 59	10 03		10 09	10 18	10 33			10 39		
Watton-at-Stone	d	10 06										
Hertford North	d	10 12							10 32			10 52
Bayford	d	10 16							10 36			10 56
Cuffley	d	10 21							10 41			
Crews Hill	d	10 24										11 04
Gordon Hill	d	10 27							10 47			11 07
Enfield Chase	d	10 29							10 49			11 09
Grange Park	d	10 31							10 51			11 11
Winchmore Hill	d	10 33							10 53			11 13
Palmers Green	d	[illegible]							10 55			11 15
Bowes Park	d	10 38							10 58			11 18
Knebworth	d				10 13					10 43		
Welwyn North	d				[illegible]					10 47		
Welwyn Garden City [4]	d			10 03	10 20			10 23		10 50	10 43	
Hatfield	d			10 07	10 23			10 27		10 53	10 47	
Welham Green	d			10 11				10 31			10 51	
Brookmans Park	d			10 13				10 33			10 53	
Potters Bar	d			10 16	10 29			10 36		10 59	10 56	
Hadley Wood	d			10 20				10 40			11 00	
New Barnet	d			10 22				10 42			11 02	
Oakleigh Park	d			10 24				10 44			11 04	
New Southgate	d			10 27				10 47			11 07	
Alexandra Palace	d	10 40		10 30				10 50	11 00		11 10	11 20
Hornsey	d	10 42		10 32				10 52	11 02		11 12	11 22
Harringay	d	10 44		10 34				10 54	11 04		11 14	11 24
Finsbury Park ⊖	d	10 47	10 21	10 37	10 41		10 54	10 57	11 07	11 08	11 17	11 27
Drayton Park	d	10 49		10 39				10 59	11 09		11 19	11 29
Highbury & Islington ⊖	d	10 50		10 40				11 00	11 10		11 20	11 30
Essex Road	d	10 52		10 42				11 02	11 12		11 22	11 32
Old Street ⊖	d	10 55		10 45				11 05	11 15		11 25	11 35
Moorgate ⊖	a	11 00		10 50				11 10	11 20		11 30	11 40
London Kings Cross [15] ⊖	a		10 30		10 49	10 45	11 02			11 19		

Table 24

Mondays to Fridays

Letchworth Garden City, Hertford North and Welwyn Garden City - London

		FC	FC [1]	FC	FC [1]	FC [1]	FC	FC	FC [1]	FC	FC	FC
Letchworth Garden City	d	10 50	10 54						11 29			11 50
Hitchin [4]	d	10 54	10 58		11 03	11 28			11 33			11 54
Stevenage [4]	d	10 59	11 03		11 09	11 33			11 39			11 59
Watton-at-Stone	d	11 06										12 06
Hertford North	d	11 12						11 32			11 52	12 12
Bayford	d	11 16						11 36			11 56	12 16
Cuffley	d	11 21						11 41			12 01	12 21
Crews Hill	d	11 24						11 44			12 04	12 24
Gordon Hill	d	11 27						11 47			12 07	12 27
Enfield Chase	d	11 29						11 49			12 09	12 29
Grange Park	d	11 31						11 51			12 11	12 31
Winchmore Hill	d	11 33						11 53			12 13	12 33
Palmers Green	d	11 35						11 55			12 15	12 35
Bowes Park	d	11 38						11 58			12 18	12 38
Knebworth	d				11 13				11 43			
Welwyn North	d				11 17				11 47			
Welwyn Garden City [4]	d			11 03	11 20		11 23		11 50	11 43		
Hatfield	d			11 07	11 23		11 27		11 53	11 47		
Welham Green	d			11 11			11 31			11 51		
Brookmans Park	d			11 13			11 33			11 53		
Potters Bar	d			11 16	11 29		11 36		11 59	11 56		
Hadley Wood	d			11 20			11 40			12 00		
New Barnet	d			11 22			11 42			12 02		
Oakleigh Park	d			11 24			11 44			12 04		
New Southgate	d			11 27			11 47			12 07		
Alexandra Palace	d	11 40		11 30			11 50	12 00		12 10	12 20	12 40
Hornsey	d	11 42		11 32			11 52	12 02		12 12	12 22	12 42
Harringay	d	11 44		11 34			11 54	12 04		12 14	12 24	12 44
Finsbury Park ⊖	d	11 47	11 21	11 37	11 41	11 52	11 57	12 07	12 11	12 17	12 27	12 47
Drayton Park	d	11 49		11 39			11 59	12 09		12 19	12 29	12 49
Highbury & Islington ⊖	d	11 50		11 40			12 00	12 10		12 20	12 30	12 50
Essex Road	d	11 52		11 42			12 02	12 12		12 22	12 32	12 52
Old Street ⊖	d	11 55		11 45			12 05	12 15		12 25	12 35	12 55
Moorgate ⊖	a	12 00		11 50			12 10	12 20		12 30	12 40	13 00
London Kings Cross [15] ⊖	a		11 30		11 49	12 00			12 19			

		FC [1]	FC	FC [1]	FC [1]	FC	FC	FC [1]	FC	FC	FC
Letchworth Garden City	d	11 54						12 29			12 50
Hitchin [4]	d	11 58		12 03	12 28			12 33			12 54
Stevenage [4]	d	12 03		12 09	12 33			12 39			12 59
Watton-at-Stone	d										13 06
Hertford North	d						12 32			12 52	13 12
Bayford	d						12 36			12 56	13 16
Cuffley	d						12 41			13 01	13 21
Crews Hill	d						12 44			13 04	13 24
Gordon Hill	d						12 47			13 07	13 27
Enfield Chase	d						12 49			13 09	13 29
Grange Park	d						12 51			13 11	13 31
Winchmore Hill	d						12 53			13 13	13 33
Palmers Green	d						12 55			13 15	13 35
Bowes Park	d						12 58			13 18	13 38
Knebworth	d			12 13				12 43			
Welwyn North	d			12 17				12 47			
Welwyn Garden City [4]	d		12 03	12 20		12 23		12 50	12 43		
Hatfield	d		12 07	12 23		12 27		12 53	12 47		
Welham Green	d		12 11			12 31			12 51		
Brookmans Park	d		12 13			12 33			12 53		
Potters Bar	d		12 16	12 29		12 36		12 59	12 56		
Hadley Wood	d		12 20			12 40			13 00		
New Barnet	d		12 22			12 42			13 02		
Oakleigh Park	d		12 24			12 44			13 04		
New Southgate	d		12 27			12 47			13 07		
Alexandra Palace	d		12 30			12 50	13 00		13 10	13 20	13 40
Hornsey	d		12 32			12 52	13 02		13 12	13 22	13 42
Harringay	d		12 34			12 54	13 04		13 14	13 24	13 44
Finsbury Park ⊖	d	12 21	12 37	12 41	12 51	12 57	13 07	13 08	13 17	13 27	13 47
Drayton Park	d		12 39			12 59	13 09		13 19	13 29	13 49
Highbury & Islington ⊖	d		12 40			13 00	13 10		13 20	13 30	13 50
Essex Road	d		12 42			13 02	13 12		13 22	13 32	13 52
Old Street ⊖	d		12 45			13 05	13 15		13 25	13 35	13 55
Moorgate ⊖	a		12 50			13 10	13 20		13 30	13 40	14 00
London Kings Cross [15] ⊖	a	12 30		12 49	13 00			13 19			

		FC [1]	FC	FC [1]	FC [1]	FC	FC	FC [1]	FC	FC	FC	FC [1]
Letchworth Garden City	d	12 54						13 29			13 50	13 54
Hitchin [4]	d	12 58		13 03	13 28			13 33			13 54	13 58
Stevenage [4]	d	13 03		13 09	13 33			13 39			13 59	14 03
Watton-at-Stone	d										14 06	
Hertford North	d						13 32			13 52	14 12	
Bayford	d						13 36			13 56	14 16	
Cuffley	d						13 41			14 01	14 21	
Crews Hill	d						13 44			14 04	14 24	
Gordon Hill	d						13 47			14 07	14 27	
[illegible]	d						13 49			14 09	14 29	
Grange Park	d						13 51			14 11	14 31	
Winchmore Hill	d						13 53			14 13	14 33	
Palmers Green	d						13 55			14 15	14 35	
Bowes Park	d						13 58			14 18	14 38	
Knebworth	d			13 13				13 43				
Welwyn North	d			13 17				13 47				
Welwyn Garden City [4]	d		13 03	13 20		13 23		13 50	13 43			
Hatfield	d		13 07	13 23		13 27		13 53	13 47			
Welham Green	d		13 11			13 31			[illegible]			
Brookmans Park	d		13 13			13 33			13 53			
Potters Bar	d		13 16	13 29		13 36		13 59	13 56			
Hadley Wood	d		13 20			13 40			14 00			
New Barnet	d		13 22			13 42			14 02			
Oakleigh Park	d		13 24			13 44			14 04			
New Southgate	d		13 27			13 47			14 07			
Alexandra Palace	d		13 30			13 50	14 00		14 10	14 20	14 40	
Hornsey	d		13 32			13 52	14 02		14 12	14 22	14 42	
Harringay	d		13 34			13 54	14 04		14 14	14 24	14 44	
Finsbury Park ⊖	d	13 21	13 37	13 41	13 51	13 57	14 07	14 08	14 17	14 27	14 47	14 21
Drayton Park	d		13 39			13 59	14 09		14 19	14 29	14 49	
Highbury & Islington ⊖	d		13 40			14 00	14 10		14 20	14 30	14 50	
Essex Road	d		13 42			14 02	14 12		14 22	14 32	14 52	
Old Street ⊖	d		13 45			14 05	14 15		14 25	14 35	14 55	
Moorgate ⊖	a		13 50			14 10	14 20		14 30	14 40	15 00	
London Kings Cross [15] ⊖	a	13 30		13 49	14 00			14 19				14 30

		FC	FC [1]	FC [1]	FC	FC	FC [1]	FC	FC	FC	FC [1]	FC
Letchworth Garden City	d						14 29			14 50	14 54	
Hitchin [4]	d		14 04	14 28			14 33			14 54	14 58	
Stevenage [4]	d		14 10	14 33			14 39			14 59	15 03	
Watton-at-Stone	d									15 06		
Hertford North	d					14 32			14 52	15 12		
Bayford	d					14 36			14 56	15 16		
Cuffley	d					14 41			15 01	15 21		
Crews Hill	d					14 44			15 04	15 24		
Gordon Hill	d					14 47			15 07	15 27		
[illegible]	d					14 49			15 09	15 29		
Grange Park	d					14 51			15 11	15 31		
Winchmore Hill	d					14 53			15 13	15 33		
Palmers Green	d					14 55			15 15	15 35		
Bowes Park	d					14 58			15 18	15 38		
Knebworth	d		14 14				14 43					
Welwyn North	d		14 18				14 47					
Welwyn Garden City [4]	d	14 03	14 21		14 23		14 50	14 43				15 03
Hatfield	d	14 07	14 24		14 27		14 53	14 47				15 07
Welham Green	d	14 11			14 31			14 51				15 11
Brookmans Park	d	14 13			14 33			14 53				15 13
Potters Bar	d	14 16	14 30		14 36		14 59	14 56				15 16
Hadley Wood	d	14 20			14 40			15 00				15 20
New Barnet	d	14 22			14 42			15 02				15 22
Oakleigh Park	d	14 24			14 44			15 04				15 24
New Southgate	d	14 27			14 47			15 07				15 27
Alexandra Palace	d	14 30			14 50	15 00		15 10	15 20	15 40		15 30
Hornsey	d	14 32			14 52	15 02		15 12	15 22	15 42		15 32
Harringay	d	14 34			14 54	15 04		15 14	15 24	15 44		15 34
Finsbury Park ⊖	d	14 37	14 42	14 52	14 57	15 07	15 11	15 17	15 27	15 47	15 21	15 37
Drayton Park	d	14 39			14 59	15 09		15 19	15 29	15 49		15 39
Highbury & Islington ⊖	d	14 40			15 00	15 10		15 20	15 30	15 50		15 40
Essex Road	d	14 42			15 02	15 12		15 22	15 32	15 52		15 42
Old Street ⊖	d	14 45			15 05	15 15		15 25	15 35	15 55		15 45
Moorgate ⊖	a	14 50			15 10	15 20		15 30	15 40	16 00		15 50
London Kings Cross [15] ⊖	a		14 50	15 01			15 20				15 30	

Table 24

Mondays to Fridays

Letchworth Garden City, Hertford North and Welwyn Garden City - London

		FC [1]	FC [1]	FC	FC	FC [1]	FC	FC	FC	FC [1]	FC	FC [1]	FC	FC	FC [1]	FC	FC	FC [1]	FC	FC	FC	FC [1]	FC
Letchworth Garden City	d					15 29			15 50	15 54				16 20				16 29				16 55	
Hitchin [4]	d	15 03	15 30			15 33			15 54	15 58		16 04		16 24	16 28			16 33				17 00	
Stevenage [4]	d	15 09	15 36			15 39			15 59	16 03		16 10		16 29	16 33			16 39			16 59	17 05	
Watton-at-Stone	d								16 06					16 36							17 06		
Hertford North	d				15 33			15 53	16 13				16 33	16 43						16 53	17 13		
Bayford	d				15 37			15 57	16 17				16 37	16 47						16 57	17 17		
Cuffley	d				15 42			16 02	16 22				16 42	16 52						17 02	17 22		
Crews Hill	d				15 45			16 05	16 25				16 45	16 55						17 05	17 25		
Gordon Hill	d				15 48			16 08	16 28				16 48	16 58						17 08	17 28		
Enfield Chase	d				15 50			16 10	16 30				16 50	17 00						17 10	17 30		
Grange Park	d				15 52			16 12	16 32				16 52							17 12	17 32		
Winchmore Hill	d				15 54			16 14	16 34				16 54	17 02						17 14	17 34		
Palmers Green	d				15 56			16 16	16 36				16 56	17 05						17 16	17 36		
Bowes Park	d				15 59			16 19	16 39				16 59							17 19	17 39		
Knebworth	d	15 13				15 43						16 14						16 43					
Welwyn North	d	15 17				15 47						16 18						16 47					
Welwyn Garden City [4]	d	15 20		15 24		15 50	15 44				16 04	16 21				16 24	16 40	16 51	16 44				17 04
Hatfield	d	15 23		15 28		15 53	15 48				16 08	16 24				16 28	16 43	16 55	16 48				17 08
Welham Green	d			15 32			15 52				16 12					16 32			16 52				17 12
Brookmans Park	d			15 34			15 54				16 14					16 34			16 54				17 14
Potters Bar	d	15 29		15 37		15 59	15 57				16 17	16 30				16 37	16 49	17 01	16 57				17 17
Hadley Wood	d			15 41			16 01				16 21					16 41			17 01				17 21
New Barnet	d			15 43			16 03				16 23					16 43			17 03				17 23
Oakleigh Park	d			15 45			16 05				16 25					16 45			17 05				17 25
New Southgate	d			15 48			16 08				16 28					16 48			17 08				17 28
Alexandra Palace	d			15 51	16 01		16 11	16 21	16 41		16 31		17 01			16 51			17 11	17 21	17 41		17 31
Hornsey	d			15 53	16 03		16 13	16 23	16 43		16 33		17 03			16 53			17 13	17 23	17 43		17 33
Harringay	d			15 55	16 05		16 15	16 25	16 45		16 35		17 05			16 55			17 15	17 25	17 45		17 35
Finsbury Park ⊖	d	15 41	15 53	15 58	16 08	16 10	16 18	16 28	16 48	16 21	16 38	16 39	17 08	17 12	16 51	16 58	17 01	17 11	17 18	17 28	17 48	17 23	17 38
Drayton Park	d			16 00	16 10		16 20	16 30	16 50		16 40		17 10	17 14		17 00			17 20	17 30	17 50		17 40
Highbury & Islington ⊖	d			16 01	16 11		16 21	16 31	16 51		16 41		17 11	17 15		17 01			17 21	17 31	17 51		17 41
Essex Road	d			16 03	16 13		16 23	16 33	16 53		16 43		17 13	17 17		17 03			17 23	17 33	17 53		17 43
Old Street ⊖	d			16 06	16 16		16 26	16 36	16 56		16 46		17 16	17 20		17 06			17 26	17 36	17 56		17 46
Moorgate ⊖	a			16 12	16 21		16 31	16 41	17 01		16 51		17 21	17 26		17 11			17 31	17 41	18 01		17 51
London Kings Cross [15] ⊖	a	15 50	16 02			16 17				16 30		16 50			17 01		17 10	17 21				17 35	

		FC [1]	FC	FC	FC [1]	FC	FC	FC	FC [1]	FC	FC [1]	FC	FC [1]	FC	FC	FC [1]	FC [1]	FC	FC [1]	FC	FC	FC [1]	FC
Letchworth Garden City	d								17 29		17 59								18 29			18 59	
Hitchin [4]	d	17 03			17 28				17 33		18 03		18 11			18 29	18 42		18 33			19 03	
Stevenage [4]	d	17 09		17 29	17 33				17 39	17 53	18 09		18 17		18 23	18 35	18 48		18 39		18 53	19 09	
Watton-at-Stone	d			17 36						18 00					18 30						19 00		
Hertford North	d		17 36	17 43						18 06				18 18	18 36					18 48	19 06		
Bayford	d			17 47										18 22						18 52			
Cuffley	d		17 43	17 52						18 13				18 27	18 43					18 57	19 13		
Crews Hill	d			17 55										18 30						19 00			
Gordon Hill	d		17 48	17 58		17 38				18 18				18 33	18 48					19 03	19 18		
Enfield Chase	d		17 50	18 00		17 40				18 20				18 35	18 50					19 05	19 20		
Grange Park	d			18 02		17 42								18 37						19 07			
Winchmore Hill	d		17 52	18 04		17 44				18 22				18 39	18 52					19 09	19 22		
Palmers Green	d		17 55	18 06		17 46				18 25				18 41	18 55					19 11	19 25		
Bowes Park	d			18 09		17 49								18 44						19 14			
Knebworth	d	17 13							17 43				18 21						18 43				
Welwyn North	d	17 17							17 47				18 25						18 47				
Welwyn Garden City [4]	d	17 21					17 44	17 34	17 51			18 04	18 28					18 34	18 51				19 04
Hatfield	d	17 25					17 48	17 38	17 55			18 08	18 32					18 38	18 55				19 08
Welham Green	d							17 42				18 12						18 42					19 12
Brookmans Park	d							17 44				18 14						18 44					19 14
Potters Bar	d	17 31					17 55	17 47	18 01			18 17	18 38					18 47	19 01				19 17
Hadley Wood	d							17 51				18 21						18 51					19 21
New Barnet	d							17 53				18 23						18 53					19 23
Oakleigh Park	d							17 55				18 25						18 55					19 25
New Southgate	d							17 58				18 28						18 58					19 28
Alexandra Palace	d			18 11		17 51		18 01				18 31		18 46				19 01		19 16			19 31
Hornsey	d			18 13		17 53		18 03				18 33		18 48				19 03		19 18			19 33
Harringay	d			18 15		17 55		18 05				18 35		18 50				19 05		19 20			19 35
Finsbury Park ⊖	d	17 41	18 02	18 18	17 51	17 58	18 07	18 08	18 11	18 32	18 27	18 38	18 47	18 53	19 02	18 54	19 06	19 08	19 11	19 23	19 32	19 27	19 38
Drayton Park	d		18 04	18 20		18 00		18 10		18 34		18 40		18 55	19 04			19 10		19 25	19 34		19 40
Highbury & Islington ⊖	d		18 05	18 21		18 01		18 11		18 35		18 41		18 56	19 05			19 11		19 26	19 35		19 41
Essex Road	d		18 07	18 23		18 03		18 13		18 37		18 43		18 58	19 07			19 13		19 28	19 37		19 43
Old Street ⊖	d		18 10	18 26		18 06		18 16		18 40		18 46		19 01	19 10			19 16		19 31	19 40		19 46
Moorgate ⊖	a		18 16	18 31		18 12		18 22		18 45		18 51		19 06	19 15			19 21		19 36	19 45		19 51
London Kings Cross [15] ⊖	a	17 50			18 00		18 17		18 20		18 35		18 58			19 01	19 15		19 22			19 34	

Table 24

Mondays to Fridays

Letchworth Garden City, Hertford North and Welwyn Garden City - London

		FC [1]	FC	FC	FC	FC [1]	FC	FC	FC [1]	FC	FC [1]	FC	FC [1]	FC	FC [1]	FC	FC [1]	FC	FC [1]	FC	FC [1]	FC	FC [1]
Letchworth Garden City	d					19 29			19 55			20 20			20 29		20 54			21 20	21 29		
Hitchin [4]	d	19 11				19 33			20 00		20 03	20 24	20 28		20 33		20 58		21 03	21 24	21 33		21 41
Stevenage [4]	d	19 17				19 39		19 59	20 05		20 09	20 29	20 33		20 39	20 59	21 03		21 09	21 29	21 39		21 47
Watton-at-Stone	d							20 06				20 36				21 06				21 36			
Hertford North	d		19 18	19 36			19 48	20 12				20 42				21 12				21 42			
Bayford	d		19 22				19 52	20 16				20 46				21 16				21 46			
Cuffley	d		19 27	19 43			19 57	20 21				20 51				21 21				21 51			
Crews Hill	d		19 30				20 00	20 24				20 54				21 24				21 54			
Gordon Hill	d		19 33	19 48			20 03	20 27				20 57				21 27				21 57			
Enfield Chase	d		19 35	19 50			20 05	20 29				20 59				21 29				21 59			
Grange Park	d		19 37				20 07	20 31				21 01				21 31				22 01			
Winchmore Hill	d		19 39	19 52			20 09	20 33				21 03				21 33				22 03			
Palmers Green	d		19 41	19 55			20 11	20 35				21 05				21 35				22 05			
Bowes Park	d		19 44				20 14	20 38				21 08				21 38				22 08			
Knebworth	d	19 21				19 43					20 13				20 43				21 13		21 43		
Welwyn North	d	19 25				19 47					20 17				20 47				21 17		21 47		
Welwyn Garden City [4]	d	19 28			19 34	19 50				19 58	20 20			20 28	20 50			20 58	21 20		21 50	21 28	
Hatfield	d	19 32			19 38	19 53				20 02	20 23			20 32	20 53			21 02	21 23		21 53	21 32	
Welham Green	d				19 42					20 06				20 36				21 06				21 36	
Brookmans Park	d				19 44					20 08				20 38				21 08				21 38	
Potters Bar	d	19 38			19 47	19 59				20 11	20 29			20 41	20 59			21 11	21 29		21 59	21 41	
Hadley Wood	d				19 51					20 15				20 45				21 15				21 45	
New Barnet	d				19 53					20 17				20 47				21 17				21 47	
Oakleigh Park	d				19 55					20 19				20 49				21 19				21 49	
New Southgate	d				19 58					20 22				20 52				21 22				21 52	
Alexandra Palace	d		19 46		20 01		20 16	20 40		20 25		21 10		20 55		21 40		21 25		22 10		21 55	
Hornsey	d		19 48		20 03		20 18	20 42		20 27		21 12		20 57		21 42		21 27		22 12		21 57	
Harringay	d		19 50		20 05		20 20	20 44		20 29		21 14		20 59		21 44		21 29		22 14		21 59	
Finsbury Park ⊖	d	19 47	19 53	20 02	20 08	20 11	20 23	20 47	20 23	20 32	20 38	21 17	20 51	21 02	21 11	21 47	21 21	21 32	21 38	22 17	22 11	22 02	22 05
Drayton Park	d		19 55	20 04	20 10		20 25	20 49		20 34		21 19		21 04		21 49		21 34					
Highbury & Islington ⊖	d		19 56	20 05	20 11		20 26	20 50		20 35		21 20		21 05		21 50		21 35					
Essex Road	d		19 58	20 07	20 13		20 28	20 52		20 37		21 22		21 07		21 52		21 37					
Old Street ⊖	d		20 01	20 10	20 16		20 31	20 55		20 40		21 25		21 10		21 55		21 40					
Moorgate ⊖	a		20 06	20 15	20 21		20 36	21 00		20 45		21 30		21 15		22 00		21 45					
London Kings Cross [15] ⊖	a	19 59				20 19			20 33		20 49		21 00		21 19		21 29		21 49	22 25	22 19	22 10	22 14

		FC [1]	FC	FC [1]	FC	FC	FC	FC [1]	FC [1]	FC	FC	FC [1]	FC	FC [1]
Letchworth Garden City	d	21 54				22 20		22 29	22 54				23 18	23 47
Hitchin [4]	d	21 58		22 11		22 24		22 33	22 58			23 16	23 22	23 54
Stevenage [4]	d	22 03		22 17		22 29		22 39	23 03			23 22	23 27	23 59
Watton-at-Stone	d					22 36							23 34	
Hertford North	d				22 12	22 42					23 10		23 40	
Bayford	d				22 16	22 46					23 14		23 44	
Cuffley	d				22 21	22 51					23 19		23 49	
Crews Hill	d				22 24	22 54					23 22		23 52	
Gordon Hill	d				22 27	22 57					23 25		23 55	
Enfield Chase	d				22 29	22 59					23 27		23 57	
Grange Park	d				22 31	23 01					23 29		23 59	
Winchmore Hill	d				22 33	23 03					23 31		00 01	
Palmers Green	d				22 35	23 05					23 33		00 03	
Bowes Park	d				22 38	23 08					23 36		00 06	
Knebworth	d			22 20				22 43				23 25		00 02
Welwyn North	d			22 24				22 46				23 29		00 06
Welwyn Garden City [4]	d		21 58	22 27			22 30	22 49		23 00		23 32		00 09
Hatfield	d		22 02	22 30			22 34	22 52		23 04		23 35		00 12
Welham Green	d		22 06				22 38			23 08				
Brookmans Park	d		22 08				22 40			23 10				
Potters Bar	d		22 11	22 36			22 43	22 58		23 13		23 41		00 18
Hadley Wood	d		22 15				22 47			23 17				
New Barnet	d		22 17				22 49			23 19				
Oakleigh Park	d		22 19				22 51			23 21				
New Southgate	d		22 22				22 54			23 24				
Alexandra Palace	d		22 25		22 40	23 10	22 57			23 27	23 38		00 08	
Hornsey	d		22 27		22 42	23 12	22 59			23 29	23 40		00 10	
Harringay	d		22 29		22 44	23 14	23 01			23 31	23 42		00 12	
Finsbury Park ⊖	d	22 21	22 32	22 44	22 47	23 17	23 04	23 10	23 21	23 34	23 45	23s52	00 15	00 29
Drayton Park	d													
Highbury & Islington ⊖	d													
Essex Road	d													
Old Street ⊖	d													
Moorgate ⊖	a													
London Kings Cross [15] ⊖	a	22 30	22 40	22 56	22 55	23 25	23 12	23 21	23 30	23 42	23 53	00 01	00 26	00 42

Table 24

Letchworth Garden City, Hertford North and Welwyn Garden City - London

			FC	FC ■	FC	FC ■	FC	FC ■	FC	FC ■		FC	FC ■	FC	FC	FC ■	FC	FC ■	FC ■	FC		FC ■	FC	FC	FC ■
Letchworth Garden City	d		23p18	23p47			04 50		05 20	05 29					06 20			06 29	06 54						
Hitchin ■	d		23p22	23p54		04 08	04 54	04 58	05 24	05 33			06 03		06 24	06 28		06 33	06 58			07 03			07 28
Stevenage ■	d		23p27	23p59		04 13	04 59	05 05	05 29	05 39			06 09		06 29	06 33		06 39	07 03			07 09		07 29	07 33
Watton-at-Stone	d		23p34				05 06		05 36						06 36									07 36	
Hertford North	d		23p40			04 23	05 12		05 42					06 12	06 42								07 12	07 42	
Bayford	d		23p44				05 16		05 46					06 16	06 46								07 16	07 46	
Cuffley	d		23p49			04 30	05 21		05 51					06 21	06 51								07 21	07 51	
Crews Hill	d		23p52				05 24		05 54					06 24	06 54								07 24	07 54	
Gordon Hill	d		23p55			04 34	05 27		05 57					06 27	06 57								07 27	07 57	
Enfield Chase	d		23p57			04 36	05 29		05 59					06 29	06 59								07 29	07 59	
Grange Park	d		23p59				05 31		06 01					06 31	07 01								07 31	08 01	
Winchmore Hill	d		00 01				05 33		06 03					06 33	07 03								07 33	08 03	
Palmers Green	d		00 03				05 35		06 05					06 35	07 05								07 35	08 05	
Bowes Park	d		00 06				05 38		06 08					06 38	07 08								07 38	08 08	
Knebworth	d			00 02				05 07		05 43			06 13					06 43				07 13			
Welwyn North	d			00 06				05 11		05 47			06 17					06 47				07 17			
Welwyn Garden City ■	d			00 09	04 10			05 15		05 50		05 58	06 20				06 28	06 50		06 58		07 20			
Hatfield	d			00 12	04 14			05 19		05 53		06 02	06 23				06 32	06 53		07 02		07 23			
Welham Green	d											06 06					06 36			07 06					
Brookmans Park	d				04 19							06 08					06 38			07 08					
Potters Bar	d			00 18	04 22			05 24		05 59		06 11	06 29				06 41	06 59		07 11		07 29			
Hadley Wood	d											06 15					06 45			07 15					
New Barnet	d				04 27			05 29				06 17					06 47			07 17					
Oakleigh Park	d				04 29			05 31				06 19					06 49			07 19					
New Southgate	d				04 32			05 34				06 22					06 52			07 22					
Alexandra Palace	d		00 08		04 35		05 40	05 37	06 10			06 25		06 40	07 10		06 55			07 25			07 40	08 10	
Hornsey	d		00 10		04 37	04 43	05 42		06 12			06 27		06 42	07 12		06 57			07 27			07 42	08 12	
Harringay	d		00 12		04 39		05 44		06 14			06 29		06 44	07 14		06 59			07 29			07 44	08 14	
Finsbury Park	⊖ d		00 15	00 29	04 42	04s46	05 47	05 41	06 17	06 08		06 32	06 38	06 47	07 17	06 51	07 02	07 08	07 21	07 32		07 38	07 47	08 17	07 51
Drayton Park	d																								
Highbury & Islington	⊖ d																								
Essex Road	d																								
Old Street	⊖ d																								
Moorgate	⊖ a																								
London Kings Cross ■	⊖ a		00 26	00 42	04 51	04 59	05 58	05 56	06 25	06 19		06 40	06 49	06 55	07 25	07 01	07 10	07 19	07 31	07 40		07 49	07 55	08 25	08 01

		FC	FC ■	FC ■	FC	FC ■		FC	FC	FC ■	FC	FC ■	FC ■	FC	FC ■	FC		FC	FC	FC ■	FC ■	FC	FC ■	FC	FC
Letchworth Garden City	d		07 29	07 54								08 29	08 54							09 29	09 54				
Hitchin ■	d		07 33	07 58		08 03				08 28		08 33	08 58		09 03					09 33	09 58		10 03		
Stevenage ■	d		07 39	08 03		08 09			08 29	08 33		08 39	09 03		09 09				09 29	09 39	10 03		10 09		10 29
Watton-at-Stone	d								08 36										09 36						10 36
Hertford North	d							08 12	08 42							09 12			09 42					10 12	10 42
Bayford	d							08 16	08 46							09 16			09 46					10 16	10 46
Cuffley	d							08 21	08 51							09 21			09 51					10 21	10 51
Crews Hill	d							08 24	08 54							09 24			09 54					10 24	10 54
Gordon Hill	d							08 27	08 57							09 27			09 57					10 27	10 57
Enfield Chase	d							08 29	08 59							09 29			09 59					10 29	10 59
Grange Park	d							08 31	09 01							09 31			10 01					10 31	11 01
Winchmore Hill	d							08 33	09 03							09 33			10 03					10 33	11 03
Palmers Green	d							08 35	09 05							09 35			10 05					10 35	11 05
Bowes Park	d							08 38	09 08							09 38			10 08					10 38	11 08
Knebworth	d		07 43			08 13						08 43			09 13					09 43			10 13		
Welwyn North	d		07 47			08 17						08 47			09 17					09 47			10 17		
Welwyn Garden City ■	d	07 28	07 50		07 58	08 20					08 28	08 50		08 58	09 20			09 28		09 50		09 58	10 20		
Hatfield	d	07 32	07 53		08 02	08 23					08 32	08 53		09 02	09 23			09 32		09 53		10 02	10 23		
Welham Green	d	07 36			08 06						08 36			09 06				09 36				10 06			
Brookmans Park	d	07 38			08 08						08 38			09 08				09 38				10 08			
Potters Bar	d	07 41	07 59		08 11	08 29					08 41	08 59		09 11	09 29			09 41		09 59		10 11	10 29		
Hadley Wood	d	07 45			08 15						08 45			09 15				09 45				10 15			
New Barnet	d	07 47			08 17						08 47			09 17				09 47				10 17			
Oakleigh Park	d	07 49			08 19						08 49			09 19				09 49				10 19			
New Southgate	d	07 52			08 22						08 52			09 22				09 52				10 22			
Alexandra Palace	d	07 55			08 25			08 40	09 10		08 55			09 25		09 40		09 55	10 10			10 25		10 40	11 10
Hornsey	d	07 57			08 27			08 42	09 12		08 57			09 27		09 42		09 57	10 12			10 27		10 42	11 12
Harringay	d	07 59			08 29			08 44	09 14		08 59			09 29		09 44		09 59	10 14			10 29		10 44	11 14
Finsbury Park	⊖ d	08 02	08 08	08 21	08 32	08 38		08 47	09 17	08 51	09 02	09 08	09 21	09 32	09 38	09 47		10 02	10 17	10 08	10 21	10 32	10 38	10 47	11 17
Drayton Park	d																								
Highbury & Islington	⊖ d																								
Essex Road	d																								
Old Street	⊖ d																								
Moorgate	⊖ a																								
London Kings Cross ■	⊖ a	08 10	08 19	08 31	08 40	08 49		08 55	09 25	09 01	09 10	09 19	09 31	09 38	09 49	09 55		10 10	10 25	10 19	10 31	10 40	10 49	10 55	11 25

b previous night, stops to set down only

Table 24

Letchworth Garden City, Hertford North and Welwyn Garden City - London

		FC ■		FC	FC ■	FC ■	FC	FC ■	FC	FC	FC ■	FC		FC ■	FC ■	FC	FC ■	FC	FC	FC	FC ■	FC ■		FC	FC ■
Letchworth Garden City	d				10 29	10 54								11 29	11 54						12 29	12 54			
Hitchin ■	d	10 28			10 33	10 58		11 03			11 28			11 33	11 58		12 03				12 33	12 58			13 03
Stevenage ■	d	10 33			10 39	11 03		11 09		11 29	11 33			11 39	12 03		12 09			12 29	12 39	13 03			13 09
Watton-at-Stone	d									11 36										12 36					
Hertford North	d								11 12	11 42								12 12		12 42					
Bayford	d								11 16	11 46								12 16		12 46					
Cuffley	d								11 21	11 51								12 21		12 51					
Crews Hill	d								11 24	11 54								12 24		12 54					
Gordon Hill	d								11 27	11 57								12 27		12 57					
Enfield Chase	d								11 29	11 59								12 29		12 59					
Grange Park	d								11 31	12 01								12 31		13 01					
Winchmore Hill	d								11 33	12 03								12 33		13 03					
Palmers Green	d								11 35	12 05								12 35		13 05					
Bowes Park	d								11 38	12 08								12 38		13 08					
Knebworth	d				10 43			11 13						11 43			12 13				12 43				13 13
Welwyn North	d				10 47			11 17						11 47			12 17				12 47				13 17
Welwyn Garden City ■	d			10 28	10 50		10 58	11 20				11 28		11 50		11 58	12 20		12 28		12 50			12 58	13 20
Hatfield	d			10 32	10 53		11 02	11 23				11 32		11 53		12 02	12 23		12 32		12 53			13 02	13 23
Welham Green	d			10 36			11 06					11 36				12 06			12 36					13 06	
Brookmans Park	d			10 38			11 08					11 38				12 08			12 38					13 08	
Potters Bar	d			10 41	10 59		11 11	11 29				11 41		11 59		12 11	12 29		12 41		12 59			13 11	13 30
Hadley Wood	d			10 45			11 15					11 45				12 15			12 45					13 15	
New Barnet	d			10 47			11 17					11 47				12 17			12 47					13 17	
Oakleigh Park	d			10 49			11 19					11 49				12 19			12 49					13 19	
New Southgate	d			10 52			11 22					11 52				12 22			12 52					13 22	
Alexandra Palace	d			10 55			11 25		11 40	12 10		11 55				12 25		12 40	12 55	13 10				13 25	
Hornsey	d			10 57			11 27		11 42	12 12		11 57				12 27		12 42	12 57	13 12				13 27	
Harringay	d			10 59			11 29		11 44	12 14		11 59				12 29		12 44	12 59	13 14				13 29	
Finsbury Park	⊖ d	10 51		11 02	11 08	11 21	11 32	11 38	11 47	12 17	11 51	12 02		12 08	12 21	12 32	12 38	12 47	13 02	13 17	13 08	13 21		13 32	13 38
Drayton Park	d																								
Highbury & Islington	⊖ d																								
Essex Road	d																								
Old Street	⊖ d																								
Moorgate	⊖ a																								
London Kings Cross ■	⊖ a	11 01		11 10	11 19	11 31	11 40	11 48	11 55	12 25	12 01	12 10		12 19	12 31	12 40	12 49	12 55	13 10	13 25	13 21	13 31		13 40	13 49

		FC	FC	FC ■	FC	FC ■	FC ■	FC		FC ■	FC	FC	FC ■	FC	FC ■	FC ■	FC	FC ■	FC	FC	FC ■	FC	FC ■	FC ■	FC
Letchworth Garden City	d					13 29	13 54								14 29	14 54							15 29	15 54	
Hitchin ■	d			13 28		13 33	13 58			14 03			14 28		14 33	14 58		15 03			15 28		15 33	15 58	
Stevenage ■	d		13 29	13 33		13 39	14 03			14 09		14 29	14 33		14 39	15 03		15 09		15 29	15 33		15 39	16 03	
Watton-at-Stone	d		13 36									14 36								15 36					
Hertford North	d	13 12	13 42								14 12	14 42							15 12	15 42					
Bayford	d	13 16	13 46								14 16	14 46							15 16	15 46					
Cuffley	d	13 21	13 51								14 21	14 51							15 21	15 51					
Crews Hill	d	13 24	13 54								14 24	14 54							15 24	15 54					
Gordon Hill	d	13 27	13 57								14 27	14 57							15 27	15 57					
Enfield Chase	d	13 29	13 59								14 29	14 59							15 29	15 59					
Grange Park	d	13 31	14 01								14 31	15 01							15 31	16 01					
Winchmore Hill	d	13 33	14 03								14 33	15 03							15 33	16 03					
Palmers Green	d	13 35	14 05								14 35	15 05							15 35	16 05					
Bowes Park	d	13 38	14 08								14 38	15 08							15 38	16 08					
Knebworth	d					13 43				14 13					14 43			15 13					15 43		
Welwyn North	d					13 47				14 17					14 47			15 17					15 47		
Welwyn Garden City ■	d				13 28	13 50		13 58		14 20				14 28	14 50		14 58	15 20				15 28	15 50		15 58
Hatfield	d				13 32	13 53		14 02		14 23				14 32	14 53		15 02	15 23				15 32	15 53		16 02
Welham Green	d				13 36			14 06						14 36			15 06					15 36			16 06
Brookmans Park	d				13 38			14 08						14 38			15 08					15 38			16 08
Potters Bar	d				13 41	13 59		14 11		14 29				14 41	14 59		15 11	15 29				15 41	15 59		16 11
Hadley Wood	d				13 45			14 15						14 45			15 15					15 45			16 15
New Barnet	d				13 47			14 17						14 47			15 17					15 47			16 17
Oakleigh Park	d				13 49			14 19						14 49			15 19					15 49			16 19
New Southgate	d				13 52			14 22						14 52			15 22					15 52			16 22
Alexandra Palace	d	13 39	14 10		13 55			14 25			14 40	15 10		14 55			15 25		15 40	16 10		15 55			16 25
Hornsey	d	13 41	14 12		13 57			14 27			14 42	15 12		14 57			15 27		15 42	16 12		15 57			16 27
Harringay	d	13 43	14 14		13 59			14 29			14 44	15 14		14 59			15 29		15 44	16 14		15 59			16 29
Finsbury Park	⊖ d	13 46	14 17	13 51	14 02	14 08	14 21	14 32		14 38	14 47	15 17	14 51	15 02	15 08	15 21	15 32	15 38	15 47	16 17	15 51	16 02	16 08	16 21	16 32
Drayton Park	d																								
Highbury & Islington	⊖ d																								
Essex Road	d																								
Old Street	⊖ d																								
Moorgate	⊖ a																								
London Kings Cross ■	⊖ a	13 54	14 25	14 01	14 10	14 19	14 31	14 40		14 49	14 55	15 25	15 01	15 10	15 19	15 31	15 40	15 49	15 55	16 25	16 00	16 10	16 19	16 31	16 40

Table 24

Letchworth Garden City, Hertford North and Welwyn Garden City - London

Saturdays
until 10 July

	FC 1	FC	FC	FC 1	FC	FC 1	FC 1	FC	FC 1	FC	FC	FC 1	FC	FC 1	FC 1	FC	FC 1	FC	FC	FC 1	FC
Letchworth Garden City d						16 29	16 54							17 29	17 54						
Hitchin 4 d	16 03			16 28		16 33	16 58		17 03			17 28		17 33	17 58		18 03			18 28	
Stevenage 4 d	16 09		16 29	16 33		16 39	17 03		17 09		17 29	17 33		17 39	18 03		18 09		18 29	18 33	
Watton-at-Stone d			16 36								17 36								18 36		
Hertford North d		16 12	16 42							17 12	17 42							18 12	18 42		
Bayford d		16 16	16 46							17 16	17 46							18 16	18 46		
Cuffley d		16 21	16 51							17 21	17 51							18 21	18 51		
Crews Hill d		16 24	16 54							17 24	17 54							18 24	18 54		
Gordon Hill d		16 27	16 57							17 27	17 57							18 27	18 57		
Enfield Chase d		16 29	16 59							17 29	17 59							18 29	18 59		
Grange Park d		16 31	17 01							17 31	18 01							18 31	19 01		
Winchmore Hill d		16 33	17 03							17 33	18 03							18 33	19 03		
Palmers Green d		16 35	17 05							17 35	18 05							18 35	19 05		
Bowes Park d		16 38	17 08							17 38	18 08							18 38	19 08		
Knebworth d	16 13					16 43			17 12					17 42			18 13				
Welwyn North d	16 17					16 47			17 17					17 47			18 17				
Welwyn Garden City 4 d	16 20				16 28	16 50		16 58	17 20				17 28	17 50		17 58	18 20				18 28
Hatfield d	16 23				16 32	16 53		17 02	17 23				17 32	17 53		18 02	18 23				18 32
Welham Green d					16 36			17 06					17 36			18 06					18 36
Brookmans Park d					16 38			17 08					17 38			18 08					18 38
Potters Bar d	16 29				16 41	16 59		17 11	17 29				17 41	17 59		18 11	18 29				18 41
Hadley Wood d					16 45			17 15					17 45			18 15					18 45
New Barnet d					16 47			17 17					17 47			18 17					18 47
Oakleigh Park d					16 49			17 19					17 49			18 19					18 49
New Southgate d					16 52			17 22					17 52			18 22					18 52
Alexandra Palace d		16 40	17 10		16 55			17 25		17 40	18 10		17 55			18 25		18 40	19 10		18 55
Hornsey d		16 42	17 12		16 57			17 27		17 42	18 12		17 57			18 27		18 42	19 12		18 57
Harringay d		16 44	17 14		16 59			17 29		17 44	18 14		17 59			18 29		18 44	19 14		18 59
Finsbury Park ⊖ d	16 38	16 47	17 17	16 51	17 02	17 08	17 21	17 32	17 38	17 47	18 17	17 51	18 02	18 08	18 21	18 32	18 38	18 47	19 17	18 51	19 02
Drayton Park d																					
Highbury & Islington ⊖ d																					
Essex Road d																					
Old Street ⊖ d																					
Moorgate ⊖ a																					
London Kings Cross 15 ⊖ a	16 49	16 55	17 25	17 01	17 10	17 19	17 31	17 40	17 49	17 55	18 25	18 01	18 10	18 19	18 31	18 40	18 49	18 55	19 25	19 01	19 10

	FC 1	FC 1	FC	FC 1	FC	FC	FC 1	FC	FC 1	FC 1	FC	FC 1	FC	FC	FC 1	FC	FC 1	FC 1	FC	FC 1	FC	FC
Letchworth Garden City d	18 29	18 54							19 29	19 54							20 29	20 54				
Hitchin 4 d	18 33	18 58		19 03			19 28		19 33	19 58		20 03			20 28		20 33	20 58		21 03		
Stevenage 4 d	18 39	19 03		19 09		19 29	19 33		19 39	20 03		20 09		20 29	20 33		20 39	21 03		21 09		21 29
Watton-at-Stone d						19 36								20 36								21 36
Hertford North d					19 12	19 42							20 12	20 42							21 12	21 42
Bayford d					19 16	19 46							20 16	20 46							21 16	21 46
Cuffley d					19 21	19 51							20 21	20 51							21 21	21 51
Crews Hill d					19 24	19 54							20 24	20 54							21 24	21 54
Gordon Hill d					19 27	19 57							20 27	20 57							21 27	21 57
Enfield Chase d					19 29	19 59							20 29	20 59							21 29	21 59
Grange Park d					19 31	20 01							20 31	21 01							21 31	22 01
Winchmore Hill d					19 33	20 03							20 33	21 03							21 33	22 03
Palmers Green d					19 35	20 05							20 35	21 05							21 35	22 05
Bowes Park d					19 38	20 08							20 38	21 08							21 38	22 08
Knebworth d	18 43			19 13					19 43			20 13					20 43			21 13		
Welwyn North d	18 47			19 17					19 47			20 17					20 47			21 17		
Welwyn Garden City 4 d	18 50		18 58	19 20				19 28	19 50		19 58	20 20				20 28	20 50		20 58	21 20		
Hatfield d	18 53		19 02	19 23				19 32	19 53		20 02	20 23				20 32	20 53		21 02	21 23		
Welham Green d			19 06					19 36			20 06					20 36			21 06			
Brookmans Park d			19 08					19 38			20 08					20 38			21 08			
Potters Bar d	18 59		19 11	19 29				19 41	19 59		20 11	20 29				20 41	20 59		21 11	21 29		
Hadley Wood d			19 15					19 45			20 15					20 45			21 15			
New Barnet d			19 17					19 47			20 17					20 47			21 17			
Oakleigh Park d			19 19					19 49			20 19					20 49			21 19			
New Southgate d			19 22					19 52			20 22					20 52			21 22			
Alexandra Palace d			19 25		19 40	20 10		19 55			20 25		20 40	21 10		20 55			21 25		21 40	22 10
Hornsey d			19 27		19 42	20 12		19 57			20 27		20 42	21 12		20 57			21 27		21 42	22 12
Harringay d			19 29		19 44	20 14		19 59			20 29		20 44	21 14		20 59			21 29		21 44	22 14
Finsbury Park ⊖ d	19 08	19 21	19 32	19 38	19 47	20 17	19 51	20 02	20 08	20 21	20 32	20 38	20 47	21 17	20 51	21 02	21 08	21 21	21 32	21 38	21 47	22 17
Drayton Park d																						
Highbury & Islington ⊖ d																						
Essex Road d																						
Old Street ⊖ d																						
Moorgate ⊖ a																						
London Kings Cross 15 ⊖ a	19 19	19 31	19 40	19 49	19 55	20 25	20 01	20 10	20 19	20 31	20 40	20 49	20 55	21 25	21 01	21 10	21 19	21 31	21 40	21 49	21 55	22 25

Table 24

Letchworth Garden City, Hertford North and Welwyn Garden City - London

Saturdays
until 10 July

	FC 1	FC	FC 1	FC 1	FC	FC 1	FC	FC	FC 1	FC	FC 1	FC 1	FC	FC 1	FC	FC	FC 1	FC 1
Letchworth Garden City d			21 29	21 54							22 29	22 54						23 41
Hitchin 4 d	21 28		21 33	21 58		22 03			22 28		22 33	22 58		23 03			23 31	23 45
Stevenage 4 d	21 33		21 39	22 03		22 09		22 29	22 33		22 39	23 03		23 09		23 29	23 34	23 50
Watton-at-Stone d								22 36								23 36		
Hertford North d							22 12	22 42							23 12	23 42		
Bayford d							22 16	22 46							23 16	23 46		
Cuffley d							22 21	22 51							23 21	23 51		
Crews Hill d							22 24	22 54							23 24	23 54		
Gordon Hill d							22 27	22 57							23 27	23 57		
Enfield Chase d							22 29	22 59							23 29	23 59		
Grange Park d							22 31	23 01							23 31	00 01		
Winchmore Hill d							22 33	23 03							23 33	00 03		
Palmers Green d							22 35	23 05							23 35	00 05		
Bowes Park d							22 38	23 08							23 38	00 08		
Knebworth d			21 43			22 13					22 43			23 13				23 53
Welwyn North d			21 47			22 17					22 47			23 17				23 57
Welwyn Garden City 4 d		21 28	21 50		21 58	22 20				22 28	22 50		22 58	23 20				00 01
Hatfield d		21 32	21 53		22 02	22 23				22 32	22 53		23 02	23 23				00 04
Welham Green d		21 36			22 06					22 36			23 06					
Brookmans Park d		21 38			22 08					22 38			23 08					
Potters Bar d		21 41	21 59		22 11	22 29				22 41	22 59		23 11	23 29				00 10
Hadley Wood d		21 45			22 15					22 45			23 15					
New Barnet d		21 47			22 17					22 47			23 17					
Oakleigh Park d		21 49			22 19					22 49			23 19					
New Southgate d		21 52			22 22					22 52			23 22					
Alexandra Palace d		21 55			22 25		22 40	23 10		22 55			23 25		23 41	00 10		
Hornsey d		21 57			22 27		22 42	23 12		22 57			23 27		23 43	00 12		
Harringay d		21 59			22 29		22 44	23 14		22 59			23 29		23 45	00 14		
Finsbury Park ⊖ d	21 51	22 02	22 08	22 21	22 32	22 38	22 47	23 17	22 52	23 02	23 08	23 21	23 32	23 41	23 47	00 17	00 01	00s27
Drayton Park d																		
Highbury & Islington ⊖ d																		
Essex Road d																		
Old Street ⊖ d																		
Moorgate ⊖ a																		
London Kings Cross 15 ⊖ a	22 01	22 10	22 19	22 31	22 40	22 49	22 55	23 25	23 01	23 10	23 19	23 31	23 40	23 52	23 56	00 25	00 09	00 35

Saturdays
17 July to 04 September

	FC	FC 1	FC	FC 1	FC	FC 1	FC	FC 1	FC	FC 1	FC	FC	FC 1	FC	FC 1	FC 1	FC	FC 1	FC	FC	FC 1
Letchworth Garden City d	23p18	23p47			04 50		05 20	05 29				06 20			06 29	06 54					
Hitchin 4 d	23p22	23p54		04 08	04 54	04 58	05 24	05 33		06 03		06 24	06 28		06 33	06 58		07 03			07 28
Stevenage 4 d	23p27	23p59		04 13	04 59	05 05	05 29	05 39		06 09		06 29	06 33		06 39	07 03		07 09		07 29	07 33
Watton-at-Stone d	23p34				05 06		05 36					06 36								07 36	
Hertford North d	23p40			04 23	05 12		05 42				06 12	06 42							07 12	07 42	
Bayford d	23p44				05 16		05 46				06 16	06 46							07 16	07 46	
Cuffley d	23p49			04 30	05 21		05 51				06 21	06 51							07 21	07 51	
Crews Hill d	23p52				05 24		05 54				06 24	06 54							07 24	07 54	
Gordon Hill d	23p55			04 34	05 27		05 57				06 27	06 57							07 27	07 57	
Enfield Chase d	23p57			04 36	05 29		05 59				06 29	06 59							07 29	07 59	
Grange Park d	23p59				05 31		06 01				06 31	07 01							07 31	08 01	
Winchmore Hill d	00 01				05 33		06 03				06 33	07 03							07 33	08 03	
Palmers Green d	00 03				05 35		06 05				06 35	07 05							07 35	08 05	
Bowes Park d	00 06				05 38		06 08				06 38	07 08							07 38	08 08	
Knebworth d		00 02				05 07		05 43		06 13					06 43			07 13			
Welwyn North d		00 06				05 11		05 47		06 17					06 47			07 17			
Welwyn Garden City 4 d		00 09	04 10			05 15		05 50	05 58	06 20				06 28	06 50		06 58	07 20			
Hatfield d		00 12	04 14			05 19		05 53	06 02	06 23				06 32	06 53		07 02	07 23			
Welham Green d									06 06					06 36			07 06				
Brookmans Park d			04 19						06 08					06 38			07 08				
Potters Bar d		00 18	04 22			05 24		05 59	06 11	06 29				06 41	06 59		07 11	07 29			
Hadley Wood d									06 15					06 45			07 15				
New Barnet d			04 27			05 29			06 17					06 47			07 17				
Oakleigh Park d			04 29			05 31			06 19					06 49			07 19				
New Southgate d			04 32			05 34			06 22					06 52			07 22				
Alexandra Palace d	00 08		04 35		05 40	05 37	06 10		06 25		06 40	07 10		06 55			07 25		07 40	08 10	
Hornsey d	00 10		04 37	04 43	05 42		06 12		06 27		06 42	07 12		06 57			07 27		07 42	08 12	
Harringay d	00 12		04 39		05 44		06 14		06 29		06 44	07 14		06 59			07 29		07 44	08 14	
Finsbury Park ⊖ d	00 15	00 29	04 42	04s46	05 47	05 41	06 17	06 08	06 32	06 38	06 47	07 17	06 51	07 02	07 08	07 21	07 32	07 38	07 47	08 17	07 51
Drayton Park d																					
Highbury & Islington ⊖ d																					
Essex Road d																					
Old Street ⊖ d																					
Moorgate ⊖ a																					
London Kings Cross 15 ⊖ a	00 26	00 42	04 51	04 59	05 58	05 56	06 25	06 19	06 40	06 49	06 55	07 25	07 01	07 10	07 19	07 31	07 40	07 49	07 55	08 25	08 01

b previous night, stops to set down only

Table 24

Letchworth Garden City, Hertford North and Welwyn Garden City - London

Saturdays

17 July to 04 September

		FC	FC ■	FC ■	FC	FC ■		FC	FC	FC ■	FC	FC ■	FC ■	FC	FC ■	FC		FC	FC	FC ■	FC ■	FC	FC ■	FC	FC
Letchworth Garden City	d		07 29	07 54								08 29	08 54							09 29	09 54				
Hitchin ■	d		07 33	07 58		08 03				08 28		08 33	08 58		09 03					09 33	09 58		10 03		
Stevenage ■	d		07 39	08 03		08 09			08 29	08 33		08 39	09 03		09 09				09 29	09 39	10 03		10 09		10 29
Watton-at-Stone	d								08 36										09 36						10 36
Hertford North	d							08 12	08 42							09 12			09 42					10 12	10 42
Bayford	d							08 16	08 46							09 16			09 46					10 16	10 46
Cuffley	d							08 21	08 51							09 21			09 51					10 21	10 51
Crews Hill	d							08 24	08 54							09 24			09 54					10 24	10 54
Gordon Hill	d							08 27	08 57							09 27			09 57					10 27	10 57
Enfield Chase	d							08 29	08 59							09 29			09 59					10 29	10 59
Grange Park	d							08 31	09 01							09 31			10 01					10 31	11 01
Winchmore Hill	d							08 33	09 03							09 33			10 03					10 33	11 03
Palmers Green	d							08 35	09 05							09 35			10 05					10 35	11 05
Bowes Park	d							08 38	09 08							09 38			10 08					10 38	11 08
Knebworth	d		07 43			08 13						08 43			09 13					09 43			10 13		
Welwyn North	d		07 47			08 17						08 47			09 17					09 47			10 17		
Welwyn Garden City ■	d	07 28	07 50		07 58	08 20					08 28	08 50		08 58	09 20			09 28		09 50		09 58	10 20		
Hatfield	d	07 32	07 53		08 02	08 23					08 32	08 53		09 02	09 23			09 32		09 53		10 02	10 23		
Welham Green	d	07 36			08 06						08 36			09 06				09 36				10 06			
Brookmans Park	d	07 38			08 08						08 38			09 08				09 38				10 08			
Potters Bar	d	07 41	07 59		08 11	08 29					08 41	08 59		09 11	09 29			09 41		09 59		10 11	10 29		
Hadley Wood	d	07 45			08 15						08 45			09 15				09 45				10 15			
New Barnet	d	07 47			08 17						08 47			09 17				09 47				10 17			
Oakleigh Park	d	07 49			08 19						08 49			09 19				09 49				10 19			
New Southgate	d	07 52			08 22						08 52			09 22				09 52				10 22			
Alexandra Palace	d	07 55			08 25			08 40	09 10		08 55			09 25		09 40		09 55	10 10			10 25		10 40	11 10
Hornsey	d	07 57			08 27			08 42	09 12		08 57			09 27		09 42		09 57	10 12			10 27		10 42	11 12
Harringay	d	07 59			08 29			08 44	09 14		08 59			09 29		09 44		09 59	10 14			10 29		10 44	11 14
Finsbury Park ⊖	d	08 02	08 08	08 21	08 32	08 38		08 47	09 17	08 51	09 02	09 08	09 21	09 32	09 38	09 47		10 02	10 17	10 08	10 21	10 32	10 38	10 47	11 17
Drayton Park	d																								
Highbury & Islington ⊖	d																								
Essex Road	d																								
Old Street ⊖	d																								
Moorgate ⊖	a																								
London Kings Cross ■ ⊖	a	08 10	08 19	08 31	08 40	08 49		08 55	09 25	09 01	09 10	09 19	09 31	09 38	09 49	09 55		10 10	10 25	10 19	10 31	10 40	10 49	10 55	11 25

		FC ■		FC	FC ■	FC ■	FC	FC ■	FC	FC	FC ■	FC		FC ■	FC ■	FC	FC ■	FC	FC	FC	FC ■	FC ■		FC	FC ■
Letchworth Garden City	d				10 29	10 54								11 29	11 54						12 29	12 54			
Hitchin ■	d	10 28			10 33	10 58		11 03			11 28			11 33	11 58		12 03				12 33	12 58			13 03
Stevenage ■	d	10 33			10 39	11 03		11 09		11 29	11 33			11 39	12 03		12 09			12 29	12 39	13 03			13 09
Watton-at-Stone	d									11 36										12 36					
Hertford North	d								11 12	11 42								12 12		12 42					
Bayford	d								11 16	11 46								12 16		12 46					
Cuffley	d								11 21	11 51								12 21		12 51					
Crews Hill	d								11 24	11 54								12 24		12 54					
Gordon Hill	d								11 27	11 57								12 27		12 57					
Enfield Chase	d								11 29	11 59								12 29		12 59					
Grange Park	d								11 31	12 01								12 31		13 01					
Winchmore Hill	d								11 33	12 03								12 33		13 03					
Palmers Green	d								11 35	12 05								12 35		13 05					
Bowes Park	d								11 38	12 08								12 38		13 08					
Knebworth	d				10 43			11 13						11 43			12 13				12 43				13 13
Welwyn North	d				10 47			11 17						11 47			12 17				12 47				13 17
Welwyn Garden City ■	d			10 28	10 50		10 58	11 20				11 28		11 50		11 58	12 20		12 28		12 50			12 58	13 20
Hatfield	d			10 32	10 53		11 02	11 23				11 32		11 53		12 02	12 23		12 32		12 53			13 02	13 23
Welham Green	d			10 36			11 06					11 36				12 06			12 36					13 06	
Brookmans Park	d			10 38			11 08					11 38				12 08			12 38					13 08	
Potters Bar	d			10 41	10 59		11 11	11 29				11 41		11 59		12 11	12 29		12 41		12 59			13 11	13 30
Hadley Wood	d			10 45			11 15					11 45				12 15			12 45					13 15	
New Barnet	d			10 47			11 17					11 47				12 17			12 47					13 17	
Oakleigh Park	d			10 49			11 19					11 49				12 19			12 49					13 19	
New Southgate	d			10 52			11 22					11 52				12 22			12 52					13 22	
Alexandra Palace	d			10 55			11 25		11 40	12 10		11 55				12 25		12 40	12 55	13 10				13 25	
Hornsey	d			10 57			11 27		11 42	12 12		11 57				12 27		12 42	12 57	13 12				13 27	
Harringay	d			10 59			11 29		11 44	12 14		11 59				12 29		12 44	12 59	13 14				13 29	
Finsbury Park ⊖	d	10 51		11 02	11 08	11 21	11 32	11 38	11 47	12 17	11 51	12 02		12 08	12 21	12 32	12 38	12 47	13 02	13 17	13 08	13 21		13 32	13 38
Drayton Park	d																								
Highbury & Islington ⊖	d																								
Essex Road	d																								
Old Street ⊖	d																								
Moorgate ⊖	a																								
London Kings Cross ■ ⊖	a	11 01		11 10	11 19	11 31	11 40	11 48	11 55	12 25	12 01	12 10		12 19	12 31	12 40	12 49	12 55	13 10	13 25	13 21	13 31		13 40	13 49

Table 24

Letchworth Garden City, Hertford North and Welwyn Garden City - London

Saturdays

17 July to 04 September

		FC	FC	FC ■	FC	FC ■	FC ■	FC ■		FC ■	FC	FC ■	FC	FC	FC ■	FC	FC ■	FC ■		FC ■	FC ■	FC	FC ■	FC ■	FC ■
Letchworth Garden City	d					13 29	13 29	13 54		13 54							14 29	14 29			14 54			15 29	
Hitchin ■	d			13 28		13 33	13 33	13 58		13 58		14 03			14 28		14 33	14 33		14 54	14 58		15 28	15 33	15 54
Stevenage ■	d		13 29	13 33		13 39	13 39	14 03		14 03		14 09		14 29	14 33		14 39	14 39		15a01	15 04		15 33	15 38	16a01
Watton-at-Stone	d		13 36											14 36											
Hertford North	d	13 12	13 42										14 12	14 42								15 22			
Bayford	d	13 16	13 46										14 16	14 46								15 26			
Cuffley	d	13 21	13 51										14 21	14 51								15 31			
Crews Hill	d	13 24	13 54										14 24	14 54								15 34			
Gordon Hill	d	13 27	13 57										14 27	14 57								15 37			
Enfield Chase	d	13 29	13 59										14 29	14 59								15 39			
Grange Park	d	13 31	14 01										14 31	15 01								15 41			
Winchmore Hill	d	13 33	14 03										14 33	15 03								15 43			
Palmers Green	d	13 35	14 05										14 35	15 05								15 45			
Bowes Park	d	13 38	14 08										14 38	15 08								15 48			
Knebworth	d					13 43	13 43					14 13					14 43	14 43							
Welwyn North	d					13 47	13 47					14 17					14 47	14 47							
Welwyn Garden City ■	d				13 28	13 50	13 50				13 58	14 20				14 28	14 50	14 50							
Hatfield	d				13 32	13 53	13 53				14 02	14 23				14 32	14 53	14 53							
Welham Green	d				13 36						14 06					14 36									
Brookmans Park	d				13 38						14 08					14 38									
Potters Bar	d				13 41	13 59	13 59				14 11	14 29				14 41	14 59	14 59							
Hadley Wood	d				13 45						14 15					14 45									
New Barnet	d				13 47						14 17					14 47									
Oakleigh Park	d				13 49						14 19					14 49									
New Southgate	d				13 52						14 22					14 52									
Alexandra Palace	d	13 39	14 10		13 55						14 25		14 40	15 10		14 55						15 50			
Hornsey	d	13 41	14 12		13 57						14 27		14 42	15 12		14 57						15 52			
Harringay	d	13 43	14 14		13 59						14 29		14 44	15 14		14 59						15 54			
Finsbury Park ⊖	d	13 46	14 17	13 51	14 02	14 08	14 08	14 21		14 21	14 32	14 38	14 47	15 17	14 51	15 02	15 08	15 08			15 22	15 57	16 05	16 14	
Drayton Park	d																								
Highbury & Islington ⊖	d																								
Essex Road	d																								
Old Street ⊖	d																								
Moorgate ⊖	a																								
London Kings Cross ■ ⊖	a	13 55	14 25	14 01	14 10	14 19	14 19	14 31		14 31	14 40	14 49	14 55	15 25	15 01	15 10	15 19	15 19			15 31	16 05	16 15	16 21	

		FC ■	FC	FC ■		FC ■	FC ■	FC ■	FC	FC ■	FC ■	FC ■	FC ■	FC		FC ■	FC ■	FC ■	FC ■	FC	FC ■	FC ■	FC ■	FC ■	
Letchworth Garden City	d	15 54				16 29		16 54			17 29		17 54				18 29		18 54			19 29		19 54	
Hitchin ■	d	15 58		16 28		16 33	16 54	16 58		17 28	17 33	17 54	17 58			18 28	18 33	18 54	18 58		19 28	19 33	19 54	19 58	
Stevenage ■	d	16 04		16 33		16 38	17a01	17 04		17 33	17 38	18a01	18 04			18 33	18 38	19a01	19 04		19 33	19 38	20a01	20 04	
Watton-at-Stone	d																								
Hertford North	d		16 22						17 22					18 22						19 22					
Bayford	d		16 26						17 26					18 26						19 26					
Cuffley	d		16 31						17 31					18 31						19 31					
Crews Hill	d		16 34						17 34					18 34						19 34					
Gordon Hill	d		16 37						17 37					18 37						19 37					
Enfield Chase	d		16 39						17 39					18 39						19 39					
Grange Park	d		16 41						17 41					18 41						19 41					
Winchmore Hill	d		16 43						17 43					18 43						19 43					
Palmers Green	d		16 45						17 45					18 45						19 45					
Bowes Park	d		16 48						17 48					18 48						19 48					
Knebworth	d																								
Welwyn North	d																								
Welwyn Garden City ■	d																								
Hatfield	d																								
Welham Green	d																								
Brookmans Park	d																								
Potters Bar	d																								
Hadley Wood	d																								
New Barnet	d																								
Oakleigh Park	d																								
New Southgate	d																								
Alexandra Palace	d		16 50						17 50					18 50						19 50					
Hornsey	d		16 52						17 52					18 52						19 52					
Harringay	d		16 54						17 54					18 54						19 54					
Finsbury Park ⊖	d	16 32	16 57	17 00		17 12		17 32	17 57	18 04	18 08		18 32	18 57		19 03	19 08		19 32	19 57	19 59	20 06		20 32	
Drayton Park	d																								
Highbury & Islington ⊖	d																								
Essex Road	d																								
Old Street ⊖	d																								
Moorgate ⊖	a																								
London Kings Cross ■ ⊖	a	16 39	17 04	17 11		17 19		17 39	18 04	18 14	18 15		18 39	19 04		19 12	19 14		19 39	20 04	20 09	20 13		20 41	

Table 24

Saturdays
17 July to 04 September

Letchworth Garden City, Hertford North and Welwyn Garden City - London

		FC	FC ■	FC ■	FC ■	FC ■	FC	FC ■	FC ■	FC ■	FC ■	FC	FC ■	FC ■	FC ■	FC ■	FC ■	FC	FC ■	FC ■
Letchworth Garden City	d			20 29		20 54			21 29		21 54			22 29		22 54	23 01			23 41
Hitchin ■	d		20 28	20 33	20 54	20 58		21 28	21 33	21 54	21 58		22 28	22 33	22 54	22 58	23 05		23 28	23 45
Stevenage ■	d		20 33	20 38	21a01	21 04		21 33	21 38	22a01	22 04		22 33	22 38	23a01	23 04	23 11		23 33	23 52
Watton-at-Stone	d																			23 58
Hertford North	d	20 22					21 22					22 22						23 22		00 03
Bayford	d	20 26					21 26					22 26						23 26		
Cuffley	d	20 31					21 31					22 31						23 31		
Crews Hill	d	20 34					21 34					22 34						23 34		
Gordon Hill	d	20 37					21 37					22 37						23 37		
Enfield Chase	d	20 39					21 39					22 39						23 39		
Grange Park	d	20 41					21 41					22 41						23 41		
Winchmore Hill	d	20 43					21 43					22 43						23 43		
Palmers Green	d	20 45					21 45					22 45						23 45		
Bowes Park	d	20 48					21 48					22 48						23 48		
Knebworth	d																			
Welwyn North	d																			
Welwyn Garden City ■	d																			
Hatfield	d																			
Welham Green	d																			
Brookmans Park	d																			
Potters Bar	d																			
Hadley Wood	d																			
New Barnet	d																			
Oakleigh Park	d																			
New Southgate	d																			
Alexandra Palace	d	20 50					21 50					22 50						23 50		
Hornsey	d	20 52					21 52					22 52						23 52		
Harringay	d	20 54					21 54					22 54						23 54		
Finsbury Park ⊖	d	20 57	21 00	21 08		21 32	21 57	22 00	22 07		22 32	22 57	23 01	23 07		23 32	23 38	23 57	00 04	00s22
Drayton Park	d																			
Highbury & Islington ⊖	d																			
Essex Road	d																			
Old Street ⊖	d																			
Moorgate ⊖	a																			
London Kings Cross ■ ⊖	a	21 04	21 10	21 15		21 40	22 04	22 10	22 14		22 39	23 04	23 10	23 14		23 39	23 45	00 04	00 12	00 31

Saturdays
from 11 September

		FC ■	FC	FC ■	FC	FC ■	FC	FC ■	FC	FC ■	FC	FC ■	FC	FC	FC ■	FC	FC ■	FC ■	FC	FC ■	FC	FC	FC ■
Letchworth Garden City	d		23p18	23p47			04 50		05 20	05 29				06 20			06 29	06 54					
Hitchin ■	d	23p16	23p22	23p54		04 08	04 54	04 58	05 24	05 33		06 03		06 24	06 28		06 33	06 58		07 03			07 28
Stevenage ■	d	23p22	23p27	23p59		04 13	04 59	05 05	05 29	05 39		06 09		06 29	06 33		06 39	07 03		07 09		07 29	07 33
Watton-at-Stone	d		23p34				05 06		05 36					06 36								07 36	
Hertford North	d		23p40			04 23	05 12		05 42				06 12	06 42							07 12	07 42	
Bayford	d		23p44				05 16		05 46				06 16	06 46							07 16	07 46	
Cuffley	d		23p49			04 30	05 21		05 51				06 21	06 51							07 21	07 51	
Crews Hill	d		23p52				05 24		05 54				06 24	06 54							07 24	07 54	
Gordon Hill	d		23p55			04 34	05 27		05 57				06 27	06 57							07 27	07 57	
Enfield Chase	d		23p57			04 36	05 29		05 59				06 29	06 59							07 29	07 59	
Grange Park	d		23p59				05 31		06 01				06 31	07 01							07 31	08 01	
Winchmore Hill	d		00 01				05 33		06 03				06 33	07 03							07 33	08 03	
Palmers Green	d		00 03				05 35		06 05				06 35	07 05							07 35	08 05	
Bowes Park	d		00 06				05 38		06 08				06 38	07 08							07 38	08 08	
Knebworth	d	23p25		00 02				05 07		05 43		06 13					06 43			07 13			
Welwyn North	d	23p29		00 06				05 11		05 47		06 17					06 47			07 17			
Welwyn Garden City ■	d	23p32		00 09	04 10			05 15		05 50	05 58	06 20				06 28	06 50		06 58	07 20			
Hatfield	d	23p35		00 12	04 14			05 19		05 53	06 02	06 23				06 32	06 53		07 02	07 23			
Welham Green	d										06 06					06 36			07 06				
Brookmans Park	d				04 19						06 08					06 38			07 08				
Potters Bar	d	23p41		00 18	04 22			05 24		05 59	06 11	06 29				06 41	06 59		07 11	07 29			
Hadley Wood	d										06 15					06 45			07 15				
New Barnet	d				04 27			05 29			06 17					06 47			07 17				
Oakleigh Park	d				04 29			05 31			06 19					06 49			07 19				
New Southgate	d				04 32			05 34			06 22					06 52			07 22				
Alexandra Palace	d		00 08		04 35		05 40	05 37	06 10		06 25		06 40	07 10		06 55			07 25		07 40	08 10	
Hornsey	d		00 10		04 37	04 43	05 42		06 12		06 27		06 42	07 12		06 57			07 27		07 42	08 12	
Harringay	d		00 12		04 39		05 44		06 14		06 29		06 44	07 14		06 59			07 29		07 44	08 14	
Finsbury Park ⊖	d	23b52	00 15	00 29	04 42	04s46	05 47	05 41	06 17	06 08	06 32	06 38	06 47	07 17	06 51	07 02	07 08	07 21	07 32	07 38	07 47	08 17	07 51
Drayton Park	d																						
Highbury & Islington ⊖	d																						
Essex Road	d																						
Old Street ⊖	d																						
Moorgate ⊖	a																						
London Kings Cross ■ ⊖	a	00 01	00 26	00 42	04 51	04 59	05 58	05 56	06 25	06 19	06 40	06 49	06 55	07 25	07 01	07 10	07 19	07 31	07 40	07 49	07 55	08 25	08 01

b previous night, stops to set down only

Table 24

Saturdays
from 11 September

Letchworth Garden City, Hertford North and Welwyn Garden City - London

		FC	FC ■	FC ■	FC	FC ■	FC	FC	FC ■	FC	FC ■	FC ■	FC	FC ■	FC	FC	FC	FC ■	FC ■	FC	FC ■	FC	FC
Letchworth Garden City	d		07 29	07 54							08 29	08 54						09 29	09 54				
Hitchin ■	d		07 33	07 58		08 03			08 28		08 33	08 58		09 03				09 33	09 58		10 03		
Stevenage ■	d		07 39	08 03		08 09		08 29	08 33		08 39	09 03		09 09			09 29	09 39	10 03		10 09		10 29
Watton-at-Stone	d							08 36									09 36						10 36
Hertford North	d						08 12	08 42							09 12		09 42					10 12	10 42
Bayford	d						08 16	08 46							09 16		09 46					10 16	10 46
Cuffley	d						08 21	08 51							09 21		09 51					10 21	10 51
Crews Hill	d						08 24	08 54							09 24		09 54					10 24	10 54
Gordon Hill	d						08 27	08 57							09 27		09 57					10 27	10 57
Enfield Chase	d						08 29	08 59							09 29		09 59					10 29	10 59
Grange Park	d						08 31	09 01							09 31		10 01					10 31	11 01
Winchmore Hill	d						08 33	09 03							09 33		10 03					10 33	11 03
Palmers Green	d						08 35	09 05							09 35		10 05					10 35	11 05
Bowes Park	d						08 38	09 08							09 38		10 08					10 38	11 08
Knebworth	d		07 43			08 13					08 43			09 13				09 43			10 13		
Welwyn North	d		07 47			08 17					08 47			09 17				09 47			10 17		
Welwyn Garden City ■	d	07 28	07 50		07 58	08 20				08 28	08 50		08 58	09 20		09 28		09 50		09 58	10 20		
Hatfield	d	07 32	07 53		08 02	08 23				08 32	08 53		09 02	09 23		09 32		09 53		10 02	10 23		
Welham Green	d	07 36			08 06					08 36			09 06			09 36				10 06			
Brookmans Park	d	07 38			08 08					08 38			09 08			09 38				10 08			
Potters Bar	d	07 41	07 59		08 11	08 29				08 41	08 59		09 11	09 29		09 41		09 59		10 11	10 29		
Hadley Wood	d	07 45			08 15					08 45			09 15			09 45				10 15			
New Barnet	d	07 47			08 17					08 47			09 17			09 47				10 17			
Oakleigh Park	d	07 49			08 19					08 49			09 19			09 49				10 19			
New Southgate	d	07 52			08 22					08 52			09 22			09 52				10 22			
Alexandra Palace	d	07 55			08 25		08 40	09 10		08 55			09 25		09 40	09 55	10 10			10 25		10 40	11 10
Hornsey	d	07 57			08 27		08 42	09 12		08 57			09 27		09 42	09 57	10 12			10 27		10 42	11 12
Harringay	d	07 59			08 29		08 44	09 14		08 59			09 29		09 44	09 59	10 14			10 29		10 44	11 14
Finsbury Park ⊖	d	08 02	08 08	08 21	08 32	08 38	08 47	09 17	08 51	09 02	09 08	09 21	09 32	09 38	09 47	10 02	10 17	10 08	10 21	10 32	10 38	10 47	11 17
Drayton Park	d																						
Highbury & Islington ⊖	d																						
Essex Road	d																						
Old Street ⊖	d																						
Moorgate ⊖	a																						
London Kings Cross ■ ⊖	a	08 10	08 19	08 31	08 40	08 49	08 55	09 25	09 01	09 10	09 19	09 31	09 38	09 49	09 55	10 10	10 25	10 19	10 31	10 40	10 49	10 55	11 25

		FC ■	FC	FC ■	FC ■	FC	FC ■	FC	FC	FC ■	FC	FC ■	FC ■	FC	FC ■	FC	FC	FC	FC ■	FC ■	FC	FC ■
Letchworth Garden City	d			10 29	10 54							11 29	11 54						12 29	12 54		
Hitchin ■	d	10 28		10 33	10 58		11 03			11 28		11 33	11 58		12 03				12 33	12 58		13 03
Stevenage ■	d	10 33		10 39	11 03		11 09		11 29	11 33		11 39	12 03		12 09			12 29	12 39	13 03		13 09
Watton-at-Stone	d								11 36									12 36				
Hertford North	d							11 12	11 42							12 12		12 42				
Bayford	d							11 16	11 46							12 16		12 46				
Cuffley	d							11 21	11 51							12 21		12 51				
Crews Hill	d							11 24	11 54							12 24		12 54				
Gordon Hill	d							11 27	11 57							12 27		12 57				
Enfield Chase	d							11 29	11 59							12 29		12 59				
Grange Park	d							11 31	12 01							12 31		13 01				
Winchmore Hill	d							11 33	12 03							12 33		13 03				
Palmers Green	d							11 35	12 05							12 35		13 05				
Bowes Park	d							11 38	12 08							12 38		13 08				
Knebworth	d			10 43			11 13					11 43			12 13				12 43			13 13
Welwyn North	d			10 47			11 17					11 47			12 17				12 47			13 17
Welwyn Garden City ■	d		10 28	10 50		10 58	11 20				11 28	11 50		11 58	12 20		12 28		12 50		12 58	13 20
Hatfield	d		10 32	10 53		11 02	11 23				11 32	11 53		12 02	12 23		12 32		12 53		13 02	13 23
Welham Green	d		10 36			11 06					11 36			12 06			12 36				13 06	
Brookmans Park	d		10 38			11 08					11 38			12 08			12 38				13 08	
Potters Bar	d		10 41	10 59		11 11	11 29				11 41	11 59		12 11	12 29		12 41		12 59		13 11	13 30
Hadley Wood	d		10 45			11 15					11 45			12 15			12 45				13 15	
New Barnet	d		10 47			11 17					11 47			12 17			12 47				13 17	
Oakleigh Park	d		10 49			11 19					11 49			12 19			12 49				13 19	
New Southgate	d		10 52			11 22					11 52			12 22			12 52				13 22	
Alexandra Palace	d		10 55			11 25		11 40	12 10		11 55			12 25		12 40	12 55	13 10			13 25	
Hornsey	d		10 57			11 27		11 42	12 12		11 57			12 27		12 42	12 57	13 12			13 27	
Harringay	d		10 59			11 29		11 44	12 14		11 59			12 29		12 44	12 59	13 14			13 29	
Finsbury Park ⊖	d	10 51	11 02	11 08	11 21	11 32	11 38	11 47	12 17	11 51	12 02	12 08	12 21	12 32	12 38	12 47	13 02	13 17	13 08	13 21	13 32	13 38
Drayton Park	d																					
Highbury & Islington ⊖	d																					
Essex Road	d																					
Old Street ⊖	d																					
Moorgate ⊖	a																					
London Kings Cross ■ ⊖	a	11 01	11 10	11 19	11 31	11 40	11 48	11 55	12 25	12 01	12 10	12 19	12 31	12 40	12 49	12 55	13 10	13 25	13 21	13 31	13 40	13 49

Letchworth Garden City, Hertford North and Welwyn Garden City - London

		FC	FC	FC [1]	FC	FC [1]	FC [1]	FC		FC [1]	FC	FC	FC [1]	FC	FC [1]	FC [1]	FC	FC [1]	FC	FC [1]	FC	FC [1]	FC	FC [1]	FC
Letchworth Garden City	d					13 29	13 54								14 29	14 54				15 29				15 54	
Hitchin [4]	d			13 28		13 33	13 58			14 03			14 28		14 33	14 58		15 03		15 33		15 28		15 58	
Stevenage [4]	d		13 29	13 33		13 39	14 03			14 09		14 29	14 33		14 39	15 03		15 09		15 39	15 29	15 33		16 03	
Watton-at-Stone	d		13 36									14 36									15 36				
Hertford North	d	13 12	13 42								14 12	14 42							15 12		15 42				
Bayford	d	13 16	13 46								14 16	14 46							15 16		15 46				
Cuffley	d	13 21	13 51								14 21	14 51							15 21		15 51				
Crews Hill	d	13 24	13 54								14 24	14 54							15 24		15 54				
Gordon Hill	d	13 27	13 57								14 27	14 57							15 27		15 57				
Enfield Chase	d	13 29	13 59								14 29	14 59							15 29		15 59				
Grange Park	d	13 31	14 01								14 31	15 01							15 31		16 01				
Winchmore Hill	d	13 33	14 03								14 33	15 03							15 33		16 03				
Palmers Green	d	13 35	14 05								14 35	15 05							15 35		16 05				
Bowes Park	d	13 38	14 08								14 38	15 08							15 38		16 08				
Knebworth	d					13 43				14 13					14 43			15 13		15 43					
Welwyn North	d					13 47				14 17					14 47			15 17		15 47					
Welwyn Garden City [4]	d				13 28	13 50		13 58		14 20				14 28	14 50		14 58	15 20		15 50			15 28		15 58
Hatfield	d				13 32	13 53		14 02		14 23				14 32	14 53		15 02	15 23		15 53			15 32		16 02
Welham Green	d				13 36			14 06						14 36			15 06						15 36		16 06
Brookmans Park	d				13 38			14 08						14 38			15 08						15 38		16 08
Potters Bar	d				13 41	13 59		14 11		14 29				14 41	14 59		15 11	15 29		15 59			15 41		16 11
Hadley Wood	d				13 45			14 15						14 45			15 15						15 45		16 15
New Barnet	d				13 47			14 17						14 47			15 17						15 47		16 17
Oakleigh Park	d				13 49			14 19						14 49			15 19						15 49		16 19
New Southgate	d				13 52			14 22						14 52			15 22						15 52		16 22
Alexandra Palace	d	13 39	14 10		13 55			14 25			14 40	15 10		14 55			15 25		15 40		16 10		15 55		16 25
Hornsey	d	13 41	14 12		13 57			14 27			14 42	15 12		14 57			15 27		15 42		16 12		15 57		16 27
Harringay	d	13 43	14 14		13 59			14 29			14 44	15 14		14 59			15 29		15 44		16 14		15 59		16 29
Finsbury Park ⊖	d	13 46	14 17	13 51	14 02	14 08	14 21	14 32		14 38	14 47	15 17	14 51	15 02	15 08	15 21	15 32	15 38	15 47	16 08	16 17	15 51	16 02	16 21	16 32
Drayton Park	d																								
Highbury & Islington ⊖	d																								
Essex Road	d																								
Old Street ⊖	d																								
Moorgate ⊖	a																								
London Kings Cross [15] ⊖	a	13 54	14 25	14 01	14 10	14 19	14 31	14 40		14 49	14 55	15 25	15 01	15 10	15 19	15 31	15 40	15 49	15 55	16 19	16 25	16 00	16 10	16 31	16 40

		FC [1]	FC	FC		FC [1]	FC	FC [1]	FC [1]	FC	FC [1]	FC	FC	FC [1]		FC	FC [1]	FC [1]	FC	FC [1]	FC	FC	FC [1]	FC	
Letchworth Garden City	d							16 29	16 54								17 29	17 54							
Hitchin [4]	d	16 03				16 28		16 33	16 58		17 03			17 28			17 33	17 58		18 03			18 28		
Stevenage [4]	d	16 09		16 29		16 33		16 39	17 03		17 09		17 29	17 33			17 39	18 03		18 09		18 29	18 33		
Watton-at-Stone	d			16 36									17 36									18 36			
Hertford North	d		16 12	16 42								17 12	17 42								18 12	18 42			
Bayford	d		16 16	16 46								17 16	17 46								18 16	18 46			
Cuffley	d		16 21	16 51								17 21	17 51								18 21	18 51			
Crews Hill	d		16 24	16 54								17 24	17 54								18 24	18 54			
Gordon Hill	d		16 27	16 57								17 27	17 57								18 27	18 57			
Enfield Chase	d		16 29	16 59								17 29	17 59								18 29	18 59			
Grange Park	d		16 31	17 01								17 31	18 01								18 31	19 01			
Winchmore Hill	d		16 33	17 03								17 33	18 03								18 33	19 03			
Palmers Green	d		16 35	17 05								17 35	18 05								18 35	19 05			
Bowes Park	d		16 38	17 08								17 38	18 08								18 38	19 08			
Knebworth	d	16 13						16 43			17 12						17 42			18 13					
Welwyn North	d	16 17						16 47			17 17						17 47			18 17					
Welwyn Garden City [4]	d	16 20					16 28	16 50		16 58	17 20					17 28	17 50		17 58	18 20				18 28	
Hatfield	d	16 23					16 32	16 53		17 02	17 23					17 32	17 53		18 02	18 23				18 32	
Welham Green	d						16 36			17 06						17 36			18 06					18 36	
Brookmans Park	d						16 38			17 08						17 38			18 08					18 38	
Potters Bar	d	16 29					16 41	16 59		17 11	17 29					17 41	17 59		18 11	18 29				18 41	
Hadley Wood	d						16 45			17 15						17 45			18 15					18 45	
New Barnet	d						16 47			17 17						17 47			18 17					18 47	
Oakleigh Park	d						16 49			17 19						17 49			18 19					18 49	
New Southgate	d						16 52			17 22						17 52			18 22					18 52	
Alexandra Palace	d		16 40	17 10			16 55			17 25		17 40	18 10			17 55			18 25		18 40	19 10		18 55	
Hornsey	d		16 42	17 12			16 57			17 27		17 42	18 12			17 57			18 27		18 42	19 12		18 57	
Harringay	d		16 44	17 14			16 59			17 29		17 44	18 14			17 59			18 29		18 44	19 14		18 59	
Finsbury Park ⊖	d	16 38	16 47	17 17		16 51	17 02	17 08	17 21	17 32	17 38	17 47	18 17	17 51		18 02	18 08	18 21	18 32	18 38	18 47	19 17	18 51	19 02	
Drayton Park	d																								
Highbury & Islington ⊖	d																								
Essex Road	d																								
Old Street ⊖	d																								
Moorgate ⊖	a																								
London Kings Cross [15] ⊖	a	16 49	16 55	17 25		17 01	17 10	17 19	17 31	17 40	17 49	17 55	18 25	18 01		18 10	18 19	18 31	18 40	18 49	18 55	19 25	19 01	19 10	

Letchworth Garden City, Hertford North and Welwyn Garden City - London

		FC [1]	FC [1]	FC	FC [1]	FC	FC	FC [1]	FC	FC [1]		FC [1]	FC	FC [1]	FC	FC	FC [1]	FC	FC [1]	FC [1]		FC	FC [1]	FC	FC
Letchworth Garden City	d	18 29	18 54							19 29		19 54							20 29	20 54					
Hitchin [4]	d	18 33	18 58		19 03			19 28		19 33		19 58		20 03			20 28		20 33	20 58			21 03		
Stevenage [4]	d	18 39	19 03		19 09		19 29	19 33		19 39		20 03		20 09		20 29	20 33		20 39	21 03			21 09		21 29
Watton-at-Stone	d						19 36									20 36									21 36
Hertford North	d					19 12	19 42								20 12	20 42								21 12	21 42
Bayford	d					19 16	19 46								20 16	20 46								21 16	21 46
Cuffley	d					19 21	19 51								20 21	20 51								21 21	21 51
Crews Hill	d					19 24	19 54								20 24	20 54								21 24	21 54
Gordon Hill	d					19 27	19 57								20 27	20 57								21 27	21 57
Enfield Chase	d					19 29	19 59								20 29	20 59								21 29	21 59
Grange Park	d					19 31	20 01								20 31	21 01								21 31	22 01
Winchmore Hill	d					19 33	20 03								20 33	21 03								21 33	22 03
Palmers Green	d					19 35	20 05								20 35	21 05								21 35	22 05
Bowes Park	d					19 38	20 08								20 38	21 08								21 38	22 08
Knebworth	d	18 43			19 13					19 43				20 13					20 43				21 13		
Welwyn North	d	18 47			19 17					19 47				20 17					20 47				21 17		
Welwyn Garden City [4]	d	18 50		18 58	19 20				19 28	19 50			19 58	20 20				20 28	20 50			20 58	21 20		
Hatfield	d	18 53		19 02	19 23				19 32	19 53			20 02	20 23				20 32	20 53			21 02	21 23		
Welham Green	d			19 06					19 36				20 06					20 36				21 06			
Brookmans Park	d			19 08					19 38				20 08					20 38				21 08			
Potters Bar	d	18 59		19 11	19 29				19 41	19 59			20 11	20 29				20 41	20 59			21 11	21 29		
Hadley Wood	d			19 15					19 45				20 15					20 45				21 15			
New Barnet	d			19 17					19 47				20 17					20 47				21 17			
Oakleigh Park	d			19 19					19 49				20 19					20 49				21 19			
New Southgate	d			19 22					19 52				20 22					20 52				21 22			
Alexandra Palace	d			19 25		19 40	20 10		19 55				20 25		20 40	21 10		20 55				21 25		21 40	22 10
Hornsey	d			19 27		19 42	20 12		19 57				20 27		20 42	21 12		20 57				21 27		21 42	22 12
Harringay	d			19 29		19 44	20 14		19 59				20 29		20 44	21 14		20 59				21 29		21 44	22 14
Finsbury Park ⊖	d	19 08	19 21	19 32	19 38	19 47	20 17	19 51	20 02	20 08		20 21	20 32	20 38	20 47	21 17	20 51	21 02	21 08	21 21		21 32	21 38	21 47	22 17
Drayton Park	d																								
Highbury & Islington ⊖	d																								
Essex Road	d																								
Old Street ⊖	d																								
Moorgate ⊖	a																								
London Kings Cross [15] ⊖	a	19 19	19 31	19 40	19 49	19 55	20 25	20 01	20 10	20 19		20 31	20 40	20 49	20 55	21 25	21 01	21 10	21 19	21 31		21 40	21 49	21 55	22 25

		FC [1]	FC	FC [1]	FC [1]	FC		FC [1]	FC	FC	FC [1]	FC	FC [1]	FC [1]	FC	FC [1]		FC	FC	FC [1]	FC [1]				
Letchworth Garden City	d			21 29	21 54								22 29	22 54							23 41				
Hitchin [4]	d	21 28		21 33	21 58			22 03			22 28		22 33	22 58		23 03				23 31	23 45				
Stevenage [4]	d	21 33		21 39	22 03			22 09		22 29	22 33		22 39	23 03		23 09			23 29	23 34	23 50				
Watton-at-Stone	d									22 36									23 36						
Hertford North	d								22 12	22 42								23 12	23 42						
Bayford	d								22 16	22 46								23 16	23 46						
Cuffley	d								22 21	22 51								23 21	23 51						
Crews Hill	d								22 24	22 54								23 24	23 54						
Gordon Hill	d								22 27	22 57								23 27	23 57						
Enfield Chase	d								22 29	22 59								23 29	23 59						
Grange Park	d								22 31	23 01								23 31	00 01						
Winchmore Hill	d								22 33	23 03								23 33	00 03						
Palmers Green	d								22 35	23 05								23 35	00 05						
Bowes Park	d								22 38	23 08								23 38	00 08						
Knebworth	d			21 43				22 13					22 43			23 13					23 53				
Welwyn North	d			21 47				22 17					22 47			23 17					23 57				
Welwyn Garden City [4]	d		21 28	21 50		21 58		22 20				22 28	22 50		22 58	23 20					00 01				
Hatfield	d		21 32	21 53		22 02		22 23				22 32	22 53		23 02	23 23					00 04				
Welham Green	d		21 36			22 06						22 36			23 06										
Brookmans Park	d		21 38			22 08						22 38			23 08										
Potters Bar	d		21 41	21 59		22 11		22 29				22 41	22 59		23 11	23 29					00 10				
Hadley Wood	d		21 45			22 15						22 45			23 15										
New Barnet	d		21 47			22 17						22 47			23 17										
Oakleigh Park	d		21 49			22 19						22 49			23 19										
New Southgate	d		21 52			22 22						22 52			23 22										
Alexandra Palace	d		21 55			22 25			22 40	23 10		22 55			23 25			23 41	00 10						
Hornsey	d		21 57			22 27			22 42	23 12		22 57			23 27			23 43	00 12						
Harringay	d		21 59			22 29			22 44	23 14		22 59			23 29			23 45	00 14						
Finsbury Park ⊖	d	21 51	22 02	22 08	22 21	22 32		22 38	22 47	23 17	22 52	23 02	23 08	23 21	23 32	23 41		23 47	00 17	00 01	00s25				
Drayton Park	d																								
Highbury & Islington ⊖	d																								
Essex Road	d																								
Old Street ⊖	d																								
Moorgate ⊖	a																								
London Kings Cross [15] ⊖	a	22 01	22 10	22 19	22 31	22 40		22 49	22 55	23 25	23 01	23 10	23 19	23 31	23 40	23 52		23 56	00 25	00 09	00 35				

Table 24

Sundays until 11 July

Letchworth Garden City, Hertford North and Welwyn Garden City - London

		FC	FC ■1	FC	FC	FC	FC ■1	FC	FC ■1	FC		FC	FC	FC	FC	FC ■1	FC	FC ■1	FC	FC		FC ■1	FC ■1	FC	FC ■1
Letchworth Garden City	d								06 54							07 54						08 29	08 54		
Hitchin ■4	d		23p31				06 33		06 58							07 58		08 28				08 33	08 58		09 28
Stevenage ■4	d	23p29	23p34				06 39		07 03					07 35		08 03		08 33		08 35		08 39	09 03		09 33
Watton-at-Stone	d	23p36												07 42						08 42					
Hertford North	d	23p42		05 48	06 18			06 48				07 18		07 48			08 18			08 48					
Bayford	d	23p46		05 52	06 22			06 49				07 19		07 52			08 19			08 52					
Cuffley	d	23p51		05a58	06a28			06a55				07a25		07a58			08a25			08a58					
Crews Hill	d	23p54																							
Gordon Hill	d	23p57																							
Enfield Chase	d	23p59																							
Grange Park	d	00 01																							
Winchmore Hill	d	00 03																							
Palmers Green	d	00 05																							
Bowes Park	d	00 08																							
Knebworth	d						06 43															08 43			
Welwyn North	d						06 47															08 47			
Welwyn Garden City ■4	d					06 28	06 50			06 58			07 28		07 58				08 28			08 50		08 58	
Hatfield	d					06 32	06 53			07 02			07 32		08 02				08 32			08 53		09 02	
Welham Green	d					06 36				07 06			07 36		08 06				08 36					09 06	
Brookmans Park	d					06 38				07 10			07 38		08 08				08 39					09 09	
Potters Bar	d					06 41	06 59			07 14			07 41		08 11				08 43			08 59		09 13	
Hadley Wood	d					06 45				07 18			07 45		08 15				08 47					09 17	
New Barnet	d					06 47				07 21			07 47		08 17				08 49					09 19	
Oakleigh Park	d					06 49				07 23			07 49		08 19				08 51					09 21	
New Southgate	d					06 52				07 26			07 52		08 22				08 54					09 24	
Alexandra Palace	d	00 10				06 58				07 32			07 58		08 28				09 00					09 30	
Hornsey	d	00 12																							
Harringay	d	00 14																							
Finsbury Park ⊖	d	00 17	00 01			07 02	07 11		07 32	07 37			08 04		08 34	08s40		08 56	09 06			09 13	09 26	09 36	09 56
Drayton Park	d																								
Highbury & Islington ⊖	d																								
Essex Road	d																								
Old Street ⊖	d																								
Moorgate ⊖	a																								
London Kings Cross ■15 ⊖	a	00 25	00 09			07 13	07 19		07 42	07 48			08 15		08 43	08 47		09 05	09 15			09 22	09 35	09 45	10 05

		FC	FC ■1	FC ■1	FC	FC		FC ■1	FC	FC	FC ■1	FC ■1	FC	FC	FC ■1	FC		FC	FC ■1	FC ■1	FC	FC	FC ■1	FC	FC
Letchworth Garden City	d		09 29	09 54							10 29	10 54							11 29	11 54					
Hitchin ■4	d		09 33	09 58				10 28			10 33	10 58			11 28				11 33	11 58			12 28		
Stevenage ■4	d		09 39	10 03				10 33		10 35	10 39	11 03			11 33			11 35	11 39	12 03			12 33		12 35
Watton-at-Stone	d									10 42								11 42							12 42
Hertford North	d					10 18				10 48				11 18				11 48				12 18			12 48
Bayford	d					10 19				10 52				11 19				11 52				12 19			12 52
Cuffley	d					10a25				10a58				11a25				11a58				12a25			12a58
Crews Hill	d																								
Gordon Hill	d																								
Enfield Chase	d																								
Grange Park	d																								
Winchmore Hill	d																								
Palmers Green	d																								
Bowes Park	d																								
Knebworth	d		09 43								10 43								11 43						
Welwyn North	d		09 47								10 47								11 47						
Welwyn Garden City ■4	d	09 28	09 50		09 58				10 28		10 50		10 58			11 28			11 50		11 58			12 28	
Hatfield	d	09 32	09 53		10 02				10 32		10 53		11 02			11 32			11 53		12 02			12 32	
Welham Green	d	09 36			10 06				10 36				11 06			11 36					12 06			12 36	
Brookmans Park	d	09 39			10 10				10 39				11 08			11 38					12 08			12 38	
Potters Bar	d	09 43	09 59		10 14				10 43		10 59		11 11			11 41			11 59		12 11			12 41	
Hadley Wood	d	09 47			10 18				10 47				11 15			11 45					12 15			12 45	
New Barnet	d	09 49			10 20				10 50				11 17			11 47					12 17			12 47	
Oakleigh Park	d	09 51			10 22				10 52				11 19			11 49					12 19			12 49	
New Southgate	d	09 54			10 25				10 55				11 22			11 52					12 22			12 52	
Alexandra Palace	d	10 00			10 31				11 01				11 25			11 55					12 25			12 55	
Hornsey	d												11 27			11 57					12 27			12 57	
Harringay	d												11 29			11 59					12 29			12 59	
Finsbury Park ⊖	d	10 07	10 13	10 26	10 37			10 56	11 06		11 13	11 21	11 32		11 51	12 02			12 11	12 21	12 32		12 51	13 02	
Drayton Park	d																								
Highbury & Islington ⊖	d																								
Essex Road	d																								
Old Street ⊖	d																								
Moorgate ⊖	a																								
London Kings Cross ■15 ⊖	a	10 14	10 22	10 35	10 48			11 05	11 12		11 22	11 30	11 40		12 00	12 10			12 19	12 30	12 40		13 00	13 10	

Table 24

Sundays until 11 July

Letchworth Garden City, Hertford North and Welwyn Garden City - London

		FC ■1		FC ■1	FC	FC	FC ■1	FC	FC	FC ■1	FC	FC		FC ■1	FC	FC	FC ■1	FC ■1	FC	FC	FC ■1	FC		FC	FC ■1
Letchworth Garden City	d	12 29		12 54						13 29							14 29	14 54							15 29
Hitchin ■4	d	12 33		12 58			13 28			13 33				14 28			14 33	14 58			15 28				15 33
Stevenage ■4	d	12 39		13 03			13 33		13 35	13 39				14 33		14 35	14 39	15 03			15 33			15 35	15 39
Watton-at-Stone	d								13 42							14 42								15 42	
Hertford North	d					13 18			13 48			14 18				14 48				15 18				15 48	
Bayford	d					13 19			13 52			14 19				14 52				15 19				15 52	
Cuffley	d					13a25			13a58			14a25				14a58				15a25				15a58	
Crews Hill	d																								
Gordon Hill	d																								
Enfield Chase	d																								
Grange Park	d																								
Winchmore Hill	d																								
Palmers Green	d																								
Bowes Park	d																								
Knebworth	d	12 43								13 43							14 43								15 43
Welwyn North	d	12 47								13 47							14 47								15 47
Welwyn Garden City ■4	d	12 50			12 58			13 28		13 50	13 58				14 28		14 50		14 58			15 28			15 50
Hatfield	d	12 53			13 02			13 32		13 53	14 02				14 32		14 53		15 02			15 32			15 53
Welham Green	d				13 06			13 36			14 06				14 36				15 06			15 36			
Brookmans Park	d				13 08			13 38			14 08				14 38				15 08			15 38			
Potters Bar	d	12 59			13 11			13 41		13 59	14 11				14 41		14 59		15 11			15 41			15 59
Hadley Wood	d				13 15			13 45			14 15				14 45				15 15			15 45			
New Barnet	d				13 17			13 47			14 17				14 47				15 17			15 47			
Oakleigh Park	d				13 19			13 49			14 19				14 49				15 19			15 49			
New Southgate	d				13 22			13 52			14 22				14 52				15 22			15 52			
Alexandra Palace	d				13 25			13 55			14 25				14 55				15 25			15 55			
Hornsey	d				13 27			13 57			14 27				14 57				15 27			15 57			
Harringay	d				13 29			13 59			14 29				14 59				15 29			15 59			
Finsbury Park ⊖	d	13 11		13 21	13 32		13 51	14 02		14 11	14 32			14 51	15 02		15 11	15 21	15 32		15 51	16 02			16 11
Drayton Park	d																								
Highbury & Islington ⊖	d																								
Essex Road	d																								
Old Street ⊖	d																								
Moorgate ⊖	a																								
London Kings Cross ■15 ⊖	a	13 19		13 30	13 40		14 00	14 10		14 19	14 40			15 00	15 10		15 19	15 30	15 40		16 00	16 10			16 19

		FC ■1	FC	FC	FC ■1	FC	FC	FC ■1		FC ■1	FC	FC	FC ■1	FC	FC	FC ■1	FC ■1	FC		FC	FC ■1	FC	FC	FC ■1	FC ■1
Letchworth Garden City	d	15 54						16 29		16 54						17 29	17 54							18 29	18 54
Hitchin ■4	d	15 58			16 28			16 33		16 58			17 28			17 33	17 58				18 28			18 33	18 58
Stevenage ■4	d	16 03			16 33		16 35	16 39		17 03			17 33		17 35	17 39	18 03				18 33		18 35	18 39	19 03
Watton-at-Stone	d						16 42								17 42								18 42		
Hertford North	d			16 18			16 48					17 18			17 48					18 18			18 48		
Bayford	d			16 19			16 52					17 19			17 52					18 19			18 52		
Cuffley	d			16a25			16a58					17a25			17a58					18a25			18a58		
Crews Hill	d																								
Gordon Hill	d																								
Enfield Chase	d																								
Grange Park	d																								
Winchmore Hill	d																								
Palmers Green	d																								
Bowes Park	d																								
Knebworth	d							16 43								17 43								18 43	
Welwyn North	d							16 47								17 47								18 47	
Welwyn Garden City ■4	d		15 58			16 28		16 50			16 58			17 28		17 50		17 58				18 28		18 50	
Hatfield	d		16 02			16 32		16 53			17 02			17 32		17 53		18 02				18 32		18 53	
Welham Green	d		16 06			16 36					17 06			17 36				18 06				18 36			
Brookmans Park	d		16 08			16 38					17 08			17 38				18 08				18 38			
Potters Bar	d		16 11			16 41		16 59			17 11			17 41		17 59		18 11				18 41		18 59	
Hadley Wood	d		16 15			16 45					17 15			17 45				18 15				18 45			
New Barnet	d		16 17			16 47					17 17			17 47				18 17				18 47			
Oakleigh Park	d		16 19			16 49					17 19			17 49				18 19				18 49			
New Southgate	d		16 22			16 52					17 22			17 52				18 22				18 52			
Alexandra Palace	d		16 25			16 55					17 25			17 55				18 25				18 55			
Hornsey	d		16 27			16 57					17 27			17 57				18 27				18 57			
Harringay	d		16 29			16 59					17 29			17 59				18 29				18 59			
Finsbury Park ⊖	d	16 21	16 32		16 52	17 02		17 11		17 21	17 32		17 51	18 02		18 11	18 21	18 32			18 51	19 02		19 11	19 21
Drayton Park	d																								
Highbury & Islington ⊖	d																								
Essex Road	d																								
Old Street ⊖	d																								
Moorgate ⊖	a																								
London Kings Cross ■15 ⊖	a	16 30	16 40		17 00	17 10		17 19		17 30	17 40		18 00	18 10		18 19	18 30	18 40			19 00	19 10		19 19	19 29

Sundays
until 11 July

Letchworth Garden City, Hertford North and Welwyn Garden City - London

		FC	FC	FC ■	FC	FC	FC ■	FC ■	FC	FC	FC ■	FC	FC	FC ■	FC ■	FC	FC	FC ■	FC	FC	FC ■	FC ■
Letchworth Garden City	d						19 29	19 54						20 29	20 54						21 29	21 54
Hitchin ■	d			19 28			19 33	19 58			20 28			20 33	20 58			21 28			21 33	21 58
Stevenage ■	d			19 33		19 35	19 39	20 03			20 33		20 35	20 39	21 03			21 33		21 35	21 39	22 03
Watton-at-Stone	d					19 42							20 42							21 42		
Hertford North	d		19 18			19 48				20 18			20 48				21 18			21 48		
Bayford	d		19 19			19 52				20 19			20 52				21 19			21 52		
Cuffley	d		19a25			19a58				20a25			20a58				21a25			21a58		
Crews Hill	d																					
Gordon Hill	d																					
Enfield Chase	d																					
Grange Park	d																					
Winchmore Hill	d																					
Palmers Green	d																					
Bowes Park	d																					
Knebworth	d						19 43							20 43							21 43	
Welwyn North	d						19 47							20 47							21 47	
Welwyn Garden City ■	d	18 58			19 28		19 50		19 58			20 28		20 50		20 58			21 28		21 50	
Hatfield	d	19 02			19 32		19 53		20 02			20 32		20 53		21 02			21 32		21 53	
Welham Green	d	19 06			19 36				20 06			20 36				21 06			21 36			
Brookmans Park	d	19 08			19 38				20 08			20 38				21 08			21 38			
Potters Bar	d	19 11			19 41		19 59		20 11			20 41		20 59		21 11			21 41		21 59	
Hadley Wood	d	19 15			19 45				20 15			20 45				21 15			21 45			
New Barnet	d	19 17			19 47				20 17			20 47				21 17			21 47			
Oakleigh Park	d	19 19			19 49				20 19			20 49				21 19			21 49			
New Southgate	d	19 22			19 52				20 22			20 52				21 22			21 52			
Alexandra Palace	d	19 25			19 55				20 25			20 55				21 25			21 55			
Hornsey	d	19 27			19 57				20 27			20 57				21 27			21 57			
Harringay	d	19 29			19 59				20 29			20 59				21 29			21 59			
Finsbury Park	⊖ d	19 32		19 51	20 02		20 11	20 21	20 32		20 51	21 02		21 11	21 21	21 32		21 51	22 02		22 11	22 21
Drayton Park	d																					
Highbury & Islington	⊖ d																					
Essex Road	d																					
Old Street	⊖ d																					
Moorgate	⊖ a																					
London Kings Cross ■	⊖ a	19 40		20 00	20 10		20 19	20 30	20 40		21 00	21 10		21 19	21 30	21 40		22 00	22 10		22 19	22 30

		FC	FC	FC ■	FC	FC	FC ■	FC	FC	FC	FC ■	FC ■
Letchworth Garden City	d						22 29					23 39
Hitchin ■	d			22 28			22 33				23 34	23 43
Stevenage ■	d			22 33		22 35	22 39			23 35	23 39	23 48
Watton-at-Stone	d					22 42				23 42		
Hertford North	d		22 18			22 48			23 18	23 48		
Bayford	d		22 19			22 52			23 19	23 52		
Cuffley	d		22a25			22a58			23a25	23a58		
Crews Hill	d											
Gordon Hill	d											
Enfield Chase	d											
Grange Park	d											
Winchmore Hill	d											
Palmers Green	d											
Bowes Park	d											
Knebworth	d						22 43					23 51
Welwyn North	d						22 47					23 55
Welwyn Garden City ■	d	21 58			22 28		22 50	22 58				23 58
Hatfield	d	22 02			22 32		22 53	23 02				00 01
Welham Green	d	22 06			22 36			23 06				
Brookmans Park	d	22 08			22 38			23 08				
Potters Bar	d	22 11			22 41		22 59	23 11				00 07
Hadley Wood	d	22 15			22 45			23 15				
New Barnet	d	22 17			22 47			23 17				
Oakleigh Park	d	22 19			22 49			23 19				
New Southgate	d	22 22			22 52			23 22				
Alexandra Palace	d	22 25			22 55			23 25				
Hornsey	d	22 27			22 57			23 27				
Harringay	d	22 29			22 59			23 29				
Finsbury Park	⊖ d	22 32		22 51	23 02		23 11	23 32			00 05	00 20
Drayton Park	d											
Highbury & Islington	⊖ d											
Essex Road	d											
Old Street	⊖ d											
Moorgate	⊖ a											
London Kings Cross ■	⊖ a	22 40		23 00	23 12		23 19	23 44			00 14	00 32

Sundays
18 July to 05 September

Letchworth Garden City, Hertford North and Welwyn Garden City - London

		FC	FC ■	FC ■	FC	FC ■	FC ■	FC	FC ■	FC ■	FC	FC	FC ■	FC ■	FC ■	FC	FC ■	FC ■	FC ■	FC	FC ■	FC ■	FC ■	FC
Letchworth Garden City	d			23p41			06 54			07 54				08 30	08 54			09 29	09 54			10 29	10 54	
Hitchin ■	d		23p28	23p45		06 28	06 58		07 28	07 58			08 28	08 34	08 58		09 28	09 33	09 58		10 28	10 33	10 58	
Stevenage ■	d		23p33	23p52		06 36	07 04		07 36	08 04			08 33	08 39	09 04		09 33	09 38	10 04		10 34	10 38	11 04	
Watton-at-Stone	d			23p52																				
Hertford North	d	23p22		00 03	06 22			07 22			00 08	08 22				09 22				10 22				11 22
Bayford	d	23p26			06 26			07 26			00 12	08 26				09 26				10 26				11 26
Cuffley	d	23p31			06 31			07 31			00 17	08 31				09 31				10 31				11 31
Crews Hill	d	23p34			06 34			07 34			00 20	08 34				09 34				10 34				11 34
Gordon Hill	d	23p37			06 37			07 37			00 23	08 37				09 37				10 37				11 37
Enfield Chase	d	23p39			06 39			07 39			00 25	08 39				09 39				10 39				11 39
Grange Park	d	23p41			06 41			07 41			00 27	08 41				09 41				10 41				11 41
Winchmore Hill	d	23p43			06 43			07 43			00 29	08 43				09 43				10 43				11 43
Palmers Green	d	23p45			06 45			07 45			00 31	08 45				09 45				10 45				11 45
Bowes Park	d	23p48			06 48			07 48			00 34	08 48				09 48				10 48				11 48
Knebworth	d																							
Welwyn North	d																							
Welwyn Garden City ■	d																							
Hatfield	d																							
Welham Green	d																							
Brookmans Park	d																							
Potters Bar	d																							
Hadley Wood	d																							
New Barnet	d																							
Oakleigh Park	d																							
New Southgate	d																							
Alexandra Palace	d	23p50			06 50			07 50			00 36	08 50				09 50				10 50				11 50
Hornsey	d	23p52			06 52			07 52			00 38	08 52				09 52				10 52				11 52
Harringay	d	23p54			06 54			07 54			00 40	08 54				09 54				10 54				11 54
Finsbury Park	⊖ d	23p57	00 04	00s22	06 57	07 02	07 32	07 57	08 02	08 32	00 43	08 57	08 59	09 06	09 32	09 57	09 59	10 06	10 32	10 57	11 04	11 11	11 32	11 57
Drayton Park	d																							
Highbury & Islington	⊖ d																							
Essex Road	d																							
Old Street	⊖ d																							
Moorgate	⊖ a																							
London Kings Cross ■	⊖ a	00 04	00 12	00 31	07 06	07 12	07 42	08 06	08 12	08 40	00 53	09 04	09 09	09 13	09 39	10 04	10 08	10 13	10 39	11 04	11 12	11 18	11 41	12 04

		FC ■	FC ■	FC ■	FC	FC ■	FC ■	FC ■	FC	FC ■	FC ■	FC ■	FC	FC ■	FC ■	FC ■	FC	FC ■	FC ■	FC ■	FC	FC ■	FC ■
Letchworth Garden City	d		11 29	11 54			12 29	12 54			13 29	13 54			14 29	14 54			15 29	15 54			16 29
Hitchin ■	d	11 28	11 33	11 58		12 28	12 33	12 58		13 28	13 33	13 58		14 28	14 33	14 58		15 28	15 33	15 58		16 28	16 33
Stevenage ■	d	11 33	11 38	12 04		12 33	12 38	13 04		13 33	13 38	14 04		14 35	14 38	15 04		15 36	15 38	16 04		16 35	16 38
Watton-at-Stone	d																						
Hertford North	d				12 22				13 22				14 22				15 22				16 22		
Bayford	d				12 26				13 26				14 26				15 26				16 26		
Cuffley	d				12 31				13 31				14 31				15 31				16 31		
Crews Hill	d				12 34				13 34				14 34				15 34				16 34		
Gordon Hill	d				12 37				13 37				14 37				15 37				16 37		
Enfield Chase	d				12 39				13 39				14 39				15 39				16 39		
Grange Park	d				12 41				13 41				14 41				15 41				16 41		
Winchmore Hill	d				12 43				13 43				14 43				15 43				16 43		
Palmers Green	d				12 45				13 45				14 45				15 45				16 45		
Bowes Park	d				12 48				13 48				14 48				15 48				16 48		
Knebworth	d																						
Welwyn North	d																						
Welwyn Garden City ■	d																						
Hatfield	d																						
Welham Green	d																						
Brookmans Park	d																						
Potters Bar	d																						
Hadley Wood	d																						
New Barnet	d																						
Oakleigh Park	d																						
New Southgate	d																						
Alexandra Palace	d				12 50				13 50				14 50				15 50				16 50		
Hornsey	d				12 52				13 52				14 52				15 52				16 52		
Harringay	d				12 54				13 54				14 54				15 54				16 54		
Finsbury Park	⊖ d	12 01	12 12	12 32	12 57	13 05	13 09	13 32	13 57	14 04	14 08	14 32	14 57	15 05	15 11	15 33	15 57	16 06	16 12	16 32	16 57	17 05	17 11
Drayton Park	d																						
Highbury & Islington	⊖ d																						
Essex Road	d																						
Old Street	⊖ d																						
Moorgate	⊖ a																						
London Kings Cross ■	⊖ a	12 09	12 19	12 40	13 08	13 13	13 16	13 40	14 04	14 12	14 16	14 40	15 04	15 14	15 18	15 43	16 04	16 15	16 19	16 40	17 04	17 14	17 18

Table 24

Sundays
18 July to 05 September

Letchworth Garden City, Hertford North and Welwyn Garden City - London

	FC ■1	FC	FC ■1	FC ■1	FC ■1	FC	FC ■1	FC ■1	FC ■1	FC	FC ■1	FC ■1	FC ■1	FC	FC ■1	FC ■1	FC ■1	FC	FC ■1	FC ■1	FC ■1
Letchworth Garden City d	16 54			17 29	17 54			18 29	18 54			19 29	19 54			20 29	20 54			21 29	21 54
Hitchin ■4 d	16 58		17 28	17 33	17 58		18 28	18 33	18 58		19 28	19 33	19 58		20 28	20 33	20 58		21 28	21 33	21 58
Stevenage ■4 d	17 04		17 33	17 38	18 04		18 33	18 38	19 04		19 33	19 38	20 04		20 33	20 38	21 04		21 33	21 38	22 04
Watton-at-Stone d																					
Hertford North d		17 22				18 22				19 22				20 22				21 22			
Bayford d		17 26				18 26				19 26				20 26				21 26			
Cuffley d		17 31				18 31				19 31				20 31				21 31			
Crews Hill d		17 34				18 34				19 34				20 34				21 34			
Gordon Hill d		17 37				18 37				19 37				20 37				21 37			
Enfield Chase d		17 39				18 39				19 39				20 39				21 39			
Grange Park d		17 41				18 41				19 41				20 41				21 41			
Winchmore Hill d		17 43				18 43				19 43				20 43				21 43			
Palmers Green d		17 45				18 45				19 45				20 45				21 45			
Bowes Park d		17 48				18 48				19 48				20 48				21 48			
Knebworth d																					
Welwyn North d																					
Welwyn Garden City ■4 d																					
Hatfield d																					
Welham Green d																					
Brookmans Park d																					
Potters Bar d																					
Hadley Wood d																					
New Barnet d																					
Oakleigh Park d																					
New Southgate d																					
Alexandra Palace d		17 50				18 50				19 50				20 50				21 50			
Hornsey d		17 52				18 52				19 52				20 52				21 52			
Harringay d		17 54				18 54				19 54				20 54				21 54			
Finsbury Park ⊖ d	17 32	17 57	18 01	18 12	18 32	18 57	19 02	19 07	19 32	19 57	20 01	20 14	20 32	20 57	21 01	21 12	21 32	21 57	22 01	22 11	22 32
Drayton Park d																					
Highbury & Islington ⊖ d																					
Essex Road d																					
Old Street ⊖ d																					
Moorgate ⊖ a																					
London Kings Cross ■15 ⊖ a	17 40	18 04	18 09	18 19	18 40	19 08	19 12	19 15	19 40	20 04	20 09	20 21	20 40	21 04	21 09	21 19	21 40	22 04	22 09	22 18	22 40

	FC	FC ■1	FC ■1	FC ■1	FC	FC ■1	FC ■1
Letchworth Garden City d			22 29	22 54			23 54
Hitchin ■4 d		22 28	22 33	22 58		23 34	23 58
Stevenage ■4 d		22 33	22 38	23 04		23 40	00 03
Watton-at-Stone d							00 08
Hertford North d	22 22				23 22		00 14
Bayford d	22 26				23 26		
Cuffley d	22 31				23 31		
Crews Hill d	22 34				23 34		
Gordon Hill d	22 37				23 37		
Enfield Chase d	22 39				23 39		
Grange Park d	22 41				23 41		
Winchmore Hill d	22 43				23 43		
Palmers Green d	22 45				23 45		
Bowes Park d	22 48				23 48		
Knebworth d							
Welwyn North d							
Welwyn Garden City ■4 d							
Hatfield d							
Welham Green d							
Brookmans Park d							
Potters Bar d							
Hadley Wood d							
New Barnet d							
Oakleigh Park d							
New Southgate d							
Alexandra Palace d	22 50				23 50		
Hornsey d	22 52				23 52		
Harringay d	22 54				23 54		
Finsbury Park ⊖ d	22 57	23 01	23 11	23 32	23 57	00 09	00 30
Drayton Park d							
Highbury & Islington ⊖ d							
Essex Road d							
Old Street ⊖ d							
Moorgate ⊖ a							
London Kings Cross ■15 ⊖ a	23 04	23 09	23 18	23 40	00 04	00 17	00 42

Table 24

Sundays
from 12 September

Letchworth Garden City, Hertford North and Welwyn Garden City - London

	FC	FC ■1	FC ■1	FC 🚌	FC	FC	FC ■1	FC 🚌	FC	FC	FC ■1	FC	FC	FC	FC 🚌	FC ■1	FC 🚌	FC	FC ■1	FC	FC	FC	FC 🚌
Letchworth Garden City d			23p41												07 00								08 00
Hitchin ■4 d		23p31	23p45	06 10				06 33							07 15		07 45						08 15
Stevenage ■4 d	23p29	23p34	23p50	06a30			06 39	06a53			07 08			07 29	07a35	07 40	08a05		08 10			08 29	08a35
Watton-at-Stone d	23p36													07 36								08 36	
Hertford North d	23p42				06 12				06 42			07 12		07 42						08 12		08 42	
Bayford d	23p46				06 16				06 46			07 16		07 46						08 16		08 46	
Cuffley d	23p51				06 21				06 51			07 21		07 51						08 21		08 51	
Crews Hill d	23p54				06 24				06 54			07 24		07 54						08 24		08 54	
Gordon Hill d	23p57				06 27				06 57			07 27		07 57						08 27		08 57	
Enfield Chase d	23p59				06 29				06 59			07 29		07 59						08 29		08 59	
Grange Park d	00 01				06 31				07 01			07 31		08 01						08 31		09 01	
Winchmore Hill d	00 03				06 33				07 03			07 33		08 03						08 33		09 03	
Palmers Green d	00 05				06 35				07 05			07 35		08 05						08 35		09 05	
Bowes Park d	00 08				06 38				07 08			07 38		08 08						08 38		09 08	
Knebworth d			23p53				06 43									07 43			08 13				
Welwyn North d			23p57				06 47									07 47			08 17				
Welwyn Garden City ■4 d			00 01			06 28	06 50			06 58			07 28			07 50		07 58	08 20		08 28		
Hatfield d			00 04			06 32	06 53			07 02			07 32			07 54		08 02	08 24		08 32		
Welham Green d						06 36				07 06			07 36					08 06			08 36		
Brookmans Park d						06 38				07 08			07 38					08 08			08 38		
Potters Bar d			00 10			06 41	06 59			07 11			07 41			08 00		08 11	08 30		08 41		
Hadley Wood d						06 45				07 15			07 45					08 15			08 45		
New Barnet d						06 47				07 17			07 47					08 17			08 47		
Oakleigh Park d						06 49				07 19			07 49					08 19			08 49		
New Southgate d						06 52				07 22			07 52					08 22			08 52		
Alexandra Palace d	00 10				06 40	06 55			07 10	07 25		07 40	07 55	08 10				08 25		08 40	08 55	09 10	
Hornsey d	00 12				06 42	06 57			07 12	07 27		07 42	07 57	08 12				08 27		08 42	08 57	09 12	
Harringay d	00 14				06 44	06 59			07 14	07 29		07 44	07 59	08 14				08 29		08 44	08 59	09 14	
Finsbury Park ⊖ d	00 17	00 01	00 26		06 47	07 02	07s11		07 17	07 32	07s40	07 47	08 02	08 17		08 11		08 32	08 42	08 47	09 02	09 17	
Drayton Park d																							
Highbury & Islington ⊖ d																							
Essex Road d																							
Old Street ⊖ d																							
Moorgate ⊖ a																							
London Kings Cross ■15 ⊖ a	00 25	00 09	00 35		06 57	07 13	07 19		07 29	07 45	07 48	07 57	08 15	08 27		08 23		08 40	08 49	08 55	09 10	09 25	

	FC ■1	FC 🚌	FC 🚌	FC	FC ■1	FC 🚌	FC	FC ■1	FC	FC ■1	FC	FC ■1	FC ■1	FC	FC	FC	FC ■1	FC	FC ■1	FC ■1	FC	FC
Letchworth Garden City d			08 35			08 46						09 29	09 54						10 29	10 54		
Hitchin ■4 d		08 45	08 50			09 01				09 28		09 33	09 58				10 28		10 33	10 58		
Stevenage ■4 d	08 40	09a05	09a10		09 15	09a21		09 28	09 29	09 33		09 39	10 03			10 29	10 33		10 39	11 03		
Watton-at-Stone d									09 36							10 36						
Hertford North d							09 12		09 42						10 12	10 42						11 12
Bayford d							09 16		09 46						10 16	10 46						11 16
Cuffley d							09 21		09 51						10 21	10 51						11 21
Crews Hill d							09 24		09 54						10 24	10 54						11 24
Gordon Hill d							09 27		09 57						10 27	10 57						11 27
Enfield Chase d							09 29		09 59						10 29	10 59						11 29
Grange Park d							09 31		10 01						10 31	11 01						11 31
Winchmore Hill d							09 33		10 03						10 33	11 03						11 33
Palmers Green d							09 35		10 05						10 35	11 05						11 35
Bowes Park d							09 38		10 08						10 38	11 08						11 38
Knebworth d	08 43				09 18							09 43							10 43			
Welwyn North d	08 47				09 22							09 47							10 47			
Welwyn Garden City ■4 d	08 50			08 58	09 25						09 28	09 50		09 58				10 28	10 50		10 58	
Hatfield d	08 54			09 02	09 29						09 32	09 53		10 02				10 32	10 53		11 02	
Welham Green d				09 06							09 36			10 06				10 36			11 06	
Brookmans Park d				09 08							09 38			10 08				10 38			11 08	
Potters Bar d	09 00			09 11	09 35						09 41	09 59		10 11				10 41	10 59		11 11	
Hadley Wood d				09 15							09 45			10 15				10 45			11 15	
New Barnet d				09 17							09 47			10 17				10 47			11 17	
Oakleigh Park d				09 19							09 49			10 19				10 49			11 19	
New Southgate d				09 22							09 52			10 22				10 52			11 22	
Alexandra Palace d				09 25			09 40		10 10		09 55			10 25	10 40	11 10		10 55			11 25	11 40
Hornsey d				09 27			09 42		10 12		09 57			10 27	10 42	11 12		10 57			11 27	11 42
Harringay d				09 29			09 44		10 14		09 59			10 29	10 44	11 14		10 59			11 29	11 44
Finsbury Park ⊖ d	09 11			09 32	09 44		09 47	09 47	10 17	09 51	10 02	10 11	10 21	10 32	10 47	11 17	10 51	11 02	11 11	11 21	11 32	11 47
Drayton Park d																						
Highbury & Islington ⊖ d																						
Essex Road d																						
Old Street ⊖ d																						
Moorgate ⊖ a																						
London Kings Cross ■15 ⊖ a	09 18			09 40	09 51		09 55	09 56	10 25	10 00	10 10	10 19	10 30	10 40	10 55	11 25	11 00	11 10	11 19	11 30	11 40	11 55

Table 24

Sundays from 12 September

Letchworth Garden City, Hertford North and Welwyn Garden City - London

		FC	FC ■	FC	FC ■	FC ■	FC	FC	FC	FC ■	FC	FC ■	FC ■	FC	FC	FC	FC ■	FC	FC ■	FC	FC	FC
Letchworth Garden City	d				11 29	11 54						12 29	12 54						13 29			
Hitchin ■	d		11 28		11 33	11 58				12 28		12 33	12 58				13 28		13 33			
Stevenage ■	d	11 29	11 33		11 39	12 03			12 29	12 33		12 39	13 03			13 29	13 33		13 39			14 29
Watton-at-Stone	d	11 36							12 36							13 36						14 36
Hertford North	d	11 42						12 12	12 42						13 12	13 42					14 12	14 42
Bayford	d	11 46						12 16	12 46						13 16	13 46					14 16	14 46
Cuffley	d	11 51						12 21	12 51						13 21	13 51					14 21	14 51
Crews Hill	d	11 54						12 24	12 54						13 24	13 54					14 24	14 54
Gordon Hill	d	11 57						12 27	12 57						13 27	13 57					14 27	14 57
Enfield Chase	d	11 59						12 29	12 59						13 29	13 59					14 29	14 59
Grange Park	d	12 01						12 31	13 01						13 31	14 01					14 31	15 01
Winchmore Hill	d	12 03						12 33	13 03						13 33	14 03					14 33	15 03
Palmers Green	d	12 05						12 35	13 05						13 35	14 05					14 35	15 05
Bowes Park	d	12 08						12 38	13 08						13 38	14 08					14 38	15 08
Knebworth	d				11 43							12 43							13 43			
Welwyn North	d				11 47							12 47							13 47			
Welwyn Garden City ■	d			11 28	11 50		11 58				12 28	12 50		12 58				13 28	13 50	13 58		
Hatfield	d			11 32	11 53		12 02				12 32	12 53		13 02				13 32	13 53	14 02		
Welham Green	d			11 36			12 06				12 36			13 06				13 36		14 06		
Brookmans Park	d			11 38			12 08				12 38			13 08				13 38		14 08		
Potters Bar	d			11 41	11 59		12 11				12 41	12 59		13 11				13 41	13 59	14 11		
Hadley Wood	d			11 45			12 15				12 45			13 15				13 45		14 15		
New Barnet	d			11 47			12 17				12 47			13 17				13 47		14 17		
Oakleigh Park	d			11 49			12 19				12 49			13 19				13 49		14 19		
New Southgate	d			11 52			12 22				12 52			13 22				13 52		14 22		
Alexandra Palace	d	12 10		11 55			12 25	12 40	13 10		12 55			13 25	13 40	14 10		13 55		14 25	14 40	15 10
Hornsey	d	12 12		11 57			12 27	12 42	13 12		12 57			13 27	13 42	14 12		13 57		14 27	14 42	15 12
Harringay	d	12 14		11 59			12 29	12 44	13 14		12 59			13 29	13 44	14 14		13 59		14 29	14 44	15 14
Finsbury Park ⊖	d	12 17	11 51	12 02	12 11	12 21	12 32	12 47	13 17	12 51	13 02	13 11	13 21	13 32	13 47	14 17	13 51	14 02	14 11	14 32	14 47	15 17
Drayton Park	d																					
Highbury & Islington ⊖	d																					
Essex Road	d																					
Old Street ⊖	d																					
Moorgate ⊖	a																					
London Kings Cross ■ ⊖	a	12 25	12 00	12 10	12 19	12 30	12 40	12 55	13 25	13 00	13 10	13 19	13 30	13 40	13 55	14 25	14 00	14 10	14 19	14 40	14 55	15 25

		FC ■	FC	FC ■	FC ■	FC	FC	FC	FC ■	FC	FC ■	FC ■	FC	FC	FC	FC ■	FC	FC ■	FC ■	FC	FC	FC	FC ■
Letchworth Garden City	d			14 29	14 54						15 29	15 54						16 29	16 54				
Hitchin ■	d	14 28		14 33	14 58				15 28		15 33	15 58				16 28		16 33	16 58				17 28
Stevenage ■	d	14 33		14 39	15 03			15 29	15 33		15 39	16 03			16 29	16 33		16 39	17 03			17 29	17 33
Watton-at-Stone	d							15 36							16 36							17 36	
Hertford North	d						15 12	15 42						16 12	16 42						17 12	17 42	
Bayford	d						15 16	15 46						16 16	16 46						17 16	17 46	
Cuffley	d						15 21	15 51						16 21	16 51						17 21	17 51	
Crews Hill	d						15 24	15 54						16 24	16 54						17 24	17 54	
Gordon Hill	d						15 27	15 57						16 27	16 57						17 27	17 57	
Enfield Chase	d						15 29	15 59						16 29	16 59						17 29	17 59	
Grange Park	d						15 31	16 01						16 31	17 01						17 31	18 01	
Winchmore Hill	d						15 33	16 03						16 33	17 03						17 33	18 03	
Palmers Green	d						15 35	16 05						16 35	17 05						17 35	18 05	
Bowes Park	d						15 38	16 08						16 38	17 08						17 38	18 08	
Knebworth	d			14 43							15 43							16 43					
Welwyn North	d			14 47							15 47							16 47					
Welwyn Garden City ■	d		14 28	14 50		14 58				15 28	15 50		15 58				16 28	16 50		16 58			
Hatfield	d		14 32	14 53		15 02				15 32	15 53		16 02				16 32	16 53		17 02			
Welham Green	d		14 36			15 06				15 36			16 06				16 36			17 06			
Brookmans Park	d		14 38			15 08				15 38			16 08				16 38			17 08			
Potters Bar	d		14 41	14 59		15 11				15 41	15 59		16 11				16 41	16 59		17 11			
Hadley Wood	d		14 45			15 15				15 45			16 15				16 45			17 15			
New Barnet	d		14 47			15 17				15 47			16 17				16 47			17 17			
Oakleigh Park	d		14 49			15 19				15 49			16 19				16 49			17 19			
New Southgate	d		14 52			15 22				15 52			16 22				16 52			17 22			
Alexandra Palace	d		14 55			15 25	15 40	16 10		15 55			16 25	16 40	17 10		16 55			17 25	17 40	18 10	
Hornsey	d		14 57			15 27	15 42	16 12		15 57			16 27	16 42	17 12		16 57			17 27	17 42	18 12	
Harringay	d		14 59			15 29	15 44	16 14		15 59			16 29	16 44	17 14		16 59			17 29	17 44	18 14	
Finsbury Park ⊖	d	14 51	15 02	15 11	15 21	15 32	15 47	16 17	15 51	16 02	16 11	16 21	16 32	16 47	17 17	16 52	17 02	17 11	17 21	17 32	17 47	18 17	17 51
Drayton Park	d																						
Highbury & Islington ⊖	d																						
Essex Road	d																						
Old Street ⊖	d																						
Moorgate ⊖	a																						
London Kings Cross ■ ⊖	a	15 00	15 10	15 19	15 30	15 40	15 55	16 25	16 00	16 10	16 19	16 30	16 40	16 55	17 25	17 00	17 10	17 19	17 30	17 40	17 55	18 25	18 00

Table 24

Sundays from 12 September

Letchworth Garden City, Hertford North and Welwyn Garden City - London

		FC	FC ■	FC ■	FC	FC	FC	FC ■	FC	FC ■	FC ■	FC	FC	FC	FC ■	FC	FC ■	FC ■	FC	FC	FC	FC ■
Letchworth Garden City	d		17 29	17 54						18 29	18 54						19 29	19 54				
Hitchin ■	d		17 33	17 58				18 28		18 33	18 58				19 28		19 33	19 58				20 28
Stevenage ■	d		17 39	18 03			18 29	18 33		18 39	19 03			19 29	19 33		19 39	20 03			20 29	20 33
Watton-at-Stone	d						18 36							19 36							20 36	
Hertford North	d					18 12	18 42						19 12	19 42						20 12	20 42	
Bayford	d					18 16	18 46						19 16	19 46						20 16	20 46	
Cuffley	d					18 21	18 51						19 21	19 51						20 21	20 51	
Crews Hill	d					18 24	18 54						19 24	19 54						20 24	20 54	
Gordon Hill	d					18 27	18 57						19 27	19 57						20 27	20 57	
Enfield Chase	d					18 29	18 59						19 29	19 59						20 29	20 59	
Grange Park	d					18 31	19 01						19 31	20 01						20 31	21 01	
Winchmore Hill	d					18 33	19 03						19 33	20 03						20 33	21 03	
Palmers Green	d					18 35	19 05						19 35	20 05						20 35	21 05	
Bowes Park	d					18 38	19 08						19 38	20 08						20 38	21 08	
Knebworth	d		17 43							18 43							19 43					
Welwyn North	d		17 47							18 47							19 47					
Welwyn Garden City ■	d	17 28	17 50		17 58				18 28	18 50		18 58				19 28	19 50		19 58			
Hatfield	d	17 32	17 53		18 02				18 32	18 53		19 02				19 32	19 53		20 02			
Welham Green	d	17 36			18 06				18 36			19 06				19 36			20 06			
Brookmans Park	d	17 38			18 08				18 38			19 08				19 38			20 08			
Potters Bar	d	17 41	17 59		18 11				18 41	18 59		19 11				19 41	19 59		20 11			
Hadley Wood	d	17 45			18 15				18 45			19 15				19 45			20 15			
New Barnet	d	17 47			18 17				18 47			19 17				19 47			20 17			
Oakleigh Park	d	17 49			18 19				18 49			19 19				19 49			20 19			
New Southgate	d	17 52			18 22				18 52			19 22				19 52			20 22			
Alexandra Palace	d	17 55			18 25	18 40	19 10		18 55			19 25	19 40	20 10		19 55			20 25	20 40	21 10	
Hornsey	d	17 57			18 27	18 42	19 12		18 57			19 27	19 42	20 12		19 57			20 27	20 42	21 12	
Harringay	d	17 59			18 29	18 44	19 14		18 59			19 29	19 44	20 14		19 59			20 29	20 44	21 14	
Finsbury Park ⊖	d	18 02	18 11	18 21	18 32	18 47	19 17	18 51	19 02	19 11	19 21	19 32	19 47	20 17	19 51	20 02	20 11	20 21	20 32	20 47	21 17	20 51
Drayton Park	d																					
Highbury & Islington ⊖	d																					
Essex Road	d																					
Old Street ⊖	d																					
Moorgate ⊖	a																					
London Kings Cross ■ ⊖	a	18 10	18 19	18 30	18 40	18 55	19 25	19 00	19 10	19 19	19 29	19 40	19 55	20 25	20 00	20 10	20 19	20 30	20 40	20 55	21 25	21 00

		FC	FC ■	FC ■	FC	FC	FC	FC ■	FC	FC ■	FC ■	FC	FC	FC	FC ■	FC	FC ■	FC	FC	FC	FC ■	FC ■
Letchworth Garden City	d		20 29	20 54						21 29	21 54						22 29					23 39
Hitchin ■	d		20 33	20 58				21 28		21 33	21 58				22 28		22 33				23 34	23 43
Stevenage ■	d		20 39	21 03			21 29	21 33		21 39	22 03			22 29	22 33		22 39			23 29	23 39	23 48
Watton-at-Stone	d						21 36							22 36						23 36		
Hertford North	d					21 12	21 42						22 12	22 42					23 12	23 42		
Bayford	d					21 16	21 46						22 16	22 46					23 16	23 46		
Cuffley	d					21 21	21 51						22 21	22 51					23 21	23 51		
Crews Hill	d					21 24	21 54						22 24	22 54					23 24	23 54		
Gordon Hill	d					21 27	21 57						22 27	22 57					23 27	23 57		
Enfield Chase	d					21 29	21 59						22 29	22 59					23 29	23 59		
Grange Park	d					21 31	22 01						22 31	23 01					23 31	00 01		
Winchmore Hill	d					21 33	22 03						22 33	23 03					23 33	00 03		
Palmers Green	d					21 35	22 05						22 35	23 05					23 35	00 05		
Bowes Park	d					21 38	22 08						22 38	23 08					23 38	00 08		
Knebworth	d		20 43							21 43							22 43					23 51
Welwyn North	d		20 47							21 47							22 47					23 55
Welwyn Garden City ■	d	20 28	20 50		20 58				21 28	21 50		21 58				22 28	22 50	22 58				23 58
Hatfield	d	20 32	20 53		21 02				21 32	21 53		22 02				22 32	22 53	23 02				00 01
Welham Green	d	20 36			21 06				21 36			22 06				22 36		23 06				
Brookmans Park	d	20 38			21 08				21 38			22 08				22 38		23 08				
Potters Bar	d	20 41	20 59		21 11				21 41	21 59		22 11				22 41	22 59	23 11				00 07
Hadley Wood	d	20 45			21 15				21 45			22 15				22 45		23 15				
New Barnet	d	20 47			21 17				21 47			22 17				22 47		23 17				
Oakleigh Park	d	20 49			21 19				21 49			22 19				22 49		23 19				
New Southgate	d	20 52			21 22				21 52			22 22				22 52		23 22				
Alexandra Palace	d	20 55			21 25	21 40	22 10		21 55			22 25	22 40	23 10		22 55		23 25	23 40	00 10		
Hornsey	d	20 57			21 27	21 42	22 12		21 57			22 27	22 42	23 12		22 57		23 27	23 42	00 12		
Harringay	d	20 59			21 29	21 44	22 14		21 59			22 29	22 44	23 14		22 59		23 29	23 44	00 14		
Finsbury Park ⊖	d	21 02	21 11	21 21	21 32	21 47	22 17	21 51	22 02	22 11	22 21	22 32	22 47	23 17	22 51	23 02	23 11	23 32	23 47	00 17	00 05	00 20
Drayton Park	d																					
Highbury & Islington ⊖	d																					
Essex Road	d																					
Old Street ⊖	d																					
Moorgate ⊖	a																					
London Kings Cross ■ ⊖	a	21 10	21 19	21 30	21 40	21 55	22 25	22 00	22 10	22 19	22 30	22 40	22 58	23 27	23 00	23 12	23 19	23 44	23 57	00 27	00 14	00 32

London - Stevenage, Cambridge and Peterborough

					FC ■ A	FC ■ B	FC MX ■			FC ■ B	FC MX ■	FC C	FC MX	FC MX ■	FC MX	FC D	FC ■ A	FC ■ B	FC MX ■		FC MX	FC ■ D	FC ■ E	FC MX
London Kings Cross ⊖	d				23p05	23p06	23p06			23p22	23p22	23p26	23p26	23p36				23p41	00 04		00 06	00 07	00 07	
Finsbury Park ⊖	d				23p10	23p11	23p11			23p27	23p27	23p31	23p32	23p41				23p47	00 09		00 12	00 12	00 12	
Potters Bar	d					23p21	23p21							23p51										
Hatfield	d					23p27	23p27							23p57				00 08						
Welwyn Garden City	d					23p31	23p31							00 01				00 20						
Welwyn North	d					23p34	23p34							00 04				00 23						
Knebworth	d					23p38	23p38							00 08				00 28						
Hertford North	d											00 07	00 07		←	00 07					00 47		00 39	←
Stevenage	d				23p40	23p42	23p42			23p46	23p46	00a20	00 20	00 12	00 20	00a20		00 31	00 31		01 00	00 48	00 48	01 00
Hitchin	d				23p45	23p50	23p50			23p54	23p54		→	00 20	00 26			00 37	00 39		→	00 56	00 56	01 06
Letchworth Garden City	d					23p54	23p54							00a29	00a36			00a52	00 43			01 00	01 00	01a16
Baldock	d					23p57	23p58												00 46			01 04	01 04	
Ashwell & Morden	d					00 02	00 03												00 51			01 09	01 09	
Royston	d					00 07	00 07										00 10		00 56			01 13	01 13	
Meldreth	d					00 11	00 11										00 13		00 59			01 17	01 17	
Shepreth	d					00 14	00 14										00 16		01 02			01 20	01 20	
Foxton	d					00 16	00 17										00 19		01 05			01 23	01 23	
Cambridge	a					00 29	00 29										00 32		01 22			01 39	01 39	
Arlesey	d				23p50					23p59	23p59													
Biggleswade	d				23p55					00 04	00 04													
Sandy	d				23p59					00 08	00 08													
St Neots	d				00 06					00 15	00 15													
Huntingdon	d				00 14					00 23	00 26													
Peterborough	a				00 34					00 42	00 42													

		FC ■ B	FC ■ A	FC MX ■	FC MX ■	FC ■ D	FC ■ B	FC D	FC ■ F	FC ■ A	FC D	FC ■	FC	FC ■	FC	GR ■		FC ■	GR ■	FC ■	FC ■	FC	FC ■	FC ■	GR ■
London Kings Cross ⊖	d	00 36	00 36	00 36	01 06	01 06	01 06		01 36	01 36		05 22		05 45	05 56	06 00		06 06	06 15		06 22	06 26	06 36	06 52	07 00
Finsbury Park ⊖	d	00 41	00 41	00 41	01 11	01 11	01 11		01 41	01 41		05 27		05 50	06 02			06 11			06 27	06 32	06 41	06 57	
Potters Bar	d	00 51		00 51					01 58			05 37						06 21					06 51		
Hatfield	d	00 57		00 57					02 04			05 43						06 27					06 57		
Welwyn Garden City	d	01 01		01 01					02 08			05 47						06 31					07 01		
Welwyn North	d	01s04		01s04					02s11			05 50						06 34					07 04		
Knebworth	d	01s08		01s08					02s15			05 54						06 38					07 08		
Hertford North	d				01 38		01 38	01 38			02 38		05 50		06 40					←		07 10			
Stevenage	d	01 12	01 12	01 12	01 47	01 47	01 47	02a00	02 18	02 18	03a00	05 58	06a05	06 08	06a55	06 19		06 42	06 34	06 42	06 46	07a25	07 12	07 17	07 19
Hitchin	d	01 17	01 17	01 17	01 52	01 52	01 52		02 23	02 23		06 06		06 13				→		06 47	06 51		07 17	07 22	
Letchworth Garden City	d				02a06	02a06	02a06							06 17						06 51				07 26	
Baldock	d													06 20						06 55				07 29	
Ashwell & Morden	d													06 25						07 00				07 34	
Royston	d													06 30						07 06				07 39	
Meldreth	d													06 34						07 10				07 43	
Shepreth	d													06 37						07 13				07 46	
Foxton	d													06 40						07 16				07 48	
Cambridge	a													06 55						07 29				08 02	
Arlesey	d	01s25	01s25	01s25								06 11									06 56		07 23		
Biggleswade	d	01s30	01s30	01s30					02s35	02s35		06 16									07 01		07 28		
Sandy	d	01s34	01s34	01s34								06 20									07 05		07 32		
St Neots	d	01s42	01s42	01s42					02s45	02s45		06 28									07 12		07 39		
Huntingdon	d	01s52	01s52	01s52					02s56	02s56		06 35									07 20		07 47		
Peterborough	a	02 11	02 11	02 13					03 14	03 14		06 54				06 50			07 05		07 38		08 09		07 51

A MO from 19 July until 6 September
B MO until 12 July, MO from 13 September
C MO from 13 September
D MO until 12 July
E MO from 19 July
F until 16 July, MX from 20 July until 3 September, from 7 September

London - Stevenage, Cambridge and Peterborough

		FC ■		GR ■	FC ■		FC ■	GR ■	GR ■	FC ■	FC ■	FC ■		FC ■	GR ■	FC ■	FC ■	FC ■	FC ■	GR ■	GR ■	FC ■			FC ■
London Kings Cross ⊖	d	07 06		07 10			07 22	07 30	07 35	07 36	07 52	08 03		08 22	08 30	08 33	08 52	09 06	09 22	09 30	09 35	09 36			09 52
Finsbury Park ⊖	d	07 11					07 27			07 41	07 57	08 08		08 27		08 38	08 57	09 11	09 27			09 41			09 57
Potters Bar	d	07 21								07 51		08 19				08 49		09 21				09 51			
Hatfield	d	07 27								07 57		08 25				08 55		09 27				09 57			
Welwyn Garden City	d	07 31								08 01		08 31				09 01		09 31				10 01			
Welwyn North	d	07 34								08 04		08 34				09 04		09 34				10 04			
Knebworth	d	07 38								08 08		08 38				09 08		09 38				10 08			
Hertford North	d				←																				
Stevenage	d	07 42		07 29	07 42		07 46	07 50	07 56	08 12	08 17	08 42		08 46	08 49	09 12	09 16	09 42	09 46	09 49	09 54	10 12			10 16
Hitchin	d	→			07 47		07 51			08 17	08 22	08 47		08 51		09 17	09 21	09 47	09 51			10 17			10 21
Letchworth Garden City	d				07 51						08 26	08 54					09 25	09 51							10 25
Baldock	d				07 55						08 29	08 57					09 28	09 55							10 28
Ashwell & Morden	d				08 00						08 34	09 02						10 00							
Royston	d				08 06						08 39	09 07					09 36	10 04							10 36
Meldreth	d				08 10						08 43	09 11						10 08							
Shepreth	d				08 13						08 46	09 14						10 11							
Foxton	d				08 16						08 48	09 16						10 14							
Cambridge	a				08 29						09 02	09 29					09 55	10 29							10 54
Arlesey	d						07 56			08 23				08 56		09 23						10 23			
Biggleswade	d						08 01			08 28				09 01		09 28			09 59			10 28			
Sandy	d						08 05			08 32				09 05		09 32			10 03			10 32			
St Neots	d						08 12			08 39				09 12		09 39			10 10			10 39			
Huntingdon	d						08 20			08 47				09 20		09 47			10 18			10 47			
Peterborough	a			08 00			08 38	08 21		09 14				09 38	09 20	10 04			10 35	10 20	10 26	11 05			

		FC ■	FC ■	FC ■	FC ■	FC ■	FC ■	GR ■		GR ■	FC ■	FC ■	FC ■	GR ■	FC ■	FC ■	GR ■	FC ■		FC ■	FC ■	FC ■	FC ■	FC ■	FC ■
London Kings Cross ⊖	d	10 06	10 22	10 36	10 52	11 06	11 22	11 30		11 35	11 36	11 52	12 06	12 10		12 22	12 35	12 36		12 52	13 06	13 22	13 36	13 52	14 06
Finsbury Park ⊖	d	10 11	10 27	10 41	10 57	11 11	11 27				11 41	11 57	12 11			12 27		12 41		12 57	13 11	13 27	13 41	13 57	14 11
Potters Bar	d	10 21		10 51		11 21					11 51		12 21					12 51			13 21		13 51		14 21
Hatfield	d	10 27		10 57		11 27					11 57		12 27					12 57			13 27		13 57		14 27
Welwyn Garden City	d	10 31		11 01		11 31					12 01		12 31					13 01			13 31		14 01		14 31
Welwyn North	d	10 34		11 04		11 34					12 04		12 34					13 04			13 34		14 04		14 34
Knebworth	d	10 38		11 08		11 38					12 08		12 38					13 08			13 38		14 08		14 38
Hertford North	d														←										
Stevenage	d	10 42	10 46	11 12	11 16	11 42	11 46	11 50		11 54	12 12	12 16	12 42	12 29	12 42	12 46	12 54	13 12		13 16	13 42	13 46	14 12	14 16	14 42
Hitchin	d	10 47	10 51	11 17	11 21	11 47	11 51				12 17	12 21	→		12 47	12 51		13 17		13 21	13 47	13 51	14 17	14 21	14 47
Letchworth Garden City	d	10 51			11 25	11 51						12 25			12 51					13 25	13 51			14 25	14 51
Baldock	d	10 55			11 28	11 55						12 28			12 55					13 28	13 55			14 28	14 55
Ashwell & Morden	d	11 00				12 00									13 00						14 00				15 00
Royston	d	11 04			11 36	12 04						12 36			13 04					13 36	14 04			14 36	15 04
Meldreth	d	11 08				12 08									13 08						14 08				15 08
Shepreth	d	11 11				12 11									13 11						14 11				15 11
Foxton	d	11 14				12 14									13 14						14 14				15 14
Cambridge	a	11 29			11 54	12 27						12 54			13 27					13 54	14 27			14 54	15 29
Arlesey	d			11 23			11 56				12 23					12 56		13 23				13 56	14 23		
Biggleswade	d		10 59	11 28			12 01				12 28					13 01		13 28				14 01	14 28		
Sandy	d		11 03	11 32			12 05				12 32					13 05		13 32				14 05	14 32		
St Neots	d		11 10	11 39			12 12				12 39					13 12		13 39				14 12	14 39		
Huntingdon	d		11 18	11 47			12 20				12 47					13 20		13 47				14 20	14 47		
Peterborough	a		11 34	12 06			12 40	12 21		12 27	13 07			13 00		13 36		14 05				14 36	15 05		

		FC ■	GR ■	FC ■		FC ■	FC ■	FC ■	GR ■	FC ■	FC ■	FC ■	FC ■	FC ■		FC ■	GR ■	FC ■	FC ■	FC ■	FC ■	FC ■	FC ■	FC ■	
London Kings Cross ⊖	d	14 22	14 35	14 36		14 52	15 06	15 22	15 35	15 36	15 52	16 06	16 17			16 22	16 30	16 32	16 40	16 44	16 50	16 54	17 10	17 14	
Finsbury Park ⊖	d	14 27		14 41		14 57	15 11	15 27		15 41	15 57	16 11				16 27		16 37			16 55	16 59			
Potters Bar	d			14 51			15 21			15 51		16 21						16 48							
Hatfield	d			14 57			15 27			15 57		16 27						16 54				17 15			
Welwyn Garden City	d			15 01			15 31			16 01		16 32						16 59				17 19			
Welwyn North	d			15 04			15 34			16 04		16 35						17 03			17 11	17 22			
Knebworth	d			15 08			15 38			16 08		16 39						17 07				17 26			
Hertford North	d													←											
Stevenage	d	14 46	14 54	15 12		15 16	15 42	15 46	15 54	16 12	16 16	16 43	16 38	16 43		16 47	16 49	17 11			17 17	17 36			
Hitchin	d	14 51		15 17		15 21	15 47	15 51		16 17	16 21	→		16 49		16 53		17 17			17 23	17 42	17 33		
Letchworth Garden City	d					15 25	15 51				16 25		16 47	16 53				17 24		17 10		17 47			
Baldock	d					15 28	15 55				16 28		16 50	16 57				17 28				17 51			
Ashwell & Morden	d						16 00				16 33		16 55	17 02				17 33				17 56			
Royston	d					15 36	16 04				16 37		17a03	17 06				17 37		17 20		18 01		17 48	
Meldreth	d						16 08							17 10				17 41				18 05			
Shepreth	d						16 11							17 13				17 44				18 08			
Foxton	d						16 14							17 16				17 47				18 10			
Cambridge	a					15 54	16 30				16 54			17 30				18 02		17 35		18 24		18 03	
Arlesey	d	14 56		15 23				15 56		16 23						16 58					17 28				
Biggleswade	d	15 01		15 28				16 01		16 28						17 03			17 07		17 33				
Sandy	d	15 05		15 32				16 05		16 32						17 07					17 37				
St Neots	d	15 12		15 39				16 12		16 39						17 22			17 17		17 45		17 50		
Huntingdon	d	15 20		15 47				16 20		16 47						17a31			17 25		17 53		17 58		
Peterborough	a	15 36		16 04				16 37	16 26	17 04									17 43		18 12		18 22		

London - Stevenage, Cambridge and Peterborough

		FC	FC	FC	GR	FC	FC	FC	FC	FC		FC	FC	FC	FC	FC	GR	FC	FC	FC		FC	FC	FC	FC
		1	1	1	R 1	1	1	1	1	1		1	1	1	1	1	R 1	1	1	1		1	1	1	1
London Kings Cross 15 ⊖	d	17 14	17 22	17 23	17 33		17 40	17 44	17 52	17 53			18 10	18 14	18 22	18 23	18 30	18 40	18 44	18 44		18 52	18 53	19 10	19 15
Finsbury Park ⊖	d	17 19	17 28					17 49	17 58					18 19	18 28				18 49			18 58			
Potters Bar	d																								
Hatfield	d																					19 14			
Welwyn Garden City 4	d		17 47						18 17						18 47							19 18			
Welwyn North	d		17 51						18 21						18 51	18 41						19 22			
Knebworth	d	17 35	17 55						18 25						18 55				19 05			19 26			
Hertford North	d					←						←													
Stevenage 4	d	17 40	18 04	17 43	17 52	18 04		18 09	18 34	18 13		18 34		18 39	19 04		18 50		19 10			19 36	19 13		
Hitchin 4	d	17 46	→			18 10	18 03	18 16	→			18 40	18 33	18 46	19 10	18 51			19 16			→		19 34	
Letchworth Garden City	d			17 52		18 16				18 22		18 46			19 16	18 55							19 22		19 41
Baldock	d			17 55						18 25						18 59							19 25		
Ashwell & Morden	d			18 00						18 30						19 04							19 30		
Royston	d			18a07		18 28				18a38		18 58			19 28	19a11				19 18			19a37		19 51
Meldreth	d					18 32						19 02			19 32										
Shepreth	d					18 35						19 05			19 35										
Foxton	d					18 37						19 07			19 37										
Cambridge	a					18 54						19 22			19 52					19 33					20 08
Arlesey	d	17 51						18 21						18 51					19 21						
Biggleswade	d	17 56						18 26						18 56				19 07	19 26						
Sandy	d	18 00						18 30						19 00					19 30						
St Neots	d	18 08					18 20	18 38					18 50	19 08				19 17	19 38					19 52	
Huntingdon	d	18 16					18 28	18 46					18 58	19 16				19 25	19 46					20 00	
Peterborough 8	a	18 33					18 50	19 03					19 14	19 33				19 42	20 03					20 24	

		FC	FC	FC	FC	FC		FC	FC	FC	FC	FC	FC	FC	FC	GR		FC	FC	FC	FC	FC	FC	FC	FC
		1	1	1	1	1		1	1	1	1	1	1	1	1	R 1		1	1	1	1	1	1	1	1
London Kings Cross 15 ⊖	d		19 18	19 22		19 34		19 45	19 52	20 06	20 07	20 15	20 22	20 36	20 52	21 00		21 06	21 07	21 15	21 22	21 36	21 52	22 06	22 07
Finsbury Park ⊖	d		19 23	19 27		19 39			19 57	20 11			20 27	20 41	20 57			21 11			21 27	21 41	21 57	22 11	
Potters Bar	d		19 34							20 21				20 51				21 21				21 51		22 21	
Hatfield	d		19 42			19 53				20 27				20 57				21 27				21 57		22 27	
Welwyn Garden City 4	d		19 48			20 00				20 31				21 01				21 31				22 01		22 31	
Welwyn North	d		19 52			20 04				20 34				21 04				21 34				22 04		22 34	
Knebworth	d		19 56			20 08				20 38				21 08				21 38				22 08		22 38	
Hertford North	d	←			←																				
Stevenage 4	d	19b36	20 04	19 47	20 04	20 12			20 17	20 42			20 47	21 12	21 16	21 20		21 42			21 47	22 12	22 16	22 42	
Hitchin 4	d	19 42	→	19 53	20 10	20 17			20 23	20 47			20 53	21 17	21 21			21 47			21 53	22 17	22 21	22 47	
Letchworth Garden City	d	19 47			20 15	20a23		20 10		20 51		20 40		21a23	21 28			21 51		21 40		22a23	22 28	22 51	
Baldock	d	19 51			20 19					20 55					21 31			21 55					22 31	22 55	
Ashwell & Morden	d	19 56			20 24					21 00					21 36			22 00					22 36	23 00	
Royston	d	20 01			20 29			20 20		21 04		20 50			21 41			22 04		21 50			22 41	23 04	
Meldreth	d	20 05			20 33					21 08					21 44			22 08						23 08	
Shepreth	d	20 08			20 36					21 11					21 47			22 11						23 11	
Foxton	d	20 10			20 38					21 14					21 50			22 14						23 14	
Cambridge	a	20 24			20 52			20 35		21 27		21 05			22 03			22 27		22 05			22 58	23 27	
Arlesey	d			19 58					20 28				20 58								21 58				
Biggleswade	d			20 03					20 33				21 03						21 35		22 03				22 35
Sandy	d			20 07					20 37				21 07								22 07				
St Neots	d			20 15					20 45		20 41		21 15						21 44		22 15				22 44
Huntingdon	d			20 23					20 55		20 49		21 23						21 51		22 23				22 51
Peterborough 8	a			20 40					21 26		21 05		21 40			21 53			22 07		22 40				23 07

		FC		FC	FC	FC	FC	FC	FC	FC	FC	FC		FC	FC	FC
		1		1		1	1		1	1	1	1			1	
London Kings Cross 15 ⊖	d	22 15		22 22	22 26	22 36	22 52		23 01	23 06	23 15	23 22		23 26	23 36	
Finsbury Park ⊖	d			22 27	22 32	22 41	22 57			23 11		23 27		23 32	23 41	
Potters Bar	d					22 51				23 21					23 51	
Hatfield	d					22 57				23 27					23 57	
Welwyn Garden City 4	d					23 01				23 31					00 01	
Welwyn North	d					23 04				23 34					00 04	
Knebworth	d					23 08				23 38					00 08	
Hertford North	d				23 07			←						00 07		←
Stevenage 4	d			22 48	23 20	23 12	23 16	23 20		23 42		23 46		00 20	00 12	00 20
Hitchin 4	d			22 53	→	23 17	23 24	23 28		23 50		23 54		→	00 20	00 26
Letchworth Garden City	d	22 40				23a26	23 31	23a36		23 54	23 44				00a29	00a36
Baldock	d						23 34			23 58						
Ashwell & Morden	d						23 39			00 03						
Royston	d	22 50					23 44			00 07	23 54					
Meldreth	d									00 11						
Shepreth	d									00 14						
Foxton	d									00 17						
Cambridge	a	23 05					00 01			00 29	00 10					
Arlesey	d			22 58								23 59				
Biggleswade	d			23 03					23 29			00 04				
Sandy	d			23 07								00 08				
St Neots	d			23 15					23 38			00 15				
Huntingdon	d			23 23					23 45			00 26				
Peterborough 8	a			23 43					00 12			00 42				

London - Stevenage, Cambridge and Peterborough

		FC	FC	FC	FC	FC	FC	FC	FC	FC		FC	FC	FC	FC	FC	FC	FC	FC	FC		FC	GR	FC	FC
		1	1	1	1	1		1		1		1		1		1	1	1	1	1		1	R 1	1	1
London Kings Cross 15 ⊖	d	22p52	23p01	23p06	23p15	23p22	23p26	23p36		00 01		00 04	00 06	00 31		00 36	01 06	01 36	05 22	05 45		06 06	06 15		06 22
Finsbury Park ⊖	d	22p57		23p11		23p27	23p32	23p41				00 09	00 12			00 41	01 11	01 41	05 27	05 50		06 11			06 27
Potters Bar	d			23p21				23p51								00 51		01 58	05 37			06 21			
Hatfield	d			23p27				23p57								00 57		02 04	05 43			06 27			
Welwyn Garden City 4	d			23p31				00 01								01 01		02 08	05 47			06 31			
Welwyn North	d			23p34				00 04								01s04		02s11	05 50			06 34			
Knebworth	d			23p38				00 08								01s08		02s15	05 54			06 38			
Hertford North	d						00 07		←				00 47		←		01 38							←	
Stevenage 4	d	23p16		23p42		23p46	00 20	00 12	00 20	00s21		00 31	01 00	00s50	01 00	01 12	01 47	02 18	05 58	06 08		06 42	06 34	06 42	06 46
Hitchin 4	d	23p24		23p50		23p54	→	00 20	00 26	00s35		00 39	→	01s05	01 06	01 17	01 52	02 23	06 06	06 13		→		06 47	06 51
Letchworth Garden City	d	23p31		23p54	23p44			00a29	00a36			00 43		01s08	01a16		02a06			06 16				06 51	
Baldock	d	23p34		23p58								00 46								06 19				06 55	
Ashwell & Morden	d	23p39		00 03								00 51								06 24				07 00	
Royston	d	23p44		00 07	23p54							00 56		01s17						06 29				07 04	
Meldreth	d			00 11								00 59								06 32				07 08	
Shepreth	d			00 14								01 02								06 35				07 11	
Foxton	d			00 17								01 05								06 38				07 14	
Cambridge	a	00 01		00 29	00 10							01 22		01 34						06 50				07 27	
Arlesey	d					23p59										01s25			06 11						06 56
Biggleswade	d		23p29			00 04				00s44						01s30		02s35	06 16						07 01
Sandy	d					00 08										01s34			06 20						07 05
St Neots	d		23p38			00 15				00s53						01s42		02s45	06 28						07 12
Huntingdon	d		23p45			00 26				01s04						01s52		02s56	06 35						07 20
Peterborough 8	a		00 12			00 42				01 24						02 13		03 14	06 56				07 05		07 36

		FC	FC	FC	FC	FC		FC	FC	FC	GR	FC	FC	FC	GR	FC		FC	FC	GR	FC	FC	GR		FC
			1	1	1	1			1	1	R 1	1	1		R 1	1		1	1	R 1	1		R 1		1
London Kings Cross 15 ⊖	d	06 26	06 36	06 52	07 06	07 22		07 26	07 36	07 52	08 00	08 06	08 22	08 26	08 30	08 36		08 52	09 06	09 10	09 22	09 26	09 30		09 36
Finsbury Park ⊖	d	06 32	06 41	06 57	07 11	07 27		07 32	07 41	07 57		08 11	08 27	08 32		08 41		08 57	09 11		09 27	09 32			09 41
Potters Bar	d		06 51		07 21				07 51			08 21				08 51			09 21						09 51
Hatfield	d		06 57		07 27				07 57			08 27				08 57			09 27						09 57
Welwyn Garden City 4	d		07 01		07 31				08 01			08 31				09 01			09 31						10 01
Welwyn North	d		07 04		07 34				08 04			08 34				09 04			09 34						10 04
Knebworth	d		07 08		07 38				08 08			08 38				09 08			09 38						10 08
Hertford North	d	07 07						08 07						09 07								10 07			
Stevenage 4	d	07a20	07 12	07 16	07 42	07 46		08a20	08 12	08 16	08 20	08 42	08 46	09a20	08 49	09 12		09 16	09 42	09 29	09 46	10a20	09 49		10 12
Hitchin 4	d		07 17	07 21	07 47	07 51			08 17	08 21		08 47	08 51			09 17		09 21	09 47		09 51				10 17
Letchworth Garden City	d			07 25	07 51					08 25		08 51						09 25	09 51						
Baldock	d			07 28	07 55					08 28		08 55						09 28	09 55						
Ashwell & Morden	d			07 33	08 00							09 00							10 00						
Royston	d			07 37	08 04					08 36		09 04						09 36	10 04						
Meldreth	d			07 41	08 08							09 08							10 08						
Shepreth	d			07 44	08 11							09 11							10 11						
Foxton	d			07 46	08 14							09 14							10 14						
Cambridge	a			07 59	08 27					08 54		09 27						09 54	10 27						
Arlesey	d		07 23			07 56			08 23				08 56			09 23					09 56				10 23
Biggleswade	d		07 28			08 01			08 28				09 01			09 28					10 01				10 28
Sandy	d		07 32			08 05			08 32				09 05			09 32					10 05				10 32
St Neots	d		07 39			08 12			08 39				09 12			09 39					10 12				10 39
Huntingdon	d		07 47			08 20			08 47				09 20			09 47					10 20				10 47
Peterborough 8	a		08 04			08 38			09 05		08 51		09 38		09 20	10 05					10 36		10 20		11 04

		FC		FC	FC	FC	FC	FC	FC	FC	FC	GR		FC	FC	FC	FC	FC	FC	FC	FC	FC		FC	GR
		1		1	1		1	1	1	1		R 1		1	1	1	1		1	1	1	1			R 1
London Kings Cross 15 ⊖	d	09 52		10 06	10 22	10 26	10 36	10 52	11 06	11 22	11 26	11 30		11 36	11 52	12 06	12 22	12 26	12 36	12 52	13 06	13 22		13 26	13 30
Finsbury Park ⊖	d	09 57		10 11	10 27	10 32	10 41	10 57	11 11	11 27	11 32			11 41	11 57	12 11	12 27	12 32	12 41	12 57	13 11	13 27		13 32	
Potters Bar	d			10 21			10 51		11 21					11 51		12 21			12 51		13 21				
Hatfield	d			10 27			10 57		11 27					11 57		12 27			12 57		13 27				
Welwyn Garden City 4	d			10 31			11 01		11 31					12 01		12 31			13 01		13 31				
Welwyn North	d			10 34			11 04		11 34					12 04		12 34			13 04		13 34				
Knebworth	d			10 38			11 08		11 38					12 08		12 38			13 08		13 38				
Hertford North	d					11 08					12 07							13 07						14 07	
Stevenage 4	d	10 16		10 42	10 46	11a21	11 12	11 16	11 42	11 46	12a20	11 50		12 12	12 16	12 42	12 46	13a20	13 12	13 16	13 42	13 46		14a20	13 49
Hitchin 4	d	10 21		10 47	10 51		11 17	11 21	11 47	11 51				12 17	12 21	12 47	12 51		13 17	13 21	13 47	13 51			
Letchworth Garden City	d	10 25		10 51				11 25	11 51						12 25	12 51				13 25	13 51				
Baldock	d	10 28		10 55				11 28	11 55						12 28	12 55				13 28	13 55				
Ashwell & Morden	d			11 00					12 00							13 00					14 00				
Royston	d	10 36		11 04				11 36	12 04						12 36	13 04				13 36	14 04				
Meldreth	d			11 08					12 08							13 08					14 08				
Shepreth	d			11 11					12 11							13 11					14 11				
Foxton	d			11 14					12 14							13 14					14 14				
Cambridge	a	10 54		11 27				11 54	12 27						12 54	13 27				13 54	14 27				
Arlesey	d				10 56		11 23			11 56				12 23			12 56		13 23			13 56			
Biggleswade	d				11 01		11 28			12 01				12 28			13 01		13 28			14 01			
Sandy	d				11 05		11 32			12 05				12 32			13 05		13 32			14 05			
St Neots	d				11 12		11 39			12 12				12 39			13 12		13 39			14 12			
Huntingdon	d				11 20		11 47			12 20				12 47			13 20		13 47			14 20			
Peterborough 8	a				11 38		12 05			12 39		12 21		13 05			13 36		14 05			14 38			14 20

Table 25

London - Stevenage, Cambridge and Peterborough

Saturdays
until 10 July

		FC ■	FC ■	FC ■	FC ■	FC	FC ■	FC ■	FC ■	FC ■	FC	GR ■	FC ■	FC ■	FC ■	FC ■	FC	FC ■	FC ■	FC ■	FC ■
London Kings Cross ⊖	d	13 36	13 52	14 06	14 22	14 26	14 36	14 52	15 06	15 22	15 26	15 30	15 36	15 52	16 06	16 22	16 26	16 36	16 52	17 06	17 10
Finsbury Park ⊖	d	13 42	13 57	14 11	14 27	14 32	14 41	14 56	15 11	15 27	15 32		15 41	15 57	16 11	16 27	16 32	16 41	16 57	17 11	
Potters Bar	d	13 52		14 21			14 51		15 21				15 51		16 21			16 51		17 21	
Hatfield	d	13 58		14 27			14 57		15 27				15 57		16 27			16 57		17 27	
Welwyn Garden City	d	14 02		14 31			15 01		15 31				16 01		16 31			17 01		17 31	
Welwyn North	d	14 05		14 34			15 04		15 34				16 04		16 34			17 04		17 34	
Knebworth	d	14 09		14 38			15 08		15 38				16 08		16 38			17 08		17 38	
Hertford North	d					15 07					16 07						17 07				
Stevenage	d	14 12	14 16	14 42	14 46	15a20	15 12	15 16	15 42	15 46	16a20	15 49	16 12	16 16	16 42	16 46	17a20	17 12	17 16	17 42	
Hitchin	d	14 17	14 21	14 47	14 51		15 17	15 21	15 47	15 51			16 17	16 22	16 47	16 51		17 17	17 21	17 47	
Letchworth Garden City	d		14 25	14 51				15 25	15 51					16 25	16 51				17 25	17 51	
Baldock	d		14 28	14 55				15 28	15 55					16 28	16 55				17 28	17 55	
Ashwell & Morden	d			15 00					16 00						17 00					18 00	
Royston	d		14 36	15 04				15 36	16 04					16 36	17 04				17 36	18 04	
Meldreth	d			15 08					16 08						17 08					18 08	
Shepreth	d			15 11					16 11						17 11					18 11	
Foxton	d			15 14					16 14						17 14					18 14	
Cambridge	a		14 54	15 27				15 54	16 27					16 54	17 27				17 54	18 27	
Arlesey	d	14 24			14 56		15 23			15 56			16 23			16 56		17 23			
Biggleswade	d	14 29			15 01		15 28			16 01			16 28			17 01		17 28			
Sandy	d	14 33			15 05		15 32			16 05			16 32			17 05		17 32			
St Neots	d	14 39			15 12		15 39			16 12			16 39			17 12		17 39			17 44
Huntingdon	d	14 48			15 20		15 47			16 20			16 47			17 20		17 47			17 52
Peterborough	a	15 06			15 36		16 04			16 36		16 20	17 04			17 36		18 04			18 08

		FC ■	FC	GR ■	FC ■	FC ■	FC ■	FC ■	FC ■	FC ■	FC ■	FC	FC ■	FC ■	FC ■	GR ■	FC ■	FC ■	FC	FC ■	FC ■
London Kings Cross ⊖	d	17 22	17 26	17 30	17 36	17 45	17 52	18 06	18 10		18 22	18 26	18 36	18 45	18 52	19 00	19 06	19 22	19 26	19 36	19 45
Finsbury Park ⊖	d	17 27	17 32		17 41		17 57	18 11			18 27	18 32	18 41		18 57		19 11	19 27	19 32	19 41	
Potters Bar	d				17 51			18 21					18 51				19 21			19 51	
Hatfield	d				17 57			18 27					18 57				19 27			19 57	
Welwyn Garden City	d				18 01			18 31					19 01				19 31			20 01	
Welwyn North	d				18 04			18 34					19 04				19 34			20 04	
Knebworth	d				18 08			18 38					19 08				19 38			20 08	
Hertford North	d		18 07							←		19 07							20 07		
Stevenage	d	17 46	18a20	17 50	18 12		18 15	18 42		18 42	18 46	19a20	19 12		19 16	19 19	19 42	19 46	20a20	20 12	
Hitchin	d	17 51			18 17		18 21	→		18 47	18 51		19 17		19 21		19 47	19 51		20 17	
Letchworth Garden City	d						18 25			18 51					19 25		19 51				
Baldock	d						18 28			18 55					19 28		19 55				
Ashwell & Morden	d									19 00							20 00				
Royston	d					18 18	18 36			19 04				19 18	19 36		20 04				20 18
Meldreth	d									19 08							20 08				
Shepreth	d									19 11							20 11				
Foxton	d									19 14							20 14				
Cambridge	a					18 35	18 54			19 27				19 35	19 54		20 27				20 35
Arlesey	d	17 56			18 23						18 56		19 23					19 56		20 23	
Biggleswade	d	18 01			18 28						19 01		19 28					20 01		20 28	
Sandy	d	18 05			18 32						19 05		19 32					20 05		20 32	
St Neots	d	18 12			18 39				18 44		19 12		19 39					20 12		20 39	
Huntingdon	d	18 20			18 47				18 52		19 20		19 47					20 20		20 47	
Peterborough	a	18 36		18 21	19 05				19 10		19 36		20 04			19 50		20 36		21 05	

		FC ■	FC ■	FC ■	FC	FC ■	FC ■	FC ■	FC ■	FC ■	FC	FC ■	FC ■	FC ■	FC ■	FC ■	FC	FC ■	FC ■	FC ■	FC ■	FC ■	FC	FC
London Kings Cross ⊖	d	19 52	20 06	20 22	20 26	20 36	20 45	20 52	21 06	21 22	21 26	21 36	21 52	22 06	22 15	22 22	22 26	22 36	22 52	23 06	23 15	23 22	23 26	23 41
Finsbury Park ⊖	d	19 57	20 11	20 27	20 32	20 41		20 57	21 11	21 27	21 32	21 41	21 57	22 11		22 27	22 32	22 41	22 57	23 11		23 27	23 32	23 47
Potters Bar	d		20 21			20 51			21 21			21 51		22 21				22 51		23 21				00 08
Hatfield	d		20 27			20 57			21 27			21 57		22 27				22 57		23 27				00 16
Welwyn Garden City	d		20 31			21 01			21 31			22 01		22 31				23 01		23 31				00 31
Welwyn North	d		20 34			21 04			21 34			22 04		22 34				23 04		23 34				00 34
Knebworth	d		20 38			21 08			21 38			22 08		22 38				23 08		23 38				00 38
Hertford North	d				21 07						22 07						23 07						00 07	
Stevenage	d	20 16	20 42	20 46	21a20	21 12		21 16	21 42	21 46	22a20	22 12	22 16	22 42		22 46	23a20	23 12	23 16	23 42		23 56	00 20	00 42
Hitchin	d	20 21	20 47	20 51		21 17		21 21	21 47	21 51		22 17	22 21	22 47		22 54		23 20	23 24	23 50		00 04	00 28	00 50
Letchworth Garden City	d	20 25	20 51					21 25	21 51				22 25	22 51	22 40			23a26		23 54	23 44		00a35	00a59
Baldock	d	20 28	20 55					21 28	21 55				22 28	22 55						23 57				
Ashwell & Morden	d		21 00						22 00					23 00						00 02				
Royston	d	20 36	21 04				21 18	21 36	22 04				22 36	23 04	22 50					00 07	23 54			
Meldreth	d		21 08						22 08					23 08						00 11				
Shepreth	d		21 11						22 11					23 11						00 14				
Foxton	d		21 14						22 14					23 14						00 16				
Cambridge	a	20 54	21 27				21 35	21 54	22 27				22 54	23 27	23 05					00 29	00 10			
Arlesey	d			20 56		21 23				21 56		22 23				22 59			23 29			[illegible]		
Biggleswade	d			21 01		21 28				22 01		[illegible]				23 04			23 34			00 14		
Sandy	d			21 05		21 32				22 05		22 32				23 08			23 38			00 18		
St Neots	d			21 12		21 39				22 12		22 39				23 15			23 45			00 25		
Huntingdon	d			21 20		21 47				22 20		22 47				23 23			23 53			00 33		
Peterborough	a			21 36		22 05				22 36		23 05				23 43			00 13			00 53		

Table 25

London - Stevenage, Cambridge and Peterborough

Saturdays
until 10 July

		FC ■	
London Kings Cross ⊖	d	23 52	
Finsbury Park ⊖	d	23 57	
Potters Bar	d		
Hatfield	d		
Welwyn Garden City	d		
Welwyn North	d		
Knebworth	d		
Hertford North	d		
Stevenage	d	00 34	00 26
Hitchin	d	00s36	00s34
Letchworth Garden City	d		
Baldock	d		
Ashwell & Morden	d		
Royston	d		
Meldreth	d		
Shepreth	d		
Foxton	d		
Cambridge	a		
Arlesey	d		00 39
Biggleswade	d	00s45	00s44
Sandy	d		00s48
St Neots	d	00s54	00s56
Huntingdon	d	01s02	01s03
Peterborough	a	01 21	01 24

Saturdays
17 July to 04 September

		FC ■	FC ■	FC ■	FC ■	FC ■	FC	FC ■	FC	FC ■	FC ■	FC	FC ■	FC	FC ■	FC ■	FC ■	FC ■	FC ■	FC ■	GR ■	FC ■	FC ■
London Kings Cross ⊖	d	22p52	23p01	23p06	23p15	23p22	23p26	23p36		00 01	00 04	00 06	00 31		00 36	01 06	01 36	05 22	05 45	06 06	06 15		06 22
Finsbury Park ⊖	d	22p57		23p11		23p27	23p32	23p41			00 09	00 12			00 41	01 11	01 41	05 27	05 50	06 11			06 27
Potters Bar	d			23p21				23p51							00 51		01 58	05 37		06 21			
Hatfield	d			23p27				23p57							00 57		02 04	05 43		06 27			
Welwyn Garden City	d			23p31				00 01							01 01		02 08	05 47		06 31			
Welwyn North	d			23p34				00 04							01s04		02s11	05 50		06 34			
Knebworth	d			23p38				00 08							01s08		02s15	05 54		06 38			
Hertford North	d						00 07		←			00 47		←		01 38						←	
Stevenage	d	23p16		23p42		23p46	00 20	00 12	00 20	00s21	00 31	01 00	00s50	01 00	01 12	01 47	02 18	05 58	06 08	06 42	06 34	06 42	06 46
Hitchin	d	23p24		23p50		23p54	→	00 20	00 26	00s35	00 39	→	01s05	01 06	01 17	01 52	02 23	06 06	06 13	→		06 47	06 51
Letchworth Garden City	d	23p31		23p54	23p44			00a29	00a36		00 43		01s08	01a16		02a06			06 16			06 51	
Baldock	d	23p34		23p58							00 46								06 19			06 55	
Ashwell & Morden	d	23p39		00 03							00 51								06 24			07 00	
Royston	d	23p44		00 07	23p54						00 56		01s17						06 29			07 04	
Meldreth	d			00 11							00 59								06 32			07 08	
Shepreth	d			00 14							01 02								06 35			07 11	
Foxton	d			00 17							01 05								06 38			07 14	
Cambridge	a	00 01		00 29	00 10						01 22		01 34						06 50			07 27	
Arlesey	d					23p59									01s25			06 11					06 56
Biggleswade	d		23p29			00 04				00s44					01s30		02s35	06 16					07 01
Sandy	d					00 08									01s34			06 20					07 05
St Neots	d		23p38			00 15				00s53					01s42		02s45	06 28					07 12
Huntingdon	d		23p45			00 26				01s04					01s52		02s56	06 35					07 20
Peterborough	a		00 12			00 42				01 24					02 13		03 14	06 56			07 05		07 36

		FC	FC ■	FC ■	FC ■	FC ■	FC	FC ■	FC ■	GR ■	FC ■	FC ■	FC	GR ■	FC ■	FC ■	FC ■	GR ■	FC ■	FC	GR ■	FC ■
London Kings Cross ⊖	d	06 26	06 36	06 52	07 06	07 22	07 26	07 36	07 52	08 00	08 06	08 22	08 26	08 30	08 36	08 52	09 06	09 10	09 22	09 26	09 30	09 36
Finsbury Park ⊖	d	06 32	06 41	06 57	07 11	07 27	07 32	07 41	07 57		08 11	08 27	08 32		08 41	08 57	09 11		09 27	09 32		09 41
Potters Bar	d		06 51		07 21			07 51			08 21				08 51		09 21					09 51
Hatfield	d		06 57		07 27			07 57			08 27				08 57		09 27					09 57
Welwyn Garden City	d		07 01		07 31			08 01			08 31				09 01		09 31					10 01
Welwyn North	d		07 04		07 34			08 04			08 34				09 04		09 34					10 04
Knebworth	d		07 08		07 38			08 08			08 38				09 08		09 38					10 08
Hertford North	d	07 07					08 07						09 07							10 07		
Stevenage	d	07a20	07 12	07 16	07 42	07 46	08a20	08 12	08 16	08 20	08 42	08 46	09a20	08 49	09 12	09 16	09 42	09 29	09 46	10a20	09 49	10 12
Hitchin	d		07 17	07 21	07 47	07 51		08 17	08 21		08 47	08 51			09 17	09 21	09 47		09 51			10 17
Letchworth Garden City	d			07 25	07 51				08 25		08 51					09 25	09 51					
Baldock	d			07 28	07 55				08 28		08 55					09 28	09 55					
Ashwell & Morden	d			07 33	08 00						09 00						10 00					
Royston	d			07 37	08 04				[illegible]		[illegible]					09 36	10 04					
Meldreth	d			07 41	08 08						09 08						10 08					
Shepreth	d			07 44	08 11						09 11						10 11					
Foxton	d			07 46	08 14						09 14						10 14					
Cambridge	a			07 59	08 27				08 54		09 27					09 54	10 27					
Arlesey	d		07 23			07 56		08 23				08 56			09 23				09 56			10 23
Biggleswade	d		07 28			08 01		08 28				09 01			09 28				10 01			10 28
Sandy	d		07 32			08 05		08 32				09 05			09 32				10 05			10 32
St Neots	d		07 39			08 12		08 39				09 12			09 39				10 12			10 39
Huntingdon	d		07 47			08 20		08 47				09 20			09 47				10 20			10 47
Peterborough	a		08 04			08 38		09 05		08 51		09 38		09 20	10 05				10 36		10 20	11 04

Table 25

London - Stevenage, Cambridge and Peterborough

Saturdays
17 July to 04 September

	FC	FC	FC	FC	FC	FC	FC	FC	FC	GR	FC	FC	FC	FC	FC	FC	FC	FC	FC	FC	GR
	1	1	1		1	1	1	1		1	1	1	1	1		1	1	1	1		1
London Kings Cross ⊖ d	09 52	10 06	10 22	10 26	10 36	10 52	11 06	11 22	11 26	11 30	11 36	11 52	12 06	12 22	12 26	12 36	12 52	13 06	13 22	13 26	13 30
Finsbury Park ⊖ d	09 57	10 11	10 27	10 32	10 41	10 57	11 11	11 27	11 32		11 41	11 57	12 11	12 27	12 32	12 41	12 57	13 11	13 27	13 32	
Potters Bar d		10 21			10 51		11 21				11 51		12 21			12 51		13 21			
Hatfield d		10 27			10 57		11 27				11 57		12 27			12 57		13 27			
Welwyn Garden City d		10 31			11 01		11 31				12 01		12 31			13 01		13 31			
Welwyn North d		10 34			11 04		11 34				12 04		12 34			13 04		13 34			
Knebworth d		10 38			11 08		11 38				12 08		12 38			13 08		13 38			
Hertford North d				11 08					12 07						13 07					14 07	
Stevenage d	10 16	10 42	10 46	11a21	11 12	11 16	11 42	11 46	12a20	11 50	12 12	12 16	12 42	12 46	13a20	13 12	13 16	13 42	13 46	14a20	13 49
Hitchin d	10 21	10 47	10 51		11 17	11 21	11 47	11 51			12 17	12 21	12 47	12 51		13 17	13 21	13 47	13 51		
Letchworth Garden City d	10 25	10 51				11 25	11 51					12 25	12 51				13 25	13 51			
Baldock d	10 28	10 55				11 28	11 55					12 28	12 55				13 28	13 55			
Ashwell & Morden d		11 00					12 00						13 00					14 00			
Royston d	10 36	11 04				11 36	12 04					12 36	13 04				13 36	14 04			
Meldreth d		11 08					12 08						13 08					14 08			
Shepreth d		11 11					12 11						13 11					14 11			
Foxton d		11 14					12 14						13 14					14 14			
Cambridge a	10 54	11 27				11 54	12 27					12 54	13 27				13 54	14 27			
Arlesey d			10 56		11 23			11 56			12 23			12 56		13 23			13 56		
Biggleswade d			11 01		11 28			12 01			12 28			13 01		13 28			14 01		
Sandy d			11 05		11 32			12 05			12 32			13 05		13 32			14 05		
St Neots d			11 12		11 39			12 12			12 39			13 12		13 39			14 12		
Huntingdon d			11 20		11 47			12 20			12 47			13 20		13 47			14 20		
Peterborough a			11 38		12 05			12 39		12 21	13 05			13 36		14 05			14 38		14 20

	FC	FC	FC	FC	FC	FC	FC	FC	FC	FC	GR	FC	FC	FC	FC	FC	FC	FC	FC	FC
	1	1	1	1		1	1		1	1	1	1	1	1	1	1	1	1	1	1
London Kings Cross ⊖ d	13 36	13 52	14 06	14 22	14 26	14 36	14 52		15 04	15 09	15 15		15 38		16 04	16 09		16 38		17 04
Finsbury Park ⊖ d	13 42	13 57	14 11	14 28	14 32	14 41	14 56			15 14			15 43			16 14		16 43		
Potters Bar d	13 52		14 21			14 51														
Hatfield d	13 58		14 27			14 57														
Welwyn Garden City d	14 02		14 31			15 01														
Welwyn North d	14 05		14 34			15 04														
Knebworth d	14 09		14 38			15 08														
Hertford North d					15 07			←												
Stevenage d	14 12	14 16	14 42	14 46	15 21	15 12	15 16	15 21	15 25	15 40	15 49		16 09	16 13	16 34	16 40		17 09	17 13	17 36
Hitchin d	14 17	14 21	14 47	14 51	→	15 17	15 21	15 28	15 39	15 45			16 14	16 18	16 39	16 45		17 14	17 18	17 41
Letchworth Garden City d		14 25	14 51				15 25	15a33	15 43				16 18		16 43			17 18		17 45
Baldock d		14 28	14 55				15 28		15 46				16 21		16 46			17 21		17 48
Ashwell & Morden d			15 00						15 51				16 26		16 51			17 26		17 53
Royston d		14 36	15 04				15 36		15 55			16 10	16 30		16 55		17 10	17 30		17 57
Meldreth d			15 08									16 13					17 13			
Shepreth d			15 11									16 16					17 16			
Foxton d			15 14									16 19					17 19			
Cambridge a		14 54	15 27				15 54		16 14			16 32	16 46		17 12		17 32	17 46		18 14
Arlesey d	14 24			14 57		15 23				15 50				16 23		16 50			17 23	
Biggleswade d	14 29			15 02		15 28				15 55				16 28		16 55			17 28	
Sandy d	14 33			15 05		15 32				15 59				16 32		16 59			17 32	
St Neots d	14 39			15 13		15 39				16 06				16 39		17 06			17 39	
Huntingdon d	14 48			15 20		15 47				16 14				16 47		17 14			17 47	
Peterborough a	15 06			15 36		16 04				16 34	16 20			17 03		17 34			18 05	

	FC	GR	FC	FC	FC	FC	FC	FC	FC	FC	GR	FC	FC	FC	FC	FC	FC	FC	FC	FC
	1	1	1	1	1	1	1	1	1	1	1	1	1	1	1	1	1	1	1	1
London Kings Cross ⊖ d	17 09	17 15		17 38		18 04	18 09		18 38		18 50	19 04	19 09		19 38		20 04	20 09		20 38
Finsbury Park ⊖ d	17 14			17 43			18 14		18 43				19 14		19 43			20 14		20 43
Potters Bar d																				
Hatfield d																				
Welwyn Garden City d																				
Welwyn North d																				
Knebworth d																				
Hertford North d																				
Stevenage d	17 42	17 48		18 09	18 13	18 35	18 40		19 09	19 13	19 23	19 35	19 40		20 09	20 13	20 34	20 40		21 09
Hitchin d	17 47			18 14	18 18	18 40	18 45		19 14	19 18		19 40	19 45		20 14	20 18	20 39	20 45		21 14
Letchworth Garden City d				18 18		18 43			19 18			19 44			20 18		20 43			21 18
Baldock d				18 21		18 46			19 21			19 47			20 21		20 46			21 21
Ashwell & Morden d				18 26		18 51			19 26			19 52			20 26		20 51			21 26
Royston d			18 10	18 30		18 56		19 10	19 30			19 56		20 10	20 30		20 55		21 10	21 30
Meldreth d			18 13					19 13						20 13					21 13	
Shepreth d			18 16					19 16						20 16					21 16	
Foxton d			18 19					19 19						20 19					21 19	
Cambridge a			18 32	18 46		19 13		19 32	19 46			20 13		20 32	20 46		21 12		21 32	21 46
Arlesey d	17 52				18 23		18 50			19 23			19 51			20 23		20 50		
Biggleswade d	17 57				18 28		18 55			19 28			19 56			20 28		20 55		
Sandy d	18 01				18 32		18 59			19 32			19 59			20 32		20 59		
St Neots d	18 08				18 39		19 06			19 39			20 07			20 39		21 06		
Huntingdon d	18 16				18 47		19 14			19 47			20 14			20 47		21 14		
Peterborough a	18 36	18 20			19 03		19 34			20 03			20 34			21 03		21 34		

Table 25

London - Stevenage, Cambridge and Peterborough

Saturdays
17 July to 04 September

	FC	FC	FC	FC	FC	FC	FC	FC	FC	FC	FC	FC	FC	FC	FC	FC
	1	1	1	1	1	1	1	1	1	1	1	1	1	1	1	1
London Kings Cross ⊖ d		20 54	21 04	21 09		21 38		21 54	22 04	22 09		22 38		23 04	23 09	23 38
Finsbury Park ⊖ d		20 59		21 14		21 43		21 59		22 14		22 43			23 14	23 43
Potters Bar d																
Hatfield d																
Welwyn Garden City d																
Welwyn North d																
Knebworth d																
Hertford North d																
Stevenage d	21 13	21 25	21 34	21 40		22 09	22 13	22 25	22 34	22 40		23 09	23 13	23 34	23 40	00 08
Hitchin d	21 18	21 30	21 39	21 45		22 14	22 18	22 30	22 39	22 45		23 14	23 18	23 39	23 45	00 11
Letchworth Garden City d			21 43			22 18			22 43			23 18		23 43		00 16
Baldock d			21 46			22 21			22 46			23 21		23 46		00 21
Ashwell & Morden d			21 51			22 26			22 51			23 26		23 51		00 26
Royston d			21 55		22 10	22 30			22 55		23 10	23 30		23 55		00 28
Meldreth d					22 13						23 13					
Shepreth d					22 16						23 16					
Foxton d					22 19						23 19					
Cambridge a			22 12		22 32	22 47			23 12		23 32	23 46		00 12		00 46
Arlesey d	21 23			21 50			22 23			22 50			23 23		23 50	
Biggleswade d	21 28	21 38		21 55			22 28	22 38		22 55			23 28		23 55	
Sandy d	21 32			21 59			22 32			22 59			23 32		23 59	
St Neots d	21 39	21 47		22 06			22 39	22 47		23 06			23 39		00 06	
Huntingdon d	21 47	21 54		22 14			22 47	22 54		23 14			23 47		00 14	
Peterborough a	22 03	22 14		22 34			23 03	23 14		23 34			00 03		00 34	

Saturdays
from 11 September

	FC	FC	FC	FC	FC	FC	FC	FC	FC	FC	FC	FC	FC	FC	FC	FC	FC	FC	FC	GR	FC	FC
	1	1	1	1	1		1		1	1		1		1	1	1	1	1	1	1	1	1
London Kings Cross ⊖ d	22p52	23p01	23p06	23p15	23p22	23p26	23p36		00 01	00 04	00 06	00 31		00 36	01 06	01 36	05 22	05 45	06 06	06 15		06 22
Finsbury Park ⊖ d	22p57		23p11		23p27	23p32	23p41			00 09	00 12			00 41	01 11	01 41	05 27	05 50	06 11			06 27
Potters Bar d			23p21				23p51							00 51		01 58	05 37		06 21			
Hatfield d			23p27				23p57							00 57		02 04	05 43		06 27			
Welwyn Garden City d			23p31				00 01							01 01		02 08	05 47		06 31			
Welwyn North d			23p34				00 04							01s04		02s11	05 50		06 34			
Knebworth d			23p38				00 08							01s08		02s15	05 54		06 38			
Hertford North d						00 07		←			00 47		←		01 38						←	
Stevenage d	23p16		23p42		23p46	00 20	00 12	00 20	00s21	00 31	01 00	00s50	01 00	01 12	01 47	02 18	05 58	06 08	06 42	06 34	06 42	06 46
Hitchin d	23p24		23p50		23p54	→	00 20	00 26	00s35	00 39	→	01s05	01 06	01 17	01 52	02 23	06 06	06 13	→		06 47	06 51
Letchworth Garden City d	23p31		23p54	23p44			00a29	00a36		00 43		01s08	01a16		02a06			06 16			06 51	
Baldock d	23p34		23p58							00 46								06 19			06 55	
Ashwell & Morden d	23p39		00 03							00 51								06 24			07 00	
Royston d	23p44		00 07	23p54						00 56		01s17						06 29			07 04	
Meldreth d			00 11							00 59								06 32			07 08	
Shepreth d			00 14							01 02								06 35			07 11	
Foxton d			00 17							01 05								06 38			07 14	
Cambridge a	00 01		00 29	00 10						01 22		01 34						06 50			07 27	
Arlesey d					23p59									01s25			06 11					06 56
Biggleswade d		23p29			00 04				00s44					01s30		02s35	06 16					07 01
Sandy d					00 08									01s34			06 20					07 05
St Neots d		23p38			00 15				00s53					01s42		02s45	06 28					07 12
Huntingdon d		23p45			00 26				01s04					01s52		02s56	06 35					07 20
Peterborough a		00 12			00 42				01 24					02 13		03 14	06 56			07 05		07 36

	FC	FC	FC	FC	FC	FC	FC	FC	GR	FC	FC	FC	GR	FC	FC	FC	GR	FC	FC	GR	FC
		1	1	1	1		1	1	1	1	1		1	1	1	1	1	1		1	1
London Kings Cross ⊖ d	06 26	06 36	06 52	07 06	07 22	07 26	07 36	07 52	08 00	08 06	08 22	08 26	08 30	08 36	08 52	09 06	09 10	09 22	09 26	09 30	09 36
Finsbury Park ⊖ d	06 32	06 41	06 57	07 11	07 27	07 32	07 41	07 57		08 11	08 27	08 32		08 41	08 57	09 11		09 27	09 32		09 41
Potters Bar d		06 51		07 21			07 51			08 21				08 51		09 21					09 51
Hatfield d		06 57		07 27			07 57			08 27				08 57		09 27					09 57
Welwyn Garden City d		07 01		07 31			08 01			08 31				09 01		09 31					10 01
Welwyn North d		07 04		07 34			08 04			08 34				09 04		09 34					10 04
Knebworth d		07 08		07 38			08 08			08 38				09 08		09 38					10 08
Hertford North d	07 07					08 07						09 07							10 07		
Stevenage d	07a20	07 12	07 16	07 42	07 46	08a20	08 12	08 16	08 20	08 42	08 46	09a20	08 49	09 12	09 16	09 42	09 29	09 46	10a20	09 49	10 12
Hitchin d		07 17	07 21	07 47	07 51		08 17	08 21		08 47	08 51			09 17	09 21	09 47		09 51			10 17
Letchworth Garden City d			07 25	07 51				08 25		08 51					09 25	09 51					
Baldock d			07 28	07 55				08 28		08 55					09 28	09 55					
Ashwell & Morden d			07 33	08 00						09 00						10 00					
Royston d			07 37	08 04				08 36		09 04					09 36	10 04					
Meldreth d			07 41	08 08						09 08						10 08					
Shepreth d			07 44	08 11						09 11						10 11					
Foxton d			07 46	08 14						09 14						10 14					
Cambridge a			07 59	08 27				08 54		09 27					09 54	10 27					
Arlesey d		07 23			07 56		08 23				08 56			09 23				09 56			10 23
Biggleswade d		07 28			08 01		08 28				09 01			09 28				10 01			10 28
Sandy d		07 32			08 05		08 32				09 05			09 32				10 05			10 32
St Neots d		07 39			08 12		08 39				09 12			09 39				10 12			10 39
Huntingdon d		07 47			08 20		08 47				09 20			09 47				10 20			10 47
Peterborough a		08 04			08 38		09 05		08 51		09 38		09 20	10 05				10 36		10 20	11 04

Table 25

London - Stevenage, Cambridge and Peterborough

Saturdays from 11 September

Station		FC	FC	FC	FC	FC	FC	FC	FC	FC	GR	FC
		1	1	1		1	1	1	1		1	1
London Kings Cross	⊖ d	09 52	10 06	10 22	10 26	10 36	10 52	11 06	11 22	11 26	11 30	11 36
Finsbury Park	⊖ d	09 57	10 11	10 27	10 32	10 41	10 57	11 11	11 27	11 32		11 41
Potters Bar	d		10 21			10 51		11 21				11 51
Hatfield	d		10 27			10 57		11 27				11 57
Welwyn Garden City	d		10 31			11 01		11 31				12 01
Welwyn North	d		10 34			11 04		11 34				12 04
Knebworth	d		10 38			11 08		11 38				12 08
Hertford North	d				11 08					12 07		
Stevenage	d	10 16	10 42	10 46	11a21	11 12	11 16	11 42	11 46	12a20	11 50	12 12
Hitchin	d	10 21	10 47	10 51		11 17	11 21	11 47	11 51			12 17
Letchworth Garden City	d	10 25	10 51				11 25	11 51				
Baldock	d	10 28	10 55				11 28	11 55				
Ashwell & Morden	d		11 00					12 00				
Royston	d	10 36	11 04				11 36	12 04				
Meldreth	d		11 08					12 08				
Shepreth	d		11 11					12 11				
Foxton	d		11 14					12 14				
Cambridge	a	10 54	11 27				11 54	12 27				
Arlesey	d			10 56		11 23			11 56			12 23
Biggleswade	d			11 01		11 28			12 01			12 28
Sandy	d			11 05		11 32			12 05			12 32
St Neots	d			11 12		11 39			12 12			12 39
Huntingdon	d			11 20		11 47			12 20			12 47
Peterborough	a			11 38		12 05			12 39		12 21	13 05

Station		FC	FC	FC	FC	FC	FC	FC	FC	FC	GR
		1	1	1		1	1	1	1		1
London Kings Cross	⊖ d	11 52	12 06	12 22	12 26	12 36	12 52	13 06	13 22	13 26	13 30
Finsbury Park	⊖ d	11 57	12 11	12 27	12 32	12 41	12 57	13 11	13 27	13 32	
Potters Bar	d		12 21			12 51		13 21			
Hatfield	d		12 27			12 57		13 27			
Welwyn Garden City	d		12 31			13 01		13 31			
Welwyn North	d		12 34			13 04		13 34			
Knebworth	d		12 38			13 08		13 38			
Hertford North	d				13 07					14 07	
Stevenage	d	12 16	12 42	12 46	13a20	13 12	13 16	13 42	13 46	14a20	13 49
Hitchin	d	12 21	12 47	12 51		13 17	13 21	13 47	13 51		
Letchworth Garden City	d	12 25	12 51				13 25	13 51			
Baldock	d	12 28	12 55				13 28	13 55			
Ashwell & Morden	d		13 00					14 00			
Royston	d	12 36	13 04				13 36	14 04			
Meldreth	d		13 08					14 08			
Shepreth	d		13 11					14 11			
Foxton	d		13 14					14 14			
Cambridge	a	12 54	13 27				13 54	14 27			
Arlesey	d			12 56		13 23			13 56		
Biggleswade	d			13 01		13 28			14 01		
Sandy	d			13 05		13 32			14 05		
St Neots	d			13 12		13 39			14 12		
Huntingdon	d			13 20		13 47			14 20		
Peterborough	a			13 36		14 05			14 38		14 20

Station		FC	FC	FC	FC	FC	FC	FC	FC	FC	FC	GR	FC
		1	1	1	1		1	1	1	1		1	1
London Kings Cross	⊖ d	13 36	13 52	14 06	14 22	14 26	14 36	14 52	15 06	15 22	15 26	15 30	15 36
Finsbury Park	⊖ d	13 42	13 57	14 11	14 27	14 32	14 41	14 56	15 11	15 27	15 32		15 41
Potters Bar	d	13 52		14 21			14 51		15 21				15 51
Hatfield	d	13 58		14 27			14 57		15 27				15 57
Welwyn Garden City	d	14 02		14 31			15 01		15 31				16 01
Welwyn North	d	14 05		14 34			15 04		15 34				16 04
Knebworth	d	14 09		14 38			15 08		15 38				16 08
Hertford North	d					15 07					16 07		
Stevenage	d	14 12	14 16	14 42	14 46	15a20	15 12	15 16	15 42	15 46	16a20	15 49	16 12
Hitchin	d	14 17	14 21	14 47	14 51		15 17	15 21	15 47	15 51			16 17
Letchworth Garden City	d		14 25	14 51				15 25	15 51				
Baldock	d		14 28	14 55				15 28	15 55				
Ashwell & Morden	d			15 00					16 00				
Royston	d		14 36	15 04				15 36	16 04				
Meldreth	d			15 08					16 08				
Shepreth	d			15 11					16 11				
Foxton	d			15 14					16 14				
Cambridge	a		14 54	15 27				15 54	16 27				
Arlesey	d	14 24			14 56		15 23			15 56			16 23
Biggleswade	d	14 29			15 01		15 28			16 01			16 28
Sandy	d	14 33			15 05		15 32			16 05			16 32
St Neots	d	14 39			15 12		15 39			16 12			16 39
Huntingdon	d	14 48			15 20		15 47			16 20			16 47
Peterborough	a	15 06			15 36		16 04			16 36		16 20	17 04

Station		FC	FC	FC	FC	FC	FC	FC	FC
		1	1	1		1	1	1	1
London Kings Cross	⊖ d	15 52	16 06	16 22	16 26	16 36	16 52	17 06	17 10
Finsbury Park	⊖ d	15 57	16 11	16 27	16 32	16 41	16 57	17 11	
Potters Bar	d		16 21			16 51		17 21	
Hatfield	d		16 27			16 57		17 27	
Welwyn Garden City	d		16 31			17 01		17 31	
Welwyn North	d		16 34			17 04		17 34	
Knebworth	d		16 38			17 08		17 38	
Hertford North	d				17 07				
Stevenage	d	16 16	16 42	16 46	17a20	17 12	17 16	17 42	
Hitchin	d	16 22	16 47	16 51		17 17	17 21	17 47	
Letchworth Garden City	d	16 25	16 51				17 25	17 51	
Baldock	d	16 28	16 55				17 28	17 55	
Ashwell & Morden	d		17 00					18 00	
Royston	d	16 36	17 04				17 36	18 04	
Meldreth	d		17 08					18 08	
Shepreth	d		17 11					18 11	
Foxton	d		17 14					18 14	
Cambridge	a	16 54	17 27				17 54	18 27	
Arlesey	d			16 56		17 23			
Biggleswade	d			17 01		17 28			
Sandy	d			17 05		17 32			
St Neots	d			17 12		17 39			17 44
Huntingdon	d			17 20		17 47			17 52
Peterborough	a			17 36		18 04			18 08

Station		FC	FC	GR	FC	FC	FC	FC	FC
		1		1	1	1	1	1	1
London Kings Cross	⊖ d	17 22	17 26	17 30	17 36	17 45	17 52	18 06	18 08
Finsbury Park	⊖ d	17 27	17 32		17 41		17 57	18 11	
Potters Bar	d				17 51			18 21	
Hatfield	d				17 57			18 27	
Welwyn Garden City	d				18 01			18 31	
Welwyn North	d				18 04			18 34	
Knebworth	d				18 08			18 38	
Hertford North	d		18 07						
Stevenage	d	17 46	18a20	17 50	18 12		18 15	18 42	18 27
Hitchin	d	17 51			18 17		18 21	→	18 32
Letchworth Garden City	d						18 25		
Baldock	d						18 28		
Ashwell & Morden	d								
Royston	d					18 18	18 36		
Meldreth	d								
Shepreth	d								
Foxton	d								
Cambridge	a					18 35	18 54		
Arlesey	d	17 58			18 23				
Biggleswade	d	18 01			18 28				
Sandy	d	18 05			18 32				
St Neots	d	18 12			18 39				18 46
Huntingdon	d	18 20			18 47				18 53
Peterborough	a	18 36		18 21	19 05				19 09

Station		FC	FC	FC	FC	FC	FC	GR	FC	FC	FC	FC	FC
		1	1		1	1	1	1	1	1		1	1
London Kings Cross	⊖ d		18 22	18 26	18 36	18 45	18 52	19 00	19 06	19 22	19 26	19 36	19 45
Finsbury Park	⊖ d		18 27	18 32	18 41		18 57		19 11	19 27	19 32	19 41	
Potters Bar	d				18 51				19 21			19 51	
Hatfield	d				18 57				19 27			19 57	
Welwyn Garden City	d				19 01				19 31			20 01	
Welwyn North	d				19 04				19 34			20 04	
Knebworth	d				19 08				19 38			20 08	
Hertford North	d	←		19 07							20 07		
Stevenage	d	18 42	18 46	19a20	19 12		19 16	19 19	19 42	19 46	20a20	20 12	
Hitchin	d	18 47	18 51		19 17		19 21		19 47	19 51		20 17	
Letchworth Garden City	d	18 51					19 25		19 51				
Baldock	d	18 55					19 28		19 55				
Ashwell & Morden	d	19 00							20 00				
Royston	d	19 04				19 18	19 36		20 04				20 18
Meldreth	d	19 08							20 08				
Shepreth	d	19 11							20 11				
Foxton	d	19 14							20 14				
Cambridge	a	19 27				19 35	19 54		20 27				20 35
Arlesey	d		18 56		19 23					19 56		20 23	
Biggleswade	d		19 01		19 28					20 01		20 28	
Sandy	d		19 05		19 32					20 05		20 32	
St Neots	d		19 12		19 39					20 12		20 39	
Huntingdon	d		19 20		19 47					20 20		20 47	
Peterborough	a		19 36		20 04			19 50		20 36		21 05	

Table 25

London - Stevenage, Cambridge and Peterborough

Saturdays from 11 September

Station		FC	FC	FC	FC	FC	FC	FC	FC	FC	FC	FC	FC
		1	1	1		1	1	1	1	1		1	1
London Kings Cross	⊖ d	19 52	20 06	20 22	20 26	20 36	20 45	20 52	21 06	21 22	21 26	21 36	21 52
Finsbury Park	⊖ d	19 57	20 11	20 27	20 32	20 41		20 57	21 11	21 27	21 32	21 41	21 57
Potters Bar	d		20 21			20 51			21 21			21 51	
Hatfield	d		20 27			20 57			21 27			21 57	
Welwyn Garden City	d		20 31			21 01			21 31			22 01	
Welwyn North	d		20 34			21 04			21 34			22 04	
Knebworth	d		20 38			21 08			21 38			22 08	
Hertford North	d				21 07						22 07		
Stevenage	d	20 16	20 42	20 46	21a20	21 12		21 16	21 42	21 46	22a20	22 12	22 16
Hitchin	d	20 21	20 47	20 51		21 17		21 21	21 47	21 51		22 17	22 21
Letchworth Garden City	d	20 25	20 51					21 25	21 51				22 25
Baldock	d	20 28	20 55					21 28	21 55				22 28
Ashwell & Morden	d		21 00						22 00				
Royston	d	20 36	21 04				21 18	21 36	22 04				22 36
Meldreth	d		21 08						22 08				
Shepreth	d		21 11						22 11				
Foxton	d		21 14						22 14				
Cambridge	a	20 54	21 27				21 35	21 54	22 27				22 54
Arlesey	d			20 56		21 23				21 56		22 23	
Biggleswade	d			21 01		21 28				22 01		22 28	
Sandy	d			21 05		21 32				22 05		22 32	
St Neots	d			21 12		21 39				22 12		22 39	
Huntingdon	d			21 20		21 47				22 20		22 47	
Peterborough	a			21 36		22 05				22 36		23 05	

Station		FC	FC	FC	FC	FC	FC	FC	FC	FC	FC	FC
		1	1	1		1	1	1	1	1		
London Kings Cross	⊖ d	22 06	22 15	22 22	22 26	22 36	22 52	23 06	23 15	23 22	23 26	23 41
Finsbury Park	⊖ d	22 11		22 27	22 32	22 41	22 57	23 11		23 27	23 32	23 47
Potters Bar	d	22 21				22 51		23 21				00 08
Hatfield	d	22 27				22 57		23 27				00 16
Welwyn Garden City	d	22 31				23 01		23 31				00b31
Welwyn North	d	22 34				23 04		23 34				00 34
Knebworth	d	22 38				23 08		23 38				00 38
Hertford North	d				23 07						00 07	
Stevenage	d	22 42		22 46	23a20	23 12	23 16	23 42		23 56	00 20	00 42
Hitchin	d	22 47		22 54		23 20	23 24	23 50		00 04	00 28	00 50
Letchworth Garden City	d	22 51	22 40			23a26		23 54	23 44		00a35	00a59
Baldock	d	22 55						23 57				
Ashwell & Morden	d	23 00						00 02				
Royston	d	23 04	22 50					00 07	23 54			
Meldreth	d	23 08						00 11				
Shepreth	d	23 11						00 14				
Foxton	d	23 14						00 16				
Cambridge	a	23 27	23 05					00 29	00 10			
Arlesey	d			22 59			23 29			00 09		
Biggleswade	d			23 04			23 34			00 14		
Sandy	d			23 08			23 38			00 18		
St Neots	d			23 15			23 45			00 25		
Huntingdon	d			23 23			23 53			00 33		
Peterborough	a			23 43			00 13			00 53		

Station		FC
		1
London Kings Cross	⊖ d	23 52
Finsbury Park	⊖ d	23 57
Potters Bar	d	
Hatfield	d	
Welwyn Garden City	d	
Welwyn North	d	
Knebworth	d	
Hertford North	d	
Stevenage	d	
Hitchin	d	00s36
Letchworth Garden City	d	
Baldock	d	
Ashwell & Morden	d	
Royston	d	
Meldreth	d	
Shepreth	d	
Foxton	d	
Cambridge	a	
Arlesey	d	
Biggleswade	d	00s45
Sandy	d	
St Neots	d	00s54
Huntingdon	d	01s02
Peterborough	a	01 21

Sundays until 11 July

Station		FC	FC	FC	FC	FC	FC	FC	FC	FC	FC	FC	FC
		1	1			1	1	1	1		1	1	1
London Kings Cross	⊖ d	23p06	23p22	23p26	23p41	23p52	00 04	00 07	06 52		07 06	07 22	07 52
Finsbury Park	⊖ d	23p11	23p27	23p32	23p47	23p57	00 09	00 12	06 57		07 11	07 27	07 58
Potters Bar	d	23p21			00 08						07 21		
Hatfield	d	23p27			00 16						07 27		
Welwyn Garden City	d	23p31			00b31		00 27				07 33		
Welwyn North	d	23p34			00 34						07 36		
Knebworth	d	23p38			00 38						07 40		
Hertford North	d			00 07			00 39			07 07			
Stevenage	d	23p42	23p56	00 20	00 42		00 48	07 45	07 17	07a22	07 45	07 50	08 16
Hitchin	d	23p50	00 04	00 28	00 50	00s36	00 56	07 52	07 26		07 52	08 00	08 30
Letchworth Garden City	d	23p54		00a35	00a59		01 01	07 56	07 34		07 56		08 33
Baldock	d	23p57					01 05	07 59	07 37		07 59		08 36
Ashwell & Morden	d	00 02					01 10	08 04			08 04		
Royston	d	00 07					01 14	08 09	07 45		08 09		08 44
Meldreth	d	00 11					01 18	08 13			08 13		
Shepreth	d	00 14					01 21	08 16			08 16		
Foxton	d	00 16					01 24	08 18			08 18		
Cambridge	a	00 29					01 40	08 34	08 03		08 34		09 03
Arlesey	d		00 09									08 05	
Biggleswade	d		00 14			00s45						08 10	
Sandy	d		00 18									08 14	
St Neots	d		00 25			00s54						08 21	
Huntingdon	d		00 33			01s02						08 29	
Peterborough	a		00 53			01 21						08 50	

Station		FC	FC	FC	FC	GR	FC	FC	FC	FC	FC	FC
			1	1	1	1		1	1	1		1
London Kings Cross	⊖ d		08 06	08 22	08 52	09 00		09 06	09 22	09 52		10 06
Finsbury Park	⊖ d		08 11	08 27	08 57			09 11	09 27	09 57		10 11
Potters Bar	d		08 21					09 21				10 21
Hatfield	d		08 27					09 27				10 27
Welwyn Garden City	d		08 31					09 31				10 31
Welwyn North	d		08 34					09 34				10 34
Knebworth	d		08 38					09 38				10 38
Hertford North	d	08 15					09 15				10 15	
Stevenage	d	08a28	08 42	08 46	09 16	09 19	09a28	09 42	09 46	10 16	10a28	10 42
Hitchin	d		08 47	08 51	09 21			09 47	09 51	10 21		10 47
Letchworth Garden City	d		08 54		09 25			09 51		10 25		10 51
Baldock	d		08 57		09 28			09 55		10 28		10 55
Ashwell & Morden	d		09 02					10 00				11 00
Royston	d		09 07		09 36			10 04		10 36		11 04
Meldreth	d		09 13					10 08				11 08
Shepreth	d		09 16					10 11				11 11
Foxton	d		09 18					10 14				11 14
Cambridge	a		09 31		09 54			10 27		10 54		11 27
Arlesey	d			08 56					09 58			
Biggleswade	d			09 01					10 04			
Sandy	d			09 05					10 09			
St Neots	d			09 12					10 16			
Huntingdon	d			09 20					10 24			
Peterborough	a			09 39		09 48			10 40			

Table 25

London - Stevenage, Cambridge and Peterborough

Sundays until 11 July

		FC	FC	FC	FC	FC	FC	FC	FC	GR	FC	FC	FC	GR	FC	FC	FC	GR	FC	FC	FC	FC
		1	1		1	1	1	1		R 1 trolley	1	1	1	R 1 restaurant		1	1	R 1 restaurant	1		1	1
London Kings Cross [15] ⊖	d	10 22	10 52		11 06	11 22	11 52	12 06		12 10		12 22	12 52	13 00		13 06	13 22	13 30	13 52		14 06	14 22
Finsbury Park ⊖	d	10 27	10 57		11 11	11 27	11 57	12 11				12 27	12 57			13 11	13 27		13 57		14 11	14 27
Potters Bar	d				11 21			12 21								13 21					14 21	
Hatfield	d				11 27			12 27								13 27					14 27	
Welwyn Garden City [4]	d				11 31			12 31								13 31					14 31	
Welwyn North	d				11 34			12 34								13 34					14 34	
Knebworth	d				11 38			12 38								13 38					14 38	
Hertford North	d			11 15					12 15		←				13 15					14 15		
Stevenage [4]	d	10 46	11 16	11a28	11 42	11 46	12 16	12 42	12a28	12 29	12 42	12 46	13 16	13 19	13a28	13 42	13 46	13 49	14 16	14a28	14 42	14 46
Hitchin [4]	d	10 51	11 21		11 47	11 51	12 21	→			12 47	12 51	13 21			13 47	13 51		14 21		14 47	14 51
Letchworth Garden City	d		11 25		11 51		12 25				12 51		13 25			13 51			14 25		14 51	
Baldock	d		11 28		11 55		12 28				12 55		13 28			13 55			14 28		14 55	
Ashwell & Morden	d				12 00						13 00					14 00					15 00	
Royston	d		11 36		12 04		12 36				13 04		13 36			14 04			14 36		15 04	
Meldreth	d				12 08						13 08					14 08					15 08	
Shepreth	d				12 11						13 11					14 11					15 11	
Foxton	d				12 14						13 14					14 14					15 14	
Cambridge	a		11 54		12 27		12 54				13 27		13 54			14 27			14 54		15 27	
Arlesey	d	10 56				11 56						12 56					13 56					14 56
Biggleswade	d	11 01				12 01						13 01					14 01					15 01
Sandy	d	11 05				12 05						13 05					14 05					15 05
St Neots	d	11 12				12 12						13 12					14 12					15 12
Huntingdon	d	11 20				12 20						13 20					14 20					15 20
Peterborough [8]	a	11 36				12 36				12 58		13 36		13 50			14 36	14 18				15 36

		FC	GR	FC	FC	FC	FC	FC	FC	GR	FC	FC	GR	FC	FC	FC	FC	FC	GR	FC
		1	R 1 trolley		1	1	1	1		R 1 trolley	1	1	R 1 trolley	1	1		1	1	R 1 trolley	1
London Kings Cross [15] ⊖	d	14 52	15 00		15 06	15 22	15 52	16 06		16 10		16 22	16 30	16 36	16 52		17 06	17 22	17 30	17 36
Finsbury Park ⊖	d	14 57			15 11	15 27	15 57	16 11				16 27		16 41	16 57		17 11	17 27		17 41
Potters Bar	d				15 21			16 21						16 51			17 21			17 51
Hatfield	d				15 27			16 27						16 57			17 27			17 57
Welwyn Garden City [4]	d				15 31			16 31						17 01			17 31			18 01
Welwyn North	d				15 34			16 34						17 04			17 34			18 04
Knebworth	d				15 38			16 38						17 08			17 38			18 08
Hertford North	d			15 15					16 15		←					17 15				
Stevenage [4]	d	15 16	15 19	15a28	15 42	15 46	16 16	16 42	16a28	16 29	16 42	16 46	16 49	17 12	17 16	17a28	17 42	17 46	17 49	18 12
Hitchin [4]	d	15 21			15 47	15 51	16 21	→			16 47	16 51		17 17	17 21		17 47	17 51		18 17
Letchworth Garden City	d	15 25			15 51		16 25				16 51				17 25		17 51			
Baldock	d	15 28			15 55		16 28				16 55				17 28		17 55			
Ashwell & Morden	d				16 00						17 00						18 00			
Royston	d	15 36			16 04		16 36				17 04				17 36		18 04			
Meldreth	d				16 08						17 08						18 08			
Shepreth	d				16 11						17 11						18 11			
Foxton	d				16 14						17 14						18 14			
Cambridge	a	15 54			16 27		16 54				17 27				17 54		18 27			
Arlesey	d					15 56						16 56		17 23				17 56		18 23
Biggleswade	d					16 01						17 01		17 28				18 01		18 28
Sandy	d					16 05						17 05		17 32				18 05		18 32
St Neots	d					16 12						17 12		17 39				18 12		18 39
Huntingdon	d					16 20						17 20		17 47				18 20		18 47
Peterborough [8]	a		15 49			16 38				16 58		17 36	17 18	18 06				18 38	18 18	19 05

		FC	FC	FC	FC	GR	FC	FC	FC	FC	GR	GR	FC	FC	FC	FC	FC	FC	FC	FC	FC	FC
		1		1	1	R 1 trolley	1		1	1	R 1 trolley	R 1 restaurant	1	1		1	1		1	1	1	
London Kings Cross [15] ⊖	d	17 52		18 06	18 22	18 30	18 52		19 06	19 22	19 30	19 35	19 52	20 06		20 22	20 52		21 06	21 22	21 52	
Finsbury Park ⊖	d	17 57		18 11	18 27		18 57		19 11	19 27			19 57	20 11		20 27	20 57		21 11	21 27	21 57	
Potters Bar	d			18 21					19 21					20 21					21 21			
Hatfield	d			18 27					19 27					20 27					21 27			
Welwyn Garden City [4]	d			18 31					19 31					20 31					21 31			
Welwyn North	d			18 34					19 34					20 34					21 34			
Knebworth	d			18 38					19 38					20 38					21 38			
Hertford North	d		18 15					19 15							20 15			21 15				22 15
Stevenage [4]	d	18 16	18a28	18 42	18 46	18 50	19 16	19a28	19 42	19 46	19 50	19 54	20 16	20 42	20a28	20 46	21 16	21a28	21 42	21 46	22 16	22a28
Hitchin [4]	d	18 21		18 47	18 51		19 21		19 47	19 51			20 21	20 47		20 51	21 21		21 47	21 51	22 21	
Letchworth Garden City	d	18 25		18 51			19 25		19 51				20 25	20 51			21 25		21 51		22 25	
Baldock	d	18 28		18 55			19 28		19 55				20 28	20 55			21 28		21 55		22 28	
Ashwell & Morden	d			19 00					20 00					21 00					22 00			
Royston	d	18 36		19 04			19 36		20 04				20 36	21 04			21 36		22 04		22 36	
Meldreth	d			19 08					20 08					21 08					22 08			
Shepreth	d			19 11					20 11					21 11					22 11			
Foxton	d			19 14					20 14					21 14					22 14			
Cambridge	a	18 54		19 27			19 54		20 27				20 54	21 27			21 54		22 27		22 54	
Arlesey	d				18 56					19 56						20 56				21 56		
Biggleswade	d				19 01					20 01						21 01				22 01		
Sandy	d				19 05					20 05						21 05				22 05		
St Neots	d				19 12					20 12						21 12				22 12		
Huntingdon	d				19 20					20 20						21 20				22 20		
Peterborough [8]	a				19 36	19 19				20 36	20 19	20 23				21 36				22 36		

Table 25

London - Stevenage, Cambridge and Peterborough

Sundays until 11 July

		FC	FC	FC	FC	FC	FC	FC	FC
		1	1	1		1	1	1	
London Kings Cross [15] ⊖	d	22 06	22 22	22 52		23 06	23 15	23 22	23 41
Finsbury Park ⊖	d	22 11	22 27	22 57		23 11		23 27	23 47
Potters Bar	d	22 21				23 21			00 08
Hatfield	d	22 27				23 27			00 16
Welwyn Garden City [4]	d	22 31				23 31			00 20
Welwyn North	d	22 34				23 34			00 23
Knebworth	d	22 38				23 38			00 28
Hertford North	d				23 15				
Stevenage [4]	d	22 42	22 46	23 16	23a28	23 42		23 46	00 31
Hitchin [4]	d	22 47	22 51	23 21		23 50		23 54	00 37
Letchworth Garden City	d	22 51		23 25		23 54	23 44		00a52
Baldock	d	22 55		23 28		23 57			
Ashwell & Morden	d	23 00				00 02			
Royston	d	23 04		23 36		00 07	23 54		
Meldreth	d	23 08				00 11			
Shepreth	d	23 11				00 14			
Foxton	d	23 14				00 16			
Cambridge	a	23 27		23 54		00 29	00 10		
Arlesey	d		22 56					23 59	
Biggleswade	d		23 01					00 04	
Sandy	d		23 05					00 08	
St Neots	d		23 12					00 15	
Huntingdon	d		23 20					00 23	
Peterborough [8]	a		23 40					00 42	

Sundays 18 July to 05 September

		FC	FC	FC	FC	FC	FC	FC	FC	FC	FC	FC	FC	FC	FC	FC	FC	GR	FC	FC	FC	FC
		1	1	1	1	1	1	1	1	1	1	1	1	1	1	1	1	R 1 trolley	1	1	1	1
London Kings Cross [15] ⊖	d	23p09		23p38	00 01	00 04	00 07	00 36	06 38	07 04	07 09		07 38	08 04	08 09		08 38	08 45	09 04	09 09		09 38
Finsbury Park ⊖	d	23p14		23p43	00 06	00 10	00 12	00 41	06 43		07 14		07 43		08 14		08 43			09 14		09 43
Potters Bar	d																					
Hatfield	d																					
Welwyn Garden City [4]	d																					
Welwyn North	d																					
Knebworth	d																					
Hertford North	d						00 39															
Stevenage [4]	d	23p40		00 08		00 40	00 48	01 16	07 11	07 35	07 42		08 11	08 35	08 41		09 09	09 19	09 35	09 41		10 09
Hitchin [4]	d	23p45		00 11	00 39	00 41	00 56	01 23	07 16	07 40	07 51		08 16	08 40	08 46		09 12		09 40	09 46		10 14
Letchworth Garden City	d			00 16		00 45	01 01		07 20	07 44			08 20	08 44			09 17		09 44			10 18
Baldock	d			00 21			01 05		07 23	07 47			08 23	08 47					09 47			10 21
Ashwell & Morden	d			00 26			01 10		07 28	07 52			08 28	08 52					09 52			10 26
Royston	d		00 07	00 28		00 55	01 14		07 34	07 56		08 10	08 32	08 56		09 10	09 26		09 56		10 10	10 30
Meldreth	d		00 10				01 18					08 13				09 13					10 13	
Shepreth	d		00 13				01 21					08 16				09 16					10 16	
Foxton	d		00 16				01 24					08 19				09 19					10 19	
Cambridge	a		00 29	00 46		01 16	01 40		07 51	08 13		08 32	08 48	09 13		09 32	09 45		10 13		10 32	10 46
Arlesey	d	23p50			00 45			01s30			07 56				08 52					09 51		
Biggleswade	d	23p55			00 50			01s35			08 01				08 57					09 56		
Sandy	d	23p59			00 53			01s39			08 05				09 00					10 00		
St Neots	d	00 06			01 01			01s47			08 12				09 08					10 07		
Huntingdon	d	00 14			01 08			01s54			08 20				09 15					10 15		
Peterborough [8]	a	00 34			01 32			02 16			08 39				09 34			09 48		10 35		

		FC	FC	GR	FC	FC	FC	FC	FC	FC	GR	FC	FC	FC	FC	GR	FC	FC	GR	FC	FC
		1	1	R 1 trolley	1	1	1	1	1	1	R 1 trolley	1	1	1	1	R 1 restaurant	1	1	R 1 restaurant	1	1
London Kings Cross [15] ⊖	d	10 04	10 09	10 15		10 38	11 04	11 09		11 38	11 57	12 04	12 09		12 38	12 45	13 04	13 09	13 15		13 38
Finsbury Park ⊖	d		10 14			10 43		11 14		11 43			12 14		12 43			13 14			13 43
Potters Bar	d																				
Hatfield	d																				
Welwyn Garden City [4]	d																				
Welwyn North	d																				
Knebworth	d																				
Hertford North	d																				
Stevenage [4]	d	10 34	10 40	10 49		11 09	11 35	11 41		12 09	12 29	12 34	12 40		13 09	13 16	13 34	13 40	13 49		14 09
Hitchin [4]	d	10 39	10 45			11 14	11 40	11 46		12 14		12 39	12 45		13 14		13 39	13 45			14 14
Letchworth Garden City	d	10 43				11 18	11 44			12 18		12 43			13 18		13 43				14 18
Baldock	d	10 46				11 21	11 47			12 21		12 46			13 21		13 46				14 21
Ashwell & Morden	d	10 51				11 26	11 52			12 26		12 51			13 26		13 51				14 26
Royston	d	10 55			11 10	11 30	11 56		12 10	12 30		12 55		13 10	13 30		13 55			14 10	14 30
Meldreth	d				11 13				12 13					13 13						14 13	
Shepreth	d				11 16				12 16					13 16						14 16	
Foxton	d				11 19				12 19					13 19						14 19	
Cambridge	a	11 12			11 32	11 46	12 13		12 32	12 46		13 12		13 32	13 46		14 12			14 32	14 46
Arlesey	d		10 50					11 51					12 50					13 50			
Biggleswade	d		10 55					11 56					12 55					13 55			
Sandy	d		10 59					12 00					12 59					13 59			
St Neots	d		11 06					12 07					13 06					14 06			
Huntingdon	d		11 14					12 15					13 14					14 14			
Peterborough [8]	a		11 34	11 18				12 35			12 58		13 34			13 48		14 34	14 18		

Table 25

Sundays
18 July to 05 September

London - Stevenage, Cambridge and Peterborough

		FC	FC	FC	FC	GR	FC	FC	FC	FC	GR	FC	FC	GR	FC	FC	FC	FC	GR	FC	FC
London Kings Cross ⊖	d	14 04	14 09		14 38	14 45	15 04	15 09		15 38	15 55	16 04	16 09	16 15		16 38	17 04	17 09	17 15		17 38
Finsbury Park ⊖	d		14 14		14 43			15 14		15 43			16 14			16 43		17 14			17 43
Potters Bar	d																				
Hatfield	d																				
Welwyn Garden City	d																				
Welwyn North	d																				
Knebworth	d																				
Hertford North	d																				
Stevenage	d	14 35	14 41		15 09	15 19	15 34	15 40		16 09	16 29	16 34	16 40	16 49		17 09	17 34	17 40	17 49		18 09
Hitchin	d	14 40	14 46		15 14		15 39	15 45		16 14		16 39	16 45			17 14	17 39	17 45			18 14
Letchworth Garden City	d	14 44			15 18		15 43			16 18		16 43				17 18	17 43				18 18
Baldock	d	14 47			15 21		15 46			16 21		16 46				17 21	17 46				18 21
Ashwell & Morden	d	14 52			15 26		15 51			16 26		16 51				17 26	17 51				18 26
Royston	d	14 56		15 10	15 30		15 55		16 10	16 30		16 55			17 10	17 30	17 55			18 10	18 30
Meldreth	d			15 13					16 13						17 13					18 13	
Shepreth	d			15 16					16 16						17 16					18 16	
Foxton	d			15 19					16 19						17 19					18 19	
Cambridge	a	15 13		15 32	15 46		16 12		16 32	16 46		17 12			17 32	17 46	18 12			18 32	18 46
Arlesey	d		14 51					15 50					16 50					17 50			
Biggleswade	d		14 56					15 55					16 55					17 55			
Sandy	d		15 00					15 59					16 59					17 59			
St Neots	d		15 07					16 06					17 06					18 06			
Huntingdon	d		15 15					16 14					17 14					18 14			
Peterborough	a		15 35			15 49		16 34			16 59		17 34	17 18				18 34	18 18		

		FC	FC	GR	FC	FC	GR	FC	FC	FC	FC	GR	FC	FC	FC	FC	FC	FC	FC	FC	FC
London Kings Cross ⊖	d	18 04	18 09	18 15		18 38	18 55	19 04	19 09		19 38	19 45	20 04	20 09		20 38	21 04	21 09		21 38	22 04
Finsbury Park ⊖	d		18 14			18 43			19 14		19 43			20 14		20 43		21 14		21 43	
Potters Bar	d																				
Hatfield	d																				
Welwyn Garden City	d																				
Welwyn North	d																				
Knebworth	d																				
Hertford North	d																				
Stevenage	d	18 34	18 40	18 50		19 09	19 28	19 34	19 40		20 09	20 17	20 34	20 40		21 09	21 34	21 40		22 09	22 34
Hitchin	d	18 39	18 45			19 14		19 39	19 45		20 14		20 39	20 45		21 14	21 39	21 45		22 14	22 39
Letchworth Garden City	d	18 43				19 18		19 43			20 18		20 43			21 18	21 43			22 18	22 43
Baldock	d	18 46				19 21		19 46			20 21		20 46			21 21	21 46			22 21	22 46
Ashwell & Morden	d	18 51				19 26		19 51			20 26		20 51			21 26	21 51			22 26	22 51
Royston	d	18 55			19 10	19 30		19 55		20 10	20 30		20 55		21 10	21 30	21 55		22 10	22 30	22 55
Meldreth	d				19 13					20 13					21 13				22 13		
Shepreth	d				19 16					20 16					21 16				22 16		
Foxton	d				19 19					20 19					21 19				22 19		
Cambridge	a	19 12			19 32	19 46		20 12		20 32	20 46		21 12		21 32	21 46	22 12		22 32	22 47	23 12
Arlesey	d		18 50						19 50					20 50				21 50			
Biggleswade	d		18 55						19 55					20 55				21 55			
Sandy	d		18 59						19 59					20 59				21 59			
St Neots	d		19 06						20 06					21 06				22 06			
Huntingdon	d		19 14						20 14					21 14				22 14			
Peterborough	a		19 34	19 19			19 58		20 34			20 46		21 34				22 34			

		FC	FC	FC	FC	FC	FC
London Kings Cross ⊖	d	22 09		22 38	23 02	23 02	23 05
Finsbury Park ⊖	d	22 14		22 43			23 10
Potters Bar	d						
Hatfield	d						
Welwyn Garden City	d						
Welwyn North	d						
Knebworth	d						
Hertford North	d						
Stevenage	d	22 40		23 09	23 34	23 34	23 40
Hitchin	d	22 45		23 14	23 39	23 39	23 45
Letchworth Garden City	d			23 18	23 43	23 43	
Baldock	d			23 21	23 46	23 46	
Ashwell & Morden	d			23 26	23 51	23 51	
Royston	d		23 10	23 30	23 55	23 55	
Meldreth	d		23 13				
Shepreth	d		23 16				
Foxton	d		23 19				
Cambridge	a		23 32	23 47	00 12	00 12	
Arlesey	d	22 50					23 50
Biggleswade	d	22 55					23 55
Sandy	d	22 59					23 59
St Neots	d	23 06					00 06
Huntingdon	d	23 14					00 14
Peterborough	a	23 34					00 34

Table 25

Sundays
from 12 September

London - Stevenage, Cambridge and Peterborough

		FC	FC	FC	FC	FC	FC	FC	FC	FC	FC	FC	FC	FC	FC	FC	FC	FC	FC	FC	FC	FC	FC	FC	FC
London Kings Cross ⊖	d	23p06	23p22	23p26	23p41	00 04	00 07	00 36		06 06			06 26	06 36			07 06			07 26		07 36			
Finsbury Park ⊖	d	23p11	23p27	23p32	23p47	00 09	00 12	00 41		06 11			06 32	06 41			07 11			07 32		07 41			
Potters Bar	d	23p21			00 08			00 51		06 21				06 51			07 21					07 51			
Hatfield	d	23p27			00 16			00 57		06 27				06 57			07 27					07 57			
Welwyn Garden City	d	23p31			00 31	00 27		01 03		06 31				07 01			07 31					08 01			
Welwyn North	d	23p34			00 34			01s06		06 37				07 07			07 37					08 07			
Knebworth	d	23p38			00 38			01s10		06 41				07 11			07 41					08 11			
Hertford North	d			00 07			00 39						07 07							08 07					
Stevenage	d	23p42	23p56	00 20	00 42	00 33	00 48	01a18	01 23	06a49	06 57	06 57	07a22	07a19	07 27		07a49	07 57	07 57	08a23		08a19	08 27		08 57
Hitchin	d	23p50	00 04	00 28	00 50	00 41	00 56		01 43		07 17	07 17			07 47			08 17	08 17				08 47		09 17
Letchworth Garden City	d	23p54		00a35	00a59	00 44	01 01					07 32			08a02	07 37		08a32			08 07		09a02	08 37	
Baldock	d	23p57					01 05									07 40					08 10			08 40	
Ashwell & Morden	d	00 02					01 10														08 15				
Royston	d	00 07				00 54	01 14									07 48					08 20			08 48	
Meldreth	d	00 11					01 18														08 24				
Shepreth	d	00 14					01 21														08 27				
Foxton	d	00 16					01 24														08 29				
Cambridge	a	00 29				01 15	01 40									08 04					08 41			09 04	
Arlesey	d		00 09						02s01			07 44							08 35						09 35
Biggleswade	d		00 14						02s21			08 04							08 55						09a55
Sandy	d		00 18						02s31			08 14							09 05						
St Neots	d		00 25						02s51			08 34							09 25						
Huntingdon	d		00 33						03s21		08 09	09 04							09 55						
Peterborough	a		00 53						04 01		08 49	09 44							10 35						

		FC	FC	FC	FC	GR	FC	FC	FC	FC	FC	FC	FC	GR	FC	FC	FC	FC	FC	FC	GR	FC	FC	FC
London Kings Cross ⊖	d	08 30		08 26	08 52	09 00	09 06	09 22	09 26	09 52	10 06	10 22	10 26	10 30	10 52	11 06	11 22	11 26	11 52	12 06	12 10		12 22	12 26
Finsbury Park ⊖	d	08 35		08 32	08 57		09 11	09 27	09 32	09 57	10 11	10 27	10 32		10 57	11 11	11 27	11 32	11 57	12 11			12 27	12 32
Potters Bar	d	08 44					09 21				10 21					11 21				12 21				
Hatfield	d	08 49					09 27				10 27					11 27				12 27				
Welwyn Garden City	d	08 53					09 31				10 31					11 31				12 31				
Welwyn North	d	08 56					09 34				10 34					11 34				12 34				
Knebworth	d	09 00					09 38				10 38					11 38				12 38				
Hertford North	d			09 07					10 07				11 07					12 07				←		13 07
Stevenage	d	09a06		09a20	09 16	09 19	09 42	09 46	10a20	10 16	10 42	10 46	11a20	10 49	11 16	11 42	11 46	12a20	12 16	12 42	12 29	12 42	12 46	13a20
Hitchin	d				09 21		09 47	09 51		10 21	10 47	10 51			11 21	11 47	11 51		12 21	→		12 47	12 51	
Letchworth Garden City	d		09 07		09 25		09 51			10 25	10 51				11 25	11 51			12 25			12 51		
Baldock	d		09 10		09 28		09 55			10 28	10 55				11 28	11 55			12 28			12 55		
Ashwell & Morden	d		09 15				10 00				11 00					12 00						13 00		
Royston	d		09 20		09 36		10 04			10 36	11 04				11 36	12 04			12 36			13 04		
Meldreth	d		09 24				10 08				11 08					12 08						13 08		
Shepreth	d		09 27				10 11				11 11					12 11						13 11		
Foxton	d		09 29				10 14				11 14					12 14						13 14		
Cambridge	a		09 43		09 54		10 27			10 54	11 27				11 54	12 27			12 54			13 27		
Arlesey	d							09 56				10 56					11 56						12 56	
Biggleswade	d							10 01				11 01					12 01						13 01	
Sandy	d							10 05				11 05					12 05						13 05	
St Neots	d							10 12				11 12					12 12						13 12	
Huntingdon	d							10 20				11 20					12 20						13 20	
Peterborough	a					09 48		10 36				11 36		11 18			12 36				12 58		13 36	

		FC	GR	FC	FC	FC	GR	FC	FC	FC	FC	FC	GR	FC	FC	FC	FC	FC	GR	FC	FC
London Kings Cross ⊖	d	12 52	13 00	13 06	13 22	13 26	13 30	13 52	14 06	14 22	14 26	14 52	15 00	15 06	15 22	15 26	15 52	16 06	16 10		16 22
Finsbury Park ⊖	d	12 57		13 11	13 27	13 32		13 57	14 11	14 27	14 32	14 57		15 11	15 27	15 32	15 57	16 11			16 27
Potters Bar	d			13 21					14 21					15 21				16 21			
Hatfield	d			13 27					14 27					15 27				16 27			
Welwyn Garden City	d			13 31					14 31					15 31				16 31			
Welwyn North	d			13 34					14 34					15 34				16 34			
Knebworth	d			13 38					14 38					15 38				16 38			
Hertford North	d					14 07					15 07					16 07				←	
Stevenage	d	13 16	13 19	13 42	13 46	14a20	13 49	14 16	14 42	14 46	15a20	15 16	15 19	15 42	15 46	16a20	16 16	16 42	16 29	16 42	16 46
Hitchin	d	13 21		13 47	13 51			14 21	14 47	14 51		15 21		15 47	15 51		16 21	→		16 47	16 51
Letchworth Garden City	d	13 25		13 51				14 25	14 51			15 25		15 51			16 25			16 51	
Baldock	d	13 28		13 55				14 28	14 55			15 28		15 55			16 28			16 55	
Ashwell & Morden	d			14 00					15 00					16 00						17 00	
Royston	d	13 36		14 04				14 36	15 04			15 36		16 04			16 36			17 04	
Meldreth	d			14 08					15 08					16 08						17 08	
Shepreth	d			14 11					15 11					16 11						17 11	
Foxton	d			14 14					15 14					16 14						17 14	
Cambridge	a	13 54		14 27				14 54	15 27			15 54		16 27			16 54			17 27	
Arlesey	d				13 56					14 56					15 56						16 56
Biggleswade	d				14 01					15 01					16 01						17 01
Sandy	d				14 05					15 05					16 05						17 05
St Neots	d				14 12					15 12					16 12						17 12
Huntingdon	d				14 20					15 20					16 20						17 20
Peterborough	a		13 50		14 36		14 18			15 36			15 49		16 38				16 58		17 36

London - Stevenage, Cambridge and Peterborough

Sundays from 12 September

		FC	GR	FC	FC	FC	FC	FC	GR	FC	FC	FC	FC	FC	GR	FC	FC	FC	FC	GR	GR	FC
			R 1 ☕	1	1	1	1		R 1 ☕	1	1	1	1		R 1 ☕	1	1	1		R 1 ☕	R 1 ☕	1
London Kings Cross ⊖	d	16 26	16 30	16 36	16 52	17 06	17 22	17 26	17 30	17 36	17 52	18 06	18 22	18 26	18 30	18 52	19 06	19 22	19 26	19 30	19 35	19 52
Finsbury Park ⊖	d	16 32		16 41	16 57	17 11	17 27	17 32		17 41	17 57	18 11	18 27	18 32		18 57	19 11	19 27	19 32			19 57
Potters Bar	d			16 51		17 21				17 51		18 21					19 21					
Hatfield	d			16 57		17 27				17 57		18 27					19 27					
Welwyn Garden City	d			17 01		17 31				18 01		18 31					19 31					
Welwyn North	d			17 04		17 34				18 04		18 34					19 34					
Knebworth	d			17 08		17 38				18 08		18 38					19 38					
Hertford North	d	17 07						18 07						19 07					20 07			
Stevenage	d	17a20	16 49	17 12	17 16	17 42	17 46	18a20	17 49	18 12	18 16	18 42	18 46	19a20	18 50	19 16	19 42	19 46	20a20	19 50	19 54	20 16
Hitchin	d			17 17	17 21	17 47	17 51			18 17	18 21	18 47	18 51			19 21	19 47	19 51				20 21
Letchworth Garden City	d				17 25	17 51					18 25	18 51				19 25	19 51					20 25
Baldock	d				17 28	17 55					18 28	18 55				19 28	19 55					20 28
Ashwell & Morden	d					18 00						19 00					20 00					
Royston	d				17 36	18 04					18 36	19 04				19 36	20 04					20 36
Meldreth	d					18 08						19 08					20 08					
Shepreth	d					18 11						19 11					20 11					
Foxton	d					18 14						19 14					20 14					
Cambridge	a				17 54	18 27					18 54	19 27				19 54	20 27					20 54
Arlesey	d			17 23			17 56			18 23			18 56					19 56				
Biggleswade	d			17 28			18 01			18 28			19 01					20 01				
Sandy	d			17 32			18 05			18 32			19 05					20 05				
St Neots	d			17 39			18 12			18 39			19 12					20 12				
Huntingdon	d			17 47			18 20			18 47			19 20					20 20				
Peterborough	a		17 18	18 06			18 38		18 18	19 05			19 36		19 19			20 36		20 19	20 23	

		FC	FC	FC	FC	FC	FC	FC	FC	FC	FC	FC	FC	FC	FC	FC	FC	FC
		1	1		1	1	1		1	1	1		1	1	1	1		
London Kings Cross ⊖	d	20 06	20 22	20 26	20 52	21 06	21 22	21 26	21 52	22 06	22 22	22 26	22 52	23 06	23 15	23 22	23 26	23 41
Finsbury Park ⊖	d	20 11	20 27	20 32	20 57	21 11	21 27	21 32	21 57	22 11	22 27	22 32	22 57	23 11		23 27	23 31	23 47
Potters Bar	d	20 21				21 21				22 21				23 21				00 08
Hatfield	d	20 27				21 27				22 27				23 27				00 16
Welwyn Garden City	d	20 31				21 31				22 31				23 31				00 20
Welwyn North	d	20 34				21 34				22 34				23 34				00 23
Knebworth	d	20 38				21 38				22 38				23 38				00 28
Hertford North	d			21 07				22 07				23 07					00 07	
Stevenage	d	20 42	20 46	21a20	21 16	21 42	21 46	22a20	22 16	22 42	22 46	23a20	23 16	23 42		23 46	00a20	00 31
Hitchin	d	20 47	20 51		21 21	21 47	21 51		22 21	22 47	22 51		23 21	23 50		23 54		00 37
Letchworth Garden City	d	20 51			21 25	21 51			22 25	22 51			23 25	23 54	23 44			00a52
Baldock	d	20 55			21 28	21 55			22 28	22 55			23 28	23 57				
Ashwell & Morden	d	21 00				22 00				23 00				00 02				
Royston	d	21 04			21 36	22 04			22 36	23 04			23 36	00 07	23 54			
Meldreth	d	21 08				22 08				23 08				00 11				
Shepreth	d	21 11				22 11				23 11				00 14				
Foxton	d	21 14				22 14				23 14				00 16				
Cambridge	a	21 27			21 54	22 27			22 54	23 27			23 54	00 29	00 10			
Arlesey	d		20 56				21 56				22 56					23 59		
Biggleswade	d		21 01				22 01				23 01					00 04		
Sandy	d		21 05				22 05				23 05					00 08		
St Neots	d		21 12				22 12				23 12					00 15		
Huntingdon	d		21 20				22 20				23 20					00 23		
Peterborough	a		21 36				22 36				23 40					00 42		

Peterborough, Cambridge and Stevenage - London

		FC	FC	FC	FC	FC	FC	FC	FC	FC	FC	FC	FC	FC	FC	FC	FC	FC	FC	FC	FC	FC	FC
		1 A	MX	B	1 C	1 A	1 C	MX 1	1		1	1	1	1	1	1	1	1	1	1		1	1
Peterborough	d	22p50			22p51				03 25		04 12		05 12		05 40				06 00	06 21			
Huntingdon	d	23p04			23p05				03 39		04 26		05 26		05 55				06 15	06 37			
St Neots	d	23p11			23p12				03 46		04 34		05 34		06 03				06 23	06 45			
Sandy	d	23p19			23p20						04 41		05 41						06 31				
Biggleswade	d	23p22			23p23				03 56		04 45		05 45						06 35	06 54			
Arlesey	d	23p27			23p28						04 50		05 50						06 40				
Cambridge	d						23p15	23p15								05 35	05 45	06 15					06 27
Foxton	d							23p25								05 44							06 37
Shepreth	d							23p27								05 46							06 40
Meldreth	d							23p30								05 49							06 43
Royston	d						23p29	23p35				05 16		05 46		06 05	05 59	06 29				06 44	06 50
Ashwell & Morden	d							23p39				05 21		05 51		06 10						06 48	06 55
Baldock	d							23p44				05 26		05 56		06 15						06 53	07 00
Letchworth Garden City	d		23p18				23p39	23p47		04 50		05 29		05 59		06 19	06 09	06 39			06 48	06 57	07 04
Hitchin	d	23p34	23p22		23p34	←	23p43	23p54	04 08	04 54	04 58	05 33	05 58	06 03	06 19	06 23		06 43	06 46		06 52	07 01	07 08
Stevenage	d	23p40	23p27	23p29	23p39	23p40	23p48	23p59	04 13	04 59	05 04	05 39	06 03	06 09	06 25	06 29		06 48	06 52		06 58	07 07	07 14
Hertford North	a	→	23p40	23p42					04 23	05 12													
Knebworth	d						23p51	00 02			05 07	05 43		06 13		06 33			06 55			07 11	07 18
Welwyn North	d						23p55	00 06			05 11	05 47		06 17		06 37			06 59				07 22
Welwyn Garden City	d						23p58	00 09			05 15	05 50		06 20		06 40			07 03		07 08		07 26
Hatfield	d						00 01	00 12			05 19	05 53		06 23		06 44					07 12		07 30
Potters Bar	d						00 07	00 18			05 25	05 59		06 29		06 49					07 18		
Finsbury Park ⊖	d		00 15	00 17	00 05	00 09	00 20	00 29	04s46	05 47	05 41	06 08	06 21	06 38	06 44	06 58		07 06	07 17		07 34	07 27	07 46
London Kings Cross ⊖	a		00 26	00 27	00 14	00 17	00 32	00 42	04 59	05 58	05 55	06 18	06 30	06 48	06 52	07 07	06 38	07 15	07 25	07 28	07 42	07 35	07 56

		FC	FC	FC	FC	FC	FC	FC	FC	FC	FC	FC	FC	FC	FC	FC	FC	FC	FC	FC	FC	FC	FC
		1	1		1	1	1	1	1	1	1	1	1	1	1	1	1	1	1	1		1	1
Peterborough	d		06 32		06 53	07 04					07 14		07 26				07 33		07 58				08 16
Huntingdon	d		06 47		07 09	07 23					07 32		07 40				07 50		08 12				08 31
St Neots	d		06 55		07 17	07 32					07 40		07 48				07 58		08 20				08 38
Sandy	d		07 03			07 40											08 06						08 46
Biggleswade	d		07 07			07 44							07 56				08 10						08 49
Arlesey	d		07 12			07 49											08 15						08 54
Cambridge	d	06 45						06 57	07 15						07 26	07 45		07 54		08 15			
Foxton	d							07 07							07 36			08 04					
Shepreth	d							07 10							07 39			08 06					
Meldreth	d							07 13							07 43			08 09					
Royston	d	06 59					07 14	07 21	07 29	07 34				07 43	07 51	07 59		08 14		08 29		08 34	
Ashwell & Morden	d						07 18			07 38				07 48				08 18				08 38	
Baldock	d						07 23			07 43				07 53				08 23				08 43	
Letchworth Garden City	d	07 09		07 20			07 27	07 32		07 47				07 57	08 02			08 27		08 39		08 47	
Hitchin	d		07 18	07 24		07 55	07 31	07 36		07 51		←		08 01	08 06		08 21	08 31			08 39	08 51	09 00
Stevenage	d		07 24	07 30	07 36	08 01	07 37	07 42			07 59	08 01		08 07	08 12		08 27		08 39		08 45	08 57	09 05
Hertford North	a					→																	
Knebworth	d							07 46						08 11	08 16						08 49		
Welwyn North	d							07 50		07 59					08 20						08 53		
Welwyn Garden City	d			07 42				07 54							08 24						08 58		
Hatfield	d			07 46																	09 02		
Potters Bar	d			07 52																			
Finsbury Park ⊖	d		07 41	08 09			07 56	08 09				08 19			08 39		08 46				09 19	09 15	09 23
London Kings Cross ⊖	a	07 39	07 50	08 17	07 59		08 04	08 18	08 06	08 19	08 22	08 28	08 31	08 36	08 49	08 39	08 56	09 00	09 03	09 12	09 27	09 23	09 32

		GR	FC	FC	FC	FC	FC	FC	GR	FC	FC	FC	FC	FC	FC	FC	FC	GR	FC	FC	FC	GR
		R 1 ✕	1	1	1	1	1	1	R 1 ☕	1	1	1	1	1	1	1	1	R 1 ☕	1	1	1	R 1 ✕
Peterborough	d				08 45		09 15	09 23	09 26					09 44		10 15		10 36		10 46		11 17
Huntingdon	d				09 00		09 30	09 41						09 59		10 33				11 00		
St Neots	d				09 07		09 37	09 49						10 06		10 41				11 07		
Sandy	d				09 15			09 57						10 14		10 48				11 15		
Biggleswade	d				09 18		09 45	10 01						10 17		10 52				11 18		
Arlesey	d				09 23			10 06						10 22		10 57						
Cambridge	d		08 25	08 45		08 54				09 26			09 50		09 55		10 26				10 55	
Foxton	d		08 35			09 04									10 05						11 05	
Shepreth	d		08 37			09 06									10 07						11 07	
Meldreth	d		08 40			09 09									10 10						11 10	
Royston	d		08 46	08 59		09 15				09 43			10 04		10 15		10 43				11 15	
Ashwell & Morden	d		08 51			09 20									10 20						11 20	
Baldock	d		08 56			09 25				09 51					10 25		10 51				11 25	
Letchworth Garden City	d		09 00	09 09		09 29				09 54	09 59		10 14		10 29		10 54				11 29	
Hitchin	d		09 04		09 29	09 33		10 12		09 58	10 03	←		10 28	10 33	11 03	10 58		←	11 28	11 33	
Stevenage	d	09 06	09 10		09 34	09 39	09 56	10 18	09 57	10 03	10 09	10 18		10 33	10 39	11 09	11 03	11 05	11 09	11 33	11 39	11 47
Hertford North	a							→								→						
Knebworth	d		09 13			09 43					10 13				10 43				11 13		11 43	
Welwyn North	d		09 17			09 47					10 17				10 47				11 17		11 47	
Welwyn Garden City	d		09 20			09 50					10 20				10 50				11 20		11 50	
Hatfield	d		09 24			09 54					10 23				10 53				11 23		11 53	
Potters Bar	d		09 30			10 00					10 29				10 59				11 29		11 59	
Finsbury Park ⊖	d		09 41		09 52	10 09				10 21	10 41			10 54	11 08		11 21		11 41	11 52	12 11	
London Kings Cross ⊖	a	09 35	09 50	09 41	10 02	10 18	10 22		10 25	10 30	10 49	10 45	10 46	11 02	11 19		11 30	11 34	11 49	12 00	12 19	12 15

A MO from 19 July until 6 September
B MO from 13 September
C MO until 12 July, MO from 13 September
b previous night, stops to set down only

Peterborough, Cambridge and Stevenage - London

		FC	FC	FC	FC	GR	FC	FC		FC	GR	FC	FC	FC	FC	FC	GR	FC		FC	FC	FC	GR	FC	FC
		1	1	1	1	1	1	1		1	1	1	1	1	1	1	1	1		1	1	1	1	1	1
Peterborough 8	d		11 17	11 44		12 14		12 18		12 43	12 47				13 19	13 43	13 47					14 18	14 43	14 45	
Huntingdon	d		11 33	12 00				12 33		13 00					13 34	13 59						14 33		15 01	
St Neots	d		11 41	12 07				12 41		13 07					13 42	14 06						14 41		15 08	
Sandy	d		11 48	12 15				12 48		13 15					13 49	14 14						14 48		15 16	
Biggleswade	d		11 52	12 18				12 52		13 18					13 53	14 17						14 52		15 19	
Arlesey	d		11 57					12 57							13 58	14 22						14 57		15 24	
Cambridge	d	11 26			11 55		12 28						12 55	13 28						13 55	14 28				14 55
Foxton	d				12 05								13 05							14 05					15 05
Shepreth	d				12 07								13 07							14 07					15 07
Meldreth	d				12 10								13 10							14 10					15 10
Royston	d	11 43			12 15		12 43						13 15	13 43						14 15	14 43				15 15
Ashwell & Morden	d				12 20								13 20							14 20					15 20
Baldock	d	11 51			12 25		12 51						13 25	13 51						14 25	14 51				15 25
Letchworth Garden City	d	11 54			12 29		12 54						13 29	13 54						14 29	14 54				15 29
Hitchin 4	d	11 58	12 03	12 28	12 33		12 58	13 03		13 28		←	13 33	13 58	14 04	14 28		←		14 33	14 58	15 03		15 30	15 33
Stevenage 4	d	12 03	12 09	12 33	12 39	12 43	13 03	13 09		13 33	13 16	13 33	13 39	14 03	14 10	14 33	14 17	14 33		14 39	15 03	15 09	15 12	15 35	15 39
Hertford North	a									→						→									
Knebworth	d		12 13		12 43			13 13					13 43		14 14					14 43		15 13			15 43
Welwyn North	d		12 17		12 47			13 17					13 47		14 18					14 47		15 17			15 47
Welwyn Garden City 4	d		12 20		12 50			13 20					13 50		14 21					14 50		15 20			15 50
Hatfield	d		12 23		12 53			13 23					13 53		14 24					14 53		15 23			15 53
Potters Bar	d		12 29		12 59			13 29					13 59		14 30					14 59		15 29			15 59
Finsbury Park ⊖	d	12 21	12 41	12 51	13 08		13 21	13 41				13 51	14 08	14 21	14 42			14 52		15 11	15 21	15 41		15 53	16 10
London Kings Cross 15 ⊖	a	12 30	12 49	13 00	13 19	13 10	13 30	13 49			13 43	14 00	14 19	14 30	14 50		14 44	15 01		15 20	15 30	15 50	15 40	16 02	16 17

		FC	GR	FC		FC	FC	GR	FC	FC	FC	GR	FC	FC		FC	GR	FC		FC	FC	FC	GR	FC	FC
		1	1	1		1	1	1	1	1	1	1	1	1		1	1	1		1	1	1	1	1	1
Peterborough 8	d	15 19	15 23				15 44	15 49			16 14	16 19				16 45	17 04				17 20			17 56	
Huntingdon	d	15 34					15 59				16 33					16 59					17 41	18 04		18 12	
St Neots	d	15 42					16 06				16 41					17 06					17 48	18 11		18 19	
Sandy	d	15 49					16 14				16 48					17 14					17 56			18 27	
Biggleswade	d	15 53					16 17				16 52					17 17					18 00			18 30	
Arlesey	d	15 58					16 22				16 57					17 22					18 05			18 35	
Cambridge	d			15 26						15 55			16 24					16 55		17 26					17 55
Foxton	d									16 05			16 33					17 05		17 35					18 05
Shepreth	d									16 07			16 35					17 07		17 37					18 07
Meldreth	d									16 10			16 38					17 10		17 40					18 10
Royston	d			15 43						16 15			16 43					17 15		17 46					18 15
Ashwell & Morden	d									16 20			16 47					17 20		17 51					18 20
Baldock	d			15 51						16 25			16 52					17 25		17 56					18 25
Letchworth Garden City	d			15 54						16 29			16 55					17 29		17 59					18 29
Hitchin 4	d	16 04		15 58		←	16 28		←	16 33	17 03		17 00	←		17 28		17 33		18 03	18 11	18 29		18 42	18 33
Stevenage 4	d	16 10	15 53	16 03		16 10	16 33	16 18	16 33	16 39	17 09	16 48	17 05	17 09		17 33	17 34	17 39		18 09	18 17	18 35	18 42	18 48	18 39
Hertford North	a	→					→				→														
Knebworth	d					16 14				16 43				17 13				17 43			18 21				18 43
Welwyn North	d					16 18				16 47				17 17				17 47			18 25				18 47
Welwyn Garden City 4	d					16 21				16 51				17 21				17 51			18 28				18 51
Hatfield	d					16 24				16 55				17 25				17 55			18 32				18 55
Potters Bar	d					16 30				17 01				17 31				18 01			18 38				19 01
Finsbury Park ⊖	d			16 21		16 39			16 51	17 11			17 23	17 41		17 51		18 11		18 27	18 47	18 54		19 06	19 11
London Kings Cross 15 ⊖	a		16 22	16 30		16 50		16 45	17 01	17 21		17 15	17 35	17 50		18 00	18 04	18 20		18 35	18 58	19 01	19 12	19 15	19 22

		GR	FC	FC	FC	FC		GR	FC			FC	FC	GR	FC	GR	FC	FC	FC	GR		FC		FC	FC
		1	1	1	1	1		1	1			1	1	1	1	1	1	1	1	1				1	1
Peterborough 8	d			18 20		19 17		19 20					19 41	19 47					20 16	20 46					20 55
Huntingdon	d			18 41		19 33							19 59						20 33						21 12
St Neots	d			18 48		19 41							20 06						20 41						21 19
Sandy	d			18 56		19 48							20 14						20 48						21 27
Biggleswade	d			19 00		19 52							20 17						20 52						21 30
Arlesey	d			19 05		19 57							20 22						20 57						21 35
Cambridge	d		18 26		18 55				19 24								19 55	20 28						20 55	
Foxton	d		18 35		19 05				19 33								20 05							21 05	
Shepreth	d		18 37		19 07				19 35								20 07							21 07	
Meldreth	d		18 40		19 10				19 38								20 10							21 10	
Royston	d		18 46		19 15				19 43								20 15	20 43						21 15	
Ashwell & Morden	d		18 51		19 20				19 47								20 20							21 20	
Baldock	d		18 56		19 25				19 52								20 25	20 51						21 25	
Letchworth Garden City	d		18 59		19 29				19 55								20 29	20 54				21 20		21 29	
Hitchin 4	d		19 03	19 11	19 33	20 03			20 00			←	20 28		←		20 33	20 58	21 03			21 24		21 33	21 41
Stevenage 4	d	19 02	19 09	19 17	19 39	20 09		19 50	20 05			20 09	20 33	20 16	20 33	20 35	20 39	21 03	21 09	21 17		21 29		21 39	21 47
Hertford North	a					→							→									21 42			
Knebworth	d			19 21	19 43							20 13					20 43		21 13					21 43	
Welwyn North	d			19 25	19 47							20 17					20 47		21 17					21 47	
Welwyn Garden City 4	d			19 28	19 50							20 20					20 50		21 20					21 50	
Hatfield	d			19 32	19 53							20 23					20 53		21 23					21 53	
Potters Bar	d			19 38	19 59							20 29					20 59		21 29					21 59	
Finsbury Park ⊖	d		19 27	19 47	20 11				20 23			20 38			20 51		21 11	21 21	21 38			22 17		22 11	22 05
London Kings Cross 15 ⊖	a	19 29	19 34	19 59	20 19			20 18	20 33			20 49		20 44	21 00	21 03	21 19	21 29	21 49	21 44		22 25		22 19	22 14

Table 25 Mondays to Fridays

Peterborough, Cambridge and Stevenage - London

		GR	FC	FC	FC	FC		GR	FC	FC	GR	FC	FC
		1	1	1		1		1	1	1	1		1
Peterborough 8	d	21 21		21 28				22 15		22 30	22 59		
Huntingdon	d			21 42						22 44			
St Neots	d			21 49						22 51			
Sandy	d			21 57						22 59			
Biggleswade	d			22 00						23 02			
Arlesey	d			22 05						23 07			
Cambridge	d		21 28			21 55			22 28				23 15
Foxton	d					22 05							23 25
Shepreth	d					22 07							23 27
Meldreth	d					22 10							23 30
Royston	d		21 43			22 15			22 43				23 35
Ashwell & Morden	d					22 20							23 39
Baldock	d		21 51			22 25			22 51				23 44
Letchworth Garden City	d		21 54		22 20	22 29			22 54			23 18	23 47
Hitchin 4	d		21 58	22 11	22 24	22 33			22 58	23 16		23 22	23 54
Stevenage 4	d	21 52	22 03	22 17	22 29	22 39		22s47	23 03	23 22	23s33	23 27	23 59
Hertford North	a				22 42							23 40	
Knebworth	d			22 20		22 43				23 25			00 02
Welwyn North	d			22 24		22 46				23 29			00 06
Welwyn Garden City 4	d			22 27		22 49				23 32			00 09
Hatfield	d			22 30		22 52				23 35			00 12
Potters Bar	d			22 36		22 58				23 41			00 18
Finsbury Park ⊖	d		22 21	22 44	23 17	23 10			23 21	23s52		00 15	00 29
London Kings Cross 15 ⊖	a	22 20	22 30	22 56	23 25	23 21		23 11	23 30	00 01	00 05	00 26	00 42

Saturdays
until 10 July

		FC	FC	FC	FC	FC	FC	FC	FC	FC		FC	FC	FC	FC	FC	FC	FC	FC	FC		FC	FC	FC	FC
		1		1	1		1		1	1		1		1	1	1	1		1	1		1	1		1
Peterborough 8	d	22p30			03 25		04 12					05 14		05 45			06 18		06 45				07 18		07 44
Huntingdon	d	22p44			03 39		04 26					05 28		05 59			06 33		06 59				07 33		07 59
St Neots	d	22p51			03 46		04 34					05 36		06 06			06 41		07 06				07 41		08 06
Sandy	d	22p59					04 41					05 43		06 14			06 48		07 14				07 48		08 14
Biggleswade	d	23p02			03 56		04 45					05 47		06 17			06 52		07 17				07 52		08 17
Arlesey	d	23p07					04 50					05 52		06 22			06 57		07 22				07 57		08 22
Cambridge	d			23p15						05 45					05 55	06 28				06 55		07 28			
Foxton	d			23p25											06 05					07 05					
Shepreth	d			23p27											06 07					07 07					
Meldreth	d			23p30											06 10					07 10					
Royston	d			23p35					05 16	05 59					06 15	06 43				07 15		07 43			
Ashwell & Morden	d			23p39					05 21						06 20					07 20					
Baldock	d			23p44					05 26						06 25	06 51				07 25		07 51			
Letchworth Garden City	d		23p18	23p47		04 50		05 20	05 29	06 09			06 20		06 29	06 54				07 29		07 54			
Hitchin 4	d	23p16	23p22	23p54	04 08	04 54	04 58	05 24	05 33			06 03	06 24	06 28	06 33	06 58	07 03		07 28	07 33		07 58	08 03		08 28
Stevenage 4	d	23p22	23p27	23p59	04 13	04 59	05 05	05 29	05 39			06 09	06 29	06 33	06 39	07 03	07 09	07 29	07 33	07 39		08 03	08 09	08 29	08 33
Hertford North	a		23p40		04 23	05 12		05 42					06 42					07 42						08 42	
Knebworth	d	23p25		00 02			05 07		05 43			06 13			06 43		07 13			07 43			08 13		
Welwyn North	d	23p29		00 06			05 11		05 47			06 17			06 47		07 17			07 47			08 17		
Welwyn Garden City 4	d	23p32		00 09			05 15		05 50			06 20			06 50		07 20			07 50			08 20		
Hatfield	d	23p35		00 12			05 19		05 53			06 23			06 53		07 23			07 53			08 23		
Potters Bar	d	23p41		00 18			05 24		05 59			06 29			06 59		07 29			07 59			08 29		
Finsbury Park ⊖	d	23b52	00 15	00 29	04s46	05 47	05 41	06 17	06 08			06 38	07 17	06 51	07 08	07 21	07 38	08 17	07 51	08 08		08 21	08 38	09 17	08 51
London Kings Cross 15 ⊖	a	00 01	00 26	00 42	04 59	05 58	05 56	06 25	06 19	06 38		06 49	07 25	07 01	07 19	07 31	07 49	08 25	08 01	08 19		08 31	08 49	09 25	09 01

		FC	FC	FC	FC	FC	FC	FC	GR	FC	FC	FC	FC	FC	FC	FC		FC	GR	FC	FC	FC	FC	FC	GR
		1	1	1	1	1		1	1	1	1		1	1	1	1		1	1	1		1	1	1	1
Peterborough 8	d			08 18	08 45	09 12			09 16				09 45	10 14		10 18			10 33			10 45		11 16	11 21
Huntingdon	d			08 33	08 59	09 28					09 33		09 59	10 28		10 33						10 59		11 33	
St Neots	d			08 41	09 06	09 35					09 41		10 06	10 35		10 41						11 06		11 41	
Sandy	d			08 48	09 14						09 48		10 14			10 48						11 14		11 48	
Biggleswade	d			08 52	09 17	09 43					09 52		10 17	10 43		10 52						11 17		11 52	
Arlesey	d			08 57	09 22						09 57		10 22			10 57						11 22		11 57	
Cambridge	d	07 55	08 28					08 55		09 28					09 55			10 28					10 55		
Foxton	d	08 05						09 05							10 05								11 05		
Shepreth	d	08 07						09 07							10 07								11 07		
Meldreth	d	08 10						09 10							10 10								11 10		
Royston	d	08 15	08 43					09 15		09 43					10 15			10 43					11 15		
Ashwell & Morden	d	08 20						09 20							10 20								11 20		
Baldock	d	08 25	08 51					09 25		09 51					10 25			10 51					11 25		
Letchworth Garden City	d	08 29	08 54					09 29		09 54					10 29			10 54					11 29		
Hitchin 4	d	08 33	08 58	09 03	09 28			09 33		09 58	10 03		10 28		10 33	11 03		10 58		←		11 28	11 33	12 03	
Stevenage 4	d	08 39	09 03	09 09	09 33		09 29	09 39	09 45	10 03	10 09	10 29	10 33		10 39	11 09		11 03	11 03	11 09	11 29	11 33	11 39	12 09	11 52
Hertford North	a						09 42					10 42				→					11 42			→	
Knebworth	d	08 43		09 13				09 43			10 13				10 43					11 13			11 43		
Welwyn North	d	08 47		09 17				09 47			10 17				10 47					11 17			11 47		
Welwyn Garden City 4	d	08 50		09 20				09 50			10 20				10 50					11 20			11 50		
Hatfield	d	08 53		09 23				09 53			10 23				10 53					11 23			11 53		
Potters Bar	d	08 59		09 29				09 59			10 29				10 59					11 29			11 59		
Finsbury Park ⊖	d	09 08	09 21	09 38	09 51		10 17	10 08		10 21	10 38	11 17	10 51		11 08			11 21		11 38	12 17	11 51	12 08		
London Kings Cross 15 ⊖	a	09 19	09 31	09 49	10 01	10 15	10 25	10 19	10 13	10 31	10 49	11 25	11 01	11 15	11 19			11 31	11 33	11 48	12 25	12 01	12 19		12 20

b previous night, stops to set down only

Table 25

Peterborough, Cambridge and Stevenage - London

Saturdays until 10 July

		FC	FC	FC	FC	FC	FC	GR	FC	FC	FC	FC	FC	FC	FC	GR	FC	FC	FC	FC	FC
		1	1	1		1	1	■ 1 ✕	1		1	1	1	1	1	■ 1 ✕		1	1	1	1
Peterborough ■	d			12 15				12 34			12 45			13 18	13 42	13 47					14 18
Huntingdon	d			12 33							12 59			13 33	13 59						14 33
St Neots	d			12 41							13 06			13 41	14 06						14 41
Sandy	d			12 48							13 14			13 48	14 14						14 48
Biggleswade	d			12 52							13 17			13 52	14 17						14 52
Arlesey	d			12 57							13 22			13 57	14 22						14 57
Cambridge	d	11 28				11 55	12 28					12 55	13 28						13 55	14 28	
Foxton	d					12 05						13 05							14 05		
Shepreth	d					12 07						13 07							14 07		
Meldreth	d					12 10						13 10							14 10		
Royston	d	11 43				12 15	12 43					13 15	13 43						14 15	14 43	
Ashwell & Morden	d					12 20						13 20							14 20		
Baldock	d	11 51				12 25	12 51					13 25	13 51						14 25	14 51	
Letchworth Garden City	d	11 54				12 29	12 54					13 29	13 54						14 29	14 54	
Hitchin ■	d	11 58	←	13 03		12 33	12 58		←		13 28	13 33	13 58	14 03	14 28			←	14 33	14 58	15 03
Stevenage ■	d	12 03	12 09	13 09	12 29	12 39	13 03	13 03	13 09	13 29	13 33	13 39	14 03	14 09	14 33	14 16	14 29	14 33	14 39	15 03	15 09
Hertford North	a			→	12 42					13 42					→		14 42				
Knebworth	d		12 13			12 43			13 13			13 43		14 13					14 43		15 13
Welwyn North	d		12 17			12 47			13 17			13 47		14 17					14 47		15 17
Welwyn Garden City ■	d		12 20			12 50			13 20			13 50		14 20					14 50		15 20
Hatfield	d		12 23			12 53			13 23			13 53		14 23					14 53		15 23
Potters Bar	d		12 29			12 59			13 30			13 59		14 29					14 59		15 29
Finsbury Park ⊖	d	12 21	12 38		13 17	13 08	13 21		13 38	14 17	13 51	14 08	14 21	14 38			15 17	14 51	15 08	15 21	15 38
London Kings Cross ■ ⊖	a	12 31	12 49		13 25	13 21	13 31	13 33	13 49	14 25	14 01	14 19	14 31	14 49		14 43	15 25	15 01	15 19	15 31	15 49

		FC	FC	FC	FC	FC	FC	GR	FC	FC	FC	FC	FC	GR	FC	FC	GR	FC	FC	FC	FC	FC
			1	1	1	1	1	■ 1 ✕	1		1	1	1	■ 1 ✕	1	1	■ 1 A ✕		1	1	1	1
Peterborough ■	d		14 45			15 18	15 45	15 50	16 18					16 35		16 43	16 47					17 18
Huntingdon	d		14 59			15 33	15 59		16 33							16 59						17 33
St Neots	d		15 06			15 41	16 06		16 41							17 06						17 41
Sandy	d		15 14			15 48	16 14		16 48							17 14						17 48
Biggleswade	d		15 17			15 52	16 17		16 52							17 17						17 52
Arlesey	d		15 22			15 57	16 22		16 57							17 22						17 57
Cambridge	d			14 55	15 28							15 55	16 28							16 55	17 28	
Foxton	d			15 05								16 05								17 05		
Shepreth	d			15 07								16 07								17 07		
Meldreth	d			15 10								16 10								17 10		
Royston	d			15 15	15 43							16 15	16 43							17 15	17 43	
Ashwell & Morden	d			15 20								16 20								17 20		
Baldock	d			15 25	15 51							16 25	16 51							17 25	17 51	
Letchworth Garden City	d			15 29	15 54							16 29	16 54							17 29	17 54	
Hitchin ■	d		15 28	15 33	15 58	16 03	16 28		17 03		←	16 33	16 58		←	17 28			←	17 33	17 58	18 03
Stevenage ■	d	15 29	15 33	15 39	16 03	16 09	16 33	16 19	17 09	16 29	16 33	16 39	17 03	17 04	17 09	17 33	17 16	17 29	17 33	17 39	18 03	18 09
Hertford North	a	15 42					→		→	16 42						→		17 42				
Knebworth	d			15 43		16 13						16 43			17 12					17 42		18 13
Welwyn North	d			15 47		16 17						16 47			17 17					17 47		18 17
Welwyn Garden City ■	d			15 50		16 20						16 50			17 20					17 50		18 20
Hatfield	d			15 53		16 23						16 53			17 23					17 53		18 23
Potters Bar	d			15 59		16 29						16 59			17 29					17 59		18 29
Finsbury Park ⊖	d	16 17	15 51	16 10	16 21	16 38				17 17	16 51	17 08	17 21		17 38			18 17	17 51	18 08	18 21	18 38
London Kings Cross ■ ⊖	a	16 25	16 00	16 17	16 31	16 49		16 47		17 25	17 01	17 19	17 31	17 33	17 49		17 43	18 25	18 01	18 19	18 31	18 49

		FC	GR	FC	FC	FC	FC	FC	FC	FC	FC	GR	FC	FC	GR	FC	FC	FC	FC	FC	GR
		1	■ 1 ✕		1	1	1	1		1	1	■ 1 ✕	1	1	■ 1 ✕	1		1	1	1	■ 1 ✕
Peterborough ■	d	17 45	17 50					18 18		18 43		19 12	19 18		19 38			19 45		20 14	20 19
Huntingdon	d	17 59						18 33		18 59			19 33					19 59		20 33	
St Neots	d	18 06						18 41		19 06			19 41					20 06		20 41	
Sandy	d	18 14						18 48		19 14			19 48					20 14		20 48	
Biggleswade	d	18 17						18 52		19 17			19 52					20 17		20 52	
Arlesey	d	18 22						18 57		19 22			19 57					20 22		20 57	
Cambridge	d					17 55	18 28				18 55			19 28					19 55		
Foxton	d					18 05					19 05								20 05		
Shepreth	d					18 07					19 07								20 07		
Meldreth	d					18 10					19 10								20 10		
Royston	d					18 15	18 43				19 15			19 43					20 15		
Ashwell & Morden	d					18 20					19 20								20 20		
Baldock	d					18 25	18 51				19 25			19 51					20 25		
Letchworth Garden City	d					18 29	18 54				19 29			19 54					20 29		
Hitchin ■	d	18 28			←	18 33	18 58	19 03		19 28	19 33		20 03	19 58		←		20 28	20 33	21 03	
Stevenage ■	d	18 33	18 19	18 29	18 33	18 39	19 03	19 09	19 29	19 33	19 39	19 41	20 09	20 03	20 07	20 09	20 29	20 33	20 39	21 09	20 48
Hertford North	a	→		18 42					19 42				→				20 42			→	
Knebworth	d					18 43		19 13			19 43					20 13			20 43		
Welwyn North	d					18 47		19 17			19 47					20 17			20 47		
Welwyn Garden City ■	d					18 50		19 20			19 50					20 20			20 50		
Hatfield	d					18 53		19 23			19 53					20 23			20 53		
Potters Bar	d					18 59		19 29			19 59					20 29			20 59		
Finsbury Park ⊖	d			19 17	18 51	19 08	19 21	19 38	20 17	19 51	20 08			20 21		20 38	21 17	20 51	21 08		
London Kings Cross ■ ⊖	a		18 47	19 25	19 01	19 19	19 31	19 49	20 25	20 01	20 19	20 10		20 31	20 35	20 49	21 25	21 01	21 19		21 15

A The Flying Scotsman

Table 25

Peterborough, Cambridge and Stevenage - London

Saturdays until 10 July

		FC	FC	FC	CR	FC	FC	FC	FC	GR	FC	FC	FC	GR	FC	FC	FC	FC	FC	FC	FC	FC
		1	1	1	■ 1 ✕	1		1	1	■ 1 ✕	1	1	1	■ 1		1	1	1	1		1	1
Peterborough ■	d			20 45	20 49	21 18				21 22			21 45	21 51					22 18		22 45	
Huntingdon	d			20 59		21 33							21 59						22 33		22 59	
St Neots	d			21 06		21 41							22 06						22 41		23 06	
Sandy	d			21 14		21 48							22 14						22 48		23 14	
Biggleswade	d			21 17		21 52							22 17						22 52		23 17	
Arlesey	d			21 22		21 57							22 22						22 57		23 22	
Cambridge	d	20 28							20 55		21 28						21 55	22 28				23 10
Foxton	d								21 05								22 05					23 19
Shepreth	d								21 07								22 07					23 22
Meldreth	d								21 10								22 10					23 25
Royston	d	20 43							21 15		21 43						22 15	22 43				23 29
Ashwell & Morden	d								21 20								22 20					23 33
Baldock	d	20 51							21 25		21 51						22 25	22 51				23 38
Letchworth Garden City	d	20 54							21 29		21 54						22 29	22 54				23 41
Hitchin ■	d	20 58	←	21 28		22 03		←	21 33		21 58	←	22 28			←	22 33	22 58	23 03		23 31	23 45
Stevenage ■	d	21 03	21 09	21 33	21 18	22 09	21 29	21 33	21 39	21 52	22 03	22 09	22 33	22 20	22 29	22 33	22 39	23 03	23 09	23 29	23 34	23 50
Hertford North	a			→		→	21 42						→		22 42					23 42		
Knebworth	d		21 13						21 43			22 13					22 43		23 13			23 53
Welwyn North	d		21 17						21 47			22 17					22 47		23 17			23 57
Welwyn Garden City ■	d		21 20						21 50			22 20					22 50		23 20			00 01
Hatfield	d		21 23						21 53			22 23					22 53		23 23			00 04
Potters Bar	d		21 29						21 59			22 29					22 59		23 29			00 10
Finsbury Park ⊖	d	21 21	21 38				22 17	21 51	22 08		22 21	22 38			23 17	22 52	23 08	23 21	23 41	00 17	00 01	00s27
London Kings Cross ■ ⊖	a	21 31	21 49		21 45		22 25	22 01	22 19	22 20	22 31	22 49		22 47	23 25	23 01	23 19	23 31	23 52	00 25	00 09	00 35

Saturdays 17 July to 04 September

		FC	FC	FC	FC	FC	FC	FC	FC	FC	FC	FC	FC	FC	FC	FC	FC	FC	FC	FC	FC	FC	FC
		1		1	1		1		1	1	1		1	1	1	1		1	1	1	1		1
Peterborough ■	d	22p30			03 25		04 12				05 14		05 45			06 18		06 45			07 18		07 44
Huntingdon	d	22p44			03 39		04 26				05 28		05 59			06 33		06 59			07 33		07 59
St Neots	d	22p51			03 46		04 34				05 36		06 06			06 41		07 06			07 41		08 06
Sandy	d	22p59					04 41				05 43		06 14			06 48		07 14			07 48		08 14
Biggleswade	d	23p02			03 56		04 45				05 47		06 17			06 52		07 17			07 52		08 17
Arlesey	d	23p07					04 50				05 52		06 22			06 57		07 22			07 57		08 22
Cambridge	d			23p15						05 45				05 55	06 28				06 55	07 28			
Foxton	d			23p25										06 05					07 05				
Shepreth	d			23p27										06 07					07 07				
Meldreth	d			23p30										06 10					07 10				
Royston	d			23p35					05 16	05 59				06 15	06 43				07 15	07 43			
Ashwell & Morden	d			23p39					05 21					06 20					07 20				
Baldock	d			23p44					05 26					06 25	06 51				07 25	07 51			
Letchworth Garden City	d		23p18	23p47		04 50		05 20	05 29	06 09		06 20		06 29	06 54				07 29	07 54			
Hitchin ■	d	23p16	23p22	23p54	04 08	04 54	04 58	05 24	05 33		06 03	06 24	06 28	06 33	06 58	07 03		07 28	07 33	07 58	08 03		08 28
Stevenage ■	d	23p22	23p27	23p59	04 13	04 59	05 03	05 29	05 39		06 09	06 29	06 33	06 39	07 03	07 09	07 29	07 33	07 39	08 03	08 09	08 29	08 33
Hertford North	a		23p40		04 23	05 12		05 42				06 42					07 42					08 42	
Knebworth	d	23p25		00 02			05 07		05 43		06 13			06 43		07 13			07 43		08 13		
Welwyn North	d	23p29		00 06			05 11		05 47		06 17			06 47		07 17			07 47		08 17		
Welwyn Garden City ■	d	23p32		00 09			05 15		05 50		06 20			06 50		07 20			07 50		08 20		
Hatfield	d	23p35		00 12			05 19		05 53		06 23			06 53		07 23			07 53		08 23		
Potters Bar	d	23p41		00 18			05 24		05 59		06 29			06 59		07 29			07 59		08 29		
Finsbury Park ⊖	d	23f52	00 15	00 29	04s46	05 47	05 41	06 17	06 08		06 38	07 17	06 51	07 08	07 21	07 38	08 17	07 51	08 08	08 21	08 38	09 17	08 51
London Kings Cross ■ ⊖	a	00 01	00 26	00 42	04 59	05 58	05 56	06 25	06 19	06 38	06 49	07 25	07 01	07 19	07 31	07 49	08 25	08 01	08 19	08 31	08 49	09 25	09 01

		FC	FC	FC	FC	FC	FC	GR	FC	FC	FC	FC	FC	FC	FC	FC	GR	FC	FC	FC	FC	FC	GR
		1	1	1	1		1	■ 1 ✕	1	1		1	1	1	1	1	■ 1 ✕	1		1	1	1	■ 1 ✕
Peterborough ■	d			08 18	08 45			09 16				09 45	10 14		10 18		10 33			10 45		11 16	11 21
Huntingdon	d			08 33	08 59					09 33		09 59	10 28		10 33					10 59		11 33	
St Neots	d			08 41	09 06					09 41		10 06	10 35		10 41					11 06		11 41	
Sandy	d			08 48	09 14					09 48		10 14			10 48					11 14		11 48	
Biggleswade	d			08 52	09 17					09 52		10 17	10 43		10 52					11 17		11 52	
Arlesey	d			08 57	09 22					09 57		10 22			10 57					11 22		11 57	
Cambridge	d	07 55	08 28				08 55		09 28					09 55		10 28					10 55		
Foxton	d	08 05					09 05							10 05							11 05		
Shepreth	d	08 07					09 07							10 07							11 07		
Meldreth	d	08 10					09 10							10 10							11 10		
Royston	d	08 15	08 43				09 15		09 43					10 15		10 43					11 15		
Ashwell & Morden	d	08 20					09 20							10 20							11 20		
Baldock	d	08 25	08 51				09 25		09 51					10 25		10 51					11 25		
Letchworth Garden City	d	08 29	08 54				09 29		09 54					10 29		10 54					11 29		
Hitchin ■	d	08 33	08 58	09 03	09 28		09 33		09 58	10 03		10 28		10 33	11 03	10 58		←		11 28	11 33	12 03	
Stevenage ■	d	08 39	09 03	09 09	09 33	09 29	09 39	09 45	10 03	10 09	10 29	10 33		10 39	11 09	11 03	11 03	11 09	11 29	11 33	11 39	12 09	11 52
Hertford North	a					09 42					10 42				→				11 42			→	
Knebworth	d	08 43		09 13			09 43			10 13				10 43				11 13			11 43		
Welwyn North	d	08 47		09 17			09 47			10 17				10 47				11 17			11 47		
Welwyn Garden City ■	d	08 50		09 20			09 50			10 20				10 50				11 20			11 50		
Hatfield	d	08 53		09 23			09 53			10 23				10 53				11 23			11 53		
Potters Bar	d	08 59		09 29			09 59			10 29				10 59				11 29			11 59		
Finsbury Park ⊖	d	09 08	09 21	09 38	09 51	10 17	10 08		10 21	10 38	11 17	10 51		11 08		11 21		11 38	12 17	11 51	12 08		
London Kings Cross ■ ⊖	a	09 19	09 31	09 49	10 01	10 25	10 19	10 13	10 31	10 49	11 25	11 01	11 15	11 19		11 31	11 33	11 48	12 25	12 01	12 19		12 20

f previous night, stops to set down only

Table 25

Peterborough, Cambridge and Stevenage - London

Saturdays
17 July to 04 September

		FC	FC	FC	FC	FC	FC	GR	FC	FC	FC	FC	FC	FC	FC	FC	FC	GR	FC	FC
		1	1	1		1	1	1	1		1	1	1	1	1	1	1	1		1
Peterborough	d			12 15				12 34			12 45					13 18	13 42	13 47		
Huntingdon	d			12 33							12 59					13 33	13 59			
St Neots	d			12 41							13 06					13 41	14 06			
Sandy	d			12 48							13 14					13 48	14 14			
Biggleswade	d			12 52							13 17					13 52	14 17			
Arlesey	d			12 57							13 22					13 57	14 22			
Cambridge	d	11 28				11 55	12 28					12 55	12 55	13 28	13 28					
Foxton	d					12 05						13 05	13 05							
Shepreth	d					12 07						13 07	13 07							
Meldreth	d					12 10						13 10	13 10							
Royston	d	11 43				12 15	12 43					13 15	13 15	13 43	13 43					
Ashwell & Morden	d					12 20						13 20	13 20							
Baldock	d	11 51				12 25	12 51					13 25	13 25	13 51	13 51					
Letchworth Garden City	d	11 54				12 29	12 54					13 29	13 29	13 54	13 54					
Hitchin	d	11 58	←	13 03		12 33	12 58		←		13 28	13 33	13 33	13 58	13 58	14 03	14 28			←
Stevenage	d	12 03	12 09	13 09	12 29	12 39	13 03	13 03	13 09	13 29	13 33	13 39	13 39	14 03	14 03	14 09	14 33	14 16	14 29	14 33
Hertford North	a			→	12 42					13 42							→		14 42	
Knebworth	d		12 13			12 43			13 13			13 43	13 43			14 13				
Welwyn North	d		12 17			12 47			13 17			13 47	13 47			14 17				
Welwyn Garden City	d		12 20			12 50			13 20			13 50	13 50			14 20				
Hatfield	d		12 23			12 53			13 23			13 53	13 53			14 23				
Potters Bar	d		12 29			12 59			13 30			13 59	13 59			14 29				
Finsbury Park ⊖	d	12 21	12 38		13 17	13 08	13 21		13 38	14 17	13 51	14 08	14 08	14 21	14 21	14 38			15 17	14 51
London Kings Cross ⊖	a	12 31	12 49		13 25	13 21	13 31	13 33	13 49	14 25	14 01	14 19	14 19	14 31	14 31	14 49		14 43	15 25	15 01

		FC	FC	FC	FC	FC	FC	FC	FC	FC	FC	FC	GR	FC	FC	FC	FC	GR	FC	GR	FC	FC
		1	1	1	1	1	1	1	1	1	1	1	1	1	1	1	1	1	1	1 A	1	1
Peterborough	d			14 10			14 45		15 10			15 45	15 50			16 10		16 35	16 43	16 47		
Huntingdon	d			14 25			14 59		15 25			15 59				16 25			16 59			
St Neots	d			14 32			15 06		15 32			16 06				16 32			17 06			
Sandy	d			14 40			15 14		15 40			16 14				16 40			17 14			
Biggleswade	d			14 43			15 17		15 43			16 17				16 43			17 17			
Arlesey	d			14 48			15 22		15 48			16 22				16 48			17 22			
Cambridge	d	13 55	13 55		14 28	14 44		15 04		15 28	15 44				16 04		16 28				16 44	
Foxton	d	14 05	14 05			14 53					15 53										16 53	
Shepreth	d	14 07	14 07			14 55					15 55										16 55	
Meldreth	d	14 10	14 10			14 59					15 59										16 59	
Royston	d	14 15	14 15		14 42	15a04		15 18		15 42	16a04				16 18		16 42				17a04	
Ashwell & Morden	d	14 20	14 20		14 47					15 47							16 47					
Baldock	d	14 25	14 25		14 51			15 26		15 51					16 26		16 51					
Letchworth Garden City	d	14 29	14 29		14 54			15 29		15 54					16 29		16 54					
Hitchin	d	14 33	14 33	14 54	14 58		15 28	15 33	15 54	15 58		16 28		←	16 33	16 54	16 58		17 28			←
Stevenage	d	14 39	14 39	15a01	15 04		15 33	15 38	16a01	16 04		16 33	16 21	16 33	16 38	17a01	17 04	17 08	17 33	17 17		17 33
Hertford North	a											→							→			
Knebworth	d	14 42	14 43																			
Welwyn North	d	14 47	14 47																			
Welwyn Garden City	d	14 50	14 50																			
Hatfield	d	14 53	14 53																			
Potters Bar	d	14 59	14 59																			
Finsbury Park ⊖	d	15 08	15 08		15 22		16 05	16 14		16 32				17 00	17 12		17 32					18 04
London Kings Cross ⊖	a	15 19	15 19		15 31		16 15	16 21		16 39			17 06	17 11	17 19		17 39	17 48		18 06		18 14

		FC	FC	FC	FC	FC	GR	FC	FC	FC	FC	FC	FC	FC	FC	GR	FC	GR	FC	FC	FC
		1	1	1	1	1	1	1	1	1	1	1	1	1	1	1	1	1	1	1	1
Peterborough	d		17 10			17 45	17 50			18 10		18 43			19 10	19 12		19 38		19 45	
Huntingdon	d		17 25			17 59				18 25		18 59			19 25					19 59	
St Neots	d		17 32			18 06				18 32		19 06			19 32					20 06	
Sandy	d		17 40			18 14				18 40		19 14			19 40					20 14	
Biggleswade	d		17 43			18 17				18 43		19 17			19 43					20 17	
Arlesey	d		17 48			18 22				18 48		19 22			19 48					20 22	
Cambridge	d	17 04		17 28	17 44				18 04		18 28		18 44	19 04			19 28		19 44		20 04
Foxton	d				17 53								18 53						19 53		
Shepreth	d				17 55								18 55						19 55		
Meldreth	d				17 59								18 59						19 59		
Royston	d	17 18		17 42	18a04				18 18		18 42		19a04	19 18			19 42		20a04		20 18
Ashwell & Morden	d			17 47							18 47						19 47				
Baldock	d	17 26		17 51					18 26		18 51			19 26			19 51				20 26
Letchworth Garden City	d	17 29		17 54					18 29		18 54			19 29			19 54				20 29
Hitchin	d	17 33	17 54	17 58		18 28		←	18 33	18 54	18 58	19 28		19 33	19 54		19 58			20 28	20 33
Stevenage	d	17 38	18a01	18 04		18 33	18 23	18 33	18 38	19a01	19 04	19 33		19 38	20a01	19 44	20 04	20 09		20 33	20 38
Hertford North	a					→															
Knebworth	d																				
Welwyn North	d																				
Welwyn Garden City	d																				
Hatfield	d																				
Potters Bar	d																				
Finsbury Park ⊖	d	18 08		18 32				19 03	19 08		19 32	19 59		20 06			20 32			21 00	21 08
London Kings Cross ⊖	a	18 15		18 39			19 09	19 12	19 14		19 39	20 09		20 13		20 22	20 41	20 45		21 10	21 15

A The Flying Scotsman

Table 25

Peterborough, Cambridge and Stevenage - London

Saturdays
17 July to 04 September

		FC	GR	FC	FC	FC	GR	FC	FC	FC	GR	FC	FC	FC	GR	FC	FC	FC	FC	FC	FC	FC
		1	1	1	1	1	1	1	1	1	1	1	1	1	1	1	1	1	1	1	1	1
Peterborough	d	20 10	20 19			20 45	20 49			21 10	21 22			21 45	21 51			22 10			22 45	
Huntingdon	d	20 25				20 59				21 25				21 59				22 25			22 59	
St Neots	d	20 32				21 06				21 32				22 06				22 32			23 06	
Sandy	d	20 40				21 14				21 40				22 14				22 40			23 14	
Biggleswade	d	20 43				21 17				21 43				22 17				22 43			23 17	
Arlesey	d	20 48				21 22				21 48				22 22				22 48			23 22	
Cambridge	d			20 28	20 44				21 04			21 28	21 44				22 04		22 28	22 35		23 10
Foxton	d				20 53								21 53									23 19
Shepreth	d				20 55								21 55									23 22
Meldreth	d				20 59								21 59									23 25
Royston	d			20 42	21a04				21 18			21 42	22a04				22 18		22 42	22 49		23 29
Ashwell & Morden	d			20 47								21 47							22 47	22 54		23 33
Baldock	d			20 51					21 26			21 51					22 26		22 51	22 58		23 38
Letchworth Garden City	d			20 54					21 29			21 54					22 29		22 54	23 01		23 41
Hitchin	d	20 54		20 58		21 28		←	21 33	21 54		21 58		22 28		←	22 33	22 54	22 58	23 05	23 28	23 45
Stevenage	d	21a01	20 49	21 04		21 33	21 21	21 33	21 38	22a01	21 54	22 04		22 33	22 21	22 33	22 38	23a01	23 04	23 11	23 33	23 52
Hertford North	a					→								→								00 03
Knebworth	d																					
Welwyn North	d																					
Welwyn Garden City	d																					
Hatfield	d																					
Potters Bar	d																					
Finsbury Park ⊖	d			21 32				22 00	22 07			22 32				23 01	23 07		23 32	23 38	00 04	00s22
London Kings Cross ⊖	a		21 27	21 40			22 06	22 10	22 14		22 32	22 39			23 06	23 10	23 14		23 39	23 45	00 12	00 37

Saturdays
from 11 September

		FC	FC	FC	FC	FC	FC	FC	FC	FC	FC	FC	FC	FC	FC	FC	FC	FC	FC	FC	FC	FC	FC
		1		1	1		1		1	1	1		1	1	1	1		1	1	1	1		1
Peterborough	d	22p30			03 25		04 12				05 14		05 45			06 18		06 45			07 18		07 44
Huntingdon	d	22p44			03 39		04 26				05 28		05 59			06 33		06 59			07 33		07 59
St Neots	d	22p51			03 46		04 34				05 36		06 06			06 41		07 06			07 41		08 06
Sandy	d	22p59					04 41				05 43		06 14			06 48		07 14			07 48		08 14
Biggleswade	d	23p02			03 56		04 45				05 47		06 17			06 52		07 17			07 52		08 17
Arlesey	d	23p07					04 50				05 52		06 22			06 57		07 22			07 57		08 22
Cambridge	d			23p15						05 45				05 55	06 28				06 55	07 28			
Foxton	d			23p25										06 05					07 05				
Shepreth	d			23p27										06 07					07 07				
Meldreth	d			23p30										06 10					07 10				
Royston	d			23p35					05 16	05 59				06 15	06 43				07 15	07 43			
Ashwell & Morden	d			23p39					05 21					06 20					07 20				
Baldock	d			23p44					05 26					06 25	06 51				07 25	07 51			
Letchworth Garden City	d		23p18	23p47		04 50		05 20	05 29	06 09		06 20		06 29	06 54				07 29	07 54			
Hitchin	d	23p16	23p22	23p54	04 08	04 54	04 58	05 24	05 33		06 03	06 24	06 28	06 33	06 58	07 03		07 28	07 33	07 58	08 03		08 28
Stevenage	d	23p22	23p27	23p59	04 13	04 59	05 05	05 29	05 39		06 09	06 29	06 33	06 39	07 03	07 09	07 29	07 33	07 39	08 03	08 09	08 29	08 33
Hertford North	a		23p40		04 23	05 12		05 42				06 42					07 42					08 42	
Knebworth	d	23p25		00 02			05 07		05 43		06 13			06 43		07 13			07 43		08 13		
Welwyn North	d	23p29		00 06			05 11		05 47		06 17			06 47		07 17			07 47		08 17		
Welwyn Garden City	d	23p32		00 09			05 15		05 50		06 20			06 50		07 20			07 50		08 20		
Hatfield	d	23p35		00 12			05 19		05 53		06 23			06 53		07 23			07 53		08 23		
Potters Bar	d	23p41		00 18			05 24		05 59		06 29			06 59		07 29			07 59		08 29		
Finsbury Park ⊖	d	23b52	00 15	00 29	04s46	05 47	05 41	06 17	06 08		06 38	07 17	06 51	07 08	07 21	07 38	08 17	07 51	08 08	08 21	08 38	09 17	08 51
London Kings Cross ⊖	a	00 01	00 26	00 42	04 59	05 58	05 56	06 25	06 19	06 38	06 49	07 25	07 01	07 19	07 31	07 49	08 25	08 01	08 19	08 31	08 49	09 25	09 01

		FC	FC	FC	FC	FC	FC	GR	FC	FC	FC	FC	FC	FC	FC	FC	GR	FC	FC	FC	FC	FC	GR
		1	1	1	1		1	1	1	1		1	1	1	1	1	1	1		1	1	1	1
Peterborough	d			08 18	08 45			09 16				09 45	10 14		10 18		10 33			10 45		11 16	11 21
Huntingdon	d			08 33	08 59					09 33		09 59	10 28		10 33					10 59		11 33	
St Neots	d			08 41	09 06					09 41		10 06	10 35		10 41					11 06		11 41	
Sandy	d			08 48	09 14					09 48		10 14			10 48					11 14		11 48	
Biggleswade	d			08 52	09 17					09 52		10 17	10 43		10 52					11 17		11 52	
Arlesey	d			08 57	09 22					09 57		10 22			10 57					11 22		11 57	
Cambridge	d	07 55	08 28				08 55		09 28					09 55		10 28					10 55		
Foxton	d	08 05					09 05							10 05							11 05		
Shepreth	d	08 07					09 07							10 07							11 07		
Meldreth	d	08 10					09 10							10 10							11 10		
Royston	d	08 15	08 43				09 15		09 43					10 15		10 43					11 15		
Ashwell & Morden	d	08 20					09 20							10 20							11 20		
Baldock	d	08 25	08 51				09 25		09 51					10 25		10 51					11 25		
Letchworth Garden City	d	08 29	08 54				09 29		09 54					10 29		10 54					11 29		
Hitchin	d	08 33	08 58	09 03	09 28		09 33		09 58	10 03		10 28		10 33	11 03	10 58		←		11 28	11 33	12 03	
Stevenage	d	08 39	09 03	09 09	09 33	09 29	09 39	09 45	10 03	10 09	10 29	10 33		10 39	11 09	11 03	11 03	11 09	11 29	11 33	11 39	12 09	11 52
Hertford North	a					09 42					10 42				→				11 42			→	
Knebworth	d	08 43		09 13			09 43			10 13				10 43				11 13			11 43		
Welwyn North	d	08 47		09 17			09 47			10 17				10 47				11 17			11 47		
Welwyn Garden City	d	08 50		09 20			09 50			10 20				10 50				11 20			11 50		
Hatfield	d	08 53		09 23			09 53			10 23				10 53				11 23			11 53		
Potters Bar	d	08 59		09 29			09 59			10 29				10 59				11 29			11 59		
Finsbury Park ⊖	d	09 08	09 21	09 38	09 51	10 17	10 08		10 21	10 38	11 17	10 51		11 08		11 21		11 38	12 17	11 51	12 08		
London Kings Cross ⊖	a	09 19	09 31	09 49	10 01	10 25	10 19	10 13	10 31	10 49	11 25	11 01	11 15	11 19		11 31	11 33	11 48	12 25	12 01	12 19		12 20

b previous night, stops to set down only

Peterborough, Cambridge and Stevenage - London

Saturdays from 11 September

		FC 1	FC 1	FC 1	FC	FC 1	FC 1	GR ■ 1	FC 1	FC	FC 1	FC 1	FC 1	FC 1	FC 1	GR ■ 1	FC	FC 1	FC 1	FC 1	FC 1
Peterborough 8	d			12 15				12 34			12 45			13 18	13 42	13 47					14 18
Huntingdon	d			12 33							12 59			13 33	13 59						14 33
St Neots	d			12 41							13 06			13 41	14 06						14 41
Sandy	d			12 48							13 14			13 48	14 14						14 48
Biggleswade	d			12 52							13 17			13 52	14 17						14 52
Arlesey	d			12 57							13 22			13 57	14 22						14 57
Cambridge	d	11 28				11 55	12 28					12 55	13 28						13 55	14 20	
Foxton	d					12 05						13 05							14 05		
Shepreth	d					12 07						13 07							14 07		
Meldreth	d					12 10						13 10							14 10		
Royston	d	11 43				12 15	12 43					13 15	13 43						14 15	14 43	
Ashwell & Morden	d					12 20						13 20							14 20		
Baldock	d	11 51				12 25	12 51					13 25	13 51						14 25	14 51	
Letchworth Garden City	d	11 54				12 29	12 54					13 29	13 54						14 29	14 54	
Hitchin 4	d	11 58	←	13 03		12 33	12 58		←		13 28	13 33	13 58	14 03	14 28			←	14 33	14 58	15 03
Stevenage 4	d	17 03	12 09	13 09	12 29	12 39	13 03	13 03	13 09	13 29	13 33	13 39	14 03	14 09	14 33	14 16	14 29	14 33	14 39	15 03	15 09
Hertford North	a			→	12 42					13 42					→		14 42				
Knebworth	d		12 13			12 43			13 13			13 43		14 13					14 43		15 13
Welwyn North	d		12 17			12 47			13 17			13 47		14 17					14 47		15 17
Welwyn Garden City 4	d		12 20			12 50			13 20			13 50		14 20					14 50		15 20
Hatfield	d		12 23			12 53			13 23			13 53		14 23					14 53		15 23
Potters Bar	d		12 29			12 59			13 30			13 59		14 29					14 59		15 29
Finsbury Park ⊖	d	12 21	12 38		13 17	13 08	13 21		13 38	14 17	13 51	14 08	14 21	14 38			15 17	14 51	15 08	15 21	15 38
London Kings Cross 15 ⊖	a	12 31	12 49		13 25	13 21	13 31	13 33	13 49	14 25	14 01	14 19	14 31	14 49		14 43	15 25	15 01	15 19	15 31	15 49

		FC	FC 1	FC 1	FC 1	FC 1	FC 1	GR ■ 1	FC 1	FC	FC 1	FC 1	FC 1	GR ■ 1	FC 1	FC 1	GR ■ 1 A	FC	FC 1	FC 1	FC 1	FC 1
Peterborough 8	d		14 45			15 18	15 45	15 50	16 18					16 35		16 43	16 47					17 18
Huntingdon	d		14 59			15 33	15 59		16 33							16 59						17 33
St Neots	d		15 06			15 41	16 06		16 41							17 06						17 41
Sandy	d		15 14			15 48	16 14		16 48							17 14						17 48
Biggleswade	d		15 17			15 52	16 17		16 52							17 17						17 52
Arlesey	d		15 22			15 57	16 22		16 57							17 22						17 57
Cambridge	d			14 55	15 28							15 55	16 28							16 55	17 28	
Foxton	d			15 05								16 05								17 05		
Shepreth	d			15 07								16 07								17 07		
Meldreth	d			15 10								16 10								17 10		
Royston	d			15 15	15 43							16 15	16 43							17 15	17 43	
Ashwell & Morden	d			15 20								16 20								17 20		
Baldock	d			15 25	15 51							16 25	16 51							17 25	17 51	
Letchworth Garden City	d			15 29	15 54							16 29	16 54							17 29	17 54	
Hitchin 4	d		15 28	15 33	15 58	16 03	16 28		17 03		←	16 33	16 58		←	17 28			←	17 33	17 58	18 03
Stevenage 4	d	15 29	15 33	15 39	16 03	16 09	16 33	16 19	17 09	16 29	16 33	16 39	17 03	17 04	17 09	17 33	17 16	17 29	17 33	17 39	18 03	18 09
Hertford North	a	15 42					→		→	16 42						→		17 42				
Knebworth	d			15 43		16 13						16 43			17 12					17 42		18 13
Welwyn North	d			15 47		16 17						16 47			17 17					17 47		18 17
Welwyn Garden City 4	d			15 50		16 20						16 50			17 20					17 50		18 20
Hatfield	d			15 53		16 23						16 53			17 23					17 53		18 23
Potters Bar	d			15 59		16 29						16 59			17 29					17 59		18 29
Finsbury Park ⊖	d	16 17	15 51	16 10	16 21	16 38				17 17	16 51	17 08	17 21		17 38			18 17	17 51	18 08	18 21	18 38
London Kings Cross 15 ⊖	a	16 25	16 00	16 17	16 31	16 49		16 47		17 25	17 01	17 19	17 31	17 33	17 49		17 43	18 25	18 01	18 19	18 31	18 49

		FC 1	GR ■ 1	FC	FC 1	FC 1	FC 1	FC 1	FC	FC 1	FC 1	GR ■ 1	FC 1	FC 1	GR ■ 1	FC 1	FC	FC 1	FC 1	FC 1	GR ■ 1
Peterborough 8	d	17 45	17 50					18 18		18 43		19 12	19 18		19 38			19 45		20 14	20 19
Huntingdon	d	17 59						18 33		18 59			19 33					19 59		20 33	
St Neots	d	18 06						18 41		19 06			19 41					20 06		20 41	
Sandy	d	18 14						18 48		19 14			19 48					20 14		20 48	
Biggleswade	d	18 17						18 52		19 17			19 52					20 17		20 52	
Arlesey	d	18 22						18 57		19 22			19 57					20 22		20 57	
Cambridge	d					17 55	18 28				18 55			19 28					19 55		
Foxton	d					18 05					19 05								20 05		
Shepreth	d					18 07					19 07								20 07		
Meldreth	d					18 10					19 10								20 10		
Royston	d					18 15	18 43				19 15			19 43					20 15		
Ashwell & Morden	d					18 20					19 20								20 20		
Baldock	d					18 25	18 51				19 25			19 51					20 25		
Letchworth Garden City	d					18 29	18 54				19 29			19 54					20 29		
Hitchin 4	d	18 28			←	18 33	18 58	19 03		19 28	19 33		20 03	19 58		←		20 28	20 33	21 03	
Stevenage 4	d	18 33	18 19	18 29	18 33	18 39	19 03	19 09	19 29	19 33	19 39	19 41	20 09	20 03	20 07	20 09	20 29	20 33	20 39	21 09	20 48
Hertford North	a	→		18 42					19 42				→				20 42			→	
Knebworth	d					18 43		19 13			19 43					20 13			20 43		
Welwyn North	d					18 47		19 17			19 47					20 17			20 47		
Welwyn Garden City 4	d					18 50		19 20			19 50					20 20			20 50		
Hatfield	d					18 53		19 23			19 53					20 23			20 53		
Potters Bar	d					18 59		19 29			19 59					20 29			20 59		
Finsbury Park ⊖	d			19 17	18 51	19 08	19 21	19 38	20 17	19 51	20 08			20 21		20 38	21 17	20 51	21 08		
London Kings Cross 15 ⊖	a		18 47	19 25	19 01	19 19	19 31	19 49	20 25	20 01	20 19	20 10		20 31	20 35	20 49	21 25	21 01	21 19		21 15

A The Flying Scotsman

Peterborough, Cambridge and Stevenage - London

Saturdays from 11 September

		FC 1	FC 1	FC 1	GR ■ 1	FC 1	FC	FC 1	FC 1	GR ■ 1	FC 1	FC 1	FC 1	GR ■ 1	FC	FC 1	FC 1	FC 1	FC 1	FC	FC 1	FC 1
Peterborough 8	d			20 45	20 49	21 18				21 22			21 45	21 51					22 18		22 45	
Huntingdon	d			20 59		21 33							21 59						22 33		22 59	
St Neots	d			21 06		21 41							22 06						22 41		23 06	
Sandy	d			21 14		21 48							22 14						22 48		23 14	
Biggleswade	d			21 17		21 52							22 17						22 52		23 17	
Arlesey	d			21 22		21 57							22 22						22 57		23 22	
Cambridge	d	20 28							20 55		21 28						21 55	22 28				23 10
Foxton	d								21 05								22 05					23 19
Shepreth	d								21 07								22 07					23 22
Meldreth	d								21 10								22 10					23 25
Royston	d	20 43							21 15		21 43						22 15	22 43				23 29
Ashwell & Morden	d								21 20								22 20					23 33
Baldock	d	20 51							21 25		21 51						22 25	22 51				23 38
Letchworth Garden City	d	20 54							21 29		21 54						22 29	22 54				23 41
Hitchin 4	d	20 58	←	21 28		22 03		←	21 33		21 58	←	22 28			←	22 33	22 58	23 03		23 31	23 45
Stevenage 4	d	21 03	21 09	21 33	21 18	22 09	21 29	21 33	21 39	21 52	22 03	22 09	22 33	22 20	22 29	22 33	22 39	23 03	23 09	23 29	23 34	23 50
Hertford North	a			→		→	21 42						→		22 42					23 42		
Knebworth	d		21 13						21 43			22 13					22 43		23 13			23 53
Welwyn North	d		21 17						21 47			22 17					22 47		23 17			23 57
Welwyn Garden City 4	d		21 20						21 50			22 20					22 50		23 20			00 01
Hatfield	d		21 23						21 53			22 23					22 53		23 23			00 04
Potters Bar	d		21 29						21 59			22 29					22 59		23 29			00 10
Finsbury Park ⊖	d	21 21	21 38				22 17	21 51	22 08		22 21	22 38			23 17	22 52	23 08	23 21	23 41	00 17	00 01	00s27
London Kings Cross 15 ⊖	a	21 31	21 49		21 45		22 25	22 01	22 19	22 20	22 31	22 49		22 47	23 25	23 01	23 19	23 31	23 52	00 25	00 09	00 35

Sundays until 11 July

		FC	FC 1	FC 1	FC 1	FC	FC 1	FC 1	FC 1	FC	FC 1	FC 1	FC 1	FC 1	FC 1	FC 1	FC 1	FC	FC 1	GR ■ 1	FC 1	FC 1	FC
Peterborough 8	d		22p45	05 45			06 45		07 45				08 45		09 14		09 45			10 24		10 45	
Huntingdon	d		22p59	05 59			06 59		07 59				08 59		09 28		09 59					10 59	
St Neots	d		23p06	06 07			07 06		08 06				09 06		09 35		10 06					11 06	
Sandy	d		23p14	06 14			07 14		08 14				09 14				10 14					11 14	
Biggleswade	d		23p17	06 18			07 18		08 17				09 17		09 43		10 17					11 17	
Arlesey	d		23p22	06 23			07 23		08 22				09 22				10 22					11 22	
Cambridge	d				06 28			07 28			07 55	08 28		08 55		09 28			09 55		10 28		
Foxton	d										08 05			09 05					10 05				
Shepreth	d										08 07			09 07					10 07				
Meldreth	d										08 10			09 10					10 10				
Royston	d				06 43			07 43			08 15	08 43		09 15		09 43			10 15		10 43		
Ashwell & Morden	d										08 20			09 20					10 20				
Baldock	d				06 51			07 51			08 25	08 51		09 25		09 51			10 25		10 51		
Letchworth Garden City	d				06 54			07 54			08 29	08 54		09 29		09 54			10 29		10 54		
Hitchin 4	d		23p31	06 33	06 58		07 33	07 58	08 28		08 33	08 58	09 28	09 33		09 58	10 28		10 33		10 58	11 28	
Stevenage 4	d	23p29	23p34	06 39	07 03	07 35	07 39	08 03	08 33	08 35	08 39	09 03	09 33	09 39		10 03	10 33	10 35	10 39	10 55	11 03	11 33	11 35
Hertford North	a	23p42				07 48				08 48								10 48					11 48
Knebworth	d			06 43			07 43				08 43			09 43					10 43				
Welwyn North	d			06 47			07 47				08 47			09 47					10 47				
Welwyn Garden City 4	d			06 50			07 50				08 50			09 50					10 50				
Hatfield	d			06 53			07 53				08 53			09 53					10 53				
Potters Bar	d			06 59			07 59				08 59			09 59					10 59				
Finsbury Park ⊖	d	00 17	00 01	07 11	07 32		08 05	08s40	08 56		09 13	09 26	09 56	10 13		10 26	10 56		11 13		11 21	11 51	
London Kings Cross 15 ⊖	a	00 25	00 09	07 19	07 42		08 19	08 47	09 05		09 22	09 35	10 05	10 22	10 23	10 35	11 05		11 22	11 27	11 30	12 00	

Peterborough, Cambridge and Stevenage - London

Sundays until 11 July

		FC	GR	FC	FC	FC		FC	FC	FC	FC	GR	FC	GR		FC		FC	FC	FC	GR	FC	FC	FC	FC
		1	R 1	1	1			1	1	1		R 1	1	R 1		1			1	1	R 1	1		1	1
Peterborough 8	d		11 25		11 42					12 42		13 06				13 42						14 45			
Huntingdon	d				11 59					12 59						13 59						14 59			
St Neots	d				12 06					13 06						14 06						15 06			
Sandy	d				12 14					13 14						14 14						15 14			
Biggleswade	d				12 17					13 17						14 17						15 17			
Arlesey	d				12 22					13 22						14 22						15 22			
Cambridge	d	10 55		11 28				11 55	12 28				12 55						13 55	14 28				14 55	15 28
Foxton	d	11 05						12 05					13 05						14 05					15 05	
Shepreth	d	11 07						12 07					13 07						14 07					15 07	
Meldreth	d	11 10						12 10					13 10						14 10					15 10	
Royston	d	11 15		11 43				12 15	12 43				13 15						14 15	14 43				15 15	15 43
Ashwell & Morden	d	11 20						12 20					13 20						14 20					15 20	
Baldock	d	11 25		11 51				12 25	12 51				13 25						14 25	14 51				15 25	15 51
Letchworth Garden City	d	11 29		11 54				12 29	12 54				13 29						14 29	14 54				15 29	15 54
Hitchin 4	d	11 33		11 58	12 28			12 33	12 58	13 28			13 33			14 28			14 33	14 58		15 28		15 33	15 58
Stevenage 4	d	11 39	11 55	12 03	12 33	12 35		12 39	13 03	13 33	13 35	13 36	13 39	14 16		14 33		14 35	14 39	15 03	15 28	15 33	15 35	15 39	16 03
Hertford North	a					12 48					13 48							14 48					15 48		
Knebworth	d	11 43						12 43					13 43						14 43					15 43	
Welwyn North	d	11 47						12 47					13 47						14 47					15 47	
Welwyn Garden City 4	d	11 50						12 50					13 50						14 50					15 50	
Hatfield	d	11 53						12 53					13 53						14 53					15 53	
Potters Bar	d	11 59						12 59					13 59						14 59					15 59	
Finsbury Park ⊖	d	12 11		12 21	12 51			13 11	13 21	13 51			14 11			14 51			15 11	15 21		15 51		16 11	16 21
London Kings Cross 15 ⊖	a	12 19	12 23	12 30	13 00			13 19	13 30	14 00		14 04	14 19	14 44		15 00			15 19	15 30	15 55	16 00		16 19	16 30

		FC		GR		FC	FC	FC	GR	FC	FC	GR		FC	FC	FC	FC	GR	FC	FC	FC	GR		FC	GR
		1		R 1		1		1	R 1	1	1	R 1 A		1		1	1	R 1	1		1	R 1		1	R 1
Peterborough 8	d	15 44		15 47					16 18		16 45	16 51						17 40	17 45					18 45	
Huntingdon	d	15 59									16 59								17 59					18 59	
St Neots	d	16 06									17 06								18 06					19 06	
Sandy	d	16 14									17 14								18 14					19 14	
Biggleswade	d	16 17									17 17								18 17					19 17	
Arlesey	d	16 22									17 22								18 22					19 22	
Cambridge	d							15 55		16 28						16 55	17 28				17 55				
Foxton	d							16 05								17 05					18 05				
Shepreth	d							16 07								17 07					18 07				
Meldreth	d							16 10								17 10					18 10				
Royston	d							16 15		16 43						17 15	17 43				18 15				
Ashwell & Morden	d							16 20								17 20					18 20				
Baldock	d							16 25		16 51						17 25	17 51				18 25				
Letchworth Garden City	d							16 29		16 54						17 29	17 54				18 29				
Hitchin 4	d	16 28				←		16 33		16 58	17 28			←		17 33	17 58		18 28		18 33			19 28	
Stevenage 4	d	16 33		16 18		16 33	16 35	16 39	16 48	17 03	17 33	17 21		17 33	17 35	17 39	18 03	18 10	18 33	18 35	18 39	18 42		19 33	19 02
Hertford North	a	→					16 48				→				17 48					18 48				→	
Knebworth	d							16 43								17 43					18 43				
Welwyn North	d							16 47								17 47					18 47				
Welwyn Garden City 4	d							16 50								17 50					18 50				
Hatfield	d							16 53								17 53					18 53				
Potters Bar	d							16 59								17 59					18 59				
Finsbury Park ⊖	d					16 52		17 11		17 21				17 51		18 11	18 21		18 51		19 11				
London Kings Cross 15 ⊖	a			16 46		17 00		17 19	17 17	17 30		17 49		18 00		18 19	18 33	18 37	19 00		19 19	19 14			19 34

		FC	FC	GR	FC	FC	FC	FC		GR	FC	GR	FC	GR	FC	FC	GR	FC		FC		GR	FC	FC	FC
		1	1	R 1	1		1	1		R 1	1	R 1	1	R 1		1	R 1	1		1		R 1	1		1
Peterborough 8	d			18 51						19 34	19 42	19 45		20 02			20 20			20 45		20 48			
Huntingdon	d										19 59									20 59					
St Neots	d										20 06									21 06					
Sandy	d										20 14									21 14					
Biggleswade	d										20 17									21 17					
Arlesey	d										20 22									21 22					
Cambridge	d	18 28	18 45				18 55	19 28								19 55		20 28							20 55
Foxton	d						19 05									20 05									21 05
Shepreth	d						19 07									20 07									21 07
Meldreth	d						19 10									20 10									21 10
Royston	d	18 43	18 58				19 15	19 43								20 15		20 43							21 15
Ashwell & Morden	d						19 20									20 20									21 20
Baldock	d	18 51					19 25	19 51								20 25		20 51							21 25
Letchworth Garden City	d	18 54					19 29	19 54								20 29		20 54							21 29
Hitchin 4	d	18 58			←		19 33	19 58			20 28		←			20 33		20 58		21 28			←		21 33
Stevenage 4	d	19 03		19 21	19 33	19 35	19 39	20 03		20 08	20 33	20 18	20 33	20 33	20 35	20 39	20 52	21 03		21 33		21 20	21 33	21 35	21 39
Hertford North	a					19 48					→				20 48					→				21 48	
Knebworth	d						19 43									20 43									21 43
Welwyn North	d						19 47									20 47									21 47
Welwyn Garden City 4	d						19 50									20 50									21 50
Hatfield	d						19 53									20 53									21 53
Potters Bar	d						19 59									20 59									21 59
Finsbury Park ⊖	d	19 21			19 51		20 11	20 21					20 51			21 11		21 21					21 51		22 11
London Kings Cross 15 ⊖	a	19 29	19 35	19 48	20 00		20 19	20 30		20 34		20 43	21 00	21 02		21 19	21 20	21 30				21 47	22 00		22 19

A The Flying Scotsman

Peterborough, Cambridge and Stevenage - London

Sundays until 11 July

		GR	FC	GR		FC	GR	FC	FC	FC	FC	FC
		R 1	1	R 1		1	R 1		1		1	1
Peterborough 8	d	21 18		21 37		21 45	22 04				22 51	
Huntingdon	d					21 59					23 05	
St Neots	d					22 06					23 12	
Sandy	d					22 14					23 20	
Biggleswade	d					22 17					23 23	
Arlesey	d					22 22					23 28	
Cambridge	d		21 28						21 55			23 15
Foxton	d								22 05			
Shepreth	d								22 07			
Meldreth	d								22 10			
Royston	d		21 43						22 15			23 29
Ashwell & Morden	d								22 20			
Baldock	d		21 51						22 25			
Letchworth Garden City	d		21 54						22 29			23 39
Hitchin 4	d		21 58			22 28			22 33		23 34	23 48
Stevenage 4	d	21 48	22 03	22 07		22 33	22 34	22 35	22 39	23 35	23 39	23 51
Hertford North	a							22 48		23 48		
Knebworth	d								22 43			23 51
Welwyn North	d								22 47			23 55
Welwyn Garden City 4	d								22 50			23 58
Hatfield	d								22 53			00 01
Potters Bar	d								22 59			00 07
Finsbury Park ⊖	d		22 21			22 51			23 11		00 05	00 20
London Kings Cross 15 ⊖	a	22 16	22 30	22 34		23 00	23 04		23 19		00 14	00 32

Sundays 18 July to 05 September

		FC		FC	FC	FC	FC	FC	FC	FC		FC	FC	FC	FC	FC	FC	FC	FC	FC		GR	FC	FC
		1		1	1	1	1	1	1	1		1	1	1	1	1	1	1	1	1		R 1	1	1
Peterborough 8	d	22p45		05 45		06 42		07 42						08 45		09 14			09 45			10 24		
Huntingdon	d	22p59		05 59		06 59		07 59						08 59		09 28			09 59					
St Neots	d	23p06		06 06		07 06		08 06						09 06		09 35			10 06					
Sandy	d	23p14		06 14		07 14		08 14						09 14					10 14					
Biggleswade	d	23p17		06 17		07 17		08 17						09 17		09 43			10 17					
Arlesey	d	23p22		06 22		07 22		08 22						09 22					10 22					
Cambridge	d				06 28		07 28		07 45	08 04		08 28	08 45		09 04		09 28	09 45		10 04			10 28	10 44
Foxton	d								07 53				08 54					09 54						10 53
Shepreth	d								07 56				08 56					09 56						10 55
Meldreth	d								07 59				08 59					09 59						10 59
Royston	d				06 42		07 42		08a04	08 18		08 42	09a04		09 18		09 42	10a04		10 18			10 42	11a04
Ashwell & Morden	d				06 47		07 47					08 47					09 47						10 47	
Baldock	d				06 51		07 51			08 26		08 51			09 26		09 51			10 26			10 51	
Letchworth Garden City	d				06 54		07 54			08 30		08 54			09 29		09 54			10 29			10 54	
Hitchin 4	d	23p28		06 28	06 58	07 28	07 58	08 28		08 34		08 58		09 28	09 33		09 58		10 28	10 33			10 58	
Stevenage 4	d	23p33		06 36	07 04	07 36	08 04	08 33		08 39		09 04		09 33	09 33		10 04		10 34	10 38		10 57	11 04	
Hertford North	a																							
Knebworth	d																							
Welwyn North	d																							
Welwyn Garden City 4	d																							
Hatfield	d																							
Potters Bar	d																							
Finsbury Park ⊖	d	00 04		07 02	07 32	08 02	08 32	08 59		09 06		09 32		09 59	10 06		10 32		11 04	11 11			11 32	
London Kings Cross 15 ⊖	a	00 12		07 12	07 42	08 12	08 40	09 09		09 13		09 39		10 08	10 13	10 26	10 39		11 12	11 18		11 33	11 41	

		FC	FC	GR	FC	FC		FC	FC	FC	FC	FC	FC	GR	FC	FC		GR		FC	FC	FC	FC	GR	FC
		1	1	R 1	1	1		1	1	1	1	1	1	R 1	1	1		R 1		1	1	1	1	R 1	1
Peterborough 8	d	10 45		11 25				11 45			12 42			13 06						13 45					14 45
Huntingdon	d	10 59						11 59			12 59									13 59					14 59
St Neots	d	11 06						12 06			13 06									14 06					15 06
Sandy	d	11 14						12 14			13 14									14 14					15 14
Biggleswade	d	11 17						12 17			13 17									14 17					15 17
Arlesey	d	11 22						12 22			13 22									14 22					15 22
Cambridge	d		11 04		11 28	11 44			12 04	12 28		12 44	13 04		13 28	13 44					14 04	14 28	14 44		
Foxton	d					11 53						12 53				13 53							14 53		
Shepreth	d					11 55						12 55				13 55							14 55		
Meldreth	d					11 59						12 59				13 59							14 59		
Royston	d		11 18		11 42	12a04			12 18	12 42		13a04	13 18		13 42	14a04					14 18	14 42	15a04		
Ashwell & Morden	d				11 47					12 47					13 47							14 47			
Baldock	d		11 26		11 51				12 26	12 51			13 26		13 51						14 26	14 51			
Letchworth Garden City	d		11 29		11 54				12 29	12 54			13 29		13 54						14 29	14 54			
Hitchin 4	d	11 28	11 33		11 58			12 28	12 33	12 58	13 28		13 33		13 58					14 28	14 33	14 58			15 28
Stevenage 4	d	11 33	11 38	11 57	12 04			12 33	12 38	13 04	13 33		13 38	13 40	14 04			14 21		14 35	14 38	15 04		15 29	15 36
Hertford North	a																								
Knebworth	d																								
Welwyn North	d																								
Welwyn Garden City 4	d																								
Hatfield	d																								
Potters Bar	d																								
Finsbury Park ⊖	d	12 01	12 12		12 32			13 05	13 09	13 32	14 04		14 08		14 32					15 05	15 11	15 33			16 06
London Kings Cross 15 ⊖	a	12 09	12 19	12 33	12 40			13 13	13 16	13 40	14 12		14 16	14 22	14 40			15 05		15 14	15 18	15 43		16 09	16 15

Table 25

Sundays 18 July to 05 September

Peterborough, Cambridge and Stevenage - London

		FC	FC	FC	FC	GR	FC	FC	GR	FC	FC	FC	GR	FC	FC	FC	GR	FC	FC	FC	GR
													A								
Peterborough	d				15 45	15 47			16 18			16 45	16 51				17 40		17 45		18 07
Huntingdon	d				15 59							16 59							17 59		
St Neots	d				16 06							17 06							18 06		
Sandy	d				16 14							17 14							18 14		
Biggleswade	d				16 17							17 17							18 17		
Arlesey	d				16 22							17 22							18 22		
Cambridge	d	15 04	15 28	15 44				16 04		16 28	16 44				17 04	17 28		17 44		18 04	
Foxton	d			15 53							16 53							17 53			
Shepreth	d			15 55							16 55							17 55			
Meldreth	d			15 59							16 59							17 59			
Royston	d	15 18	15 42	16a04				16 18		16 42	17a04				17 18	17 42		18a04		18 18	
Ashwell & Morden	d		15 47							16 47						17 47					
Baldock	d	15 26	15 51					16 26		16 51					17 26	17 51				18 26	
Letchworth Garden City	d	15 29	15 54					16 29		16 54					17 29	17 54				18 29	
Hitchin	d	15 33	15 58		16 28		←	16 33		16 58		17 28		←	17 33	17 58			18 28	18 33	
Stevenage	d	15 38	16 04		16 35	16 20	16 35	16 38	16 51	17 04		17 33	17 23	17 33	17 38	18 04	18 11		18 33	18 38	18 42
Hertford North	a				→							→									
Knebworth	d																				
Welwyn North	d																				
Welwyn Garden City	d																				
Hatfield	d																				
Potters Bar	d																				
Finsbury Park	d	16 12	16 32				17 05	17 11		17 32				18 01	18 12	18 32			19 02	19 07	
London Kings Cross	a	16 19	16 40			17 06	17 14	17 18	17 33	17 40			18 06	18 09	18 19	18 40	18 49		19 12	19 15	19 20

		FC	FC	FC	GR	FC	GR	FC	FC	FC	FC	GR	FC	GR	FC	GR	FC	FC	FC	GR	FC	FC
Peterborough	d			18 45	18 54		19 01			19 42		19 47		20 02		20 20			20 45	20 48		
Huntingdon	d			18 59						19 59									20 59			
St Neots	d			19 06						20 06									21 06			
Sandy	d			19 14						20 14									21 14			
Biggleswade	d			19 17						20 17									21 17			
Arlesey	d			19 22						20 22									21 22			
Cambridge	d	18 28	18 44					19 04	19 28		19 44				20 04		20 28	20 44				21 04
Foxton	d		18 53								19 53							20 53				
Shepreth	d		18 55								19 55							20 55				
Meldreth	d		18 59								19 59							20 59				
Royston	d	18 42	19a04					19 18	19 42		20a04				20 18		20 42	21a04				21 18
Ashwell & Morden	d	18 47							19 47								20 47					
Baldock	d	18 51						19 26	19 51						20 26		20 51					21 26
Letchworth Garden City	d	18 54						19 29	19 54						20 29		20 54					21 29
Hitchin	d	18 58		19 28		←		19 33	19 58	20 28			←		20 33		20 58		21 28		←	21 33
Stevenage	d	19 04		19 33	19 25	19 33	19 38	19 38	20 04	20 33		20 20	20 33	20 35	20 38	20 53	21 04		21 33	21 21	21 33	21 38
Hertford North	a			→						→									→			
Knebworth	d																					
Welwyn North	d																					
Welwyn Garden City	d																					
Hatfield	d																					
Potters Bar	d																					
Finsbury Park	d	19 32				20 01		20 14	20 32				21 01		21 12		21 32				22 01	22 11
London Kings Cross	a	19 40			20 06	20 09	20 15	20 21	20 40			21 06	21 09	21 14	21 19	21 32	21 40			22 06	22 09	22 18

		GR	FC	GR	FC	FC	GR	FC	FC	FC	FC	FC
Peterborough	d	21 18		21 37		21 45	22 04				22 50	
Huntingdon	d					21 59					23 04	
St Neots	d					22 06					23 11	
Sandy	d					22 14					23 19	
Biggleswade	d					22 17					23 22	
Arlesey	d					22 22					23 27	
Cambridge	d		21 28		21 44			22 04	22 28	22 44		23 25
Foxton	d				21 53					22 53		23 35
Shepreth	d				21 55					22 55		23 37
Meldreth	d				21 59					22 59		23 40
Royston	d		21 42		22a04			22 18	22 42	23a04		23 44
Ashwell & Morden	d		21 47						22 47			
Baldock	d		21 51					22 26	22 51			
Letchworth Garden City	d		21 54					22 29	22 54			23 54
Hitchin	d		21 58			22 28		22 33	22 58		23 34	23 58
Stevenage	d	21 49	22 04	22 08		22 33	22 36	22 38	23 04		23 40	00 03
Hertford North	a											
Knebworth	d											
Welwyn North	d											
Welwyn Garden City	d											
Hatfield	d											
Potters Bar	d											
Finsbury Park	d		22 32			23 01		23 11	23 32		00 09	00 30
London Kings Cross	a	22 29	22 40	22 46		23 09	23 15	23 18	23 40		00 17	00 42

A The Flying Scotsman

Table 25

Sundays from 12 September

Peterborough, Cambridge and Stevenage - London

		FC	FC	FC	FC	FC	FC	FC	FC	FC	FC	FC	FC	FC	FC	FC	FC	FC	FC	FC	FC	FC	FC	FC
Peterborough	d		22p45					04 15						05 27							06 27	07 27		
Huntingdon	d		22p59					04 55						06 07							07 07	08 07		
St Neots	d		23p06					05 25						06 37							07 37	08 37		
Sandy	d		23p14					05 45						06 57							07 57	08 57		
Biggleswade	d		23p17					05 55						07 07							08 07	09a07		
Arlesey	d		23p22					06 15						07 27							08 27			
Cambridge	d			23p10		06 28				07 20					07 55		08 15							
Foxton	d			23p19						07 30					08 05									
Shepreth	d			23p22						07 32					08 07									
Meldreth	d			23p25						07 35					08 10									
Royston	d			23p29		06 43				07 39					08 15		08 29							
Ashwell & Morden	d			23p33						07 44					08 20									
Baldock	d			23p38		06 51				07 49					08 25		08 37							
Letchworth Garden City	d			23p41		06a55				07a54		07 00			08a30		08a41		08 00				08 35	
Hitchin	d		23p31	23p45	06 10			06 33				07 15		07 45					08 15		08 45		08 50	
Stevenage	d	23p29	23p34	23p50	06a30		06 39	06a53	07 08		07 29	07a35	07 40	08a05		08 10		08 29	08a35	08 40	09a05		09a10	09 15
Hertford North	a	23p42									07 42							08 42						
Knebworth	d			23p53			06 43						07 43			08 13				08 43				09 18
Welwyn North	d			23p57			06 47						07 47			08 17				08 47				09 22
Welwyn Garden City	d			00 01			06 50						07 50			08 20				08 50				09 25
Hatfield	d			00 04			06 53						07 54			08 24				08 54				09 29
Potters Bar	d			00 10			06 59						08 00			08 30				09 00				09 35
Finsbury Park	d	00 17	00 01	00s27			07s11		07s40		08 17		08 11			08 42		09 17		09 11				09 44
London Kings Cross	a	00 25	00 09	00 35			07 19		07 48		08 27		08 23			08 49		09 25		09 18				09 51

		FC	FC	FC	FC	FC	FC	FC	FC	FC	FC	GR	FC	FC	FC	FC	GR	FC	FC	FC	FC	FC
Peterborough	d				08 45	09 14				09 45		10 24			10 45		11 25			11 42		
Huntingdon	d				08 59	09 28				09 59					10 59					11 59		
St Neots	d				09 06	09 35				10 06					11 06					12 06		
Sandy	d				09 14					10 14					11 14					12 14		
Biggleswade	d				09 17	09 43				10 17					11 17					12 17		
Arlesey	d				09 22					10 22					11 22					12 22		
Cambridge	d						08 55	09 28			09 55		10 28			10 55		11 28			11 55	12 28
Foxton	d						09 05				10 05					11 05					12 05	
Shepreth	d						09 07				10 07					11 07					12 07	
Meldreth	d						09 10				10 10					11 10					12 10	
Royston	d						09 15	09 43			10 15		10 43			11 15		11 43			12 15	12 43
Ashwell & Morden	d						09 20				10 20					11 20					12 20	
Baldock	d						09 25	09 51			10 25		10 51			11 25		11 51			12 25	12 51
Letchworth Garden City	d	08 46					09 29	09 54			10 29		10 54			11 29		11 54			12 29	12 54
Hitchin	d	09 01			09 28		09 33	09 58		10 28	10 33		10 58		11 28	11 33		11 58		12 28	12 33	12 58
Stevenage	d	09a21	09 28	09 29	09 33		09 39	10 03	10 29	10 33	10 39	10 55	11 03	11 29	11 33	11 39	11 55	12 03	12 29	12 33	12 39	13 03
Hertford North	a			09 42					10 42					11 42					12 42			
Knebworth	d						09 43				10 43					11 43					12 43	
Welwyn North	d						09 47				10 47					11 47					12 47	
Welwyn Garden City	d						09 50				10 50					11 50					12 50	
Hatfield	d						09 53				10 53					11 53					12 53	
Potters Bar	d						09 59				10 59					11 59					12 59	
Finsbury Park	d		09 47	10 17	09 51		10 11	10 21	11 17	10 51	11 11		11 21	12 17	11 51	12 11		12 21	13 17	12 51	13 11	13 21
London Kings Cross	a		09 56	10 25	10 00	10 15	10 19	10 30	11 25	11 00	11 19	11 28	11 30	12 25	12 00	12 19	12 23	12 30	13 25	13 00	13 19	13 30

		FC	FC	GR	FC	GR	FC	FC	FC	FC	GR	FC	FC	FC	FC	FC	GR	FC	FC	FC
Peterborough	d		12 42	13 06				13 42					14 45			15 44	15 47			
Huntingdon	d		12 59					13 59					14 59			15 59				
St Neots	d		13 06					14 06					15 06			16 06				
Sandy	d		13 14					14 14					15 14			16 14				
Biggleswade	d		13 17					14 17					15 17			16 17				
Arlesey	d		13 22					14 22					15 22			16 22				
Cambridge	d				12 55				13 55	14 28				14 55	15 28					15 55
Foxton	d				13 05				14 05					15 05						16 05
Shepreth	d				13 07				14 07					15 07						16 07
Meldreth	d				13 10				14 10					15 10						16 10
Royston	d				13 15				14 15	14 43				15 15	15 43					16 15
Ashwell & Morden	d				13 20				14 20					15 20						16 20
Baldock	d				13 25				14 25	14 51				15 25	15 51					16 25
Letchworth Garden City	d				13 29				14 29	14 54				15 29	15 54					16 29
Hitchin	d		13 28		13 33			14 28	14 33	14 58			15 28	15 33	15 58	16 28			←	16 33
Stevenage	d	13 29	13 33	13 36	13 39	14 16	14 29	14 33	14 39	15 03	15 28	15 29	15 33	15 39	16 03	16 33	16 18	16 29	16 33	16 39
Hertford North	a	13 42					14 42					15 42				→		16 42		
Knebworth	d				13 43				14 43					15 43						16 43
Welwyn North	d				13 47				14 47					15 47						16 47
Welwyn Garden City	d				13 50				14 50					15 50						16 50
Hatfield	d				13 53				14 53					15 53						16 53
Potters Bar	d				13 59				14 59					15 59						16 59
Finsbury Park	d	14 17	13 51		14 11		15 17	14 51	15 11	15 21		16 17	15 51	16 11	16 21			17 17	16 52	17 11
London Kings Cross	a	14 25	14 00	14 04	14 19	14 44	15 25	15 00	15 19	15 30	15 55	16 25	16 00	16 19	16 30		16 46	17 25	17 00	17 19

Table 25

Sundays
from 12 September

Peterborough, Cambridge and Stevenage - London

		GR	FC	FC	GR	FC	FC	FC		FC	GR	FC	FC	FC	GR	FC	GR	FC		FC	GR	FC	FC	FC	FC
					A																				
Peterborough 8	d	16 18		16 45	16 51						17 40		17 45			18 45					18 51				
Huntingdon	d			16 59									17 59			18 59									
St Neots	d			17 06									18 06			19 06									
Sandy	d			17 14									18 14			19 14									
Biggleswade	d			17 17									18 17			19 17									
Arlesey	d			17 22									18 22			19 22									
Cambridge	d		16 28					16 55		17 28				17 55				18 28		18 45				18 55	19 28
Foxton	d							17 05						18 05										19 05	
Shepreth	d							17 07						18 07										19 07	
Meldreth	d							17 10						18 10										19 10	
Royston	d		16 43					17 15		17 43				18 15				18 43		18 58				19 15	19 43
Ashwell & Morden	d							17 20						18 20										19 20	
Baldock	d		16 51					17 25		17 51				18 25				18 51						19 25	19 51
Letchworth Garden City	d		16 54					17 29		17 54				18 29				18 54						19 29	19 54
Hitchin 4	d		16 58	17 28			←	17 33		17 58			18 28	18 33		19 28		18 58					←	19 33	19 58
Stevenage 4	d	16 48	17 03	17 33	17 21	17 29	17 33	17 39		18 03	18 10	18 29	18 33	18 39	18 42	19 33	19 02	19 03			19 21	19 29	19 33	19 39	20 03
Hertford North	a			→		17 42						18 42				→						19 42			
Knebworth	d							17 43						18 43										19 43	
Welwyn North	d							17 47						18 47										19 47	
Welwyn Garden City 4	d							17 50						18 50										19 50	
Hatfield	d							17 53						18 53										19 53	
Potters Bar	d							17 59						18 59										19 59	
Finsbury Park ⊖	d		17 21			18 17	17 51	18 11		18 21		19 17	18 51	19 11				19 21				20 17	19 51	20 11	20 21
London Kings Cross 15 ⊖	a	17 17	17 30		17 49	18 25	18 00	18 19		18 30	18 37	19 25	19 00	19 19	19 14		19 34	19 29		19 35	19 48	20 25	20 00	20 19	20 30

		GR	FC	GR		FC	FC	GR	FC	GR	FC	FC	HT	GR		FC	FC	FC	GR	FC	GR	FC	FC	GR	
Peterborough 8	d	19 34	19 42	19 45				20 02		20 20		20 45		20 48					21 18		21 37		21 45	22 04	
Huntingdon	d		19 59									20 59											21 59		
St Neots	d		20 06									21 06											22 06		
Sandy	d		20 14									21 14											22 14		
Biggleswade	d		20 17									21 17											22 17		
Arlesey	d		20 22									21 22											22 22		
Cambridge	d								19 55		20 28							20 55		21 28					
Foxton	d								20 05									21 05							
Shepreth	d								20 07									21 07							
Meldreth	d								20 10									21 10							
Royston	d								20 15		20 43							21 15		21 43					
Ashwell & Morden	d								20 20									21 20							
Baldock	d								20 25		20 51							21 25		21 51					
Letchworth Garden City	d								20 29		20 54							21 29		21 54					
Hitchin 4	d		20 28				←		20 33		20 58	21 28					←	21 33		21 58			22 28		
Stevenage 4	d	20 08	20 33	20 18		20 29	20 33	20 33	20 39	20 52	21 03	21 33	21s10	21 20		21 29	21 33	21 39	21 48	22 03	22 07	22 29	22 33	22 34	
Hertford North	a		→			20 42						→				21 42						22 42			
Knebworth	d								20 43									21 43							
Welwyn North	d								20 47									21 47							
Welwyn Garden City 4	d								20 50									21 50							
Hatfield	d								20 53									21 53							
Potters Bar	d								20 59									21 59							
Finsbury Park ⊖	d					21 17	20 51		21 11		21 21					22 17	21 51	22 11		22 21		23 17	22 51		
London Kings Cross 15 ⊖	a	20 34		20 43		21 25	21 00	21 02	21 19	21 20	21 30		21 35	21 47		22 25	22 00	22 19	22 16	22 30	22 34	23 27	23 00	23 04	

		FC	FC	FC	FC
Peterborough 8	d			22 51	
Huntingdon	d			23 05	
St Neots	d			23 12	
Sandy	d			23 20	
Biggleswade	d			23 23	
Arlesey	d			23 28	
Cambridge	d	21 55			23 15
Foxton	d	22 05			
Shepreth	d	22 07			
Meldreth	d	22 10			
Royston	d	22 15			23 29
Ashwell & Morden	d	22 20			
Baldock	d	22 25			
Letchworth Garden City	d	22 29			23 39
Hitchin 4	d	22 33		23 34	23 48
Stevenage 4	d	22 39	23 29	23 39	23 51
Hertford North	a		23 42		
Knebworth	d	22 43			23 51
Welwyn North	d	22 47			23 55
Welwyn Garden City 4	d	22 50			23 58
Hatfield	d	22 53			00 01
Potters Bar	d	22 59			00 07
Finsbury Park ⊖	d	23 11	00 17	00 05	00 20
London Kings Cross 15 ⊖	a	23 19	00 27	00 14	00 32

A The Flying Scotsman

Route Diagram for Table 26

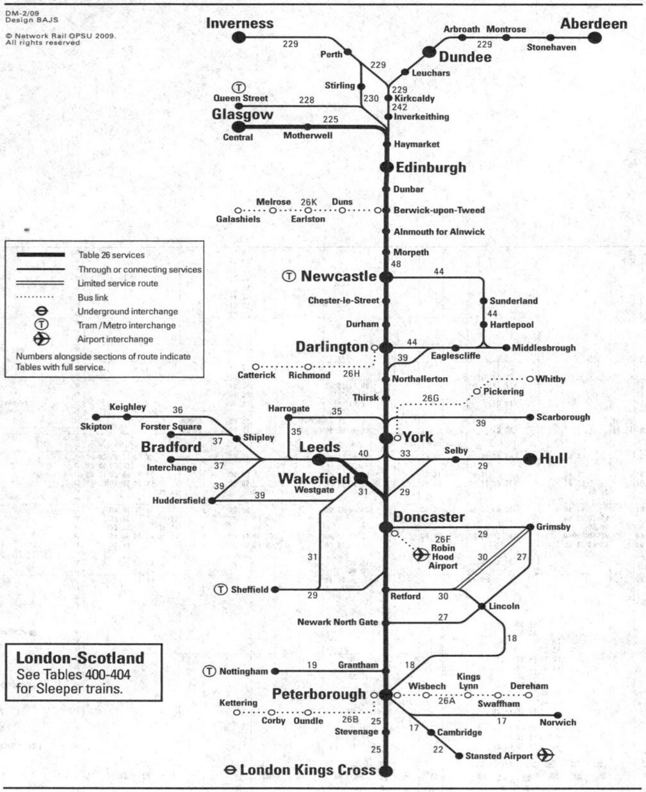

London - Humberside, Yorkshire, North East England and Scotland

		GR MO A	GR MO B	GR MO	GR MX	GR MX C	GR MX D	NT	TP ◇	GR	NT	GR	GR
London Kings Cross 15 ⊖	d	21p45	22p00		22p00					06 00			
Stevenage 4	d									06 19			
Peterborough 8	a	22p43	22p44		22p46					06 50			
Norwich	d												
Peterborough 8	d	22p45	22p45		22p47					06 51			
Grantham 7	a				23p08					07 10			
	d				23p08					07 10			
Newark North Gate 7	a				23p19					07 22			
	d				23p19					07 22			
Retford 10	d									07 37			
Doncaster 7	a	23p42	23p42		23p49					07 51			
Selby	a												
Hull	a												
Wakefield Westgate 7	a									08 10			
Leeds 10	a									08 32			
Shipley	a												
Bradford Forster Square	a												
Keighley	a												
Skipton	a												
Sheffield 7	d												
Doncaster 7	d	23p45	23p45		23p49								06 15
York 8	a	00 39	00 39		00 41								06 35
Scarborough	a												
Leeds 10	d												
York 8	d			00 50		00 50	00 50		05 54				06 37
Thirsk	d								06 10				
Northallerton	d								06 18				
Darlington 7	a			01s32		01s26	01s41		06 29				07 05
Eaglescliffe	a												
Middlesbrough	a								07 01				
Darlington 7	d			01s34		01s28	01s43				06 15		07 06
Durham	d			01s51		01s45	02s00				06 36		07 23
Chester-le-Street	d										06 43		
Newcastle 8	a			02 23		02 18	02 18				06 55		07 39
Hartlepool	a												
Sunderland	a												
Newcastle 8	d							05 45				06 25	07 41
Morpeth	d							06 05				06 38	
Alnmouth for Alnwick	d							06a22				06 52	08 07
Berwick-upon-Tweed	d											07 14	08 29
Dunbar	d											07 38	08 52
Edinburgh 10	a											08 05	09 19
Edinburgh	d											08 08	09 22
Haymarket	d											08 13	09 27
Motherwell	a											08 59	10 05
Glasgow Central 15	a											09 22	10 30
Stirling	a												
Perth	a												
Inverness	a												
Inverkeithing	a												
Kirkcaldy	a												
Leuchars 8	a												
Dundee	a												
Arbroath	a												
Montrose	a												
Stonehaven	a												
Aberdeen	a												

A 19 July until 6 September
B until 12 July and from 13 September
C MX until 6 July and from 31 August. TO from 13 July until 24 August.
D WTHFO from 7 July until 27 August

Table 26

Mondays to Fridays

London - Humberside, Yorkshire, North East England and Scotland

		NT	TP ◇	XC ◇	TP ◇	NT	GR	TP ◇	NT	NT	XC ◇	GR	GR	EM ◇	TP ◇	XC ◇	GR	GR	HT BHX ◇	TP ◇	TP ◇	NT	XC ◇
London Kings Cross 15 ⊖	d											06 15	06 35				07 00	07 10	07 20				
Stevenage 4	d											06 34					07 19	07 29	07u44				
Peterborough 8	a											07 05	07 21				07 51	08 00					
Norwich	d													05 50									
Peterborough 8	d											07 07	07 21	07 27			07 51	08 01					
Grantham 7	a											07 26	07 40	07 58					08 29				
	d											07 26	07 40						08 30				
Newark North Gate 7	a											07 38						08 28					
	d											07 38						08 28					
Retford 10	d											07 53							08 51				
Doncaster 7	a											08 08	08 12					08 56	09 05				
Selby	a																		09 21				
Hull	a																		10 03				
Wakefield Westgate 7	a												08 31					09 17					
Leeds 10	a												08 50					09 35					
Shipley	a																						
Bradford Forster Square	a																						
Keighley	a																						
Skipton	a																						
Sheffield 7	d			06 40							07 12					07 54							08 21
Doncaster 7	d			07 06								08 08				08 27							
York 8	a			07 27								08 31				08 47	08 56						
Scarborough	a																						
Leeds 10	d		06 35				07 10	07 50			07 57									08 27	08 57		09 07
York 8	d		07 06	07 29	07 32		07 37	08 23			08 27	08 35			08 42	08 50	08 58			09e03	09 26		09 37
Thirsk	d		07 22		07 54			08 39													09 46		
Northallerton	d		07 30		08 02			08 49							09 03					09 24	09 55		
Darlington 7	a		07 41	07 55			08 05				08 55	09 02			09 14	09 20	09 26			09 36			10 04
Eaglescliffe	a																						
Middlesbrough	a				08 34			09 20													10 30		
Darlington 7	d	07 20	07 42	07 56			08 05		08 15		08 56	09 03			09 15	09 22	09 28			09 37			10 05
Durham	d	07 41	07 59	08 16			08 23		08 36		09 13	09 20			09 31	09 38				09 54			10 22
Chester-le-Street	d	07 48	08 05						08 43							09 45							
Newcastle 8	a	08 02	08 17	08 37			08 39		09 00		09 26	09 36			09 48	09 55	09 59			10 09			10 36
Hartlepool	a																						
Sunderland	a																						
Newcastle 8	d					07 58	08 41			09 00	09 29	09 39					10 04					10 15	10 39
Morpeth	d					08a20	08 55			09a20	09 42											10a35	
Alnmouth for Alnwick	d										09 56												
Berwick-upon-Tweed	d						09 30					10 22					10 47						11 21
Dunbar	d						09 53																11 44
Edinburgh 10	a						10 20				10 57	11 08					11 32						12 11
Edinburgh	d						10 27										11 38						
Haymarket	d						10 32										11 43						
Motherwell	a																12 25						
Glasgow Central 15	a																12 47						
Stirling	a																						
Perth	a																						
Inverness	a																						
Inverkeithing	a						10 47																
Kirkcaldy	a						11 04																
Leuchars 8	a						11 28																
Dundee	a						11 43																
Arbroath	a						12 01																
Montrose	a						12 17																
Stonehaven	a						12 40																
Aberdeen	a						13 03																

e arr. 0857

London - Humberside, Yorkshire, North East England and Scotland

		GR	GR	XC	GR	GR	GC	TP	NT	XC	GR	GR	EM	XC	TP	GR	GR	TP	NT	XC	GR	GR
				◇				◇		◇			◇	◇	◇			◇		◇		
London Kings Cross 15 ⊖	d	07 30	07 35		08 00	08 10	08 19				08 30	08 40				09 00	09 10				09 30	09 35
Stevenage 4	d	07 50	07 56								08 49										09 49	09 54
Peterborough 8	a	08 21			08 46	09 00					09 20	09 27				09 45	09 57				10 20	10 26
Norwich	d												07 57									
Peterborough 8	d	08 26			08 46	09 01					09 21	09 27	09 27			09 46	09 57				10 21	10 27
Grantham 7	a	08 45										09 46	09 57									10 46
	d	08 45										09 46										10 46
Newark North Gate 7	a										09 48										10 48	
	d										09 48										10 48	
Retford 10	d											10 08										
Doncaster 7	a	09 16										10 23				10 34					11 12	11 17
Selby	a																					
Hull	a																					
Wakefield Westgate 7	a		09 30			10 03						10 50					10 57					11 36
Leeds 10	a		09 46			10 23						11 09					11 18					11 55
Shipley	a																					
Bradford Forster Square	a																					
Keighley	a																					
Skipton	a																					
Sheffield 7	d			08 54						09 21				09 54						10 21		
Doncaster 7	d	09 17		09 22										10 17		10 35					11 12	
York 8	a	09 40		09 48	09 53		10 43				10 34			10 40		10 58					11 37	
Scarborough	a																					
Leeds 10	d							09 27		10 05					10 27			10 57		11 05		
York 8	d	09 44		09 51	09 55		10 46	10 00		10 31	10 36			10 43	10 54	11 05		11 26		11 32	11 41	
Thirsk	d						11 02											11 46				
Northallerton	d						11 10	10 21							11 15			11 55			12 00	
Darlington 7	a	10 12		10 17	10 22			10 32		10 59	11 05			11 12	11 27	11 33				11 58	12 13	
Eaglescliffe	a						11 28															
Middlesbrough	a																	12 28				
Darlington 7	d	10 12		10 19	10 23			10 33		11 01	11 06			11 14	11 28	11 33				12 00	12 13	
Durham	d			10 35	10 40			10 51		11 18	11 23			11 30	11 45					12 23	12 31	
Chester-le-Street	d							10 57														
Newcastle 8	a	10 44		10 52	10 57			11 08		11 32	11 41			11 49	11 59	12 03				12 36	12 49	
Hartlepool	a						11 47															
Sunderland	a						12 24															
Newcastle 8	d				10 59				11 15	11 34						12 05			12 15	12 40		
Morpeth	d								11a35										12a36			
Alnmouth for Alnwick	d									12 01						12 31						
Berwick-upon-Tweed	d				11 42											12 53				13 22		
Dunbar	d																			13 45		
Edinburgh 10	a				12 31					13 05						13 37				14 14		
Edinburgh	d															13 40						
Haymarket	d															13 45						
Motherwell	a															14 26						
Glasgow Central 15	a															14 47						
Stirling	a																					
Perth	a																					
Inverness	a																					
Inverkeithing	a																					
Kirkcaldy	a																					
Leuchars 3	a																					
Dundee	a																					
Arbroath	a																					
Montrose	a																					
Stonehaven	a																					
Aberdeen	a																					

London - Humberside, Yorkshire, North East England and Scotland

		HT	EM	XC	GR	GR	TP	TP	NT	GR	GR	EM	GC	XC	XC	GR	GR	GC	TP	TP	NT	XC
		◇	◇	◇	A		◇	◇		B		◇		◇	◇				◇	◇		◇
London Kings Cross 15 ⊖	d	09 48			10 00	10 10				10 30	10 35		10 50			11 00	11 10	11 27				
Stevenage 4	d	10u09																				
Peterborough 8	a				10 45	10 56				11 16	11 22					11 46	11 56					
Norwich	d		08 57									09 57										
Peterborough 8	d		10 30		10 45	10 56				11 17	11 23	11 27				11 46	11 58					
Grantham 7	a	10 54	11 12			11 16					11 42	11 55					12 19					
	d	10 55				11 16					11 42						12 19					
Newark North Gate 7	a					11 28					11 55						12 30					
	d					11 28					11 55						12 30					
Retford 10	d	11 17				11 43																
Doncaster 7	a	11 32				11 58					12 18		12 28				12 58					
Selby	a	11 51																				
Hull	a	12 32																				
Wakefield Westgate 7	a					12 16					12 36						13 17					
Leeds 10	a					12 36					12 54						13 41					
Shipley	a																					
Bradford Forster Square	a																					
Keighley	a																					
Skipton	a																					
Sheffield 7	d			10 54										11 21	11 54							12 21
Doncaster 7	d			11 17											12 17							
York 8	a			11 45	11 53					12 25					12 45	12 51		13 19				
Scarborough	a																					
Leeds 10	d						11 27	11 57						12 05					12 27	12 57		13 05
York 8	d			11 47	11 55		12e01	12 26		12 29				12 34	12 45	12 52		13 22	12h59	13 26		13 32
Thirsk	d							12 46										13 38		13 46		
Northallerton	d						12 22	12 55										13 47	13 20	13 55		
Darlington 7	a			12 20	12 25		12 33							13 00	13 13	13 20			13 31			14 00
Eaglescliffe	a																	14 05				
Middlesbrough	a							13 30												14 28		
Darlington 7	d			12 21	12 26		12 34							13 02	13 15	13 20			13 32			14 02
Durham	d			12 45			12 50							13 19	13 31				13 48			14 19
Chester-le-Street	d			12 51															13 54			
Newcastle 8	a			13 01	12 55		13 06			13 22				13 33	13 46	13 50			14 07			14 37
Hartlepool	a																	14 24				
Sunderland	a																	14 53				
Newcastle 8	d				12 57				13 03	13 27				13 35		13 51					14 15	14 40
Morpeth	d								13a23												14a34	
Alnmouth for Alnwick	d													14 01								
Berwick-upon-Tweed	d															14 34						15 22
Dunbar	d																					15 45
Edinburgh 10	a				14 25					14 53				15 10		15 19						16 16
Edinburgh	d									15 00						15 22						
Haymarket	d									15 04												
Motherwell	a															16 06						
Glasgow Central 15	a															16 28						
Stirling	a																					
Perth	a																					
Inverness	a																					
Inverkeithing	a									15 18												
Kirkcaldy	a									15 35												
Leuchars 3	a									16 00												
Dundee	a									16 18												
Arbroath	a									16 35												
Montrose	a									16 51												
Stonehaven	a									17 14												
Aberdeen	a									17 37												

A The Flying Scotsman
B The Northern Lights

e arr. 1152

h arr. 1252

London - Humberside, Yorkshire, North East England and Scotland

		GR	EM	GR	HT	XC	GR	GR	TP	TP	NT	XC	GR	GR	EM	XC	GR	GR	TP	TP	NT
							A														
London Kings Cross 15 ⊖	d	11 30		11 35	11 48		12 00	12 10					12 30	12 35			13 00	13 10			
Stevenage 4	d	11 50		11 54				12 29						12 54							
Peterborough 8	a	12 21		12 27			12 46	13 00					13 16				13 45	13 56			
Norwich	d		10 57												11 57						
Peterborough 8	d	12 21	12 25	12 27			12 47	13 01					13 17		13 26		13 46	13 58			
Grantham 7	a		12 58	12 46	12 53			13 20						13 41	13 56			14 17			
	d			12 46	12 54			13 20						13 41				14 17			
Newark North Gate 7	a	12 50		12 58										13 55				14 29			
	d	12 50		12 58										13 55				14 29			
Retford 10	d				13 16			13 42													
Doncaster 7	a	13 14			13 29			13 57					14 06	14 20			14 33	14 53			
Selby	a				13 44																
Hull	a				14 25																
Wakefield Westgate 7	a			13 37				14 14						14 39				15 14			
Leeds 10	a			13 55				14 35						15 01				15 35			
Shipley	a																				
Bradford Forster Square	a																				
Keighley	a																				
Skipton	a																				
Sheffield 7	d					12 54						13 21				13 54					
Doncaster 7	d	13 15				13 24							14 07			14 19	14 34				
York 8	a	13 39				13 46	13 58						14 34			14 43	14 57				
Scarborough	a																				
Leeds 10	d								13 27	13 57		14 06							14 27	14 57	
York 8	d	13 42				13 50	14 04		13 54	14 26		14 33	14 36			14 48	15 00		14 54	15 26	
Thirsk	d									14 46										15 46	
Northallerton	d								14 16	14 55			14 58						15 23	15 55	
Darlington 7	a	14 10				14 16			14 27			14 58	15 11			15 16	15 27		15 34		
Eaglescliffe	a																				
Middlesbrough	a									15 30										16 30	
Darlington 7	d	14 10				14 18			14 34			15 00	15 11			15 18	15 28		15 34		
Durham	d	14 28				14 35			14 50			15 16	15 29			15 35			15 50		
Chester-le-Street	d					14 42													15 57		
Newcastle 8	a	14 46				14 51	14 58		15 04			15 31	15 47			15 53	15 57		16 12		
Hartlepool	a																				
Sunderland	a																				
Newcastle 8	d						15 00				15 15	15 35					15 59				16 15
Morpeth	d										15a35	15 48									16a36
Alnmouth for Alnwick	d											16 02									
Berwick-upon-Tweed	d																16 42				
Dunbar	d																				
Edinburgh 10	a						16 27					17 04					17 33				
Edinburgh	d						16 33										17 40				
Haymarket	d						16 38										17 45				
Motherwell	a																18 23				
Glasgow Central 15	a																18 41				
Stirling	a						17 19														
Perth	a						18 00														
Inverness	a						20 08														
Inverkeithing	a																				
Kirkcaldy	a																				
Leuchars 3	a																				
Dundee	a																				
Arbroath	a																				
Montrose	a																				
Stonehaven	a																				
Aberdeen	a																				

A The Highland Chieftain

London - Humberside, Yorkshire, North East England and Scotland

		GR	HT	GR	EM	XC	XC	GR	GR	GC	GR	EM	GR	TP	NT	XC	XC	GR	GR	TP	NT	NT	XC
						A																	A
London Kings Cross 15 ⊖	d	13 30	13 33	13 35				14 00	14 10	14 20	14 30		14 35					15 00	15 10				
Stevenage 4	d												14 54										
Peterborough 8	a			14 24					14 56		15 16								15 56				
Norwich	d				12 57							13 57											
Peterborough 8	d			14 25	14 26				14 56		15 17	15 26							15 57				
Grantham 7	a		14 34	14 44	14 56				15 15			15 55							16 18				
	d		14 35	14 44					15 15										16 18				
Newark North Gate 7	a			14 56					15 27										16 29				
	d			14 58					15 27										16 29				
Retford 10	d	14 48	14 56																16 45				
Doncaster 7	a	15 02	15 11	15 22				15 29	15 52	16 00			16 08						17 00				
Selby	a		15 27																				
Hull	a		16 10																				
Wakefield Westgate 7	a			15 51					16 15				16 30						17 18				
Leeds 10	a			16 09					16 35				16 48						17 36				
Shipley	a																						
Bradford Forster Square	a																						
Keighley	a																						
Skipton	a																						
Sheffield 7	d					14 21	14 54									15 21	15 54						16 21
Doncaster 7	d	15 03					15 18	15 30									16 17						
York 8	a	15 25					15 40	15 53			16 21						16 39	16 44					
Scarborough	a																						
Leeds 10	d					15 07								15 57		16 05				16 27			17 07
York 8	d	15 28				15 34	15 44	15 55			16 23			16 26		16 32	16 43	16 46		16h58			17 33
Thirsk	d													16 46						17 14			
Northallerton	d													16 55						17 22			
Darlington 7	a	16 01				16 06	16 11	16 23			16 50					16 57	17 10	17 14		17 37			17 59
Eaglescliffe	a																						
Middlesbrough	a													17 30									
Darlington 7	d	16 01				16 07	16 13	16 23			16 51					16 59	17 12	17 15		17 38			18 02
Durham	d					16 25	16 30				17 08					17 15	17g33			17 55			18 18
Chester-le-Street	d																17 39			18 01			
Newcastle 8	a	16 31				16 37	16 46	16 53			17 26					17 34	17 50	17 44		18 15			18 36
Hartlepool	a																						
Sunderland	a																						
Newcastle 8	d	16 32				16 40		16 54							17 15	17 37		17 46			17 50	18 28	18 43
Morpeth	d														17 36						18a11	18a49	
Alnmouth for Alnwick	d	16 58													18a20	18 02							
Berwick-upon-Tweed	d					17 26		17 38										18 29					19 25
Dunbar	d					17 49																	19 48
Edinburgh 10	a	18 03				18 13		18 26								19 03		19 13					20 12
Edinburgh	d					18 16		18 30								19 07		19 18					20 15
Haymarket	d					18 21		18 35								19 12		19 22					20 20
Motherwell	a															19 55		19 59					
Glasgow Central 15	a															20 26		20 20					
Stirling	a																						
Perth	a																						
Inverness	a																						
Inverkeithing	a					18 36		18 54															20 33
Kirkcaldy	a					18 58		19 11															20 49
Leuchars 3	a					19 29		19 38															21 21
Dundee	a					19 44		19 53															21 40
Arbroath	a					20 01		20 10															
Montrose	a					20 15		20 26															
Stonehaven	a					20 35		20 49															
Aberdeen	a					20 55		21 12															

A to Dunbar

g arr. 1728

h arr. 1652

London - Humberside, Yorkshire, North East England and Scotland

Station		GR	GR	EM	XC	GR	HT	GR	TP	TP	XC	GR	GR	GR	EM	GC	GR	GR	GR	TP	XC	XC	GR
											A	FX	FO			B			C		FX	FO	
London Kings Cross 15 ⊖	d	15 30	15 35			16 00	15 05	16 10				16 30	16 30	16 35		16 50	17 00	17 03	17 19				17 30
Stevenage 4	d		15 54									16 49	16 49										
Peterborough 8	a	16 16	16 26					16 56						17 24				17 51	18 06				18 16
Norwich	d			14 57											15 52								
Peterborough 8	d	16 17	16 26	16 27				16 56						17 25	17 27			17 51	18 07				18 17
Grantham 7	a		16 45	16 58			17 06	17 15				17 34	17 34		17 58			18 10					
	d		16 45				17 07	17 15				17 34	17 34					18 10					
Newark North Gate 7	a							17 27				17 46	17 46						18 35				
	d							17 27				17 46	17 46						18 35				
Retford 10	d						17 28							18 04									
Doncaster 7	a	17 08	17 19			17 29	17 41					18 09	18 09	18 19				18 41	19 03				
Selby	a						17 59												19 20				
Hull	a						18 40												20 00				
Wakefield Westgate 7	a		17 36					18 04						18 36				19 00					
Leeds 10	a		17 55					18 23						18 55				19 20					
Shipley	a																						
Bradford Forster Square	a																						
Keighley	a																						
Skipton	a																						
Sheffield 7	d				16 54						17 22										17 47	17 47	
Doncaster 7	d	17 09			17 17	17 30						18 10	18 10										
York 8	a	17 31			17 40	17 54						18 33	18 33			18 44	18 51						19 23
Scarborough	a																						
Leeds 10	d								17 12	17 57	18 06									18 27	18 35	18 35	
York 8	d	17 34			17 46	17 58			17c43	18 26	18 33	18 39	18 39			18 47	18 53			18 56	19 01	19 01	19 25
Thirsk	d								18 02	18 46						19 05							
Northallerton	d	17 54							18 10	18 55		19 00	19 00			19 15				19 21			
Darlington 7	a	18 06			18 15	18 27					19 00	19 13	19 13				19 21			19 33	19 38	19 38	19 52
Eaglescliffe	a															19 32							
Middlesbrough	a								18 41	19 30													
Darlington 7	d	18 07			18 17	18 27					19 02	19 13	19 13				19 21			19 34	19 39	19 39	19 53
Durham	d	18 24			18 34						19 19	19 31	19 31							19 50	19 56	19 56	20 10
Chester-le-Street	d																				20 02	20 02	
Newcastle 8	a	18 40			18 50	18 57					19 34	19 49	19 49				19 51			20 09	20 13	20 13	20 26
Hartlepool	a															20 00							
Sunderland	a															20 37							
Newcastle 8	d	18 50				18 59					19 38		19 49				19 53				20 16	20 16	20 29
Morpeth	d																						20 44
Alnmouth for Alnwick	d	19 16									20 06												21 00
Berwick-upon-Tweed	d					19 43																	21 22
Dunbar	d																						21 46
Edinburgh 10	a	20 26				20 28					21 08		21 15				21 21				21 40	21 57	22 14
Edinburgh	d					20 32					21 14												
Haymarket	d					20 37					21 19												
Motherwell	a										22 03												
Glasgow Central 15	a										22 30												
Stirling	a																						
Perth	a																						
Inverness	a																						
Inverkeithing	a					20 51																	
Kirkcaldy	a					21 08																	
Leuchars 3	a					21 33																	
Dundee	a					21 47																	
Arbroath	a					22 05																	
Montrose	a					22 21																	
Stonehaven	a					22 44																	
Aberdeen	a					23 07																	

A to Alnmouth for Alnwick
B The 21st Century Limited
C The Hull Executive
c arr. 1736

Table 26 Mondays to Fridays

London - Humberside, Yorkshire, North East England and Scotland

Station		GR	EM	GR	XC	XC	GR	GR	GR	TP	NT	XC	GR	GR	GR	HT	EM	XC	GR	GR	GR
					A								FX	FO					FX	FO	
London Kings Cross 15 ⊖	d	17 33		17 49			18 00	18 03	18 19				18 30	18 30	18 35	18 50			19 00	19 00	19 03
Stevenage 4	d	17 52											18 50	18 50							
Peterborough 8	a			18 37				18 54	19 06						19 25				19 46	19 46	19 52
Norwich	d		16 57														17 54				
Peterborough 8	d		18 26	18 39				18 54	19 07						19 25		19 31		19 47	19 47	19 53
Grantham 7	a	18 40	18 52	19 04				19 15					19 35	19 35		19 55	20 01				20 12
	d	18 40		19 05				19 15					19 35	19 35		19 56					20 12
Newark North Gate 7	a			19 17					19 34						19 52				20 14	20 14	
	d			19 17					19 34						19 54				20 14	20 14	
Retford 10	d	19 02											19 57	19 57		20 18					
Doncaster 7	a	19 17		19 41			19 28	19 48					20 14	20 14	20 18	20 30			20 38	20 38	20 49
Selby	a															20 46					
Hull	a															21 27					
Wakefield Westgate 7	a	19 34		20 01				20 07							20 36						21 13
Leeds 10	a	19 52		20 21				20 24							20 54						21 34
Shipley	a	20s11																			
Bradford Forster Square	a	20 22																			
Keighley	a							20s57													
Skipton	a							21 13													
Sheffield 7	d				18 21	18 54						19 26						19 54			
Doncaster 7	d					19 20	19 28						20 15	20 15				20 22	20 38	20 38	
York 8	a					19 44	19 51		20 20				20 39	20 39				20 46	21 01	21 01	
Scarborough	a																				
Leeds 10	d				19 05					19 57		20 09									
York 8	d				19b37	19 47	19 53		20 23	20c29		20f37	20 44	20 44				20 51	21 03	21 03	
Thirsk	d									20 45											
Northallerton	d									20 53			21 03	21 03							
Darlington 7	a				20 04	20 12	20 22		20 51			21 07	21 16	21 16				21 20	21 30	21 30	
Eaglescliffe	a																				
Middlesbrough	a									21 25											
Darlington 7	d				20 05	20 14	20 23		20 51			21 09	21 16	21 16				21 22	21 31	21 31	
Durham	d				20 23	20 31			21 09			21 26	21 34	21 34				21 40	21 49	21 49	
Chester-le-Street	d																	21 46			
Newcastle 8	a				20 38	20 48	20 52		21 27			21 39	21 52	21 52				21 55	22 07	22 07	
Hartlepool	a																				
Sunderland	a																				
Newcastle 8	d				20 40		20 54				21 05	21 48		21 53						22 07	
Morpeth	d										21a26									22 22	
Alnmouth for Alnwick	d											22 12								22 38	
Berwick-upon-Tweed	d				21 28		21 37					22 33		22 37						23 00	
Dunbar	d				21 52																
Edinburgh 10	a				22 17		22 23					23 23		23 30						23 53	
Edinburgh	d						22 26														
Haymarket	d						22 30														
Motherwell	a						23 10														
Glasgow Central 15	a						23 33														
Stirling	a																				
Perth	a																				
Inverness	a																				
Inverkeithing	a																				
Kirkcaldy	a																				
Leuchars 3	a																				
Dundee	a																				
Arbroath	a																				
Montrose	a																				
Stonehaven	a																				
Aberdeen	a																				

A to Durham
b arr. 1930
c arr. 2023
f arr. 2031

Table 26

London - Humberside, Yorkshire, North East England and Scotland

		GC	TP	GR FO	GR FX	GR FO	EM	GC	XC	GR	GR MX	GR	HT BHX	GR	XC	GR	GR MX	TP
										A	B					A	B	
London Kings Cross 15 ⊖	d	19 18		19 30	19 33	19 33		19 48		20 00	20 00	20 03	20 30	20 33		21 00	21 00	
Stevenage 4	d															21 20	21 20	
Peterborough 8	a				20 20	20 20				20 46	20 46	20 52		21 20		21 53	21 53	
Norwich	d						18 57											
Peterborough 8	d				20 21	20 21	20 28			20 46	20 46	20 53		21 20		21 54	21 54	
Grantham 7	a				20 41	20 41	20 56					21 12	21 30	21 39				
	d				20 41	20 41						21 12	21 32	21 39				
Newark North Gate 7	a				20 53	20 53						21 24		21 51		22 23	22 23	
	d				20 53	20 53						21 24		21 51		22 23	22 23	
Retford 10	d									21 23	21 23		21 53					
Doncaster 7	a				21 19	21 19		21 29		21 38	21 38	21 53	22 07	22 17		22 47	22 47	
Selby	a												22 29					
Hull	a												23 11					
Wakefield Westgate 7	a				21 37	21 37						22 13		22 35				
Leeds 10	a				21 55	21 55						22 33		22 53				
Shipley	a																	
Bradford Forster Square	a																	
Keighley	a																	
Skipton	a																	
Sheffield 7 ⇌	d								20 54						21 54			
Doncaster 7	d								21 23	21 39	21 39				22 31	22 48	22 48	
York 8	a	21 15		21 21					21 45	22 01	22 01				22 54	23 13	23 13	
Scarborough	a																	
Leeds 10	d		20 45															22 42
York 8	d	21 18	21 14	21 23					21 47	22 03	22 03					23 14	23 14	23g21
Thirsk	d	21 38	21 30															23 35
Northallerton	d	21 47	21 38							22 23	22 23							23 55
Darlington 7	a		21 49	21 53					22 13	22 35	22 50					23 49	00 08	00 06
Eaglescliffe	a	22 05																
Middlesbrough	a																	
Darlington 7	d		21 50	21 54					22 14	22 36	22 51					23 50	00 09	00 08
Durham	d		22 08	22 11					22 31	22 53	23 08					00 07	00 26	00 24
Chester-le-Street	d								22 37									
Newcastle 8 ⇌	a		22 22	22 29					22 51	23 13	23 26					00 41	00 45	00 56
Hartlepool	a	22 27																
Sunderland ⇌	a	22 54																
Newcastle 8 ⇌	d																	
Morpeth	d																	
Alnmouth for Alnwick	d																	
Berwick-upon-Tweed	d																	
Dunbar	d																	
Edinburgh 10	a																	
Edinburgh	d																	
Haymarket	d																	
Motherwell	a																	
Glasgow Central 15	a																	
Stirling	a																	
Perth	a																	
Inverness	a																	
Inverkeithing	a																	
Kirkcaldy	a																	
Leuchars 3	a																	
Dundee	a																	
Arbroath	a																	
Montrose	a																	
Stonehaven	a																	
Aberdeen	a																	

A until 5 July and from 30 August, also Mondays from 12 July until 23 August.
B 6 July until 27 August

g arr. 2312

Table 26

London - Humberside, Yorkshire, North East England and Scotland

		GR	GR	GR MX	GR MTX	GR
				A	B	
London Kings Cross 15 ⊖	d	21 30	22 00			23 30
Stevenage 4	d					
Peterborough 8	a	22 16	22 46			00s23
Norwich	d					
Peterborough 8	d	22 17	22 47			
Grantham 7	a	22 38	23 08			00s44
	d	22 38	23 08			
Newark North Gate 7	a	22 49	23 19			00s56
	d	22 49	23 19			
Retford 10	d	23 05				
Doncaster 7	a	23 24	23 49			01s24
Selby	a					
Hull	a					
Wakefield Westgate 7	a	23 42				
Leeds 10	a	23 59				02 37
Shipley	a					
Bradford Forster Square	a					
Keighley	a					
Skipton	a					
Sheffield 7 ⇌	d					
Doncaster 7	d		23 49			
York 8	a		00 41			
Scarborough	a					
Leeds 10	d					
York 8	d			00 50	00 50	
Thirsk	d					
Northallerton	d					
Darlington 7	a			01s26	01s41	
Eaglescliffe	a					
Middlesbrough	a					
Darlington 7	d			01s28	01s43	
Durham	d			01s45	02s00	
Chester-le-Street	d					
Newcastle 8 ⇌	a			02 18	02 18	
Hartlepool	a					
Sunderland ⇌	a					
Newcastle 8 ⇌	d					
Morpeth	d					
Alnmouth for Alnwick	d					
Berwick-upon-Tweed	d					
Dunbar	d					
Edinburgh 10	a					
Edinburgh	d					
Haymarket	d					
Motherwell	a					
Glasgow Central 15	a					
Stirling	a					
Perth	a					
Inverness	a					
Inverkeithing	a					
Kirkcaldy	a					
Leuchars 3	a					
Dundee	a					
Arbroath	a					
Montrose	a					
Stonehaven	a					
Aberdeen	a					

A until 6 July and from 31 August, also Tuesdays from 13 July until 24 August.
B 7 July until 27 August

Table 26

London - Humberside, Yorkshire, North East England and Scotland

		GR	GR	GR	TP	NT	GR	GR	NT	TP	TP	NT	GR	XC	TP	NT	XC	GR	EM	TP
		■ [1] ⊏	■ [1] A	■ [1] B	◇[1]		■ [1] ⊏	■ [1] ⊏✕		◇[1]	◇[1]		■ [1] ⊏✕	◇[1] ✕	◇[1] ✕		◇[1] ✕	■ [1] ⊏✕	◇	◇[1]
London Kings Cross [15] ⊖	d	22p00																06 15		
Stevenage [4]	d																	06 34		
Peterborough [8]	a	22p46																07 05		
Norwich	d																		05 52	
Peterborough [8]	d	22p47																07 06	07 27	
Grantham [7]	a	23p08																07 25	07 56	
	d	23p08																07 25		
Newark North Gate [7]	a	23p19																07 37		
	d	23p19																07 37		
Retford [10]	d																	07 52		
Doncaster [7]	a	23p49																08 07		
Selby	a																			
Hull	a																			
Wakefield Westgate [7]	a																			
Leeds [10]	a																			
Shipley	a																			
Bradford Forster Square	a																			
Keighley	a																			
Skipton	a																			
Sheffield [7]	d													06 49			07 12			
Doncaster [7]	d	23p49						06 20						07 17				08 08		
York [8]	a	00 41						06 40						07 39				08 31		
Scarborough	a																			
Leeds [10]	d									06 35			07 10		07 50		07 57			
York [8]	d		00 50	00 50	05 54			06 42		07 06	07 32		07 35	07 42	08 23		08 28	08 33		08 42
Thirsk	d				06 10					07 22	07 54				08 46					
Northallerton	d				06 18			07 01		07 30	08 02				08 55					09 03
Darlington [7]	a		01s26	01s41	06 29			07 15		07 41			08 04	08 09			08 54	09 00		09 14
Eaglescliffe	a																			
Middlesbrough	a				07 01						08 34				09 32					
Darlington [7]	d		01s28	01s43				07 15	07 20	07 42			08 05	08 11		08 15	08 55	09 01		09 15
Durham	d		01s45	02s00				07 33	07 41	07 59			08 22	08 29		08 36	09 12	09 18		09 31
Chester-le-Street	d								07 48	08 05						08 43				
Newcastle [8]	a		02 18	02 18				07 50	08 02	08 17			08 39	08 46		09 00	09 26	09 34		09 48
Hartlepool	a																			
Sunderland	a																			
Newcastle [8]	d					06 00	06 25	07 52				08 24	08 45				09 29	09 39		
Morpeth	d					06 20	06 38	08 06				08a44					09 42			
Alnmouth for Alnwick	d					06 38	06 52	08 20									09 56			
Berwick-upon-Tweed	d						07 14	08 42					09 29					10 22		
Dunbar	d						07 38	09 06					09 52							
Edinburgh [10]	a						08 05	09 31					10 21				10 57	11 08		
Edinburgh	d						08 08	09 38					10 26							
Haymarket	d						08 13	09 42					10 31							
Motherwell	a						08 57	10 28												
Glasgow Central [15]	a						09 16	10 48												
Stirling	a																			
Perth	a																			
Inverness	a																			
Inverkeithing	a												10 46							
Kirkcaldy	a												11 03							
Leuchars [3]	a												11 27							
Dundee	a												11 43							
Arbroath	a												12 01							
Montrose	a												12 17							
Stonehaven	a												12 40							
Aberdeen	a												13 03							

A until 3 July　　**B** 10 July

Table 26

London - Humberside, Yorkshire, North East England and Scotland

		XC	TP	GR	GR	XC	GC	TP	NT	GR	GR	EM	TP	TP	NT	XC	GR	EM	XC	TP	GR	GR	TP
		◇[1] ✕	◇[1] ✕	■ [1] ✕⊘	■ [1] ⊏✕	◇[1] ✕	■ [1] ⊏	◇[1] ✕		■ [1] ✕⊘	■ [1] ⊏✕	◇[1] ⊏	◇[1] ✕	◇[1] ✕		◇[1] ✕	■ [1] ⊏✕	◇	◇[1] ✕	◇[1] ✕	■ [1] ✕⊘	■ [1] ⊏✕	◇[1] ✕
London Kings Cross [15] ⊖	d			07 00	07 10		07 57			08 00	08 10						08 30				09 00	09 10	
Stevenage [4]	d									08 20							08 49					09 29	
Peterborough [8]	a			07 45	07 56		08 43			08 51	08 57						09 20				09 45		
Norwich	d																	07 57					
Peterborough [8]	d			07 46	07 56		08 44			08 51	08 57						09 21	09 30			09 46		
Grantham [7]	a			08 05	08 15						09 16						09 40	09 58					
	d			08 05	08 15						09 16						09 40						
Newark North Gate [7]	a			08 17	08 27						09 28											10 22	
	d			08 17	08 27						09 28											10 22	
Retford [10]	d				08 42																10 23		
Doncaster [7]	a			08 40	08 57					09 37	09 56						10 11				10 38	10 47	
Selby	a																						
Hull	a																						
Wakefield Westgate [7]	a				09 15						10 14											11 11	
Leeds [10]	a				09 35						10 35											11 35	
Shipley	a																						
Bradford Forster Square	a																						
Keighley	a																						
Skipton	a																						
Sheffield [7]	d	07 54				08 54						09 21				09 21			09 54				
Doncaster [7]	d	08 25		08 42		09 23				09 37		09 55					10 12		10 20		10 39		
York [8]	a	08 49		09 04		09 45	09 58			10 00		10 16					10 39		10 44		11 01		
Scarborough	a											11 06											
Leeds [10]	d		08 27					08 57					09 27	09 57		10 07				10 27			10 57
York [8]	d	08 51	08 57	09 06		09 47	09 59	09 26		10 03			09 56	10 26		10 34	10 42		10 47	10 54	11 04		11 26
Thirsk	d						10 21	09 46						10 46									11 46
Northallerton	d		09 18				10 31	09 55					10 25	10 55						11 15			11 55
Darlington [7]	a	09 18	09 29	09 35		10 13				10 30			10 36			10 59	11 11		11 16	11 27	11 32		
Eaglescliffe	a						10 48																
Middlesbrough	a							10 30						11 31									12 28
Darlington [7]	d	09 20	09 30	09 36		10 14				10 31			10 37			11 01	11 11		11 17	11 28	11 32		
Durham	d	09 36	09 46			10 31				10 48			10 54			11 17			11 34	11 45			
Chester-le-Street	d	09 43											11 00										
Newcastle [8]	a	09 54	10 02	10 05		10 46				11 04			11 12			11 32	11 41		11 49	11 59	12 02		
Hartlepool	a						11 20																
Sunderland	a						11 50																
Newcastle [8]	d			10 08					10 15	11 08					11 15	11 36	11 43				12 03		
Morpeth	d								10a35						11a35								
Alnmouth for Alnwick	d									11 34						12 00							
Berwick-upon-Tweed	d			10 51													12 26						
Dunbar	d																						
Edinburgh [10]	a			11 35						12 39						13 01	13 13				13 27		
Edinburgh	d			11 40																	13 40		
Haymarket	d			11 44																	13 44		
Motherwell	a			12 25																	14 27		
Glasgow Central [15]	a			12 47																	14 47		
Stirling	a																						
Perth	a																						
Inverness	a																						
Inverkeithing	a																						
Kirkcaldy	a																						
Leuchars [3]	a																						
Dundee	a																						
Arbroath	a																						
Montrose	a																						
Stonehaven	a																						
Aberdeen	a																						

London - Humberside, Yorkshire, North East England and Scotland

		NT	XC	GR	HT	EM	XC	TP	GR	GR	TP	NT	GR	EM	GC	XC	XC	GR	GR	GR	GC	TP
									A				B									
London Kings Cross 15 ⊖	d			09 30	09 34				10 00	10 10			10 30		10 36			10 40	11 00	11 10	11 27	
Stevenage 4	d			09 49	09u55																	
Peterborough 8	a			10 20					10 46	10 56			11 16					11 26	11 46	11 56		
Norwich	d					08 57								09 57								
Peterborough 8	d			10 21		10 28			10 46	10 56			11 17	11 25				11 27	11 46	11 56		
Grantham 7	a			10 40	10 45	10 57				11 15				11 57				11 48		12 15		
	d			10 40	10 46					11 15								11 48		12 16		
Newark North Gate 7	a									11 27										12 28		
	d									11 27										12 28		
Retford 10	d				11 06															12 43		
Doncaster 7	a			11 13	11 24				11 32	11 53					12 12			12 19	12 33	12 58		
Selby	a				11 39																	
Hull	a				12 22																	
Wakefield Westgate 7	a									12 16										13 17		
Leeds 10	a									12 35										13 35		
Shipley	a																					
Bradford Forster Square	a																					
Keighley	a																					
Skipton	a																					
Sheffield 7 ⇌	d		10 21				10 54									11 21	11 54					
Doncaster 7	d			11 14			11 20		11 32								12 18	12 21	12 34			
York 8	a			11 39			11 44		11 56				12 27				12 44	12 47	12 56		13 25	
Scarborough	a																					
Leeds 10	d		11 07					11 27			11 57					12 07						12 27
York 8	d		11 34	11 41			11 47	11 54	11 59		12 26		12 29			12 34	12 47	12 49	12 58		13 30	12 54
Thirsk	d										12 46										13 51	
Northallerton	d							12 15	12 20		12 55										14 09	13 23
Darlington 7	a		11 59	12 08			12 14	12 27	12 32							13 01	13 12	13 17	13 25			13 34
Eaglescliffe	a																				14 27	
Middlesbrough	a										13 30											
Darlington 7	d		12 01	12 09			12 16	12 28	12 33							13 03	13 14	13 17	13 26			13 34
Durham	d		12 17	12 27			12 35	12 45								13 19	13 30	13 35				13 50
Chester-le-Street	d						12 42															13 57
Newcastle 8 ⇌	a		12 33	12 43			12 50	12 59	13 02				13 25			13 33	13 45	13 53	13 57			14 10
Hartlepool	a																				14 46	
Sunderland ⇌	a																				15 17	
Newcastle 8 ⇌	d	12 15	12 36	12 45					13 05			13 15	13 26			13 36			13 59			
Morpeth	d	12a35										13a36										
Alnmouth for Alnwick	d															14 00						
Berwick-upon-Tweed	d		13 18	13 28															14 42			
Dunbar	d		13 41																			
Edinburgh 10	a		14 07	14 15					14 31				14 53			15 04			15 27			
Edinburgh	d												15 00						15 36			
Haymarket	d												15 04						15 45			
Motherwell	a																		16 27			
Glasgow Central 15	a																		16 51			
Stirling	a																					
Perth	a																					
Inverness	a																					
Inverkeithing	a												15 18									
Kirkcaldy	a												15 35									
Leuchars 3	a												16 00									
Dundee	a												16 19									
Arbroath	a												16 36									
Montrose	a												16 52									
Stonehaven	a												17 15									
Aberdeen	a												17 38									

A The Flying Scotsman B The Northern Lights

Table 26

London - Humberside, Yorkshire, North East England and Scotland

Saturdays
until 10 July

		TP	NT	XC	GR	HT	EM	XC	GR	GR	TP	TP	NT	XC	GR	EM	XC	GR	GR	TP	TP	NT
									A													
London Kings Cross 15 ⊖	d				11 30	11 48			12 00	12 10					12 30			13 00	13 10			
Stevenage 4	d				11 50																	
Peterborough 8	a				12 21				12 46	12 56					13 16			13 46	13 56			
Norwich	d						10 57									11 57						
Peterborough 8	d				12 21		12 25		12 47	12 56					13 16	13 28		13 46	13 56			
Grantham 7	a				12 42	12 49	12 58			13 15					13 35	13 56			14 16			
	d				12 42	12 49				13 15					13 35				14 16			
Newark North Gate 7	a									13 27									14 28			
	d									13 27									14 28			
Retford 10	d					13 13													14 43			
Doncaster 7	a				13 14	13 26				13 52					14 07			14 33	14 58			
Selby	a					13 42																
Hull	a					14 22																
Wakefield Westgate 7	a									14 16									15 15			
Leeds 10	a									14 35									15 35			
Shipley	a																					
Bradford Forster Square	a																					
Keighley	a																					
Skipton	a																					
Sheffield 7 ⇌	d			12 21				12 54						13 21			13 54					
Doncaster 7	d				13 15			13 21							14 07		14 18	14 34				
York 8	a				13 39			13 44	13 55						14 34		14 44	14 58				
Scarborough	a																					
Leeds 10	d	12 57		13 07							13 27	13 57		14 07						14 27	14 57	
York 8	d	13 26		13 34	13 41			13 49	13 59		13 54	14 26		14 34	14 36		14 47	15 00		14 54	15 26	
Thirsk	d	13 46										14 46									15 46	
Northallerton	d	13 55									14 23	15 00			14 55					15 23	15 55	
Darlington 7	a			13 59	14 09			14 16			14 34			14 59	15 08		15 15	15 27		15 34		
Eaglescliffe	a																					
Middlesbrough	a	14 28										15 35									16 30	
Darlington 7	d			14 01	14 09			14 17			14 34			15 01	15 08		15 16	15 28		15 34		
Durham	d			14 17	14 27			14 35			14 50			15 17	15 26		15 33	15 45		15 50		
Chester-le-Street	d							14 42												15 57		
Newcastle 8 ⇌	a			14 32	14 43			14 50	14 54		15 06			15 32	15 42		15 46	16 01		16 12		
Hartlepool	a																					
Sunderland ⇌	a																					
Newcastle 8 ⇌	d		14 15	14 36	14 45				14 59				15 15	15 36	15 47			16 03				16 15
Morpeth	d		14a36										15a35	15 49								16a36
Alnmouth for Alnwick	d													16 03				16 30				
Berwick-upon-Tweed	d			15 18					15 43									16 52				
Dunbar	d			15 41																		
Edinburgh 10	a			16 05	16 13				16 29					17 05	17 14			17 37				
Edinburgh	d								16 33									17 40				
Haymarket	d								16 38									17 45				
Motherwell	a																	18 28				
Glasgow Central 15	a																	18 50				
Stirling	a								17 19													
Perth	a								18 00													
Inverness	a								20 08													
Inverkeithing	a																					
Kirkcaldy	a																					
Leuchars 3	a																					
Dundee	a																					
Arbroath	a																					
Montrose	a																					
Stonehaven	a																					
Aberdeen	a																					

A The Highland Chieftain

Table 26

Saturdays until 10 July

London - Humberside, Yorkshire, North East England and Scotland

		XC	GR	EM	XC	GR	GR	EM	GC	TP	XC	XC	NT	GR	HT	GR	EM	TP	TP	NT	XC	XC
		◇1	1	◇	◇1	1	1	◇		◇1	◇1	◇1		1	◇1	1	◇	◇1	◇1		◇1	◇1
London Kings Cross ⊖	d		13 30			14 00	14 30		14 39					15 00	15 08	15 30						
Stevenage	d		13 49												15u28	15 49						
Peterborough	a		14 20			14 46	15 16							15 45		16 20						
Norwich	d			12 57				13 57									14 57					
Peterborough	d		14 21	14 26		14 47	15 16	15 26						15 46		16 21	16 27					
Grantham	a		14 40	14 57			15 35	15 55							16 11	16 40	16 55					
	d		14 40				15 35								16 11	16 40						
Newark North Gate	a		14 52				15 47									16 52						
	d		14 52				15 47									16 52						
Retford	d						16 02								16 32							
Doncaster	a					15 35	16 18		16 21					16 32	16 47	17 16						
Selby	a														17 05							
Hull	a														17 47							
Wakefield Westgate	a						16 36									17 33						
Leeds	a						16 54									17 53						
Shipley	a																					
Bradford Forster Square	a																					
Keighley	a																					
Skipton	a																					
Sheffield	d	14 21			14 54						15 21	15 54									16 21	16 54
Doncaster	d				15 18	15 36						16 17		16 33								17 21
York	a		15 39		15 44	15 59						16 39		16 56								17 44
Scarborough	a																					
Leeds	d	15 07								15 57	16 07							16 27	16 57		17 07	
York	d	15 34	15 42		15 47	16 01				16 26	16 34	16 43		16 57				17g02	17 26		17 32	17 47
Thirsk	d									16 46								17 20	17 43			
Northallerton	d									16 55								17 28	17 53			
Darlington	a	15 59	16 09		16 13	16 29					16 59	17 10		17 27				17 37			17 59	18 12
Eaglescliffe	a																					
Middlesbrough	a									17 33									18 32			
Darlington	d	16 01	16 10		16 15	16 29					17 01	17 12		17 27				17 38			18 01	18 14
Durham	d	16 17	16 27		16 33						17 17	17f33		17 45				17 55			18 18	18 30
Chester-le-Street	d											17 39						18 01				
Newcastle	a	16 32	16 43		16 46	16 59					17 32	17 51		18 01				18 15			18 33	18 45
Hartlepool	a																					
Sunderland	a																					
Newcastle	d	16 36	16 45			17 01					17 36		17 44	18 02						18 28	18 42	
Morpeth	d												18a06							18a49		
Alnmouth for Alnwick	d										18 02											
Berwick-upon-Tweed	d	17 18												18 45							19 26	
Dunbar	d	17 41																			19 50	
Edinburgh	a	18 05	18 13			18 27					19 07			19 34							20 15	
Edinburgh	d	18 08				18 32					19 10			19 39							20 22	
Haymarket	d	18 13				18 37					19 14			19 43							20 26	
Motherwell	a										19 55			20 22								
Glasgow Central	a										20 24			20 45								
Stirling	a																					
Perth	a																					
Inverness	a																					
Inverkeithing	a	18 25				18 54															20 43	
Kirkcaldy	a	18 40				19 11															21 00	
Leuchars	a	19 11				19 38															21 35	
Dundee	a	19 24				19 53															21 52	
Arbroath	a	19 41				20 10																
Montrose	a	20 01				20 26																
Stonehaven	a	20 22				20 49																
Aberdeen	a	20 41				21 12																

c arr. 1734

f arr. 1728

g arr. 1652

Table 26

Saturdays until 10 July

London - Humberside, Yorkshire, North East England and Scotland

		GR	GR	EM	GC	TP	XC	GR	HT	GR	EM	TP	XC	NT	TP	NT	XC	XC	GR	GR	GR	GR	TP
		1	1	◇	1 A	◇1	◇1	1	◇1	1	◇	◇1	◇1		◇1		◇1	◇1	1	1	1	1	◇1
London Kings Cross ⊖	d	16 00	16 30		16 50			17 00	17 04	17 30									17 40	18 00	18 03	18 30	
Stevenage	d								17u24	17 50													
Peterborough	a	16 46	17 16					17 45		18 21									18 27	18 46	18 52		
Norwich	d			15 52							16 57												
Peterborough	d	16 46	17 16	17 27				17 46		18 21	18 26								18 27	18 46	18 52		
Grantham	a		17 35	18 01					18 10	18 42	18 55								18 48			19 30	
	d		17 35	18 03					18 10	18 42									18 48			19 30	
Newark North Gate	a		17 47							18 54									19 00		19 20		
	d		17 47							18 54									19 00		19 20		
Retford	d		18 02						18 31														
Doncaster	a	17 35	18 17					18 33	18 46	19 17									19 24	19 33		20 01	
Selby	a								19 07														
Hull	a								19 47														
Wakefield Westgate	a		18 35							19 35											20 00	20 19	
Leeds	a		18 53							19 51											20 22	20 35	
Shipley	a																					20s56	
Bradford Forster Square	a																					21 06	
Keighley	a									20s17													
Skipton	a									20 31													
Sheffield	d						17 21						17 47				18 21	18 54					
Doncaster	d	17 35						18 34										19 22	19 25	19 34			
York	a	17 58			18 45			18 56										19 44	19 48	19 57			
Scarborough	a																						
Leeds	d					17 57	18 07					18 27	18 35	18 41	18 57		19c07						19 57
York	d	18 02			18 46	18 26	18 34	18 58				18 56	19 04	19b29	19 26		19 34	19 47	19 50	20 02			20 27
Thirsk	d				19 03	18 46									19 42								20 43
Northallerton	d	18 21			19 10	18 55						19 21			19 50								20 51
Darlington	a	18 34					19 01	19 25				19 33	19 37				20 03	20 12	20 18	20 30			
Eaglescliffe	a				19 28																		
Middlesbrough	a					19 28									20 23								21 25
Darlington	d	18 34					19 02	19 26				19 34	19 39				20 04	20 14	20 19	20 31			
Durham	d						19 20	19 43				19 50	19 55				20 22	20 30	20 36				
Chester-le-Street	d																	20 37					
Newcastle	a	19 04					19 35	19 59				20 09	20 10				20 33	20 51	20 57	21 00			
Hartlepool	a				19 56																		
Sunderland	a				20 35																		
Newcastle	d	19 06					19 37	20 01					20 14			20 24	20 36			21 02			
Morpeth	d															20a45				21 17			
Alnmouth for Alnwick	d						20 04													21 33			
Berwick-upon-Tweed	d	19 49											20 56				21 20			21 55			
Dunbar	d							21 05									21 43						
Edinburgh	a	20 35					21 06	21 30					21 39				22 10			22 42			
Edinburgh	d						21 10	21 45															
Haymarket	d						21 14	21 49															
Motherwell	a						21 55	22 26															
Glasgow Central	a						22 18	22 46															
Stirling	a																						
Perth	a																						
Inverness	a																						
Inverkeithing	a																						
Kirkcaldy	a																						
Leuchars	a																						
Dundee	a																						
Arbroath	a																						
Montrose	a																						
Stonehaven	a																						
Aberdeen	a																						

A The 21st Century Limited

b arr. 1918

c arr. 1901

Table 26

Saturdays
until 10 July

London - Humberside, Yorkshire, North East England and Scotland

		XC	GR	GR	EM	XC		GR	GC	TP	GR	HT	EM	GC	GR	XC		XC	GR	GR			EM	XC	XC
																			A	B					
London Kings Cross 15 ⊖	d		18 35	18 40				19 00	19 07		19 30	19 37		19 48	20 00				20 30	20 30					
Stevenage 4	d							19 19				19u57													
Peterborough 8	a		19 21	19 26				19 50			20 16				20 46				21 16	21 16					
Norwich	d				17 54								18 57												
Peterborough 8	d		19 21	19 27	19 30			19 51			20 16		20 27		20 46				21 17	21 17			21 27		
Grantham 7	a				19 59						20 35	20 41	20 58		21 05				21 38	21 38			22 00		
	d										20 35	20 43			21 05				21 38	21 38					
Newark North Gate 7	a			19 55							20 47				21 17				21 49	21 49					
	d			19 55							20 47				21 17				21 49	21 49					
Retford 10	d			20 11								21 05			21 32										
Doncaster 7	a		20 08	20 27				20 37			21 11	21 20		21 29	21 47				22 14	22 14					
Selby	a			20 43								21 35													
Hull	a			21 27								22 16													
Wakefield Westgate 7	a														22 05										
Leeds 10	a														22 24										
Shipley	a																								
Bradford Forster Square	a																								
Keighley	a																								
Skipton	a																								
Sheffield 7	d	19 21				19 54										20 54		20 23						21 54	22 26
Doncaster 7	d		20 08			20 18		20 38			21 12					21 26			22 14	22 14				22 20	22 49
York 8	a		20 34			20 40		21 00	21 15		21 36					21 48			22 38	22 38				22 43	
Scarborough	a																								
Leeds 10	d	20 07								20 45								21b15							23a24
York 8	d	20 34	20 41			20 45		21 02	21 17	21 11	21 42					21 51		21a58	22 39	22 39					
Thirsk	d								21 36	21 28															
Northallerton	d							21 23	21 46	21 36															
Darlington 7	a	21 04	21 09			21 14		21 36		21 47	22 09					22 21			23 07	23 44					
Eaglescliffe	a								22 06																
Middlesbrough	a																								
Darlington 7	d	21 05	21 09			21 15		21 36		21 48	22 10					22 23			23 08	23 45					
Durham	d	21 22	21 27			21 33		21 54		22 05	22 27					22 44			23 25	00 02					
Chester-le-Street	d					21 40										22 51									
Newcastle 8	a	21 33	21 45			21 50		22 12		22 19	22 45					23 05			23 46	00 33					
Hartlepool	a								22 25																
Sunderland	a								22 54																
Newcastle 8	d	21 36																							
Morpeth	d																								
Alnmouth for Alnwick	d	22 00																							
Berwick-upon-Tweed	d	22 21																							
Dunbar	d																								
Edinburgh 10	a	23 04																							
Edinburgh	d																								
Haymarket	d																								
Motherwell	a																								
Glasgow Central 15	a																								
Stirling	a																								
Perth	a																								
Inverness	a																								
Inverkeithing	a																								
Kirkcaldy	a																								
Leuchars 3	a																								
Dundee	a																								
Arbroath	a																								
Montrose	a																								
Stonehaven	a																								
Aberdeen	a																								

A Until 26 June
B 3 and 10 July
b arr. 2104

Table 26

Saturdays
17 July to 04 September

London - Humberside, Yorkshire, North East England and Scotland

					GR	GR	GR	TP	NT	GR		GR	NT	TP	TP	NT	GR	XC	TP	NT		XC	GR	EM	TP
						A	B																		
London Kings Cross 15 ⊖	d				22p00																		06 15		
Stevenage 4	d																						06 34		
Peterborough 8	a				22p46																		07 05		
Norwich	d																							05 52	
Peterborough 8	d				22p47																		07 06	07 27	
Grantham 7	a				23p08																		07 25	07 56	
	d				23p08																		07 25		
Newark North Gate 7	a				23p19																		07 37		
	d				23p19																		07 37		
Retford 10	d																						07 52		
Doncaster 7	a				23p49																		08 07		
Selby	a																								
Hull	a																								
Wakefield Westgate 7	a																								
Leeds 10	a																								
Shipley	a																								
Bradford Forster Square	a																								
Keighley	a																								
Skipton	a																								
Sheffield 7	d																	06 49				07 12			
Doncaster 7	d				23p49							06 20						07 17					08 08		
York 8	a				00 41							06 40						07 39					08 31		
Scarborough	a																								
Leeds 10	d													06 35			07 10		07 50			07 57			
York 8	d					00 50	00 50	05 54				06 42		07 06	07 32		07 35	07 42	08 23			08 28	08 33		08 42
Thirsk	d							06 10						07 22	07 54				08 46						
Northallerton	d							06 18				07 01		07 30	08 02				08 55						09 03
Darlington 7	a					01s26	01s41	06 29				07 15		07 41			08 04	08 09				08 54	09 00		09 14
Eaglescliffe	a																								
Middlesbrough	a							07 01							08 34				09 32						
Darlington 7	d					01s28	01s43					07 15	07 20	07 42			08 05	08 11		08 15		08 55	09 01		09 15
Durham	d					01s45	02s00					07 33	07 41	07 59			08 22	08 29		08 36		09 12	09 18		09 31
Chester-le-Street	d												07 48	08 05						08 43					
Newcastle 8	a					02 18	02 18					07 50	08 02	08 17			08 39	08 46		09 00		09 26	09 34		09 48
Hartlepool	a																								
Sunderland	a																								
Newcastle 8	d								06 00	06 25		07 52				08 24	08 45					09 29	09 39		
Morpeth	d								06 20	06 38		08 06				08a44						09 42			
Alnmouth for Alnwick	d								06a38	06 52		08 20										09 56			
Berwick-upon-Tweed	d									07 14		08 42					09 29						10 22		
Dunbar	d									07 38		09 06					09 52								
Edinburgh 10	a									08 05		09 31					10 21					10 57	11 08		
Edinburgh	d									08 08		09 38					10 26								
Haymarket	d									08 13		09 42					10 31								
Motherwell	a									08 57		10 28													
Glasgow Central 15	a									09 16		10 48													
Stirling	a																								
Perth	a																								
Inverness	a																								
Inverkeithing	a																10 46								
Kirkcaldy	a																11 03								
Leuchars 3	a																11 27								
Dundee	a																11 43								
Arbroath	a																12 01								
Montrose	a																12 17								
Stonehaven	a																12 40								
Aberdeen	a																13 03								

A 4 September
B until 28 August

Table 26

Saturdays
17 July to 04 September

London - Humberside, Yorkshire, North East England and Scotland

		XC	TP	GR	GR	HT	XC	GC	TP	NT	GR	GR	EM	TP	TP	NT	XC	GR	EM	XC	TP	GR	GR
London Kings Cross ⊖	d			07 00	07 10	07 36		07 57			08 00	08 10						08 30				09 00	09 10
Stevenage	d					07u56					08 20							08 49					09 29
Peterborough	a			07 45	07 56			08 43			08 51	08 57						09 20				09 45	
Norwich	d																		07 57				
Peterborough	d			07 46	07 56			08 44			08 51	08 57						09 21	09 30			09 46	
Grantham	a			08 05	08 15	08 37						09 16						09 40	09 58				
	d			08 05	08 15	08 38						09 16						09 40					
Newark North Gate	a			08 17	08 27							09 28											10 22
	d			08 17	08 27							09 28											10 22
Retford	d				08 42	08 59																10 23	
Doncaster	a			08 40	08 57	09 16					09 37	09 56						10 11				10 38	10 47
Selby	a					09 32																	
Hull	a					10 16																	
Wakefield Westgate	a				09 15							10 14											11 11
Leeds	a				09 35							10 35											11 35
Shipley	a																						
Bradford Forster Square	a																						
Keighley	a																						
Skipton	a																						
Sheffield	d	07 54					08 54						09 21				09 21			09 54			
Doncaster	d	08 25		08 42			09 23				09 37		09 55					10 12		10 20		10 39	
York	a	08 49		09 04			09 45	09 58			10 00		10 16					10 39		10 44		11 01	
Scarborough	a												11 06										
Leeds	d		08 27						08 57					09 27	09 57		10 07				10 27		
York	d	08 51	08 57	09 06			09 47	09 59	09 26		10 03			09 56	10 26		10 34	10 42		10 47	10 54	11 04	
Thirsk	d							10 21	09 46						10 46								
Northallerton	d		09 18					10 31	09 55					10 25	10 55						11 15		
Darlington	a	09 18	09 29	09 35			10 13				10 30			10 36			10 59	11 11		11 16	11 27	11 32	
Eaglescliffe	a							10 48															
Middlesbrough	a								10 30						11 31								
Darlington	d	09 20	09 30	09 36			10 14				10 31			10 37			11 01	11 11		11 17	11 28	11 32	
Durham	d	09 36	09 46				10 31				10 48			10 54			11 17			11 34	11 45		
Chester-le-Street	d	09 43												11 00									
Newcastle	a	09 54	10 02	10 05			10 46				11 04			11 12			11 32	11 41		11 49	11 59	12 02	
Hartlepool	a							11 20															
Sunderland	a							11 50															
Newcastle	d			10 08						10 15	11 08					11 15	11 36	11 43				12 03	
Morpeth	d									10a35						11a35							
Alnmouth for Alnwick	d										11 34						12 00						
Berwick-upon-Tweed	d			10 51														12 26					
Dunbar	d																						
Edinburgh	a			11 35							12 39						13 01	13 13				13 27	
Edinburgh	d			11 40																		13 40	
Haymarket	d			11 44																		13 44	
Motherwell	a			12 25																		14 27	
Glasgow Central	a			12 47																		14 47	
Stirling	a																						
Perth	a																						
Inverness	a																						
Inverkeithing	a																						
Kirkcaldy	a																						
Leuchars	a																						
Dundee	a																						
Arbroath	a																						
Montrose	a																						
Stonehaven	a																						
Aberdeen	a																						

Table 26

Saturdays
17 July to 04 September

London - Humberside, Yorkshire, North East England and Scotland

		TP	NT	XC	GR	EM	XC	TP	GR A	GR	TP	NT	GR B	EM	GC	XC	XC	GR	GR	GR	GC	TP
London Kings Cross ⊖	d				09 30				10 00	10 10			10 30		10 36			10 40	11 00	11 10	11 27	
Stevenage	d				09 49																	
Peterborough	a				10 20				10 46	10 56			11 16					11 26	11 46	11 56		
Norwich	d					08 57								09 57								
Peterborough	d				10 21	10 28			10 46	10 56			11 17	11 25				11 27	11 46	11 56		
Grantham	a				10 40	10 57				11 15				11 57				11 48		12 15		
	d				10 40					11 15								11 48		12 16		
Newark North Gate	a									11 27										12 28		
	d									11 27										12 28		
Retford	d																			12 43		
Doncaster	a				11 13				11 32	11 53					12 12			12 19	12 33	12 58		
Selby	a																					
Hull	a																					
Wakefield Westgate	a									12 16										13 17		
Leeds	a									12 35										13 35		
Shipley	a																					
Bradford Forster Square	a																					
Keighley	a																					
Skipton	a																					
Sheffield	d			10 21			10 54									11 21	11 54					
Doncaster	d				11 14		11 20		11 32								12 18	12 21	12 34			
York	a				11 39		11 44		11 56				12 27				12 44	12 47	12 56		13 25	
Scarborough	a																					
Leeds	d	10 57		11 07				11 27			11 57					12 07						12 27
York	d	11 26		11 34	11 41		11 47	11 54	11 59		12 26		12 29			12 34	12 47	12 49	12 58		13 30	12 54
Thirsk	d	11 46									12 46										13 51	
Northallerton	d	11 55						12 15	12 20		12 55										14 09	13 23
Darlington	a			11 59	12 08		12 14	12 27	12 32							13 01	13 12	13 17	13 25			13 34
Eaglescliffe	a																				14 27	
Middlesbrough	a	12 28									13 30											
Darlington	d			12 01	12 09		12 16	12 28	12 33							13 03	13 14	13 17	13 26			13 34
Durham	d			12 17	12 27		12 35	12 45								13 19	13 30	13 35				13 50
Chester-le-Street	d						12 42															13 57
Newcastle	a			12 33	12 43		12 50	12 59	13 02				13 25			13 33	13 45	13 53	13 57			14 10
Hartlepool	a																				14 46	
Sunderland	a																				15 17	
Newcastle	d		12 15	12 36	12 45				13 05			13 15	13 26			13 36			13 59			
Morpeth	d		12a35									13a36										
Alnmouth for Alnwick	d															14 00						
Berwick-upon-Tweed	d			13 18	13 28														14 42			
Dunbar	d			13 41																		
Edinburgh	a			14 07	14 15				14 31				14 53			15 04			15 27			
Edinburgh	d												15 00						15 36			
Haymarket	d												15 04						15 45			
Motherwell	a																		16 27			
Glasgow Central	a																		16 51			
Stirling	a																					
Perth	a																					
Inverness	a																					
Inverkeithing	a												15 18									
Kirkcaldy	a												15 35									
Leuchars	a												16 00									
Dundee	a												16 19									
Arbroath	a												16 36									
Montrose	a												16 52									
Stonehaven	a												17 15									
Aberdeen	a												17 38									

A The Flying Scotsman
B The Northern Lights

Table 26

London - Humberside, Yorkshire, North East England and Scotland

Station		TP	NT	XC	GR	HT	EM	XC	GR	GR	TP	TP	NT	XC	GR	EM	XC	GR	GR	TP	TP	NT
									A													
London Kings Cross ⊖	d				11 30	11 48			12 00	12 10					12 30			13 00	13 10			
Stevenage	d				11 50																	
Peterborough	a				12 21				12 46	12 56					13 16			13 46	13 56			
Norwich	d						10 57									11 57						
Peterborough	d				12 21		12 25		12 47	12 56					13 16	13 28		13 46	13 56			
Grantham	a				12 42	12 49	12 58			13 15					13 35	13 56			14 16			
	d				12 42	12 49				13 15					13 35				14 16			
Newark North Gate	a									13 27									14 28			
	d									13 27									14 28			
Retford	d					13 13													14 43			
Doncaster	a				13 14	13 26				13 52					14 07			14 33	14 58			
Selby	a					13 42																
Hull	a					14 22																
Wakefield Westgate	a									14 16									15 15			
Leeds	a									14 35									15 35			
Shipley	a																					
Bradford Forster Square	a																					
Keighley	a																					
Skipton	a																					
Sheffield ⇌	d			12 21				12 54						13 21			13 54					
Doncaster	d				13 15			13 21							14 07		14 18	14 34				
York	a				13 39			13 44	13 55						14 34		14 44	14 58				
Scarborough	a																					
Leeds	d	12 57		13 07							13 27	13 57		14 07						14 27	14 57	
York	d	13 26		13 34	13 41			13 49	13 59		13 54	14 26		14 34	14 36		14 47	15 00		14 54	15 26	
Thirsk	d	13 46										14 46									15 46	
Northallerton	d	13 55									14 23	15 00			14 55					15 23	15 55	
Darlington	a			13 59	14 09			14 16			14 34			14 59	15 08		15 15	15 27		15 34		
Eaglescliffe	a																					
Middlesbrough	a	14 28										15 35									16 30	
Darlington	d			14 01	14 09			14 17			14 34			15 01	15 08		15 16	15 28		15 34		
Durham	d			14 17	14 27			14 35			14 50			15 17	15 26		15 33	15 45		15 50		
Chester-le-Street	d							14 42												15 57		
Newcastle ⇌	a			14 32	14 43			14 50	14 54		15 06			15 32	15 42		15 46	16 01		16 12		
Hartlepool	a																					
Sunderland ⇌	a																					
Newcastle ⇌	d		14 15	14 36	14 45				14 59				15 15	15 36	15 47			16 03				16 15
Morpeth	d		14a36										15a35	15 49								16a36
Alnmouth for Alnwick	d													16 03				16 30				
Berwick-upon-Tweed	d			15 18					15 43									16 52				
Dunbar	d			15 41																		
Edinburgh	a			16 05	16 13				16 29					17 05	17 14			17 37				
Edinburgh	d								16 33									17 40				
Haymarket	d								16 38									17 45				
Motherwell	a																	18 28				
Glasgow Central	a																	18 50				
Stirling	a								17 19													
Perth	a								18 00													
Inverness	a								20 08													
Inverkeithing	a																					
Kirkcaldy	a																					
Leuchars	a																					
Dundee	a																					
Arbroath	a																					
Montrose	a																					
Stonehaven	a																					
Aberdeen	a																					

A The Highland Chieftain

Table 26

London - Humberside, Yorkshire, North East England and Scotland

Station		XC	GR	EM	XC	GR	GR	EM	GC	TP	XC	XC	NT	GC	GR	HT	GR	EM	TP	TP	NT	XC	XC
London Kings Cross ⊖	d		13 30			14 00	14 30		14 39					14 48	15 00	15 08	15 15						
Stevenage	d		13 49													15u28	15 49						
Peterborough	a		14 20			14 46	15 16								15 45		16 20						
Norwich	d			12 57				13 57										14 57					
Peterborough	d		14 21	14 26		14 47	15 16	15 26							15 46		16 21	16 27					
Grantham	a		14 40	14 57			15 35	15 55								16 10	16 40	16 55					
	d		14 40				15 35									16 10	16 40						
Newark North Gate	a		14 52				15 47										16 52						
	d		14 52				15 47										16 52						
Retford	d						16 02									16 30							
Doncaster	a					15 35	16 18		16 21						16 32	16 47	17 16						
Selby	a															17 05							
Hull	a															17 47							
Wakefield Westgate	a						16 36										17 33						
Leeds	a						16 54										17 53						
Shipley	a																						
Bradford Forster Square	a																						
Keighley	a																						
Skipton	a																						
Sheffield ⇌	d	14 21			14 54						15 21	15 54										16 21	16 54
Doncaster	d				15 18	15 36						16 17			16 33								17 21
York	a		15 39		15 44	15 59						16 39		16 49	16 56								17 44
Scarborough	a																						
Leeds	d	15 07								15 57	16 07								16 27	16 57		17 07	
York	d	15 34	15 42		15 47	16 01				16 26	16 34	16 43		16 51	16 57				17g02	17 26		17 32	17 47
Thirsk	d									16 46				17 08					17 20	17 43			
Northallerton	d									16 55				17 23					17 28	17 53			
Darlington	a	15 59	16 09		16 13	16 29					16 59	17 10			17 27				17 37			17 59	18 12
Eaglescliffe	a													17 50									
Middlesbrough	a									17 33										18 32			
Darlington	d	16 01	16 10		16 15	16 29					17 01	17 12			17 27				17 38			18 01	18 14
Durham	d	16 17	16 27		16 33						17 17	17f33			17 45				17 55			18 18	18 30
Chester-le-Street	d											17 39							18 01				
Newcastle ⇌	a	16 32	16 43		16 46	16 59					17 32	17 51			18 01				18 15			18 33	18 45
Hartlepool	a													18 19									
Sunderland ⇌	a													18 51									
Newcastle ⇌	d	16 36	16 45			17 01					17 36		17 44		18 02						18 28	18 42	
Morpeth	d												18a06								18a49		
Alnmouth for Alnwick	d										18 02												
Berwick-upon-Tweed	d	17 18													18 45							19 26	
Dunbar	d	17 41																				19 50	
Edinburgh	a	18 05	18 13			18 27					19 07				19 34							20 15	
Edinburgh	d	18 08				18 32					19 10				19 39							20 22	
Haymarket	d	18 13				18 37					19 14				19 43							20 26	
Motherwell	a										19 55				20 22								
Glasgow Central	a										20 24				20 45								
Stirling	a																						
Perth	a																						
Inverness	a																						
Inverkeithing	a	18 25				18 54																20 43	
Kirkcaldy	a	18 40				19 11																21 00	
Leuchars	a	19 11				19 38																21 35	
Dundee	a	19 24				19 53																21 52	
Arbroath	a	19 41				20 10																	
Montrose	a	20 01				20 26																	
Stonehaven	a	20 22				20 49																	
Aberdeen	a	20 41				21 12																	

f arr. 1728

g arr. 1652

Table 26

Saturdays
17 July to 04 September

London - Humberside, Yorkshire, North East England and Scotland

		GR	HT	GR	EM	TP	XC	GR	GC	GR	TP	XC	TP	NT	XC	XC	GR	EM	GR	GR	GR	TP
									A													
London Kings Cross ⊖	d	15 45	15 58	16 15				16 45	16 53	16 57							17 15		17 45	17 50	17 58	
Stevenage	d		16u30														17 48					
Peterborough	a	16 46		17 16				17 46		18 01							18 20		18 46	18 52	18 58	
Norwich	d				15 52													16 57				
Peterborough	d	16 46		17 16	17 27			17 47		18 02							18 20	18 26	18 46	18 52	18 58	
Grantham	a		17 22	17 35	18 01					18 22							18 39	18 55			19 19	
	d		17 23	17 35						18 22							18 40				19 19	
Newark North Gate	a			17 47						18 34							18 52			19 20	19 31	
	d			17 47						18 34							18 52			19 20	19 31	
Retford	d		17 44							18 49											19 46	
Doncaster	a	17 35	17 59	18 11				18 33		19 03							19 16		19 33		20 02	
Selby	a		18 15																		20 18	
Hull	a		19 03																		21 00	
Wakefield Westgate	a			18 29						19 23										20 00		
Leeds	a			18 47						19 45										20 22		
Shipley	a																			20s56		
Bradford Forster Square	a																			21 06		
Keighley	a									20s17												
Skipton	a									20 31												
Sheffield	d						17 21					17 47			18 21	18 54						
Doncaster	d	17 35						18 34								19 22	19 25		19 34			
York	a	17 58						18 56	19 02							19 44	19 48		19 57			
Scarborough	a																					
Leeds	d					17 57	18 07				18 27	18 35	18 57		19c07							19 57
York	d	18 02				18 26	18 34	18 58	19 08		18 56	19 04	19 26		19 34	19 47	19 50		20 02			20 27
Thirsk	d					18 46			19 24				19 42									20 43
Northallerton	d	18 21				18 55			19 32		19 21		19 50									20 51
Darlington	a	18 34					19 01	19 25			19 33	19 37			20 03	20 12	20 18		20 30			
Eaglescliffe	a								19 50													
Middlesbrough	a					19 28							20 23									21 25
Darlington	d	18 34					19 02	19 26			19 34	19 39			20 04	20 14	20 19		20 31			
Durham	d						19 20	19 43			19 50	19 55			20 22	20 30	20 36					
Chester-le-Street	d															20 37						
Newcastle	a	19 04					19 35	19 59			20 09	20 10			20 33	20 51	20 57		21 00			
Hartlepool	a								20 20													
Sunderland	a								20 50													
Newcastle	d	19 06					19 37	20 01				20 14		20 24	20 36				21 02			
Morpeth	d													20a45					21 17			
Alnmouth for Alnwick	d						20 04												21 33			
Berwick-upon-Tweed	d	19 49										20 56			21 20				21 55			
Dunbar	d							21 05							21 43							
Edinburgh	a	20 35					21 06	21 30				21 39			22 10				22 42			
Edinburgh	d						21 10	21 45														
Haymarket	d						21 14	21 49														
Motherwell	a						21 55	22 26														
Glasgow Central	a						22 18	22 46														
Stirling	a																					
Perth	a																					
Inverness	a																					
Inverkeithing	a																					
Kirkcaldy	a																					
Leuchars	a																					
Dundee	a																					
Arbroath	a																					
Montrose	a																					
Stonehaven	a																					
Aberdeen	a																					

A The 21st Century Limited

c arr. 1901

Table 26

Saturdays
17 July to 04 September

London - Humberside, Yorkshire, North East England and Scotland

		XC	GR	EM	XC	GR	GR	HT	TP	GR	EM	GC	GR	XC	GR	EM	XC
London Kings Cross ⊖	d		18 15			18 45	18 50	18 58		19 15		19 45	19 50		20 15		
Stevenage	d						19 23	19u30									
Peterborough	a		19 16			19 46				20 16			20 52		21 16		
Norwich	d			17 54							18 57						
Peterborough	d		19 16	19 30		19 46				20 16	20 27		20 52		21 17	21 27	
Grantham	a			19 59				20 22		20 35	20 58		21 11		21 38	22 00	
	d							20 24		20 35			21 11		21 38		
Newark North Gate	a									20 47			21 23		21 49		
	d									20 47			21 23		21 49		
Retford	d							20 45					21 38				
Doncaster	a		20 05			20 33	20 38	20 59		21 11		21 29	21 53		22 14		
Selby	a							21 15									
Hull	a							21 55									
Wakefield Westgate	a						20 55						22 11				
Leeds	a						21 21						22 34				
Shipley	a																
Bradford Forster Square	a																
Keighley	a																
Skipton	a																
Sheffield	d	19 21			19 54									20 54			21 54
Doncaster	d		20 07		20 18	20 33				21 12				21 26	22 14		22 20
York	a		20 34		20 40	20 58				21 36				21 48	22 38		22 43
Scarborough	a																
Leeds	d	20 07							20 45								
York	d	20 34	20 41		20 45	21 02			21 11	21 42				21 51	22 39		
Thirsk	d								21 28								
Northallerton	d					21 23			21 36								
Darlington	a	21 04	21 09		21 14	21 36			21 47	22 09				22 21	23 44		
Eaglescliffe	a																
Middlesbrough	a																
Darlington	d	21 05	21 09		21 15	21 36			21 48	22 10				22 23	23 45		
Durham	d	21 22	21 27		21 33	21 54			22 05	22 27				22 44	00 02		
Chester-le-Street	d				21 40									22 51			
Newcastle	a	21 33	21 45		21 50	22 12			22 19	22 45				23 05	00 26		
Hartlepool	a																
Sunderland	a																
Newcastle	d	21 36															
Morpeth	d																
Alnmouth for Alnwick	d	22 00															
Berwick-upon-Tweed	d	22 21															
Dunbar	d																
Edinburgh	a	23 04															
Edinburgh	d																
Haymarket	d																
Motherwell	a																
Glasgow Central	a																
Stirling	a																
Perth	a																
Inverness	a																
Inverkeithing	a																
Kirkcaldy	a																
Leuchars	a																
Dundee	a																
Arbroath	a																
Montrose	a																
Stonehaven	a																
Aberdeen	a																

Table 26

Saturdays
from 11 September

London - Humberside, Yorkshire, North East England and Scotland

		GR	GR	TP	NT	GR	GR	NT	TP	TP	NT	GR	XC	TP	NT	XC	GR	EM	TP	XC	TP
		■1	■1	◇1		■1	■1		◇1	◇1		■1	◇1	◇1		◇1	■1	◇	◇1	◇1	◇1
London Kings Cross 15 ⊖	d	22p00															06 15				
Stevenage 4	d																06 34				
Peterborough 8	a	22p46															07 05				
Norwich	d																	05 52			
Peterborough 8	d	22p47															07 06	07 27			
Grantham 7	a	23p08															07 25	07 56			
	d	23p08															07 25				
Newark North Gate 7	a	23p19															07 37				
	d	23p19															07 37				
Retford 10	d																07 52				
Doncaster 7	a	23p49															08 07				
Selby	a																				
Hull	a																				
Wakefield Westgate 7	a																				
Leeds 10	a																				
Shipley	a																				
Bradford Forster Square	a																				
Keighley	a																				
Skipton	a																				
Sheffield 7 ⇌	d												06 49			07 12		09 42		07 54	
Doncaster 7	d	23p49					06 20						07 17				08 08			08 25	
York 8	a	00 41					06 40						07 39				08 31			08 49	
Scarborough	a																				
Leeds 10	d								06 35			07 10		07 50		07 57					08 27
York 8	d		00 50	05 54			06 42		07 06	07 32		07 35	07 42	08 23		08 28	08 33		08 42	08 51	08 57
Thirsk	d			06 10					07 22	07 54				08 46							
Northallerton	d			06 18			07 01		07 30	08 02				08 55					09 03		09 18
Darlington 7	a		01s26	06 29			07 15		07 41			08 04	08 09			08 54	09 00		09 14	09 18	09 29
Eaglescliffe	a																				
Middlesbrough	a			07 01						08 34				09 32							
Darlington 7	d		01s28				07 15	07 20	07 42			08 05	08 11		08 15	08 55	09 01		09 15	09 20	09 30
Durham	d		01s45				07 33	07 41	07 59			08 22	08 29		08 36	09 12	09 18		09 31	09 36	09 46
Chester-le-Street	d							07 48	08 05						08 43					09 43	
Newcastle 8 ⇌	a		02 18				07 50	08 02	08 17			08 39	08 46		09 00	09 26	09 34		09 48	09 54	10 02
Hartlepool	a																				
Sunderland ⇌	a																				
Newcastle 8 ⇌	d				06 00	06 25	07 52				08 24	08 45				09 29	09 39				
Morpeth	d				06 20	06 38	08 06				08a44					09 42					
Alnmouth for Alnwick	d				06a38	06 52	08 20									09 56					
Berwick-upon-Tweed	d					07 14	08 42					09 29					10 22				
Dunbar	d					07 38	09 06					09 52									
Edinburgh 10	a					08 05	09 31					10 21				10 57	11 08				
Edinburgh	d					08 08	09 38					10 26									
Haymarket	d					08 13	09 42					10 31									
Motherwell	a					08 57	10 28														
Glasgow Central 15	a					09 16	10 48														
Stirling	a																				
Perth	a																				
Inverness	a																				
Inverkeithing	a											10 46									
Kirkcaldy	a											11 03									
Leuchars 8	a											11 27									
Dundee	a											11 43									
Arbroath	a											12 01									
Montrose	a											12 17									
Stonehaven	a											12 40									
Aberdeen	a											13 03									

Table 26

Saturdays
from 11 September

London - Humberside, Yorkshire, North East England and Scotland

		GR	GR	XC	GC	TP	NT	GR	GR	EM	TP	TP	NT	XC	GR	EM	XC	TP	GR	GR	TP	NT	XC
		■1	■1	◇1	■1	◇1		■1	■1	◇1	◇1	◇1		◇1	■1	◇	◇1	◇1	■1	■1	◇1		◇1
London Kings Cross 15 ⊖	d	07 00	07 10		07 57			08 00	08 10						08 30				09 00	09 10			
Stevenage 4	d							08 20							08 49					09 29			
Peterborough 8	a	07 45	07 56		08 43			08 51	08 57						09 20				09 45				
Norwich	d															07 57							
Peterborough 8	d	07 46	07 56		08 44			08 51	08 57						09 21	09 30			09 46				
Grantham 7	a	08 05	08 15						09 16						09 40	09 58							
	d	08 05	08 15						09 16						09 40								
Newark North Gate 7	a	08 17	08 27						09 28											10 22			
	d	08 17	08 27						09 28											10 22			
Retford 10	d		08 42																10 23				
Doncaster 7	a	08 40	08 57					09 37	09 56						10 11				10 38	10 47			
Selby	a																						
Hull	a																						
Wakefield Westgate 7	a		09 15						10 14											11 11			
Leeds 10	a		09 35						10 35											11 35			
Shipley	a																						
Bradford Forster Square	a																						
Keighley	a																						
Skipton	a																						
Sheffield 7 ⇌	d			08 54						09 21				09 21			09 54						10 21
Doncaster 7	d	08 42		09 23				09 37		09 55					10 12		10 20		10 39				
York 8	a	09 04		09 45	09 58			10 00		10 16					10 39		10 44		11 01				
Scarborough	a																						
Leeds 10	d					08 57					09 27	09 57		10 07				10 27			10 57		11 07
York 8	d	09 06		09 47	09 59	09 26		10 03			09 56	10 26		10 34	10 42		10 47	10 54	11 04		11 26		11 34
Thirsk	d				10 21	09 46						10 46									11 46		
Northallerton	d				10 31	09 55					10 25	10 55						11 15			11 55		
Darlington 7	a	09 35		10 13				10 30			10 36			10 59	11 11		11 16	11 27	11 32				11 59
Eaglescliffe	a				10 48																		
Middlesbrough	a					10 30						11 31									12 28		
Darlington 7	d	09 36		10 14				10 31			10 37			11 01	11 11		11 17	11 28	11 32				12 01
Durham	d			10 31				10 48			10 54			11 17			11 34	11 45					12 17
Chester-le-Street	d										11 00												
Newcastle 8 ⇌	a	10 05		10 46				11 04			11 12			11 32	11 41		11 49	11 59	12 02				12 33
Hartlepool	a				11 20																		
Sunderland ⇌	a				11 50																		
Newcastle 8 ⇌	d	10 08					10 15	11 08					11 15	11 36	11 43				12 03			12 15	12 36
Morpeth	d						10a35						11a35									12a35	
Alnmouth for Alnwick	d							11 34						12 00									
Berwick-upon-Tweed	d	10 51													12 26								13 18
Dunbar	d																						13 41
Edinburgh 10	a	11 35						12 39						13 01	13 13				13 27				14 07
Edinburgh	d	11 40																	13 40				
Haymarket	d	11 44																	13 44				
Motherwell	a	12 25																	14 27				
Glasgow Central 15	a	12 47																	14 47				
Stirling	a																						
Perth	a																						
Inverness	a																						
Inverkeithing	a																						
Kirkcaldy	a																						
Leuchars 8	a																						
Dundee	a																						
Arbroath	a																						
Montrose	a																						
Stonehaven	a																						
Aberdeen	a																						

Table 26

Saturdays from 11 September

London - Humberside, Yorkshire, North East England and Scotland

Station		GR	HT	EM	XC	TP	GR	GR	TP	NT	GR	EM	GC	XC	XC	GR	GR	GR	GC	TP	TP	NT
							A				B											
London Kings Cross ⊖	d	09 30	09 34				10 00	10 10			10 30		10 36			10 40	11 00	11 10	11 27			
Stevenage	d	09 49	09u55																			
Peterborough	a	10 20					10 46	10 56			11 16					11 26	11 46	11 56				
Norwich	d			08 57								09 57										
Peterborough	d	10 21		10 28			10 46	10 56			11 17	11 25				11 27	11 46	11 56				
Grantham	a	10 40	10 45	10 57				11 15				11 57				11 48		12 15				
	d	10 40	10 46					11 15								11 48		12 16				
Newark North Gate	a							11 27										12 28				
	d							11 27										12 28				
Retford	d		11 06															12 43				
Doncaster	a	11 13	11 24				11 32	11 53					12 11			12 19	12 33	12 58				
Selby	a		11 39																			
Hull	a		12 22																			
Wakefield Westgate	a							12 16										13 17				
Leeds	a							12 35										13 35				
Shipley	a																					
Bradford Forster Square	a																					
Keighley	a																					
Skipton	a																					
Sheffield	d				10 54									11 21	11 54							
Doncaster	d	11 14			11 20		11 32								12 18	12 21	12 34					
York	a	11 39			11 44		11 56				12 27				12 44	12 47	12 56		13 25			
Scarborough	a																					
Leeds	d					11 27			11 57					12 07						12 27	12 57	
York	d	11 41			11 47	11 54	11 59		12 26		12 29			12 34	12 47	12 49	12 58		13 30	12 54	13 26	
Thirsk	d								12 46										13 51		13 46	
Northallerton	d					12 15	12 20		12 55										14 09	13 23	13 55	
Darlington	a	12 08			12 14	12 27	12 32							13 01	13 12	13 17	13 25			13 34		
Eaglescliffe	a																		14 27			
Middlesbrough	a								13 30												14 28	
Darlington	d	12 09			12 16	12 28	12 33							13 03	13 14	13 17	13 26			13 34		
Durham	d	12 27			12 35	12 45								13 19	13 30	13 35				13 50		
Chester-le-Street	d				12 42															13 57		
Newcastle	a	12 43			12 50	12 59	13 02				13 25			13 33	13 45	13 53	13 57			14 10		
Hartlepool	a																		14 46			
Sunderland	a																		15 17			
Newcastle	d	12 45					13 05			13 15	13 26			13 36			13 59					14 15
Morpeth	d									13a36												14a36
Alnmouth for Alnwick	d													14 00								
Berwick-upon-Tweed	d	13 28															14 42					
Dunbar	d																					
Edinburgh	a	14 15					14 31				14 53			15 34			15 27					
Edinburgh	d										15 00						15 36					
Haymarket	d										15 04						15 45					
Motherwell	a																16 27					
Glasgow Central	a																16 51					
Stirling	a																					
Perth	a																					
Inverness	a																					
Inverkeithing	a										15 18											
Kirkcaldy	a										15 35											
Leuchars	a										16 00											
Dundee	a										16 19											
Arbroath	a										16 36											
Montrose	a										16 52											
Stonehaven	a										17 15											
Aberdeen	a										17 38											

A The Flying Scotsman
B The Northern Lights

Table 26

Saturdays from 11 September

London - Humberside, Yorkshire, North East England and Scotland

Station		XC	GR	HT	EM	XC	GR	GR	TP	TP	NT	XC	GR	EM	XC	GR	GR	TP	TP	NT	XC	GR
							A															
London Kings Cross ⊖	d		11 30	11 48			12 00	12 10					12 30			13 00	13 10					13 30
Stevenage	d		11 50																			13 49
Peterborough	a		12 21				12 46	12 56					13 16			13 46	13 56					14 20
Norwich	d				10 57									11 57								
Peterborough	d		12 21		12 25		12 47	12 56					13 16	13 28		13 46	13 56					14 21
Grantham	a		12 42	12 49	12 58			13 15					13 35	13 56			14 16					14 40
	d		12 42	12 49				13 15					13 35	13 58			14 16					14 40
Newark North Gate	a							13 27									14 28					14 52
	d							13 27									14 28					14 52
Retford	d			13 13													14 43					
Doncaster	a		13 14	13 26				13 52					14 07			14 33	14 58					
Selby	a			13 42																		
Hull	a			14 22																		
Wakefield Westgate	a							14 16									15 15					
Leeds	a							14 35									15 35					
Shipley	a																					
Bradford Forster Square	a																					
Keighley	a																					
Skipton	a																					
Sheffield	d	12 21				12 54						13 21			13 54						14 21	
Doncaster	d		13 15			13 21							14 07		14 18	14 34						
York	a		13 39			13 44	13 55						14 34		14 44	14 58						15 39
Scarborough	a																					
Leeds	d	13 07							13 27	13 57		14 07						14 27	14 57		15 07	
York	d	13 34	13 41			13 49	13 59		13 54	14 26		14 34	14 36		14 47	15 00		14 54	15 26		15 34	15 42
Thirsk	d									14 46									15 46			
Northallerton	d								14 23	15 00			14 55					15 23	15 55			
Darlington	a	13 59	14 09			14 16			14 34			14 59	15 08		15 15	15 27		15 34			15 59	16 09
Eaglescliffe	a																					
Middlesbrough	a									15 35									16 30			
Darlington	d	14 01	14 09			14 17			14 34			15 01	15 08		15 16	15 28		15 34			16 01	16 10
Durham	d	14 17	14 27			14 35			14 50			15 17	15 26		15 33	15 45		15 50			16 17	16 27
Chester-le-Street	d					14 42												15 57				
Newcastle	a	14 32	14 43			14 50	14 54		15 06			15 32	15 42		15 46	16 01		16 12			16 32	16 43
Hartlepool	a																					
Sunderland	a																					
Newcastle	d	14 36	14 45				14 59				15 15	15 36	15 47			16 03				16 15	16 36	16 45
Morpeth	d										15a35	15 49								16a36		
Alnmouth for Alnwick	d											16 03				16 30						
Berwick-upon-Tweed	d	15 18					15 43									16 52					17 18	
Dunbar	d	15 41																			17 41	
Edinburgh	a	16 05	16 13				16 29					17 05	17 14			17 37					18 05	18 13
Edinburgh	d						16 33									17 40					18 08	
Haymarket	d						16 38									17 45					18 13	
Motherwell	a															18 28						
Glasgow Central	a															18 50						
Stirling	a						17 19															
Perth	a						18 00															
Inverness	a						20 08															
Inverkeithing	a																				18 25	
Kirkcaldy	a																				18 40	
Leuchars	a																				19 11	
Dundee	a																				19 24	
Arbroath	a																				19 41	
Montrose	a																				20 01	
Stonehaven	a																				20 22	
Aberdeen	a																				20 41	

A The Highland Chieftain

Table 26

Saturdays
from 11 September

London - Humberside, Yorkshire, North East England and Scotland

		EM	XC	GR	GR	EM	GC	TP	XC	XC	NT	GR	HT	GR	EM	TP	TP	NT	XC	XC	GR	GR
		◇	◇			◇		◇	◇	◇			◇		◇	◇	◇		◇	◇		
London Kings Cross	d			14 00	14 30		14 39					15 00	15 08	15 30							16 00	16 30
Stevenage	d												15u28	15 49								
Peterborough	a			14 46	15 16							15 45		16 20							16 46	17 16
Norwich	d	12 57				13 57									14 57							
Peterborough	d	14 26		14 47	15 16	15 26						15 46		16 21	16 27						16 46	17 16
Grantham	a	14 57			15 35	15 55							16 11	16 40	16 55							17 35
	d				15 35								16 11	16 40								17 35
Newark North Gate	a				15 47									16 52								17 47
	d				15 47									16 52								17 47
Retford	d				16 02								16 32									18 02
Doncaster	a			15 35	16 18		16 21					16 32	16 47	17 16							17 35	18 17
Selby	a												17 05									
Hull	a												17 47									
Wakefield Westgate	a				16 36									17 33								18 35
Leeds	a				16 54									17 53								18 53
Shipley	a																					
Bradford Forster Square	a																					
Keighley	a																					
Skipton	a																					
Sheffield	d		14b54						15 21	15 54									16 21	16 54		
Doncaster	d		15 18	15 36						16 17		16 33								17 21	17 35	
York	a		15 44	15 59						16 39		16 56								17 44	17 58	
Scarborough	a																					
Leeds	d							15 57	16 07							16 27	16 57		17 07			
York	d		15 47	16 01				16 26	16 34	16 43		16 57				17g02	17 26		17 33	17 47	18 02	
Thirsk	d							16 46								17 20	17 43					
Northallerton	d							16 55								17 28	17 53				18 21	
Darlington	a		16 13	16 29					16 59	17 10		17 27				17 37			17 59	18 12	18 34	
Eaglescliffe	a																					
Middlesbrough	a							17 33									18 32					
Darlington	d		16 15	16 29					17 01	17 12		17 27				17 38			18 01	18 14	18 34	
Durham	d		16 33						17 17	17f33		17 45				17 55			18 17	18 30		
Chester-le-Street	d									17 39						18 01						
Newcastle	a		16 46	16 59					17 32	17 51		18 01				18 15			18 36	18 45	19 04	
Hartlepool	a																					
Sunderland	a																					
Newcastle	d			17 01					17 36		17 44	18 02						18 28	18 43		19 06	
Morpeth	d										18a06							18a49				
Alnmouth for Alnwick	d								18 02													
Berwick-upon-Tweed	d											18 45							19 26		19 49	
Dunbar	d																		19 50			
Edinburgh	a			18 27					19 07			19 34							20 15		20 35	
Edinburgh	d			18 32					19 10			19 39							20 22			
Haymarket	d			18 37					19 14			19 43							20 26			
Motherwell	a								19 55			20 22										
Glasgow Central	a								20 24			20 45										
Stirling	a																					
Perth	a																					
Inverness	a																					
Inverkeithing	a			18 54															20 43			
Kirkcaldy	a			19 11															20 59			
Leuchars	a			19 38															21 31			
Dundee	a			19 53															21 47			
Arbroath	a			20 10																		
Montrose	a			20 26																		
Stonehaven	a			20 49																		
Aberdeen	a			21 12																		

f arr. 1728

g arr. 1652

Table 26

Saturdays
from 11 September

London - Humberside, Yorkshire, North East England and Scotland

		EM	GC	TP	XC	GR	HT	GR	EM	TP	XC	NT	TP	NT	XC	XC	GR	GR	GR	GR	TP	XC	GR
		◇	A	◇	◇		◇		◇	◇	◇		◇		◇	◇					◇	◇	
London Kings Cross	d		16 50			17 00	17 04	17 30									17 40	18 00	18 03	18 30			18 35
Stevenage	d						17u24	17 50															
Peterborough	a					17 45		18 21									18 27	18 46	18 52				19 21
Norwich	d	15 52							16 57														
Peterborough	d	17 27				17 46		18 21	18 26								18 27	18 46	18 52				19 21
Grantham	a	18 01					18 10	18 42	18 55								18 48			19 30			
	d						18 10	18 42									18 48			19 30			
Newark North Gate	a							18 54									19 00		19 20				
	d							18 54									19 00		19 20				
Retford	d						18 31																
Doncaster	a					18 33	18 46	19 17									19 24	19 33		20 01			20 08
Selby	a						19 07																
Hull	a						19 47																
Wakefield Westgate	a							19 35											20 00	20 19			
Leeds	a							19 51											20 22	20 35			
Shipley	a																			20s56			
Bradford Forster Square	a																			21 06			
Keighley	a							20s17															
Skipton	a							20 31															
Sheffield	d				17 21						17 47				18 21	18 54						19 21	
Doncaster	d					18 34										19 22	19 25	19 34					20 08
York	a		18 45			18 56										19 44	19 48	19 57					20 34
Scarborough	a																						
Leeds	d			17 57	18 07					18 27	18 35	18 41	18 57		19 07						19 57	20 07	
York	d		18 46	18 26	18 34	18 58				18 56	19 04	19b29	19 26		19 34	19 47	19 50	20 02			20 27	20 34	20 41
Thirsk	d		19 03	18 46									19 42								20 43		
Northallerton	d		19 10	18 55						19 21			19 50								20 51		
Darlington	a				19 01	19 25				19 33	19 37				20 03	20 12	20 18	20 30				21 04	21 09
Eaglescliffe	a		19 28																				
Middlesbrough	a			19 28									20 23								21 25		
Darlington	d				19 02	19 26				19 34	19 39				20 04	20 14	20 19	20 31				21 05	21 09
Durham	d				19 20	19 43				19 50	19 55				20 22	20 30	20 36					21 22	21 27
Chester-le-Street	d															20 37							
Newcastle	a				19 35	19 59				20 09	20 10				20 33	20 51	20 57	21 00				21 33	21 45
Hartlepool	a		19 56																				
Sunderland	a		20 35																				
Newcastle	d				19 37	20 01					20 14			20 24	20 36			21 02				21 36	
Morpeth	d													20a45				21 17					
Alnmouth for Alnwick	d				20 04													21 33				22 00	
Berwick-upon-Tweed	d										20 56				21 20			21 55				22 21	
Dunbar	d					21 05									21 43								
Edinburgh	a				21 06	21 30					21 39				22 10			22 42				23 04	
Edinburgh	d				21 10	21 45																	
Haymarket	d				21 14	21 49																	
Motherwell	a				21 55	22 26																	
Glasgow Central	a				22 18	22 46																	
Stirling	a																						
Perth	a																						
Inverness	a																						
Inverkeithing	a																						
Kirkcaldy	a																						
Leuchars	a																						
Dundee	a																						
Arbroath	a																						
Montrose	a																						
Stonehaven	a																						
Aberdeen	a																						

A The 21st Century Limited
b arr. 1918

Table 26

Saturdays from 11 September

London - Humberside, Yorkshire, North East England and Scotland

Station		GR	EM	XC	GR	GC	TP	GR	HT	EM	GC	GR	XC	GR A	GR B	EM	XC
London Kings Cross ⊖	d	18 40			19 00	19 07		19 30	19 37		19 48	20 00		20 30	20 30		
Stevenage	d				19 19				19u57								
Peterborough	a	19 26			19 50			20 16				20 46		21 16	21 16		
Norwich	d		17 54							18 57							
Peterborough	d	19 27	19 30		19 51			20 16		20 27		20 46		21 17	21 17	21 27	
Grantham	a		19 59					20 35	20 41	20 58		21 05		21 38	21 38	22 00	
	d		20 03					20 35	20 43	20 58		21 05		21 38	21 38	22 02	
Newark North Gate	a	19 55						20 47				21 17		21 49	21 49		
	d	19 55						20 47				21 17		21 49	21 49		
Retford	d	20 11							21 05			21 32					
Doncaster	a	20 27			20 37			21 11	21 20		21 29	21 47		22 14	22 14		
Selby	a	20 43							21 35								
Hull	a	21 27							22 16								
Wakefield Westgate	a											22 05					
Leeds	a											22 24					
Shipley	a																
Bradford Forster Square	a																
Keighley	a																
Skipton	a																
Sheffield	d			19 54									20 54				21 54
Doncaster	d			20 18	20 38			21 12					21 26	22 14	22 14		22 20
York	a			20 40	21 00	21 15		21 36					21 48	22 38	22 38		22 43
Scarborough	a																
Leeds	d						20 45										
York	d			20 45	21 02	21 17	21 11	21 42					21 51	22 39	22 39		
Thirsk	d					21 36	21 28										
Northallerton	d				21 23	21 46	21 36										
Darlington	a			21 14	21 36		21 47	22 09					22 21	23 07	23 44		
Eaglescliffe	a					22 06											
Middlesbrough	a																
Darlington	d			21 15	21 36		21 48	22 10					22 23	23 09	23 45		
Durham	d			21 33	21 54		22 05	22 27					22 44	23 25	00 02		
Chester-le-Street	d			21 40									22 51				
Newcastle	a			21 50	22 12		22 19	22 45					23 05	23 46	00 26		
Hartlepool	a					22 25											
Sunderland	a					22 54											
Newcastle	d																
Morpeth	d																
Alnmouth for Alnwick	d																
Berwick-upon-Tweed	d																
Dunbar	d																
Edinburgh	a																
Edinburgh	d																
Haymarket	d																
Motherwell	a																
Glasgow Central	a																
Stirling	a																
Perth	a																
Inverness	a																
Inverkeithing	a																
Kirkcaldy	a																
Leuchars	a																
Dundee	a																
Arbroath	a																
Montrose	a																
Stonehaven	a																
Aberdeen	a																

A From 18 September

B 11 September

Table 26

Sundays until 11 July

London - Humberside, Yorkshire, North East England and Scotland

Station		TP	XC	GR	TP	XC	GR	TP	XC	GR	GC	GR	TP	TP	GR	XC	GR B	GR	EM	TP	EM
London Kings Cross ⊖	d									09 00	09 07	09 10			09 30		10 00	10 10			
Stevenage	d									09 19											
Peterborough	a									09 48	09 52	09 57			10 14		10 44	10 54			
Norwich	d																		09 33		
Peterborough	d									09 49	09 54	09 57			10 14		10 45	10 54	11 11		
Grantham	a											10 19					11 07		11 52		
	d											10 19					11 07		11 56		
Newark North Gate	a									10 19								11 24			
	d									10 19								11 24			
Retford	d											10 41						11 39			
Doncaster	a									10 44		10 57			11 05		11 39	11 55			
Selby	a																				
Hull	a																				
Wakefield Westgate	a											11 15						12 13			
Leeds	a											11 34						12 32			
Shipley	a																				
Bradford Forster Square	a																				
Keighley	a																				
Skipton	a																				
Sheffield	d								09 21							10 21					11 45
Doncaster	d						09 43			10 44					11 06		11 41				12 07
York	a						10 05			11 07	11 14				11 29		12 05				12 29
Scarborough	a																				
Leeds	d	07 40			08 40	09 08		09 40	10 08					10 40		1108				11 40	
York	d	08 21		09 00	09 10	09 37	10 06	10 13	10 36	11 09	11 18		10 45	11 15	11 30	11 36	12 06			12 15	
Thirsk	d	08 37									11 35		11 02								
Northallerton	d	08 45		09 20	09 30			10 35			11 44		11 10	11 35						12 35	
Darlington	a	08 56		09 32	09 41	10 03	10 34	10 46	11 02	11 36				11 46	11 58	12 03	12 34			12 46	
Eaglescliffe	a										12 03										
Middlesbrough	a	09 25											11 43								
Darlington	d			09 33	09 42	10 04	10 34	10 47	11 04	11 37				11 47	11 58	12 04	12 34			12 47	
Durham	d			09 50	10 00	10 21	10 52	11 08	11 20	11 54				12 03		12 21	12 52			13 03	
Chester-le-Street	d																				
Newcastle	a			10 06	10 18	10 35	11 08	11 24	11 35	12 10				12 20	12 28	12 35	13 08			13 20	
Hartlepool	a										12 22										
Sunderland	a										12 52										
Newcastle	d		09 45	10 15		10 38	11 11		11 38	12 15					12 31	12 38	13 09				
Morpeth	d		09 57	10 30																	
Alnmouth for Alnwick	d		10 11	10 46					12 02												
Berwick-upon-Tweed	d			11 08		11 20	11 54			12 58						13 20					
Dunbar	d			11 32		11 43										13 41					
Edinburgh	a		11 13	11 57		12 07	12 38		13 03	13 46					14 02	14 10	14 35				
Edinburgh	d			12 04		12 12	12 41														
Haymarket	d			12 08		12 16	12 45														
Motherwell	a			12 46		12 53	13 33														
Glasgow Central	a			13 08		13 12	13 56														
Stirling	a																				
Perth	a																				
Inverness	a																				
Inverkeithing	a																				
Kirkcaldy	a																				
Leuchars	a																				
Dundee	a																				
Arbroath	a																				
Montrose	a																				
Stonehaven	a																				
Aberdeen	a																				

B The Flying Scotsman

Table 26

Sundays
until 11 July

London - Humberside, Yorkshire, North East England and Scotland

		GR	HT	XC	GR	GR	EM	GC	TP	TP	XC	GR	GR	TP	GR	HT	XC	XC	GR	GR	TP	XC	GR
		◇	◇	◇	A		◇		◇	◇	◇			◇	B	◇	◇	◇			◇	◇	
London Kings Cross 15 ⊖	d	10 30	10 41		11 00	11 10		11 35				12 00	12 10		12 30	12 40			13 00	13 10			13 30
Stevenage 4	d	10 49	11u01										12 29			13u00			13 19				13 49
Peterborough 8	a	11 18			11 44	11 54						12 44	12 58		13 14				13 50	13 56			14 18
Norwich	d						10 47																
Peterborough 8	d	11 19			11 45	11 54	12 18					12 44	12 59		13 15				13 51	13 57			14 19
Grantham 7	a		11 45			12 16	12 48						13 21			13 44				14 19			
	d		11 46			12 16							13 21			13 45				14 19			
Newark North Gate 7	a					12 28						13 14								14 31			
	d					12 28						13 14								14 31			
Retford 10	d		12 07			12 43							13 43			14 06							
Doncaster 7	a	12 09	12 23		12 37	12 59		13 08				13 39	13 59		14 07	14 20			14 41	14 56			15 09
Selby	a		12 41													14 36							
Hull	a		13 23													15 16							
Wakefield Westgate 7	a					13 17							14 16							15 13			
Leeds 10	a					13 36							14 36							15 33			
Shipley	a																						
Bradford Forster Square	a																						
Keighley	a																						
Skipton	a																						
Sheffield 7 ⇌	d			11 21							12 21						13 21	13 51				14 21	
Doncaster 7	d	12 10			12 38							13 40			14 09			14 15	14 42				15 10
York 8	a	12 33			13 02							14 04			14 33			14 43	15 05				15 34
Scarborough	a																						
Leeds 10	d			12 08					12 12	12 40	13 08			13 40			14 08				14 40	15 08	
York 8	d	12 35		12 40	13 09				12 45	13 15	13 36	14 06		14 15	14 35		14 39	14 46	15 07		1515	15 36	15 38
Thirsk	d								13 02														
Northallerton	d								13 10	13 35		14 25		14 35							15 35		
Darlington 7	a	13 02		13 08	13 37					13 46	14 02	14 38		14 46	15 03		15 07	15 15	15 34		15 46	16 01	16 07
Eaglescliffe	a																						
Middlesbrough	a								13 43														
Darlington 7	d	13 03		13 10	13 37					13 47	14 04	14 38		14 47	15 03		15 09	15 17	15 35		15 47	16 03	16 07
Durham	d			13 26	13 55					14 03	14 20	14 56		15 03			15 25	15 33	15 54		16 03	16 19	16 25
Chester-le-Street	d									14 09													
Newcastle 8 ⇌	a	13 32		13 41	14 12					14 22	14 35	15 12		15 20	15 33		15 38	15 46	16 10		16 20	16 34	16 41
Hartlepool	a																						
Sunderland ⇌	a																						
Newcastle 8 ⇌	d	13 34		13 43	14 14						14 37	15 14			15 34		15 41		16 11			16 38	16 42
Morpeth	d																15 54						16 58
Alnmouth for Alnwick	d			14 08													16 08						17 14
Berwick-upon-Tweed	d	14 17									15 20	15 57										17 20	17 36
Dunbar	d										15 43											17 43	
Edinburgh 10	a	15 02		15 09	15 40						16 07	16 43			17 00		17 09		17 37			18 07	18 22
Edinburgh	d	15 11			16 00										17 11				17 42			18 10	
Haymarket	d	15 16			16 04										17 16				17 46			18 15	
Motherwell	a	15 55																	18 24				
Glasgow Central 15	a	16 15																	18 45				
Stirling	a														17 52								
Perth	a														18 28								
Inverness	a														20 44								
Inverkeithing	a				16 24																	18 27	
Kirkcaldy	a				16 41																	18 43	
Leuchars 3	a				17 05																	19 13	
Dundee	a				17 24																	19 28	
Arbroath	a				17 41																	19 45	
Montrose	a				17 59																	19 59	
Stonehaven	a				18 22																	20 22	
Aberdeen	a				18 46																	20 42	

A The Northern Lights
B The Highland Chieftain

Table 26

Sundays
until 11 July

London - Humberside, Yorkshire, North East England and Scotland

		XC	GC	GR	GR	TP	XC	GR	EM	XC	GR	GR	TP	TP	XC	XC	GR	HT	EM	GC	GR	GR
		◇				◇	◇		◇	◇			◇	◇	◇	◇		◇	◇			
London Kings Cross 15 ⊖	d		13 45	14 00	14 10			14 30			15 00	15 10					15 30	15 44		15 57	16 00	16 10
Stevenage 4	d										15 19							16u04				16 29
Peterborough 8	a			14 44	14 54			15 14			15 49	15 54					16 14				16 46	16 58
Norwich	d								13 49										14 47			
Peterborough 8	d			14 45	14 54			15 14	15 26		15 49	15 55					16 15		16 24		16 47	16 59
Grantham 7	a				15 16				15 56			16 17					16 39	16 48	16 54			
	d				15 16							16 18					16 39	16 49				
Newark North Gate 7	a				15 28							16 30					16 50					
	d				15 28							16 31					16 50					
Retford 10	d				15 43													17 10				17 39
Doncaster 7	a			15 38	15 59			16 07				16 57					17 16	17 25		17 30	17 39	17 55
Selby	a																	17 49				
Hull	a																	18 32				
Wakefield Westgate 7	a				16 17							17 14										18 12
Leeds 10	a				16 36							17 34										18 30
Shipley	a																					
Bradford Forster Square	a																					
Keighley	a																					
Skipton	a																					
Sheffield 7 ⇌	d	14 51					15 21			15 51					16 21	16 51						
Doncaster 7	d	15 15		15 39				16 09		16 17						17 15	17 20				17 40	
York 8	a	15 40	15 44	16 04				16 32		16 40	17 03					17 42	17 46				18 04	
Scarborough	a																					
Leeds 10	d					15 40	16 08						16 12	16 40	17 08							
York 8	d	15 46	15 50	16 06		16 15	16 36	16 42		16 46	17 05		16 40	1714	17 36	17 44	17 47				18 07	
Thirsk	d		16 06										17 02									
Northallerton	d		16 16			16 35							17 10	17 35								
Darlington 7	a	16 12		16 34		16 46	17 01	17 09		17 14	17 32			17 46	18 01	18 10	18 15				18 35	
Eaglescliffe	a		16 36																			
Middlesbrough	a												17 43									
Darlington 7	d	16 14		16 34		16 47	17 03	17 10		17 15	17 33			17 47	18 03	18 11	18 16				18 36	
Durham	d	16 31				17 03	17 19			17 33				18 03	18 19	18 28	18 33					
Chester-le-Street	d													18 09								
Newcastle 8 ⇌	a	16 45		17 04		17 20	17 34	17 39		17 48	18 02			18 22	18 34	18 42	18 52				19 05	
Hartlepool	a		16 55																			
Sunderland ⇌	a		17 35																			
Newcastle 8 ⇌	d			17 07			17 38	17 45			18 05				18 38						19 07	
Morpeth	d																					
Alnmouth for Alnwick	d						18 02															
Berwick-upon-Tweed	d							18 28			18 48				19 20							
Dunbar	d														19 43							
Edinburgh 10	a			18 33			19 03	19 14			19 33				20 07						20 35	
Edinburgh	d			18 42							19 37				20 12							
Haymarket	d			18 47							19 42				20 16							
Motherwell	a										20 19				20 53							
Glasgow Central 15	a										20 38				21 12							
Stirling	a																					
Perth	a																					
Inverness	a																					
Inverkeithing	a			19 01																		
Kirkcaldy	a			19 18																		
Leuchars 3	a			19 43																		
Dundee	a			19 57																		
Arbroath	a			20 15																		
Montrose	a			20 31																		
Stonehaven	a			20 54																		
Aberdeen	a			21 17																		

Table 26

Sundays until 11 July

London - Humberside, Yorkshire, North East England and Scotland

		EM	TP	XC	GR	GR	GR	TP	TP	XC	XC	XC	GR	HT	EM	GR	GR	GC	TP	XC	GR	GR
London Kings Cross ⊖	d				16 30	16 40	17 10						17 30	17 41		18 00	18 10	18 20			18 30	18 40
Stevenage	d				16 49								17 49	18u01							18 50	
Peterborough	a				17 18	17 24	17 54						18 18			18 44	18 54				19 19	19 25
Norwich	d	15 53													16 57							
Peterborough	d	17 14			17 19	17 25	17 54						18 19		18 30	18 45	18 55				19 19	19 25
Grantham	a	17 52				17 47	18 17							18 45	18 59	19 06						19 47
	d	17 55				17 47	18 17							18 46	19 01	19 06						19 47
Newark North Gate	a												18 49				19 25					
	d												18 49				19 26					
Retford	d													19 07			19 42					
Doncaster	a				18 10		18 50						19 14	19 23		19 42	19 58				20 12	20 20
Selby	a													19 39								
Hull	a													20 25								
Wakefield Westgate	a					18 38	19 07										20 16					20 38
Leeds	a					18 59	19 27										20 35					20 59
Shipley	a																					
Bradford Forster Square	a																					
Keighley	a																					
Skipton	a																					
Sheffield	d			17 21						17 51	18 21	18 51								19 21		
Doncaster	d				18 11					18 15		19 17	19 20			19 42					20 12	
York	a				18 34							19 42	19 45			20 07		20 23			20 39	
Scarborough	a																					
Leeds	d		17 40	18c08				18e12	18 40	18g57	19 08								19 40	20 08		
York	d		18b14	18 36	18 42			18 40	19f14	19 24	19 36	19 45	19 47			20 08		20 25	20h13	20 35	20 40	
Thirsk	d							18 59										20 42	20 30			
Northallerton	d		18 35		19 01			19 07	19 35				20 08					20 50	20 38		21 00	
Darlington	a		18 46	19 01	19 15				19 46	19 51	20 03	20 10	20 20			20 36				21 03	21 13	
Eaglescliffe	a																	21 13				
Middlesbrough	a							19 40											21 12			
Darlington	d		18 47	19 03	19 15				19 47	19 53	20 04	20 12	20 21			20 36				21 04	21 13	
Durham	d		19 03	19 19	19 33				20 03	20 09	20 22	20 28	20 38							21 22	21 31	
Chester-le-Street	d								20 09	20 18												
Newcastle	a		19 20	19 34	19 51				20 22	20 26	20 37	20 43	20 56			21 06				21 37	21 47	
Hartlepool	a																	21 33				
Sunderland	a																	22 05				
Newcastle	d			19 40							20 39	20 49				21 07				21 39	21 52	
Morpeth	d											21 02										
Alnmouth for Alnwick	d			20 05								21 16				21 35				22 07		
Berwick-upon-Tweed	d										21 25	21 37				21 57				22 30	22 36	
Dunbar	d										21 50										22 59	
Edinburgh	a			21 06							22 15	22 20				22 44				23 14	23 27	
Edinburgh	d			21 12																		
Haymarket	d			21 16																		
Motherwell	a			21 53																		
Glasgow Central	a			22 14																		
Stirling	a																					
Perth	a																					
Inverness	a																					
Inverkeithing	a																					
Kirkcaldy	a																					
Leuchars	a																					
Dundee	a																					
Arbroath	a																					
Montrose	a																					
Stonehaven	a																					
Aberdeen	a																					

b arr. 1806
c arr. 1802
e arr. 1804
f arr. 1906
g arr. 1851
h arr. 2006

Table 26

Sundays until 11 July

London - Humberside, Yorkshire, North East England and Scotland

		EM	XC	GR	GR	GC	GR	TP	XC	GR	EM	GR	GR	HT	GR	EM	TP	GR	GR	GR	GR
London Kings Cross ⊖	d			19 00	19 10	19 27	19 30			19 35		20 00	20 03	20 10	20 30			21 00	21 30	22 00	22 10
Stevenage	d						19 50			19 54				20u30							
Peterborough	a			19 44	19 55		20 19			20 23		20 44	20 50		21 14			21 45	22 14	22 44	22s59
Norwich	d	17 56									18 57					20 52					
Peterborough	d	19 26		19 44	19 56		20 19			20 24	20 31	20 44	20 50		21 14	22 22		21 46	22 15	22 45	
Grantham	a	19 56			20 19						21 01			21 18	21 36	22 50			22 39		23s31
	d				20 19									21 19	21 36				22 39		
Newark North Gate	a				20 30										21 48				22 50		23s42
	d				20 30										21 48				22 50		
Retford	d													21 40	22 03				23 06		
Doncaster	a			20 35	20 56	21 02	21 10			21 14		21 36		21 54	22 19			22 42	23 27	23 42	00s12
Selby	a				21 15									22s09							
Hull	a				21 56									22 50							
Wakefield Westgate	a						21 27						21 57		22 37						
Leeds	a						21 47						22 16		23 00				00 24		00 18
Shipley	a																				
Bradford Forster Square	a																				
Keighley	a																				
Skipton	a																				
Sheffield	d		19 51						20 51												
Doncaster	d		20 18	20 35					21 21	21 23		21 36						22 43		23 45	
York	a		20 44	21 00					21 42	21 46		22 00						23 09		00 39	
Scarborough	a																				
Leeds	d							20 40									22e12				
York	d		20 47	21 02				21 08	21 44	21 48		22 02					22 42	23 11			
Thirsk	d							21 26									23 06				
Northallerton	d							21 34									23 16	23 47			
Darlington	a		21 18	21 30				21 46	22 22	22 28		22 43					23 32	23 59			
Eaglescliffe	a																				
Middlesbrough	a																				
Darlington	d		21 19	21 30				21 46	22 23	22 29		22 43					23 33	23 59			
Durham	d		21 37					22 03	22 40	22 46		23 01					23 49	00 17			
Chester-le-Street	d																				
Newcastle	a		21 54	22 02				22 20	23 07	23 16		23 34					00 21	00 50			
Hartlepool	a																				
Sunderland	a																				
Newcastle	d																				
Morpeth	d																				
Alnmouth for Alnwick	d																				
Berwick-upon-Tweed	d																				
Dunbar	d																				
Edinburgh	a																				
Edinburgh	d																				
Haymarket	d																				
Motherwell	a																				
Glasgow Central	a																				
Stirling	a																				
Perth	a																				
Inverness	a																				
Inverkeithing	a																				
Kirkcaldy	a																				
Leuchars	a																				
Dundee	a																				
Arbroath	a																				
Montrose	a																				
Stonehaven	a																				
Aberdeen	a																				

Table 26

Sundays
18 July to 05 September

London - Humberside, Yorkshire, North East England and Scotland

		TP	XC	GR	TP	XC	GR	TP	XC	GR	GC	GR	TP	TP	GR	XC	GR	GR	EM	EM	TP
																	A				
London Kings Cross 15 ⊖	d									08 45	08 53	08 58			09 15		09 45	09 55			
Stevenage 4	d									09 19											
Peterborough 6	a									09 48		09 56			10 15		10 44	10 53			
Norwich	d																		09 33		
Peterborough 6	d									09 49		09 57			10 16		10 45	10 54	11 11		
Grantham 7	a											10 19					11 07		11 52		
	d											10 19					11 07				
Newark North Gate 7	a									10 19								11 24			
	d									10 19								11 24			
Retford 10	d											10 41						11 39			
Doncaster 7	a									10 44		10 57			11 06		11 39	11 55			
Selby	a																				
Hull	a																				
Wakefield Westgate 7	a											11 15						12 13			
Leeds 10	a											11 34						12 32			
Shipley	a																				
Bradford Forster Square	a																				
Keighley	a																				
Skipton	a																				
Sheffield 7	d								09 21							10 21				11 31	
Doncaster 7	d						09 43			10 44					11 07		11 41			11 53	
York 8	a						10 05			11 07	11 14				11 30		12 05			12 15	
Scarborough	a																				
Leeds 10	d	07 40			08 40	09 08		09 40	10 08					10 40		11 08					11 40
York 8	d	08 21		09 00	09 10	09 37	10 06	1013	10 36	11 09	11 18		10 45	11 15	11 31	11 36	12 06				12 15
Thirsk	d	08 37									11 35		11 02								
Northallerton	d	08 45		09 20	09 30			10 35			11 44		11 10	11 35							12 35
Darlington 7	a	08 56		09 32	09 41	10 03	10 34	10 46	11 02	11 36				11 46	11 59	12 03	12 34				12 46
Eaglescliffe	a										12 03										
Middlesbrough	a	09 25											11 43								
Darlington 7	d			09 33	09 42	10 04	10 34	10 47	11 04	11 37				11 47	11 59	12 04	12 34				12 47
Durham	d			09 50	10 00	10 21	10 52	11 08	11 20	11 54				12 03		12 21	12 52				13 03
Chester-le-Street	d																				
Newcastle 8	a			10 06	10 18	10 35	11 08	11 24	11 35	12 10				12 20	12 29	12 35	13 08				13 20
Hartlepool	a										12 22										
Sunderland	a										12 52										
Newcastle 8	d		09 45	10 15		10 38	11 11		11 38	12 15					12 31	12 38	13 09				
Morpeth	d		09 57	10 30																	
Alnmouth for Alnwick	d		10 11	10 46					12 02												
Berwick-upon-Tweed	d			11 08		11 20	11 54			12 58						13 20					
Dunbar	d			11 32		11 43										13 41					
Edinburgh 10	a		11 13	11 57		12 07	12 38		13 03	13 46					14 02	14 10	14 35				
Edinburgh	d			12 04		12 12	12 41														
Haymarket	d			12 08		12 16	12 45														
Motherwell	a			12 46		12 53	13 33														
Glasgow Central 15	a			13 08		13 12	13 56														
Stirling	a																				
Perth	a																				
Inverness	a																				
Inverkeithing	a																				
Kirkcaldy	a																				
Leuchars 3	a																				
Dundee	a																				
Arbroath	a																				
Montrose	a																				
Stonehaven	a																				
Aberdeen	a																				

A The Flying Scotsman

Table 26

Sundays
18 July to 05 September

London - Humberside, Yorkshire, North East England and Scotland

		GR	XC	GR	HT	GR	EM	TP	TP	XC	GR	GC	GR	TP	GR	XC	XC	GR	HT	GR	TP	XC	GR
				A											B								
London Kings Cross 15 ⊖	d	10 15		10 45	10 53	10 58					11 45	11 51	11 57		12 15			12 45	12 50	12 55			13 15
Stevenage 4	d	10 49			11u25								12 29					13 16	13u23				13 49
Peterborough 6	a	11 18		11 44		11 56					12 43		12 58		13 13			13 48		13 56			14 18
Norwich	d						10 47																
Peterborough 6	d	11 19		11 45		11 57	12 18				12 44		12 59		13 15			13 48		13 57			14 19
Grantham 7	a				12 13	12 19	12 46						13 21						14 15	14 20			
	d				12 14	12 19							13 21						14 16	14 20			
Newark North Gate 7	a					12 31					13 14									14 32			
	d					12 31					13 14									14 32			
Retford 10	d				12 34	12 46							13 43						14 36				
Doncaster 7	a	12 09		12 37	12 50	13 02					13 39	13 47	13 59		14 07			14 39	14 51	14 57			15 09
Selby	a				13 08														15 07				
Hull	a				13 53														15 48				
Wakefield Westgate 7	a					13 19							14 16							15 15			
Leeds 10	a					13 39							14 36							15 35			
Shipley	a																						
Bradford Forster Square	a																						
Keighley	a																						
Skipton	a																						
Sheffield 7	d		11 21							12 21						13 21	13 51					14 21	
Doncaster 7	d	12 10		12 38							13 40				14 09		14 15	14 42					15 10
York 8	a	12 33		13 02							14 04				14 33		14 43	15 05					15 34
Scarborough	a																						
Leeds 10	d		12 08					12 12	12 40	13 08				13 40		14 08					14 40	15 08	
York 8	d	12 35	12 40	13 09				12 45	1315	13 36	14 06			14 15	14 35	14 39	14 46	15 07			15 15	15 36	15 38
Thirsk	d							13 02															
Northallerton	d							13 10	13 35		14 25			14 35							15 35		
Darlington 7	a	13 02	13 08	13 37					13 46	14 02	14 38			14 46	15 03	15 07	15 15	15 34			15 46	16 01	16 07
Eaglescliffe	a																						
Middlesbrough	a							13 43															
Darlington 7	d	13 03	13 10	13 37					13 47	14 04	14 38			14 47	15 03	15 09	15 17	15 35			15 47	16 03	16 07
Durham	d		13 26	13 55					14 03	14 20	14 56			15 03		15 25	15 33	15 54			16 03	16 19	16 25
Chester-le-Street	d								14 09														
Newcastle 8	a	13 32	13 41	14 12					14 22	14 35	15 12			15 20	15 33	15 38	15 46	16 10			16 20	16 34	16 41
Hartlepool	a																						
Sunderland	a																						
Newcastle 8	d	13 34	13 43	14 14						14 37	15 14				15 34	15 41		16 11				16 38	16 42
Morpeth	d															15 54							16 58
Alnmouth for Alnwick	d		14 08													16 08							17 14
Berwick-upon-Tweed	d	14 17								15 20	15 57											17 20	17 36
Dunbar	d									15 43												17 43	
Edinburgh 10	a	15 02	15 09	15 40						16 07	16 43				17 00	17 09		17 37				18 07	18 22
Edinburgh	d	15 11		16 00											17 11			17 42				18 10	
Haymarket	d	15 16		16 04											17 16			17 46				18 15	
Motherwell	a	15 55																18 24					
Glasgow Central 15	a	16 15																18 45					
Stirling	a														17 52								
Perth	a														18 28								
Inverness	a														20 44								
Inverkeithing	a			16 24																		18 27	
Kirkcaldy	a			16 41																		18 43	
Leuchars 3	a			17 05																		19 13	
Dundee	a			17 24																		19 28	
Arbroath	a			17 41																		19 45	
Montrose	a			17 59																		19 59	
Stonehaven	a			18 22																		20 22	
Aberdeen	a			18 46																		20 42	

A The Northern Lights
B The Highland Chieftain

Table 26

Sundays

18 July to 05 September

London - Humberside, Yorkshire, North East England and Scotland

		XC	GR	GC	GR	TP	XC	GR	EM	XC	GR	GR	TP	TP	XC	XC	GR	EM	GR	HT	GR	EM
		◇1	R 1	R 1	R 1	◇1	◇1	R 1	◇	◇1	R 1	R 1	◇1	◇1	◇1	◇1	R 1	◇	R 1	◇1	R 1	◇
London Kings Cross 15 ⊖	d		13 45	13 51	13 55			14 15			14 45	14 55					15 15		15 45	15 51	15 55	
Stevenage 4	d										15 19									16u24	16 29	
Peterborough 8	a		14 43		14 56			15 14			15 49	15 55					16 14		16 45		16 59	
Norwich	d								13 49									14 47				15 53
Peterborough 8	d		14 45		14 57			15 15	15 26		15 49	15 55					16 15	16 24	16 47		16 59	17 14
Grantham 7	a				15 19				15 56			16 17					16 39	16 54		17 15		17 52
	d				15 19							16 18					16 39			17 16		
Newark North Gate 7	a				15 31							16 30					16 50					
	d				15 31							16 31					16 50					
Retford 10	d				15 46															17 36	17 41	
Doncaster 7	a		15 38		16 02			16 07				16 57					17 16		17 39	17 54	18 00	
Selby	a																			18 07		
Hull	a																			18 50		
Wakefield Westgate 7	a				16 19							17 14									18 17	
Leeds 10	a				16 41							17 34									18 35	
Shipley	a																					
Bradford Forster Square	a																					
Keighley	a																					
Skipton	a																					
Sheffield 7	d	14 51					15 21			15 51					16 21	16 51						
Doncaster 7	d	15 15	15 39					16 09		16 17						17 15	17 21		17 40			
York 8	a	15 40	16 04	16 11				16 32		16 40	17 03					17 42	17 45		18 04			
Scarborough	a																					
Leeds 10	d					15 40	16 08						16 12	16 40	17 08							
York 8	d	15 46	16 06	16 23		16 15	16 36	16 42		16 46	17 05		16 40	1714	17 36	17 44	17 47		18 07			
Thirsk	d			16 39									17 02									
Northallerton	d			16 49		16 35							17 10	17 35								
Darlington 7	a	16 12	16 34			16 46	17 01	17 09		17 14	17 32			17 46	18 01	18 10	18 14		18 35			
Eaglescliffe	a			17 08																		
Middlesbrough	a												17 43									
Darlington 7	d	16 14	16 34			16 47	17 03	17 10		17 15	17 33			17 47	18 03	18 11	18 15		18 36			
Durham	d	16 31				17 03	17 19			17 33				18 03	18 19	18 28	18 32					
Chester-le-Street	d													18 09								
Newcastle 8	a	16 45	17 04			17 20	17 34	17 39		17 48	18 02			18 22	18 34	18 42	18 50		19 05			
Hartlepool	a			17 28																		
Sunderland	a			17 55																		
Newcastle 8	d		17 07				17 38	17 45			18 05				18 38				19 07			
Morpeth	d																					
Alnmouth for Alnwick	d						18 02															
Berwick-upon-Tweed	d							18 28			18 48				19 20							
Dunbar	d														19 43							
Edinburgh 10	a		18 33				19 03	19 14			19 33				20 07				20 35			
Edinburgh	d		18 42								19 37				20 12							
Haymarket	d		18 47								19 42				20 16							
Motherwell	a										20 19				20 53							
Glasgow Central 15	a										20 38				21 12							
Stirling	a																					
Perth	a																					
Inverness	a																					
Inverkeithing	a		19 01																			
Kirkcaldy	a		19 18																			
Leuchars 3	a		19 43																			
Dundee	a		19 57																			
Arbroath	a		20 15																			
Montrose	a		20 31																			
Stonehaven	a		20 54																			
Aberdeen	a		21 17																			

Table 26

Sundays

18 July to 05 September

London - Humberside, Yorkshire, North East England and Scotland

		TP	XC	XC	GR	GR	GC	GR	TP	TP	XC	XC	XC	GR	EM	GR	HT	GR	TP	XC	GR	GR	EM
		◇1	◇1	◇1	R 1	R 1		R 1	◇1	◇1	◇1	◇1	◇1	R 1	◇	R 1	◇1	R 1	◇1	◇1	R 1	R 1	◇
London Kings Cross 15 ⊖	d				16 15	16 45	16 51	16 55						17 15		17 45	17 51	17 55			18 15		
Stevenage 4	d				16 49									17 49			18u23				18 50		
Peterborough 8	a				17 18	17 43		17 55						18 18		18 44		18 56			19 19		
Norwich	d														16 57								17 56
Peterborough 8	d				17 19	17 44		17 56						18 19	18 30	18 45		18 57			19 19	19 25	19 26
Grantham 7	a				17 41			18 19							18 59	19 06	19 12					19 47	19 56
	d				17 41			18 19								19 06	19 13					19 47	
Newark North Gate 7	a					18 14								18 49				19 27					
	d													18 49				19 27					
Retford 10	d																19 33	19 42					
Doncaster 7	a				18 17	18 40	18 46	18 54						19 14		19 42	19 49	19 58			20 12	20 22	
Selby	a																20 20						
Hull	a																21 04						
Wakefield Westgate 7	a							19 12										20 16				20 40	
Leeds 10	a							19 35										20 35				21 01	
Shipley	a																						
Bradford Forster Square	a																						
Keighley	a																						
Skipton	a																						
Sheffield 7	d		17 21	17 51								18 21	18 51							19 21			
Doncaster 7	d			18 15	18 18	18 43							19 17	19 20		19 42					20 12		
York 8	a				18 40	19 05							19 42	19 45		20 07					20 39		
Scarborough	a																						
Leeds 10	d	17 40	18 08	1857					18 12	18 40	←	19 08							19 40	20 08			
York 8	d	1814	18 36	19 24	18 42	19 07			18 40	19 14	19 24	19 36	19 45	19 47		20 08			2013	20 35	20 40		
Thirsk	d			→					18 59										20 30				
Northallerton	d	18 35			19 01				19 07	19 35				20 08					20 38		21 00		
Darlington 7	a	18 46	19 01		19 15	19 35				19 46	19 51	20 03	20 10	20 20		20 36				21 03	21 13		
Eaglescliffe	a																						
Middlesbrough	a								19 40										21 12				
Darlington 7	d	18 47	19 03		19 15	19 36				19 47	19 53	20 04	20 12	20 21		20 36				21 04	21 13		
Durham	d	19 03	19 19		19 33	19 53				20 03	20 09	20 22	20 28	20 38						21 22	21 31		
Chester-le-Street	d									20 09	20 18												
Newcastle 8	a	19 20	19 34		19 51	20 09				20 22	20 26	20 37	20 43	20 56		21 06				21 37	21 47		
Hartlepool	a																						
Sunderland	a																						
Newcastle 8	d		19 40			20 11						20 39	20 49			21 07				21 39	21 52		
Morpeth	d												21 02										
Alnmouth for Alnwick	d		20 05										21 16			21 35				22 07			
Berwick-upon-Tweed	d					20 54						21 25	21 37			21 57				22 30	22 36		
Dunbar	d											21 50									22 59		
Edinburgh 10	a		21 06			21 38						22 15	22 20			22 44				23 14	23 27		
Edinburgh	d		21 12			21 41																	
Haymarket	d		21 16			21 45																	
Motherwell	a		21 53			22 23																	
Glasgow Central 15	a		22 14			22 45																	
Stirling	a																						
Perth	a																						
Inverness	a																						
Inverkeithing	a																						
Kirkcaldy	a																						
Leuchars 3	a																						
Dundee	a																						
Arbroath	a																						
Montrose	a																						
Stonehaven	a																						
Aberdeen	a																						

Table 26

London - Humberside, Yorkshire, North East England and Scotland

Sundays
18 July to 05 September

Station		XC	GR	GR	GR	TP	XC	XC	GR	EM	GR	GR	HT	GR	TP	GR	GC	GR	EM	GR	GR
London Kings Cross ⊖	d		18 45	18 55	19 15						19 45	19 50	19 57	20 15		20 45	20 58	21 15		21 45	22 15
Stevenage	d			19 28							20 17		20u29								
Peterborough	a		19 43	19 58	20 14						20 46	20 50		21 14		21 45		22 14		22 43	
Norwich	d									18 57									20 52		
Peterborough	d		19 44	19 58	20 14				20 25	20 31	20 46	20 51		21 14		21 46		22 15	22 22	22 45	23 28
Grantham	a				20 38					21 01			21 17	21 36				22 39	22 50		23 42
	d				20 38								21 19	21 36				22 39			23 52
Newark North Gate	a				20 50									21 48				22 50			23 54
	d				20 50									21 48				22 50			00 04
Retford	d												21 40	22 03				23 06			
Doncaster	a		20 35	20 49	21 15				21 22		21 37		21 54	22 19		22 42	22 47	23 27		23 42	00 23
Selby	a				21 31								22s09								
Hull	a				22 11								22 50								
Wakefield Westgate	a			21 06								21 57		22 37							
Leeds	a			21 30								22 16		23 00				00 24			01 35
Shipley	a																				
Bradford Forster Square	a																				
Keighley	a																				
Skipton	a																				
Sheffield	d	19 51					20 21	20 51													
Doncaster	d	20 18	20 35					21 21	21 23		21 37					22 43				23 45	
York	a	20 44	21 00					21 42	21 47		22 01					23 09				00 39	
Scarborough	a																				
Leeds	d					20 40	21 08								22 12						
York	d	20 47	21 02			21 08	21a32	21 44	21 49		22 02				22 42	23 11					
Thirsk	d					21 26									23 06						
Northallerton	d					21 34									23 16	23 47					
Darlington	a	21 18	21 30			21 46		22 22	22 28		22 43				23 32	23 59					
Eaglescliffe	a																				
Middlesbrough	a																				
Darlington	d	21 19	21 30			21 46		22 23	22 29		22 43				23 33	23 59					
Durham	d	21 37				22 03		22 40	22 46		23 01				23 49	00 17					
Chester-le-Street	d																				
Newcastle	a	21 54	22 02			22 20		23 07	23 17		23 34				00 21	00 50					
Hartlepool	a																				
Sunderland	a																				
Newcastle	d																				
Morpeth	d																				
Alnmouth for Alnwick	d																				
Berwick-upon-Tweed	d																				
Dunbar	d																				
Edinburgh	a																				
Edinburgh	d																				
Haymarket	d																				
Motherwell	a																				
Glasgow Central	a																				
Stirling	a																				
Perth	a																				
Inverness	a																				
Inverkeithing	a																				
Kirkcaldy	a																				
Leuchars	a																				
Dundee	a																				
Arbroath	a																				
Montrose	a																				
Stonehaven	a																				
Aberdeen	a																				

Table 26

London - Humberside, Yorkshire, North East England and Scotland

Sundays
from 12 September

Station		TP	XC	GR	TP	XC	GR	TP	XC	GR	GC	GR	TP	TP	GR	XC	GR	GR	EM	TP	GR	HT
																	A					
London Kings Cross ⊖	d									09 00	09 07	09 10			09 30		10 00	10 10			10 30	10 41
Stevenage	d									09 19											10 49	11u01
Peterborough	a									09 48	09 52	09 57			10 14		10 44	10 54			11 18	
Norwich	d																					
Peterborough	d									09 49	09 54	09 57			10 14		10 45	10 54			11 19	
Grantham	a											10 19					11 07					11 45
	d											10 19					11 07					11 46
Newark North Gate	a									10 19								11 24				
	d									10 19								11 24				
Retford	d											10 41						11 39				12 07
Doncaster	a									10 44		10 57			11 05		11 39	11 55			12 09	12 23
Selby	a																					12 41
Hull	a																					13 23
Wakefield Westgate	a											11 15						12 13				
Leeds	a											11 34						12 32				
Shipley	a																					
Bradford Forster Square	a																					
Keighley	a																					
Skipton	a																					
Sheffield	d								09 21							10 21			11 31			
Doncaster	d						09 43			10 44					11 06		11 41		11 53		12 10	
York	a						10 05			11 07	11 14				11 29		12 05		12 15		12 33	
Scarborough	a																					
Leeds	d				08 40	09 08		09 47	10 08				10 18	10 40		11 08				11 40		
York	d	08 21		09 00	09 10	09 37	10 06	10 13	10 36	11 09	11 18		10 45	1115	11 30	11 36	12 06			1215	12 35	
Thirsk	d	08 37									11 35		11 02									
Northallerton	d	08 45		09 20	09 30			10 35			11 44		11 10	11 35						12 35		
Darlington	a	08 56		09 32	09 41	10 03	10 34	10 46	11 02	11 36				11 46	11 58	12 03	12 34			12 46	13 02	
Eaglescliffe	a										12 03											
Middlesbrough	a	09 25											11 43									
Darlington	d			09 33	09 42	10 04	10 34	10 47	11 04	11 37				11 47	11 58	12 04	12 34			12 47	13 03	
Durham	d			09 50	10 00	10 21	10 52	11 08	11 20	11 54				12 03		12 21	12 52			13 03		
Chester-le-Street	d																					
Newcastle	a			10 06	10 18	10 35	11 08	11 24	11 35	12 10				12 20	12 28	12 35	13 08			13 20	13 32	
Hartlepool	a										12 22											
Sunderland	a										12 52											
Newcastle	d		09 45	10 15		10 38	11 11		11 38	12 15					12 31	12 38	13 09				13 34	
Morpeth	d		09 57	10 30																		
Alnmouth for Alnwick	d		10 11	10 46					12 02													
Berwick-upon-Tweed	d			11 08		11 20	11 54			12 58						13 20					14 17	
Dunbar	d			11 32		11 43										13 41						
Edinburgh	a		11 13	11 57		12 07	12 38		13 03	13 46					14 02	14 10	14 35				15 02	
Edinburgh	d			12 04		12 12	12 41														15 11	
Haymarket	d			12 08		12 16	12 45														15 16	
Motherwell	a			12 46		12 53	13 33														15 55	
Glasgow Central	a			13 08		13 12	13 56														16 15	
Stirling	a																					
Perth	a																					
Inverness	a																					
Inverkeithing	a																					
Kirkcaldy	a																					
Leuchars	a																					
Dundee	a																					
Arbroath	a																					
Montrose	a																					
Stonehaven	a																					
Aberdeen	a																					

A The Flying Scotsman

Table 26

Sundays from 12 September

London - Humberside, Yorkshire, North East England and Scotland

		XC	GR	GR	EM	GC	TP	TP	XC	GR	GR	TP	GR	HT	XC	XC	GR	GR	TP	XC	GR	XC
			A		B								D									
London Kings Cross ⊖	d		11 00	11 10		11 35				12 00	12 10		12 30	12 40			13 00	13 10			13 30	
Stevenage	d										12 29			13u00			13 19				13 49	
Peterborough	a		11 44	11 54						12 44	12 58		13 14				13 50	13 56			14 18	
Norwich	d				10 47																	
Peterborough	d		11 45	11 54	12 18					12 44	12 59		13 15				13 51	13 57			14 19	
Grantham	a			12 16	12 48						13 21			13 44				14 19				
	d			12 16	12 50						13 21			13 45				14 19				
Newark North Gate	a			12 28						13 14								14 31				
	d			12 28						13 14								14 31				
Retford	d			12 43							13 43			14 06								
Doncaster	a		12 37	12 59		13 08				13 39	13 59		14 07	14 20			14 41	14 56			15 09	
Selby	a													14 36								
Hull	a													15 16								
Wakefield Westgate	a			13 17							14 16							15 13				
Leeds	a			13 36							14 36							15 33				
Shipley	a																					
Bradford Forster Square	a																					
Keighley	a																					
Skipton	a																					
Sheffield	d	11 21							12 21						13 21	13 51				14 21		14 51
Doncaster	d		12 38							13 40			14 09			14 15	14 42				15 10	15 15
York	a		13 02							14 04			14 33			14 43	15 05				15 34	15 40
Scarborough	a																					
Leeds	d	12 08					12 12	12 40	13 08			13 40			14 08				14 40	15 08		
York	d	12 40	13 09				12 45	13 15	13 36	14 06		1415	14 35		1439	14 46	15 07		1515	15 36	15 38	15 46
Thirsk	d						13 02															
Northallerton	d						13 10	13 35		14 25		14 35							15 35			
Darlington	a	13 08	13 37					13 46	14 02	14 38		14 46	15 03		15 07	15 15	15 34		15 46	16 01	16 07	16 12
Eaglescliffe	a																					
Middlesbrough	a						13 43															
Darlington	d	13 10	13 37					13 47	14 04	14 38		14 47	15 03		15 09	15 17	15 35		15 47	16 03	16 07	16 14
Durham	d	13 26	13 55					14 03	14 20	14 56		15 03			15 25	15 33	15 54		16 03	16 19	16 25	16 31
Chester-le-Street	d							14 09														
Newcastle	a	13 41	14 12					14 22	14 35	15 12		15 20	15 33		15 38	15 46	16 10		16 20	16 34	16 41	16 45
Hartlepool	a																					
Sunderland	a																					
Newcastle	d	13 43	14 14						14 37	15 14			15 34		15 41		16 11			16 38	16 42	
Morpeth	d														15 54						16 58	
Alnmouth for Alnwick	d	14 08													16 08						17 14	
Berwick-upon-Tweed	d								15 20	15 57										17 20	17 36	
Dunbar	d								15 43											17 43		
Edinburgh	a	15 09	15 40						16 07	16 43			17 00		17 09		17 37			18 07	18 22	
Edinburgh	d		16 00										17 11				17 42			18 10		
Haymarket	d		16 04										17 16				17 46			18 15		
Motherwell	a																18 24					
Glasgow Central	a																18 45					
Stirling	a												17 52									
Perth	a												18 28									
Inverness	a												20 44									
Inverkeithing	a		16 24																	18 27		
Kirkcaldy	a		16 41																	18 43		
Leuchars	a		17 05																	19 13		
Dundee	a		17 24																	19 28		
Arbroath	a		17 41																	19 45		
Montrose	a		17 59																	19 59		
Stonehaven	a		18 22																	20 22		
Aberdeen	a		18 46																	20 42		

A The Northern Lights
B from 24 October

D The Highland Chieftain

Table 26

Sundays from 12 September

London - Humberside, Yorkshire, North East England and Scotland

		GC	GR	GR	TP	XC	GR	EM	XC	GR	GR	TP	TP	XC	XC	GR	HT	EM	GC	GR
								A										A		
London Kings Cross ⊖	d	13 45	14 00	14 10			14 30			15 00	15 10					15 30	15 44		15 57	16 00
Stevenage	d									15 19							16u04			
Peterborough	a		14 44	14 54			15 14			15 49	15 54					16 14				16 46
Norwich	d							13 49										14 49		
Peterborough	d		14 45	14 54			15 14	15 26		15 49	15 55					16 15		16 24		16 47
Grantham	a			15 16				15 56			16 17					16 39	16 48	16 54		
	d			15 16							16 18					16 39	16 49			
Newark North Gate	a			15 28							16 30					16 50				
	d			15 28							16 31					16 50				
Retford	d			15 43													17 10			
Doncaster	a		15 38	15 59			16 07				16 57					17 16	17 25		17 30	17 39
Selby	a																17 49			
Hull	a																18 32			
Wakefield Westgate	a			16 17							17 14									
Leeds	a			16 36							17 34									
Shipley	a																			
Bradford Forster Square	a																			
Keighley	a																			
Skipton	a																			
Sheffield	d					15 21			15 51					16 21	16 51					
Doncaster	d		15 39				16 09		16 17						17 15	17 20				17 40
York	a	15 44	16 04				16 32		16 40	17 03					17 42	17 46				18 04
Scarborough	a																			
Leeds	d				15 40	16 08						16 12	16 40	17 08						
York	d	15 50	16 06		16 15	16 36	16 42		16 46	17 05		16 40	1714	17 36	17 44	17 47				18 07
Thirsk	d	16 06										17 02								
Northallerton	d	16 16			16 35							17 10	17 35							
Darlington	a		16 34		16 46	17 01	17 09		17 14	17 32			17 46	18 01	18 10	18 15				18 35
Eaglescliffe	a	16 36																		
Middlesbrough	a											17 43								
Darlington	d		16 34		16 47	17 03	17 10		17 15	17 33			17 47	18 03	18 11	18 16				18 36
Durham	d				17 03	17 19			17 33				18 03	18 19	18 28	18 33				
Chester-le-Street	d												18 09							
Newcastle	a		17 04		17 20	17 34	17 39		17 48	18 02			18 22	18 34	18 42	18 52				19 05
Hartlepool	a	16 55																		
Sunderland	a	17 35																		
Newcastle	d		17 07			17 38	17 45			18 05				18 38						19 07
Morpeth	d																			
Alnmouth for Alnwick	d					18 02														
Berwick-upon-Tweed	d						18 28			18 48				19 20						
Dunbar	d													19 43						
Edinburgh	a		18 33			19 03	19 14			19 33				20 07						20 35
Edinburgh	d		18 42							19 37				20 12						
Haymarket	d		18 47							19 42				20 16						
Motherwell	a									20 19				20 53						
Glasgow Central	a									20 38				21 12						
Stirling	a																			
Perth	a																			
Inverness	a																			
Inverkeithing	a		19 01																	
Kirkcaldy	a		19 18																	
Leuchars	a		19 43																	
Dundee	a		19 57																	
Arbroath	a		20 15																	
Montrose	a		20 31																	
Stonehaven	a		20 54																	
Aberdeen	a		21 17																	

A from 24 October

Table 26

Sundays from 12 September

London - Humberside, Yorkshire, North East England and Scotland

		GR	EM			TP	XC	GR	GR	GR	GR	TP	TP	XC	XC	XC	GR			HT	EM	GR	GR	GC	TP
		1	◇ A			◇1	◇1	1	1	1	1	◇1	◇1	◇1	◇1	◇1	1			◇1	◇ A	1	1		◇1
London Kings Cross 15 ⊖	d	16 10						16 30	16 40	17 00	17 10						17 30			17 41		18 00	18 10	18 20	
Stevenage 4	d	16 29						16 49									17 49			18u01					
Peterborough 8	a	16 58						17 18	17 24	17 44	17 54						18 18					18 44	18 54		
Norwich	d		15 53																		16 57				
Peterborough 8	d	16 59	17 14					17 19	17 25	17 44	17 54						18 19				18 30	18 45	18 55		
Grantham 7	a		17 52						17 47		18 17									18 45	18 59	19 06			
	d								17 47		18 17									18 46		19 06			
Newark North Gate 7	a									18 14							18 49						19 25		
	d									18 14							18 49						19 26		
Retford 10	d	17 39																		19 07			19 42		
Doncaster 7	a	17 55						18 10		18 40	18 50						19 14			19 23		19 42	19 58		
Selby	a																			19 39					
Hull	a																			20 25					
Wakefield Westgate 7	a	18 12							18 38		19 07												20 16		
Leeds 10	a	18 30							18 59		19 27												20 35		
Shipley	a																								
Bradford Forster Square	a																								
Keighley	a																								
Skipton	a																								
Sheffield 7	d						17 21							17 51	18 21	18 51									
Doncaster 7	d							18 11		18 43				18 15		19 17	19 20					19 42			
York 8	a							18 34		19 05						19 42	19 45					20 07		20 23	
Scarborough	a																								
Leeds 10	d					17 40	18 08					18 12	18 40	18 57	19 08										19 40
York 8	d					18 14	18 36	18 42		19 07		18 40	19 14	19 24	19 36	19 45	19 47					20 08		20 25	20 13
Thirsk	d											18 59												20 42	20 30
Northallerton	d					18 35		19 01				19 07	19 35				20 08							20 50	20 38
Darlington 7	a					18 46	19 01	19 15		19 35			19 46	19 51	20 03	20 10	20 20					20 36			
Eaglescliffe	a																							21 13	
Middlesbrough	a											19 40													21 12
Darlington 7	d					18 47	19 03	19 15		19 36			19 47	19 53	20 04	20 12	20 21					20 36			
Durham	d					19 03	19 19	19 33		19 53			20 03	20 09	20 22	20 28	20 38								
Chester-le-Street	d												20 09	20 18											
Newcastle 8	a					19 20	19 34	19 51		20 09			20 22	20 26	20 37	20 43	20 56					21 06			
Hartlepool	a																							21 33	
Sunderland	a																							22 05	
Newcastle 8	d						19 40			20 11					20 39	20 49						21 07			
Morpeth	d															21 02									
Alnmouth for Alnwick	d						20 05									21 16						21 35			
Berwick-upon-Tweed	d									20 54					21 25	21 37						21 57			
Dunbar	d														21 50										
Edinburgh 10	a						21 06			21 38					22 15	22 20						22 44			
Edinburgh	d						21 12			21 41															
Haymarket	d						21 16			21 45															
Motherwell	a						21 53			22 23															
Glasgow Central 15	a						22 14			22 45															
Stirling	a																								
Perth	a																								
Inverness	a																								
Inverkeithing	a																								
Kirkcaldy	a																								
Leuchars 3	a																								
Dundee	a																								
Arbroath	a																								
Montrose	a																								
Stonehaven	a																								
Aberdeen	a																								

A from 24 October

Table 26

Sundays from 12 September

London - Humberside, Yorkshire, North East England and Scotland

		XC	GR	GR		EM	XC	GR	GR	GC	GR	TP		XC		GR	EM	GR	GR	HT	GR			TP
		◇1	1	1		◇ A	◇1	1	1		1	◇1		◇1		1	◇ A	1	1	◇1	1			◇1
London Kings Cross 15 ⊖	d		18 30	18 40				19 00	19 10	19 27	19 30					19 35		20 00	20 03	20 10	20 30			
Stevenage 4	d		18 50								19 50					19 54				20u30				
Peterborough 8	a		19 19	19 25				19 44	19 55		20 19					20 23		20 44	20 50		21 14			
Norwich	d					17 56											18 57							
Peterborough 8	d		19 19	19 25		19 26		19 44	19 56		20 19					20 24	20 31	20 44	20 50		21 14			
Grantham 7	a			19 47		19 56			20 19								21 01			21 18	21 36			
	d			19 47					20 19											21 19	21 36			
Newark North Gate 7	a								20 30												21 48			
	d								20 30												21 48			
Retford 10	d																			21 40	22 03			
Doncaster 7	a		20 12	20 20				20 35	20 56	21 02	21 10					21 14		21 36		21 54	22 19			
Selby	a								21 15											22s09				
Hull	a								21 56											22 50				
Wakefield Westgate 7	a			20 38							21 27								21 57		22 37			
Leeds 10	a			20 59							21 47								22 16		23 00			
Shipley	a																							
Bradford Forster Square	a																							
Keighley	a																							
Skipton	a																							
Sheffield 7	d	19 21					19 51							20 51										
Doncaster 7	d		20 12				20 18	20 35						21 21		21 23		21 36						
York 8	a		20 39				20 44	21 00						21 42		21 46		22 00						
Scarborough	a																							
Leeds 10	d	20 08										20 40												22e12
York 8	d	20 35	20 40				20 47	21 02				21 08		21 44		21 48		22 02						22 42
Thirsk	d											21 26												23 06
Northallerton	d		21 00									21 34												23 16
Darlington 7	a	21 03	21 13				21 18	21 30				21 46		22 22		22 28		22 43						23 32
Eaglescliffe	a																							
Middlesbrough	a																							
Darlington 7	d	21 04	21 13				21 19	21 30				21 46		22 23		22 29		22 43						23 33
Durham	d	21 22	21 31				21 37					22 03		22 40		22 46		23 01						23 49
Chester-le-Street	d																							
Newcastle 8	a	21 37	21 47				21 54	22 02				22 20		23 07		23 16		23 34						00 21
Hartlepool	a																							
Sunderland	a																							
Newcastle 8	d	21 39	21 52																					
Morpeth	d																							
Alnmouth for Alnwick	d	22 07																						
Berwick-upon-Tweed	d	22 30	22 36																					
Dunbar	d		22 59																					
Edinburgh 10	a	23 14	23 27																					
Edinburgh	d																							
Haymarket	d																							
Motherwell	a																							
Glasgow Central 15	a																							
Stirling	a																							
Perth	a																							
Inverness	a																							
Inverkeithing	a																							
Kirkcaldy	a																							
Leuchars 3	a																							
Dundee	a																							
Arbroath	a																							
Montrose	a																							
Stonehaven	a																							
Aberdeen	a																							

A from 24 October

Table 26

Sundays from 12 September

London - Humberside, Yorkshire, North East England and Scotland

Station		GR	GR	EM	GR	GR
		◇A				
London Kings Cross ⊖	d	21 00	21 30		22 00	22 10
Stevenage	d					
Peterborough	a	21 45	22 14		22 44	22s59
Norwich	d			20 52		
Peterborough	d	21 46	22 15	22 22	22 45	
Grantham	a		22 39	22 50		23s31
	d		22 39			
Newark North Gate	a		22 50			23s42
	d		22 50			
Retford	d		23 06			
Doncaster	a	22 42	23 27		23 42	00s12
Selby	a					
Hull	a					
Wakefield Westgate	a					
Leeds	a		00 24			01 18
Shipley	a					
Bradford Forster Square	a					
Keighley	a					
Skipton	a					
Sheffield	d					
Doncaster	d	22 43			23 45	
York	a	23 09			00 39	
Scarborough	a					
Leeds	d					
York	d	23 11				
Thirsk	d					
Northallerton	d	23 47				
Darlington	a	23 59				
Eaglescliffe	a					
Middlesbrough	a					
Darlington	d	23 59				
Durham	d	00 17				
Chester-le-Street	d					
Newcastle	a	00 50				
Hartlepool	a					
Sunderland	a					
Newcastle	d					
Morpeth	d					
Alnmouth for Alnwick	d					
Berwick-upon-Tweed	d					
Dunbar	d					
Edinburgh	a					
Edinburgh	d					
Haymarket	d					
Motherwell	a					
Glasgow Central	a					
Stirling	a					
Perth	a					
Inverness	a					
Inverkeithing	a					
Kirkcaldy	a					
Leuchars	a					
Dundee	a					
Arbroath	a					
Montrose	a					
Stonehaven	a					
Aberdeen	a					

A from 24 October

Table 26

Mondays to Fridays

Scotland, North East England, Yorkshire and Humberside - London

Station		EM	TP	GR	GR	GR	GR MO	GR MX	GR	GR
			◇							
Aberdeen	d									
Stonehaven	d									
Montrose	d									
Arbroath	d									
Dundee	d									
Leuchars	d									
Kirkcaldy	d									
Inverkeithing	d									
Inverness	d									
Perth	d									
Stirling	d									
Glasgow Central	d									
Motherwell	d									
Haymarket	d									
Edinburgh	a									
Edinburgh	d									
Dunbar	d									
Berwick-upon-Tweed	d									
Alnmouth for Alnwick	d									
Morpeth	d									
Newcastle	a									
Sunderland	d									
Hartlepool	d									
Newcastle	d						04 20	04 30		05 25
Chester-le-Street	d									
Durham	d						04 34	04 44		05 38
Darlington	a						04 51	05 01		05 55
Middlesbrough	d		05 57							
Eaglescliffe	d									
Darlington	d						04 52	05 02		05 56
Northallerton	d		06 25				05 18	05 28		06 08
Thirsk	d		06 33							
York	a		06 51				05 53	05 54		06 28
Leeds	a		07 20							
Harrogate	d									
Scarborough	d									
York	d						06 00	06 00		06 30
Doncaster	a						06 22	06 22		06 53
Skipton	d									
Keighley	d									
Bradford Forster Square	d									
Shipley	d									
Leeds	d				05 05	05 30			06 05	
Wakefield Westgate	d				05 17	05 42			06 18	
Sheffield	a									
Hull	d									
Selby	d									
Doncaster	d				05 35	06 00	06 23	06 23		06 54
Retford	d				05 50				06 48	
Newark North Gate	a				06 05	06 24	06 46	06 46	07 03	
	d				06 05	06 24	06 46	06 46	07 04	
Grantham	a				06 18	06 37	06 59	06 59	07 16	07 25
	d	05 51			06 18	06 37	06 59	06 59	07 17	07 25
Peterborough	a	06 25			06 37	06 58	07 18	07 18	07 37	07 45
Norwich	a									
Peterborough	d			06 10	06 40	07 00	07 20	07 20	07 40	07 50
Stevenage	a									
London Kings Cross ⊖	a			07 00	07 30	07 53	08 13	08 13	08 32	08 43

Scotland, North East England, Yorkshire and Humberside - London

		HT	GR	GR	XC	GR	TP	XC	GR	GR	EM	GR	GR	GC	GR	XC	GR	GR	EM	GC
		BHX										A								B
Aberdeen	d																			
Stonehaven	d																			
Montrose	d																			
Arbroath	d																			
Dundee	d																			
Leuchars	d																			
Kirkcaldy	d																			
Inverkeithing	d																			
Inverness	d																			
Perth	d																			
Stirling	d																			
Glasgow Central	d																			
Motherwell	d																			
Haymarket	d																			
Edinburgh	a																			
Edinburgh	d																	05 50		
Dunbar	d																			
Berwick-upon-Tweed	d																	06 29		
Alnmouth for Alnwick	d																			
Morpeth	d																			
Newcastle	a																	07 16		
Sunderland	d																			06 41
Hartlepool	d																			07 08
Newcastle	d					06 00	06 13	06 21		06 30						06 44	07 00	07 20		
Chester-le-Street	d							06 32												
Durham	d					06 12	06 29	06 39		06 44						06 56	07 12			
Darlington	a					06 29	06 45	06 55		07 01						07 12	07 29			
Middlesbrough	d																			
Eaglescliffe	d																			07 28
Darlington	d					06 30	06 46	06 56		07 02						07 14	07 30			
Northallerton	d						06 58			07 13										07 46
Thirsk	d						07 06													07 57
York	a					06 57	07 30	07 22		07 34						07 40	07 58	08 09		08 17
Leeds	a						08 04									08 08				
Harrogate	d														07 28					
Scarborough	d																			
York	d				06 32	07 00		07 27		07 36							08 00	08 11		08 20
Doncaster	a							07 49												
Skipton	d												06 55							
Keighley	d												07u05							
Bradford Forster Square	d			06 30																
Shipley	d			06u35									07u14							
Leeds	d		06 40	07b00	07 05				07 20				07e40		08f05	08 11				
Wakefield Westgate	d		06 52	07 12	07 18				07 32				07 52		08 17	08 23				
Sheffield	a				07 50			08 18								08 51				
Hull	d	06 25										07 00								
Selby	d	07 00										07 32								
Doncaster	d	07 18		07 30								07 55		08 28	08 37					
Retford	d	07 32											08 19							
Newark North Gate	a		07 29										08 34							
	d		07 29										08 34							
Grantham	a	07 56										08 29						09 02		
	d	07 57									08 25	08 29						09 02	09 11	
Peterborough	a					08 03			08 32		08 57	08 50			09 26				09 38	
Norwich	a										10 43								11 13	
Peterborough	d					08 04			08 33			08 51			09 26					
Stevenage	a									09 06					09 57					
London Kings Cross	a	09 17	08 46	09 08		08 59			09 26	09 35		09 45	09 52	10 06	10 25		09 55	10 11		10 31

A The Hull Executive
B The Zephyr
e arr. 0729

Table 26 Mondays to Fridays

Scotland, North East England, Yorkshire and Humberside - London

		TP	XC	TP	GR	HT	GR	GR	XC	NT	GR	XC	EM	GR	GR	EM	GR	XC	NT	TP
Aberdeen	d																			
Stonehaven	d																			
Montrose	d																			
Arbroath	d																			
Dundee	d																			
Leuchars	d																			
Kirkcaldy	d																			
Inverkeithing	d																			
Inverness	d																			
Perth	d																			
Stirling	d																			
Glasgow Central	d																	06 01		
Motherwell	d																			
Haymarket	d																	06 55		
Edinburgh	a																	06 59		
Edinburgh	d				06 00				06 08			06 44		07 00				07 08		
Dunbar	d				06 20													07 28		
Berwick-upon-Tweed	d				06 43				06 49			07 23		07 42				07 51		
Alnmouth for Alnwick	d				07 03				07 10	07 23		07 47								
Morpeth	d				07 19					07 49		08 02							08 32	
Newcastle	a				07 38				07 43	08 14		08 20		08 30				08 38	08 57	
Sunderland	d																			
Hartlepool	d																			
Newcastle	d		07 23	07 26	07 40				07 45		07 52	08 24		08 32				08 43		
Chester-le-Street	d			07 36								08 33								
Durham	d		07 37	07 43							08 04	08 40		08 45				08 55		
Darlington	a		07 52	07 59					08 11		08 22	08 55		09 04				09 11		
Middlesbrough	d	07 23																		09 00
Eaglescliffe	d																			
Darlington	d		07 55	08 00					08 13		08 22	08 57		09 05				09 12		
Northallerton	d	07 53		08 12																09 27
Thirsk	d	08 01		08 20																09 35
York	a	08 19	08 24	08 55	08 34				08 42		08 50	09 24		09 34				09 40		09 55
Leeds	a	08 52		09 23					09 08									10 08		10 23
Harrogate	d																			
Scarborough	d																			
York	d		08 27		08 36						08 52	09 27		09 36						
Doncaster	a		08 50								09 16	09 54		10 03						
Skipton	d																			
Keighley	d																			
Bradford Forster Square	d																			
Shipley	d																			
Leeds	d						08 40	09 05	09 11						09 40		10 05	10 12		
Wakefield Westgate	d						08 52	09 18	09 24						09 52		10 18	10 24		
Sheffield	a		09 20						09 51			10 20						10 51		
Hull	d					08 12														
Selby	d					08 45														
Doncaster	d					09 04	09 14	09 36			09 21			10 03	10 11		10 35			
Retford	d					09 16		09 51												
Newark North Gate	a						09 37	10 06			09 46				10 35		10 59			
	d						09 37	10 06			09 46				10 35		10 59			
Grantham	a				09 25	09 41					09 58		10 06	10 36		11 05	11 11			
	d				09 26	09 42					09 58		10 08	10 37		11 07	11 11			
Peterborough	a				09 46		10 05	10 35			10 18		10 42	10 56	11 03	11 36	11 31			
Norwich	a												12 13			13 13				
Peterborough	d				09 48		10 05	10 36			10 19			10 57	11 03		11 31			
Stevenage	a							11 05												
London Kings Cross	a				10 40	10 51	10 58	11 34			11 14			11 51	11 56		12 25			

Table 26

Mondays to Fridays

Scotland, North East England, Yorkshire and Humberside - London

Station		GR	TP	GR	XC	HT	GC	TP	GR	EM	GR	XC	NT	TF	XC	GR	GC	TP	GR	EM	GR
Aberdeen	d																				
Stonehaven	d																				
Montrose	d																				
Arbroath	d																				
Dundee	d											06 32									
Leuchars 3	d											06 46									
Kirkcaldy	d											07 21									
Inverkeithing	d											07 42									
Inverness	d																				
Perth	d																				
Stirling	d																				
Glasgow Central 15	d			06 50												07 50					
Motherwell	d			07 04												08 04					
Haymarket	d			07 46								08 01				08 49					
Edinburgh 10	a			07 52								08 05				08 55					
Edinburgh	d			08 00								08 11				09 00					
Dunbar	d																				
Berwick-upon-Tweed	d											08 52				09 39					
Alnmouth for Alnwick	d			08 56																	
Morpeth	d												09 32								
Newcastle 8	a			09 27								09 40	09 55			10 29					
Sunderland	d						09 18														
Hartlepool	d						09 42														
Newcastle 8	d	09 00	09 12	09 30	09 35							09 43		10 15	10 25	10 34					
Chester-le-Street	d		09 21																		
Durham	d	09 12	09 27		09 48							09 56		10 27	10 37	10 47					
Darlington 7	a	09 32	09 43	09 58	10 04							10 12		10 43	10 53	11 04					
Middlesbrough	d							09 59										11 00			
Eaglescliffe	d						10 01														
Darlington 7	d	09 32	09 44	09 58	10 05							10 13		10 44	10 54	11 05					
Northallerton	d	09 45	09 56				10 19	10 27						10 56				11 27			
Thirsk	d						10 29	10 35										11 35			
York 8	a	10 05	10 21	10 27	10 32		10 51	10 55				10 41		11 21	11 24	11 33		11 55			
Leeds 10	a		10 53					11 23				11 08		11 33				12 23			
Harrogate	d																				
Scarborough	d																				
York 8	d	10 06		10 29	10 34		10 53								11 27	11 35					
Doncaster 7	a	10 30		10 53	10 57										11 51	12 00					
Skipton	d																				
Keighley	d																				
Bradford Forster Square	d																				
Shipley	d																				
Leeds 10	d								10 40		11 05	11 11							11 40		12 05
Wakefield Westgate 7	d								10 52		11 17	11 24							11 52		12 17
Sheffield 7	a				11 20							11 51			12 20						
Hull	d					10 12															
Selby	d					10 47															
Doncaster 7	d	10 30		10 53		11 05			11b16		11 37					12 00	12 06		12 12		12 36
Retford 10	d			11 08		11 20															12 51
Newark North Gate 7	a								11 41												
	d								11 41												
Grantham 7	a					11 40			11 53		12 09										13 14
	d					11 40			11 54	12 07	12 09									13 07	13 14
Peterborough 8	a	11 16		11 48					12 13	12 42	12 28					12 46			13 00	13 38	
Norwich	a									14 13										15 13	
Peterborough 8	d	11 17		11 49					12 14		12 29					12 47			13 01		
Stevenage 4	a	11 47							12 43							13 16					
London Kings Cross 15 ⊖	a	12 15		12 42		12 47	12 49		13 10		13 22					13 43	13 46		13 54		14 20

b arr. 1109

Table 26

Mondays to Fridays

Scotland, North East England, Yorkshire and Humberside - London

Station		XC	GR	NT	TP	XC	GR	GR	EM	HT	GR	XC	GR	NT	TP	TP	XC	GR	GR	GR	TP	XC
Aberdeen	d												07 52									08 20
Stonehaven	d												08 09									08 38
Montrose	d												08 32									08 59
Arbroath	d												08 48									09 15
Dundee	d	07 35											09 06									09 32
Leuchars 3	d	07 48											09 20									09 47
Kirkcaldy	d	08 20											09 44									10 17
Inverkeithing	d	08 35											10 01									10 32
Inverness	d																					
Perth	d																					
Stirling	d																					
Glasgow Central 15	d											09 00						09 50				
Motherwell	d											09 15						10 04				
Haymarket	d	08 54										09 53	10 19					10 48				10 54
Edinburgh 10	a	08 58										09 58	10 25					10 55				11 01
Edinburgh	d	09 07	09 30									10 08	10 30					11 00				11 08
Dunbar	d	09 28																				11 28
Berwick-upon-Tweed	d	09 51	10 10															11 39				11 51
Alnmouth for Alnwick	d											11 05						11 59				
Morpeth	d			10 50								11 20		11 50								
Newcastle 8	a	10 38	10 59	11 14								11 37	11 57	12 13				12 30				12 38
Sunderland	d																					
Hartlepool	d																					
Newcastle 8	d	10 44	11 01		11 15	11 27	11 30					11 40	11 59			12 15	12 19	12 35				12 44
Chester-le-Street	d																12 28					
Durham	d	10 56			11 27	11 39	11 44					11 52				12 27	12 35	12 48				12 56
Darlington 7	a	11 12	11 28		11 43	11 55	12 01					12 09				12 43	12 51	13 05				13 12
Middlesbrough	d														12 00						12 50	
Eaglescliffe	d																					
Darlington 7	d	11 13	11 29		11 44	11 56	12 02					12 11				12 44	12 53	13 06				13 13
Northallerton	d				11 56										12 27	12 56					13 17	
Thirsk	d														12 35						13 25	
York 8	a	11 41	11 58		12 21	12 24	12 30					12 41	12 50		12 55	13 21	13 24	13 34			13 50	13 41
Leeds 10	a	12 08			12 53							13 08			13 23	13 53					14 23	14 07
Harrogate	d																					
Scarborough	d																					
York 8	d		12 00			12 27	12 32						12 53				13 26	13 36				
Doncaster 7	a					12 50	12 54										13 53	14 02				
Skipton	d																					
Keighley	d																					
Bradford Forster Square	d																					
Shipley	d																					
Leeds 10	d	12 12						12 40			13 05	13 12							13 40	14 05		14 12
Wakefield Westgate 7	d	12 24						12 52			13 18	13 24							13 53	14 18		14 24
Sheffield 7	a	12 51				13 20						13 51					14 20					14 51
Hull	d									12 45												
Selby	d									13 20												
Doncaster 7	d						12 55	13 11		13 37	13 39							14 03	14 17			
Retford 10	d										13 55											
Newark North Gate 7	a		12 43								14 10		13 40									
	d		12 43								14 10		13 40									
Grantham 7	a									14 08	14 23									15 03		
	d								14 07	14 09	14 23									15 03		
Peterborough 8	a		13 11				13 42	13 59	14 38		14 42		14 08					14 49	15 05	15 23		
Norwich	a								16 13													
Peterborough 8	d		13 13				13 47	13 59			14 43		14 09					14 50	15 06	15 23		
Stevenage 4	a						14 17				15 12									15 53		
London Kings Cross 15 ⊖	a		14 10				14 44	14 51		15 20	15 40		15 05					15 44	15 58	16 22		

Scotland, North East England, Yorkshire and Humberside - London

		GR	GC	NT	TP	TP	EM	GR	XC	GR	GR	XC	GR	EM	GR	TP	XC	GR	HT	TP FO	TP FX
		A											B					C			
Aberdeen	d												09 52								
Stonehaven	d												10 09								
Montrose	d												10 32								
Arbroath	d												10 49								
Dundee	d												11 06								
Leuchars	d												11 20								
Kirkcaldy	d												11 44								
Inverkeithing	d												12 01								
Inverness	d	07 55																			
Perth	d	09 56																			
Stirling	d	10 30																			
Glasgow Central	d																	11 50			
Motherwell	d																	12 06			
Haymarket	d	11 11											12 19					12 49			
Edinburgh	a	11 16											12 25					12 56			
Edinburgh	d	11 30						12 00				12 05	12 30					13 00			
Dunbar	d																				
Berwick-upon-Tweed	d							12 39										13 39			
Alnmouth for Alnwick	d											13 05									
Morpeth	d			12 50																	
Newcastle	a	12 56		13 13				13 26				13 38	13 56					14 26			
Sunderland	d		12 30																		
Hartlepool	d		12 54																		
Newcastle	d	13 01			13 15			13 29	13 34			13 44	14 00		14 05	14 12	14 26	14 34			
Chester-le-Street	d																				
Durham	d				13 27				13 46			13 56			14 17	14 24	14 40				
Darlington	a				13 43			13 55	14 02			14 12			14 34	14 43	14 55	15 00			
Middlesbrough	d					13 50														14 50	14 50
Eaglescliffe	d		13 16																		
Darlington	d				13 44			13 56	14 03			14 13			14 35	14 44	14 57	15 02			
Northallerton	d		13 39		13 56	14 17									14 46	14 56				15 17	15 17
Thirsk	d		13 48			14 25														15 25	15 25
York	a	13 52	14 06		14 21	14 50		14 24	14 29			14 41	14 51		15 06	15 21	15 26	15 33		15 50	15 50
Leeds	a				14 53	15 23						15 08				15 53					16 22
Harrogate	d																				
Scarborough	d																				
York	d	13 54	14 08					14 26	14 32				14 53		15 11		15 29	15 35			
Doncaster	a							14 49	14 55						15 35		15 54	15 59			
Skipton	d																				
Keighley	d																				
Bradford Forster Square	d																				
Shipley	d																				
Leeds	d									14 40	15 05	15 12									
Wakefield Westgate	d									14 52	15 17	15 24									
Sheffield	a								15 20			15 51					16 20				
Hull	d																		15 18		
Selby	d																		15 57		
Doncaster	d							14 50		15 15					15 36			16 00	16 15		
Retford	d														15 51				16 33		
Newark North Gate	a							15 13		15 41					16 06						
	d							15 13		15 41					16 06						
Grantham	a							15 26		15 54					16 19				16 55		
	d						15 07	15 26		15 54				16 07	16 19				16 55		
Peterborough	a						15 34	15 45			16 18		16 01	16 34				16 47			
Norwich	a						17 13							18 13							
Peterborough	d							15 49			16 19		16 02					16 48			
Stevenage	a							16 18			16 48								17s46		
London Kings Cross	a	15 50	16 05					16 45		17 04	17 15		16 57		17 28			17 41	18 13		

A The Highland Chieftain

B The Northern Lights

C The Flying Scotsman

Scotland, North East England, Yorkshire and Humberside - London

		GR	GR	XC FO	XC FX	NT	GR	TP	XC	GR	GC	GR	GR	XC	TP	NT	GR	TP	GR	XC	TP	HT	GR
Aberdeen	d																						
Stonehaven	d																						
Montrose	d																						
Arbroath	d																						
Dundee	d																						
Leuchars	d																						
Kirkcaldy	d																						
Inverkeithing	d																						
Inverness	d																						
Perth	d																						
Stirling	d																						
Glasgow Central	d																		13 50				
Motherwell	d																		14 05				
Haymarket	d																		14 49				
Edinburgh	a																		14 56				
Edinburgh	d			13 07	13 07					14 00				14 08					15 00				
Dunbar	d			13 28	13 28																		
Berwick-upon-Tweed	d			13 51	13 51					14 39													
Alnmouth for Alnwick	d													15 05									
Morpeth	d					14 50										15 50							
Newcastle	a			14 38	14 38	15 13				15 28				15 35		16 13			16 24				
Sunderland	d																						
Hartlepool	d																						
Newcastle	d			14 40	14 40		14 55	15 12	15 22	15 30				15 42			15 55	16 06	16 28	16 32			
Chester-le-Street	d							15 21										16 15		16 41			
Durham	d			14 52	14 52		15 07	15 27	15 34					15 54			16 08	16 21		16 48			
Darlington	a			15 10	15 10		15 24	15 43	15 50	16 01				16 10			16 26	16 39		17 04			
Middlesbrough	d														15 50						16 50		
Eaglescliffe	d																						
Darlington	d			15 12	15 12		15 25	15 44	15 51	16 02				16 12			16 26	16 39		17 05			
Northallerton	d							15 56							16 17			16 50			17 17		
Thirsk	d														16 25			16 58			17 25		
York	a			15 41	15 41		15 52	16 21	16 23	16 30				16 41	16 50		16 54	17 25	17 20	17 31	17 50		
Leeds	a			16 07	16 08			16 53						17 07	17 23			17 53			18 23		
Harrogate	d																						
Scarborough	d																						
York	d						15 54		16 25	16 32							16 56		17 21	17 34			
Doncaster	a								16 48								17 19			17 57			
Skipton	d																						
Keighley	d																						
Bradford Forster Square	d																						
Shipley	d																						
Leeds	d	15 40	16 05	16 11	16 11							16 40	17 05	17 12									17 40
Wakefield Westgate	d	15 52	16 17	16 23	16 23							16 52	17 17	17 24									17 52
Sheffield	a			16 51	16 51				17 18					17 51						18 20			
Hull	d																					17 06	
Selby	d																					17 43	
Doncaster	d		16 36								17 00	17 10	17 37				17 20					18 03	18 11
Retford	d												17 57									18 17	
Newark North Gate	a		17 00									17 33					17 44						18 34
	d		17 00									17 33					17 44						18 34
Grantham	a						16 44										17 57					18 37	18 47
	d						16 44										17 57					18 37	18 47
Peterborough	a	16 51	17 27				17 04					18 01							18 26				19 06
Norwich	a																						
Peterborough	d	16 52	17 28				17 04					18 02							18 26				19 07
Stevenage	a						17 34						19 02				18 42					19s24	
London Kings Cross	a	17 47	18 25				18 04			18 28	18 46	18 54	19 29				19 12		19 19			19 49	19 59

Table 26

Scotland, North East England, Yorkshire and Humberside - London

		GR	XC	NT	GR	TP	XC	GR	EM	TP	GR	GC	GR	XC	GR	XC	GR	HT BHX
		1	◇1		1	◇1	◇1	1	◇	◇1	1	1	1	◇1	1	◇1	1	◇1
Aberdeen	d																	
Stonehaven	d																	
Montrose	d																	
Arbroath	d																	
Dundee	d																	
Leuchars 3	d																	
Kirkcaldy	d																	
Inverkeithing	d																	
Inverness	d																	
Perth	d																	
Stirling	d																	
Glasgow Central 15	d																15 50	
Motherwell	d																16 04	
Haymarket	d																16 50	
Edinburgh 10	a																16 56	
Edinburgh	d		15 07					16 00						16 08			17 00	
Dunbar	d		15 28					16 20										
Berwick-upon-Tweed	d		15 51					16 43										
Alnmouth for Alnwick	d													17 09			18 00	
Morpeth	d			16 50										17 24				
Newcastle 8	a		16 38	17 12				17 31						17 40			18 32	
Sunderland	d											17 30						
Hartlepool	d											17 56						
Newcastle 8	d		16 40		16 55	17 01	17 17	17 32						17 44	18 10	18 20	18 35	
Chester-le-Street	d						17 26									18 29		
Durham	d		16 52		17 07	17 13	17 33							17 56	18 22	18 36		
Darlington 7	a		17 11		17 25	17 29	17 48	17 59						18 12	18 39	18 54	19 03	
Middlesbrough	d									17 50								
Eaglescliffe	d											18 15						
Darlington 7	d		17 12		17 25	17 30	17 50	17 59						18 13	18 40	18 56	19 04	
Northallerton	d					17 42				18 17		18 37			18 51			
Thirsk	d									18 25		18 46						
York 8	a		17 41		17 53	18 06	18 16	18 28		18 50		19 05		18 42	19 11	19 25	19 33	
Leeds 10	a		18 08			18 35				19 35				19 08				
Harrogate	d																	
Scarborough	d																	
York 8	d				17 55		18 24	18 31				19 08			19 13	19 29	19 35	
Doncaster 7	a				18 20		18 49	18 53							19 37	19 55	19 59	
Skipton	d																	
Keighley	d																	
Bradford Forster Square	d																	
Shipley	d																	
Leeds 10	d	18 05	18 11								18 40		19 05	19 11				
Wakefield Westgate 7	d	18 17	18 23								18 52		19 17	19 23				
Sheffield 7	a		18 51				19 20							19 51		20 20		
Hull	d																	19 18
Selby	d																	19 53
Doncaster 7	d	18 35			18 21			18 54			19 13		19 35		19 39		20 00	20 10
Retford 10	d				18 36													
Newark North Gate 7	a				18 51			19 17			19 38				20 02			
	d				18 51			19 17			19 38				20 02			
Grantham 7	a										19 51		20 06					20 41
	d								19 07		19 51		20 06					20 41
Peterborough 8	a	19 25			19 19			19 46	19 36				20 27		20 32		20 46	
Norwich	a								21 13									
Peterborough 8	d	19 26			19 20			19 47					20 28		20 33		20 46	
Stevenage 4	a				19 50			20 16			20 35						21 17	21s30
London Kings Cross 15 ⊖	a	20 21			20 18			20 44			21 03	21 09	21 20		21 25		21 44	21 58

Table 26

Scotland, North East England, Yorkshire and Humberside - London

		GR	XC	TP	NT	TP	GR	NT	XC	EM	GR	XC	TP FO	TP FX	NT	GR	GR	TP	TP	NT
		1	◇1 A	◇1		◇1	1		◇1 B	◇	1	◇1 A	◇1	◇1		1	1	◇1	◇1	
Aberdeen	d						14 50													
Stonehaven	d						15 07													
Montrose	d						15 30													
Arbroath	d						15 46													
Dundee	d						16 04													
Leuchars 3	d						16 18													
Kirkcaldy	d						16 45													
Inverkeithing	d						17 01													
Inverness	d																			
Perth	d																			
Stirling	d																			
Glasgow Central 15	d																17 50			
Motherwell	d																18 05			
Haymarket	d						17 20										18 49			
Edinburgh 10	a						17 27										18 55			
Edinburgh	d		17 08				17 30					18 08				18 35	19 00			
Dunbar	d		17 28				17 54					18 28				18 55	19 20			
Berwick-upon-Tweed	d		17 51				18 17					18 51				19 18	19 43			
Alnmouth for Alnwick	d											19 11			19 21	19 40				
Morpeth	d				18 33			19 01							19 46	19 57				21 34
Newcastle 8	a		18 39		18 56		19 06	19 25				19 40			20 07	20 18	20 33			21 56
Sunderland	d																			
Hartlepool	d																			
Newcastle 8	d		18 40			18 58	19 08		19 25			19 43					20 38		21 33	22 00
Chester-le-Street	d								19 37											22 09
Durham	d		18 52			19 10			19 44			19 55					20 51		21 46	22 18
Darlington 7	a		19 11			19 26	19 36		20 02			20 12					21 08		22 02	22 38
Middlesbrough	d			19 00									20 00	20 00				21 30		
Eaglescliffe	d																			22 55
Darlington 7	d		19 12			19 27	19 36		20 04			20 12	20 31	20 31			21 09	21 58	22 03	
Northallerton	d			19 27		19 38							20 42	20 42				22 09	22 30	
Thirsk	d			19 35									20 50	20 50				22 17		
York 8	a		19 41	19 58		20 02	20 05		20 30			20 41	21 10	21 10			21 38	22 44	22 57	
Leeds 10	a		20 08			20 35						21 07		21 35					23 33	
Harrogate	d																			
Scarborough	d																			
York 8	d						20 09		20 32								21 40			
Doncaster 7	a						20 31		20 55								22 02			
Skipton	d																			
Keighley	d																			
Bradford Forster Square	d																			
Shipley	d																			
Leeds 10	d	19 40	20 11								20 40	21 11								
Wakefield Westgate 7	d	19 52	20 23								20 55	21 23								
Sheffield 7	a		20 51						21 24			21 51								
Hull	d																			
Selby	d																			
Doncaster 7	d	20 14					20 32				21 12						22 03			
Retford 10	d										21 27									
Newark North Gate 7	a	20 37									21 42						22 26			
	d	20 37									21 42						22 26			
Grantham 7	a	20 50								21 05	21 55						22 39			
	d	20 50								21 07	21 55						22 39			
Peterborough 8	a	21 09					21 20			21 35	22 14						22 58			
Norwich	a									23 18										
Peterborough 8	d	21 10					21 21				22 15						22 59			
Stevenage 4	a						21 52				22s46						23 33			
London Kings Cross 15 ⊖	a	22 04					22 20				23 11						00 05			

A — to York

B — to Darlington

Table 26

Scotland, North East England, Yorkshire and Humberside - London

		GR	GR	XC FO
Aberdeen	d	18 16		
Stonehaven	d	18 33		
Montrose	d	18 56		
Arbroath	d	19 12		
Dundee	d	19 30		
Leuchars	d	19 44		
Kirkcaldy	d	20 08		
Inverkeithing	d	20 24		
Inverness	d			
Perth	d			
Stirling	d			
Glasgow Central	d		19 50	
Motherwell	d		20 04	
Haymarket	d	20 44	20 49	
Edinburgh	a	20 50	20 55	
Edinburgh	d		21 00	23 17
Dunbar	d		21 20	23a53
Berwick-upon-Tweed	d		21 43	
Alnmouth for Alnwick	d		22 05	
Morpeth	d		22 22	
Newcastle	a		22 41	
Sunderland	d			
Hartlepool	d			
Newcastle	d		22 43	
Chester-le-Street	d			
Durham	d		22 58	
Darlington	a		23 15	
Middlesbrough	d			
Eaglescliffe	d			
Darlington	d		23 16	
Northallerton	d		23s45	
Thirsk	d			
York	a		00 14	
Leeds	a			
Harrogate	d			
Scarborough	d			
York	d			
Doncaster	a			
Skipton	d			
Keighley	d			
Bradford Forster Square	d			
Shipley	d			
Leeds	d			
Wakefield Westgate	d			
Sheffield	a			
Hull	d			
Selby	d			
Doncaster	d			
Retford	d			
Newark North Gate	a			
	d			
Grantham	a			
	d			
Peterborough	a			
Norwich	a			
Peterborough	d			
Stevenage	a			
London Kings Cross	a			

Table 26

Scotland, North East England, Yorkshire and Humberside - London

		EM	GR	GR	TP	GR	NT	GR	XC	GR	TP	XC	GR	TP	GC	EM	GR
Aberdeen	d																
Stonehaven	d																
Montrose	d																
Arbroath	d																
Dundee	d																
Leuchars	d																
Kirkcaldy	d																
Inverkeithing	d																
Inverness	d																
Perth	d																
Stirling	d																
Glasgow Central	d																
Motherwell	d																
Haymarket	d																
Edinburgh	a																
Edinburgh	d																
Dunbar	d																
Berwick-upon-Tweed	d																
Alnmouth for Alnwick	d																
Morpeth	d																
Newcastle	a																
Sunderland	d						06 20										
Hartlepool	d						06a46										
Newcastle	d			04 30						06 00	06 13	06 21					06 35
Chester-le-Street	d											06 32					
Durham	d			04 45						06 12	06 29	06 39					06 47
Darlington	a			05 02						06 29	06 45	06 55					07 04
Middlesbrough	d				05 57									07 21			
Eaglescliffe	d																
Darlington	d			05 03						06 30	06 46	06 56					07 05
Northallerton	d			05 30	06 25						06 58			07 48			
Thirsk	d				06 33						07 06			07 56			
York	a			05 57	06 51					06 57	07 30	07 23		08 16			07 33
Leeds	a				07 20						08 04			08 52			
Harrogate	d																
Scarborough	d																
York	d			06 00					06 09	07 00		07 25					07 36
Doncaster	a			06 22						07 22		07 48					07 59
Skipton	d																
Keighley	d																
Bradford Forster Square	d																
Shipley	d																
Leeds	d		05 05			06 10		07 00	07 05								
Wakefield Westgate	d		05 17			06 22		07 12	07 18								
Sheffield	a								07 51			08 18					
Hull	d												06 50				
Selby	d												07 23				
Doncaster	d		05 35	06 23		06 40		07 30		07 23			07 43		07 55		07 59
Retford	d		05 50			06 55											
Newark North Gate	a		06 05			07 10		07 53									08 23
	d		06 05			07 10		07 53									08 23
Grantham	a		06 17			07 23		08 06									08 35
	d	05 51	06 17			07 23		08 06								08 16	08 35
Peterborough	a	06 25	06 37	07 09		07 42		08 25		08 09			08 31			08 44	08 56
Norwich	a															10 19	
Peterborough	d		06 37	07 09		07 48		08 26		08 09			08 32				08 57
Stevenage	a																
London Kings Cross	a		07 29	08 03		08 40		09 18		09 03			09 25		09 43		09 51

Table 26

Saturdays
until 10 July

Scotland, North East England, Yorkshire and Humberside - London

Station		GR	GR	XC	GR	XC	EM	GR	GR	GC	TP	HT	EM	XC	GR	GR	NT	XC
										A								
Aberdeen	d																	
Stonehaven	d																	
Montrose	d																	
Arbroath	d																	
Dundee	d																	
Leuchars	d																	
Kirkcaldy	d																	
Inverkeithing	d																	
Inverness	d																	
Perth	d																	
Stirling	d																	
Glasgow Central	d																	
Motherwell	d																	
Haymarket	d																	
Edinburgh	a																	
Edinburgh	d													06 12	06 15			06 55
Dunbar	d														06 35			
Berwick-upon-Tweed	d													06 51	06 58			07 35
Alnmouth for Alnwick	d													07 11	07 18		07 33	07 55
Morpeth	d														07 34		07 59	08 09
Newcastle	a													07 41	07 53		08 24	08 27
Sunderland	d									06 53								
Hartlepool	d									07 17								
Newcastle	d			06 42	07 00	07 25			07 30		07 33			07 44	07 54			08 30
Chester-le-Street	d										07 42							
Durham	d			06 56	07 12	07 38			07 42		07 48			07 56				08 42
Darlington	a			07 11	07 29	07 53			08 00		08 05			08 12	08 21			08 58
Middlesbrough	d																	
Eaglescliffe	d									07 45								
Darlington	d			07 13	07 30	07 55			08 00		08 06			08 13	08 21			08 59
Northallerton	d				07 41					08 05	08 18							
Thirsk	d									08 16	08 26							
York	a			07 41	08 01	08 22			08 28	08 44	08 55			08 41	08 50			09 26
Leeds	a			08 08							09 23			09 07				
Harrogate	d							07 44										
Scarborough	d																	
York	d				08 04	08 27			08 30	08 47					08 51			09 28
Doncaster	a					08 50			08 54						09 15			09 51
Skipton	d	06 55																
Keighley	d	07u07																
Bradford Forster Square	d		07 33															
Shipley	d	07u18	07u38															
Leeds	d	0740	0805	08 12				08 15						09 11		09 05		
Wakefield Westgate	d	07 52	08 18	08 24										09 24		09 17		
Sheffield	a			08 51		09 20								09 51				10 20
Hull	d											08 02						
Selby	d											08 37						
Doncaster	d							08 45	08 55			09 01			09 15	09 35		
Retford	d	08 20							09 10			09 21						
Newark North Gate	a	08 34	08 54													10 00		
	d	08 34	08 54													10 00		
Grantham	a	08 46	09 06									09 42				10 12		
	d	08 46	09 06				09 11					09 42	10 08			10 12		
Peterborough	a	09 06	09 26		09 12		09 43	09 32	09 49				10 37		10 06	10 32		
Norwich	a						11 18						12 18					
Peterborough	d	09 07	09 26		09 16			09 33	09 49						10 06	10 33		
Stevenage	a				09 45											11 03		
London Kings Cross	a	10 04	10 20		10 13			10 26	10 43	10 48		10 52			10 59	11 33		

A The Zephyr

Table 26

Saturdays
until 10 July

Scotland, North East England, Yorkshire and Humberside - London

Station		TP	GR	EM	GR	XC	GR	TP	XC	GR	HT	TP	GC	XC	NT	GR	TP	XC	GR	EM	GR	TP
Aberdeen	d																					
Stonehaven	d																					
Montrose	d																					
Arbroath	d																					
Dundee	d																					
Leuchars	d																					
Kirkcaldy	d																					
Inverkeithing	d																					
Inverness	d																					
Perth	d																					
Stirling	d																					
Glasgow Central	d									06 50				07 00							07 50	
Motherwell	d									07 05											08 04	
Haymarket	d									07 47				07 54							08 49	
Edinburgh	a									07 52				07 59							08 56	
Edinburgh	d		07 00			07 07	07 30			08 00				08 05		08 35					09 00	
Dunbar	d					07 27																
Berwick-upon-Tweed	d		07 40			07 50	08 09							08 47		09 14					09 41	
Alnmouth for Alnwick	d									08 58				09 09								
Morpeth	d														09 32							
Newcastle	a		08 31			08 38	08 57			09 29				09 39	09 55	10 02					10 29	
Sunderland	d												09 29									
Hartlepool	d												09 53									
Newcastle	d		08 33			08 40	08 59	09 12	09 25	09 32				09 41		10 05	10 12	10 25			10 32	
Chester-le-Street	d					08 49		09 21														
Durham	d		08 46			08 56	09 12	09 27	09 37					09 55			10 27	10 38			10 45	
Darlington	a		09 04			09 12	09 30	09 43	09 54	10 00				10 10		10 31	10 43	10 54			11 03	
Middlesbrough	d	09 00										10 00										11 00
Eaglescliffe	d												10 15									
Darlington	d		09 04			09 13	09 30	09 44	09 56	10 01				10 12		10 35	10 44	10 56			11 03	
Northallerton	d	09 27					09 43	09 56				10 27	10 35				10 56					11 27
Thirsk	d	09 35										10 35	10 44									11 35
York	a	09 55	09 33			09 41	10 05	10 21	10 22	10 29		10 55	11 02	10 41		11 05	11 21	11 24			11 32	11 55
Leeds	a	10 23				10 08		10 53				11 23		11 08			11 53					12 23
Harrogate	d																					
Scarborough	d																					
York	d		09 35				10 06		10 25	10 31			11 04			11 07		11 27			11 33	
Doncaster	a		10 01				10 31		10 48	10 52						11 28		11 50			11 57	
Skipton	d																					
Keighley	d																					
Bradford Forster Square	d																					
Shipley	d																					
Leeds	d				10 05	10 12								11 11					11 05			
Wakefield Westgate	d				10 18	10 24								11 24					11 17			
Sheffield	a					10 51			11 20					11 51				12 20				
Hull	d										10 06											
Selby	d										10 41											
Doncaster	d		10 01		10 36		10 31			10 55	11 02					11 29			11 39		11 57	
Retford	d									11 10	11 17											
Newark North Gate	a				11 00														12 01			
	d				11 00														12 01			
Grantham	a				11 12						11 38					12 00			12 14		12 28	
	d			11 07	11 12						11 38					12 00			12 14	12 07	12 28	
Peterborough	a		10 48	11 36	11 32		11 20			11 49						12 19			12 33	12 38	12 48	
Norwich	a			13 13																14 13		
Peterborough	d		10 49		11 32		11 21			11 50						12 20			12 34		12 48	
Stevenage	a						11 52				12s25								13 03			
London Kings Cross	a	🍴	11 41		12 24		12 20			12 42	12 52		12 56			13 12			13 33		13 41	

Table 26

Saturdays until 10 July

Scotland, North East England, Yorkshire and Humberside - London

		GC	EM	XC	GR	NT	GR	TP	XC	GR	TP	GR	XC	GR	NT	TP	XC	EM	GR	HT	EM	GR	XC	TP
		◇1	◇	◇1	1		1	◇1	◇1	1	◇1	1	◇1	1		◇1	◇1	◇	1	◇1	◇	1	◇1	◇1
Aberdeen	d													07 52									08 20	
Stonehaven	d													08 09									08 38	
Montrose	d													08 32									08 59	
Arbroath	d													08 48									09 15	
Dundee	d			07 35										09 06									09 32	
Leuchars 3	d			07 48										09 20									09 47	
Kirkcaldy	d			08 20										09 44									10 17	
Inverkeithing	d			08 35										10 01									10 32	
Inverness	d																							
Perth	d																							
Stirling	d																							
Glasgow Central 15	d									08 50			09 00						09 50					
Motherwell	d									09 04									10 04					
Haymarket	d			08 54						09 46			09 55	10 21					10 48				10 51	
Edinburgh 10	a			08 58						09 53			09 59	10 26					10 55				10 58	
Edinburgh	d			09 05	09 30					10 00			10 05	10 30					11 00				11 05	
Dunbar	d			09 26																			11 25	
Berwick-upon-Tweed	d			09 49	10 09														11 39				11 48	
Alnmouth for Alnwick	d												11 04											
Morpeth	d					10 50							11 19		11 50									
Newcastle 8 ⇌	a			10 38	10 56	11 14				11 27			11 39	11 55	12 13				12 26				12 38	
Sunderland ⇌	d																							
Hartlepool	d																							
Newcastle 8 ⇌	d			10 44	11 00			11 15	11 25	11 29			11 41	12 00		12 15	12 22		12 33				12 44	
Chester-le-Street	d																12 31							
Durham	d			10 56				11 27	11 37	11 42			11 55	12 13		12 27	12 38		12 46				12 56	
Darlington 7	a			11 12	11 26			11 43	11 54	12 00			12 10	12 31		12 43	12 53		13 03				13 12	
Middlesbrough	d										12 00													12 50
Eaglescliffe	d																							
Darlington 7	d			11 13	11 27			11 44	11 56	12 01			12 12	12 31		12 44	12 55		13 04				13 13	
Northallerton	d							11 56			12 27					12 56								13 17
Thirsk	d										12 35													13 25
York 8	a			11 41	11 57			12 21	12 22	12 29	12 55		12 41	13 00		13 21	13 24		13 32				13 41	13 50
Leeds 10	a			12 08				12 53			13 23		13 08			13 53							14 08	14 23
Harrogate	d																							
Scarborough	d																							
York 8	d				11 59				12 25	12 33				13 02			13 27		13 34					
Doncaster 7	a				12 20				12 50	12 56							13 52		13 58					
Skipton	d																							
Keighley	d																							
Bradford Forster Square	d																							
Shipley	d																							
Leeds 10	d			12 11			12 05					13 05	13 11									14 05	14 11	
Wakefield Westgate 7	d			12 24			12 17					13 17	13 23									14 17	14 24	
Sheffield 7 ⇌	a			12 51					13 20				13 51				14 20						14 51	
Hull	d																			13 05				
Selby	d																			13 40				
Doncaster 7	d	12 06			12 21		12 38			12 57		13 38							13 58	14 04		14 36		
Retford 10	d						12 53													14 19		14 51		
Newark North Gate 7	a						13 08					14 01										15 06		
	d						13 08					14 01										15 06		
Grantham 7	a						13 20												14 29	14 39		15 19		
	d		13 08				13 20											14 07	14 29	14 39	15 07	15 19		
Peterborough 8	a		13 35		13 07					13 45		14 29		14 09				14 39	14 49		15 34	15 38		
Norwich	a		15 13															16 13			17 13			
Peterborough 8	d				13 07					13 47		14 29		14 14					14 49			15 39		
Stevenage 4	a									14 16										15s26				
London Kings Cross 15 ⊖	a	13 45			14 00		14 27			14 43		15 21		15 10					15 42	15 52		16 34		

Table 26

Saturdays until 10 July

Scotland, North East England, Yorkshire and Humberside - London

		GR	GC	NT	TP	XC	GR	TP	EM	XC	GR	NT	GR	TP	XC	GR	HT	GR	XC	GR	TP
		1 A	1		◇1	◇1	1	◇1	◇	◇1	1 B		1	◇1	◇1	1 C	◇1	1	◇1	1	◇1
Aberdeen	d										09 52										
Stonehaven	d										10 09										
Montrose	d										10 32										
Arbroath	d										10 49										
Dundee	d										11 06										
Leuchars 3	d										11 20										
Kirkcaldy	d										11 44										
Inverkeithing	d										12 01										
Inverness	d	07 55																			
Perth	d	09 56																			
Stirling	d	10 30																			
Glasgow Central 15	d															11 50					
Motherwell	d															12 06					
Haymarket	d	11 09									12 19					12 49					
Edinburgh 10	a	11 15									12 25					12 55					
Edinburgh	d	11 30					12 00			12 05	12 30					13 00			13 05	13 30	
Dunbar	d																		13 26		
Berwick-upon-Tweed	d						12 39												13 48	14 09	
Alnmouth for Alnwick	d	12 28								13 05											
Morpeth	d			12 50								13 50									
Newcastle 8 ⇌	a	12 59		13 13			13 26			13 35	13 57	14 13				14 25			14 38	14 57	
Sunderland ⇌	d		12 30																		
Hartlepool	d		12 54																		
Newcastle 8 ⇌	d	13 03			13 15	13 27	13 31			13 44	13 59			14 15	14 22	14 29			14 44	14 59	
Chester-le-Street	d																				
Durham	d				13 27	13 39	13 44			13 56	14 12			14 27	14 34	14 42			14 56		
Darlington 7	a				13 43	13 56	14 01			14 12	14 30			14 43	14 51	14 59			15 12	15 25	
Middlesbrough	d							14 00													14 50
Eaglescliffe	d		13 13																		
Darlington 7	d				13 44	13 58	14 02			14 13	14 30			14 44	14 52	15 00			15 13	15 26	
Northallerton	d		13 32		13 56		14 13	14 27						14 56							15 17
Thirsk	d		13 43					14 35													15 25
York 8	a	13 54	14 03		14 21	14 24	14 34	14 55		14 41	14 59			15 21	15 23	15 28			15 41	15 55	15 50
Leeds 10	a				14 53			15 23		15 08				15 53					16 08		16 23
Harrogate	d																				
Scarborough	d																				
York 8	d	13 57	14 05			14 27	14 37				15 01				15 26	15 30				15 57	
Doncaster 7	a					14 50	15 03								15 51	15 55				16 21	
Skipton	d																				
Keighley	d																				
Bradford Forster Square	d																				
Shipley	d																				
Leeds 10	d									15 12			15 05					16 05	16 12		
Wakefield Westgate 7	d									15 24			15 17					16 17	16 24		
Sheffield 7 ⇌	a					15 20				15 51					16 20				16 51		
Hull	d																15 06				
Selby	d																15 42				
Doncaster 7	d						15 04						15 35			15 55	16 02	16 39		16 21	
Retford 10	d																16 17	16 54			
Newark North Gate 7	a												16 02					17 09			
	d												16 02					17 09			
Grantham 7	a												16 15				16 37			16 52	
	d								16 07				16 15				16 37			16 52	
Peterborough 8	a	15 04					15 50		16 38				16 34			16 42		17 36		17 11	
Norwich	a								18 18												
Peterborough 8	d	15 04					15 50						16 35			16 47		17 37		17 13	
Stevenage 4	a						16 19						17 04			17 16	17s25				
London Kings Cross 15 ⊖	a	16 03	16 07				16 47				16 58		17 33			17 43	17 52	18 29		18 10	

A The Highland Chieftain

B The Northern Lights

C The Flying Scotsman

Table 26

Saturdays
until 10 July

Scotland, North East England, Yorkshire and Humberside - London

		NT	TP	XC	GC	GR	XC	NT	TP	TP	XC	GR	EM	EM	GR	XC	NT	NT	TP	XC	GR	HT	TP
Aberdeen	d																						
Stonehaven	d																						
Montrose	d																						
Arbroath	d																						
Dundee	d																						
Leuchars 3	d																						
Kirkcaldy	d																						
Inverkeithing	d																						
Inverness	d																						
Perth	d																						
Stirling	d																						
Glasgow Central 15	d											13 50											
Motherwell	d											14 06											
Haymarket	d											14 49											
Edinburgh 10	a											14 56											
Edinburgh	d					14 00	14 05					15 00				15 05					16 00		
Dunbar	d															15 26							
Berwick-upon-Tweed	d					14 39										15 48					16 39		
Alnmouth for Alnwick	d						15 05																
Morpeth	d	14 50						15 50										16 50					
Newcastle 8	a	15 13				15 26	15 35	16 13				16 25				16 38		17 13			17 26		
Sunderland	d																						
Hartlepool	d																						
Newcastle 8	d		15 09	15 25		15 28	15 44			16 06	16 22	16 29				16 44			17 01	17 22	17 30		
Chester-le-Street	d		15 18							16 15	16 31									17 31			
Durham	d		15 24	15 38		15 42	15 56			16 21	16 38	16 42				16 56			17 13	17 38			
Darlington 7	a		15 41	15 54		16 03	16 12			16 39	16 54	16 59				17 12			17 29	17 53	17 58		
Middlesbrough	d								15 50														18 07
Eaglescliffe	d																						
Darlington 7	d		15 42	15 56		16 04	16 13			16 39	16 56	17 00				17 13			17 30	17 55	17 59		
Northallerton	d		15 53						16 17	16 50									17 42				18 35
Thirsk	d								16 25	16 58													18 43
York 8	a		16 17	16 22		16 32	16 41		16 50	17 18	17 22	17 29				17 41			18 06	18 22	18 27		19 03
Leeds 10	a		16 53				17 08			17 53						18 08			18 35				19 35
Harrogate	d																						
Scarborough	d												17 03				16 22						
York 8	d			16 25		16 34					17 25	17 31	17 49							18 25	18 29		
Doncaster 7	a			16 50		16 58					17 50	17 54	18 15							18 48	18 51		
Skipton	d																						
Keighley	d																						
Bradford Forster Square	d																						
Shipley	d																						
Leeds 10	d						17 12								17 40	18 11							
Wakefield Westgate 7	d						17 24								17 52	18 24							
Sheffield 7	a			17 20			17 51				18 20		18 44			18 51				19 21			
Hull	d																17 52					18 12	
Selby	d																18 24					18 47	
Doncaster 7	d				16 56	16 59						17 55			18 10		18 47				18 52	19 05	
Retford 10	d														18 25							19 20	
Newark North Gate 7	a											18 18			18 40								
	d											18 18			18 40								
Grantham 7	a					17 30									18 52							19 40	
	d					17 30								18 15	18 52							19 40	
Peterborough 8	a					17 49						18 46		18 42	19 12						19 38		
Norwich	a													20 18									
Peterborough 8	d					17 50						18 48			19 12						19 38		
Stevenage 4	a					18 19									19 41						20 07	20s25	
London Kings Cross 15 ⊖	a				18 40	18 47						19 40			20 10						20 35	20 52	

Table 26

Saturdays
until 10 July

Scotland, North East England, Yorkshire and Humberside - London

		TP	GR	XC	GC	XC	GR	XC	NT	TP	GR	TP	NT	XC	EM	GR	XC	TP	NT	GR	NT	NT
Aberdeen	d										14 50											
Stonehaven	d										15 07											
Montrose	d										15 30											
Arbroath	d										15 46											
Dundee	d										16 04											
Leuchars 3	d										16 18											
Kirkcaldy	d										16 45											
Inverkeithing	d										17 01											
Inverness	d																					
Perth	d																					
Stirling	d																					
Glasgow Central 15	d						15 50													17 50		
Motherwell	d						16 06													18 06		
Haymarket	d						16 50				17 20									18 47		
Edinburgh 10	a						16 56				17 25									18 55		
Edinburgh	d			16 05			17 00	17 05			17 30						18 05			19 00		
Dunbar	d							17 25			17 50						18 25			19 20		
Berwick-upon-Tweed	d							17 48			18 13						18 48			19 43		
Alnmouth for Alnwick	d			17 05			17 58										19 08		19 24	20 05		
Morpeth	d			17 20					18 32				19 04						19 49	20 22	21 15	
Newcastle 8	a			17 38			18 30	18 40	18 56		19 03		19 26				19 41		20 12	20 41	21 40	
Sunderland	d				17 30																	
Hartlepool	d				17 56																	
Newcastle 8	d			17 44		18 22	18 33	18 44			19 06	18 52		19 25			19 43			20 47		21 50
Chester-le-Street	d					18 31																21 59
Durham	d			17 56		18 38	18 46	18 56				19 04		19 37			19 56			21 00		22 08
Darlington 7	a			18 12		18 54	19 03	19 12			19 34	19 20		19 53			20 12			21 18		22 29
Middlesbrough	d	17 00								19 00								20 10				
Eaglescliffe	d				18 28																	22 43
Darlington 7	d			18 13		18 56	19 05	19 13			19 34	19 21		19 54			20 13			21 18		
Northallerton	d	17 27			18 46					19 27		19 36						20 37		21 30		
Thirsk	d	17 35			18 55					19 35								20 45				
York 8	a	17 55		18 41	19 13	19 22	19 34	19 41		19 58	20 04	20 02		20 20			20 41	21 07		21 51		
Leeds 10	a	18 23		19 08				20 08				20 35					21 08	21 35				
Harrogate	d																					
Scarborough	d																					
York 8	d				19 15	19 25	19 36				20 06			20 23						21 52		
Doncaster 7	a					19 50	19 59				20 29									22 17		
Skipton	d																					
Keighley	d																					
Bradford Forster Square	d																					
Shipley	d																					
Leeds 10	d		18 40	19 11				20 11								20 15	21 11					
Wakefield Westgate 7	d		18 54	19 24				20 23								20 31	21 23			22 39		
Sheffield 7	a			19 50		20 20		20 52						21 20			21 51					
Hull	d																					
Selby	d																					
Doncaster 7	d		19 14				20 00				20 30					20 48						
Retford 10	d		19 29													21 03						
Newark North Gate 7	a		19 44													21 18						
	d		19 44													21 18						
Grantham 7	a		19 56													21 31						
	d		19 56												21 07	21 31						
Peterborough 8	a		20 16				20 46				21 18				21 34	21 50						
Norwich	a														23 18							
Peterborough 8	d		20 19				20 49				21 22					21 51						
Stevenage 4	a		20 48				21 18				21 52					22 20						
London Kings Cross 15 ⊖	a		21 15		21 30		21 45				22 20					22 47						

Scotland, North East England, Yorkshire and Humberside - London

		EM	GR	GR	GR	XC	TP	GR	XC	GR	TP	XC	GR	EM	GC	EM	GR
Aberdeen	d																
Stonehaven	d																
Montrose	d																
Arbroath	d																
Dundee	d																
Leuchars	d																
Kirkcaldy	d																
Inverkeithing	d																
Inverness	d																
Perth	d																
Stirling	d																
Glasgow Central	d																
Motherwell	d																
Haymarket	d																
Edinburgh	a																
Edinburgh	d																
Dunbar	d																
Berwick-upon-Tweed	d																
Alnmouth for Alnwick	d																
Morpeth	d																
Newcastle	a																
Sunderland	d																
Hartlepool	d																
Newcastle	d			04 30						06 00	06 13	06 21					06 35
Chester-le-Street	d											06 32					
Durham	d			04 45						06 12	06 29	06 39					06 47
Darlington	a			05 02						06 29	06 45	06 55					07 04
Middlesbrough	d						05 57										
Eaglescliffe	d																
Darlington	d			05 03						06 30	06 46	06 56					07 05
Northallerton	d			05 30			06 25				06 58						
Thirsk	d						06 33				07 06						
York	a			05 57			06 51			06 57	07 30	07 23					07 33
Leeds	a						07 20				08 04						
Harrogate	d																
Scarborough	d																
York	d			06 00					06 09	07 00		07 25					07 36
Doncaster	a			06 22						07 22		07 48					07 59
Skipton	d																
Keighley	d																
Bradford Forster Square	d																
Shipley	d																
Leeds	d		05 05		06 10	06 15		07 00	07 05					07 34			
Wakefield Westgate	d		05 17		06 22	06 29		07 12	07 18					07 46			
Sheffield	a								07 51			08 18		08 21			
Hull	d												06 50				
Selby	d												07 23				
Doncaster	d		05 35	06 23	06 40	06 47		07 30		07 23			07 43		07 55		07 59
Retford	d		05 50		06 55												
Newark North Gate	a		06 05		07 10			07 53									08 23
	d		06 05		07 10			07 53									08 23
Grantham	a		06 17		07 23			08 06									08 35
	d	05 51	06 17		07 23			08 06								08 16	08 35
Peterborough	a	06 25	06 37	07 09	07 42			08 25		08 09			08 31			08 44	08 56
Norwich	a															10 19	
Peterborough	d		06 37	07 09	07 48			08 26		08 09			08 32				08 57
Stevenage	a																
London Kings Cross	a		07 29	08 03	08 40			09 18		09 03			09 25		09 43		09 51

Scotland, North East England, Yorkshire and Humberside - London

		GR	GR	XC	TP		XC	EM	GR	GR	GC	HT	TP	EM	XC	GR	GR	NT	XC
											A								
Aberdeen	d																		
Stonehaven	d																		
Montrose	d																		
Arbroath	d																		
Dundee	d																		
Leuchars	d																		
Kirkcaldy	d																		
Inverkeithing	d																		
Inverness	d																		
Perth	d																		
Stirling	d																		
Glasgow Central	d																		
Motherwell	d																		
Haymarket	d																		
Edinburgh	a																		
Edinburgh	d														06 12	06 15			06 55
Dunbar	d															06 35			
Berwick-upon-Tweed	d														06 51	06 58			07 35
Alnmouth for Alnwick	d														07 11	07 18		07 33	07 55
Morpeth	d															07 34		07 59	08 09
Newcastle	a														07 41	07 53		08 24	08 27
Sunderland	d										06 53								
Hartlepool	d										07 17								
Newcastle	d			06 42	07 00		07 25			07 30			07 33		07 44	07 54			08 30
Chester-le-Street	d												07 42						
Durham	d			06 56	07 12		07 38			07 42			07 48		07 56				08 42
Darlington	a			07 11	07 29		07 53			08 00			08 05		08 12	08 21			08 58
Middlesbrough	d					07 21													
Eaglescliffe	d										07 45								
Darlington	d			07 13	07 30		07 55			08 00			08 06		08 13	08 21			08 59
Northallerton	d				07 41	07 48					08 05		08 18						
Thirsk	d					07 56					08 16		08 26						
York	a			07 41	08 01	08 16	08 22			08 28	08 44		08 55		08 41	08 50			09 26
Leeds	a			08 08									09 23		09 07				
Harrogate	d								07 44										
Scarborough	d																		
York	d				08 04		08 27			08 30	08 47					08 51			09 28
Doncaster	a						08 50			08 54						09 15			09 51
Skipton	d	06 55																	
Keighley	d	07u07																	
Bradford Forster Square	d		07 33																
Shipley	d	07u18	07u38																
Leeds	d	0740	0805	08 12					08 15						09 11		09 05		
Wakefield Westgate	d	07 52	08 18	08 24											09 24		09 17		
Sheffield	a			08 51			09 20								09 51				10 20
Hull	d											08 02							
Selby	d											08 37							
Doncaster	d								08 45	08 55		09 01				09 15	09 35		
Retford	d	08 20								09 10		09 21							
Newark North Gate	a	08 34	08 54														10 00		
	d	08 34	08 54														10 00		
Grantham	a	08 46	09 06									09 42					10 12		
	d	08 46	09 06					09 11				09 42		10 08			10 12		
Peterborough	a	09 06	09 26		09 12			09 43	09 32	09 49				10 37		10 06	10 32		
Norwich	a							11 18						12 18					
Peterborough	d	09 07	09 26		09 16				09 33	09 49						10 06	10 33		
Stevenage	a				09 45												11 03		
London Kings Cross	a	10 04	10 20		10 13				10 26	10 43	10 48	10 52				10 59	11 33		

A The Zephyr

Table 26

Saturdays
17 July to 04 September

Scotland, North East England, Yorkshire and Humberside - London

		TP	GR	EM	GR	XC	GR	TP	XC	GR	HT	GC	XC	NT	GR	TP	GR	TP	XC	EM	GR
Aberdeen	d																				
Stonehaven	d																				
Montrose	d																				
Arbroath	d																				
Dundee	d																				
Leuchars 3	d																				
Kirkcaldy	d																				
Inverkeithing	d																				
Inverness	d																				
Perth	d																				
Stirling	d																				
Glasgow Central 15	d									06 50			07 00								07 50
Motherwell	d									07 05											08 04
Haymarket	d									07 47			07 54								08 49
Edinburgh 10	a									07 52			07 59								08 56
Edinburgh	d		07 00			07 07	07 30			08 00			08 05		08 35						09 00
Dunbar	d					07 27															
Berwick-upon-Tweed	d		07 40			07 50	08 09						08 47		09 14						09 41
Alnmouth for Alnwick	d									08 58			09 05								
Morpeth	d													09 32							
Newcastle 8	a		08 31			08 38	08 57			09 29			09 39	09 55	10 02						10 29
Sunderland	d											09 29									
Hartlepool	d											09 53									
Newcastle 8	d		08 33			08 40	08 59	09 12	09 25	09 32			09 41		10 05			10 12	10 25		10 32
Chester-le-Street	d					08 49		09 21													
Durham	d		08 46			08 56	09 12	09 27	09 37				09 55					10 27	10 38		10 45
Darlington 7	a		09 04			09 12	09 30	09 43	09 54	10 00			10 10		10 31			10 43	10 54		11 03
Middlesbrough	d	09 00														10 00					
Eaglescliffe	d											10 15									
Darlington 7	d		09 04			09 13	09 30	09 44	09 56	10 01			10 12		10 35			10 44	10 56		11 03
Northallerton	d	09 27					09 43	09 56				10 35				10 27		10 56			
Thirsk	d	09 35										10 44				10 35					
York 8	a	09 55	09 33			09 41	10 05	10 21	10 22	10 29		11 02	10 41		11 05	10 55		11 21	11 24		11 32
Leeds 10	a	10 23				10 08		10 53					11 08			11 23		11 53			
Harrogate	d																				
Scarborough	d																				
York 8	d		09 35				10 06		10 25	10 31		11 04			11 07				11 27		11 33
Doncaster 7	a		10 01				10 31		10 48	10 52					11 28				11 50		11 57
Skipton	d																				
Keighley	d																				
Bradford Forster Square	d																				
Shipley	d																				
Leeds 10	d				10 05	10 12							11 11				11 05				
Wakefield Westgate 7	d				10 18	10 24							11 24				11 17				
Sheffield 7	a					10 51			11 20				11 51						12 20		
Hull	d										10 06										
Selby	d										10 41										
Doncaster 7	d		10 01		10 36		10 31			10 55	11 02				11 29		11 39				11 57
Retford 10	d									11 10	11 17										
Newark North Gate 7	a				11 00												12 01				
	d				11 00												12 01				
Grantham 7	a				11 12						11 38				12 00		12 14				12 28
	d			11 07	11 12						11 38				12 00		12 14			12 07	12 28
Peterborough 8	a		10 48	11 36	11 32		11 20			11 49					12 19		12 33			12 38	12 48
Norwich	a			13 13																14 13	
Peterborough 8	d		10 49		11 32		11 21			11 50					12 20		12 34				12 48
Stevenage 4	a						11 52				12s25						13 03				
London Kings Cross 15 ⊖	a		11 41		12 24		12 20			12 42	12 52	12 56			13 12		13 33				13 41

Table 26

Saturdays
17 July to 04 September

Scotland, North East England, Yorkshire and Humberside - London

		GC	EM	XC	TP	GR	NT	GR	TP	XC	GR	HT	XC	TP	GR	NT	GR	TP	XC	EM	GR	EM	XC
Aberdeen	d														07 52								08 20
Stonehaven	d														08 09								08 38
Montrose	d														08 32								08 59
Arbroath	d														08 48								09 15
Dundee	d			07 35											09 06								09 32
Leuchars 3	d			07 48											09 20								09 47
Kirkcaldy	d			08 20											09 44								10 17
Inverkeithing	d			08 35											10 01								10 32
Inverness	d																						
Perth	d																						
Stirling	d																						
Glasgow Central 15	d										08 50		09 00								09 50		
Motherwell	d										09 04										10 04		
Haymarket	d			08 54							09 46		09 55		10 21						10 48		10 51
Edinburgh 10	a			08 58							09 53		09 59		10 26						10 55		10 58
Edinburgh	d			09 05		09 30					10 00		10 05		10 30						11 00		11 05
Dunbar	d			09 26																			11 25
Berwick-upon-Tweed	d			09 49		10 09															11 39		11 48
Alnmouth for Alnwick	d												11 04										
Morpeth	d						10 50						11 19			11 50							
Newcastle 8	a			10 38		10 56	11 14				11 27		11 39		11 55	12 13					12 26		12 38
Sunderland	d																						
Hartlepool	d																						
Newcastle 8	d			10 44		11 00			11 15	11 25	11 29		11 41		12 00			12 15	12 22		12 33		12 44
Chester-le-Street	d																		12 31				
Durham	d			10 56					11 27	11 37	11 42		11 55		12 13			12 27	12 38		12 46		12 56
Darlington 7	a			11 12		11 26			11 43	11 54	12 00		12 10		12 31			12 43	12 53		13 03		13 12
Middlesbrough	d				11 00									12 00									
Eaglescliffe	d																						
Darlington 7	d			11 13		11 27			11 44	11 56	12 01		12 12		12 31			12 44	12 55		13 04		13 13
Northallerton	d				11 27				11 56					12 27				12 56					
Thirsk	d				11 35									12 35									
York 8	a			11 41	11 55	11 57			12 21	12 22	12 29		12 41	12 55	13 00			13 21	13 24		13 32		13 41
Leeds 10	a			12 08	12 23				12 53				13 08	13 23				13 53					14 08
Harrogate	d																						
Scarborough	d																						
York 8	d					11 59				12 25	12 33				13 02				13 27		13 34		
Doncaster 7	a					12 20				12 50	12 56								13 52		13 58		
Skipton	d																						
Keighley	d																						
Bradford Forster Square	d																						
Shipley	d																						
Leeds 10	d			12 11				12 05					13 11				13 05						14 11
Wakefield Westgate 7	d			12 24				12 17					13 23				13 17						14 24
Sheffield 7	a			12 51						13 20			13 51						14 20				14 51
Hull	d											12 05											
Selby	d											12 40											
Doncaster 7	d	12 06				12 21		12 38			12 57	13 04					13 38				13 58		
Retford 10	d							12 53				13 19											
Newark North Gate 7	a							13 08									14 01						
	d							13 08									14 01						
Grantham 7	a							13 20				13 39									14 29		
	d		13 08					13 20				13 39								14 07	14 29	15 07	
Peterborough 8	a		13 35			13 07					13 45				14 09		14 29			14 39	14 49	15 34	
Norwich	a		15 13																	16 13		17 13	
Peterborough 8	d					13 07					13 47				14 14		14 29				14 49		
Stevenage 4	a										14 16	14s24											
London Kings Cross 15 ⊖	a	13 45				14 00		14 27			14 43	14 50			15 10		15 21				16 07		

Scotland, North East England, Yorkshire and Humberside - London

		TP	GR	GC	NT	GR	TP	XC	GR	TP	EM	XC	GR	NT	TP	XC	GR	GR	HT	XC	TP	GR	GR
			A										B					C					
Aberdeen	d												09 52										
Stonehaven	d												10 09										
Montrose	d												10 32										
Arbroath	d												10 49										
Dundee	d												11 06										
Leuchars	d												11 20										
Kirkcaldy	d												11 44										
Inverkeithing	d												12 01										
Inverness	d		07 55																				
Perth	d		09 56																				
Stirling	d		10 30																				
Glasgow Central	d																	11 50					
Motherwell	d																	12 06					
Haymarket	d		11 09										12 19					12 49					
Edinburgh	a		11 15										12 25					12 55					
Edinburgh	d		11 30						12 00			12 05	12 30					13 00		13 05		13 30	
Dunbar	d																			13 26			
Berwick-upon-Tweed	d								12 39											13 48		14 09	
Alnmouth for Alnwick	d		12 28									13 05											
Morpeth	d				12 50									13 50									
Newcastle	a		12 59		13 13				13 26			13 35	13 57	14 13				14 25		14 38		14 57	
Sunderland	d			12 30																			
Hartlepool	d			12 54																			
Newcastle	d		13 03				13 15	13 27	13 31			13 44	13 59		14 15	14 22		14 29		14 44		14 59	
Chester-le-Street	d																						
Durham	d						13 27	13 39	13 44			13 56	14 12		14 27	14 34		14 42		14 56			
Darlington	a						13 43	13 56	14 01			14 12	14 30		14 43	14 51		14 59		15 12		15 25	
Middlesbrough	d	12 50								14 00											14 50		
Eaglescliffe	d			13 13																			
Darlington	d						13 44	13 58	14 02			14 13	14 30		14 44	14 52		15 00		15 13		15 26	
Northallerton	d	13 17		13 32			13 56		14 13	14 27					14 56						15 17		
Thirsk	d	13 25		13 43						14 35											15 25		
York	a	13 50	13 54	14 03			14 21	14 24	14 34	14 55		14 41	14 59		15 21	15 23		15 28		15 41	15 50	15 55	
Leeds	a	14 23					14 53			15 23		15 08			15 53					16 08	16 23		
Harrogate	d																						
Scarborough	d																						
York	d		13 57	14 05				14 27	14 37				15 01			15 26		15 30				15 57	
Doncaster	a							14 50	15 03							15 51		15 55				16 21	
Skipton	d																						
Keighley	d																						
Bradford Forster Square	d																						
Shipley	d																						
Leeds	d					14 05						15 12					15 05			16 12			16 05
Wakefield Westgate	d					14 17						15 24					15 17			16 24			16 17
Sheffield	a							15 20				15 51				16 20				16 51			
Hull	d																		15 06				
Selby	d																		15 42				
Doncaster	d					14 36			15 04								15 35	15 55	16 02			16 21	16 39
Retford	d					14 51													16 17				16 54
Newark North Gate	a					15 06											16 02						17 09
	d					15 06											16 02						17 09
Grantham	a					15 19											16 15		16 37			16 52	
	d					15 19					16 07						16 15		16 37			16 52	
Peterborough	a		15 04			15 38			15 50		16 38						16 34	16 41				17 11	17 36
Norwich	a										18 18												
Peterborough	d		15 04			15 39			15 50								16 35	16 47				17 13	17 37
Stevenage	a								16 21								17 08	17 17	17s24				
London Kings Cross	a		16 16	16 25		16 48			17 06				17 16				17 48	18 06	18 11			18 20	18 44

A The Highland Chieftain

B The Northern Lights

C The Flying Scotsman

Table 26

Saturdays
17 July to 04 September

Scotland, North East England, Yorkshire and Humberside - London

		NT	TP	XC	GC	GR	XC	TP	NT	TP	XC	GR	EM	EM	GR	XC	NT	NT	TP	TP	XC	GR	HT
Aberdeen	d																						
Stonehaven	d																						
Montrose	d																						
Arbroath	d																						
Dundee	d																						
Leuchars	d																						
Kirkcaldy	d																						
Inverkeithing	d																						
Inverness	d																						
Perth	d																						
Stirling	d																						
Glasgow Central	d											13 50											
Motherwell	d											14 06											
Haymarket	d											14 49											
Edinburgh	a											14 56											
Edinburgh	d					14 00	14 05					15 00				15 05						16 00	
Dunbar	d															15 26							
Berwick-upon-Tweed	d					14 39										15 48						16 39	
Alnmouth for Alnwick	d						15 05																
Morpeth	d	14 50							15 50									16 50					
Newcastle	a	15 13				15 26	15 35		16 13			16 25				16 38		17 13				17 26	
Sunderland	d																						
Hartlepool	d																						
Newcastle	d		15 09	15 25		15 28	15 44			16 06	16 22	16 29				16 44				17 01	17 22	17 30	
Chester-le-Street	d		15 18							16 15	16 31										17 31		
Durham	d		15 24	15 38		15 42	15 56			16 21	16 38	16 42				16 56				17 13	17 38		
Darlington	a		15 41	15 54		16 03	16 12			16 39	16 54	16 59				17 12				17 29	17 53	17 58	
Middlesbrough	d							15 50											17 00				
Eaglescliffe	d																						
Darlington	d		15 42	15 56		16 04	16 13			16 39	16 56	17 00				17 13				17 30	17 55	17 59	
Northallerton	d		15 53					16 17		16 50									17 27	17 42			
Thirsk	d							16 25		16 58									17 35				
York	a		16 17	16 22		16 32	16 41	16 50		17 18	17 22	17 29				17 41			17 55	18 06	18 22	18 27	
Leeds	a		16 53				17 08	17 23		17 53						18 08			18 23	18 35			
Harrogate	d																						
Scarborough	d												17 03				16 22						
York	d			16 25		16 34					17 25	17 31	17 49								18 25	18 29	
Doncaster	a			16 50		16 58					17 50	17 54	18 15								18 48	18 51	
Skipton	d																						
Keighley	d																						
Bradford Forster Square	d																						
Shipley	d																						
Leeds	d						17 12								17 40	18 11							
Wakefield Westgate	d						17 24								17 52	18 24							
Sheffield	a			17 20			17 51				18 20		18 44			18 51					19 21		
Hull	d																17 52						18 12
Selby	d																18 24						18 47
Doncaster	d				16 56	16 59						17 55			18 10		18 47					18 52	19 05
Retford	d														18 25								19 20
Newark North Gate	a											18 18			18 40								
	d											18 18			18 40								
Grantham	a					17 30									18 52								19 40
	d					17 30								18 15	18 52								19 40
Peterborough	a					17 49						18 46		18 42	19 12							19 38	
Norwich	a													20 18									
Peterborough	d					17 50						18 48			19 12							19 38	
Stevenage	a					18 23									19 44							20 09	20s27
London Kings Cross	a				19 06	19 09						20 06			20 22							20 45	21 07

Table 26

Saturdays
17 July to 04 September

Scotland, North East England, Yorkshire and Humberside - London

		GR	XC	TP	GC	XC	GR	XC	NT	TP	TP	GR	NT	XC	EM	GR	XC	NT	TP	GR	NT	NT
Aberdeen	d											14 50										
Stonehaven	d											15 07										
Montrose	d											15 30										
Arbroath	d											15 46										
Dundee	d											16 04										
Leuchars	d											16 18										
Kirkcaldy	d											16 45										
Inverkeithing	d											17 01										
Inverness	d																					
Perth	d																					
Stirling	d																					
Glasgow Central	d						15 50													17 50		
Motherwell	d						16 06													18 06		
Haymarket	d						16 50					17 20								18 47		
Edinburgh	a						16 56					17 25								18 55		
Edinburgh	d		16 05				17 00	17 05				17 30					18 05			19 00		
Dunbar	d							17 25				17 50					18 25			19 20		
Berwick-upon-Tweed	d							17 48				18 13					18 48			19 43		
Alnmouth for Alnwick	d		17 05				17 58										19 08	19 24		20 05		
Morpeth	d		17 20						18 32				19 04					19 49		20 22	21 15	
Newcastle	a		17 38				18 30	18 40	18 56			19 03	19 26				19 41	20 12		20 41	21 40	
Sunderland	d				17 30																	
Hartlepool	d				17 56																	
Newcastle	d		17 44			18 22	18 33	18 44			18 52	19 06		19 25			19 43			20 47		21 50
Chester-le-Street	d					18 31																21 59
Durham	d		17 56			18 38	18 46	18 56			19 04			19 37			19 56			21 00		22 08
Darlington	a		18 12			18 54	19 03	19 12			19 20	19 34		19 53			20 12			21 18		22 29
Middlesbrough	d			18 07						19 00									20 10			
Eaglescliffe	d				18 28																	22 43
Darlington	d		18 13			18 56	19 05	19 13			19 21	19 34		19 54			20 13			21 18		
Northallerton	d			18 35	18 46					19 27	19 36								20 37	21 30		
Thirsk	d			18 43	18 55					19 35									20 45			
York	a		18 41	19 03	19 13	19 22	19 34	19 41		19 58	20 02	20 04		20 20			20 41		21 07	21 51		
Leeds	a		19 08	19 35				20 08			20 35						21 08		21 35			
Harrogate	d																					
Scarborough	d																					
York	d				19 15	19 25	19 36					20 06		20 23						21 52		
Doncaster	a					19 50	19 59					20 29								22 17		
Skipton	d																					
Keighley	d																					
Bradford Forster Square	d																					
Shipley	d																					
Leeds	d	18 40	19 11					20 11								20 15	21 11					
Wakefield Westgate	d	18 54	19 24					20 23								20 31	21 23			22 39		
Sheffield	a		19 50			20 20		20 52						21 20			21 51					
Hull	d																					
Selby	d																					
Doncaster	d	19 14					20 00					20 30				20 48						
Retford	d	19 29														21 03						
Newark North Gate	a	19 44														21 18						
	d	19 44														21 18						
Grantham	a	19 56														21 31						
	d	19 56													21 07	21 31						
Peterborough	a	20 16					20 46					21 18			21 34	21 50						
Norwich	a														23 18							
Peterborough	d	20 19					20 49					21 22				21 51						
Stevenage	a	20 49					21 21					21 54				22 21						
London Kings Cross	a	21 27			21 30		22 06					22 32				23 06						

Table 26

Saturdays
from 11 September

Scotland, North East England, Yorkshire and Humberside - London

		EM	GR	GR	TP	GR	XC	GR	XC	GR	TP	XC	GR	TP	GC	EM	GR
Aberdeen	d																
Stonehaven	d																
Montrose	d																
Arbroath	d																
Dundee	d																
Leuchars	d																
Kirkcaldy	d																
Inverkeithing	d																
Inverness	d																
Perth	d																
Stirling	d																
Glasgow Central	d																
Motherwell	d																
Haymarket	d																
Edinburgh	a																
Edinburgh	d																
Dunbar	d																
Berwick-upon-Tweed	d																
Alnmouth for Alnwick	d																
Morpeth	d																
Newcastle	a																
Sunderland	d																
Hartlepool	d																
Newcastle	d			04 30						06 00	06 13	06 21					06 35
Chester-le-Street	d											06 32					
Durham	d			04 45						06 12	06 29	06 39					06 47
Darlington	a			05 02						06 29	06 45	06 55					07 04
Middlesbrough	d				05 57									07 21			
Eaglescliffe	d																
Darlington	d			05 03						06 30	06 46	06 56					07 05
Northallerton	d			05 30	06 25						06 58			07 48			
Thirsk	d				06 33						07 06			07 56			
York	a			05 57	06 51					06 57	07 30	07 23		08 16			07 33
Leeds	a				07 20						08 04			08 52			
Harrogate	d																
Scarborough	d																
York	d			06 00					06 09	07 00		07 25					07 36
Doncaster	a			06 22						07 22		07 48					07 59
Skipton	d																
Keighley	d																
Bradford Forster Square	d																
Shipley	d																
Leeds	d		05 05			06 10	06 15	07 00	07 05								
Wakefield Westgate	d		05 17			06 22	06 29	07 12	07 18								
Sheffield	a								07 51			08 18					
Hull	d												06 50				
Selby	d												07 23				
Doncaster	d		05 35	06 23		06 40	06 47	07 30		07 23			07 43		07 55		07 59
Retford	d		05 50			06 55											
Newark North Gate	a		06 05			07 10		07 53									08 23
	d		06 05			07 10		07 53									08 23
Grantham	a		06 17			07 23		08 06									08 35
	d	05 51	06 17			07 23		08 06								08 16	08 35
Peterborough	a	06 25	06 37	07 09		07 42		08 25		08 09			08 31			08 44	08 56
Norwich	a															10 19	
Peterborough	d		06 37	07 09		07 48		08 26		08 09			08 32				08 57
Stevenage	a																
London Kings Cross	a		07 29	08 03		08 40		09 18		09 03			09 25		09 43		09 51

Table 26

Saturdays from 11 September

Scotland, North East England, Yorkshire and Humberside - London

		GR	GR	XC	GR	XC		EM		GR	GR	GC	TP	HT			EM	GR	XC	GR			NT	XC	TP
		1	1	◇1	1	◇1		◇		1	1	1 A	◇1	◇1			◇	1	◇1	1				◇1	◇1
Aberdeen	d																								
Stonehaven	d																								
Montrose	d																								
Arbroath	d																								
Dundee	d																								
Leuchars 3	d																								
Kirkcaldy	d																								
Inverkeithing	d																								
Inverness	d																								
Perth	d																								
Stirling	d																								
Glasgow Central 15	d																								
Motherwell	d																								
Haymarket	d																								
Edinburgh 10	a																								
Edinburgh	d																		06 12	06 15				06 55	
Dunbar	d																			06 35					
Berwick-upon-Tweed	d																		06 51	06 58				07 35	
Alnmouth for Alnwick	d																		07 11	07 18			07 33	07 55	
Morpeth	d																			07 34			07 59	08 09	
Newcastle 8	a																		07 41	07 53			08 24	08 27	
Sunderland	d											06 53													
Hartlepool	d											07 17													
Newcastle 8	d			06 42	07 00	07 25					07 30		07 33						07 44	07 54				08 30	
Chester-le-Street	d												07 42												
Durham	d			06 56	07 12	07 38					07 42		07 48						07 56					08 42	
Darlington 7	a			07 11	07 29	07 53					08 00		08 05						08 12	08 21				08 58	
Middlesbrough	d																								09 00
Eaglescliffe	d											07 45													
Darlington 7	d			07 13	07 30	07 55					08 00		08 06						08 13	08 21				08 59	
Northallerton	d				07 41							08 05	08 18												09 27
Thirsk	d											08 16	08 26												09 35
York 8	a			07 41	08 01	08 22					08 28	08 44	08 55						08 41	08 50				09 26	09 55
Leeds 10	a			08 08									09 23						09 07						10 23
Harrogate	d									07 44															
Scarborough	d																								
York 8	d				08 04	08 27					08 30	08 47								08 51				09 28	
Doncaster 7	a					08 50					08 54									09 15				09 51	
Skipton	d	06 55																							
Keighley	d	07u07																							
Bradford Forster Square	d		07 33																						
Shipley	d	07u18	07u38																						
Leeds 10	d	07b40	08c05	08 12						08 15								09 05	09 11						
Wakefield Westgate 7	d	07 52	08 18	08 24														09 17	09 24						
Sheffield 7	a			08 51		09 20													09 51					10 20	
Hull	d													08 02											
Selby	d													08 37											
Doncaster 7	d									08 45	08 55			09 01				09 35		09 15					
Retford 10	d	08 20									09 10			09 21											
Newark North Gate 7	a	08 34	08 54															10 00							
	d	08 34	08 54															10 00							
Grantham 7	a	08 46	09 06											09 42				10 12							
	d	08 46	09 06					09 11						09 42			10 08	10 12							
Peterborough 8	a	09 06	09 26		09 12			09 43		09 32	09 49						10 37	10 32		10 06					
Norwich	a							11 18									12 18								
Peterborough 8	d	09 07	09 26		09 16					09 33	09 49							10 33		10 06					
Stevenage 4	a				09 45													11 03							
London Kings Cross 15 ⊖	a	10 04	10 20		10 13					10 26	10 43	10 48		10 52				11 33		10 59					

A The Zephyr

b arr. 0733

c arr. 0753

Table 26

Saturdays from 11 September

Scotland, North East England, Yorkshire and Humberside - London

				GR	EM	GR	XC	GR	TP	XC	GR	HT	TP	GC	GR	XC	NT	GR	TP	XC			EM	GR	TP
				1	◇	1	◇1	1	◇1	◇1	1	◇1	◇1	1	1	◇1		1	◇1	◇1			◇	1	◇1
Aberdeen	d																								
Stonehaven	d																								
Montrose	d																								
Arbroath	d																								
Dundee	d																								
Leuchars 3	d																								
Kirkcaldy	d																								
Inverkeithing	d																								
Inverness	d																								
Perth	d																								
Stirling	d																								
Glasgow Central 15	d										06 50					07 00								07 50	
Motherwell	d										07 05													08 04	
Haymarket	d										07 47					07 54								08 49	
Edinburgh 10	a										07 52					07 59								08 56	
Edinburgh	d			07 00			07 07	07 30			08 00					08 05		08 35						09 00	
Dunbar	d						07 27																		
Berwick-upon-Tweed	d			07 40			07 50	08 09								08 47		09 14						09 41	
Alnmouth for Alnwick	d										08 58					09 09									
Morpeth	d																09 32								
Newcastle 8	a			08 31			08 38	08 57			09 29					09 39	09 55	10 02						10 29	
Sunderland	d													09 29											
Hartlepool	d													09 53											
Newcastle 8	d			08 33			08 40	08 59	09 12	09 25	09 32					09 41		10 05	10 12	10 25				10 32	
Chester-le-Street	d						08 49		09 21																
Durham	d			08 46			08 56	09 12	09 27	09 37						09 55			10 27	10 38				10 45	
Darlington 7	a			09 04			09 12	09 30	09 43	09 54	10 00					10 10		10 31	10 43	10 54				11 03	
Middlesbrough	d												10 00												11 00
Eaglescliffe	d													10 15											
Darlington 7	d			09 04			09 13	09 30	09 44	09 56	10 01					10 12		10 35	10 44	10 56				11 03	
Northallerton	d							09 43	09 56				10 27	10 35					10 56						11 27
Thirsk	d												10 35	10 44											11 35
York 8	a			09 33			09 41	10 05	10 21	10 22	10 29		10 55	11 02		10 41		11 05	11 21	11 24				11 32	11 55
Leeds 10	a						10 08		10 53				11 23			11 08			11 53						12 23
Harrogate	d																								
Scarborough	d																								
York 8	d			09 35				10 06		10 25	10 31			11 04				11 07		11 27				11 33	
Doncaster 7	a			10 01				10 31		10 48	10 52							11 28		11 50				11 57	
Skipton	d																								
Keighley	d																								
Bradford Forster Square	d																								
Shipley	d																								
Leeds 10	d					10 05	10 12								11 05	11 11									
Wakefield Westgate 7	d					10 18	10 24								11 17	11 24									
Sheffield 7	a						10 51			11 20						11 51				12 20					
Hull	d											10 06													
Selby	d											10 41													
Doncaster 7	d			10 01		10 36		10 31			10 55	11 02			11 39			11 29						11 57	
Retford 10	d										11 10	11 17													
Newark North Gate 7	a					11 00									12 01										
	d					11 00									12 01										
Grantham 7	a					11 12						11 38			12 14			12 00						12 28	
	d				11 07	11 12						11 38			12 14			12 00					12 07	12 28	
Peterborough 8	a			10 48	11 36	11 32		11 20			11 49				12 33			12 19					12 38	12 48	
Norwich	a				13 13																		14 13		
Peterborough 8	d			10 49		11 32		11 21			11 50				12 34			12 20						12 48	
Stevenage 4	a							11 52				12s25			13 03										
London Kings Cross 15 ⊖	a			11 41		12 24		12 20			12 42	12 52		12 56	13 33			13 12						13 41	

Table 26

Saturdays from 11 September

Scotland, North East England, Yorkshire and Humberside - London

		GC	EM	GR	XC	XC	GR	TP	NT	TP	XC	GR	GR	XC	GR	NT	TP	XC	EM	GR	HT	EM	GR	TP
					A	B																		
Aberdeen	d														07 52									
Stonehaven	d														08 09									
Montrose	d														08 32									
Arbroath	d														08 48									
Dundee	d				07 35	07 35									09 06									
Leuchars 3	d				07 48	07 48									09 20									
Kirkcaldy	d				08 20	08 20									09 44									
Inverkeithing	d				08 35	08 35									10 01									
Inverness	d																							
Perth	d																							
Stirling	d																							
Glasgow Central 15	d											08 50		09 00						09 50				
Motherwell	d											09 04								10 04				
Haymarket	d				08 54	08 57						09 46		09 55	10 21					10 48				
Edinburgh 10	a				08 58	09 01						09 53		09 59	10 26					10 55				
Edinburgh	d				09 05	09 05	09 30					10 00		10 05	10 30					11 00				
Dunbar	d				09 26	09 26																		
Berwick-upon-Tweed	d				09 49	09 49	10 09													11 39				
Alnmouth for Alnwick	d													11 04										
Morpeth	d								10 50					11 19		11 50								
Newcastle 8	a				10 38	10 38	10 56		11 14			11 27		11 39	11 55	12 13				12 26				
Sunderland	d																							
Hartlepool	d																							
Newcastle 8	d				10 44	10 44	11 00			11 15	11 25	11 29		11 41	12 00		12 15	12 22		12 33				
Chester-le-Street	d																	12 31						
Durham	d				10 56	10 56				11 27	11 37	11 42		11 55	12 13		12 27	12 38		12 46				
Darlington 7	a				11 12	11 12	11 26			11 43	11 54	12 00		12 10	12 31		12 43	12 53		13 03				
Middlesbrough	d							12 00																12 50
Eaglescliffe	d																							
Darlington 7	d				11 13	11 13	11 27			11 44	11 56	12 01		12 12	12 31		12 44	12 55		13 04				
Northallerton	d							12 27		11 56							12 56							13 17
Thirsk	d							12 35																13 25
York 8	a				11 41	11 41	11 57	12 55		12 21	12 22	12 29		12 41	13 00		13 21	13 24		13 32				13 50
Leeds 10	a				12 08	12 08		13 23		12 53				13 08			13 53							14 23
Harrogate	d																							
Scarborough	d																							
York 8	d						11 59				12 25	12 33			13 02			13 27		13 34				
Doncaster 7	a						12 20				12 50	12 56						13 52		13 58				
Skipton	d																							
Keighley	d																							
Bradford Forster Square	d																							
Shipley	d																							
Leeds 10	d			12 05	12 11	12 11							13 05	13 11									14 05	
Wakefield Westgate 7	d			12 17	12 24	12 24							13 17	13 23									14 17	
Sheffield 7	a				12 51	12 51					13 20			13 51				14 20						
Hull	d																				13 05			
Selby	d																				13 40			
Doncaster 7	d	12 06		12 38			12 21					12 57	13 38							13 58	14 04		14 36	
Retford 10	d			12 53																	14 19		14 51	
Newark North Gate 7	a			13 08									14 01										15 06	
	d			13 08									14 01										15 06	
Grantham 7	a			13 20																14 29	14 39		15 19	
	d		13 08	13 20															14 07	14 29	14 39	15 07	15 19	
Peterborough 8	a		13 35				13 07					13 45	14 29		14 09				14 39	14 49		15 34	15 38	
Norwich	a		15 13																16 13			17 13		
Peterborough 8	d						13 07					13 47	14 29		14 14					14 49			15 39	
Stevenage 4	a											14 16									15s26			
London Kings Cross 15	a	13 45		14 27			14 00					14 43	15 21		15 10					15 42	15 52		16 34	

A Until 18 September

B From 25 September

Table 26

Saturdays from 11 September

Scotland, North East England, Yorkshire and Humberside - London

		XC	GR	GC	NT	TP	XC	GR	TP	EM	GR	XC	GR	NT	TP	XC	GR	HT	GR	XC	TP
			A										B				C				
Aberdeen	d	08 20											09 52								
Stonehaven	d	08 38											10 09								
Montrose	d	08 59											10 32								
Arbroath	d	09 15											10 49								
Dundee	d	09 32											11 06								
Leuchars 3	d	09 47											11 20								
Kirkcaldy	d	10 17											11 44								
Inverkeithing	d	10 32											12 01								
Inverness	d		07 55																		
Perth	d		09 56																		
Stirling	d		10 30																		
Glasgow Central 15	d																11 50				
Motherwell	d																12 06				
Haymarket	d	10 51	11 09										12 19				12 49				
Edinburgh 10	a	10 58	11 15										12 25				12 55				
Edinburgh	d	11 05	11 30					12 00				12 05	12 30				13 00			13 05	
Dunbar	d	11 25																		13 26	
Berwick-upon-Tweed	d	11 48						12 39												13 48	
Alnmouth for Alnwick	d		12 28									13 05									
Morpeth	d				12 50									13 50							
Newcastle 8	a	12 38	12 59		13 13			13 26				13 35	13 57	14 13			14 25			14 38	
Sunderland	d			12 30																	
Hartlepool	d			12 54																	
Newcastle 8	d	12 44	13 03			13 15	13 27	13 31				13 44	13 59		14 15	14 22	14 29			14 44	
Chester-le-Street	d																				
Durham	d	12 56				13 27	13 39	13 44				13 56	14 12		14 27	14 34	14 42			14 56	
Darlington 7	a	13 12				13 43	13 56	14 01				14 12	14 30		14 43	14 51	14 59			15 12	
Middlesbrough	d								14 00												14 50
Eaglescliffe	d			13 13																	
Darlington 7	d	13 13				13 44	13 58	14 02				14 13	14 30		14 44	14 52	15 00			15 13	
Northallerton	d			13 32		13 56		14 13	14 27						14 56						15 17
Thirsk	d			13 43					14 35												15 25
York 8	a	13 41	13 54	14 03		14 21	14 24	14 34	14 55			14 41	14 59		15 21	15 23	15 28			15 41	15 50
Leeds 10	a	14 08				14 53			15 23			15 08			15 53					16 08	16 23
Harrogate	d																				
Scarborough	d																				
York 8	d		13 57	14 05			14 27	14 37					15 01			15 26	15 30				
Doncaster 7	a						14 50	15 03								15 51	15 55				
Skipton	d																				
Keighley	d																				
Bradford Forster Square	d																				
Shipley	d																				
Leeds 10	d	14 11									15 05	15 12							16 05	16 12	
Wakefield Westgate 7	d	14 24									15 17	15 24							16 17	16 24	
Sheffield 7	a	14 51					15 20					15 51				16 20				16 51	
Hull	d																	15 06			
Selby	d																	15 42			
Doncaster 7	d							15 04			15 35						15 55	16 02	16 39		
Retford 10	d																	16 17	16 54		
Newark North Gate 7	a										16 02								17 09		
	d										16 02								17 09		
Grantham 7	a										16 15							16 37			
	d									16 07	16 15							16 37			
Peterborough 8	a		15 04					15 50		16 38	16 34						16 42		17 36		
Norwich	a									18 18											
Peterborough 8	d		15 04					15 50			16 35						16 47		17 37		
Stevenage 4	a							16 19			17 04						17 16	17s25			
London Kings Cross 15	a		16 03	16 07				16 47			17 33		16 58				17 43	17 52	18 29		

A The Highland Chieftain

B The Northern Lights

C The Flying Scotsman

Table 26

Scotland, North East England, Yorkshire and Humberside - London

		GR	NT	TP	XC	GC	GR	XC	NT	TP	TP	XC	GR	EM		EM	GR	XC	NT		NT	TP	TP	XC	GR
Aberdeen	d																								
Stonehaven	d																								
Montrose	d																								
Arbroath	d																								
Dundee	d																								
Leuchars	d																								
Kirkcaldy	d																								
Inverkeithing	d																								
Inverness	d																								
Perth	d																								
Stirling	d																								
Glasgow Central	d												13 50												
Motherwell	d												14 06												
Haymarket	d												14 49												
Edinburgh	a												14 56												
Edinburgh	d	13 30					14 00	14 05					15 00					15 05							16 00
Dunbar	d																	15 26							
Berwick-upon-Tweed	d	14 09					14 39											15 48							16 39
Alnmouth for Alnwick	d							15 05																	
Morpeth	d		14 50						15 50												16 50				
Newcastle	a	14 57	15 13				15 26	15 35	16 13				16 25					16 38			17 13				17 26
Sunderland	d																								
Hartlepool	d																								
Newcastle	d	14 59		15 09	15 25		15 28	15 44			16 06	16 22	16 29					16 44					17 01	17 22	17 30
Chester-le-Street	d			15 18							16 15	16 31												17 31	
Durham	d			15 24	15 38		15 42	15 56			16 21	16 38	16 42					16 56					17 13	17 38	
Darlington	a	15 25		15 41	15 54		16 03	16 12			16 39	16 54	16 59					17 12					17 29	17 53	17 58
Middlesbrough	d									15 50												17 00			
Eaglescliffe	d																								
Darlington	d	15 26		15 42	15 56		16 04	16 13			16 39	16 56	17 00					17 13					17 30	17 55	17 59
Northallerton	d			15 53						16 17	16 50											17 27	17 42		
Thirsk	d									16 25	16 58											17 35			
York	a	15 55		16 17	16 22		16 32	16 41		16 50	17 18	17 22	17 29					17 41				17 55	18 06	18 22	18 27
Leeds	a			16 53				17 08		17 23	17 53							18 08				18 23	18 35		
Harrogate	d																								
Scarborough	d																		16 20						
York	d	15 57			16 25		16 34					17 25	17 31	17 49										18 25	18 29
Doncaster	a	16 21			16 50		16 58					17 50	17 54	18 16										18 48	18 51
Skipton	d																								
Keighley	d																								
Bradford Forster Square	d																								
Shipley	d																								
Leeds	d							17 12									17 40	18 11							
Wakefield Westgate	d							17 24									17 52	18 24							
Sheffield	a				17 20			17 51				18 20		18 44				18 51						19 21	
Hull	d																		17 52						
Selby	d																		18 24						
Doncaster	d	16 21				16 56	16 59						17 55				18 10		18 47						18 52
Retford	d																18 25								
Newark North Gate	a												18 18				18 40								
	d												18 18				18 40								
Grantham	a	16 52					17 30										18 52								
	d	16 52					17 30									18 15	18 52								
Peterborough	a	17 11					17 49						18 46			18 42	19 12								19 38
Norwich	a															20 18									
Peterborough	d	17 13					17 50						18 48				19 12								19 38
Stevenage	a						18 19										19 41								20 07
London Kings Cross ⊖	a	18 10				18 40	18 47						19 40				20 10								20 35

Table 26

Scotland, North East England, Yorkshire and Humberside - London

		HT	GR	XC		GC	TP	XC	GR	XC	NT	TP	GR	TP	NT	XC		EM	GR	XC	NT	GR		TP	NT
Aberdeen	d												14 50												
Stonehaven	d												15 07												
Montrose	d												15 30												
Arbroath	d												15 46												
Dundee	d												16 04												
Leuchars	d												16 18												
Kirkcaldy	d												16 45												
Inverkeithing	d												17 01												
Inverness	d																								
Perth	d																								
Stirling	d																								
Glasgow Central	d								15 50													17 50			
Motherwell	d								16 06													18 06			
Haymarket	d								16 50				17 20									18 47			
Edinburgh	a								16 56				17 25									18 55			
Edinburgh	d			16 05					17 00	17 05			17 30							18 05		19 00			
Dunbar	d									17 25			17 50							18 25		19 20			
Berwick-upon-Tweed	d									17 48			18 13							18 48		19 43			
Alnmouth for Alnwick	d			17 05					17 58											19 08	19 24	20 05			
Morpeth	d			17 20							18 32				19 04						19 49	20 22			21 15
Newcastle	a			17 38					18 30	18 40	18 56		19 03		19 26					19 41	20 12	20 41			21 40
Sunderland	d					17 30																			
Hartlepool	d					17 56																			
Newcastle	d			17 44				18 22	18 33	18 44		18 52	19 06			19 25				19 43		20 47			
Chester-le-Street	d							18 31																	
Durham	d			17 56				18 38	18 46	18 56		19 04				19 37				19 56		21 00			
Darlington	a			18 12				18 54	19 03	19 12		19 20	19 34			19 53				20 12		21 18			
Middlesbrough	d						18 07							19 00										20 10	
Eaglescliffe	d					18 28																			
Darlington	d			18 13				18 56	19 05	19 13		19 21	19 34			19 54				20 13		21 18			
Northallerton	d					18 46	18 35					19 36		19 27								21 30		20 37	
Thirsk	d					18 55	18 43							19 35										20 45	
York	a			18 41		19 13	19 03	19 22	19 34	19 41		20 02	20 04	19 58		20 20				20 41		21 51		21 07	
Leeds	a			19 08			19 35			20 08		20 35								21 08				21 35	
Harrogate	d																								
Scarborough	d																								
York	d					19 15		19 25	19 36				20 06			20 23						21 52			
Doncaster	a							19 50	19 59				20 29									22 17			
Skipton	d																								
Keighley	d																								
Bradford Forster Square	d																								
Shipley	d																								
Leeds	d		18 40	19 11						20 11									20 15	21 11					
Wakefield Westgate	d		18 54	19 24						20 23									20 31	21 23		22 39			
Sheffield	a			19 50				20 20		20 52						21 20				21 51					
Hull	d	18 12																							
Selby	d	18 47																							
Doncaster	d	19 05	19 14						20 00				20 30						20 48						
Retford	d	19 20	19 29																21 03						
Newark North Gate	a		19 44																21 18						
	d		19 44																21 18						
Grantham	a	19 40	19 56																21 31						
	d	19 40	19 56															21 07	21 31						
Peterborough	a		20 16						20 46				21 18					21 34	21 50						
Norwich	a																	23 18							
Peterborough	d		20 19						20 49				21 22						21 51						
Stevenage	a	20s25	20 48						21 18				21 52						22 20						
London Kings Cross ⊖	a	20 52	21 15			21 30			21 45				22 20						22 47						

Table 26

Saturdays from 11 September

Scotland, North East England, Yorkshire and Humberside - London

Station		NT	TP
Aberdeen	d		
Stonehaven	d		
Montrose	d		
Arbroath	d		
Dundee	d		
Leuchars	d		
Kirkcaldy	d		
Inverkeithing	d		
Inverness	d		
Perth	d		
Stirling	d		
Glasgow Central	d		
Motherwell	d		
Haymarket	d		
Edinburgh	a		
Edinburgh	d		
Dunbar	d		
Berwick-upon-Tweed	d		
Alnmouth for Alnwick	d		
Morpeth	d		
Newcastle	a		
Sunderland	d		
Hartlepool	d		
Newcastle	d	21 50	
Chester-le-Street	d	21 59	
Durham	d	22 08	
Darlington	a	22 29	
Middlesbrough	d		21 50
Eaglescliffe	d		
Darlington	d		22 19
Northallerton	d		22 30
Thirsk	d		22 38
York	a		22 57
Leeds	a		23 33
Harrogate	d		
Scarborough	d		
York	d		
Doncaster	a		
Skipton	d		
Keighley	d		
Bradford Forster Square	d		
Shipley	d		
Leeds	d		
Wakefield Westgate	d		
Sheffield	a		
Hull	d		
Selby	d		
Doncaster	d		
Retford	d		
Newark North Gate	a		
	d		
Grantham	a		
	d		
Peterborough	a		
Norwich	a		
Peterborough	d		
Stevenage	a		
London Kings Cross	a		

Table 26

Sundays until 11 July

Scotland, North East England, Yorkshire and Humberside - London

Station		GR	GC	GR	TP	XC	EM	HT	GR	XC	GR	GR	XC	GR	GC	TP	TP	EM	GR	XC
Aberdeen	d																			
Stonehaven	d																			
Montrose	d																			
Arbroath	d																			
Dundee	d																			
Leuchars	d																			
Kirkcaldy	d																			
Inverkeithing	d																			
Inverness	d																			
Perth	d																			
Stirling	d																			
Glasgow Central	d																			
Motherwell	d																			
Haymarket	d																			
Edinburgh	a																			
Edinburgh	d																			08 50
Dunbar	d																			
Berwick-upon-Tweed	d																			09 33
Alnmouth for Alnwick	d																			
Morpeth	d																			
Newcastle	a																			10 21
Sunderland	d														09 10					
Hartlepool	d														09 34					
Newcastle	d			08 00	08 06						09 00		09 25	09 30		09 33				10 25
Chester-le-Street	d															09 42				
Durham	d			08 12	08 18						09 12		09 38			09 48				10 37
Darlington	a			08 30	08 35						09 29		09 53	09 58		10 04				10 54
Middlesbrough	d																10 15			
Eaglescliffe	d														09 55					
Darlington	d			08 30	08 35						09 30		09 55	09 59		10 05				10 54
Northallerton	d				08 47						09 43				10 13	10 16	10 42			
Thirsk	d														10 27		10 51			
York	a			08 58	09 11						10 03		10 22	10 27	10 46	10 41	11 11			11 24
Leeds	a				09 38								10 51			11 08	11 38			11 51
Harrogate	d																			
Scarborough	d																			
York	d			09 00						09 28	10 04			10 28	10 49					
Doncaster	a			09 24							10 28			10 53						
Skipton	d																			
Keighley	d																			
Bradford Forster Square	d																			
Shipley	d																			
Leeds	d	08 25				09 00			09 40	10 00		10 40	11 00						11 40	12 00
Wakefield Westgate	d	08 37				09 11			09 52	10 12		10 52	11 12						11 52	12 12
Sheffield	a																			
Hull	d							09 07												
Selby	d							09 42												
Doncaster	d	08 55	09 05	09 25		09 32		09 59	10 10	10 30	10 28	11 13	11 30	10 53					12 10	12 30
Retford	d			09 40				10 14				11 28								
Newark North Gate	a	09 18							10 32		10 51	11 42								
	d	09 18							10 32		10 51	11 42								
Grantham	a	09 31		10 02				10 34			11 03	11 54							12 40	
	d	09 31		10 02			10 29	10 34			11 03	11 54						12 18	12 40	
Peterborough	a	09 53		10 24			11 06		11 02		11 25	12 16		11 43				12 50		
Norwich	a						13 11											14 35		
Peterborough	d	09 53		10 24					11 02		11 25	12 16		11 45						
Stevenage	a			10 55				11s23			11 55									
London Kings Cross	a	10 53	10 57	11 27				11 49	11 55		12 23	13 14		12 40	12 48				13 50	

Table 26

Sundays until 11 July

Scotland, North East England, Yorkshire and Humberside - London

		GR	GR	TP	GR	XC	EM	GR	HT	GR	TP	GR	XC	GC	TP	GR	XC	EM	GR	TP	GR	GR
Aberdeen	d																					
Stonehaven	d																					
Montrose	d																					
Arbroath	d																					
Dundee	d																					
Leuchars 3	d																					
Kirkcaldy	d																					
Inverkeithing	d																					
Inverness	d																					
Perth	d																					
Stirling	d																					
Glasgow Central 15	d																					
Motherwell	d																					
Haymarket	d																					
Edinburgh 10	a																					
Edinburgh	d	09 00	09 30			09 50		10 00		10 30			10 50			11 00	11 25		11 30			
Dunbar	d												11 10									
Berwick-upon-Tweed	d	09 39						10 39		11 09			11 33									
Alnmouth for Alnwick	d					10 47																
Morpeth	d					11 02													12 40			
Newcastle 8	a	10 26	10 53			11 19		11 27		11 56			12 20			12 24	12 47		12 59			
Sunderland	d																					
Hartlepool	d																					
Newcastle 8	d	10 32	10 55	11 03		11 25		11 34		11 58	12 05		12 25			12 33	13 18		13 01	13 06	13 10	
Chester-le-Street	d																13 27					
Durham	d		11 08	11 15		11 37					12 17		12 37			12 46	13 34			13 18	13 23	
Darlington 7	a	10 59		11 31		11 53				12 24	12 33		12 53			13 03	13 50		13 27	13 34	13 40	
Middlesbrough	d														12 45							
Eaglescliffe	d																					
Darlington 7	d	10 59		11 32		11 54				12 25	12 34		12 54			13 04	13 52		13 28	13 35	13 41	
Northallerton	d			11 44											13 12						13 52	
Thirsk	d														13 21							
York 8	a	11 28	11 49	12 07		12 22		12 25		12 53	13 07		13 22		13 41	13 35	14 19		13 56	14 10	14 12	
Leeds 10	a			12 38		12 51					13 38		13 51		14 08					14 38		
Harrogate	d																					
Scarborough	d																					
York 8	d	11 29	11 53					12 29		12 55						13 37	14 22		14 00		14 14	
Doncaster 7	a	11 53						12 54		13 18						14 00	14 47		14 24		14 37	
Skipton	d																					
Keighley	d																					
Bradford Forster Square	d																					
Shipley	d																					
Leeds 10	d				12 40	13 00						13 40	14 00									14 40
Wakefield Westgate 7	d				12 52	13 12						13 52	14 12									14 52
Sheffield 7	a												14 45				15 18					
Hull	d								12 12													
Selby	d								12 47													
Doncaster 7	d	11 53			13 11	13 30		12 54	13 06	13 19		14 10		13 45		14 01			14 24		14 38	15 10
Retford 10	d				13b34				13 21													15 25
Newark North Gate 7	a		12 36		13 48							14 33										15 39
	d		12 36		13 48							14 33										15 39
Grantham 7	a				14 00			13 26	13 40										14 54			15 52
	d				14 00		13 14	13 26	13 40									14 14	14 54			15 52
Peterborough 8	a	12 40	13 06		14 22		13 41			14 06						14 48		14 41			15 25	16 13
Norwich	a						15 28											16 35				
Peterborough 8	d	12 45	13 06		14 22					14 06						14 48					15 25	16 18
Stevenage 4	a		13 36					14 16	14s29			15 28										16 48
London Kings Cross 15 ⊖	a	13 39	14 04		15 16			14 44	14 55	15 04		15 55		15 20		15 42			16 04		16 19	17 17

b arr. 1326

Table 26

Sundays until 11 July

Scotland, North East England, Yorkshire and Humberside - London

		XC	GR	HT	GR	TP	XC	GC	TP	EM	GR	XC	GR	GR	TP	XC	EM	GR	XC	GR	GC	TP
					A								B	C								
Aberdeen	d				09 48														11 12			
Stonehaven	d				10 05														11 29			
Montrose	d				10 28														11 50			
Arbroath	d				10 44														12 06			
Dundee	d				11 02														12 25			
Leuchars 3	d				11 16														12 38			
Kirkcaldy	d				11 40														13 03			
Inverkeithing	d				11 56														13 18			
Inverness	d													09 40								
Perth	d													11 57								
Stirling	d													12 33								
Glasgow Central 15	d		10 50									11 37								12 50		
Motherwell	d		11 05									11 54								13 05		
Haymarket	d		11 48		12 18							12 39		13 13					13 37	13 50		
Edinburgh 10	a		11 54		12 24							12 44		13 18					13 42	13 55		
Edinburgh	d	11 50	12 00		12 30							12 50	13 00	13 30		13 33			13 50	14 00		
Dunbar	d											13 10										
Berwick-upon-Tweed	d		12 39									13 33	13 39	14 09		14 18						
Alnmouth for Alnwick	d	12 47			13 29											14 38			14 47			
Morpeth	d																					
Newcastle 8	a	13 17	13 26		14 00							14 22	14 29	14 58		15 08			15 19	15 23		
Sunderland	d							13 42														
Hartlepool	d							14 06														
Newcastle 8	d	13 25	13 38		14 03	14 08	14 18					14 25	14 32	14 59	15 07	15 18			15 25	15 30		
Chester-le-Street	d														15 16							
Durham	d	13 37				14 20	14 30					14 37		15 13	15 22	15 30			15 37			
Darlington 7	a	13 54	14 04		14 30	14 36	14 46					14 53	14 58	15 30	15 39	15 46			15 53	15 57		
Middlesbrough	d								14 45													16 45
Eaglescliffe	d							14 34														
Darlington 7	d	13 54	14 05		14 31	14 37	14 47					14 54	14 59	15 31	15 40	15 47			15 54	15 57		
Northallerton	d					14 48		14 54	15 12				15 10									17 12
Thirsk	d							15 04	15 21													17 21
York 8	a	14 25	14 33		15 00	15 12	15 16	15 26	15 41			15 22	15 31	16 00	16 13	16 15			16 22	16 26		17 41
Leeds 10	a	14 51				15 38			16 08			15 51			16 38				16 51			18 08
Harrogate	d																					
Scarborough	d																					
York 8	d		14 36		15 07		15 20	15 31					15 34	16 03		16 20				16 28		
Doncaster 7	a		14 59				15 46						15 57	16 28		16 48				16 52		
Skipton	d																					
Keighley	d																					
Bradford Forster Square	d																					
Shipley	d																					
Leeds 10	d	15 00									15 40	16 00						16 40	17 00			
Wakefield Westgate 7	d	15 12									15 52	16 12						16 52	17 12			
Sheffield 7	a	15 42					16 15					16 41				17 18			17 41			
Hull	d			14 10																		
Selby	d			14 45																		
Doncaster 7	d		15 00	15 05							16 10		15 58	16 28				17 10		16 52	17 03	
Retford 10	d			15 20																		
Newark North Gate 7	a												16 20									
	d												16 20									
Grantham 7	a			15 40							16 40							17 40				
	d			15 40						16 25	16 40						17 25	17 40				
Peterborough 8	a		15 47							16 56	17 01		16 51	17 18			17 52	18 02		17 39		
Norwich	a									18 29							19 29					
Peterborough 8	d		15 47								17 02		16 51	17 18				18 02		17 40		
Stevenage 4	a		16 18	16s29									17 21							18 10		
London Kings Cross 15 ⊖	a		16 46	16 55	17 10			17 24			17 57		17 49	18 14				18 55		18 37	18 47	

A The Northern Lights

B The Flying Scotsman

C The Highland Chieftain

Table 26

Sundays until 11 July

Scotland, North East England, Yorkshire and Humberside - London

		HT	GR	GR	TP	XC	GR	GR	TP	EM	EM	GR	GR	GR	CR	XC	EM	GR	XC	GR	TP	GR	TP
Aberdeen	d			11 47																		13 50	
Stonehaven	d			12 04																		14 07	
Montrose	d			12 27																		14 30	
Arbroath	d			12 43																		14 46	
Dundee	d			13 01																		15 04	
Leuchars	d			13 15																		15 18	
Kirkcaldy	d			13 39																		15 42	
Inverkeithing	d			13 55																		15 58	
Inverness	d																						
Perth	d																						
Stirling	d																						
Glasgow Central	d																			14 50			
Motherwell	d																			15 05			
Haymarket	d			14 19																15 50		16 20	
Edinburgh	a			14 24																15 55		16 25	
Edinburgh	d			14 30				15 00						15 30					15 50	16 00		16 30	
Dunbar	d																						
Berwick-upon-Tweed	d							15 39						16 09								17 09	
Alnmouth for Alnwick	d																		16 47			17 32	
Morpeth	d													16 43					17 02				
Newcastle	a			15 55				16 26						17 02					17 20	17 25		18 04	
Sunderland	d																						
Hartlepool	d																						
Newcastle	d		15 50	16 03	16 08	16 18		16 33	16 52					17 04	17 10	17 18			17 25	17 32	17 53	18 10	
Chester-le-Street	d								17 01														
Durham	d		16 02		16 20	16 30		16 46	17 08						17 22	17 33			17 37		18 07		
Darlington	a		16 20	16 30	16 36	16 46		17 03	17 25					17 30	17 40	17 49			17 54	17 58	18 23		
Middlesbrough	d																						18 45
Eaglescliffe	d																						
Darlington	d		16 20	16 31	16 37	16 47		17 04	17 26					17 31	17 40	17 50			17 55	17 59	18 24		
Northallerton	d		16 32		16 48				17 37						17 52						18 35		19 12
Thirsk	d																						19 21
York	a		16 52	17 00	17 12	17 17		17 34	18 00					18 04	18 13	18 17			18 23	18 28	18 58	19 01	19 41
Leeds	a				17 38				18 38										18 51		19 38		20 08
Harrogate	d																						
Scarborough	d																						
York	d		16 55	17 04		17 21		17 36		17 40				18 05	18 14	18 20				18 29		19 03	
Doncaster	a		17 19	17 28		17 47		18 00		18 05				18 29	18 39	18 48				18 53		19 28	
Skipton	d																						
Keighley	d																						
Bradford Forster Square	d																						
Shipley	d																						
Leeds	d						17 05					17 40						18 40	19 00				
Wakefield Westgate	d						17 18					17 52						18 52	19 12				
Sheffield	a					18 18				18 28						19 15			19 40				
Hull	d	16 23											17 30										
Selby	d	16 58											18 05										
Doncaster	d	17 15	17 22	17 30			17 36	18 03					18 23	18 31	18 39			19 10		18 53		19 29	
Retford	d	17 30					17 51						18b44										
Newark North Gate	a		17 46				18 05								19 03								
	d		17 46				18 05								19 03								
Grantham	a	17 49										18 37	19 06					19 40					
	d	17 49									18 18	18 37	19 06				19 23	19 40					
Peterborough	a			18 21				18 50			18 45	18 59	19 28	19 18	19 33		19 56	20 01		19 42		20 19	
Norwich	a										20 28						21 35						
Peterborough	d			18 23				18 51				18 59	19 29	19 19	19 34			20 02		19 45		20 20	
Stevenage	a		18 42				19 02	19 21							20 08			20 32		20 18		20 52	
London Kings Cross	a	19 06	19 14	19 17			19 34	19 48				19 57	20 23	20 14	20 34			21 02		20 43		21 20	

b arr. 1838

Table 26

Sundays until 11 July

Scotland, North East England, Yorkshire and Humberside - London

		XC	XC	HT	GR	GR	GC	TP	XC	GR	XC	GR	TP	TP	EM	GR	NT	GR	GR
Aberdeen	d																		
Stonehaven	d																		
Montrose	d																		
Arbroath	d																		
Dundee	d																		
Leuchars	d																		
Kirkcaldy	d																		
Inverkeithing	d																		
Inverness	d																		
Perth	d																		
Stirling	d																		
Glasgow Central	d				15 50											17 50			19 50
Motherwell	d				16 05											18 05			20 05
Haymarket	d				16 46											18 46			20 46
Edinburgh	a				16 51											18 52			20 51
Edinburgh	d		16 50		17 00	17 30					17 50	18 00				19 00		20 00	21 00
Dunbar	d		17 10								18 10					19 20		20 20	21 21
Berwick-upon-Tweed	d		17 33									18 39						20 43	21 44
Alnmouth for Alnwick	d										18 51	19 01							22 06
Morpeth	d																	21 17	
Newcastle	a		18 20		18 24	18 53					19 20	19 31				20 27		21 36	22 39
Sunderland	d						18 42												
Hartlepool	d						19 06												
Newcastle	d	18 18	18 25		18 29	18 57		19 06	19 18		19 25	19 35		20 07		20 31	21 06	21 40	
Chester-le-Street	d																21 15		
Durham	d	18 33	18 38		18 43	19 10		19 18	19 33		19 39	19 48		20 19			21 24	21 53	
Darlington	a	18 49	18 54		19 00	19 27		19 34	19 49		19 55	20 05		20 35		20 57	21 44	22 10	
Middlesbrough	d												20 07						
Eaglescliffe	d						19 25										21 57		
Darlington	d	18 50	18 54		19 01	19 28		19 35	19 50		19 56	20 06		20 36		20 58		22 11	
Northallerton	d					19 39	19 47						20 34	20 48				22s42	
Thirsk	d						19 56						20 42						
York	a	19 16	19 25		19 29	20 00	20 13	20 09	20 17		20 24	20 34	21 02	21 12		21 26		23 19	
Leeds	a		19 51					20 38			20 51			21 38					
Harrogate	d																		
Scarborough	d																		
York	d	19 20			19 31	20 02	20 15		20 20			20 36				21 28			
Doncaster	a	19 48			19 54	20 25			20 43			20 59				21 51			
Skipton	d																		
Keighley	d																		
Bradford Forster Square	d																		
Shipley	d																		
Leeds	d		20 00							20 15	21 00								
Wakefield Westgate	d		20 12							20 28	21 12								
Sheffield	a	20 16	20 40						21 17		21 44								
Hull	d			18 48															
Selby	d			19 23															
Doncaster	d			19 43	19 55	20 26				20 48		21 00				21 52			
Retford	d			19 58								21 15							
Newark North Gate	a				20 17							21 29							
	d				20 17							21 34							
Grantham	a			20 18		20 56									21 18	22 22			
	d			20 18		20 56									21 19	22 22			
Peterborough	a				20 47	21 17				21 35		22 03			21 46	22 43			
Norwich	a														23 25				
Peterborough	d				20 48	21 18				21 37		22 04				22 44			
Stevenage	a			21s09	21 20	21 48				22 07		22 34							
London Kings Cross	a			21 35	21 47	22 16	22 17			22 34		23 04				23 42			

Table 26

Sundays until 11 July

Scotland, North East England, Yorkshire and Humberside - London

Station		TP ◇1
Aberdeen	d	
Stonehaven	d	
Montrose	d	
Arbroath	d	
Dundee	d	
Leuchars 3	d	
Kirkcaldy	d	
Inverkeithing	d	
Inverness	d	
Perth	d	
Stirling	d	
Glasgow Central 15	d	
Motherwell	d	
Haymarket	d	
Edinburgh 10	a	
Edinburgh	d	
Dunbar	d	
Berwick-upon-Tweed	d	
Alnmouth for Alnwick	d	
Morpeth	d	
Newcastle 8	a	
Sunderland	d	
Hartlepool	d	
Newcastle 8	d	
Chester-le-Street	d	
Durham	d	
Darlington 7	a	
Middlesbrough	d	22 07
Eaglescliffe	d	
Darlington 7	d	
Northallerton	d	22 34
Thirsk	d	22 42
York 8	a	23 09
Leeds 10	a	23 38
Harrogate	d	
Scarborough	d	
York 8	d	
Doncaster 7	a	
Skipton	d	
Keighley	d	
Bradford Forster Square	d	
Shipley	d	
Leeds 10	d	
Wakefield Westgate 7	d	
Sheffield 7	a	
Hull	d	
Selby	d	
Doncaster 7	d	
Retford 10	d	
Newark North Gate 7	a	
	d	
Grantham 7	a	
	d	
Peterborough 8	a	
Norwich	a	
Peterborough 8	d	
Stevenage 4	a	
London Kings Cross 15 ⊖	a	

Table 26

Sundays 18 July to 05 September

Scotland, North East England, Yorkshire and Humberside - London

Station		GR	GC	GR	TP	XC	EM	HT	GR	XC	GR	GR	XC	GR	GC	TP	TP	EM	GR	XC
		■ 1	◇1	■ 1	◇1	◇1	◇	◇1	■ 1	◇1	■ 1	■ 1	◇1	■ 1	■ 1	◇1	◇1	◇	■ 1	◇1
Aberdeen	d																			
Stonehaven	d																			
Montrose	d																			
Arbroath	d																			
Dundee	d																			
Leuchars 3	d																			
Kirkcaldy	d																			
Inverkeithing	d																			
Inverness	d																			
Perth	d																			
Stirling	d																			
Glasgow Central 15	d																			
Motherwell	d																			
Haymarket	d																			
Edinburgh 10	a																			
Edinburgh	d																			08 50
Dunbar	d																			
Berwick-upon-Tweed	d																			09 33
Alnmouth for Alnwick	d																			
Morpeth	d																			
Newcastle 8	a																			10 21
Sunderland	d														09 10					
Hartlepool	d														09 34					
Newcastle 8	d			08 00	08 06						09 00		09 25	09 30		09 33				10 25
Chester-le-Street	d															09 42				
Durham	d			08 12	08 18						09 12		09 38			09 48				10 37
Darlington 7	a			08 30	08 35						09 29		09 53	09 58		10 04				10 54
Middlesbrough	d																10 15			
Eaglescliffe	d														09 55					
Darlington 7	d			08 30	08 35						09 30		09 55	09 59		10 05				10 54
Northallerton	d				08 47						09 43				10 13	10 16	10 42			
Thirsk	d														10 27		10 51			
York 8	a			08 58	09 11						10 03		10 22	10 27	10 46	10 41	11 11			11 24
Leeds 10	a				09 38								10 51			11 08	11 38			11 51
Harrogate	d																			
Scarborough	d																			
York 8	d			09 00						09 28	10 04			10 28	10 49					
Doncaster 7	a			09 24							10 28			10 52						
Skipton	d																			
Keighley	d																			
Bradford Forster Square	d																			
Shipley	d																			
Leeds 10	d	08 25				09 00			09 40	10b00		10 40	11 00						11 40	12 00
Wakefield Westgate 7	d	08 37				09 11			09 52	10 12		10 52	11 12						11 52	12 12
Sheffield 7	a																			
Hull	d							09 07												
Selby	d							09 42												
Doncaster 7	d	08 55	09 05	09 25		09 32		09 59	10 10	10 30	10 28	11 13	11 30	10 53					12 10	12 30
Retford 10	d			09 40				10 14				11 28								
Newark North Gate 7	a	09 18							10 32		10 51	11 42								
	d	09 18							10 32		10 51	11 42								
Grantham 7	a	09 31		10 02				10 34			11 03	11 54							12 40	
	d	09 31		10 02				10 34			11 03	11 54						12 18	12 40	
Peterborough 8	a	09 53		10 24			11 06		11 02		11 25	12 16		11 39				12 50		
Norwich	a						13 11											14 35		
Peterborough 8	d	09 53		10 24					11 02		11 25	12 16		11 40						
Stevenage 4	a			10 57				11s24			11 57									
London Kings Cross 15 ⊖	a	11 06	11 09	11 33				12 07	12 12		12 33	13 24		12 45	13 07				14 09	

b arr. 0951

Table 26

Sundays

18 July to 05 September

Scotland, North East England, Yorkshire and Humberside - London

		GR	GR	TP	GR	XC	EM	GR	HT	GR	TP	GR	XC	GC	GR	TP	XC	EM	GR	TP	GR	GR
Aberdeen	d																					
Stonehaven	d																					
Montrose	d																					
Arbroath	d																					
Dundee	d																					
Leuchars 3	d																					
Kirkcaldy	d																					
Inverkeithing	d																					
Inverness	d																					
Perth	d																					
Stirling	d																					
Glasgow Central 15	d																					
Motherwell	d																					
Haymarket	d																					
Edinburgh 10	a																					
Edinburgh	d	09 00	09 30			09 50		10 00		10 30			10 50		11 00		11 25		11 30			
Dunbar	d												11 10									
Berwick-upon-Tweed	d	09 39						10 39		11 09			11 33									
Alnmouth for Alnwick	d					10 47																
Morpeth	d					11 02													12 40			
Newcastle 8	a	10 26	10 53			11 19		11 27		11 56			12 20		12 24		12 47		12 59			
Sunderland	d																					
Hartlepool	d																					
Newcastle 8	d	10 32	10 55	11 03		11 25		11 34		11 58	12 05		12 25		12 33		13 18		13 01	13 06	13 10	
Chester-le-Street	d																13 27					
Durham	d		11 08	11 15		11 37					12 17		12 37		12 46		13 34			13 18	13 23	
Darlington 7	a	10 59		11 31		11 53				12 24	12 33		12 53		13 03		13 50		13 27	13 34	13 40	
Middlesbrough	d															12 45						
Eaglescliffe	d																					
Darlington 7	d	10 59		11 32		11 54				12 25	12 34		12 54		13 04		13 52		13 28	13 35	13 41	
Northallerton	d			11 44												13 12					13 52	
Thirsk	d															13 21						
York 8	a	11 28	11 49	12 07		12 22		12 25		12 53	13 07		13 22		13 35	13 41	14 19		13 56	14 10	14 12	
Leeds 10	a			12 38		12 51					13 38		13 51			14 08				14 38		
Harrogate	d																					
Scarborough	d																					
York 8	d	11 29	11 53					12 29		12 55					13 37		14 22		14 00		14 14	
Doncaster 7	a	11 53						12 54		13 18					14 00		14 47		14 24		14 37	
Skipton	d																					
Keighley	d																					
Bradford Forster Square	d																					
Shipley	d																					
Leeds 10	d				12 40	13 00						13 40	14 00									14 40
Wakefield Westgate 7	d				12 52	13 12						13 52	14 12									14 52
Sheffield 7	a												14 45				15 18					
Hull	d								12 12													
Selby	d								12 47													
Doncaster 7	d	11 53			13 11	13 30		12 54	13 06	13 19		14 10		13 45	14 01				14 24		14 38	15 10
Retford 10	d				13b34				13 21													15 25
Newark North Gate 7	a		12 36		13 48							14 33										15 39
	d		12 36		13 48							14 33										15 39
Grantham 7	a				14 00			13 26	13 40										14 54			15 52
	d				14 00		13 14	13 26	13 40									14 14	14 54			15 52
Peterborough 8	a	12 40	13 06		14 22		13 41			14 06					14 48			14 41			15 25	16 13
Norwich	a						15 28											16 35				
Peterborough 8	d	12 45	13 06		14 22					14 16					14 48						15 25	16 18
Stevenage 4	a		13 39					14 21	14s30			15 29										16 51
London Kings Cross 15 ⊖	a	14 06	14 22		15 31			15 06	15 10	15 24		16 09		15 36	16 06				16 26		16 32	17 33

b arr. 1326

Table 26

Sundays

18 July to 05 September

Scotland, North East England, Yorkshire and Humberside - London

		XC	GR	HT	GR A	TP	XC	GC	TP	EM	GR	XC	GR B	GR C	TP	XC	EM	GR	XC	GR	HT
Aberdeen	d				09 48														11 12		
Stonehaven	d				10 05														11 29		
Montrose	d				10 28														11 50		
Arbroath	d				10 44														12 06		
Dundee	d				11 02														12 25		
Leuchars 3	d				11 16														12 38		
Kirkcaldy	d				11 40														13 03		
Inverkeithing	d				11 56														13 18		
Inverness	d													09 40							
Perth	d													11 57							
Stirling	d													12 33							
Glasgow Central 15	d		10 50									11 37								12 50	
Motherwell	d		11 05									11 54								13 05	
Haymarket	d		11 48		12 18							12 39		13 13					13 37	13 50	
Edinburgh 10	a		11 54		12 24							12 44		13 18					13 42	13 55	
Edinburgh	d	11 50	12 00		12 30							12 50	13 00	13 30		13 33			13 50	14 00	
Dunbar	d											13 10									
Berwick-upon-Tweed	d		12 39									13 33	13 39	14 09		14 18					
Alnmouth for Alnwick	d	12 47			13 29											14 38			14 47		
Morpeth	d																				
Newcastle 8	a	13 17	13 26		14 00							14 22	14 29	14 58		15 08			15 19	15 23	
Sunderland	d							13 42													
Hartlepool	d							14 06													
Newcastle 8	d	13 25	13 38		14 03	14 08	14 18					14 25	14 32	14 59	15 07	15 18			15 25	15 27	
Chester-le-Street	d														15 16						
Durham	d	13 37				14 20	14 30					14 37		15 13	15 22	15 30			15 37	15 41	
Darlington 7	a	13 54	14 04		14 30	14 36	14 46					14 53	14 58	15 30	15 39	15 46			15 53	15 58	
Middlesbrough	d								14 45												
Eaglescliffe	d							14 34													
Darlington 7	d	13 54	14 05		14 31	14 37	14 47					14 54	14 59	15 31	15 40	15 47			15 54	15 58	
Northallerton	d					14 48		14 54	15 12				15 10								
Thirsk	d							15 04	15 21												
York 8	a	14 25	14 33		15 00	15 12	15 16	15 26	15 41			15 22	15 31	16 00	16 13	16 15			16 22	16 27	
Leeds 10	a	14 51				15 38			16 08			15 51			16 38				16 51		
Harrogate	d																				
Scarborough	d																				
York 8	d		14 36		15 07		15 20	15 31					15 34	16 03		16 20				16 28	
Doncaster 7	a		14 59				15 46						15 57	16 28		16 48				16 52	
Skipton	d																				
Keighley	d																				
Bradford Forster Square	d																				
Shipley	d																				
Leeds 10	d	15 00									15 40	16 00						16 40	17 00		
Wakefield Westgate 7	d	15 12									15 52	16 12						16 52	17 12		
Sheffield 7	a	15 42					16 15					16 41				17 18			17 41		
Hull	d			14 10																	16 23
Selby	d			14 45																	16 58
Doncaster 7	d		15 00	15 05							16 10		15 58	16 28				17 10		16 52	17 15
Retford 10	d			15 20																	17 30
Newark North Gate 7	a												16 20					17 33			
	d												16 20					17 34			
Grantham 7	a			15 40							16 40							17 45			17 51
	d			15 40						16 25	16 40						17 25	17 45			17 51
Peterborough 8	a		15 47							16 56	17 01		16 51	17 18			17 52	18 07		17 39	
Norwich	a									18 29							19 29				
Peterborough 8	d		15 47								17 02		16 51	17 18				18 07		17 40	
Stevenage 4	a		16 20	16s30									17 23					18 41		18 11	
London Kings Cross 15 ⊖	a		17 06	17 10	17 26			17 43			18 14		18 06	18 26				19 20		18 49	19 29

A The Northern Lights

B The Flying Scotsman

C The Highland Chieftain

Table 26

Sundays

18 July to 05 September

Scotland, North East England, Yorkshire and Humberside - London

		GR	TP	XC	GR	GC	GR	TP	TP	EM	EM	GR	GR	GR	GR	XC	EM	GR	XC	GR	TP	GR	XC	TP
		1	◇1	◇1	1	◇1	1	◇1	◇1	◇1	◇	1	1	1	1	◇1	◇	1	◇1	1	◇1	1	◇1	◇1
Aberdeen	d	11 47																				13 50		
Stonehaven	d	12 04																				14 07		
Montrose	d	12 27																				14 30		
Arbroath	d	12 43																				14 46		
Dundee	d	13 01																				15 04		
Leuchars 3	d	13 15																				15 18		
Kirkcaldy	d	13 39																				15 42		
Inverkeithing	d	13 55																				15 58		
Inverness	d																							
Perth	d																							
Stirling	d																							
Glasgow Central 15	d																			14 50				
Motherwell	d																			15 05				
Haymarket	d	14 19																		15 50		16 20		
Edinburgh 10	a	14 24																		15 55		16 25		
Edinburgh	d	14 30					15 00							15 30					15 50	16 00		16 30		
Dunbar	d																							
Berwick-upon-Tweed	d						15 39							16 09								17 09		
Alnmouth for Alnwick	d																		16 47			17 32		
Morpeth	d													16 43					17 02					
Newcastle 8	a	15 55					16 26							17 02					17 20	17 25		18 04		
Sunderland	d																							
Hartlepool	d																							
Newcastle 8	d	16 00	16 08	16 18			16 33		16 52					17 04	17 10	17 18			17 25	17 32	17 53	18 10	18 18	
Chester-le-Street	d								17 01															
Durham	d		16 20	16 30			16 46		17 08						17 22	17 33			17 37		18 07		18 33	
Darlington 7	a	16 28	16 36	16 46			17 03		17 25					17 30	17 40	17 49			17 54	17 58	18 23		18 49	
Middlesbrough	d							16 45																18 45
Eaglescliffe	d																							
Darlington 7	d	16 28	16 37	16 47			17 04		17 26					17 31	17 40	17 50			17 55	17 59	18 24		18 50	
Northallerton	d	16 43	16 48					17 12	17 37						17 52						18 35			19 12
Thirsk	d							17 21																19 21
York 8	a	17 03	17 12	17 17			17 34	17 41	18 00					18 04	18 13	18 17			18 23	18 28	18 58	19 01	19 16	19 41
Leeds 10	a		17 38					18 08	18 38										18 51		19 38			20 08
Harrogate	d																							
Scarborough	d																							
York 8	d	17 05		17 21			17 36			17 40				18 05	18 14	18 20				18 29		19 03	19 20	
Doncaster 7	a	17 29		17 47			18 00			18 05				18 29	18 39	18 48				18 53		19 28	19 48	
Skipton	d																							
Keighley	d																							
Bradford Forster Square	d																							
Shipley	d																							
Leeds 10	d				17 05							17 40						18 40	19 00					
Wakefield Westgate 7	d				17 18							17 52						18 52	19 12					
Sheffield 7	a			18 18						18 28						19 15			19 40				20 16	
Hull	d												17 30											
Selby	d												18 05											
Doncaster 7	d	17 30			17 36	1744	18 03						18 23	18 31	18 39			19 10		18 53		19 29		
Retford 10	d				17 51								18c44											
Newark North Gate 7	a				18 05										19 03									
	d				18 05										19 03									
Grantham 7	a											18 39	19 06					19 40						
	d										18 18	18 39	19 06				19 23	19 40						
Peterborough 8	a	18 21			18 36		18 53				18 49	19 01	19 30	19 18	19 38		19 56	20 01		19 46		20 19		
Norwich	a										20 32						21 35							
Peterborough 8	d	18 23					18 54					19 01	19 31	19 19				20 02		19 47		20 20		
Stevenage 4	a						19 25					19 37						20 35		20 20		20 53		
London Kings Cross 15 ⊖	a	19 32				19 44	20 06					20 15	20 44	20 27				21 14		21 06		21 32		

c arr. 1838

Table 26

Sundays

18 July to 05 September

Scotland, North East England, Yorkshire and Humberside - London

		XC	GR	HT	GR	GC	TP	XC	GR	XC	GR	TP	TP	EM	GR	NT	GR	GR	TP
		◇1	1	◇1	1	1	◇1	◇1	1	◇1	1	◇1	◇1	◇	1		1	1	◇1
Aberdeen	d																		
Stonehaven	d																		
Montrose	d																		
Arbroath	d																		
Dundee	d																		
Leuchars 3	d																		
Kirkcaldy	d																		
Inverkeithing	d																		
Inverness	d																		
Perth	d																		
Stirling	d																		
Glasgow Central 15	d		15 50												17 50			19 50	
Motherwell	d		16 05												18 05			20 05	
Haymarket	d		16 46												18 46			20 46	
Edinburgh 10	a		16 51												18 52			20 51	
Edinburgh	d	16 50	17 00		17 30					17 50	18 00				19 00		20 00	21 00	
Dunbar	d	17 10								18 10					19 20		20 20	21 21	
Berwick-upon-Tweed	d	17 33									18 39						20 43	21 44	
Alnmouth for Alnwick	d									18 51	19 01							22 06	
Morpeth	d																21 17		
Newcastle 8	a	18 20	18 24		18 53					19 20	19 31				20 27		21 36	22 39	
Sunderland	d					18 42													
Hartlepool	d					19 06													
Newcastle 8	d	18 25	18 29		18 57		19 06	19 18		19 25	19 35		20 07		20 31	21 06	21 40		
Chester-le-Street	d															21 15			
Durham	d	18 38	18 43		19 10		19 18	19 33		19 39	19 48		20 19			21 24	21 53		
Darlington 7	a	18 54	19 00		19 27		19 34	19 49		19 55	20 05		20 35		20 57	21 44	22 10		
Middlesbrough	d											20 07							22 07
Eaglescliffe	d					19 25										21 57			
Darlington 7	d	18 54	19 01		19 28		19 35	19 50		19 56	20 06		20 36		20 58		22 11		
Northallerton	d				19 39	19 47						20 34	20 48				22s42		22 34
Thirsk	d					19 56						20 42							22 42
York 8	a	19 25	19 29		20 00	20 13	20 09	20 17		20 24	20 34	21 02	21 12		21 26		23 19		23 09
Leeds 10	a	19 51					20 38			20 51			21 38						23 38
Harrogate	d																		
Scarborough	d																		
York 8	d		19 31		20 02	20 15		20 20			20 36				21 28				
Doncaster 7	a		19 54		20 25			20 43			20 59				21 51				
Skipton	d																		
Keighley	d																		
Bradford Forster Square	d																		
Shipley	d																		
Leeds 10	d	20 00							20 15	21 00									
Wakefield Westgate 7	d	20 12							20 28	21 12									
Sheffield 7	a	20 40						21 17		21 44									
Hull	d			19 15															
Selby	d			19 50															
Doncaster 7	d		19 55	20 10	20 26				20 48		21 00				21 52				
Retford 10	d			20 25							21 15								
Newark North Gate 7	a		20 17								21 29								
	d		20 17								21 34								
Grantham 7	a			20 44	20 56										22 22				
	d			20 45	20 56									21 19	22 22				
Peterborough 8	a		20 47		21 17				21 35		22 03			21 46	22 43				
Norwich	a													23 25					
Peterborough 8	d		20 48		21 18				21 37		22 04				22 44				
Stevenage 4	a		21 21	21s37	21 49				22 08		22 36								
London Kings Cross 15 ⊖	a		22 06	22 14	22 28	22 32			22 46		23 15				00 06				

Table 26

Sundays from 12 September

Scotland, North East England, Yorkshire and Humberside - London

		GR	GC	GR	TP	HT	GR	XC	GR	GR	XC	GR	GC	TP	TP	GR	XC	GR
		■ 1	◇1	■ 1	◇1	◇1	■ 1	◇1	■ 1	■ 1	◇1	■ 1	◇1	◇1	◇1	■ 1	◇1	■ 1
Aberdeen	d																	
Stonehaven	d																	
Montrose	d																	
Arbroath	d																	
Dundee	d																	
Leuchars 3	d																	
Kirkcaldy	d																	
Inverkeithing	d																	
Inverness	d																	
Perth	d																	
Stirling	d																	
Glasgow Central 15	d																	
Motherwell	d																	
Haymarket	d																	
Edinburgh 10	a																	
Edinburgh	d																08 50	09 00
Dunbar	d																	
Berwick-upon-Tweed	d																09 33	09 39
Alnmouth for Alnwick	d																	
Morpeth	d																	
Newcastle 8	a																10 21	10 26
Sunderland	d												09 10					
Hartlepool	d												09 34					
Newcastle 8	d			08 00	08 06				09 00		09 25	09 30		09 33			10 25	10 32
Chester-le-Street	d													09 42				
Durham	d			08 12	08 18				09 12		09 38			09 48			10 37	
Darlington 7	a			08 30	08 35				09 29		09 53	09 58		10 04			10 54	10 59
Middlesbrough	d														10 15			
Eaglescliffe	d												09 55					
Darlington 7	d			08 30	08 35				09 30		09 55	09 59		10 05			10 54	10 59
Northallerton	d				08 47				09 43				10 13	10 16	10 42			
Thirsk	d												10 27		10 51			
York 8	a			08 58	09 11				10 03		10 22	10 27	10 46	10 41	11 11		11 24	11 28
Leeds 10	a				09 38						10 51			11 08	11 38		11 51	
Harrogate	d																	
Scarborough	d																	
York 8	d			09 00				09 28	10 04			10 28	10 49					11 29
Doncaster 7	a			09 24					10 28			10 53						11 53
Skipton	d																	
Keighley	d																	
Bradford Forster Square	d																	
Shipley	d																	
Leeds 10	d	08 25	08 28				09 40	10 00		10 40	11 00					11 40	12 00	
Wakefield Westgate 7	d	08 37					09 52	10 12		10 52	11 12					11 52	12 12	
Sheffield 7	a																	
Hull	d					09 07												
Selby	d					09 42												
Doncaster 7	d	08 55	09 10	09 25		09 59	10 10	10 30	10 28	11 13	11 30	10 53				12 10	12 30	11 53
Retford 10	d			09 40		10 14				11 28								
Newark North Gate 7	a	09 18					10 32		10 51	11 42								
	d	09 18					10 32		10 51	11 42								
Grantham 7	a	09 31		10 02		10 34			11 03	11 54						12 40		
	d	09 31		10 02		10 34			11 03	11 54						12 40		
Peterborough 8	a	09 53		10 24			11 02		11 25	12 16		11 43						12 40
Norwich	a																	
Peterborough 8	d	09 53		10 24			11 02		11 25	12 16		11 45						12 45
Stevenage 4	a			10 55		11s23			11 55									
London Kings Cross 15 ⊖	a	10 52	10 52	11 28		11 49	11 55		12 23	13 14		12 40	12 48			13 50		13 39

Table 26

Sundays from 12 September

Scotland, North East England, Yorkshire and Humberside - London

		GR	TP	GR	XC	EM	GR	HT	GR	TP	GR	XC	GC	GR	TP	XC	EM	GR	TP	GR	GR	XC
		■ 1	◇1	■ 1	◇1	◇ A	■ 1	◇1	■ 1	◇1	■ 1	◇1	◇1	■ 1	◇1	◇1	◇ A	■ 1	◇1	■ 1	■ 1	◇1
Aberdeen	d																					
Stonehaven	d																					
Montrose	d																					
Arbroath	d																					
Dundee	d																					
Leuchars 3	d																					
Kirkcaldy	d																					
Inverkeithing	d																					
Inverness	d																					
Perth	d																					
Stirling	d																					
Glasgow Central 15	d																					
Motherwell	d																					
Haymarket	d																					
Edinburgh 10	a																					
Edinburgh	d	09 30			09 50		10 00		10 30			10 50		11 00		11 25		11 30				11 50
Dunbar	d											11 10										
Berwick-upon-Tweed	d						10 39		11 09			11 33										
Alnmouth for Alnwick	d				10 47																	12 47
Morpeth	d				11 02													12 40				
Newcastle 8	a	10 53			11 19		11 27		11 56			12 20		12 24		12 47		12 59				13 17
Sunderland	d																					
Hartlepool	d																					
Newcastle 8	d	10 55	11 03		11 25		11 34		11 58	12 05		12 25		12 33		13 18		13 01	13 06	13 10		13 25
Chester-le-Street	d															13 27						
Durham	d	11 08	11 15		11 37					12 17		12 37		12 46		13 34			13 18	13 23		13 37
Darlington 7	a		11 31		11 53				12 24	12 33		12 53		13 03		13 50		13 27	13 34	13 40		13 54
Middlesbrough	d														12 45							
Eaglescliffe	d																					
Darlington 7	d		11 32		11 54				12 25	12 34		12 54		13 04		13 52		13 28	13 35	13 41		13 54
Northallerton	d		11 44												13 12					13 52		
Thirsk	d														13 21							
York 8	a	11 49	12 07		12 22		12 25		12 53	13 07		13 22		13 35	13 41	14 19		13 56	14 10	14 12		14 25
Leeds 10	a		12 38		12 51					13 38		13 51			14 08				14 38			14 51
Harrogate	d																					
Scarborough	d																					
York 8	d	11 53					12 29		12 55					13 37		14 22		14 00		14 14		
Doncaster 7	a						12 54		13 18					14 00		14 47		14 24		14 37		
Skipton	d																					
Keighley	d																					
Bradford Forster Square	d																					
Shipley	d																					
Leeds 10	d			12 40	13 00						13 40	14 00									14 40	15 00
Wakefield Westgate 7	d			12 52	13 12						13 52	14 12									14 52	15 12
Sheffield 7	a											14 45				15 18						15 42
Hull	d							12 12														
Selby	d							12 47														
Doncaster 7	d			13 11	13 30		12 54	13 06	13 19		14 10		13 45	14 01				14 24		14 38	15 10	
Retford 10	d			13b34				13 21													15 25	
Newark North Gate 7	a	12 36		13 48							14 33										15 39	
	d	12 36		13 48							14 33										15 39	
Grantham 7	a			14 00			13 26	13 40										14 54			15 52	
	d			14 00		13 14	13 26	13 40									14 22	14 54			15 52	
Peterborough 8	a	13 06		14 22		13 41			14 06					14 48			14 52			15 25	16 13	
Norwich	a					15 31											16 35					
Peterborough 8	d	13 06		14 22					14 06					14 48						15 25	16 18	
Stevenage 4	a	13 36					14 16	14s29			15 28										16 48	
London Kings Cross 15 ⊖	a	14 04		15 16			14 44	14 55	15 04		15 55		15 20	15 42				16 04		16 19	17 17	

A from 24 October

b arr. 1326

Table 26

Sundays
from 12 September

Scotland, North East England, Yorkshire and Humberside - London

		GR	HT	GR	TP	XC	GC	TP	EM	GR	XC	GR	GR	TP	XC	EM	GR	XC	GR	GC	HT
		■1	◇1	■1	◇1	◇1	■1	◇1	◇	■1	◇1	■1	■1	◇1	◇1	◇	■1	◇1	■1	◇1	◇1
				A					B			C	D			B					
Aberdeen	d			09 48														11 12			
Stonehaven	d			10 05														11 29			
Montrose	d			10 28														11 50			
Arbroath	d			10 44														12 06			
Dundee	d			11 02														12 25			
Leuchars 3	d			11 16														12 38			
Kirkcaldy	d			11 40														13 03			
Inverkeithing	d			11 56														13 18			
Inverness	d												09 40								
Perth	d												11 57								
Stirling	d												12 33								
Glasgow Central 15	d	10 50									11 37								12 50		
Motherwell	d	11 05									11 54								13 05		
Haymarket	d	11 48		12 18							12 39		13 13					13 37	13 50		
Edinburgh 10	a	11 54		12 24							12 44		13 18					13 42	13 55		
Edinburgh	d	12 00		12 30							12 50	13 00	13 30		13 33			13 50	14 00		
Dunbar	d										13 10										
Berwick-upon-Tweed	d	12 39									13 33	13 39	14 09		14 18						
Alnmouth for Alnwick	d			13 29											14 38			14 47			
Morpeth	d																				
Newcastle 8 ⇌	a	13 26		14 00							14 22	14 29	14 58		15 08			15 19	15 23		
Sunderland ⇌	d						13 42														
Hartlepool	d						14 06														
Newcastle 8 ⇌	d	13 38		14 03	14 08	14 18					14 25	14 32	14 59	15 07	15 18			15 25	15 30		
Chester-le-Street	d													15 16							
Durham	d				14 20	14 30					14 37		15 13	15 22	15 30			15 37			
Darlington 7	a	14 04		14 30	14 36	14 46					14 53	14 58	15 30	15 39	15 46			15 53	15 57		
Middlesbrough	d							14 45													
Eaglescliffe	d						14 34														
Darlington 7	d	14 05		14 31	14 37	14 47					14 54	14 59	15 31	15 40	15 47			15 54	15 57		
Northallerton	d				14 48		14 54	15 12				15 10									
Thirsk	d						15 04	15 21													
York 8	a	14 33		15 00	15 12	15 16	15 26	15 41			15 22	15 31	16 00	16 13	16 15			16 22	16 26		
Leeds 10	a				15 38			16 08			15 51			16 38				16 51			
Harrogate	d																				
Scarborough	d																				
York 8	d	14 36		15 07		15 20	15 31					15 34	16 03		16 20				16 28		
Doncaster 7	a	14 59				15 46						15 57	16 28		16 48				16 52		
Skipton	d																				
Keighley	d																				
Bradford Forster Square	d																				
Shipley	d																				
Leeds 10	d									15 40	16 00						16 40	17 00			
Wakefield Westgate 7	d									15 52	16 12						16 52	17 12			
Sheffield 7 ⇌	a					16 15					16 41				17 18			17 41			
Hull	d		14 10																		16 23
Selby	d		14 45																		16 58
Doncaster 7	d	15 00	15 05							16 10		15 58	16 28				17 10		16 52	17 03	17 15
Retford 10	d		15 20																		17 30
Newark North Gate 7	a											16 20									
	d											16 20									
Grantham 7	a		15 40							16 40							17 40				17 49
	d		15 40						16 25	16 40						17 23	17 40				17 49
Peterborough 8	a	15 47							16 56	17 01		16 51	17 18			17 53	18 02		17 39		
Norwich	a								18 29							19 29					
Peterborough 8	d	15 47								17 02		16 51	17 18				18 02		17 40		
Stevenage 4	a	16 18	16s29									17 21							18 10		
London Kings Cross 15 ⊖	a	16 46	16 55	17 10			17 24			17 57		17 49	18 14				18 55		18 37	18 47	19 06

A The Northern Lights
B from 24 October
C The Flying Scotsman
D The Highland Chieftain

Table 26

Sundays
from 12 September

Scotland, North East England, Yorkshire and Humberside - London

		GR	GR	TP	XC	GR	GR	TP	TP	EM	EM	GR	GR	GR	GR	XC	EM	GR	XC	GR	TP	GR	XC	TP
		■1	■1	◇1	◇1	■1	■1	◇1	◇1	◇1	◇	■1	■1	■1	■1	◇1	◇	■1	◇1	■1	◇1	■1	◇1	◇1
											A						A							
Aberdeen	d		11 47																			13 50		
Stonehaven	d		12 04																			14 07		
Montrose	d		12 27																			14 30		
Arbroath	d		12 43																			14 46		
Dundee	d		13 01																			15 04		
Leuchars 3	d		13 15																			15 18		
Kirkcaldy	d		13 39																			15 42		
Inverkeithing	d		13 55																			15 58		
Inverness	d																							
Perth	d																							
Stirling	d																							
Glasgow Central 15	d																			14 50				
Motherwell	d																			15 05				
Haymarket	d		14 19																	15 50		16 20		
Edinburgh 10	a		14 24																	15 55		16 25		
Edinburgh	d		14 30				15 00							15 30					15 50	16 00		16 30		
Dunbar	d																							
Berwick-upon-Tweed	d						15 39							16 09								17 09		
Alnmouth for Alnwick	d																		16 47			17 32		
Morpeth	d													16 43					17 02					
Newcastle 8 ⇌	a		15 55				16 26							17 02					17 20	17 25		18 04		
Sunderland ⇌	d																							
Hartlepool	d																							
Newcastle 8 ⇌	d	15 50	16 03	16 08	16 18		16 33		16 52					17 04	17 10	17 18			17 25	17 32	17 53	18 10	18 18	
Chester-le-Street	d								17 01															
Durham	d	16 02		16 20	16 30		16 46		17 08						17 22	17 33			17 37		18 07		18 33	
Darlington 7	a	16 20	16 30	16 36	16 46		17 03		17 25					17 30	17 40	17 49			17 54	17 58	18 23		18 49	
Middlesbrough	d							16 45																18 45
Eaglescliffe	d																							
Darlington 7	d	16 20	16 31	16 37	16 47		17 04		17 26					17 31	17 40	17 50			17 55	17 59	18 24		18 50	
Northallerton	d	16 32		16 48				17 12	17 37						17 52						18 35			19 12
Thirsk	d							17 21																19 21
York 8	a	16 52	17 00	17 12	17 17		17 34	17 41	18 00					18 04	18 13	18 17			18 23	18 28	18 58	19 01	19 16	19 41
Leeds 10	a			17 38				18 08	18 38										18 51		19 38			20 08
Harrogate	d																							
Scarborough	d																							
York 8	d	16 55	17 04		17 21		17 36			17 40				18 05	18 14	18 20				18 29		19 03	19 20	
Doncaster 7	a	17 19	17 28		17 47		18 00			18 05				18 29	18 39	18 48				18 53		19 28	19 48	
Skipton	d																							
Keighley	d																							
Bradford Forster Square	d																							
Shipley	d																							
Leeds 10	d					17 05						17 40						18 40	19 00					
Wakefield Westgate 7	d					17 18						17 52						18 52	19 12					
Sheffield 7 ⇌	a				18 18					18 28						19 15			19 40				20 16	
Hull	d												17 30											
Selby	d												18 05											
Doncaster 7	d	17 22	17 30			17 36	18 03						18 23	18 31	18 39			19 10		18 53		19 29		
Retford 10	d					17 51							18b44											
Newark North Gate 7	a	17 46				18 05									19 03									
	d	17 46				18 05									19 03									
Grantham 7	a											18 37	19 06					19 40						
	d										18 18	18 37	19 06				19 23	19 40						
Peterborough 8	a		18 21				18 50				18 45	18 59	19 28	19 18	19 33		19 56	20 01		19 42		20 19		
Norwich	a										20 28						21 35							
Peterborough 8	d		18 23				18 51					18 59	19 29	19 19	19 34			20 02		19 45		20 20		
Stevenage 4	a	18 42				19 02	19 21								20 08			20 32		20 18		20 52		
London Kings Cross 15 ⊖	a	19 14	19 17			19 34	19 48					19 57	20 23	20 14	20 34			21 02		20 43		21 20		

A from 24 October
b arr. 1838

Table 26

Sundays from 12 September

Scotland, North East England, Yorkshire and Humberside - London

		XC	HT	GR	GR	GC	TP	XC	GR	XC	GR	TP	TP	EM	GR	NT	GR	GR	TP
		◇1	◇1	1	1	1	◇1	◇1	1	◇1	1	◇1	◇1	◇ A	1		1	1	◇1
Aberdeen	d																		
Stonehaven	d																		
Montrose	d																		
Arbroath	d																		
Dundee	d																		
Leuchars 3	d																		
Kirkcaldy	d																		
Inverkeithing	d																		
Inverness	d																		
Perth	d																		
Stirling	d																		
Glasgow Central 15	d			15 50											17 50			19 50	
Motherwell	d			16 05											18 05			20 05	
Haymarket	d			16 46											18 46			20 46	
Edinburgh 10	a			16 51											18 52			20 51	
Edinburgh	d	16 50		17 00	17 30					17 50	18 00				19 00		20 00	21 00	
Dunbar	d	17 10								18 10					19 20		20 20	21 21	
Berwick-upon-Tweed	d	17 33									18 39						20 43	21 44	
Alnmouth for Alnwick	d									18 51	19 01							22 06	
Morpeth	d																21 17		
Newcastle 8	a	18 20		18 24	18 53					19 20	19 31				20 27		21 36	22 39	
Sunderland	d					18 42													
Hartlepool	d					19 06													
Newcastle 8	d	18 25		18 29	18 57		19 06	19 18		19 25	19 35		20 07		20 31	21 06	21 40		
Chester-le-Street	d															21 15			
Durham	d	18 38		18 43	19 10		19 18	19 33		19 39	19 48		20 19			21 24	21 53		
Darlington 7	a	18 54		19 00	19 27		19 34	19 49		19 55	20 05		20 35		20 57	21 44	22 10		
Middlesbrough	d											20 07							22 07
Eaglescliffe	d					19 25										21 57			
Darlington 7	d	18 54		19 01	19 28		19 35	19 50		19 56	20 06		20 36		20 58		22 11		
Northallerton	d				19 39	19 47						20 34	20 48				22s42		22 34
Thirsk	d					19 56						20 42							22 42
York 8	a	19 25		19 29	20 00	20 13	20 09	20 17		20 24	20 34	21 02	21 12		21 26		23 19		23 09
Leeds 10	a	19 51					20 38			20 51			21 38						23 38
Harrogate	d																		
Scarborough	d																		
York 8	d			19 31	20 02	20 15		20 20			20 36				21 28				
Doncaster 7	a			19 54	20 25			20 43			20 59				21 51				
Skipton	d																		
Keighley	d																		
Bradford Forster Square	d																		
Shipley	d																		
Leeds 10	d	20 00							20 15	21 00									
Wakefield Westgate 7	d	20 12							20 28	21 12									
Sheffield 7	a	20 40						21 17		21 44									
Hull	d		18 48																
Selby	d		19 23																
Doncaster 7	d		19 43	19 55	20 26				20 48		21 00				21 52				
Retford 10	d		19 58								21 15								
Newark North Gate 7	a			20 17							21 29								
	d			20 17							21 34								
Grantham 7	a		20 18		20 56										22 22				
	d		20 18		20 56									21 19	22 22				
Peterborough 8	a			20 47	21 17				21 35		22 03			21 46	22 43				
Norwich	a													23 25					
Peterborough 8	d			20 48	21 18				21 37		22 04				22 44				
Stevenage 4	a		21s09	21 20	21 48				22 07		22 34								
London Kings Cross 15 ⊖	a		21 35	21 47	22 16	22 17			22 34		23 04				23 42				

A from 24 October

Table 26A

Mondays to Saturdays

Peterborough - Wisbech, Kings Lynn, Swaffham and Dereham

Bus Service

		GR SX	GR SX	GR SO	GR	GR	GR	GR	GR	GR	GR	GR	GR	GR	GR	GR	GR	GR	GR	GR	GR	GR	GR
Peterborough	d	07 00	07 30	07 35	08 05	08 35	09 05	09 35	10 05	10 35	11 05	11 35	12 05	12 35	13 05	13 35	14 05	14 35	15 05	15 35	16 05	16 35	17 10
Wisbech Bus Station	d	07 51	08 21	08 26	08 56	09 26	09 56	10 26	10 56	11 26	11 56	12 26	12 56	13 26	13 56	14 26	14 56	15 26	15 56	16 26	16 56	17 26	18 00
Kings Lynn Bus Station	d	08 32	09 02	09 02	09 32	10 02	10 32	11 02	11 32	12 02	12 32	13 02	13 32	14 02	14 32	15 02	15 32	16 02	16 32	17 02	17 32	18 02	18 35
Swaffham Market Place	d	09 04	09 34	09 34	10 04	10 34	11 04	11 34	12 04	12 34	13 04	13 34	14 04	14 34	15 04	15 34	16 04	16 34	17 04	17 34	18 04	18 34	19 06
Dereham Market Place	a	09 37	10 07	10 07	10 37	11 07	11 37	12 07	12 37	13 07	13 37	14 07	14 37	15 07	15 37	16 07	16 37	17 07	17 37	18 07	18 37	19 07	19 37

		GR	GR	GR	GR	GR	GR	GR
Peterborough	d	17 40	18 10	18 40	19 10	20 10	21 10	22 10
Wisbech Bus Station	d	18 30	19 00	19 30	20 00	21 00	22 00	23 00
Kings Lynn Bus Station	d	18a58	19 35	19a58	20 35	21 35	22a28	23a28
Swaffham Market Place	d		20 06		21 06	22 06		
Dereham Market Place	a		20 37		21 37	22 37		

Sundays

		GR	GR	GR	GR	GR	GR	GR	GR	GR	GR	GR	GR	GR	GR	GR
Peterborough	d	08 10	09 10	10 10	11 10	12 10	13 10	14 10	15 10	16 10	17 10	18 10	19 10	20 10	21 10	22 10
Wisbech Bus Station	d	09 00	10 00	11 00	12 00	13 00	14 00	15 00	16 00	17 00	18 00	19 00	20 00	21 00	22 00	23 00
Kings Lynn Bus Station	d	09 35	10 35	11 35	12 35	13 35	14 35	15 35	16 35	17 35	18 35	19 35	20 35	21 35	22a28	23a28
Swaffham Market Place	d	10 06	11 06	12 06	13 06	14 06	15 06	16 06	17 06	18 06	19 06	20 06	21 06	22 06		
Dereham Market Place	a	10 37	11 37	12 37	13 37	14 37	15 37	16 37	17 37	18 37	19 37	20 37	21 37	22 37		

Table 26A

Mondays to Saturdays

Dereham, Swaffham, Kings Lynn and Wisbech - Peterborough

Bus Service

		GR SX	GR SX	GR	GR	GR	GR SX	GR SO	GR SX	GR SO	GR SX	GR SO	GR SX	GR SO	GR	GR	GR	GR	GR	GR	GR	GR	GR
Dereham Market Place	d						07 05	07 09	07 30	07 39	08 00	08 09	08 35	08 36	09 05	09 35	10 05	10 35	11 05	11 35	12 05	12 35	13 05
Swaffham Market Place	d						07 35	07 39	08 02	08 09	08 32	08 39	09 07	09 07	09 37	10 07	10 37	11 07	11 35	12 07	12 37	13 07	13 37
Kings Lynn Bus Station	d	05 40	06 10	06 45	07 15	07 45	08 15	08 15	08 45	08 45	09 15	09 15	09 45	09 45	10 15	10 45	11 15	11 45	12 15	12 45	13 15	13 45	14 15
Wisbech Bus Station	d	06 13	06 43	07 18	07 48	08 18	08 48	08 48	09 18	09 18	09 48	09 48	10 18	10 18	10 48	11 18	11 48	12 18	12 48	13 18	13 48	14 18	14 48
Peterborough	a	06 54	07 24	07 59	08 29	08 59	09 29	09 29	09 59	09 59	10 29	10 29	10 59	10 59	11 29	11 59	12 29	12 59	13 29	13 59	14 29	14 59	15 29

		GR	GR	GR	GR	GR	GR	GR	GR SO	GR SX	GR SO	GR SX	GR	GR
Dereham Market Place	d	13 35	14 05	14 35	15 05	15 35	16 05	16 35	17 40	17 44	18 40	18 44	19 44	20 44
Swaffham Market Place	d	14 07	14 37	15 07	15 37	16 07	16 37	17 07	18 12	18 14	19 12	19 14	20 14	21 14
Kings Lynn Bus Station	d	14 45	15 15	15 45	16 15	16 45	17 15	17 45	18 50	18 50	19 50	19 50	20 50	21 50
Wisbech Bus Station	d	15 18	15 48	16 18	16 48	17 18	17 48	18 18	19 22	19 22	20 22	20 22	21 22	22 22
Peterborough	a	15 59	16 29	16 59	17 29	17 59	18 29	18 59	20 01	20 01	21 01	21 01	22 01	23 01

Sundays

		GR	GR	GR	GR	GR	GR	GR	GR	GR	GR	GR	GR	GR	GR	GR	GR
Dereham Market Place	d				08 44	09 44	10 44	11 44	12 44	13 44	14 44	15 44	16 44	17 44	18 44	19 44	20 44
Swaffham Market Place	d				09 14	10 14	11 14	12 14	13 14	14 14	15 14	16 14	17 14	18 14	19 14	20 14	21 14
Kings Lynn Bus Station	d	06 50	07 50	08 50	09 50	10 50	11 50	12 50	13 50	14 50	15 50	16 50	17 50	18 50	19 50	20 50	21 50
Wisbech Bus Station	d	07 22	08 22	09 22	10 22	11 22	12 22	13 22	14 22	15 22	16 22	17 22	18 22	19 22	20 22	21 22	22 22
Peterborough	a	08 01	09 01	10 01	11 01	12 01	13 01	14 01	15 01	16 01	17 01	18 01	19 01	20 01	21 01	22 01	23 01

Table 26B

Mondays to Saturdays

Peterborough - Oundle, Corby and Kettering

Bus Service

		GR	GR	GR	GR	GR	GR	GR	GR	GR	GR	GR	GR	GR	GR
Peterborough Queensgate	d	07 05	07 40	09 10	10 10	11 10	12 10	13 10	14 10	15 10	16 10	17 10	18 30	19 30	20 30
Oundle Market Place	a	07 27	08 22	09 32	10 32	11 32	12 32	13 32	14 32	15 32	16 32	17 32	18 57	19 57	20 57
Corby George Street	a	08 05	09 05	10 05	11 05	12 05	13 05	14 05	15 05	16 05	17 05	18 05	19 25	20 25	21 25
Kettering Library	a	08 35	09 35	10 35	11 35	12 35	13 35	14 35	15 35	16 35	17 35	18 35	19 55	20 55	21 55

Sundays

		GR	GR	GR	GR	GR	GR
Peterborough Queensgate	d	10 10	12 10	14 10	16 10	18 10	20 10
Oundle Market Place	a	10 37	12 37	14 37	16 37	18 37	20 37
Corby George Street	a	11 05	13 05	15 05	17 05	19 05	21 05
Kettering Library	a	11 35	13 35	15 35	17 35	19 35	21 33

Table 26B

Mondays to Saturdays

Kettering and Corby, Oundle - Peterborough

Bus Service

		GR	GR	GR	GR	GR	GR	GR	GR	GR	GR	GR	GR	GR	GR	GR
Kettering Library	d	05 30	06 00	07 05		08 45	09 45	10 45	11 45	12 45	13 45	14 45	15 45	16 50	17 55	18 55
Corby George Street	d	05 55	06 25	07 30		09 10	10 10	11 10	12 10	13 10	14 10	15 10	16 10	17 15	18 20	19 20
Oundle Market Place	d	06 23	06 53	07 58	08 38	09 38	10 38	11 38	12 38	13 38	14 38	15 38	16 38	17 43	18 48	19 48
Peterborough Queensgate	a	06 40	07 25	08 30	09 00	10 00	11 00	12 00	13 00	14 00	15 00	16 00	17 00	18 05	19 10	20 20

Sundays

		GR	GR	GR	GR	GR	GR
Kettering Library	d	08 15	10 15	12 15	14 15	16 15	18 15
Corby George Street	d	08 40	10 40	12 40	14 40	16 40	18 40
Oundle Market Place	d	09 08	11 08	13 08	15 08	17 08	19 08
Peterborough Queensgate	a	09 40	11 40	13 40	15 40	17 40	19 40

Table 26F

Mondays to Saturdays

Doncaster - Robin Hood Airport

Bus Service

		GR	GR	GR	GR	GR	GR	GR	GR	GR	GR	GR	GR	GR	GR	GR	GR	GR	GR
Doncaster Interchange	d	05 35	06 35	07 35	08 35	09 35	10 35	11 35	12 35	13 35	14 35	15 35	16 35	17 35	18 35	19 35	20 35	21 35	22 35
Robin Hood Airport	a	05 59	06 59	07 59	08 59	09 59	10 59	11 59	12 59	13 59	14 59	15 59	16 59	17 59	18 59	19 59	20 59	21 59	22 59

Sundays

		GR	GR	GR	GR	GR	GR	GR	GR	GR
Doncaster Interchange	d	08 35	09 35	10 35	11 35	12 35	13 35	15 35	16 35	17 35
Robin Hood Airport	a	08 59	09 59	10 59	11 59	12 59	13 59	15 59	16 59	17 59

Table 26F

Mondays to Saturdays

Robin Hood Airport - Doncaster

Bus Service

		GR	GR	GR	GR	GR	GR	GR	GR	GR	GR	GR	GR	GR	GR	GR	GR	GR	GR
Robin Hood Airport	d	06 05	07 05	08 05	09 05	10 05	11 05	12 05	13 05	14 05	15 05	16 05	17 05	18 05	19 05	20 05	21 05	22 05	23 05
Doncaster Interchange	a	06 30	07 30	08 30	09 30	10 30	11 30	12 30	13 30	14 30	15 30	16 30	17 30	18 30	19 30	20 30	21 30	22 30	23 30

Sundays

		GR	GR	GR	GR	GR	GR	GR	GR	GR	GR
Robin Hood Airport	d	09 05	10 05	11 05	12 05	13 05	14 05	15 05	16 05	17 05	18 05
Doncaster Interchange	a	09 30	10 30	11 30	12 30	13 30	14 30	15 30	16 30	17 30	18 30

Table 26G

Mondays to Fridays

York - Pickering and Whitby

Bus Service

		GR	GR	GR	GR	GR	GR	GR	GR	GR	GR	GR	GR	GR
York	d	06 46	08 18	09 20	10 01	10 22	11 22	12 22	13 22	14 22	15 22	16 24	17 34	18 31
Eden Camp	a	08 02	09 22	10 22	10 57	11 22	12 22	13 22	14 22	15 22	16 22	17 27	18 32	19 27
Flamingo Land	a			10 35		11 35								
Pickering Eastgate	a	08 16	09 36	10 43	11 09	11 43	12 36	13 36	14 36	15 36	16 36	17 41	18 46	19 41
Whitby Bus Station	a		10 37		11 51	12 44		14 37		16 37	17 37		19 41	

Saturdays

		GR	GR	GR	GR	GR	GR	GR	GR	GR	GR	GR	GR
York	d	08 22	09 22	09 56	10 22	11 22	12 22	13 22	14 22	15 22	16 22	17 34	18 27
Eden Camp	a	09 22	10 22	10 52	11 22	12 22	13 22	14 22	15 22	16 22	17 22	18 27	19 27
Flamingo Land	a		10 35		11 35								
Pickering Eastgate	a	09 36	10 43	11 04	11 43	12 36	13 36	14 36	15 36	16 36	17 36	18 41	19 41
Whitby Bus Station	a	10 37		11 46	12 44		14 37		16 37	17 37		19 42	

Sundays

		GR	GR	GR	GR	GR	GR
York	d	09 22	09 52	09 56	12 52	14 52	16 12
Eden Camp	a	10 22	10 52	10 52	13 52	15 52	17 12
Flamingo Land	a	10 35	11 05				
Pickering Eastgate	a	10 48		11 06	14 06	16 06	17 26
Whitby Bus Station	a			12 07	15 07	17 07	18 27

Table 26G

Mondays to Fridays

Whitby and Pickering - York

Bus Service

		GR	GR	GR	GR	GR	GR	GR	GR	GR	GR	GR	GR	GR	GR	GR
Whitby Bus Station	d					11 06	12 31	13 06		15 06		17 31		18 16		20 16
Pickering Eastgate	d	06 47	08 37	09 07	11 07	12 07	13 13	14 07	15 07	16 07		18 13	17 57	19 17	19 57	21 17
Flamingo Land	d										17 12		18 15			
Eden Camp	d	07 03	08 53	09 23	11 23	12 23	13 23	14 23	15 23	16 23	17 23	18 23	18 26	19 33	20 13	21 33
York	a	08 06	09 56	10 26	12 26	13 26	14 26	15 26	16 26	17 27	18 27	19 23	19 23	20 30	21 30	22 30

Saturdays

		GR	GR	GR	GR	GR	GR	GR	GR	GR	GR	GR	GR	GR	GR	GR
Whitby Bus Station	d					11 06	12 31	13 06		15 06		17 31		18 16		20 16
Pickering Eastgate	d	07 07	08 37	09 07	11 07	12 07	13 13	14 07	15 07	16 07		18 13	17 57	19 17	19 57	21 17
Flamingo Land	d										17 12		18 15			
Eden Camp	d	07 23	08 53	09 23	11 23	12 23	13 23	14 23	15 23	16 23	17 23	18 23	18 26	19 33	20 13	21 33
York	a	08 26	09 56	10 26	12 26	13 26	14 26	15 26	16 26	17 26	18 25	19 23	19 23	20 30	21 30	22 30

Sundays

		GR	GR	GR	GR	GR	GR	GR
Whitby Bus Station	d			12 26	15 46		17 46	18 46
Pickering Eastgate	d	08 57	10 57	13 27	16 47		18 47	19 47
Flamingo Land	d					17 52		
Eden Camp	d	09 13	11 13	13 43	17 03	18 03	19 03	20 03
York	a	10 26	12 26	14 46	18 06	19 03	20 03	21 00

Table 26H

Mondays to Saturdays

Darlington - Richmond and Catterick

Bus Service

		GR SX	GR SX	GR	GR	GR	GR	GR	GR	GR	GR	GR	GR	GR	GR	GR	GR	GR	GR	GR	GR	GR	GR
Darlington	d	06 23	06 53	07 33	08 03	08 33	09 03	09 33	10 03	10 33	11 03	11 33	12 03	12 33	13 03	13 33	14 03	14 33	15 03	15 33	16 03	16 33	17 03
Richmond (Market)	a	06 54	07 24	08 04	08 34	09 04	09 34	10 04	10 34	11 04	11 34	12 04	12 34	13 04	13 34	14 04	14 34	15 04	15 34	16 04	16 34	17 04	17 34
Catterick Garrison Tesco	a	07 05	07 35	08 15	08 45	09 15	09 45	10 15	10 45	11 15	11 45	12 15	12 45	13 15	13 45	14 15	14 45	15 15	15 45	16 15	16 45	17 15	17 45
Catterick Camp Centre	a	07 07	07 37	08 17	08 47	09 17	09 47	10 17	10 47	11 17	11 47	12 17	12 47	13 17	13 47	14 17	14 47	15 17	15 47	16 17	16 47	17 17	17 47
Catterick Garrison Kemmel	a	07 15	07 45	08 25	08 55	09 25	09 55	10 25	10 55	11 25	11 55	12 25	12 55	13 25	13 55	14 25	14 55	15 25	15 55	16 25	16 55	17 25	17 55

		GR	GR	GR	GR	GR		GR
Darlington	d	17 33	18 03	19 03	20 03	21 03		23 03
Richmond (Market)	a	18 04	18 36	19 36	20 36	21 36		23 36
Catterick Garrison Tesco	a	18 15	18 47	19 47	20 47	21 47		23 47
Catterick Camp Centre	a	18 17	18 49	19 49	20 49	21 49		23 49
Catterick Garrison Kemmel	a	18 25	18 57	19 57	20 57	21 57		23 57

Sundays

		GR	GR	GR	GR	GR	GR	GR	GR	GR	GR	GR	GR	GR	GR	GR	GR	GR
Darlington	d	09 03	10 03	11 03	12 03	13 03	14 03	15 03	16 03	17 03	18 03	18 33	19 03	19 33	20 03	21 03	22 03	23 03
Richmond (Market)	a	09 34	10 34	11 34	12 34	13 34	14 34	15 34	16 34	17 34	18 36	19 06	19 36	20 06	20 36	21 36	22 36	23 36
Catterick Garrison Tesco	a	09 45	10 45	11 45	12 45	13 45	14 45	15 45	16 45	17 45	18 47	19 17	19 47	20 17	20 47	21 47	22 47	23 47
Catterick Camp Centre	a	09 47	10 47	11 47	12 47	13 47	14 47	15 47	16 47	17 47	18 49	19 19	19 49	20 19	20 49	21 49	22 49	23 49
Catterick Garrison Kemmel	a	09 55	10 55	11 55	12 55	13 55	14 55	15 55	16 55	17 55	18 57	19 27	19 57	20 27	20 57	21 57	22 57	23 57

Table 26H

Mondays to Saturdays

Catterick and Richmond - Darlington

Bus Service

		GR SX	GR SX	GR SX	GR SO	GR SX	GR SO	GR	GR	GR	GR	GR
Catterick Garrison Kemmel	d	06 22	06 52	07 22	07 27	07 52	07 57	08 32	09 02	09 32	10 02	10 32
Catterick Camp Centre	d	06 30	07 00	07 30	07 35	08 00	08 05	08 40	09 10	09 40	10 10	10 40
Catterick Garrison Tesco	d	06 32	07 02	07 32	07 37	08 02	08 07	08 42	09 12	09 42	10 12	10 42
Richmond (Market)	d	06 44	07 14	07 44	07 49	08 14	08 19	08 54	09 24	09 54	10 24	10 54
Darlington	a	07 15	07 45	08 20	08 20	08 45	08 50	09 25	09 55	10 25	10 55	11 25

		GR	GR	GR	GR	GR	GR	GR	GR	GR	GR	GR
Catterick Garrison Kemmel	d	11 02	11 32	12 02	12 32	13 02	13 32	14 02	14 32	15 02	15 32	16 02
Catterick Camp Centre	d	11 10	11 40	12 10	12 40	13 10	13 40	14 10	14 40	15 10	15 40	16 10
Catterick Garrison Tesco	d	11 12	11 42	12 12	12 42	13 12	13 42	14 12	14 42	15 12	15 42	16 12
Richmond (Market)	d	11 24	11 54	12 24	12 54	13 24	13 54	14 24	14 54	15 24	15 54	16 24
Darlington	a	11 55	12 25	12 55	13 25	13 55	14 25	14 55	15 25	15 55	16 25	16 55

		GR	GR	GR	GR	GR	GR	GR	GR	GR
Catterick Garrison Kemmel	d	16 32	17 02	17 32	18 02	18 32	19 02	20 02	21 02	22 02
Catterick Camp Centre	d	16 40	17 10	17 40	18 10	18 40	19 10	20 10	21 10	22 10
Catterick Garrison Tesco	d	16 42	17 12	17 42	18 12	18 42	19 12	20 12	21 12	22 12
Richmond (Market)	d	16 54	17 24	17 54	18 24	18 54	19 24	20 24	21 24	22 24
Darlington	a	17 25	17 55	18 25	18 55	19 25	19 57	20 57	21 57	22 57

Sundays

		GR	GR	GR	GR	GR	GR	GR
Catterick Garrison Kemmel	d	09 02	10 02	11 02	12 02	13 02	14 02	15 02
Catterick Camp Centre	d	09 10	10 10	11 10	12 10	13 10	14 10	15 10
Catterick Garrison Tesco	d	09 12	10 12	11 12	12 12	13 12	14 12	15 12
Richmond (Market)	d	09 24	10 24	11 24	12 24	13 24	14 24	15 24
Darlington	a	09 55	10 55	11 55	12 55	13 55	14 55	15 55

		GR	GR	GR	GR	GR	GR	GR
Catterick Garrison Kemmel	d	16 02	17 02	18 02	19 02	20 02	21 02	22 02
Catterick Camp Centre	d	16 10	17 10	18 10	19 10	20 10	21 10	22 10
Catterick Garrison Tesco	d	16 12	17 12	18 12	19 12	20 12	21 12	22 12
Richmond (Market)	d	16 24	17 24	18 24	19 24	20 24	21 24	22 24
Darlington	a	16 55	17 55	18 55	19 57	20 57	21 57	22 57

Table 26K

Mondays to Fridays

Berwick-upon-Tweed - Scottish Border Towns

Bus Service

This service is operated by First Lowland under contract to Scottish Borders Council. Telephone 01835 824000

		XC	XC	XC	XC	XC	XC	XC	XC	XC
Berwick-upon-Tweed	d	06 57	08 12	09 52	10 52	12 52	15 07	17 47	18 47	20 22
Duns	a	07 30	08 45	10 25	11 25	13 25	15 40	18 20	19 20	20 55
Earlston	a	08 08	09 33	11 03	12 03	14 03	16 28	18 58	19 58	21 33
Melrose	a	08 22	09 47	11 15	12 15	14 15	16 40	19 10	20 10	21 45
Galashiels Bus Station	a	08 40	10 02	11 30	12 30	14 30	16 55	19 25	20 25	22 00

Saturdays

		XC	XC	XC	XC	XC	XC
Berwick-upon-Tweed	d	08 22	10 52	12 52	15 17	17 17	19 17
Duns	a	08 55	11 25	13 25	15 50	17 50	19 50
Earlston	a	09 33	12 03	14 03	16 28	18 28	20 28
Melrose	a	09 47	12 15	14 15	16 40	18 40	20 40
Galashiels Bus Station	a	10 02	12 30	14 30	16 55	18 55	20 55

Sundays

		XC	XC	XC	XC	XC	XC
Berwick-upon-Tweed	d	10 52	12 52	15 17	17 42	19 07	20 37
Duns	a	11 25	13 40	15 50	18 30	19 55	21 10
Earlston	a	12 03	14 18	16 28	19 08	20 33	21 48
Melrose	a	12 15	14 30	16 40	19 20	20 45	22 00
Galashiels Bus Station	a	12 30	14 45	16 55	19 35	21 00	22 15

Table 26K

Mondays to Fridays

Scottish Border Towns - Berwick-upon-Tweed

This service is operated by First Lowland under contract to Scottish Borders Council. Telephone 01835 824000

Bus Service

		XC	XC	XC	XC	XC	XC	XC	XC
Galashiels Bus Station	d	06 25	07 40	08 10	10 50	12 50	14 40	16 32	17 20
Melrose	d	06 40	07 55	08 28	11 05	13 05	14 55	16 50	17 35
Earlston	d	06 52	08 07	08 40	11 17	13 17	15 07	17 02	17 47
Duns	d	07 30	08 50	09 20	11 55	13 55	15 55	17 40	18 30
Berwick-upon-Tweed	a	08 01	09 26	09 56	12 26	14 26	16 26	18 11	19 01

Saturdays

		XC	XC	XC	XC	XC	XC
Galashiels Bus Station	d	06 35	08 20	10 50	12 50	14 50	17 20
Melrose	d	06 50	08 35	11 05	13 05	15 05	17 35
Earlston	d	07 02	08 47	11 17	13 17	15 17	17 52
Duns	d	07 40	09 25	11 55	13 55	15 55	18 30
Berwick-upon-Tweed	a	08 11	09 56	12 26	14 26	16 26	19 01

Sundays

		XC	XC	XC	XC	XC	XC
Galashiels Bus Station	d	08 50	10 50	12 35	14 50	16 35	18 35
Melrose	d	09 05	11 05	12 50	15 05	16 50	18 50
Earlston	d	09 17	11 17	13 02	15 17	17 02	19 02
Duns	d	09 55	11 55	13 40	15 55	17 40	19 40
Berwick-upon-Tweed	a	10 26	12 26	14 26	16 26	18 26	20 26

Table 27

Mondays to Fridays

Cleethorpes - Lincoln - Newark - Nottingham

		EM A	EM B	EM	EM ◇1	EM A	EM B	EM	EM A	EM B	EM		EM A	EM B	EM	EM A	EM B	EM A	EM B	EM	EM A	EM B	EM B	EM A	EM
Cleethorpes	d			05 49																					
Grimsby Town	d			05 56				07 03							09 28					11 28					
Habrough	d			06 06				07 13							09 38					11 38					
Barnetby	d			06 15				07 22							09 47					11 47					
Market Rasen	d			06 32				07 39							10 03					12 03					
Lincoln	a			06 51				07 57							10 22					12 22					
	d	05 26	05 26	06 53	07 08	07 26	07 26	07 59	08 35	08 35	09 11		09 31	09 31	10 23	10 36	10 36	11 42	11 42	12 23	12 30	12 30	13 40	13 40	14 05
Hykeham	d	05 34	05 34	07 01		07 34	07 34		08 43	08 43						10 44	10 44				12 38	12 38			
Swinderby	d	05 40	05 40	07 07		07 40	07 40		08 49	08 49						10 50	10 50				12 44	12 44			
Collingham	d	05 45	05 45	07 12	07 23	07 45	07 45	08 15	08 54	08 54	09 26				10 40	10 55	10 55			12 40	12 48	12 48			14 21
Newark North Gate 7	a	05 56	05 56	07 22				08 25			09 36				10 52					12 52					14 33
	d	05 59	05 59																						
Newark Castle	d	06 10	06 10		07 33	07 56	07 56		09 05	09 05			09 55	09 55		11 04	11 04	12 05	12 05		12 57	12 57	14 05	14 05	
Rolleston	d	06 16	06 16			08 03	08 03						10 01	10 01							13 04	13 04			
Fiskerton	d	06 18	06 18			08 05	08 05						10 03	10 03							13 06	13 06			
Bleasby	d	06 22	06 22			08 08	08 08						10 07	10 07							13 09	13 09			
Thurgarton	d	06 25	06 25			08 11	08 11						10 10	10 10							13 12	13 12			
Lowdham	d	06 29	06 29			08 15	08 15		09 18	09 18			10 14	10 14		11 17	11 17	12 18	12 18		13 17	13 17	14 17	14 17	
Burton Joyce	d	06 34	06 34			08 19	08 19						10 19	10 19											
Carlton	d	06 38	06 38			08 23	08 23						10 23	10 23							13 23	13 23			
Nottingham 8	a	06 47	06 45		07 57	08 32	08 30		09 32	09 30			10 32	10 30		11 32	11 29	12 32	12 30		13 32	13 30	14 30	14 32	

		EM A	EM B	EM	EM A	EM B	EM A	EM B		EM	EM A	EM B	EM	EM A	EM B	EM	EM	EM		EM	EM
Cleethorpes	d																			21 15	
Grimsby Town	d			13 52						16 03						18 28				21 22	
Habrough	d			14 02						16 12						18 38				21 31	
Barnetby	d			14 11						16 21						18 49				21 40	
Market Rasen	d			14 27						16 36						19 04				21 55	
Lincoln	a			14 47						16 55						19 23				22 18	
	d	14 35	14 35	14 48	15 30	15 30	16 35	16 35		16 57	17 28	17 28	18 18	18 35	18 35	19 25	20 42	21 40			22 28
Hykeham	d				15 37	15 37	16 43	16 43			17 36	17 36				19 33					22 36
Swinderby	d				15 43	15 43	16 49	16 49			17 42	17 42				19 39					22 42
Collingham	d			15 04	15 48	15 48	16 54	16 54		17 12	17 47	17 47	18 34			19 44	20 57				22 47
Newark North Gate 7	a			15 14						17 25			18 44			19 54					
	d																				
Newark Castle	d	15 00	15 00		15 58	15 58	17 04	17 04			17 57	17 57		19 03	19 03		21 10	22 05			22 58
Rolleston	d				16 04	16 04					18 03	18 03									
Fiskerton	d				16 06	16 06					18 05	18 05									23 05
Bleasby	d				16 10	16 10					18 09	18 09									23 08
Thurgarton	d				16 12	16 12					18 12	18 12									
Lowdham	d	15 13	15 13		16 16	16 16	17 17	17 17			18 16	18 16		19 16	19 16		21 23	22 18			23 13
Burton Joyce	d	15 17	15 17								18 20	18 20									23 17
Carlton	d	15 21	15 21		16 23	16 23					18 23	18 23									23 21
Nottingham 8	a	15 32	15 29		16 32	16 30	17 32	17 30			18 32	18 31		19 31	19 29		21 39	22 34			23 33

Saturdays

		EM C	EM D	EM ◇1	EM C	EM D	EM	EM C	EM D	EM		EM C	EM D	EM	EM C	EM D	EM C	EM D	EM	EM C		EM D	EM C	EM D	EM
Cleethorpes	d																								
Grimsby Town	d						07 03							09 28					11 28						
Habrough	d						07 13							09 38					11 38						
Barnetby	d						07 22							09 47					11 47						
Market Rasen	d						07 39							10 03					12 03						
Lincoln	a						07 57							10 22					12 22						
	d	05 26	05 26	07 08	07 26	07 26	07 59	08 35	08 35	09 11		09 31	09 31	10 23	10 36	10 36	11 42	11 42	12 23	12 30		12 30	13 40	13 40	14 05
Hykeham	d	05 34	05 34		07 34	07 34		08 43	08 43						10 44	10 44				12 38		12 38			
Swinderby	d	05 40	05 40		07 40	07 40		08 49	08 49						10 50	10 50				12 44		12 44			
Collingham	d	05 45	05 45	07 23	07 45	07 45	08 15	08 54	08 54	09 26				10 40	10 55	10 55			12 40	12 48		12 48			14 21
Newark North Gate 7	a	05 56	05 56				08 25			09 36				10 52					12 52						14 33
	d	05 59	05 59																						
Newark Castle	d	06 10	06 10	07 35	07 56	07 56		09 04	09 04			09 55	09 55		11 04	11 04	12 05	12 05		12 57		12 57	14 05	14 05	
Rolleston	d	06 16	06 16		08 03	08 03						10 01	10 01							13 04		13 04			
Fiskerton	d	06 18	06 18		08 05	08 05						10 03	10 03							13 06		13 06			
Bleasby	d	06 22	06 22		08 08	08 08						10 07	10 07							13 09		13 09			
Thurgarton	d	06 25	06 25		08 11	08 11						10 10	10 10							13 12		13 12			
Lowdham	d	06 29	06 29		08 15	08 15		09 18	09 18			10 14	10 14		11 17	11 17	12 18	12 18		13 17		13 17	14 17	14 17	
Burton Joyce	d	06 34	06 34		08 19	08 19						10 19	10 19												
Carlton	d	06 38	06 38		08 23	08 23						10 23	10 23							13 23		13 23			
Nottingham 8	a	06 47	06 45	07 58	08 32	08 30		09 32	09 30			10 32	10 30		11 32	11 29	12 32	12 30		13 32		13 30	14 32	14 30	

A from 27 September
B until 24 September
C from 2 October
D until 25 September

For connections to London Kings Cross please refer to Table 26

Table 27

Saturdays

Cleethorpes - Lincoln - Newark - Nottingham

		EM A	EM B	EM	EM A	EM B	EM A	EM B	EM	EM A	EM B	EM A	EM B	EM	EM	EM	EM
Cleethorpes	d																
Grimsby Town	d			13 52					16 03					18 28		19 45	
Habrough	d			14 02					16 12					18 38		19 54	
Barnetby	d			14 11					16 21					18 49		20 03	
Market Rasen	d			14 27					16 36					19 04		20 18	
Lincoln	a			14 47					16 55					19 23		20 37	
	d	14 35	14 35	14 48	15 30	15 30	16 35	16 35	16 57	17 28	17 28	18 35	18 35	19 25	19 35		20 45
Hykeham	d				15 37	15 37	16 43	16 43		17 36	17 36			19 33			
Swinderby	d				15 43	15 43	16 49	16 49		17 42	17 42			19 39			
Collingham	d			15 04	15 48	15 48	16 54	16 54	17 12	17 47	17 47			19 44			21 00
Newark North Gate 7	a			15 14					17 25					19 54			
	d																
Newark Castle	d	15 01	15 01		15 58	15 58	17 04	17 04		17 57	17 57	19 02	19 02		20 03		21 10
Rolleston	d				16 04	16 04				18 03	18 03						
Fiskerton	d				16 06	16 06				18 05	18 05						
Bleasby	d				16 10	16 10				18 09	18 09						
Thurgarton	d				16 12	16 12				18 12	18 12						
Lowdham	d	15 14	15 14		16 16	16 16	17 17	17 17		18 16	18 16	19 16	19 16		20 16		21 23
Burton Joyce	d	15 19	15 19							18 20	18 20						
Carlton	d	15 23	15 23		16 23	16 23				18 23	18 23						
Nottingham 8	a	15 32	15 30		16 32	16 30	17 32	17 30		18 32	18 31	19 31	19 29		20 30		21 39

Sundays
until 05 September

		EM	EM	EM	EM	EM	EM	EM	EM	EM	EM	EM	EM	EM
Cleethorpes	d			13 56						18 18		19 54		
Grimsby Town	d			14 03						18 25		20 07		
Habrough	d			14 13						18 35		20 17		
Barnetby	d			14 22						18 44		20 26		
Market Rasen	d			14 37						18 59		20 41		
Lincoln	a			14 56						19 18		20 58		
	d	11 05	13 00	15 00	15 50	17 10	17 25	18 10	19 10	19 24	20 10	21 00	21 26	22 10
Hykeham	d			15 08		17 18		18 18	19 18		20 18	21 08		22 18
Swinderby	d			15 14		17 24		18 24	19 24		20 24	21 14		22 24
Collingham	d	11 20	13 15	15 18		17 28		18 28	19 28		20 28	21 18		22 28
Newark North Gate 7	a	11 30	13 25	15 28	16 14		17 49			19 48		21 27	21 50	
	d			15 32								21 31		
Newark Castle	d			15 42		17 38		18 39	19 40		20 40	21 40		22 39
Rolleston	d							18 45						22 45
Fiskerton	d							18 47						22 47
Bleasby	d							18 51						22 50
Thurgarton	d							18 54						22 53
Lowdham	d			15 55		17 51		18 58	19 52		20 52	21 53		22 58
Burton Joyce	d							19 02						23 02
Carlton	d							19 06						23 05
Nottingham 8	a			16 11		18 08		19 17	20 08		21 08	22 09		23 17

Sundays
12 September to 17 October

		EM	EM	EM	EM	EM	EM	EM	EM
Cleethorpes	d								
Grimsby Town	d								
Habrough	d								
Barnetby	d								
Market Rasen	d								
Lincoln	a								
	d	11 05	13 00	15 00	18 09	19 10	20 10	21 00	22 10
Hykeham	d			15 08	18 17	19 18	20 18	21 08	22 18
Swinderby	d			15 14	18 23	19 24	20 24	21 14	22 24
Collingham	d	11 20	13 15	15 18	18 27	19 28	20 28	21 18	22 28
Newark North Gate 7	a	11 30	13 25	15 28	18 37	19 38	20 38	21 28	22 38
	d								
Newark Castle	d								
Rolleston	d								
Fiskerton	d								
Bleasby	d								
Thurgarton	d								
Lowdham	d								
Burton Joyce	d								
Carlton	d								
Nottingham 8	a								

A from 2 October

B until 25 September

For connections to London Kings Cross please refer to Table 26

Table 27

Sundays
from 24 October

Cleethorpes - Lincoln - Newark - Nottingham

		EM	EM	EM	EM	EM	EM	EM	EM
Cleethorpes	d								
Grimsby Town	d								
Habrough	d								
Barnetby	d								
Market Rasen	d								
Lincoln	a								
	d	11 05	13 00	15 00	18 10	19 10	20 10	21 00	22 10
Hykeham	d			15 08	18 18	19 18	20 18	21 08	22 18
Swinderby	d			15 14	18 24	19 24	20 24	21 14	22 24
Collingham	d	11 20	13 15	15 18	18 28	19 28	20 28	21 18	22 28
Newark North Gate 7	a	11 30	13 25	15 28				21 27	
	d			15 32				21 31	
Newark Castle	d			15 42	18 39	19 40	20 40	21 40	22 39
Rolleston	d				18 45				22 45
Fiskerton	d				18 47				22 47
Bleasby	d				18 51				22 50
Thurgarton	d				18 54				22 53
Lowdham	d			15 55	18 58	19 52	20 52	21 53	22 58
Burton Joyce	d				19 02				23 02
Carlton	d				19 06				23 05
Nottingham 8	a			16 11	19 17	20 08	21 08	22 09	23 17

For connections to London Kings Cross please refer to Table 26

Table 27

Mondays to Fridays

Nottingham - Newark - Lincoln - Cleethorpes

		EM	EM A	EM B	EM B	EM A	EM	EM	EM A	EM B	EM B	EM A	EM	EM A	EM B	EM A	EM B	EM	EM A	EM B	EM	EM A	EM B
Nottingham 8	d		05 55	05 55	06 53	06 55			08 05	08 05	09 21	09 23		10 29	10 29	11 17	11 15		12 27	12 27		13 17	13 17
Carlton	d		06 01	06 01	06 59	07 01			08 13	08 13	09 28	09 30				11 23	11 21					13 23	13 23
Burton Joyce	d		06 05	06 05	07 03	07 05			08 17	08 17						11 27	11 25					13 27	13 27
Lowdham	d		06 10	06 10	07 09	07 10			08 21	08 21	09 35	09 36		10 40	10 41	11 32	11 31		12 38	12 39		13 32	13 32
Thurgarton	d		06 14	06 14	07 13	07 14			08 25	08 25						11 36	11 35					13 36	13 36
Bleasby	d		06 17	06 17	07 16	07 17			08 28	08 28						11 39	11 38					13 39	13 39
Fiskerton	d		06 20	06 20	07 19	07 20			08 32	08 32						11 42	11 41					13 42	13 42
Rolleston	d		06 22	06 22	07 21	07 22			08 34	08 34						11 45	11 44					13 44	13 44
Newark Castle	d		06 30	06 30	07 29	07 29			08 41	08 41	09 51	09 51		10 58	10 58	11 52	11 52		12 53	12 53		13 51	13 51
Newark North Gate 7	a																						
	d						07 45	08 31					09 57					12 04			13 02		
Collingham	d		06 40	06 40	07 39	07 39	07 54	08 40					10 05	11 08	11 08	12 01	12 01	12 13			13 11	14 01	14 01
Swinderby	d		06 44	06 44			07 59	08 45						11 12	11 12			12 17				14 05	14 05
Hykeham	d		06 50	06 50			08 05	08 51						11 18	11 18			12 24				14 11	14 11
Lincoln	a		07 04	07 06	07 58	07 58	08 15	09 02	09 08	09 10	10 17	10 18	10 21	11 30	11 31	12 21	12 22	12 35	13 20	13 22	13 30	14 23	14 26
	d	05 57					08 17						10 23					12 37					
Market Rasen	d	06 13					08 34						10 40					12 54					
Barnetby	a	06 30					08 51						10 56					13 11					
Habrough	a	06 41					09 01						11 06					13 21					
Grimsby Town	a	06 56					09 15						11 21					13 36					
Cleethorpes	a																						

		EM	EM A	EM B	EM	EM A	EM B	EM B	EM A	EM	EM	EM A	EM B	EM A	EM B	EM A	EM B	EM	EM	EM ◇1 ⊏⊐	EM
Nottingham 8	d		14 29	14 29		15 27	15 25	16 13	16 14			17 17	17 17	17 50	17 50	18 15	18 14			20 29	22 25
Carlton	d					15 33	15 31	16 19	16 20			17 23	17 23			18 21	18 20				22 31
Burton Joyce	d							16 23	16 24			17 27	17 27			18 25	18 24				22 35
Lowdham	d		14 40	14 40		15 40	15 39	16 29	16 29			17 32	17 33	18 01	18 01	18 30	18 30			20 40	22 40
Thurgarton	d							16 33	16 33			17 36	17 37			18 34	18 34				
Bleasby	d							16 36	16 36			17 39	17 40			18 37	18 37				22 45
Fiskerton	d							16 39	16 39			17 42	17 43			18 40	18 40				22 48
Rolleston	d							16 42	16 42			17 45	17 46			18 43	18 43				
Newark Castle	d		14 55	14 55		15 54	15 54	16 49	16 49			17 53	17 53	18 15	18 15	18 51	18 51			20 57	22 56
Newark North Gate 7	a																				23 05
	d	14 36			15 36						17 34							19 24	20 32		23 08
Collingham	d	14 44			15 45	16 03	16 03	16 58	16 58		17 42	18 02	18 02	18 25	18 25	19 00	19 00	19 33	20 41	21 05	23 17
Swinderby	d					16 07	16 07					18 07	18 07	18 29	18 29	19 04	19 04				23 22
Hykeham	d					16 13	16 13					18 13	18 13	18 35	18 35	19 10	19 10				23 28
Lincoln	a	15 00	15 22	15 24	16 03	16 25	16 27	17 15	17 14		18 03	18 26	18 27	18 48	18 49	19 22	19 23	19 51	20 56	21 24	23 40
	d	15 01								17 21								19 55			
Market Rasen	d	15 17								17 37								20 12			
Barnetby	a	15 33								17 53								20 30			
Habrough	a	15 42								18 02								20 40			
Grimsby Town	a	15 57								18 17								20 52			
Cleethorpes	a																	21 02			

Saturdays

		EM	EM C	EM D	EM D	EM C	EM	EM	EM C	EM D	EM D	EM C	EM	EM C	EM D	EM C	EM D	EM	EM C	EM D	EM	EM C	EM D
Nottingham 8	d		05 55	05 55	06 53	06 55			08 01	08 01	09 21	09 23		10 29	10 29	11 17	11 15		12 27	12 27		13 17	13 17
Carlton	d		06 01	06 01	06 59	07 01			08 08	08 08	09 27	09 29				11 23	11 21					13 23	13 23
Burton Joyce	d		06 05	06 05	07 03	07 05			08 12	08 12						11 27	11 25					13 27	13 27
Lowdham	d		06 10	06 10	07 09	07 10			08 17	08 17	09 35	09 36		10 40	10 41	11 32	11 31		12 38	12 39		13 32	13 32
Thurgarton	d		06 14	06 14	07 13	07 14			08 21	08 21						11 36	11 35					13 36	13 36
Bleasby	d		06 17	06 17	07 16	07 17			08 24	08 24						11 39	11 38					13 39	13 39
Fiskerton	d		06 20	06 20	07 19	07 20			08 27	08 27						11 42	11 41					13 42	13 42
Rolleston	d		06 22	06 22	07 21	07 22			08 30	08 30						11 45	11 44					13 44	13 44
Newark Castle	d		06 30	06 30	07 29	07 29			08 37	08 37	09 50	09 50		10 58	10 58	11 52	11 52		12 53	12 53		13 51	13 51
Newark North Gate 7	a																						
	d							08 31					09 57					12 04			13 02		
Collingham	d		06 40	06 40	07 39	07 39		08 40					10 05	11 08	11 08	12 01	12 01	12 13			13 11	14 00	14 00
Swinderby	d		06 44	06 44				08 45						11 12	11 12			12 17				14 05	14 05
Hykeham	d		06 50	06 50				08 51						11 18	11 18			12 24				14 11	14 11
Lincoln	a		07 04	07 06	07 58	07 58		09 02	09 08	09 10	10 17	10 17	10 21	11 30	11 31	12 21	12 22	12 35	13 20	13 22	13 30	14 23	14 26
	d	05 57					08 17						10 23					12 37					
Market Rasen	d	06 13					08 34						10 40					12 54					
Barnetby	a	06 30					08 51						10 56					13 11					
Habrough	a	06 41					09 01						11 06					13 21					
Grimsby Town	a	06 56					09 15						11 21					13 36					
Cleethorpes	a																						

A until 24 September
B from 27 September
C until 25 September
D from 2 October

For connections from London Kings Cross please refer to Table 26

Table 27

Saturdays

Nottingham - Newark - Lincoln - Cleethorpes

		EM	EM A	EM B	EM	EM B	EM A	EM A	EM B	EM	EM A	EM B	EM	EM A	EM B	EM ◇1 ⊏⊐	EM	EM	EM
Nottingham 8	d		14 29	14 29		15 25	15 27	16 14	16 13		17 17	17 17		18 15	18 14	19 29		20 29	21 25
Carlton	d					15 31	15 33	16 20	16 19		17 23	17 23		18 21	18 20				
Burton Joyce	d							16 24	16 23		17 27	17 27		18 25	18 24				21 33
Lowdham	d		14 40	14 41		15 39	15 40	16 29	16 29		17 32	17 33		18 30	18 30	19 40		20 40	21 37
Thurgarton	d							16 33	16 33		17 36	17 37		18 34	18 34				
Bleasby	d							16 36	16 36		17 39	17 40		18 37	18 37				21 42
Fiskerton	d							16 39	16 39		17 42	17 43		18 40	18 40				21 46
Rolleston	d							16 42	16 42		17 45	17 46		18 43	18 43				
Newark Castle	d		14 55	14 55		15 54	15 54	16 49	16 49		17 53	17 53		18 50	18 50	19e59		20 57	21 57
Newark North Gate 7	a																		22 06
	d	14 36			15 36								18 05				20 32		22 09
Collingham	d	14 44			15 45	16 03	16 03	16 58	16 58		18 02	18 02	18 14	18 59	18 59	20 08	20 41	21 05	22 18
Swinderby	d					16 07	16 07				18 07	18 07		19 04	19 04				22 22
Hykeham	d					16 13	16 13				18 13	18 13		19 10	19 10				22 28
Lincoln	a	15 00	15 22	15 23	16 03	16 25	16 25	17 14	17 15		18 26	18 27	18 33	19 22	19 23	20 26	20 56	21 24	22 40
	d	15 01								17 21			18 33				20 58		
Market Rasen	d	15 17								17 37			18 49				21a15		
Barnetby	a	15 33								17 53			19 05						
Habrough	a	15 42								18 02			19 14						
Grimsby Town	a	15 57								18 17			19 29						
Cleethorpes	a																		

Sundays
until 05 September

		EM	EM	EM	EM	EM	EM	EM	EM	EM	EM	EM	EM	EM
Nottingham 8	d			15 29		16 35		17 30	18 37		19 37	20 37		22 26
Carlton	d							17 36						22 32
Burton Joyce	d							17 39						22 35
Lowdham	d			15 39		16 45		17 43	18 47		19 47	20 47		22 40
Thurgarton	d							17 47						22 44
Bleasby	d							17 50						22 47
Fiskerton	d							17 54						22 50
Rolleston	d							17 56						22 52
Newark Castle	d			15 55		17 00		18 05	19 02		20 02	21 02		23 01
Newark North Gate 7	a								19 12					23 11
	d	11 35	13 35		16 37		17 56		19 17	19 55			22 00	23 15
Collingham	d	11 43	13 43	16 04	16 45	17 09		18 14	19 25		20 11	21 11	22 09	23 23
Swinderby	d				16 50	17 14		18 19	19 30		20 16	21 16		23 28
Hykeham	d				16 56	17 20		18 25	19 36		20 22	21 22		23 34
Lincoln	a	12 00	14 02	16 21	17 08	17 32	18 20	18 38	19 48	20 21	20 34	21 34	22 27	23 46
	d	12 02		16 23			18 22							
Market Rasen	d	12 18		16 39			18 38							
Barnetby	a	12 33		16 54			18 53							
Habrough	a	12 41		17 02			19 01							
Grimsby Town	a	12 53		17 14			19 13							
Cleethorpes	a	13 16		17 23			19 24							

Sundays
12 September to 17 October

		EM	EM	EM	EM	EM	EM	EM	EM
Nottingham 8	d								
Carlton	d								
Burton Joyce	d								
Lowdham	d								
Thurgarton	d								
Bleasby	d								
Fiskerton	d								
Rolleston	d								
Newark Castle	d								
Newark North Gate 7	a								
	d	11 35	13 35	17 01	18 06	19 17	20 03	21 03	23 15
Collingham	d	11 43	13 43	17 09	18 14	19 25	20 11	21 11	23 23
Swinderby	d			17 14	18 19	19 30	20 16	21 16	23 28
Hykeham	d			17 20	18 25	19 36	20 22	21 22	23 34
Lincoln	a	12 02	14 02	17 32	18 37	19 48	20 34	21 34	23 46
	d								
Market Rasen	d								
Barnetby	a								
Habrough	a								
Grimsby Town	a								
Cleethorpes	a								

A until 25 September
B from 2 October

For connections from London Kings Cross please refer to Table 26

Table 27

Sundays
from 24 October

Nottingham - Newark - Lincoln - Cleethorpes

		EM	EM	EM	EM	EM	EM	EM	EM
Nottingham 8 ⇌	d			16 35	17 30	18 37	19 37	20 37	22 26
Carlton	d				17 36				22 32
Burton Joyce	d				17 39				22 35
Lowdham	d			16 45	17 43	18 47	19 47	20 47	22 40
Thurgarton	d				17 47				22 44
Bleasby	d				17 50				22 47
Fiskerton	d				17 54				22 50
Rolleston	d				17 56				22 52
Newark Castle	d			17 00	18 05	19 02	20 02	21 02	23 01
Newark North Gate 7	a					19 12			23 11
	d	11 35	13 35			19 17			23 15
Collingham	d	11 43	13 43	17 09	18 14	19 25	20 11	21 11	23 23
Swinderby	d			17 14	18 19	19 30	20 16	21 16	23 28
Hykeham	d			17 20	18 25	19 36	20 22	21 22	23 34
Lincoln	a	12 02	14 02	17 32	18 38	19 48	20 34	21 34	23 46
	d								
Market Rasen	d								
Barnetby	a								
Habrough	a								
Grimsby Town	a								
Cleethorpes	a								

Table 29

Mondays to Fridays

Hull and Cleethorpes - Doncaster - Meadowhall, Sheffield, Manchester and Manchester Airport
Cleethorpes - Barton-on-Humber

		TP	NT	NT	NT	TP	EM	NT	NT	TP	NT	HT	TP	TP	XC	NT	NT
												BHX				BHX	
		◇1				◇1				◇1		◇1	◇1	◇1	◇1		
						⊼				⊼		⊠	⊼	⊼	⊼	🚌	
Hull	d				05 20					06 00	06 07	06 25		06 35			
Hessle	d										06 14						
Ferriby	d										06 19						
Brough	d				05 32					06 12	06 24	06 37		06 47			
Broomfleet	d																
Gilberdyke	d									06 19	06 31						
Eastrington	d																
Howden	d									06 26		06 49					
Wressle	d																
Selby	a									06 36		06 59		07 07			
	d								06 18	06 36		07 00		07 07			
York 8 33	a																
Saltmarshe	d										06 37						
Goole	d				05 47						06 42						
Thorne North	d				05 56						06 51						
Cleethorpes	d					05 18	05 49	06 00									
New Clee	d																
Grimsby Docks	d																
Grimsby Town	a					05 25	05 55	06 08									
	d					05 26	05 56	06 08									
Great Coates	d																
Healing	d							06 15									
Stallingborough	d							06 18									
Habrough	d					05 36	06 06	06 24									
Ulceby	d							06 28									
Thornton Abbey	d																
Goxhill	d							06 35									
New Holland	d							06 40									
Barrow Haven	d							06 43									
Barton-on-Humber	a							06 48									
Barton-on-Humber	d															06 53	
Hull Paragon Interchange	a															07 20	
Barnetby	d					05 45	06a15										
Scunthorpe	a					06 00											
	d					06 00											
Althorpe	d					06 05											
Crowle	d					06 11											
Thorne South	d					06 20											
Hatfield & Stainforth	d				06 03	06 25					06 57						
Kirk Sandall	d				06 10						07 01						
Adwick 31	d																
Bentley (S.Yorks) 31	d																
Doncaster 7 31	a				06 16	06 38			06 38		07 12	07 16					
London Kings Cross 15 ⊖26	a											09 17					
York 8 26	d												06 28				
Doncaster 7	d	05 40	06 00		06 25	06 39									06 45		07 02
Conisbrough	d		06 07		06 32												07 09
Mexborough	d		06 11		06 36												07 13
Swinton (S.Yorks)	d		06 14	06 22	06 39												07 16
Rotherham Central	d		06 22	06 31	06 46												07 27
Meadowhall ⇌	d	05 58	06 28	06 37	06 52	06 58											07 33
Sheffield 7 ⇌	a	06 08	06 38	06 47	07 07	07 06									07 11		07 40
	d	06 11				07 09											
Stockport 78	a	06 53				07 53											
Manchester Piccadilly 10 ⇌	a	07 02				08 02				08 05			07 51	08 36			
Manchester Airport 85 ✈	a	07 29				08 26							08 12				

Hull and Cleethorpes - Doncaster - Meadowhall, Sheffield, Manchester and Manchester Airport
Cleethorpes - Barton-on-Humber

		XC	NT	TP	EM	NT	NT	NT	GR	NT	XC	TP	XC	NT	NT	NT BHX	NT	TP	NT	XC	NT	NT	NT
		◇■ ✠		◇■ ✠					■ ■ A ✠		◇■ ✠	◇■ ✠	◇■ ✠			🚌		◇■ ✠		◇■ ✠			
Hull	d							06 40	07 00	07 07		07 33							07 36				08 04
Hessle	d							06 47											07 43				
Ferriby	d							06 52											07 48				
Brough	d							06 57	07 12	07 19		07 45							07 53				08 16
Broomfleet	d																		07 58				
Gilberdyke	d							07 04		07 26									08 03				
Eastrington	d									07 31													
Howden	d									07 35		07 56											
Wressle	d									07 40													
Selby	a								07 32	07 48		08 06											
	d								07 32	07 48		08 07											
York ■ 33	a									08 21													
Saltmarshe	d							07 10											08 08				
Goole	d							07 15											08 13				08 30
Thorne North	d							07 24											08 22				
Cleethorpes	d			06 18		07 00												07 18					
New Clee	d																						
Grimsby Docks	d					07 05																	
Grimsby Town	a			06 25		07 08												07 25					
	d			06 26	07 03	07 09												07 26					
Great Coates	d					07 13																	
Healing	d					07 16																	
Stallingborough	d					07 19																	
Habrough	d			06 36	07 13	07 25												07 36					
Ulceby	d					07 28																	
Thornton Abbey	d					07 33																	
Goxhill	d					07 36																	
New Holland	d					07 40																	
Barrow Haven	d					07 43																	
Barton-on-Humber	a					07 49																	
Barton-on-Humber	d															08 20							
Hull Paragon Interchange	a															08 52							
Barnetby	d			06 45	07a22													07 45					
Scunthorpe	a			07 00														08 00					
	d			07 00											07 34			08 00				08 10	
Althorpe	d														07 39							08 15	
Crowle	d														07 45							08 21	
Thorne South	d														07 53							08 30	
Hatfield & Stainforth	d							07 30							07 59				08 28			08 35	
Kirk Sandall	d							07 34							08 03				08 32			08 40	
Adwick 31	d						07 29							07 54							08 35		
Bentley (S.Yorks) 31	d						07 33							07 57							08 39		
Doncaster ■ 31	a			07 33			07 37	07 45	07 53					08 01	08 14			08 30	08 43		08 44	08 52	08 55
London Kings Cross ■ ⊖26	a								09 45														
York ■ 26	d	06 32									07 27		07 44							08 27			
Doncaster ■	d			07 35			07 39	07 46			07 52			08 13				08 42		08 51		09 01	08 56
Conisbrough	d						07 46	07 53						08 20								09 08	
Mexborough	d						07 50	07 57						08 24								09 12	
Swinton (S.Yorks)	d		07 29				07 53	08 00						08 30			08 34					09 15	
Rotherham Central	d		07 41				08 00	08 12						08 42			08 47					09 27	
Meadowhall 🚊	d		07 47	07 53			08 06	08 22						08 49			08 55	09 01				09 33	09 15
Sheffield ■ 🚊	a	07 50	07 57	08 00			08 18	08 32			08 18		08 51	08 58			09 05	09 08		09 20		09 41	09 26
	d			08 05														09 11					
Stockport 78	a			08 53														09 53					
Manchester Piccadilly ■ 🚊	a			09 02								09 36						10 02					
Manchester Airport 85 ✈	a			09 33														10 26					

A The Hull Executive

Hull and Cleethorpes - Doncaster - Meadowhall, Sheffield, Manchester and Manchester Airport
Cleethorpes - Barton-on-Humber

		HT	XC	TP	NT	NT	NT	TP	TP	NT	NT	NT	XC	NT	EM	XC	NT BHX	NT	NT	NT	TP
		◇■ ⊠	◇■ ✠	◇■ ✠				◇■ ✠	◇■ ✠				◇■ ✠			◇■ ✠	🚌				◇■ ✠
Hull	d	08 12					08 28		08 40	08 56		09 02								09 25	
Hessle	d						08 35													09 32	
Ferriby	d						08 40													09 37	
Brough	d	08 24					08 45		08 52	09 08		09 14								09 42	
Broomfleet	d																				
Gilberdyke	d						08 52					09 21								09 49	
Eastrington	d																				
Howden	d	08 36										09 28									
Wressle	d																				
Selby	a	08 44							09 10			09 38									
	d	08 45							09 11			09 38									
York ■ 33	a											10 11									
Saltmarshe	d																				
Goole	d						09 01			09 23										09 58	
Thorne North	d						09 09													10 06	
Cleethorpes	d							08 28			09 00										09 28
New Clee	d										09x03										
Grimsby Docks	d										09 05										
Grimsby Town	a							08 35			09 08										09 35
	d							08 36			09 08				09 28						09 36
Great Coates	d										09 12										
Healing	d										09 15										
Stallingborough	d										09 18										
Habrough	d							08 46			09 24				09 38						
Ulceby	d										09 28										
Thornton Abbey	d										09 32										
Goxhill	d										09 35										
New Holland	d										09 40										
Barrow Haven	d										09 43										
Barton-on-Humber	a										09 48										
Barton-on-Humber	d																10 00				
Hull Paragon Interchange	a																10 27				
Barnetby	d							08 55							09a47						09 55
Scunthorpe	a							09 10													10 10
	d							09 10						09 17							10 10
Althorpe	d													09 22							
Crowle	d													09 29							
Thorne South	d													09 37							
Hatfield & Stainforth	d						09 16							09 43						10 12	
Kirk Sandall	d						09 20							09 47						10 17	
Adwick 31	d					09 13													10 13		
Bentley (S.Yorks) 31	d					09 17													10 17		
Doncaster ■ 31	a	09 04				09 22	09 31	09 40		09 46				09 58					10 22	10 27	10 40
London Kings Cross ■ ⊖26	a	10 51																			
York ■ 26	d		08 45	09 28									09 27			09 44					
Doncaster ■	d					09 24		09 42		09 48			09 56	10 02					10 24		10 42
Conisbrough	d					09 31								10 09					10 31		
Mexborough	d					09 35								10 13					10 35		
Swinton (S.Yorks)	d				09 35	09 42								10 16				10 34	10 41		
Rotherham Central	d				09 44	09 50								10 27				10 44	10 49		
Meadowhall 🚊	d				09 50	09 55		10 01		10 07				10 33				10 50	10 57		11 01
Sheffield ■ 🚊	a		09 51		10 00	10 05		10 08		10 20			10 20	10 41		10 51		11 00	11 05		11 08
	d							10 11													11 11
Stockport 78	a							10 53													11 53
Manchester Piccadilly ■ 🚊	a			10 49				11 02	10 36												12 02
Manchester Airport 85 ✈	a			11 12				11 26													12 26

Hull and Cleethorpes - Doncaster - Meadowhall, Sheffield, Manchester and Manchester Airport
Cleethorpes - Barton-on-Humber

		TP	NT	XC	NT	HT	NT	TP	XC	NT	NT	TP	NT	NT	NT	XC	NT	NT	EM	XC	NT BHX	NT
		◇1		◇1		◇1		◇1	◇1			◇1				◇1				◇1		
		⊼		⊼		⊠		⊼	⊼			⊼				⊼				⊼	🚌	
Hull	d	09 40	09 56			10 12	10 22	10 38					10 57		11 05							
Hessle	d						10 29															
Ferriby	d						10 34															
Brough	d	09 52	10 08			10 24	10 39	10 50					11 09		11 17							
Broomfleet	d																					
Gilberdyke	d						10 46															
Eastrington	d																					
Howden	d					10 36									11 29							
Wressle	d																					
Selby	a	10 10				10 46		11 08							11 39							
	d	10 11				10 47		11 09							11 39							
York 8 33	a														12 09							
Saltmarshe	d																					
Goole	d		10 22				10 55						11 23									
Thorne North	d						11 03															
Cleethorpes	d											10 28		11 00								
New Clee	d													11x03								
Grimsby Docks	d													11 05								
Grimsby Town	a											10 35		11 08								
	d											10 36		11 08					11 28			
Great Coates	d													11 12								
Healing	d													11 15								
Stallingborough	d													11 18								
Habrough	d											10 46		11 24					11 38			
Ulceby	d													11 28								
Thornton Abbey	d													11 32								
Goxhill	d													11 35								
New Holland	d													11 40								
Barrow Haven	d													11 43								
Barton-on-Humber	a													11 48								
Barton-on-Humber	d																				12 00	
Hull Paragon Interchange	a																				12 27	
Barnetby	d											10 55							11a47			
Scunthorpe	a											11 10										
	d				10 18							11 10						11 17				
Althorpe	d				10 23													11 22				
Crowle	d				10 29													11 28				
Thorne South	d				10 38													11 37				
Hatfield & Stainforth	d				10 43		11 09											11 42				
Kirk Sandall	d				10 48		11 14											11 47				
Adwick 31	d										11 16											
Bentley (S.Yorks) 31	d										11 20											
Doncaster 7 31	a		10 46		10 58	11 04	11 23				11 25	11 40	11 46					11 58				
London Kings Cross 15 ⊖26	a					12 47																
York 8 26	d			10 34					10 44							11 27	11 01			11 45		
Doncaster 7	d		10 48	10 58	11 02						11 27	11 42	11 48			11 54		11 59				
Conisbrough	d				11 09						11 34							12 06				
Mexborough	d				11 13						11 38							12 10				
Swinton (S.Yorks)	d				11 16					11 34	11 41						12 02	12 16				12 34
Rotherham Central	d				11 27					11 45	11 50						12 11	12 27				12 45
Meadowhall 🚊	d		11 06		11 33					11 50	11 55	12 01	12 06				12 16	12 33				12 50
Sheffield 7 🚊	a		11 20	11 20	11 41				11 51	12 00	12 05	12 08	12 19			12 20	12 26	12 41		12 51		13 00
	d											1211										
Stockport 78	a											12 53										
Manchester Piccadilly 10 🚊	a	11 36						12 36				13 02										
Manchester Airport 85 ✈	a											13 26										

Hull and Cleethorpes - Doncaster - Meadowhall, Sheffield, Manchester and Manchester Airport
Cleethorpes - Barton-on-Humber

		NT	NT	TP	TP	NT	XC	NT	XC	NT	NT	NT	TP	HT	TP	NT	NT	NT	XC	NT	XC
				◇1	◇1		◇1		◇1				◇1	◇1	◇1				◇1		◇1
				⊼	⊼		⊼		⊼				⊼	⊠	⊼				⊼		⊼
Hull	d		11 22		11 38	11 55						12 22	12 38	12 45		12 57		13 12			
Hessle	d		11 29									12 29									
Ferriby	d		11 34									12 34									
Brough	d		11 39		11 50	12 07						12 39	12 50	12 57		13 09		13 24			
Broomfleet	d											12 44									
Gilberdyke	d		11 46									12 49						13 31			
Eastrington	d																	13 36			
Howden	d													13 09				13 40			
Wressle	d																	13 46			
Selby	a				12 08								13 08	13 19				13 54			
	d				12 09								13 09	13 20				13 54			
York 8 33	a																	14 25			
Saltmarshe	d		11 52																		
Goole	d		11 58			12 22						12 58				13 23					
Thorne North	d		12 06									13 06									
Cleethorpes	d			11 28											12 28		13 00				
New Clee	d																13x03				
Grimsby Docks	d																13 05				
Grimsby Town	a			11 35											12 35		13 08				
	d			11 36											12 36		13 08				
Great Coates	d																13 12				
Healing	d																13 15				
Stallingborough	d																13 18				
Habrough	d																13 24				
Ulceby	d																13 28				
Thornton Abbey	d																13 32				
Goxhill	d																13 35				
New Holland	d																13 40				
Barrow Haven	d																13 43				
Barton-on-Humber	a																13 48				
Barton-on-Humber	d																				
Hull Paragon Interchange	a																				
Barnetby	d			11 55											12 55						
Scunthorpe	a			12 10											13 10						
	d			12 10				12 17							13 10					13 18	
Althorpe	d							12 22												13 23	
Crowle	d							12 28												13 29	
Thorne South	d							12 37												13 38	
Hatfield & Stainforth	d		12 12					12 42				13 12								13 43	
Kirk Sandall	d		12 17					12 47				13 17								13 48	
Adwick 31	d	12 12									13 12										
Bentley (S.Yorks) 31	d	12 16									13 16										
Doncaster 7 31	a	12 24	12 27	12 40		12 46		12 59			13 23	13 29		13 37	13 40	13 46				13 58	
London Kings Cross 15 ⊖26	a													15 20							
York 8 26	d						12 27		12 45										13 26		13 44
Doncaster 7	d	12 25		12 42		12 48	12 55	12 59			13 23				13 42	13 48			13 55	14 01	
Conisbrough	d	12 32						13 09			13 31									14 09	
Mexborough	d	12 36						13 13			13 35									14 13	
Swinton (S.Yorks)	d	12 42						13 16		13 34	13 41									14 16	
Rotherham Central	d	12 50						13 27		13 45	13 50									14 27	
Meadowhall 🚊	d	12 55		13 01		13 06		13 33		13 50	13 55				14 01	14 06				14 33	
Sheffield 7 🚊	a	13 05		13 08		13 20	13 20	13 41	13 51	14 00	14 05				14 08	14 20			14 20	14 41	14 51
	d			13 11											14 11						
Stockport 78	a			13 53											14 53						
Manchester Piccadilly 10 🚊	a			14 02	13 36								14 36		15 02						
Manchester Airport 85 ✈	a			14 26											15 26						

Table 29

Mondays to Fridays

Hull and Cleethorpes - Doncaster - Meadowhall, Sheffield, Manchester and Manchester Airport Cleethorpes - Barton-on-Humber

		NT BHX	NT	NT	NT	TP	TP	EM	NT	XC		NT	XC	NT	NT	NT	TP	TP	NT	NT		NT	XC	NT	NT
						◇1	◇1			◇1			◇1				◇1	◇1					◇1		
		🚌				🛒	🛒			🛒			🛒				🛒	🛒					🛒		
Hull	d				13 25		13 38		13 57							14 25		14 38	14 56			15 02			
Hessle	d				13 32											14 32									
Ferriby	d				13 37											14 37									
Brough	d				13 42		13 50		14 09							14 42		14 50	15 08			15 14			
Broomfleet	d																								
Gilberdyke	d				13 49											14 49						15 22			
Eastrington	d																								
Howden	d																					15 28			
Wressle	d																								
Selby	a						14 08											15 08				15 38			
	d						14 09											15 09				15 38			
York 8 33	a																					16 05			
Saltmarshe	d																								
Goole	d				13 58				14 23							14 58			15 23						
Thorne North	d				14 06											15 06									
Cleethorpes	d					13 28											14 28			15 00					
New Clee	d																			15x03					
Grimsby Docks	d																			15 05					
Grimsby Town	a					13 35											14 35			15 08					
	d					13 36		13 52									14 36			15 08					
Great Coates	d																			15 12					
Healing	d																			15 15					
Stallingborough	d																			15 18					
Habrough	d							14 02									14 46			15 24					
Ulceby	d																			15 28					
Thornton Abbey	d																			15 32					
Goxhill	d																			15 35					
New Holland	d																			15 40					
Barrow Haven	d																			15 43					
Barton-on-Humber	a																			15 48					
Barton-on-Humber	d	14 00																							
Hull Paragon Interchange	a	14 27																							
Barnetby	d					13 55		14a11									14 55								
Scunthorpe	a					14 10											15 10								
	d					14 10						14 18					15 10								15 17
Althorpe	d											14 23													15 22
Crowle	d											14 29													15 28
Thorne South	d											14 38													15 37
Hatfield & Stainforth	d				14 12							14 43				15 12									15 42
Kirk Sandall	d				14 17							14 48				15 17									15 47
Adwick 31	d			14 14											15 13										
Bentley (S.Yorks) 31	d			14 18											15 17										
Doncaster 7 31	a			14 22	14 29	14 40			14 46			14 58			15 22	15 27	15 40		15 46						15 58
London Kings Cross 15 ⊖26	a																								
York 8 26	d									14 32			14 44										15 29	15 02	
Doncaster 7	d			14 24		14 42			14 48	14 57		15 02			15 24		15 42		15 48				15 55		16 02
Conisbrough	d			14 31								15 10			15 31										16 09
Mexborough	d			14 35								15 14			15 35										16 13
Swinton (S.Yorks)	d		14 34	14 41								15 17		15 34	15 41									16 01	16 16
Rotherham Central	d		14 45	14 50								15 27		15 43	15 50									16 10	16 27
Meadowhall 🚋	d		14 50	14 55		15 01			15 06			15 33		15 50	15 55		16 01		16 07					16 18	16 33
Sheffield 7 🚋	a		15 00	15 05		15 08			15 19	15 20		15 41	15 51	16 00	16 05		16 08		16 20				16 20	16 25	16 41
	d					15 11											16 10								
Stockport 78	a					15 53											16 53								
Manchester Piccadilly 10 🚋	a					16 02	15 36										17 02	16 36							
Manchester Airport 85 ✈	a					16 26											17 32								

Table 29

Mondays to Fridays

Hull and Cleethorpes - Doncaster - Meadowhall, Sheffield, Manchester and Manchester Airport Cleethorpes - Barton-on-Humber

		HT	XC	TP FO	NT BHX	NT		NT	NT	TP	TP	NT	EM	NT	XC	NT	NT	TP	XC	NT	NT		TP		NT
		◇1	◇1	◇1						◇1	◇1				◇1			◇1	◇1				◇1		
					🚌																				
		⊠	🛒	🛒						🛒	🛒				🛒			🛒	🛒				🛒		
Hull	d	15 18							15 25		15 38	15 57		16 10			16 27	16 40							16 54
Hessle	d								15 32								16 34								
Ferriby	d								15 37								16 39								
Brough	d	15 30							15 42		15 50	16 09		16 22			16 44	16 52							17 06
Broomfleet	d																16 49								
Gilberdyke	d								15 49					16 29			16 54								17 13
Eastrington	d																								
Howden	d	15 42												16 36											
Wressle	d																								
Selby	a	15 56									16 08			16 46				17 10							
	d	15 57									16 09			16 47				17 11							
York 8 33	a													17 13											
Saltmarshe	d																16 59								
Goole	d								15 58			16 23					17 04								17 22
Thorne North	d								16 06								17 13								
Cleethorpes	d									15 28													16 28		
New Clee	d																								
Grimsby Docks	d																								
Grimsby Town	a									15 35													16 35		
	d									15 36			16 03										16 36		
Great Coates	d																								
Healing	d																								
Stallingborough	d																								
Habrough	d												16 12												
Ulceby	d																								
Thornton Abbey	d																								
Goxhill	d																								
New Holland	d																								
Barrow Haven	d																								
Barton-on-Humber	a																								
Barton-on-Humber	d				16 00																				
Hull Paragon Interchange	a				16 27																				
Barnetby	d									15 55			16a21										16 55		
Scunthorpe	a									16 10													17 10		
	d									16 10						16 18							17 10		
Althorpe	d															16 23									
Crowle	d															16 29									
Thorne South	d															16 38									
Hatfield & Stainforth	d								16 12							16 43	17 19								
Kirk Sandall	d								16 17							16 48	17 23								
Adwick 31	d							16 13																	
Bentley (S.Yorks) 31	d							16 17																	
Doncaster 7 31	a	16 15						16 23	16 27	16 40		16 46				17 00	17 34						17 40		17 47
London Kings Cross 15 ⊖26	a	18 13																							
York 8 26	d		15 44	15 58											16 25				16 44						
Doncaster 7	d							16 24		16 42		16 47			16 53	17 02					17 24		17 42		17 48
Conisbrough	d							16 31								17 09					17 31				
Mexborough	d							16 35								17 13					17 35				
Swinton (S.Yorks)	d					16 34		16 41								17 16				17 34	17 42				
Rotherham Central	d					16 43		16 50								17 27				17 44	17 50				
Meadowhall 🚋	d					16 50		16 55		17 01		17 06				17 33				17 50	17 57		18 01		18 06
Sheffield 7 🚋	a		16 51			17 00		17 05		17 08		17 19			17 18	17 41			17 51	18 00	18 04		18 08		18 19
	d									17 11													18 10		
Stockport 78	a									17 53													18 53		
Manchester Piccadilly 10 🚋	a			17 25						18 02	17 37							18 37					19 02		
Manchester Airport 85 ✈	a									18 26													19b28		

b Fridays 2 July to 3 September arr. 1933

Hull and Cleethorpes - Doncaster - Meadowhall, Sheffield, Manchester and Manchester Airport Cleethorpes - Barton-on-Humber

		NT		TP	XC	NT	HT	NT	XC	NT	NT BHX	NT		NT	TP	NT	TP	XC	NT	NT	NT	EM		XC	NT
				◇1	◇1 ⌶		◇1 ⊠		◇1 ⌶		🚌				◇1 ⌶		◇1 ⌶	◇1 ⌶						◇1 ⌶	
Hull	d			17 01			17 06	17 18		17 42						17 52	17 58				18 22				
Hessle	d							17 25		17 49											18 29				
Ferriby	d							17 30		17 54											18 34				
Brough	d			17 13			17 19	17 35		17 59						18 04	18 10				18 39				
Broomfleet	d							17 40																	
Gilberdyke	d							17 45		18 06											18 47				
Eastrington	d							17 49																	
Howden	d						17 32	17 54																	
Wressle	d							17 58																	
Selby	a			17 31			17 42	18 06								18 25	18 29								
	d			17 32			17 43	18 06								18 26	18 29								
York 8 33	a							18 36																	
Saltmarshe	d									18 12															
Goole	d									18 19											18 55				
Thorne North	d									18 28											19 04				
Cleethorpes	d	17 00													17 28										
New Clee	d																								
Grimsby Docks	d	17 05																							
Grimsby Town	a	17 08													17 35										
	d	17 09													17 36							18 28			
Great Coates	d	17 13																							
Healing	d	17 16																							
Stallingborough	d	17 19																							
Habrough	d	17 25													17 46							18 38			
Ulceby	d	17 28																							
Thornton Abbey	d	17 33																							
Goxhill	d	17 36																							
New Holland	d	17 40																							
Barrow Haven	d	17 43																							
Barton-on-Humber	a	17 49																							
Barton-on-Humber	d										18 00														
Hull Paragon Interchange	a										18 27														
Barnetby	d														17 55							18a49			
Scunthorpe	a														18 10										
	d					17 18									18 10					18 18					
Althorpe	d					17 23														18 23					
Crowle	d					17 29														18 29					
Thorne South	d					17 38														18 38					
Hatfield & Stainforth	d					17 43				18 34										18 46	19 12				
Kirk Sandall	d					17 48				18 39										18 50	19 16				
Adwick 31	d																								
Bentley (S.Yorks) 31	d																		←						
Doncaster 7 31	a					17 59	18 01			18 51					18 40	18 45			18 51	19 04	19 27				
London Kings Cross 15 ⊖26	a						19 49																		
York 8 26	d				17 34				17 44									18 24						18 44	
Doncaster 7	d				17 58	18 02								18 26	18 42	18 47		18 52	18 55						
Conisbrough	d					18 09				→				18 33					19 02						
Mexborough	d					18 13								18 37					19 06						
Swinton (S.Yorks)	d					18 16						18 34		18 42					19 09						19 34
Rotherham Central	d					18 27						18 45		18 49					19 19						19 45
Meadowhall 🚋	d					18 33						18 50		18 57	19 01	19 06			19 25						19 50
Sheffield 7 🚋	a				18 20	18 43			18 51			19 00		19 06	19 08	19 17		19 20	19 35					19 51	20 00
	d														19 11										
Stockport 78	a														19 53										
Manchester Piccadilly 10 🚋	a														20 02		19 57								
Manchester Airport 85 ✈	a														20 37										

Hull and Cleethorpes - Doncaster - Meadowhall, Sheffield, Manchester and Manchester Airport Cleethorpes - Barton-on-Humber

		NT	TP		NT	TP	NT	NT		NT	HT BHX	XC	NT	NT BHX	NT	XC	NT	TP		NT	XC	NT	TP FO	XC	TP FX
			◇1 ⌶			◇1					◇1 ⊠	◇1 ⌶		🚌		◇1		◇1			◇1		◇1	◇1	◇1
Hull	d				18 53	18 59		19 10			19 18		19 25									20 03	20 35		20 45
Hessle	d												19 32									20 10			
Ferriby	d												19 37									20 15			
Brough	d				19 05	19 11		19 22			19 30		19 42									20 20	20 47		20 57
Broomfleet	d																								
Gilberdyke	d							19 29					19 49									20 27			
Eastrington	d																								
Howden	d							19 36			19 43														
Wressle	d																								
Selby	a					19 29		19 46			19 52												21 06		21 16
	d					19 30		19 47			19 53												21 06		21 16
York 8 33	a							20 16																	
Saltmarshe	d																								
Goole	d				19 19								19 58									20 36			
Thorne North	d												20 06									20 44			
Cleethorpes	d		18 28				19 00											19 28							
New Clee	d																								
Grimsby Docks	d						19 05																		
Grimsby Town	a		18 35				19 08											19 35							
	d		18 36				19 09											19 36							
Great Coates	d						19 13																		
Healing	d						19 16																		
Stallingborough	d						19 19																		
Habrough	d		18 46				19 25											19 46							
Ulceby	d						19 28																		
Thornton Abbey	d						19 33																		
Goxhill	d						19 36																		
New Holland	d						19 40																		
Barrow Haven	d						19 43																		
Barton-on-Humber	a						19 49																		
Barton-on-Humber	d													19 53											
Hull Paragon Interchange	a													20 20											
Barnetby	d		18 55															19 55							
Scunthorpe	a		19 10															20 10							
	d		19 10							19 18								20 10		20 21					
Althorpe	d									19 23										20 26					
Crowle	d									19 29										20 32					
Thorne South	d									19 38										20 41					
Hatfield & Stainforth	d									19 43			20 14							20 46		20 51			
Kirk Sandall	d									19 48			20 19							20 51		20 56			
Adwick 31	d																								
Bentley (S.Yorks) 31	d																								
Doncaster 7 31	a		19 40		19 46					19 59	20 10		20 30					20 40		21 01		21 05			
London Kings Cross 15 ⊖26	a										21 58														
York 8 26	d											19 29				19 44					20 32			20 44	
Doncaster 7	d	19 28	19 42		19 49							19 57			20 03			20 42			20 57	21 07			
Conisbrough	d	19 35													20 10			20 48				21 14			
Mexborough	d	19 39													20 14			20 52				21 18			
Swinton (S.Yorks)	d	19 43													20 17		20 34	20 55				21 21			
Rotherham Central	d	19 50													20 28		20 43	21 01				21 29			
Meadowhall 🚋	d	19 57	20 01		20 07										20 33		20 51	21 07				21 36			
Sheffield 7 🚋	a	20 06	20 08		20 18							20 20			20 41	20 51	21 02	21 19			21 24	21 47		21 51	
	d		20 11																						
Stockport 78	a		20 53																						
Manchester Piccadilly 10 🚋	a		21 02																				22 33		
Manchester Airport 85 ✈	a		21 36																				22 57		

Table 29

Mondays to Fridays

Hull and Cleethorpes - Doncaster - Meadowhall, Sheffield, Manchester and Manchester Airport Cleethorpes - Barton-on-Humber

		NT	TP ◇1	NT	EM	NT	NT	TP ◇1	NT	NT	NT (bus)	NT	NT	NT	NT
Hull	d						20 56	21 33						22 20	
Hessle	d													22 27	
Ferriby	d													22 32	
Brough	d						21 08	21 45						22 37	
Broomfleet	d														
Gilberdyke	d							21 52							
Eastrington	d														
Howden	d														
Wressle	d														
Selby	a							22 07							
	d							22 07							
York 8 33	a														
Saltmarshe	d														
Goole	d						21 22		21 35					22 51	
Thorne North	d								21 44					23 00	
Cleethorpes	d		20 28	21 00	21 15										
New Clee	d														
Grimsby Docks	d			21 05											
Grimsby Town	a		20 35	21 08	21 21										
	d		20 36	21 08	21 22										
Great Coates	d			21 12											
Healing	d			21 15											
Stallingborough	d			21 18											
Habrough	d			21 24	21 31										
Ulceby	d			21 28											
Thornton Abbey	d			21 32											
Goxhill	d			21 35											
New Holland	d			21 40											
Barrow Haven	d			21 43											
Barton-on-Humber	a			21 48											
Barton-on-Humber	d										21 53				
Hull Paragon Interchange	a										22 20				
Barnetby	d		20 55		21a40										
Scunthorpe	a		21 10												
	d		21 10							21 31		22 21			
Althorpe	d									21 36		22 26			
Crowle	d									21 42		22 32			
Thorne South	d									21 51		22 41			
Hatfield & Stainforth	d								21 50	21 56		22 46		23 06	
Kirk Sandall	d								21 54	22 01		22 51		23 10	
Adwick 31	d														
Bentley (S.Yorks) 31	d														
Doncaster 7 31	a		21 40				21 45		22 07	22 11		23 03		23 21	
London Kings Cross 15 ⊖26	a														
York 8 26	d														
Doncaster 7	d		21 42			21 30	21 48			22 13				23 22	
Conisbrough	d					21 37				22 20				23 29	
Mexborough	d					21 41				22 24				23 33	
Swinton (S.Yorks)	d	21 35				21 44				22 27			22 34	23 36	23 55
Rotherham Central	d	21 44				21 55				22 38			22 46	23 45	00 03
Meadowhall ⇌	d	21 52	21 58			22 03	22 09			22 44			22 52	23 54	00 08
Sheffield 7 ⇌	a	22 05	22 08			22 11	22 21			22 54			23 02	00 04	00 22
	d		22 11												
Stockport 78	a		22 53												
Manchester Piccadilly 10 ⇌	a		23 02					23 37							
Manchester Airport 85 ✈	a		23 26												

Table 29

Saturdays

Hull and Cleethorpes - Doncaster - Meadowhall, Sheffield, Manchester and Manchester Airport Cleethorpes - Barton-on-Humber

		TP ◇1	NT	NT	NT	TP ◇1 ⌶	TP ◇1 ⌶	NT	NT	TP ◇1	TP ◇1	NT	XC ◇1 ⌶	NT	XC ◇1 ⌶	NT	TP ◇1 ⌶	EM
Hull	d			05 20			06 00		06 07		06 35	06 40						
Hessle	d								06 14			06 47						
Ferriby	d								06 19			06 52						
Brough	d			05 32			06 12		06 24		06 47	06 57						
Broomfleet	d																	
Gilberdyke	d						06 19		06 31			07 04						
Eastrington	d																	
Howden	d						06 26											
Wressle	d																	
Selby	a						06 36				07 07							
	d				06 15		06 36				07 07							
York 8 33	a																	
Saltmarshe	d								06 37			07 10						
Goole	d			05 47					06 42			07 15						
Thorne North	d			05 56					06 51			07 24						
Cleethorpes	d					05 18		06 00									06 18	
New Clee	d																	
Grimsby Docks	d																	
Grimsby Town	a					05 25		06 08									06 25	
	d					05 26		06 08									06 26	07 03
Great Coates	d																	
Healing	d							06 15										
Stallingborough	d							06 18										
Habrough	d					05 36		06 24									06 36	07 13
Ulceby	d							06 28										
Thornton Abbey	d																	
Goxhill	d							06 35										
New Holland	d							06 40										
Barrow Haven	d							06 43										
Barton-on-Humber	a							06 48										
Barton-on-Humber	d																	
Hull Paragon Interchange	a																	
Barnetby	d					05 45											06 45	07a22
Scunthorpe	a					06 00											07 00	
	d					06 00											07 00	
Althorpe	d					06 05												
Crowle	d					06 11												
Thorne South	d					06 20												
Hatfield & Stainforth	d			06 03		06 25			06 57			07 30						
Kirk Sandall	d			06 10					07 01			07 34						
Adwick 31	d																	
Bentley (S.Yorks) 31	d																	
Doncaster 7 31	a			06 16	06 36	06 38			07 12			07 45					07 33	
London Kings Cross 15 ⊖26	a																	
York 8 26	d									06 28					06 09			
Doncaster 7	d	05 40	06 00	06 25		06 39						→	06 47	07 02			07 35	
Conisbrough	d		06 07	06 32										07 09				
Mexborough	d		06 11	06 36										07 13				
Swinton (S.Yorks)	d		06 14	06 39										07 16		07 29		
Rotherham Central	d		06 22	06 46										07 27		07 41		
Meadowhall ⇌	d	05 58	06 27	06 52		06 58								07 33		07 47	07 53	
Sheffield 7 ⇌	a	06 08	06 38	07 07		07 06							07 15	07 45	07 51	07 57	08 00	
	d	06 11				07 09											08 05	
Stockport 78	a	06 53				07 53											08 53	
Manchester Piccadilly 10 ⇌	a	07 02				08 02	08 05			07 51	08 36						09 02	
Manchester Airport 85 ✈	a	07 29				08 26				08 12							09 26	

Table 29

Hull and Cleethorpes - Doncaster - Meadowhall, Sheffield, Manchester and Manchester Airport Cleethorpes - Barton-on-Humber

	NT	NT	GR	NT	NT	XC	TP	NT	XC	NT	NT	NT	TP	NT	HT	XC	NT	NT	NT	HT	XC	TP
			8 1 🍴			◇1 🍴	◇1 🍴		◇1 🍴		🚌		◇1 🍴		◇1 ⊠	◇1 🍴				◇1 ⊠	◇1 🍴	◇1 🍴
Hull d			06 50		06 57		07 33							07 36	08 02				08 08			
Hessle d														07 43								
Ferriby d														07 48								
Brough d			07 02		07 09		07 45							07 53	08 14				08 20			
Broomfleet d														07 58								
Gilberdyke d					07 17									08 03								
Eastrington d					07 21																	
Howden d					07 26		07 56								08 26							
Wressle d					07 31																	
Selby a			07 23		07 40		08 06								08 36							
d			07 23		07 40		08 07								08 37							
York 8 33 a					08 15																	
Saltmarshe d														08 08								
Goole d														08 13					08 34			
Thorne North d														08 22								
Cleethorpes d	07 00												07 18									
New Clee d																						
Grimsby Docks d	07 05																					
Grimsby Town a	07 08												07 25									
d	07 09												07 26									
Great Coates d	07 13																					
Healing d	07 16																					
Stallingborough d	07 19																					
Habrough d	07 25												07 36									
Ulceby d	07 28																					
Thornton Abbey d	07 33																					
Goxhill d	07 36																					
New Holland d	07 40																					
Barrow Haven d	07 43																					
Barton-on-Humber a	07 49																					
Barton-on-Humber d											08 20											
Hull Paragon Interchange a											08 52											
Barnetby d													07 45									
Scunthorpe a													08 00									
d								07 34					08 00					08 10				
Althorpe d								07 39										08 15				
Crowle d								07 45										08 21				
Thorne South d								07 53										08 30				
Hatfield & Stainforth d								07 59						08 28				08 35				
Kirk Sandall d								08 03						08 32				08 40				
Adwick 31 d		07 29								08 07							08 35					
Bentley (S.Yorks) 31 d		07 33		←						08 11							08 39			←		
Doncaster 7 31 a		07 37	07 40	07 45				08 14		08 15			08 30	08 43	09 00		08 44	08 52	08 57	09 00		
London Kings Cross 15 ⊖26 a			09 25												→					10 52		
York 8 26 d						07 25			07 44							08 27					08 44	09 28
Doncaster 7 d		07 39		07 46		07 52				08 17			08 41			08 53		09 01	08 59			
Conisbrough d		07 46		07 53						08 24								09 08				
Mexborough d		07 50		07 57						08 28								09 12				
Swinton (S.Yorks) d		07 53		08 00						08 31		08 34						09 15				
Rotherham Central d		08 00		08 12						08 41		08 47						09 27				
Meadowhall ⇌ d		08 06		08 22						08 49		08 55	09 01					09 33	09 19			
Sheffield 7 ⇌ a		08 18		08 32		08 18			08 51	08 58		09 05	09 08			09 20		09 41	09 28		09 51	
d													09 11									
Stockport 78 a													09 53									
Manchester Piccadilly 10 ⇌ a							09 36						10 02									10 49
Manchester Airport 85 ✈ a													10 26									11 12

Table 29

Hull and Cleethorpes - Doncaster - Meadowhall, Sheffield, Manchester and Manchester Airport Cleethorpes - Barton-on-Humber

	NT	NT	NT	TP	TP	NT	NT	NT	XC	NT	EM	XC	NT	NT	NT	NT	TP	TP	NT	XC	NT
				◇1 🍴	◇1 🍴				◇1 🍴			◇1 🍴	🚌				◇1 🍴	◇1		◇1 🍴	
Hull d			08 28		08 40	08 56		09 02								09 25		09 40	09 56		
Hessle d			08 35													09 32					
Ferriby d			08 40													09 37					
Brough d			08 45		08 52	09 08		09 14								09 42		09 52	10 08		
Broomfleet d																					
Gilberdyke d			08 52					09 21								09 49					
Eastrington d																					
Howden d								09 28													
Wressle d																					
Selby a					09 10			09 38										10 10			
d					09 11			09 38										10 11			
York 8 33 a								10 10													
Saltmarshe d																					
Goole d			09 01			09 23										09 58			10 22		
Thorne North d			09 09													10 06					
Cleethorpes d				08 28			09 00										09 28				
New Clee d							09x03														
Grimsby Docks d							09 05														
Grimsby Town a				08 35			09 08										09 35				
d				08 36			09 08				09 28						09 36				
Great Coates d							09 12														
Healing d							09 15														
Stallingborough d							09 18														
Habrough d				08 46			09 24				09 38										
Ulceby d							09 28														
Thornton Abbey d							09 32														
Goxhill d							09 35														
New Holland d							09 40														
Barrow Haven d							09 43														
Barton-on-Humber a							09 48														
Barton-on-Humber d													10 00								
Hull Paragon Interchange a													10 27								
Barnetby d				08 55							09a47						09 55				
Scunthorpe a				09 10													10 10				
d				09 10						09 17							10 10				10 18
Althorpe d										09 22											10 23
Crowle d										09 29											10 29
Thorne South d										09 37											10 38
Hatfield & Stainforth d			09 15							09 43						10 12					10 43
Kirk Sandall d			09 20							09 47						10 17					10 48
Adwick 31 d		09 13													10 10						
Bentley (S.Yorks) 31 d		09 17													10 14						
Doncaster 7 31 a		09 22	09 31	09 40		09 46				09 58					10 19	10 27	10 40		10 46		10 58
London Kings Cross 15 ⊖26 a																					
York 8 26 d									09 28			09 44								10 25	
Doncaster 7 d		09 24		09 42		09 48			09 53	10 02					10 23		10 42		10 48	10 53	11 02
Conisbrough d		09 31								10 09					10 31						11 09
Mexborough d		09 35								10 13					10 35						11 13
Swinton (S.Yorks) d	09 35	09 42								10 16				10 34	10 41						11 16
Rotherham Central d	09 44	09 50								10 27				10 44	10 50						11 27
Meadowhall ⇌ d	09 50	09 55		10 01		10 07				10 33				10 50	10 57		11 01		11 06		11 33
Sheffield 7 ⇌ a	10 00	10 05		10 08		10 20			10 20	10 41		10 51		11 00	11 06		11 08		11 20	11 20	11 41
d				10 11													11 11				
Stockport 78 a				10 53													11 53				
Manchester Piccadilly 10 ⇌ a				11 02	10 36												12 02	11 36			
Manchester Airport 85 ✈ a				11 26													12 26				

Table 29

Saturdays

Hull and Cleethorpes - Doncaster - Meadowhall, Sheffield, Manchester and Manchester Airport
Cleethorpes - Barton-on-Humber

		HT	XC	NT	NT	NT	TP	TP	NT	NT	NT	NT	XC	NT	NT	EM	XC	NT	NT	NT	NT	TP	TP
		◇1 ⊠	◇1 🛒				◇1 🛒	◇1					◇1 🛒				◇1 🛒	🚌				◇1 🛒	◇1 🛒
Hull	d	10 06				10 22		10 38	10 57		11 05										11 22		11 38
Hessle	d					10 29															11 29		
Ferriby	d					10 34															11 34		
Brough	d	10 18				10 39		10 50	11 09		11 17										11 39		11 50
Broomfleet	d																						
Gilberdyke	d					10 46															11 46		
Eastrington	d																						
Howden	d	10 30									11 29												
Wressle	d																						
Selby	a	10 40						11 08			11 39												12 08
	d	10 41						11 09			11 39												12 09
York 8 33	a										12 09												
Saltmarshe	d																				11 52		
Goole	d					10 55			11 23												11 58		
Thorne North	d					11 03															12 06		
Cleethorpes	d						10 28			11 00		11 13										11 28	
New Clee	d									11x03													
Grimsby Docks	d									11 05													
Grimsby Town	a						10 35			11 08		11 20										11 35	
	d						10 36			11 08		11 21				11 28						11 36	
Great Coates	d									11 12													
Healing	d									11 15													
Stallingborough	d									11 18													
Habrough	d						10 46			11 24		11 31				11 38							
Ulceby	d									11 28													
Thornton Abbey	d									11 32													
Goxhill	d									11 35													
New Holland	d									11 40													
Barrow Haven	d									11 43													
Barton-on-Humber	a									11 48													
Barton-on-Humber	d																	12 00					
Hull Paragon Interchange	a																	12 27					
Barnetby	d						10 55					11 40				11a47						11 55	
Scunthorpe	a						11 10															12 10	
	d						11 10								11 17							12 10	
Althorpe	d														11 22								
Crowle	d														11 28								
Thorne South	d														11 37								
Hatfield & Stainforth	d					11 08									11 42						12 12		
Kirk Sandall	d					11 14									11 47						12 17		
Adwick 31	d				11 08															12 12			
Bentley (S.Yorks) 31	d				11 12															12 16			
Doncaster 7 31	a	11 01			11 19	11 25	11 40		11 46						11 59					12 22	12 27	12 40	
London Kings Cross 15 ⊖26	a	12 52																					
York 8 26	d		10 45										11 27	11 01			11 45						
Doncaster 7	d				11 24		11 42		11 48				11 55		12 02					12 24		12 42	
Conisbrough	d				11 32										12 09					12 31			
Mexborough	d				11 36										12 13					12 35			
Swinton (S.Yorks)	d			11 34	11 41									12 01	12 16				12 34	12 42			
Rotherham Central	d			11 45	11 55									12 11	12 27				12 45	12 50			
Meadowhall 🚋	d			11 50	12 00		11 59		12 06					12 16	12 33				12 50	12 55		13 01	
Sheffield 7 🚋	a		11 51	12 00	12 10		12 08		12 20			13 23	12 20	12 25	12 41		12 51		13 00	13 05		13 08	
	d						12 11															13 11	
Stockport 78	a						12 53															13 53	
Manchester Piccadilly 10 🚋	a						13 02	12 36														14 02	13 36
Manchester Airport 85 ✈	a						13 33															14 26	

Table 29

Saturdays

Hull and Cleethorpes - Doncaster - Meadowhall, Sheffield, Manchester and Manchester Airport
Cleethorpes - Barton-on-Humber

		NT	HT	XC	NT	XC	NT	NT	NT	TP	TP	NT	NT	XC	NT	HT	NT	XC	NT	NT	NT	NT	TP
			◇1 A ⊠	◇1 🛒		◇1 🛒				◇1 🛒	◇1 🛒			◇1 🛒		◇1 B ⊠		◇1 🛒	🚌				◇1 🛒
Hull	d	11 55	12 05						12 22		12 38	12 57				13 05	13 12					13 25	
Hessle	d								12 29													13 32	
Ferriby	d								12 34													13 37	
Brough	d	12 07	12 17						12 39		12 50	13 09				13 17	13 24					13 42	
Broomfleet	d								12 44														
Gilberdyke	d								12 49								13 31					13 49	
Eastrington	d																13 36						
Howden	d		12 30													13 29	13 40						
Wressle	d																13 45						
Selby	a		12 39								13 08					13 39	13 53						
	d		12 40								13 09					13 40	13 54						
York 8 33	a																14 25						
Saltmarshe	d																						
Goole	d	12 22							12 58			13 23										13 58	
Thorne North	d								13 06													14 06	
Cleethorpes	d									12 28			13 00										13 28
New Clee	d												13x03										
Grimsby Docks	d												13 05										
Grimsby Town	a									12 35			13 08										13 35
	d									12 36			13 08										13 36
Great Coates	d												13 12										
Healing	d												13 15										
Stallingborough	d												13 18										
Habrough	d												13 24										
Ulceby	d												13 28										
Thornton Abbey	d												13 32										
Goxhill	d												13 35										
New Holland	d												13 40										
Barrow Haven	d												13 43										
Barton-on-Humber	a												13 48										
Barton-on-Humber	d																		14 00				
Hull Paragon Interchange	a																		14 27				
Barnetby	d									12 55													13 55
Scunthorpe	a									13 10													14 10
	d				12 18					13 10					13 18								14 10
Althorpe	d				12 22										13 23								
Crowle	d				12 28										13 29								
Thorne South	d				12 37										13 38								
Hatfield & Stainforth	d				12 42				13 12						13 43							14 12	
Kirk Sandall	d				12 47				13 17						13 48							14 17	
Adwick 31	d							13 12													14 14		
Bentley (S.Yorks) 31	d							13 16													14 18		
Doncaster 7 31	a	12 46	13 03		12 59			13 23	13 29	13 40		13 46			13 58	14 03					14 22	14 29	14 40
London Kings Cross 15 ⊖26	a		14 50													15 52							
York 8 26	d			12 25		12 45								13 27				13 44					
Doncaster 7	d	12 48		12 52	13 01			13 23		13 42		13 48		13 54	14 01						14 24		14 42
Conisbrough	d				13 09			13 31							14 09						14 31		
Mexborough	d				13 13			13 35							14 13						14 35		
Swinton (S.Yorks)	d				13 16		13 34	13 41							14 16					14 34	14 41		
Rotherham Central	d				13 27		13 45	13 50							14 27					14 45	14 50		
Meadowhall 🚋	d	13 06			13 33		13 50	13 55		14 01		14 06			14 33					14 50	14 55		15 01
Sheffield 7 🚋	a	13 20		13 20	13 41	13 51	14 00	14 05		14 08		14 20		14 20	14 41			14 51		15 00	15 05		15 08
	d									14 11													15 11
Stockport 78	a									14 53													15 53
Manchester Piccadilly 10 🚋	a									15 02	14 36												16 02
Manchester Airport 85 ✈	a									15 26													16 26

A from 17 July until 4 September

B until 10 July and from 11 September

Hull and Cleethorpes - Doncaster - Meadowhall, Sheffield, Manchester and Manchester Airport
Cleethorpes - Barton-on-Humber

		TP	EM	NT	XC	NT	XC	NT	NT	NT	TP	TP	NT	NT	NT	NT	XC	NT	NT	HT	HT	XC	NT
		◇1			◇1		◇1				◇1	◇1					◇1			◇1 A	◇1 B	◇1	
					⊼		⊼				⊼						⊼			⊠	⊠	⊼	🚌
Hull	d	13 38		13 57						14 25		14 38	14 51	14 56						15 06	15 06		
Hessle	d									14 32													
Ferriby	d									14 37													
Brough	d	13 50		14 09						14 42		14 50	15 03	15 08						15 18	15 18		
Broomfleet	d																						
Gilberdyke	d									14 49													
Eastrington	d																						
Howden	d												15 15							15 31	15 31		
Wressle	d																						
Selby	a	14 08										15 08	15 24							15 41	15 41		
	d	14 09										15 09	15 25							15 42	15 42		
York 8 33	a												15 54										
Saltmarshe	d																						
Goole	d			14 23						14 58				15 23									
Thorne North	d									15 06													
Cleethorpes	d										14 28				15 00	15 21							
New Clee	d														15x03								
Grimsby Docks	d														15 05								
Grimsby Town	a										14 35				15 08	15 27							
	d		13 52								14 36				15 08	15 28							
Great Coates	d														15 12								
Healing	d														15 15								
Stallingborough	d														15 18								
Habrough	d		14 02								14 46				15 24	15 38							
Ulceby	d														15 28								
Thornton Abbey	d														15 32								
Goxhill	d														15 35								
New Holland	d														15 40								
Barrow Haven	d														15 43								
Barton-on-Humber	a														15 48								
Barton-on-Humber	d																						16 00
Hull Paragon Interchange	a																						16 27
Barnetby	d		14a11								14 55					15 48							
Scunthorpe	a										15 10												
	d					14 18					15 10								15 17				
Althorpe	d					14 23													15 22				
Crowle	d					14 29													15 28				
Thorne South	d					14 38													15 37				
Hatfield & Stainforth	d					14 43				15 12									15 42				
Kirk Sandall	d					14 48				15 17									15 47				
Adwick 31	d								15 13														
Bentley (S.Yorks) 31	d								15 17														
Doncaster 7 31	a			14 46		14 58			15 22	15 27	15 40			15 46					15 58	16 02	16 02		
London Kings Cross 15 ⊖26	a																			17 52	18 11		
York 8 26	d				14 27		14 44										15 26	15 11				15 45	
Doncaster 7	d			14 48	14b56	15 02			15 24		15 42			15 48			15 55		16 00				
Conisbrough	d					15 10			15 31										16 09				
Mexborough	d					15 14			15 35										16 13				
Swinton (S.Yorks)	d					15 17		15 34	15 41									16 10	16 16				
Rotherham Central	d					15 27		15 43	15 55									16 18	16 27				
Meadowhall ⇌	d			15 06		15 33		15 50	16 00		15 58			16 07				16 24	16 33				
Sheffield 7 ⇌	a			15 20	15 20	15 41	15 51	16 00	16 10		16 08			16 20		17 23	16 20	16 35	16 41			16 51	
	d										16 10												
Stockport 78	a										16 53												
Manchester Piccadilly 10 ⇌	a	15 36									17 02	16 36											
Manchester Airport 85 ✈	a										17 32												

A until 10 July and from 11 September

B from 17 July until 4 September

b arr. 1450

Hull and Cleethorpes - Doncaster - Meadowhall, Sheffield, Manchester and Manchester Airport
Cleethorpes - Barton-on-Humber

		NT	NT	NT	TP	TP	NT	EM	NT	XC	NT	NT	TP	XC	NT	NT	TP	NT	NT	TP	NT	XC	NT
					◇1	◇1				◇1			◇1	◇1			◇1			◇1		◇1	
					⊼	⊼				⊼				⊼			⊼					⊼	
Hull	d			15 25		15 40	15 57		16 10			16 27	16 40					16 54		17 01	17 18		
Hessle	d			15 32								16 34									17 25		
Ferriby	d			15 37								16 39									17 30		
Brough	d			15 42		15 52	16 09		16 22			16 44	16 52					17 06		17 13	17 35		
Broomfleet	d											16 49									17 40		
Gilberdyke	d			15 49					16 29			16 54						17 13			17 45		
Eastrington	d																				17 49		
Howden	d								16 36												17 54		
Wressle	d																				17 58		
Selby	a					16 10			16 46				17 10							17 31	18 06		
	d					16 11			16 47				17 11							17 32	18 06		
York 8 33	a								17 13												18 35		
Saltmarshe	d											16 59											
Goole	d			15 58			16 23					17 04						17 22					
Thorne North	d			16 06								17 13											
Cleethorpes	d				15 28												16 28		17 00				
New Clee	d																						
Grimsby Docks	d																		17 05				
Grimsby Town	a				15 35												16 35		17 08				
	d				15 36			16 03									16 36		17 09				
Great Coates	d																		17 13				
Healing	d																		17 16				
Stallingborough	d																		17 19				
Habrough	d							16 12											17 25				
Ulceby	d																		17 28				
Thornton Abbey	d																		17 33				
Goxhill	d																		17 36				
New Holland	d																		17 40				
Barrow Haven	d																		17 43				
Barton-on-Humber	a																		17 49				
Barton-on-Humber	d																						
Hull Paragon Interchange	a																						
Barnetby	d				15 55			16a21									16 55						
Scunthorpe	a				16 10												17 10						
	d				16 10						16 18						17 10						17 18
Althorpe	d										16 23												17 23
Crowle	d										16 29												17 29
Thorne South	d										16 38												17 38
Hatfield & Stainforth	d			16 12							16 43	17 19											17 43
Kirk Sandall	d			16 17							16 48	17 23											17 48
Adwick 31	d		16 13																				
Bentley (S.Yorks) 31	d		16 16																				
Doncaster 7 31	a		16 22	16 27	16 40		16 46				16 58	17 34					17 40	17 47					17 58
London Kings Cross 15 ⊖26	a																						
York 8 26	d									16 25				16 45								17 25	
Doncaster 7	d		16 23		16 42		16 47			16 53	17 01					17 24	17 42	17 48				17 55	18 02
Conisbrough	d		16 30								17 09					17 31							18 09
Mexborough	d		16 35								17 13					17 35							18 13
Swinton (S.Yorks)	d	16 34	16 41								17 16				17 34	17 42							18 16
Rotherham Central	d	16 43	16 50								17 27				17 44	17 50							18 27
Meadowhall ⇌	d	16 50	16 55		17 01		17 06				17 33				17 50	17 57	18 01	18 06					18 33
Sheffield 7 ⇌	a	17 00	17 05		17 08		17 19			17 20	17 41			17 51	18 00	18 05	18 08	18 19				18 20	18 41
	d				17 11												18 10						
Stockport 78	a				17 53												18 53						
Manchester Piccadilly 10 ⇌	a				18 02	17 37							18 37				19 02						
Manchester Airport 85 ✈	a				18 26												19 28						

Table 29

Hull and Cleethorpes - Doncaster - Meadowhall, Sheffield, Manchester and Manchester Airport
Cleethorpes - Barton-on-Humber

		NT	EM	XC	NT	NT	NT	TP	NT	TP	TP	TP	XC	NT	HT	HT	NT	EM	XC	NT	NT	NT
			◇■	◇■				◇■		◇■	◇■	◇■	◇■		◇■	◇■			◇■			
										A	B	C			D	B						
			☕	⌶	🚌			⌶					⌶		⊠	⊠			⌶			
Hull	d	17 40							17 52	17 58	18 03	18 03			18 12	18 12	18 22			18 46		
Hessle	d	17 47															18 29					
Ferriby	d	17 52															18 34					
Brough	d	17 57							18 04	18 10	18 15	18 15			18 25	18 25	18 39			18 58		
Broomfleet	d																					
Gilberdyke	d	18 04															18 46			19 05		
Eastrington	d																					
Howden	d														18 37	18 37				19 12		
Wressle	d																					
Selby	a								18 24	18 29	18 33	18 33			18 46	18 46				19 22		
	d								18 24	18 29	18 34	18 34			18 47	18 47				19 22		
York ■ 33	a																			19 56		
Saltmarshe	d	18 10																				
Goole	d	18 19															18 55					
Thorne North	d	18 28															19 04					
Cleethorpes	d							17 28														
New Clee	d																					
Grimsby Docks	d																					
Grimsby Town	a							17 35														
	d							17 36										18 28				
Great Coates	d																					
Healing	d																					
Stallingborough	d																					
Habrough	d							17 46										18 38				
Ulceby	d																					
Thornton Abbey	d																					
Goxhill	d																					
New Holland	d																					
Barrow Haven	d																					
Barton-on-Humber	a																					
Barton-on-Humber	d				18 00																	
Hull Paragon Interchange	a				18 27																	
Barnetby	d							17 55										18a49				
Scunthorpe	a							18 10														
	d							18 10						18 18								
Althorpe	d													18 23								
Crowle	d													18 29								
Thorne South	d													18 38								
Hatfield & Stainforth	d	18 34												18 46			19 12					
Kirk Sandall	d	18 39												18 50			19 16					
Adwick 31	d																					
Bentley (S.Yorks) 31	d																					
Doncaster ■ 31	a	18 51						18 40	18 45					19 01	19 04	19 04	19 27					
London Kings Cross ■ ⊖26	a														20 52	21 07						
York ■ 26	d		17 49	17 45									18 25						18 44			
Doncaster ■	d		18 17				18 24	18 42	18 47				18b54	19 03								19 25
Conisbrough	d						18 31							19 11								19 32
Mexborough	d						18 35							19 15								19 36
Swinton (S.Yorks)	d					18 34	18 41							19 18							19 34	19 43
Rotherham Central	d					18 43	18 48							19 28							19 43	19 51
Meadowhall 🚋	d					18 50	18 56	19 01	19 06					19 33							19 50	19 57
Sheffield ■ 🚋	a		18 44	18 51		19 00	19 05	19 08	19 17				19 21	19 43					19 50		20 00	20 06
	d							19 11														
Stockport 78	a							19 53														
Manchester Piccadilly ■ 🚋	a							20 02		19 57		20 05										
Manchester Airport 85 ✈	a							20 36														

A from 11 September
B from 17 July until 4 September
C until 10 July
D until 10 July and from 11 September
b arr. 1848

Table 29

Hull and Cleethorpes - Doncaster - Meadowhall, Sheffield, Manchester and Manchester Airport
Cleethorpes - Barton-on-Humber

		TP	NT	TP	NT	NT	NT	XC	NT	NT	TP	NT	XC	NT	TP	EM	NT	XC	NT	XC	NT	TP	NT
		◇■		◇■				◇■			◇■		◇■		◇■			◇■		◇■		◇■	
		⌶						⌶		🚌			⌶					⌶		⌶			
Hull	d		18 53	18 59					19 25		19 56								20 03				20 51
Hessle	d								19 32										20 10				
Ferriby	d								19 37										20 15				
Brough	d		19 05	19 11					19 42		20 08								20 20				21 03
Broomfleet	d																						
Gilberdyke	d								19 49										20 27				
Eastrington	d																						
Howden	d																						
Wressle	d																						
Selby	a			19 29							20 26												
	d			19 30							20 27												
York ■ 33	a																						
Saltmarshe	d																						
Goole	d		19 19						19 58										20 36				21 17
Thorne North	d								20 06										20 44				21 26
Cleethorpes	d	18 28			19 00	19 13									19 28							20 28	
New Clee	d																						
Grimsby Docks	d				19 05																		
Grimsby Town	a	18 35			19 08	19 19									19 35							20 35	
	d	18 36			19 09	19 20									19 36	19 45						20 36	
Great Coates	d				19 13																		
Healing	d				19 16																		
Stallingborough	d				19 19																		
Habrough	d	18 46			19 25	19 30									19 46	19 54							
Ulceby	d				19 28																		
Thornton Abbey	d				19 33																		
Goxhill	d				19 36																		
New Holland	d				19 40																		
Barrow Haven	d				19 43																		
Barton-on-Humber	a				19 49																		
Barton-on-Humber	d									19 53													
Hull Paragon Interchange	a									20 20													
Barnetby	d	18 55				19 39									19 55	20a03						20 55	
Scunthorpe	a	19 10													20 10							21 10	
	d	19 10					19 18								20 10		20 18					21 10	
Althorpe	d						19 23										20 23						
Crowle	d						19 29										20 30						
Thorne South	d						19 38										20 38						
Hatfield & Stainforth	d						19 43		20 13								20 44		20 51				21 32
Kirk Sandall	d						19 48		20 17								20 48		20 56				21 37
Adwick 31	d																						
Bentley (S.Yorks) 31	d																						
Doncaster ■ 31	a	19 40	19 46				19 58		20 30						20 40		21 00		21 05			21 40	21 45
London Kings Cross ■ ⊖26	a																						
York ■ 26	d							19 25					19 44					20 23		20 44			
Doncaster ■	d	19 42	19 49					19 53				20 03			20 42				21 07			21 42	21 48
Conisbrough	d											20 10			20 48				21 14				
Mexborough	d											20 14			20 52				21 18				
Swinton (S.Yorks)	d											20 17		20 34	20 55				21 21		21 35		
Rotherham Central	d											20 29		20 43	21 01				21 28		21 44		
Meadowhall 🚋	d	20 01	20 07									20 35		20 51	21 07				21 35		21 52	21 58	22 09
Sheffield ■ 🚋	a	20 08	20 18			21 22		20 20				20 42	20 52	21 02	21 19			21 20	21 46	21 51	22 05	22 10	22 21
	d	20 11																					
Stockport 78	a	20 53																					
Manchester Piccadilly ■ 🚋	a	21 02																					
Manchester Airport 85 ✈	a	21 36																					

Table 29

Saturdays

Hull and Cleethorpes - Doncaster - Meadowhall, Sheffield, Manchester and Manchester Airport Cleethorpes - Barton-on-Humber

			NT	NT	TP		NT	NT	NT	NT	NT	NT	NT
					◇■		🚌						
Hull		d			21 33								22 17
Hessle		d											22 24
Ferriby		d											22 29
Brough		d			21 45								22 34
Broomfleet		d											
Gilberdyke		d			21 52								
Eastrington		d											
Howden		d											
Wressle		d											
Selby		a			22 07								
		d			22 07								
York ■	33	a											
Saltmarshe		d											
Goole		d											22 48
Thorne North		d											22 57
Cleethorpes		d	21 00										
New Clee		d											
Grimsby Docks		d	21 05										
Grimsby Town		a	21 08										
		d	21 08										
Great Coates		d	21 12										
Healing		d	21 15										
Stallingborough		d	21 18										
Habrough		d	21 24										
Ulceby		d	21 28										
Thornton Abbey		d	21 32										
Goxhill		d	21 35										
New Holland		d	21 40										
Barrow Haven		d	21 43										
Barton-on-Humber		a	21 48										
Barton-on-Humber		d					21 53						
Hull Paragon Interchange		a					22 20						
Barnetby		d											
Scunthorpe		a											
		d		21 21					22 21				
Althorpe		d		21 26					22 26				
Crowle		d		21 32					22 32				
Thorne South		d		21 40					22 41				
Hatfield & Stainforth		d		21 46					22 46				23 03
Kirk Sandall		d		21 51					22 51				23 07
Adwick	31	d											
Bentley (S.Yorks)	31	d											
Doncaster ■	31	a		22 01					23 02				23 18
London Kings Cross ■	⊖26	a											
York ■	26	d											
Doncaster ■		d						21 54			22 24		23 19
Conisbrough		d						22 01			22 31		23 26
Mexborough		d						22 05			22 35		23 30
Swinton (S.Yorks)		d						22 08		22 40	22 42	23 30	23 33
Rotherham Central		d						22 16		22 46	22 52	23 38	23 43
Meadowhall	⇌	d						22 22		22 52	22 58	23 44	23 49
Sheffield ■	⇌	a						22 32		23 02	23 05	23 58	23 59
		d											
Stockport	78	a											
Manchester Piccadilly ■	⇌	a			23 37								
Manchester Airport	85 ✈	a											

Table 29

Sundays
until 11 July

Hull and Cleethorpes - Doncaster - Meadowhall, Sheffield, Manchester and Manchester Airport Cleethorpes - Barton-on-Humber

								NT			NT		XC	NT	NT	NT	TP	HT	NT	XC	NT		TP	NT	NT	NT
													◇■				◇■	◇■		◇■			◇■		🚌	
													✠					⊠		✠						
Hull		d													08 42	08 54	09 00	09 07			09 41					
Hessle		d													08 49											
Ferriby		d													08 54											
Brough		d													08 59	09 06	09 12	09 19			09 53					
Broomfleet		d																								
Gilberdyke		d													09 06						10 00					
Eastrington		d																								
Howden		d														09 18		09 31								
Wressle		d																								
Selby		a														09 27	09 32	09 41								
		d														09 28	09 33	09 42								
York ■	33	a														09 56										
Saltmarshe		d																								
Goole		d													09 15				09 43		10 09					
Thorne North		d																	09 51							
Cleethorpes		d																					09 28	09 55		
New Clee		d																						09 59		
Grimsby Docks		d																						10 01		
Grimsby Town		a																					09 35	10 04		
		d																					09 36	10 04		
Great Coates		d																						10 08		
Healing		d																						10 11		
Stallingborough		d																						10 12		
Habrough		d																					09 46	10 19		
Ulceby		d																						10 23		
Thornton Abbey		d																						10 28		
Goxhill		d																						10 31		
New Holland		d																						10 36		
Barrow Haven		d																						10 39		
Barton-on-Humber		a																						10 44		
Barton-on-Humber		d																							10 55	
Hull Paragon Interchange		a																							11 19	
Barnetby		d																					09 55			
Scunthorpe		a																					10 10			
		d																					10 10			
Althorpe		d																								
Crowle		d																								
Thorne South		d																								
Hatfield & Stainforth		d																	09 57		10 21					
Kirk Sandall		d																	10 02		10 26					
Adwick	31	d																								
Bentley (S.Yorks)	31	d																								
Doncaster ■	31	a													09 38			09 58	10 11		10 36		10 40			
London Kings Cross ■	⊖26	a																11 49								
York ■	26	d																		09 28						
Doncaster ■		d						08 03			09 13		09 32		09 39				10 13	10 30			10 42			11 13
Conisbrough		d						08 10			09 20								10 20							11 20
Mexborough		d						08 14			09 24								10 24							11 24
Swinton (S.Yorks)		d						08 17			09 28			09 35					10 27							11 27
Rotherham Central		d						08 25			09 35			09 48					10 35							11 35
Meadowhall	⇌	d						08 30			09 41			09 54	10 00				10 40				11 00			11 40
Sheffield ■	⇌	a						08 41			09 51		09 55	10 03	10 09				10 52	10 54			11 07			11 51
		d																					11 10			
Stockport	78	a																					11 53			
Manchester Piccadilly ■	⇌	a															11 05						12 06			
Manchester Airport	85 ✈	a																					12 29			

Table 29

Sundays
until 11 July

Hull and Cleethorpes - Doncaster - Meadowhall, Sheffield, Manchester and Manchester Airport
Cleethorpes - Barton-on-Humber

		XC	NT	TP	TP	NT		NT	XC	NT	TP	NT	TP	HT	NT	TP		NT	XC	NT	TP	NT	TP	NT	NT
		◇■		◇■	◇■				◇■		◇■		◇■	◇■		◇■			◇■		◇■		◇■		
		🛒							🛒					⊠					🛒					🚌	
Hull	d		10 41		10 58					11 41		11 53	12 00	12 12						12 41	12 58	13 24			
Hessle	d																								
Ferriby	d																								
Brough	d		10 53		11 10					11 53		12 05	12 12	12 24						12 53	13 10	13 36			
Broomfleet	d																								
Gilberdyke	d		11 00							12 00										13 00					
Eastrington	d																								
Howden	d											12 17		12 36								13 48			
Wressle	d																								
Selby	a				11 28							12 26	12 32	12 46							13 28	13 57			
	d				11 29							12 27	12 33	12 47							13 29	13 58			
York ■ 33	a											12 51										14 22			
Saltmarshe	d																								
Goole	d		11 09					11 43		12 09										13 09					
Thorne North	d							11 51																	
Cleethorpes	d			10 28							11 28				12 55										
New Clee	d														12 59										
Grimsby Docks	d														13 01										
Grimsby Town	a			10 35							11 35				13 04										
	d			10 36							11 36				13 04										
Great Coates	d														13 08										
Healing	d														13 11										
Stallingborough	d														13 12										
Habrough	d			10 46											13 19										
Ulceby	d														13 23										
Thornton Abbey	d														13 28										
Goxhill	d														13 31										
New Holland	d														13 36										
Barrow Haven	d														13 39										
Barton-on-Humber	a														13 44										
Barton-on-Humber	d																							13 55	
Hull Paragon Interchange	a																							14 19	
Barnetby	d			10 55							11 55														
Scunthorpe	a			11 10							12 10														
	d			11 10							12 10														
Althorpe	d																								
Crowle	d																								
Thorne South	d																								
Hatfield & Stainforth	d							11 57																	
Kirk Sandall	d							12 02																	
Adwick 31	d																								
Bentley (S.Yorks) 31	d																								
Doncaster ■ 31	a		11 32	11 40				12 14		12 32	12 40			13 05						13 32					
London Kings Cross ■ ⊖26	a													14 55											
York ■ 26	d	10 28							11 28							13 15			12 28						
Doncaster ■	d	11 30	11 33	11 42				12 16	12 30		12 42							13 13	13 30	13 34			13 42		
Conisbrough	d							12 23										13 20							
Mexborough	d							12 27										13 24							
Swinton (S.Yorks)	d					11 55		12 30										13 27							14 01
Rotherham Central	d					12 06		12 38										13 36							14 09
Meadowhall ⇌	d		11 52	12 00		12 11		12 43			13 00							13 44		13 53			14 00		14 17
Sheffield ■ ⇌	a	11 53	12 03	12 07		12 20		12 55	12 54		13 07							13 52	13 54	14 04			14 07		14 25
	d			12 10							13 10												14 11		
Stockport 78	a			12 53							13 53												14 53		
Manchester Piccadilly ■ ⇌	a			13 06	12 54						14 06		13 54			14 34					14 54		15 06		
Manchester Airport 85 ✈	a			13 29							14 29					14 55							15 29		

Table 29

Sundays
until 11 July

Hull and Cleethorpes - Doncaster - Meadowhall, Sheffield, Manchester and Manchester Airport
Cleethorpes - Barton-on-Humber

		XC		NT	NT	TP	EM		HT	XC	XC	NT			NT	NT	TP	TP	NT	XC	NT	XC		NT	NT
		◇■				◇■			◇■	◇■	◇■						◇■	◇■		◇■		◇■			
		🛒							⊠	🛒	🛒									🛒		🛒			
Hull	d				13 35				14 10			14 28				14 41		14 58							15 41
Hessle	d				13 42																				
Ferriby	d				13 47																				
Brough	d				13 52				14 22			14 40				14 53		15 10							15 53
Broomfleet	d																								
Gilberdyke	d				14 00											15 00									16 00
Eastrington	d																								
Howden	d								14 34			14 52													
Wressle	d																								
Selby	a								14 44			15 01						15 28							
	d								14 45			15 02						15 29							
York ■ 33	a											15 27													
Saltmarshe	d																								
Goole	d			13 43	14 08											15 09								15 43	16 09
Thorne North	d			13 51																				15 51	
Cleethorpes	d					13 28	13 56										14 28		15 01						
New Clee	d																		15 05						
Grimsby Docks	d																		15 07						
Grimsby Town	a					13 35	14 02										14 35		15 10						
	d					13 36	14 03										14 36		15 10						
Great Coates	d																		15 14						
Healing	d																		15 17						
Stallingborough	d																		15 18						
Habrough	d						14 13										14 46		15 25						
Ulceby	d																		15 29						
Thornton Abbey	d																		15 34						
Goxhill	d																		15 37						
New Holland	d																		15 42						
Barrow Haven	d																		15 45						
Barton-on-Humber	a																		15 50						
Barton-on-Humber	d																								
Hull Paragon Interchange	a																								
Barnetby	d					13 55	14a22										14 55								
Scunthorpe	a					14 10											15 10								
	d					14 10											15 10								
Althorpe	d																								
Crowle	d																								
Thorne South	d																								
Hatfield & Stainforth	d			13 57																				15 57	
Kirk Sandall	d			14 02																				16 02	
Adwick 31	d																								
Bentley (S.Yorks) 31	d																								
Doncaster ■ 31	a			14 11	14 31	14 40			15 05							15 32	15 40							16 11	16 32
London Kings Cross ■ ⊖26	a								16 55																
York ■ 26	d	13 28								14 22	14 28									15 20		15 28			
Doncaster ■	d			14 13	14 33	14 42				14 50					15 13	15 33	15 42			15 50				16 13	16 33
Conisbrough	d			14 20											15 20									16 20	
Mexborough	d			14 24											15 24									16 24	
Swinton (S.Yorks)	d			14 30											15 30						15 55			16 29	
Rotherham Central	d			14 37											15 37						16 05			16 37	
Meadowhall ⇌	d			14 43	14 52	15 00									15 43	15 52	16 00				16 11			16 43	16 53
Sheffield ■ ⇌	a	14 45		14 52	15 03	15 07				15 18	15 42				15 51	16 01	16 07			16 15	16 21	16 41		16 52	17 03
	d					15 11											16 11								
Stockport 78	a					15 53											16 53								
Manchester Piccadilly ■ ⇌	a					16 06											17 06	16 54							
Manchester Airport 85 ✈	a					16 29											17 29								

Table 29

Sundays until 11 July

Hull and Cleethorpes - Doncaster - Meadowhall, Sheffield, Manchester and Manchester Airport Cleethorpes - Barton-on-Humber

		TP	NT	NT	XC	XC	HT	NT	NT	TP	XC	NT	NT	EM	NT	TP	NT	GR	NT	TP	NT	XC
		◇1	🚌		◇1 ⊼	◇1 ⊼	◇1 ⊠			◇1	◇1 ⊼			◇1 ⊏		◇1		1 ⊏⊼		◇1		◇1 ⊼
Hull	d			16 00			16 23		16 41	16 58		17 23						17 30	17 41			
Hessle	d																					
Ferriby	d																					
Brough	d			16 12			16 35		16 53	17 10		17 35						17 42	17 53			
Broomfleet	d																					
Gilberdyke	d								17 00										18 00			
Eastrington	d																					
Howden	d			16 24			16 47					17 47										
Wressle	d																					
Selby	a			16 33			16 57			17 28		17 56						18 05				
	d			16 34			16 58			17 29		17 57						18 05				
York 8 33	a			16 58								18 23										
Saltmarshe	d																					
Goole	d								17 09								17 43		18 09			
Thorne North	d																17 51					
Cleethorpes	d	15 28														16 28				17 28	17 55	
New Clee	d																				17 59	
Grimsby Docks	d																				18 01	
Grimsby Town	a	15 35														16 35				17 35	18 04	
	d	15 36														16 36				17 36	18 04	
Great Coates	d																				18 08	
Healing	d																				18 11	
Stallingborough	d																				18 12	
Habrough	d																			17 46	18 19	
Ulceby	d																				18 23	
Thornton Abbey	d																				18 28	
Goxhill	d																				18 31	
New Holland	d																				18 36	
Barrow Haven	d																				18 39	
Barton-on-Humber	a																				18 44	
Barton-on-Humber	d		15 55																			
Hull Paragon Interchange	a		16 19																			
Barnetby	d	15 55														16 55				17 55		
Scunthorpe	a	16 10														17 10				18 10		
	d	16 10														17 10				18 10		
Althorpe	d																					
Crowle	d																					
Thorne South	d																					
Hatfield & Stainforth	d																17 57					
Kirk Sandall	d																18 02					
Adwick 31	d																					
Bentley (S.Yorks) 31	d																					
Doncaster 7 31	a	16 40					17 14		17 31							17 40	18 11	18 23	18 33	18 40		
London Kings Cross 15 ⊖26	a						19 06											20 23				
York 8 26	d				16 20	16 28					17 21			17 40	17 17							18 20
Doncaster 7	d	16 42			16 50			17 13	17 32		17 50			18 06		17 42	18 13		18 34	18 42		18 50
Conisbrough	d							17 21									18 20					
Mexborough	d							17 25									18 24					
Swinton (S.Yorks)	d							17 30					17 55		18 11		18 30					
Rotherham Central	d							17 38					18 06		18 18		18 37					
Meadowhall ⇌	d	17 00						17 43	17 53				18 12		18 24	18 00	18 43		18 53	19 00		
Sheffield 7 ⇌	a	17 07			17 18	17 41		17 54	18 01		18 18		18 23	18 28	18 35	18 07	18 52		19 03	19 07		19 15
	d	17 11														18 11				19 11		
Stockport 78	a	17 53														18 53				19 53		
Manchester Piccadilly 10 ⇌	a	18 06								18 54						19 06				20 06		
Manchester Airport 85 ✈	a	18 29														19 29				20 29		

Table 29

Sundays until 11 July

Hull and Cleethorpes - Doncaster - Meadowhall, Sheffield, Manchester and Manchester Airport Cleethorpes - Barton-on-Humber

		EM	XC	TP	NT	NT	NT	HT	TP	NT	XC	NT	XC	TP	NT	TP	EM	XC	NT	XC	NT	NT
			◇1 ⊼	◇1	🚌			◇1 ⊠	◇1		◇1 ⊼		◇1 ⊼	◇1		◇1		◇1 ⊼		◇1 ⊼		
Hull	d						18 38	18 48	18 58	19 04									20 22		20 30	
Hessle	d																					
Ferriby	d																					
Brough	d						18 50	19 00	19 10	19 16									20 34		20 42	
Broomfleet	d																					
Gilberdyke	d						18 57														20 49	
Eastrington	d																					
Howden	d							19 12		19 28									20 46			
Wressle	d																					
Selby	a							19 22	19 28	19 37									20 55			
	d							19 23	19 29	19 38									20 56			
York 8 33	a									20 02									21 20			
Saltmarshe	d																					
Goole	d						19 06														20 58	
Thorne North	d						19 14															
Cleethorpes	d	18 18		18 28												19 28	19 54					
New Clee	d																					
Grimsby Docks	d																					
Grimsby Town	a	18 24		18 35												19 35	20 00					
	d	18 25		18 36												19 36	20 07					
Great Coates	d																					
Healing	d																					
Stallingborough	d																					
Habrough	d	18 35															20 17					
Ulceby	d																					
Thornton Abbey	d																					
Goxhill	d																					
New Holland	d																					
Barrow Haven	d																					
Barton-on-Humber	a																					
Barton-on-Humber	d				18 55																	
Hull Paragon Interchange	a				19 19																	
Barnetby	d	18a44		18 55												19 55	20a26					
Scunthorpe	a			19 10												20 10						
	d			19 10												20 10						
Althorpe	d																					
Crowle	d																					
Thorne South	d																					
Hatfield & Stainforth	d						19 20															
Kirk Sandall	d						19 25															
Adwick 31	d																					
Bentley (S.Yorks) 31	d																					
Doncaster 7 31	a			19 40			19 35	19 43								20 40					21 21	
London Kings Cross 15 ⊖26	a							21 35														
York 8 26	d		18 28								19 20		19 28	20 15				20 20		20 28		20 42
Doncaster 7	d			19 42		19 15	19 37				19 50				20 14	20 42		20c50			21 23	
Conisbrough	d					19 22									20 21							
Mexborough	d					19 26									20 25							
Swinton (S.Yorks)	d					19 30						19 55			20 32							21 38
Rotherham Central	d					19 41						20 06			20 39						21 39	21 49
Meadowhall ⇌	d			20 00		19 47	19 57					20 11			20 45	21 00					21 45	21 54
Sheffield 7 ⇌	a		19 40	20 07		19 55	20 06				20 16	20 23	20 40		20 53	21 07		21 17		21 44	21 56	22 05
	d			20 11												21 11						
Stockport 78	a			20 53												21 53						
Manchester Piccadilly 10 ⇌	a			21 06					20 54					21 36		22 06						
Manchester Airport 85 ✈	a			21 29												22 29						

c arr. 2043

Table 29

Sundays until 11 July

Hull and Cleethorpes - Doncaster - Meadowhall, Sheffield, Manchester and Manchester Airport
Cleethorpes - Barton-on-Humber

			TP	TP	NT	NT
			◇1	◇1		
Hull		d		21 00		21 15
Hessle		d				21 22
Ferriby		d				21 27
Brough		d		21 12		21 32
Broomfleet		d				
Gilberdyke		d				21 39
Eastrington		d				
Howden		d				
Wressle		d				
Selby		a		21 30		
		d		21 31		
York	33	a				
Saltmarshe		d				
Goole		d				21 48
Thorne North		d				21 56
Cleethorpes		d	20 28			
New Clee		d				
Grimsby Docks		d				
Grimsby Town		a	20 35			
		d	20 36			
Great Coates		d				
Healing		d				
Stallingborough		d				
Habrough		d	20 46			
Ulceby		d				
Thornton Abbey		d				
Goxhill		d				
New Holland		d				
Barrow Haven		d				
Barton-on-Humber		a				
Barton-on-Humber		d				
Hull Paragon Interchange		a				
Barnetby		d	20 55			
Scunthorpe		a	21 10			
		d	21 10			
Althorpe		d				
Crowle		d				
Thorne South		d				
Hatfield & Stainforth		d				22 02
Kirk Sandall		d				22 07
Adwick	31	d				
Bentley (S.Yorks)	31	d				
Doncaster	31	a	21 40			22 17
London Kings Cross	26	a				
York	26	d				
Doncaster		d	21 42			22 20
Conisbrough		d				22 27
Mexborough		d				22 31
Swinton (S.Yorks)		d	21 52		22 32	22 37
Rotherham Central		d	21 58		22 40	22 44
Meadowhall		d	22 04		22 45	22 50
Sheffield		a	22 15		22 54	22 58
		d				
Stockport	78	a				
Manchester Piccadilly		a				
Manchester Airport	85	a				

Table 29

Sundays 18 July to 05 September

Hull and Cleethorpes - Doncaster - Meadowhall, Sheffield, Manchester and Manchester Airport
Cleethorpes - Barton-on-Humber

			NT	NT	XC	NT	NT	NT	TP	HT	NT	XC	NT	TP	NT	NT	NT
					◇1				◇1	◇1		◇1		◇1			
					[trolley]					[boxed cross]		[trolley]				[bus]	
Hull		d					08 42	08 54	09 00	09 07			09 41				
Hessle		d					08 49										
Ferriby		d					08 54										
Brough		d					08 59	09 06	09 12	09 19			09 53				
Broomfleet		d															
Gilberdyke		d					09 06						10 00				
Eastrington		d															
Howden		d						09 18		09 31							
Wressle		d															
Selby		a						09 27	09 32	09 41							
		d						09 28	09 33	09 42							
York	33	a						09 56									
Saltmarshe		d															
Goole		d					09 15				09 43		10 09				
Thorne North		d									09 51						
Cleethorpes		d												09 28	09 55		
New Clee		d													09 59		
Grimsby Docks		d													10 01		
Grimsby Town		a												09 35	10 04		
		d												09 36	10 04		
Great Coates		d													10 08		
Healing		d													10 11		
Stallingborough		d													10 12		
Habrough		d												09 46	10 19		
Ulceby		d													10 23		
Thornton Abbey		d													10 28		
Goxhill		d													10 31		
New Holland		d													10 36		
Barrow Haven		d													10 39		
Barton-on-Humber		a													10 44		
Barton-on-Humber		d														10 55	
Hull Paragon Interchange		a														11 19	
Barnetby		d												09 55			
Scunthorpe		a												10 10			
		d												10 10			
Althorpe		d															
Crowle		d															
Thorne South		d															
Hatfield & Stainforth		d									09 57		10 21				
Kirk Sandall		d									10 02		10 26				
Adwick	31	d															
Bentley (S.Yorks)	31	d															
Doncaster	31	a					09 38			09 58	10 11		10 36	10 40			
London Kings Cross	26	a								12 07							
York	26	d										09 28					
Doncaster		d	08 03	09 13	09 32		09 39				10 13	10 30		10 42			11 13
Conisbrough		d	08 10	09 20							10 20						11 20
Mexborough		d	08 14	09 24							10 24						11 24
Swinton (S.Yorks)		d	08 17	09 28		09 35					10 27						11 27
Rotherham Central		d	08 25	09 35		09 48					10 35						11 35
Meadowhall		d	08 30	09 41		09 54	10 00				10 40			11 00			11 40
Sheffield		a	08 41	09 51	09 55	10 03	10 09				10 52	10 54		11 07			11 51
		d												11 10			
Stockport	78	a												11 53			
Manchester Piccadilly		a							11 05					12 06			
Manchester Airport	85	a												12 29			

Table 29

Sundays
18 July to 05 September

Hull and Cleethorpes - Doncaster - Meadowhall, Sheffield, Manchester and Manchester Airport
Cleethorpes - Barton-on-Humber

		XC	NT	TP	TP	NT	NT	XC	NT	TP	NT	TP
		◇1 ⊤		◇1	◇1			◇1 ⊤		◇1		◇1
Hull	d		10 41		10 58				11 41		11 53	12 00
Hessle	d											
Ferriby	d											
Brough	d		10 53		11 10				11 53		12 05	12 12
Broomfleet	d											
Gilberdyke	d		11 00						12 00			
Eastrington	d											
Howden	d										12 17	
Wressle	d											
Selby	a				11 28						12 26	12 32
	d				11 29						12 27	12 33
York 8	33 a										12 51	
Saltmarshe	d											
Goole	d		11 09				11 43		12 09			
Thorne North	d						11 51					
Cleethorpes	d			10 28						11 28		
New Clee	d											
Grimsby Docks	d											
Grimsby Town	a			10 35						11 35		
	d			10 36						11 36		
Great Coates	d											
Healing	d											
Stallingborough	d											
Habrough	d			10 46								
Ulceby	d											
Thornton Abbey	d											
Goxhill	d											
New Holland	d											
Barrow Haven	d											
Barton-on-Humber	a											
Barton-on-Humber	d											
Hull Paragon Interchange	a											
Barnetby	d			10 55						11 55		
Scunthorpe	a			11 10						12 10		
	d			11 10						12 10		
Althorpe	d											
Crowle	d											
Thorne South	d											
Hatfield & Stainforth	d						11 57					
Kirk Sandall	d						12 02					
Adwick	31 d											
Bentley (S.Yorks)	31 d											
Doncaster 7	31 a		11 32	11 40			12 14		12 32	12 40		
London Kings Cross 15	⊖26 a											
York 8	26 d	10 28						11 28				
Doncaster 7	d	11 30	11 33	11 42			12 16	12 30		12 42		
Conisbrough	d						12 23					
Mexborough	d						12 27					
Swinton (S.Yorks)	d					11 55	12 30					
Rotherham Central	d					12 06	12 38					
Meadowhall	⇌ d		11 52	12 00		12 11	12 43			13 00		
Sheffield 7	⇌ a	11 53	12 03	12 07		12 20	12 55	12 54		13 07		
	d			12 10						13 10		
Stockport	78 a			12 53						13 53		
Manchester Piccadilly 10	⇌ a			13 06	12 54					14 06		13 54
Manchester Airport	85 ✈ a			13 29						14 29		

		HT	NT	TP	NT	XC	NT	TP	NT	TP	NT	NT
		◇1 ⊠		◇1		◇1 ⊤		◇1		◇1	🚌	
Hull	d	12 12					12 41	12 58	13 24			
Hessle	d											
Ferriby	d											
Brough	d	12 24					12 53	13 10	13 36			
Broomfleet	d											
Gilberdyke	d						13 00					
Eastrington	d											
Howden	d	12 36							13 48			
Wressle	d											
Selby	a	12 46						13 28	13 57			
	d	12 47						13 29	13 58			
York 8	33 a								14 22			
Saltmarshe	d											
Goole	d						13 09					
Thorne North	d											
Cleethorpes	d		12 55									
New Clee	d		12 59									
Grimsby Docks	d		13 01									
Grimsby Town	a		13 04									
	d		13 04									
Great Coates	d		13 08									
Healing	d		13 11									
Stallingborough	d		13 12									
Habrough	d		13 19									
Ulceby	d		13 23									
Thornton Abbey	d		13 28									
Goxhill	d		13 31									
New Holland	d		13 36									
Barrow Haven	d		13 39									
Barton-on-Humber	a		13 44									
Barton-on-Humber	d										13 55	
Hull Paragon Interchange	a										14 19	
Barnetby	d											
Scunthorpe	a											
	d											
Althorpe	d											
Crowle	d											
Thorne South	d											
Hatfield & Stainforth	d											
Kirk Sandall	d											
Adwick	31 d											
Bentley (S.Yorks)	31 d											
Doncaster 7	31 a	13 05					13 32					
London Kings Cross 15	⊖26 a	15 10										
York 8	26 d			13 15		12 28						
Doncaster 7	d				13 13	13 30	13 34			13 42		
Conisbrough	d				13 20							
Mexborough	d				13 24							
Swinton (S.Yorks)	d				13 27							14 01
Rotherham Central	d				13 36							14 09
Meadowhall	⇌ d				13 44		13 53			14 00		14 17
Sheffield 7	⇌ a				13 52	13 54	14 04			14 07		14 25
	d									14 11		
Stockport	78 a									14 53		
Manchester Piccadilly 10	⇌ a			14 34				14 54		15 06		
Manchester Airport	85 ✈ a			14 55						15 29		

Table 29

Sundays
18 July to 05 September

Hull and Cleethorpes - Doncaster - Meadowhall, Sheffield, Manchester and Manchester Airport
Cleethorpes - Barton-on-Humber

		XC	NT	NT	TP	EM	HT	XC	XC	NT
		◇1 ⊤			◇1		◇1 ⊠	◇1 ⊤	◇1 ⊤	
Hull	d			13 35			14 10			14 28
Hessle	d			13 42						
Ferriby	d			13 47						
Brough	d			13 52			14 22			14 40
Broomfleet	d									
Gilberdyke	d			14 00						
Eastrington	d									
Howden	d						14 34			14 52
Wressle	d									
Selby	a						14 44			15 01
	d						14 45			15 02
York 8	33 a									15 27
Saltmarshe	d									
Goole	d		13 43	14 08						
Thorne North	d		13 51							
Cleethorpes	d				13 28	13 56				
New Clee	d									
Grimsby Docks	d									
Grimsby Town	a				13 35	14 02				
	d				13 36	14 03				
Great Coates	d									
Healing	d									
Stallingborough	d									
Habrough	d					14 13				
Ulceby	d									
Thornton Abbey	d									
Goxhill	d									
New Holland	d									
Barrow Haven	d									
Barton-on-Humber	a									
Barton-on-Humber	d									
Hull Paragon Interchange	a									
Barnetby	d				13 55	14a22				
Scunthorpe	a				14 10					
	d				14 10					
Althorpe	d									
Crowle	d									
Thorne South	d									
Hatfield & Stainforth	d		13 57							
Kirk Sandall	d		14 02							
Adwick	31 d									
Bentley (S.Yorks)	31 d									
Doncaster 7	31 a		14 11	14 31	14 40		15 05			
London Kings Cross 15	⊖26 a						17 10			
York 8	26 d	13 28						14 22	14 28	
Doncaster 7	d		14 13	14 33	14 42			14 50		
Conisbrough	d		14 20							
Mexborough	d		14 24							
Swinton (S.Yorks)	d		14 30							
Rotherham Central	d		14 37							
Meadowhall	⇌ d		14 43	14 52	15 00					
Sheffield 7	⇌ a	14 45	14 52	15 03	15 07			15 18	15 42	
	d				15 11					
Stockport	78 a				15 53					
Manchester Piccadilly 10	⇌ a				16 06					
Manchester Airport	85 ✈ a				16 29					

		NT	NT	TP	TP	NT	XC	NT	XC	NT	NT
				◇1	◇1		◇1 ⊤		◇1 ⊤		
Hull	d		14 41		14 58						15 41
Hessle	d										
Ferriby	d										
Brough	d		14 53		15 10						15 53
Broomfleet	d										
Gilberdyke	d		15 00								16 00
Eastrington	d										
Howden	d										
Wressle	d										
Selby	a				15 28						
	d				15 29						
York 8	33 a										
Saltmarshe	d										
Goole	d		15 09							15 43	16 09
Thorne North	d									15 51	
Cleethorpes	d			14 28		15 01					
New Clee	d					15 05					
Grimsby Docks	d					15 07					
Grimsby Town	a			14 35		15 10					
	d			14 36		15 10					
Great Coates	d					15 14					
Healing	d					15 17					
Stallingborough	d					15 18					
Habrough	d			14 46		15 25					
Ulceby	d					15 29					
Thornton Abbey	d					15 34					
Goxhill	d					15 37					
New Holland	d					15 42					
Barrow Haven	d					15 45					
Barton-on-Humber	a					15 50					
Barton-on-Humber	d										
Hull Paragon Interchange	a										
Barnetby	d			14 55							
Scunthorpe	a			15 10							
	d			15 10							
Althorpe	d										
Crowle	d										
Thorne South	d										
Hatfield & Stainforth	d									15 57	
Kirk Sandall	d									16 02	
Adwick	31 d										
Bentley (S.Yorks)	31 d										
Doncaster 7	31 a		15 32	15 40						16 11	16 32
London Kings Cross 15	⊖26 a										
York 8	26 d						15 20		15 28		
Doncaster 7	d	15 13	15 33	15 42			15 50			16 13	16 33
Conisbrough	d	15 20								16 20	
Mexborough	d	15 24								16 24	
Swinton (S.Yorks)	d	15 30						15 55		16 29	
Rotherham Central	d	15 37						16 05		16 37	
Meadowhall	⇌ d	15 43	15 52	16 00				16 11		16 43	16 53
Sheffield 7	⇌ a	15 51	16 01	16 07			16 15	16 21	16 41	16 52	17 03
	d			16 11							
Stockport	78 a			16 53							
Manchester Piccadilly 10	⇌ a			17 06	16 54						
Manchester Airport	85 ✈ a			17 29							

Table 29

Sundays

18 July to 05 September

Hull and Cleethorpes - Doncaster - Meadowhall, Sheffield, Manchester and Manchester Airport
Cleethorpes - Barton-on-Humber

Station			TP	NT	NT	TP	XC	XC	HT	NT	NT	TP	XC	NT	NT	EM	NT	TP	NT	GR	NT	TP	NT	XC
			◇1			◇1	◇1	◇1	◇1			◇1	◇1			◇1		◇1		1		◇1		◇1
Hull		d			16 00				16 23		16 41	16 58		17 23						17 30	17 41			
Hessle		d																						
Ferriby		d																						
Brough		d			16 12				16 35		16 53	17 10		17 35						17 42	17 53			
Broomfleet		d																						
Gilberdyke		d									17 00										18 00			
Eastrington		d																						
Howden		d			16 24				16 47					17 47										
Wressle		d																						
Selby		a			16 33				16 57			17 28		17 56						18 05				
		d			16 34				16 58			17 29		17 57						18 05				
York 8	33	a			16 58									18 23										
Saltmarshe		d																						
Goole		d									17 09								17 43		18 09			
Thorne North		d																	17 51					
Cleethorpes		d	15 28															16 28				17 28	17 55	
New Clee		d																					17 59	
Grimsby Docks		d																					18 01	
Grimsby Town		a	15 35															16 35				17 35	18 04	
		d	15 36															16 36				17 36	18 04	
Great Coates		d																					18 08	
Healing		d																					18 11	
Stallingborough		d																					18 12	
Habrough		d																				17 46	18 19	
Ulceby		d																					18 23	
Thornton Abbey		d																					18 28	
Goxhill		d																					18 31	
New Holland		d																					18 36	
Barrow Haven		d																					18 39	
Barton-on-Humber		a																					18 44	
Barton-on-Humber		d		15 55																				
Hull Paragon Interchange		a		16 19																				
Barnetby		d	15 55															16 55				17 55		
Scunthorpe		a	16 10															17 10				18 10		
		d	16 10															17 10				18 10		
Althorpe		d																						
Crowle		d																						
Thorne South		d																						
Hatfield & Stainforth		d																	17 57					
Kirk Sandall		d																	18 02					
Adwick	31	d																						
Bentley (S.Yorks)	31	d																						
Doncaster 7	31	a	16 40						17 14		17 31							17 40	18 11	18 23	18 33	18 40		
London Kings Cross 15	⊖26	a							19 29											20 44				
York 8	26	d				16 15	16 20	16 28					17 21			17 40	17 17							18 20
Doncaster 7		d	16 42				16 50			17 13	17 32		17 50			18 06		17 42	18 13		18 34	18 42		18 50
Conisbrough		d								17 21									18 20					
Mexborough		d								17 25									18 24					
Swinton (S.Yorks)		d								17 30					17 55		18 11		18 30					
Rotherham Central		d								17 38					18 06		18 18		18 37					
Meadowhall	⇌	d	17 00							17 43	17 53				18 12		18 24	18 00	18 43		18 53	19 00		
Sheffield 7	⇌	a	17 07				17 18	17 41		17 54	18 01		18 18		18 23	18 28	18 35	18 07	18 52		19 03	19 07		19 15
		d	17 11															18 11				19 11		
Stockport	78	a	17 53															18 53				19 53		
Manchester Piccadilly 10	⇌	a	18 06			17 34						18 54						19 06				20 06		
Manchester Airport	85 ✈	a	18 29			17 55												19 29				20 29		

Table 29

Sundays

18 July to 05 September

Hull and Cleethorpes - Doncaster - Meadowhall, Sheffield, Manchester and Manchester Airport
Cleethorpes - Barton-on-Humber

Station			EM	XC	TP	NT	NT	NT	TP	NT	HT	XC	NT	XC	NT	TP	EM	XC	NT	XC	NT	NT
				◇1	◇1				◇1		◇1	◇1		◇1		◇1		◇1		◇1		
Hull		d						18 38	18 58	19 04	19 15								20 22		20 30	
Hessle		d																				
Ferriby		d																				
Brough		d						18 50	19 10	19 16	19 27								20 34		20 42	
Broomfleet		d																				
Gilberdyke		d						18 57													20 49	
Eastrington		d																				
Howden		d								19 28	19 39								20 46			
Wressle		d																				
Selby		a							19 28	19 37	19 49								20 55			
		d							19 29	19 38	19 50								20 56			
York 8	33	a								20 02									21 20			
Saltmarshe		d																				
Goole		d						19 06													20 58	
Thorne North		d						19 14														
Cleethorpes		d	18 18		18 28											19 28	19 54					
New Clee		d																				
Grimsby Docks		d																				
Grimsby Town		a	18 24		18 35											19 35	20 00					
		d	18 25		18 36											19 36	20 07					
Great Coates		d																				
Healing		d																				
Stallingborough		d																				
Habrough		d	18 35														20 17					
Ulceby		d																				
Thornton Abbey		d																				
Goxhill		d																				
New Holland		d																				
Barrow Haven		d																				
Barton-on-Humber		a																				
Barton-on-Humber		d				18 55																
Hull Paragon Interchange		a				19 19																
Barnetby		d	18a44		18 55											19 55	20a26					
Scunthorpe		a			19 10											20 10						
		d			19 10											20 10						
Althorpe		d																				
Crowle		d																				
Thorne South		d																				
Hatfield & Stainforth		d						19 20														
Kirk Sandall		d						19 25														
Adwick	31	d																				
Bentley (S.Yorks)	31	d																				
Doncaster 7	31	a			19 40			19 35			20 09					20 40					21 21	
London Kings Cross 15	⊖26	a									22 14											
York 8	26	d		18 28								19 20		19 28				20 20		20 28		20 42
Doncaster 7		d			19 42		19 15	19 37				19 50			20 14	20 42		20c50			21 23	
Conisbrough		d					19 22								20 21							
Mexborough		d					19 26								20 25							
Swinton (S.Yorks)		d					19 30						19 55		20 32							21 38
Rotherham Central		d					19 41						20 06		20 39						21 39	21 49
Meadowhall	⇌	d			20 00		19 47	19 57					20 11		20 45	21 00					21 45	21 54
Sheffield 7	⇌	a		19 40	20 07		19 55	20 06				20 16	20 23	20 40	20 53	21 07		21 17		21 44	21 56	22 05
		d			20 11											21 11						
Stockport	78	a			20 53											21 53						
Manchester Piccadilly 10	⇌	a			21 06				20 54							22 06						
Manchester Airport	85 ✈	a			21 29											22 29						

c arr. 2043

Table 29

Sundays
18 July to 05 September

Hull and Cleethorpes - Doncaster - Meadowhall, Sheffield, Manchester and Manchester Airport
Cleethorpes - Barton-on-Humber

		TP	TP	NT	NT
		◇1	◇1		
Hull	d		21 00		21 15
Hessle	d				21 22
Ferriby	d				21 27
Brough	d		21 12		21 32
Broomfleet	d				
Gilberdyke	d				21 39
Eastrington	d				
Howden	d				
Wressle	d				
Selby	a		21 30		
	d		21 31		
York 8	33 a				
Saltmarshe	d				
Goole	d				21 48
Thorne North	d				21 56
Cleethorpes	d	20 28			
New Clee	d				
Grimsby Docks	d				
Grimsby Town	a	20 35			
	d	20 36			
Great Coates	d				
Healing	d				
Stallingborough	d				
Habrough	d	20 46			
Ulceby	d				
Thornton Abbey	d				
Goxhill	d				
New Holland	d				
Barrow Haven	d				
Barton-on-Humber	a				
Barton-on-Humber	d				
Hull Paragon Interchange	a				
Barnetby	d	20 55			
Scunthorpe	a	21 10			
	d	21 10			
Althorpe	d				
Crowle	d				
Thorne South	d				
Hatfield & Stainforth	d				22 02
Kirk Sandall	d				22 07
Adwick	31 d				
Bentley (S.Yorks)	31 d				
Doncaster 7	31 a	21 40			22 17
London Kings Cross 15	⊖26 a				
York 8	26 d				
Doncaster 7	d	21 42			22 20
Conisbrough	d				22 27
Mexborough	d				22 31
Swinton (S.Yorks)	d	21 52		22 32	22 37
Rotherham Central	d	21 58		22 40	22 44
Meadowhall	⇌ d	22 04		22 45	22 50
Sheffield 7	⇌ a	22 15		22 54	22 58
	d				
Stockport	78 a				
Manchester Piccadilly 10	⇌ a				
Manchester Airport	85 ✈ a				

Table 29

Sundays
from 12 September

Hull and Cleethorpes - Doncaster - Meadowhall, Sheffield, Manchester and Manchester Airport
Cleethorpes - Barton-on-Humber

		NT	NT	XC	NT	NT	NT	TP	HT	NT	XC	NT	TP	NT	NT	NT	XC	NT	TP	TP
				◇1				◇1	◇1		◇1		◇1				◇1		◇1	◇1
				A										B	B					
				🍴					☒		🍴				🚌		🍴			
Hull	d					08 42	08 54	09 00	09 07			09 41						10 41		10 58
Hessle	d					08 49														
Ferriby	d					08 54														
Brough	d					08 59	09 06	09 12	09 19			09 53						10 53		11 10
Broomfleet	d																			
Gilberdyke	d					09 06						10 00						11 00		
Eastrington	d																			
Howden	d						09 18		09 31											
Wressle	d																			
Selby	a						09 27	09 32	09 41											11 28
	d						09 28	09 33	09 42											11 29
York 8	33 a						09 56													
Saltmarshe	d																			
Goole	d					09 15				09 43		10 09						11 09		
Thorne North	d									09 51										
Cleethorpes	d												09 28	09 55					10 28	
New Clee	d													09 59						
Grimsby Docks	d													10 01						
Grimsby Town	a												09 35	10 04					10 35	
	d												09 36	10 04					10 36	
Great Coates	d													10 08						
Healing	d													10 11						
Stallingborough	d													10 12						
Habrough	d												09 46	10 19					10 46	
Ulceby	d													10 23						
Thornton Abbey	d													10 28						
Goxhill	d													10 31						
New Holland	d													10 36						
Barrow Haven	d													10 39						
Barton-on-Humber	a													10 44						
Barton-on-Humber	d														10 55					
Hull Paragon Interchange	a														11 19					
Barnetby	d												09 55						10 55	
Scunthorpe	a												10 10						11 10	
	d												10 10						11 10	
Althorpe	d																			
Crowle	d																			
Thorne South	d																			
Hatfield & Stainforth	d									09 57		10 21								
Kirk Sandall	d									10 02		10 26								
Adwick	31 d																			
Bentley (S.Yorks)	31 d																			
Doncaster 7	31 a					09 38			09 58	10 11		10 36	10 40					11 32	11 40	
London Kings Cross 15	⊖26 a								11 49											
York 8	26 d										09 28						10 28			
Doncaster 7	d	08 03	09 13	09 32		09 39				10 13	10 30		10 42			11 13	11 30	11 33	11 42	
Conisbrough	d	08 10	09 20							10 20						11 20				
Mexborough	d	08 14	09 24							10 24						11 24				
Swinton (S.Yorks)	d	08 17	09 28		09 35					10 27						11 27				
Rotherham Central	d	08 25	09 35		09 48					10 35						11 35				
Meadowhall	⇌ d	08 30	09 41		09 54	10 00				10 40			11 00			11 40		11 52	12 00	
Sheffield 7	⇌ a	08 41	09 51	09 55	10 03	10 09				10 52	10 54		11 07			11 51	11 53	12 03	12 07	
	d												11 10						12 10	
Stockport	78 a												11 53						12 53	
Manchester Piccadilly 10	⇌ a												12 06						13 02	
Manchester Airport	85 ✈ a												12 29						13 29	

A Until 17 October

B 12 September

Table 29

Sundays
from 12 September

Hull and Cleethorpes - Doncaster - Meadowhall, Sheffield, Manchester and Manchester Airport
Cleethorpes - Barton-on-Humber

	NT	NT	XC	NT	TP	NT	TP	HT	NT	NT	XC	NT	TP	NT	TP	NT	NT	XC	NT	NT	TP	TP
			◇1		◇1		◇1	◇1			◇1		◇1		◇1			◇1			◇1	◇1
									A					A		A 🚌						
			⊼					⊠			⊼							⊼				
Hull d				11 41		11 53	12 00	12 12				12 41	12 58	13 24						13 35		
Hessle d																				13 42		
Ferriby d																				13 47		
Brough d				11 53		12 05	12 12	12 24				12 53	13 10	13 36						13 52		
Broomfleet d																						
Gilberdyke d				12 00								13 00								14 00		
Eastrington d																						
Howden d						12 17		12 36						13 48								
Wressle d																						
Selby a						12 26	12 32	12 46					13 28	13 57								
d						12 27	12 33	12 47					13 29	13 58								
York 8 33 a						12 51								14 22								
Saltmarshe d																						
Goole d		11 43		12 09								13 09							13 43	14 08		
Thorne North d		11 51																	13 51			
Cleethorpes d					11 28				12 55												13 28	
New Clee d									12 59													
Grimsby Docks d									13 01													
Grimsby Town a					11 35				13 04												13 35	
d					11 36				13 04												13 36	
Great Coates d									13 08													
Healing d									13 11													
Stallingborough d									13 12													
Habrough d									13 19													
Ulceby d									13 23													
Thornton Abbey d									13 28													
Goxhill d									13 31													
New Holland d									13 36													
Barrow Haven d									13 39													
Barton-on-Humber a									13 44													
Barton-on-Humber d																13 55						
Hull Paragon Interchange a																14 19						
Barnetby d					11 55																13 55	
Scunthorpe a					12 10																14 10	
d					12 10																14 10	
Althorpe d																						
Crowle d																						
Thorne South d																						
Hatfield & Stainforth d		11 57																	13 57			
Kirk Sandall d		12 02																	14 02			
Adwick 31 d																						
Bentley (S.Yorks) 31 d																						
Doncaster 7 31 a		12 14		12 32	12 40			13 05				13 32							14 11	14 31	14 40	
London Kings Cross 15 ⊖26 a								14 55														
York 8 26 d			11 28								12 28							13 28				14 15
Doncaster 7 d		12 16	12 30		12 42					13 13	13 30	13 34			13 42				14 13	14 33	14 42	
Conisbrough d		12 23								13 20									14 20			
Mexborough d		12 27								13 24									14 24			
Swinton (S.Yorks) d	11 55	12 30								13 27							14 01		14 30			
Rotherham Central d	12 06	12 38								13 36							14 09		14 37			
Meadowhall 🚋 d	12 11	12 43			13 00					13 44		13 53			14 00		14 17		14 43	14 52	15 00	
Sheffield 7 🚋 a	12 20	12 55	12 54		13 07					13 52	13 54	14 04			14 07		14 25	14 45	14 52	15 03	15 07	
d					13 10										14 11						15 11	
Stockport 78 a					13 53										14 53						15 53	
Manchester Piccadilly 10 🚋 a					14 06										15 06						16 06	15 34
Manchester Airport 85 ✈ a					14 29										15 29						16 29	15 55

A 12 September

Table 29

Sundays
from 12 September

Hull and Cleethorpes - Doncaster - Meadowhall, Sheffield, Manchester and Manchester Airport
Cleethorpes - Barton-on-Humber

	HT	XC	XC	NT	NT	NT	TP	TP	NT	XC	NT	XC	NT	NT	TP	NT	NT	XC	XC
	◇1	◇1	◇1				◇1	◇1		◇1		◇1			◇1			◇1	◇1
									A							A 🚌	A		
	⊠	⊼	⊼							⊼		⊼						⊼	⊼
Hull d	14 10			14 28		14 41		14 58						15 41			16 00		
Hessle d																			
Ferriby d																			
Brough d	14 22			14 40		14 53		15 10						15 53			16 12		
Broomfleet d																			
Gilberdyke d						15 00								16 00					
Eastrington d																			
Howden d	14 34			14 52													16 24		
Wressle d																			
Selby a	14 44			15 01				15 28									16 33		
d	14 45			15 02				15 29									16 34		
York 8 33 a				15 27													16 58		
Saltmarshe d																			
Goole d						15 09							15 43	16 09					
Thorne North d													15 51						
Cleethorpes d							14 28		15 01						15 28				
New Clee d									15 05										
Grimsby Docks d									15 07										
Grimsby Town a							14 35		15 10						15 35				
d							14 36		15 10						15 36				
Great Coates d									15 14										
Healing d									15 17										
Stallingborough d									15 18										
Habrough d							14 46		15 25										
Ulceby d									15 29										
Thornton Abbey d									15 34										
Goxhill d									15 37										
New Holland d									15 42										
Barrow Haven d									15 45										
Barton-on-Humber a									15 50										
Barton-on-Humber d																15 55			
Hull Paragon Interchange a																16 19			
Barnetby d							14 55								15 55				
Scunthorpe a							15 10								16 10				
d							15 10								16 10				
Althorpe d																			
Crowle d																			
Thorne South d																			
Hatfield & Stainforth d													15 57						
Kirk Sandall d													16 02						
Adwick 31 d																			
Bentley (S.Yorks) 31 d																			
Doncaster 7 31 a	15 05					15 32	15 40						16 11	16 32	16 40				
London Kings Cross 15 ⊖26 a	16 55																		
York 8 26 d		14 22	14 28							15 20		15 28						16 20	16 28
Doncaster 7 d		14 50			15 13	15 33	15 42			15 50			16 13	16 33	16 42			16 50	
Conisbrough d					15 20								16 20						
Mexborough d					15 24								16 24						
Swinton (S.Yorks) d					15 30						15 55		16 29						
Rotherham Central d					15 37						16 05		16 37						
Meadowhall 🚋 d					15 43	15 52	16 00				16 11		16 43	16 53	17 00				
Sheffield 7 🚋 a		15 18	15 42		15 51	16 01	16 07			16 15	16 21	16 41	16 52	17 03	17 07			17 18	17 41
d							16 11								17 11				
Stockport 78 a							16 53								17 53				
Manchester Piccadilly 10 🚋 a							17 06	16 54							18 06				
Manchester Airport 85 ✈ a							17 29								18 29				

A 12 September

Hull and Cleethorpes - Doncaster - Meadowhall, Sheffield, Manchester and Manchester Airport
Cleethorpes - Barton-on-Humber

		HT		NT	NT	TP	XC	NT	NT	EM	NT	TP	NT	GR	NT	TP	NT	XC		XC	TP	TP	NT	NT
		◇■				◇■	◇■			◇■		◇■		■		◇■	A	◇■		◇■	◇■	◇■	A	
Hull	d	16 23			16 41	16 58		17 23						17 30	17 41									
Hessle	d																							
Ferriby	d																							
Brough	d	16 35			16 53	17 10		17 35						17 42	17 53									
Broomfleet	d																							
Gilberdyke	d				17 00										18 00									
Eastrington	d																							
Howden	d	16 47						17 47																
Wressle	d																							
Selby	a	16 57				17 28		17 56						18 05										
	d	16 58				17 29		17 57						18 05										
York 8 33	a							18 23																
Saltmarshe	d																							
Goole	d				17 09								17 43		18 09									
Thorne North	d												17 51											
Cleethorpes	d											16 28				17 28	17 55					18 28		
New Clee	d																17 59							
Grimsby Docks	d																18 01							
Grimsby Town	a											16 35				17 35	18 04					18 35		
	d											16 36				17 36	18 04					18 36		
Great Coates	d																18 08							
Healing	d																18 11							
Stallingborough	d																18 12							
Habrough	d															17 46	18 19							
Ulceby	d																18 23							
Thornton Abbey	d																18 28							
Goxhill	d																18 31							
New Holland	d																18 36							
Barrow Haven	d																18 39							
Barton-on-Humber	a																18 44							
Barton-on-Humber	d																						18 55	
Hull Paragon Interchange	a																						19 19	
Barnetby	d											16 55				17 55						18 55		
Scunthorpe	a											17 10				18 10						19 10		
	d											17 10				18 10						19 10		
Althorpe	d																							
Crowle	d																							
Thorne South	d																							
Hatfield & Stainforth	d												17 57											
Kirk Sandall	d												18 02											
Adwick 31	d																							
Bentley (S.Yorks) 31	d																							
Doncaster 7 31	a	17 14			17 31							17 40	18 11	18 23	18 33	18 40						19 40		
London Kings Cross 15 ⊖26	a	19 06												20 23										
York 8 26	d						17 21			17 40	17 17							18 20		18 28	18 33			
Doncaster 7	d			17 13	17 32		17 50			18 06		17 42	18 13		18 34	18 42		18 50				19 42		19 15
Conisbrough	d			17 21									18 20											19 22
Mexborough	d			17 25									18 24											19 26
Swinton (S.Yorks)	d			17 30					17 55		18 11		18 30											19 30
Rotherham Central	d			17 38					18 06		18 18		18 37											19 41
Meadowhall	d			17 43	17 53				18 12		18 24	18 00	18 43		18 53	19 00						20 00		19 47
Sheffield 7	a			17 54	18 01		18 18		18 23	18 28	18 35	18 07	18 52		19 03	19 07		19 15		19 40		20 07		19 55
	d											18 11				19 11						20 11		
Stockport 78	a											18 53				19 53						20 53		
Manchester Piccadilly 10	a					18 54						19 06				20 06					19 54	21 06		
Manchester Airport 85	a											19 29				20 29						21 29		

A 12 September

Table 29

Sundays
from 12 September

Hull and Cleethorpes - Doncaster - Meadowhall, Sheffield, Manchester and Manchester Airport
Cleethorpes - Barton-on-Humber

		NT	HT	TP	NT	XC		NT	XC		NT	TP	XC	NT	XC	NT		NT	TP	TP	NT	NT
			◇■	◇■	A	◇■			◇■			◇■	◇■		◇■				◇■	◇■		
Hull	d	18 38	18 48	18 58	19 04									20 22		20 30				21 00		21 15
Hessle	d																					21 22
Ferriby	d																					21 27
Brough	d	18 50	19 00	19 10	19 16									20 34		20 42				21 12		21 32
Broomfleet	d																					
Gilberdyke	d	18 57														20 49						21 39
Eastrington	d																					
Howden	d		19 12		19 28									20 46								
Wressle	d																					
Selby	a		19 22	19 28	19 37									20 55						21 30		
	d		19 23	19 29	19 38									20 56						21 31		
York 8 33	a				20 02									21 20								
Saltmarshe	d																					
Goole	d	19 06														20 58						21 48
Thorne North	d	19 14																				21 56
Cleethorpes	d											19 28							20 28			
New Clee	d																					
Grimsby Docks	d																					
Grimsby Town	a											19 35							20 35			
	d											19 36							20 36			
Great Coates	d																					
Healing	d																					
Stallingborough	d																					
Habrough	d																		20 46			
Ulceby	d																					
Thornton Abbey	d																					
Goxhill	d																					
New Holland	d																					
Barrow Haven	d																					
Barton-on-Humber	a																					
Barton-on-Humber	d																					
Hull Paragon Interchange	a																					
Barnetby	d											19 55							20 55			
Scunthorpe	a											20 10							21 10			
	d											20 10							21 10			
Althorpe	d																					
Crowle	d																					
Thorne South	d																					
Hatfield & Stainforth	d	19 20																				22 02
Kirk Sandall	d	19 25																				22 07
Adwick 31	d																					
Bentley (S.Yorks) 31	d																					
Doncaster 7 31	a	19 35	19 43									20 40				21 21			21 40			22 17
London Kings Cross 15 ⊖26	a		21 35																			
York 8 26	d					19 20			19 28				20 20		20 28			20 42				
Doncaster 7	d	19 37				19 50					20 14	20 42	20c50			21 23			21 42			22 20
Conisbrough	d										20 21											22 27
Mexborough	d										20 25											22 31
Swinton (S.Yorks)	d							19 55			20 32							21 38	21 52		22 32	22 37
Rotherham Central	d							20 06			20 39					21 39		21 49	21 58		22 40	22 44
Meadowhall	d	19 57						20 11			20 45	21 00				21 45		21 54	22 04		22 45	22 50
Sheffield 7	a	20 06				20 16		20 23	20 40		20 53	21 07	21 17		21 44	21 56		22 05	22 15		22 54	22 58
	d											21 11										
Stockport 78	a											21 53										
Manchester Piccadilly 10	a			20 54								22 06										
Manchester Airport 85	a											22 29										

A 12 September

c arr. 2043

Table 29

Manchester Airport, Manchester, Sheffield and Meadowhall - Doncaster - Cleethorpes and Hull Barton-on-Humber - Cleethorpes

		NT	NT	NT	NT	NT	EM	NT	NT	NT	XC	NT	NT
					bus						◇1 ✕		bus
Manchester Airport 85 ✈	d												
Manchester Piccadilly 10	d												
Stockport 78	d												
Sheffield 7	a												
	d	05 22		05 29					06 18	06 28	06 40	06 52	
Meadowhall	d	05 28		05 35					06 24	06 34		06 58	
Rotherham Central	d	05 34		05 41					06 30	06 40		07 04	
Swinton (S.Yorks)	d	05a42		05 49					06 38	06a51		07 14	
Mexborough	d			05 52					06 41			07 17	
Conisbrough	d			05 56					06 45			07 21	
London Kings Cross	d												
Doncaster 7	a			06 06					06 56		07 04	07 30	
York 8 26	a										07 27		
Doncaster 31	d		05 52	06 14		06 25		06 47	06 59			07 32	
Bentley (S.Yorks) 31	a					06 28			07 02			07 35	
Adwick 31	a					06 32			07 08			07 40	
Kirk Sandall	d			06 20				06 53					
Hatfield & Stainforth	d			06 25				06 58					
Thorne South	d							07 03					
Crowle	d							07 11					
Althorpe	d							07 17					
Scunthorpe	a							07 26					
	d												
Barnetby	d						06 31						
Hull Paragon Interchange	d				06 20								06 55
Barton-on-Humber	a				06 52								07 30
Barton-on-Humber	d												
Barrow Haven	d												
New Holland	d												
Goxhill	d												
Thornton Abbey	d												
Ulceby	d												
Habrough	d						06 41						
Stallingborough	d												
Healing	d												
Great Coates	d												
Grimsby Town	a						06 56						
	d												
Grimsby Docks	d												
New Clee	d												
Cleethorpes	a												
Thorne North	d			06 31									
Goole	d			06 42									
Saltmarshe	d			06 46									
York 8 33	d												
Selby	a		06 14										
Wressle	d												
Howden	d												
Eastrington	d												
Gilberdyke	d			06 53									
Broomfleet	d			06 57									
Brough	d			07 03									
Ferriby	d			07 07									
Hessle	d			07 12									
Hull	a			07 22									

Table 29

Manchester Airport, Manchester, Sheffield and Meadowhall - Doncaster - Cleethorpes and Hull Barton-on-Humber - Cleethorpes

		NT	NT	TP	XC	NT	NT	TP	NT	NT	NT	NT	NT	TP	NT	XC	EM	NT	NT	TP	NT	XC
				◇1	◇1 ✕			◇1 ✕						◇1 ✕		◇1 ✕				◇1 ✕		◇1 ✕
Manchester Airport 85 ✈	d			05 15																06 55		
Manchester Piccadilly 10	d			05b44				06 21						07 36						07c20		
Stockport 78	d			05 52																07 28		
Sheffield 7	a			06 49	07 06											07 48				08 10		08 17
	d			06 55	07 12	07 14						07 24	07 41			07 54				08 11	08 14	08 21
Meadowhall	d			07 01		07 21						07 30	07 47							08 17	08 23	
Rotherham Central	d					07 27						07 36	07 55								08 29	
Swinton (S.Yorks)	d					07a35						07 44	08 03								08a38	
Mexborough	d											07 47	08 06									
Conisbrough	d											07 51	08 10									
London Kings Cross	d																					
Doncaster 7	a			07 22								08 01	08 20			08 25				08 40		
York 8 26	a				08 23											08 47						09 33
Doncaster 31	d		07 14	07 24					07 28		07 58	08 03	08 22					08 26	08 52	08 42		
Bentley (S.Yorks) 31	a		07 17								08 01							08 29	08 55			
Adwick 31	a		07 21								08 05							08 33	09 01			
Kirk Sandall	d								07 34			08 09										
Hatfield & Stainforth	d								07 39			08 14										
Thorne South	d											08 18										
Crowle	d											08 27										
Althorpe	d											08 33										
Scunthorpe	a			07 49								08 43								09 07		
	d			07 50																09 08		
Barnetby	d			08 04													08 52			09 22		
Hull Paragon Interchange	d																					
Barton-on-Humber	a																					
Barton-on-Humber	d	06 58													08 00							
Barrow Haven	d	07 03													08 05							
New Holland	d	07 07													08 08							
Goxhill	d	07 11													08 13							
Thornton Abbey	d														08 16							
Ulceby	d	07 19													08 20							
Habrough	d	07 23		08 12											08 25		09 01					
Stallingborough	d	07 28													08 30							
Healing	d	07 31													08 33							
Great Coates	d														08 36							
Grimsby Town	a	07 38		08 26											08 41		09 15			09 42		
	d	07 38		08 35											08 41					09 43		
Grimsby Docks	d														08 44							
New Clee	d														08x46							
Cleethorpes	a	07 50		08 46											08 51					09 54		
Thorne North	d								07 44													
Goole	d								07 53				08 42									
Saltmarshe	d								07 58													
York 8 33	d									07 30												
Selby	a							07 43		07 50				08 58								
Wressle	d									07 58												
Howden	d							07 52		08 03												
Eastrington	d									08 08												
Gilberdyke	d						07 39		08 04	08 12												
Broomfleet	d						07 43			08 16												
Brough	d						07 49	08 04	08 12	08 22			08 56									
Ferriby	d						07 53		08 16	08 27												
Hessle	d						07 58		08 21	08 31												
Hull	a						08 11	08 20	08 34	08 46			09 12	09 31								

b arr. 0533 c arr. 0713

Table 29

Mondays to Fridays

Manchester Airport, Manchester, Sheffield and Meadowhall - Doncaster - Cleethorpes and Hull Barton-on-Humber - Cleethorpes

	NT	HT BHX	NT	NT	NT	NT	TP	XC	NT	TP	NT	XC	NT	NT	NT	NT	NT	NT	NT	TP
		◇1 ⊠		🚌			◇1 ✠	◇1 ✠		◇1 ✠		◇1 ✠								◇1 ✠
Manchester Airport 85 ✈ d										07 54										
Manchester Piccadilly 10 ⇌ d							08 42			08b20										09 42
Stockport 78 d										08 28										
Sheffield 7 ⇌ a								08 46	08 49	09 08		09 17								
d			08 25			08 41		08 54	08 57	09 11	09 14	09 21		09 24	09 29				09 41	
Meadowhall ⇌ d			08 31			08 47			09 03	09 17	09 21			09 30	09 35				09 47	
Rotherham Central d			08 37						09 11		09 27			09 37	09 42					
Swinton (S.Yorks) d			08 48						09 19		09a36			09 48	09 51					
Mexborough d			08 51						09 22					09 51						
Conisbrough d			08 55						09 26					09 55						
London Kings Cross d		07 20																		
Doncaster 7 a		09 05	09 05			09 12		09 20	09 36	09 40				10 04					10 11	
York 8 26 a								09 48				10 27			10 52					
Doncaster 31 d	08 56	09 06	09 10		09 14	09 16			09 38	09 42			09 46	10 06				10 14	10 16	
Bentley (S.Yorks) 31 a					09 17				09 41									10 17		
Adwick 31 a					09 21				09 47									10 21		
Kirk Sandall d	09 02		09 18										09 52	10 12						
Hatfield & Stainforth d	09 07		09 23										09 57	10 17						
Thorne South d			09 28											10 22						
Crowle d			09 36											10 31						
Althorpe d			09 42											10 37						
Scunthorpe a			09 50							10 07				10 45						
d										10 08										
Barnetby d										10 22										
Hull Paragon Interchange d				09 05																
Barton-on-Humber a				09 40																
Barton-on-Humber d																	09 58			
Barrow Haven d																	10 03			
New Holland d																	10 06			
Goxhill d																	10 11			
Thornton Abbey d																	10 14			
Ulceby d																	10 18			
Habrough d										10 31							10 23			
Stallingborough d																	10 28			
Healing d																	10 31			
Great Coates d																	10 34			
Grimsby Town a										10 44							10 39			
d										10 45							10 39			
Grimsby Docks d																	10 42			
New Clee d																	10x44			
Cleethorpes a										10 59							10 49			
Thorne North d	09 12												10 02							
Goole d	09 21					09 39							10 11						10 35	
Saltmarshe d																				
York 8 33 d																09 53				
Selby a		09 21					09 57									10 12				10 57
Wressle d																				
Howden d		09 32														10 22				
Eastrington d																				
Gilberdyke d	09 29												10 19			10 29				
Broomfleet d																				
Brough d	09 37	09 44				09 53	10 16						10 27			10 37			10 49	11 16
Ferriby d	09 42												10 32							
Hessle d	09 46												10 36							
Hull a	09 59	10 03				10 10	10 34						10 49			10 56			11 06	11 34

b arr. 0813

Table 29

Mondays to Fridays

Manchester Airport, Manchester, Sheffield and Meadowhall - Doncaster - Cleethorpes and Hull Barton-on-Humber - Cleethorpes

	XC	NT	TP	NT	XC	NT	NT	NT	XC	EM	NT	NT	HT	TP	NT	TP	NT	XC	NT	NT
	◇1 ✠		◇1 ✠		◇1 ✠				◇1 ✠		🚌		◇1 ⊠	◇1 ✠		◇1 ✠		◇1 ✠		
Manchester Airport 85 ✈ d			08 55													09 55				
Manchester Piccadilly 10 ⇌ d			09b20											10 42		10c20				
Stockport 78 d			09 28													10 28				
Sheffield 7 ⇌ a	09 46	09 49	10 08		10 17				10 46						10 49	11 08		11 17		
d	09 54	09 57	10 11	10 14	10 21		10 24	10 41	10 54						10 57	11 11	11 14	11 21		11 24
Meadowhall ⇌ d		10 03	10 17	10 21			10 30	10 47							11 03	11 17	11 21			11 30
Rotherham Central d		10 10		10 27			10 36								11 10		11 27			11 37
Swinton (S.Yorks) d		10 18		10a36			10 44								11 20		11a36			11 48
Mexborough d		10 21					10 47								11 23					11 51
Conisbrough d		10 25					10 51								11 27					11 55
London Kings Cross d													09 48							
Doncaster 7 a	10 15	10 36	10 40				11 05	11 07	11 15				11 32		11 35	11 40				12 04
York 8 26 a	10 40				11 28				11 45									12 29		
Doncaster 31 d		10 46	10 42			10 46	11 07	11 17				11 26	11 36		11 38	11 42			11 49	12 07
Bentley (S.Yorks) 31 a		10 49										11 29			11 41					
Adwick 31 a		10 55										11 33			11 47					
Kirk Sandall d						10 52	11 13												11 55	12 14
Hatfield & Stainforth d						10 57	11 18												12 00	12 19
Thorne South d							11 23													12 24
Crowle d							11 31													12 32
Althorpe d							11 37													12 38
Scunthorpe a			11 07				11 45									12 07				12 46
d			11 08													12 08				
Barnetby d			11 22							10 57						12 22				
Hull Paragon Interchange d											11 05									
Barton-on-Humber a											11 40									
Barton-on-Humber d																				
Barrow Haven d																				
New Holland d																				
Goxhill d																				
Thornton Abbey d																				
Ulceby d																				
Habrough d										11 06						12 31				
Stallingborough d																				
Healing d																				
Great Coates d																				
Grimsby Town a			11 42							11 21						12 44				
d			11 43													12 45				
Grimsby Docks d																				
New Clee d																				
Cleethorpes a			11 54													12 57				
Thorne North d						11 02													12 05	
Goole d						11 11		11 37											12 14	
Saltmarshe d																				
York 8 33 d																				
Selby a													11 51	11 57						
Wressle d																				
Howden d													12 02							
Eastrington d																				
Gilberdyke d						11 19													12 22	
Broomfleet d						11 24														
Brough d						11 30		11 51					12 15	12 19					12 30	
Ferriby d						11 34													12 35	
Hessle d						11 39													12 39	
Hull a						11 52		12 09					12 32	12 36					12 52	

b arr. 0913

c arr. 1013

Table 29

Mondays to Fridays

Manchester Airport, Manchester, Sheffield and Meadowhall - Doncaster - Cleethorpes and Hull Barton-on-Humber - Cleethorpes

		NT	NT	TP	XC	NT	NT	NT	TP	NT	XC	NT	NT	NT	XC	NT	EM	NT	HT	TP	NT	NT
				◇1 ⊼	◇1 ⊼				◇1 ⊼		◇1 ⊼				◇1 ⊼	🚌			◇1 ⊠	◇1 ⊼		
Manchester Airport 85 ✈	d								10 55													
Manchester Piccadilly 10	d			11 42					11b20											12 42		
Stockport 78	d								11 28													
Sheffield 7	a				11 46			11 49	12 08		12 17				12 46						12 49	
	d		11 41		11 54			11 57	12 11	12 14	12 21		12 24	12 41	12 54						12 57	
Meadowhall	d		11 47					12 03	12 17	12 21			12 30	12 47							13 03	
Rotherham Central	d							12 10		12 27			12 37								13 10	
Swinton (S.Yorks)	d							12 19		12a36			12 47								13 18	
Mexborough	d							12 22					12 50								13 21	
Conisbrough	d							12 26					12 54								13 25	
London Kings Cross	d																		11 48			
Doncaster 7	a		12 11		12 15			12 35	12 40				13 04	13 11	13 20				13 29		13 35	
York 8 26	a				12 45						13 29				13 46							
Doncaster 31	d		12 14				12 25	12 38	12 42			12 49	13 06	13 18				13 27	13 29		13 38	
Bentley (S.Yorks) 31	a						12 28	12 41										13 30			13 41	
Adwick 31	a						12 32	12 46										13 34			13 47	
Kirk Sandall	d											12 55	13 12									
Hatfield & Stainforth	d											13 00	13 17									
Thorne South	d												13 22									
Crowle	d												13 31									
Althorpe	d												13 37									
Scunthorpe	a								13 07				13 45									
	d								13 08													
Barnetby	d								13 22								13 12					
Hull Paragon Interchange	d															13 05						
Barton-on-Humber	a															13 40						
Barton-on-Humber	d					11 58																13 58
Barrow Haven	d					12 03																14 03
New Holland	d					12 06																14 06
Goxhill	d					12 11																14 11
Thornton Abbey	d					12 14																14 14
Ulceby	d					12 18																14 18
Habrough	d					12 23											13 21					14 23
Stallingborough	d					12 28																14 28
Healing	d					12 31																14 31
Great Coates	d					12 34																14 34
Grimsby Town	a					12 39			13 42								13 36					14 39
	d					12 39			13 43													14 39
Grimsby Docks	d					12 42																14 42
New Clee	d					12x44																14x44
Cleethorpes	a					12 49			13 54													14 49
Thorne North	d											13 05										
Goole	d		12 35									13 14		13 37								
Saltmarshe	d																					
York 8 33	d	11 53																				
Selby	a	12 17		12 57															13 44	13 57		
Wressle	d																					
Howden	d	12 27																	13 55			
Eastrington	d																					
Gilberdyke	d	12 34										13 22										
Broomfleet	d																					
Brough	d	12 42	12 49	13 16								13 30		13 51					14 08	14 16		
Ferriby	d											13 35										
Hessle	d											13 39										
Hull	a	13 02	13 06	13 34								13 52		14 08					14 25	14 34		

b arr. 1113

Table 29

Mondays to Fridays

Manchester Airport, Manchester, Sheffield and Meadowhall - Doncaster - Cleethorpes and Hull Barton-on-Humber - Cleethorpes

		TP	NT	XC	NT	NT	NT	NT	NT	TP	XC	NT	NT	TP	EM	NT	XC	NT	NT
		◇1 ⊼		◇1 ⊼						◇1 ⊼	◇1 ⊼			◇1 ⊼			◇1 ⊼		
Manchester Airport 85 ✈	d	11 55												12 55					
Manchester Piccadilly 10	d	12b20								13 42				13c20					
Stockport 78	d	12 28												13 28					
Sheffield 7	a	13 08		13 17							13 46		13 49	14 08			14 17		
	d	13 11	13 14	13 21			13 24	13 28	13 41		13 54		13 57	14 11		14 14	14 21		14 24
Meadowhall	d	13 17	13 21				13 30	13 35	13 46				14 03	14 17		14 21			14 30
Rotherham Central	d		13 27				13 37	13 41					14 10			14 27			14 37
Swinton (S.Yorks)	d		13 36				13 47	13 50					14 18			14a36			14 48
Mexborough	d						13 50						14 21						14 51
Conisbrough	d						13 54						14 25						14 55
London Kings Cross	d																		
Doncaster 7	a	13 40					14 04		14 13		14 17		14 35	14 40					15 04
York 8 26	a			14 29				14 51			14 43						15 29		
Doncaster 31	d	13 42				13 46	14 06		14 17			14 27	14 38	14 42				14 46	15 06
Bentley (S.Yorks) 31	a											14 30	14 41						
Adwick 31	a											14 34	14 47						
Kirk Sandall	d					13 52	14 13											14 53	15 12
Hatfield & Stainforth	d					13 57	14 18											14 58	15 17
Thorne South	d						14 23												15 22
Crowle	d						14 32												15 30
Althorpe	d						14 38												15 36
Scunthorpe	a	14 07					14 45							15 07					15 45
	d	14 08												15 08					
Barnetby	d	14 22												15 22	15 34				
Hull Paragon Interchange	d																		
Barton-on-Humber	a																		
Barton-on-Humber	d																		
Barrow Haven	d																		
New Holland	d																		
Goxhill	d																		
Thornton Abbey	d																		
Ulceby	d																		
Habrough	d	14 31													15 42				
Stallingborough	d																		
Healing	d																		
Great Coates	d																		
Grimsby Town	a	14 44												15 42	15 57				
	d	14 45												15 43					
Grimsby Docks	d																		
New Clee	d																		
Cleethorpes	a	14 57												15 54					
Thorne North	d					14 02												15 03	
Goole	d					14 12			14 37									15 12	
Saltmarshe	d					14 17													
York 8 33	d				13 44														
Selby	a				14 08					14 57									
Wressle	d																		
Howden	d				14 17														
Eastrington	d																		
Gilberdyke	d					14 28												15 20	
Broomfleet	d																		
Brough	d				14 29	14 36			14 52	15 16								15 28	
Ferriby	d					14 40												15 33	
Hessle	d					14 45												15 37	
Hull	a				14 49	14 56			15 10	15 34								15 50	

b arr. 1213

c arr. 1313

Table 29

Manchester Airport, Manchester, Sheffield and Meadowhall - Doncaster - Cleethorpes and Hull Barton-on-Humber - Cleethorpes

	NT	NT	HT	TP	XC	NT	NT	NT	NT	TP	NT	XC	NT	NT	NT	NT	XC	NT	TP	NT
			◇1	◇1	◇1					◇1		◇1					◇1		◇1	
			⊠	⊤	⊤	🚌				⊤		⊤					⊤		⊤	
Manchester Airport 85 ✈ d										13 55									14 55	
Manchester Piccadilly 10 d				14 42						14b20									15c20	
Stockport 78 d										14 28									15 28	
Sheffield 7 a					14 46				14 49	15 08		15 17					15 46	15 49	16 08	
d		14 41			14 54				14 57	15 11	15 14	15 21		15 24		15 41	15 54	15 57	16 11	
Meadowhall d		14 47							15 03	15 17	15 21			15 30		15 47		16 03	16 17	
Rotherham Central d									15 10		15 27			15 37				16 10		
Swinton (S.Yorks) d									15 18		15a36			15 47				16 18		
Mexborough d									15 21					15 50				16 21		
Conisbrough d									15 25					15 54				16 25		
London Kings Cross d			13 33																	
Doncaster 7 a		15 09	15 11		15 16				15 36	15 40				16 04		16 12	16 15	16 35	16 40	
York 8 26 a					15 40							16 29					16 39			
Doncaster 31 d		15 14	15 12					15 14	15 38	15 42			15 46	16 09	16 14	16 18		16 38	16 42	
Bentley (S.Yorks) 31 a								15 17	15 41						16 17			16 41		
Adwick 31 a								15 21	15 47						16 21			16 47		
Kirk Sandall d													15 52	16 15						
Hatfield & Stainforth d													15 57	16 20						
Thorne South d														16 25						
Crowle d														16 34						
Althorpe d														16 40						
Scunthorpe a										16 07				16 48					17 07	
d										16 08									17 08	
Barnetby d										16 22									17 22	
Hull Paragon Interchange d						15 05														
Barton-on-Humber a						15 40														
Barton-on-Humber d							15 58													
Barrow Haven d							16 03													
New Holland d							16 06													
Goxhill d							16 11													
Thornton Abbey d							16 14													
Ulceby d							16 18													
Habrough d							16 23			16 31										
Stallingborough d							16 28													
Healing d							16 31													
Great Coates d							16 34													
Grimsby Town a							16 39			16 44									17 42	
d							16 39			16 45									17 43	
Grimsby Docks d							16 42													
New Clee d																				
Cleethorpes a							16 48			16 57									17 54	
Thorne North d													16 02							
Goole d		15 33											16 11			16 36				
Saltmarshe d																				
York 8 33 d	14 59																			16 12
Selby a	15 18		15 27	15 57																16 38
Wressle d																				16 46
Howden d	15 28		15 38																	16 51
Eastrington d																				
Gilberdyke d													16 20							16 58
Broomfleet d																				
Brough d	15 40	15 47	15 53	16 16									16 28			16 49				17 06
Ferriby d													16 32							17 10
Hessle d													16 37							
Hull a	15 59	16 04	16 10	16 34									16 49			17 11				17 27

b arr. 1413 c arr. 1513

Table 29

Manchester Airport, Manchester, Sheffield and Meadowhall - Doncaster - Cleethorpes and Hull Barton-on-Humber - Cleethorpes

	TP	NT	XC	NT	NT	NT	XC	EM	NT	NT	NT	NT	TP	NT	XC	NT	HT	NT	TP
	◇1		◇1				◇1						◇1		◇1		◇1		◇1
	⊤		⊤				⊤		🚌				⊤		⊤		⊠		⊤
Manchester Airport 85 ✈ d													15 55						
Manchester Piccadilly 10 d	15 42												16b20						16 42
Stockport 78 d													16 28						
Sheffield 7 a			16 17				16 46					16 49	17 08		17 19				
d		16 14	16 21	16 24		16 41	16 54					16 57	17 11	17 14	17 22			17 25	
Meadowhall d		16 21		16 30		16 47						17 03	17 17	17 21				17 31	
Rotherham Central d		16 27		16 37								17 10		17 27				17 39	
Swinton (S.Yorks) d		16a36		16 47								17 18		17a36				17 47	
Mexborough d				16 50								17 21						17 50	
Conisbrough d				16 54								17 25						17 54	
London Kings Cross d																	16 05		
Doncaster 7 a				17 07		17 12	17 15					17 35	17 40				17 41	18 07	
York 8 26 a			17 30				17 40								18 31				
Doncaster 31 d					16 46	17 14				17 22	17 27	17 38	17 42				17 42		
Bentley (S.Yorks) 31 a											17 30	17 41							
Adwick 31 a											17 34	17 47							
Kirk Sandall d					16 52					17 29									
Hatfield & Stainforth d					16 57					17 34									
Thorne South d										17 39									
Crowle d										17 47									
Althorpe d										17 53									
Scunthorpe a										18 01			18 07						
d													18 08						
Barnetby d								17 54					18 22						
Hull Paragon Interchange d									17 10										
Barton-on-Humber a									17 45										
Barton-on-Humber d																			
Barrow Haven d																			
New Holland d																			
Goxhill d																			
Thornton Abbey d																			
Ulceby d																			
Habrough d								18 02					18 32						
Stallingborough d																			
Healing d																			
Great Coates d																			
Grimsby Town a								18 17					18 48						
d													18 49						
Grimsby Docks d																			
New Clee d																			
Cleethorpes a													18 59						
Thorne North d					17 02	17 26													
Goole d					17 11	17 35													
Saltmarshe d					17 16														
York 8 33 d																17 27			
Selby a	17 00															17 45	17 59		18 04
Wressle d																			
Howden d																17 55	18 10		18 16
Eastrington d																			
Gilberdyke d					17 23											18 01			
Broomfleet d																			
Brough d	17 18				17 31	17 49										18 09	18 23		18 28
Ferriby d					17 36														
Hessle d					17 40														
Hull a	17 37				17 53	18 06										18 29	18 40		18 46

b arr. 1613

Table 29

Mondays to Fridays

Manchester Airport, Manchester, Sheffield and Meadowhall - Doncaster - Cleethorpes and Hull Barton-on-Humber - Cleethorpes

	NT	NT	XC	NT	NT	TP	NT		NT	NT	NT	XC	TP	GR	NT	NT	TP		XC	TP	NT	NT	XC	NT
			◇1			◇1						◇1	◇1	1			◇1		◇1	◇1			◇1	
														A										
			🛒			🛒						🛒	🛒	🛒			🛒		🛒	🛒				
Manchester Airport 85 ✈ d													16 55							17 55				
Manchester Piccadilly 10 ⇌ d						17 42							17b20				18 42			18 20				
Stockport 78 d													17 28							18 28				
Sheffield 7 ⇌ a			17 44							17 49		18 18	18 15						18 49	19 10	18 57		19 19	
d		17 41	17 47							17 57	18 14	18 21	18 24		18 29	18 41			18 54	19 11	19 00	19 18	19 26	
Meadowhall ⇌ d		17 47								18 03	18 21		18 29		18 35	18 47				19 17	19 06	19 25		
Rotherham Central d										18 10	18 27				18 42						19 12	19 31		
Swinton (S.Yorks) d										18 18	18a36				18 50						19 20	19a40		
Mexborough d										18 21					18 53						19 23			
Conisbrough d										18 25					18 57						19 27			
London Kings Cross d														17 19										
Doncaster 7 a		18 14								18 38			18 53	19 33	19 08	19 11			19 17	19 40	19 39			
York 8 26 a			18 58									19 30							19 44				20 31	
Doncaster 31 d	17 56	18 16					18 27		18 28	18 41			18 55	19 05		19 13				19 42				19 20
Bentley (S.Yorks) 31 a							18 30																	
Adwick 31 a							18 34																	
Kirk Sandall d	18 02								18 36	18 48														19 27
Hatfield & Stainforth d	18 07								18 41	18 53														19 32
Thorne South d									18 46															19 36
Crowle d									18 54															19 45
Althorpe d									19 00															19 51
Scunthorpe a									19 09				19 22							20 07				19 59
d													19 23							20 08				
Barnetby d													19 37							20 22				
Hull Paragon Interchange d																								
Barton-on-Humber a																								
Barton-on-Humber d				18 00																				
Barrow Haven d				18 05																				
New Holland d				18 08																				
Goxhill d				18 13																				
Thornton Abbey d				18 16																				
Ulceby d				18 20																				
Habrough d				18 25																				
Stallingborough d				18 30																				
Healing d				18 33																				
Great Coates d				18 36																				
Grimsby Town a				18 41									19 57							20 42				
d				18 41									19 58							20 43				
Grimsby Docks d				18 44																				
New Clee d																								
Cleethorpes a				18 50									20 09							20 55				
Thorne North d	18 12									18 58														
Goole d	18 21	18 36								19 07						19 34								
Saltmarshe d	18 26																							
York 8 33 d					18 20																			
Selby a					18 45	19 00								19 20			20 00							
Wressle d					18 53																			
Howden d					18 57												20 10							
Eastrington d					19 02																			
Gilberdyke d	18 32				19 06					19 21														
Broomfleet d	18 36																							
Brough d	18 42	18 53			19 13	19 19				19 29				19 43		19 49	20 22							
Ferriby d	18 46									19 34														
Hessle d	18 51									19 38														
Hull a	19 04	19 09			19 32	19 37				19 48				20 00		20 07	20 40							

A The Hull Executive

b arr. 1713

Table 29

Mondays to Fridays

Manchester Airport, Manchester, Sheffield and Meadowhall - Doncaster - Cleethorpes and Hull Barton-on-Humber - Cleethorpes

	NT	NT	NT	NT	NT	NT	EM	XC	NT	NT	HT	NT	TP		EM	NT	NT	TP	NT	NT	NT	XC	NT	NT
								◇1			◇1		◇1					◇1				◇1		
	🚌										⊠												🚌	
Manchester Airport 85 ✈ d													18 55											
Manchester Piccadilly 10 ⇌ d													19 18					20 11						
Stockport 78 d													19 26											
Sheffield 7 ⇌ a								19 47					20 08									20 49		
d			19 30			19 44		19 54				19 57	20 11						20 15	20 27	20 38	20 54		
Meadowhall ⇌ d			19 36			19 50						20 03	20 17						20 21	20 35	20 45			
Rotherham Central d			19 42									20 10							20 27	20 41	20 52			
Swinton (S.Yorks) d			19 51									20 19							20 36	20a50	21 00			
Mexborough d			19 54									20 22							20 39		21 03			
Conisbrough d			19 58									20 26							20 43		21 07			
London Kings Cross d											18 50													
Doncaster 7 a			20 08			20 11		20 20			20 30	20 36	20 40						20 56		21 18	21 21		
York 8 26 a								20 46														21 45		
Doncaster 31 d		19 27			19 51	20 14				20 25	20 31		20 42			20 38	20 44		20 57		21 18			
Bentley (S.Yorks) 31 a		19 30														20 41								
Adwick 31 a		19 34														20 45								
Kirk Sandall d					19 57					20 31									21 04		21 26			
Hatfield & Stainforth d					20 02					20 36									21 09		21 31			
Thorne South d										20 41											21 38			
Crowle d										20 50											21 46			
Althorpe d										20 56											21 52			
Scunthorpe a										21 04			21 07								22 01			
d													21 08											
Barnetby d							20 31						21 22		20 31									
Hull Paragon Interchange d	19 25																						21 25	
Barton-on-Humber a	19 52																						21 52	
Barton-on-Humber d				19 58					19 58															21 58
Barrow Haven d				20 03					20 03															22 03
New Holland d				20 06					20 06															22 06
Goxhill d				20 11					20 11															22 11
Thornton Abbey d				20 14					20 14															22 14
Ulceby d				20 18					20 18															22 18
Habrough d				20 23			20 40		20 23				21 31		20 40									22 23
Stallingborough d				20 28					20 28															22 28
Healing d				20 31					20 31															22 31
Great Coates d				20 34					20 34															22 34
Grimsby Town a				20 39			20 52		20 39				21 44		20 52									22 39
d				20 39			20 52		20 39				21 45		20 52									22 39
Grimsby Docks d				20 42					20 42															22 42
New Clee d																								
Cleethorpes a				20 48			21 02		20 48				21 57		21 02									22 48
Thorne North d					20 08														21 15					
Goole d					20 17	20 33													21a23					
Saltmarshe d																								
York 8 33 d																								
Selby a											20 46						21 01	21 34						
Wressle d																								
Howden d											20 57							21 43						
Eastrington d																								
Gilberdyke d					20 25												21 15							
Broomfleet d																								
Brough d					20 33	20 47					21 09						21 23	21 55						
Ferriby d					20 37												21 28							
Hessle d					20 42												21 32							
Hull a					20 55	21 06					21 27						21 45	22 12						

Table 29 — Mondays to Fridays

Manchester Airport, Manchester, Sheffield and Meadowhall - Doncaster - Cleethorpes and Hull Barton-on-Humber - Cleethorpes

		NT	TP	NT	NT	TP	NT	HT	XC	NT	TP	NT	NT	TP	NT	NT	NT
			FO			FX		BHX									
			◇■			◇■		◇■	◇■		◇■			◇■			
								⊠									
Manchester Airport 85 ✈	d		19 55								20 47						
Manchester Piccadilly ■ ⇌	d		20b20								21c20						
Stockport 78	d		20 28								21 28						
Sheffield ■ ⇌	a		21 10						21 48		22 08						
	d		21 11	21 15	21 30	21 34			21 54		22 11	22 24	22 34		23 15		23 27
Meadowhall ⇌	d		21 17	21 21	21 36	21 40					22 17	22 31	22 40		23 21		23 33
Rotherham Central	d			21 27	21 42							22 37	22 46		23 27		23 39
Swinton (S.Yorks)	d			21 36	21a50							22a46	22 54		23a36		23 48
Mexborough	d			21 39									22 57				23 51
Conisbrough	d			21 43									23 01				23 55
London Kings Cross	d							20 30									
Doncaster ■	a		21 40	21 52		22 01		22 07	22 29		22 40		23 13				00 07
York ■ 26	a								22 54								
Doncaster 31	d	21 38	21 42	21 54		22 15		22 12		22 38	22 42					23 25	
Bentley (S.Yorks) 31	a	21 41								22 41							
Adwick 31	a	21 45								22 45							
Kirk Sandall	d			22 02							22 49					23 31	
Hatfield & Stainforth	d			22 07							22 53					23 36	
Thorne South	d										22 58						
Crowle	d										23 07						
Althorpe	d										23 13						
Scunthorpe	a		22 07			22 40					23 18						
	d		22 08			22 41					23 18						
Barnetby	d		22 22			22 58					23 35						
Hull Paragon Interchange	d																
Barton-on-Humber	a																
Barton-on-Humber	d																
Barrow Haven	d																
New Holland	d																
Goxhill	d																
Thornton Abbey	d																
Ulceby	d																
Habrough	d		22 31			23 07					23 43						
Stallingborough	d																
Healing	d																
Great Coates	d																
Grimsby Town	a		22 44			23 22					23 57						
	d		22 45			23 23					23 58						
Grimsby Docks	d																
New Clee	d																
Cleethorpes	a		22 57			23 32					00 09						
Thorne North	d			22 13												23 42	
Goole	d			22 22												23a53	
Saltmarshe	d			22 26													
York ■ 33	d						22 03										
Selby	a						22 21	22 29									
Wressle	d																
Howden	d						22 31	22 40									
Eastrington	d																
Gilberdyke	d			22 32			22 39										
Broomfleet	d																
Brough	d			22 39			22 46	22 54						23 05			
Ferriby	d						22 51										
Hessle	d						22 56										
Hull	a			22 58			23 09	23 11						23 23			

b arr. 2013 c arr. 2113

Table 29 — Saturdays

Manchester Airport, Manchester, Sheffield and Meadowhall - Doncaster - Cleethorpes and Hull Barton-on-Humber - Cleethorpes

		NT	NT	EM	NT	NT	NT	XC	NT	NT	NT	NT	TP	XC	NT	NT	TP	NT
								◇■					◇■	◇■			◇■	
								✠		⇌				✠				
Manchester Airport 85 ✈	d												05 15					
Manchester Piccadilly ■ ⇌	d												05c44				06 21	
Stockport 78	d												05 52					
Sheffield ■ ⇌	a							06 44					06 49	07 09				
	d		05 29			06 18	06 28	06 49	06 52				06 55	07 12	07 14			
Meadowhall ⇌	d		05 35			06 24	06 34		06 58				07 01		07 21			
Rotherham Central	d		05 41			06 30	06 40		07 04						07 27			
Swinton (S.Yorks)	d		05 49			06 38	06a48		07 14						07a35			
Mexborough	d		05 52			06 41			07 17									
Conisbrough	d		05 56			06 45			07 21									
London Kings Cross	d																	
Doncaster ■	a		06 06			06 57		07 16	07 31				07 22					
York ■ 26	a							07 39						08 25				
Doncaster 31	d	05 50	06 14		06 47	07 00			07 32			07 14	07 24					07 30
Bentley (S.Yorks) 31	a					07 03			07 35			07 17						
Adwick 31	a					07 09			07 41			07 21						
Kirk Sandall	d		06 20		06 53													07 36
Hatfield & Stainforth	d		06 25		06 58													07 41
Thorne South	d				07 03													
Crowle	d				07 11													
Althorpe	d				07 17													
Scunthorpe	a				07 25								07 49					
	d												07 50					
Barnetby	d			06 31									08 04					
Hull Paragon Interchange	d									06 55								
Barton-on-Humber	a									07 30								
Barton-on-Humber	d										06 58							
Barrow Haven	d										07 03							
New Holland	d										07 07							
Goxhill	d										07 11							
Thornton Abbey	d																	
Ulceby	d										07 19							
Habrough	d			06 41							07 23							
Stallingborough	d										07 28							
Healing	d										07 31							
Great Coates	d																	
Grimsby Town	a			06 56							07 37		08 24					
	d										07 38		08 35					
Grimsby Docks	d																	
New Clee	d																	
Cleethorpes	a										07 50		08 46					
Thorne North	d		06 30															07 46
Goole	d		06 39															07 55
Saltmarshe	d		06 44															08 00
York ■ 33	d																	
Selby	a	06 10															07 43	
Wressle	d																	
Howden	d																07 52	
Eastrington	d																	
Gilberdyke	d		06 50													07 39		08 06
Broomfleet	d		06 54													07 43		
Brough	d		07 00													07 49	08 04	08 14
Ferriby	d		07 04													07 53		08 18
Hessle	d		07 09													07 58		08 23
Hull	a		07 22													08 11	08 20	08 36

c arr. 0533

Table 29

Saturdays

Manchester Airport, Manchester, Sheffield and Meadowhall - Doncaster - Cleethorpes and Hull Barton-on-Humber - Cleethorpes

		NT	NT	NT	NT	EM	TP	XC	TP	NT	NT	NT	NT	NT	NT	NT	NT	NT	HT	TP	XC
							◇1	◇1	◇1							🚌			◇1 A	◇1	◇1
							🛒	🛒	🛒										⊠		🛒
Manchester Airport 85 ✈	d								06 55												
Manchester Piccadilly 10	d						07 36		07 20											08 42	
Stockport 78	d								07 26												
Sheffield 7	a							07 48	08 10												08 46
	d	07 24		07 41				07 54	08 11		08 14				08 25			08 41			08 54
Meadowhall	d	07 30		07 47					08 17		08 23				08 31			08 47			
Rotherham Central	d	07 36		07 55							08 29				08 37						
Swinton (S.Yorks)	d	07 44		08 03							08a38				08 48						
Mexborough	d	07 47		08 06											08 51						
Conisbrough	d	07 51		08 10											08 55						
London Kings Cross	d																		07 36		
Doncaster 7	a	08 01		08 20				08 23	08 40						09 05			09 09	09 16		09 21
York 8 26	a							08 49													09 45
Doncaster 31	d	08 03		08 22					08 42			08 26	08 48	08 50	09 10		09 14	09 16	09 18		
Bentley (S.Yorks) 31	a											08 29		08 53			09 17				
Adwick 31	a											08 33		08 59			09 21				
Kirk Sandall	d	08 09											08 55		09 18						
Hatfield & Stainforth	d	08 14											09 00		09 23						
Thorne South	d	08 18													09 28						
Crowle	d	08 27													09 36						
Althorpe	d	08 33													09 42						
Scunthorpe	a	08 43							09 07						09 50						
	d								09 08												
Barnetby	d					08 52			09 22	09 39											
Hull Paragon Interchange	d															09 05					
Barton-on-Humber	a															09 40					
Barton-on-Humber	d				08 00																
Barrow Haven	d				08 05																
New Holland	d				08 08																
Goxhill	d				08 13																
Thornton Abbey	d				08 16																
Ulceby	d				08 20																
Habrough	d				08 25	09 01			09 31	09 48											
Stallingborough	d				08 30																
Healing	d				08 33																
Great Coates	d				08 36																
Grimsby Town	a				08 41	09 15			09 44	10 00											
	d				08 43				09 45	10 01											
Grimsby Docks	d				08 45																
New Clee	d				08x48																
Cleethorpes	a				08 52				09 59	10 13											
Thorne North	d												09 05								
Goole	d			08 42									09 14					09 39			
Saltmarshe	d																				
York 8 33	d		07 30																		
Selby	a		07 50				08 58												09 32	09 57	
Wressle	d		07 58																		
Howden	d		08 03																09 43		
Eastrington	d		08 08																		
Gilberdyke	d		08 12										09 22								
Broomfleet	d		08 16																		
Brough	d		08 22	08 56									09 30					09 53	10 00	10 16	
Ferriby	d		08 27										09 35								
Hessle	d		08 31										09 39								
Hull	a		08 46	09 12			09 31						09 55					10 10	10 16	10 34	

A from 17 July until 4 September

Table 29

Saturdays

Manchester Airport, Manchester, Sheffield and Meadowhall - Doncaster - Cleethorpes and Hull Barton-on-Humber - Cleethorpes

		NT	TP	NT	EM	XC	NT	NT	NT	NT	NT	NT	NT	TP	XC	NT	TP	NT	XC
			◇1		◇1	◇1								◇1	◇1		◇1		◇1
			🛒		🍴	🛒								🛒	🛒		🛒		🛒
Manchester Airport 85 ✈	d		07 54														08 55		
Manchester Piccadilly 10	d		08b20											09 42			09c20		
Stockport 78	d		08 28														09 28		
Sheffield 7	a		09 08		09 07	09 17									09 46	09 49	10 08		10 17
	d	08 57	09 11	09 14	09 21	09 21		09 25	09 31				09 41		09 54	09 57	10 11	10 14	10 21
Meadowhall	d	09 03	09 17	09 21				09 32	09 37				09 47			10 03	10 17	10 21	
Rotherham Central	d	09 10		09 27				09 39	09 44							10 10		10 27	
Swinton (S.Yorks)	d	09 19		09a36				09 48	09 52							10 18		10a36	
Mexborough	d	09 22						09 51								10 21			
Conisbrough	d	09 26						09 55								10 25			
London Kings Cross	d																		
Doncaster 7	a	09 36	09 40		09 53			10 05					10 11		10 18	10 36	10 40		
York 8 26	a				10 16	10 30			10 52						10 44				11 30
Doncaster 31	d	09 37	09 42				09 46	10 07				10 14	10 22			10 37	10 42		
Bentley (S.Yorks) 31	a	09 44										10 17				10 41			
Adwick 31	a	09 50										10 21				10 47			
Kirk Sandall	d						09 53	10 14											
Hatfield & Stainforth	d						09 58	10 19											
Thorne South	d							10 24											
Crowle	d							10 33											
Althorpe	d							10 39											
Scunthorpe	a		10 07					10 46									11 07		
	d		10 08														11 08		
Barnetby	d		10 22														11 22		
Hull Paragon Interchange	d																		
Barton-on-Humber	a																		
Barton-on-Humber	d										09 58								
Barrow Haven	d										10 03								
New Holland	d										10 06								
Goxhill	d										10 11								
Thornton Abbey	d										10 14								
Ulceby	d										10 18								
Habrough	d		10 31								10 23								
Stallingborough	d										10 28								
Healing	d										10 31								
Great Coates	d										10 34								
Grimsby Town	a		10 44								10 39						11 42		
	d		10 45								10 39						11 43		
Grimsby Docks	d										10 42								
New Clee	d										10x44								
Cleethorpes	a		10 59								10 49						11 54		
Thorne North	d						10 03												
Goole	d						10 12						10 41						
Saltmarshe	d																		
York 8 33	d									09 53									
Selby	a									10 12				10 57					
Wressle	d																		
Howden	d									10 22									
Eastrington	d																		
Gilberdyke	d						10 20			10 29									
Broomfleet	d																		
Brough	d						10 28			10 37			10 54	11 16					
Ferriby	d						10 33												
Hessle	d						10 37												
Hull	a						10 50			10 56			11 12	11 34					

b arr. 0813

c arr. 0913

Table 29

Saturdays

Manchester Airport, Manchester, Sheffield and Meadowhall - Doncaster - Cleethorpes and Hull Barton-on-Humber - Cleethorpes

		NT	NT	EM	NT	NT	NT	NT	XC	HT	TP	NT	TP	NT	XC	NT	NT	NT	NT	TP	XC
									◇1	◇1	◇1		◇1		◇1					◇1	◇1
										A											
					🚌				🛒	⊠	🛒		🛒		🛒						🛒
Manchester Airport 85 ✈	d												09 55								
Manchester Piccadilly 10	d										10 42		10b20							11 42	
Stockport 78	d												10 28								
Sheffield 7	a								10 46			10 49	11 08		11 17						11 46
	d		10 24				10 41		10 54			10 57	11 11	11 14	11 21		11 24		11 41		11 54
Meadowhall	d		10 31				10 47					11 03	11 17	11 21			11 31		11 47		
Rotherham Central	d		10 37									11 10		11 27			11 37				
Swinton (S.Yorks)	d		10 47									11 20		11a36			11 48				
Mexborough	d		10 50									11 23					11 51				
Conisbrough	d		10 54									11 27					11 55				
London Kings Cross	d									09 34											
Doncaster 7	a		11 04				11 09		11 16	11 24		11 35	11 40				12 04		12 11		12 16
York 8 26	a								11 44						12 30						12 44
Doncaster 31	d	10 46	11 07			11 14	11 17			11 25		11 38	11 42			11 46	12 08		12 14		
Bentley (S.Yorks) 31	a					11 17						11 41									
Adwick 31	a					11 21						11 47									
Kirk Sandall	d	10 52	11 13													11 52	12 14				
Hatfield & Stainforth	d	10 57	11 18													11 57	12 19				
Thorne South	d		11 23														12 24				
Crowle	d		11 31														12 32				
Althorpe	d		11 37														12 38				
Scunthorpe	a		11 45										12 07				12 47				
	d												12 08								
Barnetby	d			10 57									12 22								
Hull Paragon Interchange	d				11 05																
Barton-on-Humber	a				11 40																
Barton-on-Humber	d							11 58													
Barrow Haven	d							12 03													
New Holland	d							12 06													
Goxhill	d							12 11													
Thornton Abbey	d							12 14													
Ulceby	d							12 18													
Habrough	d			11 06				12 23					12 31								
Stallingborough	d							12 28													
Healing	d							12 31													
Great Coates	d							12 34													
Grimsby Town	a			11 21				12 39					12 44								
	d							12 39					12 45								
Grimsby Docks	d							12 42													
New Clee	d							12x44													
Cleethorpes	a							12 49					12 57								
Thorne North	d	11 02														12 02					
Goole	d	11 12					11 37									12 12			12 35		
Saltmarshe	d																				
York 8 33	d																	11 50			
Selby	a									11 39	11 57							12 09		12 57	
Wressle	d																				
Howden	d									11 50								12 19			
Eastrington	d																				
Gilberdyke	d	11 20														12 20		12 27			
Broomfleet	d	11 25																			
Brough	d	11 31					11 51			12 03	12 16					12 28		12 35	12 49	13 16	
Ferriby	d	11 35														12 33					
Hessle	d	11 40														12 37					
Hull	a	11 53					12 09			12 22	12 34					12 50		12 54	13 06	13 34	

A until 10 July and from 11 September

b arr. 1013

Table 29

Saturdays

Manchester Airport, Manchester, Sheffield and Meadowhall - Doncaster - Cleethorpes and Hull Barton-on-Humber - Cleethorpes

		NT	NT	EM	TP	NT	XC	NT	NT	NT	NT	NT	NT	NT	XC	HT	TP	NT	TP	NT
					◇1		◇1								◇1	◇1	◇1		◇1	
					🛒		🛒			🚌					🛒	⊠			🛒	
Manchester Airport 85 ✈	d				10 55														11 55	
Manchester Piccadilly 10	d				11b20												12 42		12c20	
Stockport 78	d				11 28														12 28	
Sheffield 7	a		11 49		12 08		12 16								12 46			12 49	13 08	
	d		11 57		12 11	12 14	12 21		12 24				12 41	14 14	12 54			12 57	13 11	13 14
Meadowhall	d		12 03		12 17	12 21			12 31				12 47	14 21				13 03	13 17	13 21
Rotherham Central	d		12 10			12 27			12 37					14 27				13 10		13 27
Swinton (S.Yorks)	d		12 19			12a36			12 47					14a36				13 18		13a36
Mexborough	d		12 22						12 50									13 21		
Conisbrough	d		12 26						12 54									13 25		
London Kings Cross	d															11 48				
Doncaster 7	a		12 35		12 40				13 04				13 11		13 19	13 26		13 35	13 40	
York 8 26	a						13 32								13 44					
Doncaster 31	d	12 14	12 36		12 42			12 46	13 06			13 14	13 18			13 27		13 38	13 42	
Bentley (S.Yorks) 31	a	12 17	12 40									13 17						13 41		
Adwick 31	a	12 21	12 45									13 21						13 47		
Kirk Sandall	d							12 52	13 12											
Hatfield & Stainforth	d							12 57	13 17											
Thorne South	d								13 22											
Crowle	d								13 31											
Althorpe	d								13 37											
Scunthorpe	a				13 07				13 45										14 07	
	d				13 08														14 08	
Barnetby	d			13 12	13 22						13 38								14 22	
Hull Paragon Interchange	d									13 05										
Barton-on-Humber	a									13 40										
Barton-on-Humber	d																			
Barrow Haven	d																			
New Holland	d																			
Goxhill	d																			
Thornton Abbey	d																			
Ulceby	d																			
Habrough	d			13 21							13 47								14 31	
Stallingborough	d																			
Healing	d																			
Great Coates	d																			
Grimsby Town	a			13 36	13 42						14 00								14 44	
	d				13 43						14 00								14 45	
Grimsby Docks	d																			
New Clee	d																			
Cleethorpes	a				13 54						14 11								14 57	
Thorne North	d							13 02												
Goole	d							13 11					13 37							
Saltmarshe	d																			
York 8 33	d																			
Selby	a															13 42	13 57			
Wressle	d																			
Howden	d															13 53				
Eastrington	d																			
Gilberdyke	d							13 20												
Broomfleet	d																			
Brough	d							13 28					13 51			14 05	14 16			
Ferriby	d							13 32												
Hessle	d							13 37												
Hull	a							13 50					14 08			14 22	14 34			

b arr. 1113

c arr. 1213

Table 29

Saturdays

Manchester Airport, Manchester, Sheffield and Meadowhall - Doncaster - Cleethorpes and Hull Barton-on-Humber - Cleethorpes

		XC	NT	NT	NT	NT	NT	NT	NT	TP	XC	NT	TP	XC	NT	NT	NT	NT	NT	TP
		◇1								◇1	◇1		◇1	◇1			🚌			◇1
		⊼								⊼	⊼		⊼	⊼						
Manchester Airport 85 ✈	d												12 55							
Manchester Piccadilly 10 ⇌	d									13 42			13b20							14 42
Stockport 78	d												13 28							
Sheffield 7 ⇌	a	13 17									13 46	13 49	14 08	14 17						
	d	13 21			13 24	13 28			13 41		13 54	13 57	14 11	14 21		14 24			14 41	
Meadowhall ⇌	d				13 31	13 35			13 47			14 03	14 17			14 31			14 47	
Rotherham Central	d				13 37	13 42						14 10				14 37				
Swinton (S.Yorks)	d				13 47	13 50						14 18				14 47				
Mexborough	d				13 50							14 21				14 50				
Conisbrough	d				13 54							14 25				14 54				
London Kings Cross	d																			
Doncaster 7	a				14 04				14 13		14 16	14 35	14 40			15 04			15 11	
York 8 26	a	14 30				14 51					14 44			15 32						
Doncaster 31	d			13 46	14 06			14 14	14 17			14 38	14 42		14 46	15 07			15 14	
Bentley (S.Yorks) 31	a							14 17				14 41								
Adwick 31	a							14 21				14 47								
Kirk Sandall	d			13 52	14 12										14 52	15 13				
Hatfield & Stainforth	d			13 57	14 17										14 57	15 18				
Thorne South	d				14 22											15 23				
Crowle	d				14 31											15 31				
Althorpe	d				14 37											15 37				
Scunthorpe	a				14 45								15 07			15 46				
	d												15 08							
Barnetby	d												15 22							
Hull Paragon Interchange	d																15 05			
Barton-on-Humber	a																15 40			
Barton-on-Humber	d						13 58													
Barrow Haven	d						14 03													
New Holland	d						14 06													
Goxhill	d						14 11													
Thornton Abbey	d						14 14													
Ulceby	d						14 18													
Habrough	d						14 23													
Stallingborough	d						14 28													
Healing	d						14 31													
Great Coates	d						14 34													
Grimsby Town	a						14 39						15 42							
	d						14 39						15 43							
Grimsby Docks	d						14 42													
New Clee	d						14x44													
Cleethorpes	a						14 49						15 54							
Thorne North	d			14 02											15 02					
Goole	d			14 12					14 37						15 13				15 37	
Saltmarshe	d			14 17																
York 8 33	d		13 38															15 05		
Selby	a		14 03							14 57								15 23		15 57
Wressle	d																			
Howden	d		14 13															15 33		
Eastrington	d																			
Gilberdyke	d			14 26											15 21					
Broomfleet	d																			
Brough	d		14 25	14 34					14 52	15 16					15 29			15 44	15 51	16 16
Ferriby	d			14 39											15 34					
Hessle	d			14 43											15 38					
Hull	a		14 45	14 56					15 10	15 34					15 51			16 03	16 07	16 34

b arr. 1313

Table 29

Saturdays

Manchester Airport, Manchester, Sheffield and Meadowhall - Doncaster - Cleethorpes and Hull Barton-on-Humber - Cleethorpes

		XC	EM	NT	NT	NT	TP	NT	XC	NT	NT	NT	XC	NT	TP	NT	NT	TP	NT	NT	XC
		◇1					◇1		◇1				◇1		◇1			◇1			◇1
		⊼					⊼		⊼				⊼					⊼			⊼
Manchester Airport 85 ✈	d						13 55											14 55			
Manchester Piccadilly 10 ⇌	d						14b20								15 42			15c20			
Stockport 78	d						14 28											15 28			
Sheffield 7 ⇌	a	14 46				14 49	15 08		15 17				15 46				15 49	16 08			16 18
	d	14 54				14 57	15 11	15 14	15 21		15 24	15 41	15 54				15 57	16 11		16 14	16 21
Meadowhall ⇌	d					15 03	15 17	15 21			15 31	15 47					16 03	16 17		16 21	
Rotherham Central	d					15 10		15 27			15 37						16 10			16 27	
Swinton (S.Yorks)	d					15 18		15a36			15 47						16 18			16a36	
Mexborough	d					15 21					15 50						16 21				
Conisbrough	d					15 25					15 54						16 25				
London Kings Cross	d																				
Doncaster 7	a	15 16				15 36	15 40				16 04	16 12	16 15				16 35	16 40			
York 8 26	a	15 44							16 30				16 39								17 29
Doncaster 31	d				15 14	15 38	15 42			15 46	16 06	16 14				16 27	16 38	16 42			
Bentley (S.Yorks) 31	a				15 17	15 41										16 30	16 41				
Adwick 31	a				15 21	15 47										16 34	16 47				
Kirk Sandall	d									15 52	16 13										
Hatfield & Stainforth	d									15 57	16 18										
Thorne South	d										16 24										
Crowle	d										16 33										
Althorpe	d										16 39										
Scunthorpe	a						16 07				16 46							17 07			
	d						16 08											17 08			
Barnetby	d		15 34				16 22											17 22	17 38		
Hull Paragon Interchange	d																				
Barton-on-Humber	a																				
Barton-on-Humber	d			15 58																	
Barrow Haven	d			16 03																	
New Holland	d			16 06																	
Goxhill	d			16 11																	
Thornton Abbey	d			16 14																	
Ulceby	d			16 18																	
Habrough	d		15 42	16 23			16 31												17 47		
Stallingborough	d			16 28																	
Healing	d			16 31																	
Great Coates	d			16 34																	
Grimsby Town	a		15 57	16 39			16 44											17 42	18 01		
	d			16 39			16 45											17 43	18 02		
Grimsby Docks	d			16 42																	
New Clee	d																				
Cleethorpes	a			16 48			16 57											17 54	18 11		
Thorne North	d									16 02											
Goole	d									16 12		16 36									
Saltmarshe	d																				
York 8 33	d													16 12							
Selby	a													16 38	17 00						
Wressle	d													16 46							
Howden	d													16 51							
Eastrington	d																				
Gilberdyke	d									16 20				16 58							
Broomfleet	d																				
Brough	d									16 28		16 50		17 06	17 18						
Ferriby	d									16 33				17 10							
Hessle	d									16 37											
Hull	a									16 52		17 05		17 27	17 37						

b arr. 1413

c arr. 1513

Table 29

Saturdays

Manchester Airport, Manchester, Sheffield and Meadowhall - Doncaster - Cleethorpes and Hull Barton-on-Humber - Cleethorpes

			NT	HT	NT	NT	XC	NT	NT	NT	TP	NT	NT	TP	NT	XC	NT	HT	NT	NT
				◇1			◇1				◇1			◇1		◇1		◇1 A		
				⊠			⌶	🚌						⌶		⌶		⊠		
Manchester Airport	85 ✈	d												15 55						
Manchester Piccadilly 10	🚇	d									16 42			16c20						
Stockport	78	d												16 28						
Sheffield 7	🚇	a					16 46						16 49	17 08		17 19				
		d			16 24	16 41	16 54						16 57	17 11	17 14	17 21			17 41	17 27
Meadowhall	🚇	d			16 31	16 47							17 03	17 17	17 21				17 47	17 33
Rotherham Central		d			16 37								17 10		17 27					17 39
Swinton (S.Yorks)		d			16 47								17 18		17a36					17 47
Mexborough		d			16 50								17 21							17 50
Conisbrough		d			16 54								17 25							17 54
London Kings Cross		d		15 08														15 58		
Doncaster 7		a		16 47	17 08	17 12	17 19						17 35	17 40				17 59	18 14	18 07
York 8	26	a					17 44									18 31				
Doncaster	31	d	16 47	16 48		17 14			17 22			17 27	17 38	17 42			17 48	18 00	18 24	
Bentley (S.Yorks)	31	a										17 30	17 41							
Adwick	31	a										17 34	17 47							
Kirk Sandall		d	16 53						17 28								17 54			
Hatfield & Stainforth		d	16 58						17 33								17 59			
Thorne South		d							17 38											
Crowle		d							17 47											
Althorpe		d							17 53											
Scunthorpe		a							18 01					18 07						
		d												18 08						
Barnetby		d												18 22						
Hull Paragon Interchange		d						17 10												
Barton-on-Humber		a						17 45												
Barton-on-Humber		d																		
Barrow Haven		d																		
New Holland		d																		
Goxhill		d																		
Thornton Abbey		d																		
Ulceby		d																		
Habrough		d												18 32						
Stallingborough		d																		
Healing		d																		
Great Coates		d																		
Grimsby Town		a												18 48						
		d												18 49						
Grimsby Docks		d																		
New Clee		d																		
Cleethorpes		a												18 59						
Thorne North		d	17 03			17 26											18 04			
Goole		d	17 12			17 35											18 13		18 44	
Saltmarshe		d	17 17														18 18			
York 8	33	d								17 18										
Selby		a		17 05						17 37	17 57							18 15		
Wressle		d																		
Howden		d		17 16						17 47	18 07							18 26		
Eastrington		d																		
Gilberdyke		d	17 23							17 57							18 25			
Broomfleet		d															18 29			
Brough		d	17 31	17 28		17 53				18 05	18 19						18 35	18 43	18 58	
Ferriby		d	17 36														18 40			
Hessle		d	17 40														18 45			
Hull		a	17 53	17 47		18 10				18 22	18 37						18 56	19 03	19 16	

A from 17 July until 4 September

c arr. 1613

Table 29

Saturdays

Manchester Airport, Manchester, Sheffield and Meadowhall - Doncaster - Cleethorpes and Hull Barton-on-Humber - Cleethorpes

			XC	NT	EM	NT	NT	TP	NT	XC	NT	NT	HT	TP	NT	NT	NT	TP	XC	NT
			◇1					◇1		◇1			◇1 A	◇1				◇1	◇1	
			⌶							⌶			⊠	⌶					⌶	
Manchester Airport	85 ✈	d												16 55						
Manchester Piccadilly 10	🚇	d						17 42						17b20				18 42		
Stockport	78	d												17 28						
Sheffield 7	🚇	a	17 44	17 49						18 18				18 15					18 47	18 57
		d	17 47	17 57					18 14	18 21				18 24		18 29	18 41		18 54	19 00
Meadowhall	🚇	d		18 03					18 21					18 29		18 35	18 47			19 06
Rotherham Central		d		18 10					18 27							18 42				19 12
Swinton (S.Yorks)		d		18 18					18a36							18 50				19 20
Mexborough		d		18 21												18 53				19 23
Conisbrough		d		18 25												18 57				19 27
London Kings Cross		d											17 04							
Doncaster 7		a		18 38									18 46	18 53		19 08	19 11		19 18	19 39
York 8	26	a	18 59							19 31									19 44	
Doncaster	31	d									18 27	18 27	18 48	18 55	18 58	19 13	19 13			
Bentley (S.Yorks)	31	a										18 30								
Adwick	31	a										18 34								
Kirk Sandall		d									18 34				19 06	19 20				
Hatfield & Stainforth		d									18 39				19 11	19 25				
Thorne South		d									18 44					19 30				
Crowle		d									18 52					19 39				
Althorpe		d									18 58					19 45				
Scunthorpe		a									19 07			19 22		19 52				
		d												19 23						
Barnetby		d			17 54									19 37						
Hull Paragon Interchange		d																		
Barton-on-Humber		a																		
Barton-on-Humber		d				18 00														
Barrow Haven		d				18 05														
New Holland		d				18 08														
Goxhill		d				18 13														
Thornton Abbey		d				18 16														
Ulceby		d				18 20														
Habrough		d			18 02	18 25														
Stallingborough		d				18 30														
Healing		d				18 33														
Great Coates		d				18 36														
Grimsby Town		a			18 17	18 41								19 57						
		d				18 41								19 58						
Grimsby Docks		d				18 44														
New Clee		d																		
Cleethorpes		a				18 50								20 09						
Thorne North		d													19 16					
Goole		d													19 25					
Saltmarshe		d																		
York 8	33	d					18 13													
Selby		a					18 41	19 00					19 07				19 34	20 00		
Wressle		d																		
Howden		d					18 51						19 18					20 10		
Eastrington		d					18 56													
Gilberdyke		d					19 00								19 33					
Broomfleet		d																		
Brough		d					19 08	19 19					19 30		19 41		19 54	20 22		
Ferriby		d													19 46					
Hessle		d													19 50					
Hull		a					19 28	19 37					19 47		20 03		20 11	20 40		

A until 10 July and from 11 September

b arr. 1713

Table 29

Saturdays

Manchester Airport, Manchester, Sheffield and Meadowhall - Doncaster - Cleethorpes and Hull Barton-on-Humber - Cleethorpes

		EM	NT	NT	NT	TP	NT	XC	NT	GR	NT	NT	XC	NT	NT	GR	NT	NT	XC
						◇1		◇1		1 A			◇1			1 B			◇1
Manchester Airport 85	d					17 55													
Manchester Piccadilly 10	d					18b20													
Stockport 78	d					18 28													
Sheffield 7	a					19 10		19 18					19 51						20 18
	d					19 11	19 14	19 21			19 30	19 44	19 54				19 57	20 15	20 23
Meadowhall	d					19 17	19 21				19 36	19 50					20 03	20 20	
Rotherham Central	d						19 27				19 42						20 09	20 26	
Swinton (S.Yorks)	d						19a40				19 51						20 17	20 36	
Mexborough	d										19 54						20 20	20 39	
Conisbrough	d										19 58						20 24	20 43	
London Kings Cross	d									17 58						18 40			
Doncaster 7	a					19 40				20 02	20 09	20 11	20 16			20 27	20 36	20 56	
York 8 26	a							20 31					20 40						21 58
Doncaster 31	d			19 27		19 42			19 47	20 03		20 14			20 25	20 27			
Bentley (S.Yorks) 31	a			19 30															
Adwick 31	a			19 34															
Kirk Sandall	d								19 53						20 31				
Hatfield & Stainforth	d								19 58						20 36				
Thorne South	d														20 41				
Crowle	d														20 50				
Althorpe	d														20 56				
Scunthorpe	a					20 07									21 04				
	d					20 08													
Barnetby	d	19 06				20 22													
Hull Paragon Interchange	d		19 25																
Barton-on-Humber	a		19 52																
Barton-on-Humber	d				19 58														
Barrow Haven	d				20 03														
New Holland	d				20 06														
Goxhill	d				20 11														
Thornton Abbey	d				20 14														
Ulceby	d				20 18														
Habrough	d	19 14			20 23														
Stallingborough	d				20 28														
Healing	d				20 31														
Great Coates	d				20 34														
Grimsby Town	a	19 29			20 39	20 42													
	d				20 39	20 43													
Grimsby Docks	d				20 42														
New Clee	d																		
Cleethorpes	a				20 48	20 55													
Thorne North	d								20 03										
Goole	d								20 12			20 33							
Saltmarshe	d																		
York 8 33	d													20 17					
Selby	a									20 18				20 35		20 43			
Wressle	d																		
Howden	d													20 45					
Eastrington	d																		
Gilberdyke	d								20 22					20 51					
Broomfleet	d																		
Brough	d								20 30	20 42		20 47		20 59		21 06			
Ferriby	d								20 35					21 04					
Hessle	d								20 39					21 08					
Hull	a								20 52	21 00		21 06		21 23		21 27			

A from 17 July until 4 September

B until 10 July and from 11 September

b arr. 1813

Table 29

Saturdays

Manchester Airport, Manchester, Sheffield and Meadowhall - Doncaster - Cleethorpes and Hull Barton-on-Humber - Cleethorpes

		NT	NT	NT	HT	TP	NT	NT	TP	NT	HT	NT	XC	NT	NT	TP	NT	TP	XC	TP
					◇1 A	◇1			◇1		◇1 B		◇1			◇1 B		◇1	◇1	◇1
Manchester Airport 85	d					18 55														20 47
Manchester Piccadilly 10	d					19 18										21 11				21b20
Stockport 78	d					19 26														21 28
Sheffield 7	a					20 08							20 49						21 44	22 08
	d	20 27				20 11						20 38	20 54		21 15		21 30	21 34	21 54	22 11
Meadowhall	d	20 35				20 17						20 44			21 21		21 36	21 40		22 17
Rotherham Central	d	20 42										20 53			21 27		21 42			
Swinton (S.Yorks)	d	20a50										21 05			21 36		21a50			
Mexborough	d											21 08			21 39					
Conisbrough	d											21 12			21 43					
London Kings Cross	d				18 58						19 37									
Doncaster 7	a				20 59	20 40					21 20	21 21	21 25		21 55			22 01	22 19	22 36
York 8 26	a												21 48						22 43	
Doncaster 31	d		20 45	20 46	21 00	20 42	21 07				21 20			21 28	21 57			22 11		22 38
Bentley (S.Yorks) 31	a		20 48											21 31						
Adwick 31	a		20 52											21 35						
Kirk Sandall	d			20 52			21 13								22 02					22 43
Hatfield & Stainforth	d			20 57			21 18								22 07					22 47
Thorne South	d						21 23													22 52
Crowle	d						21 31													23 00
Althorpe	d						21 37													23 06
Scunthorpe	a					21 07	21 46											22 36		23 11
	d					21 08												22 37		23 12
Barnetby	d					21 22												22 54		23 26
Hull Paragon Interchange	d							21 25												
Barton-on-Humber	a							21 52												
Barton-on-Humber	d									21 58										
Barrow Haven	d									22 03										
New Holland	d									22 06										
Goxhill	d									22 11										
Thornton Abbey	d									22 14										
Ulceby	d									22 18										
Habrough	d					21 31				22 23								23 03		23 34
Stallingborough	d									22 28										
Healing	d									22 31										
Great Coates	d									22 34										
Grimsby Town	a					21 44				22 39								23 18		23 48
	d					21 45				22 39								23 19		23 49
Grimsby Docks	d									22 42										
New Clee	d																			
Cleethorpes	a					21 57				22 48								23 28		23 59
Thorne North	d			21 02											22 13					
Goole	d			21 11											22 22					
Saltmarshe	d														22 26					
York 8 33	d																			
Selby	a				21 15						21 35					22 45				
Wressle	d																			
Howden	d				21 26				21 39		21 47									
Eastrington	d																			
Gilberdyke	d			21 19											22 32					
Broomfleet	d																			
Brough	d			21 27	21 39				21 51		21 59				22 41	23 05				
Ferriby	d																			
Hessle	d																			
Hull	a			21 45	21 55				22 08		22 16				22 58	23 23				

A from 17 July until 4 September

B until 10 July and from 11 September

b arr. 2113

Table 29

Saturdays

Manchester Airport, Manchester, Sheffield and Meadowhall - Doncaster - Cleethorpes and Hull Barton-on-Humber - Cleethorpes

			XC	NT	NT	NT	TP	NT
			◇1				◇1	
							A	
			✕					
Manchester Airport	85 ✈	d						
Manchester Piccadilly 10	⇌	d						
Stockport	78	d						
Sheffield 7	⇌	a	22 23					
		d	22 26		22 30	22 34		23 26
Meadowhall	⇌	d			22 36	22 40		23 32
Rotherham Central		d			22 42	22 46		23 38
Swinton (S.Yorks)		d			22 50	22a54		23 46
Mexborough		d			22 53			23 49
Conisbrough		d			22 57			23 53
London Kings Cross		d						
Doncaster 7		a	22 47		23 08			00 05
York 8	26	a						
Doncaster	31	d		22 52	23 09			
Bentley (S.Yorks)	31	a		22 55				
Adwick	31	a		22 59				
Kirk Sandall		d			23 16			
Hatfield & Stainforth		d			23 21			
Thorne South		d						
Crowle		d						
Althorpe		d						
Scunthorpe		a						
		d						
Barnetby		d						
Hull Paragon Interchange		d						
Barton-on-Humber		a						
Barton-on-Humber		d						
Barrow Haven		d						
New Holland		d						
Goxhill		d						
Thornton Abbey		d						
Ulceby		d						
Habrough		d						
Stallingborough		d						
Healing		d						
Great Coates		d						
Grimsby Town		a						
		d						
Grimsby Docks		d						
New Clee		d						
Cleethorpes		a						
Thorne North		d			23 26			
Goole		d			23a37			
Saltmarshe		d						
York 8	33	d						
Selby		a						
Wressle		d						
Howden		d						
Eastrington		d						
Gilberdyke		d						
Broomfleet		d						
Brough		d					23 05	
Ferriby		d						
Hessle		d						
Hull		a					23 23	

A from 17 July until 4 September

Table 29

Sundays until 11 July

Manchester Airport, Manchester, Sheffield and Meadowhall - Doncaster - Cleethorpes and Hull Barton-on-Humber - Cleethorpes

			NT	NT	NT	XC	NT	NT	TP	TP	XC	NT	NT	NT	NT	NT	NT
						◇1			◇1	◇1	◇1						
												🚌					
						✕					✕						
Manchester Airport	85 ✈	d															
Manchester Piccadilly 10	⇌	d							09 11								
Stockport	78	d															
Sheffield 7	⇌	a									10 16						
		d	08 00		08 45	09 21	09 36			09 52	10 21			10 26		11 05	
Meadowhall	⇌	d	08 06		08 51		09 42			09 57				10 32		11 11	
Rotherham Central		d	08 12		08 57		09 48			10 02						11 17	
Swinton (S.Yorks)		d	08 20		09 05		09a58			10 09						11 25	
Mexborough		d	08 23		09 08					10 12						11 28	
Conisbrough		d	08 27		09 12					10 17						11 32	
London Kings Cross		d															
Doncaster 7		a	08 38		09 22					10 26				10 51		11 43	
York 8	26	a				10 33					11 34						
Doncaster	31	d		09 07	09 26			10 19		10 28				10 53			11 07
Bentley (S.Yorks)	31	a															
Adwick	31	a															
Kirk Sandall		d		09 13													11 13
Hatfield & Stainforth		d		09 18													11 18
Thorne South		d															
Crowle		d															
Althorpe		d															
Scunthorpe		a								10 54							
		d								10 55							
Barnetby		d								11 09							
Hull Paragon Interchange		d										10 25					
Barton-on-Humber		a										10 50					
Barton-on-Humber		d													11 00		
Barrow Haven		d													11 05		
New Holland		d													11 08		
Goxhill		d													11 13		
Thornton Abbey		d													11 16		
Ulceby		d													11 20		
Habrough		d													11 25		
Stallingborough		d													11 30		
Healing		d													11 33		
Great Coates		d													11 36		
Grimsby Town		a								11 29					11 41		
		d								11 35					11 41		
Grimsby Docks		d													11 44		
New Clee		d													11 46		
Cleethorpes		a								11 44					11 55		
Thorne North		d		09 24	09 38												11 25
Goole		d		09a35	09 47			10 38						11 13			11a36
Saltmarshe		d															
York 8	33	d											10 40				
Selby		a							10 43				10 58				
Wressle		d															
Howden		d											11 08				
Eastrington		d															
Gilberdyke		d			09 58			10 46						11 24			
Broomfleet		d															
Brough		d			10 06			10 54	11 03				11 19	11 32			
Ferriby		d															
Hessle		d															
Hull		a			10 21			11 11	11 20				11 38	11 47			

Table 29

Sundays until 11 July

Manchester Airport, Manchester, Sheffield and Meadowhall - Doncaster - Cleethorpes and Hull Barton-on-Humber - Cleethorpes

		XC	NT	EM	EM	NT	HT	TP	XC	NT	NT	TP	TP	NT	XC	NT	NT	NT	NT
		◇1		◇1			◇1	◇1	◇1			◇1	◇1		◇1				
		⊥		◻			⊠		⊥						⊥			🚌	
Manchester Airport 85 ✈	d							10 44											
Manchester Piccadilly 10 ⇌	d							11b18				12 02	12 18						
Stockport 78	d							11 27					12 28						
Sheffield 7 ⇌	a	11 17		11 42				12 08	12 18				13 08		13 17				
	d	11 21	11 36	11 45				12 11	12 21	12 24	12 28		13 11		13 21		13 24		13 36
Meadowhall ⇌	d		11 42					12 16		12 30	12 34		13 16				13 30		13 42
Rotherham Central	d		11 49							12 36							13 36		13 49
Swinton (S.Yorks)	d		12a00							12 49							13 47		13a57
Mexborough	d									12 52							13 50		
Conisbrough	d									12 56							13 54		
London Kings Cross	d						10 41												
Doncaster 7	a			12 06			12 23	12 39		13 04	12 54		13 35				14 02		
York 8 26	a	12 32		12 29					13 32						14 32				
Doncaster 31	d						12 24	12 42		13 06	12 55			13 10			14 04		
Bentley (S.Yorks) 31	a													13 13					
Adwick 31	a													13 17					
Kirk Sandall	d									13 12									
Hatfield & Stainforth	d									13 17									
Thorne South	d																		
Crowle	d																		
Althorpe	d																		
Scunthorpe	a							13 07											
	d							13 08											
Barnetby	d				12 33			13 22											
Hull Paragon Interchange	d																	13 25	
Barton-on-Humber	a																	13 50	
Barton-on-Humber	d																		
Barrow Haven	d																		
New Holland	d																		
Goxhill	d																		
Thornton Abbey	d																		
Ulceby	d																		
Habrough	d				12 41			13 31											
Stallingborough	d																		
Healing	d																		
Great Coates	d																		
Grimsby Town	a				12 53			13 44											
	d				13 05			13 45											
Grimsby Docks	d																		
New Clee	d																		
Cleethorpes	a				13 16			13 57											
Thorne North	d									13 25									
Goole	d									13a35	13 15						14 25		
Saltmarshe	d																		
York 8 33	d					12 05										13 23			
Selby	a					12 23	12 41					13 23				13 42			
Wressle	d																		
Howden	d					12 33	12 52									13 52			
Eastrington	d																		
Gilberdyke	d										13 23						14 33		
Broomfleet	d																		
Brough	d					12 44	13 04				13 31	13 41				14 04	14 41		
Ferriby	d																		
Hessle	d																		
Hull	a					13 03	13 23				13 48	14 00				14 23	14 59		

b arr. 1058

Table 29

Sundays until 11 July

Manchester Airport, Manchester, Sheffield and Meadowhall - Doncaster - Cleethorpes and Hull Barton-on-Humber - Cleethorpes

		EM	XC	NT	HT	TP	XC	NT	NT	NT	TP	XC	NT	TP	XC	NT	NT		NT	NT
		◇	◇1		◇1	◇1	◇1				◇1	◇1		◇1	◇1					
			⊥		⊠		⊥					⊥			⊥		🚌			
Manchester Airport 85 ✈	d					12 55								13 55						
Manchester Piccadilly 10 ⇌	d	12 44				13b20					14 02			14c20						
Stockport 78	d	12 54				13 28								14 28						
Sheffield 7 ⇌	a	13 37	13 43			14 08	14 17					14 46		15 08	15 17					
	d		13 51			14 11	14 21		14 28	14 22		14 51		15 11	15 21	15 24				15 28
Meadowhall ⇌	d					14 16			14 34	14 28				15 16		15 30				15 34
Rotherham Central	d									14 34						15 37				
Swinton (S.Yorks)	d									14 46						15 47				
Mexborough	d									14 49						15 50				
Conisbrough	d									14 53						15 54				
London Kings Cross	d				12 40															
Doncaster 7	a		14 13		14 20	14 35			14 56	15 03		15 13		15 39		16 04				15 55
York 8 26	a		14 43				15 32					15 40			16 32					
Doncaster 31	d				14 21	14 42			14 59	15 05			15 10	15 42						15 56
Bentley (S.Yorks) 31	a												15 13							
Adwick 31	a												15 17							
Kirk Sandall	d									15 13										
Hatfield & Stainforth	d									15 18										
Thorne South	d																			
Crowle	d																			
Althorpe	d																			
Scunthorpe	a					15 07								16 07						
	d					15 08								16 08						
Barnetby	d					15 22								16 22						
Hull Paragon Interchange	d																15 30			
Barton-on-Humber	a																15 55			
Barton-on-Humber	d			14 00														16 15		
Barrow Haven	d			14 05														16 20		
New Holland	d			14 08														16 23		
Goxhill	d			14 13														16 28		
Thornton Abbey	d			14 16														16 31		
Ulceby	d			14 20														16 35		
Habrough	d			14 25										16 31				16 40		
Stallingborough	d			14 30														16 45		
Healing	d			14 33														16 48		
Great Coates	d			14 36														16 51		
Grimsby Town	a			14 41		15 42								16 44				16 56		
	d			14 41		15 43								16 45				16 56		
Grimsby Docks	d			14 44														16 59		
New Clee	d			14 46														17 01		
Cleethorpes	a			14 55		15 54								16 57				17 10		
Thorne North	d									15 25										
Goole	d								15 19	15 33										16 17
Saltmarshe	d																			
York 8 33	d							14 42											15 43	
Selby	a				14 36			15 01			15 22								16 01	
Wressle	d																			
Howden	d				14 47			15 11											16 11	
Eastrington	d																			
Gilberdyke	d								15 27											16 25
Broomfleet	d																			
Brough	d				14 59			15 23	15 35		15 42								16 23	16 33
Ferriby	d								15 40											
Hessle	d								15 44											
Hull	a				15 16			15 42	15 57		16 00								16 42	16 50

b arr. 1309

c arr. 1409

Table 29

Sundays until 11 July

Manchester Airport, Manchester, Sheffield and Meadowhall - Doncaster - Cleethorpes and Hull Barton-on-Humber - Cleethorpes

Station		NT	NT	XC	EM	TP	XC	NT	NT	TP	XC	NT	NT	HT	TP	XC	NT	NT	NT	EM
				◇1 H		◇1	◇1 H			◇1	◇1 H			◇1 ⊠	◇1	◇1 H				
Manchester Airport 85 ✈	d					14 55									15 55					
Manchester Piccadilly 10 ⇌	d					15b20				16 02					16c20					
Stockport 78	d					15 28									16 28					
Sheffield 7 ⇌	a			15 47		16 08	16 18				16 48				17 08	17 17				
	d	15 36	15 46	15 51		16 11	16 21	16 24	16 28		16 51				17 11	17 21	17 24	17 28	17 36	
Meadowhall ⇌	d	15 42	15 52			16 16		16 30	16 34						17 16		17 30	17 34	17 43	
Rotherham Central	d	15 48	15 58					16 37									17 37		17 49	
Swinton (S.Yorks)	d	15a56	16 08					16 47									17 47		17a57	
Mexborough	d							16 50									17 50			
Conisbrough	d							16 54									17 54			
London Kings Cross	d													15 44						
Doncaster 7	a			16 15		16 35		17 04	16 54		17 13			17 25	17 35		18 05	17 57		
York 8 26	a		17 01	16 40			17 32				17 42					18 32				
Doncaster 31	d					16 42		17 05	16 56			17 10		17 35	17 42			18 03		
Bentley (S.Yorks) 31	a											17 13								
Adwick 31	a											17 17								
Kirk Sandall	d							17 13												
Hatfield & Stainforth	d							17 18												
Thorne South	d																			
Crowle	d																			
Althorpe	d																			
Scunthorpe	a					17 07									18 07					
	d					17 08									18 08					
Barnetby	d				16 54	17 22									18 22					18 53
Hull Paragon Interchange	d																			
Barton-on-Humber	a																			
Barton-on-Humber	d																			
Barrow Haven	d																			
New Holland	d																			
Goxhill	d																			
Thornton Abbey	d																			
Ulceby	d																			
Habrough	d				17 02															19 01
Stallingborough	d																			
Healing	d																			
Great Coates	d																			
Grimsby Town	a				17 14	17 42									18 42					19 13
	d				17 14	17 43									18 43					19 13
Grimsby Docks	d																			
New Clee	d																			
Cleethorpes	a				17 23	17 54									18 54					19 24
Thorne North	d							17 25												
Goole	d							17a34	17 15									18 22		
Saltmarshe	d																			
York 8 33	d											17 10								
Selby	a									17 23		17 30		17 49						
Wressle	d																			
Howden	d											17 41		18 02						
Eastrington	d																			
Gilberdyke	d								17 23									18 35		
Broomfleet	d																			
Brough	d								17 31	17 41		17 53		18 13				18 43		
Ferriby	d																			
Hessle	d																			
Hull	a								17 49	18 00		18 12		18 32				18 57		

b arr. 1509 c arr. 1609

Table 29

Sundays until 11 July

Manchester Airport, Manchester, Sheffield and Meadowhall - Doncaster - Cleethorpes and Hull Barton-on-Humber - Cleethorpes

Station		XC	TP	XC	NT	NT	TP	NT	XC	NT	NT	HT	TP	NT	XC	NT	TP	NT	NT
		◇1 H	◇1	◇1 H			◇1	🚌	◇1 H			◇1 ⊠	◇1		◇1 H		◇1		
Manchester Airport 85 ✈	d		16 55														17 55		
Manchester Piccadilly 10 ⇌	d		17b20				18 02						19 02				18 20		
Stockport 78	d		17 28														18 28		
Sheffield 7 ⇌	a	17 48	18 08	18 19					18 46						19 20		19 08		
	d	17 51	18 11	18 21	18 25	18 28			18 51	18 57					19 21	19 29	19 11		19 36
Meadowhall ⇌	d		18 16		18 31	18 35				19 04						19 35	19 16		19 42
Rotherham Central	d				18 37					19 10						19 41			19 49
Swinton (S.Yorks)	d				18 47					19 18						19 49			19a57
Mexborough	d				18 50											19 52			
Conisbrough	d				18 54											19 56			
London Kings Cross	d											17 41							
Doncaster 7	a	18 13	18 35		19 04	18 54			19 13			19 23				20 07	19 35		
York 8 26	a	19 21		19 32					19 42	20 17					20 32				
Doncaster 31	d		18 42			18 55						19 24					19 42	19 30	
Bentley (S.Yorks) 31	a																	19 33	
Adwick 31	a																	19 37	
Kirk Sandall	d					19 01													
Hatfield & Stainforth	d					19 06													
Thorne South	d																		
Crowle	d																		
Althorpe	d																		
Scunthorpe	a		19 07														20 07		
	d		19 08														20 08		
Barnetby	d		19 22														20 22		
Hull Paragon Interchange	d							18 30											
Barton-on-Humber	a							18 55											
Barton-on-Humber	d													19 15					
Barrow Haven	d													19 20					
New Holland	d													19 23					
Goxhill	d													19 28					
Thornton Abbey	d													19 31					
Ulceby	d													19 35					
Habrough	d		19 31											19 40					
Stallingborough	d													19 45					
Healing	d													19 48					
Great Coates	d													19 51					
Grimsby Town	a		19 44											19 56			20 42		
	d		19 45											20 01			20 43		
Grimsby Docks	d													20 03					
New Clee	d													20 06					
Cleethorpes	a		19 57											20 14			20 55		
Thorne North	d					19 12													
Goole	d					19 21													
Saltmarshe	d																		
York 8 33	d										19 10								
Selby	a						19 23				19 29	19 39	20 17						
Wressle	d																		
Howden	d										19 39	19 52							
Eastrington	d																		
Gilberdyke	d					19 29													
Broomfleet	d																		
Brough	d					19 37	19 41				19 52	20 03	20 36						
Ferriby	d																		
Hessle	d																		
Hull	a					19 55	20 00				20 10	20 25	20 56						

b arr. 1709

Table 29

Sundays
until 11 July

Manchester Airport, Manchester, Sheffield and Meadowhall - Doncaster - Cleethorpes and Hull Barton-on-Humber - Cleethorpes

		XC	NT	TP	GR	TP	XC	NT	XC	TP	NT	NT	HT	NT	NT	TP	NT	TP	NT
		◇1		◇1	1	◇1	◇1		◇1	◇1			◇1			◇1		◇1	
Manchester Airport 85	d			18 55						19 55									
Manchester Piccadilly 10	d			19 20		20 06				20b18									
Stockport 78	d			19 28						20 27									
Sheffield 7	a	19 39		20 08			20 17		20 38	21 08									
	d	19 51	20 02	20 11			20 21	20 28	20 51	21 11				21 24	21 36		22 26	22 30	23 34
Meadowhall	d		20 09	20 16				20 34		21 16				21 30	21 42		22 32	22 36	23 40
Rotherham Central	d							20 40						21 37	21 48		22 38		23 47
Swinton (S.Yorks)	d							20 48						21 47	21a56		22 48		23 55
Mexborough	d							20 51						21 50			22 51		23 58
Conisbrough	d							20 55						21 54			22 55		00 02
London Kings Cross	d				19 10								20 10						
Doncaster 7	a	20 16	20 30	20 39	20 56			21 05	21 19	21 35			21 54	22 03			23 04	22 56	00 13
York 8 26	a	20 44					21 32		21 42										
Doncaster 31	d		20 30	20 42	20 58			21 07		21 42		21 49	21 55	22 04			23 07	22 58	
Bentley (S.Yorks) 31	a											21 52							
Adwick 31	a											21 56							
Kirk Sandall	d							21 13											
Hatfield & Stainforth	d							21 18											
Thorne South	d																		
Crowle	d																		
Althorpe	d																		
Scunthorpe	a			21 07						22 07								23 23	
	d			21 08						22 08								23 24	
Barnetby	d			21 22						22 22								23 38	
Hull Paragon Interchange	d																		
Barton-on-Humber	a																		
Barton-on-Humber	d																		
Barrow Haven	d																		
New Holland	d																		
Goxhill	d																		
Thornton Abbey	d																		
Ulceby	d																		
Habrough	d			21 31						22 31									
Stallingborough	d																		
Healing	d																		
Great Coates	d																		
Grimsby Town	a			21 44						22 44								23 57	
	d			21 45						22 45								23 58	
Grimsby Docks	d																		
New Clee	d																		
Cleethorpes	a			21 57						22 57								00 09	
Thorne North	d							21 24									23 19		
Goole	d		20 49					21a34						22 23			23 28		
Saltmarshe	d																		
York 8 33	d										21 41								
Selby	a				21 15	21 38					22 00		22s09						
Wressle	d																		
Howden	d										22 10		22s21						
Eastrington	d																		
Gilberdyke	d		20 57											22 32			23 36		
Broomfleet	d																		
Brough	d		21 05		21 36	21 58					22 22		22 31	22 40		23 00	23 44		
Ferriby	d																		
Hessle	d																		
Hull	a		21 23		21 56	22 15					22 41		22 50	22 57		23 18	00 02		

b arr. 2009

Table 29

Sundays
18 July to 05 September

Manchester Airport, Manchester, Sheffield and Meadowhall - Doncaster - Cleethorpes and Hull Barton-on-Humber - Cleethorpes

		NT	NT	NT	XC	NT	NT	TP	TP	XC	NT	NT	NT	NT	NT	NT
					◇1			◇1	◇1	◇1						
Manchester Airport 85	d															
Manchester Piccadilly 10	d							09 11								
Stockport 78	d															
Sheffield 7	a									10 16						
	d	08 00		08 45	09 21	09 36			09 52	10 21			10 26		11 05	
Meadowhall	d	08 06		08 51		09 42			09 57				10 32		11 11	
Rotherham Central	d	08 12		08 57		09 48			10 02						11 17	
Swinton (S.Yorks)	d	08 20		09 05		09a58			10 09						11 25	
Mexborough	d	08 23		09 08					10 12						11 28	
Conisbrough	d	08 27		09 12					10 17						11 32	
London Kings Cross	d															
Doncaster 7	a	08 38		09 22					10 26				10 51		11 43	
York 8 26	a				10 33					11 34						
Doncaster 31	d		09 07	09 26			10 19		10 28				10 53			11 07
Bentley (S.Yorks) 31	a															
Adwick 31	a															
Kirk Sandall	d		09 13													11 13
Hatfield & Stainforth	d		09 18													11 18
Thorne South	d															
Crowle	d															
Althorpe	d															
Scunthorpe	a								10 54							
	d								10 55							
Barnetby	d								11 09							
Hull Paragon Interchange	d										10 25					
Barton-on-Humber	a										10 50					
Barton-on-Humber	d													11 00		
Barrow Haven	d													11 05		
New Holland	d													11 08		
Goxhill	d													11 13		
Thornton Abbey	d													11 16		
Ulceby	d													11 20		
Habrough	d													11 25		
Stallingborough	d													11 30		
Healing	d													11 33		
Great Coates	d													11 36		
Grimsby Town	a								11 29					11 41		
	d								11 35					11 41		
Grimsby Docks	d													11 44		
New Clee	d													11 46		
Cleethorpes	a								11 44					11 55		
Thorne North	d		09 24	09 38												11 25
Goole	d		09a35	09 47			10 38						11 13			11a36
Saltmarshe	d															
York 8 33	d											10 40				
Selby	a							10 43				10 58				
Wressle	d															
Howden	d											11 08				
Eastrington	d															
Gilberdyke	d			09 58			10 46						11 24			
Broomfleet	d															
Brough	d			10 06			10 54	11 03				11 19	11 32			
Ferriby	d															
Hessle	d															
Hull	a			10 21			11 11	11 20				11 38	11 47			

b arr. 0936

Table 29

Sundays
18 July to 05 September

Manchester Airport, Manchester, Sheffield and Meadowhall - Doncaster - Cleethorpes and Hull Barton-on-Humber - Cleethorpes

		XC	EM	EM	NT	TP	HT	NT	XC	NT	NT	TP	TP	NT	XC	NT	NT	NT	NT
		◇1	◇1			◇1	◇1		◇1			◇1	◇1		◇1				
		⌶	⊐				⊠		⌶						⌶			🚌	
Manchester Airport 85 ✈	d					10 44													
Manchester Piccadilly [10]	d					11b18						12 02	12 18						
Stockport 78	d					11 27							12 28						
Sheffield [7]	a	11 17	11 28			12 08			12 18				13 08		13 17				
	d	11 21	11 31		11 36	12 11			12 21	12 24	12 28		13 11		13 21		13 24		13 36
Meadowhall	d				11 42	12 16				12 30	12 34		13 16				13 30		13 42
Rotherham Central	d				11 49					12 36							13 36		13 49
Swinton (S.Yorks)	d				12a00					12 49							13 47		13a57
Mexborough	d									12 52							13 50		
Conisbrough	d									12 56							13 54		
London Kings Cross	d						10 53												
Doncaster [7]	a		11 52			12 39	12 50			13 04	12 54		13 35				14 02		
York [8] 26	a	12 32	12 15						13 32						14 32				
Doncaster 31	d					12 42	12 52			13 06	12 55			13 10			14 04		
Bentley (S.Yorks) 31	a													13 13					
Adwick 31	a													13 17					
Kirk Sandall	d									13 12									
Hatfield & Stainforth	d									13 17									
Thorne South	d																		
Crowle	d																		
Althorpe	d																		
Scunthorpe	a					13 07													
	d					13 08													
Barnetby	d			12 33		13 22													
Hull Paragon Interchange	d																	13 25	
Barton-on-Humber	a																	13 50	
Barton-on-Humber	d																		
Barrow Haven	d																		
New Holland	d																		
Goxhill	d																		
Thornton Abbey	d																		
Ulceby	d																		
Habrough	d			12 41		13 31													
Stallingborough	d																		
Healing	d																		
Great Coates	d																		
Grimsby Town	a			12 53		13 44													
	d			13 05		13 45													
Grimsby Docks	d																		
New Clee	d																		
Cleethorpes	a			13 16		13 57													
Thorne North	d									13 25									
Goole	d									13a35	13 15						14 25		
Saltmarshe	d																		
York [8] 33	d							12 05								13 23			
Selby	a						13 08	12 23				13 23				13 42			
Wressle	d																		
Howden	d						13 20	12 33								13 52			
Eastrington	d																		
Gilberdyke	d										13 23						14 33		
Broomfleet	d																		
Brough	d						13 38	12 44			13 31	13 41				14 04	14 41		
Ferriby	d																		
Hessle	d																		
Hull	a						13 53	13 03			13 48	14 00				14 23	14 59		

b arr. 1058

Table 29

Sundays
18 July to 05 September

Manchester Airport, Manchester, Sheffield and Meadowhall - Doncaster - Cleethorpes and Hull Barton-on-Humber - Cleethorpes

		EM	NT	XC	TP	XC	NT	HT	NT	TP	XC	NT	TP	XC	NT	NT	NT	NT	NT	EM
		◇		◇1	◇1	◇1		◇1		◇1	◇1		◇1	◇1						
				⌶		⌶		⊠			⌶			⌶			🚌			
Manchester Airport 85 ✈	d				12 55								13 55							
Manchester Piccadilly [10]	d	12 44			13b20					14 02			14c20							
Stockport 78	d	12 54			13 28								14 28							
Sheffield [7]	a	13 37		13 43	14 08	14 17					14 46		15 08	15 17						
	d			13 51	14 11	14 21			14 28		14 51		15 11	15 21		15 24			15 28	
Meadowhall	d				14 16				14 34				15 16			15 30			15 34	
Rotherham Central	d															15 37				
Swinton (S.Yorks)	d															15 47				
Mexborough	d															15 50				
Conisbrough	d															15 54				
London Kings Cross	d							12 50												
Doncaster [7]	a			14 13	14 35			14 51	14 56		15 13		15 39			16 04			15 55	
York [8] 26	a			14 43		15 32					15 40			16 32						
Doncaster 31	d				14 42			14 51	14 59			15 10	15 42						15 56	
Bentley (S.Yorks) 31	a											15 13								
Adwick 31	a											15 17								
Kirk Sandall	d																			
Hatfield & Stainforth	d																			
Thorne South	d																			
Crowle	d																			
Althorpe	d																			
Scunthorpe	a				15 07								16 07							
	d				15 08								16 08							
Barnetby	d				15 22								16 22							16 54
Hull Paragon Interchange	d																15 30			
Barton-on-Humber	a																15 55			
Barton-on-Humber	d		14 00												16 15					
Barrow Haven	d		14 05												16 20					
New Holland	d		14 08												16 23					
Goxhill	d		14 13												16 28					
Thornton Abbey	d		14 16												16 31					
Ulceby	d		14 20												16 35					
Habrough	d		14 25										16 31		16 40					17 02
Stallingborough	d		14 30												16 45					
Healing	d		14 33												16 48					
Great Coates	d		14 36												16 51					
Grimsby Town	a		14 41		15 42								16 44		16 56					17 14
	d		14 41		15 43								16 45		16 56					17 14
Grimsby Docks	d		14 44												16 59					
New Clee	d		14 46												17 01					
Cleethorpes	a		14 55		15 54								16 57		17 10					17 23
Thorne North	d																			
Goole	d								15 19										16 17	
Saltmarshe	d																			
York [8] 33	d						14 42											15 43		
Selby	a						15 01	15 07		15 23								16 01		
Wressle	d																			
Howden	d						15 11	15 17										16 11		
Eastrington	d																			
Gilberdyke	d								15 27										16 25	
Broomfleet	d																			
Brough	d						15 23	15 29	15 35	15 41								16 23	16 33	
Ferriby	d								15 40											
Hessle	d								15 44											
Hull	a						15 42	15 48	15 57	16 00								16 42	16 50	

b arr. 1309

c arr. 1409

Table 29

Sundays
18 July to 05 September

Manchester Airport, Manchester, Sheffield and Meadowhall - Doncaster - Cleethorpes and Hull Barton-on-Humber - Cleethorpes

	NT	NT	XC	TP	XC	NT	NT	TP	XC	NT	TP	NT	HT	XC	NT	NT	NT	XC
			◇1 🍴	◇1	◇1 🍴			◇1	◇1 🍴		◇1		◇1 ⊠	◇1 🍴				◇1 🍴
Manchester Airport 85 ✈ d				14 55							15 55							
Manchester Piccadilly 10 ⇌ d				15b20				16 02			16c20							
Stockport 78 d				15 28							16 28							
Sheffield 7 ⇌ a			15 47	16 08	16 18				16 48		17 08			17 17				17 48
d	15 36	15 46	15 51	16 11	16 21	16 24	16 28		16 51		17 11			17 21	17 24	17 28	17 36	17 51
Meadowhall ⇌ d	15 42	15 52		16 16		16 30	16 34				17 16				17 30	17 34	17 43	
Rotherham Central d	15 48	15 58				16 37									17 37		17 49	
Swinton (S.Yorks) d	15a56	16 08				16 47									17 47		17a57	
Mexborough d						16 50									17 50			
Conisbrough d						16 54									17 54			
London Kings Cross d													15 51					
Doncaster 7 a			16 15	16 35		17 04	16 54		17 13		17 35		17 54		18 05	17 57		18 13
York 8 26 a		17 01	16 40		17 32				17 42					18 32				19 21
Doncaster 31 d				16 42		17 05	16 56			17 10	17 42		17 54			18 03		
Bentley (S.Yorks) 31 a										17 13								
Adwick 31 a										17 17								
Kirk Sandall d						17 13												
Hatfield & Stainforth d						17 18												
Thorne South d																		
Crowle d																		
Althorpe d																		
Scunthorpe a				17 07							18 07							
d				17 08							18 08							
Barnetby d				17 22							18 22							
Hull Paragon Interchange d																		
Barton-on-Humber a																		
Barton-on-Humber d																		
Barrow Haven d																		
New Holland d																		
Goxhill d																		
Thornton Abbey d																		
Ulceby d																		
Habrough d																		
Stallingborough d																		
Healing d																		
Great Coates d																		
Grimsby Town a				17 42							18 42							
d				17 43							18 43							
Grimsby Docks d																		
New Clee d																		
Cleethorpes a				17 54							18 54							
Thorne North d						17 25												
Goole d						17a34	17 15									18 22		
Saltmarshe d																		
York 8 33 d												17 10						
Selby a								17 23				17 30	18 07					
Wressle d																		
Howden d												17 41	18 20					
Eastrington d																		
Gilberdyke d							17 23									18 35		
Broomfleet d																		
Brough d							17 31	17 41				17 53	18 31			18 43		
Ferriby d																		
Hessle d																		
Hull a							17 49	18 00				18 12	18 50			18 57		

b arr. 1509
c arr. 1609

Table 29

Sundays
18 July to 05 September

Manchester Airport, Manchester, Sheffield and Meadowhall - Doncaster - Cleethorpes and Hull Barton-on-Humber - Cleethorpes

	EM	TP	XC	NT	NT	TP	NT	XC	NT	NT	TP	NT	XC	NT	HT	NT	TP	NT
		◇1	◇1 🍴			◇1	🚌	◇1 🍴			◇1		◇1 🍴		◇1 ⊠		◇1	
Manchester Airport 85 ✈ d		16 55															17 55	
Manchester Piccadilly 10 ⇌ d		17b20				18 02					19 02						18 20	
Stockport 78 d		17 28															18 28	
Sheffield 7 ⇌ a		18 08	18 19					18 46					19 20				19 08	
d		18 11	18 21	18 25	18 28			18 51	18 57				19 21			19 29	19 11	19 36
Meadowhall ⇌ d		18 16		18 31	18 35				19 04							19 35	19 16	19 42
Rotherham Central d				18 37					19 10							19 41		19 49
Swinton (S.Yorks) d				18 47					19 18							19 49		19a57
Mexborough d				18 50												19 52		
Conisbrough d				18 54												19 56		
London Kings Cross d															17 51			
Doncaster 7 a		18 35		19 04	18 54			19 13							19 49	20 07	19 35	
York 8 26 a			19 32					19 42	20 17				20 32					
Doncaster 31 d		18 42			18 55									19 30	19 54		19 42	
Bentley (S.Yorks) 31 a														19 33				
Adwick 31 a														19 37				
Kirk Sandall d					19 01													
Hatfield & Stainforth d					19 06													
Thorne South d																		
Crowle d																		
Althorpe d																		
Scunthorpe a		19 07															20 07	
d		19 08															20 08	
Barnetby d	18 53	19 22															20 22	
Hull Paragon Interchange d							18 30											
Barton-on-Humber a							18 55											
Barton-on-Humber d												19 15						
Barrow Haven d												19 20						
New Holland d												19 23						
Goxhill d												19 28						
Thornton Abbey d												19 31						
Ulceby d												19 35						
Habrough d	19 01	19 31										19 40						
Stallingborough d												19 45						
Healing d												19 48						
Great Coates d												19 51						
Grimsby Town a	19 13	19 44										19 56					20 42	
d	19 13	19 45										20 01					20 43	
Grimsby Docks d												20 03						
New Clee d												20 06						
Cleethorpes a	19 24	19 57										20 14					20 55	
Thorne North d					19 12													
Goole d					19 21													
Saltmarshe d																		
York 8 33 d										19 10								
Selby a						19 23				19 29	20 17				20 20			
Wressle d																		
Howden d										19 39					20 33			
Eastrington d																		
Gilberdyke d					19 29													
Broomfleet d																		
Brough d					19 37	19 41				19 52	20 36				20 44			
Ferriby d																		
Hessle d																		
Hull a					19 55	20 00				20 10	20 56				21 04			

b arr. 1709

Table 29

Sundays
18 July to 05 September

Manchester Airport, Manchester, Sheffield and Meadowhall - Doncaster - Cleethorpes and Hull Barton-on-Humber - Cleethorpes

		XC	NT	TP	XC	NT	GR	TP	XC	TP	NT	NT	HT	NT	NT	TP	NT	TP	NT
		◇■		◇■	◇■		■ ■	◇■	◇■	◇■			◇■ ⊠			◇■		◇■	
Manchester Airport 85 ✈	d			18 55						19 55									
Manchester Piccadilly	d			19 20				20 06		20b18									
Stockport 78	d			19 28						20 27									
Sheffield	a	19 39		20 08	20 17				20 38	21 08									
	d	19 51	20 02	20 11	20 21	20 28			20 51	21 11				21 24	21 36		22 26	22 30	23 34
Meadowhall	d		20 09	20 16		20 34				21 16				21 30	21 42		22 32	22 36	23 40
Rotherham Central	d					20 40								21 37	21 48		22 38		23 47
Swinton (S.Yorks)	d					20 48								21 47	21a56		22 48		23 55
Mexborough	d					20 51								21 50			22 51		23 58
Conisbrough	d					20 55								21 54			22 55		00 02
London Kings Cross	d						19 15						19 57						
Doncaster	a	20 16	20 30	20 39		21 05	21 15		21 19	21 35			21 54	22 03			23 04	22 56	00 13
York 26	a	20 44			21 32				21 42										
Doncaster 31	d		20 30	20 42		21 07	21 16			21 42		21 49	21 55	22 04			23 07	22 58	
Bentley (S.Yorks) 31	a											21 52							
Adwick 31	a											21 56							
Kirk Sandall	d					21 13													
Hatfield & Stainforth	d					21 18													
Thorne South	d																		
Crowle	d																		
Althorpe	d																		
Scunthorpe	a			21 07						22 07								23 23	
	d			21 08						22 08								23 24	
Barnetby	d			21 22						22 22								23 38	
Hull Paragon Interchange	d																		
Barton-on-Humber	a																		
Barton-on-Humber	d																		
Barrow Haven	d																		
New Holland	d																		
Goxhill	d																		
Thornton Abbey	d																		
Ulceby	d																		
Habrough	d			21 31						22 31									
Stallingborough	d																		
Healing	d																		
Great Coates	d																		
Grimsby Town	a			21 44						22 44								23 57	
	d			21 45						22 45								23 58	
Grimsby Docks	d																		
New Clee	d																		
Cleethorpes	a			21 57						22 57								00 09	
Thorne North	d					21 24											23 19		
Goole	d		20 49			21a34								22 23			23 28		
Saltmarshe	d																		
York 33	d										21 41								
Selby	a						21 31	21 38			22 00		22s09						
Wressle	d																		
Howden	d										22 10		22s21						
Eastrington	d																		
Gilberdyke	d		20 57											22 32			23 36		
Broomfleet	d																		
Brough	d		21 05				21 52	21 58			22 22		22 31	22 40		23 00	23 44		
Ferriby	d																		
Hessle	d																		
Hull	a		21 23				22 11	22 15			22 41		22 50	22 57		23 18	00 02		

b arr. 2009

Table 29

Sundays
from 12 September

Manchester Airport, Manchester, Sheffield and Meadowhall - Doncaster - Cleethorpes and Hull Barton-on-Humber - Cleethorpes

		NT	NT	NT	XC	NT	NT	TP	XC	NT	NT	TP	NT	NT	NT	NT	NT
					◇■			◇■	◇■	A	A	◇■					
Manchester Airport 85 ✈	d																
Manchester Piccadilly	d																
Stockport 78	d																
Sheffield	a								10 16								
	d	08 00		08 45	09 21	09 36		09 52	10 21					10 26	11 05		
Meadowhall	d	08 06		08 51		09 42		09 57						10 32	11 11		
Rotherham Central	d	08 12		08 57		09 48		10 02							11 17		
Swinton (S.Yorks)	d	08 20		09 05		09a58		10 09							11 25		
Mexborough	d	08 23		09 08				10 12							11 28		
Conisbrough	d	08 27		09 12				10 17							11 32		
London Kings Cross	d																
Doncaster	a	08 38		09 22				10 26						10 51	11 43		
York 26	a				10 33				11 34								
Doncaster 31	d		09 07	09 26			10 19	10 28						10 53		11 07	11 10
Bentley (S.Yorks) 31	a																11 13
Adwick 31	a																11 17
Kirk Sandall	d		09 13													11 13	
Hatfield & Stainforth	d		09 18													11 18	
Thorne South	d																
Crowle	d																
Althorpe	d																
Scunthorpe	a							10 54									
	d							10 55									
Barnetby	d							11 09									
Hull Paragon Interchange	d									10 25							
Barton-on-Humber	a									10 50							
Barton-on-Humber	d										11 00						
Barrow Haven	d										11 05						
New Holland	d										11 08						
Goxhill	d										11 13						
Thornton Abbey	d										11 16						
Ulceby	d										11 20						
Habrough	d										11 25						
Stallingborough	d										11 30						
Healing	d										11 33						
Great Coates	d										11 36						
Grimsby Town	a							11 29			11 41						
	d							11 35			11 41						
Grimsby Docks	d										11 44						
New Clee	d										11 46						
Cleethorpes	a							11 44			11 55						
Thorne North	d		09 24	09 38												11 25	
Goole	d		09a35	09 47			10 38							11 13		11a36	
Saltmarshe	d																
York 33	d												10 40				
Selby	a												10 58				
Wressle	d																
Howden	d												11 08				
Eastrington	d																
Gilberdyke	d			09 58			10 46							11 24			
Broomfleet	d																
Brough	d			10 06			10 54					11 04	11 19	11 32			
Ferriby	d																
Hessle	d																
Hull	a			10 21			11 11					11 22	11 38	11 47			

A 12 September

b arr. 0936

Table 29

Sundays from 12 September

Manchester Airport, Manchester, Sheffield and Meadowhall - Doncaster - Cleethorpes and Hull Barton-on-Humber - Cleethorpes

	XC	EM	NT	NT	HT	TP	XC	NT	NT	TP	NT	XC	NT	TP	NT	NT	NT	NT	EM
	◇1	◇1		A	◇1	◇1	◇1			◇1		◇1	A	◇1			A		◇
Manchester Airport 85 d						10 44													
Manchester Piccadilly 10 d						11b18				12 18									12 44
Stockport 78 d						11 27				12 28									12 55
Sheffield 7 a	11 17	11 28				12 08	12 18			13 08		13 17							13 37
d	11 21	11 31	11 36			12 11	12 21	12 24	12 28	13 11		13 21				13 24		13 36	13 49
Meadowhall d			11 42			12 16		12 30	12 34	13 16						13 30		13 42	
Rotherham Central d			11 49					12 36								13 36		13 49	
Swinton (S.Yorks) d			12a00					12 49								13 47		13a57	
Mexborough d								12 52								13 50			
Conisbrough d								12 56								13 54			
London Kings Cross d					10 41														
Doncaster 7 a		11 52			12 23	12 39		13 04	12 54	13 35						14 02			
York 8 26 a	12 32	12 15					13 32					14 32							
Doncaster 31 d					12 24	12 42		13 06	12 55		13 10					14 04			
Bentley (S.Yorks) 31 a											13 13								
Adwick 31 a											13 17								
Kirk Sandall d								13 12											
Hatfield & Stainforth d								13 17											
Thorne South d																			
Crowle d																			
Althorpe d																			
Scunthorpe a						13 07													
d						13 08													
Barnetby d						13 22													
Hull Paragon Interchange d													13 25						
Barton-on-Humber a													13 50						
Barton-on-Humber d																	14 00		
Barrow Haven d																	14 05		
New Holland d																	14 08		
Goxhill d																	14 13		
Thornton Abbey d																	14 16		
Ulceby d																	14 20		
Habrough d						13 31											14 25		
Stallingborough d																	14 30		
Healing d																	14 33		
Great Coates d																	14 36		
Grimsby Town a						13 44											14 41		
d						13 45											14 41		
Grimsby Docks d																	14 44		
New Clee d																	14 46		
Cleethorpes a						13 57											14 55		
Thorne North d								13 25											
Goole d								13a35	13 15							14 25			
Saltmarshe d																			
York 8 33 d				12 05											13 23				
Selby a				12 23	12 41										13 42				
Wressle d																			
Howden d				12 33	12 52										13 52				
Eastrington d																			
Gilberdyke d									13 23							14 33			
Broomfleet d																			
Brough d				12 44	13 04				13 31					13 41	14 04	14 41			
Ferriby d																			
Hessle d																			
Hull a				13 03	13 23				13 48					14 01	14 23	14 59			

A 12 September

b arr. 1058

Table 29

Sundays from 12 September

Manchester Airport, Manchester, Sheffield and Meadowhall - Doncaster - Cleethorpes and Hull Barton-on-Humber - Cleethorpes

	XC	HT	TP	XC	NT	NT	XC	NT	TP	XC	NT	NT	TP	NT	NT	NT	NT
	◇1	◇1	◇1	◇1	A		◇1		◇1	◇1		A	◇1			A	
Manchester Airport 85 d			12 55						13 55								
Manchester Piccadilly 10 d			13b20						14c20								
Stockport 78 d			13 28						14 28								
Sheffield 7 a	13 43		14 08	14 17			14 46		15 08	15 17							
d	13 51		14 11	14 21		14 28	14 51		15 11	15 21	15 24				15 28		15 36
Meadowhall d			14 16			14 34			15 16		15 30				15 34		15 42
Rotherham Central d											15 37						15 48
Swinton (S.Yorks) d											15 47						15a56
Mexborough d											15 50						
Conisbrough d											15 54						
London Kings Cross d		12 40															
Doncaster 7 a	14 13	14 20	14 35			14 56	15 13		15 39		16 04				15 55		
York 8 26 a	14 43			15 32			15 40			16 32							
Doncaster 31 d		14 21	14 42			14 59		15 10	15 42						15 56		
Bentley (S.Yorks) 31 a								15 13									
Adwick 31 a								15 17									
Kirk Sandall d																	
Hatfield & Stainforth d																	
Thorne South d																	
Crowle d																	
Althorpe d																	
Scunthorpe a			15 07						16 07								
d			15 08						16 08								
Barnetby d			15 22						16 22								
Hull Paragon Interchange d												15 30					
Barton-on-Humber a												15 55					
Barton-on-Humber d																16 15	
Barrow Haven d																16 20	
New Holland d																16 23	
Goxhill d																16 28	
Thornton Abbey d																16 31	
Ulceby d																16 35	
Habrough d									16 31							16 40	
Stallingborough d																16 45	
Healing d																16 48	
Great Coates d																16 51	
Grimsby Town a			15 42						16 44							16 56	
d			15 43						16 45							16 56	
Grimsby Docks d																16 59	
New Clee d																17 01	
Cleethorpes a			15 54						16 57							17 10	
Thorne North d																	
Goole d						15 19									16 17		
Saltmarshe d																	
York 8 33 d					14 42									15 43			
Selby a		14 36			15 01									16 01			
Wressle d																	
Howden d		14 47			15 11									16 11			
Eastrington d																	
Gilberdyke d						15 27									16 25		
Broomfleet d																	
Brough d		14 59			15 23	15 35							15 41	16 23	16 33		
Ferriby d						15 40											
Hessle d						15 44											
Hull a		15 16			15 42	15 57							16 00	16 42	16 50		

A 12 September

b arr. 1309

c arr. 1409

Manchester Airport, Manchester, Sheffield and Meadowhall - Doncaster - Cleethorpes and Hull Barton-on-Humber - Cleethorpes

	NT	XC	TP	XC	NT	NT	TP	XC	NT	NT	HT	TP	XC	NT	NT	NT	XC	TP
		◇1	◇1	◇1			◇1	◇1		A	◇1	◇1	◇1				◇1	◇1
		⌶		⌶				⌶			⊠		⌶				⌶	
Manchester Airport 85 ✈ d			14 55									15 55						16 55
Manchester Piccadilly 10 ⇌ d			15b20				16 02					16c20						17e20
Stockport 78 d			15 28									16 28						17 28
Sheffield 7 ⇌ a		15 47	16 08	16 18				16 48				17 08	17 17				17 48	18 08
d	15 46	15 51	16 11	16 21	16 24	16 28		16 51				17 11	17 21	17 24	17 28	17 36	17 51	18 11
Meadowhall ⇌ d	15 52		16 16		16 30	16 34						17 16		17 30	17 34	17 43		18 16
Rotherham Central d	15 58				16 37									17 37		17 49		
Swinton (S.Yorks) d	16 08				16 47									17 47		17a57		
Mexborough d					16 50									17 50				
Conisbrough d					16 54									17 54				
London Kings Cross d											15 44							
Doncaster 7 a		16 15	16 35		17 04	16 54		17 13			17 25	17 35		18 05	17 57		18 13	18 35
York 8 26 a	17 01	16 40		17 32				17 42					18 32				19 21	
Doncaster 31 d			16 42		17 05	16 56			17 10		17 35	17 42			18 03			18 42
Bentley (S.Yorks) 31 a									17 13									
Adwick 31 a									17 17									
Kirk Sandall d					17 13													
Hatfield & Stainforth d					17 18													
Thorne South d																		
Crowle d																		
Althorpe d																		
Scunthorpe a			17 07									18 07						19 07
d			17 08									18 08						19 08
Barnetby d			17 22									18 22						19 22
Hull Paragon Interchange d																		
Barton-on-Humber a																		
Barton-on-Humber d																		
Barrow Haven d																		
New Holland d																		
Goxhill d																		
Thornton Abbey d																		
Ulceby d																		
Habrough d																		19 31
Stallingborough d																		
Healing d																		
Great Coates d																		
Grimsby Town a			17 42									18 42						19 44
d			17 43									18 43						19 45
Grimsby Docks d																		
New Clee d																		
Cleethorpes a			17 54									18 54						19 57
Thorne North d					17 25													
Goole d					17a34	17 15									18 22			
Saltmarshe d																		
York 8 33 d										17 10								
Selby a							17 23			17 30	17 49							
Wressle d																		
Howden d										17 41	18 02							
Eastrington d																		
Gilberdyke d						17 23									18 35			
Broomfleet d																		
Brough d						17 31	17 41			17 53	18 13				18 43			
Ferriby d																		
Hessle d																		
Hull a						17 49	18 00			18 12	18 32				18 57			

A 12 September
b arr. 1509
c arr. 1609
e arr. 1709

Table 29

Sundays
from 12 September

Manchester Airport, Manchester, Sheffield and Meadowhall - Doncaster - Cleethorpes and Hull Barton-on-Humber - Cleethorpes

	XC	NT	NT	TP	NT	XC	NT	NT	HT	TP	NT	XC	NT	TP	NT	NT	XC	NT	TP
	◇1			◇1	A	◇1			◇1	◇1	A	◇1		◇1			◇1		◇1
	⌶				🚌	⌶			⊠			⌶					⌶		
Manchester Airport 85 ✈ d														17 55					18 55
Manchester Piccadilly 10 ⇌ d				18 02						19 02				18 20					19 20
Stockport 78 d														18 28					19 28
Sheffield 7 ⇌ a	18 19					18 46						19 20		19 08			19 39		20 08
d	18 21	18 25	18 28			18 51	18 57					19 21	19 29	19 11		19 36	19 51	20 02	20 11
Meadowhall ⇌ d		18 31	18 35				19 04						19 35	19 16		19 42		20 09	20 16
Rotherham Central d		18 37					19 10						19 41			19 49			
Swinton (S.Yorks) d		18 47					19 18						19 49			19a57			
Mexborough d		18 50											19 52						
Conisbrough d		18 54											19 56						
London Kings Cross d									17 41										
Doncaster 7 a		19 04	18 54			19 13			19 23				20 07	19 35			20 16	20 30	20 39
York 8 26 a	19 32					19 42	20 17					20 32					20 44		
Doncaster 31 d			18 55						19 24					19 42	19 30			20 30	20 42
Bentley (S.Yorks) 31 a															19 33				
Adwick 31 a															19 37				
Kirk Sandall d			19 01																
Hatfield & Stainforth d			19 06																
Thorne South d																			
Crowle d																			
Althorpe d																			
Scunthorpe a														20 07					21 07
d														20 08					21 08
Barnetby d														20 22					21 22
Hull Paragon Interchange d					18 30														
Barton-on-Humber a					18 55														
Barton-on-Humber d											19 15								
Barrow Haven d											19 20								
New Holland d											19 23								
Goxhill d											19 28								
Thornton Abbey d											19 31								
Ulceby d											19 35								
Habrough d											19 40								21 31
Stallingborough d											19 45								
Healing d											19 48								
Great Coates d											19 51								
Grimsby Town a											19 56			20 42					21 44
d											20 01			20 43					21 45
Grimsby Docks d											20 03								
New Clee d											20 06								
Cleethorpes a											20 14			20 55					21 57
Thorne North d			19 12																
Goole d			19 21															20 49	
Saltmarshe d																			
York 8 33 d								19 10											
Selby a				19 23				19 29	19 39	20 17									
Wressle d																			
Howden d								19 39	19 52										
Eastrington d																			
Gilberdyke d			19 29															20 57	
Broomfleet d																			
Brough d			19 37	19 41				19 52	20 03	20 36								21 05	
Ferriby d																			
Hessle d																			
Hull a			19 55	20 00				20 10	20 25	20 56								21 23	

A 12 September

Manchester Airport, Manchester, Sheffield and Meadowhall - Doncaster - Cleethorpes and Hull Barton-on-Humber - Cleethorpes

Sundays
from 12 September

		GR	TP	XC	NT	XC	TP	NT	NT	HT	NT	NT	TP	NT	TP	NT
		8 1 ⊥⊥	◇1	◇1 ⊥		◇1 ⊥	◇1			◇1 ⊠			◇1		◇1	
Manchester Airport 85	d						19 55									
Manchester Piccadilly 10	d		20 06				20b18									
Stockport 78	d						20 27									
Sheffield 7	a			20 17		20 38	21 08									
	d			20 21	20 28	20 51	21 11				21 24	21 36		22 26	22 30	23 34
Meadowhall	d				20 34		21 16				21 30	21 42		22 32	22 36	23 40
Rotherham Central	d				20 40						21 37	21 48		22 38		23 47
Swinton (S.Yorks)	d				20 48						21 47	21a56		22 48		23 55
Mexborough	d				20 51						21 50			22 51		23 58
Conisbrough	d				20 55						21 54			22 55		00 02
London Kings Cross	d	19 10								20 10						
Doncaster 7	a	20 56			21 05	21 19	21 35			21 54	22 03			23 04	22 56	00 13
York 8 26	a			21 32		21 42										
Doncaster 31	d	20 58			21 07		21 42		21 49	21 55	22 04			23 07	22 58	
Bentley (S.Yorks) 31	a								21 52							
Adwick 31	a								21 56							
Kirk Sandall	d				21 13											
Hatfield & Stainforth	d				21 18											
Thorne South	d															
Crowle	d															
Althorpe	d															
Scunthorpe	a						22 07								23 23	
	d						22 08								23 24	
Barnetby	d						22 22								23 38	
Hull Paragon Interchange	d															
Barton-on-Humber	a															
Barton-on-Humber	d															
Barrow Haven	d															
New Holland	d															
Goxhill	d															
Thornton Abbey	d															
Ulceby	d															
Habrough	d						22 31									
Stallingborough	d															
Healing	d															
Great Coates	d															
Grimsby Town	a						22 44								23 57	
	d						22 45								23 58	
Grimsby Docks	d															
New Clee	d															
Cleethorpes	a						22 57								00 09	
Thorne North	d				21 24									23 19		
Goole	d				21a34						22 23			23 28		
Saltmarshe	d															
York 8 33	d							21 41								
Selby	a	21 15	21 38					22 00		22s09						
Wressle	d															
Howden	d							22 10		22s21						
Eastrington	d															
Gilberdyke	d										22 32			23 36		
Broomfleet	d															
Brough	d	21 36	21 58					22 22		22 31	22 40		23 00	23 44		
Ferriby	d															
Hessle	d															
Hull	a	21 56	22 15					22 41		22 50	22 57		23 18	00 02		

b arr. 2009

Sheffield - Retford and Lincoln

Mondays to Fridays

		NT	NT	NT	NT	NT	NT	NT	NT	NT	NT
Huddersfield 34	d										
Barnsley 34	d										
Meadowhall 34	d					07 33		09 33	10 33	11 33	12 33
Sheffield 7	d	05 39	05 46	06 43	07 30	07 44	08 44	09 44	10 44	11 44	12 44
Darnall	d		05 51	06 48	07 35		08 49	09 49	10 49	11 49	12 49
Woodhouse	d		05 56	06 53	07 40		08 54	09 54	10 54	11 54	12 54
Kiveton Bridge	d		06 03	07 00	07 47		09 01	10 01	11 01	12 01	13 01
Kiveton Park	d	05 54	06 06	07 03	07 50	07 59	09 04	10 04	11 04	12 04	13 04
Shireoaks	d		06 11	07 08	07 55		09 09	10 09	11 09	12 09	13 09
Worksop	d	06 01	06 23	07 14	07 59	08a10	09 13	10 13	11 13	12 13	13 13
Retford 10	a	06 10	06 38	07 23	08 09		09 23	10 23	11 23	12 23	13 23
	d	06 10		07 24	08 09		09 23	10 23	11 23	12 23	13 23
Gainsborough Lea Road 18	d	06 25		07 38	08 24		09 38	10 38	11 38	12 38	13 41
Saxilby 18	d	06 37		07 51	08 37		09 51	10 51	11 51	12 51	13 53
Lincoln 18	a	06 53		08 06	08 52		10 06	11 06	12 06	13 06	14 09

		NT	NT	NT	NT	NT	NT	NT	NT	NT	NT	NT
Huddersfield 34	d										20 18	
Barnsley 34	d										21 11	
Meadowhall 34	d	13 33	14 33	15 33	16 33	16 55	17 33			20 33	21 29	
Sheffield 7	d	13 44	14 44	15 44	16 44	17 24	17 44	18 45	19 48	20 44	21 44	22 44
Darnall	d	13 49	14 49	15 49	16 49	17 29	17 49	18 50	19 53	20 49	21 49	22 49
Woodhouse	d	13 54	14 54	15 54	16 54	17 34	17 54	18 55	19 58	20 54	21 54	22 54
Kiveton Bridge	d	14 01	15 01	16 01	17 01	17 41	18 01	19 02	20 05	21 01	22 01	23 01
Kiveton Park	d	14 04	15 04	16 04	17 04	17 44	18 04	19 05	20 08	21 04	22 04	23 04
Shireoaks	d	14 09	15 09	16 09	17 09	17 48	18 09	19 10	20 13	21 09	22 08	23 09
Worksop	d	14 13	15 13	16 13	17 13	17 52	18 13	19 14	20 17	21a21	22 14	23a22
Retford 10	a	14 23	15 23	16 23	17 23	18 07	18 23	19 24	20 27		22 28	
	d	14 23	15 23	16 23	17 23		18 23	19 24	20 27			
Gainsborough Lea Road 18	d	14 38	15 38	16 38	17 38		18 38	19 39	20 42			
Saxilby 18	d	14 51	15 51	16 51	17 51		18 51	19 52	20 55			
Lincoln 18	a	15 06	16 06	17 06	18 06		19 07	20 06	21 10			

Sundays
until 11 July

		NT	NT	NT	NT	NT	NT
Huddersfield 34	d						
Barnsley 34	d						
Meadowhall 34	d						
Sheffield 7	d	13 42	13 57	16 02	18 02	19 26	21 06
Darnall	d		14 03	16 07	18 07	19 31	21 11
Woodhouse	d		14 08	16 12	18 12	19 36	21 16
Kiveton Bridge	d		14 14	16 19	18 19	19 43	21 23
Kiveton Park	d		14 17	16 22	18 22	19 46	21 26
Shireoaks	d		14 22	16 26	18 26	19 50	21 30
Worksop	d	14 02	14 26	16 30	18 30	19 54	21 34
Retford 10	a	14 11	14 39	16 39	18 39	20 03	21 48
	d	14 12		16 40	18 40	20 04	
Gainsborough Lea Road 18	d	14 26		16 54	18 54	20 18	
Saxilby 18	d	14 39		17 07	19 07	20 31	
Lincoln 18	a	14 54		17 21	19 22	20 45	

Sundays
18 July to 05 September

		NT	NT	NT	NT	NT	NT
Huddersfield 34	d						
Barnsley 34	d						
Meadowhall 34	d						
Sheffield 7	d	13 42	13 57	16 02	18 02	19 26	21 06
Darnall	d		14 03	16 07	18 07	19 31	21 11
Woodhouse	d		14 08	16 12	18 12	19 36	21 16
Kiveton Bridge	d		14 14	16 19	18 19	19 43	21 23
Kiveton Park	d		14 17	16 22	18 22	19 46	21 26
Shireoaks	d		14 22	16 26	18 26	19 50	21 30
Worksop	d	14 02	14 26	16 30	18 30	19 54	21 34
Retford 10	a	14 11	14 39	16 39	18 39	20 03	21 48
	d						
Gainsborough Lea Road 18	d						
Saxilby 18	d						
Lincoln 18	a						

Sundays
from 12 September

		NT	NT	NT	NT	NT	NT
Huddersfield 34	d						
Barnsley 34	d						
Meadowhall 34	d						
Sheffield 7	d	13 42	13 57	16 02	18 02	19 26	21 06
Darnall	d		14 03	16 07	18 07	19 31	21 11
Woodhouse	d		14 08	16 12	18 12	19 36	21 16
Kiveton Bridge	d		14 14	16 19	18 19	19 43	21 23
Kiveton Park	d		14 17	16 22	18 22	19 46	21 26
Shireoaks	d		14 22	16 26	18 26	19 50	21 30
Worksop	d	14 02	14 26	16 30	18 30	19 54	21 34
Retford 10	a	14 11	14 39	16 39	18 39	20 03	21 48
	d	14 12		16 40	18 40	20 04	
Gainsborough Lea Road 18	d	14 26		16 54	18 54	20 18	
Saxilby 18	d	14 39		17 07	19 07	20 31	
Lincoln 18	a	14 54		17 21	19 22	20 45	

For connections to London Kings Cross please refer to Table 26

Table 30

Saturdays

Sheffield - Retford and Lincoln

Station			NT	NT	NT	NT	NT	NT	NT	NT	NT	NT	NT
Huddersfield	34	d											
Barnsley	34	d											
Meadowhall	34	d							09 33	10 33	11 33		12 33
Sheffield 7		d	05 39	05 46	06 43	07 30	08 03	08 44	09 44	10 44	11 44	12 00	12 44
Darnall		d		05 51	06 48	07 35	08 08	08 49	09 49	10 49	11 49	12 05	12 49
Woodhouse		d		05 56	06 53	07 40	08 13	08 54	09 54	10 54	11 54	12 10	12 54
Kiveton Bridge		d		06 03	07 00	07 47	08 20	09 01	10 01	11 01	12 01	12 17	13 01
Kiveton Park		d	05 54	06 06	07 03	07 50	08 23	09 04	10 04	11 04	12 04	12 20	13 04
Shireoaks		d		06 11	07 08	07 55	08 28	09 09	10 09	11 09	12 09	12 25	13 09
Worksop		d	06 01	06 23	07 14	07 59	08 32	09 13	10 13	11 13	12 13	12 35	13 13
Retford 10		a	06 10	06 38	07 23	08 09	08 42	09 23	10 23	11 23	12 23	12 44	13 23
		d	06 10		07 24	08 09	08 42	09 23	10 23	11 23	12 23	12 45	13 23
Gainsborough Lea Road	18	d	06 25		07 38	08 24		09 38	10 38	11 38	12 38		13 38
Saxilby	18	d	06 37		07 51	08 37		09 51	10 51	11 51	12 51		13 51
Lincoln	18	a	06 53		08 06	08 52		10 06	11 06	12 06	13 06		14 06
Gainsborough Central		d					08 57					13 00	
Kirton Lindsey		d					09 11					13 13	
Brigg		d					09 24					13 22	
Barnetby	29	a					09 38					13 37	
Habrough	29	a					09 48					13 47	
Grimsby Town	29	a					10 00					14 00	
Cleethorpes	29	a					10 13					14 11	

Station			NT	NT	NT	NT	NT	NT	NT	NT	NT	NT
Huddersfield	34	d										
Barnsley	34	d										
Meadowhall	34	d	13 33	14 33	15 33		16 33	16 55	17 33	18 33		20 35
Sheffield 7		d	13 44	14 44	15 44	16 00	16 44	17 24	17 44	18 45	19 48	20 44
Darnall		d	13 49	14 49	15 49	16 05	16 49	17 29	17 49	18 50	19 53	20 49
Woodhouse		d	13 54	14 54	15 54	16 10	16 54	17 34	17 54	18 55	19 58	20 54
Kiveton Bridge		d	14 01	15 01	16 01	16 17	17 01	17 41	18 01	19 02	20 05	21 01
Kiveton Park		d	14 04	15 04	16 04	16 20	17 04	17 44	18 04	19 05	20 08	21 04
Shireoaks		d	14 09	15 09	16 09	16 25	17 09	17 48	18 09	19 10	20 13	21 09
Worksop		d	14 13	15 13	16 13	16 36	17 13	17 52	18 13	19 14	20 17	21a23
Retford 10		a	14 23	15 23	16 23	16 46	17 23	18 07	18 23	19 24	20 27	
		d	14 23	15 23	16 23	16 46	17 23		18 23	19 24	20 27	
Gainsborough Lea Road	18	d	14 38	15 45	16 38		17 38		18 38	19 39	20 42	
Saxilby	18	d	14 51	15 58	16 51		17 51		18 51	19 52	20 55	
Lincoln	18	a	15 06	16 09	17 06		18 06		19 07	20 06	21 10	
Gainsborough Central		d				17 01						
Kirton Lindsey		d				17 15						
Brigg		d				17 27						
Barnetby	29	a				17 37						
Habrough	29	a				17 47						
Grimsby Town	29	a				18 01						
Cleethorpes	29	a				18 11						

Station			NT A	NT B	NT
Huddersfield	34	d	20s13	20s18	
Barnsley	34	d	21s11	21s11	
Meadowhall	34	d	21s29	21s29	
Sheffield 7		d	21s44	21s44	22 44
Darnall		d	21s49	21s49	22 49
Woodhouse		d	21s54	21s54	22 54
Kiveton Bridge		d	22s01	22s01	23 01
Kiveton Park		d	22s04	22s04	23 04
Shireoaks		d	22s08	22s08	23 09
Worksop		d	22s14	22s14	23a22
Retford 10		a	22 28	22 28	
		d			
Gainsborough Lea Road	18	d			
Saxilby	18	d			
Lincoln	18	a			
Gainsborough Central		d			
Kirton Lindsey		d			
Brigg		d			
Barnetby	29	a			
Habrough	29	a			
Grimsby Town	29	a			
Cleethorpes	29	a			

A from 11 September
B until 4 September

For connections to London Kings Cross please refer to Table 26

Table 30

Mondays to Fridays

Lincoln and Retford - Sheffield

Station			NT	NT	NT	NT	NT	NT	NT	NT	NT	NT	NT
Lincoln	18	d			07 04		08 27	09 27	10 27	11 27	12 27	13 27	14 27
Saxilby	18	d			07 14		08 36	09 36	10 36	11 36	12 36	13 36	14 36
Gainsborough Lea Road	18	d			07 26		08 49	09 49	10 49	11 49	12 49	13 49	14 49
Retford 10		a			07 40		09 03	10 03	11 03	12 03	13 03	14 03	15 03
		d		07 03	07 40		09 03	10 03	11 03	12 03	13 03	14 03	15 03
Worksop		d	06 30	07 16	07 52	08 14	09 15	10 15	11 15	12 15	13 15	14 15	15 15
Shireoaks		d	06 33	07 20	07 55	08 19	09 19	10 19	11 19	12 19	13 19	14 19	15 19
Kiveton Park		d	06 39	07 25	08 01	08 25	09 25	10 25	11 25	12 25	13 25	14 25	15 25
Kiveton Bridge		d	06 42	07 28	08 04	08 28	09 28	10 28	11 28	12 28	13 28	14 28	15 28
Woodhouse		d	06 48	07 35	08 10	08 34	09 34	10 34	11 34	12 34	13 34	14 34	15 34
Darnall		d	06 53	07 40	08 15	08 39	09 39	10 39	11 39	12 39	13 39	14 39	15 39
Sheffield 7		a	07 02	07 48	08 26	08 49	09 49	10 49	11 49	12 49	13 49	14 49	15 49
Meadowhall	34	a		07 57		09 03	10 03	11 03	12 03	13 03	14 03	15 03	16 03
Barnsley	34	a		08 11									
Huddersfield	34	a											

Station			NT	NT	NT	NT	NT	NT	NT	NT	NT	NT	NT
Lincoln	18	d	15 27	16 27	17 22		18 24	19 43	20 27		21 27		
Saxilby	18	d	15 36	16 36	17 31		18 33	19 52	20 36		21 36		
Gainsborough Lea Road	18	d	15 49	16 49	17 44		18 46	20 05	20 49		21 49		
Retford 10		a	16 03	17 03	17 58		19 04	20 19	21 03		22 03		
		d	16 03	17 03	17 58	18 14	19 05	20 19	21 03		22 03	22 45	
Worksop		d	16 15	17 15	18 10	18 25	19 16	20 32	21 15	21 28	22 15	22 58	23 28
Shireoaks		d	16 19	17 19		18 29	19 20	20 36		21 32	22 19	23 02	23 32
Kiveton Park		d	16 25	17 25		18 34	19 26	20 42	21 23	21 38	22 25	23 08	23 38
Kiveton Bridge		d	16 28	17 28		18 37	19 29	20 45		21 41	22 28	23 11	23 41
Woodhouse		d	16 34	17 34		18 43	19 36	20 50		21 48	22 34	23 18	23 52
Darnall		d	16 39	17 39		18 48	19 41	20 55		21 53	22 39	23 23	23 57
Sheffield 7		a	16 49	17 49	18 35	18 57	19 55	21 05	21 47	22 02	22 50	23 33	00 04
Meadowhall	34	a	17 03	18 03		19 06							
Barnsley	34	a											
Huddersfield	34	a											

Sundays
until 11 July

Station			NT	NT	NT	NT	NT
Lincoln	18	d		15 15	17 35	19 35	
Saxilby	18	d		15 25	17 45	19 45	
Gainsborough Lea Road	18	d		15 37	17 57	19 57	
Retford 10		a		15 51	18 11	20 11	
		d	14 50	15 51	18 11	20 11	22 24
Worksop		d	15 01	16 03	18 23	20 23	22 35
Shireoaks		d	15 05	16 06	18 26	20 26	22 39
Kiveton Park		d	15 10	16 12	18 32	20 32	22 44
Kiveton Bridge		d	15 13	16 15	18 35	20 35	22 47
Woodhouse		d	15 19	16 21	18 41	20 41	22 53
Darnall		d	15 24	16 26	18 46	20 46	22 58
Sheffield 7		a	15 33	16 36	18 55	20 56	23 07
Meadowhall	34	a	15 42	16 44			
Barnsley	34	a	16 03	17 05			
Huddersfield	34	a	16 53				

Sundays
18 July to 05 September

Station			NT	NT	NT	NT	NT
Lincoln	18	d					
Saxilby	18	d					
Gainsborough Lea Road	18	d					
Retford 10		a					
		d	14 50	15 51	18 11	20 11	22 24
Worksop		d	15 01	16 03	18 23	20 23	22 35
Shireoaks		d	15 05	16 06	18 26	20 26	22 39
Kiveton Park		d	15 10	16 12	18 32	20 32	22 44
Kiveton Bridge		d	15 13	16 15	18 35	20 35	22 47
Woodhouse		d	15 19	16 21	18 41	20 41	22 53
Darnall		d	15 24	16 26	18 46	20 46	22 58
Sheffield 7		a	15 33	16 36	18 55	20 56	23 07
Meadowhall	34	a	15 42	16 44			
Barnsley	34	a	16 03	17 05			
Huddersfield	34	a	16 53				

Sundays
from 12 September

Station			NT	NT	NT	NT	NT
Lincoln	18	d		15 15	17 35	19 35	
Saxilby	18	d		15 25	17 45	19 45	
Gainsborough Lea Road	18	d		15 37	17 57	19 57	
Retford 10		a		15 51	18 11	20 11	
		d	14 50	15 51	18 11	20 11	22 24
Worksop		d	15 01	16 03	18 23	20 23	22 35
Shireoaks		d	15 05	16 06	18 26	20 26	22 39
Kiveton Park		d	15 10	16 12	18 32	20 32	22 44
Kiveton Bridge		d	15 13	16 15	18 35	20 35	22 47
Woodhouse		d	15 19	16 21	18 41	20 41	22 53
Darnall		d	15 24	16 26	18 46	20 46	22 58
Sheffield 7		a	15 33	16 36	18 55	20 56	23 07
Meadowhall	34	a	15 42	16 44			
Barnsley	34	a	16 03	17 05			
Huddersfield	34	a	16 57				

For connections from London Kings Cross please refer to Table 26

Table 30

Saturdays

Lincoln and Retford - Sheffield

	NT	NT	NT	NT	NT	NT	NT	NT	NT		NT	NT	NT	NT	NT	NT	NT	NT	NT		NT	NT	NT	NT
Cleethorpes 29 d								11 13						15 21							19 13			
Grimsby Town 29 d								11 21						15 28							19 20			
Habrough 29 d								11 31						15 38							19 30			
Barnetby 29 d								11 40						15 48							19 39			
Brigg d								11 46						15 53							19 45			
Kirton Lindsey d								11 55						16 02							19 54			
Gainsborough Central d								12 21						16 20							20 12			
Lincoln 18 d			07 04	08 27	09 27	10 27	11 27		12 27		13 27	14 27	15 27		16 27	17 22		18 24	19 43			20 27		21 24
Saxilby 18 d			07 14	08 36	09 36	10 36	11 36		12 36		13 36	14 36	15 36		16 36	17 31		18 33	19 52			20 36		21 33
Gainsborough Lea Road 18 d			07 26	08 49	09 49	10 49	11 49		12 49		13 49	14 49	15 49		16 49	17 44		18 46	20 05			20 49		21 46
Retford 10 a			07 40	09 03	10 03	11 03	12 03	12 35	13 03		14 03	15 03	16 03	16 35	17 03	17 58		19 04	20 19		20 26	21 03		22 00
d		07 03	07 40	09 03	10 03	11 03	12 03	12 36	13 03		14 03	15 03	16 03	16 35	17 03	17 58	18 14	19 04	20 19		20 27	21 04		22 00
Worksop d	06 30	07 16	07 52	09 15	10 15	11 15	12 15	12 47	13 15		14 15	15 15	16 15	16 47	17 15	18 10	18 25	19 16	20 31		20 38	21 15	21 28	22 12
Shireoaks d	06 33	07 20	07 55	09 19	10 19	11 19	12 19	12 51	13 19		14 19	15 19	16 19	16 51	17 19		18 29	19 20	20 35		20 42		21 32	22 16
Kiveton Park d	06 39	07 25	08 01	09 25	10 25	11 25	12 25	12 57	13 25		14 25	15 25	16 25	16 57	17 25		18 34	19 26	20 41		20 48	21 23	21 38	22 22
Kiveton Bridge d	06 42	07 28	08 04	09 28	10 28	11 28	12 28	13 00	13 28		14 28	15 28	16 28	17 00	17 28		18 37	19 29	20 44		20 53		21 41	22 25
Woodhouse d	06 48	07 35	08 10	09 34	10 34	11 34	12 34	13 07	13 34		14 34	15 34	16 34	17 06	17 34		18 43	19 35	20 50		21 01		21 48	22 31
Darnall d	06 53	07 40	08 15	09 39	10 39	11 39	12 39	13 12	13 39		14 39	15 39	16 39	17 11	17 39		18 48	19 40	20 55		21 06		21 53	22 36
Sheffield 7 a	07 02	07 48	08 26	09 49	10 49	11 49	12 49	13 23	13 49		14 49	15 49	16 49	17 23	17 49	18 35	18 57	19 55	21 05		21 22	21 46	22 02	22 46
Meadowhall 34 a		07 57		10 03	11 03	12 03	13 03		14 03		15 03	16 03	17 03		18 03		19 06							
Barnsley 34 a		08 11																						
Huddersfield 34 a																								

	NT	NT
Cleethorpes 29 d		
Grimsby Town 29 d		
Habrough 29 d		
Barnetby 29 d		
Brigg d		
Kirton Lindsey d		
Gainsborough Central d		
Lincoln 18 d		
Saxilby 18 d		
Gainsborough Lea Road 18 d		
Retford 10 a		
d	22 45	
Worksop d	22 58	23 28
Shireoaks d	23 02	23 32
Kiveton Park d	23 08	23 38
Kiveton Bridge d	23 11	23 41
Woodhouse d	23 18	23 47
Darnall d	23 23	23 52
Sheffield 7 a	23 33	00 01
Meadowhall 34 a		
Barnsley 34 a		
Huddersfield 34 a		

For connections from London Kings Cross please refer to Table 26

Network Diagram for Tables 31, 32, 33, 34

DM-3/09(2)
Design BAJS

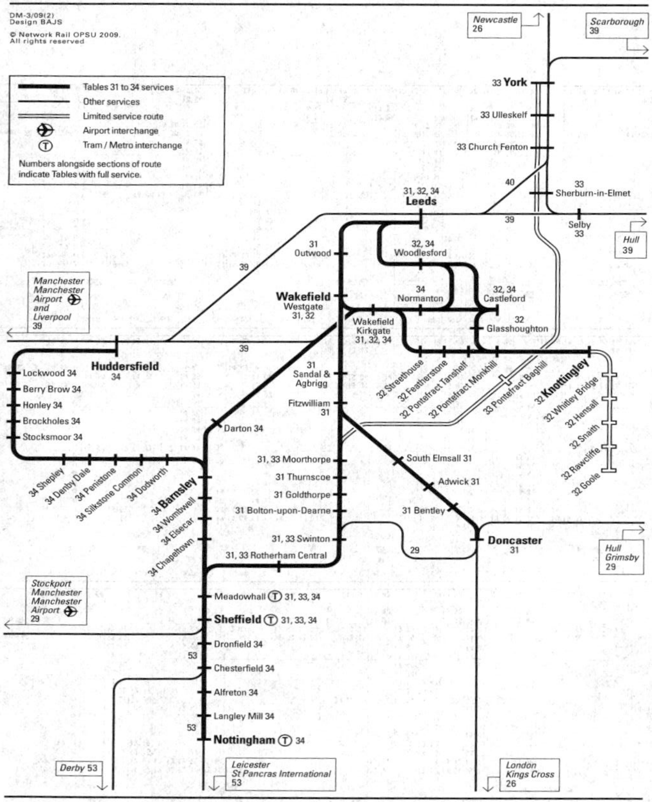

Table 31

Mondays to Fridays

Sheffield, Doncaster and Wakefield - Leeds

				NT	NT		NT				NT		NT	NT	NT	NT	NT	NT	XC	NT	NT		NT	GR	NT	NT
																			◇1 ✠					R 1 ⊏		
Sheffield 7	29 ⇌	d		05 22	05 50						06 06		06 18	06 28	06 49		06 52	07 06	07 12		07 14		07 20			07 51
Meadowhall	29 ⇌	d		05 28	05 56						06 12		06 24	06 34	06 55		06 58	07 12			07 21		07 26			07 57
Rotherham Central	29	d		05 34									06 30	06 40			07 04				07 27					
Swinton (S.Yorks)	29	d		05 42									06 38	06 51			07 14				07 35					
Bolton-upon-Dearne		d		05 46										06 56							07 39					
Goldthorpe		d		05 49										06 58							07 42					
Thurnscoe		d		05 52										07 01							07 45					
Moorthorpe		d		05 57										07 06							07 50					
Doncaster 7		d					06 25						06 59			07 14	07 32							07 51	07 58	
Bentley (S.Yorks)		d					06 28						07 02			07 17	07 35								08 01	
Adwick		a					06 32						07 08			07 21	07 40								08 05	
		d					06 32									07 21									08 05	
South Elmsall		d					06 38									07 27									08 11	
Fitzwilliam		d		06 02			06 43							07 12		07 35					07 56				08 16	
Sandal & Agbrigg		d		06 08			06 49							07 18		07 41				←	08 02				08 22	
Wakefield Westgate 7	32,39	a		06 12			06 53							07 22		07 45			07 36	07 45	08 06			08 10	08 26	
		d		06 13			06 53							07 23		07 45			07 37	07 45	08 07			08 10	08 27	
Wakefield Kirkgate 4	32,34,39	a			06 27						06 49				07 27	→		07 49					07 57			08 27
		d			06 28						06 50				07 28			07 50					07 58			08 28
Outwood		d		06 18			06 58							07 28						07 50	08 12				08 31	
Leeds 10	32,34	a		06 35	06 49		07 14				07 28			07 44	07 51			08 25	07 52	08 04	08 30		08 21	08 32	08 46	08 49

			NT	GR	NT	NT	NT		XC	NT	NT	NT	GR	GR	NT	NT	NT		NT	NT	NT	XC	NT	GR	NT	NT
				R 1 ⊏					◇1 ✠				R 1 ⊏✠	R 1 ⊏✠								◇1 ✠		R 1 ⊏✠		
Sheffield 7	29 ⇌	d	08 06			08 14	08 18		08 21						08 51		08 57		09 06	09 14	09 18	09 21	09 29			09 51
Meadowhall	29 ⇌	d	08 12			08 23	08 24								08 57		09 03		09 12	09 21	09 24		09 35			09 57
Rotherham Central	29	d				08 29											09 11			09 27			09 42			
Swinton (S.Yorks)	29	d				08 38											09 19			09 36			09 51			
Bolton-upon-Dearne		d				08 42														09 41						
Goldthorpe		d				08 45														09 43						
Thurnscoe		d				08 48														09 46						
Moorthorpe		d				08 53														09 51			10 01			
Doncaster 7		d		08 12	08 16					08 26		08 52	09 00			09 14	09 38									
Bentley (S.Yorks)		d			08 19					08 29		08 55				09 17	09 41									
Adwick		a			08 25					08 33		09 01				09 21	09 47									
		d								08 33						09 21										
South Elmsall		d								08 39						09 27										
Fitzwilliam		d				08 59				08 47						09 32				10 01						
Sandal & Agbrigg		d				09 05				08 53	←					09 38				10 07					←	
Wakefield Westgate 7	32,39	a		08 31		09 09			08 48	08 57	09 09		09 17			09 42				10 11		09 46			10 11	
		d		08 31		09 09			08 49	08 57	09 09		09 17	09 30		09 42				10 11		09 47		10 03	10 11	
Wakefield Kirkgate 4	32,34,39	a	08 49			→	08 57								09 27				09 49	→	09 57					10 27
		d	08 50				08 58								09 28				09 50		09 58					10 28
Outwood		d								09 02	09 14					09 47									10 16	
Leeds 10	32,34	a	09 25	08 50			09 19		09 03	09 14	09 30		09 35	09 46	09 49	10 02			10 25		10 18	10 02		10 23	10 33	10 48

			NT		NT	NT	NT	NT	XC	GR	GR	NT	NT		GR	NT	NT	NT	NT	NT	XC	NT	NT		GR	NT
									◇1 ✠	R 1 ⊏	R 1 ⊏				R 1 ⊏✠						◇1 ✠				R 1 ⊏✠	
Sheffield 7	29 ⇌	d			09 57	10 06	10 14	10 18	10 21				10 51				10 57	11 06	11 14	11 18	11 21					11 51
Meadowhall	29 ⇌	d			10 03	10 12	10 21	10 24					10 57				11 03	11 12	11 21	11 24						11 57
Rotherham Central	29	d			10 10		10 27										11 10		11 27							
Swinton (S.Yorks)	29	d			10 18		10 36										11 20		11 36							
Bolton-upon-Dearne		d					10 41												11 41							
Goldthorpe		d					10 43												11 43							
Thurnscoe		d					10 46												11 46							
Moorthorpe		d					10 51												11 51							
Doncaster 7		d	10 14		10 46					10 30					11 19	11 26	11 38								11 59	
Bentley (S.Yorks)		d	10 17		10 49											11 29	11 41									
Adwick		a	10 21		10 55											11 33	11 47									
		d	10 21													11 33										
South Elmsall		d	10 27													11 39										
Fitzwilliam		d	10 32				10 57									11 45			11 57							
Sandal & Agbrigg		d	10 38				11 03					←				11 51			12 03			←	←			
Wakefield Westgate 7	32,39	a	10 42				11 07		10 46	10 50		11 07			11 36	11 55			12 07		11 46	11 55	12 07		12 16	
		d	10 42				11 08		10 47	10 50	10 57	11 08			11 36	11 55			12 08		11 47	11 55	12 08		12 16	
Wakefield Kirkgate 4	32,34,39	a				10 49	→	10 57					11 27			→		11 49	→	11 57						12 27
		d				10 50		10 58					11 28					11 50		11 58						12 28
Outwood		d	10 47									11 13										12 00	12 13			
Leeds 10	32,34	a	11 02			11 25		11 18	11 02	11 09	11 18	11 30	11 48		11 55			12 25		12 18	12 01	12 14	12 30		12 36	12 48

Table 31

Mondays to Fridays

Sheffield, Doncaster and Wakefield - Leeds

			GR	NT	NT	NT	NT	NT	XC		NT	NT	GC	GR	NT	NT	NT	NT	NT		NT	GR	XC	NT	NT	NT
			R 1 ⊏						◇1 ✠					R 1 ⊏✠								R 1 ⊏	◇1 ✠			
Sheffield 7	29 ⇌	d			11 57	12 06	12 14	12 18	12 21						12 51		12 57	13 06	13 14		13 18		13 21			13 28
Meadowhall	29 ⇌	d			12 03	12 12	12 21	12 24							12 57		13 03	13 12	13 21		13 24					13 35
Rotherham Central	29	d			12 10		12 27										13 10		13 27							13 41
Swinton (S.Yorks)	29	d			12 19		12 36										13 18		13 36							13 50
Bolton-upon-Dearne		d					12 41												13 41							
Goldthorpe		d					12 43												13 43							
Thurnscoe		d					12 46												13 46							
Moorthorpe		d					12 51												13 51							14 01
Doncaster 7		d	12 19	12 25	12 38								12 34	12 59		13 27	13 38									
Bentley (S.Yorks)		d		12 28	12 41											13 30	13 41									
Adwick		a		12 32	12 46											13 34	13 47									
		d		12 32												13 34										
South Elmsall		d		12 38												13 40										
Fitzwilliam		d		12 43			12 57									13 45			13 57							
Sandal & Agbrigg		d		12 49			13 03				←	←				13 51			14 03					←	←	
Wakefield Westgate 7	32,39	a	12 36	12 53			13 07		12 46		12 53	13 07		13 17		13 55			14 07				13 46	13 55	14 07	
		d	12 36	12 53			13 08		12 47		12 53	13 08		13 17		13 55			14 08			13 37	13 47	13 55	14 08	
Wakefield Kirkgate 4	32,34,39	a		→		12 49	→	12 57					12 59		13 27	→		13 50	→		13 57					
		d				12 50		12 58							13 28			13 50			13 58					
Outwood		d									12 58	13 13												14 00	14 13	
Leeds 10	32,34	a	12 54			13 25		13 18	13 02		13 13	13 33		13 41	13 48			14 25			14 18	13 55	14 02	14 14	14 30	

			GR	NT	GR		NT	NT	NT	NT	NT	XC	NT	NT	GR		NT	NT	NT	NT	NT	NT	XC	GR	NT	
			R 1 ✠⊘		R 1 ⊏✠							◇1 ✠			R 1 ✠⊘								◇1 ✠	R 1 ⊏✠		
Sheffield 7	29 ⇌	d		13 51				13 57	14 06	14 14	14 18	14 21					14 51		14 57	15 06	15 14	15 18	15 21			
Meadowhall	29 ⇌	d		13 57				14 03	14 12	14 21	14 24						14 57		15 03	15 12	15 21	15 24				
Rotherham Central	29	d						14 10		14 27									15 10		15 27					
Swinton (S.Yorks)	29	d						14 18		14 36									15 18		15 36					
Bolton-upon-Dearne		d								14 41											15 41					
Goldthorpe		d								14 43											15 43					
Thurnscoe		d								14 46											15 46					
Moorthorpe		d								14 51											15 51					
Doncaster 7		d	13 57		14 21		14 27	14 38							14 53			15 14	15 38					15 29		
Bentley (S.Yorks)		d					14 30	14 41										15 17	15 41							
Adwick		a					14 34	14 47										15 21	15 47							
		d					14 34											15 21								
South Elmsall		d					14 40											15 27								
Fitzwilliam		d					14 45			14 57								15 32			15 57					
Sandal & Agbrigg		d					14 51			15 03			←	←				15 38			16 03				←	
Wakefield Westgate 7	32,39	a	14 14		14 39		14 55			15 07		14 46	14 55	15 07	15 14			15 42			16 08		15 46	15 51	16 08	
		d	14 14		14 39		14 55			15 08		14 47	14 55	15 08	15 14			15 42			16 08		15 47	15 51	16 08	
Wakefield Kirkgate 4	32,34,39	a		14 27			→		14 49	→	14 57						15 27			15 49	→	15 57				
		d		14 28					14 50		14 58						15 28			15 50		15 58				
Outwood		d											15 00	15 13				15 47							16 13	
Leeds 10	32,34	a	14 35	14 48	15 01				15 25		15 18	15 04	15 15	15 30	15 35		15 48	16 02		16 25		16 19	16 02	16 09	16 30	

			GR	NT	GC	GR	NT	NT	NT	NT	XC	NT	NT	GR	NT	GR	NT	NT	NT	NT	XC		NT	GR	XC	NT
			R 1 ⊏✠			R 1 ⊏✠					◇1 ✠			R 1 ✠⊘		R 1 ⊏✠					◇1 ✠			R 1 ⊏✠	◇1 ✠	
Sheffield 7	29 ⇌	d		15 51				15 57	16 06	16 14	16 21	16 18			16 51			16 57	17 06	17 14	17 22				17 47	
Meadowhall	29 ⇌	d		15 57				16 03	16 12	16 21		16 24			16 57			17 03	17 12	17 21						
Rotherham Central	29	d						16 10		16 27								17 10		17 27						
Swinton (S.Yorks)	29	d						16 18		16 36								17 18		17 36						
Bolton-upon-Dearne		d								16 41										17 40						
Goldthorpe		d								16 43										17 43						
Thurnscoe		d								16 46										17 46						
Moorthorpe		d								16 51										17 51						
Doncaster 7		d	15 55		16 04	16 10	16 14	16 38						17 01		17 19	17 27	17 38								
Bentley (S.Yorks)		d					16 17	16 41									17 30	17 41								
Adwick		a					16 21	16 47									17 34	17 47								
		d					16 21										17 34									
South Elmsall		d					16 27										17 40									
Fitzwilliam		d					16 32			16 57							17 45			18 10						
Sandal & Agbrigg		d					16 38			17 03			←				17 51			18 16			←			←
Wakefield Westgate 7	32,39	a	16 15			16 30	16 42			17 07	16 47		17 07	17 18		17 36	17 55			18 20	17 47		17 55		18 12	18 20
		d	16 15			16 30	16 42			17 08	16 48		17 08	17 18		17 36	17 55			18 20	17 48		17 55	18 04	18 13	18 20
Wakefield Kirkgate 4	32,34,39	a		16 27	16 46				16 49	→		16 57			17 28		→		17 49	→						
		d		16 28					16 50			16 58			17 28				17 50							
Outwood		d					16 50						17 13										18 00			18 25
Leeds 10	32,34	a	16 35	16 48		16 48	17 02		17 25		17 02	17 18	17 30	17 36	17 48	17 55			18 25		18 03		18 15	18 23	18 30	18 42

Table 31

Mondays to Fridays

Sheffield, Doncaster and Wakefield - Leeds

			NT	NT	NT	NT	GR		XC	NT	GR	NT	GR	NT	NT	NT	NT		XC	NT	GR	GR	NT	NT	NT	NT
																			A							
Sheffield	29	d	17 51	18 06	18 14	18 18			18 21					18 51	19 06	15 18	19 22		19 26					19 51	20 06	20 18
Meadowhall	29	d	17 57	18 12	18 21	18 24								18 57	19 12	19 25	19 28							19 57	20 12	20 24
Rotherham Central	29	d			18 27											19 31										
Swinton (S.Yorks)	29	d			18 36											19 40										
Bolton-upon-Dearne		d			18 41											19 44										
Goldthorpe		d			18 43											19 47										
Thurnscoe		d			18 46											19 50										
Moorthorpe		d			18 51											19 55										
Doncaster		d					18 19			18 27	18 43		19 17							19 27	19 42	19 48				
Bentley (S.Yorks)		d								18 30										19 30						
Adwick		a								18 34										19 34						
		d								18 34										19 34						
South Elmsall		d								18 40										19 40						
Fitzwilliam		d			19 01					18 46						20 05				19 46						
Sandal & Agbrigg		d			19 07					18 51		←				20 11				19 51			←			
Wakefield Westgate	32,39	a			19 12		18 36		18 47	18 55	19 00	19 12	19 34			20 15			19 49	19 55	20 01	20 07	20 15			
		d			19 12		18 36		18 48	18 56	19 00	19 12	19 34			20 16			19 50	19 56	20 01	20 07	20 16			
Wakefield Kirkgate	32,34,39	a	18 28	18 50	→	18 58								19 29	19 50	←	19 58							20 28	20 49	20 57
		d	18 32	18 50		18 58								19 32	19 50		19 58							20 28	20 50	20 58
Outwood		d								19 00		19 17								20 00			20 21			
Leeds	32,34	a	18 51	19 27		19 23	18 55		19 02	19 15	19 20	19 33	19 52	19 55	20 26		20 19		20 05	20 17	20 21	20 24	20 36	20 48	21 26	21 22

			GR		XC	NT	GR	NT	GR	GR	XC	EM	GC			NT	GR	NT	NT	GR	EM	NT	XC			NT
									FO	FX									FX							
Sheffield	29	d			20 21			20 27			21 21	21 25						21 30	22 06		22 19	22 24	22 30			
Meadowhall	29	d						20 35										21 36	22 12			22 31				
Rotherham Central	29	d						20 41										21 42				22 37				
Swinton (S.Yorks)	29	d						20 50										21 50				22 46				
Bolton-upon-Dearne		d						20 55										21 55				22 51				
Goldthorpe		d						20 57										21 57				22 53				
Thurnscoe		d						21 00										22 00				22 56				
Moorthorpe		d						21 05										22 05				23 01				
Doncaster		d	20 19			20 38	20 54		21 20	21 20			21 32			21 38	21 55			22 18						22 38
Bentley (S.Yorks)		d				20 41										21 41										22 41
Adwick		a				20 45										21 45										22 45
		d				20 45										21 45										22 45
South Elmsall		d				20 51										21 51										22 51
Fitzwilliam		d				20 59		21 11								21 58		22 11				23 07				22 56
Sandal & Agbrigg		d				21 04		21 17								22 04		22 17				23 13				23 02
Wakefield Westgate	32,39	a	20 36		20 53	21 08	21 13	21 22	21 37	21 37	21 50	21 54				22 08	22 13	22 21		22 35	22 46	23 17	22 57			23 06
		d	20 36		20 54	21 09	21 15	21 22	21 37	21 37	21 51	21 55				22 09	22 13	22 21		22 35	22 47	23 18	22 58			23 06
Wakefield Kirkgate	32,34,39	a											22 20						22 49			→				
		d																	22 50							
Outwood		d				21 13		21 27								22 14		22 26								23 11
Leeds	32,34	a	20 54		21 10	21 27	21 34	21 47	21 55	21 55	22 04	22 12				22 28	22 33	22 46	23 28	22 53	23 05		23 16			23 26

			NT	NT	EM	GR	NT	NT	NT
			FO				FO	FX	FX
Sheffield	29	d			22 48		23 15	23 15	23 24
Meadowhall	29	d					23 21	23 21	23 30
Rotherham Central	29	d					23 27	23 27	
Swinton (S.Yorks)	29	d					23 36	23 36	
Bolton-upon-Dearne		d					23 41	23 41	
Goldthorpe		d					23 44	23 44	
Thurnscoe		d					23 47	23 47	
Moorthorpe		d					23 52	23 52	
Doncaster		d				23 24			
Bentley (S.Yorks)		d							
Adwick		a							
		d							
South Elmsall		d							
Fitzwilliam		d							
Sandal & Agbrigg		d		←					
Wakefield Westgate	32,39	a		23 17	23 21	23 42		00 09	
		d		23 18	23 22	23 42		00 09	
Wakefield Kirkgate	32,34,39	a							00s10
		d	22 50						
Outwood		d		23 24					
Leeds	32,34	a	23 28	23 38	23 38	23 59	00 29	00 30	

A to Wakefield Westgate

Table 31

Saturdays

Sheffield, Doncaster and Wakefield - Leeds

					NT	NT	NT	NT	NT	NT	NT		XC	NT	NT	NT	NT	NT	NT	NT	NT		NT	GR	NT	NT
Sheffield	29	d				06 06	06 18	06 28		06 52	07 06		07 12		07 14	07 51	08 06			08 14	08 18				08 51	
Meadowhall	29	d				06 12	06 24	06 34		06 58	07 12				07 21	07 57	08 12			08 23	08 24				08 57	
Rotherham Central	29	d					06 30	06 40		07 04					07 27					08 29						
Swinton (S.Yorks)	29	d					06 38	06 48		07 14					07 35					08 38						
Bolton-upon-Dearne		d						06 52							07 39					08 42						
Goldthorpe		d						06 55							07 42					08 45						
Thurnscoe		d						06 58							07 45					08 48						
Moorthorpe		d						07 03							07 50					08 53						
Doncaster		d			06 25		07 00		07 14	07 32								08 17	08 26				08 50	08 58		09 14
Bentley (S.Yorks)		d			06 28		07 03		07 17	07 35								08 20	08 29				08 53			09 17
Adwick		a			06 32		07 09		07 21	07 41								08 26	08 33				08 59			09 21
		d			06 32				07 21										08 33							09 21
South Elmsall		d			06 38				07 27										08 39							09 27
Fitzwilliam		d			06 43			07 09	07 35						07 56				08 46	08 59						09 32
Sandal & Agbrigg		d			06 49			07 15	07 41					←	08 02				08 52	09 05						09 38
Wakefield Westgate	32,39	a			06 53			07 19	07 45				07 36	07 45	08 06				08 56	09 09				09 15		09 42
		d			06 53			07 19	07 45				07 37	07 45	08 07				08 56	09 09				09 15		09 42
Wakefield Kirkgate	32,34,39	a				06 49			→		07 49					08 27	08 49				08 57				09 27	
		d				06 50					07 50					08 28	08 50				08 58				09 28	
Outwood		d			06 58			07 24						07 50	08 12				09 01	09 14						09 47
Leeds	32,34	a			07 14	07 28		07 44			08 25		07 52	08 04	08 30	08 49	09 25		09 14	09 30	09 19			09 35	09 49	10 02

			NT	NT	NT	NT	XC		NT	NT	GR	NT	NT	NT	NT	NT	NT	NT		XC	NT	GR	NT	NT	NT	NT	NT
Sheffield	29	d	08 57	09 06	09 14	09 18	09 21			09 31		09 51		09 57	10 06	10 14	10 18		10 21			10 51		10 57	11 06	11 14
Meadowhall	29	d	09 03	09 12	09 21	09 24				09 37		09 57		10 03	10 12	10 21	10 24					10 57		11 03	11 12	11 21
Rotherham Central	29	d	09 10		09 27					09 44				10 10		10 27								11 10		11 27
Swinton (S.Yorks)	29	d	09 19		09 36					09 52				10 18		10 36								11 20		11 36
Bolton-upon-Dearne		d			09 41											10 41										11 41
Goldthorpe		d			09 43											10 43										11 43
Thurnscoe		d			09 46											10 46										11 46
Moorthorpe		d			09 51					10 02						10 51										11 51
Doncaster		d	09 37								09 57		10 14	10 37							10 48		11 14	11 38		
Bentley (S.Yorks)		d	09 44										10 17	10 41									11 17	11 41		
Adwick		a	09 50										10 21	10 47									11 21	11 47		
		d											10 21										11 21			
South Elmsall		d											10 27										11 27			
Fitzwilliam		d			09 57								10 32			10 57							11 32			11 57
Sandal & Agbrigg		d			10 03				←				10 38			11 03				←			11 38			12 03
Wakefield Westgate	32,39	a			10 07		09 46		10 07		10 14		10 42			11 07			10 46	11 07	11 11		11 42			12 07
		d			10 08		09 47		10 08		10 16		10 42			11 08			10 47	11 08	11 13		11 42			12 08
Wakefield Kirkgate	32,34,39	a		09 49	→	09 57						10 27			10 49	→	10 57					11 27			11 49	→
		d		09 50		09 58						10 28			10 50		10 58					11 28			11 50	
Outwood		d							10 13				10 47							11 13			11 47			
Leeds	32,34	a		10 25		10 18	10 02		10 30		10 35	10 48	11 02		11 25		11 18		11 02	11 30	11 35	11 48	12 02		12 25	

			NT		XC	NT	GR	NT	GC	NT	NT	NT	NT		NT	XC	NT	GR	NT	NT	NT	NT	NT		NT	XC
Sheffield	29	d	11 18		11 21			11 51			11 57	12 06	12 14		12 18	12 21			12 51		12 57	13 06	13 14		13 18	13 21
Meadowhall	29	d	11 24					11 57			12 03	12 12	12 21		12 24				12 57		13 03	13 12	13 21		13 24	
Rotherham Central	29	d									12 10		12 27								13 10		13 27			
Swinton (S.Yorks)	29	d									12 19		12 36								13 18		13 36			
Bolton-upon-Dearne		d											12 41										13 41			
Goldthorpe		d											12 43										13 43			
Thurnscoe		d											12 46										13 46			
Moorthorpe		d											12 51										13 51			
Doncaster		d					11 59		12 13	12 14	12 36							12 59		13 14	13 38					
Bentley (S.Yorks)		d								12 17	12 40									13 17	13 41					
Adwick		a								12 21	12 45									13 21	13 47					
		d								12 21										13 21						
South Elmsall		d								12 27										13 27						
Fitzwilliam		d								12 32			12 57							13 32			13 57			
Sandal & Agbrigg		d				←				12 38			13 03				←			13 38			14 03			
Wakefield Westgate	32,39	a			11 46	12 07	12 16			12 42			13 07			12 46	13 07	13 17		13 42			14 07			13 46
		d			11 47	12 08	12 16			12 42			13 08			12 47	13 08	13 17		13 42			14 08			13 47
Wakefield Kirkgate	32,34,39	a	11 57					12 27	12 56			12 49	→		12 57				13 27			13 50	→		13 57	
		d	11 58					12 28				12 50			12 58				13 28			13 50			13 58	
Outwood		d				12 13				12 47							13 13			13 47						
Leeds	32,34	a	12 18		12 02	12 30	12 35	12 48		13 02		13 25			13 18	13 02	13 33	13 35	13 48	14 02		14 25			14 18	14 02

Sheffield, Doncaster and Wakefield - Leeds

		NT	NT	GR	NT	NT	NT	NT		NT	NT	XC	NT	GR	NT	NT	NT	NT		NT	NT	XC	NT	NT	GR
				■ 1 ✕								◇1 ✕		■ 1 ✕								◇1 ✕			■ 1 ✕
Sheffield 7	29 ⇌ d		13 28		13 51		13 57	14 06		14 14	14 18	14 21			14 51		14 57	15 06		15 14	15 18	15 21		15 51	
Meadowhall	29 ⇌ d		13 35		13 57		14 03	14 12		14 21	14 24				14 57		15 03	15 12		15 21	15 24			15 57	
Rotherham Central	29 d		13 42				14 10			14 27							15 10			15 27					
Swinton (S.Yorks)	29 d		13 50				14 18			14 36							15 18			15 36					
Bolton-upon-Dearne	d									14 41										15 41					
Goldthorpe	d									14 43										15 43					
Thurnscoe	d									14 46										15 46					
Moorthorpe	d		14 00							14 51										15 51					
Doncaster 7	d			13 59		14 14	14 38							14 58		15 14	15 38								16 19
Bentley (S.Yorks)	d					14 17	14 41									15 17	15 41								
Adwick	a					14 21	14 47									15 21	15 47								
	d					14 21										15 21									
South Elmsall	d					14 27										15 27									
Fitzwilliam	d					14 32				14 57						15 32				15 57					
Sandal & Agbrigg	d	←				14 38				15 03			←			15 38				16 03			←		
Wakefield Westgate 7	32,39 a	14 07		14 16		14 42				15 07		14 46	15 07	15 15		15 42				16 08		15 46	16 08		16 36
	d	14 08		14 16		14 42				15 08		14 47	15 08	15 15		15 42				16 08		15 47	16 08		16 36
Wakefield Kirkgate 4	32,34,39 a				14 27			14 49		→	14 57				15 27			15 49		→	15 57			16 27	
	d				14 28			14 50			14 58				15 28			15 50			15 58			16 28	
Outwood	d	14 13				14 47							15 13			15 47							16 13		
Leeds 10	32,34 a	14 30		14 35	14 48	15 02		15 25			15 18	15 02	15 30	15 35	15 48	16 02		16 25			16 19	16 02	16 30	16 48	16 54

		GC	NT	NT		NT	NT	NT	XC	NT	NT	NT	GR	NT		NT	NT	NT	NT	XC	NT	NT	XC	GR	
									◇1 ✕				■ 1 ✕							◇1 ✕			◇1 ✕	■ 1 A ✕	
Sheffield 7	29 ⇌ d			15 57		16 06	16 14	16 18	16 21			16 51				16 57	17 06	17 14	17 18	17 21			17 47		
Meadowhall	29 ⇌ d			16 03		16 12	16 21	16 24				16 57				17 03	17 12	17 21	17 24						
Rotherham Central	29 d			16 10			16 27									17 10		17 27							
Swinton (S.Yorks)	29 d			16 18			16 36									17 18		17 36							
Bolton-upon-Dearne	d						16 41											17 41							
Goldthorpe	d						16 43											17 43							
Thurnscoe	d						16 46											17 46							
Moorthorpe	d						16 51											17 51							
Doncaster 7	d	16 23	16 27	16 38									17 16	17 27		17 38								18 12	
Bentley (S.Yorks)	d		16 30	16 41										17 30		17 41									
Adwick	a		16 34	16 47										17 34		17 47									
	d		16 34											17 34											
South Elmsall	d		16 40											17 40											
Fitzwilliam	d		16 45				16 57							17 46				17 57							
Sandal & Agbrigg	d		16 51				17 03			←	←			17 51				18 03			←	←			
Wakefield Westgate 7	32,39 a		16 55				17 07		16 49	16 55	17 07		17 33	17 55				18 07		17 47	17 55	18 07	18 14	18 29	
	d		16 55				17 08		16 50	16 55	17 08		17 33	17 56				18 08		17 47	17 56	18 08	18 15	18 29	
Wakefield Kirkgate 4	32,34,39 a	17 10	→			16 49	→	16 57				17 28		→			17 49	→	17 57						
	d					16 50		16 58				17 28					17 50		17 58						
Outwood	d									17 02	17 13										18 00	18 13			
Leeds 10	32,34 a					17 25		17 18	17 04	17 16	17 30	17 48	17 53				18 25		18 18	18 02	18 15	18 30	18 32	18 47	

		NT	NT	NT	NT	GR	XC	NT	NT	GR		GR	NT	NT	NT	NT	XC	NT	GR	NT		GR	NT	NT	XC
						■ 1 B ✕	◇1 ✕			■ 1 A ✕		■ 1 B ✕					◇1 ✕		■ 1 ✕			■ 1 B ✕			◇1 ✕
Sheffield 7	29 ⇌ d	17 51	18 06	18 14	18 18		18 21						18 51	19 06	19 14	19 18	19 21						19 51	20 06	20 23
Meadowhall	29 ⇌ d	17 57	18 12	18 21	18 24								18 57	19 12	19 21	19 24							19 57	20 12	
Rotherham Central	29 d			18 27											19 27										
Swinton (S.Yorks)	29 d			18 36											19 40										
Bolton-upon-Dearne	d			18 41											19 44										
Goldthorpe	d			18 43											19 47										
Thurnscoe	d			18 46											19 50										
Moorthorpe	d			18 51											19 55										
Doncaster 7	d					18 18		18 27		19 06		19 18						19 27				20 02			
Bentley (S.Yorks)	d							18 30										19 30							
Adwick	a							18 34										19 34							
	d							18 34										19 34							
South Elmsall	d							18 40										19 40							
Fitzwilliam	d			18 57				18 45							20 01			19 45							
Sandal & Agbrigg	d			19 03				18 51	←						20 07			19 51		←					
Wakefield Westgate 7	32,39 a			19 07		18 35	18 46	18 55	19 07	19 23		19 35			20 11		19 46	19 55	20 00	20 11		20 19			20 48
	d			19 08		18 35	18 47	18 55	19 08	19 26		19 35			20 11		19 47	19 55	20 00	20 11		20 19			20 49
Wakefield Kirkgate 4	32,34,39 a	18 28	18 50	→	18 58								19 29	19 50	→	19 58							20 28	20 49	
	d	18 32	18 50		18 58								19 32	19 50		19 58							20 28	20 50	
Outwood	d							19 00	19 13									20 00		20 16					
Leeds 10	32,34 a	18 51	19 27		19 23	18 53	19 01	19 17	19 28	19 45		19 51	19 55	20 26		20 19	20 02	20 13	20 22	20 32		20 35	20 48	21 26	21 04

A from 17 July until 4 September

B until 10 July and from 11 September

Sheffield, Doncaster and Wakefield - Leeds

		GR	NT	NT	NT	XC		EM	GC		NT	GR	GR	NT	GR	EM			XC	NT	NT	NT
		■ 1 A ✕				◇1 ✕		◇1 ⊡				■ 1 B ✕	■ 1 A ✕		■ 1 ✕	◇1 ⊡			◇1 ✕			
Sheffield 7	29 ⇌ d			20 27	21 06	21 21		21 24						21 30		22 19			22 26			22 34
Meadowhall	29 ⇌ d			20 35	21 12									21 36								22 40
Rotherham Central	29 d			20 42										21 42								22 46
Swinton (S.Yorks)	29 d			20 50										21 50								22 54
Bolton-upon-Dearne	d			20 55										21 54								22 58
Goldthorpe	d			20 57										21 57								23 01
Thurnscoe	d			21 00										22 00								23 04
Moorthorpe	d			21 05										22 05								23 09
Doncaster 7	d	20 38	20 45						21 30		21 28	21 48	21 54		22 22				22 49		22 52	
Bentley (S.Yorks)	d		20 48								21 31										22 55	
Adwick	a		20 52								21 35										22 59	
	d		20 52								21 35										22 59	
South Elmsall	d		20 58								21 41										23 05	
Fitzwilliam	d		21 03	21 11							21 51			22 11							23 10	23 15
Sandal & Agbrigg	d		21 09	21 17							21 56			22 17							23 16	23 21
Wakefield Westgate 7	32,39 a	20 55	21 13	21 22		21 48		21 53			22 00	22 05	22 11	22 21	22 39	22 44			23 09		23 20	23 25
	d	20 58	21 13	21 22		21 49		21 54			22 01	22 05	22 11	22 21	22 39	22 45			23 10		23 20	23 26
Wakefield Kirkgate 4	32,34,39 a				21 52				22 15													
	d				21 52				22 17											22 50		
Outwood	d		21 18	21 27							22 05			22 26							23 25	23 31
Leeds 10	32,34 a	21 21	21 33	21 47	22 29	22 02		22 10			22 18	22 24	22 34	22 46	22 58	23 04			23 24	23 28	23 38	23 46

Sundays

		NT	NT	NT	XC	NT	XC	NT	GR	NT		NT	XC	GR	NT	NT	XC	NT	GR	GR		GC	NT	NT	XC
				◇	◇1 ✕		◇1 ✕		■ 1 ✕				◇1 ✕	■ 1 ✕			◇1 ✕		■ 1 C ✕	■ 1 D ✕		C			◇1 ✕
Sheffield 7	29 ⇌ d	08 39		09 17	09 21	09 36	10 21	10 39				11 17	11 21		11 36	12 16	12 21	12 39						13 17	13 21
Meadowhall	29 ⇌ d	08 45		09 23		09 42		10 45				11 23			11 42	12 23		12 45						13 23	
Rotherham Central	29 d					09 48									11 49										
Swinton (S.Yorks)	29 d					09 58									12 00										
Bolton-upon-Dearne	d					10 03									12 04										
Goldthorpe	d					10 05									12 07										
Thurnscoe	d					10 08									12 10										
Moorthorpe	d					10 13									12 15										
Doncaster 7	d		09 10						10 58	11 10				11 56					13 00	13 02		13 09	13 10		
Bentley (S.Yorks)	d		09 13							11 13													13 13		
Adwick	a		09 17							11 17													13 17		
	d		09 17							11 17													13 17		
South Elmsall	d		09 23							11 23													13 23		
Fitzwilliam	d		09 28			10 19				11 28					12 21								13 28		
Sandal & Agbrigg	d		09 34			10 25				11 34					12 27								13 34		
Wakefield Westgate 7	32,39 a		09 38		09 44	10 29	10 44		11 15	11 38			11 44	12 13	12 31		12 44		13 17	13 19			13 38		13 44
	d		09 38		09 45	10 30	10 45		11 15	11 38			11 45	12 13	12 31		12 45		13 17	13 19			13 38		13 45
Wakefield Kirkgate 4	32,34,39 a	09 29		09 55				11 29				11 52				12 52		13 29				13 52		13 52	
	d	09 30		09 55				11 30				11 53				12 53		13 30						13 53	
Outwood	d		09 43			10 35				11 43					12 36								13 43		
Leeds 10	32,34 a	10 04	09 52	10 15	10 02	10 52	11 02	12 05	11 34	11 56		12 18	12 02	12 32	12 53	13 18	13 02	14 04	13 36	13 39			13 57	14 18	14 02

		GC	GR	NT	NT	XC		NT	GR	GR	NT	NT	XC	GR	GR	NT		NT	NT	XC	NT	GR	NT	NT	XC
		D	■ 1 ✕			◇1 ✕			■ 1 C ✕	■ 1 D ✕			◇1 ✕	■ 1 C ✕	■ 1 D ✕					◇1 ✕		■ 1 ✕			◇1 ✕
Sheffield 7	29 ⇌ d			13 36	14 17	14 21		14 39				15 17	15 21			15 36		15 46	16 17	16 21	16 39			17 17	17 21
Meadowhall	29 ⇌ d			13 42	14 23			14 45				15 23				15 42		15 52	16 23		16 45			17 23	
Rotherham Central	29 d			13 49												15 48		15 58							
Swinton (S.Yorks)	29 d			13 57												15 56		16 08							
Bolton-upon-Dearne	d			14 01												16 00									
Goldthorpe	d			14 04												16 03									
Thurnscoe	d			14 07												16 06									
Moorthorpe	d			14 12												16 11		16 18							
Doncaster 7	d	13 49	13 59						14 56	14 58	15 10			16 00	16 02							16 57	17 10		
Bentley (S.Yorks)	d										15 13												17 13		
Adwick	a										15 17												17 17		
	d										15 17												17 17		
South Elmsall	d										15 23												17 23		
Fitzwilliam	d			14 17							15 28					16 17							17 28		
Sandal & Agbrigg	d			14 23							15 34					16 23							17 34		
Wakefield Westgate 7	32,39 a		14 16	14 27		14 44			15 13	15 15	15 38		15 44	16 17	16 19	16 27				16 44		17 14	17 38		17 45
	d		14 16	14 28		14 45			15 13	15 15	15 38		15 45	16 17	16 19	16 27				16 45		17 14	17 38		17 45
Wakefield Kirkgate 4	32,34,39 a	14 34			14 52			15 29				15 52							16 52		17 29			17 52	
	d				14 53			15 30				15 53							16 53		17 30			17 53	
Outwood	d			14 33							15 43					16 32							17 43		
Leeds 10	32,34 a		14 36	14 47	15 18	15 02		16 04	15 33	15 35	15 57	16 18	16 02	16 36	16 41	16 52			17 18	17 02	18 05	17 34	17 56	18 18	18 02

A from 17 July until 4 September

B until 10 July and from 11 September

C until 11 July and from 12 September

D from 18 July until 5 September

Sheffield, Doncaster and Wakefield - Leeds

		GC A	EM	GR A	GR B	NT	XC	NT	GR A	XC	NT	GC B	GR A	GR B	NT	NT	XC	NT	GR	NT	NT	GR A
Sheffield 7	29 d		17 34			17 36	17 51	18 17		18 21	18 39				18 57	19 16	19 21			19 36	20 17	
Meadowhall	29 d					17 43		18 23			18 45				19 04	19 23				19 42	20 23	
Rotherham Central	29 d					17 49									19 10					19 49		
Swinton (S.Yorks)	29 d					17 57									19 18					19 57		
Bolton-upon-Dearne	d					18 02														20 02		
Goldthorpe	d					18 04														20 04		
Thurnscoe	d					18 07														20 07		
Moorthorpe	d					18 12									19 28					20 12		
Doncaster 7	d	17 31		17 55	18 00		18 15					18 47	18 50	18 54				19 30	19 59			20 20
Bentley (S.Yorks)	d																	19 33				
Adwick	a																	19 37				
	d																	19 37				
South Elmsall	d																	19 43				
Fitzwilliam	d					18 18												19 48		20 18		
Sandal & Agbrigg	d					18 24												19 54		20 24		
Wakefield Westgate 7	32,39 a		18 06	18 12	18 17	18 28	18 33		18 38	18 47			19 07	19 12			19 48	19 58	20 16	20 28		20 38
	d		18 07	18 12	18 17	18 29	18 34		18 38	18 48			19 07	19 12			19 49	19 58	20 16	20 28		20 38
Wakefield Kirkgate 4	32,34,39 a	18 15						18 52			19 29	19 31				19 52					20 52	
	d							18 53			19 30					19 53					20 53	
Outwood	d					18 34												20 03		20 33		
Leeds 10	32,34 a		18 24	18 30	18 35	18 49	18 51	19 18	18 59	19 04	20 05		19 27	19 35		20 18	20 05	20 16	20 35	20 52	21 16	20 59

		GR B	XC	NT	GR B	GC A	GR A	EM	XC	GR	NT	NT	GR	XC	NT	GC B	EM
Sheffield 7	29 d		20 21	20 39				21 03	21 21			21 36		22 21	22 39		23 30
Meadowhall	29 d			20 45								21 42			22 45		
Rotherham Central	29 d											21 48					
Swinton (S.Yorks)	29 d											21 56					
Bolton-upon-Dearne	d											22 00					
Goldthorpe	d											22 03					
Thurnscoe	d											22 06					
Moorthorpe	d											22 11					
Doncaster 7	d	20 22			20 49	21 04	21 10				21 49		22 20			22 48	
Bentley (S.Yorks)	d										21 52						
Adwick	a										21 56						
	d										21 56						
South Elmsall	d										22 02						
Fitzwilliam	d										22 09	22 16					
Sandal & Agbrigg	d										22 15	22 22					
Wakefield Westgate 7	32,39 a	20 40	20 46		21 06		21 27	21 32	21 44		22 19	22 26	22 37	22 45			00 15
	d	20 40	20 47		21 06		21 27	21 33	21 45	21 57	22 20	22 27	22 37	22 45			00 16
Wakefield Kirkgate 4	32,34,39 a			21 29		21 46									23 28	23 30	
	d			21 30											23 30		
Outwood	d										22 25	22 32					
Leeds 10	32,34 a	21 01	21 03	22 04	21 30		21 47	21 49	22 01	22 16	22 39	22 52	23 03	23 04	00 04		00 32

A until 11 July and from 12 September

B from 18 July until 5 September

Leeds - Wakefield, Doncaster and Sheffield

		GR	EM	GR	NT	XC	NT	NT	GR	XC	NT	EM	NT	GR	NT	GR	XC	NT	NT	GR	NT	GC	NT
Leeds 10	32,34 d	05 05	05 25	05 30	05 33	06 00		06 05	06 05	06 15	06 19	06 34	06 38	06 40	06 43	07 00	07 05		07 05	07 20			
Outwood	d				05 44						06 28				06 54								
Wakefield Kirkgate 4	32,34,39 a							06 21					07 07						07 25				
	d						06 04	06 21					07 08						07 25			07 42	
Wakefield Westgate 7	32,39 a	05 17	05 36	05 42	05 49	06 11			06 18	06 26	06 32	06 45		06 52	06 58	07 12	07 17			07 32			
	d	05 17	05 37	05 42	05 49	06 12				06 27	06 33	06 46			06 58	07 12	07 18						
Sandal & Agbrigg	d				05 53						06 36				07 02								
Fitzwilliam	d				06 00						06 42				07 09								
South Elmsall	d										06 47												
Adwick	a										06 53												
	d										06 53										07 29		07 54
Bentley (S.Yorks)	d										06 57										07 33		07 57
Doncaster 7	a	05 35	05 55	06 00						06 43	07 07					07 29					07 37	08 26	08 01
Moorthorpe	d				06 06										07 14								
Thurnscoe	d				06 12										07 20								
Goldthorpe	d				06 14										07 22								
Bolton-upon-Dearne	d				06 17										07 25								
Swinton (S.Yorks)	29 a				06 22										07 29						07 53		08 30
Rotherham Central	29 a				06 30										07 39			←			08 00		08 40
Meadowhall	29 a				06 37		06 41	06 49					07 48		07 46			07 48	07 53		08 05		08 49
Sheffield 7	29 a		06 18		06 47	06 39	06 55	07 00		07 11		07 25	→		07 57		07 50	07 57	08 05		08 18		→

		NT	NT	NT	NT	NT	GR	NT	NT	GR	XC	NT	NT	NT	NT	NT	NT	GR	NT	NT	GR	XC	NT
Leeds 10	32,34 d	07 27	07 29	07 35			07 40	07 47	08 02	08 05	08 11			08 19	08 32	08 37		08 40	08 48	09 05	09 05	09 11	
Outwood	d	07 36			←			07 59						08 28			←		08 59				
Wakefield Kirkgate 4	32,34,39 a		08 00	07 54	08 00				08 23						09 03	08 54	09 03			09 23			
	d		08 04	07 55	08 04				08 23						09 04	08 55	09 04			09 23			
Wakefield Westgate 7	32,39 a	07 42	→				07 52	08 03		08 17	08 22			08 34	→			08 52	09 03		09 18	09 23	
	d	07 42						08 03		08 17	08 23			08 35				08 52	09 03		09 18	09 24	
Sandal & Agbrigg	d	07 45						08 07						08 39					09 07				
Fitzwilliam	d	07 51						08 14						08 43					09 14				
South Elmsall	d	08 06												08 48									
Adwick	a	08 11												08 54									
	d	08 11											08 35	08 54									09 13
Bentley (S.Yorks)	d	08 15											08 39	08 58									09 17
Doncaster 7	a	08 24								08 36			08 44	09 07				09 11			09 35		09 22
Moorthorpe	d							08 19											09 20				
Thurnscoe	d							08 25											09 26				
Goldthorpe	d							08 27											09 28				
Bolton-upon-Dearne	d							08 30											09 31				
Swinton (S.Yorks)	29 a							08 34											09 35				09 42
Rotherham Central	29 a					←		08 47				←							09 44				09 50
Meadowhall	29 a			08 31	08 45	08 49		08 54	08 52			08 54				09 27	09 46		09 50	09 52			09 55
Sheffield 7	29 a			08 39	08 55	08 58		→	09 02		08 51	09 05				09 37	09 56		10 00	10 02		09 51	10 05

		NT	NT	NT	GR	NT	NT	GR	XC	NT	NT	NT	NT	NT	GR	NT	GR	GC	NT	XC	NT	NT
Leeds 10	32,34 d	09 32	09 37		09 40	09 48	10 05	10 05	10 12		10 19	10 32	10 37		10 40	10 48	11 05		11 05	11 11		11 19
Outwood	d			←		09 59					10 28			←		10 59						11 28
Wakefield Kirkgate 4	32,34,39 a	10 01	09 54	10 01			10 23					11 01	10 54	11 01					11 23			
	d	10 04	09 55	10 04			10 23					11 04	10 55	11 04				11 13	11 23			
Wakefield Westgate 7	32,39 a	→			09 52	10 03		10 18	10 23		10 32	→			10 52	11 03	11 17			11 23		11 32
	d				09 52	10 03		10 18	10 24		10 32				10 52	11 03	11 17			11 24		11 32
Sandal & Agbrigg	d					10 07					10 35					11 07						11 35
Fitzwilliam	d					10 14					10 42					11 14						11 42
South Elmsall	d										10 47											11 47
Adwick	a										10 52											11 52
	d									10 13	10 53										11 16	11 53
Bentley (S.Yorks)	d									10 17	10 57										11 20	11 57
Doncaster 7	a				10 11			10 35		10 22	11 07				11 09		11 37	12 04			11 25	12 07
Moorthorpe	d					10 19										11 19						
Thurnscoe	d					10 25										11 25						
Goldthorpe	d					10 27										11 27						
Bolton-upon-Dearne	d					10 30										11 30						
Swinton (S.Yorks)	29 a					10 34				10 38						11 34					11 41	
Rotherham Central	29 a					10 44				10 48						11 44					11 50	
Meadowhall	29 a		10 27	10 46		10 50	10 52			10 57			11 27	11 46		11 50			11 52		11 55	
Sheffield 7	29 a		10 37	10 56		11 00	11 02		10 51	11 05			11 37	11 56		12 00			12 02	11 51	12 05	

Leeds - Wakefield, Doncaster and Sheffield

			NT	NT	NT	NT	GR	NT	NT	GR	XC	NT	NT	NT	NT	NT	GR	NT	NT	GR	XC	NT	NT	NT	NT
Leeds 10	32,34	d	11 32		11 37		11 40	11 48	12 05	12 05	12 12		12 19	12 32	12 37		12 40	12 48	13 05	13 05	13 12		13 19	13 32	13 37
Outwood		d				←		11 59					12 28			←		12 59					13 28		
Wakefield Kirkgate 4	32,34,39	a	12 01		11 54	12 01			12 23					13 02	12 54	13 02			13 23					14 01	13 54
		d	12 04		11 55	12 04			12 23					13 04	12 55	13 04			13 23					14 04	13 55
Wakefield Westgate 7	32,39	a	→				11 52	12 03		12 17	12 23		12 32	→			12 52	13 03		13 18	13 23		13 32	→	
		d					11 52	12 03		12 17	12 24		12 32				12 52	13 03		13 18	13 24		13 32		
Sandal & Agbrigg		d						12 07					12 35					13 07					13 35		
Fitzwilliam		d						12 14					12 42					13 14					13 42		
South Elmsall		d											12 47										13 47		
Adwick		a											12 52										13 52		
		d										12 12	12 53									13 12	13 53		
Bentley (S.Yorks)		d										12 16	12 57									13 16	13 57		
Doncaster 7		a					12 12			12 36		12 24	13 07				13 11			13 37		13 23	14 07		
Moorthorpe		d		11 51				12 19										13 19							
Thurnscoe		d						12 25										13 25							
Goldthorpe		d						12 27										13 27							
Bolton-upon-Dearne		d						12 30										13 30							
Swinton (S.Yorks)	29	a		12 01				12 34				12 41						13 34				13 41			
Rotherham Central	29	a		12 10				12 44				12 50						13 44				13 50			
Meadowhall	29	a		12 16	12 27	12 46		12 50	12 52			12 55			13 27	13 46		13 50	13 52			13 55			14 27
Sheffield 7	29	a		12 26	12 37	12 56		13 00	13 02		12 51	13 05			13 37	13 56		14 00	14 02		13 51	14 05			14 37

			NT	GR	NT	NT	GR	XC	NT	NT	NT	NT	NT	GR	NT	NT	GR	XC	NT	NT	NT	NT	NT	NT
Leeds 10	32,34	d		13 40	13 48	14 05	14 05	14 12		14 19	14 32	14 37		14 40	14 48	15 05	15 05	15 12		15 19	15 32		15 37	
Outwood		d	←		13 59					14 28			←		14 59					15 28				←
Wakefield Kirkgate 4	32,34,39	a	14 01			14 23					15 01	14 54	15 01			15 23					16 01		15 54	16 01
		d	14 04			14 23					15 04	14 55	15 04			15 23					16 04		15 55	16 04
Wakefield Westgate 7	32,39	a		13 53	14 03		14 18	14 23		14 32	→			14 52	15 03		15 17	15 23		15 32	→			
		d		13 53	14 03			14 24		14 32				14 52	15 03			15 24		15 32				
Sandal & Agbrigg		d			14 07					14 35					15 07					15 35				
Fitzwilliam		d			14 14					14 42					15 14					15 42				
South Elmsall		d								14 47										15 47				
Adwick		a								14 52										15 52				
		d							14 14	14 53									15 13	15 53				
Bentley (S.Yorks)		d							14 18	14 57									15 17	15 57				
Doncaster 7		a		14 13					14 22	15 07				15 11					15 22	16 07				
Moorthorpe		d			14 19										15 19							15 51		
Thurnscoe		d			14 25										15 25									
Goldthorpe		d			14 27										15 27									
Bolton-upon-Dearne		d			14 30										15 30									
Swinton (S.Yorks)	29	a			14 34				14 41						15 34				15 41			16 01		
Rotherham Central	29	a			14 44				14 50						15 42				15 50			16 10		
Meadowhall	29	a	14 46		14 50	14 52			14 55			15 27	15 46		15 50	15 52			15 55			16 17	16 27	16 46
Sheffield 7	29	a	14 56		15 00	15 02		14 51	15 05			15 37	15 56		16 00	16 02		15 51	16 05			16 25	16 37	16 56

			GR	NT	GR	GC	NT	XC	NT	NT	NT	NT	NT	GR	NT	NT	GR	XC	NT	NT	NT	NT	NT
Leeds 10	32,34	d	15 40	15 48	16 05		16 05	16 11		16 19	16 32	16 37		16 40	16 48	17 05	17 05	17 12		17 19	17 32	17 37	
Outwood		d		15 59						16 28			←		16 59					17 28			←
Wakefield Kirkgate 4	32,34,39	a					16 23				17 01	16 54	17 01			17 22					18 01	17 54	18 01
		d				16 11	16 23				17 04	16 55	17 04			17 23					18 04	17 55	18 04
Wakefield Westgate 7	32,39	a	15 52	16 03	16 17			16 23		16 32	→			16 52	17 03		17 17	17 23		17 32	→		
		d	15 52	16 03	16 17			16 23		16 32				16 52	17 03		17 17	17 24		17 32			
Sandal & Agbrigg		d		16 07						16 35					17 07					17 35			
Fitzwilliam		d		16 14						16 42					17 14					17 42			
South Elmsall		d								16 47										17 47			
Adwick		a								16 52										17 52			
		d							16 13	16 53									17 09	17 53			
Bentley (S.Yorks)		d							16 17	16 57									17 14	17 57			
Doncaster 7		a			16 36	16 58			16 23	17 07				17 10			17 36		17 19	18 07			
Moorthorpe		d		16 19											17 19								
Thurnscoe		d		16 25											17 25								
Goldthorpe		d		16 27											17 27								
Bolton-upon-Dearne		d		16 30											17 30								
Swinton (S.Yorks)	29	a		16 34					16 41						17 34								
Rotherham Central	29	a		16 43					16 50						17 44								
Meadowhall	29	a		16 50			16 52		16 55			17 27	17 46		17 50	17 51						18 27	18 46
Sheffield 7	29	a		17 00			17 02	16 51	17 05			17 37	17 56		18 00	18 02		17 51				18 38	18 56

Leeds - Wakefield, Doncaster and Sheffield

			GR	NT	NT	GR	XC	NT	NT	NT	GR	NT	NT	NT	NT	GR	XC	NT	NT	GR	NT	NT	NT	XC	NT	NT
Leeds 10	32,34	d	17 40	17 46	18 05	18 05	18 11		18 19	18 32	18 40	18 43	18 48		19 05	19 05	19 11	19 19	19 37	19 40	19 43		19 48	20 11	20 21	20 30
Outwood		d		17 57					18 28				18 59	←				19 28				←	19 59		20 30	
Wakefield Kirkgate 4	32,34,39	a			18 23					19 04		18 59		19 04	19 22				20 06		19 59	20 06				20 46
		d			18 23					19 04		18 59		19 04	19 24				20 07		20 00	20 07				20 46
Wakefield Westgate 7	32,39	a	17 52	18 01		18 17	18 22		18 32	→	18 52		19 03			19 17	19 23	19 32	→	19 52			20 03	20 22	20 34	
		d	17 52	18 01		18 17	18 23		18 32		18 52		19 03			19 17	19 23	19 32		19 52			20 03	20 23	20 34	
Sandal & Agbrigg		d		18 07					18 35				19 07					19 35					20 07		20 37	
Fitzwilliam		d		18 14					18 42				19 14					19 42					20 14		20 44	
South Elmsall		d							18 47									19 47							20 49	
Adwick		a							18 52									19 52							20 54	
		d						18 14	18 53									19 53							20 55	
Bentley (S.Yorks)		d						18 18	18 57									19 57							20 59	
Doncaster 7		a	18 10			18 34		18 25	19 07		19 10					19 34		20 07		20 13					21 09	
Moorthorpe		d		18 19									19 19										20 19			
Thurnscoe		d		18 25									19 25										20 25			
Goldthorpe		d		18 27									19 27										20 27			
Bolton-upon-Dearne		d		18 30									19 30										20 30			
Swinton (S.Yorks)	29	a		18 34									19 34										20 34			
Rotherham Central	29	a		18 44									19 44										20 42			
Meadowhall	29	a		18 50	18 52							19 33	19 50	19 46	19 52						20 32	20 45	20 51			21 17
Sheffield 7	29	a		19 00	19 03		18 51					19 43	20 00	19 57	20 03		19 51				20 44	20 58	21 02	20 51		21 30

			NT	GR	NT	XC	NT	NT	NT	NT	NT	NT	NT
Leeds 10	32,34	d	20 37	20 40	20 48	21 11	21 28		21 37	21 48	22 37	22 39	23 09
Outwood		d			20 59		21 37			21 59		22 48	23 20
Wakefield Kirkgate 4	32,34,39	a	21 06					21 47	22 06		23 10		
		d	21 07					21 47	22 07		23 10		
Wakefield Westgate 7	32,39	a		20 55	21 03	21 22	21 41	21 53		22 03		22 53	23 24
		d		20 55	21 03	21 23	21 42			22 03		22 54	23 24
Sandal & Agbrigg		d			21 07		21 45			22 07		22 57	23 28
Fitzwilliam		d			21 13		21 51			22 14		23 03	23 35
South Elmsall		d					21 56					23 08	
Adwick		a					22 02					23 14	
		d					22 02					23 14	
Bentley (S.Yorks)		d					22 06					23 18	
Doncaster 7		a		21 12			22 16					23 27	
Moorthorpe		d			21 20					22 19			23 40
Thurnscoe		d			21 26					22 25			23 46
Goldthorpe		d			21 28					22 27			23 48
Bolton-upon-Dearne		d			21 31					22 30			23 51
Swinton (S.Yorks)	29	a			21 35					22 34			23 55
Rotherham Central	29	a			21 44					22 46			00 02
Meadowhall	29	a	21 45		21 52				22 47	22 52	23 51		00 08
Sheffield 7	29	a	21 58		22 05	21 51			22 58	23 02	00 02		00 22

Saturdays

			GR	XC	GR	XC	EM	GC	NT	NT	GR	XC	NT	NT	NT	NT	NT	NT	EM	NT	NT	NT	GR
Leeds 10	32,34	d	05 05	06 00	06 10	06 15	06 34		06 38	06 43	07 00	07 05		07 05			07 26	07 29	07 34	07 35			07 40
Outwood		d								06 54							07 35				←		
Wakefield Kirkgate 4	32,34,39	a						07 04	07 07					07 25				08 00		07 54	08 00		
		d						07 06	07 08					07 25				08 04		07 55	08 04		
Wakefield Westgate 7	32,39	a	05 17	06 11	06 22	06 28	06 45			06 58	07 12	07 17					07 39	→	07 45				07 52
		d	05 17	06 12	06 22	06 29	06 46			06 58	07 12	07 18					07 39		07 46				07 52
Sandal & Agbrigg		d								07 02							07 42						
Fitzwilliam		d								07 09							07 49						
South Elmsall		d															08 06						
Adwick		a															08 12						
		d													07 29	08 07	08 12						
Bentley (S.Yorks)		d													07 33	08 11	08 16						
Doncaster 7		a	05 34		06 40	06 46		07 52			07 29				07 37	08 15	08 24						
Moorthorpe		d								07 14													
Thurnscoe		d								07 20													
Goldthorpe		d								07 22													
Bolton-upon-Dearne		d								07 25													
Swinton (S.Yorks)	29	a								07 29					07 53	08 31							
Rotherham Central	29	a								07 39			←		08 00	08 41						←	
Meadowhall	29	a							07 48	07 46			07 48	07 53	08 05	08 48				08 31	08 45	08 48	
Sheffield 7	29	a		06 45		07 15	07 22		→	07 57		07 51	07 57	08 05	08 18	→			08 21	08 39	08 55	08 58	

Table 31

Leeds - Wakefield, Doncaster and Sheffield

		NT	GR	NT	XC			NT	NT	NT	NT	NT	NT	NT	NT	GR		XC	NT	NT	NT	NT	NT	NT	GR
Leeds 10	32,34 d	07 47	08 05	08 05	0812					08 19	08 32	08 37		08 48	09 05	09 05		09 11		09 19	09 32	09 37		09 48	10 05
Outwood	d	07 59								08 28			←	08 59						09 28			←	09 59	
Wakefield Kirkgate 4	32,34,39 a			08 23							09 03	08 54	09 03		09 23						10 01	09 54	10 01		
	d			08 23							09 04	08 55	09 04		09 23						10 04	09 55	10 04		
Wakefield Westgate 7	32,39 a	08 03	08 18		08 23					08 33	→			09 03		09 17		09 23		09 33	→			10 03	10 18
	d	08 03	08 18		08 24					08 34				09 03		09 17		09 24		09 33				10 03	10 18
Sandal & Agbrigg	d	08 07								08 37				09 07						09 36				10 07	
Fitzwilliam	d	08 14								08 43				09 14						09 42				10 14	
South Elmsall	d									08 48										09 47					
Adwick	a									08 54										09 52					
	d								08 35	08 54									09 13	09 53					
Bentley (S.Yorks)	d								08 39	08 58									09 17	09 57					
Doncaster 7	a								08 44	09 07						09 35			09 22	10 07					10 36
Moorthorpe	d	08 19												09 20										10 19	
Thurnscoe	d	08 25												09 26										10 25	
Goldthorpe	d	08 27												09 28										10 27	
Bolton-upon-Dearne	d	08 30												09 31										10 30	
Swinton (S.Yorks)	29 a	08 34												09 35					09 42					10 34	
Rotherham Central	29 a	08 47						←						09 44					09 50					10 43	
Meadowhall	29 a	08 54		08 52				08 54				09 27	09 46	09 50	09 52				09 55			10 27	10 46	10 50	
Sheffield 7	29 a	→		09 02	08 51			09 05				09 37	09 56	10 00	10 02			09 51	10 05			10 37	10 56	11 00	

		NT	XC	NT	NT	NT	NT	NT	NT	GR	GC	NT		XC	NT	NT	NT	NT	NT	NT	NT	NT		GR	XC
Leeds 10	32,34 d	10 05	10 12		10 19	10 32	10 37		10 48	11 05		11 05		11 11		11 19	11 32		11 37		11 48	12 05		12 05	12 11
Outwood	d				10 28			←	10 59							11 28				←	11 59				
Wakefield Kirkgate 4	32,34,39 a	10 23				11 01	10 54	11 01				11 23					12 01		11 54	12 01		12 23			
	d	10 23				11 04	10 55	11 04			11 13	11 23					12 04		11 55	12 04		12 23			
Wakefield Westgate 7	32,39 a		10 23		10 32	→			11 03	11 17				11 23		11 32	→				12 03			12 17	12 23
	d		10 24		10 32				11 03	11 17				11 24		11 32					12 03			12 17	12 24
Sandal & Agbrigg	d				10 35				11 07							11 35					12 07				
Fitzwilliam	d				10 42				11 14							11 42					12 14				
South Elmsall	d				10 47											11 47									
Adwick	a				10 52											11 52									
	d			10 10	10 53										11 08	11 53									
Bentley (S.Yorks)	d			10 14	10 57										11 12	11 57									
Doncaster 7	a			10 19	11 07					11 38	12 04				11 19	12 07								12 34	
Moorthorpe	d								11 19									11 49			12 19				
Thurnscoe	d								11 25												12 25				
Goldthorpe	d								11 27												12 27				
Bolton-upon-Dearne	d								11 30												12 30				
Swinton (S.Yorks)	29 a			10 38					11 34						11 [illegible]9			11 59			12 34				
Rotherham Central	29 a			10 49					11 44						11 [illegible]1			12 10			12 44				
Meadowhall	29 a	10 52		10 56			11 27	11 46	11 50			11 52			12 00			12 16	12 27	12 46	12 50	12 52			
Sheffield 7	29 a	11 02	10 51	11 06			11 37	11 56	12 00			12 02		11 51	12 10			12 25	12 37	12 56	13 00	13 02			12 51

		NT	NT	NT	NT	NT	NT	NT		GR	XC	NT	NT	NT	NT	NT	NT	NT		GR	XC	NT	NT	NT	NT
Leeds 10	32,34 d		12 19	12 32	12 37		12 48	13 05		13 05	13 11		13 19	13 32	13 37		13 48	14 05		14 05	14 11		14 19	14 32	14 37
Outwood	d		12 28			←	12 59						13 28			←	13 59						14 28		
Wakefield Kirkgate 4	32,34,39 a			13 02	12 54	13 02		13 23						14 01	13 54	14 01		14 23						15 01	14 54
	d			13 04	12 55	13 04		13 23						14 04	13 55	14 04		14 23						15 04	14 55
Wakefield Westgate 7	32,39 a		12 32	→			13 03			13 17	13 22		13 32	→			14 03			14 17	14 23		14 32	→	
	d		12 32				13 03			13 17	13 23		13 32				14 03			14 17	14 24		14 32		
Sandal & Agbrigg	d		12 35				13 07						13 35				14 07						14 35		
Fitzwilliam	d		12 42				13 14						13 42				14 14						14 42		
South Elmsall	d		12 47										13 47										14 47		
Adwick	a		12 52										13 52										14 52		
	d	12 12	12 53									13 12	13 53									14 14	14 53		
Bentley (S.Yorks)	d	12 16	12 57									13 16	13 57									14 18	14 57		
Doncaster 7	a	12 22	13 07							13 37		13 23	14 07							14 34		14 22	15 07		
Moorthorpe	d						13 19										14 19								
Thurnscoe	d						13 25										14 25								
Goldthorpe	d						13 27										14 27								
Bolton-upon-Dearne	d						13 30										14 30								
Swinton (S.Yorks)	29 a	12 41					13 34					13 41					14 34					14 41			
Rotherham Central	29 a	12 50					13 44					13 50					14 44					14 50			
Meadowhall	29 a	12 55			13 27	13 46	13 50	13 52				13 55			14 27	14 46	14 50	14 52				14 55			15 27
Sheffield 7	29 a	13 05			13 37	13 56	14 00	14 02			13 51	14 05			14 37	14 56	15 00	15 02			14 51	15 05			15 37

Table 31

Leeds - Wakefield, Doncaster and Sheffield

		NT	NT	NT		GR	XC	NT	NT	NT	NT	NT	NT	NT		GR	GC	NT	XC	NT	NT	NT	NT	NT
Leeds 10	32,34 d		14 48	15 05		15 05	15 12		15 19	15 32		15 37		15 48		16 05		16 05	16 12		16 19	16 32	16 37	
Outwood	d	←	14 59						15 28				←	15 59							16 28			←
Wakefield Kirkgate 4	32,34,39 a	15 01		15 23						16 01		15 54	16 01					16 23				17 01	16 54	17 01
	d	15 04		15 23						16 04		15 55	16 04				16 10	16 23				17 04	16 55	17 04
Wakefield Westgate 7	32,39 a		15 03			15 17	15 23		15 32	→				16 03		16 17			16 23		16 32	→		
	d		15 03			15 17	15 24		15 32					16 03		16 17			16 24		16 32			
Sandal & Agbrigg	d		15 07						15 35					16 07							16 35			
Fitzwilliam	d		15 14						15 42					16 14							16 42			
South Elmsall	d								15 47												16 47			
Adwick	a								15 52												16 52			
	d							15 13	15 53											16 13	16 53			
Bentley (S.Yorks)	d							15 17	15 57											16 16	16 57			
Doncaster 7	a					15 35		15 22	16 07							16 38	16 54			16 22	17 07			
Moorthorpe	d		15 19								16 01			16 19										
Thurnscoe	d		15 25											16 25										
Goldthorpe	d		15 27											16 27										
Bolton-upon-Dearne	d		15 30											16 30										
Swinton (S.Yorks)	29 a		15 34					15 41			16 10			16 34						16 41				
Rotherham Central	29 a		15 42					15 50			16 17			16 43						16 50				
Meadowhall	29 a	15 46	15 50	15 52				16 00			16 23	16 27	16 46	16 50				16 52		16 55			17 27	17 46
Sheffield 7	29 a	15 56	16 00	16 02			15 51	16 10			16 35	16 37	16 56	17 00				17 02	16 51	17 05			17 37	17 56

		NT	NT	NT	XC	NT	NT	NT	NT	GR		NT	NT	XC	NT	NT	NT	NT	NT	GR	NT	NT	XC	NT	NT
Leeds 10	32,34 d	16 48		17 05	17 12	17 19	17 32	17 37		17 40		17 46	18 05	18 11		18 19	18 32	18 37		18 40	18 48	19 05	19 11	19 22	19 37
Outwood	d	16 59				17 28			←			17 57				18 27			←		18 59			19 28	
Wakefield Kirkgate 4	32,34,39 a			17 22			18 01	17 54	18 01				18 23				19 04	18 54	19 04			19 24			20 06
	d			17 23			18 04	17 55	18 04				18 23				19 04	18 55	19 04			19 24			20 07
Wakefield Westgate 7	32,39 a	17 03			17 23	17 32	→			17 52		18 01		18 23		18 31	→			18 54	19 03		19 23	19 32	→
	d	17 03			17 24	17 32				17 52		18 01		18 24		18 32				18 54	19 03		19 24	19 32	
Sandal & Agbrigg	d	17 07				17 35						18 05				18 35					19 07			19 35	
Fitzwilliam	d	17 14				17 42						18 12				18 42					19 14			19 42	
South Elmsall	d					17 47										18 47								19 47	
Adwick	a					17 52										18 53								19 53	
	d		17 05			17 53									18 12	18 53								19 53	
Bentley (S.Yorks)	d		17 09			17 57									18 16	18 57								19 57	
Doncaster 7	a		17 14			18 07				18 09					18 23	19 07				19 12				20 10	
Moorthorpe	d	17 19										18 17									19 19				
Thurnscoe	d	17 25										18 23									19 25				
Goldthorpe	d	17 27										18 25									19 27				
Bolton-upon-Dearne	d	17 30										18 28									19 30				
Swinton (S.Yorks)	29 a	17 34										18 34									19 34				
Rotherham Central	29 a	17 44										18 43									19 43				
Meadowhall	29 a	17 50		17 51				18 27	18 46			18 50	18 52					19 27	19 46		19 50	19 52			
Sheffield 7	29 a	18 00		18 02	17 51			18 38	18 56			19 00	19 03	18 51				19 37	19 57		20 00	20 03	19 50		

		NT	NT	NT	XC	GR		NT	NT	NT	NT	XC	NT	NT	NT	NT		NT		NT	NT
Leeds 10	32,34 d	19 43		19 48	20 11	20 15		20 21	20 30	20 37	20 48	21 11	21 34		21 37	21 48		22 16		22 37	22 44
Outwood	d		←	19 59				20 30			20 59		21 43			21 59		22 25			22 55
Wakefield Kirkgate 4	32,34,39 a	19 59	20 06						20 46	21 06				21 47	22 06					23 10	
	d	20 00	20 07						20 46	21 07				21 48	22 07						
Wakefield Westgate 7	32,39 a			20 03	20 22	20 30		20 36			21 03	21 22	21 47	21 53		22 03		22 29			22 59
	d			20 03	20 23	20 31		20 36			21 03	21 23	21 47			22 03		22 30			22 59
Sandal & Agbrigg	d			20 07				20 39			21 07		21 50			22 07		22 33			23 03
Fitzwilliam	d			20 14				20 46			21 13		21 57			22 14		22 39			23 10
South Elmsall	d							20 51					22 02					22 44			
Adwick	a							20 56					22 07					22 50			
	d							20 57					22 08					22 50			
Bentley (S.Yorks)	d							21 01					22 12					22 54			
Doncaster 7	a					20 48		21 09					22 22					23 04			
Moorthorpe	d			20 19							21 20					22 19					23 15
Thurnscoe	d			20 25							21 26					22 25					23 21
Goldthorpe	d			20 27							21 28					22 27					23 23
Bolton-upon-Dearne	d			20 30							21 31					22 30					23 26
Swinton (S.Yorks)	29 a			20 34							21 35					22 40					23 30
Rotherham Central	29 a			20 42							21 44					22 46					23 37
Meadowhall	29 a	20 32	20 45	20 51					21 17	21 45	21 52				22 47	22 52					23 43
Sheffield 7	29 a	20 44	20 58	21 02	20 52				21 30	21 58	22 05	21 51			22 58	23 02					23 58

Leeds - Wakefield, Doncaster and Sheffield

Station	Table		XC	GR	GC	GC	NT	NT	XC	NT	GR	GR	EM	XC	NT	NT	NT	EM	GR	NT	XC	NT	NT
			◇1	1	◇1	◇1			◇1		1	1	◇1	◇1				◇1	1		◇1		
					A	B			C									B					
Leeds 10	32,34	d	08 10	08 25			08 34	08 49	09 00	09 05	09 05	09 40	09 44	10 00	10 02	10 09	10 17	10 20	10 40	10 57	11 00	11 09	11 29
Outwood		d						09 00								10 18						11 20	
Wakefield Kirkgate 4	32,34,39	a					09 03			09 21					10 18		10 46			11 13			11 46
		d			08 41	08 48	09 03			09 21					10 18		10 46			11 13			11 46
Wakefield Westgate 7	32,39	a	08 21	08 37				09 04	09 11		09 17	09 52	09 57	10 11		10 22		10 31	10 52		11 11	11 24	
		d	08 22	08 37				09 04	09 11		09 17	09 52	09 58	10 12		10 22		10 32	10 52		11 12	11 24	
Sandal & Agbrigg		d						09 08								10 25						11 28	
Fitzwilliam		d						09 15								10 32						11 35	
South Elmsall		d														10 37							
Adwick		a														10 42							
		d														10 43							
Bentley (S.Yorks)		d														10 47							
Doncaster 7		a		08 54	09 04	09 09			09 31		09 36	10 09		10 28		10 57			11 12		11 28		
Moorthorpe		d						09 20														11 40	
Thurnscoe		d						09 26														11 46	
Goldthorpe		d						09 28														11 48	
Bolton-upon-Dearne		d						09 31														11 51	
Swinton (S.Yorks)	29	a						09 35														11 55	
Rotherham Central	29	a						09 44														12 05	
Meadowhall	29 ⇌	a					09 44	09 53		09 57					10 51		11 32			11 46		12 11	12 17
Sheffield 7	29 ⇌	a	08 52				09 55	10 03	09 55	10 04			10 25	10 54	11 02		11 44	11 03		11 56	11 53	12 20	12 29

Station	Table		GR	XC	NT	NT	GC	NT	GR	XC	NT	GR	XC	EM	NT	NT	NT	GR	XC	NT	NT	GR	XC	GC
			1	◇1			◇1		1	◇1		1	◇1	◇1				1	◇1			1	◇1	◇1
																								F
Leeds 10	32,34	d	11 40	12 00	12 09	12 29		12 34	12 40	13 00	13 09	13 40	14h00	14 05	14 05	14 09	14 17	14 40	15 00	15 05	15 09	15 40	16 00	
Outwood		d			12 18						13 20					14 18					15 20			
Wakefield Kirkgate 4	32,34,39	a				12 46		13 03							14 21		14 46			15 22				
		d				12 46	13 02	13 04							14 21		14 46			15 22				16 19
Wakefield Westgate 7	32,39	a	11 52	12 11	12 22				12 52	13 11	13 24	13 52	14 11	14 17		14 22		14 52	15 11		15 24	15 52	16 11	
		d	11 52	12 12	12 22				12 52	13 12	13 24	13 52	14 12	14 18		14 23		14 52	15 12		15 24	15 52	16 12	
Sandal & Agbrigg		d			12 25						13 28					14 26					15 28			
Fitzwilliam		d			12 32						13 35					14 32					15 35			
South Elmsall		d			12 37											14 37								
Adwick		a			12 42											14 43								
		d			12 43											14 43								
Bentley (S.Yorks)		d			12 47											14 47								
Doncaster 7		a	12 09	12 28	12 57		13 43		13 11	13 28		14 09				14 58		15 10				16 09		17 00
Moorthorpe		d									13 40										15 40			
Thurnscoe		d									13 46										15 46			
Goldthorpe		d									13 48										15 48			
Bolton-upon-Dearne		d									13 51										15 51			
Swinton (S.Yorks)	29	a									14 00										15 55			
Rotherham Central	29	a									14 08										16 05			
Meadowhall	29 ⇌	a				13 18		13 47			14 14				14 54		15 35			15 55	16 10			
Sheffield 7	29 ⇌	a		12 54		13 29		13 58		13 54	14 25		14 45	14 55	15 06		15 45		15 42	16 05	16 21		16 41	

Station	Table		NT	NT	NT	GR	GC	XC	NT	GR	NT	GR	XC	NT	NT	NT	NT	GR	XC	NT	NT	XC	GR
						1	◇1	◇1		1		1	◇1					1	◇1			◇1	1
							G																
Leeds 10	32,34	d	16 05	16 09	16 17	16 40		17 00	17 05	17 05	17 09	17 40	18 00		18 05	18 09	18 17	18 40	19 00	19 04	19 09	20 00	20 15
Outwood		d		16 18							17 20					18 18					19 20		
Wakefield Kirkgate 4	32,34,39	a	16 21		16 46				17 21						18 21		18 45			19 21			
		d	16 22		16 46		16 48		17 21						18 22		18 45			19 21			
Wakefield Westgate 7	32,39	a		16 22		16 52		17 11		17 18	17 24	17 52	18 11			18 22		18 52	19 11		19 24	20 11	20 28
		d		16 22		16 52		17 12		17 18	17 24	17 52	18 12			18 22		18 52	19 12		19 24	20 12	20 28
Sandal & Agbrigg		d		16 25							17 28					18 25					19 28		
Fitzwilliam		d		16 32							17 35					18 32					19 35		
South Elmsall		d		16 37												18 37							
Adwick		a		16 42												18 42							
		d		16 43												18 43							
Bentley (S.Yorks)		d		16 47												18 47							
Doncaster 7		a		16 57		17 10	17 38			17 35						18 57		19 09					20 47
Moorthorpe		d									17 40			18 02							19 40		
Thurnscoe		d									17 46										19 46		
Goldthorpe		d									17 48										19 48		
Bolton-upon-Dearne		d									17 51										19 51		
Swinton (S.Yorks)	29	a									17 55			18 11							19 55		
Rotherham Central	29	a									18 05			18 18							20 04		
Meadowhall	29 ⇌	a	16 56		17 34				17 55		18 11			18 23	18 56		19 32			19 54	20 10		
Sheffield 7	29 ⇌	a	17 05		17 44			17 41	18 05		18 23		18 40	18 35	19 05		19 43		19 40	20 04	20 23	20 40	

A until 5 September
B from 12 September
C until 17 October
F until 11 July and from 12 September
G from 18 July until 5 September

Leeds - Wakefield, Doncaster and Sheffield

Station	Table		NT	NT	XC	NT	NT	NT	NT
					◇1				
Leeds 10	32,34	d	20 17	20 20	21 00	21 09		21 40	22 17
Outwood		d		20 29		21 18		21 51	
Wakefield Kirkgate 4	32,34,39	a	20 46						22 46
		d	20 46						22 46
Wakefield Westgate 7	32,39	a		20 33	21 11	21 22		21 55	
		d		20 34	21 12	21 22		21 55	
Sandal & Agbrigg		d		20 37		21 25		21 59	
Fitzwilliam		d		20 43		21 32		22 06	
South Elmsall		d		20 48		21 37			
Adwick		a		20 54		21 42			
		d		20 54		21 43			
Bentley (S.Yorks)		d		20 58		21 47			
Doncaster 7		a		21 08		21 55			
Moorthorpe		d					21 29	22 11	
Thurnscoe		d						22 17	
Goldthorpe		d						22 19	
Bolton-upon-Dearne		d						22 22	
Swinton (S.Yorks)	29	a					21 38	22 32	
Rotherham Central	29	a					21 48	22 39	
Meadowhall	29 ⇌	a	21 33				21 54	22 45	23 30
Sheffield 7	29 ⇌	a	21 42		21 44		22 05	22 54	23 43

Table 32

Mondays to Saturdays

Leeds and Wakefield - Pontefract, Knottingley and Goole

			NT SX	NT SX	NT SO	NT	NT	NT	NT SX	NT SO	NT SO	NT SX	NT	NT	NT SX	NT SO	NT	NT	NT SX	NT SO
Leeds 10	31,34	d	05 46			06 38	07 00	07 29			08 00	08 05		08 32	09 00	09 00		09 32	10 00	10 00
Woodlesford	34	d	05 54			06 46	07 08	07 37			08 08	08 15		08 40	09 08	09 08		09 40	10 08	10 08
Castleford	34	a	06 03			06 54	07 19	07 45			08 17	08 24		08 48	09 17	09 17		09 48	10 18	10 18
		d	06 05			06 57	07 19	07 48			08 19	08 26		08 51	09 19	09 19		09 51	10 19	10 19
Glasshoughton		d	06 10				07 24				08 24	08 31			09 24	09 24			10 24	10 24
Wakefield Westgate 7	31,39	d		06 24	06 24															
Wakefield Kirkgate 4	31,34,39	a		06 29	06 29	07 07		08 00						09 03				10 01		
		d		06 29	06 29				07 31	07 31			08 31				09 31			
Streethouse		d		06 36	06 36				07 39	07 39			08 39				09 39			
Featherstone		d		06 40	06 40				07 43	07 43			08 43				09 43			
Pontefract Tanshelf		d		06 44	06 44				07 46	07 46			08 46				09 46			
Pontefract Monkhill		a	06 14	06 46	06 46		07 28		07 50	07 50	08 28	08 35	08 49		09 28	09 28	09 49		10 28	10 28
		d	06 14	06 47	06 47		07 28		07 50	07 50	08 28	08 35	08 49		09 28	09 28	09 49		10 28	10 28
Knottingley		a	06 20	06 55	06 55		07 36		07 59	07 59	08 36	08 44	08 56		09 37	09 37	09 56		10 35	10 36
		d																		
Whitley Bridge		d																		
Hensall		d																		
Snaith		d																		
Rawcliffe		d																		
Goole		a																		

			NT	NT	NT SX	NT SO	NT	NT	NT	NT	NT	NT	NT	NT	NT	NT	NT	NT	NT
Leeds 10	31,34	d		10 32	11 00	11 00		11 32	12 00		12 32	13 00		13 32	14 00		14 32	15 00	
Woodlesford	34	d		10 40	11 08	11 08		11 40	12 08		12 40	13 08		13 40	14 08		14 40	15 08	
Castleford	34	a		10 48	11 17	11 17		11 48	12 17		12 48	13 17		13 48	14 17		14 48	15 17	
		d		10 51	11 19	11 19		11 51	12 19		12 51	13 19		13 51	14 19		14 51	15 19	
Glasshoughton		d			11 24	11 24			12 24			13 24			14 24			15 24	
Wakefield Westgate 7	31,39	d																	
Wakefield Kirkgate 4	31,34,39	a		11 01				12 01			13 02			14 01			15 01		
		d	10 31				11 31			12 31			13 31			14 31			15 31
Streethouse		d	10 39				11 39			12 39			13 39			14 39			15 39
Featherstone		d	10 43				11 43			12 43			13 43			14 43			15 43
Pontefract Tanshelf		d	10 46				11 46			12 46			13 46			14 46			15 46
Pontefract Monkhill		a	10 49		11 29	11 28	11 49		12 28	12 49		13 28	13 49		14 28	14 49		15 28	15 49
		d	10 49		11 29	11 28	11 49		12 28	12 49		13 28	13 49		14 28	14 49		15 28	15 49
Knottingley		a	10 56		11 35	11 35	11 56		12 35	12 56		13 35	13 56		14 35	14 56		15 35	15 56
		d																	
Whitley Bridge		d																	
Hensall		d																	
Snaith		d																	
Rawcliffe		d																	
Goole		a																	

			NT	NT	NT	NT	NT	NT	NT	NT	NT SO	NT	NT SO	NT SX	NT	NT
Leeds 10	31,34	d	15 32	16 00		16 32	17 16		17 32	18 00	18 32		19 00	19 10		19 37
Woodlesford	34	d	15 40	16 08		16 40	17 24		17 40	18 08	18 40		19 08	19 18		19 45
Castleford	34	a	15 48	16 17		16 48	17 33		17 48	18 17	18 48		19 18	19 28		19 53
		d	15 51	16 19		16 51	17 35		17 51	18 19	18 51		19 20	19 30		19 56
Glasshoughton		d		16 24			17 40			18 24			19 24	19 34		
Wakefield Westgate 7	31,39	d														
Wakefield Kirkgate 4	31,34,39	a	16 01			17 01			18 01		19 04					20 06
		d			16 31			17 31				18 33			19 33	
Streethouse		d			16 39			17 39				18 41			19 41	
Featherstone		d			16 43			17 43				18 45			19 45	
Pontefract Tanshelf		d			16 46			17 46				18 48			19 48	
Pontefract Monkhill		a		16 28	16 49		17 44	17 49		18 28		18 51	19 28	19 38	19 51	
		d		16 28	16 49		17 44	17 49		18 28		18 51	19 28	19 38	19 51	
Knottingley		a		16 35	16 56		17 50	17 57		18 35		18 58	19 35	19 45	19 58	
		d					17 51									
Whitley Bridge		d					17 57									
Hensall		d					18 01									
Snaith		d					18 08									
Rawcliffe		d					18 12									
Goole		a					18 26									

			NT	NT	NT	NT	NT	NT	NT	NT SO	NT SX	NT SX	NT SO
Leeds 10	31,34	d	20 05		20 37	21 05		21 37	22 05			22 37	22 37
Woodlesford	34	d	20 13		20 45	21 13		21 45	22 13			22 45	22 45
Castleford	34	a	20 22		20 53	21 22		21 53	22 24			22 53	22 53
		d	20 24		20 56	21 24		21 56	22 24			22 56	22 56
Glasshoughton		d	20 29			21 29			22 29				
Wakefield Westgate 7	31,39	d					21 57			23 04	23 04		
Wakefield Kirkgate 4	31,34,39	a			21 06		22 00	22 06		23 07	23 07	23 10	23 10
		d		20 54			22 00			23 07	23 07	23 10	
Streethouse		d		21 02			22 08			23 15	23 15		
Featherstone		d		21 06			22 12			23 19	23 19		
Pontefract Tanshelf		d		21 09			22 16			23 23	23 23		
Pontefract Monkhill		a	20 33	21 12		21 33	22 18		22 33	23 29	23 25		
		d	20 33	21 12		21 33	22 19		22 33		23 26		
Knottingley		a	20 40	21 19		21 40	22 25		22 42		23 32		
		d											
Whitley Bridge		d											
Hensall		d											
Snaith		d											
Rawcliffe		d											
Goole		a											

Table 32

Sundays

Leeds and Wakefield - Pontefract, Knottingley and Goole

			NT	NT	NT	NT	NT	NT	NT	NT	NT	NT	NT	NT	NT	NT	NT
Leeds 10	31,34	d	08 34	09 34	10 17	11 17	12 34	13 17	14 17	15 17	16 17	17 17	18 17	19 17	20 17	21 17	22 17
Woodlesford	34	d	08 42	09 42	10 25	11 25	12 42	13 25	14 25	15 25	16 25	17 25	18 25	19 25	20 25	21 25	22 25
Castleford	34	a	08 50	09 50	10 33	11 33	12 50	13 33	14 33	15 33	16 33	17 33	18 33	19 35	20 33	21 33	22 33
		d	08 53	09 53	10 36	11 36	12 53	13 36	14 36	15 36	16 36	17 36	18 36	19 36	20 36	21 36	22 36
Glasshoughton		d		09 57		11 40		13 40		15 40		17 40		19 40		21 40	
Wakefield Westgate 7	31,39	d															
Wakefield Kirkgate 4	31,34,39	a	09 03		10 46		13 03		14 46		16 46		18 45		20 46		22 46
		d			|												
Streethouse		d															
Featherstone		d															
Pontefract Tanshelf		d															
Pontefract Monkhill		a		10 02		11 45		13 45		15 45		17 45		19 45		21 45	
		d		10 02		11 45		13 45		15 45		17 45		19 45		21 45	
Knottingley		a		10 08		11 52		13 52		15 52		17 52		19 52		21 52	
		d															
Whitley Bridge		d															
Hensall		d															
Snaith		d															
Rawcliffe		d															
Goole		a															

Goole, Knottingley and Pontefract - Wakefield and Leeds

		NT MSX	NT SX	NT	NT	NT SX	NT SX	NT SO	NT	NT	NT	NT	NT	NT
Goole	d						07 04	07 06						
Rawcliffe	d						07 11	07 13						
Snaith	d						07 16	07 18						
Hensall	d						07 23	07 25						
Whitley Bridge	d						07 29	07 29						
Knottingley	a						07 37	07 37						
	d		06 25		06 56		07 37	07 37		07 53	08 16		08 53	09 16
Pontefract Monkhill	a		06 29		07 00		07 42	07 42		07 57	08 20		08 57	09 20
	d		06 29		07 00		07 42	07 42		07 57	08 20		08 57	09 20
Pontefract Tanshelf	d				07 03					08 00			09 00	
Featherstone	d				07 06					08 03			09 03	
Streethouse	d				07 10					08 07			09 07	
Wakefield Kirkgate [4] 31,34,39	a	00s10			07 21					08 18			09 18	
	d	00s13		06 50					07 50			08 50		
Wakefield Westgate [7] 31,39	a	00 17												
Glasshoughton 34	d		06 34				07 47	07 47			08 25			09 25
Castleford	a		06 38	07 00			07 51	07 51	08 00		08 30	09 00		09 29
	d		06 41	07 02		07 38	07 54	07 54	08 02		08 32	09 02		09 32
Woodlesford 34	d		06 50	07 12		07 47	08 03	08 03	08 12		08 41	09 12		09 41
Leeds [10] 31,34	a		07 04	07 28		08 01	08 18	08 19	08 25		08 54	09 25		09 53

		NT	NT	NT SO	NT SX	NT	NT	NT	NT	NT	NT SO	NT SX	NT	NT	NT	NT
Goole	d															
Rawcliffe	d															
Snaith	d															
Hensall	d															
Whitley Bridge	d															
Knottingley	a															
	d		09 53	10 16	10 16		10 53	11 16		11 53	12 16	12 16		12 53	13 16	
Pontefract Monkhill	a		09 57	10 20	10 20		10 57	11 20		11 57	12 20	12 20		12 57	13 20	
	d		09 57	10 20	10 20		10 57	11 20		11 57	12 20	12 20		12 57	13 20	
Pontefract Tanshelf	d		10 00				11 00			12 00				13 00		
Featherstone	d		10 03				11 03			12 03				13 03		
Streethouse	d		10 07				11 07			12 07				13 07		
Wakefield Kirkgate [4] 31,34,39	a		10 20				11 18			12 18				13 18		
	d	09 50				10 50			11 50				12 50			13 50
Wakefield Westgate [7] 31,39	a															
Glasshoughton 34	d			10 25	10 25			11 25			12 25	12 25			13 25	
Castleford	a	10 00		10 30	10 30	11 00		11 29	12 00		12 29	12 29	13 00		13 29	14 00
	d	10 02		10 32	10 32	11 02		11 32	12 02		12 32	12 32	13 02		13 32	14 02
Woodlesford 34	d	10 12		10 41	10 39	11 12		11 41	12 12		12 41	12 41	13 12		13 41	14 12
Leeds [10] 31,34	a	10 25		10 54	10 56	11 25		11 53	12 25		12 53	12 54	13 25		13 53	14 25

		NT	NT	NT	NT	NT	NT	NT	NT	NT	NT	NT	NT	NT	NT
Goole	d														
Rawcliffe	d														
Snaith	d														
Hensall	d														
Whitley Bridge	d														
Knottingley	a														
	d	13 53	14 16		14 53	15 16		15 53	16 16		16 53	17 14		18 02	18 39
Pontefract Monkhill	a	13 57	14 20		14 57	15 20		15 57	16 20		16 57	17 18		18 06	18 43
	d	13 57	14 20		14 57	15 20		15 57	16 20		16 57	17 18		18 06	18 43
Pontefract Tanshelf	d	14 00			15 00			16 00			17 00			18 09	
Featherstone	d	14 03			15 03			16 03			17 03			18 12	
Streethouse	d	14 07			15 07			16 07			17 07			18 16	
Wakefield Kirkgate [4] 31,34,39	a	14 18			15 18			16 19			17 18			18 27	
	d			14 50			15 50			16 50			17 50		
Wakefield Westgate [7] 31,39	a														
Glasshoughton 34	d		14 25			15 25			16 25			17 23			18 48
Castleford	a		14 29	15 00		15 29	16 00		16 29	17 00		17 27	18 00		18 54
	d		14 32	15 02		15 32	16 02		16 32	17 02		17 30	18 02		18 57
Woodlesford 34	d		14 41	15 12		15 41	16 12		16 41	17 12		17 41	18 12		19 06
Leeds [10] 31,34	a		14 53	15 25		15 53	16 25		16 55	17 25		17 53	18 25		19 20

		NT	NT	NT	NT	NT	NT	NT	NT	NT	NT	NT	NT	NT
Goole	d			18 49										
Rawcliffe	d			18 56										
Snaith	d			19 01										
Hensall	d			19 08										
Whitley Bridge	d			19 12										
Knottingley	a			19 20										
	d		19 02	19 21		19 55	20 16		21 16	21 23		22 16		22 30
Pontefract Monkhill	a		19 06	19 25		19 59	20 20		21 20	21 27		22 22		22 34
	d		19 06	19 25		19 59	20 20		21 20	21 27		22 22		22 34
Pontefract Tanshelf	d		19 09			20 02				21 30				22 37
Featherstone	d		19 12			20 05				21 33				22 40
Streethouse	d		19 16			20 09				21 37				22 44
Wakefield Kirkgate [4] 31,34,39	a		19 27			20 20				21 47				22 55
	d	18 50			19 50			20 50		21 47	21 52		22 50	22 55
Wakefield Westgate [7] 31,39	a									21 53				23 01
Glasshoughton 34	d			19 30			20 25		21 25			22 27		
Castleford	a	19 00		19 34	20 00		20 29	21 00	21 29		22 04	22 31	23 00	
	d	19 03		19 37	20 02		20 32	21 02	21 32		22 05	22 34	23 02	
Woodlesford 34	d	19 13		19 46	20 12		20 44	21 12	21 41		22 15	22 43	23 13	
Leeds [10] 31,34	a	19 27		20 00	20 26		20 57	21 26	21 53		22 29	22 57	23 28	

Table 32 Mondays to Saturdays

Goole, Knottingley and Pontefract - Wakefield and Leeds

		NT
Goole	d	
Rawcliffe	d	
Snaith	d	
Hensall	d	
Whitley Bridge	d	
Knottingley	a	
	d	23 05
Pontefract Monkhill	a	23 09
	d	23 09
Pontefract Tanshelf	d	
Featherstone	d	
Streethouse	d	
Wakefield Kirkgate [4] 31,34,39	a	
	d	
Wakefield Westgate [7] 31,39	a	
Glasshoughton 34	d	23 14
Castleford	a	23 18
	d	23 21
Woodlesford 34	d	23 30
Leeds [10] 31,34	a	23 44

Sundays

		NT	NT	NT	NT	NT	NT	NT	NT	NT	NT	NT	NT	NT	NT	NT
Goole	d															
Rawcliffe	d															
Snaith	d															
Hensall	d															
Whitley Bridge	d															
Knottingley	a															
	d		10 26		12 26		14 26		16 26		18 26		20 26		22 26	
Pontefract Monkhill	a		10 30		12 30		14 30		16 30		18 30		20 30		22 30	
	d		10 30		12 30		14 30		16 30		18 30		20 30		22 30	
Pontefract Tanshelf	d															
Featherstone	d															
Streethouse	d															
Wakefield Kirkgate [4] 31,34,39	a															
	d	09 30		11 30		13 30		15 30		17 30		19 30		21 30		23 30
Wakefield Westgate [7] 31,39	a															
Glasshoughton 34	d		10 35		12 35		14 35		16 35		18 35		20 35		22 35	
Castleford	a	09 40	10 39	11 40	12 39	13 40	14 39	15 40	16 39	17 40	18 39	19 41	20 39	21 40	22 39	23 40
	d	09 42	10 42	11 41	12 42	13 42	14 42	15 41	16 42	17 42	18 42	19 44	20 42	21 42	22 42	23 42
Woodlesford 34	d	09 52	10 51	11 51	12 52	13 51	14 51	15 51	16 51	17 51	18 51	19 53	20 51	21 51	22 51	23 51
Leeds [10] 31,34	a	10 04	11 04	12 05	13 04	14 04	15 04	16 04	17 04	18 05	19 04	20 05	21 03	22 04	23 04	00 04

Table 33

Sheffield and Selby - York

Local services only

Mondays to Fridays

		NT	NT	NT	NT	NT	NT	NT	NT	NT	NT	NT	NT	NT	NT	NT	NT	NT	NT	NT	NT	NT
Sheffield 7	29,31 ⇌ d								09 29							13 28						
Meadowhall	29,31 ⇌ d								09 35							13 35						
Rotherham Central	29,31 d								09 42							13 41						
Swinton (S.Yorks)	29,31 d								09 51							13 50						
Moorthorpe	31 d								10 01							14 01						
Pontefract Baghill	d								10 10							14 10						
Hull	29 d		07 07				09 02				11 05				13 12		15 02		16 10		17 18	
Selby	d	06 48	07 48			09 15	09 38			10 54	11 39		12 51		13 54		15 38		16 47		18 06	
Sherburn-in-Elmet	d	07 00	08 02			09 26			10 28						14 08	14 28						
Church Fenton	d	07 04		08 05	09 05			10 05	10 32			12 05		14 05		14 32		16 05		17 53		19 05
Ulleskelf	d		08 08						10 36							14 36				17 58		
York 8	29 a	07 20	08 21	08 21	09 21	09 46	10 11	10 21	10 52	11 20	12 09	12 21	13 15	14 21	14 25	14 51	16 05	16 21	17 13	18 10	18 36	19 21

		NT	NT	NT	NT
Sheffield 7	29,31 ⇌ d				
Meadowhall	29,31 ⇌ d				
Rotherham Central	29,31 d				
Swinton (S.Yorks)	29,31 d				
Moorthorpe	31 d				
Pontefract Baghill	d				
Hull	29 d	19 10			
Selby	d	19 47		21 21	
Sherburn-in-Elmet	d				
Church Fenton	d		21 12		23 16
Ulleskelf	d		21 16		
York 8	29 a	20 16	21 31	21 51	23 33

Saturdays

		NT	NT	NT	NT	NT	NT	NT	NT	NT	NT	NT	NT	NT	NT	NT	NT	NT	NT	NT	NT
Sheffield 7	29,31 ⇌ d								09 31							13 28					
Meadowhall	29,31 ⇌ d								09 37							13 35					
Rotherham Central	29,31 d								09 44							13 42					
Swinton (S.Yorks)	29,31 d								09 52							13 50					
Moorthorpe	31 d								10 02							14 00					
Pontefract Baghill	d								10 11							14 09					
Hull	29 d		06 57				09 02				11 05				13 12		14 51		16 10		17 18
Selby	d	06 48	07 40			09 15	09 38			10 54	11 39		12 51		13 54		15 25		16 47		18 06
Sherburn-in-Elmet	d	07 00	07 54			09 26			10 28				13 03			14 27					
Church Fenton	d	07 04		08 05	09 05			10 05	10 32			12 05		14 05		14 31		16 05		18 06	
Ulleskelf	d		08 00						10 36							14 35				18 10	
York 8	29 a	07 20	08 15	08 20	09 21	09 46	10 10	10 21	10 52	11 20	12 09	12 21	13 22	14 21	14 25	14 51	15 54	16 21	17 13	18 24	18 35

		NT	NT	NT	NT	NT	NT
Sheffield 7	29,31 ⇌ d						
Meadowhall	29,31 ⇌ d						
Rotherham Central	29,31 d						
Swinton (S.Yorks)	29,31 d						
Moorthorpe	31 d						
Pontefract Baghill	d						
Hull	29 d		18 46				
Selby	d		19 22	20 35		22 28	
Sherburn-in-Elmet	d						
Church Fenton	d	19 05			21 12		23 19
Ulleskelf	d				21 16		
York 8	29 a	19 18	19 56	21 00	21 31	22 53	23 36

Sundays

		NT	NT	NT B	NT C	NT	NT	NT D	NT	NT	NT D	NT	NT	NT	NT	NT D	NT	NT	NT	NT
Sheffield 7	29,31 ⇌ d											15 46					18 57			
Meadowhall	29,31 ⇌ d											15 52					19 04			
Rotherham Central	29,31 d											15 58					19 10			
Swinton (S.Yorks)	29,31 d											16 08					19 18			
Moorthorpe	31 d											16 18					19 28			
Pontefract Baghill	d											16 26					19 37			
Hull	29 d		08 54			11 53		13 24		14 28	16 00			17 23		19 04			20 22	
Selby	d		09 28			12 27		13 58		15 02	16 34			17 57		19 38			20 56	
Sherburn-in-Elmet	d											16 43					19 55			
Church Fenton	d	09 18		10 51	10 52		12 49		14 49			16 47	16 49		18 47		19 59	20 49		23 07
Ulleskelf	d																			
York 8	29 a	09 34	09 56	11 07	11 08	12 51	13 02	14 22	15 02	15 27	16 58	17 01	17 06	18 23	19 03	20 02	20 17	21 03	21 20	23 18

A from 17 July until 4 September
B until 5 September
C from 12 September
D until 12 September

Table 33

York - Selby and Sheffield

Local services only

Mondays to Fridays

		NT	NT	NT	NT	NT	NT	NT	NT	NT	NT	NT	NT	NT	NT	NT	NT	NT	NT	NT	NT	NT	NT
York 8	29 d	06 09	07 06	07 30	07 48	08 43	09 09	09 53	10 20	11 01	11 09	11 53	12 18	13 09	13 44	14 59	15 02	15 08	16 12	17 08	17 27	18 05	18 20
Ulleskelf	d		07 15							11 11							15 12					18 14	
Church Fenton	a		07 20		08 00		09 20			11 15	11 20			13 20			15 16	15 20	16 23	17 20		18 19	
	d		07 21		08 05		09 21			11 15	11 21			13 21			15 16	15 20	16 23	17 20		18 20	
Sherburn-in-Elmet	d									11 19					13 56		15 20		16 27				18 34
Selby	a	06 30		07 50		09 06		10 12	10 40			12 17	12 38		14 08	15 18			16 38		17 45		18 45
Hull	29 a			08 46				10 56				13 02			14 49	15 59			17 27		18 29		19 32
Pontefract Baghill	d									11 39							15 39						
Moorthorpe	31 a									11 51							15 51						
Swinton (S.Yorks)	29,31 a									12 01							16 01						
Rotherham Central	29,31 a									12 10							16 10						
Meadowhall	29,31 ⇌ a									12 16							16 17						
Sheffield 7	29,31 ⇌ a									12 26							16 25						

		NT	NT	NT	NT	NT	NT
York 8	29 d	19 04	20 21	21 16	22 03	22 09	23 13
Ulleskelf	d			21 25			
Church Fenton	a	19 15		21 30		22 21	23 28
	d	19 21		21 31		22 21	23 28
Sherburn-in-Elmet	d						
Selby	a		20 43		22 21		
Hull	29 a				23 09		
Pontefract Baghill	d						
Moorthorpe	31 a						
Swinton (S.Yorks)	29,31 a						
Rotherham Central	29,31 a						
Meadowhall	29,31 ⇌ a						
Sheffield 7	29,31 ⇌ a						

Saturdays

		NT	NT	NT	NT	NT	NT	NT	NT	NT	NT	NT	NT	NT	NT	NT	NT	NT	NT	NT	NT	NT	NT
York 8	29 d	06 05	07 06	07 30	08 09	08 34	09 09	09 53	10 17	11 01	11 09	11 50	12 18	13 09	13 38	15 05	15 08	15 11	16 12	17 08	17 18	18 13	19 04
Ulleskelf	d		07 15							11 11								15 22				18 22	
Church Fenton	a		07 20		08 21		09 20			11 15	11 20			13 20			15 20	15 26	16 23	17 20		18 26	19 15
	d		07 21		08 22		09 21			11 15	11 21			13 21			15 20	15 26	16 23	17 20		18 27	19 21
Sherburn-in-Elmet	d									11 19					13 52			15 30	16 27			18 30	
Selby	a	06 26		07 50		08 55		10 12	10 37			12 09	12 38		14 03	15 23			16 38		17 37	18 41	
Hull	29 a			08 46				10 56				12 54			14 45	16 03			17 27		18 22	19 28	
Pontefract Baghill	d									11 37								15 49					
Moorthorpe	31 a									11 49								16 01					
Swinton (S.Yorks)	29,31 a									11 59								16 10					
Rotherham Central	29,31 a									12 10								16 17					
Meadowhall	29,31 ⇌ a									12 16								16 23					
Sheffield 7	29,31 ⇌ a									12 25								16 35					

		NT	NT	NT	NT	NT	NT
York 8	29 d	19 29	20 17	21 18	21 45	22 09	23 13
Ulleskelf	d			21 27			
Church Fenton	a			21 33		22 20	23 28
	d			21 33		22 21	23 28
Sherburn-in-Elmet	d						
Selby	a	19 49	20 35		22 05		
Hull	29 a		21 23				
Pontefract Baghill	d						
Moorthorpe	31 a						
Swinton (S.Yorks)	29,31 a						
Rotherham Central	29,31 a						
Meadowhall	29,31 ⇌ a						
Sheffield 7	29,31 ⇌ a						

Sundays

		NT	NT	NT	NT	NT A	NT	NT	NT A	NT	NT	NT A	NT	NT	NT	NT	NT	NT	NT
York 8	29 d	08 50	09 52	10 40	11 52	12 05	13 23	13 52	14 42	15 43	15 52	17 10	17 17	17 52	19 10	19 52	20 42	21 41	21 52
Ulleskelf	d																		
Church Fenton	a	09 01	10 03		12 03			14 03			16 03		17 28	18 03		20 03	20 55		22 04
	d	09 02	10 04		12 04			14 04			16 04		17 28	18 04		20 04	20 55		22 04
Sherburn-in-Elmet	d												17 32				20 59		
Selby	a			10 58		12 23	13 42		15 01	16 01		17 30			19 29			22 00	
Hull	29 a			11 38		13 03	14 23		15 42	16 42		18 12			20 10			22 41	
Pontefract Baghill	d												17 49				21 17		
Moorthorpe	31 a												18 01				21 29		
Swinton (S.Yorks)	29,31 a												18 11				21 38		
Rotherham Central	29,31 a												18 18				21 48		
Meadowhall	29,31 ⇌ a												18 23				21 54		
Sheffield 7	29,31 ⇌ a												18 35				22 05		

A until 12 September

Table 34

Mondays to Fridays

until 03 September

Nottingham, Sheffield - Barnsley - Huddersfield and Leeds

		NT	NT	NT	NT	NT	NT	NT	NT	NT	NT	NT	TP	NT	NT	NT	NT	EM	NT	NT
													◇1					◇		
Nottingham 6 ⇌	d															06 23		06 40		
Langley Mill	d															06 38				
Alfreton	d															06 46		07 02		
Chesterfield	d										06 26					06 58		07 13		
Dronfield	d										06 33					07 05		07 20		
Sheffield 7 29,31 ⇌	a										06 46					07 18		07 31		
	d	05 16	05 22	05 29	05 36	05 50	06 06	06 18	06 28	06 36	06 49	06 52	06 55	07 06	07 14	07 20	07 24	07 35	07 36	07 41
Meadowhall 4 29,31 ⇌	a	05 22	05 27	05 34	05 41	05 55	06 11	06 23	06 33	06 41	06 54	06 57	07 00	07 11	07 20	07 25	07 30		07 41	07 46
	d	05 22			05 42	05 56	06 12			06 42	06 55			07 12		07 26			07 42	
Chapeltown	d	05 28			05 48		06 18			06 48				07 18					07 48	
Elsecar	d	05 33					06 23							07 23						
Wombwell	d	05 37			05 55		06 27			06 55				07 27					07 55	
Barnsley	a	05 43			06 00	06 10	06 32			07 00	07 09			07 32		07 41			08 00	
	d				06 01	06 10	06 33			07 01	07 12			07 33		07 42			08 01	
Dodworth	d				06 07					07 07									08 07	
Silkstone Common	d				06 11					07 11									08 11	
Penistone	d				06 18					07 18									08 18	
Denby Dale	d				06 24					07 24									08 24	
Shepley	d				06 29					07 29									08 29	
Stocksmoor	d				06 32					07 32									08 32	
Brockholes	d				06 36					07 36									08 36	
Honley	d				06 38					07 38									08 38	
Berry Brow	d				06 41					07 41									08 41	
Lockwood	d				06 44					07 44									08 44	
Huddersfield	a				06 49					07 49									08 49	
Darton	d						06 38							07 38						
Wakefield Kirkgate 4 31	a					06 27	06 49				07 27			07 49		07 57				
	d					06 28	06 50				07 28			07 50		07 58				
Normanton	d					06 33	06 54				07 33			07 54						
Castleford	a						07 00							08 00						
Woodlesford	a						07 11							08 12						
Leeds 10 31	a					06 49	07 28				07 51			08 25		08 21				

		NT	EM	NT	TP	NT	NT	NT	NT	EM	NT	NT	NT	NT	TP	NT	NT	NT	NT	NT	NT	NT	NT
			◇1		◇1					◇					◇1								
Nottingham 6 ⇌	d						07 13			07 45							08 11						
Langley Mill	d						07 29										08 31						
Alfreton	d						07 37			08 07							08 39						
Chesterfield	d		07 42				07 50			08 18							08 51						
Dronfield	d		07 49							08 25							08 58						
Sheffield 7 29,31 ⇌	a		08 00				08 08			08 38							09 15						
	d	07 51		08 06	08 11	08 14	08 18	08 25	08 36	08 42	08 41	08 51	08 57	09 06	09 11	09 14	09 18	09 24	09 29	09 36	09 41	09 51	09 57
Meadowhall 4 29,31 ⇌	a	07 57		08 11	08 16	08 20	08 24	08 30	08 41		08 46	08 56	09 03	09 11	09 16	09 20	09 23	09 29	09 34	09 41	09 46	09 56	10 03
	d	07 57		08 12			08 24		08 42			08 57		09 12			09 24			09 42		09 57	
Chapeltown	d			08 18					08 48					09 18						09 48			
Elsecar	d			08 23										09 23									
Wombwell	d			08 27					08 55					09 27						09 55			
Barnsley	a	08 11		08 32			08 40		09 00			09 11		09 32			09 40			10 00		10 11	
	d	08 12		08 33			08 42		09 01			09 12		09 33			09 42			10 01		10 12	
Dodworth	d								09 07											10 07			
Silkstone Common	d								09 11											10 11			
Penistone	d								09 18											10 18			
Denby Dale	d								09 24											10 24			
Shepley	d								09 29											10 29			
Stocksmoor	d								09 32											10 32			
Brockholes	d								09 36											10 36			
Honley	d								09 38											10 38			
Berry Brow	d								09 41											10 41			
Lockwood	d								09 44											10 44			
Huddersfield	a								09 49											10 49			
Darton	d			08 38										09 38									
Wakefield Kirkgate 4 31	a	08 27		08 49			08 57					09 27		09 49			09 57					10 27	
	d	08 28		08 50			08 58					09 28		09 50			09 58					10 28	
Normanton	d			08 54										09 54									
Castleford	a			09 00										10 00									
Woodlesford	a			09 12										10 12									
Leeds 10 31	a	08 49		09 25			09 19					09 49		10 25			10 18					10 48	

Table 34

Mondays to Fridays

until 03 September

Nottingham, Sheffield - Barnsley - Huddersfield and Leeds

		NT	TP	NT	NT	NT	NT	NT	NT	NT	NT	TP	NT	NT	NT	NT	NT	NT	NT	NT	TP	NT
			◇1									◇1									◇1	
Nottingham 6 ⇌	d				09 15									10 15								
Langley Mill	d				09 32									10 32								
Alfreton	d				09 40									10 40								
Chesterfield	d				09 52									10 52								
Dronfield	d				09 59									10 59								
Sheffield 7 29,31 ⇌	a				10 15									11 15								
	d	10 06	10 11	10 14	10 18	10 24	10 36	10 41	10 51	10 57	11 06	11 11	11 14	11 18	11 24	11 36	11 41	11 51	11 57	12 06	12 11	12 14
Meadowhall 4 29,31 ⇌	a	10 11	10 16	10 20	10 23	10 29	10 41	10 46	10 56	11 03	11 11	11 16	11 20	11 23	11 29	11 41	11 46	11 56	12 03	12 11	12 16	12 20
	d	10 12			10 24		10 42		10 57		11 12			11 24		11 42		11 57		12 12		
Chapeltown	d	10 18					10 48				11 18					11 48				12 18		
Elsecar	d	10 23									11 23									12 23		
Wombwell	d	10 27					10 55				11 27					11 55				12 27		
Barnsley	a	10 32			10 40		11 00		11 11		11 32			11 40		12 00		12 11		12 32		
	d	10 33			10 42		11 01		11 12		11 33			11 42		12 01		12 12		12 33		
Dodworth	d						11 07									12 07						
Silkstone Common	d						11 11									12 11						
Penistone	d						11 18									12 18						
Denby Dale	d						11 24									12 24						
Shepley	d						11 29									12 29						
Stocksmoor	d						11 32									12 32						
Brockholes	d						11 36									12 36						
Honley	d						11 38									12 38						
Berry Brow	d						11 41									12 41						
Lockwood	d						11 44									12 44						
Huddersfield	a						11 49									12 49						
Darton	d	10 38									11 38									12 38		
Wakefield Kirkgate 4 31	a	10 49			10 57				11 27		11 49			11 57				12 27		12 49		
	d	10 50			10 58				11 28		11 50			11 58				12 28		12 50		
Normanton	d	10 54									11 54									12 54		
Castleford	a	11 00									12 00									13 00		
Woodlesford	a	11 12									12 12									13 12		
Leeds 10 31	a	11 25			11 18				11 48		12 25			12 18				12 48		13 25		

		NT	NT	NT	NT	NT	NT	NT	TP	NT	NT	NT	NT	NT	NT	NT	NT	NT	TP	NT	NT	NT	NT
									◇1										◇1				
Nottingham 6 ⇌	d	11 15									12 15										13 15		
Langley Mill	d	11 31									12 32										13 32		
Alfreton	d	11 39									12 40										13 40		
Chesterfield	d	11 52									12 52										13 52		
Dronfield	d	11 59									12 59										13 59		
Sheffield 7 29,31 ⇌	a	12 16									13 15										14 15		
	d	12 18	12 24	12 36	12 41	12 51	12 57	13 06	13 11	13 14	13 18	13 24	13 28	13 36	13 41	13 51	13 57	14 06	14 11	14 14	14 18	14 24	14 36
Meadowhall 4 29,31 ⇌	a	12 23	12 29	12 41	12 46	12 56	13 03	13 11	13 16	13 20	13 23	13 29	13 34	13 41	13 46	13 56	14 03	14 11	14 16	14 20	14 23	14 29	14 41
	d	12 24		12 42		12 57		13 12			13 24			13 42		13 57		14 12			14 24		14 42
Chapeltown	d			12 48				13 18						13 48				14 18					14 48
Elsecar	d							13 23										14 23					
Wombwell	d			12 55				13 27						13 55				14 27					14 55
Barnsley	a	12 40		13 00		13 11		13 32			13 40			14 00		14 11		14 32			14 40		15 00
	d	12 42		13 01		13 12		13 33			13 42			14 01		14 12		14 33			14 42		15 01
Dodworth	d			13 07										14 07									15 07
Silkstone Common	d			13 11										14 11									15 11
Penistone	d			13 18										14 18									15 18
Denby Dale	d			13 24										14 24									15 24
Shepley	d			13 29										14 29									15 29
Stocksmoor	d			13 32										14 32									15 32
Brockholes	d			13 36										14 36									15 36
Honley	d			13 38										14 38									15 38
Berry Brow	d			13 41										14 41									15 41
Lockwood	d			13 44										14 44									15 44
Huddersfield	a			13 49										14 49									15 49
Darton	d							13 38										14 38					
Wakefield Kirkgate 4 31	a	12 57				13 27		13 50			13 57					14 27		14 49			14 57		
	d	12 58				13 28		13 50			13 58					14 28		14 50			14 58		
Normanton	d							13 54										14 54					
Castleford	a							14 00										15 00					
Woodlesford	a							14 12										15 12					
Leeds 10 31	a	13 18				13 48		14 25			14 18					14 48		15 25			15 18		

Nottingham, Sheffield - Barnsley - Huddersfield and Leeds

			NT	NT	NT		NT	TP ◇1 🍴	NT	NT	NT	NT	NT	NT	NT		NT	TP ◇1 🍴	NT	NT	NT	NT	NT	NT	NT	NT
Nottingham 8		d								14 15										15 15						
Langley Mill		d								14 30										15 32						
Alfreton		d								14 38										15 40						
Chesterfield		d								14 52										15 51						
Dronfield		d								14 59										15 58						
Sheffield 7	29,31	a								15 15										16 15						
		d	14 41	14 51	14 57		15 06	15 11	15 14	15 18	15 24	15 36	15 41	15 51	15 57		16 06	16 11	16 14	16 18	16 24	16 36	16 41	16 51	16 57	17 06
Meadowhall 4	29,31	a	14 46	14 56	15 03		15 11	15 16	15 20	15 23	15 29	15 41	15 46	15 56	16 03		16 11	16 16	16 20	16 23	16 29	16 41	16 46	16 56	17 03	17 11
		d		14 57			15 12			15 24		15 42		15 57			16 12			16 24		16 42		16 57		17 12
Chapeltown		d					15 18					15 48					16 18					16 48				17 18
Elsecar		d					15 23										16 23					16 53				17 23
Wombwell		d					15 27					15 55					16 27					16 57				17 27
Barnsley		a		15 11			15 32			15 40		16 00		16 11			16 32			16 40		17 02		17 11		17 32
		d		15 12			15 33			15 42		16 01		16 12			16 33			16 42		17 03		17 12		17 33
Dodworth		d										16 07										17 09				
Silkstone Common		d										16 11										17 13				
Penistone		d										16 18										17 20				
Denby Dale		d										16 24										17 26				
Shepley		d										16 29										17 31				
Stocksmoor		d										16 32										17 34				
Brockholes		d										16 36										17 38				
Honley		d										16 38										17 40				
Berry Brow		d										16 41										17 43				
Lockwood		d										16 44										17 46				
Huddersfield		a										16 49										17 50				
Darton		d					15 38										16 38									17 38
Wakefield Kirkgate 4	31	a		15 27			15 49			15 57				16 27			16 49			16 57				17 28		17 49
		d		15 28			15 50			15 58				16 28			16 50			16 58				17 28		17 50
Normanton		d					15 54										16 54									17 54
Castleford		a					16 00										17 00									18 00
Woodlesford		a					16 12										17 12									18 12
Leeds 10	31	a		15 48			16 25			16 19				16 48			17 25			17 19				17 48		18 25

			TP ◇1 🍴	NT	NT	NT	NT	NT	NT	NT	NT	NT	NT	TP ◇1 🍴	NT	NT	NT	NT	NT	NT	NT	NT	NT	NT	NT	NT
Nottingham 8		d		16 15									17 15									18 15				
Langley Mill		d		16 32									17 31									18 32				
Alfreton		d		16 40									17 39									18 40				
Chesterfield		d		16 54									17 52									18 52				
Dronfield		d		17 01									17 59									18 59				
Sheffield 7	29,31	a		17 17									18 15									19 15				
		d	17 11	17 18	17 14	17 27	17 36	17 41	17 51	17 57	18 06	18 14	18 18	18 24	18 29	18 36	18 41	18 51	19 00	19 06	19 18	19 22	19 30	19 36	19 44	19 51
Meadowhall 4	29,31	a	17 16	17 23	17 20	17 32	17 41	17 46	17 56	18 03	18 12	18 20	18 23	18 29	18 35	18 41	18 46	18 56	19 06	19 11	19 24	19 27	19 35	19 41	19 49	19 56
		d		17 24			17 42		17 57		18 12		18 24			18 42		18 57		19 12		19 28		19 42	19 50	19 57
Chapeltown		d					17 48				18 18					18 48				19 18				19 48		
Elsecar		d					17 53				18 23					18 53				19 23				19 53		
Wombwell		d					17 57				18 27					18 57				19 27				19 57		
Barnsley		a		17 40			18 02		18 11		18 33		18 42			19 02		19 14		19 33		19 42		20 02		20 12
		d		17 42			18 03		18 12		18 33		18 42			19 08		19 14		19 33		19 42		20 08		20 12
Dodworth		d					18 09									19 14								20 14		
Silkstone Common		d					18 13									19 18								20 18		
Penistone		d					18b27									19 25								20 25		
Denby Dale		d					18 33									19 31								20 31		
Shepley		d					18 38									19 34								20 36		
Stocksmoor		d					18 41									19 39								20 39		
Brockholes		d					18 45									19 43								20 43		
Honley		d					18 47									19 45								20 45		
Berry Brow		d					18 50									19 48								20 48		
Lockwood		d					18 53									19 51								20 51		
Huddersfield		a					18 57									19 56								20 55		
Darton		d									18 38									19 38						
Wakefield Kirkgate 4	31	a		17 57					18 28		18 50		18 58					19 29		19 50		19 58				20 28
		d		17 58					18 32		18 50		18 58					19 32		19 50		19 58				20 28
Normanton		d									18 54									19 54						
Castleford		a									19 00									20 00						
Woodlesford		a									19 13									20 12						
Leeds 10	31	a		18 18					18 51		19 27		19 23					19 55		20 26		20 19				20 48

b arr. 1820

Nottingham, Sheffield - Barnsley - Huddersfield and Leeds

			NT	NT	TP ◇1	NT	NT	NT	NT	NT	TP FO ◇1	NT	NT	TP FX ◇1	NT	NT FO	NT FX		TP ◇1	NT	NT FO	NT	NT	NT	NT	NT FX
Nottingham 8		d					19 15													21 11						
Langley Mill		d					19 32													21 31						
Alfreton		d					19 40													21 39						
Chesterfield		d					19 52													22 00						
Dronfield		d					19 59													22 07						
Sheffield 7	29,31	a					20 15													22 19						
		d	19 57	20 06	20 11	20 15	20 18	20 27	20 38	20 41	21 11	21 15	21 30	21 34	21 41	22 06	22 06		22 11			22 24	22 34	22 41	23 15	23 24
Meadowhall 4	29,31	a	20 03	20 11	20 16	20 20	20 24	20 34	20 44	20 47	21 16	21 21	21 35	21 39	21 46	22 11	22 11		22 16			22 30	22 39	22 46	23 20	23 29
		d		20 12			20 24			20 47					21 47	22 12	22 12						22 40	22 47		23 30
Chapeltown		d		20 18						20 53					21 53	22 18	22 18							22 53		23 36
Elsecar		d		20 23												22 23	22 23							22 58		23 41
Wombwell		d		20 27						21 00					22 00	22 27	22 27							23 02		23 45
Barnsley		a		20 32			20 40			21 06					22 05	22 32	22 32							23 07		23 50
		d		20 33			20 42			21 08					22 08		22 33							23 08		23 51
Dodworth		d								21 14					22 14									23 14		
Silkstone Common		d								21 18					22 18									23 18		
Penistone		d								21 25					22 25									23 25		
Denby Dale		d								21 31					22 31									23 31		
Shepley		d								21 36					22 36									23 36		
Stocksmoor		d								21 39					22 39									23 39		
Brockholes		d								21 43					22 43									23 43		
Honley		d								21 45					22 45									23 45		
Berry Brow		d								21 48					22 48									23 48		
Lockwood		d								21 51					22 51									23 51		
Huddersfield		a								21 56					22 57									23 55		
Darton		d		20 38													22 38									23 56
Wakefield Kirkgate 4	31	a		20 49			20 57										22 49									00s10
		d		20 50			20 58										22 50				22 50					
Normanton		d		20 54													22 54				22 54					
Castleford		a		21 00													23 00				23 00					
Woodlesford		a		21 12													23 13				23 13					
Leeds 10	31	a		21 26			21 22										23 28				23 28					

			NT
Nottingham 8		d	
Langley Mill		d	
Alfreton		d	
Chesterfield		d	
Dronfield		d	
Sheffield 7	29,31	a	
		d	23 27
Meadowhall 4	29,31	a	23 32
		d	
Chapeltown		d	
Elsecar		d	
Wombwell		d	
Barnsley		a	
		d	
Dodworth		d	
Silkstone Common		d	
Penistone		d	
Denby Dale		d	
Shepley		d	
Stocksmoor		d	
Brockholes		d	
Honley		d	
Berry Brow		d	
Lockwood		d	
Huddersfield		a	
Darton		d	
Wakefield Kirkgate 4	31	a	
		d	
Normanton		d	
Castleford		a	
Woodlesford		a	
Leeds 10	31	a	

Table 34

Nottingham, Sheffield - Barnsley - Huddersfield and Leeds

			NT	NT			NT	NT	NT	NT		NT	NT	NT	NT	NT	TP ◇1	NT	NT	NT		NT	EM ◇	NT	NT
Nottingham 8	d																			06 23			06 40		
Langley Mill	d																			06 38					
Alfreton	d																			06 46			07 02		
Chesterfield	d														06 26					06 58			07 13		
Dronfield	d														06 33					07 05			07 20		
Sheffield 7 29,31	a														06 46					07 18			07 31		
	d		05 16	05 22			05 29	05 36	05 50	06 06		06 18	06 28	06 36	06 49	06 52	06 55	07 06	07 14	07 20		07 24	07 35	07 36	07 41
Meadowhall 4 29,31	a		05 22	05 27			05 34	05 41	05 55	06 11		06 23	06 33	06 41	06 54	06 57	07 00	07 11	07 20	07 25		07 30		07 41	07 46
	d		05 22					05 42	05 56	06 12				06 42	06 55			07 12		07 26				07 42	
Chapeltown	d		05 28					05 48		06 18				06 48				07 18						07 48	
Elsecar	d		05 33							06 23								07 23							
Wombwell	d		05 37					05 55		06 27				06 55				07 27						07 55	
Barnsley	a		05 43					06 00	06 10	06 32				07 00	07 09			07 32		07 41				08 00	
	d							06 01	06 10	06 33				07 01	07 12			07 33		07 42				08 01	
Dodworth	d							06 07						07 07										08 07	
Silkstone Common	d							06 11						07 11										08 11	
Penistone	d							06 18						07 18										08 18	
Denby Dale	d							06 24						07 24										08 24	
Shepley	d							06 29						07 29										08 29	
Stocksmoor	d							06 32						07 32										08 32	
Brockholes	d							06 36						07 36										08 36	
Honley	d							06 38						07 38										08 38	
Berry Brow	d							06 41						07 41										08 41	
Lockwood	d							06 44						07 44										08 44	
Huddersfield	a							06 54						07 54										08 53	
Darton	d									06 38								07 38							
Wakefield Kirkgate 4 31	a								06 27	06 49					07 27			07 49		07 57					
	d								06 28	06 50					07 28			07 50		07 58					
Normanton	d								06 33	06 54					07 33			07 54							
Castleford	a									07 00								08 00							
Woodlesford	a									07 11								08 12							
Leeds 10 31	a								06 49	07 28					07 51			08 25	08 30	08 21					

		NT	EM ◇1	NT	TP ◇1	NT		NT	NT	NT	EM ◇	NT	NT	NT	NT	TP ◇1		NT	NT	NT	NT	NT	NT	NT	NT
Nottingham 8	d							07 13			07 45								08 11						
Langley Mill	d							07 29											08 31						
Alfreton	d							07 37			08 07								08 39						
Chesterfield	d		07 42					07 50			08 18								08 51						
Dronfield	d		07 49								08 25								08 58						
Sheffield 7 29,31	a		08 00					08 08			08 38								09 15						
	d	07 51		08 06	08 11	08 14		08 18	08 25	08 36	08 42	08 41	08 51	08 57	09 06	09 11		09 14	09 18	09 24	09 29	09 36	09 41	09 51	09 57
Meadowhall 4 29,31	a	07 57		08 11	08 16	08 20		08 24	08 30	08 41		08 46	08 56	09 03	09 11	09 16		09 20	09 23	09 29	09 34	09 41	09 46	09 56	10 03
	d	07 57		08 12				08 24		08 42			08 57		09 12				09 24			09 42		09 57	
Chapeltown	d			08 18						08 48					09 18							09 48			
Elsecar	d			08 23											09 23										
Wombwell	d			08 27						08 55					09 27							09 55			
Barnsley	a	08 11		08 32				08 40		09 00			09 11		09 32				09 40			10 00		10 11	
	d	08 12		08 33				08 42		09 01			09 12		09 33				09 42			10 01		10 12	
Dodworth	d									09 07												10 07			
Silkstone Common	d									09 11												10 11			
Penistone	d									09 18												10 18			
Denby Dale	d									09 24												10 24			
Shepley	d									09 29												10 29			
Stocksmoor	d									09 32												10 32			
Brockholes	d									09 36												10 36			
Honley	d									09 38												10 38			
Berry Brow	d									09 41												10 41			
Lockwood	d									09 44												10 44			
Huddersfield	a									09 50												10 53			
Darton	d			08 38											09 38										
Wakefield Kirkgate 4 31	a	08 27		08 49				08 57					09 27		09 49				09 57					10 27	
	d	08 28		08 50				08 58					09 28		09 50				09 58					10 28	
Normanton	d			08 54											09 54										
Castleford	a			09 00											10 00										
Woodlesford	a			09 12											10 12										
Leeds 10 31	a	08 49		09 25				09 19					09 49		10 25				10 18					10 48	

Table 34

Nottingham, Sheffield - Barnsley - Huddersfield and Leeds

		NT		TP ◇1	NT	NT	NT	NT	NT	NT	NT	NT		TP ◇1	NT	NT	NT	NT	NT	NT	NT	NT		TP ◇1	NT
Nottingham 8	d					09 15										10 15									
Langley Mill	d					09 32										10 32									
Alfreton	d					09 40										10 40									
Chesterfield	d					09 52										10 52									
Dronfield	d					09 59										10 59									
Sheffield 7 29,31	a					10 15										11 15									
	d	10 06		10 11	10 14	10 18	10 24	10 36	10 41	10 51	10 57	11 06		11 11	11 14	11 18	11 24	11 36	11 41	11 51	11 57	12 06		12 11	12 14
Meadowhall 4 29,31	a	10 11		10 16	10 20	10 23	10 29	10 41	10 46	10 56	11 03	11 11		11 16	11 20	11 23	11 29	11 41	11 46	11 56	12 03	12 11		12 16	12 20
	d	10 12				10 24		10 42		10 57		11 12				11 24		11 42		11 57		12 12			
Chapeltown	d	10 18						10 48				11 18						11 48				12 18			
Elsecar	d	10 23										11 23										12 23			
Wombwell	d	10 27						10 55				11 27						11 55				12 27			
Barnsley	a	10 32				10 40		11 00		11 11		11 32				11 40		12 00		12 11		12 32			
	d	10 33				10 42		11 01		11 12		11 33				11 42		12 01		12 12		12 33			
Dodworth	d							11 07										12 07							
Silkstone Common	d							11 11										12 11							
Penistone	d							11 18										12 18							
Denby Dale	d							11 24										12 24							
Shepley	d							11 29										12 29							
Stocksmoor	d							11 32										12 32							
Brockholes	d							11 36										12 36							
Honley	d							11 38										12 38							
Berry Brow	d							11 41										12 41							
Lockwood	d							11 44										12 44							
Huddersfield	a							11 53										12 52							
Darton	d	10 38										11 38										12 38			
Wakefield Kirkgate 4 31	a	10 49				10 57				11 27		11 49				11 57				12 27		12 49			
	d	10 50				10 58				11 28		11 50				11 58				12 28		12 50			
Normanton	d	10 54										11 54										12 54			
Castleford	a	11 00										12 00										13 00			
Woodlesford	a	11 12										12 12										13 12			
Leeds 10 31	a	11 25				11 18				11 48		12 25				12 18				12 48		13 25			

		NT	NT	NT	NT	NT	NT	NT		TP ◇1	NT	NT	NT	NT	NT	NT	NT	NT		NT	TP ◇1	NT	NT	NT	NT
Nottingham 8	d	11 15										12 15											13 15		
Langley Mill	d	11 31										12 32											13 32		
Alfreton	d	11 39										12 40											13 40		
Chesterfield	d	11 52										12 52											13 52		
Dronfield	d	11 59										12 59											13 59		
Sheffield 7 29,31	a	12 16										13 15											14 15		
	d	12 18	12 24	12 36	12 41	12 51	12 57	13 06		13 11	13 14	13 18	13 24	13 28	13 36	13 41	13 51	13 57		14 06	14 11	14 14	14 18	14 24	14 36
Meadowhall 4 29,31	a	12 23	12 29	12 41	12 46	12 56	13 03	13 11		13 16	13 20	13 23	13 29	13 34	13 41	13 46	13 56	14 03		14 11	14 16	14 20	14 23	14 29	14 41
	d	12 24		12 42		12 57		13 12				13 24			13 42		13 57			14 12			14 24		14 42
Chapeltown	d			12 48				13 18							13 48					14 18					14 48
Elsecar	d							13 23												14 23					
Wombwell	d			12 55				13 27							13 55					14 27					14 55
Barnsley	a	12 40		13 00		13 11		13 32				13 40			14 00		14 11			14 32			14 40		15 00
	d	12 42		13 01		13 12		13 33				13 42			14 01		14 12			14 33			14 42		15 01
Dodworth	d			13 07											14 07										15 07
Silkstone Common	d			13 11											14 11										15 11
Penistone	d			13 18											14 18										15 18
Denby Dale	d			13 24											14 24										15 24
Shepley	d			13 29											14 29										15 29
Stocksmoor	d			13 32											14 32										15 32
Brockholes	d			13 36											14 36										15 36
Honley	d			13 38											14 38										15 38
Berry Brow	d			13 41											14 41										15 41
Lockwood	d			13 44											14 44										15 44
Huddersfield	a			13 53											14 53										15 53
Darton	d							13 38												14 38					
Wakefield Kirkgate 4 31	a	12 57				13 27		13 50				13 57					14 27			14 49			14 57		
	d	12 58				13 28		13 50				13 58					14 28			14 50			14 58		
Normanton	d							13 54												14 54					
Castleford	a							14 00												15 00					
Woodlesford	a							14 12												15 12					
Leeds 10 31	a	13 18				13 48		14 25				14 18					14 48			15 25			15 18		

Nottingham, Sheffield - Barnsley - Huddersfield and Leeds

Mondays to Fridays
from 06 September

		NT	NT	NT	NT	TP ◇1 ⚒	NT	NT	NT	NT	NT	NT	NT	NT	TP ◇1 ⚒	NT	NT	NT	NT	NT	NT	NT	NT
Nottingham 8	d							14 15								15 15							
Langley Mill	d							14 30								15 32							
Alfreton	d							14 38								15 40							
Chesterfield	d							14 52								15 51							
Dronfield	d							14 59								15 58							
Sheffield 7 29,31	a							15 15								16 15							
	d	14 41	14 51	14 57	15 06	15 11	15 14	15 18	15 24	15 36	15 41	15 51	15 57	16 06	16 11	16 18	16 14	16 24	16 36	16 41	16 51	16 57	17 06
Meadowhall 4 29,31	a	14 46	14 56	15 03	15 11	15 16	15 20	15 23	15 29	15 41	15 46	15 56	16 03	16 11	16 16	16 23	16 20	16 29	16 41	16 46	16 56	17 03	17 11
	d		14 57		15 12			15 24		15 42		15 57		16 12		16 24			16 42		16 57		17 12
Chapeltown	d				15 18					15 48				16 18					16 48				17 18
Elsecar	d				15 23									16 23					16 53				17 23
Wombwell	d				15 27					15 55				16 27					16 57				17 27
Barnsley	a		15 11		15 32			15 40		16 00		16 11		16 32		16 40			17 02		17 11		17 32
	d		15 12		15 33			15 42		16 01		16 12		16 33		16 42			17 03		17 12		17 33
Dodworth	d									16 07									17 09				
Silkstone Common	d									16 11									17 13				
Penistone	d									16 18									17 20				
Denby Dale	d									16 24									17 26				
Shepley	d									16 29									17 31				
Stocksmoor	d									16 32									17 34				
Brockholes	d									16 36									17 38				
Honley	d									16 38									17 40				
Berry Brow	d									16 41									17 43				
Lockwood	d									16 44									17 46				
Huddersfield	a									16 52									17 51				
Darton	d				15 38									16 38									17 38
Wakefield Kirkgate 4 31	a		15 27		15 49			15 57				16 27		16 49		16 57					17 28		17 49
	d		15 28		15 50			15 58				16 28		16 50		16 58					17 28		17 50
Normanton	d				15 54									16 54									17 54
Castleford	a				16 00									17 00									18 00
Woodlesford	a				16 12									17 12									18 12
Leeds 10 31	a		15 48		16 25			16 19				16 48		17 25		17 19					17 48		18 25

		TP ◇1 ⚒	NT	NT	NT	NT	NT	NT	NT	NT	NT	NT	TP ◇1 ⚒	NT	NT	NT	NT	NT	NT	NT	NT	NT	NT	NT	NT
Nottingham 8	d			16 15								17 15									18 15				
Langley Mill	d			16 32								17 31									18 32				
Alfreton	d			16 40								17 39									18 40				
Chesterfield	d			16 54								17 52									18 52				
Dronfield	d			17 01								17 59									18 59				
Sheffield 7 29,31	a			17 17								18 15									19 15				
	d	17 11	17 14	17 18	17 27	17 36	17 41	17 51	17 57	18 06	18 14	18 18	18 24	18 29	18 36	18 41	18 51	19 00	19 06	19 18	19 22	19 30	19 36	19 44	19 51
Meadowhall 4 29,31	a	17 16	17 20	17 23	17 32	17 41	17 46	17 56	18 03	18 12	18 20	18 23	18 29	18 35	18 41	18 46	18 56	19 06	19 11	19 24	19 27	19 35	19 41	19 49	19 56
	d			17 24		17 42		17 57		18 12		18 24			18 42		18 57		19 12		19 28		19 42		19 57
Chapeltown	d					17 48				18 18					18 48				19 18				19 48		
Elsecar	d					17 53				18 23					18 53				19 23				19 53		
Wombwell	d					17 57				18 27					18 57				19 27				19 57		
Barnsley	a			17 40		18 02		18 11		18 33		18 42			19 02		19 14		19 33		19 42		20 02		20 12
	d			17 42		18 03		18 12		18 33		18 42			19 08		19 14		19 33		19 42		20 08		20 12
Dodworth	d					18 09									19 14								20 14		
Silkstone Common	d					18 13									19 18								20 18		
Penistone	d					18b27									19 25								20 25		
Denby Dale	d					18 33									19 31								20 31		
Shepley	d					18 38									19 36								20 36		
Stocksmoor	d					18 41									19 39								20 39		
Brockholes	d					18 45									19 43								20 43		
Honley	d					18 47									19 45								20 45		
Berry Brow	d					18 50									19 48								20 48		
Lockwood	d					18 53									19 51								20 51		
Huddersfield	a					19 02									20 01								21 00		
Darton	d									18 38									19 38						
Wakefield Kirkgate 4 31	a			17 57				18 28		18 50		18 58					19 29		19 50		19 58				20 28
	d			17 58				18 32		18 50		18 58					19 32		19 50		19 58				20 28
Normanton	d									18 54									19 54						
Castleford	a									19 00									20 00						
Woodlesford	a									19 13									20 12						
Leeds 10 31	a			18 18				18 51		19 27	19 33	19 23					19 55		20 26	20 36	20 19				20 48

b arr. 1820

Table 34

Nottingham, Sheffield - Barnsley - Huddersfield and Leeds

Mondays to Fridays
from 06 September

		NT	NT	TP ◇1	NT	NT	NT	NT	NT	TP FO ◇1	NT	NT	TP FX ◇1	NT	NT FO	NT FX	TP ◇1	NT	NT FO	NT	NT	NT	NT	NT FX
Nottingham 8	d					19 15												21 11						
Langley Mill	d					19 32												21 31						
Alfreton	d					19 40												21 39						
Chesterfield	d					19 52												22 00						
Dronfield	d					19 59												22 07						
Sheffield 7 29,31	a					20 15												22 19						
	d	19 57	20 06	20 11	20 15	20 18	20 27	20 38	20 41	21 11	21 15	21 30	21 34	21 41	22 06	22 06	22 11			22 24	22 34	22 41	23 15	23 24
Meadowhall 4 29,31	a	20 03	20 11	20 16	20 20	20 24	20 34	20 44	20 47	21 16	21 21	21 35	21 39	21 46	22 11	22 11	22 16			22 30	22 39	22 46	23 20	23 29
	d		20 12			20 24			20 47					21 47	22 12	22 12						22 47		23 30
Chapeltown	d		20 18						20 53					21 53	22 18	22 18						22 53		23 36
Elsecar	d		20 23												22 23	22 23						22 58		23 41
Wombwell	d		20 27						21 00					22 00	22 27	22 27						23 02		23 45
Barnsley	a		20 32			20 40			21 06					22 05	22 32	22 32						23 07		23 50
	d		20 33			20 42			21 08					22 08		22 33						23 08		23 51
Dodworth	d								21 14					22 14								23 14		
Silkstone Common	d								21 18					22 18								23 18		
Penistone	d								21 25					22 25								23 25		
Denby Dale	d								21 31					22 31								23 31		
Shepley	d								21 36					22 36								23 36		
Stocksmoor	d								21 39					22 39								23 39		
Brockholes	d								21 43					22 43								23 43		
Honley	d								21 45					22 45								23 45		
Berry Brow	d								21 48					22 48								23 48		
Lockwood	d								21 51					22 51								23 51		
Huddersfield	a								22 00					23 01								23 55		
Darton	d		20 38													22 38								23 56
Wakefield Kirkgate 4 31	a		20 49			20 57										22 49								00s10
	d		20 50			20 58										22 50			22 50					00s13
Normanton	d		20 54													22 54			22 54					
Castleford	a		21 00													23 00			23 00					
Woodlesford	a		21 12													23 13			23 13					
Leeds 10 31	a		21 26			21 22										23 28			23 28					

		NT
Nottingham 8	d	
Langley Mill	d	
Alfreton	d	
Chesterfield	d	
Dronfield	d	
Sheffield 7 29,31	a	
	d	23 27
Meadowhall 4 29,31	a	23 32
	d	
Chapeltown	d	
Elsecar	d	
Wombwell	d	
Barnsley	a	
	d	
Dodworth	d	
Silkstone Common	d	
Penistone	d	
Denby Dale	d	
Shepley	d	
Stocksmoor	d	
Brockholes	d	
Honley	d	
Berry Brow	d	
Lockwood	d	
Huddersfield	a	
Darton	d	
Wakefield Kirkgate 4 31	a	
	d	
Normanton	d	
Castleford	a	
Woodlesford	a	
Leeds 10 31	a	

Nottingham, Sheffield - Barnsley - Huddersfield and Leeds

		NT	NT	NT	NT	NT	NT	NT	NT	TP	NT	NT	NT	EM	NT	NT	NT	EM	NT	TP	NT	NT	NT
										◇1				◇				◇1 ⌷		◇1			
Nottingham 8	d													06 40								07 13	
Langley Mill	d																					07 29	
Alfreton	d													07 02								07 37	
Chesterfield	d													07 13				07 42				07 50	
Dronfield	d													07 20				07 49					
Sheffield 7 29,31	a													07 31				07 59				08 08	
	d	05 16	05 29	05 43	06 06	06 18	06 28	06 36	06 52	06 55	07 06	07 14	07 24		07 36	07 41	07 51		08 06	08 11	08 14	08 18	08 25
Meadowhall 4 29,31	a	05 21	05 34	05 48	06 11	06 23	06 33	06 41	06 57	07 00	07 11	07 20	07 30		07 41	07 46	07 57		08 11	08 16	08 20	08 24	08 30
	d	05 22		05 49	06 12			06 42			07 12				07 42		07 57		08 12			08 24	
Chapeltown	d	05 28		05 55	06 18			06 48			07 18				07 48				08 18				
Elsecar	d	05 33		06 01	06 23						07 23								08 23				
Wombwell	d	05 37		06 05	06 27			06 55			07 27				07 55				08 27				
Barnsley	a	05 43		06 11	06 32			07 00			07 32				08 00		08 11		08 32			08 40	
	d				06 33			07 01			07 33				08 01		08 12		08 33			08 42	
Dodworth	d							07 07							08 07								
Silkstone Common	d							07 11							08 11								
Penistone	d							07 18							08 18								
Denby Dale	d							07 24							08 24								
Shepley	d							07 29							08 29								
Stocksmoor	d							07 32							08 32								
Brockholes	d							07 36							08 36								
Honley	d							07 38							08 38								
Berry Brow	d							07 41							08 41								
Lockwood	d							07 44							08 44								
Huddersfield	a							07 49							08 49								
Darton	d				06 38						07 38								08 38				
Wakefield Kirkgate 4 31	a				06 49						07 49						08 27		08 49			08 57	
	d				06 50						07 50						08 28		08 50			08 58	
Normanton	d				06 54						07 54								08 54				
Castleford	a				07 00						08 00								09 00				
Woodlesford	a				07 12						08 12								09 12				
Leeds 10 31	a				07 28						08 25						08 49		09 25			09 19	

		NT	EM	NT	NT	NT	NT	TP	NT	NT	NT	NT	NT	NT	NT	NT	NT	TP	NT	NT	NT	NT	NT
			◇					◇1 ⌶										◇1 ⌶					
Nottingham 8	d		07 45							08 11										09 15			
Langley Mill	d									08 31										09 32			
Alfreton	d		08 07							08 39										09 40			
Chesterfield	d		08 18							08 51										09 52			
Dronfield	d		08 25							08 58										09 59			
Sheffield 7 29,31	a		08 38							09 15										10 15			
	d	08 36	08 42	08 41	08 51	08 57	09 06	09 11	09 14	09 18	09 25	09 31	09 36	09 41	09 51	09 57	10 06	10 11	10 14	10 18	10 24	10 36	10 41
Meadowhall 4 29,31	a	08 41		08 46	08 56	09 03	09 11	09 16	09 20	09 23	09 32	09 37	09 41	09 46	09 56	10 03	10 11	10 16	10 20	10 23	10 29	10 41	10 46
	d	08 42			08 57		09 12			09 24			09 42		09 57		10 12			10 24		10 42	
Chapeltown	d	08 48					09 18						09 48				10 18					10 48	
Elsecar	d						09 23										10 23						
Wombwell	d	08 55					09 27						09 55				10 27					10 55	
Barnsley	a	09 00			09 11		09 32			09 40			10 00		10 11		10 32			10 40		11 00	
	d	09 01			09 12		09 33			09 42			10 01		10 12		10 33			10 42		11 01	
Dodworth	d	09 07											10 07									11 07	
Silkstone Common	d	09 11											10 11									11 11	
Penistone	d	09 18											10 18									11 18	
Denby Dale	d	09 24											10 24									11 24	
Shepley	d	09 29											10 29									11 29	
Stocksmoor	d	09 32											10 32									11 32	
Brockholes	d	09 36											10 36									11 36	
Honley	d	09 38											10 38									11 38	
Berry Brow	d	09 41											10 41									11 41	
Lockwood	d	09 44											10 44									11 44	
Huddersfield	a	09 49											10 49									11 49	
Darton	d						09 38										10 38						
Wakefield Kirkgate 4 31	a				09 27		09 49			09 57					10 27		10 49			10 57			
	d				09 28		09 50			09 58					10 28		10 50			10 58			
Normanton	d						09 54										10 54						
Castleford	a						10 00										11 00						
Woodlesford	a						10 12										11 12						
Leeds 10 31	a				09 49		10 25			10 18					10 48		11 25			11 18			

Table 34

Saturdays
until 04 September

Nottingham, Sheffield - Barnsley - Huddersfield and Leeds

		NT	NT	NT	TP	NT	NT	NT	NT	NT	NT	NT	NT	TP	NT	NT	NT	NT	NT	NT	NT	NT
					◇1 ⌶									◇1 ⌶								
Nottingham 8	d						10 15									11 15						
Langley Mill	d						10 32									11 31						
Alfreton	d						10 40									11 39						
Chesterfield	d						10 52									11 52						
Dronfield	d						10 59															
Sheffield 7 29,31	a						11 15									12 16						
	d	10 51	10 57	11 06	11 11	11 14	11 18	11 24	11 36	11 41	11 51	11 57	12 06	12 11	12 14	12 18	12 24	12 36	12 41	12 51	12 57	13 06
Meadowhall 4 29,31	a	10 56	11 03	11 11	11 16	11 20	11 23	11 29	11 41	11 46	11 56	12 03	12 11	12 16	12 20	12 23	12 29	12 41	12 46	12 56	13 03	13 11
	d	10 57		11 12			11 24		11 42		11 57		12 12			12 24		12 42		12 57		13 12
Chapeltown	d			11 18					11 48				12 18					12 48				13 18
Elsecar	d			11 23									12 23									13 23
Wombwell	d			11 27					11 55				12 27					12 55				13 27
Barnsley	a	11 11		11 32			11 40		12 00		12 11		12 32			12 40		13 00		13 11		13 32
	d	11 12		11 33			11 42		12 01		12 12		12 33			12 42		13 01		13 12		13 33
Dodworth	d								12 07									13 07				
Silkstone Common	d								12 11									13 11				
Penistone	d								12 18									13 18				
Denby Dale	d								12 24									13 24				
Shepley	d								12 29									13 29				
Stocksmoor	d								12 32									13 32				
Brockholes	d								12 36									13 36				
Honley	d								12 38									13 38				
Berry Brow	d								12 41									13 41				
Lockwood	d								12 44									13 44				
Huddersfield	a								12 49									13 49				
Darton	d			11 38									12 38									13 38
Wakefield Kirkgate 4 31	a	11 27		11 49			11 57				12 27		12 49			12 57				13 27		13 50
	d	11 28		11 50			11 58				12 28		12 50			12 58				13 28		13 50
Normanton	d			11 54									12 54									13 54
Castleford	a			12 00									12 59									14 00
Woodlesford	a			12 12									13 12									14 12
Leeds 10 31	a	11 48		12 25			12 18				12 48		13 25			13 18				13 48		14 25

		TP	NT	NT	NT	NT	NT	NT	NT	NT	NT	TP	NT	NT	NT	NT	NT	NT	NT	NT	TP	NT	NT
		◇1 ⌶										◇1 ⌶									◇1 ⌶		
Nottingham 8	d			12 15										13 15									14 15
Langley Mill	d			12 32										13 32									14 30
Alfreton	d			12 40										13 40									14 38
Chesterfield	d			12 52										13 52									14 52
Dronfield	d			12 59										13 59									14 59
Sheffield 7 29,31	a			13 15										14 15									15 15
	d	13 11	13 14	13 18	13 24	13 28	13 36	13 41	13 51	13 57	14 06	14 11	14 14	14 18	14 24	14 36	14 41	14 51	14 57	15 06	15 11	15 14	15 18
Meadowhall 4 29,31	a	13 16	13 20	13 23	13 29	13 34	13 41	13 46	13 56	14 03	14 11	14 16	14 20	14 23	14 29	14 41	14 46	14 56	15 03	15 11	15 16	15 20	15 23
	d			13 24			13 42		13 57		14 12			14 24		14 42		14 57		15 12			15 24
Chapeltown	d						13 48				14 18					14 48				15 18			
Elsecar	d										14 23									15 23			
Wombwell	d						13 55				14 27					14 55				15 27			
Barnsley	a			13 40			14 00		14 11		14 32			14 40		15 00		15 11		15 32			15 40
	d			13 42			14 01		14 12		14 33			14 42		15 01		15 12		15 33			15 42
Dodworth	d						14 07									15 07							
Silkstone Common	d						14 11									15 11							
Penistone	d						14 18									15 18							
Denby Dale	d						14 24									15 24							
Shepley	d						14 29									15 29							
Stocksmoor	d						14 32									15 32							
Brockholes	d						14 36									15 36							
Honley	d						14 38									15 38							
Berry Brow	d						14 41									15 41							
Lockwood	d						14 44									15 44							
Huddersfield	a						14 49									15 49							
Darton	d										14 38									15 38			
Wakefield Kirkgate 4 31	a			13 57					14 27		14 49			14 57				15 27		15 49			15 57
	d			13 58					14 28		14 50			14 58				15 28		15 50			15 58
Normanton	d										14 54									15 54			
Castleford	a										15 00									16 00			
Woodlesford	a										15 12									16 12			
Leeds 10 31	a			14 18					14 48		15 25			15 18				15 48		16 25		16 30	16 19

Table 34

Saturdays
until 04 September

Nottingham, Sheffield - Barnsley - Huddersfield and Leeds

		NT	NT	NT		NT	NT	NT	TP ◇1	NT	NT	NT	NT	NT		NT	NT	NT	TP ◇1	NT	NT	NT	NT	NT	NT
Nottingham 8	d										15 15										16 15				
Langley Mill	d										15 32										16 32				
Alfreton	d										15 40										16 40				
Chesterfield	d										15 51										16 54				
Dronfield	d										15 58										17 01				
Sheffield 7 29,31	a										16 15										17 15				
	d	15 24	15 36	15 41		15 51	15 57	16 06	16 11	16 14	16 18	16 24	16 36	16 41		16 51	16 57	17 06	17 11	17 14	17 18	17 27	17 36	17 41	17 51
Meadowhall 4 29,31	a	15 29	15 41	15 46		15 56	16 03	16 11	16 16	16 20	16 23	16 29	16 41	16 46		16 56	17 03	17 11	17 16	17 21	17 23	17 32	17 41	17 46	17 56
	d		15 42			15 57		16 12			16 24		16 42			16 57		17 12			17 24		17 42		17 57
Chapeltown	d		15 48					16 18					16 48					17 18					17 48		
Elsecar	d							16 23					16 53					17 23					17 53		
Wombwell	d		15 55					16 27					16 57					17 27					17 57		
Barnsley	a		16 00			16 11		16 32			16 40		17 02			17 11		17 32			17 40		18 02		18 11
	d		16 01			16 12		16 33			16 42		17 03			17 12		17 33			17 42		18 03		18 12
Dodworth	d		16 07										17 09										18 09		
Silkstone Common	d		16 11										17 13										18 13		
Penistone	d		16 18										17 20										18 20		
Denby Dale	d		16 24										17 26										18 26		
Shepley	d		16 29										17 31										18 31		
Stocksmoor	d		16 32										17 34										18 34		
Brockholes	d		16 36										17 38										18 38		
Honley	d		16 38										17 40										18 40		
Berry Brow	d		16 41										17 43										18 43		
Lockwood	d		16 44										17 46										18 46		
Huddersfield	a		16 49										17 50										18 51		
Darton	d							16 38										17 38							
Wakefield Kirkgate 4 31	a					16 27		16 49			16 57					17 28		17 49			17 57				18 28
	d					16 28		16 50			16 58					17 28		17 50			17 58				18 32
Normanton	d							16 54										17 54							
Castleford	a							17 00										18 00							
Woodlesford	a							17 12										18 12							
Leeds 10 31	a					16 48		17 25			17 18					17 48		18 25			18 18				18 51

		NT	NT	NT	NT	TP ◇1	NT	NT	NT	NT	NT	NT	TP ◇1	NT	NT	NT	NT	NT	NT	NT	NT	TP ◇1	NT	NT	NT
Nottingham 8	d				17 15										18 15									19 15	
Langley Mill	d				17 31										18 32									19 32	
Alfreton	d				17 39										18 40									19 40	
Chesterfield	d				17 52										18 52									19 52	
Dronfield	d				17 59										18 59									19 59	
Sheffield 7 29,31	a				18 15										19 15									20 15	
	d	17 57	18 06	18 14	18 18	18 24	18 29	18 36	18 41	18 51	19 00	19 06	19 11	19 14	19 18	19 30	19 36	19 44	19 51	19 57	20 06	20 11	20 15	20 18	20 27
Meadowhall 4 29,31	a	18 03	18 12	18 20	18 23	18 29	18 34	18 41	18 46	18 56	19 06	19 11	19 16	19 20	19 23	19 35	19 41	19 49	19 56	20 03	20 11	20 16	20 20	20 24	20 35
	d		18 12		18 24			18 42		18 57		19 12			19 24		19 42		19 57		20 12			20 24	
Chapeltown	d		18 18					18 48				19 18					19 48				20 18				
Elsecar	d		18 23					18 53				19 23					19 53				20 23				
Wombwell	d		18 27					18 57				19 27					19 57				20 27				
Barnsley	a		18 33		18 42			19 02		19 14		19 33			19 42		20 02		20 12		20 32			20 42	
	d		18 33		18 42			19 03		19 14		19 33			19 42		20 08		20 12		20 33			20 42	
Dodworth	d							19 09									20 14								
Silkstone Common	d							19 13									20 18								
Penistone	d							19 20									20 25								
Denby Dale	d							19 26									20 31								
Shepley	d							19 31									20 36								
Stocksmoor	d							19 34									20 39								
Brockholes	d							19 38									20 43								
Honley	d							19 41									20 45								
Berry Brow	d							19 44									20 48								
Lockwood	d							19 46									20 51								
Huddersfield	a							19 51									20 55								
Darton	d		18 38									19 38									20 38				
Wakefield Kirkgate 4 31	a		18 50		18 58					19 29		19 50			19 58				20 28		20 49			20 57	
	d		18 50		18 58					19 32		19 50			19 58				20 28		20 50			20 58	
Normanton	d		18 54									19 54									20 54				
Castleford	a		19 00									20 00									21 00				
Woodlesford	a		19 13									20 12									21 12				
Leeds 10 31	a		19 27		19 23					19 55		20 26			20 19				20 48		21 26			21 22	

Table 34

Saturdays
until 04 September

Nottingham, Sheffield - Barnsley - Huddersfield and Leeds

		NT	NT	NT	NT	NT	TP ◇1	NT	NT	TP ◇1	NT	NT	NT	NT	NT	NT
Nottingham 8	d										21 15					
Langley Mill	d										21 31					
Alfreton	d										21 39					
Chesterfield	d										21 50					
Dronfield	d										21 57					
Sheffield 7 29,31	a										22 13					
	d	20 38	20 41	21 06	21 15	21 30	21 34	21 41	22 06	22 11		22 30		22 34	22 41	23 26
Meadowhall 4 29,31	a	20 43	20 47	21 11	21 21	21 36	21 39	21 46	22 11	22 16		22 35		22 39	22 46	23 31
	d		20 47	21 12				21 47	22 12						22 47	
Chapeltown	d		20 53	21 18				21 53	22 18						22 53	
Elsecar	d			21 23					22 23						22 58	
Wombwell	d		21 00	21 27				22 00	22 27						23 02	
Barnsley	a		21 07	21 33				22 05	22 32						23 07	
	d		21 08	21 33				22 08							23 08	
Dodworth	d		21 14					22 14							23 14	
Silkstone Common	d		21 18					22 18							23 18	
Penistone	d		21 25					22 25							23 25	
Denby Dale	d		21 31					22 31							23 31	
Shepley	d		21 36					22 36							23 36	
Stocksmoor	d		21 39					22 39							23 39	
Brockholes	d		21 43					22 43							23 43	
Honley	d		21 45					22 45							23 45	
Berry Brow	d		21 48					22 48							23 48	
Lockwood	d		21 51					22 51							23 51	
Huddersfield	a		21 56					22 56							23 59	
Darton	d			21 38												
Wakefield Kirkgate 4 31	a			21 52												
	d			21 52									22 50			
Normanton	d			21 57									22 54			
Castleford	a			22 04									23 00			
Woodlesford	a			22 14									23 13			
Leeds 10 31	a			22 29									23 28			

Saturdays
from 11 September

		NT	NT	NT	NT	NT	NT	NT	NT	TP ◇1	NT	NT	NT	EM ◇	NT	NT	NT	EM ◇1	NT	TP ◇1	NT	NT	NT
Nottingham 8	d													06 40								07 13	
Langley Mill	d																					07 29	
Alfreton	d													07 02								07 37	
Chesterfield	d													07 13				07 42				07 50	
Dronfield	d													07 20				07 49					
Sheffield 7 29,31	a													07 31				07 59				08 08	
	d	05 16	05 29	05 43	06 06	06 18	06 28	06 36	06 52	06 55	07 06	07 14	07 24	07 35	07 36	07 41	07 51		08 06	08 11	08 14	08 18	08 25
Meadowhall 4 29,31	a	05 21	05 34	05 48	06 11	06 23	06 33	06 41	06 57	07 00	07 11	07 20	07 30		07 41	07 46	07 57		08 11	08 16	08 20	08 24	08 30
	d	05 22		05 49	06 12			06 42			07 12				07 42		07 57		08 12			08 24	
Chapeltown	d	05 28		05 55	06 18			06 48			07 18				07 48				08 18				
Elsecar	d	05 33		06 01	06 23						07 23								08 23				
Wombwell	d	05 37		06 05	06 27			06 55			07 27				07 55				08 27				
Barnsley	a	05 43		06 11	06 32			07 00			07 32				08 00		08 11		08 32			08 40	
	d				06 33			07 01			07 33				08 01		08 12		08 33			08 42	
Dodworth	d							07 07							08 07								
Silkstone Common	d							07 11							08 11								
Penistone	d							07 18							08 18								
Denby Dale	d							07 24							08 24								
Shepley	d							07 29							08 29								
Stocksmoor	d							07 32							08 32								
Brockholes	d							07 36							08 36								
Honley	d							07 38							08 38								
Berry Brow	d							07 41							08 41								
Lockwood	d							07 44							08 44								
Huddersfield	a							07 54							08 53								
Darton	d				06 38						07 38								08 38				
Wakefield Kirkgate 4 31	a				06 49						07 49						08 27		08 49			08 57	
	d				06 50						07 50						08 28		08 50			08 58	
Normanton	d				06 54						07 54								08 54				
Castleford	a				07 00						08 00								09 00				
Woodlesford	a				07 12						08 12								09 12				
Leeds 10 31	a				07 28						08 25						08 49		09 25		09 30	09 19	

Table 34

Saturdays from 11 September

Nottingham, Sheffield - Barnsley - Huddersfield and Leeds

		NT	EM ◇	NT	NT	NT	NT	TP ◇1 ✠	NT	NT	NT	NT	NT	NT	NT	NT	NT	TP ◇1 ✠	NT	NT	NT	NT	NT
Nottingham 8	d		07 45							08 11										09 15			
Langley Mill	d									08 31										09 32			
Alfreton	d		08 07							08 39										09 40			
Chesterfield	d		08 18							08 51										09 52			
Dronfield	d		08 25							08 58										09 59			
Sheffield 7 29,31	a		08 38							09 15										10 15			
	d	08 36		08 41	08 51	08 57	09 06	09 11	09 14	09 18	09 25	09 31	09 36	09 41	09 51	09 57	10 06	10 11	10 14	10 18	10 24	10 36	10 41
Meadowhall 4 29,31	a	08 41		08 46	08 56	09 03	09 11	09 16	09 20	09 23	09 32	09 37	09 41	09 46	09 56	10 03	10 11	10 16	10 20	10 23	10 29	10 41	10 46
	d	08 42			08 57		09 12			09 24			09 42		09 57		10 12			10 24		10 42	
Chapeltown	d	08 48					09 18						09 48				10 18					10 48	
Elsecar	d						09 23										10 23						
Wombwell	d	08 55					09 27						09 55				10 27					10 55	
Barnsley	a	09 00			09 11		09 32			09 40			10 00		10 11		10 32			10 40		11 00	
	d	09 01			09 12		09 33			09 42			10 01		10 12		10 33			10 42		11 01	
Dodworth	d	09 07											10 07									11 07	
Silkstone Common	d	09 11											10 11									11 11	
Penistone	d	09 18											10 18									11 18	
Denby Dale	d	09 24											10 24									11 24	
Shepley	d	09 29											10 29									11 29	
Stocksmoor	d	09 32											10 32									11 32	
Brockholes	d	09 36											10 36									11 36	
Honley	d	09 38											10 38									11 38	
Berry Brow	d	09 41											10 41									11 41	
Lockwood	d	09 44											10 44									11 44	
Huddersfield	a	09 52											10 53									11 53	
Darton	d						09 38										10 38						
Wakefield Kirkgate 4 31	a				09 27		09 49			09 57					10 27		10 49			10 57			
	d				09 28		09 50			09 58					10 28		10 50			10 58			
Normanton	d						09 54										10 54						
Castleford	a						10 00										11 00						
Woodlesford	a						10 12										11 12						
Leeds 10 31	a				09 49		10 25		10 30	10 18					10 48		11 25		11 30	11 18			

		NT	NT	NT	TP ◇1 ✠	NT	NT	NT	NT	NT	NT	NT	NT	TP ◇1 ✠	NT	NT	NT	NT	NT	NT	NT	NT
Nottingham 8	d						10 15									11 15						
Langley Mill	d						10 32									11 31						
Alfreton	d						10 40									11 39						
Chesterfield	d						10 52									11 52						
Dronfield	d						10 59															
Sheffield 7 29,31	a						11 15									12 16						
	d	10 51	10 57	11 06	11 11	11 14	11 18	11 24	11 36	11 41	11 51	11 57	12 06	12 11	12 14	12 18	12 24	12 36	12 41	12 51	12 57	13 06
Meadowhall 4 29,31	a	10 56	11 03	11 11	11 16	11 20	11 23	11 29	11 41	11 46	11 56	12 03	12 11	12 16	12 20	12 23	12 29	12 41	12 46	12 56	13 03	13 11
	d	10 57		11 12			11 24		11 42		11 57		12 12			12 24		12 42		12 57		13 12
Chapeltown	d			11 18					11 48				12 18					12 48				13 18
Elsecar	d			11 23									12 23									13 23
Wombwell	d			11 27					11 55				12 27					12 55				13 27
Barnsley	a	11 11		11 32			11 40		12 00		12 11		12 32			12 40		13 00		13 11		13 32
	d	11 12		11 33			11 42		12 01		12 12		12 33			12 42		13 01		13 12		13 33
Dodworth	d								12 07									13 07				
Silkstone Common	d								12 11									13 11				
Penistone	d								12 18									13 18				
Denby Dale	d								12 24									13 24				
Shepley	d								12 29									13 29				
Stocksmoor	d								12 32									13 32				
Brockholes	d								12 36									13 36				
Honley	d								12 38									13 38				
Berry Brow	d								12 41									13 41				
Lockwood	d								12 44									13 44				
Huddersfield	a								12 52									13 53				
Darton	d			11 38									12 38									13 38
Wakefield Kirkgate 4 31	a	11 27		11 49			11 57				12 27		12 49			12 57				13 27		13 50
	d	11 28		11 50			11 58				12 28		12 50			12 58				13 28		13 50
Normanton	d			11 54									12 54									13 54
Castleford	a			12 00									12 59									14 00
Woodlesford	a			12 12									13 12									14 12
Leeds 10 31	a	11 48		12 25			12 18				12 48		13 25			13 18				13 48		14 25

Table 34

Saturdays from 11 September

Nottingham, Sheffield - Barnsley - Huddersfield and Leeds

		TP ◇1 ✠	NT	NT	NT	NT	NT	NT	NT	NT	NT	TP ◇1 ✠	NT	NT	NT	NT	NT	NT	NT	NT	TP ◇1 ✠	NT	NT
Nottingham 8	d			12 15										13 15									14 15
Langley Mill	d			12 32										13 32									14 30
Alfreton	d			12 40										13 40									14 38
Chesterfield	d			12 52										13 52									14 52
Dronfield	d			12 59										13 59									14 59
Sheffield 7 29,31	a			13 15										14 15									15 15
	d	13 11	13 14	13 18	13 24	13 28	13 36	13 41	13 51	13 57	14 06	14 11	14 14	14 18	14 24	14 36	14 41	14 51	14 57	15 06	15 11	15 14	15 18
Meadowhall 4 29,31	a	13 16	13 20	13 23	13 29	13 34	13 41	13 46	13 56	14 03	14 11	14 16	14 20	14 23	14 29	14 41	14 46	14 56	15 03	15 11	15 16	15 20	15 23
	d			13 24			13 42		13 57		14 12			14 24		14 42		14 57		15 12			15 24
Chapeltown	d						13 48				14 18					14 48				15 18			
Elsecar	d										14 23									15 23			
Wombwell	d						13 55				14 27					14 55				15 27			
Barnsley	a			13 40			14 00		14 11		14 32			14 40		15 00		15 11		15 32			15 40
	d			13 42			14 01		14 12		14 33			14 42		15 01		15 12		15 33			15 42
Dodworth	d						14 07									15 07							
Silkstone Common	d						14 11									15 11							
Penistone	d						14 18									15 18							
Denby Dale	d						14 24									15 24							
Shepley	d						14 29									15 29							
Stocksmoor	d						14 32									15 32							
Brockholes	d						14 36									15 36							
Honley	d						14 38									15 38							
Berry Brow	d						14 41									15 41							
Lockwood	d						14 44									15 44							
Huddersfield	a						14 53									15 53							
Darton	d										14 38									15 38			
Wakefield Kirkgate 4 31	a			13 57					14 27		14 49			14 57				15 27		15 49			15 57
	d			13 58					14 28		14 50			14 58				15 28		15 50			15 58
Normanton	d										14 54									15 54			
Castleford	a										15 00									16 00			
Woodlesford	a										15 12									16 12			
Leeds 10 31	a			14 18					14 48		15 25			15 18				15 48		16 25			16 19

		NT	NT	NT	NT	NT	NT	TP ◇1 ✠	NT	NT	NT	NT	NT	NT	NT	NT	TP ◇1 ✠	NT	NT	NT	NT	NT
Nottingham 8	d									15 15									16 15			
Langley Mill	d									15 32									16 32			
Alfreton	d									15 40									16 40			
Chesterfield	d									15 51									16 54			
Dronfield	d									15 58									17 01			
Sheffield 7 29,31	a									16 15									17 15			
	d	15 24	15 36	15 41	15 51	15 57	16 06	16 11	16 14	16 18	16 24	16 36	16 41	16 51	16 57	17 06	17 11	17 14	17 18	17 36	17 41	17 51
Meadowhall 4 29,31	a	15 29	15 41	15 46	15 56	16 03	16 11	16 16	16 20	16 23	16 29	16 41	16 46	16 56	17 03	17 11	17 16	17 21	17 23	17 41	17 46	17 56
	d		15 42		15 57		16 12			16 24		16 42		16 57		17 12			17 24	17 42		17 57
Chapeltown	d		15 48				16 18					16 48				17 18				17 48		
Elsecar	d						16 23					16 53				17 23				17 53		
Wombwell	d		15 55				16 27					16 57				17 27				17 57		
Barnsley	a		16 00		16 11		16 32			16 40		17 02		17 11		17 32			17 40	18 02		18 11
	d		16 01		16 12		16 33			16 42		17 03		17 12		17 33			17 42	18 03		18 12
Dodworth	d		16 07									17 09								18 09		
Silkstone Common	d		16 11									17 13								18 13		
Penistone	d		16 18									17 20								18 20		
Denby Dale	d		16 24									17 26								18 26		
Shepley	d		16 29									17 31								18 31		
Stocksmoor	d		16 32									17 34								18 34		
Brockholes	d		16 36									17 38								18 38		
Honley	d		16 38									17 40								18 40		
Berry Brow	d		16 41									17 43								18 43		
Lockwood	d		16 44									17 46								18 46		
Huddersfield	a		16 52									17 54								18 56		
Darton	d						16 38									17 38						
Wakefield Kirkgate 4 31	a				16 27		16 49			16 57				17 28		17 49			17 57			18 28
	d				16 28		16 50			16 58				17 28		17 50			17 58			18 32
Normanton	d						16 54									17 54						
Castleford	a						17 00									18 00						
Woodlesford	a						17 12									18 12						
Leeds 10 31	a				16 48		17 25		17 30	17 18				17 48		18 25		18 30	18 18			18 51

Table 34

Nottingham, Sheffield - Barnsley - Huddersfield and Leeds

Saturdays
from 11 September

		NT	NT	NT	NT	TP	NT	NT	NT	NT	NT	NT	TP	NT	NT	NT	NT	NT	NT	NT	NT	TP	NT	NT	NT
						◇1							◇1									◇1			
Nottingham 8	d				17 15										18 15									19 15	
Langley Mill	d				17 31										18 32									19 32	
Alfreton	d				17 39										18 40									19 40	
Chesterfield	d				17 52										18 52									19 52	
Dronfield	d				17 59										18 59									19 59	
Sheffield 7 29,31	a				18 15										19 15									20 15	
	d	17 57	18 06	18 14	18 18	18 24	18 29	18 36	18 41	18 51	19 00	19 06	19 11	19 14	19 18	19 30	19 36	19 44	19 51	19 57	20 06	20 11	20 15	20 18	20 27
Meadowhall 4 29,31	a	18 03	18 12	18 20	18 23	18 29	18 34	18 41	18 46	18 56	19 06	19 11	19 16	19 20	19 23	19 35	19 41	19 49	19 56	20 03	20 11	20 16	20 20	20 24	20 35
	d		18 12		18 24			18 42		18 57		19 12			19 24		19 42		19 57		20 12			20 24	
Chapeltown	d		18 18					18 48				19 18					19 48				20 18				
Elsecar	d		18 23					18 53				19 23					19 53				20 23				
Wombwell	d		18 27					18 57				19 27					19 57				20 27				
Barnsley	a		18 33		18 42			19 02		19 14		19 33			19 42		20 02		20 12		20 32			20 42	
	d		18 33		18 42			19 03		19 14		19 33			19 42		20 08		20 12		20 33			20 42	
Dodworth	d							19 09									20 14								
Silkstone Common	d							19 13									20 18								
Penistone	d							19 20									20 25								
Denby Dale	d							19 26									20 31								
Shepley	d							19 31									20 36								
Stocksmoor	d							19 34									20 39								
Brockholes	d							19 38									20 43								
Honley	d							19 41									20 45								
Berry Brow	d							19 44									20 48								
Lockwood	d							19 46									20 51								
Huddersfield	a							19 54									21 00								
Darton	d		18 38									19 38									20 38				
Wakefield Kirkgate 4 31	a		18 50		18 58					19 29		19 50			19 58				20 28		20 49			20 57	
	d		18 50		18 58					19 32		19 50			19 58				20 28		20 50			20 58	
Normanton	d		18 54									19 54									20 54				
Castleford	a		19 00									20 00									21 00				
Woodlesford	a		19 13									20 12									21 12				
Leeds 10 31	a		19 27		19 23					19 55		20 26			20 19				20 48		21 26			21 22	

		NT	NT	NT	NT	NT	TP	NT	NT	TP	NT	NT	NT	NT	NT	NT
							◇1			◇1						
Nottingham 8	d										21 15					
Langley Mill	d										21 31					
Alfreton	d										21 39					
Chesterfield	d										21 50					
Dronfield	d										21 57					
Sheffield 7 29,31	a										22 13					
	d	20 38	20 41	21 06	21 15	21 30	21 34	21 41	22 06	22 11		22 30		22 34	22 41	23 26
Meadowhall 4 29,31	a	20 43	20 47	21 11	21 21	21 36	21 39	21 46	22 11	22 16		22 35		22 39	22 46	23 31
	d		20 47	21 12				21 47	22 12						22 47	
Chapeltown	d		20 53	21 18				21 53	22 18						22 53	
Elsecar	d			21 23					22 23						22 58	
Wombwell	d		21 00	21 27				22 00	22 27						23 02	
Barnsley	a		21 07	21 33				22 05	22 32						23 07	
	d		21 08	21 33				22 08							23 08	
Dodworth	d		21 14					22 14							23 14	
Silkstone Common	d		21 18					22 18							23 18	
Penistone	d		21 25					22 25							23 25	
Denby Dale	d		21 31					22 31							23 31	
Shepley	d		21 36					22 36							23 36	
Stocksmoor	d		21 39					22 39							23 39	
Brockholes	d		21 43					22 43							23 43	
Honley	d		21 45					22 45							23 45	
Berry Brow	d		21 48					22 48							23 48	
Lockwood	d		21 51					22 51							23 5[illegible]	
Huddersfield	a		22 01					23 01							00 0[illegible]	
Darton	d			21 38												
Wakefield Kirkgate 4 31	a			21 52												
	d			21 52									22 50			
Normanton	d			21 57									22 54			
Castleford	a			22 04									23 00			
Woodlesford	a			22 14									23 13			
Leeds 10 31	a			22 29									23 28			

Table 34

Nottingham, Sheffield - Barnsley - Huddersfield and Leeds

Sundays
until 11 July

		NT	NT	NT	NT	NT	NT	TP	NT	NT		NT	NT	NT	NT	TP	NT	NT	NT	NT		NT	TP	NT	NT
								◇1								◇1							◇1		
Nottingham 8	d												10 06				11 15							12 19	
Langley Mill	d												10 27				11 31							12 35	
Alfreton	d												10 35				11 39							12 43	
Chesterfield	d												10 54				11 51							12 54	
Dronfield	d												11 01				11 58							13 01	
Sheffield 7 29,31	a												11 15				12 15							13 15	
	d	08 00	08 39	08 45	09 17	09 36	09 39	09 52	10 26	10 39		11 05	11 17	11 36	11 49	12 11	12 16	12 24	12 28	12 35		12 39	13 11	13 17	13 24
Meadowhall 4 29,31	a	08 05	08 44	08 50	09 22	09 41	09 44	09 57	10 31	10 44		11 10	11 22	11 41	11 54	12 16	12 22	12 29	12 33	12 40		12 44	13 16	13 22	13 29
	d		08 45		09 23		09 45			10 45			11 23		11 55		12 23			12 41		12 45		13 23	
Chapeltown	d		08 51				09 51			10 51					12 01							12 55			
Elsecar	d		08 56				09 56			10 56					12 06							13 00			
Wombwell	d		09 00				10 00			11 00					12 10							13 04			
Barnsley	a		09 05		09 37		10 05			11 05			11 37		12 15		12 37			12 55		13 09		13 37	
	d		09 10		09 37		10 06			11 10			11 37		12 16		12 37			13 06		13 10		13 37	
Dodworth	d						10 12								12 22					13 12					
Silkstone Common	d						10 16								12 26					13 16					
Penistone	d						10 23								12 33					13 23					
Denby Dale	d						10 29								12 39					13 29					
Shepley	d						10 34								12 44					13 34					
Stocksmoor	d						10 37								12 47					13 37					
Brockholes	d						10 41								12 51					13 41					
Honley	d						10 43								12 53					13 43					
Berry Brow	d						10 46								12 56					13 46					
Lockwood	d						10 49								12 59					13 49					
Huddersfield	a						10 53								13 03					13 53					
Darton	d		09 15							11 15												13 15			
Wakefield Kirkgate 4 31	a		09 29		09 55					11 29			11 52				12 52					13 29		13 52	
	d		09 30		09 55					11 30			11 53				12 53					13 30		13 53	
Normanton	d		09 34							11 34												13 34			
Castleford	a		09 40							11 40												13 40			
Woodlesford	a		09 52							11 51												13 51			
Leeds 10 31	a		10 04		10 15					12 05			12 18				13 18					14 04		14 18	

		NT	NT	TP	NT	NT	NT	NT	TP	NT	NT	NT	NT	NT	NT	TP	NT	NT	NT	NT	NT	TP	NT	NT	NT
				◇1					◇1							◇1						◇1			
Nottingham 8	d				13 09					14 19							15 14						16 14		
Langley Mill	d				13 27					14 35							15 36						16 30		
Alfreton	d				13 35					14 43							15 44						16 38		
Chesterfield	d				13 51					14 54							15 53						16 50		
Dronfield	d				13 58					15 01							16 00						16 57		
Sheffield 7 29,31	a				14 15					15 15							16 15						17 15		
	d	13 36	13 39	14 11	14 17	14 22	14 28	14 39	15 11	15 17	15 24	15 28	15 36	15 39	15 46	16 11	16 17	16 24	16 28	16 39	16 54	17 11	17 17	17 24	17 28
Meadowhall 4 29,31	a	13 41	13 44	14 16	14 22	14 27	14 33	14 44	15 16	15 22	15 29	15 33	15 41	15 42	15 51	16 16	16 22	16 29	16 33	16 44	16 59	17 16	17 22	17 29	17 33
	d		13 45		14 23			14 45		15 23				15 43			16 23			16 45	17 00		17 23		
Chapeltown	d		13 51					14 51						15 49						16 51					
Elsecar	d		13 56					14 56						15 54						16 56					
Wombwell	d		14 00					15 00						15 58						17 00					
Barnsley	a		14 05		14 37			15 05		15 37				16 03			16 37			17 05	17 14		17 37		
	d		14 06		14 37			15 10		15 37				16 04			16 37			17 10	17 15		17 37		
Dodworth	d		14 12											16 10							17 21				
Silkstone Common	d		14 16											16 14							17 25				
Penistone	d		14 23											16 21							17 32				
Denby Dale	d		14 29											16 27							17 38				
Shepley	d		14 34											16 32							17 43				
Stocksmoor	d		14 37											16 35							17 46				
Brockholes	d		14 41											16 39							17 50				
Honley	d		14 43											16 41							17 52				
Berry Brow	d		14 46											16 44							17 55				
Lockwood	d		14 49											16 47							17 58				
Huddersfield	a		14 53											16 53							18 05				
Darton	d							15 15												17 15					
Wakefield Kirkgate 4 31	a				14 52			15 29		15 52							16 52			17 29			17 52		
	d				14 53			15 30		15 53							16 53			17 30			17 53		
Normanton	d							15 34												17 34					
Castleford	a							15 40												17 40					
Woodlesford	a							15 51												17 51					
Leeds 10 31	a				15 18			16 04		16 18							17 18			18 05			18 18		

Table 34

Sundays
until 11 July

Nottingham, Sheffield - Barnsley - Huddersfield and Leeds

		NT		NT	TP ◇1	NT	NT	NT	NT	NT	TP ◇1	NT	NT	NT	NT	NT	TP ◇1	NT	NT	NT	TP ◇1	NT	NT	NT	NT
Nottingham [8] ⇌	d					17 14						18 14						19 19							
Langley Mill	d					17 30						18 30						19 35							
Alfreton	d					17 38						18 38						19 43							
Chesterfield	d					17 49						18 50						19 54							
Dronfield	d					17 56						18 56						20 01							
Sheffield [7] 29,31 ⇌	a					18 15						19 15						20 15							
	d			17 39	18 11	18 17	18 25	18 28	18 39	18 57	19 11	19 16	19 29	19 36	19 39	20 02	20 11	20 17	20 28	20 39	21 11	21 24	21 36	21 43	22 26
Meadowhall [4] 29,31 ⇌	a	17 36		17 46	18 16	18 22	18 30	18 34	18 44	19 03	19 16	19 22	19 34	19 41	19 44	20 08	20 16	20 22	20 33	20 44	21 16	21 29	21 41	21 48	22 31
	d	17 43		17 46		18 23			18 45			19 23			19 45			20 23		20 45				21 49	
Chapeltown	d			17 52					18 51						19 51					20 51				21 55	
Elsecar	d			17 58					18 56						19 56					20 56				22 00	
Wombwell	d			18 01					19 00						20 00					21 00				22 04	
Barnsley	a			18 08		18 37			19 05			19 37			20 05			20 37		21 06				22 09	
	d			18 10		18 37			19 10			19 37			20 06			20 37		21 10					
Dodworth	d			18 16											20 12										
Silkstone Common	d			18 20											20 16										
Penistone	d			18 27											20 23										
Denby Dale	d			18 34											20 29										
Shepley	d			18 39											20 34										
Stocksmoor	d			18 41											20 37										
Brockholes	d			18 45											20 41										
Honley	d			18 48											20 43										
Berry Brow	d			18 51											20 46										
Lockwood	d			18 53											20 49										
Huddersfield	a			18 58											20 53										
Darton	d								19 15											21 15					
Wakefield Kirkgate [4] 31	a					18 52			19 29			19 52						20 52		21 29					
	d					18 53			19 30			19 53						20 53		21 30					
Normanton	d								19 34											21 34					
Castleford	a								19 41											21 40					
Woodlesford	a								19 53											21 51					
Leeds [10] 31	a					19 18			20 05			20 18					TP	21 16		22 04					

		TP ◇1	NT	NT	NT
Nottingham [8] ⇌	d		21 20		
Langley Mill	d		21 41		
Alfreton	d		21 49		
Chesterfield	d		22 08		
Dronfield	d		22 15		
Sheffield [7] 29,31 ⇌	a		22 32		
	d	22 30		22 39	23 34
Meadowhall [4] 29,31 ⇌	a	22 35		22 44	23 39
	d			22 45	
Chapeltown	d			22 51	
Elsecar	d			22 56	
Wombwell	d			23 00	
Barnsley	a			23 05	
	d			23 10	
Dodworth	d				
Silkstone Common	d				
Penistone	d				
Denby Dale	d				
Shepley	d				
Stocksmoor	d				
Brockholes	d				
Honley	d				
Berry Brow	d				
Lockwood	d				
Huddersfield	a				
Darton	d			23 15	
Wakefield Kirkgate [4] 31	a			23 28	
	d			23 30	
Normanton	d			23 34	
Castleford	a			23 40	
Woodlesford	a			23 51	
Leeds [10] 31	a			00 04	

Table 34

Sundays
18 July to 05 September

Nottingham, Sheffield - Barnsley - Huddersfield and Leeds

		NT	NT	NT	NT	NT	NT	TP ◇1	NT	NT		NT	NT	NT	NT	TP ◇1	NT	NT	NT	NT		NT	TP ◇1	NT	NT
Nottingham [8] ⇌	d												10 06				11 15							12 19	
Langley Mill	d												10 27				11 31							12 35	
Alfreton	d												10 35				11 39							12 43	
Chesterfield	d												10 54				11 51							12 54	
Dronfield	d												11 01				11 58							13 01	
Sheffield [7] 29,31 ⇌	a												11 15				12 15							13 15	
	d	08 00	08 39	08 45	09 17	09 36	09 39	09 52	10 26	10 39		11 05	11 17	11 36	11 49	12 11	12 16	12 24	12 28	12 35		12 39	13 11	13 17	13 24
Meadowhall [4] 29,31 ⇌	a	08 05	08 44	08 50	09 22	09 41	09 44	09 57	10 31	10 44		11 10	11 22	11 41	11 54	12 16	12 22	12 29	12 33	12 40		12 44	13 16	13 22	13 29
	d		08 45		09 23		09 45			10 45			11 23		11 55		12 23			12 41		12 45		13 23	
Chapeltown	d		08 51				09 51			10 51					12 01							12 55			
Elsecar	d		08 56				09 56			10 56					12 06							13 00			
Wombwell	d		09 00				10 00			11 00					12 10							13 04			
Barnsley	a		09 05		09 37		10 05			11 05			11 37		12 15		12 37			12 55		13 09		13 37	
	d		09 10		09 37		10 06			11 10			11 37		12 16		12 37			13 06		13 10		13 37	
Dodworth	d						10 12								12 22					13 12					
Silkstone Common	d						10 16								12 26					13 16					
Penistone	d						10 23								12 33					13 23					
Denby Dale	d						10 29								12 39					13 29					
Shepley	d						10 34								12 44					13 34					
Stocksmoor	d						10 37								12 47					13 37					
Brockholes	d						10 41								12 51					13 41					
Honley	d						10 43								12 53					13 43					
Berry Brow	d						10 46								12 56					13 46					
Lockwood	d						10 49								12 59					13 49					
Huddersfield	a						10 53								13 03					13 53					
Darton	d		09 15							11 15												13 15			
Wakefield Kirkgate [4] 31	a		09 29		09 55					11 29			11 52				12 52					13 29		13 52	
	d		09 30		09 55					11 30			11 53				12 53					13 30		13 53	
Normanton	d		09 34							11 34												13 34			
Castleford	a		09 40							11 40												13 40			
Woodlesford	a		09 52							11 51												13 51			
Leeds [10] 31	a		10 04		10 15					12 05			12 18				13 18					14 04		14 18	

		NT	NT	TP ◇1	NT	NT	NT	NT	TP ◇1	NT	NT	NT	NT	NT	NT	TP ◇1	NT	NT	NT	NT	NT	TP ◇1	NT	NT	NT
Nottingham [8] ⇌	d				13 09					14 19							15 14						16 14		
Langley Mill	d				13 27					14 35							15 36						16 30		
Alfreton	d				13 35					14 43							15 44						16 38		
Chesterfield	d				13 51					14 54							15 53						16 50		
Dronfield	d				13 58					15 01							16 00						16 57		
Sheffield [7] 29,31 ⇌	a				14 15					15 15							16 15						17 15		
	d	13 36	13 39	14 11	14 17	14 28		14 39	15 11	15 17	15 24	15 28	15 39	15 36	15 46	16 11	16 17	16 24	16 28	16 39	16 54	17 11	17 17	17 24	17 28
Meadowhall [4] 29,31 ⇌	a	13 41	13 44	14 16	14 22	14 33		14 44	15 16	15 22	15 29	15 33	15 42	15 41	15 51	16 16	16 22	16 29	16 33	16 44	16 59	17 16	17 22	17 29	17 33
	d		13 45		14 23			14 45		15 23			15 43				16 23			16 45	17 00		17 23		
Chapeltown	d		13 51					14 51					15 49							16 51					
Elsecar	d		13 56					14 56					15 54							16 56					
Wombwell	d		14 00					15 00					15 58							17 00					
Barnsley	a		14 05		14 37			15 05		15 37			16 03				16 37			17 05	17 14		17 37		
	d		14 06		14 37			15 10		15 37			16 04				16 37			17 10	17 15		17 37		
Dodworth	d		14 12										16 10								17 21				
Silkstone Common	d		14 16										16 14								17 25				
Penistone	d		14 23										16 21								17 32				
Denby Dale	d		14 29										16 27								17 38				
Shepley	d		14 34										16 32								17 43				
Stocksmoor	d		14 37										16 35								17 46				
Brockholes	d		14 41										16 39								17 50				
Honley	d		14 43										16 41								17 52				
Berry Brow	d		14 46										16 44								17 55				
Lockwood	d		14 49										16 47								17 58				
Huddersfield	a		14 53										16 53								18 05				
Darton	d							15 15												17 15					
Wakefield Kirkgate [4] 31	a				14 52			15 29		15 52							16 52			17 29			17 52		
	d				14 53			15 30		15 53							16 53			17 30			17 53		
Normanton	d							15 34												17 34					
Castleford	a							15 40												17 40					
Woodlesford	a							15 51												17 51					
Leeds [10] 31	a				15 18			16 04		16 18							17 18			18 05			18 18		

Table 34

Sundays

18 July to 05 September

Nottingham, Sheffield - Barnsley - Huddersfield and Leeds

		NT		NT	TP ◇1	NT	NT	NT	NT	NT	TP ◇1	NT	NT	NT	NT	NT	TP ◇1	NT	NT	NT	TP ◇1	NT	NT	NT	NT
Nottingham 8	d					17 14						18 14						19 19							
Langley Mill	d					17 30						18 30						19 35							
Alfreton	d					17 38						18 38						19 43							
Chesterfield	d					17 49						18 50						19 54							
Dronfield	d					17 56						18 56						20 01							
Sheffield 7 29,31	a					18 15						19 15						20 15							
	d	17 36		17 39	18 11	18 17	18 25	18 28	18 39	18 57	19 11	19 16	19 29	19 36	19 39	20 02	20 11	20 17	20 28	20 39	21 11	21 24	21 36	21 43	22 26
Meadowhall 4 29,31	a	17 43		17 46	18 16	18 22	18 30	18 34	18 44	19 03	19 16	19 22	19 34	19 41	19 44	20 08	20 16	20 22	20 33	20 44	21 16	21 29	21 41	21 48	22 31
	d			17 46		18 23			18 45			19 23			19 45			20 23		20 45	21 16			21 49	
Chapeltown	d			17 52					18 51						19 51					20 51				21 55	
Elsecar	d			17 58					18 56						19 56					20 56				22 00	
Wombwell	d			18 01					19 00						20 00					21 00				22 04	
Barnsley	a			18 08		18 37			19 05			19 37			20 05			20 37		21 06				22 09	
	d			18 10		18 37			19 10			19 37			20 06			20 37		21 10					
Dodworth	d			18 16											20 12										
Silkstone Common	d			18 20											20 16										
Penistone	d			18 27											20 23										
Denby Dale	d			18 34											20 29										
Shepley	d			18 39											20 34										
Stocksmoor	d			18 41											20 37										
Brockholes	d			18 45											20 41										
Honley	d			18 48											20 43										
Berry Brow	d			18 51											20 46										
Lockwood	d			18 53											20 49										
Huddersfield	a			18 58											20 53										
Darton	d								19 15											21 15					
Wakefield Kirkgate 4 31	a					18 52			19 29			19 52						20 52		21 29					
	d					18 53			19 30			19 53						20 53		21 30					
Normanton	d								19 34											21 34					
Castleford	a								19 41											21 40					
Woodlesford	a								19 53											21 51					
Leeds 10 31	a					19 18			20 05			20 18						21 16		22 04					

		TP ◇1	NT	NT	NT
Nottingham 8	d		21 20		
Langley Mill	d		21 41		
Alfreton	d		21 49		
Chesterfield	d		22 08		
Dronfield	d		22 15		
Sheffield 7 29,31	a		22 32		
	d	22 30		22 39	23 34
Meadowhall 4 29,31	a	22 35		22 44	23 39
	d			22 45	
Chapeltown	d			22 51	
Elsecar	d			22 56	
Wombwell	d			23 00	
Barnsley	a			23 05	
	d			23 10	
Dodworth	d				
Silkstone Common	d				
Penistone	d				
Denby Dale	d				
Shepley	d				
Stocksmoor	d				
Brockholes	d				
Honley	d				
Berry Brow	d				
Lockwood	d				
Huddersfield	a				
Darton	d			23 15	
Wakefield Kirkgate 4 31	a			23 28	
	d			23 30	
Normanton	d			23 34	
Castleford	a			23 40	
Woodlesford	a			23 51	
Leeds 10 31	a			00 04	

Table 34

Sundays

from 12 September

Nottingham, Sheffield - Barnsley - Huddersfield and Leeds

			NT	NT	NT	NT	NT	NT	TP ◇1	NT		NT	NT	NT	NT	NT	TP ◇1	NT	NT	NT		NT	NT	TP ◇1	NT
Nottingham 8	d													10 06				11 15							12 19
Langley Mill	d													10 27				11 31							12 35
Alfreton	d													10 35				11 39							12 43
Chesterfield	d													10 54				11 51							12 54
Dronfield	d													11 01				11 58							13 01
Sheffield 7 29,31	a													11 15				12 15							13 15
	d		08 00	08 39	08 45	09 17	09 36	09 39	09 52	10 26		10 39	11 05	11 17	11 36	11 49	12 11	12 16	12 24	12 28		12 35	12 39	13 11	13 17
Meadowhall 4 29,31	a		08 05	08 44	08 50	09 22	09 41	09 44	09 57	10 31		10 44	11 10	11 22	11 41	11 54	12 16	12 22	12 29	12 33		12 40	12 44	13 16	13 22
	d			08 45		09 23		09 45				10 45		11 23		11 55		12 23				12 41	12 45		13 23
Chapeltown	d			08 51				09 51				10 51				12 01							12 55		
Elsecar	d			08 56				09 56				10 56				12 06							13 00		
Wombwell	d			09 00				10 00				11 00				12 10							13 04		
Barnsley	a			09 05		09 37		10 05				11 05		11 37		12 15		12 37				12 55	13 09		13 37
	d			09 10		09 37		10 06				11 10		11 37		12 16		12 37				13 06	13 10		13 37
Dodworth	d							10 12								12 22						13 12			
Silkstone Common	d							10 16								12 26						13 16			
Penistone	d							10 23								12 33						13 23			
Denby Dale	d							10 29								12 39						13 29			
Shepley	d							10 34								12 44						13 34			
Stocksmoor	d							10 37								12 47						13 37			
Brockholes	d							10 41								12 51						13 41			
Honley	d							10 43								12 53						13 43			
Berry Brow	d							10 46								12 56						13 46			
Lockwood	d							10 49								12 59						13 49			
Huddersfield	a							10 58								13 07						13 58			
Darton	d			09 15								11 15											13 15		
Wakefield Kirkgate 4 31	a			09 29		09 55						11 29		11 52				12 52					13 29		13 52
	d			09 30		09 55						11 30		11 53				12 53					13 30		13 53
Normanton	d			09 34								11 34											13 34		
Castleford	a			09 40								11 40											13 40		
Woodlesford	a			09 52								11 51											13 51		
Leeds 10 31	a			10 04		10 15						12 05		12 18				13 18					14 04		14 18

		NT	NT	NT	TP ◇1	NT		NT	NT	TP ◇1	NT	NT	NT	NT	NT	NT	TP ◇1	NT	NT	NT	NT	NT	TP ◇1	NT	NT
Nottingham 8	d					13 09					14 19							15 14						16 14	
Langley Mill	d					13 27					14 35							15 36						16 30	
Alfreton	d					13 35					14 43							15 44						16 38	
Chesterfield	d					13 51					14 54							15 53						16 50	
Dronfield	d					13 58					15 01							16 00						16 57	
Sheffield 7 29,31	a					14 15					15 15							16 15			16 36			17 15	
	d	13 24	13 36	13 39	14 11	14 17		14 28	14 39	15 11	15 17	15 24	15 28	15 36	15 39	15 46	16 11	16 17	16 24	16 28	16 39	16 54	17 11	17 17	17 24
Meadowhall 4 29,31	a	13 29	13 41	13 44	14 16	14 22		14 33	14 44	15 16	15 22	15 29	15 33	15 41	15 42	15 51	16 16	16 22	16 29	16 33	16 44	16 59	17 16	17 22	17 29
	d			13 45					14 45		15 23				15 43			16 23			16 45	17 00		17 23	
Chapeltown	d			13 51					14 51						15 49						16 51				
Elsecar	d			13 56					14 56						15 54						16 56				
Wombwell	d			14 00					15 00						15 58						17 00				
Barnsley	a			14 05		14 37			15 05		15 37				16 03			16 37			17 05	17 14		17 37	
	d			14 06		14 37			15 10		15 37				16 04			16 37			17 10	17 15		17 37	
Dodworth	d			14 12											16 10							17 21			
Silkstone Common	d			14 16											16 14							17 25			
Penistone	d			14 23											16 21							17 32			
Denby Dale	d			14 29											16 27							17 38			
Shepley	d			14 34											16 32							17 43			
Stocksmoor	d			14 37											16 35							17 46			
Brockholes	d			14 41											16 39							17 50			
Honley	d			14 43											16 41							17 52			
Berry Brow	d			14 46											16 44							17 55			
Lockwood	d			14 49											16 47							17 58			
Huddersfield	a			14 58											16 57							18 07			
Darton	d								15 15												17 15				
Wakefield Kirkgate 4 31	a					14 52			15 29		15 52							16 52			17 29			17 52	
	d					14 53			15 30		15 53							16 53			17 30			17 53	
Normanton	d								15 34												17 34				
Castleford	a								15 40												17 40				
Woodlesford	a								15 51												17 51				
Leeds 10 31	a					15 18			16 04		16 18							17 18			18 05			18 18	

Table 34

Sundays
from 12 September

Nottingham, Sheffield - Barnsley - Huddersfield and Leeds

	NT		NT	NT	TP ◇1	NT	NT	NT	NT	NT	TP ◇1	NT	NT	NT	NT	NT	TP ◇1	NT	NT	NT	TP ◇1	NT	NT	NT
Nottingham 8 d						17 14						18 14						19 19						
Langley Mill d						17 30						18 30						19 35						
Alfreton d						17 38						18 38						19 43						
Chesterfield d						17 49						18 50						19 54						
Dronfield d						17 56						18 56						20 01						
Sheffield 7 29,31 a						18 15						19 15						20 15						
d	17 28		17 36	17 39	18 11	18 17	18 25	18 28	18 39	18 57	19 11	19 16	19 29	19 36	19 39	20 02	20 11	20 17	20 28	20 39	21 11	21 24	21 36	21 43
Meadowhall 4 29,31 a	17 33		17 43	17 46	18 16	18 22	18 30	18 34	18 44	19 03	19 16	19 22	19 34	19 41	19 44	20 08	20 16	20 22	20 33	20 44	21 16	21 29	21 41	21 48
d				17 46		18 23			18 45			19 23			19 45			20 23		20 45				21 49
Chapeltown d				17 52					18 51						19 51					20 51				21 55
Elsecar d				17 58					18 56						19 56					20 56				22 00
Wombwell d				18 01					19 00						20 00					21 00				22 04
Barnsley a				18 08		18 37			19 05			19 37			20 05			20 37		21 06				22 09
d				18 10		18 37			19 10			19 37			20 06			20 37		21 10				
Dodworth d				18 16											20 12									
Silkstone Common d				18 20											20 16									
Penistone d				18 27											20 23									
Denby Dale d				18 34											20 29									
Shepley d				18 39											20 34									
Stocksmoor d				18 41											20 41									
Brockholes d				18 45											20 45									
Honley d				18 48											20 48									
Berry Brow d				18 51											20 51									
Lockwood d				18 53											20 53									
Huddersfield a				19 02											20 58									
Darton d									19 15											21 15				
Wakefield Kirkgate 4 31 a						18 52			19 29			19 52						20 52		21 29				
d						18 53			19 30			19 53						20 53		21 30				
Normanton d									19 34											21 34				
Castleford a									19 41											21 40				
Woodlesford a									19 53											21 51				
Leeds 10 31 a						19 18			20 05			20 18						21 16		22 04				

	NT	TP ◇1	NT	NT	NT
Nottingham 8 d			21 20		
Langley Mill d			21 41		
Alfreton d			21 49		
Chesterfield d			22 08		
Dronfield d			22 15		
Sheffield 7 29,31 a			22 32	22 34	
d	22 26	22 30		22 39	23 34
Meadowhall 4 29,31 a	22 31	22 35		22 44	23 39
d				22 45	
Chapeltown d				22 51	
Elsecar d				22 56	
Wombwell d				23 00	
Barnsley a				23 05	
d				23 10	
Dodworth d					
Silkstone Common d					
Penistone d					
Denby Dale d					
Shepley d					
Stocksmoor d					
Brockholes d					
Honley d					
Berry Brow d					
Lockwood d					
Huddersfield a					
Darton d				23 15	
Wakefield Kirkgate 4 31 a				23 28	
d				23 30	
Normanton d				23 34	
Castleford a				23 40	
Woodlesford a				23 51	
Leeds 10 31 a				00 04	

Table 34

Mondays to Fridays
until 03 September

Leeds and Huddersfield - Barnsley - Sheffield, Nottingham

	NT	NT	NT			TP ◇1	NT	NT	NT			NT	NT	NT	TP ◇1 ⌶	NT	NT	NT	NT		TP ◇1 ⌶			NT
Leeds 10 31 d													06 05					06 38						
Woodlesford d																		06 46						
Castleford d																		06 57						
Normanton d																		07 03						
Wakefield Kirkgate 4 31 a													06 21					07 07						
d												06 04	06 21					07 08						
Darton d												06 15						07 19						
Huddersfield d																06 10								
Lockwood d																06 13								
Berry Brow d																06 16								
Honley d																06 19								
Brockholes d																06 22								
Stocksmoor d																06 26								
Shepley d																06 28								
Denby Dale d																06 34								
Penistone d																06 42								
Silkstone Common d																06 47								
Dodworth d																06 51								
Barnsley a												06 20	06 37			06 57		07 25						
d		05 23					05 50					06 21	06 38			06 58		07 25						
Wombwell d		05 28					05 55					06 26				07 03		07 30						
Elsecar d		05 32					05 59					06 30				07 07		07 34						
Chapeltown d		05 37					06 04					06 35				07 12		07 39						
Meadowhall 29,31 a		05 43					06 10					06 41	06 49			07 20		07 48						
d		05 43				05 58	06 10	06 28	06 37			06 42	06 49	06 52	06 58	07 20	07 33	07 48	07 47		07 53			08 06
Sheffield 7 29,31 a		05 53				06 08	06 25	06 38	06 47			06 55	07 00	07 07	07 06	07 29	07 40	07 57	07 57		08 00			08 18
d			06 00										07 03											
Dronfield d			06 10										07 13											
Chesterfield d			06 16										07 20											
Alfreton d			06 30										07 33											
Langley Mill d			06 37										07 40											
Nottingham a			07 08										08 02											

	NT	NT	NT	NT	NT		NT	NT		TP ◇1 ⌶	NT	NT	NT	NT		NT	NT	NT		NT	TP ◇1 ⌶	NT	NT	NT
Leeds 10 31 d			07 35	07 29			08 02						08 37			08 32		09 05						09 37
Woodlesford d				07 37												08 40								
Castleford d				07 48												08 51								
Normanton d				07 54												08 57								
Wakefield Kirkgate 4 31 a			07 54	08 00			08 23						08 54			09 03		09 23						09 54
d			07 55	08 04			08 23						08 55			09 04		09 23						09 55
Darton d				08 15												09 15								
Huddersfield d	07 10											08 10											09 13	
Lockwood d	07 13											08 13											09 16	
Berry Brow d	07 16											08 16											09 19	
Honley d	07 19											08 19											09 22	
Brockholes d	07 22											08 22											09 25	
Stocksmoor d	07 26											08 26											09 29	
Shepley d	07 28											08 28											09 31	
Denby Dale d	07 34											08 34											09 36	
Penistone d	07 42											08 42											09 44	
Silkstone Common d	07 47											08 47											09 49	
Dodworth d	07 51											08 51											09 53	
Barnsley a	07 57		08 11	08 21			08 39					08 57	09 11			09 23		09 39					10 00	10 12
d	07 58		08 14	08 24			08 40					08 58	09 14			09 24		09 40					10 01	10 14
Wombwell d	08 03			08 29								09 03				09 29							10 06	
Elsecar d	08 07			08 33								09 07				09 33								
Chapeltown d	08 12			10 38								09 12				09 38							10 13	
Meadowhall 29,31 a	08 20		08 31	08 46			08 52					09 20	09 27			09 46		09 52		09 55	10 01	10 06	10 20	10 27
d	08 20	08 22	08 31	08 47	08 49		08 52	08 55		09 01	09 15	09 21	09 28	09 33		09 46	09 50	09 52		09 55	10 01	10 07	10 21	10 28
Sheffield 7 29,31 a	08 29	08 32	08 39	08 56	08 58		09 02	09 05		09 08	09 26	09 30	09 37	09 41		09 56	10 00	10 02		10 05	10 08	10 20	10 30	10 37
d							09 05											10 05						
Dronfield d							09 15											10 15						
Chesterfield d							09 22											10 22						
Alfreton d							09 33											10 33						
Langley Mill d							09 40											10 40						
Nottingham a							10 00											11 00						

Table 34

Mondays to Fridays
until 03 September

Leeds and Huddersfield - Barnsley - Sheffield, Nottingham

		NT	NT	NT	NT	NT	TP ◇■	NT	NT	NT	NT	NT	NT	NT	NT	TP ◇■	NT	NT	NT	NT
Leeds ■	31 d		09 32		10 05					10 37		10 32		11 05						11 37
Woodlesford	d		09 40									10 40								
Castleford	d		09 51									10 51								
Normanton	d		09 57									10 57								
Wakefield Kirkgate ■	31 a		10 01		10 23					10 54		11 01		11 23						11 54
	d		10 04		10 23					10 55		11 04		11 23						11 55
Darton	d		10 15									11 15								
Huddersfield	d								10 13										11 13	
Lockwood	d								10 16										11 16	
Berry Brow	d								10 19										11 19	
Honley	d								10 22										11 22	
Brockholes	d								10 25										11 25	
Stocksmoor	d								10 29										11 29	
Shepley	d								10 31										11 31	
Denby Dale	d								10 36										11 36	
Penistone	d								10 44										11 44	
Silkstone Common	d								10 49										11 49	
Dodworth	d								10 53										11 53	
Barnsley	a		10 21		10 39				11 00	11 11		11 21		11 39					12 00	12 11
	d		10 24		10 40				11 01	11 14		11 24		11 40					12 01	12 14
Wombwell	d		10 29						11 06			11 29							12 06	
Elsecar	d		10 33									11 33								
Chapeltown	d		10 38						11 13			11 38							12 13	
Meadowhall	29,31 a		10 46		10 52				11 19	11 27		11 46		11 52					12 20	12 27
	d	10 33	10 46	10 50	10 52	10 57	11 01	11 06	11 19	11 28	11 33	11 46	11 50	11 52	11 55	12 01	12 06	12 16	12 21	12 28
Sheffield ■	29,31 a	10 41	10 56	11 00	11 02	11 05	11 08	11 20	11 30	11 37	11 41	11 56	12 00	12 02	12 05	12 08	12 19	12 26	12 30	12 37
	d				11 05									12 05						
Dronfield	d				11 15									12 15						
Chesterfield	d				11 22									12 22						
Alfreton	d				11 33									12 33						
Langley Mill	d				11 40									12 40						
Nottingham	a				12 02									13 00						

		NT	NT	NT	NT	NT	TP ◇■	NT	NT	NT	NT	NT	NT	NT	NT	TP ◇■	NT	NT	NT	NT	NT	NT
Leeds ■	31 d			11 32	12 05					12 37		12 32		13 05					13 37		13 32	
Woodlesford	d			11 40								12 40									13 40	
Castleford	d			11 51								12 51									13 51	
Normanton	d			11 57								12 57									13 57	
Wakefield Kirkgate ■	31 a			12 01	12 23					12 54		13 02		13 23					13 54		14 01	
	d			12 04	12 23					12 55		13 04		13 23					13 55		14 04	
Darton	d			12 15								13 15									14 15	
Huddersfield	d								12 13									13 13				
Lockwood	d								12 16									13 16				
Berry Brow	d								12 19									13 19				
Honley	d								12 22									13 22				
Brockholes	d								12 25									13 25				
Stocksmoor	d								12 29									13 29				
Shepley	d								12 31									13 31				
Denby Dale	d								12 36									13 36				
Penistone	d								12 44									13 44				
Silkstone Common	d								12 49									13 49				
Dodworth	d								12 53									13 53				
Barnsley	a			12 21	12 39				13 00	13 11		13 21		13 39				14 00	14 11		14 21	
	d			12 24	12 40				13 01	13 14		13 24		13 40				14 01	14 14		14 24	
Wombwell	d			12 29					13 06			13 29						14 06			14 29	
Elsecar	d			12 33								13 33									14 33	
Chapeltown	d			12 38					13 13			13 38						14 13			14 38	
Meadowhall	29,31 a			12 46	12 52				13 20	13 27		13 46		13 52				14 20	14 27		14 46	
	d	12 33	12 50	12 46	12 52	12 55	13 01	13 06	13 20	13 28	13 33	13 46	13 50	3 52	13 55	14 01	14 06	14 20	14 28	14 33	14 46	14 50
Sheffield ■	29,31 a	12 41	13 00	12 56	13 02	13 05	13 08	13 20	13 30	13 37	13 41	13 56	14 00	4 02	14 05	14 08	14 20	14 30	14 37	14 41	14 56	15 00
	d				13 05									14 05								
Dronfield	d				13 15									14 15								
Chesterfield	d				13 22									14 22								
Alfreton	d				13 33									14 33								
Langley Mill	d				13 40									14 40								
Nottingham	a				14 00									15 00								

Table 34

Mondays to Fridays
until 03 September

Leeds and Huddersfield - Barnsley - Sheffield, Nottingham

		NT	NT	TP ◇■	NT	NT	NT	NT	NT	NT	NT	NT	NT	TP ◇■	NT	NT	NT	NT	EM ◇	NT
Leeds ■	31 d	14 05					14 37		14 32		15 05	15 32						15 37		
Woodlesford	d								14 40			15 40								
Castleford	d								14 51			15 51								
Normanton	d								14 57			15 57								
Wakefield Kirkgate ■	31 a	14 23					14 54		15 01		15 23	16 01						15 54		
	d	14 23					14 55		15 04		15 23	16 04						15 55		
Darton	d								15 15			16 15								
Huddersfield	d					14 13											15 13			
Lockwood	d					14 16											15 16			
Berry Brow	d					14 19											15 19			
Honley	d					14 22											15 22			
Brockholes	d					14 25											15 25			
Stocksmoor	d					14 29											15 29			
Shepley	d					14 31											15 31			
Denby Dale	d					14 36											15 36			
Penistone	d					14 44											15 44			
Silkstone Common	d					14 49											15 49			
Dodworth	d					14 53											15 53			
Barnsley	a	14 39				15 00	15 11		15 21		15 39	16 21					16 00	16 11		
	d	14 40				15 01	15 14		15 24		15 40	16 24					16 01	16 14		
Wombwell	d					15 06			15 29			16 29					16 06			
Elsecar	d								15 33			16 33								
Chapeltown	d					15 13			15 38			16 38					16 13			
Meadowhall	29,31 a	14 52				15 20	15 27		15 46		15 52	16 46					16 20	16 27		
	d	14 52	14 55	15 01	15 06	15 20	15 28	15 33	15 46	15 50	15 52	16 46	15 55	16 01	16 07	16 18	16 20	16 28		16 33
Sheffield ■	29,31 a	15 02	15 05	15 08	15 19	15 30	15 37	15 41	15 56	16 00	16 02	16 56	16 05	16 08	16 20	16 25	16 30	16 37		16 41
	d	15 05									16 05								16 38	
Dronfield	d	15 15									16 15								16 48	
Chesterfield	d	15 22									16 22								16 56	
Alfreton	d	15 33									16 33								17 07	
Langley Mill	d	15 40									16 40									
Nottingham	a	16 00									17 00								17 31	

		NT	NT	NT	TP ◇■	NT	NT	NT	NT	EM ◇	NT	NT	NT	NT	TP ◇■	NT	NT	NT	NT	NT	NT
Leeds ■	31 d		16 05					16 37			16 32		17 05					17 37		17 32	
Woodlesford	d										16 40									17 40	
Castleford	d										16 51									17 51	
Normanton	d										16 57		17 18							17 57	
Wakefield Kirkgate ■	31 a		16 23					16 54			17 01		17 22					17 54		18 01	
	d		16 23					16 55			17 04		17 23					17 55		18 04	
Darton	d										17 15									18 15	
Huddersfield	d						16 13										17 13				
Lockwood	d						16 16										17 16				
Berry Brow	d						16 19										17 19				
Honley	d						16 22										17 22				
Brockholes	d						16 25										17 25				
Stocksmoor	d						16 29										17 29				
Shepley	d						16 31										17 31				
Denby Dale	d						16 36										17 36				
Penistone	d						16 44										17 44				
Silkstone Common	d						16 49										17 49				
Dodworth	d						16 53										17 53				
Barnsley	a		16 39				17 00	17 11			17 21		17 39				18 00	18 11		18 21	
	d		16 40				17 01	17 14			17 24		17 40				18 01	18 14		18 24	
Wombwell	d						17 06				17 29						18 06			18 29	
Elsecar	d										17 33									18 33	
Chapeltown	d						17 13				17 38						18 13			18 38	
Meadowhall	29,31 a		16 52				17 20	17 27			17 46		17 51				18 20	18 27		18 46	
	d	16 50	16 52	16 55	17 01	17 06	17 21	17 28	17 33		17 46	17 50	17 52	17 57	18 01	18 06	18 20	18 28	18 33	18 46	18 50
Sheffield ■	29,31 a	17 00	17 02	17 05	17 08	17 19	17 31	17 37	17 41		17 56	18 00	18 02	18 04	18 08	18 19	18 30	18 38	18 43	18 56	19 00
	d		17 05							17 44			18 05								
Dronfield	d		17 15							17 56			18 15								
Chesterfield	d		17 22							18 02			18 22								
Alfreton	d		17 33							18 12			18 33								
Langley Mill	d		17 40										18 40								
Nottingham	a		18 00							18 34			19 00								

Table 34

Leeds and Huddersfield - Barnsley - Sheffield, Nottingham

Mondays to Fridays
until 03 September

		NT	NT	TP ◇1	NT	NT	NT	NT	NT	NT	NT		NT	NT	TP ◇1	NT		NT	NT	NT	NT	NT	TP ◇1	NT	EM ◇
Leeds 10 31	d	18 05							18 43	18 32			19 05						19 43		19 37			20 30	
Woodlesford	d									18 40											19 45				
Castleford	d									18 51											19 56				
Normanton	d									18 57											20 02				
Wakefield Kirkgate 4 31	a	18 23							18 59	19 04			19 22						19 59		20 06			20 46	
	d	18 23							18 59	19 04			19 24						20 00		20 07			20 46	
Darton	d									19 15											20 19				
Huddersfield	d					17 56		18 22										19 18							
Lockwood	d					17 59		18 25										19 21							
Berry Brow	d					18 02		18 28										19 24							
Honley	d					18 05		18 31										19 27							
Brockholes	d					18 08		18 34										19 30							
Stocksmoor	d					18 12		18 38										19 34							
Shepley	d					18 14		18 40										19 36							
Denby Dale	d					18 19		18 45										19 43							
Penistone	d					18 31		18 53										19 49							
Silkstone Common	d					18 36		18 58										19 54							
Dodworth	d					18 40		19 02										19 58							
Barnsley	a	18 39				18 47		19 09	19 15	19 24			19 40					20 05	20 16		20 24			21 02	
	d	18 40				18 55		19 10	19 18	19 24			19 40					20 06	20 16		20 24			21 03	
Wombwell	d					19 00		19 15		19 29								20 11			20 29				
Elsecar	d					19 04				19 33											20 33				
Chapeltown	d					19 09		19 22		19 38								20 18			20 38				
Meadowhall 29,31	a	18 52				19 16		19 29		19 46			19 52					20 24	20 32		20 45			21 17	
	d	18 52	18 57	19 01	19 06	19 16	19 25	19 30	19 34	19 46	19 50		19 52	19 57	20 01	20 07		20 26	20 32	20 33	20 46	20 51	21 07	21 19	
Sheffield 7 29,31	a	19 03	19 06	19 08	19 17	19 27	19 35	19 40	19 43	19 57	20 00		20 03	20 06	20 08	20 18		20 36	20 44	20 41	20 58	21 02	21 19	21 30	21 35
	d	19 05											20 05												21 39
Dronfield	d	19 15											20 15												21 49
Chesterfield	d	19 22											20 22												21 55
Alfreton	d	19 33											20 33												22 05
Langley Mill	d	19 40											20 40												22 12
Nottingham	a	20 00											21 00												22 38

		NT		NT	NT	NT		TP ◇1	NT	NT	NT	NT		NT	NT		NT	NT	NT						
Leeds 10 31	d				20 37									21 37				22 37							
Woodlesford	d				20 45									21 45				22 45							
Castleford	d				20 56									21 56				22 56							
Normanton	d				21 02									22 02				23 01							
Wakefield Kirkgate 4 31	a				21 06									22 06				23 10							
	d				21 07									22 07				23 10							
Darton	d				21 18									22 18				23 24							
Huddersfield	d	20 18									21 18						22 18								
Lockwood	d	20 21									21 21						22 21								
Berry Brow	d	20 24									21 24						22 24								
Honley	d	20 27									21 27						22 27								
Brockholes	d	20 30									21 30						22 30								
Stocksmoor	d	20 34									21 34						22 34								
Shepley	d	20 36									21 36						22 36								
Denby Dale	d	20 41									21 41						22 41								
Penistone	d	20 49									21 49						22 49								
Silkstone Common	d	20 54									21 54						22 54								
Dodworth	d	20 58									21 58						22 58								
Barnsley	a	21 08			21 24						22 05			22 25			23 05	23 31							
	d	21 11			21 24						22 06			22 25			23 06	23 31							
Wombwell	d	21 16			21 29						22 11			22 30			23 11	23 36							
Elsecar	d				21 33									22 34			23 15	23 40							
Chapeltown	d	21 23			21 38						22 18			22 39			23 20	23 45							
Meadowhall 29,31	a	21 28			21 45						22 23			22 47			23 25	23 51							
	d	21 29		21 36	21 46	21 52		21 58	22 03	22 09	22 25	22 44		22 47	22 52		23 26	23 51	23 54						
Sheffield 7 29,31	a	21 41		21 47	21 58	22 05		22 08	22 11	22 21	22 36	22 54		22 58	23 02		23 36	00 02	00 04						
	d	21 44																							
Dronfield	d																								
Chesterfield	d																								
Alfreton	d																								
Langley Mill	d																								
Nottingham	a																								

Table 34

Leeds and Huddersfield - Barnsley - Sheffield, Nottingham

Mondays to Fridays
from 06 September

					NT	NT	TP ◇1	NT	NT	NT			NT	NT	NT	TP ◇1	NT	NT	NT	NT				TP ◇1	NT
Leeds 10 31	d													06 05						06 38						
Woodlesford	d																		06 46						
Castleford	d																		06 57						
Normanton	d																		07 03						
Wakefield Kirkgate 4 31	a													06 21						07 07						
	d												06 04	06 21						07 08						
Darton	d												06 15							07 19						
Huddersfield	d																06 05								
Lockwood	d																06 08								
Berry Brow	d																06 11								
Honley	d																06 14								
Brockholes	d																06 17								
Stocksmoor	d																06 21								
Shepley	d																06 23								
Denby Dale	d																06 34								
Penistone	d																06 42								
Silkstone Common	d																06 47								
Dodworth	d																06 51								
Barnsley	a												06 20	06 37			06 57		07 25						
	d				05 23			05 50					06 21	06 38			06 58		07 25						
Wombwell	d				05 28			05 55					06 26				07 03		07 30						
Elsecar	d				05 32			05 59					06 30				07 07		07 34						
Chapeltown	d				05 37			06 04					06 35				07 12		07 39						
Meadowhall 29,31	a				05 43			06 10					06 41	06 49			07 20		07 48						
	d			00 08	05 43		05 58	06 10	06 28	06 37			06 42	06 49	06 52	06 58	07 20	07 33	07 48	07 47				07 53	08 06
Sheffield 7 29,31	a			00 22	05 53		06 08	06 25	06 38	06 47			06 55	07 00	07 07	07 06	07 29	07 40	07 57	07 57				08 00	08 18
	d					06 00								07 03											
Dronfield	d					06 10								07 13											
Chesterfield	d					06 16								07 20											
Alfreton	d					06 30								07 33											
Langley Mill	d					06 37								07 40											
Nottingham	a					07 08								08 02											

		NT	NT	NT		NT		NT	NT		TP ◇1	NT	NT	NT	NT		NT	NT	NT		NT	TP ◇1	NT	NT	NT
Leeds 10 31	d			07 35	07 29			08 02						08 37			08 32		09 05						09 37
Woodlesford	d				07 37												08 40								
Castleford	d				07 48												08 51								
Normanton	d				07 54												08 57								
Wakefield Kirkgate 4 31	a			07 54	08 00			08 23						08 54			09 03		09 23						09 54
	d			07 55	08 04			08 23						08 55			09 04		09 23						09 55
Darton	d				08 15												09 15								
Huddersfield	d	07 08											08 07											09 08	
Lockwood	d	07 11											08 10											09 11	
Berry Brow	d	07 14											08 13											09 14	
Honley	d	07 17											08 16											09 17	
Brockholes	d	07 20											08 19											09 20	
Stocksmoor	d	07 24											08 23											09 24	
Shepley	d	07 26											08 25											09 26	
Denby Dale	d	07 34											08 34											09 36	
Penistone	d	07 42											08 42											09 44	
Silkstone Common	d	07 47											08 47											09 49	
Dodworth	d	07 51											08 51											09 53	
Barnsley	a	07 57		08 11	08 21			08 39					09 00	09 11			09 23		09 39					10 00	10 12
	d	07 58		08 14	08 24			08 40					09 01	09 14			09 24		09 40					10 01	10 14
Wombwell	d	08 03			08 29								09 06				09 29							10 06	
Elsecar	d	08 07			08 33								09 10				09 33								
Chapeltown	d	08 12			08 38								09 15				09 38							10 13	
Meadowhall 29,31	a	08 20		08 31	08 45			08 52					09 21	09 27			09 46		09 52					10 20	10 27
	d	08 20	08 22	08 31	08 45	08 49		08 52	08 55		09 01	09 15	09 21	09 28	09 33		09 46	09 50	09 52		09 55	10 01	10 07	10 21	10 28
Sheffield 7 29,31	a	08 29	08 32	08 39	08 55	08 58		09 02	09 05		09 08	09 26	09 30	09 37	09 41		09 56	10 00	10 02		10 05	10 08	10 20	10 30	10 37
	d							09 05											10 05						
Dronfield	d							09 15											10 15						
Chesterfield	d							09 22											10 22						
Alfreton	d							09 33											10 33						
Langley Mill	d							09 40											10 40						
Nottingham	a							10 00											11 00						

Table 34

Mondays to Fridays

from 06 September

Leeds and Huddersfield - Barnsley - Sheffield, Nottingham

			NT		NT	NT			NT	TP	NT	NT	NT	NT	NT	NT		NT		NT	TP	NT	NT		NT	NT
										◇1											◇1					
Leeds 10	31	d				10 05	09 32						10 37		10 32			11 05								11 37
Woodlesford		d					09 40								10 40											
Castleford		d					09 51								10 51											
Normanton		d					09 57								10 57											
Wakefield Kirkgate 4	31	a				10 23	10 01						10 54		11 01			11 23								11 54
		d				10 23	10 04						10 55		11 04			11 23								11 55
Darton		d					10 15								11 15											
Huddersfield		d										10 08													11 08	
Lockwood		d										10 11													11 11	
Berry Brow		d										10 14													11 14	
Honley		d										10 17													11 17	
Brockholes		d										10 20													11 20	
Stocksmoor		d										10 24													11 24	
Shepley		d										10 26													11 26	
Denby Dale		d										10 36													11 36	
Penistone		d										10 44													11 44	
Silkstone Common		d										10 49													11 49	
Dodworth		d										10 53													11 53	
Barnsley		a				10 39	10 21					11 00	11 11		11 21			11 39							12 00	12 11
		d				10 40	10 24					11 01	11 14		11 24			11 40							12 01	12 14
Wombwell		d					10 29					11 06			11 29										12 06	
Elsecar		d					10 33								11 33											
Chapeltown		d					10 38					11 13			11 38										12 13	
Meadowhall	29,31	a				10 52	10 46					11 19	11 27		11 46			11 52							12 20	12 27
		d	10 33		10 50	10 52	10 47		10 57	11 01	11 06	11 19	11 28	11 33	11 46	11 50		11 52		11 55	12 01	12 06	12 16		12 21	12 28
Sheffield 7	29,31	a	10 41		11 00	11 02	10 56		11 05	11 08	11 20	11 30	11 37	11 41	11 56	12 00		12 02		12 05	12 08	12 19	12 26		12 30	12 37
		d				11 05												12 05								
Dronfield		d				11 15												12 15								
Chesterfield		d				11 22												12 22								
Alfreton		d				11 33												12 33								
Langley Mill		d				11 40												12 40								
Nottingham		a				12 02												13 00								

			NT	NT	NT	NT	NT	TP		NT	NT	NT	NT	NT	NT	NT		NT		TP	NT	NT	NT	NT	NT	NT
								◇1												◇1						
Leeds 10	31	d		11 32		12 05						12 37		12 32		13 05							13 37		13 32	
Woodlesford		d		11 40										12 40											13 40	
Castleford		d		11 51										12 51											13 51	
Normanton		d		11 57										12 57											13 57	
Wakefield Kirkgate 4	31	a		12 01		12 23						12 54		13 02		13 23							13 54		14 01	
		d		12 04		12 23						12 55		13 04		13 23							13 55		14 04	
Darton		d		12 15										13 15											14 15	
Huddersfield		d									12 08											13 08				
Lockwood		d									12 11											13 11				
Berry Brow		d									12 14											13 14				
Honley		d									12 17											13 17				
Brockholes		d									12 20											13 20				
Stocksmoor		d									12 24											13 24				
Shepley		d									12 26											13 26				
Denby Dale		d									12 36											13 36				
Penistone		d									12 44											13 44				
Silkstone Common		d									12 49											13 49				
Dodworth		d									12 53											13 53				
Barnsley		a		12 21		12 39					13 00	13 11		13 21		13 39						14 00	14 11		14 21	
		d		12 24		12 40					13 01	13 14		13 24		13 40						14 01	14 14		14 24	
Wombwell		d		12 29							13 06			13 29								14 06			14 29	
Elsecar		d		12 33										13 33											14 33	
Chapeltown		d		12 38							13 13			13 38								14 13			14 38	
Meadowhall	29,31	a		12 46		12 52					13 20	13 27		13 46		13 52						14 20	14 27		14 46	
		d	12 33	12 46	12 50	12 52	12 55	13 01		13 06	13 20	13 28	13 33	13 46	13 50	13 52		13 55		14 01	14 06	14 20	14 28	14 33	14 46	14 50
Sheffield 7	29,31	a	12 41	12 56	13 00	13 02	13 05	13 08		13 20	13 30	13 37	13 41	13 56	14 00	14 02		14 05		14 08	14 20	14 30	14 37	14 41	14 56	15 00
		d				13 05										14 05										
Dronfield		d				13 15										14 15										
Chesterfield		d				13 22										14 22										
Alfreton		d				13 33										14 33										
Langley Mill		d				13 40										14 40										
Nottingham		a				14 00										15 00										

Table 34

Mondays to Fridays

from 06 September

Leeds and Huddersfield - Barnsley - Sheffield, Nottingham

				NT			NT	TP	NT	NT	NT	NT	NT	NT	NT		NT	TP	NT	NT	NT	NT	NT	EM	NT	NT
								◇1										◇1						◇		
Leeds 10	31	d		14 05							14 37		14 32		15 05							15 37			15 32	
Woodlesford		d											14 40												15 40	
Castleford		d											14 51												15 51	
Normanton		d											14 57												15 57	
Wakefield Kirkgate 4	31	a		14 23							14 54		15 01		15 23							15 54			16 01	
		d		14 23							14 55		15 04		15 23							15 55			16 04	
Darton		d											15 15												16 15	
Huddersfield		d								14 08											15 08					
Lockwood		d								14 11											15 11					
Berry Brow		d								14 14											15 14					
Honley		d								14 17											15 17					
Brockholes		d								14 20											15 20					
Stocksmoor		d								14 24											15 24					
Shepley		d								14 26											15 26					
Denby Dale		d								14 36											15 36					
Penistone		d								14 44											15 44					
Silkstone Common		d								14 49											15 49					
Dodworth		d								14 53											15 53					
Barnsley		a		14 39						15 00	15 11		15 21		15 39						16 00	16 11			16 21	
		d		14 40						15 01	15 14		15 24		15 40						16 01	16 14			16 24	
Wombwell		d								15 06			15 29								16 06				16 29	
Elsecar		d											15 33												16 33	
Chapeltown		d								15 13			15 38								16 13				16 38	
Meadowhall	29,31	a		14 52						15 20	15 27		15 46		15 52						16 20	16 27			16 46	
		d		14 52			14 55	15 01	15 06	15 20	15 28	15 33	15 46	15 50	15 52		15 55	16 01	16 07	16 18	16 20	16 28	16 33		16 46	16 50
Sheffield 7	29,31	a		15 02			15 05	15 08	15 19	15 30	15 37	15 41	15 56	16 00	16 02		16 05	16 08	16 20	16 25	16 30	16 37	16 41		16 56	17 00
		d		15 05											16 05									16 38		
Dronfield		d		15 15											16 15									16 48		
Chesterfield		d		15 22											16 22									16 56		
Alfreton		d		15 33											16 33									17 07		
Langley Mill		d		15 40											16 40											
Nottingham		a		16 00											17 00									17 31		

				NT		NT	TP	NT	NT	NT	EM	NT	NT	NT			NT	TP	NT	NT	NT		NT	NT		NT
							◇1				◇							◇1								
Leeds 10	31	d		16 05						16 37		16 32		17 05							17 37			17 32		
Woodlesford		d										16 40												17 40		
Castleford		d										16 51												17 51		
Normanton		d										16 57		17 18										17 57		
Wakefield Kirkgate 4	31	a		16 23						16 54		17 01		17 22							17 54			18 01		
		d		16 23						16 55		17 04		17 23							17 55			18 04		
Darton		d										17 15												18 15		
Huddersfield		d							16 08											17 08						
Lockwood		d							16 11											17 11						
Berry Brow		d							16 14											17 14						
Honley		d							16 17											17 17						
Brockholes		d							16 20											17 20						
Stocksmoor		d							16 24											17 24						
Shepley		d							16 26											17 26						
Denby Dale		d							16 36											17 36						
Penistone		d							16 44											17 44						
Silkstone Common		d							16 49											17 49						
Dodworth		d							16 53											17 53						
Barnsley		a		16 39					17 00	17 11		17 21		17 39						18 00	18 11			18 21		
		d		16 40					17 01	17 14		17 24		17 40						18 01	18 14			18 24		
Wombwell		d							17 06			17 29								18 06				18 29		
Elsecar		d										17 33												18 33		
Chapeltown		d							17 13			17 38								18 13				18 38		
Meadowhall	29,31	a		16 52					17 20	17 27		17 46		17 51						18 20	18 27			18 46		
		d		16 52		16 55	17 01	17 06	17 21	17 28		17 46	17 50	17 52			17 57	18 01	18 06	18 20	18 28		18 33	18 46		18 50
Sheffield 7	29,31	a		17 02		17 05	17 08	17 19	17 31	17 37	17 37	17 56	18 00	18 02			18 04	18 08	18 19	18 30	18 38		18 43	18 56		19 00
		d		17 05							17 44			18 05												
Dronfield		d		17 15							17 56			18 15												
Chesterfield		d		17 22							18 02			18 22												
Alfreton		d		17 33							18 12			18 33												
Langley Mill		d		17 40										18 40												
Nottingham		a		18 00							18 34			19 00												

Table 34

Mondays to Fridays
from 06 September

Leeds and Huddersfield - Barnsley - Sheffield, Nottingham

Station		NT	NT	TP ◇1 ⌶	NT	NT	NT	NT	NT	NT	NT	NT	TP ◇1 ⌶	NT	NT	NT	NT	NT	NT	TP ◇1	NT	EM ◇
Leeds 10	31 d	18 05							18 43		19 05					19 43		19 37			20 30	
Woodlesford	d																	19 45				
Castleford	d																	19 56				
Normanton	d																	20 02				
Wakefield Kirkgate 4	31 a	18 23							18 59		19 22					19 59		20 06			20 46	
	d	18 23							18 59		19 24					20 00		20 07			20 46	
Darton	d																	20 19				
Huddersfield	d					17 56		18 22							19 15							
Lockwood	d					17 59		18 25							19 18							
Berry Brow	d					18 02		18 28							19 21							
Honley	d					18 05		18 31							19 24							
Brockholes	d					18 08		18 34							19 27							
Stocksmoor	d					18 12		18 38							19 31							
Shepley	d					18 14		18 40							19 33							
Denby Dale	d					18 19		18 45							19 43							
Penistone	d					18 31		18 53							19 49							
Silkstone Common	d					18 36		18 58							19 54							
Dodworth	d					18 40		19 02							19 58							
Barnsley	a	18 39				18 47		19 09	19 15		19 40				20 05	20 16		20 24			21 02	
	d	18 40				18 55		19 10	19 18		19 40				20 06	20 16		20 24			21 03	
Wombwell	d					19 00		19 15							20 11			20 29				
Elsecar	d					19 04												20 33				
Chapeltown	d					19 09		19 22							20 18			20 38				
Meadowhall	29,31 ⇌ a	18 52				19 16		19 29	19 33		19 52				20 24	20 32		20 45			21 17	
	d	18 52	18 57	19 01	19 06	19 16	19 25	19 30	19 34	19 50	19 52	19 57	20 01	20 07	20 26	20 32	20 33	20 46	20 51	21 07	21 19	
Sheffield 7	29,31 ⇌ a	19 03	19 06	19 08	19 17	19 27	19 35	19 40	19 43	20 00	20 03	20 06	20 08	20 18	20 36	20 44	20 41	20 58	21 02	21 19	21 30	21 35
	d	19 05									20 05											21 39
Dronfield	d	19 15									20 15											21 49
Chesterfield	d	19 22									20 22											21 55
Alfreton	d	19 33									20 33											22 05
Langley Mill	d	19 40									20 40											22 12
Nottingham	a	20 00									21 00											22 38

Station		NT	NT	NT	NT	TP ◇1	NT	NT	NT	NT	NT	NT	NT	NT	NT	NT
Leeds 10	31 d			20 37							21 37			22 37		
Woodlesford	d			20 45							21 45			22 45		
Castleford	d			20 56							21 56			22 56		
Normanton	d			21 02							22 02			23 01		
Wakefield Kirkgate 4	31 a			21 06							22 06			23 10		
	d			21 07							22 07			23 10		
Darton	d			21 18							22 18			23 24		
Huddersfield	d	20 18							21 18				22 15			
Lockwood	d	20 21							21 21				22 18			
Berry Brow	d	20 24							21 24				22 21			
Honley	d	20 27							21 27				22 24			
Brockholes	d	20 30							21 30				22 27			
Stocksmoor	d	20 34							21 34				22 31			
Shepley	d	20 36							21 36				22 33			
Denby Dale	d	20 41							21 41				22 41			
Penistone	d	20 52							21 49				22 49			
Silkstone Common	d	20 54							21 54				22 54			
Dodworth	d	20 58							21 58				22 58			
Barnsley	a	21 08		21 24					22 05		22 25		23 05	23 31		
	d	21 11		21 24					22 06		22 25		23 06	23 31		
Wombwell	d	21 16		21 29					22 11		22 30		23 11	23 36		
Elsecar	d			21 33							22 34		23 15	23 40		
Chapeltown	d	21 23		21 38					22 18		22 39		23 20	23 45		
Meadowhall	29,31 ⇌ a	21 28		21 45					22 23		22 47		23 25	23 51		
	d	21 29	21 36	21 46	21 52	21 58	22 03	22 09	22 25	22 44	22 47	22 52	23 26	23 51	23 54	00 08
Sheffield 7	29,31 ⇌ a	21 41	21 47	21 58	22 05	22 08	22 11	22 21	22 36	22 54	22 58	23 02	23 36	00 02	00 04	00 22
	d	21 44														
Dronfield	d															
Chesterfield	d															
Alfreton	d															
Langley Mill	d															
Nottingham	a															

Table 34

Saturdays
until 04 September

Leeds and Huddersfield - Barnsley - Sheffield, Nottingham

Station		NT	NT	TP ◇1	NT	NT	NT	NT	TP ◇1 ⌶	NT	NT	NT	NT	TP ◇1 ⌶	NT	NT	NT	NT	NT	NT
Leeds 10	31 d											06 38						07 35	07 29	
Woodlesford	d											06 46							07 37	
Castleford	d											06 57							07 48	
Normanton	d											07 03							07 54	
Wakefield Kirkgate 4	31 a											07 07						07 54	08 00	
	d											07 08						07 55	08 04	
Darton	d											07 19							08 15	
Huddersfield	d									06 10						07 10				
Lockwood	d									06 13						07 13				
Berry Brow	d									06 16						07 16				
Honley	d									06 19						07 19				
Brockholes	d									06 22						07 22				
Stocksmoor	d									06 26						07 26				
Shepley	d									06 28						07 28				
Denby Dale	d									06 34						07 34				
Penistone	d									06 42						07 42				
Silkstone Common	d									06 47						07 47				
Dodworth	d									06 51						07 51				
Barnsley	a									06 57		07 25				07 57		08 11	08 21	
	d		05 23		05 50		06 21			06 58		07 25				07 58		08 14	08 24	
Wombwell	d		05 28		05 55		06 26			07 03		07 30				08 03			08 29	
Elsecar	d		05 32		05 59		06 30			07 07		07 34				08 07			08 33	
Chapeltown	d		05 37		06 04		06 35			07 12		07 39				08 12			08 38	
Meadowhall	29,31 ⇌ a		05 43		06 10		06 41			07 20		07 48				08 18		08 31	08 45	
	d	00 08	05 43	05 58	06 10	06 27	06 42	06 52	06 58	07 20	07 33	07 48	07 47	07 53	08 06	08 18	08 22	08 31	08 45	08 55
Sheffield 7	29,31 ⇌ a	00 22	05 54	06 08	06 25	06 38	06 55	07 07	07 06	07 29	07 45	07 57	07 57	08 00	08 18	08 29	08 32	08 39	08 55	09 05
	d						07 03													
Dronfield	d						07 13													
Chesterfield	d						07 20													
Alfreton	d						07 33													
Langley Mill	d						07 40													
Nottingham	a						08 02													

Station		NT	NT	TP ◇1 ⌶	NT	NT	NT	NT	NT	NT	NT	NT	TP ◇1 ⌶	NT	NT	NT	NT	NT	NT
Leeds 10	31 d		08 05				08 37		08 32		09 05					09 37		09 32	
Woodlesford	d								08 40									09 40	
Castleford	d								08 51									09 51	
Normanton	d								08 57									09 57	
Wakefield Kirkgate 4	31 a		08 23				08 54		09 03		09 23					09 54		10 01	
	d		08 23				08 55		09 04		09 23					09 55		10 04	
Darton	d								09 15									10 15	
Huddersfield	d					08 10									09 13				
Lockwood	d					08 13									09 16				
Berry Brow	d					08 16									09 19				
Honley	d					08 19									09 22				
Brockholes	d					08 22									09 25				
Stocksmoor	d					08 26									09 29				
Shepley	d					08 28									09 31				
Denby Dale	d					08 34									09 36				
Penistone	d					08 42									09 44				
Silkstone Common	d					08 47									09 49				
Dodworth	d					08 51									09 53				
Barnsley	a		08 39			08 57	09 11		09 23		09 39				10 00	10 12		10 21	
	d		08 40			08 58	09 14		09 24		09 40				10 01	10 14		10 24	
Wombwell	d					09 03			09 29						10 06			10 29	
Elsecar	d					09 07			09 33									10 33	
Chapeltown	d					09 12			09 38						10 13			10 38	
Meadowhall	29,31 ⇌ a		08 52			09 20	09 27		09 46		09 52				10 20	10 27		10 46	
	d	08 49	08 52	09 01	09 19	09 21	09 28	09 33	09 46	09 50	09 52	09 55	10 01	10 07	10 21	10 28	10 33	10 47	10 50
Sheffield 7	29,31 ⇌ a	08 58	09 02	09 08	09 28	09 30	09 37	09 41	09 56	10 00	10 02	10 05	10 08	10 20	10 30	10 37	10 41	10 56	11 00
	d		09 05								10 05								
Dronfield	d		09 15								10 15								
Chesterfield	d		09 22								10 22								
Alfreton	d		09 33								10 33								
Langley Mill	d		09 40								10 40								
Nottingham	a		10 00								11 00								

Table 34

Saturdays
until 04 September

Leeds and Huddersfield - Barnsley - Sheffield, Nottingham

	NT	TP ◇1	NT	NT	NT	NT	NT	NT	NT	TP ◇1	NT	NT	NT	NT	NT	NT	NT	NT	NT
Leeds 10 31 d					10 37		10 32		11 05						11 37		11 32		12 05
Woodlesford d							10 40										11 40		
Castleford d							10 51										11 51		
Normanton d							10 57										11 57		
Wakefield Kirkgate 4 31 a					10 54		11 01		11 23						11 54		12 01		12 23
d					10 55		11 04		11 23						11 55		12 04		12 23
Darton d							11 15										12 15		
Huddersfield d				10 13										11 13					
Lockwood d				10 16										11 16					
Berry Brow d				10 19										11 19					
Honley d				10 22										11 22					
Brockholes d				10 25										11 25					
Stocksmoor d				10 29										11 29					
Shepley d				10 31										11 31					
Denby Dale d				10 36										11 36					
Penistone d				10 44										11 44					
Silkstone Common d				10 49										11 49					
Dodworth d				10 53										11 53					
Barnsley a				11 00	11 11		11 21		11 39					12 00	12 11		12 21		12 39
d				11 01	11 14		11 24		11 40					12 01	12 14		12 24		12 40
Wombwell d				11 06			11 29							12 06			12 29		
Elsecar d							11 33										12 33		
Chapeltown d				11 13			11 38							12 13			12 38		
Meadowhall 29,31 ⇌ a				11 18	11 27		11 46		11 52					12 20	12 27		12 46		12 52
d	10 57	11 01	11 06	11 19	11 28	11 33	11 46	11 50	11 52	11 59	12 00	12 06	12 16	12 21	12 28	12 33	12 46	12 50	12 52
Sheffield 7 29,31 ⇌ a	11 06	11 08	11 20	11 29	11 37	11 41	11 56	12 00	12 02	12 08	12 10	12 20	12 25	12 30	12 37	12 41	12 56	13 00	13 02
d									12 05										13 05
Dronfield d									12 15										13 15
Chesterfield d									12 22										13 22
Alfreton d									12 33										13 33
Langley Mill d									12 40										13 40
Nottingham a									13 00										14 00

	NT	TP ◇1	NT	NT	NT	NT	NT	NT	NT	TP ◇1	NT	NT	NT	NT	NT	NT	NT	NT	TP ◇1	NT
Leeds 10 31 d					12 37	12 32		13 05					13 37		13 32		14 05			
Woodlesford d						12 40									13 40					
Castleford d						12 51									13 51					
Normanton d						12 57									13 57					
Wakefield Kirkgate 4 31 a					12 54	13 02		13 23					13 54		14 01		14 23			
d					12 55	13 04		13 23					13 55		14 04		14 23			
Darton d						13 15									14 15					
Huddersfield d				12 13								13 13								
Lockwood d				12 16								13 16								
Berry Brow d				12 19								13 19								
Honley d				12 22								13 22								
Brockholes d				12 25								13 25								
Stocksmoor d				12 29								13 29								
Shepley d				12 31								13 31								
Denby Dale d				12 36								13 34								
Penistone d				12 44								13 44								
Silkstone Common d				12 49								13 49								
Dodworth d				12 53								13 53								
Barnsley a				13 00	13 11	13 21		13 39				14 00	14 11		14 21		14 39			
d				13 01	13 14	13 24		13 40				14 01	14 14		14 24		14 40			
Wombwell d				13 06		13 29						14 06			14 29					
Elsecar d						13 33									14 33					
Chapeltown d				13 13		13 38						14 13			14 38					
Meadowhall 29,31 ⇌ a				13 20	13 27	13 46		13 52				14 20	14 27		14 46		14 52			
d	12 55	13 01	13 06	13 20	13 28	13 46	13 50	13 52	13 55	14 01	14 06	14 20	14 28	14 33	14 46	14 50	14 52	14 55	15 01	15 06
Sheffield 7 29,31 ⇌ a	13 05	13 08	13 20	13 30	13 37	13 56	14 00	14 02	14 05	14 08	14 20	14 30	14 37	14 41	14 56	15 00	15 02	15 05	15 08	15 20
d								14 05									15 05			
Dronfield d								14 15									15 15			
Chesterfield d								14 22									15 22			
Alfreton d								14 33									15 33			
Langley Mill d								14 40									15 40			
Nottingham a								15 00									16 00			

Table 34

Saturdays
until 04 September

Leeds and Huddersfield - Barnsley - Sheffield, Nottingham

	NT	NT	NT	NT	NT	NT	TP ◇1	NT	NT	NT	NT	NT	EM ◇	NT	NT	NT	NT	NT	TP ◇1
Leeds 10 31 d		14 37		14 32		15 05						15 37			15 32		16 05		
Woodlesford d				14 40											15 40				
Castleford d				14 51											15 51				
Normanton d				14 57											15 57				
Wakefield Kirkgate 4 31 a		14 54		15 01		15 23						15 54			16 01		16 23		
d		14 55		15 04		15 23						15 55			16 04		16 23		
Darton d				15 15											16 15				
Huddersfield d	14 13									15 13									
Lockwood d	14 16									15 16									
Berry Brow d	14 19									15 19									
Honley d	14 22									15 22									
Brockholes d	14 25									15 25									
Stocksmoor d	14 29									15 29									
Shepley d	14 31									15 31									
Denby Dale d	14 36									15 36									
Penistone d	14 44									15 44									
Silkstone Common d	14 49									15 49									
Dodworth d	14 53									15 53									
Barnsley a	15 00	15 11		15 21		15 39				16 00		16 11			16 21		16 39		
d	15 01	15 14		15 24		15 40				16 01		16 14			16 24		16 40		
Wombwell d	15 06			15 29						16 06					16 29				
Elsecar d				15 33											16 33				
Chapeltown d	15 13			15 38						16 13					16 38				
Meadowhall 29,31 ⇌ a	15 20	15 27		15 46		15 52				16 20		16 27			16 46		16 52		
d	15 20	15 28	15 33	15 46	15 50	15 52	15 58	16 00	16 07	16 20	16 24	16 28		16 33	16 46	16 50	16 52	16 55	17 01
Sheffield 7 29,31 ⇌ a	15 30	15 37	15 41	15 56	16 00	16 02	16 08	16 10	16 20	16 30	16 35	16 37	16 35	16 41	16 56	17 00	17 02	17 05	17 08
d						16 05							16 38				17 05		
Dronfield d						16 15							16 48				17 15		
Chesterfield d						16 22							16 53				17 22		
Alfreton d						16 33							17 04				17 33		
Langley Mill d						16 40											17 40		
Nottingham a						17 00							17 29				18 00		

	NT	NT	NT	NT	NT	NT	NT	NT	TP ◇1	NT	NT	NT	NT	NT	NT	NT	NT	TP ◇1	NT	NT
Leeds 10 31 d			16 37		16 32		17 05					17 37		17 32		18 05				
Woodlesford d					16 40									17 40						
Castleford d					16 51									17 51						
Normanton d					16 57		17 18							17 57						
Wakefield Kirkgate 4 31 a			16 54		17 01		17 22					17 54		18 01		18 23				
d			16 55		17 04		17 23					17 55		18 04		18 23				
Darton d					17 15									18 15						
Huddersfield d		16 13									17 13									18 13
Lockwood d		16 16									17 16									18 16
Berry Brow d		16 19									17 19									18 19
Honley d		16 22									17 22									18 22
Brockholes d		16 25									17 25									18 25
Stocksmoor d		16 29									17 29									18 29
Shepley d		16 31									17 31									18 31
Denby Dale d		16 36									17 36									18 36
Penistone d		16 44									17 44									18 44
Silkstone Common d		16 49									17 49									18 49
Dodworth d		16 53									17 53									18 53
Barnsley a		17 00	17 11		17 21		17 39				18 00	18 11		18 21		18 39				19 01
d		17 01	17 14		17 24		17 40				18 01	18 14		18 24		18 40				19 01
Wombwell d		17 06			17 29						18 06			18 29						19 06
Elsecar d					17 33									18 33						
Chapeltown d		17 13			17 38						18 13			18 38						19 13
Meadowhall 29,31 ⇌ a		17 20	17 27		17 46		17 51				18 20	18 27		18 46		18 52				19 20
d	17 06	17 21	17 28	17 33	17 46	17 50	17 52	17 57	18 01	18 06	18 20	18 28	18 33	18 46	18 50	18 52	18 56	19 01	19 06	19 20
Sheffield 7 29,31 ⇌ a	17 19	17 32	17 37	17 41	17 56	18 00	18 02	18 05	18 08	18 19	18 30	18 38	18 41	18 56	19 00	19 03	19 05	19 08	19 17	19 30
d							18 05									19 05				
Dronfield d							18 15									19 15				
Chesterfield d							18 22									19 22				
Alfreton d							18 33									19 33				
Langley Mill d							18 40									19 40				
Nottingham a							19 00									20 00				

Table 34

Saturdays until 04 September

Leeds and Huddersfield - Barnsley - Sheffield, Nottingham

		NT	NT	NT	NT	NT	NT	TP	NT	NT	NT	NT	NT	NT	TP	NT	EM	NT	NT	NT	NT
								◇1 🛒							◇1		◇				
Leeds 10	31 d	18 37		18 32		19 05					19 43		19 37			20 30				20 37	
Woodlesford	d			18 40									19 45							20 45	
Castleford	d			18 51									19 56							20 56	
Normanton	d			18 57									20 02							21 02	
Wakefield Kirkgate 4	31 a	18 54		19 04		19 24					19 59		20 06			20 46				21 06	
	d	18 55		19 04		19 24					20 00		20 07			20 46				21 07	
Darton	d			19 15									20 19							21 18	
Huddersfield	d									19 18								20 18			
Lockwood	d									19 21								20 21			
Berry Brow	d									19 24								20 24			
Honley	d									19 27								20 27			
Brockholes	d									19 30								20 30			
Stocksmoor	d									19 34								20 34			
Shepley	d									19 36								20 36			
Denby Dale	d									19 41								20 41			
Penistone	d									19 49								20 49			
Silkstone Common	d									19 54								20 54			
Dodworth	d									19 58								20 58			
Barnsley	a	19 11		19 24		19 40				20 05	20 16		20 24			21 02		21 08		21 24	
	d	19 14		19 24		19 40				20 06	20 16		20 24			21 03		21 11		21 24	
Wombwell	d			19 29						20 11			20 29					21 16		21 29	
Elsecar	d			19 33									20 33							21 33	
Chapeltown	d			19 38						20 18			20 38					21 23		21 38	
Meadowhall	29,31 a	19 27		19 46		19 52				20 24	20 32		20 45			21 17		21 28		21 45	
	d	19 28	19 33	19 46	19 50	19 52	19 57	20 01	20 07	20 24	20 32	20 35	20 46	20 51	21 07	21 19		21 29	21 35	21 46	21 52
Sheffield 7	29,31 a	19 37	19 43	19 57	20 00	20 03	20 06	20 08	20 18	20 36	20 44	20 42	20 58	21 02	21 19	21 30	21 34	21 40	21 46	21 58	22 05
	d					20 05											21 38	21 44			
Dronfield	d					20 15											21 48				
Chesterfield	d					20 22											21 54				
Alfreton	d					20 33											22 05				
Langley Mill	d					20 40											22 12				
Nottingham	a					21 00											22 33				

		TP	NT	NT	NT	NT	NT	NT	NT	NT	NT	NT
		◇1										
Leeds 10	31 d					21 37		22 37				
Woodlesford	d					21 45		22 45				
Castleford	d					21 56		22 56				
Normanton	d					22 02		23 01				
Wakefield Kirkgate 4	31 a					22 06		23 10				
	d					22 07						
Darton	d					22 18						
Huddersfield	d				21 18					22 18		
Lockwood	d				21 21					22 21		
Berry Brow	d				21 24					22 24		
Honley	d				21 27					22 27		
Brockholes	d				21 30					22 30		
Stocksmoor	d				21 34					22 34		
Shepley	d				21 36					22 36		
Denby Dale	d				21 41					22 41		
Penistone	d				21 49					22 49		
Silkstone Common	d				21 54					22 54		
Dodworth	d				21 58					22 58		
Barnsley	a				22 05	22 25				23 05		
	d				22 06	22 25				23 06		
Wombwell	d				22 11	22 30				23 11		
Elsecar	d					22 34				23 15		
Chapeltown	d				22 18	22 39				23 20		
Meadowhall	29,31 a				22 23	22 47				23 26		
	d	21 58	22 09	22 22	22 25	22 47	22 52		22 58	23 27	23 44	23 49
Sheffield 7	29,31 a	22 10	22 21	22 32	22 36	22 58	23 02		23 05	23 36	23 58	23 59
	d											
Dronfield	d											
Chesterfield	d											
Alfreton	d											
Langley Mill	d											
Nottingham	a											

Table 34

Saturdays from 11 September

Leeds and Huddersfield - Barnsley - Sheffield, Nottingham

		NT	NT	TP	NT	NT	NT	NT	TP	NT	NT	NT	NT	TP	NT	NT	NT	NT	NT	NT
				◇1					◇1 🛒					◇1 🛒						
Leeds 10	31 d											06 38						07 35	07 29	
Woodlesford	d											06 46							07 37	
Castleford	d											06 57							07 48	
Normanton	d											07 03							07 54	
Wakefield Kirkgate 4	31 a											07 07						07 54	08 00	
	d											07 08						07 55	08 04	
Darton	d											07 19							08 15	
Huddersfield	d									06 05						07 05				
Lockwood	d									06 08						07 08				
Berry Brow	d									06 11						07 11				
Honley	d									06 14						07 14				
Brockholes	d									06 17						07 17				
Stocksmoor	d									06 21						07 21				
Shepley	d									06 23						07 23				
Denby Dale	d									06 34						07 34				
Penistone	d									06 42						07 42				
Silkstone Common	d									06 47						07 47				
Dodworth	d									06 51						07 51				
Barnsley	a									06 57		07 25				07 57		08 11	08 21	
	d		05 23		05 50		06 21			06 58		07 25				07 58		08 14	08 24	
Wombwell	d		05 28		05 55		06 26			07 03		07 30				08 03			08 29	
Elsecar	d		05 32		05 59		06 30			07 07		07 34				08 07			08 33	
Chapeltown	d		05 37		06 04		06 35			07 12		07 39				08 12			08 38	
Meadowhall	29,31 a		05 43		06 10		06 41			07 20		07 48				08 18		08 31	08 45	
	d	00 08	05 43	05 58	06 10	06 27	06 42	06 52	06 58	07 20	07 33	07 48	07 47	07 53	08 06	08 18	08 22	08 31	08 45	08 55
Sheffield 7	29,31 a	00 22	05 54	06 08	06 25	06 38	06 55	07 07	07 06	07 29	07 45	07 57	07 57	08 00	08 18	08 29	08 32	08 39	08 55	09 05
	d						07 03													
Dronfield	d						07 13													
Chesterfield	d						07 20													
Alfreton	d						07 33													
Langley Mill	d						07 40													
Nottingham	a						08 02													

		NT	NT	TP	NT	NT	NT	NT	NT	NT	NT	NT	TP	NT	NT	NT	NT	NT	NT
				◇1 🛒									◇1 🛒						
Leeds 10	31 d		08 05				08 37		08 32		09 05					09 37		09 32	
Woodlesford	d								08 40									09 40	
Castleford	d								08 51									09 51	
Normanton	d								08 57									09 57	
Wakefield Kirkgate 4	31 a		08 23				08 54		09 03		09 23					09 54		10 01	
	d		08 23				08 55		09 04		09 23					09 55		10 04	
Darton	d								09 15									10 15	
Huddersfield	d					08 07									09 08				
Lockwood	d					08 10									09 11				
Berry Brow	d					08 13									09 14				
Honley	d					08 16									09 17				
Brockholes	d					08 19									09 20				
Stocksmoor	d					08 23									09 24				
Shepley	d					08 25									09 26				
Denby Dale	d					08 34									09 36				
Penistone	d					08 42									09 44				
Silkstone Common	d					08 47									09 49				
Dodworth	d					08 51									09 53				
Barnsley	a		08 39			08 57	09 11		09 23		09 39				10 00	10 12		10 21	
	d		08 40			08 58	09 14		09 24		09 40				10 01	10 14		10 24	
Wombwell	d					09 03			09 29						10 06			10 29	
Elsecar	d					09 07			09 33									10 33	
Chapeltown	d					09 12			09 38						10 13			10 38	
Meadowhall	29,31 a		08 52			09 20	09 27		09 46		09 52				10 20	10 27		10 46	
	d	08 49	08 52	09 01	09 19	09 21	09 28	09 33	09 46	09 50	09 52	09 55	10 01	10 07	10 21	10 28	10 33	10 47	10 50
Sheffield 7	29,31 a	08 58	09 02	09 08	09 28	09 30	09 37	09 41	09 56	10 00	10 02	10 05	10 08	10 20	10 30	10 37	10 41	10 56	11 00
	d		09 05								10 05								
Dronfield	d		09 15								10 15								
Chesterfield	d		09 22								10 22								
Alfreton	d		09 33								10 33								
Langley Mill	d		09 40								10 40								
Nottingham	a		10 00								11 00								

Table 34

Saturdays from 11 September

Leeds and Huddersfield - Barnsley - Sheffield, Nottingham

Station			NT	TP ◇1 ⌶	NT	NT	NT	NT	NT	NT	NT	TP ◇1 ⌶	NT	NT	NT	NT	NT	NT	NT	NT	NT
Leeds 10	31	d					10 37		10 32		11 05						11 37		11 32		12 05
Woodlesford		d							10 40										11 40		
Castleford		d							10 51										11 51		
Normanton		d							10 57										11 57		
Wakefield Kirkgate 4	31	a					10 54		11 01		11 23						11 54		12 01		12 23
		d					10 55		11 04		11 23						11 55		12 04		12 23
Darton		d							11 15										12 15		
Huddersfield		d				10 08										11 08					
Lockwood		d				10 11										11 11					
Berry Brow		d				10 14										11 14					
Honley		d				10 17										11 17					
Brockholes		d				10 20										11 20					
Stocksmoor		d				10 24										11 24					
Shepley		d				10 26										11 26					
Denby Dale		d				10 36										11 36					
Penistone		d				10 44										11 44					
Silkstone Common		d				10 49										11 49					
Dodworth		d				10 53										11 53					
Barnsley		a				11 00	11 11		11 21		11 39					12 00	12 11		12 21		12 39
		d				11 01	11 14		11 24		11 40					12 01	12 14		12 24		12 40
Wombwell		d				11 06			11 29							12 06			12 29		
Elsecar		d							11 33										12 33		
Chapeltown		d				11 13			11 38							12 13			12 38		
Meadowhall	29,31	a				11 18	11 27		11 46		11 52					12 20	12 27		12 46		12 52
		d	10 57	11 01	11 06	11 19	11 28	11 33	11 46	11 50	11 52	11 59	12 00	12 06	12 16	12 21	12 28	12 33	12 46	12 50	12 52
Sheffield 7	29,31	a	11 06	11 08	11 20	11 29	11 37	11 41	11 56	12 00	12 02	12 08	12 10	12 20	12 25	12 30	12 37	12 41	12 56	13 00	13 02
		d									12 05										13 05
Dronfield		d									12 15										13 15
Chesterfield		d									12 22										13 22
Alfreton		d									12 33										13 33
Langley Mill		d									12 40										13 40
Nottingham		a									13 00										14 00

Station			NT	TP ◇1 ⌶	NT	NT	NT	NT	NT	NT	NT	TP ◇1 ⌶	NT	NT	NT	NT	NT	NT	NT	NT	TP ◇1 ⌶	NT
Leeds 10	31	d					12 37	12 32		13 05					13 37		13 32		14 05			
Woodlesford		d						12 40									13 40					
Castleford		d						12 51									13 51					
Normanton		d						12 57									13 57					
Wakefield Kirkgate 4	31	a					12 54	13 02		13 23					13 54		14 01		14 23			
		d					12 55	13 04		13 23					13 55		14 04		14 23			
Darton		d						13 15									14 15					
Huddersfield		d				12 08								13 08								
Lockwood		d				12 11								13 11								
Berry Brow		d				12 14								13 14								
Honley		d				12 17								13 17								
Brockholes		d				12 20								13 20								
Stocksmoor		d				12 24								13 24								
Shepley		d				12 26								13 25								
Denby Dale		d				12 36								13 36								
Penistone		d				12 44								13 44								
Silkstone Common		d				12 49								13 49								
Dodworth		d				12 53								13 53								
Barnsley		a				13 00	13 11	13 21		13 39				14 00	14 11		14 21		14 39			
		d				13 01	13 14	13 24		13 40				14 01	14 14		14 24		14 40			
Wombwell		d				13 06		13 29						14 06			14 29					
Elsecar		d						13 33									14 33					
Chapeltown		d				13 13		13 38						14 13			14 38					
Meadowhall	29,31	a				13 20	13 27	13 46		13 52				14 20	14 27		14 46		14 52			
		d	12 55	13 01	13 06	13 20	13 28	13 46	13 50	13 52	13 55	14 01	14 06	14 20	14 28	14 33	14 46	14 50	14 52	14 55	15 01	15 06
Sheffield 7	29,31	a	13 05	13 08	13 20	13 30	13 37	13 56	14 00	14 02	14 05	14 08	14 20	14 30	14 37	14 41	14 56	15 00	15 02	15 05	15 08	15 20
		d								14 05									15 05			
Dronfield		d								14 15									15 15			
Chesterfield		d								14 22									15 22			
Alfreton		d								14 33									15 33			
Langley Mill		d								14 40									15 40			
Nottingham		a								15 00									16 00			

Table 34

Saturdays from 11 September

Leeds and Huddersfield - Barnsley - Sheffield, Nottingham

Station			NT	NT	NT	NT	NT	NT	TP ◇1 ⌶	NT	NT	NT	NT	NT	EM ◇	NT	NT	NT	NT	NT	TP ◇1 ⌶
Leeds 10	31	d		14 37		14 32		15 05						15 37			15 32		16 05		
Woodlesford		d				14 40											15 40				
Castleford		d				14 51											15 51				
Normanton		d				14 57											15 57				
Wakefield Kirkgate 4	31	a		14 54		15 01		15 23						15 54			16 01		16 23		
		d		14 55		15 04		15 23						15 55			16 04		16 23		
Darton		d				15 15											16 15				
Huddersfield		d	14 08									15 08									
Lockwood		d	14 11									15 11									
Berry Brow		d	14 14									15 14									
Honley		d	14 17									15 17									
Brockholes		d	14 20									15 20									
Stocksmoor		d	14 24									15 24									
Shepley		d	14 26									15 26									
Denby Dale		d	14 36									15 36									
Penistone		d	14 44									15 44									
Silkstone Common		d	14 49									15 49									
Dodworth		d	14 53									15 53									
Barnsley		a	15 00	15 11		15 21		15 39				16 00		16 11			16 21		16 39		
		d	15 01	15 14		15 24		15 40				16 01		16 14			16 24		16 40		
Wombwell		d	15 06			15 29						16 06					16 29				
Elsecar		d				15 33											16 33				
Chapeltown		d	15 13			15 38						16 13					16 38				
Meadowhall	29,31	a	15 20	15 27		15 46		15 52				16 20		16 27			16 46				
		d	15 20	15 28	15 33	15 46	15 50	15 52	15 58	16 00	16 07	16 20	16 24	16 28		16 33	16 46	16 50	16 52	16 55	17 01
Sheffield 7	29,31	a	15 30	15 37	15 41	15 56	16 00	16 02	16 08	16 10	16 20	16 30	16 35	16 37	16 35	16 41	16 56	17 00	17 02	17 05	17 08
		d						16 05							16 38				17 05		
Dronfield		d						16 15							16 48				17 15		
Chesterfield		d						16 22							16 53				17 22		
Alfreton		d						16 33							17 04				17 33		
Langley Mill		d						16 40											17 40		
Nottingham		a						17 00							17 29				18 00		

Station			NT	NT	NT	NT	NT	NT	NT	NT	TP ◇1 ⌶	NT	NT	NT	NT	NT	NT	NT	NT	TP ◇1 ⌶	NT	NT
Leeds 10	31	d			16 37		16 32		17 05					17 37		17 32		18 05				
Woodlesford		d					16 40									17 40						
Castleford		d					16 51									17 51						
Normanton		d					16 57		17 18							17 57						
Wakefield Kirkgate 4	31	a			16 54		17 01		17 22					17 54		18 01		18 23				
		d			16 55		17 04		17 23					17 55		18 04		18 23				
Darton		d					17 15									18 15						
Huddersfield		d		16 08									17 08									18 08
Lockwood		d		16 11									17 11									18 11
Berry Brow		d		16 14									17 14									18 14
Honley		d		16 17									17 17									18 17
Brockholes		d		16 20									17 20									18 20
Stocksmoor		d		16 24									17 24									18 24
Shepley		d		16 26									17 26									18 26
Denby Dale		d		16 36									17 36									18 36
Penistone		d		16 44									17 44									18 44
Silkstone Common		d		16 49									17 49									18 49
Dodworth		d		16 53									17 53									18 53
Barnsley		a		17 00	17 11		17 21		17 39				18 00	18 11		18 21		18 39				19 01
		d		17 01	17 14		17 24		17 40				18 01	18 14		18 24		18 40				19 01
Wombwell		d		17 06			17 29						18 06			18 29						19 06
Elsecar		d					17 33									18 33						
Chapeltown		d		17 13			17 38						18 13			18 38						19 13
Meadowhall	29,31	a		17 20	17 27		17 46		17 51				18 20	18 27		18 46		18 52				19 20
		d	17 06	17 21	17 28	17 33	17 46	17 50	17 52	17 57	18 01	18 06	18 20	18 28	18 33	18 46	18 50	18 52	18 56	19 01	19 06	19 20
Sheffield 7	29,31	a	17 19	17 32	17 37	17 41	17 56	18 00	18 02	18 05	18 08	18 19	18 30	18 38	18 41	18 56	19 00	19 03	19 05	19 08	19 17	19 30
		d							18 05									19 05				
Dronfield		d							18 15									19 15				
Chesterfield		d							18 22									19 22				
Alfreton		d							18 33									19 33				
Langley Mill		d							18 40									19 40				
Nottingham		a							19 00									20 00				

Table 34

Saturdays from 11 September

Leeds and Huddersfield - Barnsley - Sheffield, Nottingham

		NT	NT	NT	NT	NT	NT	TP	NT	NT	NT	NT	NT	NT	TP	NT	EM	NT	NT	NT	NT
								◇1							◇1		◇				
Leeds 10 31	d	18 37		18 32		19 05					19 43		19 37			20 30				20 37	
Woodlesford	d			18 40									19 45							20 45	
Castleford	d			18 51									19 56							20 56	
Normanton	d			18 57									20 02							21 02	
Wakefield Kirkgate 4 31	a	18 54		19 04		19 24					19 59		20 06			20 46				21 06	
	d	18 55		19 04		19 24					20 00		20 07			20 46				21 07	
Darton	d			19 15									20 19							21 18	
Huddersfield	d									19 15								20 13			
Lockwood	d									19 18								20 16			
Berry Brow	d									19 21								20 19			
Honley	d									19 24								20 22			
Brockholes	d									19 27								20 25			
Stocksmoor	d									19 31								20 29			
Shepley	d									19 33								20 31			
Denby Dale	d									19 41								20 41			
Penistone	d									19 49								20 49			
Silkstone Common	d									19 54								20 54			
Dodworth	d									19 58								20 58			
Barnsley	a	19 11		19 24		19 40				20 05	20 16		20 24			21 02		21 08		21 24	
	d	19 14		19 24		19 40				20 06	20 16		20 24			21 03		21 11		21 24	
Wombwell	d			19 29						20 11			20 29					21 16		21 29	
Elsecar	d			19 33									20 33							21 33	
Chapeltown	d			19 38						20 18			20 38					21 23		21 38	
Meadowhall 29,31	a	19 27		19 46		19 52				20 24	20 32		20 45			21 17		21 28		21 45	
	d	19 28	19 33	19 46	19 50	19 52	19 57	20 01	20 07	20 24	20 32	20 35	20 46	20 51	21 07	21 19		21 29	21 35	21 46	21 52
Sheffield 7 29,31	a	19 37	19 43	19 57	20 00	20 03	20 06	20 08	20 18	20 36	20 44	20 42	20 58	21 02	21 19	21 30	21 34	21 40	21 46	21 58	22 05
	d					20 05											21 38				
Dronfield	d					20 15											21 48				
Chesterfield	d					20 22											21 54				
Alfreton	d					20 33											22 05				
Langley Mill	d					20 40											22 12				
Nottingham	a					21 00											22 33				

		TP	NT	NT	NT	NT	NT	NT	NT	NT	NT	NT
		◇1										
Leeds 10 31	d					21 37		22 37				
Woodlesford	d					21 45		22 45				
Castleford	d					21 56		22 56				
Normanton	d					22 02		23 01				
Wakefield Kirkgate 4 31	a					22 06		23 10				
	d					22 07						
Darton	d					22 18						
Huddersfield	d				21 15					22 15		
Lockwood	d				21 18					22 18		
Berry Brow	d				21 21					22 21		
Honley	d				21 24					22 24		
Brockholes	d				21 27					22 27		
Stocksmoor	d				21 31					22 31		
Shepley	d				21 33					22 33		
Denby Dale	d				21 41					22 41		
Penistone	d				21 49					22 49		
Silkstone Common	d				21 54					22 54		
Dodworth	d				21 58					22 58		
Barnsley	a				22 05	22 25				23 05		
	d				22 06	22 25				23 06		
Wombwell	d				22 11	22 30				23 11		
Elsecar	d					22 34				23 15		
Chapeltown	d				22 18	22 39				23 20		
Meadowhall 29,31	a				22 23	22 47				23 26		
	d	21 58	22 09	22 22	22 25	22 47	22 52		22 58	23 27	23 44	23 49
Sheffield 7 29,31	a	22 10	22 21	22 32	22 36	22 58	23 02		23 05	23 36	23 58	23 59
	d											
Dronfield	d											
Chesterfield	d											
Alfreton	d											
Langley Mill	d											
Nottingham	a											

Table 34

Sundays until 11 July

Leeds and Huddersfield - Barnsley - Sheffield, Nottingham

		NT	NT	TP	NT	NT	NT	NT	NT	NT	NT	NT	TP	NT	NT	NT	NT	NT	TP	NT	NT
				◇1									◇1						◇1		
Leeds 10 31	d					08 34		09 05				10 02			10 17		10 57				11 29
Woodlesford	d					08 42									10 25						
Castleford	d					08 53									10 36						
Normanton	d					08 58									10 41						
Wakefield Kirkgate 4 31	a					09 03		09 21				10 18			10 46		11 13				11 46
	d					09 03		09 21				10 18			10 46		11 13				11 46
Darton	d					09 17									11 00						
Huddersfield	d									09 19				10 15							
Lockwood	d									09 22				10 18							
Berry Brow	d									09 25				10 21							
Honley	d									09 28				10 24							
Brockholes	d									09 31				10 27							
Stocksmoor	d									09 35				10 31							
Shepley	d									09 37				10 33							
Denby Dale	d									09 42				10 39							
Penistone	d									09 50				10 46							
Silkstone Common	d									09 55				10 52							
Dodworth	d									09 59				10 55							
Barnsley	a					09 24		09 40		10 06		10 37		11 03	11 08		11 32				12 05
	d					09 24		09 41		10 12		10 38		11 03	11 12		11 33				12 06
Wombwell	d					09 29				10 17					11 17						
Elsecar	d					09 33				10 21					11 21						
Chapeltown	d					09 38				10 26					11 26						
Meadowhall 29,31	a					09 44		09 57		10 32		10 51		11 20	11 32		11 46				12 17
	d	08 30		09 00	09 41	09 44	09 54	09 57	10 00	10 33	10 40	10 51	11 00	11 20	11 35	11 40	11 46	11 52	12 00	12 11	12 17
Sheffield 7 29,31	a	08 41		09 07	09 51	09 55	10 03	10 04	10 09	10 43	10 52	11 02	11 07	11 28	11 44	11 51	11 56	12 03	12 07	12 20	12 29
	d		09 00					10 07				11 03					12 00				12 31
Dronfield	d		09 10					10 17				11 13					12 10				12 42
Chesterfield	d		09 17					10 23				11 20					12 18				12 49
Alfreton	d		09 28					10 33				11 30					12 28				12 59
Langley Mill	d		09 35					10 41				11 38					12 36				13 07
Nottingham	a		09 53					10 59				11 54					12 53				13 25

		NT	NT	TP	NT	NT	NT	NT	TP	NT	NT	NT	NT	NT	TP	NT	NT	NT	NT	NT	TP	NT
				◇1					◇1						◇1						◇1	
Leeds 10 31	d				12 29		12 34							14 05			14 17			15 05		
Woodlesford	d						12 42										14 25					
Castleford	d						12 53										14 36					
Normanton	d						12 58										14 41					
Wakefield Kirkgate 4 31	a				12 46		13 03							14 21			14 46			15 22		
	d				12 46		13 04							14 21			14 46			15 22		
Darton	d						13 18										15 00					
Huddersfield	d	11 29									13 19					14 15						
Lockwood	d	11 32									13 22					14 18						
Berry Brow	d	11 35									13 25					14 21						
Honley	d	11 38									13 28					14 24						
Brockholes	d	11 41									13 31					14 27						
Stocksmoor	d	11 45									13 35					14 31						
Shepley	d	11 47									13 37					14 33						
Denby Dale	d	11 52									13 42					14 39						
Penistone	d	12 00									13 50					14 46						
Silkstone Common	d	12 05									13 55					14 52						
Dodworth	d	12 09									13 59					14 55						
Barnsley	a	12 16			13 05		13 24				14 06			14 40		15 03	15 07			15 41		
	d	12 17			13 06		13 24				14 12			14 41		15 03	15 12			15 42		
Wombwell	d	12 22					13 29				14 17						15 17					
Elsecar	d	12 26					13 33				14 21						15 21					
Chapeltown	d	12 31					13 38				14 26						15 26					
Meadowhall 29,31	a	12 34			13 18		13 47				14 32			14 54		15 20	15 35			15 55		
	d	12 35	12 43	13 00	13 18	13 44	13 50	13 53	14 00	14 17	14 33	14 43	14 52	14 56	15 00	15 21	15 35	15 43	15 52	15 56	16 00	16 11
Sheffield 7 29,31	a	12 47	12 55	13 07	13 29	13 52	13 58	14 04	14 07	14 25	14 48	14 52	15 03	15 06	15 07	15 28	15 45	15 51	16 01	16 05	16 07	16 21
	d				13 31									15 07						16 07		
Dronfield	d				13 42									15 17						16 17		
Chesterfield	d				13 48									15 24						16 23		
Alfreton	d				13 59									15 34						16 33		
Langley Mill	d				14 06									15 42						16 41		
Nottingham	a				14 22									16 00						16 59		

Table 34

Sundays
until 11 July

Leeds and Huddersfield - Barnsley - Sheffield, Nottingham

					NT	NT	NT	NT	TP	NT	NT	NT	NT	TP	NT		NT	NT	NT	NT	NT	TP	NT		NT	NT
									◇1					◇1								◇1				
Leeds ■10	31	d						16 05		16 17			17 05								18 05		18 17			19 04
Woodlesford		d								16 25													18 25			
Castleford		d								16 36													18 36			
Normanton		d								16 41													18 40			
Wakefield Kirkgate ■4	31	a						16 21		16 46			17 21								18 21		18 45			19 21
		d						16 22		16 46			17 21								18 22		18 45			19 21
Darton		d								17 00													18 59			
Huddersfield		d			15 19													17 19								
Lockwood		d			15 22													17 22								
Berry Brow		d			15 25													17 25								
Honley		d			15 28													17 28								
Brockholes		d			15 31													17 31								
Stocksmoor		d			15 35													17 35								
Shepley		d			15 37													17 37								
Denby Dale		d			15 42													17 47								
Penistone		d			15 50													17 54								
Silkstone Common		d			15 55													18 00								
Dodworth		d			15 59													18 03								
Barnsley		a			16 06			16 41		17 07			17 40					18 11			18 41		19 05			19 40
		d			16 12			16 42		17 12			17 41					18 12			18 42		19 11			19 40
Wombwell		d			16 17					17 17								18 17					19 17			
Elsecar		d			16 21					17 21								18 21					19 21			
Chapeltown		d			16 26					17 26								18 26					19 26			
Meadowhall	29,31 ⇌	a			16 32			16 56		17 34			17 55					18 32			18 56		19 32			19 54
		d			16 34	16 43	16 53	16 56	17 00	17 35	17 43	17 53	17 56	18 00	18 12		18 24	18 33	18 43	18 53	18 56	19 00	19 33		19 47	19 54
Sheffield ■7	29,31 ⇌	a			16 44	16 52	17 03	17 05	17 07	17 44	17 54	18 01	18 05	18 07	18 23		18 35	18 44	18 52	19 03	19 05	19 07	19 43		19 55	20 04
		d						17 07					18 07								19 07					20 06
Dronfield		d						17 17					18 17								19 17					20 16
Chesterfield		d						17 23					18 25								19 25					20 23
Alfreton		d						17 33					18 36								19 36					20 34
Langley Mill		d						17 41					18 43								19 43					20 41
Nottingham		a						17 59					19 00								19 59					20 57

			NT	TP	NT	NT	NT	TP	NT			NT	NT	TP	NT	NT	NT	NT								
				◇1				◇1						◇1												
Leeds ■10	31	d							20 17									22 17								
Woodlesford		d							20 25									22 25								
Castleford		d							20 36									22 36								
Normanton		d							20 41									22 41								
Wakefield Kirkgate ■4	31	a							20 46									22 46								
		d							20 46									22 46								
Darton		d							21 00									23 00								
Huddersfield		d				19 19																				
Lockwood		d				19 22																				
Berry Brow		d				19 25																				
Honley		d				19 28																				
Brockholes		d				19 31																				
Stocksmoor		d				19 35																				
Shepley		d				19 37																				
Denby Dale		d				19 42																				
Penistone		d				19 50																				
Silkstone Common		d				19 55																				
Dodworth		d				19 59																				
Barnsley		a				20 06			21 07									23 07								
		d				20 12			21 12						22 21			23 12								
Wombwell		d				20 17			21 17						22 26			23 17								
Elsecar		d				20 21			21 21						22 30			23 21								
Chapeltown		d				20 26			21 26						22 35			23 26								
Meadowhall	29,31 ⇌	a				20 34			21 33						22 40			23 30								
		d	19 57	20 00	20 11	20 34	20 45	21 00	21 33			21 45	21 54	22 04	22 41	22 45	22 50	23 32								
Sheffield ■7	29,31 ⇌	a	20 06	20 07	20 23	20 43	20 53	21 07	21 42			21 56	22 05	22 15	22 51	22 54	22 58	23 43								
		d																								
Dronfield		d																								
Chesterfield		d																								
Alfreton		d																								
Langley Mill		d																								
Nottingham		a																								

Table 34

Sundays
18 July to 05 September

Leeds and Huddersfield - Barnsley - Sheffield, Nottingham

			NT	NT	TP	NT	NT	NT	NT		NT		NT	NT	NT	TP	NT	NT	NT	NT	NT		TP	NT		NT
					◇1											◇1							◇1			
Leeds ■10	31	d					08 34		09 05						10 02			10 17		10 57						11 29
Woodlesford		d					08 42											10 25								
Castleford		d					08 53											10 36								
Normanton		d					08 58											10 41								
Wakefield Kirkgate ■4	31	a					09 03		09 21						10 18			10 46		11 13						11 46
		d					09 03		09 21						10 18			10 46		11 13						11 46
Darton		d					09 17											11 00								
Huddersfield		d											09 19				10 15									
Lockwood		d											09 22				10 18									
Berry Brow		d											09 25				10 21									
Honley		d											09 28				10 24									
Brockholes		d											09 31				10 27									
Stocksmoor		d											09 35				10 31									
Shepley		d											09 37				10 33									
Denby Dale		d											09 42				10 39									
Penistone		d											09 50				10 46									
Silkstone Common		d											09 55				10 52									
Dodworth		d											09 59				10 55									
Barnsley		a					09 24		09 40				10 06		10 37		11 03	11 08		11 32						12 05
		d					09 24		09 41				10 12		10 38		11 03	11 12		11 33						12 06
Wombwell		d					09 29						10 17					11 17								
Elsecar		d					09 33						10 21					11 21								
Chapeltown		d					09 38						10 26					11 26								
Meadowhall	29,31 ⇌	a					09 44		09 57				10 32		10 51		11 20	11 32		11 46						12 17
		d	08 30		09 00	09 41	09 44	09 54	09 57		10 00		10 33	10 40	10 51	11 00	11 20	11 35	11 40	11 46	11 52		12 00	12 11		12 17
Sheffield ■7	29,31 ⇌	a	08 41		09 07	09 51	09 55	10 03	10 04		10 09		10 43	10 52	11 02	11 07	11 28	11 44	11 51	11 56	12 03		12 07	12 20		12 29
		d		09 00					10 07						11 03					12 00						12 31
Dronfield		d		09 10					10 17						11 13					12 10						12 42
Chesterfield		d		09 17					10 23						11 20					12 18						12 49
Alfreton		d		09 28					10 33						11 30					12 28						12 59
Langley Mill		d		09 35					10 41						11 38					12 36						13 07
Nottingham		a		09 53					10 59						11 54					12 53						13 25

			NT	NT	TP	NT	NT		NT	NT	TP	NT		NT	NT	NT	NT		TP	NT	NT	NT	NT	NT	TP	NT
					◇1						◇1								◇1						◇1	
Leeds ■10	31	d				12 29			12 34								14 05				14 17			15 05		
Woodlesford		d							12 42												14 25					
Castleford		d							12 53												14 36					
Normanton		d							12 58												14 41					
Wakefield Kirkgate ■4	31	a				12 46			13 03								14 21				14 46			15 22		
		d				12 46			13 04								14 21				14 46			15 22		
Darton		d							13 18												15 00					
Huddersfield		d	11 29											13 19						14 15						
Lockwood		d	11 32											13 22						14 18						
Berry Brow		d	11 35											13 25						14 21						
Honley		d	11 38											13 28						14 24						
Brockholes		d	11 41											13 31						14 27						
Stocksmoor		d	11 45											13 35						14 31						
Shepley		d	11 47											13 37						14 33						
Denby Dale		d	11 52											13 42						14 39						
Penistone		d	12 00											13 50						14 46						
Silkstone Common		d	12 05											13 55						14 52						
Dodworth		d	12 09											13 59						14 55						
Barnsley		a	12 16			13 05			13 24					14 06			14 40			15 03	15 07			15 41		
		d	12 17			13 06			13 24					14 12			14 41			15 03	15 12			15 42		
Wombwell		d	12 22						13 29					14 17							15 17					
Elsecar		d	12 26						13 33					14 21							15 21					
Chapeltown		d	12 31						13 38					14 26							15 26					
Meadowhall	29,31 ⇌	a	12 34			13 18			13 47					14 32			14 54			15 20	15 35			15 55		
		d	12 35	12 43	13 00	13 18	13 44		13 50	13 53	14 00	14 17		14 33	14 43	14 52	14 56		15 00	15 21	15 35	15 43	15 52	15 56	16 00	16 11
Sheffield ■7	29,31 ⇌	a	12 47	12 55	13 07	13 29	13 52		13 58	14 04	14 07	14 25		14 48	14 52	15 03	15 06		15 07	15 28	15 45	15 51	16 01	16 05	16 07	16 21
		d				13 31											15 07							16 07		
Dronfield		d				13 42											15 17							16 17		
Chesterfield		d				13 48											15 24							16 23		
Alfreton		d				13 59											15 34							16 33		
Langley Mill		d				14 06											15 42							16 41		
Nottingham		a				14 22											16 00							16 59		

Table 34

Sundays

18 July to 05 September

Leeds and Huddersfield - Barnsley - Sheffield, Nottingham

			NT	NT	NT	NT	TP ◇1	NT	NT	NT	NT	TP ◇1	NT	NT	NT	NT	NT	NT	TP ◇1	NT	NT	NT
Leeds 10	31	d				16 05		16 17			17 05							18 05		18 17		19 04
Woodlesford		d						16 25												18 25		
Castleford		d						16 36												18 36		
Normanton		d						16 41												18 40		
Wakefield Kirkgate 4	31	a				16 21		16 46			17 21							18 21		18 45		19 21
		d				16 22		16 46			17 21							18 22		18 45		19 21
Darton		d						17 00												18 59		
Huddersfield		d	15 19												17 19							
Lockwood		d	15 22												17 22							
Berry Brow		d	15 25												17 25							
Honley		d	15 28												17 28							
Brockholes		d	15 31												17 31							
Stocksmoor		d	15 35												17 35							
Shepley		d	15 37												17 37							
Denby Dale		d	15 42												17 47							
Penistone		d	15 50												17 54							
Silkstone Common		d	15 55												18 00							
Dodworth		d	15 59												18 03							
Barnsley		a	16 06			16 41		17 07			17 40				18 11			18 41		19 05		19 40
		d	16 12			16 42		17 12			17 41				18 12			18 42		19 11		19 40
Wombwell		d	16 17					17 17							18 17					19 17		
Elsecar		d	16 21					17 21							18 21					19 21		
Chapeltown		d	16 26					17 26							18 26					19 26		
Meadowhall	29,31	a	16 32			16 56		17 34			17 55				18 32			18 56		19 32		19 54
		d	16 34	16 43	16 53	16 56	17 00	17 35	17 43	17 53	17 56	18 00	18 12	18 24	18 33	18 43	18 53	18 56	19 00	19 33	19 47	19 54
Sheffield 7	29,31	a	16 44	16 52	17 03	17 05	17 07	17 44	17 54	18 01	18 05	18 07	18 23	18 35	18 44	18 52	19 03	19 05	19 07	19 43	19 55	20 04
		d				17 07					18 07							19 07				20 06
Dronfield		d				17 17					18 17							19 17				20 16
Chesterfield		d				17 23					18 25							19 25				20 23
Alfreton		d				17 33					18 36							19 36				20 34
Langley Mill		d				17 41					18 43							19 43				20 41
Nottingham		a				17 59					19 00							19 59				20 57

			NT	TP ◇1	NT	NT	NT	TP ◇1	NT	NT	NT	TP ◇1	NT	NT	NT	NT
Leeds 10	31	d							20 17							22 17
Woodlesford		d							20 25							22 25
Castleford		d							20 36							22 36
Normanton		d							20 41							22 41
Wakefield Kirkgate 4	31	a							20 46							22 46
		d							20 46							22 46
Darton		d							21 00							23 00
Huddersfield		d				19 19										
Lockwood		d				19 22										
Berry Brow		d				19 25										
Honley		d				19 28										
Brockholes		d				19 31										
Stocksmoor		d				19 35										
Shepley		d				19 37										
Denby Dale		d				19 42										
Penistone		d				19 50										
Silkstone Common		d				19 55										
Dodworth		d				19 59										
Barnsley		a				20 06			21 07							23 07
		d				20 12			21 12				22 21			23 12
Wombwell		d				20 17			21 17				22 26			23 17
Elsecar		d				20 21			21 21				22 30			23 21
Chapeltown		d				20 26			21 26				22 35			23 26
Meadowhall	29,31	a				20 34			21 33				22 40			23 30
		d	19 57	20 00	20 11	20 34	20 45	21 00	21 33	21 45	21 54	22 04	22 41	22 45	22 50	23 32
Sheffield 7	29,31	a	20 06	20 07	20 23	20 43	20 53	21 07	21 42	21 56	22 05	22 15	22 51	22 54	22 58	23 43
		d														
Dronfield		d														
Chesterfield		d														
Alfreton		d														
Langley Mill		d														
Nottingham		a														

Table 34

Sundays

from 12 September

Leeds and Huddersfield - Barnsley - Sheffield, Nottingham

			NT	NT	TP ◇1	NT	NT	NT	NT	NT	NT	NT	NT	NT	NT	NT	NT	NT	TP ◇1	NT	NT	NT	NT	NT
Leeds 10	31	d					08 34		09 05	09 34			10 02		10 17		10 57				11 17	11 29		
Woodlesford		d					08 42			09 42					10 25						11 25			
Castleford		d					08 53			09 53					10 36						11 36			
Normanton		d					08 58								10 41									
Wakefield Kirkgate 4	31	a					09 03		09 21				10 18		10 46		11 13					11 46		
		d					09 03		09 21				10 18		10 46		11 13					11 46		
Darton		d					09 17								11 00									
Huddersfield		d												10 11									11 24	
Lockwood		d												10 14									11 27	
Berry Brow		d												10 17									11 30	
Honley		d												10 20									11 33	
Brockholes		d												10 23									11 36	
Stocksmoor		d												10 27									11 40	
Shepley		d												10 29									11 42	
Denby Dale		d												10 39									11 52	
Penistone		d												10 46									12 00	
Silkstone Common		d												10 52									12 05	
Dodworth		d												10 55									12 09	
Barnsley		a					09 24		09 40				10 37	11 03	11 08		11 32					12 05	12 16	
		d					09 24		09 41				10 38	11 03	11 12		11 33					12 06	12 17	
Wombwell		d					09 29								11 17								12 22	
Elsecar		d					09 33								11 21								12 26	
Chapeltown		d					09 38								11 26								12 31	
Meadowhall	29,31	a					09 44		09 57				10 51	11 20	11 32		11 46					12 17	12 34	
		d	08 30		09 00	09 41	09 44	09 54	09 57		10 00	10 40	10 51	11 20	11 35	11 40	11 46	11 52	12 00	12 11		12 17	12 35	12 43
Sheffield 7	29,31	a	08 41		09 07	09 51	09 55	10 03	10 04		10 09	10 52	11 02	11 28	11 44	11 51	11 56	12 03	12 07	12 20		12 29	12 47	12 55
		d		09 00					10 07				11 03				12 00					12 31		
Dronfield		d		09 10					10 17				11 13				12 10					12 42		
Chesterfield		d		09 17					10 23				11 20				12 18					12 49		
Alfreton		d		09 28					10 33				11 30				12 28					12 59		
Langley Mill		d		09 35					10 41				11 38				12 36					13 07		
Nottingham		a		09 53					10 59				11 54				12 53					13 25		

			TP ◇1	NT	NT	NT	NT	TP ◇1	NT	NT	NT	NT	NT	TP ◇1	NT	NT	NT	NT	NT	TP ◇1	NT	NT
Leeds 10	31	d		12 29		12 34							14 05			14 17			15 05			
Woodlesford		d				12 42										14 25						
Castleford		d				12 53										14 36						
Normanton		d				12 58										14 41						
Wakefield Kirkgate 4	31	a		12 46		13 03							14 21			14 46			15 22			
		d		12 46		13 04							14 21			14 46			15 22			
Darton		d				13 18										15 00						
Huddersfield		d								13 14					14 11							15 14
Lockwood		d								13 17					14 14							15 17
Berry Brow		d								13 20					14 17							15 20
Honley		d								13 23					14 20							15 23
Brockholes		d								13 26					14 23							15 26
Stocksmoor		d								13 30					14 27							15 30
Shepley		d								13 32					14 29							15 32
Denby Dale		d								13 42					14 39							15 42
Penistone		d								13 50					14 46							15 50
Silkstone Common		d								13 55					14 52							15 55
Dodworth		d								13 59					14 55							15 59
Barnsley		a		13 05		13 24				14 06			14 40		15 03	15 07			15 41			16 06
		d		13 06		13 24				14 12			14 41		15 03	15 12			15 42			16 12
Wombwell		d				13 29				14 17						15 17						16 17
Elsecar		d				13 33				14 21						15 21						16 21
Chapeltown		d				13 38				14 26						15 26						16 26
Meadowhall	29,31	a		13 18		13 47				14 32			14 54		15 20	15 35			15 55			16 32
		d	13 00	13 18	13 44	13 50	13 53	14 00	14 17	14 33	14 43	14 52	14 56	15 00	15 21	15 35	15 43	15 52	15 56	16 00	16 11	16 34
Sheffield 7	29,31	a	13 07	13 29	13 52	13 58	14 04	14 07	14 25	14 48	14 52	15 03	15 06	15 07	15 28	15 45	15 51	16 01	16 05	16 07	16 21	16 44
		d		13 31									15 07						16 07			
Dronfield		d		13 42									15 17						16 17			
Chesterfield		d		13 48									15 24						16 23			
Alfreton		d		13 59									15 34						16 33			
Langley Mill		d		14 06									15 42						16 41			
Nottingham		a		14 22									16 00						16 59			

Table 34

Sundays
from 12 September

Leeds and Huddersfield - Barnsley - Sheffield, Nottingham

Station	Table		NT		NT	NT	TP ◇1	NT	NT	NT	NT		TP ◇1	NT	NT	NT	NT	NT	NT	TP ◇1	NT	NT	NT	NT	TP ◇1	NT
Leeds 10	31	d				16 05		16 17			17 05								18 05		18 17		19 04			
Woodlesford		d						16 25													18 25					
Castleford		d						16 36													18 36					
Normanton		d						16 41													18 40					
Wakefield Kirkgate 4	31	a				16 21		16 46			17 21								18 21		18 45		19 21			
		d				16 22		16 46			17 21								18 22		18 45		19 21			
Darton		d						17 00													18 59					
Huddersfield		d														17 19										
Lockwood		d														17 22										
Berry Brow		d														17 25										
Honley		d														17 28										
Brockholes		d														17 31										
Stocksmoor		d														17 35										
Shepley		d														17 37										
Denby Dale		d														17 47										
Penistone		d														17 54										
Silkstone Common		d														18 00										
Dodworth		d														18 03										
Barnsley		a				16 41		17 07			17 40					18 11			18 41		19 05		19 40			
		d				16 42		17 12			17 41					18 12			18 42		19 11		19 40			
Wombwell		d						17 17								18 17					19 17					
Elsecar		d						17 21								18 21					19 21					
Chapeltown		d						17 26								18 26					19 26					
Meadowhall	29,31	a				16 56		17 34			17 55					18 32			18 56		19 32		19 54			
		d	16 43		16 53	16 56	17 00	17 35	17 43	17 53	17 56		18 00	18 12	18 24	18 33	18 43	18 53	18 56	19 00	19 33	19 47	19 54	19 57	20 00	20 11
Sheffield 7	29,31	a	16 52		17 03	17 05	17 07	17 44	17 54	18 01	18 05		18 07	18 23	18 35	18 44	18 52	19 03	19 05	19 07	19 43	19 55	20 04	20 06	20 07	20 23
		d				17 07					18 07								19 07				20 06			
Dronfield		d				17 17					18 17								19 17				20 16			
Chesterfield		d				17 23					18 25								19 25				20 23			
Alfreton		d				17 33					18 36								19 36				20 34			
Langley Mill		d				17 41					18 43								19 43				20 41			
Nottingham		a				17 59					19 00								19 59				20 57			

Station	Table		NT		NT	TP ◇1	NT		NT		NT	TP ◇1	NT	NT	NT	NT
Leeds 10	31	d					20 17									22 17
Woodlesford		d					20 25									22 25
Castleford		d					20 36									22 36
Normanton		d					20 41									22 41
Wakefield Kirkgate 4	31	a					20 46									22 46
		d					20 46									22 46
Darton		d					21 00									23 00
Huddersfield		d	19 14													
Lockwood		d	19 17													
Berry Brow		d	19 20													
Honley		d	19 23													
Brockholes		d	19 26													
Stocksmoor		d	19 30													
Shepley		d	19 32													
Denby Dale		d	19 42													
Penistone		d	19 51													
Silkstone Common		d	19 56													
Dodworth		d	20 00													
Barnsley		a	20 06				21 07									23 07
		d	20 12				21 12						22 21			23 12
Wombwell		d	20 17				21 17						22 26			23 17
Elsecar		d	20 21				21 21						22 30			23 21
Chapeltown		d	20 26				21 26						22 35			23 26
Meadowhall	29,31	a	20 34				21 33						22 40			23 30
		d	20 34		20 45	21 00	21 33		21 45		21 54	22 04	22 41	22 45	22 50	23 32
Sheffield 7	29,31	a	20 43		20 53	21 07	21 42		21 56		22 05	22 15	22 51	22 54	22 58	23 43
		d														
Dronfield		d														
Chesterfield		d														
Alfreton		d														
Langley Mill		d														
Nottingham		a														

Network Diagram for Tables 35, 36, 37, 38

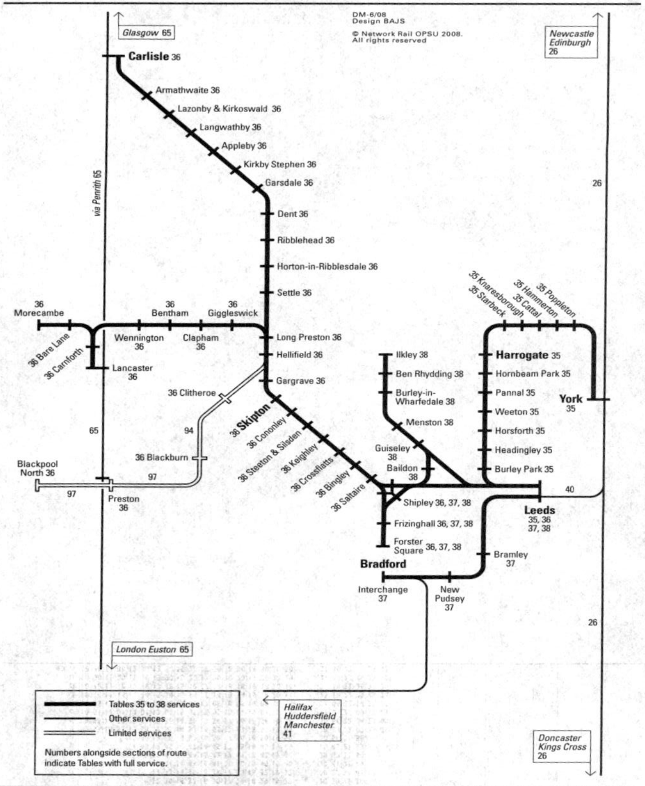

Table 35

York - Harrogate - Leeds

Mondays to Fridays

			NT	NT	NT	GR	NT	NT	NT	NT	NT	NT	NT	NT	NT	NT	NT	NT	NT	NT	NT	NT	NT	NT
York	40	d					06 52				07 57		08 45	09 10		10 11		11 11		12 11		13 11		14 11
Poppleton		d					06 56				08 01		08 50	09 14		10 15		11 15		12 15		13 15		14 15
Hammerton		d					07 04				08 09		08 58	09 22		10 23		11 23		12 23		13 23		14 23
Cattal		d					07 07				08 12		09 01	09 26		10 26		11 26		12 26		13 26		14 26
Knaresborough		a					07 15				08 21		09 09	09 34		10 34		11 34		12 34		13 34		14 34
		d			07 00		07 24	07 42	07 56		08 21	08 56	09 10	09 35	10 05	10 35	11 05	11 35	12 05	12 35	13 05	13 35	14 05	14 35
Starbeck		d			07 03		07 27	07 45	07 59		08 24	08 59	09 13	09 38	10 08	10 38	11 08	11 38	12 08	12 38	13 08	13 38	14 08	14 38
Harrogate		a			07 08		07 32	07 50	08 04		08 29	09 04	09 18	09 43	10 13	10 43	11 13	11 43	12 13	12 43	13 13	13 43	14 13	14 43
		d	06 06	06 30	07 11	07 28	07 40	07 51	08 06	08 14	08 30	09 05	09 19	09 44	10 14	10 44	11 14	11 44	12 14	12 44	13 14	13 44	14 14	14 44
Hornbeam Park		d	06 08	06 32	07 14		07 42	07 54		08 17	08 33		09 22	09 47	10 17	10 47	11 17	11 47	12 17	12 47	13 17	13 47	14 17	14 47
Pannal		d	06 13	06 37	07 19		07 47	07 59		08 22	08 38		09 27	09 52	10 22	10 52	11 22	11 52	12 22	12 52	13 22	13 52	14 22	14 52
Weeton		d	06 18	06 42	07 23		07 51	08 03		08 26	08 42		09 31	09 56	10 26	10 56	11 26	11 56	12 26	12 56	13 26	13 56	14 26	14 56
Horsforth		d	06 28	06 50	07 32	07u45	08 00	08 12	08 22	08 35	08 51	09 21	09 40	10 05	10 35	11 05	11 35	12 05	12 35	13 05	13 35	14 05	14 35	15 05
Headingley		d	06 32	06 54	07 36		08 04	08 16	08 26	08 39	08 55	09 25	09 44	10 09	10 39	11 09	11 39	12 09	12 39	13 09	13 39	14 09	14 39	15 09
Burley Park		d	06 34	06 56	07 38		08 06	08 18	08 29	08 41	08 57	09 27	09 47	10 11	10 41	11 11	11 41	12 11	12 41	13 11	13 41	14 11	14 41	15 11
Leeds	40	a	06 44	07 08	07 48	07 57	08 17	08 31	08 40	08 52	09 08	09 37	09 56	10 22	10 52	11 22	11 52	12 22	12 52	13 22	13 52	14 22	14 52	15 22

			NT	NT	NT	NT	NT	NT	NT	NT	NT	NT	NT	NT	NT	NT
York	40	d		15 11		16 11		16 54	17 17		18 11		19 11	20 11	21 11	22 11
Poppleton		d		15 15		16 15		16 58	17 21		18 15		19 15	20 15	21 16	22 15
Hammerton		d		15 23		16 23		17 06	17 29		18 23		19 23	20 23	21 23	22 23
Cattal		d		15 26		16 26		17 09	17 32		18 26		19 26	20 26	21 27	22 27
Knaresborough		a		15 34		16 34		17 17	17 40		18 34		19 34	20 34	21 34	22 35
		d	15 05	15 35	16 05	16 35	17 05	17 18	17 41	18 05	18 35	19 05	19 35	20 35	21 35	22 36
Starbeck		d	15 08	15 38	16 08	16 38	17 08	17 21	17 44	18 12	18 38	19 08	19 38	20 38	21 39	22 40
Harrogate		a	15 13	15 43	16 13	16 43	17 13	17 26	17 49	18 17	18 43	19 13	19 43	20 43	21 43	22 45
		d	15 14	15 44	16 14	16 44	17 14	17 37	17 50	18 18	18 44	19 14	19 44	20 44	21 45	22 47
Hornbeam Park		d	15 17	15 47	16 17	16 47	17 17	17 39	17 53	18 21	18 47	19 17	19 47	20 47	21 48	22 49
Pannal		d	15 22	15 52	16 22	16 52	17 22	17 44	17 58	18 26	18 52	19 22	19 52	20 52	21 53	22 54
Weeton		d	15 26	15 56	16 26	16 56	17 26	17 49	18 02	18 30	18 56	19 26	19 56	20 56	21 58	22 59
Horsforth		d	15 35	16 05	16 35	17 05	17 38	17 57	18 11	18 39	19 05	19 35	20 05	21 05	22 06	23 08
Headingley		d	15 39	16 09	16 39	17 09	17 42	18 01	18 15	18 43	19 09	19 39	20 09	21 09	22 10	23 12
Burley Park		d	15 41	16 11	16 41	17 11	17 44	18 03	18 17	18 45	19 11	19 41	20 11	21 11	22 13	23 15
Leeds	40	a	15 52	16 22	16 52	17 22	17 55	18 17	18 28	18 55	19 22	19 52	20 22	21 22	22 23	23 24

Saturdays

			NT	NT	NT	GR	NT	NT	NT	NT	NT	NT	NT	NT	NT	NT	NT	NT	NT	NT	NT	NT	NT	NT
York	40	d			06 53			07 57		08 45	09 10		10 11		11 11		12 11		13 11		14 11		15 11	
Poppleton		d			06 57			08 01		08 49	09 14		10 15		11 15		12 15		13 15		14 15		15 15	
Hammerton		d			07 05			08 09		08 57	09 22		10 23		11 23		12 23		13 23		14 23		15 23	
Cattal		d			07 08			08 12		09 00	09 26		10 26		11 26		12 26		13 26		14 26		15 26	
Knaresborough		a			07 16			08 20		09 08	09 34		10 34		11 34		12 34		13 34		14 34		15 34	
		d		06 47	07 21		07 51	08 21	08 51	09 09	09 35	10 05	10 35	11 05	11 35	12 05	12 35	13 05	13 35	14 05	14 35	15 05	15 35	16 05
Starbeck		d		06 50	07 24		07 54	08 24	08 54	09 12	09 38	10 08	10 38	11 08	11 38	12 08	12 38	13 08	13 38	14 08	14 38	15 08	15 38	16 08
Harrogate		a		06 55	07 29		07 59	08 29	08 59	09 17	09 43	10 13	10 43	11 13	11 43	12 13	12 43	13 13	13 43	14 13	14 43	15 13	15 43	16 13
		d	06 06	06 56	07 31	07 44	08 00	08 30	09 00	09 18	09 44	10 14	10 44	11 14	11 44	12 14	12 44	13 14	13 44	14 14	14 44	15 14	15 44	16 14
Hornbeam Park		d	06 08	06 59	07 33		08 03	08 33	09 03	09 21	09 47	10 17	10 47	11 17	11 47	12 17	12 47	13 17	13 47	14 17	14 47	15 17	15 47	16 17
Pannal		d	06 13	07 04	07 38		08 08	08 38	09 08	09 26	09 52	10 22	10 52	11 22	11 52	12 22	12 52	13 22	13 52	14 22	14 52	15 22	15 52	16 22
Weeton		d	06 18	07 08	07 42		08 12	08 42	09 12	09 30	09 56	10 26	10 56	11 26	11 56	12 26	12 56	13 26	13 56	14 26	14 56	15 26	15 56	16 26
Horsforth		d	06 28	07 17	07 51		08 21	08 51	09 21	09 39	10 05	10 35	11 05	11 35	12 05	12 35	13 05	13 35	14 05	14 35	15 05	15 35	16 05	16 35
Headingley		d	06 32	07 21	07 55		08 25	08 55	09 25	09 43	10 09	10 39	11 09	11 39	12 09	12 39	13 09	13 39	14 09	14 39	15 09	15 39	16 09	16 39
Burley Park		d	06 34	07 23	07 57		08 27	08 57	09 27	09 47	10 11	10 41	11 11	11 41	12 11	12 41	13 11	13 41	14 11	14 41	15 11	15 41	16 11	16 41
Leeds	40	a	06 44	07 34	08 08	08 10	08 38	09 08	09 37	09 55	10 22	10 52	11 22	11 52	12 22	12 52	13 22	13 52	14 22	14 52	15 22	15 52	16 22	16 52

			NT	NT	NT	NT	NT	NT	NT	NT	NT
York	40	d	16 11		16 54	17 17		18 11	19 11	20 11	21 57
Poppleton		d	16 15		16 58	17 21		18 15	19 15	20 15	22 01
Hammerton		d	16 23		17 06	17 29		18 23	19 23	20 23	22 09
Cattal		d	16 26		17 09	17 32		18 26	19 26	20 26	22 12
Knaresborough		a	16 34		17 17	17 40		18 34	19 34	20 34	22 20
		d	16 35	17 05	17 18	17 41	18 05	18 35	19 35	20 35	22 21
Starbeck		d	16 38	17 08	17 21	17 44	18 12	18 38	19 38	20 38	22 24
Harrogate		a	16 43	17 13	17 26	17 49	18 17	18 43	19 43	20 43	22 29
		d	16 44	17 14	17 30	17 50	18 18	18 44	19 44	20 44	22 37
Hornbeam Park		d	16 47	17 17	17 32	17 53	18 21	18 47	19 47	20 47	22 39
Pannal		d	16 52	17 22	17 37	17 58	18 26	18 52	19 52	20 52	22 44
Weeton		d	16 56	17 26	17 42	18 02	18 30	18 56	19 56	20 56	22 49
Horsforth		d	17 05	17 38	17 50	18 11	18 39	19 05	20 05	21 05	22 57
Headingley		d	17 09	17 42	17 54	18 15	18 43	19 09	20 09	21 09	23 01
Burley Park		d	17 11	17 44	17 57	18 17	18 45	19 11	20 11	21 11	23 04
Leeds	40	a	17 22	17 55	18 07	18 28	18 55	19 22	20 22	21 22	23 14

Table 35

York - Harrogate - Leeds

Sundays

			NT	NT	NT	NT	NT	NT	NT	NT	NT	NT	NT	NT
York	40	d				12 18	14 20	16 18	17 17	18 17	19 17	20 18	21 26	
Poppleton		d				12 22	14 24	16 22	17 21	18 21	19 21	20 22	21 30	
Hammerton		d				12 30	14 32	16 30	17 29	18 29	19 29	20 30	21 38	
Cattal		d				12 33	14 35	16 33	17 32	18 32	19 32	20 33	21 41	
Knaresborough		a				12 41	14 43	16 41	17 40	18 40	19 40	20 41	21 49	
		d			11 42	12 42	14 44	16 42	17 42	18 42	19 42	20 42	21 50	
Starbeck		d			11 45	12 45	14 47	16 45	17 45	18 45	19 45	20 45	21 53	
Harrogate		a			11 50	12 50	14 52	16 50	17 50	18 50	19 50	20 50	21 58	
		d	09 53	10 53	11 53	12 53	14 53	16 53	17 53	18 53	19 53	20 53	22 02	23 05
Hornbeam Park		d	09 56	10 56	11 56	12 56	14 56	16 56	17 56	18 56	19 56	20 56	22 04	23 08
Pannal		d	10 01	11 01	12 01	13 01	15 01	17 01	18 01	19 01	20 01	21 01	22 09	23 13
Weeton		d	10 05	11 05	12 05	13 05	15 05	17 05	18 05	19 05	20 05	21 05	22 14	23 17
Horsforth		d	10 14	11 14	12 14	13 14	15 14	17 14	18 14	19 14	20 14	21 14	22 22	23 26
Headingley		d	10 18	11 18	12 18	13 18	15 18	17 18	18 18	19 18	20 18	21 18	22 26	23 30
Burley Park		d	10 20	11 20	12 20	13 20	15 20	17 20	18 20	19 20	20 20	21 20	22 29	23 32
Leeds	40	a	10 30	11 30	12 30	13 30	15 30	17 30	18 30	19 30	20 30	21 30	22 40	23 43

Table 35

Mondays to Fridays

Leeds - Harrogate - York

			NT MX	NT	NT	NT	NT	NT	NT	NT	NT	NT	NT	NT	NT	NT	NT	NT	NT	NT	NT	NT	NT	NT
Leeds 10	40	d	23p29	06 09	06 29	07 13	07 43	07 59	08 29	08 59	09 29	09 59	10 29	10 59	11 29	11 59	12 29	12 59	13 29	13 59	14 29	14 59	15 29	15 59
Burley Park		d	23p33	06 13	06 33	07 17	07 47	08 03	08 33	09 03	09 33	10 03	10 33	11 03	11 33	12 03	12 33	13 03	13 33	14 03	14 33	15 03	15 33	16 03
Headingley		d	23p36	06 16	06 36	07 20	07 50	08 06	08 36	09 06	09 36	10 06	10 36	11 06	11 36	12 06	12 36	13 06	13 36	14 06	14 36	15 06	15 36	16 06
Horsforth		d	23p41	06 21	06 41	07 25	07 55	08 11	08 41	09 11	09 41	10 11	10 41	11 11	11 41	12 11	12 41	13 11	13 41	14 11	14 41	15 11	15 41	16 11
Weeton		d	23p49	06 29	06 49	07 33		08 19	08 49	09 19	09 49	10 19	10 49	11 19	11 49	12 19	12 49	13 19	13 49	14 19	14 49	15 19	15 49	16 19
Pannal		d	23p55	06 35	06 55	07 39		08 25	08 55	09 25	09 55	10 25	10 55	11 25	11 55	12 25	12 55	13 25	13 55	14 25	14 55	15 25	15 55	16 25
Hornbeam Park		d	23p58	06 40	07 00	07 44	08 10	08 30	09 00	09 30	10 00	10 30	11 00	11 30	12 00	12 30	13 00	13 30	14 00	14 30	15 00	15 30	16 00	16 30
Harrogate		a	00 06	06 43	07 04	07 49	08 13	08 33	09 03	09 33	10 03	10 33	11 03	11 33	12 03	12 33	13 03	13 33	14 03	14 33	15 03	15 33	16 03	16 33
		d		06 45	07 05	07 49	08 16	08 34	09 05	09 35	10 05	10 35	11 05	11 35	12 05	12 35	13 05	13 35	14 05	14 35	15 05	15 35	16 05	16 35
Starbeck		d		06 49	07 08	07 52	08 19	08 38	09 08	09 38	10 08	10 38	11 08	11 38	12 08	12 38	13 08	13 38	14 08	14 38	15 08	15 38	16 08	16 38
Knaresborough		a		06 54	07 15	07 59	08 25	08 45	09 14	09 45	10 14	10 45	11 14	11 45	12 14	12 45	13 14	13 45	14 14	14 45	15 14	15 45	16 14	16 45
		d		06 55	07 19	07 59	08 28		09 15		10 14		11 14		12 14		13 14		14 14		15 14		16 14	
Cattal		d		07 03	07 27	08 07	08 36		09 23		10 22		11 22		12 22		13 22		14 22		15 22		16 22	
Hammerton		d		07 06	07 30	08 11	08 39		09 27		10 26		11 26		12 26		13 26		14 26		15 26		16 26	
Poppleton		d		07 13	07 37	08 18	08 46		09 34		10 33		11 33		12 33		13 33		14 33		15 33		16 33	
York 8	40	a		07 21	07 48	08 28	08 58		09 47		10 46		11 45		12 45		13 45		14 45		15 47		16 45	

			NT	NT	NT	NT	NT	NT	NT	NT	NT	NT	NT	NT	NT	NT
Leeds 10	40	d	16 29	16 42	16 59	17 13	17 29	17 44	17 59	18 29	18 59	19 29	20 29	21 29	22 29	23 29
Burley Park		d	16 33	16 46	17 03	17 17	17 33	17 48	18 03	18 33	19 03	19 33	20 33	21 33	22 33	23 33
Headingley		d	16 36	16 49	17 06	17 20	17 36	17 51	18 06	18 36	19 06	19 36	20 36	21 36	22 36	23 36
Horsforth		d	16 41	16a55	17 11	17 25	17 41	17 56	18 11	18 41	19 11	19 41	20 41	21 41	22 41	23 41
Weeton		d	16 49		17 19	17 33	17 49		18 19	18 49	19 19	19 49	20 49	21 49	22 49	23 49
Pannal		d	16 55		17 25	17 39	17 55		18 25	18 55	19 25	19 55	20 55	21 55	22 55	23 55
Hornbeam Park		d	17 00		17 30	17 44	18 00		18 30	19 00	19 30	20 00	21 00	22 00	23 01	23 58
Harrogate		a	17 03		17 33	17 47	18 03	18 15	18 33	19 03	19 33	20 03	21 03	22 03	23 08	00 06
		d	17 08		17 35	17 49	18 05	18 16	18 35	19 05	19 35	20 05	21 05	22 05		
Starbeck		d	17 11		17 38	17 52	18 08	18 20	18 39	19 08	19 38	20 08	21 08	22 08		
Knaresborough		a	17 17		17 45	18 00	18 14	18 26	18 45	19 14	19 45	20 14	21 14	22 15		
		d	17 21				18 14			19 14		20 14	21 14			
Cattal		d	17 29				18 22			19 22		20 22	21 22			
Hammerton		d	17 32				18 26			19 26		20 26	21 26			
Poppleton		d	17 39				18 33			19 33		20 33	21 33			
York 8	40	a	17 48				18 46			19 45		20 44	21 47			

Saturdays

			NT	NT	NT	NT	NT	NT	NT	NT	NT	NT	NT	NT	NT	NT	NT	NT	NT	NT	NT	NT	NT	NT
Leeds 10	40	d	23p29	06 07	06 37	07 13	07 39	07 54	08 29	08 59	09 29	09 59	10 29	10 59	11 29	11 59	12 29	12 59	13 29	13 59	14 29	14 59	15 29	15 59
Burley Park		d	23p33	06 11	06 41	07 17	07 43	07 58	08 33	09 03	09 33	10 03	10 33	11 03	11 33	12 03	12 33	13 03	13 33	14 03	14 33	15 03	15 33	16 03
Headingley		d	23p36	06 14	06 44	07 20	07 46	08 01	08 36	09 06	09 36	10 06	10 36	11 06	11 36	12 06	12 36	13 06	13 36	14 06	14 36	15 06	15 36	16 06
Horsforth		d	23p41	06 19	06 49	07 25	07 51	08 06	08 41	09 11	09 41	10 11	10 41	11 11	11 41	12 11	12 41	13 11	13 41	14 11	14 41	15 11	15 41	16 11
Weeton		d	23p49	06 27	06 57	07 33	07 59	08 14	08 49	09 19	09 49	10 19	10 49	11 19	11 49	12 19	12 49	13 19	13 49	14 19	14 49	15 19	15 49	16 19
Pannal		d	23p55	06 33	07 03	07 39	08 05	08 20	08 55	09 25	09 55	10 25	10 55	11 25	11 55	12 25	12 55	13 25	13 55	14 25	14 55	15 25	15 55	16 25
Hornbeam Park		d	23p58	06 38	07 08	07 44	08 10	08 25	09 00	09 30	10 00	10 30	11 00	11 30	12 00	12 30	13 00	13 30	14 00	14 30	15 00	15 30	16 00	16 30
Harrogate		a	00 06	06 41	07 11	07 47	08 13	08 28	09 03	09 33	10 03	10 33	11 03	11 33	12 03	12 33	13 03	13 33	14 03	14 33	15 03	15 33	16 03	16 33
		d		06 45	07 14	07 49	08 16	08 29	09 05	09 35	10 05	10 35	11 05	11 35	12 05	12 35	13 05	13 35	14 05	14 35	15 05	15 35	16 05	16 35
Starbeck		d		06 49	07 17	07 52	08 19	08 33	09 08	09 38	10 08	10 38	11 08	11 38	12 08	12 38	13 08	13 38	14 08	14 38	15 08	15 38	16 08	16 38
Knaresborough		a		06 54	07 23	07 59	08 25	08 40	09 14	09 45	10 14	10 45	11 14	11 45	12 14	12 45	13 14	13 45	14 14	14 45	15 14	15 45	16 14	16 45
		d		06 55	07 23	07 59	08 28		09 15		10 14		11 14		12 14		13 14		14 14		15 14		16 14	
Cattal		d		07 03	07 31	08 07	08 36		09 23		10 22		11 22		12 22		13 22		14 22		15 22		16 22	
Hammerton		d		07 07	07 35	08 11	08 39		09 27		10 26		11 26		12 26		13 26		14 26		15 26		16 26	
Poppleton		d		07 14	07 42	08 19	08 46		09 34		10 33		11 33		12 33		13 33		14 33		15 33		16 33	
York 8	40	a		07 21	07 51	08 27	08 59		09 45		10 45		11 45		12 45		13 42		14 46		15 46		16 45	

			NT	NT	NT	NT	NT	NT	NT	NT	NT	NT	NT
Leeds 10	40	d	16 29	16 59	17 13	17 29	17 59	18 29	19 29	20 29	21 20	22 29	23 21
Burley Park		d	16 33	17 03	17 17	17 33	18 03	18 33	19 33	20 33	21 24	22 33	23 25
Headingley		d	16 36	17 06	17 20	17 36	18 06	18 36	19 36	20 36	21 27	22 36	23 28
Horsforth		d	16 41	17 11	17 25	17 41	18 11	18 41	19 41	20 41	21 32	22 41	23 33
Weeton		d	16 49	17 19	17 33	17 49	18 19	18 49	19 49	20 49	21 40	22 49	23 41
Pannal		d	16 55	17 25	17 39	17 55	18 25	18 55	19 55	20 55	21 46	22 55	23 47
Hornbeam Park		d	17 00	17 30	17 44	18 00	18 30	19 00	20 00	21 00	21 51	23 00	23 52
Harrogate		a	17 03	17 33	17 47	18 03	18 33	19 03	20 03	21 03	21 54	23 06	23 58
		d	17 08	17 35	17 49	18 05	18 35	19 05	20 05	21 05	21 56		
Starbeck		d	17 11	17 38	17 52	18 08	18 38	19 08	20 08	21 08	21 59		
Knaresborough		a	17 17	17 45	18 00	18 14	18 45	19 14	20 14	21 14	22 06		
		d	17 21			18 14		19 14	20 14	21 14			
Cattal		d	17 29			18 22		19 22	20 22	21 22			
Hammerton		d	17 33			18 26		19 26	20 26	21 31			
Poppleton		d	17 40			18 33		19 33	20 33	21 38			
York 8	40	a	17 47			18 46		19 45	20 45	21 48			

Table 35

Sundays

Leeds - Harrogate - York

			NT	NT	NT	NT	NT	NT	NT	NT	NT	NT	NT	NT
Leeds 10	40	d	09 54	10 54	12 54	14 54	15 54	16 54	17 54	18 54	19 54	21 16	22 23	23 22
Burley Park		d	09 59	10 59	12 59	14 59	15 59	16 59	17 59	18 59	19 59	21 21	22 28	23 27
Headingley		d	10 01	11 01	13 01	15 01	16 01	17 01	18 01	19 01	20 01	21 23	22 30	23 29
Horsforth		d	10 07	11 07	13 07	15 07	16 07	17 07	18 07	19 07	20 07	21 29	22 36	23 35
Weeton		d	10 14	11 14	13 14	15 14	16 14	17 14	18 14	19 14	20 14	21 37	22 43	23 42
Pannal		d	10 20	11 20	13 20	15 20	16 20	17 20	18 20	19 20	20 20	21 43	22 49	23 48
Hornbeam Park		d	10 25	11 25	13 25	15 25	16 25	17 25	18 25	19 25	20 25	21 48	22 54	23 53
Harrogate		a	10 31	11 28	13 28	15 28	16 28	17 28	18 28	19 28	20 28	21 51	23 00	23 59
		d		11 30	13 30	15 30	16 30	17 30	18 30	19 30	20 30	21 53		
Starbeck		d		11 34	13 34	15 34	16 34	17 34	18 34	19 34	20 34	21 57		
Knaresborough		a		11 39	13 39	15 39	16 39	17 39	18 39	19 39	20 39	22 03		
		d		11 40	13 40	15 40	16 45	17 44	18 44	19 44	20 45			
Cattal		d		11 48	13 48	15 48	16 53	17 52	18 52	19 52	20 53			
Hammerton		d		11 51	13 51	15 51	16 56	17 55	18 55	19 55	20 56			
Poppleton		d		11 58	13 58	15 58	17 03	18 02	19 02	20 02	21 03			
York 8	40	a		12 07	14 08	16 08	17 10	18 10	19 12	20 12	21 15			

Leeds and Bradford - Skipton, Lancaster, Morecambe and Carlisle

			NT	NT	NT	NT	NT	NT	NT	NT	NT	NT	NT	NT	NT	NT	NT	NT	NT	NT	NT	NT
London Kings Cross ■15	⊖26	d																				
Leeds ■10	37	d		05 55		06 21		06 56		07 25			07 51		08 19	08 25		08 49	08 56		09 26	
Bradford Forster Square	37	d			06 10		06 40		07 15			07 42		08 11			08 41			09 11		09 41
Frizinghall	37	d			06 13		06 43		07 18			07 45		08 14			08 44			09 14		09 44
Shipley	37	a		06 07	06 17	06 32	06 47	07 08	07 22	07 36		07 49	08 02	08 18	08 31	08 37	08 48	09 01	09 07	09 18	09 37	09 48
		d		06 08	06 19	06 33	06 48	07 08	07 23	07 37		07 50	08 03	08 19	08 32	08 37	08 49	09 02	09 08	09 19	09 38	09 49
Saltaire		d		06 10	06 22	06 35	06 50	07 10	07 26	07 39		07 53	08 05	08 22		08 40	08 52		09 10	09 22	09 40	09 52
Bingley		d		06 15	06 26	06 39	06 54	07 14	07 30	07 43		07 57	08 09	08 26	08 37	08 44	08 56	09 06	09 14	09 26	09 44	09 56
Crossflatts		d		06 17	06 28	06 41	06 56	07 17	07 32	07 46		07 59	08 12	08 28		08 46	08 58		09 17	09 28	09 47	09 58
Keighley		d		06 22	06 33	06 45	07 01	07 21	07 37	07 50		08 04	08 17	08 33	08 43	08 50	09 03	09 12	09 21	09 33	09 51	10 03
Steeton & Silsden		d		06 26	06 37	06 49	07 05	07 26	07 41	07 55		08 08	08 22	08 37		08 54	09 07		09 26	09 37	09 56	10 07
Cononley		d		06 31	06 42	06 53	07 09	07 30	07 46	07 59		08 13	08 26	08 42		08 59	09 12		09 30	09 42	10 00	10 12
Skipton		a		06 40	06 49	07 03	07 19	07 39	07 54	08 08		08 21	08 34	08 50	08 55	09 09	09 20	09 24	09 40	09 50	10 11	10 20
		d	05 40												09 00			09 26				
Gargrave		d	05 45												09 05			09 32				
Blackpool North	94	d																				
Preston		d																				
Blackburn	97	d																				
Clitheroe	94	d																				
Hellifield		d	05 55												09 14			09 40				
Long Preston		d	05 58												09 17			09 43				
Giggleswick		d	06 08												09 24							
Clapham (Nth Yorkshire)		d	06 16												09 33							
Bentham		d	06 22												09 39							
Wennington		d	06 27												09 44							
Carnforth	82	a	06 43												10 00							
Lancaster ■	65,82,98	a	06 53												10 12							
Bare Lane	98	a													10 25							
Morecambe	98	a													10 32							
Settle		d																09 50				
Horton-in-Ribblesdale		d																09 58				
Ribblehead		d																10 06				
Dent		d																10 16				
Garsdale		d																10 21				
Kirkby Stephen		d									07 28							10 34				
Appleby		d									07 40							10 47				
Langwathby		d									07 54							11 01				
Lazonby & Kirkoswald		d									08 00							11 07				
Armathwaite		d									08 08							11 15				
Carlisle ■	65	a									08 24							11 34				

			NT	NT	NT	NT	NT	NT	NT	NT	NT	NT	NT	NT	NT	NT	NT	NT	NT	NT	NT	NT	NT	NT
London Kings Cross ■15	⊖26	d																						
Leeds ■10	37	d	09 47	09 56		10 19	10 26		10 49	10 56		11 26		11 56		12 26		12 49	12 56		13 26		13 49	13 56
Bradford Forster Square	37	d			10 11			10 41			11 11		11 41		12 11		12 41			13 11		13 41		
Frizinghall	37	d			10 14			10 44			11 14		11 44		12 14		12 44			13 14		13 44		
Shipley	37	a	10 01	10 07	10 18	10 31	10 37	10 48	11 01	11 07	11 18	11 38	11 48	12 07	12 18	12 37	12 48	13 01	13 07	13 18	13 37	13 48	14 03	14 07
		d	10 02	10 08	10 19	10 32	10 38	10 49	11 02	11 08	11 19	11 38	11 49	12 08	12 19	12 38	12 49	13 02	13 08	13 19	13 38	13 49	14 03	14 08
Saltaire		d		10 10	10 22		10 40	10 52		11 10	11 21	11 40	11 52	12 10	12 22	12 40	12 52		13 10	13 22	13 40	13 52		14 10
Bingley		d	10 06	10 14	10 26	10 37	10 44	10 56	11 06	11 14	11 25	11 44	11 56	12 14	12 26	12 44	12 56	13 06	13 14	13 26	13 44	13 56	14 08	14 14
Crossflatts		d		10 17	10 28		10 47	10 58		11 17	11 27	11 47	11 58	12 17	12 28	12 47	12 58		13 17	13 28	13 47	13 58		14 17
Keighley		d	10 12	10 21	10 33	10 42	10 51	11 03	11 12	11 21	11 32	11 51	12 03	12 21	12 33	12 51	13 03	13 12	13 21	13 33	13 51	14 03	14 14	14 21
Steeton & Silsden		d		10 26	10 37		10 56	11 07		11 26	11 36	11 56	12 07	12 26	12 37	12 56	13 07		13 26	13 37	13 56	14 07		14 26
Cononley		d		10 30	10 42		11 00	11 12		11 30	11 40	12 00	12 12	12 30	12 42	13 00	13 11		13 30	13 42	14 00	14 11		14 30
Skipton		a	10 24	10 39	10 50	10 55	11 11	11 20	11 24	11 40	11 50	12 11	12 20	12 40	12 50	13 10	13 20	13 24	13 40	13 50	14 10	14 20	14 26	14 40
		d	10 26			11 00			11 26									13 26					14 34	
Gargrave		d				11 05												13 31					14 39	
Blackpool North	94	d																						
Preston		d																						
Blackburn	97	d																						
Clitheroe	94	d																						
Hellifield		d				11 14			11 37									13 40					14 48	
Long Preston		d				11 17												13 42					14 51	
Giggleswick		d				11 25																	14 59	
Clapham (Nth Yorkshire)		d				11 33																	15 07	
Bentham		d				11 39																	15 13	
Wennington		d				11 44																	15 18	
Carnforth	82	a				12 00																	15 34	
Lancaster ■	65,82,98	a				12 11																	15 47	
Bare Lane	98	a				12 34																	16 09	
Morecambe	98	a				12 39																	16 13	
Settle		d	10 44						11 46									13 48						
Horton-in-Ribblesdale		d							11 54									13 57						
Ribblehead		d							12 02									14 05						
Dent		d							12 12									14 14						
Garsdale		d							12 17									14 20						
Kirkby Stephen		d	11 22						12 30									14 32						
Appleby		d	11 36						12 43									14 45						
Langwathby		d							12 57									14 59						
Lazonby & Kirkoswald		d							13 03									15 04						
Armathwaite		d							13 11									15 12						
Carlisle ■	65	a	12 17						13 29									15 32						

Leeds and Bradford - Skipton, Lancaster, Morecambe and Carlisle

			NT	NT	NT	NT	NT	NT	NT	NT	NT	NT	NT	NT	NT	NT	NT	NT	NT	NT	NT	NT	NT	NT
London Kings Cross ■15	⊖26	d																						
Leeds ■10	37	d		14 26		14 49	14 56		15 26		15 56		16 26		16 39	16 56		17 26		17 50	17 56		18 26	
Bradford Forster Square	37	d	14 11		14 41			15 11		15 41		16 11		16 40			17 11		17 38			18 11		18 41
Frizinghall	37	d	14 14		14 44			15 14		15 44		16 14		16 43			17 14		17 41			18 14		18 44
Shipley	37	a	14 18	14 37	14 48	15 01	15 07	15 18	15 37	15 48	16 07	16 18	16 37	16 48	16 53	17 07	17 18	17 37	17 45	18 02	18 08	18 18	18 38	18 48
		d	14 19	14 38	14 49	15 02	15 08	15 19	15 38	15 49	16 08	16 19	16 38	16 49	16 55	17 08	17 19	17 38	17 46	18 03	18 08	18 19	18 38	18 49
Saltaire		d	14 22	14 40	14 52		15 10	15 22	15 40	15 52	16 10	16 22	16 40	16 52		17 10	17 22	17 40	17 49	18 05		18 22	18 40	18 51
Bingley		d	14 26	14 44	14 56	15 06	15 14	15 26	15 44	15 56	16 14	16 26	16 44	16 56	17 03	17 14	17 26	17 44	17 53	18 09	18 17	18 26	18 44	18 55
Crossflatts		d	14 28	14 47	14 58		15 17	15 28	15 47	15 58	16 17	16 28	16 47	16 58		17 17	17 28	17 47	17 55	18 12		18 28	18 47	18 57
Keighley		d	14 33	14 51	15 03	15 12	15 21	15 33	15 51	16 03	16 21	16 33	16 51	17 03	17 10	17 21	17 33	17 51	18 00	18 16	18 24	18 33	18 51	19 02
Steeton & Silsden		d	14 37	14 56	15 07		15 26	15 37	15 56	16 07	16 26	16 37	16 56	17 07		17 26	17 37	17 56	18 04	18 21	18 29	18 37	18 56	19 06
Cononley		d	14 41	15 00	15 12		15 30	15 42	16 00	16 11	16 30	16 42	17 00	17 11		17 30	17 42	18 00	18 09	18 25		18 42	19 00	19 10
Skipton		a	14 50	15 10	15 20	15 24	15 40	15 50	16 10	16 20	16 40	16 50	17 10	17 19	17 24	17 40	17 50	18 10	18 17	18 34	18 40	18 50	19 10	19 20
		d				15 26									17 24						18 41			
Gargrave		d													17 30						18 46			
Blackpool North	94	d																						
Preston		d																						
Blackburn	97	d																						
Clitheroe	94	d																						
Hellifield		d				15 37									17 39						18 55			
Long Preston		d													17 42						18 57			
Giggleswick		d													17 49									
Clapham (Nth Yorkshire)		d													17 57									
Bentham		d													18 04									
Wennington		d													18 09									
Carnforth	82	a													18 29									
Lancaster ■	65,82,98	a													18 42									
Bare Lane	98	a													18 55									
Morecambe	98	a													19 01									
Settle		d				15 45															19 03			
Horton-in-Ribblesdale		d				15 53															19 12			
Ribblehead		d				16 01															19 20			
Dent		d				16 11															19 29			
Garsdale		d				16 16															19 35			
Kirkby Stephen		d				16 29															19 47			
Appleby		d				16 41															20 00			
Langwathby		d				16 55															20 14			
Lazonby & Kirkoswald		d				17 01															20 19			
Armathwaite		d				17 09															20 27			
Carlisle ■	65	a				17 28															20 48			

			NT	NT	NT	NT	NT	NT	NT	NT	GR ■ 1	NT	NT	NT	NT	NT	NT	NT	NT	NT
London Kings Cross ■15	⊖26	d									18 03									
Leeds ■10	37	d	18 50		19 19	19 26		19 56		20 26	20 33	20 56		21 26	21 56		22 26	22 56		23 18
Bradford Forster Square	37	d		19 07			19 36		20 11				21 05			22 05			23 09	
Frizinghall	37	d		19 10			19 39		20 14				21 08			22 08			23 12	
Shipley	37	a	19 03	19 14	19 31	19 37	19 43	20 07	20 18	20 37		21 07	21 12	21 38	22 07	22 12	22 37	23 07	23 16	23 31
		d	19 03	19 15	19 32	19 38	19 44	20 08	20 19	20 38		21 08	21 14	21 38	22 08	22 14	22 38	23 08	23 17	23 32
Saltaire		d	19 05	19 18		19 40	19 47	20 10	20 22	20 40		21 10	21 17	21 40	22 10	22 17	22 40	23 10	23 20	23 34
Bingley		d	19 09	19 22	19 36	19 44	19 51	20 14	20 26	20 44		21 14	21 21	21 44	22 14	22 21	22 44	23 14	23 24	23 38
Crossflatts		d	19 11	19 24		19 47	19 53	20 17	20 28	20 47		21 17	21 23	21 47	22 17	22 23	22 46	23 17	23 26	23 40
Keighley		d	19 15	19 29	19 42	19 51	19 58	20 21	20 33	20 51	20s58	21 21	21 28	21 51	22 21	22 28	22 51	23 21	23 31	23 44
Steeton & Silsden		d	19 19	19 33		19 56	20 02	20 26	20 37	20 55		21 26	21 32	21 56	22 26	22 32	22 56	23 26	23 35	23 48
Cononley		d	19 23	19 38		20 00	20 07	20 30	20 42	20 59		21 30	21 36	22 00	22 30	22 36	23 00	23 30	23 40	23 52
Skipton		a	19 33	19 46	19 54	20 10	20 15	20 40	20 50	21 10	21 13	21 39	21 44	22 10	22 40	22 44	23 11	23 41	23 48	00 02
		d			20 00															
Gargrave		d			20 06															
Blackpool North	94	d																		
Preston		d																		
Blackburn	97	d																		
Clitheroe	94	d																		
Hellifield		d			20 15															
Long Preston		d			20 18															
Giggleswick		d																		
Clapham (Nth Yorkshire)		d																		
Bentham		d																		
Wennington		d																		
Carnforth	82	a																		
Lancaster ■	65,82,98	a																		
Bare Lane	98	a																		
Morecambe	98	a																		
Settle		d			20 24															
Horton-in-Ribblesdale		d			20 32															
Ribblehead		d			20a42															
Dent		d																		
Garsdale		d																		
Kirkby Stephen		d																		
Appleby		d																		
Langwathby		d																		
Lazonby & Kirkoswald		d																		
Armathwaite		d																		
Carlisle ■	65	a																		

Table 36

Saturdays

Leeds and Bradford - Skipton, Lancaster, Morecambe and Carlisle

Station		NT	NT	NT	NT	NT	NT	NT	NT	NT	NT	NT	NT	NT	NT	NT	NT	NT	NT	NT	NT	NT
London Kings Cross 15	⊖26 d																					
Leeds 10	37 d	05 55		06 19	06 56		07 56		08 19	08 25		08 49	08 56		09 26		09 47		09 56		10 19	10 26
Bradford Forster Square	37 d		06 10			07 11		08 11			08 41			09 11		09 41				10 11		
Frizinghall	37 d		06 13			07 14		08 14			08 44			09 14		09 44				10 14		
Shipley	37 a	06 07	06 17	06 31	07 08	07 18	08 08	08 18	08 31	08 37	08 44	09 01	09 07	09 18	09 37	09 48	10 01		10 07	10 18	10 31	10 37
	d	06 08	06 19	06 32	07 08	07 19	08 08	08 19	08 32	08 37	08 45	09 02	09 08	09 19	09 38	09 49	10 02		10 08	10 19	10 32	10 38
Saltaire	d	06 10	06 22		07 10	07 22	08 10	08 22		08 40	08 52		09 10	09 22	09 40	09 52			10 10	10 22		10 40
Bingley	d	06 15	06 26	06 36	07 14	07 26	08 14	08 26	08 37	08 44	08 56	09 06	09 14	09 26	09 44	09 56	10 06		10 14	10 26	10 37	10 44
Crossflatts	d	06 17	06 28		07 17	07 28	08 16	08 28		08 46	08 58		09 17	09 28	09 47	09 58			10 17	10 28		10 47
Keighley	d	06 22	06 33	06 42	07 21	07 33	08 20	08 33	08 43	08 50	09 03	09 12	09 21	09 33	09 51	10 03	10 12		10 21	10 33	10 42	10 51
Steeton & Silsden	d	06 26	06 37		07 26	07 37	08 24	08 37		08 54	09 07		09 26	09 37	09 56	10 07			10 26	10 37		10 56
Cononley	d	06 31	06 42		07 30	07 42	08 28	08 42		08 59	09 12		09 30	09 42	10 00	10 12			10 30	10 42		11 00
Skipton	a	06 40	06 49	06 55	07 39	07 50	08 39	08 50	08 55	09 09	09 20	09 24	09 40	09 50	10 11	10 20	10 24		10 39	10 50	10 55	11 11
	d	06 40		06 56					09 00			09 26					10 26				11 00	
Gargrave	d	06 45							09 05			09 32									11 05	
Blackpool North	94 d																					
Preston	d																	08 42				
Blackburn	97 d																					
Clitheroe	94 d																					
Hellifield	d	06 54		07 08					09 14			09 40									11 14	
Long Preston	d	06 57							09 17			09 43									11 17	
Giggleswick	d	07 07							09 24												11 25	
Clapham (Nth Yorkshire)	d	07 15							09 33												11 33	
Bentham	d	07 21							09 39												11 39	
Wennington	d	07 26							09 44												11 44	
Carnforth	82 a	07 42							10 00												12 00	
Lancaster 6	65,82,98 a	07 52							10 12									09 02			12 11	
Bare Lane	98 a								10 25												12 31	
Morecambe	98 a								10 32												12 36	
Settle	d			07 15								09 50					10 44					
Horton-in-Ribblesdale	d			07 24								09 58										
Ribblehead	d			07 32								10 05										
Dent	d			07 41								10 14										
Garsdale	d			07 47								10 2[illegible]										
Kirkby Stephen	d			07 59								10 34					11 22					
Appleby	d			08 12								10 47					11 36					
Langwathby	d			08 26								11 01										
Lazonby & Kirkoswald	d			08 31								11 07										
Armathwaite	d			08 39								11 15										
Carlisle 8	65 a			08 58								11 34					12 17	12 39				

Station		NT	NT	NT	NT	NT	NT	NT	NT	NT	NT	NT	NT	NT	NT	NT	NT	NT	NT	NT	NT	NT	NT
London Kings Cross 15	⊖26 d																						
Leeds 10	37 d		10 49	10 56		11 26		11 56		12 26		12 49	12 56		13 26		13 49	13 56		14 26		14 49	14 56
Bradford Forster Square	37 d	10 41			11 11		11 41		12 11		12 41			13 11		13 41			14 11		14 41		
Frizinghall	37 d	10 44			11 14		11 44		12 14		12 44			13 14		13 44			14 14		14 44		
Shipley	37 a	10 48	11 01	11 07	11 18	11 38	11 48	12 07	12 18	12 37	12 48	13 01	13 07	13 18	13 37	13 48	14 03	14 07	14 18	14 37	14 48	15 01	15 07
	d	10 49	11 02	11 08	11 19	11 38	11 49	12 08	12 19	12 38	12 49	13 02	13 08	13 19	13 38	13 49	14 03	14 08	14 19	14 38	14 49	15 02	15 08
Saltaire	d	10 52		11 10	11 21	11 40	11 52	12 10	12 22	12 40	12 52		13 10	13 22	13 40	13 52		14 10	14 22	14 40	14 52		15 10
Bingley	d	10 56	11 06	11 14	11 25	11 44	11 56	12 14	12 26	12 44	12 56	13 06	13 14	13 26	13 44	13 56	14 08	14 14	14 26	14 44	14 56	15 06	15 14
Crossflatts	d	10 58		11 17	11 27	11 47	11 58	12 17	12 28	12 47	12 58		13 17	13 28	13 47	13 58		14 17	14 28	14 47	14 58		15 17
Keighley	d	11 03	11 12	11 21	11 32	11 51	12 03	12 21	12 33	12 51	13 03	13 12	13 21	13 33	13 51	14 03	14 14	14 21	14 33	14 51	15 03	15 12	15 21
Steeton & Silsden	d	11 07		11 26	11 36	11 56	12 07	12 26	12 37	12 56	13 07		13 26	13 37	13 56	14 07		14 26	14 37	14 56	15 07		15 26
Cononley	d	11 12		11 30	11 40	12 00	12 12	12 30	12 42	13 00	13 11		13 30	13 42	14 00	14 11		14 30	14 41	15 00	15 12		15 30
Skipton	a	11 20	11 24	11 40	11 50	12 10	12 20	12 40	12 50	13 10	13 20	13 24	13 40	13 50	14 10	14 20	14 26	14 40	14 50	15 10	15 20	15 24	15 40
	d		11 26									13 26					14 34					15 26	
Gargrave	d											13 31					14 39						
Blackpool North	94 d																						
Preston	d																						
Blackburn	97 d																						
Clitheroe	94 d																						
Hellifield	d		11 37									13 40					14 48					15 37	
Long Preston	d											13 42					14 51						
Giggleswick	d																14 59						
Clapham (Nth Yorkshire)	d																15 07						
Bentham	d																15 13						
Wennington	d																15 18						
Carnforth	82 a																15 34						
Lancaster 6	65,82,98 a																15 45						
Bare Lane	98 a																15 55						
Morecambe	98 a																16 02						
Settle	d		11 46									13 48										15 45	
Horton-in-Ribblesdale	d		11 54									13 57										15 53	
Ribblehead	d		12 02									14 05										16 01	
Dent	d		12 12									14 14										16 11	
Garsdale	d		12 17									14 20										16 16	
Kirkby Stephen	d		12 30									14 32										16 29	
Appleby	d		12 43									14 45										16 41	
Langwathby	d		12 57									14 59										16 55	
Lazonby & Kirkoswald	d		13 03									15 04										17 01	
Armathwaite	d		13 11									15 12										17 09	
Carlisle 8	65 a		13 29									15 27										17 28	

Table 36

Saturdays

Leeds and Bradford - Skipton, Lancaster, Morecambe and Carlisle

Station		NT	NT	NT	NT	NT	NT	NT	NT	NT	NT	NT	NT	NT A	NT B	NT A 🚌	NT	NT A 🚌	NT	NT	NT	NT
London Kings Cross 15	⊖26 d																					
Leeds 10	37 d		15 26		15 56		16 26		16 39	16 56		17 26		17 50	17 50		17 56			18 26		18 56
Bradford Forster Square	37 d	15 11		15 41		16 11		16 40			17 11		17 41						18 11		18 41	
Frizinghall	37 d	15 14		15 44		16 14		16 43			17 14		17 44						18 14		18 44	
Shipley	37 a	15 18	15 37	15 48	16 07	16 18	16 37	16 48	16 53	17 07	17 18	17 37	17 48	18 02	18 02		18 08		18 18	18 38	18 48	19 07
	d	15 19	15 38	15 49	16 08	16 19	16 38	16 49	16 55	17 08	17 19	17 38	17 49	18 03	18 03		18 08		18 19	18 38	18 49	19 08
Saltaire	d	15 22	15 40	15 52	16 10	16 22	16 40	16 52		17 10	17 22	17 40	17 51				18 10		18 22	18 40	18 51	19 10
Bingley	d	15 26	15 44	15 56	16 14	16 26	16 44	16 56	17 03	17 14	17 26	17 44	17 55	18 08	18 08		18 14		18 26	18 44	18 55	19 14
Crossflatts	d	15 28	15 47	15 58	16 17	16 28	16 47	16 58		17 17	17 28	17 47	17 57				18 17		18 28	18 47	18 57	19 17
Keighley	d	15 33	15 51	16 03	16 21	16 33	16 51	17 03	17 10	17 21	17 33	17 51	18 02	18 14	18 14		18 21		18 33	18 51	19 02	19 21
Steeton & Silsden	d	15 37	15 56	16 07	16 26	16 37	16 56	17 07		17 26	17 37	17 56	18 06	18 19	18 19		18 26		18 37	18 56	19 06	19 26
Cononley	d	15 42	16 00	16 11	16 30	16 42	17 00	17 11		17 30	17 42	18 00	18 10				18 30		18 42	19 00	19 10	19 30
Skipton	a	15 50	16 10	16 20	16 40	16 50	17 10	17 19	17 24	17 40	17 50	18 10	18 17	18 29	18 29		18 40		18 50	19 10	19 20	19 40
	d								17 24					18 35	18 35	18 35		18 40				
Gargrave	d								17 30					18 40	18 40			18u55				
Blackpool North	94 d																					
Preston	d																					
Blackburn	97 d																					
Clitheroe	94 d																					
Hellifield	d								17 39					18 49	18 49			19u10				
Long Preston	d								17 42					18a51	18 51			19u18				
Giggleswick	d								17 49													
Clapham (Nth Yorkshire)	d								17 57													
Bentham	d								18 04													
Wennington	d								18 09													
Carnforth	82 a								18 26													
Lancaster 6	65,82,98 a								18 38													
Bare Lane	98 a								18 53													
Morecambe	98 a								18 59													
Settle	d														18 57	19 05		19 28				
Horton-in-Ribblesdale	d														19 06			19 43				
Ribblehead	d														19 14			19 58				
Dent	d														19 23							
Garsdale	d														19 29			20 43				
Kirkby Stephen	d														19 41	20 15		21 18				
Appleby	d														19 54	20 40		21 43				
Langwathby	d														20 08			22 08				
Lazonby & Kirkoswald	d														20 13			22 18				
Armathwaite	d														20 21			22 33				
Carlisle 8	65 a														20 41	21 40		22 58				

A from 23 October

B until 16 October

Table 36

Leeds and Bradford - Skipton, Lancaster, Morecambe and Carlisle

Saturdays

		NT	NT	NT	NT	NT	NT	GR	GR	NT	NT	NT	NT	NT	NT	NT	NT	NT	NT	NT	NT
			A	B		A 🚌		1 C	1 D												
London Kings Cross ⊖26	d							16 57	17 30												
Leeds 37	d		19 19	19 19	19 26			19 57	19 57		20 06	20 26	20 56		21 26	21 56		22 26	22 56		23 18
Bradford Forster Square 37	d	19 07					19 36			20 07				21 05			22 05			23 05	
Frizinghall 37	d	19 10					19 39			20 10				21 08			22 08			23 08	
Shipley 37	a	19 14	19 31	19 31	19 37		19 43			20 15	20 17	20 37	21 07	21 12	21 38	22 07	22 12	22 37	23 07	23 12	23 31
	d	19 15	19 32	19 32	19 38		19 44			20 15	20 20	20 38	21 08	21 14	21 38	22 08	22 14	22 38	23 08	23 14	23 32
Saltaire	d	19 18			19 40		19 47			20 17	20 22	20 40	21 10	21 17	21 40	22 10	22 17	22 40	23 10	23 17	23 34
Bingley	d	19 22	19 36	19 36	19 44		19 51			20 21	20 26	20 44	21 14	21 21	21 44	22 14	22 21	22 44	23 14	23 21	23 38
Crossflatts	d	19 24			19 47		19 53			20 23	20 28	20 47	21 17	21 23	21 47	22 17	22 23	22 46	23 17	23 23	23 40
Keighley	d	19 29	19 42	19 42	19 51		19 58	20s18	20s18	20 28	20 33	20 51	21 21	21 28	21 51	22 21	22 28	22 51	23 21	23 28	23 44
Steeton & Silsden	d	19 33			19 56		20 02			20 32	20 37	20 56	21 26	21 32	21 56	22 26	22 32	22 56	23 26	23 32	23 48
Cononley	d	19 38			20 00		20 07			20 36	20 41	20 59	21 30	21 36	22 00	22 30	22 36	23 00	23 30	23 37	23 52
Skipton	a	19 46	19 54	19 54	20 10		20 15	20 31	20 31	20 47	20 49	21 10	21 39	21 44	22 10	22 40	22 44	23 11	23 41	23 44	00 02
	d		20 00	20 00		20 10															
Gargrave	d		20 06	20 06		20u25															
Blackpool North 94	d																				
Preston	d																				
Blackburn 97	d																				
Clitheroe 94	d																				
Hellifield	d		20 15	20 15		20u40															
Long Preston	d		20a18	20 18		20u48															
Giggleswick	d																				
Clapham (Nth Yorkshire)	d																				
Bentham	d																				
Wennington	d																				
Carnforth 82	a																				
Lancaster 65,82,98	a																				
Bare Lane 98	a																				
Morecambe 98	a																				
Settle	d			20 24		20 58															
Horton-in-Ribblesdale	d			20 32		21 13															
Ribblehead	d			20a42		21a28															
Dent	d																				
Garsdale	d																				
Kirkby Stephen	d																				
Appleby	d																				
Langwathby	d																				
Lazonby & Kirkoswald	d																				
Armathwaite	d																				
Carlisle 65	a																				

A from 23 October
B until 16 October
C 17 July until 4 September
D until 10 July and from 11 September

Table 36

Leeds and Bradford - Skipton, Lancaster, Morecambe and Carlisle

Sundays

		NT	NT	NT	NT	NT	NT	NT	NT	NT	NT	NT	NT	NT	NT	NT	NT	NT	NT	NT	NT	NT
		B	C	D	D	C 🚌	E	C 🚌			B					C	D	C 🚌	C 🚌			
London Kings Cross ⊖26	d																					
Leeds 37	d	08 40	09 00	09 00					10 08		10 51	11 08	12 08		13 08	13 15	13 15			14 08		14 57
Bradford Forster Square 37	d									10 48				12 48							14 48	
Frizinghall 37	d									10 51				12 51							14 51	
Shipley 37	a	08 52	09 13	09 13					10 19	10 54	11 03	11 19	12 19	12 54	13 19	13 28	13 28			14 19	14 54	15 09
	d	08 53	09 14	09 14					10 20	10 55	11 04	11 20	12 20	12 55	13 20	13 29	13 29			14 20	14 55	15 10
Saltaire	d	08 55	09 16	09 16					10 22	10 57		11 22	12 22	12 57	13 22					14 22	14 57	
Bingley	d	09 00	09 21	09 21					10 26	11 01	11 09	11 26	12 26	13 01	13 26	13 34	13 34			14 26	15 01	15 15
Crossflatts	d	09 02	09 23	09 23					10 28	11 03		11 28	12 28	13 03	13 28					14 28	15 03	
Keighley	d	09 07	09 28	09 28					10 32	11 08	11 14	11 32	12 32	13 08	13 32	13 39	13 39			14 32	15 08	15 20
Steeton & Silsden	d	09 11	09 32	09 32					10 36	11 12		11 36	12 36	13 12	13 36					14 36	15 12	
Cononley	d	09 16	09 37	09 37					10 40	11 16		11 40	12 40	13 16	13 40					14 40	15 16	
Skipton	a	09 23	09 44	09 44					10 48	11 23	11 27	11 48	12 48	13 23	13 48	13 53	13 53			14 48	15 23	15 33
	d	09 26	09 46	09 46		09 55		09 55			11 29					13 54	13 54	14 05	14 05			15 36
Gargrave	d	09 31	09 51	09 51							11 35					14 00	14 00		14 20			15 41
Blackpool North 94	d				08 36																	
Preston	d				09 05		10 00															
Blackburn 97	d				09 27		10 22															
Clitheroe 94	d				09 51		10 45															
Hellifield	d	09 40	10a00	10 00	10 15		11 08	10 15			11 44					14 08	14 08		14 35			15 50
Long Preston	d	09 43									11 46					14a11	14 11		14 45			15 53
Giggleswick	d	09 52									11 54											16 00
Clapham (Nth Yorkshire)	d	10 00									12 02											16 08
Bentham	d	10 06									12 08											16 15
Wennington	d	10 11									12 13											16 20
Carnforth 82	a	10 28									12 30											16 36
Lancaster 65,82,98	a	10 40									12 44											16 46
Bare Lane 98	a	10 51									13 07											16 56
Morecambe 98	a	10 57									13 11											17 03
Settle	d			10 08	10 23	10 25	11 17	10 27									14 17	14 35	14 55			
Horton-in-Ribblesdale	d			10 17	10 32		11 26	10 42									14 26		15 10			
Ribblehead	d			10 25	10 40		11 34	10 57									14 34		15 25			
Dent	d			10 35	10 50		11 44										14 44					
Garsdale	d			10 41	10 56		11 49	11 42									14 50		16 10			
Kirkby Stephen	d			10 54	11 09	11 35	12 02	12 17									15 03	15 45	16 45			
Appleby	d			11 07	11 22	12 00	12 16	12 42									15 15	16 10	17 10			
Langwathby	d			11 21	11 36		12 30	13 07									15 29		17 35			
Lazonby & Kirkoswald	d			11 27	11 42		12 36	13 17									15 35		17 45			
Armathwaite	d			11 35	11 50		12 44	13 32									15 43		18 00			
Carlisle 65	a			11 52	12 10	13 00	13 05	13 57									16 00	17 10	18 25			

		NT	NT	NT	NT	NT	NT	NT	NT	NT	NT	NT	NT	NT	NT	NT	NT	NT	NT
							C	D	C 🚌	C 🚌									
London Kings Cross ⊖26	d																		
Leeds 37	d	15 08	16 08		17 08	17 21	17 33	17 33			18 08		19 08	20 08		21 08	22 08		23 10
Bradford Forster Square 37	d			16 48								18 48			20 48			22 48	
Frizinghall 37	d			16 51								18 51			20 51			22 51	
Shipley 37	a	15 19	16 19	16 54	17 19	17 33	17 45	17 45			18 19	18 54	19 19	20 19	20 54	21 19	22 19	22 54	23 21
	d	15 20	16 20	16 55	17 20	17 34	17 46	17 46			18 20	18 55	19 20	20 20	20 55	21 20	22 20	22 55	23 22
Saltaire	d	15 22	16 22	16 57	17 22						18 22	18 57	19 22	20 22	20 57	21 22	22 22	22 57	23 24
Bingley	d	15 26	16 26	17 01	17 26	17 39	17 50	17 50			18 26	19 01	19 26	20 26	21 01	21 26	22 26	23 01	23 28
Crossflatts	d	15 28	16 28	17 03	17 28						18 28	19 03	19 28	20 28	21 03	21 28	22 28	23 03	23 30
Keighley	d	15 32	16 32	17 08	17 32	17 44	17 56	17 56			18 32	19 08	19 32	20 32	21 08	21 32	22 32	23 08	23 34
Steeton & Silsden	d	15 36	16 36	17 12	17 36						18 36	19 12	19 36	20 36	21 12	21 36	22 36	23 12	23 38
Cononley	d	15 40	16 40	17 16	17 40						18 40	19 16	19 40	20 40	21 16	21 40	22 40	23 16	23 42
Skipton	a	15 48	16 48	17 23	17 48	17 57	18 08	18 08			18 48	19 23	19 48	20 48	21 23	21 48	22 48	23 23	23 50
	d					18 00	18 11	18 11	18 20	18 20									
Gargrave	d					18 05													
Blackpool North 94	d																		
Preston	d																		
Blackburn 97	d																		
Clitheroe 94	d																		
Hellifield	d					18 14	18a22	18 22		18u40									
Long Preston	d					18 18													
Giggleswick	d					18 25													
Clapham (Nth Yorkshire)	d					18 33													
Bentham	d					18 39													
Wennington	d					18 44													
Carnforth 82	a					19 00													
Lancaster 65,82,98	a					19 13													
Bare Lane 98	a					19 29													
Morecambe 98	a					19 35													
Settle	d							18 30	18 50	18 55									
Horton-in-Ribblesdale	d							18 39		19 10									
Ribblehead	d							18 47		19 25									
Dent	d							18 57											
Garsdale	d							19 02		20 10									
Kirkby Stephen	d							19 15	20 00	20 45									
Appleby	d							19 28	20 25	21 10									
Langwathby	d							19 42		21 35									
Lazonby & Kirkoswald	d							19 48		21 45									
Armathwaite	d							19 56		22 00									
Carlisle 65	a							20 13	21 25	22 25									

B until 12 September
C from 24 October
D until 17 October
E until 5 September

Carlisle, Morecambe, Lancaster and Skipton - Bradford and Leeds

	NT	NT	NT	NT	NT	NT	GR	NT	NT		NT	NT	NT	NT	NT	NT	NT	NT	NT		NT	NT	NT	NT
Carlisle ■ 65 d				06 20																				
Armathwaite d				06 34																				
Lazonby & Kirkoswald d				06 41																				
Langwathby d				06 47																				
Appleby d				07 02																				
Kirkby Stephen d				07a17																				
Garsdale d																								
Dent d																								
Ribblehead d														07 14										
Horton-in-Ribblesdale d														07 21										
Settle d														07 29										
Morecambe 98 d																								
Bare Lane 98 d																								
Lancaster ■ 65,82,98 d																	07 10							
Carnforth 82 d																	07 20							
Wennington d																	07 34							
Bentham d																	07 39							
Clapham (Nth Yorkshire) d																	07 46							
Giggleswick d																	07 54							
Long Preston d														07 34			08 02							
Hellifield d														07 37			08 06							
Clitheroe 94 a																								
Blackburn 94,97 a																								
Preston ■ 97 a																								
Blackpool North 97 a																								
Gargrave d														07 46			08 14							
Skipton a														07 54			08 23							
Skipton d	05 48	06 02	06 18		06 27	06 42	06 55	07 01	07 08		07 24	07 32	07 47	07 56	08 01	08 15	08 27	08 32	08 43		09 02	09 18	09 32	09 48
Cononley d	05 52	06 06	06 22		06 31	06 46		07 05	07 12		07 28	07 36	07 51		08 05	08 19		08 36	08 47		09 06	09 22	09 36	09 52
Steeton & Silsden d	05 56	06 10	06 26		06 35	06 51		07 10	07 17		07 33	07 41	07 56	08 04	08 10	08 24		08 40	08 51		09 10	09 26	09 40	09 56
Keighley d	06 01	06 15	06 31		06 40	06 56	07u05	07 15	07 21		07 37	07 45	08 00	08 09	08 14	08 28	08 37	08 45	08 56		09 15	09 31	09 45	10 01
Crossflatts d	06 04	06 18	06 34		06 43	07 00		07 19	07 26		07 41	07 49	08 04		08 18	08 32		08 48	08 59		09 18	09 34	09 48	10 04
Bingley d	06 07	06 21	06 37		06 46	07 02		07 22	07 28		07 44	07 52	08 07	08 14	08 21	08 35	08 42	08 51	09 02		09 21	09 37	09 51	10 07
Saltaire d	06 10	06 24	06 40		06 49	07 06		07 25	07 32		07 48	07 56	08 11		08 25	08 39		08 54	09 05		09 24	09 40	09 54	10 10
Shipley a	06 12	06 27	06 42		06 53	07 08		07 27	07 34		07 50	07 58	08 13	08 18	08 27	08 41	08 46	08 58	09 07		09 27	09 42	09 58	10 12
Shipley d	06 13	06 28	06 44		06 53	07 09	07u14	07 28	07 35		07 50	08 00	08 13	08 19	08 28	08 41	08 47	08 58	09 08		09 28	09 44	09 58	10 14
Frizinghall 37 a		06 32			06 57			07 32				08 03			08 31			09 02			09 32		10 02	
Bradford Forster Square 37 a		06 38			07 03			07 39				08 09			08 38			09 09			09 38		10 08	
Leeds ■ 37 a	06 27		06 58			07 23	07 29		07 49		08 05		08 27	08 37		08 56	09 04		09 23			09 59		10 28
London Kings Cross ■ ⊖26 a							09 52																	

	NT	NT	NT	NT	NT			NT	NT	NT	NT	NT	NT	NT	NT		NT	NT	NT	NT	NT	NT	NT	NT
Carlisle ■ 65 d					08 53																	11 51		
Armathwaite d					09 07																	12 05		
Lazonby & Kirkoswald d					09 14																	12 12		
Langwathby d					09 20																	12 18		
Appleby d					09 35																	12 33		
Kirkby Stephen d					09 48																	12 46		
Garsdale d					10 02																	13 00		
Dent d					10 07																	13 05		
Ribblehead d					10 17																	13 14		
Horton-in-Ribblesdale d					10 24																	13 21		
Settle d					10 32																	13 29		
Morecambe 98 d													10 34											
Bare Lane 98 d													10 38											
Lancaster ■ 65,82,98 d													10 49											
Carnforth 82 d													11b09											
Wennington d													11 23											
Bentham d													11 29											
Clapham (Nth Yorkshire) d													11 36											
Giggleswick d													11 44											
Long Preston d													11 52									13 34		
Hellifield d					10 39								11 56									13 37		
Clitheroe 94 a																								
Blackburn 94,97 a																								
Preston ■ 97 a																								
Blackpool North 97 a																								
Gargrave d													12 04									13 45		
Skipton a					10 54								12 13									13 56		
Skipton d	10 02	10 18	10 32	10 48	10 59			11 02	11 18	11 33	11 48	12 02	12 13	12 18	12 32		12 48	13 02	13 18	13 32	13 48	13 58	14 02	14 18
Cononley d	10 06	10 22	10 36	10 52				11 06	11 22	11 37	11 52	12 06		12 22	12 36		12 52	13 06	13 22	13 36	13 52		14 06	14 22
Steeton & Silsden d	10 10	10 26	10 40	10 56				11 10	11 26	11 41	11 56	12 10		12 26	12 40		12 56	13 10	13 26	13 40	13 56		14 10	14 27
Keighley d	10 15	10 31	10 45	11 01	11 09			11 15	11 31	11 46	12 01	12 15	12 23	12 31	12 45		13 01	13 15	13 31	13 45	14 01	14 09	14 15	14 31
Crossflatts d	10 18	10 34	10 48	11 04				11 18	11 34	11 49	12 04	12 18		12 34	12 48		13 04	13 18	13 34	13 48	14 04		14 18	14 35
Bingley d	10 21	10 37	10 51	11 07	11 13			11 21	11 37	11 52	12 07	12 21		12 37	12 51		13 07	13 21	13 37	13 51	14 07	14 13	14 21	14 38
Saltaire d	10 24	10 40	10 54	11 10				11 24	11 40	11 55	12 10	12 24		12 40	12 54		13 10	13 24	13 40	13 54	14 10		14 24	14 42
Shipley a	10 27	10 42	10 57	11 12	11 18			11 28	11 42	11 58	12 14	12 27	12 33	12 42	12 57		13 12	13 27	13 42	13 57	14 12	14 18	14 28	14 44
Shipley d	10 28	10 44	10 58	11 14	11 18			11 28	11 44	11 58	12 14	12 28	12 33	12 44	12 58		13 14	13 28	13 44	13 58	14 14	14 18	14 28	14 45
Frizinghall 37 a	10 32		11 02					11 32		12 02		12 32			13 02			13 32		14 02			14 32	
Bradford Forster Square 37 a	10 38		11 08					11 38		12 10		12 38			13 08			13 38		14 08			14 38	
Leeds ■ 37 a		10 58		11 28	11 36				11 58		12 29		12 55	12 58			13 28		13 58		14 28	14 37		15 00
London Kings Cross ■ ⊖26 a																								

b arr. 1058

Table 36

Mondays to Fridays

Carlisle, Morecambe, Lancaster and Skipton - Bradford and Leeds

	NT		NT	NT	NT	NT	NT	NT	NT	NT	NT		NT	NT	NT		NT	NT	NT	NT	NT		NT	NT
Carlisle ■ 65 d										14 00					15 03									
Armathwaite d										14 14														
Lazonby & Kirkoswald d										14 21														
Langwathby d										14 27														
Appleby d										14 43					15 40									
Kirkby Stephen d										14 56					15 53									
Garsdale d										15 09														
Dent d										15 14														
Ribblehead d										15 23														
Horton-in-Ribblesdale d										15 30														
Settle d										15 39					16 35									
Morecambe 98 d					13 29															16 19				
Bare Lane 98 d					13 36															16 23				
Lancaster ■ 65,82,98 d					13b48																			
Carnforth 82 d					13 58															16 32				
Wennington d					14 12															16 46				
Bentham d					14 18															16 52				
Clapham (Nth Yorkshire) d					14 25															16 59				
Giggleswick d					14 33															17 10				
Long Preston d					14 40															17 18				
Hellifield d					14 44					15 48										17 22				
Clitheroe 94 a																								
Blackburn 94,97 a																								
Preston ■ 97 a																								
Blackpool North 97 a																								
Gargrave d					14 52															17 30				
Skipton a					15 03					16 05					16 55					17 39				
Skipton d	14 32		14 48	15 00	15 10	15 18	15 32	15 48	16 02	16 12	16 18		16 36	16 49	16 58		17 02	17 19	17 28	17 41	17 49		18 02	18 16
Cononley d	14 36		14 52	15 04		15 22	15 36	15 52	16 06		16 22		16 40	16 53			17 06	17 23	17 32		17 53		18 06	18 20
Steeton & Silsden d	14 40		14 56	15 08		15 26	15 40	15 56	16 10		16 26		16 44	16 57			17 10	17 27	17 36		17 57		18 10	18 25
Keighley d	14 45		15 01	15 13	15 20	15 31	15 45	16 01	16 15	16 22	16 31		16 49	17 02	17 08		17 15	17 32	17 41	17 51	18 02		18 15	18 29
Crossflatts d	14 48		15 04	15 16		15 34	15 48	16 04	16 18		16 34		16 52	17 05			17 18	17 35	17 44		18 05		18 18	18 33
Bingley d	14 51		15 07	15 19	15 25	15 37	15 51	16 07	16 21	16 26	16 37		16 55	17 08	17 15		17 21	17 38	17 47		18 08		18 21	18 35
Saltaire d	14 54		15 10	15 22		15 40	15 54	16 10	16 24		16 40		16 58	17 11			17 24	17 41	17 50		18 11		18 24	18 39
Shipley a	14 57		15 12	15 25	15 30	15 42	15 57	16 12	16 27	16 31	16 42		17 02	17 13	17 20		17 28	17 43	17 55	17 58	18 13		18 28	18 42
Shipley d	14 58		15 14	15 28	15 30	15 44	15 58	16 14	16 28	16 31	16 44		17 02	17 15	17 20		17 28	17 45	17 56	17 58	18 14		18 28	18 44
Frizinghall 37 a	15 02			15 32			16 02		16 31				17 06				17 32		17 59				18 32	
Bradford Forster Square 37 a	15 08			15 38			16 08		16 38				17 12				17 38		18 05				18 38	
Leeds ■ 37 a			15 28		15 47	15 58		16 28		16 51	16 58			17 29	17 40			18 00		18 15	18 29			18 59
London Kings Cross ■ ⊖26 a																								

	NT	NT	NT	NT	NT	NT	NT		NT	NT	NT	NT	NT	NT	NT	NT	NT		NT	NT
Carlisle ■ 65 d	16 18									18 16										
Armathwaite d	16 32									18 30										
Lazonby & Kirkoswald d	16 39									18 37										
Langwathby d	16 45									18 43										
Appleby d	17 01									18 58										
Kirkby Stephen d	17 14									19 11										
Garsdale d	17 27									19 24										
Dent d	17 32									19 29										
Ribblehead d	17 42									19 39						21 00				
Horton-in-Ribblesdale d	17 48									19 45						21 06				
Settle d	17 57									19 53						21 14				
Morecambe 98 d												19 08								
Bare Lane 98 d												19 12								
Lancaster ■ 65,82,98 d												19c24								
Carnforth 82 d												19 34								
Wennington d												19 48								
Bentham d												19 54								
Clapham (Nth Yorkshire) d												20 01								
Giggleswick d												20 09								
Long Preston d	18 03											20 17				21 20				
Hellifield d	18 06									20 01		20 21				21 23				
Clitheroe 94 a																				
Blackburn 94,97 a																				
Preston ■ 97 a																				
Blackpool North 97 a																				
Gargrave d	18 14											20 29				21 31				
Skipton a	18 23									20 16		20 38				21 40				
Skipton d	18 28	18 32	18 48	19 00	19 18	19 32	19 48		19 54	20 16	20 24	20 42	20 48	20 54	21 18		21 48		21 54	22 18
Cononley d		18 36	18 52	19 04	19 22	19 36	19 52		19 58		20 28		20 52	20 58	21 22		21 52		21 58	22 22
Steeton & Silsden d		18 40	18 56	19 08	19 26	19 40	19 56		20 02		20 32		20 56	21 02	21 26		21 56		22 02	22 26
Keighley d	18 38	18 45	19 01	19 13	19 31	19 45	20 01		20 07	20 26	20 37	20 52	21 01	21 07	21 31		22 01		22 07	22 31
Crossflatts d		18 48	19 04	19 16	19 34	19 48	20 04		20 10		20 40		21 04	21 10	21 34		22 04		22 10	22 34
Bingley d	18 42	18 51	19 07	19 19	19 37	19 51	20 07		20 13	20 31	20 43		21 07	21 13	21 37		22 07		22 13	22 37
Saltaire d		18 54	19 10	19 22	19 40	19 54	20 10		20 16		20 46		21 10	21 16	21 40		22 10		22 16	22 40
Shipley a	18 48	18 58	19 12	19 25	19 42	19 57	20 12		20 19	20 35	20 48	20 59	21 12	21 19	21 42		22 13		22 19	22 42
Shipley d	18 48	18 58	19 14	19 26	19 44	19 58	20 14		20 20	20 36	20 49	20 59	21 14	21 19	21 43		22 14		22 19	22 43
Frizinghall 37 a		19 02		19 29		20 01			20 24					21 23					22 23	
Bradford Forster Square 37 a		19 08		19 35		20 08			20 32					21 29					22 31	
Leeds ■ 37 a	19 07		19 29		19 59		20 28			20 57	21 03	21 17	21 30		21 59		22 32			23 01
London Kings Cross ■ ⊖26 a																				

b arr. 1342

c arr. 1919

Table 36

Carlisle, Morecambe, Lancaster and Skipton - Bradford and Leeds

	NT	NT	NT	GR	NT	NT	NT	NT	NT	NT	NT	NT	NT	NT	NT	NT	NT	NT	NT	NT	NT	NT
Carlisle 65 d																		07 52				
Armathwaite d																		08 06				
Lazonby & Kirkoswald d																		08 13				
Langwathby d																		08 19				
Appleby d																		08 34				
Kirkby Stephen d																		08 47				
Garsdale d																		09 00				
Dent d																		09 05				
Ribblehead d								07 14										09 15				
Horton-in-Ribblesdale d								07 21										09 21				
Settle d								07 29										09 29				
Morecambe 98 d																						
Bare Lane 98 d																						
Lancaster 65,82,98 d																08 24						
Carnforth 82 d																08 34						
Wennington d																08 48						
Bentham d																08 53						
Clapham (Nth Yorkshire) d																09 00						
Giggleswick d																09 08						
Long Preston d								07 34								09 16						
Hellifield d								07 37								09 20		09 37				
Clitheroe 94 a																						
Blackburn 94,97 a																						
Preston 97 a																						
Blackpool North 97 a																						
Gargrave d								07 46								09 28						
Skipton a								07 54								09 37		09 53				
Skipton d	05 48	06 02	06 47	06 55	07 01	07 32	07 47	07 56	08 01	08 18	08 32	08 48	09 02	09 18	09 32	09 42	09 48	09 57	10 02	10 18	10 32	10 48
Cononley d	05 52	06 06	06 51		07 05	07 36	07 51		08 05	08 22	08 36	08 52	09 06	09 22	09 36		09 52		10 06	10 22	10 36	10 52
Steeton & Silsden d	05 56	06 10	06 56		07 10	07 41	07 56	08 04	08 10	08 27	08 40	08 56	09 10	09 26	09 40		09 56		10 10	10 26	10 40	10 56
Keighley d	06 01	06 15	07 00	07u07	07 15	07 45	08 00	08 09	08 14	08 31	08 45	09 01	09 15	09 31	09 45	09 52	10 01	10 08	10 15	10 31	10 45	11 01
Crossflatts d	06 04	06 18	07 04		07 19	07 49	08 04		08 18	08 35	08 48	09 04	09 18	09 34	09 48		10 04		10 18	10 34	10 48	11 04
Bingley d	06 07	06 21	07 07		07 22	07 52	08 07	08 14	08 21	08 38	08 51	09 07	09 21	09 37	09 51	09 58	10 07	10 12	10 21	10 37	10 51	11 07
Saltaire d	06 10	06 24	07 11		07 25	07 56	08 11		08 25	08 42	08 54	09 10	09 24	09 40	09 54		10 10		10 24	10 40	10 54	11 10
Shipley a	06 12	06 27	07 13		07 28	07 58	08 13	08 18	08 27	08 44	08 57	09 12	09 27	09 42	09 58	10 02	10 12	10 18	10 27	10 42	10 57	11 12
Shipley d	06 13	06 28	07 13	07u18	07 28	08 00	08 13	08 19	08 28	08 44	08 58	09 14	09 28	09 44	09 58	10 02	10 14	10 19	10 28	10 44	10 58	11 14
Frizinghall 37 a		06 32			07 32	08 03			08 31		09 02		09 32		10 02				10 32		11 02	
Bradford Forster Square 37 a		06 38			07 39	08 09			08 38		09 09		09 38		10 08				10 38		11 08	
Leeds 37 a	06 27		07 27	07 33			08 27	08 37		08 58		09 28		09 59		10 22	10 28	10 34		10 58		11 28
London Kings Cross ⊖26 a				10 04																		

	NT	NT	NT	NT	NT	NT	NT	NT	NT	NT	NT	NT	NT	NT	NT	NT	NT	NT
Carlisle 65 d			09 26												11 51			
Armathwaite d			09 40												12 05			
Lazonby & Kirkoswald d			09 47												12 12			
Langwathby d			09 53												12 18			
Appleby d			10 08												12 33			
Kirkby Stephen d			10 21												12 46			
Garsdale d			10 35												12 59			
Dent d			10 40												13 04			
Ribblehead d			10 49												13 14			
Horton-in-Ribblesdale d			10 56												13 20			
Settle d			11 04												13 28			
Morecambe 98 d							10 34											
Bare Lane 98 d							10 38											
Lancaster 65,82,98 d							10 49											
Carnforth 82 d							11b09											
Wennington d							11 23											
Bentham d							11 29											
Clapham (Nth Yorkshire) d							11 36											
Giggleswick d							11 44											
Long Preston d							11 52								13 34			
Hellifield d			11 11				11 56								13 37			
Clitheroe 94 a																		
Blackburn 94,97 a																		
Preston 97 a																		
Blackpool North 97 a																		
Gargrave d							12 04								13 45			
Skipton a			11 26				12 13								13 55			
Skipton d	11 02	11 18	11 28	11 33	11 48	12 02	12 13	12 18	12 32	12 48	13 02	13 18	13 32	13 48	13 58	14 02	14 18	14 32
Cononley d	11 06	11 22		11 37	11 52	12 06		12 22	12 36	12 52	13 06	13 22	13 36	13 52		14 06	14 22	14 36
Steeton & Silsden d	11 10	11 26		11 41	11 56	12 10		12 26	12 40	12 56	13 10	13 26	13 40	13 56		14 10	14 27	14 40
Keighley d	11 15	11 31	11 38	11 46	12 01	12 15	12 23	12 31	12 45	13 01	13 15	13 31	13 45	14 01	14 09	14 15	14 31	14 45
Crossflatts d	11 18	11 34		11 49	12 04	12 18		12 34	12 48	13 04	13 18	13 34	13 48	14 04		14 18	14 35	14 48
Bingley d	11 21	11 37	11 42	11 52	12 07	12 21		12 37	12 51	13 07	13 21	13 37	13 51	14 07	14 13	14 21	14 38	14 51
Saltaire d	11 24	11 40		11 55	12 10	12 24		12 40	12 54	13 10	13 24	13 40	13 54	14 10		14 24	14 42	14 54
Shipley a	11 27	11 42	11 49	11 58	12 14	12 27	12 33	12 42	12 57	13 12	13 27	13 42	13 57	14 12	14 18	14 28	14 44	14 58
Shipley d	11 28	11 44	11 49	11 58	12 14	12 28	12 33	12 44	12 58	13 14	13 28	13 44	13 58	14 14	14 18	14 28	14 45	14 58
Frizinghall 37 a	11 32			12 02		12 32			13 02		13 32		14 02			14 32		15 02
Bradford Forster Square 37 a	11 38			12 10		12 38			13 08		13 38		14 08			14 38		15 08
Leeds 37 a		11 58	12 07		12 29		12 55	12 58		13 28		13 58		14 28	14 37		15 00	
London Kings Cross ⊖26 a																		

b arr. 1058

Table 36

Saturdays

Carlisle, Morecambe, Lancaster and Skipton - Bradford and Leeds

	NT	NT	NT	NT	NT	NT	NT	NT	NT	NT	NT	NT	NT	NT	NT	NT	NT	NT	NT	NT	NT
Carlisle 65 d									14 26	15 25						15 49					16 18
Armathwaite d									14 40												16 32
Lazonby & Kirkoswald d									14 47												16 39
Langwathby d									14 53												16 45
Appleby d									15 09							16 26					17 01
Kirkby Stephen d									15 22							16 39					17 14
Garsdale d									15 35												17 27
Dent d									15 40												17 32
Ribblehead d									15 49												17 42
Horton-in-Ribblesdale d									15 56												17 48
Settle d									16 04							17 16					17 57
Morecambe 98 d			13 29															16 19			
Bare Lane 98 d			13 36															16 24			
Lancaster 65,82,98 d			13b48							19 05								16c40			
Carnforth 82 d			13 58															16 50			
Wennington d			14 12															17 04			
Bentham d			14 18															17 09			
Clapham (Nth Yorkshire) d			14 25															17 16			
Giggleswick d			14 33															17 25			
Long Preston d			14 40															17 33			18 03
Hellifield d			14 44						16 11									17 36			18 06
Clitheroe 94 a																					
Blackburn 94,97 a																					
Preston 97 a										19 30											
Blackpool North 97 a																					
Gargrave d			14 52															17 44			18 14
Skipton a			15 03						16 26							17 38		17 54			18 23
Skipton d	14 48	15 00	15 10	15 18	15 32	15 48	16 02	16 18	16 28		16 33	16 49	17 02	17 19	17 28	17 41	17 49	17 58	18 02	18 16	18 28
Cononley d	14 52	15 04		15 22	15 36	15 52	16 06	16 22			16 37	16 53	17 06	17 23	17 32		17 53		18 06	18 20	
Steeton & Silsden d	14 56	15 08		15 26	15 40	15 56	16 10	16 26			16 41	16 57	17 10	17 27	17 36		17 57		18 10	18 25	
Keighley d	15 01	15 13	15 20	15 31	15 45	16 01	16 15	16 31	16 38		16 46	17 02	17 15	17 32	17 41	17 51	18 02	18 08	18 15	18 29	18 38
Crossflatts d	15 04	15 16		15 34	15 48	16 04	16 18	16 34			16 49	17 05	17 18	17 35	17 44		18 05		18 18	18 33	
Bingley d	15 07	15 19	15 25	15 37	15 51	16 07	16 21	16 37	16 42		16 52	17 08	17 21	17 38	17 47	17 55	18 08	18 14	18 21	18 35	18 42
Saltaire d	15 10	15 22		15 40	15 54	16 10	16 24	16 40			16 55	17 11	17 24	17 41	17 50		18 11		18 24	18 39	
Shipley a	15 12	15 26	15 30	15 43	15 57	16 12	16 27	16 42	16 49		16 59	17 13	17 27	17 43	17 55	18 00	18 13	18 19	18 28	18 42	18 48
Shipley d	15 14	15 28	15 30	15 44	15 58	16 14	16 28	16 44	16 49		16 59	17 15	17 28	17 45	17 56	18 00	18 14	18 19	18 28	18 44	18 48
Frizinghall 37 a		15 32			16 02		16 31				17 03		17 32		17 59				18 32		
Bradford Forster Square 37 a		15 38			16 08		16 38				17 08		17 38		18 05				18 38		
Leeds 37 a	15 28		15 47	15 58		16 28		16 58	17 07			17 29		18 00		18 17	18 29	18 36		18 59	19 07
London Kings Cross ⊖26 a																					

	NT	NT	NT	NT	NT	NT A 🚌	NT A 🚌	NT A 🚌	NT A 🚌	NT	NT	NT B	NT A	NT	NT	NT	NT	NT	NT B	NT A	NT	NT
Carlisle 65 d						16 40	16 45	18 15	18 15			18 16										
Armathwaite d							17 10		18 40			18 30										
Lazonby & Kirkoswald d							17 25		18 55			18 37										
Langwathby d							17 35		19 05			18 43										
Appleby d						17 40	18 00	19 15	19 30			18 58										
Kirkby Stephen d						18 05	18 25	19 40	19 55			19 11										
Garsdale d							19 00		20 30			19 24										
Dent d												19 29										
Ribblehead d							19 40		21 15			19 39							21 00			
Horton-in-Ribblesdale d							19 55		21 30			19 45							21 06			
Settle d						19 15	20 10	20 50	21 45			19 53							21 14			
Morecambe 98 d															19 09							
Bare Lane 98 d															19 13							
Lancaster 65,82,98 d															19 24							
Carnforth 82 d															19 35							
Wennington d															19 49							
Bentham d															19 54							
Clapham (Nth Yorkshire) d															20 01							
Giggleswick d															20 10							
Long Preston d															20 18				21 20	21 20		
Hellifield d							20 22		21 57			20 01	20 01		20 21				21 23	21 23		
Clitheroe 94 a																						
Blackburn 94,97 a																						
Preston 97 a																						
Blackpool North 97 a																						
Gargrave d															20 29				21 31	21 31		
Skipton a						19 45	20 42	21 20	22s20			20 16	20 16		20 38				21 40	21 40		
Skipton d	18 32	18 48	19 00	19 18	19 32				22s20	19 48	19 54	20 16	20 16	20 24	20 38	20 48	20 54	21 18			21 48	21 54
Cononley d	18 36	18 52	19 04	19 22	19 36				22s30	19 52	19 58			20 28		20 52	20 58	21 22			21 52	21 58
Steeton & Silsden d	18 40	18 56	19 08	19 26	19 40				22s38	19 56	20 02			20 32		20 56	21 02	21 26			21 56	22 02
Keighley d	18 45	19 01	19 13	19 31	19 45				22s45	20 01	20 07	20 26	20 26	20 37	20 48	21 01	21 07	21 31			22 01	22 07
Crossflatts d	18 48	19 04	19 16	19 34	19 48				22s53	20 04	20 10			20 39		21 04	21 10	21 34			22 04	22 10
Bingley d	18 51	19 07	19 19	19 37	19 51				22s56	20 07	20 13	20 31	20 31	20 43	20 53	21 07	21 13	21 37			22 07	22 13
Saltaire d	18 54	19 10	19 22	19 40	19 54				23s00	20 10	20 16			20 45		21 10	21 16	21 40			22 10	22 16
Shipley a	18 58	19 12	19 25	19 42	19 57				23s10	20 12	20 20	20 35	20 35	20 47	20 57	21 12	21 19	21 42			22 13	22 19
Shipley d	18 58	19 14	19 26	19 44	19 58				23s10	20 14	20 20	20 36	20 36	20 49	20 57	21 14	21 19	21 43			22 14	22 19
Frizinghall 37 a	19 02		19 29		20 01						20 24						21 23					22 23
Bradford Forster Square 37 a	19 08		19 35		20 08						20 32						21 29					22 31
Leeds 37 a		19 29		19 59					23 45	20 28		20 55	20 55	21 03	21 16	21 30		21 59			22 32	
London Kings Cross ⊖26 a																						

A from 23 October
B until 16 October
b arr. 1342
c arr. 1630

Table 36

Saturdays

Carlisle, Morecambe, Lancaster and Skipton - Bradford and Leeds

Station		NT
Carlisle	65 d	
Armathwaite	d	
Lazonby & Kirkoswald	d	
Langwathby	d	
Appleby	d	
Kirkby Stephen	d	
Garsdale	d	
Dent	d	
Ribblehead	d	
Horton-in-Ribblesdale	d	
Settle	d	
Morecambe	98 d	
Bare Lane	98 d	
Lancaster	65,82,98 d	
Carnforth	82 d	
Wennington	d	
Bentham	d	
Clapham (Nth Yorkshire)	d	
Giggleswick	d	
Long Preston	d	
Hellifield	d	
Clitheroe	94 a	
Blackburn	94,97 a	
Preston	97 a	
Blackpool North	97 a	
Gargrave	d	
Skipton	a	
	d	22 18
Cononley	d	22 22
Steeton & Silsden	d	22 26
Keighley	d	22 31
Crossflatts	d	22 34
Bingley	d	22 37
Saltaire	d	22 40
Shipley	a	22 42
	d	22 43
Frizinghall	37 a	
Bradford Forster Square	37 a	
Leeds	37 a	23 01
London Kings Cross	⊖26 a	

Sundays

Station		NT	NT A	NT A	NT	NT	NT	NT	NT B	NT A	NT	NT	NT	NT	NT C	NT	NT	NT	NT B	NT A	NT C	NT	NT A
Carlisle	65 d		08 45	09 00					09 25										13 51				14 00
Armathwaite	d		09 10						09 39										14 05				
Lazonby & Kirkoswald	d		09 25						09 46										14 12				
Langwathby	d		09 35						09 53										14 19				
Appleby	d		10 00	10 00					10 07										14 33				15 00
Kirkby Stephen	d		10 25	10 25					10 21										14 47				15 25
Garsdale	d		11 00						10 34										15 00				
Dent	d								10 40										15 06				
Ribblehead	d		11 45						10 49										15 15				
Horton-in-Ribblesdale	d		12 00						10 56										15 22				
Settle	d		12 15	11 35					11 04										15 30				16 35
Morecambe	98 d														12 20						14c46		
Bare Lane	98 d														12 24						14 50		
Lancaster	65,82,98 d														12b48								
Carnforth	82 d														12 58						15 00		
Wennington	d														13 12						15 14		
Bentham	d														13 17						15 20		
Clapham (Nth Yorkshire)	d														13 24						15 26		
Giggleswick	d														13 32						15 35		
Long Preston	d		12 25						11 10	11 10					13 40				15 36	15 36	15 45		
Hellifield	d		12 33						11 13	11 13					13 44				15 39	15 39	15 48		
Clitheroe	94 a																						
Blackburn	94,97 a																						
Preston	97 a																						
Blackpool North	97 a																						
Gargrave	d		12 48						11 21	11 21					13 52				15 47	15 47	15 57		
Skipton	a		13 03	12 05					11 30	11 30					14 01				15 55	15 55	16 05		17 05
	d	08 35			09 15	09 36	10 15	11 15	11 30	11 30	11 37	12 15	13 15	13 37	14 02	14 15	15 15	15 37	15 57	15 57	16 08	16 15	
Cononley	d	08 39			09 19	09 40	10 19	11 19			11 41	12 19	13 19	13 41		14 19	15 19	15 41				16 19	
Steeton & Silsden	d	08 44			09 23	09 44	10 23	11 23			11 45	12 23	13 23	13 45		14 23	15 23	15 45				16 23	
Keighley	d	08 48			09 28	09 49	10 28	11 28	11 40	11 40	11 50	12 28	13 28	13 50	14 12	14 28	15 28	15 50	16 07	16 07	16 18	16 28	
Crossflatts	d	08 52			09 31	09 52	10 31	11 31			11 53	12 31	13 31	13 53		14 31	15 31	15 53				16 31	
Bingley	d	08 54			09 34	09 55	10 34	11 34	11 44	11 44	11 56	12 34	13 34	13 56	14 16	14 34	15 34	15 56	16 11	16 11	16 23	16 34	
Saltaire	d	08 58			09 37	09 58	10 37	11 37			11 59	12 37	13 37	13 59		14 37	15 37	15 59				16 37	
Shipley	a	09 00			09 39	10 01	10 39	11 39	11 49	11 49	12 02	12 39	13 39	14 02	14 21	14 39	15 39	16 02	16 16	16 16	16 27	16 39	
	d	09 00			09 40	10 01	10 40	11 40	11 49	11 49	12 02	12 40	13 40	14 02	14 21	14 40	15 40	16 02	16 16	16 16	16 29	16 40	
Frizinghall	37 a					10 05					12 06			14 06				16 06					
Bradford Forster Square	37 a					10 12					12 12			14 12				16 12					
Leeds	37 a	09 14			09 54		10 54	11 54	12 06	12 06		12 54	13 54		14 39	14 54	15 54		16 33	16 33	16 47	16 54	
London Kings Cross	⊖26 a																						

A from 24 October
B until 17 October
C until 12 September
b arr. 1230
c arr. 1438

Table 36

Sundays

Carlisle, Morecambe, Lancaster and Skipton - Bradford and Leeds

Station		NT	NT	NT	NT A	NT B	NT C	NT A	NT A	NT	NT	NT	NT A	NT C	NT	NT	NT	NT	NT	NT
Carlisle	65 d				14 15	15 35	16 37	16 45					16 55	17 41						
Armathwaite	d				14 40	15 51	16 51	17 10						17 55						
Lazonby & Kirkoswald	d				14 55	15 58	16 58	17 25						18 03						
Langwathby	d				15 05	16 05	17 05	17 35						18 09						
Appleby	d				15 30	16 20	17 20	18 00					17 55	18 25						
Kirkby Stephen	d				15 55	16 34	17 34	18 25					18 20	18 38						
Garsdale	d				16 30	16 47	17 47	19 00						18 52						
Dent	d					16 53	17 53							18 57						
Ribblehead	d				17 15	17 02	18 02	19 45						19 07						
Horton-in-Ribblesdale	d				17 30	17 09	18 09	20 00						19 14						
Settle	d				17 45	17 21	18 19	20 15					19 30	19 22						
Morecambe	98 d									17 45							20 00			
Bare Lane	98 d									17 49							20 04			
Lancaster	65,82,98 d									18b04							20c20			
Carnforth	82 d									18 14							20 30			
Wennington	d									18 28							20 44			
Bentham	d									18 33							20 49			
Clapham (Nth Yorkshire)	d									18 40							20 56			
Giggleswick	d									18 49							21 05			
Long Preston	d							20 25		18 57							21 13			
Hellifield	d				18 03	17 30	18 26	20 33	18 40	19 00				19 32			21 16			
Clitheroe	94 a					17 55								19 56						
Blackburn	94,97 a					18 23								20 22						
Preston	97 a					18 50								20 47						
Blackpool North	97 a													21 16						
Gargrave	d				18 18			20 48		19 09							21 24			
Skipton	a				18 33		18 41	21 03	18 55	19 17			20 00				21 33			
	d	17 15	17 37	18 15			18 43		18 56	19 18	19 24	19 37			20 15	21 15	21 33	21 39	22 15	23 15
Cononley	d	17 19	17 41	18 19							19 28	19 41			20 19	21 19		21 43	22 19	23 19
Steeton & Silsden	d	17 23	17 45	18 23							19 32	19 45			20 23	21 23		21 47	22 23	23 23
Keighley	d	17 28	17 50	18 28			18 53		19 06	19 28	19 37	19 50			20 28	21 28	21 43	21 52	22 28	23 29
Crossflatts	d	17 31	17 53	18 31							19 40	19 53			20 31	21 31		21 55	22 31	23 31
Bingley	d	17 34	17 56	18 34			18 57		19 11	19 32	19 43	19 56			20 34	21 34	21 48	21 58	22 34	23 34
Saltaire	d	17 37	17 59	18 37							19 46	19 59			20 37	21 37		22 01	22 37	23 37
Shipley	a	17 39	18 02	18 39			19 02		19 15	19 37	19 48	20 02			20 39	21 39	21 53	22 04	22 39	23 41
	d	17 40	18 02	18 40			19 03		19 17	19 38	19 49	20 02			20 40	21 40	21 54	22 04	22 40	23 41
Frizinghall	37 a		18 06									20 06						22 08		
Bradford Forster Square	37 a		18 12									20 12						22 14		
Leeds	37 a	17 54		18 54			19 20		19 35	19 56	20 03				20 54	21 54	22 10		22 54	23 58
London Kings Cross	⊖26 a																			

A from 24 October
B until 5 September
C until 17 October
b arr. 1755
c arr. 2011

Leeds - Shipley and Bradford

Station		NT	NT	NT	NT	NT	NT	NT	NT	NT		NT	NT	NT	NT	NT	NT	NT	NT	NT		NT	NT	NT	NT
Leeds	d	05 08	05 51	05 55	06 03		06 21	06 22	06 37				06 49	06 51	06 56	07 08		07 22		07 25		07 37		07 39	07 51
Shipley	a			06 07			06 32						07 01		07 08					07 36				07 50	
	d					06 28				06 41		06 53	07 02				07 15		07 28				07 47	07 51	
Frizinghall	d					06 32				06 44		06 57	07 04				07 17		07 32				07 49	07 53	
Bramley	d	05 15	05 58					06 29	06 44							07 15		07 29				07 44			
New Pudsey	d	05 20	06 02		06 13			06 34	06 49					07 01		07 20		07 34				07 49			08 01
Bradford Interchange	a	05 28	06 13		06 21			06 42	06 57					07 11		07 28		07 43				07 57			08 09
Bradford Forster Square	a					06 38				06 50		07 03	07 10				07 22		07 39				07 56	07 59	

Station		NT	NT	NT	NT	NT		NT	NT	NT	NT	NT	NT	NT	NT	NT		NT	NT	NT	NT	NT	NT	NT	NT
Leeds	d		07 51	08 08		08 10			08 19	08 22	08 25	08 37		08 40		08 49		08 51	08 56	09 08		09 10	09 22		09 26
Shipley	a		08 02			08 22			08 31		08 37			08 51		09 01			09 07			09 21			09 37
	d	08 00			08 13	08 23		08 28					08 48	08 52	08 58						09 18	09 22		09 28	
Frizinghall	d	08 03			08 16	08 25		08 31					08 50	08 54	09 02						09 21	09 24		09 32	
Bramley	d			08 15						08 29		08 44								09 15			09 29		
New Pudsey	d			08 20						08 34		08 49						09 00		09 20			09 34		
Bradford Interchange	a			08 28						08 42		08 57						09 10		09 28			09 42		
Bradford Forster Square	a	08 09			08 22	08 31		08 38					08 56	09 00	09 09						09 27	09 31		09 38	

Station		NT		NT	NT	NT	NT	NT	NT	NT	NT	NT		NT	NT	NT	NT	NT	NT	NT	NT	NT		NT	NT
Leeds	d	09 37			09 40		09 47	09 51	09 56	10 08		10 10			10 19	10 22	10 26	10 37		10 40		10 49		10 51	10 56
Shipley	a				09 52		10 01		10 07			10 21			10 31		10 37			10 51		11 01			11 07
	d			09 44	09 52	09 58					10 14	10 22		10 28					10 44	10 52	10 58				
Frizinghall	d			09 47	09 54	10 02					10 17	10 24		10 32					10 47	10 54	11 02				
Bramley	d	09 44								10 15						10 29		10 44							
New Pudsey	d	09 49						10 01		10 20						10 34		10 49						11 01	
Bradford Interchange	a	09 57						10 10		10 28						10 42		10 57						11 10	
Bradford Forster Square	a			09 53	10 02	10 08					10 23	10 30		10 38					10 53	11 00	11 08				

Station		NT	NT	NT	NT	NT	NT	NT		NT	NT	NT	NT	NT	NT	NT	NT	NT		NT	NT	NT	NT	NT	NT
Leeds	d	11 08		11 10	11 22		11 26	11 37			11 40	11 51		12 08		12 10	12 22			12 26	12 37		12 40		12 49
Shipley	a			11 21			11 38				11 51					12 21				12 37			12 51		13 01
	d		11 14	11 22		11 28				11 44	11 52		11 58		12 14	12 22		12 28				12 44	12 52	12 58	
Frizinghall	d		11 17	11 24		11 32				11 47	11 54		12 02		12 17	12 24		12 32				12 47	12 54	13 02	
Bramley	d	11 15			11 29			11 44						12 15			12 29				12 44				
New Pudsey	d	11 20			11 34			11 49				12 01		12 20			12 34				12 49				
Bradford Interchange	a	11 28			11 42			11 57				12 10		12 28			12 42				12 57				
Bradford Forster Square	a		11 23	11 30		11 38				11 53	12 00		12 10		12 24	12 30		12 38				12 53	13 00	13 08	

Station		NT	NT	NT		NT	NT	NT	NT	NT	NT	NT	NT	NT		NT	NT	NT	NT	NT	NT	NT	NT	NT	
Leeds	d	12 51	12 56	13 08			13 10	13 22		13 26	13 37		13 40			13 49	13 51	13 56	14 08		14 10	14 22		14 26	
Shipley	a		13 07				13 21			13 37			13 51			14 03		14 07			14 21			14 37	
	d					13 14	13 22		13 28			13 44	13 52	13 58						14 14	14 22		14 28		
Frizinghall	d					13 17	13 24		13 32			13 47	13 54	14 02						14 17	14 24		14 32		
Bramley	d			13 15				13 29			13 44								14 15			14 29			
New Pudsey	d	13 01		13 20				13 34			13 49						14 01		14 20			14 34			
Bradford Interchange	a	13 11		13 28				13 42			13 57						14 11		14 28			14 42			
Bradford Forster Square	a					13 23	13 30		13 38			13 53	14 00	14 08						14 23	14 30		14 38		

Station		NT	NT	NT	NT	NT	NT	NT	NT	NT		NT	NT	NT	NT	NT	NT	NT	NT	NT		NT	NT	NT	NT
Leeds	d	14 37		14 40		14 49	14 51	14 56	15 08			15 10	15 22		15 26	15 37		15 40	15 51			15 56	16 08		16 10
Shipley	a			14 51		15 01		15 07				15 21			15 37			15 52				16 07			16 21
	d		14 44	14 52	14 58					15 14		15 22		15 28			15 44	15 52		15 58				16 14	16 22
Frizinghall	d		14 47	14 54	15 02					15 17		15 24		15 32			15 47	15 55		16 02				16 17	16 24
Bramley	d	14 44							15 15				15 29			15 44							16 15		
New Pudsey	d	14 49					15 01		15 20				15 34			15 49			16 01				16 20		
Bradford Interchange	a	14 57					15 11		15 28				15 42			15 57			16 10				16 28		
Bradford Forster Square	a		14 53	15 00	15 08					15 23		15 30		15 38			15 53	16 01		16 08				16 23	16 30

Station		NT	NT	NT	NT	NT		NT	NT	NT	NT	NT	NT	NT	NT	NT		NT	NT	NT	NT	NT	NT	NT	NT
Leeds	d	16 22		16 26		16 35		16 37	16 39	16 51		16 56	17 08		17 10	17 22			17 26		17 36		17 50	17 51	17 56
Shipley	a			16 37		16 49			16 53			17 07			17 21				17 37		17 49		18 02		18 08
	d		16 28		16 44	16 49					17 02			17 15	17 22			17 28		17 44	17 50	17 56			
Frizinghall	d		16 31		16 47	16 52					17 06			17 17	17 24			17 32		17 46	17 52	17 59			
Bramley	d	16 29						16 44					17 15			17 29									
New Pudsey	d	16 34						16 49		17 01			17 20			17 34								18 01	
Bradford Interchange	a	16 42						16 57		17 10			17 28			17 42								18 10	
Bradford Forster Square	a		16 38		16 53	16 58					17 12			17 23	17 30			17 38		17 53	17 58	18 05			

Station		NT		NT	NT	NT	NT	NT	NT	NT	NT	NT	NT	NT	NT	NT	NT	NT	NT	NT	NT	NT		NT	NT
Leeds	d	18 08			18 10	18 22		18 26	18 37		18 40	18 50	18 51		19 08		19 10		19 19	19 26	19 37				19 56
Shipley	a				18 21			18 38			18 52	19 02					19 21		19 31	19 37					20 07
	d			18 14	18 22		18 28			18 44	18 52			18 58		19 14	19 22	19 26				19 44		19 58	
Frizinghall	d			18 17	18 24		18 32			18 46	18 55			19 02		19 17	19 24	19 29				19 47		20 01	
Bramley	d	18 15				18 30			18 44						19 15						19 44				
New Pudsey	d	18 20				18 35			18 49				19 01		19 20						19 49				
Bradford Interchange	a	18 28				18 43			18 58				19 10		19 28						19 57				
Bradford Forster Square	a			18 23	18 31		18 38			18 52	19 01			19 08		19 23	19 30	19 35				19 53		20 08	

Table 37 Mondays to Fridays

Leeds - Shipley and Bradford

Station		GR	NT	NT	NT	NT	NT	NT		NT	NT	NT	NT	NT	NT	NT	NT	NT		NT	NT	NT	NT	NT	NT
Leeds	d	19 59	20 08			20 26	20 37	20 51				20 56	21 08		21 26	21 37				21 56	22 08		22 26	22 37	
Shipley	a	20s11				20 37						21 07			21 38					22 07			22 37		
	d	20s12		20 20	20 28					20 48	21 03			21 19			21 48	22 03				22 19			22 48
Frizinghall	d			20 24	20 30					20 51	21 05			21 23			21 51	22 05				22 23			22 51
Bramley	d		20 15				20 44						21 15			21 44					22 15			22 44	
New Pudsey	d		20 20				20 49	21 01					21 20			21 49					22 20			22 49	
Bradford Interchange	a		20 28				20 57	21 10					21 28			21 57					22 28			22 57	
Bradford Forster Square	a	20 22		20 32	20 36					20 57	21 12			21 29			21 57	22 11				22 31			22 57

Station		NT	NT	NT		NT
Leeds	d		22 56	23 08		23 18
Shipley	a		23 07			23 31
	d	23 03				
Frizinghall	d	23 05				
Bramley	d			23 15		
New Pudsey	d			23 20		
Bradford Interchange	a			23 29		
Bradford Forster Square	a	23 13				

Saturdays

Station		NT	NT	NT	NT	NT	NT	NT	NT	NT		NT	NT	NT	NT	NT	NT	NT	NT	NT		NT	NT	NT	NT
Leeds	d	05 37	05 51	05 55	06 16		06 19	06 37	06 51	06 56		07 08	07 10		07 37		07 51		07 56	08 08		08 10		08 19	08 22
Shipley	a			06 07			06 31			07 08			07 21						08 08			08 22		08 31	
	d					06 28							07 22	07 28		07 47		08 00				08 23	08 28		
Frizinghall	d					06 32							07 24	07 32		07 49		08 03				08 25	08 31		
Bramley	d	05 44	05 58		06 23			06 44				07 15			07 44					08 15					08 29
New Pudsey	d	05 49	06 02		06 28			06 49	07 01			07 20			07 49		08 01			08 20					08 34
Bradford Interchange	a	05 57	06 13		06 36			06 57	07 11			07 28			07 57		08 09			08 28					08 42
Bradford Forster Square	a					06 38							07 30	07 39		07 56		08 09				08 31	08 38		

Station		NT	NT	NT	NT	NT		NT	NT	NT	NT	NT	NT	NT	NT	NT		NT	NT	NT	NT	NT	NT	NT	NT
Leeds	d	08 25	08 37		08 40			08 49	08 51	08 56	09 08		09 10	09 22		09 26		09 37		09 40		09 47	09 51	09 56	10 08
Shipley	a	08 37			08 51			09 01		09 07			09 21			09 37				09 52		10 01		10 07	
	d			08 44	08 52	08 58						09 14	09 22		09 28				09 44	09 52	09 58				
Frizinghall	d			08 46	08 54	09 02						09 17	09 24		09 32				09 47	09 54	10 02				
Bramley	d		08 44								09 15			09 29				09 44							10 15
New Pudsey	d		08 49						09 00		09 20			09 34				09 49					10 01		10 20
Bradford Interchange	a		08 57						09 12		09 28			09 42				09 57					10 10		10 28
Bradford Forster Square	a			08 53	09 00	09 09						09 24	09 31		09 38				09 53	10 02	10 08				

Station		NT		NT	NT	NT	NT	NT	NT	NT	NT	NT		NT	NT	NT	NT	NT	NT	NT	NT	NT		NT	NT
Leeds	d			10 10		10 19	10 22	10 26	10 37		10 40			10 49	10 51	10 56	11 08		11 10	11 22		11 26		11 37	
Shipley	a			10 21		10 31		10 37			10 51			11 01		11 07			11 21			11 38			
	d	10 14		10 22	10 28					10 44	10 52	10 58						11 14	11 22		11 28				11 44
Frizinghall	d	10 17		10 24	10 32					10 47	10 54	11 02						11 17	11 24		11 32				11 47
Bramley	d						10 29		10 44								11 15			11 29				11 44	
New Pudsey	d						10 34		10 49						11 01		11 20			11 34				11 49	
Bradford Interchange	a						10 42		10 57						11 10		11 28			11 42				11 57	
Bradford Forster Square	a	10 23		10 30	10 38					10 53	11 00	11 08						11 23	11 30		11 38				11 53

Station		NT	NT	NT	NT	NT	NT	NT		NT	NT	NT	NT	NT	NT	NT	NT	NT		NT	NT	NT	NT	NT	NT
Leeds	d	11 40	11 51		11 56	12 08		12 10		12 22		12 26	12 37		12 40		12 49	12 51		12 56	13 08		13 10	13 22	
Shipley	a	11 51			12 07			12 21				12 37			12 51		13 01			13 07			13 21		
	d	11 52		11 58			12 14	12 22			12 28			12 44	12 52	12 58						13 14	13 22		13 28
Frizinghall	d	11 54		12 02			12 17	12 24			12 32			12 47	12 54	13 02						13 17	13 24		13 32
Bramley	d					12 15				12 29			12 44								13 15			13 29	
New Pudsey	d		12 01			12 20				12 34			12 49					13 01			13 20			13 34	
Bradford Interchange	a		12 10			12 28				12 42			12 57					13 11			13 28			13 42	
Bradford Forster Square	a	12 00		12 10			12 24	12 30			12 38			12 53	13 00	13 08						13 23	13 30		13 38

Station		NT	NT	NT		NT	NT	NT	NT	NT	NT	NT	NT	NT		NT	NT	NT	NT	NT	NT	NT	NT	NT	
Leeds	d	13 26	13 37			13 40		13 49	13 51	13 56	14 08		14 10	14 22			14 26	14 37		14 40		14 49	14 51	14 56	
Shipley	a	13 37				13 51		14 03		14 07			14 21				14 37			14 51		15 01		15 07	
	d			13 44		13 52	13 58					14 14	14 22			14 28			14 44	14 52	14 58				
Frizinghall	d			13 47		13 54	14 02					14 17	14 24			14 32			14 47	14 54	15 02				
Bramley	d		13 44								14 15			14 29				14 44							
New Pudsey	d		13 49						14 01		14 20			14 34				14 49					15 01		
Bradford Interchange	a		13 57						14 11		14 28			14 42				14 57					15 11		
Bradford Forster Square	a			13 53		14 00	14 08					14 23	14 30			14 38			14 53	15 00	15 08				

Station		NT	NT	NT	NT	NT	NT	NT	NT	NT		NT	NT	NT	NT	NT	NT	NT	NT	NT		NT	NT	NT	NT
Leeds	d	15 08		15 10	15 22		15 26	15 37		15 40		15 51		15 56	16 08		16 10	16 22		16 26			16 35	16 37	16 39
Shipley	a			15 21			15 37			15 52				16 07			16 21			16 37			16 49		16 53
	d		15 14	15 22		15 28			15 44	15 52			15 58			16 14	16 22		16 28			16 44	16 49		
Frizinghall	d		15 17	15 24		15 32			15 47	15 55			16 02			16 17	16 24		16 31			16 47	16 52		
Bramley	d	15 15			15 29			15 44							16 15			16 29						16 44	
New Pudsey	d	15 20			15 34			15 49				16 01			16 20			16 34						16 49	
Bradford Interchange	a	15 28			15 42			15 57				16 10			16 28			16 42						16 57	
Bradford Forster Square	a		15 23	15 30		15 38			15 53	16 01			16 08			16 23	16 30		16 38			16 53	16 58		

Table 37

Saturdays

Leeds - Shipley and Bradford

		NT	NT	NT	NT	NT		NT	NT	NT	NT	NT A	NT	NT	NT	NT		NT	NT	NT	NT	NT	NT	NT	NT
Leeds 10	d	16 51		16 56	17 08			17 10	17 22		17 26	17 37	17 37		17 40			17 50	17 51	17 56	18 08		18 10	18 22	
Shipley	a			17 07				17 21			17 37				17 51			18 02		18 08			18 21		
	d		16 59			17 15		17 22		17 28				17 44	17 52	17 56						18 14	18 22		18 28
Frizinghall	d		17 03			17 17		17 24		17 32				17 46	17 54	17 59						18 17	18 24		18 32
Bramley	d				17 15				17 29			17 44	17 44								18 15			18 30	
New Pudsey	d	17 01			17 20				17 34			17 49	7 49						18 01		18 20			18 35	
Bradford Interchange	a	17 10			17 28				17 42			17 57	17 57						18 10		18 28			18 43	
Bradford Forster Square	a		17 08			17 23		17 30		17 38				17 53	18 00	18 05						18 23	18 31		18 38

		NT		NT	NT	NT	NT	NT	NT	NT	NT	NT		NT	NT	NT	NT	NT	NT	NT	NT	NT		NT	NT
Leeds 10	d	18 26		18 37		18 40	18 51		18 56	19 08		19 10			19 19	19 22	19 26	19 37			20 06	20 08			
Shipley	a	18 38				18 52			19 07			19 21			19 31		19 37				20 17				
	d	8			18 44	18 52		18 58			19 14	19 22		19 26					19 44	19 58				20 20	20 28
Frizinghall	d				18 46	18 55		19 02			19 17	19 24		19 29					19 47	20 01				20 24	20 30
Bramley	d			18 44						19 15						19 30		19 44				20 15			
New Pudsey	d			18 49			19 01			19 20						19 35		19 49				20 20			
Bradford Interchange	a			18 58			19 10			19 28						19 44		19 57				20 28			
Bradford Forster Square	a				18 52	19 01		19 08			19 23	19 30		19 35					19 53	20 08				20 32	20 36

		NT	NT	NT	GR	NT	NT	NT		NT	NT	NT	NT	NT	NT	NT	NT	NT		NT	NT	NT	NT	NT	NT
Leeds 10	d	20 26	20 37		20 43	20 51		20 56		21 08		21 26	21 37			21 56	22 08			22 26	22 37			22 56	23 00
Shipley	a	20 37			20s56			21 07				21 38				22 07				22 37				23 07	
	d			20 48	20s57		21 03				21 19			21 48	22 03			22 19				22 48	23 03		
Frizinghall	d			20 51			21 05				21 23			2l 51	22 05			22 23				22 51	23 05		
Bramley	d		20 44							21 15			21 44				22 15				22 44				23 07
New Pudsey	d		20 49			21 01				21 20			21 49				22 20				22 49				23 12
Bradford Interchange	a		20 57			21 10				21 28			21 57				22 28				22 57				23 21
Bradford Forster Square	a			20 57	21 06		21 12				21 29			21 57	22 11			22 31				22 57	23 13		

		NT
Leeds 10	d	23 18
Shipley	a	23 31
	d	23 32
Frizinghall	d	
Bramley	d	
New Pudsey	d	
Bradford Interchange	a	
Bradford Forster Square	a	

Sundays

		NT B	NT C	NT B	NT	NT D	NT	NT	NT	NT		NT	NT	NT	NT	NT	NT	NT	NT	NT		NT D	NT	NT	NT
Leeds 10	d	08 02	08 03	08 21	08 34	08 40	08 45	09 00	09 02	09 18		09 34	09 35	09 54			10 08	10 12	10 34	10 35		10 51	10 54	11 08	11 12
Shipley	a				08 45	08 52		09 13				09 45					10 19		10 45			11 03		11 19	
	d				08 46							09 46			10 01	10 15			10 46						
Frizinghall	d				08 48							09 48			10 05	10 18			10 48						
Bramley	d	08 10	08 10	08 28					09 09	09 25				10 01				10 19					11 01		11 19
New Pudsey	d	08 15	08 15	08 33			08 54		09 14	09 30			09 44	10 06				10 24		10 44			11 06		11 24
Bradford Interchange	a	08 23	08 23	08 41			09 03		09 22	09 38			09 53	10 14				10 32		10 53			11 14		11 32
Bradford Forster Square	a				08 54							09 54			10 2	10 24			10 54						

		NT	NT	NT	NT	NT		NT	NT	NT	NT	NT	NT	NT	NT	NT		NT	NT	NT	NT	NT	NT	NT	NT
Leeds 10	d	11 34	11 35	11 54				12 08	12 12	12 34	12 35	12 54	13 08	13 12	13 15	13 34		13 35	13 54			14 08	14 12	14 34	14 35
Shipley	a	11 45						12 19		12 45			13 19		13 28	13 45						14 19		14 45	
	d	11 46			12 02	12 15				12 46						13 46				14 02	14 15			14 46	
Frizinghall	d	11 48			12 06	12 18				12 48						13 48				14 06	14 18			14 48	
Bramley	d			12 01					12 19			13 01		13 19					14 01				14 19		
New Pudsey	d		11 44	12 06					12 24		12 44	13 06		13 24				13 44	14 06				14 24		14 44
Bradford Interchange	a		11 53	12 14					12 32		12 53	13 14		13 32				13 53	14 14				14 32		14 53
Bradford Forster Square	a	11 54			12 12	12 24				12 54						13 54				14 12	14 24			14 54	

		NT		NT	NT	NT	NT	NT	NT	NT	NT	NT		NT	NT	NT	NT	NT	NT	NT	NT	NT		NT	NT
Leeds 10	d	14 54		14 57	15 08	15 12	15 34	15 35	15 54			16 08		16 12	16 35	16 35	16 54	17 08	17 12	17 21	17 33	17 35		17 37	17 54
Shipley	a			15 09	15 19		15 45					16 19				16 46		17 19		17 33	17 45			17 48	
	d						15 46			16 02	16 15					16 46								17 49	
Frizinghall	d						15 48			16 06	16 18					16 48								17 51	
Bramley	d	15 01				15 19			16 01					16 19			17 01		17 19						18 01
New Pudsey	d	15 06				15 24		15 44	16 06					16 24	16 44		17 06		17 24			17 44			18 06
Bradford Interchange	a	15 14				15 32		15 53	16 14					16 32	16 53		17 14		17 32			17 53			18 14
Bradford Forster Square	a						15 54			16 12	16 24					16 55								17 58	

A from 23 October
B until 11 July and from 12 September
C from 18 July until 5 September
D until 12 September

Table 37

Sundays

Leeds - Shipley and Bradford

		NT	NT	NT	NT	NT	NT	NT		NT	NT	NT	NT	NT	NT	NT	NT	NT		NT	NT	NT	NT	NT	NT
Leeds 10	d			18 08	18 12	18 34	18 35	19 03		19 08	19 34	19 35	19 54			20 08	20 12	20 34		20 35	21 04	21 08	21 34	21 35	
Shipley	a			18 19		18 45				19 19	19 45					20 19		20 45				21 19	21 45		
	d	18 02	18 15	18 20		18 46					19 46			20 02	20 15			20 46					21 46		22 04
Frizinghall	d	18 06	18 18			18 48					19 48			20 06	20 18			20 48					21 48		22 08
Bramley	d				18 19			19 10					20 01				20 20				21 12			21 43	
New Pudsey	d				18 24		18 44	19 15				19 44	20 06				20 25			20 44	21 17			21 47	
Bradford Interchange	a				18 32		18 53	19 23				19 53	20 14				20 34			20 53	21 25			21 56	
Bradford Forster Square	a	18 12	18 24			18 54					19 54			20 12	20 24			20 54					21 54		22 14

		NT	NT	NT		NT	NT	NT	NT
Leeds 10	d	22 05		22 08		22 34	22 35	23 10	23 22
Shipley	a			22 19		22 45		23 21	
	d		22 15	22 20		22 46		23 22	
Frizinghall	d		22 18			22 48			
Bramley	d	22 12					22 43		23 29
New Pudsey	d	22 17					22 47		23 34
Bradford Interchange	a	22 27					22 56		23 43
Bradford Forster Square	a		22 24			22 54			

Table 37

Mondays to Fridays

Bradford and Shipley - Leeds

					NT MX	NT	NT	NT	NT	NT		GR	NT	NT	NT	NT	NT	NT	NT	GR		NT	NT	NT	NT
												■ 1 ✕								■ 1					
Bradford Forster Square	d					06 01		06 10		06 15		06 30		06 40	06 44		06 55					07 11	07 15		
Bradford Interchange	d				00 37				06 18							06 48			07 02					07 20	
New Pudsey	d								06 27							06 57			07 11					07 28	
Bramley	d								06 31							07 01			07 15						
Frizinghall	d					06 04		06 13		06 18				06 43	06 47		06 58					07 14	07 18		
Shipley	a					06 08		06 17		06 22				06 47	06 51		07 02					07 18	07 22		
	d					06 08	06 13					06u35	06 44				07 02	07 09		07u14					07 35
Leeds 10	a				00 55	06 22	06 27		06 42			06 52	06 58			07 09	07 16	07 23	07 27	07 29				07 39	07 49

		NT	NT	NT	NT	NT		NT	NT	NT	NT	NT	NT	NT	NT	NT		NT	NT	NT	NT	NT	NT	NT	NT
Bradford Forster Square	d		07 42		07 46			07 59			08 11		08 16		08 26					08 41	08 46				09 01
Bradford Interchange	d	07 34				07 50				08 05				08 20				08 34				08 50		09 04	
New Pudsey	d	07 42				07 58				08 14				08 28				08 42				08 58		09 12	
Bramley	d	07 46				08 02				08 18								08 46				09 02		09 16	
Frizinghall	d		07 45		07 49			08 02			08 14		08 19		08 29					08 44	08 49				09 04
Shipley	a		07 49		07 53			08 06			08 18		08 23		08 33					08 48	08 53				09 08
	d			07 50				08 07	08 13			08 19			08 33	08 41			08 47				09 08		09 09
Leeds 10	a	07 57		08 05		08 12		08 24	08 27	08 30		08 37		08 39	08 49	08 56		08 56	09 04			09 12	09 23	09 27	09 26

		NT		NT	NT	NT	NT	NT	NT	NT	NT	NT		NT	NT	NT	NT	NT	NT	NT	NT	NT		NT	NT
Bradford Forster Square	d	09 11		09 16		09 31			09 41	09 46		10 01				10 11	10 16		10 31			10 41		10 46	
Bradford Interchange	d				09 20		09 34				09 50			10 04				10 19		10 34					10 50
New Pudsey	d				09 27		09 42				09 58			10 12				10 28		10 42					10 58
Bramley	d						09 46				10 02			10 16						10 46					11 02
Frizinghall	d	09 14		09 19		09 34			09 44	09 49		10 04				10 14	10 19		10 34			10 44		10 49	
Shipley	a	09 18		09 23		09 38			09 48	09 53		10 08				10 18	10 23		10 38			10 48		10 53	
	d					09 39		09 44				10 09			10 14				10 39		10 44				
Leeds 10	a				09 39	09 53	09 58	09 59			10 12	10 25		10 27	10 28			10 39	10 53	10 58	10 58				11 13

		NT	NT	NT	NT	NT	NT	NT		NT	NT	NT	NT	NT	NT	NT	NT	NT		NT	NT	NT	NT	NT	NT
Bradford Forster Square	d	11 01				11 11	11 16			11 31			11 41	11 46		12 01				12 11		12 16		12 31	
Bradford Interchange	d		11 05					11 20				11 34			11 50		12 05				12 19				12 34
New Pudsey	d		11 13					11 28				11 42			11 58		12 13				12 28				12 42
Bramley	d		11 17									11 46			12 02		12 17								12 46
Frizinghall	d	11 04				11 14	11 19			11 34			11 44	11 49		12 04				12 14		12 19		12 34	
Shipley	a	11 08				11 18	11 23			11 38			11 48	11 53		12 08				12 18		12 23		12 38	
	d	11 09		11 14	11 18					11 39	11 44					12 09		12 14					12 33	12 39	
Leeds 10	a	11 24	11 27	11 28	11 36			11 39		11 55	11 58	11 58			12 12	12 24	12 27	12 29			12 39		12 55	12 55	12 58

		NT	NT	NT		NT	NT	NT	NT	NT	NT	NT	NT	NT		NT	NT	NT	NT	NT	NT	NT	NT	NT	NT
Bradford Forster Square	d		12 41	12 46			13 01			13 11		13 16	13 31				13 41	13 46		14 01				14 11	
Bradford Interchange	d					12 50		13 05			13 19			13 34					13 50		14 05				14 19
New Pudsey	d					12 58		13 13			13 28			13 42					13 58		14 13				14 28
Bramley	d					13 02		13 17						13 46					14 02		14 17				
Frizinghall	d		12 44	12 49			13 04			13 14		13 19	13 34				13 44	13 49		14 04				14 14	
Shipley	a		12 48	12 53			13 08			13 18		13 23	13 38				13 48	13 53		14 08				14 18	
	d	12 44					13 09		13 14				13 39			13 44				14 09		14 14	14 18		
Leeds 10	a	12 58				13 12	13 24	13 27	13 28		13 39		13 54	13 58		13 58			14 12	14 24	14 27	14 28	14 37		14 39

		NT	NT	NT	NT	NT	NT	NT	NT	NT		NT	NT	NT	NT	NT	NT	NT	NT	NT		NT	NT	NT	NT
Bradford Forster Square	d	14 16	14 31			14 41	14 46		15 01				15 11		15 16		15 31			15 41		15 46		16 01	
Bradford Interchange	d			14 34				14 50		15 05				15 19				15 34					15 50		16 05
New Pudsey	d			14 42				14 58		15 13				15 28				15 42					15 58		16 13
Bramley	d			14 46				15 02		15 17								15 46					16 02		16 17
Frizinghall	d	14 19	14 34			14 44	14 49		15 04				15 14		15 19		15 34			15 44		15 49		16 04	
Shipley	a	14 23	14 38			14 48	14 53		15 08				15 18		15 23		15 38			15 48		15 53		16 08	
	d		14 39		14 45				15 09			15 14				15 30	15 39		15 44					16 09	
Leeds 10	a		14 53	14 58	15 00			15 12	15 24	15 27		15 28		15 39		15 47	15 53	15 58	15 58				16 12	16 24	16 27

		NT	NT	NT	NT	NT		NT	NT	NT	NT	NT	NT	NT	NT	NT		NT	NT	NT	NT	NT	NT	NT	NT
Bradford Forster Square	d		16 11		16 16			16 31			16 40	16 44		17 01				17 11			17 16	17 31			17 38
Bradford Interchange	d			16 19					16 34				16 50		17 04				17 19				17 34		
New Pudsey	d			16 28					16 42				16 58		17 13				17 28				17 42		
Bramley	d								16 46				17 02		17 17								17 46		
Frizinghall	d		16 14		16 19			16 34			16 43	16 48		17 04				17 14			17 19	17 34			17 41
Shipley	a		16 18		16 23			16 38			16 48	16 52		17 08				17 18			17 23	17 38			17 45
	d	16 14				16 31		16 39		16 44				17 09		17 15		17 19		17 20		17 39		17 45	
Leeds 10	a	16 28		16 39		16 51		16 53	16 58	16 58			17 12	17 24	17 27	17 29			17 39	17 40		17 55	17 58	18 00	

		NT		NT	NT	NT	NT	NT	NT	NT	NT	NT		NT	NT	NT	NT	NT	NT	NT	NT	NT		NT	NT
Bradford Forster Square	d	17 46				18 01		18 11	18 16		18 27					18 41	18 46		19 01			19 07			19 31
Bradford Interchange	d			17 50						18 19		18 34						18 52		19 05				19 19	
New Pudsey	d			17 58						18 28		18 42						19 00		19 13				19 28	
Bramley	d			18 02								18 46						19 04		19 17					
Frizinghall	d	17 49				18 04		18 14	18 19		18 30					18 44	18 49		19 04			19 10			19 34
Shipley	a	17 53				18 08		18 18	18 23		18 34					18 48	18 53		19 08			19 14			19 38
	d				17 58	18 09	18 14				18 34			18 44	18 48				19 09		19 14				19 39
Leeds 10	a			18 12	18 15	18 24	18 29			18 39	18 48	18 56		18 59	19 07			19 13	19 26	19 28	19 29			19 39	19 55

Table 37

Mondays to Fridays

Bradford and Shipley - Leeds

		NT	NT	NT	NT	NT	NT	NT		NT	NT	NT	NT	NT	NT	NT	NT	NT		NT	NT	NT	NT	NT	NT
Bradford Forster Square	d		19 36		19 41					20 11		20 25			20 38					21 05		21 25			21 38
Bradford Interchange	d	19 34				19 50		20 04			20 19			20 37				21 04						21 37	
New Pudsey	d	19 42				19 59		20 13			20 28			20 46				21 13						21 46	
Bramley	d	19 46				20 03		20 17						20 50				21 17						21 50	
Frizinghall	d		19 39		19 44					20 14		20 28			20 41					21 08		21 28			21 41
Shipley	a		19 43		19 48					20 18		20 32			20 45					21 12		21 32			21 45
	d			19 44			20 14						20 36			20 49	20 59				21 14		21 43		
Leeds 10	a	19 58		19 59		20 13	20 28	20 29			20 41		20 57	21 01		21 03	21 17	21 25			21 30		21 59	22 01	

		NT	NT	NT		NT	NT	NT	NT	NT	NT	NT	NT	NT
Bradford Forster Square	d		22 05				22 25			22 38		23 09	23 20	
Bradford Interchange	d	22 04				22 19			22 37		23 04			23 46
New Pudsey	d	22 13				22 28			22 46		23 13			23 54
Bramley	d	22 17							22 50		23 17			23 58
Frizinghall	d		22 08				22 28			22 41		23 12	23 23	
Shipley	a		22 12				22 32			22 45		23 16	23 27	
	d			22 14				22 43						
Leeds 10	a	22 25		22 32		22 41		23 01	23 01		23 27			00 09

Saturdays

			NT	NT	NT	NT	NT	NT	NT	NT		NT	GR	NT	NT	NT	GR	NT	NT	NT		NT	NT	NT	NT
													■ 1				■ 1								
Bradford Forster Square	d			06 01		06 10	06 15		07 01					07 11	07 15		07 33			07 59				08 11	
Bradford Interchange	d		00 37					06 26		07 05						07 20		07 34	07 50				08 05		
New Pudsey	d							06 35		07 14						07 28		07 42	07 58				08 14		
Bramley	d							06 39		07 18								07 46	08 02				08 18		
Frizinghall	d			06 04		06 13	06 18		07 04					07 14	07 18					08 02				08 14	
Shipley	a			06 08		06 17	06 22		07 08					07 18	07 22					08 06				08 18	
	d			06 08	06 13				07 09			07 13	07u18				07u38			08 07		08 13			08 19
Leeds 10	a		00 55	06 22	06 27			06 48	07 23	07 27		07 27	07 33			07 39	07 53	07 57	08 12	08 24		08 27	08 30		08 37

		NT	NT	NT	NT	NT		NT	NT	NT	NT	NT	NT	NT	NT	NT		NT	NT	NT	NT	NT	NT	NT	NT
Bradford Forster Square	d	08 16		08 31				08 41	08 46		09 01			09 11	09 16			09 31			09 41	09 46			10 01
Bradford Interchange	d		08 20		08 34					08 50		09 04				09 20			09 34				09 50		
New Pudsey	d		08 28		08 42					08 58		09 12				09 27			09 42				09 58		
Bramley	d				08 46					09 02		09 16							09 46				10 02		
Frizinghall	d	08 19		08 34				08 44	08 49		09 04			09 14	09 19			09 34			09 44	09 49			10 04
Shipley	a	08 23		08 38				08 48	08 53		09 08			09 18	09 23			09 38			09 48	09 53			10 08
	d			08 38		08 44					09 09		09 14					09 39		09 44				10 02	10 09
Leeds 10	a		08 39	08 54	08 57	08 58				09 12	09 26	09 27	09 28			09 39		09 53	09 58	09 59			10 12	10 22	10 25

		NT		NT	NT	NT	NT	NT	NT	NT	NT	NT		NT	NT	NT	NT	NT	NT	NT	NT	NT		NT	NT
Bradford Forster Square	d				10 11			10 16	10 31			10 41		10 46		11 01			11 11		11 16	11 31			
Bradford Interchange	d	10 04					10 19			10 34					10 50		11 05			11 20				11 34	
New Pudsey	d	10 12					10 28			10 42					10 58		11 13			11 28				11 42	
Bramley	d	10 16								10 46					11 02		11 17							11 46	
Frizinghall	d				10 14			10 19	10 34			10 44		10 49		11 04			11 14		11 19	11 34			
Shipley	a				10 18			10 23	10 38			10 48		10 53		11 08			11 18		11 23	11 38			
	d			10 14		10 19			10 39		10 44					11 09		11 14				11 39			11 44
Leeds 10	a	10 27		10 28		10 34	10 39		10 53	10 58	10 58				11 13	11 24	11 27	11 28		11 39		11 55		11 58	11 58

		NT	NT	NT	NT	NT	NT	NT		NT	NT	NT	NT	NT	NT	NT	NT	NT		NT	NT	NT	NT	NT	NT
Bradford Forster Square	d	11 41		11 46		12 01				12 11		12 16		12 31			12 41	12 46			13 01			13 11	
Bradford Interchange	d				11 50		12 05				12 19				12 34					12 50		13 05			13 19
New Pudsey	d				11 58		12 13				12 28				12 42					12 58		13 13			13 28
Bramley	d				12 02		12 17								12 46					13 02		13 17			
Frizinghall	d	11 44		11 49		12 04				12 14		12 19		12 34			12 44	12 49			13 04			13 14	
Shipley	a	11 48		11 53		12 08				12 18		12 23		12 38			12 48	12 53			13 08			13 18	
	d		11 49	3		12 09		12 14					12 33	12 39		12 44					13 09		13 14		
Leeds 10	a		12 07		12 12	12 24	12 27	12 29			12 39		12 55	12 55	12 58	12 58				13 12	13 24	13 27	13 28		13 39

		NT	NT	NT		NT	NT	NT	NT	NT	NT	NT	NT	NT		NT	NT	NT	NT	NT	NT	NT	NT	NT	
Bradford Forster Square	d	13 16	13 31				13 41	13 46		14 01				14 11			14 16	14 31			14 41	14 46		15 01	
Bradford Interchange	d			13 34					13 50		14 05					14 19			14 34				14 50		
New Pudsey	d			13 42					13 58		14 13					14 28			14 42				14 58		
Bramley	d			13 46					14 02		14 17								14 46				15 02		
Frizinghall	d	13 19	13 34				13 44	13 49		14 04				14 14			14 19	14 34			14 44	14 49		15 04	
Shipley	a	13 23	13 38				13 48	13 53		14 08				14 18			14 23	14 38			14 48	14 53		15 08	
	d		13 39			13 44				14 09		14 14	14 18					14 39		14 45				15 09	
Leeds 10	a		13 54	13 58		13 58			14 12	14 24	14 27	14 28	14 37			14 39		14 53	14 58	15 00			15 12	15 24	

		NT	NT	NT	NT	NT	NT	NT	NT	NT		NT	NT	NT	NT	NT	NT	NT	NT	NT		NT	NT	NT	NT
Bradford Forster Square	d			15 11		15 16		15 31				15 41	15 46		16 01			16 11		16 16		16 31			16 40
Bradford Interchange	d	15 05			15 19				15 34					15 50		16 05			16 19				16 34		
New Pudsey	d	15 13			15 28				15 42					15 58		16 13			16 28				16 42		
Bramley	d	15 17							15 46					16 02		16 17							16 46		
Frizinghall	d			15 14		15 19		15 34				15 44	15 49		16 04			16 14		16 19		16 34			16 43
Shipley	a			15 18		15 23		15 38				15 48	15 53		16 08			16 18		16 23		16 38			16 48
	d		15 14				15 30	15 39		15 44					16 09		16 14					16 39		16 44	
Leeds 10	a	15 27	15 28		15 39		15 47	15 54	15 58	15 58				16 12	16 24	16 27	16 28		16 39			16 53	16 58	16 58	

Table 37

Saturdays

Bradford and Shipley - Leeds

		NT	NT	NT	NT	NT		NT	NT	NT	NT	NT	NT	NT	NT	NT		NT	NT	NT	NT	NT	NT	NT	NT
Bradford Forster Square	d		16 44		17 01				17 11	17 16		17 31			17 41	17 46				18 01			18 11		18 16
Bradford Interchange	d			16 50		17 04					17 19		17 34					17 50			18 04				
New Pudsey	d			16 58		17 13					17 28		17 42					17 58			18 13				
Bramley	d			17 02		17 17							17 46					18 02			18 17				
Frizinghall	d		16 48		17 04				17 14	17 19		17 34			17 44	17 49				18 04			18 14		18 19
Shipley	a		16 52		17 08				17 18	17 23		17 38			17 48	17 53				18 08			18 18		18 23
	d	16 49			17 09			17 15				17 39		17 45					18 00	18 09		18 14		18 19	
Leeds 10	a	17 07		17 12	17 24	17 27		17 29			17 39	17 55	17 53	18 00				18 12	18 17	18 24	18 28	18 29		18 36	

		NT		NT	NT	NT	NT	NT	NT	NT	NT	NT		NT	NT	NT	NT	NT	NT	NT	NT	NT		NT	NT
Bradford Forster Square	d			18 31				18 41	18 46		19 01				19 07		19 31		19 36		19 41				
Bradford Interchange	d	18 19			18 34					18 50		19 05				19 19		19 34				19 50			20 04
New Pudsey	d	18 28			18 42					18 58		19 13				19 28		19 42				19 58			20 13
Bramley	d				18 46					19 02		19 17						19 46				20 03			20 17
Frizinghall	d			18 34				18 44	18 49		19 04				19 10		19 34		19 39		19 44				
Shipley	a			18 38				18 48	18 53		19 08				19 14		19 38		19 43		19 48				
	d			18 38		18 44	18 48				19 09			19 14			19 39			19 44				20 14	
Leeds 10	a	18 39		18 52	18 56	18 59	19 07			19 13	19 26	19 28		19 29		19 39	19 55	19 58		19 59		20 13		20 28	20 29

		NT	NT	NT	NT	NT	NT	NT		NT	NT	NT	NT	NT	NT	NT	NT	NT		NT	NT	NT	NT	NT	NT
Bradford Forster Square	d	20 07		20 25			20 38					21 05		21 25			21 38			22 05			22 25		
Bradford Interchange	d		20 19			20 37					21 04					21 37		22 04				22 19		22 37	
New Pudsey	d		20 28			20 46					21 13					21 46		22 13				22 28		22 46	
Bramley	d					20 50					21 17					21 50		22 17						22 50	
Frizinghall	d	20 10		20 28			20 41					21 08		21 28			21 41			22 08			22 28		
Shipley	a	20 15		20 32			20 45					21 12		21 32			21 45			22 12			22 32		
	d				20 36			20 49		20 57			21 14		21 43						22 14				22 43
Leeds 10	a		20 41		20 55	21 01		21 03		21 16	21 25		21 30		21 59	22 01		22 25			22 32	22 41		23 01	23 01

		NT	NT			NT	NT
Bradford Forster Square	d	22 38				23 05	23 20
Bradford Interchange	d		23 06				
New Pudsey	d		23 14				
Bramley	d		23 18				
Frizinghall	d	22 41				23 08	23 23
Shipley	a	22 45				23 12	23 27
	d						
Leeds 10	a		23 27				

Sundays

		NT B	GC ◇1 C	NT	NT	NT	NT	NT	NT	NT D		NT C	NT	NT	NT	NT	NT	NT	NT	NT		NT	NT	NT	NT
Bradford Forster Square	d					09 02			10 02						10 38	10 48		11 02							12 02
Bradford Interchange	d	00 04	08 05	08 31			09 20			10 02		10 04	10 25				11 02		11 25			11 44		12 02	
New Pudsey	d	00 12		08 39			09 29			10 10		10 12	10 33				11 10		11 33			11 53		12 10	
Bramley	d	00 16		08 43			09 33			10 14		10 16	10 37						11 37			11 57			
Frizinghall	d					09 05			10 05						10 41	10 51		11 05							12 05
Shipley	a					09 08			10 08						10 44	10 54		11 09							12 08
	d				09 00	09 10		09 40	10 08					10 40				11 10		11 40			11 49		12 08
Leeds 10	a	00 27	08 20	08 51	09 14	09 24	09 42	09 54	10 22	10 24		10 25	10 46	10 54			11 21	11 24	11 48	11 54		12 05	12 06	12 22	12 22

		NT	NT	NT	NT	NT		NT	NT	NT	NT	NT	NT	NT	NT E	NT		NT	NT	NT	NT	NT	NT	NT	NT
Bradford Forster Square	d			12 38		12 48			13 02					14 02					14 38		14 48		15 02		
Bradford Interchange	d	12 25			12 44			13 02		13 25		13 44	14 02			14 25				14 44		15 02		15 25	
New Pudsey	d	12 33			12 53			13 10		13 33		13 53	14 11			14 33				14 53		15 10		15 33	
Bramley	d	12 37			12 57					13 37		13 57				14 37				14 57				15 37	
Frizinghall	d			12 41		12 51			13 05					14 05					14 41		14 51		15 05		
Shipley	a			12 44		12 54			13 08					14 08					14 44		14 54		15 08		
	d		12 40						13 08		13 40			14 08	14 21			14 40					15 08		15 40
Leeds 10	a	12 47	12 54		13 06			13 22	13 22	13 46	13 54	14 06	14 22	14 22	14 39	14 48		14 54		15 06		15 22	15 24	15 46	15 54

		NT		NT	NT	NT	NT E	NT	NT	NT	NT	NT		NT	NT	NT	NT	NT	NT	NT	NT	NT		NT	NT
Bradford Forster Square	d				16 02					16 38		16 48			17 02					18 02				18 38	
Bradford Interchange	d	15 44		16 03				16 26			16 44			17 02		17 25		17 44	18 02		18 25				18 44
New Pudsey	d	15 53		16 11				16 34			16 53			17 10		17 33		17 53	18 10		18 33				18 53
Bramley	d	15 57						16 38			16 57					17 37		17 57			18 37				18 57
Frizinghall	d				16 05					16 41		16 51			17 05					18 05				18 41	
Shipley	a				16 08					16 44		16 54			17 08					18 08				18 44	
	d				16 08	16 16	16 29		16 40						17 09		17 40			18 08		18 40			
Leeds 10	a	16 06		16 22	16 22	16 33	16 47	16 48	16 54		17 05			17 21	17 23	17 46	17 54	18 05	18 21	18 23	18 46	18 54			19 07

A from 23 October
C from 12 September
D until 5 September
E until 12 September

Table 37

Sundays

Bradford and Shipley - Leeds

		NT	NT A	NT	NT	NT B	NT	NT		NT	NT	NT	NT	NT	NT	NT	NT	NT		NT	NT	NT	NT	NT	NT
Bradford Forster Square	d	18 48			19 02								20 02			20 38	20 48			21 02					
Bradford Interchange	d			19 02			19 25				19 44	20 02		20 25				21 02			21 26		21 44		22 02
New Pudsey	d			19 10			19 33				19 53	20 10		20 33				21 10			21 34		21 53		22 10
Bramley	d						19 37				19 57			20 37							21 38		21 57		
Frizinghall	d	18 51			19 05								20 05			20 41	20 51			21 05					
Shipley	a	18 54			19 08								20 08			20 44	20 54			21 08					
	d		19 03		19 08	19 17		19 38		19 49			20 08		20 40					21 08		21 40		21 54	
Leeds 10	a		19 20	19 21	19 22	19 35	19 47	19 56		20 03	20 08	20 23	20 22	20 47	20 54			21 22		21 24	21 48	21 54	22 05	22 10	22 22

		NT	NT	NT		NT	NT	NT	NT	NT C	NT	NT	NT D
Bradford Forster Square	d	22 02				22 38	22 48		23 02				
Bradford Interchange	d		22 26					23 04		23 25		23 47	23 57
New Pudsey	d		22 35					23 12		23 33		23 55	00 05
Bramley	d		22 39							23 37		23 59	00 09
Frizinghall	d	22 05				22 41	22 51		23 05				
Shipley	a	22 08				22 44	22 54		23 08				
	d	22 08		22 40					23 08		23 41		
Leeds 10	a	22 22	22 47	22 54				23 23	23 22	23 46	23 58	00 08	00 18

A until 17 October
B from 24 October
C until 11 July and from 12 September
D from 18 July until 5 September

Leeds and Bradford - Ilkley

		NT	NT	NT SX	NT SX	NT	NT SX	NT SO	NT SX	NT SX	NT SX	NT SO	NT SX	NT	NT	NT	NT SO	NT SX	NT	NT	NT	NT	NT
Leeds 10	d	06 02		06 27		07 02			07 29	07 35		08 02	08 02		08 32		09 02	09 02		09 32		10 02	
Bradford Forster Square	37 d		06 15		06 44		07 11	07 15			07 46			08 16		08 46			09 16		09 46		10 16
Frizinghall	37 d		06 18		06 47		07 14	07 18			07 49			08 19		08 49			09 19		09 49		10 19
Shipley	37 d		06 22		06 51		07 18	07 23			07 53			08 23		08 53			09 23		09 53		10 23
Baildon	d		06 25		06 54		07 21	07 26			07 56			08 26		08 56			09 26		09 56		10 26
Guiseley	d	06 14	06 31	06 41	07 00	07 14	07 27	07 32	07 42	07 50	08 02	08 14	08 14	08 32	08 44	09 02	09 14	09 14	09 32	09 45	10 02	10 14	10 32
Menston	d	06 17	06 34	06 44	07 03	07 17	07 30	07 35	07 45	07 53	08 05	08 17	08 17	08 35	08 47	09 05	09 17	09 17	09 35	09 48	10 05	10 17	10 35
Burley-in-Wharfedale	d	06 20	06 37	06 47	07 06	07 20	07 33	07 38	07 48	07 56	08 09	08 20	08 20	08 38	08 50	09 08	09 20	09 20	09 38	09 52	10 08	10 20	10 38
Ben Rhydding	d	06 23	06 40	06 51	07 09	07 24	07 36	07 41	07 52	07 59	08 12	08 23	08 23	08 41	08 53	09 11	09 24	09 24	09 41	09 55	10 11	10 23	10 41
Ilkley	a	06 29	06 46	06 56	07 15	07 29	07 42	07 47	07 57	08 05	08 18	08 29	08 29	08 49	09 02	09 17	09 33	09 33	09 47	10 01	10 17	10 30	10 47

		NT	NT	NT	NT	NT	NT	NT	NT	NT	NT	NT	NT	NT	NT	NT	NT	NT	NT	NT	NT	NT	NT
Leeds 10	d	10 32		11 02		11 32		12 02		12 32		13 02		13 32		14 02		14 32		15 02		15 32	
Bradford Forster Square	37 d		10 46		11 16		11 46		12 16		12 46		13 16		13 46		14 16		14 46		15 16		15 46
Frizinghall	37 d		10 49		11 19		11 49		12 19		12 49		13 19		13 49		14 19		14 49		15 19		15 49
Shipley	37 d		10 53		11 23		11 53		12 23		12 53		13 23		13 53		14 23		14 53		15 23		15 53
Baildon	d		10 56		11 26		11 56		12 26		12 56		13 26		13 56		14 26		14 56		15 26		15 56
Guiseley	d	10 44	11 02	11 14	11 32	11 44	12 02	12 14	12 32	12 44	13 02	13 14	13 32	13 44	14 02	14 14	14 32	14 44	15 02	15 14	15 32	15 44	16 02
Menston	d	10 47	11 05	11 17	11 35	11 47	12 05	12 17	12 35	12 47	13 05	13 17	13 35	13 47	14 05	14 17	14 35	14 47	15 05	15 17	15 35	15 47	16 05
Burley-in-Wharfedale	d	10 50	11 08	11 20	11 38	11 50	12 08	12 20	12 38	12 50	13 08	13 20	13 38	13 50	14 08	14 20	14 38	14 50	15 08	15 20	15 38	15 50	16 08
Ben Rhydding	d	10 53	11 11	11 23	11 41	11 53	12 11	12 23	12 41	12 53	13 11	13 23	13 41	13 53	14 11	14 23	14 41	14 53	15 11	15 23	15 41	15 53	16 11
Ilkley	a	10 59	11 17	11 29	11 47	12 00	12 17	12 29	12 47	13 01	13 17	13 29	13 47	13 59	14 17	14 29	14 47	15 01	15 17	15 29	15 47	15 59	16 17

		NT	NT	NT	NT SO	NT SX	NT	NT SX	NT SO	NT SX	NT	NT	NT	NT	NT SO	NT SX	NT	NT	NT	NT	NT	NT SX
Leeds 10	d	16 02		16 32			17 02	17 15			17 32		18 02		18 32	18 32		19 02	19 32		20 02	
Bradford Forster Square	37 d		16 16		16 44	16 44			17 16	17 16		17 46		18 16			18 46			19 41		20 38
Frizinghall	37 d		16 19		16 48	16 48			17 19	17 19		17 49		18 19			18 49			19 44		20 41
Shipley	37 d		16 23		16 52	16 52			17 23	17 25		17 53		18 23			18 53			19 48		20 45
Baildon	d		16 26		16 55	16 55			17 26	17 28		17 57		18 26			18 56			19 51		20 48
Guiseley	d	16 14	16 32	16 44	17 01	17 01	17 14	17 28	17 32	17 35	17 44	18 02	18 14	18 32	18 44	18 44	19 02	19 14	19 44	19 56	20 14	20 54
Menston	d	16 17	16 35	16 47	17 04	17 04	17 17	17 31	17 35	17 38	17 47	18 05	18 17	18 35	18 47	18 47	19 05	19 17	19 47	19 59	20 17	20 57
Burley-in-Wharfedale	d	16 20	16 38	16 50	17 07	17 07	17 20	17 34	17 38	17 42	17 51	18 08	18 20	18 38	18 50	18 50	19 08	19 20	19 50	20 02	20 20	21 00
Ben Rhydding	d	16 23	16 41	16 53	17 10	17 10	17 23	17 37	17 41	17 46	17 54	18 12	18 23	18 41	18 53	18 53	19 11	19 24	19 53	20 06	20 23	21 03
Ilkley	a	16 29	16 47	17 00	17 17	17 17	17 29	17 43	17 47	17 51	18 00	18 17	18 30	18 47	19 01	19 01	19 17	19 29	20 00	20 12	20 30	21 09

		NT SO	NT	NT	NT SX	NT SO	NT	NT	NT SX	NT SO
Leeds 10	d		21 06		22 06	22 06		23 15		
Bradford Forster Square	37 d	20 38		21 38			22 38		23 20	23 20
Frizinghall	37 d	20 41		21 41			22 41		23 23	23 23
Shipley	37 d	20 45		21 45			22 45		23 27	23 27
Baildon	d	20 48		21 48			22 48		23 30	23 30
Guiseley	d	20 54	21 18	21 54	22 18	22 18	22 54	23 27	23 36	23 36
Menston	d	20 57	21 21	21 57	22 21	22 21	22 57	23 30	23 39	23 39
Burley-in-Wharfedale	d	21 00	21 24	22 00	22 24	22 24	23 00	23 33	23 42	23 42
Ben Rhydding	d	21 03	21 27	22 03	22 27	22 27	23 03	23 36	23 45	23 45
Ilkley	a	21 09	21 33	22 09	22 34	22 34	23 09	23 42	23 51	23 51

Sundays

		NT	NT	NT	NT	NT	NT	NT	NT	NT	NT	NT	NT	NT	NT	NT	NT	NT	NT	NT	NT	NT	NT
Leeds 10	d	09 12	10 12		11 12	12 12		13 12	14 12		15 12	16 12		17 12	18 12		19 12	20 12		21 12	22 12		23 14
Bradford Forster Square	37 d			10 38			12 38			14 38			16 38			18 38			20 38			22 38	
Frizinghall	37 d			10 41			12 41			14 41			16 41			18 41			20 41			22 41	
Shipley	37 d			10 44			12 44			14 44			16 44			18 44			20 44			22 44	
Baildon	d			10 47			12 47			14 47			16 47			18 47			20 47			22 47	
Guiseley	d	09 23	10 23	10 52	11 23	12 23	12 52	13 23	14 23	14 52	15 23	16 23	16 52	17 23	18 23	18 52	19 23	20 23	20 52	21 23	22 23	22 52	23 25
Menston	d	09 26	10 26	10 55	11 26	12 26	12 55	13 26	14 26	14 55	15 26	16 26	16 55	17 26	18 26	18 55	19 26	20 26	20 55	21 26	22 26	22 55	23 28
Burley-in-Wharfedale	d	09 29	10 29	10 58	11 29	12 29	12 58	13 29	14 29	14 58	15 29	16 29	16 58	17 29	18 29	18 58	19 29	20 29	20 58	21 29	22 29	22 58	23 31
Ben Rhydding	d	09 33	10 33	11 02	11 33	12 33	13 02	13 33	14 33	15 02	15 33	16 33	17 02	17 33	18 33	19 02	19 33	20 33	21 02	21 33	22 33	23 02	23 35
Ilkley	a	09 38	10 38	11 07	11 38	12 38	13 07	13 38	14 38	15 07	15 38	16 38	17 07	17 38	18 38	19 07	19 38	20 38	21 07	21 38	22 38	23 07	23 40

Ilkley - Bradford and Leeds

		NT SX	NT SO	NT SX	NT SO	NT SX	NT SX	NT	NT	NT SX	NT SX	NT SX	NT SO	NT SX	NT SO	NT SX	NT SO	NT SX	NT SO	NT SX	NT	NT SO	NT SX	NT SX
Ilkley	d	06 09	06 09	06 17	06 19	06 40	06 50	07 10	07 22	07 40	07 50	08 05	08 10	08 17	08 21	08 24	08 40	08 40	08 51	08 54	09 10	09 21	09 21	09 40
Ben Rhydding	d	06 11	06 11	06 19	06 21	06 42	06 52	07 12	07 24	07 42	07 52	08 07	08 12	08 19	08 23	08 26	08 42	08 42	08 53	08 56	09 12	09 23	09 23	09 42
Burley-in-Wharfedale	d	06 17	06 17	06 25	06 27	06 48	06 58	07 18	07 30	07 48	07 58	08 13	08 18	08 25	08 29	08 32	08 48	08 48	08 59	09 02	09 18	09 29	09 29	09 48
Menston	d	06 20	06 20	06 28	06 30	06 51	07 01	07 21	07 33	07 51	08 01	08 16	08 21	08 28	08 32	08 35	08 51	08 51	09 02	09 05	09 21	09 32	09 32	09 51
Guiseley	d	06 23	06 23	06 31	06 34	06 54	07 04	07 24	07 36	07 54	08 04	08 19	08 24	08 31	08 35	08 39	08 54	08 54	09 05	09 08	09 24	09 35	09 35	09 54
Baildon	d			06 36	06 39		07 09		07 41		08 09				08 40	08 44			09 10	09 13		09 40	09 40	
Shipley	37 a			06 41	06 44		07 14		07 47		08 12				08 43	08 47			09 14	09 18		09 44	09 44	
Frizinghall	37 a			06 44	06 47		07 17		07 49		08 16				08 46	08 50			09 17	09 21		09 47	09 47	
Bradford Forster Square	37 a			06 50	06 55		07 22		07 56		08 22				08 53	08 56			09 24	09 27		09 53	09 53	
Leeds 10	a	06 39	06 39			07 10		07 38		08 09		08 34	08 39	08 46			09 11	09 11			09 39			10 11

		NT SO	NT	NT SX	NT SO	NT	NT	NT	NT	NT SO	NT SX	NT	NT SO	NT SX	NT	NT	NT	NT	NT	NT	NT SO	NT SX	NT
Ilkley	d	09 40	09 51	10 10	10 10	10 21	10 40	10 51	11 10	11 21	11 21	11 40	11 51	11 51	12 10	12 21	12 40	12 51	13 10	13 21	13 40	13 40	13 51
Ben Rhydding	d	09 42	09 53	10 12	10 12	10 23	10 42	10 53	11 12	11 23	11 23	11 42	11 53	11 53	12 12	12 23	12 42	12 53	13 12	13 23	13 42	13 42	13 53
Burley-in-Wharfedale	d	09 48	09 59	10 18	10 18	10 29	10 48	10 59	11 18	11 29	11 29	11 48	11 59	11 59	12 18	12 29	12 48	12 59	13 18	13 29	13 48	13 48	13 59
Menston	d	09 51	10 02	10 21	10 21	10 32	10 51	11 02	11 21	11 32	11 32	11 51	12 02	12 02	12 21	12 32	12 51	13 02	13 21	13 32	13 51	13 51	14 02
Guiseley	d	09 54	10 05	10 25	10 25	10 35	10 54	11 05	11 24	11 35	11 35	11 54	12 05	12 05	12 24	12 35	12 54	13 05	13 24	13 35	13 54	13 54	14 05
Baildon	d		10 10			10 40		11 10		11 40	11 40		12 10	12 10		12 40		13 10		13 40			14 10
Shipley	37 a		10 14			10 44		11 14		11 44	11 44		12 14	12 14		12 44		13 14		13 44			14 14
Frizinghall	37 a		10 17			10 47		11 17		11 47	11 47		12 17	12 17		12 47		13 17		13 47			14 17
Bradford Forster Square	37 a		10 23			10 53		11 23		11 53	11 53		12 24	12 24		12 53		13 23		13 53			14 23
Leeds 10	a	10 11		10 41	10 41		11 08		11 39			12 08			12 39		13 08		13 38		14 09	14 09	

		NT SO	NT SX	NT	NT	NT	NT	NT	NT	NT	NT SO	NT SX	NT	NT SX	NT SO	NT	NT SO	NT SX	NT	NT SO	NT SX	NT
Ilkley	d	14 10	14 10	14 21	14 40	14 51	15 10	15 21	15 40	15 51	16 10	16 12	16 21	16 40	16 40	16 51	17 10	17 14	17 21	17 40	17 42	17 51
Ben Rhydding	d	14 12	14 12	14 23	14 42	14 53	15 12	15 23	15 42	15 53	16 12	16 14	16 23	16 42	16 42	16 53	17 12	17 16	17 23	17 42	17 44	17 53
Burley-in-Wharfedale	d	14 18	14 18	14 29	14 48	14 59	15 18	15 29	15 48	15 59	16 18	16 20	16 29	16 48	16 48	16 59	17 18	17 22	17 29	17 48	17 50	17 59
Menston	d	14 21	14 21	14 32	14 51	15 02	15 21	15 32	15 51	16 02	16 21	16 23	16 32	16 51	16 51	17 02	17 21	17 25	17 32	17 51	17 53	18 02
Guiseley	d	14 24	14 24	14 35	14 54	15 05	15 24	15 35	15 54	16 05	16 24	16 27	16 35	16 54	16 54	17 05	17 24	17 29	17 35	17 54	17 56	18 05
Baildon	d			14 40		15 10		15 40		16 10			16 40			17 10			17 40			18 10
Shipley	37 a			14 44		15 14		15 44		16 14			16 44			17 14			17 43			18 14
Frizinghall	37 a			14 47		15 17		15 47		16 17			16 47			17 17			17 46			18 17
Bradford Forster Square	37 a			14 53		15 23		15 53		16 23			16 53			17 23			17 53			18 23
Leeds 10	a	14 39	14 39		15 10		15 40		16 08		16 38	16 41		17 09	17 09		17 38	17 44		18 09	18 16	

		NT SX	NT	NT	NT	NT	NT	NT	NT SO	NT SX	NT	NT SO	NT SX	NT	NT	NT	NT	NT	NT
Ilkley	d	18 04	18 10	18 21	18 40	18 51	19 10	19 21	19 40	19 40	20 05	20 21	20 21	20 40	21 21	21 40	22 21	22 40	23 21
Ben Rhydding	d	18 06	18 12	18 23	18 42	18 53	19 12	19 23	19 42	19 42	20 07	20 23	20 23	20 42	21 23	21 42	22 23	22 42	23 23
Burley-in-Wharfedale	d	18 12	18 18	18 29	18 48	18 59	19 18	19 29	19 48	19 48	20 13	20 29	20 29	20 48	21 29	21 48	22 29	22 48	23 29
Menston	d	18 15	18 21	18 32	18 51	19 02	19 21	19 32	19 51	19 51	20 16	20 32	20 32	20 51	21 32	21 51	22 32	22 51	23 32
Guiseley	d	18 18	18 24	18 35	18 54	19 05	19 24	19 35	19 54	19 54	20 19	20 35	20 35	20 54	21 35	21 54	22 35	22 54	23 35
Baildon	d			18 40		19 10		19 40			20 24			20 59		21 59		22 59	
Shipley	37 a			18 43		19 14		19 44			20 27			21 03		22 02		23 02	
Frizinghall	37 a			18 46		19 17		19 47			20 30			21 05		22 05		23 05	
Bradford Forster Square	37 a			18 52		19 23		19 53			20 36			21 12		22 11		23 13	
Leeds 10	a	18 35	18 40		19 09		19 40		20 09	20 09		20 53	20 53		21 49		22 49		23 49

Sundays

		NT	NT	NT	NT	NT	NT	NT	NT	NT	NT	NT	NT	NT	NT	NT	NT	NT	NT	NT	NT	NT	NT
Ilkley	d	09 30	09 53	10 21	11 21	11 53	12 21	13 21	13 53	14 21	15 21	15 53	16 21	17 21	17 53	18 21	19 21	19 53	20 21	21 21	21 53	22 21	23 21
Ben Rhydding	d	09 32	09 55	10 23	11 23	11 55	12 23	13 23	13 55	14 23	15 23	15 55	16 23	17 23	17 55	18 23	19 23	19 55	20 23	21 23	21 55	22 23	23 23
Burley-in-Wharfedale	d	09 38	10 01	10 29	11 29	12 01	12 29	13 29	14 01	14 29	15 29	16 01	16 29	17 29	18 01	18 29	19 29	20 01	20 29	21 29	22 01	22 29	23 29
Menston	d	09 41	10 04	10 32	11 32	12 04	12 32	13 32	14 04	14 32	15 32	16 04	16 32	17 32	18 04	18 32	19 32	20 04	20 32	21 32	22 04	22 32	23 32
Guiseley	d	09 44	10 07	10 35	11 35	12 07	12 35	13 35	14 07	14 35	15 35	16 07	16 35	17 35	18 07	18 35	19 35	20 07	20 35	21 35	22 07	22 35	23 35
Baildon	d		10 12			12 12			14 12			16 12			18 12			20 12			22 12		
Shipley	37 a		10 15			12 15			14 15			16 15			18 15			20 15			22 15		
Frizinghall	37 a		10 18			12 18			14 18			16 18			18 18			20 18			22 18		
Bradford Forster Square	37 a		10 24			12 24			14 24			16 24			18 24			20 24			22 24		
Leeds 10	a	09 58		10 49	11 49		12 49	13 49		14 49	15 49		16 49	17 49		18 49	19 49		20 49	21 49		22 49	23 49

Network Diagram for Tables 39, 40, 41, 43

DM-25/09
Design BAJS

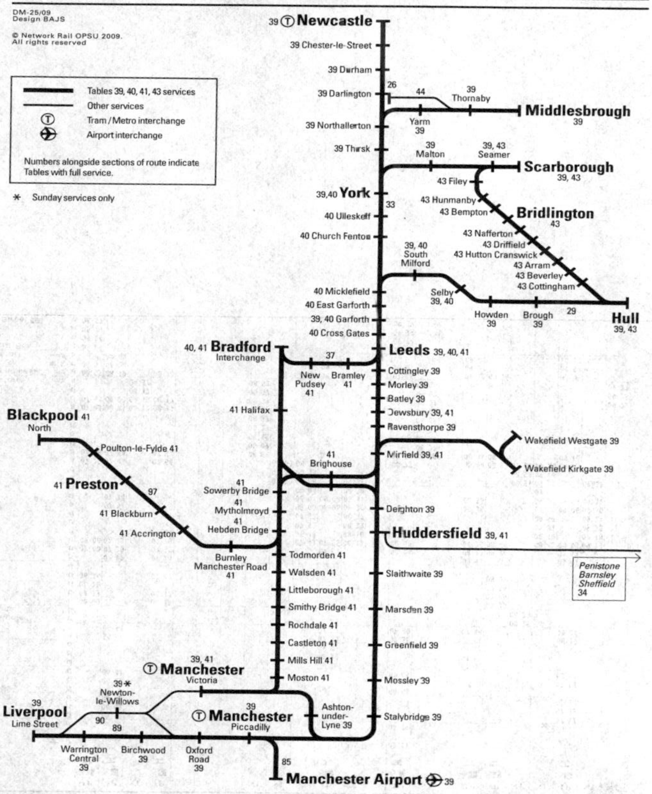

Table 39

Mondays to Fridays

Newcastle, Middlesbrough, Scarborough, York, Hull, Leeds and Wakefield - Huddersfield - Manchester, Manchester Airport and Liverpool

					TP MO ◇1	TP MX ◇1		TP MO ◇1	TP MX ◇1	TP FO ◇1		TP ◇1	NT	NT		TP ◇1	TP ◇1	NT	NT	NT		TP ◇1	NT	NT	
Newcastle [8]	d																								
Chester-le-Street	d																								
Durham	d																								
Middlesbrough	d																								
Thornaby	d																								
Yarm	d																								
Darlington [7]	d																								
Northallerton	d																								
Thirsk	d																								
Scarborough	d																								
Seamer	d																								
Malton	d																								
York [8]	a																								
	d				01 38	01 38		02 47	02 52	04 00		05 26					05 57					06 28			
Wakefield Westgate	d																		06 30						
Wakefield Kirkgate	d																		06 35						
Hull	d																								
Brough	d																								
Howden	d																								
Selby	d																								
South Milford	d																								
Garforth	d																06 12								
Leeds [10]	a				02 04	02 19		03 13	03 33	04 42		05 52					06 22					06 52			
	d				02 05	02 20		03 15	03 35	04 52		05 55	06 13				06 25			06 43		06 55	07 13		
Cottingley	d																			06 48					
Morley	d												06 21							06 52			07 21		
Batley	d												06 26							06 57			07 26		
Dewsbury	a											06 06	06 29				06 36			07 00		07 06	07 29		
	d											06 06	06 29				06 36			07 01		07 06	07 29		
Ravensthorpe	d																			07 04					
Mirfield	d												06a35						06 48	07 08			07a35		
Deighton	d																		06 55	07 16					
Huddersfield	a				02 42	02 42		03 56	03 56	05 27		06 14					06 44		06 59	07 20		07 15			
	d				02 45	02 45		03 59	03 59	05 28		06 15		06 29			06 45	06 57				07 16		07 33	
Slaithwaite	d													06 36				07 04						07 40	
Marsden	d													06 42				07 12						07b55	
Greenfield	d													06 50				07 20						08 03	
Mossley (Grtr Manchester)	d													06 54				07 24						08 07	
Stalybridge	a											06 33		06 59			07 03	07 29				07 34		08 12	
	d											06 33		07 00			07 04	07 30				07 34		08 13	
Ashton-under-Lyne	d													07 04				07 34						→	
Manchester Victoria	a													07 17				07 47							
Manchester Piccadilly [10]	a				03 44	03 44		04 58	04 58	06 02		06 50					07 19					07 51			
	d				03 44	03 44		05 00	05 00	06 08		06 54				07 07	07 23					07 54			
Manchester Airport	a				04 00	04 00		05 19	05 19	06 24		07 12					07 42					08 12			
Manchester Oxford Road	a															07 09									
Birchwood	a															07 24									
Warrington Central	a															07 29									
Liverpool Lime Street [10]	a															07 57									

Newcastle, Middlesbrough, Scarborough, York, Hull, Leeds and Wakefield - Huddersfield - Manchester, Manchester Airport and Liverpool

		TP	TP	NT	TP	NT	NT	NT	TP	NT	TP	NT	TP	TP	NT	NT	TP	NT	NT
		◇1	◇1		◇1				◇1		◇1		◇1	◇1			◇1		
Newcastle 8 ⛴	d										06 13								
Chester-le-Street	d																		
Durham	d										06 29								
Middlesbrough	d		05 57														07 23		
Thornaby	d		06 02														07 28		
Yarm	d		06 10														07 38		
Darlington 7	d										06 46								
Northallerton	d		06 25								06 58						07 53		
Thirsk	d		06 33								07 06						08 01		
Scarborough	d								06 30				07 00						
Seamer	d								06 35				07 05						
Malton	d								06 53				07 23						
York 8	a		06 51						07 20		07 30		07 51				08 19		
	d		06 54						07 23		07 40		07 54				08 24		
Wakefield Westgate	d						07 29								08 29				
Wakefield Kirkgate	d						07 35								08 35				
Hull	d	06 00			06 35									07 33					
Brough	d	06 12			06 47									07 45					
Howden	d	06 26												07 56					
Selby	d	06 36			07 07									08 07					
South Milford	d																		
Garforth	d		07 09		07 24								08 13				08 41		
Leeds 10	a	07 00	07 20		07 35				07 52		08 04		08 23	08 36			08 52		
	d	07 08	07 23		07 38			07 43	07 55	08 13	08 08		08 25	08 40		08 43	08 55	09 13	
Cottingley	d							07 48		08 18						08 48		09 18	
Morley	d							07 52		08 22						08 52		09 22	
Batley	d							07 57		08 27						08 57		09 27	
Dewsbury	a		07 34					08 00	08 06	08 30			08 36			09 00	09 06	09 30	
	d		07 34					08 01	08 06	08 31			08 36			09 01	09 06	09 31	
Ravensthorpe	d							08 04		08 34						09 04			
Mirfield	d						07 50	08 08		08a38					08 51	09 08		09a37	
Deighton	d						07 56	08 13							08 58	09 16			
Huddersfield	a	07 25	07 43		07 56		08 03	08 20	08 15		08 25		08 44	08 58	09 05	09 20	09 15		
	d	07 26	07 44		07 57	08 02			08 16		08 26	08 30	08 45	08 59			09 16		
Slaithwaite	d					08 09						08 37							
Marsden	d					08 15						08 43							
Greenfield	d					08 23						08 51							
Mossley (Grtr Manchester)	d			←		08 27						08 55							
Stalybridge	a	07 43	08 01	08 12	08 17	08 32					08 43	09 00							
	d	07 44	08 02	08 13	08 17	08 33					08 44	09 01							09 22
Ashton-under-Lyne	d			08 17		08 37						09 05							09 26
Manchester Victoria ⛴	a			08 31		08 52						09 20							09 37
Manchester Piccadilly 10 ⛴	a	08 05	08 19		08 36				08 51		09 05		09 19	09 36			09 49		
	d	08 07	08 24						08 54		09 07		09 24				09 54		
Manchester Airport ✈	a		08 42						09 12				09 42				10 12		
Manchester Oxford Road	a	08 09									09 09								
Birchwood	a	08 24									09 24								
Warrington Central	a	08 29									09 29								
Liverpool Lime Street 10	a	08 57									09 57								10 43

b arr. 0653

Newcastle, Middlesbrough, Scarborough, York, Hull, Leeds and Wakefield - Huddersfield - Manchester, Manchester Airport and Liverpool

		TP	NT	TP	TP	NT	NT	TP	NT	NT	TP	NT	TP	TP	NT	NT	TP	NT	NT
		◇1		◇1	◇1			◇1			◇1		◇1	◇1			◇1		
Newcastle 8 ⛴	d			07 26													09 12		
Chester-le-Street	d			07 36													09 21		
Durham	d			07 43													09 27		
Middlesbrough	d												09 00						
Thornaby	d												09 05						
Yarm	d												09 13						
Darlington 7	d			08 00													09 44		
Northallerton	d			08 12									09 27				09 56		
Thirsk	d			08 20									09 35						
Scarborough	d	07 38									08 47								
Seamer	d	07 43									08 52								
Malton	d	08 01									09 10								
York 8	a	08 28		08 55							09 37		09 55				10 21		
	d	08 40		08 58				09 28			09 40		09 58				10 28		
Wakefield Westgate	d					09 29									10 29				
Wakefield Kirkgate	d					09 35									10 35				
Hull	d				08 40									09 40					
Brough	d				08 52									09 52					
Howden	d																		
Selby	d				09 11									10 11					
South Milford	d																		
Garforth	d			09 13									10 13						
Leeds 10	a	09 04		09 23	09 34			09 53			10 04		10 23	10 36			10 53		
	d	09 08		09 25	09 40		09 43	09 55	10 13		10 08		10 25	10 40		10 43	10 55	11 13	
Cottingley	d						09 48									10 48			
Morley	d						09 52		10 21							10 52		11 21	
Batley	d						09 57		10 26							10 57		11 26	
Dewsbury	a			09 36			10 00	10 06	10 29				10 36			11 00	11 06	11 29	
	d			09 36			10 01	10 06	10 29				10 36			11 01	11 06	11 29	
Ravensthorpe	d						10 04									11 04			
Mirfield	d					09 51	10 08		10a35						10 51	11 08		11a35	
Deighton	d					09 58	10 14								10 58	11 14			
Huddersfield	a	09 25		09 45	09 58	10 05	10 21	10 15			10 25		10 45	10 58	11 05	11 22	11 15		
	d	09 26	09 30	09 46	09 59			10 16			10 26	10 30	10 46	10 59			11 16		
Slaithwaite	d		09 37									10 37							
Marsden	d		09 43									10 43							
Greenfield	d		09 51									10 51							
Mossley (Grtr Manchester)	d		09 55									10 55							
Stalybridge	a	09 43	10 00								10 43	11 00							
	d	09 44	10 01							10 22	10 44	11 01							11 22
Ashton-under-Lyne	d		10 05							10 26		11 05							11 26
Manchester Victoria ⛴	a		10 20							10 36		11 20							11 35
Manchester Piccadilly 10 ⛴	a	10 05		10 19	10 36			10 49			11 05		11 19	11 36			11 49		
	d	10 07		10 24				10 54			11 07		11 24				11 54		
Manchester Airport ✈	a			10 42				11 12					11 45				12 12		
Manchester Oxford Road	a	10 09									11 09								
Birchwood	a	10 24									11 24								
Warrington Central	a	10 29									11 29								
Liverpool Lime Street 10	a	10 57								11 43	11 57								12 43

Table 39

Mondays to Fridays

Newcastle, Middlesbrough, Scarborough, York, Hull, Leeds and Wakefield - Huddersfield - Manchester, Manchester Airport and Liverpool

		TP ◇1	NT	TP ◇1	TP ◇1	NT	NT	TP ◇1	NT	NT	TP ◇1	NT	TP ◇1	TP ◇1	NT	NT	TP ◇1	NT	NT	TP ◇1
Newcastle 8	d							10 15									11 15			
Chester-le-Street	d																			
Durham	d							10 27									11 27			
Middlesbrough	d			09 59									11 00							
Thornaby	d			10 04									11 05							
Yarm	d			10 12									11 13							
Darlington 7	d							10 44									11 44			
Northallerton	d			10 27				10 56					11 27				11 56			
Thirsk	d			10 35									11 35							
Scarborough	d	09 47									10 47									11 47
Seamer	d	09 52									10 52									11 52
Malton	d	10 10									11 10									12 10
York 8	a	10 37		10 55				11 21			11 37		11 55				12 21			12 37
	d	10 40		10 58				11 28			11 40		11 58				12 28			12 39
Wakefield Westgate	d					11 29									12 29					
Wakefield Kirkgate	d					11 35									12 35					
Hull	d				10 38									11 38						
Brough	d				10 50									11 50						
Howden	d																			
Selby	d				11 09									12 09						
South Milford	d																			
Garforth	d			11 13									12 13							
Leeds 10	a	11 04		11 23	11 34			11 53			12 04		12 23	12 34			12 53			13 03
	d	11 08		11 25	11 40		11 43	11 55	12 13		12 08		12 25	12 40		12 43	12 55	13 13		13 08
Cottingley	d						11 48									12 48				
Morley	d						11 52		12 21							12 52		13 21		
Batley	d						11 57		12 26							12 57		13 26		
Dewsbury	a			11 36			12 00	12 06	12 29				12 36			13 00	13 06	13 29		
	d			11 36			12 01	12 06	12 29				12 36			13 01	13 06	13 29		
Ravensthorpe	d						12 04									13 04				
Mirfield	d					11 49	12 08		12a35						12 49	13 08		13a35		
Deighton	d					11 58	12 17								12 58	13 14				
Huddersfield	a	11 25		11 45	11 58	12 05	12 21	12 15			12 25		12 45	12 58	13 05	13 21	13 15			13 25
	d	11 26	11 30	11 46	11 59			12 16			12 26	12 30	12 46	12 59			13 16			13 26
Slaithwaite	d		11 37									12 37								
Marsden	d		11 43									12 43								
Greenfield	d		11 51									12 51								
Mossley (Grtr Manchester)	d		11 55									12 55								
Stalybridge	a	11 43	12 00								2 43	13 00								13 43
	d	11 44	12 01							12 22	12 44	13 01							13 22	13 44
Ashton-under-Lyne	d		12 05							12 26		13 05							13 26	
Manchester Victoria	a		12 20							12 35		13 20							13 35	
Manchester Piccadilly 10	a	12 05		12 19	12 36			12 49			13 05		13 19	13 36			13 49			14 05
	d	12 07		12 24				12 54			13 07		13 24				13 54			14 07
Manchester Airport	a			12 42				13 12					13 42				14 12			
Manchester Oxford Road	a	12 09									13 09									14 09
Birchwood	a	12 24									13 24									14 24
Warrington Central	a	12 29									13 29									14 29
Liverpool Lime Street 10	a	12 57								13 43	13 57								14 43	14 57

Table 39

Mondays to Fridays

Newcastle, Middlesbrough, Scarborough, York, Hull, Leeds and Wakefield - Huddersfield - Manchester, Manchester Airport and Liverpool

		NT	TP ◇1	TP ◇1	NT	NT	TP ◇1	NT	NT	TP ◇1	NT	TP ◇1	TP ◇1	NT	NT	TP ◇1	NT	NT	TP ◇1
Newcastle 8	d						12 15									13 15			
Chester-le-Street	d																		
Durham	d						12 27									13 27			
Middlesbrough	d		12 00									12 50							
Thornaby	d		12 05									12 55							
Yarm	d		12 13									13 03							
Darlington 7	d						12 44									13 44			
Northallerton	d		12 27				12 56					13 17				13 56			
Thirsk	d		12 35									13 25							
Scarborough	d									12 47									13 47
Seamer	d									12 52									13 52
Malton	d									13 10									14 10
York 8	a		12 55				13 21			13 37		13 50				14 21			14 37
	d		12 58				13 28			13 40		13 58				14 28			14 40
Wakefield Westgate	d				13 29									14 29					
Wakefield Kirkgate	d				13 35									14 35					
Hull	d			12 38									13 38						
Brough	d			12 50									13 50						
Howden	d																		
Selby	d			13 09									14 09						
South Milford	d																		
Garforth	d		13 13									14 13							
Leeds 10	a		13 23	13 34			13 53			14 04		14 23	14 34			14 53			15 04
	d		13 25	13 40		13 43	13 55	14 13		14 08		14 25	14 40		14 43	14 55	15 13		15 08
Cottingley	d					13 48									14 48				
Morley	d					13 52		14 21							14 52		15 21		
Batley	d					13 57		14 26							14 57		15 26		
Dewsbury	a		13 36			14 00	14 06	14 29				14 36			15 00	15 06	15 29		
	d		13 36			14 01	14 06	14 29				14 36			15 01	15 06	15 29		
Ravensthorpe	d					14 04									15 04				
Mirfield	d				13 51	14 08		14a35						14 51	15 08		15a35		
Deighton	d				13 58	14 14								14 58	15 16				
Huddersfield	a		13 45	13 58	14 05	14 21	14 15			14 25		14 45	14 58	15 05	15 21	15 15			15 25
	d	13 30	13 46	13 59			14 16			14 26	14 30	14 46	14 59			15 16			15 26
Slaithwaite	d	13 37									14 37								
Marsden	d	13 43									14 43								
Greenfield	d	13 51									14 51								
Mossley (Grtr Manchester)	d	13 55									14 55								
Stalybridge	a	14 00								14 43	15 00								15 43
	d	14 01							14 22	14 44	15 01							15 22	15 44
Ashton-under-Lyne	d	14 05							14 26		15 05							15 26	
Manchester Victoria	a	14 20							14 35		15 20							15 35	
Manchester Piccadilly 10	a		14 19	14 36			14 49			15 05		15 19	15 36			15 49			16 05
	d		14 24				14 54			15 07		15 24				15 54			16 07
Manchester Airport	a		14 42				15 12					15 42				16 12			
Manchester Oxford Road	a									15 09									16 09
Birchwood	a									15 24									16 24
Warrington Central	a									15 29									16 29
Liverpool Lime Street 10	a								15 43	15 57								16 43	16 57

Newcastle, Middlesbrough, Scarborough, York, Hull, Leeds and Wakefield - Huddersfield - Manchester, Manchester Airport and Liverpool

		NT	TP ◇1 ⊼	TP ◇1 ⊼			NT	NT	TP ◇1 ⊼	NT	TP FO ◇1	NT	NT	NT	TP FX ◇1 ⊼	TP FO ◇1 ⊼	TP ◇1 ⊼	NT	NT	NT		TP ◇1 ⊼	NT		TP ◇1 ⊼
Newcastle 8 ⇌	d								14 12													15 12			
Chester-le-Street	d																					15 21			
Durham	d								14 24													15 27			
Middlesbrough	d		13 50								14 50				14 50										
Thornaby	d		13 55								14 55				14 55										
Yarm	d		14 03								15 03				15 03										
Darlington 7	d								14 44													15 44			
Northallerton	d		14 17						14 56		15 17				15 17							15 56			
Thirsk	d		14 25								15 25				15 25										
Scarborough	d																								15 47
Seamer	d																								15 52
Malton	d																								16 10
York 8	a		14 50						15 21		15 50				15 50							16 21			16 37
	d		14 58						15 28						15 58	15 58						16 28			16 40
Wakefield Westgate	d						15 29											16 29							
Wakefield Kirkgate	d						15 35											16 35							
Hull	d			14 38													15 38								
Brough	d			14 50													15 50								
Howden	d																								
Selby	d			15 09													16 09								
South Milford	d																								
Garforth	d		15 13														16 23								
Leeds 10	a		15 23	15 34					15 53						16 22	16 22	16 36					16 53			17 04
	d		15 25	15 40				15 43	15 55	16 13					16 25	16 25	16 40		16 43			16 55	17 13		17 08
Cottingley	d							15 48		16 18									16 48				17 18		
Morley	d							15 52		16 22									16 52				17 22		
Batley	d							15 57		16 27									16 57				17 27		
Dewsbury	a		15 36					16 00	16 06	16 30					16 36	16 36			17 00			17 06	17 30		
	d		15 36					16 01	16 06	16 31					16 36	16 36			17 01			17 06	17 31		
Ravensthorpe	d							16 04		16 34									17 04				17 34		
Mirfield	d						15 51	16 08		16a38								16 51	17 08				17a38		
Deighton	d						15 58	16 14										16 58	17 14						
Huddersfield	a		15 45	15 58			16 05	16 21	16 15						16 45	16 45	16 58	17 05	17 21			17 15			17 25
	d	15 30	15 46	15 59					16 16					16 30	16 46	16 46	16 59					17 16			17 26
Slaithwaite	d	15 37												16 37											
Marsden	d	15 43												16 43											
Greenfield	d	15 51												16 51											
Mossley (Grtr Manchester)	d	15 55												16 55											
Stalybridge	a	16 00												17 00			17 18								17 43
	d	16 01										16 22	16 42	17 01			17 18								17 44
Ashton-under-Lyne	d	16 05										16 26	16 46	17 05											
Manchester Victoria ⇌	a	16 21										16 35	16 58	17 24											
Manchester Piccadilly 10 ⇌	a		16 19	16 36					16 49						17 25	17 25	17 37					17 49			18 05
	d		16 24						16 54													17 54			18 07
Manchester Airport ✈	a		16 42						17 12													18 12			
Manchester Oxford Road	a																								18 09
Birchwood	a																								18 24
Warrington Central	a																								18 29
Liverpool Lime Street 10	a											17 43													18 59

Newcastle, Middlesbrough, Scarborough, York, Hull, Leeds and Wakefield - Huddersfield - Manchester, Manchester Airport and Liverpool

		NT	TP ◇1 ⊼	TP ◇1 ⊼	NT	NT		NT	TP ◇1 ⊼	TP ◇1		NT		TP ◇1 ⊼	NT	TP ◇1 ⊼		TP ◇1 ⊼	NT	NT	TP ◇1 ⊼		TP ◇1	NT	NT
Newcastle 8 ⇌	d								16 06									17 01							
Chester-le-Street	d								16 15																
Durham	d								16 21									17 13							
Middlesbrough	d		15 50													16 50									
Thornaby	d		15 55													16 55									
Yarm	d		16 03													17 03									
Darlington 7	d								16 39									17 30							
Northallerton	d		16 17						16 50							17 17		17 42							
Thirsk	d		16 25						16 58							17 25									
Scarborough	d													16 47									17 47		
Seamer	d													16 52									17 52		
Malton	d													17 10									18 10		
York 8	a		16 50						17 25					17 37		17 50		18 06					18 37		
	d		16 58						17 28					17 40		17 58		18 09					18 40		
Wakefield Westgate	d					17 29													18 29						
Wakefield Kirkgate	d					17 35													18 35						
Hull	d			16 40						17 01											17 58				
Brough	d			16 52						17 13											18 10				
Howden	d																								
Selby	d			17 11						17 32											18 29				
South Milford	d																								
Garforth	d		17 13													18 13									
Leeds 10	a		17 23	17 36					17 53	17 58				18 04		18 23		18 35			18 53		19 04		
	d		17 26	17 40				17 43	17 55	18 02		18 13		18 08		18 25		18 40		18 43	18 55		19 08		19 13
Cottingley	d							17 48				18 18								18 48					19 18
Morley	d							17 52				18 22								18 52					19 22
Batley	d							17 57				18 27								18 57					19 27
Dewsbury	a		17 37					18 00	18 06	18 13		18 30				18 36				19 00	19 06				19 31
	d		17 37					18 01	18 06	18 13		18 31				18 36				19 01	19 06				19 31
Ravensthorpe	d							18 04				18 34								19 04					19 34
Mirfield	d					17 51		18 08				18a38							18 51	19 08					19 38
Deighton	d					17 58		18 13											18 58	19 13					19 45
Huddersfield	a		17 46	17 58		18 05		18 21	18 15	18 23				18 25		18 45		18 58	19 05	19 20	19 15		19 25		19 50
	d	17 30	17 46	17 59	18 04				18 16					18 26	18 30	18 46		18 59			19 16		19 26	19 30	
Slaithwaite	d	17 37			18 11										18 37									19 37	
Marsden	d	17 43			18 17										18 43									19 43	
Greenfield	d	17 51													18 51									19 51	
Mossley (Grtr Manchester)	d	17 55													18 55									19 55	
Stalybridge	a	18 00		18 18	18 30									18 43	19 01								19 43	20 00	
	d	18 01		18 18	18 31									18 44	19 01								19 44	20 01	
Ashton-under-Lyne	d	18 05			18 35										19 05									20 05	
Manchester Victoria ⇌	a	18 20			18 48										19 20									20 20	
Manchester Piccadilly 10 ⇌	a		18 19	18 37					18 49					19 05		19 21		19 32			19 57		20 05		
	d		18 24						18 54					19 07				19 40					20 07		
Manchester Airport ✈	a		18 42						19 13									19 59							
Manchester Oxford Road	a													19 09									20 09		
Birchwood	a													19 24									20 24		
Warrington Central	a													19 29									20 29		
Liverpool Lime Street 10	a													19 57									20 59		

Newcastle, Middlesbrough, Scarborough, York, Hull, Leeds and Wakefield - Huddersfield - Manchester, Manchester Airport and Liverpool

		TP	TP	TP	NT	TP	NT	NT	TP	NT	TP	NT	NT	TP FX	TP FO	TP FO	TP FX	TP	NT	TP
		◇1	◇1	◇1		◇1			◇1		◇1			◇1	◇1	◇1	◇1	◇1		◇1
Newcastle 8	d								18 58											
Chester-le-Street	d																			
Durham	d								19 10											
Middlesbrough	d	17 50		19 00										20 00	20 00					20 50
Thornaby	d	17 55		19 05										20 05	20 05					20 55
Yarm	d	18 03		19 13																21 03
Darlington 7	d								19 27					20 31	20 31					
Northallerton	d	18 17		19 27					19 38					20 42	20 42					21 17
Thirsk	d	18 25		19 35										20 50	20 50					
Scarborough	d					18 47					19 47							20 37		
Seamer	d					18 52					19 52							20 42		
Malton	d					19 10					20 10							21 00		
York 8	a	18 50		19 58		19 37			20 02		20 37			21 10	21 10			21 28		21 44
	d	19 10				19 39			20 10		20 40			21 10						21 45
Wakefield Westgate	d				19 29					20 29									21 29	
Wakefield Kirkgate	d				19 35					20 35									21 35	
Hull	d		18 59													20 35	20 45			
Brough	d		19 11													20 47	20 57			
Howden	d																			
Selby	d		19 30													21 06	21 16			
South Milford	d															21 16	21 26			
Garforth	d	19 24																		
Leeds 10	a	19 35	19 56			20 03			20 35		21 04			21 35		21 35	21 44			22 07
	d	19 40				20 08		20 13	20 40		21 08		21 13	21 40		21 40				22 08
Cottingley	d							20 18					21 18							
Morley	d							20 22					21 22							
Batley	d							20 27					21 27							
Dewsbury	a	19 51						20 30	20 51				21 30	21 51		21 51				
	d	19 51						20 31	20 51				21 31	21 51		21 51				
Ravensthorpe	d							20 34					21 34							
Mirfield	d				19 51			20 37		20 50			21 38						21 48	
Deighton	d				19 58			20 44		20 58			21 45						22 01	
Huddersfield	a	19 59			20 05	20 25		20 51	20 59	21 05	21 25		21 49	21 59		21 59			22 05	22 25
	d	20 00				20 26	20 30		21 00		21 26	21 30		22 00		22 00				22 26
Slaithwaite	d						20 37					21 37								
Marsden	d						20 43					21 43								
Greenfield	d						20 51					21 51								
Mossley (Grtr Manchester)	d						20 55					21 55								
Stalybridge	a					20 43	21 00				21 43	22 00								22 43
	d					20 44	21 01				21 44	22 01								22 44
Ashton-under-Lyne	d						21 05					22 05								
Manchester Victoria	a						21 20					22 20								
Manchester Piccadilly 10	a	20 33				21 05			21 33		22 05			22 33		22 33				23 05
	d	20 40				21 07			21 40		22 07			22 40		22 40				
Manchester Airport	a	20 57							21 57					22 57		22 57				
Manchester Oxford Road	a					21 09					22 09									
Birchwood	a					21 24					22 24									
Warrington Central	a					21 29					22 29									
Liverpool Lime Street 10	a					21 57					22 59									

Newcastle, Middlesbrough, Scarborough, York, Hull, Leeds and Wakefield - Huddersfield - Manchester, Manchester Airport and Liverpool

		TP	TP	NT	NT	TP	NT	NT	NT	TP
		◇1	◇1			◇1				◇1
Newcastle 8	d									21 33
Chester-le-Street	d									
Durham	d									21 46
Middlesbrough	d	21 30								
Thornaby	d	21 35								
Yarm	d									
Darlington 7	d	21 58								22 03
Northallerton	d	22 09								22 30
Thirsk	d	22 17								
Scarborough	d		22 07							
Seamer	d		22 12							
Malton	d		22 30							
York 8	a	22 44	22 57							22 57
	d									23 07
Wakefield Westgate	d							22 42		
Wakefield Kirkgate	d							22 47		
Hull	d					21 33				
Brough	d					21 45				
Howden	d									
Selby	d					22 07				
South Milford	d					22 16				
Garforth	d									
Leeds 10	a					22 35				23 33
	d				22 18	22 40			23 13	23 35
Cottingley	d				22 23				23 18	
Morley	d				22 27				23 22	
Batley	d				22 32				23 27	
Dewsbury	a				22 35	22 51			23 30	23 46
	d				22 36	22 51			23 31	23 46
Ravensthorpe	d				22 39				23 34	
Mirfield	d				22 44			23 00	23 38	
Deighton	d				22 49			23 08	23 45	
Huddersfield	a				22 54	22 59		23 15	23 49	23 55
	d			22 34		23 00	23 05			23 56
Slaithwaite	d			22 41			23 12			
Marsden	d			22 47			23 18			
Greenfield	d			22 55			23 26			
Mossley (Grtr Manchester)	d			22 59			23 30			
Stalybridge	a			23 04			23 35			
	d			23 05			23 36			
Ashton-under-Lyne	d			23 09			23 40			
Manchester Victoria	a			23 24			23 53			
Manchester Piccadilly 10	a					23 37				00 54
	d									00 54
Manchester Airport	a									01 10
Manchester Oxford Road	a									
Birchwood	a									
Warrington Central	a									
Liverpool Lime Street 10	a									

Table 39

Saturdays

Newcastle, Middlesbrough, Scarborough, York, Hull, Leeds and Wakefield - Huddersfield - Manchester, Manchester Airport and Liverpool

		TP	TP	TP	TP	TP	TP	TP	NT	NT	TP	TP	NT	TP	NT	NT	NT	NT
		◇■	◇■	◇■	◇■	◇■	◇■	◇■			◇■ ⌶	◇■		◇■				
Newcastle ■ ⇌	d																	
Chester-le-Street	d																	
Durham	d																	
Middlesbrough	d											05 57						
Thornaby	d											06 02						
Yarm	d											06 10						
Darlington ■	d																	
Northallerton	d											06 25						
Thirsk	d											06 33						
Scarborough	d																	
Seamer	d																	
Malton	d																	
York ■	a											06 51						
	d	01 52	02 40	03 52	05 26		05 57	06 28				06 54						
Wakefield Westgate	d																07 29	
Wakefield Kirkgate	d																07 35	
Hull	d										06 00			06 35				
Brough	d										06 12			06 47				
Howden	d										06 26							
Selby	d										06 36			07 07				
South Milford	d																	
Garforth	d						06 12					07 09						
Leeds ■	a	02 18	03 06	04 34	05 52		06 22	06 52			07 00	07 20		07 35				
	d	02 20	03 09	04 45	05 55		06 25	06 55	07 13		07 08	07 23		07 38				07 43
Cottingley	d																	07 48
Morley	d								07 21									07 52
Batley	d								07 26									07 57
Dewsbury	a				06 06		06 36	07 06	07 29			07 34						08 00
	d				06 06		06 36	07 06	07 29			07 34						08 01
Ravensthorpe	d																	08 04
Mirfield	d								07a35								07 50	08 08
Deighton	d																07 56	08 13
Huddersfield	a	02 56	03 47	05 27	06 14		06 44	07 15			07 25	07 43		07 56			08 03	08 20
	d	02 56	03 59	05 28	06 15		06 45	07 16		07 33	07 26	07 44		07 57		08 02		
Slaithwaite	d									07 40						08 09		
Marsden	d									07b55						08 15		
Greenfield	d									08 03						08 23		
Mossley (Grtr Manchester)	d									08 07			←			08 27		
Stalybridge	a				06 33		07 03	07 34		08 12	07 43	08 01	08 12	08 17		08 32		
	d				06 33		07 04	07 34		08 13	07 44	08 02	08 13	08 17	08 22	08 33		
Ashton-under-Lyne	d									→			08 17		08 26	08 37		
Manchester Victoria ⇌	a												08 31		08 35	08 52		
Manchester Piccadilly ■ ⇌	a	03 44	04 52	06 02	06 50		07 19	07 51			08 05	08 19		08 36				
	d	03 44	04 54	06 08	06 54	07 07	07 23	07 54			08 07	08 24						
Manchester Airport ✈	a	04 00	05 10	06 24	07 12		07 42	08 12				08 42						
Manchester Oxford Road	a					07 09					08 09							
Birchwood	a					07 24					08 24							
Warrington Central	a					07 29					08 29							
Liverpool Lime Street ■	a					07 57					08 57				09 43			

b arr. 0745

Table 39

Saturdays

Newcastle, Middlesbrough, Scarborough, York, Hull, Leeds and Wakefield - Huddersfield - Manchester, Manchester Airport and Liverpool

		TP	NT	TP	NT	TP	TP	NT	NT	TP	NT	NT	TP	NT	TP	TP	NT	NT	TP	NT
		◇■		◇■ ⌶		◇■ ⌶	◇■ ⌶			◇■ ⌶			◇■ ⌶		◇■ ⌶	◇■ ⌶			◇■ ⌶	
Newcastle ■ ⇌	d			06 13											07 33					
Chester-le-Street	d														07 42					
Durham	d			06 29											07 48					
Middlesbrough	d									07 21										
Thornaby	d									07 26										
Yarm	d									07 34										
Darlington ■	d			06 46											08 06					
Northallerton	d			06 58						07 48					08 18					
Thirsk	d			07 06						07 56					08 26					
Scarborough	d	06 34				07 04							07 47							
Seamer	d	06 39				07 09							07 52							
Malton	d	06 57				07 27							08 10							
York ■	a	07 24		07 30		07 55				08 16			08 37		08 55					
	d	07 28		07 40		07 58				08 26			08 40		08 58				09 28	
Wakefield Westgate	d							08 29									09 29			
Wakefield Kirkgate	d							08 35									09 35			
Hull	d						07 33									08 40				
Brough	d						07 45									08 52				
Howden	d						07 56													
Selby	d						08 07									09 11				
South Milford	d																			
Garforth	d					08 13									09 13					
Leeds ■	a	07 52		08 04		08 23	08 36			08 52			09 04		09 23	09 34			09 53	
	d	07 55	08 13	08 08		08 25	08 40		08 43	08 55	09 13		09 08		09 25	09 40		09 43	09 55	10 13
Cottingley	d		08 18						08 48		09 18							09 48		
Morley	d		08 22						08 52		09 22							09 52		10 21
Batley	d		08 27						08 57		09 27							09 57		10 26
Dewsbury	a	08 06	08 30			08 36			09 00	09 06	09 30				09 36			10 00	10 06	10 29
	d	08 06	08 31			08 36			09 01	09 06	09 31				09 36			10 01	10 06	10 29
Ravensthorpe	d		08 34						09 04									10 04		
Mirfield	d		08a38					08 51	09 08		09a37						09 51	10 08		10a35
Deighton	d							08 58	09 17								09 58	10 14		
Huddersfield	a	08 15		08 25		08 44	08 58	09 05	09 21	09 15			09 25		09 45	09 58	10 05	10 21	10 15	
	d	08 16		08 26	08 30	08 45	08 59			09 16			09 26	09 30	09 46	09 59			10 16	
Slaithwaite	d				08 37									09 37						
Marsden	d				08 43									09 43						
Greenfield	d				08 51									09 51						
Mossley (Grtr Manchester)	d				08 55									09 55						
Stalybridge	a			08 43	09 00								09 43	10 00						
	d			08 44	09 01							09 22	09 44	10 01						
Ashton-under-Lyne	d				09 05							09 26		10 05						
Manchester Victoria ⇌	a				09 20							09 35		10 20						
Manchester Piccadilly ■ ⇌	a	08 51		09 05		09 19	09 36			09 49			10 05		10 19	10 36			10 49	
	d	08 54		09 07		09 24				09 54			10 07		10 24				10 54	
Manchester Airport ✈	a	09 12				09 42				10 12					10 42				11 12	
Manchester Oxford Road	a			09 09									10 09							
Birchwood	a			09 24									10 24							
Warrington Central	a			09 29									10 29							
Liverpool Lime Street ■	a			09 57								10 43	10 57							

Table 39

Saturdays

Newcastle, Middlesbrough, Scarborough, York, Hull, Leeds and Wakefield - Huddersfield - Manchester, Manchester Airport and Liverpool

		NT	TP	NT	TP	TP	NT	NT	TP	NT	NT	TP	TP	NT	TP	TP	NT	NT	TP
			◇1		◇1 🛒	◇1			◇1 🛒			◇1 🛒	◇1 A		◇1 🛒	◇1			◇1 🛒
Newcastle ■	d								09 12										10 12
Chester-le-Street	d								09 21										
Durham	d								09 27										10 27
Middlesbrough	d				09 00										10 00				
Thornaby	d				09 05										10 05				
Yarm	d				09 13										10 13				
Darlington ■	d								09 44										10 44
Northallerton	d				09 27				09 56						10 27				10 56
Thirsk	d				09 35										10 35				
Scarborough	d		08 47									09 47	10 30						
Seamer	d		08 52									09 52							
Malton	d		09 10									10 10	10 51						
York ■	a		09 37		09 55				10 21			10 37	11 18		10 55				11 21
	d		09 40		09 58				10 28			10 40			10 58				11 28
Wakefield Westgate	d						10 29										11 29		
Wakefield Kirkgate	d						10 35										11 35		
Hull	d					09 40										10 38			
Brough	d					09 52										10 50			
Howden	d																		
Selby	d					10 11										11 09			
South Milford	d																		
Garforth	d				10 13										11 13				
Leeds ■	a		10 04		10 23	10 36			10 53			11 04			11 23	11 34			11 53
	d		10 08		10 25	10 40		10 43	10 55	11 13		11 08			11 25	11 40		11 43	11 55
Cottingley	d							10 48										11 48	
Morley	d							10 52		11 21								11 52	
Batley	d							10 57		11 26								11 57	
Dewsbury	a				10 36			11 00	11 06	11 29					11 36			12 00	12 06
	d				10 36			11 01	11 06	11 29					11 36			12 01	12 06
Ravensthorpe	d							11 04										12 04	
Mirfield	d						10 51	11 08		11a35							11 49	12 08	
Deighton	d						10 58	11 14									11 58	12 14	
Huddersfield	a		10 25		10 45	10 58	11 05	11 21	11 15			11 25			11 45	11 58	12 05	12 21	12 15
	d		10 26	10 30	10 46	10 59			11 16			11 26		11 30	11 46	11 59			12 16
Slaithwaite	d			10 37										11 37					
Marsden	d			10 43										11 43					
Greenfield	d			10 51										11 51					
Mossley (Grtr Manchester)	d			10 55										11 55					
Stalybridge	a		10 43	11 00								11 43		12 00					
	d	10 22	10 44	11 01							11 22	11 44		12 01					
Ashton-under-Lyne	d	10 26		11 05							11 26			12 05					
Manchester Victoria	a	10 35		11 20							11 35			12 20					
Manchester Piccadilly ■	a		11 05		11 19	11 36			11 49			12 05			12 19	12 36			12 49
	d		11 07		11 24				11 54			12 07			12 24				12 54
Manchester Airport ✈	a				11 42				12 12						12 42				13 12
Manchester Oxford Road	a		11 09									12 09							
Birchwood	a		11 24									12 24							
Warrington Central	a		11 29									12 29							
Liverpool Lime Street ■	a	11 43	11 57								12 43	12 57							

A from 17 July until 4 September

Table 39

Saturdays

Newcastle, Middlesbrough, Scarborough, York, Hull, Leeds and Wakefield - Huddersfield - Manchester, Manchester Airport and Liverpool

		NT	NT	TP	NT	TP	TP	NT	NT	TP	NT	NT	TP	NT	TP	TP	NT	NT	TP	NT
				◇1 🛒		◇1 🛒	◇1 🛒			◇1 🛒			◇1		◇1 🛒	◇1 🛒			◇1 🛒	
Newcastle ■	d									11 15									12 15	
Chester-le-Street	d																			
Durham	d									11 27									12 27	
Middlesbrough	d					11 00									12 00					
Thornaby	d					11 05									12 05					
Yarm	d					11 13									12 13					
Darlington ■	d									11 44									12 44	
Northallerton	d					11 27				11 56					12 27				12 56	
Thirsk	d					11 35									12 35					
Scarborough	d			10 47									11 47							
Seamer	d			10 52									11 52							
Malton	d			11 10									12 10							
York ■	a			11 37		11 55				12 21			12 37		12 55				13 21	
	d			11 40		11 58				12 28			12 40		12 58				13 28	
Wakefield Westgate	d							12 29									13 29			
Wakefield Kirkgate	d							12 35									13 35			
Hull	d						11 38									12 38				
Brough	d						11 50									12 50				
Howden	d																			
Selby	d						12 09									13 09				
South Milford	d																			
Garforth	d					12 13									13 13					
Leeds ■	a			12 04		12 23	12 34			12 53			13 04		13 23	13 34			13 53	
	d	12 13		12 08		12 25	12 40		12 43	12 55	13 13		13 08		13 25	13 40		13 43	13 55	14 13
Cottingley	d								12 48									13 48		
Morley	d	12 21							12 52		13 21							13 52		14 21
Batley	d	12 26							12 57		13 26							13 57		14 26
Dewsbury	a	12 29				12 36			13 00	13 06	13 29				13 36			14 00	14 06	14 29
	d	12 29				12 36			13 01	13 06	13 29				13 36			14 01	14 06	14 29
Ravensthorpe	d								13 04									14 04		
Mirfield	d	12a35						12 49	13 08		13a35						13 51	14 08		14a35
Deighton	d							12 58	13 14								13 58	14 14		
Huddersfield	a			12 25		12 45	12 58	13 05	13 21	13 15			13 25		13 45	13 58	14 05	14 21	14 15	
	d			12 26	12 30	12 46	12 59			13 16			13 26	13 30	13 46	13 59			14 16	
Slaithwaite	d				12 37									13 37						
Marsden	d				12 43									13 43						
Greenfield	d				12 51									13 51						
Mossley (Grtr Manchester)	d				12 55									13 55						
Stalybridge	a			12 43	13 00								13 43	14 00						
	d		12 22	12 44	13 01							13 22	13 44	14 01						
Ashton-under-Lyne	d		12 26		13 05							13 26		14 05						
Manchester Victoria	a		12 36		13 20							13 35		14 20						
Manchester Piccadilly ■	a			13 05		13 19	13 36			13 49			14 05		14 19	14 36			14 49	
	d			13 07		13 24				13 54			14 07		14 24				14 54	
Manchester Airport ✈	a					13 42				14 12					14 42				15 12	
Manchester Oxford Road	a			13 09									14 09							
Birchwood	a			13 24									14 24							
Warrington Central	a			13 29									14 29							
Liverpool Lime Street ■	a		13 43	13 57								14 43	14 57							

Table 39

Saturdays

Newcastle, Middlesbrough, Scarborough, York, Hull, Leeds and Wakefield - Huddersfield - Manchester, Manchester Airport and Liverpool

		NT	TP	NT	TP	TP	NT	NT	TP	NT	NT	TP	NT	TP	TP	NT	NT	NT	TP	NT
			◇1 🛒		◇1 🛒	◇1			◇1 🛒			◇1 🛒		◇1 🛒	◇1				◇1 🛒	
Newcastle 8 ⇌	d								13 15										14 15	
Chester-le-Street	d																			
Durham	d								13 27										14 27	
Middlesbrough	d				12 50									14 00						
Thornaby	d				12 55									14 05						
Yarm	d				13 03									14 13						
Darlington 7	d								13 44										14 44	
Northallerton	d				13 17				13 56					14 27					14 56	
Thirsk	d				13 25									14 35						
Scarborough	d		12 47									13 47								
Seamer	d		12 52									13 52								
Malton	d		13 10									14 10								
York 8	a		13 37		13 50				14 21			14 37		14 55					15 21	
	d		13 40		13 58				14 28			14 40		14 58					15 28	
Wakefield Westgate	d						14 38										15 29			
Wakefield Kirkgate	d						14 44										15 35			
Hull	d					13 38									14 38	14 51				
Brough	d					13 50									14 50	15 03				
Howden	d															15 15				
Selby	d					14 09									15 09	15 25				
South Milford	d																			
Garforth	d				14 13									15 13						
Leeds 10	a		14 04		14 23	14 34			14 53			15 04		15 23	15 34				15 53	
	d		14 08		14 25	14 37		14 43	14 55	15 13		15 08		15 25	15 40			15 43	15 55	16 13
Cottingley	d							14 48										15 48		16 18
Morley	d							14 52		15 21								15 52		16 22
Batley	d							14 57		15 26								15 57		16 27
Dewsbury	a				14 36			15 00	15 06	15 29				15 36				16 00	16 06	16 30
	d				14 36			15 01	15 06	15 29				15 36				16 01	16 06	16 31
Ravensthorpe	d							15 04										16 04		16 34
Mirfield	d						14 57	15 08		15a35							15 51	16 08		16a38
Deighton	d						15 03	15 14									15 58	16 15		
Huddersfield	a		14 25		14 45	14 55	15 10	15 21	15 15			15 25		15 45	15 58		16 05	16 21	16 15	
	d		14 26	14 30	14 46	14 56			15 16			15 26	15 30	15 46	15 59				16 16	
Slaithwaite	d			14 37									15 37							
Marsden	d			14 43									15 43							
Greenfield	d			14 51									15 51							
Mossley (Grtr Manchester)	d			14 55									15 55							
Stalybridge	a		14 43	15 00								15 43	16 00							
	d	14 22	14 44	15 01							15 22	15 44	16 01							
Ashton-under-Lyne	d	14 26		15 05							15 26		16 05							
Manchester Victoria ⇌	a	14 35		15 20						16 53	15 35		16 20							17 53
Manchester Piccadilly 10 ⇌	a		15 05		15 19	15 36			15 49			16 05		16 19	16 36				16 49	
	d		15 07		15 24				15 54			16 07		16 24					16 54	
Manchester Airport ✈	a				15 42				16 12					16 42					17 12	
Manchester Oxford Road	a		15 09									16 09								
Birchwood	a		15 24									16 24								
Warrington Central	a		15 29									16 29								
Liverpool Lime Street 10	a	15 43	15 57								16 43	16 57								

Table 39

Saturdays

Newcastle, Middlesbrough, Scarborough, York, Hull, Leeds and Wakefield - Huddersfield - Manchester, Manchester Airport and Liverpool

		NT	NT	TP	TP	NT	NT	NT	TP	NT	NT	TP	NT	TP	TP	NT	NT	TP	TP
				◇1 🛒	◇1 🛒				◇1 🛒			◇1 🛒		◇1 🛒	◇1			◇1 🛒	◇1
Newcastle 8 ⇌	d								15 09									16 06	
Chester-le-Street	d								15 18									16 15	
Durham	d								15 24									16 21	
Middlesbrough	d			14 50										15 50					
Thornaby	d			14 55										15 55					
Yarm	d			15 03										16 03					
Darlington 7	d								15 42									16 39	
Northallerton	d			15 17					15 53					16 17				16 50	
Thirsk	d			15 25										16 25				16 58	
Scarborough	d											15 47							
Seamer	d											15 52							
Malton	d											16 10							
York 8	a			15 50					16 17			16 37		16 50				17 18	
	d			15 58					16 28			16 40		16 58				17 28	
Wakefield Westgate	d						16 29									17 29			
Wakefield Kirkgate	d						16 35									17 35			
Hull	d				15 40										16 40				17 01
Brough	d				15 52										16 52				17 13
Howden	d																		
Selby	d				16 11										17 11				17 32
South Milford	d																		
Garforth	d			16 13										17 13					
Leeds 10	a			16 23	16 36				16 53			17 04		17 23	17 36			17 53	17 58
	d			16 25	16 40			16 43	16 55	17 13		17 08		17 26	17 40		17 43	17 55	
Cottingley	d							16 48		17 18							17 48		
Morley	d							16 52		17 22							17 52		
Batley	d							16 57		17 27							17 57		
Dewsbury	a			16 36				17 00	17 06	17 30				17 37			18 00	18 06	
	d			16 36				17 01	17 06	17 31				17 37			18 01	18 06	
Ravensthorpe	d							17 04		17 34							18 04		
Mirfield	d						16 51	17 08		17a38						17 51	18 08		
Deighton	d						16 58	17 14								17 58	18 13		
Huddersfield	a			16 45	16 58		17 05	17 21	17 15			17 25		17 46	17 58	18 05	18 21	18 15	
	d		16 30	16 46	16 59	17 04			17 16			17 26	17 30	17 46	17 59			18 16	
Slaithwaite	d		16 37			17 11							17 37						
Marsden	d		16 43			17a17							17 43						
Greenfield	d		16 51										17 51						
Mossley (Grtr Manchester)	d		16 55										17 55						
Stalybridge	a		17 00		17 18							17 43	18 00		18 18				
	d	16 22	17 01		17 18						17 22	17 44	18 01		18 18				
Ashton-under-Lyne	d	16 26	17 05								17 26		18 05						
Manchester Victoria ⇌	a	16 35	17 20								17 35		18 20						
Manchester Piccadilly 10 ⇌	a			17 21	17 37				17 49			18 05		18 19	18 37			18 49	
	d								17 54			18 07		18 24				18 54	
Manchester Airport ✈	a								18 12					18 42				19 13	
Manchester Oxford Road	a											18 09							
Birchwood	a											18 24							
Warrington Central	a											18 29							
Liverpool Lime Street 10	a	17 43									18 43	18 59							

Table 39

Saturdays

Newcastle, Middlesbrough, Scarborough, York, Hull, Leeds and Wakefield - Huddersfield - Manchester, Manchester Airport and Liverpool

		NT	NT	TP ◇1	NT	TP ◇1	TP ◇1	NT	NT	TP ◇1 A	TP ◇1 C	TP ◇1 D	TP ◇1 E	TP ◇1 D	NT	NT	TP ◇1	TP ◇1	TP ◇1
Newcastle 8	d						17 01												
Chester-le-Street	d																		
Durham	d						17 13												
Middlesbrough	d					17 00											18 07		19 00
Thornaby	d					17 05											18 12		19 05
Yarm	d					17 13											18 20		19 13
Darlington 7	d						17 30												
Northallerton	d					17 27	17 42										18 35		19 27
Thirsk	d					17 35											18 43		19 35
Scarborough	d			16 47								17 45	17 45						
Seamer	d			16 52								17 50	17 50						
Malton	d			17 10								18 08	18 08						
York 8	a			17 37		17 55	18 06					18 35	18 35				19 03		19 58
	d			17 40		17 58	18 09					18 38	18 38				19 10		
Wakefield Westgate	d							18 29											
Wakefield Kirkgate	d							18 35											
Hull	d									17 58	18 03			18 03				18 59	
Brough	d									18 10	18 15			18 15				19 11	
Howden	d																		
Selby	d									18 29	18 34			18 34				19 30	
South Milford	d																		
Garforth	d					18 13											19 24		
Leeds 10	a			18 04		18 23	18 35			18 53	18 58	19 04	19 04	18 58			19 35	19 56	
	d	18 13		18 08		18 25	18 40		18 43	18 55			19 08	19 08		19 13	19 40		
Cottingley	d	18 18							18 48							19 18			
Morley	d	18 22							18 52							19 22			
Batley	d	18 27							18 57							19 27			
Dewsbury	a	18 30				18 36	18 51		19 00	19 06						19 30	19 51		
	d	18 31				18 36	18 51		19 01	19 06						19 31	19 51		
Ravensthorpe	d	18 34							19 04							19 34			
Mirfield	d	18a38						18 51	19 08							19 38			
Deighton	d							18 58	19 13							19 45			
Huddersfield	a			18 25		18 45	18 59	19 05	19 20	19 15			19 25	19 25		19 49	19 59		
	d			18 26	18 30	18 46	19 00			19 16			19 26	19 26	19 30		20 00		
Slaithwaite	d				18 37										19 37				
Marsden	d				18 43										19 43				
Greenfield	d				18 51										19 51				
Mossley (Grtr Manchester)	d				18 55										19 55				
Stalybridge	a			18 43	19 00								19 43	19 43	20 00				
	d		18 22	18 44	19 01								19 44	19 44	20 01				
Ashton-under-Lyne	d		18 26		19 05										20 05				
Manchester Victoria	a		18 35		19 20										20 20				
Manchester Piccadilly 10	a			19 05		19 21	19 33			19 57			20 05	20 05			20 33		
	d			19 07			19 40						20 07	20 07			20 40		
Manchester Airport ✈	a						19 59										20 57		
Manchester Oxford Road	a			19 09									20 09	20 09					
Birchwood	a			19 24									20 24	20 24					
Warrington Central	a			19 29									20 29	20 29					
Liverpool Lime Street 10	a		19 43	19 57									20 59	20 59					

A from 11 September
C from 17 July until 4 September
D until 10 July
E from 17 July

Table 39

Saturdays

Newcastle, Middlesbrough, Scarborough, York, Hull, Leeds and Wakefield - Huddersfield - Manchester, Manchester Airport and Liverpool

		NT	TP ◇1	NT	NT	TP ◇1	TP ◇1	NT	NT	TP ◇1	NT	NT	TP ◇1	NT	TP ◇1	TP ◇1	NT	NT	TP ◇1	NT A	NT B
Newcastle 8	d					18 52			21 50												
Chester-le-Street	d								21 59												
Durham	d					19 04			22 08												
Middlesbrough	d												20 10		20 50						
Thornaby	d												20 15		20 55						
Yarm	d												20 23		21 03						
Darlington 7	d					19 21			22 30												
Northallerton	d					19 36							20 37		21 17						
Thirsk	d												20 45								
Scarborough	d		18 47							19 47						22 07					
Seamer	d		18 52							19 52						22 12					
Malton	d		19 10							20 10						22 30					
York 8	a		19 37			20 02				20 37			21 07		21 41	22 57					
	d		19 40			20 10				20 40			21 10		21 45						
Wakefield Westgate	d	19 29						20 29						21 29							
Wakefield Kirkgate	d	19 35						20 35						21 35							
Hull	d						19 56												21 33		
Brough	d						20 08												21 45		
Howden	d																				
Selby	d						20 27												22 07		
South Milford	d						20 36												22 16		
Garforth	d																				
Leeds 10	a		20 04			20 35	20 56			21 04			21 35		22 07				22 35		
	d		20 08		20 13	20 40				21 08		21 13	21 40		22 08			22 17	22 40		
Cottingley	d				20 18							21 18						22 22			
Morley	d				20 22							21 22						22 26			
Batley	d				20 27							21 27						22 31			
Dewsbury	a				20 30	20 51						21 30	21 51					22 34	22 51		
	d				20 31	20 51						21 31	21 51					22 35	22 51		
Ravensthorpe	d				20 34							21 34						22 38			
Mirfield	d	19 51			20 38			20 50				21 38		21 48				22 42			
Deighton	d	19 58			20 44			20 58				21 45		22 01				22 48			
Huddersfield	a	20 05	20 25		20 48	20 59		21 05		21 25		21 49	21 59	22 05	22 25			22 53	22 59		
	d		20 26	20 30	20 48	21 00				21 26	21 30		22 00		22 26		22 34		23 00		23 05
Slaithwaite	d			20 37	20 55						21 37						22 41				23 12
Marsden	d			20 43	21a02						21 43						22 47				23 18
Greenfield	d			20 51							21 51						22 55				23 26
Mossley (Grtr Manchester)	d			20 55							21 55						22 59				23 30
Stalybridge	a		20 43	21 00						21 43	22 01				22 43		23 04				23 35
	d		20 44	21 01						21 44	22 01				22 44		23 05			23 32	23 36
Ashton-under-Lyne	d			21 05							22 06						23 09			23 36	23 40
Manchester Victoria	a			21 20							22 20						23 24			23 49	23 53
Manchester Piccadilly 10	a		21 05			21 33				22 05			22 33		23 05				23 37		
	d		21 07			21 40				22 07			22 40								
Manchester Airport ✈	a					21 57							22 57								
Manchester Oxford Road	a		21 09							22 09											
Birchwood	a		21 24							22 24											
Warrington Central	a		21 29							22 29											
Liverpool Lime Street 10	a		21 57							22 58											

A from 11 September
B until 4 September

Table 39

Saturdays

Newcastle, Middlesbrough, Scarborough, York, Hull, Leeds and Wakefield - Huddersfield - Manchester, Manchester Airport and Liverpool

		NT	NT	NT	TP	TP	TP	TP
					◇■	◇■		
			A	B	B	A	A	A
Newcastle	d							
Chester-le-Street	d							
Durham	d							
Middlesbrough	d				21 50	21 50		
Thornaby	d				21 55	21 55		
Yarm	d							
Darlington	d				22 19	22 19		
Northallerton	d				22 30	22 30		
Thirsk	d				22 38	22 38		
Scarborough	d							
Seamer	d							
Malton	d							
York	a				22 57	22 57		
	d				23 07	23 07		
Wakefield Westgate	d	22 42						
Wakefield Kirkgate	d	22 47						
Hull	d							
Brough	d							
Howden	d							
Selby	d							
South Milford	d							
Garforth	d							
Leeds	a				23 33	23 33		
	d		23 05	23 13	23 35		23 45	23 45
Cottingley	d		23 10	23 18				
Morley	d		23 14	23 22				
Batley	d		23 19	23 27				
Dewsbury	a		23 22	23 30	23 46			00 10
	d		23 23	23 31	23 46			00 10
Ravensthorpe	d		23 26	23 34				
Mirfield	d	23 00	23 30	23 38				
Deighton	d	23 08	23 37	23 45				
Huddersfield	a	23 15	23 41	23 49	23 55		00 20	00 35
	d				23 56		00 20	00 35
Slaithwaite	d							
Marsden	d							
Greenfield	d							
Mossley (Grtr Manchester)	d							
Stalybridge	a							
	d							
Ashton-under-Lyne	d							
Manchester Victoria	a							
Manchester Piccadilly	a				00 41		01 20	
	d				00 45			
Manchester Airport	a				01 00			01 35
Manchester Oxford Road	a							
Birchwood	a							
Warrington Central	a							
Liverpool Lime Street	a							

A from 11 September

B until 4 September

Table 39

Sundays
until 11 July

Newcastle, Middlesbrough, Scarborough, York, Hull and Leeds - Huddersfield - Manchester, Manchester Airport and Liverpool

		TP	TP	TP	TP	TP	TP	TP	NT	TP	NT	TP	TP	NT	TP	TP	NT	TP	NT	TP	TP
		◇■	◇■	◇■	◇■	◇■	◇■	◇■		◇■		◇■	◇■		◇■	◇■		◇■		◇■	◇■
Newcastle	d											08 06						09 33			
Chester-le-Street	d																	09 42			
Durham	d											08 18						09 48			
Middlesbrough	d																			10 15	
Thornaby	d																			10 20	
Yarm	d																			10 28	
Darlington	d											08 35						10 05			
Northallerton	d											08 47						10 16		10 42	
Thirsk	d																			10 51	
Scarborough	d															09 20					
Seamer	d															09 25					
Malton	d															09 43					
York	a											09 11				10 09		10 41		11 10	
	d	02 44	03 59	05 12	06 12	07 12		08 10		08 40		09 15				10 15		10 45		11 15	
Hull	d												09 00								10 58
Brough	d												09 12								11 10
Howden	d																				
Selby	d												09 33								11 29
South Milford	d												09 42								11 38
Garforth	d																				
Leeds	a	03 09	04 24	05 37	06 37	07 37		08 37		09 04		09 37	10 00			10 38		11 07		11 37	11 56
	d	03 10	04 25	05 40	06 40	07 40		08 40	08 44	09 10		09 40	10 06			10 40	10 44	11 10		11 40	11 59
Cottingley	d								08 49								10 49				
Morley	d								08 53								10 53				
Batley	d								08 58								10 58				
Dewsbury	a			05 51	06 50	07 50		08 50	09 01			09 50				10 51	11 01			11 50	
	d			05 51	06 51	07 51		08 51	09 02			09 51				10 51	11 02			11 51	
Ravensthorpe	d								09 05								11 05				
Mirfield	d								09 09								11 09				
Deighton	d								09 16								11 15				
Huddersfield	a	03 29	04 44	06 00	06 59	07 59		08 59	09 20	09 26		09 59	10 25			11 00	11 20	11 26		11 59	12 16
	d	03 30	04 45	06 01	07 01	08 01		09 01		09 28	09 37	10 01	10 26	10 37		11 00		11 28	11 37	12 01	12 17
Slaithwaite	d										09 44			10 44					11 44		
Marsden	d										09 50			10 50					11 50		
Greenfield	d										09 58			10 58					11 58		
Mossley (Grtr Manchester)	d										10 02			11 02					12 02		
Stalybridge	a				07 18	08 18		09 18		09 44	10 07		10 45	11 07				11 45	12 07		
	d				07 19	08 19		09 19		09 46	10 08		10 46	11 08				11 46	12 08		
Ashton-under-Lyne	d										10 12			11 12					12 12		
Manchester Victoria	a										10 26			11 26					12 26		
	d																				
Manchester Piccadilly	a	04 02	05 17	06 34	07 34	08 34		09 34		10 05		10 34	11 05			11 34		12 05		12 34	12 54
	d	04 06	05 21	06 38	07 38	08 38	09 07	09 38		10 07		10 38			11 07	11 38		12 07		12 38	
Manchester Airport	a	04 23	05 38	06 55	07 55	08 55		09 55				10 55				11 55				12 55	
Manchester Oxford Road	a						09 08			10 08					11 08			12 08			
Newton-le-Willows	a																				
Birchwood	a						09 23			10 23					11 24			12 23			
Warrington Central	a						09 28			10 28					11 29			12 28			
Liverpool Lime Street	a						09 57			10 57					11 57			12 57			

Table 39

Sundays
until 11 July

Newcastle, Middlesbrough, Scarborough, York, Hull and Leeds - Huddersfield - Manchester, Manchester Airport and Liverpool

		TP	NT	TP	NT	TP	TP	NT	TP	TP	TP	NT	TP	NT	TP	TP	NT	TP	TP	TP
		◇1		◇1		◇1	◇1		◇1	◇1	◇1		◇1		◇1	◇1		◇1	◇1	◇1
Newcastle 8	d			11 03					12 05				13 06					14 08		
Chester-le-Street	d																			
Durham	d			11 15					12 17				13 18					14 20		
Middlesbrough	d										12 45									14 45
Thornaby	d										12 50									14 50
Yarm	d										12 58									14 58
Darlington 7	d			11 32					12 34				13 35					14 37		
Northallerton	d			11 44							13 12							14 48		15 12
Thirsk	d										13 21									15 21
Scarborough	d	10 50					11 50									13 50				
Seamer	d	10 55					11 55									13 55				
Malton	d	11 13					12 13									14 13				
York 8	a	11 39		12 06			12 39		13 07		13 41		14 10			14 39		15 11		15 41
	d	11 45		12 15			12 45		13 15		13 45		14 15		14 33	14 45		15 15		15 45
Hull	d					12 00				12 58									14 58	
Brough	d					12 12				13 10									15 10	
Howden	d																			
Selby	d					12 33				13 29									15 29	
South Milford	d									13 38									15 38	
Garforth	d																			
Leeds 10	a	12 07		12 37		12 56	13 07		13 37	13 55	14 07		14 37		14 56	15 08		15 38	15 56	16 07
	d	12 10		12 40	12 44	12 59	13 10		13 40	13 59	14 10		14 40	14 44	14 59	15 10		15 40	15 59	16 10
Cottingley	d				12 49									14 49						
Morley	d				12 53									14 53						
Batley	d				12 58									14 58						
Dewsbury	a			12 50	13 01				13 50				14 51	15 01				15 51		
	d			12 51	13 02				13 51				14 51	15 02				15 51		
Ravensthorpe	d				13 05									15 05						
Mirfield	d				13 09									15 09						
Deighton	d				13 20									15 20						
Huddersfield	a	12 26		12 59	13 24	13 16	13 27		13 59	14 16	14 26		15 00	15 24	15 16	15 26		16 00	16 16	16 27
	d	12 28	12 37	13 01		13 17	13 28	13 37	14 01	14 18	14 28	14 37	15 01		15 17	15 28	15 37	16 01	16 17	16 28
Slaithwaite	d		12 44					13 44				14 44					15 44			
Marsden	d		12 50					13 50				14 50					15 50			
Greenfield	d		12 58					13 58				14 58					15 58			
Mossley (Grtr Manchester)	d		13 02					14 02				15 02					16 02			
Stalybridge	a	12 45	13 07				13 44	14 07			14 45	15 07				15 45	16 07			16 44
	d	12 46	13 08				13 46	14 08			14 46	15 08				15 46	16 08			16 46
Ashton-under-Lyne	d		13 12					14 12				15 12					16 12			
Manchester Victoria	a		13 26					14 26				15 26					16 26			
	d																			
Manchester Piccadilly 10	a	13 04		13 34		13 54	14 05		14 34	14 54	15 04		15 34		15 54	16 04		16 34	16 54	17 04
	d	13 07		13 38			14 07		14 38		15 07		15 38			16 07		16 38		17 07
Manchester Airport	a			13 55					14 55				15 55					16 55		
Manchester Oxford Road	a	13 08					14 08				15 08					16 08				17 08
Newton-le-Willows	a																			
Birchwood	a	13 23					14 23				15 23					16 23				17 23
Warrington Central	a	13 28					14 28				15 28					16 28				17 28
Liverpool Lime Street 10	a	13 57					14 57				15 57					16 57				17 57

Table 39

Sundays
until 11 July

Newcastle, Middlesbrough, Scarborough, York, Hull and Leeds - Huddersfield - Manchester, Manchester Airport and Liverpool

		NT	TP	NT	TP	TP	NT	TP	TP	TP	NT	TP	NT	TP	TP	NT	TP	TP	TP	NT
			◇1		◇1	◇1		◇1	◇1	◇1		◇1		◇1	◇1		◇1	◇1	◇1	
Newcastle 8	d		15 07					16 08				16 52					17 53			
Chester-le-Street	d		15 16									17 01								
Durham	d		15 22					16 20				17 08					18 07			
Middlesbrough	d									16 45									18 45	
Thornaby	d									16 50									18 50	
Yarm	d									16 58									18 58	
Darlington 7	d		15 40					16 37				17 26					18 24			
Northallerton	d							16 48		17 12		17 37					18 35		19 12	
Thirsk	d									17 21									19 21	
Scarborough	d					15 50									17 50					
Seamer	d					15 55									17 55					
Malton	d					16 13									18 13					
York 8	a		16 12			16 39		17 11		17 41		17 59			18 39		18 58		19 40	
	d		16 15		16 33	16 45		17 15		17 45		18 15		18 33	18 45		19 15		19 45	
Hull	d								16 58									18 58		19 04
Brough	d								17 10									19 10		19 16
Howden	d																			19 28
Selby	d								17 29									19 29		19 38
South Milford	d								17 39									19 38		
Garforth	d																			
Leeds 10	a		16 37		16 56	17 07		17 38	17 56	18 07		18 37		18 56	19 07		19 37	19 56	20 07	
	d		16 40	16 44	16 59	17 10		17 40	17 59	18 10		18 40	18 44	18 59	19 10		19 40	19 59	20 10	
Cottingley	d			16 49									18 49							
Morley	d			16 53									18 53							
Batley	d			16 58									18 58							
Dewsbury	a		16 51	17 01				17 51				18 51	19 01				19 51			
	d		16 51	17 02				17 51				18 51	19 02				19 51			
Ravensthorpe	d			17 05									19 05							
Mirfield	d			17 09									19 09							
Deighton	d			17 20									19 20							
Huddersfield	a		17 00	17 24	17 16	17 27		18 00	18 16	18 27		19 00	19 24	19 16	19 27		20 00	20 16	20 27	
	d	16 37	17 01		17 17	17 28	17 37	18 01	18 17	18 28	18 37	19 01		19 17	19 28	19 37	20 01	20 17	20 28	
Slaithwaite	d	16 44					17 44				18 44					19 44				
Marsden	d	16 50					17 50				18 50					19 50				
Greenfield	d	16 58					17 58				18 58					19 58				
Mossley (Grtr Manchester)	d	17 02					18 02				19 02					20 02				
Stalybridge	a	17 07				17 44	18 07			18 44	19 07				19 44	20 07			20 44	
	d	17 08				17 46	18 08			18 46	19 08				19 46	20 08			20 46	
Ashton-under-Lyne	d	17 12					18 12				19 12					20 12				
Manchester Victoria	a	17 26					18 26				19 26					20 26				
	d																			
Manchester Piccadilly 10	a		17 34		17 54	18 04		18 34	18 54	19 04		19 34		19 54	20 04		20 34	20 54	21 04	
	d		17 38			18 07		18 38		19 07		19 38			20 07		20 38		21 07	
Manchester Airport	a		17 55					18 55				19 55					20 55			
Manchester Oxford Road	a					18 08				19 08					20 08				21 08	
Newton-le-Willows	a																			
Birchwood	a					18 23				19 23					20 23				21 23	
Warrington Central	a					18 28				19 28					20 28				21 28	
Liverpool Lime Street 10	a					18 57				19 57					20 57				21 57	

Table 39

Sundays until 11 July

Newcastle, Middlesbrough, Scarborough, York, Hull and Leeds - Huddersfield - Manchester, Manchester Airport and Liverpool

		TP ◇1	NT	TP ◇1	NT	TP ◇1	NT	TP ◇1	TP ◇1	TP ◇1	NT	TP ◇1
Newcastle 8	d			19 06				20 07				
Chester-le-Street	d											
Durham	d			19 18				20 19				
Middlesbrough	d	20 07										22 07
Thornaby	d	20 12										22 12
Yarm	d	20 20										22 20
Darlington 7	d			19 35				20 36				
Northallerton	d	20 34						20 48				22 34
Thirsk	d	20 42										22 42
Scarborough	d					19 50				21 20		
Seamer	d					19 55				21 25		
Malton	d					20 13				21 43		
York 8	a	21 02		20 09		20 39		21 12		22 09		23 09
	d			20 15		20 45		21 15		22 12		23 12
Hull	d								21 00			
Brough	d								21 12			
Howden	d											
Selby	d								21 31			
South Milford	d								21 40			
Garforth	d											
Leeds 10	a			20 37		21 07		21 38	21 59	22 38		23 37
	d			20 40	20 44	21 10		21 40		22 40	22 44	23 40
Cottingley	d				20 49						22 49	
Morley	d				20 53						22 53	
Batley	d				20 58						22 58	
Dewsbury	a			20 51	21 01			21 51			23 01	23 50
	d			20 51	21 02			21 51			23 02	23 51
Ravensthorpe	d				21 05						23 05	
Mirfield	d				21 09						23 09	
Deighton	d				21 15						23 16	
Huddersfield	a			21 00	21 18	21 27		22 00		22 56	23 20	23 58
	d		20 37	21 01	21 19	21 28	21 37	22 01		22 58		00 01
Slaithwaite	d		20 44		21 26		21 44					
Marsden	d		20 50		21a33		21 50					
Greenfield	d		20 58				21 58					
Mossley (Grtr Manchester)	d		21 02				22 02					
Stalybridge	a		21 07	21 18			22 07	22 18		23 18		
	d		21 08	21 19			22 08	22 19		23 19		
Ashton-under-Lyne	d		21 12				22 12					
Manchester Victoria	a		21 26				22 26					
	d											
Manchester Piccadilly 10	a			21 36		22 04		22 36		23 36		00 42
	d					22 07		22 38				00 44
Manchester Airport	a							22 55				01 00
Manchester Oxford Road	a					22 08						
Newton-le-Willows	a											
Birchwood	a					22 23						
Warrington Central	a					22 28						
Liverpool Lime Street 10	a					22 57						

Table 39

Sundays 18 July to 05 September

Newcastle, Middlesbrough, Scarborough, York, Hull and Leeds - Huddersfield - Manchester, Manchester Airport and Liverpool

		TP ◇1	TP ◇1	TP ◇1	TP ◇1	TP ◇1	TP ◇1	TP ◇1	NT	TP ◇1	NT	TP ◇1	TP ◇1	NT	TP ◇1	TP ◇1	NT	TP ◇1	NT	TP ◇1	TP ◇1
Newcastle 8	d											08 06						09 33			
Chester-le-Street	d																	09 42			
Durham	d											08 18						09 48			
Middlesbrough	d																			10 15	
Thornaby	d																			10 20	
Yarm	d																			10 28	
Darlington 7	d											08 35						10 05			
Northallerton	d											08 47						10 16		10 42	
Thirsk	d																			10 51	
Scarborough	d															09 20					
Seamer	d															09 25					
Malton	d															09 43					
York 8	a											09 11				10 09		10 41		11 10	
	d	02 44	03 59	05 12	06 12	07 12		08 10		08 40		09 15				10 15		10 45		11 15	
Hull	d												09 00								10 58
Brough	d												09 12								11 10
Howden	d																				
Selby	d												09 33								11 29
South Milford	d												09 42								11 38
Garforth	d																				
Leeds 10	a	03 09	04 24	05 37	06 37	07 37		08 37		09 04		09 37	10 00			10 38		11 07		11 37	11 56
	d	03 10	04 25	05 40	06 40	07 40		08 40	08 44	09 10		09 40	10 06			10 40	10 44	11 10		11 40	11 59
Cottingley	d								08 49								10 49				
Morley	d								08 53								10 53				
Batley	d								08 58								10 58				
Dewsbury	a			05 51	06 50	07 50		08 50	09 01			09 50				10 51	11 01			11 50	
	d			05 51	06 51	07 51		08 51	09 02			09 51				10 51	11 02			11 51	
Ravensthorpe	d								09 05								11 05				
Mirfield	d								09 09								11 09				
Deighton	d								09 16								11 15				
Huddersfield	a	03 29	04 44	06 00	06 59	07 59		08 59	09 20	09 26		09 59	10 25			11 00	11 20	11 26		11 59	12 16
	d	03 30	04 45	06 01	07 01	08 01		09 01		09 28	09 37	10 01	10 26	10 37		11 00		11 28	11 37	12 01	12 17
Slaithwaite	d										09 44			10 44					11 44		
Marsden	d										09 50			10 50					11 50		
Greenfield	d										09 58			10 58					11 58		
Mossley (Grtr Manchester)	d										10 02			11 02					12 02		
Stalybridge	a				07 18	08 18		09 18		09 44	10 06		10 45	11 06				11 45	12 06		
	d				07 19	08 19		09 19		09 46	10 07		10 46	11 07				11 46	12 07		
Ashton-under-Lyne	d																				
Manchester Victoria	a																				
	d																				
Manchester Piccadilly 10	a	04 02	05 17	06 34	07 34	08 34		09 34		10 05	10 25	10 34	11 05	11 25		11 34		12 04	12 25	12 34	12 54
	d	04 06	05 21	06 38	07 38	08 38	09 07	09 38		10 07		10 38			11 07	11 38		12 07		12 38	
Manchester Airport	a	04 23	05 38	06 55	07 55	08 55		09 55				10 55				11 55				12 55	
Manchester Oxford Road	a						09 08			10 08					11 08			12 08			
Newton-le-Willows	a																				
Birchwood	a						09 23			10 23					11 24			12 23			
Warrington Central	a						09 28			10 28					11 29			12 28			
Liverpool Lime Street 10	a						09 57			10 57					11 57			12 57			

Table 39

Sundays
18 July to 05 September

Newcastle, Middlesbrough, Scarborough, York, Hull and Leeds - Huddersfield - Manchester, Manchester Airport and Liverpool

		TP ◇1	NT	TP ◇1	NT	TP ◇1	TP ◇1	NT	TP ◇1	TP ◇1	TP ◇1	NT	TP ◇1	NT	TP ◇1	TP ◇1	NT	TP ◇1	TP ◇1	TP ◇1
Newcastle 8	d			11 03					12 05				13 06					14 08		
Chester-le-Street	d																			
Durham	d			11 15					12 17				13 18					14 20		
Middlesbrough	d										12 45									14 45
Thornaby	d										12 50									14 50
Yarm	d										12 58									14 58
Darlington 7	d			11 32					12 34				13 35					14 37		
Northallerton	d			11 44							13 12							14 48		15 12
Thirsk	d										13 21									15 21
Scarborough	d	10 50					11 50									13 50				
Seamer	d	10 55					11 55									13 55				
Malton	d	11 13					12 13									14 13				
York 8	a	11 39		12 06			12 39		13 07		13 41		14 10			14 39		15 11		15 41
	d	11 45		12 15			12 45		13 15		13 45		14 15		14 33	14 45		15 15		15 45
Hull	d					12 00				12 58									14 58	
Brough	d					12 12				13 10									15 10	
Howden	d																			
Selby	d					12 33				13 29									15 29	
South Milford	d									13 38									15 38	
Garforth	d																			
Leeds 10	a	12 07		12 37		12 56	13 07		13 37	13 55	14 07		14 37		14 56	15 08		15 38	15 56	16 07
	d	12 10		12 40	12 44	12 59	13 10		13 40	13 59	14 10		14 40	14 44	14 59	15 10		15 40	15 59	16 10
Cottingley	d				12 49									14 49						
Morley	d				12 53									14 53						
Batley	d				12 58									14 58						
Dewsbury	a			12 50	13 01				13 50				14 51	15 01				15 51		
	d			12 51	13 02				13 51				14 51	15 02				15 51		
Ravensthorpe	d				13 05									15 05						
Mirfield	d				13 09									15 09						
Deighton	d				13 20									15 20						
Huddersfield	a	12 26		12 59	13 24	13 16	13 27		13 59	14 16	14 26		15 00	15 24	15 16	15 26		16 00	16 16	16 27
	d	12 28	12 37	13 01		13 17	13 28	13 37	14 01	14 18	14 28	14 37	15 01		15 17	15 28	15 37	16 01	16 17	16 28
Slaithwaite	d		12 44					13 44				14 44					15 44			
Marsden	d		12 50					13 50				14 50					15 50			
Greenfield	d		12 58					13 58				14 58					15 58			
Mossley (Grtr Manchester)	d		13 02					14 02				15 02					16 02			
Stalybridge	a	12 45	13 06				13 44	14 06			14 45	15 06				15 45	16 07			16 44
	d	12 46	13 07				13 46	14 07			14 46	15 07				15 46	16 08			16 46
Ashton-under-Lyne	d																			
Manchester Victoria	a																			
	d																			
Manchester Piccadilly 10	a	13 04	13 25	13 34		13 54	14 05	14 25	14 34	14 54	15 04	15 25	15 34		15 54	16 04	16 21	16 34	16 54	17 04
	d	13 07		13 38			14 07		14 38		15 07		15 38			16 07		16 38		17 07
Manchester Airport	a			13 55					14 55				15 55					16 55		
Manchester Oxford Road	a	13 08					14 08				15 08					16 08				17 08
Newton-le-Willows	a																			
Birchwood	a	13 23					14 23				15 23					16 23				17 23
Warrington Central	a	13 28					14 28				15 28					16 28				17 28
Liverpool Lime Street 10	a	13 57					14 57				15 57					16 57				17 57

Table 39

Sundays
18 July to 05 September

Newcastle, Middlesbrough, Scarborough, York, Hull and Leeds - Huddersfield - Manchester, Manchester Airport and Liverpool

		NT	TP ◇1	NT	TP ◇1	TP ◇1	NT	TP ◇1	TP ◇1	TP ◇1	NT	TP ◇1	NT	TP ◇1	TP ◇1	NT	TP ◇1	TP ◇1	TP ◇1
Newcastle 8	d		15 07					16 08				16 52					17 53		
Chester-le-Street	d		15 16									17 01							
Durham	d		15 22					16 20				17 08					18 07		
Middlesbrough	d									16 45									18 45
Thornaby	d									16 50									18 50
Yarm	d									16 58									18 58
Darlington 7	d		15 40					16 37				17 26					18 24		
Northallerton	d							16 48		17 12		17 37					18 35		19 12
Thirsk	d									17 21									19 21
Scarborough	d					15 50									17 50				
Seamer	d					15 55									17 55				
Malton	d					16 13									18 13				
York 8	a		16 12			16 39		17 11		17 41		17 59			18 39		18 58		19 40
	d		16 15		16 33	16 45		17 15		17 45		18 15		18 33	18 45		19 15		19 45
Hull	d								16 58									18 58	
Brough	d								17 10									19 10	
Howden	d																		
Selby	d								17 29									19 29	
South Milford	d								17 39									19 38	
Garforth	d																		
Leeds 10	a		16 37		16 56	17 07		17 38	17 56	18 07		18 37		18 56	19 07		19 37	19 56	20 07
	d		16 40	16 44	16 59	17 10		17 40	17 59	18 10		18 40	18 44	18 59	19 10		19 40	19 59	20 10
Cottingley	d			16 49									18 49						
Morley	d			16 53									18 53						
Batley	d			16 58									18 58						
Dewsbury	a		16 51	17 01				17 51				18 51	19 01				19 51		
	d		16 51	17 02				17 51				18 51	19 02				19 51		
Ravensthorpe	d			17 05									19 05						
Mirfield	d			17 09									19 09						
Deighton	d			17 20									19 20						
Huddersfield	a		17 00	17 24	17 16	17 27		18 00	18 16	18 27		19 00	19 24	19 16	19 27		20 00	20 16	20 27
	d	16 37	17 01		17 17	17 28	17 37	18 01	18 17	18 28	18 37	19 01		19 17	19 28	19 37	20 01	20 17	20 28
Slaithwaite	d	16 44					17 44				18 44					19 44			
Marsden	d	16 50					17 50				18 50					19 50			
Greenfield	d	16 58					17 58				18 58					19 58			
Mossley (Grtr Manchester)	d	17 02					18 02				19 02					20 02			
Stalybridge	a	17 07				17 44	18 07			18 44	19 07				19 44	20 07			20 44
	d	17 08				17 46	18 08			18 46	19 08				19 46	20 08			20 46
Ashton-under-Lyne	d																		
Manchester Victoria	a																		
	d																		
Manchester Piccadilly 10	a	17 25	17 34		17 54	18 04	18 25	18 34	18 54	19 04	19 25	19 34		19 54	20 04	20 25	20 34	20 54	21 04
	d		17 38			18 07		18 38		19 07		19 38			20 07		20 38		21 07
Manchester Airport	a		17 55					18 55				19 55					20 55		
Manchester Oxford Road	a					18 08				19 08					20 08				21 08
Newton-le-Willows	a																		
Birchwood	a					18 23				19 23					20 23				21 23
Warrington Central	a					18 28				19 28					20 28				21 28
Liverpool Lime Street 10	a					18 57				19 57					20 57				21 57

Table 39

Sundays
18 July to 05 September

Newcastle, Middlesbrough, Scarborough, York, Hull and Leeds - Huddersfield - Manchester, Manchester Airport and Liverpool

		TP ◇1		NT	TP ◇1	NT	TP ◇1	NT		TP ◇1	TP ◇1		TP ◇1	NT	TP ◇1
Newcastle 8 ⇌	d				19 06					20 07					
Chester-le-Street	d														
Durham	d				19 18					20 19					
Middlesbrough	d	20 07													22 07
Thornaby	d	20 12													22 12
Yarm	d	20 20													22 20
Darlington 7	d				19 35					20 36					
Northallerton	d	20 34								20 48					22 34
Thirsk	d	20 42													22 42
Scarborough	d						19 50						21 20		
Seamer	d						19 55						21 25		
Malton	d						20 13						21 43		
York 8	a	21 02			20 09		20 39			21 12			22 09		23 09
	d				20 15		20 45			21 15			22 12		23 12
Hull	d										21 00				
Brough	d										21 12				
Howden	d														
Selby	d										21 31				
South Milford	d										21 40				
Garforth	d														
Leeds 10	a				20 37		21 07			21 38	21 59		22 38		23 37
	d				20 40	20 44	21 10			21 40			22 40	22 44	23 40
Cottingley	d					20 49								22 49	
Morley	d					20 53								22 53	
Batley	d					20 58								22 58	
Dewsbury	a				20 51	21 01				21 51				23 01	23 50
	d				20 51	21 02				21 51				23 02	23 51
Ravensthorpe	d					21 05								23 05	
Mirfield	d					21 09								23 09	
Deighton	d					21 15								23 16	
Huddersfield	a				21 00	21 18	21 27			22 00			22 56	23 20	23 58
	d			20 37	21 01	21 19	21 28	21 37		22 01			22 58		00 01
Slaithwaite	d			20 44		21 26		21 44							
Marsden	d			20 50		21a33		21 50							
Greenfield	d			20 58				21 58							
Mossley (Grtr Manchester)	d			21 02				22 02							
Stalybridge	a			21 07	21 18			22 07		22 18			23 18		
	d			21 08	21 19			22 08		22 19			23 19		
Ashton-under-Lyne	d														
Manchester Victoria ⇌	a														
	d														
Manchester Piccadilly 10 ⇌	a			21 25	21 36		22 04	22 25		22 36			23 36		00 42
	d						22 07			22 38					00 44
Manchester Airport ✈	a									22 55					01 00
Manchester Oxford Road	a						22 08								
Newton-le-Willows	a														
Birchwood	a						22 23								
Warrington Central	a						22 28								
Liverpool Lime Street 10	a						22 57								

Table 39

Sundays
from 12 September

Newcastle, Middlesbrough, Scarborough, York, Hull and Leeds - Huddersfield - Manchester, Manchester Airport and Liverpool

			TP ◇1	TP ◇1	NT	TP ◇1	TP ◇1	TP ◇1	NT	TP ◇1		NT	TP ◇1	NT	TP ◇1	TP ◇1	TP ◇1		NT	TP ◇1	NT	TP ◇1	TP ◇1	NT	TP ◇1
Newcastle 8 ⇌	d					08 06							09 33							11 03					12 05
Chester-le-Street	d												09 42												
Durham	d					08 18							09 48							11 15					12 17
Middlesbrough	d														10 15										
Thornaby	d														10 20										
Yarm	d														10 28										
Darlington 7	d					08 35							10 05							11 32					12 34
Northallerton	d					08 47							10 16		10 42					11 44					
Thirsk	d														10 51										
Scarborough	d									09 20							10 50						11 50		
Seamer	d									09 25							10 55						11 55		
Malton	d									09 43							11 13						12 13		
York 8	a					09 11				10 09			10 41		11 10		11 39			12 06			12 39		13 07
	d			08 30		09 15		09 45		10 15			10 45		11 15		11 45			12 15			12 45		13 15
Hull	d						09 00									10 58						12 00			
Brough	d						09 12									11 10						12 12			
Howden	d																								
Selby	d						09 33									11 29						12 33			
South Milford	d						09 42									11 38									
Garforth	d																								
Leeds 10	a			08 54		09 37	10 00	10 08		10 38			11 07		11 37	11 56	12 07			12 37		12 56	13 07		13 37
	d			09 00		09 40		10 10		10 40		10 44	11 10		11 40	11 59	12 10			12 40	12 44	12 59	13 10		13 40
Cottingley	d											10 49									12 49				
Morley	d											10 53									12 53				
Batley	d											10 58									12 58				
Dewsbury	a			09 10		09 50				10 51		11 01			11 50	12 09				12 50	13 01	13 09			13 50
	d			09 10		09 51				10 51		11 02			11 51	12 10				12 51	13 02	13 10			13 51
Ravensthorpe	d											11 05									13 05				
Mirfield	d											11 09									13 09				
Deighton	d											11 15									13 20				
Huddersfield	a			09 19		10 02				11 01		11 20			12 02	12 20				13 01	13 24	13 20			14 02
	d			09 22		10 04				11 04					12 04					13 04					14 04
Slaithwaite	d																								
Marsden	d																								
Greenfield	d																								
Mossley (Grtr Manchester)	d																								
Stalybridge	a																								
	d				10 08				11 08					12 08					13 08					14 08	
Ashton-under-Lyne	d				10 12				11 12					12 12					13 12					14 12	
Manchester Victoria ⇌	a			10 10	10 26	10 52		11 04	11 26	11 52			12 03	12 26	12 52		13 03		13 26	13 52			14 04	14 26	14 52
	d		09 15	10 15		10 54		11 09		11 54			12 09		12 54		13 09			13 54			14 09		14 54
Manchester Piccadilly 10 ⇌	a					11 08				12 08					13 08					14 08					15 14
	d					11 10				12 10					13 10					14 10					15 18
Manchester Airport ✈	a					11 25				12 25					13 25					14 25					15 35
Manchester Oxford Road	a																								
Newton-le-Willows	a		09 32	10 32				11 27					12 27				13 27						14 27		
Birchwood	a																								
Warrington Central	a		10 b05	11 b05				12 b00					13 b00				14 b00						15 b00		
Liverpool Lime Street 10	a		09 57	10 57				11 57					12 57				13 57						14 57		

b by bus

Table 39

Sundays from 12 September

Newcastle, Middlesbrough, Scarborough, York, Hull and Leeds - Huddersfield - Manchester, Manchester Airport and Liverpool

		TP ◇1	TP ◇1	TP ◇1	NT	TP ◇1	NT	TP ◇1	NT	TP ◇1	TP ◇1	TP ◇1	NT	TP ◇1	NT	TP ◇1	TP ◇1	NT
Newcastle 8	d			13 06						14 08				15 07				
Chester-le-Street	d													15 16				
Durham	d			13 18						14 20				15 22				
Middlesbrough	d		12 45									14 45						
Thornaby	d		12 50									14 50						
Yarm	d		12 58									14 58						
Darlington 7	d			13 35						14 37				15 40				
Northallerton	d		13 12							14 48		15 12						
Thirsk	d		13 21									15 21						
Scarborough	d							13 50									15 50	
Seamer	d							13 55									15 55	
Malton	d							14 13									16 13	
York 8	a		13 41	14 10				14 39		15 11		15 41		16 12			16 39	
	d		13 45	14 15		14 33		14 45		15 15		15 45		16 15		16 33	16 45	
Hull	d	12 58									14 58							
Brough	d	13 10									15 10							
Howden	d																	
Selby	d	13 29									15 29							
South Milford	d	13 38									15 38							
Garforth	d																	
Leeds 10	a	13 55	14 07	14 37		14 56		15 08		15 38	15 56	16 07		16 37		16 56	17 07	
	d	13 59	14 10	14 40	14 44	14 59		15 10		15 40	15 59	16 10		16 40	16 44	16 59	17 10	
Cottingley	d				14 49										16 49			
Morley	d				14 53										16 53			
Batley	d				14 58										16 58			
Dewsbury	a	14 09		14 51	15 01					15 51				16 51	17 01			
	d	14 10		14 51	15 02					15 51				16 51	17 02			
Ravensthorpe	d				15 05										17 05			
Mirfield	d				15 09										17 09			
Deighton	d				15 20										17 20			
Huddersfield	a	14 20		15 00	15 24	15 16		15 26		16 00	16 16	16 27		17 00	17 24	17 16	17 27	
	d			15 01		15 17		15 28	15 37	16 01	16 17	16 28	16 37	17 01		17 17	17 28	17 37
Slaithwaite	d								15 44				16 44					17 44
Marsden	d								15 50				16 50					17 50
Greenfield	d								15 58				16 58					17 58
Mossley (Grtr Manchester)	d								16 02				17 02					18 02
Stalybridge	a							15 45	16 07			16 44	17 07				17 44	18 07
	d						15 08	15 46	16 08			16 46	17 08				17 46	18 08
Ashton-under-Lyne	d						15 12		16 12				17 12					18 12
Manchester Victoria	a		15 03				15 26		16 26				17 26					18 26
	d		15 09															
Manchester Piccadilly 10	a			15 34		15 54		16 04		16 34	16 54	17 04		17 34		17 54	18 04	
	d			15 38				16 07		16 38		17 07		17 38			18 07	
Manchester Airport ✈	a			15 55						16 55				17 55				
Manchester Oxford Road	a							16 08				17 08					18 08	
Newton-le-Willows	a		15 27															
Birchwood	a							16 23				17 23					18 23	
Warrington Central	a		16b00					16 28				17 28					18 28	
Liverpool Lime Street 10	a		15 57					16 57				17 57					18 57	

b by bus

Table 39

Sundays from 12 September

Newcastle, Middlesbrough, Scarborough, York, Hull and Leeds - Huddersfield - Manchester, Manchester Airport and Liverpool

		TP ◇1	TP ◇1	TP ◇1	NT	TP ◇1	NT	TP ◇1	TP ◇1	NT	TP ◇1	TP ◇1	TP ◇1	TP ◇1	NT	TP ◇1	NT	TP ◇1	NT
Newcastle 8	d	16 08				16 52					17 53					19 06			
Chester-le-Street	d					17 01													
Durham	d	16 20				17 08					18 07					19 18			
Middlesbrough	d			16 45									18 45	20 07					
Thornaby	d			16 50									18 50	20 12					
Yarm	d			16 58									18 58	20 20					
Darlington 7	d	16 37				17 26					18 24					19 35			
Northallerton	d	16 48		17 12		17 37					18 35		19 12	20 34					
Thirsk	d			17 21									19 21	20 42					
Scarborough	d								17 50									19 50	
Seamer	d								17 55									19 55	
Malton	d								18 13									20 13	
York 8	a	17 11		17 41		17 59			18 39		18 58		19 40	21 02		20 09		20 39	
	d	17 15		17 45		18 15		18 33	18 45		19 15		19 45			20 15		20 45	
Hull	d		16 58									18 58							
Brough	d		17 10									19 10							
Howden	d																		
Selby	d		17 29									19 29							
South Milford	d		17 38									19 38							
Garforth	d																		
Leeds 10	a	17 38	17 56	18 07		18 37		18 56	19 07		19 37	19 56	20 07			20 37		21 07	
	d	17 40	17 59	18 10		18 40	18 44	18 59	19 10		19 40	19 59	20 10			20 40	20 44	21 10	
Cottingley	d						18 49										20 49		
Morley	d						18 53										20 53		
Batley	d						18 58										20 58		
Dewsbury	a	17 51				18 51	19 01				19 51					20 51	21 01		
	d	17 51				18 51	19 02				19 51					20 51	21 02		
Ravensthorpe	d						19 05										21 05		
Mirfield	d						19 09										21 09		
Deighton	d						19 20										21 15		
Huddersfield	a	18 00	18 16	18 27		19 00	19 24	19 16	19 27		20 00	20 16	20 27			21 00	21 18	21 27	
	d	18 01	18 17	18 28	18 37	19 01		19 17	19 28	19 37	20 01	20 17	20 28		20 37	21 01	21 19	21 28	21 37
Slaithwaite	d				18 44					19 44					20 44		21 26		21 44
Marsden	d				18 50					19 50					20 50		21a33		21 50
Greenfield	d				18 58					19 58					20 58				21 58
Mossley (Grtr Manchester)	d				19 02					20 02					21 02				22 02
Stalybridge	a			18 44	19 07				19 44	20 07			20 44		21 07	21 18			22 07
	d			18 46	19 08				19 46	20 08			20 46		21 08	21 19			22 08
Ashton-under-Lyne	d				19 12					20 12					21 12				22 12
Manchester Victoria	a				19 26					20 26					21 26				22 26
	d																		
Manchester Piccadilly 10	a	18 34	18 54	19 04		19 34		19 54	20 04		20 34	20 54	21 04			21 36		22 04	
	d	18 38		19 07		19 38			20 07		20 38		21 07					22 07	
Manchester Airport ✈	a	18 55				19 55					20 55								
Manchester Oxford Road	a			19 08					20 08				21 08					22 08	
Newton-le-Willows	a																		
Birchwood	a			19 23					20 23				21 23					22 23	
Warrington Central	a			19 28					20 28				21 28					22 28	
Liverpool Lime Street 10	a			19 57					20 57				21 57					22 57	

Table 39

Sundays
from 12 September

Newcastle, Middlesbrough, Scarborough, York, Hull and Leeds - Huddersfield - Manchester, Manchester Airport and Liverpool

		TP ◇■	TP ◇■	NT	TP ◇■	NT	TP ◇■
Newcastle ■ ⇌	d	20 07		21 06			
Chester-le-Street	d			21 15			
Durham	d	20 19		21 24			
Middlesbrough	d						22 07
Thornaby	d						22 12
Yarm	d						22 20
Darlington ■	d	20 36		21 45			
Northallerton	d	20 48					22 34
Thirsk	d						22 42
Scarborough	d				21 20		
Seamer	d				21 25		
Malton	d				21 43		
York ■	a	21 12			22 09		23 09
	d	21 15			22 12		23 12
Hull	d		21 00				
Brough	d		21 12				
Howden	d						
Selby	d		21 31				
South Milford	d		21 40				
Garforth	d						
Leeds ■	a	21 38	21 59		22 38		23 37
	d	21 40			22 40	22 44	23 40
Cottingley	d					22 49	
Morley	d					22 53	
Batley	d					22 58	
Dewsbury	a	21 51				23 01	23 50
	d	21 51				23 02	23 51
Ravensthorpe	d					23 05	
Mirfield	d					23 09	
Deighton	d					23 16	
Huddersfield	a	22 00			22 56	23 20	23 58
	d	22 01			22 58		00 01
Slaithwaite	d						
Marsden	d						
Greenfield	d						
Mossley (Grtr Manchester)	d						
Stalybridge	a	22 18			23 18		
	d	22 19			23 19		
Ashton-under-Lyne	d						
Manchester Victoria ⇌	a						
	d						
Manchester Piccadilly ■ ⇌	a	22 36			23 36		00 42
	d	22 38					00 44
Manchester Airport ✈	a	22 55					01 00
Manchester Oxford Road	a						
Newton-le-Willows	a						
Birchwood	a						
Warrington Central	a						
Liverpool Lime Street ■	a						

Table 39

Mondays to Fridays

Liverpool, Manchester Airport and Manchester - Huddersfield - Wakefield, Leeds, Hull, York, Scarborough, Middlesbrough and Newcastle

		TP MX ◇■	TP MO ◇■	NT	TP ◇■	TP ◇■	TP ◇■	TP ◇■	NT	TP ◇■	NT
Liverpool Lime Street ■	d										
Warrington Central	d										
Birchwood	d										
Manchester Oxford Road	d										
Manchester Airport ✈	d	00 38	00 48			04 12				05 37	
Manchester Piccadilly ■ ⇌	a	00 51	01 01			04 27				05 51	
	d	00 53	01 03			04 30		05 39		05 57	
Manchester Victoria ⇌	d										
Ashton-under-Lyne	d										
Stalybridge	a							05 52			
	d							05 52	06 41		
Mossley (Grtr Manchester)	d								06 45		
Greenfield	d								06 49		
Marsden	d								06 58		
Slaithwaite	d								07 02		
Huddersfield	a					05 31		06 10	07 10	06 26	
	d			05 32		05 38		06 11		06 27	06 31
Deighton	d			05 36							06 34
Mirfield	d			05 41							06 39
Ravensthorpe	d										06 42
Dewsbury	a									06 36	06 46
	d									06 37	06 46
Batley	d										06 49
Morley	d										06 55
Cottingley	d										06 59
Leeds ■	a	02 03	02 32			06 01		06 32		06 52	07 08
	d	02 08	02 34			06 02		06 35		06 55	
Garforth	d										
South Milford	a										
Selby	a										
Howden	a										
Brough	a										
Hull	a										
Wakefield Kirkgate	a			05 57							
Wakefield Westgate	a			06 05							
York ■	a	02 47	03 04			06 27		07 01		07 22	
	d				05 54		06 40	07 06		07 25	
Malton	d						07 04			07 49	
Seamer	a						07 21			08 06	
Scarborough	a						07 30			08 15	
Thirsk	a				06 10			07 22			
Northallerton	a				06 18			07 30			
Darlington ■	a				06 29			07 41			
Yarm	d										
Thornaby	a				06 53						
Middlesbrough	a				07 01						
Durham	a							07 58			
Chester-le-Street	a							08 04			
Newcastle ■ ⇌	a							08 17			

Table 39

Mondays to Fridays

Liverpool, Manchester Airport and Manchester - Huddersfield - Wakefield, Leeds, Hull, York, Scarborough, Middlesbrough and Newcastle

		NT	TP ◇1 ⌶	TP ◇1	NT	TP ◇1 ⌶	NT	NT	TP ◇1 ⌶ A	TP ◇1	NT	TP ◇1 ⌶	NT	TP ◇1 ⌶	NT	NT	TP ◇1 ⌶
Liverpool Lime Street 10	d								06 16								
Warrington Central	d								06 38								
Birchwood	d								06 43								
Manchester Oxford Road	d								07b07								
Manchester Airport ✈	d					06 23						07 05					07 35
Manchester Piccadilly 10	a					06 39			07 09			07 22					07 49
	d		06 21			06 54			07 11			07 26		07 36			07 56
Manchester Victoria	d						06 55								07 40		
Ashton-under-Lyne	d						07 05								07 49		
Stalybridge	a					07 07	07 10		07 26					07 49	07 54		08 09
	d					07 07	07 11		07 26					07 49	07 54		08 09
Mossley (Grtr Manchester)	d						07 15								07 59		
Greenfield	d						07 19								08 03		
Marsden	d				06 48		07 28								08 11		
Slaithwaite	d				06 52		07 32								08 16		
Huddersfield	a		06 54		07 00	07 25	07 41		07 44			07 56		08 09	08 24		08 28
	d	06 41	06 56		07 00	07 26			07 45		07 49	07 57		08 10		08 13	08 30
Deighton	d	06 45			07 03						07 53					08 16	
Mirfield	d	06 50			07 08			07 20			07 58		08 06			08 21	
Ravensthorpe	d				07 11			07 23								08 24	
Dewsbury	a		07 05		07 15			07 27	07 54			08 06	08 11	08 19		08 27	08 39
	d		07 06		07 15			07 35	07 55			08 07	08 12	08 20		08 27	08 39
Batley	d				07 18			07 38					08 15			08 30	
Morley	d				07 24			07 44					08 21			08 36	
Cottingley	d				07 28			07 47					08 24			08 39	
Leeds 10	a		07 19		07 38	07 48		07 55	08 10			08 24	08 33	08 36		08 52	08 54
	d		07 23			07 50			08 12			08 27		08 38			08 57
Garforth	d					08 00											09 05
South Milford	a																
Selby	a		07 43											08 58			
Howden	a		07 52														
Brough	a		08 04														
Hull	a		08 20											09 31			
Wakefield Kirkgate	a	07 03									08 13						
Wakefield Westgate	a	07 10									08 23						
York 8	a					08 21			08 34			08 57					09 23
	d			07 32		08 23			08 38	08 42		09 03					09 26
Malton	d								09 02								
Seamer	a								09 19								
Scarborough	a								09 33								
Thirsk	a			07 54		08 39											09 46
Northallerton	a			08 02		08 49				09 02		09 24					09 55
Darlington 7	a									09 14		09 36					
Yarm	d			08 16		09 03											10 10
Thornaby	a			08 26		09 11											10 22
Middlesbrough	a			08 34		09 20											10 30
Durham	a									09 31		09 53					
Chester-le-Street	a																
Newcastle 8	a									09 48		10 09					

A Conveys through portion to Newcastle

b arr. 0700

Table 39

Mondays to Fridays

Liverpool, Manchester Airport and Manchester - Huddersfield - Wakefield, Leeds, Hull, York, Scarborough, Middlesbrough and Newcastle

		NT	NT	NT	TP ◇1 ⌶	NT	TP ◇1 ⌶	NT	TP ◇1 ⌶	NT	TP ◇1 ⌶	NT	NT	TP ◇1 ⌶	TP ◇1 ⌶	NT	NT	TP ◇1 ⌶	NT	TP ◇1 ⌶	NT
Liverpool Lime Street 10	d				07 16	07 16								08 22					08 44		
Warrington Central	d				07 40									08 44							
Birchwood	d				07 45									08 49							
Manchester Oxford Road	d				08 06									09 07							
Manchester Airport ✈	d						08 05				08 35				09 05					09 35	
Manchester Piccadilly 10	a				08 08		08 22				08 49			09 09	09 22					09 52	
	d				08 10		08 26		08 42		08 55			09 11	09 26			09 42		09 57	
Manchester Victoria	d		08 02			08b27				08 57							09 27		09c57		
Ashton-under-Lyne	d		08 12			08 37				09 07							09 37		10 07		
Stalybridge	a		08 18		08 26	08 41				09 13				09 26			09 42		10 13		
	d				08 26	08 42								09 26			09 42				
Mossley (Grtr Manchester)	d					08 46											09 47				
Greenfield	d					08 50											09 51				
Marsden	d					08 59											09 59				
Slaithwaite	d					09 03											10 04				
Huddersfield	a				08 44	09 12	08 56		09 15		09 26			09 44	09 56		10 12	10 15		10 26	
	d	08 33		08 37	08 45		08 57		09 16		09 27	09 31	09 35	09 45	09 57			10 16		10 27	10 31
Deighton	d	08 36		08 40								09 34	09 38								10 34
Mirfield	d	08 41		08 45				09 07				09 39	09 43			10 07					10 39
Ravensthorpe	d	08 44										09 42									10 42
Dewsbury	a	08 48					09 06	09 12			09 36	09 46			10 06	10 12				10 36	10 46
	d	08 53					09 07	09 12			09 37	09 46			10 07	10 12				10 37	10 46
Batley	d	08 56						09 15				09 49				10 15					10 49
Morley	d	09 02						09 21				09 55				10 21					10 55
Cottingley	d	09 06										09 59									10 59
Leeds 10	a	09 17			09 06		09 22	09 31	09 36		09 52	10 07		10 09	10 22	10 31		10 36		10 52	11 07
	d				09 12		09 27		09 38		09 57			10 12	10 27			10 38		10 57	
Garforth	d										10 05									11 05	
South Milford	a																				
Selby	a								09 57									10 57			
Howden	a																				
Brough	a								10 15									11 15			
Hull	a								10 34									11 34			
Wakefield Kirkgate	a			09 02									10 03								
Wakefield Westgate	a			09 08									10 09								
York 8	a				09 35		09 55				10 23			10 35	10 52					11 23	
	d				09 38		10 00				10 26			10 38	10 54					11 26	
Malton	d				10 02									11 02							
Seamer	a				10 19									11 19							
Scarborough	a				10 30									11 30							
Thirsk	a										10 46									11 46	
Northallerton	a						10 21				10 55				11 15					11 55	
Darlington 7	a						10 32								11 27						
Yarm	d										11 10									12 10	
Thornaby	a										11 22									12 19	
Middlesbrough	a										11 31									12 28	
Durham	a						10 50								11 44						
Chester-le-Street	a						10 56														
Newcastle 8	a						11 08								11 59						

b arr. 0819

c arr. 0947

Liverpool, Manchester Airport and Manchester - Huddersfield - Wakefield, Leeds, Hull, York, Scarborough, Middlesbrough and Newcastle

Station		NT	TP ◇1		TP ◇1	NT	NT	NT	TP ◇1	TP ◇1	NT	NT	TP ◇1			TP ◇1	NT		NT	TP ◇1	NT	TP ◇1	NT	NT	NT
Liverpool Lime Street 10	d		09 22					09 46					10 22											10 46	
Warrington Central	d		09 44										10 44												
Birchwood	d		09 49										10 49												
Manchester Oxford Road	d		10 07										11 07												
Manchester Airport ✈	d				10 05					10 35						11 05						11 35			
Manchester Piccadilly 10	a		10 09		10 22					10 52			11 09			11 22						11 52			
	d		10 11		10 27				10 42	10 57			11 11			11 27				11 42		11 57			
Manchester Victoria	d						10 27	10b57											11 27					11c57	
Ashton-under-Lyne	d						10 37	11 07											11 37					12 07	
Stalybridge	a		10 26				10 42	11 13					11 26						11 42					12 13	
	d		10 26				10 42						11 26						11 42						
Mossley (Grtr Manchester)	d						10 47												11 47						
Greenfield	d						10 51												11 51						
Marsden	d						10 59												11 59						
Slaithwaite	d						11 04												12 04						
Huddersfield	a		10 44		10 56		11 12		11 15	11 26			11 44			11 56			12 12	12 15		12 26			12 30
	d	10 35	10 45		10 57				11 16	11 27	11 31	11 35	11 45			11 57				12 16		12 27	12 31		12 35
Deighton	d	10 38									11 34	11 38											12 34		12 38
Mirfield	d	10 43				11 07					11 39	11 43					12 07						12 39		12 43
Ravensthorpe	d										11 42												12 42		
Dewsbury	a				11 06	11 12				11 36	11 46					12 06	12 12					12 36	12 46		
	d				11 07	11 12				11 37	11 46					12 07	12 12					12 37	12 46		
Batley	d					11 15					11 49						12 15						12 49		
Morley	d					11 21					11 55						12 21						12 55		
Cottingley	d										11 59												12 59		
Leeds 10	a		11 09		11 22	11 33			11 36	11 52	12 07		12 09			12 22	12 31			12 36	12 39	12 52	13 07		
	d		11 12		11 27				11 38	11 57			12 12			12 27				12 38	12 41	12 57			
Garforth	d									12 05											12 53	13 05			
South Milford	a																								
Selby	a								11 57											12 57					
Howden	a																								
Brough	a								12 18											13 15					
Hull	a								12 36											13 34					
Wakefield Kirkgate	a	11 02										12 02													13 02
Wakefield Westgate	a	11 08										12 08													13 08
York 8	a		11 35		11 52					12 23			12 35			12 52					13 19	13 23			
	d		11 38		12 01					12 26			12 38			12 59						13 26			
Malton	d		12 02										13 02												
Seamer	a		12 19										13 19												
Scarborough	a		12 30										13 30												
Thirsk	a									12 46												13 46			
Northallerton	a				12 21					12 55						13 19						13 55			
Darlington 7	a				12 33											13 31									
Yarm	d									13 10												14 10			
Thornaby	a									13 21												14 19			
Middlesbrough	a									13 30												14 28			
Durham	a				12 50											13 48									
Chester-le-Street	a															13 54									
Newcastle 8	a				13 06											14 07									

b arr. 1049

c arr. 1149

Liverpool, Manchester Airport and Manchester - Huddersfield - Wakefield, Leeds, Hull, York, Scarborough, Middlesbrough and Newcastle

Station		TP ◇1			TP ◇1	NT	NT	TP ◇1	TP ◇1	NT	NT	NT	TP ◇1		TP ◇1			NT	NT	TP ◇1		TP ◇1	NT	NT	NT
Liverpool Lime Street 10	d	11 22										11 46	12 22												12 46
Warrington Central	d	11 44											12 44												
Birchwood	d	11 49											12 49												
Manchester Oxford Road	d	12 07											13 07												
Manchester Airport ✈	d				12 05				12 35						13 05							13 35			
Manchester Piccadilly 10	a	12 09			12 22				12 52				13 09		13 22							13 52			
	d	12 11			12 27			12 42	12 57				13 11		13 27					13 42		13 57			
Manchester Victoria	d						12 27					12b57							13 27						13c57
Ashton-under-Lyne	d						12 37					13 07							13 37						14 07
Stalybridge	a	12 26					12 42					13 13	13 26						13 42						14 13
	d	12 26					12 42						13 26						13 42						
Mossley (Grtr Manchester)	d						12 47												13 47						
Greenfield	d						12 51												13 51						
Marsden	d						12 59												13 59						
Slaithwaite	d						13 04												14 04						
Huddersfield	a	12 44			12 56		13 12	13 15	13 26				13 44		13 56				14 12	14 15		14 26			
	d	12 45			12 57			13 16	13 27	13 31	13 35		13 45		13 57					14 16		14 27	14 31	14 35	
Deighton	d									13 34	13 38												14 34	14 38	
Mirfield	d					13 07				13 39	13 43							14 07					14 39	14 43	
Ravensthorpe	d									13 42													14 42		
Dewsbury	a				13 06	13 12			13 36	13 46					14 06			14 12				14 36	14 46		
	d				13 07	13 12			13 37	13 46					14 07			14 12				14 37	14 46		
Batley	d					13 15				13 49								14 15					14 49		
Morley	d					13 21				13 55								14 21					14 55		
Cottingley	d									13 59													14 59		
Leeds 10	a	13 09			13 22	13 31		13 36	13 52	14 07			14 09		14 22			14 31		14 36		14 52	15 07		
	d	13 12			13 27			13 38	13 57				14 12		14 27					14 38		14 57			
Garforth	d								14 05													15 05			
South Milford	a																								
Selby	a							13 57												14 57					
Howden	a																								
Brough	a							14 15												15 15					
Hull	a							14 34												15 34					
Wakefield Kirkgate	a										14 02													15 02	
Wakefield Westgate	a										14 08													15 08	
York 8	a	13 35			13 52				14 23				14 35		14 52							15 23			
	d	13 38			13 54				14 26				14 38		14 54							15 26			
Malton	d	14 02											15 02												
Seamer	a	14 19											15 19												
Scarborough	a	14 30											15 30												
Thirsk	a								14 46													15 46			
Northallerton	a				14 15				14 55						15 22							15 55			
Darlington 7	a				14 27										15 34										
Yarm	d								15 10													16 10			
Thornaby	a								15 22													16 22			
Middlesbrough	a								15 30													16 30			
Durham	a				14 50										15 50										
Chester-le-Street	a														15 57										
Newcastle 8	a				15 04										16 12										

b arr. 1250

c arr. 1347

Liverpool, Manchester Airport and Manchester - Huddersfield - Wakefield, Leeds, Hull, York, Scarborough, Middlesbrough and Newcastle

		TP ◇1 ✠	TP ◇1 ✠	NT	NT	TP ◇1 ✠	TP ◇1 ✠	NT	NT	NT	TP ◇1 ✠	TP ◇1 ✠	NT	NT	TP ◇1 ✠	NT	TP ◇1 ✠	NT
Liverpool Lime Street 10	d	13 22						13 46			14 22					14 46		
Warrington Central	d	13 44									14 44							
Birchwood	d	13 49									14 49							
Manchester Oxford Road	d	14 07									15 07							
Manchester Airport ✈	d		14 05				14 35					15 05					15 35	
Manchester Piccadilly 10	a	14 09	14 22				14 52				15 09	15 22					15 52	
	d	14 11	14 27			14 42	14 57				15 11	15 27			15 42		15 57	
Manchester Victoria	d				14 27			14b57						15 27		15c57		
Ashton-under-Lyne	d				14 37			15 07						15 37		16 07		
Stalybridge	a	14 26			14 42			15 13			15 26			15 42		16 13		
	d	14 26			14 42						15 26			15 42				
Mossley (Grtr Manchester)	d				14 47									15 47				
Greenfield	d				14 51									15 51				
Marsden	d				14 59									15 59				
Slaithwaite	d				15 04									16 04				
Huddersfield	a	14 44	14 56		15 12	15 15	15 26				15 44	15 56		16 12	16 15		16 26	
	d	14 45	14 57			15 16	15 27		15 31	15 35	15 45	15 57			16 16		16 27	16 31
Deighton	d								15 34	15 38								16 34
Mirfield	d			15 07					15 39	15 43			16 07					16 39
Ravensthorpe	d								15 42									16 42
Dewsbury	a		15 06	15 12			15 36		15 46			16 06	16 12				16 36	16 46
	d		15 07	15 12			15 37		15 46			16 07	16 12				16 37	16 46
Batley	d			15 15					15 49				16 15					16 49
Morley	d			15 21					15 55				16 21					16 55
Cottingley	d								15 59									16 59
Leeds 10	a	15 09	15 22	15 31		15 36	15 52		16 07		16 09	16 22	16 31		16 36		16 52	17 07
	d	15 12	15 27			15 38	15 57				16 12	16 27			16 38		16 57	
Garforth	d						16 05										17 05	
South Milford	a																	
Selby	a					15 57									17 00			
Howden	a																	
Brough	a					16 15									17 18			
Hull	a					16 34									17 37			
Wakefield Kirkgate	a									16 02								
Wakefield Westgate	a									16 08								
York 8	a	15 35	15 52				16 23				16 35	16 52					17 23	
	d	15 38					16 26				16 38	16 58					17 26	
Malton	d	16 02									17 02						17 50	
Seamer	a	16 19									17 19						18 07	
Scarborough	a	16 30									17 30						18 17	
Thirsk	a						16 46					17 14						
Northallerton	a						16 55					17 22						
Darlington 7	a											17 37						
Yarm	d						17 10											
Thornaby	a						17 22											
Middlesbrough	a						17 30											
Durham	a											17 55						
Chester-le-Street	a											18 01						
Newcastle 8	a											18 15						

b arr. 1450 c arr. 1549

Liverpool, Manchester Airport and Manchester - Huddersfield - Wakefield, Leeds, Hull, York, Scarborough, Middlesbrough and Newcastle

		NT	TP ◇1 ✠	NT	TP ◇1 ✠	NT	NT	TP ◇1 ✠	TP ◇1 ✠	NT	NT	NT	TP ◇1 ✠	NT	TP ◇1 ✠	NT	NT	TP ◇1 ✠	NT
Liverpool Lime Street 10	d		15 22							15 46			16 22						
Warrington Central	d		15 44										16 44						
Birchwood	d		15 49										16 49						
Manchester Oxford Road	d		16 07										17 07						
Manchester Airport ✈	d				16 05				16 35						17 05				
Manchester Piccadilly 10	a		16 09		16 22				16 52				17 09		17 22				
	d		16 11		16 27			16 42	16 56				17 11		17 26			17 42	
Manchester Victoria	d			16 17			16 27			16b57				17 15			17 27		
Ashton-under-Lyne	d			16 27			16 37			17 07				17 24			17 38		
Stalybridge	a		16 26	16 33			16 42		17 09	17 12			17 26	17 29	17 39		17 43		
	d		16 26				16 42		17 09	17 12			17 26	17 29	17 39		17 43		
Mossley (Grtr Manchester)	d						16 47			17 17				17 34			17 48		
Greenfield	d						16 51			17 21				17 38			17 52		
Marsden	d						16 59			17 29							18 01		
Slaithwaite	d						17 04			17 34									
Huddersfield	a		16 44		16 56		17 12	17 15	17 27	17 42			17 44	17 54	17 57		18 12	18 15	
	d	16 35	16 45		16 57			17 16	17 28		17 31	17 35	17 45		17 58			18 16	18 36
Deighton	d	16 38									17 34	17 38							18 39
Mirfield	d	16 43				17 07					17 39	17 43				18 07			18 44
Ravensthorpe	d										17 42								18 47
Dewsbury	a				17 06	17 12			17 36		17 46				18 06	18 13			18 51
	d				17 07	17 12			17 37		17 46				18 07	18 13			18 56
Batley	d					17 15					17 49					18 16			18 59
Morley	d					17 21					17 55					18 22			19 05
Cottingley	d										17 59								19 09
Leeds 10	a		17 09		17 22	17 31		17 36	17 52		18 06		18 09		18 22	18 33		18 36	19 18
	d		17 12		17 24			17 38	17 57				18 12		18 27			18 38	
Garforth	d				17 34				18 05										
South Milford	a																	18 51	
Selby	a							18 04										19 00	
Howden	a							18 15											
Brough	a							18 27										19 18	
Hull	a							18 46										19 37	
Wakefield Kirkgate	a	17 02										18 02							
Wakefield Westgate	a	17 08										18 08							
York 8	a		17 36		17 57				18 23				18 35		18 52				
	d		17 43		18 00				18 26				18 43		18 56				
Malton	d				18 24								19 07						
Seamer	a				18 41								19 24						
Scarborough	a				18 52								19 33						
Thirsk	a		18 02						18 46										
Northallerton	a		18 10						18 55						19 20				
Darlington 7	a														19 33				
Yarm	d		18 24						19 10										
Thornaby	a		18 32						19 22										
Middlesbrough	a		18 41						19 30										
Durham	a														19 50				
Chester-le-Street	a																		
Newcastle 8	a														20 09				

b arr. 1649

Liverpool, Manchester Airport and Manchester - Huddersfield - Wakefield, Leeds, Hull, York, Scarborough, Middlesbrough and Newcastle

		NT	NT	TP		NT	TP		NT					TP	NT	NT	TP	NT	TP	NT		NT	NT	TP	TP
				◇1 ⊼			◇1 ⊼							◇1			◇1		◇1					◇1	◇1
Liverpool Lime Street 10	d		16 46	17 22													18 22							19 22	
Warrington Central	d			17 44													18 44							19 44	
Birchwood	d			17 49													18 49							19 49	
Manchester Oxford Road	d			18 07													19 07							20 07	
Manchester Airport	d													18 35					19 20						20 20
Manchester Piccadilly 10	a			18 09										18 52			19 09		19 36					20 09	20 36
	d			18 11			18 27				18 42			18 57			19 11		19 42					20 11	20 42
Manchester Victoria	d		17c57			18 27														19 27					
Ashton-under-Lyne	d		18 07			18 37														19 37					
Stalybridge	a		18 12	18 26		18 42											19 26			19 42				20 26	
	d		18 12	18 26		18 42											19 26			19 42				20 26	
Mossley (Grtr Manchester)	d		18 17			18 47														19 47					
Greenfield	d		18 21			18 51														19 51					
Marsden	d		18 29			18 59														19 59					
Slaithwaite	d		18 34			19 04														20 04					
Huddersfield	a		18 43	18 44		19 12	18 56				19 15			19 26			19 44		20 15	20 12				20 44	21 15
	d	18 40		18 45			18 57				19 16			19 27	19 31	19 35	19 45		20 16			20 31	20 35	20 45	21 16
Deighton	d	18 43													19 34	19 38						20 34	20 38		
Mirfield	d	18 48							19 08						19 39	19 43		20 07				20 39	20 43		
Ravensthorpe	d														19 42							20 42			
Dewsbury	a						19 06		19 13					19 36	19 46			20 12	20 25			20 46			21 25
	d						19 07		19 13					19 37	19 46			20 12	20 26			20 46			21 26
Batley	d								19 16						19 49			20 15				20 49			
Morley	d								19 22						19 55			20 21				20 55			
Cottingley	d														19 59							20 59			
Leeds 10	a			19 09			19 22		19 33		19 36			19 52	20 07		20 09	20 34	20 41			21 07		21 09	21 41
	d			19 12			19 27				19 38			19 57			20 12		20 45					21 12	21 42
Garforth	d													20 05											
South Milford	a										19 51													21 24	
Selby	a										20 00													21 34	
Howden	a										20 09													21 43	
Brough	a										20 21													21 55	
Hull	a										20 40													22 12	
Wakefield Kirkgate	a	19 02														20 03							21 02		
Wakefield Westgate	a	19 08														20 09							21 08		
York 8	a			19 35			19 55							20 23			20 35		21 09						22 08
	d			19 38										20 29			20 38		21 14						22 15
Malton	d			20 02													21 02								22 39
Seamer	a			20 19													21 19								22 56
Scarborough	a			20 30													21 30								23 06
Thirsk	a													20 45					21 30						
Northallerton	a													20 53					21 38						
Darlington 7	a																		21 49						
Yarm	d													21 07											
Thornaby	a													21 16											
Middlesbrough	a													21 25											
Durham	a																		22 07						
Chester-le-Street	a																								
Newcastle 8	a																		22 22						

c arr. 1747

Table 39 Mondays to Fridays

Liverpool, Manchester Airport and Manchester - Huddersfield - Wakefield, Leeds, Hull, York, Scarborough, Middlesbrough and Newcastle

		NT			NT		TP	NT		TP	TP	NT		NT	TP	NT	TP	TP FX	TP FO
							◇1			◇1	◇1				◇1		◇1	◇1	◇1
Liverpool Lime Street 10	d						20 22										22 30		
Warrington Central	d						20 44										22 52		
Birchwood	d						20 49										22 57		
Manchester Oxford Road	d						21 07										23 17		
Manchester Airport	d										21 20				22 22			23 18	23 18
Manchester Piccadilly 10	a						21 09				21 36				22 36		23 19	23 34	23 34
	d						21 11				21 42				22 42		23 21	23 38	23 38
Manchester Victoria	d	20 27						21 27				22 08				23 00			
Ashton-under-Lyne	d	20 37						21 37				22 18				23 10			
Stalybridge	a	20 42					21 26	21 42			21 55	22 22			22 55	23 14	23 34		
	d	20 42					21 26	21 42			21 55	22 23			22 55	23 15	23 34		
Mossley (Grtr Manchester)	d	20 47						21 47				22 27				23 19			
Greenfield	d	20 51						21 51				22 31				23 23			
Marsden	d	20 59						21 59				22 40				23 32			
Slaithwaite	d	21 04						22 04				22 44				23 36			
Huddersfield	a	21 12					21 44	22 12			22 15	22 53			23 15	23 44	23 52	00 25	00 09
	d				21 31		21 45				22 16			22 31	23 16		23 53	00 27	00 09
Deighton	d				21 34									22 34					
Mirfield	d				21 39									22 39					
Ravensthorpe	d				21 42									22 42					
Dewsbury	a				21 46						22 25			22 46	23 25			00s35	00s18
	d				21 46						22 26			22 46	23 26			00s35	00s18
Batley	d				21 49									22 49					
Morley	d				21 55									22 55					
Cottingley	d				21 59									22 59					
Leeds 10	a				22 08		22 09				22 41			23 07	23 41		00 31	00 50	00 35
	d						22 12			22 22	22 42				23 42		00 34	00 54	00 37
Garforth	d																		
South Milford	a									22 36									
Selby	a									22 45									
Howden	a																		
Brough	a									23 05									
Hull	a									23 23									
Wakefield Kirkgate	a																		
Wakefield Westgate	a																		
York 8	a						22 35				23 12				00 10		01 16	01 43	01 20
	d										23 21								
Malton	d																		
Seamer	a																		
Scarborough	a																		
Thirsk	a										23 35								
Northallerton	a										23 55								
Darlington 7	a										00 06								
Yarm	d																		
Thornaby	a																		
Middlesbrough	a																		
Durham	a										00 24								
Chester-le-Street	a																		
Newcastle 8	a										00 56								

Table 39

Liverpool, Manchester Airport and Manchester - Huddersfield - Wakefield, Leeds, Hull, York, Scarborough, Middlesbrough and Newcastle

		TP	TP	TP	NT	TP	TP	TP	NT	NT	TP	TP	NT	TP	NT	NT
		◇1	◇1	◇1		◇1	◇1	◇1			◇1	◇1		◇1 ℸ		
Liverpool Lime Street 10	d															
Warrington Central	d															
Birchwood	d															
Manchester Oxford Road	d															
Manchester Airport ✈	d	00 38	04 15					05 37						06 23		
Manchester Piccadilly 10 ⇌	a	00 51	04 29					05 51						06 39		
	d	00 53	04 30				05 39	05 57				06 21		06 54		
Manchester Victoria ⇌	d															06 55
Ashton-under-Lyne	d															07 05
Stalybridge	a						05 52							07 07		07 10
	d						05 52							07 07		07 11
Mossley (Grtr Manchester)	d															07 15
Greenfield	d															07 19
Marsden	d												07 00			07 28
Slaithwaite	d												07 04			07 32
Huddersfield	a	01 34	05 11				06 10	06 26				06 54	07 12	07 25		07 41
	d	01 35	05 12				06 11	06 27	06 31	06 37		06 56		07 26	07 32	
Deighton	d								06 34	06 41					07 36	
Mirfield	d								06 39	06 46					07 41	
Ravensthorpe	d								06 42							
Dewsbury	a							06 36	06 46			07 05				
	d							06 37	06 46			07 06				
Batley	d								06 49							
Morley	d								06 55							
Cottingley	d								06 59							
Leeds 10	a	02 13	05 32				06 32	06 52	07 07			07 19		07 48		
	d	02 16	05 34		06 38		06 35	06 55				07 23		07 50		
Garforth	d				06 50									08 00		
South Milford	a															
Selby	a											07 43				
Howden	a											07 52				
Brough	a											08 04				
Hull	a											08 20				
Wakefield Kirkgate	a									06 59					07 57	
Wakefield Westgate	a									07 06					08 08	
York 8	a	02 47	06 01		07 15		07 01	07 22						08 21		
	d			05 54		06 40	07 06	07 25			07 32			08 23		
Malton	d					07 04		07 49								
Seamer	a					07 21		08 06								
Scarborough	a					07 30		08 15								
Thirsk	a			06 10			07 22				07 54			08 46		
Northallerton	a			06 18			07 30				08 02			08 55		
Darlington 7	a			06 29			07 41									
Yarm	d										08 16			09 10		
Thornaby	a			06 53							08 26			09 22		
Middlesbrough	a			07 01							08 34			09 32		
Durham	a						07 58									
Chester-le-Street	a						08 04									
Newcastle 8 ⇌	a						08 17									

Table 39

Liverpool, Manchester Airport and Manchester - Huddersfield - Wakefield, Leeds, Hull, York, Scarborough, Middlesbrough and Newcastle

		TP	TP	TP	NT	TP	NT	NT	NT	TP	NT	NT	TP	TP	NT	TP	NT	TP	TP	NT	NT
		◇1 ℸ	◇1	◇1 ℸ		◇1 ℸ				◇1 ℸ			◇1 A	◇1 ℸ		◇1 ℸ		◇1	◇1 ℸ		
Liverpool Lime Street 10	d	06 16						06 46						07 16	07 16						
Warrington Central	d	06 38												07 40							
Birchwood	d	06 43												07 45							
Manchester Oxford Road	d	07b07												08 06							
Manchester Airport ✈	d			07 05						07 33						08 05			08 35		
Manchester Piccadilly 10 ⇌	a	07 09		07 22						07 48				08 08		08 22			08 49		
	d	07 11		07 26		07 36				07 55				08 10		08 26		08 42	08 57		
Manchester Victoria ⇌	d						07 40	07c57							08e27						
Ashton-under-Lyne	d						07 49	08 07							08 37						
Stalybridge	a	07 26				07 49	07 54	08 13		08 08				08 26	08 41						
	d	07 26				07 49	07 54			08 09				08 26	08 42						
Mossley (Grtr Manchester)	d						07 59								08 46						
Greenfield	d						08 03								08 50						
Marsden	d						08 11								08 59						
Slaithwaite	d						08 16								09 03						
Huddersfield	a	07 44		07 56		08 09	08 24			08 28				08 44	09 12	08 56		09 15	09 26		
	d	07 45		07 57		08 10			08 14	08 30	08 33	08 37		08 45		08 57		09 16	09 27	09 31	09 35
Deighton	d								08 17		08 36	08 40								09 34	09 38
Mirfield	d				08 06				08 23		08 41	08 45					09 07			09 39	09 43
Ravensthorpe	d								08 26		08 44									09 42	
Dewsbury	a	07 54		08 06	08 11	08 19			08 29	08 39	08 48					09 06	09 12		09 36	09 46	
	d	07 55		08 07	08 12	08 20			08 30	08 39	08 53					09 07	09 12		09 37	09 46	
Batley	d				08 15				08 33		08 56						09 15			09 49	
Morley	d				08 21				08 39		09 02						09 21			09 55	
Cottingley	d				08 24				08 42		09 06									09 59	
Leeds 10	a	08 10		08 24	08 33	08 36			08 51	08 54	09 16			09 06		09 22	09 31	09 36	09 52	10 07	
	d	08 12		08 27		08 38				08 57				09 12		09 27		09 38	09 57		
Garforth	d									09 05									10 05		
South Milford	a																				
Selby	a					08 58												09 57			
Howden	a																				
Brough	a																	10 15			
Hull	a					09 31												10 34			
Wakefield Kirkgate	a											09 05									10 03
Wakefield Westgate	a											09 12									10 10
York 8	a	08 34		08 54						09 23				09 35		09 52			10 23		
	d	08 38	08 42	08 57						09 26			09 28	09 38		09 56			10 26		
Malton	d	09 02												10 02							
Seamer	a	09 19												10 19							
Scarborough	a	09 30											10 14	10 30							
Thirsk	a									09 46									10 46		
Northallerton	a		09 02	09 17						09 55						10 25			10 55		
Darlington 7	a		09 14	09 29												10 36					
Yarm	d									10 10									11 10		
Thornaby	a									10 22									11 22		
Middlesbrough	a									10 30									11 31		
Durham	a		09 31	09 46												10 53					
Chester-le-Street	a															10 59					
Newcastle 8 ⇌	a		09 48	10 02												11 12					

A from 17 July until 4 September
b arr. 0700
c arr. 0749
e arr. 0819

Table 39

Saturdays

Liverpool, Manchester Airport and Manchester - Huddersfield - Wakefield, Leeds, Hull, York, Scarborough, Middlesbrough and Newcastle

		TP	NT	TP	NT	NT	TP	TP	NT	NT	NT	TP	TP	TP	NT	NT	TP	TP	NT
		◇1		◇1			◇1	◇1				◇1 A	◇1	◇1			◇1	◇1	
Liverpool Lime Street 10	d	08 22								08 44			09 22						
Warrington Central	d	08 44											09 44						
Birchwood	d	08 49											09 49						
Manchester Oxford Road	d	09 07											10 07						
Manchester Airport	d			09 05				09 35						10 05				10 35	
Manchester Piccadilly 10	a	09 09		09 22				09 52					10 09	10 22				10 52	
	d	09 11		09 26			09 42	09 57					10 11	10 27			10 42	10 57	
Manchester Victoria	d		08 57			09 27				09b57						10 27			
Ashton-under-Lyne	d		09 07			09 37				10 07						10 37			
Stalybridge	a	09 26	09 13			09 42				10 13			10 26			10 42			
	d	09 26				09 42							10 26			10 42			
Mossley (Grtr Manchester)	d					09 47										10 47			
Greenfield	d					09 51										10 51			
Marsden	d					09 59										10 59			
Slaithwaite	d					10 04										11 04			
Huddersfield	a	09 44		09 56		10 12	10 15	10 26					10 44	10 56		11 12	11 15	11 26	
	d	09 45		09 57			10 16	10 27	10 31		10 35		10 45	10 57			11 16	11 27	11 31
Deighton	d								10 34		10 38								11 34
Mirfield	d				10 07				10 39		10 43				11 07				11 39
Ravensthorpe	d								10 42										11 42
Dewsbury	a			10 06	10 12			10 36	10 46					11 06	11 12			11 36	11 46
	d			10 07	10 12			10 37	10 46					11 07	11 12			11 37	11 46
Batley	d				10 15				10 49						11 15				11 49
Morley	d				10 21				10 55						11 21				11 55
Cottingley	d								10 59										11 59
Leeds 10	a	10 09		10 22	10 31		10 36	10 52	11 07				11 09	11 22	11 33		11 36	11 52	12 07
	d	10 12		10 27			10 38	10 57					11 12	11 27			11 38	11 57	
Garforth	d							11 05										12 05	
South Milford	a																		
Selby	a						10 57										11 57		
Howden	a																		
Brough	a						11 15										12 15		
Hull	a						11 34										12 34		
Wakefield Kirkgate	a										11 02								
Wakefield Westgate	a										11 08								
York 8	a	10 35		10 52				11 23					11 35	11 52				12 23	
	d	10 38		10 54				11 26				11 28	11 38	11 54				12 26	
Malton	d	11 02											12 02						
Seamer	a	11 19											12 19						
Scarborough	a	11 30										12 14	12 30						
Thirsk	a							11 46										12 46	
Northallerton	a			11 15				11 55						12 15				12 55	
Darlington 7	a			11 27										12 27					
Yarm	d							12 10										13 10	
Thornaby	a							12 19										13 21	
Middlesbrough	a							12 28										13 30	
Durham	a			11 44										12 44					
Chester-le-Street	a																		
Newcastle 8	a			11 59										12 59					

A from 17 July until 4 September

b arr. 0947

Table 39

Saturdays

Liverpool, Manchester Airport and Manchester - Huddersfield - Wakefield, Leeds, Hull, York, Scarborough, Middlesbrough and Newcastle

		NT	TP	TP	NT	TP	NT	NT	TP	NT	TP	NT	NT	NT	TP	TP	NT	NT	TP	TP	NT
			◇1 A	◇1		◇1			◇1		◇1				◇1	◇1			◇1	◇1	
Liverpool Lime Street 10	d			10 22	09 46							10 46			11 22						
Warrington Central	d			10 44											11 44						
Birchwood	d			10 49											11 49						
Manchester Oxford Road	d			11 07											12 07						
Manchester Airport	d					11 05					11 35					12 05				12 35	
Manchester Piccadilly 10	a			11 09		11 22					11 52				12 09	12 22				12 52	
	d			11 11		11 27			11 42		11 57				12 11	12 27			12 42	12 57	
Manchester Victoria	d				10c57			11 27				11b57						12 27			
Ashton-under-Lyne	d				11 07			11 37				12 07						12 37			
Stalybridge	a			11 26	11 13			11 42				12 13			12 26			12 42			
	d			11 26				11 42							12 26			12 42			
Mossley (Grtr Manchester)	d							11 47										12 47			
Greenfield	d							11 51										12 51			
Marsden	d							11 59										12 59			
Slaithwaite	d							12 04										13 04			
Huddersfield	a			11 44		11 56		12 12	12 15		12 26				12 44	12 56		13 12	13 15	13 26	
	d	11 35		11 45		11 57			12 16		12 27		12 31	12 35	12 45	12 57			13 16	13 27	13 31
Deighton	d	11 38											12 34	12 38							13 34
Mirfield	d	11 43					12 07						12 39	12 43			13 07				13 39
Ravensthorpe	d												12 42								13 42
Dewsbury	a					12 06	12 12				12 36		12 46			13 06	13 12			13 36	13 46
	d					12 07	12 12				12 37		12 46			13 07	13 12			13 37	13 46
Batley	d						12 15						12 49				13 15				13 49
Morley	d						12 21						12 55				13 21				13 55
Cottingley	d												12 59								13 59
Leeds 10	a			12 09		12 22	12 31		12 36	12 39	12 52		13 07		13 09	13 22	13 31		13 36	13 52	14 07
	d			12 12		12 27			12 38	12 41	12 57				13 12	13 27			13 38	13 57	
Garforth	d									12 53	13 05									14 05	
South Milford	a																				
Selby	a								12 57										13 57		
Howden	a																				
Brough	a								13 15										14 15		
Hull	a								13 34										14 34		
Wakefield Kirkgate	a	12 02												13 02							
Wakefield Westgate	a	12 08												13 08							
York 8	a			12 35		12 52				13 19	13 23				13 35	13 52				14 23	
	d		12 28	12 38		12 54					13 26				13 38	13 54				14 26	
Malton	d			13 02											14 02						
Seamer	a			13 19											14 19						
Scarborough	a		13 14	13 30											14 30						
Thirsk	a										13 43									14 46	
Northallerton	a					13 23					13 55					14 22				15 00	
Darlington 7	a					13 34										14 34					
Yarm	d										14 10									15 14	
Thornaby	a										14 19									15 28	
Middlesbrough	a										14 28									15 35	
Durham	a					13 50										14 50					
Chester-le-Street	a					13 57															
Newcastle 8	a					14 10										15 06					

A from 17 July until 4 September

b arr. 1149

c arr. 1049

Table 39

Saturdays

Liverpool, Manchester Airport and Manchester - Huddersfield - Wakefield, Leeds, Hull, York, Scarborough, Middlesbrough and Newcastle

		NT	TP	NT	TP	NT	NT	TP	TP	NT	NT	NT	TP	TP	NT	NT	TP	TP	NT	NT
			◇1		◇1			◇1	◇1				◇1	◇1			◇1	◇1		
Liverpool Lime Street 10	d		12 22	11 46								12 46	13 22							13 46
Warrington Central	d		12 44										13 44							
Birchwood	d		12 49										13 49							
Manchester Oxford Road	d		13 07										14 07							
Manchester Airport ✈	d				13 05				13 35					14 05				14 35		
Manchester Piccadilly 10	a		13 09		13 22				13 52				14 09	14 22				14 52		
	d		13 11		13 27			13 42	13 57				14 11	14 27			14 42	14 57		
Manchester Victoria	d			12e57			13 27					13b57				14 27				14c57
Ashton-under-Lyne	d			13 07			13 37					14 07				14 37				15 07
Stalybridge	a		13 26	13 13			13 42					14 13	14 26			14 42				15 13
	d		13 26				13 42						14 26			14 42				
Mossley (Grtr Manchester)	d						13 47									14 47				
Greenfield	d						13 51									14 51				
Marsden	d						13 59									14 59				
Slaithwaite	d						14 04									15 04				
Huddersfield	a	13 29	13 44		13 56		14 12	14 15	14 26		14 29		14 44	14 56		15 12	15 15	15 26		
	d	13 35	13 45		13 57			14 16	14 27	14 31	14 35		14 45	14 57			15 16	15 27	15 31	
Deighton	d	13 38								14 34	14 38								15 34	
Mirfield	d	13 43				14 07				14 39	14 43				15 07				15 39	
Ravensthorpe	d									14 42									15 42	
Dewsbury	a				14 06	14 12			14 36	14 46				15 06	15 12			15 36	15 46	
	d				14 07	14 12			14 37	14 46				15 07	15 12			15 37	15 46	
Batley	d					14 15				14 49					15 15				15 49	
Morley	d					14 21				14 55					15 21				15 55	
Cottingley	d									14 59									15 59	
Leeds 10	a		14 09		14 22	14 31		14 36	14 52	15 07			15 09	15 22	15 31		15 36	15 52	16 07	
	d		14 12		14 27			14 38	14 57				15 12	15 27			15 38	15 57		
Garforth	d								15 05									16 05		
South Milford	a																			
Selby	a							14 57									15 57			
Howden	a																			
Brough	a							15 15									16 15			
Hull	a							15 34									16 34			
Wakefield Kirkgate	a	14 02									15 02									
Wakefield Westgate	a	14 08									15 08									
York 8	a		14 35		14 52				15 23				15 35	15 54				16 23		
	d		14 38		14 54				15 26				15 38					16 26		
Malton	d		15 02										16 02							
Seamer	a		15 19										16 19							
Scarborough	a		15 30										16 30							
Thirsk	a								15 46									16 46		
Northallerton	a				15 22				15 55									16 55		
Darlington 7	a				15 34															
Yarm	d								16 10									17 10		
Thornaby	a								16 22									17 22		
Middlesbrough	a								16 30									17 33		
Durham	a				15 50															
Chester-le-Street	a				15 57															
Newcastle 8	a				16 12															

b arr. 1349
e arr. 1249

b arr. 1349

Table 39

Saturdays

Liverpool, Manchester Airport and Manchester - Huddersfield - Wakefield, Leeds, Hull, York, Scarborough, Middlesbrough and Newcastle

		NT	TP	TP	NT	NT	TP	NT	TP	NT	NT	TP	TP	NT	NT	NT	TP	TP	NT	NT
			◇1	◇1			◇1		◇1			◇1	◇1				◇1	◇1		
Liverpool Lime Street 10	d		14 22					14 46				15 22				15 46				
Warrington Central	d		14 44									15 44								
Birchwood	d		14 49									15 49								
Manchester Oxford Road	d		15 07									16 07								
Manchester Airport ✈	d			15 05					15 35				16 05					16 35		
Manchester Piccadilly 10	a		15 09	15 22					15 52			16 09	16 22					16 52		
	d		15 11	15 27			15 42		15 57			16 11	16 27				16 42	16 56		
Manchester Victoria	d					15 27		15b57							16 27	16c57				
Ashton-under-Lyne	d					15 37		16 07							16 37	17 07				
Stalybridge	a		15 26			15 42		16 13				16 26			16 42	17 13		17 09		
	d		15 26			15 42						16 26			16 42			17 09		
Mossley (Grtr Manchester)	d					15 47									16 47					
Greenfield	d					15 51									16 51					
Marsden	d					15 59									16 59				17 29	
Slaithwaite	d					16 04									17 04				17 33	
Huddersfield	a		15 44	15 56		16 12	16 15		16 26			16 44	16 56		17 12		17 15	17 27	17 41	
	d	15 35	15 45	15 57			16 16		16 27	16 31	16 35	16 45	16 57				17 16	17 28		17 31
Deighton	d	15 38								16 34	16 38									17 34
Mirfield	d	15 43			16 07					16 39	16 43			17 07						17 39
Ravensthorpe	d									16 42										17 42
Dewsbury	a			16 06	16 12				16 36	16 46			17 06	17 12				17 36		17 46
	d			16 07	16 12				16 37	16 46			17 07	17 12				17 37		17 46
Batley	d				16 15					16 49				17 15						17 49
Morley	d				16 21					16 55				17 21						17 55
Cottingley	d									16 59										17 59
Leeds 10	a		16 09	16 22	16 31		16 36		16 52	17 07		17 09	17 22	17 31			17 36	17 52		18 06
	d		16 12	16 27			16 38		16 57			17 12	17 24				17 38	17 57		
Garforth	d								17 05				17 34					18 05		
South Milford	a																			
Selby	a						17 00										17 57			
Howden	a																18 06			
Brough	a						17 18										18 18			
Hull	a						17 37										18 37			
Wakefield Kirkgate	a	16 02									17 02									
Wakefield Westgate	a	16 08									17 08									
York 8	a		16 35	16 52					17 23			17 35	17 57					18 23		
	d		16 38	17 02					17 26			17 38						18 26		
Malton	d		17 02									18 02								
Seamer	a		17 19									18 19								
Scarborough	a		17 30									18 30								
Thirsk	a			17 20					17 42									18 46		
Northallerton	a			17 28					17 52									18 55		
Darlington 7	a			17 37																
Yarm	d								18 07									19 09		
Thornaby	a								18 26									19 18		
Middlesbrough	a								18 32									19 28		
Durham	a			17 55																
Chester-le-Street	a			18 01																
Newcastle 8	a			18 15																

b arr. 1549

c arr. 1649

Table 39

Saturdays

Liverpool, Manchester Airport and Manchester - Huddersfield - Wakefield, Leeds, Hull, York, Scarborough, Middlesbrough and Newcastle

		NT	TP	TP	NT	NT	TP	TP	NT	NT	NT	TP	NT	TP	TP	NT	TP	TP	NT
			◇1	◇1			◇1	◇1				◇1		◇1 A	◇1 B		◇1	◇1	
Liverpool Lime Street 10	d		16 22								16 46	17 22							
Warrington Central	d		16 44									17 44							
Birchwood	d		16 49									17 49							
Manchester Oxford Road	d		17 07									18 07							
Manchester Airport ✈	d			17 05				17 35										18 35	
Manchester Piccadilly 10	a		17 09	17 22				17 52				18 09						18 52	
	d		17 11	17 26			17 42	17 56				18 11					18 42	18 57	
Manchester Victoria	d					17 27					17b57		18 27						
Ashton-under-Lyne	d					17 37					18 07		18 37						
Stalybridge	a		17 26	17 39		17 42		18 09			18 13	18 26	18 42						
	d		17 26	17 39		17 42		18 09				18 26	18 42						
Mossley (Grtr Manchester)	d					17 47							18 47						
Greenfield	d					17 51							18 51						
Marsden	d					17 59							18 59						
Slaithwaite	d					18 04							19 04						
Huddersfield	a		17 44	17 57		18 12	18 15	18 27				18 44	19 12				19 15	19 26	
	d	17 35	17 45	17 58			18 16	18 28	18 31	18 35		18 45					19 16	19 27	19 31
Deighton	d	17 38							18 34	18 39									19 34
Mirfield	d	17 43			18 07				18 39	18 44						19 08			19 39
Ravensthorpe	d								18 42										19 42
Dewsbury	a			18 06	18 12			18 36	18 46			18 55				19 13		19 36	19 46
	d			18 07	18 13			18 37	18 46			18 55				19 13		19 37	19 46
Batley	d				18 16				18 49							19 16			19 49
Morley	d				18 22				18 55							19 22			19 55
Cottingley	d								18 59										19 59
Leeds 10	a		18 09	18 22	18 33		18 36	18 52	19 07			19 10				19 33	19 36	19 52	20 07
	d		18 12	18 27			18 38	18 57				19 12		19 27	19 27		19 38	19 57	
Garforth	d							19 05										20 05	
South Milford	a						18 51										19 51		
Selby	a						19 00										20 00		
Howden	a																20 09		
Brough	a						19 18										20 21		
Hull	a						19 37										20 40		
Wakefield Kirkgate	a	18 02								19 02									
Wakefield Westgate	a	18 08								19 08									
York 8	a		18 35	18 52				19 23				19 35		19 59	20 05			20 23	
	d		18 38	18 56				19 26				19 38						20 27	
Malton	d		19 02									20 02							
Seamer	a		19 19									20 19							
Scarborough	a		19 30									20 30							
Thirsk	a							19 42										20 43	
Northallerton	a			19 20				19 50										20 51	
Darlington 7	a			19 33															
Yarm	d							20 04										21 05	
Thornaby	a							20 12										21 14	
Middlesbrough	a							20 23										21 25	
Durham	a			19 50															
Chester-le-Street	a																		
Newcastle 8	a			20 09															

A from 17 July   B until 10 July   b arr. 1747

Table 39

Saturdays

Liverpool, Manchester Airport and Manchester - Huddersfield - Wakefield, Leeds, Hull, York, Scarborough, Middlesbrough and Newcastle

		NT	TP	NT	TP	NT	NT	NT	NT	TP	TP	TP	NT	NT	NT	TP	TP	NT	NT
			◇1		◇1					◇1	◇1	◇1				◇1 A	◇1 B		C
Liverpool Lime Street 10	d		18 22								19 22					20 22	20 22		
Warrington Central	d		18 44								19 44					20 44	20 44		
Birchwood	d		18 49								19 49					20 49	20 49		
Manchester Oxford Road	d		19 07								20 07					21 07	21 07		
Manchester Airport ✈	d				19 19							20 20							
Manchester Piccadilly 10	a		19 09		19 36						20 09	20 36				21 09	21 09		
	d		19 11		19 42						20 11	20 42				21 11	21 11		
Manchester Victoria	d					19 27							20 27					21 27	22 08
Ashton-under-Lyne	d					19 37							20 37					21 37	22 18
Stalybridge	a		19 26			19 42					20 26		20 42			21 26	21 26	21 41	22 25
	d		19 26			19 42					20 26		20 42			21 26	21 26	21 42	
Mossley (Grtr Manchester)	d					19 47							20 47					21 46	
Greenfield	d					19 51							20 51					21 50	
Marsden	d					19 59							20 59	21 19				21 59	
Slaithwaite	d					20 04							21 04	21 23				22 03	
Huddersfield	a		19 44		20 15	20 12					20 44	21 15	21 12	21 30		21 44	21 44	22 12	
	d	19 35	19 45		20 16		20 25	20 31	20 35		20 45	21 16		21 31	21 35	21 45	21 45		
Deighton	d	19 38						20 34	20 38					21 34	21 39				
Mirfield	d	19 43		20 07				20 39	20 43					21 39	21 44				
Ravensthorpe	d							20 42						21 42					
Dewsbury	a			20 12	20 25			20 46				21 25		21 46					
	d			20 12	20 26			20 46				21 26		21 46					
Batley	d			20 15				20 49						21 49					
Morley	d			20 21				20 55						21 55					
Cottingley	d							20 59						21 59					
Leeds 10	a		20 09	20 34	20 41		21 25	21 07			21 09	21 41		22 07		22 09	22 09		
	d		20 12		20 45					21 08	21 12	21 42				22 12	22 22		
Garforth	d																		
South Milford	a									21 20							22 36		
Selby	a									21 30							22 45		
Howden	a									21 39									
Brough	a									21 51							23 05		
Hull	a									22 08							23 23		
Wakefield Kirkgate	a	20 03							21 02						21 58				
Wakefield Westgate	a	20 09							21 08						22 10				
York 8	a		20 35		21 09						21 40	22 08				22 35			
	d		20 38		21 11							22 11							
Malton	d		21 02									22 35							
Seamer	a		21 19									22 52							
Scarborough	a		21 30									23 01							
Thirsk	a				21 28														
Northallerton	a				21 36														
Darlington 7	a				21 47														
Yarm	d																		
Thornaby	a																		
Middlesbrough	a																		
Durham	a				22 04														
Chester-le-Street	a																		
Newcastle 8	a				22 19														

A from 17 July until 4 September   B until 10 July and from 11 September   C from 11 September

Table 39

Saturdays

Liverpool, Manchester Airport and Manchester - Huddersfield - Wakefield, Leeds, Hull, York, Scarborough, Middlesbrough and Newcastle

		TP ◇1 A	TP ◇1	NT B	NT C	NT B	TP ◇1	TP ◇1 C	NT C	NT B	TP ◇1 B	TP ◇1 B	TP C 🚌	TP C 🚌	TP C 🚌
Liverpool Lime Street 10	d							22 30			22 30				
Warrington Central	d							22 52			22 52				
Birchwood	d							22 57			22 57				
Manchester Oxford Road	d							23 17			23 17				
Manchester Airport ✈	d		21 20				22 22					23 24		23 24	
Manchester Piccadilly 10 🚌	a		21 36				22 36	23 19			23 19	23 39		23u49	
	d		21 42				22 42	23 21			23 21	23 41		23u49	23 49
Manchester Victoria 🚌	d			22 08					23 00	23 00		23 56			
Ashton-under-Lyne	d			22 18					23 10	23 10					
Stalybridge	a		21 55	22 22			22 55	23 36	23 16	23 14	23 34				
	d		21 55	22 23			22 55			23 15	23 34		23 50		
Mossley (Grtr Manchester)	d			22 27						23 19					
Greenfield	d			22 31						23 23					
Marsden	d			22 40						23 32					
Slaithwaite	d			22 44						23 34					
Huddersfield	a		22 15	22 53			23 15			23 44	23 52	00 25	00 35	00s49	00 49
	d		22 16		22 19	22 31	23 16				23 53	00 26	00 35	00s49	00 49
Deighton	d				22 23	22 34									
Mirfield	d				22 28	22 39									
Ravensthorpe	d				22 31	22 42									
Dewsbury	a		22 25		22 34	22 46	23 25					00s35	00s55		
	d		22 26		22 35	22 46	23 26					00s35	00s55		
Batley	d				22 38	22 49									
Morley	d				22 44	22 55									
Cottingley	d				22 47	22 59									
Leeds 10	a		22 41		22 55	23 07	23 41				00 14	00 50	01 20	01s24	01 24
	d	22 22	22 42				23 42				00 15	00 54		01s24	01 30
Garforth	d														
South Milford	a	22 36													
Selby	a	22 45													
Howden	a														
Brough	a	23 05													
Hull	a	23 23													
Wakefield Kirkgate	a														
Wakefield Westgate	a														
York 8	a		23 08				00 10				00 42	01 22		02 09	02 15
	d														
Malton	d														
Seamer	a														
Scarborough	a														
Thirsk	a														
Northallerton	a														
Darlington 7	a														
Yarm	d														
Thornaby	a														
Middlesbrough	a														
Durham	a														
Chester-le-Street	a														
Newcastle 8 🚌	a														

A from 17 July until 4 September
B until 4 September
C from 11 September

Table 39

Sundays
until 11 July

Liverpool, Manchester Airport and Manchester - Huddersfield, Leeds, Hull, York, Scarborough, Middlesbrough and Newcastle

		TP ◇1	TP ◇1	TP ◇1	NT	TP ◇1	TP ◇1	TP ◇1	TP ◇1	NT	TP ◇1	NT	NT	TP ◇1	TP ◇1	TP ◇1	TP ◇1	NT	TP ◇1	NT
Liverpool Lime Street 10	d										08 22					09 22			10 22	
Warrington Central	d										08 44					09 44			10 44	
Birchwood	d										08 49					09 49			10 49	
Newton-le-Willows	d																			
Manchester Oxford Road	d										09 07					10 07			11 07	
Manchester Airport ✈	d	01 22	04 43	06 24		07 24		08 06							09 20		10 19			
Manchester Piccadilly 10 🚌	a	01 35	04 56	06 37		07 37		08 24			09 09				09 37	10 09	10 34		11 09	
	d	01 42	05 02	06 42		07 42		08 28			09 11				09 42	10 11	10 42		11 11	
Manchester Victoria 🚌	a																			
	d									08 43		09 43						10 43		11 43
Ashton-under-Lyne	d									08 53		09 53						10 53		11 53
Stalybridge	a			06 54		07 54		08 39		08 56	09 23	09 57				10 23		10 57	11 23	11 57
	d			06 55		07 55		08 41		08 58	09 24	09 58				10 24		10 58	11 24	11 58
Mossley (Grtr Manchester)	d									09 02		10 02						11 02		12 02
Greenfield	d									09 06		10 06						11 06		12 06
Marsden	d									09 15		10 15						11 15		12 15
Slaithwaite	d									09 19		10 19						11 19		12 19
Huddersfield	a	02 10	05 30	07 11		08 11		08 58		09 28	09 41	10 28			10 11	10 41	11 11	11 28	11 41	12 28
	d	02 12	05 32	07 12	07 51	08 12		09 04			09 43		09 51		10 12	10 43	11 12		11 43	
Deighton	d				07 54								09 54							
Mirfield	d				07 59								09 59							
Ravensthorpe	d				08 02								10 02							
Dewsbury	a			07 21	08 05	08 21		09 11					10 05		10 20		11 21			
	d			07 22	08 06	08 22		09 12					10 06		10 21		11 21			
Batley	d				08 09								10 09							
Morley	d				08 15								10 15							
Cottingley	d				08 19								10 19							
Leeds 10	a	02 32	05 52	07 36	08 27	08 37		09 28			10 08		10 27		10 37	11 03	11 36		12 03	
	d	02 35	05 55	07 40		08 40	09 12	09 40	10 12		10 20				10 40	11 12	11 40		12 12	
Garforth	d																			
South Milford	a										10 33									
Selby	a										10 42									
Howden	a																			
Brough	a										11 03									
Hull	a										11 20									
York 8	a	03 03	06 23	08 08		09 07	09 36	10 06	10 37						11 05	11 37	12 05		12 37	
	d			08 21		09 10	09 40	10 13	10 40					10 45	11 15	11 43	12 15		12 45	
Malton	d						10 04									12 08				
Seamer	a						10 21									12 24				
Scarborough	a						10 32		11 28							12 32				
Thirsk	a			08 36										11 02					13 01	
Northallerton	a			08 44		09 29		10 35						11 10	11 35		12 35		13 09	
Darlington 7	a			08 56		09 41		10 45							11 45		12 46			
Yarm	d													11 24					13 24	
Thornaby	a			09 16										11 33					13 33	
Middlesbrough	a			09 25										11 43					13 43	
Durham	a					10 00		11 07							12 02		13 03			
Chester-le-Street	a																			
Newcastle 8 🚌	a					10 18		11 24							12 20		13 20			

Table 39

Liverpool, Manchester Airport and Manchester - Huddersfield, Leeds, Hull, York, Scarborough, Middlesbrough and Newcastle

		NT	TP ◇1	TP ◇1	TP ◇1	TP ◇1	TP ◇1	NT	TP ◇1	TP ◇1	NT	NT	TP ◇1	TP ◇1	TP ◇1	TP ◇1	NT	TP ◇1	TP ◇1	NT	NT	TP ◇1	TP ◇1	TP ◇1
Liverpool Lime Street 10	d					11 22				12 22					13 22				14 22					15 22
Warrington Central	d					11 44				12 44					13 44				14 44					15 44
Birchwood	d					11 49				12 49					13 49				14 49					15 49
Newton-le-Willows	d																							
Manchester Oxford Road	d					12 07				13 07					14 07				15 07					16 07
Manchester Airport ✈	d			11 17			12 20						13 20			14 20						15 20		
Manchester Piccadilly 10	a			11 34		12 09	12 37			13 09			13 37		14 09	14 37			15 09			15 37		16 09
	d			11 42	12 02	12 11	12 42		13 02	13 11			13 42	14 02	14 11	14 42		15 02	15 11			15 42	16 02	16 11
Manchester Victoria	a																							
	d							12 43			13 43						14 43			15 43				
Ashton-under-Lyne	d							12 53			13 53						14 53			15 53				
Stalybridge	a					12 23		12 57		13 24	13 57				14 23		14 57		15 24	15 57				16 23
	d					12 24		12 58		13 24	13 58				14 24		14 58		15 24	15 58				16 24
Mossley (Grtr Manchester)	d							13 02			14 02						15 02			16 02				
Greenfield	d							13 06			14 06						15 06			16 06				
Marsden	d							13 15			14 15						15 15			16 15				
Slaithwaite	d							13 19			14 19						15 19			16 19				
Huddersfield	a			12 11	12 32	12 41	13 11	13 28	13 31	13 42	14 28		14 11	14 31	14 41	15 11	15 28	15 31	15 42	16 28		16 11	16 31	16 41
	d	11 58		12 12	12 33	12 43	13 12		13 33	13 43		13 58	14 12	14 33	14 43	15 12		15 33	15 43		15 58	16 12	16 33	16 43
Deighton	d	12 01										14 01									16 01			
Mirfield	d	12 06										14 06									16 06			
Ravensthorpe	d	12 09										14 09									16 09			
Dewsbury	a	12 12		12 21			13 21					14 12	14 21			15 21					16 12	16 21		
	d	12 13		12 21			13 21					14 13	14 21			15 21					16 13	16 21		
Batley	d	12 16										14 16									16 16			
Morley	d	12 22										14 22									16 22			
Cottingley	d	12 26										14 26									16 26			
Leeds 10	a	12 34		12 36	12 54	13 04	13 36		13 54	14 04		14 34	14 36	14 54	15 04	15 36		15 54	16 04		16 34	16 37	16 54	17 04
	d			12 40	13 00	13 12	13 40		13 57	14 12			14 40	15 00	15 12	15 40		15 57	16 12			16 40	17 00	17 12
Garforth	d																							
South Milford	a				13 12									15 13									17 13	
Selby	a				13 23									15 22									17 22	
Howden	a																							
Brough	a				13 41									15 41									17 40	
Hull	a				14 00									16 00									18 00	
York 8	a			13 05		13 36	14 06		14 24	14 37			15 05		15 36	16 06		16 24	16 37			17 06		17 36
	d		12 49	13 15		13 40	14 15			14 40			15 15		15 40	16 15			16 40			17 14		17 40
Malton	d					14 04									16 04									18 04
Seamer	a					14 20									16 20									18 20
Scarborough	a		13 35			14 32									16 32									18 32
Thirsk	a									15 02									17 01					
Northallerton	a			13 35			14 35			15 10			15 35			16 35			17 09			17 35		
Darlington 7	a			13 45			14 45						15 45			16 45						17 45		
Yarm	d									15 24									17 24					
Thornaby	a									15 40									17 33					
Middlesbrough	a									15 52									17 43					
Durham	a			14 02			15 02						16 02			17 02						18 02		
Chester-le-Street	a			14 08																		18 08		
Newcastle 8	a			14 22			15 20						16 20			17 20						18 22		

Table 39

Liverpool, Manchester Airport and Manchester - Huddersfield, Leeds, Hull, York, Scarborough, Middlesbrough and Newcastle

		TP ◇1	NT	TP ◇1	TP ◇1	NT	NT	TP ◇1	TP ◇1	TP ◇1	TP ◇1	TP ◇1	NT	TP ◇1	TP ◇1	NT	NT	TP ◇1	TP ◇1	TP ◇1	TP ◇1	NT
Liverpool Lime Street 10	d				16 22						17 22				18 22					19 22		
Warrington Central	d				16 44						17 44				18 44					19 44		
Birchwood	d				16 49						17 49				18 49					19 49		
Newton-le-Willows	d																					
Manchester Oxford Road	d				17 07						18 07				19 07					20 07		
Manchester Airport ✈	d	16 20							17 20			18 20						19 20			20 20	
Manchester Piccadilly 10	a	16 37			17 09				17 37		18 09	18 37			19 09			19 37		20 09	20 37	
	d	16 42		17 02	17 11				17 42	18 02	18 11	18 42		19 02	19 11			19 42	20 06	20 11	20 42	
Manchester Victoria	a																					
	d		16 43			17 43							18 43			19 43						20 43
Ashton-under-Lyne	d		16 53			17 53							18 53			19 53						20 53
Stalybridge	a		16 57		17 23	17 57					18 23		18 57		19 23	19 57				20 23		20 57
	d		16 58		17 24	17 58					18 24		18 58		19 24	19 58				20 24		20 58
Mossley (Grtr Manchester)	d		17 02			18 02							19 02			20 02						21 02
Greenfield	d		17 06			18 06							19 06			20 06						21 06
Marsden	d		17 15			18 15							19 15			20 15						21 15
Slaithwaite	d		17 19			18 19							19 19			20 19						21 19
Huddersfield	a	17 11	17 28	17 31	17 41	18 28			18 11	18 31	18 41	19 11	19 28	19 31	19 41	20 28		20 11	20 35	20 41	21 11	21 28
	d	17 12		17 33	17 43		17 58		18 12	18 33	18 43	19 12		19 33	19 43		19 58	20 12	20 37	20 43	21 12	
Deighton	d						18 01										20 01					
Mirfield	d						18 06										20 06					
Ravensthorpe	d						18 09										20 09					
Dewsbury	a	17 21					18 12		18 21			19 21					20 12	20 21			21 21	
	d	17 21					18 13		18 21			19 21					20 13	20 21			21 21	
Batley	d						18 16										20 16					
Morley	d						18 22										20 22					
Cottingley	d						18 26										20 26					
Leeds 10	a	17 36		17 54	18 04		18 34		18 36	18 54	19 03	19 36		19 54	20 03		20 34	20 37	20 58	21 03	21 36	
	d	17 40		17 57	18 12				18 40	19 00	19 12	19 40		19 57	20 12			20 40	21 04	21 12	21 40	
Garforth	d																					
South Milford	a									19 13												
Selby	a									19 22				20 16					21 38			
Howden	a																					
Brough	a									19 41				20 36					21 57			
Hull	a									20 00				20 56					22 15			
York 8	a	18 06		18 24	18 37				19 06		19 37	20 06			20 37			21 06		21 37	22 05	
	d	18 14			18 40			18 45	19 14		19 40	20 13			20 40			21 08			22 10	
Malton	d										20 04				21 04						22 34	
Seamer	a										20 20				21 20						22 51	
Scarborough	a							19 34			20 32				21 32						23 02	
Thirsk	a				18 58							20 29						21 25				
Northallerton	a	18 35			19 06				19 35			20 37						21 33				
Darlington 7	a	18 45							19 45									21 46				
Yarm	d				19 21							20 52										
Thornaby	a				19 30							21 01										
Middlesbrough	a				19 40							21 12										
Durham	a	19 02							20 02									22 03				
Chester-le-Street	a								20 08													
Newcastle 8	a	19 20							20 22									22 20				

Table 39

Sundays
until 11 July

Liverpool, Manchester Airport and Manchester - Huddersfield, Leeds, Hull, York, Scarborough, Middlesbrough and Newcastle

		TP	NT	TP	NT	TP	TP	TP
		◇1		◇1		◇1	◇1	◇1
Liverpool Lime Street 10	d	20 22					21 52	
Warrington Central	d	20 44					22 14	
Birchwood	d	20 49					22 19	
Newton-le-Willows	d							
Manchester Oxford Road	d	21 07					22 37	
Manchester Airport	d					21 20		23 20
Manchester Piccadilly 10	a	21 09				21 37	22 38	23 37
	d	21 11				21 42	22 42	23 42
Manchester Victoria	a							
	d		21 43					
Ashton-under-Lyne	d		21 53					
Stalybridge	a	21 23	21 57				22 55	
	d	21 24					22 55	
Mossley (Grtr Manchester)	d							
Greenfield	d							
Marsden	d				21 47			
Slaithwaite	d				21 51			
Huddersfield	a	21 41			21 56	22 11	23 13	00 11
	d	21 43			21 57	22 12	23 14	00 12
Deighton	d				22 01			
Mirfield	d				22 06			
Ravensthorpe	d				22 09			
Dewsbury	a				22 12	22 21	23 23	
	d				22 13	22 21	23 23	
Batley	d				22 16			
Morley	d				22 22			
Cottingley	d				22 25			
Leeds 10	a	22 03			22 34	22 37	23 36	00 50
	d	22 12		22 20		22 40	23 40	00 53
Garforth	d							
South Milford	a			22 33				
Selby	a			22 41				
Howden	a							
Brough	a			22 59				
Hull	a			23 18				
York 8	a	22 36				23 11	00 11	01 22
	d	22 42						
Malton	d							
Seamer	a							
Scarborough	a							
Thirsk	a	23 06						
Northallerton	a	23 16						
Darlington 7	a	23 31						
Yarm	d							
Thornaby	a							
Middlesbrough	a							
Durham	a	23 48						
Chester-le-Street	a							
Newcastle 8	a	00 21						

Table 39

Sundays
18 July to 05 September

Liverpool, Manchester Airport and Manchester - Huddersfield, Leeds, Hull, York, Scarborough, Middlesbrough and Newcastle

			TP			TP	TP	NT	TP	TP	TP	NT	TP
			◇1			◇1	◇1		◇1	◇1	◇1		◇1
Liverpool Lime Street 10	d												
Warrington Central	d												
Birchwood	d												
Newton-le-Willows	d												
Manchester Oxford Road	d												
Manchester Airport	d		01 22			04 43	06 24		07 24		08 06		
Manchester Piccadilly 10	a		01 35			04 56	06 37		07 37		08 24		
	d		01 42			05 02	06 42		07 42		08 28	08 32	
Manchester Victoria	a												
	d												
Ashton-under-Lyne	d												
Stalybridge	a						06 54		07 54		08 39	08 44	
	d						06 55		07 55		08 41	08 46	
Mossley (Grtr Manchester)	d											08 49	
Greenfield	d											08 53	
Marsden	d											09 03	
Slaithwaite	d											09 06	
Huddersfield	a		02 10			05 30	07 11		08 11		08 58	09 16	
	d		02 12			05 32	07 12	07 51	08 12		09 04		
Deighton	d							07 54					
Mirfield	d							07 59					
Ravensthorpe	d							08 02					
Dewsbury	a						07 21	08 05	08 21		09 11		
	d						07 22	08 06	08 22		09 12		
Batley	d							08 09					
Morley	d							08 15					
Cottingley	d							08 19					
Leeds 10	a		02 32			05 52	07 36	08 27	08 37		09 28		
	d		02 35			05 55	07 40		08 40	09 12	09 40		10 12
Garforth	d												
South Milford	a												
Selby	a												
Howden	a												
Brough	a												
Hull	a												
York 8	a		03 03			06 23	08 08		09 07	09 36	10 06		10 37
	d						08 21		09 10	09 40	10 13		10 40
Malton	d									10 04			
Seamer	a									10 21			
Scarborough	a									10 32			11 28
Thirsk	a						08 36						
Northallerton	a						08 44		09 29		10 35		
Darlington 7	a						08 56		09 41		10 45		
Yarm	d												
Thornaby	a						09 16						
Middlesbrough	a						09 25						
Durham	a								10 00		11 07		
Chester-le-Street	a												
Newcastle 8	a								10 18		11 24		

		TP		NT	TP	TP	NT	TP		TP	NT	TP	NT
		◇1			◇1	◇1		◇1		◇1		◇1	
Liverpool Lime Street 10	d	08 22						09 22				10 22	
Warrington Central	d	08 44						09 44				10 44	
Birchwood	d	08 49						09 49				10 49	
Newton-le-Willows	d												
Manchester Oxford Road	d	09 07						10 07				11 07	
Manchester Airport	d					09 20				10 19			
Manchester Piccadilly 10	a	09 09				09 37		10 09		10 34		11 09	
	d	09 11				09 42	09 45	10 11		10 42	10 45	11 11	
Manchester Victoria	a												
	d												
Ashton-under-Lyne	d												
Stalybridge	a	09 23					09 58	10 23			10 58	11 23	
	d	09 24					09 59	10 24			10 59	11 24	
Mossley (Grtr Manchester)	d						10 04				11 04		
Greenfield	d						10 08				11 08		
Marsden	d						10 17				11 17		
Slaithwaite	d						10 21				11 21		
Huddersfield	a	09 41				10 11	10 29	10 41		11 11	11 29	11 41	
	d	09 43		09 51		10 12		10 43		11 12		11 43	11 58
Deighton	d			09 54									12 01
Mirfield	d			09 59									12 06
Ravensthorpe	d			10 02									12 09
Dewsbury	a			10 05		10 20				11 21			12 12
	d			10 06		10 21				11 21			12 13
Batley	d			10 09									12 16
Morley	d			10 15									12 22
Cottingley	d			10 19									12 26
Leeds 10	a	10 08		10 27		10 37		11 03		11 36		12 03	12 34
	d	10 20				10 40		11 12		11 40		12 12	
Garforth	d												
South Milford	a	10 33											
Selby	a	10 42											
Howden	a												
Brough	a	11 03											
Hull	a	11 20											
York 8	a					11 05		11 37		12 05		12 37	
	d				10 45	11 15		11 43		12 15		12 45	
Malton	d							12 08					
Seamer	a							12 24					
Scarborough	a							12 32					
Thirsk	a				11 02							13 01	
Northallerton	a				11 10	11 35				12 35		13 09	
Darlington 7	a					11 45				12 46			
Yarm	d				11 24							13 24	
Thornaby	a				11 33							13 33	
Middlesbrough	a				11 43							13 43	
Durham	a					12 02				13 03			
Chester-le-Street	a												
Newcastle 8	a					12 20				13 20			

Table 39

Sundays
18 July to 05 September

Liverpool, Manchester Airport and Manchester - Huddersfield, Leeds, Hull, York, Scarborough, Middlesbrough and Newcastle

		TP ◇1	TP ◇1	NT	TP ◇1	TP ◇1	TP ◇1	NT	TP ◇1	TP ◇1	NT	TP ◇1	NT
Liverpool Lime Street 10	d					11 22				12 22			
Warrington Central	d					11 44				12 44			
Birchwood	d					11 49				12 49			
Newton-le-Willows	d												
Manchester Oxford Road	d					12 07				13 07			
Manchester Airport ✈	d		11 17				12 20					13 20	
Manchester Piccadilly 10 ⇌	a		11 34			12 09	12 37			13 09		13 37	
	d		11 42	11 45	12 02	12 11	12 42	12 45	13 02	13 11		13 42	13 45
Manchester Victoria ⇌	a												
	d												
Ashton-under-Lyne	d												
Stalybridge	a			11 58		12 23		12 58		13 24			13 58
	d			11 59		12 24		12 59		13 24			13 59
Mossley (Grtr Manchester)	d			12 04				13 04					14 04
Greenfield	d			12 08				13 08					14 08
Marsden	d			12 17				13 16					14 17
Slaithwaite	d			12 21				13 20					14 21
Huddersfield	a		12 11	12 29	12 32	12 41	13 11	13 29	13 31	13 42		14 11	14 29
	d		12 12		12 33	12 43	13 12		13 33	13 43	13 58	14 12	
Deighton	d										14 01		
Mirfield	d										14 06		
Ravensthorpe	d										14 09		
Dewsbury	a		12 21				13 21				14 12	14 21	
	d		12 21				13 21				14 13	14 21	
Batley	d										14 16		
Morley	d										14 22		
Cottingley	d										14 26		
Leeds 10	a		12 36		12 54	13 04	13 36		13 54	14 04	14 34	14 36	
	d		12 40		13 00	13 12	13 40		13 57	14 12		14 40	
Garforth	d												
South Milford	a				13 12								
Selby	a				13 23								
Howden	a												
Brough	a				13 41								
Hull	a				14 00								
York 8	a		13 05			13 36	14 06		14 24	14 37		15 05	
	d	12 49	13 15			13 40	14 15			14 40		15 15	
Malton	d					14 04							
Seamer	a					14 20							
Scarborough	a	13 35				14 32							
Thirsk	a									15 02			
Northallerton	a		13 35				14 35			15 10		15 35	
Darlington 7	a		13 45				14 45					15 45	
Yarm	d									15 24			
Thornaby	a									15 40			
Middlesbrough	a									15 52			
Durham	a		14 02				15 02					16 02	
Chester-le-Street	a		14 08										
Newcastle 8 ⇌	a		14 22				15 20					16 20	

		TP ◇1	TP ◇1	TP ◇1		NT	TP ◇1	TP ◇1	NT	TP ◇1	NT	TP ◇1	TP ◇1
Liverpool Lime Street 10	d		13 22					14 22					15 22
Warrington Central	d		13 44					14 44					15 44
Birchwood	d		13 49					14 49					15 49
Newton-le-Willows	d												
Manchester Oxford Road	d		14 07					15 07					16 07
Manchester Airport ✈	d			14 20						15 20			
Manchester Piccadilly 10 ⇌	a		14 09	14 37				15 09		15 37			16 09
	d	14 02	14 11	14 42		14 45	15 02	15 11		15 42	15 45	16 02	16 11
Manchester Victoria ⇌	a												
	d												
Ashton-under-Lyne	d												
Stalybridge	a		14 23			14 58		15 24			15 58		16 23
	d		14 24			14 59		15 24			15 59		16 24
Mossley (Grtr Manchester)	d					15 04					16 04		
Greenfield	d					15 08					16 08		
Marsden	d					15 17					16 17		
Slaithwaite	d					15 21					16 21		
Huddersfield	a	14 32	14 41	15 11		15 29	15 32	15 42		16 11	16 29	16 32	16 41
	d	14 33	14 43	15 12			15 33	15 43	15 58	16 12		16 33	16 43
Deighton	d								16 01				
Mirfield	d								16 06				
Ravensthorpe	d								16 09				
Dewsbury	a			15 21					16 12	16 21			
	d			15 21					16 13	16 21			
Batley	d								16 16				
Morley	d								16 22				
Cottingley	d								16 26				
Leeds 10	a	14 53	15 04	15 36			15 53	16 04	16 34	16 37		16 53	17 04
	d	15 00	15 12	15 40			15 57	16 12		16 40		17 00	17 12
Garforth	d												
South Milford	a	15 12										17 13	
Selby	a	15 23										17 22	
Howden	a												
Brough	a	15 40										17 40	
Hull	a	16 00										18 00	
York 8	a		15 36	16 06			16 24	16 37		17 06			17 36
	d		15 40	16 15				16 40		17 14			17 40
Malton	d		16 04										18 04
Seamer	a		16 20										18 20
Scarborough	a		16 32										18 32
Thirsk	a							17 01					
Northallerton	a			16 35				17 09		17 35			
Darlington 7	a			16 45						17 45			
Yarm	d							17 24					
Thornaby	a							17 33					
Middlesbrough	a							17 43					
Durham	a			17 02						18 02			
Chester-le-Street	a									18 08			
Newcastle 8 ⇌	a			17 20						18 22			

Table 39

Sundays
18 July to 05 September

Liverpool, Manchester Airport and Manchester - Huddersfield, Leeds, Hull, York, Scarborough, Middlesbrough and Newcastle

		TP ◇1		NT	TP ◇1	TP ◇1	NT	TP ◇1	TP ◇1	NT	TP ◇1	TP ◇1	
Liverpool Lime Street 10	d					16 22						17 22	
Warrington Central	d					16 44						17 44	
Birchwood	d					16 49						17 49	
Newton-le-Willows	d												
Manchester Oxford Road	d					17 07						18 07	
Manchester Airport ✈	d	16 20							17 20				
Manchester Piccadilly 10 ⇌	a	16 37				17 09			17 37			18 09	
	d	16 42		16 45	17 02	17 11			17 42	17 45	18 02	18 11	
Manchester Victoria ⇌	a												
	d												
Ashton-under-Lyne	d												
Stalybridge	a			16 58		17 23				17 58		18 23	
	d			16 59		17 24				17 59		18 24	
Mossley (Grtr Manchester)	d			17 04						18 04			
Greenfield	d			17 08						18 08			
Marsden	d			17 17						18 17			
Slaithwaite	d			17 21						18 21			
Huddersfield	a	17 11		17 29	17 31	17 41			18 11	18 29	18 31	18 41	
	d	17 12			17 33	17 43	17 58		18 12		18 33	18 43	
Deighton	d						18 01						
Mirfield	d						18 06						
Ravensthorpe	d						18 09						
Dewsbury	a	17 21					18 12		18 21				
	d	17 21					18 13		18 21				
Batley	d						18 16						
Morley	d						18 22						
Cottingley	d						18 26						
Leeds 10	a	17 36			17 54	18 04	18 34		18 36		18 54	19 03	
	d	17 40			17 57	18 12			18 40		19 00	19 12	
Garforth	d												
South Milford	a										19 13		
Selby	a										19 22		
Howden	a												
Brough	a										19 41		
Hull	a										20 00		
York 8	a	18 06			18 24	18 37			19 06			19 37	
	d	18 14				18 40		18 45	19 14			19 40	
Malton	d											20 04	
Seamer	a											20 20	
Scarborough	a							19 34				20 32	
Thirsk	a					18 58							
Northallerton	a	18 35				19 06			19 35				
Darlington 7	a	18 45							19 45				
Yarm	d					19 21							
Thornaby	a					19 30							
Middlesbrough	a					19 40							
Durham	a	19 02							20 02				
Chester-le-Street	a								20 08				
Newcastle 8 ⇌	a	19 20							20 22				

		TP ◇1	NT	TP ◇1	TP ◇1	NT	TP ◇1	NT	TP ◇1	TP ◇1		TP ◇1	NT
Liverpool Lime Street 10	d				18 22					19 22			
Warrington Central	d				18 44					19 44			
Birchwood	d				18 49					19 49			
Newton-le-Willows	d												
Manchester Oxford Road	d				19 07					20 07			
Manchester Airport ✈	d	18 20					19 20					20 20	
Manchester Piccadilly 10 ⇌	a	18 37			19 09		19 37			20 09		20 37	
	d	18 42	18 45	19 02	19 11		19 42	19 45	20 06	20 11		20 42	20 45
Manchester Victoria ⇌	a												
	d												
Ashton-under-Lyne	d												
Stalybridge	a		18 58		19 23			19 58		20 23			20 58
	d		18 59		19 24			19 59		20 24			20 59
Mossley (Grtr Manchester)	d		19 04					20 04					21 04
Greenfield	d		19 08					20 08					21 08
Marsden	d		19 17					20 17					21 17
Slaithwaite	d		19 21					20 21					21 21
Huddersfield	a	19 11	19 29	19 32	19 41		20 11	20 29	20 35	20 41		21 11	21 29
	d	19 12		19 33	19 43	19 58	20 12		20 37	20 43		21 12	
Deighton	d					20 01							
Mirfield	d					20 06							
Ravensthorpe	d					20 09							
Dewsbury	a	19 21				20 12	20 21					21 21	
	d	19 21				20 13	20 21					21 21	
Batley	d					20 16							
Morley	d					20 22							
Cottingley	d					20 26							
Leeds 10	a	19 36		19 53	20 03	20 34	20 37		20 58	21 03		21 36	
	d	19 40		19 57	20 12		20 40		21 04	21 12		21 40	
Garforth	d												
South Milford	a												
Selby	a			20 16					21 38				
Howden	a												
Brough	a			20 36					21 57				
Hull	a			20 56					22 15				
York 8	a	20 06			20 37		21 06			21 37		22 05	
	d	20 13			20 40		21 08					22 10	
Malton	d				21 04							22 34	
Seamer	a				21 20							22 51	
Scarborough	a				21 32							23 02	
Thirsk	a	20 29					21 25						
Northallerton	a	20 37					21 33						
Darlington 7	a						21 46						
Yarm	d	20 52											
Thornaby	a	21 01											
Middlesbrough	a	21 12											
Durham	a						22 03						
Chester-le-Street	a												
Newcastle 8 ⇌	a						22 20						

Table 39

Sundays
18 July to 05 September

Liverpool, Manchester Airport and Manchester - Huddersfield, Leeds, Hull, York, Scarborough, Middlesbrough and Newcastle

		TP ◇1	NT	TP ◇1	NT	TP ◇1	TP ◇1	TP ◇1
Liverpool Lime Street 10	d	20 22					21 52	
Warrington Central	d	20 44					22 14	
Birchwood	d	20 49					22 19	
Newton-le-Willows	d							
Manchester Oxford Road	d	21 07					22 37	
Manchester Airport ✈	d					21 20		23 20
Manchester Piccadilly 10	a	21 09				21 37	22 38	23 37
	d	21 11				21 42	22 42	23 42
Manchester Victoria	a							
	d		21 43					
Ashton-under-Lyne	d		21 53					
Stalybridge	a	21 23	21 57				22 55	
	d	21 24					22 55	
Mossley (Grtr Manchester)	d							
Greenfield	d							
Marsden	d				21 47			
Slaithwaite	d				21 51			
Huddersfield	a	21 41			21 56	22 11	23 13	00 11
	d	21 43			21 57	22 12	23 14	00 12
Deighton	d				22 01			
Mirfield	d				22 06			
Ravensthorpe	d				22 09			
Dewsbury	a				22 12	22 21	23 23	
	d				22 13	22 21	23 23	
Batley	d				22 16			
Morley	d				22 22			
Cottingley	d				22 25			
Leeds 10	a	22 03			22 34	22 37	23 36	00 50
	d	22 12		22 20		22 40	23 40	00 53
Garforth	d							
South Milford	a			22 33				
Selby	a			22 41				
Howden	a							
Brough	a			22 59				
Hull	a			23 18				
York 8	a	22 36				23 11	00 11	01 22
	d	22 42						
Malton	d							
Seamer	a							
Scarborough	a							
Thirsk	a	23 06						
Northallerton	a	23 16						
Darlington 7	a	23 31						
Yarm	d							
Thornaby	a							
Middlesbrough	a							
Durham	a	23 48						
Chester-le-Street	a							
Newcastle 8	a	00 21						

Table 39

Sundays
from 12 September

Liverpool, Manchester Airport and Manchester - Huddersfield, Leeds, Hull, York, Scarborough, Middlesbrough and Newcastle

		TP ◇1	TP ◇1	NT	TP ◇1	TP ◇1	NT	TP ◇1	TP ◇1	TP ◇1	NT	TP ◇1	TP ◇1	NT	TP ◇1	NT	TP ◇1	NT	TP ◇1	TP ◇1	TP ◇1	NT
Liverpool Lime Street 10	d							08 19				09 22			10 22					11 22		
Warrington Central	d							08 b05				09 b10			10 b10					11 b10		
Birchwood	d																					
Newton-le-Willows	d							08 35				09 40			10 40					11 40		
Manchester Oxford Road	d																					
Manchester Airport ✈	d					07 40				09 03			10 03				11 03				12 03	
Manchester Piccadilly 10	a					07 53				09 18			10 18				11 17				12 18	
	d					07 55				09 20			10 20				11 20				12 20	
Manchester Victoria	a					08 09		08 56		09 35		10 03	10 35		11 03		11 34			12 03	12 34	
	d			08 43		08 30		09 05		09 38	09 43	10 05	10 38	10 43	11 05		11 38	11 43		12 05	12 38	12 43
Ashton-under-Lyne	d			08 53							09 53			10 53				11 53				12 53
Stalybridge	a			08 58							09 59			10 59				11 59				12 59
	d																					
Mossley (Grtr Manchester)	d																					
Greenfield	d																					
Marsden	d																					
Slaithwaite	d																					
Huddersfield	a					09 15		09 53				10 52										
	d					09 20	09 44	09 54				10 54				11 58			12 30			
Deighton	d						09 47									12 01						
Mirfield	d						09 52									12 06						
Ravensthorpe	d						09 55									12 09						
Dewsbury	a					09 28	09 58			10 20			11 20		11 58	12 12			12 39	12 58		
	d					09 29	10 03			10 21			11 21		11 58	12 13			12 39	12 58		
Batley	d						10 06									12 16						
Morley	d						10 12									12 22						
Cottingley	d						10 15									12 26						
Leeds 10	a					09 44	10 23	10 13		10 37		11 15	11 37		12 10	12 34	12 36		12 54	13 10	13 36	
	d		08 40		09 12	09 47		10 18	10 24	10 40		11 18	11 40		12 12		12 40		13 00	13 12	13 40	
Garforth	d																					
South Milford	a								10 36										13 12			
Selby	a								10 45										13 23			
Howden	a																					
Brough	a								11 03										13 41			
Hull	a								11 22										14 01			
York 8	a		09 07		09 36	10 10		10 41		11 05		11 40	12 05		12 37		13 05			13 37	14 06	
	d	08 21	09 10		09 40	10 13		10 45		11 15		11 43	12 15		12 45		13 15			13 40	14 15	
Malton	d				10 04							12 08								14 04		
Seamer	a				10 21							12 24								14 20		
Scarborough	a				10 32							12 32								14 32		
Thirsk	a	08 36						11 02							13 01							
Northallerton	a	08 44	09 29			10 35		11 10		11 35			12 35		13 09		13 35				14 35	
Darlington 7	a	08 56	09 41			10 45				11 45			12 46				13 45				14 45	
Yarm	d							11 24							13 24							
Thornaby	a	09 16						11 33							13 33							
Middlesbrough	a	09 25						11 43							13 43							
Durham	a		10 00			11 07				12 02			13 03				14 02				15 02	
Chester-le-Street	a																14 08					
Newcastle 8	a		10 18			11 24				12 20			13 20				14 22				15 20	

b by bus

Table 39

Sundays from 12 September

Liverpool, Manchester Airport and Manchester - Huddersfield, Leeds, Hull, York, Scarborough, Middlesbrough and Newcastle

		TP ◇1	TP ◇1	NT	TP ◇1	TP ◇1	NT	TP ◇1	TP ◇1	NT	TP ◇1	TP ◇1	NT	NT	TP ◇1	TP ◇1	TP ◇1	TP ◇1	NT	TP ◇1	TP ◇1	NT	NT	TP ◇1
Liverpool Lime Street 10	d		12 22					13 22				14 22					15 22				16 22			
Warrington Central	d		*12* b *10*					*13* b *10*				14 44					15 44				16 44			
Birchwood	d											14 49					15 49				16 49			
Newton-le-Willows	d		12 40					13 40																
Manchester Oxford Road	d											15 07					16 07				17 07			
Manchester Airport ✈	d				13 03				14 20						15 20			16 20						17 20
Manchester Piccadilly 10	a				13 18				14 37			15 09			15 37		16 09	16 37			17 09			17 37
	d				13 20				14 42		15 02	15 11			15 42	16 02	16 11	16 42		17 02	17 11			17 42
Manchester Victoria	a		13 03		13 34			14 03																
	d		13 05		13 38		13 43	14 05		14 43			15 43						16 43			17 43		
Ashton-under-Lyne	d						13 53			14 53			15 53						16 53			17 53		
Stalybridge	a						13 59			14 57		15 24	15 57				16 23		16 57		17 23	17 57		
	d									14 58		15 24	15 58				16 24		16 58		17 24	17 58		
Mossley (Grtr Manchester)	d									15 02			16 02						17 02			18 02		
Greenfield	d									15 06			16 06						17 06			18 06		
Marsden	d									15 15			16 15						17 15			18 15		
Slaithwaite	d									15 19			16 19						17 19			18 19		
Huddersfield	a								15 11	15 28	15 31	15 42	16 28		16 11	16 31	16 41	17 11	17 28	17 31	17 41	18 28		18 11
	d	13 30		13 58		14 30			15 12		15 33	15 43		15 58	16 12	16 33	16 43	17 12		17 33	17 43		17 58	18 12
Deighton	d			14 01										16 01									18 01	
Mirfield	d			14 06										16 06									18 06	
Ravensthorpe	d			14 09										16 09									18 09	
Dewsbury	a	13 39	13 58	14 12		14 39		14 58	15 21					16 12	16 21			17 21					18 12	18 21
	d	13 39	13 58	14 13		14 39		14 58	15 21					16 13	16 21			17 21					18 13	18 21
Batley	d			14 16										16 16									18 16	
Morley	d			14 22										16 22									18 22	
Cottingley	d			14 26										16 26									18 26	
Leeds 10	a	13 54	14 11	14 34	14 36	14 53		15 10	15 36		15 54	16 04		16 34	16 37	16 54	17 04	17 36		17 54	18 04		18 34	18 36
	d	13 57	14 12		14 40	15 00		15 12	15 40		15 57	16 12			16 40	17 00	17 12	17 40		17 57	18 12			18 40
Garforth	d																							
South Milford	a					15 13										17 13								
Selby	a					15 22										17 22								
Howden	a																							
Brough	a					15 41										17 40								
Hull	a					16 00										18 00								
York 8	a	14 24	14 37		15 05			15 37	16 06		16 24	16 37			17 06		17 36	18 06		18 24	18 37			19 06
	d		14 40		15 15			15 40	16 15			16 40			17 14		17 40	18 14			18 40			19 14
Malton	d							16 04									18 04							
Seamer	a							16 20									18 20							
Scarborough	a							16 32									18 32							
Thirsk	a		15 02									17 01									18 58			
Northallerton	a		15 10		15 35				16 35			17 09			17 35			18 35			19 06			19 35
Darlington 7	a				15 45				16 45						17 45			18 45						19 45
Yarm	d		15 24									17 24									19 21			
Thornaby	a		15 40									17 33									19 30			
Middlesbrough	a		15 52									17 43									19 40			
Durham	a				16 02				17 02						18 02			19 02						20 02
Chester-le-Street	a														18 08									20 08
Newcastle 8	a				16 20				17 20						18 22			19 20						20 22

b by bus

Table 39

Sundays from 12 September

Liverpool, Manchester Airport and Manchester - Huddersfield, Leeds, Hull, York, Scarborough, Middlesbrough and Newcastle

		TP ◇1	TP ◇1	TP ◇1	NT	TP ◇1	TP ◇1	NT	NT	TP ◇1	TP ◇1	TP ◇1	TP ◇1	NT	TP ◇1	NT	TP ◇1	NT	TP ◇1	TP ◇1	TP ◇1
Liverpool Lime Street 10	d		17 22				18 22					19 22			20 22					21 52	
Warrington Central	d		17 44				18 44					19 44			20 44					22 14	
Birchwood	d		17 49				18 49					19 49			20 49					22 19	
Newton-le-Willows	d																				
Manchester Oxford Road	d		18 07				19 07					20 07			21 07					22 37	
Manchester Airport ✈	d			18 20						19 20			20 20						21 20		23 20
Manchester Piccadilly 10	a		18 09	18 37			19 09			19 37		20 09	20 37		21 09				21 37	22 38	23 37
	d	18 02	18 11	18 42		19 02	19 11			19 42	20 06	20 11	20 42		21 11				21 42	22 42	23 42
Manchester Victoria	a																				
	d				18 43			19 43						20 43		21 43					
Ashton-under-Lyne	d				18 53			19 53						20 53		21 53					
Stalybridge	a		18 23		18 57		19 23	19 57				20 23		20 57	21 23	21 57				22 55	
	d		18 24		18 58		19 24	19 58				20 24		20 58	21 24					22 55	
Mossley (Grtr Manchester)	d				19 02			20 02						21 02							
Greenfield	d				19 06			20 06						21 06							
Marsden	d				19 15			20 15						21 15				21 47			
Slaithwaite	d				19 19			20 19						21 19				21 51			
Huddersfield	a	18 31	18 41	19 11	19 28	19 31	19 41	20 28		20 11	20 35	20 41	21 11	21 28	21 41			21 56	22 11	23 13	00 11
	d	18 33	18 43	19 12		19 33	19 43		19 58	20 12	20 37	20 43	21 12		21 43			21 57	22 12	23 14	00 12
Deighton	d								20 01									22 01			
Mirfield	d								20 06									22 06			
Ravensthorpe	d								20 09									22 09			
Dewsbury	a			19 21					20 12	20 21			21 21					22 12	22 21	23 23	
	d			19 21					20 13	20 21			21 21					22 13	22 21	23 23	
Batley	d								20 16									22 16			
Morley	d								20 22									22 22			
Cottingley	d								20 26									22 25			
Leeds 10	a	18 54	19 03	19 36		19 54	20 03		20 34	20 37	20 58	21 03	21 36		22 03			22 34	22 37	23 36	00 50
	d	19 00	19 12	19 40		19 57	20 12			20 40	21 04	21 12	21 40		22 12		22 20		22 40	23 40	00 53
Garforth	d																				
South Milford	a	19 13															22 33				
Selby	a	19 22				20 16					21 38						22 41				
Howden	a																				
Brough	a	19 41				20 36					21 57						22 59				
Hull	a	20 00				20 56					22 15						23 18				
York 8	a		19 37	20 06			20 37			21 06		21 37	22 05		22 36				23 11	00 11	01 22
	d		19 40	20 13			20 40			21 08			22 10		22 42						
Malton	d		20 04				21 04						22 34								
Seamer	a		20 20				21 20						22 51								
Scarborough	a		20 32				21 32						23 02								
Thirsk	a			20 29						21 25					23 06						
Northallerton	a			20 37						21 33					23 16						
Darlington 7	a									21 46					23 31						
Yarm	d			20 52																	
Thornaby	a			21 01																	
Middlesbrough	a			21 12																	
Durham	a									22 03					23 48						
Chester-le-Street	a																				
Newcastle 8	a									22 20					00 21						

Table 40

York and Selby - Leeds

	TP MO	TP MX	TP MO	TP MX	TP MX	TP	NT	TP	NT	NT	TP	XC	TP	NT	TP	TP	NT	TP	NT	NT	NT	TP
York 33 d	01 38	01 38	02 47	02 52	04 00	05 26	05 40	05 57	06 09	06 13	06 23	06 32			06 54		07 06	07 23			07 30	07 40
Ulleskelf 33 d																	07 15					
Church Fenton 33 d																	07 21					
Selby d									06a30				06 36	06 41		07 07			07 22	07 43	07a50	
South Milford d														06 50					07 31	07 53		
Micklefield d							05 58			06 28				06 56			07 28		07 40	07 58		
East Garforth d							06 02			06 32				07 00			07 32		07 44	08 02		
Garforth d							06 05	06 12		06 35				07 02	07 09	07 24	07 35		07 47	08 05		
Cross Gates d							06 09			06 40				07 07			07 40	07 44	07 52	08 10		
Leeds a	02 04	02 19	03 13	03 33	04 42	05 52	06 19	06 22		06 49	06 52	06 56	07 00	07 18	07 20	07 35	07 49	07 52	08 01	08 19		08 04
Bradford Interchange 37 a										07 11				07 43			08 09		08 28	08 42		

	XC	NT	TP	TP	NT	TP	NT	TP	NT	XC	NT	TP	TP	NT	TP	TP	XC	NT	TP	NT	TP	NT
York 33 d	07 44	07 48	07 54		08 12	08 24		08 40	08 43	08 45		08 58		09 09	09 28	09 40	09 44			09 53	09 58	10 11
Ulleskelf 33 d																						
Church Fenton 33 d		08 05												09 21								
Selby d				08 07			08 26		09a06		08 43		09 11					09 43	10 11	10 12		
South Milford d							08 35				08 53							09 52				
Micklefield d		08 13			08 28		08 41				08 58			09 28				09 58				10 29
East Garforth d		08 17			08 32		08 45				09 02			09 32				10 02				10 33
Garforth d		08 20	08 13		08 34	08 41	08 47				09 05	09 13		09 35				10 05			10 13	10 35
Cross Gates d		08 25			08 39		08 52				09 10			09 40				10 10				10 40
Leeds a	08 08	08 35	08 23	08 36	08 48	08 52	09 02	09 04		09 08	09 19	09 23	09 34	09 49	09 53	10 04	10 08	10 19	10 36		10 23	10 49
Bradford Interchange 37 a					09 10						09 42			10 10				10 42				11 10

	NT	TP	TP	XC	NT	TP	NT	TP	NT	TP	TP	XC	NT	TP	NT	TP	NT	NT	TP	TP	XC
York 33 d	10 20	10 28	10 40	10 44		10 58	11 01		11 09	11 28	11 40	11 45			11 53	11 58	12 13	12 18	12 28	12 39	12 45
Ulleskelf 33 d							11 11														
Church Fenton 33 d							11a15		11 21												
Selby d	10a40				10 43			11 09					11 43	12 09	12a18			12a38			
South Milford d					10 53								11 52								
Micklefield d					10 58				11 29				11 58				12 28				
East Garforth d					11 02				11 33				12 02				12 32				
Garforth d					11 05	11 13			11 35				12 05			12 13	12 35				
Cross Gates d					11 10				11 40				12 10				12 40				
Leeds a		10 53	11 04	11 08	11 19	11 23		11 34	11 49	11 53	12 04	12 08	12 19	12 34		12 23	12 49		12 53	13 03	13 08
Bradford Interchange 37 a					11 42				12 10				12 42				13 11				

	NT	TP	TP	NT	TP	TP	XC	NT	NT	TP	TP	NT	TP	TP	XC	NT	TP	TP	NT	NT	NT	TP
York 33 d		12 58		13 09	13 28	13 40	13 44		13 44	13 58		14 13	14 28	14 40	14 44		14 58		14 59	15 02	15 08	15 28
Ulleskelf 33 d																				15 12		
Church Fenton 33 d				13 21																15 16	15 20	
Selby d	12 43		13 09					13 43	14a08		14 09					14 43		15 09	15a18			
South Milford d	12 53							13 53								14 53						
Micklefield d	12 58			13 29				13 58				14 29				14 58					15 29	
East Garforth d	13 02			13 33				14 02				14 33				15 02					15 33	
Garforth d	13 05	13 13		13 35				14 05		14 13		14 35				15 05	15 13				15 35	
Cross Gates d	13 10			13 40				14 10				14 40				15 10					15 40	
Leeds a	13 19	13 23	13 34	13 49	13 53	14 04	14 07	14 19		14 23	14 34	14 49	14 53	15 04	15 08	15 19	15 23	15 34			15 49	15 53
Bradford Interchange 37 a	13 42			14 11				14 42				15 11				15 42					16 10	

	TP	XC FO	XC FX	NT	TP	TP	NT	NT	TP	TP	XC	NT	TP	TP	NT	TP	NT	NT	TP	TP	XC
York 33 d	15 40	15 44	15 44		15 58		16 12	16 13	16 28	16 40	16 44		16 58		17 08			17 27	17 28	17 40	17 44
Ulleskelf 33 d																					
Church Fenton 33 d							16 23								17 20						
Selby d				15 43		16 09	16a39					16 43		17 11		17 32	17 43	17a46			
South Milford d				15 53								16 53					17 53				
Micklefield d				15 58				16 29				16 58			17 28		17 58				
East Garforth d				16 02				16 33				17 02			17 32		18 02				
Garforth d				16 05		16 23		16 35				17 05	17 13		17 35		18 05				
Cross Gates d				16 10				16 40				17 10			17 40		18 10				
Leeds a	16 04	16 07	16 08	16 19	16 22	16 36		16 49	16 53	17 04	17 07	17 19	17 23	17 36	17 49	17 58	18 19		17 53	18 04	18 08
Bradford Interchange 37 a				16 42				17 10							18 10		18 43				

Table 40

York and Selby - Leeds

	TP	NT	NT	TP	TP	NT	TP	XC	NT	NT	NT	TP	TP	TP	XC	TP	NT	NT	TP	XC	TP FO	TP FX	TP FX
York 33 d	17 58		18 05	18 09		18 20	18 40	18 44			19 04	19 10		19 39	19 44	20 10	20 13	20 21	20 40	20 44		21 10	
Ulleskelf 33 d			18 14																				
Church Fenton 33 d			18 20								19 21												
Selby d		18 00			18 29	18a46			18 43	19 00			19 30					20a43			21 06		21 16
South Milford d									18 53												21 16		21 26
Micklefield d			18 29						18 58		19 28						20 27						
East Garforth d			18 33						19 02		19 32						20 31						
Garforth d	18 13	18 18	18 35						19 05	19 15	19 35	19 24					20 34						
Cross Gates d			18 40						19 10		19 40						20 39						
Leeds a	18 23	18 31	18 47	18 35	18 53		19 04	19 08	19 20	19 27	19 48	19 35	19 56	20 03	20 08	20 35	20 48		21 04	21 07	21 35	21 35	21 44
Bradford Interchange 37 a		18 58	19 10						19 44								21 10						

	NT	TP	TP	NT	NT	TP	NT
York 33 d	21 16	21 45		22 03	22 09	23 07	23 13
Ulleskelf 33 d	21 25						
Church Fenton 33 d	21 31				22 21		23 28
Selby d			22 07	22a22			
South Milford d			22 16				
Micklefield d	21 38				22 29		23 35
East Garforth d	21 42				22 33		23 39
Garforth d	21 45				22 36		23 42
Cross Gates d	21 50				22 40		23 47
Leeds a	21 59	22 07	22 35		22 51	23 33	23 56
Bradford Interchange 37 a							

Saturdays

	TP	TP	TP	TP	TP	NT	XC	NT	TP	TP	NT	TP	TP	NT	TP	NT	NT	TP	XC	TP	TP	NT	TP
York 33 d	01 52	02 40	03 52	05 26	05 57	06 05	06 09	06 13	06 28			06 54		07 06	07 28		07 30	07 40	07 44	07 58		08 09	08 26
Ulleskelf 33 d														07 15									
Church Fenton 33 d														07 21								08 22	
Selby d						06a26				06 36	06 41		07 07			07 43	07a50				08 07		
South Milford d											06 50					07 53							
Micklefield d								06 28			06 56			07 28		07 58						08 28	
East Garforth d								06 32			07 00			07 32		08 02						08 32	
Garforth d					06 12			06 35			07 02	07 09		07 35		08 05				08 13		08 35	
Cross Gates d								06 40			07 07			07 40		08 10						08 40	
Leeds a	02 18	03 06	04 34	05 52	06 22		06 54	06 49	06 52	07 00	07 18	07 20	07 35	07 49	07 52	08 19		08 04	08 08	08 23	08 36	08 49	08 52
Bradford Interchange 37 a								07 11			07 43			08 09		08 42						09 12	

	NT	TP	XC	NT	TP	TP	NT	TP	TP	XC	NT	TP	NT	TP	NT	NT	TP	TP	XC	NT	TP	NT
York 33 d	08 34	08 40	08 44		08 58		09 09	09 28	09 40	09 44			09 53	09 58	10 11	10 17	10 28	10 40	10 45		10 58	11 01
Ulleskelf 33 d																						11 11
Church Fenton 33 d							09 21															11 15
Selby d	08a55			08 43		09 11					09 43	10 11	10a12			10a37				10 43		
South Milford d				08 53							09 53									10 53		
Micklefield d				08 58			09 28				09 58				10 29					10 58		
East Garforth d				09 02			09 32				10 02				10 33					11 02		
Garforth d				09 05	09 13		09 35				10 05			10 13	10 35					11 05	11 13	
Cross Gates d				09 10			09 40				10 10				10 41					11 10		
Leeds a		09 04	09 07	09 19	09 23	09 34	09 49	09 53	10 04	10 08	10 19	10 36		10 23	10 49		10 53	11 04	11 08	11 19	11 23	
Bradford Interchange 37 a				09 42			10 10				10 42				11 10					11 42		

	TP	NT	TP	TP	XC	NT	NT	TP	TP	NT	NT	TP	TP	XC	NT	TP	TP	NT	TP	NT	NT
York 33 d		11 09	11 28	11 40	11 45		11 50	11 58		12 13	12 18	12 28	12 40	12 45		12 58		13 09	13 28		13 38
Ulleskelf 33 d																					
Church Fenton 33 d		11 21																13 21			
Selby d	11 09					11 43	12a09		12 09		12a38				12 43		13 09			13 43	14a04
South Milford d						11 53									12 53					13 53	
Micklefield d		11 29				11 58				12 28					12 58			13 29		13 58	
East Garforth d		11 33				12 02				12 32					13 02			13 33		14 02	
Garforth d		11 35				12 05		12 13		12 35					13 05	13 13		13 35		14 05	
Cross Gates d		11 40				12 10				12 40					13 10			13 40		14 10	
Leeds a	11 34	11 49	11 53	12 04	12 08	12 19		12 23	12 34	12 49		12 53	13 04	13 08	13 19	13 23	13 34	13 49	13 53	14 19	
Bradford Interchange 37 a		12 10				12 42				13 11					13 42			14 11		14 42	

York and Selby - Leeds

Saturdays

			TP ◇1 ⌶	XC ◇1 ⌶	TP ◇1 ⌶	TP ◇1	NT	TP ◇1 ⌶	TP ◇1 ⌶	XC ◇1 ⌶	NT	TP ◇1 ⌶	TP ◇1	NT	NT	NT	TP ◇1 ⌶	TP ◇1 ⌶	XC ◇1 ⌶	NT	TP ◇1 ⌶	TP ◇1 ⌶	NT	NT
York	33	d	13 40	13 44	13 58		14 13	14 28	14 40	14 44		14 58		15 05	15 08	15 11	15 28	15 40	15 45		15 58		16 12	16 13
Ulleskelf	33	d														15 22								
Church Fenton	33	d													15 20	15 26							16 23	
Selby		d				14 09					14 43		15 09	15a24						15 43		16 11	16a39	
South Milford		d									14 53									15 53				
Micklefield		d					14 29				14 58				15 29					15 58				16 29
East Garforth		d					14 33				15 02				15 33					16 03				16 33
Garforth		d			14 13		14 35				15 05	15 13			15 35					16 05	16 13			16 35
Cross Gates		d					14 40				15 10				15 40					16 10				16 40
Leeds		a	14 04	14 08	14 23	14 34	14 49	14 53	15 04	15 08	15 19	15 23	15 34		15 49		15 53	16 04	16 08	16 19	16 23	16 36		16 49
Bradford Interchange	37	a					15 11				15 42				16 10					16 42				17 10

			TP ◇1 ⌶	TP ◇1 ⌶	XC ◇1 ⌶	NT	TP ◇1 ⌶	TP ◇1	NT	TP ◇1	NT	TP ◇1 ⌶	TP ◇1	XC ◇1 ⌶	NT	TP ◇1	TP ◇1	NT	TP ◇1 A	TP ◇1 B	NT	TP ◇1
York	33	d	16 28	16 40	16 45		16 58		17 08		17 18	17 28	17 40	17 45		17 58	18 09	18 12			18 13	18 38
Ulleskelf	33	d																			18 22	
Church Fenton	33	d							17 20												18 27	
Selby		d				16 43		17 11		17 32	17a37				17 43				18 29	18 34	18 42	
South Milford		d				16 53									17 53							
Micklefield		d				16 58			17 28						17 58			18 28				
East Garforth		d				17 02			17 32						18 02			18 32				
Garforth		d				17 05	17 13		17 35						18 05	18 13		18 35				
Cross Gates		d				17 10			17 40						18 10			18 40				
Leeds		a	16 53	17 04	17 08	17 19	17 23	17 36	17 49	17 58		17 53	18 04	18 08	18 19	18 23	18 35	18 49	18 53	18 58		19 04
Bradford Interchange	37	a				17 42			18 10						18 43			19 10				

			XC ◇1 ⌶	NT	NT	NT	TP ◇1	TP ◇1	TP ◇1	XC ◇1 ⌶	TP ◇1	NT	TP ◇1	NT	TP ◇1	XC ◇1 ⌶	TP ◇1	NT	TP ◇1	NT	TP ◇1	NT
York	33	d	18 44			19 04	19 10		19 40	19 44	20 10	20 13		20 17	20 40	20 44	21 10	21 18	21 45	21 45		22 09
Ulleskelf	33	d																21 27				
Church Fenton	33	d				19 21												21 33				22 21
Selby		d		18 43	18 55			19 30					20 27	20a36						22a05	22 07	
South Milford		d		18 53									20 36								22 16	
Micklefield		d		18 58		19 28						20 27						21 41				22 28
East Garforth		d		19 02		19 32						20 31						21 45				22 32
Garforth		d		19 05	19 12	19 35	19 24					20 34						21 47				22 35
Cross Gates		d		19 10		19 40						20 39						21 52				22 40
Leeds		a	19 08	19 20	19 25	19 51	19 35	19 56	20 04	20 08	20 35	20 48	20 56		21 04	21 08	21 35	21 57	22 07		22 35	22 51
Bradford Interchange	37	a		19 44								21 10										

			TP ◇1	NT
York	33	d	23 07	23 13
Ulleskelf	33	d		
Church Fenton	33	d		23 28
Selby		d		
South Milford		d		
Micklefield		d		23 35
East Garforth		d		23 39
Garforth		d		23 42
Cross Gates		d		23 47
Leeds		a	23 33	23 56
Bradford Interchange	37	a		

A from 11 September
B until 4 September

Table 40

York and Selby - Leeds

Sundays

			TP A 🚌	TP ◇1 B	TP A 🚌	TP ◇1 B	TP A 🚌	TP ◇1 B	TP A 🚌	TP ◇1 B	TP ◇1 B	TP ◇1	TP ◇1 A	TP ◇1 B	NT	TP ◇1	XC ◇1 ⌶	TP ◇1	TP ◇1 A	NT	TP ◇1	XC ◇1 ⌶	NT	TP ◇1
York	33	d	01 35	02 44	03 40	03 59	04 45	05 12	06 00	06 12	07 12	08 10	08 30	08 40	08 50	09 15	09 28		09 45	09 52	10 15	10 28	10 40	10 45
Ulleskelf	33	d																						
Church Fenton	33	d													09 02					10 04				
Selby		d																09 33					10a59	
South Milford		d																09 42						
Micklefield		d													09 09					10 12				
East Garforth		d													09 13					10 16				
Garforth		d													09 16					10 18				
Cross Gates		d													09 21					10 23				
Leeds		a	02 20	03 10	04 25	04 25	05 30	05 38	06 45	06 38	07 38	08 37	08 55	09 05	09 30	09 38	09 51	10 00	10 08	10 32	10 38	10 51		11 08
Bradford Interchange	37	a													09 53					10 53				

			NT	TP ◇1	XC ◇1 ⌶	TP ◇1	TP ◇1	NT	NT C	TP ◇1	XC ◇1 ⌶	TP ◇1	TP ◇1	NT	TP ◇1	TP ◇1	NT	XC ◇1 ⌶	TP ◇1	NT	TP ◇1	XC ◇1 ⌶	TP ◇1	NT C
York	33	d	10 57	11 15	11 28		11 45	11 52	12 05	12 15	12 28		12 45	12 52	13 15		13 23	13 28	13 45	13 52	14 15	14 28	14 33	14 42
Ulleskelf	33	d																						
Church Fenton	33	d						12 04												14 04				
Selby		d				11 29			12a24			12 33				13 29	13a42							15a01
South Milford		d				11 38										13 38								
Micklefield		d	11 12					12 11						13 07						14 11				
East Garforth		d	11 16					12 15						13 11						14 15				
Garforth		d	11 18					12 18						13 13						14 18				
Cross Gates		d	11 23					12 23						13 18						14 23				
Leeds		a	11 32	11 38	11 51	11 56	12 08	12 32		12 38	12 51	12 56	13 08	13 27	13 38	13 56		13 51	14 08	14 32	14 38	14 51	14 56	
Bradford Interchange	37	a	11 53					12 53						13 53						14 53				

			TP ◇1	NT	TP ◇1	XC ◇1 ⌶	TP ◇1	NT	TP ◇1	NT	TP ◇1	XC ◇1 ⌶	TP ◇1	TP ◇1	NT	TP ◇1	NT C	TP ◇1	NT	XC ◇1 ⌶	TP ◇1	NT	TP ◇1	XC ◇1 ⌶
York	33	d	14 45	14 52	15 15	15 28		15 43	15 45	15 52	16 15	16 28	16 33	16 45	16 52		17 10	17 15	17 17	17 28	17 45	17 52	18 15	18 28
Ulleskelf	33	d																						
Church Fenton	33	d								16 04									17a28			18 04		
Selby		d					15 29	16a02								17 29	17a31							
South Milford		d					15 38									17 38								
Micklefield		d		15 07						16 11					17 07							18 11		
East Garforth		d		15 11						16 15					17 11							18 15		
Garforth		d		15 13						16 18					17 13							18 18		
Cross Gates		d		15 18						16 23					17 18							18 23		
Leeds		a	15 08	15 27	15 38	15 51	15 56		16 08	16 32	16 38	16 51	16 56	17 08	17 27	17 56		17 38		17 51	18 08	18 32	18 38	18 51
Bradford Interchange	37	a		15 53						16 53					17 53							18 53		

			TP ◇1	TP ◇1	NT	TP ◇1	NT	TP ◇1	XC ◇1 ⌶	TP ◇1	NT	TP ◇1	XC ◇1 ⌶	NT	TP ◇1	NT	TP ◇1	TP ◇1	NT	NT	TP ◇1	TP ◇1
York	33	d	18 33	18 45	18 52		19 10	19 15	19 28	19 45	19 52	20 15	20 28	20 42	20 45	20 57	21 15		21 41	21 52	22 12	23 12
Ulleskelf	33	d																				
Church Fenton	33	d									20 04			20a55						22 04		
Selby		d				19 29	19a30											21 31	22a00			
South Milford		d				19 38												21 40				
Micklefield		d			19 07						20 12					21 12				22 12		
East Garforth		d			19 11						20 16					21 17				22 16		
Garforth		d			19 13						20 18					21 19				22 19		
Cross Gates		d			19 18						20 23					21 24				22 23		
Leeds		a	18 56	19 08	19 27	19 56		19 38	19 51	20 08	20 32	20 38	20 51		21 08	21 33	21 38	21 59		22 32	22 38	23 38
Bradford Interchange	37	a			19 53						20 53					21 56						

A from 12 September
B until 5 September
C until 12 September

Table 40

Leeds - Selby and York

		TP MX	TP MO	TP MX	TP MX	TP MO	TP	TP	NT	NT	TP	GR	NT	TP	NT	NT	TP	XC
		◇1	◇1	◇1	◇1	◇1	◇1	◇1			◇1	1 🍴		◇1 ⌶			◇1 ⌶	◇1 ⌶
Bradford Interchange	37 d														07 02	07 20		
Leeds 10	d	00 34	00 54	00 54	02 08	02 34	06 02	06 35	06 38	06 48	06 55	07 10	07 13	07 23	07 29	07 41	07 50	07 57
Cross Gates	d								06 44						07 36	07 48		
Garforth	d								06 50	06 58					07 41	07 53	08 00	
East Garforth	d								06 52						07 43	07 56		
Micklefield	d								06 56						07 47	07 59		
South Milford	d									07 04								
Selby	a									07 20			07 40	07 43				
Church Fenton	33 a															08 05		
Ulleskelf	33 a																	
York 8	33 a	01 16	01 22	01 43	02 47	03 04	06 27	07 31	07 15		07 22	07 33			08 06	08 21	08 21	08 23

		NT	TP	NT	TP	TP	NT	TP	XC	TP	NT	TP	TP	NT	TP	XC	TP	NT	TP
			◇1 ⌶		◇1 ⌶	◇1 ⌶		◇1 ⌶	◇1 ⌶	◇1 ⌶		◇1 ⌶	◇1 ⌶		◇1 ⌶	◇1 ⌶	◇1 ⌶		◇1 ⌶
Bradford Interchange	37 d	07 34		07 50			08 20				08 50			09 20				09 50	
Leeds 10	d	08 00	08 12	08 15	08 27	08 38	08 41	08 57	09 07	09 12	09 15	09 27	09 38	09 41	09 57	10 05	10 12	10 15	10 27
Cross Gates	d	08 06		08 22			08 48				09 22			09 48				10 22	
Garforth	d	08 12		08 27			08 53	09 05			09 27			09 53	10 05			10 27	
East Garforth	d	08 14		08 29			08 56				09 29			09 56				10 29	
Micklefield	d	08 18		08 33			08 59				09 33			09 59				10 33	
South Milford	d	08 22		08 38							09 38							10 38	
Selby	a	08 36		08 55		08 58					09 53		09 57					10 54	
Church Fenton	33 a						09 05							10 05					
Ulleskelf	33 a																		
York 8	33 a		08 34		08 57		09 21	09 23	09 33	09 35		09 55		10 21	10 23	10 27	10 35		10 52

		TP	NT	TP	XC	TP	NT	TP	TP	NT	TP	XC	TP	NT	TP	TP	NT
		◇1 ⌶		◇1 ⌶	◇1 ⌶	◇1 ⌶		◇1 ⌶	◇1 ⌶		◇1 ⌶	◇1 ⌶	◇1 ⌶		◇1 ⌶	◇1 ⌶	
Bradford Interchange	37 d		10 19				10 50			11 20				11 50			12 19
Leeds 10	d	10 38	10 41	10 57	11 05	11 12	11 15	11 27	11 38	11 41	11 57	12 05	12 12	12 15	12 27	12 38	12 41
Cross Gates	d		10 48				11 22			11 48				12 22			12 48
Garforth	d		10 53	11 05			11 27			11 53	12 05			12 27			12 53
East Garforth	d		10 56				11 29			11 56				12 29			12 56
Micklefield	d		10 59				11 33			11 59				12 33			12 59
South Milford	d						11 38							12 38			
Selby	a	10 57					11 55		11 57					12 50		12 57	
Church Fenton	33 a									12 05							
Ulleskelf	33 a																
York 8	33 a		11 19	11 23	11 28	11 35		11 52		12 21	12 23	12 29	12 35		12 52		13 19

		TP	XC	TP	NT	TP	TP	NT	TP	XC	TP	NT	TP	TP	NT	TP	XC	TP	NT
		◇1 ⌶	◇1 ⌶	◇1 ⌶		◇1 ⌶	◇1 ⌶		◇1 ⌶	◇1 ⌶	◇1 ⌶		◇1 ⌶	◇1 ⌶		◇1 ⌶	◇1 ⌶	◇1 ⌶	
Bradford Interchange	37 d				12 50			13 19				13 50			14 19				14 50
Leeds 10	d	12 57	13 05	13 12	13 15	13 27	13 38	13 41	13 57	14 06	14 12	14 15	14 27	14 38	14 41	14 57	15 07	15 12	15 15
Cross Gates	d				13 22			13 48				14 22			14 48				15 22
Garforth	d	13 05			13 27			13 53	14 05			14 27			14 53	15 05			15 27
East Garforth	d				13 29			13 56				14 29			14 56				15 29
Micklefield	d				13 33			13 59				14 33			14 59				15 33
South Milford	d				13 38							14 38							15 38
Selby	a				13 51		13 57					14 50		14 57					15 52
Church Fenton	33 a							14 05											
Ulleskelf	33 a																		
York 8	33 a	13 23	13 29	13 35		13 52		14 21	14 23	14 29	14 35		14 52		15 19	15 23	15 29	15 35	

		TP	TP	NT	TP	XC	TP	NT	TP	TP	NT	TP	XC	TP	NT	TP	NT	TP
		◇1 ⌶	◇1 ⌶		◇1 ⌶	◇1 ⌶	◇1 ⌶		◇1 ⌶	◇1 ⌶		◇1 ⌶	◇1 ⌶	◇1 ⌶		◇1 ⌶		◇1 ⌶
Bradford Interchange	37 d			15 19				15 50			16 19				16 50			
Leeds 10	d	15 27	15 38	15 41	15 57	16 05	16 12	16 15	16 27	16 38	16 41	16 57	17 07	17 12	17 15	17 24	17 28	17 38
Cross Gates	d			15 48				16 22			16 48			17 18	17 23		17 35	
Garforth	d			15 53	16 05			16 27			16 53	17 05			17 29	17 34	17 40	
East Garforth	d			15 56				16 30			16 56				17 31		17 42	
Micklefield	d			15 59				16 34			16 59				17 35		17 46	
South Milford	d							16 39							17 40			
Selby	a		15 57					16 54		17 00					17 53			18 04
Church Fenton	33 a			16 05													17 51	
Ulleskelf	33 a																17 57	
York 8	33 a	15 52		16 21	16 23	16 29	16 35		16 52		17 19	17 23	17 30	17 36		17 57	18 10	

Table 40

Leeds - Selby and York

		NT	NT	TP	XC	TP	NT	TP	XC	TP	NT	TP	XC	TP	NT	TP	TP	NT	TP
				◇1 ⌶	◇1 ⌶	◇1 ⌶		◇1 ⌶	◇1 ⌶	◇1 ⌶		◇1 ⌶	◇1 ⌶	◇1 ⌶		◇1 ⌶	◇1 ⌶		◇1
Bradford Interchange	37 d	17 19					17 50				18 19				18 52			19 19	
Leeds 10	d	17 41	17 49	17 57	18 06	18 12	18 15	18 27	18 35	18 38	18 41	18 57	19 05	19 12	19 15	19 27	19 38	19 41	19 57
Cross Gates	d	17 48	17 56				18 22				18 48				19 22			19 48	
Garforth	d	17 53	18 01	18 05			18 27				18 53	19 05			19 27			19 53	20 05
East Garforth	d	17 56	18 04				18 29				18 56				19 29			19 56	
Micklefield	d	17 59	18 08				18 33				18 59				19 33			19 59	
South Milford	d		18 12				18 38			18 51							19 51		
Selby	a		18 24				18 50			19 00							20 00		
Church Fenton	33 a										19 05								
Ulleskelf	33 a																		
York 8	33 a	18 19		18 23	18 31	18 35		18 52	18 58		19 21	19 23	19 30	19 35	19 54	19 55		20 21	20 23

		XC	TP	TP	NT	TP	TP	NT	TP	TP	TP	NT	TP
		◇1	◇1	◇1		◇1	◇1		◇1	◇1	◇1		◇1
Bradford Interchange	37 d				20 19							22 19	
Leeds 10	d	20 09	20 12	20 45	20 48	21 12	21 42	21 51	22 12	22 22	22 42	22 51	23 42
Cross Gates	d				20 55			21 58				22 58	
Garforth	d				21 00			22 03				23 03	
East Garforth	d				21 02			22 06				23 06	
Micklefield	d				21 06			22 10				23 10	
South Milford	d					21 24				22 36			
Selby	a					21 34				22 45			
Church Fenton	33 a				21 12							23 16	
Ulleskelf	33 a				21 16								
York 8	33 a	20 31	20 35	21 09	21 31		22 08	22 28	22 35		23 12	23 33	00 10

Saturdays

		TP	TP	TP	TP	NT	TP	GR	NT	TP	NT	TP	XC	NT	TP	NT	TP	TP
		◇1	◇1	◇1	◇1		◇1	1 🍴		◇1		◇1 ⌶	◇1 ⌶		◇1 ⌶		◇1 ⌶	◇1 ⌶
Bradford Interchange	37 d										07 20			07 34				
Leeds 10	d	00 34	02 16	05 34	06 35	06 38	06 55	07 10	07 14	07 23	07 41	07 50	07 57	08 00	08 12	08 15	08 27	08 38
Cross Gates	d					06 44					07 48			08 06		08 22		
Garforth	d					06 50					07 53	08 00		08 12		08 27		
East Garforth	d					06 52					07 56			08 14		08 29		
Micklefield	d					06 56					07 59			08 18		08 33		
South Milford	d													08 22		08 38		
Selby	a								07 37	07 43				08 36		08 52		08 58
Church Fenton	33 a										08 05							
Ulleskelf	33 a																	
York 8	33 a	01 16	02 47	06 01	07 01	07 15	07 22	07 34			08 20	08 21	08 25		08 34		08 54	

		NT	TP	TP	NT	TP	TP	NT	TP	XC	TP	NT	TP	TP	NT	TP	XC	TP
			◇1 ⌶	◇1 ⌶		◇1 ⌶	◇1		◇1 ⌶	◇1 ⌶	◇1 ⌶		◇1 ⌶	◇1 ⌶		◇1 ⌶	◇1 ⌶	◇1 ⌶
Bradford Interchange	37 d	08 20			08 50			09 20				09 50			10 19			
Leeds 10	d	08 41	08 57	09 12	09 15	09 27	09 38	09 41	09 57	10 07	10 12	10 15	10 27	10 38	10 41	10 57	11 07	11 12
Cross Gates	d	08 48			09 22			09 48				10 22			10 48			
Garforth	d	08 53	09 05		09 27			09 53	10 05			10 27			10 53	11 05		
East Garforth	d	08 56			09 29			09 56				10 29			10 56			
Micklefield	d	08 59			09 33			09 59				10 33			10 59			
South Milford	d				09 38							10 38						
Selby	a				09 53		09 57					10 53		10 57				
Church Fenton	33 a	09 05						10 05										
Ulleskelf	33 a																	
York 8	33 a	09 21	09 23	09 35		09 52		10 21	10 23	10 30	10 35		10 52		11 19	11 23	11 30	11 35

		NT	TP	TP	NT	TP	XC	TP	NT	TP	TP	NT	TP	XC	TP	NT	TP
			◇1	◇1 ⌶		◇1 ⌶	◇1 ⌶	◇1 ⌶		◇1 ⌶	◇1		◇1 ⌶	◇1 ⌶	◇1 ⌶		◇1 ⌶
Bradford Interchange	37 d	10 50			11 20				11 50			12 19				12 50	
Leeds 10	d	11 15	11 27	11 38	11 41	11 57	12 07	12 12	12 15	12 27	12 38	12 41	12 57	13 07	13 12	13 15	13 27
Cross Gates	d	11 22			11 48				12 22			12 48				13 22	
Garforth	d	11 27			11 53	12 05			12 27			12 53	13 05			13 27	
East Garforth	d	11 29			11 56				12 29			12 56				13 29	
Micklefield	d	11 33			11 59				12 33			12 59				13 33	
South Milford	d	11 38							12 38							13 38	
Selby	a	11 55		11 57					12 50		12 57					13 51	
Church Fenton	33 a				12 05												
Ulleskelf	33 a																
York 8	33 a		11 52		12 21	12 23	12 30	12 35		12 52		13 19	13 23	13 32	13 35		13 52

Table 40

Leeds - Selby and York

Saturdays

	TP	NT	TP	XC	TP	NT	TP	TP	NT	TP	XC	TP	NT	TP	TP	NT	TP
	◇1		◇1 🍴	◇1 🍴	◇1 🍴		◇1 🍴	◇1 🍴		◇1 🍴	◇1 🍴	◇1 🍴		◇1 🍴	◇1		◇1
Bradford Interchange 37 d		13 19				13 50			14 19				14 50			15 19	
Leeds 10 d	13 38	13 41	13 57	14 07	14 12	14 15	14 27	14 38	14 41	14 57	15 07	15 12	15 15	15 27	15 38	15 41	15 57
Cross Gates d		13 48				14 22			14 48				15 22			15 48	
Garforth d		13 53	14 05			14 27			14 53	15 05			15 27			15 53	16 05
East Garforth d		13 56				14 29			14 56				15 29			15 56	
Micklefield d		13 59				14 33			14 59				15 33			15 59	
South Milford d						14 38							15 38				
Selby a	13 57					14 50		14 57					15 52		15 57		
Church Fenton 33 a		14 05														16 05	
Ulleskelf 33 a																	
York 8 33 a		14 21	14 23	14 30	14 35		14 52		15 19	15 23	15 32	15 35		15 54		16 21	16 23

	XC	TP	NT	TP	TP	NT	TP	XC	TP	NT	TP	TP	NT	TP	XC	TP	NT
	◇1 🍴	◇1 🍴		◇1 🍴	◇1		◇1 🍴	◇1 🍴	◇1		◇1	◇1		◇1	◇1 🍴	◇1	
Bradford Interchange 37 d			15 50			16 19				16 50			17 19				17 50
Leeds 10 d	16 07	16 12	16 15	16 27	16 38	16 41	16 57	17 07	17 12	17 15	17 24	17 38	17 41	17 57	18 07	18 12	18 15
Cross Gates d			16 22			16 48				17 23			17 48				18 22
Garforth d			16 27			16 53	17 05			17 29	17 34		17 53	18 05			18 27
East Garforth d			16 30			16 56				17 31			17 56				18 29
Micklefield d			16 34			16 59				17 35			17 59				18 33
South Milford d			16 39							17 40							18 38
Selby a			16 54		17 00					17 53		17 57					18 50
Church Fenton 33 a													18 06				
Ulleskelf 33 a													18 10				
York 8 33 a	16 30	16 35		16 52		17 19	17 23	17 29	17 35		17 57		18 24	18 23	18 31	18 35	

	TP	XC	TP	NT	TP	XC	TP	NT	TP	TP	TP	NT	TP	XC	TP	TP
	◇1	◇1 🍴	◇1		◇1	◇1 🍴	◇1		◇1 A	◇1 B	◇1		◇1	◇1 🍴	◇1	◇1
Bradford Interchange 37 d				18 19				18 50				19 19				
Leeds 10 d	18 27	18 35	18 38	18 41	18 57	19 07	19 12	19 15	19 27	19 27	19 38	19 41	19 57	20 07	20 12	20 45
Cross Gates d				18 48				19 22				19 48				
Garforth d				18 53	19 05			19 27				19 53	20 05			
East Garforth d				18 56				19 29				19 56				
Micklefield d				18 59				19 33				19 59				
South Milford d			18 51								19 51					
Selby a			19 00								20 00					
Church Fenton 33 a				19 05												
Ulleskelf 33 a																
York 8 33 a	18 52	18 59		19 18	19 23	19 31	19 35	19 57	19 59	20 05		20 21	20 23	20 31	20 35	21 09

	NT	TP	TP	XC	TP	NT	TP	TP	TP	NT	TP
		◇1	◇1	◇1 🍴	◇1		◇1 C	◇1	◇1		◇1
Bradford Interchange 37 d	20 19									22 19	
Leeds 10 d	20 48	21 08	21 12	21 15	21 42	21 45	22 12	22 22	22 42	22 54	23 42
Cross Gates d	20 55					21 52				23 01	
Garforth d	21 00					21 57				23 06	
East Garforth d	21 02					21 59				23 09	
Micklefield d	21 06					22 03				23 13	
South Milford d		21 21						22 36			
Selby a		21 30						22 45			
Church Fenton 33 a	21 12									23 19	
Ulleskelf 33 a	21 16										
York 8 33 a	21 31		21 40	21 58	22 08	22 22	22 35		23 08	23 36	00 10

Sundays

	TP	TP	TP	TP	TP	TP	TP	TP	TP	TP	TP	NT	GR	XC	TP	TP	TP	NT	XC	TP
	◇1 E	◇1 F	◇1 E	F 🚌	F 🚌	◇1 G	F 🚌	◇1 G	F 🚌	◇1 G	◇1		■ 1 🍴	◇1 🍴	◇1	◇1 G	◇1 F		◇1 🍴	◇1 G 🍴
Bradford Interchange 37 d												08 31						09 20		
Leeds 10 d	00 15	00 15	00 54	01s24	01 30	02 35	03 50	05 55	07 26	07 40	08 40	08 54	09 05	09 08	09 12	09 40	09 47	09 50	10 08	10 12
Cross Gates d												09 00						09 56		
Garforth d												09 06						10 02		
East Garforth d												09 08						10 04		
Micklefield d												09 12						10 08		
South Milford d																				
Selby a																				
Church Fenton 33 a												09 18								
Ulleskelf 33 a																				
York 8 33 a	00 42	00 44	01 22	02 09	02 15	03 03	04 35	06 23	08 10	08 09	09 08	09 34	10 05	09 35	09 37	10 06	10 11	10 29	10 33	10 37

A from 17 July
B until 10 July
C from 17 July until 4 September
E from 30 May until 5 September
F from 12 September
G until 5 September

Table 40

Leeds - Selby and York

Sundays

	TP	TP	TP	NT	NT	TP	XC	TP	TP	NT	TP	XC	TP	NT	TP	TP	XC
	◇1 A	◇1 B	◇1 A	B	A	◇1	◇1 🍴	◇1 B	◇1 A		◇1	◇1 🍴	◇1		◇1	◇1	◇1 🍴
Bradford Interchange 37 d				10 02	10 04					11 02				12 02			
Leeds 10 d	10 16	10 20	10 24	10 27	10 28	10 40	11 08	11 12	11 18	11 25	11 40	12 08	12 12	12 25	12 40	13 00	13 08
Cross Gates d				10 33	10 34					11 32				12 32			
Garforth d				10 39	10 40					11 37				12 37			
East Garforth d				10 41	10 42					11 39				12 39			
Micklefield d				10 45	10 46					11 43				12 43			
South Milford d		10 34	10 36													13 13	
Selby a		10 43	10 46													13 23	
Church Fenton 33 a				10 51	10 52									12 48			
Ulleskelf 33 a																	
York 8 33 a	10 41			11 07	11 08	11 06	11 34	11 38	11 41	11 59	12 06	12 32	12 37	13 02	13 06		13 32

	TP	NT	TP	TP	XC	TP	NT	TP	TP	XC	TP	NT	TP
	◇1		◇1	◇1	◇1 🍴	◇1		◇1	◇1	◇1 🍴	◇1		◇1
Bradford Interchange 37 d		13 02					14 02					15 02	
Leeds 10 d	13 12	13 25	13 40	13 57	14 08	14 12	14 25	14 40	15 00	15 08	15 12	15 25	15 40
Cross Gates d		13 32					14 32					15 32	
Garforth d		13 37					14 37					15 37	
East Garforth d		13 39					14 39					15 39	
Micklefield d		13 43					14 43					15 43	
South Milford d									15 13				
Selby a									15 23				
Church Fenton 33 a							14 48						
Ulleskelf 33 a													
York 8 33 a	13 37	13 59	14 06	14 24	14 32	14 37	15 02	15 06		15 32	15 37	15 59	16 06

	TP	XC	TP	NT	TP	TP	XC	TP	NT	TP	TP	XC	TP	NT	TP
	◇1	◇1 🍴	◇1		◇1	◇1	◇1 🍴	◇1		◇1	◇1	◇1 🍴	◇1		◇1
Bradford Interchange 37 d				16 03					17 02					18 02	
Leeds 10 d	15 57	16 08	16 12	16 25	16 40	17 00	17 08	17 12	17 25	17 40	17 57	18 08	18 12	18 23	18 40
Cross Gates d				16 32					17 32					18 30	
Garforth d				16 37					17 37					18 35	
East Garforth d				16 39					17 39					18 38	
Micklefield d				16 43					17 43					18 41	
South Milford d						17 13									
Selby a						17 23									
Church Fenton 33 a				16 48										18 47	
Ulleskelf 33 a															
York 8 33 a	16 24	16 32	16 37	17 06	17 06		17 32	17 37	18 02	18 06	18 24	18 32	18 37	19 03	19 06

	XC	TP	XC	TP	NT	TP	TP	XC	TP	NT	TP	TP	XC	TP	NT	TP
	◇1 🍴	◇1	◇1 🍴	◇1		◇1	◇1	◇1 🍴	◇1		◇1	◇1	◇1 🍴	◇1		◇1
Bradford Interchange 37 d					19 02					20 02					21 02	
Leeds 10 d	18 57	19 00	19 08	19 12	19 25	19 40	19 57	20 08	20 12	20 25	20 40	21 04	21 08	21 12	21 25	21 40
Cross Gates d					19 32					20 32					21 32	
Garforth d					19 37					20 37					21 37	
East Garforth d					19 39					20 40					21 39	
Micklefield d					19 43					20 43					21 43	
South Milford d		19 13														
Selby a		19 23					20 17					21 38				
Church Fenton 33 a										20 49						
Ulleskelf 33 a																
York 8 33 a	19 21		19 32	19 37	20 01	20 06		20 32	20 37	21 03	21 06		21 32	21 37	21 59	22 06

	TP	TP	TP	NT	TP
	◇1	◇1	◇1		◇1
Bradford Interchange 37 d					
Leeds 10 d	22 12	22 20	22 40	22 43	23 40
Cross Gates d				22 49	
Garforth d				22 55	
East Garforth d				22 57	
Micklefield d				23 01	
South Milford d		22 33			
Selby a		22 42			
Church Fenton 33 a				23 07	
Ulleskelf 33 a					
York 8 33 a	22 37		23 11	23 18	00 11

A from 12 September
B until 5 September

Leeds and Bradford - Huddersfield, Blackpool North, Rochdale and Manchester Victoria via Halifax and Brighouse

		NT	NT	NT	NT	NT	NT	GC ◇1	NT	NT	NT	NT	NT	NT	NT	NT	NT	NT	NT	NT	NT	NT
York	40 d									06 13						07 06						08 12
Selby	40 d													06 41				07 22		07 43		
Leeds	37,39 d	05 08	05 51	06 03	06 13	06 22			06 37	06 51		07 08	07 13	07 22	07 37	07 51		08 08	08 13	08 22	08 37	08 51
Bramley	37 d	05 15	05 58			06 29			06 44			07 15		07 29	07 44			08 15		08 29	08 44	
New Pudsey	37 d	05 20	06 02	06 13		06 34			06 49	07 01		07 20		07 34	07 49	08 01		08 20		08 34	08 49	09 00
Bradford Interchange	37 a	05 28	06 13	06 21		06 42			06 57	07 11		07 28		07 43	07 57	08 09		08 28		08 42	08 57	09 10
	d	05 32	06 14	06 24		06 45		06 51	07 00	07 14		07 31		07 45	08 00	08 12		08 32		08 45	09 00	09 12
Halifax	a	05 44	06 25	06 36		06 58		07 06	07 13	07 25		07 43		08 00	08 12	08 23		08 44		09 00	09 12	09 24
	d	05 44	06 26	06 36			07 03	07 08	07 13	07 26		07 44		08 06	08 12	08 24		08 44		09 06	09 12	09 24
Dewsbury	39 d				06 29								07 29						08 31			
Mirfield	39 d				06 35								07 35						08 38			
Brighouse	d				06 49		07a13	07a20					07 49	08 16					08 49	09 16		
Huddersfield	39 a													08 29						09 29		
Sowerby Bridge	d	05 51		06 43	06 59				07 20				07 59		08 19				08 59		09 19	
Mytholmroyd	d	05 57		06 49	07 05				07 26				08 05		08 25				09 05		09 25	
Hebden Bridge	a	06 00	06 37	06 52	07 08				07 29	07 37		07 55	08 08		08 28	08 35		08 56	09 08		09 28	09 36
	d	06 00	06 38	06 52	07 08				07 29	07 38		07 56	08 08		08 28	08 36		08 56	09 08		09 28	09 36
Burnley Manchester Road	97 a		06 57							07 57						08 57						09 56
Accrington	97 a		07 06							08 06						09 06						10 06
Blackburn	97 a		07 16							08 14						09 14						10 14
Preston	97 a		07 36							08 38						09 32						10 32
Poulton-le-Fylde	97 a		07 54							08 56						09 50						10 50
Blackpool North	97 a		08 05							09 05						10 00						11 00
Todmorden	d	06 08		06 59	07 15				07 37		07 44	08 04	08 15		08 36			09 04	09 15		09 36	
Walsden	d	06 11		07 02					07 40		07 47				08 39						09 39	
Littleborough	d	06 17		07 09	07 23				07 46		07 53		08 23		08 45				09 23		09 45	
Smithy Bridge	d	06 20		07 11	07 25				07 49		07 56		08 25		08 48				09 25		09 48	
Rochdale	a	06 24		07 15	07 29				07 53		08 00	08 14	08 29		08 51			09 14	09 29		09 51	
	d	06 24		07 16	07 30				07 53		08 00	08 14	08 30		08 51		09 04	09 14	09 30		09 51	
Castleton	d	06 27		07 19	07 33				07 56		08 03	08 17	08 33				09 07		09 33			
Mills Hill	d	06 32		07 24	07 38				08 01		08 08	08 22	08 37				09 12		09 37			
Moston	d	06 35		07 27	07 41				08 04		08 11	08 25	08 40				09 15		09 40			
Manchester Victoria	a	06 48		07 37	07 53				08 14		08 22	08 38	08 53		09 08		09 26	09 32	09 53		10 07	

		NT	NT	NT	NT	NT	NT	GC ◇1	NT	NT	NT	NT	NT	NT	NT	NT	NT	NT	NT	NT	NT	NT	NT
York	40 d						09 09							10 11						11 09			
Selby	40 d				08 43							09 43						10 43					
Leeds	37,39 d		09 08	09 13	09 22	09 37	09 51			10 08	10 13	10 22	10 37	10 51		11 08	11 13	11 22	11 37	11 51		12 08	12 13
Bramley	37 d		09 15		09 29	09 44				10 15		10 29	10 44			11 15		11 29	11 44			12 15	
New Pudsey	37 d		09 20		09 34	09 49	10 01			10 20		10 34	10 49	11 01		11 20		11 34	11 49	12 01		12 20	
Bradford Interchange	37 a		09 28		09 42	09 57	10 10			10 28		10 42	10 57	11 10		11 28		11 42	11 57	12 10		12 28	
	d		09 32		09 45	10 00	10 12	10 22		10 32		10 45	11 00	11 12		11 32		11 45	12 00	12 14		12 32	
Halifax	a		09 44		10 00	10 12	10 24	10 34		10 44		11 00	11 12	11 24		11 44		11 58	12 12	12 25		12 44	
	d		09 44		10 06	10 12	10 24	10 38		10 44		11 06	11 12	11 24		11 44		12 06	12 12	12 26		12 44	
Dewsbury	39 d			09 31							10 29						11 29						12 29
Mirfield	39 d			09 37							10 35						11 35						12 35
Brighouse	d			09 49	10 16			10a50			10 49	11 16					11 49	12 16					12 49
Huddersfield	39 a				10 29							11 29						12 30					
Sowerby Bridge	d			09 59		10 19					10 59		11 19				11 59		12 19				12 59
Mytholmroyd	d			10 05		10 25					11 05		11 25				12 05		12 25				13 05
Hebden Bridge	a		09 56	10 08		10 28	10 36			10 56	11 08		11 28	11 36		11 56	12 08		12 28	12 37		12 56	13 08
	d		09 56	10 08		10 28	10 36			10 56	11 08		11 28	11 36		11 56	12 08		12 28	12 38		12 56	13 08
Burnley Manchester Road	97 a						10 57							11 57						12 57			
Accrington	97 a						11 06							12 06						13 06			
Blackburn	97 a						11 14							12 14						13 14			
Preston	97 a						11 32							12 32						13 32			
Poulton-le-Fylde	97 a						11 50							12 50						13 50			
Blackpool North	97 a						12 00							13 00						14 00			
Todmorden	d		10 04	10 15		10 36				11 04	11 15		11 36			12 04	12 15		12 36			13 04	13 15
Walsden	d					10 39							11 39						12 39				
Littleborough	d			10 23		10 45					11 23		11 45				12 23		12 45				13 23
Smithy Bridge	d			10 25		10 48					11 25		11 48				12 25		12 48				13 25
Rochdale	a		10 14	10 29		10 51				11 14	11 29		11 51			12 14	12 29		12 51			13 14	13 29
	d	10 04	10 14	10 30		10 51			11 04	11 14	11 30		11 51		12 04	12 14	12 30		12 51		13 04	13 14	13 30
Castleton	d	10 07		10 33					11 07		11 33				12 07		12 33				13 07		13 33
Mills Hill	d	10 12		10 38					11 12		11 38				12 12		12 38				13 12		13 38
Moston	d	10 15		10 41					11 15		11 41				12 15		12 41				13 15		13 41
Manchester Victoria	a	10 26	10 32	10 53		11 07			11 26	11 32	11 53		12 07		12 25	12 32	12 53		13 07		13 25	13 32	13 53

For connections to Liverpool Lime Street please refer to Table 90

Table 41

Mondays to Fridays

Leeds and Bradford - Huddersfield, Blackpool North, Rochdale and Manchester Victoria via Halifax and Brighouse

		NT	NT	NT	NT	NT	NT	NT	NT	NT	NT	NT	NT	NT	NT	NT	GC ◇1	NT	NT	NT	NT	NT
York	40 d			12 13						13 09						14 13						
Selby	40 d	11 43						12 43						13 43							14 43	
Leeds	37,39 d	12 22	12 37	12 51		13 08	13 13	13 22	13 37	13 51		14 08	14 13	14 22	14 37	14 51			15 08	15 13	15 22	15 37
Bramley	37 d	12 29	12 44			13 15		13 29	13 44			14 15		14 29	14 44				15 15		15 29	15 44
New Pudsey	37 d	12 34	12 49	13 01		13 20		13 34	13 49	14 01		14 20		14 34	14 49	15 01			15 20		15 34	15 49
Bradford Interchange	37 a	12 42	12 57	13 11		13 28		13 42	13 57	14 11		14 28		14 42	14 57	15 11			15 28		15 42	15 57
	d	12 45	13 00	13 14		13 32		13 45	14 00	14 14		14 32		14 45	15 00	15 14	15 22		15 32		15 45	16 00
Halifax	a	13 00	13 12	13 25		13 44		14 00	14 12	14 25		14 44		14 59	15 12	15 25	15 33		15 44		16 00	16 12
	d	13 06	13 12	13 26		13 44		14 06	14 12	14 26		14 44		15 06	15 12	15 26	15 36		15 44		16 06	16 12
Dewsbury	39 d						13 29						14 29							15 29		
Mirfield	39 d						13 35						14 35							15 35		
Brighouse	d	13 16					13 49	14 16					14 49	15 16			15a47			15 49	16 16	
Huddersfield	39 a	13 29						14 29						15 29							16 29	
Sowerby Bridge	d		13 19				13 59		14 19				14 59		15 19					15 59		16 19
Mytholmroyd	d		13 25				14 05		14 25				15 05		15 25					16 05		16 25
Hebden Bridge	a		13 28	13 37		13 56	14 08		14 28	14 37		14 56	15 08		15 28	15 37			15 56	16 08		16 28
	d		13 28	13 38		13 56	14 08		14 28	14 38		14 56	15 08		15 28	15 38			15 56	16 08		16 28
Burnley Manchester Road	97 a			13 57						14 57						15 57						
Accrington	97 a			14 06						15 06						16 06						
Blackburn	97 a			14 14						15 14						16 14						
Preston	97 a			14 32						15 32						16 32						
Poulton-le-Fylde	97 a			14 50						15 50						16 50						
Blackpool North	97 a			15 00						16 00						17 00						
Todmorden	d		13 36			14 04	14 15		14 36			15 04	15 15		15 36				16 04	16 15		16 36
Walsden	d		13 39						14 39						15 39							16 39
Littleborough	d		13 45				14 23		14 45				15 23		15 45					16 23		16 45
Smithy Bridge	d		13 48				14 25		14 48				15 25		15 48					16 25		16 48
Rochdale	a		13 51			14 14	14 29		14 51			15 14	15 29		15 51				16 14	16 29		16 51
	d		13 51		14 04	14 14	14 30		14 51		15 04	15 14	15 30		15 51			16 04	16 14	16 30		16 51
Castleton	d				14 07		14 33				15 07		15 33					16 07		16 33		
Mills Hill	d				14 12		14 38				15 12		15 38					16 12		16 38		
Moston	d				14 15		14 41				15 15		15 41					16 15		16 41		
Manchester Victoria	a		14 07		14 25	14 32	14 53		15 08		15 26	15 32	15 53		16 08			16 27	16 32	16 53		17 07

		NT	NT	NT	NT	NT	NT	NT	NT	NT	NT	NT	NT	NT	NT	NT	NT	NT	NT	NT	NT	NT	NT	NT	NT
York	40 d	15 08						16 13						17 08						18 05					
Selby	40 d					15 43												17 43	18 00			18 43			
Leeds	37,39 d	15 51		16 08	16 13	16 22	16 37	16 51		17 08	17 13	17 22	17 37	17 51		18 08	18 13	18 22	18 37	18 51	19 08	19 22	19 37	20 08	20 37
Bramley	37 d			16 15		16 29	16 44			17 15		17 29	17 44			18 15		18 30	18 44		19 15	19 30	19 44	20 15	20 44
New Pudsey	37 d	16 01		16 20		16 34	16 49	17 01		17 20		17 34	17 49	18 01		18 20		18 35	18 49	19 01	19 20	19 35	19 49	20 20	20 49
Bradford Interchange	37 a	16 10		16 28		16 42	16 57	17 10		17 28		17 42	17 57	18 10		18 28		18 43	18 58	19 10	19 28	19 43	19 57	20 28	20 57
	d	16 13		16 32		16 45	17 00	17 12		17 32		17 45	18 00	18 12		18 32		18 46	19 00	19 12	19 32	19 46	20 00	20 31	21 00
Halifax	a	16 24		16 44		17 00	17 12	17 24		17 44		17 58	18 12	18 24		18 44		19 00	19 12	19 24	19 44	20 00	20 12	20 44	21 12
	d	16 25		16 44		17 06	17 12	17 24		17 44		18 06	18 12	18 24		18 44		19 06	19 12	19 24	19 44	20 06	20 12	20 44	21 12
Dewsbury	39 d				16 31						17 31						18 31								
Mirfield	39 d				16 38						17 38						18 38								
Brighouse	d				16 49	17 16					17 49	18 16					18 49	19 16				20 16		20 55	
Huddersfield	39 a					17 29						18 31						19 29				20 29		21 08	
Sowerby Bridge	d	16 31			16 59		17 19	17 31			17 59		18 19	18 31			18 59		19 19				20 19		21 19
Mytholmroyd	d				17 05		17 25				18 05		18 25				19 05		19 25				20 25		21 25
Hebden Bridge	a	16 38		16 56	17 08		17 28	17 37		17 56	18 08		18 28	18 37		18 56	19 08		19 28	19 36	19 56		20 28		21 28
	d	16 38		16 56	17 08		17 28	17 38		17 56	18 08		18 28	18 38		18 56	19 08		19 28	19 36	19 56		20 28		21 28
Burnley Manchester Road	97 a	16 57						17 57						18 57						19 56					
Accrington	97 a	17 06						18 06						19 06						20 05					
Blackburn	97 a	17 14						18 14						19 14						20 14					
Preston	97 a	17 32						18 33						19 32						20 32					
Poulton-le-Fylde	97 a	17 56						18 50						19 50						20 50					
Blackpool North	97 a	18 06						19 00						20 00						21 00					
Todmorden	d			17 04	17 15		17 36			18 04	18 15		18 36			19 04	19 15		19 36		20 04		20 36		21 36
Walsden	d						17 39				18 19		18 39				19 19		19 39				20 39		21 39
Littleborough	d				17 23		17 45				18 25		18 45				19 25		19 45				20 45		21 45
Smithy Bridge	d				17 25		17 48				18 28		18 48				19 28		19 48				20 48		21 48
Rochdale	a			17 14	17 29		17 51			18 14	18 32		18 51			19 15	19 32		19 52		20 14		20 52		21 52
	d		17 03	17 14	17 30		17 51		18 02	18 14	18 32		18 51		19 00	19 15	19 32		19 52		20 14		20 52		21 52
Castleton	d		17 06		17 33				18 05		18 35				19 03		19 35		19 55				20 55		21 55
Mills Hill	d		17 11		17 38				18 10		18 40				19 08		19 40		20 00				21 00		22 00
Moston	d		17 14		17 41				18 13		18 43				19 11		19 43		20 03				21 03		22 03
Manchester Victoria	a		17 23	17 32	17 53		18 07		18 21	18 32	18 53		19 08		19 21	19 31	19 54		20 15		20 32		21 14		22 14

For connections to Liverpool Lime Street please refer to Table 90

Leeds and Bradford - Huddersfield, Blackpool North, Rochdale and Manchester Victoria via Halifax and Brighouse

		NT	NT	NT	NT	NT	NT
York ■	40 d	20 13					
Selby	40 d						
Leeds ■	37,39 d	20 51	21 08	21 37	22 08	22 37	23 08
Bramley	37 d		21 15	21 44	22 15	22 44	23 15
New Pudsey	37 d	21 01	21 20	21 49	22 20	22 49	23 20
Bradford Interchange	37 a	21 10	21 28	21 57	22 28	22 57	23 29
	d	21 13	21 31	22 00	22 31	23 00	23 31
Halifax	a	21 24	21 44	22 12	22 44	23 12	23 44
	d	21 25	21 44	22 12	22 44	23 12	23 44
Dewsbury	39 d						
Mirfield	39 d						
Brighouse	d		21 55		22 55		23 55
Huddersfield	39 a		22 08		23 08		00 08
Sowerby Bridge	d			22 19		23 19	
Mytholmroyd	d			22 25		23 25	
Hebden Bridge	a	21 36		22 28		23 28	
	d	21 37		22 28		23 28	
Burnley Manchester Road	97 a	21 56					
Accrington	97 a	22 05					
Blackburn	97 a	22 13					
Preston ■	97 a	22 31					
Poulton-le-Fylde	97 a	22 49					
Blackpool North	97 a	22 59					
Todmorden	d			22 36		23 36	
Walsden	d			22 39		23 39	
Littleborough	d			22 45		23 45	
Smithy Bridge	d			22 48		23 48	
Rochdale	a			22 52		23 52	
	d			22 52		23 52	
Castleton	d			22 55			
Mills Hill	d			23 00			
Moston	d			23 03			
Manchester Victoria	a			23 14		00 08	

Saturdays

		NT	NT	GC ◇1	NT	NT	NT	NT	NT	NT	NT	NT	NT	NT	NT	NT	NT	NT	NT	NT	NT	NT
York ■	40 d							06 13					07 06						08 09			
Selby	40 d										06 41						07 43					
Leeds ■	37,39 d	05 37	05 51		06 16	06 37		06 51	07 08	07 13	07 22	07 37	07 51		08 08	08 13	08 22	08 37	08 51		09 08	09 13
Bramley	37 d	05 44	05 58		06 23	06 44			07 15		07 29	07 44			08 15		08 29	08 44			09 15	
New Pudsey	37 d	05 49	06 02		06 28	06 49		07 01	07 20		07 34	07 49	08 01		08 20		08 34	08 49	09 00		09 20	
Bradford Interchange	37 a	05 57	06 13		06 36	06 57		07 11	07 28		07 43	07 57	08 09		08 28		08 42	08 57	09 12		09 28	
	d	06 00	06 14	06 20	06 40	07 00		07 14	07 31		07 45	08 00	08 12		08 32		08 45	09 00	09 12		09 32	
Halifax	a	06 12	06 25	06 31	06 52	07 12		07 25	07 43		08 00	08 12	08 24		08 44		09 00	09 12	09 24		09 44	
	d	06 12	06 26	06 34	06 52	07 12		07 26	07 44		08 06	08 12	08 24		08 44		09 06	09 12	09 24		09 44	
Dewsbury	39 d									07 29						08 31						09 31
Mirfield	39 d									07 35						08 38						09 37
Brighouse	d			06a46						07 49	08 16					08 49	09 16					09 49
Huddersfield	39 a										08 29						09 29					
Sowerby Bridge	d	06 19			06 59	07 19				07 59		08 19				08 59		09 19				09 59
Mytholmroyd	d	06 25			07 05	07 25				08 05		08 25				09 05		09 25				10 05
Hebden Bridge	a	06 28	06 37		07 08	07 28		07 37	07 55	08 08		08 28	08 36		08 56	09 08		09 28	09 36		09 56	10 08
	d	06 28	06 38		07 08	07 28	07 33	07 38	07 56	08 08		08 28	08 36		08 56	09 08		09 28	09 36		09 56	10 08
Burnley Manchester Road	97 a		06 57					07 57					08 57						09 56			
Accrington	97 a		07 06					08 06					09 06						10 06			
Blackburn	97 a		07 16					08 14					09 14						10 14			
Preston ■	97 a		07 36					08 38					09 32						10 32			
Poulton-le-Fylde	97 a		07 54					08 56					09 50						10 50			
Blackpool North	97 a		08 05					09 05					10 00						11 00			
Todmorden	d	06 35			07 15	07 36	07 44		08 04	08 15		08 36			09 04	09 15		09 36			10 04	10 15
Walsden	d	06 38				07 39	07 47					08 39						09 39				
Littleborough	d	06 45			07 23	07 45	07 53			08 23		08 45				09 23		09 45				10 23
Smithy Bridge	d	06 47			07 25	07 48	07 56			08 25		08 48				09 25		09 48				10 25
Rochdale	a	06 54			07 29	07 52	08 00		08 14	08 29		08 51			09 14	09 29		09 51			10 14	10 29
	d	06 55			07 30	07 52	08 00		08 14	08 30		08 51		09 04	09 14	09 30		09 51		10 04	10 14	10 30
Castleton	d	06 58			07 33	07 55	08 03		08 17	08 33				09 07		09 33				10 07		10 33
Mills Hill	d	07 03			07 38	08 00	08 08		08 22	08 37				09 12		09 37				10 12		10 38
Moston	d	07 06			07 41	08 03	08 11		08 25	08 40				09 15		09 40				10 15		10 41
Manchester Victoria	a	07 17			07 53	08 14	08 22		08 38	08 53		09 08		09 26	09 32	09 53		10 07		10 26	10 32	10 53

For connections to Liverpool Lime Street please refer to Table 90

Leeds and Bradford - Huddersfield, Blackpool North, Rochdale and Manchester Victoria via Halifax and Brighouse

		NT	NT	NT	GC ◇1	NT	NT	NT	NT	NT	NT	NT	NT	NT	NT	NT	NT	NT	NT	NT	NT	NT	NT
York ■	40 d			09 09							10 11						11 09						12 13
Selby	40 d	08 43							09 43						10 43						11 43		
Leeds ■	37,39 d	09 22	09 37	09 51			10 08	10 13	10 22	10 37	10 51		11 08	11 13	11 22	11 37	11 51		12 08	12 13	12 22	12 37	12 51
Bramley	37 d	09 29	09 44				10 15		10 29	10 44			11 15		11 29	11 44			12 15		12 29	12 44	
New Pudsey	37 d	09 34	09 49	10 01			10 20		10 34	10 49	11 01		11 20		11 34	11 49	12 01		12 20		12 34	12 49	13 01
Bradford Interchange	37 a	09 42	09 57	10 10			10 28		10 42	10 57	11 10		11 28		11 42	11 57	12 10		12 28		12 42	12 57	13 11
	d	09 45	10 00	10 12	10 22		10 32		10 45	11 00	11 12		11 32		11 45	12 00	12 14		12 32		12 45	13 00	13 14
Halifax	a	10 00	10 12	10 24	10 34		10 44		11 00	11 12	11 24		11 44		11 58	12 12	12 25		12 44		13 00	13 12	13 25
	d	10 06	10 12	10 24	10 38		10 44		11 06	11 12	11 24		11 44		12 06	12 12	12 26		12 44		13 06	13 12	13 26
Dewsbury	39 d							10 29						11 29						12 29			
Mirfield	39 d							10 35						11 35						12 35			
Brighouse	d	10 16			10a49			10 49	11 16					11 49	12 16					12 49	13 16		
Huddersfield	39 a	10 29							11 29						12 29						13 29		
Sowerby Bridge	d		10 19					10 59		11 19				11 59		12 19				12 59		13 19	
Mytholmroyd	d		10 25					11 05		11 25				12 05		12 25				13 05		13 25	
Hebden Bridge	a		10 28	10 36			10 56	11 08		11 28	11 36		11 56	12 08		12 28	12 37		12 56	13 08		13 28	13 37
	d		10 28	10 36			10 56	11 08		11 28	11 36		11 56	12 08		12 28	12 38		12 56	13 08		13 28	13 38
Burnley Manchester Road	97 a			10 57							11 57						12 57						13 57
Accrington	97 a			11 06							12 06						13 06						14 06
Blackburn	97 a			11 14							12 14						13 14						14 14
Preston ■	97 a			11 32							12 32						13 32						14 32
Poulton-le-Fylde	97 a			11 50							12 50						13 50						14 50
Blackpool North	97 a			12 00							13 00						14 00						15 00
Todmorden	d		10 36				11 04	11 15		11 36			12 04	12 15		12 36			13 04	13 15		13 36	
Walsden	d		10 39							11 39						12 39						13 39	
Littleborough	d		10 45					11 23		11 45				12 23		12 45				13 23		13 45	
Smithy Bridge	d		10 48					11 25		11 48				12 25		12 48				13 25		13 48	
Rochdale	a		10 51				11 14	11 29		11 51			12 14	12 29		12 51			13 14	13 29		13 51	
	d		10 51			11 04	11 14	11 30		11 51		12 04	12 14	12 30		12 51		13 04	13 14	13 30		13 51	
Castleton	d					11 07		11 33				12 07		12 33				13 07		13 33			
Mills Hill	d					11 12		11 38				12 12		12 38				13 12		13 38			
Moston	d					11 15		11 41				12 15		12 41				13 15		13 41			
Manchester Victoria	a		11 08			11 26	11 32	11 53		12 08		12 25	12 32	12 53		13 08		13 25	13 32	13 53		14 07	

		NT	NT	NT	NT	NT	NT	NT	NT	NT	NT	NT	NT	GC ◇1	NT	NT	NT	NT	NT	NT	NT	NT
York ■	40 d						13 09						14 13							15 08		
Selby	40 d				12 43						13 43							14 43				
Leeds ■	37,39 d		13 08	13 13	13 22	13 37	13 51		14 08	14 13	14 22	14 37	14 51			15 08	15 13	15 22	15 37	15 51		16 08
Bramley	37 d		13 15		13 29	13 44			14 15		14 29	14 44				15 15		15 29	15 44			16 15
New Pudsey	37 d		13 20		13 34	13 49	14 01		14 20		14 34	14 49	15 01			15 20		15 34	15 49	16 01		16 20
Bradford Interchange	37 a		13 28		13 42	13 57	14 11		14 28		14 42	14 57	15 11			15 28		15 42	15 57	16 10		16 28
	d		13 32		13 45	14 00	14 14		14 32		14 45	15 00	15 14	15 22		15 32		15 45	16 00	16 13		16 32
Halifax	a		13 44		14 00	14 12	14 25		14 44		14 59	15 12	15 25	15 33		15 44		15 58	16 12	16 24		16 44
	d		13 44		14 06	14 12	14 26		14 44		15 06	15 12	15 26	15 35		15 44		16 06	16 12	16 25		16 44
Dewsbury	39 d			13 29						14 29							15 29					
Mirfield	39 d			13 35						14 35							15 35					
Brighouse	d			13 49	14 16					14 49	15 16			15a46			15 49	16 16				
Huddersfield	39 a				14 29						15 29							16 29				
Sowerby Bridge	d			13 59		14 19				14 59		15 19					15 59		16 19	16 31		
Mytholmroyd	d			14 05		14 25				15 05		15 25					16 05		16 25			
Hebden Bridge	a		13 56	14 08		14 28	14 37		14 56	15 08		15 28	15 37			15 56	16 08		16 28	16 38		16 56
	d		13 56	14 08		14 28	14 38		14 56	15 08		15 28	15 38			15 56	16 08		16 28	16 38		16 56
Burnley Manchester Road	97 a						14 57						15 57							16 57		
Accrington	97 a						15 06						16 06							17 06		
Blackburn	97 a						15 14						16 14							17 14		
Preston ■	97 a						15 32						16 32							17 32		
Poulton-le-Fylde	97 a						15 50						16 50							17 56		
Blackpool North	97 a						16 00						17 00							18 06		
Todmorden	d		14 04	14 15		14 36			15 04	15 15		15 36				16 04	16 15		16 36			17 04
Walsden	d					14 39						15 39							16 39			
Littleborough	d			14 23		14 45				15 23		15 45					16 23		16 45			
Smithy Bridge	d			14 25		14 48				15 25		15 48					16 25		16 48			
Rochdale	a		14 14	14 29		14 51			15 14	15 29		15 51				16 14	16 29		16 51			17 14
	d	14 04	14 14	14 30		14 51		15 04	15 14	15 30		15 51			16 04	16 14	16 30		16 51		17 03	17 14
Castleton	d	14 07		14 33				15 07		15 33					16 07		16 33				17 06	
Mills Hill	d	14 12		14 38				15 12		15 38					16 12		16 38				17 11	
Moston	d	14 15		14 41				15 15		15 41					16 15		16 41				17 14	
Manchester Victoria	a	14 25	14 32	14 53		15 08		15 26	15 32	15 53		16 08			16 25	16 32	16 53		17 07		17 23	17 32

For connections to Liverpool Lime Street please refer to Table 90

Table 41

Saturdays

Leeds and Bradford - Huddersfield, Blackpool North, Rochdale and Manchester Victoria via Halifax and Brighouse

Station	Table		NT	NT	NT	NT	NT	NT	NT	NT	NT	NT	NT	NT	NT	NT	NT	NT	NT	NT	NT	NT	NT
York [8]	40	d				16 13						17 08						18 12					
Selby	40	d		15 43						16 43						17 43				18 43			
Leeds [10]	37,39	d	16 13	16 22	16 37	16 51		17 08	17 13	17 22	17 37	17 51		18 08	18 13	18 22	18 37	18 51	19 08	19 22	19 37	20 08	20 37
Bramley	37	d		16 29	16 44			17 15		17 29	17 44			18 15		18 30	18 44		19 15	19 30	19 44	20 15	20 44
New Pudsey	37	d		16 34	16 49	17 01		17 20		17 34	17 49	18 01		18 20		18 35	18 49	19 01	19 20	19 35	19 49	20 20	20 49
Bradford Interchange	37	a		16 42	16 57	17 10		17 28		17 42	17 57	18 10		18 28		18 43	18 58	19 10	19 28	19 44	19 57	20 28	20 57
		d		16 45	17 00	17 12		17 32		17 45	18 00	18 12		18 32		18 46	19 00	19 12	19 32	19 46	20 00	20 31	21 00
Halifax		a		17 00	17 12	17 24		17 44		17 58	18 12	18 24		18 44		19 00	19 12	19 24	19 44	20 00	20 12	20 44	21 12
		d		17 06	17 12	17 24		17 44		18 06	18 12	18 24		18 44		19 06	19 12	19 24	19 44	20 06	20 12	20 44	21 12
Dewsbury	39	d	16 31						17 31						18 31								
Mirfield	39	d	16 38						17 38						18 38								
Brighouse		d	16 49	17 16					17 49	18 16					18 49	19 16				20 16		20 55	
Huddersfield	39	a		17 29						18 30						19 29				20 29		21 08	
Sowerby Bridge		d	16 59		17 19	17 31			17 59		18 19	18 31			18 59		19 19				20 19		21 19
Mytholmroyd		d	17 05		17 25				18 05		18 25				19 05		19 25				20 25		21 25
Hebden Bridge		a	17 08		17 28	17 37		17 56	18 08		18 28	18 38		18 56	19 08		19 29	19 36	19 56		20 28		21 28
		d	17 08		17 28	17 38		17 56	18 08		18 28	18 38		18 56	19 08		19 29	19 36	19 56		20 28		21 28
Burnley Manchester Road	97	a				17 57						18 57						19 56					
Accrington	97	a				18 06						19 06						20 05					
Blackburn	97	a				18 14						19 14						20 14					
Preston [8]	97	a				18 33						19 32						20 32					
Poulton-le-Fylde	97	a				18 50						19 50						20 50					
Blackpool North	97	a				19 00						20 00						21 00					
Todmorden		d	17 15		17 36			18 04	18 15		18 36			19 04	19 15		19 36		20 04		20 36		21 36
Walsden		d			17 39				18 19		18 39				19 19		19 39				20 39		21 39
Littleborough		d	17 23		17 45				18 25		18 45				19 25		19 45				20 45		21 45
Smithy Bridge		d	17 25		17 48				18 28		18 48				19 28		19 48				20 48		21 48
Rochdale		a	17 29		17 51			18 14	18 32		18 51			19 15	19 32		19 52		20 14		20 52		21 52
		d	17 30		17 51		18 02	18 14	18 32		18 51		19 02	19 16	19 32		19 52		20 14		20 52		21 52
Castleton		d	17 33				18 05		18 35				19 05		19 35		19 55				20 55		21 55
Mills Hill		d	17 38				18 10		18 40				19 10		19 40		20 00				21 00		22 00
Moston		d	17 41				18 13		18 43				19 13		19 43		20 03				21 03		22 03
Manchester Victoria		a	17 53		18 07		18 21	18 32	18 54		19 07		19 22	9 32	19 54		20 15		20 32		21 14		22 14

Station	Table		NT	NT	NT	NT	NT	NT	NT
York [8]	40	d	20 13						
Selby	40	d							
Leeds [10]	37,39	d	20 51	21 08	21 37	22 08		22 37	23 00
Bramley	37	d		21 15	21 44	22 15		22 44	23 07
New Pudsey	37	d	21 01	21 20	21 49	22 20		22 49	23 12
Bradford Interchange	37	a	21 10	21 28	21 57	22 28		22 57	23 21
		d	21 13	21 31	22 00	22 31		23 00	23 23
Halifax		a	21 24	21 44	22 12	22 44		23 12	23 36
		d	21 25	21 44	22 12	22 44		23 12	23 36
Dewsbury	39	d							
Mirfield	39	d							
Brighouse		d		21 55		22 55			23 47
Huddersfield	39	a		22 08		23 07			23 59
Sowerby Bridge		d			22 19			23 19	
Mytholmroyd		d			22 25			23 25	
Hebden Bridge		a	21 36		22 28			23 28	
		d	21 37		22 28			23 28	
Burnley Manchester Road	97	a	21 56						
Accrington	97	a	22 05						
Blackburn	97	a	22 13						
Preston [8]	97	a	22 31						
Poulton-le-Fylde	97	a	22 49						
Blackpool North	97	a	22 59						
Todmorden		d			22 36			23 36	
Walsden		d			22 39			23 39	
Littleborough		d			22 45			23 45	
Smithy Bridge		d			22 48			23 48	
Rochdale		a			22 52			23 52	
		d			22 52		23 04	23 52	
Castleton		d					23 07		
Mills Hill		d					23 12		
Moston		d					23 15		
Manchester Victoria		a			23 08		23 27	00 08	

For connections to Liverpool Lime Street please refer to Table 90

Table 41

Sundays
until 11 July

Leeds and Bradford - Huddersfield, Blackpool North, Rochdale and Manchester Victoria via Halifax and Brighouse

Station	Table		GC ◇1	NT	NT	NT	NT	NT	NT	NT	NT	NT	NT	NT	GC ◇1	NT	NT	NT	NT	NT	NT	NT	NT	NT	NT
York [8]	40	d						08 50			09 52			10 57				11 52			12 52			13 52	
Selby	40	d																							
Leeds [10]	37,39	d		08 21	08 45	09 02	09 18	09 35	09 54	10 12	10 35	10 54	11 12	11 35		11 54	12 12	12 35	12 54	13 12	13 35	13 54	14 12	14 35	14 54
Bramley	37	d		08 28		09 09	09 25		10 01	10 19		11 01	11 19			12 01	12 19		13 01	13 19		14 01	14 19		15 01
New Pudsey	37	d		08 33	08 54	09 14	09 30	09 44	10 06	10 24	10 44	11 06	11 24	11 44		12 06	12 24	12 44	13 06	13 24	13 44	14 06	14 24	14 44	15 06
Bradford Interchange	37	a		08 41	09 03	09 22	09 38	09 53	10 14	10 32	10 53	11 14	11 32	11 53		12 14	12 32	12 53	13 14	13 32	13 53	14 14	14 32	14 53	15 14
		d	07 52	08 45	09 05	09 25	09 41	09 55	10 17	10 35	10 55	11 17	11 35	11 55	12 08	12 17	12 35	12 55	13 17	13 35	13 55	14 17	14 35	14 55	15 17
Halifax		a	08 03	08 57	09 17	09 37	09 54	10 07	10 29	10 48	11 07	11 29	11 48	12 07	12 19	12 29	12 48	13 07	13 29	13 48	14 07	14 29	14 48	15 07	15 29
		d	08 06	09 01	09 17	09 37	09 54	10 07	10 29	10 48	11 07	11 29		12 07	12 22	12 29	12 48	13 07	13 29		14 07	14 29	14 48	15 07	15 29
Dewsbury	39	d																							
Mirfield	39	d																							
Brighouse		d	08a18				10 04			10 58					12a34		12 58						14 58		
Huddersfield	39	a					10 17			11 12							13 12						15 12		
Sowerby Bridge		d		09 08		09 44			10 36			11 36				12 36			13 36			14 36			15 36
Mytholmroyd		d		09 14		09 50			10 42			11 42				12 42			13 42			14 42			15 42
Hebden Bridge		a		09 17	09 29	09 53		10 19	10 45		11 19	11 45		12 19		12 45		13 19	13 45		14 19	14 45		15 19	15 45
		d		09 17	09 29	09 53		10 19	10 45		11 19	11 45		12 19		12 45		13 19	13 45		14 19	14 45		15 19	15 45
Burnley Manchester Road	97	a			09 50			10 38			11 38			12 38				13 38			14 38			15 38	
Accrington	97	a			09 59			10 47			11 47			12 47				13 47			14 47			15 47	
Blackburn	97	a			10 07			10 56			11 55			12 55				13 55			14 55			15 55	
Preston [8]	97	a			10 27			11 13			12 13			13 13				14 13			15 13			16 13	
Poulton-le-Fylde	97	a			10 45			11 31			12 31			13 31				14 30			15 32			16 31	
Blackpool North	97	a			10 53			11 39			12 38			13 38				14 38			15 39			16 38	
Todmorden		d		09 24		10 00			10 52			11 52				12 52			13 52			14 52			15 52
Walsden		d		09 27		10 03			10 55			11 55				12 55			13 55			14 55			15 55
Littleborough		d		09 34		10 10			11 02			12 02				13 02			14 02			15 02			16 02
Smithy Bridge		d		09 36		10 12			11 04			12 04				13 04			14 04			15 04			16 04
Rochdale		a		09 41		10 16			11 08			12 08				13 08			14 08			15 08			16 08
		d		09 41		10 17			11 09			12 09				13 09			14 09			15 09			16 09
Castleton		d		09 44		10 20			11 12			12 12				13 12			14 12			15 12			16 12
Mills Hill		d		09 49		10 25			11 17			12 17				13 17			14 17			15 17			16 17
Moston		d		09 52		10 28			11 20			12 20				13 20			14 20			15 20			16 20
Manchester Victoria		a		10 02		10 38			11 30			12 30				13 30			14 30			15 30			16 30

Station	Table		GC ◇1	NT	NT	NT	NT	NT	NT	NT	NT	NT	NT	NT	NT	NT	NT	NT	NT	NT	NT	NT	NT	NT
York [8]	40	d			14 52			15 52			16 52			17 52		18 52			19 52		20 57			
Selby	40	d																						
Leeds [10]	37,39	d		15 12	15 35	15 54	16 12	16 35	16 54	17 12	17 35	17 54	18 12	18 35	19 03	19 35	19 54	20 12	20 35	21 04	21 35	22 05	22 35	23 22
Bramley	37	d		15 19		16 01	16 19		17 01	17 19		18 01	18 19		19 10		20 01	20 20		21 12	21 43	22 12	22 43	23 29
New Pudsey	37	d		15 24	15 44	16 06	16 24	16 44	17 06	17 24	17 44	18 06	18 24	18 44	19 15	19 44	20 06	20 25	20 44	21 17	21 47	22 17	22 47	23 34
Bradford Interchange	37	a		15 32	15 53	16 14	16 32	16 53	17 14	17 32	17 53	18 14	18 32	18 53	19 23	19 53	20 14	20 34	20 53	21 25	21 56	22 27	22 56	23 43
		d	15 33	15 39	15 55	16 17	16 35	16 55	17 17	17 39	17 55	18 17	18 35	18 55	19 27	19 55	20 19	20 35	20 55	21 28	21 58	22 29	22 58	
Halifax		a	15 44	15 51	16 07	16 29	16 48	17 07	17 29	17 48	18 07	18 29	18 48	19 07	19 39	20 07	20 31	20 47	21 07	21 40	22 10	22 42	23 12	
		d	15 46		16 07	16 29	16 48	17 07	17 29		18 07	18 29	18 48	19 07	19 39	20 07	20 31	20 48	21 07	21 41	22 11	22 42	23 12	
Dewsbury	39	d																						
Mirfield	39	d																						
Brighouse		d	15a56				16 58						18 58					20 58				22 52	23a23	
Huddersfield	39	a					17 12						19 12					21 13				23 04		
Sowerby Bridge		d				16 36			17 36			18 36			19 46		20 38			21 47	22 17			
Mytholmroyd		d				16 42			17 42			18 42			19 52		20 44			21 53	22 23			
Hebden Bridge		a			16 19	16 45		17 19	17 45		18 19	18 45		19 19	19 55	20 19	20 47		21 19	21 57	22 27			
		d			16 19	16 45		17 19	17 45		18 19	18 45		19 19	19 55	20 19	20 47		21 19		22 27			
Burnley Manchester Road	97	a			16 38			17 38			18 38			19 38		20 38			21 38					
Accrington	97	a			16 47			17 47			18 47			19 47		20 47			21 47					
Blackburn	97	a			16 55			17 55			18 55			19 56		20 55			21 55					
Preston [8]	97	a			17 13			18 13			19 13			20 14		21 13			22 13					
Poulton-le-Fylde	97	a			17 31			18 31			19 31			20 32		21 31			22 31					
Blackpool North	97	a			17 38			18 38			19 38			20 39		21 38			22 38					
Todmorden		d				16 52			17 52			18 52			20 02		20 54				22 34			
Walsden		d				16 55			17 55			18 55			20 05		20 57				22 37			
Littleborough		d				17 02			18 02			19 02			20 11		21 03				22 44			
Smithy Bridge		d				17 04			18 04			19 04			20 14		21 06				22 46			
Rochdale		a				17 08			18 08			19 08			20 18		21 10				22 50			
		d				17 09			18 09			19 09			20 19		21 11				22 51			
Castleton		d				17 12			18 12			19 12			20 22		21 14				22 54			
Mills Hill		d				17 17			18 17			19 17			20 27		21 19				22 59			
Moston		d				17 20			18 20			19 20			20 30		21 22				23 02			
Manchester Victoria		a				17 30			18 30			19 30			20 41		21 33				23 12			

For connections to Liverpool Lime Street please refer to Table 90

Leeds and Bradford - Huddersfield, Blackpool North, Rochdale and Manchester Victoria via Halifax and Brighouse

Station			GC ◇1	NT	NT	NT	NT	NT	NT (bus)	NT (bus)	NT	NT	NT	NT (bus)	NT (bus)	NT	NT	NT (bus)	NT (bus)	GC ◇1	NT	NT	NT
York	40	d						08 50					09 52				10 57						11 52
Selby	40	d																					
Leeds	37,39	d		08 03	08 45	09 02	09 18	09 35			09 54	10 12	10 35			10 54	11 35				11 54	12 12	12 35
Bramley	37	d		08 10		09 09	09 25				10 01	10 19				11 01					12 01	12 19	
New Pudsey	37	d		08 15	08 54	09 14	09 30	09 44			10 06	10 24	10 44			11 06	11 44				12 06	12 24	12 44
Bradford Interchange	37	a		08 23	09 03	09 22	09 38	09 53			10 14	10 32	10 53			11 14	11 53				12 14	12 32	12 53
		d	07 52	08 28	09 05	09 25	09 41	09 55			10 17	10 35	10 55			11 17	11 55			12 08	12 17	12 35	12 55
Halifax		a	08 03	08 40	09 17	09 37	09 54	10 07			10 29	10 48	11 07			11 29	12 07			12 19	12 29	12 48	13 07
		d	08 06	08 40	09 17	09 37	09 54	10 07			10 29	10 48	11 07			11 29	12 07			12 22	12 29	12 48	13 07
Dewsbury	39	d																					
Mirfield	39	d																					
Brighouse		d	08a18				10 04					10 58								12a34		12 58	
Huddersfield	39	a					10 17					11 12										13 12	
Sowerby Bridge		d		08 47		09 44					10 36					11 36					12 36		
Mytholmroyd		d		08 53		09 50					10 42					11 42					12 42		
Hebden Bridge		a		08 56	09 29	09 53		10 19			10 45		11 19			11 45	12 19				12 45		13 19
		d		08 56	09 29	09 53		10 19			10 45		11 19			11 45	12 19				12 45		13 19
Burnley Manchester Road	97	a			09 50			10 38					11 38				12 38						13 38
Accrington	97	a			09 59			10 47					11 47				12 47						13 47
Blackburn	97	a			10 07			10 56					11 55				12 55						13 55
Preston	97	a			10 27			11 13					12 13				13 13						14 13
Poulton-le-Fylde	97	a			10 45			11 31					12 31				13 31						14 30
Blackpool North	97	a			10 53			11 39					12 38				13 38						14 38
Todmorden		d		09 03		10 00					10 52					11 52					12 52		
Walsden		d		09 06		10 03					10 55					11 55					12 55		
Littleborough		d		09 13		10 10					11 02					12 02					13 02		
Smithy Bridge		d		09 15		10 12					11 04					12 04					13 04		
Rochdale		a		09 23		10 20					11 12					12 12					13 12		
		d							09 30	09 30				10 25	10 25			11 20	11 20				
Castleton		d								09 36					10 31				11 26				
Mills Hill		d								09 46					10 41				11 36				
Moston		d								10 01					10 56				11 51				
Manchester Victoria		a							09 52	10 21				10 47	11 16			11 42	12 11				

Station			NT (bus)	NT (bus)	NT	NT	NT (bus)	NT (bus)	NT	NT	NT	NT (bus)	NT (bus)	NT	NT	NT (bus)	NT (bus)	GC ◇1	NT	NT	NT	NT (bus)	NT (bus)	NT
York	40	d				12 52					13 52				14 52						15 52			
Selby	40	d																						
Leeds	37,39	d			12 54	13 35			13 54	14 12	14 35			14 54	15 35				15 54	16 12	16 35			16 54
Bramley	37	d			13 01				14 01	14 19				15 01					16 01	16 19				17 01
New Pudsey	37	d			13 06	13 44			14 06	14 24	14 44			15 06	15 44				16 06	16 24	16 44			17 06
Bradford Interchange	37	a			13 14	13 53			14 14	14 32	14 53			15 14	15 53				16 14	16 32	16 53			17 14
		d			13 17	13 55			14 17	14 35	14 55			15 17	15 55			16 00	16 17	16 35	16 55			17 17
Halifax		a			13 29	14 07			14 29	14 48	15 07			15 29	16 07			16 13	16 29	16 48	17 07			17 29
		d			13 29	14 07			14 29	14 48	15 07			15 29	16 07			16 14	16 29	16 48	17 07			17 29
Dewsbury	39	d																						
Mirfield	39	d																						
Brighouse		d								14 58								16a25		16 58				
Huddersfield	39	a								15 12										17 12				
Sowerby Bridge		d			13 36				14 36					15 36					16 36					17 36
Mytholmroyd		d			13 42				14 42					15 42					16 42					17 42
Hebden Bridge		a			13 45	14 19			14 45		15 19			15 45	16 19				16 45		17 19			17 45
		d			13 45	14 19			14 45		15 19			15 45	16 19				16 45		17 19			17 45
Burnley Manchester Road	97	a				14 38					15 38				16 38						17 38			
Accrington	97	a				14 47					15 47				16 47						17 47			
Blackburn	97	a				14 55					15 55				16 55						17 55			
Preston	97	a				15 13					16 13				17 13						18 13			
Poulton-le-Fylde	97	a				15 32					16 31				17 31						18 31			
Blackpool North	97	a				15 39					16 38				17 38						18 38			
Todmorden		d			13 52				14 52					15 52					16 52					17 52
Walsden		d			13 55				14 55					15 55					16 55					17 55
Littleborough		d			14 02				15 02					16 02					17 02					18 02
Smithy Bridge		d			14 04				15 04					16 04					17 04					18 04
Rochdale		a			14 12				15 12					16 12					17 12					18 12
		d	12 20	12 20			13 20	13 20				14 20	14 20			15 20	15 20					16 20	16 20	
Castleton		d		12 26				13 26					14 26				15 26						16 26	
Mills Hill		d		12 36				13 36					14 36				15 36						16 36	
Moston		d		12 51				13 51					14 51				15 51						16 51	
Manchester Victoria		a	12 42	13 11			13 42	14 11				14 42	15 11			15 42	16 11					16 42	17 11	

For connections to Liverpool Lime Street please refer to Table 90

Table 41

Sundays
18 July to 05 September

Leeds and Bradford - Huddersfield, Blackpool North, Rochdale and Manchester Victoria via Halifax and Brighouse

Station			NT	NT (bus)	NT (bus)	NT	NT	NT	NT (bus)	NT (bus)	NT	NT	NT (bus)	NT (bus)	NT	NT	NT	NT (bus)	NT (bus)	NT	NT	NT (bus)	NT (bus)
York	40	d	16 52					17 52				18 52					19 52				20 57		
Selby	40	d																					
Leeds	37,39	d	17 35			17 54	18 12	18 35			19 03	19 35			19 54	20 12	20 35			21 04	21 35		
Bramley	37	d				18 01	18 19				19 10				20 01	20 20				21 12	21 43		
New Pudsey	37	d	17 44			18 06	18 24	18 44			19 15	19 44			20 06	20 25	20 44			21 17	21 47		
Bradford Interchange	37	a	17 53			18 14	18 32	18 53			19 23	19 53			20 14	20 34	20 53			21 25	21 56		
		d	17 55			18 17	18 35	18 55			19 27	19 55			20 19	20 35	20 55			21 28	21 58		
Halifax		a	18 07			18 29	18 48	19 07			19 39	20 07			20 31	20 47	21 07			21 40	22 10		
		d	18 07			18 29	18 48	19 07			19 39	20 07			20 31	20 48	21 07			21 41	22 11		
Dewsbury	39	d																					
Mirfield	39	d																					
Brighouse		d					18 58									20 58							
Huddersfield	39	a					19 12									21 13							
Sowerby Bridge		d				18 36					19 46				20 38					21 47	22 17		
Mytholmroyd		d				18 42					19 52				20 44					21 53	22 23		
Hebden Bridge		a	18 19			18 45		19 19			19 55	20 19			20 47		21 19			21 57	22 27		
		d	18 19			18 45		19 19			19 55	20 19			20 47		21 19				22 27		
Burnley Manchester Road	97	a	18 38					19 38				20 38					21 38						
Accrington	97	a	18 47					19 47				20 47					21 47						
Blackburn	97	a	18 55					19 56				20 55					21 55						
Preston	97	a	19 13					20 14				21 13					22 13						
Poulton-le-Fylde	97	a	19 31					20 32				21 31					22 31						
Blackpool North	97	a	19 38					20 39				21 38					22 38						
Todmorden		d				18 52					20 02				20 54						22 34		
Walsden		d				18 55					20 05				20 57						22 37		
Littleborough		d				19 02					20 11				21 03						22 44		
Smithy Bridge		d				19 04					20 14				21 06						22 46		
Rochdale		a				19 12					20 22				21 14						22 54		
		d		17 20	17 20				18 20	18 20			19 20	19 20				20 30	20 30			21 20	21 20
Castleton		d			17 26					18 26				19 26					20 36				21 26
Mills Hill		d			17 36					18 36				19 36					20 46				21 36
Moston		d			17 51					18 51				19 51					21 01				21 51
Manchester Victoria		a		17 42	18 11				18 42	19 11			19 42	20 11				20 52	21 21			21 42	22 11

Station			NT	NT	NT (bus)	NT (bus)
York	40	d				
Selby	40	d				
Leeds	37,39	d	22 05	22 35		
Bramley	37	d	22 12	22 43		
New Pudsey	37	d	22 17	22 47		
Bradford Interchange	37	a	22 27	22 56		
		d	22 29	22 58		
Halifax		a	22 42	23 12		
		d	22 42	23 12		
Dewsbury	39	d				
Mirfield	39	d				
Brighouse		d	22 52	23a23		
Huddersfield	39	a	23 04			
Sowerby Bridge		d				
Mytholmroyd		d				
Hebden Bridge		a				
		d				
Burnley Manchester Road	97	a				
Accrington	97	a				
Blackburn	97	a				
Preston	97	a				
Poulton-le-Fylde	97	a				
Blackpool North	97	a				
Todmorden		d				
Walsden		d				
Littleborough		d				
Smithy Bridge		d				
Rochdale		a				
		d			23 00	23 00
Castleton		d				23 06
Mills Hill		d				23 16
Moston		d				23 31
Manchester Victoria		a			23 22	23 51

For connections to Liverpool Lime Street please refer to Table 90

Table 41

Sundays from 12 September

Leeds and Bradford - Huddersfield, Blackpool North, Rochdale and Manchester Victoria via Halifax and Brighouse

Station			NT	NT	NT	NT	NT	NT	NT	NT	NT	NT	NT	GC ◇1	NT	NT	NT	NT	NT	NT	NT	NT	NT	NT	GC ◇1
York 8	40	d					08 50			09 52			10 57				11 52			12 52			13 52		
Selby	40	d																							
Leeds 10	37,39	d	08 21	08 45	09 02	09 18	09 35	09 54	10 12	10 35	10 54	11 12	11 35		11 54	12 12	12 35	12 54	13 12	13 35	13 54	14 12	14 35	14 54	
Bramley	37	d	08 28		09 09	09 25		10 01	10 19		11 01	11 19			12 01	12 19		13 01	13 19		14 01	14 19		15 01	
New Pudsey	37	d	08 33	08 54	09 14	09 30	09 44	10 06	10 24	10 44	11 06	11 24	11 44		12 06	12 24	12 44	13 06	13 24	13 44	14 06	14 24	14 44	15 06	
Bradford Interchange	37	a	08 41	09 03	09 22	09 38	09 53	10 14	10 32	10 53	11 14	11 32	11 53		12 14	12 32	12 53	13 14	13 32	13 53	14 14	14 32	14 53	15 14	
		d	08 45	09 05	09 25	09 41	09 55	10 17	10 35	10 55	11 17	11 35	11 55	12 08	12 17	12 35	12 55	13 17	13 35	13 55	14 17	14 35	14 55	15 17	15 33
Halifax		a	08 57	09 17	09 37	09 54	10 07	10 29	10 48	11 07	11 29	11 48	12 07	12 19	12 29	12 48	13 07	13 29	13 48	14 07	14 29	14 48	15 07	15 29	15 44
		d	09 01	09 17	09 37	09 54	10 07	10 29	10 48	11 07	11 29		12 07	12 22	12 29	12 48	13 07	13 29		14 07	14 29	14 48	15 07	15 29	15 46
Dewsbury	39	d																							
Mirfield	39	d																							
Brighouse		d				10 04			10 58					12a34		12 58						14 58			15a56
Huddersfield	39	a				10 17			11 12							13 12						15 12			
Sowerby Bridge		d	09 08		09 44			10 36			11 36				12 36			13 36			14 36			15 36	
Mytholmroyd		d	09 14		09 50			10 42			11 42				12 42			13 42			14 42			15 42	
Hebden Bridge		a	09 17	09 29	09 53		10 19	10 45		11 19	11 45		12 19		12 45		13 19	13 45		14 19	14 45		15 19	15 45	
		d	09 17	09 29	09 53		10 19	10 45		11 19	11 45		12 19		12 45		13 19	13 45		14 19	14 45		15 19	15 45	
Burnley Manchester Road	97	a		09 50			10 38			11 38			12 38				13 38			14 38			15 38		
Accrington	97	a		09 59			10 47			11 47			12 47				13 47			14 47			15 47		
Blackburn	97	a		10 07			10 56			11 55			12 55				13 55			14 55			15 55		
Preston 8	97	a		10 27			11 13			12 13			13 13				14 13			15 13			16 13		
Poulton-le-Fylde	97	a		10 45			11 31			12 31			13 31				14 30			15 32			16 31		
Blackpool North	97	a		10 53			11 39			12 38			13 38				14 38			15 39			16 38		
Todmorden		d	09 24		10 00			10 52			11 52				12 52			13 52			14 52			15 52	
Walsden		d	09 27		10 03			10 55			11 55				12 55			13 55			14 55			15 55	
Littleborough		d	09 34		10 10			11 02			12 02				13 02			14 02			15 02			16 02	
Smithy Bridge		d	09 36		10 12			11 04			12 04				13 04			14 04			15 04			16 04	
Rochdale		a	09 41		10 16			11 08			12 08				13 08			14 08			15 08			16 08	
		d	09 41		10 17			11 09			12 09				13 09			14 09			15 09			16 09	
Castleton		d	09 44		10 20			11 12			12 12				13 12			14 12			15 12			16 12	
Mills Hill		d	09 49		10 25			11 17			12 17				13 17			14 17			15 17			16 17	
Moston		d	09 52		10 28			11 20			12 20				13 20			14 20			15 20			16 20	
Manchester Victoria		a	10 02		10 38			11 30			12 30				13 30			14 30			15 30			16 30	

Station			NT	NT	NT	NT	NT	NT	NT	NT	NT	NT	NT	NT	NT	NT	NT	NT	NT	NT	NT	NT	NT
York 8	40	d		14 52			15 52			16 52			17 52		18 52			19 52		20 57			
Selby	40	d																					
Leeds 10	37,39	d	15 12	15 35	15 54	16 12	16 35	16 54	17 12	17 35	17 54	18 12	18 35	19 03	19 33	19 54	20 12	20 35	21 04	21 35	22 05	22 35	23 22
Bramley	37	d	15 19		16 01	16 19		17 01	17 19		18 01	18 19		19 10		20 01	20 20		21 12	21 43	22 12	22 43	23 29
New Pudsey	37	d	15 24	15 44	16 06	16 24	16 44	17 06	17 24	17 44	18 06	18 24	18 44	19 15	19 44	20 06	20 25	20 44	21 17	21 47	22 17	22 47	23 34
Bradford Interchange	37	a	15 32	15 53	16 14	16 32	16 53	17 14	17 32	17 53	18 14	18 32	18 53	19 23	19 53	20 14	20 34	20 53	21 25	21 56	22 27	22 56	23 43
		d	15 35	15 55	16 17	16 35	16 55	17 17	17 35	17 55	18 17	18 35	18 55	19 27	19 55	20 19	20 35	20 55	21 28	21 58	22 29	22 58	
Halifax		a	15 51	16 07	16 29	16 48	17 07	17 29	17 48	18 07	18 29	18 48	19 07	19 39	20 07	20 31	20 47	21 07	21 40	22 10	22 42	23 12	
		d		16 07	16 29	16 48	17 07	17 29		18 07	18 29	18 48	19 07	19 39	20 07	20 31	20 48	21 07	21 41	22 11	22 42	23 12	
Dewsbury	39	d																					
Mirfield	39	d																					
Brighouse		d				16 58						18 58					20 58				22 52	23a23	
Huddersfield	39	a				17 12						19 12					21 13				23 04		
Sowerby Bridge		d			16 36			17 36			18 36			19 46		20 38			21 47	22 17			
Mytholmroyd		d			16 42			17 42			18 42			19 52		20 44			21 53	22 23			
Hebden Bridge		a		16 19	16 45		17 19	17 45		18 19	18 45		19 19	19 55	20 19	20 47		21 19	21 57	22 27			
		d		16 19	16 45		17 19	17 45		18 19	18 45		19 19	19 55	20 19	20 47		21 19		22 27			
Burnley Manchester Road	97	a		16 38			17 38			18 38			19 38		20 38			21 38					
Accrington	97	a		16 47			17 47			18 47			19 47		20 47			21 47					
Blackburn	97	a		16 55			17 55			18 55			19 56		20 55			21 55					
Preston 8	97	a		17 13			18 13			19 13			20 14		21 13			22 13					
Poulton-le-Fylde	97	a		17 31			18 31			19 31			20 32		21 31			22 31					
Blackpool North	97	a		17 38			18 38			19 38			20 39		21 38			22 38					
Todmorden		d			16 52			17 52			18 52			20 02		20 54				22 34			
Walsden		d			16 55			17 55			18 55			20 05		20 57				22 37			
Littleborough		d			17 02			18 02			19 02			20 11		21 03				22 44			
Smithy Bridge		d			17 04			18 04			19 04			20 14		21 06				22 46			
Rochdale		a			17 08			18 08			19 08			20 18		21 10				22 50			
		d			17 09			18 09			19 09			20 19		21 11				22 51			
Castleton		d			17 12			18 12			19 12			20 22		21 14				22 54			
Mills Hill		d			17 17			18 17			19 17			20 27		21 19				22 59			
Moston		d			17 20			18 20			19 20			20 30		21 22				23 02			
Manchester Victoria		a			17 30			18 30			19 30			20 41		21 33				23 12			

For connections to Liverpool Lime Street please refer to Table 90

Table 41

Mondays to Fridays

Manchester Victoria, Rochdale, Blackpool North and Huddersfield - Bradford and Leeds via Brighouse and Halifax

Station			NT	NT	NT	NT	NT	NT	NT	NT	NT	NT	NT	NT	NT	NT	NT	NT	NT	NT
Manchester Victoria		d			05 51			06 17	06 43		06 58		07 17	07 48		08 00		08 22	08 30	08 48
Moston		d						06 23			07 04		07 23			08 06			08 36	
Mills Hill		d						06 28			07 09		07 28			08 11			08 40	
Castleton		d						06 33			07 14		07 33			08 16			08 45	
Rochdale		a			06 05			06 36	06 56		07 17		07 36	08 01		08 19		08 34	08 51	09 02
		d			06 05			06 37	06 56		07 18		07 37	08 01		08 20		08 35		09 02
Smithy Bridge		d			06 09			06 41			07 22		07 41			08 24		08 39		
Littleborough		d			06 13			06 44			07 25		07 44			08 27		08 42		
Walsden		d			06 19			06 50			07 31		07 50					08 48		
Todmorden		d			06 22			06 54	07 08		07 35		07 54	08 13		08 34		08 52		09 14
Blackpool North	97	d				05 29						06 28					07 29			
Poulton-le-Fylde	97	d				05 35						06 34					07 35			
Preston 8	97	d				05 54						06 54					07 54			
Blackburn	97	d				06 10						07 10					08 10			
Accrington	97	d				06 17						07 17					08 17			
Burnley Manchester Road	97	d				06 26						07 26					08 26			
Hebden Bridge		a			06 29	06 49		07 00	07 14		07 41	07 49	08 00	08 19		08 41	08 49	08 58		09 20
		d	05 47	06 17	06 29	06 50		07 00	07 16		07 41	07 50	08 00	08 21		08 41	08 50	09 00		09 21
Mytholmroyd		d	05 50	06 20	06 32			07 03	07 19		07 45		08 04			08 44		09 03		
Sowerby Bridge		d	05 56	06 26	06 38	06 57		07 09	07 25		07 50	07 57	08 09			08 50	08 57	09 09		
Huddersfield	39	d								07 29					08 21					
Brighouse		d								07 39	07 59				08 33	08 58				
Mirfield	39	a									08 06					09 06				
Dewsbury	39	a									08 11					09 12				
Halifax		a	06 02	06 32	06 45	07 03		07 16	07 32	07 50		08 03	08 16	08 33	08 43		09 03	09 15		09 33
		d	06 03	06 33	06 45	07 03	07 03	07 16	07 33	07 50		08 03	08 16	08 33	08 48		09 03	09 16		09 33
Bradford Interchange		a	06 16	06 46	07 00	07 17		07 31	07 47	08 04		08 17	08 31	08 47	09 01		09 17	09 31		09 47
		d	06 18	06 48	07 02	07 20		07 34	07 50	08 05		08 20	08 34	08 50	09 04		09 20	09 34		09 50
New Pudsey	37	a	06 27	06 57	07 11	07 28		07 42	07 58	08 14		08 28	08 42	08 58	09 12		09 27	09 42		09 58
Bramley	37	a	06 30	07 00	07 14			07 46	08 02	08 18			08 46	09 02	09 16			09 46		10 02
Leeds 10	37,39	a	06 42	07 09	07 27	07 39	07 55	07 57	08 12	08 30	08 33	08 39	08 56	09 12	09 27	09 31	09 39	09 58		10 12
Selby	40	a						08 36	08 55					09 53						10 54
York 8	40	a			08 06	08 21						09 21					10 21			

Station			NT	NT	NT	NT	NT	NT	NT	NT	NT	NT	NT	NT	NT	NT	NT	NT	NT	NT	NT	NT	NT	NT
Manchester Victoria		d		09 00		09 22	09 33	09 48		10 00		10 21	10 30	10 48		11 00		11 21	11 30	11 48		12 00		12 21
Moston		d		09 06			09 39			10 06			10 36			11 06			11 36			12 06		
Mills Hill		d		09 11			09 44			10 11			10 40			11 11			11 40			12 11		
Castleton		d		09 16			09 49			10 16			10 45			11 16			11 45			12 16		
Rochdale		a		09 19		09 35	09 54	10 02		10 19		10 34	10 51	11 02		11 19		11 34	11 51	12 02		12 19		12 34
		d		09 20		09 36		10 02		10 20		10 35		11 02		11 20		11 35		12 02		12 20		12 35
Smithy Bridge		d		09 24		09 40				10 24		10 39				11 24		11 39				12 24		12 39
Littleborough		d		09 27		09 43				10 27		10 42				11 27		11 42				12 27		12 42
Walsden		d				09 49						10 48						11 48						12 48
Todmorden		d		09 34		09 53		10 14		10 34		10 52		11 14		11 34		11 52		12 14		12 34		12 52
Blackpool North	97	d			08 29						09 29						10 29						11 29	
Poulton-le-Fylde	97	d			08 35						09 35						10 35						11 35	
Preston 8	97	d			08 54						09 54						10 54						11 54	
Blackburn	97	d			09 10						10 10						11 10						12 10	
Accrington	97	d			09 17						10 17						11 17						12 17	
Burnley Manchester Road	97	d			09 26						10 26						11 28						12 26	
Hebden Bridge		a		09 41	09 49	09 59		10 20		10 41	10 49	10 58		11 20		11 41	11 49	11 58		12 20		12 41	12 49	12 58
		d		09 41	09 50	10 00		10 21		10 41	10 50	11 00		11 21		11 41	11 50	12 00		12 21		12 41	12 50	13 00
Mytholmroyd		d		09 44		10 03				10 44		11 03				11 44		12 03				12 44		13 03
Sowerby Bridge		d		09 50		10 09				10 50		11 09				11 50		12 09				12 50		13 09
Huddersfield	39	d	09 23						10 23						11 23						12 23			
Brighouse		d	09 34	09 58					10 33	10 58					11 33	11 58					12 33	12 58		
Mirfield	39	a		10 06						11 06						12 06						13 06		
Dewsbury	39	a		10 12						11 12						12 12						13 12		
Halifax		a	09 44		10 02	10 15		10 33	10 43		11 02	11 15		11 33	11 43		12 02	12 15		12 33	12 43		13 02	13 15
		d	09 48		10 03	10 16		10 33	10 49		11 03	11 16		11 33	11 49		12 03	12 16		12 33	12 49		13 03	13 16
Bradford Interchange		a	10 02		10 17	10 31		10 47	11 02		11 17	11 31		11 47	12 02		12 17	12 31		12 47	13 02		13 17	13 31
		d	10 04		10 19	10 34		10 50	11 05		11 20	11 34		11 50	12 05		12 19	12 34		12 50	13 05		13 19	13 34
New Pudsey	37	a	10 12		10 28	10 42		10 58	11 13		11 28	11 42		11 58	12 13		12 27	12 42		12 58	13 13		13 27	13 42
Bramley	37	a	10 16			10 46		11 02	11 17			11 46		12 02	12 17			12 46		13 02	13 17			13 46
Leeds 10	37,39	a	10 27	10 31	10 39	10 58		11 13	11 27	11 33	11 39	11 58		12 12	12 27	12 31	12 39	12 58		13 12	13 27	13 31	13 39	13 58
Selby	40	a						11 55						12 50						13 51				
York 8	40	a			11 19						12 21						13 19						14 21	

For connections from Liverpool Lime Street please refer to Table 90

Table 41

Mondays to Fridays

Manchester Victoria, Rochdale, Blackpool North and Huddersfield - Bradford and Leeds via Brighouse and Halifax

Station			NT	NT	NT	NT	GC	NT	NT	NT	NT	NT	NT		NT	NT	NT	NT	NT	NT	NT	NT	NT		NT	NT
Manchester Victoria ⇌		d	12 30	12 48		13 00			13 21	13 30	13 48		14 00			14 21	14 30	14 48		15 00		15 21	15 30		15 48	
Moston		d	12 36			13 06				13 36			14 06				14 36			15 06			15 36			
Mills Hill		d	12 40			13 11				13 40			14 11				14 40			15 11			15 40			
Castleton		d	12 45			13 16				13 45			14 16				14 45			15 16			15 45			
Rochdale		a	12 51	13 02		13 19			13 34	13 51	14 02		14 19			14 34	14 51	15 02		15 19		15 34	15 51		16 02	
		d		13 02		13 20			13 35		14 02		14 20			14 35		15 02		15 20		15 35			16 02	
Smithy Bridge		d				13 24			13 39				14 24			14 39				15 24		15 39				
Littleborough		d				13 27			13 42				14 27			14 42				15 27		15 42				
Walsden		d							13 48							14 48						15 48				
Todmorden		d		13 14		13 34			13 52		14 14		14 34			14 52		15 14		15 34		15 52			16 14	
Blackpool North	97	d						12 29							13 29						14 29					
Poulton-le-Fylde	97	d						12 35							13 35						14 35					
Preston ■	97	d						12 54							13 54						14 54					
Blackburn	97	d						13 10							14 10						15 10					
Accrington	97	d						13 17							14 17						15 17					
Burnley Manchester Road	97	d						13 26							14 26						15 26					
Hebden Bridge		a		13 20		13 41		13 49	13 58		14 20		14 41		14 49	14 58		15 20		15 41	15 49	16 00			16 20	
		d		13 21		13 41		13 50	14 00		14 21		14 41		14 50	15 00		15 21		15 41	15 50	16 01			16 21	
Mytholmroyd		d				13 44			14 03				14 44			15 03				15 44		16 04				
Sowerby Bridge		d				13 50			14 09				14 50			15 09				15 50		16 10				
Huddersfield	39	d			13 23							14 23							15 23							16 23
Brighouse		d			13 34	13 58	13 26					14 33	14 58						15 33	15 58						16 33
Mirfield	39	a				14 06							15 06							16 06						
Dewsbury	39	a				14 12							15 12							16 12						
Halifax		a		13 33	13 44		13 37	14 02	14 15		14 33	14 43			15 02	15 15		15 33	15 43		16 02	16 16			16 33	16 46
		d		13 33	13 49		13 41	14 03	14 16		14 33	14 49			15 03	15 16		15 33	15 49		16 03	16 17			16 33	16 49
Bradford Interchange		a		13 47	14 02		13 54	14 17	14 31		14 47	15 02			15 17	15 31		15 47	16 02		16 17	16 31			16 47	17 02
		d		13 50	14 05			14 19	14 34		14 50	15 05			15 19	15 34		15 50	16 05		16 19	16 34			16 50	17 04
New Pudsey	37	a		13 58	14 13			14 28	14 42		14 58	15 13			15 27	15 42		15 58	16 13		16 27	16 42			16 58	17 13
Bramley	37	a		14 02	14 17				14 46		15 02	15 17				15 46		16 02	16 17			16 46			17 02	17 17
Leeds ■	37,39	a		14 12	14 27	14 31		14 39	14 58		15 12	15 27	15 31		15 39	15 58		16 12	16 27	16 31	16 39	16 58			17 12	17 27
Selby	40	a		14 50							15 52							16 54							17 53	
York ■	40	a						15 19							16 21						17 19					

Station			NT	NT	NT	NT		GC	NT	NT	NT	NT	NT	NT		NT	NT	NT	NT	NT	NT	NT	NT	NT	NT	NT
Manchester Victoria ⇌		d	16 00		16 24	16 30			16 48		17 00		17 18	17 30		17 43		18 00		18 21	18 26	18 48		19 00		19 21
Moston		d	16 06			16 36					17 06		17 24	17 36		17 49					18 32			19 06		19 27
Mills Hill		d	16 11			16 40					17 11		17 29	17 40		17 54		18 09			18 36			19 11		19 32
Castleton		d	16 16			16 45					17 16		17 34	17 45		17 59		18 14			18 41			19 16		19 37
Rochdale		a	16 19		16 37	16 51			17 02		17 19		17 37	17 51		18 02		18 18		18 35	18 47	19 01		19 19		19 40
		d	16 20		16 37				17 02		17 20		17 38			18 03		18 18		18 36		19 01		19 19		19 41
Smithy Bridge		d	16 24		16 41						17 24		17 42					18 22		18 40				19 23		19 45
Littleborough		d	16 27		16 45						17 27		17 46			18 08		18 26		18 43				19 27		19 48
Walsden		d			16 51								17 52					18 32		18 49						19 54
Todmorden		d	16 34		16 54				17 14		17 34		17 55			18 16		18 35		18 53		19 13		19 34		19 58
Blackpool North	97	d		15 29								16 29							17 14						18 29	
Poulton-le-Fylde	97	d		15 35								16 35							17 20						18 35	
Preston ■	97	d		15 54								16 54							17 44						18 54	
Blackburn	97	d		16 10								17 10							18 11						19 10	
Accrington	97	d		16 17								17 17							18 19						19 17	
Burnley Manchester Road	97	d		16 26								17 26							18 28						19 26	
Hebden Bridge		a	16 41	16 49	17 01				17 20		17 41	17 49	18 01			18 22		18 42	18 49	18 59		19 20		19 41	19 49	20 04
		d	16 41	16 50	17 01				17 21		17 41	17 50	18 01			18 23		18 42	18 50	19 00		19 20		19 41	19 50	20 05
Mytholmroyd		d	16 44		17 04						17 44		18 05					18 45		19 03				19 44		20 08
Sowerby Bridge		d	16 50		17 10						17 50		18 11					18 51		19 09				19 50		20 14
Huddersfield	39	d								17 23							18 23						19 23			
Brighouse		d	16 58					17 07		17 34	17 58						18 34	18 59					19 33	19 58		
Mirfield	39	a	17 06								18 07							19 07						20 07		
Dewsbury	39	a	17 12								18 13							19 13						20 12		
Halifax		a		17 02	17 17			17 22	17 33	17 49		18 02	18 17			18 35	18 45		19 03	19 15		19 32	19 43		20 03	20 20
		d		17 03	17 17			17 24	17 33	17 49		18 03	18 17			18 35	18 49		19 03	19 16		19 32	19 49		20 03	20 21
Bradford Interchange		a		17 17	17 31			17 39	17 47	18 04		18 17	18 32			18 49	19 02		19 17	19 31		19 48	20 02		20 17	20 35
		d		17 19	17 34				17 50	18 04		18 19	18 34			18 52	19 05		19 19	19 34		19 50	20 04		20 19	20 37
New Pudsey	37	a		17 28	17 42				17 58	18 13		18 28	18 42			19 00	19 13		19 28	19 42		19 59	20 13		20 28	20 46
Bramley	37	a			17 46				18 02	18 13			18 46			19 04	19 17			19 46		20 03	20 16			20 49
Leeds ■	37,39	a	17 31	17 39	17 58				18 12	18 28	18 33	18 39	18 56			19 13	19 28	19 33	19 39	19 58		20 13	20 29	20 34	20 41	21 01
Selby	40	a							18 50																	
York ■	40	a		18 19								19 21				19 54			20 21						21 31	

For connections from Liverpool Lime Street please refer to Table 90

Table 41

Mondays to Fridays

Manchester Victoria, Rochdale, Blackpool North and Huddersfield - Bradford and Leeds via Brighouse and Halifax

Station			NT	NT	NT		NT	NT	NT	GC	NT	NT
Manchester Victoria ⇌		d		20 21				21 21			22 28	23 20
Moston		d		20 27				21 27			22 34	23 27
Mills Hill		d		20 32				21 32			22 39	23 32
Castleton		d		20 37				21 37			22 44	23 37
Rochdale		a		20 40				21 40			22 47	23 40
		d		20 41				21 41			22 48	23 41
Smithy Bridge		d		20 45				21 45			22 52	23 45
Littleborough		d		20 48				21 48			22 55	23 48
Walsden		d		20 54				21 54			23 01	23 54
Todmorden		d		20 58				21 58			23 05	23 58
Blackpool North	97	d					20 29					
Poulton-le-Fylde	97	d					20 35					
Preston ■	97	d					20 54					
Blackburn	97	d					21 10					
Accrington	97	d					21 17					
Burnley Manchester Road	97	d					21 28					
Hebden Bridge		a		21 04			21 50	22 04			23 11	00 04
		d		21 05			21 51	22 05			23 11	00 04
Mytholmroyd		d		21 08				22 08			23 15	00 08
Sowerby Bridge		d		21 14				22 14			23 20	00 13
Huddersfield	39	d	20 25		21 27				22 25			
Brighouse		d	20 35		21 37				22 35	22 46		
Mirfield	39	a										
Dewsbury	39	a										
Halifax		a	20 45	21 20	21 47		22 03	22 20	22 45	22 56	23 29	00 20
		d	20 49	21 21	21 49		22 03	22 21	22 49	22 58	23 29	00 20
Bradford Interchange		a	21 02	21 35	22 02		22 17	22 35	23 02	23 12	23 43	00 34
		d	21 04	21 37	22 04		22 19	22 37	23 04		23 46	00 37
New Pudsey	37	a	21 13	21 46	22 13		22 28	22 46	23 13		23 54	
Bramley	37	a	21 16	21 49	22 16			22 49	23 16		23 58	
Leeds ■	37,39	a	21 25	22 01	22 25		22 41	23 01	23 27		00 09	00 55
Selby	40	a										
York ■	40	a					23 33					

Saturdays

Station					NT	NT	NT	NT	NT	NT	NT		NT	NT	NT	NT	NT	NT	NT	NT	NT		NT	NT	NT	NT
Manchester Victoria ⇌		d				05 54		06 21	06 43		06 58			07 17	07 48		08 00		08 22	08 30	08 48			09 00		09 22
Moston		d									07 04			07 23			08 06			08 36				09 06		
Mills Hill		d									07 09			07 28			08 11			08 40				09 11		
Castleton		d									07 14			07 33			08 16			08 45				09 16		
Rochdale		a				06 08		06 34	06 56		07 17			07 36	08 01		08 19		08 34	08 51	09 02			09 19		09 35
		d				06 09		06 35	06 56		07 18			07 37	08 01		08 20		08 35		09 02			09 20		09 36
Smithy Bridge		d				06 13		06 39			07 22			07 41			08 24		08 39					09 24		09 40
Littleborough		d				06 16		06 42			07 25			07 44			08 27		08 42					09 27		09 43
Walsden		d				06 22		06 48			07 31			07 50					08 48							09 49
Todmorden		d				06 26		06 52	07 08		07 35			07 54	08 13		08 34		08 52		09 14			09 34		09 53
Blackpool North	97	d					05 29						06 28					07 29							08 29	
Poulton-le-Fylde	97	d					05 35						06 34					07 35							08 35	
Preston ■	97	d					05 54						06 54					07 54							08 54	
Blackburn	97	d					06 10						07 10					08 10							09 10	
Accrington	97	d					06 17						07 17					08 17							09 17	
Burnley Manchester Road	97	d					06 26						07 26					08 26							09 26	
Hebden Bridge		a				06 32	06 49	06 58	07 14		07 41		07 49	08 00	08 19		08 41	08 49	08 58		09 20			09 41	09 49	09 59
		d			05 55	06 33	06 50	07 00	07 16		07 41		07 50	08 00	08 21		08 41	08 50	09 00		09 21			09 41	09 50	10 00
Mytholmroyd		d			05 58	06 36		07 03	07 19		07 45			08 04			08 44		09 03					09 44		10 03
Sowerby Bridge		d			06 04	06 42	06 57	07 09	07 25		07 50		07 57	08 09			08 50	08 57	09 09					09 50		10 09
Huddersfield	39	d								07 29						08 21							09 23			
Brighouse		d								07 39	07 59					08 33	08 58						09 34	09 58		
Mirfield	39	a									08 06						09 06							10 06		
Dewsbury	39	a									08 11						09 12							10 12		
Halifax		a			06 10	06 48	07 03	07 15	07 32	07 50			08 03	08 16	08 33	08 43		09 03	09 15		09 33		09 44		10 02	10 15
		d			06 11	06 49	07 03	07 16	07 33	07 50			08 03	08 16	08 33	08 49		09 03	09 16		09 33		09 48		10 03	10 16
Bradford Interchange		a			06 24	07 03	07 17	07 31	07 47	08 04			08 17	08 31	08 47	09 02		09 17	09 31		09 47		10 02		10 17	10 31
		d			06 26	07 05	07 20	07 34	07 50	08 05			08 20	08 34	08 50	09 04		09 20	09 34		09 50		10 04		10 19	10 34
New Pudsey	37	a			06 35	07 14	07 28	07 42	07 58	08 14			08 28	08 42	08 58	09 12		09 27	09 42		09 58		10 12		10 27	10 42
Bramley	37	a			06 38	07 17		07 46	08 02	08 18				08 46	09 02	09 16			09 46		10 02		10 16			10 46
Leeds ■	37,39	a			06 48	07 27	07 39	07 57	08 12	08 30	08 33		08 39	08 57	09 12	09 27	09 31	09 39	09 58		10 12		10 27	10 31	10 39	10 58
Selby	40	a						08 36							09 53						10 53					
York ■	40	a					08 20						09 21					10 21							11 19	

For connections from Liverpool Lime Street please refer to Table 90

Table 41

Saturdays

Manchester Victoria, Rochdale, Blackpool North and Huddersfield - Bradford and Leeds via Brighouse and Halifax

	NT	NT	NT	NT	NT		NT	NT	NT	NT	NT	NT
Manchester Victoria d	09 33	09 48		10 00			10 21	10 30	10 48		11 00	
Moston d	09 39			10 06				10 36			11 06	
Mills Hill d	09 44			10 11				10 40			11 11	
Castleton d	09 49			10 16				10 45			11 16	
Rochdale a	09 54	10 02		10 19			10 34	10 51	11 02		11 19	
d		10 02		10 20			10 35		11 02		11 20	
Smithy Bridge d				10 24			10 39				11 24	
Littleborough d				10 27			10 42				11 27	
Walsden d							10 48					
Todmorden d		10 14		10 34			10 52		11 14		11 34	
Blackpool North 97 d					09 29							10 29
Poulton-le-Fylde 97 d					09 35							10 35
Preston 8 97 d					09 54							10 54
Blackburn 97 d					10 10							11 10
Accrington 97 d					10 17							11 17
Burnley Manchester Road 97 d					10 26							11 28
Hebden Bridge a		10 20		10 41	10 49		10 58		11 20		11 41	11 49
d		10 21		10 41	10 50		11 00		11 21		11 41	11 50
Mytholmroyd d				10 44			11 03				11 44	
Sowerby Bridge d				10 50			11 09				11 50	
Huddersfield 39 d			10 23							11 23		
Brighouse d			10 33	10 58						11 33	11 58	
Mirfield 39 a				11 06							12 06	
Dewsbury 39 a				11 12							12 12	
Halifax a		10 33	10 43		11 02		11 15		11 33	11 43		12 02
d		10 33	10 49		11 03		11 16		11 33	11 49		12 03
Bradford Interchange a		10 47	11 02		11 17		11 31		11 47	12 02		12 17
d		10 50	11 05		11 20		11 34		11 50	12 05		12 19
New Pudsey 37 a		10 58	11 13		11 28		11 42		11 58	12 13		12 27
Bramley 37 a		11 02	11 17				11 46		12 02	12 17		
Leeds 10 37,39 a		11 13	11 27	11 33	11 39		11 58		12 12	12 27	12 31	12 39
Selby 40 a		11 55							12 50			
York 8 40 a					12 21							13 19

	NT	NT	NT		NT	NT	NT	NT	NT	NT	GC	NT
Manchester Victoria d	11 21	11 30	11 48			12 00		12 21	12 30	12 48		
Moston d		11 36				12 06			12 36			
Mills Hill d		11 40				12 11			12 40			
Castleton d		11 45				12 16			12 45			
Rochdale a	11 34	11 51	12 02			12 19		12 34	12 51	13 02		
d	11 35		12 02			12 20		12 35		13 02		
Smithy Bridge d	11 39					12 24		12 39				
Littleborough d	11 42					12 27		12 42				
Walsden d	11 48							12 48				
Todmorden d	11 52		12 14			12 34		12 52		13 14		
Blackpool North 97 d							11 24					
Poulton-le-Fylde 97 d							11 31					
Preston 8 97 d							11 54					
Blackburn 97 d							12 10					
Accrington 97 d							12 17					
Burnley Manchester Road 97 d							12 26					
Hebden Bridge a	11 58		12 20			12 41	12 49	12 58		13 20		
d	12 00		12 21			12 41	12 50	13 00		13 21		
Mytholmroyd d	12 03					12 44		13 03				
Sowerby Bridge d	12 09					12 50		13 09				
Huddersfield 39 d					12 23							13 23
Brighouse d					12 33	12 58					13 28	13 34
Mirfield 39 a						13 06						
Dewsbury 39 a						13 12						
Halifax a	12 15		12 33		12 43		13 02	13 15		13 33	13 37	13 44
d	12 16		12 33		12 49		13 03	13 16		13 33	13 40	13 49
Bradford Interchange a	12 31		12 47		13 02		13 17	13 31		13 47	13 53	14 02
d	12 34		12 50		13 05		13 19	13 34		13 50		14 05
New Pudsey 37 a	12 42		12 58		13 13		13 27	13 42		13 58		14 13
Bramley 37 a	12 46		13 02		13 17			13 46		14 02		14 17
Leeds 10 37,39 a	12 58		13 12		13 27	13 31	13 39	13 58		14 12		14 27
Selby 40 a			13 51							14 50		
York 8 40 a							14 21					

	NT		NT	NT	NT	NT	NT	NT	NT	NT	NT	
Manchester Victoria d	13 00			13 21	13 30	13 48		14 00		14 21	14 30	
Moston d	13 06				13 36			14 06			14 36	
Mills Hill d	13 11				13 40			14 11			14 40	
Castleton d	13 16				13 45			14 16			14 45	
Rochdale a	13 19			13 34	13 51	14 02		14 19		14 34	14 51	
d	13 20			13 35		14 02		14 20		14 35		
Smithy Bridge d	13 24			13 39				14 24		14 39		
Littleborough d	13 27			13 42				14 27		14 42		
Walsden d				13 48						14 48		
Todmorden d	13 34			13 52		14 14		14 34		14 52		
Blackpool North 97 d			12 29						13 29			
Poulton-le-Fylde 97 d			12 35						13 35			
Preston 8 97 d			12 54						13 54			
Blackburn 97 d			13 10						14 10			
Accrington 97 d			13 17						14 17			
Burnley Manchester Road 97 d			13 26						14 26			
Hebden Bridge a	13 41		13 49	13 58		14 20		14 41	14 49	14 58		
d	13 41		13 50	14 00		14 21		14 41	14 50	15 00		
Mytholmroyd d	13 44			14 03				14 44		15 03		
Sowerby Bridge d	13 50			14 09				14 50		15 09		
Huddersfield 39 d							14 23					
Brighouse d	13 58						14 33	14 58				
Mirfield 39 a	14 06							15 06				
Dewsbury 39 a	14 12							15 12				
Halifax a			14 02	14 15		14 33	14 43		15 02	15 15		
d			14 03	14 16		14 33	14 49		15 03	15 16		
Bradford Interchange a			14 17	14 31		14 47	15 02		15 17	15 31		
d			14 19	14 34		14 50	15 05		15 19	15 34		
New Pudsey 37 a			14 27	14 42		14 58	15 13		15 27	15 42		
Bramley 37 a				14 46		15 02	15 17			15 46		
Leeds 10 37,39 a	14 31		14 39	14 58		15 12	15 27	15 31	15 39	15 58		
Selby 40 a						15 52						
York 8 40 a			15 19						16 21			

	NT	NT	NT	NT	NT	NT	NT	NT	NT		NT	NT
Manchester Victoria d	14 48		15 00		15 21	15 30	15 48		16 00			16 21
Moston d			15 06			15 36			16 06			
Mills Hill d			15 11			15 40			16 11			
Castleton d			15 16			15 45			16 16			
Rochdale a	15 02		15 19		15 34	15 51	16 02		16 19			16 34
d	15 02		15 20		15 35		16 02		16 20			16 35
Smithy Bridge d			15 24		15 39				16 24			16 39
Littleborough d			15 27		15 42				16 27			16 42
Walsden d					15 48							16 48
Todmorden d	15 14		15 34		15 52		16 14		16 34			16 52
Blackpool North 97 d				14 29							15 29	
Poulton-le-Fylde 97 d				14 35							15 35	
Preston 8 97 d				14 54							15 54	
Blackburn 97 d				15 10							16 10	
Accrington 97 d				15 17							16 17	
Burnley Manchester Road 97 d				15 26							16 26	
Hebden Bridge a	15 20		15 41	15 49	16 00		16 20		16 41		16 49	16 58
d	15 21		15 41	15 50	16 01		16 21		16 41		16 50	17 00
Mytholmroyd d			15 44		16 04				16 44			17 03
Sowerby Bridge d			15 50		16 10				16 50			17 09
Huddersfield 39 d		15 23						16 23				
Brighouse d		15 33	15 58					16 33	16 58			
Mirfield 39 a			16 06						17 06			
Dewsbury 39 a			16 12						17 12			
Halifax a	15 33	15 43		16 02	16 16		16 33	16 46			17 02	17 15
d	15 33	15 49		16 03	16 17		16 33	16 49			17 03	17 16
Bradford Interchange a	15 47	16 02		16 17	16 31		16 47	17 02			17 17	17 31
d	15 50	16 05		16 19	16 34		16 50	17 04			17 19	17 34
New Pudsey 37 a	15 58	16 13		16 27	16 42		16 58	17 13			17 28	17 42
Bramley 37 a	16 02	16 17			16 46		17 02	17 17				17 46
Leeds 10 37,39 a	16 12	16 27	16 31	16 39	16 58		17 12	17 27	17 31		17 39	17 58
Selby 40 a	16 54						17 53					
York 8 40 a				17 19							18 24	

For connections from Liverpool Lime Street please refer to Table 90

Table 41

Saturdays

Manchester Victoria, Rochdale, Blackpool North and Huddersfield - Bradford and Leeds via Brighouse and Halifax

	NT	NT		GC	NT	NT	NT		NT	NT		NT
Manchester Victoria d	16 30	16 48				17 00			17 18	17 30		17 43
Moston d	16 36					17 06			17 24	17 36		17 49
Mills Hill d	16 40					17 11			17 29	17 40		17 54
Castleton d	16 45					17 16			17 34	17 45		17 59
Rochdale a	16 51	17 02				17 19			17 37	17 51		18 02
d		17 02				17 20			17 38			18 03
Smithy Bridge d						17 24			17 42			
Littleborough d						17 27			17 45			18 08
Walsden d									17 51			
Todmorden d		17 14				17 34			17 55			18 16
Blackpool North 97 d							16 29					
Poulton-le-Fylde 97 d							16 35					
Preston 8 97 d							16 54					
Blackburn 97 d							17 10					
Accrington 97 d							17 17					
Burnley Manchester Road 97 d							17 26					
Hebden Bridge a		17 20				17 41	17 49		18 01			18 22
d		17 21				17 41	17 50		18 01			18 23
Mytholmroyd d						17 44			18 05			
Sowerby Bridge d						17 50			18 10			
Huddersfield 39 d					17 23							
Brighouse d				17 30	17 34	17 58						
Mirfield 39 a						18 07						
Dewsbury 39 a						18 12						
Halifax a		17 33		17 39	17 49		18 02		18 17			18 35
d		17 33		17 41	17 49		18 03		18 17			18 35
Bradford Interchange a		17 47		17 54	18 04		18 17		18 32			18 49
d		17 50			18 04		18 19		18 34			18 50
New Pudsey 37 a		17 58			18 13		18 28		18 42			18 58
Bramley 37 a		18 02			18 17				18 46			19 02
Leeds 10 37,39 a		18 12			18 28	18 33	18 39		18 56			19 13
Selby 40 a		18 50					19 49					
York 8 40 a												19 57

	NT	NT	NT	NT	NT	NT	NT	NT	NT	NT	NT	NT
Manchester Victoria d		18 00		18 21	18 28	18 48		19 00		19 21		20 21
Moston d					18 34			19 06		19 27		20 27
Mills Hill d		18 09			18 38			19 10		19 32		20 32
Castleton d		18 14			18 43			19 15		19 37		20 37
Rochdale a		18 18		18 35	18 49	19 01		19 19		19 40		20 40
d		18 18		18 36		19 01		19 19		19 41		20 41
Smithy Bridge d		18 22		18 40				19 23		19 45		20 45
Littleborough d		18 26		18 43				19 27		19 48		20 48
Walsden d		18 32		18 49						19 54		20 54
Todmorden d		18 35		18 53		19 13		19 34		19 58		20 58
Blackpool North 97 d			17 14						18 29			
Poulton-le-Fylde 97 d			17 20						18 35			
Preston 8 97 d			17 44						18 54			
Blackburn 97 d			18 11						19 10			
Accrington 97 d			18 19						19 17			
Burnley Manchester Road 97 d			18 28						19 26			
Hebden Bridge a		18 42	18 49	18 59		19 20		19 41	19 49	20 04		21 04
d		18 42	18 50	19 00		19 20		19 41	19 50	20 05		21 05
Mytholmroyd d		18 45		19 03				19 44		20 08		21 08
Sowerby Bridge d		18 51		19 09				19 50		20 14		21 14
Huddersfield 39 d	18 23						19 23				20 25	
Brighouse d	18 34	18 59					19 33	19 58			20 35	
Mirfield 39 a		19 07						20 07				
Dewsbury 39 a		19 13						20 12				
Halifax a	18 45		19 03	19 15		19 32	19 43		20 03	20 20	20 45	21 20
d	18 49		19 03	19 16		19 32	19 49		20 03	20 21	20 49	21 21
Bradford Interchange a	19 02		19 17	19 31		19 48	20 02		20 17	20 35	21 02	21 35
d	19 05		19 19	19 34		19 50	20 04		20 19	20 37	21 04	21 37
New Pudsey 37 a	19 13		19 28	19 42		19 58	20 13		20 28	20 46	21 13	21 46
Bramley 37 a	19 17			19 46		20 03	20 16			20 49	21 16	21 49
Leeds 10 37,39 a	19 28	19 33	19 39	19 58		20 13	20 29	20 34	20 41	21 01	21 25	22 01
Selby 40 a												
York 8 40 a			20 21						21 31			

	NT	NT	NT		NT	NT	GC	NT	NT
Manchester Victoria d			21 21		22 21			22 54	23 20
Moston d			21 27		22 27				23 26
Mills Hill d			21 32		22 32				23 31
Castleton d			21 37		22 37				23 36
Rochdale a			21 40		22 42			23 07	23 41
d			21 41					23 07	
Smithy Bridge d			21 45					23 11	
Littleborough d			21 48					23 15	
Walsden d			21 54					23 21	
Todmorden d			21 58					23 24	
Blackpool North 97 d		20 29							
Poulton-le-Fylde 97 d		20 35							
Preston 8 97 d		20 54							
Blackburn 97 d		21 10							
Accrington 97 d		21 17							
Burnley Manchester Road 97 d		21 28							
Hebden Bridge a		21 50	22 04					23 31	
d		21 51	22 05					23 31	
Mytholmroyd d			22 08					23 34	
Sowerby Bridge d			22 14					23 40	
Huddersfield 39 d	21 25					22 25			
Brighouse d	21 35					22 37	22 44		
Mirfield 39 a									
Dewsbury 39 a									
Halifax a	21 45	22 03	22 20			22 48	22 53	23 46	
d	21 49	22 03	22 21			22 50	22 56	23 47	
Bradford Interchange a	22 02	22 17	22 35			23 03	23 10	00 02	
d	22 04	22 19	22 37			23 06		00 04	
New Pudsey 37 a	22 13	22 28	22 46			23 14		00 12	
Bramley 37 a	22 16		22 49			23 18		00 15	
Leeds 10 37,39 a	22 25	22 41	23 01			23 27		00 27	
Selby 40 a									
York 8 40 a		23 36							

For connections from Liverpool Lime Street please refer to Table 90

Table 41

Sundays until 11 July

Manchester Victoria, Rochdale, Blackpool North and Huddersfield - Bradford and Leeds via Brighouse and Halifax

		NT	NT	NT	NT	NT	NT	NT	NT	NT
Manchester Victoria	d				09 08		10 08			11 08
Moston	d				09 15		10 15			11 15
Mills Hill	d				09 19		10 19			11 19
Castleton	d				09 24		10 24			11 24
Rochdale	a				09 28		10 28			11 28
	d				09 28		10 28			11 28
Smithy Bridge	d				09 32		10 32			11 32
Littleborough	d				09 36		10 36			11 36
Walsden	d				09 42		10 42			11 42
Todmorden	d				09 45		10 45			11 45
Blackpool North	97 d					09 11			10 11	
Poulton-le-Fylde	97 d					09 17			10 17	
Preston 8	97 d					09 37			10 37	
Blackburn	97 d					09 54			10 54	
Accrington	97 d					10 01			11 01	
Burnley Manchester Road	97 d					10 10			11 10	
Hebden Bridge	a				09 52	10 32	10 52		11 32	11 52
	d				09 52	10 32	10 52		11 32	11 52
Mytholmroyd	d				09 55		10 55			11 55
Sowerby Bridge	d				10 01		11 01			12 01
Huddersfield	39 d			09 25				11 08		
Brighouse	d			09 35				11 18		
Mirfield	39 a									
Dewsbury	39 a									
Halifax	a			09 46	10 08	10 44	11 08	11 28	11 44	12 08
	d		09 05	09 46	10 08	10 45	11 08	11 29	11 45	12 08
Bradford Interchange	a		09 18	09 59	10 22	10 59	11 22	11 42	11 59	12 22
	d	08 31	09 20	10 02	10 25	11 02	11 25	11 44	12 02	12 25
New Pudsey	37 a	08 39	09 29	10 10	10 33	11 10	11 33	11 53	12 10	12 33
Bramley	37 a	08 43	09 32	10 14	10 37		11 37	11 56		12 37
Leeds 10	37,39 a	08 51	09 42	10 24	10 46	11 21	11 48	12 05	12 22	12 47
Selby	40 a									
York 8	40 a	09 34	10 29	11 07		11 59			13 02	

		NT	NT	NT	NT	NT	NT	NT	GC	NT	NT	NT	NT	NT
Manchester Victoria	d			12 08			13 08				14 08			15 08
Moston	d			12 15			13 15				14 15			15 15
Mills Hill	d			12 19			13 19				14 19			15 19
Castleton	d			12 24			13 24				14 24			15 24
Rochdale	a			12 28			13 28				14 28			15 28
	d			12 28			13 28				14 28			15 28
Smithy Bridge	d			12 32			13 32				14 32			15 32
Littleborough	d			12 36			13 36				14 36			15 36
Walsden	d			12 42			13 42				14 42			15 42
Todmorden	d			12 45			13 45				14 45			15 45
Blackpool North	97 d		11 13			12 11				13 13			14 11	
Poulton-le-Fylde	97 d		11 19			12 17				13 19			14 17	
Preston 8	97 d		11 37			12 37				13 37			14 37	
Blackburn	97 d		11 54			12 54				13 54			14 54	
Accrington	97 d		12 01			13 01				14 01			15 01	
Burnley Manchester Road	97 d		12 10			13 10				14 10			15 10	
Hebden Bridge	a		12 32	12 52		13 32	13 52			14 32	14 52		15 32	15 52
	d		12 32	12 52		13 32	13 52			14 32	14 52		15 32	15 52
Mytholmroyd	d			12 55			13 55				14 55			15 55
Sowerby Bridge	d			13 01			14 01				15 01			16 01
Huddersfield	39 d				13 08							15 08		
Brighouse	d				13 18				14 20			15 18		
Mirfield	39 a													
Dewsbury	39 a													
Halifax	a		12 44	13 08	13 28	13 44	14 08		14 35	14 44	15 08	15 28	15 44	16 08
	d	12 29	12 45	13 08	13 29	13 46	14 08	14 29	14 36	14 45	15 08	15 29	15 46	16 08
Bradford Interchange	a	12 42	12 59	13 22	13 42	14 00	14 22	14 42	14 49	14 59	15 22	15 42	16 00	16 22
	d	12 44	13 02	13 25	13 44	14 02	14 25	14 44		15 02	15 25	15 44	16 03	16 26
New Pudsey	37 a	12 53	13 10	13 33	13 53	14 10	14 33	14 53		15 10	15 33	15 53	16 11	16 34
Bramley	37 a	12 56		13 37	13 56		14 37	14 56			15 37	15 56		16 38
Leeds 10	37,39 a	13 06	13 22	13 46	14 06	14 22	14 48	15 06		15 22	15 46	16 06	16 22	16 48
Selby	40 a													
York 8	40 a		13 59			15 02				15 59			17 06	

		NT	NT	NT	NT	NT	NT	NT	NT	GC
Manchester Victoria	d			16 08			17 08			
Moston	d			16 15			17 15			
Mills Hill	d			16 19			17 19			
Castleton	d			16 24			17 24			
Rochdale	a			16 28			17 28			
	d			16 28			17 28			
Smithy Bridge	d			16 32			17 32			
Littleborough	d			16 36			17 36			
Walsden	d			16 42			17 42			
Todmorden	d			16 45			17 45			
Blackpool North	97 d		15 13			16 11			17 11	
Poulton-le-Fylde	97 d		15 19			16 17			17 17	
Preston 8	97 d		15 37			16 37			17 37	
Blackburn	97 d		15 54			16 54			17 54	
Accrington	97 d		16 01			17 01			18 01	
Burnley Manchester Road	97 d		16 10			17 10			18 10	
Hebden Bridge	a		16 32	16 52		17 32	17 52		18 32	
	d		16 32	16 52		17 32	17 52		18 32	
Mytholmroyd	d			16 55			17 55			
Sowerby Bridge	d			17 01			18 01			
Huddersfield	39 d				17 08					
Brighouse	d				17 17					18 39
Mirfield	39 a									
Dewsbury	39 a									
Halifax	a		16 44	17 08	17 27	17 44	18 08		18 44	18 51
	d	16 29	16 45	17 08	17 29	17 45	18 08	18 29	18 45	18 54
Bradford Interchange	a	16 42	16 59	17 22	17 42	17 59	18 22	18 42	18 59	19 09
	d	16 44	17 02	17 25	17 44	18 02	18 25	18 44	19 02	
New Pudsey	37 a	16 53	17 10	17 33	17 53	18 10	18 33	18 53	19 10	
Bramley	37 a	16 56		17 37	17 56		18 37	18 56		
Leeds 10	37,39 a	17 05	17 21	17 46	18 05	18 21	18 46	19 07	19 21	
Selby	40 a									
York 8	40 a		18 02			19 03			20 01	

		NT	NT	NT	NT	NT	NT	NT	NT	NT	GC	NT	NT	NT
Manchester Victoria	d	18 08			19 08		20 08			21 08			22 08	
Moston	d	18 15			19 15		20 15			21 15			22 15	
Mills Hill	d	18 19			19 19		20 19			21 19			22 19	
Castleton	d	18 24			19 24		20 24			21 24			22 24	
Rochdale	a	18 28			19 28		20 28			21 28			22 28	
	d	18 28			19 28		20 28			21 28			22 28	
Smithy Bridge	d	18 32			19 32		20 32			21 32			22 32	
Littleborough	d	18 36			19 36		20 36			21 36			22 36	
Walsden	d	18 42			19 42		20 42			21 42			22 42	
Todmorden	d	18 45			19 45		20 45			21 45			22 45	
Blackpool North	97 d			18 11		19 13			20 11			21 13		
Poulton-le-Fylde	97 d			18 17		19 19			20 17			21 19		
Preston 8	97 d			18 37		19 37			20 37			21 39		
Blackburn	97 d			18 54		19 54			20 54			21 55		
Accrington	97 d			19 01		20 01			21 01			22 02		
Burnley Manchester Road	97 d			19 10		20 10			21 10			22 12		
Hebden Bridge	a	18 52		19 32	19 52	20 32	20 52		21 32	21 52		22 34	22 52	
	d	18 52		19 32	19 52	20 32	20 52		21 32	21 52		22 34	22 52	
Mytholmroyd	d	18 55			19 55		20 55			21 55			22 55	
Sowerby Bridge	d	19 01			20 01		21 01			22 01			23 01	
Huddersfield	39 d		19 08					21 08						
Brighouse	d		19 18					21 18			22 10			
Mirfield	39 a													
Dewsbury	39 a													
Halifax	a	19 08	19 28	19 44	20 08	20 44	21 08	21 28	21 44	22 08	22 21	22 46	23 08	
	d	19 08	19 29	19 45	20 08	20 45	21 08	21 29	21 45	22 10	22 23	22 47	23 08	
Bradford Interchange	a	19 22	19 42	19 59	20 22	20 59	21 22	21 42	21 59	22 24	22 36	23 01	23 22	
	d	19 25	19 44	20 02	20 25	21 02	21 26	21 44	22 02	22 26		23 04	23 25	23 47
New Pudsey	37 a	19 33	19 53	20 10	20 33	21 10	21 34	21 53	22 10	22 35		23 12	23 33	23 55
Bramley	37 a	19 37	19 56		20 37		21 38	21 56		22 39			23 37	23 59
Leeds 10	37,39 a	19 47	20 08	20 23	20 47	21 22	21 48	22 05	22 22	22 47		23 23	23 46	00 08
Selby	40 a													
York 8	40 a			21 03		21 59								

For connections from Liverpool Lime Street please refer to Table 90

Table 41

Sundays 18 July to 05 September

Manchester Victoria, Rochdale, Blackpool North and Huddersfield - Bradford and Leeds via Brighouse and Halifax

		NT 🚌	NT 🚌	NT	NT	NT	NT	NT 🚌	NT 🚌
Manchester Victoria	d	08 25	08 55					09 25	09 55
Moston	d	08 45						09 45	
Mills Hill	d	09 00						10 00	
Castleton	d	09 10						10 10	
Rochdale	a	09 16	09 17					10 16	10 17
	d					09 28			
Smithy Bridge	d					09 32			
Littleborough	d					09 36			
Walsden	d					09 42			
Todmorden	d					09 45			
Blackpool North	97 d						09 11		
Poulton-le-Fylde	97 d						09 17		
Preston 8	97 d						09 37		
Blackburn	97 d						09 54		
Accrington	97 d						10 01		
Burnley Manchester Road	97 d						10 10		
Hebden Bridge	a					09 52	10 32		
	d					09 52	10 32		
Mytholmroyd	d					09 55			
Sowerby Bridge	d					10 01			
Huddersfield	39 d				09 25				
Brighouse	d				09 35				
Mirfield	39 a								
Dewsbury	39 a								
Halifax	a				09 46	10 08	10 44		
	d			09 05	09 46	10 08	10 45		
Bradford Interchange	a			09 18	09 59	10 22	10 59		
	d			09 20	10 02	10 25	11 02		
New Pudsey	37 a			09 29	10 10	10 33	11 10		
Bramley	37 a			09 32	10 14	10 37			
Leeds 10	37,39 a			09 42	10 24	10 46	11 21		
Selby	40 a								
York 8	40 a			10 29	11 07		11 59		

		NT	NT 🚌	NT 🚌	NT	NT	NT	NT 🚌	NT 🚌	NT	NT	NT	NT 🚌	NT 🚌
Manchester Victoria	d		10 25	10 55				11 25	11 55				12 25	12 55
Moston	d		10 45					11 45					12 45	
Mills Hill	d		11 00					12 00					13 00	
Castleton	d		11 10					12 10					13 10	
Rochdale	a		11 16	11 17				12 16	12 17				13 16	13 17
	d	10 28					11 28					12 28		
Smithy Bridge	d	10 32					11 32					12 32		
Littleborough	d	10 36					11 36					12 36		
Walsden	d	10 42					11 42					12 42		
Todmorden	d	10 45					11 45					12 45		
Blackpool North	97 d					10 11					11 13			
Poulton-le-Fylde	97 d					10 17					11 19			
Preston 8	97 d					10 37					11 37			
Blackburn	97 d					10 54					11 54			
Accrington	97 d					11 01					12 01			
Burnley Manchester Road	97 d					11 10					12 10			
Hebden Bridge	a	10 52				11 32	11 52				12 32	12 52		
	d	10 52				11 32	11 52				12 32	12 52		
Mytholmroyd	d	10 55					11 55					12 55		
Sowerby Bridge	d	11 01					12 01					13 01		
Huddersfield	39 d				11 08									
Brighouse	d				11 18									
Mirfield	39 a													
Dewsbury	39 a													
Halifax	a	11 08			11 28	11 44	12 08				12 44	13 08		
	d	11 08			11 29	11 45	12 08			12 29	12 45	13 08		
Bradford Interchange	a	11 22			11 42	11 59	12 22			12 42	12 59	13 22		
	d	11 25			11 44	12 02	12 25			12 44	13 02	13 25		
New Pudsey	37 a	11 33			11 53	12 10	12 33			12 53	13 10	13 33		
Bramley	37 a	11 37			11 56		12 37			12 56		13 37		
Leeds 10	37,39 a	11 48			12 05	12 22	12 47			13 06	13 22	13 46		
Selby	40 a													
York 8	40 a					13 02					13 59			

		NT	NT	NT	NT 🚌	NT 🚌	NT	NT	NT	NT 🚌
Manchester Victoria	d				13 25	13 55				14 25
Moston	d				13 45					14 45
Mills Hill	d				14 00					15 00
Castleton	d				14 10					15 10
Rochdale	a				14 16	14 17				15 16
	d			13 28					14 28	
Smithy Bridge	d			13 32					14 32	
Littleborough	d			13 36					14 36	
Walsden	d			13 42					14 42	
Todmorden	d			13 45					14 45	
Blackpool North	97 d		12 11					13 13		
Poulton-le-Fylde	97 d		12 17					13 19		
Preston 8	97 d		12 37					13 37		
Blackburn	97 d		12 54					13 54		
Accrington	97 d		13 01					14 01		
Burnley Manchester Road	97 d		13 10					14 10		
Hebden Bridge	a		13 32	13 52				14 32	14 52	
	d		13 32	13 52				14 32	14 52	
Mytholmroyd	d			13 55					14 55	
Sowerby Bridge	d			14 01					15 01	
Huddersfield	39 d	13 08								
Brighouse	d	13 18								
Mirfield	39 a									
Dewsbury	39 a									
Halifax	a	13 28	13 44	14 08				14 44	15 08	
	d	13 29	13 46	14 08			14 29	14 45	15 08	
Bradford Interchange	a	13 42	14 00	14 22			14 42	14 59	15 22	
	d	13 44	14 02	14 25			14 44	15 02	15 25	
New Pudsey	37 a	13 53	14 10	14 33			14 53	15 10	15 33	
Bramley	37 a	13 56		14 37			14 56		15 37	
Leeds 10	37,39 a	14 06	14 22	14 48			15 06	15 22	15 46	
Selby	40 a									
York 8	40 a		15 02					15 59		

		GC	NT 🚌	NT	NT	NT	NT 🚌	NT 🚌	NT	NT	NT	NT 🚌	NT 🚌	NT
Manchester Victoria	d		14 55				15 25	15 55				16 25	16 55	
Moston	d						15 45					16 45		
Mills Hill	d						16 00					17 00		
Castleton	d						16 10					17 10		
Rochdale	a		15 17				16 16	16 17				17 16	17 17	
	d					15 28					16 28			
Smithy Bridge	d					15 32					16 32			
Littleborough	d					15 36					16 36			
Walsden	d					15 42					16 42			
Todmorden	d					15 45					16 45			
Blackpool North	97 d				14 11					15 13				
Poulton-le-Fylde	97 d				14 17					15 19				
Preston 8	97 d				14 37					15 37				
Blackburn	97 d				14 54					15 54				
Accrington	97 d				15 01					16 01				
Burnley Manchester Road	97 d				15 10					16 10				
Hebden Bridge	a				15 32	15 52				16 32	16 52			
	d				15 32	15 52				16 32	16 52			
Mytholmroyd	d					15 55					16 55			
Sowerby Bridge	d					16 01					17 01			
Huddersfield	39 d			15 08										17 08
Brighouse	d	14 57		15 18										17 17
Mirfield	39 a													
Dewsbury	39 a													
Halifax	a	15 13		15 28	15 44	16 08				16 44	17 08			17 27
	d	15 14		15 29	15 46	16 08			16 29	16 45	17 08			17 29
Bradford Interchange	a	15 28		15 42	16 00	16 22			16 42	16 59	17 22			17 42
	d			15 44	16 03	16 26			16 44	17 02	17 25			17 44
New Pudsey	37 a			15 53	16 11	16 34			16 53	17 10	17 33			17 53
Bramley	37 a			15 56		16 38			16 56		17 37			17 56
Leeds 10	37,39 a			16 06	16 22	16 48			17 05	17 21	17 46			18 05
Selby	40 a													
York 8	40 a				17 06					18 02				

For connections from Liverpool Lime Street please refer to Table 90

Table 41

Sundays
18 July to 05 September

Manchester Victoria, Rochdale, Blackpool North and Huddersfield - Bradford and Leeds via Brighouse and Halifax

	NT	NT	NT (bus)	NT (bus)	NT	NT	NT	NT (bus)	NT (bus)	NT	NT	NT	NT (bus)	GC	NT	NT (bus)	NT	NT (bus)	NT (bus)	NT	NT
Manchester Victoria d			17 25	17 55				18 25	18 55				19 25			19 55		20 25	20 55		
Moston d			17 45					18 45					19 45					20 45			
Mills Hill d			18 00					19 00					20 00					21 00			
Castleton d			18 10					19 10					20 10					21 10			
Rochdale a			18 16	18 17				19 16	19 17				20 16			20 17		21 16	21 17		
d		17 28					18 28					19 28					20 28				
Smithy Bridge d		17 32					18 32					19 32					20 32				
Littleborough d		17 36					18 36					19 36					20 36				
Walsden d		17 42					18 42					19 42					20 42				
Todmorden d		17 45					18 45					19 45					20 45				
Blackpool North 97 d	16 11					17 11					18 11				19 13						20 11
Poulton-le-Fylde 97 d	16 17					17 17					18 17				19 19						20 17
Preston 8 97 d	16 37					17 37					18 37				19 37						20 37
Blackburn 97 d	16 54					17 54					18 54				19 54						20 54
Accrington 97 d	17 01					18 01					19 01				20 01						21 01
Burnley Manchester Road 97 d	17 10					18 10					19 10				20 10						21 10
Hebden Bridge a	17 32	17 52				18 32	18 52				19 32	19 52			20 32		20 52				21 32
d	17 32	17 52				18 32	18 52				19 32	19 52			20 32		20 52				21 32
Mytholmroyd d		17 55					18 55					19 55					20 55				
Sowerby Bridge d		18 01					19 01					20 01					21 01				
Huddersfield 39 d										19 08										21 08	
Brighouse d										19 18				19 55						21 18	
Mirfield 39 a																					
Dewsbury 39 a																					
Halifax a	17 44	18 08				18 44	19 08			19 28	19 44	20 08		20 13	20 44		21 08			21 28	21 44
d	17 45	18 08			18 29	18 45	19 08			19 29	19 45	20 08		20 15	20 45		21 08			21 29	21 45
Bradford Interchange a	17 59	18 22			18 42	18 59	19 22			19 42	19 59	20 22		20 30	20 59		21 22			21 42	21 59
d	18 02	18 25			18 44	19 02	19 25			19 44	20 02	20 25			21 02		21 26			21 44	22 02
New Pudsey 37 a	18 10	18 33			18 53	19 10	19 33			19 53	20 10	20 33			21 10		21 34			21 53	22 10
Bramley 37 a		18 37			18 56		19 37			19 56		20 37					21 38			21 56	
Leeds 10 37,39 a	18 21	18 46			19 07	19 21	19 47			20 08	20 23	20 47			21 22		21 48			22 05	22 22
Selby 40 a																					
York 8 40 a	19 03					20 01					21 03				21 59						

	NT	NT	NT (bus)	NT (bus)	NT	GC
Manchester Victoria d			21 55	22 25		
Moston d			22 15			
Mills Hill d			22 30			
Castleton d			22 40			
Rochdale a			22 46	22 47		
d	21 28				23 00	
Smithy Bridge d	21 32				23 04	
Littleborough d	21 36				23 08	
Walsden d	21 42				23 14	
Todmorden d	21 45				23 17	
Blackpool North 97 d		21 13				
Poulton-le-Fylde 97 d		21 19				
Preston 8 97 d		21 39				
Blackburn 97 d		21 55				
Accrington 97 d		22 02				
Burnley Manchester Road 97 d		22 12				
Hebden Bridge a	21 52	22 34			23 24	
d	21 52	22 34			23 24	
Mytholmroyd d	21 55				23 27	
Sowerby Bridge d	22 01				23 33	
Huddersfield 39 d						
Brighouse d						23 54
Mirfield 39 a						
Dewsbury 39 a						
Halifax a	22 08	22 46			23 40	00 05
d	22 10	22 47			23 40	00 07
Bradford Interchange a	22 24	23 01			23 54	00 20
d	22 26	23 04			23 57	
New Pudsey 37 a	22 35	23 12			00 05	
Bramley 37 a	22 39				00 09	
Leeds 10 37,39 a	22 47	23 23			00 18	
Selby 40 a						
York 8 40 a						

For connections from Liverpool Lime Street please refer tc Table 90

Table 41

Sundays
from 12 September

Manchester Victoria, Rochdale, Blackpool North and Huddersfield - Bradford and Leeds via Brighouse and Halifax

	NT	NT	NT	NT	NT	NT	NT	NT	NT	NT	NT	NT	NT	NT	NT	NT	GC	NT	NT	NT	NT	NT
Manchester Victoria d				09 08		10 08			11 08			12 08			13 08				14 08			15 08
Moston d				09 15		10 15			11 15			12 15			13 15				14 15			15 15
Mills Hill d				09 19		10 19			11 19			12 19			13 19				14 19			15 19
Castleton d				09 24		10 24			11 24			12 24			13 24				14 24			15 24
Rochdale a				09 28		10 28			11 28			12 28			13 28				14 28			15 28
d				09 28		10 28			11 28			12 28			13 28				14 28			15 28
Smithy Bridge d				09 32		10 32			11 32			12 32			13 32				14 32			15 32
Littleborough d				09 36		10 36			11 36			12 36			13 36				14 36			15 36
Walsden d				09 42		10 42			11 42			12 42			13 42				14 42			15 42
Todmorden d				09 45		10 45			11 45			12 45			13 45				14 45			15 45
Blackpool North 97 d					09 01			10 11			11 13			12 11				13 13			14 11	
Poulton-le-Fylde 97 d					09 07			10 17			11 19			12 17				13 19			14 17	
Preston 8 97 d					09 27			10 37			11 37			12 37				13 37			14 37	
Blackburn 97 d					09 44			10 54			11 54			12 54				13 54			14 54	
Accrington 97 d					09 51			11 01			12 01			13 01				14 01			15 01	
Burnley Manchester Road 97 d					10 00			11 10			12 10			13 10				14 10			15 10	
Hebden Bridge a				09 52	10 22	10 52		11 32	11 52		12 32	12 52		13 32	13 52			14 32	14 52		15 32	15 52
d				09 52	10 22	10 52		11 32	11 52		12 32	12 52		13 32	13 52			14 32	14 52		15 32	15 52
Mytholmroyd d				09 55		10 55			11 55			12 55			13 55				14 55			15 55
Sowerby Bridge d				10 01		11 01			12 01			13 01			14 01				15 01			16 01
Huddersfield 39 d			09 27				11 08						13 08							15 08		
Brighouse d			09 37				11 18						13 18				14 20			15 18		
Mirfield 39 a																						
Dewsbury 39 a																						
Halifax a			09 48	10 08	10 34	11 08	11 28	11 44	12 08		12 44	13 08	13 28	13 44	14 08		14 35	14 44	15 08	15 28	15 44	16 08
d		09 05	09 48	10 08	10 45	11 08	11 29	11 45	12 08	12 29	12 45	13 08	13 29	13 46	14 08	14 29	14 36	14 45	15 08	15 29	15 46	16 08
Bradford Interchange a		09 18	10 01	10 22	10 59	11 22	11 42	11 59	12 22	12 42	12 59	13 22	13 42	14 00	14 22	14 42	14 49	14 59	15 22	15 42	16 00	16 22
d	08 31	09 20	10 04	10 25	11 02	11 25	11 44	12 02	12 25	12 44	13 02	13 25	13 44	14 02	14 25	14 44		15 02	15 25	15 44	16 03	16 26
New Pudsey 37 a	08 39	09 29	10 12	10 33	11 10	11 33	11 53	12 10	12 33	12 53	13 10	13 33	13 53	14 10	14 33	14 53		15 10	15 33	15 53	16 11	16 34
Bramley 37 a	08 43	09 32	10 16	10 37		11 37	11 56		12 37	12 56		13 37	13 56		14 37	14 56			15 37	15 56		16 38
Leeds 10 37,39 a	08 51	09 42	10 25	10 46	11 21	11 48	12 05	12 22	12 47	13 06	13 22	13 46	14 06	14 22	14 48	15 06		15 22	15 46	16 06	16 22	16 48
Selby 40 a																						
York 8 40 a	09 34	10 29	11 08		11 59			13 02			13 59			15 02				15 59			17 06	

	NT	NT	NT	NT	NT	NT	NT	NT	GC	NT	NT	NT	NT	NT	NT	NT	NT	GC	NT	NT	NT
Manchester Victoria d			16 08			17 08				18 08			19 08		20 08			21 08			22 08	
Moston d			16 15			17 15				18 15			19 15		20 15			21 15			22 15	
Mills Hill d			16 19			17 19				18 19			19 19		20 19			21 19			22 19	
Castleton d			16 24			17 24				18 24			19 24		20 24			21 24			22 24	
Rochdale a			16 28			17 28				18 28			19 28		20 28			21 28			22 28	
d			16 28			17 28				18 28			19 28		20 28			21 28			22 28	
Smithy Bridge d			16 32			17 32				18 32			19 32		20 32			21 32			22 32	
Littleborough d			16 36			17 36				18 36			19 36		20 36			21 36			22 36	
Walsden d			16 42			17 42				18 42			19 42		20 42			21 42			22 42	
Todmorden d			16 45			17 45				18 45			19 45		20 45			21 45			22 45	
Blackpool North 97 d		15 13			16 11			17 11				18 11		19 13			20 11			21 13		
Poulton-le-Fylde 97 d		15 19			16 17			17 17				18 17		19 19			20 17			21 19		
Preston 8 97 d		15 37			16 37			17 37				18 37		19 37			20 37			21 39		
Blackburn 97 d		15 54			16 54			17 54				18 54		19 54			20 54			21 55		
Accrington 97 d		16 01			17 01			18 01				19 01		20 01			21 01			22 02		
Burnley Manchester Road 97 d		16 10			17 10			18 10				19 10		20 10			21 10			22 12		
Hebden Bridge a		16 32	16 52		17 32	17 52		18 32		18 52		19 32	19 52	20 32	20 52		21 32	21 52		22 34	22 52	
d		16 32	16 52		17 32	17 52		18 32		18 52		19 32	19 52	20 32	20 52		21 32	21 52		22 34	22 52	
Mytholmroyd d			16 55			17 55				18 55			19 55		20 55			21 55			22 55	
Sowerby Bridge d			17 01			18 01				19 01			20 01		21 01			22 01			23 01	
Huddersfield 39 d				17 08							19 08					21 08						
Brighouse d				17 17					18 39		19 18					21 18			22 10			
Mirfield 39 a																						
Dewsbury 39 a																						
Halifax a		16 44	17 08	17 27	17 44	18 08		18 44	18 51	19 08	19 28	19 44	20 08	20 44	21 08	21 28	21 44	22 08	22 21	22 46	23 08	
d	16 29	16 45	17 08	17 29	17 45	18 08	18 29	18 45	18 54	19 08	19 29	19 45	20 08	20 45	21 08	21 29	21 45	22 10	22 23	22 47	23 08	
Bradford Interchange a	16 42	16 59	17 22	17 42	17 59	18 22	18 42	18 59	19 09	19 22	19 42	19 59	20 22	20 59	21 22	21 42	21 59	22 24	22 36	23 01	23 22	
d	16 44	17 02	17 25	17 44	18 02	18 25	18 44	19 02		19 25	19 44	20 02	20 25	21 02	21 26	21 44	22 02	22 26		23 04	23 25	23 47
New Pudsey 37 a	16 53	17 10	17 33	17 53	18 10	18 33	18 53	19 10		19 33	19 53	20 10	20 33	21 10	21 34	21 53	22 10	22 35		23 12	23 33	23 55
Bramley 37 a	16 56		17 37	17 56		18 37	18 56			19 37	19 56		20 37		21 38	21 56		22 39			23 37	23 59
Leeds 10 37,39 a	17 05	17 21	17 46	18 05	18 21	18 46	19 07	19 21		19 47	20 08	20 23	20 47	21 22	21 48	22 05	22 22	22 47		23 23	23 46	00 08
Selby 40 a																						
York 8 40 a		18 02			19 03			20 01				21 03		21 59								

For connections from Liverpool Lime Street please refer to Table 90

Table 43

Hull - Beverley, Bridlington and Scarborough

Mondays to Saturdays
until 04 September

		NT	TP ◇1	TP ◇1	NT	NT	NT	NT	TP ◇1	NT	NT	NT	TP ◇1	NT	NT	NT	TP ◇1	TP ◇1	NT	NT	NT	NT	TP ◇1
Hull	d	06 23			06 54	07 14	07 36	07 52		08 14	08 37	09 17		09 47	10 14	10 44			11 14	11 44	12 14	12 44	
Cottingham	d	06 30			07 01	07 21	07 43	07 59		08 21	08 44	09 24		09 54	10 21	10 51			11 21	11 51	12 21	12 51	
Beverley	d	06 36			07 07	07 27	07a51	08 05		08 27	08a52	09 30		10 00	10 27	10 57			11 27	11 57	12 27	12 57	
Arram	d				07 12			08 10														13 02	
Hutton Cranswick	d				07 19	07 36		08 17		08 36		09 39		10 09		11 06				12 06		13 09	
Driffield	d	06 48			07 24	07 42		08 22		08 42		09 45		10 15	10 39	11 12			11 39	12 12	12 39	13 14	
Nafferton	d				07 28	07 46		08 26		08 46		09 49		10 19		11 16				12 16		13 18	
Bridlington	a	07 04			07 40	07 59		08 41		08 57		10 02		10 30	10 56	11 29			11 53	12 29	12 56	13 33	
	d				07 49					09 00				10 37					12 05				
Bempton	d				07 56					09 07				10 44					12 12				
Hunmanby	d				08 06					09 17				10 54					12 22				
Filey	d				08 11					09 22				10 59					12 27				
Seamer	d		07 21	08 06	08 22				09 19	09 34			10 19	11 10			11 19	12 19	12 38				13 19
Scarborough	a		07 30	08 15	08 29				09 30	09 39			10 30	11 17			11 30	12 30	12 45				13 30

		TP ◇1	NT	NT	NT	TP ◇1	NT	NT	NT	NT SX	TP ◇1	TP ◇1	NT	NT	NT	TP SX ◇1	TP SO ◇1	TP SX ◇1	NT	NT	NT	NT SX	NT SO
Hull	d		13 14	13 44	14 14		14 44	15 14	15 44	16 00			16 19	16 44	17 14				17 38	17 56	18 14	18 44	18 59
Cottingham	d		13 21	13 51	14 21		14 51	15 21	15 51	16 07			16 26	16 51	17 21				17 45	18 03	18 21	18 51	19 06
Beverley	d		13 27	13 57	14 27		14 57	15 27	15 57	16a15			16 32	16 57	17 27				17 51	18a11	18 27	18a58	19a13
Arram	d								16 02										17 56				
Hutton Cranswick	d			14 06			15 06		16 09				16 41		17 36				18 03		18 36		
Driffield	d		13 39	14 12	14 39		15 12	15 39	16 14				16 46	17 09	17 42				18 08		18 42		
Nafferton	d			14 16			15 16		16 18				16 50		17 46				18 12		18 46		
Bridlington	a		13 53	14 29	14 55		15 27	15 56	16 33				17 01	17 26	18 00				18 24		18 59		
	d		14 05				15 31						17 04						18 30				
Bempton	d		14 12				15 38						17 10						18 37				
Hunmanby	d		14 22				15 48						17 20						18 47				
Filey	d		14 27				15 53						17 25						18 52				
Seamer	d	14 19	14 38			15 19	16 04				16 19	17 19	17 36			18 07	18 19	18 41	19 03				
Scarborough	a	14 30	14 45			15 30	16 10				16 30	17 30	17 43			18 17	18 30	18 52	19 09				

		TP SO ◇1	TP SX ◇1	TP SO ◇1	TP SX ◇1	NT SX	NT SO	NT	NT	TP ◇1	NT	TP SO ◇1	TP SX ◇1	NT
Hull	d					19 14	19 20	20 14	21 09		21 48			23 00
Cottingham	d					19 21	19 27	20 21	21 16		21 55			23 07
Beverley	d					19 27	19 33	20 27	21a24		22 01			23a15
Arram	d							20 32						
Hutton Cranswick	d					19 36	19 42	20 39			22 10			
Driffield	d					19 41	19 47	20 44			22 16			
Nafferton	d					19 46	19 52	20 48			22 20			
Bridlington	a					19 57	20 03	21 02			22 33			
	d					20 00	20 06							
Bempton	d					20 07	20 13							
Hunmanby	d					20 17	20 23							
Filey	d					20 22	20 28							
Seamer	d	19 19	19 24	20 19	20 19	20 33	20 39			21 19		22 52	22 56	
Scarborough	a	19 30	19 33	20 30	20 30	20 39	20 45			21 30		23 01	23 06	

Mondays to Saturdays
from 06 September

		NT	TP ◇1	TP ◇1	NT	NT	NT	NT	TP ◇1	NT	NT	NT	TP ◇1	NT	NT	NT	TP ◇1	TP ◇1	NT	NT	NT	NT	TP ◇1
Hull	d	06 23			06 54	07 14	07 36	07 52		08 14	08 37	09 17		09 47	10 14	10 44			11 14	11 44	12 14	12 44	
Cottingham	d	06 30			07 01	07 21	07 43	07 59		08 21	08 44	09 24		09 54	10 21	10 51			11 21	11 51	12 21	12 51	
Beverley	d	06 37			07 08	07 28	07a52	08 06		08 28	08a53	09 31		10 01	10 28	10 58			11 28	11 58	12 28	12 58	
Arram	d				07 12			08 10														13 02	
Hutton Cranswick	d				07 19	07 37		08 17		08 37		09 40		10 10		11 07				12 07		13 09	
Driffield	d	06 49			07 25	07 42		08 23		08 42		09 45		10 15	10 40	11 12			11 40	12 12	12 40	13 15	
Nafferton	d				07 29	07 46		08 27		08 46		09 49		10 19		11 16				12 16		13 19	
Bridlington	a	07 07			07 42	08 01		08 42		09 00		10 04		10 32	10 58	11 31			11 56	12 31	12 58	13 34	
	d				07 47					09 02				10 36					12 05				
Bempton	d				07 54					09 09				10 43					12 12				
Hunmanby	d				08 04					09 19				10 53					12 22				
Filey	d				08 09					09 24				10 58					12 27				
Seamer	d		07 21	08 06	08 22				09 19	09 36			10 19	11 10			11 19	12 19	12 39				13 19
Scarborough	a		07 30	08 15	08 30				09 30	09 44			10 30	11 17			11 30	12 30	12 46				13 30

Table 43

Hull - Beverley, Bridlington and Scarborough

Mondays to Saturdays
from 06 September

		TP ◇1	NT	NT	NT	TP ◇1	NT	NT	NT	NT SX	TP ◇1	TP ◇1	NT	NT	NT	TP SX ◇1	TP SO ◇1	TP SX ◇1	NT	NT	NT	NT SX	NT SO
Hull	d		13 14	13 44	14 14		14 44	15 14	15 44	16 00			16 19	16 44	17 14				17 38	17 56	18 14	18 44	18 59
Cottingham	d		13 21	13 51	14 21		14 51	15 21	15 51	16 07			16 26	16 51	17 21				17 45	18 03	18 21	18 51	19 06
Beverley	d		13 28	13 58	14 28		14 58	15 28	15 58	16a15			16 32	16 58	17 28				17 52	18a11	18 28	18a59	19a14
Arram	d								16 02										17 56				
Hutton Cranswick	d			14 07			15 07		16 09				16 41		17 37				18 03		18 37		
Driffield	d		13 40	14 12	14 40		15 12	15 40	16 15				16 47	17 10	17 42				18 09		18 42		
Nafferton	d			14 16			15 16		16 19				16 51		17 46				18 13		18 46		
Bridlington	a		13 55	14 31	14 58		15 28	15 58	16 34				17 02	17 28	18 01				18 25		19 01		
	d		14 05				15 31						17 04						18 30				
Bempton	d		14 12				15 38						17 11						18 37				
Hunmanby	d		14 22				15 48						17 21						18 47				
Filey	d		14 27				15 53						17 26						18 52				
Seamer	d	14 19	14 39			15 19	16 05				16 19	17 19	17 38			18 07	18 19	18 41	19 03				
Scarborough	a	14 30	14 46			15 30	16 13				16 30	17 30	17 46			18 17	18 30	18 52	19 12				

		TP SO ◇1	TP SX ◇1	TP SO ◇1	TP SX ◇1	NT SX	NT SO	NT	NT	TP ◇1	NT	TP SO ◇1	TP SX ◇1	NT
Hull	d					19 14	19 20	20 14	21 09		21 48			23 00
Cottingham	d					19 21	19 27	20 21	21 16		21 55			23 07
Beverley	d					19 28	19 33	20 28	21a25		22 02			23a15
Arram	d							20 32						
Hutton Cranswick	d					19 37	19 42	20 39			22 11			
Driffield	d					19 41	19 47	20 45			22 17			
Nafferton	d					19 46	19 52	20 49			22 21			
Bridlington	a					19 58	20 03	21 04			22 35			
	d					20 01	20 06							
Bempton	d					20 08	20 13							
Hunmanby	d					20 18	20 23							
Filey	d					20 23	20 28							
Seamer	d	19 19	19 24	20 19	20 19	20 35	20 39			21 19		22 52	22 56	
Scarborough	a	19 30	19 33	20 30	20 30	20 43	20 48			21 30		23 01	23 06	

Sundays
until 05 September

		NT	TP ◇1	NT	NT	NT	TP ◇1	NT	NT	TP ◇1	NT	NT	TP ◇1	NT	NT	NT	TP ◇1	NT	NT	NT	TP ◇1	TP ◇1	TP ◇1
Hull	d	09 00		09 25	10 25	11 25		12 00	13 00		14 05	15 05		16 05	16 55	17 15		18 00	19 00	20 00			
Cottingham	d	09 07		09 32	10 32	11 32		12 07	13 07		14 12	15 12		16 12	17 02	17 22		18 07	19 07	20 06			
Beverley	d	09 13		09 38	10 38	11 38		12 13	13 13		14 18	15 18		16 18	17 08	17 28		18 13	19 13	20a12			
Arram	d			09 43																			
Hutton Cranswick	d			09 50	10 47			12 22			14 27			16 27		17 37			19 22				
Driffield	d	09 25		09 55	10 53	11 50		12 28	13 25		14 33	15 30		16 33	17 20	17 43		18 25	19 28				
Nafferton	d			09 59	10 57			12 32			14 37			16 37		17 47			19 32				
Bridlington	a	09 41		10 11	11 08	12 06		12 43	13 42		14 48	15 46		16 48	17 37	18 00		18 39	19 45				
	d			10 13	11 11			12 46			14 51			16 53				18 45					
Bempton	d			10 20	11 18			12 53			14 58			17 00				18 52					
Hunmanby	d			10 30	11 28			13 03			15 08			17 10				19 02					
Filey	d			10 35	11 33			13 08			15 13			17 15				19 07					
Seamer	d		10 21	10 46	11 44		12 25	13 20		14 21	15 24		16 21	17 26			18 21	19 19			20 21	21 21	22 51
Scarborough	a		10 32	10 54	11 50		12 34	13 25		14 32	15 30		16 32	17 32			18 32	19 24			20 32	21 32	23 02

Sundays
from 12 September

		NT	TP ◇1	NT	NT	NT	TP ◇1	NT	NT	TP ◇1	NT	NT	TP ◇1	NT	NT	NT	TP ◇1	NT	NT	NT	TP ◇1	TP ◇1	TP ◇1
Hull	d	08 58		09 25	10 25	11 25		12 00	12 58		14 05	15 05		16 05	16 55	17 15		18 00	19 00	20 00			
Cottingham	d	09 05		09 32	10 32	11 32		12 07	13 05		14 12	15 12		16 12	17 02	17 22		18 07	19 07	20 06			
Beverley	d	09 12		09 39	10 38	11 39		12 14	13 12		14 18	15 19		16 19	17 09	17 29		18 14	19 14	20a14			
Arram	d			09 43																			
Hutton Cranswick	d			09 50	10 47			12 23			14 27			16 28		17 38			19 23				
Driffield	d	09 24		09 56	10 53	11 51		12 28	13 24		14 33	15 31		16 33	17 21	17 43		18 26	19 28				
Nafferton	d			10 00	10 57			12 32			14 37			16 37		17 47			19 32				
Bridlington	a	09 40		10 13	11 09	12 08		12 45	13 42		14 50	15 48		16 50	17 39	18 02		18 40	19 47				
	d			10 15	11 11			12 47			14 52			16 53				18 45					
Bempton	d			10 22	11 18			12 54			14 59			17 00				18 52					
Hunmanby	d			10 32	11 28			13 04			15 09			17 10				19 02					
Filey	d			10 37	11 33			13 09			15 14			17 15				19 07					
Seamer	d		10 21	10 49	11 45		12 25	13 20		14 21	15 26		16 21	17 27			18 21	19 19			20 21	21 21	22 51
Scarborough	a		10 32	10 57	11 53		12 34	13 27		14 32	15 35		16 32	17 35			18 32	19 24			20 32	21 32	23 02

Table 43

Scarborough, Bridlington and Beverley - Hull

Mondays to Saturdays
until 04 September

		NT SO	TP SX ◇1	TP SO ◇1	NT SX	NT SX	NT	NT SO	NT SX	NT	NT	TP SX ◇1	TP SO ◇1	TP SX ◇1	TP SO ◇1	NT	TP ◇1	NT SO	NT SX	NT	NT	TP ◇1
Scarborough	d		06 30	06 34							06 50	07 00	07 04	07 38	07 47		08 47				09 02	09 47
Seamer	d		06a35	06a39							06 55	07a05	07a09	07a43	07a52		08a52				09 07	09a52
Filey	d										07 04										09 16	
Hunmanby	d										07 09										09 21	
Bempton	d										07 19										09 31	
Bridlington	a										07 27										09 38	
	d						06 46	07 12	07 14		07 34					08 08				09 05	09 41	
Nafferton	d						06 57	07 23	07 25		07 45					08 19				09 16	09 52	
Driffield	d						07 01	07 27	07 29		07 49					08 23				09 20	09 56	
Hutton Cranswick	d						07 06	07 32	07 34		07 54					08 28				09 25	10 01	
Arram	d										08 01									09 32		
Beverley	d	06 30			06 38	06 58	07 16	07 42	07 44	07 57	08 07					08 38		09 00	09 00	09 37	10 11	
Cottingham	d	06 36			06 43	07 03	07 22	07 48	07 50	08 03	08 13					08 44		09 06	09 06	09 43	10 17	
Hull	a	06 45			06 53	07 12	07 33	08 00	08 00	08 13	08 23					08 54		09 15	09 15	09 53	10 27	

		NT	NT	TP ◇1	NT	NT	NT SO	NT SX	TP ◇1	NT	TP ◇1	NT SX	NT SO	NT	NT SO	NT SX	TP ◇1	NT	TP ◇1	NT	NT SO
Scarborough	d		10 00	10 47			11 27	11 27	11 47		12 47				13 28	13 28	13 47		14 47		14 54
Seamer	d		10 05	10a52			11 32	11 32	11a52		12a52				13 33	13 33	13a52		14a52		14 59
Filey	d		10 14				11 41	11 41							13 42	13 42					15 08
Hunmanby	d		10 19				11 46	11 46							13 46	13 47					15 12
Bempton	d		10 29				11 56	11 56							13 56	13 57					15 22
Bridlington	a		10 36				12 03	12 03							14 04	14 04					15 30
	d	10 11	10 41		11 11	11 41	12 11	12 11		12 41		13 11	13 11	13 41	14 11	14 11		14 41		15 11	15 38
Nafferton	d		10 52			11 52				12 52				13 52				14 52			15 49
Driffield	d	10 24	10 56		11 24	11 56	12 24	12 24		12 56		13 24	13 24	13 56	14 24	14 24		14 56		15 24	15 53
Hutton Cranswick	d		11 01			12 01				13 01				14 01				15 01			15 58
Arram	d					12 08															
Beverley	d	10 37	11 11		11 37	12 13	12 37	12 37		13 11		13 37	13 37	14 11	14 37	14 37		15 11		15 37	16 08
Cottingham	d	10 43	11 17		11 43	12 19	12 43	12 43		13 17		13 43	13 43	14 17	14 43	14 43		15 17		15 43	16 14
Hull	a	10 53	11 27		11 53	12 29	12 54	12 54		13 27		13 53	13 54	14 27	14 53	14 53		15 30		15 53	16 24

		NT SX	TP ◇1	NT SO	NT SX	NT	NT	TP ◇1	NT	TP SO ◇1	TP SX ◇1	NT	NT	NT	TP ◇1	NT	TP ◇1	NT	TP SX ◇1	NT	NT
Scarborough	d	14 54	15 47				16 22	16 47		17 45	17 47			17 53	18 47		19 47	20 06	20 37		
Seamer	d	14 59	15a52				16 27	16a52		17a50	17a52			17 58	18a52		19a52	20 11	20a42		
Filey	d	15 08					16 36							18 07				20 20			
Hunmanby	d	15 13					16 41							18 12				20 26			
Bempton	d	15 23					16 51							18 22				20 35			
Bridlington	a	15 30					16 58							18 29				20 43			
	d	15 38		16 09	16 09	16 41	17 06		17 34				18 15	18 40		19 10		20 45			21 28
Nafferton	d	15 49				16 52			17 45					18 51		19 21		20 56			21 39
Driffield	d	15 53		16 22	16 22	16 56	17 19		17 49				18 28	18 55		19 25		21 01			21 43
Hutton Cranswick	d	15 58				17 01			17 54					19 00		19 30		21 06			21 48
Arram	d					17 08															
Beverley	d	16 08		16 35	16 35	17 13	17 32		18 04			18 20	18 41	19 10		19 40		21 15		21 40	21 58
Cottingham	d	16 14		16 41	16 41	17 19	17 38		18 10			18 25	18 47	19 16		19 46		21 21		21 46	22 04
Hull	a	16 24		16 50	16 51	17 30	17 49		18 20			18 35	18 58	19 27		19 58		21 31		21 57	22 14

		TP ◇1	NT
Scarborough	d	22 07	
Seamer	d	22a12	
Filey	d		
Hunmanby	d		
Bempton	d		
Bridlington	a		
	d		22 42
Nafferton	d		22 53
Driffield	d		22 58
Hutton Cranswick	d		23 03
Arram	d		
Beverley	d		23 12
Cottingham	d		23 18
Hull	a		23 28

Table 43

Scarborough, Bridlington and Beverley - Hull

Mondays to Saturdays
from 06 September

		NT SO	TP SX ◇1	TP SO ◇1	NT SX	NT SX	NT	NT SO	NT SX	NT	NT	TP SX ◇1	TP SO ◇1	TP SX ◇1	TP SO ◇1	NT	TP ◇1	NT SO	NT SX	NT	NT	TP ◇1
Scarborough	d		06 30	06 34							06 50	07 00	07 04	07 38	07 47		08 47				09 00	09 47
Seamer	d		06a35	06a39							06 55	07a05	07a09	07a43	07a52		08a52				09 05	09a52
Filey	d										07 04										09 14	
Hunmanby	d										07 09										09 20	
Bempton	d										07 19										09 30	
Bridlington	a										07 27										09 37	
	d						06 44	07 12	07 14		07 32					08 06				09 03	09 40	
Nafferton	d						06 55	07 23	07 25		07 43					08 17				09 14	09 51	
Driffield	d						06 59	07 27	07 29		07 47					08 21				09 18	09 55	
Hutton Cranswick	d						07 04	07 32	07 34		07 52					08 26				09 23	10 00	
Arram	d										07 59									09 30		
Beverley	d	06 30			06 38	06 58	07 15	07 42	07 44	07 57	08 06					08 36		09 00	09 00	09 36	10 10	
Cottingham	d	06 36			06 43	07 03	07 21	07 48	07 50	08 03	08 12					08 42		09 06	09 06	09 42	10 16	
Hull	a	06 46			06 53	07 15	07 33	07 59	08 00	08 13	08 23					08 54		09 15	09 15	09 53	10 27	

		NT	NT	TP ◇1	NT	NT	NT	TP ◇1	NT	TP ◇1	NT SX	NT SO	NT	NT	TP ◇1	NT	TP ◇1	NT	NT	TP ◇1	NT
Scarborough	d		09 58	10 47			11 27	11 47		12 47				13 28	13 47		14 47		14 54	15 47	
Seamer	d		10 03	10a52			11 32	11a52		12a52				13 33	13a52		14a52		14 59	15a52	
Filey	d		10 12				11 41							13 42					15 08		
Hunmanby	d		10 17				11 46							13 47					15 13		
Bempton	d		10 27				11 56							13 57					15 23		
Bridlington	a		10 35				12 03							14 05					15 30		
	d	10 09	10 40		11 09	11 40	12 09		12 40		13 09	13 09	13 40	14 09		14 40		15 09	15 36		16 09
Nafferton	d		10 51			11 51			12 51				13 51			14 51			15 47		
Driffield	d	10 22	10 55		11 22	11 55	12 22		12 55		13 22	13 22	13 55	14 22		14 55		15 22	15 51		16 22
Hutton Cranswick	d		11 00			12 00			13 00				14 00			15 00			15 56		
Arram	d					12 07															
Beverley	d	10 36	11 10		11 36	12 12	12 36		13 10		13 36	13 36	14 10	14 36		15 10		15 36	16 07		16 35
Cottingham	d	10 42	11 16		11 42	12 18	12 42		13 16		13 42	13 42	14 16	14 42		15 16		15 42	16 13		16 41
Hull	a	10 53	11 27		11 53	12 29	12 54		13 27		13 53	13 54	14 27	14 53		15 30		15 53	16 24		16 51

		NT	NT	TP ◇1	NT	TP SO ◇1	TP SX ◇1	NT	NT	NT	TP ◇1	NT	TP ◇1	NT	TP SX ◇1	NT	NT SO	NT SX	TP ◇1	NT
Scarborough	d		16 20	16 47		17 45	17 47			17 53	18 47		19 47	20 05	20 37				22 07	
Seamer	d		16 25	16a52		17a50	17a52			17 58	18a52		19a52	20 10	20a42				22a12	
Filey	d		16 34							18 07				20 20						
Hunmanby	d		16 39							18 12				20 26						
Bempton	d		16 49							18 22				20 35						
Bridlington	a		16 58							18 29				20 43						
	d	16 40	17 04		17 32				18 13	18 40		19 09		20 45			21 26	21 26		22 40
Nafferton	d	16 51			17 43					18 51		19 20		20 56			21 37	21 37		22 51
Driffield	d	16 55	17 17		17 47				18 26	18 55		19 24		21 01			21 41	21 41		22 56
Hutton Cranswick	d	17 00			17 52					19 00		19 29		21 06			21 46	21 46		23 01
Arram	d	17 07																		
Beverley	d	17 12	17 30		18 03			18 20	18 40	19 10		19 39		21 15		21 40	21 57	21 57		23 11
Cottingham	d	17 18	17 36		18 09			18 25	18 46	19 16		19 45		21 21		21 46	22 03	22 03		23 17
Hull	a	17 30	17 49		18 20			18 35	18 58	19 27		19 58		21 32		21 59	22 14	22 14		23 28

Sundays
until 05 September

		TP ◇1	NT	TP ◇1	NT	TP ◇1	NT	TP ◇1	NT	NT	TP ◇1	NT	NT	NT	TP ◇1	NT	NT	NT	NT	NT	TP ◇1	TP ◇1
Scarborough	d	09 20		10 50	11 12	11 50	12 08	13 50		14 08	15 50		16 08		17 50			18 08		19 37	19 50	21 20
Seamer	d	09a25		10a55	11 17	11a55	12 13	13a55		14 13	15a55		16 13		17a55			18 13		19 42	19a55	21a25
Filey	d				11 26		12 22			14 22			16 22					18 22		19 51		
Hunmanby	d				11 31		12 27			14 27			16 27					18 27		19 56		
Bempton	d				11 41		12 37			14 37			16 37					18 37		20 06		
Bridlington	a				11 48		12 44			14 45			16 44					18 44		20 13		
	d		09 51		11 51		12 51		13 51	14 49		15 51	16 51	17 21		17 51	18 11	18 51	19 55	20 17		
Nafferton	d		10 02		12 01				14 02			16 02		17 32				19 02	20 06			
Driffield	d		10 06		12 06		13 04		14 06	15 02		16 06	17 04	17 36		18 04	18 24	19 06	20 10	20 30		
Hutton Cranswick	d		10 11		12 10				14 11			16 11		17 41				19 11	20 15			
Arram	d																	19 18				
Beverley	d		10 21		12 20		13 17		14 21	15 16		16 21	17 17	17 51		18 17	18 37	19 23	20 25	20 43		
Cottingham	d		10 27		12 25		13 23		14 27	15 22		16 27	17 23	17 57		18 23	18 43	19 29	20 31	20 49		
Hull	a		10 37		12 35		13 33		14 37	15 33		16 37	17 34	18 07		18 33	18 53	19 39	20 41	20 59		

Table 43

Sundays
from 12 September

Scarborough, Bridlington and Beverley - Hull

		TP	NT	TP	NT	TP	NT	NT	TP	NT	NT	TP	NT	NT	NT	TP	NT	NT	NT	NT	TP	TP
		◇1		◇1		◇1			◇1			◇1				◇1					◇1	◇1
Scarborough	d	09 20		10 50	11 11	11 50	12 08		13 50	14 08		15 50	16 08			17 50		18 08		19 36	19 50	21 20
Seamer	d	09a25		10a55	11 16	11a55	12 13		13a55	14 13		15a55	16 13			17a55		18 13		19 41	19a55	21a25
Filey	d				11 26		12 22			14 22			16 22					18 22		19 50		
Hunmanby	d				11 30		12 27			14 27			16 27					18 27		19 55		
Bempton	d				11 40		12 37			14 37			16 37					18 37		20 05		
Bridlington	a				11 48		12 45			14 44			16 45					18 45		20 13		
	d		09 49		11 50		12 49	13 49		14 51	15 49		16 49	17 19	17 49		18 09	18 49	19 53	20 15		
Nafferton	d		10 00		12 01			14 00			16 00			17 30				19 00	20 04			
Driffield	d		10 04		12 06		13 02	14 04		15 04	16 04		17 02	17 34	18 02		18 22	19 04	20 08	20 28		
Hutton Cranswick	d		10 09		12 10			14 09			16 09			17 39				19 09	20 13			
Arram	d																	19 16				
Beverley	d		10 20		12 20		13 16	14 20		15 17	16 20		17 16	17 50	18 16		18 36	19 22	20 24	20 42		
Cottingham	d		10 26		12 25		13 22	14 26		15 23	16 26		17 22	17 56	18 22		18 42	19 28	20 30	20 48		
Hull	a		10 37		12 36		13 33	14 37		15 33	16 37		17 34	18 07	18 33		18 53	19 39	20 41	20 59		

Network Diagram for Tables 44, 45, 48

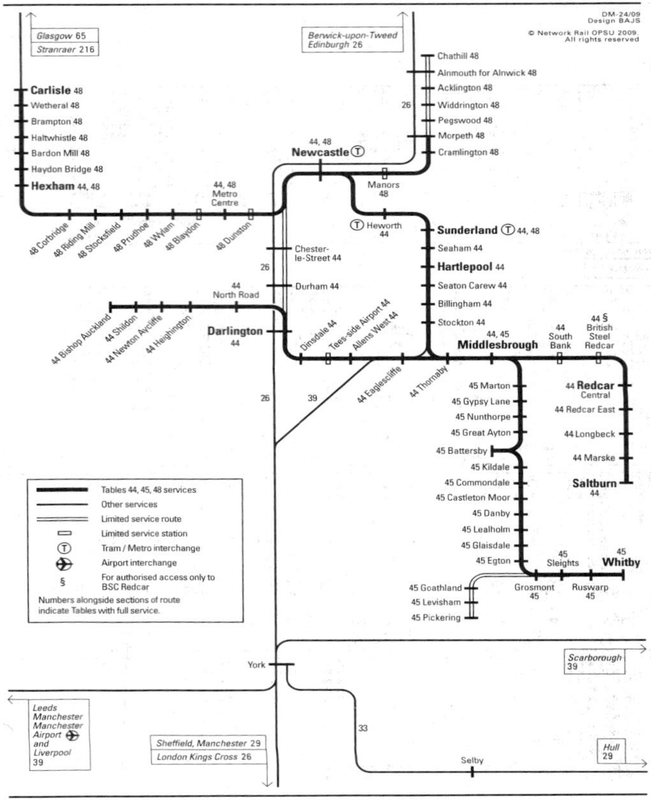

Table 44

Mondays to Fridays
until 03 September

Newcastle, Sunderland, Bishop Auckland and Darlington - Middlesbrough and Saltburn

	NT	NT	TP	NT	NT	GC	NT	NT	NT	TP	NT	NT	TP	NT	NT	GC	NT	NT	TP	NT
			◇1			2 1 A ✕				◇1			◇1 ⊼			2 1 ✕			◇1 ⊼	
Hexham 48 d									06 13						07 41					08 44
Metrocentre 48 d															08 15					09 15
Newcastle 26 d	06 00								07b00			07 30			08 30					09 30
Heworth d	06 07								07 07			07 37			08 37					09 37
Sunderland a	06 19								07 19			07 49			08 49					09 49
d	06 20					06 41			07 20			07 50			08 50	09 18				09 50
Seaham d	06 28								07 28			07 58			08 58					09 58
Hartlepool d	06a46					07 08			07 45			08 15			09 15	09 42				10 15
Seaton Carew d									07 49			08 19			09 19					10 19
Billingham d									07 56			08 26			09 26					10 26
Stockton d									08 04			08 33			09 33					10 33
Bishop Auckland d								07 21										09 25		
Shildon d								07 26										09 30		
Newton Aycliffe d								07 31										09 35		
Heighington d								07 34										09 38		
North Road d								07 43										09 47		
Chester-le-Street 26 d																				
Durham 26 d																				
Darlington 26 a								07 46										09 50		
d			06 36	06 40	07 05		07 24	07 48			08 10			09 00			09 36	09 53		
Dinsdale d				06 46			07 29				08 15			09 05				09 58		
Tees-side Airport d																				
Allens West d				06 53	07 15		07 36	07 59			08 22			09 12				10 05		
Eaglescliffe a				06 55	07 17	07 27	07 38	08 01			08 24			09 14		10 00		10 07		
d				06 57	07 18	07 28	07 38	08 01			08 24			09 14				10 07		
Thornaby d			06 53	07 03	07 23		07 44	08 07	08 12	08 26	08 33	08 39	09 12	09 20	09 39		09 52	10 18	10 22	10 39
Middlesbrough a			07 01	07 08	07 28		07 50	08 12	08 20	08 34	08 38	08 46	09 20	09 27	09 48		09 57	10 23	10 30	10 48
d		06 34		07 08	07 30		07 51	08 13			08 39	08 47		09 28			09 57	10 24		
South Bank d							07 56				08 43									
British Steel Redcar § d					07 38															
Redcar Central d		06 45		07 19	07 42		08 03				08 51			09 38			10 08	10 35		
Redcar East d		06 48		07 21	07 45		08 06				08 53			09 41			10 10	10 37		
Longbeck d		06 52		07 25	07 49		08 10				08 57			09 45			10 14	10 41		
Marske d		06 54		07 27	07 50		08 11				08 59			09 46			10 16	10 43		
Saltburn a		07 03		07 35	07 58		08 19				09 07			09 54			10 24	10 52		

	NT	NT	NT	NT	TP	NT	NT	NT	GC	NT	TP	NT	NT	TP	NT	NT	NT
					◇1 ⊼				2 1 ✕		◇1 ⊼			◇1 ⊼			
Hexham 48 d			09 44				10 44					11 44				12 44	
Metrocentre 48 d			10 15				11 15					12 15				13 15	
Newcastle 26 d			10 30				11 30					12 30				13 30	
Heworth d			10 37				11 37					12 37				13 37	
Sunderland a			10 49				11 49					12 49				13 49	
d			10 50				11 50		12 30			12 50				13 50	
Seaham d			10 58				11 58					12 58				13 58	
Hartlepool d			11 15				12 15		12 54			13 15				14 15	
Seaton Carew d			11 19				12 19					13 19				14 19	
Billingham d			11 26				12 26					13 26				14 26	
Stockton d			11 33				12 33					13 33				14 33	
Bishop Auckland d	10 03					11 40									13 40		
Shildon d	10 08					11 45									13 45		
Newton Aycliffe d	10 13					11 50									13 50		
Heighington d	10 16					11 53									13 53		
North Road d	10 25					12 02									14 02		
Chester-le-Street 26 d																	
Durham 26 d																	
Darlington 26 a	10 28					12 06									14 06		
d	10 30	11 00		11 35		12 07		12 30		12 56			13 30		14 08		14 32
Dinsdale d				11 40									13 35				
Tees-side Airport d																	
Allens West d	10 41			11 47				12 40					13 42		14 18		14 42
Eaglescliffe a	10 43	11 11		11 49				12 42	13 15				13 44		14 20		14 44
d	10 43	11 12		11 49				12 43					13 44		14 21		14 45
Thornaby d	10 48	11 17	11 39	11 55	12 19	12 25	12 39	12 48		13 12	13 21	13 39	13 51	14 19	14 26	14 39	14 50
Middlesbrough a	10 54	11 22	11 48	12 00	12 28	12 31	12 49	12 53		13 17	13 30	13 48	13 56	14 28	14 32	14 48	14 55
d	10 55	11 23		12 01		12 32		12 54		13 20			13 57		14 33		14 56
South Bank d																	
British Steel Redcar § d																	
Redcar Central d	11 05	11 33		12 11		12 42		13 04		13 30			14 07		14 43		15 06
Redcar East d	11 08	11 36		12 14		12 45		13 07		13 33			14 10		14 46		15 09
Longbeck d	11 12	11 40		12 18		12 49		13 11		13 37			14 14		14 50		15 13
Marske d	11 13	11 41		12 19		12 50		13 12		13 38			14 15		14 51		15 14
Saltburn a	11 22	11 49		12 27		12 58		13 20		13 46			14 23		14 59		15 22

§ For authorised access only to BSC Redcar
A The Zephyr
b arr. 0652

Table 44

Mondays to Fridays
until 03 September

Newcastle, Sunderland, Bishop Auckland and Darlington - Middlesbrough and Saltburn

	NT	TP	NT	NT	NT	TP	NT	NT	NT	TP	NT	NT	NT	GC	NT	TP	NT	NT	TP
		◇1 ⊼				◇1 ⊼				◇1 ⊼				2 1 ✕		◇1 ⊼			◇1 ⊼
Hexham 48 d			13 44				14 44				15 44		16 14				16 44		
Metrocentre 48 d			14 15				15 15				16 15		16 42				17 15		
Newcastle 26 d			14 30				15 30				16 30		16 53				17 30		
Heworth d			14 37				15 37				16 37		17 00				17 37		
Sunderland a			14 49				15 49				16 49		17 14				17 50		
d			14 50				15 50				16 50		17 15	17 30			17 50		
Seaham d			14 58				15 58				16 58		17 22				17 58		
Hartlepool d			15 15				16 15				17 15		17 39	17 56			18 15		
Seaton Carew d			15 19				16 19				17 19		17 43				18 19		
Billingham d			15 26				16 26				17 26		17 50				18 26		
Stockton d			15 33				16 33				17 33		17 57				18 33		
Bishop Auckland d					15 30				16 30									18 03	
Shildon d					15 35				16 35									18 08	
Newton Aycliffe d					15 40				16 40									18 13	
Heighington d					15 43				16 43									18 16	
North Road d					15 52				16 52									18 25	
Chester-le-Street 26 d																			
Durham 26 d																			
Darlington 26 a					15 55				16 57									18 31	
d	15 00			15 30	15 57			16 30	16 59			17 34			18 03			18 33	
Dinsdale d				15 35	16 03							17 39			18 08				
Tees-side Airport d																			
Allens West d				15 42	16 10			16 41	17 09			17 46			18 15			18 43	
Eaglescliffe a	15 11			15 44	16 12			16 43	17 11			17 48		18 14	18 17			18 45	
d	15 11			15 44	16 12			16 44	17 12			17 48		18 15	18 17			18 46	
Thornaby d	15 17	15 22	15 39	15 50	16 18	16 22	16 41	16 49	17 17	17 22	17 39	17 54	18 03		18 23	18 32	18 39	18 51	19 22
Middlesbrough a	15 22	15 30	15 48	15 55	16 23	16 30	16 47	16 54	17 23	17 30	17 49	17 59	18 15		18 28	18 41	18 48	18 56	19 30
d	15 23			15 56	16 24			16 56	17 24			17 59			18 30			18 59	
South Bank d					16 29							18 04							
British Steel Redcar § d																			
Redcar Central d	15 33			16 06	16 36			17 06	17 35			18 11			18 40			19 09	
Redcar East d	15 36			16 09	16 39			17 09	17 37			18 14			18 43			19 12	
Longbeck d	15 40			16 13	16 43			17 13	17 41			18 18			18 47			19 16	
Marske d	15 41			16 14	16 44			17 14	17 43			18 19			18 48			19 17	
Saltburn a	15 49			16 22	16 55			17 22	17 52			18 27			18 56			19 26	

	NT	NT	NT	NT	NT	TP	NT	NT	NT
						◇1			
Hexham 48 d	17 42			18 44					
Metrocentre 48 d	18 13			19 17			20 30		
Newcastle 26 d	18b30			19 30			20c45		22 00
Heworth d	18 37			19 37			20 52		
Sunderland a	18 49			19 50			21 04		
d	18 50			19 50			21 05		
Seaham d	18 58			19 58			21 13		
Hartlepool d	19 15			20 15			21 29		
Seaton Carew d	19 19			20 19			21 33		
Billingham d	19 26			20 26			21 40		
Stockton d	19 33			20 33			21 47		
Bishop Auckland d		19 03						21 15	
Shildon d		19 08						21 20	
Newton Aycliffe d		19 13						21 25	
Heighington d		19 16						21 28	
North Road d		19 25						21 37	
Chester-le-Street 26 d									22 09
Durham 26 d									22 18
Darlington 26 a		19 30						21 40	22 38
d		19 31	20 07		20 30			21 44	22 42
Dinsdale d			20 12					21 49	
Tees-side Airport d									
Allens West d		19 42	20 19					21 56	22 53
Eaglescliffe a		19 44	20 21		20 41			21 58	22 55
d		19 44	20 21		20 41			21 58	22 55
Thornaby d	19 40	19 50	20 26	20 39	20 50	21 17	21 53	22 04	23 00
Middlesbrough a	19 48	19 55	20 35	20 50	20 55	21 25	22 02	22 09	23 10
d		19 56			20 55			22 09	
South Bank d									
British Steel Redcar § d									
Redcar Central d		20 06			21 05			22 20	
Redcar East d		20 09			21 08			22 22	
Longbeck d		20 13			21 12			22 26	
Marske d		20 14			21 13			22 28	
Saltburn a		20 23			21 22			22 37	

§ For authorised access only to BSC Redcar
b arr. 1823
c arr. 2038

Newcastle, Sunderland, Bishop Auckland and Darlington - Middlesbrough and Saltburn

		NT	NT	TP	NT	NT	GC	NT	NT	NT	TP	NT	NT	TP	NT	NT	GC	NT	NT	TP	NT
				◇1			■ 1 A ✕				◇1			◇1 H			■ 1 ✕			◇1 H	
Hexham	48 d									06 13						07 39					08 44
Metrocentre	48 d															08 17					09 15
Newcastle 8	26 d	06 00								07 00			07 30			08 30					09 30
Heworth	d	06 07								07 07			07 37			08 37					09 37
Sunderland	a	06 19								07 19			07 49			08 49					09 49
	d	06 20					06 41			07 20			07 50			08 50	09 18				09 50
Seaham	d	06 28								07 28			07 58			08 58					09 58
Hartlepool	d	06a46					07 08			07 45			08 15			09 15	09 42				10 15
Seaton Carew	d									07 49			08 19			09 19					10 19
Billingham	d									07 56			08 26			09 26					10 26
Stockton	d									08 04			08 33			09 33					10 33
Bishop Auckland	d								07 21										09 25		
Shildon	d								07 26										09 30		
Newton Aycliffe	d								07 31										09 35		
Heighington	d								07 34										09 38		
North Road	d								07 43										09 47		
Chester-le-Street	26 d																				
Durham	26 d																				
Darlington 7	26 a								07 46										09 50		
	d			06 36	06 40	07 05		07 24	07 48			08 10			09 00			09 36	09 53		
Dinsdale	d				06 46			07 29				08 15			09 05				09 58		
Tees-side Airport	d																				
Allens West	d				06 53	07 15		07 36	07 59			08 22			09 12				10 05		
Eaglescliffe	a				06 55	07 17	07 27	07 38	08 01			08 24			09 14		10 00		10 07		
	d				06 57	07 18	07 28	07 38	08 01			08 24			09 14				10 07		
Thornaby	d			06 53	07 03	07 23		07 44	08 07	08 12	08 26	08 33	08 39	09 12	09 20	09 39		09 52	10 18	10 22	10 39
Middlesbrough	a			07 01	07 08	07 28		07 50	08 12	08 20	08 34	08 38	08 46	09 20	09 27	09 48		09 57	10 23	10 30	10 48
	d		06 34		07 08	07 30		07 51				08 39			09 28			09 57	10 24		
South Bank	d							07 56				08 43									
British Steel Redcar §	d					07 38															
Redcar Central	d		06 45		07 19	07 42		08 03				08 51			09 38			10 08	10 35		
Redcar East	d		06 48		07 21	07 45		08 06				08 53			09 41			10 10	10 37		
Longbeck	d		06 52		07 25	07 49		08 10				08 57			09 45			10 14	10 41		
Marske	d		06 54		07 27	07 50		08 11				08 59			09 46			10 16	10 43		
Saltburn	a		07 03		07 35	07 58		08 19				09 07			09 54			10 24	10 52		

		NT	NT	NT	NT	TP	NT	NT	NT	GC	NT	TP	NT	NT	TP	NT	NT	NT
						◇1 H				■ 1 ✕		◇1 H			◇1 H			
Hexham	48 d			09 42				10 44					11 42				12 42	
Metrocentre	48 d			10 15				11 15					12 15				13 15	
Newcastle 8	26 d			10 30				11 30					12 30				13 30	
Heworth	d			10 37				11 37					12 37				13 37	
Sunderland	a			10 49				11 49					12 49				13 49	
	d			10 50				11 50		12 30			12 50				13 50	
Seaham	d			10 58				11 58					12 58				13 58	
Hartlepool	d			11 15				12 15		12 54			13 15				14 15	
Seaton Carew	d			11 19				12 19					13 19				14 19	
Billingham	d			11 26				12 26					13 26				14 26	
Stockton	d			11 33				12 33					13 33				14 33	
Bishop Auckland	d	10 03					11 40									13 40		
Shildon	d	10 08					11 45									13 45		
Newton Aycliffe	d	10 13					11 50									13 50		
Heighington	d	10 16					11 53									13 53		
North Road	d	10 25					12 02									14 02		
Chester-le-Street	26 d																	
Durham	26 d																	
Darlington 7	26 a	10 28					12 06									14 06		
	d	10 30	11 00		11 35		12 07		12 30		12 56			13 30		14 08		14 32
Dinsdale	d				11 40									13 35				
Tees-side Airport	d																	
Allens West	d	10 41			11 47				12 40					13 42		14 18		14 42
Eaglescliffe	a	10 43	11 11		11 49				12 42	13 15				13 44		14 20		14 44
	d	10 43	11 12		11 49				12 43					13 44		14 21		14 45
Thornaby	d	10 48	11 17	11 39	11 55	12 19	12 25	12 39	12 48		13 12	13 21	13 39	13 51	14 19	14 26	14 39	14 50
Middlesbrough	a	10 54	11 22	11 48	12 00	12 28	12 31	12 49	12 53		13 17	13 30	13 48	13 56	14 28	14 32	14 48	14 55
	d	10 55	11 23		12 01		12 32		12 54		13 20			13 57		14 33		14 56
South Bank	d																	
British Steel Redcar §	d																	
Redcar Central	d	11 05	11 33		12 11		12 42		13 04		13 30			14 07		14 43		15 06
Redcar East	d	11 08	11 36		12 14		12 45		13 07		13 33			14 10		14 46		15 09
Longbeck	d	11 12	11 40		12 18		12 49		13 11		13 37			14 14		14 50		15 13
Marske	d	11 13	11 41		12 19		12 50		13 12		13 38			14 15		14 51		15 14
Saltburn	a	11 22	11 49		12 27		12 58		13 20		13 46			14 23		14 59		15 22

§ For authorised access only to BSC Redcar

A The Zephyr

Newcastle, Sunderland, Bishop Auckland and Darlington - Middlesbrough and Saltburn

		NT	TP	NT	NT	NT	TP	NT	NT	NT	TP	NT	NT	NT	GC	NT	TP	NT	NT	TP
			◇1 H				◇1 H				◇1 H				■ 1 ✕		◇1 H			◇1 H
Hexham	48 d			13 42				14 42				15 42		16 12				16 42		
Metrocentre	48 d			14 15				15 15				16 15		16 40				17 15		
Newcastle 8	26 d			14 30				15 30				16 30		16 53				17 30		
Heworth	d			14 37				15 37				16 37		17 00				17 37		
Sunderland	a			14 49				15 49				16 49		17 14				17 50		
	d			14 50				15 50				16 50		17 15	17 30			17 50		
Seaham	d			14 58				15 58				16 58		17 22				17 58		
Hartlepool	d			15 15				16 15				17 15		17 39	17 56			18 15		
Seaton Carew	d			15 19				16 19				17 19		17 43				18 19		
Billingham	d			15 26				16 26				17 26		17 50				18 26		
Stockton	d			15 33				16 33				17 33		17 57				18 33		
Bishop Auckland	d					15 30				16 30									18 03	
Shildon	d					15 35				16 35									18 08	
Newton Aycliffe	d					15 40				16 40									18 13	
Heighington	d					15 43				16 43									18 16	
North Road	d					15 52				16 52									18 25	
Chester-le-Street	26 d																			
Durham	26 d																			
Darlington 7	26 a					15 55				16 57									18 31	
	d	15 00			15 30	15 57			16 30	16 59			17 34			18 03			18 33	
Dinsdale	d				15 35	16 03							17 39			18 08				
Tees-side Airport	d																			
Allens West	d				15 42	16 10			16 41	17 09			17 46			18 15			18 43	
Eaglescliffe	a	15 11			15 44	16 12			16 43	17 11			17 48		18 14	18 17			18 45	
	d	15 11			15 44	16 12			16 44	17 12			17 48			18 17			18 46	
Thornaby	d	15 17	15 22	15 39	15 50	16 18	16 22	16 41	16 49	17 17	17 22	17 39	17 54	18 03		18 23	18 32	18 39	18 51	19 22
Middlesbrough	a	15 22	15 30	15 48	15 55	16 23	16 30	16 47	16 54	17 23	17 30	17 49	17 59	18 15		18 28	18 41	18 48	18 56	19 30
	d	15 23			15 56	16 24			16 56	17 24			17 59			18 30			18 59	
South Bank	d					16 29							18 04							
British Steel Redcar §	d																			
Redcar Central	d	15 33			16 06	16 36			17 06	17 35			18 11			18 40			19 09	
Redcar East	d	15 36			16 09	16 39			17 09	17 37			18 14			18 43			19 12	
Longbeck	d	15 40			16 13	16 43			17 13	17 41			18 18			18 47			19 16	
Marske	d	15 41			16 14	16 44			17 14	17 43			18 19			18 48			19 17	
Saltburn	a	15 49			16 22	16 55			17 22	17 52			18 27			18 56			19 26	

		NT	NT	NT	NT	NT	TP	NT	NT	NT
							◇1			
Hexham	48 d	17 42			18 40					
Metrocentre	48 d	18 13			19 17			20 30		
Newcastle 8	26 d	18b30			19 30			20c45		22 00
Heworth	d	18 37			19 37			20 52		
Sunderland	a	18 49			19 50			21 04		
	d	18 50			19 50			21 05		
Seaham	d	18 58			19 58			21 13		
Hartlepool	d	19 15			20 15			21 29		
Seaton Carew	d	19 19			20 19			21 33		
Billingham	d	19 26			20 26			21 40		
Stockton	d	19 33			20 33			21 47		
Bishop Auckland	d		19 03						21 15	
Shildon	d		19 08						21 20	
Newton Aycliffe	d		19 13						21 25	
Heighington	d		19 16						21 28	
North Road	d		19 25						21 37	
Chester-le-Street	26 d									22 09
Durham	26 d									22 18
Darlington 7	26 a		19 30						21 40	22 38
	d		19 31	20 07		20 30			21 44	22 42
Dinsdale	d			20 12					21 49	
Tees-side Airport	d									
Allens West	d		19 42	20 19					21 56	22 53
Eaglescliffe	a		19 44	20 21		20 41			21 58	22 55
	d		19 44	20 21		20 41			21 58	22 55
Thornaby	d	19 40	19 50	20 26	20 39	20 50	21 17	21 53	22 04	23 00
Middlesbrough	a	19 48	19 55	20 35	20 50	20 55	21 25	22 02	22 09	
	d		19 56			20 55			22 09	
South Bank	d									
British Steel Redcar §	d									
Redcar Central	d		20 06			21 05			22 20	
Redcar East	d		20 09			21 08			22 22	
Longbeck	d		20 13			21 12			22 26	
Marske	d		20 14			21 13			22 28	
Saltburn	a		20 23			21 22			22 37	

§ For authorised access only to BSC Redcar

b arr. 1823

c arr. 2038

Newcastle, Sunderland, Bishop Auckland and Darlington - Middlesbrough and Saltburn

Station			NT	NT	TP	NT	NT	NT	GC	NT	NT	TP	NT	NT	NT	TP	NT	NT	NT	GC	TP	NT
					◇1				A			◇1				◇1					◇1	
Hexham	48	d									06 13											08 44
Metrocentre	48	d																				09 15
Newcastle 8	26	d	06 00								07b00			07 30			08 30					09 30
Heworth		d	06 07								07 07			07 37			08 37					09 37
Sunderland		a	06 19								07 19			07 49			08 49					09 49
		d	06 20						06 53		07 20			07 50			08 50			09 29		09 50
Seaham		d	06 28								07 28			07 58			08 58					09 58
Hartlepool		d	06a46						07 17		07 45			08 15			09 15			09 53		10 15
Seaton Carew		d									07 49			08 19			09 19					10 19
Billingham		d									07 56			08 26			09 26					10 26
Stockton		d									08 04			08 33			09 33					10 33
Bishop Auckland		d											07 35						09 23			
Shildon		d											07 40						09 28			
Newton Aycliffe		d											07 45						09 33			
Heighington		d											07 48						09 37			
North Road		d											07 57						09 45			
Chester-le-Street	26	d																				
Durham	26	d																				
Darlington 7	26	a											08 00						09 49			
		d			06 36	06 40	06 58	07 19		07 38			08 09		08 56			09 23	09 51			
Dinsdale		d				06 46		07 24					08 15		09 01			09 28	09 56			
Tees-side Airport		d																				
Allens West		d				06 53	07 08	07 31		07 49			08 22		09 08			09 35	10 03			
Eaglescliffe		a				06 55	07 10	07 32	07 44	07 51			08 27		09 10			09 37	10 05	10 14		
		d				06 55	07 11	07 32		07 51			08 27		09 10			09 37	10 05			
Thornaby		d			06 53	07 01	07 16	07 39		07 56	08 12	08 24	08 33	08 39	09 16	09 22	09 39	09 45	10 11		10 22	10 39
Middlesbrough		a			07 01	07 09	07 21	07 44		08 02	08 22	08 34	08 38	08 48	09 21	09 32	09 48	09 53	10 16		10 30	10 48
		d		06 40		07 10	07 22	07 45					08 39		09 26			09 54	10 20			
South Bank		d						07 49					08 43									
British Steel Redcar §		d																				
Redcar Central		d		06 50		07 20	07 32	07 57					08 51		09 36			10 04	10 30			
Redcar East		d		06 53		07 23	07 35	07 59					08 53		09 39			10 07	10 33			
Longbeck		d		06 57		07 27	07 39	08 03					08 57		09 43			10 11	10 37			
Marske		d		06 58		07 28	07 40	08 05					08 59		09 44			10 12	10 38			
Saltburn		a		07 05		07 35	07 48	08 14					09 08		09 52			10 20	10 47			

Station			NT	NT	TP	NT	NT	TP	NT	NT	NT	GC	NT	TP	NT	NT	NT	TP	NT
					◇1			◇1						◇1				◇1	
Hexham	48	d				09 44				10 44					11 44				12 44
Metrocentre	48	d				10 15				11 15					12 15				13 15
Newcastle 8	26	d				10 30				11 30					12 30				13 30
Heworth		d				10 37				11 37					12 37				13 37
Sunderland		a				10 49				11 49					12 49				13 49
		d				10 50				11 50		12 30			12 50				13 50
Seaham		d				10 58				11 58					12 58				13 58
Hartlepool		d				11 15				12 15		12 54			13 15				14 15
Seaton Carew		d				11 19				12 19					13 19				14 19
Billingham		d				11 26				12 26					13 26				14 26
Stockton		d				11 33				12 33					13 33				14 33
Bishop Auckland		d	09 53						11 40								13 26		
Shildon		d	09 58						11 45								13 31		
Newton Aycliffe		d	10 03						11 50								13 36		
Heighington		d	10 06						11 53								13 39		
North Road		d	10 15						12 02								13 48		
Chester-le-Street	26	d																	
Durham	26	d																	
Darlington 7	26	a	10 18						12 06								13 51		
		d	10 20	10 47			11 30		12 06		12 35		12 58			13 31	13 53		
Dinsdale		d					11 35						13 03			13 36			
Tees-side Airport		d	10 28																
Allens West		d	10 33				11 42				12 45		13 10			13 43	14 04		
Eaglescliffe		a	10 35	10 58			11 44				12 47	13 12	13 12			13 45	14 06		
		d	10 35	10 59			11 44				12 48	13 13	13 12			13 45	14 06		
Thornaby		d	10 45	11 04	11 22	11 39	11 50	12 19	12 25	12 39	12 53		13 18	13 21	13 39	13 52	14 13	14 19	14 39
Middlesbrough		a	10 52	11 09	11 31	11 48	11 55	12 28	12 32	12 49	12 58		13 23	13 30	13 48	13 57	14 18	14 28	14 48
		d	10 54	11 14			11 56		12 33		12 58		13 24			13 58	14 21		
South Bank		d																	
British Steel Redcar §		d																	
Redcar Central		d	11 04	11 24			12 06		12 43		13 09		13 34			14 08	14 31		
Redcar East		d	11 07	11 27			12 09		12 46		13 11		13 37			14 11	14 34		
Longbeck		d	11 11	11 31			12 13		12 50		13 15		13 41			14 15	14 38		
Marske		d	11 12	11 32			12 14		12 51		13 17		13 42			14 16	14 39		
Saltburn		a	11 20	11 40			12 22		12 59		13 25		13 50			14 24	14 48		

§ For authorised access only to BSC Redcar

A The Zephyr

b arr. 0652

Table 44

Saturdays until 04 September

Newcastle, Sunderland, Bishop Auckland and Darlington - Middlesbrough and Saltburn

Station			NT	NT	TP	NT	NT	NT	TP	NT	NT	NT	TP	NT	NT	NT	NT	GC	TP	NT
					◇1				◇1				◇1						◇1	
Hexham	48	d				13 44				14 44				15 44		16 16				16 44
Metrocentre	48	d				14 15				15 15				16 15		16 40				17 15
Newcastle 8	26	d				14 30				15 30				16 30		16 53				17 30
Heworth		d				14 37				15 37				16 37		17 00				17 37
Sunderland		a				14 49				15 50				16 49		17 14				17 50
		d				14 50				15 50				16 50		17 15		17 30		17 50
Seaham		d				14 58				15 58				16 58		17 22				17 58
Hartlepool		d				15 15				16 15				17 15		17 39		17 56		18 15
Seaton Carew		d				15 19				16 19				17 19		17 43				18 19
Billingham		d				15 26				16 26				17 26		17 50				18 26
Stockton		d				15 33				16 33				17 33		17 57				18 33
Bishop Auckland		d						15 32							17 00					
Shildon		d						15 37							17 05					
Newton Aycliffe		d						15 42							17 10					
Heighington		d						15 45							17 13					
North Road		d						15 54							17 22					
Chester-le-Street	26	d																		
Durham	26	d																		
Darlington 7	26	a						15 58							17 26					
		d	14 35	15 04			15 32	16 00			16 27	17 04			17 27		18 02			
Dinsdale		d					15 37								17 33		18 07			
Tees-side Airport		d																		
Allens West		d	14 45	15 14			15 44				16 37				17 40		18 14			
Eaglescliffe		a	14 47	15 16			15 46	16 11			16 39	17 15			17 42		18 16	18 27		
		d	14 48	15 17			15 46	16 12			16 40	17 15			17 42		18 16			
Thornaby		d	14 53	15 22	15 28	15 39	15 52	16 17	16 22	16 39	16 45	17 21	17 22	17 39	17 47	18 03	18 22		18 26	18 39
Middlesbrough		a	14 58	15 27	15 35	15 48	15 57	16 22	16 30	16 47	16 52	17 26	17 33	17 49	17 54	18 15	18 27		18 32	18 48
		d	14 58	15 28			15 58	16 23			16 54	17 28			17 54		18 27			
South Bank		d						16 27							17 59					
British Steel Redcar §		d																		
Redcar Central		d	15 09	15 39			16 08	16 35			17 04	17 38			18 06		18 38			
Redcar East		d	15 11	15 41			16 11	16 37			17 07	17 41			18 09		18 40			
Longbeck		d	15 15	15 45			16 15	16 41			17 11	17 45			18 13		18 44			
Marske		d	15 17	15 47			16 16	16 43			17 12	17 46			18 14		18 46			
Saltburn		a	15 25	15 55			16 24	16 52			17 20	17 54			18 23		18 54			

Station			NT	TP	NT	NT	TP	NT	NT	NT	TP	NT	NT	NT
				◇1			◇1				◇1			
Hexham	48	d			17 42				18 44					
Metrocentre	48	d			18 13				19 17				20 47	
Newcastle 8	26	d			18b30				19 30				21 00	21 50
Heworth		d			18 37				19 37				21 08	
Sunderland		a			18 49				19 50				21 20	
		d			18 50				19 50				21 20	
Seaham		d			18 58				19 58				21 28	
Hartlepool		d			19 15				20 15				21 45	
Seaton Carew		d			19 19				20 19				21 49	
Billingham		d			19 26				20 26				21 56	
Stockton		d			19 33				20 33				22 03	
Bishop Auckland		d	18 00			18 59						21 17		
Shildon		d	18 05			19 04						21 22		
Newton Aycliffe		d	18 10			19 09						21 27		
Heighington		d	18 13			19 12						21 30		
North Road		d	18 22			19 21						21 39		
Chester-le-Street	26	d												21 59
Durham	26	d												22 08
Darlington 7	26	a	18 25			19 25						21 42		22 29
		d	18 30			19 27		20 07		20 30		21 44		22 30
Dinsdale		d						20 12				21 49		
Tees-side Airport		d												
Allens West		d	18 41			19 38		20 19				21 56		22 41
Eaglescliffe		a	18 43			19 40		20 21		20 41		21 58		22 43
		d	18 45			19 40		20 21		20 41		21 58		22 43
Thornaby		d	18 50	19 18	19 39	19 45	20 13	20 27	20 39	20 48	21 15	22 04	22 09	22 48
Middlesbrough		a	19 00	19 28	19 48	19 52	20 23	20 38	20 50	20 55	21 25	22 09	22 18	22 57
		d	19 01		19 48	19 54				20 55		22 09		
South Bank		d												
British Steel Redcar §		d												
Redcar Central		d	19 11			20 04				21 05		22 20		
Redcar East		d	19 14			20 07				21 08		22 22		
Longbeck		d	19 18			20 11				21 12		22 26		
Marske		d	19 19			20 12				21 13		22 28		
Saltburn		a	19 28			20 21				21 22		22 37		

§ For authorised access only to BSC Redcar

b arr. 1823

Table 44

Saturdays
from 11 September

Newcastle, Sunderland, Bishop Auckland and Darlington - Middlesbrough and Saltburn

	NT	NT	TP ◇1	NT	NT	NT	GC 1 A	NT	NT	TP ◇1	NT	NT	NT	TP ◇1	NT	NT	NT	GC 1	TP ◇1	NT
Hexham 48 d									06 13											08 43
Metrocentre 48 d																				09 15
Newcastle 8 26 d	06 00								07 00			07 30			08 30					09 30
Heworth d	06 07								07 07			07 37			08 37					09 37
Sunderland a	06 19								07 19			07 49			08 49					09 49
d	06 20						06 53		07 20			07 50			08 50			09 29		09 50
Seaham d	06 28								07 28			07 58			08 58					09 58
Hartlepool d	06a46						07 17		07 45			08 15			09 15			09 53		10 15
Seaton Carew d									07 49			08 19			09 19					10 19
Billingham d									07 56			08 26			09 26					10 26
Stockton d									08 04			08 33			09 33					10 33
Bishop Auckland d											07 35						09 23			
Shildon d											07 40						09 28			
Newton Aycliffe d											07 45						09 33			
Heighington d											07 48						09 37			
North Road d											07 57						09 45			
Chester-le-Street 26 d																				
Durham 26 d																				
Darlington 7 26 a											08 00						09 49			
d			06 36	06 40	06 58	07 19		07 38			08 09		08 56			09 23	09 51			
Dinsdale d				06 46		07 24					08 15		09 01			09 28	09 56			
Tees-side Airport d																				
Allens West d				06 53	07 08	07 31		07 49			08 22		09 08			09 35	10 03			
Eaglescliffe a				06 55	07 10	07 32	07 44	07 51			08 27		09 10			09 37	10 05	10 14		
d				06 55	07 11	07 32		07 51			08 27		09 10			09 37	10 05	10 15		
Thornaby d			06 53	07 01	07 16	07 39		07 56	08 12	08 26	08 33	08 39	09 16	09 22	09 39	09 45	10 11		10 22	10 39
Middlesbrough a			07 01	07 09	07 21	07 44		08 02	08 22	08 34	08 38	08 48	09 21	09 32	09 48	09 53	10 16		10 30	10 48
d		06 40		07 10	07 22	07 45					08 39		09 26			09 54	10 20			
South Bank d						07 49					08 43									
British Steel Redcar § d																				
Redcar Central d		06 50		07 20	07 32	07 57					08 51		09 36			10 04	10 30			
Redcar East d		06 53		07 23	07 35	07 59					08 53		09 39			10 07	10 33			
Longbeck d		06 57		07 27	07 39	08 03					08 57		09 43			10 11	10 37			
Marske d		06 58		07 28	07 40	08 05					08 59		09 44			10 12	10 38			
Saltburn a		07 05		07 35	07 48	08 14					09 08		09 52			10 20	10 47			

	NT	NT	TP ◇1	NT	NT	TP ◇1	NT	NT	NT	GC 1	NT	TP ◇1	NT	NT	NT	TP ◇1	NT
Hexham 48 d				09 43				10 44					11 42				12 42
Metrocentre 48 d				10 14				11 15					12 14				13 15
Newcastle 8 26 d				10b30				11 30					12 30				13 30
Heworth d				10 37				11 37					12 37				13 37
Sunderland a				10 49				11 49					12 49				13 49
d				10 50				11 50		12 30			12 50				13 50
Seaham d				10 58				11 58					12 58				13 58
Hartlepool d				11 15				12 15		12 54			13 15				14 15
Seaton Carew d				11 19				12 19					13 19				14 19
Billingham d				11 26				12 26					13 26				14 26
Stockton d				11 33				12 33					13 33				14 33
Bishop Auckland d	09 53						11 40								13 26		
Shildon d	09 58						11 45								13 31		
Newton Aycliffe d	10 03						11 50								13 36		
Heighington d	10 06						11 53								13 39		
North Road d	10 15						12 02								13 48		
Chester-le-Street 26 d																	
Durham 26 d																	
Darlington 7 26 a	10 18						12 06								13 51		
d	10 20	10 47			11 30		12 06		12 35		12 58			13 31	13 53		
Dinsdale d					11 35						13 03			13 36			
Tees-side Airport d	10 28																
Allens West d	10 33				11 42				12 45		13 10			13 43	14 04		
Eaglescliffe a	10 35	10 58			11 44				12 47	13 12	13 12			13 45	14 06		
d	10 35	10 59			11 44				12 48		13 12			13 45	14 06		
Thornaby d	10 45	11 04	11 22	11 39	11 50	12 19	12 25	12 39	12 53		13 18	13 21	13 39	13 52	14 13	14 19	14 39
Middlesbrough a	10 52	11 09	11 31	11 48	11 55	12 28	12 32	12 49	12 58		13 23	13 30	13 48	13 57	14 18	14 28	14 48
d	10 54	11 14			11 56		12 33		12 58		13 24			13 58	14 21		
South Bank d																	
British Steel Redcar § d																	
Redcar Central d	11 04	11 24			12 06		12 43		13 09		13 34			14 08	14 31		
Redcar East d	11 07	11 27			12 09		12 46		13 11		13 37			14 11	14 34		
Longbeck d	11 11	11 31			12 13		12 50		13 15		13 41			14 15	14 38		
Marske d	11 12	11 32			12 14		12 51		13 17		13 42			14 16	14 39		
Saltburn a	11 20	11 40			12 22		12 59		13 25		13 50			14 24	14 48		

§ For authorised access only to BSC Redcar

A The Zephyr

b arr. 1024

Table 44

Saturdays
from 11 September

Newcastle, Sunderland, Bishop Auckland and Darlington - Middlesbrough and Saltburn

	NT	NT	TP ◇1	NT	NT	NT	TP ◇1	NT	NT	NT	TP ◇1	NT	NT	NT	NT	GC 1	TP ◇1	NT
Hexham 48 d				13 42				14 44				15 42		16 12				16 42
Metrocentre 48 d				14 15				15 15				16 15		16 40				17 15
Newcastle 8 26 d				14 30				15 30				16 30		16 53				17 30
Heworth d				14 37				15 37				16 37		17 00				17 37
Sunderland a				14 49				15 50				16 49		17 14				17 50
d				14 50				15 50				16 50		17 15		17 30		17 50
Seaham d				14 58				15 58				16 58		17 22				17 58
Hartlepool d				15 15				16 15				17 15		17 39		17 56		18 15
Seaton Carew d				15 19				16 19				17 19		17 43				18 19
Billingham d				15 26				16 26				17 26		17 50				18 26
Stockton d				15 33				16 33				17 33		17 57				18 33
Bishop Auckland d						15 32							17 00					
Shildon d						15 37							17 05					
Newton Aycliffe d						15 42							17 10					
Heighington d						15 45							17 13					
North Road d						15 54							17 22					
Chester-le-Street 26 d																		
Durham 26 d																		
Darlington 7 26 a						15 58							17 26					
d	14 35	15 04			15 32	16 00			16 27	17 04			17 27		18 02			
Dinsdale d					15 37								17 33		18 07			
Tees-side Airport d																		
Allens West d	14 45	15 14			15 44				16 37				17 40		18 14			
Eaglescliffe a	14 47	15 16			15 46	16 11			16 39	17 15			17 42		18 16	18 27		
d	14 48	15 17			15 46	16 12			16 40	17 15			17 42		18 16			
Thornaby d	14 53	15 22	15 28	15 39	15 52	16 17	16 22	16 39	16 45	17 21	17 22	17 39	17 47	18 03	18 22		18 26	18 39
Middlesbrough a	14 58	15 27	15 35	15 48	15 57	16 22	16 30	16 47	16 52	17 26	17 33	17 49	17 54	18 15	18 27		18 32	18 48
d	14 58	15 28			15 58	16 23			16 54	17 28			17 54		18 27			
South Bank d						16 27							17 59					
British Steel Redcar § d																		
Redcar Central d	15 09	15 39			16 08	16 35			17 04	17 38			18 06		18 38			
Redcar East d	15 11	15 41			16 11	16 37			17 07	17 41			18 09		18 40			
Longbeck d	15 15	15 45			16 15	16 41			17 11	17 45			18 13		18 44			
Marske d	15 17	15 47			16 16	16 43			17 12	17 46			18 14		18 46			
Saltburn a	15 25	15 55			16 24	16 52			17 20	17 54			18 23		18 54			

	NT	TP ◇1	NT	NT	TP ◇1	NT	NT	NT	TP ◇1	NT	NT	NT
Hexham 48 d			17 42				18 42					
Metrocentre 48 d			18 13				19 17				20 47	
Newcastle 8 26 d			18b30				19 30				21 00	21 50
Heworth d			18 37				19 37				21 08	
Sunderland a			18 49				19 50				21 20	
d			18 50				19 50				21 20	
Seaham d			18 58				19 58				21 28	
Hartlepool d			19 15				20 15				21 45	
Seaton Carew d			19 19				20 19				21 49	
Billingham d			19 26				20 26				21 56	
Stockton d			19 33				20 33				22 03	
Bishop Auckland d	18 00			18 59						21 17		
Shildon d	18 05			19 04						21 22		
Newton Aycliffe d	18 10			19 09						21 27		
Heighington d	18 13			19 12						21 30		
North Road d	18 22			19 21						21 39		
Chester-le-Street 26 d												21 59
Durham 26 d												22 08
Darlington 7 26 a	18 25			19 25						21 42		22 29
d	18 30			19 27		20 07		20 30		21 44		22 30
Dinsdale d						20 12				21 49		
Tees-side Airport d												
Allens West d	18 41			19 38		20 19				21 56		22 41
Eaglescliffe a	18 43			19 40		20 21		20 41		21 58		22 43
d	18 45			19 40		20 21		20 41		21 58		22 43
Thornaby d	18 50	19 18	19 39	19 45	20 13	20 27	20 39	20 48	21 15	22 04	22 09	22 48
Middlesbrough a	19 00	19 28	19 48	19 52	20 23	20 38	20 50	20 55	21 25	22 09	22 18	22 57
d	19 01			19 54				20 55		22 09		
South Bank d												
British Steel Redcar § d												
Redcar Central d	19 11			20 04				21 05		22 20		
Redcar East d	19 14			20 07				21 08		22 22		
Longbeck d	19 18			20 11				21 12		22 26		
Marske d	19 19			20 12				21 13		22 28		
Saltburn a	19 28			20 21				21 22		22 37		

§ For authorised access only to BSC Redcar

b arr. 1823

Table 44

Sundays
until 05 September

Newcastle, Sunderland, Bishop Auckland and Darlington - Middlesbrough and Saltburn

		NT	NT	TP	NT	NT	GC	NT	NT	NT	NT	NT	TP	NT	NT	NT	NT	NT	TP
				◇1			1 ✕						◇1						◇1
Hexham	48 d																		
Metrocentre	48 d											10 48			11 48		12 48		
Newcastle 8	26 d							09 00		09 45		11 00			12 00		13 00		
Heworth	d							09 07		09 52		11 06			12 06		13 06		
Sunderland	a							09 22		10 05		11 22			12 21		13 22		
	d						09 10			10 06					12 21				
Seaham	d									10 14					12 29				
Hartlepool	d						09 34			10 31					12 45			13 30	
Seaton Carew	d									10 35					12 50			13 34	
Billingham	d									10 42					12 57			13 41	
Stockton	d									10 49					13 04			13 48	
Bishop Auckland	d				08 40						10 29					12 40			
Shildon	d				08 45						10 34					12 45			
Newton Aycliffe	d				08 50						10 39					12 50			
Heighington	d				08 54						10 42					12 53			
North Road	d				09 02						10 51					13 02			
Chester-le-Street	26 d																		
Durham	26 d																		
Darlington 7	26 a				09 05						10 54					13 08		14 08	
	d	08 18	08 41	09 00	09 07	09 20			10 03		11 04			12 02		13 10			
Dinsdale	d	08 23	08 46		09 12	09 25					11 09					13 15			
Tees-side Airport	d																		
Allens West	d	08 30	08 53		09 19	09 32					11 16					13 22			
Eaglescliffe	a	08 32	08 55		09 21	09 34	09 54		10 14		11 18			12 13		13 24			
	d	08 32	08 55		09 21	09 34			10 14		11 18			12 13		13 24			
Thornaby	d	08 38	09 01	09 16	09 31	09 43			10 20	10 55	11 24		11 33	12 19	13 09	13 30			13 33
Middlesbrough	a	08 44	09 06	09 25	09 40	09 49			10 25	11 02	11 30		11 43	12 24	13 20	13 35			13 43
	d	08 47	09 07			09 50			10 29		11 30			12 25		13 35			
South Bank	d																		
British Steel Redcar §	d																		
Redcar Central	d		09 17			10 00			10 40		11 41			12 35		13 46			
Redcar East	d		09 20			10 03			10 42		11 43			12 38		13 48			
Longbeck	d		09 24			10 07			10 46		11 47			12 42		13 52			
Marske	d		09 25			10 08			10 48		11 49			12 43		13 54			
Saltburn	a		09 32			10 15			10 55		11 57			12 50		14 02			

		NT	GC	NT	NT	NT	NT	NT	NT	NT	NT	NT	TP	NT	NT	NT	GC	NT
			1 ✕										◇1				1 ✕	
Hexham	48 d																	
Metrocentre	48 d			13 48	14 48						15 48	16 48				17 48		18 48
Newcastle 8	26 d			14 00	15 00						16 00	17 00				18 00		19 00
Heworth	d			14 06	15 06						16 06	17 06				18 06		19 06
Sunderland	a			14 21	15 22						16 21	17 22				18 21		19 22
	d		13 42	14 21							16 21					18 21	18 42	
Seaham	d			14 29							16 29					18 29		
Hartlepool	d		14 06	14 45						16 22	16 45					18 45	19 06	
Seaton Carew	d			14 50						16 26	16 50					18 50		
Billingham	d			14 57						16 33	16 57					18 57		
Stockton	d			15 04						16 40	17 04					19 04		
Bishop Auckland	d						14 49							16 56				
Shildon	d						14 54							17 01				
Newton Aycliffe	d						14 59							17 06				
Heighington	d						15 02							17 09				
North Road	d						15 11							17 18				
Chester-le-Street	26 d																	
Durham	26 d																	
Darlington 7	26 a						15 14			17 00				17 22				
	d	14 10				15 06	15 16	15 42	16 19					17 24	18 31			
Dinsdale	d						15 21							17 29				
Tees-side Airport	d																	
Allens West	d						15 28							17 37				
Eaglescliffe	a	14 21	14 33				15 30	15 53	16 30					17 39	18 42		19 24	
	d	14 21					15 30	15 53	16 30					17 39	18 42			
Thornaby	d	14 27		15 09		15 22	15 36	15 59	16 36		17 09		17 33	17 44	18 48	19 09		
Middlesbrough	a	14 32		15 18		15 27	15 41	16 04	16 41		17 18		17 43	17 49	18 53	19 18		
	d	14 33					15 42	16 05	16 45					17 50	18 54			
South Bank	d																	
British Steel Redcar §	d																	
Redcar Central	d	14 43					15 52	16 15	16 55					18 01	19 04			
Redcar East	d	14 46					15 55	16 18	16 58					18 03	19 07			
Longbeck	d	14 50					15 59	16 22	17 02					18 07	19 11			
Marske	d	14 51					16 00	16 23	17 03					18 09	19 12			
Saltburn	a	14 59					16 08	16 30	17 11					18 17	19 19			

§ For authorised access only to BSC Redcar

Table 44

Sundays
until 05 September

Newcastle, Sunderland, Bishop Auckland and Darlington - Middlesbrough and Saltburn

		NT	TP	NT	NT	TP	NT	NT	NT
			◇1			◇1			
Hexham	48 d								
Metrocentre	48 d								
Newcastle 8	26 d						20 00	21 06	
Heworth	d						20 07		
Sunderland	a						20 21		
	d						20 21		
Seaham	d						20 29		
Hartlepool	d						20 45		
Seaton Carew	d						20 50		
Billingham	d						20 57		
Stockton	d						21 04		
Bishop Auckland	d	18 49			19 55				
Shildon	d	18 54			20 00				
Newton Aycliffe	d	18 59			20 05				
Heighington	d	19 02			20 08				
North Road	d	19 11			20 17				
Chester-le-Street	26 d							21 15	
Durham	26 d							21 24	
Darlington 7	26 a	19 16			20 20			21 44	
	d			19 32	20 22			21 45	22 45
Dinsdale	d			19 37					
Tees-side Airport	d								
Allens West	d			19 44	20 33				
Eaglescliffe	a			19 46	20 35			21 57	22 56
	d			19 46	20 35			21 57	22 56
Thornaby	d		19 30	19 52	20 42	21 01	21 08	22 02	23 02
Middlesbrough	a		19 40	19 57	20 47	21 12	21 20	22 07	23 10
	d			19 58	20 50			22 08	
South Bank	d								
British Steel Redcar §	d								
Redcar Central	d			20 08	21 00			22 18	
Redcar East	d			20 11	21 03			22 21	
Longbeck	d			20 15	21 07			22 25	
Marske	d			20 16	21 08			22 26	
Saltburn	a			20 23	21 17			22 34	

Sundays
from 12 September

		NT	NT	TP	NT	NT	GC	NT	NT	NT	NT	NT	NT	TP	NT	NT	NT	NT	NT
		A	A	◇1	A		1 ✕			A	B			◇1					
Hexham	48 d																		
Metrocentre	48 d												10 48			11 48		12 48	
Newcastle 8	26 d							09 00		09 45	10 00		11 00			12 00		13 00	
Heworth	d							09 07		09 52	10 07		11 06			12 06		13 06	
Sunderland	a							09 22		10 05	10 19		11 22			12 21		13 22	
	d						09 10			10 06	10 20					12 21			
Seaham	d									10 14	10 28					12 29			
Hartlepool	d						09 34			10 31	10 45					12 45			13 30
Seaton Carew	d									10 35	10 49					12 50			13 34
Billingham	d									10 42	10 56					12 57			13 41
Stockton	d									10 49	11 03					13 04			13 48
Bishop Auckland	d				08 40							10 29					12 40		
Shildon	d				08 45							10 34					12 45		
Newton Aycliffe	d				08 50							10 39					12 50		
Heighington	d				08 54							10 42					12 53		
North Road	d				09 02							10 51					13 02		
Chester-le-Street	26 d																		
Durham	26 d																		
Darlington 7	26 a				09 05							10 54					13 08		14 08
	d	08 18	08 41	09 00	09 07	09 20			10 03			11 04			12 02		13 10		
Dinsdale	d	08 23	08 46		09 12	09 25						11 09					13 15		
Tees-side Airport	d																		
Allens West	d	08 30	08 53		09 19	09 32						11 16					13 22		
Eaglescliffe	a	08 32	08 55		09 21	09 34	09 54		10 14			11 18			12 13		13 24		
	d	08 32	08 55		09 21	09 34			10 14			11 18			12 13		13 24		
Thornaby	d	08 38	09 01	09 16	09 31	09 43			10 20	10 55	11 09	11 24		11 33	12 19	13 09	13 30		
Middlesbrough	a	08 44	09 06	09 25	09 40	09 49			10 25	11 02	11 18	11 30		11 43	12 24	13 20	13 35		
	d	08 47	09 07		09 45	09 50			10 29			11 30			12 25		13 35		
South Bank	d																		
British Steel Redcar §	d																		
Redcar Central	d		09 17			10 00			10 40			11 41			12 35		13 46		
Redcar East	d		09 20			10 03			10 42			11 43			12 38		13 48		
Longbeck	d		09 24			10 07			10 46			11 47			12 42		13 52		
Marske	d		09 25			10 08			10 48			11 49			12 43		13 54		
Saltburn	a		09 32			10 15			10 55			11 57			12 50		14 02		

§ For authorised access only to BSC Redcar
A 12 September
B not 12 September

Table 44

Sundays from 12 September

Newcastle, Sunderland, Bishop Auckland and Darlington - Middlesbrough and Saltburn

	TP	NT	GC	NT	NT	NT	NT	NT	NT	NT	NT	NT	TP	NT	NT	NT	GC
	◇1		▪ 1 ☕			A							◇1				▪ 1 ☕
Hexham 48 d																	
Metrocentre 48 d				13 48	14 48						15 48	16 48				17 48	
Newcastle 26 d				14 00	15 00						16 00	17 00				18 00	
Heworth d				14 06	15 06						16 06	17 06				18 06	
Sunderland a				14 21	15 22						16 21	17 22				18 21	
d			13 42	14 21							16 21					18 21	18 42
Seaham d				14 29							16 29					18 29	
Hartlepool d			14 06	14 45						16 22	16 45					18 45	19 06
Seaton Carew d				14 50						16 26	16 50					18 50	
Billingham d				14 57						16 33	16 57					18 57	
Stockton d				15 04						16 40	17 04					19 04	
Bishop Auckland d							14 49							16 56			
Shildon d							14 54							17 01			
Newton Aycliffe d							14 59							17 06			
Heighington d							15 02							17 09			
North Road d							15 11							17 18			
Chester-le-Street 26 d																	
Durham 26 d																	
Darlington 26 a							15 14			17 00				17 22			
d		14 10				15 06	15 16	15 42	16 19					17 24	18 31		
Dinsdale d							15 21							17 29			
Tees-side Airport d																	
Allens West d							15 28							17 37			
Eaglescliffe a		14 21	14 33				15 30	15 53	16 30					17 39	18 42		19 24
d		14 21					15 30	15 53	16 30					17 39	18 42		
Thornaby d	13 33	14 27		15 09		15 22	15 36	15 59	16 36		17 09		17 33	17 44	18 48	19 09	
Middlesbrough a	13 43	14 32		15 18		15 27	15 41	16 04	16 41		17 18		17 43	17 49	18 53	19 18	
d		14 33					15 42	16 05	16 45					17 50	18 54		
South Bank d																	
British Steel Redcar § d																	
Redcar Central d		14 43					15 52	16 15	16 55					18 01	19 04		
Redcar East d		14 46					15 55	16 18	16 58					18 03	19 07		
Longbeck d		14 50					15 59	16 22	17 02					18 07	19 11		
Marske d		14 51					16 00	16 23	17 03					18 09	19 12		
Saltburn a		14 59					16 08	16 30	17 11					18 17	19 19		

	NT	NT	TP	NT	NT	NT	TP	NT	NT	NT
			◇1		A	B	◇1			
Hexham 48 d										
Metrocentre 48 d	18 48									
Newcastle 26 d	19 00							20 00	21 06	
Heworth d	19 06							20 07		
Sunderland a	19 22							20 21		
d								20 21		
Seaham d								20 29		
Hartlepool d								20 45		
Seaton Carew d								20 50		
Billingham d								20 57		
Stockton d								21 04		
Bishop Auckland d		18 49			19 55					
Shildon d		18 54			20 00					
Newton Aycliffe d		18 59			20 05					
Heighington d		19 02			20 08					
North Road d		19 11			20 17					
Chester-le-Street 26 d									21 15	
Durham 26 d									21 24	
Darlington 26 a		19 16			20 20				21 44	
d				19 32	20 22	20 32			21 45	22 45
Dinsdale d				19 37		20 37				
Tees-side Airport d										
Allens West d				19 44	20 33	20 44				
Eaglescliffe a				19 46	20 35	20 46			21 57	22 56
d				19 46	20 35	20 46			21 57	22 56
Thornaby d			19 30	19 52	20 42	20 52	21 01	21 08	22 02	23 02
Middlesbrough a			19 40	19 57	20 47	20 57	21 12	21 20	22 07	
d				19 58	20 50	20 58			22 08	
South Bank d										
British Steel Redcar § d										
Redcar Central d				20 08	21 00	21 08			22 18	
Redcar East d				20 11	21 03	21 11			22 21	
Longbeck d				20 15	21 07	21 15			22 25	
Marske d				20 16	21 08	21 16			22 26	
Saltburn a				20 23	21 17	21 24			22 34	

§ For authorised access only to BSC Redcar

A 12 September

B not 12 September

Table 44

Mondays to Fridays until 03 September

Saltburn and Middlesbrough - Darlington, Bishop Auckland, Sunderland and Newcastle

	NT	TP	NT	NT	NT	NT	TP	NT	NT	NT	NT	NT	NT	TP	NT	NT	TP	NT	NT	NT	TP	GC	NT	NT
		◇1 🛒					◇1 🛒							◇1 🛒			◇1 🛒				◇1 🛒	▪ 1 ✕		
Saltburn d				06 24					07 17	07 38	08 00		08 30			09 21		10 00		10 30			11 00	
Marske d				06 28					07 21	07 42	08 04		08 34			09 25		10 04		10 34			11 04	
Longbeck d				06 31					07 24	07 45	08 07		08 37			09 28		10 07		10 37			11 07	
Redcar East d				06 34					07 27	07 48	08 10		08 40			09 31		10 10		10 40			11 10	
Redcar Central d				06 37					07 30	07 51	08 13		08 43			09 34		10 13		10 43			11 13	
British Steel Redcar § d																								
South Bank d													08 50											
Middlesbrough a				06 47					07 40	08 02	08 25		08 55			09 45		10 24		10 54			11 23	
d	05 45	05 57		06 49		06 56	07 23	07 32	07 42	08 02	08 25	08 32	08 55	09 00	09 32	09 46	09 59	10 24	10 32	10 54	11 00		11 24	11 32
Thornaby d	05 50	06 02		06 54		07 02	07 28	07 37	07 47	08 07	08 30	08 37	09 00	09 05	09 37	09 51	10 04	10 29	10 37	10 59	11 05		11 30	11 37
Eaglescliffe a	05 55			06 59					07 52	08 12	08 35		09 06			09 56		10 34				11 28	11 35	
d	05 56			06 59					07 52	08 13	08 35		09 06			09 57		10 34				11 29	11 35	
Allens West d	05 58			07 02					07 55	08 15	08 38		09 08			09 59		10 37					11 38	
Tees-side Airport d																								
Dinsdale d				07 08					08 01	08 22								10 43						
Darlington 26 a	06 14			07 20					08 11	08 31	08 54		09 24			10 17		10 54		11 19			11 52	
d	06 15			07 20	06 47				08 15	08 33			09 26					10 55						
North Road d					06 50					08 36			09 29					10 58						
Heighington d					06 58					08 44			09 37					11 06						
Newton Aycliffe d					07 02					08 48			09 40					11 10						
Shildon d					07 06					08 52			09 45					11 14						
Bishop Auckland a					07 18					08 59			09 52					11 21						
Stockton d						07 08		07 43				08 43			09 43				10 43					11 43
Billingham d						07 15		07 50				08 50			09 50				10 50					11 50
Seaton Carew d						07 21		07 56				08 56			09 56				10 56					11 56
Hartlepool d			07 03			07 27		08 02				09 02			10 02				11 02			11 48		12 02
Seaham d			07 18			07 42		08 17				09 17			10 17				11 17					12 17
Sunderland a			07 28			07 53		08 28				09 28			10 28				11 28			12 24		12 29
d			07 30			07 55		08 29				09 30			10 30				11 30					12 30
Heworth d			07 41			08 06		08 42				09 42			10 42				11 42					12 42
Newcastle 26 a	06 55		07 51	08 02		08 16		08 52	09 00			09 52			10 52				11 52					12 50
Metrocentre 48 a			08 03			08 31		09 01							11 01				12 01					13 01
Hexham 48 a			08 40			08 58		09 37							11 36				12 36					13 36

	NT	TP	NT	NT	TP	NT	NT	NT	TP	NT	GC	NT	NT	TP FO	TP FX	NT	NT	NT	TP	NT	NT	NT
		◇1 🛒			◇1 🛒				◇1 🛒		▪ 1 ✕			◇1	◇1 🛒				◇1 🛒			
Saltburn d	11 30		12 00			12 30	13 00			13 30		14 00				14 30	15 03			15 30	15 55	
Marske d	11 34		12 04			12 34	13 04			13 34		14 04				14 35	15 07			15 34	15 59	
Longbeck d	11 37		12 07			12 37	13 07			13 37		14 07				14 38	15 10			15 37	16 02	
Redcar East d	11 40		12 10			12 40	13 10			13 40		14 10				14 41	15 13			15 40	16 05	
Redcar Central d	11 43		12 13			12 43	13 13			13 43		14 13				14 44	15 16			15 43	16 08	
British Steel Redcar § d																						
South Bank d																						
Middlesbrough a	11 55		12 23	12 28		12 56	13 24			13 54		14 23				14 54	15 26			15 54	16 18	
d	11 55	12 00	12 24	12 32	12 50	12 57	13 25	13 32	13 50	13 55		14 24	14 32	14 50	14 50	14 55	15 27	15 32	15 50	15 55	16 19	16 32
Thornaby d	12 00	12 05	12 29	12 37	12 55	13 02	13 30	13 37	13 55	14 00		14 29	14 37	14 55	14 55	15 00	15 32	15 37	15 55	16 00	16 24	16 37
Eaglescliffe a			12 34			13 07	13 35			14 05	14 05	14 34					15 37			16 05	16 29	
d			12 35			13 07	13 35			14 05	14 06	14 35					15 37			16 05	16 30	
Allens West d			12 37				13 38					14 37					15 40			16 08	16 32	
Tees-side Airport d																						
Dinsdale d			12 44				13 44										15 46			16 14		
Darlington 26 a	12 19		12 53			13 23	13 54			14 21		14 52				15 20	15 56			16 24	16 52	
d			12 55									14 54					15 57					
North Road d			12 58									14 57					16 01					
Heighington d			13 06									15 05					16 09					
Newton Aycliffe d			13 10									15 09					16 12					
Shildon d			13 14									15 13					16 16					
Bishop Auckland a			13 21									15 19					16 24					
Stockton d				12 43				13 43					14 43					15 43				16 44
Billingham d				12 50				13 50					14 50					15 50				16 51
Seaton Carew d				12 56				13 56					14 56					15 56				16 57
Hartlepool d				13 02				14 00			14 26		15 02					16 02				17 03
Seaham d				13 17				14 15					15 17					16 17				17 18
Sunderland a				13 28				14 26			14 53		15 28					16 27				17 29
d				13 30				14 28					15 30					16 30				17 30
Heworth d				13 42				14 40					15 42					16 42				17 42
Newcastle 26 a				13 51				14 49					15 51					16 51				17 51
Metrocentre 48 a				14 01				15 01					16 01					17 01				18 01
Hexham 48 a				14 36				15 36					16 36					17 36				18 32

§ For authorised access only to BSC Redcar

Table 44

Mondays to Fridays
until 03 September

Saltburn and Middlesbrough - Darlington, Bishop Auckland, Sunderland and Newcastle

	TP	NT	NT	NT	TP	NT	NT	NT		NT	TP	NT	GC	NT	NT	TP	NT	TP		NT	TP	NT	GC	NT
	◇1 Ħ				◇1						◇1		▣ 1 A ✕			◇1		◇1			◇1		▣ 1 ✕	
Saltburn d		16 30	17 00			17 30	18 00			18 30				19 00	19 30					20 30		21 30		22 40
Marske d		16 34	17 04			17 34	18 04			18 34				19 04	19 34					20 34		21 34		22 44
Longbeck d		16 37	17 07			17 37	18 07			18 37				19 07	19 37					20 37		21 37		22 47
Redcar East d		16 40	17 10			17 40	18 10			18 40				19 10	19 40					20 40		21 40		22 50
Redcar Central d		16 43	17 13			17 43	18 13			18 43				19 13	19 43					20 43		21 43		22 53
British Steel Redcar § d		16 46																						
South Bank d		16 52																						
Middlesbrough a		16 57	17 23			17 54	18 23			18 53				19 23	19 54		20 25			20 54		21 54		23 03
d	16 50	16 57	17 24	17 32	17 50	17 55	18 24	18 30		18 54	19 00	19 20		19 25	19 55	20 00	20 30	20 50		20 55	21 30	21 55		23 05
Thornaby d	16 55	17 02	17 29	17 37	17 55	18 00	18 29	18 35		18 59	19 05	19 25		19 30	20 00	20 05	20 35	20 55		21 00	21 35	22 00		23 10
Eaglescliffe a		17 07	17 34			18 05				19 04				19 35	20 05					21 05		22 05		
d		17 08	17 35			18 05				19 05			19 33	19 35	20 05					21 06		22 05	22 06	
Allens West d		17 10	17 37			18 08				19 07				19 38	20 08					21 08		22 08		
Tees-side Airport d																								
Dinsdale d		17 17	17 44			18 14				19 14				19 44						21 15		22 14		
Darlington 7 26 a		17 26	17 54			18 24	18 49			19 26				19 56	20 25	20 29				21 24	21 54	22 24		23 31
d		17 28				18 32									20 30	20 31					21 58			
North Road d		17 31				18 35									20 33									
Heighington d		17 39				18 43									20 41									
Newton Aycliffe d		17 43				18 47									20 45									
Shildon d		17 47				18 51									20 49									
Bishop Auckland a		17 55				18 58									20 56									
Stockton d				17 43				18 41				19 31					20 41							
Billingham d				17 50				18 48				19 38					20 48							
Seaton Carew d				17 56				18 54				19 44					20 54							
Hartlepool d				18 02				19 00				19 49	20 01				21 00						22 28	
Seaham d				18 18				19 15				20 10					21 15							
Sunderland ⇌ a				18 28				19 26				20 21	20 37				21 26						22 54	
d				18 30				19 27				20 27					21 27							
Heworth ⇌ d				18 41				19 38				20 38					21 38							
Newcastle 8 26 ⇌ a				18 53				19 47				20 49					21 47							
Metrocentre 48 a								19 57																
Hexham 48 a																								

Mondays to Fridays
from 06 September

	NT	TP	NT	NT	NT	NT	TP	NT	NT	NT	NT	NT	NT	TP	NT	NT	TP	NT	NT	NT	TP	GC	NT	NT
		◇1 Ħ					◇1 Ħ							◇1 Ħ			◇1 Ħ				◇1 Ħ	▣ 1 ✕		
Saltburn d				06 24					07 17	07 38	08 00		08 30			09 21		10 00		10 30			11 00	
Marske d				06 28					07 21	07 42	08 04		08 34			09 25		10 04		10 34			11 04	
Longbeck d				06 31					07 24	07 45	08 07		08 37			09 28		10 07		10 37			11 07	
Redcar East d				06 34					07 27	07 48	08 10		08 40			09 31		10 10		10 40			11 10	
Redcar Central d				06 37					07 30	07 51	08 13		08 43			09 34		10 13		10 43			11 13	
British Steel Redcar § d																								
South Bank d													08 50											
Middlesbrough a				06 47				07 29	07 40	08 02	08 25		08 55		09 29	09 45		10 24		10 54			11 23	
d	05 45	05 57		06 49		06 56	07 23	07 32	07 42	08 02	08 25	08 32	08 55	09 00	09 32	09 46	09 59	10 24	10 32	10 54	11 00		11 24	11 32
Thornaby d	05 50	06 02		06 54		07 02	07 28	07 37	07 47	08 07	08 30	08 37	09 00	09 05	09 37	09 51	10 04	10 29	10 37	10 59	11 05		11 30	11 37
Eaglescliffe a	05 55			06 59					07 52	08 12	08 35		09 06			09 56		10 34				11 28	11 35	
d	05 56			06 59					07 52	08 13	08 35		09 06			09 57		10 34				11 29	11 35	
Allens West d	05 58			07 02					07 55	08 15	08 38		09 08			09 59		10 37					11 38	
Tees-side Airport d																								
Dinsdale d				07 08					08 01	08 22								10 43						
Darlington 7 26 a	06 14			07 20					08 11	08 31	08 54		09 24			10 17		10 54		11 19			11 52	
d	06 15			07 20	06 47				08 15	08 33			09 26					10 55						
North Road d					06 50					08 36			09 29					10 58						
Heighington d					06 58					08 44			09 37					11 06						
Newton Aycliffe d					07 02					08 48			09 40					11 10						
Shildon d					07 06					08 52			09 45					11 14						
Bishop Auckland a					07 18					08 59			09 52					11 21						
Stockton d						07 08		07 43				08 43			09 43				10 43					11 43
Billingham d						07 15		07 50				08 50			09 50				10 50					11 50
Seaton Carew d						07 21		07 56				08 56			09 56				10 56					11 56
Hartlepool d			07 03			07 27		08 02				09 02			10 02				11 02			11 48		12 02
Seaham d			07 18			07 42		08 17				09 17			10 17				11 17					12 17
Sunderland ⇌ a			07 28			07 53		08 28				09 28			10 28				11 28			12 24		12 29
d			07 30			07 55		08 29				09 30			10 30				11 30					12 30
Heworth ⇌ d			07 41			08 06		08 42				09 42			10 42				11 42					12 42
Newcastle 8 26 ⇌ a	06 55		07 51	08 02		08 16		08 52	09 00			09 52			10 52				11 52					12 50
Metrocentre 48 a			08 03			08 31		09 01							11 01				12 01					13 01
Hexham 48 a			08 40			09 01		09 39							11 39				12 39					13 39

§ For authorised access only to BSC Redcar
A The 21st Century Limited

Table 44

Mondays to Fridays
from 06 September

Saltburn and Middlesbrough - Darlington, Bishop Auckland, Sunderland and Newcastle

	NT	TP	NT	NT	TP	NT	NT	NT	TP	NT	GC	NT	NT	TP	TP	NT	NT	NT	TP	NT	NT	NT	TP	NT
														FO	FX									
		◇1 Ħ			◇1 Ħ				◇1 Ħ		▣ 1 ✕			◇1	◇1 Ħ				◇1 Ħ				◇1 Ħ	
Saltburn d	11 30		12 00			12 30	13 00			13 30		14 00				14 30	15 03			15 30	15 55			16 30
Marske d	11 34		12 04			12 34	13 04			13 34		14 04				14 35	15 07			15 34	15 59			16 34
Longbeck d	11 37		12 07			12 37	13 07			13 37		14 07				14 38	15 10			15 37	16 02			16 37
Redcar East d	11 40		12 10			12 40	13 10			13 40		14 10				14 41	15 13			15 40	16 05			16 40
Redcar Central d	11 43		12 13			12 43	13 13			13 43		14 13				14 44	15 16			15 43	16 08			16 43
British Steel Redcar § d																								16 46
South Bank d																								16 52
Middlesbrough a	11 55		12 23			12 56	13 24			13 54		14 23				14 54	15 26			15 54	16 18			16 57
d	11 55	12 00	12 24	12 32	12 50	12 57	13 25	13 32	13 50	13 55		14 24	14 32	14 50	14 50	14 55	15 27	15 32	15 50	15 55	16 19	16 32	16 50	16 57
Thornaby d	12 00	12 05	12 29	12 37	12 55	13 02	13 30	13 37	13 55	14 00		14 29	14 37	14 55	14 55	15 00	15 32	15 37	15 55	16 00	16 24	16 37	16 55	17 02
Eaglescliffe a			12 34			13 07	13 35			14 05		14 34					15 37			16 05	16 29			17 07
d			12 35			13 07	13 35			14 05	14 06	14 35					15 37			16 05	16 30			17 08
Allens West d			12 37				13 38					14 37					15 40			16 08	16 32			17 10
Tees-side Airport d																								
Dinsdale d			12 44				13 44										15 46			16 14				17 17
Darlington 7 26 a	12 19		12 53			13 23	13 54			14 21		14 52				15 20	15 56			16 24	16 52			17 26
d			12 55									14 54					15 57							17 28
North Road d			12 58									14 57					16 01							17 31
Heighington d			13 06									15 05					16 09							17 39
Newton Aycliffe d			13 10									15 09					16 12							17 43
Shildon d			13 14									15 13					16 16							17 47
Bishop Auckland a			13 21									15 19					16 24							17 55
Stockton d				12 43				13 43					14 43					15 43				16 44		
Billingham d				12 50				13 50					14 50					15 50				16 51		
Seaton Carew d				12 56				13 56					14 56					15 56				16 57		
Hartlepool d				13 02				14 00			14 26		15 02					16 02				17 03		
Seaham d				13 17				14 15					15 17					16 17				17 18		
Sunderland ⇌ a				13 28				14 26			14 53		15 28					16 27				17 29		
d				13 30				14 28					15 30					16 30				17 30		
Heworth ⇌ d				13 42				14 40					15 42					16 42				17 42		
Newcastle 8 26 ⇌ a				13 51				14 49					15 51					16 51				17 51		
Metrocentre 48 a				14 01				15 01					16 01					17 01				18 01		
Hexham 48 a				14 39				15 39					16 39					17 39				18 32		

	NT	NT	TP	NT	NT	NT		NT	TP	NT	GC	NT	NT	TP	NT	TP	NT	TP	NT	GC	NT			
			◇1						◇1		▣ 1 A ✕			◇1		◇1		◇1		▣ 1 ✕				
Saltburn d	17 00			17 30	18 00			18 30				19 00	19 30				20 30		21 30		22 40			
Marske d	17 04			17 34	18 04			18 34				19 04	19 34				20 34		21 34		22 44			
Longbeck d	17 07			17 37	18 07			18 37				19 07	19 37				20 37		21 37		22 47			
Redcar East d	17 10			17 40	18 10			18 40				19 10	19 40				20 40		21 40		22 50			
Redcar Central d	17 13			17 43	18 13			18 43				19 13	19 43				20 43		21 43		22 53			
British Steel Redcar § d																								
South Bank d																								
Middlesbrough a	17 23			17 54	18 23			18 53				19 23	19 54		20 25		20 54		21 54		23 03			
d	17 24	17 32	17 50	17 55	18 24	18 30		18 54	19 00	19 20		19 25	19 55	20 00	20 30	20 50	20 55	21 30	21 55		23 05			
Thornaby d	17 29	17 37	17 55	18 00	18 29	18 35		18 59	19 05	19 25		19 30	20 00	20 05	20 35	20 55	21 00	21 35	22 00		23 10			
Eaglescliffe a	17 34			18 05				19 04				19 35	20 05				21 05		22 05					
d	17 35			18 05				19 05			19 33	19 35	20 05				21 06		22 05	22 06				
Allens West d	17 37			18 08				19 07				19 38	20 08				21 08		22 08					
Tees-side Airport d																								
Dinsdale d	17 44			18 14				19 14				19 44					21 15		22 14					
Darlington 7 26 a	17 54			18 24	18 49			19 26				19 56	20 25	20 29			21 24	21 54	22 24		23 31			
d				18 32									20 30											
North Road d				18 35									20 33											
Heighington d				18 43									20 41											
Newton Aycliffe d				18 47									20 45											
Shildon d				18 51									20 49											
Bishop Auckland a				18 58									20 56											
Stockton d		17 43				18 41				19 31					20 41									
Billingham d		17 50				18 48				19 38					20 48									
Seaton Carew d		17 56				18 54				19 44					20 54									
Hartlepool d		18 02				19 00				19 49	20 01				21 00					22 28				
Seaham d		18 18				19 15				20 10					21 15									
Sunderland ⇌ a		18 28				19 26				20 21	20 37				21 26					22 54				
d		18 30				19 27				20 27					21 27									
Heworth ⇌ d		18 41				19 38				20 38					21 38									
Newcastle 8 26 ⇌ a		18 53				19 47				20 49					21 47									
Metrocentre 48 a						19 57																		
Hexham 48 a																								

§ For authorised access only to BSC Redcar
A The 21st Century Limited

Saturdays until 04 September

Saltburn and Middlesbrough - Darlington, Bishop Auckland, Sunderland and Newcastle

		NT	TP	NT	NT	NT	NT	TP	NT	NT	NT	NT	NT	TP	NT	NT	TP	NT	NT	NT	GC	TP	NT	NT
			◇■					◇■ ✕						◇■ ✕			◇■ ✕				■	◇■ ✕		
Saltburn	d			06 24						07 17	08 00		08 30			09 13		10 00		10 30			11 00	
Marske	d			06 28						07 21	08 04		08 34			09 17		10 04		10 34			11 04	
Longbeck	d			06 31						07 24	08 07		08 37			09 20		10 07		10 37			11 07	
Redcar East	d			06 34						07 27	08 10		08 40			09 23		10 10		10 40			11 10	
Redcar Central	d			06 37						07 30	08 13		08 43			09 26		10 13		10 43			11 13	
British Steel Redcar §	d																							
South Bank	d												08 50											
Middlesbrough	a			06 47						07 40	08 24		08 55			09 36		10 23		10 54			11 23	
	d	05 50	05 57	06 49			06 56	07 21	07 32	07 42	08 25	08 32	08 55	09 00	09 32	09 39	10 00	10 24	10 32	10 54		11 00	11 24	11 32
Thornaby	d	05 55	06 02	06 54			07 02	07 26	07 37	07 47	08 30	08 37	09 00	09 05	09 37	09 44	10 05	10 29	10 37	10 59		11 05	11 29	11 37
Eaglescliffe	a	06 00		06 59						07 56	08 35		09 05			09 49		10 34			10 48		11 34	
	d	06 00		06 59						07 56	08 35		09 06			09 49		10 34			10 49		11 35	
Allens West	d	06 03		07 02						07 59	08 38		09 08			09 52		10 37					11 37	
Tees-side Airport	d																							
Dinsdale	d			07 08						08 07								10 43						
Darlington ■ 26	a	06 18		07 20						08 14	08 54		09 24			10 06		10 54		11 19			11 54	
	d			07 20	06 48					08 15			09 24					10 57						
North Road	d				06 51								09 27					11 00						
Heighington	d				06 59								09 35					11 08						
Newton Aycliffe	d				07 02								09 39					11 12						
Shildon	d				07 07								09 43					11 16						
Bishop Auckland	a				07 19								09 50					11 23						
Stockton	d						07 08		07 43			08 43			09 43				10 43					11 43
Billingham	d						07 15		07 50			08 50			09 50				10 50					11 50
Seaton Carew	d						07 21		07 56			08 56			09 56				10 56					11 56
Hartlepool	d					07 03	07 27		08 02			09 02			10 02				11 02		11 21			21 02
Seaham	d					07 18	07 42		08 17			09 17			10 17				11 17					12 17
Sunderland ⇌	a					07 28	07 53		08 28			09 28			10 28				11 28		11 50			12 29
	d					07 30	07 55		08 29			09 29			10 30				11 30					12 30
Heworth ⇌	d					07 42	08 07		08 42			09 42			10 42				11 42					12 42
Newcastle ■ 26 ⇌	a			08 02		07 53	08 17		08 52	09 00		09 54			10 52				11 52					12 52
Metrocentre 48	a					08 03	08 31		09 01						11 01				12 01					13 01
Hexham 48	a					08 40	08 58		09 37						11 36				12 36					13 36

		NT	TP	NT	NT	TP	NT	NT	NT	NT	TP	GC	NT	NT	TP	NT	NT	NT	TP	NT	NT	NT	NT	TP	NT
			◇■ ✕			◇■ ✕					◇■ ✕	■			◇■ ✕				◇■ ✕					◇■	
Saltburn	d	11 30		11 56			12 30	13 00		13 30			13 58			14 30	15 00			15 30	16 00		16 30		16 59
Marske	d	11 34		12 00			12 34	13 04		13 34			14 02			14 34	15 04			15 34	16 04		16 34		17 03
Longbeck	d	11 37		12 03			12 37	13 07		13 37			14 05			14 37	15 07			15 37	16 07		16 37		17 06
Redcar East	d	11 40		12 06			12 40	13 10		13 40			14 08			14 40	15 10			15 40	16 10		16 40		17 09
Redcar Central	d	11 43		12 09			12 43	13 13		13 43			14 11			14 43	15 13			15 43	16 13		16 43		17 12
British Steel Redcar §	d																								
South Bank	d																								17 19
Middlesbrough	a	11 54		12 19			12 54	13 23		13 53			14 21			14 54	15 23			15 53	16 23		16 54		17 24
	d	11 55	12 00	12 20	12 32	12 50	12 55	13 24	13 32	13 55	14 00		14 23	14 32	14 50	14 55	15 27	15 32	15 50	15 55	16 24	16 32	16 55	17 00	17 25
Thornaby	d	12 00	12 05	12 25	12 37	12 55	13 00	13 29	13 37	14 00	14 05		14 28	14 37	14 55	15 00	15 32	15 37	15 55	16 00	16 29	16 37	17 00	17 05	17 30
Eaglescliffe	a			12 30			13 05	13 34					14 33				15 37			16 05	16 34		17 05		17 35
	d			12 30			13 05	13 34				14 28	14 33				15 37			16 05	16 34		17 05		17 35
Allens West	d			12 33				13 37					14 36				15 40			16 08	16 37		17 08		17 38
Tees-side Airport	d							13 41																	
Dinsdale	d			12 39				13 45									15 46			16 14			17 14		
Darlington ■ 26	a	12 20		12 49			13 21	13 55		14 20			14 50			15 20	15 55			16 24	16 51		17 25		17 52
	d			12 50									14 53							16 25			17 30		
North Road	d			12 54									14 57							16 28			17 34		
Heighington	d			13 02									15 05							16 37			17 42		
Newton Aycliffe	d			13 05									15 08							16 40			17 45		
Shildon	d			13 09									15 12							16 44			17 49		
Bishop Auckland	a			13 16									15 20							16 52			17 58		
Stockton	d				12 43				13 44					14 43				15 43				16 44			
Billingham	d				12 50				13 51					14 50				15 50				16 51			
Seaton Carew	d				12 56				13 57					14 56				15 56				16 57			
Hartlepool	d				13 02				14 03			14 47		15 02				16 02				17 03			
Seaham	d				13 17				14 18					15 17				16 17				17 18			
Sunderland ⇌	a				13 28				14 29			15 17		15 28				16 27				17 29			
	d				13 30				14 31					15 30				16 30				17 30			
Heworth ⇌	d				13 42				14 42					15 42				16 42				17 42			
Newcastle ■ 26 ⇌	a				13 52				14 51					15 51				16 52				17 51			
Metrocentre 48	a				14 01				15 01					16 00				17 01				18 01			
Hexham 48	a				14 36				15 36					16 35				17 36				18 32			

§ For authorised access only to BSC Redcar

A from 17 July until 4 September

Saturdays until 04 September

Saltburn and Middlesbrough - Darlington, Bishop Auckland, Sunderland and Newcastle

		NT	GC	NT	TP	NT	NT	NT	TP	NT	GC	NT	GC	NT	TP	NT	TP	NT	TP	NT	GC	NT
			■ A		◇■				◇■		■ A		■ B		◇■		◇■		◇■		■ C	
Saltburn	d			17 28		18 00		18 28				19 00		19 35				20 30		21 30		22 40
Marske	d			17 32		18 04		18 32				19 04		19 39				20 34		21 34		22 44
Longbeck	d			17 35		18 07		18 35				19 07		19 42				20 37		21 37		22 47
Redcar East	d			17 38		18 10		18 38				19 10		19 45				20 40		21 40		22 50
Redcar Central	d			17 41		18 13		18 41				19 13		19 48				20 43		21 43		22 53
British Steel Redcar §	d																					
South Bank	d																					
Middlesbrough	a			17 55		18 23		18 51				19 23		19 58				20 54		21 53		23 04
	d	17 30		17 56	18 07	18 24	18 30	18 53	19 00	19 20		19 25		19 59	20 10	20 30	20 50	20 55	21 50	21 55		23 05
Thornaby	d	17 35		18 01	18 12	18 29	18 35	18 58	19 05	19 25		19 30		20 04	20 15	20 35	20 55	21 00	21 55	22 00		23 10
Eaglescliffe	a			18 06				19 03				19 35		20 09				21 05		22 05		
	d		17 57	18 06				19 03			19 31	19 35	19 53	20 10				21 06		22 05	22 07	
Allens West	d			18 09				19 06				19 38		20 12				21 08		22 08		
Tees-side Airport	d																					
Dinsdale	d			18 15				19 12				19 44		20 19				21 15		22 14		
Darlington ■ 26	a			18 26		18 49		19 23				19 54		20 28				21 24	22 15	22 24		23 30
	d			18 26										20 36								
North Road	d			18 30										20 39								
Heighington	d			18 38										20 47								
Newton Aycliffe	d			18 41										20 51								
Shildon	d			18 45										20 55								
Bishop Auckland	a			18 53										21 02								
Stockton	d	17 41					18 41			19 31						20 41						
Billingham	d	17 48					18 48			19 38						20 48						
Seaton Carew	d	17 54					18 54			19 44						20 54						
Hartlepool	d	18 02	18 20				19 00			19 49	20b06		20 21			21 00					22 26	
Seaham	d	18 18					19 15			20 10						21 15						
Sunderland ⇌	a	18 28	18 51				19 26			20 20	20 35		20 50			21 26					22 54	
	d	18 30					19 27			20 27						21 27						
Heworth ⇌	d	18 42					19 38			20 38						21 38						
Newcastle ■ 26 ⇌	a	18 53					19 48			20 48						21 48						
Metrocentre 48	a						19 58															
Hexham 48	a																					

Saturdays from 11 September

		NT	TP	NT	NT	NT	NT	TP	NT	NT	NT	NT	NT	TP	NT	NT	TP	NT	NT	NT	GC	TP	NT	NT
			◇■					◇■ ✕						◇■ ✕			◇■ ✕				■	◇■ ✕		
Saltburn	d			06 24						07 17	08 00		08 30			09 13		10 00		10 30			11 00	
Marske	d			06 28						07 21	08 04		08 34			09 17		10 04		10 34			11 04	
Longbeck	d			06 31						07 24	08 07		08 37			09 20		10 07		10 37			11 07	
Redcar East	d			06 34						07 27	08 10		08 40			09 23		10 10		10 40			11 10	
Redcar Central	d			06 37						07 30	08 13		08 43			09 26		10 13		10 43			11 13	
British Steel Redcar §	d																							
South Bank	d												08 50											
Middlesbrough	a			06 47						07 40	08 24		08 55			09 36		10 23		10 54			11 23	
	d	05 50	05 57	06 49			06 56	07 21	07 32	07 42	08 25	08 32	08 55	09 00	09 32	09 39	10 00	10 24	10 32	10 54		11 00	11 24	11 32
Thornaby	d	05 55	06 02	06 54			07 02	07 26	07 37	07 47	08 30	08 37	09 00	09 05	09 37	09 44	10 05	10 29	10 37	10 59		11 05	11 29	11 37
Eaglescliffe	a	06 00		06 59						07 56	08 35		09 05			09 49		10 34			10 48		11 34	
	d	06 00		06 59						07 56	08 35		09 06			09 49		10 34			10 49		11 35	
Allens West	d	06 03		07 02						07 59	08 38		09 08			09 52		10 37					11 37	
Tees-side Airport	d																							
Dinsdale	d			07 08						08 07								10 43						
Darlington ■ 26	a	06 18		07 20						08 14	08 54		09 24			10 06		10 54		11 19			11 54	
	d			07 20	06 48					08 15			09 24					10 57						
North Road	d				06 51								09 27					11 00						
Heighington	d				06 59								09 35					11 08						
Newton Aycliffe	d				07 02								09 39					11 12						
Shildon	d				07 07								09 43					11 16						
Bishop Auckland	a				07 19								09 50					11 23						
Stockton	d						07 08		07 43			08 43			09 43				10 43					11 43
Billingham	d						07 15		07 50			08 50			09 50				10 50					11 50
Seaton Carew	d						07 21		07 56			08 56			09 56				10 56					11 56
Hartlepool	d					07 03	07 27		08 02			09 02			10 02				11 02		11 21			12 02
Seaham	d					07 18	07 42		08 17			09 17			10 17				11 17					12 17
Sunderland ⇌	a					07 28	07 53		08 28			09 28			10 28				11 28		11 50			12 29
	d					07 30	07 55		08 29			09 29			10 30				11 30					12 30
Heworth ⇌	d					07 42	08 07		08 42			09 42			10 42				11 42					12 42
Newcastle ■ 26 ⇌	a			08 02		07 53	08 17		08 52	09 00		09 54			10 52				11 52					12 52
Metrocentre 48	a					08 03	08 31		09 01						11 01				12 01					13 01
Hexham 48	a					08 40	09 00		09 39						11 38				12 38					13 39

§ For authorised access only to BSC Redcar

A until 10 July. **The 21st Century Limited**

B from 17 July until 4 September. **The 21st Century Limited**

C until 10 July

Table 44

Saturdays from 11 September

Saltburn and Middlesbrough - Darlington, Bishop Auckland, Sunderland and Newcastle

	NT	TP	NT	NT	TP	NT	NT	NT	NT	TP	GC	NT	NT	TP	NT	NT	NT	TP	NT	NT	NT	NT	TP	NT
		◇1			◇1					◇1	1			◇1				◇1					◇1	
Saltburn d	11 30		11 56			12 30	13 00		13 30			13 58			14 30	15 00			15 30	16 00		16 30		16 59
Marske d	11 34		12 00			12 34	13 04		13 34			14 02			14 34	15 04			15 34	16 04		16 34		17 03
Longbeck d	11 37		12 03			12 37	13 07		13 37			14 05			14 37	15 07			15 37	16 07		16 37		17 06
Redcar East d	11 40		12 06			12 40	13 10		13 40			14 08			14 40	15 10			15 40	16 10		16 40		17 09
Redcar Central d	11 43		12 09			12 43	13 13		13 43			14 11			14 43	15 13			15 43	16 13		16 43		17 12
British Steel Redcar § d																								
South Bank d																								17 19
Middlesbrough a	11 54		12 19			12 54	13 23		13 53			14 21			14 54	15 23			15 53	16 23		16 54		17 24
d	11 55	12 00	12 20	12 32	12 50	12 55	13 24	13 32	13 55	14 00		14 23	14 32	14 50	14 55	15 27	15 32	15 50	15 55	16 24	16 32	16 55	17 00	17 25
Thornaby d	12 00	12 05	12 25	12 37	12 55	13 00	13 29	13 37	14 00	14 05		14 28	14 37	14 55	15 00	15 32	15 37	15 55	16 00	16 29	16 37	17 00	17 05	17 30
Eaglescliffe a			12 30			13 05	13 34				14 27	14 33				15 37			16 05	16 34		17 05		17 35
d			12 30			13 05	13 34				14 28	14 33				15 37			16 05	16 34		17 05		17 35
Allens West d			12 33				13 37					14 36				15 40			16 08	16 37		17 08		17 38
Tees-side Airport d							13 41																	
Dinsdale d			12 39				13 45									15 46			16 14			17 14		
Darlington 26 a	12 20		12 49			13 21	13 55		14 20			14 50			15 20	15 55			16 24	16 51		17 25		17 52
d			12 50									14 53							16 25			17 30		
North Road d			12 54									14 57							16 28			17 34		
Heighington d			13 02									15 05							16 37			17 42		
Newton Aycliffe d			13 05									15 08							16 40			17 45		
Shildon d			13 09									15 12							16 44			17 49		
Bishop Auckland a			13 16									15 20							16 52			17 58		
Stockton d				12 43				13 44					14 43				15 43				16 44			
Billingham d				12 50				13 51					14 50				15 50				16 51			
Seaton Carew d				12 56				13 57					14 56				15 56				16 57			
Hartlepool d				13 02				14 03			14 47		15 02				16 02				17 03			
Seaham d				13 17				14 18					15 17				16 17				17 18			
Sunderland a				13 28				14 29			15 17		15 28				16 27				17 29			
d				13 30				14 31					15 30				16 30				17 30			
Heworth d				13 42				14 42					15 42				16 42				17 42			
Newcastle 26 a				13 52				14 51					15 51				16 52				17 51			
Metrocentre 48 a				14 01				15 01					16 00				17 01				18 01			
Hexham 48 a				14 38				15 38					16 37				17 37				18 34			

	NT	NT	TP	NT	NT	NT	TP	NT	GC	NT	NT	TP	NT	TP	NT	TP	NT	GC	NT
			◇1				◇1		1 A			◇1		◇1		◇1		1	
Saltburn d		17 28		18 00		18 28				19 00	19 35				20 30		21 30		22 40
Marske d		17 32		18 04		18 32				19 04	19 39				20 34		21 34		22 44
Longbeck d		17 35		18 07		18 35				19 07	19 42				20 37		21 37		22 47
Redcar East d		17 38		18 10		18 38				19 10	19 45				20 40		21 40		22 50
Redcar Central d		17 41		18 13		18 41				19 13	19 48				20 43		21 43		22 53
British Steel Redcar § d																			
South Bank d																			
Middlesbrough a		17 55		18 23		18 51				19 23	19 58				20 54		21 53		23 04
d	17 30	17 56	18 07	18 24	18 30	18 53	19 00	19 20		19 25	19 59	20 10	20 30	20 50	20 55	21 50	21 55		23 05
Thornaby d	17 35	18 01	18 12	18 29	18 35	18 58	19 05	19 25		19 30	20 04	20 15	20 35	20 55	21 00	21 55	22 00		23 10
Eaglescliffe a		18 06				19 03			19 28	19 35	20 09				21 05		22 05	22 06	
d		18 06				19 03			19 31	19 35	20 10				21 06		22 05	22 07	
Allens West d		18 09				19 06				19 38	20 12				21 08		22 08		
Tees-side Airport d																			
Dinsdale d		18 15				19 12				19 44	20 19				21 15		22 14		
Darlington 26 a		18 26		18 49		19 23				19 54	20 28				21 24	22 15	22 24		23 30
d		18 26									20 36								
North Road d		18 30									20 39								
Heighington d		18 38									20 47								
Newton Aycliffe d		18 41									20 51								
Shildon d		18 45									20 55								
Bishop Auckland a		18 53									21 02								
Stockton d	17 41				18 41			19 31					20 41						
Billingham d	17 48				18 48			19 38					20 48						
Seaton Carew d	17 54				18 54			19 44					20 54						
Hartlepool d	18 02				19 00			19 49	20b06				21 00					22 26	
Seaham d	18 18				19 15			20 10					21 15						
Sunderland a	18 28				19 26			20 20	20 35				21 26					22 54	
d	18 30				19 27			20 27					21 27						
Heworth d	18 42				19 38			20 38					21 38						
Newcastle 26 a	18 53				19 48			20 48					21 48						
Metrocentre 48 a					19 58														
Hexham 48 a																			

§ For authorised access only to BSC Redcar

A The 21st Century Limited

b arr. 1956

Table 44

Sundays until 05 September

Saltburn and Middlesbrough - Darlington, Bishop Auckland, Sunderland and Newcastle

	NT	NT	NT	NT	NT	NT	TP	NT	NT	NT	NT	GC	NT	NT	TP	NT	NT	NT	NT	TP	NT	NT	NT	NT
							◇1					1			◇1					◇1				
Saltburn d						09 36		10 28		11 00				12 01		13 00			14 14				15 25	
Marske d						09 40		10 32		11 04				12 05		13 04			14 18				15 29	
Longbeck d						09 43		10 35		11 07				12 08		13 07			14 21				15 32	
Redcar East d						09 46		10 38		11 10				12 11		13 10			14 24				15 35	
Redcar Central d						09 49		10 41		11 13				12 14		13 13			14 27				15 38	
British Steel Redcar § d																								
South Bank d																								
Middlesbrough a						09 59		10 51		11 23				12 24		13 23			14 37				15 48	
d		08 45	09 15		09 30	10 00	10 15	10 53		11 24	11 30			12 25	12 45	13 25		13 30	14 38	14 45	15 30		15 50	
Thornaby d		08 50	09 20		09 35	10 05	10 20	10 58		11 29	11 35			12 30	12 50	13 30		13 35	14 43	14 50	15 35		15 55	
Eaglescliffe a		08 55	09 25			10 10		11 03		11 34		12 03		12 35		13 35			14 48				16 00	
d		08 55	09 25			10 10		11 03		11 34		12 04		12 36		13 35			14 49				16 00	
Allens West d		08 58	09 28							11 37						13 38							16 03	
Tees-side Airport d																								
Dinsdale d			09 34							11 43						13 44							16 09	
Darlington 26 a		09 15	09 49			10 30		11 22		11 53				12 53		13 54			15 06				16 20	
d	08 05		09 51							11 54			12 20			14 06						15 37	16 22	
North Road d	08 08		09 54							11 57						14 09							16 25	
Heighington d	08 16		10 02							12 06						14 18							16 33	
Newton Aycliffe d	08 19		10 05							12 09						14 21							16 36	
Shildon d	08 24		10 10							12 13						14 25							16 41	
Bishop Auckland a	08 34		10 20							12 19						14 31							16 46	
Stockton d					09 41						11 41		12 36					13 41			15 41	15 53		
Billingham d					09 48						11 48		12 43					13 48			15 48	16 00		
Seaton Carew d					09 54						11 54		12 49					13 54			15 54	16 06		
Hartlepool d					10 00						12 00	12 24	12a57					14 00			16 00	16a14		
Seaham d					10 15						12 15							14 15			16 16			
Sunderland a					10 26						12 26	12 52						14 26			16 26			
d				09 28	10 28				11 28		12 28						13 28	14 28			16 28			15 28
Heworth d				09 39	10 39				11 37		12 37						13 39	14 39			16 40			15 39
Newcastle 26 a				09 50	10 50				11 48		12 48						13 49	14 48			16 49			15 48
Metrocentre 48 a				10 01	11 01				11 57		12 59						13 59	14 59			16 58			15 59
Hexham 48 a																								

	TP	NT	GC	NT	GC	NT	NT	NT	NT	NT	TP	NT	NT	NT	NT	TP	NT	GC	NT	TP	NT
	◇1		1 A		1 B						◇1					◇1		A		◇1	
Saltburn d				16 25		16 48			17 20			18 27			19 23		20 31		21 30		22 38
Marske d				16 29		16 52			17 24			18 31			19 27		20 35		21 34		22 42
Longbeck d				16 32		16 55			17 27			18 34			19 30		20 38		21 37		22 45
Redcar East d				16 35		16 58			17 30			18 37			19 33		20 41		21 40		22 48
Redcar Central d				16 38		17 01			17 33			18 40			19 36		20 44		21 43		22 51
British Steel Redcar § d																					
South Bank d																					
Middlesbrough a				16 48		17 11			17 48			18 52			19 46		20 55		21 53		23 01
d	16 45			16 49		17 14	17 25	17 30	17 49	18 37	18 45	18 55		19 30	19 47	20 07	20 56		21 55	22 07	23 02
Thornaby d	16 50			16 54		17 19	17 30	17 35	17 54	18 42	18 50	19 00		19 35	19 52	20 12	21 01		22 00	22 12	23 07
Eaglescliffe a			16 36	16 59	17 08	17 24	17 37		17 59	18 47		19 05			19 57		21 06	21 13	22 05		23 12
d			16 37	17 00	17 09	17 25	17 37		17 59	18 48		19 06			19 58		21 07	21 14	22 05		23 12
Allens West d							17 40		18 02	18 51					20 00				22 08		
Tees-side Airport d																					
Dinsdale d							17 50		18 08	18 57					20 07				22 14		
Darlington 26 a				17 18		17 43	18 05		18 15	19 07		19 25			20 17		21 24		22 26		23 30
d							18 15			19 23											
North Road d							18 18			19 26											
Heighington d							18 26			19 34											
Newton Aycliffe d							18 29			19 37											
Shildon d							18 34			19 42											
Bishop Auckland a							18 39			19 47											
Stockton d								17 41						19 41							
Billingham d								17 48						19 48							
Seaton Carew d								17 54						19 54							
Hartlepool d			17b03		17 29			18 00						20 00				21 36			
Seaham d								18 15						20 15							
Sunderland a			17 35		17 55			18 26						20 25				22 05			
d		17 28						18 28					19 28	20 28							
Heworth d		17 39						18 39					19 39	20 39							
Newcastle 26 a		17 48						18 48					19 52	20 47							
Metrocentre 48 a		17 59						18 59													
Hexham 48 a																					

§ For authorised access only to BSC Redcar

A until 11 July

B from 18 July until 5 September

b arr. 1655

Table 44

Saltburn and Middlesbrough - Darlington, Bishop Auckland, Sunderland and Newcastle

	NT	NT	NT	NT	NT	NT	NT	TP	NT	NT	NT	NT
	A					A	B	◇1				
Saltburn d						09 36			10 28		11 00	
Marske d						09 40			10 32		11 04	
Longbeck d						09 43			10 35		11 07	
Redcar East d						09 46			10 38		11 10	
Redcar Central d						09 49			10 41		11 13	
British Steel Redcar § d												
South Bank d												
Middlesbrough a						09 59			10 51		11 23	
d		08 45	09 15		09 30	10 00	10 00	10 15	10 53		11 24	11 30
Thornaby d		08 50	09 20		09 35	10 05	10 05	10 20	10 58		11 29	11 35
Eaglescliffe a		08 55	09 25			10 10	10 10		11 03		11 34	
d		08 55	09 25			10 10	10 10		11 03		11 34	
Allens West d		08 58	09 28								11 37	
Tees-side Airport d												
Dinsdale d			09 34								11 43	
Darlington 7 26 a		09 15	09 49			10 30	10 28		11 22		11 53	
d	08 05		09 51								11 54	
North Road d	08 08		09 54								11 57	
Heighington d	08 16		10 02								12 06	
Newton Aycliffe d	08 19		10 05								12 09	
Shildon d	08 24		10 10								12 13	
Bishop Auckland a	08 34		10 20								12 19	
Stockton d					09 41							11 41
Billingham d					09 48							11 48
Seaton Carew d					09 54							11 54
Hartlepool d					10 00							12 00
Seaham d					10 15							12 15
Sunderland ⇌ a					10 26							12 26
d				09 28	10 28					11 28		12 28
Heworth ⇌ d				09 39	10 39					11 37		12 37
Newcastle 8 26 ⇌ a				09 50	10 50					11 48		12 48
Metrocentre 48 a				10 01	11 01					11 57		12 59
Hexham 48 a												

	GC	NT	NT	TP	NT	NT	NT	NT	NT	TP	NT	NT
	■ 1 ⊏			◇1						◇1		
Saltburn d			12 01		13 00				14 14			15 25
Marske d			12 05		13 04				14 18			15 29
Longbeck d			12 08		13 07				14 21			15 32
Redcar East d			12 11		13 10				14 24			15 35
Redcar Central d			12 14		13 13				14 27			15 38
British Steel Redcar § d												
South Bank d												
Middlesbrough a			12 24		13 23				14 37			15 48
d			12 25	12 45	13 25		13 30		14 38	14 45	15 30	15 50
Thornaby d			12 30	12 50	13 30		13 35		14 43	14 50	15 35	15 55
Eaglescliffe a	12 03		12 35		13 35				14 48			16 00
d	12 04		12 36		13 35				14 49			16 00
Allens West d					13 38							16 03
Tees-side Airport d												
Dinsdale d					13 44							16 09
Darlington 7 26 a			12 53		13 54				15 06			16 20
d		12 20			14 06			15 37				16 22
North Road d					14 09							16 25
Heighington d					14 18							16 33
Newton Aycliffe d					14 21							16 36
Shildon d					14 25							16 41
Bishop Auckland a					14 31							16 46
Stockton d		12 36					13 41	15 53			15 41	
Billingham d		12 43					13 48	16 00			15 48	
Seaton Carew d		12 49					13 54	16 06			15 54	
Hartlepool d	12 24	12a57					14 00	16a14			16 00	
Seaham d							14 15				16 16	
Sunderland ⇌ a	12 52						14 26				16 26	
d						13 28	14 28				16 28	
Heworth ⇌ d						13 39	14 39				16 40	
Newcastle 8 26 ⇌ a						13 49	14 48				16 49	
Metrocentre 48 a						13 59	14 59				16 58	
Hexham 48 a												

	NT	TP	NT	GC	NT	NT	NT	NT	NT	NT	NT	TP
		◇1		■ 1 ⊏			A		A	B	A	◇1
Saltburn d					16 25	16 48			17 20	17 20		
Marske d					16 29	16 52			17 24	17 24		
Longbeck d					16 32	16 55			17 27	17 27		
Redcar East d					16 35	16 58			17 30	17 30		
Redcar Central d					16 38	17 01			17 33	17 33		
British Steel Redcar § d												
South Bank d												
Middlesbrough a					16 48	17 11			17 48	17 48		
d		16 45			16 49	17 14	17 25	17 30	17 49	17 49	18 37	18 45
Thornaby d		16 50			16 54	17 19	17 30	17 35	17 54	17 54	18 42	18 50
Eaglescliffe a				16 36	16 59	17 24	17 37		17 59	17 59	18 47	
d				16 37	17 00	17 25	17 37		17 59	17 59	18 48	
Allens West d							17 40		18 02	18 02	18 51	
Tees-side Airport d												
Dinsdale d							17 50		18 08	18 08	18 57	
Darlington 7 26 a					17 18	17 43	18 05		18 15	18 18	19 07	
d							18 15			18 20	19 23	
North Road d							18 18			18 23	19 26	
Heighington d							18 26			18 31	19 34	
Newton Aycliffe d							18 29			18 34	19 37	
Shildon d							18 34			18 39	19 42	
Bishop Auckland a							18 39			18 44	19 47	
Stockton d								17 41				
Billingham d								17 48				
Seaton Carew d								17 54				
Hartlepool d				17b03				18 00				
Seaham d								18 15				
Sunderland ⇌ a				17 35				18 26				
d	15 28		17 28					18 28				
Heworth ⇌ d	15 39		17 39					18 39				
Newcastle 8 26 ⇌ a	15 48		17 48					18 48				
Metrocentre 48 a	15 59		17 59					18 59				
Hexham 48 a												

	NT	NT	NT	NT	NT	TP	NT	GC	NT	TP	NT
			A	B		◇1				◇1	
Saltburn d	18 27				19 23		20 31		21 30		22 38
Marske d	18 31				19 27		20 35		21 34		22 42
Longbeck d	18 34				19 30		20 38		21 37		22 45
Redcar East d	18 37				19 33		20 41		21 40		22 48
Redcar Central d	18 40				19 36		20 44		21 43		22 51
British Steel Redcar § d											
South Bank d											
Middlesbrough a	18 52				19 46		20 55		21 53		23 01
d	18 55		19 30	19 30	19 47	20 07	20 56		21 55	22 07	23 02
Thornaby d	19 00		19 35	19 35	19 52	20 12	21 01		22 00	22 12	23 07
Eaglescliffe a	19 05				19 57		21 06	21 13	22 05		23 12
d	19 06				19 58		21 07	21 14	22 05		23 12
Allens West d					20 00				22 08		
Tees-side Airport d											
Dinsdale d					20 07				22 14		
Darlington 7 26 a	19 25				20 17		21 24		22 26		23 30
d											
North Road d											
Heighington d											
Newton Aycliffe d											
Shildon d											
Bishop Auckland a											
Stockton d			19 41	19 41							
Billingham d			19 48	19 48							
Seaton Carew d			19 54	19 54							
Hartlepool d			20 00	20 00				21 36			
Seaham d			20 15	20 15							
Sunderland ⇌ a			20 25	20 25				22 05			
d		19 28	20 28	20 28							
Heworth ⇌ d		19 39	20 39	20 39							
Newcastle 8 26 ⇌ a		19 52	20 47	20 47							
Metrocentre 48 a											
Hexham 48 a											

§ For authorised access only to BSC Redcar
A 12 September
B not 12 September
b arr. 1655

Table 45

Middlesbrough and Pickering - Whitby

	NT	NT	NT	NY	NT	NT	NY	NT	NT	NT	NY	NY	NT	NT	NT
				A ⊏			A ⊏				B ⊏	C ⊏			
Newcastle 8 44 ⇌ d			07 30			10 30			13 30	15 30				18b30	18b30
Middlesbrough d	07 06	08 13	08 47		10 38	11 49		14 16	14 49	16 47			17 40	19 49	19 49
Marton d	07 11	08 18	08 52		10 43	11 54		14 21	14 54	16 52			17 45	19 54	19 54
Gypsy Lane d	07 14	08 21	08 55		10 46	11 57		14 24	14 57	16 55			17 48	19 57	19 57
Nunthorpe d	07 19	08a28	08a59		10 49	12a01		14 27	15a03	16a59			17 51	20a03	20a03
Great Ayton d	07 25				10 55			14 33					17 57		
Battersby a	07 31				11 01			14 39					18 03		
d	07 39				11 05			14 43					18 07		
Kildale d	07 44				11 10			14 48					18 12		
Commondale d	07 51				11 17			14 55					18 19		
Castleton Moor d	07 55				11 20			14 58					18 22		
Danby d	07 58				11 23			15 01					18 25		
Lealholm d	08 05				11 30			15 08					18 32		
Glaisdale a	08 10				11 34			15 12					18 36		
d	08 12				11 37			15 15					18 39		
Egton d	08 16				11 40			15 18					18 42		
Pickering § d				09 00			12 00				*15 00*	16 00			
Levisham § d				09 20			12 20				*15 20*	16 20			
Goathland § d				09 48			12 50				16 10	16 50			
Grosmont d	08 20			10 10	11 44		13 10	15 22			16 35	17 10	18 46		
Sleights d	08 29			10 24	11 53		13 24	15 31			16 49	17 24	18 55		
Ruswarp d	08 34				11 58			15 36					19 00		
Whitby a	08 41			10 35	12 05		13 35	15 43			17 00	17 35	19 07		

Saturdays

	NT	NT	NT	NY	NT	NT	NY	NT	NT	NT	NY	NY	NT	NT	NT
				D ⊏			D ⊏				E ⊏	F ⊏			
Newcastle 8 44 ⇌ d			07 30			10d30			13 30	15 30				16b30	18c30
Middlesbrough d	07 06	08 04	08 49		10 38	11 49		14 16	14 49	16 47			17 40	17 54	19 48
Marton d	07 11	08 09	08 54		10 43	11 54		14 21	14 54	16 52			17 45	17 59	19 53
Gypsy Lane d	07 14	08 12	08 58		10 46	11 57		14 24	14 57	16 55			17 48	18 02	19 56
Nunthorpe d	07 19	08a18	09a01		10 49	12a01		14 27	15a01	16a59			17 51	18a08	20a01
Great Ayton d	07 25				10 55			14 33					17 57		
Battersby a	07 31				11 01			14 39					18 03		
d	07 39				11 05			14 43					18 07		
Kildale d	07 44				11 10			14 48					18 12		
Commondale d	07 51				11 17			14 55					18 19		
Castleton Moor d	07 55				11 20			14 58					18 22		
Danby d	07 58				11 23			15 01					18 25		
Lealholm d	08 05				11 30			15 08					18 32		
Glaisdale a	08 10				11 34			15 12					18 36		
d	08 12				11 37			15 15					18 39		
Egton d	08 16				11 40			15 18					18 42		
Pickering § d				09 00			12 00				*15 00*	16 00			
Levisham § d				09 20			12 20				*15 20*	16 20			
Goathland § d				09 48			12 50				16 10	16 50			
Grosmont d	08 20			10 10	11 44		13 10	15 22			16 35	17 10	18 46		
Sleights d	08 29			10 24	11 53		13 24	15 31			16 49	17 24	18 55		
Ruswarp d	08 34				11 58			15 36					19 00		
Whitby a	08 41			10 35	12 05		13 35	15 43			17 00	17 35	19 07		

Sundays until 12 September

	NT	NY	NT	NT	NY	NT	NT
		⊏			⊏		
Newcastle 8 44 ⇌ d				09 45			
Middlesbrough d	08 47		09 45	11 06		14 17	15 29
Marton d	08 52		09 50	11 11		14 23	15 34
Gypsy Lane d	08 55		09 53	11 14		14 26	15 37
Nunthorpe d	08 58		09 56	11 17		14 29	15 40
Great Ayton d	09 04		10 02	11 24		14 35	15 46
Battersby a	09 10		10 08	11 29		14 41	15 52
d	09 14		10 12	11 34		14 45	15 56
Kildale d	09 19		10 17	11 38		14 50	16 01
Commondale d	09 26		10 24	11 45		14 57	16 08
Castleton Moor d	09 29		10 27	11 49		15 00	16 11
Danby d	09 32		10 30	11 52		15 03	16 14
Lealholm d	09 39		10 37	11 58		15 10	16 21
Glaisdale a	09 43		10 41	12 03		15 14	16 25
d	09 46		10 50	12 05		15 17	16 30
Egton d	09 49		10 53	12 09		15 20	16 33
Pickering § d		09 00			12 00		
Levisham § d		09 20			12 20		
Goathland § d		09 48			12 50		
Grosmont d	09 53	10 10	10 57	12 13	13 10	15 24	16 37
Sleights d	10 02	10 24	11 06	12 22	13 24	15 33	16 46
Ruswarp d	10 07		11 11	12 26		15 38	16 51
Whitby a	10 12	10 35	11 16	12 31	13 35	15 42	16 56

§ North Yorkshire Moors Railway. For full service between Grosmont and Pickering please refer to separate publicity
A FX until 28 October also 4 June and 29 October
B FX until 24 June (excluding 31 May until 3 June), from 28 June until 16 July and from 4 until 28 October. From 6 until 30 September, also 29 October
C from 31 May until 4 June, from 19 July until 3 September
D until 30 October
E from 19 June until 17 July, 11, 18 and 25 September, 9, 23 and 30 October
F 29 May, 5 and 12 June, from 24 July until 4 September, 2 and 16 October
b arr. 1625
c arr. 1823
d arr. 1024

Table 45

Whitby - Pickering and Middlesbrough

		NT	NT	NT	NT	NY A 🚂	NT	NT	NY A 🚂	NT	NT	NY B 🚂	NY C 🚂	NT	NT	NT
Whitby	d				08 52	11 00		12 41	14 00		16 05	17 30	18 00			19 15
Ruswarp	d				08 56	11 08		12 45	14 08		16 09	17 36	18 08			19 19
Sleights	d				09 01			12 50			16 14					19 24
Grosmont	d				09 09	11b30		12 58	14c30		16 22	18d00	18e25			19 32
Goathland §	a					11 45			14 45			18 15	18 40			
Levisham §	a					12 16			15 16			18 40	19 05			
Pickering §	a					12 40			15 40			19 00	19 30			
Egton	d				09 12			13 01			16 26					19 35
Glaisdale	a				09 16			13 05			16 30					19 39
	d				09 19			13 08			16 33					19 42
Lealholm	d				09 24			13 13			16 38					19 47
Danby	d				09 30			13 19			16 45					19 53
Castleton Moor	d				09 33			13 22			16 49					19 56
Commondale	d				09 37			13 26			16 52					20 00
Kildale	d				09 44			13 33			16 59					20 07
Battersby	a				09 49			13 38			17 04					20 12
	d				09 53			13 42			17 09					20 16
Great Ayton	d				09 58			13 47			17 14					20 21
Nunthorpe	d	07 19	08 30	09 16	10 05		12 16	13 54		17 02	17 21			18 24	20 14	20 28
Gypsy Lane	d	07 21	08 32	09 18	10 07		12 18	13 56		17 04	17 23			18 26	20 16	20 30
Marton	d	07 23	08 34	09 21	10 10		12 21	13 59		17 06	17 25			18 29	20 19	20 33
Middlesbrough	a	07 29	08 43	09 29	10 18		12 28	14 07		17 15	17 35			18 35	20 25	20 41
Newcastle 8 (44 ⛴)	a	08 52		10 52			13 51								21 47	

Saturdays

		NT	NT	NT	NT	NY D 🚂	NT	NT	NY D 🚂	NT	NT	NT	NY E 🚂	NY F 🚂	NT	NT	NT
Whitby	d				08 52	11 00		12 41	14 00			16 05	17 30	18 00			19 15
Ruswarp	d				08 56	11 08		12 45	14 08			16 09	17 36	18 08			19 19
Sleights	d				09 01			12 50				16 14					19 24
Grosmont	d				09 09	11b30		12 58	14c30			16 22	18d00	18e25			19 32
Goathland §	a					11 45			14 45				18 15	18 40			
Levisham §	a					12 16			15 16				18 40	19 05			
Pickering §	a					12 40			15 40				19 00	19 30			
Egton	d				09 12			13 01				16 26					19 35
Glaisdale	a				09 16			13 05				16 30					19 39
	d				09 19			13 08				16 33					19 42
Lealholm	d				09 24			13 13				16 38					19 47
Danby	d				09 30			13 19				16 45					19 53
Castleton Moor	d				09 33			13 22				16 49					19 56
Commondale	d				09 37			13 26				16 52					20 00
Kildale	d				09 44			13 33				16 59					20 07
Battersby	a				09 49			13 38				17 04					20 12
	d				09 53			13 42				17 09					20 16
Great Ayton	d				09 58			13 47				17 14					20 21
Nunthorpe	d	07 19	08 26	09 16	10 05		12 16	13 54		15 16	17 02	17 21			18 24	20 14	20 28
Gypsy Lane	d	07 21	08 28	09 18	10 07		12 18	13 56		15 18	17 04	17 23			18 26	20 16	20 30
Marton	d	07 23	08 30	09 21	10 10		12 21	13 59		15 21	17 06	17 25			18 29	20 19	20 33
Middlesbrough	a	07 29	08 39	09 27	10 18		12 27	14 07		15 30	17 15	17 35			18 37	20 27	20 41
Newcastle 8 (44 ⛴)	a	08 52		10 52			13 52			16 52						21 48	

Sundays
until 12 September

		NT	NY 🚂	NT	NY 🚂	NT	NT	NT
Whitby	d	10 24	11 00	12 43	14 00	15 57	17 09	18 00
Ruswarp	d	10 28	11 08	12 47	14 08	16 01	17 13	18 04
Sleights	d	10 33		12 52		16 06	17 18	18 09
Grosmont	d	10 41	11b30	13 00	14c30	16 14	17 26	18 17
Goathland §	a		11 45		14 45			
Levisham §	a		12 16		15 16			
Pickering §	a		12 40		15 40			
Egton	d	10 44		13 03		16 17	17 29	18 20
Glaisdale	a	10 48		13 07		16 21	17 33	18 24
	d	10 53		13 10		16 26	17 36	18 27
Lealholm	d	10 58		13 15		16 31	17 41	18 32
Danby	d	11 04		13 21		16 37	17 47	18 38
Castleton Moor	d	11 07		13 24		16 40	17 50	18 41
Commondale	d	11 11		13 28		16 44	17 54	18 45
Kildale	d	11 18		13 35		16 51	18 01	18 52
Battersby	a	11 23		13 40		16 56	18 06	18 57
	d	11 39		13 44		17 00	18 10	19 01
Great Ayton	d	11 44		13 49		17 05	18 15	19 06
Nunthorpe	d	11 51		13 56		17 12	18 22	19 13
Gypsy Lane	d	11 53		13 58		17 14	18 24	19 15
Marton	d	11 55		14 01		17 17	18 27	19 18
Middlesbrough	a	12 02		14 07		17 23	18 35	19 26
Newcastle 8 (44 ⛴)	a							20 47

§ North Yorkshire Moors Railway. For full service between Grosmont and Pickering please refer to separate publicity

A FX until 28 October also 4 June and 29 October

B FX until 24 June (excluding 31 May until 3 June), from 28 June until 16 July and from 4 until 28 October. From 6 until 30 September, also 29 October

C from 31 May until 4 June, from 19 July until 3 September

D until 30 October, not 31 July

E from 19 June until 17 July, 11, 18 and 25 September, 9, 23 and 30 October

F 29 May, 5 and 12 June, from 24 July until 4 September, 2 and 16 October

b Arr. 1122

c Arr. 1420

d Arr. 1745

e Arr. 1820

Table 48

Chathill and Morpeth - Newcastle - Metrocentre, Hexham and Carlisle

		NT	NT	GR 1 ✕	XC ◇1 ✕	NT	NT	NT	XC ◇1 ✕	NT	NT	GR 1 ✕	NT	NT	NT	NT	NT	NT	NT	NT	XC ◇1 ✕	NT	NT	NT	NT
Chathill	d						07 11																		
Alnmouth for Alnwick 26	d			07 03	07 10		07 23		07 47			08 56									11 05				
Acklington	d						07 31																		
Widdrington	d						07 38																		
Pegswood	d						07 44																		
Morpeth 26	d			07 19			07 49		08 02		08 32					09 32				10 50	11 20				11 50
Cramlington	d						07 57				08 40					09 41				10 58					11 58
Manors	d						08 10				08 53														
Newcastle 8 (26 ⛴)	a			07 38	07 43		08 14		08 20		08 57	09 27				09 55				11 14	11 37				12 13
Sunderland (44 ⛴)	d					07 30		07 55		08 29				09 30					10 30					11 30	
Newcastle 8 (⛴)	d	06 30	06 49			07 56		08 24		08 54			09 23	09a52	09 40	10 00	10 24	10 44	10 54	11 14		11 24	11 44	11 54	12 14
Dunston	d															10 05									
Metrocentre	a					08 03		08 31		09 01			09 31		09 47	10 08	10 32	10 52	11 01	11 21		11 32	11 53	12 01	12 22
	d					08 04		08 32		09 02			09 32			10 09	10 32		11 02			11 33		12 02	
Blaydon	d					08 08				09 05															
Wylam	d	06 44				08 14		08 40		09 12						10 17			11 10					12 10	
Prudhoe	d	06 48	07 05			08 18		08 44		09 15			09 42			10 21	10 43		11 14			11 43		12 14	
Stocksfield	d	06 53				08 23		08 48		09 20						10 25			11 18					12 18	
Riding Mill	d	06 57				08 27				09 24						10 30			11 23					12 23	
Corbridge	d	07 01				08 31				09 28						10 33			11 26					12 26	
Hexham	a	07 10	07 17			08 40		08 58		09 37			09 55			10 42	10 55		11 36			11 56		12 36	
	d		07 17					08 59					09 55				10 55					11 56			
Haydon Bridge	d		07 26					09 08					10 04									12 05			
Bardon Mill	d		07 33					09 14														12 12			
Haltwhistle	d		07 40					09 21					10 16				11 14					12 19			
Brampton (Cumbria)	d		07 55					09 37														12 34			
Wetheral	d		08 04					09 45														12 43			
Carlisle 8	a		08 13					09 56					10 50				11 46					12 53			

		GR 1 ✕	NT	NT	NT	NT	NT	XC ◇1 ✕	NT	NT	NT	NT	NT	NT	NT	NT	XC ◇1 ✕	NT	NT	NT	NT	NT	NT	NT	NT
Chathill	d																								
Alnmouth for Alnwick 26	d	11 59						13 05									15 05								
Acklington	d																								
Widdrington	d																								
Pegswood	d																								
Morpeth 26	d						12 50					13 50				14 50					15 50				16 50
Cramlington	d						12 58					13 58				14 58					15 58				16 58
Manors	d						13 11					14 10													
Newcastle 8 (26 ⛴)	a	12 30					13 13	13 38				14 13				15 13	15 35				16 13				17 12
Sunderland (44 ⛴)	d					12 30					13 30				14 28					15 30				16 30	
Newcastle 8 (⛴)	d		12 24	12 39	12 44	12 54	13 14		13 24	13 44	13 54	14 14	14 24	14 44	14 54	15 14		15 24	15 44	15 54	16 14	16 26	16 44	16 54	
Dunston	d																								
Metrocentre	a		12 32	12 46	12 52	13 01	13 22		13 31	13 51	14 01	14 22	14 31	14 52	15 01	15 21		15 32	15 51	16 01	16 21	16 33	16 51	17 01	
	d			12 47		13 02			13 32		14 02		14 32		15 02			15 32		16 02		16 34		17 02	
Blaydon	d																								
Wylam	d					13 10					14 10		14 40		15 10					16 10		16 42		17 10	
Prudhoe	d			12 58		13 14			13 43		14 14		14 44		15 14			15 43		16 14		16 46		17 14	
Stocksfield	d					13 18					14 18				15 18					16 18		16 50		17 18	
Riding Mill	d					13 23					14 23				15 23					16 23		16 55		17 23	
Corbridge	d					13 26					14 26				15 26					16 26		16 58		17 26	
Hexham	a			13 10		13 36			13 55		14 36		14 56		15 36			15 55		16 36		17 04		17 36	
	d			13 11					14 01				14 57					15 55				17 05			
Haydon Bridge	d												15 06					16 05				17 14			
Bardon Mill	d																	16 11							
Haltwhistle	d			13 29					14 19				15 17					16 19				17 25			
Brampton (Cumbria)	d																	16 34							
Wetheral	d																	16 43							
Carlisle 8	a			14 00					14 56				15 49					16 54				17 57			

For connections from London Kings Cross please refer to Table 26

Table 48

Mondays to Fridays
until 03 September

Chathill and Morpeth - Newcastle - Metrocentre, Hexham and Carlisle

		XC	NT	NT	NT	GR	NT	NT	NT	NT	NT	XC	NT	NT	NT	GR	NT	NT	NT	NT	NT	NT	GR	NT
		◇1	◇			1						◇1				1							1	
Chathill	d														19 09									
Alnmouth for Alnwick 26	d	17 09				18 00						19 11			19 21	19 40							22 05	
Acklington	d														19 29									
Widdrington	d														19 36									
Pegswood	d														19 42									
Morpeth 26	d	17 24								18 33	19 01				19 46	19 57					21 34		22 22	
Cramlington	d									18 41	19 09				19 55						21 42			
Manors	d																							
Newcastle 26	a	17 40				18 32				18 56	19 25	19 40			20 07	20 18					21 56		22 41	
Sunderland 44	d				17 30				18 30					19 27			20 27			21 27				
Newcastle	d		17 12	17 24	17 54		18 01	18 24	18a53				19 10	19 50	20 15		20a49	21 03	21 22	21a47		21 55		22 30
Dunston	d						18 07																	
Metrocentre	a		17 20	17 32	18 01		18 10	18 31					19 17	19 57	20 22			21 11	21 29			22 04		22 37
	d		17 20	17 33	18 02			18 32					19 18		20 23				21 30					22 38
Blaydon	d			17 37																				
Wylam	d		17 29	17 44	18 10			18 40					19 26		20 31				21 38					22 46
Prudhoe	d		17 32	17 47	18 14			18 44					19 30		20 35				21 42					22 50
Stocksfield	d			17 52	18 18			18 48					19 34		20 39				21 46					22 54
Riding Mill	d			17 56	18 23			18 53					19 39		20 44				21 51					22 59
Corbridge	d			18 00	18 26			18 56					19 42		20 47				21 54					23 02
Hexham	a		17 46	18 07	18 32			19 02					19 48		20 56				22 00					23 11
	d		17 47		18 33			19 03					19 49						22 01					
Haydon Bridge	d		17 56		18 42								19 58						22 10					
Bardon Mill	d		18 02		18 48														22 16					
Haltwhistle	d		18 09		18 55			19 21					20 09						22 23					
Brampton (Cumbria)	d		18 25					19 37											22 39					
Wetheral	d		18 33					19 45											22 47					
Carlisle	a		18 45		19 28			19 57					20 42						22 58					

Mondays to Fridays
from 06 September

		NT	NT	GR	XC	NT	NT	NT	XC	NT	NT	GR	NT	NT	NT	NT	NT	NT	NT	NT	XC	NT	NT	NT	NT
				1	◇1				◇1			1									◇1				
Chathill	d						07 11																		
Alnmouth for Alnwick 26	d			07 03	07 10		07 23		07 47			08 56									11 05				
Acklington	d						07 31																		
Widdrington	d						07 38																		
Pegswood	d						07 44																		
Morpeth 26	d			07 19			07 49		08 02		08 32					09 32				10 50	11 20				11 50
Cramlington	d						07 57				08 40					09 41				10 58					11 58
Manors	d						08 10				08 53														
Newcastle 26	a			07 38	07 43		08 14		08 20		08 57	09 27				09 55				11 14	11 37				12 13
Sunderland 44	d					07 30		07 55		08 29				09 30					10 30					11 30	
Newcastle	d	06 25	06 49			07 56		08 24		08 54			09 23	09a52	09 40	10 00	10 24	10 44	10 54	11 14		11 24	11 44	11 54	12 14
Dunston	d															10 05									
Metrocentre	a					08 03		08 31		09 01			09 31		09 47	10 08	10 32	10 52	11 01	11 21		11 32	11 53	12 01	12 22
	d					08 04		08 32		09 02			09 32			10 09	10 32		11 02			11 33		12 02	
Blaydon	d					08 08				09 05															
Wylam	d	06 39				08 14		08 40		09 12						10 17			11 10					12 10	
Prudhoe	d	06 43	07 05			08 18		08 44		09 15			09 42			10 21	10 43		11 14			11 43		12 14	
Stocksfield	d	06 48				08 23		08 48		09 20						10 25			11 18					12 18	
Riding Mill	d	06 52				08 27				09 24						10 30			11 23					12 23	
Corbridge	d	06 56				08 31				09 28						10 33			11 26					12 26	
Hexham	a	07 08	07 17			08 40		09 01		09 39			09 55			10 42	10 55		11 39			11 56		12 38	
	d		07 17					09 02					09 55				10 55					11 57			
Haydon Bridge	d		07 26					09 11					10 04									12 06			
Bardon Mill	d		07 33					09 17														12 12			
Haltwhistle	d		07 40					09 24					10 18				11 14					12 19			
Brampton (Cumbria)	d		07 55					09 40														12 35			
Wetheral	d		08 04					09 48														12 43			
Carlisle	a		08 13					10 01					10 48				11 46					12 55			

For connections from London Kings Cross please refer to Table 26

Table 48

Mondays to Fridays
from 06 September

Chathill and Morpeth - Newcastle - Metrocentre, Hexham and Carlisle

		GR	NT	NT	NT	NT	NT	XC	NT	NT	NT	NT	NT	NT	NT	NT	XC	NT	NT	NT	NT	NT	NT	NT	NT
		1						◇1									◇1								
Chathill	d																								
Alnmouth for Alnwick 26	d	11 59						13 05									15 05								
Acklington	d																								
Widdrington	d																								
Pegswood	d																								
Morpeth 26	d						12 50					13 50				14 50					15 50				16 50
Cramlington	d						12 58					13 58				14 58					15 58				16 58
Manors	d						13 11					14 10													
Newcastle 26	a	12 30					13 13	13 38				14 13				15 13	15 35				16 13				17 12
Sunderland 44	d					12 30					13 30				14 28					15 30				16 30	
Newcastle	d		12 24	12 39	12 44	12 54	13 14		13 24	13 44	13 54	14 14	14 24	14 44	14 54	15 14		15 24	15 44	15 54	16 14	16 26	16 44	16 54	
Dunston	d																								
Metrocentre	a		12 32	12 46	12 52	13 01	13 22		13 31	13 51	14 01	14 22	14 31	14 52	15 01	15 21		15 32	15 51	16 01	16 21	16 33	16 51	17 01	
	d			12 47		13 02			13 32		14 02		14 32		15 02			15 32		16 02		16 34		17 02	
Blaydon	d																								
Wylam	d					13 10					14 10		14 40		15 10					16 10		16 42		17 10	
Prudhoe	d			12 58		13 14			13 43		14 14		14 44		15 14			15 43		16 14		16 46		17 14	
Stocksfield	d					13 18					14 18				15 18					16 18		16 50		17 18	
Riding Mill	d					13 23					14 23				15 23					16 23		16 55		17 23	
Corbridge	d					13 26					14 26				15 26					16 26		16 58		17 26	
Hexham	a			13 12		13 39			13 55		14 39		14 56		15 39			15 55		16 39		17 04		17 36	
	d			13 13					14 01				14 57					15 55				17 05			
Haydon Bridge	d												15 06					16 05				17 14			
Bardon Mill	d																	16 11							
Haltwhistle	d			13 31					14 19				15 17					16 19				17 25			
Brampton (Cumbria)	d																	16 34							
Wetheral	d																	16 43							
Carlisle	a			14 07					14 56				15 51					16 55				18 00			

		XC	NT	NT	NT	GR	NT	NT	NT	NT	NT	XC	NT	NT	NT	GR	NT	NT	NT	NT	NT	NT	GR	NT
		◇1	◇			1						◇1				1							1	
Chathill	d														19 09									
Alnmouth for Alnwick 26	d	17 09				18 00						19 11			19 21	19 40							22 05	
Acklington	d														19 29									
Widdrington	d														19 36									
Pegswood	d														19 42									
Morpeth 26	d	17 24								18 33	19 01				19 46	19 57					21 34		22 22	
Cramlington	d									18 41	19 09				19 55						21 42			
Manors	d																							
Newcastle 26	a	17 40				18 32				18 56	19 25	19 40			20 07	20 18					21 56		22 41	
Sunderland 44	d				17 30				18 30					19 27			20 27			21 27				
Newcastle	d		17 12	17 24	17 54		18 01	18 24	18a53				19 10	19 50	20 15		20a49	21 03	21 22	21a47		21 55		22 27
Dunston	d						18 07																	
Metrocentre	a		17 20	17 32	18 01		18 10	18 31					19 17	19 57	20 22			21 11	21 29			22 04		22 34
	d		17 20	17 33	18 02			18 32					19 18		20 23				21 30					22 35
Blaydon	d			17 37																				
Wylam	d		17 29	17 44	18 10			18 40					19 26		20 31				21 38					22 43
Prudhoe	d		17 32	17 47	18 14			18 44					19 30		20 35				21 42					22 47
Stocksfield	d			17 52	18 18			18 48					19 34		20 39				21 46					22 51
Riding Mill	d			17 56	18 23			18 53					19 39		20 44				21 51					22 56
Corbridge	d			18 00	18 26			18 56					19 42		20 47				21 54					22 59
Hexham	a		17 46	18 07	18 32			19 04					19 48		20 59				22 01					23 11
	d		17 47		18 33			19 05					19 49						22 02					
Haydon Bridge	d		17 56		18 42								19 58						22 11					
Bardon Mill	d		18 02		18 48														22 17					
Haltwhistle	d		18 09		18 55			19 23					20 09						22 24					
Brampton (Cumbria)	d		18 25					19 39											22 40					
Wetheral	d		18 33					19 47											22 48					
Carlisle	a		18 45		19 28			19 59					20 42						23 01					

For connections from London Kings Cross please refer to Table 26

Table 48

Chathill and Morpeth - Newcastle - Metrocentre, Hexham and Carlisle

Saturdays
until 04 September

	NT	XC	GR	NT	NT	NT	XC	NT	GR	XC	NT	NT	NT	NT	NT	NT	NT	NT	XC	NT	NT	NT
		◇1	1				◇1		1	◇1									◇1			
Chathill d				07 21																		
Alnmouth for Alnwick 26 d		07 11	07 18	07 33			07 55		08 58	09 09									11 04			
Acklington d				07 41																		
Widdrington d				07 48																		
Pegswood d				07 54																		
Morpeth 26 d			07 34	07 59			08 09							09 32				10 50	11 19			
Cramlington d				08 07										09 40				10 58				
Manors d				08 20																		
Newcastle 26 a		07 41	07 53	08 24			08 27		09 29	09 39				09 55				11 14	11 39			
Sunderland 44 d					07 30	07 55		08 29				09 29					10 30					11 30
Newcastle d	06 34				07 56	08 24		08 54			09 24	09a54	09 44	09 58	10 24	10 44	10 54	11 14		11 24	11 44	11 54
Dunston d														10 05								
Metrocentre a					08 03	08 31		09 01			09 31		09 51	10 08	10 31	10 53	11 01	11 21		11 32	11 52	12 01
Metrocentre d					08 04	08 32		09 02			09 32			10 09	10 32		11 02			11 33		12 02
Blaydon d					08 08			09 05														
Wylam d	06 49				08 14	08 40		09 12						10 17			11 10					12 10
Prudhoe d	06 53				08 18	08 44		09 15			09 42			10 21	10 42		11 14			11 44		12 14
Stocksfield d	06 57				08 23	08 48		09 20						10 25			11 18					12 18
Riding Mill d	07 02				08 27			09 24						10 30			11 23					12 23
Corbridge d	07 05				08 31			09 28						10 33			11 26					12 26
Hexham a	07 10				08 40	08 58		09 37			09 55			10 42	10 55		11 36			11 56		12 36
Hexham d	07 11					08 59					09 55				10 55					11 57		
Haydon Bridge d	07 20					09 08					10 04									12 06		
Bardon Mill d	07 26					09 14														12 12		
Haltwhistle d	07 33					09 21					10 16				11 14					12 19		
Brampton (Cumbria) d	07 49					09 37														12 35		
Wetheral d	07 57					09 45														12 43		
Carlisle a	08 07					09 56					10 46				11 45					12 54		

	NT	NT	GR	NT	NT	NT	NT	XC	NT	NT	NT	NT	NT	NT	NT	NT	XC	NT	NT	NT	NT	NT	NT	NT
			1 A					◇1									◇1							
Chathill d																								
Alnmouth for Alnwick 26 d			12 28					13 05									15 05							
Acklington d																								
Widdrington d																								
Pegswood d																								
Morpeth 26 d	11 50						12 50					13 50				14 50					15 50			
Cramlington d	11 58						12 58					13 58				14 58					15 58			
Manors d	12 11						13 11																	
Newcastle 26 a	12 13		12 59				13 13	13 35				14 13				15 13	15 35				16 13			
Sunderland 44 d						12 30					13 30				14 31					15 30				16 30
Newcastle d	12 14	12 24		12 39	12 44	12 54	13 14		13 24	13 44	13 54	14 14	14 24	14 44	14 54	15 14		15 24	15 44	15 53	16 14	16 26	16 44	16 54
Dunston d																								
Metrocentre a	12 22	12 31		12 46	12 52	13 01	13 22		13 31	13 51	14 01	14 22	14 31	14 52	15 01	15 21		15 31	15 51	16 00	16 21	16 33	16 51	17 01
Metrocentre d				12 47		13 02			13 32		14 02		14 33		15 02			15 32		16 01		16 34		17 02
Blaydon d																								
Wylam d						13 10					14 10		14 41		15 10					16 09		16 42		17 10
Prudhoe d				12 57		13 14			13 43		14 14		14 45		15 14			15 42		16 13		16 46		17 14
Stocksfield d						13 18					14 18				15 18					16 17		16 50		17 18
Riding Mill d						13 23					14 23				15 23					16 22		16 55		17 23
Corbridge d						13 26					14 26				15 26					16 25		16 58		17 26
Hexham a				13 10		13 36			13 55		14 36		14 56		15 36			15 55		16 35		17 04		17 36
Hexham d				13 11					14 01				14 58					15 56				17 05		
Haydon Bridge d													15 07					16 05				17 14		
Bardon Mill d																		16 11						
Haltwhistle d				13 29					14 19				15 18					16 18				17 25		
Brampton (Cumbria) d																		16 34						
Wetheral d																		16 43						
Carlisle a				14 00					14 56				15 49					16 54				17 58		

A The Highland Chieftain

For connections from London Kings Cross please refer to Table 26

Table 48

Chathill and Morpeth - Newcastle - Metrocentre, Hexham and Carlisle

Saturdays
until 04 September

	NT	NT	NT	NT	XC	NT	NT	NT	GR	NT	NT	NT	NT	XC	NT	GR	NT	NT	NT	NT	NT	NT
	◇				◇1				1					◇1		1						
Chathill d															19 12							
Alnmouth for Alnwick 26 d					17 05				17 58					19 08	19 24	20 05						
Acklington d															19 32							
Widdrington d															19 39							
Pegswood d															19 45							
Morpeth 26 d		16 50			17 20					18 32		19 04			19 49	20 22			21 15			
Cramlington d		16 58								18 40		19 12			19 58				21 23			
Manors d																						
Newcastle 26 a		17 13			17 38				18 30	18 56		19 26		19 41	20 12	20 41			21 40			
Sunderland 44 d				17 30				18 30					19 27				20 27				21 27	
Newcastle d	17 12		17 24	17 54		18 01	18 24	18a53			19 10		19 50		20 14		20a48	20 30		21 22	21a48	21 56
Dunston d			17 30			18 07																
Metrocentre a	17 20		17 32	18 01		18 10	18 31				19 17		19 58		20 21			20 39		21 29		22 04
Metrocentre d	17 20		17 33	18 02			18 32				19 18				20 22					21 30		
Blaydon d			17 37																			
Wylam d	17 29		17 44	18 10			18 40				19 26				20 30					21 38		
Prudhoe d	17 32		17 47	18 14			18 44				19 30				20 34					21 42		
Stocksfield d			17 52	18 18			18 48				19 34				20 38					21 46		
Riding Mill d			17 56	18 23			18 53				19 39				20 43					21 51		
Corbridge d			18 00	18 26			18 56				19 42				20 46					21 54		
Hexham a	17 46		18 07	18 32			19 02				19 48				20 55					22 00		
Hexham d	17 47			18 33			19 03				19 49									22 01		
Haydon Bridge d	17 56			18 42							19 58									22 10		
Bardon Mill d	18 02			18 48																22 16		
Haltwhistle d	18 09			18 55			19 21				20 09									22 23		
Brampton (Cumbria) d	18 25						19 37													22 39		
Wetheral d	18 33						19 45													22 47		
Carlisle a	18 53			19 28			19 57				20 42									22 58		

Saturdays
from 11 September

	NT	XC	GR	NT	NT	NT	XC	NT	GR	XC	NT	NT	NT	NT	NT	NT	NT	NT	XC	NT	NT	NT	NT
		◇1	1				◇1		1	◇1									◇1				
Chathill d				07 21																			
Alnmouth for Alnwick 26 d		07 11	07 18	07 33			07 55		08 58	09 09									11 04				
Acklington d				07 41																			
Widdrington d				07 48																			
Pegswood d				07 54																			
Morpeth 26 d			07 34	07 59			08 09							09 32				10 50	11 19				11 50
Cramlington d				08 07										09 40				10 58					11 58
Manors d				08 20																			
Newcastle 26 a		07 41	07 53	08 24			08 27		09 29	09 39				09 55				11 14	11 39				12 13
Sunderland 44 d					07 30	07 55		08 29				09 29					10 30					11 30	
Newcastle d	06 34				07 56	08 24		08 54			09 24	09a54	09 44	09 58	10 24	10 44	10 54	11 14		11 24	11 44	11 54	12 14
Dunston d														10 05									
Metrocentre a					08 03	08 31		09 01			09 31		09 51	10 08	10 31	10 53	11 01	11 21		11 32	11 52	12 01	12 22
Metrocentre d					08 04	08 32		09 02			09 32			10 08	10 32		11 02			11 33		12 02	
Blaydon d					08 08			09 05															
Wylam d	06 49				08 14	08 40		09 12						10 17			11 10					12 10	
Prudhoe d	06 53				08 18	08 44		09 15			09 42			10 21	10 43		11 14			11 44		12 14	
Stocksfield d	06 57				08 23	08 48		09 20						10 25			11 18					12 18	
Riding Mill d	07 02				08 27			09 24						10 30			11 23					12 23	
Corbridge d	07 05				08 31			09 28						10 33			11 26					12 26	
Hexham a	07 10				08 40	09 00		09 39			09 57			10 42	10 55		11 38			11 57		12 39	
Hexham d	07 11					09 01					09 57				10 55					11 58			
Haydon Bridge d	07 20					09 10					10 06									12 07			
Bardon Mill d	07 26					09 16														12 13			
Haltwhistle d	07 33					09 23					10 18				11 14					12 20			
Brampton (Cumbria) d	07 49					09 39														12 36			
Wetheral d	07 57					09 47														12 44			
Carlisle a	08 07					09 58					10 50				11 47					12 56			

For connections from London Kings Cross please refer to Table 26

Chathill and Morpeth - Newcastle - Metrocentre, Hexham and Carlisle

Saturdays from 11 September

	NT	GR	NT	NT	NT	NT	XC	NT	NT	NT	NT	NT	NT	NT	NT		XC	NT	NT	NT	NT	NT	NT	NT
		A					◇										◇							
Chathill d																								
Alnmouth for Alnwick 26 d		12 28					13 05										15 05							
Acklington d																								
Widdrington d																								
Pegswood d																								
Morpeth 26 d						12 50					13 50				14 50						15 50			
Cramlington d						12 58					13 58				14 58						15 58			
Manors d						13 11																		
Newcastle 26 a		12 59				13 13	13 35				14 13				15 13		15 35				16 13			
Sunderland 44 d					12 30					13 30				14 31						15 30				16 30
Newcastle d	12 24		12 39	12 44	12 54	13 14		13 24	13 44	13 54	14 14	14 24	14 44	14 54	15 14			15 24	15 44	15 53	16 14	16 24	16 44	16 54
Dunston d																								
Metrocentre a	12 31		12 46	12 52	13 01	13 22		13 31	13 51	14 01	14 22	14 31	14 52	15 01	15 21			15 31	15 51	16 00	16 21	16 31	16 51	17 01
d			12 47		13 02			13 32		14 02		14 33		15 02				15 32		16 01		16 32		17 02
Blaydon d																								
Wylam d					13 10					14 10		14 41		15 10						16 09		16 40		17 10
Prudhoe d			12 57		13 14			13 43		14 14		14 45		15 14				15 42		16 13		16 44		17 14
Stocksfield d					13 18					14 18				15 18						16 17		16 48		17 18
Riding Mill d					13 23					14 23				15 23						16 22		16 53		17 23
Corbridge d					13 26					14 26				15 26						16 25		16 56		17 26
Hexham a			13 10		13 39			13 55		14 38		14 56		15 38				15 55		16 37		17 04		17 37
d			13 11					14 01				14 58						15 56				17 05		
Haydon Bridge d												15 07						16 05				17 14		
Bardon Mill d																		16 11						
Haltwhistle d			13 29					14 19				15 18						16 18				17 25		
Brampton (Cumbria) d																		16 34						
Wetheral d																		16 43						
Carlisle a			14 03					14 56				15 49						16 58				17 58		

	NT	NT	NT	NT	XC	NT	NT	NT	GR	NT	NT	NT	NT	XC	NT		GR	NT	NT	NT	NT	NT	NT	
	◇				◇									◇										
Chathill d															19 12									
Alnmouth for Alnwick 26 d					17 05				17 58					19 08	19 24		20 05							
Acklington d															19 32									
Widdrington d															19 39									
Pegswood d															19 45									
Morpeth 26 d		16 50			17 20					18 32		19 04			19 49		20 22			21 15				
Cramlington d		16 58								18 40		19 12			19 58					21 23				
Manors d																								
Newcastle 26 a		17 13			17 38				18 30	18 56		19 26		19 41	20 12		20 41			21 40				
Sunderland 44 d				17 30				18 30					19 27					20 27				21 27		
Newcastle d	17 12		17 24	17 54		18 01	18 24	18a53			19 10		19 50		20 15			20a48	20 30		21 22	21a48	21 56	
Dunston d			17 30			18 07																		
Metrocentre a	17 20		17 32	18 01		18 10	18 31				19 17		19 58		20 22				20 39		21 29		22 04	
d	17 20		17 33	18 02			18 32				19 18				20 23						21 30			
Blaydon d			17 37																					
Wylam d	17 29		17 44	18 10			18 40				19 26				20 31						21 38			
Prudhoe d	17 32		17 47	18 14			18 44				19 30				20 35						21 42			
Stocksfield d			17 52	18 18			18 48				19 34				20 39						21 46			
Riding Mill d			17 56	18 23			18 53				19 39				20 44						21 51			
Corbridge d			18 00	18 26			18 56				19 42				20 47						21 54			
Hexham a	17 46		18 09	18 34			19 02				19 48				20 58						22 00			
d	17 47			18 35			19 03				19 49										22 01			
Haydon Bridge d	17 56			18 44							19 58										22 10			
Bardon Mill d	18 02			18 50																	22 16			
Haltwhistle d	18 09			18 57			19 21				20 09										22 23			
Brampton (Cumbria) d	18 25						19 37														22 39			
Wetheral d	18 33						19 45														22 47			
Carlisle a	18 53			19 30			19 58				20 42										22 58			

A The Highland Chieftain

For connections from London Kings Cross please refer to Table 26

Chathill and Morpeth - Newcastle - Metrocentre, Hexham and Carlisle

Sundays until 05 September

	NT	NT	NT	NT	NT	NT	XC	NT	NT	NT	NT	NT	GR	NT	XC	NT	NT	GR	NT	NT	NT	XC	NT	XC
							◇								◇			A				◇		◇
Chathill d																								
Alnmouth for Alnwick 26 d							10 47								12 47			13 29				14 38		14 47
Acklington d																								
Widdrington d																								
Pegswood d																								
Morpeth 26 d							11 02						12 40											
Cramlington d																								
Manors d																								
Newcastle 26 a							11 19						12 59		13 17			14 00				15 08		15 19
Sunderland 44 d		09 28			10 28				11 28			12 28					13 28				14 28			
Newcastle d	09 10	09 53	10 10	10 30	10 51	11 10		11 30	11 50	12 10	12 30	12 50		13 10		13 30	13 50		14 10	14 30	14 50		15 10	
Dunston d																								
Metrocentre a	09 17	10 01	10 17	10 37	11 01	11 17		11 37	11 57	12 17	12 37	12 59		13 17		13 37	13 59		14 17	14 37	14 59		15 17	
d	09 18		10 18			11 18				12 18				13 18					14 18				15 18	
Blaydon d																								
Wylam d	09 26		10 26			11 26				12 26				13 26					14 26				15 26	
Prudhoe d	09 30		10 30			11 30				12 30				13 30					14 30				15 30	
Stocksfield d	09 34		10 34			11 34				12 34				13 34					14 34				15 34	
Riding Mill d	09 39		10 39			11 39				12 39				13 39					14 39				15 39	
Corbridge d	09 42		10 42			11 42				12 42				13 42					14 42				15 42	
Hexham a	09 48		10 48			11 48				12 48				13 48					14 48				15 48	
d	09 49		10 49			11 49				12 49				13 49					14 49				15 49	
Haydon Bridge d	09 58		10 58							12 58													15 58	
Bardon Mill d	10 04		11 04							12 04													16 04	
Haltwhistle d	10 11		11 11			12 08				13 11				14 08					15 08				16 11	
Brampton (Cumbria) d	10 27		11 27							13 27													16 27	
Wetheral d	10 35		11 35							13 35													16 35	
Carlisle a	10 44		11 45			12 38				13 45				14 38					15 40				16 45	

	NT	NT	NT	NT	NT	GR	NT	XC	NT	NT	GR	NT	NT	NT	XC	NT	GR	NT	NT	GR	GR			
								◇							◇									
Chathill d																								
Alnmouth for Alnwick 26 d								16 47			17 32				18 51		19 01				22 06			
Acklington d																								
Widdrington d																								
Pegswood d																								
Morpeth 26 d						16 43		17 02												21 17				
Cramlington d																								
Manors d																								
Newcastle 26 a						17 02		17 20			18 04				19 20		19 31			21 36	22 39			
Sunderland 44 d		15 28			16 28					17 28				18 28		19 28			20 28					
Newcastle d	15 30	15 50	16 10	16 30	16 50		17 10		17 30	17 50		18 10	18 30	18 50		19a52		20 15	20a47					
Dunston d																								
Metrocentre a	15 37	15 59	16 19	16 37	16 58		17 17		17 37	17 59		18 17	18 37	18 59				20 22						
d			16 20				17 18					18 18						20 23						
Blaydon d																								
Wylam d			16 28				17 26					18 26						20 31						
Prudhoe d			16 32				17 30					18 30						20 35						
Stocksfield d			16 36				17 34					18 34						20 39						
Riding Mill d			16 41				17 39					18 39						20 44						
Corbridge d			16 44				17 42					18 42						20 47						
Hexham a			16 50				17 48					18 48						20 53						
d			16 51				17 49					18 49						20 54						
Haydon Bridge d												18 58						21 03						
Bardon Mill d												19 04						21 09						
Haltwhistle d			17 10				18 08					19 11						21 16						
Brampton (Cumbria) d												19 27						21 32						
Wetheral d												19 35						21 40						
Carlisle a			17 40				18 38					19 45						21 50						

A The Northern Lights

For connections from London Kings Cross please refer to Table 26

Table 48

Sundays from 12 September

Chathill and Morpeth - Newcastle - Metrocentre, Hexham and Carlisle

		NT	NT	NT	NT	NT	NT	XC	NT	NT	NT	NT	NT	GR	NT	XC	NT	NT	GR	NT	NT	NT	XC	NT	XC
								◇1						1		◇1			1 A				◇1		◇1
Chathill	d																								
Alnmouth for Alnwick 26	d							10 47								12 47			13 29				14 38		14 47
Acklington	d																								
Widdrington	d																								
Pegswood	d																								
Morpeth 26	d							11 02						12 40											
Cramlington	d																								
Manors	d																								
Newcastle 26 ⇌	a							11 19						12 59		13 17			14 00				15 08		15 19
Sunderland 44 ⇌	d		09 28			10 28				11 28			12 28					13 28				14 28			
Newcastle ⇌	d	09 10	09 53	10 06	10 30	10 51	11 06		11 30	11 50	12 06	12 30	12 50		13 07		13 30	13 50		14 10	14 30	14 50		15 07	
Dunston	d																								
Metrocentre	a	09 17	10 01	10 13	10 37	11 01	11 13		11 37	11 57	12 13	12 37	12 59		13 14		13 37	13 59		14 17	14 37	14 59		15 14	
	d	09 18		10 14			11 14				12 14				13 15					14 18				15 15	
Blaydon	d																								
Wylam	d	09 26		10 22			11 22				12 22				13 23					14 26				15 23	
Prudhoe	d	09 30		10 26			11 26				12 26				13 27					14 30				15 27	
Stocksfield	d	09 34		10 30			11 30				12 30				13 31					14 34				15 31	
Riding Mill	d	09 39		10 35			11 35				12 35				13 36					14 39				15 36	
Corbridge	d	09 42		10 38			11 38				12 38				13 39					14 42				15 39	
Hexham	a	09 48		10 44			11 44				12 44				13 45					14 48				15 45	
	d	09 49		10 45			11 45				12 45				13 46					14 49				15 46	
Haydon Bridge	d	09 58		10 54							12 54													15 55	
Bardon Mill	d	10 04		11 00							13 00													16 01	
Haltwhistle	d	10 11		11 07			12 04				13 07				14 05					15 08				16 08	
Brampton (Cumbria)	d	10 27		11 23							13 23													16 24	
Wetheral	d	10 35		11 31							13 31													16 32	
Carlisle	a	10 46		11 42			12 39				13 42				14 39					15 40				16 45	

		NT	NT	NT	NT	NT	GR	NT	XC	NT	NT	GR	NT	NT	NT	XC	NT	GR	NT	NT	GR	GR
							1		◇1			1				◇1		1			1	1
Chathill	d																					
Alnmouth for Alnwick 26	d								16 47			17 32				18 51		19 01				22 06
Acklington	d																					
Widdrington	d																					
Pegswood	d																					
Morpeth 26	d						16 43		17 02												21 17	
Cramlington	d																					
Manors	d																					
Newcastle 26 ⇌	a						17 02		17 20			18 04				19 20		19 31			21 36	22 39
Sunderland 44 ⇌	d		15 28			16 28					17 28				18 28		19 28			20 28		
Newcastle ⇌	d	15 30	15 50	16 10	16 30	16 50		17 10		17 30	17 50		18 10	18 30	18 50		19a52		20 15	20a47		
Dunston	d																					
Metrocentre	a	15 37	15 59	16 19	16 37	16 58		17 17		17 37	17 59		18 17	18 37	18 59				20 22			
	d			16 20				17 18					18 18						20 23			
Blaydon	d																					
Wylam	d			16 28				17 26					18 26						20 31			
Prudhoe	d			16 32				17 30					18 30						20 35			
Stocksfield	d			16 36				17 34					18 34						20 39			
Riding Mill	d			16 41				17 39					18 39						20 44			
Corbridge	d			16 44				17 42					18 42						20 47			
Hexham	a			16 50				17 48					18 48						20 53			
	d			16 51				17 49					18 49						20 54			
Haydon Bridge	d												18 58						21 03			
Bardon Mill	d												19 04						21 09			
Haltwhistle	d			17 10				18 08					19 11						21 16			
Brampton (Cumbria)	d												19 27						21 32			
Wetheral	d												19 35						21 40			
Carlisle	a			17 43				18 38					19 46						21 52			

A The Northern Lights

For connections from London Kings Cross please refer to Table 26

Table 48

Mondays to Fridays until 03 September

Carlisle, Hexham and Metrocentre - Newcastle - Morpeth and Chathill

		NT	NT	NT	GR	GR	NT	NT	NT	GR		NT	NT	NT	XC	NT	NT	NT	NT	NT		NT	NT	XC	GR
					1	1				1					◇1									◇1	1
Carlisle	d			06 25				07 13					08 29				09 37						10 33		
Wetheral	d			06 32				07 20					08 37												
Brampton (Cumbria)	d			06 42				07 30					08 47												
Haltwhistle	d			06 56				07 45					09 01				10 10						11 01		
Bardon Mill	d			07 04				07 52					09 09												
Haydon Bridge	d			07 09				07 57					09 14										11 12		
Hexham	a			07 18				08 06					09 23				10 28						11 21		
	d		06 13	07 18			07 41	08 07				08 44	09 23			09 44	10 28			10 44			11 21		
Corbridge	d		06 17	07 23			07 45	08 11				08 48				09 48				10 48					
Riding Mill	d		06 22	07 26			07 50	08 16				08 53				09 53				10 53					
Stocksfield	d		06 26	07 30			07 54	08 20				08 57				09 57				10 57					
Prudhoe	d		06 30	07 36			07 58	08 24				09 01	09 35			10 01	10 40			11 01			11 33		
Wylam	d		06 34	07 40			08 02	08 28				09 05				10 05				11 05					
Blaydon	d						08 08	08 34																	
Metrocentre	a			07 48			08 13	08 39				09 14	09 46			10 14	10 51			11 15			11 45		
	d			07 48			08 15	08 40				09 15	09 47			10 15	10 51		11 00	11 15		11 30	11 45		
Dunston	d							08 43																	
Newcastle ⇌	a		06 52	08 03			08 25	08 54				09 27	09 59			10 25	11 01		11 10	11 25		11 38	11 57		
Sunderland 44 ⇌	a		07 19				08 49					09 49				10 49				11 49					
Newcastle 26 ⇌	d	05 45			06 25	07 41			07 58	08 41				09 00	09 29			10 15	11 15					11 34	12 05
Manors	d																								
Cramlington	d	05 57							08 11					09 12				10 27	11 27						
Morpeth 26	d	06 05			06 38				08a20	08 55				09a20	09 42			10a35	11a35						
Pegswood	d																								
Widdrington	d																								
Acklington	d																								
Alnmouth for Alnwick 26	d	06 22			06 52	08 07									09 56									12 01	12 31
Chathill	a	06 36																							

		NT	NT	NT	NT	NT		NT	NT	NT	NT	XC	NT	NT	NT	NT		NT	NT	XC	NT	NT	NT	NT	GR
												◇1								◇1		◇			1
Carlisle	d					11 34					12 30					13 35						14 34			
Wetheral	d										12 37														
Brampton (Cumbria)	d										12 47														
Haltwhistle	d					12 02					13 01					14 03						15 03			
Bardon Mill	d										13 09														
Haydon Bridge	d					12 13					13 14														
Hexham	a					12 22					13 23					14 21						15 21			
	d		11 44			12 23			12 44		13 23			13 44		14 21			14 44			15 22		15 44	
Corbridge	d		11 48						12 48					13 48					14 48					15 48	
Riding Mill	d		11 53						12 53					13 53					14 53					15 53	
Stocksfield	d		11 57						12 57					13 57					14 57					15 57	
Prudhoe	d		12 01			12 34			13 01		13 35			14 01		14 33			15 01			15 33		16 01	
Wylam	d		12 05						13 05					14 05					15 05					16 05	
Blaydon	d																								
Metrocentre	a		12 14			12 45			13 14		13 46			14 14		14 44			15 14			15 45		16 14	
	d	12 05	12 15	12 30	12 40	12 45		13 00	13 15	13 30	13 47		14 00	14 15	14 29	14 44		15 00	15 15		15 30	15 46	16 00	16 15	
Dunston	d																		15 18						
Newcastle ⇌	a	12 12	12 28	12 39	12 51	13 03		13 10	13 26	13 38	13 59		14 09	14 26	14 40	14 56		15 09	15 27		15 38	15 58	16 12	16 25	
Sunderland 44 ⇌	a		12 49						13 49					14 49					15 49					16 49	
Newcastle 26 ⇌	d	12 15			13 03							13 35	14 15					15 15		15 35			16 15		16 32
Manors	d																						16 17		
Cramlington	d	12 26			13 14								14 27					15 27					16 28		
Morpeth 26	d	12a36			13a23								14a34					15a35		15 48			16a36		
Pegswood	d																								
Widdrington	d																								
Acklington	d																								
Alnmouth for Alnwick 26	d											14 01								16 02				16 58	16 58
Chathill	a																								

For connections to London Kings Cross please refer to Table 26

Table 48

Mondays to Fridays
until 03 September

Carlisle, Hexham and Metrocentre - Newcastle - Morpeth and Chathill

		NT	NT	NT	NT	XC	NT	NT	NT	NT	NT	GR	NT	NT	XC	GR	NT	NT	NT	NT	NT	XC	GR FO
						◇1						1			◇1	1						◇1	1
Carlisle	d		15 26					16 37			17 20			18 37				19 45					
Wetheral	d							16 44			17 27			18 44									
Brampton (Cumbria)	d							16 54			17 37			18 53									
Haltwhistle	d		15 54					17 08			17 52			19 08				20 13					
Bardon Mill	d							17 16			17 59												
Haydon Bridge	d		16 05					17 21			18 04												
Hexham	a		16 14					17 30			18 13			19 26				20 31					
	d		16 14		16 44			17 31	17 42		18 14		18 44	19 26				20 31			21 14		
Corbridge	d				16 48				17 46		18 18		18 48	19 31				20 36			21 18		
Riding Mill	d				16 53				17 51		18 23		18 53	19 35				20 40			21 23		
Stocksfield	d				16 57			17 40	17 55		18 27		18 57	19 39				20 44			21 27		
Prudhoe	d		16 26		17 01			17 44	17 59		18 31		19 01	19 44				20 49			21 31		
Wylam	d				17 05				18 03		18 35		19 05	19 48				20 52			21 35		
Blaydon	d												19 11										
Metrocentre	a		16 42		17 14			17 56	18 12		18 43		19 16	19 56				21 01			21 44		
	d	16 30	16 42	17 00	17 15		17 35	17 56	18 13	18 18	18 44		19 17	19 56			20 30	21 02		21 22	21 45		
Dunston	d																						
Newcastle	a	16 40	16 51	17 08	17 25		17 43	18 08	18 23	18 26	18 56		19 27	20 09			20 38	21 14		21 30	21 56		
Sunderland 44	a		17 14		17 50				18 49				19 50				21 04						
Newcastle 26	d			17 15		17 37	17 50			18 28		18b50			19 38	20 29			21 05			21c48	22 07
Manors	d			17 17			17 52			18 30													
Cramlington	d			17 28			18 03			18 41									21 17				
Morpeth 26	d			17 36			18a11			18a49						20 44			21a26				22 22
Pegswood	d			17 40																			
Widdrington	d			17 46																			
Acklington	d			18 12																			
Alnmouth for Alnwick 26	d			18 20		18 02						19 16			20 06	21 00						22 12	22 38
Chathill	a			18 34																			

		NT	NT	NT
Carlisle	d		21 25	
Wetheral	d		21 32	
Brampton (Cumbria)	d		21 42	
Haltwhistle	d		21 57	
Bardon Mill	d		22 04	
Haydon Bridge	d		22 09	
Hexham	a		22 18	
	d		22 19	23 14
Corbridge	d		22 23	23 18
Riding Mill	d		22 28	23 23
Stocksfield	d		22 32	23 27
Prudhoe	d		22 36	23 31
Wylam	d		22 40	23 35
Blaydon	d			
Metrocentre	a		22 49	23 45
	d	22 15	22 50	23 45
Dunston	d			
Newcastle	a	22 23	23 03	23 57
Sunderland 44	a			
Newcastle 26	d			
Manors	d			
Cramlington	d			
Morpeth 26	d			
Pegswood	d			
Widdrington	d			
Acklington	d			
Alnmouth for Alnwick 26	d			
Chathill	a			

b arr. 1840

c arr. 2139

For connections to London Kings Cross please refer to Table 26

Table 48

Mondays to Fridays
from 06 September

Carlisle, Hexham and Metrocentre - Newcastle - Morpeth and Chathill

		NT	NT	NT	GR	GR	NT	NT	NT	GR	NT	NT	NT	XC	NT	NT	NT	NT	NT	NT	NT	XC	GR
					1	1				1				◇1								◇1	1
Carlisle	d			06 25				07 13				08 29				09 37					10 30		
Wetheral	d			06 32				07 20				08 37											
Brampton (Cumbria)	d			06 42				07 30				08 47											
Haltwhistle	d			06 56				07 45				09 01				10 10					10 58		
Bardon Mill	d			07 04				07 52				09 09											
Haydon Bridge	d			07 09				07 57				09 14									11 09		
Hexham	a			07 18				08 06				09 23				10 28					11 21		
	d		06 13	07 18			07 39	08 07			08 44	09 23			09 42	10 28			10 44		11 21		
Corbridge	d		06 17	07 23			07 43	08 11			08 48				09 46				10 48				
Riding Mill	d		06 22	07 26			07 50	08 16			08 53				09 51				10 53				
Stocksfield	d		06 26	07 30			07 54	08 20			08 57				09 55				10 57				
Prudhoe	d		06 31	07 36			07 58	08 24			09 01	09 35			10 00	10 40			11 01		11 33		
Wylam	d		06 35	07 40			08 02	08 28			09 05				10 04				11 05				
Blaydon	d						08 08	08 34															
Metrocentre	a			07 48			08 16	08 43			09 14	09 46			10 14	10 51			11 15		11 46		
	d			07 48			08 17	08 44			09 15	09 47			10 15	10 51		11 00	11 15	11 30	11 46		
Dunston	d							08 47															
Newcastle	a		06 55	08 09			08 27	09 01			09 27	09 59			10 25	11 03		11 10	11 25	11 38	12 00		
Sunderland 44	a		07 19				08 49				09 49				10 49				11 49				
Newcastle 26	d	05 45			06 25	07 41			07 58	08 41			09 00	09 29			10 15	11 15				11 34	12 05
Manors	d																						
Cramlington	d	05 57							08 11				09 12				10 27	11 27					
Morpeth 26	d	06 05			06 38				08a20	08 55			09a20	09 42			10a35	11a35					
Pegswood	d																						
Widdrington	d																						
Acklington	d																						
Alnmouth for Alnwick 26	d	06 22			06 52	08 07								09 56								12 01	12 31
Chathill	a	06 36																					

		NT	NT	NT	NT	NT	NT	NT	NT	NT	XC	NT	NT	NT	NT	NT	NT	XC	NT	NT	NT	GR	NT
											◇1							◇1		◇		1	
Carlisle	d					11 34				12 26					13 35					14 34			
Wetheral	d									12 33													
Brampton (Cumbria)	d									12 43													
Haltwhistle	d					12 02				12 57					14 03					15 03			
Bardon Mill	d									13 05													
Haydon Bridge	d					12 13				13 10													
Hexham	a					12 23				13 19					14 21					15 21			
	d		11 42			12 24		12 42		13 19			13 42		14 21		14 42			15 22			15 42
Corbridge	d		11 46					12 46					13 46				14 46						15 46
Riding Mill	d		11 51					12 51					13 51				14 51						15 51
Stocksfield	d		11 55					12 55					13 55				14 55						15 55
Prudhoe	d		12 00			12 35		13 00		13 31			14 00		14 33		15 00			15 33			16 00
Wylam	d		12 04					13 04					14 04				15 04						16 04
Blaydon	d																						
Metrocentre	a		12 14			12 45		13 14		13 46			14 14		14 44		15 14			15 45			16 14
	d	12 05	12 15	12 30	12 40	12 45	13 00	13 15	13 30	13 47		14 00	14 15	14 29	14 44	15 00	15 15		15 30	15 46	16 00		16 15
Dunston	d																15 18						
Newcastle	a	12 12	12 28	12 39	12 51	13 03	13 10	13 26	13 38	14 00		14 09	14 26	14 40	14 57	15 09	15 27		15 38	15 58	16 12		16 25
Sunderland 44	a		12 49					13 49					14 49				15 49						16 49
Newcastle 26	d	12 15			13 03						13 35	14 15				15 15		15 35			16 15	16 32	
Manors	d																				16 17		
Cramlington	d	12 26			13 14							14 27				15 27					16 28		
Morpeth 26	d	12a36			13a23							14a34				15a35		15 48			16a36		
Pegswood	d																						
Widdrington	d																						
Acklington	d																						
Alnmouth for Alnwick 26	d										14 01							16 02				16 58	
Chathill	a																						

For connections to London Kings Cross please refer to Table 26

Table 48

Carlisle, Hexham and Metrocentre - Newcastle - Morpeth and Chathill

Mondays to Fridays
from 06 September

		NT	NT	NT	NT	XC	NT	NT	NT	NT	NT	GR	NT	NT	XC	GR	NT	NT	NT	NT	NT	XC	GR FO
						◇ 1						■ 1			◇ 1	■ 1						◇ 1	■ 1
Carlisle [8]	d		15 22					16 33			17 12			18 37				19 41					
Wetheral	d							16 40			17 19			18 44									
Brampton (Cumbria)	d							16 50			17 29			18 53									
Haltwhistle	d		15 50					17 04			17 44			19 08				20 09					
Bardon Mill	d							17 12			17 51												
Haydon Bridge	d		16 01					17 17			17 56												
Hexham	a		16 12					17 26			18 09			19 27				20 27					
	d		16 12		16 42			17 27	17 42		18 10		18 40	19 27				20 27			21 10		
Corbridge	d				16 46				17 46		18 14		18 44	19 32				20 32			21 14		
Riding Mill	d				16 51				17 51		18 19		18 49	19 36				20 36			21 19		
Stocksfield	d				16 55			17 36	17 55		18 23		18 53	19 40				20 40			21 23		
Prudhoe	d		16 24		17 00			17 40	17 59		18 27		18 59	19 45				20 45			21 29		
Wylam	d				17 04				18 03		18 31		19 03	19 49				20 48			21 33		
Blaydon	d												19 09										
Metrocentre	a		16 40		17 14			17 56	18 12		18 43		19 16	19 57				21 01			21 44		
	d	16 30	16 40	17 00	17 15		17 35	17 56	18 13	18 18	18 44		19 17	19 57			20 30	21 02		21 22	21 45		
Dunston	d																						
Newcastle [8] ⇌	a	16 40	16 50	17 08	17 25		17 43	18 08	18 23	18 26	18 56		19 27	20 12			20 38	21 14		21 30	21 56		
Sunderland 44 ⇌	a		17 14		17 50				18 49				19 50				21 04						
Newcastle [8] 26 ⇌	d			17 15		17 37	17 50			18 28		18b50			19 38	20 29			21 05			21c48	22 07
Manors	d			17 17			17 52			18 30													
Cramlington	d			17 28			18 03			18 41									21 17				
Morpeth 26	d			17 36			18a11			18a49						20 44			21a26				22 22
Pegswood	d			17 40																			
Widdrington	d			17 46																			
Acklington	d			18 12																			
Alnmouth for Alnwick 26	d			18 20		18 02						19 16			20 06	21 00						22 12	22 38
Chathill	a			18 34																			

		NT	NT	NT
Carlisle [8]	d		21 18	
Wetheral	d		21 25	
Brampton (Cumbria)	d		21 35	
Haltwhistle	d		21 50	
Bardon Mill	d		21 57	
Haydon Bridge	d		22 02	
Hexham	a		22 13	
	d		22 14	23 14
Corbridge	d		22 18	23 18
Riding Mill	d		22 23	23 23
Stocksfield	d		22 27	23 27
Prudhoe	d		22 31	23 31
Wylam	d		22 35	23 35
Blaydon	d			
Metrocentre	a		22 44	23 45
	d	22 15	22 45	23 45
Dunston	d			
Newcastle [8] ⇌	a	22 23	23 00	23 57
Sunderland 44 ⇌	a			
Newcastle [8] 26 ⇌	d			
Manors	d			
Cramlington	d			
Morpeth 26	d			
Pegswood	d			
Widdrington	d			
Acklington	d			
Alnmouth for Alnwick 26	d			
Chathill	a			

b arr. 1840

c arr. 2139

For connections to London Kings Cross please refer to Table 26

Table 48

Carlisle, Hexham and Metrocentre - Newcastle - Morpeth and Chathill

Saturdays
until 04 September

		NT	NT	NT	GR	NT	GR	NT	NT	NT	XC	NT	NT	NT	GR	NT	NT	NT	NT	XC	NT	NT	NT
					■ 1		■ 1				◇ 1				■ 1					◇ 1			
Carlisle [8]	d			06 25		07 13				08 29			09 37						10 33				
Wetheral	d			06 32		07 20				08 37													
Brampton (Cumbria)	d			06 42		07 30				08 47													
Haltwhistle	d			06 56		07 45				09 01			10 05						11 02				
Bardon Mill	d			07 04		07 52				09 09													
Haydon Bridge	d			07 09		07 57				09 14									11 12				
Hexham	a			07 18		08 06				09 23			10 23						11 21				
	d		06 13	07 18		08 07			08 44	09 23		09 44	10 23				10 44		11 22			11 44	
Corbridge	d		06 17	07 23		08 11			08 48			09 48					10 48					11 48	
Riding Mill	d		06 22	07 27		08 16			08 53			09 53					10 53					11 53	
Stocksfield	d		06 26	07 31		08 20			08 57			09 57					10 57					11 57	
Prudhoe	d		06 30	07 36		08 24			09 01	09 35		10 01	10 35				11 01		11 33			12 01	
Wylam	d		06 34	07 40		08 28			09 05	09 39		10 05					11 05					12 05	
Blaydon	d					08 34																	
Metrocentre	a			07 49		08 39			09 14	09 48		10 14	10 46				11 14		11 45			12 14	
	d			07 49		08 40			09 15	09 49		10 15	10 46			11 00	11 15	11 30	11 45		12 00	12 15	12 30
Dunston	d					08 43																	
Newcastle [8] ⇌	a		06 52	08 03		08 54			09 28	10 01		10 25	11 01			11 10	11 25	11 38	11 59		12 08	12 25	12 38
Sunderland 44 ⇌	a		07 19						09 49			10 49					11 49					12 49	
Newcastle [8] 26 ⇌	d	06 00			06 25		07 52	08 24			09 29			10 15	11 08	11 15				11 36	12 15		
Manors	d																						
Cramlington	d	06 12						08 36						10 27		11 27					12 27		
Morpeth 26	d	06 20			06 38		08 06	08a44			09 42			10a35		11a35					12a35		
Pegswood	d																						
Widdrington	d																						
Acklington	d																						
Alnmouth for Alnwick 26	d	06 38			06 52		08 20				09 56				11 34					12 00			
Chathill	a	06 53																					

		NT	NT	NT	NT	NT	NT	NT	XC	NT	NT	NT	NT	NT	NT	NT	NT	XC	GR	NT	NT	NT	NT
									◇ 1								◇	◇ 1	■ 1				
Carlisle [8]	d		11 34					12 30					13 35				14 34						15 26
Wetheral	d							12 37															
Brampton (Cumbria)	d							12 47															
Haltwhistle	d		12 02					13 01					14 04				15 04						15 56
Bardon Mill	d							13 09															
Haydon Bridge	d		12 13					13 14															16 07
Hexham	a		12 22					13 23					14 21				15 22						16 16
	d		12 23		12 44			13 23			13 44		14 22		14 44		15 22				15 44		16 16
Corbridge	d				12 48						13 48				14 48						15 48		
Riding Mill	d				12 53						13 53				14 53						15 53		
Stocksfield	d				12 57						13 57				14 57						15 57		
Prudhoe	d		12 34		13 01			13 35			14 01		14 34		15 01		15 33				16 01		16 28
Wylam	d				13 05						14 05				15 05						16 05		
Blaydon	d																						
Metrocentre	a		12 45		13 14			13 46			14 14		14 44		15 14		15 45				16 14		16 40
	d	12 40	12 45	13 00	13 15		13 30	13 47		14 00	14 15	14 30	14 46	15 00	15 15	15 30	15 46			16 00	16 15	16 30	16 40
Dunston	d														15 18								
Newcastle [8] ⇌	a	12 52	12 57	13 11	13 26		13 39	14 00		14 13	14 26	14 40	14 57	15 09	15 27	15 38	15 58			16 08	16 25	16 38	16 50
Sunderland 44 ⇌	a				13 49						14 49				15 50						16 49		17 14
Newcastle [8] 26 ⇌	d					13 15			13 36	14 15				15 15				15 36	16 03	16 15			
Manors	d																			16 17			
Cramlington	d					13 26				14 26				15 27						16 28			
Morpeth 26	d					13a36				14a36				15a35				15 49		16a36			
Pegswood	d																						
Widdrington	d																						
Acklington	d																						
Alnmouth for Alnwick 26	d								14 00									16 03	16 30				
Chathill	a																						

For connections to London Kings Cross please refer to Table 26

Table 48

Saturdays until 04 September

Carlisle, Hexham and Metrocentre - Newcastle - Morpeth and Chathill

		NT	NT	XC	NT	NT	NT	NT	NT	NT	XC	NT	NT	NT	NT	NT	GR	NT	XC	NT	NT
				◇1							◇1						■1		◇1		
Carlisle 8	d					16 37			17 20			18 37				19 45					21 20
Wetheral	d					16 44			17 27			18 44									21 27
Brampton (Cumbria)	d					16 54			17 37			18 53									21 37
Haltwhistle	d					17 08			17 52			19 08				20 13					21 52
Bardon Mill	d					17 16			17 59												21 59
Haydon Bridge	d					17 21			18 04												22 04
Hexham	a					17 30			18 13			19 26				20 31					22 13
	d		16 44			17 31	17 42		18 14	18 44		19 26				20 31		21 14			22 14
Corbridge	d		16 48				17 46		18 18	18 48		19 31				20 36		21 18			22 18
Riding Mill	d		16 53				17 51		18 23	18 53		19 35				20 40		21 23			22 23
Stocksfield	d		16 57			17 40	17 55		18 27	18 57		19 39				20 44		21 27			22 27
Prudhoe	d		17 01			17 44	17 59		18 31	19 01		19 44				20 49		21 31			22 31
Wylam	d		17 05				18 03		18 35	19 05		19 48				20 52		21 35			22 35
Blaydon	d									19 11											
Metrocentre	a		17 14			17 55	18 12		18 43	19 16		19 56				21 01		21 44			22 44
	d	17 00	17 15		17 35	17 55	18 13	18 18	18 44	19 17		19 56	20 15		20 47	21 02		21 45		22 10	22 45
Dunston	d																				
Newcastle 8	a	17 08	17 26		17 43	18 08	18 23	18 26	18 56	19 27		20 11	20 23		20 55	21 14		21 56		22 20	22 59
Sunderland 44	a		17 50				18 49			19 50					21 20						
Newcastle 8 26	d	17 10		17 36	17 44			18 28			19 37			20 24			21 02		21 36		
Manors	d	17 13			17 47			18 30													
Cramlington	d	17 24			17 58			18 41						20 36							
Morpeth 26	d	17 32			18a06			18a49						20a45			21 17				
Pegswood	d	17 35																			
Widdrington	d	17 41																			
Acklington	d	17 48																			
Alnmouth for Alnwick 26	d	18 00		18 02							20 04						21 33		22 00		
Chathill	a	18 19																			

Saturdays from 11 September

		NT	NT	NT	GR	NT	GR	NT	NT	NT	XC	NT	NT	NT	GR	NT	NT	NT	NT	XC	NT	NT	NT
					■1		■1				◇1				■1					◇1			
Carlisle 8	d			06 25		07 13				08 27			09 37						10 33				
Wetheral	d			06 32		07 20				08 35													
Brampton (Cumbria)	d			06 42		07 30				08 45													
Haltwhistle	d			06 56		07 45				08 59			10 05						11 02				
Bardon Mill	d			07 04		07 52				09 07													
Haydon Bridge	d			07 09		07 57				09 12									11 12				
Hexham	a			07 22		08 06				09 21			10 23						11 25				
	d		06 13	07 22		08 07			08 43	09 21		09 43	10 23				10 44		11 26			11 42	
Corbridge	d		06 17	07 27		08 11			08 47			09 47					10 48					11 46	
Riding Mill	d		06 22	07 31		08 16			08 52			09 52					10 53					11 51	
Stocksfield	d		06 26	07 35		08 20			08 56			09 56					10 57					11 55	
Prudhoe	d		06 32	07 40		08 24			09 00	09 33		10 00	10 35				11 01		11 37			11 59	
Wylam	d		06 36	07 44		08 28			09 04	09 37		10 04					11 05					12 03	
Blaydon	d					08 34																	
Metrocentre	a			07 56		08 39			09 14	09 48		10 13	10 46				11 14		11 51			12 13	
	d			07 56		08 40			09 15	09 49		10 14	10 46			11 00	11 15	11 30	11 51		12 00	12 14	12 30
Dunston	d					08 43																	
Newcastle 8	a		06 55	08 10		08 54			09 28	10 01		10 24	11 01			11 10	11 25	11 38	12 05		12 08	12 25	12 38
Sunderland 44	a		07 19						09 49			10 49					11 49					12 49	
Newcastle 8 26	d	06 00			06 25		07 52	08 24			09 29			10 15	11 08	11 15				11 36	12 15		
Manors	d																						
Cramlington	d	06 12						08 36						10 27		11 27					12 27		
Morpeth 26	d	06 20			06 38		08 06	08a44			09 42			10a35		11a35					12a35		
Pegswood	d																						
Widdrington	d																						
Acklington	d																						
Alnmouth for Alnwick 26	d	06 38			06 52		08 20				09 56				11 34					12 00			
Chathill	a	06 53																					

For connections to London Kings Cross please refer to Table 26

Table 48

Saturdays from 11 September

Carlisle, Hexham and Metrocentre - Newcastle - Morpeth and Chathill

		NT	NT	NT	NT	NT	NT	NT	XC	NT	NT	NT	NT	NT	NT	NT	NT	XC	GR	NT	NT	NT	NT
									◇1								◇	◇1	■1				
Carlisle 8	d		11 34					12 26					13 35				14 34						15 19
Wetheral	d							12 33															
Brampton (Cumbria)	d							12 43															
Haltwhistle	d		12 02					12 57					14 04				15 05						15 50
Bardon Mill	d							13 05															
Haydon Bridge	d		12 13					13 10															16 01
Hexham	a		12 23					13 19					14 21				15 22						16 12
	d		12 24		12 42			13 19			13 42		14 22		14 44		15 22				15 42		16 12
Corbridge	d				12 46						13 46				14 48						15 46		
Riding Mill	d				12 51						13 51				14 53						15 51		
Stocksfield	d				12 55						13 55				14 57						15 55		
Prudhoe	d		12 35		12 59			13 31			13 59		14 34		15 01		15 34				15 59		16 24
Wylam	d				13 03						14 03				15 05						16 03		
Blaydon	d																						
Metrocentre	a		12 47		13 14			13 46			14 14		14 48		15 14		15 49				16 14		16 40
	d	12 40	12 48	13 00	13 15		13 30	13 47		14 00	14 15	14 30	14 50	15 00	15 15	15 30	15 50			16 00	16 15	16 30	16 40
Dunston	d														15 18								
Newcastle 8	a	12 52	12 59	13 11	13 26		13 39	14 00		14 13	14 26	14 40	15 01	15 09	15 27	15 38	16 01			16 08	16 25	16 38	16 50
Sunderland 44	a				13 49						14 49				15 50						16 49		17 14
Newcastle 8 26	d					13 15			13 36	14 15				15 15				15 36	16 03	16 15			
Manors	d																			16 17			
Cramlington	d					13 26				14 26				15 27						16 28			
Morpeth 26	d					13a36				14a36				15a35				15 49		16a36			
Pegswood	d																						
Widdrington	d																						
Acklington	d																						
Alnmouth for Alnwick 26	d								14 00									16 03	16 30				
Chathill	a																						

		NT	NT	XC	NT	NT	NT	NT	NT	NT	XC	NT	NT	NT	NT	NT	GR	NT	XC	NT	NT
				◇1							◇1						■1		◇1		
Carlisle 8	d					16 33			17 16			18 37				19 45					21 14
Wetheral	d					16 40			17 23			18 44									21 21
Brampton (Cumbria)	d					16 50			17 33			18 53									21 31
Haltwhistle	d					17 04			17 48			19 08				20 13					21 46
Bardon Mill	d					17 12			17 55												21 53
Haydon Bridge	d					17 17			18 00												21 58
Hexham	a					17 26			18 09			19 26				20 31					22 11
	d		16 42			17 27	17 42		18 10	18 42		19 26				20 31		21 12			22 12
Corbridge	d		16 46				17 46		18 14	18 46		19 31				20 36		21 16			22 16
Riding Mill	d		16 51				17 51		18 19	18 51		19 35				20 40		21 21			22 21
Stocksfield	d		16 55			17 36	17 55		18 23	18 55		19 39				20 44		21 25			22 25
Prudhoe	d		16 59			17 40	17 59		18 27	18 59		19 44				20 49		21 29			22 29
Wylam	d		17 03				18 03		18 31	19 03		19 48				20 52		21 33			22 33
Blaydon	d									19 09											
Metrocentre	a		17 14			17 55	18 12		18 43	19 16		19 59				21 01		21 44			22 44
	d	17 00	17 15		17 35	17 55	18 13	18 18	18 44	19 17		19 59	20 15		20 47	21 02		21 45		22 10	22 45
Dunston	d																				
Newcastle 8	a	17 08	17 26		17 43	18 08	18 23	18 26	18 56	19 27		20 14	20 23		20 55	21 14		21 56		22 20	22 59
Sunderland 44	a		17 50				18 49			19 50					21 20						
Newcastle 8 26	d	17 10		17 36	17 44			18 28			19 37			20 24			21 02		21 36		
Manors	d	17 13			17 47			18 30													
Cramlington	d	17 24			17 58			18 41						20 36							
Morpeth 26	d	17 32			18a06			18a49						20a45			21 17				
Pegswood	d	17 35																			
Widdrington	d	17 41																			
Acklington	d	17 48																			
Alnmouth for Alnwick 26	d	18 00		18 02							20 04						21 33		22 00		
Chathill	a	18 19																			

For connections to London Kings Cross please refer to Table 26

Table 48

Sundays until 05 September

Carlisle, Hexham and Metrocentre - Newcastle - Morpeth and Chathill

		XC	GR	NT	NT	NT	NT	NT	XC	NT	NT	NT	NT	NT	NT	XC	NT	NT	NT	NT	NT	NT	XC
Carlisle	d				09 05			10 05				11 12			12 05				13 12			14 12	
Wetheral	d				09 12			10 12							12 12								
Brampton (Cumbria)	d				09 22			10 22							12 22								
Haltwhistle	d				09 36			10 36				11 40			12 36				13 40			14 40	
Bardon Mill	d				09 44			10 44							12 44								
Haydon Bridge	d				09 49			10 49							12 49								
Hexham	a				09 58			10 58				11 58			12 58				13 58			14 58	
	d				09 59			10 59				11 59			12 59				13 59			14 59	
Corbridge	d				10 03			11 03				12 03			13 03				14 03			15 03	
Riding Mill	d				10 08			11 08				12 08			13 08				14 08			15 08	
Stocksfield	d				10 12			11 12				12 12			13 12				14 12			15 12	
Prudhoe	d				10 16			11 16				12 16			13 16				14 16			15 16	
Wylam	d				10 20			11 20				12 20			13 20				14 20			15 20	
Blaydon	d																						
Metrocentre	a				10 29			11 29				12 29			13 29				14 29			15 29	
	d			10 10	10 30	10 48	11 10	11 30		11 48	12 10	12 30	12 48	13 10	13 30		13 48	14 10	14 30	14 48	15 10	15 30	
Dunston	d																						
Newcastle	a			10 18	10 40	10 56	11 18	11 40		11 56	12 18	12 40	12 56	13 18	13 40		13 56	14 18	14 40	14 56	15 18	15 40	
Sunderland 44	a					11 22				12 21			13 22				14 21			15 22			
Newcastle 26	d	09 45	10b15						11 38							13 43							15 41
Manors	d																						
Cramlington	d																						
Morpeth 26	d	09 57	10 30																				15 54
Pegswood	d																						
Widdrington	d																						
Acklington	d																						
Alnmouth for Alnwick 26	d	10 11	10 46						12 02							14 08							16 08
Chathill	a																						

		NT	NT	NT	GR	NT	NT	NT	XC	NT	NT	NT	NT	NT	NT	XC	NT	XC	GR	XC
Carlisle	d			15 05				16 12				17 12			18 05		20 15			
Wetheral	d			15 12											18 12					
Brampton (Cumbria)	d			15 22											18 22					
Haltwhistle	d			15 36				16 40				17 40			18 36		20 43			
Bardon Mill	d			15 44											18 44					
Haydon Bridge	d			15 49											18 49					
Hexham	a			15 58				16 58				17 58			18 58		21 01			
	d			15 59				16 59				17 59			18 59		21 01			
Corbridge	d			16 03				17 03				18 03			19 03		21 05			
Riding Mill	d			16 08				17 08				18 08			19 08		21 10			
Stocksfield	d			16 12				17 12				18 12			19 12		21 14			
Prudhoe	d			16 16				17 16				18 16			19 16		21 18			
Wylam	d			16 20				17 20				18 20			19 20		21 22			
Blaydon	d																			
Metrocentre	a			16 29				17 29				18 29			19 29		21 31			
	d	15 48	16 10	16 30		16 48	17 10	17 30		17 48	18 10	18 30	18 48	19 10	19 30		21 31			
Dunston	d																			
Newcastle	a	15 58	16 18	16 40		16 56	17 18	17 40		17 55	18 18	18 40	18 56	19 18	19 40		21 43			
Sunderland 44	a	16 21				17 22				18 21			19 22							
Newcastle 26	d				16 42				17 38							19c40		20e49	21 07	21 39
Manors	d																			
Cramlington	d																			
Morpeth 26	d				16 58													21 02		
Pegswood	d																			
Widdrington	d																			
Acklington	d																			
Alnmouth for Alnwick 26	d				17 14				18 02							20 05		21 16	21 35	22 07
Chathill	a																			

b arr. 1006 c arr. 1934 e arr. 2043

For connections to London Kings Cross please refer to Table 26

Table 48

Sundays from 12 September

Carlisle, Hexham and Metrocentre - Newcastle - Morpeth and Chathill

		XC	GR	NT	NT	NT	NT	NT	XC	NT	NT	NT	NT	NT	NT	XC	NT	NT	NT	NT	NT	NT	XC
Carlisle	d				09 05			10 01				11 08			12 05				13 09			14 09	
Wetheral	d				09 12			10 08							12 12								
Brampton (Cumbria)	d				09 22			10 18							12 22								
Haltwhistle	d				09 36			10 32				11 36			12 36				13 37			14 37	
Bardon Mill	d				09 44			10 40							12 44								
Haydon Bridge	d				09 49			10 45							12 49								
Hexham	a				09 58			10 54				11 54			12 58				13 55			14 55	
	d				09 59			10 55				11 55			12 59				13 56			14 56	
Corbridge	d				10 03			10 59				11 59			13 03				14 00			15 00	
Riding Mill	d				10 08			11 04				12 04			13 08				14 05			15 05	
Stocksfield	d				10 12			11 08				12 08			13 12				14 09			15 09	
Prudhoe	d				10 16			11 12				12 12			13 16				14 13			15 13	
Wylam	d				10 20			11 16				12 16			13 20				14 17			15 17	
Blaydon	d																						
Metrocentre	a				10 33			11 29				12 29			13 33				14 29			15 29	
	d			10 10	10 33	10 48	11 10	11 29		11 48	12 10	12 30	12 48	13 10	13 33		13 48	14 10	14 30	14 48	15 10	15 30	
Dunston	d																						
Newcastle	a			10 18	10 43	10 56	11 18	11 39		11 56	12 18	12 40	12 56	13 18	13 43		13 56	14 18	14 40	14 56	15 18	15 40	
Sunderland 44	a					11 22				12 21			13 22				14 21			15 22			
Newcastle 26	d	09 45	10b15						11 38							13 43							15 41
Manors	d																						
Cramlington	d																						
Morpeth 26	d	09 57	10 30																				15 54
Pegswood	d																						
Widdrington	d																						
Acklington	d																						
Alnmouth for Alnwick 26	d	10 11	10 46						12 02							14 08							16 08
Chathill	a																						

		NT	NT	NT	GR	NT	NT	NT	XC	NT	NT	NT	NT	NT	NT	XC	NT	XC	GR	XC
Carlisle	d			15 05				16 11				17 10			18 01		20 15			
Wetheral	d			15 12											18 08					
Brampton (Cumbria)	d			15 22											18 18					
Haltwhistle	d			15 36				16 39				17 38			18 32		20 43			
Bardon Mill	d			15 44											18 40					
Haydon Bridge	d			15 49											18 45					
Hexham	a			15 58				16 57				17 56			18 54		20 58			
	d			15 59				16 58				17 57			18 55		20 59			
Corbridge	d			16 03				17 02				18 01			18 59		21 03			
Riding Mill	d			16 08				17 07				18 06			19 04		21 08			
Stocksfield	d			16 12				17 11				18 10			19 08		21 12			
Prudhoe	d			16 16				17 15				18 14			19 12		21 16			
Wylam	d			16 20				17 19				18 18			19 16		21 20			
Blaydon	d																			
Metrocentre	a			16 33				17 32				18 31			19 29		21 32			
	d	15 48	16 10	16 33		16 48	17 10	17 33		17 48	18 10	18 32	18 48	19 10	19 29		21 33			
Dunston	d																			
Newcastle	a	15 58	16 18	16 43		16 56	17 18	17 43		17 55	18 18	18 42	18 56	19 18	19 39		21 46			
Sunderland 44	a	16 21				17 22				18 21			19 22							
Newcastle 26	d				16 42				17 38							19c40		20e49	21 07	21 39
Manors	d																			
Cramlington	d																			
Morpeth 26	d				16 58													21 02		
Pegswood	d																			
Widdrington	d																			
Acklington	d																			
Alnmouth for Alnwick 26	d				17 14				18 02							20 05		21 16	21 35	22 07
Chathill	a																			

b arr. 1006 c arr. 1934 e arr. 2043

For connections to London Kings Cross please refer to Table 26

Route Diagram for Table 49

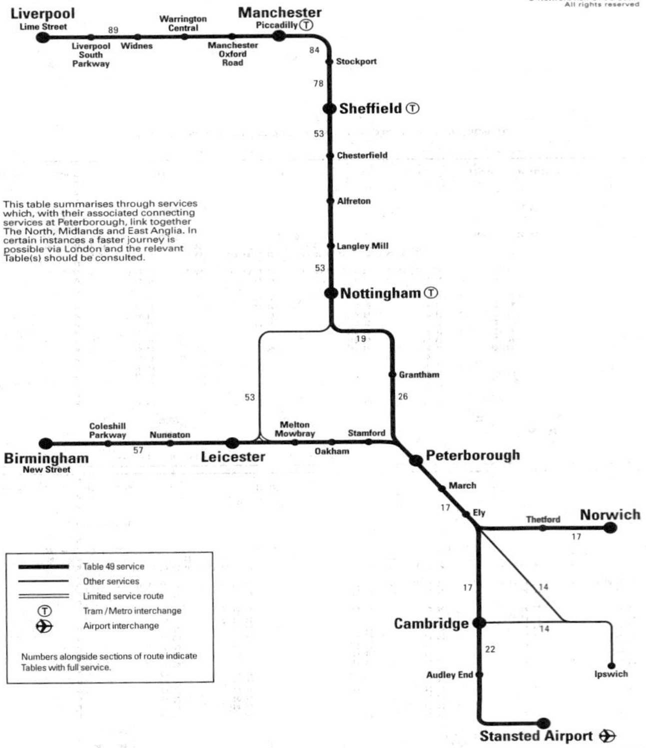

This table summarises through services which, with their associated connecting services at Peterborough, link together The North, Midlands and East Anglia. In certain instances a faster journey is possible via London and the relevant Table(s) should be consulted.

Stansted Airport - East Anglia - East Midlands - Birmingham and North West England

		XC ◇1	XC ◇1	EM ◇	EM ◇	EM ◇	EM ◇	XC ◇1	EM ◇	XC ◇1	EM ◇	XC ◇1
Norwich	d						05 50		06 52		07 57	
Thetford	d						06 23		07 20		08 24	
Stansted Airport	d		05 15					06 06		07 21		08 21
Audley End	d		05 36					06 23		07 37		08 37
Cambridge	d	05 15	05 55					06 52		08 00		09 00
Ely	d	05 30	06 10				06 51	07 08	07 45	08 15	08 50	09 15
March	d	05 46	06 28				07 07	07 26	08 01	08 31	09 07	09 31
Peterborough	a	06 08	06 50				07 25	07 50	08 24	08 50	09 25	09 50
	d	06 10	06 52				07 27	07 50	08 27	08 52	09 27	09 52
Stamford	d	06 23	07 05					08 05		09 05		10 05
Oakham	d	06 39	07 21					08 21		09 21		10 21
Melton Mowbray	d	06 50	07 33					08 33		09 33		10 33
Leicester	d	07 10	07 49					08 49		09 49		10 49
Nuneaton	a	07 29	08 15					09 08		10 08		11 08
Coleshill Parkway	a	07 45	08 32					09 25		10 25		11 25
Birmingham New Street	a	08 00	08 45					09 38		10 38		11 38
Grantham	d						07 58		08 58		09 58	
Nottingham	a						08 38		09 36		10 36	
	d			05 20	06 40	07 45	08 45		09 45		10 45	
Langley Mill	d											
Alfreton	d				07 02	08 07	09 07		10 07		11 07	
Chesterfield	d			05 49	07 13	08 18	09 18		10 18		11 18	
Sheffield	a			06 15	07 31	08 38	09 38		10 38		11 38	
	d			06 20	07 35	08 42	09 42		10 42		11 42	
Stockport	a			07 22	08 24	09 25	10 25		11 25		12 25	
Manchester Piccadilly	a			07 34	08 36	09 36	10 36		11 36		12 36	
Manchester Oxford Road	a			07 37	08 40	09 40	10 40		11 40		12 40	
Warrington Central	a			07 53	08 57	09 57	10 57		11 57		12 57	
Widnes	a			08 01	09 05	10 05	11 05		12 05		13 05	
Liverpool South Parkway	a			08 18	09 15	10 15	11 15		12 15		13 15	
Liverpool Lime Street	a			08 31	09 31	10 31	11 31		12 31		13 31	

		EM ◇	XC ◇1	EM ◇	XC ◇1	EM ◇	XC ◇1	EM ◇	XC ◇1	EM ◇	XC ◇1	EM ◇
Norwich	d	08 57		09 57		10 57		11 57		12 57		13 57
Thetford	d	09 24		10 24		11 24		12 24		13 24		14 24
Stansted Airport	d		09 21		10 21		11 25		12 25		13 25	
Audley End	d		09 37		10 37		11 37		12 37		13 37	
Cambridge	d		10 00		11 00		12 00		13 00		14 00	
Ely	d	09 52	10 15	10 52	11 15	11 52	12 15	12 52	13 15	13 52	14 15	14 52
March	d		10 31		11 31		12 31		13 31		14 31	
Peterborough	a	10 26	10 50	11 25	11 50	12 24	12 50	13 25	13 50	14 25	14 50	15 25
	d	10 30	10 52	11 27	11 52	12 25	12 52	13 26	13 52	14 26	14 52	15 26
Stamford	d		11 05		12 05		13 05		14 05		15 05	
Oakham	d		11 21		12 21		13 21		14 21		15 21	
Melton Mowbray	d		11 33		12 33		13 33		14 33		15 33	
Leicester	d		11 49		12 49		13 49		14 49		15 49	
Nuneaton	a		12 08		13 08		14 08		15 08		16 08	
Coleshill Parkway	a		12 25		13 25		14 25		15 25		16 25	
Birmingham New Street	a		12 39		13 39		14 44		15 44		16 39	
Grantham	d	11 13		11 56		12 58		13 58		14 58		15 58
Nottingham	a	11 43		12 36		13 36		14 36		15 36		16 36
	d	11 45		12 45		13 45		14 45		15 45		16 45
Langley Mill	d											
Alfreton	d	12 07		13 07		14 07		15 07		16 07		17 07
Chesterfield	d	12 18		13 18		14 19		15 20		16 18		17 18
Sheffield	a	12 38		13 38		14 38		15 38		16 38		17 34
	d	12 42		13 42		14 42		15 42		16 42		17 40
Stockport	a	13 25		14 25		15 25		16 25		17 25		18 25
Manchester Piccadilly	a	13 36		14 36		15 36		16 36		17 37		18 36
Manchester Oxford Road	a	13 40		14 40		15 40		16 40		17 40		18 40
Warrington Central	a	13 57		14 57		15 57		16 57		18 03		18 57
Widnes	a	14 05		15 05		16 05		17 05		18 11		19 05
Liverpool South Parkway	a	14 15		15 15		16 15		17 15		18 21		19 18
Liverpool Lime Street	a	14 31		15 31		16 31		17 31		18 35		19 35

		XC ◇1	EM ◇	XC ◇1	EM ◇	XC ◇1	EM ◇	XC ◇1	EM ◇	XC ◇1	EM ◇	XC ◇1	NT	NT	EM	XC ◇1
Norwich	d		14 57		15 52		16 57		17 54		18 57					
Thetford	d		15 24		16 27		17 27		18 27		19 24					
Stansted Airport	d	14 25		15 20		16 25		17 18		18 21		19 21				20 21
Audley End	d	14 37		15 37		16 37		17 33		18 37		19 37				20 37
Cambridge	d	15 00		16 00		17 00		17 51		19 00		20 00				21 00
Ely	d	15 15	15 52	16 15	16 52	17 15	17 52	18 06	18 52	19 15	19 52	20 15				21 15
March	d	15 31		16 31		17 31		18 25	19 08	19 31		20 31				21 31
Peterborough	a	15 50	16 25	16 50	17 26	17 50	18 25	18 50	19 31	19 50	20 26	20 50				21 50
	d	15 52	16 27	16 52	17 27	17 52	18 26	18 52	19 31	19 52	20 28	20 52			21 30	21 52
Stamford	d	16 05		17 05		18 05		19 05		20 05		21 05			21 43	22 05
Oakham	d	16 21		17 21		18 21		19 21		20 21		21 21			21 58	22 21
Melton Mowbray	d	16 33		17 33		18 33		19 33		20 33		21 33			22 11	22 33
Leicester	d	16 49		17 49		18 49		19 49		20 49		21 49				22 49
Nuneaton	a	17 08		18 16		19 08		20 08		21 08		22 08				23 08
Coleshill Parkway	a	17 25		18 32		19 25		20 25		21 25		22 25				23 25
Birmingham New Street	a	17 38		18 45		19 39		20 43		21 39		22 45				23 39
Grantham	d		16 58		17 58		18 58		20 03		20 58					
Nottingham	a		17 36		18 36		19 36		20 37		21 35				22 50	
	d		17 45		18 45		19 40						20 45	21 11		
Langley Mill	d		18 02											21 31		
Alfreton	d		18 09		19 07		20 01							21 39		
Chesterfield	d		18 21		19 18		20 12						21 28	22 00		
Sheffield	a		18 38		19 39		20 28						21 54	22 19		
	d		18 42		19 42		20 32									
Stockport	a		19 25		20 25		21 20									
Manchester Piccadilly	a		19 36		20 36		21 32									
Manchester Oxford Road	a		19 40		20 40											
Warrington Central	a		19 57		20 57											
Widnes	a		20 05		21 05											
Liverpool South Parkway	a		20 15		21 19											
Liverpool Lime Street	a		20 35		21 35											

For connections from Ipswich please refer to Table 14

Table 49

Saturdays

Stansted Airport - East Anglia - East Midlands - Birmingham and North West England

		XC	EM	XC	EM	EM	EM	XC	EM	XC	EM	XC	EM	XC	EM	XC	EM	XC	EM	XC	EM	XC	EM
		◇1	◇	◇1	◇	◇	◇	◇1	◇	◇1	◇	◇1	◇	◇1	◇	◇1	◇	◇1	◇	◇1	◇	◇1	◇
Norwich	d						05 52		06 52		07 57		08 57		09 57		10 57		11 57		12 57		13 57
Thetford	d						06 25		07 20		08 24		09 24		10 24		11 24		12 24		13 24		14 24
Stansted Airport	d			05 25				06 25		07 25		08 25		09 25		10 25		11 25		12 25		13 25	
Audley End	d			05 37				06 37		07 37		08 37		09 37		10 37		11 37		12 37		13 37	
Cambridge	d	05 15		05 55				06 56		08 00		09 00		10 00		11 00		12 00		13 00		14 00	
Ely	d	05 30		06 10			06 51	07 11	07 44	08 15	08 54	09 15	09 51	10 15	10 53	11 15	11 53	12 15	12 54	13 15	13 53	14 15	14 53
March	d	05 46		06 28			07 07	07 29	08 01	08 31	09 11	09 31		10 31		11 31		12 31		13 31		14 31	
Peterborough	a	06 08		06 50			07 25	07 50	08 26	08 50	09 28	09 50	10 25	10 50	11 24	11 50	12 24	12 50	13 26	13 50	14 25	14 50	15 25
	d	06 10		06 52			07 27	07 52	08 30	08 52	09 30	09 52	10 28	10 52	11 25	11 52	12 25	12 52	13 28	13 52	14 26	14 52	15 26
Stamford	d	06 23		07 05				08 05		09 05		10 05		11 05		12 05		13 05		14 05		15 05	
Oakham	d	06 39		07 21				08 21		09 21		10 21		11 21		12 21		13 21		14 21		15 21	
Melton Mowbray	d	06 50		07 33				08 33		09 33		10 33		11 33		12 33		13 33		14 33		15 33	
Leicester	d	07 16		07 49				08 49		09 49		10 49		11 49		12 49		13 49		14 49		15 49	
Nuneaton	a	07 35		08 08				09 08		10 08		11 08		12 08		13 08		14 08		15 08		16 08	
Coleshill Parkway	a	07 51		08 24				09 25		10 25		11 25		12 25		13 25		14 25		15 25		16 25	
Birmingham New Street	a	08 04		08 38				09 38		10 38		11 38		12 33		13 38		14 38		15 38		16 38	
Grantham	d						07 58		08 58		09 58		10 58		11 58		12 58		13 58		14 58		15 58
Nottingham	a						08 39		09 36		10 36		11 35		12 36		13 36		14 36		15 36		16 36
	d		05 18		06 40	07 45	08 45		09 45		10 45		11 45		12 45		13 45		14 45		15 45		16 45
Langley Mill	d																						
Alfreton	d				07 02	08 07	09 07		10 07		11 07		12 07		13 07		14 07		15 07		16 07		17 07
Chesterfield	d		05 49		07 13	08 18	09 18		10 18		11 18		12 18		13 18		14 18		15 18		16 18		17 18
Sheffield	a		06 15		07 31	08 38	09 38		10 38		11 38		12 38		13 38		14 38		15 38		16 38		17 34
	d		06 20		07 35	08 42	09 42		10 42		11 42		12 42		13 42		14 42		15 42		16 42		17 40
Stockport	a		07 22		08 24	09 25	10 25		11 25		12 25		13 25		14 25		15 25		16 25		17 25		18 25
Manchester Piccadilly	a		07 34		08 36	09 36	10 36		11 36		12 36		13 36		14 36		15 36		16 36		17 37		18 36
Manchester Oxford Road	a		07 37		08 40	09 40	10 40		11 40		12 40		13 40		14 40		15 40		16 40		17 40		18 40
Warrington Central	a		07 53		08 57	09 57	10 57		11 57		12 57		13 57		14 57		15 57		16 57		18 03		18 57
Widnes	a		08 01		09 05	10 05	11 05		12 05		13 05		14 05		15 05		16 05		17 05		18 11		19 05
Liverpool South Parkway	a		08 18		09 15	10 15	11 15		12 15		13 15		14 15		15 15		16 15		17 15		18 21		19 18
Liverpool Lime Street	a		08 31		09 31	10 31	11 31		12 31		13 31		14 31		15 31		16 31		17 31		18 35		19 35

		XC	EM	XC	EM	XC	EM	XC	EM	XC	EM	XC	NT	NT	EM
		◇1	◇	◇1	◇	◇1	◇	◇1	◇	◇1	◇	◇1			
Norwich	d		14 57		15 52		16 57		17 54		18 57				
Thetford	d		15 24		16 23		17 27		18 27		19 24				
Stansted Airport	d	14 25		15 25		16 25		17 25		18 25		19 25			
Audley End	d	14 37		15 37		16 37		17 37		18 37		19 37			
Cambridge	d	15 00		16 00		17 00		18 00		19 00		20 00			
Ely	d	15 15	15 52	16 15	16 52	17 15	17 52	18 15	18 53	19 15	19 53	20 15			
March	d	15 31		16 31		17 31		18 33	19 09	19 31		20 31			
Peterborough	a	15 50	16 25	16 50	17 26	17 50	18 25	18 50	19 29	19 50	20 25	20 50			
	d	15 52	16 27	16 52	17 27	17 52	18 26	18 52	19 30	19 52	20 27	20 52			21 27
Stamford	d	16 05		17 05		18 05		19 05		20 05		21 05			
Oakham	d	16 21		17 21		18 21		19 21		20 21		21 21			
Melton Mowbray	d	16 33		17 33		18 33		19 33		20 33		21 33			
Leicester	d	16 49		17 49		18 49		19 49		20 49		21 49			
Nuneaton	a	17 08		18 08		19 08		20 08		21 08		22 08			
Coleshill Parkway	a	17 25		18 25		19 25		20 25		21 25		22 25			
Birmingham New Street	a	17 38		18 38		19 38		20 38		21 38		22 38			
Grantham	d		16 58		18 03		18 58		20 03		20 58				22 02
Nottingham	a		17 36		18 36		19 36		20 37		21 32				22 32
	d		17 45		18 45		19 40						20 39	21 15	
Langley Mill	d		18 03										21 02	21 31	
Alfreton	d		18 10		19 07		20 01						21 10	21 39	
Chesterfield	d		18 22		19 18		20 11						21 22	21 50	
Sheffield	a		18 39		19 39		20 27						21 40	22 13	
	d		18 42		19 42		20 31								
Stockport	a		19 25		20 25		21 20								
Manchester Piccadilly	a		19 36		20 37		21 32								
Manchester Oxford Road	a		19 40												
Warrington Central	a		19 57												
Widnes	a		20 05												
Liverpool South Parkway	a		20 19												
Liverpool Lime Street	a		20 34												

For connections from Ipswich please refer to Table 14

Table 49

Sundays
until 05 September

Stansted Airport - East Anglia - East Midlands - Birmingham and North West England

		EM	EM	EM	EM	EM	EM	XC	EM	EM	XC	XC	XC	XC	EM	EM	EM	XC	EM	XC	XC	EM	XC
		◇ A	◇ B	◇	◇ A	◇ B	◇	◇1	◇ B	◇ A	◇1	◇1 B	◇1 A	◇1	◇	◇	◇	◇1	◇	◇1 B	◇1 A	◇	◇1
Norwich	d						09 33		10 47	10 47							13 49		14 47			15 53	
Thetford	d						10 00		11 14	11 14							14 16		15 14			16 20	
Stansted Airport	d							10 25			11 25	12 25	12 25	13 25				14 25		15 25	15 25		16 25
Audley End	d							10 39			11 39	12 39	12 39	13 39				14 39		15 39	15 39		16 39
Cambridge	d							10 56			11 57	12 57	12 57	13 57				14 57		15 57	15 57		16 56
Ely	d						10 32	11 11	11 39	11 39	12 15	13 15	13 15	14 15			14 45	15 15	15 48	16 15	16 15		17 15
March	d							11 27			12 31	13 31	13 31	14 31				15 31		16 31	16 31		17 31
Peterborough	a						11 09	11 50	12 16	12 16	12 50	13 50	13 50	14 50			15 24	15 50	16 22	16 50	16 50	17 10	17 50
	d						11 11	11 52	12 18	12 18	12 52	13 52	13 52	14 52			15 26	15 52	16 24	16 52	16 52	17 14	17 52
Stamford	d							12 05			13 05	14 05	14 05	15 05				16 05		17 05	17 05		18 05
Oakham	d							12 21			13 21	14 21	14 20	15 21				16 21		17 21	17 21		18 21
Melton Mowbray	d							12 33			13 33	14 33	14 32	15 33				16 32		17 32	17 32		18 33
Leicester	d							12 49			13 49	14 49	14 49	15 49				16 48		17 48	17 49		18 49
Nuneaton	a							13 08			14 08	15 08	15 08	16 08				17 08		18 08	18 08		19 08
Coleshill Parkway	a							13 24			14 24	15 24	15 24	16 24				17 24		18 24	18 24		19 24
Birmingham New Street	a							13 39			14 37	15 39	15 39	16 39				17 37		18 39	18 39		19 37
Grantham	d						11 56		12 50	12 47							15 59		16 56			17 55	
Nottingham	a						12 33		13 28	13 26							16 28		17 25			18 29	
	d	09 31	09 31	10 41	11 46	11 46	12 39		13 38	13 38					14 37	15 44	16 40		17 37			18 37	
Langley Mill	d						12 56		13 55	13 55					14 54		17 00		17 54			18 54	
Alfreton	d	09 53	09 55	11 03	12 08	12 08	13 04		14 03	14 03					15 02	16 06	17 08		18 02			19 02	
Chesterfield	d	10 08	10 08	11 15	12 18	12 19	13 17		14 18	14 18					15 13	16 23	17 22		18 17			19 12	
Sheffield	a	10 33	10 33	11 35	12 36	12 36	13 33		14 36	14 36					15 31	16 39	17 40		18 34			19 31	
	d	10 41	10 41	11 38	12 41	12 41	13 38		14 39	14 39					15 38	16 44	17 44		18 37			19 35	
Stockport	a	11 25	11 25	12 25	13 25	13 25	14 25		15 25	15 25					16 25	17 26	18 25		19 25			20 25	
Manchester Piccadilly	a	11 37	11 37	12 37	13 37	13 37	14 37		15 37	15 37					16 37	17 37	18 37		19 37			20 38	
Manchester Oxford Road	a	11 41	11 41	12 41	13 41	13 41	14 41		15 41	15 41					16 41	17 41	18 41		19 41				
Warrington Central	a	11 58	11 58	12 58	13 58	13 58	14 58		15 58	15 58					16 58	17 58	18 58		19 58				
Widnes	a	12 06	12 06	13 06	14 06	14 06	15 06		16 06	16 06					17 06	18 06	19 06		20 06				
Liverpool South Parkway	a	12 16	12 16	13 16	14 16	14 16	15 16		16 16	16 16					17 16	18 16	19 16		20 16				
Liverpool Lime Street	a	12 30	12 30	13 30	14 30	14 30	15 30		16 30	16 30					17 30	18 30	19 30		20 30				

		EM	XC	XC	EM	XC	EM	XC	NT	EM	EM	NT
		◇	◇1 B	◇1 A	◇	◇1	◇	◇1			◇	
Norwich	d	16 57			17 56		18 57				20 52	
Thetford	d	17 24			18 23		19 24				21 19	
Stansted Airport	d		17 25	17 25		18 25		19 25				
Audley End	d		17 39	17 39		18 39		19 39				
Cambridge	d		17 57	17 57		18 57		19 57				
Ely	d	17 48	18 15	18 15	18 48	19 15	19 49	20 15			21 44	
March	d		18 31	18 31		19 31		20 31				
Peterborough	a	18 25	18 50	18 50	19 24	19 50	20 28	20 50			22 20	
	d	18 30	18 52	18 52	19 26	19 52	20 31	20 52			22 22	
Stamford	d		19 05	19 05		20 05		21 05				
Oakham	d		19 21	19 21		20 21		21 21				
Melton Mowbray	d		19 33	19 33		20 33		21 33				
Leicester	d		19 49	19 50		20 49		21 49				
Nuneaton	a		20 08	20 09		21 08		22 08				
Coleshill Parkway	a		20 24	20 25		21 24		22 24				
Birmingham New Street	a		20 39	20 40		21 37		22 38				
Grantham	d	19 01			19 57		21 03			19 37	22 51	
Nottingham	a	19 30			20 31		21 35			20 14	23 26	
	d	19 38							20 13	20 26		21 20
Langley Mill	d								20 29			21 41
Alfreton	d	20 00							20 37			21 49
Chesterfield	d	20 10							20 48			22 08
Sheffield	a	20 31							21 14			22 32
	d	20 35										
Stockport	a	21 24										
Manchester Piccadilly	a	21 36										
Manchester Oxford Road	a											
Warrington Central	a											
Widnes	a											
Liverpool South Parkway	a											
Liverpool Lime Street	a											

A from 18 July until 5 September
B until 11 July

For connections from Ipswich please refer to Table 14

Table 49

Sundays

12 September to 17 October

Stansted Airport - East Anglia - East Midlands - Birmingham and North West England

		EM	XC	EM	EM	EM	EM	XC	XC	XC	EM	EM	EM	XC	EM	XC	EM	XC	EM	XC		EM	XC	EM	XC
		◇	◇1 ⊥	◇	◇	◇	◇	◇1 ⊥	◇1 ⊥	◇1 ⊥	◇	◇	◇	◇1 ⊥	◇	◇1 ⊥	◇	◇1 ⊥	◇	◇1 ⊥		◇	◇1 ⊥	◇	◇1 ⊥
Norwich	d						10 47						13 49		14 49		15 53		16 57			17 56		18 57	
Thetford	d						11 14						14 16		15 16		16 20		17 24			18 23		19 24	
Stansted Airport ✈	d		10 25					11 25	12 25	13 25				14 25		15 25		16 25		17 25			18 25		19 25
Audley End	d		10 39					11 39	12 39	13 39				14 39		15 39		16 39		17 39			18 39		19 39
Cambridge	d		10 56					11 57	12 57	13 57				14 57		15 57		16 56		17 57			18 57		19 57
Ely 6	d		11 11				11 39	12 15	13 15	14 15			14 45	15 15	15 48	16 15		17 15	17 50	18 15		18 48	19 15	19 49	20 15
March	d		11 27					12 31	13 31	14 31				15 31		16 31		17 31		18 31			19 31		20 31
Peterborough 8	a		11 50				12 16	12 50	13 50	14 50			15 24	15 50	16 22	16 50	17 10	17 50	18 25	18 50		19 24	19 50	20 29	20 50
	d		11 52				12 18	12 52	13 52	14 52			15 26	15 52	16 24	16 52	17 14	17 52	18 30	18 52		19 26	19 52	20 31	20 52
Stamford	d		12 05					13 05	14 05	15 05				16 05		17 05		18 05		19 05			20 05		21 05
Oakham	d		12 21					13 21	14 21	15 21				16 21		17 21		18 21		19 21			20 21		21 21
Melton Mowbray	d		12 33					13 33	14 33	15 33				16 32		17 32		18 33		19 33			20 33		21 33
Leicester	d		12 49					13 49	14 49	15 49				16 48		17 48		18 49		19 49			20 49		21 49
Nuneaton	a		13 08					14 08	15 08	16 08				17 08		18 08		19 08		20 08			21 08		22 08
Coleshill Parkway	a		13 24					14 24	15 24	16 24				17 24		18 24		19 24		20 24			21 24		22 24
Birmingham New Street 12	a		13 39					14 37	15 39	16 39				17 37		18 39		19 37		20 39			21 37		22 38
Grantham 7	d																								
Nottingham 8 🚊	a						13 26						16 34		17 30		18 21		19 38			20 42		21 41	
	d	09 31		10 41	11 46	12 39	13 38				14 37	15 44	16 41		17 37		18 35		19 41						
Langley Mill	d						13 55				14 54		17 00		17 54		18 54								
Alfreton	d	09 53		11 03	12 08	13 04	14 03				15 02	16 06	17 08		18 02		19 02		20 03						
Chesterfield	d	10 08		11 15	12 18	13 17	14 18				15 13	16 23	17 22		18 17		19 13		20 13						
Sheffield 7 🚊	a	10 33		11 35	12 36	13 33	14 36				15 31	16 39	17 40		18 34		19 31		20 31						
	d	10 41		11 38	12 41	13 38	14 39				15 38	16 44	17 44		18 37		19 35		20 35						
Stockport	a	11 25		12 25	13 25	14 25	15 25				16 25	17 26	18 25		19 25		20 25		21 24						
Manchester Piccadilly 10 🚊	a	11 37		12 37	13 37	14 37	15 37				16 37	17 37	18 37		19 37		20 38		21 36						
Manchester Oxford Road	a	11 41		12 41	13 41	14 41	15 41				16 41	17 41	18 41		19 41										
Warrington Central	a	11 58		12 58	13 58	14 58	15 58				16 58	17 58	18 58		19 58										
Widnes	a	12 06		13 06	14 06	15 06	16 06				17 06	18 06	19 06		20 06										
Liverpool South Parkway 7	a	12 16		13 16	14 16	1516	16 16				17 16	18 16	19 16		20 16										
Liverpool Lime Street 10	a	12 30		13 30	14 30	15 28	16 30				17 30	18 30	19 30		20 30										

		NT	EM	NT
			◇	
Norwich	d		20 52	
Thetford	d		21 19	
Stansted Airport ✈	d			
Audley End	d			
Cambridge	d			
Ely 6	d		21 44	
March	d			
Peterborough 8	a		22 20	
	d		22 22	
Stamford	d			
Oakham	d			
Melton Mowbray	d			
Leicester	d			
Nuneaton	a			
Coleshill Parkway	a			
Birmingham New Street 12	a			
Grantham 7	d			
Nottingham 8 🚊	a		23 41	
	d	20 13		21 20
Langley Mill	d	20 29		21 41
Alfreton	d	20 37		21 49
Chesterfield	d	20 48		22 08
Sheffield 7 🚊	a	21 14		22 32
	d			
Stockport	a			
Manchester Piccadilly 10 🚊	a			
Manchester Oxford Road	a			
Warrington Central	a			
Widnes	a			
Liverpool South Parkway 7	a			
Liverpool Lime Street 10	a			

For connections from Ipswich please refer to Table 14

Table 49

Sundays

from 24 October

Stansted Airport - East Anglia - East Midlands - Birmingham and North West England

		EM	XC	EM	EM	EM	EM	XC	XC	XC	EM		EM	EM	XC	EM	XC	EM	XC	EM	XC		EM	XC	EM	XC
		◇	◇1 ⊥	◇	◇	◇	◇	◇1 ⊥	◇1 ⊥	◇1 ⊥	◇		◇	◇	◇1 ⊥	◇	◇1 ⊥	◇	◇1 ⊥	◇	◇1 ⊥		◇	◇1 ⊥	◇	◇1 ⊥
Norwich	d						10 47							13 49		14 49		15 53		16 57			17 56		18 57	
Thetford	d						11 14							14 16		15 16		16 20		17 24			18 23		19 24	
Stansted Airport ✈	d		10 25					11 25	12 25	13 25					14 25		15 25		16 25		17 25			18 25		19 25
Audley End	d		10 39					11 39	12 39	13 39					14 39		15 39		16 39		17 39			18 39		19 39
Cambridge	d		10 56					11 57	12 57	13 57					14 57		15 57		16 56		17 57			18 57		19 57
Ely 6	d		11 11				11 39	12 15	13 15	14 15				14 45	15 15	15 48	16 15		17 15	17 48	18 15		18 48	19 15	19 49	20 15
March	d		11 27					12 31	13 31	14 31					15 31		16 31		17 31		18 31			19 31		20 31
Peterborough 8	a		11 50				12 16	12 50	13 50	14 50				15 24	15 50	16 22	16 50	17 10	17 50	18 25	18 50		19 24	19 50	20 29	20 50
	d		11 52				12 18	12 52	13 52	14 52				15 26	15 52	16 24	16 52	17 14	17 52	18 30	18 52		19 26	19 52	20 31	20 52
Stamford	d		12 05					13 05	14 05	15 05					16 05		17 05		18 05		19 05			20 05		21 05
Oakham	d		12 21					13 21	14 21	15 21					16 21		17 21		18 21		19 21			20 21		21 21
Melton Mowbray	d		12 33					13 33	14 33	15 33					16 32		17 32		18 33		19 33			20 33		21 33
Leicester	d		12 49					13 49	14 49	15 49					16 48		17 48		18 49		19 49			20 49		21 49
Nuneaton	a		13 08					14 08	15 08	16 08					17 08		18 08		19 08		20 08			21 08		22 08
Coleshill Parkway	a		13 24					14 24	15 24	16 24					17 24		18 24		19 24		20 24			21 24		22 24
Birmingham New Street 12	a		13 39					14 37	15 39	16 39					17 37		18 39		19 37		20 39			21 37		22 38
Grantham 7	d						12 50							15 59		16 56		17 55		19 01			19 57		21 03	
Nottingham 8 🚊	a						13 28							16 28		17 25		18 29		19 30			20 31		21 35	
	d	09 31		10 41	11 46	12 39	13 38				14 37		15 44	16 41		17 37		18 37		19 38						
Langley Mill	d						13 55				14 54			17 00		17 54		18 54								
Alfreton	d	09 53		11 03	12 08	13 04	14 03				15 02		16 06	17 08		18 02		19 02		20 00						
Chesterfield	d	10 08		11 15	12 18	13 17	14 18				15 13		16 23	17 22		18 17		19 13		20 10						
Sheffield 7 🚊	a	10 33		11 35	12 36	13 33	14 36				15 31		16 39	17 40		18 34		19 31		20 31						
	d	10 41		11 38	12 41	13 38	14 39				15 38		16 44	17 44		18 37		19 35		20 35						
Stockport	a	11 25		12 25	13 25	14 25	15 25				16 25		17 26	18 25		19 25		20 25		21 24						
Manchester Piccadilly 10 🚊	a	11 37		12 37	13 37	14 37	15 37				16 37		17 37	18 37		19 37		20 38		21 36						
Manchester Oxford Road	a	11 41		12 41	13 41	14 41	15 41				16 41		17 41	18 41		19 41										
Warrington Central	a	11 58		12 58	13 58	14 58	15 58				16 58		17 58	18 58		19 58										
Widnes	a	12 06		13 06	14 06	15 06	16 06				17 06		18 06	19 06		20 06										
Liverpool South Parkway 7	a	12 16		13 16	14 16	1516	16 16				17 16		18 16	19 16		20 16										
Liverpool Lime Street 10	a	12 30		13 30	14 30	15 28	16 30				17 30		18 30	19 30		20 30										

		NT	EM	NT
			◇	
Norwich	d		20 52	
Thetford	d		21 19	
Stansted Airport ✈	d			
Audley End	d			
Cambridge	d			
Ely 6	d		21 44	
March	d			
Peterborough 8	a		22 20	
	d		22 22	
Stamford	d			
Oakham	d			
Melton Mowbray	d			
Leicester	d			
Nuneaton	a			
Coleshill Parkway	a			
Birmingham New Street 12	a			
Grantham 7	d		22 51	
Nottingham 8 🚊	a		23 26	
	d	20 13		21 20
Langley Mill	d	20 29		21 41
Alfreton	d	20 37		21 49
Chesterfield	d	20 48		22 08
Sheffield 7 🚊	a	21 14		22 32
	d			
Stockport	a			
Manchester Piccadilly 10 🚊	a			
Manchester Oxford Road	a			
Warrington Central	a			
Widnes	a			
Liverpool South Parkway 7	a			
Liverpool Lime Street 10	a			

For connections from Ipswich please refer to Table 14

Table 49

Mondays to Fridays

North West England and Birmingham - East Midlands - East Anglia- Stansted Airport

		EM	EM	EM	EM	EM	EM	XC	EM	NT		XC	EM	EM	NT	EM	XC	EM	XC	EM		XC	EM	XC	EM
		◇ A	◇ B	◇ C	MX ◇	◇		◇1	◇			◇1	D	E		◇	◇1	◇	◇1	◇		◇1	◇	◇1	◇
Liverpool Lime Street [10]	d	21p22	21p22	21p22	21p37															06 47			07 43		08 52
Liverpool South Parkway [7] ✈	d	~	~	~	21p47															06 57			07 53		09 03
Widnes	d	21p39	21p39	21p39	21p55															07 07			08 05		09 11
Warrington Central	d	21p47	21p47	21p47	22p03															07 15			08 13		09 19
Manchester Oxford Road	d	22p07	22p07	22p07	22p24															07 38			08 39		09 39
Manchester Piccadilly [10]	d	22p11	22p11	22p11	22p28															07 42			08 43		09 43
Stockport	d	22p28	22p28	22p28	22p37															07 54			08 54		09 54
Sheffield [7]	a	23p25	23p25	23p25	23p35															08 34			09 35		10 33
	d	23p29	23p29	23p29	23p37					05 05					06 [illegible]					08 38			09 38		10 38
Chesterfield	d	23p43	23p43	23p43	00 02					05 20					06 [illegible]					08 53			09 53		10 52
Alfreton	d	23p54	23p54	23p54											06 30					09 03			10 04		11 03
Langley Mill	d	00 02	00 03	00 02											06 37										
Nottingham [8]	a	00 30	00 30	00 33	00 41					06 12					07 08	07 48				09 30			10 30		11 30
	d					04 51	05 10		05 56				06 53	06 55		07 52		08 34		09 34			10 34		11 34
Grantham [7]	d						05 51									08 25		09 11		10 08			11 07		12 07
Birmingham New Street [12]	d							05 22				06 22					07 22		08 22			09 22		10 22	
Coleshill Parkway	d											06 35					07 35		08 35			09 35		10 35	
Nuneaton	d							05 50				06 52					07 51		08 51			09 52		10 52	
Leicester	d							06 11				07 17					08 17		09 17			10 17		11 17	
Melton Mowbray	d					05 29		06 27	06 52			07 33					08 33		09 33			10 33		11 33	
Oakham	d					05 41		06 40	07 04			07 45					08 45		09 45			10 45		11 45	
Stamford	d					06 02		06 54	07 18			08 01					09 01		10 01			11 01		12 01	
Peterborough [8]	a					06 17	06 25	07 07	07 33			08 16	09 27	09 27		08 57	09 16	09 38	10 16	10 42		11 16	11 36	12 16	12 42
	d					06 27		07 09	07 35			08 18				08 59	09 18	09 40	10 18	10 44		11 18	11 38	12 18	12 43
March	a					06 42		07 28	07 50			08 33					09 34		10 33			11 33		12 33	
Ely [6]	a					07 01		07 51	08 11			08 50				09 41	09 52	10 13	10 52	11 16		11 52	12 11	12 52	13 16
Cambridge	a							08 08				09 08					10 08		11 08			12 08		13 08	
Audley End	a							08 23				09 23					10 23		11 23			12 23		13 23	
Stansted Airport ✈	a							08 38				09 38					10 45		11 45			12 45		13 45	
Thetford	a					07 28			08 36							10 05		10 38		11 41			12 36		13 40
Norwich	a					08 13			09 13							10 43		11 13		12 13			13 13		14 13

		XC	EM	XC	EM	XC		EM	XC	EM	EM	EM	XC	XC	XC	XC	EM	XC	EM	XC	EM	EM	EM	XC	EM
		◇1	◇	◇1	◇	◇1		◇	◇1	◇	◇	◇	◇1	◇1	◇1	◇1	◇	◇1	◇	◇1	◇	◇	◇	◇1	◇
Liverpool Lime Street [10]	d		09 52		10 52			11 52		12 52	13 52	14 52					15 52		16 52		17 52	18 52	19 52		21 37
Liverpool South Parkway [7] ✈	d		10 03		11 03			12 03		13 03	14 03	15 03					16 03		17 03		18 03	19 03	20 03		21 47
Widnes	d		10 11		11 11			12 11		13 11	14 11	15 11					16 11		17 11		18 11	19 11	20 11		21 55
Warrington Central	d		10 19		11 19			12 19		13 19	14 19	15 19					16 19		17 19		18 19	19 19	20 19		22 03
Manchester Oxford Road	d		10 39		11 39			12 39		13 39	14 39	15 39					16 39		17 39		18 39	19 39	20 39		22 24
Manchester Piccadilly [10]	d		10 43		11 43			12 43		13 43	14 43	15 43					16 43		17 43		18 43	19 43	20 43		22 28
Stockport	d		10 54		11 54			12 54		13 54	14 54	15 54					16 54		17 54		18 54	19 54	20 54		22 37
Sheffield [7]	a		11 34		12 34			13 34		14 35	15 34	16 34					17 37		18 41		19 33	20 36	21 35		23 35
	d		11 38		12 38			13 38		14 38	15 38	16 38					17 44		18 45		19 38	20 41	21 39		23 37
Chesterfield	d		11 53		12 53			13 52		14 53	15 53	16 56					18 02		19 01		19 53	20 58	21 55		00 02
Alfreton	d		12 03		13 03			14 03		15 07	16 03	17 07					18 12		19 11		20 04	21 09	22 05		
Langley Mill	d																						22 12		
Nottingham [8]	a		12 30		13 30			14 31		15 28	16 33	17 31					18 34		19 38		20 31	21 38	22 38		00 41
	d		12 34		13 34			14 34		15 34		17 34					18 35				20 34				
Grantham [7]	d		13 07		14 07			15 07		16 07		18 12					19 07				21 07				
Birmingham New Street [12]	d	11 22		12 22		13 22			14 22				15 22	16 22	16 52	17 22		18 22		19 22				20 22	
Coleshill Parkway	d	11 35		12 35		13 35			14 35				15 35	16 35	17 05	17 35		18 35		19 35				20 35	
Nuneaton	d	11 52		12 52		13 52			14 52				15 52	16 52	12 52	17 22		18 52		19 52				20 52	
Leicester	d	12 17		13 17		14 17			15 17				16 17	17 17	13 17	17 50		19 17		20 17				21 17	
Melton Mowbray	d	12 33		13 33		14 33			15 33				16 33	17 33	13 33	13 07		19 33		20 33				21 33	
Oakham	d	12 45		13 45		14 45			15 45				16 45	17 45	13 45	13 19		19 45		20 45				21 45	
Stamford	d	13 01		14 01		15 01			16 01				17 01	18 01	14 01	13 40		20 01		21 01				22 01	
Peterborough [8]	a	13 16	13 38	14 16	14 38	15 16		15 34	16 16	16 34		18 41	17 16	18 16	14 16	13 57	19 36	20 16		21 16	21 35			22 16	
	d	13 16	13 40	14 18	14 40	15 16		15 35	16 18	16 36		18 42	17 18	18 18	14 18	13 59	19 37	20 18		21 16	21 37			22 18	
March	a	13 33		14 33		15 34			16 33			18 58	17 36	18 33	14 33	1[illegible] 14		20 33		21 34				22 35	
Ely [6]	a	13 52	14 13	14 52	15 13	15 52		16 08	16 52	17 09			17 58	18 52	14 52	1[illegible] 32	20 13	20 52		21 52	22 10			22 54	
Cambridge	a	14 08		15 08		16 08			17 08				18 16	19 08	15 08	1[illegible] 50		21 08		22 08				23 11	
Audley End	a	14 23		15 23		16 23			17 23				18 31	19 23	15 23			21 03		22 23					
Stansted Airport ✈	a	14 45		15 45		16 45			17 39				18 45	19 42	15 45			21 45		22 53					
Thetford	a		14 37		15 37			16 33		17 33		19 49					20 36				22 34				
Norwich	a		15 13		16 13			17 13		18 13		20 22					21 13				23 18				

A MO from 13 September
B MO from 19 July until 6 September
C MO until 12 July
D from 27 September
E until 24 September

For connections to Ipswich please refer to Table 14

Table 49

Saturdays

North West England and Birmingham - East Midlands - East Anglia- Stansted Airport

		EM	EM	EM	XC	EM	XC	EM	EM	NT		EM	XC	EM	XC	EM	XC	EM	XC	EM		XC	EM	XC	EM
		◇	◇		◇1	◇	◇1	A	B			◇	◇1	◇	◇1	◇	◇1	◇	◇1	◇		◇1	◇	◇1	◇
Liverpool Lime Street [10]	d	21p37														06 49		07 42		08 52			09 52		10 52
Liverpool South Parkway [7] ✈	d	21p47														06 59		07 52		09 03			10 03		11 03
Widnes	d	21p55														07 07		08 05		09 11			10 11		11 11
Warrington Central	d	22p03														07 15		08 13		09 19			10 19		11 19
Manchester Oxford Road	d	22p24														07 38		08 39		09 39			10 39		11 39
Manchester Piccadilly [10]	d	22p28														07 42		08 43		09 43			10 43		11 43
Stockport	d	22p37														07 54		08 54		09 54			10 54		11 54
Sheffield [7]	a	23p35														08 34		09 34		10 34			11 34		12 34
	d	23p37								05 54						08 38		09 38		10 38			11 38		12 38
Chesterfield	d	00 02								06 20						08 53		09 53		10 53			11 53		12 53
Alfreton	d									06 30						09 03		10 03		11 03			12 03		13 03
Langley Mill	d									06 38															
Nottingham [8]	a	00 41								07 04						09 30		10 30		11 29			12 29		13 30
	d		05 04	05 10		05 54		06 53	06 55			07 45		08 34		09 34		10 34		11 34			12 34		13 34
Grantham [7]	d			05 51								08 16		09 11		10 08		11 07		12 07			13 08		14 07
Birmingham New Street [12]	d				05 22		06 22						07 22		08 22		09 22		10 22			11 22		12 22	
Coleshill Parkway	d				05 35		06 35						07 35		08 35		09 35		10 35			11 35		12 35	
Nuneaton	d				05 52		06 52						07 52		08 52		09 52		10 52			11 52		12 52	
Leicester	d				06 13		07 15						08 15		09 15		10 15		11 15			12 15		13 15	
Melton Mowbray	d		05 37		06 31	06 50	07 31						08 31		09 31		10 31		11 31			12 31		13 31	
Oakham	d		05 49		06 43	07 02	07 43						08 43		09 43		10 43		11 43			12 43		13 43	
Stamford	d		06 06		06 57	07 16	07 59						08 59		09 59		10 59		11 59			12 59		13 59	
Peterborough [8]	a		06 19	06 25	07 11	07 33	08 16	09 27	09 27			08 44	09 16	09 43	10 14	10 37	11 16	11 36	12 14	12 38		13 16	13 35	14 16	14 39
	d		06 27		07 13	07 35	08 18					08 46	09 18	09 46	10 18	10 44	11 16	11 38	12 18	12 40		13 18	13 38	14 18	14 41
March	a		06 42		07 31	07 50	08 33						09 33		10 33		11 34		12 33			13 34		14 33	
Ely [6]	a		07 01		07 52	08 11	08 52					09 19	09 52	10 19	10 52	11 17	11 52	12 11	12 52	13 13		13 52	14 11	14 52	15 14
Cambridge	a				08 08		09 08						10 08		11 08		12 08		13 08			14 08		15 08	
Audley End	a				08 23		09 23						10 23		11 23		12 23		13 23			14 23		15 23	
Stansted Airport ✈	a				08 45		09 45						10 45		11 45		12 45		13 45			14 45		15 45	
Thetford	a		07 30			08 36						09 44		10 44		11 44		12 35		13 39			14 35		15 38
Norwich	a		08 13			09 15						10 19		11 18		12 18		13 13		14 13			15 13		16 13

		XC	EM	XC	EM	EM		XC	XC	EM	EM	XC	XC	XC	EM	EM		EM	XC	EM
		◇1	◇	◇1	◇	◇		◇1	◇1	◇	◇	◇1	◇1	◇1	◇	◇		◇	◇1	◇
Liverpool Lime Street [10]	d		11 52		12 52	13 52				14 52	16 52				17 52	18 52		19 52		20 52
Liverpool South Parkway [7] ✈	d		12 03		13 03	14 03				15 03	17 03				18 03	19 03		20 03		21 03
Widnes	d		12 11		13 11	14 11				15 11	17 11				18 11	19 11		20 11		21 11
Warrington Central	d		12 19		13 19	14 19				15 19	17 19				18 19	19 19		20 19		21 19
Manchester Oxford Road	d		12 39		13 39	14 39				15 39	17 39				18 39	19 39		20 39		21 39
Manchester Piccadilly [10]	d		12 43		13 43	14 43				15 43	17 43				18 43	19 43		20 43		21 43
Stockport	d		12 54		13 54	14 54				15 54	17 54				18 54	19 54		20 54		21 52
Sheffield [7]	a		13 34		14 34	15 34				16 35	18 35				19 35	20 35		21 34		22 31
	d		13 38		14 38	15 38				16 38	18 38				19 38	20 41		21 38		22 35
Chesterfield	d		13 53		14 53	15 53				16 53	18 53				19 53	20 59		21 54		22 51
Alfreton	d		14 03		15 04	16 03				17 04	19 03				20 04	21 09		22 05		
Langley Mill	d																	22 12		
Nottingham [8]	a		14 29		15 29	16 33				17 29	19 33				20 31	21 33		22 33		23 31
	d		14 34		15 34					17 34					20 34					
Grantham [7]	d		15 07		16 07					18 15					21 07					
Birmingham New Street [12]	d	13 22		14 22				15 22	16 22			17 22	18 22	19 22					20 22	
Coleshill Parkway	d	13 35		14 35				15 35	16 35			17 35	18 35	19 35					20 35	
Nuneaton	d	13 52		14 52				15 52	16 52			17 52	18 52	19 52					20 52	
Leicester	d	14 15		15 15				16 15	17 15			18 15	19 15	20 15					21 15	
Melton Mowbray	d	14 31		15 31				16 31	17 31			18 31	19 31	20 31					21 31	
Oakham	d	14 43		15 43				16 43	17 43			18 43	19 43	20 43					21 43	
Stamford	d	14 59		15 59				16 59	17 59			18 59	19 59	20 59					21 59	
Peterborough [8]	a	15 16	15 34	16 16	16 38			17 16	18 14	18 42		19 16	20 14	21 16	21 34				22 16	
	d	15 18	15 36	16 18	16 39			17 18	18 18	18 42		19 18	20 18	21 18	21 36				22 18	
March	a	15 34		16 33				17 37	18 33	19 01		19 33	20 33	21 34					22 33	
Ely [6]	a	15 52	16 09	16 52	17 13			17 59	18 52	19 19		19 52	20 52	21 52	22 10				22 53	
Cambridge	a	16 08		17 08				18 16	19 08			20 08	21 08	22 08					23 10	
Audley End	a	16 23		17 23				18 33	19 24			20 23	21 23	22 23						
Stansted Airport ✈	a	16 45		17 45				18 53	19 45			20 45	21 45	22 45						
Thetford	a		16 34		17 37					19 44					22 34					
Norwich	a		17 13		18 18					20 18					23 18					

A from 2 October
B until 25 September

For connections to Ipswich please refer to Table 14

Table 49

Sundays until 05 September

North West England and Birmingham - East Midlands - East Anglia- Stansted Airport

Station		EM	EM ◇	NT	EM ◇ 🍴	XC ◇1 B 🍴	XC ◇1 C 🍴	EM ◇	XC ◇1 B 🍴	XC ◇1 C 🍴	EM ◇	XC ◇1 B 🍴	XC ◇1 C 🍴	EM ◇	XC ◇1 🍴	EM ◇ B	EM ◇ C	XC ◇1 🍴	EM ◇	XC ◇1 B 🍴	XC ◇1 C 🍴	EM ◇ C	EM ◇ B
Liverpool Lime Street 10	d															12 52	12 52		13 52			14 52	14 52
Liverpool South Parkway 7 ✈	d															13 03	13 03		14 03			15 03	15 03
Widnes	d															13 11	13 11		14 11			15 11	15 11
Warrington Central	d															13 19	13 19		14 19			15 19	15 19
Manchester Oxford Road	d															13 39	13 39		14 39			15 39	15 39
Manchester Piccadilly 10 ⛴	d													12 44		13 44	13 44		14 44			15 44	15 44
Stockport	d													12 54		13 54	13 54		14 54			15 54	15 54
Sheffield 7 ⛴	a													13 37		14 42	14 39		15 33			16 36	16 36
	d			09 00	10 49						12 49			13 49		14 53	14 53		15 43			16 40	16 40
Chesterfield	d			09 17	11 04						13 03			14 03		15 07	15 07		15 57			16 56	16 56
Alfreton	d			09 28	11 14						13 14			14 14		15 18	15 18		16 08			17 07	17 07
Langley Mill	d			09 35												15 25	15 25		16 15			17 14	17 14
Nottingham 8 ⛴	a			09 53	11 38						13 39			14 40		15 44	15 44		16 33			17 32	17 32
	d	09 40	09 52		11 45			12 39			13 41			14 45		15 52	15 52		16 45			17 36	17 36
Grantham 7	d	10 18	10 29		12 18			13 14			14 14					16 25	16 25		17 25			18 18	18 18
Birmingham New Street 12	d					11 22	11 22		12 22	12 22		13 22	13 22		14 22			15 22		16 22	16 22		
Coleshill Parkway	d					11 35	11 35		12 35	12 35		13 35	13 35		14 35			15 35		16 35	16 35		
Nuneaton	d					11 52	11 52		12 52	12 52		13 52	13 52		14 52			15 52		16 52	16 52		
Leicester	d					12 15	12 14		13 15	13 14		14 15	14 14		15 15			16 13		17 16	17 18		
Melton Mowbray	d					12 33	12 30		13 33	13 33		14 33	14 33		15 33			16 31		17 33	17 33		
Oakham	d					12 45	12 42		13 45	13 45		14 45	14 45		15 45			16 43		17 45	17 45		
Stamford	d					13 01	12 58		14 01	14 01		15 01	15 01		16 01			16 59		18 01	18 01		
Peterborough 8	a		11 06		12 50	13 16	13 16	13 41	14 16	14 16	14 41	15 16	15 16	16 04	16 16	16 56	16 56	17 14	17 52	18 16	18 16	18 45	18 49
	d		11 09		12 53	13 18	13 18	13 43	14 18	14 18	14 42	15 18	15 18	16 05	16 18	16 58	16 58	17 18	17 53	18 18	18 18	18 47	18 51
March	a		11 25			13 33	13 33		14 33	14 33		15 33	15 33		16 33			17 33	18 12	18 33	18 33		
Ely 8	a		11 48		13 32	13 52	13 52	14 21	14 52	14 52	15 21	15 52	15 52	16 38	16 52	17 31	17 31	17 52	18 31	18 52	18 52	19 20	19 24
Cambridge	a					14 08	14 08		15 08	15 08		16 08	16 08		17 07			18 07		19 07	19 07		
Audley End	a					14 23	14 23		15 23	15 23		16 23	16 23		17 23			18 23		19 23	19 23		
Stansted Airport ✈	a					14 43	14 43		15 43	15 43		16 37	16 37		17 43			18 43		19 43	19 43		
Thetford	a		12 23		13 57			14 48			15 48			17 02		17 56	17 56		18 55			19 48	19 52
Norwich	a		13 11		14 35			15 28			16 35			17 35		18 29	18 29		19 29			20 28	20 32

Station		XC ◇1 🍴	EM ◇ A	EM ◇	XC ◇1 B 🍴	XC ◇1 C 🍴	XC ◇1 B 🍴	XC ◇1 C 🍴	EM ◇	EM ◇	EM ◇	XC ◇1 B 🍴	XC ◇1 C 🍴	EM ◇ B	EM ◇ C
Liverpool Lime Street 10	d		15 52	16 52					17 52	18 52	19 52			21 22	21 22
Liverpool South Parkway 7 ✈	d		16 03	17 03					18 03	19 03	20 03				
Widnes	d		16 11	17 11					18 11	19 11	20 11			21 39	21 39
Warrington Central	d		16 19	17 19					18 19	19 19	20 19			21 47	21 47
Manchester Oxford Road	d		16 39	17 39					18 39	19 39	20 39			22 07	22 07
Manchester Piccadilly 10 ⛴	d		16 43	17 44					18 44	19 44	20 44			22 11	22 11
Stockport	d		16 54	17 54					18 54	19 54	20 54			22 28	22 28
Sheffield 7 ⛴	a		17 37	18 37					19 34	20 34	21 36			23 25	23 25
	d		17 44	18 41					19 40	20 40	21 40			23 29	23 29
Chesterfield	d		17 58	18 56					19 55	20 55	21 54			23 43	23 43
Alfreton	d		18 11	19 06					20 06	21 06	22 05			23 54	23 54
Langley Mill	d			19 14					20 14	21 14	22 12			00 03	00 02
Nottingham 8 ⛴	a		18 33	19 36					20 31	21 36	22 35			00 30	00 33
	d		18 34						20 44						
Grantham 7	d		19 05						21 19						
Birmingham New Street 12	d	17 22			18 22	18 22	19 22	19 22				20 22	20 22		
Coleshill Parkway	d	17 35			18 35	18 35	19 35	19 35				20 35	20 35		
Nuneaton	d	17 52			18 52	18 52	19 52	19 52				20 51	20 51		
Leicester	d	18 15			19 14	19 15	20 15	20 14				21 15	21 13		
Melton Mowbray	d	18 31			19 31	19 31	20 31	20 31				21 31	21 31		
Oakham	d	18 43			19 43	19 43	20 43	20 43				21 43	21 43		
Stamford	d	18 59			19 59	19 59	20 59	20 59				21 59	21 59		
Peterborough 8	a	19 14	19 34		20 14	20 14	21 14	21 14	21 46			22 14	22 14		
	d	19 18	19 37		20 18	20 18	21 18	21 18	21 48			22 18	22 18		
March	a	19 33			20 33	20 33	21 33	21 33				22 33	22 33		
Ely 8	a	19 52	20 13		20 52	20 52	21 52	21 52	22 21			22 52	22 52		
Cambridge	a	20 07			21 07	21 07	22 07	22 07				23 07	23 07		
Audley End	a	20 23			21 23	21 23	22 23	22 23							
Stansted Airport ✈	a	20 43			21 43	21 43	22 43	22 43							
Thetford	a		20 35						22 45						
Norwich	a		21 13						23 25						

A until 10 December
B from 18 July until 5 September
C until 11 July

For connections to Ipswich please refer to Table 14

Table 49

Sundays 12 September to 17 October

North West England and Birmingham - East Midlands - East Anglia- Stansted Airport

Station		NT	XC ◇1 🍴	EM ◇	XC ◇1 🍴	EM ◇	XC ◇1 🍴	EM ◇	XC ◇1 🍴	EM ◇	XC ◇1 🍴	EM ◇	XC ◇1 🍴	EM ◇	XC ◇1 🍴	EM ◇ A	EM ◇	XC ◇1 🍴	XC ◇1 🍴	EM ◇	EM ◇	EM ◇	XC ◇1 🍴
Liverpool Lime Street 10	d									12 52		13 52		14 52		15 52	16 52			17 52	18 52	19 52	
Liverpool South Parkway 7 ✈	d									13 03		14 03		15 03		16 03	17 03			18 03	19 03	20 03	
Widnes	d									13 11		14 11		15 11		16 11	17 11			18 11	19 11	20 11	
Warrington Central	d									13 19		14 19		15 19		16 19	17 19			18 19	19 19	20 19	
Manchester Oxford Road	d									13 39		14 39		15 39		16 39	17 39			18 39	19 39	20 39	
Manchester Piccadilly 10 ⛴	d							12 44		13 44		14 44		15 44		16 43	17 44			18 44	19 44	20 44	
Stockport	d							12 55		13 54		14 54		15 54		16 54	17 54			18 54	19 54	20 54	
Sheffield 7 ⛴	a							13 37		14 39		15 37		16 36		17 37	18 37			19 34	20 34	21 36	
	d	09 00				12 49		13 49		14 53		15 43		16 40		17 44	18 41			19 40	20 40	21 40	
Chesterfield	d	09 17				13 03		14 03		15 07		15 57		16 56		17 58	18 56			19 55	20 55	21 54	
Alfreton	d	09 28				13 14		14 14		15 19		16 08		17 08		18 11	19 06			20 06	21 06	22 05	
Langley Mill	d	09 35								15 26		16 15		17 16			19 14			20 14	21 13	22 12	
Nottingham 8 ⛴	a	09 53				13 39		14 38		15 44		16 33		17 32		18 33	19 35			20 31	21 36	22 35	
	d			12 35		13 43		14 43		15 48		16 38		17 35		18 34				20 40			
Grantham 7	d															19 05							
Birmingham New Street 12	d		11 22		12 22		13 22		14 22		15 22		16 22		17 22			18 22	19 22				20 22
Coleshill Parkway	d		11 35		12 35		13 35		14 35		15 35		16 35		17 35			18 35	19 35				20 35
Nuneaton	d		11 52		12 52		13 52		14 52		15 52		16 52		17 52			18 52	19 52				20 51
Leicester	d		12 15		13 15		14 15		15 15		16 15		17 15		18 14			19 15	20 15				21 15
Melton Mowbray	d		12 33		13 33		14 33		15 33		16 32		17 33		18 30			19 31	20 31				21 31
Oakham	d		12 45		13 45		14 45		15 45		16 43		17 45		18 42			19 43	20 43				21 43
Stamford	d		13 01		14 01		15 01		16 01		16 59		18 01		18 58			19 59	20 59				21 59
Peterborough 8	a		13 16	13 41	14 16	14 50	15 16	16 02	16 16	16 59	17 14	17 50	18 16	18 45	19 14	19 34		20 14	21 14	21 46			22 14
	d		13 18	13 43	14 18	14 53	15 18	16 03	16 18	17 00	17 18	17 56	18 18	18 47	19 18	19 37		20 18	21 18	21 48			22 18
March	a		13 33		14 33		15 33		16 33		17 33	18 11	18 33		19 33			20 33	21 33				22 33
Ely 8	a		13 52	14 16	14 52	15 29	15 52	16 38	16 52	17 33	17 52	18 31	18 52	19 20	19 52	20 13		20 52	21 52	22 21			22 52
Cambridge	a		14 08		15 08		16 08		17 07		18 07		19 07		20 07			21 07	22 07				23 07
Audley End	a		14 23		15 23		16 23		17 23		18 23		19 23		20 23			21 23	22 23				
Stansted Airport ✈	a		14 43		15 43		16 37		17 43		18 43		19 43		20 43			21 43	22 43				
Thetford	a			14 50		15 53		17 02		17 58		18 55		19 48		20 35				22 45			
Norwich	a			15 31		16 35		17 35		18 32		19 29		20 28		21 13				23 25			

Station		EM ◇
Liverpool Lime Street 10	d	21 22
Liverpool South Parkway 7 ✈	d	
Widnes	d	21 39
Warrington Central	d	21 47
Manchester Oxford Road	d	22 07
Manchester Piccadilly 10 ⛴	d	22 11
Stockport	d	22 28
Sheffield 7 ⛴	a	23 25
	d	23 29
Chesterfield	d	23 43
Alfreton	d	23 54
Langley Mill	d	00 02
Nottingham 8 ⛴	a	00 30
	d	
Grantham 7	d	
Birmingham New Street 12	d	
Coleshill Parkway	d	
Nuneaton	d	
Leicester	d	
Melton Mowbray	d	
Oakham	d	
Stamford	d	
Peterborough 8	a	
	d	
March	a	
Ely 8	a	
Cambridge	a	
Audley End	a	
Stansted Airport ✈	a	
Thetford	a	
Norwich	a	

A until 10 December

For connections to Ipswich please refer to Table 14

Table 49

Sundays
from 24 October

North West England and Birmingham - East Midlands - East Anglia- Stansted Airport

		NT	XC ◇1 ☕	EM ◇	XC ◇1 ☕	EM ◇	XC ◇1 ☕	EM ◇	XC ◇1 ☕	EM ◇
Liverpool Lime Street 10	d									12 52
Liverpool South Parkway 7 ✈	d									13 03
Widnes	d									13 11
Warrington Central	d									13 19
Manchester Oxford Road	d									13 39
Manchester Piccadilly 10	d							12 44		13 44
Stockport	d							12 55		13 54
Sheffield 7	a							13 37		14 39
	d	09 00				12 49		13 49		14 53
Chesterfield	d	09 17				13 03		14 03		15 07
Alfreton	d	09 28				13 14		14 14		15 19
Langley Mill	d	09 35								15 26
Nottingham 8	a	09 53				13 39		14 38		15 45
	d			12 39		13 49		14 43		15 52
Grantham 7	d			13 14		14 22				16 25
Birmingham New Street 12	d		11 22		12 22		13 22		14 22	
Coleshill Parkway	d		11 35		12 35		13 35		14 35	
Nuneaton	d		11 52		12 52		13 52		14 52	
Leicester	d		12 15		13 15		14 15		15 15	
Melton Mowbray	d		12 33		13 33		14 33		15 33	
Oakham	d		12 45		13 45		14 45		15 45	
Stamford	d		13 01		14 01		15 01		16 01	
Peterborough 8	a		13 16	13 41	14 16	14 52	15 16	16 02	16 16	16 56
	d		13 18	13 43	14 18	14 53	15 18	16 03	16 18	16 58
March	a		13 33		14 33		15 33		16 33	
Ely 8	a		13 52	14 16	14 52	15 29	15 52	16 38	16 52	17 31
Cambridge	a		14 08		15 08		16 08		17 07	
Audley End	a		14 23		15 23		16 23		17 23	
Stansted Airport ✈	a		14 43		15 43		16 37		17 43	
Thetford	a			14 50		15 53		17 02		17 56
Norwich	a			15 31		16 35		17 35		18 29

		XC ◇1 ☕	EM ◇	XC ◇1 ☕	EM ◇	XC ◇1 ☕	EM ◇ A	EM ◇	XC ◇1 ☕	XC ◇1 ☕	EM ◇	EM ◇	EM ◇	XC ◇1 ☕
Liverpool Lime Street 10	d		13 52		14 52		15 52	16 52			17 52	18 52	19 52	
Liverpool South Parkway 7 ✈	d		14 03		15 03		16 03	17 03			18 03	19 03	20 03	
Widnes	d		14 11		15 11		16 11	17 11			18 11	19 11	20 11	
Warrington Central	d		14 19		15 19		16 19	17 19			18 19	19 19	20 19	
Manchester Oxford Road	d		14 39		15 39		16 39	17 39			18 39	19 39	20 39	
Manchester Piccadilly 10	d		14 44		15 44		16 43	17 44			18 44	19 44	20 44	
Stockport	d		14 54		15 54		16 54	17 54			18 54	19 54	20 54	
Sheffield 7	a		15 37		16 36		17 37	18 37			19 34	20 34	21 36	
	d		15 43		16 40		17 44	18 41			19 40	20 40	21 40	
Chesterfield	d		15 57		16 56		17 58	18 56			19 55	20 55	21 54	
Alfreton	d		16 08		17 07		18 11	19 06			20 06	21 06	22 05	
Langley Mill	d		16 15		17 14			19 14			20 14	21 13	22 12	
Nottingham 8	a		16 33		17 32		18 33	19 35			20 31	21 36	22 35	
	d		16 45		17 36		18 34				20 44			
Grantham 7	d		17 23		18 18		19 05				21 19			
Birmingham New Street 12	d	15 22		16 22		7 22			18 22	19 22				20 22
Coleshill Parkway	d	15 35		16 35		7 35			18 35	19 35				20 35
Nuneaton	d	15 52		16 52		7 52			18 52	19 52				20 51
Leicester	d	16 15		17 15		8 14			19 15	20 15				21 15
Melton Mowbray	d	16 32		17 33		8 30			19 31	20 31				21 31
Oakham	d	16 43		17 45		8 42			19 43	20 43				21 43
Stamford	d	16 59		18 01		8 58			19 59	20 59				21 59
Peterborough 8	a	17 14	17 53	18 16	18 45	9 14	19 34		20 14	21 14	21 46			22 14
	d	17 18	17 56	18 18	18 47	9 18	19 37		20 18	21 18	21 48			22 18
March	a	17 33	18 11	18 33		9 33			20 33	21 33				22 33
Ely 8	a	17 52	18 31	18 52	19 20	9 52	20 13		20 52	21 52	22 21			22 52
Cambridge	a	18 07		19 07		20 07			21 07	22 07				23 07
Audley End	a	18 23		19 23		20 23			21 23	22 23				
Stansted Airport ✈	a	18 43		19 43		20 43			21 43	22 43				
Thetford	a		18 55		19 48		20 35				22 45			
Norwich	a		19 29		20 28		21 13				23 25			

		EM ◇
Liverpool Lime Street 10	d	21 22
Liverpool South Parkway 7 ✈	d	
Widnes	d	21 39
Warrington Central	d	21 47
Manchester Oxford Road	d	22 07
Manchester Piccadilly 10	d	22 11
Stockport	d	22 28
Sheffield 7	a	23 25
	d	23 29
Chesterfield	d	23 43
Alfreton	d	23 54
Langley Mill	d	00 02
Nottingham 8	a	00 30
	d	
Grantham 7	d	
Birmingham New Street 12	d	
Coleshill Parkway	d	
Nuneaton	d	
Leicester	d	
Melton Mowbray	d	
Oakham	d	
Stamford	d	
Peterborough 8	a	
	d	
March	a	
Ely 8	a	
Cambridge	a	
Audley End	a	
Stansted Airport ✈	a	
Thetford	a	
Norwich	a	

A until 10 December

Network Diagram for Tables 50, 55, 56, 57

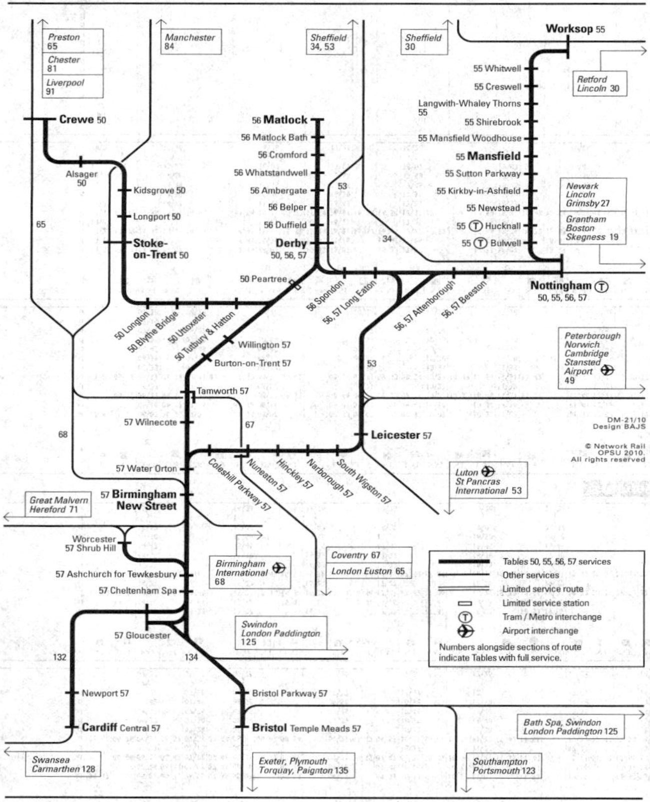

Table 50

Mondays to Fridays

Derby - Stoke-on-Trent and Crewe

		NT	NT	LM	NT	LM	NT	LM	NT	LM	NT	LM	NT	LM	NT	LM	NT	LM	NT	LM	NT	LM	NT
				◇1		◇1		1		◇1		◇1		◇1		1		◇1		◇1		1	
Derby 6	d																						
Peartree	d																						
Tutbury & Hatton	d																						
Uttoxeter	d																						
Blythe Bridge	d																						
Longton	d																						
Stoke-on-Trent	a																						
	d	06 30	07 17	07 26	07 57	08 13	08 58	09 13	09 58	10 13	10 58	11 13	11 58	12 13	12 58	13 13	13 58	14 13	14 58	15 13	15 58	16 13	16 58
Longport	d	06 34	07 21																				
Kidsgrove	d	06a38	07a25	07 34	08a04	08 21	09a05	09 21	10a05	10 21	11a05	11 21	12a05	12 21	13a05	13 21	14a05	14 21	15a05	15 21	16a05	16 21	17a05
Alsager	d			07 39		08 26		09 26		10 26		11 26		12 26		13 26		14 26		15 26		16 26	
Crewe 10	a			07 49		08 38		09 38		10 38		11 38		12 38		13 38		14 38		15 39		16 38	

		LM	NT	LM	NT	NT	NT	LM	NT
		◇1		◇1				◇1	
Derby 6	d								
Peartree	d								
Tutbury & Hatton	d								
Uttoxeter	d								
Blythe Bridge	d								
Longton	d								
Stoke-on-Trent	a								
	d	17 13	17 58	18 41	18 58	19 58	20 58	21 05	22 18
Longport	d								
Kidsgrove	d	17 21	18a05	18 49	19a05	20a05	21a05	21 14	22a25
Alsager	d	17 26		18 54				21 18	
Crewe 10	a	17 38		19 05				21 27	

Saturdays

		NT	LM	NT	LM	NT	LM	NT	LM	NT	LM	NT	LM	NT	LM	NT	LM	NT	LM	NT	LM	NT	LM
			◇1		◇1		◇1		◇1		◇1		1		◇1		◇1		◇1		◇1		◇1
Derby 6	d																						
Peartree	d																						
Tutbury & Hatton	d																						
Uttoxeter	d																						
Blythe Bridge	d																						
Longton	d																						
Stoke-on-Trent	a																						
	d	06 57	07 13	07 57	08 13	08 58	09 13	09 58	10 13	10 58	11 13	11 58	12 13	12 58	13 13	13 58	14 13	14 58	15 13	15 58	16 13	16 58	17 13
Longport	d																						
Kidsgrove	d	07a04	07 21	08a04	08 21	09a05	09 21	10a05	10 21	11a05	11 21	12a05	12 21	13a05	13 21	14a05	14 21	15a05	15 21	16a05	16 21	17a05	17 21
Alsager	d		07 26		08 26		09 26		10 26		11 26		12 26		13 26		14 26		15 26		16 26		17 26
Crewe 10	a		07 36		08 37		09 38		10 38		11 38		12 38		13 38		14 38		15 38		16 38		17 38

		NT	LM	NT	LM	NT	LM	NT	LM	NT
			◇1		◇1		◇1		◇1	
										A
Derby 6	d									
Peartree	d									
Tutbury & Hatton	d									
Uttoxeter	d									
Blythe Bridge	d									
Longton	d									
Stoke-on-Trent	a									
	d	17 58	18 41	18 58	19 13	19 58	20 13	20 58	21 16	22 18
Longport	d									
Kidsgrove	d	18a05	18 50	19a05	19 21	20a05	20 21	21a05	21 24	22a25
Alsager	d		18 54		19 26		20 25		21 28	
Crewe 10	a		19 05		19 36		20 35		21 38	

Sundays

		LM	LM	LM	LM	LM	NT	LM	LM	NT	LM	NT
		1		◇1	◇1	◇1		◇1	◇1		◇1	
		B	C (bus)	C	B							
Derby 6	d											
Peartree	d											
Tutbury & Hatton	d											
Uttoxeter	d											
Blythe Bridge	d											
Longton	d											
Stoke - on-Trent	a											
	d	12 03	12 20	13 18	13 20	15 41	16 01	17 42	19 41	20 01	21 43	22 39
Longport	d											
Kidsgrove	d	12 11	12 38	13 26	13 28	15 52	16a08	17 50	19 52	20a08	21 54	22a46
Alsager	d	12 15	12 52	13 30	13 32	15 58		17 54	19 59		22 01	
Crewe 10	a	12 26	13 07	13 41	13 43	16 07		18 06	20 08		22 12	

A from 17 July **B** from 18 July **C** until 11 July

Table 50

Mondays to Fridays

Crewe and Stoke-on-Trent - Derby

		XC	NT	EM	LM	EM	LM	EM	NT	LM	EM	NT	LM	EM	NT	LM	EM	NT	LM	EM	NT	LM	EM
		◇1	1		◇1		◇1		1	◇1		1	◇1		1	◇1		1	◇1		1	◇1	
		(trolley)		A		A		A			A			A			A			A			A
Crewe 10	d	05 47		06 07	06 35	06 58	07 33	08 07		08 33	09 07		09 33	10 07		10 33	11 07		11 33	12 07		12 33	13 07
Alsager	d			06 16	06 44	07 07	07 41	08 16		08 41	09 16		09 41	10 16		10 41	11 16		11 41	12 16		12 41	13 16
Kidsgrove	d		06 16	06 21	06 48	07 12	07 46	08 21	08 32	08 46	09 21	09 32	09 47	10 21	10 32	10 46	11 21	11 32	11 47	12 21	12 32	12 46	13 21
Longport	d			06 27		07 18		08 27			09 27			10 27			11 27			12 27			13 27
Stoke-on-Trent	a	06 06	06 26	06 31	06 57	07 23	07 54	08 31	08 42	08 54	09 31	09 42	09 55	10 31	10 42	10 54	11 31	11 42	11 55	12 31	12 42	12 54	13 31
	d			06 33		07 24		08 33			09 33			10 33			11 33			12 33			13 33
Longton	d			06 39		07 30		08 39			09 39			10 39			11 40			12 39			13 39
Blythe Bridge	d			06 45		07 36		08 45			09 45			10 45			11 46			12 45			13 45
Uttoxeter	d			06 58		07 49		08 58			09 58			10 58			11 58			12 58			13 58
Tutbury & Hatton	d			07 07		07 58		09 07			10 07			11 07			12 07			13 07			14 07
Peartree	d			07 20																			
Derby 6	a			07 27		08 17		09 26			10 26			11 26			12 26			13 26			14 26

		NT	LM	EM	NT	LM	EM	NT	LM	EM	NT	LM	EM	NT	LM	EM	NT	LM	EM	NT	NT	NT	NT
		1	◇1		1	◇1		1	◇1		1	◇1		1	◇1		1	◇1		1	1	1	1
				A			A			A			A			A			A				
Crewe 10	d		13 33	14 07		14 33	15 07		15 33	16 07		16 33	17 07		17 33	18 07		18 33	19 07				
Alsager	d		13 41	14 16		14 41	15 16		15 41	16 16		16 41	17 16		17 41	18 16		18 41	19 16				
Kidsgrove	d	13 32	13 46	14 21	14 32	14 46	15 21	15 32	15 46	16 21	16 32	16 46	17 21	17 32	17 46	18 21	18 32	18 46	19 21	19 32	20 32	21 32	22 32
Longport	d			14 27			15 27			16 27			17 27			18 27			19 27				
Stoke-on-Trent	a	13 42	13 54	14 31	14 42	14 54	15 31	15 42	15 54	16 31	16 42	16 54	17 31	17 42	17 54	18 31	18 42	18 54	19 31	19 42	20 42	21 42	22 42
	d			14 33			15 33			16 33			17 33			18 33			19 33				
Longton	d			14 39			15 39			16 39			17 39			18 39			19 39				
Blythe Bridge	d			14 45			15 45			16 45			17 45			18 45			19 45				
Uttoxeter	d			14 58			15 58			16 58			17 58			18 58			19 58				
Tutbury & Hatton	d			15 07			16 07			17 07			18 07			19 07			20 07				
Peartree	d						16 18																
Derby 6	a			15 26			16 26			17 26			18 26			19 26			20 26				

Saturdays

		XC	NT	EM	LM	EM	NT	LM	EM	NT	LM	EM	NT	LM	EM	NT	LM	EM	NT	LM	EM	NT	LM
		◇1	1		◇1		1	◇1		1	◇1		1	◇1		1	◇1		1	◇1		1	◇1
		(trolley)		B		B			B			B			B			B			B		
Crewe 10	d	05 47		06 07	06 38	07 07		07 38	08 07		08 33	09 07		09 33	10 07		10 33	11 07		11 33	12 07		12 33
Alsager	d			06 16	06 47	07 16		07 46	08 16		08 41	09 16		09 41	10 16		10 41	11 16		11 41	12 16		12 41
Kidsgrove	d		06 16	06 21	06 51	07 21	07 28	07 51	08 21	08 32	08 46	09 21	09 32	09 46	10 21	10 32	10 46	11 21	11 32	11 46	12 21	12 32	12 46
Longport	d			06 27		07 27			08 27			09 27			10 27			11 27			12 27		
Stoke-on-Trent	a	06 07	06 26	06 31	06 59	07 31	07 40	07 59	08 31	08 42	08 54	09 31	09 42	09 54	10 31	10 42	10 54	11 31	11 42	11 54	12 31	12 42	12 54
	d			06 33		07 33			08 33			09 33			10 33			11 33			12 33		
Longton	d			06 39		07 39			08 39			09 39			10 39			11 39			12 39		
Blythe Bridge	d			06 45		07 45			08 45			09 45			10 45			11 45			12 45		
Uttoxeter	d			06 58		07 58			08 58			09 58			10 58			11 58			12 58		
Tutbury & Hatton	d			07 07		08 07			09 07			10 07			11 07			12 07			13 07		
Peartree	d			07 19																			
Derby 6	a			07 28		08 24			09 26			10 26			11 26			12 26			13 26		

		EM	NT	LM	EM	NT	LM	EM	NT	LM	EM	NT	LM	EM	NT	LM	EM	NT	LM	EM	NT	NT	NT
			1	◇1		1	◇1		1	◇1		1	◇1		1	◇1		1	◇1		1	1	1
		B			B			B			B			B			B			B			
Crewe 10	d	13 07		13 33	14 07		14 33	15 07		15 33	16 07		16 33	17 07		17 33	18 07		18 33	19 07			
Alsager	d	13 16		13 41	14 16		14 41	15 16		15 41	16 16		16 41	17 16		17 41	18 16		18 41	19 16			
Kidsgrove	d	13 21	13 32	13 46	14 21	14 32	14 46	15 21	15 32	15 46	16 21	16 32	16 46	17 21	17 32	17 46	18 21	18 32	18 46	19 21	19 32	20 32	21 32
Longport	d	13 27			14 27			15 27			16 27			17 27			18 27			19 27			
Stoke-on-Trent	a	13 31	13 42	13 54	14 31	14 42	14 54	15 31	15 42	15 54	16 31	16 42	16 54	17 31	17 42	17 54	18 31	18 42	18 54	19 31	19 42	20 42	21 42
	d	13 33			14 33			15 33			16 33			17 33			18 33			19 33			
Longton	d	13 39			14 39			15 39			16 39			17 39			18 39			19 39			
Blythe Bridge	d	13 45			14 45			15 45			16 45			17 45			18 45			19 45			
Uttoxeter	d	13 58			14 58			15 58			16 58			17 58			18 58			19 58			
Tutbury & Hatton	d	14 07			15 07			16 07			17 07			18 07			19 07			20 07			
Peartree	d							16 19															
Derby 6	a	14 26			15 26			16 26			17 26			18 26			19 25			20 26			

		NT
		1
		C
Crewe 10	d	
Alsager	d	
Kidsgrove	d	22 32
Longport	d	
Stoke-on-Trent	a	22 42
	d	
Longton	d	
Blythe Bridge	d	
Uttoxeter	d	
Tutbury & Hatton	d	
Peartree	d	
Derby 6	a	

A from 27 September **B** from 2 October **C** from 17 July

Table 50

Sundays

Crewe and Stoke-on-Trent - Derby

		LM	LM	LM	LM	LM	NT	LM	LM	NT	LM	NT
			1		◇1	◇1	1	◇1	◇1	1	◇1	1
			A	B	A							
		🚌		🚌								
Crewe 10	d	09 53	10 37	10 45	11 38	13 38		15 38	17 38		19 36	
Alsager	d	10 10	10 46	11 02	11 46	13 46		15 46	17 46		19 44	
Kidsgrove	d	10 24	10 50	11 16	11 52	13 51	15 25	15 52	17 51	19 28	19 50	22 26
Longport	d											
Stoke-on-Trent	a	10 39	10 57	11 32	11 59	13 58	15 37	15 59	17 58	19 40	19 57	22 36
	d											
Longton	d											
Blythe Bridge	d											
Uttoxeter	d											
Tutbury & Hatton	d											
Peartree	d											
Derby 6	a											

A from 18 July

B until 11 July

Route Diagram for Table 51

DM-5/10
Design BAJS

This Table summarises through services which, with their associated connecting services at Birmingham New Street, link centres in the North and South of the country. In certain instances a faster journey is possible via London and the relevant Table(s) should be consulted.

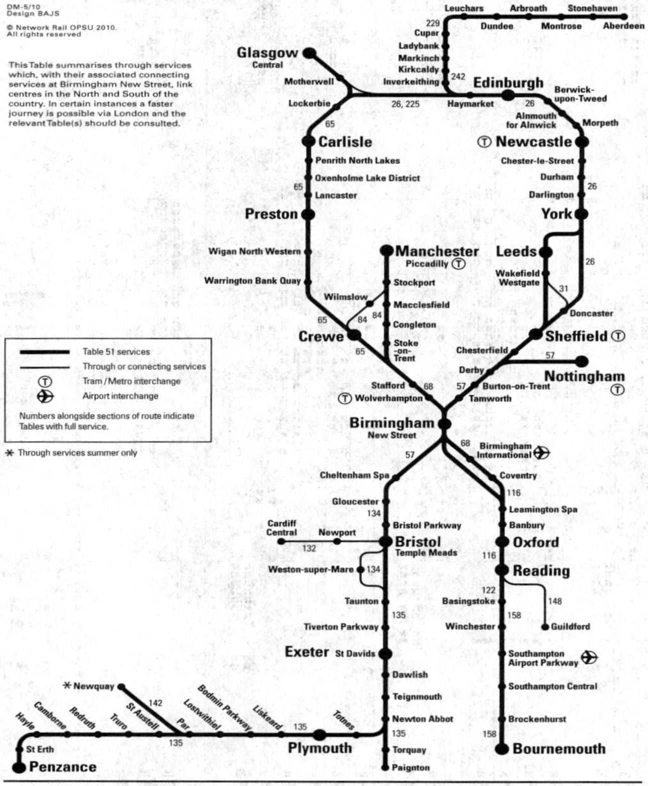

* Through services summer only

Scotland, The North East, North West England - The South West and South Coast

		XC	XC	XC	XC	XC	XC	XC	XC	XC	VT	XC	XC	XC	XC	XC	XC	XC	VT	XC
		◇1	◇1	◇1	◇1	◇1	◇1	◇1	◇1	◇1	◇1	◇1	■ 1	◇1	◇1	◇1	◇1	1	◇1	◇1
		⌶	⌶	⌶	⌶	⌶	⌶	⌶	⌶	⌶	⊠	⌶	⌶	⌶	⌶	⌶	⌶		⊠	⌶
Aberdeen	d																			
Stonehaven	d																			
Montrose	d																			
Arbroath	d																			
Dundee	d																			
Leuchars 3	d																			
Cupar	d																			
Ladybank	d																			
Markinch	d																			
Kirkcaldy	d																			
Inverkeithing	d																			
Glasgow Central 15	d																			
Motherwell	d																			
Haymarket	d																			
Edinburgh 10	d																			
Haymarket	d																			
Lockerbie	d																			
Carlisle 8	d																			
Penrith North Lakes	d																			
Oxenholme Lake District	d																			
Lancaster 6	d																		06 58	
Preston 8	d										06 16								07 17	
Wigan North Western	d										06 27								07 28	
Warrington Bank Quay	d										06 38								07 39	
Manchester Piccadilly 10 ⇌	d						05 00			06 00							07 06			07 26
Stockport	d									06 08							07 16			07 35
Wilmslow	d																			
Crewe 10	d						05 47			06 38	07 01								08 01	
Macclesfield	d																			07 49
Congleton	d																			
Stoke-on-Trent	d						06 07										07 44			08 07
Stafford	d						06 25			06 58										08 25
Wolverhampton 7 ⇌	d						06 41			07 15	07 31						08 15		08 32	08 41
Dunbar	d																			
Berwick-upon-Tweed	d																			
Alnmouth for Alnwick	d																			
Morpeth	d																			
Newcastle 8	d																			
Chester-le-Street	d																			
Durham	d																			
Darlington 7	d																			
York 8	d																			
Leeds 10	d				06 00											06 15				
Wakefield Westgate 7	d				06 12											06 27				
Doncaster 7	d															06 45				
Sheffield 7 ⇌	d				06 50				06 01							07 18				
Chesterfield	d				07 04				06 27							07 30				
Nottingham 8 ⇌	d							06 00					06 37		06 56			07 37		
Derby 6	d				07 26	06 10		06 36	06 48				07 06		07 36	07 50		08 06		
Burton-on-Trent	d				07 37	06 20		06 48	06 58				07 18		07 49	08 00		08 18		
Tamworth	d				07 49	06 31		07 00	07 09				07 30		08 01	08 11		08 30		
Birmingham New Street 12	a				08 09	06 52	06 58	07 24	07 27	07 31	07 55		07 55		08 24	08 29	08 31	08 54	08 55	08 58
Birmingham New Street 12	d	05 00	05 42	06 03	08 12	07 12	07 03	07 30	07 33	07 42		06 33	08 03	06 42	08 30	08 33	08 42			09 03
Cheltenham Spa	a	06 01	06 43		08 51	07 51		08 14		08 23				07 20	09 10		09 23			
Gloucester 7	a	06 16	06 53					08 27							09 22					
Bristol Parkway 7	a				09 24	08 25				08 56				07 56			09 56			
Bristol Temple Meads 10	a				09 39	08 40				09 14				08 08			10 08			
Newport (South Wales)	a	07 09	07 52					09 12							10 09					
Cardiff Central 7	a	07 26	08 08					09 30							10 25					
Weston-super-Mare	a																			
Taunton	a				10 16	09 15								08 42						
Tiverton Parkway	a				10 29	09 28								08 54						
Exeter St Davids 6	a				10 46	09 43								09 10						
Dawlish	a																			
Teignmouth	a																			
Newton Abbot	a				11 08	10 03														
Torquay	a													09 39						
Paignton	a													09 46						
Totnes	a				11 22	10 16														
Plymouth	a				11 51	10 46														
Liskeard 6	a																			
Bodmin Parkway	a																			
Lostwithiel	a																			
Par	a																			
Newquay	a																			
St Austell	a																			
Truro	a																			
Redruth	a																			
Camborne	a																			
Hayle	a																			
St Erth	a																			
Penzance	a																			
Birmingham International ✈	d			06 14			07 14						08 14							09 14
Coventry	d			06 25			07 25						08 25							09 25
Leamington Spa 8	d			06 38			07 38		08 04			07 00	08 38			09 00				09 38
Banbury	a			06 56			07 54		08 20			07 21	08 54			09 18				09 54
Oxford	a			07 14			08 14		08 40			07 41	09 14			09 41				10 14
Reading 7	a			07 39			08 40		09 08			08 08	09 39			10 08				10 39
Guildford	a																			
Basingstoke	a			08 08			09 08						10 08							11 08
Winchester	a			08 24			09 24						10 24							11 24
Southampton Airport Parkway ✈	a			08 32			09 32						10 32							11 32
Southampton Central	a			08 44			09 41						10 43							11 43
Brockenhurst 3	a			08 59			09 56						10 58							11 58
Bournemouth	a			09 15			10 12						11 12							12 12

Scotland, The North East, North West England - The South West and South Coast

		XC	XC	XC	XC	XC	VT	XC	XC	XC	XC	XC	XC	VT	XC	XC	XC	XC	XC	XC	VT	XC	XC
		◇1	◇1	◇1	◇1	1	◇1	◇1	◇1	◇1	◇1	◇1	1	◇1	◇1	◇1	◇1	◇1	◇1	1	◇1	◇1	◇1
		⌶	⌶	⌶	⌶		⊠	⌶	⌶	⌶	⌶	⌶		⊠	⌶	⌶	⌶	⌶	⌶		⊠	⌶	⌶
Aberdeen	d																						
Stonehaven	d																						
Montrose	d																						
Arbroath	d																						
Dundee	d																						
Leuchars 3	d																						
Cupar	d																						
Ladybank	d																						
Markinch	d																						
Kirkcaldy	d																						
Inverkeithing	d																						
Glasgow Central 15	d						05 50														08 00		06 01
Motherwell	d						06 04																
Haymarket	d																						06 55
Edinburgh 10	d													06 52		06 08		06 44					07e08
Haymarket	d													06 56									
Lockerbie	d																						
Carlisle 8	d						07 04							08 08							09 09		
Penrith North Lakes	d						07 19							08 23									
Oxenholme Lake District	d						07 42																
Lancaster 6	d						07 57							08 57							09 57		
Preston 8	d						08 17							09 17							10 17		
Wigan North Western	d						08 28							09 28							10 28		
Warrington Bank Quay	d						08 39							09 39							10 39		
Manchester Piccadilly 10 ⇌	d				08 07			08 27				09 07			09 27				10 07			10 27	
Stockport	d				08 16			08 35				09 16			09 35				10 16			10 35	
Wilmslow	d																						
Crewe 10	d						09 01							10 01							11 01		
Macclesfield	d							08 49							09 49							10 49	
Congleton	d																						
Stoke-on-Trent	d				08 44			09 07				09 44			10 07				10 44			11 07	
Stafford	d				09 03			09 25				10 03			10 25							11 25	
Wolverhampton 7 ⇌	d				09 16		09 32	09 41				10 17		10 32	10 41				11 17		11 32	11 41	
Dunbar	d																						07 28
Berwick-upon-Tweed	d															06 49		07 23					07 51
Alnmouth for Alnwick	d															07 10		07 47					
Morpeth	d																	08 02					
Newcastle 8	d			06 21					06 44		07 23					07 45		08 24					08 43
Chester-le-Street	d			06 32														08 33					
Durham	d			06 39					06 56		07 37							08 40					08 55
Darlington 7	d			06 56					07 14		07 55					08 13		08 57					09 12
York 8	d	06 32		07c27					07 44		08 27					08 45		09 27					09 44
Leeds 10	d	07b05							08 11							09 11							10 12
Wakefield Westgate 7	d	07 18							08 23							09 24							10 24
Doncaster 7	d			07 52							08 51							09 56					
Sheffield 7 ⇌	d	07 53		08 20					08 54		09 23					09 54		10 23					10 54
Chesterfield	d	08 06		08 32					09 06							10 06							11 06
Nottingham 8 ⇌	d		08 08			08 37				09 11			09 37				10 11			10 37			
Derby 6	d	08 28	08 36	08 53		09 06			09 28	09 36	09 53		10 06			10 28	10 37	10 53		11 06			11 28
Burton-on-Trent	d	08 38	08 49			09 17			09 38	09 49			10 18				10 49			11 17			
Tamworth	d	08 49	09 01			09 30				10 01			10 30			10 48	11 01			11 30			
Birmingham New Street 12	a	09 09	09 24	09 27	09 39	09 54	09 55	09 58	10 07	10 24	10 27	10 39	10 54	10 55	10 58	11 09	11 24	11 27	11 39	11 54	11 55	11 58	12 07
Birmingham New Street 12	d	09 12	09 30	09 33	09 42			10 03	10 12	10 30	10 33	10 42			11 03	11 12	11 30	11 33	11 42			12 03	12 12
Cheltenham Spa	a	09 51	10 10		10 23				10 50	11 10		11 23				11 51	12 10		12 23				12 50
Gloucester 7	a		10 22							11 22							12 22						
Bristol Parkway 7	a	10 26			10 56				11 26			11 56				12 28			12 56				13 24
Bristol Temple Meads 10	a	10 41			11 12				11 38			12 08				12 41			13 10				13 39
Newport (South Wales)	a		11 11							12 09							13 11						
Cardiff Central 7	a		11 27							12 27							13 29						
Weston-super-Mare	a				11 32																		
Taunton	a	11 16			12 00				12 15							13 16							14 15
Tiverton Parkway	a	11 29			12 13				12 28							13 29							14 28
Exeter St Davids 6	a	11 46			12 30				12 43							13 46							14 43
Dawlish	a				12 43																		
Teignmouth	a				12 48																		
Newton Abbot	a	12 07			12 55				13 03							14 07							15 03
Torquay	a				13 06																		
Paignton	a				13 14																		
Totnes	a	12 21							13 16							14 21							15 16
Plymouth	a	12 50							13 43							14 50							15 43
Liskeard 6	a																						
Bodmin Parkway	a																						
Lostwithiel	a																						
Par	a																						
Newquay	a																						
St Austell	a																						
Truro	a																						
Redruth	a																						
Camborne	a																						
Hayle	a																						
St Erth	a																						
Penzance	a																						
Birmingham International ✈	d							10 14							11 14							12 14	
Coventry	d							10 25							11 25							12 25	
Leamington Spa 8	d			10 00				10 38			11 00				11 38			12 00				12 38	
Banbury	a			10 17				10 54			11 17				11 54			12 17				12 54	
Oxford	a			10 41				11 14			11 40				12 14			12 40				13 14	
Reading 7	a			11 08				11 39			12 08				12 39			13 08				13 39	
Guildford	a																						
Basingstoke	a							12 08							13 08							14 08	
Winchester	a							12 24							13 24							14 24	
Southampton Airport Parkway ✈	a							12 32							13 32							14 34	
Southampton Central	a							12 41							13 41							14 42	
Brockenhurst 3	a							12 56							13 56							14 56	
Bournemouth	a							13 10							14 10							15 11	

Table 51

Mondays to Fridays

Scotland, The North East, North West England - The South West and South Coast

		XC	XC	XC	XC	VT	XC	XC	XC	XC	XC	XC	VT	XC	XC	XC	XC	XC	XC	VT	XC	XC
		◇1 ⊼	◇1 ⊼	◇1 ⊼	1	◇1 ⊏	◇1 ⊼	◇1 ⊼	◇1 ⊼	◇1 ⊼	◇1 ⊼	1	◇1 ⊏	◇1 ⊼	◇1 ⊼	◇1 ⊼	◇1 ⊼	◇1 ⊼	1	◇1 ⊏	◇1 ⊼	◇1 ⊼
Aberdeen	d																					
Stonehaven	d																					
Montrose	d																					
Arbroath	d																					
Dundee	d							06 32							07 35							
Leuchars	d							06 46							07 48							
Cupar	d							06 54							07 55							
Ladybank	d							07 03							08 03							
Markinch	d							07 11							08 11							
Kirkcaldy	d							07 21							08 20							
Inverkeithing	d							07 42							08 35							
Glasgow Central	d												10 00									09 00
Motherwell	d																					09 15
Haymarket	d							08 01							08 54							09 53
Edinburgh	d					08 52		08 11							09 07					10 52		10 08
Haymarket	d					08 57														10 57		
Lockerbie	d																					
Carlisle	d					10 07							11 09							12 07		
Penrith North Lakes	d												11 24									
Oxenholme Lake District	d					10 42														12 43		
Lancaster	d					10 57														12 57		
Preston	d					11 17							12 17							13 17		
Wigan North Western	d					11 28							12 28							13 28		
Warrington Bank Quay	d					11 39							12 39							13 39		
Manchester Piccadilly	d			11 07			11 27				12 07			12 27				13 07			13 27	
Stockport	d			11 16			11 35				12 16			12 35				13 16			13 35	
Wilmslow	d																					
Crewe	d					12 01							13 01							14 01		
Macclesfield	d						11 49							12 49							13 49	
Congleton	d																					
Stoke-on-Trent	d			11 44			12 07				12 44			13 07				13 44			14 07	
Stafford	d			12 03			12 25							13 25							14 25	
Wolverhampton	d			12 17		12 32	12 41				13 14		13 32	13 41				14 15		14 32	14 41	
Dunbar	d														09 28							
Berwick-upon-Tweed	d							08 52							09 51							
Alnmouth for Alnwick	d																					11 05
Morpeth	d																					11 20
Newcastle	d		09 35					09 43		10 25					10 44		11 27					11 40
Chester-le-Street	d																					
Durham	d		09 48					09 56		10 37					10 56		11 39					11 52
Darlington	d		10 05					10 13		10 54					11 13		11 56					12 11
York	d		10 34					10 44		11 27					11 45		12 27					12 45
Leeds	d							11 11							12 12							13 12
Wakefield Westgate	d							11 24							12 24							13 24
Doncaster	d		10 58							11 54							12 55					
Sheffield	d		11 23					11 54		12 23					12 54		13 23					13 54
Chesterfield	d							12 06							13 06							14 06
Nottingham	d	11 08			11 37				12 08			12 37				13 11			13 37			
Derby	d	11 36	11 53		12 06			12 28	12 37	12 53		13 06			13 28	13 36	13 53		14 06			14 28
Burton-on-Trent	d	11 49			12 18				12 49			13 20			13 38	13 49			14 18			
Tamworth	d	12 01			12 30			12 48	13 01			13 32				14 01			14 30			14 48
Birmingham New Street	a	12 24	12 27	12 39	12 54	12 55	12 58	13 09	13 24	13 27	13 31	13 54	13 55	13 58	14 07	14 24	14 27	14 31	14 54	14 55	14 58	15 07
Birmingham New Street	d	12 30	12 33	12 42			13 03	13 12	13 30	13 33	13 42			14 03	14 12	14 30	14 33	14 42			15 03	15 12
Cheltenham Spa	a	13 10		13 23				13 55	14 10		14 23				14 50	15 10		15 23				15 50
Gloucester	a	13 22							14 22							15 22						
Bristol Parkway	a			13 57				14 27			14 56				15 24			15 56				16 26
Bristol Temple Meads	a			14 09				14 41			15 10				15 40			16 08				16 41
Newport (South Wales)	a	14 09							15 12							16 10						
Cardiff Central	a	14 27							15 29							16 29						
Weston-super-Mare	a																					
Taunton	a							15 16			15 44				16 15							17 15
Tiverton Parkway	a							15 29			15 57				16 28							17 28
Exeter St Davids	a							15 46			16 13				16 43							17 43
Dawlish	a																					
Teignmouth	a																					
Newton Abbot	a							16 07							17 03							18 10
Torquay	a																					
Paignton	a																					
Totnes	a							16 21							17 16							18 23
Plymouth	a							16 50							17 43							18 51
Liskeard	a																					19 22
Bodmin Parkway	a																					19 34
Lostwithiel	a																					
Par	a																					19 44
Newquay	a																					
St Austell	a																					19 51
Truro	a																					20 08
Redruth	a																					20 24
Camborne	a																					20 32
Hayle	a																					
St Erth	a																					20 42
Penzance	a																					20 54
Birmingham International ✈	d						13 14							14 14							15 14	
Coventry	d						13 25							14 25							15 25	
Leamington Spa	d		13 00				13 38			14 00				14 38			15 00				15 38	
Banbury	a		13 17				13 54			14 17				14 54			15 17				15 54	
Oxford	a		13 40				14 14			14 40				15 14			15 41				16 14	
Reading	a		14 08				14 39			15 08				15 39			16 08				16 39	
Guildford	a																					
Basingstoke	a						15 08							16 08							17 08	
Winchester	a						15 24							16 24							17 24	
Southampton Airport Parkway ✈	a						15 32							16 32							17 32	
Southampton Central	a						15 41							16 41							17 41	
Brockenhurst	a						15 56							16 56							17 56	
Bournemouth	a						16 10							17 10							18 15	

Table 51

Mondays to Fridays

Scotland, The North East, North West England - The South West and South Coast

		XC	XC	XC	XC	VT	XC	XC	XC	XC	XC	XC	VT	XC	XC	XC	XC	XC	XC	VT	XC	XC FO	XC FX
		◇1 ⊼	◇1 ⊼	◇1 ⊼	1	◇1 ⊏	◇1 ⊼	◇1 ⊼	◇1 ⊼	◇1 ⊼	◇1 ⊼	1	◇1 ⊏	◇1 ⊼	◇1 ⊼	◇1 ⊼	◇1 ⊼	◇1 ⊼	1	◇1 ⊏	◇1 ⊼	◇1 ⊼	◇1 ⊼
Aberdeen	d							08 20															
Stonehaven	d							08 38															
Montrose	d							08 59															
Arbroath	d							09 15															
Dundee	d							09 32															
Leuchars	d							09 47															
Cupar	d							09 54															
Ladybank	d							10 01															
Markinch	d							10 09															
Kirkcaldy	d							10 17															
Inverkeithing	d							10 32															
Glasgow Central	d					12 00														14 00			
Motherwell	d																						
Haymarket	d							10 54															
Edinburgh	d							11 08					12 52		12 05							13 07	13 07
Haymarket	d												12 57										
Lockerbie	d																						
Carlisle	d					13 09							14 07							15 09			
Penrith North Lakes	d												14 22										
Oxenholme Lake District	d																			15 44			
Lancaster	d					13 58							14 57										
Preston	d					14 17							15 17							16 17			
Wigan North Western	d					14 28							15 28							16 28			
Warrington Bank Quay	d					14 39							15 39							16 39			
Manchester Piccadilly	d			14 07			14 27				15 07			15 27				16 07			16 27		
Stockport	d			14 16			14 35				15 16			15 35				16 16			16 35		
Wilmslow	d																						
Crewe	d					15 01							16 01							17 01			
Macclesfield	d						14 49							15 49							16 49		
Congleton	d																						
Stoke-on-Trent	d			14 44			15 07				15 44			16 07				16 44			17 07		
Stafford	d			15 03			15 25				16 03			16 25				17 03			17 25		
Wolverhampton	d			15 17		15 32	15 41				16 17		16 32	16 41				17 16		17 32	17 41		
Dunbar	d							11 28														13 28	13 28
Berwick-upon-Tweed	d							11 51														13 51	13 51
Alnmouth for Alnwick	d														13 05								
Morpeth	d																						
Newcastle	d		12 19					12 44		13 34					13 44		14 26					14 40	14 40
Chester-le-Street	d		12 28																				
Durham	d		12 35					12 56		13 46					13 56		14 40					14 52	14 52
Darlington	d		12 53					13 13		14 03					14 13		14 57					15 12	15 12
York	d		13 26					13 44		14 32					14 44		15 29					15 44	15 44
Leeds	d							14 12							15 12							16 11	16 11
Wakefield Westgate	d							14 24							15 24							16 23	16 23
Doncaster	d		13 55							14 57							15 55						
Sheffield	d		14 23					14 54		15 23					15 54		16 23					16 54	16 54
Chesterfield	d							15 06							16 06							17 06	17 06
Nottingham	d	14 08			14 37				15 11			15 37				16 08			16 37				
Derby	d	14 36	14 53		15 06			15 28	15 36	15 53		16 06			16 28	16 36	16 53		17 06			17 28	17 28
Burton-on-Trent	d	14 49			15 20			15 38	15 49			16 18				16 49			17 20			17 38	17 38
Tamworth	d	15 01			15 31				16 01			16 30			16 48	17 01			17 31				
Birmingham New Street	a	15 24	15 27	15 39	15 54	15 55	15 58	16 08	16 24	16 27	16 39	16 54	16 55	16 58	17 09	17 25	17 28	17 39	17 54	17 55	17 58	18 07	18 07
Birmingham New Street	d	15 30	15 33	15 42			16 03	16 12	16 30	16 33	16 42			17 03	17 12	17 30	17 33	17 42			18 03	18 12	18 12
Cheltenham Spa	a	16 10		16 23				16 51	17 13		17 23				17 50	18 18		18 23				18 51	18 51
Gloucester	a	16 22							17 26							18 30							
Bristol Parkway	a			16 56				17 24			17 58				18 27			18 55				19 27	19 27
Bristol Temple Meads	a			17 11				17 40			18 10				18 40			19 07				19 39	19 39
Newport (South Wales)	a	17 11							18 10							19 16							
Cardiff Central	a	17 28							18 27							19 33							
Weston-super-Mare	a																						
Taunton	a			17 45				18 16							19 15							20 16	20 16
Tiverton Parkway	a			17 57				18 29							19 28							20 29	20 29
Exeter St Davids	a			18 13				18 44							19 43							20 44	20 44
Dawlish	a			18 26																			
Teignmouth	a			18 31																			
Newton Abbot	a			18 38				19 06							20 04							21 03	21 03
Torquay	a			18 49																			
Paignton	a			18 57																			
Totnes	a							19 19							20 17							21 17	21 17
Plymouth	a							19 45							20 45							21 50	21 50
Liskeard	a							20 12							21 14								
Bodmin Parkway	a							20 24							21 26								
Lostwithiel	a														21 32								
Par	a							20 35							21 39								
Newquay	a																						
St Austell	a							20 41							21 45								
Truro	a							20 59							22 03								
Redruth	a							21 14							22 14								
Camborne	a							21 21							22 22								
Hayle	a														22 30								
St Erth	a							21 32							22 34								
Penzance	a							21 42							22 45								
Birmingham International ✈	d						16 14							17 14							18 14		
Coventry	d						16 25							17 25							18 25		
Leamington Spa	d		16 00				16 38			17 00				17 38			18 00				18 38		
Banbury	a		16 17				16 54			17 17				17 54			18 18				18 54		
Oxford	a		16 40				17 14			17 41				18 14			18 40				19 14		
Reading	a		17 08				17 39			18 08				18 39			19 08				19 39		
Guildford	a																						
Basingstoke	a						18 08							19 08							20 09		
Winchester	a						18 24							19 24							20 24		
Southampton Airport Parkway ✈	a						18 33							19 33							20 33		
Southampton Central	a						18 44							19 41							20 41		
Brockenhurst	a						18 58							19 56							20 58		
Bournemouth	a						19 13							20 12							21 15		

Scotland, The North East, North West England - The South West and South Coast

		XC	XC	XC	VT	XC	XC	XC	XC	XC	XC	XC	VT	XC	XC	XC FO	XC FX	XC	XC	XC	LM	VT	XC
		◇1 ✕	◇1 ✕	◇1 ✕	1 B ⊟	1	◇1 ✕	◇1 ✕	◇1 ✕	◇1 ✕	◇1 ✕	1	◇1 ⊟	◇1 ✕	◇1 ✕	◇1 ✕	◇1 ✕	◇1 ✕	◇1 G ✕	◇1 H ✕	1	1 ⊟	1
Aberdeen	d																						
Stonehaven	d																						
Montrose	d																						
Arbroath	d																						
Dundee	d																						
Leuchars	d																						
Cupar	d																						
Ladybank	d																						
Markinch	d																						
Kirkcaldy	d																						
Inverkeithing	d																						
Glasgow Central	d												16 00										
Motherwell	d																						
Haymarket	d																						
Edinburgh	d				14 52			14 08							15 07							16 52	
Haymarket	d				14 56																	16 57	
Lockerbie	d																						
Carlisle	d				16 06								17 09									18 07	
Penrith North Lakes	d				16 21																		
Oxenholme Lake District	d												17 44									18 42	
Lancaster	d				16 56																	18 57	
Preston	d				17 17								18 17									19 17	
Wigan North Western	d				17 28								18 28									19 28	
Warrington Bank Quay	d				17 39								18 39									19 39	
Manchester Piccadilly	d			17 06			17 27				18 05			18 27					19 07	19 07			
Stockport	d						17 35				18 13			18 35					19 16	19 16			
Wilmslow	d						17 44																
Crewe	d				18 01		18 07						19 01								19 55	20 01	
Macclesfield	d			17 27							18 26												
Congleton	d													18 54									
Stoke-on-Trent	d			17 44							18 44			19 07					19 44	19 44			
Stafford	d			18 04			18 28							19 25					20 04	20 04	20 16		
Wolverhampton	d			18 16	18 31		18 41				19 15		19 32	19 41					20 17	20 17	20 29	20 34	
Dunbar	d														15 28								
Berwick-upon-Tweed	d														15 51								
Alnmouth for Alnwick	d							15 05															
Morpeth	d																						
Newcastle	d		15 22					15 42		16 32					16 40			17 17					
Chester-le-Street	d									16 41								17 26					
Durham	d		15 34					15 54		16 48					16 52			17 33					
Darlington	d		15 51					16 12		17 05					17 12			17 50					
York	d		16 25					16 44		17 34					17 44			18 24					
Leeds	d							17 12							18 11								
Wakefield Westgate	d							17 24							18 23								
Doncaster	d		16 53							17 58								18 52					
Sheffield	d		17 23					17 54		18 23					18 54			19 23					
Chesterfield	d							18 07							19 06								
Nottingham	d	17 08				17 37			18 08			18 37				19 08	19 08						19 37
Derby	d	17 36	17 53			18 05		18 28	18 37	18 53		19 06			19 28	19 37	19 36	19 54					20 05
Burton-on-Trent	d	17 49				18 20			18 49			19 17			19 38	19 49	19 49						20 17
Tamworth	d	18 04				18 32		18 48	19 01			19 29				20 01	20 01						20 29
Birmingham New Street	a	18 25	18 28	18 38	18 55	18 57	18 58	19 08	19 24	19 28	19 31	19 54	19 55	19 58	20 09	20 24	20 24	20 27	20 33	20 33	20 47	20 55	20 57
Birmingham New Street	d	18 30	18 33	18 42			19 03	19 12	19 30	19 33	19 42			20 03	20 12	20 30	20 30	20 33	20 42	20 42			
Cheltenham Spa	a	19 13		19 23				19 50	20 10		20 23				20 51	21 10	21 10		21 25	21 25			
Gloucester	a	19 27							20 22							21 22	21 22						
Bristol Parkway	a			19 56				20 27			20 56				21 25				21 57	21 57			
Bristol Temple Meads	a			20 13				20 41			21 08				21 38				22 14	22 14			
Newport (South Wales)	a	20 12		20 47					21 08							22 15	22 15						
Cardiff Central	a	20 31		21 02					21 27							22 31	22 35						
Weston-super-Mare	a																						
Taunton	a							21 18			21 44				22 15								
Tiverton Parkway	a							21 31			21 57				22 28								
Exeter St Davids	a							21 46			22 13				22 44								
Dawlish	a																						
Teignmouth	a																						
Newton Abbot	a							22 05			22 33				23 05								
Torquay	a																						
Paignton	a																						
Totnes	a							22 19			22 46				23 18								
Plymouth	a							22 46			23 12				23 44								
Liskeard	a																						
Bodmin Parkway	a																						
Lostwithiel	a																						
Par	a																						
Newquay	a																						
St Austell	a																						
Truro	a																						
Redruth	a																						
Camborne	a																						
Hayle	a																						
St Erth	a																						
Penzance	a																						
Birmingham International	d						19 14							20 14									
Coventry	d						19 25							20 25									
Leamington Spa	d		19 00				19 38			20 05				20 38				21 00					
Banbury	a		19 17				19 54			20 21				20 54				21 17					
Oxford	a		19 41				20 14			20 41				21 14				21 40					
Reading	a		20 08				20 39			21 07				21 40				22 16					
Guildford	a																	22 59					
Basingstoke	a						21 09							22 09									
Winchester	a						21 24							22 24									
Southampton Airport Parkway	a						21 33							22 33									
Southampton Central	a						21 41							22 42									
Brockenhurst	a						21 56							22 56									
Bournemouth	a						22 16							23 21									

B until 16 July, from 6 September

G until 3 September

H from 6 September

Scotland, The North East, North West England - The South West and South Coast

		XC	XC	XC	XC	VT	XC	XC	XC FO	XC FX	XC	VT	XC	XC	XC	XC	XC
		◇1 ✕	◇1 ✕	◇1	◇1 ✕	◇1 ⊟	1	◇1	◇1 ✕	◇1 ✕	◇1 ✕	◇1 ⊟	◇1	1	◇1 ✕	◇1 ✕	◇1
Aberdeen	d																
Stonehaven	d																
Montrose	d																
Arbroath	d																
Dundee	d																
Leuchars	d																
Cupar	d																
Ladybank	d																
Markinch	d																
Kirkcaldy	d																
Inverkeithing	d																
Glasgow Central	d					17 40											
Motherwell	d																
Haymarket	d																
Edinburgh	d		16 08						17 08	17 08		18 52			18 08		
Haymarket	d											18 57					
Lockerbie	d					18 33											
Carlisle	d					18 54						20 08					
Penrith North Lakes	d					19 09											
Oxenholme Lake District	d					19 32						20 42					
Lancaster	d					19 47						20 57					
Preston	d					20 08						21 17					
Wigan North Western	d					20 19						21 28					
Warrington Bank Quay	d					20 31						21 39					
Manchester Piccadilly	d	19 27		20 07				20 27					21 28				22 07
Stockport	d	19 35		20 16				20 35					21 36				22 16
Wilmslow	d																
Crewe	d					20 53						22 01					
Macclesfield	d	19 49						20 49					21 50				22 29
Congleton	d																
Stoke-on-Trent	d	20 07		20 44				21 08					22 08				22 47
Stafford	d	20 26				21 14		21 26					22 26				23 07
Wolverhampton	d	20 43		21 15		21 32		21 41				22 32	22 41				23 21
Dunbar	d								17 28	17 28					18 28		
Berwick-upon-Tweed	d								17 51	17 51					18 51		
Alnmouth for Alnwick	d		17 09												19 11		
Morpeth	d		17 24														
Newcastle	d		17 44		18 20				18 40	18 40	19 25				19 43		
Chester-le-Street	d				18 29						19 37						
Durham	d		17 56		18 36				18 52	18 52	19 44				19 55		
Darlington	d		18 13		18 56				19 12	19 12	20 04				20 12		
York	d		18 44		19 29				19 44	19 44	20 32				20 44		
Leeds	d		19 11						20 11	20 11					21 11		
Wakefield Westgate	d		19 23						20 23	20 23					21 23		
Doncaster	d				19 57						20 57						
Sheffield	d		19 54		20 23				20 54	20 54	21 27				22 00		
Chesterfield	d		20 06						21 06	21 06	21 39				22 24		
Nottingham	d						20 37							21 37			
Derby	d		20 28		20 54		21 06		21 28	21 28	22 00			22 10	22 45		
Burton-on-Trent	d						21 20		21 38	21 38				22 21	22 55		
Tamworth	d		20 48				21 33		21 49	21 49				22 33	23 06		
Birmingham New Street	a	21 00	21 07	21 31	21 35	21 50	21 58	22 00	22 07	22 07	22 54	22 55	22 58	23 02	23 34		23 38
Birmingham New Street	d	21 03	21 12						22 12	22 12						22 03	
Cheltenham Spa	a		21 51						22 50	22 50							
Gloucester	a		22 02														
Bristol Parkway	a		22 52						23 53	23 54							
Bristol Temple Meads	a		23 04						00 16	00 17							
Newport (South Wales)	a																
Cardiff Central	a																
Weston-super-Mare	a																
Taunton	a																
Tiverton Parkway	a																
Exeter St Davids	a																
Dawlish	a																
Teignmouth	a																
Newton Abbot	a																
Torquay	a																
Paignton	a																
Totnes	a																
Plymouth	a																
Liskeard	a																
Bodmin Parkway	a																
Lostwithiel	a																
Par	a																
Newquay	a																
St Austell	a																
Truro	a																
Redruth	a																
Camborne	a																
Hayle	a																
St Erth	a																
Penzance	a																
Birmingham International	d	21 14														22 14	
Coventry	d	21 25														22 25	
Leamington Spa	d	21 38														22 38	
Banbury	a	21 54														22 54	
Oxford	a	22 14														23 14	
Reading	a	22 41														23 52	
Guildford	a																
Basingstoke	a	23 12															
Winchester	a	23 28															
Southampton Airport Parkway	a	23 37															
Southampton Central	a	23 47															
Brockenhurst	a																
Bournemouth	a																

Table 51

Saturdays until 04 September

Scotland, The North East, North West England - The South West and South Coast

Station		XC	XC	XC	XC	XC	XC	XC	XC	VT	XC	XC	XC	XC	XC	VT	XC	XC	XC	VT	XC	XC
		◇■ ⊼	◇■ ⊼	◇■ ⊼	◇■ ⊼	◇■ ⊼	◇■ ⊼	◇■ ⊼	◇■ ⊼	◇■ ⊔	◇■ ⊼	■ ■ ⊼	◇■ ⊼	◇■ ⊼	◇■ ⊼	◇■ ⊔	◇■ ⊼	◇■ ⊼	■	◇■ ⊔	◇■ ⊼	◇■ ⊼
Aberdeen	d																					
Stonehaven	d																					
Montrose	d																					
Arbroath	d																					
Dundee	d																					
Leuchars	d																					
Cupar	d																					
Ladybank	d																					
Markinch	d																					
Kirkcaldy	d																					
Inverkeithing	d																					
Glasgow Central	d																					
Motherwell	d																					
Haymarket	d																					
Edinburgh	d																					
Haymarket	d																					
Lockerbie	d																					
Carlisle	d																					
Penrith North Lakes	d																					
Oxenholme Lake District	d																					
Lancaster	d																			06 58		
Preston	d									06 17										07 17		
Wigan North Western	d									06 28										07 28		
Warrington Bank Quay	d									06 39										07 39		
Manchester Piccadilly	d					05 11			06 00									07 00			07 27	
Stockport	d								06 08									07 09			07 35	
Wilmslow	d																					
Crewe	d					05 47				07 01										08 01		
Macclesfield	d								06 21									07 25			07 49	
Congleton	d																					
Stoke-on-Trent	d					06 08			06 39									07 44			08 07	
Stafford	d					06 26			06 58									08 04			08 26	
Wolverhampton	d					06 41			07 15	07 32						08 06		08 18		08 32	08 41	
Dunbar	d																					
Berwick-upon-Tweed	d																					
Alnmouth for Alnwick	d																					
Morpeth	d																					
Newcastle	d																					
Chester-le-Street	d																					
Durham	d																					
Darlington	d																					
York	d																					06 09
Leeds	d												06 0[illegible]				06 15					07 05
Wakefield Westgate	d												06 12				06 29					07 18
Doncaster	d																06 47					
Sheffield	d							05 42					06 5[illegible]				07 18					07 54
Chesterfield	d							05 54					07 03				07 30					08 06
Nottingham	d						05 57					06 37			06 56				07 34			
Derby	d				06 10		06 36	06 47				07 06	07 25		07 36		07 50		08 03			08 28
Burton-on-Trent	d				06 20		06 48	06 57				07 18	07 3[illegible]		07 49		08 00		08 18			08 38
Tamworth	d				06 31		07 00	07 08				07 30	07 4[illegible]		08 01		08 11		08 30			08 50
Birmingham New Street	a				06 50	06 57	07 24	07 27	07 31	07 55		07 55	08 0[illegible]		08 24	08 24	08 29	08 38	08 54	08 55	08 58	09 07
Birmingham New Street	d	05 00	05 42	06 03	07 12	07 03	07 30	07 33	07 42		06 33	08 03	08 12	06 42	08 30	08 30	08 33	08 42			09 03	09 12
Cheltenham Spa	a	06 02	06 41		07 50		08 10		08 23				08 5[illegible]	07 23	09 10			09 25				09 50
Gloucester	a	06 13	06 54				08 22								09 22							
Bristol Parkway	a				08 24				08 56				09 24	07 56				09 58				10 29
Bristol Temple Meads	a				08 38				09 08				09 3[illegible]	08 08				10 11				10 42
Newport (South Wales)	a	07 06	07 52				09 07								10 05							
Cardiff Central	a	07 22	08 08				09 23								10 21							
Weston-super-Mare	a																					
Taunton	a				09 15								10 15	08 42				11 01				11 15
Tiverton Parkway	a				09 28								10 29	08 54				11 14				11 28
Exeter St Davids	a				09 43								10 45	09 10				11 31				11 43
Dawlish	a																					
Teignmouth	a																					
Newton Abbot	a				10 03								11 08					11 53				12 04
Torquay	a													09 38								
Paignton	a													09 46								
Totnes	a				10 16								11 22					12 07				12 17
Plymouth	a				10 44								11 5[illegible]					12 34				12 45
Liskeard	a																	13 03				
Bodmin Parkway	a																	13 18				
Lostwithiel	a																					
Par	a																	13 31				
Newquay	a																	14 37				
St Austell	a																					
Truro	a																					
Redruth	a																					
Camborne	a																					
Hayle	a																					
St Erth	a																					
Penzance	a																					
Birmingham International ✈	d			06 14		07 15						08 14				08 39					09 14	
Coventry	d			06 25		07 25						08 25				08 51					09 25	
Leamington Spa	d			06 38		07 38		08 00			07 00	08 38					09 00				09 38	
Banbury	a			06 54		07 54		08 17			07 17	08 54					09 17				09 54	
Oxford	a			07 14		08 14		08 40			07 40	09 14					09 40				10 14	
Reading	a			07 39		08 39		09 08			08 08	09 39					10 08				10 39	
Guildford	a																					
Basingstoke	a			08 08		09 08						10 08									11 08	
Winchester	a			08 24		09 24						10 24									11 24	
Southampton Airport Parkway ✈	a			08 32		09 32						10 32									11 32	
Southampton Central	a			08 41		09 40						10 43									11 41	
Brockenhurst	a			08 56		09 57						10 58									11 57	
Bournemouth	a			09 14		10 11						11 12									12 11	

Table 51

Saturdays until 04 September

Scotland, The North East, North West England - The South West and South Coast

Station		XC	XC	XC	XC	VT	XC	XC	XC	XC	XC	XC	VT	XC	XC	XC	XC	XC	XC	VT	XC	XC	XC
		◇■ ⊼	◇■ ⊼	◇■ ⊼	■	◇■ ⊔	◇■ ⊼	◇■ ⊼	◇■ ⊼	◇■ ⊼	◇■ ⊼	■	◇■ ⊔	◇■ ⊼	◇■ ⊼	◇■ ⊼	◇■ ⊼	◇■ ⊼	■	◇■ ⊔	◇■ ⊼	◇■ ⊼	◇■ ⊼
Aberdeen	d																						
Stonehaven	d																						
Montrose	d																						
Arbroath	d																						
Dundee	d																						
Leuchars	d																						
Cupar	d																						
Ladybank	d																						
Markinch	d																						
Kirkcaldy	d																						
Inverkeithing	d																						
Glasgow Central	d					05 50														08 00			
Motherwell	d					06 05																	
Haymarket	d																						
Edinburgh	d												06 52		06 12		06 55					07 07	
Haymarket	d												06 56										
Lockerbie	d																						
Carlisle	d					07 03							08 07							09 09			
Penrith North Lakes	d					07 18							08 22										
Oxenholme Lake District	d					07 42																	
Lancaster	d					07 57							08 57							09 57			
Preston	d					08 17							09 17							10 17			
Wigan North Western	d					08 28							09 28							10 28			
Warrington Bank Quay	d					08 39							09 39							10 39			
Manchester Piccadilly	d			07 58			08 27				09 07			09 27				10 07			10 27		
Stockport	d			08 08			08 35				09 16			09 35				10 16			10 35		
Wilmslow	d																						
Crewe	d					09 01							10 01							11 01			
Macclesfield	d			08 25			08 49							09 49							10 49		
Congleton	d																						
Stoke-on-Trent	d			08 44			09 07				09 44			10 07				10 44			11 07		
Stafford	d			09 04			09 26				10 03			10 26				11 03			11 26		
Wolverhampton	d			09 18		09 32	09 41				10 17		10 32	10 41				11 17		11 32	11 41		
Dunbar	d																					07 27	
Berwick-upon-Tweed	d														06 51		07 35					07 50	
Alnmouth for Alnwick	d														07 11		07 55						
Morpeth	d																08 09						
Newcastle	d		06 21					06 42		07 25					07 44		08 30					08 40	
Chester-le-Street	d		06 32																			08 49	
Durham	d		06 39					06 56		07 38					07 56		08 42					08 56	
Darlington	d		06 56					07 13		07 55					08 13		08 59					09 13	
York	d		07 25					07 44		08 27					08 44		09 28					09 44	
Leeds	d							08 12							09 11							10 12	
Wakefield Westgate	d							08 24							09 24							10 24	
Doncaster	d		07 52							08 53							09 53						
Sheffield	d		08 20					08 54		09 23					09 54		10 23					10 54	
Chesterfield	d		08 32					09 08							10 06							11 06	
Nottingham	d	08 08			08 37				09 08			09 37				10 08			10 37				11 11
Derby	d	08 35	08 53		09 06			09 30	09 36	09 53		10 06			10 28	10 36	10 53		11 06			11 28	11 36
Burton-on-Trent	d	08 48			09 18			09 41	09 48			10 18				10 48			11 17			11 38	11 48
Tamworth	d	09 00			09 29				10 00			10 30			10 48	11 00			11 29				12 00
Birmingham New Street	a	09 24	09 29	09 39	09 54	09 55	09 58	10 08	10 24	10 27	10 39	10 54	10 55	10 58	11 07	11 24	11 27	11 39	11 54	11 55	11 58	12 07	12 24
Birmingham New Street	d	09 30	09 33	09 42			10 03	10 12	10 30	10 33	10 42			11 03	11 12	11 30	11 33	11 42			12 03	12 12	12 30
Cheltenham Spa	a	10 10		10 25				10 52	11 10		11 23				11 50	12 10		12 23				12 50	13 10
Gloucester	a	10 22							11 23							12 22							13 22
Bristol Parkway	a			10 58				11 25			11 56				12 29			12 56				13 24	
Bristol Temple Meads	a			11 11				11 39			12 08				12 42			13 08				13 38	
Newport (South Wales)	a	11 05							12 06							13 06							14 05
Cardiff Central	a	11 24							12 22							13 22							14 21
Weston-super-Mare	a			11 31																			
Taunton	a			12 00				12 15							13 15							14 15	
Tiverton Parkway	a			12 13				12 29							13 28							14 28	
Exeter St Davids	a			12 30				12 45							13 43							14 43	
Dawlish	a			12 44																			
Teignmouth	a			12 51																			
Newton Abbot	a			12 59				13 07							14 04							15 04	
Torquay	a			13 10																			
Paignton	a			13 20																			
Totnes	a							13 21							14 17							15 17	
Plymouth	a							13 48							14 45							15 45	
Liskeard	a							14 13															
Bodmin Parkway	a							14 26															
Lostwithiel	a																						
Par	a							14 37															
Newquay	a																						
St Austell	a							14 44															
Truro	a							15 03															
Redruth	a							15 15															
Camborne	a							15 23															
Hayle	a																						
St Erth	a							15 33															
Penzance	a							15 47															
Birmingham International ✈	d						10 14							11 14							12 14		
Coventry	d						10 25							11 25							12 25		
Leamington Spa	d		10 00				10 38			11 00				11 38			12 00				12 38		
Banbury	a		10 17				10 54			11 17				11 54			12 17				12 54		
Oxford	a		10 40				11 14			11 40				12 14			12 40				13 14		
Reading	a		11 09				11 39			12 08				12 39			13 08				13 39		
Guildford	a																						
Basingstoke	a						12 08							13 08							14 08		
Winchester	a						12 24							13 24							14 24		
Southampton Airport Parkway ✈	a						12 32							13 32							14 33		
Southampton Central	a						12 41							13 41							14 41		
Brockenhurst	a						12 57							13 57							14 57		
Bournemouth	a						13 11							14 11							15 11		

Scotland, The North East, North West England - The South West and South Coast

Station		XC ◇1	XC ◇1	XC 1	VT ◇1	XC ◇1	XC ◇1	XC ◇1	XC ◇1	XC ◇1	XC 1	VT ◇1	XC ◇1	XC ◇1	XC ◇1	XC ◇1	XC ◇1	XC 1	VT ◇1	XC ◇1	XC ◇1	XC ◇1
Aberdeen	d																					
Stonehaven	d																					
Montrose	d																					
Arbroath	d																					
Dundee	d													07 35								
Leuchars	d													07 48								
Cupar	d													07 55								
Ladybank	d													08 03								
Markinch	d													08 11								
Kirkcaldy	d													08 20								
Inverkeithing	d													08 35								
Glasgow Central	d						07 00					10 00									09 00	
Motherwell	d																					
Haymarket	d						07 54							08 54							09 55	
Edinburgh	d				08 52		08 05							09 05					10 52		10 05	
Haymarket	d				08 57														10 57			
Lockerbie	d																					
Carlisle	d				10 07							11 09							12 07			
Penrith North Lakes	d											11 24										
Oxenholme Lake District	d				10 42														12 43			
Lancaster	d				10 57														12 57			
Preston	d				11 17							12 17							13 17			
Wigan North Western	d				11 28							12 28							13 28			
Warrington Bank Quay	d				11 39							12 39							13 39			
Manchester Piccadilly	d		11 07			11 27				12 07			12 27				13 07			13 27		
Stockport	d		11 16			11 35				12 16			12 35				13 16			13 35		
Wilmslow	d																					
Crewe	d				12 01							13 01							14 01			
Macclesfield	d					11 49							12 49							13 49		
Congleton	d																					
Stoke-on-Trent	d		11 44			12 07				12 44			13 07				13 44			14 07		
Stafford	d		12 03			12 25				13 03			13 26				14 03			14 26		
Wolverhampton	d		12 17		12 32	12 41				13 16		13 32	13 41				14 17		14 32	14 41		
Dunbar	d													09 26								
Berwick-upon-Tweed	d						08 47							09 49								
Alnmouth for Alnwick	d						09 09														11 04	
Morpeth	d																				11 19	
Newcastle	d	09 25					09 41		10 25					10 44		11 25					11 41	
Chester-le-Street	d																					
Durham	d	09 37					09 55		10 38					10 56		11 37					11 55	
Darlington	d	09 56					10 12		10 56					11 13		11 56					12 12	
York	d	10 25					10 45		11 27					11 45		12 25					12 45	
Leeds	d						11 11							12 11							13 11	
Wakefield Westgate	d						11 24							12 24							13 23	
Doncaster	d	10 53							11 55							12 52						
Sheffield	d	11 23					11 54		12 23					12 54		13 23					13 54	
Chesterfield	d						12 07							13 06							14 07	
Nottingham	d			11 37				12 08			12 37				13 08			13 37				14 08
Derby	d	11 53		12 06			12 29	12 36	12 53		13 06			13 28	13 36	13 53		14 06			14 29	14 36
Burton-on-Trent	d			12 18				12 48			13 20			13 38	13 48			14 18				14 48
Tamworth	d			12 30			12 49	13 00			13 32				14 00			14 30			14 48	15 00
Birmingham New Street	a	12 27	12 39	12 54	12 55	12 58	13 09	13 24	13 27	13 39	13 54	13 55	13 58	14 07	14 24	14 27	14 39	14 54	14 55	14 58	15 08	15 24
Birmingham New Street	d	12 33	12 42			13 03	13 12	13 30	13 33	13 42			14 03	14 12	14 30	14 33	14 42			15 03	15 12	15 30
Cheltenham Spa	a		13 25				13 51	14 10		14 23				14 50	15 10		15 23				15 50	16 10
Gloucester	a							14 22							15 22							16 22
Bristol Parkway	a		13 58				14 26			14 57				15 24			15 56				16 29	
Bristol Temple Meads	a		14 10				14 41			15 10				15 38			16 08				16 42	
Newport (South Wales)	a							15 06							16 06							17 06
Cardiff Central	a							15 22							16 22							17 24
Weston-super-Mare	a																					
Taunton	a						15 16			15 44				16 15							17 17	
Tiverton Parkway	a						15 29			15 56											17 30	
Exeter St Davids	a						15 46			16 12				16 40							17 47	
Dawlish	a																					
Teignmouth	a																					
Newton Abbot	a						16 08			16 34											18 08	
Torquay	a									16 50												
Paignton	a									16 59												
Totnes	a						16 22							17 13							18 22	
Plymouth	a						16 49							17 40							18 50	
Liskeard	a						17 14							18 04							19 16	
Bodmin Parkway	a						17 27							18 16							19 29	
Lostwithiel	a																					
Par	a						17 40							18 27							19 40	
Newquay	a						18 45															
St Austell	a													18 33							19 47	
Truro	a													18 50							20 06	
Redruth	a													19 08							20 18	
Camborne	a													19 15							20 26	
Hayle	a																					
St Erth	a													19 25							20 36	
Penzance	a													19 36							20 49	
Birmingham International	d					13 15							14 14							15 14		
Coventry	d					13 25							14 25							15 25		
Leamington Spa	d	13 02				13 38			14 00				14 38			15 00				15 38		
Banbury	a	13 19				13 54			14 17				14 54			15 19				15 54		
Oxford	a	13 40				14 14			14 40				15 14			15 41				16 14		
Reading	a	14 08				14 39			15 08				15 39			16 08				16 39		
Guildford	a																					
Basingstoke	a					15 08							16 08							17 08		
Winchester	a					15 24							16 24							17 24		
Southampton Airport Parkway	a					15 32							16 32							17 32		
Southampton Central	a					15 41							16 41							17 41		
Brockenhurst	a					15 57							16 57							17 57		
Bournemouth	a					16 11							17 11							18 11		

Scotland, The North East, North West England - The South West and South Coast

Station		XC ◇1	XC ◇1	XC 1	VT ◇1	XC ◇1	XC ◇1	XC ◇1	XC ◇1	XC ◇1	XC 1	VT ◇1	XC ◇1	XC ◇1	XC ◇1	XC ◇1	XC ◇1	XC 1	VT ◇1	XC ◇1	XC ◇1	XC ◇1	XC ◇1
Aberdeen	d						08 20																
Stonehaven	d						08 38																
Montrose	d						08 59																
Arbroath	d						09 15																
Dundee	d						09 32																
Leuchars	d						09 47																
Cupar	d						09 54																
Ladybank	d						10 01																
Markinch	d						10 08																
Kirkcaldy	d						10 17																
Inverkeithing	d						10 32																
Glasgow Central	d				12 00														14 00				
Motherwell	d																						
Haymarket	d						10 51																
Edinburgh	d						11 05					12 52		12 05							13 05		
Haymarket	d											12 57											
Lockerbie	d																						
Carlisle	d				13 09							14 07							15 11				
Penrith North Lakes	d											14 22											
Oxenholme Lake District	d																		15 46				
Lancaster	d				13 58							14 57											
Preston	d				14 17							15 17							16 17				
Wigan North Western	d				14 28							15 28							16 28				
Warrington Bank Quay	d				14 39							15 39							16 39				
Manchester Piccadilly	d		14 07			14 27				15 07			15 27				16 07			16 27			
Stockport	d		14 16			14 35				15 16			15 35				16 16			16 35			
Wilmslow	d																						
Crewe	d				15 01							16 01							17 01				
Macclesfield	d					14 49							15 49							16 49			
Congleton	d																						
Stoke-on-Trent	d		14 44			15 07				15 44			16 07				16 44			17 07			
Stafford	d		15 03			15 26				16 03			16 25				17 03			17 26			
Wolverhampton	d		15 17		15 32	15 41				16 17		16 32	16 41				17 17		17 32	17 41			
Dunbar	d						11 25														13 26		
Berwick-upon-Tweed	d						11 48														13 48		
Alnmouth for Alnwick	d													13 05									
Morpeth	d																						
Newcastle	d	12 22					12 44		13 27					13 44		14 22					14 44		15 25
Chester-le-Street	d	12 31																					
Durham	d	12 38					12 56		13 39					13 56		14 34					14 56		15 38
Darlington	d	12 55					13 13		13 58					14 13		14 52					15 13		15 56
York	d	13 27					13 44		14 27					14 44		15 26					15 45		16 25
Leeds	d						14 11							15 12							16 12		
Wakefield Westgate	d						14 24							15 24							16 24		
Doncaster	d	13 54							14 56							15 55							16 53
Sheffield	d	14 23					14 54		15 23					15 54		16 23					16 54		17 23
Chesterfield	d						15 06							16 07							17 06		
Nottingham	d			14 37				15 08			15 37				16 08			16 37				17 08	
Derby	d	14 53		15 06			15 28	15 36	15 53		16 06			16 28	16 36	16 53		17 06			17 28	17 36	17 53
Burton-on-Trent	d			15 20			15 38	15 48			16 18				16 48			17 20			17 38	17 48	
Tamworth	d			15 32				16 00			16 30			16 48	17 00			17 32				18 00	
Birmingham New Street	a	15 27	15 39	15 54	15 55	15 58	16 07	16 24	16 27	16 39	16 54	16 55	16 58	17 07	17 24	17 27	17 39	17 54	17 55	17 58	18 07	18 24	18 27
Birmingham New Street	d	15 33	15 42			16 03	16 12	16 30	16 33	16 42			17 03	17 12	17 30	17 33	17 42			18 03	18 12	18 30	18 33
Cheltenham Spa	a		16 23				16 50	17 10		17 23				17 50	18 17		18 23				18 50	19 10	
Gloucester	a							17 22							18 29							19 22	
Bristol Parkway	a		16 56				17 24			17 56				18 29			18 55				19 27		
Bristol Temple Meads	a		17 10				17 38			18 08				18 43			19 08				19 41		
Newport (South Wales)	a							18 05							19 12							20 05	
Cardiff Central	a							18 21							19 29							20 21	
Weston-super-Mare	a																						
Taunton	a						18 15							19 16							20 15		
Tiverton Parkway	a						18 28							19 29							20 28		
Exeter St Davids	a						18 43							19 44							20 43		
Dawlish	a																						
Teignmouth	a																						
Newton Abbot	a						19 04							20 04							21 03		
Torquay	a																						
Paignton	a																						
Totnes	a						19 17							20 17							21 16		
Plymouth	a						19 43							20 45							21 44		
Liskeard	a						20 10																
Bodmin Parkway	a						20 22																
Lostwithiel	a						20 28																
Par	a						20 35																
Newquay	a																						
St Austell	a						20 41																
Truro	a						20 59																
Redruth	a						21 10																
Camborne	a						21 17																
Hayle	a						21 25																
St Erth	a						21 29																
Penzance	a						21 43																
Birmingham International	d					16 14							17 14							18 14			
Coventry	d					16 25							17 25							18 25			
Leamington Spa	d	16 02				16 38			17 00				17 38			18 00				18 38			19 00
Banbury	a	16 18				16 54			17 17				17 54			18 17				18 54			19 17
Oxford	a	16 40				17 14			17 41				18 14			18 40				19 14			19 40
Reading	a	17 08				17 39			18 08				18 39			19 08				19 39			20 08
Guildford	a																						
Basingstoke	a					18 08							19 08							20 08			
Winchester	a					18 24							19 24							20 24			
Southampton Airport Parkway	a					18 32							19 32							20 32			
Southampton Central	a					18 40							19 41							20 41			
Brockenhurst	a					18 57							19 57							20 57			
Bournemouth	a					19 11							20 11							21 11			

Table 51

Saturdays until 04 September

Scotland, The North East, North West England - The South West and South Coast

		XC	VT	XC	XC	XC	XC	XC	XC	XC	VT	XC	XC	XC	XC	XC	LM	VT	XC	XC	XC	XC	XC
		◇1	◇1	1	◇1	◇1	◇1	◇1	◇1	1	◇1	◇1	◇1	◇1	◇1	◇1	1	◇1	1	◇1	◇1	◇1	◇1
Aberdeen	d																						
Stonehaven	d																						
Montrose	d																						
Arbroath	d																						
Dundee	d																						
Leuchars	d																						
Cupar	d																						
Ladybank	d																						
Markinch	d																						
Kirkcaldy	d																						
Inverkeithing	d																						
Glasgow Central	d										16 00												
Motherwell	d																						
Haymarket	d																						
Edinburgh	d		14 52			14 05							15 05					16 52			16 05		
Haymarket	d		14 57															16 57					
Lockerbie	d																						
Carlisle	d		16 07								17 09							18 07					
Penrith North Lakes	d		16 22																				
Oxenholme Lake District	d										17 44							18 42					
Lancaster	d		16 57															18 57					
Preston	d		17 17								18 17							19 17					
Wigan North Western	d		17 28								18 28							19 28					
Warrington Bank Quay	d		17 39								18 39							19 39					
Manchester Piccadilly	d	17 06			17 27				18 05			18 27				19 07				19 27			20 07
Stockport	d				17 36				18 13			18 35				19 16				19 35			20 16
Wilmslow	d																						
Crewe	d		18 01								19 01						19 51	20 01					
Macclesfield	d	17 26							18 26											19 49			
Congleton	d				17 54							18 54											
Stoke-on-Trent	d	17 43			18 08				18 44			19 07				19 44				20 07			20 44
Stafford	d	18 04			18 27				19 03			19 25				20 03	20 12			20 26			21 03
Wolverhampton	d	18 17	18 32		18 41				19 17		19 32	19 41				20 17	20 28	20 32		20 41			21 16
Dunbar	d												15 25										
Berwick-upon-Tweed	d												15 48										
Alnmouth for Alnwick	d					15 05															17 05		
Morpeth	d																				17 20		
Newcastle	d					15b44		16 22					16c44		17 22						17f44	18 22	
Chester-le-Street	d							16 31							17 31							18 31	
Durham	d					15 56		16 38					16 56		17 38						17 56	18 38	
Darlington	d					16 13		16 56					17 13		17 55						18 13	18 56	
York	d					16 45		17 25					17 45		18 25						18 44	19 25	
Leeds	d					17 12							18 11								19 11		
Wakefield Westgate	d					17 24							18 24								19 24		
Doncaster	d							17 55							18e54							19 53	
Sheffield	d					17 54		18 23					18 54		19 24						19 54	20 23	
Chesterfield	d					18 06							19 06								20 06		
Nottingham	d			17 37			18 08			18 37				19 08					19 37				
Derby	d			18 05		18 28	18 36	18 53		19 06			19 28	19 36	19 54				20 05		20 28	20 53	
Burton-on-Trent	d			18 20			18 48			19 18			19 38	19 48					20 17				
Tamworth	d			18 33		18 48	19 00			19 30				20 00					20 29		20 49		
Birmingham New Street	a	18 38	18 55	18 57	18 58	19 07	19 24	19 27	19 33	19 54	19 55	19 58	20 07	20 24	20 27	20 33	20 47	20 55	20 56	20 58	21 07	21 27	21 32
Birmingham New Street	d	18 42			19 03	19 12	19 30	19 33	19 42			20 03	20 12	20 30	20 33	20 42				21 03	21 12		
Cheltenham Spa	a	19 23				19 50	20 10		20 23				20 50	21 10		21 23					21 50		
Gloucester	a						20 22							21 22							22 02		
Bristol Parkway	a	19 56				20 29			20 56				21 23			21 58					22 33		
Bristol Temple Meads	a	20 08				20 42			21 08				21 35			22 12					22 46		
Newport (South Wales)	a	20 55					21 10							22 21									
Cardiff Central	a	21 11					21 28							22 44									
Weston-super-Mare	a																						
Taunton	a					21 15							22 16										
Tiverton Parkway	a					21 28							22 28										
Exeter St Davids	a					21 43							22 44										
Dawlish	a																						
Teignmouth	a																						
Newton Abbot	a					22 05							23 11										
Torquay	a																						
Paignton	a																						
Totnes	a					22 21							23 26										
Plymouth	a					22 49							23 54										
Liskeard	a																						
Bodmin Parkway	a																						
Lostwithiel	a																						
Par	a																						
Newquay	a																						
St Austell	a																						
Truro	a																						
Redruth	a																						
Camborne	a																						
Hayle	a																						
St Erth	a																						
Penzance	a																						
Birmingham International ✈	d				19 14							20 14								21 14			
Coventry	d				19 25							20 25								21 25			
Leamington Spa	d				19 38			20 03				20 38			21 00					21 38			
Banbury	a				19 54			20 19				20 54			21 19					21 54			
Oxford	a				20 14			20 40				21 14			21 41					22 16			
Reading	a				20 39			21 08				21 39			22 10					22 41			
Guildford	a														22 59								
Basingstoke	a				21 08							22 08								23 11			
Winchester	a				21 24							22 24								23 27			
Southampton Airport Parkway ✈	a				21 33							22 32								23 35			
Southampton Central	a				21 41							22 41								23 43			
Brockenhurst	a				21 57							22 57											
Bournemouth	a				22 15							23 21											

Table 51

Saturdays until 04 September

Scotland, The North East, North West England - The South West and South Coast

		VT	XC	XC	XC	XC	XC	VT	VT	XC	XC	XC	XC
		◇1	1	◇1	◇1	◇1	◇1	◇1	◇1	1	◇1	◇1	◇1
												A	B
Aberdeen	d												
Stonehaven	d												
Montrose	d												
Arbroath	d												
Dundee	d												
Leuchars	d												
Cupar	d												
Ladybank	d												
Markinch	d												
Kirkcaldy	d												
Inverkeithing	d												
Glasgow Central	d	18 00						18 40					
Motherwell	d												
Haymarket	d												
Edinburgh	d				17 05				18 52		18 05		
Haymarket	d								18 57				
Lockerbie	d												
Carlisle	d	19 09						19 48	20 07				
Penrith North Lakes	d							20 02	20 22				
Oxenholme Lake District	d							20 25	20 45				
Lancaster	d	19 56						20 40	21 00				
Preston	d	20 17						21 00	21 20				
Wigan North Western	d	20 28						21 11	21 31				
Warrington Bank Quay	d	20 39						21 22	21 42				
Manchester Piccadilly	d			20 27		21 07						21 28	21 28
Stockport	d			20 35								21 36	21 36
Wilmslow	d												21 45
Crewe	d	21 01						21 43	22 04				22 09
Macclesfield	d			20 49								21 50	
Congleton	d												
Stoke-on-Trent	d			21 07		21 45						22 08	
Stafford	d			21 27		22 03		22 08	22 29			22 34	22 34
Wolverhampton	d	21 33		21 41		22 16		22 23	22 41			22 53	22 53
Dunbar	d				17 25						18 25		
Berwick-upon-Tweed	d				17 48						18 48		
Alnmouth for Alnwick	d										19 08		
Morpeth	d												
Newcastle	d				18 44		19 25				19 43		
Chester-le-Street	d												
Durham	d				18 56		19 37				19 56		
Darlington	d				19 13		19 54				20 13		
York	d				19 44		20 23				20 44		
Leeds	d				20 11						21 11		
Wakefield Westgate	d				20 23						21 23		
Doncaster	d												
Sheffield	d				20 54		21 23				21 54		
Chesterfield	d				21 06		21 35				22 06		
Nottingham	d		20 36							21 37			
Derby	d		21 06		21 28		21 57			22 10	22 27		
Burton-on-Trent	d		21 20		21 38		22 07			22 21	22 37		
Tamworth	d		21 33		21 49		22 18			22 33	22 48		
Birmingham New Street	a	21 54	21 55	21 58	22 07	22 32	22 45	22 46	22 59	23 02	23 06	23 17	23 17
Birmingham New Street	d												
Cheltenham Spa	a												
Gloucester	a												
Bristol Parkway	a												
Bristol Temple Meads	a												
Newport (South Wales)	a												
Cardiff Central	a												
Weston-super-Mare	a												
Taunton	a												
Tiverton Parkway	a												
Exeter St Davids	a												
Dawlish	a												
Teignmouth	a												
Newton Abbot	a												
Torquay	a												
Paignton	a												
Totnes	a												
Plymouth	a												
Liskeard	a												
Bodmin Parkway	a												
Lostwithiel	a												
Par	a												
Newquay	a												
St Austell	a												
Truro	a												
Redruth	a												
Camborne	a												
Hayle	a												
St Erth	a												
Penzance	a												
Birmingham International ✈	d												
Coventry	d												
Leamington Spa	d												
Banbury	a												
Oxford	a												
Reading	a												
Guildford	a												
Basingstoke	a												
Winchester	a												
Southampton Airport Parkway ✈	a												
Southampton Central	a												
Brockenhurst	a												
Bournemouth	a												

A from 17 July until 4 September

B until 10 July

Table 51

Saturdays from 11 September

Scotland, The North East, North West England - The South West and South Coast

Station		XC	XC	XC	XC	XC	XC	XC	XC	XC	XC	VT	XC	XC	XC	VT	XC	XC	XC	VT	XC	XC
Aberdeen	d																					
Stonehaven	d																					
Montrose	d																					
Arbroath	d																					
Dundee	d																					
Leuchars	d																					
Cupar	d																					
Ladybank	d																					
Markinch	d																					
Kirkcaldy	d																					
Inverkeithing	d																					
Glasgow Central	d																					
Motherwell	d																					
Haymarket	d																					
Edinburgh	d																					
Haymarket	d																					
Lockerbie	d																					
Carlisle	d																					
Penrith North Lakes	d																					
Oxenholme Lake District	d																					
Lancaster	d																			06 58		
Preston	d											06 17								07 17		
Wigan North Western	d											06 28								07 28		
Warrington Bank Quay	d											06 39								07 39		
Manchester Piccadilly	d							05 11			06 00							07 07			07 27	
Stockport	d										06 08							07 16			07 35	
Wilmslow	d																					
Crewe	d							05 47				07 01								08 01		
Macclesfield	d										06 21										07 49	
Congleton	d																					
Stoke-on-Trent	d							06 08			06 39							07 44			08 07	
Stafford	d							06 26			06 58							08 03			08 26	
Wolverhampton	d							06 41			07 15	07 32				08 06		08 18		08 32	08 41	
Dunbar	d																					
Berwick-upon-Tweed	d																					
Alnmouth for Alnwick	d																					
Morpeth	d																					
Newcastle	d																					
Chester-le-Street	d																					
Durham	d																					
Darlington	d																					
York	d																					06 09
Leeds	d													06 00			06 15					07 05
Wakefield Westgate	d													06 12			06 29					07 18
Doncaster	d																06 47					
Sheffield	d													06 50			07 18					07 54
Chesterfield	d													07 03			07 30					08 06
Nottingham	d								05 57				06 37		06 56				07 34			
Derby	d						06 10		06 36	06 47			07 06	07 25	07 36		07 50		08 03			08 28
Burton-on-Trent	d						06 20		06 48	06 57			07 18	07 36	07 49		08 00		08 18			08 38
Tamworth	d						06 31		07 00	07 08			07 30	07 48	08 01		08 11		08 30			08 50
Birmingham New Street	a						06 50	06 57	07 24	07 27	07 31	07 55	07 55	08 08	08 24	08 24	08 29	08 38	08 54	08 55	08 58	09 07
Birmingham New Street	d	05 00	05 42	06 03	06 33	06 42	07 12	07 03	07 30	07 33	07 42		08 03	08 12	08 30	08 30	08 33	08 42			09 03	09 12
Cheltenham Spa	a	06 02	06 41			07 23	07 50		08 10		08 23			08 51	09 10			09 23				09 50
Gloucester	a	06 13	06 54						08 22						09 22							
Bristol Parkway	a					07 56	08 24				08 56			09 24				09 56				10 29
Bristol Temple Meads	a					08 08	08 38				09 08			09 38				10 08				10 42
Newport (South Wales)	a	07 06	07 52						09 07						10 05							
Cardiff Central	a	07 22	08 08						09 23						10 21							
Weston-super-Mare	a																					
Taunton	a					08 42	09 15							10 16								11 15
Tiverton Parkway	a					08 54	09 28							10 29								11 28
Exeter St Davids	a					09 10	09 43							10 46								11 43
Dawlish	a																					
Teignmouth	a																					
Newton Abbot	a						10 03							11 07								12 03
Torquay	a					09 38																
Paignton	a					09 46																
Totnes	a						10 16							11 21								12 16
Plymouth	a						10 44							11 51								12 44
Liskeard	a																					
Bodmin Parkway	a																					
Lostwithiel	a																					
Par	a																					
Newquay	a																					
St Austell	a																					
Truro	a																					
Redruth	a																					
Camborne	a																					
Hayle	a																					
St Erth	a																					
Penzance	a																					
Birmingham International	d			06 14				07 15					08 14			08 39					09 14	
Coventry	d			06 25				07 25					08 25			08 51					09 25	
Leamington Spa	d			06 38	07 00			07 38		08 00			08 38				09 00				09 38	
Banbury	a			06 54	07 17			07 54		08 17			08 54				09 17				09 54	
Oxford	a			07 14	07 40			08 14		08 40			09 14				09 40				10 14	
Reading	a			07 39	08 08			08 39		09 08			09 39				10 08				10 39	
Guildford	a																					
Basingstoke	a			08 08				09 08					10 08								11 08	
Winchester	a			08 24				09 24					10 24								11 24	
Southampton Airport Parkway	a			08 32				09 32					10 32								11 32	
Southampton Central	a			08 41				09 40					10 43								11 41	
Brockenhurst	a			08 56				09 57					10 58								11 57	
Bournemouth	a			09 14				10 11					11 12								12 11	

Table 51

Saturdays from 11 September

Scotland, The North East, North West England - The South West and South Coast

Station		XC	XC	XC	XC	VT	XC	XC	XC	XC	XC	XC	VT	XC	XC	XC	XC	XC	XC	VT	XC	XC	XC
Aberdeen	d																						
Stonehaven	d																						
Montrose	d																						
Arbroath	d																						
Dundee	d																						
Leuchars	d																						
Cupar	d																						
Ladybank	d																						
Markinch	d																						
Kirkcaldy	d																						
Inverkeithing	d																						
Glasgow Central	d					05 50														08 00			
Motherwell	d					06 05																	
Haymarket	d																						
Edinburgh	d												06 52		06 12		06 55					07 07	
Haymarket	d												06 56										
Lockerbie	d																						
Carlisle	d					07 03							08 07							09 09			
Penrith North Lakes	d					07 18							08 22										
Oxenholme Lake District	d					07 42																	
Lancaster	d					07 57							08 57							09 57			
Preston	d					08 17							09 17							10 17			
Wigan North Western	d					08 28							09 28							10 28			
Warrington Bank Quay	d					08 39							09 39							10 39			
Manchester Piccadilly	d			08 07			08 27				09 07			09 27				10 07			10 27		
Stockport	d			08 16			08 35				09 16			09 35				10 16			10 35		
Wilmslow	d																						
Crewe	d					09 01							10 01							11 01			
Macclesfield	d						08 49							09 49							10 49		
Congleton	d																						
Stoke-on-Trent	d			08 44			09 07				09 44			10 07				10 44			11 07		
Stafford	d			09 03			09 26				10 03			10 26				11 03			11 26		
Wolverhampton	d			09 17		09 32	09 41				10 17		10 32	10 41				11 17		11 32	11 41		
Dunbar	d																					07 27	
Berwick-upon-Tweed	d														06 51		07 35					07 50	
Alnmouth for Alnwick	d														07 11		07 55						
Morpeth	d																08 09						
Newcastle	d		06 21					06 42		07 25					07 44		08 30					08 40	
Chester-le-Street	d		06 32																			08 49	
Durham	d		06 39					06 56		07 38					07 56		08 42					08 56	
Darlington	d		06 56					07 13		07 55					08 13		08 59					09 13	
York	d		07 25					07 44		08 27					08 44		09 28					09 44	
Leeds	d							08 12							09 11							10 12	
Wakefield Westgate	d							08 24							09 24							10 24	
Doncaster	d		07 52							08 53							09 53						
Sheffield	d		08 20					08 54		09 23					09 54		10 23					10 54	
Chesterfield	d		08 32					09 06							10 06							11 06	
Nottingham	d	08 08			08 37				09 08			09 37				10 08			10 37				11 11
Derby	d	08 35	08 53		09 06			09 28	09 36	09 53		10 06			10 28	10 36	10 53		11 06			11 28	11 36
Burton-on-Trent	d	08 48			09 18			09 38	09 48			10 18				10 48			11 17			11 38	11 48
Tamworth	d	09 00			09 29				10 00			10 30			10 48	11 00			11 29				12 00
Birmingham New Street	a	09 24	09 29	09 39	09 54	09 55	09 58	10 07	10 24	10 27	10 39	10 54	10 55	10 58	11 07	11 24	11 27	11 39	11 54	11 55	11 58	12 07	12 24
Birmingham New Street	d	09 30	09 33	09 42			10 03	10 12	10 30	10 33	10 42			11 03	11 12	11 30	11 33	11 42			12 03	12 12	12 30
Cheltenham Spa	a	10 10		10 23				10 50	11 10		11 23				11 50	12 10		12 23				12 50	13 10
Gloucester	a	10 22							11 23							12 22							13 22
Bristol Parkway	a			10 57				11 24			11 56				12 29			12 56				13 24	
Bristol Temple Meads	a			11 10				11 38			12 08				12 42			13 08				13 38	
Newport (South Wales)	a	11 05							12 06							13 06							14 05
Cardiff Central	a	11 24							12 22							13 22							14 21
Weston-super-Mare	a			11 31																			
Taunton	a			11 59				12 15							13 15							14 15	
Tiverton Parkway	a			12 12				12 28							13 28							14 28	
Exeter St Davids	a			12 27				12 43							13 43							14 43	
Dawlish	a			12 40																			
Teignmouth	a			12 45																			
Newton Abbot	a			12 52				13 03							14 03							15 03	
Torquay	a			13 03																			
Paignton	a			13 11																			
Totnes	a							13 16							14 16							15 16	
Plymouth	a							13 44							14 44							15 44	
Liskeard	a																						
Bodmin Parkway	a																						
Lostwithiel	a																						
Par	a																						
Newquay	a																						
St Austell	a																						
Truro	a																						
Redruth	a																						
Camborne	a																						
Hayle	a																						
St Erth	a																						
Penzance	a																						
Birmingham International	d						10 14							11 14							12 14		
Coventry	d						10 25							11 25							12 25		
Leamington Spa	d		10 00				10 38			11 00				11 38			12 00				12 38		
Banbury	a		10 17				10 54			11 17				11 54			12 17				12 54		
Oxford	a		10 40				11 14			11 40				12 14			12 40				13 14		
Reading	a		11 09				11 39			12 08				12 39			13 08				13 39		
Guildford	a																						
Basingstoke	a						12 08							13 08							14 08		
Winchester	a						12 24							13 24							14 24		
Southampton Airport Parkway	a						12 32							13 32							14 33		
Southampton Central	a						12 41							13 41							14 41		
Brockenhurst	a						12 57							13 57							14 57		
Bournemouth	a						13 11							14 11							15 11		

Table 51

Saturdays
from 11 September

Scotland, The North East, North West England - The South West and South Coast

		XC	XC	XC	VT	XC	XC	XC	XC	XC	XC	VT	XC	XC	XC	XC	XC	XC	VT	XC	XC
		◇1	◇1	1	◇1	◇1	◇1	◇1	◇1	◇1	1	◇1	◇1	◇1	◇1	◇1	◇1	1	◇1	◇1	◇1
Aberdeen	d																				
Stonehaven	d																				
Montrose	d																				
Arbroath	d																				
Dundee	d													07 35							
Leuchars 3	d													07 48							
Cupar	d													07 55							
Ladybank	d													08 03							
Markinch	d													08 11							
Kirkcaldy	d													08 20							
Inverkeithing	d													08 35							
Glasgow Central 15	d						07 00					10 00									09 00
Motherwell	d																				
Haymarket	d						07 54							08 57							09 55
Edinburgh 10	d				08 52		08 05							09 05					10 52		10 05
Haymarket	d				08 57														10 57		
Lockerbie	d																				
Carlisle 8	d				10 07							11 09							12 07		
Penrith North Lakes	d											11 24									
Oxenholme Lake District	d				10 42														12 43		
Lancaster 6	d				10 57														12 57		
Preston 8	d				11 17							12 17							13 17		
Wigan North Western	d				11 28							12 28							13 28		
Warrington Bank Quay	d				11 39							12 39							13 39		
Manchester Piccadilly 10	d		11 07			11 27				12 07			12 27				13 07			13 27	
Stockport	d		11 16			11 35				12 16			12 35				13 16			13 35	
Wilmslow	d																				
Crewe 10	d				12 01							13 01							14 01		
Macclesfield	d					11 49							12 49							13 49	
Congleton	d																				
Stoke-on-Trent	d		11 44			12 07				12 44			13 07				13 44			14 07	
Stafford	d		12 03			12 25				13 03			13 26				14 03			14 26	
Wolverhampton 7	d		12 17		12 32	12 41				13 16		13 32	13 41				14 17		14 32	14 41	
Dunbar	d													09 26							
Berwick-upon-Tweed	d						08 47							09 49							
Alnmouth for Alnwick	d						09 09														11 04
Morpeth	d																				11 19
Newcastle 8	d	09 25					09 41		10 25					10 44		11 25					11 41
Chester-le-Street	d																				
Durham	d	09 37					09 55		10 38					10 56		11 37					11 55
Darlington 7	d	09 56					10 12		10 56					11 13		11 56					12 12
York 8	d	10 25					10 45		11 27					11 45		12 25					12 45
Leeds 10	d						11 11							12 11							13 11
Wakefield Westgate 7	d						11 24							12 24							13 23
Doncaster 7	d	10 53							11 55							12 52					
Sheffield 7	d	11 23					11 54		12 23					12 54		13 23					13 54
Chesterfield	d						12 07							13 06							14 07
Nottingham 8	d			11 37				12 08			12 37				13 08			13 37			
Derby 6	d	11 53		12 06			12 29	12 36	12 53		13 06			13 28	13 36	13 53		14 06			14 29
Burton-on-Trent	d			12 18				12 48			13 20			13 38	13 48			14 18			
Tamworth	d			12 30			12 49	13 00			13 32				14 00			14 30			14 48
Birmingham New Street 12	a	12 27	12 39	12 54	12 55	12 58	13 09	13 24	13 27	13 39	13 54	13 55	13 58	14 07	14 24	14 27	14 39	14 54	14 55	14 58	15 08
Birmingham New Street 12	d	12 33	12 42			13 03	13 12	13 30	13 33	13 42			14 03	14 12	14 30	14 33	14 42			15 03	15 12
Cheltenham Spa	a		13 25				13 51	14 10		14 23				14 50	15 10		15 23				15 50
Gloucester 7	a							14 22							15 22						
Bristol Parkway 7	a		13 58				14 26			14 57				15 24			15 56				16 29
Bristol Temple Meads 10	a		14 10				14 41			15 10				15 38			16 08				16 42
Newport (South Wales)	a							15 06							16 06						
Cardiff Central 7	a							15 22							16 22						
Weston-super-Mare	a																				
Taunton	a						15 16							16 15							17 17
Tiverton Parkway	a						15 29							16 28							17 30
Exeter St Davids 6	a						15 46							16 43							17 47
Dawlish	a																				
Teignmouth	a																				
Newton Abbot	a						16 07							17 03							18 10
Torquay	a																				
Paignton	a																				
Totnes	a						16 21							17 16							18 24
Plymouth	a						16 50							17 44							18 52
Liskeard 6	a																				19 22
Bodmin Parkway	a																				19 35
Lostwithiel	a																				
Par	a																				19 46
Newquay	a																				
St Austell	a																				19 53
Truro	a																				20 12
Redruth	a																				20 24
Camborne	a																				20 32
Hayle	a																				
St Erth	a																				20 42
Penzance	a																				20 55
Birmingham International	d					13 15							14 14							15 14	
Coventry	d					13 25							14 25							15 25	
Leamington Spa 6	d	13 02				13 38			14 00				14 38			15 00				15 38	
Banbury	a	13 19				13 54			14 17				14 54			15 19				15 54	
Oxford	a	13 40				14 14			14 40				15 14			15 41				16 14	
Reading 7	a	14 08				14 39			15 08				15 39			16 08				16 39	
Guildford	a																				
Basingstoke	a					15 08							16 08							17 08	
Winchester	a					15 24							16 24							17 24	
Southampton Airport Parkway	a					15 32							16 32							17 32	
Southampton Central	a					15 41							16 41							17 41	
Brockenhurst 3	a					15 57							16 57							17 57	
Bournemouth	a					16 11							17 11							18 11	

Table 51

Saturdays
from 11 September

Scotland, The North East, North West England - The South West and South Coast

		XC	XC	XC	XC	VT	XC	XC	XC	XC	XC	XC	VT	XC	XC	XC	XC	XC	XC	VT	XC
		◇1	◇1	◇1	1	◇1	◇1	◇1	◇1	◇1	◇1	1	◇1	◇1	◇1	◇1	◇1	◇1	1	◇1	◇1
Aberdeen	d							08 20													
Stonehaven	d							08 38													
Montrose	d							08 59													
Arbroath	d							09 15													
Dundee	d							09 32													
Leuchars 3	d							09 47													
Cupar	d							09 54													
Ladybank	d							10 01													
Markinch	d							10 08													
Kirkcaldy	d							10 17													
Inverkeithing	d							10 32													
Glasgow Central 15	d					12 00														14 00	
Motherwell	d																				
Haymarket	d							10 51													
Edinburgh 10	d							11 05					12 52		12 05						
Haymarket	d												12 57								
Lockerbie	d																				
Carlisle 8	d					13 09							14 07							15 11	
Penrith North Lakes	d												14 22								
Oxenholme Lake District	d																			15 46	
Lancaster 6	d					13 58							14 57								
Preston 8	d					14 17							15 17							16 17	
Wigan North Western	d					14 28							15 28							16 28	
Warrington Bank Quay	d					14 39							15 39							16 39	
Manchester Piccadilly 10	d			14 07			14 27				15 07			15 27				16 07			16 27
Stockport	d			14 16			14 35				15 16			15 35				16 16			16 35
Wilmslow	d																				
Crewe 10	d					15 01							16 01							17 01	
Macclesfield	d						14 49							15 49							16 49
Congleton	d																				
Stoke-on-Trent	d			14 44			15 07				15 44			16 07				16 44			17 07
Stafford	d			15 03			15 26				16 03			16 25				17 03			17 26
Wolverhampton 7	d			15 17		15 32	15 41				16 17		16 32	16 41				17 17		17 32	17 41
Dunbar	d							11 25													
Berwick-upon-Tweed	d							11 48													
Alnmouth for Alnwick	d														13 05						
Morpeth	d																				
Newcastle 8	d		12 22					12 44		13 27					13 44		14 22				
Chester-le-Street	d		12 31																		
Durham	d		12 38					12 56		13 39					13 56		14 34				
Darlington 7	d		12 55					13 13		13 58					14 13		14 52				
York 8	d		13 27					13 44		14 27					14 44		15 26				
Leeds 10	d							14 11							15 12						
Wakefield Westgate 7	d							14 24							15 24						
Doncaster 7	d		13 54							14 56							15 55				
Sheffield 7	d		14 23					14 54		15 23					15 54		16 23				
Chesterfield	d							15 06							16 07						
Nottingham 8	d	14 08			14 37				15 08			15 37				16 08			16 37		
Derby 6	d	14 36	14 53		15 06			15 28	15 36	15 53		16 06			16 28	16 36	16 53		17 06		
Burton-on-Trent	d	14 48			15 20			15 38	15 48			16 18				16 48			17 20		
Tamworth	d	15 00			15 32				16 00			16 30			16 48	17 00			17 32		
Birmingham New Street 12	a	15 24	15 27	15 39	15 54	15 55	15 58	16 07	16 24	16 27	16 39	16 54	16 55	16 58	17 07	17 24	17 27	17 39	17 54	17 55	17 58
Birmingham New Street 12	d	15 30	15 33	15 42			16 03	16 12	16 30	16 33	16 42			17 03	17 12	17 30	17 33	17 42			18 03
Cheltenham Spa	a	16 10		16 23				16 50	17 10		17 23				17 50	18 17		18 23			
Gloucester 7	a	16 22							17 22							18 29					
Bristol Parkway 7	a			16 56				17 24			17 56				18 29			18 55			
Bristol Temple Meads 10	a			17 08				17 38			18 08				18 42			19 07			
Newport (South Wales)	a	17 06							18 05							19 12					
Cardiff Central 7	a	17 24							18 21							19 29					
Weston-super-Mare	a																				
Taunton	a			17 42				18 15							19 14						
Tiverton Parkway	a			17 54				18 28							19 27						
Exeter St Davids 6	a			18 10				18 43							19 42						
Dawlish	a			18 22																	
Teignmouth	a			18 27																	
Newton Abbot	a			18 34				19 04							20 02						
Torquay	a			18 46																	
Paignton	a			18 54																	
Totnes	a							19 17							20 15						
Plymouth	a							19 43							20 43						
Liskeard 6	a							20 10							21 22						
Bodmin Parkway	a							20 22							21 35						
Lostwithiel	a							20 28													
Par	a							20 35							21 45						
Newquay	a																				
St Austell	a							20 41							21 52						
Truro	a							20 59							22 10						
Redruth	a							21 10							22 27						
Camborne	a							21 17							22 34						
Hayle	a							21 25													
St Erth	a							21 29							22 44						
Penzance	a							21 43							22 55						
Birmingham International	d						16 14							17 14							18 14
Coventry	d						16 25							17 25							18 25
Leamington Spa 6	d		16 02				16 38			17 00				17 38			18 00				18 38
Banbury	a		16 18				16 54			17 17				17 54			18 17				18 54
Oxford	a		16 40				17 14			17 41				18 14			18 40				19 14
Reading 7	a		17 08				17 39			18 08				18 39			19 08				19 39
Guildford	a																				
Basingstoke	a						18 08							19 08							20 08
Winchester	a						18 24							19 24							20 24
Southampton Airport Parkway	a						18 32							19 32							20 32
Southampton Central	a						18 40							19 41							20 41
Brockenhurst 3	a						18 57							19 57							20 57
Bournemouth	a						19 11							20 11							21 11

Scotland, The North East, North West England - The South West and South Coast

	XC	XC	XC	XC	XC	VT	XC	XC	XC	XC	XC	XC	XC	VT	XC	XC	XC	XC	XC	LM	VT	XC
	◇■	◇■	◇■	◇■	◇■	◇■	■	◇■	◇■	◇■	◇■	◇■	■	◇■	◇■	◇■	◇■	◇■	◇■	■	◇■	■
				A	B																	
	🛒	🛒	🛒	🛒	🛒	🍴		🛒	🛒	🛒	🛒	🛒		🍴	🛒	🛒	🛒	🛒	🛒		🍴	
Aberdeen d																						
Stonehaven d																						
Montrose d																						
Arbroath d																						
Dundee d																						
Leuchars [3] d																						
Cupar d																						
Ladybank d																						
Markinch d																						
Kirkcaldy d																						
Inverkeithing d																						
Glasgow Central [15] d														16 00								
Motherwell d																						
Haymarket d																						
Edinburgh [10] d	13 05					14 52			14 05							15 05					16 52	
Haymarket d						14 57															16 57	
Lockerbie d																						
Carlisle [8] d						16 07								17 09							18 07	
Penrith North Lakes d						16 22																
Oxenholme Lake District d														17 44							18 42	
Lancaster [6] d						16 57															18 57	
Preston [8] d						17 17								18 17							19 17	
Wigan North Western d						17 28								18 28							19 28	
Warrington Bank Quay d						17 39								18 39							19 39	
Manchester Piccadilly [10] d				17 06	17 06			17 27				18 05			18 27				19 07			
Stockport d								17 36				18 13			18 35				19 16			
Wilmslow d																						
Crewe [10] d						18 01								19 01						19 51	20 01	
Macclesfield d				17 26	17 26							18 26										
Congleton d								17 54							18 54							
Stoke-on-Trent d				17 43	17 44			18 08				18 44			19 07				19 44			
Stafford d				18 04	18 04			18 27				19 03			19 25				20 03	20 12		
Wolverhampton [7] d				18 17	18 17	18 32		18 41				19 17		19 32	19 41				20 17	20 28	20 32	
Dunbar d	13 26															15 26						
Berwick-upon-Tweed d	13 48															15 48						
Alnmouth for Alnwick d									15 05													
Morpeth d																						
Newcastle [8] d	14 44		15 25						15 44		16 22					16 44		17 22				
Chester-le-Street d											16 31							17 31				
Durham d	14 56		15 38						15 56		16 38					16 56		17 38				
Darlington [7] d	15 13		15 56						16 13		16 56					17 13		17 55				
York [8] d	15 45		16 25						16 45		17 25					17 45		18 25				
Leeds [10] d	16 12								17 12							18 11						
Wakefield Westgate [7] d	16 24								17 24							18 24						
Doncaster [7] d			16 53								17 55							18 54				
Sheffield [7] d	16 54		17 23						17 54		18 23					18 54		19 24				
Chesterfield d	17 06								18 06							19 06						
Nottingham [8] d		17 08					17 37			18 08			18 37				19 08					19 37
Derby [6] d	17 28	17 36	17 53				18 05		18 28	18 36	18 53		19 06			19 28	19 36	19 54				20 05
Burton-on-Trent d	17 38	17 48					18 20			18 48			19 18			19 38	19 48					20 17
Tamworth d		18 00					18 33		18 48	19 00			19 30				20 00					20 29
Birmingham New Street [12] a	18 07	18 24	18 27	18 38	18 38	18 55	18 57	18 58	19 07	19 24	19 27	19 33	19 54	19 55	19 58	20 07	20 24	20 27	20 33	20 47	20 55	20 56
Birmingham New Street [12] d	18 12	18 30	18 33	18 42	18 42			19 03	19 12	19 30	19 33	19 42			20 03	20 12	20 30	20 33	20 42			
Cheltenham Spa a	18 50	19 10		19 23	19 23				19 50	20 10		20 23				20 50	21 10		21 23			
Gloucester [7] a		19 22								20 22							21 22					
Bristol Parkway [7] a	19 27			19 56	19 56				20 29			20 56				21 23			21 58			
Bristol Temple Meads [10] a	19 41			20 08	20 08				20 42			21 08				21 35			22 12			
Newport (South Wales) a		20 05		20 55	20 55					21 10							22 21					
Cardiff Central [7] a		20 21		21 11	21 11					21 28							22 44					
Weston-super-Mare a																						
Taunton a	20 15								21 15			21 44				22 16						
Tiverton Parkway a	20 28								21 28			21 56				22 28						
Exeter St Davids [6] a	20 43								21 43			22 12				22 44						
Dawlish a																						
Teignmouth a																						
Newton Abbot a	21 03								22 05			22 31				23 11						
Torquay a																						
Paignton a																						
Totnes a	21 16								22 21			22 44				23 26						
Plymouth a	21 44								22 49			23 12				23 54						
Liskeard [6] a																						
Bodmin Parkway a																						
Lostwithiel a																						
Par a																						
Newquay a																						
St Austell a																						
Truro a																						
Redruth a																						
Camborne a																						
Hayle a																						
St Erth a																						
Penzance a																						
Birmingham International ✈ d								19 14							20 14							
Coventry d								19 25							20 25							
Leamington Spa [6] d			19 00					19 38			20 03				20 38			21 00				
Banbury a			19 17					19 54			20 19				20 54			21 19				
Oxford a			19 40					20 14			20 40				21 14			21 41				
Reading [7] a			20 08					20 39			21 08				21 39			22 10				
Guildford a																		22 59				
Basingstoke a								21 08							22 08							
Winchester a								21 24							22 24							
Southampton Airport Parkway ✈ a								21 33							22 32							
Southampton Central a								21 41							22 41							
Brockenhurst [3] a								21 57							22 57							
Bournemouth a								22 15							23 21							

A from 11 September until 16 October **B** from 23 October

Scotland, The North East, North West England - The South West and South Coast

	XC	XC	XC	XC	VT	XC	XC	XC	XC	XC	VT	VT	XC	XC	XC
	◇■	◇■	◇■	◇■	◇■	■	◇■	◇■	◇■	◇■	◇■	◇■	■	◇■	◇■
	🛒	🛒	🛒	🛒	🍴		🛒	🛒	🛒	🛒	🍴	🍴		🛒	🛒
Aberdeen d															
Stonehaven d															
Montrose d															
Arbroath d															
Dundee d															
Leuchars [3] d															
Cupar d															
Ladybank d															
Markinch d															
Kirkcaldy d															
Inverkeithing d															
Glasgow Central [15] d					18 00						18 40				
Motherwell d															
Haymarket d															
Edinburgh [10] d		16 05						17 05				18 52		18 05	
Haymarket d												18 57			
Lockerbie d															
Carlisle [8] d					19 09						19 48	20 07			
Penrith North Lakes d											20 02	20 22			
Oxenholme Lake District d											20 25	20 45			
Lancaster [6] d					19 56						20 40	21 00			
Preston [8] d					20 17						21 00	21 20			
Wigan North Western d					20 28						21 11	21 31			
Warrington Bank Quay d					20 39						21 22	21 42			
Manchester Piccadilly [10] d	19 27			20 07			20 27		21 07						21 28
Stockport d	19 35			20 16			20 35								21 36
Wilmslow d															
Crewe [10] d					21 01						21 43	22 04			
Macclesfield d	19 49						20 49								21 50
Congleton d															
Stoke-on-Trent d	20 07			20 44			21 07		21 45						22 08
Stafford d	20 26			21 03			21 27		22 03		22 08	22 29			22 34
Wolverhampton [7] d	20 41			21 16	21 33		21 41		22 16		22 23	22 41			22 53
Dunbar d								17 25						18 25	
Berwick-upon-Tweed d								17 48						18 48	
Alnmouth for Alnwick d		17 05												19 08	
Morpeth d		17 20													
Newcastle [8] d		17 44	18 22					18 44		19 25				19 43	
Chester-le-Street d			18 31												
Durham d		17 56	18 38					18 56		19 37				19 56	
Darlington [7] d		18 13	18 56					19 13		19 54				20 13	
York [8] d		18 44	19 25					19 44		20 23				20 44	
Leeds [10] d		19 11						20 11						21 11	
Wakefield Westgate [7] d		19 24						20 23						21 23	
Doncaster [7] d			19 53												
Sheffield [7] d		19 54	20 23					20 54		21 23				21 54	
Chesterfield d		20 06						21 06		21 35				22 06	
Nottingham [8] d						20 36							21 37		
Derby [6] d		20 28	20 53			21 06		21 28		21 57			22 10	22 27	
Burton-on-Trent d						21 20		21 38		22 07			22 21	22 37	
Tamworth d		20 49				21 33		21 49		22 18			22 33	22 48	
Birmingham New Street [12] a	20 58	21 07	21 27	21 32	21 54	21 55	21 58	22 07	22 32	22 45	22 46	22 59	23 02	23 06	23 17
Birmingham New Street [12] d	21 03	21 12													
Cheltenham Spa a		21 50													
Gloucester [7] a		22 02													
Bristol Parkway [7] a		22 33													
Bristol Temple Meads [10] a		22 46													
Newport (South Wales) a															
Cardiff Central [7] a															
Weston-super-Mare a															
Taunton a															
Tiverton Parkway a															
Exeter St Davids [6] a															
Dawlish a															
Teignmouth a															
Newton Abbot a															
Torquay a															
Paignton a															
Totnes a															
Plymouth a															
Liskeard [6] a															
Bodmin Parkway a															
Lostwithiel a															
Par a															
Newquay a															
St Austell a															
Truro a															
Redruth a															
Camborne a															
Hayle a															
St Erth a															
Penzance a															
Birmingham International ✈ d	21 14														
Coventry d	21 25														
Leamington Spa [6] d	21 38														
Banbury a	21 54														
Oxford a	22 16														
Reading [7] a	22 41														
Guildford a															
Basingstoke a	23 11														
Winchester a	23 27														
Southampton Airport Parkway ✈ a	23 35														
Southampton Central a	23 43														
Brockenhurst [3] a															
Bournemouth a															

Table 51

Sundays until 11 July

Scotland, The North East, North West England - The South West and South Coast

		XC	XC	XC	XC	XC	XC	VT	XC	XC	XC	XC	XC	VT	XC	XC	XC	XC	VT	XC	XC	XC	XC	XC	VT
		◇1	◇1	◇1	◇1	◇1	◇1	◇1	◇1	◇1	◇1	◇1	◇1	◇1	◇1	◇1	◇1	◇1	◇1	◇1	◇1	◇1	◇1	◇1	◇1
Aberdeen	d																								
Stonehaven	d																								
Montrose	d																								
Arbroath	d																								
Dundee	d																								
Leuchars	d																								
Cupar	d																								
Ladybank	d																								
Markinch	d																								
Kirkcaldy	d																								
Inverkeithing	d																								
Glasgow Central	d																								
Motherwell	d																								
Haymarket	d																								
Edinburgh	d																				08 50				10 52
Haymarket	d																								10 57
Lockerbie	d																								
Carlisle	d																								12 07
Penrith North Lakes	d																								
Oxenholme Lake District	d																								12 43
Lancaster	d																		12 00						12 57
Preston	d							10 17						11 17					12 17						13 17
Wigan North Western	d							10 28						11 28					12 28						13 28
Warrington Bank Quay	d							10 39						11 39					12 39						13 39
Manchester Piccadilly	d		08 27		09 27				10 24						11 27					12 26				13 07	
Stockport	d		08 36		09 36				10 33						11 36										
Wilmslow	d		08 43		09 44				10 43						11 44					12 43					
Crewe	d		09 05					11 03						12 01					13 01						14 01
Macclesfield	d																								
Congleton	d																								
Stoke-on-Trent	d																							13 43	
Stafford	d		09 26		10 26				11 24						12 25					13 26					
Wolverhampton	d		09 41		10 41			11 33	11 41					12 33	12 41				13 32	13 41				14 15	14 33
Dunbar	d																								
Berwick-upon-Tweed	d																				09 33				
Alnmouth for Alnwick	d																								
Morpeth	d																								
Newcastle	d															09 25					10 25				
Chester-le-Street	d																								
Durham	d															09 38					10 37				
Darlington	d															09 55					10 54				
York	d										09 28					10 28					11 28				
Leeds	d			08 10		09 00					10 00					11 00					12 00				
Wakefield Westgate	d			08 22		09 11					10 12					11 12					12 12				
Doncaster	d					09 32					10 30					11 30					12 30				
Sheffield	d			08 54		09 57					10 57					11 57					12 57				
Chesterfield	d			09 07		10 09					11 09					12 09					13 09				
Nottingham	d											11 10										13 05			
Derby	d			09 28		10 33					11 30	11 36				12 30					13 32	13 36	13 52		
Burton-on-Trent	d										11 41	11 48									13 43	13 48			
Tamworth	d											12 00				12 48						14 00			
Birmingham New Street	a		09 58	10 21	10 58	11 31		11 56	11 58		12 16	12 26		12 55	12 58	13 07			13 55	13 58	14 10	14 22	14 27	14 31	14 55
Birmingham New Street	d	09 03	10 03	10 28	11 03		11 33		12 03	12 12		12 30	12 33		13 03	13 12	13 33	13 42		14 03	14 12	14 30	14 33	14 42	
Cheltenham Spa	a			12 04						12 50		13 10				13 50		14 23			14 51	15 10		15 24	
Gloucester	a											13 21										15 21			
Bristol Parkway	a			12 37						13 23						14 23		14 56			15 25			15 57	
Bristol Temple Meads	a			12 50						13 35						14 39		15 08			15 38			16 10	
Newport (South Wales)	a											14 10										16 06			
Cardiff Central	a											14 30										16 26			
Weston-super-Mare	a																								
Taunton	a			13 25						14 15						15 15					16 16			16 45	
Tiverton Parkway	a			13 36						14 28						15 28					16 27			16 57	
Exeter St Davids	a			13 55						14 44						15 44					16 47			17 13	
Dawlish	a																							17 25	
Teignmouth	a																							17 30	
Newton Abbot	a			14 18						15 03						16 03					17 07			17 37	
Torquay	a																							17 49	
Paignton	a																							17 58	
Totnes	a			14 32						15 16						16 16					17 21				
Plymouth	a			15 01						15 44						16 44					17 50				
Liskeard	a																								
Bodmin Parkway	a																								
Lostwithiel	a																								
Par	a																								
Newquay	a																								
St Austell	a																								
Truro	a																								
Redruth	a																								
Camborne	a																								
Hayle	a																								
St Erth	a																								
Penzance	a																								
Birmingham International ✈	d	09 14	10 14		11 14				12 14						13 14					14 14					
Coventry	d	09 25	10 25		11 25				12 25						13 25					14 25					
Leamington Spa	d	09 38	10 38		11 38		12 00		12 38				13 00		13 38		14 00			14 38			15 00		
Banbury	a	09 54	10 54		11 54		12 17		12 54				13 17		13 55		14 17			14 54			15 18		
Oxford	a	10 14	11 14		12 14		12 48		13 14				13 41		14 14		14 45			15 14			15 41		
Reading	a	10 42	11 42		12 42		13 15		13 42				14 10		14 42		15 15			15 42			16 09		
Guildford	a																								
Basingstoke	a	11 09	12 09		13 09				14 09						15 09					16 09					
Winchester	a	11 24	12 24		13 24				14 24						15 24					16 24					
Southampton Airport Parkway ✈	a	11 33	12 33		13 33				14 33						15 33					16 33					
Southampton Central	a	11 42	12 42		13 42				14 42						15 42					16 42					
Brockenhurst	a	12 02	13 02		14 01				15 02						16 02					17 02					
Bournemouth	a	12 27	13 27		14 27				15 27						16 27					17 27					

Table 51

Sundays until 11 July

Scotland, The North East, North West England - The South West and South Coast

		XC	XC	XC	XC	XC	VT	XC	XC	XC	XC	XC	VT	XC	XC	XC	XC	XC	VT	XC	XC	XC	XC	XC	VT	XC
		◇1	◇1	◇1	◇1	◇1	◇1	◇1	◇1	◇1	◇1	◇1	◇1	◇1	◇1	◇1	◇1	◇1	◇1	◇1	◇1	◇1	◇1	◇1	◇1	◇1
Aberdeen	d																									
Stonehaven	d																									
Montrose	d																									
Arbroath	d																									
Dundee	d																									
Leuchars	d																									
Cupar	d																									
Ladybank	d																									
Markinch	d																									
Kirkcaldy	d																									
Inverkeithing	d																									
Glasgow Central	d						11 52												13 55		11 37					
Motherwell	d																				11 54					
Haymarket	d																				12 39					
Edinburgh	d		09 50						10 50		11 25		12 52		11 50						12 50		13 33		14 52	
Haymarket	d												12 56												14 57	
Lockerbie	d																									
Carlisle	d						13 10						14 07						15 09						16 07	
Penrith North Lakes	d												14 22												16 22	
Oxenholme Lake District	d																		15 44							
Lancaster	d						13 58						14 57												16 57	
Preston	d						14 17						15 17						16 15						17 17	
Wigan North Western	d						14 28						15 28						16 26						17 28	
Warrington Bank Quay	d						14 39						15 39						16 37						17 39	
Manchester Piccadilly	d	13 27				14 07		14 27				15 07		15 27				16 07		16 27				17 07		17 27
Stockport	d	13 36						14 36						15 36						16 36						17 36
Wilmslow	d																									
Crewe	d						15 01						16 01						16 59						18 01	
Macclesfield	d	13 49						14 49						15 49						16 49						17 49
Congleton	d																									
Stoke-on-Trent	d	14 07				14 43		15 07				15 43		16 07				16 43		17 08				17 43		18 08
Stafford	d	14 25						15 25						16 25						17 26						18 26
Wolverhampton	d	14 41				15 15	15 32	15 41				16 15	16 33	16 41				17 15	17 32	17 41				18 15	18 33	18 41
Dunbar	d								11 10												13 10					
Berwick-upon-Tweed	d								11 33												13 33		14 18			
Alnmouth for Alnwick	d		10 47												12 47								14 38			
Morpeth	d		11 02																							
Newcastle	d		11 25						12 25		13 18				13 25		14 18				14 25		15 18			
Chester-le-Street	d										13 27															
Durham	d		11 37						12 37		13 34				13 37		14 30				14 37		15 30			
Darlington	d		11 54						12 54		13 52				13 54		14 47				14 54		15 47			
York	d		12 28						13 28		14 22				14 28		15 20				15 28		16 20			
Leeds	d		13 00						14 00						15 00						16 00					
Wakefield Westgate	d		13 12						14 12						15 12						16 12					
Doncaster	d		13 30								14 50						15 50						16 50			
Sheffield	d		13 57		14 20				14 50		15 20				15 50		16 20				16 50		17 20			
Chesterfield	d		14 09		14 32				15 02						16 02						17 02					
Nottingham	d			14 10						15 05						16 05						17 10				
Derby	d		14 30	14 35	14 53				15 23	15 35	15 51				16 23	16 35	16 51				17 25	17 36	17 51			
Burton-on-Trent	d			14 48					15 35	15 48						16 48					17 35	17 48				
Tamworth	d		14 49	15 00						16 00					16 43	17 00						18 00				
Birmingham New Street	a	14 58	15 07	15 21	15 27	15 31	15 55	15 58	16 00	16 23	16 27	16 31	16 56	16 58	17 02	17 21	17 27	17 31	17 55	17 58	18 00	18 21	18 27	18 31	18 56	18 58
Birmingham New Street	d	15 03	15 12	15 30	15 33	15 42		16 04	16 12	16 30	16 33	16 42		17 03	17 12	17 30	17 33	17 42		18 03	18 12	18 30	18 33	18 42		19 03
Cheltenham Spa	a		15 50	16 10		16 24			16 50	17 10		17 24			17 50	18 10		18 24			18 50	19 11		19 24		
Gloucester	a			16 21						17 21						18 21						19 24				
Bristol Parkway	a		16 23			16 57			17 23			18 01			18 23			18 57			19 23			20 02		
Bristol Temple Meads	a		16 35			17 09			17 35			18 13			18 37			19 09			19 35			20 14		
Newport (South Wales)	a			17 06						18 06						19 06						20 09				
Cardiff Central	a			17 26						18 28						19 26						20 29				
Weston-super-Mare	a																							20 36		
Taunton	a		17 15						18 19						19 15						20 16			20 58		
Tiverton Parkway	a		17 28						18 32						19 28						20 29			21 11		
Exeter St Davids	a		17 44						18 48						19 48						20 45			21 27		
Dawlish	a																							21 42		
Teignmouth	a																							21 47		
Newton Abbot	a		18 03						19 07						20 07						21 04			21 54		
Torquay	a																							22 06		
Paignton	a																							22 11		
Totnes	a		18 16						19 20						20 20						21 17					
Plymouth	a		18 44						19 48						20 48						21 45					
Liskeard	a		19 17												21 12											
Bodmin Parkway	a		19 29												21 24											
Lostwithiel	a																									
Par	a		19 39												21 34											
Newquay	a																									
St Austell	a		19 46												21 41											
Truro	a		20 07												21 58											
Redruth	a		20 18												22 10											
Camborne	a		20 25												22 19											
Hayle	a																									
St Erth	a		20 36												22 30											
Penzance	a		20 47												22 41											
Birmingham International ✈	d	15 14						16 14						17 14						18 14						19 14
Coventry	d	15 25						16 25						17 25						18 25						19 25
Leamington Spa	d	15 38			16 00			16 38			17 00			17 38			18 00			18 38			19 00			19 38
Banbury	a	15 54			16 17			16 54			17 17			17 54			18 17			18 54			19 17			19 54
Oxford	a	16 14			16 41			17 14			17 38			18 14			18 44			19 14			19 38			20 14
Reading	a	16 42			17 09			17 39			18 09			18 42			19 15			19 42			20 09			20 42
Guildford	a																									
Basingstoke	a	17 09						18 09						19 09						20 09						21 09
Winchester	a	17 24						18 24						19 24						20 24						21 24
Southampton Airport Parkway ✈	a	17 33						18 33						19 33						20 33						21 33
Southampton Central	a	17 40						18 42						19 40						20 43						21 43
Brockenhurst	a	18 02						19 01						20 02						21 02						22 02
Bournemouth	a	18 27						19 27						20 27						21 27						22 27

Table 51

Sundays until 11 July

Scotland, The North East, North West England - The South West and South Coast

		XC	XC	XC	XC	VT	XC	XC	XC	XC	XC	VT	XC	XC	XC	XC	XC	XC	XC	XC	VT	XC	VT	XC	XC
Aberdeen	d	11 12																							
Stonehaven	d	11 29																							
Montrose	d	11 50																							
Arbroath	d	12 06																							
Dundee	d	12 25																							
Leuchars	d	12 38																							
Cupar	d	12 45																							
Ladybank	d																								
Markinch	d																								
Kirkcaldy	d	13 03																							
Inverkeithing	d	13 18																							
Glasgow Central	d					15 56		13 45													18 30				
Motherwell	d							14 03																	
Haymarket	d	13 37						14 43																	
Edinburgh	d	13 50						14 50				16 52		15 50				16 50					18 52	17 50	
Haymarket	d											16 56											18 57		
Lockerbie	d																								
Carlisle	d					17 09						18 07									19 44		20 07		
Penrith North Lakes	d																						20 22		
Oxenholme Lake District	d					17 44						18 42									20 19				
Lancaster	d											18 57									20 34		20 57		
Preston	d					18 17						19 17									20 55		21 17		
Wigan North Western	d					18 28						19 28									21 07		21 28		
Warrington Bank Quay	d					18 39						19 39									21 18		21 39		
Manchester Piccadilly	d				18 07		18 27				19 07		19 27				20 07					21 07			22 07
Stockport	d						18 36						19 36				20 16					21 16			22 16
Wilmslow	d																								
Crewe	d					19 01						20 01									21 40		22 01		
Macclesfield	d						18 49						19 49				20 29					21 29			22 29
Congleton	d																								
Stoke-on-Trent	d				18 43		19 07				19 43		20 07				20 47					21 47			22 47
Stafford	d						19 25						20 25				21 09				22 02	22 06			23 05
Wolverhampton	d				19 15	19 32	19 41				20 15	20 32	20 41				21 22				22 16	22 22	22 32		23 19
Dunbar	d							15 10										17 10						18 10	
Berwick-upon-Tweed	d							15 33										17 33							
Alnmouth for Alnwick	d	14 47												16 47										18 51	
Morpeth	d													17 02											
Newcastle	d	15 25		16 18				16 25		17 18				17 25		18 18		18 25		19 18				19 25	
Chester-le-Street	d																								
Durham	d	15 37		16 30				16 37		17 33				17 37		18 33		18 38		19 33				19 39	
Darlington	d	15 54		16 47				16 54		17 50				17 55		18 50		18 54		19 50				19 56	
York	d	16 28		17 21				17 28		18 20				18 28		19 20		19 28		20 20				20 28	
Leeds	d	17 00						18 00						19 00				20 00						21 00	
Wakefield Westgate	d	17 12						18 12						19 12				20 12						21 12	
Doncaster	d			17 50						18 50						19 50				20 50					
Sheffield	d	17 50		18 20				18 50		19 20				19 50		20 20		20 50		21 20				21 50	
Chesterfield	d	18 02						19 02						20 02				21 02		21 32				22 02	
Nottingham	d		18 05						19 10						20 10				21 08						
Derby	d	18 23	18 35	18 51				19 23	19 34	19 51				20 23	20 35	20 51		21 23	21 35	21 53				22 23	
Burton-on-Trent	d		18 48					19 35	19 48						20 48			21 35	21 48	22 04				22 35	
Tamworth	d	18 43	19 00						20 00					20 43	21 00			21 46	22 00	22 14				22 46	
Birmingham New Street	a	19 02	19 21	19 27	19 31	19 55	19 58	20 00	20 23	20 27	20 31	20 55	21 00	21 02	21 18	21 24	21 39	22 04	22 23	22 33	22 40	22 40	22 57	23 04	23 36
Birmingham New Street	d	19 12	19 30	19 33	19 42		20 03	20 12		20 33	20 42		21 03	21 12			21 42	22 12							
Cheltenham Spa	a	19 50	20 10		20 24			20 50			21 24			21 50			22 24	22 50							
Gloucester	a		20 21											22 01											
Bristol Parkway	a	20 23			20 57			21 23			21 59			22 35			23 00	23 23							
Bristol Temple Meads	a	20 35			21 09			21 35			22 11			22 47			23 13	23 35							
Newport (South Wales)	a		21 06																						
Cardiff Central	a		21 26																						
Weston-super-Mare	a																								
Taunton	a	21 15						22 15																	
Tiverton Parkway	a	21 28						22 28																	
Exeter St Davids	a	21 44						22 44																	
Dawlish	a																								
Teignmouth	a																								
Newton Abbot	a	22 03						23 04																	
Torquay	a																								
Paignton	a																								
Totnes	a	22 16						23 20																	
Plymouth	a	22 46						23 49																	
Liskeard	a																								
Bodmin Parkway	a																								
Lostwithiel	a																								
Par	a																								
Newquay	a																								
St Austell	a																								
Truro	a																								
Redruth	a																								
Camborne	a																								
Hayle	a																								
St Erth	a																								
Penzance	a																								
Birmingham International	d						20 14						21 14												
Coventry	d						20 25						21 24												
Leamington Spa	d			20 00			20 38			21 00			21 35												
Banbury	a			20 18			20 54			21 17															
Oxford	a			20 40			21 14			21 38			22 08												
Reading	a			21 09			21 42			22 05			22 35												
Guildford	a									22 42															
Basingstoke	a						22 11																		
Winchester	a						22 26																		
Southampton Airport Parkway	a						22 35																		
Southampton Central	a						22 43																		
Brockenhurst	a																								
Bournemouth	a																								

Table 51

Sundays 18 July to 05 September

Scotland, The North East, North West England - The South West and South Coast

		XC	XC	XC	XC	XC	XC	VT	XC	XC	XC	XC	XC	VT	XC	XC	XC	XC	VT	XC	XC	XC	XC	XC	XC
Aberdeen	d																								
Stonehaven	d																								
Montrose	d																								
Arbroath	d																								
Dundee	d																								
Leuchars	d																								
Cupar	d																								
Ladybank	d																								
Markinch	d																								
Kirkcaldy	d																								
Inverkeithing	d																								
Glasgow Central	d																								
Motherwell	d																								
Haymarket	d																								
Edinburgh	d																				08 50				
Haymarket	d																								
Lockerbie	d																								
Carlisle	d																								
Penrith North Lakes	d																								
Oxenholme Lake District	d																								
Lancaster	d																		12 00						
Preston	d							10 17						11 17					12 17						
Wigan North Western	d							10 28						11 28					12 28						
Warrington Bank Quay	d							10 39						11 39					12 39						
Manchester Piccadilly	d		08 27		09 27				10 24						11 27					12 26					13 07
Stockport	d		08 36		09 36				10 34						11 36					12 36					
Wilmslow	d		08 43																						
Crewe	d		09 05					11 03						12 01					13 01						
Macclesfield	d				09 49				10 47						11 49					12 49					
Congleton	d																								
Stoke-on-Trent	d				10 07				11 07						12 07					13 07					13 43
Stafford	d		09 26		10 27				11 28						12 25					13 25					
Wolverhampton	d		09 41		10 43			11 33	11 43					12 33	12 41				13 32	13 41					14 15
Dunbar	d																								
Berwick-upon-Tweed	d																				09 33				
Alnmouth for Alnwick	d																								
Morpeth	d																								
Newcastle	d															09 25					10 25				
Chester-le-Street	d																								
Durham	d															09 38					10 37				
Darlington	d															09 55					10 54				
York	d									09 28						10 28					11 28				
Leeds	d			08 10		09 00				10 00						11 00					12 00				
Wakefield Westgate	d			08 22		09 11				10 12						11 12					12 12				
Doncaster	d					09 32				10 30						11 30					12 30				
Sheffield	d			08 54		09 57				10 57						11 57					12 57				
Chesterfield	d			09 07		10 09				11 09						12 09					13 09				
Nottingham	d											11 10					12 10					13 05			
Derby	d			09 28		10 33				11 30		11 36				12 30	12 36				13 32	13 36		13 52	
Burton-on-Trent	d									11 41		11 48					12 48				13 43	13 48			
Tamworth	d											12 00				12 48	13 00					14 00			
Birmingham New Street	a		09 58	10 21	10 59	11 31		11 56	12 00	12 07		12 26		12 55	12 58	13 07	13 21		13 55	13 58	14 10	14 22		14 27	14 31
Birmingham New Street	d	09 03	10 03	10 28	11 03		11 33		12 03		12 12	12 30	12 33		13 03	13 12	13 30	13 33		14 03	14 12	14 30	13 42	14 33	14 42
Cheltenham Spa	a			11 50							12 50	13 10				13 50	14 12				14 51	15 10	14 23		15 24
Gloucester	a											13 21					14 22					15 21			
Bristol Parkway	a			12 23							13 23					14 23					15 25		14 56		16 00
Bristol Temple Meads	a			12 37							13 35					14 39					15 38		15 08		16 11
Newport (South Wales)	a																15 03					16 06			
Cardiff Central	a																15 28					16 26			
Weston-super-Mare	a																								
Taunton	a			13 16							14 15					15 15					16 16				16 45
Tiverton Parkway	a			13 27							14 28					15 28					16 27				16 57
Exeter St Davids	a			13 46							14 44					15 44					16 47				17 13
Dawlish	a																								17 25
Teignmouth	a																								17 30
Newton Abbot	a			14 07							15 03					16 03					17 07				17 37
Torquay	a																								17 49
Paignton	a																								17 58
Totnes	a			14 21							15 16					16 16					17 21				
Plymouth	a			14 50							15 44					16 44					17 50				
Liskeard	a																								
Bodmin Parkway	a																								
Lostwithiel	a																								
Par	a																								
Newquay	a																								
St Austell	a																								
Truro	a																								
Redruth	a																								
Camborne	a																								
Hayle	a																								
St Erth	a																								
Penzance	a																								
Birmingham International	d	09 14	10 14		11 14				12 14						13 14					14 14					
Coventry	d	09 25	10 25		11 25				12 25						13 25					14 25					
Leamington Spa	d	09 38	10 38		11 38		12 00		12 38				13 00		13 38			14 00		14 38				15 00	
Banbury	a	09 54	10 54		11 54		12 17		12 54				13 18		13 54			14 17		14 54				15 18	
Oxford	a	10 14	11 14		12 14		12 48		13 14				13 41		14 14			14 45		15 14				15 41	
Reading	a	10 42	11 42		12 42		13 15		13 42				14 10		14 42			15 15		15 42				16 09	
Guildford	a																								
Basingstoke	a	11 09	12 09		13 09				14 09						15 09					16 09					
Winchester	a	11 24	12 24		13 24				14 24						15 24					16 24					
Southampton Airport Parkway	a	11 33	12 33		13 33				14 33						15 33					16 33					
Southampton Central	a	11 42	12 42		13 42				14 42						15 42					16 42					
Brockenhurst	a	12 02	13 02		14 01				15 02						16 02					17 02					
Bournemouth	a	12 27	13 27		14 27				15 27						16 27					17 27					

Table 51

Sundays
18 July to 05 September

Scotland, The North East, North West England - The South West and South Coast

		VT ◇1	XC ◇1	XC ◇1	XC ◇1	XC ◇1	XC ◇1	VT ◇1	XC ◇1	XC ◇1	XC ◇1	XC ◇1	XC ◇1	VT ◇1	XC ◇1	XC ◇1	XC ◇1	XC ◇1	XC ◇1	VT ◇1	XC ◇1	XC ◇1	XC ◇1	XC ◇1	XC ◇1	VT ◇1
Aberdeen	d																									
Stonehaven	d																									
Montrose	d																									
Arbroath	d																									
Dundee	d																									
Leuchars 3	d																									
Cupar	d																									
Ladybank	d																									
Markinch	d																									
Kirkcaldy	d																									
Inverkeithing	d																									
Glasgow Central 15	d							11 52												13 55		11 37				
Motherwell	d																					11 54				
Haymarket	d																					12 39				
Edinburgh 10	d	10 52		09 50						10 50		11 25		12 52		11 50						12 50		13 33		14 52
Haymarket	d	10 57												12 56												14 57
Lockerbie	d																									
Carlisle 8	d	12 07						13 10						14 07						15 09						16 07
Penrith North Lakes	d													14 22												16 22
Oxenholme Lake District	d	12 43																		15 44						
Lancaster 6	d	12 57						13 58						14 57												16 57
Preston 8	d	13 17						14 17						15 17						16 15						17 17
Wigan North Western	d	13 28						14 28						15 28						16 26						17 28
Warrington Bank Quay	d	13 39						14 39						15 39						16 37						17 39
Manchester Piccadilly 10 ⇌	d		13 27				14 07		14 27				15 07		15 27				16 07		16 27				17 07	
Stockport	d		13 36						14 36						15 36						16 36					
Wilmslow	d																									
Crewe 10	d	14 01						15 01						16 01						16 59						18 01
Macclesfield	d		13 49						14 49						15 49						16 49					
Congleton	d																									
Stoke-on-Trent	d		14 07				14 43		15 07				15 43		16 07				16 43		17 08				17 43	
Stafford	d		14 25						15 25						16 25						17 26					
Wolverhampton 7 ⇌	d	14 33	14 41				15 15	15 32	15 41				16 15	16 33	16 41				17 15	17 32	17 41				18 15	18 33
Dunbar	d									11 10												13 10				
Berwick-upon-Tweed	d									11 33												13 33				
Alnmouth for Alnwick	d			10 47												12 47								14 18		
Morpeth	d			11 02																				14 38		
Newcastle 8	d			11 25						12 25		13 18				13 25		14 18				14 25		15 18		
Chester-le-Street	d											13 27														
Durham	d			11 37						12 37		13 34				13 37		14 30				14 37		15 30		
Darlington 7	d			11 54						12 54		13 52				13 54		14 47				14 54		15 47		
York 8	d			12 28						13 28		14 22				14 28		15 20				15 28		16 20		
Leeds 10	d			13 00						14 00						15 00						16 00				
Wakefield Westgate 7	d			13 12						14 12						15 12						16 12				
Doncaster 7	d			13 30								14 50						15 50						16 50		
Sheffield 7 ⇌	d			13 57		14 20				14 50		15 20				15 50		16 20				16 50		17 20		
Chesterfield	d			14 09		14 32				15 02						16 02						17 02				
Nottingham 8 ⇌	d				14 10						15 05						16 05						17 10			
Derby 6	d			14 30	14 35	14 53				15 23	15 35	15 51				16 23	16 35	16 51				17 25	17 36	17 51		
Burton-on-Trent	d				14 48					15 35	15 48						16 48					17 35	17 48			
Tamworth	d			14 49	15 00						16 00					16 43	17 00						18 00			
Birmingham New Street 12	a	14 55	14 58	15 07	15 21	15 27	15 31	15 55	15 58	16 00	16 23	16 27	16 31	16 56	16 58	17 02	17 21	17 27	17 31	17 55	17 58	18 00	18 21	18 27	18 31	18 56
Birmingham New Street 12	d		15 03	15 12	15 30	15 33	15 42		16 04	16 12	16 30	16 33	16 42		17 03	17 12	17 30	17 33	17 42		18 03	18 12	18 30	18 33	18 42	
Cheltenham Spa	a			15 50	16 10		16 24			16 50	17 10		17 24			17 50	18 10		18 24			18 50	19 11		19 24	
Gloucester 7	a				16 21						17 21						18 21						19 24			
Bristol Parkway 7	a			16 23			16 57			17 23			18 01			18 23			18 57			19 23			20 02	
Bristol Temple Meads 10	a			16 35			17 09			17 35			18 13			18 37			19 09			19 35			20 14	
Newport (South Wales)	a				17 02						18 02						19 02						20 05			
Cardiff Central 7	a				17 26						18 28						19 26						20 29			
Weston-super-Mare	a																								20 36	
Taunton	a			17 15						18 19						19 15						20 16			20 58	
Tiverton Parkway	a			17 28						18 32						19 28						20 29			21 11	
Exeter St Davids 6	a			17 44						18 48						19 48						20 45			21 27	
Dawlish	a																								21 42	
Teignmouth	a																								21 47	
Newton Abbot	a			18 03						19 07						20 07						21 04			21 54	
Torquay	a																								22 06	
Paignton	a																								22 11	
Totnes	a			18 16						19 20						20 20						21 17				
Plymouth	a			18 44						19 48						20 48						21 45				
Liskeard 6	a			19 17												21 12										
Bodmin Parkway	a			19 29												21 24										
Lostwithiel	a																									
Par	a			19 39												21 34										
Newquay	a																									
St Austell	a			19 46												21 41										
Truro	a			20 07												21 58										
Redruth	a			20 18												22 10										
Camborne	a			20 25												22 19										
Hayle	a																									
St Erth	a			20 36												22 30										
Penzance	a			20 47												22 41										
Birmingham International ✈	d		15 14						16 14						17 14						18 14					
Coventry	d		15 25						16 25						17 25						18 25					
Leamington Spa 8	d		15 38			16 00			16 38			17 00			17 38			18 00			18 38			19 00		
Banbury	a		15 54			16 17			16 54			17 17			17 54			18 17			18 54			19 17		
Oxford	a		16 14			16 41			17 14			17 38			18 14			18 44			19 14			19 38		
Reading 7	a		16 42			17 09			17 39			18 09			18 42			19 15			19 42			20 09		
Guildford	a																									
Basingstoke	a		17 09						18 09						19 09						20 09					
Winchester	a		17 24						18 24						19 24						20 24					
Southampton Airport Parkway ✈	a		17 33						18 33						19 33						20 33					
Southampton Central	a		17 40						18 42						19 40						20 43					
Brockenhurst 3	a		18 02						19 01						20 02						21 02					
Bournemouth	a		18 27						19 27						20 27						21 27					

Table 51

Sundays
18 July to 05 September

Scotland, The North East, North West England - The South West and South Coast

		VT ◇1	XC ◇1	XC ◇1	XC ◇1	XC ◇1	XC ◇1	VT ◇1	XC ◇1	XC ◇1	XC ◇1	XC ◇1	XC ◇1	VT ◇1	XC ◇1	XC ◇1	XC ◇1	XC ◇1	XC ◇1	XC ◇1	XC ◇1	XC ◇1	VT ◇1	XC ◇1	VT ◇1
Aberdeen	d			11 12																					
Stonehaven	d			11 29																					
Montrose	d			11 50																					
Arbroath	d			12 06																					
Dundee	d			12 25																					
Leuchars 3	d			12 38																					
Cupar	d			12 45																					
Ladybank	d																								
Markinch	d																								
Kirkcaldy	d			13 03																					
Inverkeithing	d			13 18																					
Glasgow Central 15	d							15 56	13 45														18 30		
Motherwell	d								14 03																
Haymarket	d			13 37					14 43																
Edinburgh 10	d	14 52		13 50					14 50					16 52		15 50				16 50					18 52
Haymarket	d	14 57												16 56											18 57
Lockerbie	d																								
Carlisle 8	d	16 07						17 09						18 07									19 44		20 07
Penrith North Lakes	d	16 22																							20 22
Oxenholme Lake District	d							17 44						18 42									20 19		
Lancaster 6	d	16 57												18 57									20 34		20 57
Preston 8	d	17 17						18 17						19 17									20 55		21 17
Wigan North Western	d	17 28						18 28						19 28									21 07		21 28
Warrington Bank Quay	d	17 39						18 39						19 39									21 18		21 39
Manchester Piccadilly 10 ⇌	d		17 27				18 07			18 27			19 07		19 27				20 07					21 07	
Stockport	d		17 36							18 36					19 36				20 16					21 16	
Wilmslow	d																								
Crewe 10	d	18 01						19 01						20 01									21 40		22 01
Macclesfield	d		17 49							18 49					19 49				20 29					21 29	
Congleton	d																								
Stoke-on-Trent	d		18 08				18 43			19 07			19 43		20 07				20 47					21 47	
Stafford	d		18 26							19 25					20 25				21 09				22 02	22 06	
Wolverhampton 7 ⇌	d	18 33	18 41				19 15	19 32		19 41			20 15	20 32	20 41				21 22				22 16	22 22	22 32
Dunbar	d								15 10											17 10					
Berwick-upon-Tweed	d								15 33											17 33					
Alnmouth for Alnwick	d			14 47												16 47									
Morpeth	d															17 02									
Newcastle 8	d			15 25		16 18			16 25			17 18				17 25		18 18		18 25		19 18			
Chester-le-Street	d																								
Durham	d			15 37		16 30			16 37			17 33				17 37		18 33		18 38		19 33			
Darlington 7	d			15 54		16 47			16 54			17 50				17 55		18 50		18 54		19 50			
York 8	d			16 28		17 21			17 28			18 20				18 28		19 20		19 28		20 20			
Leeds 10	d			17 00					18 00							19 00				20 00					
Wakefield Westgate 7	d			17 12					18 12							19 12				20 12					
Doncaster 7	d					17 50						18 50						19 50				20 50			
Sheffield 7 ⇌	d			17 50		18 20			18 50			19 20				19 50		20 20		20 50		21 20			
Chesterfield	d			18 02					19 02							20 02				21 02		21 32			
Nottingham 8 ⇌	d				18 05						19 10						20 10				21 08				
Derby 6	d			18 23	18 35	18 51			19 23		19 34	19 51				20 23	20 35	20 51		21 23	21 35	21 53			
Burton-on-Trent	d				18 48				19 35		19 48						20 48			21 35	21 48	22 04			
Tamworth	d			18 43	19 00						20 00					20 43	21 00			21 46	22 00	22 14			
Birmingham New Street 12	a	18 56	18 58	19 02	19 21	19 27	19 31	19 55	20 00	19 58	20 23	20 27	20 31	20 55	21 00	21 02	21 18	21 24	21 39	22 04	22 23	22 33	22 40	22 40	22 57
Birmingham New Street 12	d		19 03	19 12	19 30	19 33	19 42		20 12	20 03		20 33	20 42		21 03	21 12			21 42	22 12					
Cheltenham Spa	a			19 50	20 10		20 24		20 50				21 24			21 50			22 24	22 50					
Gloucester 7	a				20 21											22 01									
Bristol Parkway 7	a			20 23			20 57		21 23				21 59			22 35			23 00	23 23					
Bristol Temple Meads 10	a			20 35			21 09		21 35				22 11			22 47			23 13	23 35					
Newport (South Wales)	a				21 05																				
Cardiff Central 7	a				21 29																				
Weston-super-Mare	a																								
Taunton	a			21 15					22 15																
Tiverton Parkway	a			21 28					22 28																
Exeter St Davids 6	a			21 44					22 44																
Dawlish	a																								
Teignmouth	a																								
Newton Abbot	a			22 03					23 04																
Torquay	a																								
Paignton	a																								
Totnes	a			22 16					23 20																
Plymouth	a			22 46					23 49																
Liskeard 6	a																								
Bodmin Parkway	a																								
Lostwithiel	a																								
Par	a																								
Newquay	a																								
St Austell	a																								
Truro	a																								
Redruth	a																								
Camborne	a																								
Hayle	a																								
St Erth	a																								
Penzance	a																								
Birmingham International ✈	d		19 14							20 14					21 14										
Coventry	d		19 25							20 25					21 24										
Leamington Spa 8	d		19 38			20 00				20 38		21 00			21 35										
Banbury	a		19 54			20 18				20 54		21 17													
Oxford	a		20 14			20 40				21 14		21 38			22 08										
Reading 7	a		20 42			21 09				21 42		22 05			22 35										
Guildford	a											22 42													
Basingstoke	a		21 09							22 11															
Winchester	a		21 24							22 26															
Southampton Airport Parkway ✈	a		21 33							22 35															
Southampton Central	a		21 43							22 43															
Brockenhurst 3	a		22 02																						
Bournemouth	a		22 27																						

Table 51

Sundays
18 July to 05 September

Scotland, The North East, North West England - The South West and South Coast

		XC	XC
		◇■	◇■
Aberdeen	d		
Stonehaven	d		
Montrose	d		
Arbroath	d		
Dundee	d		
Leuchars ■	d		
Cupar	d		
Ladybank	d		
Markinch	d		
Kirkcaldy	d		
Inverkeithing	d		
Glasgow Central ■	d		
Motherwell	d		
Haymarket	d		
Edinburgh ■	d	17 50	
Haymarket	d		
Lockerbie	d		
Carlisle ■	d		
Penrith North Lakes	d		
Oxenholme Lake District	d		
Lancaster ■	d		
Preston ■	d		
Wigan North Western	d		
Warrington Bank Quay	d		
Manchester Piccadilly ■	d		22 07
Stockport	d		22 16
Wilmslow	d		
Crewe ■	d		
Macclesfield	d		22 29
Congleton	d		
Stoke-on-Trent	d		22 47
Stafford	d		23 05
Wolverhampton ■	d		23 19
Dunbar	d	18 10	
Berwick-upon-Tweed	d		
Alnmouth for Alnwick	d	18 51	
Morpeth	d		
Newcastle ■	d	19 25	
Chester-le-Street	d		
Durham	d	19 39	
Darlington ■	d	19 56	
York ■	d	20 28	
Leeds ■	d	21 00	
Wakefield Westgate ■	d	21 12	
Doncaster ■	d		
Sheffield ■	d	21 50	
Chesterfield	d	22 02	
Nottingham ■	d		
Derby ■	d	22 23	
Burton-on-Trent	d	22 35	
Tamworth	d	22 46	
Birmingham New Street ■	a	23 04	23 36
Birmingham New Street ■	d		
Cheltenham Spa	a		
Gloucester ■	a		
Bristol Parkway ■	a		
Bristol Temple Meads ■	a		
Newport (South Wales)	a		
Cardiff Central ■	a		
Weston-super-Mare	a		
Taunton	a		
Tiverton Parkway	a		
Exeter St Davids ■	a		
Dawlish	a		
Teignmouth	a		
Newton Abbot	a		
Torquay	a		
Paignton	a		
Totnes	a		
Plymouth	a		
Liskeard ■	a		
Bodmin Parkway	a		
Lostwithiel	a		
Par	a		
Newquay	a		
St Austell	a		
Truro	a		
Redruth	a		
Camborne	a		
Hayle	a		
St Erth	a		
Penzance	a		
Birmingham International	d		
Coventry	d		
Leamington Spa ■	d		
Banbury	a		
Oxford	a		
Reading ■	a		
Guildford	a		
Basingstoke	a		
Winchester	a		
Southampton Airport Parkway	a		
Southampton Central	a		
Brockenhurst ■	a		
Bournemouth	a		

Table 51

Sundays
12 September to 17 October

Scotland, The North East, North West England - The South West and South Coast

		XC	XC	XC	XC	XC	XC	XC	XC	XC	VT	XC	XC	XC	XC	VT	XC	XC	XC	XC	XC	VT	XC	XC	XC	XC	XC
		◇■	◇■	◇■	◇■	◇■	◇■	◇■	◇■	◇■	◇■	◇■	◇■	◇■	◇■	◇■	◇■	◇■	◇■	◇■	◇■	◇■	◇■	◇■	◇■	◇■	◇■
Aberdeen	d																										
Stonehaven	d																										
Montrose	d																										
Arbroath	d																										
Dundee	d																										
Leuchars ■	d																										
Cupar	d																										
Ladybank	d																										
Markinch	d																										
Kirkcaldy	d																										
Inverkeithing	d																										
Glasgow Central ■	d																										
Motherwell	d																										
Haymarket	d																										
Edinburgh ■	d																						08 50				
Haymarket	d																										
Lockerbie	d																										
Carlisle ■	d																										
Penrith North Lakes	d																										
Oxenholme Lake District	d																										
Lancaster ■	d																					12 00					
Preston ■	d										10 17					11 17						12 17					
Wigan North Western	d										10 28					11 28						12 28					
Warrington Bank Quay	d										10 39					11 39						12 39					
Manchester Piccadilly ■	d			08 26			09 27					10 27					11 27						12 26				13 07
Stockport	d			08 35			09 36					10 36					11 36						12 35				
Wilmslow	d			08 41																							
Crewe ■	d			09 05							11 03					12 01						13 01					
Macclesfield	d						09 49					10 49					11 49						12 49				
Congleton	d																										
Stoke-on-Trent	d						10 07					11 07					12 07						13 07				13 43
Stafford	d			09 26			10 27					11 27					12 25						13 25				
Wolverhampton ■	d			09 41			10 43				11 33	11 42				12 33	12 41					13 32	13 41				14 15
Dunbar	d																										
Berwick-upon-Tweed	d																							09 33			
Alnmouth for Alnwick	d																										
Morpeth	d																										
Newcastle ■	d																	09 25						10 25			
Chester-le-Street	d																										
Durham	d																	09 38						10 37			
Darlington ■	d																	09 55						10 54			
York ■	d												09 28					10 28						11 28			
Leeds ■	d				08 10			09 00					10 00					11 00						12 00			
Wakefield Westgate ■	d				08 22			09 11					10 12					11 12						12 12			
Doncaster ■	d							09 32					10 30					11 30						12 30			
Sheffield ■	d				08 54			09 57					10 57					11 57						12 57			
Chesterfield	d				09 07			10 09					11 09					12 09						13 09			
Nottingham ■	d													11 10					12 10						13 05		
Derby ■	d				09 28			10 33					11 30	11 36				12 30	12 36					13 32	13 36	13 52	
Burton-on-Trent	d												11 41	11 48					12 48					13 43	13 48		
Tamworth	d				09 47									12 00				12 48	13 00						14 00		
Birmingham New Street ■	a			09 58	10 09		10 59	11 08			11 56	12 00	12 07	12 26		12 55	12 58	13 07	13 21			13 55	13 58	14 10	14 22	14 27	14 31
Birmingham New Street ■	d	09 03	09 12	10 03	10 12	10 30	11 03	11 12	11 30	11 33		12 03	12 12	12 30	12 33		13 03	13 12	13 30	13 33	13 42		14 03	14 12	14 30	14 33	14 42
Cheltenham Spa	a		09 49		10 55	11 10		11 50	12 10				12 50	13 10				13 50	14 12		14 23			14 51	15 10		15 24
Gloucester ■	a					11 21			12 20					13 21					14 22						15 21		
Bristol Parkway ■	a		10 23		11 28			12 23					13 23					14 23			14 56			15 25			16 00
Bristol Temple Meads ■	a		10 35		11 41			12 36					13 35					14 39			15 08			15 38			16 11
Newport (South Wales)	a					12 06			13 06					14 10					15 07						16 06		
Cardiff Central ■	a					12 26			13 26					14 30					15 28						16 26		
Weston-super-Mare	a																										
Taunton	a		11 19		12 16			13 16					14 15					15 15						16 16			16 45
Tiverton Parkway	a		11 33		12 27			13 28					14 28					15 28						16 27			16 57
Exeter St Davids ■	a		11 48		12 46			13 46					14 44					15 44						16 47			17 13
Dawlish	a																										17 25
Teignmouth	a																										17 30
Newton Abbot	a		12 08		13 09			14 07					15 03					16 03						17 07			17 37
Torquay	a																										17 49
Paignton	a																										17 58
Totnes	a		12 22		13 23			14 21					15 16					16 16						17 21			
Plymouth	a		12 49		13 52			14 50					15 44					16 44						17 50			
Liskeard ■	a		13 17																								
Bodmin Parkway	a		13 29																								
Lostwithiel	a																										
Par	a		13 39																								
Newquay	a																										
St Austell	a		13 46																								
Truro	a		14 03																								
Redruth	a		14 15																								
Camborne	a		14 22																								
Hayle	a																										
St Erth	a		14 32																								
Penzance	a		14 43																								
Birmingham International	d	09 14		10 14			11 14					12 14					13 14						14 14				
Coventry	d	09 25		10 25			11 25					12 25					13 25						14 25				
Leamington Spa ■	d	09 38		10 38			11 38			12 00		12 38			13 00		13 38			14 00			14 38			15 00	
Banbury	a	09 54		10 54			11 54			12 17		12 54			13 17		13 54			14 17			14 54			15 18	
Oxford	a	10 14		11 14			12 14			12 38		13 14			13 41		14 14			14 37			15 14			15 41	
Reading ■	a	10 42		11 42			12 42			13 09		13 42			14 10		14 42			15 09			15 42			16 09	
Guildford	a																										
Basingstoke	a	11 09		12 09			13 09					14 09					15 09						16 09				
Winchester	a	11 24		12 24			13 24					14 24					15 24						16 24				
Southampton Airport Parkway	a	11 33		12 33			13 33					14 33					15 33						16 33				
Southampton Central	a	11 42		12 42			13 42					14 42					15 42						16 42				
Brockenhurst ■	a	12 02		13 02			14 01					15 02					16 02						17 02				
Bournemouth	a	12 27		13 27			14 27					15 27					16 27						17 27				

Table 51

Scotland, The North East, North West England - The South West and South Coast

Sundays

12 September to 17 October

		VT	XC	XC	XC	XC	XC	VT	XC	XC	XC	XC	XC	VT	XC	XC	XC	XC	XC	VT	XC	XC	XC	XC	XC	VT	XC
		◇1	◇1	◇1	◇1	◇1	◇1	◇1	◇1	◇1	◇1	◇1	◇1	◇1	◇1	◇1	◇1	◇1	◇1	◇1	◇1	◇1	◇1	◇1	◇1	◇1	◇1
Aberdeen	d																										
Stonehaven	d																										
Montrose	d																										
Arbroath	d																										
Dundee	d																										
Leuchars 3	d																										
Cupar	d																										
Ladybank	d																										
Markinch	d																										
Kirkcaldy	d																										
Inverkeithing	d																										
Glasgow Central 15	d							11 52												13 55		11 37					
Motherwell	d																					11 54					
Haymarket	d																					12 39					
Edinburgh 10	d	10 52		09 50						10 50		11 25		12 52		11 50						12 50		13 33		14 52	
Haymarket	d	10 57												12 56												14 57	
Lockerbie	d																										
Carlisle 8	d	12 07						13 10						14 07						15 09						16 07	
Penrith North Lakes	d													14 22												16 22	
Oxenholme Lake District	d	12 43																		15 44							
Lancaster 6	d	12 57						13 58						14 57												16 57	
Preston 8	d	13 17						14 17						15 17						16 15						17 17	
Wigan North Western	d	13 28						14 28						15 28						16 26						17 28	
Warrington Bank Quay	d	13 39						14 39						15 39						16 37						17 39	
Manchester Piccadilly 10	d		13 27				14 07		14 27				15 07		15 27				16 07		16 27				17 07		17 27
Stockport	d		13 36						14 36						15 36						16 36						17 36
Wilmslow	d																										
Crewe 10	d	14 01						15 01						16 01						16 59						18 01	
Macclesfield	d		13 49						14 49						15 49						16 49						17 49
Congleton	d																										
Stoke-on-Trent	d		14 07				14 43		15 07				15 43		16 07				16 43		17 08				17 43		18 08
Stafford	d		14 25						15 25						16 25						17 26						18 26
Wolverhampton 7	d	14 33	14 41				15 15	15 32	15 41				16 15	16 33	16 41				17 15	17 32	17 41				18 15	18 33	18 41
Dunbar	d									11 10												13 10					
Berwick-upon-Tweed	d									11 33												13 33					
Alnmouth for Alnwick	d			10 47												12 47								14 18			
Morpeth	d			11 02																				14 38			
Newcastle 8	d			11b25						12 25		13 18				13 25		14 18				14 25		15 18			
Chester-le-Street	d											13 27															
Durham	d			11 37						12 37		13 34				13 37		14 30				14 37		15 30			
Darlington 7	d			11 54						12 54		13 52				13 54		14 47				14 54		15 47			
York 8	d			12 28						13 28		14 22				14 28		15 20				15 28		16 20			
Leeds 10	d			13 00						14 00						15 00						16 00					
Wakefield Westgate 7	d			13 12						14 12						15 12						16 12					
Doncaster 7	d			13 30								14 50						15 50						16 50			
Sheffield 7	d			13 57		14 20				14 50		15 20				15 50		16 20				16 50		17 20			
Chesterfield	d			14 09		14 32				15 02						16 02						17 02					
Nottingham 8	d				14 10						15 05						16 05						17 10				
Derby 6	d			14 30	14 35	14 53				15 23	15 35	15 51				16 23	16 35	16 51				17 25	17 36	17 51			
Burton-on-Trent	d				14 48					15 35	15 48						16 48					17 35	17 48				
Tamworth	d			14 49	15 00						16 00					16 43	17 00						18 00				
Birmingham New Street 12	a	14 55	14 58	15 07	15 21	15 27	15 31	15 55	15 58	16 00	16 23	16 27	16 31	16 56	16 58	17 02	17 21	17 27	17 31	17 55	17 58	18 00	18 21	18 27	18 31	18 56	18 58
Birmingham New Street 12	d		15 03	15 12	15 30	15 33	15 42		16 04	16 12	16 30	16 33	16 42		17 03	17 12	17 30	17 33	17 42		18 03	18 12	18 30	18 33	18 42		19 03
Cheltenham Spa	a			15 50	16 10		16 24			16 50	17 10		17 24			17 50	18 10		18 24			18 50	19 11		19 24		
Gloucester 7	a				16 21						17 21						18 21						19 24				
Bristol Parkway 7	a			16 23			16 57			17 23			18 01			18 23			18 57			19 23			20 02		
Bristol Temple Meads 10	a			16 35			17 09			17 35			18 13			18 37			19 09			19 35			20 14		
Newport (South Wales)	a				17 06						18 06						19 06						20 09				
Cardiff Central 7	a				17 26						18 28						19 26						20 11				
Weston-super-Mare	a																								20 36		
Taunton	a			17 15						18 19						19 15						20 16			20 58		
Tiverton Parkway	a			17 28						18 32						19 28						20 29			21 11		
Exeter St Davids 6	a			17 44						18 48						19 48						20 45			21 26		
Dawlish	a																								21 42		
Teignmouth	a																								21 47		
Newton Abbot	a			18 03						19 07						20 07						21 04			21 54		
Torquay	a																										
Paignton	a																										
Totnes	a			18 16						19 20						20 20						21 17					
Plymouth	a			18 44						19 48						20 48						21 45			22 38		
Liskeard 6	a			19 17												21 12											
Bodmin Parkway	a			19 29												21 24											
Lostwithiel	a																										
Par	a			19 39												21 34											
Newquay	a																										
St Austell	a			19 46												21 41											
Truro	a			20 07												21 58											
Redruth	a			20 18												22 10											
Camborne	a			20 25												22 19											
Hayle	a																										
St Erth	a			20 36												22 30											
Penzance	a			20 47												22 41											
Birmingham International ✈	d		15 14						16 14						17 14						18 14						19 14
Coventry	d		15 25						16 25						17 25						18 25						19 25
Leamington Spa 8	d		15 38			16 00			16 38			17 00			17 38			18 00			18 38			19 00			19 38
Banbury	a		15 54			16 17			16 54			17 17			17 54			18 17			18 54			19 17			19 54
Oxford	a		16 14			16 41			17 14			17 38			18 14			18 39			19 14			19 38			20 14
Reading 7	a		16 42			17 09			17 39			18 09			18 42			19 09			19 42			20 09			20 42
Guildford	a																										
Basingstoke	a		17 09						18 09						19 09						20 09						21 09
Winchester	a		17 24						18 24						19 24						20 24						21 24
Southampton Airport Parkway ✈	a		17 33						18 33						19 33						20 33						21 33
Southampton Central	a		17 40						18 42						19 40						20 43						21 43
Brockenhurst 3	a		18 02						19 01						20 02						21 02						22 02
Bournemouth	a		18 27						19 27						20 27						21 27						22 27

Table 51

Scotland, The North East, North West England - The South West and South Coast

Sundays

12 September to 17 October

		XC	XC	XC	XC	VT	XC	XC	XC	XC	XC	VT	XC	XC	XC	XC	XC	XC	XC	XC	VT	XC	VT	XC	XC
		◇1	◇1	◇1	◇1	◇1	◇1	◇1	◇1	◇1	◇1	◇1	◇1	◇1	◇1	◇1	◇1	◇1	◇1	◇1	◇1	◇1	◇1	◇1	◇1
Aberdeen	d	11 12																							
Stonehaven	d	11 29																							
Montrose	d	11 50																							
Arbroath	d	12 06																							
Dundee	d	12 25																							
Leuchars 3	d	12 38																							
Cupar	d	12 45																							
Ladybank	d																								
Markinch	d																								
Kirkcaldy	d	13 03																							
Inverkeithing	d	13 18																							
Glasgow Central 15	d					15 56		13 45													18 30				
Motherwell	d							14 03																	
Haymarket	d	13 37						14 43																	
Edinburgh 10	d	13 50						14 50				16 52		15 50				16 50					18 52	17 50	
Haymarket	d											16 56											18 57		
Lockerbie	d																								
Carlisle 8	d					17 09						18 07									19 44		20 07		
Penrith North Lakes	d																						20 22		
Oxenholme Lake District	d					17 44						18 42									20 19				
Lancaster 6	d											18 57									20 34		20 57		
Preston 8	d					18 17						19 17									20 55		21 17		
Wigan North Western	d					18 28						19 28									21 07		21 28		
Warrington Bank Quay	d					18 39						19 39									21 18		21 39		
Manchester Piccadilly 10	d				18 07		18 27				19 07		19 27				20 07					21 07			22 07
Stockport	d						18 36						19 36				20 16					21 16			22 16
Wilmslow	d																								
Crewe 10	d					19 01						20 01									21 40		22 01		
Macclesfield	d						18 49						19 49				20 29					21 29			22 29
Congleton	d																								
Stoke-on-Trent	d				18 43		19 07				19 43		20 07				20 47					21 47			22 47
Stafford	d						19 25						20 25				21 09				22 02	22 06			23 05
Wolverhampton 7	d				19 15	19 32	19 41				20 15	20 32	20 41				21 22				22 16	22 22	22 32		23 19
Dunbar	d							15 10										17 10						18 10	
Berwick-upon-Tweed	d							15 33										17 33							
Alnmouth for Alnwick	d	14 47												16 47										18 51	
Morpeth	d													17 02											
Newcastle 8	d	15 25		16 18				16 25		17 18				17 25		18 18		18 25		19 18				19 25	
Chester-le-Street	d																								
Durham	d	15 37		16 30				16 37		17 33				17 37		18 33		18 38		19 33				19 39	
Darlington 7	d	15 54		16 47				16 54		17 50				17 55		18 50		18 54		19 50				19 56	
York 8	d	16 28		17 21				17 28		18 20				18 28		19 20		19 28		20 20				20 28	
Leeds 10	d	17 00						18 00						19 00				20 00						21 00	
Wakefield Westgate 7	d	17 12						18 12						19 12				20 12						21 12	
Doncaster 7	d			17 50						18 50						19 50				20 50					
Sheffield 7	d	17 50		18 20				18 50		19 20				19 50		20 20		20 50		21 20				21 50	
Chesterfield	d	18 02						19 02						20 02				21 02		21 32				22 02	
Nottingham 8	d		18 05						19 10						20 10				21 08						
Derby 6	d	18 23	18 35	18 51				19 23	19 34	19 51				20 23	20 35	20 51		21 23	21 35	21 53				22 23	
Burton-on-Trent	d		18 48					19 35	19 48						20 48			21 35	21 48	22 04				22 35	
Tamworth	d	18 43	19 00						20 00					20 43	21 00			21 46	22 00	22 14				22 46	
Birmingham New Street 12	a	19 02	19 21	19 27	19 31	19 55	19 58	20 00	20 23	20 27	20 31	20 55	21 00	21 02	21 18	21 24	21 39	22 04	22 23	22 33	22 40	22 40	22 57	23 04	23 36
Birmingham New Street 12	d	19 12	19 30	19 33	19 42		20 03	20 12		20 33	20 42		21 03	21 12			21 42	22 12							
Cheltenham Spa	a	19 50	20 10		20 24			20 50			21 24			21 50			22 24	22 50							
Gloucester 7	a		20 18											22 01											
Bristol Parkway 7	a	20 23			20 57			21 23			21 59			22 35			23 00	23 23							
Bristol Temple Meads 10	a	20 35			21 09			21 35			22 11			22 47			23 13	23 35							
Newport (South Wales)	a		21 06																						
Cardiff Central 7	a		21 26																						
Weston-super-Mare	a																								
Taunton	a	21 15						22 15																	
Tiverton Parkway	a	21 28						22 28																	
Exeter St Davids 6	a	21 44						22 44																	
Dawlish	a																								
Teignmouth	a																								
Newton Abbot	a	22 03						23 04																	
Torquay	a																								
Paignton	a																								
Totnes	a	22 16						23 20																	
Plymouth	a	22 46						23 49																	
Liskeard 6	a																								
Bodmin Parkway	a																								
Lostwithiel	a																								
Par	a																								
Newquay	a																								
St Austell	a																								
Truro	a																								
Redruth	a																								
Camborne	a																								
Hayle	a																								
St Erth	a																								
Penzance	a																								
Birmingham International ✈	d						20 14						21 14												
Coventry	d						20 25						21 24												
Leamington Spa 8	d			20 00			20 38			21 00			21 35												
Banbury	a			20 18			20 54			21 17															
Oxford	a			20 40			21 14			21 38			22 08												
Reading 7	a			21 09			21 42			22 05			22 35												
Guildford	a									22 42															
Basingstoke	a						22 11																		
Winchester	a						22 26																		
Southampton Airport Parkway ✈	a						22 35																		
Southampton Central	a						22 43																		
Brockenhurst 3	a																								
Bournemouth	a																								

Table 51

Sundays
from 24 October

Scotland, The North East, North West England - The South West and South Coast

		XC	XC	XC	XC	XC	XC	VT	XC	XC	XC	XC	XC	XC	XC	XC	VT	XC	XC	XC	XC	XC	XC	VT	XC
		◇1	◇1	◇1	◇1	◇1	◇1	◇1	◇1	◇1	◇1	◇1	◇1	◇1	◇1	◇1	◇1	◇1	◇1	◇1	◇1	◇1	◇1	◇1	◇1
Aberdeen	d																								
Stonehaven	d																								
Montrose	d																								
Arbroath	d																								
Dundee	d																								
Leuchars 3	d																								
Cupar	d																								
Ladybank	d																								
Markinch	d																								
Kirkcaldy	d																								
Inverkeithing	d																								
Glasgow Central 15	d																								
Motherwell	d																								
Haymarket	d																								
Edinburgh 10	d																		08 50						
Haymarket	d																								
Lockerbie	d																								
Carlisle 8	d																								
Penrith North Lakes	d																								
Oxenholme Lake District	d																								
Lancaster 6	d																							12 10	
Preston 8	d																							12 30	
Wigan North Western	d																								
Warrington Bank Quay	d																								
Manchester Piccadilly 10	d	08 26				09 27			10 27			11 27						12 26					13 07		13 27
Stockport	d	08 35				09 36			10 36			11 36						12 35							13 36
Wilmslow	d	08 41																							
Crewe 10	d	09 05						11 03									13 01							14 01	
Macclesfield	d					09 49			10 49			11 49						12 49							13 49
Congleton	d																								
Stoke-on-Trent	d					10 07			11 07			12 07						13 07					13 43		14 07
Stafford	d	09 26				10 27			11 27			12 25						13 25							14 25
Wolverhampton 7	d	09 41				10 43		11 33	11 42			12 41					13 32	13 41					14 15	14 32	14 41
Dunbar	d																								
Berwick-upon-Tweed	d																		09 33						
Alnmouth for Alnwick	d																								
Morpeth	d																								
Newcastle 8	d												09 25						10 25						
Chester-le-Street	d																								
Durham	d												09 38						10 37						
Darlington 7	d												09 55						10 54						
York 8	d									09 28			10 28						11 28						
Leeds 10	d		08 10							10 00			11 00						12 00						
Wakefield Westgate 7	d		08 22							10 12			11 12						12 12						
Doncaster 7	d									10 30			11 30						12 30						
Sheffield 7	d		08 54							10 57			11 57						12 57						
Chesterfield	d		09 07							11 09			12 09						13 09						
Nottingham 8	d										11 10					12 10					13 05				
Derby 6	d		09 28							11 30	11 36		12 30			12 36			13 32		13 36	13 52			
Burton-on-Trent	d									11 41	11 48					12 48			13 43		13 48				
Tamworth	d		09 47								12 00		12 48			13 00					14 00				
Birmingham New Street 12	a	09 58	10 09			10 59		11 56	12 00	12 07	12 26	12 58	13 07			13 21	13 55	13 58	14 10		14 22	14 27	14 31	14 55	14 58
Birmingham New Street 12	d	10 03	10 12	09 03	09 12	11 03	11 30		12 03	12 12	12 30	13 03	13 12	11 33	12 33	13 30		14 03	14 12	13 33	14 30	14 33	14 42		15 03
Cheltenham Spa	a		10 54		09 49		12 10			12 50	13 10		13 50			14 12			14 51		15 10		15 24		
Gloucester 7	a		11 04		10 01		12 20			13 01	13 21		14 02			14 22					15 21				
Bristol Parkway 7	a		12 19		11 15					14 25			15 11						15 25				16 00		
Bristol Temple Meads 10	a		12 41		11 40					14 40			15 26						15 38				16 11		
Newport (South Wales)	a						13 09				14 10					15 07					16 06				
Cardiff Central 7	a						13 29				14 30					15 28					16 26				
Weston-super-Mare	a																								
Taunton	a		13 16		12 15					15 15									16 16				16 45		
Tiverton Parkway	a		13 27		12 28					15 28									16 27				16 57		
Exeter St Davids 6	a		13 46		12 44					15 44									16 47				17 13		
Dawlish	a																						17 25		
Teignmouth	a																						17 30		
Newton Abbot	a		14 07		13 03					16 03									17 07				17 37		
Torquay	a																						17 49		
Paignton	a																						17 58		
Totnes	a		14 21		13 17					16 16									17 21						
Plymouth	a		14 50		13 45					16 44									17 50						
Liskeard 8	a																								
Bodmin Parkway	a																								
Lostwithiel	a																								
Par	a																								
Newquay	a																								
St Austell	a																								
Truro	a																								
Redruth	a																								
Camborne	a																								
Hayle	a																								
St Erth	a																								
Penzance	a																								
Birmingham International ✈	d	10 14		09 14		11 14			12 14			13 14						14 14							15 14
Coventry	d	10 25		09 25		11 25			12 25			13 25						14 25							15 25
Leamington Spa 8	d	10 38		09 38		11 38			12 38			13 38		12 00	13 00			14 38		14 00		15 00			15 38
Banbury	a	10 54		09 54		11 54			12 54			13 54		12 17	13 17			14 54		14 17		15 18			15 54
Oxford	a	11 14		10 14		12 14			13 14			14 14		12 38	13 41			15 14		14 37		15 41			16 14
Reading 7	a	11 42		10 42		12 42			13 42			14 42		13 09	14 10			15 42		15 09		16 09			16 42
Guildford	a																								
Basingstoke	a	12 09		11 09		13 09			14 09			15 09						16 09							17 09
Winchester	a	12 24		11 24		13 24			14 24			15 24						16 24							17 24
Southampton Airport Parkway ✈	a	12 33		11 33		13 33			14 33			15 33						16 33							17 33
Southampton Central	a	12 42		11 42		13 42			14 42			15 42						16 42							17 40
Brockenhurst 3	a	13 02		12 02		14 01			15 02			16 02						17 02							18 02
Bournemouth	a	13 27		12 27		14 27			15 27			16 27						17 27							18 27

Table 51

Sundays
from 24 October

Scotland, The North East, North West England - The South West and South Coast

		XC	XC	XC	XC	VT	XC	XC	XC	XC	XC	VT	XC	XC	XC	XC	XC	VT	XC	XC	XC	XC	XC	VT	XC
		◇1	◇1	◇1	◇1	◇1	◇1	◇1	◇1	◇1	◇1	◇1	◇1	◇1	◇1	◇1	◇1	◇1	◇1	◇1	◇1	◇1	◇1	◇1	◇1
Aberdeen	d																								
Stonehaven	d																								
Montrose	d																								
Arbroath	d																								
Dundee	d																								
Leuchars 3	d																								
Cupar	d																								
Ladybank	d																								
Markinch	d																								
Kirkcaldy	d																								
Inverkeithing	d																								
Glasgow Central 15	d																	13 55		11 37					
Motherwell	d																			11 54					
Haymarket	d																			12 39					
Edinburgh 10	d	09 50				10 52		10 50		11 25		12 52		11 50						12 50		13 33		14 52	
Haymarket	d					10 57						12 56												14 57	
Lockerbie	d																								
Carlisle 8	d					12 07						14 07						15 09						16 07	
Penrith North Lakes	d											14 22												16 22	
Oxenholme Lake District	d					12 43												15 44							
Lancaster 6	d					12 57						14 57												16 57	
Preston 8	d					13 30						15 17						16 15						17 17	
Wigan North Western	d											15 28						16 26						17 28	
Warrington Bank Quay	d											15 39						16 37						17 39	
Manchester Piccadilly 10	d				14 07		14 27				15 07		15 27				16 07		16 27				17 07		17 27
Stockport	d						14 36						15 36						16 36						17 36
Wilmslow	d																								
Crewe 10	d					15 01						16 01						16 59						18 01	
Macclesfield	d						14 49						15 49						16 49						17 49
Congleton	d																								
Stoke-on-Trent	d				14 43		15 07				15 43		16 07				16 43		17 08				17 43		18 08
Stafford	d						15 25						16 25						17 26						18 26
Wolverhampton 7	d				15 15	15 32	15 41				16 15	16 33	16 41				17 15	17 32	17 41				18 15	18 33	18 41
Dunbar	d							11 10												13 10					
Berwick-upon-Tweed	d							11 33												13 33		14 18			
Alnmouth for Alnwick	d	10 47												12 47								14 38			
Morpeth	d	11 02																							
Newcastle 8	d	11 25						12 25		13 18				13 25		14 18				14 25		15 18			
Chester-le-Street	d									13 27															
Durham	d	11 37						12 37		13 34				13 37		14 30				14 37		15 30			
Darlington 7	d	11 54						12 54		13 52				13 54		14 47				14 54		15 47			
York 8	d	12 28						13 28		14 22				14 28		15 20				15 28		16 20			
Leeds 10	d	13 00						14 00						15 00						16 00					
Wakefield Westgate 7	d	13 12						14 12						15 12						16 12					
Doncaster 7	d	13 30								14 50						15 50						16 50			
Sheffield 7	d	13 57		14 20				14 50		15 20				15 50		16 20				16 50		17 20			
Chesterfield	d	14 09		14 32				15 02						16 02						17 02					
Nottingham 8	d		14 10						15 05						16 05						17 10				
Derby 6	d	14 30	14 35	14 53				15 23	15 35	15 51				16 23	16 35	16 51				17 25	17 36	17 51			
Burton-on-Trent	d		14 48					15 35	15 48						16 48					17 35	17 48				
Tamworth	d	14 49	15 00						16 00					16 43	17 00						18 00				
Birmingham New Street 12	a	15 07	15 21	15 27	15 31	15 54	15 58	16 00	16 23	16 27	16 31	16 56	16 58	17 02	17 21	17 27	17 31	17 55	17 58	18 00	18 21	18 27	18 31	18 56	18 58
Birmingham New Street 12	d	15 12	15 30	15 33	15 42		16 04	16 12	16 30	16 33	16 42		17 03	17 12	17 30	17 33	17 42		18 03	18 12	18 30	18 33	18 42		19 03
Cheltenham Spa	a	15 50	16 10		16 24			16 50	17 10		17 24			17 50	18 10		18 24			18 50	19 11		19 24		
Gloucester 7	a		16 21						17 21						18 21						19 24				
Bristol Parkway 7	a	16 23			16 57			17 23			18 01			18 23			18 57			19 23			20 02		
Bristol Temple Meads 10	a	16 35			17 09			17 35			18 13			18 37			19 09			19 35			20 14		
Newport (South Wales)	a		17 06						18 06						19 06						20 09				
Cardiff Central 7	a		17 26						18 28						19 26						20 11				
Weston-super-Mare	a																						20 36		
Taunton	a	17 15						18 19						19 15						20 16			20 58		
Tiverton Parkway	a	17 28						18 32						19 28						20 29			21 11		
Exeter St Davids 6	a	17 44						18 48						19 48						20 45			21 26		
Dawlish	a																						21 42		
Teignmouth	a																						21 47		
Newton Abbot	a	18 03						19 07						20 07						21 04			21 54		
Torquay	a																								
Paignton	a																								
Totnes	a	18 16						19 20						20 20						21 17					
Plymouth	a	18 44						19 48						20 48						21 45			22 38		
Liskeard 8	a	19 17												21 12											
Bodmin Parkway	a	19 29												21 24											
Lostwithiel	a																								
Par	a	19 39												21 34											
Newquay	a																								
St Austell	a	19 46												21 41											
Truro	a	20 07												21 58											
Redruth	a	20 18												22 10											
Camborne	a	20 25												22 19											
Hayle	a																								
St Erth	a	20 36												22 30											
Penzance	a	20 47												22 41											
Birmingham International ✈	d						16 14						17 14						18 14						19 14
Coventry	d						16 25						17 25						18 25						19 25
Leamington Spa 8	d			16 00			16 38			17 00			17 38			18 00			18 38			19 00			19 38
Banbury	a			16 17			16 54			17 17			17 54			18 17			18 54			19 17			19 54
Oxford	a			16 41			17 14			17 38			18 14			18 39			19 14			19 38			20 14
Reading 7	a			17 09			17 39			18 09			18 42			19 09			19 42			20 09			20 42
Guildford	a																								
Basingstoke	a						18 09						19 09						20 09						21 09
Winchester	a						18 24						19 24						20 24						21 24
Southampton Airport Parkway ✈	a						18 33						19 33						20 33						21 33
Southampton Central	a						18 42						19 40						20 43						21 43
Brockenhurst 3	a						19 01						20 02						21 02						22 02
Bournemouth	a						19 27						20 27						21 27						22 27

Table 51

Sundays from 24 October

Scotland, The North East, North West England - The South West and South Coast

		XC	XC	XC	XC	VT	XC	XC	XC	XC	XC	VT	XC	XC	XC	XC	XC	XC	XC	XC	VT	XC	VT	XC	XC
		◇1	◇1	◇1	◇1	◇1	◇1	◇1	◇1	◇1	◇1	◇1	◇1	◇1	◇1	◇1	◇1	◇1	◇1	◇1	◇1	◇1	◇1	◇1	◇1
Aberdeen	d	11 12																							
Stonehaven	d	11 29																							
Montrose	d	11 50																							
Arbroath	d	12 06																							
Dundee	d	12 25																							
Leuchars	d	12 38																							
Cupar	d	12 45																							
Ladybank	d																								
Markinch	d																								
Kirkcaldy	d	13 03																							
Inverkeithing	d	13 18																							
Glasgow Central	d					15 56		13 45													18 30				
Motherwell	d							14 03																	
Haymarket	d	13 37						14 43																	
Edinburgh	d	13 50						14 50				16 52		15 50				16 50					18 52	17 50	
Haymarket	d											16 56											18 57		
Lockerbie	d																								
Carlisle	d					17 09						18 07									19 44		20 07		
Penrith North Lakes	d																						20 22		
Oxenholme Lake District	d					17 44						18 42									20 19				
Lancaster	d											18 57									20 34		20 57		
Preston	d					18 17						19 17									20 55		21 17		
Wigan North Western	d					18 28						19 28									21 07		21 28		
Warrington Bank Quay	d					18 39						19 39									21 18		21 39		
Manchester Piccadilly	d				18 07		18 27				19 07		19 27				20 07					21 07			22 07
Stockport	d						18 36						19 36				20 16					21 16			22 16
Wilmslow	d																								
Crewe	d					19 01						20 01									21 40		22 01		
Macclesfield	d						18 49						19 49				20 29					21 29			22 29
Congleton	d																								
Stoke-on-Trent	d				18 43		19 07				19 43		20 07				20 48					21 47			22 47
Stafford	d						19 25						20 25				21 09				22 02	22 06			23 05
Wolverhampton	d				19 15	19 32	19 41				20 15	20 32	20 41				21 23				22 16	22 22	22 32		23 19
Dunbar	d							15 10										17 10						18 10	
Berwick-upon-Tweed	d							15 33										17 33							
Alnmouth for Alnwick	d	14 47												16 47										18 51	
Morpeth	d													17 02											
Newcastle	d	15 25		16 18				16 25		17 18				17 25		18 18		18 25		19 18				19 25	
Chester-le-Street	d																								
Durham	d	15 37		16 30				16 37		17 33				17 37		18 33		18 38		19 33				19 39	
Darlington	d	15 54		16 47				16 54		17 50				17 55		18 50		18 54		19 50				19 56	
York	d	16 28		17 21				17 28		18 20				18 28		19 20		19 28		20 20				20 28	
Leeds	d	17 00						18 00						19b00				20f00						21i00	
Wakefield Westgate	d	17 12						18 12						19 12				20 12						21 12	
Doncaster	d			17 50						18 50						19 50				20h50					
Sheffield	d	17 50		18 20				18 50		19 20				19c50		20 20		20g50		21 20				21j50	
Chesterfield	d	18 02						19 02						20 02				21 02		21 32				22 02	
Nottingham	d		18 05						19 10						20 10				21 08						
Derby	d	18 23	18 35	18 51				19 23	19 34	19 51				20 23	20 35	20 51		21 23	21 35	21 53				22 23	
Burton-on-Trent	d		18 48					19 35	19 48						20 48			21 35	21 48	22 04				22 35	
Tamworth	d	18 43	19 00						20 00					20 43	21 00			21 46	22 00	22 14				22 46	
Birmingham New Street	a	19 02	19 21	19 27	19 31	19 55	19 58	20 00	20 23	20 27	20 31	20 55	21 00	21 02	21 18	21 24	21 39	22 04	22 23	22 33	22 40	22 40	22 57	23 04	23 36
Birmingham New Street	d	19 12	19 30	19 33	19 42		20 03	20 12		20 33	20 42		21 03	21 12				22 12							
Cheltenham Spa	a	19 50	20 10		20 24			20 50			21 24			21 50				22 50							
Gloucester	a		20 18											22 01											
Bristol Parkway	a	20 23			20 57			21 23			21 59			22 35				23 59							
Bristol Temple Meads	a	20 35			21 09			21 35			22 11			22 47				00 14							
Newport (South Wales)	a		21 06																						
Cardiff Central	a		21 26																						
Weston-super-Mare	a																								
Taunton	a	21 15						22 15																	
Tiverton Parkway	a	21 28						22 28																	
Exeter St Davids	a	21 44						22 44																	
Dawlish	a																								
Teignmouth	a																								
Newton Abbot	a	22 03						23 04																	
Torquay	a																								
Paignton	a																								
Totnes	a	22 16						23 20																	
Plymouth	a	22 46						23 49																	
Liskeard	a																								
Bodmin Parkway	a																								
Lostwithiel	a																								
Par	a																								
Newquay	a																								
St Austell	a																								
Truro	a																								
Redruth	a																								
Camborne	a																								
Hayle	a																								
St Erth	a																								
Penzance	a																								
Birmingham International	d						20 14						21 14												
Coventry	d						20 25						21 24												
Leamington Spa	d			20 00			20 38			21 00			21 35												
Banbury	a			20 18			20 54			21 17															
Oxford	a			20 40			21 14			21 38			22 08												
Reading	a			21 09			21 42			22 05			22 35												
Guildford	a									22 42															
Basingstoke	a						22 11																		
Winchester	a						22 26																		
Southampton Airport Parkway	a						22 35																		
Southampton Central	a						22 43																		
Brockenhurst	a																								
Bournemouth	a																								

Table 51

Mondays to Fridays

South Coast and the South West - North West England, The North East and Scotland

		XC	XC	VT	VT	XC	XC	XC	XC	XC	XC	XC	VT
		◇1	◇1	◇1	◇1	1	◇1	◇1	1	◇1	◇1	1	◇1
				F	G								
Bournemouth	d												
Brockenhurst	d												
Southampton Central	d												
Southampton Airport Parkway	d												
Winchester	d												
Basingstoke	d												
Guildford	d												
Reading	d												
Oxford	d												
Banbury	d												
Leamington Spa	d												
Coventry	d												
Birmingham International	d												
Penzance	d												
St Erth	d												
Hayle	d												
Camborne	d												
Redruth	d												
Truro	d												
St Austell	d												
Newquay	d												
Par	d												
Lostwithiel	d												
Bodmin Parkway	d												
Liskeard	d												
Plymouth	d												
Totnes	d												
Paignton	d												
Torquay	d												
Newton Abbot	d												
Teignmouth	d												
Dawlish	d												
Exeter St Davids	d												
Tiverton Parkway	d												
Taunton	d												
Weston-super-Mare	d												
Cardiff Central	d												
Newport (South Wales)	d												
Bristol Temple Meads	d												
Bristol Parkway	d												
Gloucester	d												
Cheltenham Spa	d												
Birmingham New Street	a												
Birmingham New Street	d	05 57	06 00	06 17	06 17	06 19	06 20	06 30	06 49	06 57	07 03	07 19	07 19
Tamworth	a					06 39			07 07		07 19	07 38	
Burton-on-Trent	a					06 50			07 19		07 29	07 50	
Derby	a		06 32			07 04		07 11	07 34		07 42	08 05	
Nottingham	a					07 41			08 08			08 33	
Chesterfield	a		06 52					07 31			08 02		
Sheffield	a		07 06					07 48			08 17		
Doncaster	a							08 25					
Wakefield Westgate	a		07 36								08 48		
Leeds	a		07 52								09 03		
York	a		08 23					08 47			09 33		
Darlington	a		08 55					09 20			10 04		
Durham	a		09 13					09 37			10 21		
Chester-le-Street	a							09 44					
Newcastle	a		09 26					09 55			10 36		
Morpeth	a		09 41										
Alnmouth for Alnwick	a		09 55										
Berwick-upon-Tweed	a										11 20		
Dunbar	a										11 43		
Wolverhampton	d	06 16		06 34	06 35		06 40			07 16			07 36
Stafford	a	06 29					06 53			07 29			
Stoke-on-Trent	a	06 50					07 12						
Congleton	a	07 02											
Macclesfield	a	07 11					07 30						
Crewe	a			07 07	07 06					07 50			08 07
Wilmslow	a									08 08			
Stockport	a	07 27					07 45			08 20			
Manchester Piccadilly	a	07 37					08 00			08 34			
Warrington Bank Quay	a			07 26	07 25								08 26
Wigan North Western	a			07 37	07 36								08 37
Preston	a			07 51	07 50								08 51
Lancaster	a			08 08	08 07								09 08
Oxenholme Lake District	a			08 21	08 20								
Penrith North Lakes	a												09 44
Carlisle	a			09 01	09 01								09 59
Lockerbie	a												
Haymarket	a			10 15	10 15								
Edinburgh	a		10 57	10 20	10 20						12 11		
Haymarket	a												
Motherwell	a												
Glasgow Central	a												11 16
Inverkeithing	a												
Kirkcaldy	a												
Markinch	a												
Ladybank	a												
Cupar	a												
Leuchars	a												
Dundee	a												
Arbroath	a												
Montrose	a												
Stonehaven	a												
Aberdeen	a												

F until 16 July, from 6 September **G** from 19 July until 3 September

Table 51

South Coast and the South West - North West England, The North East and Scotland

Station		XC	XC	XC	XC	XC	XC	XC	VT	XC	XC	XC	XC	XC	XC	VT	XC	XC	XC	XC
		◇■ ⊼	◇■ ⊼	■	◇■ ⊼	◇■ ⊼	◇■	■	◇■ ⊠	◇■ ⊼	◇■ ⊼	◇■	◇■ ⊼	◇■ ⊼	■	◇■ ⊠	◇■ ⊼	◇■ ⊼	◇■	◇■ ⊼
Bournemouth	d																			06 30
Brockenhurst	d																			06 49
Southampton Central	d				05 15								06 15							07 15
Southampton Airport Parkway ✈	d				05 22								06 22							07 22
Winchester	d				05 31								06 31							07 31
Basingstoke	d				05 47								06 47							07 47
Guildford	d									06 02										
Reading	d				06 11					06 41			07 11				07 41			08 11
Oxford	d				06 36					07 07			07 36				08 07			08 36
Banbury	d				06 54					07 26			07 55				08 27			08 54
Leamington Spa	d				07 12					07 43			08 12				08 44			09 12
Coventry	d				07 27								08 27							09 27
Birmingham International ✈	d				07 38								08 38							09 38
Penzance	d																			
St Erth	d																			
Hayle	d																			
Camborne	d																			
Redruth	d																			
Truro	d																			
St Austell	d																			
Newquay	d																			
Par	d																			
Lostwithiel	d																			
Bodmin Parkway	d																			
Liskeard	d																			
Plymouth	d													05 20						
Totnes	d													05 45						
Paignton	d																			
Torquay	d																			
Newton Abbot	d													06 03						
Teignmouth	d																			
Dawlish	d																			
Exeter St Davids	d													06 23						
Tiverton Parkway	d													06 37						
Taunton	d													06 51						
Weston-super-Mare	d																			
Cardiff Central	d											06 40						07 00	07 45	
Newport (South Wales)	d											06 55						07 15	08 02	
Bristol Temple Meads	d					06 27					07 00			07 30				08 00		
Bristol Parkway	d					06 40					07 10			07 40				08 10		
Gloucester	d						07 10					07 46							08 46	
Cheltenham Spa	d					07 12	07 21				07 42	07 57		08 12				08 42	08 58	
Birmingham New Street	a				07 48	07 56	08 16			08 16	08 26	08 45	08 48	08 56			09 18	09 26	09 45	09 48
Birmingham New Street	d	07 30	07 31	07 49	07 57	08 03		08 19	08 20	08 30	08 31	08 49	08 57	09 03	09 19	09 20	09 30	09 31	09 49	09 57
Tamworth	d			08 07		08 19		08 37				09 07			09 39				10 07	
Burton-on-Trent	d			08 19		08 29		08 49				09 19		09 26	09 50				10 19	
Derby	a	08 11		08 34		08 42		09 05		09 11		09 34		09 39	10 05		10 08		10 36	
Nottingham	a			09 05				09 35				10 05			10 33				11 04	
Chesterfield	a	08 32				09 02								10 02						
Sheffield	a	08 46				09 17				09 46				10 17			10 46			
Doncaster	a	09 20								10 15							11 15			
Wakefield Westgate	a					09 46								10 46						
Leeds	a					10 02								11 02						
York	a	09 48				10 27				10 40				11 28			11 45			
Darlington	a	10 17				10 59				11 12				11 58			12 20			
Durham	a	10 34				11 17				11 29				12 22			12 38			
Chester-le-Street	a																12 50			
Newcastle	a	10 52				11 32				11 49				12 36			13 01			
Morpeth	a																			
Alnmouth for Alnwick	a					12 00														
Berwick-upon-Tweed	a													13 21						
Dunbar	a													13 44						
Wolverhampton	d		07 49		08 15				08 37		08 49		09 15			09 37		09 49		10 15
Stafford	a				08 29						09 00		09 29					10 00		10 29
Stoke-on-Trent	a		08 18		08 54						09 19		09 54					10 19		10 54
Congleton	a																			
Macclesfield	a		08 35		09 11								10 11							11 11
Crewe	a								09 07							10 07				
Wilmslow	a																			
Stockport	a		08 49		09 27						09 49		10 27					10 49		11 27
Manchester Piccadilly	a		08 59		09 39						09 59		10 39					10 59		11 39
Warrington Bank Quay	a								09 26							10 26				
Wigan North Western	a								09 37							10 37				
Preston	a								09 51							10 51				
Lancaster	a								10 09							11 08				
Oxenholme Lake District	a								10 24											
Penrith North Lakes	a															11 44				
Carlisle	a								11 02							12 00				
Lockerbie	a																			
Haymarket	a								12 17											
Edinburgh	a					13 05			12 22					14 14						
Haymarket	a																			
Motherwell	a																			
Glasgow Central	a															13 17				
Inverkeithing	a																			
Kirkcaldy	a																			
Markinch	a																			
Ladybank	a																			
Cupar	a																			
Leuchars	a																			
Dundee	a																			
Arbroath	a																			
Montrose	a																			
Stonehaven	a																			
Aberdeen	a																			

Table 51

South Coast and the South West - North West England, The North East and Scotland

Station		XC	XC	VT	VT	XC	XC	XC	XC	XC	XC	VT	XC	XC	XC	XC	XC	XC	VT	XC
		◇■ ⊼	■	◇■ B ⊡	◇■ A ⊡	◇■ ⊼	◇■ ⊼	◇■	◇■ ⊼	◇■ ⊼	■	◇■ ⊡	◇■ ⊼	◇■ ⊼	◇■	◇■ ⊼	◇■ ⊼	■	◇■ ⊡	◇■ ⊼
Bournemouth	d								07 30							08 45				
Brockenhurst	d								07 49							09 00				
Southampton Central	d								08 15							09 15				
Southampton Airport Parkway ✈	d								08 22							09 22				
Winchester	d								08 31							09 31				
Basingstoke	d								08 47							09 47				
Guildford	d																			
Reading	d					08 41			09 11				09 41			10 11				10 41
Oxford	d					09 07			09 36				10 07			10 36				11 07
Banbury	d					09 26			09 54				10 25			10 54				11 25
Leamington Spa	d					09 43			10 12				10 45			11 12				11 43
Coventry	d			09 43					10 27							11 27				
Birmingham International ✈	d			09 54					10 38							11 38				
Penzance	d																06 28			
St Erth	d																06 36			
Hayle	d																			
Camborne	d																06 46			
Redruth	d																06 52			
Truro	d																07 04			
St Austell	d																07 20			
Newquay	d																			
Par	d																07 28			
Lostwithiel	d																			
Bodmin Parkway	d																07 39			
Liskeard	d																07 51			
Plymouth	d	06 25								07 25							08 25			
Totnes	d	06 50								07 50							08 50			
Paignton	d						07 01													
Torquay	d						07 07													
Newton Abbot	d	07 03					07 18			08 03							09 03			
Teignmouth	d						07 25													
Dawlish	d						07 30													
Exeter St Davids	d	07 23					07 44			08 23							09 24			
Tiverton Parkway	d	07 37					07 57			08 37							09 38			
Taunton	d	07 51					08 12			08 51							09 52			
Weston-super-Mare	d						08 33													
Cardiff Central	d							08 45							09 45					
Newport (South Wales)	d							09 02							10 00					
Bristol Temple Meads	d	08 30					09 00			09 30				10 00			10 30			
Bristol Parkway	d	08 40					09 10			09 40				10 10			10 40			
Gloucester	d							09 46							10 46					
Cheltenham Spa	d	09 12					09 42	09 57		10 12				10 42	10 57		11 12			
Birmingham New Street	a	09 56		10 08		10 18	10 26	10 45	10 48	10 56			11 18	11 26	11 45	11 48	11 58			12 18
Birmingham New Street	d	10 03	10 19	10 19	10 20	10 30	10 31	10 49	10 57	11 03	11 19	11 20	11 30	11 31	11 49	11 57	12 03	12 19	12 20	12 30
Tamworth	d	10 19	10 36					11 07			11 39				12 07		12 19	12 38		
Burton-on-Trent	d		10 48					11 19		11 26	11 50				12 19			12 49		
Derby	a	10 39	11 05			11 08		11 34		11 39	12 05		12 08		12 36		12 41	13 05		13 09
Nottingham	a		11 33					12 05			12 33				13 05			13 33		
Chesterfield	a	11 02								12 02							13 02			
Sheffield	a	11 17				11 46				12 17			12 46				13 17			13 46
Doncaster	a					12 15							13 20							14 17
Wakefield Westgate	a	11 46								12 46							13 46			
Leeds	a	12 01								13 02							14 02			
York	a	12 29				12 45				13 29			13 46				14 29			14 43
Darlington	a	13 00				13 13				14 00			14 16				14 58			15 16
Durham	a	13 18				13 30				14 18			14 34				15 15			15 34
Chester-le-Street	a												14 41							
Newcastle	a	13 33				13 46				14 37			14 51				15 31			15 53
Morpeth	a																15 47			
Alnmouth for Alnwick	a	14 00															16 01			
Berwick-upon-Tweed	a									15 21										
Dunbar	a									15 44										
Wolverhampton	d			10 38	10 37		10 49		11 15			11 37		11 49		12 15			12 37	
Stafford	a						11 00		11 28					12 00		12 29				
Stoke-on-Trent	a						11 19		11 54					12 19		12 54				
Congleton	a																			
Macclesfield	a								12 11							13 11				
Crewe	a			11 07	11 07							12 07							13 07	
Wilmslow	a																			
Stockport	a						11 49		12 27					12 49		13 27				
Manchester Piccadilly	a						11 59		12 39					12 59		13 39				
Warrington Bank Quay	a			11 26	11 26							12 26							13 26	
Wigan North Western	a			11 37	11 37							12 37							13 37	
Preston	a			11 51	11 51							12 51							13 51	
Lancaster	a			12 07	12 08							13 08							14 08	
Oxenholme Lake District	a			12 22	12 22							13 22								
Penrith North Lakes	a																		14 44	
Carlisle	a			13 01	13 01							14 01							15 00	
Lockerbie	a																			
Haymarket	a			14 16	14 16														16 17	
Edinburgh	a	15 10		14 22	14 22					16 16							17 04		16 22	
Haymarket	a																			
Motherwell	a																			
Glasgow Central	a											15 17								
Inverkeithing	a																			
Kirkcaldy	a																			
Markinch	a																			
Ladybank	a																			
Cupar	a																			
Leuchars	a																			
Dundee	a																			
Arbroath	a																			
Montrose	a																			
Stonehaven	a																			
Aberdeen	a																			

A until 16 July, from 6 September

B from 19 July until 3 September

Table 51

Mondays to Fridays

South Coast and the South West - North West England, The North East and Scotland

		XC	XC	XC	XC	XC	VT	XC	XC	XC	XC	XC	XC	VT	XC	XC	XC	XC	XC	XC
		◇1 (trolley)	◇1	◇1 (trolley)	◇1 (trolley)	1	◇1 (shop)	◇1 (trolley)	◇1 (trolley)	◇1	◇1 (trolley)	◇1 (trolley)	1	◇1 (shop)	◇1 (trolley)	◇1 (trolley)	◇1	◇1 (trolley)	◇1 (trolley)	◇1 (trolley)
Bournemouth	d			09 45							10 45							11 45		
Brockenhurst 3	d			10 00							11 00							12 00		
Southampton Central	d			10 15							11 15							12 15		
Southampton Airport Parkway ✈	d			10 22							11 22							12 22		
Winchester	d			10 31							11 31							12 31		
Basingstoke	d			10 47							11 47							12 47		
Guildford	d																			
Reading 7	d			11 11				11 41			12 11				12 41			13 11		13 41
Oxford	d			11 36				12 07			12 36				13 07			13 36		14 07
Banbury	d			11 56				12 27			12 54				13 25			13 54		14 28
Leamington Spa 8	d			12 13				12 45			13 12				13 43			14 12		14 45
Coventry	d			12 27							13 27							14 27		
Birmingham International ✈	d			12 38							13 38							14 38		
Penzance	d											08 28								
St Erth	d											08 36								
Hayle	d																			
Camborne	d											08 46								
Redruth	d											08 52								
Truro	d											09 04								
St Austell	d											09 20								
Newquay	d																			
Par	d											09 28								
Lostwithiel	d																			
Bodmin Parkway	d											09 39								
Liskeard 6	d											09 51								
Plymouth	d				09 25							10 25							11 25	
Totnes	d				09 50							10 50							11 50	
Paignton	d								10 06											
Torquay	d								10 12											
Newton Abbot	d				10 03				10 23			11 03							12 03	
Teignmouth	d								10 30											
Dawlish	d								10 35											
Exeter St Davids 6	d				10 23				10 49			11 23							12 23	
Tiverton Parkway	d				10 37				11 02			11 37							12 37	
Taunton	d				10 51				11 17			11 51							12 51	
Weston-super-Mare	d																			
Cardiff Central 7	d		10 45							11 45							12 45			
Newport (South Wales)	d		11 00							12 00							13 01			
Bristol Temple Meads 10	d	11 00			11 30				12 00			12 30				13 00			13 30	
Bristol Parkway 7	d	11 10			11 40				12 10			12 40				13 10			13 40	
Gloucester 7	d		11 46							12 46							13 46			
Cheltenham Spa	d	11 42	11 57		12 12				12 42	12 57		13 12				13 42	13 57		14 12	
Birmingham New Street 12	a	12 26	12 45	12 48	12 56			13 18	13 26	13 45	13 48	13 56			14 18	14 26	14 45	14 48	14 56	15 18
Birmingham New Street 12	d	12 31	12 49	12 57	13 03	13 19	13 20	13 30	13 31	13 49	13 57	14 03	14 19	14 20	14 30	14 31	14 49	14 57	15 03	15 30
Tamworth	d		13 07			13 39				14 07		14 19	14 39				15 07			
Burton-on-Trent	d		13 19		13 28	13 50				14 19			14 50				15 19		15 26	
Derby 6	a		13 35		13 40	14 05		14 08		14 34		14 39	15 05		15 08		15 34		15 39	16 08
Nottingham 6	a		14 05			14 35				15 05			15 33				16 05			
Chesterfield	a				14 02							15 02							16 02	
Sheffield 7	a				14 17			14 46				15 17			15 46				16 17	16 46
Doncaster 7	a							15 16							16 15					17 15
Wakefield Westgate 7	a				14 46							15 46							16 47	
Leeds 10	a				15 04							16 02							17 02	
York 8	a				15 29			15 40				16 29			16 39				17 30	17 40
Darlington 7	a				16 06			16 11				16 57			17 10				17 59	18 15
Durham	a				16 24			16 29				17 14			17 28				18 17	18 33
Chester-le-Street	a														17 39					
Newcastle 8	a				16 37			16 46				17 34			17 50				18 36	18 50
Morpeth	a																			
Alnmouth for Alnwick	a											18 01								
Berwick-upon-Tweed	a				17 25														19 24	
Dunbar	a				17 48														19 47	
Wolverhampton 7	d	12 49		13 15			13 37		13 49		14 15			14 37		14 49		15 15		
Stafford	a	13 00		13 29					14 00		14 29					15 00		15 29		
Stoke-on-Trent	a	13 19		13 54					14 19		14 54					15 19		15 54		
Congleton	a																			
Macclesfield	a			14 11							15 11							16 11		
Crewe 10	a						14 07							15 07						
Wilmslow	a																			
Stockport	a	13 49		14 27					14 49		15 27					15 49		16 27		
Manchester Piccadilly 10	a	13 59		14 39					14 59		15 39					15 59		16 39		
Warrington Bank Quay	a						14 26							15 26						
Wigan North Western	a						14 37							15 37						
Preston 8	a						14 51							15 51						
Lancaster 6	a						15 08							16 08						
Oxenholme Lake District	a						15 22													
Penrith North Lakes	a													16 44						
Carlisle 8	a						16 01							17 00						
Lockerbie	a																			
Haymarket	a													18 14						
Edinburgh 10	a				18 13							19 03		18 22					20 12	
Haymarket	a				18 19							19 11							20 19	
Motherwell	a											19 55								
Glasgow Central 15	a						17 13					20 26								
Inverkeithing	a				18 36														20 33	
Kirkcaldy	a				18 58														20 49	
Markinch	a				19 08														20 59	
Ladybank	a				19 15														21 07	
Cupar	a				19 22														21 14	
Leuchars 3	a				19 29														21 21	
Dundee	a				19 44														21 40	
Arbroath	a				20 01															
Montrose	a				20 15															
Stonehaven	a				20 35															
Aberdeen	a				20 55															

Table 51

Mondays to Fridays

South Coast and the South West - North West England, The North East and Scotland

		XC	VT	VT	XC	XC	XC	XC	XC	XC	XC	VT	XC	XC	XC	XC	XC	XC	VT	XC	XC
			A	B					FX	FO											
		1	◇1 (shop)	◇1 (shop)	◇1 (trolley)	◇1 (trolley)	◇1	◇1 (trolley)	◇1 (trolley)	◇1 (trolley)	1	■ 1 (shop)	◇1 (trolley)	◇1 (trolley)	◇1	◇1 (trolley)	◇1 (trolley)	1	■ 1 (shop)	◇1 (trolley)	◇1 (trolley)
Bournemouth	d							12 45								13 45					
Brockenhurst 3	d							13 00								14 00					
Southampton Central	d							13 15								14 15					
Southampton Airport Parkway ✈	d							13 22								14 22					
Winchester	d							13 31								14 31					
Basingstoke	d							13 47								14 47					
Guildford	d																				
Reading 7	d				13 41			14 11	14 41	14 41						15 11				15 41	
Oxford	d				14 07			14 36	15 07	15 07						15 36				16 07	
Banbury	d				14 28			14 56	15 25	15 25						15 54				16 30	
Leamington Spa 8	d				14 45			15 14	15 43	15 43						16 12				16 49	
Coventry	d			14 43				15 27								16 27					
Birmingham International ✈	d			14 54				15 38								16 39					
Penzance	d					09 40															
St Erth	d					09 48															
Hayle	d					09 52															
Camborne	d					10 01															
Redruth	d					10 08															
Truro	d					10 19															
St Austell	d					10 35															
Newquay	d																				
Par	d					10 43															
Lostwithiel	d					10 50															
Bodmin Parkway	d					10 57															
Liskeard 6	d					11 09															
Plymouth	d					11 50							12 23				13 23				
Totnes	d					12 15							12 49				13 49				
Paignton	d																				14 01
Torquay	d																				14 07
Newton Abbot	d					12 28							13 03				14 03				14 18
Teignmouth	d																				14 25
Dawlish	d																				14 30
Exeter St Davids 6	d					12 48							13 25				14 25				14 44
Tiverton Parkway	d					13 02							13 39				14 39				14 57
Taunton	d					13 16							13 54				14 54				15 12
Weston-super-Mare	d																				15 38
Cardiff Central 7	d						13 45								14 45						
Newport (South Wales)	d						14 00								15 01						
Bristol Temple Meads 10	d					14 00							14 30	15 00			15 30				16 00
Bristol Parkway 7	d					14 10							14 40	15 10			15 40				16 10
Gloucester 7	d						14 46								15 46						
Cheltenham Spa	d					14 42	14 57						15 12	15 42	15 57		16 12				16 42
Birmingham New Street 12	a			15 08	15 18	15 26	15 45	15 48	16 18	16 18			15 56	16 26	16 45	16 48	16 58			17 18	17 26
Birmingham New Street 12	d	15 19	15 20	15 20	15 30	15 31	15 49	15 57	16 30	16 30	16 19	16 20	16 03	16 31	16 49	16 57	17 03	17 19	17 20	17 30	17 31
Tamworth	d	15 39					16 07				16 39		16 19		17 07			17 39			
Burton-on-Trent	d	15 50					16 19				16 50				17 19		17 26	17 51			
Derby 6	a	16 05			16 08		16 34		17 08	17 08	17 05		16 40		17 34		17 40	18 05		18 08	
Nottingham 6	a	16 33					17 05				17 33				18 05			18 33			
Chesterfield	a												17 02				18 01				
Sheffield 7	a				16 46				17 44	17 44			17 19				18 18			18 49	
Doncaster 7	a				17 15															19 17	
Wakefield Westgate 7	a								18 12	18 12			17 47				18 47				
Leeds 10	a								18 30	18 30			18 03				19 02				
York 8	a				17 40				18 58	18 58			18 31				19 30			19 44	
Darlington 7	a				18 15				19 38	19 38			19 00				20 04			20 12	
Durham	a				18 33				19 55	19 55			19 18				20 22			20 30	
Chester-le-Street	a								20 01	20 01											
Newcastle 8	a				18 50				20 13	20 13			19 34				20 38			20 48	
Morpeth	a																				
Alnmouth for Alnwick	a												20 04								
Berwick-upon-Tweed	a																21 27				
Dunbar	a																21 51				
Wolverhampton 7	d		15 37	15 37		15 50		16 15				16 37		16 49		17 15			17 37		17 50
Stafford	a							16 29						17 00		17 29					18 01
Stoke-on-Trent	a					16 18		16 54						17 19		17 54					18 20
Congleton	a																				
Macclesfield	a							17 11								18 11					
Crewe 10	a		16 07	16 07								17 07							18 07		
Wilmslow	a																				
Stockport	a					16 47		17 27						17 49		18 27					18 49
Manchester Piccadilly 10	a					16 59		17 39						17 59		18 39					18 59
Warrington Bank Quay	a		16 26	16 26								17 26							18 26		
Wigan North Western	a		16 37	16 37								17 37							18 37		
Preston 8	a		16 51	16 51								17 51							18 51		
Lancaster 6	a		17 09	17 09								18 08							19 08		
Oxenholme Lake District	a		17 24	17 24								18 22							19 23		
Penrith North Lakes	a		17 50	17 50								18 48									
Carlisle 8	a		18 06	18 06								19 04							20 02		
Lockerbie	a																				
Haymarket	a											20 16									
Edinburgh 10	a								21 40	21 57		20 22	21 08				22 17				
Haymarket	a												21 17								
Motherwell	a												22 03								
Glasgow Central 15	a		19 19	19 19									22 30						21 17		
Inverkeithing	a																				
Kirkcaldy	a																				
Markinch	a																				
Ladybank	a																				
Cupar	a																				
Leuchars 3	a																				
Dundee	a																				
Arbroath	a																				
Montrose	a																				
Stonehaven	a																				
Aberdeen	a																				

A until 16 July, from 6 September

B from 19 July until 3 September

South Coast and the South West - North West England, The North East and Scotland

		XC	XC	XC	XC	XC	VT	XC	XC	XC	XC	XC	XC	VT	XC	XC	XC	XC	XC	XC
		1	◇1	◇1	◇1	1	◇1	◇1	◇1	◇1	◇1	◇1	1	◇1	◇1	◇1	◇1	◇1	◇1	◇1
				H	H		B	H	H		H	H		B	H	H		H	H	H
Bournemouth	d			14 45							15 45							16 45		
Brockenhurst 3	d			15 00							16 00							17 00		
Southampton Central	d			15 15							16 15							17 15		
Southampton Airport Parkway ✈	d			15 22							16 22							17 22		
Winchester	d			15 31							16 31							17 31		
Basingstoke	d			15 47							16 47							17 47		
Guildford	d																			
Reading 7	d			16 11				16 41			17 11				17 41			18 11		18 41
Oxford	d			16 36				17 07			17 36				18 07			18 36		19 12
Banbury	d			16 55				17 28			17 55				18 27			18 55		19 31
Leamington Spa 8	d			17 13				17 45			18 12				18 45			19 12		19 48
Coventry	d			17 27							18 27							19 27		
Birmingham International ✈	d			17 38							18 38							19 38		
Penzance	d																			
St Erth	d																			
Hayle	d																			
Camborne	d																			
Redruth	d																			
Truro	d																			
St Austell	d																			
Newquay	d																			
Par	d																			
Lostwithiel	d																			
Bodmin Parkway	d																			
Liskeard 6	d																			
Plymouth	d				14 25							15 23							16 25	
Totnes	d				14 50							15 49							16 50	
Paignton	d																			
Torquay	d																			
Newton Abbot	d				15 03							16 03							17 03	
Teignmouth	d																			
Dawlish	d																			
Exeter St Davids 6	d				15 23							16 25				16 53			17 23	
Tiverton Parkway	d				15 37							16 39				17 07			17 37	
Taunton	d				15 51							16 54				17 21			17 51	
Weston-super-Mare	d																			
Cardiff Central 7	d		15 45							16 45							17 45			
Newport (South Wales)	d		16 00							17 00							18 00			
Bristol Temple Meads 10	d				16 30				17 00			17 30				18 00			18 30	
Bristol Parkway 7	d				16 40				17 10			17 40				18 10			18 40	
Gloucester 7	d		16 46							17 46							18 46			
Cheltenham Spa	d		16 57		17 12				17 42	17 57		18 12				18 42	18 57		19 12	
Birmingham New Street 12	a		17 45	17 48	17 56			18 18	18 26	18 45	18 48	18 55			19 18	19 26	19 45	19 48	19 56	20 18
Birmingham New Street 12	d	17 39	17 49	17 57	18 03	18 19	18 20	18 30	18 31	18 49	18 57	19 03	19 19	19 20	19 30	19 31	19 49	19 57	20 03	20 30
Tamworth	d	18 00	13 07		18 19	18 39				19 07			19 39				20 07		20 19	
Burton-on-Trent	d	18 12	13 19			18 50				19 19		19 26	19 50				20 19			
Derby 6	a	18 31	13 35		18 42	19 05		19 08		19 34		19 39	20 05		20 08		20 34		20 42	21 11
Nottingham 8 ⇌	a		19 05			19 35				20 03			20 35				21 06			
Chesterfield	a				19 02			19 29				20 02							21 02	21 33
Sheffield 7 ⇌	a				19 19			19 47				20 19			20 49				21 18	21 48
Doncaster 7	a							20 20							21 21					22 29
Wakefield Westgate 7	a				19 49							20 53							21 50	
Leeds 10	a				20 05							21 10							22 04	
York 8	a				20 31			20 46							21 45					22 54
Darlington 7	a				21 07			21 20							22 13					
Durham	a				21 25			21 39							22 30					
Chester-le-Street	a							21 45							22 36					
Newcastle 8	a				21 39			21 55							22 51					
Morpeth	a																			
Alnmouth for Alnwick	a				22 11															
Berwick-upon-Tweed	a				22 32															
Dunbar	a																			
Wolverhampton 7 ⇌	d			18 15			18 37		18 49		19 15			19 37		19 49		20 16		
Stafford	a			18 29							19 27					20 00		20 29		
Stoke-on-Trent	a			18 54					19 18		19 54					20 19		20 54		
Congleton	a																			
Macclesfield	a			19 11							20 11							21 11		
Crewe 10	a						19 07							20 07						
Wilmslow	a																			
Stockport	a			19 27					19 47		20 27					20 48		21 27		
Manchester Piccadilly 10 ⇌	a			19 39					20 00		20 39					20 58		21 40		
Warrington Bank Quay	a						19 26							20 26						
Wigan North Western	a						19 37							20 37						
Preston 8	a						19 51							20 51						
Lancaster 6	a						20 08							21 08						
Oxenholme Lake District	a													21 22						
Penrith North Lakes	a						20 44													
Carlisle 8	a						21 00							22 01						
Lockerbie	a																			
Haymarket	a						22 14													
Edinburgh 10	a				23 23		22 22													
Haymarket	a																			
Motherwell	a																			
Glasgow Central 15	a													23 17						
Inverkeithing	a																			
Kirkcaldy	a																			
Markinch	a																			
Ladybank	a																			
Cupar	a																			
Leuchars 5	a																			
Dundee	a																			
Arbroath	a																			
Montrose	a																			
Stonehaven	a																			
Aberdeen	a																			

South Coast and the South West - North West England, The North East and Scotland

		XC	XC	XC	XC	XC	XC	VT	XC	XC	XC	XC	XC MTX	XC MTO	XC	XC	XC	XC	XC	XC	XC
		◇1	◇1	◇1	◇1	◇1	◇1	◇1	◇1	◇1	◇1	◇1	◇1	◇1	◇1	◇1	1	◇1	◇1	◇1	◇1
		H		H	H	H		B	H			H									
Bournemouth	d			17 45					18 45							19 45					
Brockenhurst 3	d			18 00					19 00							20 00					
Southampton Central	d			18 15					19 15							20 15					
Southampton Airport Parkway ✈	d			18 22					19 22							20 22					
Winchester	d			18 31					19 31							20 31					
Basingstoke	d			18 47					19 47							20 47					
Guildford	d																				
Reading 7	d			19 11		19 41			20 11						20 41	21 11			21 46		
Oxford	d			19 36		20 07			20 36						21 23	21 36			22 30		
Banbury	d			19 54		20 28			20 54						21 41	21 54			22 53		
Leamington Spa 8	d			20 12		20 46			21 12						22 00	22 12			23 13		
Coventry	d			20 27					21 27							22 24			23 27		
Birmingham International ✈	d			20 38					21 38							22 34			23 37		
Penzance	d																				
St Erth	d																				
Hayle	d																				
Camborne	d																				
Redruth	d																				
Truro	d																				
St Austell	d																				
NEWQUAY	d																				
Par	d																				
Lostwithiel	d																				
Bodmin Parkway	d																				
Liskeard 6	d																				
Plymouth	d				17 23							18 25									
Totnes	d				17 49							18 50									
Paignton	d																				20 12
Torquay	d																				20 18
Newton Abbot	d				18 03							19 03									20 29
Teignmouth	d																				
Dawlish	d																				
Exeter St Davids 6	d				18 25							19 23									20 50
Tiverton Parkway	d				18 39							19 37									21 03
Taunton	d				18 54							19 51									21 18
Weston-super-Mare	d																				
Cardiff Central 7	d		18 45							19 50								21 05		21 50	
Newport (South Wales)	d		19 01							20 05								21 20		22 05	
Bristol Temple Meads 10	d	19 00			19 30		20 00					20 30									22 00
Bristol Parkway 7	d	19 10			19 40		20 10					20 40									22 15
Gloucester 7	d		19 46				20 46			20 58								22 06		22 47	
Cheltenham Spa	d	19 42	19 57		20 12		20 56			21 09		21 17						22 17		22 59	23 27
Birmingham New Street 12	a	20 28	20 45	20 48	20 52	21 22	21 46		21 48	21 53		22 09			22 30	22 45		23 27	23 49	00 04	00 10
Birmingham New Street 12	d	20 31	20 49	20 58	21 03			21 20	21 57		22 02		22 28	22 28			23 09				
Tamworth	d		21 09		21 19						22 28						23 28				
Burton-on-Trent	d		21 21		21 30						22 40						23 39				
Derby 6	a		21 36		21 44						22 54						23 55				
Nottingham 8 ⇌	a		22 08								23 27						00 18				
Chesterfield	a				22 05																
Sheffield 7 ⇌	a				22 24																
Doncaster 7	a																				
Wakefield Westgate 7	a				22 57																
Leeds 10	a				23 16																
York 8	a																				
Darlington 7	a																				
Durham	a																				
Chester-le-Street	a																				
Newcastle 8	a																				
Morpeth	a																				
Alnmouth for Alnwick	a																				
Berwick-upon-Tweed	a																				
Dunbar	a																				
Wolverhampton 7 ⇌	d	20 49		21 17				21 42	22 16				22 46	22 46							
Stafford	a			21 31				21 54	22 29				22 58	22 58							
Stoke-on-Trent	a	21 18		21 54					22 53				23 20	23 20							
Congleton	a																				
Macclesfield	a			22 11					23 11												
Crewe 10	a							22 17													
Wilmslow	a																				
Stockport	a	21 47		22 25					23 25												
Manchester Piccadilly 10 ⇌	a	22 00		22 35					23 37				00 12	00 32							
Warrington Bank Quay	a							22 36													
Wigan North Western	a							22 46													
Preston 8	a							23 02													
Lancaster 6	a																				
Oxenholme Lake District	a																				
Penrith North Lakes	a																				
Carlisle 8	a																				
Lockerbie	a																				
Haymarket	a																				
Edinburgh 10	a																				
Haymarket	a																				
Motherwell	a																				
Glasgow Central 15	a																				
Inverkeithing	a																				
Kirkcaldy	a																				
Markinch	a																				
Ladybank	a																				
Cupar	a																				
Leuchars 5	a																				
Dundee	a																				
Arbroath	a																				
Montrose	a																				
Stonehaven	a																				
Aberdeen	a																				

Table 51

Saturdays until 04 September

South Coast and the South West - North West England, The North East and Scotland

		XC	XC	XC	VT	VT	XC	XC	XC	XC	XC	XC	VT	AW	XC	XC	XC	XC	XC	XC
		◇1	◇1	1	◇1	◇1	◇1	◇1	1	◇1	◇1	1	◇1	◇	◇1	◇1	1	◇1	◇1	1
					A	B														
		⊼	⊼		⊏	⊏	⊼	⊼		⊼	⊼		⊏	⊼	⊼	⊼		⊼	⊼	
Bournemouth	d																			
Brockenhurst 3	d																			
Southampton Central	d																	05 09		
Southampton Airport Parkway ✈	d																	05 16		
Winchester	d																	05 25		
Basingstoke	d																	05 41		
Guildford	d																			
Reading 7	d																	06 10		
Oxford	d																	06 38		
Banbury	d																	06 56		
Leamington Spa 8	d																	07 14		
Coventry	d																	07 27		
Birmingham International ✈	d													07 09				07 40		
Penzance	d																			
St Erth	d																			
Hayle	d																			
Camborne	d																			
Redruth	d																			
Truro	d																			
St Austell	d																			
Newquay	d																			
Par	d																			
Lostwithiel	d																			
Bodmin Parkway	d																			
Liskeard 6	d																			
Plymouth	d																			
Totnes	d																			
Paignton	d																			
Torquay	d																			
Newton Abbot	d																			
Teignmouth	d																			
Dawlish	d																			
Exeter St Davids 6	d																			
Tiverton Parkway	d																			
Taunton	d																			
Weston-super-Mare	d																			
Cardiff Central 7	d																			
Newport (South Wales)	d																			
Bristol Temple Meads 10	d																		06 27	
Bristol Parkway 7	d																		06 40	
Gloucester 7	d																			07 06
Cheltenham Spa	d																		07 12	07 18
Birmingham New Street 12	a													07 20				07 51	07 56	08 08
Birmingham New Street 12	d	05 55	05 57	06 19	06 20	06 20	06 30	06 31	06 49	06 57	07 03	07 19	07 20	07 24	07 30	07 31	07 49	07 57	08 03	
Tamworth	d	06 12		06 39			06 46		07 07		07 19	07 38			07 46		08 07		08 19	
Burton-on-Trent	d	06 22		06 50			06 56		07 19		07 29	07 50			07 56		08 22		08 29	
Derby 6	a	06 35		07 06			07 09		07 37		07 42	08 05			08 09		08 34		08 42	
Nottingham 8	a			07 38					08 08			08 34					09 05			
Chesterfield	a	06 55					07 29				08 02				08 29				09 02	
Sheffield 7	a	07 09					07 48				08 17				08 46				09 17	
Doncaster 7	a						08 23								09 21					
Wakefield Westgate 7	a	07 36									08 46								09 46	
Leeds 10	a	07 52									09 02								10 02	
York 8	a	08 25					08 49				09 30				09 45				10 30	
Darlington 7	a	08 54					09 18				09 59				10 13				10 59	
Durham	a	09 11					09 35				10 16				10 30				11 16	
Chester-le-Street	a						09 42													
Newcastle 8	a	09 26					09 54				10 33				10 46				11 32	
Morpeth	a	09 41																		
Alnmouth for Alnwick	a	09 55																	11 59	
Berwick-upon-Tweed	a										11.17									
Dunbar	a										11 40									
Wolverhampton 7	d		06 16		06 37	06 36		06 49		07 14			07 37	07 42		07 49		08 15		
Stafford	a		06 29					07 00		07 29						08 00		08 29		
Stoke-on-Trent	a		06 50					07 18								08 19		08 54		
Congleton	a		07 02																	
Macclesfield	a		07 11					07 36								08 36		09 11		
Crewe 10	a				07 07	07 07				07 50			08 07							
Wilmslow	a									08 09										
Stockport	a		07 27					07 49		08 20						08 49		09 27		
Manchester Piccadilly 10	a		07 38					08 00		08 35						08 59		09 39		
Warrington Bank Quay	a				07 26	07 26							08 27							
Wigan North Western	a				07 37	07 37							08 38							
Preston 8	a				07 51	07 50							08 52							
Lancaster 6	a				08 08	08 08							09 09							
Oxenholme Lake District	a				08 22	08 22														
Penrith North Lakes	a												09 45							
Carlisle 8	a				09 01	09 01							10 01							
Lockerbie	a																			
Haymarket	a				10 16	10 16														
Edinburgh 10	a	10 57			10 22	10 22					12 07								13 01	
Haymarket	a																			
Motherwell	a																			
Glasgow Central 15	a												11 17							
Inverkeithing	a																			
Kirkcaldy	a																			
Markinch	a																			
Ladybank	a																			
Cupar	a																			
Leuchars 3	a																			
Dundee	a																			
Arbroath	a																			
Montrose	a																			
Stonehaven	a																			
Aberdeen	a																			

A until 10 July

B from 17 July until 4 September

Table 51

Saturdays until 04 September

South Coast and the South West - North West England, The North East and Scotland

		XC	VT	XC	XC	XC	XC	XC	XC	VT	XC	XC	XC	XC	XC	XC	VT	VT	XC	XC	XC
		1	◇1	◇1	◇1	◇1	◇1	◇1	1	◇1	◇1	◇1	◇1	◇1	◇1	1	◇1	◇1	◇1	◇1	◇1
																	A	B			
			⊏	⊼	⊼		⊼	⊼		⊏	⊼	⊼		⊼	⊼		⊏	⊏	⊼	⊼	
Bournemouth	d										06 25			06 37							
Brockenhurst 3	d										06 39			06 55							
Southampton Central	d						06 15				06 53			07e15							
Southampton Airport Parkway ✈	d						06 22				07 01			07 22							
Winchester	d						06 31				07 09			07 31							
Basingstoke	d						06 47				07 25			07 47							
Guildford	d			06 09																	
Reading 7	d			06 46			07 11				07 47			08 11					08 40		
Oxford	d			07 12			07 36				08 15			08 36					09 07		
Banbury	d			07 33			07 54				08 35			08 54					09 25		
Leamington Spa 8	d			07 51			08 12				08 55			09 12					09 43		
Coventry	d						08 27							09 27				09 42			
Birmingham International ✈	d						08 38							09 39				09 53			
Penzance	d																				
St Erth	d																				
Hayle	d																				
Camborne	d																				
Redruth	d																				
Truro	d																				
St Austell	d																				
Newquay	d																				
Par	d																				
Lostwithiel	d																				
Bodmin Parkway	d																				
Liskeard 6	d																				
Plymouth	d							05 25							06 25						
Totnes	d							05 50							06 50						
Paignton	d																			07 00	
Torquay	d																			07 06	
Newton Abbot	d							06 03							07 03					07 18	
Teignmouth	d																			07 25	
Dawlish	d																			07 30	
Exeter St Davids 6	d							06 23							07 23					07 48	
Tiverton Parkway	d							06 37							07 37						
Taunton	d							06 51							07 51					08 12	
Weston-super-Mare	d																				
Cardiff Central 7	d					06 40						07 00	07 45								08 45
Newport (South Wales)	d					06 55						07 15	08 00								09 02
Bristol Temple Meads 10	d				07 00			07 30				08 00			08 30					09 00	
Bristol Parkway 7	d				07 10			07 40				08 10			08 40					09 10	
Gloucester 7	d					07 46							08 46								09 46
Cheltenham Spa	d				07 42	07 57		08 12				08 42	08 57		09 12					09 42	09 57
Birmingham New Street 12	a			08 17	08 26	08 45	08 48	08 56			09 19	09 26	09 45	09 48	09 56			10 08	10 17	10 26	10 45
Birmingham New Street 12	d	08 19	08 20	08 30	08 31	08 49	08 57	09 03	09 19	09 20	09 30	09 31	09 49	09 57	10 03	10 19	10 20	10 20	10 30	10 31	10 49
Tamworth	d	08 36				09 07			09 39				10 07		10 19	10 36					11 07
Burton-on-Trent	d	08 48				09 19		09 26	09 52				10 20			10 48					11 19
Derby 6	a	09 05		09 08		09 34		09 41	10 06		10 09		10 34		10 41	11 05			11 09		11 34
Nottingham 8	a	09 35				10 05			10 33				11 05			11 33					12 05
Chesterfield	a							10 02							11 02						
Sheffield 7	a			09 46				10 17			10 46				11 17				11 46		
Doncaster 7	a			10 18							11 16								12 16		
Wakefield Westgate 7	a							10 46							11 46						
Leeds 10	a							11 02							12 02						
York 8	a			10 44				11 30			11 44				12 30				12 44		
Darlington 7	a			11 16				11 59			12 14				13 01				13 12		
Durham	a			11 33				12 16			12 34				13 18				13 29		
Chester-le-Street	a										12 41										
Newcastle 8	a			11 49				12 33			12 50				13 33				13 45		
Morpeth	a																				
Alnmouth for Alnwick	a														13 59						
Berwick-upon-Tweed	a							13 17													
Dunbar	a							13 40													
Wolverhampton 7	d		08 37		08 49		09 15			09 37		09 49		10 15			10 37	10 37		10 49	
Stafford	a				09 00		09 29					10 00		10 29						11 00	
Stoke-on-Trent	a				09 19		09 54					10 19		10 54						11 19	
Congleton	a																				
Macclesfield	a						10 11							11 11							
Crewe 10	a		09 07							10 07							11 07	11 07			
Wilmslow	a																				
Stockport	a				09 49		10 27					10 49		11 27						11 49	
Manchester Piccadilly 10	a				09 59		10 39					10 59		11 39						11 59	
Warrington Bank Quay	a		09 26							10 26							11 26	11 27			
Wigan North Western	a		09 37							10 37							11 37	11 38			
Preston 8	a		09 51							10 51							11 51	11 52			
Lancaster 6	a		10 08							11 08							12 08	12 08			
Oxenholme Lake District	a		10 22														12 22	12 22			
Penrith North Lakes	a									11 44											
Carlisle 8	a		11 01							12 00							13 01	13 01			
Lockerbie	a																				
Haymarket	a		12 16														14 16	14 16			
Edinburgh 10	a		12 22					14 07							15 04		14 22	14 22			
Haymarket	a																				
Motherwell	a																				
Glasgow Central 15	a									13 17											
Inverkeithing	a																				
Kirkcaldy	a																				
Markinch	a																				
Ladybank	a																				
Cupar	a																				
Leuchars 3	a																				
Dundee	a																				
Arbroath	a																				
Montrose	a																				
Stonehaven	a																				
Aberdeen	a																				

A until 10 July

B from 17 July until 4 September

Table 51

South Coast and the South West - North West England, The North East and Scotland

	XC	XC	XC	VT	XC	XC	XC	XC	XC	XC	VT	XC	XC	XC	XC	XC	XC	VT	XC
	◇1 🛒	◇1 🛒	1	◇1 ☕	◇1 🛒	◇1 🛒	◇1	◇1 🛒	◇1 🛒	1	◇1 ☕	◇1 🛒	◇1 🛒	◇1	◇1 🛒	◇1 🛒	1	◇1 ☕	◇1 🛒
Bournemouth d	07 45							08 45							09 45				
Brockenhurst d	08 00							09 00							10 00				
Southampton Central d	08 15							09 15							10 15				
Southampton Airport Parkway ✈ d	08 22							09 22							10 22				
Winchester d	08 31							09 31							10 31				
Basingstoke d	08 47							09 47							10 47				
Guildford d																			
Reading d	09 11				09 40			10 11				10 40			11 11				11 40
Oxford d	09 36				10 07			10 36				11 07			11 36				12 07
Banbury d	09 54				10 25			10 54				11 25			11 54				12 25
Leamington Spa d	10 12				10 43			11 12				11 43			12 12				12 45
Coventry d	10 27							11 27							12 27				
Birmingham International ✈ d	10 38							11 38							12 38				
Penzance d									06 30										
St Erth d									06 38										
Hayle d									06 41										
Camborne d									06 51										
Redruth d									06 57										
Truro d									07 09										
St Austell d									07 25										
Newquay d																			
Par d									07 32										
Lostwithiel d									07 39										
Bodmin Parkway d									07 46										
Liskeard d									07 58										
Plymouth d		07 25							08 25				08 40			09 25			
Totnes d		07 50							08 50				09 05			09 50			
Paignton d																			
Torquay d																			
Newton Abbot d		08 03							09 03				09 18			10 03			
Teignmouth d																			
Dawlish d																			
Exeter St Davids d		08 23							09 23				09 39			10 23			
Tiverton Parkway d		08 37							09 37				09 52			10 37			
Taunton d		08 51							09 51				10 07			10 51			
Weston-super-Mare d													10 34						
Cardiff Central d							09 45							10 45					
Newport (South Wales) d							10 00							11 00					
Bristol Temple Meads d		09 30				10 00			10 30				11 00			11 30			
Bristol Parkway d		09 40				10 10			10 40				11 10			11 40			
Gloucester d							10 46							11 46					
Cheltenham Spa d		10 12				10 42	10 57		11 12				11 42	11 57		12 12			
Birmingham New Street a	10 48	10 56			11 17	11 26	11 45	11 48	11 56			12 17	12 26	12 45	12 48	12 56			13 17
Birmingham New Street d	10 57	11 03	11 19	11 20	11 30	11 31	11 49	11 57	12 03	12 19	12 20	12 30	12 31	12 49	12 57	13 03	13 19	13 20	13 30
Tamworth d			11 39				12 07			12 38				13 07			13 39		
Burton-on-Trent d		11 26	11 51				12 19			12 51				13 19		13 26	13 51		
Derby a		11 41	12 05		12 09		12 35		12 41	13 05		13 09		13 34		13 41	14 05		14 09
Nottingham a			12 33				13 05			13 35				14 06			14 33		
Chesterfield a		12 02							13 02							14 02			
Sheffield a		12 16			12 46				13 17			13 46				14 17			14 46
Doncaster a					13 19							14 16							15 16
Wakefield Westgate a		12 46							13 46							14 46			
Leeds a		13 02							14 02							15 02			
York a		13 32			13 44				14 30			14 44				15 32			15 44
Darlington a		13 59			14 16				14 59			15 15				15 59			16 13
Durham a		14 16			14 34				15 16			15 32				16 16			16 32
Chester-le-Street a					14 41														
Newcastle a		14 32			14 50				15 32			15 46				16 32			16 46
Morpeth a									15 48										
Alnmouth for Alnwick a									16 02										
Berwick-upon-Tweed a		15 17														17 17			
Dunbar a		15 40														17 40			
Wolverhampton d	11 15			11 37		11 49		12 15			12 37		12 49		13 15			13 37	
Stafford a	11 29					12 00		12 29					13 00		13 29				
Stoke-on-Trent a	11 54					12 19		12 54					13 19		13 54				
Congleton a																			
Macclesfield a	12 11							13 11							14 11				
Crewe a				12 07							13 07							14 07	
Wilmslow a																			
Stockport a	12 27					12 49		13 27					13 49		14 27				
Manchester Piccadilly a	12 39					12 59		13 39					13 59		14 39				
Warrington Bank Quay a				12 26							13 26							14 26	
Wigan North Western a				12 37							13 37							14 37	
Preston a				12 51							13 51							14 51	
Lancaster a				13 08							14 08							15 08	
Oxenholme Lake District a				13 22														15 22	
Penrith North Lakes a											14 44								
Carlisle a				14 01							15 00							16 01	
Lockerbie a																			
Haymarket a											16 15								
Edinburgh a		16 05							17 05		16 22					18 05			
Haymarket a																18 11			
Motherwell a																		17 17	
Glasgow Central a				15 17															
Inverkeithing a																18 25			
Kirkcaldy a																18 40			
Markinch a																18 50			
Ladybank a																18 57			
Cupar a																19 04			
Leuchars a																19 11			
Dundee a																19 24			
Arbroath a																19 41			
Montrose a																20 01			
Stonehaven a																20 22			
Aberdeen a																20 41			

Table 51

Saturdays
until 04 September

South Coast and the South West - North West England, The North East and Scotland

	XC	XC	XC	XC	XC	VT	XC	XC	XC	XC	XC	XC	VT	VT	XC	XC	XC	XC	XC
	◇1 ☕🛒	◇1	◇1 🛒	◇1 🛒	1	◇1 ☕	◇1 🛒	◇1 ☕🛒	◇1	◇1 🛒	◇1 🛒	1	◇1 A ☕	◇1 B ☕	◇1 🛒	◇1 ☕🛒	◇1	◇1 🛒	◇1 🛒
Bournemouth d			10 45							11 45								12 45	
Brockenhurst d			11 00							12 00								13 00	
Southampton Central d			11 15							12 15								13 15	
Southampton Airport Parkway ✈ d			11 22							12 22								13 22	
Winchester d			11 31							12 31								13 31	
Basingstoke d			11 47							12 47								13 47	
Guildford d																			
Reading d			12 11				12 40			13 11					13 40			14 11	
Oxford d			12 36				13 07			13 36					14 07			14 36	
Banbury d			12 54				13 25			13 54					14 25			14 54	
Leamington Spa d			13 12				13 43			14 12					14 45			15 12	
Coventry d			13 27							14 27				14 43				15 27	
Birmingham International ✈ d			13 38							14 38				14 54				15 38	
Penzance d				08 25															
St Erth d				08 33															
Hayle d																			
Camborne d				08 43															
Redruth d				08 50															
Truro d				09 02															
St Austell d				09 19															
Newquay d											09 27								
Par d				09 26							10 29								
Lostwithiel d																			
Bodmin Parkway d				09 37							10 42								
Liskeard d				09 50							10 55								
Plymouth d				10 25							11 23								12 23
Totnes d				10 50							11 49								12 49
Paignton d	10 06																		
Torquay d	10 13																		
Newton Abbot d	10 24			11 03							12 03								13 03
Teignmouth d	10 33																		
Dawlish d	10 39																		
Exeter St Davids d	10 53			11 24							12 25								13 25
Tiverton Parkway d	11 07			11 37							12 39								13 39
Taunton d	11 21			11 52							12 54								13 54
Weston-super-Mare d																			
Cardiff Central d		11 45							12 45								13 45		
Newport (South Wales) d		12 00							13 01								14 00		
Bristol Temple Meads d	12 00			12 30				13 00			13 30					14 00			14 30
Bristol Parkway d	12 10			12 40				13 10			13 40					14 10			14 40
Gloucester d		12 46							13 46								14 46		
Cheltenham Spa d	12 42	12 57		13 12				13 42	13 57		14 13					14 42	14 57		15 12
Birmingham New Street a	13 26	13 45	13 48	13 56			14 17	14 26	14 45	14 48	14 56			15 08	15 17	15 26	15 45	15 48	15 54
Birmingham New Street d	13 31	13 49	13 57	14 03	14 19	14 20	14 30	14 31	14 49	14 57	15 03	15 19	15 20	15 20	15 30	15 31	15 49	15 57	16 03
Tamworth d		14 07		14 19	14 38				15 07			15 39					16 07		16 17
Burton-on-Trent d		14 19			14 50				15 19		15 26	15 50					16 19		
Derby a		14 35		14 41	15 05		15 08		15 34		15 43	16 05			16 08		16 34		16 40
Nottingham a		15 05			15 33				16 05			16 33					17 05		
Chesterfield a				15 02							16 02								17 01
Sheffield a				15 17			15 46				16 18				16 46				17 19
Doncaster a							16 15								17 19				
Wakefield Westgate a				15 46							16 49								17 47
Leeds a				16 02							17 04								18 02
York a				16 30			16 39				17 29				17 44				18 31
Darlington a				16 59			17 10				17 59				18 12				19 01
Durham a				17 16			17 28				18 17				18 29				19 19
Chester-le-Street a							17 39												
Newcastle a				17 32			17 51				18 33				18 45				19 35
Morpeth a																			
Alnmouth for Alnwick a				18 01															20 03
Berwick-upon-Tweed a											19 25								
Dunbar a											19 49								
Wolverhampton d	13 49		14 15			14 37		14 49		15 15			15 37	15 37		15 49		16 15	
Stafford a	14 00		14 29					15 00		15 29						16 00		16 29	
Stoke-on-Trent a	14 19		14 54					15 19		15 54						16 19		16 54	
Congleton a																			
Macclesfield a			15 11							16 11								17 11	
Crewe a						15 07							16 08	16 08					
Wilmslow a																			
Stockport a	14 49		15 27					15 49		16 27						16 49		17 27	
Manchester Piccadilly a	14 59		15 39					15 59		16 39						16 59		17 39	
Warrington Bank Quay a						15 26							16 26	16 26					
Wigan North Western a						15 37							16 37	16 37					
Preston a						15 51							16 51	16 51					
Lancaster a						16 08							17 09	17 09					
Oxenholme Lake District a													17 24	17 24					
Penrith North Lakes a						16 45													
Carlisle a						17 00							18 03	18 03					
Lockerbie a																			
Haymarket a						18 14													
Edinburgh a				19 07		18 22					20 15								21 06
Haymarket a				19 13							20 25								21 13
Motherwell a				19 55															21 55
Glasgow Central a				20 24									19 17	19 17					22 18
Inverkeithing a											20 43								
Kirkcaldy a											21 00								
Markinch a											21 10								
Ladybank a											21 18								
Cupar a											21 26								
Leuchars a											21 35								
Dundee a											21 52								
Arbroath a																			
Montrose a																			
Stonehaven a																			
Aberdeen a																			

A until 10 July

B from 17 July until 4 September

Table 51

South Coast and the South West - North West England, The North East and Scotland

		XC 1	VT ◇1 ⊡	XC ◇1 ⊼	XC ◇1 ⊼	XC ◇1	XC ◇1 ⊼	XC ◇1 ⊼	XC 1	VT ◇1 ⊡	XC ◇1 ⊼	XC ◇1 ⊼	XC ◇1	XC ◇1 ⊼	XC ◇1 ⊼	XC 1	VT ◇1 ⊡	XC ◇1 ⊼	XC ◇1 ⊼	XC ◇1
Bournemouth	d						13 45							14 45						
Brockenhurst ■3	d						14 00							15 00						
Southampton Central	d						14 15							15 15						
Southampton Airport Parkway ✈	d						14 22							15 22						
Winchester	d						14 31							15 31						
Basingstoke	d						14 47							15 47						
Guildford	d																			
Reading ■7	d			14 40			15 11				15 40			16 11				16 40		
Oxford	d			15 07			15 36				16 07			16 36				17 07		
Banbury	d			15 25			15 54				16 25			16 54				17 25		
Leamington Spa ■8	d			15 43			16 12				16 48			17 12				17 43		
Coventry	d						16 27							17 27						
Birmingham International ✈	d						16 38							17 38						
Penzance	d																			
St Erth	d																			
Hayle	d																			
Camborne	d																			
Redruth	d																			
Truro	d																			
St Austell	d																			
Newquay	d																			
Par	d																			
Lostwithiel	d																			
Bodmin Parkway	d																			
Liskeard ■6	d																			
Plymouth	d							13 25							14 25					
Totnes	d							13 50							14 50					
Paignton	d											13 47								
Torquay	d											13 54								
Newton Abbot	d							14 03				14 06			15 03					
Teignmouth	d											14 15								
Dawlish	d											14 22								
Exeter St Davids ■6	d							14 24				14 38			15 23					
Tiverton Parkway	d							14 37							15 37					
Taunton	d							14 52				15 03			15 51					
Weston-super-Mare	d											15 30								
Cardiff Central ■7	d					14 45							15 45							16 45
Newport (South Wales)	d					15 01							16 00							17 01
Bristol Temple Meads ■10	d				15 00			15 30				16 00			16 30				17 00	
Bristol Parkway ■7	d				15 10			15 40				16 10			16 40				17 10	
Gloucester ■7	d					15 46							16 46							17 46
Cheltenham Spa	d				15 42	15 57		16 12				16 42	16 57		17 12				17 42	17 57
Birmingham New Street ■12	a			16 17	16 26	16 45	16 48	16 56			17 17	17 26	17 45	17 48	17 56			18 17	18 26	18 45
Birmingham New Street ■12	d	16 19	16 20	16 30	16 31	16 49	16 57	17 03	17 19	17 20	17 30	17 31	17 49	17 57	18 03	18 19	18 20	18 30	18 31	18 49
Tamworth	d	16 39				17 07			17 39				18 07		18 19	18 39				19 07
Burton-on-Trent	d	16 50				17 19		17 26	17 51				18 19			18 50				19 19
Derby ■6	a	17 05		17 08		17 34		17 41	18 05		18 08		18 35		18 41	19 05		19 08		19 35
Nottingham ■8 🚌	a	17 33				18 05			18 33				19 05			19 33				20 05
Chesterfield	a							18 02							19 02			19 29		
Sheffield ■7 🚌	a			17 44				18 18			18 47				19 18			19 51		
Doncaster ■7	a										19 18							20 16		
Wakefield Westgate ■7	a			18 14				18 46							19 46					
Leeds ■10	a			18 32				19 01							20 02					
York ■8	a			18 59				19 31			19 44				20 31			20 40		
Darlington ■7	a			19 37				20 03			20 12				21 04			21 14		
Durham	a			19 54				20 21			20 29				21 21			21 32		
Chester-le-Street	a										20 36							21 39		
Newcastle ■8	a			20 10				20 33			20 51				21 33			21 50		
Morpeth	a																			
Alnmouth for Alnwick	a														21 59					
Berwick-upon-Tweed	a			20 55				21 19							22 20					
Dunbar	a							21 42												
Wolverhampton ■7 🚌	d		16 37		16 49		17 15			17 37		17 48		18 15			18 37		18 49	
Stafford	a				17 00		17 29					18 01		18 29					19 00	
Stoke-on-Trent	a				17 19		17 54					18 19		18 54					19 19	
Congleton	a																			
Macclesfield	a						18 11							19 11						
Crewe ■10	a		17 07							18 07							19 07			
Wilmslow	a																			
Stockport	a				17 49		18 27							19 27					19 49	
Manchester Piccadilly ■10 🚌	a				17 59		18 39					18 59		19 40					19 59	
Warrington Bank Quay	a		17 26							18 26							19 26			
Wigan North Western	a		17 37							18 37							19 37			
Preston ■8	a		17 51							18 51							19 59			
Lancaster ■6	a		18 08							19 08										
Oxenholme Lake District	a		18 22							19 22										
Penrith North Lakes	a		18 48																	
Carlisle ■8	a		19 04							20 01										
Lockerbie	a																			
Haymarket	a		20 19																	
Edinburgh ■10	a		20 24	21 39				22 10							23 04					
Haymarket	a																			
Motherwell	a																			
Glasgow Central ■15	a									21 17										
Inverkeithing	a																			
Kirkcaldy	a																			
Markinch	a																			
Ladybank	a																			
Cupar	a																			
Leuchars ■3	a																			
Dundee	a																			
Arbroath	a																			
Montrose	a																			
Stonehaven	a																			
Aberdeen	a																			

Table 51

South Coast and the South West - North West England, The North East and Scotland

		XC ◇1 ⊼	XC ◇1 ⊼	XC ◇1 ⊼	XC 1	VT ◇1 ⊡	XC ◇1 ⊼	XC ◇1	XC ◇1 ⊼	XC ◇1 ⊼	VT ◇1 ⊡	XC ◇1 ⊼	XC ◇1 ⊼	XC ◇1	XC ◇1 ⊼	XC ◇1 B ⊼	XC ◇1 C ⊼	XC ◇1 ⊼	XC ◇1 ⊼	XC ◇1 B ⊼
Bournemouth	d	15 45							16 45						17 45					18 45
Brockenhurst ■3	d	16 00							17 00						18 00					19 00
Southampton Central	d	16 15							17 15						18 15					19 15
Southampton Airport Parkway ✈	d	16 22							17 22						18 22					19 22
Winchester	d	16 31							17 31						18 31					19 31
Basingstoke	d	16 47							17 47						18 47					19 47
Guildford	d																			
Reading ■7	d	17 11		17 40					18 11			18 40			19 11			19 40		20 11
Oxford	d	17 36		18 07					18 36			19 07			19 36			20 07		20 36
Banbury	d	17 54		18 25					18 54			19 25			19 54			20 30		20 54
Leamington Spa ■8	d	18 12		18 45					19 12			19 43			20 12			20 47		21 12
Coventry	d	18 27							19 27						20 27					21 27
Birmingham International ✈	d	18 38							19 38						20 39					21 38
Penzance	d																			
St Erth	d																			
Hayle	d																			
Camborne	d																			
Redruth	d																			
Truro	d																			
St Austell	d																			
Newquay	d															15 24	15 24			
Par	d															16 28	16 28			
Lostwithiel	d																			
Bodmin Parkway	d															16 40	16 40			
Liskeard ■6	d															16 53	16 53			
Plymouth	d		15 25							16 25						17 23	17 23			
Totnes	d		15 50							16 50						17 49	17 49			
Paignton	d																		18 10	
Torquay	d																		18 17	
Newton Abbot	d		16 03							17 03						18 03	18 03		18 28	
Teignmouth	d																			
Dawlish	d																			
Exeter St Davids ■6	d		16 23							17 23						18 25	18 25		18 50	
Tiverton Parkway	d		16 37							17 37						18 39	18 39		19 03	
Taunton	d		16 51							17 51						18 54	18 54		19 18	
Weston-super-Mare	d																			
Cardiff Central ■7	d							17 45						18 45						
Newport (South Wales)	d							18 00						19 01						
Bristol Temple Meads ■10	d		17 30				18 00			18 30			19 00			19 30	19 30		20 00	
Bristol Parkway ■7	d		17 40				18 10			18 40			19 10			19 40	19 40		20 10	
Gloucester ■7	d							18 46						19 46						
Cheltenham Spa	d		18 12				18 42	18 57		19 12			19 42	19 57		20 12	20 12		20 42	
Birmingham New Street ■12	a	18 48	18 56	19 17			19 26	19 45	19 48	19 56		20 18	20 26	20 40	20 48	20 50	20 50	21 16	21 38	21 48
Birmingham New Street ■12	d	18 57	19 03	19 30	19 19	19 20	19 31	19 49	19 57	20 03	20 20	20 30	20 31	20 49	21 03	21 01	21 03			21 57
Tamworth	d				19 39			20 07		20 19				21 08	21 20					
Burton-on-Trent	d		19 26		19 50			20 19						21 20	21 30					
Derby ■6	a		19 41	20 08	20 05			20 34		20 41		21 25		21 35	21 45					
Nottingham ■8 🚌	a				20 35			21 04						22 08						
Chesterfield	a		20 02	20 29						21 02					22 07					
Sheffield ■7 🚌	a		20 18	20 49						21 18		21 57			22 23					
Doncaster ■7	a			21 25								22 30			22 47					
Wakefield Westgate ■7	a		20 48							21 48					23 09					
Leeds ■10	a		21 04							22 02					23 24					
York ■8	a		21 58	21 48								22 55								
Darlington ■7	a			22 21																
Durham	a			22 41																
Chester-le-Street	a			22 50																
Newcastle ■8	a			23 05																
Morpeth	a																			
Alnmouth for Alnwick	a																			
Berwick-upon-Tweed	a																			
Dunbar	a																			
Wolverhampton ■7 🚌	d	19 15				19 37	19 49		20 16		20 37		20 49			21 18	21 19			22 16
Stafford	a	19 29					20 00		20 29		20 49		21 00			21 31	21 32			22 29
Stoke-on-Trent	a	19 54					20 19		20 54				21 20				21 50			
Congleton	a																			
Macclesfield	a	20 11					20 36		21 11				21 38							
Crewe ■10	a					20 07					21 09					21 58				
Wilmslow	a															22 20				23 11
Stockport	a	20 27					20 49		21 27				21 53			22 36	22 24			23 21
Manchester Piccadilly ■10 🚌	a	20 39					20 59		21 39				22 04			22 48	22 39			23 32
Warrington Bank Quay	a					20 26														
Wigan North Western	a					20 37														
Preston ■8	a					20 59														
Lancaster ■6	a																			
Oxenholme Lake District	a																			
Penrith North Lakes	a																			
Carlisle ■8	a																			
Lockerbie	a																			
Haymarket	a																			
Edinburgh ■10	a																			
Haymarket	a																			
Motherwell	a																			
Glasgow Central ■15	a																			
Inverkeithing	a																			
Kirkcaldy	a																			
Markinch	a																			
Ladybank	a																			
Cupar	a																			
Leuchars ■3	a																			
Dundee	a																			
Arbroath	a																			
Montrose	a																			
Stonehaven	a																			
Aberdeen	a																			

B until 10 July

C from 17 July until 4 September

Table 51

Saturdays
until 04 September

South Coast and the South West - North West England, The North East and Scotland

Station		XC ◇1 A H	XC ◇1	XC ◇1 H	XC ◇1 H	XC ◇1 A H	XC ◇1 B H	XC ◇1	XC ◇1 H	XC ◇1	XC ◇1 H
Bournemouth	d	18 45							19 45		
Brockenhurst	d	19 00							20 00		
Southampton Central	d	19 15							20 15		
Southampton Airport Parkway ✈	d	19 22							20 22		
Winchester	d	19 31							20 31		
Basingstoke	d	19 47							20 47		
Guildford	d										
Reading	d	20 11			20 40				21 11		21 40
Oxford	d	20 36			21 07				21 36		22 07
Banbury	d	20 54			21 25				21 54		22 25
Leamington Spa	d	21 12			21 45				22 12		22 43
Coventry	d	21 27			21 56				22 27		
Birmingham International ✈	d	21 38			22 13				22 39		
Penzance	d			16 25							
St Erth	d			16 36							
Hayle	d										
Camborne	d			16 47							
Redruth	d			16 54							
Truro	d			17 06							
St Austell	d			17 24							
NEWQUAY	d										
Par	d										
Lostwithiel	d										
Bodmin Parkway	d			17 40							
Liskeard	d			17 53							
Plymouth	d			18 23							
Totnes	d			18 49							
Paignton	d										
Torquay	d										
Newton Abbot	d			19 03							
Teignmouth	d										
Dawlish	d										
Exeter St Davids	d			19 25							
Tiverton Parkway	d										
Taunton	d			19 49							
Weston-super-Mare	d										
Cardiff Central	d		20 00					20 50			
Newport (South Wales)	d		20 15					21 05			
Bristol Temple Meads	d			20 30							
Bristol Parkway	d			20 40							
Gloucester	d		21 07	21 14				21 49			
Cheltenham Spa	d		21 18	21 25				22 00			
Birmingham New Street	a	21 48	22 07	22 11	22 25			22 42	22 48		23 09
Birmingham New Street	d	21 57	22 10			22 31	22 31			22 49	
Tamworth	d		22 28							23 08	
Burton-on-Trent	d		22 39							23 20	
Derby	a		22 55							23 33	
Nottingham ⇌	a		23 28								
Chesterfield	a										
Sheffield ⇌	a										
Doncaster	a										
Wakefield Westgate	a										
Leeds	a										
York	a										
Darlington	a										
Durham	a										
Chester-le-Street	a										
Newcastle	a										
Morpeth	a										
Alnmouth for Alnwick	a										
Berwick-upon-Tweed	a										
Dunbar	a										
Wolverhampton ⇌	d	22 16				22 49	22 49				
Stafford	a	22 29				23 02	23 02				
Stoke-on-Trent	a	22 50				23 20					
Congleton	a										
Macclesfield	a	23 07				23 38					
Crewe	a										
Wilmslow	a						23 42				
Stockport	a	23 21				23 53	23 53				
Manchester Piccadilly ⇌	a	23 32				00 10	00 10				
Warrington Bank Quay	a										
Wigan North Western	a										
Preston	a										
Lancaster	a										
Oxenholme Lake District	a										
Penrith North Lakes	a										
Carlisle	a										
Lockerbie	a										
Haymarket	a										
Edinburgh	a										
Haymarket	a										
Motherwell	a										
Glasgow Central	a										
Inverkeithing	a										
Kirkcaldy	a										
Markinch	a										
Ladybank	a										
Cupar	a										
Leuchars	a										
Dundee	a										
Arbroath	a										
Montrose	a										
Stonehaven	a										
Aberdeen	a										

A from 17 July until 4 September **B** until 10 July

Table 51

Saturdays
from 11 September

South Coast and the South West - North West England, The North East and Scotland

Station		XC ◇1 H	XC ◇1 H	XC 1	VT ◇1	XC ◇1 H	XC ◇1 H	XC 1	XC ◇1 H	XC ◇1 H	XC 1	VT ◇1	XC ◇1 H	XC ◇1 H	XC 1	XC ◇1 H	XC ◇1 H	XC 1
Bournemouth	d																	
Brockenhurst	d																	
Southampton Central	d															05 09		
Southampton Airport Parkway ✈	d															05 16		
Winchester	d															05 25		
Basingstoke	d															05 41		
Guildford	d																	
Reading	d															06e10		
Oxford	d															06 38		
Banbury	d															06 56		
Leamington Spa	d															07 14		
Coventry	d															07 27		
Birmingham International ✈	d															07 40		
Penzance	d																	
St Erth	d																	
Hayle	d																	
Camborne	d																	
Redruth	d																	
Truro	d																	
St Austell	d																	
Newquay	d																	
Par	d																	
Lostwithiel	d																	
Bodmin Parkway	d																	
Liskeard	d																	
Plymouth	d																	
Totnes	d																	
Paignton	d																	
Torquay	d																	
Newton Abbot	d																	
Teignmouth	d																	
Dawlish	d																	
Exeter St Davids	d																	
Tiverton Parkway	d																	
Taunton	d																	
Weston-super-Mare	d																	
Cardiff Central	d																	
Newport (South Wales)	d																	
Bristol Temple Meads	d																06 27	
Bristol Parkway	d																06 40	
Gloucester	d																	07 06
Cheltenham Spa	d																07 12	07 18
Birmingham New Street	a															07 51	07 56	08 08
Birmingham New Street	d	05 55	05 57	06 19	06 20	06 30	06 31	06 49	06 57	07 03	07 19	07 20	07 30	07 31	07 49	07 57	08 03	
Tamworth	d	06 12		06 39		06 46		07 07		07 19	07 38		07 46		08 07		08 19	
Burton-on-Trent	d	06 22		06 50		06 56		07 19		07 29	07 50		07 56		08 22		08 29	
Derby	a	06 35		07 06		07 09		07 37		07 42	08 05		08 09		08 34		08 42	
Nottingham ⇌	a			07 38				08 08			08 34				09 05			
Chesterfield	a	06 55				07 29				08 02			08 29				09 02	
Sheffield ⇌	a	07 09				07 48				08 17			08 46				09 17	
Doncaster	a					08 23							09 21					
Wakefield Westgate	a	07 36								08 46							09 46	
Leeds	a	07 52								09 02							10 02	
York	a	08 25				08 49				09 30			09 45				10 30	
Darlington	a	08 54				09 18				09 59			10 13				10 59	
Durham	a	09 11				09 35				10 16			10 30				11 16	
Chester-le-Street	a					09 42												
Newcastle	a	09 26				09 54				10 33			10 46				11 32	
Morpeth	a	09 41																
Alnmouth for Alnwick	a	09 55															11 59	
Berwick-upon-Tweed	a									11 17								
Dunbar	a									11 40								
Wolverhampton ⇌	d		06 16		06 37		06 49		07 14			07 37		07 49		08 15		
Stafford	a		06 29				07 00		07 29					08 00		08 29		
Stoke-on-Trent	a		06 50				07 18							08 19		08 54		
Congleton	a		07 02															
Macclesfield	a		07 11				07 36							08 36		09 11		
Crewe	a				07 07				07 50			08 07						
Wilmslow	a								08 09									
Stockport	a		07 27				07 49		08 20					08 49		09 27		
Manchester Piccadilly ⇌	a		07 38				07 59		08 35					08 59		09 39		
Warrington Bank Quay	a				07 26							08 27						
Wigan North Western	a				07 37							08 38						
Preston	a				07 51							08 52						
Lancaster	a				08 08							09 09						
Oxenholme Lake District	a				08 22													
Penrith North Lakes	a											09 45						
Carlisle	a				09 01							10 01						
Lockerbie	a																	
Haymarket	a				10 16													
Edinburgh	a	10 57			10 22					12 07							13 01	
Haymarket	a																	
Motherwell	a																	
Glasgow Central	a											11 17						
Inverkeithing	a																	
Kirkcaldy	a																	
Markinch	a																	
Ladybank	a																	
Cupar	a																	
Leuchars	a																	
Dundee	a																	
Arbroath	a																	
Montrose	a																	
Stonehaven	a																	
Aberdeen	a																	

Table 51

Saturdays from 11 September

South Coast and the South West - North West England, The North East and Scotland

		XC	VT	XC	XC	XC	XC	XC	XC	VT	XC	XC	XC	XC	XC	XC	VT	XC	XC	XC	XC
		1	◇1	◇1	◇1	◇1	◇1	◇1	1	◇1	◇1	◇1	◇1	◇1	◇1	1	◇1	◇1	◇1	◇1	◇1
Bournemouth	d										06 25			06 37							07 45
Brockenhurst	d										06 39			06 55							08 00
Southampton Central	d						06 15				06 53			07 15							08 15
Southampton Airport Parkway	d						06 22				07 01			07 22							08 22
Winchester	d						06 31				07 09			07 31							08 31
Basingstoke	d						06 47				07 25			07 47							08 47
Guildford	d			06 09																	
Reading	d			06 46			07 11				07 47			08 11				08 40			09 11
Oxford	d			07 12			07 36				08 15			08 36				09 07			09 36
Banbury	d			07 33			07 54				08 35			08 54				09 25			09 54
Leamington Spa	d			07 51			08 12				08 55			09 12				09 43			10 12
Coventry	d						08 27							09 27							10 27
Birmingham International	d						08 38							09 39							10 38
Penzance	d																				
St Erth	d																				
Hayle	d																				
Camborne	d																				
Redruth	d																				
Truro	d																				
St Austell	d																				
Newquay	d																				
Par	d																				
Lostwithiel	d																				
Bodmin Parkway	d																				
Liskeard	d																				
Plymouth	d							05 25							06 25						
Totnes	d							05 50							06 50						
Paignton	d																		07 00		
Torquay	d																		07 06		
Newton Abbot	d							06 03							07 03				07 18		
Teignmouth	d																		07 25		
Dawlish	d																		07 30		
Exeter St Davids	d							06 23							07 23				07 48		
Tiverton Parkway	d							06 37							07 37						
Taunton	d							06 51							07 51				08 12		
Weston-super-Mare	d																				
Cardiff Central	d					06 40						07 00	07 45							08 45	
Newport (South Wales)	d					06 55						07 15	08 00							09 02	
Bristol Temple Meads	d				07 00			07 30				08 00			08 30				09 00		
Bristol Parkway	d				07 10			07 40				08 10			08 40				09 10		
Gloucester	d					07 46							08 46							09 46	
Cheltenham Spa	d				07 42	07 57		08 12				08 42	08 57		09 12				09 42	09 57	
Birmingham New Street	a			08 17	08 26	08 45	08 48	08 56			09 19	09 26	09 45	09 48	09 56			10 17	10 26	10 45	10 48
Birmingham New Street	d	08 19	08 20	08 30	08 31	08 49	08 57	09 03	09 19	09 20	09 30	09 31	09 49	09 57	10 03	10 19	10 20	10 30	10 31	10 49	10 57
Tamworth	d	08 36				09 07			09 39				10 07		10 19	10 36				11 07	
Burton-on-Trent	d	08 48				09 19		09 26	09 52				10 20			10 48				11 19	
Derby	a	09 05		09 08		09 34		09 41	10 06		10 09		10 34		10 41	11 05		11 09		11 34	
Nottingham	a	09 35				10 05			10 33				11 05			11 33				12 05	
Chesterfield	a							10 02							11 02						
Sheffield	a			09 46				10 17			10 46				11 17			11 46			
Doncaster	a			10 18							11 16							12 16			
Wakefield Westgate	a							10 46							11 46						
Leeds	a							11 02							12 02						
York	a			10 44				11 30			11 44				12 30			12 44			
Darlington	a			11 16				11 59			12 14				13 01			13 12			
Durham	a			11 33				12 16			12 34				13 18			13 29			
Chester-le-Street	a										12 41										
Newcastle	a			11 49				12 33			12 50				13 33			13 45			
Morpeth	a																				
Alnmouth for Alnwick	a														13 59						
Berwick-upon-Tweed	a							13 17													
Dunbar	a							13 40													
Wolverhampton	d		08 37		08 49		09 15			09 37		09 49		10 15			10 37		10 49		11 15
Stafford	a				09 00		09 29					10 00		10 29					11 00		11 29
Stoke-on-Trent	a				09 19		09 54					10 19		10 54					11 19		11 54
Congleton	a																				
Macclesfield	a						10 11							11 11							12 11
Crewe	a		09 07							10 07							11 07				
Wilmslow	a																				
Stockport	a				09 49		10 27					10 49		11 27					11 49		12 27
Manchester Piccadilly	a				09 59		10 39					10 59		11 39					11 59		12 39
Warrington Bank Quay	a		09 26							10 26							11 26				
Wigan North Western	a		09 37							10 37							11 37				
Preston	a		09 51							10 51							11 51				
Lancaster	a		10 08							11 08							12 08				
Oxenholme Lake District	a		10 22														12 22				
Penrith North Lakes	a									11 44											
Carlisle	a		11 01							12 00							13 01				
Lockerbie	a																				
Haymarket	a		12 16														14 16				
Edinburgh	a		12 22					14 07							15 04		14 22				
Haymarket	a																				
Motherwell	a																				
Glasgow Central	a									13 17											
Inverkeithing	a																				
Kirkcaldy	a																				
Markinch	a																				
Ladybank	a																				
Cupar	a																				
Leuchars	a																				
Dundee	a																				
Arbroath	a																				
Montrose	a																				
Stonehaven	a																				
Aberdeen	a																				

Table 51

Saturdays from 11 September

South Coast and the South West - North West England, The North East and Scotland

		XC	XC	VT	XC	XC	XC	XC	XC	XC	VT	XC	XC	XC	XC	XC	XC	VT	XC
		◇1	1	◇1	◇1	◇1	◇1	◇1	◇1	1	◇1	◇1	◇1	◇1	◇1	◇1	1	◇1	◇1
Bournemouth	d							08 45							09 45				
Brockenhurst	d							09 00							10 00				
Southampton Central	d							09 15							10 15				
Southampton Airport Parkway	d							09 22							10 22				
Winchester	d							09 31							10 31				
Basingstoke	d							09 47							10 47				
Guildford	d																		
Reading	d				09 40			10 11				10 40			11 11				11 40
Oxford	d				10 07			10 36				11 07			11 36				12 07
Banbury	d				10 25			10 54				11 25			11 54				12 25
Leamington Spa	d				10 43			11 12				11 43			12 12				12 45
Coventry	d							11 27							12 27				
Birmingham International	d							11 38							12 38				
Penzance	d								06 30										
St Erth	d								06 38										
Hayle	d								06 41										
Camborne	d								06 51										
Redruth	d								06 57										
Truro	d								07 09										
St Austell	d								07 25										
Newquay	d																		
Par	d								07 32										
Lostwithiel	d								07 39										
Bodmin Parkway	d								07 46										
Liskeard	d								07 58										
Plymouth	d	07 25							08 25							09 25			
Totnes	d	07 50							08 50							09 50			
Paignton	d																		
Torquay	d																		
Newton Abbot	d	08 03							09 03							10 03			
Teignmouth	d																		
Dawlish	d																		
Exeter St Davids	d	08 23							09 23							10 23			
Tiverton Parkway	d	08 37							09 37							10 37			
Taunton	d	08 51							09 51							10 51			
Weston-super-Mare	d																		
Cardiff Central	d						09 45							10 45					
Newport (South Wales)	d						10 00							11 00					
Bristol Temple Meads	d	09 30				10 00			10 30				11 00			11 30			
Bristol Parkway	d	09 40				10 10			10 40				11 10			11 40			
Gloucester	d						10 46							11 46					
Cheltenham Spa	d	10 12				10 42	10 57		11 12				11 42	11 57		12 12			
Birmingham New Street	a	10 56			11 17	11 26	11 45	11 48	11 56			12 17	12 26	12 45	12 48	12 56			13 17
Birmingham New Street	d	11 03	11 19	11 20	11 30	11 31	11 49	11 57	12 03	12 19	12 20	12 30	12 31	12 49	12 57	13 03	13 19	13 20	13 30
Tamworth	d		11 39				12 07		12 19	12 38				13 07			13 39		
Burton-on-Trent	d	11 26	11 51				12 19			12 51				13 19		13 26	13 51		
Derby	a	11 41	12 05		12 09		12 35		12 41	13 05		13 09		13 34		13 41	14 05		14 09
Nottingham	a		12 33				13 05			13 35				14 06			14 33		
Chesterfield	a	12 02							13 02							14 02			
Sheffield	a	12 16			12 46				13 17			13 46				14 17			14 46
Doncaster	a				13 19							14 16							15 16
Wakefield Westgate	a	12 46							13 46							14 46			
Leeds	a	13 02							14 02							15 02			
York	a	13 32			13 44				14 30			14 44				15 32			15 44
Darlington	a	13 59			14 16				14 59			15 15				15 59			16 13
Durham	a	14 16			14 34				15 16			15 32				16 16			16 32
Chester-le-Street	a				14 41														
Newcastle	a	14 32			14 50				15 32			15 46				16 32			16 46
Morpeth	a								15 48										
Alnmouth for Alnwick	a								16 02										
Berwick-upon-Tweed	a	15 17														17 17			
Dunbar	a	15 40														17 40			
Wolverhampton	d			11 37		11 49		12 15			12 37		12 49		13 15			13 37	
Stafford	a					12 00		12 29					13 00		13 29				
Stoke-on-Trent	a					12 19		12 54					13 19		13 54				
Congleton	a																		
Macclesfield	a							13 11							14 11				
Crewe	a			12 07							13 07							14 07	
Wilmslow	a																		
Stockport	a					12 49		13 27					13 49		14 27				
Manchester Piccadilly	a					12 59		13 39					13 59		14 39				
Warrington Bank Quay	a			12 26							13 26							14 26	
Wigan North Western	a			12 37							13 37							14 37	
Preston	a			12 51							13 51							14 51	
Lancaster	a			13 08							14 08							15 08	
Oxenholme Lake District	a			13 22														15 22	
Penrith North Lakes	a										14 44								
Carlisle	a			14 01							15 00							16 01	
Lockerbie	a																		
Haymarket	a										16 15								
Edinburgh	a	16 05							17 05		16 22					18 05			
Haymarket	a															18 11			
Motherwell	a																		
Glasgow Central	a			15 17														17 17	
Inverkeithing	a															18 25			
Kirkcaldy	a															18 40			
Markinch	a															18 50			
Ladybank	a															18 57			
Cupar	a															19 04			
Leuchars	a															19 11			
Dundee	a															19 24			
Arbroath	a															19 41			
Montrose	a															20 01			
Stonehaven	a															20 22			
Aberdeen	a															20 41			

Table 51

South Coast and the South West - North West England, The North East and Scotland

		XC ◇1 🍴	XC ◇1	XC ◇1 🍴	XC ◇1 🍴	XC 1	VT ◇1 🛒	XC ◇1 🍴	XC ◇1 🍴	XC ◇1	XC ◇1 🍴	XC ◇1 🍴	XC 1	VT ◇1 🛒	XC ◇1 🍴	XC ◇1 🍴	XC ◇1	XC ◇1 🍴
Bournemouth	d			10 45							11 45							12 45
Brockenhurst 3	d			11 00							12 00							13 00
Southampton Central	d			11 15							12 15							13 15
Southampton Airport Parkway ✈	d			11 22							12 22							13 22
Winchester	d			11 31							12 31							13 31
Basingstoke	d			11 47							12 47							13 47
Guildford	d																	
Reading 7	d			12 11				12 40			13 11				13 40			14 11
Oxford	d			12 36				13 07			13 36				14 07			14 36
Banbury	d			12 54				13 25			13 54				14 25			14 54
Leamington Spa 8	d			13 12				13 43			14 12				14 45			15 12
Coventry	d			13 27							14 27							15 27
Birmingham International ✈	d			13 38							14 38							15 38
Penzance	d				08 28											09 43		
St Erth	d				08 36											09 51		
Hayle	d																	
Camborne	d				08 46											10 01		
Redruth	d				08 52											10 07		
Truro	d				09 04											10 19		
St Austell	d				09 20											10 35		
Newquay	d																	
Par	d				09 28											10 42		
Lostwithiel	d															10 49		
Bodmin Parkway	d				09 39											10 56		
Liskeard 6	d				09 51											11 09		
Plymouth	d				10 25							11 25				11 48		
Totnes	d				10 50							11 50				12 13		
Paignton	d	10 06																
Torquay	d	10 12																
Newton Abbot	d	10 23			11 03							12 03				12 25		
Teignmouth	d	10 30																
Dawlish	d	10 35																
Exeter St Davids 6	d	10 49			11 23							12 23				12 48		
Tiverton Parkway	d	11 02			11 37							12 37				13 02		
Taunton	d	11 17			11 51							12 51				13 16		
Weston-super-Mare	d																	
Cardiff Central 7	d		11 45							12 45							13 45	
Newport (South Wales)	d		12 00							13 01							14 00	
Bristol Temple Meads 10	d	12 00			12 30				13 00			13 30				14 00		
Bristol Parkway 7	d	12 10			12 40				13 10			13 40				14 10		
Gloucester 7	d		12 46							13 46							14 46	
Cheltenham Spa	d	12 42	12 57		13 12				13 42	13 57		14 12				14 42	14 57	
Birmingham New Street 12	a	13 26	13 45	13 48	13 56			14 17	14 26	14 45	14 48	14 56			15 17	15 26	15 45	15 48
Birmingham New Street 12	d	13 31	13 49	13 57	14 03	14 19	14 20	14 30	14 31	14 49	14 57	15 03	15 19	15 20	15 30	15 31	15 49	15 57
Tamworth	d		14 07		14 19	14 38				15 07			15 39				16 07	
Burton-on-Trent	d		14 19			14 50				15 19		15 26	15 50				16 19	
Derby 6	a		14 35		14 41	15 05		15 08		15 34		15 41	16 05		16 08		16 34	
Nottingham 8 🚌	a		15 05			15 33				16 05			16 33				17 05	
Chesterfield	a				15 02							16 02						
Sheffield 7 🚌	a				15 17			15 46				16 18			16 46			
Doncaster 7	a							16 15							17 19			
Wakefield Westgate 7	a				15 46							16 49						
Leeds 10	a				16 02							17 04						
York 8	a				16 30			16 39				17 29			17 44			
Darlington 7	a				16 59			17 10				17 59			18 12			
Durham	a				17 16			17 28				18 16			18 29			
Chester-le-Street	a							17 39										
Newcastle 8	a				17 32			17 51				18 36			18 45			
Morpeth	a																	
Alnmouth for Alnwick	a				18 01													
Berwick-upon-Tweed	a											19 25						
Dunbar	a											19 49						
Wolverhampton 7 🚌	d	13 49		14 15			14 37		14 49		15 15			15 37		15 49		16 15
Stafford	a	14 00		14 29					15 00		15 29					16 00		16 29
Stoke-on-Trent	a	14 19		14 54					15 19		15 54					16 19		16 54
Congleton	a																	
Macclesfield	a			15 11							16 11							17 11
Crewe 10	a						15 07							16 08				
Wilmslow	a																	
Stockport	a	14 49		15 27					15 49		16 27					16 49		17 27
Manchester Piccadilly 10 🚌	a	14 59		15 39					15 59		16 39					16 59		17 39
Warrington Bank Quay	a						15 26							16 26				
Wigan North Western	a						15 37							16 37				
Preston 8	a						15 51							16 51				
Lancaster 6	a						16 08							17 09				
Oxenholme Lake District	a													17 24				
Penrith North Lakes	a						16 45											
Carlisle 8	a						17 00							18 03				
Lockerbie	a																	
Haymarket	a						18 14											
Edinburgh 10	a				19 07		18 22					20 15						
Haymarket	a				19 13							20 25						
Motherwell	a				19 55													
Glasgow Central 15	a				20 24									19 17				
Inverkeithing	a											20 43						
Kirkcaldy	a											20 59						
Markinch	a											21 08						
Ladybank	a											21 16						
Cupar	a											21 23						
Leuchars 3	a											21 31						
Dundee	a											21 47						
Arbroath	a																	
Montrose	a																	
Stonehaven	a																	
Aberdeen	a																	

Table 51

South Coast and the South West - North West England, The North East and Scotland

		XC ◇1 🍴	XC ◇1 🍴	XC 1	VT ◇1 🛒	XC ◇1 🍴	XC ◇1	XC ◇1 🍴	XC ◇1 🍴	XC ◇1 🍴	XC 1	VT ◇1 🛒	XC ◇1 🍴	XC ◇1	XC ◇1 🍴	XC ◇1 🍴	XC ◇1 🍴	XC 1
Bournemouth	d							13 45							14 45			
Brockenhurst 3	d							14 00							15 00			
Southampton Central	d							14 15							15 15			
Southampton Airport Parkway ✈	d							14 22							15 22			
Winchester	d							14 31							15 31			
Basingstoke	d							14 47							15 47			
Guildford	d																	
Reading 7	d		14 40					15 11		15 40					16 11		16 40	
Oxford	d		15 07					15 36		16 07					16 36		17 07	
Banbury	d		15 25					15 54		16 25					16 54		17 25	
Leamington Spa 8	d		15 43					16 12		16 48					17 12		17 43	
Coventry	d							16 27							17 27			
Birmingham International ✈	d							16 38							17 38			
Penzance	d																	
St Erth	d																	
Hayle	d																	
Camborne	d																	
Redruth	d																	
Truro	d																	
St Austell	d																	
Newquay	d																	
Par	d																	
Lostwithiel	d																	
Bodmin Parkway	d																	
Liskeard 6	d																	
Plymouth	d	12 23							13 25							14 25		
Totnes	d	12 49							13 50							14 50		
Paignton	d												13 53					
Torquay	d												13 59					
Newton Abbot	d	13 03							14 03				14 10			15 03		
Teignmouth	d												14 17					
Dawlish	d												14 22					
Exeter St Davids 6	d	13 25							14 24				14 36			15 23		
Tiverton Parkway	d	13 39							14 37				14 49			15 37		
Taunton	d	13 54							14 52				15 04			15 51		
Weston-super-Mare	d												15 30					
Cardiff Central 7	d						14 45							15 45				
Newport (South Wales)	d						15 01							16 00				
Bristol Temple Meads 10	d	14 30				15 00			15 30				16 00			16 30		
Bristol Parkway 7	d	14 40				15 10			15 40				16 10			16 40		
Gloucester 7	d						15 46							16 46				
Cheltenham Spa	d	15 12				15 42	15 57		16 12				16 42	16 57		17 12		
Birmingham New Street 12	a	15 55	16 17			16 26	16 45	16 48	16 56	17 17			17 26	17 45	17 48	17 56	18 17	
Birmingham New Street 12	d	16 03	16 30	16 19	16 20	16 31	16 49	16 57	17 03	17 30	17 19	17 20	17 31	17 49	17 57	18 03	18 30	18 19
Tamworth	d	16 17		16 39			17 07				17 39			18 07		18 19		18 39
Burton-on-Trent	d			16 50			17 19		17 26		17 51			18 19				18 50
Derby 6	a	16 40	17 08	17 05			17 34		17 41	18 08	18 05			18 35		18 41	19 08	19 05
Nottingham 8 🚌	a			17 33			18 05				18 33			19 05				19 33
Chesterfield	a	17 00							18 02							19 02	19 29	
Sheffield 7 🚌	a	17 18	17 44						18 18	18 47						19 18	19 51	
Doncaster 7	a									19 18							20 16	
Wakefield Westgate 7	a	17 47	18 14						18 46							19 46		
Leeds 10	a	18 02	18 32						19 01							20 02		
York 8	a	18 31	18 59						19 31	19 44						20 31	20 40	
Darlington 7	a	19 01	19 37						20 03	20 12						21 04	21 14	
Durham	a	19 19	19 54						20 21	20 29						21 21	21 32	
Chester-le-Street	a									20 36							21 39	
Newcastle 8	a	19 35	20 10						20 33	20 51						21 33	21 50	
Morpeth	a																	
Alnmouth for Alnwick	a	20 03														21 59		
Berwick-upon-Tweed	a		20 55						21 19							22 20		
Dunbar	a								21 42									
Wolverhampton 7 🚌	d				16 37	16 49		17 15				17 37	17 49		18 15			
Stafford	a					17 00		17 29					18 00		18 29			
Stoke-on-Trent	a					17 19		17 54					18 19		18 54			
Congleton	a																	
Macclesfield	a							18 11							19 11			
Crewe 10	a				17 07							18 07						
Wilmslow	a																	
Stockport	a					17 49		18 27					18 49		19 27			
Manchester Piccadilly 10 🚌	a					17 59		18 39					18 59		19 40			
Warrington Bank Quay	a				17 26							18 26						
Wigan North Western	a				17 37							18 37						
Preston 8	a				17 51							18 51						
Lancaster 6	a				18 08							19 08						
Oxenholme Lake District	a				18 22							19 22						
Penrith North Lakes	a				18 48													
Carlisle 8	a				19 04							20 01						
Lockerbie	a																	
Haymarket	a				20 19													
Edinburgh 10	a	21 06	21 39		20 24				22 10							23 04		
Haymarket	a	21 13																
Motherwell	a	21 55																
Glasgow Central 15	a	22 18										21 17						
Inverkeithing	a																	
Kirkcaldy	a																	
Markinch	a																	
Ladybank	a																	
Cupar	a																	
Leuchars 3	a																	
Dundee	a																	
Arbroath	a																	
Montrose	a																	
Stonehaven	a																	
Aberdeen	a																	

Table 51

Saturdays
from 11 September

South Coast and the South West - North West England, The North East and Scotland

		VT	XC	XC	XC	XC	XC	VT	XC	XC	XC	XC	XC	XC	VT	XC	XC	XC
		◇1	◇1	◇1	◇1	◇1	1	◇1	◇1	◇1	◇1	◇1	◇1	◇1	◇1	◇1	◇1	◇1
Bournemouth	d				15 45							16 45						17 45
Brockenhurst 3	d				16 00							17 00						18 00
Southampton Central	d				16 15							17 15						18 15
Southampton Airport Parkway ✈	d				16 22							17 22						18 22
Winchester	d				16 31							17 31						18 31
Basingstoke	d				16 47							17 47						18 47
Guildford	d																	
Reading 7	d				17 11				17 40			18 11		18 40				19 11
Oxford	d				17 36				18 07			18 36		19 07				19 36
Banbury	d				17 54				18 25			18 54		19 25				19 54
Leamington Spa 6	d				18 12				18 45			19 12		19 43				20 12
Coventry	d				18 27							19 27						20 27
Birmingham International ✈	d				18 38							19 38						20 39
Penzance	d																	
St Erth	d																	
Hayle	d																	
Camborne	d																	
Redruth	d																	
Truro	d																	
St Austell	d																	
Newquay	d																	
Par	d																	
Lostwithiel	d																	
Bodmin Parkway	d																	
Liskeard 6	d																	
Plymouth	d					15 25							16 25					
Totnes	d					15 50							16 50					
Paignton	d																	
Torquay	d																	
Newton Abbot	d					16 03							17 03					
Teignmouth	d																	
Dawlish	d																	
Exeter St Davids 6	d					16 23							17 23					
Tiverton Parkway	d					16 37							17 37					
Taunton	d					16 51							17 51					
Weston-super-Mare	d																	
Cardiff Central 7	d			16 45							17 45						18 45	
Newport (South Wales)	d			17 01							18 00						19 01	
Bristol Temple Meads 10	d		17 00			17 30				18 00			18 30			19 00		
Bristol Parkway 7	d		17 10			17 40				18 10			18 40			19 10		
Gloucester 7	d			17 46							18 46						19 46	
Cheltenham Spa	d		17 42	17 57		18 12				18 42	18 57		19 12			19 42	19 57	
Birmingham New Street 12	a		18 26	18 45	18 48	18 56			19 17	19 26	19 45	19 48	19 56	20 18		20 26	20 40	20 48
Birmingham New Street 12	d	18 20	18 31	18 49	18 57	19 03	19 19	19 20	19 30	19 31	19 49	19 57	20 03	20 30	20 20	20 31	20 49	20 57
Tamworth	d			19 07			19 39				20 07		20 19				21 08	
Burton-on-Trent	d			19 19		19 26	19 50				20 19						21 20	
Derby 6	a			19 35		19 41	20 05		20 08		20 34		20 42	21 27			21 35	
Nottingham 5	a			20 05			20 35				21 04						22 08	
Chesterfield	a					20 02			20 29				21 02					
Sheffield 7	a					20 18			20 49				21 18	21 59				
Doncaster 7	a								21 25					22 32				
Wakefield Westgate 7	a					20 48							21 48					
Leeds 10	a					21 04							22 02					
York 8	a					21 58			21 48					22 55				
Darlington 7	a								22 21									
Durham	a								22 41									
Chester-le-Street	a								22 50									
Newcastle 8	a								23 05									
Morpeth	a																	
Alnmouth for Alnwick	a																	
Berwick-upon-Tweed	a																	
Dunbar	a																	
Wolverhampton 7	d	18 37	18 49		19 15			19 37		19 49		20 16			20 37	20 49		21 17
Stafford	a		19 00		19 29					20 00		20 29			20 49	21 00		21 29
Stoke-on-Trent	a		19 19		19 54					20 19		20 54				21 20		21 54
Congleton	a																	
Macclesfield	a				20 11					20 36		21 11				21 38		22 11
Crewe 10	a	19 07						20 07							21 09			
Wilmslow	a																	
Stockport	a		19 49		20 27					20 49		21 27				21 53		22 27
Manchester Piccadilly 10	a		19 59		20 39					20 59		21 39				22 04		22 39
Warrington Bank Quay	a	19 26						20 26										
Wigan North Western	a	19 37						20 37										
Preston 8	a	19 59						20 59										
Lancaster 6	a																	
Oxenholme Lake District	a																	
Penrith North Lakes	a																	
Carlisle 8	a																	
Lockerbie	a																	
Haymarket	a																	
Edinburgh 10	a																	
Haymarket	a																	
Motherwell	a																	
Glasgow Central 15	a																	
Inverkeithing	a																	
Kirkcaldy	a																	
Markinch	a																	
Ladybank	a																	
Cupar	a																	
Leuchars 3	a																	
Dundee	a																	
Arbroath	a																	
Montrose	a																	
Stonehaven	a																	
Aberdeen	a																	

Table 51

Saturdays
from 11 September

South Coast and the South West - North West England, The North East and Scotland

		XC	XC	XC	XC	XC	XC	XC	XC	XC	XC	XC	XC
		◇1	◇1	◇1	◇1	◇1	◇1	◇1	◇1	◇1	◇1	◇1	◇1
Bournemouth	d				18 45						19 45		
Brockenhurst 3	d				19 00						20 00		
Southampton Central	d				19 15						20 15		
Southampton Airport Parkway ✈	d				19 22						20 22		
Winchester	d				19 31						20 31		
Basingstoke	d				19 47						20 47		
Guildford	d												
Reading 7	d		19 40		20 11			20 40			21 11		21 40
Oxford	d		20 07		20 36			21 07			21 36		22 07
Banbury	d		20 30		20 54			21 25			21 54		22 25
Leamington Spa 6	d		20 47		21 12			21 45			22 12		22 43
Coventry	d				21 27			21 56			22 27		
Birmingham International ✈	d				21 38			22 13			22 39		
Penzance	d												
St Erth	d												
Hayle	d												
Camborne	d												
Redruth	d												
Truro	d												
St Austell	d												
Newquay	d												
Par	d												
Lostwithiel	d												
Bodmin Parkway	d												
Liskeard 6	d												
Plymouth	d	17 23					18 25						
Totnes	d	17 49					18 50						
Paignton	d												
Torquay	d												
Newton Abbot	d	18 03					19 03						
Teignmouth	d												
Dawlish	d												
Exeter St Davids 6	d	18 25					19 23						
Tiverton Parkway	d	18 39					19 37						
Taunton	d	18 54					19 51						
Weston-super-Mare	d												
Cardiff Central 7	d					20 00				20 50			
Newport (South Wales)	d					20 15				21 05			
Bristol Temple Meads 10	d	19 30		20 00			20 30						
Bristol Parkway 7	d	19 40		20 10			20 40						
Gloucester 7	d					21 07	21 14			21 49			
Cheltenham Spa	d	20 12		20 42		21 18	21 24			22 00			
Birmingham New Street 12	a	20 53	21 16	21 38	21 48	22 07	22 11	22 25		22 42	22 48		23 09
Birmingham New Street 12	d	21 03			21 57	22 10			22 31			22 49	
Tamworth	d	21 19				22 28						23 08	
Burton-on-Trent	d	21 30				22 39						23 20	
Derby 6	a	21 44				22 55						23 33	
Nottingham 5	a					23 28							
Chesterfield	a	22 07											
Sheffield 7	a	22 23											
Doncaster 7	a	22 47											
Wakefield Westgate 7	a	23 09											
Leeds 10	a	23 24											
York 8	a												
Darlington 7	a												
Durham	a												
Chester-le-Street	a												
Newcastle 8	a												
Morpeth	a												
Alnmouth for Alnwick	a												
Berwick-upon-Tweed	a												
Dunbar	a												
Wolverhampton 7	d				22 16				22 49				
Stafford	a				22 29				23 02				
Stoke-on-Trent	a				22 50				23 20				
Congleton	a												
Macclesfield	a				23 07				23 38				
Crewe 10	a												
Wilmslow	a												
Stockport	a				23 21				23 53				
Manchester Piccadilly 10	a				23 32				00 10				
Warrington Bank Quay	a												
Wigan North Western	a												
Preston 8	a												
Lancaster 6	a												
Oxenholme Lake District	a												
Penrith North Lakes	a												
Carlisle 8	a												
Lockerbie	a												
Haymarket	a												
Edinburgh 10	a												
Haymarket	a												
Motherwell	a												
Glasgow Central 15	a												
Inverkeithing	a												
Kirkcaldy	a												
Markinch	a												
Ladybank	a												
Cupar	a												
Leuchars 3	a												
Dundee	a												
Arbroath	a												
Montrose	a												
Stonehaven	a												
Aberdeen	a												

Table 51

Sundays until 11 July

South Coast and the South West - North West England, The North East and Scotland

		VT	XC	VT	XC	XC	VT	XC	XC	XC	VT	XC	XC	XC	VT	XC	XC	XC
		◇1	◇1	◇1	◇1	◇1	◇1	◇1	◇1	◇1	◇1	◇1	◇1	◇1	◇1	◇1	◇1	◇1
Bournemouth	d																	09 40
Brockenhurst 3	d																	09 57
Southampton Central	d													09 15				10 15
Southampton Airport Parkway ✈	d													09 22				10 22
Winchester	d													09 31				10 31
Basingstoke	d													09 47				10 47
Guildford	d																	
Reading 7	d									09 11				10 11				11 11
Oxford	d									09 37				10 37				11 37
Banbury	d									09 54				10 54				11 54
Leamington Spa 8	d									10 12				11 12				12 12
Coventry	d									10 28				11 28				12 28
Birmingham International ✈	d									10 40				11 40				12 40
Penzance	d																	
St Erth	d																	
Hayle	d																	
Camborne	d																	
Redruth	d																	
Truro	d																	
St Austell	d																	
Newquay	d																	
Par	d																	
Lostwithiel	d																	
Bodmin Parkway	d																	
Liskeard 6	d																	
Plymouth	d																	
Totnes	d																	
Paignton	d																	
Torquay	d																	
Newton Abbot	d																	
Teignmouth	d																	
Dawlish	d																	
Exeter St Davids 6	d																	
Tiverton Parkway	d																	
Taunton	d																	
Weston-super-Mare	d																	
Cardiff Central 7	d																	
Newport (South Wales)	d																	
Bristol Temple Meads 10	d								08 45			09 30						
Bristol Parkway 7	d								08 55			09 40						
Gloucester 7	d											10 12						
Cheltenham Spa	d								09 27			10 21						
Birmingham New Street 12	a								10 40	10 50		11 36		11 50				12 50
Birmingham New Street 12	d	08 45	09 01	09 20	09 30	10 00	10 20	10 30		11 01	11 20	12 03	11 49	12 01	12 20	12 30	12 49	13 01
Tamworth	d											12 19	12 07				13 07	
Burton-on-Trent	d				10 30			11 26					12 19				13 19	
Derby 6	a				10 42			11 42				12 42	12 34			13 09	13 38	
Nottingham 8	a												13 02				14 02	
Chesterfield	a				11 02			12 02				13 02				13 29		
Sheffield 7	a				11 17			12 18				13 17				13 43		
Doncaster 7	a															14 13		
Wakefield Westgate 7	a				11 44			12 44				13 44						
Leeds 10	a				12 02			13 02				14 02						
York 8	a				12 32			13 32				14 32				14 43		
Darlington 7	a				13 08			14 02				15 07				15 15		
Durham	a				13 25			14 19				15 24				15 32		
Chester-le-Street	a																	
Newcastle 8	a				13 41			14 35				15 38				15 46		
Morpeth	a											15 53						
Alnmouth for Alnwick	a				14 07							16 07						
Berwick-upon-Tweed	a							15 19										
Dunbar	a							15 42										
Wolverhampton 7	d	09 04	09 19	09 37		10 18	10 37			11 19	11 37			12 20	12 37			13 19
Stafford	a	09 17	09 33			10 32				11 32				12 33				13 33
Stoke-on-Trent	a																	13 56
Congleton	a																	
Macclesfield	a																	14 14
Crewe 10	a	09 38	09 54	10 06			11 08				12 07				13 07			
Wilmslow	a		10 12			11 06				12 07				13 08				
Stockport	a		10 22			11 16				12 20				13 19				14 28
Manchester Piccadilly 10	a		10 39			11 32				12 40				13 40				14 40
Warrington Bank Quay	a	09 57		10 26			11 27				12 26				13 26			
Wigan North Western	a	10 08		10 37			11 38				12 37				13 37			
Preston 8	a	10 25		10 51			11 52				12 51				13 51			
Lancaster 6	a			11 07			12 09				13 08				14 08			
Oxenholme Lake District	a			11 22			12 23				13 22							
Penrith North Lakes	a														14 44			
Carlisle 8	a			12 01			13 02				14 01				15 00			
Lockerbie	a																	
Haymarket	a						14 14								16 14			
Edinburgh 10	a				15 09		14 22	16 07				17 09			16 22			
Haymarket	a																	
Motherwell	a																	
Glasgow Central 15	a			13 19							15 16							
Inverkeithing	a																	
Kirkcaldy	a																	
Markinch	a																	
Ladybank	a																	
Cupar	a																	
Leuchars 3	a																	
Dundee	a																	
Arbroath	a																	
Montrose	a																	
Stonehaven	a																	
Aberdeen	a																	

Table 51

Sundays until 11 July

South Coast and the South West - North West England, The North East and Scotland

		XC	XC	VT	XC	XC	XC	XC	VT	XC	XC	XC	XC	XC	XC	VT	XC	XC	XC	XC
		◇1	◇1	◇1	◇1	◇1	◇1	◇1	◇1	◇1	◇1	◇1	◇1	◇1	◇1	◇1	◇1	◇1	◇1	◇1
Bournemouth	d						10 40						11 40						12 40	
Brockenhurst 3	d						10 57						11 57						12 57	
Southampton Central	d						11 15						12 15						13 15	
Southampton Airport Parkway ✈	d						11 22						12 22						13 22	
Winchester	d						11 31						12 31						13 31	
Basingstoke	d						11 47						12 47						13 47	
Guildford	d									12 14										
Reading 7	d						12 11			12 54			13 11		13 40				14 11	
Oxford	d						12 37			13 17			13 37		14 06				14 37	
Banbury	d						12 54			13 35			13 54		14 25				14 54	
Leamington Spa 8	d						13 12			13 53			14 12		14 43				15 12	
Coventry	d						13 26						14 26						15 26	
Birmingham International ✈	d						13 38						14 38						15 38	
Penzance	d													09 30						
St Erth	d													09 38						
Hayle	d																			
Camborne	d													09 48						
Redruth	d													09 54						
Truro	d													10 06						
St Austell	d													10 24						
Newquay	d																			
Par	d													10 31						
Lostwithiel	d																			
Bodmin Parkway	d													10 42						
Liskeard 6	d													10 54						
Plymouth	d	09 25						10 25						11 25			12 00			12 25
Totnes	d	09 50						10 50						11 50						12 50
Paignton	d										10 50									
Torquay	d										10 56									
Newton Abbot	d	10 03						11 03			11 08			12 03			12 36			13 03
Teignmouth	d										11 15									
Dawlish	d										11 20									
Exeter St Davids 6	d	10 23						11 23			11 32			12 23			12 57			13 26
Tiverton Parkway	d	10 38						11 37			11 46			12 37			13 10			13 40
Taunton	d	10 51						11 51			12 00			12 51			13 25			13 54
Weston-super-Mare	d										12 21									
Cardiff Central 7	d					11 45												13 45		
Newport (South Wales)	d					11 59												13 59		
Bristol Temple Meads 10	d	11 30						12 30			13 00			13 30			14 00			14 30
Bristol Parkway 7	d	11 40						12 40			13 10			13 40			14 10			14 40
Gloucester 7	d	12 25				12 47						13 51						14 47		
Cheltenham Spa	d	12 35				12 58		13 12			13 42	14 02		14 12			14 42	14 58		15 12
Birmingham New Street 12	a	13 11				13 41	13 48	13 50		14 19	14 26	14 45	14 48	14 50	15 10		15 27	15 41	15 48	15 50
Birmingham New Street 12	d	13 30	13 03	13 20	13 31	13 49	14 01	14 03	14 20	14 30	14 31	14 49	15 01	15 03	15 30	15 20	15 31	15 49	16 01	16 03
Tamworth	d					14 07		14 19				15 09						16 07		16 19
Burton-on-Trent	d		13 26			14 19						15 21		15 26				16 19		
Derby 6	a	14 09	13 44			14 34		14 42		15 04		15 34		15 42	16 02			16 34		16 42
Nottingham 8	a					15 07						16 08						17 03		
Chesterfield	a	14 29	14 02					15 02						16 02						17 02
Sheffield 7	a	14 46	14 17					15 17		15 47				16 18	16 48					17 17
Doncaster 7	a	15 13								16 15					17 13					
Wakefield Westgate 7	a		14 44					15 44						16 44						17 45
Leeds 10	a		15 02					16 02						17 02						18 02
York 8	a	15 40	15 32					16 32		16 40				17 32	17 42					18 32
Darlington 7	a	16 12	16 01					17 01		17 14				18 01	18 10					19 01
Durham	a	16 30	16 18					17 18		17 32				18 18	18 27					19 18
Chester-le-Street	a																			
Newcastle 8	a	16 45	16 34					17 34		17 48				18 34	18 42					19 34
Morpeth	a																			
Alnmouth for Alnwick	a							18 01												20 04
Berwick-upon-Tweed	a		17 19											19 19						
Dunbar	a		17 42											19 42						
Wolverhampton 7	d			13 37	13 49		14 19		14 37		14 49		15 19			15 37	15 49		16 19	
Stafford	a						14 33						15 33						16 35	
Stoke-on-Trent	a				14 19		14 56				15 19		15 56				16 19		16 56	
Congleton	a																			
Macclesfield	a						15 14						16 14						17 14	
Crewe 10	a			14 09					15 09							16 09				
Wilmslow	a																			
Stockport	a						15 28						16 28						17 28	
Manchester Piccadilly 10	a				14 57		15 40				15 59		16 40				16 59		17 40	
Warrington Bank Quay	a			14 28					15 28							16 28				
Wigan North Western	a			14 39					15 39							16 39				
Preston 8	a			14 52					15 53							16 53				
Lancaster 6	a			15 10					16 10							17 10				
Oxenholme Lake District	a			15 24												17 24				
Penrith North Lakes	a								16 46											
Carlisle 8	a			16 03					17 02							18 03				
Lockerbie	a																			
Haymarket	a								18 13											
Edinburgh 10	a		18 07					19 03	18 22					20 07						21 06
Haymarket	a		18 13											20 15						21 15
Motherwell	a													20 53						21 53
Glasgow Central 15	a			17 18										21 12		19 18				22 14
Inverkeithing	a		18 27																	
Kirkcaldy	a		18 43																	
Markinch	a		18 52																	
Ladybank	a		19 00																	
Cupar	a		19 06																	
Leuchars 3	a		19 13																	
Dundee	a		19 28																	
Arbroath	a		19 45																	
Montrose	a		19 59																	
Stonehaven	a		20 22																	
Aberdeen	a		20 42																	

Table 51

South Coast and the South West - North West England, The North East and Scotland

		XC ◇1 ✠	VT ◇1 ⊐	XC ◇1 ✠	XC ◇1	XC ◇1 ✠	XC ◇1 ✠	XC ◇1 ✠	VT ◇1 ⊐	XC ◇1 ✠	XC ◇1	XC ◇1 ✠	XC ◇1 ✠	XC ◇1 ✠	VT ◇1 ⊐	XC ◇1 ✠	XC ◇1	XC ◇1 ✠	XC ◇1 ✠
Bournemouth	d					13 40						14 40						15 40	
Brockenhurst 3	d					13 57						14 57						15 57	
Southampton Central	d					14 15						15 15						16 15	
Southampton Airport Parkway ✈	d					14 22						15 22						16 22	
Winchester	d					14 31						15 31						16 31	
Basingstoke	d					14 47						15 47						16 47	
Guildford	d																		
Reading 7	d	14 40				15 11		15 40				16 11		16 40				17 11	
Oxford	d	15 06				15 37		16 06				16 37		17 06				17 37	
Banbury	d	15 25				15 54		16 25				16 54		17 25				17 54	
Leamington Spa 6	d	15 43				16 12		16 43				17 12		17 43				18 12	
Coventry	d					16 26						17 26						18 26	
Birmingham International ✈	d					16 38						17 38						18 38	
Penzance	d															12 30			
St Erth	d															12 40			
Hayle	d															12 44			
Camborne	d															12 56			
Redruth	d															13 02			
Truro	d															13 14			
St Austell	d															13 31			
Newquay	d						11 35												
Par	d															13 38			
Lostwithiel	d															13 45			
Bodmin Parkway	d						12 41									13 52			
Liskeard 6	d						12 54									14 04			
Plymouth	d						13 23						14 23			14 35			15 23
Totnes	d						13 49						14 49			15 00			15 49
Paignton	d			12 55															
Torquay	d			13 01															
Newton Abbot	d			13 16			14 03						15 03			15 12			16 03
Teignmouth	d			13 23															
Dawlish	d			13 28															
Exeter St Davids 6	d			13 42			14 25						15 25			15 33			16 25
Tiverton Parkway	d			13 55			14 39						15 38			15 46			16 38
Taunton	d			14 10			14 54						15 54			16 01			16 54
Weston-super-Mare	d															16 30			
Cardiff Central 7	d				14 45						15 45						16 45		
Newport (South Wales)	d				14 59						15 59						16 59		
Bristol Temple Meads 10	d			15 00			15 30			16 00			16 30			17 00			17 30
Bristol Parkway 7	d			15 10			15 40			16 10			16 40			17 10			17 40
Gloucester 7	d				15 47						16 47						17 47		
Cheltenham Spa	d			15 42	15 58		16 11			16 42	16 58		17 11			17 42	17 58		18 11
Birmingham New Street 12	a	16 09		16 26	16 41	16 48	16 50	17 09		17 26	17 41	17 48	17 49	18 09		18 27	18 41	18 48	18 51
Birmingham New Street 12	d	16 30	16 20	16 31	16 49	17 01	17 03	17 30	17 20	17 31	17 49	18 01	18 03	18 30	18 20	18 31	18 49	19 01	19 03
Tamworth	d				17 07						18 07		18 19				19 09		
Burton-on-Trent	d				17 19		17 29				18 19						19 21		19 26
Derby 6	a	17 04			17 35		17 42	18 05			18 34		18 42	19 02			19 33		19 40
Nottingham 5	a				18 02						19 04						19 56		
Chesterfield	a						18 03						19 04						
Sheffield 7	a	17 48					18 19	18 46					19 20	19 39					20 01
Doncaster 7	a	18 13						19 13						20 16					20 17
Wakefield Westgate 7	a	18 33					18 47						19 48						
Leeds 10	a	18 51					19 04						20 05						20 46
York 8	a	19 21					19 32	19 42					20 32	20 44					21 03
Darlington 7	a	19 51					20 03	20 10					21 03	21 18					21 32
Durham	a	20 08					20 21	20 27					21 21	21 36					
Chester-le-Street	a	20 18																	
Newcastle 8	a	20 26					20 37	20 43					21 37	21 54					
Morpeth	a							21 01											
Alnmouth for Alnwick	a							21 15					22 05						
Berwick-upon-Tweed	a						21 23	21 36					22 28						
Dunbar	a						21 48												
Wolverhampton 7	d		16u37	16 49		17 19			17u37	17 49		18 19			18 37	18 49		19 19	
Stafford	a					17 35						18 35						19 37	
Stoke-on-Trent	a			17 19		17 56				18 19		18 56				19 19		19 56	
Congleton	a																		
Macclesfield	a					18 14						19 15						20 14	
Crewe 10	a		17 09						18 09						19 09				
Wilmslow	a																		
Stockport	a					18 28						19 28						20 28	
Manchester Piccadilly 10	a			17 56		18 40				18 56		19 40				19 58		20 40	
Warrington Bank Quay	a		17 28						18 28						19 28				
Wigan North Western	a		17 39						18 39						19 39				
Preston 8	a		17 53						18 53						19 53				
Lancaster 6	a		18 10						19 10						20 10				
Oxenholme Lake District	a		18 24						19 24										
Penrith North Lakes	a		18 50												20 46				
Carlisle 8	a		19 06						20 03						21 02				
Lockerbie	a																		
Haymarket	a														22 15				
Edinburgh 10	a		20 25				22 15	22 20					23 14		22 23				
Haymarket	a																		
Motherwell	a																		
Glasgow Central 15	a								21 18										
Inverkeithing	a																		
Kirkcaldy	a																		
Markinch	a																		
Ladybank	a																		
Cupar	a																		
Leuchars 3	a																		
Dundee	a																		
Arbroath	a																		
Montrose	a																		
Stonehaven	a																		
Aberdeen	a																		

Table 51

South Coast and the South West - North West England, The North East and Scotland

		XC ◇1 ✠	VT ■ 1 ⊐	XC ◇1 ✠	XC ◇1	XC ◇1 ✠	XC ◇1 ✠	XC ◇1 ✠	VT ◇1 ⊐	XC ◇1 ✠	XC ◇1	XC ◇1 ✠	XC ◇1 ✠	XC ◇1 ✠	VT ◇1 ⊐	XC ◇1 ✠	XC ◇1	XC ◇1 ✠	XC ◇1	XC ◇1 ✠
Bournemouth	d					16 40						17 40						18 40		
Brockenhurst 3	d					16 57						17 57						18 57		
Southampton Central	d					17 15						18 15						19 15		
Southampton Airport Parkway ✈	d					17 22						18 22						19 22		
Winchester	d					17 31						18 31						19 31		
Basingstoke	d					17 47						18 47						19 47		
Guildford	d																			
Reading 7	d	17 40				18 11		18 40				19 11		19 40				20 11		20 40
Oxford	d	18 06				18 37		19 06				19 37		20 06				20 37		21 06
Banbury	d	18 25				18 54		19 25				19 54		20 25				20 54		21 25
Leamington Spa 6	d	18 43				19 12		19 43				20 12		20 43				21 12		21 43
Coventry	d					19 26		19 54				20 26		20 54				21 26		21 54
Birmingham International ✈	d					19 38		20 04				20 38		21 04				21 38		22 04
Penzance	d												15 30							
St Erth	d												15 38							
Hayle	d																			
Camborne	d												15 51							
Redruth	d												15 57							
Truro	d												16 09							
St Austell	d												16 25							
Newquay	d																			
Par	d												16 33							
Lostwithiel	d																			
Bodmin Parkway	d												16 44							
Liskeard 6	d												16 56							
Plymouth	d						16 25						17 26						18 23	
Totnes	d						16 50						17 52						18 49	
Paignton	d															18 18				
Torquay	d															18 24				
Newton Abbot	d						17 03						18 04			18 35			19 03	
Teignmouth	d																			
Dawlish	d																			
Exeter St Davids 6	d						17 23						18 24			18 56			19 25	
Tiverton Parkway	d						17 37						18 39			19 09			19 38	
Taunton	d						17 51						18 52			19 23			19 54	
Weston-super-Mare	d																			
Cardiff Central 7	d				17 45						18 45						19 45			
Newport (South Wales)	d				17 59						18 59						20 00			
Bristol Temple Meads 10	d			18 00			18 30			19 00			19 30			20 00			20 30	
Bristol Parkway 7	d			18 10			18 40			19 10			19 40			20 10			20 40	
Gloucester 7	d				18 47						19 50						20 50			
Cheltenham Spa	d			18 42	18 58		19 12			19 42	20 00		20 12			20 42	21 00		21 11	
Birmingham New Street 12	a	19 09		19 26	19 41	19 48	19 50	20 15		20 26	20 42	20 48	20 50	21 15		21 20	21 45	21 48	21 51	22 15
Birmingham New Street 12	d	19 30	19 20	19 31	19 49	20 01	20 03		20 20	20 31	20 49	21 01	21 03		21 20			22 01	22 03	
Tamworth	d				20 07		20 19				21 06		21 19						22 19	
Burton-on-Trent	d				20 19						21 18		21 29							
Derby 6	a	20 02			20 34		20 42				21 33		21 42						22 45	
Nottingham 5	a				21 01						22 00									
Chesterfield	a						21 02						22 02						23 06	
Sheffield 7	a	20 38					21 16						22 18						23 22	
Doncaster 7	a	21 19																		
Wakefield Westgate 7	a						21 44						22 45							
Leeds 10	a						22 01						23 04						00 33	
York 8	a	21 42																		
Darlington 7	a	22 22																		
Durham	a	22 39																		
Chester-le-Street	a																			
Newcastle 8	a	23 07																		
Morpeth	a																			
Alnmouth for Alnwick	a																			
Berwick-upon-Tweed	a																			
Dunbar	a																			
Wolverhampton 7	d		19 37	19 49		20 19			20 38	20 49		21 19			21 37			22 19		
Stafford	a					20 37			20 51			21 37			21 56			22 37		
Stoke-on-Trent	a			20 19		20 56				21 19		21 56						22 55		
Congleton	a																			
Macclesfield	a					21 15						22 14						23 12		
Crewe 10	a		20 09						21 10						22 15					
Wilmslow	a																			
Stockport	a					21 28						22 28						23 27		
Manchester Piccadilly 10	a			21 00		21 40				21 56		22 40						23 41		
Warrington Bank Quay	a		20 28												22 34					
Wigan North Western	a		20 39												22 45					
Preston 8	a		20 53												23 05					
Lancaster 6	a		21 10																	
Oxenholme Lake District	a		21 24																	
Penrith North Lakes	a																			
Carlisle 8	a		22 03																	
Lockerbie	a		22 22																	
Haymarket	a																			
Edinburgh 10	a																			
Haymarket	a																			
Motherwell	a		23 07																	
Glasgow Central 15	a		23 22																	
Inverkeithing	a																			
Kirkcaldy	a																			
Markinch	a																			
Ladybank	a																			
Cupar	a																			
Leuchars 3	a																			
Dundee	a																			
Arbroath	a																			
Montrose	a																			
Stonehaven	a																			
Aberdeen	a																			

Table 51

Sundays until 11 July

South Coast and the South West - North West England, The North East and Scotland

		XC	XC	XC	XC
		◇1	◇1 ✠	◇1 ✠	◇1
Bournemouth	d		19 40		
Brockenhurst 3	d		19 57		
Southampton Central	d		20 15		
Southampton Airport Parkway ✈	d		20 22		
Winchester	d		20 31		
Basingstoke	d		20 47		
Guildford	d				
Reading 7	d		21 11	21 40	
Oxford	d		21 37	22 06	
Banbury	d		21 54	22 25	
Leamington Spa 3	d		22 12	22 43	
Coventry	d		22 23	22 54	
Birmingham International ✈	d		22 33	23 04	
Penzance	d				
St Erth	d				
Hayle	d				
Camborne	d				
Redruth	d				
Truro	d				
St Austell	d				
Newquay	d				
Par	d				
Lostwithiel	d				
Bodmin Parkway	d				
Liskeard 3	d				
Plymouth	d				
Totnes	d				
Paignton	d				
Torquay	d				
Newton Abbot	d				
Teignmouth	d				
Dawlish	d				
Exeter St Davids 6	d				
Tiverton Parkway	d				
Taunton	d				
Weston-super-Mare	d				
Cardiff Central 7	d	20 45			
Newport (South Wales)	d	20 59			
Bristol Temple Meads 10	d				22 10
Bristol Parkway 7	d				22 20
Gloucester 7	d	21 47			
Cheltenham Spa	d	21 58			22 52
Birmingham New Street 12	a	22 41	22 42	23 14	23 39
Birmingham New Street 12	d				
Tamworth	d				
Burton-on-Trent	d				
Derby 6	a				
Nottingham 8 ⇌	a				
Chesterfield	a				
Sheffield 7 ⇌	a				
Doncaster 7	a				
Wakefield Westgate 7	a				
Leeds 10	a				
York 8	a				
Darlington 7	a				
Durham	a				
Chester-le-Street	a				
Newcastle 8	a				
Morpeth	a				
Alnmouth for Alnwick	a				
Berwick-upon-Tweed	a				
Dunbar	a				
Wolverhampton 7 ⇌	d				
Stafford	a				
Stoke-on-Trent	a				
Congleton	a				
Macclesfield	a				
Crewe 10	a				
Wilmslow	a				
Stockport	a				
Manchester Piccadilly 10 ⇌	a				
Warrington Bank Quay	a				
Wigan North Western	a				
Preston 8	a				
Lancaster 6	a				
Oxenholme Lake District	a				
Penrith North Lakes	a				
Carlisle 8	a				
Lockerbie	a				
Haymarket	a				
Edinburgh 10	a				
Haymarket	a				
Motherwell	a				
Glasgow Central 15	a				
Inverkeithing	a				
Kirkcaldy	a				
Markinch	a				
Ladybank	a				
Cupar	a				
Leuchars 3	a				
Dundee	a				
Arbroath	a				
Montrose	a				
Stonehaven	a				
Aberdeen	a				

Table 51

Sundays 18 July to 05 September

South Coast and the South West - North West England, The North East and Scotland

		VT	XC	VT	XC	XC	XC	VT	XC	XC	XC	VT	XC	XC	VT	XC	XC	XC	XC
		◇1 ☕	◇1 ✠	◇1 ☕	◇1 ✠	◇1 ✠	◇1 ✠	◇1 ☕	◇1 ✠	◇1 ✠	◇1 ✠	◇1 ☕	◇1	◇1 ✠	◇1 ☕	◇1 ✠	◇1	◇1 ✠	◇1 ✠
Bournemouth	d																	09 40	
Brockenhurst 3	d																	09 57	
Southampton Central	d													09 15				10 15	
Southampton Airport Parkway ✈	d													09 22				10 22	
Winchester	d													09 31				10 31	
Basingstoke	d													09 47				10 47	
Guildford	d																		
Reading 7	d									09 11				10 11				11 11	
Oxford	d									09 37				10 37				11 37	
Banbury	d									09 54				10 54				11 54	
Leamington Spa 3	d									10 12				11 12				12 12	
Coventry	d									10 28				11 28				12 28	
Birmingham International ✈	d									10 40				11 40				12 40	
Penzance	d																		
St Erth	d																		
Hayle	d																		
Camborne	d																		
Redruth	d																		
Truro	d																		
St Austell	d																		
Newquay	d																		
Par	d																		
Lostwithiel	d																		
Bodmin Parkway	d																		
Liskeard 3	d																		
Plymouth	d																		09 25
Totnes	d																		09 50
Paignton	d																		
Torquay	d																		
Newton Abbot	d																		10 03
Teignmouth	d																		
Dawlish	d																		
Exeter St Davids 6	d																		10 23
Tiverton Parkway	d																		10 38
Taunton	d																		10 51
Weston-super-Mare	d																		
Cardiff Central 7	d																		
Newport (South Wales)	d																		
Bristol Temple Meads 10	d						08 45				09 30								11 30
Bristol Parkway 7	d						08 55				09 40								11 40
Gloucester 7	d										10 12								12 25
Cheltenham Spa	d						09 30				10 24								12 35
Birmingham New Street 12	a						10 36			10 50	11 36			11 50				12 50	13 11
Birmingham New Street 12	d	08 45	09 01	09 20	09 30	10 00		10 20	10 30	11 01	12 03	11 20	11 49	12 01	12 20	12 30	12 49	13 01	13 30
Tamworth	d										12 19		12 07				13 07		
Burton-on-Trent	d				10 30				11 26				12 19				13 19		
Derby 6	a				10 42				11 42		12 42		12 34			13 09	13 38		14 09
Nottingham 8 ⇌	a												13 02				14 02		
Chesterfield	a				11 02				12 02		13 02					13 29			14 29
Sheffield 7 ⇌	a				11 17				12 18		13 17					13 43			14 46
Doncaster 7	a															14 13			15 13
Wakefield Westgate 7	a				11 44				12 44		13 44								
Leeds 10	a				12 02				13 02		14 02								
York 8	a				12 32				13 32		14 32					14 43			15 40
Darlington 7	a				13 08				14 02		15 07					15 15			16 12
Durham	a				13 25				14 19		15 24					15 32			16 30
Chester-le-Street	a																		
Newcastle 8	a				13 41				14 35		15 38					15 46			16 45
Morpeth	a										15 53								
Alnmouth for Alnwick	a				14 07						16 07								
Berwick-upon-Tweed	a								15 19										
Dunbar	a								15 42										
Wolverhampton 7 ⇌	d	09 04	09 19	09 37		10 18		10 37		11 19		11 37		12 20	12 37			13 19	
Stafford	a	09 17	09 33			10 31				11 32				12 33				13 33	
Stoke-on-Trent	a					10 51				11 52				12 51				13 56	
Congleton	a																		
Macclesfield	a					11 08				12 10				13 09				14 14	
Crewe 10	a	09 38	09 54	10 06				11 08				12 07			13 07				
Wilmslow	a		10 12																
Stockport	a		10 22			11 22				12 28				13 28				14 28	
Manchester Piccadilly 10 ⇌	a		10 39			11 32				12 40				13 40				14 40	
Warrington Bank Quay	a	09 57		10 26				11 27				12 26			13 26				
Wigan North Western	a	10 08		10 37				11 38				12 37			13 37				
Preston 8	a	10 25		10 51				11 52				12 51			13 51				
Lancaster 6	a			11 07				12 09				13 08			14 08				
Oxenholme Lake District	a			11 22				12 23				13 22							
Penrith North Lakes	a														14 44				
Carlisle 8	a			12 01				13 02				14 01			15 00				
Lockerbie	a																		
Haymarket	a							14 14							16 14				
Edinburgh 10	a				15 09			14 22	16 07		17 09				16 22				
Haymarket	a																		
Motherwell	a																		
Glasgow Central 15	a			13 19								15 16							
Inverkeithing	a																		
Kirkcaldy	a																		
Markinch	a																		
Ladybank	a																		
Cupar	a																		
Leuchars 3	a																		
Dundee	a																		
Arbroath	a																		
Montrose	a																		
Stonehaven	a																		
Aberdeen	a																		

Table 51

Sundays

18 July to 05 September

South Coast and the South West - North West England, The North East and Scotland

		XC	VT	XC	XC	XC	XC	VT	XC	XC	XC	XC	XC	XC	VT	XC	XC	XC	XC	XC
		◇1	◇1	◇1	◇1	◇1	◇1	◇1	◇1	◇1	◇1	◇1	◇1	◇1	◇1	◇1	◇1	◇1	◇1	◇1
Bournemouth	d					10 40						11 40						12 40		
Brockenhurst [3]	d					10 57						11 57						12 57		
Southampton Central	d					11 15						12 15						13 15		
Southampton Airport Parkway ✈	d					11 22						12 22						13 22		
Winchester	d					11 31						12 31						13 31		
Basingstoke	d					11 47						12 47						13 47		
Guildford	d								12 14											
Reading [7]	d					12 11			12 54			13 11		13 40				14 11		14 40
Oxford	d					12 37			13 17			13 37		14 06				14 37		15 06
Banbury	d					12 54			13 35			13 54		14 25				14 54		15 25
Leamington Spa [8]	d					13 12			13 53			14 12		14 43				15 12		15 43
Coventry	d					13 26						14 26						15 26		
Birmingham International ✈	d					13 38						14 38						15 38		
Penzance	d												09 30							
St Erth	d												09 38							
Hayle	d																			
Camborne	d												09 48							
Redruth	d												09 54							
Truro	d												10 06							
St Austell	d												10 24							
Newquay	d																			
Par	d												10 31							
Lostwithiel	d																			
Bodmin Parkway	d												10 42							
Liskeard [6]	d												10 54							
Plymouth	d						10 25						11 25			12 00			12 25	
Totnes	d						10 50						11 50						12 50	
Paignton	d									10 50										
Torquay	d									10 56										
Newton Abbot	d						11 03			11 08			12 03			12 36			13 03	
Teignmouth	d									11 15										
Dawlish	d									11 20										
Exeter St Davids [6]	d						11 23			11 32			12 23			12 57			13 26	
Tiverton Parkway	d						11 37			11 46			12 37			13 10			13 40	
Taunton	d						11 51			12 00			12 51			13 25			13 54	
Weston-super-Mare	d									12 21										
Cardiff Central [7]	d				11 25															
Newport (South Wales)	d				11 43															
Bristol Temple Meads [10]	d						12 30			13 00			13 30			14 00			14 30	
Bristol Parkway [7]	d						12 40			13 10			13 40			14 10			14 40	
Gloucester [7]	d				12 46						13 51						14 47			
Cheltenham Spa	d				12 58		13 12			13 42	14 02		14 12			14 42	14 58		15 12	
Birmingham New Street [12]	a				13 41	13 48	13 50		14 19	14 26	14 45	14 48	14 50	15 10		15 27	15 41	15 48	15 50	16 09
Birmingham New Street [12]	d	13 03	13 20	13 31	13 49	14 01	14 03	14 20	14 30	14 31	14 49	15 01	15 03	15 30	15 20	15 31	15 49	16 01	16 03	16 30
Tamworth	d				14 07		14 19				15 09						16 07			
Burton-on-Trent	d	13 26			14 19						15 21		15 26				16 19		16 19	
Derby [6]	a	13 44			14 34		14 42		15 04		15 34		15 42	16 02			16 34		16 42	17 04
Nottingham [8]	a				15 07						16 08						17 03			
Chesterfield	a	14 02					15 02						16 02						17 02	
Sheffield [7]	a	14 17					15 17		15 47				16 18	16 48					17 17	17 48
Doncaster [7]	a								16 15					17 13						18 13
Wakefield Westgate [7]	a	14 44					15 44						16 44						17 45	18 33
Leeds [10]	a	15 02					16 02						17 02						18 02	18 51
York [8]	a	15 32					16 32		16 40				17 32	17 42					18 32	19 21
Darlington [7]	a	16 01					17 01		17 14				18 01	18 10					19 01	19 51
Durham	a	16 18					17 18		17 32				18 18	18 27					19 18	20 08
Chester-le-Street	a																			20 18
Newcastle [8]	a	16 34					17 34		17 48				18 34	18 42					19 34	20 26
Morpeth	a																			
Alnmouth for Alnwick	a						18 01												20 04	
Berwick-upon-Tweed	a	17 19											19 19							
Dunbar	a	17 42											19 42							
Wolverhampton [7]	d		13 37	13 49		14 19		14 37		14 49		15 19			15 37	15 49		16 19		
Stafford	a					14 33						15 33						16 35		
Stoke-on-Trent	a			14 19		14 56				15 19		15 56				16 19		16 56		
Congleton	a																			
Macclesfield	a					15 14						16 14						17 14		
Crewe [10]	a		14 09					15 09							16 09					
Wilmslow	a																			
Stockport	a					15 28						16 28						17 28		
Manchester Piccadilly [10]	a			14 57		15 40				15 59		16 40				16 59		17 40		
Warrington Bank Quay	a		14 28					15 28							16 28					
Wigan North Western	a		14 39					15 39							16 39					
Preston [8]	a		14 52					15 53							16 53					
Lancaster [6]	a		15 10					16 10							17 10					
Oxenholme Lake District	a		15 24												17 24					
Penrith North Lakes	a							16 46												
Carlisle [8]	a		16 03					17 02							18 03					
Lockerbie	a																			
Haymarket	a							18 13												
Edinburgh [10]	a	18 07					19 03	18 22					20 07						21 06	
Haymarket	a	18 13											20 15						21 15	
Motherwell	a												20 53						21 53	
Glasgow Central [15]	a		17 18										21 12		19 18				22 14	
Inverkeithing	a	18 27																		
Kirkcaldy	a	18 43																		
Markinch	a	18 52																		
Ladybank	a	19 00																		
Cupar	a	19 06																		
Leuchars [3]	a	19 13																		
Dundee	a	19 28																		
Arbroath	a	19 45																		
Montrose	a	19 59																		
Stonehaven	a	20 22																		
Aberdeen	a	20 42																		

Table 51

Sundays

18 July to 05 September

South Coast and the South West - North West England, The North East and Scotland

		VT	XC	XC	XC	XC	XC	VT	XC	XC	XC	XC	XC	VT	XC	XC	XC	XC	XC
		◇1	◇1	◇1	◇1	◇1	◇1	◇1	◇1	◇1	◇1	◇1	◇1	◇1	◇1	◇1	◇1	◇1	◇1
Bournemouth	d				13 40						14 40						15 40		
Brockenhurst [3]	d				13 57						14 57						15 57		
Southampton Central	d				14 15						15 15						16 15		
Southampton Airport Parkway ✈	d				14 22						15 22						16 22		
Winchester	d				14 31						15 31						16 31		
Basingstoke	d				14 47						15 47						16 47		
Guildford	d																		
Reading [7]	d				15 11		15 40				16 11		16 40				17 11		17 40
Oxford	d				15 37		16 06				16 37		17 06				17 37		18 06
Banbury	d				15 54		16 25				16 54		17 25				17 54		18 25
Leamington Spa [8]	d				16 12		16 43				17 12		17 43				18 12		18 43
Coventry	d				16 26						17 26						18 26		
Birmingham International ✈	d				16 38						17 38						18 38		
Penzance	d														12 30				
St Erth	d														12 40				
Hayle	d														12 44				
Camborne	d														12 56				
Redruth	d														13 02				
Truro	d														13 14				
St Austell	d														13 31				
Newquay	d					11 35													
Par	d														13 38				
Lostwithiel	d														13 45				
Bodmin Parkway	d					12 41									13 52				
Liskeard [6]	d					12 54									14 04				
Plymouth	d					13 23						14 23			14 35			15 23	
Totnes	d					13 49						14 49			15 00			15 49	
Paignton	d		12 55																
Torquay	d		13 01																
Newton Abbot	d		13 16			14 03						15 03			15 12			16 03	
Teignmouth	d		13 23																
Dawlish	d		13 28																
Exeter St Davids [6]	d		13 42			14 25						15 25			15 33			16 25	
Tiverton Parkway	d		13 55			14 39						15 38			15 46			16 38	
Taunton	d		14 10			14 54						15 54			16 01			16 54	
Weston-super-Mare	d														16 30				
Cardiff Central [7]	d			14 45						15 45						16 45			
Newport (South Wales)	d			15 03						16 03						17 04			
Bristol Temple Meads [10]	d		15 00			15 30			16 00			16 30			17 00			17 30	
Bristol Parkway [7]	d		15 10			15 40			16 10			16 40			17 10			17 40	
Gloucester [7]	d			15 47						16 47						17 47			
Cheltenham Spa	d		15 42	15 58		16 11			16 42	16 58		17 11			17 42	17 58		18 11	
Birmingham New Street [12]	a		16 26	16 41	16 48	16 50	17 09		17 26	17 41	17 48	17 49	18 09		18 27	18 41	18 48	18 51	19 09
Birmingham New Street [12]	d	16 20	16 31	16 49	17 01	17 03	17 30	17 20	17 31	17 49	18 01	18 03	18 30	18 20	18 31	18 49	19 01	19 03	19 30
Tamworth	d			17 07						18 07		18 19				19 09			
Burton-on-Trent	d			17 19		17 29				18 19						19 21		19 26	
Derby [6]	a			17 35		17 42	18 05			18 34		18 42	19 02			19 33		19 40	20 02
Nottingham [8]	a			18 02						19 04						19 56			
Chesterfield	a					18 03						19 04						20 01	
Sheffield [7]	a					18 19	18 46					19 20	19 39					20 17	20 38
Doncaster [7]	a						19 13						20 16						21 19
Wakefield Westgate [7]	a					18 47						19 48						20 46	
Leeds [10]	a					19 04						20 05						21 03	
York [8]	a					19 32	19 42					20 32	20 44					21 32	21 42
Darlington [7]	a					20 03	20 10					21 03	21 18						22 22
Durham	a					20 21	20 27					21 21	21 36						22 39
Chester-le-Street	a																		
Newcastle [8]	a					20 37	20 43					21 37	21 54						23 07
Morpeth	a						21 01												
Alnmouth for Alnwick	a						21 15					22 05							
Berwick-upon-Tweed	a					21 23	21 36					22 28							
Dunbar	a					21 48													
Wolverhampton [7]	d	16u37	16 49		17 19			17u37	17 49		18 19			18 37	18 49		19 19		
Stafford	a				17 35						18 35						19 37		
Stoke-on-Trent	a		17 19		17 56				18 19		18 56				19 19		19 56		
Congleton	a																		
Macclesfield	a				18 14						19 15						20 14		
Crewe [10]	a	17 07						18 09						19 09					
Wilmslow	a																		
Stockport	a				18 28						19 28						20 28		
Manchester Piccadilly [10]	a		17 56		18 40				18 56		19 40				19 58		20 40		
Warrington Bank Quay	a	17 26						18 28						19 28					
Wigan North Western	a	17 37						18 39						19 39					
Preston [8]	a	17 51						18 53						19 53					
Lancaster [6]	a	18 07						19 10						20 10					
Oxenholme Lake District	a	18 22						19 24											
Penrith North Lakes	a	18 47												20 46					
Carlisle [8]	a	19 03						20 03						21 02					
Lockerbie	a																		
Haymarket	a													22 15					
Edinburgh [10]	a	20 23				22 15	22 20					23 14		22 23					
Haymarket	a																		
Motherwell	a																		
Glasgow Central [15]	a							21 18											
Inverkeithing	a																		
Kirkcaldy	a																		
Markinch	a																		
Ladybank	a																		
Cupar	a																		
Leuchars [3]	a																		
Dundee	a																		
Arbroath	a																		
Montrose	a																		
Stonehaven	a																		
Aberdeen	a																		

Table 51

Sundays 18 July to 05 September

South Coast and the South West - North West England, The North East and Scotland

		VT	XC	XC	XC	XC	XC	VT	XC	XC	XC	XC	XC	VT	XC	XC	XC	XC	XC
		1	◇1 🍴	◇1	◇1 🍴	◇1 🍴	◇1 🍴	◇1	◇1 🍴	◇1	◇1 🍴	◇1 🍴	◇1 🍴	◇1	◇1 🍴	◇1	◇1 🍴	◇1	◇1 🍴
Bournemouth	d				16 40						17 40						18 40		
Brockenhurst 3	d				16 57						17 57						18 57		
Southampton Central	d				17 15						18 15						19 15		
Southampton Airport Parkway ✈	d				17 22						18 22						19 22		
Winchester	d				17 31						18 31						19 31		
Basingstoke	d				17 47						18 47						19 47		
Guildford	d																		
Reading 7	d				18 11		18 40				19 11		19 40				20 11		20 40
Oxford	d				18 37		19 06				19 37		20 06				20 37		21 06
Banbury	d				18 54		19 25				19 54		20 25				20 54		21 25
Leamington Spa 8	d				19 12		19 43				20 12		20 43				21 12		21 43
Coventry	d				19 26		19 54				20 26		20 54				21 26		21 54
Birmingham International ✈	d				19 38		20 04				20 38		21 04				21 38		22 04
Penzance	d											15 30							
St Erth	d											15 38							
Hayle	d																		
Camborne	d											15 51							
Redruth	d											15 57							
Truro	d											16 09							
St Austell	d											16 25							
Newquay	d																		
Par	d											16 33							
Lostwithiel	d																		
Bodmin Parkway	d											16 44							
Liskeard 6	d											16 56							
Plymouth	d					16 25						17 26						18 23	
Totnes	d					16 50						17 52						18 49	
Paignton	d														18 18				
Torquay	d														18 24				
Newton Abbot	d					17 03						18 04			18 35			19 03	
Teignmouth	d																		
Dawlish	d																		
Exeter St Davids 6	d					17 23						18 24			18 56			19 25	
Tiverton Parkway	d					17 37						18 39			19 09			19 38	
Taunton	d					17 51						18 52			19 23			19 54	
Weston-super-Mare	d																		
Cardiff Central 7	d			17 45						18 45						19 45			
Newport (South Wales)	d			18 03						19 03						20 04			
Bristol Temple Meads 10	d		18 00			18 30			19 00			19 30			20 00			20 30	
Bristol Parkway 7	d		18 10			18 40			19 10			19 40			20 10			20 40	
Gloucester 7	d			18 47						19 50						20 50			
Cheltenham Spa	d		18 42	18 58		19 12			19 42	20 00		20 12			20 42	21 00		21 11	
Birmingham New Street 12	a		19 26	19 41	19 48	19 50	20 15		20 26	20 42	20 48	20 50	21 15		21 20	21 45	21 48	21 51	22 15
Birmingham New Street 12	d	19 20	19 31	19 49	20 01	20 03		20 20	20 31	20 49	21 01	21 03		21 20			22 01	22 03	
Tamworth	d			20 07		20 19				21 06		21 19						22 19	
Burton-on-Trent	d			20 19						21 18		21 29							
Derby 6	a			20 34		20 42				21 33		21 42						22 45	
Nottingham 8	a			21 01						22 00									
Chesterfield	a					21 02						22 02						23 06	
Sheffield 7	a					21 16						22 18						23 22	
Doncaster 7	a																		
Wakefield Westgate 7	a					21 44						22 45							
Leeds 10	a					22 01						23 04						00 33	
York 8	a																		
Darlington 7	a																		
Durham	a																		
Chester-le-Street	a																		
Newcastle 8	a																		
Morpeth	a																		
Alnmouth for Alnwick	a																		
Berwick-upon-Tweed	a																		
Dunbar	a																		
Wolverhampton 7	d	19 37	19 49		20 19			20 38	20 49		21 19			21 37			22 19		
Stafford	a				20 37			20 51			21 37			21 56			22 37		
Stoke-on-Trent	a		20 19		20 56				21 19		21 56						22 55		
Congleton	a																		
Macclesfield	a				21 15						22 14						23 12		
Crewe 10	a	20 09						21 10						22 15					
Wilmslow	a																		
Stockport	a				21 28						22 28						23 27		
Manchester Piccadilly 10	a		21 00		21 40				21 56		22 40						23 41		
Warrington Bank Quay	a	20 28												22 34					
Wigan North Western	a	20 39												22 45					
Preston 8	a	20 53												23 05					
Lancaster 6	a	21 10																	
Oxenholme Lake District	a	21 24																	
Penrith North Lakes	a																		
Carlisle 8	a	22 03																	
Lockerbie	a	22 22																	
Haymarket	a																		
Edinburgh 10	a																		
Haymarket	a																		
Motherwell	a	23 07																	
Glasgow Central 15	a	23 22																	
Inverkeithing	a																		
Kirkcaldy	a																		
Markinch	a																		
Ladybank	a																		
Cupar	a																		
Leuchars 8	a																		
Dundee	a																		
Arbroath	a																		
Montrose	a																		
Stonehaven	a																		
Aberdeen	a																		

Table 51

Sundays 18 July to 05 September

South Coast and the South West - North West England, The North East and Scotland

		XC	XC	XC	XC
		◇1	◇1 🍴	◇1 🍴	◇1
Bournemouth	d		19 40		
Brockenhurst 3	d		19 57		
Southampton Central	d		20 15		
Southampton Airport Parkway ✈	d		20 22		
Winchester	d		20 31		
Basingstoke	d		20 47		
Guildford	d				
Reading 7	d		21 11	21 40	
Oxford	d		21 37	22 06	
Banbury	d		21 54	22 25	
Leamington Spa 8	d		22 12	22 43	
Coventry	d		22 23	22 54	
Birmingham International ✈	d		22 33	23 04	
Penzance	d				
St Erth	d				
Hayle	d				
Camborne	d				
Redruth	d				
Truro	d				
St Austell	d				
Newquay	d				
Par	d				
Lostwithiel	d				
Bodmin Parkway	d				
Liskeard 6	d				
Plymouth	d				
Totnes	d				
Paignton	d				
Torquay	d				
Newton Abbot	d				
Teignmouth	d				
Dawlish	d				
Exeter St Davids 6	d				
Tiverton Parkway	d				
Taunton	d				
Weston-super-Mare	d				
Cardiff Central 7	d	20 45			
Newport (South Wales)	d	21 03			
Bristol Temple Meads 10	d				22 10
Bristol Parkway 7	d				22 20
Gloucester 7	d	21 47			
Cheltenham Spa	d	21 58			22 52
Birmingham New Street 12	a	22 41	22 42	23 14	23 39
Birmingham New Street 12	d				
Tamworth	d				
Burton-on-Trent	d				
Derby 6	a				
Nottingham 8	a				
Chesterfield	a				
Sheffield 7	a				
Doncaster 7	a				
Wakefield Westgate 7	a				
Leeds 10	a				
York 8	a				
Darlington 7	a				
Durham	a				
Chester-le-Street	a				
Newcastle 8	a				
Morpeth	a				
Alnmouth for Alnwick	a				
Berwick-upon-Tweed	a				
Dunbar	a				
Wolverhampton 7	d				
Stafford	a				
Stoke-on-Trent	a				
Congleton	a				
Macclesfield	a				
Crewe 10	a				
Wilmslow	a				
Stockport	a				
Manchester Piccadilly 10	a				
Warrington Bank Quay	a				
Wigan North Western	a				
Preston 8	a				
Lancaster 6	a				
Oxenholme Lake District	a				
Penrith North Lakes	a				
Carlisle 8	a				
Lockerbie	a				
Haymarket	a				
Edinburgh 10	a				
Haymarket	a				
Motherwell	a				
Glasgow Central 15	a				
Inverkeithing	a				
Kirkcaldy	a				
Markinch	a				
Ladybank	a				
Cupar	a				
Leuchars 8	a				
Dundee	a				
Arbroath	a				
Montrose	a				
Stonehaven	a				
Aberdeen	a				

Table 51

Sundays

12 September to 17 October

South Coast and the South West - North West England, The North East and Scotland

		VT ◇1	XC ◇1	XC ◇1	VT ◇1	XC ◇1	XC ◇1	VT ◇1	XC ◇1	XC ◇1	VT ◇1	XC ◇1	XC ◇1	XC ◇1	VT ◇1	XC ◇1	XC ◇1	XC ◇1	XC ◇1	VT ◇1	XC ◇1	XC ◇1
Bournemouth	d																	09 40				
Brockenhurst 3	d																	09 57				
Southampton Central	d												09 15					10 15				
Southampton Airport Parkway ✈	d												09 22					10 22				
Winchester	d												09 31					10 31				
Basingstoke	d												09 47					10 47				
Guildford	d																					
Reading 7	d								09 11				10 11					11 11				
Oxford	d								09 37				10 37					11 37				
Banbury	d								09 54				10 54					11 54				
Leamington Spa 8	d								10 12				11 12					12 12				
Coventry	d								10 28				11 28					12 28				
Birmingham International ✈	d								10 40				11 40					12 40				
Penzance	d																					
St Erth	d																					
Hayle	d																					
Camborne	d																					
Redruth	d																					
Truro	d																					
St Austell	d																					
Newquay	d																					
Par	d																					
Lostwithiel	d																					
Bodmin Parkway	d																					
Liskeard 6	d																					
Plymouth	d																		09 25			
Totnes	d																		09 50			
Paignton	d																					
Torquay	d																					
Newton Abbot	d																		10 03			
Teignmouth	d																					
Dawlish	d																					
Exeter St Davids 6	d																		10 23			
Tiverton Parkway	d																		10 37			
Taunton	d																		10 51			
Weston-super-Mare	d																					
Cardiff Central 7	d																10 45					
Newport (South Wales)	d																10 59					
Bristol Temple Meads 10	d									09 15				10 30					11 30			
Bristol Parkway 7	d									09 25				10 40					11 40			
Gloucester 7	d									10 01							11 52					
Cheltenham Spa	d									10 12				11 12			12 03		12 12			
Birmingham New Street 12	a								10 50	10 50			11 50	11 50			12 45	12 50	12 50			
Birmingham New Street 12	d	08 45	09 01	09 03	09 20	10 00	10 03	10 20	11 01	11 03	11 20	11 49	12 01	12 03	12 20	12 30	12 49	13 01	13 03	13 20	13 30	13 31
Tamworth	d			09 19			10 19					12 07		12 19			13 07					
Burton-on-Trent	d			09 29			10 29			11 26		12 19					13 19		13 26			
Derby 6	a			09 42			10 42			11 42		12 34		12 42		13 09	13 38		13 44		14 09	
Nottingham 8	a											13 02					14 04					
Chesterfield	a			10 02			11 02			12 02				13 02		13 29			14 02		14 29	
Sheffield 7	a			10 16			11 17			12 18				13 17		13 43			14 17		14 46	
Doncaster 7	a															14 13					15 13	
Wakefield Westgate 7	a			10 44			11 44			12 44				13 44					14 44			
Leeds 10	a			11 02			12 02			13 02				14 02					15 02			
York 8	a			11 34			12 32			13 32				14 32		14 43			15 32		15 40	
Darlington 7	a			12 03			13 08			14 02				15 07		15 15			16 01		16 12	
Durham	a			12 20			13 25			14 19				15 24		15 32			16 18		16 30	
Chester-le-Street	a																					
Newcastle 8	a			12 35			13 41			14 35				15 38		15 46			16 34		16 45	
Morpeth	a													15 53								
Alnmouth for Alnwick	a						14 07							16 07								
Berwick-upon-Tweed	a			13 20						15 19									17 19			
Dunbar	a			13 41						15 42									17 42			
Wolverhampton 7	d	09 04	09 19		09 37	10 18		10 37	11 19		11 37		12 20		12 37			13 19		13 37		13 49
Stafford	a	09 17	09 33			10 32			11 32				12 33					13 33				
Stoke-on-Trent	a					10 51			11 51				12 51					13 56				14 19
Congleton	a																					
Macclesfield	a					11 08			12 09				13 09					14 14				
Crewe 10	a	09 38	09 54		10 06			11 08			12 07				13 07					14 09		
Wilmslow	a		10 12																			
Stockport	a		10 21			11 22			12 22				13 28					14 28				
Manchester Piccadilly 10	a		10 34			11 34			12 34				13 40					14 40				14 57
Warrington Bank Quay	a	09 57			10 26			11 27			12 26				13 26					14 28		
Wigan North Western	a	10 08			10 37			11 38			12 37				13 37					14 39		
Preston 8	a	10 25			10 51			11 52			12 51				13 51					14 52		
Lancaster 6	a				11 07			12 09			13 08				14 08					15 10		
Oxenholme Lake District	a				11 22			12 23			13 22									15 24		
Penrith North Lakes	a														14 44							
Carlisle 8	a				12 01			13 02			14 01				15 00					16 03		
Lockerbie	a																					
Haymarket	a							14 14							16 14							
Edinburgh 10	a			14 10			15 09	14 22		16 07				17 09	16 22				18 07			
Haymarket	a																		18 13			
Motherwell	a																					
Glasgow Central 15	a				13 19						15 16									17 18		
Inverkeithing	a																		18 27			
Kirkcaldy	a																		18 43			
Markinch	a																		18 52			
Ladybank	a																		19 00			
Cupar	a																		19 06			
Leuchars 3	a																		19 13			
Dundee	a																		19 28			
Arbroath	a																		19 45			
Montrose	a																		19 59			
Stonehaven	a																		20 22			
Aberdeen	a																		20 42			

Table 51

Sundays

12 September to 17 October

South Coast and the South West - North West England, The North East and Scotland

		XC ◇1	XC ◇1	XC ◇1	VT ◇1	XC ◇1	XC ◇1	XC ◇1	XC ◇1	XC ◇1	VT ◇1	XC ◇1	XC ◇1	XC ◇1	XC ◇1	XC ◇1	VT ◇1	XC ◇1	XC ◇1	XC ◇1	XC ◇1	XC ◇1	VT ◇1
Bournemouth	d		10 40						11 40						12 40						13 40		
Brockenhurst 3	d		10 57						11 57						12 57						13 57		
Southampton Central	d		11 15						12 15						13 15						14 15		
Southampton Airport Parkway ✈	d		11 22						12 22						13 22						14 22		
Winchester	d		11 31						12 31						13 31						14 31		
Basingstoke	d		11 47						12 47						13 47						14 47		
Guildford	d					12 14																	
Reading 7	d		12 11			12 54			13 11			13 40			14 11			14 40			15 11		
Oxford	d		12 37			13 17			13 37			14 06			14 37			15 06			15 37		
Banbury	d		12 54			13 35			13 54			14 25			14 54			15 25			15 54		
Leamington Spa 8	d		13 12			13 53			14 12			14 43			15 12			15 43			16 12		
Coventry	d		13 26						14 26						15 26						16 26		
Birmingham International ✈	d		13 38						14 38						15 38						16 38		
Penzance	d									09 30												11 24	
St Erth	d									09 38												11 35	
Hayle	d																						
Camborne	d									09 48												11 46	
Redruth	d									09 54												11 53	
Truro	d									10 06												12 06	
St Austell	d									10 24												12 25	
Newquay	d																						
Par	d									10 31												12 32	
Lostwithiel	d																						
Bodmin Parkway	d									10 42												12 44	
Liskeard 6	d									10 54												12 57	
Plymouth	d			10 25						11 25			12 00			12 25						13 23	
Totnes	d			10 50						11 50						12 50						13 49	
Paignton	d						10 50																
Torquay	d						10 56																
Newton Abbot	d			11 03			11 08			12 03			12 36			13 03						14 03	
Teignmouth	d						11 15																
Dawlish	d						11 20																
Exeter St Davids 6	d			11 23			11 32			12 23			12 57			13 26						14 25	
Tiverton Parkway	d			11 37			11 46			12 37			13 10			13 40						14 39	
Taunton	d			11 51			12 00			12 51			13 25			13 54						14 54	
Weston-super-Mare	d						12 21																
Cardiff Central 7	d	11 45						12 45						13 45						14 45			
Newport (South Wales)	d	11 59						12 59						13 59						14 59			
Bristol Temple Meads 10	d			12 30			13 00			13 30			14 00			14 30			15 00			15 30	
Bristol Parkway 7	d			12 40			13 10			13 40			14 10			14 40			15 10			15 40	
Gloucester 7	d	12 47						13 51						14 47						15 47			
Cheltenham Spa	d	12 58		13 12			13 42	14 02		14 12			14 42	14 58		15 12			15 42	15 58		16 11	
Birmingham New Street 12	a	13 41	13 48	13 50		14 19	14 26	14 45	14 48	14 50		15 10	15 27	15 41	15 48	15 50		16 09	16 26	16 41	16 48	16 50	
Birmingham New Street 12	d	13 49	14 01	14 03	14 20	14 30	14 31	14 49	15 01	15 03	15 20	15 30	15 31	15 49	16 01	16 03	16 20	16 30	16 31	16 49	17 01	17 03	17 20
Tamworth	d	14 07		14 19				15 09						16 07		16 19				17 07			
Burton-on-Trent	d	14 19						15 21		15 26				16 19						17 19		17 29	
Derby 6	a	14 34		14 42		15 04		15 34		15 42		16 02		16 34		16 42		17 04		17 35		17 42	
Nottingham 8	a	15 07						16 08						17 03						18 02			
Chesterfield	a			15 02						16 02						17 02						18 03	
Sheffield 7	a			15 17		15 47				16 18		16 48				17 17		17 48				18 19	
Doncaster 7	a					16 15						17 13						18 13					
Wakefield Westgate 7	a			15 44						16 44						17 45		18 33				18 47	
Leeds 10	a			16 02						17 02						18 02		18 51				19 04	
York 8	a			16 32		16 40				17 32		17 42				18 32		19 21				19 32	
Darlington 7	a			17 01		17 14				18 01		18 10				19 01		19 51				20 03	
Durham	a			17 18		17 32				18 18		18 27				19 18		20 08				20 21	
Chester-le-Street	a																	20 18					
Newcastle 8	a			17 34		17 48				18 34		18 42				19 34		20 26				20 37	
Morpeth	a																						
Alnmouth for Alnwick	a			18 01												20 04							
Berwick-upon-Tweed	a									19 19												21 23	
Dunbar	a									19 42												21 48	
Wolverhampton 7	d		14 19		14 37		14 49		15 19		15 37		15 49		16 19		16u37		16 49		17 19		17u37
Stafford	a		14 33						15 33						16 35						17 35		
Stoke-on-Trent	a		14 56				15 19		15 56				16 19		16 56				17 19		17 56		
Congleton	a																						
Macclesfield	a		15 14						16 14						17 14						18 14		
Crewe 10	a				15 09						16 09						17 07						18 09
Wilmslow	a																						
Stockport	a		15 28						16 28						17 28						18 28		
Manchester Piccadilly 10	a		15 40				16 00		16 40				16 59		17 40				17 56		18 40		
Warrington Bank Quay	a				15 28						16 28						17 26						18 28
Wigan North Western	a				15 39						16 39						17 37						18 39
Preston 8	a				15 53						16 53						17 51						18 53
Lancaster 6	a				16 10						17 10						18 07						19 10
Oxenholme Lake District	a										17 24						18 22						19 24
Penrith North Lakes	a				16 46												18 47						
Carlisle 8	a				17 02						18 03						19 03						20 03
Lockerbie	a																						
Haymarket	a				18 13																		
Edinburgh 10	a			19 03	18 22					20 07						21 06	20 23					22 15	
Haymarket	a									20 15						21 15							
Motherwell	a									20 53						21 53							
Glasgow Central 15	a									21 12	19 18					22 14							21 18
Inverkeithing	a																						
Kirkcaldy	a																						
Markinch	a																						
Ladybank	a																						
Cupar	a																						
Leuchars 3	a																						
Dundee	a																						
Arbroath	a																						
Montrose	a																						
Stonehaven	a																						
Aberdeen	a																						

Table 51

South Coast and the South West - North West England, The North East and Scotland

		XC	XC	XC	XC	XC	VT	XC	XC	XC	XC	XC	VT	XC	XC	XC	XC	XC	XC	VT	XC	XC	XC
		◇1	◇1	◇1	◇1	◇1	◇1	◇1	◇1	◇1	◇1	◇1	1	◇1	◇1	◇1	◇1	◇1	◇1	◇1	◇1	◇1	◇1
Bournemouth	d				14 40						15 40						16 40						17 40
Brockenhurst 3	d				14 57						15 57						16 57						17 57
Southampton Central	d				15 15						16 15						17 15						18 15
Southampton Airport Parkway ✈	d				15 22						16 22						17 22						18 22
Winchester	d				15 31						16 31						17 31						18 31
Basingstoke	d				15 47						16 47						17 47						18 47
Guildford	d																						
Reading 7	d	15 40			16 11			16 40			17 11			17 40			18 11		18 40				19 11
Oxford	d	16 06			16 37			17 06			17 37			18 06			18 37		19 06				19 37
Banbury	d	16 25			16 54			17 25			17 54			18 25			18 54		19 25				19 54
Leamington Spa 6	d	16 43			17 12			17 43			18 12			18 43			19 12		19 43				20 12
Coventry	d				17 26						18 26						19 26		19 54				20 26
Birmingham International ✈	d				17 38						18 38						19 38		20 04				20 38
Penzance	d								12 30														
St Erth	d								12 40														
Hayle	d								12 44														
Camborne	d								12 56														
Redruth	d								13 02														
Truro	d								13 14														
St Austell	d								13 31														
Newquay	d																						
Par	d								13 38														
Lostwithiel	d								13 45														
Bodmin Parkway	d								13 52														
Liskeard 6	d								14 04														
Plymouth	d					14 23			14 35			15 23						16 25					
Totnes	d					14 49			15 00			15 49						16 50					
Paignton	d																						
Torquay	d																						
Newton Abbot	d					15 03			15 12			16 03						17 03					
Teignmouth	d																						
Dawlish	d																						
Exeter St Davids 6	d					15 25			15 33			16 25						17 23					
Tiverton Parkway	d					15 38			15 46			16 38						17 37					
Taunton	d					15 54			16 01			16 54						17 51					
Weston-super-Mare	d								16 30														
Cardiff Central 7	d			15 45						16 45						17 45						18 45	
Newport (South Wales)	d			15 59						16 59						17 59						18 59	
Bristol Temple Meads 10	d		16 00			16 30			17 00			17 30			18 00			18 30			19 00		
Bristol Parkway 7	d		16 10			16 40			17 10			17 40			18 10			18 40			19 10		
Gloucester 7	d			16 47						17 47						18 47						19 50	
Cheltenham Spa	d		16 42	16 58		17 11			17 42	17 58		18 11			18 42	18 58		19 12			19 42	20 00	
Birmingham New Street 12	a	17 09	17 26	17 41	17 48	17 49		18 09	18 27	18 41	18 48	18 51		19 09	19 26	19 41	19 48	19 50	20 15		20 26	20 42	20 48
Birmingham New Street 12	d	17 30	17 31	17 49	18 01	18 03	18 20	18 30	18 31	18 49	19 01	19 03	19 20	19 30	19 31	19 49	20 01	20 03		20 20	20 31	20 49	21 01
Tamworth	d			18 07		18 19				19 09						20 07		20 19				21 06	
Burton-on-Trent	d			18 19						19 21		19 26				20 19						21 19	
Derby 6	a	18 05		18 34		18 42		19 02		19 33		19 40		20 02		20 34		20 42				21 33	
Nottingham 8	a			19 04						19 56						21 01						22 00	
Chesterfield	a					19 04						20 01						21 02					
Sheffield 7	a	18 46				19 20		19 39				20 17		20 38				21 16					
Doncaster 7	a	19 13						20 16						21 19									
Wakefield Westgate 7	a					19 48						20 46						21 44					
Leeds 10	a					20 05						21 03						22 01					
York 8	a	19 42				20 32		20 44				21 32		21 42									
Darlington 7	a	20 10				21 03		21 18						22 22									
Durham	a	20 27				21 21		21 36						22 39									
Chester-le-Street	a																						
Newcastle 8	a	20 43				21 37		21 54						23 07									
Morpeth	a	21 01																					
Alnmouth for Alnwick	a	21 15				22 05																	
Berwick-upon-Tweed	a	21 36				22 28																	
Dunbar	a																						
Wolverhampton 7	d		17 49		18 19		18 37		18 49		19 19		19 37		19 49		20 19			20 38	20 49		21 19
Stafford	a				18 35						19 37						20 37			20 51			21 37
Stoke-on-Trent	a		18 19		18 56				19 19		19 56				20 19		20 56				21 19		21 56
Congleton	a																						
Macclesfield	a				19 15						20 14						21 15						22 14
Crewe 10	a						19 09						20 09							21 10			
Wilmslow	a																						
Stockport	a				19 28						20 28						21 28						22 28
Manchester Piccadilly 10	a		18 56		19 40				19 58		20 40				21 00		21 40				21 56		22 40
Warrington Bank Quay	a						19 28						20 28										
Wigan North Western	a						19 39						20 39										
Preston 8	a						19 53						20 53										
Lancaster 6	a						20 10						21 10										
Oxenholme Lake District	a												21 24										
Penrith North Lakes	a						20 46																
Carlisle 8	a						21 02						22 03										
Lockerbie	a												22 22										
Haymarket	a						22 15																
Edinburgh 10	a	22 20				23 14	22 23																
Haymarket	a																						
Motherwell	a												23 07										
Glasgow Central 15	a												23 22										
Inverkeithing	a																						
Kirkcaldy	a																						
Markinch	a																						
Ladybank	a																						
Cupar	a																						
Leuchars 3	a																						
Dundee	a																						
Arbroath	a																						
Montrose	a																						
Stonehaven	a																						
Aberdeen	a																						

Table 51

South Coast and the South West - North West England, The North East and Scotland

		XC	XC	XC	XC	VT	XC	XC	XC	XC	XC	XC	XC
		◇1	◇1	◇1	◇1	◇1	◇1	◇1	◇1	◇1	◇1	◇1	◇1
Bournemouth	d						18 40				19 40		
Brockenhurst 3	d						18 57				19 57		
Southampton Central	d						19 15				20 15		
Southampton Airport Parkway ✈	d						19 22				20 22		
Winchester	d						19 31				20 31		
Basingstoke	d						19 47				20 47		
Guildford	d												
Reading 7	d		19 40				20 11		20 40		21 11	21 40	
Oxford	d		20 06				20 37		21 06		21 37	22 06	
Banbury	d		20 25				20 54		21 25		21 54	22 25	
Leamington Spa 6	d		20 43				21 12		21 43		22 12	22 43	
Coventry	d		20 54				21 26		21 54		22 23	22 54	
Birmingham International ✈	d		21 04				21 38		22 04		22 33	23 04	
Penzance	d	15 30											
St Erth	d	15 38											
Hayle	d												
Camborne	d	15 51											
Redruth	d	15 57											
Truro	d	16 09											
St Austell	d	16 25											
Newquay	d												
Par	d	16 33											
Lostwithiel	d												
Bodmin Parkway	d	16 44											
Liskeard 6	d	16 56											
Plymouth	d	17 26						18 23					
Totnes	d	17 52						18 49					
Paignton	d			18 18									
Torquay	d			18 24									
Newton Abbot	d	18 04		18 35				19 03					
Teignmouth	d												
Dawlish	d												
Exeter St Davids 6	d	18 24		18 56				19 25					
Tiverton Parkway	d	18 39		19 09				19 38					
Taunton	d	18 52		19 23				19 54					
Weston-super-Mare	d												
Cardiff Central 7	d				19 45					20 45			
Newport (South Wales)	d				20 00					20 59			
Bristol Temple Meads 10	d	19 30		20 00				20 30					22 10
Bristol Parkway 7	d	19 40		20 10				20 40					22 20
Gloucester 7	d				20 50					21 47			
Cheltenham Spa	d	20 12		20 42	21 00			21 11		21 58			22 52
Birmingham New Street 12	a	20 50	21 15	21 20	21 45		21 48	21 51	22 15	22 41	22 42	23 14	23 39
Birmingham New Street 12	d	21 03				21 20	22 01	22 03					
Tamworth	d	21 19						22 19					
Burton-on-Trent	d	21 29											
Derby 6	a	21 42						22 45					
Nottingham 8	a												
Chesterfield	a	22 02						23 06					
Sheffield 7	a	22 18						23 22					
Doncaster 7	a												
Wakefield Westgate 7	a	22 45											
Leeds 10	a	23 04						00 33					
York 8	a												
Darlington 7	a												
Durham	a												
Chester-le-Street	a												
Newcastle 8	a												
Morpeth	a												
Alnmouth for Alnwick	a												
Berwick-upon-Tweed	a												
Dunbar	a												
Wolverhampton 7	d					21 37	22 19						
Stafford	a					21 56	22 37						
Stoke-on-Trent	a						22 55						
Congleton	a												
Macclesfield	a						23 12						
Crewe 10	a					22 15							
Wilmslow	a												
Stockport	a						23 27						
Manchester Piccadilly 10	a						23 41						
Warrington Bank Quay	a					22 34							
Wigan North Western	a					22 45							
Preston 8	a					23 05							
Lancaster 6	a												
Oxenholme Lake District	a												
Penrith North Lakes	a												
Carlisle 8	a												
Lockerbie	a												
Haymarket	a												
Edinburgh 10	a												
Haymarket	a												
Motherwell	a												
Glasgow Central 15	a												
Inverkeithing	a												
Kirkcaldy	a												
Markinch	a												
Ladybank	a												
Cupar	a												
Leuchars 3	a												
Dundee	a												
Arbroath	a												
Montrose	a												
Stonehaven	a												
Aberdeen	a												

Table 51

Sundays from 24 October

South Coast and the South West - North West England, The North East and Scotland

		XC	VT	XC	XC	VT	XC	XC	VT	XC	XC	VT	XC	XC	XC	VT	XC	XC	XC	XC	XC	XC	XC
Bournemouth	d																		09 40				
Brockenhurst	d																		09 57				
Southampton Central	d													09 15					10 15				
Southampton Airport Parkway	d													09 22					10 22				
Winchester	d													09 31					10 31				
Basingstoke	d													09 47					10 47				
Guildford	d																						
Reading	d									09 11				10 11					11 11				
Oxford	d									09 37				10 37					11 37				
Banbury	d									09 54				10 54					11 54				
Leamington Spa	d									10 12				11 12					12 12				
Coventry	d									10 28				11 28					12 28				
Birmingham International	d									10 40				11 40					12 40				
Penzance	d																						
St Erth	d																						
Hayle	d																						
Camborne	d																						
Redruth	d																						
Truro	d																						
St Austell	d																						
Newquay	d																						
Par	d																						
Lostwithiel	d																						
Bodmin Parkway	d																						
Liskeard	d																						
Plymouth	d																						
Totnes	d																						
Paignton	d																						
Torquay	d																						
Newton Abbot	d																						
Teignmouth	d																						
Dawlish	d																						
Exeter St Davids	d																						
Tiverton Parkway	d																						
Taunton	d																						
Weston-super-Mare	d																						
Cardiff Central	d																	10 45					11 45
Newport (South Wales)	d														10 13			10 59		11 15			11 59
Bristol Temple Meads	d														09 30					10 30			
Bristol Parkway	d														09 43					10 43			
Gloucester	d														10 58			11 52		12 00			12 47
Cheltenham Spa	d														11 12			12 03		12 12			12 58
Birmingham New Street	a									10 50				11 50	11 50			12 45	12 50	12 50			13 41
Birmingham New Street	d	22p31	08 45	09 01	09 03	09 20	10 00	10 03	10 20	11 01	11 03	11 20	11 49	12 01	12 03	12 20	12 30	12 49	13 01	13 03	13 30	13 31	13 49
Tamworth	d				09 19			10 19					12 07		12 19			13 07					14 07
Burton-on-Trent	d				09 29			10 29			11 26		12 19					13 19		13 26			14 19
Derby	a				09 42			10 42			11 42		12 34		12 42		13 09	13 38		13 44	14 09		14 34
Nottingham	a												13 02					14 04					15 07
Chesterfield	a				10 02			11 02			12 02				13 02		13 29			14 02	14 29		
Sheffield	a				10 16			11 17			12 18				13 17		13 43			14 17	14 46		
Doncaster	a																14 13				15 13		
Wakefield Westgate	a				10 44			11 44			12 44				13 44					14 44			
Leeds	a				11 02			12 02			13 02				14 02					15 02			
York	a				11 34			12 32			13 32				14 32		14 43			15 32	15 40		
Darlington	a				12 03			13 08			14 02				15 07		15 15			16 01	16 12		
Durham	a				12 20			13 25			14 19				15 24		15 32			16 18	16 30		
Chester-le-Street	a																						
Newcastle	a				12 35			13 41			14 35				15 38		15 46			16 34	16 45		
Morpeth	a														15 53								
Alnmouth for Alnwick	a							14 07							16 07								
Berwick-upon-Tweed	a				13 20						15 19									17 19			
Dunbar	a				13 41						15 42									17 42			
Wolverhampton	d	22p49	09 04	09 19		09 37	10 18		10 37	11 19		11 37		12 20		12 37			13 19			13 49	
Stafford	a	23p02	09 18	09 33			10 32			11 32				12 33					13 33				
Stoke-on-Trent	a	23p20					10 51			11 51				12 51					13 56			14 19	
Congleton	a																						
Macclesfield	a	23p38					11 08			12 09				13 09					14 14				
Crewe	a		09 37	09 54		10 06			11 07			12 07				13 07							
Wilmslow	a			10 12																			
Stockport	a	23p53		10 21			11 22			12 22				13 28					14 28				
Manchester Piccadilly	a	00 10		10 34			11 34			12 34				13 40					14 40			14 57	
Warrington Bank Quay	a		09 56																				
Wigan North Western	a																						
Preston	a					11 44			12 45			13 42				14 42							
Lancaster	a					12 08			13 08			14 08				15 10							
Oxenholme Lake District	a					12 22			13 22							15 24							
Penrith North Lakes	a											14 44											
Carlisle	a					13 02			14 01			15 00				16 03							
Lockerbie	a																						
Haymarket	a					14 14						16 14											
Edinburgh	a				14 10	14 22		15 09			16 07	16 22			17 09					18 07			
Haymarket	a																			18 13			
Motherwell	a																						
Glasgow Central	a								15 16							17 18							
Inverkeithing	a																			18 27			
Kirkcaldy	a																			18 43			
Markinch	a																			18 52			
Ladybank	a																			19 00			
Cupar	a																			19 06			
Leuchars	a																			19 13			
Dundee	a																			19 28			
Arbroath	a																			19 45			
Montrose	a																			19 59			
Stonehaven	a																			20 22			
Aberdeen	a																			20 42			

Table 51

Sundays from 24 October

South Coast and the South West - North West England, The North East and Scotland

		XC	XC	VT	XC	XC	XC	XC	XC	VT	XC	XC	XC	XC	XC	VT	XC	XC	XC	XC	XC	VT	XC
Bournemouth	d	10 40						11 40						12 40						13 40			
Brockenhurst	d	10 57						11 57						12 57						13 57			
Southampton Central	d	11 15						12 15						13 15						14 15			
Southampton Airport Parkway	d	11 22						12 22						13 22						14 22			
Winchester	d	11 31						12 31						13 31						14 31			
Basingstoke	d	11 47						12 47						13 47						14 47			
Guildford	d				12 14																		
Reading	d	12 11			12 54			13 11			13 40			14 11			14 40			15 11			15 40
Oxford	d	12 37			13 17			13 37			14 06			14 37			15 06			15 37			16 06
Banbury	d	12 54			13 35			13 54			14 25			14 54			15 25			15 54			16 25
Leamington Spa	d	13 12			13 53			14 12			14 43			15 12			15 43			16 12			16 43
Coventry	d	13 26						14 26						15 26						16 26			
Birmingham International	d	13 38						14 38						15 38						16 38			
Penzance	d														09 30						11 24		
St Erth	d														09 38						11 35		
Hayle	d																						
Camborne	d														09 48						11 46		
Redruth	d														09 54						11 53		
Truro	d														10 06						12 06		
St Austell	d														10 24						12 25		
Newquay	d																						
Par	d														10 31						12 32		
Lostwithiel	d																						
Bodmin Parkway	d														10 42						12 44		
Liskeard	d														10 54						12 57		
Plymouth	d		09 25						10 25						11 25			12 25			13 23		
Totnes	d		09 50						10 50						11 50			12 50			13 49		
Paignton	d																						
Torquay	d																						
Newton Abbot	d		10 03						11 03						12 03			13 02			14 03		
Teignmouth	d																						
Dawlish	d																						
Exeter St Davids	d		10 23						11 23						12 23			13 26			14 25		
Tiverton Parkway	d		10 37						11 37						12 37			13 39			14 39		
Taunton	d		10 51						11 51						12 51			13 54			14 54		
Weston-super-Mare	d																						
Cardiff Central	d						12 45						13 45						14 45				
Newport (South Wales)	d		12 18				12 59		13 13				13 59		14 10				14 59				
Bristol Temple Meads	d		11 30						12 30						13 30			15 00			15 30		
Bristol Parkway	d		11 43						12 43						13 43			15 10			15 40		
Gloucester	d		13 00				13 51		14 01				14 47		14 57				15 47				
Cheltenham Spa	d		13 12				14 02		14 12				14 58		15 12			15 42	15 58		16 11		
Birmingham New Street	a	13 48	13 50		14 19		14 45	14 48	14 53		15 10		15 41	15 48	15 50		16 09	16 26	16 41	16 48	16 50		17 09
Birmingham New Street	d	14 01	14 03	14 20	14 30	14 31	14 49	15 01	15 03	15 20	15 30	15 31	15 49	16 01	16 03	16 20	16 30	16 31	16 49	17 01	17 03	17 20	17 30
Tamworth	d		14 19				15 09						16 07		16 19				17 07				
Burton-on-Trent	d						15 21		15 26				16 19						17 19		17 29		
Derby	a		14 42		15 04		15 34		15 42		16 02		16 34		16 42		17 04		17 35		17 42		18 05
Nottingham	a						16 08						17 03						18 02				
Chesterfield	a		15 02						16 02						17 02						18 03		
Sheffield	a		15 17		15 47				16 18		16 48				17 17		17 48				18 19		18 46
Doncaster	a				16 15						17 13						18 13						19 13
Wakefield Westgate	a		15 44						16 44						17 45		18 33				18 47		
Leeds	a		16 02						17 02						18 02		18 51				19 04		
York	a		16 32		16 40				17 32		17 42				18 32		19 21				19 32		19 42
Darlington	a		17 01		17 14				18 01		18 10				19 01		19 51				20 03		20 10
Durham	a		17 18		17 32				18 18		18 27				19 18		20 08				20 21		20 27
Chester-le-Street	a																20 18						
Newcastle	a		17 34		17 48				18 34		18 42				19 34		20 26				20 37		20 43
Morpeth	a																						21 01
Alnmouth for Alnwick	a		18 01												20 04								21 15
Berwick-upon-Tweed	a								19 19												21 23		21 36
Dunbar	a								19 42												21 48		
Wolverhampton	d	14 19		14 37		14 49		15 19		15 37		15 49		16 19		16u37		16 49		17 19		17u37	
Stafford	a	14 33						15 33						16 35						17 35			
Stoke-on-Trent	a	14 56				15 19		15 56				16 19		16 56				17 19		17 56			
Congleton	a																						
Macclesfield	a	15 14						16 14						17 14						18 14			
Crewe	a			15 09						16 09						17 07						18 09	
Wilmslow	a																						
Stockport	a	15 28						16 28						17 28						18 28			
Manchester Piccadilly	a	15 40				16 00		16 40				16 59		17 40				17 56		18 40			
Warrington Bank Quay	a			15 28						16 28						17 26						18 28	
Wigan North Western	a			15 39						16 39						17 37						18 39	
Preston	a			15 53						16 53						17 51						18 53	
Lancaster	a			16 10						17 10						18 07						19 10	
Oxenholme Lake District	a									17 24						18 22						19 24	
Penrith North Lakes	a			16 46												18 47							
Carlisle	a			17 02						18 03						19 03						20 03	
Lockerbie	a																						
Haymarket	a			18 13																			
Edinburgh	a		19 03	18 22					20 07						21 06	20 23					22 15		22 20
Haymarket	a								20 15						21 15								
Motherwell	a								20 53						21 53								
Glasgow Central	a								21 12	19 18					22 14							21 18	
Inverkeithing	a																						
Kirkcaldy	a																						
Markinch	a																						
Ladybank	a																						
Cupar	a																						
Leuchars	a																						
Dundee	a																						
Arbroath	a																						
Montrose	a																						
Stonehaven	a																						
Aberdeen	a																						

Table 51

Sundays from 24 October

South Coast and the South West - North West England, The North East and Scotland

	XC	XC	XC	XC	VT	XC	XC	XC	XC	XC	VT	XC	XC	XC	XC	XC	XC	VT	XC	XC	XC	XC
	◇1 ✠	◇1	◇1 ✠	◇1 ✠	◇1 ⊡	◇1 ✠	◇1 ✠	◇1	◇1 ✠	◇1 ✠	2 1 ⊡	◇1 ✠	◇1 ✠	◇1	◇1 ✠	◇1 ✠	◇1 ✠	◇1 ⊡	◇1 ✠	◇1	◇1 ✠	◇1 ✠
Bournemouth d			14 40						15 40						16 40						17 40	
Brockenhurst 3 d			14 57						15 57						16 57						17 57	
Southampton Central d			15 15						16 15						17 15						18 15	
Southampton Airport Parkway ✈ d			15 22						16 22						17 22						18 22	
Winchester d			15 31						16 31						17 31						18 31	
Basingstoke d			15 47						16 47						17 47						18 47	
Guildford d																						
Reading 7 d			16 11			16 40			17 11			17 40			18 11		18 40				19 11	
Oxford d			16 37			17 06			17 37			18 06			18 37		19 06				19 37	
Banbury d			16 54			17 25			17 54			18 25			18 54		19 25				19 54	
Leamington Spa 8 d			17 12			17 43			18 12			18 43			19 12		19 43				20 12	
Coventry d			17 26						18 26						19 26		19 54				20 26	
Birmingham International ✈ d			17 38						18 38						19 38		20 04				20 38	
Penzance d							12 30															15 30
St Erth d							12 40															15 38
Hayle d							12 44															
Camborne d							12 56															15 51
Redruth d							13 02															15 57
Truro d							13 14															16 09
St Austell d							13 31															16 25
Newquay d																						
Par d							13 38															16 33
Lostwithiel d							13 45															
Bodmin Parkway d							13 52															16 44
Liskeard 8 d							14 04															16 56
Plymouth d				14 23			14 35			15 23						16 25						17 26
Totnes d				14 49			15 00			15 49						16 50						17 52
Paignton d																						
Torquay d																						
Newton Abbot d				15 03			15 12			16 03						17 03						18 04
Teignmouth d																						
Dawlish d																						
Exeter St Davids 6 d				15 25			15 33			16 25						17 23						18 24
Tiverton Parkway d				15 38			15 46			16 38						17 37						18 39
Taunton d				15 54			16 01			16 54						17 51						18 52
Weston-super-Mare d							16 30															
Cardiff Central 7 d		15 45						16 45						17 45						18 45		
Newport (South Wales) d		15 59						16 59						17 59						18 59		
Bristol Temple Meads 10 d	16 00			16 30			17 00			17 30			18 00			18 30			19 00			19 30
Bristol Parkway 7 d	16 10			16 40			17 10			17 40			18 10			18 40			19 10			19 40
Gloucester 7 d		16 47						17 47						18 47						19 50		
Cheltenham Spa d	16 42	16 58		17 11			17 42	17 58		18 11			18 42	18 58		19 12			19 42	20 00		20 12
Birmingham New Street 12 a	17 26	17 41	17 48	17 49		18 09	18 27	18 41	18 48	18 51		19 09	19 26	19 41	19 48	19 50	20 15		20 26	20 42	20 48	20 50
Birmingham New Street 12 d	17 31	17 49	18 01	18 03	18 20	18 30	18 31	18 49	19 01	19 03	19 20	19 30	19 31	19 49	20 01	20 03		20 20	20 31	20 49	21 01	21 03
Tamworth d		18 07		18 19				19 09						20 07		20 19				21 06		21 19
Burton-on-Trent d		18 19						19 21		19 26				20 19						21 19		21 29
Derby 6 a		18 34		18 42		19 02		19 33		19 40		20 02		20 34		20 42				21 33		21 42
Nottingham 8 ⇌ a		19 04						19 56						21 01						22 00		
Chesterfield a				19 04						20 01						21 02						22 02
Sheffield 7 ⇌ a				19 20		19 39				20 17		20 38				21 16						22 18
Doncaster 7 a						20 16						21 19										
Wakefield Westgate 7 a				19 48						20 46						21 44						22 45
Leeds 10 a				20 05						21 03						22 01						23 04
York 8 a				20 32		20 44				21 32		21 42										
Darlington 7 a				21 03		21 18						22 22										
Durham a				21 21		21 36						22 39										
Chester-le-Street a																						
Newcastle 8 a				21 37		21 54						23 07										
Morpeth a																						
Alnmouth for Alnwick a				22 05																		
Berwick-upon-Tweed a				22 28																		
Dunbar a																						
Wolverhampton 7 ⇌ d	17 49		18 19		18 37		18 49		19 19		19 37		19 49		20 19			20 38	20 49		21 19	
Stafford a			18 35						19 37						20 37			20 51			21 37	
Stoke-on-Trent a	18 19		18 56				19 19		19 56				20 19		20 56				21 19		21 56	
Congleton a																						
Macclesfield a			19 15						20 14						21 15						22 14	
Crewe 10 a					19 09						20 09							21 10				
Wilmslow a																						
Stockport a			19 28						20 28						21 28						22 28	
Manchester Piccadilly 10 ⇌ a	18 56		19 40				19 58		20 40				21 00		21 40				21 56		22 40	
Warrington Bank Quay a					19 28						20 28											
Wigan North Western a					19 39						20 39											
Preston 8 a					19 53						20 53											
Lancaster 6 a					20 10						21 10											
Oxenholme Lake District a											21 24											
Penrith North Lakes a					20 46																	
Carlisle 8 a					21 02						22 03											
Lockerbie a											22 22											
Haymarket a					22 15																	
Edinburgh 10 a				23 14	22 23																	
Haymarket a																						
Motherwell a											23 07											
Glasgow Central 15 a											23 22											
Inverkeithing a																						
Kirkcaldy a																						
Markinch a																						
Ladybank a																						
Cupar a																						
Leuchars 3 a																						
Dundee a																						
Arbroath a																						
Montrose a																						
Stonehaven a																						
Aberdeen a																						

Table 51

Sundays from 24 October

South Coast and the South West - North West England, The North East and Scotland

	XC	XC	XC	VT	XC	XC	XC	XC	XC	XC	XC
	◇1 ✠	◇1 ✠	◇1	◇1 ⊡	◇1 ✠	◇1 ✠	◇1 ✠	◇1	◇1 ✠	◇1 ✠	◇1 ✠
Bournemouth d					18 40				19 40		
Brockenhurst 3 d					18 57				19 57		
Southampton Central d					19 15				20 15		
Southampton Airport Parkway ✈					19 22				20 22		
Winchester d					19 31				20 31		
Basingstoke d					19 47				20 47		
Guildford d											
Reading 7 d	19 40				20 11		20 40		21 11	21 40	
Oxford d	20 06				20 37		21 06		21 37	22 06	
Banbury d	20 25				20 54		21 25		21 54	22 25	
Leamington Spa 8 d	20 43				21 12		21 43		22 12	22 43	
Coventry d	20 54				21 26		21 54		22 23	22 54	
Birmingham International ✈ d	21 04				21 38		22 04		22 33	23 04	
Penzance d											
St Erth d											
Hayle d											
Camborne d											
Redruth d											
Truro d											
St Austell d											
NEWQUAY d											
Par d											
Lostwithiel d											
Bodmin Parkway d											
Liskeard 8 d											
Plymouth d						18 23					
Totnes d						18 49					
Paignton d		18 18									
Torquay d		18 24									
Newton Abbot d		18 35				19 03					
Teignmouth d											
Dawlish d											
Exeter St Davids 6 d		18 56				19 25					
Tiverton Parkway d		19 09				19 38					
Taunton d		19 23				19 54					
Weston-super-Mare d											
Cardiff Central 7 d			19 45					20 45			
Newport (South Wales) d			20 00					20 59			
Bristol Temple Meads 10 d		20 00				20 30					21 39
Bristol Parkway 7 d		20 10				20 40					21 52
Gloucester 7 d			20 50					21 47			
Cheltenham Spa d		20 42	21 00			21 11		21 58			22 52
Birmingham New Street 12 a	21 15	21 20	21 45		21 48	21 51	22 15	22 41	22 42	23 14	23 39
Birmingham New Street 12 d				21 20	22 01	22 03					
Tamworth d						22 19					
Burton-on-Trent d											
Derby 6 a						22 45					
Nottingham 8 ⇌ a											
Chesterfield a						23 06					
Sheffield 7 ⇌ a						23 22					
Doncaster 7 a											
Wakefield Westgate 7 a											
Leeds 10 a						00 33					
York 8 a											
Darlington 7 a											
Durham a											
Chester-le-Street a											
Newcastle 8 a											
Morpeth a											
Alnmouth for Alnwick a											
Berwick-upon-Tweed a											
Dunbar a											
Wolverhampton 7 ⇌ d				21 37	22 19						
Stafford a				21 56	22 37						
Stoke-on-Trent a					22 55						
Congleton a											
Macclesfield a					23 12						
Crewe 10 a				22 15							
Wilmslow a											
Stockport a					23 27						
Manchester Piccadilly 10 ⇌ a					23 41						
Warrington Bank Quay a				22 34							
Wigan North Western a				22 45							
Preston 8 a				23 05							
Lancaster 6 a											
Oxenholme Lake District a											
Penrith North Lakes a											
Carlisle 8 a											
Lockerbie a											
Haymarket a											
Edinburgh 10 a											
Haymarket a											
Motherwell a											
Glasgow Central 15 a											
Inverkeithing a											
Kirkcaldy a											
Markinch a											
Ladybank a											
Cupar a											
Leuchars 3 a											
Dundee a											
Arbroath a											
Montrose a											
Stonehaven a											
Aberdeen a											

Network Diagram for Table 52

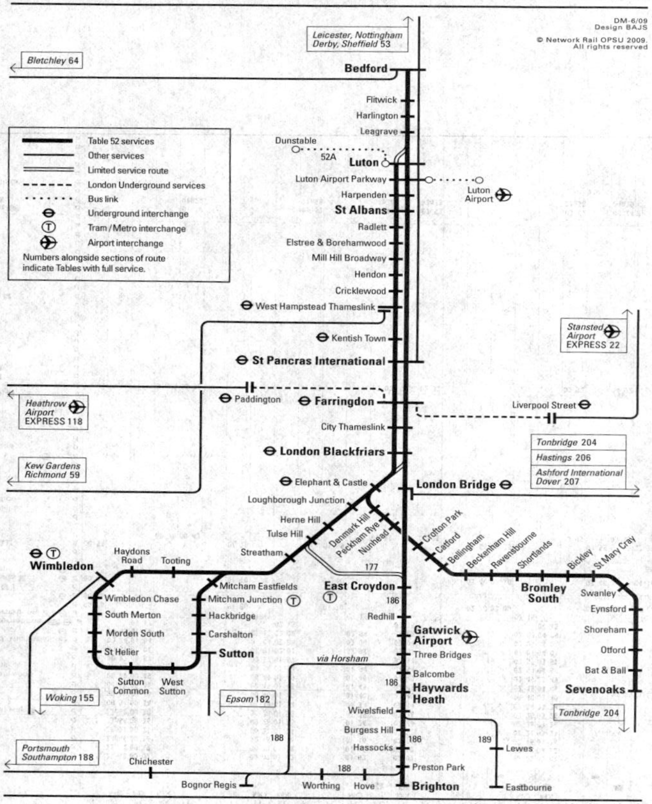

Bedford, Luton, St.Albans and City of London - South London, Gatwick Airport and Brighton

		FC MX 1	FC 1 A	FC MX 1	FC 1 B	FC MX 1	FC MX	SE MX 1	FC MX 1	FC MO 1		SN MX	SN MO	SE MO 1	SE MX 1	SE MX	SE MX 1	FC MX	FC (bus)	FC MO		FC MX 1	FC	SN MX	SE MX
Bedford 7	d	22p52				23p12														23p12		23p32			
Flitwick	d	23p02				23p22														23p22		23p42			
Harlington	d	23p06				23p26														23p26		23p46			
Leagrave	d	23p11				23p31														23p31		23p51			
Luton 10	d	23p16				23p36														23p36		23p56			
Luton Airport Parkway 7	d	23p18				23p38														23p38		23p58			
Harpenden	d	23p24				23p44														23p44		00 04			
St Albans City	d	23p30				23p50														23p50		00 10			
Radlett	d	23p35				23p55														23p55		00 15			
Elstree & Borehamwood	d	23p39				23p59														23p58		00 19			
Mill Hill Broadway	d	23p44				00 04														00 04		00 24			
Hendon	d	23p47				00 07														00 07		00 27			
Cricklewood	d	23p51				00 11														00 11		00 31			
West Hampstead Thameslink ⊖	d	23p54				00 14														00 14		00 34			
Kentish Town ⊖	d	23p58				00 18														00 18		00 42			
St Pancras International 15 ⊖	a	00 05				00 25																00 47			
St Pancras International 15 ⊖	a																			00 25					
	d																		00 01						
Farringdon 3 ⊖	d																		00 06						
City Thameslink 3	d																								
London Blackfriars 3 ⊖	d																		00 11						
Elephant & Castle ⊖	d																								
Loughborough Jn	d																								
Herne Hill 4	d																								
London Bridge 4	a																		00 26						
	d		23p12	23p12	23p12		23p28	23p37	23p42	23p42		23p36	23p39	23p45	23p48		23p52	23p58					00 12	00 06	00 17
Tulse Hill 3	d						23p40											00 10							
Streatham 4	d						23p44											00 14							
Mitcham Eastfields	d																								
Mitcham Junction	d																								
Hackbridge	d																								
Carshalton	d																								
Tooting	d						23p48											00 18							
Haydons Road	d						23p51											00 21							
Wimbledon 6 ⊖	d						23p55											00 25							
Wimbledon Chase	d						23p58											00 28							
South Merton	d						00 01											00 30							
Morden South	d						00 03											00 32							
St Helier	d						00 05											00 34							
Sutton Common	d						00 07											00 36							
West Sutton	d						00 10											00 39							
Sutton (Surrey) 4	a						00 13											00 43							
East Croydon	d		23p24	23p24	23p27				23p56	23p57		00 03	00 09										00 26	00 35	
Denmark Hill 4	d															23p52									
Peckham Rye 4	d															23p55									
Nunhead 4	d															23p57									
Crofton Park	d															23p59									
Catford	d															00 03									
Bellingham	d															00 05									
Beckenham Hill	d															00 07									
Ravensbourne	d															00 09									
Shortlands	d															00 11									
Bromley South 4	d															00 14									
Bickley 4	d															00 17									
St Mary Cray	d																								
Swanley 4	d																								
Eynsford	d																								
Shoreham (Kent)	d																								
Otford 4	d																								
Bat & Ball	d																								
Sevenoaks 4	a							00 05						00 11	00 12		00 18								00 54
Redhill	d																								
Gatwick Airport 10	d		23p41	23p41	23p50				00 18	00 19													00 48		
Three Bridges 4	d		23p47	23p47	23p54				00a24	00a24													00a54		
Balcombe	d			23p53																					
Haywards Heath 3	d		23p56	23p58	00 03																				
Wivelsfield 4	d			00 02																					
Burgess Hill 4	d		00 01	00 04	00 08																				
Hassocks 4	d			00 08																					
Preston Park	d			00 15																					
Brighton 10	a		00 13	00 19	00 22																				

A MO until 6 September

B MO from 13 September

Table 52

Bedford, Luton, St.Albans and City of London - South London, Gatwick Airport and Brighton

Station		FC bus	FC MO	FC MX	SN MX	FC		FC bus	FC MO	FC MX	FC ■	FC bus	FC MO	FC ■	FC MX ■	FC ■		FC bus	FC bus	FC MO ■	FC MX ■	FC	FC bus	FC ■	FC bus
Bedford	d		23p32	00 02					00 02	01 02			01 02		02 02					02 02	03 02				
Flitwick	d		23p42	00 12					00 12	01 12			01 12		02 12					02 12	03 12				
Harlington	d		23p46	00 16					00 16	01 16			01 16		02 16					02 16	03 16				
Leagrave	d		23p51	00 21					00 21	01 21			01 21		02 21					02 21	03 21				
Luton	d		23p56	00 26					00 26	01 26			01 26		02 26					02 26	03 26				
Luton Airport Parkway	d		23p58	00 28					00 28	01 28			01 28		02 28					02 28	03 28				
Harpenden	d		00 04	00 34					00 34	01 34			01 34		02 34					02 34	03 34				
St Albans City	d		00 10	00 40					00 40	01 40			01 40		02 40					02 40	03 40				
Radlett	d		00 15	00 45					00 45	01 45			01 45		02 45					02 45	03 45				
Elstree & Borehamwood	d		00 19	00 49					00 49	01 49			01 49		02 49					02 49	03 49				
Mill Hill Broadway	d		00 24	00 54					00 54	01 54			01 54		02 54					02 54	03 54				
Hendon	d		00 27	00 57					00 57	01 57			01 57		02 57					02 57	03 57				
Cricklewood	d		00 31	01 01					01 01	02 01			02 01		03 01					03 01	04 01				
West Hampstead Thameslink	d		00 34	01 04					01 04	02 04			02 04		03 04					03 04	04 04				
Kentish Town	d		00 42	01 12					01 12	02 08			02 08		03 08					03 08	04 09				
St Pancras International	a			01 17						02 15					03 15						04 15				
St Pancras International	a		00 47						01 17				02 15							03 15					
	d	00 30						01 00				01 30						02 30	03 00				03 30		04 00
Farringdon	d	00 35																							
City Thameslink	d																								
London Blackfriars	d	00 40						01 10				01 40						02 40	03 10				03 40		04 10
Elephant & Castle	d																								
Loughborough Jn	d																								
Herne Hill	d																								
London Bridge	a	00 55						01 25				01 55						02 55	03 25				03 55		23 25
	d				00 36	00 42					01 05			01 35		02 05						03 05		03 35	
Tulse Hill	d																								
Streatham	d																								
Mitcham Eastfields	d																								
Mitcham Junction	d																								
Hackbridge	d																								
Carshalton	d																								
Tooting	d																								
Haydons Road	d																								
Wimbledon	d																								
Wimbledon Chase	d																								
South Merton	d																								
Morden South	d																								
St Helier	d																								
Sutton Common	d																								
West Sutton	d																								
Sutton (Surrey)	a																								
East Croydon	d				01a03	00 56					01 32			02 02		02 32						03 32		04 02	
Denmark Hill	d																								
Peckham Rye	d																								
Nunhead	d																								
Crofton Park	d																								
Catford	d																								
Bellingham	d																								
Beckenham Hill	d																								
Ravensbourne	d																								
Shortlands	d																								
Bromley South	d																								
Bickley	d																								
St Mary Cray	d																								
Swanley	d																								
Eynsford	d																								
Shoreham (Kent)	d																								
Otford	d																								
Bat & Ball	d																								
Sevenoaks	a																								
Redhill	d																								
Gatwick Airport	d					01 18					01 52			02 22		02 52						03 52		04 24	
Three Bridges	d					01a24					01a58			02a28		02a58						03a58		04a30	
Balcombe	d																								
Haywards Heath	d																								
Wivelsfield	d																								
Burgess Hill	d																								
Hassocks	d																								
Preston Park	d																								
Brighton	a																								

Table 52

Bedford, Luton, St.Albans and City of London - South London, Gatwick Airport and Brighton

Station		FC MO ■		FC ■	FC bus	FC ■	FC ■	FC ■	FC ■	SN A bus	SE ■	SE		SE	SN	SN	FC	SN ■	SN	FC ■	SN	SN		EM ◇■	SE ■
Bedford	d	03 02					03 42	04 10	04 20											05 00					
Flitwick	d	03 12					03 52	04 20	04 30											05 10					
Harlington	d	03 16					03 56	04 24	04 34											05 14					
Leagrave	d	03 21					04 01	04 29	04 39											05 19					
Luton	d	03 26					04 06	04 34	04 44								05 08			05 24				06 24	
Luton Airport Parkway	d	03 28					04 08	04 36	04 46								05 10			05 26					
Harpenden	d	03 34					04 14	04 42	04 52								05 16			05 32					
St Albans City	d	03 40					04 20	04 48	04 58								05 22			05 38					
Radlett	d	03 45					04 25		05 03								05 27								
Elstree & Borehamwood	d	03 49					04 29		05 07								05 31								
Mill Hill Broadway	d	03 54					04 34		05 12								05 35								
Hendon	d	03 57					04 37		05 15								05 38								
Cricklewood	d	04 01					04 41		05 19								05 42								
West Hampstead Thameslink	d	04 04					04 44	05 04	05 22								05 46			05 54					
Kentish Town	d	04 08					04 48		05 26								05 50								
St Pancras International	a																							06 53	
St Pancras International	a	04 15					04 54	05 12	05 32								05 54			06 02					
	d				04 30		04 54	05 12	05 32								05 54			06 02					
Farringdon	d						04 59	05 17	05 37								05 58			06 07					
City Thameslink	d							05 21	05 41					05 26			06 01			06 11					
London Blackfriars	d				04a40		05 04	05 24	05 44					05 28			06 06			06 14					
Elephant & Castle	d													05 32			06 09								
Loughborough Jn	d																06 13								
Herne Hill	d																06 16								
London Bridge	a																								
	d			04 05		04 35		05 30	05 50		05 37	05 44				06 00		06 08	06 06	06 20	06 11	06 19			06 24
Tulse Hill	d															06 18	06 22								
Streatham	d															06 21	06 25								
Mitcham Eastfields	d																06 29								
Mitcham Junction	d																06 32								
Hackbridge	d																06 35								
Carshalton	d																06 38								
Tooting	d															06 25									
Haydons Road	d															06 28									
Wimbledon	d														05 56	06a31									
Wimbledon Chase	d														05 59										
South Merton	d														06 01										
Morden South	d														06 03										
St Helier	d														06 05										
Sutton Common	d														06 07										
West Sutton	d														06 10										
Sutton (Surrey)	a														06 13		06 43								
East Croydon	d			04 32		05 02	05 32	05 52	06 06									06 22	06 34	06 36					
Denmark Hill	d													05 39											
Peckham Rye	d													05 41	06 42						06 20				
Nunhead	d													05 44											
Crofton Park	d													05 47											
Catford	d													05 49											
Bellingham	d													05 52											
Beckenham Hill	d													05 54											
Ravensbourne	d													05 56											
Shortlands	d													05 58											
Bromley South	d													06 01											
Bickley	d													06 03											
St Mary Cray	d													06 08											
Swanley	d													06 12											
Eynsford	d													06 17											
Shoreham (Kent)	d													06 20											
Otford	d													06 23											
Bat & Ball	d													06 26											
Sevenoaks	a										06 05	06 27		06 29											06 49
Redhill	d																								
Gatwick Airport	d			04 52		05 22	05 56	06 10	06 22											06 52					
Three Bridges	d			05 00		05 26	06 00	06 14	06 27	05 00										06 57					
Balcombe	d							06 20	06 34																
Haywards Heath	d			05 10		05 36	06 10	06 26	06 39	05 20										07 06					
Wivelsfield	d					05 40	06 14	06 30	06 43											07 10					
Burgess Hill	d			05 15		05 42	06 16	06 32	06 45											07 12					
Hassocks	d			05 18		05 46	06 20	06 36	06 49											07 16					
Preston Park	d					05 53	06 27	06 43	06 56											07 23					
Brighton	a			05 29		05 57	06 31	06 47	07 00	05 55										07 27					

A MX until 28 May

Table 52

Mondays to Fridays

Bedford, Luton, St.Albans and City of London - South London, Gatwick Airport and Brighton

		SE	SN	FC	FC ■	EM ◇■	SN	SN	SN	SE ■	SE	SN	SN	SE ■	SE	FC	FC ■	FC	SN	SN	SN ■	SN
Bedford	d				05 20	05 32											05 40					
Flitwick	d				05 30												05 50					
Harlington	d				05 34												05 54					
Leagrave	d				05 39												05 59					
Luton	d				05 44											05 48	06 04	06 06				
Luton Airport Parkway	d				05 46	05 55										05 50	06 06	06 08				
Harpenden	d				05 52											05 56	06 12	06 14				
St Albans City	d				05 58											06 02	06 18	06 20				
Radlett	d															06 07		06 25				
Elstree & Borehamwood	d															06 11		06 29				
Mill Hill Broadway	d															06 16		06 34				
Hendon	d															06 19		06 37				
Cricklewood	d															06 23		06 41				
West Hampstead Thameslink ⊖	d			06 04	06 14											06 26	06 30	06 44				
Kentish Town ⊖	d			06 08												06 30		06 48				
St Pancras International ⊖	a					06 21																
St Pancras International ⊖	a			06 12	06 22											06 34	06 38	06 52				
	d			06 12	06 22											06 34	06 38	06 52				
Farringdon ⊖	d			06 17	06 27											06 39	06 43	→				
City Thameslink	d			06 21	06 31						06 07					06 43	06 47					
London Blackfriars ⊖	d			06 24	06 34						06 10					06 46	06 50					
Elephant & Castle ⊖	d			06 27							06 16					06 49						
Loughborough Jn	d			06 31												06 53						
Herne Hill	d			06 34												06 57						
London Bridge	a	06 13			06 41					06 37				06 52	06 44		06 56					
	d	06 14			06 42		06 30	06 33	06 36	06 38		06 41	06 51	06 53	06 44		07 00		06 58	07 03	07 03	06 54
Tulse Hill	d			06 42			06 48									07 02			07 16			
Streatham	d			06 46			06 51									07 05			07 19			
Mitcham Eastfields	d			06 50																		
Mitcham Junction	d			06 53																		
Hackbridge	d			06 56																		
Carshalton	d			06 59																		
Tooting	d						06 55									07 10			07 23			
Haydons Road	d						06 58									07 13			07 26			
Wimbledon ⊖	d		06 32				07 02									07 17			07 31			
Wimbledon Chase	d		06 35				07 05									07 20			07 34			
South Merton	d		06 37				07 07									07 22			07 36			
Morden South	d		06 39				07 09									07 24			07 38			
St Helier	d		06 41				07 11									07 26			07 40			
Sutton Common	d		06 43				07 13									07 28			07 42			
West Sutton	d		06 46				07 16									07 31			07 45			
Sutton (Surrey)	a		06 49	07 04			07 19									07 35			07 48			
East Croydon	d				06 56				07 04								07 15				07 17	07 22
Denmark Hill	d										06 22	06 50							08 16	07 12		
Peckham Rye	d		07 17				07 48	06 42			06 25											
Nunhead	d										06 27											
Crofton Park	d										06 30											
Catford	d										06 33											
Bellingham	d										06 35											
Beckenham Hill	d										06 37											
Ravensbourne	d										06 39											
Shortlands	d										06 41											
Bromley South	d										06 44											
Bickley	d										06 47											
St Mary Cray	d										06 51											
Swanley	d										06 56											
Eynsford	d										07 00											
Shoreham (Kent)	d										07 04											
Otford	d										07 07											
Bat & Ball	d										07 10											
Sevenoaks	a	06 59								07 03	07 14			07 19	07 28							
Redhill	d																					
Gatwick Airport	d				07 12												07 32					
Three Bridges	d				07 17												07 37					
Balcombe	d																					
Haywards Heath	d				07 26												07 46					
Wivelsfield	d				07 30												07 50					
Burgess Hill	d				07 32												07 52					
Hassocks	d				07 36												07 56					
Preston Park	d				07 43																	
Brighton	a				07 47												08 05					

Table 52

Mondays to Fridays

Bedford, Luton, St.Albans and City of London - South London, Gatwick Airport and Brighton

		EM ◇■	SE ■	SN	SE ■	SE	SN	SE ■	SE	FC ■	FC	FC ■	FC	FC ■	FC	SN ■	SN	SN ■	SN ■	SN	SN	SN ■
Bedford	d									05 54		05 58		06 14								
Flitwick	d									06 04		06 08		06 24								
Harlington	d											06 12										
Leagrave	d											06 17										
Luton	d									06 14		06 22		06 34	06 36							
Luton Airport Parkway	d	07 07										06 24			06 38							
Harpenden	d									06 20		06 30		06 40	06 44							
St Albans City	d									06 26		06 36	06 40	06 46	06 50							
Radlett	d												06 45		06 55							
Elstree & Borehamwood	d												06 49		07 01							
Mill Hill Broadway	d												06 54		07 06							
Hendon	d												06 57		07 09							
Cricklewood	d												07 01		07 13							
West Hampstead Thameslink ⊖	d											06 50	07 04		07 16							
Kentish Town ⊖	d												07 08		07 20							
St Pancras International ⊖	a	07 36									←											
St Pancras International ⊖	a									06 45	06 52	06 58	07 12	07 05	07 24							
	d									06 45	06 52	06 58	07 12	07 06	07 24							
Farringdon ⊖	d									06 50	06 57	07 03	→	07 11	→							
City Thameslink	d					06 39				06 54	07 01	07 07		07 15								
London Blackfriars ⊖	d					06 42				06 58	07 04	07 09		07 18								
Elephant & Castle ⊖	d					06 46				07 02	07 07			07 21								
Loughborough Jn	d										07 11			07 25								
Herne Hill	d										07 16			07 31								
London Bridge	a		07 07		07 18			07 22	07 13			07 15										
	d		07 08	07 11	07 20		07 21	07 23	07 14			07 16				07 19	07 06	07 25	07 30		07 33	07 33
Tulse Hill	d										07 20			07 37								
Streatham	d										07 23			07 40								
Mitcham Eastfields	d										07 27											
Mitcham Junction	d										07 30											
Hackbridge	d										07 33											
Carshalton	d										07 36											
Tooting	d													07 44								
Haydons Road	d													07 47								
Wimbledon ⊖	d													07 51								
Wimbledon Chase	d													07 54								
South Merton	d													07 56								
Morden South	d													07 58								
St Helier	d													08 00								
Sutton Common	d													08 02								
West Sutton	d													08 05								
Sutton (Surrey)	a										07 39			08 08								
East Croydon	d											07 31				07 35	07 38	07a40	07 46			07 49
Denmark Hill	d					06 52				07 09												
Peckham Rye	d			07 20		06 55				07 12											07 42	
Nunhead	d					06 57				07 14												
Crofton Park	d					07 00				07 17												
Catford	d					07 03				07 20												
Bellingham	d					07 05				07 22												
Beckenham Hill	d					07 07				07 24												
Ravensbourne	d					07 09				07 26												
Shortlands	d					07 11				07 28												
Bromley South	d					07 14				07 31												
Bickley	d					07 17				07 34												
St Mary Cray	d					07 21				07 38												
Swanley	d					07 26				07 44												
Eynsford	d					07 30				07 48												
Shoreham (Kent)	d					07 34				07 52												
Otford	d					07 37				07 55												
Bat & Ball	d					07 40				07 58												
Sevenoaks	a		07 35		07 42	07 43		07 48	08 00	08 01												
Redhill	d																		08 02			
Gatwick Airport	d											07 47										08 05
Three Bridges	d											07 52										08 10
Balcombe	d											07 58										
Haywards Heath	d											08 04										08 19
Wivelsfield	d											08 08										
Burgess Hill	d											08 10										08 25
Hassocks	d											08 14										
Preston Park	d											08 21										
Brighton	a											08 25										08 36

Table 52

Mondays to Fridays

Bedford, Luton, St.Albans and City of London - South London, Gatwick Airport and Brighton

		SE ■	EM ◇■ ⊠	SN	SN	SE ■	SE ■	SE	FC	FC ■	FC ■	FC	FC	EM ◇■ ⊠	FC ■	FC	SN	SN	SN	SN ■	EM ◇■ ⊠	SN ■	SE ■
Bedford [7]	d									06 18	06 22		06 26	06 32	06 36								
Flitwick	d										06 32		06 36		06 46								
Harlington	d										06 36		06 40										
Leagrave	d									06 35	06 41		06 45										
Luton [10]	d									06 40	06 46		06 50		06 56						07 56		
Luton Airport Parkway [7]	d		07 40							06 42	06 48		06 52										
Harpenden	d									06 48	06 54		06 58		07 02								
St Albans City	d									06 54	07 00		07 04		07 08	07 12							
Radlett	d												07 09			07 17							
Elstree & Borehamwood	d												07 13			07 21							
Mill Hill Broadway	d												07 17			07 26							
Hendon	d															07 29							
Cricklewood	d															07 33							
West Hampstead Thameslink ⊖	d									07 08			07 24			07 36							
Kentish Town ⊖	d															07 40							
St Pancras International [15] ⊖	a		08 09						←			←		07 13							08 26		
St Pancras International [15] ⊖	a								07 12	07 16	07 20	07 24	07 31		07 27	07 44							
	d								07 12	07 16	07 20	07 24	07 32		07 28	07 44							
Farringdon [3] ⊖	d								07 17	07 21	07 25	07 29	→		07 33	→							
City Thameslink [3]	d								07 21	07 25	07 29	07 33			07 37								
London Blackfriars [3] ⊖	d								07 24	07 28	07 32	07 36			07 40								
Elephant & Castle ⊖	d								07 28	07 33		07 40			07 44								
Loughborough Jn	d									07 37													
Herne Hill [4]	d									07 41		07 46											
London Bridge [4]	a	07 36				07 48	07 50	07 43			07 41												08 00
	d	07 38		07 41	07 46	07 49	07 51	07 44			07 42						07 29	07 36	07 51	07 53		07 56	08 01
Tulse Hill [3]	d									07 45							07 47						
Streatham [4]	d									07 48							07 51						
Mitcham Eastfields	d									07 52													
Mitcham Junction	d									07 55													
Hackbridge	d									07 58													
Carshalton	d									08 01													
Tooting	d																07 55						
Haydons Road	d																07 58						
Wimbledon [6] ⊖	d																08 02						
Wimbledon Chase	d																08 05						
South Merton	d																08 07						
Morden South	d																08 09						
St Helier	d																08 11						
Sutton Common	d																08 13						
West Sutton	d																08 16						
Sutton (Surrey) [4]	a									08 04							08 19						
East Croydon	d				08a00						07 56							08 04		08 06		08a10	
Denmark Hill [4]	d								07 34						07 50								
Peckham Rye [4]	d			07 50					07 36						07 53								
Nunhead [4]	d								07 39						07 56								
Crofton Park	d								07 42														
Catford	d								07 44						08 00								
Bellingham	d								07 47						08 02								
Beckenham Hill	d								07 49														
Ravensbourne	d								07 51														
Shortlands	d								07 54														
Bromley South [4]	d								07 57						08a10								
Bickley [4]	d								08 00														
St Mary Cray	d								08 04														
Swanley [4]	d								08 10														
Eynsford	d								08 15														
Shoreham (Kent)	d								08 18														
Otford [4]	d								08 21														
Bat & Ball	d								08 24														
Sevenoaks [4]	a	08 06				08 12	08 18	08 24	08 27														08 27
Redhill	d																			08 21			
Gatwick Airport [10]	d										08 12									08 29			
Three Bridges [4]	d										08 16									08 34			
Balcombe	d										08 22												
Haywards Heath [3]	d										08 28									08 43			
Wivelsfield [4]	d										08 32									08 47			
Burgess Hill [4]	d										08 34									08 49			
Hassocks [4]	d										08 38									08 52			
Preston Park	d										08 45									08 59			
Brighton [10]	a										08 49									09 04			

Table 52

Mondays to Fridays

Bedford, Luton, St.Albans and City of London - South London, Gatwick Airport and Brighton

		SN ■	SN	SN ■	SN	SN	FC	FC	FC	SE ■	SN ■	SN	EM ◇■ ⊠	SE ■	SN	SE ■	SE	FC	FC ■	FC	FC	SN	SN
Bedford [7]	d							06 40											06 56				
Flitwick	d							06 50											07 06				
Harlington	d							06 54															
Leagrave	d							06 59															
Luton [10]	d							07 04	07 10				08 15						07 16				
Luton Airport Parkway [7]	d							07 06	07 12														
Harpenden	d							07 12	07 18										07 22				
St Albans City	d							07 18	07 24										07 28		07 32		
Radlett	d								07 29												07 37		
Elstree & Borehamwood	d								07 33												07 41		
Mill Hill Broadway	d								07 37												07 46		
Hendon	d																				07 49		
Cricklewood	d																				07 53		
West Hampstead Thameslink ⊖	d								07 44												07 59		
Kentish Town ⊖	d																				08 03		
St Pancras International [15] ⊖	a						←						08 44					←		←			
St Pancras International [15] ⊖	a						07 31	07 38	07 51									07 44	07 47	07 51	08 07		
	d						07 32	07 38	07 52									07 44	07 48	07 52	08 08		
Farringdon [3] ⊖	d						07 37	07 43	→									07 49	07 53	07 57	→		
City Thameslink [3]	d						07 41	07 47										07 53	07 57	08 01			
London Blackfriars [3] ⊖	d						07 44	07 50										07 56	08 00	08 04			
Elephant & Castle ⊖	d						07 47	07 54										08 00		08 07			
Loughborough Jn	d						07 51													08 11			
Herne Hill [4]	d						07 56													08 15			
London Bridge [4]	a									08 08				08 20		08 24	08 12						
	d	08 00		08 02	08 03					08 09	08 08	08 10		08 21	08 20	08 25	08 13					08 06	08 14
Tulse Hill [3]	d						08 05												08 13	08 20		08 25	
Streatham [4]	d						08 09													08 24		08 28	
Mitcham Eastfields	d					08 07														08 28			
Mitcham Junction	d					08 10														08 31			
Hackbridge	d					08 13														08 34			
Carshalton	d					08 16														08 37			
Tooting	d						08 12															08 33	
Haydons Road	d						08 15															08 36	
Wimbledon [6] ⊖	d		08 02				08 19															08 39	
Wimbledon Chase	d		08 05				08 22															08 42	
South Merton	d		08 07				08 24															08 44	
Morden South	d		08 09				08 26															08 46	
St Helier	d		08 11				08 28															08 48	
Sutton Common	d		08 13				08 30															08 50	
West Sutton	d		08 16				08 33															08 53	
Sutton (Surrey) [4]	a		08 19			08 19	08 37													08 40		08 56	
East Croydon	d	08 16		08 19							08 24								08 26				08 31
Denmark Hill [4]	d							08 00										08 09					
Peckham Rye [4]	d		08 48		08 12			08 03				08 19						08 12					
Nunhead [4]	d							08 06										08 14					
Crofton Park	d							08 09										08 17					
Catford	d							08 12										08 20					
Bellingham	d							08 15										08 22					
Beckenham Hill	d							08 17										08 24					
Ravensbourne	d							08 19										08 26					
Shortlands	d							08 22										08 30					
Bromley South [4]	d							08 25										08 33					
Bickley [4]	d							08 28										08 35					
St Mary Cray	d																	08 40					
Swanley [4]	d																	08 44					
Eynsford	d																	08 49					
Shoreham (Kent)	d																	08 52					
Otford [4]	d																	08 55					
Bat & Ball	d																	08 58					
Sevenoaks [4]	a									08 35				08 44		08 51	08 59	09 01					
Redhill	d			08 41																			
Gatwick Airport [10]	d			08 54															08 42				
Three Bridges [4]	d			08 59															08 46				
Balcombe	d																		08 52				
Haywards Heath [3]	d																		08 58				
Wivelsfield [4]	d																		09 02				
Burgess Hill [4]	d																		09 04				
Hassocks [4]	d																		09 08				
Preston Park	d																		09 15				
Brighton [10]	a																		09 19				

Table 52

Bedford, Luton, St.Albans and City of London - South London, Gatwick Airport and Brighton

		SN		FC ■	EM ◇■	FC ■	FC	FC	FC	SN ■	SN ■	SN		SN ■	SN	SE ■	SN	SE ■	SN	SE ■	SE	FC ■		FC	FC ■
Bedford	d			07 00	07 08	07 12																07 16		07 22	07 28
Flitwick	d			07 10																		07 26		07 32	07 38
Harlington	d			07 14																		07 30		07 36	
Leagrave	d			07 19		07 28																07 35		07 41	
Luton	d			07 24	07 24	07 32		07 30														07 40		07 46	07 48
Luton Airport Parkway	d			07 26				07 32														07 42		07 48	
Harpenden	d			07 32		07 38		07 38														07 48		07 54	07 54
St Albans City	d			07 38		07 44		07 44	07 50													07 55		08 00	08 00
Radlett	d							07 49	07 55															08 05	
Elstree & Borehamwood	d							07 53	07 59															08 10	
Mill Hill Broadway	d							07 57	08 04																
Hendon	d								08 07																
Cricklewood	d								08 11																
West Hampstead Thameslink ⊖	d							08 04	08 15															08 20	
Kentish Town ⊖	d								08 19																
St Pancras International ⊖	a				07 53		←																		
St Pancras International ⊖	a			07 59		08 03	08 07	08 11	08 23													08 15		08 27	08 19
	d			07 59		08 04	08 08	08 12	08 24													08 16		08 28	08 20
Farringdon ⊖	d			08 03		08 09	08 13	08 17	→													08 21		→	08 25
City Thameslink	d			08 07		08 13	08 17	08 21														08 25			08 29
London Blackfriars ⊖	d			08 10		08 16	08 20	08 24														08 28			08 32
Elephant & Castle ⊖	d							08 27														08 32			
Loughborough Jn	d							08 31																	
Herne Hill	d							08 36																	
London Bridge	a			08 16												08 34		08 40		08 45	08 44				
	d	08 06		08 18						08 23	08 25	08 27		08 32	08 33	08 35		08 41	08 41	08 46	08 45				
Tulse Hill	d							08 40																	
Streatham	d							08 44																	
Mitcham Eastfields	d																								
Mitcham Junction	d																								
Hackbridge	d																								
Carshalton	d																								
Tooting	d							08 48																	
Haydons Road	d							08 51																	
Wimbledon ⊖	d							08 55									08 39								
Wimbledon Chase	d							08 58									08 42								
South Merton	d							09 00									08 44								
Morden South	d							09 02									08 46								
St Helier	d							09 04									08 48								
Sutton Common	d							09 06									08 50								
West Sutton	d							09 09									08 53								
Sutton (Surrey)	a							09 12									08 56								
East Croydon	d	08 34		08 37						08 38	08 41	08a42		08 49											08 56
Denmark Hill	d																					08 38			
Peckham Rye	d														08 42		09 23		08 50			08 41			
Nunhead	d																					08 43			
Crofton Park	d																					08 46			
Catford	d																					08 49			
Bellingham	d																					08 51			
Beckenham Hill	d																					08 53			
Ravensbourne	d																					08 55			
Shortlands	d																					08 57			
Bromley South	d						08a37															09 00			
Bickley	d																					09 03			
St Mary Cray	d																					09 07			
Swanley	d																					09 12			
Eynsford	d																					09 16			
Shoreham (Kent)	d																					09 20			
Otford	d																					09 23			
Bat & Ball	d																					09 26			
Sevenoaks	a															09 03		09 07		09 17	09 26	09 29			
Redhill	d									08 58				09 12											
Gatwick Airport	d			08 52										09 25											09 12
Three Bridges	d			08 57										09 30											09 17
Balcombe	d																								
Haywards Heath	d			09 08																					09 26
Wivelsfield	d																								09 30
Burgess Hill	d			09 13																					09 33
Hassocks	d																								09 36
Preston Park	d																								09 43
Brighton	a			09 24																					09 49

Table 52

Bedford, Luton, St.Albans and City of London - South London, Gatwick Airport and Brighton

		FC ■ A	FC	SN ■	SN	SN	SN	SE ■		SN	SN ■	SE ■	SN ■	SN	SE ■	FC	FC ■	FC ■		SN	SE ■	FC	FC	FC	FC ■
Bedford	d																07 32	07 44							07 48
Flitwick	d																07 42								07 58
Harlington	d																07 46								08 02
Leagrave	d																07 51	08 00							08 07
Luton	d																07 56	08 04					08 02		08 12
Luton Airport Parkway	d																07 58						08 04		08 14
Harpenden	d																08 04	08 10					08 10		08 20
St Albans City	d		08 06														08 11	08 16					08 16	08 22	08 27
Radlett	d		08 11																				08 21	08 27	
Elstree & Borehamwood	d		08 15																				08 25	08 31	
Mill Hill Broadway	d		08 20																				08 29	08 36	
Hendon	d		08 23																					08 39	
Cricklewood	d		08 27																					08 43	
West Hampstead Thameslink ⊖	d		08 31																				08 36	08 47	
Kentish Town ⊖	d		08 35																					08 51	
St Pancras International ⊖	a	←														←						←			
St Pancras International ⊖	a	08 23	08 39													08 27	08 31	08 35				08 39	08 43	08 55	08 47
	d	08 24	08 40													08 28	08 32	08 36				08 40	08 44	08 56	08 48
Farringdon ⊖	d	08 29	→													08 33	08 37	08 41				08 45	08 49	→	08 53
City Thameslink	d	08 33														08 37	08 41	08 45				08 49	08 53		08 57
London Blackfriars ⊖	d	08 36														08 40	08 44	08 48				08 52	08 56		09 00
Elephant & Castle ⊖	d															08 44	08 47	08a52				08 56	09 00		
Loughborough Jn	d																08 51						09 04		
Herne Hill	d	08 46															08 57						09 11		
London Bridge	a							09 00				09 07			09 20						09 24				09 11
	d			08 45	08 47	08 36	08 51	09 01		09 03	09 03	09 08	09 08	09 11	09 21					09 22	09 25				09 12
Tulse Hill	d	08 50															09 01						09 16		
Streatham	d	08 54															09 05						09 20		
Mitcham Eastfields	d	08 58																					09 24		
Mitcham Junction	d	09 01																					09 27		
Hackbridge	d	09 04																					09 30		
Carshalton	d	09 07																					09 33		
Tooting	d																09 10								
Haydons Road	d																09 13								
Wimbledon ⊖	d																09 17								
Wimbledon Chase	d																09 20								
South Merton	d																09 22								
Morden South	d																09 24								
St Helier	d																09 26								
Sutton Common	d																09 28								
West Sutton	d																09 31								
Sutton (Surrey)	a	09 10															09 37						09 36		
East Croydon	d			09 00	09 03	09 07					09 21		09 23												09 24
Denmark Hill	d															08 52						09 02			
Peckham Rye	d									09 12				09 20		08 55									
Nunhead	d															08 57									
Crofton Park	d															09 00									
Catford	d															09 03						09 09			
Bellingham	d															09 05									
Beckenham Hill	d															09 07									
Ravensbourne	d															09 09									
Shortlands	d															09 11									
Bromley South	d															09 14						09 18			
Bickley	d															09 17						09 20			
St Mary Cray	d															09 21						09 25			
Swanley	d															09 26						09b36			
Eynsford	d															09 30						09 40			
Shoreham (Kent)	d															09 34						09 44			
Otford	d															09 37						09 47			
Bat & Ball	d															09 40						09 50			
Sevenoaks	a							09 30				09 35			09 44	09 45					09 51	09 53			
Redhill	d			09 17							09 40														
Gatwick Airport	d										09 54														09 41
Three Bridges	d										10 00														09 45
Balcombe	d																								09 51
Haywards Heath	d																								09 57
Wivelsfield	d																								10 01
Burgess Hill	d																								10 03
Hassocks	d																								10 06
Preston Park	d																								10 13
Brighton	a																								10 19

A ■ from London Blackfriars

b arr. 0929

Table 52

Mondays to Fridays

Bedford, Luton, St.Albans and City of London - South London, Gatwick Airport and Brighton

Station		EM ◇■	FC ■	FC	SE	SN ■	SN	SN	SN	SE ■	SN	SE ■	FC	FC	FC ■	FC	FC	SN ■	FC ■	EM ◇■	SN ■	SN
Bedford	d	07 55	07 58												08 04				08 24	08 29		
Flitwick	d		08 08												08 14				08 34			
Harlington	d														08 18				08 38			
Leagrave	d														08 23				08 43			
Luton	d		08 20										08 20		08 28				08 48			
Luton Airport Parkway	d	08 12											08 22		08 30				08 50			
Harpenden	d		08 26										08 28		08 36				08 56			
St Albans City	d		08 32										08 34	08 42	08 43		08 58		09 03			
Radlett	d												08 39	08 47			09 03					
Elstree & Borehamwood	d												08 43	08 51			09 07					
Mill Hill Broadway	d													08 56			09 12					
Hendon	d													08 59			09 15					
Cricklewood	d													09 03			09 19					
West Hampstead Thameslink ⊖	d												08 52	09 07			09 22					
Kentish Town ⊖	d													09 11			09 26					
St Pancras International ⊖	a	08 38		←												←				09 08		
St Pancras International ⊖	a		08 51	08 55									08 59	09 15	09 03	09 15	09 30		09 23			
	d		08 52	08 56									09 00	09 16	09 04	09 16	09 30		09 24			
Farringdon ⊖	d		08 57	09 01									09 05	→	09 09	09 21	→		09 29			
City Thameslink	d		09 01	09 05									09 09		09 13	09 25			09 32			
London Blackfriars ⊖	d		09 04	09 08									09 12		09 16	09 28			09 34			
Elephant & Castle ⊖	d		09a09	09 12									09 16			09 31						
Loughborough Jn	d			09 16												09 35						
Herne Hill	d			09 25												09 41						
London Bridge	a				09 13					09 37		09 48			09 26				09 41			
	d				09 14	09 15	09 06	09 20	09 33	09 39	09 41	09 49			09 27			09 32	09 42		09 45	09 36
Tulse Hill	d			09 31												09 46						
Streatham	d			09 35												09 50						
Mitcham Eastfields	d															09 54						
Mitcham Junction	d															09 57						
Hackbridge	d															10 00						
Carshalton	d															10 03						
Tooting	d			09 40																		
Haydons Road	d			09 43																		
Wimbledon ⊖	d			09 47																		
Wimbledon Chase	d			09 50																		
South Merton	d			09 52																		
Morden South	d			09 54																		
St Helier	d			09 56																		
Sutton Common	d			09 58																		
West Sutton	d			10 01																		
Sutton (Surrey)	a			10 05												10 06						
East Croydon	d					09 30	09 34	09 37							09 39			09 51	09 54		10 00	10 04
Denmark Hill	d												09 22									
Peckham Rye	d								09 42		09 50		09 25									
Nunhead	d												09 27									
Crofton Park	d												09 30									
Catford	d												09 33									
Bellingham	d												09 35									
Beckenham Hill	d												09 37									
Ravensbourne	d												09 39									
Shortlands	d												09 41									
Bromley South	d												09 44									
Bickley	d												09 47									
St Mary Cray	d												09 51									
Swanley	d												09 56									
Eynsford	d												10 00									
Shoreham (Kent)	d												10 04									
Otford	d												10 07									
Bat & Ball	d												10 10									
Sevenoaks	a				09 58					10 05		10 12	10 13									
Redhill	d					09 53												10 10			10 17	
Gatwick Airport	d														09 57			10 24	10 11			
Three Bridges	d														10 02			10 30	10 15			
Balcombe	d																		10 21			
Haywards Heath	d														10 10				10 27			
Wivelsfield	d																		10 31			
Burgess Hill	d																		10 33			
Hassocks	d																		10 36			
Preston Park	d																		10 43			
Brighton	a														10 24				10 49			

Table 52

Mondays to Fridays

Bedford, Luton, St.Albans and City of London - South London, Gatwick Airport and Brighton

Station		SN	SE ■	SE	SN	SN	SE ■	SN	SE ■	FC	FC	FC	FC ■	FC	FC	SN ■	SN ■	FC ■	EM ◇■	FC	SN ■	SN	SN
Bedford	d												08 40					08 54	09 02				
Flitwick	d												08 50					09 04					
Harlington	d												08 54					09 08					
Leagrave	d												08 59					09 13					
Luton	d										08 54		09 04		09 14			09 18	09 19				
Luton Airport Parkway	d										08 56		09 06		09 16			09 20					
Harpenden	d										09 02		09 12		09 22			09 26					
St Albans City	d										09 08	09 14	09 18		09 29			09 34		09 44			
Radlett	d										09 13	09 19			09 34					09 49			
Elstree & Borehamwood	d										09 17	09 23			09 38					09 53			
Mill Hill Broadway	d											09 28			09 43					09 58			
Hendon	d											09 31			09 46					10 01			
Cricklewood	d											09 35			09 50					10 05			
West Hampstead Thameslink ⊖	d										09 26	09 39			09 54					10 09			
Kentish Town ⊖	d											09 43			10 00					10 13			
St Pancras International ⊖	a									←				←					09 47				
St Pancras International ⊖	a									09 30	09 33	09 48	09 39	09 48	10 04			09 53		10 18			
	d									09 30	09 34	09 48	09 40	09 48	10 04			09 54		10 18			
Farringdon ⊖	d									09 35	09 39	→	09 44	09 53	→			09 59		→			
City Thameslink	d									09 39	09 43		09 47	09 57				10 02					
London Blackfriars ⊖	d									09 42	09 46		09 50	10 00				10 05					
Elephant & Castle ⊖	d									09 46	09 49			10 03									
Loughborough Jn	d										09 53			10 07									
Herne Hill	d										09 57			10 11									
London Bridge	a		09 52	09 44			10 07		10 18				09 56					10 11					
	d	09 50	09 53	09 44	09 52	10 03	10 09	10 11	10 19				09 57			10 03	10 08	10 12			10 15	10 06	10 20
Tulse Hill	d										10 01			10 16									
Streatham	d										10 05			10 20									
Mitcham Eastfields	d													10 24									
Mitcham Junction	d													10 27									
Hackbridge	d													10 30									
Carshalton	d													10 33									
Tooting	d										10 10												
Haydons Road	d										10 13												
Wimbledon ⊖	d										10 17												
Wimbledon Chase	d										10 20												
South Merton	d										10 22												
Morden South	d										10 24												
St Helier	d										10 26												
Sutton Common	d										10 28												
West Sutton	d										10 31												
Sutton (Surrey)	a										10 35			10 36									
East Croydon	d	10 07											10 09			10 21	10 23	10 24			10 30	10 34	10 37
Denmark Hill	d									09 52													
Peckham Rye	d					10 12		10 20		09 55													
Nunhead	d									09 57													
Crofton Park	d									10 00													
Catford	d									10 03													
Bellingham	d									10 05													
Beckenham Hill	d									10 07													
Ravensbourne	d									10 09													
Shortlands	d									10 11													
Bromley South	d									10 14													
Bickley	d									10 17													
St Mary Cray	d									10 21													
Swanley	d									10 26													
Eynsford	d									10 30													
Shoreham (Kent)	d									10 34													
Otford	d									10 37													
Bat & Ball	d									10 40													
Sevenoaks	a		10 18	10 26			10 35		10 42	10 43													
Redhill	d															10 44					10 52		
Gatwick Airport	d												10 26			10 56		10 41					
Three Bridges	d															11 01		10 45					
Balcombe	d																						
Haywards Heath	d												10 38					10 55					
Wivelsfield	d																	10 59					
Burgess Hill	d																	11 01					
Hassocks	d																	11 04					
Preston Park	d																	11 11					
Brighton	a												10 54					11 17					

Table 52

Mondays to Fridays

Bedford, Luton, St.Albans and City of London - South London, Gatwick Airport and Brighton

		SE 1	SE	SN	SN	SE 1		SN	SE 1	FC	FC	FC 1	FC 1	FC	FC	SN 1		FC 1	FC	SN 1	SN	SN	SE 1	SE	SN
Bedford 7	d											09 10	09 18					09 24							
Flitwick	d											09 20	09 28					09 34							
Harlington	d											09 24						09 38							
Leagrave	d											09 29						09 43							
Luton 10	d											09 34	09 40		09 44			09 48							
Luton Airport Parkway 7	d											09 36			09 46			09 50							
Harpenden	d											09 42	09 47		09 52			09 56							
St Albans City	d											09 48	09 54		09 59			10 03	10 14						
Radlett	d														10 04				10 19						
Elstree & Borehamwood	d														10 08				10 23						
Mill Hill Broadway	d														10 13				10 28						
Hendon	d														10 16				10 31						
Cricklewood	d														10 20				10 35						
West Hampstead Thameslink ⊖	d														10 24				10 40						
Kentish Town ⊖	d									09 54					10 30				10 44						
St Pancras International 15 ⊖	a										←			←											
St Pancras International 15 ⊖	a									10 00	10 04	10 09	10 13	10 18	10 34			10 23	10 48						
	d									10 00	10 04	10 10	10 14	10 18	10 34			10 24	10 48						
Farringdon 3 ⊖	d									10 05	10 09	10 14	10 19	10 23	→			10 29	→						
City Thameslink 3	d									10 09	10 13	10 17	10 22	10 27				10 32							
London Blackfriars 3 ⊖	d									10 12	10 16	10 20	10 26	10 30				10 35							
Elephant & Castle ⊖	d									10 16	10 19		10a30	10 33											
Loughborough Jn	d										10 23			10 37											
Herne Hill 4	d										10 27			10 41											
London Bridge 4	a	10 22	10 14			10 37			10 48			10 26						10 41					10 52	10 44	
	d	10 23	10 14	10 22	10 33	10 39		10 41	10 49			10 27				10 33		10 42		10 45	10 36	10 50	10 53	10 44	10 52
Tulse Hill 3	d										10 31			10 46											
Streatham 4	d										10 35			10 50											
Mitcham Eastfields	d													10 54											
Mitcham Junction	d													10 57											
Hackbridge	d													11 00											
Carshalton	d													11 03											
Tooting	d										10 40														
Haydons Road	d										10 43														
Wimbledon 6 ⊖	d										10 47														
Wimbledon Chase	d										10 50														
South Merton	d										10 52														
Morden South	d										10 54														
St Helier	d										10 56														
Sutton Common	d										10 58														
West Sutton	d										11 01														
Sutton (Surrey) 4	a										11 05			11 06											
East Croydon	d											10 39				10 51		10 54		11 00	11 04	11 07			
Denmark Hill 4	d									10 22															
Peckham Rye 4	d				10 42			10 50		10 25															
Nunhead 4	d									10 27															
Crofton Park	d									10 30															
Catford	d									10 33															
Bellingham	d									10 35															
Beckenham Hill	d									10 37															
Ravensbourne	d									10 39															
Shortlands	d									10 41															
Bromley South 4	d									10 44															
Bickley 4	d									10 47															
St Mary Cray	d									10 51															
Swanley 4	d									10 56															
Eynsford	d									11 00															
Shoreham (Kent)	d									11 04															
Otford 4	d									11 07															
Bat & Ball	d									11 10															
Sevenoaks 4	a	10 48	10 56			11 05			11 12	11 13													11 18	11 26	
Redhill	d															11 11				11 17					
Gatwick Airport 10	d											10 56				11 24		11 11							
Three Bridges 4	d															11 30		11 15							
Balcombe	d																	11 21							
Haywards Heath 3	d											11 08						11 27							
Wivelsfield 4	d																	11 31							
Burgess Hill 4	d																	11 33							
Hassocks 4	d																	11 36							
Preston Park	d																	11 43							
Brighton 10	a											11 24						11 49							

Table 52

Mondays to Fridays

Bedford, Luton, St.Albans and City of London - South London, Gatwick Airport and Brighton

		SN		SE 1	SN	SE 1	FC	FC	FC 1	FC 1	FC	EM ◇1		FC	SN 1	FC 1	FC	SN 1	SN 1	SN	SN	SE 1		SE	SN
Bedford 7	d								09 40	09 48		09 49				09 54									
Flitwick	d								09 50	09 58						10 04									
Harlington	d								09 54							10 08									
Leagrave	d								09 59							10 13									
Luton 10	d								10 04	10 10		10 05		10 14		10 18									
Luton Airport Parkway 7	d								10 06					10 16		10 20									
Harpenden	d								10 12	10 17				10 22		10 26									
St Albans City	d								10 18	10 24				10 29		10 34	10 44								
Radlett	d													10 34			10 49								
Elstree & Borehamwood	d													10 38			10 53								
Mill Hill Broadway	d													10 43			10 58								
Hendon	d													10 46			11 01								
Cricklewood	d													10 50			11 05								
West Hampstead Thameslink ⊖	d													10 54			11 09								
Kentish Town ⊖	d						10 26							11 00			11 14								
St Pancras International 15 ⊖	a							←			←	10 30													
St Pancras International 15 ⊖	a						10 30	10 34	10 39	10 44	10 48			11 04		10 53	11 18								
	d						10 30	10 34	10 40	10 44	10 48			11 04		10 54	11 18								
Farringdon 3 ⊖	d						10 35	10 39	10 44	10 49	10 53			→		10 59	→								
City Thameslink 3	d						10 39	10 43	10 47	10 52	10 57					11 02									
London Blackfriars 3 ⊖	d						10 42	10 46	10 50	10 56	11 00					11 05									
Elephant & Castle ⊖	d						10 46	10 49		11a00	11 03														
Loughborough Jn	d							10 53			11 07														
Herne Hill 4	d							10 57			11 11														
London Bridge 4	a			11 07		11 18			10 56							11 11						11 22		11 14	
	d	11 03		11 09	11 11	11 19			10 57						11 03	11 12		11 08	11 15	11 06	11 20	11 23		11 14	11 22
Tulse Hill 3	d							11 01			11 16														
Streatham 4	d							11 05			11 20														
Mitcham Eastfields	d										11 24														
Mitcham Junction	d										11 27														
Hackbridge	d										11 30														
Carshalton	d										11 33														
Tooting	d							11 10																	
Haydons Road	d							11 13																	
Wimbledon 6 ⊖	d							11 17																	
Wimbledon Chase	d							11 20																	
South Merton	d							11 22																	
Morden South	d							11 24																	
St Helier	d							11 26																	
Sutton Common	d							11 28																	
West Sutton	d							11 31																	
Sutton (Surrey) 4	a							11 35			11 36														
East Croydon	d								11 09						11 21	11 24		11 24	11 30	11 34	11 37				
Denmark Hill 4	d						10 52																		
Peckham Rye 4	d	11 12			11 20		10 55																		
Nunhead 4	d						10 57																		
Crofton Park	d						11 00																		
Catford	d						11 03																		
Bellingham	d						11 05																		
Beckenham Hill	d						11 07																		
Ravensbourne	d						11 09																		
Shortlands	d						11 11																		
Bromley South 4	d						11 14																		
Bickley 4	d						11 17																		
St Mary Cray	d						11 21																		
Swanley 4	d						11 26																		
Eynsford	d						11 30																		
Shoreham (Kent)	d						11 34																		
Otford 4	d						11 37																		
Bat & Ball	d						11 40																		
Sevenoaks 4	a			11 35		11 42	11 43															11 48		11 56	
Redhill	d														11 44				11 52						
Gatwick Airport 10	d								11 26						11 56	11 41									
Three Bridges 4	d														12 01	11 45									
Balcombe	d																								
Haywards Heath 3	d								11 38							11 55									
Wivelsfield 4	d															11 59									
Burgess Hill 4	d															12 01									
Hassocks 4	d															12 04									
Preston Park	d															12 11									
Brighton 10	a								11 54							12 17									

Table 52 — Mondays to Fridays

Bedford, Luton, St.Albans and City of London - South London, Gatwick Airport and Brighton

Station		SN	SE 1	SN	SE 1	FC	FC	FC 1	FC	FC	FC	SN 1	FC 1	FC	SN 1	SN	SN	SE 1	SE	SN	SN	SE 1	SN
Bedford	d							10 10	10 18				10 24										
Flitwick	d							10 20	10 28				10 34										
Harlington	d							10 24					10 38										
Leagrave	d							10 29					10 43										
Luton	d							10 34	10 40		10 44		10 48										
Luton Airport Parkway	d							10 36			10 46		10 50										
Harpenden	d							10 42	10 47		10 52		10 56										
St Albans City	d							10 48	10 54		10 59		11 04	11 14									
Radlett	d										11 04			11 19									
Elstree & Borehamwood	d										11 08			11 23									
Mill Hill Broadway	d										11 13			11 28									
Hendon	d										11 16			11 31									
Cricklewood	d										11 20			11 35									
West Hampstead Thameslink ⊖	d										11 24			11 39									
Kentish Town ⊖	d					10 56					11 30			11 43									
St Pancras International ⊖	a						←			←													
St Pancras International ⊖	a					11 00	11 04	11 09	11 14	11 18	11 34		11 23	11 48									
	d					11 00	11 04	11 10	11 14	11 18	11 34		11 24	11 48									
Farringdon ⊖	d					11 05	11 09	11 14	11 19	11 23	→		11 29	→									
City Thameslink	d					11 09	11 13	11 17	11 22	11 27			11 32										
London Blackfriars ⊖	d					11 12	11 16	11 20	11 26	11 30			11 35										
Elephant & Castle ⊖	d					11 16	11 19		11a30	11 33													
Loughborough Jn	d						11 23			11 37													
Herne Hill	d						11 27			11 41													
London Bridge	a		11 37		11 48			11 26					11 41					11 52	11 44			12 07	
	d	11 33	11 39	11 41	11 49			11 27				11 33	11 42		11 45	11 36	11 50	11 53	11 44	11 52	12 03	12 09	12 11
Tulse Hill	d						11 31			11 46													
Streatham	d						11 35			11 50													
Mitcham Eastfields	d									11 54													
Mitcham Junction	d									11 57													
Hackbridge	d									12 00													
Carshalton	d									12 03													
Tooting	d						11 40																
Haydons Road	d						11 43																
Wimbledon ⊖	d						11 47																
Wimbledon Chase	d						11 50																
South Merton	d						11 52																
Morden South	d						11 54																
St Helier	d						11 56																
Sutton Common	d						11 58																
West Sutton	d						12 01																
Sutton (Surrey)	a						12 05			12 06													
East Croydon	d							11 39				11 51	11 54		12 00	12 04	12 07						
Denmark Hill	d					11 22																	
Peckham Rye	d	11 42		11 50		11 25															12 12		12 20
Nunhead	d					11 27																	
Crofton Park	d					11 30																	
Catford	d					11 33																	
Bellingham	d					11 35																	
Beckenham Hill	d					11 37																	
Ravensbourne	d					11 39																	
Shortlands	d					11 41																	
Bromley South	d					11 44																	
Bickley	d					11 47																	
St Mary Cray	d					11 51																	
Swanley	d					11 56																	
Eynsford	d					12 00																	
Shoreham (Kent)	d					12 04																	
Otford	d					12 07																	
Bat & Ball	d					12 10																	
Sevenoaks	a		12 05		12 12	12 13												12 18	12 26			12 35	
Redhill	d											12 10			12 17								
Gatwick Airport	d							11 56				12 24	12 11										
Three Bridges	d											12 30	12 15										
Balcombe	d												12 21										
Haywards Heath	d							12 08					12 27										
Wivelsfield	d												12 31										
Burgess Hill	d												12 33										
Hassocks	d												12 36										
Preston Park	d												12 43										
Brighton	a							12 24					12 49										

Table 52 — Mondays to Fridays

Bedford, Luton, St.Albans and City of London - South London, Gatwick Airport and Brighton

Station		SE 1	FC	FC	FC 1	FC	EM ◇1	FC	SN 1	SN 1	FC 1	FC	SN 1	SN	SN	SE 1	SE	SN	SN	SE 1	SN	SE 1
Bedford	d				10 40		10 49				10 54											
Flitwick	d				10 50						11 04											
Harlington	d				10 54						11 08											
Leagrave	d				10 59						11 13											
Luton	d				11 04		11 05	11 14			11 18											
Luton Airport Parkway	d				11 06			11 16			11 20											
Harpenden	d				11 12			11 22			11 26											
St Albans City	d				11 18			11 29			11 34	11 44										
Radlett	d							11 34				11 49										
Elstree & Borehamwood	d							11 38				11 53										
Mill Hill Broadway	d							11 43				11 58										
Hendon	d							11 46				12 01										
Cricklewood	d							11 50				12 05										
West Hampstead Thameslink ⊖	d							11 54				12 09										
Kentish Town ⊖	d		11 26					12 00				12 13										
St Pancras International ⊖	a			←		←	11 29															
St Pancras International ⊖	a		11 30	11 34	11 39	11 48		12 04			11 53	12 18										
	d		11 30	11 34	11 40	11 48		12 04			11 54	12 18										
Farringdon ⊖	d		11 35	11 39	11 44	11 53		→			11 59	→										
City Thameslink	d		11 39	11 43	11 47	11 57					12 02											
London Blackfriars ⊖	d		11 42	11 46	11 50	12 00					12 05											
Elephant & Castle ⊖	d		11 46	11 49		12 03																
Loughborough Jn	d			11 53		12 07																
Herne Hill	d			11 57		12 11																
London Bridge	a	12 18			11 56						12 11					12 22	12 14			12 37		12 48
	d	12 19			11 57				12 03	12 08	12 12		12 15	12 06	12 20	12 23	12 14	12 22	12 33	12 39	12 41	12 49
Tulse Hill	d			12 01		12 16																
Streatham	d			12 05		12 20																
Mitcham Eastfields	d					12 24																
Mitcham Junction	d					12 27																
Hackbridge	d					12 30																
Carshalton	d					12 33																
Tooting	d			12 10																		
Haydons Road	d			12 13																		
Wimbledon ⊖	d			12 17																		
Wimbledon Chase	d			12 20																		
South Merton	d			12 22																		
Morden South	d			12 24																		
St Helier	d			12 26																		
Sutton Common	d			12 28																		
West Sutton	d			12 31																		
Sutton (Surrey)	a			12 35		12 36																
East Croydon	d				12 09				12 21	12 23	12 24		12 30	12 34	12 37							
Denmark Hill	d		11 52																			
Peckham Rye	d		11 55																12 42		12 50	
Nunhead	d		11 57																			
Crofton Park	d		12 00																			
Catford	d		12 03																			
Bellingham	d		12 05																			
Beckenham Hill	d		12 07																			
Ravensbourne	d		12 09																			
Shortlands	d		12 11																			
Bromley South	d		12 14																			
Bickley	d		12 17																			
St Mary Cray	d		12 21																			
Swanley	d		12 26																			
Eynsford	d		12 30																			
Shoreham (Kent)	d		12 34																			
Otford	d		12 37																			
Bat & Ball	d		12 40																			
Sevenoaks	a	12 42	12 43													12 48	12 56			13 05		13 12
Redhill	d								12 44				12 52									
Gatwick Airport	d				12 26				12 56		12 41											
Three Bridges	d								13 01		12 45											
Balcombe	d																					
Haywards Heath	d				12 38						12 55											
Wivelsfield	d										12 59											
Burgess Hill	d										13 01											
Hassocks	d										13 04											
Preston Park	d										13 11											
Brighton	a				12 54						13 17											

Table 52

Mondays to Fridays

Bedford, Luton, St.Albans and City of London - South London, Gatwick Airport and Brighton

		FC	FC	FC 1	FC	FC	SN 1	FC 1	FC	SN 1		SN	SN	SE 1	SE	SN	SN	SE 1	SN	SE 1		FC	FC	FC 1	FC
Bedford 7	d			11 10				11 24																11 40	
Flitwick	d			11 20				11 34																11 50	
Harlington	d			11 24				11 38																11 54	
Leagrave	d			11 29				11 43																11 59	
Luton 10	d			11 34		11 44		11 48																12 04	
Luton Airport Parkway 7	d			11 36		11 46		11 50																12 06	
Harpenden	d			11 42		11 52		11 56																12 12	
St Albans City	d			11 48		11 59		12 04	12 14															12 18	
Radlett	d					12 04			12 19																
Elstree & Borehamwood	d					12 08			12 23																
Mill Hill Broadway	d					12 13			12 28																
Hendon	d					12 16			12 31																
Cricklewood	d					12 20			12 35																
West Hampstead Thameslink ⊖	d					12 24			12 39																
Kentish Town ⊖	d	11 56				12 30			12 43													12 26			
St Pancras International 15 ⊖	a		←		←																		←		←
St Pancras International 15 ⊖	a	12 00	12 04	12 09	12 18	12 34		12 23	12 48													12 30	12 34	12 39	12 48
	d	12 00	12 04	12 10	12 18	12 34		12 24	12 48													12 30	12 34	12 40	12 48
Farringdon 3 ⊖	d	12 05	12 09	12 14	12 23	→		12 29	→													12 35	12 39	12 44	12 53
City Thameslink 3	d	12 09	12 13	12 17	12 27			12 32														12 39	12 43	12 47	12 57
London Blackfriars 3 ⊖	d	12 12	12 16	12 20	12 30			12 35														12 42	12 46	12 50	13 00
Elephant & Castle ⊖	d	12 16	12 19		12 33																	12 46	12 49		13 03
Loughborough Jn	d		12 23		12 37																		12 53		13 07
Herne Hill 4	d		12 27		12 41																		12 57		13 11
London Bridge 4	a			12 26				12 41						12 52	12 44			13 07		13 18				12 56	
	d			12 27			12 33	12 42		12 45		12 36	12 50	12 53	12 44	12 52	13 03	13 09	13 11	13 19				12 57	
Tulse Hill 3	d		12 31		12 46																		13 01		13 16
Streatham 4	d		12 35		12 50																		13 05		13 20
Mitcham Eastfields	d				12 54																				13 24
Mitcham Junction	d				12 57																				13 27
Hackbridge	d				13 00																				13 30
Carshalton	d				13 03																				13 33
Tooting	d		12 40																				13 10		
Haydons Road	d		12 43																				13 13		
Wimbledon 6 ⊖	d		12 47																				13 17		
Wimbledon Chase	d		12 50																				13 20		
South Merton	d		12 52																				13 22		
Morden South	d		12 54																				13 24		
St Helier	d		12 56																				13 26		
Sutton Common	d		12 58																				13 28		
West Sutton	d		13 01																				13 31		
Sutton (Surrey) 4	a		13 05		13 06																		13 35		13 36
East Croydon	d			12 39			12 51	12 54		13 00		13 04	13 07											13 09	
Denmark Hill 4	d	12 22																				12 52			
Peckham Rye 4	d	12 25															13 12		13 20			12 55			
Nunhead 4	d	12 27																				12 57			
Crofton Park	d	12 30																				13 00			
Catford	d	12 33																				13 03			
Bellingham	d	12 35																				13 05			
Beckenham Hill	d	12 37																				13 07			
Ravensbourne	d	12 39																				13 09			
Shortlands	d	12 41																				13 11			
Bromley South 4	d	12 44																				13 14			
Bickley 4	d	12 47																				13 17			
St Mary Cray	d	12 51																				13 21			
Swanley 4	d	12 56																				13 26			
Eynsford	d	13 00																				13 30			
Shoreham (Kent)	d	13 04																				13 34			
Otford 4	d	13 07																				13 37			
Bat & Ball	d	13 10																				13 40			
Sevenoaks 4	a	13 13												13 18	13 26			13 35		13 42		13 43			
Redhill	d						13 10			13 17															
Gatwick Airport 10	d			12 56			13 24	13 11																13 26	
Three Bridges 4	d						13 30	13 15																	
Balcombe	d							13 21																	
Haywards Heath 3	d			13 08				13 27																13 38	
Wivelsfield 4	d							13 31																	
Burgess Hill 4	d							13 33																	
Hassocks 4	d							13 36																	
Preston Park	d							13 43																	
Brighton 10	a			13 24				13 49																13 54	

Table 52

Mondays to Fridays

Bedford, Luton, St.Albans and City of London - South London, Gatwick Airport and Brighton

		EM ◇1	FC	SN 1	SN 1	FC 1		FC	SN 1	SN	SN	SE 1	SE	SN	SN	SE 1		SN	SE 1	FC	FC	FC 1	FC	EM ◇1	FC
Bedford 7	d	11 49				11 54																12 10		12 18	
Flitwick	d					12 04																12 20			
Harlington	d					12 08																12 24			
Leagrave	d					12 13																12 29			
Luton 10	d	12 05	12 14			12 18																12 34			12 44
Luton Airport Parkway 7	d		12 16			12 20																12 36		12 34	12 46
Harpenden	d		12 22			12 26																12 42			12 52
St Albans City	d		12 29			12 34		12 44														12 48			12 59
Radlett	d		12 34					12 49																	13 04
Elstree & Borehamwood	d		12 38					12 53																	13 08
Mill Hill Broadway	d		12 43					12 58																	13 13
Hendon	d		12 46					13 01																	13 16
Cricklewood	d		12 50					13 05																	13 20
West Hampstead Thameslink ⊖	d		12 54					13 09																	13 24
Kentish Town ⊖	d		13 00					13 13												12 56					13 30
St Pancras International 15 ⊖	a	12 29																			←		←	13 01	
St Pancras International 15 ⊖	a		13 04			12 53		13 18												13 00	13 04	13 09	13 18		13 34
	d		13 04			12 54		13 18												13 00	13 04	13 10	13 18		13 34
Farringdon 3 ⊖	d		→			12 59		→												13 05	13 09	13 14	13 23		→
City Thameslink 3	d					13 02														13 09	13 13	13 17	13 27		
London Blackfriars 3 ⊖	d					13 05														13 12	13 16	13 20	13 30		
Elephant & Castle ⊖	d																			13 16	13 19		13 33		
Loughborough Jn	d																				13 23		13 37		
Herne Hill 4	d																				13 27		13 41		
London Bridge 4	a					13 11						13 22	13 14			13 37			13 48			13 26			
	d			13 03	13 08	13 12			13 15	13 06	13 20	13 23	13 14	13 22	13 33	13 39		13 41	13 49			13 27			
Tulse Hill 3	d																				13 31		13 46		
Streatham 4	d																				13 35		13 50		
Mitcham Eastfields	d																						13 54		
Mitcham Junction	d																						13 57		
Hackbridge	d																						14 00		
Carshalton	d																						14 03		
Tooting	d																				13 40				
Haydons Road	d																				13 43				
Wimbledon 6 ⊖	d																				13 47				
Wimbledon Chase	d																				13 50				
South Merton	d																				13 52				
Morden South	d																				13 54				
St Helier	d																				13 56				
Sutton Common	d																				13 58				
West Sutton	d																				14 01				
Sutton (Surrey) 4	a																				14 05		14 06		
East Croydon	d			13 21	13 23	13 24			13 30	13 34	13 37											13 39			
Denmark Hill 4	d																			13 22					
Peckham Rye 4	d														13 42			13 50		13 25					
Nunhead 4	d																			13 27					
Crofton Park	d																			13 30					
Catford	d																			13 33					
Bellingham	d																			13 35					
Beckenham Hill	d																			13 37					
Ravensbourne	d																			13 39					
Shortlands	d																			13 41					
Bromley South 4	d																			13 44					
Bickley 4	d																			13 47					
St Mary Cray	d																			13 51					
Swanley 4	d																			13 56					
Eynsford	d																			14 00					
Shoreham (Kent)	d																			14 04					
Otford 4	d																			14 07					
Bat & Ball	d																			14 10					
Sevenoaks 4	a											13 48	13 56			14 05			14 12	14 13					
Redhill	d			13 44					13 52																
Gatwick Airport 10	d			13 56		13 41																13 56			
Three Bridges 4	d			14 01		13 45																			
Balcombe	d																								
Haywards Heath 3	d					13 55																14 08			
Wivelsfield 4	d					13 59																			
Burgess Hill 4	d					14 01																			
Hassocks 4	d					14 04																			
Preston Park	d					14 11																			
Brighton 10	a					14 17																14 24			

Bedford, Luton, St.Albans and City of London - South London, Gatwick Airport and Brighton

		SN ■	FC ■	FC	SN ■	SN	SN	SE ■ ✕	SE	SN	SN	SE ■	SN	SE ■ ✕	FC	FC	FC ■	FC	EM ◇■	FC	SN ■	SN ■
Bedford ■	d		12 24														12 40		12 49			
Flitwick	d		12 34														12 50					
Harlington	d		12 38														12 54					
Leagrave	d		12 43														12 59					
Luton ■	d		12 48														13 04		13 05	13 14		
Luton Airport Parkway ■	d		12 50														13 06			13 16		
Harpenden	d		12 56														13 12			13 22		
St Albans City	d		13 04	13 14													13 18			13 29		
Radlett	d			13 19																13 34		
Elstree & Borehamwood	d			13 23																13 38		
Mill Hill Broadway	d			13 28																13 43		
Hendon	d			13 31																13 46		
Cricklewood	d			13 35																13 50		
West Hampstead Thameslink ⊖	d			13 39																13 54		
Kentish Town ⊖	d			13 43											13 26					14 00		
St Pancras International ■ ⊖	a															←		←	13 29			
St Pancras International ■ ⊖	a		13 23	13 48											13 30	13 34	13 39	13 48		14 04		
	d		13 24	13 48											13 30	13 34	13 40	13 48		14 04		
Farringdon ■ ⊖	d		13 29	→											13 35	13 39	13 44	13 53		→		
City Thameslink ■	d		13 32												13 39	13 43	13 47	13 57				
London Blackfriars ■ ⊖	d		13 35												13 42	13 46	13 50	14 00				
Elephant & Castle ⊖	d														13 46	13 49		14 03				
Loughborough Jn	d															13 53		14 07				
Herne Hill ■	d															13 57		14 11				
London Bridge ■	a		13 41					13 52	13 44			14 07		14 18			13 56					
	d	13 33	13 42		13 45	13 36	13 50	13 53	13 44	13 52	14 03	14 09	14 11	14 19			13 57				14 03	14 08
Tulse Hill ■	d															14 01		14 16				
Streatham ■	d															14 05		14 20				
Mitcham Eastfields	d																	14 24				
Mitcham Junction	d																	14 27				
Hackbridge	d																	14 30				
Carshalton	d																	14 33				
Tooting	d															14 10						
Haydons Road	d															14 13						
Wimbledon ■ ⊖	d															14 17						
Wimbledon Chase	d															14 20						
South Merton	d															14 22						
Morden South	d															14 24						
St Helier	d															14 26						
Sutton Common	d															14 28						
West Sutton	d															14 31						
Sutton (Surrey) ■	a															14 35		14 36				
East Croydon	d	13 51	13 54		14 00	14 04	14 07										14 09				14 21	14 23
Denmark Hill ■	d														13 52							
Peckham Rye ■	d										14 12		14 20		13 55							
Nunhead ■	d														13 57							
Crofton Park	d														14 00							
Catford	d														14 03							
Bellingham	d														14 05							
Beckenham Hill	d														14 07							
Ravensbourne	d														14 09							
Shortlands	d														14 11							
Bromley South ■	d														14 14							
Bickley ■	d														14 17							
St Mary Cray	d														14 21							
Swanley ■	d														14 26							
Eynsford	d														14 30							
Shoreham (Kent)	d														14 34							
Otford ■	d														14 37							
Bat & Ball	d														14 40							
Sevenoaks ■	a							14 18	14 26			14 35		14 42	14 43							
Redhill	d	14 10			14 17																14 44	
Gatwick Airport ■	d	14 24	14 11														14 26				14 56	
Three Bridges ■	d	14 30	14 15																		15 01	
Balcombe	d		14 21																			
Haywards Heath ■	d		14 27														14 38					
Wivelsfield ■	d		14 31																			
Burgess Hill ■	d		14 33																			
Hassocks ■	d		14 36																			
Preston Park	d		14 43																			
Brighton ■	a		14 49														14 54					

Bedford, Luton, St.Albans and City of London - South London, Gatwick Airport and Brighton

		FC ■	FC	SN ■	SN	SN	SE ■ ✕	SE	SN	SN	SE ■	SN	SE ■ ✕	FC	FC	FC ■	FC	FC	SN ■	FC ■	FC	SN ■	SN
Bedford ■	d	12 54														13 10				13 24			
Flitwick	d	13 04														13 20				13 34			
Harlington	d	13 08														13 24				13 38			
Leagrave	d	13 13														13 29				13 43			
Luton ■	d	13 18														13 34		13 44		13 48			
Luton Airport Parkway ■	d	13 20														13 36		13 46		13 50			
Harpenden	d	13 26														13 42		13 52		13 56			
St Albans City	d	13 34	13 44													13 48		13 59		14 04	14 14		
Radlett	d		13 49															14 04			14 19		
Elstree & Borehamwood	d		13 53															14 08			14 23		
Mill Hill Broadway	d		13 58															14 13			14 28		
Hendon	d		14 01															14 16			14 31		
Cricklewood	d		14 05															14 20			14 35		
West Hampstead Thameslink ⊖	d		14 09															14 24			14 39		
Kentish Town ⊖	d		14 13											13 56				14 30			14 43		
St Pancras International ■ ⊖	a														←		←						
St Pancras International ■ ⊖	a	13 53	14 18											14 00	14 04	14 09	14 18	14 34		14 23	14 48		
	d	13 54	14 18											14 00	14 04	14 10	14 18	14 34		14 24	14 48		
Farringdon ■ ⊖	d	13 59	→											14 05	14 09	14 14	14 23	→		14 29	→		
City Thameslink ■	d	14 02												14 09	14 13	14 17	14 27			14 32			
London Blackfriars ■ ⊖	d	14 05												14 12	14 16	14 20	14 30			14 35			
Elephant & Castle ⊖	d													14 16	14 19		14 33						
Loughborough Jn	d														14 23		14 37						
Herne Hill ■	d														14 27		14 41						
London Bridge ■	a	14 11					14 22	14 14			14 37		14 48			14 26				14 41			
	d	14 12		14 15	14 06	14 20	14 23	14 14	14 22	14 33	14 39	14 41	14 49			14 27			14 33	14 42		14 45	14 36
Tulse Hill ■	d														14 31		14 46						
Streatham ■	d														14 35		14 50						
Mitcham Eastfields	d																14 54						
Mitcham Junction	d																14 57						
Hackbridge	d																15 00						
Carshalton	d																15 03						
Tooting	d														14 40								
Haydons Road	d														14 43								
Wimbledon ■ ⊖	d														14 47								
Wimbledon Chase	d														14 50								
South Merton	d														14 52								
Morden South	d														14 54								
St Helier	d														14 56								
Sutton Common	d														14 58								
West Sutton	d														15 01								
Sutton (Surrey) ■	a														15 05		15 06						
East Croydon	d	14 24		14 30	14 34	14 37										14 39			14 51	14 54		15 00	15 04
Denmark Hill ■	d													14 22									
Peckham Rye ■	d									14 42		14 50		14 25									
Nunhead ■	d													14 27									
Crofton Park	d													14 30									
Catford	d													14 33									
Bellingham	d													14 35									
Beckenham Hill	d													14 37									
Ravensbourne	d													14 39									
Shortlands	d													14 41									
Bromley South ■	d													14 44									
Bickley ■	d													14 47									
St Mary Cray	d													14 51									
Swanley ■	d													14 56									
Eynsford	d													15 00									
Shoreham (Kent)	d													15 04									
Otford ■	d													15 07									
Bat & Ball	d													15 10									
Sevenoaks ■	a						14 48	14 56			15 05		15 12	15 13									
Redhill	d			14 52															15 10			15 17	
Gatwick Airport ■	d	14 41														14 56			15 24	15 11			
Three Bridges ■	d	14 45																	15 30	15 15			
Balcombe	d																			15 21			
Haywards Heath ■	d	14 55														15 08				15 27			
Wivelsfield ■	d	14 59																		15 31			
Burgess Hill ■	d	15 01																		15 33			
Hassocks ■	d	15 04																		15 36			
Preston Park	d	15 11																		15 43			
Brighton ■	a	15 17														15 24				15 49			

Table 52

Mondays to Fridays

Bedford, Luton, St.Albans and City of London - South London, Gatwick Airport and Brighton

		SN	SE	SE	SN	SN	SE	SN	SE	FC	FC	FC	FC	EM	FC	SN	SN	FC	FC	SN	SN	SN
			1				1		1			1		◇1		1	1	1		1		
Bedford 7	d											13 40		13 49				13 54				
Flitwick	d											13 50						14 04				
Harlington	d											13 54						14 08				
Leagrave	d											13 59						14 13				
Luton 10	d											14 04		14 05	14 14			14 18				
Luton Airport Parkway 7	d											14 06			14 16			14 20				
Harpenden	d											14 12			14 22			14 26				
St Albans City	d											14 18			14 29			14 34	14 44			
Radlett	d														14 34				14 49			
Elstree & Borehamwood	d														14 38				14 53			
Mill Hill Broadway	d														14 43				14 58			
Hendon	d														14 46				15 01			
Cricklewood	d														14 50				15 05			
West Hampstead Thameslink ⊖	d														14 54				15 09			
Kentish Town ⊖	d									14 26					15 00				15 13			
St Pancras International 15 ⊖	a										←		←	14 29								
St Pancras International 15 ⊖	a									14 30	14 34	14 39	14 48		15 04			14 53	15 18			
	d									14 30	14 34	14 40	14 48		15 04			14 54	15 18			
Farringdon 3 ⊖	d									14 35	14 39	14 44	14 53		→			14 59	→			
City Thameslink 3	d									14 39	14 43	14 47	14 57					15 02				
London Blackfriars 3 ⊖	d									14 42	14 46	14 50	15 00					15 05				
Elephant & Castle ⊖	d									14 46	14 49		15 03									
Loughborough Jn	d										14 53		15 07									
Herne Hill 4	d										14 57		15 11									
London Bridge 4	a		14 52	14 44			15 07		15 18			14 56						15 11				
	d	14 50	14 53	14 44	14 52	15 03	15 09	15 11	15 19			14 57				15 03	15 08	15 12		15 15	15 06	15 20
Tulse Hill 3	d										15 01		15 16									
Streatham 4	d										15 05		15 20									
Mitcham Eastfields	d												15 24									
Mitcham Junction	d												15 27									
Hackbridge	d												15 30									
Carshalton	d												15 33									
Tooting	d										15 10											
Haydons Road	d										15 13											
Wimbledon 6 ⊖	d										15 17											
Wimbledon Chase	d										15 20											
South Merton	d										15 22											
Morden South	d										15 24											
St Helier	d										15 26											
Sutton Common	d										15 28											
West Sutton	d										15 31											
Sutton (Surrey) 4	a										15 35		15 36									
East Croydon	d	15 07										15 09				15 21	15 23	15 24		15 30	15 34	15 37
Denmark Hill 4	d									14 52												
Peckham Rye 4	d					15 12		15 20		14 55												
Nunhead 4	d									14 57												
Crofton Park	d									15 00												
Catford	d									15 03												
Bellingham	d									15 05												
Beckenham Hill	d									15 07												
Ravensbourne	d									15 09												
Shortlands	d									15 11												
Bromley South 4	d									15 14												
Bickley 4	d									15 17												
St Mary Cray	d									15 21												
Swanley 4	d									15 26												
Eynsford	d									15 30												
Shoreham (Kent)	d									15 34												
Otford 4	d									15 37												
Bat & Ball	d									15 40												
Sevenoaks 4	a		15 18	15 26			15 35		15 42	15 43												
Redhill	d															15 44				15 52		
Gatwick Airport 10	d											15 26				15 57		15 41				
Three Bridges 4	d															16 02		15 45				
Balcombe	d																					
Haywards Heath 3	d											15 38						15 55				
Wivelsfield 4	d																	15 59				
Burgess Hill 4	d																	16 01				
Hassocks 4	d																	16 04				
Preston Park	d																	16 11				
Brighton 10	a											15 54						16 17				

Table 52

Mondays to Fridays

Bedford, Luton, St.Albans and City of London - South London, Gatwick Airport and Brighton

		SE	SE	SN	SN	SE	SN	SE	FC	FC	FC	FC	EM	FC	SN	SN	FC	FC	SN	SN	SN	SE	SE
		1				1		1			1		◇1		1	1	1		1			1	
Bedford 7	d										14 10		14 18				14 24						
Flitwick	d										14 20						14 34						
Harlington	d										14 24						14 38						
Leagrave	d										14 29						14 43						
Luton 10	d										14 34			14 44			14 48						
Luton Airport Parkway 7	d										14 36		14 34	14 46			14 50						
Harpenden	d										14 42			14 52			14 56						
St Albans City	d										14 48			14 59			15 04	15 14					
Radlett	d													15 04				15 19					
Elstree & Borehamwood	d													15 08				15 23					
Mill Hill Broadway	d													15 13				15 28					
Hendon	d													15 16				15 31					
Cricklewood	d													15 20				15 35					
West Hampstead Thameslink ⊖	d													15 24				15 39					
Kentish Town ⊖	d								14 56					15 30				15 43					
St Pancras International 15 ⊖	a									←		←	15 01										
St Pancras International 15 ⊖	a								15 00	15 04	15 09	15 18		15 34			15 23	15 48					
	d								15 00	15 04	15 10	15 18		15 34			15 24	15 48					
Farringdon 3 ⊖	d								15 05	15 09	15 14	15 23		→			15 29	→					
City Thameslink 3	d								15 09	15 13	15 17	15 27					15 32						
London Blackfriars 3 ⊖	d								15 12	15 16	15 20	15 30					15 35						
Elephant & Castle ⊖	d								15 16	15 19		15 33											
Loughborough Jn	d									15 23		15 37											
Herne Hill 4	d									15 27		15 41											
London Bridge 4	a	15 22	15 14			15 37		15 48			15 26						15 41					15 52	15 44
	d	15 23	15 14	15 22	15 33	15 39	15 41	15 49			15 27				15 33	15 38	15 42		15 45	15 36	15 50	15 53	15 44
Tulse Hill 3	d									15 31		15 46											
Streatham 4	d									15 35		15 50											
Mitcham Eastfields	d											15 54											
Mitcham Junction	d											15 57											
Hackbridge	d											16 00											
Carshalton	d											16 03											
Tooting	d									15 40													
Haydons Road	d									15 43													
Wimbledon 6 ⊖	d									15 47													
Wimbledon Chase	d									15 50													
South Merton	d									15 52													
Morden South	d									15 54													
St Helier	d									15 56													
Sutton Common	d									15 58													
West Sutton	d									16 01													
Sutton (Surrey) 4	a									16 05		16 06											
East Croydon	d										15 39				15 51	15 53	15 54		16 00	16 04	16 07		
Denmark Hill 4	d								15 22														
Peckham Rye 4	d				15 42		15 50		15 25														
Nunhead 4	d								15 27														
Crofton Park	d								15 30														
Catford	d								15 33														
Bellingham	d								15 35														
Beckenham Hill	d								15 37														
Ravensbourne	d								15 39														
Shortlands	d								15 41														
Bromley South 4	d								15 44														
Bickley 4	d								15 47														
St Mary Cray	d								15 51														
Swanley 4	d								15 56														
Eynsford	d								16 00														
Shoreham (Kent)	d								16 04														
Otford 4	d								16 07														
Bat & Ball	d								16 10														
Sevenoaks 4	a	15 48	15 56			16 05		16 12	16 13													16 18	16 26
Redhill	d														16 10				16 20				
Gatwick Airport 10	d										15 56				16 24		16 11						
Three Bridges 4	d										16 01				16 30		16 15						
Balcombe	d																16 21						
Haywards Heath 3	d										16 10						16 27						
Wivelsfield 4	d																16 31						
Burgess Hill 4	d																16 33						
Hassocks 4	d																16 36						
Preston Park	d																16 43						
Brighton 10	a										16 24						16 49						

Bedford, Luton, St.Albans and City of London - South London, Gatwick Airport and Brighton

		SN	SN	SE ■	SN	SE ■	FC	FC	FC ■	FC	EM ◇■	FC	SN ■	SN ■	FC ■	FC	SN ■	SN	SN	SE ■	SE	SN	SN
Bedford	d								14 40		14 49				14 54								
Flitwick	d								14 50						15 04								
Harlington	d								14 54						15 08								
Leagrave	d								14 59						15 13								
Luton	d								15 04		15 05	15 14			15 18								
Luton Airport Parkway	d								15 06			15 16			15 20								
Harpenden	d								15 12			15 22			15 26								
St Albans City	d								15 18			15 29			15 34	15 44							
Radlett	d											15 34				15 49							
Elstree & Borehamwood	d											15 38				15 53							
Mill Hill Broadway	d											15 43				15 58							
Hendon	d											15 46				16 01							
Cricklewood	d											15 50				16 05							
West Hampstead Thameslink ⊖	d											15 54				16 09							
Kentish Town ⊖	d						15 26					16 00				16 13							
St Pancras International ⊖	a							←		←	15 29												
St Pancras International ⊖	a						15 30	15 34	15 39	15 48		16 04			15 53	16 18							
	d						15 30	15 34	15 40	15 48		16 04			15 54	16 18							
Farringdon ⊖	d						15 35	15 39	15 44	15 53		→			15 59	→							
City Thameslink	d						15 39	15 43	15 47	15 57					16 02								
London Blackfriars ⊖	d						15 42	15 46	15 50	16 00					16 05								
Elephant & Castle ⊖	d						15 46	15 49		16 03													
Loughborough Jn	d							15 53		16 07													
Herne Hill	d							15 57		16 11													
London Bridge	a			16 07		16 18			15 56						16 11					16 22	16 13		
	d	15 52	16 03	16 09	16 11	16 19			15 57				16 03	16 08	16 12		16 15	16 06	16 20	16 23	16 14	16 22	16 33
Tulse Hill	d							16 01		16 16													
Streatham	d							16 05		16 20													
Mitcham Eastfields	d									16 24													
Mitcham Junction	d									16 27													
Hackbridge	d									16 30													
Carshalton	d									16 33													
Tooting	d							16 10															
Haydons Road	d							16 13															
Wimbledon ⊖	d							16 17															
Wimbledon Chase	d							16 20															
South Merton	d							16 22															
Morden South	d							16 24															
St Helier	d							16 26															
Sutton Common	d							16 28															
West Sutton	d							16 31															
Sutton (Surrey)	a							16 35		16 36													
East Croydon	d								16 09				16 21	16 23	16 24		16 30	16 34	16 37				
Denmark Hill	d						15 52																
Peckham Rye	d		16 12		16 20		15 55																16 42
Nunhead	d						15 57																
Crofton Park	d						16 00																
Catford	d						16 03																
Bellingham	d						16 05																
Beckenham Hill	d						16 07																
Ravensbourne	d						16 09																
Shortlands	d						16 11																
Bromley South	d						16 14																
Bickley	d						16 17																
St Mary Cray	d						16 21																
Swanley	d						16 26																
Eynsford	d						16 30																
Shoreham (Kent)	d						16 34																
Otford	d						16 37																
Bat & Ball	d						16 40																
Sevenoaks	a			16 35		16 42	16 43													16 46	16 57		
Redhill	d												16 43				16 53						
Gatwick Airport	d								16 26				16 56		16 41								
Three Bridges	d								16 31				17 02		16 46								
Balcombe	d																						
Haywards Heath	d								16 40						16 55								
Wivelsfield	d														16 59								
Burgess Hill	d														17 01								
Hassocks	d														17 04								
Preston Park	d														17 11								
Brighton	a								16 54						17 17								

Table 52 Mondays to Fridays

Bedford, Luton, St.Albans and City of London - South London, Gatwick Airport and Brighton

		SE ■	SN	SE ■	SE ■	FC	FC	FC ■	EM ◇■	FC	FC	FC	SN ■	SN ■	FC ■	FC	SE	SN	SN	SN ■	SN	SN ■
Bedford	d							15 10	15 18						15 24							
Flitwick	d							15 20							15 34							
Harlington	d							15 24							15 38							
Leagrave	d							15 29							15 43							
Luton	d							15 34		15 44					15 48							
Luton Airport Parkway	d							15 36	15 34	15 46					15 50							
Harpenden	d							15 42		15 52					15 56							
St Albans City	d							15 48		15 59					16 04	16 14						
Radlett	d									16 04						16 19						
Elstree & Borehamwood	d									16 08						16 23						
Mill Hill Broadway	d									16 13						16 28						
Hendon	d									16 16						16 31						
Cricklewood	d									16 20						16 35						
West Hampstead Thameslink ⊖	d									16 24						16 40						
Kentish Town ⊖	d					15 56				16 30	16 09					16 44						
St Pancras International ⊖	a						←		16 01			←										
St Pancras International ⊖	a					16 00	16 04	16 09		16 34	16 13	16 18			16 24	16 50						
	d					16 00	16 04	16 10		16 34	16 14	16 18			16 24	16 52						
Farringdon ⊖	d					16 05	16 09	16 14		→	16 19	16 23			16 29	→						
City Thameslink	d					16 09	16 13	16 17			16 23	16 27			16 33							
London Blackfriars ⊖	d					16 12	16 16	16 20			16 26	16 30			16 36							
Elephant & Castle ⊖	d					16 16	16 19				16 30	16 33										
Loughborough Jn	d						16 23					16 37										
Herne Hill	d						16 27					16 41										
London Bridge	a	16 35		16 44	16 48			16 26							16 42		16 39					
	d	16 36	16 41	16 45	16 49			16 27					16 33	16 38	16 43		16 40	16 48	16 52	16 57	16 58	16 59
Tulse Hill	d						16 32					16 46										
Streatham	d						16 36					16 50										
Mitcham Eastfields	d											16 56										
Mitcham Junction	d											16 59										
Hackbridge	d											17 02										
Carshalton	d											17 05										
Tooting	d						16 40															
Haydons Road	d						16 43															
Wimbledon ⊖	d						16 47															
Wimbledon Chase	d						16 50															
South Merton	d						16 52															
Morden South	d						16 54															
St Helier	d						16 56															
Sutton Common	d						16 58															
West Sutton	d						17 01															
Sutton (Surrey)	a						17 05					17 08										
East Croydon	d							16 40					16 49	16 53	17 00			17 06		17 10		17 15
Denmark Hill	d					16 22					16 39											
Peckham Rye	d		16 50			16 25					16 42										17 07	
Nunhead	d					16 27					16 44											
Crofton Park	d					16 30					16 47											
Catford	d					16 33					16 50											
Bellingham	d					16 35					16 52											
Beckenham Hill	d					16 37					16 54											
Ravensbourne	d					16 39					16 56											
Shortlands	d					16 41					16 58											
Bromley South	d					16 44					17 01											
Bickley	d					16 47					17 04											
St Mary Cray	d					16 51																
Swanley	d					16 56																
Eynsford	d					17 00																
Shoreham (Kent)	d					17 04																
Otford	d					17 07																
Bat & Ball	d					17 10																
Sevenoaks	a	17 02		17 09	17 13	17 14											17 22					
Redhill	d												17 08									17 37
Gatwick Airport	d							16 56					17 21		17 16							17 50
Three Bridges	d							17 01					17 26		17 21					17 29		17 55
Balcombe	d														17 27							
Haywards Heath	d							17 10							17 33					17 39		
Wivelsfield	d														17 37							
Burgess Hill	d							17 16							17 40					17 46		
Hassocks	d														17 44					17 49		
Preston Park	d														17 51					17 56		
Brighton	a							17 27							17 56							

Table 52

Bedford, Luton, St.Albans and City of London - South London, Gatwick Airport and Brighton

Station		SE ■	SE ■	SE	FC	FC	FC ■	EM ◇■	SN ■	FC ■	FC	FC	SN	SN	SN ■	SN	SN	SN ■	SN ■	SE ■	SN	SN ■	SE ■
Bedford	d						15 40	15 49		15 52													
Flitwick	d						15 50			16 02													
Harlington	d						15 54																
Leagrave	d						15 59																
Luton	d						16 04	16 05		16 14		16 16											
Luton Airport Parkway	d						16 06			16 17		16 18											
Harpenden	d						16 12					16 24											
St Albans City	d						16 18			16 24		16 30											
Radlett	d											16 35											
Elstree & Borehamwood	d											16 39											
Mill Hill Broadway	d											16 44											
Hendon	d											16 47											
Cricklewood	d											16 51											
West Hampstead Thameslink ⊖	d											16 54											
Kentish Town ⊖	d				16 24							16 58											
St Pancras International ⊖	a					←		16 29			←												
St Pancras International ⊖	a				16 28	16 34	16 40			16 44	16 50	17 02											
	d				16 28	16 34	16 40			16 46	16 52	17 02											
Farringdon ⊖	d				16 33	16 39	16 45			16 51	16 57	→											
City Thameslink	d				16 37	16 43	16 49			16 55	17 01												
London Blackfriars ⊖	d				16 42	16 46	16 52			17 00	17 04												
Elephant & Castle ⊖	d				16 46	16 49	16 56			17 04	17 08												
Loughborough Jn	d					16 53	17 00				17 12												
Herne Hill	d					16 57	17 06				17 16												
London Bridge	a	17 05	17 08	16 59																17 27			17 30
	d	17 06	17 09	17 00					17 09				17 06	17 11	17 15	17 17	17 21	17 23		17 28	17 28	17 29	17 31
Tulse Hill	d					17 02					17 20		17 24										
Streatham	d					17 06					17 24		17 28										
Mitcham Eastfields	d										17 28		17 32										
Mitcham Junction	d										17 31		17 35										
Hackbridge	d										17 34		17 38										
Carshalton	d										17 37		17 41										
Tooting	d					17 10																	
Haydons Road	d					17 13																	
Wimbledon ⊖	d					17 19																	
Wimbledon Chase	d					17 22																	
South Merton	d					17 24																	
Morden South	d					17 26																	
St Helier	d					17 28																	
Sutton Common	d					17 30																	
West Sutton	d					17 33																	
Sutton (Surrey)	a					17 39					17 40		17 44										
East Croydon	d								17 23	17 26					17 30	17 35		17 36				17 45	
Denmark Hill	d				16 52																		
Peckham Rye	d				16 55									17 20							17 37		
Nunhead	d				16 57																		
Crofton Park	d				17 00																		
Catford	d				17 03																		
Bellingham	d				17 05																		
Beckenham Hill	d				17 07																		
Ravensbourne	d				17 09																		
Shortlands	d				17 11																		
Bromley South	d				17 14																		
Bickley	d				17 17																		
St Mary Cray	d				17 21																		
Swanley	d				17 30																		
Eynsford	d				17 34																		
Shoreham (Kent)	d				17 38																		
Otford	d				17 41																		
Bat & Ball	d				17 44																		
Sevenoaks	a	17 31	17 37	17 43	17 48															17 53			17 59
Redhill	d																					18 07	
Gatwick Airport	d									17 41													
Three Bridges	d									17 46								17 56					
Balcombe	d									17 52													
Haywards Heath	d									17 58								18 05	17 26				
Wivelsfield	d																	18 09	17 30				
Burgess Hill	d									18 03									17 32				
Hassocks	d									18 07									17 35				
Preston Park	d									18 15									17 42				
Brighton	a									18 20									17 49				

Table 52

Bedford, Luton, St.Albans and City of London - South London, Gatwick Airport and Brighton

Station		SE	SN	EM ◇■	SE ■	SE ■	FC	FC	FC	FC ■	EM ◇■	FC ■	FC	FC	SN	SN ■	SE	SN ■	SN ■	SN	SN	SN
Bedford	d						15 56			16 10	16 18	16 22										
Flitwick	d						16 06			16 20		16 32										
Harlington	d						16 10			16 24												
Leagrave	d						16 15			16 29												
Luton	d			17 50			16 20			16 34		16 42		16 46								
Luton Airport Parkway	d						16 22			16 36	16 34	16 45		16 48								
Harpenden	d						16 28			16 42				16 54								
St Albans City	d						16 34		16 44	16 48		16 54		17 00								
Radlett	d								16 49					17 05								
Elstree & Borehamwood	d								16 53					17 09								
Mill Hill Broadway	d								16 58					17 14								
Hendon	d								17 01					17 17								
Cricklewood	d								17 05					17 21								
West Hampstead Thameslink ⊖	d						16 48		17 10					17 24								
Kentish Town ⊖	d								17 14					17 28								
St Pancras International ⊖	a			18 19				←			17 00		←									
St Pancras International ⊖	a						16 58	17 02	17 18	17 10		17 14	17 18	17 32								
	d						16 58	17 02	17 18	17 10		17 14	17 18	17 32								
Farringdon ⊖	d						17 03	17 07	→	17 15		17 19	17 23	→								
City Thameslink	d						17 07	17 11		17 19		17 23	17 27									
London Blackfriars ⊖	d						17 10	17 14		17 22		17 26	17 30									
Elephant & Castle ⊖	d						17 14	17 18				17 30	17 34									
Loughborough Jn	d							17 22					17 38									
Herne Hill	d							17 26				17 36	17 44									
London Bridge	a	17 22			17 48	17 52											17 44					
	d	17 23	17 41		17 49	17 53									17 37	17 42	17 45	17 44	17 47	17 49	17 53	17 58
Tulse Hill	d							17 31					17 48		17 55							
Streatham	d							17 36					17 52		17 58							
Mitcham Eastfields	d												17 56		18 02							
Mitcham Junction	d												17 59		18 05							
Hackbridge	d												18 02		18 09							
Carshalton	d												18 05		18 11							
Tooting	d							17 40														
Haydons Road	d							17 43														
Wimbledon ⊖	d							17 47														
Wimbledon Chase	d							17 50														
South Merton	d							17 52														
Morden South	d							17 54														
St Helier	d							17 56														
Sutton Common	d							17 58														
West Sutton	d							18 01														
Sutton (Surrey)	a							18 05					18 08		18 15							
East Croydon	d									17 46						17 55		17 58	18 00	18 06		
Denmark Hill	d						17 20															
Peckham Rye	d		17 50				17 23															18 07
Nunhead	d						17 26															
Crofton Park	d						17 29															
Catford	d						17 32															
Bellingham	d						17 35															
Beckenham Hill	d						17 37															
Ravensbourne	d						17 39															
Shortlands	d						17 43															
Bromley South	d						17 46					17 48										
Bickley	d											17 50										
St Mary Cray	d											17 55										
Swanley	d						17 55					18 00										
Eynsford	d						18 00															
Shoreham (Kent)	d						18 03															
Otford	d						18 06															
Bat & Ball	d						18 14															
Sevenoaks	a	18 06			18 15	18 21	18 22										18 27					
Redhill	d									18 00												
Gatwick Airport	d									18 14												
Three Bridges	d									18 19									18 22			
Balcombe	d									18 25												
Haywards Heath	d									18 31						18 22						
Wivelsfield	d																					
Burgess Hill	d									18 36						18 27						
Hassocks	d									18 40						18 31						
Preston Park	d									18 48						18 39						
Brighton	a									18 52												

Table 52 — Mondays to Fridays

Bedford, Luton, St.Albans and City of London - South London, Gatwick Airport and Brighton

Station		SN	SE ■	SN	EM ◇■	SE ■	FC	FC ■	FC	FC ■	EM ◇■	FC	SN ■	SN ■	SE	SN ■	SN ■	FC ■	FC	FC	SN ■	SN	SN
Bedford 7	d							16 26		16 38	16 49												
Flitwick	d							16 36		16 48													
Harlington	d							16 40		16 52													
Leagrave	d							16 45		16 57													
Luton 10	d				18 15			16 50		17 02	17 05								17 12	17 18			
Luton Airport Parkway 7	d							16 52		17 04									17 15	17 20			
Harpenden	d							16 58		17 10										17 26			
St Albans City	d							17 04		17 16		17 20							17 24	17 32			
Radlett	d											17 25								17 37			
Elstree & Borehamwood	d											17 29								17 41			
Mill Hill Broadway	d											17 34								17 46			
Hendon	d											17 37								17 49			
Cricklewood	d											17 41								17 53			
West Hampstead Thameslink ⊖	d							17 18				17 44								17 56			
Kentish Town ⊖	d						17 18					17 48								18 00			
St Pancras International 15 ⊖	a				18 39				←		17 30												
St Pancras International 15 ⊖	a						17 22	17 26	17 32	17 36		17 52							17 44	18 04			
	d						17 22	17 28	17 32	17 37		17 52						17 40	17 44	18 04			
Farringdon 3 ⊖	d						17 27	17 33	17 37	17 42		→						17 45	17 49	→			
City Thameslink 3	d						17 31	17 37	17 41	17 45								17 49	17 53				
London Blackfriars 3 ⊖	d						17 36	17 40	17 44	17 48								17 52	17 56				
Elephant & Castle ⊖	d						17 40		17 48	17 52								17 56	18 00				
Loughborough Jn	d								17 52														
Herne Hill 4	d								17 57										18 06				
London Bridge 4	a		18 11			18 14									18 06								
	d		18 12	18 11		18 15							17 57	17 59	18 07	18 08	18 12				18 16	18 18	18 21
Tulse Hill 3	d								18 02														
Streatham 4	d								18 06														
Mitcham Eastfields	d																						
Mitcham Junction	d																						
Hackbridge	d																						
Carshalton	d																						
Tooting	d								18 10														
Haydons Road	d								18 13														
Wimbledon 6 ⊖	d	18 10							18 19														
Wimbledon Chase	d								18 22														
South Merton	d								18 24														
Morden South	d								18 26														
St Helier	d								18 28														
Sutton Common	d								18 30														
West Sutton	d								18 33														
Sutton (Surrey) 4	a								18 37														
East Croydon	d							18 09					18 15	18 15		18 22	18 25	18 26			18 31	18 37	
Denmark Hill 4	d						17 47																
Peckham Rye 4	d	18 32		18 20			17 50																
Nunhead 4	d						17 52																
Crofton Park	d						17 55																
Catford	d						17 58																
Bellingham	d						18 01																
Beckenham Hill	d						18 03																
Ravensbourne	d						18 05																
Shortlands	d						18 07																
Bromley South 4	d						18 10			18 11													
Bickley 4	d						18 12																
St Mary Cray	d						18 21			18 17													
Swanley 4	d						18 26			18 22													
Eynsford	d						18 30																
Shoreham (Kent)	d						18 34																
Otford 4	d						18 37			18 30													
Bat & Ball	d						18 40																
Sevenoaks 4	a		18 37			18 42	18 44								18 49								
Redhill	d													18 34				18 39					
Gatwick Airport 10	d							18 25						18 47				18 50					
Three Bridges 4	d							18 30					18 34	18 52			18 45	18a56					
Balcombe	d																						
Haywards Heath 3	d							18 39					18 44				18 54						
Wivelsfield 4	d							18 43															
Burgess Hill 4	d							18 46					18 49				19 00						
Hassocks 4	d							18 50					18 53				19 04						
Preston Park	d							18 57					19 01				19 11						
Brighton 10	a							19 02					19 07										

Table 52 — Mondays to Fridays

Bedford, Luton, St.Albans and City of London - South London, Gatwick Airport and Brighton

Station		SN ■	SN	SE ■	SE ■	FC	FC	FC ■	FC	SN	FC	FC ■	FC	SE	SN ■	SN	SN	SE ■	SN	SE ■	SE	SE ■	FC
Bedford 7	d							16 58				17 08											
Flitwick	d							17 08				17 18											
Harlington	d							17 12				17 22											
Leagrave	d							17 17				17 27											
Luton 10	d							17 22				17 32	17 38										
Luton Airport Parkway 7	d							17 24				17 34	17 40										
Harpenden	d							17 30				17 40	17 46										
St Albans City	d							17 36	17 42			17 46	17 52										
Radlett	d								17 47				17 57										
Elstree & Borehamwood	d								17 51				18 01										
Mill Hill Broadway	d								17 56				18 06										
Hendon	d												18 09										
Cricklewood	d												18 13										
West Hampstead Thameslink ⊖	d							17 50	18 04				18 16										
Kentish Town ⊖	d					17 44							18 20										
St Pancras International 15 ⊖	a						←				←												←
St Pancras International 15 ⊖	a					17 48	17 52	17 58	18 11		18 04	18 08	18 24										18 11
	d					17 48	17 52	17 58	18 12		18 04	18 08	18 24										18 12
Farringdon 3 ⊖	d					17 53	17 57	18 03	→		18 09	18 13	→										18 17
City Thameslink 3	d					17 57	18 01	18 07			18 13	18 17											18 21
London Blackfriars 3 ⊖	d					18 00	18 04	18 10			18 16	18 20											18 24
Elephant & Castle ⊖	d					18 05	18 08	18 14			18 20												18 28
Loughborough Jn	d						18 12				18 24												
Herne Hill 4	d						18 18	18 21			18 28												
London Bridge 4	a			18 35	18 39							18 27		18 26				18 49		18 52	18 37	19 07	
	d	18 23	18 28	18 36	18 40					18 08		18 27		18 27	18 30	18 41		18 50	18 51	18 53	18 38	19 08	
Tulse Hill 3	d						18 22			18 27	18 32												
Streatham 4	d						18 26			18 30	18 36												
Mitcham Eastfields	d						18 30			18 34													
Mitcham Junction	d						18 33			18 37													
Hackbridge	d						18 36			18 41													
Carshalton	d						18 39			18 43													
Tooting	d										18 40												
Haydons Road	d										18 43												
Wimbledon 6 ⊖	d										18 47						18 43						
Wimbledon Chase	d										18 50												
South Merton	d										18 52												
Morden South	d										18 54												
St Helier	d										18 56												
Sutton Common	d										18 58												
West Sutton	d										19 01												
Sutton (Surrey) 4	a						18 42			18 47	19 07												
East Croydon	d	18 37										18 41			18 46								
Denmark Hill 4	d					18 15																	18 34
Peckham Rye 4	d		18 37			18 18										18 50	19 07						18 38
Nunhead 4	d					18 20																	18 40
Crofton Park	d					18 23																	18 43
Catford	d					18 26																	18 46
Bellingham	d					18 29																	18 49
Beckenham Hill	d					18 31																	18 51
Ravensbourne	d					18 33																	18 53
Shortlands	d					18 35																	18 57
Bromley South 4	d					18 38		18 31															19 00
Bickley 4	d					18 40																	19 03
St Mary Cray	d					18 45		18 38															19 10
Swanley 4	d					18 53		18 43															19 15
Eynsford	d					18 57																	19 19
Shoreham (Kent)	d					19 01																	19 23
Otford 4	d					19 04																	19 26
Bat & Ball	d					19 07																	19 29
Sevenoaks 4	a			19 00	19 06	19 11								19 13				19 16		19 20	19 27	19 31	19 36
Redhill	d														19 07								
Gatwick Airport 10	d											18 57			19 20								
Three Bridges 4	d	18 56										19 02			19 25								
Balcombe	d											19 08											
Haywards Heath 3	d	19 06										19 14											
Wivelsfield 4	d	19 11																					
Burgess Hill 4	d											19 19											
Hassocks 4	d											19 23											
Preston Park	d																						
Brighton 10	a											19 34											

Table 52

Bedford, Luton, St.Albans and City of London - South London, Gatwick Airport and Brighton

Station		FC ■	FC	FC	FC ■	SN ■	SN	SE ■	SN	SN	SN	SE ■	SE ■	FC ■	FC ■	FC	EM ◇■	FC	FC	SN ■	SN ■	FC ■
Bedford ■	d	17 22			17 36									17 42			17 49					17 54
Flitwick	d	17 32			17 46																	18 04
Harlington	d	17 36			17 50																	18 08
Leagrave	d	17 41			17 55																	18 13
Luton ■	d	17 46			18 00												18 05	18 08				18 18
Luton Airport Parkway ■	d	17 48			18 02									18 02				18 10				18 20
Harpenden	d	17 54			18 08													18 16				18 26
St Albans City	d	18 00		18 08	18 14													18 22	18 26			18 34
Radlett	d			18 13														18 27	18 31			
Elstree & Borehamwood	d			18 17														18 31	18 35			
Mill Hill Broadway	d			18 21															18 40			
Hendon	d			18 24															18 43			
Cricklewood	d			18 28															18 47			
West Hampstead Thameslink ⊖	d			18 30														18 40	18 50			18 46
Kentish Town ⊖	d			18 34															18 54			
St Pancras International ■ ⊖	a		←												←	←	18 29					
St Pancras International ■ ⊖	a	18 20	18 24	18 38	18 34									18 28	18 34	18 38		18 48	18 59			18 54
	d	18 20	18 24	18 38	18 34									18 30	18 34	18 38		18 48	19 00			18 54
Farringdon ■ ⊖	d	18 25	18 29	→	→									18 35	18 39	18 43		18 53	→			18 59
City Thameslink ■	d	18 29	18 33											18 39	18 43	18 47		18 57				19 03
London Blackfriars ■ ⊖	d	18 32	18 36											18 42	18 46	18 50		19 00				19 05
Elephant & Castle ⊖	d	18 36	18 40											18 46		18 54		19 04				
Loughborough Jn	d		18 44													18 58		19 08				
Herne Hill ■	d		18 48													19 02		19 12				
London Bridge ■	a							19 07				19 18	19 22		18 54							19 11
	d					18 47	18 49	19 09	19 08	19 11		19 19	19 23		18 57					19 03	19 08	19 12
Tulse Hill ■	d		18 52													19 07		19 16				
Streatham ■	d		18 56													19 11		19 20				
Mitcham Eastfields	d		19 00															19 24				
Mitcham Junction	d		19 03															19 27				
Hackbridge	d		19 06															19 30				
Carshalton	d		19 09															19 33				
Tooting	d															19 16						
Haydons Road	d															19 19						
Wimbledon ■ ⊖	d										19 17					19 23						
Wimbledon Chase	d															19 26						
South Merton	d															19 28						
Morden South	d															19 30						
St Helier	d															19 32						
Sutton Common	d															19 34						
West Sutton	d															19 37						
Sutton (Surrey) ■	a		19 12													19 40		19 36				
East Croydon	d	18 56				19 00	19 06								19 11					19 19	19 23	19 24
Denmark Hill ■	d													18 52								
Peckham Rye ■	d								19 17	19 20	19 38			18 55								
Nunhead ■	d													18 57								
Crofton Park	d													19 00								
Catford	d													19 03								
Bellingham	d													19 05								
Beckenham Hill	d													19 07								
Ravensbourne	d													19 09								
Shortlands	d													19 13								
Bromley South ■	d													19 16								
Bickley ■	d													19 19								
St Mary Cray	d													19 23								
Swanley ■	d													19 28								
Eynsford	d													19 32								
Shoreham (Kent)	d													19 36								
Otford ■	d													19 39								
Bat & Ball	d													19 42								
Sevenoaks ■	a							19 36				19 42	19 48	19 49								
Redhill	d																			19 37		
Gatwick Airport ■	d	19 11													19 26					19 50		19 41
Three Bridges ■	d														19 31					19 55		19 45
Balcombe	d	19 19																				19 51
Haywards Heath ■	d	19b31													19 40							19 57
Wivelsfield ■	d																					20 01
Burgess Hill ■	d	19 36													19 45							20 03
Hassocks ■	d	19 40													19 49							20 06
Preston Park	d	19 48																				20 13
Brighton ■	a	19 52													19 58							20 19

b arr. 1924

Table 52

Bedford, Luton, St.Albans and City of London - South London, Gatwick Airport and Brighton

Station		SN	SE	SN	SE ■	SN	SN	SE ■	FC	FC	FC ■	EM ◇■	FC	FC	FC ■	SN	SE ■	SE	SN ■	SN	SE ■	SN	SE ■
Bedford ■	d									18 04	18 10	18 18			18 24								
Flitwick	d										18 20				18 34								
Harlington	d										18 24				18 38								
Leagrave	d										18 29				18 43								
Luton ■	d									18 22	18 34			18 44	18 48								
Luton Airport Parkway ■	d									18 25	18 36	18 34		18 46	18 50								
Harpenden	d									18 30	18 42			18 52	18 56								
St Albans City	d									18 36	18 48		18 52	18 58	19 02								
Radlett	d									18 41			18 57	19 03									
Elstree & Borehamwood	d									18 45			19 01	19 07									
Mill Hill Broadway	d													19 12									
Hendon	d													19 15									
Cricklewood	d													19 19									
West Hampstead Thameslink ⊖	d									18 54			19 10	19 22									
Kentish Town ⊖	d													19 26									
St Pancras International ■ ⊖	a								←			19 01											
St Pancras International ■ ⊖	a								18 59	19 04	19 09		19 18	19 30	19 23								
	d								19 00	19 04	19 10		19 18	19 30	19 24								
Farringdon ■ ⊖	d								19 05	19 09	19 14		19 23	→	19 29								
City Thameslink ■	d								19 09	19 13	19 17		19 27		19 32								
London Blackfriars ■ ⊖	d								19 12	19 16	19 20		19 30		19 35								
Elephant & Castle ⊖	d								19 16	19 19			19 33										
Loughborough Jn	d									19 23			19 37										
Herne Hill ■	d									19 27			19 41										
London Bridge ■	a		19 14		19 37			19 48			19 26				19 41		19 52	19 44			20 07		20 18
	d	19 06	19 14	19 22	19 39	19 38	19 41	19 49			19 27				19 42	19 36	19 53	19 44	19 52	19 54	20 09	20 11	20 19
Tulse Hill ■	d									19 31			19 46										
Streatham ■	d									19 35			19 50										
Mitcham Eastfields	d												19 54										
Mitcham Junction	d												19 57										
Hackbridge	d												20 00										
Carshalton	d												20 03										
Tooting	d									19 40													
Haydons Road	d									19 43													
Wimbledon ■ ⊖	d									19 49													
Wimbledon Chase	d									19 52													
South Merton	d									19 54													
Morden South	d									19 56													
St Helier	d									19 58													
Sutton Common	d									20 00													
West Sutton	d									20 03													
Sutton (Surrey) ■	a									20 07			20 06										
East Croydon	d	19 34									19 39				19 54	20 04			20 07				
Denmark Hill ■	d								19 22														
Peckham Rye ■	d					19 47	19 50		19 25													20 20	
Nunhead ■	d								19 27														
Crofton Park	d								19 30														
Catford	d								19 33														
Bellingham	d								19 35														
Beckenham Hill	d								19 37														
Ravensbourne	d								19 39														
Shortlands	d								19 41														
Bromley South ■	d								19 44														
Bickley ■	d								19 47														
St Mary Cray	d								19 51														
Swanley ■	d								19 56														
Eynsford	d								20 00														
Shoreham (Kent)	d								20 04														
Otford ■	d								20 07														
Bat & Ball	d								20 10														
Sevenoaks ■	a		19 58		20 05			20 12	20 13								20 18	20 26			20 35		20 42
Redhill	d																		20 25				
Gatwick Airport ■	d										19 56				20 11								
Three Bridges ■	d										20 01				20 16								
Balcombe	d																						
Haywards Heath ■	d										20 10				20 26								
Wivelsfield ■	d														20 30								
Burgess Hill ■	d										20 15				20 32								
Hassocks ■	d										20 19				20 36								
Preston Park	d														20 43								
Brighton ■	a										20 28				20 47								

Bedford, Luton, St.Albans and City of London - South London, Gatwick Airport and Brighton

		FC	FC	FC ■	EM ◇■	FC	FC	SN	SN ■	FC ■	EM ◇■	SN	SE ■	SE	SN	SN ■	SN ■	SE ■	SN	SE ■	FC	FC
Bedford	d		18 36	18 40	18 49					18 54	19 18											
Flitwick	d			18 50						19 04												
Harlington	d			18 54						19 08												
Leagrave	d			18 59						19 13												
Luton	d		18 54	19 04	19 05		19 14			19 18												19 24
Luton Airport Parkway	d		18 57	19 06			19 16			19 20	19 34											19 27
Harpenden	d		19 02	19 12			19 22			19 26												19 32
St Albans City	d		19 08	19 18		19 22	19 28			19 33												19 38
Radlett	d		19 13			19 27	19 33															19 43
Elstree & Borehamwood	d		19 17			19 31	19 37															19 47
Mill Hill Broadway	d						19 42															
Hendon	d						19 45															
Cricklewood	d						19 49															
West Hampstead Thameslink ⊖	d		19 26			19 40	19 52															19 56
Kentish Town ⊖	d						19 56															
St Pancras International ⊖	a	←			19 31						20 01										←	
St Pancras International ⊖	a	19 30	19 34	19 39		19 48	20 00			19 52											20 00	20 04
	d	19 30	19 34	19 40		19 48	20 00			19 54											20 00	20 04
Farringdon ⊖	d	19 35	19 39	19 44		19 53	→			19 59											20 05	20 09
City Thameslink	d	19 39	19 43	19 47		19 57				20 02											20 09	20 13
London Blackfriars ⊖	d	19 42	19 46	19 50		20 00				20 05											20 12	20 16
Elephant & Castle ⊖	d	19 46	19 49			20 03															20 16	20 19
Loughborough Jn	d		19 53			20 07																20 23
Herne Hill	d		19 57			20 11																20 27
London Bridge	a			19 56						20 11			20 22	20 14				20 37		20 48		
	d			19 57				20 03	20 04	20 12		20 06	20 23	20 14	20 22	20 28	20 34	20 39	20 41	20 49		
Tulse Hill	d		20 01			20 16		20 20														20 31
Streatham	d		20 05			20 20		20 24														20 35
Mitcham Eastfields	d					20 24																
Mitcham Junction	d					20 27																
Hackbridge	d					20 30																
Carshalton	d					20 33																
Tooting	d		20 10																			20 40
Haydons Road	d		20 13																			20 43
Wimbledon ⊖	d		20 19																			20 47
Wimbledon Chase	d		20 22																			20 50
South Merton	d		20 24																			20 52
Morden South	d		20 26																			20 54
St Helier	d		20 28																			20 56
Sutton Common	d		20 30																			20 58
West Sutton	d		20 33																			21 01
Sutton (Surrey)	a		20 37			20 36																21 05
East Croydon	d			20 09					20 20	20 24		20 34				20 41	20a49					
Denmark Hill	d	19 52																			20 22	
Peckham Rye	d	19 55																	20 50		20 25	
Nunhead	d	19 57																			20 27	
Crofton Park	d	20 00																			20 30	
Catford	d	20 03																			20 33	
Bellingham	d	20 05																			20 35	
Beckenham Hill	d	20 07																			20 37	
Ravensbourne	d	20 09																			20 39	
Shortlands	d	20 11																			20 41	
Bromley South	d	20 14																			20 44	
Bickley	d	20 17																			20 47	
St Mary Cray	d	20 21																			20 51	
Swanley	d	20 26																			20 56	
Eynsford	d	20 30																			21 00	
Shoreham (Kent)	d	20 34																			21 04	
Otford	d	20 37																			21 07	
Bat & Ball	d	20 40																			21 10	
Sevenoaks	a	20 43											20 48	20 56				21 05		21 12	21 13	
Redhill	d																					
Gatwick Airport	d			20 26						20 41						20 56						
Three Bridges	d			20 31						20 45						21 01						
Balcombe	d									20 51												
Haywards Heath	d			20 40						20 57						21 11						
Wivelsfield	d									21 01												
Burgess Hill	d			20 45						21 03												
Hassocks	d									21 06												
Preston Park	d									21 13												
Brighton	a			20 56						21 19						21 26						

Bedford, Luton, St.Albans and City of London - South London, Gatwick Airport and Brighton

		FC	FC ■	EM ◇■	SN	SE ■	SE	SN	SN ■	SN ■	SE ■	FC	FC	FC ■	SN	SN	SE ■	SE	SN	SN ■	SE ■	SN	SE ■
Bedford	d		19 22	19 49										19 52									
Flitwick	d		19 32											20 02									
Harlington	d		19 36											20 06									
Leagrave	d		19 41											20 11									
Luton	d		19 46	20 05									19 50	20 16									
Luton Airport Parkway	d		19 48										19 52	20 18									
Harpenden	d		19 54										19 58	20 24									
St Albans City	d	19 52	20 00										20 04	20 30									
Radlett	d	19 57											20 09										
Elstree & Borehamwood	d	20 01											20 13										
Mill Hill Broadway	d												20 17										
Hendon	d												20 20										
Cricklewood	d												20 24										
West Hampstead Thameslink ⊖	d	20 10	20 14										20 26	20 44									
Kentish Town ⊖	d											20 26	20 30										
St Pancras International ⊖	a			20 29																			
St Pancras International ⊖	a	20 18	20 22									20 30	20 35	20 52									
	d	20 18	20 24									20 30	20 36	20 54									
Farringdon ⊖	d	20 23	20 29									20 35	20 40	20 59									
City Thameslink	d	20 27	20 32									20 39	20 43	21 02									
London Blackfriars ⊖	d	20 30	20 35									20 42	20 46	21 05									
Elephant & Castle ⊖	d	20 33										20 46	20 49										
Loughborough Jn	d	20 37											20 53										
Herne Hill	d	20 41											20 57										
London Bridge	a		20 41			20 52	20 44				21 07			21 11			21 18	21 13			21 37		21 48
	d		20 42		20 36	20 53	20 44	20 52	20 58	21 04	21 09			21 12	21 06	21 11	21 19	21 14	21 22	21 26	21 39	21 41	21 49
Tulse Hill	d	20 46											21 01										
Streatham	d	20 50											21 05										
Mitcham Eastfields	d	20 54																					
Mitcham Junction	d	20 57																					
Hackbridge	d	21 00																					
Carshalton	d	21 03																					
Tooting	d												21 10										
Haydons Road	d												21 13										
Wimbledon ⊖	d												21 19										
Wimbledon Chase	d												21 22										
South Merton	d												21 24										
Morden South	d												21 26										
St Helier	d												21 28										
Sutton Common	d												21 30										
West Sutton	d												21 33										
Sutton (Surrey)	a	21 06											21 39										
East Croydon	d		20 54		21 04				21 11	21 19				21 24	21 34					21a41			
Denmark Hill	d											20 52											
Peckham Rye	d											20 55				21 20						21 50	
Nunhead	d											20 57											
Crofton Park	d											21 00											
Catford	d											21 03											
Bellingham	d											21 05											
Beckenham Hill	d											21 07											
Ravensbourne	d											21 09											
Shortlands	d											21 11											
Bromley South	d											21 14											
Bickley	d											21 17											
St Mary Cray	d											21 21											
Swanley	d											21 26											
Eynsford	d											21 30											
Shoreham (Kent)	d											21 34											
Otford	d											21 37											
Bat & Ball	d											21 40											
Sevenoaks	a					21 18	21 26				21 35	21 43					21 44	21 57			22 06		22 12
Redhill	d																						
Gatwick Airport	d		21 11						21 27					21 41									
Three Bridges	d		21 15						21 32					21 45									
Balcombe	d													21 53									
Haywards Heath	d		21 26						21 41					21 58									
Wivelsfield	d		21 30											22 02									
Burgess Hill	d		21 32											22 04									
Hassocks	d		21 36											22 08									
Preston Park	d		21 43											22 15									
Brighton	a		21 47						21 55					22 19									

Table 52

Mondays to Fridays

Bedford, Luton, St.Albans and City of London - South London, Gatwick Airport and Brighton

		FC	FC	FC ■	FC	SN		SE ■	SN	SN ■	FC ■	EM ◇■	FC	FC ■	EM ◇■	EM ◇■		FC	FC ■	SE ■	SE	SN	SN	SE ■	FC
Bedford 7	d			20 22							20 52	20b54		21 22	21 25	21 49			21 52						
Flitwick	d			20 32							21 02			21 32					22 02						
Harlington	d			20 36							21 06			21 36					22 06						
Leagrave	d			20 41							21 11			21 41					22 11						
Luton 10	d		20 20	20 46	20 50						21 16	21 08	21 20	21 46		22 09		21 50	22 16						22 20
Luton Airport Parkway 7	d		20 22	20 48	20 52						21 18		21 22	21 48	21 41			21 52	22 18						22 22
Harpenden	d		20 28	20 54	20 58						21 24		21 28	21 54				21 58	22 24						22 28
St Albans City	d		20 34	21 00	21 04						21 30		21 34	22 00				22 04	22 30						22 34
Radlett	d		20 39		21 09								21 39					22 09							22 39
Elstree & Borehamwood	d		20 43		21 13								21 43					22 13							22 43
Mill Hill Broadway	d		20 47		21 17								21 47					22 18							22 48
Hendon	d		20 50		21 20								21 50					22 21							22 51
Cricklewood	d		20 54		21 24								21 54					22 25							22 55
West Hampstead Thameslink ⊖	d		20 56	21 14	21 26						21 44		21 56	22 14				22 28	22 44						22 58
Kentish Town ⊖	d	20 56	21 00		21 30								22 00					22 32							23 02
St Pancras International 15 ⊖	a											21 34		22 24	22 06	22 35		22 39	22 54						23 09
St Pancras International 15 ⊖	a	21 00	21 05	21 22	21 35						21 52		22 05												
	d	21 00	21 06	21 24	21 36						21 54		22 06												
Farringdon 3 ⊖	d	21 05	21 10	21 29	21 40						21 59		22 10												
City Thameslink 3	d	21 09	21 13	21 32	21 43						22 02		22 13												
London Blackfriars 3 ⊖	d	21 12	21 16	21 35	21 46						22 05		22 16												
Elephant & Castle ⊖	d	21 16	21 19		21 49								22 19												
Loughborough Jn	d		21 23		21 53								22 23												
Herne Hill 4	d		21 27		21 57								22 27												
London Bridge 4	a			21 41				21 52			22 11									22 07				22 18	
	d			21 42		21 36		21 53	21 52	22 04	22 12									22 09		22 08	22 11	22 19	
Tulse Hill 3	d		21 31		22 01								22 31												
Streatham 4	d		21 35		22 05								22 35												
Mitcham Eastfields	d																								
Mitcham Junction	d																								
Hackbridge	d																								
Carshalton	d																								
Tooting	d		21 40		22 10								22 40												
Haydons Road	d		21 43		22 13								22 43												
Wimbledon 6 ⊖	d		21 47		22 19								22 47												
Wimbledon Chase	d		21 50		22 22								22 50												
South Merton	d		21 52		22 24								22 52												
Morden South	d		21 54		22 26								22 54												
St Helier	d		21 56		22 28								22 56												
Sutton Common	d		21 58		22 30								22 58												
West Sutton	d		22 01		22 33								23 01												
Sutton (Surrey) 4	a		22 05		22 39								23 05												
East Croydon	d			21 54		22 04				22 19	22 24											22 36			
Denmark Hill 4	d	21 22																			21 52				
Peckham Rye 4	d	21 25																			21 55		22 20		
Nunhead 4	d	21 27																			21 57				
Crofton Park	d	21 30																			22 00				
Catford	d	21 33																			22 03				
Bellingham	d	21 35																			22 05				
Beckenham Hill	d	21 37																			22 07				
Ravensbourne	d	21 39																			22 09				
Shortlands	d	21 41																			22 11				
Bromley South 4	d	21 44																			22 14				
Bickley 4	d	21 47																			22 17				
St Mary Cray	d	21 51																			22 21				
Swanley 4	d	21 56																			22 26				
Eynsford	d	22 00																			22 30				
Shoreham (Kent)	d	22 04																			22 34				
Otford 4	d	22 07																			22 37				
Bat & Ball	d	22 10																			22 40				
Sevenoaks 4	a	22 13						22 18												22 36	22 43			22 44	
Redhill	d																								
Gatwick Airport 10	d			22 11							22 41														
Three Bridges 4	d			22 15							22 45														
Balcombe	d										22 53														
Haywards Heath 3	d			22 26							22 58														
Wivelsfield 4	d			22 30							23 02														
Burgess Hill 4	d			22 32							23 04														
Hassocks 4	d			22 36							23 08														
Preston Park	d			22 43							23 15														
Brighton 10	a			22 47							23 19														

b arr. 2048

Table 52

Mondays to Fridays

Bedford, Luton, St.Albans and City of London - South London, Gatwick Airport and Brighton

		FC ■		EM ◇■	SN	SN	FC	SE ■	SN	FC ■	SN	EM ◇■		FC	FC	SE ■	SE	SE	SE ■	FC ■	SN	SN ■		FC	FC
Bedford 7	d	22 16		22 19								22 47								22 52					
Flitwick	d	22 26																		23 02					
Harlington	d	22 30																		23 06					
Leagrave	d	22 35																		23 11					
Luton 10	d	22 40		22 34								23 05			22 46					23 16					
Luton Airport Parkway 7	d	22 42		22 38											22 48					23 18					
Harpenden	d	22 48													22 54					23 24					
St Albans City	d	22 54													23 00					23 30					
Radlett	d														23 05					23 35					
Elstree & Borehamwood	d														23 09					23 39					
Mill Hill Broadway	d														23 14					23 44					
Hendon	d														23 17					23 47					
Cricklewood	d														23 21					23 51					
West Hampstead Thameslink ⊖	d	23 12													23 24					23 54					
Kentish Town ⊖	d														23 28					23 58					
St Pancras International 15 ⊖	a	23 24		23 04								23 38			23 35					00 05					
St Pancras International 15 ⊖	a																								
	d						22 30							22 45										23 00	
Farringdon 3 ⊖	d						22 35							22 50										23 05	
City Thameslink 3	d						22 37							22 52										23 07	
London Blackfriars 3 ⊖	d						22 42							22 57										23 12	
Elephant & Castle ⊖	d																								
Loughborough Jn	d																								
Herne Hill 4	d																								
London Bridge 4	a						22 57	22 37						23 12		22 48			22 52					23 27	
	d				22 22	22 26		22 39	22 41	22 42	22 38					22 49			22 53		22 52	22 56			23 02
Tulse Hill 3	d																								23 12
Streatham 4	d																								23 16
Mitcham Eastfields	d																								
Mitcham Junction	d																								
Hackbridge	d																								
Carshalton	d																								
Tooting	d																								23 20
Haydons Road	d																								23 23
Wimbledon 6 ⊖	d																								23 27
Wimbledon Chase	d																								23 30
South Merton	d																								23 32
Morden South	d																								23 34
St Helier	d																								23 36
Sutton Common	d																								23 38
West Sutton	d																								23 41
Sutton (Surrey) 4	a																								23 45
East Croydon	d					22a42				22 56	23 06											23a11			
Denmark Hill 4	d																22 22	22 52							
Peckham Rye 4	d								22 50								22 25	22 55							
Nunhead 4	d																22 27	22 57							
Crofton Park	d																22 30	23 00							
Catford	d																22 33	23 03							
Bellingham	d																22 35	23 05							
Beckenham Hill	d																22 37	23 07							
Ravensbourne	d																22 39	23 09							
Shortlands	d																22 41	23 11							
Bromley South 4	d																22 44	23 14							
Bickley 4	d																22 47	23 17							
St Mary Cray	d																22 51								
Swanley 4	d																22 56								
Eynsford	d																23 00								
Shoreham (Kent)	d																23 04								
Otford 4	d																23 07								
Bat & Ball	d																23 10								
Sevenoaks 4	a							23 05								23 12	23 13		23 18						
Redhill	d																								
Gatwick Airport 10	d									23 11															
Three Bridges 4	d									23 15															
Balcombe	d																								
Haywards Heath 3	d									23 26															
Wivelsfield 4	d									23 30															
Burgess Hill 4	d									23 32															
Hassocks 4	d									23 36															
Preston Park	d									23 43															
Brighton 10	a									23 47															

Table 52 — Mondays to Fridays

Bedford, Luton, St.Albans and City of London - South London, Gatwick Airport and Brighton

		SE	SN	FC	SN	FC	FC	SE	SE	SN	FC	FC	FC	SE	FC	SN	SE	SN	SE	SE	FC
Bedford	d					23 12							23 32								
Flitwick	d					23 22							23 42								
Harlington	d					23 26							23 46								
Leagrave	d					23 31							23 51								
Luton	d					23 36							23 56								
Luton Airport Parkway	d					23 38							23 58								
Harpenden	d					23 44							00 04								
St Albans City	d					23 50							00 10								
Radlett	d					23 55							00 15								
Elstree & Borehamwood	d					23 59							00 19								
Mill Hill Broadway	d					00 04							00 24								
Hendon	d					00 07							00 27								
Cricklewood	d					00 11							00 31								
West Hampstead Thameslink ⊖	d					00 14							00 34								
Kentish Town ⊖	d					00 18							00 42								
St Pancras International ⊖	a					00 25							00 47								
St Pancras International ⊖	a																				
	d						23 15					23 30									
Farringdon ⊖	d						23 20					23 35									
City Thameslink	d																				
London Blackfriars ⊖	d						23 25					23 40									
Elephant & Castle ⊖	d																				
Loughborough Jn	d																				
Herne Hill	d																				
London Bridge	a	23 07					23 40	23 18				23 54		23 37			23 48			23 52	
	d	23 09	23 11	23 12	23 06			23 19		23 22	23 28			23 39	23 42	23 36	23 49	23 48		23 53	23 58
Tulse Hill	d										23 40										00 10
Streatham	d										23 44										00 14
Mitcham Eastfields	d																				
Mitcham Junction	d																				
Hackbridge	d																				
Carshalton	d																				
Tooting	d										23 48										00 18
Haydons Road	d										23 51										00 21
Wimbledon ⊖	d										23 55										00 25
Wimbledon Chase	d										23 58										00 28
South Merton	d										00 01										00 30
Morden South	d										00 03										00 32
St Helier	d										00 05										00 34
Sutton Common	d										00 07										00 36
West Sutton	d										00 10										00 39
Sutton (Surrey)	a										00 13										00 43
East Croydon	d			23 24	23 34										23 56	00 03					
Denmark Hill	d								23 22										23 52		
Peckham Rye	d		23 20						23 25									23 57	23 55		
Nunhead	d								23 27										23 57		
Crofton Park	d								23 30										23 59		
Catford	d								23 33										00 03		
Bellingham	d								23 35										00 05		
Beckenham Hill	d								23 37										00 07		
Ravensbourne	d								23 39										00 09		
Shortlands	d								23 41										00 11		
Bromley South	d								23 44										00 14		
Bickley	d								23 47										00 17		
St Mary Cray	d																				
Swanley	d																				
Eynsford	d																				
Shoreham (Kent)	d																				
Otford	d																				
Bat & Ball	d																				
Sevenoaks	a	23 35						23 44						00 05			00 12			00 18	
Redhill	d																				
Gatwick Airport	d			23 41											00 18						
Three Bridges	d			23 47											00a24						
Balcombe	d			23 53																	
Haywards Heath	d			23 58																	
Wivelsfield	d			00 02																	
Burgess Hill	d			00 04																	
Hassocks	d			00 08																	
Preston Park	d			00 15																	
Brighton	a			00 19																	

Table 52 — Saturdays

Bedford, Luton, St.Albans and City of London - South London, Gatwick Airport and Brighton

		FC	FC	FC	FC	FC	SE	FC	SN	SE	SE	SE	FC	FC	FC	FC	SN	SE	FC	SN	FC	FC	FC
Bedford	d	22p52		23p12		23p32									00 02								01 02
Flitwick	d	23p02		23p22		23p42									00 12								01 12
Harlington	d	23p06		23p26		23p46									00 16								01 16
Leagrave	d	23p11		23p31		23p51									00 21								01 21
Luton	d	23p16		23p36		23p56									00 26								01 26
Luton Airport Parkway	d	23p18		23p38		23p58									00 28								01 28
Harpenden	d	23p24		23p44		00 04									00 34								01 34
St Albans City	d	23p30		23p50		00 10									00 40								01 40
Radlett	d	23p35		23p55		00 15									00 45								01 45
Elstree & Borehamwood	d	23p39		23p59		00 19									00 49								01 49
Mill Hill Broadway	d	23p44		00 04		00 24									00 54								01 54
Hendon	d	23p47		00 07		00 27									00 57								01 57
Cricklewood	d	23p51		00 11		00 31									01 01								02 01
West Hampstead Thameslink ⊖	d	23p54		00 14		00 34									01 04								02 04
Kentish Town ⊖	d	23p58		00 18		00 42									01 12								02 08
St Pancras International ⊖	a	00 05		00 25		00 47									01 17								02 15
St Pancras International ⊖	a																						
	d													00 01					00 30			01 00	
Farringdon ⊖	d													00 06					00 35				
City Thameslink	d																						
London Blackfriars ⊖	d													00 11					00 40			01 10	
Elephant & Castle ⊖	d																						
Loughborough Jn	d																						
Herne Hill	d																						
London Bridge	a						23p37			23p48		23p52		00 26				00 17	00 55			01 25	
	d		23p12		23p28		23p39	23p42	23p36	23p49		23p53	23p58			00 12	00 06	00 18		00 36	00 42		
Tulse Hill	d				23p40								00 10										
Streatham	d				23p44								00 14										
Mitcham Eastfields	d																						
Mitcham Junction	d																						
Hackbridge	d																						
Carshalton	d																						
Tooting	d				23p48								00 18										
Haydons Road	d				23p51								00 21										
Wimbledon ⊖	d				23p55								00 25										
Wimbledon Chase	d				23p58								00 28										
South Merton	d				00 01								00 30										
Morden South	d				00 03								00 32										
St Helier	d				00 05								00 34										
Sutton Common	d				00 07								00 36										
West Sutton	d				00 10								00 39										
Sutton (Surrey)	a				00 13								00 43										
East Croydon	d		23p24					23p56	00 03							00 26	00 34			01a03	00 56		
Denmark Hill	d										23p52												
Peckham Rye	d										23p55												
Nunhead	d										23p57												
Crofton Park	d										23p59												
Catford	d										00 03												
Bellingham	d										00 05												
Beckenham Hill	d										00 07												
Ravensbourne	d										00 09												
Shortlands	d										00 11												
Bromley South	d										00 14												
Bickley	d										00 17												
St Mary Cray	d																						
Swanley	d																						
Eynsford	d																						
Shoreham (Kent)	d																						
Otford	d																						
Bat & Ball	d																						
Sevenoaks	a						00 05			00 12		00 18						00 54					
Redhill	d																						
Gatwick Airport	d		23p41					00 18								00 48					01 18		
Three Bridges	d		23p47					00a24								00a54					01a24		
Balcombe	d		23p53																				
Haywards Heath	d		23p58																				
Wivelsfield	d		00 02																				
Burgess Hill	d		00 04																				
Hassocks	d		00 08																				
Preston Park	d		00 15																				
Brighton	a		00 19																				

Table 52

Saturdays

Bedford, Luton, St.Albans and City of London - South London, Gatwick Airport and Brighton

		FC ■	FC 🚌	FC ■	FC	FC ■	FC 🚌	FC	FC ■	FC 🚌	FC ■	FC	FC 🚌	FC ■	FC	FC 🚌	FC ■	FC	FC 🚌	FC ■	FC	EM ◇■	FC 🚌
Bedford ■	d				02 02			03 02				03 42			04 12			04 42			05 12	05 32	
Flitwick	d				02 12			03 12				03 52			04 22			04 52			05 22		
Harlington	d				02 16			03 16				03 56			04 26			04 56			05 26		
Leagrave	d				02 21			03 21				04 01			04 31			05 01			05 31		
Luton ■	d				02 26			03 26				04 06			04 36			05 06			05 36		
Luton Airport Parkway ■	d				02 28			03 28				04 08			04 38			05 08			05 38	05 55	
Harpenden	d				02 34			03 34				04 14			04 44			05 14			05 44		
St Albans City	d				02 40			03 40				04 20			04 50			05 20			05 50		
Radlett	d				02 45			03 45				04 25			04 55			05 25			05 55		
Elstree & Borehamwood	d				02 49			03 49				04 29			04 59			05 29			05 59		
Mill Hill Broadway	d				02 54			03 54				04 34			05 04			05 34			06 04		
Hendon	d				02 57			03 57				04 37			05 07			05 37			06 07		
Cricklewood	d				03 01			04 01				04 41			05 11			05 41			06 11		
West Hampstead Thameslink ⊖	d				03 04			04 04				04 44			05 14			05 44			06 14		
Kentish Town ⊖	d				03 08			04 08				04 48			05 18			05 48			06 18		
St Pancras International ■ ⊖	a				03 15			04 15				04 55			05 25			05 55			06 25	06 21	
St Pancras International ■ ⊖	a																						
	d		01 30				03 00			03 30			04 00			04 30			05 00				05 30
Farringdon ■ ⊖	d																		05 05				05 35
City Thameslink ■	d																						
London Blackfriars ■ ⊖	d		01 40				03 10			03 40			04 10			04 40			05 10				05 40
Elephant & Castle ⊖	d																						
Loughborough Jn	d																						
Herne Hill ■	d																						
London Bridge ■	a		01 55				03 25			03 55			04 25			04 55			05 25				05 55
	d	01 05		01 35		02 05			03 05		03 35			04 05			04 35			05 05			
Tulse Hill ■	d																						
Streatham ■	d																						
Mitcham Eastfields	d																						
Mitcham Junction	d																						
Hackbridge	d																						
Carshalton	d																						
Tooting	d																						
Haydons Road	d																						
Wimbledon ■ ⊖ 🚋	d																						
Wimbledon Chase	d																						
South Merton	d																						
Morden South	d																						
St Helier	d																						
Sutton Common	d																						
West Sutton	d																						
Sutton (Surrey) ■	a																						
East Croydon 🚋	d	01 32		02 02		02 32			03 32		04 02			04 32			05 02			05 32			
Denmark Hill ■	d																						
Peckham Rye ■	d																						
Nunhead ■	d																						
Crofton Park	d																						
Catford	d																						
Bellingham	d																						
Beckenham Hill	d																						
Ravensbourne	d																						
Shortlands	d																						
Bromley South ■	d																						
Bickley ■	d																						
St Mary Cray	d																						
Swanley ■	d																						
Eynsford	d																						
Shoreham (Kent)	d																						
Otford ■	d																						
Bat & Ball	d																						
Sevenoaks ■	a																						
Redhill	d																						
Gatwick Airport ■	d	01 52		02 22		02 52			03 52		04 24			04 52			05 22			05 56			
Three Bridges ■	d	01a58		02a28		02a58			03a58		04a30			04a58			05 28			06 00			
Balcombe	d																05 35			06 06			
Haywards Heath ■	d																05 42			06 12			
Wivelsfield ■	d																05 46			06 16			
Burgess Hill ■	d																05 48			06 18			
Hassocks ■	d																05 52			06 22			
Preston Park	d																05 59			06 29			
Brighton ■	a																06 07			06 34			

Table 52

Saturdays

Bedford, Luton, St.Albans and City of London - South London, Gatwick Airport and Brighton

		FC ■	FC	SE	FC ■	FC 🚌	SE ■	FC ■	SN ■	SN	SE	FC 🚌	SE	FC	FC ■	FC	FC ■	FC ■	SN	FC	FC 🚌	FC 🚌
Bedford ■	d	05 38	05 42					06 08									06 24	06 38				
Flitwick	d	05 48	05 52					06 18									06 34	06 48				
Harlington	d	05 52	05 56					06 22									06 38	06 52				
Leagrave	d	05 57	06 01					06 27									06 43	06 57				
Luton ■	d	06 02	06 06					06 32								06 40	06 48	07 02				
Luton Airport Parkway ■	d	06 04	06 08					06 34								06 42	06 50	07 04				
Harpenden	d	06 10	06 14					06 40								06 48	06 56	07 10				
St Albans City	d	06 16	06 20					06 46								06 54	07 04	07 16				
Radlett	d		06 25													06 59						
Elstree & Borehamwood	d		06 29													07 03		07 23				
Mill Hill Broadway	d		06 34													07 07						
Hendon	d		06 37													07 10						
Cricklewood	d		06 41													07 14						
West Hampstead Thameslink ⊖	d	06 30	06 44					06 58								07 18		07 32				
Kentish Town ⊖	d		06 48													07a24						
St Pancras International ■ ⊖	a	06 40	06 54					07 07									07 24	07 41				
St Pancras International ■ ⊖	a																					
	d															07a31						
Farringdon ■ ⊖	d																					
City Thameslink ■	d																					
London Blackfriars ■ ⊖	d					06 00						06 19									06 16	06 37
Elephant & Castle ⊖	d					06 08						06 27									06 24	06 45
Loughborough Jn	d																				06 36	06 57
Herne Hill ■	d					06 16						06a35								06 42	06 44	07a05
London Bridge ■	a			05 43			06 07				06 13											
	d			05 44	05 52		06 08		06 08	06 11	06 14			06 21	06 27				06 41			
Tulse Hill ■	d					06a24								06 31						06 46	06a52	
Streatham ■	d													06 35						06 50		
Mitcham Eastfields	d																			06 54		
Mitcham Junction	d																			06 57		
Hackbridge	d																			07 00		
Carshalton	d																			07 03		
Tooting	d													06 40								
Haydons Road	d													06 43								
Wimbledon ■ ⊖ 🚋	d													06 47								
Wimbledon Chase	d													06 50								
South Merton	d													06 52								
Morden South	d													06 54								
St Helier	d													06 56								
Sutton Common	d													06 58								
West Sutton	d													07 01								
Sutton (Surrey) ■	a													07 05						07 06		
East Croydon 🚋	d				06 05				06 23						06 39							
Denmark Hill ■	d												06 22									
Peckham Rye ■	d									06 20			06 25						06 50			
Nunhead ■	d												06 27									
Crofton Park	d												06 30									
Catford	d												06 33									
Bellingham	d												06 35									
Beckenham Hill	d												06 37									
Ravensbourne	d												06 39									
Shortlands	d												06 41									
Bromley South ■	d												06 44									
Bickley ■	d												06 47									
St Mary Cray	d												06 51									
Swanley ■	d												06 56									
Eynsford	d												07 00									
Shoreham (Kent)	d												07 04									
Otford ■	d												07 07									
Bat & Ball	d												07 10									
Sevenoaks ■	a			06 27			06 33				06 57		07 13									
Redhill	d																					
Gatwick Airport ■	d				06 21										06 56							
Three Bridges ■	d				06 25										07 00							
Balcombe	d				06 31																	
Haywards Heath ■	d				06 38										07 10							
Wivelsfield ■	d																					
Burgess Hill ■	d																					
Hassocks ■	d																					
Preston Park	d																					
Brighton ■	a				06 52										07 24							

Table 52

Bedford, Luton, St.Albans and City of London - South London, Gatwick Airport and Brighton

		FC ■	SN	SE	FC	EM ◇■	SN	FC ■		SN ■	SE ■	SE	SN ■	FC	FC ■	FC ■	SN	FC		FC	FC	FC ■	SN	SE	FC
Bedford	d					06 49									06 54	07 08									
Flitwick	d														07 04	07 18									
Harlington	d														07 08	07 22									
Leagrave	d														07 13	07 27									
Luton	d					07 04								07 10	07 18	07 32									
Luton Airport Parkway	d													07 12	07 20	07 34									
Harpenden	d													07 18	07 26	07 40									
St Albans City	d													07 24	07 34	07 46									
Radlett	d													07 29											
Elstree & Borehamwood	d													07 33		07 53									
Mill Hill Broadway	d													07 37											
Hendon	d													07 40											
Cricklewood	d													07 44											
West Hampstead Thameslink ⊖	d													07 48		08 02									
Kentish Town ⊖	d													07a54											
St Pancras International ⊖	a					07 31									07 54	08 11									
St Pancras International ⊖	a																								
	d													08a01											
Farringdon ⊖	d																								
City Thameslink	d																								
London Blackfriars ⊖	d																			06 46	07 07				
Elephant & Castle ⊖	d																			06 54	07 15				
Loughborough Jn	d																			07 06	07 27				
Herne Hill	d																	07 12		07 14	07a35				
London Bridge	a			06 43							07 07													07 13	
	d	06 42	06 36	06 44	06 45		06 50	06 57		07 03	07 08		07 08				07 11					07 12	07 06	07 14	07 15
Tulse Hill	d				07 01													07 16		07a22					07 31
Streatham	d				07 05													07 20							07 35
Mitcham Eastfields	d																	07 24							
Mitcham Junction	d																	07 27							
Hackbridge	d																	07 30							
Carshalton	d																	07 33							
Tooting	d				07 10																				07 40
Haydons Road	d				07 13																				07 43
Wimbledon ⊖	d				07 17																				07 47
Wimbledon Chase	d				07 20																				07 50
South Merton	d				07 22																				07 52
Morden South	d				07 24																				07 54
St Helier	d				07 26																				07 56
Sutton Common	d				07 28																				07 58
West Sutton	d				07 31																				08 01
Sutton (Surrey)	a				07 35													07 36							08 05
East Croydon	d	06 54	07 04				07 07	07 09		07 21			07 23									07 24	07 34		
Denmark Hill	d											06 52													
Peckham Rye	d											06 55					07 20								
Nunhead	d											06 57													
Crofton Park	d											07 00													
Catford	d											07 03													
Bellingham	d											07 05													
Beckenham Hill	d											07 07													
Ravensbourne	d											07 09													
Shortlands	d											07 11													
Bromley South	d											07 14													
Bickley	d											07 17													
St Mary Cray	d											07 21													
Swanley	d											07 26													
Eynsford	d											07 30													
Shoreham (Kent)	d											07 34													
Otford	d											07 37													
Bat & Ball	d											07 40													
Sevenoaks	a			07 27							07 33	07 43												07 57	
Redhill	d									07 44															
Gatwick Airport	d	07 11						07 26		07 56												07 41			
Three Bridges	d	07 15								08 01												07 45			
Balcombe	d	07 21																							
Haywards Heath	d	07 27						07 38														07 55			
Wivelsfield	d	07 31																				07 59			
Burgess Hill	d	07 33																				08 01			
Hassocks	d	07 36																				08 04			
Preston Park	d	07 43																				08 11			
Brighton	a	07 49						07 54														08 17			

Table 52

Bedford, Luton, St.Albans and City of London - South London, Gatwick Airport and Brighton

		EM ◇■	SN	FC ■		SN	SN ■	SE ■	SE	FC	FC ■	FC ■	SN	FC		FC	FC	FC ■	FC	SN ■	SN	EM ◇■	SN	SE ■	
Bedford	d	07 19									07 24	07 38										07 49			
Flitwick	d										07 34	07 48													
Harlington	d										07 38	07 52													
Leagrave	d										07 43	07 57													
Luton	d									07 40	07 48	08 02										08 05			
Luton Airport Parkway	d	07 35								07 42	07 50	08 04													
Harpenden	d									07 48	07 56	08 10													
St Albans City	d									07 54	08 04	08 16													
Radlett	d									07 59															
Elstree & Borehamwood	d									08 03		08 23													
Mill Hill Broadway	d									08 07															
Hendon	d									08 10															
Cricklewood	d									08 14															
West Hampstead Thameslink ⊖	d									08 18		08 32													
Kentish Town ⊖	d									08a24															
St Pancras International ⊖	a	08 00									08 24	08 41										08 31			
St Pancras International ⊖	a																								
	d									08a31															
Farringdon ⊖	d																								
City Thameslink	d																								
London Blackfriars ⊖	d															07 16	07 37								
Elephant & Castle ⊖	d															07 24	07 45								
Loughborough Jn	d															07 36	07 57								
Herne Hill	d													07 42		07 44	08a05								
London Bridge	a							07 37																07 52	
	d		07 20	07 27		07 33	07 33	07 38					07 41					07 42	07 45	07 45	07 36		07 50	07 53	
Tulse Hill	d													07 46		07a52			08 01						
Streatham	d													07 50					08 05						
Mitcham Eastfields	d													07 54											
Mitcham Junction	d													07 57											
Hackbridge	d													08 00											
Carshalton	d													08 03											
Tooting	d																		08 10						
Haydons Road	d																		08 13						
Wimbledon ⊖	d																		08 17						
Wimbledon Chase	d																		08 20						
South Merton	d																		08 22						
Morden South	d																		08 24						
St Helier	d																		08 26						
Sutton Common	d																		08 28						
West Sutton	d																		08 31						
Sutton (Surrey)	a													08 06					08 35						
East Croydon	d		07 37	07 39			07 51											07 54		08 00	08 04		08 07		
Denmark Hill	d								07 22																
Peckham Rye	d					07 42			07 25				07 50												
Nunhead	d								07 27																
Crofton Park	d								07 30																
Catford	d								07 33																
Bellingham	d								07 35																
Beckenham Hill	d								07 37																
Ravensbourne	d								07 39																
Shortlands	d								07 41																
Bromley South	d								07 44																
Bickley	d								07 47																
St Mary Cray	d								07 51																
Swanley	d								07 56																
Eynsford	d								08 00																
Shoreham (Kent)	d								08 04																
Otford	d								08 07																
Bat & Ball	d								08 10																
Sevenoaks	a							08 02	08 13															08 18	
Redhill	d						08 10													08 17					
Gatwick Airport	d			07 56			08 24											08 11							
Three Bridges	d						08 30											08 15							
Balcombe	d																	08 21							
Haywards Heath	d			08 08														08 27							
Wivelsfield	d																	08 31							
Burgess Hill	d																	08 33							
Hassocks	d																	08 36							
Preston Park	d																	08 43							
Brighton	a			08 24														08 49							

Table 52

Bedford, Luton, St.Albans and City of London - South London, Gatwick Airport and Brighton

Station		SE	FC [1]	SN	SN [1]	SE [1]	SE	SN [1]	FC	FC [1]	FC [1]	SN	FC	FC	FC	FC [1]	SN [1]	SN	FC	EM ◇[1]	SN	SE [1]	SE
Bedford [7]	d									07 54	08 08									08 19			
Flitwick	d									08 04	08 18												
Harlington	d									08 08	08 22												
Leagrave	d									08 13	08 27												
Luton [10]	d								08 10	08 18	08 32												
Luton Airport Parkway [7]	d								08 12	08 20	08 34												
Harpenden	d								08 18	08 26	08 40									08 35			
St Albans City	d								08 24	08 34	08 46												
Radlett	d								08 29														
Elstree & Borehamwood	d								08 33		08 53												
Mill Hill Broadway	d								08 37														
Hendon	d								08 40														
Cricklewood	d								08 44														
West Hampstead Thameslink ⊖	d								08 48		09 02												
Kentish Town ⊖	d								08a54														
St Pancras International [15] ⊖	a									08 54	09 11									09 01			
St Pancras International [15] ⊖	a																						
	d								09a01														
Farringdon [3] ⊖	d																						
City Thameslink [3]	d																						
London Blackfriars [3] ⊖	d													07 46	08 06								
Elephant & Castle ⊖	d													07 54	08 15								
Loughborough Jn	d													08 06	08 27								
Herne Hill [4]	d												08 12	08 14	08a35								
London Bridge [4]	a	07 43				08 07																08 22	08 14
	d	07 44	07 57	08 03	08 03	08 08		08 08				08 11				08 12	08 15	08 06	08 15		08 20	08 23	08 14
Tulse Hill [3]	d												08 16	08a22					08 31				
Streatham [4]	d												08 20						08 35				
Mitcham Eastfields	d												08 24										
Mitcham Junction	d												08 27										
Hackbridge	d												08 30										
Carshalton	d												08 33										
Tooting	d																		08 40				
Haydons Road	d																		08 43				
Wimbledon [6] ⊖	d																		08 47				
Wimbledon Chase	d																		08 50				
South Merton	d																		08 52				
Morden South	d																		08 54				
St Helier	d																		08 56				
Sutton Common	d																		08 58				
West Sutton	d																		09 01				
Sutton (Surrey) [4]	a												08 36						09 05				
East Croydon	d		08 09		08 21			08 23								08 24	08 30	08 34			08 37		
Denmark Hill [4]	d						07 52																
Peckham Rye [4]	d			08 12			07 55					08 20											
Nunhead [4]	d						07 57																
Crofton Park	d						08 00																
Catford	d						08 03																
Bellingham	d						08 05																
Beckenham Hill	d						08 07																
Ravensbourne	d						08 09																
Shortlands	d						08 11																
Bromley South [4]	d						08 14																
Bickley [4]	d						08 17																
St Mary Cray	d						08 21																
Swanley [4]	d						08 26																
Eynsford	d						08 30																
Shoreham (Kent)	d						08 34																
Otford [4]	d						08 37																
Bat & Ball	d						08 40																
Sevenoaks [4]	a	08 27				08 33	08 43															08 48	08 56
Redhill	d				08 44												08b56						
Gatwick Airport [10]	d		08 26		08 56											08 41							
Three Bridges [4]	d				09 01											08 45							
Balcombe	d																						
Haywards Heath [3]	d		08 38													08 55							
Wivelsfield [4]	d															08 59							
Burgess Hill [4]	d															09 01							
Hassocks [4]	d															09 04							
Preston Park	d															09 11							
Brighton [10]	a		08 54													09 17							

b arr. 0848

Table 52

Bedford, Luton, St.Albans and City of London - South London, Gatwick Airport and Brighton

Station		SN	FC [1]	SN	SN [1]	SE [1]	FC	FC [1]	FC [1]	SN	FC	FC	FC	FC [1]	FC	SN [1]	SN	EM ◇[1]	SE [1]	SE	SN	SE [1]	SE
Bedford [7]	d							08 24	08 38									08 49					
Flitwick	d							08 34	08 48														
Harlington	d							08 38	08 52														
Leagrave	d							08 43	08 57														
Luton [10]	d						08 40	08 48	09 02									09 05					
Luton Airport Parkway [7]	d						08 42	08 50	09 04														
Harpenden	d						08 48	08 56	09 10														
St Albans City	d						08 54	09 04	09 16														
Radlett	d						08 59																
Elstree & Borehamwood	d						09 03		09 23														
Mill Hill Broadway	d						09 07																
Hendon	d						09 10																
Cricklewood	d						09 14																
West Hampstead Thameslink ⊖	d						09 18		09 32														
Kentish Town ⊖	d						09a24																
St Pancras International [15] ⊖	a							09 24	09 41									09 29					
St Pancras International [15] ⊖	a																						
	d						09a31																
Farringdon [3] ⊖	d																						
City Thameslink [3]	d																						
London Blackfriars [3] ⊖	d											08 16	08 37										
Elephant & Castle ⊖	d											08 24	08 45										
Loughborough Jn	d											08 36	08 57										
Herne Hill [4]	d										08 42	08 44	09a05										
London Bridge [4]	a					08 37													08 48			08 52	08 44
	d	08 22	08 27	08 33	08 33	08 39				08 41				08 42	08 45	08 45	08 36		08 49		08 50	08 53	08 44
Tulse Hill [3]	d										08 46	08a52			09 01								
Streatham [4]	d										08 50				09 05								
Mitcham Eastfields	d										08 54												
Mitcham Junction	d										08 57												
Hackbridge	d										09 00												
Carshalton	d										09 03												
Tooting	d														09 10								
Haydons Road	d														09 13								
Wimbledon [6] ⊖	d														09 17								
Wimbledon Chase	d														09 20								
South Merton	d														09 22								
Morden South	d														09 24								
St Helier	d														09 26								
Sutton Common	d														09 28								
West Sutton	d														09 31								
Sutton (Surrey) [4]	a										09 06				09 35								
East Croydon	d		08 39		08 51									08 54		09 00	09 04				09 07		
Denmark Hill [4]	d																			08 22			
Peckham Rye [4]	d			08 42						08 50										08 25			
Nunhead [4]	d																			08 27			
Crofton Park	d																			08 30			
Catford	d																			08 33			
Bellingham	d																			08 35			
Beckenham Hill	d																			08 37			
Ravensbourne	d																			08 39			
Shortlands	d																			08 41			
Bromley South [4]	d																			08 44			
Bickley [4]	d																			08 47			
St Mary Cray	d																			08 51			
Swanley [4]	d																			08 56			
Eynsford	d																			09 00			
Shoreham (Kent)	d																			09 04			
Otford [4]	d																			09 07			
Bat & Ball	d																			09 10			
Sevenoaks [4]	a					09 05													09 12	09 13		09 18	09 26
Redhill	d				09 10											09 17							
Gatwick Airport [10]	d		08 56		09 24									09 11									
Three Bridges [4]	d				09 30									09 15									
Balcombe	d													09 21									
Haywards Heath [3]	d		09 08											09 27									
Wivelsfield [4]	d													09 31									
Burgess Hill [4]	d													09 33									
Hassocks [4]	d													09 36									
Preston Park	d													09 43									
Brighton [10]	a		09 24											09 49									

Bedford, Luton, St.Albans and City of London - South London, Gatwick Airport and Brighton

Station		SN	FC 1	SN	SN 1	SE 1	SN 1	FC	FC 1	FC 1	SN	FC	FC	FC	FC 1	SN 1	SN	FC	EM ◇1	SE 1	SE	SN
Bedford	d								08 54	09 08									09 19			
Flitwick	d								09 04	09 18												
Harlington	d								09 08	09 22												
Leagrave	d								09 13	09 27												
Luton	d							09 10	09 18	09 32												
Luton Airport Parkway	d							09 12	09 20	09 34									09 35			
Harpenden	d							09 18	09 26	09 40												
St Albans City	d							09 24	09 34	09 46												
Radlett	d							09 29														
Elstree & Borehamwood	d							09 33		09 53												
Mill Hill Broadway	d							09 37														
Hendon	d							09 40														
Cricklewood	d							09 44														
West Hampstead Thameslink ⊖	d							09 48		10 02												
Kentish Town ⊖	d							09a54														
St Pancras International ⊖	a								09 54	10 11									10 00			
St Pancras International ⊖	a																					
	d							10a01														
Farringdon ⊖	d																					
City Thameslink	d																					
London Blackfriars ⊖	d												08 46	09 07								
Elephant & Castle ⊖	d												08 54	09 15								
Loughborough Jn	d												09 06	09 27								
Herne Hill	d											09 12	09 14	09a35								
London Bridge	a					09 07														09 18		
	d	08 52	08 57	09 03	09 03	09 09	09 08				09 11				09 12	09 15	09 06	09 15		09 19		09 20
Tulse Hill	d											09 16	09a22					09 31				
Streatham	d											09 20						09 35				
Mitcham Eastfields	d											09 24										
Mitcham Junction	d											09 27										
Hackbridge	d											09 30										
Carshalton	d											09 33										
Tooting	d																	09 40				
Haydons Road	d																	09 43				
Wimbledon ⊖	d																	09 47				
Wimbledon Chase	d																	09 50				
South Merton	d																	09 52				
Morden South	d																	09 54				
St Helier	d																	09 56				
Sutton Common	d																	09 58				
West Sutton	d																	10 01				
Sutton (Surrey)	a											09 36						10 05				
East Croydon	d		09 09		09 21		09 23								09 24	09 30	09 34					09 37
Denmark Hill	d																				08 52	
Peckham Rye	d			09 12							09 20										08 55	
Nunhead	d																				08 57	
Crofton Park	d																				09 00	
Catford	d																				09 03	
Bellingham	d																				09 05	
Beckenham Hill	d																				09 07	
Ravensbourne	d																				09 09	
Shortlands	d																				09 11	
Bromley South	d																				09 14	
Bickley	d																				09 17	
St Mary Cray	d																				09 21	
Swanley	d																				09 26	
Eynsford	d																				09 30	
Shoreham (Kent)	d																				09 34	
Otford	d																				09 37	
Bat & Ball	d																				09 40	
Sevenoaks	a					09 35														09 42	09 43	
Redhill	d				09 44											09 52						
Gatwick Airport	d		09 26		09 56										09 41							
Three Bridges	d				10 01										09 45							
Balcombe	d																					
Haywards Heath	d		09 38												09 55							
Wivelsfield	d														09 59							
Burgess Hill	d														10 01							
Hassocks	d														10 04							
Preston Park	d														10 11							
Brighton	a		09 54												10 17							

Bedford, Luton, St.Albans and City of London - South London, Gatwick Airport and Brighton

Station		SE 1	SE	SN	FC 1	SN	SN 1	SE 1	FC	FC 1	FC 1	SN	FC	FC	FC	FC 1	FC	SN 1	SN	EM ◇1	SE 1	SE	SN
Bedford	d									09 24	09 40									09 50			
Flitwick	d									09 34	09 50												
Harlington	d									09 38	09 54												
Leagrave	d									09 43	09 59												
Luton	d								09 40	09 48	10 04									10 05			
Luton Airport Parkway	d								09 42	09 50	10 06												
Harpenden	d								09 48	09 56	10 12												
St Albans City	d								09 54	10 04	10 18												
Radlett	d								09 59														
Elstree & Borehamwood	d								10 03		10 25												
Mill Hill Broadway	d								10 07														
Hendon	d								10 10														
Cricklewood	d								10 14														
West Hampstead Thameslink ⊖	d								10 18		10 34												
Kentish Town ⊖	d								10a24														
St Pancras International ⊖	a									10 24	10 43									10 30			
St Pancras International ⊖	a																						
	d								10a31														
Farringdon ⊖	d																						
City Thameslink	d																						
London Blackfriars ⊖	d													09 16	09 36								
Elephant & Castle ⊖	d													09 24	09 45								
Loughborough Jn	d													09 36	09 57								
Herne Hill	d												09 42	09 44	10a05								
London Bridge	a	09 22	09 14					09 37													09 48		
	d	09 23	09 14	09 22	09 27	09 33	09 33	09 39				09 41				09 42	09 45	09 45	09 36		09 49		09 50
Tulse Hill	d												09 46	09a52			10 01						
Streatham	d												09 50				10 05						
Mitcham Eastfields	d												09 54										
Mitcham Junction	d												09 57										
Hackbridge	d												10 00										
Carshalton	d												10 03										
Tooting	d																10 10						
Haydons Road	d																10 13						
Wimbledon ⊖	d																10 17						
Wimbledon Chase	d																10 20						
South Merton	d																10 22						
Morden South	d																10 24						
St Helier	d																10 26						
Sutton Common	d																10 28						
West Sutton	d																10 31						
Sutton (Surrey)	a												10 06				10 35						
East Croydon	d				09 39		09 51									09 54		10 00	10 04				10 07
Denmark Hill	d																					09 22	
Peckham Rye	d					09 42						09 50										09 25	
Nunhead	d																					09 27	
Crofton Park	d																					09 30	
Catford	d																					09 33	
Bellingham	d																					09 35	
Beckenham Hill	d																					09 37	
Ravensbourne	d																					09 39	
Shortlands	d																					09 41	
Bromley South	d																					09 44	
Bickley	d																					09 47	
St Mary Cray	d																					09 51	
Swanley	d																					09 56	
Eynsford	d																					10 00	
Shoreham (Kent)	d																					10 04	
Otford	d																					10 07	
Bat & Ball	d																					10 10	
Sevenoaks	a	09 48	09 56					10 05													10 12	10 13	
Redhill	d						10 10											10 17					
Gatwick Airport	d				09 56		10 24									10 11							
Three Bridges	d						10 30									10 15							
Balcombe	d															10 21							
Haywards Heath	d				10 08											10 27							
Wivelsfield	d															10 31							
Burgess Hill	d															10 33							
Hassocks	d															10 36							
Preston Park	d															10 43							
Brighton	a				10 24											10 49							

Table 52

Bedford, Luton, St.Albans and City of London - South London, Gatwick Airport and Brighton

	SE	SE	SN		FC	SN	SN	SE	SN	FC	FC	FC	SN		FC	FC	FC	FC	SN	SN	FC	EM	SE
Bedford d											09 54	10 08										10 19	
Flitwick d											10 04	10 18											
Harlington d											10 08	10 22											
Leagrave d											10 13	10 27											
Luton d										10 10	10 18	10 32											
Luton Airport Parkway d										10 12	10 20	10 34										10 35	
Harpenden d										10 18	10 26	10 40											
St Albans City d										10 24	10 34	10 46											
Radlett d										10 29													
Elstree & Borehamwood d										10 33		10 53											
Mill Hill Broadway d										10 37													
Hendon d										10 40													
Cricklewood d										10 44													
West Hampstead Thameslink d										10 48		11 02											
Kentish Town d										10a54													
St Pancras International a											10 54	11 11										11 01	
St Pancras International a																							
d										11a01													
Farringdon d																							
City Thameslink d																							
London Blackfriars d																09 46	10 07						
Elephant & Castle d																09 54	10 15						
Loughborough Jn d																10 06	10 27						
Herne Hill d															10 12	10 14	10a35						
London Bridge a	09 52	09 44						10 07															10 18
London Bridge d	09 53	09 44	09 52		09 57	10 03	10 03	10 09	10 08				10 11					10 12	10 15	10 06	10 15		10 19
Tulse Hill d															10 16	10a22					10 31		
Streatham d															10 20						10 35		
Mitcham Eastfields d															10 24								
Mitcham Junction d															10 27								
Hackbridge d															10 30								
Carshalton d															10 33								
Tooting d																					10 40		
Haydons Road d																					10 43		
Wimbledon d																					10 47		
Wimbledon Chase d																					10 50		
South Merton d																					10 52		
Morden South d																					10 54		
St Helier d																					10 56		
Sutton Common d																					10 58		
West Sutton d																					11 01		
Sutton (Surrey) a															10 36						11 05		
East Croydon d					10 09		10 21		10 23									10 24	10 30	10 34			
Denmark Hill d																							
Peckham Rye d						10 12							10 20										
Nunhead d																							
Crofton Park d																							
Catford d																							
Bellingham d																							
Beckenham Hill d																							
Ravensbourne d																							
Shortlands d																							
Bromley South d																							
Bickley d																							
St Mary Cray d																							
Swanley d																							
Eynsford d																							
Shoreham (Kent) d																							
Otford d																							
Bat & Ball d																							
Sevenoaks a	10 18	10 26						10 35															10 42
Redhill d							10 44												10 52				
Gatwick Airport d					10 26		10 56											10 41					
Three Bridges d							11 01											10 45					
Balcombe d																							
Haywards Heath d					10 38													10 55					
Wivelsfield d																		10 59					
Burgess Hill d																		11 01					
Hassocks d																		11 04					
Preston Park d																		11 11					
Brighton a					10 54													11 17					

Table 52

Bedford, Luton, St.Albans and City of London - South London, Gatwick Airport and Brighton

	SE	SN	SE	SE	SN	FC	SN	SN	SE		FC	FC	FC	SN	FC	FC	FC	FC	FC		SN	SN	EM	SE
Bedford d												10 24	10 38										10 50	
Flitwick d												10 34	10 48											
Harlington d												10 38	10 52											
Leagrave d												10 43	10 57											
Luton d											10 40	10 48	11 02											
Luton Airport Parkway d											10 42	10 50	11 04										11 06	
Harpenden d											10 48	10 56	11 10											
St Albans City d											10 54	11 04	11 16											
Radlett d											10 59													
Elstree & Borehamwood d											11 03		11 23											
Mill Hill Broadway d											11 07													
Hendon d											11 10													
Cricklewood d											11 14													
West Hampstead Thameslink d											11 18		11 32											
Kentish Town d											11a24													
St Pancras International a												11 24	11 41										11 29	
St Pancras International a																								
d											11a31													
Farringdon d																								
City Thameslink d																								
London Blackfriars d																10 16	10 37							
Elephant & Castle d																10 24	10 45							
Loughborough Jn d																10 36	10 57							
Herne Hill d															10 42	10 44	11a05							
London Bridge a			10 22	10 14					10 37															10 48
London Bridge d		10 20	10 23	10 14	10 22	10 27	10 33	10 33	10 39					10 41				10 42	10 45		10 45	10 36		10 49
Tulse Hill d															10 46	10a52			11 01					
Streatham d															10 50				11 05					
Mitcham Eastfields d															10 54									
Mitcham Junction d															10 57									
Hackbridge d															11 00									
Carshalton d															11 03									
Tooting d																			11 10					
Haydons Road d																			11 13					
Wimbledon d																			11 17					
Wimbledon Chase d																			11 20					
South Merton d																			11 22					
Morden South d																			11 24					
St Helier d																			11 26					
Sutton Common d																			11 28					
West Sutton d																			11 31					
Sutton (Surrey) a															11 06				11 35					
East Croydon d		10 37				10 39		10 51										10 54			11 00	11 04		
Denmark Hill d	09 52																							
Peckham Rye d	09 55						10 42							10 50										
Nunhead d	09 57																							
Crofton Park d	10 00																							
Catford d	10 03																							
Bellingham d	10 05																							
Beckenham Hill d	10 07																							
Ravensbourne d	10 09																							
Shortlands d	10 11																							
Bromley South d	10 14																							
Bickley d	10 17																							
St Mary Cray d	10 21																							
Swanley d	10 26																							
Eynsford d	10 30																							
Shoreham (Kent) d	10 34																							
Otford d	10 37																							
Bat & Ball d	10 40																							
Sevenoaks a	10 43		10 48	10 56					11 05															11 12
Redhill d								11 10													11 17			
Gatwick Airport d						10 56		11 24										11 11						
Three Bridges d								11 30										11 15						
Balcombe d																		11 21						
Haywards Heath d						11 08												11 27						
Wivelsfield d																		11 31						
Burgess Hill d																		11 33						
Hassocks d																		11 36						
Preston Park d																		11 43						
Brighton a						11 24												11 49						

Table 52

Bedford, Luton, St.Albans and City of London - South London, Gatwick Airport and Brighton

Station		SE	SN	SE 1 ✈	SE	SN	FC 1	SN	SN 1	SE 1	SN 1	FC	FC 1	FC 1	SN	FC	FC	FC	FC 1	SN 1	SN	FC	EM ◇1
Bedford 7	d												10 54	11 08									11 19
Flitwick	d												11 04	11 18									
Harlington	d												11 08	11 22									
Leagrave	d												11 13	11 27									
Luton 10	d											11 10	11 18	11 32									
Luton Airport Parkway 7	d											11 12	11 20	11 34									11 35
Harpenden	d											11 18	11 26	11 40									
St Albans City	d											11 24	11 34	11 46									
Radlett	d											11 29											
Elstree & Borehamwood	d											11 33		11 53									
Mill Hill Broadway	d											11 37											
Hendon	d											11 40											
Cricklewood	d											11 44											
West Hampstead Thameslink ⊖	d											11 48		12 02									
Kentish Town ⊖	d											11a54											
St Pancras International 15 ⊖	a												11 54	12 11									12 01
St Pancras International 15 ⊖	a																						
	d											12a01											
Farringdon 3 ⊖	d																						
City Thameslink 3	d																						
London Blackfriars 3 ⊖	d																10 46	11 07					
Elephant & Castle ⊖	d																10 54	11 15					
Loughborough Jn	d																11 06	11 27					
Herne Hill 4	d															11 12	11 14	11a35					
London Bridge 4	a			10 52	10 44					11 07													
	d		10 50	10 53	10 44	10 52	10 57	11 03	11 03	11 09	11 08				11 11				11 12	11 15	11 06	11 15	
Tulse Hill 3	d															11 16	11a22					11 31	
Streatham 4	d															11 20						11 35	
Mitcham Eastfields	d															11 24							
Mitcham Junction	d															11 27							
Hackbridge	d															11 30							
Carshalton	d															11 33							
Tooting	d																					11 40	
Haydons Road	d																					11 43	
Wimbledon 6 ⊖	d																					11 47	
Wimbledon Chase	d																					11 50	
South Merton	d																					11 52	
Morden South	d																					11 54	
St Helier	d																					11 56	
Sutton Common	d																					11 58	
West Sutton	d																					12 01	
Sutton (Surrey) 4	a															11 36						12 05	
East Croydon	d		11 07				11 09		11 21		11 23								11 24	11 30	11 34		
Denmark Hill 4	d	10 22																					
Peckham Rye 4	d	10 25						11 12							11 20								
Nunhead 4	d	10 27																					
Crofton Park	d	10 30																					
Catford	d	10 33																					
Bellingham	d	10 35																					
Beckenham Hill	d	10 37																					
Ravensbourne	d	10 39																					
Shortlands	d	10 41																					
Bromley South 4	d	10 44																					
Bickley 4	d	10 47																					
St Mary Cray	d	10 51																					
Swanley 4	d	10 56																					
Eynsford	d	11 00																					
Shoreham (Kent)	d	11 04																					
Otford 4	d	11 07																					
Bat & Ball	d	11 10																					
Sevenoaks 4	a	11 13		11 18	11 26					11 35													
Redhill	d								11 44											11 52			
Gatwick Airport 10	d						11 26		11 56										11 41				
Three Bridges 4	d								12 01										11 45				
Balcombe	d																						
Haywards Heath 3	d						11 38												11 55				
Wivelsfield 4	d																		11 59				
Burgess Hill 4	d																		12 01				
Hassocks 4	d																		12 04				
Preston Park	d																		12 11				
Brighton 10	a						11 54												12 17				

Table 52

Bedford, Luton, St.Albans and City of London - South London, Gatwick Airport and Brighton

Station		SE 1 ✈	SE	SN	SE 1 ✈	SE	SN	FC 1	SN	SN 1	SE 1	FC	FC 1	FC 1	SN	FC	FC	FC	FC 1	FC	SN 1	SN
Bedford 7	d												11 24	11 38								
Flitwick	d												11 34	11 48								
Harlington	d												11 38	11 52								
Leagrave	d												11 43	11 57								
Luton 10	d											11 40	11 48	12 02								
Luton Airport Parkway 7	d											11 42	11 50	12 04								
Harpenden	d											11 48	11 56	12 10								
St Albans City	d											11 54	12 04	12 16								
Radlett	d											11 59										
Elstree & Borehamwood	d											12 03		12 23								
Mill Hill Broadway	d											12 07										
Hendon	d											12 10										
Cricklewood	d											12 14										
West Hampstead Thameslink ⊖	d											12 18		12 32								
Kentish Town ⊖	d											12a24										
St Pancras International 15 ⊖	a												12 24	12 41								
St Pancras International 15 ⊖	a																					
	d											12a31										
Farringdon 3 ⊖	d																					
City Thameslink 3	d																					
London Blackfriars 3 ⊖	d																11 16	11 37				
Elephant & Castle ⊖	d																11 24	11 45				
Loughborough Jn	d																11 36	11 57				
Herne Hill 4	d															11 42	11 44	12a05				
London Bridge 4	a	11 18			11 22	11 14					11 37											
	d	11 19		11 20	11 23	11 14	11 22	11 27	11 33	11 33	11 39				11 41				11 42	11 45	11 45	11 36
Tulse Hill 3	d															11 46	11a52			12 01		
Streatham 4	d															11 50				12 05		
Mitcham Eastfields	d															11 54						
Mitcham Junction	d															11 57						
Hackbridge	d															12 00						
Carshalton	d															12 03						
Tooting	d																			12 10		
Haydons Road	d																			12 13		
Wimbledon 6 ⊖	d																			12 17		
Wimbledon Chase	d																			12 20		
South Merton	d																			12 22		
Morden South	d																			12 24		
St Helier	d																			12 26		
Sutton Common	d																			12 28		
West Sutton	d																			12 31		
Sutton (Surrey) 4	a															12 06				12 35		
East Croydon	d			11 37				11 39		11 51									11 54		12 00	12 04
Denmark Hill 4	d		10 52																			
Peckham Rye 4	d		10 55						11 42						11 50							
Nunhead 4	d		10 57																			
Crofton Park	d		11 00																			
Catford	d		11 03																			
Bellingham	d		11 05																			
Beckenham Hill	d		11 07																			
Ravensbourne	d		11 09																			
Shortlands	d		11 11																			
Bromley South 4	d		11 14																			
Bickley 4	d		11 17																			
St Mary Cray	d		11 21																			
Swanley 4	d		11 26																			
Eynsford	d		11 30																			
Shoreham (Kent)	d		11 34																			
Otford 4	d		11 37																			
Bat & Ball	d		11 40																			
Sevenoaks 4	a	11 42	11 43		11 48	11 56					12 05											
Redhill	d									12 10											12 17	
Gatwick Airport 10	d							11 56		12 24									12 11			
Three Bridges 4	d									12 30									12 15			
Balcombe	d																		12 21			
Haywards Heath 3	d							12 08											12 27			
Wivelsfield 4	d																		12 31			
Burgess Hill 4	d																		12 33			
Hassocks 4	d																		12 36			
Preston Park	d																		12 43			
Brighton 10	a							12 24											12 49			

Table 52

Bedford, Luton, St.Albans and City of London - South London, Gatwick Airport and Brighton

		EM ◇1	SE 1	SE	SN	SE 1	SE	SN		FC 1	SN	SN 1	SE 1	SN 1	FC	FC 1	FC 1	SN		FC	FC	FC	FC 1	SN 1	SN
Bedford 7	d	11 49														11 54	12 08								
Flitwick	d															12 04	12 18								
Harlington	d															12 08	12 22								
Leagrave	d															12 13	12 27								
Luton 10	d	12 05													12 10	12 18	12 32								
Luton Airport Parkway 7	d														12 12	12 20	12 34								
Harpenden	d														12 18	12 26	12 40								
St Albans City	d														12 24	12 34	12 46								
Radlett	d														12 29										
Elstree & Borehamwood	d														12 33		12 53								
Mill Hill Broadway	d														12 37										
Hendon	d														12 40										
Cricklewood	d														12 44										
West Hampstead Thameslink ⊖	d														12 48		13 02								
Kentish Town ⊖	d														12a54										
St Pancras International 15 ⊖	a	12 29														12 54	13 11								
St Pancras International 15 ⊖	a																								
	d														13a01										
Farringdon 3 ⊖	d																								
City Thameslink 3	d																								
London Blackfriars 3 ⊖	d																				11 46	12 07			
Elephant & Castle ⊖	d																				11 54	12 15			
Loughborough Jn	d																				12 06	12 27			
Herne Hill 4	d																			12 12	12 14	12a35			
London Bridge 4	a		11 48			11 52	11 44						12 07												
	d		11 49		11 50	11 53	11 44	11 52		11 57	12 03	12 03	12 09	12 08				12 11					12 12	12 15	12 06
Tulse Hill 3	d																			12 16	12a22				
Streatham 4	d																			12 20					
Mitcham Eastfields	d																			12 24					
Mitcham Junction	d																			12 27					
Hackbridge	d																			12 30					
Carshalton	d																			12 33					
Tooting	d																								
Haydons Road	d																								
Wimbledon 6 ⊖	d																								
Wimbledon Chase	d																								
South Merton	d																								
Morden South	d																								
St Helier	d																								
Sutton Common	d																								
West Sutton	d																								
Sutton (Surrey) 4	a																			12 36					
East Croydon	d				12 07					12 09		12 21		12 23									12 24	12 30	12 34
Denmark Hill 4	d			11 22																					
Peckham Rye 4	d			11 25							12 12							12 20							
Nunhead 4	d			11 27																					
Crofton Park	d			11 30																					
Catford	d			11 33																					
Bellingham	d			11 35																					
Beckenham Hill	d			11 37																					
Ravensbourne	d			11 39																					
Shortlands	d			11 41																					
Bromley South 4	d			11 44																					
Bickley 4	d			11 47																					
St Mary Cray	d			11 51																					
Swanley 4	d			11 56																					
Eynsford	d			12 00																					
Shoreham (Kent)	d			12 04																					
Otford 4	d			12 07																					
Bat & Ball	d			12 10																					
Sevenoaks 4	a		12 12	12 13		12 18	12 26						12 35												
Redhill	d											12 44													
Gatwick Airport 10	d									12 26		12 56											12 41	12 52	
Three Bridges 4	d											13 01											12 45		
Balcombe	d																								
Haywards Heath 3	d									12 38													12 55		
Wivelsfield 4	d																						12 59		
Burgess Hill 4	d																						13 01		
Hassocks 4	d																						13 04		
Preston Park	d																						13 11		
Brighton 10	a									12 54													13 17		

Table 52

Bedford, Luton, St.Albans and City of London - South London, Gatwick Airport and Brighton

		FC	EM ◇1	SE 1		SE	SN	SE 1	SE	SN	FC 1	SN	SN 1	SE 1		FC	FC 1	FC 1	SN	FC	FC	FC	FC 1	FC	
Bedford 7	d		12 19														12 24	12 38							
Flitwick	d																12 34	12 48							
Harlington	d																12 38	12 52							
Leagrave	d																12 43	12 57							
Luton 10	d															12 40	12 48	13 02							
Luton Airport Parkway 7	d		12 35													12 42	12 50	13 04							
Harpenden	d															12 48	12 56	13 10							
St Albans City	d															12 54	13 04	13 16							
Radlett	d															12 59									
Elstree & Borehamwood	d															13 03		13 23							
Mill Hill Broadway	d															13 07									
Hendon	d															13 10									
Cricklewood	d															13 14									
West Hampstead Thameslink ⊖	d															13 18		13 32							
Kentish Town ⊖	d															13a24									
St Pancras International 15 ⊖	a		13 01														13 24	13 41							
St Pancras International 15 ⊖	a																								
	d															13a31									
Farringdon 3 ⊖	d																								
City Thameslink 3	d																								
London Blackfriars 3 ⊖	d																				12 16	12 37			
Elephant & Castle ⊖	d																				12 24	12 45			
Loughborough Jn	d																				12 36	12 57			
Herne Hill 4	d																			12 42	12 44	13a05			
London Bridge 4	a			12 18				12 22	12 14					12 37											
	d	12 15		12 19			12 20	12 23	12 14	12 22	12 27	12 33	12 33	12 39					12 41				12 42	12 45	
Tulse Hill 3	d	12 31																		12 46	12a52			13 01	
Streatham 4	d	12 35																		12 50				13 05	
Mitcham Eastfields	d																			12 54					
Mitcham Junction	d																			12 57					
Hackbridge	d																			13 00					
Carshalton	d																			13 03					
Tooting	d	12 40																						13 10	
Haydons Road	d	12 43																						13 13	
Wimbledon 6 ⊖	d	12 47																						13 17	
Wimbledon Chase	d	12 50																						13 20	
South Merton	d	12 52																						13 22	
Morden South	d	12 54																						13 24	
St Helier	d	12 56																						13 26	
Sutton Common	d	12 58																						13 28	
West Sutton	d	13 01																						13 31	
Sutton (Surrey) 4	a	13 05																		13 06				13 35	
East Croydon	d						12 37				12 39		12 51										12 54		
Denmark Hill 4	d					11 52																			
Peckham Rye 4	d					11 55						12 42							12 50						
Nunhead 4	d					11 57																			
Crofton Park	d					12 00																			
Catford	d					12 03																			
Bellingham	d					12 05																			
Beckenham Hill	d					12 07																			
Ravensbourne	d					12 09																			
Shortlands	d					12 11																			
Bromley South 4	d					12 14																			
Bickley 4	d					12 17																			
St Mary Cray	d					12 21																			
Swanley 4	d					12 26																			
Eynsford	d					12 30																			
Shoreham (Kent)	d					12 34																			
Otford 4	d					12 37																			
Bat & Ball	d					12 40																			
Sevenoaks 4	a			12 42		12 43		12 48	12 56					13 05											
Redhill	d												13 10												
Gatwick Airport 10	d										12 56		13 24										13 11		
Three Bridges 4	d												13 30										13 15		
Balcombe	d																						13 21		
Haywards Heath 3	d										13 08												13 27		
Wivelsfield 4	d																						13 31		
Burgess Hill 4	d																						13 33		
Hassocks 4	d																						13 36		
Preston Park	d																						13 43		
Brighton 10	a										13 24												13 49		

Table 52

Saturdays

Bedford, Luton, St.Albans and City of London - South London, Gatwick Airport and Brighton

		SN ■	SN	EM ◇■	SE ■	SE	SN	SE ■	SE	SN		FC ■	SN	SN ■	SE ■	SN ■	FC	FC ■	FC ■	SN		FC	FC	FC	FC ■
Bedford	d			12 49														12 54	13 08						
Flitwick	d																	13 04	13 18						
Harlington	d																	13 08	13 22						
Leagrave	d																	13 13	13 27						
Luton	d			13 05													13 10	13 18	13 32						
Luton Airport Parkway	d																13 12	13 20	13 34						
Harpenden	d																13 18	13 26	13 40						
St Albans City	d																13 24	13 34	13 46						
Radlett	d																13 29								
Elstree & Borehamwood	d																13 33		13 53						
Mill Hill Broadway	d																13 37								
Hendon	d																13 40								
Cricklewood	d																13 44								
West Hampstead Thameslink ⊖	d																13 48		14 02						
Kentish Town ⊖	d																13a54								
St Pancras International ⊖	a			13 28														13 54	14 11						
St Pancras International ⊖	a																								
	d																14a01								
Farringdon ⊖	d																								
City Thameslink	d																								
London Blackfriars ⊖	d																						12 46	13 07	
Elephant & Castle ⊖	d																						12 54	13 15	
Loughborough Jn	d																						13 06	13 27	
Herne Hill	d																					13 12	13 14	13a35	
London Bridge	a				12 48			12 52	12 44						13 07										
	d	12 45	12 36		12 49		12 50	12 53	12 44	12 52		12 57	13 03	13 03	13 09	13 08				13 11					13 12
Tulse Hill	d																					13 16	13a22		
Streatham	d																					13 20			
Mitcham Eastfields	d																					13 24			
Mitcham Junction	d																					13 27			
Hackbridge	d																					13 30			
Carshalton	d																					13 33			
Tooting	d																								
Haydons Road	d																								
Wimbledon ⊖	d																								
Wimbledon Chase	d																								
South Merton	d																								
Morden South	d																								
St Helier	d																								
Sutton Common	d																								
West Sutton	d																								
Sutton (Surrey)	a																					13 36			
East Croydon	d	13 00	13 04				13 07					13 09		13 21		13 23									13 24
Denmark Hill	d					12 22																			
Peckham Rye	d					12 25							13 12							13 20					
Nunhead	d					12 27																			
Crofton Park	d					12 30																			
Catford	d					12 33																			
Bellingham	d					12 35																			
Beckenham Hill	d					12 37																			
Ravensbourne	d					12 39																			
Shortlands	d					12 41																			
Bromley South	d					12 44																			
Bickley	d					12 47																			
St Mary Cray	d					12 51																			
Swanley	d					12 56																			
Eynsford	d					13 00																			
Shoreham (Kent)	d					13 04																			
Otford	d					13 07																			
Bat & Ball	d					13 10																			
Sevenoaks	a				13 12	13 13		13 18	13 26						13 35										
Redhill	d	13 17												13 44											
Gatwick Airport	d											13 26		13 56											13 41
Three Bridges	d													14 01											13 45
Balcombe	d																								
Haywards Heath	d											13 38													13 55
Wivelsfield	d																								13 59
Burgess Hill	d																								14 01
Hassocks	d																								14 04
Preston Park	d																								14 11
Brighton	a											13 54													14 17

Table 52

Saturdays

Bedford, Luton, St.Albans and City of London - South London, Gatwick Airport and Brighton

		SN ■	SN	FC	EM ◇■	SE ■		SE	SN	SE ■	SE	SN	FC ■	SN	SN ■	SE ■		FC	FC ■	FC ■	SN	FC	FC	FC	FC ■
Bedford	d				13 19														13 24	13 38					
Flitwick	d																		13 34	13 48					
Harlington	d																		13 38	13 52					
Leagrave	d																		13 43	13 57					
Luton	d																	13 40	13 48	14 02					
Luton Airport Parkway	d				13 35													13 42	13 50	14 04					
Harpenden	d																	13 48	13 56	14 10					
St Albans City	d																	13 54	14 04	14 16					
Radlett	d																	13 59							
Elstree & Borehamwood	d																	14 03		14 23					
Mill Hill Broadway	d																	14 07							
Hendon	d																	14 10							
Cricklewood	d																	14 14							
West Hampstead Thameslink ⊖	d																	14 18		14 32					
Kentish Town ⊖	d																	14a24							
St Pancras International ⊖	a				14 01														14 24	14 41					
St Pancras International ⊖	a																								
	d																	14a31							
Farringdon ⊖	d																								
City Thameslink	d																								
London Blackfriars ⊖	d																						13 16	13 37	
Elephant & Castle ⊖	d																						13 24	13 45	
Loughborough Jn	d																						13 36	13 57	
Herne Hill	d																					13 42	13 44	14a05	
London Bridge	a					13 18				13 22	13 14					13 37									
	d	13 15	13 06	13 15		13 19			13 20	13 23	13 14	13 22	13 27	13 33	13 33	13 39					13 41				13 42
Tulse Hill	d			13 31																		13 46	13a52		
Streatham	d			13 35																		13 50			
Mitcham Eastfields	d																					13 54			
Mitcham Junction	d																					13 57			
Hackbridge	d																					14 00			
Carshalton	d																					14 03			
Tooting	d			13 40																					
Haydons Road	d			13 43																					
Wimbledon ⊖	d			13 47																					
Wimbledon Chase	d			13 50																					
South Merton	d			13 52																					
Morden South	d			13 54																					
St Helier	d			13 56																					
Sutton Common	d			13 58																					
West Sutton	d			14 01																					
Sutton (Surrey)	a			14 05																		14 06			
East Croydon	d	13 30	13 34						13 37				13 39		13 51										13 54
Denmark Hill	d							12 52																	
Peckham Rye	d							12 55						13 42							13 50				
Nunhead	d							12 57																	
Crofton Park	d							13 00																	
Catford	d							13 03																	
Bellingham	d							13 05																	
Beckenham Hill	d							13 07																	
Ravensbourne	d							13 09																	
Shortlands	d							13 11																	
Bromley South	d							13 14																	
Bickley	d							13 17																	
St Mary Cray	d							13 21																	
Swanley	d							13 26																	
Eynsford	d							13 30																	
Shoreham (Kent)	d							13 34																	
Otford	d							13 37																	
Bat & Ball	d							13 40																	
Sevenoaks	a					13 42		13 43		13 48	13 56					14 05									
Redhill	d	13 52													14 10										
Gatwick Airport	d												13 56		14 24										14 11
Three Bridges	d														14 30										14 15
Balcombe	d																								14 21
Haywards Heath	d												14 08												14 27
Wivelsfield	d																								14 31
Burgess Hill	d																								14 33
Hassocks	d																								14 36
Preston Park	d																								14 43
Brighton	a												14 24												14 49

Table 52

Saturdays

Bedford, Luton, St.Albans and City of London - South London, Gatwick Airport and Brighton

		FC		SN	SN	EM	SE	SE	SN	SE	SE	SN		FC	SN	SN	SE	SN	FC	FC	FC	SN		FC	FC
Bedford	d					13 49														13 54	14 08				
Flitwick	d																			14 04	14 18				
Harlington	d																			14 08	14 22				
Leagrave	d																			14 13	14 27				
Luton	d					14 05													14 10	14 18	14 32				
Luton Airport Parkway	d																		14 12	14 20	14 34				
Harpenden	d																		14 18	14 26	14 40				
St Albans City	d																		14 24	14 34	14 46				
Radlett	d																		14 29						
Elstree & Borehamwood	d																		14 33		14 53				
Mill Hill Broadway	d																		14 37						
Hendon	d																		14 40						
Cricklewood	d																		14 44						
West Hampstead Thameslink ⊖	d																		14 48		15 02				
Kentish Town ⊖	d																		14a54						
St Pancras International ⊖	a					14 28														14 54	15 11				
St Pancras International ⊖	a																								
	d																		15a01						
Farringdon ⊖	d																								
City Thameslink	d																								
London Blackfriars ⊖	d																								13 46
Elephant & Castle ⊖	d																								13 54
Loughborough Jn	d																								14 06
Herne Hill	d																							14 12	14 14
London Bridge	a						13 48			13 52	13 44						14 07								
	d	13 45		13 45	13 36		13 49		13 50	13 53	13 44	13 52		13 57	14 03	4 03	14 09	14 08				14 11			
Tulse Hill	d	14 01																						14 16	14a22
Streatham	d	14 05																						14 20	
Mitcham Eastfields	d																							14 24	
Mitcham Junction	d																							14 27	
Hackbridge	d																							14 30	
Carshalton	d																							14 33	
Tooting	d	14 10																							
Haydons Road	d	14 13																							
Wimbledon ⊖	d	14 17																							
Wimbledon Chase	d	14 20																							
South Merton	d	14 22																							
Morden South	d	14 24																							
St Helier	d	14 26																							
Sutton Common	d	14 28																							
West Sutton	d	14 31																							
Sutton (Surrey)	a	14 35																						14 36	
East Croydon	d			14 00	14 04				14 07					14 09		14 21		14 23							
Denmark Hill	d							13 22																	
Peckham Rye	d							13 25							14 12							14 20			
Nunhead	d							13 27																	
Crofton Park	d							13 30																	
Catford	d							13 33																	
Bellingham	d							13 35																	
Beckenham Hill	d							13 37																	
Ravensbourne	d							13 39																	
Shortlands	d							13 41																	
Bromley South	d							13 44																	
Bickley	d							13 47																	
St Mary Cray	d							13 51																	
Swanley	d							13 56																	
Eynsford	d							14 00																	
Shoreham (Kent)	d							14 04																	
Otford	d							14 07																	
Bat & Ball	d							14 10																	
Sevenoaks	a						14 12	14 13		14 18	14 26						14 35								
Redhill	d			14 17												14 44									
Gatwick Airport	d													14 26		14 56									
Three Bridges	d															15 01									
Balcombe	d																								
Haywards Heath	d													14 38											
Wivelsfield	d																								
Burgess Hill	d																								
Hassocks	d																								
Preston Park	d																								
Brighton	a													14 54											

Table 52

Saturdays

Bedford, Luton, St.Albans and City of London - South London, Gatwick Airport and Brighton

		FC	FC	SN	SN	FC	EM	SE		SE	SN	SE	SE	SN	FC	SN	SN	SE		FC	FC	FC	SN	FC	FC
Bedford	d						14 19														14 24	14 38			
Flitwick	d																				14 34	14 48			
Harlington	d																				14 38	14 52			
Leagrave	d																				14 43	14 57			
Luton	d																			14 40	14 48	15 02			
Luton Airport Parkway	d						14 35													14 42	14 50	15 04			
Harpenden	d																			14 48	14 56	15 10			
St Albans City	d																			14 54	15 04	15 16			
Radlett	d																			14 59					
Elstree & Borehamwood	d																			15 03		15 23			
Mill Hill Broadway	d																			15 07					
Hendon	d																			15 10					
Cricklewood	d																			15 14					
West Hampstead Thameslink ⊖	d																			15 18		15 32			
Kentish Town ⊖	d																			15a24					
St Pancras International ⊖	a						15 01														15 24	15 41			
St Pancras International ⊖	a																								
	d																			15a31					
Farringdon ⊖	d																								
City Thameslink	d																								
London Blackfriars ⊖	d	14 07																							14 16
Elephant & Castle ⊖	d	14 15																							14 24
Loughborough Jn	d	14 27																							14 36
Herne Hill	d	14a35																						14 42	14 44
London Bridge	a							14 18				14 22	14 14					14 37							
	d		14 12	14 15	14 06	14 15		14 19			14 20	14 23	14 14	14 22	14 27	14 33	14 33	14 39					14 41		
Tulse Hill	d					14 31																		14 46	14a52
Streatham	d					14 35																		14 50	
Mitcham Eastfields	d																							14 54	
Mitcham Junction	d																							14 57	
Hackbridge	d																							15 00	
Carshalton	d																							15 03	
Tooting	d					14 40																			
Haydons Road	d					14 43																			
Wimbledon ⊖	d					14 47																			
Wimbledon Chase	d					14 50																			
South Merton	d					14 52																			
Morden South	d					14 54																			
St Helier	d					14 56																			
Sutton Common	d					14 58																			
West Sutton	d					15 01																			
Sutton (Surrey)	a					15 05																		15 06	
East Croydon	d		14 24	14 30	14 34						14 37				14 39		14 51								
Denmark Hill	d									13 52															
Peckham Rye	d									13 55						14 42							14 50		
Nunhead	d									13 57															
Crofton Park	d									14 00															
Catford	d									14 03															
Bellingham	d									14 05															
Beckenham Hill	d									14 07															
Ravensbourne	d									14 09															
Shortlands	d									14 11															
Bromley South	d									14 14															
Bickley	d									14 17															
St Mary Cray	d									14 21															
Swanley	d									14 26															
Eynsford	d									14 30															
Shoreham (Kent)	d									14 34															
Otford	d									14 37															
Bat & Ball	d									14 40															
Sevenoaks	a							14 42		14 43		14 48	14 56					15 05							
Redhill	d			14 52													15 10								
Gatwick Airport	d		14 41												14 56		15 24								
Three Bridges	d		14 45														15 30								
Balcombe	d																								
Haywards Heath	d		14 55												15 08										
Wivelsfield	d		14 59																						
Burgess Hill	d		15 01																						
Hassocks	d		15 04																						
Preston Park	d		15 11																						
Brighton	a		15 17												15 24										

Table 52 — Saturdays

Bedford, Luton, St.Albans and City of London - South London, Gatwick Airport and Brighton

		FC	FC ■	FC	SN ■	SN	EM ◇■	SE ■	SE	SN	SE ■	SE	SN	FC ■	SN	SN ■	SE ■	SN ■	FC	FC ■	FC ■	SN
Bedford ■	d						14 49													14 54	15 08	
Flitwick	d																			15 04	15 18	
Harlington	d																			15 08	15 22	
Leagrave	d																			15 13	15 27	
Luton ■	d						15 05												15 10	15 18	15 32	
Luton Airport Parkway ■	d																		15 12	15 20	15 34	
Harpenden	d																		15 18	15 26	15 40	
St Albans City	d																		15 24	15 34	15 46	
Radlett	d																		15 29			
Elstree & Borehamwood	d																		15 33		15 53	
Mill Hill Broadway	d																		15 37			
Hendon	d																		15 40			
Cricklewood	d																		15 44			
West Hampstead Thameslink ⊖	d																		15 48		16 02	
Kentish Town ⊖	d																		15a54			
St Pancras International ■ ⊖	a						15 28													15 54	16 11	
St Pancras International ■ ⊖	a																					
	d																		16a01			
Farringdon ■ ⊖	d																					
City Thameslink ■	d																					
London Blackfriars ■ ⊖	d	14 37																				
Elephant & Castle ⊖	d	14 45																				
Loughborough Jn	d	14 57																				
Herne Hill ■	d	15a05																				
London Bridge ■	a							14 48			14 52	14 44					15 07					
	d		14 42	14 45	14 45	14 36		14 49		14 50	14 53	14 44	14 52	14 57	15 03	15 03	15 09	15 08				15 11
Tulse Hill ■	d			15 01																		
Streatham ■	d			15 05																		
Mitcham Eastfields	d																					
Mitcham Junction	d																					
Hackbridge	d																					
Carshalton	d																					
Tooting	d			15 10																		
Haydons Road	d			15 13																		
Wimbledon ■ ⊖	d			15 17																		
Wimbledon Chase	d			15 20																		
South Merton	d			15 22																		
Morden South	d			15 24																		
St Helier	d			15 26																		
Sutton Common	d			15 28																		
West Sutton	d			15 31																		
Sutton (Surrey) ■	a			15 35																		
East Croydon	d		14 54		15 00	15 04				15 07				15 09		15 21		15 23				
Denmark Hill ■	d								14 22													
Peckham Rye ■	d								14 25						15 12							15 20
Nunhead ■	d								14 27													
Crofton Park	d								14 30													
Catford	d								14 33													
Bellingham	d								14 35													
Beckenham Hill	d								14 37													
Ravensbourne	d								14 39													
Shortlands	d								14 41													
Bromley South ■	d								14 44													
Bickley ■	d								14 47													
St Mary Cray	d								14 51													
Swanley ■	d								14 56													
Eynsford	d								15 00													
Shoreham (Kent)	d								15 04													
Otford ■	d								15 07													
Bat & Ball	d								15 10													
Sevenoaks ■	a							15 12	15 13		15 18	15 26					15 35					
Redhill	d				15 17											15 44						
Gatwick Airport ■	d		15 11											15 26		15 56						
Three Bridges ■	d		15 15													16 01						
Balcombe	d		15 21																			
Haywards Heath ■	d		15 27											15 38								
Wivelsfield ■	d		15 31																			
Burgess Hill ■	d		15 33																			
Hassocks ■	d		15 36																			
Preston Park	d		15 43																			
Brighton ■	a		15 49											15 54								

Table 52 — Saturdays

Bedford, Luton, St.Albans and City of London - South London, Gatwick Airport and Brighton

		FC	FC	FC	FC ■	SN ■	SN	FC	EM ◇■	SE ■	SE	SN	SE ■	SE	SN	FC ■	SN	SN ■	SE ■	FC	FC ■	FC ■	SN
Bedford ■	d								15 19												15 24	15 38	
Flitwick	d																				15 34	15 48	
Harlington	d																				15 38	15 52	
Leagrave	d																				15 43	15 57	
Luton ■	d																			15 40	15 48	16 02	
Luton Airport Parkway ■	d								15 35											15 42	15 50	16 04	
Harpenden	d																			15 48	15 56	16 10	
St Albans City	d																			15 54	16 04	16 16	
Radlett	d																			15 59			
Elstree & Borehamwood	d																			16 03		16 23	
Mill Hill Broadway	d																			16 07			
Hendon	d																			16 10			
Cricklewood	d																			16 14			
West Hampstead Thameslink ⊖	d																			16 18		16 32	
Kentish Town ⊖	d																			16a24			
St Pancras International ■ ⊖	a								16 01												16 24	16 41	
St Pancras International ■ ⊖	a																						
	d																			16a31			
Farringdon ■ ⊖	d																						
City Thameslink ■	d																						
London Blackfriars ■ ⊖	d		14 46	15 07																			
Elephant & Castle ⊖	d		14 54	15 15																			
Loughborough Jn	d		15 06	15 27																			
Herne Hill ■	d	15 12	15 14	15a35																			
London Bridge ■	a									15 18			15 22	15 14					15 37				
	d				15 12	15 15	15 06	15 15		15 19		15 20	15 23	15 14	15 22	15 27	15 33	15 33	15 39				15 41
Tulse Hill ■	d	15 16	15a22					15 31															
Streatham ■	d	15 20						15 35															
Mitcham Eastfields	d	15 24																					
Mitcham Junction	d	15 27																					
Hackbridge	d	15 30																					
Carshalton	d	15 33																					
Tooting	d							15 40															
Haydons Road	d							15 43															
Wimbledon ■ ⊖	d							15 47															
Wimbledon Chase	d							15 50															
South Merton	d							15 52															
Morden South	d							15 54															
St Helier	d							15 56															
Sutton Common	d							15 58															
West Sutton	d							16 01															
Sutton (Surrey) ■	a	15 36						16 05															
East Croydon	d				15 24	15 30	15 34					15 37				15 39		15 51					
Denmark Hill ■	d										14 52												
Peckham Rye ■	d										14 55						15 42						15 50
Nunhead ■	d										14 57												
Crofton Park	d										15 00												
Catford	d										15 03												
Bellingham	d										15 05												
Beckenham Hill	d										15 07												
Ravensbourne	d										15 09												
Shortlands	d										15 11												
Bromley South ■	d										15 14												
Bickley ■	d										15 17												
St Mary Cray	d										15 21												
Swanley ■	d										15 26												
Eynsford	d										15 30												
Shoreham (Kent)	d										15 34												
Otford ■	d										15 37												
Bat & Ball	d										15 40												
Sevenoaks ■	a									15 42	15 43		15 48	15 56					16 05				
Redhill	d					15 52												16 10					
Gatwick Airport ■	d				15 41											15 56		16 24					
Three Bridges ■	d				15 45													16 30					
Balcombe	d																						
Haywards Heath ■	d				15 55											16 08							
Wivelsfield ■	d				15 59																		
Burgess Hill ■	d				16 01																		
Hassocks ■	d				16 04																		
Preston Park	d				16 11																		
Brighton ■	a				16 17											16 24							

Table 52

Saturdays

Bedford, Luton, St.Albans and City of London - South London, Gatwick Airport and Brighton

		FC	FC	FC	FC ■	FC		SN ■	SN	SE ■	SE	EM ◇■	SN	SE ■	SE	SN		FC ■	SN	SN ■	SE ■	SN ■	FC	FC ■	FC ■
Bedford	d											15 50												15 54	16 08
Flitwick	d																							16 04	16 18
Harlington	d																							16 08	16 22
Leagrave	d																							16 13	16 27
Luton	d											16 06											16 10	16 18	16 32
Luton Airport Parkway	d																						16 12	16 20	16 34
Harpenden	d																						16 18	16 26	16 40
St Albans City	d																						16 24	16 34	16 46
Radlett	d																						16 29		
Elstree & Borehamwood	d																						16 33		16 53
Mill Hill Broadway	d																						16 37		
Hendon	d																						16 40		
Cricklewood	d																						16 44		
West Hampstead Thameslink ⊖	d																						16 48		17 02
Kentish Town ⊖	d																						16a54		
St Pancras International ⊖	a											16 29												16 54	17 11
St Pancras International ⊖	a																								
	d																						17a01		
Farringdon ⊖	d																								
City Thameslink	d																								
London Blackfriars ⊖	d		15 16	15 37																					
Elephant & Castle ⊖	d		15 24	15 45																					
Loughborough Jn	d		15 36	15 57																					
Herne Hill	d	15 42	15 44	16a05																					
London Bridge	a									15 48				15 52	15 44						16 07				
	d				15 42	15 45		15 45	15 36	15 49			15 50	15 53	15 44	15 52		15 57	16 03	16 03	16 09	16 08			
Tulse Hill	d	15 46	15a52			16 01																			
Streatham	d	15 50				16 05																			
Mitcham Eastfields	d	15 54																							
Mitcham Junction	d	15 57																							
Hackbridge	d	16 00																							
Carshalton	d	16 03																							
Tooting	d					16 10																			
Haydons Road	d					16 13																			
Wimbledon ⊖	d					16 17																			
Wimbledon Chase	d					16 20																			
South Merton	d					16 22																			
Morden South	d					16 24																			
St Helier	d					16 26																			
Sutton Common	d					16 28																			
West Sutton	d					16 31																			
Sutton (Surrey)	a	16 06				16 35																			
East Croydon	d				15 54			16 00	16 04				16 07					16 09		16 21		16 23			
Denmark Hill	d										15 22														
Peckham Rye	d										15 25								16 12						
Nunhead	d										15 27														
Crofton Park	d										15 30														
Catford	d										15 33														
Bellingham	d										15 35														
Beckenham Hill	d										15 37														
Ravensbourne	d										15 39														
Shortlands	d										15 41														
Bromley South	d										15 44														
Bickley	d										15 47														
St Mary Cray	d										15 51														
Swanley	d										15 56														
Eynsford	d										16 00														
Shoreham (Kent)	d										16 04														
Otford	d										16 07														
Bat & Ball	d										16 10														
Sevenoaks	a									16 12	16 13			16 18	16 26						16 35				
Redhill	d							16 17												16 44					
Gatwick Airport	d				16 11													16 26		16 56					
Three Bridges	d				16 15															17 01					
Balcombe	d				16 21																				
Haywards Heath	d				16 27													16 38							
Wivelsfield	d				16 31																				
Burgess Hill	d				16 33																				
Hassocks	d				16 36																				
Preston Park	d				16 43																				
Brighton	a				16 49													16 54							

Table 52

Saturdays

Bedford, Luton, St.Albans and City of London - South London, Gatwick Airport and Brighton

		SN		FC	FC	FC	FC ■	SN ■	SN	FC	EM ◇■	SE ■		SE	SN	SE ■	SE	SN	FC ■	SN	SN ■	SE ■		FC	FC ■
Bedford	d										16 19														16 24
Flitwick	d																								16 34
Harlington	d																								16 38
Leagrave	d																								16 43
Luton	d																							16 40	16 48
Luton Airport Parkway	d										16 35													16 42	16 50
Harpenden	d																							16 48	16 56
St Albans City	d																							16 54	17 04
Radlett	d																							16 59	
Elstree & Borehamwood	d																							17 03	
Mill Hill Broadway	d																							17 07	
Hendon	d																							17 10	
Cricklewood	d																							17 14	
West Hampstead Thameslink ⊖	d																							17 18	
Kentish Town ⊖	d																							17a24	
St Pancras International ⊖	a										17 01														17 24
St Pancras International ⊖	a																								
	d																							17a31	
Farringdon ⊖	d																								
City Thameslink	d																								
London Blackfriars ⊖	d				15 46	16 07																			
Elephant & Castle ⊖	d				15 54	16 15																			
Loughborough Jn	d				16 06	16 27																			
Herne Hill	d			16 12	16 14	16a35																			
London Bridge	a											16 18				16 22	16 14					16 37			
	d	16 11					16 12	16 15	16 06	16 15		16 19			16 20	16 23	16 14	16 22	16 27	16 33	16 33	16 39			
Tulse Hill	d			16 16	16a22					16 31															
Streatham	d			16 20						16 35															
Mitcham Eastfields	d			16 24																					
Mitcham Junction	d			16 27																					
Hackbridge	d			16 30																					
Carshalton	d			16 33																					
Tooting	d									16 40															
Haydons Road	d									16 43															
Wimbledon ⊖	d									16 47															
Wimbledon Chase	d									16 50															
South Merton	d									16 52															
Morden South	d									16 54															
St Helier	d									16 56															
Sutton Common	d									16 58															
West Sutton	d									17 01															
Sutton (Surrey)	a			16 36						17 05															
East Croydon	d						16 24	16 30	16 34						16 37				16 39		16 51				
Denmark Hill	d													15 52											
Peckham Rye	d	16 20												15 55						16 42					
Nunhead	d													15 57											
Crofton Park	d													16 00											
Catford	d													16 03											
Bellingham	d													16 05											
Beckenham Hill	d													16 07											
Ravensbourne	d													16 09											
Shortlands	d													16 11											
Bromley South	d													16 14											
Bickley	d													16 17											
St Mary Cray	d													16 21											
Swanley	d													16 26											
Eynsford	d													16 30											
Shoreham (Kent)	d													16 34											
Otford	d													16 37											
Bat & Ball	d													16 40											
Sevenoaks	a											16 42		16 43		16 48	16 56					17 05			
Redhill	d							16 52													17 10				
Gatwick Airport	d						16 41												16 56		17 24				
Three Bridges	d						16 45														17 30				
Balcombe	d																								
Haywards Heath	d						16 55												17 08						
Wivelsfield	d						16 59																		
Burgess Hill	d						17 01																		
Hassocks	d						17 04																		
Preston Park	d						17 11																		
Brighton	a						17 17												17 24						

Bedford, Luton, St.Albans and City of London - South London, Gatwick Airport and Brighton

		FC 1	SN	FC	FC (bus)	FC (bus)	FC 1	FC	SN 1	SN	EM ◇1	SE 1	SE	SN	SE 1	SE	SN	FC 1	SN	SN 1	SE 1	SN 1	FC
Bedford	d	16 38									16 49												
Flitwick	d	16 48																					
Harlington	d	16 52																					
Leagrave	d	16 57																					
Luton	d	17 02									17 05												17 10
Luton Airport Parkway	d	17 04																					17 12
Harpenden	d	17 10																					17 18
St Albans City	d	17 16																					17 24
Radlett	d																						17 29
Elstree & Borehamwood	d	17 23																					17 33
Mill Hill Broadway	d																						17 37
Hendon	d																						17 40
Cricklewood	d																						17 44
West Hampstead Thameslink ⊖	d	17 32																					17 48
Kentish Town ⊖	d																						17a54
St Pancras International ⊖	a	17 41									17 28												
St Pancras International ⊖	a																						18a01
	d																						
Farringdon ⊖	d																						
City Thameslink	d																						
London Blackfriars ⊖	d				16 16	16 37																	
Elephant & Castle ⊖	d				16 24	16 45																	
Loughborough Jn	d				16 36	16 57																	
Herne Hill	d			16 42	16 44	17a05																	
London Bridge	a											16 48			16 52	16 44					17 07		
	d		16 41				16 42	16 45	16 45	16 36		16 49		16 50	16 53	16 44	16 52	16 57	17 03	17 03	17 09	17 08	
Tulse Hill	d			16 46	16a52			17 01															
Streatham	d			16 50				17 05															
Mitcham Eastfields	d			16 54																			
Mitcham Junction	d			16 57																			
Hackbridge	d			17 00																			
Carshalton	d			17 03																			
Tooting	d							17 10															
Haydons Road	d							17 13															
Wimbledon ⊖	d							17 17															
Wimbledon Chase	d							17 20															
South Merton	d							17 22															
Morden South	d							17 24															
St Helier	d							17 26															
Sutton Common	d							17 28															
West Sutton	d							17 31															
Sutton (Surrey)	a			17 06				17 35															
East Croydon	d						16 54		17 00	17 04				17 07				17 09		17 21		17 23	
Denmark Hill	d												16 22										
Peckham Rye	d		16 50										16 25						17 12				
Nunhead	d												16 27										
Crofton Park	d												16 30										
Catford	d												16 33										
Bellingham	d												16 35										
Beckenham Hill	d												16 37										
Ravensbourne	d												16 39										
Shortlands	d												16 41										
Bromley South	d												16 44										
Bickley	d												16 47										
St Mary Cray	d												16 51										
Swanley	d												16 56										
Eynsford	d												17 00										
Shoreham (Kent)	d												17 04										
Otford	d												17 07										
Bat & Ball	d												17 10										
Sevenoaks	a											17 12	17 13		17 18	17 26					17 35		
Redhill	d								17 17											17 44			
Gatwick Airport	d						17 11											17 26		17 56			
Three Bridges	d						17 15													18 01			
Balcombe	d						17 21																
Haywards Heath	d						17 27											17 38					
Wivelsfield	d						17 31																
Burgess Hill	d						17 33																
Hassocks	d						17 36																
Preston Park	d						17 43																
Brighton	a						17 49											17 54					

Bedford, Luton, St.Albans and City of London - South London, Gatwick Airport and Brighton

		FC 1	FC 1	SN	FC	FC (bus)	FC (bus)	FC 1	SN 1	SN	FC	EM ◇1	SE 1	SE	SN	SE 1	SE	SN	FC 1	SN	SN 1	SE 1
Bedford	d	16 54	17 08									17 19										
Flitwick	d	17 04	17 18																			
Harlington	d	17 08	17 22																			
Leagrave	d	17 13	17 27																			
Luton	d	17 18	17 32																			
Luton Airport Parkway	d	17 20	17 34									17 35										
Harpenden	d	17 26	17 40																			
St Albans City	d	17 34	17 46																			
Radlett	d																					
Elstree & Borehamwood	d		17 53																			
Mill Hill Broadway	d																					
Hendon	d																					
Cricklewood	d																					
West Hampstead Thameslink ⊖	d		18 02																			
Kentish Town ⊖	d																					
St Pancras International ⊖	a	17 54	18 11									18 01										
St Pancras International ⊖	a																					
	d																					
Farringdon ⊖	d																					
City Thameslink	d																					
London Blackfriars ⊖	d					16 46	17 07															
Elephant & Castle ⊖	d					16 54	17 15															
Loughborough Jn	d					17 06	17 27															
Herne Hill	d				17 12	17 14	17a35															
London Bridge	a												17 18			17 22	17 14					17 37
	d			17 11				17 12	17 15	17 06	17 15		17 19		17 20	17 23	17 14	17 22	17 27	17 33	17 33	17 39
Tulse Hill	d				17 16	17a22					17 31											
Streatham	d				17 20						17 35											
Mitcham Eastfields	d				17 24																	
Mitcham Junction	d				17 27																	
Hackbridge	d				17 30																	
Carshalton	d				17 33																	
Tooting	d										17 40											
Haydons Road	d										17 43											
Wimbledon ⊖	d										17 47											
Wimbledon Chase	d										17 50											
South Merton	d										17 52											
Morden South	d										17 54											
St Helier	d										17 56											
Sutton Common	d										17 58											
West Sutton	d										18 01											
Sutton (Surrey)	a				17 36						18 05											
East Croydon	d							17 24	17 30	17 34					17 37				17 39		17 51	
Denmark Hill	d													16 52								
Peckham Rye	d			17 20										16 55						17 42		
Nunhead	d													16 57								
Crofton Park	d													17 00								
Catford	d													17 03								
Bellingham	d													17 05								
Beckenham Hill	d													17 07								
Ravensbourne	d													17 09								
Shortlands	d													17 11								
Bromley South	d													17 14								
Bickley	d													17 17								
St Mary Cray	d													17 21								
Swanley	d													17 26								
Eynsford	d													17 30								
Shoreham (Kent)	d													17 34								
Otford	d													17 37								
Bat & Ball	d													17 40								
Sevenoaks	a												17 42	17 43		17 48	17 56					18 05
Redhill	d								17 52												18 10	
Gatwick Airport	d							17 41											17 56		18 24	
Three Bridges	d							17 45													18 30	
Balcombe	d																					
Haywards Heath	d							17 55											18 08			
Wivelsfield	d							17 59														
Burgess Hill	d							18 01														
Hassocks	d							18 04														
Preston Park	d							18 11														
Brighton	a							18 17											18 24			

Table 52

Saturdays

Bedford, Luton, St.Albans and City of London - South London, Gatwick Airport and Brighton

		FC	FC 1	FC 1	SN	FC	FC bus	FC bus	FC bus	FC 1	FC	SN 1	SN	EM ◇1	SE 1	SE	SN	SE 1	SE	SN	FC 1	SN	SN 1
Bedford 7	d		17 24	17 38										17 49									
Flitwick	d		17 34	17 48																			
Harlington	d		17 38	17 52																			
Leagrave	d		17 43	17 57																			
Luton 10	d	17 40	17 48	18 02										18 05									
Luton Airport Parkway 7	d	17 42	17 50	18 04																			
Harpenden	d	17 48	17 56	18 10																			
St Albans City	d	17 54	18 04	18 16																			
Radlett	d	17 59																					
Elstree & Borehamwood	d	18 03		18 23																			
Mill Hill Broadway	d	18 07																					
Hendon	d	18 10																					
Cricklewood	d	18 14																					
West Hampstead Thameslink ⊖	d	18 18		18 32																			
Kentish Town ⊖	d	18a24																					
St Pancras International 15 ⊖	a		18 24	18 41										18 28									
St Pancras International 15 ⊖	a																						
	d	18a31																					
Farringdon 3 ⊖	d																						
City Thameslink 3	d																						
London Blackfriars 3 ⊖	d						17 16	17 37	17 38														
Elephant & Castle ⊖	d						17 24	17 45	17 46														
Loughborough Jn	d						17 36	17 57	17 58														
Herne Hill 4	d					17 42	17 44	18a05	18a06														
London Bridge 4	a														17 48			17 52	17 44				
	d				17 41					17 42	17 45	17 45	17 36		17 49		17 50	17 53	17 44	17 52	17 57	18 03	18 03
Tulse Hill 3	d					17 46	17a52				18 01												
Streatham 4	d					17 50					18 05												
Mitcham Eastfields	d					17 54																	
Mitcham Junction	d					17 57																	
Hackbridge	d					18 00																	
Carshalton	d					18 03																	
Tooting	d										18 10												
Haydons Road	d										18 13												
Wimbledon 8 ⊖	d										18 17												
Wimbledon Chase	d										18 20												
South Merton	d										18 22												
Morden South	d										18 24												
St Helier	d										18 26												
Sutton Common	d										18 28												
West Sutton	d										18 31												
Sutton (Surrey) 4	a					18 06					18 35												
East Croydon	d									17 54		18 00	18 04				18 07				18 09		18 21
Denmark Hill 4	d															17 22							
Peckham Rye 4	d				17 50											17 25						18 12	
Nunhead 4	d															17 27							
Crofton Park	d															17 30							
Catford	d															17 33							
Bellingham	d															17 35							
Beckenham Hill	d															17 37							
Ravensbourne	d															17 39							
Shortlands	d															17 41							
Bromley South 4	d															17 44							
Bickley 4	d															17 47							
St Mary Cray	d															17 51							
Swanley 4	d															17 56							
Eynsford	d															18 00							
Shoreham (Kent)	d															18 04							
Otford 4	d															18 07							
Bat & Ball	d															18 10							
Sevenoaks 4	a														18 12	18 13		18 18	18 26				
Redhill	d											18 17											
Gatwick Airport 10	d									18 11													18 44
Three Bridges 4	d									18 15											18 26		18 56
Balcombe	d									18 21													19 01
Haywards Heath 3	d									18 27											18 38		
Wivelsfield 4	d									18 31													
Burgess Hill 4	d									18 33													
Hassocks 4	d									18 36													
Preston Park	d									18 43													
Brighton 10	a									18 49											18 54		

Table 52

Saturdays

Bedford, Luton, St.Albans and City of London - South London, Gatwick Airport and Brighton

		SE 1	SN 1	FC	FC 1	FC 1	SN	FC	FC bus	FC bus	FC 1	SN 1	SN	FC	EM ◇1	SE 1	SE	SN	SE 1	SE	SN	FC 1	FC 1
Bedford 7	d				17 54	18 08									18 19							18 22	
Flitwick	d				18 04	18 18																18 32	
Harlington	d				18 08	18 22																18 36	
Leagrave	d				18 13	18 27																18 41	
Luton 10	d			18 10	18 18	18 32																18 46	
Luton Airport Parkway 7	d			18 12	18 20	18 34									18 35							18 48	
Harpenden	d			18 18	18 26	18 40																18 54	
St Albans City	d			18 24	18 34	18 46																19 00	
Radlett	d			18 29																			
Elstree & Borehamwood	d			18 33		18 53																	
Mill Hill Broadway	d			18 37																			
Hendon	d			18 40																			
Cricklewood	d			18 44																			
West Hampstead Thameslink ⊖	d			18 48		19 02																19 14	
Kentish Town ⊖	d			18a54																			
St Pancras International 15 ⊖	a				18 54	19 11									18 59							19 24	
St Pancras International 15 ⊖	a																						
	d			19a01																			
Farringdon 3 ⊖	d																						
City Thameslink 3	d																						
London Blackfriars 3 ⊖	d								17 46	18 07													
Elephant & Castle ⊖	d								17 54	18 15													
Loughborough Jn	d								18 06	18 27													
Herne Hill 4	d							18 12	18 14	18a35													
London Bridge 4	a	18 07														18 18			18 22	18 14			
	d	18 09	18 08				18 11				18 12	18 15	18 06	18 15		18 19		18 20	18 23	18 14	18 22		18 27
Tulse Hill 3	d							18 16	18a22					18 31									
Streatham 4	d							18 20						18 35									
Mitcham Eastfields	d							18 24															
Mitcham Junction	d							18 27															
Hackbridge	d							18 30															
Carshalton	d							18 33															
Tooting	d													18 40									
Haydons Road	d													18 43									
Wimbledon 8 ⊖	d													18 47									
Wimbledon Chase	d													18 50									
South Merton	d													18 52									
Morden South	d													18 54									
St Helier	d													18 56									
Sutton Common	d													18 58									
West Sutton	d													19 01									
Sutton (Surrey) 4	a							18 36						19 05									
East Croydon	d		18 23								18 24	18 30	18 34					18 37					18 39
Denmark Hill 4	d																17 52						
Peckham Rye 4	d						18 20										17 55						
Nunhead 4	d																17 57						
Crofton Park	d																18 00						
Catford	d																18 03						
Bellingham	d																18 05						
Beckenham Hill	d																18 07						
Ravensbourne	d																18 09						
Shortlands	d																18 11						
Bromley South 4	d																18 14						
Bickley 4	d																18 17						
St Mary Cray	d																18 21						
Swanley 4	d																18 26						
Eynsford	d																18 30						
Shoreham (Kent)	d																18 34						
Otford 4	d																18 37						
Bat & Ball	d																18 40						
Sevenoaks 4	a	18 35														18 42	18 43		18 48	18 56			
Redhill	d											18 52											
Gatwick Airport 10	d										18 41												18 56
Three Bridges 4	d										18 45												
Balcombe	d																						
Haywards Heath 3	d										18 55												19 08
Wivelsfield 4	d										18 59												
Burgess Hill 4	d										19 01												
Hassocks 4	d										19 04												
Preston Park	d										19 11												
Brighton 10	a										19 17												19 24

Bedford, Luton, St.Albans and City of London - South London, Gatwick Airport and Brighton

		SN		SN [1]	SE [1]	SN	FC	FC	FC	FC [1]	FC	SN [1]		SN	EM ◇[1]	SE [1]	SE	FC	SN	SE [1]	SE	SN		FC [1]	FC [1]
Bedford [7]	d														18 49									18 52	
Flitwick	d																							19 02	
Harlington	d																							19 06	
Leagrave	d																							19 11	
Luton [10]	d														19 05			18 50						19 16	
Luton Airport Parkway [7]	d																	18 52						19 18	
Harpenden	d																	18 58						19 24	
St Albans City	d																	19 04						19 30	
Radlett	d																	19 09							
Elstree & Borehamwood	d																	19 13							
Mill Hill Broadway	d																	19 18							
Hendon	d																	19 21							
Cricklewood	d																	19 25							
West Hampstead Thameslink ⊖	d																	19 28						19 44	
Kentish Town ⊖	d																	19 33							
St Pancras International [15] ⊖	a														19 29			19 39						19 54	
St Pancras International [15] ⊖	a																								
	d																								
Farringdon [3] ⊖	d																								
City Thameslink [3]	d																								
London Blackfriars [3] ⊖	d							18 16	18 37																
Elephant & Castle ⊖	d							18 24	18 45																
Loughborough Jn	d							18 36	18 57																
Herne Hill [4]	d						18 42	18 44	19a05																
London Bridge [4]	a				18 37											18 48				18 52	18 44				
	d	18 33		18 33	18 39	18 41				18 42	18 45	18 45		18 36		18 49			18 50	18 53	18 44	18 52			18 57
Tulse Hill [3]	d						18 46	18a52			19 01														
Streatham [4]	d						18 50				19 05														
Mitcham Eastfields	d						18 54																		
Mitcham Junction	d						18 57																		
Hackbridge	d						19 00																		
Carshalton	d						19 03																		
Tooting	d										19 10														
Haydons Road	d										19 13														
Wimbledon [6] ⊖	d										19 17														
Wimbledon Chase	d										19 20														
South Merton	d										19 22														
Morden South	d										19 24														
St Helier	d										19 26														
Sutton Common	d										19 28														
West Sutton	d										19 31														
Sutton (Surrey) [4]	a						19 06				19 39														
East Croydon	d			18 51						18 54		19 00		19 04					19 07						19 09
Denmark Hill [4]	d																18 22								
Peckham Rye [4]	d	18 42				18 50											18 25								
Nunhead [4]	d																18 27								
Crofton Park	d																18 30								
Catford	d																18 33								
Bellingham	d																18 35								
Beckenham Hill	d																18 37								
Ravensbourne	d																18 39								
Shortlands	d																18 41								
Bromley South [4]	d																18 44								
Bickley [4]	d																18 47								
St Mary Cray	d																18 51								
Swanley [4]	d																18 56								
Eynsford	d																19 00								
Shoreham (Kent)	d																19 04								
Otford [4]	d																19 07								
Bat & Ball	d																19 10								
Sevenoaks [4]	a				19 05											19 12	19 13			19 18	19 26				
Redhill	d			19 10								19 17													
Gatwick Airport [10]	d			19 24						19 11															19 26
Three Bridges [4]	d			19 30						19 15															
Balcombe	d									19 21															
Haywards Heath [3]	d									19 27															19 38
Wivelsfield [4]	d									19 31															
Burgess Hill [4]	d									19 33															
Hassocks [4]	d									19 36															
Preston Park	d									19 43															
Brighton [10]	a									19 49															19 54

Bedford, Luton, St.Albans and City of London - South London, Gatwick Airport and Brighton

		SN	SN [1]	SE [1]	SN [1]	SN	FC	FC	EM ◇[1]	FC	FC [1]	SN	FC	SE [1]	SE	FC	SE [1]	SE		SN	FC [1]	FC [1]	SN	SN [1]	SE [1]
Bedford [7]	d								19 19												19 22				
Flitwick	d																				19 32				
Harlington	d																				19 36				
Leagrave	d																				19 41				
Luton [10]	d															19 20					19 46				
Luton Airport Parkway [7]	d								19 34							19 22					19 48				
Harpenden	d															19 28					19 54				
St Albans City	d															19 34					20 00				
Radlett	d															19 39									
Elstree & Borehamwood	d															19 43									
Mill Hill Broadway	d															19 48									
Hendon	d															19 51									
Cricklewood	d															19 55									
West Hampstead Thameslink ⊖	d															19 58					20 14				
Kentish Town ⊖	d															20 02									
St Pancras International [15] ⊖	a								20 00							20 09					20 24				
St Pancras International [15] ⊖	a																								
	d																								
Farringdon [3] ⊖	d																								
City Thameslink [3]	d																								
London Blackfriars [3] ⊖	d							18 46		19 07															
Elephant & Castle ⊖	d							18 54		19 15															
Loughborough Jn	d							19 06		19 27															
Herne Hill [4]	d						19 12	19 14		19a35															
London Bridge [4]	a			19 07										19 18			19 22	19 14							19 37
	d	19 03	19 03	19 09	19 08	19 11					19 12	19 06	19 15	19 19			19 23	19 14		19 22		19 27	19 33	19 33	19 39
Tulse Hill [3]	d						19 16	19a22					19 31												
Streatham [4]	d						19 20						19 35												
Mitcham Eastfields	d						19 24																		
Mitcham Junction	d						19 27																		
Hackbridge	d						19 30																		
Carshalton	d						19 33																		
Tooting	d												19 40												
Haydons Road	d												19 43												
Wimbledon [6] ⊖	d												19 47												
Wimbledon Chase	d												19 50												
South Merton	d												19 52												
Morden South	d												19 54												
St Helier	d												19 56												
Sutton Common	d												19 58												
West Sutton	d												20 01												
Sutton (Surrey) [4]	a						19 36						20 05												
East Croydon	d		19 21		19 23						19 24	19 34										19 39		19 51	
Denmark Hill [4]	d														18 52										
Peckham Rye [4]	d	19 12				19 20									18 55								19 42		
Nunhead [4]	d														18 57										
Crofton Park	d														19 00										
Catford	d														19 03										
Bellingham	d														19 05										
Beckenham Hill	d														19 07										
Ravensbourne	d														19 09										
Shortlands	d														19 11										
Bromley South [4]	d														19 14										
Bickley [4]	d														19 17										
St Mary Cray	d														19 21										
Swanley [4]	d														19 26										
Eynsford	d														19 30										
Shoreham (Kent)	d														19 34										
Otford [4]	d														19 37										
Bat & Ball	d														19 40										
Sevenoaks [4]	a			19 35										19 42	19 43		19 49	19 56							20 05
Redhill	d		19b46																					20 10	
Gatwick Airport [10]	d		19 56								19 41											19 56		20 24	
Three Bridges [4]	d		20 01								19 45													20 33	
Balcombe	d																								
Haywards Heath [3]	d										19 55											20 08			
Wivelsfield [4]	d										19 59														
Burgess Hill [4]	d										20 01														
Hassocks [4]	d										20 04														
Preston Park	d										20 11														
Brighton [10]	a										20 17											20 24			

b arr. 1939

Table 52

Saturdays

Bedford, Luton, St.Albans and City of London - South London, Gatwick Airport and Brighton

		SN	FC	FC		FC ■	SN	FC	FC	EM ◇■	SE ■	SE	SE	FC		SN	FC ■	FC ■	SE ■	SE	SN ■	SN	FC ■	SN	EM ◇■
Bedford ■	d									19 49							19 52								20 17
Flitwick	d																20 02								
Harlington	d																20 06								
Leagrave	d																20 11								
Luton ■	d									20 04				19 50			20 16								
Luton Airport Parkway ■	d													19 52			20 18								20 34
Harpenden	d													19 58			20 24								
St Albans City	d													20 04			20 30								
Radlett	d													20 09											
Elstree & Borehamwood	d													20 13											
Mill Hill Broadway	d													20 18											
Hendon	d													20 21											
Cricklewood	d													20 25											
West Hampstead Thameslink ⊖	d													20 28			20 44								
Kentish Town ⊖	d													20 32											
St Pancras International ■ ⊖	a									20 29				20 39			20 54								21 02
St Pancras International ■ ⊖	a																								
	d																								
Farringdon ■ ⊖	d																								
City Thameslink ■	d																								
London Blackfriars ■ ⊖	d			19 16					19 46																
Elephant & Castle ⊖	d			19 24					19 54																
Loughborough Jn	d			19 36					20 06																
Herne Hill ■	d		19 42	19 44					20 14																
London Bridge ■	a										19 48		19 43						20 02						
	d	19 41				19 42	19 36	19 45			19 49		19 44			19 52		19 57	20 03		20 08	20 11	20 12	20 06	
Tulse Hill ■	d		19 46	19a53				20 01	20a22																
Streatham ■	d		19 51					20 05																	
Mitcham Eastfields	d		19 55																						
Mitcham Junction	d		19 58																						
Hackbridge	d		20 01																						
Carshalton	d		20 04																						
Tooting	d							20 10																	
Haydons Road	d							20 13																	
Wimbledon ■ ⊖	d							20 17																	
Wimbledon Chase	d							20 20																	
South Merton	d							20 22																	
Morden South	d							20 24																	
St Helier	d							20 26																	
Sutton Common	d							20 28																	
West Sutton	d							20 31																	
Sutton (Surrey) ■	a		20 07					20 39																	
East Croydon	d					19 54	20 04											20 09			20 23		20 24	20 34	
Denmark Hill ■	d											19 22								19 52					
Peckham Rye ■	d	19 50										19 25								19 55		20 20			
Nunhead ■	d											19 27								19 57					
Crofton Park	d											19 30								20 00					
Catford	d											19 33								20 03					
Bellingham	d											19 35								20 05					
Beckenham Hill	d											19 37								20 07					
Ravensbourne	d											19 39								20 09					
Shortlands	d											19 41								20 11					
Bromley South ■	d											19 44								20 14					
Bickley ■	d											19 47								20 17					
St Mary Cray	d											19 51								20 21					
Swanley ■	d											19 56								20 26					
Eynsford	d											20 00								20 30					
Shoreham (Kent)	d											20 04								20 34					
Otford ■	d											20 07								20 37					
Bat & Ball	d											20 10								20 40					
Sevenoaks ■	a										20 12	20 13	20 27						20 30	20 43					
Redhill	d																								
Gatwick Airport ■	d					20 11												20 26					20 41		
Three Bridges ■	d					20 15																	20 45		
Balcombe	d					20 21																	20 53		
Haywards Heath ■	d					20 27												20 38					20 58		
Wivelsfield ■	d					20 31																	21 02		
Burgess Hill ■	d					20 33																	21 04		
Hassocks ■	d					20 36																	21 08		
Preston Park	d					20 43																	21 15		
Brighton ■	a					20 49												20 54					21 19		

Table 52

Saturdays

Bedford, Luton, St.Albans and City of London - South London, Gatwick Airport and Brighton

		FC	FC	SE ■	SE	FC	SN	FC ■	SE ■	SE		SN	FC ■	SN	FC	FC	EM ◇■	SE ■	SE	FC		SN	FC ■	SE ■	SE
Bedford ■	d							20 22									20 49						20 52		
Flitwick	d							20 32															21 02		
Harlington	d							20 36															21 06		
Leagrave	d							20 41															21 11		
Luton ■	d					20 20		20 46									21 03			20 50			21 16		
Luton Airport Parkway ■	d					20 22		20 48												20 52			21 18		
Harpenden	d					20 28		20 54												20 58			21 24		
St Albans City	d					20 34		21 00												21 04			21 30		
Radlett	d					20 39														21 09					
Elstree & Borehamwood	d					20 43														21 13					
Mill Hill Broadway	d					20 48														21 18					
Hendon	d					20 51														21 21					
Cricklewood	d					20 55														21 25					
West Hampstead Thameslink ⊖	d					20 58		21 14												21 28			21 44		
Kentish Town ⊖	d					21 02														21 32					
St Pancras International ■ ⊖	a					21 11		21 24									21 29			21 41			21 54		
St Pancras International ■ ⊖	a																								
	d																								
Farringdon ■ ⊖	d																								
City Thameslink ■	d																								
London Blackfriars ■ ⊖	d		20 16													20 46									
Elephant & Castle ⊖	d		20 24													20 54									
Loughborough Jn	d		20 36													21 06									
Herne Hill ■	d		20 44													21 14									
London Bridge ■	a			20 18	20 13				20 32									20 48	20 43					21 02	
	d	20 15		20 19	20 14		20 22		20 33			20 41	20 42	20 36	20 45			20 49	20 44			20 52		21 03	
Tulse Hill ■	d	20 31	20a52												21 01	21a22									
Streatham ■	d	20 35													21 05										
Mitcham Eastfields	d																								
Mitcham Junction	d																								
Hackbridge	d																								
Carshalton	d																								
Tooting	d	20 40													21 10										
Haydons Road	d	20 43													21 13										
Wimbledon ■ ⊖	d	20 47													21 17										
Wimbledon Chase	d	20 50													21 20										
South Merton	d	20 52													21 22										
Morden South	d	20 54													21 24										
St Helier	d	20 56													21 26										
Sutton Common	d	20 58													21 28										
West Sutton	d	21 01													21 31										
Sutton (Surrey) ■	a	21 05													21 39										
East Croydon	d												20 54	21 04											
Denmark Hill ■	d									20 22															20 52
Peckham Rye ■	d									20 25		20 50													20 55
Nunhead ■	d									20 27															20 57
Crofton Park	d									20 30															21 00
Catford	d									20 33															21 03
Bellingham	d									20 35															21 05
Beckenham Hill	d									20 37															21 07
Ravensbourne	d									20 39															21 09
Shortlands	d									20 41															21 11
Bromley South ■	d									20 44															21 14
Bickley ■	d									20 47															21 17
St Mary Cray	d									20 51															21 21
Swanley ■	d									20 56															21 26
Eynsford	d									21 00															21 30
Shoreham (Kent)	d									21 04															21 34
Otford ■	d									21 07															21 37
Bat & Ball	d									21 10															21 40
Sevenoaks ■	a			20 44	20 57				21 00	21 13								21 14	21 27					21 30	21 43
Redhill	d																								
Gatwick Airport ■	d												21 11												
Three Bridges ■	d												21 15												
Balcombe	d																								
Haywards Heath ■	d												21 26												
Wivelsfield ■	d												21 30												
Burgess Hill ■	d												21 32												
Hassocks ■	d												21 36												
Preston Park	d												21 43												
Brighton ■	a												21 47												

Table 52

Saturdays

Bedford, Luton, St.Albans and City of London - South London, Gatwick Airport and Brighton

		SN	SN	FC	SN	FC	FC	SE	SE	EM	FC	SN	FC	SE	SE	SN	FC	SN	EM	FC	FC	SE	FC
		1		1				1		◇1			1	1			1		◇1			1	
Bedford	d									21 22			21 22						21 47				
Flitwick	d												21 32										
Harlington	d												21 36										
Leagrave	d										21 20		21 41										
Luton	d												21 46						22 03				21 50
Luton Airport Parkway	d									21 38	21 22		21 48										21 52
Harpenden	d										21 28		21 54										21 58
St Albans City	d										21 34		22 00										22 04
Radlett	d										21 39												22 09
Elstree & Borehamwood	d										21 43												22 13
Mill Hill Broadway	d										21 48												22 18
Hendon	d										21 51												22 21
Cricklewood	d										21 55												22 25
West Hampstead Thameslink ⊖	d										21 58		22 14										22 28
Kentish Town ⊖	d										22 02												22 32
St Pancras International ⊖	a									22 05	22 09		22 24						22 30				22 41
St Pancras International ⊖	a																						
	d																						
Farringdon ⊖	d																						
City Thameslink	d																						
London Blackfriars ⊖	d						21 16														21 46		
Elephant & Castle ⊖	d						21 24														21 54		
Loughborough Jn	d						21 36														22 06		
Herne Hill	d						21 44														22 14		
London Bridge	a							21 18	21 13					21 32								21 48	
	d	21 08	21 11	21 12	21 06	21 15		21 19	21 14			21 22		21 33		21 41	21 42	21 36		21 45		21 49	
Tulse Hill	d					21 31	21a52													22 01	22a22		
Streatham	d					21 35														22 05			
Mitcham Eastfields	d																						
Mitcham Junction	d																						
Hackbridge	d																						
Carshalton	d																						
Tooting	d					21 40														22 10			
Haydons Road	d					21 43														22 13			
Wimbledon ⊖	d					21 47														22 17			
Wimbledon Chase	d					21 50														22 20			
South Merton	d					21 52														22 22			
Morden South	d					21 54														22 24			
St Helier	d					21 56														22 26			
Sutton Common	d					21 58														22 28			
West Sutton	d					22 01														22 31			
Sutton (Surrey)	a					22 05														22 39			
East Croydon	d	21 23		21 24	21 34												21 54	22 05					
Denmark Hill	d														21 22								
Peckham Rye	d		21 20												21 25	21 50							
Nunhead	d														21 27								
Crofton Park	d														21 30								
Catford	d														21 33								
Bellingham	d														21 35								
Beckenham Hill	d														21 37								
Ravensbourne	d														21 39								
Shortlands	d														21 41								
Bromley South	d														21 44								
Bickley	d														21 47								
St Mary Cray	d														21 51								
Swanley	d														21 56								
Eynsford	d														22 00								
Shoreham (Kent)	d														22 04								
Otford	d														22 07								
Bat & Ball	d														22 10								
Sevenoaks	a							21 44	21 57					22 00	22 13							22 14	
Redhill	d																						
Gatwick Airport	d			21 41													22 11						
Three Bridges	d			21 45													22 15						
Balcombe	d			21 53																			
Haywards Heath	d			21 58													22 26						
Wivelsfield	d			22 02													22 30						
Burgess Hill	d			22 04													22 32						
Hassocks	d			22 08													22 36						
Preston Park	d			22 15													22 43						
Brighton	a			22 19													22 47						

Table 52

Saturdays

Bedford, Luton, St.Albans and City of London - South London, Gatwick Airport and Brighton

		SN	FC	EM	SE	SE	SN	SN	FC	SN	FC	FC	SE	FC	FC	SN	SE	SE	EM	SN	FC	SN
			1	◇1	1		1		1				1				1		◇1		1	
Bedford	d		21 52	22 02											22 12				22 37			
Flitwick	d		22 02												22 22							
Harlington	d		22 06												22 26							
Leagrave	d		22 11												22 31							
Luton	d		22 16	22 17										22 20	22 36				22 59			
Luton Airport Parkway	d		22 18	22 20										22 22	22 38							
Harpenden	d		22 24											22 28	22 44							
St Albans City	d		22 30											22 34	22 50							
Radlett	d													22 39	22 55							
Elstree & Borehamwood	d													22 43	22 59							
Mill Hill Broadway	d													22 48	23 04							
Hendon	d													22 51	23 07							
Cricklewood	d													22 55	23 11							
West Hampstead Thameslink ⊖	d		22 44											22 58	23 14							
Kentish Town ⊖	d													23 02	23 18							
St Pancras International ⊖	a		22 54	22 47										23 09	23 25				23 35			
St Pancras International ⊖	a																					
	d																					
Farringdon ⊖	d																					
City Thameslink	d																					
London Blackfriars ⊖	d											22 16										
Elephant & Castle ⊖	d											22 24										
Loughborough Jn	d											22 36										
Herne Hill	d											22 44										
London Bridge	a				22 02								22 18				22 32					
	d	21 52			22 03		22 08	22 11	22 12	22 06	22 15		22 19			22 22	22 33			22 41	22 42	22 36
Tulse Hill	d										22 31	22a52										
Streatham	d										22 35											
Mitcham Eastfields	d																					
Mitcham Junction	d																					
Hackbridge	d																					
Carshalton	d																					
Tooting	d										22 40											
Haydons Road	d										22 43											
Wimbledon ⊖	d										22 47											
Wimbledon Chase	d										22 50											
South Merton	d										22 52											
Morden South	d										22 54											
St Helier	d										22 56											
Sutton Common	d										22 58											
West Sutton	d										23 01											
Sutton (Surrey)	a										23 05											
East Croydon	d						22 23		22 24	22 36											22 54	23 04
Denmark Hill	d					21 52												22 22				
Peckham Rye	d					21 55		22 20										22 25		22 50		
Nunhead	d					21 57												22 27				
Crofton Park	d					22 00												22 30				
Catford	d					22 03												22 33				
Bellingham	d					22 05												22 35				
Beckenham Hill	d					22 07												22 37				
Ravensbourne	d					22 09												22 39				
Shortlands	d					22 11												22 41				
Bromley South	d					22 14												22 44				
Bickley	d					22 17												22 47				
St Mary Cray	d					22 21												22 51				
Swanley	d					22 26												22 56				
Eynsford	d					22 30												23 00				
Shoreham (Kent)	d					22 34												23 04				
Otford	d					22 37												23 07				
Bat & Ball	d					22 40												23 10				
Sevenoaks	a				22 30	22 43							22 44				22 59	23 13				
Redhill	d																					
Gatwick Airport	d								22 41												23 11	
Three Bridges	d								22 45												23 15	
Balcombe	d								22 53													
Haywards Heath	d								22 58												23 26	
Wivelsfield	d								23 02												23 30	
Burgess Hill	d								23 04												23 32	
Hassocks	d								23 08												23 36	
Preston Park	d								23 15												23 43	
Brighton	a								23 19												23 47	

Table 52

Saturdays

Bedford, Luton, St.Albans and City of London - South London, Gatwick Airport and Brighton

		FC	FC	FC	SE	SE	SN	SN		SE	SN	FC	SN	FC	FC	FC	SE	SE		SN	SE	FC	SN	FC	FC
Bedford	d	22 42												23 12										23 42	
Flitwick	d	22 52												23 22										23 52	
Harlington	d	22 56												23 26										23 56	
Leagrave	d	23 01												23 31										00 01	
Luton	d	23 06												23 36										00 06	
Luton Airport Parkway	d	23 08												23 38										00 08	
Harpenden	d	23 14												23 44										00 14	
St Albans City	d	23 20												23 50										00 20	
Radlett	d	23 25												23 55										00 25	
Elstree & Borehamwood	d	23 29												23 58										00 29	
Mill Hill Broadway	d	23 34												00 04										00 34	
Hendon	d	23 37												00 07										00 37	
Cricklewood	d	23 41												00 11										00 41	
West Hampstead Thameslink ⊖	d	23 44												00 14										00 44	
Kentish Town ⊖	d	23 48												00 18										00 48	
St Pancras International ⊖	a	23 55												00 25										00 55	
St Pancras International ⊖	a																								
	d																								
Farringdon ⊖	d																								
City Thameslink	d																								
London Blackfriars ⊖	d			22 46												23 16									
Elephant & Castle ⊖	d			22 54												23 24									
Loughborough Jn	d			23 06												23 36									
Herne Hill	d			23 14												23 44									
London Bridge	a				22 48					23 02							23 18				23 32				
	d		22 45		22 49		22 52	22 56		23 03	23 11	23 12	23 06		23 15		23 19			23 22	23 33	23 42	23 36		23 45
Tulse Hill	d		23 01	23a22											23 31	23a52									00 01
Streatham	d		23 05												23 35										00 05
Mitcham Eastfields	d																								
Mitcham Junction	d																								
Hackbridge	d																								
Carshalton	d																								
Tooting	d		23 10												23 40										00 10
Haydons Road	d		23 13												23 43										00 13
Wimbledon ⊖	d		23 17												23 47										00 17
Wimbledon Chase	d		23 20												23 50										00 20
South Merton	d		23 22												23 52										00 22
Morden South	d		23 24												23 54										00 24
St Helier	d		23 26												23 56										00 26
Sutton Common	d		23 28												23 58										00 28
West Sutton	d		23 31												00 01										00 31
Sutton (Surrey)	a		23 35												00 05										00 35
East Croydon	d							23a11				23 24	23 34									23 56	00 03		
Denmark Hill	d					22 52												23 22							
Peckham Rye	d					22 55					23 20							23 25							
Nunhead	d					22 57												23 27							
Crofton Park	d					23 00												23 30							
Catford	d					23 03												23 33							
Bellingham	d					23 05												23 35							
Beckenham Hill	d					23 07												23 37							
Ravensbourne	d					23 09												23 39							
Shortlands	d					23 11												23 41							
Bromley South	d					23 14												23 44							
Bickley	d					23 17												23 47							
St Mary Cray	d																								
Swanley	d																								
Eynsford	d																								
Shoreham (Kent)	d																								
Otford	d																								
Bat & Ball	d																								
Sevenoaks	a				23 14					23 28							23 44				23 59				
Redhill	d																								
Gatwick Airport	d											23 41										00 18			
Three Bridges	d											23 47										00a24			
Balcombe	d											23 53													
Haywards Heath	d											23 58													
Wivelsfield	d											00 02													
Burgess Hill	d											00 04													
Hassocks	d											00 08													
Preston Park	d											00 15													
Brighton	a											00 19													

Table 52

Saturdays

Bedford, Luton, St.Albans and City of London - South London, Gatwick Airport and Brighton

		SE	SN	SE		SE
Bedford	d					
Flitwick	d					
Harlington	d					
Leagrave	d					
Luton	d					
Luton Airport Parkway	d					
Harpenden	d					
St Albans City	d					
Radlett	d					
Elstree & Borehamwood	d					
Mill Hill Broadway	d					
Hendon	d					
Cricklewood	d					
West Hampstead Thameslink ⊖	d					
Kentish Town ⊖	d					
St Pancras International ⊖	a					
St Pancras International ⊖	a					
	d					
Farringdon ⊖	d					
City Thameslink	d					
London Blackfriars ⊖	d					
Elephant & Castle ⊖	d					
Loughborough Jn	d					
Herne Hill	d					
London Bridge	a	23 48				23 52
	d	23 49	23 48			23 53
Tulse Hill	d					
Streatham	d					
Mitcham Eastfields	d					
Mitcham Junction	d					
Hackbridge	d					
Carshalton	d					
Tooting	d					
Haydons Road	d					
Wimbledon ⊖	d					
Wimbledon Chase	d					
South Merton	d					
Morden South	d					
St Helier	d					
Sutton Common	d					
West Sutton	d					
Sutton (Surrey)	a					
East Croydon	d					
Denmark Hill	d			23 52		
Peckham Rye	d		23 57	23 55		
Nunhead	d			23 57		
Crofton Park	d			23 59		
Catford	d			00 03		
Bellingham	d			00 05		
Beckenham Hill	d			00 07		
Ravensbourne	d			00 09		
Shortlands	d			00 11		
Bromley South	d			00 14		
Bickley	d			00 17		
St Mary Cray	d					
Swanley	d					
Eynsford	d					
Shoreham (Kent)	d					
Otford	d					
Bat & Ball	d					
Sevenoaks	a	00 14				00 18
Redhill	d					
Gatwick Airport	d					
Three Bridges	d					
Balcombe	d					
Haywards Heath	d					
Wivelsfield	d					
Burgess Hill	d					
Hassocks	d					
Preston Park	d					
Brighton	a					

Table 52

Sundays

Bedford, Luton, St.Albans and City of London - South London, Gatwick Airport and Brighton

		FC 1 A	FC 1 A	FC A	FC 1 A	SN A	FC 1 A	FC A	SE 1 A	SE A	SE 1 A	FC 1	SN	SE	SN	FC 1	FC	FC 1	SN B	FC	FC	FC	SN 1 C
Bedford 7	d		23p12				23p42													05 42	06 12	06 42	
Flitwick	d		23p22				23p52													05 52	06 22	06 52	
Harlington	d		23p26				23p56													05 56	06 26	06 56	
Leagrave	d		23p31				00 01													06 01	06 31	07 01	
Luton 10	d		23p36				00 06													06 06	06 36	07 06	
Luton Airport Parkway 7	d		23p38				00 08													06 08	06 38	07 08	
Harpenden	d		23p44				00 14													06 14	06 44	07 14	
St Albans City	d		23p50				00 20													06 20	06 50	07 20	
Radlett	d		23p55				00 25													06 25	06 55	07 25	
Elstree & Borehamwood	d		23p58				00 29													06 29	06 59	07 29	
Mill Hill Broadway	d		00 04				00 34													06 34	07 04	07 34	
Hendon	d		00 07				00 37													06 37	07 07	07 37	
Cricklewood	d		00 11				00 41													06 41	07 11	07 41	
West Hampstead Thameslink ⊖	d		00 14				00 44													06 44	07 14	07 44	
Kentish Town ⊖	d		00 18				00 48													06 48	07 18	07 48	
St Pancras International 15 ⊖	a		00 25				00 55																
St Pancras International 15 ⊖	a																			06 55	07 25	07 55	
	d																01 00						
Farringdon 3 ⊖	d																01 05						
City Thameslink 3	d																						
London Blackfriars 3 ⊖	d																01a10						
Elephant & Castle ⊖	d																						
Loughborough Jn	d																						
Herne Hill 4	d																						
London Bridge 4	a								23p48		23p52			00 17									
	d	23p12		23p15	23p42	23p36		23p45	23p49		23p53	00 12	00 06	00 18	00 36	00 42		01 05					07 05
Tulse Hill 3	d			23p31				00 01															
Streatham 4	d			23p35				00 05															
Mitcham Eastfields	d																						
Mitcham Junction	d																						
Hackbridge	d																						
Carshalton	d																						
Tooting	d			23p40				00 10															
Haydons Road	d			23p43				00 13															
Wimbledon 6 ⊖	d			23p47				00 17															
Wimbledon Chase	d			23p50				00 20															
South Merton	d			23p52				00 22															
Morden South	d			23p54				00 24															
St Helier	d			23p56				00 26															
Sutton Common	d			23p58				00 28															
West Sutton	d			00 01				00 31															
Sutton (Surrey) 4	a			00 05				00 35															
East Croydon	d	23p24			23p56	00 03						00 28	00 34		01a03	00 57		01 32					07 22
Denmark Hill 4	d									23p52													
Peckham Rye 4	d									23p55													
Nunhead 4	d									23p57													
Crofton Park	d									23p59													
Catford	d									00 03													
Bellingham	d									00 05													
Beckenham Hill	d									00 07													
Ravensbourne	d									00 09													
Shortlands	d									00 11													
Bromley South 4	d									00 14													
Bickley 4	d									00 17													
St Mary Cray	d																						
Swanley 4	d																						
Eynsford	d																						
Shoreham (Kent)	d																						
Otford 4	d																						
Bat & Ball	d																						
Sevenoaks 4	a								00 14		00 18			00 54									
Redhill	d																						07 41
Gatwick Airport 10	d	23p41			00 18							00 50				01 17		01 52					
Three Bridges 4	d	23p47			00a24							00a54				01a24		01a58	05 00				
Balcombe	d	23p53																					
Haywards Heath 3	d	23p58																	05 20				
Wivelsfield 4	d	00 02																					
Burgess Hill 4	d	00 04																					
Hassocks 4	d	00 08																					
Preston Park	d	00 15																					
Brighton 10	a	00 19																	05 55				

A not 23 May
B 23 May
C until 5 September

Table 52

Sundays

Bedford, Luton, St.Albans and City of London - South London, Gatwick Airport and Brighton

		SN	FC 1 A	FC 1 B	FC	SN	SN	FC 1 A	FC 1 B	SN	SE	FC 1	SN	SN 1 A	SN	FC 1 A	FC 1 B	SN	EM ◇1 C	SE 1	EM ◇1 D	FC	FC 1
Bedford 7	d				07 12							07 52							08 15		08 17		08 22
Flitwick	d				07 22							08 02											08 32
Harlington	d				07 26							08 06											08 36
Leagrave	d				07 31							08 11											08 41
Luton 10	d				07 36							08 16							08 34		08 37	08 20	08 46
Luton Airport Parkway 7	d				07 38							08 18										08 22	08 48
Harpenden	d				07 44							08 24										08 28	08 54
St Albans City	d				07 50							08 30										08 34	09 00
Radlett	d				07 55																	08 39	
Elstree & Borehamwood	d				07 59																	08 43	
Mill Hill Broadway	d				08 04																	08 48	
Hendon	d				08 07																	08 51	
Cricklewood	d				08 11																	08 55	
West Hampstead Thameslink ⊖	d				08 14							08 44										08 58	09 14
Kentish Town ⊖	d				08 18																	09 02	
St Pancras International 15 ⊖	a																		09 16		09 16		
St Pancras International 15 ⊖	a				08 25							08 54										09 09	09 24
	d																						
Farringdon 3 ⊖	d																						
City Thameslink 3	d																						
London Blackfriars 3 ⊖	d																						
Elephant & Castle ⊖	d																						
Loughborough Jn	d																						
Herne Hill 4	d																						
London Bridge 4	a																			08 15			
	d	07 11	07 12	07 12		07 25	07 41	07 42	07 42	07 39			07 55	08 05	08 11	08 12	08 12	08 09		08 16			
Tulse Hill 3	d					07 42							08 12										
Streatham 4	d					07 46							08 16										
Mitcham Eastfields	d																						
Mitcham Junction	d																						
Hackbridge	d																						
Carshalton	d																						
Tooting	d																						
Haydons Road	d																						
Wimbledon 6 ⊖	d																						
Wimbledon Chase	d																						
South Merton	d																						
Morden South	d																						
St Helier	d																						
Sutton Common	d																						
West Sutton	d																						
Sutton (Surrey) 4	a																						
East Croydon	d		07 24	07 27		08a02		07 54	07 57	08 07			08a32	08 21		08 24	08 27	08 37					
Denmark Hill 4	d										07 48												
Peckham Rye 4	d	07 20					07 50				07 51				08 20								
Nunhead 4	d										07 53												
Crofton Park	d										07 56												
Catford	d										07 59												
Bellingham	d										08 01												
Beckenham Hill	d										08 03												
Ravensbourne	d										08 05												
Shortlands	d										08 07												
Bromley South 4	d										08 10												
Bickley 4	d										08 13												
St Mary Cray	d										08 17												
Swanley 4	d										08 22												
Eynsford	d										08 26												
Shoreham (Kent)	d										08 30												
Otford 4	d										08 33												
Bat & Ball	d										08 36												
Sevenoaks 4	a										08 39									08 41			
Redhill	d													08 40									
Gatwick Airport 10	d		07 41	07 50				08 11	08 20							08 41	08 50						
Three Bridges 4	d		07 47	07 54				08 17	08 24							08 47	08 54						
Balcombe	d																						
Haywards Heath 3	d		07 56	08 03				08 26	08 33							08 56	09 03						
Wivelsfield 4	d																						
Burgess Hill 4	d		08 01	08 08				08 31	08 38							09 01	09 08						
Hassocks 4	d							08 35	08 42														
Preston Park	d																						
Brighton 10	a		08 13	08 22				08 44	08 52							09 13	09 22						

A until 5 September
B from 12 September
C until 11 July, from 12 September
D from 18 July until 5 September

Table 52

Sundays

Bedford, Luton, St.Albans and City of London - South London, Gatwick Airport and Brighton

		SN	SE 1	SE	SE	SN	FC 1 A	FC 1 B	SN	EM ◇1	SE 1	SE	FC	FC	FC 1	SN	SN 1 A	SN	FC 1 A	FC 1 B	SN	SE 1
Bedford 7	d									08 45					08 52							
Flitwick	d														09 02							
Harlington	d														09 06							
Leagrave	d														09 11							
Luton 10	d													08 50	09 16							
Luton Airport Parkway 7	d									09 11				08 52	09 18							
Harpenden	d													08 58	09 24							
St Albans City	d													09 04	09 30							
Radlett	d													09 09								
Elstree & Borehamwood	d													09 13								
Mill Hill Broadway	d													09 18								
Hendon	d													09 21								
Cricklewood	d													09 25								
West Hampstead Thameslink ⊖	d													09 28	09 44							
Kentish Town ⊖	d													09 32								
St Pancras International 15 ⊖	a									09 50												
St Pancras International 15 ⊖	a													09 39	09 54							
	d																					
Farringdon 3 ⊖	d																					
City Thameslink 3	d																					
London Blackfriars 3 ⊖	d												08 49									
Elephant & Castle ⊖	d												08 57									
Loughborough Jn	d												09 09									
Herne Hill 4	d												09 17									
London Bridge 4	a		08 30	08 23							08 45											09 15
	d	08 25	08 31	08 24		08 41	08 42	08 42	08 39		08 46					08 55	09 05	09 11	09 12	09 12	09 09	09 16
Tulse Hill 3	d	08 42											09a25			09 12						
Streatham 4	d	08 46														09 16						
Mitcham Eastfields	d																					
Mitcham Junction	d																					
Hackbridge	d																					
Carshalton	d																					
Tooting	d																					
Haydons Road	d																					
Wimbledon 6 ⊖	d																					
Wimbledon Chase	d																					
South Merton	d																					
Morden South	d																					
St Helier	d																					
Sutton Common	d																					
West Sutton	d																					
Sutton (Surrey) 4	a																					
East Croydon	d	09a00					08 54	08 57	09 07							09a32	09 21		09 24	09 27	09 37	
Denmark Hill 4	d				08 18							08 48										
Peckham Rye 4	d				08 21	08 50						08 51						09 20				
Nunhead 4	d				08 23							08 53										
Crofton Park	d				08 26							08 56										
Catford	d				08 29							08 59										
Bellingham	d				08 31							09 01										
Beckenham Hill	d				08 33							09 03										
Ravensbourne	d				08 35							09 05										
Shortlands	d				08 37							09 07										
Bromley South 4	d				08 40							09 10										
Bickley 4	d				08 43							09 13										
St Mary Cray	d				08 47							09 17										
Swanley 4	d				08 52							09 22										
Eynsford	d				08 56							09 26										
Shoreham (Kent)	d				09 00							09 30										
Otford 4	d				09 03							09 33										
Bat & Ball	d				09 06							09 36										
Sevenoaks 4	a		08 55	09 07	09 09						09 11	09 39										
Redhill	d																09 40					09 41
Gatwick Airport 10	d						09 11	09 20											09 41	09 50		
Three Bridges 4	d						09 17	09 24											09 47	09 54		
Balcombe	d																					
Haywards Heath 3	d						09 26	09 33											09 56	10 03		
Wivelsfield 4	d																					
Burgess Hill 4	d						09 31	09 38											10 01	10 08		
Hassocks 4	d						09 35	09 42														
Preston Park	d																					
Brighton 10	a						09 44	09 52											10 13	10 22		

A until 5 September

B from 12 September

Table 52

Sundays

Bedford, Luton, St.Albans and City of London - South London, Gatwick Airport and Brighton

		FC	FC	FC 1	EM ◇1	FC	FC 1	SN	SE 1	SE	SE	SN	FC 1 A	FC 1 B	SN	SE 1	FC	FC	FC 1	EM ◇1	FC	FC 1	SN
Bedford 7	d			09 08	09 14		09 22												09 38	09 45		09 52	
Flitwick	d			09 18			09 32												09 48			10 02	
Harlington	d			09 22			09 36												09 52			10 06	
Leagrave	d			09 27			09 41												09 57			10 11	
Luton 10	d		09 20	09 32	09 39		09 46											09 50	10 02			10 16	
Luton Airport Parkway 7	d		09 22	09 34			09 48											09 52	10 04	10 10		10 18	
Harpenden	d		09 28	09 40			09 54											09 58	10 10			10 24	
St Albans City	d		09 34	09 46			10 00											10 04	10 16			10 30	
Radlett	d		09 39															10 09					
Elstree & Borehamwood	d		09 43															10 13					
Mill Hill Broadway	d		09 48															10 18					
Hendon	d		09 51															10 21					
Cricklewood	d		09 55															10 25					
West Hampstead Thameslink ⊖	d		09 58	10 01			10 14											10 28	10 31			10 44	
Kentish Town ⊖	d		10 02															10 32					
St Pancras International 15 ⊖	a				10 20															10 49			
St Pancras International 15 ⊖	a		10 09	10 13			10 24											10 39	10 43			10 54	
	d																						
Farringdon 3 ⊖	d																						
City Thameslink 3	d																						
London Blackfriars 3 ⊖	d	09 19															09 49						
Elephant & Castle ⊖	d	09 27															09 57						
Loughborough Jn	d	09 39															10 09						
Herne Hill 4	d	09 47															10 17						
London Bridge 4	a								09 30	09 23						09 45							
	d					09 21		09 25	09 31	09 24		09 41	09 42	09 42	09 39	09 46					09 51		09 55
Tulse Hill 3	d	09a55				09 31		09 42									10a25				10 01		10 12
Streatham 4	d					09 35		09 46													10 05		10 16
Mitcham Eastfields	d																						
Mitcham Junction	d																						
Hackbridge	d																						
Carshalton	d																						
Tooting	d					09 40															10 10		
Haydons Road	d					09 43															10 13		
Wimbledon 6 ⊖	d					09 47															10 17		
Wimbledon Chase	d					09 50															10 20		
South Merton	d					09 52															10 22		
Morden South	d					09 54															10 24		
St Helier	d					09 56															10 26		
Sutton Common	d					09 58															10 28		
West Sutton	d					10 01															10 31		
Sutton (Surrey) 4	a					10 05															10 35		
East Croydon	d							10a02					09 54	09 57	10 07								10a32
Denmark Hill 4	d										09 18												
Peckham Rye 4	d										09 21	09 50											
Nunhead 4	d										09 23												
Crofton Park	d										09 26												
Catford	d										09 29												
Bellingham	d										09 31												
Beckenham Hill	d										09 33												
Ravensbourne	d										09 35												
Shortlands	d										09 37												
Bromley South 4	d										09 40												
Bickley 4	d										09 43												
St Mary Cray	d										09 47												
Swanley 4	d										09 52												
Eynsford	d										09 56												
Shoreham (Kent)	d										10 00												
Otford 4	d										10 03												
Bat & Ball	d										10 06												
Sevenoaks 4	a								09 55	10 07	10 09					10 11							
Redhill	d																						
Gatwick Airport 10	d												10 11	10 20									
Three Bridges 4	d												10 17	10 24									
Balcombe	d																						
Haywards Heath 3	d												10 26	10 33									
Wivelsfield 4	d																						
Burgess Hill 4	d												10 31	10 38									
Hassocks 4	d												10 35	10 42									
Preston Park	d																						
Brighton 10	a												10 44	10 52									

A until 5 September

B from 12 September

Table 52

Sundays

Bedford, Luton, St.Albans and City of London - South London, Gatwick Airport and Brighton

		SE 1	SE	SN 1 A	SN	FC 1 A	FC 1 B	SN	SE 1	FC	FC	FC 1	EM ◇1 C	EM ◇1 D	FC	FC 1	SN	SE 1	SE	SE	SN	FC 1 A
Bedford 7	d											10 08	10 16	10 17		10 22						
Flitwick	d											10 18				10 32						
Harlington	d											10 22				10 36						
Leagrave	d											10 27				10 41						
Luton 10	d										10 20	10 32	10 41	10 41		10 46						
Luton Airport Parkway 7	d										10 22	10 34				10 48						
Harpenden	d										10 28	10 40				10 54						
St Albans City	d										10 34	10 46				11 00						
Radlett	d										10 39											
Elstree & Borehamwood	d										10 43											
Mill Hill Broadway	d										10 48											
Hendon	d										10 51											
Cricklewood	d										10 55											
West Hampstead Thameslink ⊖	d										10 58	11 01				11 14						
Kentish Town ⊖	d										11 02											
St Pancras International 15 ⊖	a												11 20	11 20								
St Pancras International 15 ⊖	a										11 09	11 13				11 24						
	d																					
Farringdon 3 ⊖	d																					
City Thameslink 3	d																					
London Blackfriars 3 ⊖	d									10 19												
Elephant & Castle ⊖	d									10 27												
Loughborough Jn	d									10 39												
Herne Hill 4	d									10 47												
London Bridge 4	a	10 00							10 15									10 30	10 23			
	d	10 01		10 05	10 11	10 12	10 12	10 09	10 16						10 21		10 25	10 31	10 24		10 41	10 42
Tulse Hill 3	d									10a55					10 31		10 42					
Streatham 4	d														10 35		10 46					
Mitcham Eastfields	d																					
Mitcham Junction	d																					
Hackbridge	d																					
Carshalton	d																					
Tooting	d														10 40							
Haydons Road	d														10 43							
Wimbledon 6 ⊖	d														10 47							
Wimbledon Chase	d														10 50							
South Merton	d														10 52							
Morden South	d														10 54							
St Helier	d														10 56							
Sutton Common	d														10 58							
West Sutton	d														11 01							
Sutton (Surrey) 4	a														11 05							
East Croydon	d			10 21		10 24	10 27	10 37									11a02					10 54
Denmark Hill 4	d		09 48																	10 18		
Peckham Rye 4	d		09 51		10 20															10 21	10 50	
Nunhead 4	d		09 53																	10 23		
Crofton Park	d		09 56																	10 26		
Catford	d		09 59																	10 29		
Bellingham	d		10 01																	10 31		
Beckenham Hill	d		10 03																	10 33		
Ravensbourne	d		10 05																	10 35		
Shortlands	d		10 07																	10 37		
Bromley South 4	d		10 10																	10 40		
Bickley 4	d		10 13																	10 43		
St Mary Cray	d		10 17																	10 47		
Swanley 4	d		10 22																	10 52		
Eynsford	d		10 26																	10 56		
Shoreham (Kent)	d		10 30																	11 00		
Otford 4	d		10 33																	11 03		
Bat & Ball	d		10 36																	11 06		
Sevenoaks 4	a	10 25	10 39						10 41									10 55	11 07	11 09		
Redhill	d			10 40																		
Gatwick Airport 10	d					10 41	10 50															11 11
Three Bridges 4	d					10 47	10 54															11 17
Balcombe	d																					
Haywards Heath 3	d					10 56	11 03															11 26
Wivelsfield 4	d																					
Burgess Hill 4	d					11 01	11 08															11 31
Hassocks 4	d																					11 35
Preston Park	d																					
Brighton 10	a					11 13	11 22															11 44

A until 5 September
B from 12 September
C until 11 July, from 12 September
D from 18 July until 5 September

Table 52

Sundays

Bedford, Luton, St.Albans and City of London - South London, Gatwick Airport and Brighton

		FC 1 A	SN	SE 1	FC	FC	FC 1	EM ◇1	FC	FC 1	SN	SE 1	SE	SN 1 B	SN	FC 1 B	FC 1 A	SN	SE 1	FC	FC	FC 1	EM ◇1 C
Bedford 7	d						10 38	10 45		10 52												11 08	11 16
Flitwick	d						10 48			11 02												11 18	
Harlington	d						10 52			11 06												11 22	
Leagrave	d						10 57			11 11												11 27	
Luton 10	d					10 50	11 02			11 16											11 20	11 32	11 38
Luton Airport Parkway 7	d					10 52	11 04	11 10		11 18											11 22	11 34	
Harpenden	d					10 58	11 10			11 24											11 28	11 40	
St Albans City	d					11 04	11 16			11 30											11 34	11 46	
Radlett	d					11 09															11 39		
Elstree & Borehamwood	d					11 13															11 43		
Mill Hill Broadway	d					11 18															11 48		
Hendon	d					11 21															11 51		
Cricklewood	d					11 25															11 55		
West Hampstead Thameslink ⊖	d					11 28	11 31			11 44											11 58	12 01	
Kentish Town ⊖	d					11 32															12 02		
St Pancras International 15 ⊖	a							11 49															12 20
St Pancras International 15 ⊖	a					11 39	11 43			11 54											12 09	12 13	
	d																						
Farringdon 3 ⊖	d																						
City Thameslink 3	d																						
London Blackfriars 3 ⊖	d				10 49															11 19			
Elephant & Castle ⊖	d				10 57															11 27			
Loughborough Jn	d				11 09															11 39			
Herne Hill 4	d				11 17															11 47			
London Bridge 4	a			10 45								11 00							11 15				
	d	10 42	10 39	10 46					10 51		10 55	11 01		11 05	11 11	11 12	11 12	11 09	11 16				
Tulse Hill 3	d				11a25				11 01		11 12									11a55			
Streatham 4	d								11 05		11 16												
Mitcham Eastfields	d																						
Mitcham Junction	d																						
Hackbridge	d																						
Carshalton	d																						
Tooting	d								11 10														
Haydons Road	d								11 13														
Wimbledon 6 ⊖	d								11 17														
Wimbledon Chase	d								11 20														
South Merton	d								11 22														
Morden South	d								11 24														
St Helier	d								11 26														
Sutton Common	d								11 28														
West Sutton	d								11 31														
Sutton (Surrey) 4	a								11 35														
East Croydon	d	10 57	11 07								11a32			11 21		11 24	11 27	11 37					
Denmark Hill 4	d												10 48										
Peckham Rye 4	d												10 51		11 20								
Nunhead 4	d												10 53										
Crofton Park	d												10 56										
Catford	d												10 59										
Bellingham	d												11 01										
Beckenham Hill	d												11 03										
Ravensbourne	d												11 05										
Shortlands	d												11 07										
Bromley South 4	d												11 10										
Bickley 4	d												11 13										
St Mary Cray	d												11 17										
Swanley 4	d												11 22										
Eynsford	d												11 26										
Shoreham (Kent)	d												11 30										
Otford 4	d												11 33										
Bat & Ball	d												11 36										
Sevenoaks 4	a			11 11								11 25	11 39						11 41				
Redhill	d													11 40									
Gatwick Airport 10	d	11 20														11 41	11 50						
Three Bridges 4	d	11 24														11 47	11 54						
Balcombe	d																						
Haywards Heath 3	d	11 33														11 56	12 03						
Wivelsfield 4	d																						
Burgess Hill 4	d	11 38														12 01	12 08						
Hassocks 4	d	11 42																					
Preston Park	d																						
Brighton 10	a	11 52														12 13	12 22						

A from 12 September
B until 5 September
C until 11 July

Table 52

Sundays

Bedford, Luton, St.Albans and City of London - South London, Gatwick Airport and Brighton

		EM	EM	FC	FC	SN	SE	SE	SE	SN	FC	FC	SN	SE	FC	FC	FC	EM	FC	FC	SN	SE	SE
		A	B								C	A											
Bedford	d	11 16	11 17		11 22												11 38	11 45		11 52			
Flitwick	d				11 32												11 48			12 02			
Harlington	d				11 36												11 52			12 06			
Leagrave	d				11 41												11 57			12 11			
Luton	d	11 39	11 39		11 46											11 50	12 02			12 16			
Luton Airport Parkway	d				11 48											11 52	12 04	12 09		12 18			
Harpenden	d				11 54											11 58	12 10			12 24			
St Albans City	d				12 00											12 04	12 16			12 30			
Radlett	d															12 09							
Elstree & Borehamwood	d															12 13							
Mill Hill Broadway	d															12 18							
Hendon	d															12 21							
Cricklewood	d															12 25							
West Hampstead Thameslink	d				12 14											12 28	12 31			12 44			
Kentish Town	d															12 32							
St Pancras International	a	12 20	12 20															12 50					
St Pancras International	a				12 24											12 39	12 43			12 54			
	d																						
Farringdon	d																						
City Thameslink	d																						
London Blackfriars	d													11 49									
Elephant & Castle	d													11 57									
Loughborough Jn	d													12 09									
Herne Hill	d													12 17									
London Bridge	a						11 30	11 23						11 45								12 00	
	d			11 21		11 25	11 31	11 24		11 41	11 42	11 42	11 39	11 46					11 51		11 55	12 01	
Tulse Hill	d			11 31		11 42													12 01		12 12		
Streatham	d			11 35		11 46									12a25				12 05		12 16		
Mitcham Eastfields	d																						
Mitcham Junction	d																						
Hackbridge	d																						
Carshalton	d																						
Tooting	d			11 40															12 10				
Haydons Road	d			11 43															12 13				
Wimbledon	d			11 47															12 17				
Wimbledon Chase	d			11 50															12 20				
South Merton	d			11 52															12 22				
Morden South	d			11 54															12 24				
St Helier	d			11 56															12 26				
Sutton Common	d			11 58															12 28				
West Sutton	d			12 01															12 31				
Sutton (Surrey)	a			12 05															12 35				
East Croydon	d					12a02					11 54	11 57	12 07								12a32		
Denmark Hill	d								11 18														11 48
Peckham Rye	d								11 21	11 50													11 51
Nunhead	d								11 23														11 53
Crofton Park	d								11 26														11 56
Catford	d								11 29														11 59
Bellingham	d								11 31														12 01
Beckenham Hill	d								11 33														12 03
Ravensbourne	d								11 35														12 05
Shortlands	d								11 37														12 07
Bromley South	d								11 40														12 10
Bickley	d								11 43														12 13
St Mary Cray	d								11 47														12 17
Swanley	d								11 52														12 22
Eynsford	d								11 56														12 26
Shoreham (Kent)	d								12 00														12 30
Otford	d								12 03														12 33
Bat & Ball	d								12 06														12 36
Sevenoaks	a						11 55	12 07	12 09					12 11								12 25	12 39
Redhill	d																						
Gatwick Airport	d										12 11	12 20											
Three Bridges	d										12 17	12 24											
Balcombe	d																						
Haywards Heath	d										12 26	12 33											
Wivelsfield	d																						
Burgess Hill	d										12 31	12 38											
Hassocks	d										12 35	12 42											
Preston Park	d																						
Brighton	a										12 44	12 52											

A from 12 September
B from 18 July until 5 September
C until 5 September

Table 52

Sundays

Bedford, Luton, St.Albans and City of London - South London, Gatwick Airport and Brighton

		SN	SN	FC	FC	SN	SE	FC	FC	FC	EM	EM	FC	FC	SN	SE	SE	SE	SN	FC	FC	SN
		A		A	B						C	D								A	B	
Bedford	d									12 08	12 15	12 17		12 22								
Flitwick	d									12 18				12 32								
Harlington	d									12 22				12 36								
Leagrave	d									12 27				12 41								
Luton	d								12 20	12 32	12 40	12 40		12 46								
Luton Airport Parkway	d								12 22	12 34				12 48								
Harpenden	d								12 28	12 40				12 54								
St Albans City	d								12 34	12 46				13 00								
Radlett	d								12 39													
Elstree & Borehamwood	d								12 43													
Mill Hill Broadway	d								12 48													
Hendon	d								12 51													
Cricklewood	d								12 55													
West Hampstead Thameslink	d								12 58	13 01				13 14								
Kentish Town	d								13 02													
St Pancras International	a										13 20	13 20										
St Pancras International	a								13 09	13 13				13 24								
	d																					
Farringdon	d																					
City Thameslink	d																					
London Blackfriars	d							12 19														
Elephant & Castle	d							12 27														
Loughborough Jn	d							12 39														
Herne Hill	d							12 47														
London Bridge	a						12 15									12 30	12 23					
	d	12 05	12 11	12 12	12 12	12 09	12 16						12 21		12 25	12 31	12 24		12 41	12 42	12 42	12 39
Tulse Hill	d							12a55					12 31		12 42							
Streatham	d												12 35		12 46							
Mitcham Eastfields	d																					
Mitcham Junction	d																					
Hackbridge	d																					
Carshalton	d																					
Tooting	d												12 40									
Haydons Road	d												12 43									
Wimbledon	d												12 47									
Wimbledon Chase	d												12 50									
South Merton	d												12 52									
Morden South	d												12 54									
St Helier	d												12 56									
Sutton Common	d												12 58									
West Sutton	d												13 01									
Sutton (Surrey)	a												13 05									
East Croydon	d	12 21		12 24	12 27	12 37									13a02					12 54	12 57	13 07
Denmark Hill	d																	12 18				
Peckham Rye	d		12 20															12 21	12 50			
Nunhead	d																	12 23				
Crofton Park	d																	12 26				
Catford	d																	12 29				
Bellingham	d																	12 31				
Beckenham Hill	d																	12 33				
Ravensbourne	d																	12 35				
Shortlands	d																	12 37				
Bromley South	d																	12 40				
Bickley	d																	12 43				
St Mary Cray	d																	12 47				
Swanley	d																	12 52				
Eynsford	d																	12 56				
Shoreham (Kent)	d																	13 00				
Otford	d																	13 03				
Bat & Ball	d																	13 06				
Sevenoaks	a						12 41									12 55	13 07	13 09				
Redhill	d	12 40																				
Gatwick Airport	d			12 41	12 50															13 11	13 20	
Three Bridges	d			12 47	12 54															13 17	13 24	
Balcombe	d																					
Haywards Heath	d			12 56	13 03															13 26	13 33	
Wivelsfield	d																					
Burgess Hill	d			13 01	13 08															13 31	13 38	
Hassocks	d																			13 35	13 42	
Preston Park	d																					
Brighton	a			13 13	13 22															13 44	13 52	

A until 5 September
B from 12 September
C until 11 July, from 12 September
D from 18 July until 5 September

Bedford, Luton, St.Albans and City of London - South London, Gatwick Airport and Brighton

		SE	FC	FC	FC	EM	EM	FC		FC	SN	SE	SE	SN	SN	FC	FC	SN		SE	FC	FC	FC	EM	FC
		■			■	◇■	◇■			■		■		■		■	■			■			■	◇■	
						A	B							C		C	D							D	
Bedford	d				12 38	12 44	12 46			12 52													13 08	13 15	
Flitwick	d				12 48					13 02													13 18		
Harlington	d				12 52					13 06													13 22		
Leagrave	d				12 57					13 11													13 27		
Luton	d			12 50	13 02					13 16												13 20	13 32	13 39	
Luton Airport Parkway	d			12 52	13 04	13 08	13 10			13 18												13 22	13 34		
Harpenden	d			12 58	13 10					13 24												13 28	13 40		
St Albans City	d			13 04	13 16					13 30												13 34	13 46		
Radlett	d			13 09																		13 39			
Elstree & Borehamwood	d			13 13																		13 43			
Mill Hill Broadway	d			13 18																		13 48			
Hendon	d			13 21																		13 51			
Cricklewood	d			13 25																		13 55			
West Hampstead Thameslink ⊖	d			13 28	13 31					13 44												13 58	14 01		
Kentish Town ⊖	d			13 32																		14 02			
St Pancras International ⊖	a					13 50	13 50																	14 19	
St Pancras International ⊖	a			13 39	13 43					13 54												14 09	14 13		
	d																								
Farringdon ⊖	d																								
City Thameslink	d																								
London Blackfriars ⊖	d		12 49																		13 19				
Elephant & Castle ⊖	d		12 57																		13 27				
Loughborough Jn	d		13 09																		13 39				
Herne Hill	d		13 17																		13 47				
London Bridge	a	12 45										13 00								13 15					
	d	12 46						12 51			12 55	13 01		13 05	13 11	13 12	13 12	13 09		13 16					13 21
Tulse Hill	d		13a25					13 01			13 12										13a55				13 31
Streatham	d							13 05			13 16														13 35
Mitcham Eastfields	d																								
Mitcham Junction	d																								
Hackbridge	d																								
Carshalton	d																								
Tooting	d							13 10																	13 40
Haydons Road	d							13 13																	13 43
Wimbledon ⊖	d							13 17																	13 47
Wimbledon Chase	d							13 20																	13 50
South Merton	d							13 22																	13 52
Morden South	d							13 24																	13 54
St Helier	d							13 26																	13 56
Sutton Common	d							13 28																	13 58
West Sutton	d							13 31																	14 01
Sutton (Surrey)	a							13 35																	14 05
East Croydon	d										13a32			13 21		13 24	13 27	13 37							
Denmark Hill	d												12 48												
Peckham Rye	d												12 51		13 20										
Nunhead	d												12 53												
Crofton Park	d												12 56												
Catford	d												12 59												
Bellingham	d												13 01												
Beckenham Hill	d												13 03												
Ravensbourne	d												13 05												
Shortlands	d												13 07												
Bromley South	d												13 10												
Bickley	d												13 13												
St Mary Cray	d												13 17												
Swanley	d												13 22												
Eynsford	d												13 26												
Shoreham (Kent)	d												13 30												
Otford	d												13 33												
Bat & Ball	d												13 36												
Sevenoaks	a	13 11										13 25	13 39							13 41					
Redhill	d													13 40											
Gatwick Airport	d															13 41	13 50								
Three Bridges	d															13 47	13 54								
Balcombe	d																								
Haywards Heath	d															13 56	14 03								
Wivelsfield	d																								
Burgess Hill	d															14 01	14 08								
Hassocks	d																								
Preston Park	d																								
Brighton	a															14 13	14 22								

A until 11 July
B from 18 July
C until 5 September
D from 12 September

Bedford, Luton, St.Albans and City of London - South London, Gatwick Airport and Brighton

		FC	SN	SE		SE	SE	SN	FC	FC	SN	SE	FC	FC		FC	EM	FC	FC	SN	SE	SE	SN	SN
		■		■					■	■		■				■	◇■		■		■		■	
									A	B													A	
Bedford	d	13 22														13 38	13 46		13 52					
Flitwick	d	13 32														13 48			14 02					
Harlington	d	13 36														13 52			14 06					
Leagrave	d	13 41														13 57			14 11					
Luton	d	13 46												13 50		14 02			14 16					
Luton Airport Parkway	d	13 48												13 52		14 04	14 10		14 18					
Harpenden	d	13 54												13 58		14 10			14 24					
St Albans City	d	14 00												14 04		14 16			14 30					
Radlett	d													14 09										
Elstree & Borehamwood	d													14 13										
Mill Hill Broadway	d													14 18										
Hendon	d													14 21										
Cricklewood	d													14 25										
West Hampstead Thameslink ⊖	d	14 14												14 28		14 31			14 44					
Kentish Town ⊖	d													14 32										
St Pancras International ⊖	a																14 44							
St Pancras International ⊖	a	14 24												14 39		14 43			14 54					
	d																							
Farringdon ⊖	d																							
City Thameslink	d																							
London Blackfriars ⊖	d												13 49											
Elephant & Castle ⊖	d												13 57											
Loughborough Jn	d												14 09											
Herne Hill	d												14 17											
London Bridge	a			13 30		13 23						13 45									14 00			
	d		13 25	13 31		13 24		13 41	13 42	13 42	13 39	13 46						13 51		13 55	14 01		14 05	14 11
Tulse Hill	d		13 42										14a25					14 01		14 12				
Streatham	d		13 46															14 05		14 16				
Mitcham Eastfields	d																							
Mitcham Junction	d																							
Hackbridge	d																							
Carshalton	d																							
Tooting	d																	14 10						
Haydons Road	d																	14 13						
Wimbledon ⊖	d																	14 17						
Wimbledon Chase	d																	14 20						
South Merton	d																	14 22						
Morden South	d																	14 24						
St Helier	d																	14 26						
Sutton Common	d																	14 28						
West Sutton	d																	14 31						
Sutton (Surrey)	a																	14 35						
East Croydon	d		14a02						13 54	13 57	14 07									14a32			14 21	
Denmark Hill	d						13 18															13 48		
Peckham Rye	d						13 21	13 50														13 51		14 20
Nunhead	d						13 23															13 53		
Crofton Park	d						13 26															13 56		
Catford	d						13 29															13 59		
Bellingham	d						13 31															14 01		
Beckenham Hill	d						13 33															14 03		
Ravensbourne	d						13 35															14 05		
Shortlands	d						13 37															14 07		
Bromley South	d						13 40															14 10		
Bickley	d						13 43															14 13		
St Mary Cray	d						13 47															14 17		
Swanley	d						13 52															14 22		
Eynsford	d						13 56															14 26		
Shoreham (Kent)	d						14 00															14 30		
Otford	d						14 03															14 33		
Bat & Ball	d						14 06															14 36		
Sevenoaks	a			13 55		14 07	14 09					14 11									14 25	14 39		
Redhill	d																						14 40	
Gatwick Airport	d								14 11	14 20														
Three Bridges	d								14 17	14 24														
Balcombe	d																							
Haywards Heath	d								14 26	14 33														
Wivelsfield	d																							
Burgess Hill	d								14 31	14 38														
Hassocks	d								14 35	14 42														
Preston Park	d																							
Brighton	a								14 44	14 52														

A until 5 September
B from 12 September

Table 52

Sundays

Bedford, Luton, St.Albans and City of London - South London, Gatwick Airport and Brighton

		FC ■ A	FC ■ B	SN	SE ■	FC	FC	FC ■	FC	FC ■	EM ◇■ C	EM ◇■ B	SN	SE ■	SE	SE	EM ◇■ D	SN	FC ■ A	FC ■ B	SN	SE ■	FC
Bedford ■	d							14 08		14 22	14 23	14 25					14 32						
Flitwick	d							14 18		14 32													
Harlington	d							14 22		14 36													
Leagrave	d							14 27		14 41													
Luton ■	d						14 20	14 32		14 46	14 47	14 49					14 49						
Luton Airport Parkway ■	d						14 22	14 34		14 48													
Harpenden	d						14 28	14 40		14 54													
St Albans City	d						14 34	14 46		15 00													
Radlett	d						14 39																
Elstree & Borehamwood	d						14 43																
Mill Hill Broadway	d						14 48																
Hendon	d						14 51																
Cricklewood	d						14 55																
West Hampstead Thameslink ⊖	d						14 58	15 01		15 14													
Kentish Town ⊖	d						15 02																
St Pancras International ■ ⊖	a										15 22	15 22					15 22						
St Pancras International ■ ⊖	a						15 09	15 13		15 24													
	d																						
Farringdon ■ ⊖	d																						
City Thameslink ■	d																						
London Blackfriars ■ ⊖	d					14 19																	14 49
Elephant & Castle ⊖	d					14 27																	14 57
Loughborough Jn	d					14 39																	15 09
Herne Hill ■	d					14 47																	15 17
London Bridge ■	a				14 15									14 30	14 23							14 45	
	d	14 12	14 12	14 09	14 16				14 21				14 25	14 31	14 24			14 41	14 42	14 42	14 39	14 46	
Tulse Hill ■	d					14a55			14 31				14 42										15a25
Streatham ■	d								14 35				14 46										
Mitcham Eastfields	d																						
Mitcham Junction	d																						
Hackbridge	d																						
Carshalton	d																						
Tooting	d								14 40														
Haydons Road	d								14 43														
Wimbledon ■ ⊖	d								14 47														
Wimbledon Chase	d								14 50														
South Merton	d								14 52														
Morden South	d								14 54														
St Helier	d								14 56														
Sutton Common	d								14 58														
West Sutton	d								15 01														
Sutton (Surrey) ■	a								15 05														
East Croydon	d	14 24	14 27	14 37									15a02						14 54	14 57	15 07		
Denmark Hill ■	d															14 18							
Peckham Rye ■	d															14 21		14 50					
Nunhead ■	d															14 23							
Crofton Park	d															14 26							
Catford	d															14 29							
Bellingham	d															14 31							
Beckenham Hill	d															14 33							
Ravensbourne	d															14 35							
Shortlands	d															14 37							
Bromley South ■	d															14 40							
Bickley ■	d															14 43							
St Mary Cray	d															14 47							
Swanley ■	d															14 52							
Eynsford	d															14 56							
Shoreham (Kent)	d															15 00							
Otford ■	d															15 03							
Bat & Ball	d															15 06							
Sevenoaks ■	a				14 41									14 55	15 07	15 09						15 11	
Redhill	d																						
Gatwick Airport ■	d	14 41	14 50																15 11	15 20			
Three Bridges ■	d	14 47	14 54																15 17	15 24			
Balcombe	d																						
Haywards Heath ■	d	14 56	15 03																15 26	15 33			
Wivelsfield ■	d																						
Burgess Hill ■	d	15 01	15 08																15 31	15 38			
Hassocks ■	d																		15 35	15 42			
Preston Park	d																						
Brighton ■	a	15 13	15 22																15 44	15 52			

A until 5 September
B from 12 September
C until 11 July
D from 18 July until 5 September

Table 52

Sundays

Bedford, Luton, St.Albans and City of London - South London, Gatwick Airport and Brighton

		FC	FC ■	FC	FC ■	EM ◇■	SN	SE ■	SE	SN ■ A	SN	FC ■ A	FC ■ B	SN	SE ■	FC	FC	FC ■	FC	FC ■	EM ◇■	SN	SE ■
Bedford ■	d		14 38		14 52	14 54												15 08		15 22	15 25		
Flitwick	d		14 48		15 02													15 18		15 32			
Harlington	d		14 52		15 06													15 22		15 36			
Leagrave	d		14 57		15 11													15 27		15 41			
Luton ■	d	14 50	15 02		15 16												15 20	15 32		15 46	15 42		
Luton Airport Parkway ■	d	14 52	15 04		15 18	15 11											15 22	15 34		15 48			
Harpenden	d	14 58	15 10		15 24												15 28	15 40		15 54			
St Albans City	d	15 04	15 16		15 30												15 34	15 46		16 00			
Radlett	d	15 09															15 39						
Elstree & Borehamwood	d	15 13															15 43						
Mill Hill Broadway	d	15 18															15 48						
Hendon	d	15 21															15 51						
Cricklewood	d	15 25															15 55						
West Hampstead Thameslink ⊖	d	15 28	15 31		15 44												15 58	16 01		16 14			
Kentish Town ⊖	d	15 32															16 02						
St Pancras International ■ ⊖	a					15 45															16 15		
St Pancras International ■ ⊖	a	15 39	15 43		15 54												16 09	16 13		16 24			
	d																						
Farringdon ■ ⊖	d																						
City Thameslink ■	d																						
London Blackfriars ■ ⊖	d															15 19							
Elephant & Castle ⊖	d															15 27							
Loughborough Jn	d															15 39							
Herne Hill ■	d															15 47							
London Bridge ■	a							15 00							15 15								15 30
	d			14 51			14 55	15 01		15 05	15 11	15 12	15 12	15 09	15 16				15 21			15 25	15 31
Tulse Hill ■	d			15 01			15 12									15a55			15 31			15 42	
Streatham ■	d			15 05			15 16												15 35			15 46	
Mitcham Eastfields	d																						
Mitcham Junction	d																						
Hackbridge	d																						
Carshalton	d																						
Tooting	d			15 10															15 40				
Haydons Road	d			15 13															15 43				
Wimbledon ■ ⊖	d			15 17															15 47				
Wimbledon Chase	d			15 20															15 50				
South Merton	d			15 22															15 52				
Morden South	d			15 24															15 54				
St Helier	d			15 26															15 56				
Sutton Common	d			15 28															15 58				
West Sutton	d			15 31															16 01				
Sutton (Surrey) ■	a			15 35															16 05				
East Croydon	d						15a32			15 21		15 24	15 27	15 37								16a02	
Denmark Hill ■	d								14 48														
Peckham Rye ■	d								14 51		15 20												
Nunhead ■	d								14 53														
Crofton Park	d								14 56														
Catford	d								14 59														
Bellingham	d								15 01														
Beckenham Hill	d								15 03														
Ravensbourne	d								15 05														
Shortlands	d								15 07														
Bromley South ■	d								15 10														
Bickley ■	d								15 13														
St Mary Cray	d								15 17														
Swanley ■	d								15 22														
Eynsford	d								15 26														
Shoreham (Kent)	d								15 30														
Otford ■	d								15 33														
Bat & Ball	d								15 36														
Sevenoaks ■	a							15 25	15 39						15 41								15 55
Redhill	d									15 40													
Gatwick Airport ■	d											15 41	15 50										
Three Bridges ■	d											15 47	15 54										
Balcombe	d																						
Haywards Heath ■	d											15 56	16 03										
Wivelsfield ■	d																						
Burgess Hill ■	d											16 01	16 08										
Hassocks ■	d																						
Preston Park	d																						
Brighton ■	a											16 13	16 22										

A until 5 September
B from 12 September

Table 52

Sundays

Bedford, Luton, St.Albans and City of London - South London, Gatwick Airport and Brighton

		SE		SE	SN	FC ■ A	FC ■ B	SN	SE ■	FC	FC	FC ■		FC	FC ■	EM ◇■	SN	SE ■	SE	SN ■ A	SN	FC ■ A		FC ■ B	SN
Bedford ■	d											15 38			15 52	15 55									
Flitwick	d											15 48			16 02										
Harlington	d											15 52			16 06										
Leagrave	d											15 57			16 11										
Luton ■	d										15 50	16 02			16 16										
Luton Airport Parkway ■	d										15 52	16 04			16 18	16 14									
Harpenden	d										15 58	16 10			16 24										
St Albans City	d										16 04	16 16			16 30										
Radlett	d										16 09														
Elstree & Borehamwood	d										16 13														
Mill Hill Broadway	d										16 18														
Hendon	d										16 21														
Cricklewood	d										16 25														
West Hampstead Thameslink ⊖	d										16 28	16 31			16 44										
Kentish Town ⊖	d										16 32														
St Pancras International ■ ⊖	a															16 45									
St Pancras International ■ ⊖	a										16 39	16 43			16 54										
	d																								
Farringdon ■ ⊖	d																								
City Thameslink ■	d																								
London Blackfriars ■ ⊖	d								15 49																
Elephant & Castle ⊖	d								15 57																
Loughborough Jn	d								16 09																
Herne Hill ■	d								16 17																
London Bridge ■	a	15 23							15 45									16 00							
	d	15 24			15 41	15 42	15 42	15 39	15 46					15 51			15 55	16 01		16 05	16 11	16 12		16 12	16 09
Tulse Hill ■	d									16a25				16 01			16 12								
Streatham ■	d													16 05			16 16								
Mitcham Eastfields	d																								
Mitcham Junction	d																								
Hackbridge	d																								
Carshalton	d																								
Tooting	d													16 10											
Haydons Road	d													16 13											
Wimbledon ■ ⊖	d													16 17											
Wimbledon Chase	d													16 20											
South Merton	d													16 22											
Morden South	d													16 24											
St Helier	d													16 26											
Sutton Common	d													16 28											
West Sutton	d													16 31											
Sutton (Surrey) ■	a													16 35											
East Croydon	d					15 54	15 57	16 07									16a32			16 21		16 24		16 27	16 37
Denmark Hill ■	d			15 18															15 48						
Peckham Rye ■	d			15 21	15 50														15 51		16 20				
Nunhead ■	d			15 23															15 53						
Crofton Park	d			15 26															15 56						
Catford	d			15 29															15 59						
Bellingham	d			15 31															16 01						
Beckenham Hill	d			15 33															16 03						
Ravensbourne	d			15 35															16 05						
Shortlands	d			15 37															16 07						
Bromley South ■	d			15 40															16 10						
Bickley ■	d			15 43															16 13						
St Mary Cray	d			15 47															16 17						
Swanley ■	d			15 52															16 22						
Eynsford	d			15 56															16 26						
Shoreham (Kent)	d			16 00															16 30						
Otford ■	d			16 03															16 33						
Bat & Ball	d			16 06															16 36						
Sevenoaks ■	a	16 07		16 09					16 11									16 25	16 39						
Redhill	d																			16 40					
Gatwick Airport ■	d					16 11	16 20															16 41		16 50	
Three Bridges ■	d					16 17	16 24															16 47		16 54	
Balcombe	d																								
Haywards Heath ■	d					16 26	16 33															16 56		17 03	
Wivelsfield ■	d																								
Burgess Hill ■	d					16 31	16 38															17 01		17 08	
Hassocks ■	d					16 35	16 42																		
Preston Park	d																								
Brighton ■	a					16 44	16 52															17 13		17 22	

A until 5 September

B from 12 September

Table 52

Sundays

Bedford, Luton, St.Albans and City of London - South London, Gatwick Airport and Brighton

		SE ■	FC	FC	FC ■	FC	FC ■	EM ◇■		SN	SE ■	SE	SE	EM ◇■ A	EM ◇■ B	EM ◇■ C	SN	FC ■ D		FC ■ A	SN	SE ■	FC	FC	FC ■
Bedford ■	d				16 08		16 22							16 33	16 34	16 35									16 38
Flitwick	d				16 18		16 32																		16 48
Harlington	d				16 22		16 36																		16 52
Leagrave	d				16 27		16 41																		16 57
Luton ■	d			16 20	16 32		16 46	16 25																16 50	17 02
Luton Airport Parkway ■	d			16 22	16 34		16 48							16 53	16 53	16 53								16 52	17 04
Harpenden	d			16 28	16 40		16 54																	16 58	17 10
St Albans City	d			16 34	16 46		17 00																	17 04	17 16
Radlett	d			16 39																				17 09	
Elstree & Borehamwood	d			16 43																				17 13	
Mill Hill Broadway	d			16 48																				17 18	
Hendon	d			16 51																				17 21	
Cricklewood	d			16 55																				17 25	
West Hampstead Thameslink ⊖	d			16 58	17 01		17 14																	17 28	17 31
Kentish Town ⊖	d			17 02																				17 32	
St Pancras International ■ ⊖	a							16 55						17 27	17 27	17 27									
St Pancras International ■ ⊖	a			17 09	17 13		17 24																	17 39	17 43
	d																								
Farringdon ■ ⊖	d																								
City Thameslink ■	d																								
London Blackfriars ■ ⊖	d		16 19																				16 49		
Elephant & Castle ⊖	d		16 27																				16 57		
Loughborough Jn	d		16 39																				17 09		
Herne Hill ■	d		16 47																				17 17		
London Bridge ■	a	16 15									16 30	16 23										16 45			
	d	16 16				16 21				16 25	16 31	16 24					16 41	16 42		16 42	16 39	16 46			
Tulse Hill ■	d		16a55			16 31				16 42													17a25		
Streatham ■	d					16 35				16 46															
Mitcham Eastfields	d																								
Mitcham Junction	d																								
Hackbridge	d																								
Carshalton	d																								
Tooting	d					16 40																			
Haydons Road	d					16 43																			
Wimbledon ■ ⊖	d					16 47																			
Wimbledon Chase	d					16 50																			
South Merton	d					16 52																			
Morden South	d					16 54																			
St Helier	d					16 56																			
Sutton Common	d					16 58																			
West Sutton	d					17 01																			
Sutton (Surrey) ■	a					17 05																			
East Croydon	d									17a02								16 54		16 57	17 07				
Denmark Hill ■	d												16 18												
Peckham Rye ■	d												16 21				16 50								
Nunhead ■	d												16 23												
Crofton Park	d												16 26												
Catford	d												16 29												
Bellingham	d												16 31												
Beckenham Hill	d												16 33												
Ravensbourne	d												16 35												
Shortlands	d												16 37												
Bromley South ■	d												16 40												
Bickley ■	d												16 43												
St Mary Cray	d												16 47												
Swanley ■	d												16 52												
Eynsford	d												16 56												
Shoreham (Kent)	d												17 00												
Otford ■	d												17 03												
Bat & Ball	d												17 06												
Sevenoaks ■	a	16 41									16 55	17 07	17 09									17 11			
Redhill	d																								
Gatwick Airport ■	d																	17 11		17 20					
Three Bridges ■	d																	17 17		17 24					
Balcombe	d																								
Haywards Heath ■	d																	17 26		17 33					
Wivelsfield ■	d																								
Burgess Hill ■	d																	17 31		17 38					
Hassocks ■	d																	17 35		17 42					
Preston Park	d																								
Brighton ■	a																	17 44		17 52					

A from 12 September

B from 18 July until 5 September

C until 11 July

D until 5 September

Table 52

Sundays

Bedford, Luton, St.Albans and City of London - South London, Gatwick Airport and Brighton

		FC	FC 1	SN	SE 1	SE	SN 1	EM ◇1	SN	FC 1	FC 1	SN	SE 1	FC	FC	FC 1	FC	FC 1	SN	SE 1	SE	SE
							A			A	B											
Bedford 7	d		16 52					17 07								17 08		17 22				
Flitwick	d		17 02													17 18		17 32				
Harlington	d		17 06													17 22		17 36				
Leagrave	d		17 11													17 27		17 41				
Luton 10	d		17 16					17 25							17 20	17 32		17 46				
Luton Airport Parkway 7	d		17 18												17 22	17 34		17 48				
Harpenden	d		17 24												17 28	17 40		17 54				
St Albans City	d		17 30												17 34	17 46		18 00				
Radlett	d														17 39							
Elstree & Borehamwood	d														17 43							
Mill Hill Broadway	d														17 48							
Hendon	d														17 51							
Cricklewood	d														17 55							
West Hampstead Thameslink ⊖	d		17 44												17 58	18 01		18 14				
Kentish Town ⊖	d														18 02							
St Pancras International 15 ⊖	a							17 59														
St Pancras International 15 ⊖	a		17 54												18 09	18 13		18 24				
	d																					
Farringdon 3 ⊖	d																					
City Thameslink 3	d																					
London Blackfriars 3 ⊖	d													17 19								
Elephant & Castle ⊖	d													17 27								
Loughborough Jn	d													17 39								
Herne Hill 4	d													17 47								
London Bridge 4	a				17 00								17 15							17 30	17 23	
	d	16 51		16 55	17 01		17 05		17 11	17 12	17 12	17 09	17 16				17 21		17 25	17 31	17 24	
Tulse Hill 3	d	17 01		17 12										17a55			17 31		17 42			
Streatham 4	d	17 05		17 16													17 35		17 46			
Mitcham Eastfields	d																					
Mitcham Junction	d																					
Hackbridge	d																					
Carshalton	d																					
Tooting	d	17 10															17 40					
Haydons Road	d	17 13															17 43					
Wimbledon 6 ⊖	d	17 17															17 47					
Wimbledon Chase	d	17 20															17 50					
South Merton	d	17 22															17 52					
Morden South	d	17 24															17 54					
St Helier	d	17 26															17 56					
Sutton Common	d	17 28															17 58					
West Sutton	d	17 31															18 01					
Sutton (Surrey) 4	a	17 35															18 05					
East Croydon	d			17a32			17 21			17 24	17 27	17 37							18a02			
Denmark Hill 4	d					16 48																17 18
Peckham Rye 4	d					16 51			17 20													17 21
Nunhead 4	d					16 53																17 23
Crofton Park	d					16 56																17 26
Catford	d					16 59																17 29
Bellingham	d					17 01																17 31
Beckenham Hill	d					17 03																17 33
Ravensbourne	d					17 05																17 35
Shortlands	d					17 07																17 37
Bromley South 4	d					17 10																17 40
Bickley 4	d					17 13																17 43
St Mary Cray	d					17 17																17 47
Swanley 4	d					17 22																17 52
Eynsford	d					17 26																17 56
Shoreham (Kent)	d					17 30																18 00
Otford 4	d					17 33																18 03
Bat & Ball	d					17 36																18 06
Sevenoaks 4	a				17 25	17 39							17 41							17 55	18 07	18 09
Redhill	d						17 40															
Gatwick Airport 10	d									17 41	17 50											
Three Bridges 4	d									17 47	17 54											
Balcombe	d																					
Haywards Heath 3	d									17 56	18 03											
Wivelsfield 4	d																					
Burgess Hill 4	d									18 01	18 08											
Hassocks 4	d																					
Preston Park	d																					
Brighton 10	a									18 13	18 22											

A until 5 September

B from 12 September

Table 52

Sundays

Bedford, Luton, St.Albans and City of London - South London, Gatwick Airport and Brighton

		SN	FC 1	FC 1	SN	SE 1	FC	FC	FC 1	EM ◇1	FC	FC 1	SN	SE 1	SE	SN 1	EM ◇1	SN	FC 1	FC 1	SN	SE 1	FC
			A	B												A			A	B			
Bedford 7	d								17 38	17 40		17 52					18 11						
Flitwick	d								17 48			18 02											
Harlington	d								17 52			18 06											
Leagrave	d								17 57			18 11											
Luton 10	d							17 50	18 02			18 16					18 29						
Luton Airport Parkway 7	d							17 52	18 04	17 59		18 18											
Harpenden	d							17 58	18 10			18 24											
St Albans City	d							18 04	18 16			18 30											
Radlett	d							18 09															
Elstree & Borehamwood	d							18 13															
Mill Hill Broadway	d							18 18															
Hendon	d							18 21															
Cricklewood	d							18 25															
West Hampstead Thameslink ⊖	d							18 28	18 31			18 44											
Kentish Town ⊖	d							18 32															
St Pancras International 15 ⊖	a									18 29							18 59						
St Pancras International 15 ⊖	a							18 39	18 43			18 54											
	d																						
Farringdon 3 ⊖	d																						
City Thameslink 3	d																						
London Blackfriars 3 ⊖	d						17 49																18 19
Elephant & Castle ⊖	d						17 57																18 27
Loughborough Jn	d						18 09																18 39
Herne Hill 4	d						18 17																18 47
London Bridge 4	a					17 45								18 00								18 15	
	d	17 41	17 42	17 42	17 39	17 46					17 51		17 55	18 01		18 05		18 11	18 12	18 12	18 09	18 16	
Tulse Hill 3	d						18a25				18 01		18 12										18a55
Streatham 4	d										18 05		18 16										
Mitcham Eastfields	d																						
Mitcham Junction	d																						
Hackbridge	d																						
Carshalton	d																						
Tooting	d										18 10												
Haydons Road	d										18 13												
Wimbledon 6 ⊖	d										18 17												
Wimbledon Chase	d										18 20												
South Merton	d										18 22												
Morden South	d										18 24												
St Helier	d										18 26												
Sutton Common	d										18 28												
West Sutton	d										18 31												
Sutton (Surrey) 4	a										18 35												
East Croydon	d		17 54	17 57	18 07								18a32			18 21			18 24	18 27	18 37		
Denmark Hill 4	d														17 48								
Peckham Rye 4	d	17 50													17 51			18 20					
Nunhead 4	d														17 53								
Crofton Park	d														17 56								
Catford	d														17 59								
Bellingham	d														18 01								
Beckenham Hill	d														18 03								
Ravensbourne	d														18 05								
Shortlands	d														18 07								
Bromley South 4	d														18 10								
Bickley 4	d														18 13								
St Mary Cray	d														18 17								
Swanley 4	d														18 22								
Eynsford	d														18 26								
Shoreham (Kent)	d														18 30								
Otford 4	d														18 33								
Bat & Ball	d														18 36								
Sevenoaks 4	a					18 11								18 25	18 39							18 41	
Redhill	d															18 40							
Gatwick Airport 10	d		18 11	18 20															18 41	18 50			
Three Bridges 4	d		18 17	18 24															18 47	18 54			
Balcombe	d																						
Haywards Heath 3	d		18 26	18 33															18 56	19 03			
Wivelsfield 4	d																						
Burgess Hill 4	d		18 31	18 38															19 01	19 08			
Hassocks 4	d		18 35	18 42																			
Preston Park	d																						
Brighton 10	a		18 44	18 52															19 13	19 22			

A until 5 September

B from 12 September

Bedford, Luton, St.Albans and City of London - South London, Gatwick Airport and Brighton

		FC	FC	FC 1	SN	SE 1		SE	SE	EM ◇1	SN	FC 1 A	FC 1 B	SN	SE 1	FC		FC	FC	FC 1	SN	SE 1	SE	SN 1 A	EM ◇1
Bedford	d			18 22						18 40										18 52					19 10
Flitwick	d			18 32																19 02					
Harlington	d			18 36																19 06					
Leagrave	d			18 41																19 11					
Luton	d	18 20		18 46														18 50		19 16					19 29
Luton Airport Parkway	d	18 22		18 48						18 59								18 52		19 18					
Harpenden	d	18 28		18 54														18 58		19 24					
St Albans City	d	18 34		19 00														19 04		19 30					
Radlett	d	18 39																19 09							
Elstree & Borehamwood	d	18 43																19 13							
Mill Hill Broadway	d	18 48																19 18							
Hendon	d	18 51																19 21							
Cricklewood	d	18 55																19 25							
West Hampstead Thameslink ⊖	d	18 58		19 14														19 28		19 44					
Kentish Town ⊖	d	19 02																19 32							
St Pancras International ⊖	a									19 29															19 59
St Pancras International ⊖	a	19 09		19 24														19 39		19 54					
	d																								
Farringdon ⊖	d																								
City Thameslink	d																								
London Blackfriars ⊖	d															18 49									
Elephant & Castle ⊖	d															18 57									
Loughborough Jn	d															19 09									
Herne Hill	d															19 17									
London Bridge	a					18 30		18 23							18 45							19 00			
	d		18 21		18 25	18 31		18 24			18 41	18 42	18 42	18 39	18 46				18 51		18 55	19 01		19 05	
Tulse Hill	d		18 31		18 42											19a25			19 01		19 12				
Streatham	d		18 35		18 46														19 05		19 16				
Mitcham Eastfields	d																								
Mitcham Junction	d																								
Hackbridge	d																								
Carshalton	d																								
Tooting	d		18 40																19 10						
Haydons Road	d		18 43																19 13						
Wimbledon ⊖	d		18 47																19 17						
Wimbledon Chase	d		18 50																19 20						
South Merton	d		18 52																19 22						
Morden South	d		18 54																19 24						
St Helier	d		18 56																19 26						
Sutton Common	d		18 58																19 28						
West Sutton	d		19 01																19 31						
Sutton (Surrey)	a		19 05																19 35						
East Croydon	d				19a02							18 54	18 57	19 07							19a32			19 21	
Denmark Hill	d								18 18														18 48		
Peckham Rye	d								18 21		18 50												18 51		
Nunhead	d								18 23														18 53		
Crofton Park	d								18 26														18 56		
Catford	d								18 29														18 59		
Bellingham	d								18 31														19 01		
Beckenham Hill	d								18 33														19 03		
Ravensbourne	d								18 35														19 05		
Shortlands	d								18 37														19 07		
Bromley South	d								18 40														19 10		
Bickley	d								18 43														19 13		
St Mary Cray	d								18 47														19 17		
Swanley	d								18 52														19 22		
Eynsford	d								18 56														19 26		
Shoreham (Kent)	d								19 00														19 30		
Otford	d								19 03														19 33		
Bat & Ball	d								19 06														19 36		
Sevenoaks	a					18 55		19 07	19 09						19 11							19 25	19 39		
Redhill	d																							19 40	
Gatwick Airport	d											19 11	19 20												
Three Bridges	d											19 17	19 24												
Balcombe	d																								
Haywards Heath	d											19 26	19 33												
Wivelsfield	d																								
Burgess Hill	d											19 31	19 38												
Hassocks	d											19 35	19 42												
Preston Park	d																								
Brighton	a											19 44	19 52												

A until 5 September

B from 12 September

Bedford, Luton, St.Albans and City of London - South London, Gatwick Airport and Brighton

		SN		FC 1 A	FC 1 B	SN	SE 1	FC	FC	FC	FC 1	SN		SE 1	SE	SE	EM ◇1	SN	FC 1 A	FC 1 B	SN	SE 1		FC	FC
Bedford	d										19 22						19 40								
Flitwick	d										19 32														
Harlington	d										19 36														
Leagrave	d										19 41														
Luton	d								19 20		19 46														19 50
Luton Airport Parkway	d								19 22		19 48						19 59								19 52
Harpenden	d								19 28		19 54														19 58
St Albans City	d								19 34		20 00														20 04
Radlett	d								19 39																20 09
Elstree & Borehamwood	d								19 43																20 13
Mill Hill Broadway	d								19 48																20 18
Hendon	d								19 51																20 21
Cricklewood	d								19 55																20 25
West Hampstead Thameslink ⊖	d								19 58		20 14														20 28
Kentish Town ⊖	d								20 02																20 32
St Pancras International ⊖	a																20 29								
St Pancras International ⊖	a								20 09		20 24														20 39
	d																								
Farringdon ⊖	d																								
City Thameslink	d																								
London Blackfriars ⊖	d							19 19																19 49	
Elephant & Castle ⊖	d							19 27																19 57	
Loughborough Jn	d							19 39																20 09	
Herne Hill	d							19 47																20 17	
London Bridge	a						19 15							19 30	19 23							19 45			
	d	19 11		19 12	19 12	19 09	19 16			19 21		19 25		19 31	19 24			19 41	19 42	19 42	19 39	19 46			
Tulse Hill	d							19a55		19 31		19 42												20a25	
Streatham	d									19 35		19 46													
Mitcham Eastfields	d																								
Mitcham Junction	d																								
Hackbridge	d																								
Carshalton	d																								
Tooting	d									19 40															
Haydons Road	d									19 43															
Wimbledon ⊖	d									19 47															
Wimbledon Chase	d									19 50															
South Merton	d									19 52															
Morden South	d									19 54															
St Helier	d									19 56															
Sutton Common	d									19 58															
West Sutton	d									20 01															
Sutton (Surrey)	a									20 05															
East Croydon	d			19 24	19 27	19 37						20a02							19 54	19 57	20 07				
Denmark Hill	d															19 18									
Peckham Rye	d	19 20														19 21		19 50							
Nunhead	d															19 23									
Crofton Park	d															19 26									
Catford	d															19 29									
Bellingham	d															19 31									
Beckenham Hill	d															19 33									
Ravensbourne	d															19 35									
Shortlands	d															19 37									
Bromley South	d															19 40									
Bickley	d															19 43									
St Mary Cray	d															19 47									
Swanley	d															19 52									
Eynsford	d															19 56									
Shoreham (Kent)	d															20 00									
Otford	d															20 03									
Bat & Ball	d															20 06									
Sevenoaks	a						19 41							19 55	20 07	20 09						20 11			
Redhill	d																								
Gatwick Airport	d			19 41	19 50														20 11	20 20					
Three Bridges	d			19 47	19 54														20 17	20 24					
Balcombe	d																								
Haywards Heath	d			19 56	20 03														20 26	20 33					
Wivelsfield	d																								
Burgess Hill	d			20 01	20 08														20 31	20 38					
Hassocks	d																		20 35	20 42					
Preston Park	d																								
Brighton	a			20 13	20 22														20 44	20 52					

A until 5 September

B from 12 September

Table 52

Sundays

Bedford, Luton, St.Albans and City of London - South London, Gatwick Airport and Brighton

Station		FC	FC 1	SN	SE 1	SE	EM ◇1	SN 1 A		SN	FC 1 A	FC 1 B	SN	SE 1	FC	FC	FC	FC	SN	SE 1	SE	SE	EM ◇1	SN
Bedford 7	d		19 52				20 07										20 12						20 40	
Flitwick	d		20 02														20 22							
Harlington	d		20 06														20 26							
Leagrave	d		20 11														20 31							
Luton 10	d		20 16				20 26									20 20	20 36							
Luton Airport Parkway 7	d		20 18													20 22	20 38						20 55	
Harpenden	d		20 24													20 28	20 44							
St Albans City	d		20 30													20 34	20 50							
Radlett	d															20 39	20 55							
Elstree & Borehamwood	d															20 43	20 59							
Mill Hill Broadway	d															20 48	21 04							
Hendon	d															20 51	21 07							
Cricklewood	d															20 55	21 11							
West Hampstead Thameslink ⊖	d		20 44													20 58	21 14							
Kentish Town ⊖	d															21 02	21 18							
St Pancras International 15 ⊖	a						20 57																21 27	
St Pancras International 15 ⊖	a		20 54													21 09	21 25							
	d																							
Farringdon 3 ⊖	d																							
City Thameslink 3	d																							
London Blackfriars 3 ⊖	d														20 19									
Elephant & Castle ⊖	d														20 27									
Loughborough Jn	d														20 39									
Herne Hill 4	d														20 47									
London Bridge 4	a				20 00									20 15						20 30	20 23			
	d	19 51		19 55	20 01			20 05		20 11	20 12	20 12	20 09	20 16				20 21	20 25	20 31	20 24			20 41
Tulse Hill 3	d	20 01		20 12											20a55			20 31	20 42					
Streatham 4	d	20 05		20 16														20 35	20 46					
Mitcham Eastfields	d																							
Mitcham Junction	d																							
Hackbridge	d																							
Carshalton	d																							
Tooting	d	20 10																20 40						
Haydons Road	d	20 13																20 43						
Wimbledon 6 ⊖ ⇌	d	20 17																20 47						
Wimbledon Chase	d	20 20																20 50						
South Merton	d	20 22																20 52						
Morden South	d	20 24																20 54						
St Helier	d	20 26																20 56						
Sutton Common	d	20 28																20 58						
West Sutton	d	20 31																21 01						
Sutton (Surrey) 4	a	20 35																21 05						
East Croydon ⇌	d			20a32				20 21			20 24	20 27	20 37						21a02					
Denmark Hill 4	d					19 48																20 18		
Peckham Rye 4	d					19 51			20 20													20 21		20 50
Nunhead 4	d					19 53																20 23		
Crofton Park	d					19 56																20 26		
Catford	d					19 59																20 29		
Bellingham	d					20 01																20 31		
Beckenham Hill	d					20 03																20 33		
Ravensbourne	d					20 05																20 35		
Shortlands	d					20 07																20 37		
Bromley South 4	d					20 10																20 40		
Bickley 4	d					20 13																20 43		
St Mary Cray	d					20 17																20 47		
Swanley 4	d					20 22																20 52		
Eynsford	d					20 26																20 56		
Shoreham (Kent)	d					20 30																21 00		
Otford 4	d					20 33																21 03		
Bat & Ball	d					20 36																21 06		
Sevenoaks 4	a				20 25	20 39								20 41						20 55	21 07	21 09		
Redhill	d							20 40																
Gatwick Airport 10	d										20 41	20 50												
Three Bridges 4	d										20 47	20 54												
Balcombe	d																							
Haywards Heath 3	d										20 56	21 03												
Wivelsfield 4	d																							
Burgess Hill 4	d										21 01	21 08												
Hassocks 4	d																							
Preston Park	d																							
Brighton 10	a										21 13	21 22												

A until 5 September

B from 12 September

Table 52

Sundays

Bedford, Luton, St.Albans and City of London - South London, Gatwick Airport and Brighton

Station		FC 1 A	FC 1 B	SN	FC	SE 1	SE	FC	SN	SN 1 A	EM ◇1	SN	FC 1 A	FC 1 B	SN	FC	SE 1	SN	SE 1	SE	SE	EM ◇1
Bedford 7	d				20 42						21 08					21 12						21 37
Flitwick	d				20 52											21 22						
Harlington	d				20 56											21 26						
Leagrave	d				21 01											21 31						
Luton 10	d				21 06						21 23					21 36						21 52
Luton Airport Parkway 7	d				21 08											21 38						
Harpenden	d				21 14											21 44						
St Albans City	d				21 20											21 50						
Radlett	d				21 25											21 55						
Elstree & Borehamwood	d				21 29											21 59						
Mill Hill Broadway	d				21 34											22 04						
Hendon	d				21 37											22 07						
Cricklewood	d				21 41											22 11						
West Hampstead Thameslink ⊖	d				21 44											22 14						
Kentish Town ⊖	d				21 48											22 18						
St Pancras International 15 ⊖	a										21 57											22 27
St Pancras International 15 ⊖	a				21 55											22 25						
	d																					
Farringdon 3 ⊖	d																					
City Thameslink 3	d																					
London Blackfriars 3 ⊖	d																					
Elephant & Castle ⊖	d																					
Loughborough Jn	d																					
Herne Hill 4	d																					
London Bridge 4	a					20 45											21 15		21 30	21 23		
	d	20 42	20 42	20 39		20 46		20 51	20 55	21 05		21 11	21 12	21 12	21 09		21 16	21 25	21 31	21 24		
Tulse Hill 3	d							21 01	21 12									21 42				
Streatham 4	d							21 05	21 16									21 46				
Mitcham Eastfields	d																					
Mitcham Junction	d																					
Hackbridge	d																					
Carshalton	d																					
Tooting	d							21 10														
Haydons Road	d							21 13														
Wimbledon 6 ⊖ ⇌	d							21 17														
Wimbledon Chase	d							21 20														
South Merton	d							21 22														
Morden South	d							21 24														
St Helier	d							21 26														
Sutton Common	d							21 28														
West Sutton	d							21 31														
Sutton (Surrey) 4	a							21 35														
East Croydon ⇌	d	20 54	20 57	21 07					21a32	21 21			21 24	21 27	21 37			22a00				
Denmark Hill 4	d						20 48														21 18	
Peckham Rye 4	d						20 51					21 20									21 21	
Nunhead 4	d						20 53														21 23	
Crofton Park	d						20 56														21 26	
Catford	d						20 59														21 29	
Bellingham	d						21 01														21 31	
Beckenham Hill	d						21 03														21 33	
Ravensbourne	d						21 05														21 35	
Shortlands	d						21 07														21 37	
Bromley South 4	d						21 10														21 40	
Bickley 4	d						21 13														21 43	
St Mary Cray	d						21 17														21 47	
Swanley 4	d						21 22														21 52	
Eynsford	d						21 26														21 56	
Shoreham (Kent)	d						21 30														22 00	
Otford 4	d						21 33														22 03	
Bat & Ball	d						21 36														22 06	
Sevenoaks 4	a					21 11	21 39										21 41		21 55	22 07	22 09	
Redhill	d									21 40												
Gatwick Airport 10	d	21 11	21 20										21 41	21 50								
Three Bridges 4	d	21 17	21 24										21 47	21 54								
Balcombe	d																					
Haywards Heath 3	d	21 26	21 33										21 56	22 03								
Wivelsfield 4	d																					
Burgess Hill 4	d	21 31	21 38										22 01	22 08								
Hassocks 4	d	21 35	21 42																			
Preston Park	d																					
Brighton 10	a	21 44	21 52										22 13	22 22								

A until 5 September

B from 12 September

Table 52

Sundays

Bedford, Luton, St.Albans and City of London - South London, Gatwick Airport and Brighton

		SN	FC A	FC B	SN	FC	SE	SE	SN	SN A	SN	FC A	FC B	SN	FC	SE	EM	SN	SE	SE	EM	SN	FC A
Bedford	d					21 42									22 12		22 24				22 32		
Flitwick	d					21 52									22 22								
Harlington	d					21 56									22 26								
Leagrave	d					22 01									22 31								
Luton	d					22 06									22 36		22 40				22 50		
Luton Airport Parkway	d					22 08									22 38								
Harpenden	d					22 14									22 44								
St Albans City	d					22 20									22 50								
Radlett	d					22 25									22 55								
Elstree & Borehamwood	d					22 29									22 59								
Mill Hill Broadway	d					22 34									23 04								
Hendon	d					22 37									23 07								
Cricklewood	d					22 41									23 11								
West Hampstead Thameslink ⊖	d					22 44									23 14								
Kentish Town ⊖	d					22 48									23 18								
St Pancras International ⊖	a																23 13				23 27		
St Pancras International ⊖	a					22 55									23 25								
	d																						
Farringdon ⊖	d																						
City Thameslink	d																						
London Blackfriars ⊖	d																						
Elephant & Castle ⊖	d																						
Loughborough Jn	d																						
Herne Hill	d																						
London Bridge	a						21 45									22 15			22 30				
	d	21 41	21 42	21 42	21 39		21 46		21 55	22 05	22 11	22 12	22 12	22 09		22 16		22 25	22 31			22 41	22 42
Tulse Hill	d								22 12									22 42					
Streatham	d								22 16									22 46					
Mitcham Eastfields	d																						
Mitcham Junction	d																						
Hackbridge	d																						
Carshalton	d																						
Tooting	d																						
Haydons Road	d																						
Wimbledon ⊖	d																						
Wimbledon Chase	d																						
South Merton	d																						
Morden South	d																						
St Helier	d																						
Sutton Common	d																						
West Sutton	d																						
Sutton (Surrey)	a																						
East Croydon	d		21 54	21 57	22 07				22a32	22 21		22 24	22 27	22 37				23a00					22 54
Denmark Hill	d							21 48												22 18			
Peckham Rye	d	21 50						21 51			22 20									22 21		22 50	
Nunhead	d							21 53												22 23			
Crofton Park	d							21 56												22 26			
Catford	d							21 59												22 29			
Bellingham	d							22 01												22 31			
Beckenham Hill	d							22 03												22 33			
Ravensbourne	d							22 05												22 35			
Shortlands	d							22 07												22 37			
Bromley South	d							22 10												22 40			
Bickley	d							22 13												22 43			
St Mary Cray	d							22 17												22 47			
Swanley	d							22 22												22 52			
Eynsford	d							22 26												22 56			
Shoreham (Kent)	d							22 30												23 00			
Otford	d							22 33												23 03			
Bat & Ball	d							22 36												23 06			
Sevenoaks	a						22 11	22 39								22 41			22 57	23 09			
Redhill	d									22 40													
Gatwick Airport	d		22 11	22 20								22 41	22 50										23 11
Three Bridges	d		22 17	22 24								22 47	22 54										23 17
Balcombe	d																						
Haywards Heath	d		22 26	22 33								22 56	23 03										23 26
Wivelsfield	d																						
Burgess Hill	d		22 31	22 38								23 01	23 08										23 31
Hassocks	d		22 35	22 42																			23 35
Preston Park	d																						
Brighton	a		22 44	22 52								23 13	23 22										23 44

A until 5 September

B from 12 September

Table 52

Sundays

Bedford, Luton, St.Albans and City of London - South London, Gatwick Airport and Brighton

		FC A	SN	FC	SE	SE	SN	SN	FC B	FC A	SN	FC	SE	SE	SN	SE	FC	FC	SN	SE
Bedford	d			22 42								23 12					23 32			
Flitwick	d			22 52								23 22					23 42			
Harlington	d			22 56								23 26					23 46			
Leagrave	d			23 01								23 31					23 51			
Luton	d			23 06								23 36					23 56			
Luton Airport Parkway	d			23 08								23 38					23 58			
Harpenden	d			23 14								23 44					00 04			
St Albans City	d			23 20								23 50					00 10			
Radlett	d			23 25								23 55					00 15			
Elstree & Borehamwood	d			23 29								23 58					00 19			
Mill Hill Broadway	d			23 34								00 04					00 24			
Hendon	d			23 37								00 07					00 27			
Cricklewood	d			23 41								00 11					00 31			
West Hampstead Thameslink ⊖	d			23 44								00 14					00 34			
Kentish Town ⊖	d			23 48								00 18					00 42			
St Pancras International ⊖	a																			
St Pancras International ⊖	a			23 55								00 25					00 47			
	d																			
Farringdon ⊖	d																			
City Thameslink	d																			
London Blackfriars ⊖	d																			
Elephant & Castle ⊖	d																			
Loughborough Jn	d																			
Herne Hill	d																			
London Bridge	a				22 45								23 15			23 30				23 45
	d	22 42	22 39		22 46		22 55	23 11	23 12	23 12	23 09		23 16		23 25	23 31		23 42	23 39	23 46
Tulse Hill	d						23 12								23 42					
Streatham	d						23 16								23 46					
Mitcham Eastfields	d																			
Mitcham Junction	d																			
Hackbridge	d																			
Carshalton	d																			
Tooting	d																			
Haydons Road	d																			
Wimbledon ⊖	d																			
Wimbledon Chase	d																			
South Merton	d																			
Morden South	d																			
St Helier	d																			
Sutton Common	d																			
West Sutton	d																			
Sutton (Surrey)	a																			
East Croydon	d	22 57	23 07				23a32		23 24	23 27	23 37				00a01			23 57	00 09	
Denmark Hill	d					22 48								23 18						
Peckham Rye	d					22 51		23 20						23 21						
Nunhead	d					22 53								23 23						
Crofton Park	d					22 56								23 26						
Catford	d					22 59								23 29						
Bellingham	d					23 01								23 31						
Beckenham Hill	d					23 03								23 33						
Ravensbourne	d					23 05								23 35						
Shortlands	d					23 07								23 37						
Bromley South	d					23 10								23 40						
Bickley	d					23 13								23 43						
St Mary Cray	d																			
Swanley	d																			
Eynsford	d																			
Shoreham (Kent)	d																			
Otford	d																			
Bat & Ball	d																			
Sevenoaks	a				23 11								23 41			23 57				00 11
Redhill	d																			
Gatwick Airport	d	23 20							23 41	23 50								00 19		
Three Bridges	d	23 24							23 47	23 54								00a24		
Balcombe	d																			
Haywards Heath	d	23 33							23 56	00 03										
Wivelsfield	d																			
Burgess Hill	d	23 38							00 01	00 08										
Hassocks	d	23 42																		
Preston Park	d																			
Brighton	a	23 52							00 13	00 22										

A from 12 September

B until 5 September

Table 52

Mondays to Fridays

Brighton, Gatwick Airport and South London - City of London, St.Albans, Luton and Bedford

		FC	FC	FC	FC	EM	FC	FC	FC	FC		FC	FC	SN	FC	FC	SN	FC	EM	FC		FC	FC	FC	SN
		MX	MX	MO		MX	MX	MX	MO	MX		MO	MX	MX	MX	MO		MX	MX	MX		MO	MX		A
			■		■	◇■ ☕		■		■		■			■			🚌	◇■ ☕			■	■	🚌	🚌
Brighton	d				23p11					23p37		23p44					00 10								00 50
Preston Park	d									23p41															
Hassocks	d				23p19					23p47		23p52													
Burgess Hill	d				23p23					23p51		23p56													
Wivelsfield	d									23p53															
Haywards Heath	d				23p28					23p59		00 01													01 25
Balcombe	d									00 04															
Three Bridges	d				23p38					00 10		00 10													01a45
Gatwick Airport	d				23p43					00 15		00 15													
Redhill	d									00 22		00 22													
East Croydon	d				00 04					00 36		00 36													
Sevenoaks	d																								
Bat & Ball	d																								
Otford	d																								
Shoreham (Kent)	d																								
Eynsford	d																								
Swanley	d																								
St Mary Cray	d																								
Bickley	d																								
Bromley South	d																								
Shortlands	d																								
Ravensbourne	d																								
Beckenham Hill	d																								
Bellingham	d																								
Catford	d																								
Crofton Park	d																								
Nunhead	d																								
Peckham Rye	d													23p57											
Denmark Hill	d																								
Sutton (Surrey)	d																								
West Sutton	d																								
Sutton Common	d																								
St Helier	d																								
Morden South	d																								
South Merton	d																								
Wimbledon Chase	d																								
Wimbledon ⊖ 🚋	d																								
Haydons Road	d																								
Tooting	d																								
Carshalton	d																								
Hackbridge	d																								
Mitcham Junction	d																								
Mitcham Eastfields	d																								
Streatham	d																								
Tulse Hill	d													00 07											
London Bridge ⊖	a																								
	d																	23p55						00 25	
Herne Hill	d																								
Loughborough Jn	d																								
Elephant & Castle	d																								
London Blackfriars ⊖	d																	00 10						00 40	
Farringdon ⊖	d																	00 20						00 50	
St Pancras International ⊖	d	22p46	23p02			23p15	23p18	23p32					23p48		00 02				00 15	00 18			00 32		
St Pancras International ⊖	a																	00 25						00 55	
	d			23p02					23p32							00 02						00 32			
Kentish Town ⊖	d	22p51		23p06			23p23		23p36				23p53			00 07				00 23		00 37	00 37		
West Hampstead Thameslink ⊖	d	22p55	23p10	23p10			23p27	23p40	23p40				23p57		00 10	00 11				00 27		00 41	00 41		
Cricklewood	d	22p58		23p13			23p30		23p43				23p59			00 14				00 30		00 44	00 44		
Hendon	d	23p01		23p16			23p33		23p46				00 03			00 17				00 33		00 47	00 47		
Mill Hill Broadway	d	23p04		23p19			23p36		23p49				00 06			00 20				00 36		00 50	00 50		
Elstree & Borehamwood	d	23p09		23p24			23p41		23p54				00 11			00 25				00 41		00 55	00 55		
Radlett	d	23p14		23p29			23p46		23p59				00 16			00 30				00 46		01 00	01 00		
St Albans City	d	23p20	23p26	23p36			23p52	23p56	00 06				00 22		00 26	00 36				00 52		01 06	01 06		
Harpenden	d	23p26	23p32	23p42			23p58	00 02	00 12				00 28		00 32	00 42				00 58		01 12	01 12		
Luton Airport Parkway	d	23p32	23p38	23p48			00 04	00 08	00 18				00 34		00 38	00 48			00 43	01 04		01 18	01 18		
Luton	d	23p35	23p41	23p51		23p46	00 07	00 11	00 21				00 37		00 41	00 51			00 47	01 07		01 21	01 21		
Leagrave	d	23p38	23p44	23p55			00 10	00 14	00 24				00 40		00 44	00 54				01 10		01 24	01 24		
Harlington	d	23p44	23p50	00 01			00 16	00 20	00 30				00 46		00 50	01 00				01 16		01 30	01 30		
Flitwick	d	23p48	23p54	00 04			00 20	00 24	00 34				00 50		00 54	01 04				01 20		01 34	01 34		
Bedford	a	00 01	00 06	00 16		00 09	00 32	00 36	00 46				01 02		01 06	01 16			01 09	01 32		01 46	01 46		

A MX until 28 May

Table 52

Mondays to Fridays

Brighton, Gatwick Airport and South London - City of London, St.Albans, Luton and Bedford

		FC	FC	FC	FC	FC	FC	FC	FC	SN	FC	FC	FC	FC	SE	FC	FC	FC	SE	SE	EM	EM	FC	SE
		MX	MO		MO	MX	MO	MX		A	MO	MX				MO	MX							
				🚌			■	■	🚌	🚌	■	■		🚌				■			◇■ ☕	◇■ ☕	■	
Brighton	d									03 50													05 39	
Preston Park	d																						05 43	
Hassocks	d																						05 49	
Burgess Hill	d																						05 53	
Wivelsfield	d																						05 55	
Haywards Heath	d									04 25													06 00	
Balcombe	d																						06 06	
Three Bridges	d									04a45			04 25					04 55					06 11	
Gatwick Airport	d												04 30					05 00					06 16	
Redhill	d																							
East Croydon	d												04 47					05 17					06 32	
Sevenoaks	d																			05 07				05 40
Bat & Ball	d																							05 43
Otford	d																							05 46
Shoreham (Kent)	d																							05 49
Eynsford	d																							05 53
Swanley	d																							05 58
St Mary Cray	d																							06 02
Bickley	d														04 41				05 02					06 06
Bromley South	d														04 44				05 05					06 10
Shortlands	d														04 47				05 08					06 13
Ravensbourne	d														04 49									06 15
Beckenham Hill	d														04 51									06 17
Bellingham	d														04 53									06 19
Catford	d														04 56									06 22
Crofton Park	d														04 58									06 25
Nunhead	d														05 01									06 27
Peckham Rye	d														05 03									06 29
Denmark Hill	d														05 07									06 33
Sutton (Surrey)	d																							
West Sutton	d																							
Sutton Common	d																							
St Helier	d																							
Morden South	d																							
South Merton	d																							
Wimbledon Chase	d																							
Wimbledon ⊖ 🚋	d																							
Haydons Road	d																							
Tooting	d																							
Carshalton	d																							
Hackbridge	d																							
Mitcham Junction	d																							
Mitcham Eastfields	d																							
Streatham	d																							
Tulse Hill	d																							
London Bridge ⊖	a																	05 34					06 46	
	d			01 00					03 20					04 20				05 34					06 46	
Herne Hill	d																		05 23					
Loughborough Jn	d																							
Elephant & Castle	d														05 13				05 29					06 40
London Blackfriars ⊖	d			01 15					03 35				05 14	04 35	05 17			05 44	05 33				06 52	06 48
City Thameslink													05 16					05 46					06 55	06 50
Farringdon ⊖	d												05 20					05 50					06 58	06 54
St Pancras International ⊖	d	01 02				01 32		02 32				03 52					04 52							
St Pancras International ⊖	a			01 30					03 50				05 23	04 50				05 53					07 01	06 57
	d		01 02		01 32		02 32				03 52		05 24			04 52		05 54			06 10	06 37	07 02	06 58
Kentish Town ⊖	d	01 07	01 07		01 37	01 37	02 37	02 37			03 57	03 57	05 28			04 57	04 57	05 58						07 02
West Hampstead Thameslink ⊖	d	01 11	01 11		01 41	01 41	02 41	02 41			04 01	04 01	05 32			05 01	05 01	06 02					07 10	07 06
Cricklewood	d	01 14	01 14		01 44	01 44	02 44	02 44			04 04	04 04	05 35			05 04	05 04	06 05						07 09
Hendon	d	01 17	01 17		01 47	01 47	02 47	02 47			04 07	04 07	05 38			05 07	05 07	06 08						07 12
Mill Hill Broadway	d	01 20	01 20		01 50	01 50	02 50	02 50			04 10	04 10	05 41			05 10	05 10	06 11						07 15
Elstree & Borehamwood	d	01 25	01 25		01 55	01 55	02 55	02 55			04 15	04 15	05 46			05 15	05 15	06 16						07 20
Radlett	d	01 30	01 30		02 00	02 00	03 00	03 00			04 20	04 20	05 51			05 20	05 20	06 20						07 24
St Albans City	d	01 36	01 36		02 06	02 06	03 06	03 06			04 26	04 26	05 58			05 26	05 26	06 26					07 26	07a32
Harpenden	d	01 42	01 42		02 12	02 12	03 12	03 12			04 32	04 32	06 04			05 32	05 32	06 32					07 32	
Luton Airport Parkway	d	01 48	01 48		02 18	02 18	03 18	03 18			04 38	04 38	06 10			05 38	05 38	06 38					07 38	
Luton	d	01 51	01 51		02 21	02 21	03 21	03 21			04 41	04 41	06 13			05 41	05 41	06 41			06 33	06 59	07 41	
Leagrave	d	01 54	01 54		02 24	02 24	03 24	03 24			04 44	04 44	06 16			05 44	05 44	06 44					07 44	
Harlington	d	02 00	02 00		02 30	02 30	03 30	03 30			04 50	04 50	06 22			05 50	05 50	06 50					07 50	
Flitwick	d	02 04	02 04		02 34	02 34	03 34	03 34			04 54	04 54	06 26			05 54	05 54	06 54					07 54	
Bedford	a	02 16	02 16		02 46	02 46	03 46	03 46			05 06	05 06	06 40			06 06	06 06	07 08			06 47		08 06	

A MX until 28 May

Brighton, Gatwick Airport and South London - City of London, St.Albans, Luton and Bedford

Station		SE	SE ■	SN	FC	FC ■	SN	SE ■	SN ■	SN ■	SE	FC	SN	SE ■	FC	SE	SE ■	FC ■	SN ■	FC ■	SN
Brighton [10]	d			05 44		05 49			06 00	06 01								06 07	06 17	06 24	
Preston Park	d					05 53												06 11		06 28	
Hassocks [4]	d					05 59				06 09								06 18	06 25	06 35	
Burgess Hill [4]	d					06 03				06 12								06 22	06 29	06 39	
Wivelsfield [4]	d					06 05				06 15								06 25			
Haywards Heath [3]	d					06 10				06b27								06 30	06 34	06 44	
Balcombe	d																	06 35		06 50	
Three Bridges [4]	d					06 20				06 36								06 41	06a44	06 56	
Gatwick Airport [10]	d					06 24				06 41								06 46		07 01	
Redhill	d					06 33												06 56		07 11	
East Croydon	d					06 44	05 51			06 57								07 09		07 24	
Sevenoaks [4]	d		05 43					05 59			06 02			06 11		06 13	06 15				
Bat & Ball	d															06 16					
Otford [4]	d															06 19					
Shoreham (Kent)	d															06 22					
Eynsford	d															06 26					
Swanley [4]	d															06 31					
St Mary Cray [4]	d															06 35					
Bickley	d	05 41														06 39					
Bromley South	d	05 44														06 42					
Shortlands [4]	d	05 47														06 45					
Ravensbourne	d	05 49														06 47					
Beckenham Hill	d	05 51														06 49					
Bellingham	d	05 53														06 51					
Catford	d	05 56														06 54					
Crofton Park	d	05 58														06 57					
Nunhead [4]	d	06 01														06 59					
Peckham Rye [4]	d	06 07					06 15						06 09			07 01					06 27
Denmark Hill [4]	d															07 05					
Sutton (Surrey) [4]	d														06 20						
West Sutton	d														06 23						
Sutton Common	d														06 25						
St Helier	d														06 28						
Morden South	d														06 30						
South Merton	d														06 32						
Wimbledon Chase	d														06 34						
Wimbledon [5] ⊖	d														06 36						
Haydons Road	d														06 40						
Tooting	d														06 43						
Carshalton	d																				
Hackbridge	d																				
Mitcham Junction	d																				
Mitcham Eastfields	d																				
Streatham [4]	d				05 46							06 06			06 49						
Tulse Hill [3]	d				05 50							06 10	06 18		06 52						06 36
London Bridge [4] ⊖	a		06 09			06 58		06 24			06 51			06 38			06 39	07 23			
	d		06 10			06 58		06 25			06 52			06 38			06 40	07 24			
Herne Hill [4]	d				05 54							06 16			06 56					07 41	
Loughborough Jn	d											06 19			07 00						
Elephant & Castle	d	06 13			06 00							06 24			07 06	07 12					
London Blackfriars [3] ⊖	d	06 17			06 04	07 06						06 30			07 12	07 18		07 30		07 54	
City Thameslink					06 06	07 08						06 32			07 14	07 20		07 32		07 56	
Farringdon [3] ⊖	d				06 10	07 12						06 36			07 18	07 24		07 36		08 00	
St Pancras International [15] ⊖	d																				
St Pancras International [15] ⊖	a				06 13	07 15						06 39			07 21	07 27		07 39		08 03	
	d				06 14	07 18						06 40			07 22	07 28		07 40		08 04	
Kentish Town ⊖	d				06 18							06 44				07 32					
West Hampstead Thameslink ⊖	d				06 22	07 26						06 48			07 30	07 36					
Cricklewood	d				06 25							06 51				07 39					
Hendon	d				06 28							06 54				07 42					
Mill Hill Broadway	d				06 31							06 57				07 45					
Elstree & Borehamwood	d				06 36							07 02			07 40	07 50					
Radlett	d				06 40							07 06			07 44	07 54					
St Albans City	d				06 46	07 42						07 12			07a52	08a02				08 24	
Harpenden	d				06 52	07 48						07 18								08 32	
Luton Airport Parkway [7]	d				06 58	07 54						07 24						08 09		08 38	
Luton [10]	d				07 01	07 57						07 27						08a12		08 41	
Leagrave	d				07 04	08 00						07 30								08 44	
Harlington	d				07 10	08 06						07 36								08 50	
Flitwick	d				07 14	08 10						07 40								08 54	
Bedford [7]	a				07 26	08 22						07 52								09 06	

b arr. 0619

Brighton, Gatwick Airport and South London - City of London, St.Albans, Luton and Bedford

Station		EM ◇■	EM ◇■	FC	SE ■	SE	SE ■	SN ■	SN	SN	SE	SE ■	SE ■	FC	SE ■	SN	SE	SN ■	FC ■	SE ■	SE	SN
Brighton [10]	d							06 37										07 00	07 00			
Preston Park	d																		07 04			
Hassocks [4]	d																		07 10			
Burgess Hill [4]	d																		07 14			
Wivelsfield [4]	d																		07 18			
Haywards Heath [3]	d							06a56											07 23			
Balcombe	d																					
Three Bridges [4]	d																		07 32			
Gatwick Airport [10]	d																		07 38			
Redhill	d																					
East Croydon	d																		07 54			
Sevenoaks [4]	d				06 32	06 36					06 42	06 44	06 49		06 53		06 56			07 03		
Bat & Ball	d										06 48											
Otford [4]	d						06 38				06 51											
Shoreham (Kent)	d										06 54											
Eynsford	d										06 58											
Swanley [4]	d						06 48				07 03											
St Mary Cray [4]	d										07 07											
Bickley	d										07 11										07 05	
Bromley South	d						06 57				07 14										07 08	
Shortlands [4]	d										07 17										07 11	
Ravensbourne	d										07 19											
Beckenham Hill	d										07 21											
Bellingham	d										07 23											
Catford	d										07 26											
Crofton Park	d										07 29											
Nunhead [4]	d										07 31											
Peckham Rye [4]	d								06 39	06 42	07 33					06 57						07 07
Denmark Hill [4]	d										07 37											
Sutton (Surrey) [4]	d													06 48								
West Sutton	d													06 51								
Sutton Common	d													06 53								
St Helier	d													06 56								
Morden South	d													06 58								
South Merton	d													07 00								
Wimbledon Chase	d													07 02								
Wimbledon [5] ⊖	d			06 26										07 04								
Haydons Road	d			06 28										07 08								
Tooting	d			06 31										07 11								
Carshalton	d																					
Hackbridge	d																					
Mitcham Junction	d																					
Mitcham Eastfields	d																					
Streatham [4]	d			06 36										07 16								
Tulse Hill [3]	d			06 40					06 48	06 50				07 20		07 07						07 16
London Bridge [4] ⊖	a				06 54	07 18						07 09	07 14		07 22		07 37			07 29		
	d				06 55	07 19						07 10	07 15		07 23		07 38			07 30		
Herne Hill [4]	d			06 46										07 24							07 31	
Loughborough Jn	d			06 49										07 27							07 34	
Elephant & Castle	d			06 54			07 16				07 44			07 32							07 38	
London Blackfriars [3] ⊖	d			07 00			07 24				07 48			07 36					08 21		07 42	
City Thameslink				07 02			07 26				07 50			07 38					08 23		07 44	
Farringdon [3] ⊖	d			07 06			07 30				07 54			07 42					08 27		07 48	
St Pancras International [15] ⊖	d	06 55	07 00																			
St Pancras International [15] ⊖	a			07 09			07 33				07 57			07 45					08 31		07 51	
	d			07 10			07 34				07 58			07 46					08 32		07 52	
Kentish Town ⊖	d										08 02											
West Hampstead Thameslink ⊖	d			07 18							08 06			07 54							08 00	
Cricklewood	d										08 09											
Hendon	d										08 12											
Mill Hill Broadway	d										08 15											
Elstree & Borehamwood	d			07 28							08 20										08 10	
Radlett	d			07 32							08 24										08 14	
St Albans City	d			07 38			07 54				08 30			08 10					08 52		08a22	
Harpenden	d			07 44			08 00				08 36			08 16								
Luton Airport Parkway [7]	d	07 16		07 50			08 06				08 42			08 22					09 00			
Luton [10]	d		07 23	07a54			08 09				08a46			08 25					09 04			
Leagrave	d						08 12							08 28								
Harlington	d						08 18							08 34								
Flitwick	d						08 22							08 38					09 14			
Bedford [7]	a		07 38				08 34							08 50					09 26			

Table 52 — **Mondays to Fridays**

Brighton, Gatwick Airport and South London - City of London, St.Albans, Luton and Bedford

Station		EM ◇■	FC	SE ■	EM ◇■	SN	SE	SE	SE ■	SE ■	SN ■	EM ◇■	SN	SE ■	SN ■	SE	EM ◇■	SE	SN	SE	FC	FC	SN	SE ■		FC ■
Brighton ■10	d										07 22				07 33											07 24
Preston Park	d														07 37											07 28
Hassocks ■4	d																									07 35
Burgess Hill ■4	d														07 46											07 39
Wivelsfield ■4	d														07 49											
Haywards Heath ■3	d														07 54											07 46
Balcombe	d														07 59											
Three Bridges ■4	d														08 05											07 56
Gatwick Airport ■10	d																									08 01
Redhill	d																									08 09
East Croydon	d														08 25											08 21
Sevenoaks ■4	d			07 11			07 11	07 17		07 23				07 27				07 36		07 37				07 43		
Bat & Ball	d						07 14											07 39								
Otford ■4	d						07 18		07 23									07 43								
Shoreham (Kent)	d						07 21											07 46								
Eynsford	d						07 24											07 49								
Swanley ■4	d						07 30		07 32									07 54								
St Mary Cray ■4	d						07 34											07 59								
Bickley	d						07 39									07 35		08 03								
Bromley South	d						07 42		07 40							07 38		08 08								
Shortlands ■4	d						07 44									07 41		08 10								
Ravensbourne	d						07 47											08 13								
Beckenham Hill	d						07 49											08 15								
Bellingham	d						07 51											08 17								
Catford	d						07 53											08 20								
Crofton Park	d						07 56																			
Nunhead ■4	d						07 58																			
Peckham Rye ■4	d					07 12	08 00						07 25						07 38				07 42			
Denmark Hill ■4	d						08 04											08 26								
Sutton (Surrey) ■4	d		07 06																		07 37	07 40				
West Sutton	d		07 09																			07 43				
Sutton Common	d		07 11																			07 45				
St Helier	d		07 14																			07 48				
Morden South	d		07 16																			07 50				
South Merton	d		07 18																			07 52				
Wimbledon Chase	d		07 20																			07 54				
Wimbledon ■6 ⊖	d		07 22																			07 56				
Haydons Road	d		07 28																			08 00				
Tooting	d		07 31																			08 03				
Carshalton	d																				07 40					
Hackbridge	d																				07 42					
Mitcham Junction	d																				07 45					
Mitcham Eastfields	d																				07 48					
Streatham ■4	d		07 38																		07 52	08 09				
Tulse Hill ■3	d		07 42			07 20							07 34						07 47		07 57	08 13	07 50			08 36
London Bridge ■4 ⊖	a			07 36				07 59		07 50				07 53						08 18				08 09		
	d			07 37				08 00		07 51				07 54						08 20				08 10		
Herne Hill ■4	d		07 46													07 57					08 01	08 20				
Loughborough Jn	d		07 50													08 00					08 04	08 23				
Elephant & Castle	d		07 54				08 13		08 00							08 05		08 35			08 09	08 28				08 50
London Blackfriars ■3 ⊖	d		07 58				08 17		08 04							08 09		08 42			08 13	08 33				08 54
City Thameslink	d		08 00				08 19		08 06							08 11		08 44			08 15	08 35				08 56
Farringdon ■3 ⊖	d		08 04				08 23		08 10							08 15		08 48			08 19	08 39				09 00
St Pancras International ■15 ⊖	d	07 30			08 00							08 30					09 00									
St Pancras International ■15 ⊖	a		08 07				08 27		08 13							08 19		08 51			08 23	08 43				09 03
	d		08 10				08 28		08 16							08 20		08 52			08 24	08 44				09 04
Kentish Town ⊖	d		08 14															08a58			08 28	08 48				
West Hampstead Thameslink ⊖	d		08 18				08a37									08 28					08 33	08 52				
Cricklewood	d		08 21				08 39														08 36	08 55				
Hendon	d		08 24				08 42														08 39	08 58				
Mill Hill Broadway	d		08 27				08 45														08 42	09 01				
Elstree & Borehamwood	d		08 32				08 50									08 38					08 47	09 06				
Radlett	d		08 36				08 54									08 42					08 51	09 10				
St Albans City	d		08a44				08 01		08 36							08 50					08a58	09 16				09 25
Harpenden	d								08 44							08 55						09 22				09 32
Luton Airport Parkway ■7	d	07 51			|				08 50			08 51				09 01						09 28				09 38
Luton ■10	d				08 23				08 53							09a04	09 23					09a32				09 41
Leagrave	d								08 56																	09 44
Harlington	d								09 02																	09 50
Flitwick	d								09 06																	09 56
Bedford ■7	a	08 06			08 31				09 18			09 07					09 37									10 08

Table 52 — **Mondays to Fridays**

Brighton, Gatwick Airport and South London - City of London, St.Albans, Luton and Bedford

Station		SE ■	SE ■	SE	SE ■	FC ■	SN	SE	SE	SE	EM ◇■		SE ■	FC ■	SE ■	FC	FC	SE	SN	SE	SN		FC ■	SE	SE
Brighton ■10	d					07 50								08 02									08 16		
Preston Park	d					07 54								08 06									08 20		
Hassocks ■4	d					08 00								08 12									08 26		
Burgess Hill ■4	d													08 16									08 30		
Wivelsfield ■4	d													08 18									08 33		
Haywards Heath ■3	d					08 09								08 23									08 38		
Balcombe	d					08 15																			
Three Bridges ■4	d													08 34									08 47		
Gatwick Airport ■10	d					08 23								08 38									08 53		
Redhill	d																								
East Croydon	d					08 39								08 54									09 09		
Sevenoaks ■4	d				07 47			07 53		07 57			08 03		08 07									08 17	
Bat & Ball	d							07 56																	
Otford ■4	d							08 00																	
Shoreham (Kent)	d							08 03																	
Eynsford	d							08 06																	
Swanley ■4	d							08 11																	
St Mary Cray ■4	d							08 16																	
Bickley	d							08 20	07 55																
Bromley South	d		08 18					08 26	07 58																
Shortlands ■4	d		08 20					08 29	08 00																
Ravensbourne	d		08 23																						
Beckenham Hill	d		08 25																						
Bellingham	d		08 27					08 33	08 05																
Catford	d		08 30					08 36	08 08																
Crofton Park	d							08 39	08 10																
Nunhead ■4	d							08 41	08 14																
Peckham Rye ■4	d		08 36				07 53	08 43	08 16										08 12		08 16				
Denmark Hill ■4	d		08 39					08 47	08 19																
Sutton (Surrey) ■4	d															08 08	08 09								
West Sutton	d															08 11									
Sutton Common	d															08 13									
St Helier	d															08 16									
Morden South	d															08 18									
South Merton	d															08 20									
Wimbledon Chase	d															08 22									
Wimbledon ■6 ⊖	d															08 24									
Haydons Road	d															08 30									
Tooting	d															08 33									
Carshalton	d																08 12								
Hackbridge	d																08 14								
Mitcham Junction	d																08 17								
Mitcham Eastfields	d																08 20								
Streatham ■4	d															08 39	08 24								
Tulse Hill ■3	d						08 02									08 43	08 28		08 21		08 25				
London Bridge ■4 ⊖	a			07 44	08 13					08 39			08 29	09 08	08 35					08 13				08 59	08 19
	d			07 44	08 14					08 40			08 30	09 09	08 36					08 14				09 00	08 20
Herne Hill ■4	d	08 12				08 57										08 47	08 31								
Loughborough Jn	d	08 16														08 50	08 35								
Elephant & Castle	d	08 21	08 46			09 06		08 54	08 25							08 58	08 40						09g34		
London Blackfriars ■3 ⊖	d	08 25	08 50			09 10		08 58	08 29					09 22		09 02	08 46						09 38		
City Thameslink	d	08 27	08 52			09 12		09 00	08 31					09 24		09 04	08 48						09 40		
Farringdon ■3 ⊖	d	08 31	08 56			09 16		09 04	08 35					09 28		09 08	08 52						09 44		
St Pancras International ■15 ⊖	d	08 35																							
St Pancras International ■15 ⊖	a	08 36	08 59			09 19		09 07	08 39					09 32		09 11	08 55						09 47		
	d		09 00			09 20		09 08	08 40		09 30			09 32		09 12	08 56						09 48		
Kentish Town ⊖	d							09a14								09 16	09 00								
West Hampstead Thameslink ⊖	d															09 20	09 04								
Cricklewood	d															09 23	09 07								
Hendon	d															09 26	09 10								
Mill Hill Broadway	d															09 29	09 13								
Elstree & Borehamwood	d								08 57							09 34	09 18								
Radlett	d	08 57							09 01							09 40	09 22								
St Albans City	d	08 57	09 20			09 40			09 07					09 52		09 46	09a29						10 10		
Harpenden	d	09 04				09 46			09 13							09 54							10 16		
Luton Airport Parkway ■7	d	09 10	09 29			09 52			09 18		09 51			10 01		10 00							10 22		
Luton ■10	d	09 13	09 32			09 57			09a23					10 04		10a04							10 25		
Leagrave	d	09 16				10 00																	10 28		
Harlington	d	09 22				10 06																	10 34		
Flitwick	d	09 26	09 44			10 10								10 14									10 38		
Bedford ■7	a	09 38	09 58			10 22					10 07			10 28									10 50		

Brighton, Gatwick Airport and South London - City of London, St.Albans, Luton and Bedford

		SE ■	FC	SE ■	SN ■	SN	SE ■	SE ■	EM ◇■	SN	FC ■	SE	SN ■	SN	FC	SE ■	EM ◇■	SE	SE	SN	SE	SE ■	SE	SE ■
Brighton 10	d				08 22						08 36		08 38							08 44				
Preston Park	d										08 40													
Hassocks 4	d										08 46													
Burgess Hill 4	d										08 50													
Wivelsfield 4	d																							
Haywards Heath 3	d										09 00													
Balcombe	d										09 06													
Three Bridges 4	d										09 12													
Gatwick Airport 10	d										09 16													
Redhill	d																							
East Croydon	d										09 32													
Sevenoaks 4	d			08 23			08 24	08 27				08 37				08 43			08 43			08 49		08 55
Bat & Ball	d						08 27												08 46					
Otford 4	d						08 31												08 49					
Shoreham (Kent)	d						08 34												08 52					
Eynsford	d						08 37												08 56					
Swanley 4	d						08 42												09 01					
St Mary Cray 4	d						08 46												09 05					
Bickley	d						08 51												09 09					
Bromley South	d						08 54												09 12		08 44			
Shortlands 4	d						08 56												09 15		08 46			
Ravensbourne	d																		09 17		08 49			
Beckenham Hill	d																		09 19		08 51			
Bellingham	d						09 01												09 21		08 53			
Catford	d						09 04												09 24		08 56			
Crofton Park	d																		09 26		08 58			
Nunhead 4	d																		09 29		09 01			
Peckham Rye 4	d					08 23	09 09			08 33				08 42					09 31		09 03			
Denmark Hill 4	d						09 12												09 34		09 07			
Sutton (Surrey) 4	d		08 39												08 41									
West Sutton	d														08 44									
Sutton Common	d														08 46									
St Helier	d														08 49									
Morden South	d														08 51									
South Merton	d														08 53									
Wimbledon Chase	d														08 55									
Wimbledon 6 ⊖	d														08 57									
Haydons Road	d														09 00									
Tooting	d														09 03									
Carshalton	d		08 42																					
Hackbridge	d		08 44																					
Mitcham Junction	d		08 47																					
Mitcham Eastfields	d		08 50																					
Streatham 4	d		08 54												09 08									
Tulse Hill 3	d		08 58			08 32				08 47				08 50	09 16									
London Bridge 4 ⊖	a			08 49				08 55			09 46	09 20				09 11		08 42				09 14	08 50	09 22
	d			08 50				08 56			09 46	09 21				09 12		08 43				09 15	08 51	09 23
Herne Hill 4	d	08 52	09 02												09 20									
Loughborough Jn	d	08 55	09 05												09 23									
Elephant & Castle	d	09 02	09 10				09 20								09 30				09 42		09 14			
London Blackfriars 3 ⊖	d	09 06	09 14				09 26				09 54				09 34				09 46		09 18			
City Thameslink			09 16				09 28				09 56				09 36				09 48		09 20			
Farringdon 3 ⊖	d	09 12	09 20				09 32				10 00				09 40				09 52		09 24			
St Pancras International 15 ⊖	d																							
St Pancras International 15 ⊖	a	09 15	09 23				09 35				10 03				09 43				09 55		09 27			
	d	09 16	09 24				09 36		10 00		10 04				09 44		10 30		09 56		09 28			
Kentish Town ⊖	d														09 48				10 00		09 34			
West Hampstead Thameslink ⊖	d		09 31												09 54				10 04		09 40			
Cricklewood	d														09 57				10 07		09 43			
Hendon	d														10 00				10 10		09 46			
Mill Hill Broadway	d														10 03				10 13		09 49			
Elstree & Borehamwood	d		09 42												10 08				10 18		09 54			
Radlett	d		09 46												10 12				10 22		09 58			
St Albans City	d		09 52				09 57				10 25				10 18				10a29		10 04			
Harpenden	d		09 58				10 04				10 32				10 24						10 12			
Luton Airport Parkway 7	d	09 44	10 04				10 10				10 38				10 30		10 51				10 18			
Luton 10	d	09 49	10 07				10 13		10 23		10 41				10a34						10a21			
Leagrave	d		10 10				10 16				10 44													
Harlington	d		10 16				10 22				10 50													
Flitwick	d	10 00	10 22				10 26				10 54													
Bedford 7	a	10 12	10 34				10 38		10 37		11 06						11 06							

Brighton, Gatwick Airport and South London - City of London, St.Albans, Luton and Bedford

		SE	SN	SE ■	FC ■	SE	FC ■	SN	FC	SE ■	EM ◇■	SE	FC	SE	SN	SE ■	SE	SN ■	SN	SE ■	FC ■
Brighton 10	d				09 00		09 07								09 14			09 22			09 34
Preston Park	d						09 11														
Hassocks 4	d				09 08		09 17														
Burgess Hill 4	d				09 12		09 21														
Wivelsfield 4	d						09 23														
Haywards Heath 3	d				09 16		09 32														09 48
Balcombe	d						09 37														
Three Bridges 4	d				09 27		09 42														
Gatwick Airport 10	d				09 31		09 46														10 01
Redhill	d																				
East Croydon	d				09 47		10 02														10 17
Sevenoaks 4	d			08 59		09 06				09 14				09 13		09 19				09 29	
Bat & Ball	d													09 16							
Otford 4	d													09 21							
Shoreham (Kent)	d													09 24							
Eynsford	d													09 28							
Swanley 4	d													09 33							
St Mary Cray 4	d													09 37							
Bickley	d	08 55												09 42							
Bromley South	d	08 58												09 45							
Shortlands 4	d	09 00												09 48							
Ravensbourne	d	09 03												09 50							
Beckenham Hill	d	09 05												09 52							
Bellingham	d	09 07												09 54							
Catford	d	09 09												09 57							
Crofton Park	d	09 12												09 59							
Nunhead 4	d	09 14												10 02							
Peckham Rye 4	d	09 16	08 57					09 12						10 04					09 27		
Denmark Hill 4	d	09 19												10 07							
Sutton (Surrey) 4	d								09 11				09 13								
West Sutton	d								09 14												
Sutton Common	d								09 16												
St Helier	d								09 19												
Morden South	d								09 21												
South Merton	d								09 23												
Wimbledon Chase	d								09 25												
Wimbledon 6 ⊖	d								09 27												
Haydons Road	d								09 30												
Tooting	d								09 33												
Carshalton	d												09 16								
Hackbridge	d												09 18								
Mitcham Junction	d												09 21								
Mitcham Eastfields	d												09 24								
Streatham 4	d								09 38				09 28								
Tulse Hill 3	d		09 05					09 20	09 42				09 32						09 35		
London Bridge 4 ⊖	a			09 26	10 00	09 49	10 15			09 40		09 13				09 43	09 18			09 55	10 30
	d			09 27	10 00	09 50	10 16			09 41		09 14				09 44	09 19			09 55	10 30
Herne Hill 4	d								09 47				09 35								
Loughborough Jn	d								09 50				09 39								
Elephant & Castle	d	09 26							09 55				09 46	10 14							
London Blackfriars 3 ⊖	d	09 30			10 08		10 24		10 00				09 50	10 18							10 38
City Thameslink		09 32			10 10		10 26		10 02				09 52	10 20							10 40
Farringdon 3 ⊖	d	09 36			10 14		10 30		10 06				09 56	10 24							10 44
St Pancras International 15 ⊖	d																				
St Pancras International 15 ⊖	a	09 39			10 17		10 33		10 09				09 59	10 27							10 47
	d	09 40			10 18		10 34		10 10		11 00		10 00	10 28							10 48
Kentish Town ⊖	d	09a46							10 14				10a06	10a34							
West Hampstead Thameslink ⊖	d								10 18												
Cricklewood	d								10 21												
Hendon	d								10 24												
Mill Hill Broadway	d								10 27												
Elstree & Borehamwood	d								10 32												
Radlett	d								10 38												
St Albans City	d				10 40		10 55		10 46												11 10
Harpenden	d				10 46		11 00		10 54												11 16
Luton Airport Parkway 7	d				10 52		11 06		11 00												11 22
Luton 10	d				10 55		11 09		11a04		11 23										11 25
Leagrave	d				10 58		11 13														11 28
Harlington	d				11 04		11 19														11 34
Flitwick	d				11 08		11 23														11 38
Bedford 7	a				11 20		11 36				11 37										11 50

Table 52 Mondays to Fridays

Brighton, Gatwick Airport and South London - City of London, St.Albans, Luton and Bedford

		EM ◇1	SE	FC	FC 1	FC	SN	SE	SE 1	SE	SN	SE 1	SE	SN	SE 1	SE	FC 1	EM ◇1	SE	FC	FC 1	FC	SN	SE 1
Brighton 10	d				09 37						09 44						10 04				10 07			
Preston Park	d				09 41																10 11			
Hassocks 4	d				09 47																10 17			
Burgess Hill 4	d				09 51																10 21			
Wivelsfield 4	d				09 53																10 23			
Haywards Heath 3	d				09 58												10 18				10 32			
Balcombe	d																				10 37			
Three Bridges 4	d				10 10																10 42			
Gatwick Airport 10	d				10 16												10 31				10 46			
Redhill	d																							
East Croydon	d				10 32												10 47				11 02			
Sevenoaks 4	d		09 36					09 42	09 44			09 49			09 59	10 02			10 06					10 14
Bat & Ball	d							09 46								10 05								
Otford 4	d							09 50								10 08								
Shoreham (Kent)	d							09 53								10 11								
Eynsford	d							09 56								10 15								
Swanley 4	d							10 01								10 20								
St Mary Cray 4	d							10 05								10 24								
Bickley	d							10 10								10 28								
Bromley South	d							10 15								10 31								
Shortlands 4	d							10 18								10 34								
Ravensbourne	d							10 20								10 36								
Beckenham Hill	d							10 22								10 38								
Bellingham	d							10 24								10 40								
Catford	d							10 27								10 43								
Crofton Park	d							10 29								10 45								
Nunhead 4	d							10 32								10 48								
Peckham Rye 4	d						09 42	10 34						09 57		10 50							10 12	
Denmark Hill 4	d							10 37								10 54								
Sutton (Surrey) 4	d			09 37		09 38														10 07		10 08		
West Sutton	d			09 40																10 10				
Sutton Common	d			09 42																10 12				
St Helier	d			09 45																10 15				
Morden South	d			09 47																10 17				
South Merton	d			09 49																10 19				
Wimbledon Chase	d			09 51																10 21				
Wimbledon 6 ⊖	d			09 53																10 23				
Haydons Road	d			10 00																10 30				
Tooting	d			10 03																10 33				
Carshalton	d					09 41																10 11		
Hackbridge	d					09 43																10 13		
Mitcham Junction	d					09 46																10 16		
Mitcham Eastfields	d					09 49																10 19		
Streatham 4	d			10 08		09 53														10 38		10 23		
Tulse Hill 3	d			10 12		09 57	09 50							10 05						10 42		10 27	10 20	
London Bridge 4 ⊖	a		10 19		10 45				10 10	09 43		10 13	09 50		10 25		11 00		10 49		11 15			10 40
	d		10 19		10 45				10 11	09 44		10 14	09 51		10 25		11 00		10 49		11 15			10 41
Herne Hill 4	d			10 16		10 01														10 46		10 31		
Loughborough Jn	d			10 19		10 04														10 49		10 34		
Elephant & Castle	d			10 24		10 09		10 44								11 00				10 54		10 39		
London Blackfriars 5 ⊖	d			10 28	10 54	10 13		10 48								11 04	11 08			10 58	11 24	10 43		
City Thameslink	d			10 30	10 56	10 15		10 50								11 06	11 10			11 00	11 26	10 45		
Farringdon 3 ⊖	d			10 34	11 00	10 19		10 54								11 10	11 14			11 04	11 30	10 49		
St Pancras International 15 ⊖	d	11 30																12 00						
St Pancras International 15 ⊖	a			10 37	11 03	10 22		10 57								11 13	11 17			11 07	11 33	10 52		
	d			10 38	11 04	10 23		10 58								11 14	11 18			11 08	11 34	10 53		
Kentish Town ⊖	d			10 42		10 27		11a03								11a20				11 12		10 57		
West Hampstead Thameslink ⊖	d			10 46		10 31														11 16		11 01		
Cricklewood	d			10 49		10 34														11 19		11 04		
Hendon	d			10 52		10 37														11 22		11 07		
Mill Hill Broadway	d			10 55		10 41														11 25		11 11		
Elstree & Borehamwood	d			11 00		10 45														11 30		11 15		
Radlett	d			11 08		10 50														11 38		11 20		
St Albans City	d			11 15	11 25	10a57											11 40			11 45	11 55	11a27		
Harpenden	d			11 20	11 32												11 46			11 50	12 02			
Luton Airport Parkway 7	d	11 51		11 26	11 38												11 52			11 56	12 08			
Luton 10	d			11a30	11 41												11 55	12 23		12a00	12 11			
Leagrave	d				11 44												11 58				12 14			
Harlington	d				11 50												12 04				12 20			
Flitwick	d				11 54												12 08				12 24			
Bedford 7	a	12 06			12 06												12 20	12 37			12 36			

Table 52 Mondays to Fridays

Brighton, Gatwick Airport and South London - City of London, St.Albans, Luton and Bedford

		SE	SN	SE 1		SE	SN 1	SN	SE 1	SE	FC 1	SE	FC		FC 1	EM ◇1	FC	SN	SE 1	SE	SN	SE 1	SE	SN
Brighton 10	d		10 14				10 22				10 34				10 37						10 44			
Preston Park	d														10 41									
Hassocks 4	d														10 47									
Burgess Hill 4	d														10 51									
Wivelsfield 4	d														10 53									
Haywards Heath 3	d										10 48				11 02									
Balcombe	d																							
Three Bridges 4	d														11 12									
Gatwick Airport 10	d										11 01				11 16									
Redhill	d																							
East Croydon	d										11 17				11 32									
Sevenoaks 4	d			10 19					10 29	10 32		10 36							10 44			10 49		
Bat & Ball	d									10 35														
Otford 4	d									10 38														
Shoreham (Kent)	d									10 41														
Eynsford	d									10 45														
Swanley 4	d									10 50														
St Mary Cray 4	d									10 54														
Bickley	d									10 58														
Bromley South	d									11 01														
Shortlands 4	d									11 04														
Ravensbourne	d									11 06														
Beckenham Hill	d									11 08														
Bellingham	d									11 10														
Catford	d									11 13														
Crofton Park	d									11 15														
Nunhead 4	d									11 18														
Peckham Rye 4	d							10 27		11 20								10 42						10 57
Denmark Hill 4	d									11 24														
Sutton (Surrey) 4	d												10 37				10 38							
West Sutton	d												10 40											
Sutton Common	d												10 42											
St Helier	d												10 45											
Morden South	d												10 47											
South Merton	d												10 49											
Wimbledon Chase	d												10 51											
Wimbledon 6 ⊖	d												10 53											
Haydons Road	d												11 00											
Tooting	d												11 03											
Carshalton	d																10 41							
Hackbridge	d																10 43							
Mitcham Junction	d																10 46							
Mitcham Eastfields	d																10 49							
Streatham 4	d												11 08				10 53							
Tulse Hill 3	d							10 35					11 12				10 57	10 50						11 05
London Bridge 4 ⊖	a	10 13		10 43		10 20			10 55		11 30	11 19			11 45				11 10	10 43		11 13	10 50	
	d	10 14		10 44		10 21			10 55		11 30	11 19			11 45				11 11	10 44		11 14	10 51	
Herne Hill 4	d												11 16				11 01							
Loughborough Jn	d												11 19				11 04							
Elephant & Castle	d									11 30			11 24				11 09							
London Blackfriars 5 ⊖	d									11 34	11 38		11 28		11 54		11 13							
City Thameslink	d									11 36	11 40		11 30		11 56		11 15							
Farringdon 3 ⊖	d									11 40	11 44		11 34		12 00		11 19							
St Pancras International 15 ⊖	d															12 30								
St Pancras International 15 ⊖	a									11 43	11 47		11 37		12 03		11 22							
	d									11 44	11 48		11 38		12 04		11 23							
Kentish Town ⊖	d									11a50			11 42				11 27							
West Hampstead Thameslink ⊖	d												11 46				11 31							
Cricklewood	d												11 49				11 34							
Hendon	d												11 52				11 37							
Mill Hill Broadway	d												11 55				11 41							
Elstree & Borehamwood	d												12 00				11 45							
Radlett	d												12 08				11 50							
St Albans City	d										12 10		12 15		12 25		11a57							
Harpenden	d										12 16		12 20		12 32									
Luton Airport Parkway 7	d										12 22		12 26		12 38	12 51								
Luton 10	d										12 25		12a30		12 41									
Leagrave	d										12 28				12 44									
Harlington	d										12 34				12 50									
Flitwick	d										12 38				12 54									
Bedford 7	a										12 50				13 06	13 06								

Table 52

Brighton, Gatwick Airport and South London - City of London, St.Albans, Luton and Bedford

		SE 1 H	SE	FC 1	SE	FC	FC 1	EM ◇1	FC	SN		SE 1	SE	SN	SE 1 H	SE	SN 1	SN	SE 1 H		SE	FC 1	SE
Brighton 10	d			11 04			11 07							11 14			11 22					11 34	
Preston Park	d						11 11																
Hassocks 4	d						11 17																
Burgess Hill 4	d						11 21																
Wivelsfield 4	d						11 23																
Haywards Heath 3	d			11 18			11 32															11 48	
Balcombe	d						11 37																
Three Bridges 4	d						11 42																
Gatwick Airport 10	d			11 31			11 46															12 01	
Redhill	d																						
East Croydon	d			11 47			12 02															12 17	
Sevenoaks 4	d	10 59	11 02		11 06							11 14			11 19				11 29		11 32		11 36
Bat & Ball	d		11 05																		11 35		
Otford 4	d		11 08																		11 38		
Shoreham (Kent)	d		11 11																		11 41		
Eynsford	d		11 15																		11 45		
Swanley 4	d		11 20																		11 50		
St Mary Cray 4	d		11 24																		11 54		
Bickley	d		11 28																		11 58		
Bromley South	d		11 31																		12 01		
Shortlands 4	d		11 34																		12 04		
Ravensbourne	d		11 36																		12 06		
Beckenham Hill	d		11 38																		12 08		
Bellingham	d		11 40																		12 10		
Catford	d		11 43																		12 13		
Crofton Park	d		11 45																		12 15		
Nunhead 4	d		11 48																		12 18		
Peckham Rye 4	d		11 50							11 12								11 27			12 20		
Denmark Hill 4	d		11 54																		12 24		
Sutton (Surrey) 4	d					11 07			11 08														
West Sutton	d					11 10																	
Sutton Common	d					11 12																	
St Helier	d					11 15																	
Morden South	d					11 17																	
South Merton	d					11 19																	
Wimbledon Chase	d					11 21																	
Wimbledon 6 ⊖	d					11 23																	
Haydons Road	d					11 30																	
Tooting	d					11 33																	
Carshalton	d								11 11														
Hackbridge	d								11 13														
Mitcham Junction	d								11 16														
Mitcham Eastfields	d								11 19														
Streatham 4	d					11 38			11 23														
Tulse Hill 3	d					11 42			11 27	11 20								11 35					
London Bridge 4 ⊖	a	11 25		12 00	11 49		12 15					11 40	11 13		11 43	11 20			11 55			12 30	12 19
	d	11 25		12 00	11 49		12 15					11 41	11 14		11 44	11 21			11 55			12 30	12 19
Herne Hill 4	d					11 46			11 31														
Loughborough Jn	d					11 49			11 34														
Elephant & Castle	d		12 00			11 54			11 39												12 30		
London Blackfriars 3 ⊖	d		12 04	12 08		11 58	12 24		11 43												12 34	12 38	
CityThameslink			12 06	12 10		12 00	12 26		11 45												12 36	12 40	
Farringdon 3 ⊖	d		12 10	12 14		12 04	12 30		11 49												12 40	12 44	
St Pancras International 15 ⊖	d							13 00															
St Pancras International 15 ⊖	a		12 13	12 17		12 07	12 33		11 52												12 43	12 47	
	d		12 14	12 18		12 08	12 34		11 53												12 44	12 48	
Kentish Town ⊖	d		12a20			12 12			11 57												12a50		
West Hampstead Thameslink ⊖	d					12 16			12 01														
Cricklewood	d					12 19			12 04														
Hendon	d					12 22			12 07														
Mill Hill Broadway	d					12 25			12 11														
Elstree & Borehamwood	d					12 30			12 15														
Radlett	d					12 38			12 20														
St Albans City	d			12 40		12 45	12 55		12a27													13 10	
Harpenden	d			12 46		12 50	13 02															13 16	
Luton Airport Parkway 7	d			12 52		12 56	13 08															13 22	
Luton 10	d			12 55		13a00	13 11	13 23														13 25	
Leagrave	d			12 58			13 14															13 28	
Harlington	d			13 04			13 20															13 34	
Flitwick	d			13 08			13 24															13 38	
Bedford 7	a			13 20			13 36	13 37														13 50	

Table 52

Brighton, Gatwick Airport and South London - City of London, St.Albans, Luton and Bedford

		EM ◇1	FC 1	FC	SN	SE 1	SE	SN	SE 1 H	SE	SN	SE 1 H	SE	FC 1	SE		FC	FC 1	FC	SN	SE 1	SE	SN	SE 1 H
Brighton 10	d		11 37					11 44						12 04				12 07					12 14	
Preston Park	d		11 41															12 11						
Hassocks 4	d		11 47															12 17						
Burgess Hill 4	d		11 51															12 21						
Wivelsfield 4	d		11 53															12 23						
Haywards Heath 3	d		12 02											12 18				12 32						
Balcombe	d																	12 37						
Three Bridges 4	d		12 12															12 42						
Gatwick Airport 10	d		12 16											12 31				12 46						
Redhill	d																							
East Croydon	d		12 32											12 47				13 02						
Sevenoaks 4	d					11 44			11 49			11 59	12 02		12 06						12 14			12 19
Bat & Ball	d												12 05											
Otford 4	d												12 08											
Shoreham (Kent)	d												12 11											
Eynsford	d												12 15											
Swanley 4	d												12 20											
St Mary Cray 4	d												12 24											
Bickley	d												12 28											
Bromley South	d												12 31											
Shortlands 4	d												12 34											
Ravensbourne	d												12 36											
Beckenham Hill	d												12 38											
Bellingham	d												12 40											
Catford	d												12 43											
Crofton Park	d												12 45											
Nunhead 4	d												12 48											
Peckham Rye 4	d				11 42						11 57		12 50							12 12				
Denmark Hill 4	d												12 54											
Sutton (Surrey) 4	d			11 38													12 07		12 08					
West Sutton	d																12 10							
Sutton Common	d																12 12							
St Helier	d																12 15							
Morden South	d																12 17							
South Merton	d																12 19							
Wimbledon Chase	d																12 21							
Wimbledon 6 ⊖	d																12 23							
Haydons Road	d																12 30							
Tooting	d																12 33							
Carshalton	d			11 41															12 11					
Hackbridge	d			11 43															12 13					
Mitcham Junction	d			11 46															12 16					
Mitcham Eastfields	d			11 49															12 19					
Streatham 4	d			11 53													12 38		12 23					
Tulse Hill 3	d			11 57	11 50						12 05						12 42		12 27	12 20				
London Bridge 4 ⊖	a		12 45			12 10	11 43		12 13	11 50		12 25		13 00	12 49			13 15			12 40	12 13		12 43
	d		12 45			12 11	11 44		12 14	11 51		12 25		13 00	12 49			13 15			12 41	12 14		12 44
Herne Hill 4	d			12 01													12 46		12 31					
Loughborough Jn	d			12 04													12 49		12 34					
Elephant & Castle	d			12 09									13 00				12 54		12 39					
London Blackfriars 3 ⊖	d		12 54	12 13									13 04	13 08			12 58	13 24	12 43					
City Thameslink			12 56	12 15									13 06	13 10			13 00	13 26	12 45					
Farringdon 3 ⊖	d		13 00	12 19									13 10	13 14			13 04	13 30	12 49					
St Pancras International 15 ⊖	d																							
St Pancras International 15 ⊖	a		13 03	12 22									13 13	13 17			13 07	13 33	12 52					
	d	13 30	13 04	12 23									13 14	13 18			13 08	13 34	12 53					
Kentish Town ⊖	d			12 27									13a20				13 12		12 57					
West Hampstead Thameslink ⊖	d			12 31													13 16		13 01					
Cricklewood	d			12 34													13 19		13 04					
Hendon	d			12 37													13 22		13 07					
Mill Hill Broadway	d			12 41													13 25		13 11					
Elstree & Borehamwood	d			12 45													13 30		13 15					
Radlett	d			12 50													13 38		13 20					
St Albans City	d		13 25	12a57										13 40			13 45	13 55	13a27					
Harpenden	d		13 32											13 46			13 50	14 02						
Luton Airport Parkway 7	d	13 51	13 38											13 52			13 56	14 08						
Luton 10	d		13 41											13 55			14a00	14 11						
Leagrave	d		13 44											13 58				14 14						
Harlington	d		13 50											14 04				14 20						
Flitwick	d		13 54											14 08				14 24						
Bedford 7	a	14 07	14 06											14 20				14 36						

Table 52

Mondays to Fridays

Brighton, Gatwick Airport and South London - City of London, St.Albans, Luton and Bedford

		SE		SN	SN	SE	SE	EM	FC	SE	FC	FC		FC	SN	SE	SE	SN	SE	SE	SN	SE		EM	SE
				1		1 Ħ		◇1 ⊡	1			1				1			1 Ħ			1 Ħ		◇1 ⊡	
Brighton 10	d			12 22					12 34			12 37						12 44							
Preston Park	d											12 41													
Hassocks 4	d											12 47													
Burgess Hill 4	d											12 51													
Wivelsfield 4	d											12 53													
Haywards Heath 3	d								12 48			13 02													
Balcombe	d																								
Three Bridges 4	d											13 12													
Gatwick Airport 10	d								13 01			13 16													
Redhill	d																								
East Croydon	d								13 17			13 32													
Sevenoaks 4	d					12 29	12 32			12 36						12 44			12 49			12 59			13 02
Bat & Ball	d						12 35																		13 05
Otford 4	d						12 38																		13 08
Shoreham (Kent)	d						12 41																		13 11
Eynsford	d						12 45																		13 15
Swanley 4	d						12 50																		13 20
St Mary Cray 4	d						12 54																		13 24
Bickley	d						12 58																		13 28
Bromley South	d						13 01																		13 31
Shortlands 4	d						13 04																		13 34
Ravensbourne	d						13 06																		13 36
Beckenham Hill	d						13 08																		13 38
Bellingham	d						13 10																		13 40
Catford	d						13 13																		13 43
Crofton Park	d						13 15																		13 45
Nunhead 4	d						13 18																		13 48
Peckham Rye 4	d				12 27		13 20								12 42						12 57				13 50
Denmark Hill 4	d						13 24																		13 54
Sutton (Surrey) 4	d										12 37			12 38											
West Sutton	d										12 40														
Sutton Common	d										12 42														
St Helier	d										12 45														
Morden South	d										12 47														
South Merton	d										12 49														
Wimbledon Chase	d										12 51														
Wimbledon 6	d										12 53														
Haydons Road	d										13 00														
Tooting	d										13 03														
Carshalton	d													12 41											
Hackbridge	d													12 43											
Mitcham Junction	d													12 46											
Mitcham Eastfields	d													12 49											
Streatham 4	d										13 08			12 53											
Tulse Hill 3	d				12 35						13 12			12 57	12 50						13 05				
London Bridge 4	a	12 20				12 55			13 30	13 19		13 45				13 10	12 43		13 13	12 50		13 25			
	d	12 21				12 55			13 30	13 19		13 45				13 11	12 44		13 14	12 51		13 25			
Herne Hill 4	d										13 16			13 01											
Loughborough Jn	d										13 19			13 04											
Elephant & Castle	d						13 30				13 24			13 09											14 00
London Blackfriars 3	d						13 34		13 38		13 28	13 54		13 13											14 04
City Thameslink							13 36		13 40		13 30	13 56		13 15											14 06
Farringdon 3	d						13 40		13 44		13 34	14 00		13 19											14 10
St Pancras International 15	d							14 00																14 30	
St Pancras International 15	a						13 43		13 47		13 37	14 03		13 22											14 13
	d						13 44		13 48		13 38	14 04		13 23											14 14
Kentish Town	d						13a50				13 42			13 27											14a20
West Hampstead Thameslink	d										13 46			13 31											
Cricklewood	d										13 49			13 34											
Hendon	d										13 52			13 37											
Mill Hill Broadway	d										13 55			13 41											
Elstree & Borehamwood	d										14 00			13 45											
Radlett	d										14 08			13 50											
St Albans City	d								14 10		14 15	14 25		13a57											
Harpenden	d								14 16		14 20	14 32													
Luton Airport Parkway 7	d								14 22		14 26	14 38												14 51	
Luton 10	d							14 23	14 25		14a30	14 41													
Leagrave	d								14 28			14 44													
Harlington	d								14 34			14 50													
Flitwick	d								14 38			14 54													
Bedford 7	a							14 37	14 50			15 06												15 06	

Table 52

Mondays to Fridays

Brighton, Gatwick Airport and South London - City of London, St.Albans, Luton and Bedford

		FC	SE ThX	SE ThO	FC	FC	EM	FC	SN		SE	SE	SN	SE	SE	SN	SN	SE		SE	FC	SE	FC	FC	FC
		1				1	◇1 ⊡				1			1 Ħ		1		1 Ħ			1			1	
Brighton 10	d	13 04				13 07							13 14			13 22					13 34			13 37	
Preston Park	d					13 11																		13 41	
Hassocks 4	d					13 17																		13 47	
Burgess Hill 4	d					13 21																		13 51	
Wivelsfield 4	d					13 23																		13 53	
Haywards Heath 3	d	13 18				13 32															13 48			14 02	
Balcombe	d					13 37																			
Three Bridges 4	d					13 42																		14 12	
Gatwick Airport 10	d	13 31				13 46															14 01			14 16	
Redhill	d																								
East Croydon	d	13 47				14 02															14 17			14 32	
Sevenoaks 4	d		13 06	13 06							13 14			13 19				13 29		13 32		13 36			
Bat & Ball	d																			13 35					
Otford 4	d																			13 38					
Shoreham (Kent)	d																			13 41					
Eynsford	d																			13 45					
Swanley 4	d																			13 50					
St Mary Cray 4	d																			13 54					
Bickley	d																			13 58					
Bromley South	d																			14 01					
Shortlands 4	d																			14 04					
Ravensbourne	d																			14 06					
Beckenham Hill	d																			14 08					
Bellingham	d																			14 10					
Catford	d																			14 13					
Crofton Park	d																			14 15					
Nunhead 4	d																			14 18					
Peckham Rye 4	d								13 12								13 27			14 20					
Denmark Hill 4	d																			14 24					
Sutton (Surrey) 4	d				13 07			13 08															13 37		13 38
West Sutton	d				13 10																		13 40		
Sutton Common	d				13 12																		13 42		
St Helier	d				13 15																		13 45		
Morden South	d				13 17																		13 47		
South Merton	d				13 19																		13 49		
Wimbledon Chase	d				13 21																		13 51		
Wimbledon 6	d				13 23																		13 53		
Haydons Road	d				13 30																		14 00		
Tooting	d				13 33																		14 03		
Carshalton	d							13 11																	13 41
Hackbridge	d							13 13																	13 43
Mitcham Junction	d							13 16																	13 46
Mitcham Eastfields	d							13 19																	13 49
Streatham 4	d				13 38			13 23															14 08		13 53
Tulse Hill 3	d				13 42			13 27	13 20								13 35						14 12		13 57
London Bridge 4	a	14 00	13 49	13 49		14 15					13 40	13 13		13 43	13 20			13 55			14 30	14 19		14 45	
	d	14 00	13 49	13 49		14 15					13 41	13 14		13 44	13 21			13 55			14 30	14 19		14 45	
Herne Hill 4	d				13 46			13 31															14 16		14 01
Loughborough Jn	d				13 49			13 34															14 19		14 04
Elephant & Castle	d				13 54			13 39												14 30			14 24		14 09
London Blackfriars 3	d	14 08			13 58	14 24		13 43												14 34	14 38		14 28	14 54	14 13
City Thameslink		14 10			14 00	14 26		13 45												14 36	14 40		14 30	14 56	14 15
Farringdon 3	d	14 14			14 04	14 30		13 49												14 40	14 44		14 34	15 00	14 19
St Pancras International 15	d																								
St Pancras International 15	a	14 17			14 07	14 33		13 52												14 43	14 47		14 37	15 03	14 22
	d	14 18			14 08	14 34	15 00	13 53												14 44	14 48		14 38	15 04	14 23
Kentish Town	d				14 12			13 57												14a50			14 42		14 27
West Hampstead Thameslink	d				14 16			14 01															14 46		14 31
Cricklewood	d				14 19			14 04															14 49		14 34
Hendon	d				14 22			14 07															14 52		14 37
Mill Hill Broadway	d				14 25			14 11															14 55		14 41
Elstree & Borehamwood	d				14 30			14 15															15 00		14 45
Radlett	d				14 38			14 20															15 08		14 50
St Albans City	d	14 40			14 45	14 55		14a27													15 10		15 15	15 25	14a57
Harpenden	d	14 46			14 50	15 02															15 16		15 20	15 32	
Luton Airport Parkway 7	d	14 52			14 56	15 08															15 22		15 26	15 38	
Luton 10	d	14 55			15a00	15 11	15 23														15 25		15a30	15 41	
Leagrave	d	14 58				15 14															15 28			15 44	
Harlington	d	15 04				15 20															15 34			15 50	
Flitwick	d	15 08				15 24															15 38			15 54	
Bedford 7	a	15 20				15 36	15 37														15 50			16 06	

Brighton, Gatwick Airport and South London - City of London, St.Albans, Luton and Bedford

Station		SN	EM ◇1	SE 1	SE	SN	SE 1	SE	SN	SE 1	SE	FC 1	SE	FC	FC 1	EM ◇1	FC	SN	SE 1	SE	SN	SE 1	SE
Brighton 10	d					13 44						14 04			14 07						14 14		
Preston Park	d														14 11								
Hassocks 4	d														14 17								
Burgess Hill 4	d														14 21								
Wivelsfield 4	d														14 23								
Haywards Heath 3	d											14 18			14 32								
Balcombe	d														14 37								
Three Bridges 4	d														14 42								
Gatwick Airport 10	d											14 31			14 46								
Redhill	d																						
East Croydon	d											14 47			15 02								
Sevenoaks 4	d			13 44			13 49			13 59	14 02		14 06						14 14			14 19	
Bat & Ball	d										14 05												
Otford 4	d										14 08												
Shoreham (Kent)	d										14 11												
Eynsford	d										14 15												
Swanley 4	d										14 20												
St Mary Cray 4	d										14 24												
Bickley	d										14 28												
Bromley South	d										14 31												
Shortlands 4	d										14 34												
Ravensbourne	d										14 36												
Beckenham Hill	d										14 38												
Bellingham	d										14 40												
Catford	d										14 43												
Crofton Park	d										14 45												
Nunhead 4	d										14 48												
Peckham Rye 4	d	13 42							13 57		14 50							14 12					
Denmark Hill 4	d										14 54												
Sutton (Surrey) 4	d													14 07			14 08						
West Sutton	d													14 10									
Sutton Common	d													14 12									
St Helier	d													14 15									
Morden South	d													14 17									
South Merton	d													14 19									
Wimbledon Chase	d													14 21									
Wimbledon 6 ⊖	d													14 23									
Haydons Road	d													14 30									
Tooting	d													14 33									
Carshalton	d																14 11						
Hackbridge	d																14 13						
Mitcham Junction	d																14 16						
Mitcham Eastfields	d																14 19						
Streatham 4	d													14 38			14 23						
Tulse Hill 3	d	13 50							14 05					14 42			14 27	14 20					
London Bridge 4 ⊖	a			14 10	13 43		14 13	13 50		14 25		15 00	14 49		15 15				14 40	14 13		14 43	14 20
	d			14 11	13 44		14 14	13 51		14 25		15 00	14 49		15 15				14 41	14 14		14 44	14 21
Herne Hill 4	d													14 46			14 31						
Loughborough Jn	d													14 49			14 34						
Elephant & Castle	d										15 00			14 54			14 39						
London Blackfriars 3 ⊖	d										15 04	15 08		14 58	15 24		14 43						
City Thameslink											15 06	15 10		15 00	15 26		14 45						
Farringdon 3 ⊖	d										15 10	15 14		15 04	15 30		14 49						
St Pancras International 15 ⊖	d		15 30													15 59							
St Pancras International 15 ⊖	a										15 13	15 17		15 07	15 33		14 52						
	d										15 14	15 18		15 08	15 34		14 53						
Kentish Town ⊖	d										15a20			15 12			14 57						
West Hampstead Thameslink ⊖	d													15 16			15 01						
Cricklewood	d													15 19			15 04						
Hendon	d													15 22			15 07						
Mill Hill Broadway	d													15 25			15 11						
Elstree & Borehamwood	d													15 30			15 15						
Radlett	d													15 38			15 20						
St Albans City	d											15 40		15 45	15 55		15a27						
Harpenden	d											15 46		15 50	16 00								
Luton Airport Parkway 7	d		15 51									15 52		15 56	16 06								
Luton 10	d											15 55		16a00	16 09	16 22							
Leagrave	d											15 58			16 12								
Harlington	d											16 04			16 18								
Flitwick	d											16 08			16 22								
Bedford 7	a		16 06									16 20			16 36	16 37							

Brighton, Gatwick Airport and South London - City of London, St.Albans, Luton and Bedford

Station		SN 1	SN	SE 1	SE	FC 1	SE	FC	FC 1	EM ◇1	FC	SN	SE 1	SE	SN	SE 1	SE	SN	SE 1	SE	FC 1	SE
Brighton 10	d	14 22				14 34			14 37						14 44						15 04	
Preston Park	d								14 41													
Hassocks 4	d								14 47													
Burgess Hill 4	d								14 51													
Wivelsfield 4	d								14 53													
Haywards Heath 3	d					14 48			15 02												15 18	
Balcombe	d																					
Three Bridges 4	d								15 12													
Gatwick Airport 10	d					15 01			15 16												15 31	
Redhill	d																					
East Croydon	d					15 17			15 32												15 47	
Sevenoaks 4	d			14 29	14 32		14 36						14 44			14 49			14 59	15 02		15 06
Bat & Ball	d				14 35															15 05		
Otford 4	d				14 38															15 08		
Shoreham (Kent)	d				14 41															15 11		
Eynsford	d				14 45															15 15		
Swanley 4	d				14 50															15 20		
St Mary Cray 4	d				14 54															15 24		
Bickley	d				14 58															15 28		
Bromley South	d				15 01															15 31		
Shortlands 4	d				15 04															15 34		
Ravensbourne	d				15 06															15 36		
Beckenham Hill	d				15 08															15 38		
Bellingham	d				15 10															15 40		
Catford	d				15 13															15 43		
Crofton Park	d				15 15															15 45		
Nunhead 4	d				15 18															15 48		
Peckham Rye 4	d		14 27		15 20							14 42						14 57		15 50		
Denmark Hill 4	d				15 24															15 54		
Sutton (Surrey) 4	d							14 37			14 38											
West Sutton	d							14 40														
Sutton Common	d							14 42														
St Helier	d							14 45														
Morden South	d							14 47														
South Merton	d							14 49														
Wimbledon Chase	d							14 51														
Wimbledon 6 ⊖	d							14 53														
Haydons Road	d							15 00														
Tooting	d							15 03														
Carshalton	d										14 41											
Hackbridge	d										14 43											
Mitcham Junction	d										14 46											
Mitcham Eastfields	d										14 49											
Streatham 4	d							15 08			14 53											
Tulse Hill 3	d		14 35					15 12			14 57	14 50						15 05				
London Bridge 4 ⊖	a			14 55		15 30	15 19		15 45				15 10	14 43		15 13	14 50		15 25		16 00	15 49
	d			14 55		15 30	15 19		15 45				15 11	14 44		15 14	14 51		15 25		16 00	15 50
Herne Hill 4	d							15 16			15 01											
Loughborough Jn	d							15 19			15 04											
Elephant & Castle	d				15 30			15 24			15 09									16 00		
London Blackfriars 3 ⊖	d				15 34	15 38		15 28	15 54		15 13									16 04	16 08	
City Thameslink					15 36	15 40		15 30	15 56		15 15									16 06	16 10	
Farringdon 3 ⊖	d				15 40	15 44		15 34	16 00		15 19									16 10	16 13	
St Pancras International 15 ⊖	d																					
St Pancras International 15 ⊖	a				15 43	15 47		15 37	16 03		15 22									16 13	16 17	
	d				15 44	15 48		15 38	16 04	16 30	15 23									16 14	16 18	
Kentish Town ⊖	d				15a50			15 42			15 27									16a20		
West Hampstead Thameslink ⊖	d							15 46			15 31											
Cricklewood	d							15 49			15 34											
Hendon	d							15 52			15 37											
Mill Hill Broadway	d							15 55			15 41											
Elstree & Borehamwood	d							16 00			15 45											
Radlett	d							16 08			15 50											
St Albans City	d					16 10		16 15	16 25		15a57										16 40	
Harpenden	d					16 16		16 24	16 32												16 46	
Luton Airport Parkway 7	d					16 22		16 30	16 38	16 51											16 52	
Luton 10	d					16 25		16a32	16 41	16 55											16 55	
Leagrave	d					16 28			16 44												16 59	
Harlington	d					16 34			16 50												17 04	
Flitwick	d					16 38			16 54												17 08	
Bedford 7	a					16 50			17 06	17 09											17 20	

Table 52

Mondays to Fridays

Brighton, Gatwick Airport and South London - City of London, St.Albans, Luton and Bedford

Station		FC ■	EM ◇■	FC	FC ■	FC	SN	SE ■	SE	SN	SE ■	SE	SN ■	SN	SE ■	SE ■	FC ■	SE	FC	FC ■	FC	SN	SE ■	SE
Brighton 10	d				15 07					15 14			15 22				15 34			15 37				
Preston Park	d				15 11															15 41				
Hassocks 4	d				15 17															15 47				
Burgess Hill 4	d				15 21															15 51				
Wivelsfield 4	d				15 23															15 53				
Haywards Heath 3	d				15 32												15 48			15 58				
Balcombe	d				15 37																			
Three Bridges 4	d				15 42															16 07				
Gatwick Airport 10	d				15 46												16 01			16 11				
Redhill	d																							
East Croydon	d				16 02												16 17			16 28				
Sevenoaks 4	d							15 14			15 19				15 29	15 32		15 36					15 44	
Bat & Ball	d															15 35								
Otford 4	d															15 38								
Shoreham (Kent)	d															15 41								
Eynsford	d															15 45								
Swanley 4	d															15 50								
St Mary Cray 4	d															15 54								
Bickley	d															15 58								
Bromley South	d															16 01								
Shortlands 4	d															16 04								
Ravensbourne	d															16 06								
Beckenham Hill	d															16 08								
Bellingham	d															16 10								
Catford	d															16 13								
Crofton Park	d															16 15								
Nunhead 4	d															16 18								
Peckham Rye 4	d						15 12							15 27		16 20						15 42		
Denmark Hill 4	d															16 24								
Sutton (Surrey) 4	d			15 07		15 08													15 37		15 38			
West Sutton	d			15 10															15 40					
Sutton Common	d			15 12															15 42					
St Helier	d			15 15															15 45					
Morden South	d			15 17															15 47					
South Merton	d			15 19															15 49					
Wimbledon Chase	d			15 21															15 51					
Wimbledon 6 ⊖	d			15 23															15 53					
Haydons Road	d			15 30															16 00					
Tooting	d			15 33															16 03					
Carshalton	d					15 11															15 41			
Hackbridge	d					15 13															15 43			
Mitcham Junction	d					15 16															15 46			
Mitcham Eastfields	d					15 19															15 49			
Streatham 4	d			15 38		15 23													16 08		15 53			
Tulse Hill 3	d			15 42		15 27	15 20							15 35			16 33		16 12		15 57	15 50		
London Bridge 4 ⊖	a				16 15			15 40	15 13		15 43	15 20			15 55			16 19					16 11	15 43
	d				16 16			15 41	15 14		15 43	15 21			15 55			16 19					16 12	15 44
Herne Hill 4	d			15 46		15 31													16 16		16 01			
Loughborough Jn	d			15 49		15 34													16 19		16 04			
Elephant & Castle	d	16 18		15 54		15 39										16 30	16 44		16 24		16 09			
London Blackfriars 3 ⊖	d	16 22		15 58	16 26	15 43										16 36	16 52		16 30	16 56	16 14			
City Thameslink		16 24		16 00	16 28	15 45										16 38	16 54		16 32	16 58	16 16			
Farringdon 3 ⊖	d	16 27		16 04	16 31	15 49										16 41	16 57		16 35	17 01	16 19			
St Pancras International 15 ⊖	d																							
St Pancras International 15 ⊖	a	16 31		16 07	16 35	15 52										16 45	17 01		16 39	17 05	16 23			
	d	16 32	17 00	16 08	16 36	15 53										16 46	17 02		16 40	17 06	16 24			
Kentish Town ⊖	d			16 12		15 57													16 44		16 28			
West Hampstead Thameslink ⊖	d			16 16		16 01													16 48		16 32			
Cricklewood	d			16 19		16 04													16 51		16 35			
Hendon	d			16 22		16 07													16 54		16 38			
Mill Hill Broadway	d			16 26		16 11													16 58		16 42			
Elstree & Borehamwood	d			16 31		16 15													17 03		16 47			
Radlett	d			16 38		16 20													17 08		16 52			
St Albans City	d	16 52		16 45	16 56	16a27										17 08	17 22		17 15	17 26	16a59			
Harpenden	d	16 58		16 54	17 04											17 14	17 28		17 20	17 34				
Luton Airport Parkway 7	d			17 00	17 10											17 20			17 26	17 40				
Luton 10	d	17 04		17a02	17 13											17 23	17 34		17a30	17 43				
Leagrave	d				17 17											17 27				17 47				
Harlington	d				17 22											17 32				17 52				
Flitwick	d	17 14			17 26											17 36	17 44			17 56				
Bedford 7	a	17 26	17 33		17 38											17 48	17 58			18 08				

Table 52

Mondays to Fridays

Brighton, Gatwick Airport and South London - City of London, St.Albans, Luton and Bedford

Station		SN	SE ■	SE	SN	SE ■	EM ◇■	EM ◇■	SE ■	FC ■	SE	FC	FC ■	FC	SN	SE ■	SE	SN	SE ■	SE		SN ■	SE
Brighton 10	d	15 44								16 04			16 07					16 14				16 22	
Preston Park	d												16 11										
Hassocks 4	d												16 17										
Burgess Hill 4	d												16 21										
Wivelsfield 4	d																						
Haywards Heath 3	d									16 18			16 26										
Balcombe	d												16 31										
Three Bridges 4	d												16 37										
Gatwick Airport 10	d									16 31			16 41										
Redhill	d																						
East Croydon	d									16 47			16 57										
Sevenoaks 4	d		15 49			15 59			16 02		16 06					16 14			16 19				16 22
Bat & Ball	d								16 05														16 25
Otford 4	d								16 08														16 28
Shoreham (Kent)	d								16 11														
Eynsford	d								16 15														
Swanley 4	d								16 20														16 37
St Mary Cray 4	d								16 24														16 41
Bickley	d								16 28														
Bromley South	d								16 31														16 47
Shortlands 4	d								16 34														
Ravensbourne	d								16 36														
Beckenham Hill	d								16 38														
Bellingham	d								16 40														16 52
Catford	d								16 43														16 55
Crofton Park	d								16 45														
Nunhead 4	d								16 48														16 59
Peckham Rye 4	d				15 57				16 50						16 12								17 01
Denmark Hill 4	d								16 54														17 05
Sutton (Surrey) 4	d											16 07		16 08									
West Sutton	d											16 10											
Sutton Common	d											16 12											
St Helier	d											16 15											
Morden South	d											16 17											
South Merton	d											16 19											
Wimbledon Chase	d											16 21											
Wimbledon 6 ⊖	d											16 23											
Haydons Road	d											16 32											
Tooting	d											16 35											
Carshalton	d													16 11									
Hackbridge	d													16 13									
Mitcham Junction	d													16 16									
Mitcham Eastfields	d													16 19									
Streatham 4	d											16 40		16 23									
Tulse Hill 3	d				16 05					17 03		16 46		16 27	16 20								
London Bridge 4 ⊖	a		16 14	15 50		16 25					16 48					16 42	16 13		16 46	16 20			
	d		16 14	15 51		16 25					16 49					16 42	16 14		16 46	16 21			
Herne Hill 4	d											16 50		16 31									
Loughborough Jn	d											16 53		16 34									
Elephant & Castle	d								17 04	17 14		17 00		16 39									17 12
London Blackfriars 3 ⊖	d								17 08	17 22		17 04	17 26	16 44									17 16
City Thameslink									17 10	17 24		17 06	17 28	16 46									17 18
Farringdon 3 ⊖	d								17 13	17 27		17 09	17 31	16 49									17 23
St Pancras International 15 ⊖	d						17 15	17 30															
St Pancras International 15 ⊖	a								17 17	17 31		17 13	17 35	16 53									17 27
	d								17 18	17 32		17 14	17 36	16 54									17 28
Kentish Town ⊖	d											17 18		16 58									17 32
West Hampstead Thameslink ⊖	d											17 24		17 02									17 36
Cricklewood	d											17 27		17 05									17 39
Hendon	d											17 30		17 08									17 42
Mill Hill Broadway	d											17 34		17 12									17 46
Elstree & Borehamwood	d											17 39		17 17									17 51
Radlett	d											17 46		17 22									17 56
St Albans City	d								17 38	17 52		17a53	17 56	17a29									18a03
Harpenden	d									17 58			18 04										
Luton Airport Parkway 7	d								17 46				18 10										
Luton 10	d						17 41		17 49	18 04			18 13										
Leagrave	d												18 17										
Harlington	d												18 22										
Flitwick	d								18 00	18 16			18 26										
Bedford 7	a							18 07	18 12	18 28			18 38										

Brighton, Gatwick Airport and South London - City of London, St.Albans, Luton and Bedford

Station		FC	EM	EM	FC	SN	SE	FC	SE	FC		SN	SE	SE	SN	SE	SN	FC	SE	EM	SE	SE	FC	SE	SN
		A																							
Brighton	d				16 24			16 30							16 44								17 03		
Preston Park	d							16 34																	
Hassocks	d							16 40																	
Burgess Hill	d							16 44															17 13		
Wivelsfield	d							16 46																	
Haywards Heath	d				16 38			16 50															17 18		
Balcombe	d							16 57																	
Three Bridges	d				16 47			17 03															17 27		
Gatwick Airport	d				16 53			17 08															17 31		
Redhill	d																								
East Croydon	d				17 09			17 23															17 47		
Sevenoaks	d						16 29		16 32					16 44		16 52			16 59			17 02		17 05	
Bat & Ball	d								16 35													17 05			
Otford	d								16 38													17 08			
Shoreham (Kent)	d								16 41													17 11			
Eynsford	d								16 45													17 15			
Swanley	d								16 50													17 20			
St Mary Cray	d								16 54													17 24			
Bickley	d								16 58													17 28			
Bromley South	d								17 01													17 31			
Shortlands	d								17 04													17 34			
Ravensbourne	d								17 06													17 36			
Beckenham Hill	d								17 08													17 38			
Bellingham	d								17 10													17 40			
Catford	d								17 13													17 43			
Crofton Park	d								17 15													17 45			
Nunhead	d								17 18													17 48			
Peckham Rye	d					16 27			17 20			16 42					16 57					17 50			17 07
Denmark Hill	d								17 24													17 54			
Sutton (Surrey)	d	16 38								16 37															
West Sutton	d									16 40															
Sutton Common	d									16 42															
St Helier	d									16 45															
Morden South	d									16 47															
South Merton	d									16 49															
Wimbledon Chase	d									16 51															
Wimbledon	d									16 53															
Haydons Road	d									17 02															
Tooting	d									17 05															
Carshalton	d	16 41																							
Hackbridge	d	16 43																							
Mitcham Junction	d	16 46																							
Mitcham Eastfields	d	16 49																							
Streatham	d	16 53								17 10															
Tulse Hill	d	16 57				16 35				17 16		16 50					17 05								17 17
London Bridge	a				17 27		16 56						16 42	17 11		17 17			17 27		17 01		18 13	17 49	
	d				17 27		16 56						16 43	17 12		17 18			17 28		17 02		18 13	17 49	
Herne Hill	d	17 01								17 20															
Loughborough Jn	d									17 23															
Elephant & Castle	d	17 08							17 34	17 28								16 56				18 00			
London Blackfriars	d	17 12			17 36			17 52	17 40	17 32								17 00				18 06	18 22		
City Thameslink		17 14			17 38			17 54	17 42	17 34								17 02				18 08	18 24		
Farringdon	d	17 17			17 41			17 57	17 45	17 37								17 05				18 11	18 27		
St Pancras International	d			18 00																18 30					
St Pancras International	a	17 21			17 45			18 01	17 49	17 41								17 09				18 15	18 31		
	d	17 22	17 45		17 46			18 02	17 50	17 42								17 10				18 16	18 32		
Kentish Town	d									17 46															
West Hampstead Thameslink	d								17 58	17 50								17 18							
Cricklewood	d									17 53															
Hendon	d									17 56															
Mill Hill Broadway	d								18 05	18 00								17 25							
Elstree & Borehamwood	d								18 10	18 05								17 30							
Radlett	d								18 14	18 10								17 34							
St Albans City	d	17 44			18 06			18 22	18 20	18 16								17 40				18 36	18 52		
Harpenden	d	17 50			18 14			18 28	18 26	18 22								17 46					18 58		
Luton Airport Parkway	d	17 56	18 08		18 20				18 32	18 28								17 52		18 54		18 48			
Luton	d	17 59		18 23	18 23			18 34	18 37	18a32								17a55				18 51	19 04		
Leagrave	d	18 03			18 27				18 41																
Harlington	d	18 08			18 32				18 46																
Flitwick	d	18 12			18 36			18 44	18 50													19 00	19 14		
Bedford	a	18 24		18 38	18 48			18 58	19 04											19 09		19 12	19 26		

A 1 to London Blackfriars

Table 52 — Mondays to Fridays

Brighton, Gatwick Airport and South London - City of London, St.Albans, Luton and Bedford

Station		FC	EM	FC		SE	SN	SN	SE	FC	EM	FC	SN	SE	SE	SN	FC	FC	FC	SE	SN
Brighton	d	17 07						17 14				17 24					17 37				
Preston Park	d	17 11										17 28					17 41				
Hassocks	d	17 17										17 34					17 47				
Burgess Hill	d	17 21										17 38					17 51				
Wivelsfield	d											17 40					17 53				
Haywards Heath	d	17 26										17 46					18 02				
Balcombe	d																18 07				
Three Bridges	d											17 55					18 13				
Gatwick Airport	d	17 39										18 00					18 17				
Redhill	d																				
East Croydon	d	17 58										18 17					18 33				
Sevenoaks	d					17 14			17 19					17 32	17 35					17 44	
Bat & Ball	d													17 35							
Otford	d													17 38							
Shoreham (Kent)	d													17 41							
Eynsford	d													17 45							
Swanley	d													17 50							
St Mary Cray	d													17 54							
Bickley	d													17 58							
Bromley South	d													18 01							
Shortlands	d													18 04							
Ravensbourne	d													18 06							
Beckenham Hill	d													18 08							
Bellingham	d													18 10							
Catford	d													18 13							
Crofton Park	d													18 15							
Nunhead	d													18 18							
Peckham Rye	d						17 15						17 27	18 20		17 37					17 46
Denmark Hill	d													18 23							
Sutton (Surrey)	d			17 11			17 48											17 41	17 42		18 16
West Sutton	d			17 14			17 52											17 44			18 20
Sutton Common	d			17 16			17 54											17 46			18 22
St Helier	d			17 19			17 57											17 49			18 25
Morden South	d			17 21			17 59											17 51			18 27
South Merton	d			17 23			18 01											17 53			18 29
Wimbledon Chase	d			17 25			18 03											17 55			18 31
Wimbledon	d			17 27														17 57			
Haydons Road	d			17 32														18 02			
Tooting	d			17 35														18 05			
Carshalton	d																		17 45		
Hackbridge	d																		17 47		
Mitcham Junction	d																		17 50		
Mitcham Eastfields	d																		17 53		
Streatham	d			17 40														18 10	17 57		
Tulse Hill	d	18 13		17 44								18 38	17 35			17 46		18 16	18 01		
London Bridge	a					17 41			17 44						18 18		18 46			18 09	
	d					17 42			17 45						18 19		18 46			18 10	
Herne Hill	d			17 48														18 20	18 06		
Loughborough Jn	d			17 51														18 23	18 09		
Elephant & Castle	d			17 56						18 09				18 32				18 28	18 14		
London Blackfriars	d	18 26		18 00						18 14		18 52		18 36			18 56	18 32	18 18		
City Thameslink		18 28		18 02						18 16		18 54		18 38			18 58	18 34	18 20		
Farringdon	d	18 31		18 05						18 19		18 57		18 41			19 01	18 37	18 23		
St Pancras International	d		18 25								19 00										
St Pancras International	a	18 35		18 09						18 22		19 01		18 45			19 05	18 41	18 27		
	d	18 36		18 10						18 24		19 02		18 46			19 06	18 42	18 28		
Kentish Town	d			18 14														18 46	18 32		
West Hampstead Thameslink	d			18 18						18 32				18 53				18 51	18 36		
Cricklewood	d			18 21														18 54	18 39		
Hendon	d			18 24														18 57	18 42		
Mill Hill Broadway	d			18 28						18 39								19 01	18 46		
Elstree & Borehamwood	d			18 33						18 44								19 06	18 51		
Radlett	d			18 40						18 48								19 12	18 56		
St Albans City	d	18 56		18 46						18 54		19 22		19 06			19 26	19 18	19a03		
Harpenden	d	19 04		18 52						19 00		19 28		19 14			19 34	19 24			
Luton Airport Parkway	d	19 10		18 58						19 06				19 20			19 40	19 30			
Luton	d	19 13	18 51	19a02						19 09	19 23	19 34		19 23			19 43	19a34			
Leagrave	d	19 17								19 13				19 27			19 47				
Harlington	d	19 22								19 18				19 32			19 52				
Flitwick	d	19 26								19 22		19 44		19 36			19 56				
Bedford	a	19 38								19 33	19 39	19 58		19 48			20 08				

Table 52

Mondays to Fridays

Brighton, Gatwick Airport and South London - City of London, St.Albans, Luton and Bedford

		SE 1	SN	SN	SE 1	EM ◇1	FC 1	SN	SE		FC 1	SE	FC	FC	SE 1	SN	FC	SN	SE 1		SN	SE 1
Brighton 10	d		17 53				18 04				18 07					18 14						
Preston Park	d										18 11											
Hassocks 4	d										18 17											
Burgess Hill 4	d						18 14				18 21											
Wivelsfield 4	d										18 23											
Haywards Heath 3	d						18 18				18 32											
Balcombe	d										18 37											
Three Bridges 4	d										18 42											
Gatwick Airport 10	d						18 31				18 46											
Redhill	d																					
East Croydon	d						18 47				19 02											
Sevenoaks 4	d	17 49			17 59				18 06						18 14				18 19			18 32
Bat & Ball	d																					
Otford 4	d																					
Shoreham (Kent)	d																					
Eynsford	d																					
Swanley 4	d																					
St Mary Cray 4	d																					
Bickley	d																					
Bromley South	d																					
Shortlands 4	d																					
Ravensbourne	d																					
Beckenham Hill	d																					
Bellingham	d																					
Catford	d																					
Crofton Park	d																					
Nunhead 4	d																					
Peckham Rye 4	d			17 57				18 07										18 17			18 27	
Denmark Hill 4	d																					
Sutton (Surrey) 4	d												18 08	18 09			18 38	18 48				
West Sutton	d													18 12				18 54				
Sutton Common	d													18 14				18 56				
St Helier	d													18 17				18 59				
Morden South	d													18 19				19 01				
South Merton	d													18 21				19 03				
Wimbledon Chase	d													18 23				19 05				
Wimbledon 6	d													18 25				19 08				
Haydons Road	d													18 30								
Tooting	d													18 33								
Carshalton	d												18 11				18 41					
Hackbridge	d												18 13				18 43					
Mitcham Junction	d												18 16				18 46					
Mitcham Eastfields	d												18 19				18 49					
Streatham 4	d												18 23	18 40			18 53					
Tulse Hill 3	d			18 05				18 17					18 27	18 44			18 57				18 35	
London Bridge 4	a	18 16			18 25		19 00		18 48		19 15	18 08			18 40				18 43			18 55
	d	18 16			18 25		19 00		18 49		19 17	18 09			18 41				18 43			18 55
Herne Hill 4	d												18 31	18 48			19 02					
Loughborough Jn	d												18 34	18 51			19 05					
Elephant & Castle	d												18 40	18 56			19 09					
London Blackfriars 3	d						19 10				19 24		18 44	19 00			19 18					
City Thameslink							19 12				19 26		18 46	19 02			19 20					
Farringdon 3	d						19 15				19 30		18 49	19 05			19 23					
St Pancras International 15	d																19 28					
St Pancras International 15	a						19 19				19 33		18 53	19 09	19 15							
	d					19 30	19 20				19 34		18 54	19 10								
Kentish Town	d													19 14			19 32					
West Hampstead Thameslink	d						19 28				19 41		19 02	19 18			19 36					
Cricklewood	d													19 21			19 39					
Hendon	d													19 24			19 42					
Mill Hill Broadway	d												19 09	19 27			19 45					
Elstree & Borehamwood	d												19 14	19 32			19 50					
Radlett	d												19 18	19 36			19 54					
St Albans City	d						19 46				19 55		19 24	19 42			20 01					
Harpenden	d						19 52				20 02		19 30	19 48								
Luton Airport Parkway 7	d					19 53	19 58				20 08		19 36	19 54								
Luton 10	d						20 01				20 11		19a40	19a58								
Leagrave	d						20 04				20 14											
Harlington	d						20 10				20 20											
Flitwick	d						20 14				20 24											
Bedford 7	a					20 08	20 26				20 36											

A 1 from London Blackfriars

Table 52

Mondays to Fridays

Brighton, Gatwick Airport and South London - City of London, St.Albans, Luton and Bedford

		SE 1	SN	SN	SE 1	SE 1 A	FC 1	SN	SE		FC 1	SE	FC		FC	SE 1	SN	SN	SE 1			SN	EM ◇1	SE 1
Brighton 10	d		17 53				18 04				18 07						18 14							
Preston Park	d										18 11													
Hassocks 4	d										18 17													
Burgess Hill 4	d						18 14				18 21													
Wivelsfield 4	d										18 23													
Haywards Heath 3	d						18 18				18 32													
Balcombe	d										18 37													
Three Bridges 4	d										18 42													
Gatwick Airport 10	d						18 31				18 46													
Redhill	d																							
East Croydon	d						18 47				19 02													
Sevenoaks 4	d	17 49			17 59	18 02			18 06							18 14			18 19					18 32
Bat & Ball	d					18 05																		
Otford 4	d					18 08																		
Shoreham (Kent)	d					18 11																		
Eynsford	d					18 15																		
Swanley 4	d					18 20																		
St Mary Cray 4	d					18 24																		
Bickley	d					18 28																		
Bromley South	d					18 31																		
Shortlands 4	d					18 34																		
Ravensbourne	d					18 36																		
Beckenham Hill	d					18 38																		
Bellingham	d					18 40																		
Catford	d					18 43																		
Crofton Park	d					18 45																		
Nunhead 4	d					18 48																		
Peckham Rye 4	d			17 57		18 50		18 07										18 17				18 27		
Denmark Hill 4	d					18 54																		
Sutton (Surrey) 4	d												18 08		18 09			18 48						
West Sutton	d														18 12			18 54						
Sutton Common	d														18 14			18 56						
St Helier	d														18 17			18 59						
Morden South	d														18 19			19 01						
South Merton	d														18 21			19 03						
Wimbledon Chase	d														18 23			19 05						
Wimbledon 6	d														18 25			19 08						
Haydons Road	d														18 30									
Tooting	d														18 33									
Carshalton	d												18 11											
Hackbridge	d												18 13											
Mitcham Junction	d												18 16											
Mitcham Eastfields	d												18 19											
Streatham 4	d												18 23		18 40									
Tulse Hill 3	d			18 05				18 17					18 27		18 44							18 35		
London Bridge 4	a	18 16			18 25		19 00		18 48		19 15	18 08				18 40			18 43					18 55
	d	18 16			18 25		19 00		18 49		19 17	18 09				18 41			18 43					18 55
Herne Hill 4	d												18 31		18 48									
Loughborough Jn	d												18 34		18 51									
Elephant & Castle	d					19 00							18 40		18 56									
London Blackfriars 3	d					19 06	19 10				19 24		18 44		19 00									
City Thameslink						19 08	19 12				19 26		18 46		19 02									
Farringdon 3	d					19 11	19 15				19 30		18 49		19 05									
St Pancras International 15	d																							
St Pancras International 15	a					19 15	19 19				19 33		18 53		19 09									
	d					19 16	19 20				19 34		18 54		19 10								20 00	
Kentish Town	d														19 14									
West Hampstead Thameslink	d						19 28				19 41		19 02		19 18									
Cricklewood	d														19 21									
Hendon	d														19 24									
Mill Hill Broadway	d												19 09		19 27									
Elstree & Borehamwood	d												19 14		19 32									
Radlett	d												19 18		19 36									
St Albans City	d					19 36	19 46				19 55		19 24		19 42									
Harpenden	d					19 44	19 52				20 02		19 30		19 48									
Luton Airport Parkway 7	d						19 58				20 08		19 36		19 54								20 23	
Luton 10	d					19 50	20 01				20 11		19a40		19a58									
Leagrave	d					19 54	20 04				20 14													
Harlington	d						20 10				20 20													
Flitwick	d						20 14				20 24													
Bedford 7	a					20 12	20 26				20 36												20 37	

A 1 from London Blackfriars

Brighton, Gatwick Airport and South London - City of London, St.Albans, Luton and Bedford

		SE	FC ■	SE	EM ◇■	SN	FC ■		FC	SE ■	FC	FC	SN	SE ■ ✕	SN	SN	SE ■		SN ◇■	SE	SN	SE	FC ■	FC	SE ■
Brighton ■	d		18 34				18 37								18 48				18 59				19 07		
Preston Park	d						18 41												19 03				19 11		
Hassocks ■	d						18 47												19 09				19 17		
Burgess Hill ■	d						18 51												19 13				19 21		
Wivelsfield ■	d						18 53												19 15				19 23		
Haywards Heath ■	d		18 48				19 02												19 21				19 32		
Balcombe	d																						19 37		
Three Bridges ■	d						19 12																19 42		
Gatwick Airport ■	d		19 01				19 16												19a31				19 46		
Redhill	d																								
East Croydon ⇌	d		19 17				19 32																20 02		
Sevenoaks ■	d	18 32		18 35						18 44				18 49			18 59			19 02		19 06			19 14
Bat & Ball	d	18 35																		19 05					
Otford ■	d	18 38																		19 08					
Shoreham (Kent)	d	18 41																		19 11					
Eynsford	d	18 45																		19 15					
Swanley ■	d	18 50																		19 20					
St Mary Cray ■	d	18 54																		19 24					
Bickley	d	18 58																		19 28					
Bromley South	d	19 01																		19 31					
Shortlands ■	d	19 04																		19 34					
Ravensbourne	d	19 06																		19 36					
Beckenham Hill	d	19 08																		19 38					
Bellingham	d	19 10																		19 40					
Catford	d	19 13																		19 43					
Crofton Park	d	19 15																		19 45					
Nunhead ■	d	19 18																		19 48					
Peckham Rye ■	d	19 20				18 37							18 47			18 57				19 50	19 07				
Denmark Hill ■	d	19 24																		19 54					
Sutton (Surrey) ■	d								18 38		18 43													19 08	
West Sutton	d										18 46														
Sutton Common	d										18 48														
St Helier	d										18 51														
Morden South	d										18 53														
South Merton	d										18 55														
Wimbledon Chase	d										18 57														
Wimbledon ■ ⊖ ⇌	d										18 59.														
Haydons Road	d										19 02														
Tooting	d										19 05														
Carshalton	d								18 41															19 11	
Hackbridge	d								18 43															19 13	
Mitcham Junction	d								18 46															19 16	
Mitcham Eastfields	d								18 49															19 19	
Streatham ■	d								18 53		19 10													19 23	
Tulse Hill ■	d						18 47			18 57		19 14		18 56			19 05					19 17			19 27	
London Bridge ■ ⊖	a		19 30	19 19			19 45			19 10				19 13			19 25					19 52	20 15		19 40
	d		19 30	19 19			19 45			19 10				19 13			19 25					19 52	20 15		19 41
Herne Hill ■	d								19 01		19 17													19 31	
Loughborough Jn	d								19 04		19 20													19 34	
Elephant & Castle	d	19 30							19 09		19 25	18 44								20 00				19 39	
London Blackfriars ■ ⊖	d	19 34	19 38				19 54		19 18		19 30	18 48								20 04			20 24	19 46	
City Thameslink		19 36	19 40				19 56				19 32	18 50								20 06			20 26	19 48	
Farringdon ■ ⊖	d	19 40	19 44				20 00		19 23		19 36	18 53								20 10			20 30	19 52	
St Pancras International ■ ⊖	d				20 30																				
St Pancras International ■ ⊖	a	19 43	19 47				20 03		19 27		19 39	18 57								20 13			20 33	19 55	
	d	19 44	19 48				20 04		19 28		19 40	18 58								20 14			20 34	19 56	
Kentish Town ⊖	d	19a50							19 32		19 44	19 02								20a20				20 00	
West Hampstead Thameslink ⊖	d						20 11		19 36		19 49	19 06											20 41	20 04	
Cricklewood	d								19 39		19 52	19 09												20 07	
Hendon	d								19 42		19 55	19 12												20 10	
Mill Hill Broadway	d								19 45		19 59	19 16												20 13	
Elstree & Borehamwood	d								19 50		20 03	19 21												20 18	
Radlett	d								19 54		20 08	19 26												20 22	
St Albans City	d		20 10				20 25		20a01		20 15	19a33											20 55	20a29	
Harpenden	d		20 16				20 32				20 20												21 02		
Luton Airport Parkway ■	d		20 22		20 51		20 38				20 26												21 08		
Luton ■	d		20 25				20 41				20a30												21 11		
Leagrave	d		20 28				20 44																21 14		
Harlington	d		20 34				20 50																21 20		
Flitwick	d		20 38				20 54																21 24		
Bedford ■	a		20 50		21 06		21 06																21 36		

Table 52 Mondays to Fridays

Brighton, Gatwick Airport and South London - City of London, St.Albans, Luton and Bedford

		FC		SN	SN	SE ■ ✕	SN ■	SN	EM ◇■	FC ■	SE ■	SE	FC ■	SN	SE	FC ■	FC	FC	SE ■	SN	SN	EM ◇■	SE ■ ✕	SN
Brighton ■	d			19 15			19 22						19 34			19 37				19 44				
Preston Park	d															19 41								
Hassocks ■	d															19 47								
Burgess Hill ■	d															19 51								
Wivelsfield ■	d															19 53								
Haywards Heath ■	d												19 48			20 02								
Balcombe	d																							
Three Bridges ■	d									19 27						20 12								
Gatwick Airport ■	d									19 31			20 01			20 16								
Redhill	d																							
East Croydon ⇌	d									19 47			20 17			20 32								
Sevenoaks ■	d					19 19					19 29	19 32			19 36				19 44				19 49	
Bat & Ball	d											19 35												
Otford ■	d											19 38												
Shoreham (Kent)	d											19 41												
Eynsford	d											19 45												
Swanley ■	d											19 50												
St Mary Cray ■	d											19 54												
Bickley	d											19 58												
Bromley South	d											20 01												
Shortlands ■	d											20 04												
Ravensbourne	d											20 06												
Beckenham Hill	d											20 08												
Bellingham	d											20 10												
Catford	d											20 13												
Crofton Park	d											20 15												
Nunhead ■	d											20 18												
Peckham Rye ■	d				19 17			19 27				20 20		19 37							19 47			19 57
Denmark Hill ■	d											20 24												
Sutton (Surrey) ■	d	19 13															19 38	19 42						
West Sutton	d	19 16															19 41							
Sutton Common	d	19 18															19 43							
St Helier	d	19 21															19 46							
Morden South	d	19 23															19 48							
South Merton	d	19 25															19 50							
Wimbledon Chase	d	19 27															19 52							
Wimbledon ■ ⊖ ⇌	d	19 29.															19 54.							
Haydons Road	d	19 32															19 58							
Tooting	d	19 35															20 01							
Carshalton	d																	19 45						
Hackbridge	d																	19 47						
Mitcham Junction	d																	19 50						
Mitcham Eastfields	d																	19 53						
Streatham ■	d	19 40															20 06	19 57						
Tulse Hill ■	d	19 44			19 27			19 35						19 46			20 12	20 01			19 57			20 05
London Bridge ■ ⊖	a					19 43				20 00	19 54		20 30		20 22	20 45			20 10				20 13	
	d					19 43				20 00	19 55		20 30		20 22	20 45			20 11				20 13	
Herne Hill ■	d	19 47															20 16	20 05						
Loughborough Jn	d	19 50															20 19	20 08						
Elephant & Castle	d	19 55										20 30					20 24	20 13						
London Blackfriars ■ ⊖	d	20 00								20 08		20 34	20 38			20 54	20 30	20 18						
City Thameslink		20 02								20 10		20 36	20 40			20 56	20 32	20 20						
Farringdon ■ ⊖	d	20 06								20 14		20 40	20 44			21 00	20 36	20 24						
St Pancras International ■ ⊖	d								21 00													21 30		
St Pancras International ■ ⊖	a	20 09								20 17		20 43	20 47			21 03	20 39	20 27						
	d	20 10								20 18		20 44	20 48			21 04	20 40	20 28						
Kentish Town ⊖	d	20 14										20a50					20 44	20 32						
West Hampstead Thameslink ⊖	d	20 18														21 11	20 48	20 36						
Cricklewood	d	20 21															20 51	20 39						
Hendon	d	20 24															20 54	20 42						
Mill Hill Broadway	d	20 27															20 57	20 45						
Elstree & Borehamwood	d	20 32															21 02	20 50						
Radlett	d	20 38															21 08	20 54						
St Albans City	d	20 45								20 40			21 10			21 25	21 15	21a01						
Harpenden	d	20 50								20 46			21 16			21 32	21 20							
Luton Airport Parkway ■	d	20 56								20 52			21 22			21 38	21 26					21 53		
Luton ■	d	21a00							21 23	20 55			21 25			21 41	21a30							
Leagrave	d									20 58			21 28			21 44								
Harlington	d									21 04			21 34			21 50								
Flitwick	d									21 08			21 38			21 54								
Bedford ■	a								21 37	21 20			21 50			22 06						22 08		

Table 52

Mondays to Fridays

Brighton, Gatwick Airport and South London - City of London, St.Albans, Luton and Bedford

	SE 1	EM ◇1	SE	FC 1	SE	FC	FC 1	FC	SN	SE 1	SN	SE 1	SN	SE	FC 1	SE	FC	FC 1	FC	SE 1	SN
Brighton 10 d				20 04			20 07				20 14				20 34			20 37			20 44
Preston Park d							20 11											20 41			
Hassocks 4 d							20 17											20 47			
Burgess Hill 4 d							20 21											20 51			
Wivelsfield 4 d							20 23											20 53			
Haywards Heath 3 d				20 18			20 32								20 48			21 02			
Balcombe d							20 37														
Three Bridges 4 d							20 42											21 12			
Gatwick Airport 10 d				20 31			20 46								21 01			21 16			
Redhill d																					
East Croydon d				20 47			21 02								21 17			21 32			
Sevenoaks 4 d	20 00		20 02		20 06					20 14		20 19		20 32		20 35				20 44	
Bat & Ball d			20 05											20 35							
Otford 4 d			20 08											20 38							
Shoreham (Kent) d			20 11											20 41							
Eynsford d			20 15											20 45							
Swanley 4 d			20 20											20 50							
St Mary Cray 4 d			20 24											20 54							
Bickley d			20 28											20 58							
Bromley South d			20 31											21 01							
Shortlands 4 d			20 34											21 04							
Ravensbourne d			20 36											21 06							
Beckenham Hill d			20 38											21 08							
Bellingham d			20 40											21 10							
Catford d			20 43											21 13							
Crofton Park d			20 45											21 15							
Nunhead 4 d			20 48											21 18							
Peckham Rye 4 d			20 50						20 12				20 27	21 20							
Denmark Hill 4 d			20 54											21 23							
Sutton (Surrey) 4 d						20 07		20 10									20 37		20 40		
West Sutton d						20 10											20 40				
Sutton Common d						20 12											20 42				
St Helier d						20 15											20 45				
Morden South d						20 17											20 47				
South Merton d						20 19											20 49				
Wimbledon Chase d						20 21											20 51				
Wimbledon 5 ⊖ d						20 23											20 53				
Haydons Road d						20 28											20 58				
Tooting d						20 31											21 01				
Carshalton d								20 13											20 43		
Hackbridge d								20 15											20 45		
Mitcham Junction d								20 18											20 48		
Mitcham Eastfields d								20 21											20 51		
Streatham 4 d						20 36		20 25									21 06		20 55		
Tulse Hill 3 d						20 42		20 29	20 20				20 35				21 12		20 59		
London Bridge 4 ⊖ a	20 24			21 00	20 52		21 15			20 39		20 42			21 30	21 22		21 45		21 08	
d	20 25			21 00	20 52		21 15			20 40		20 43			21 30	21 22		21 45		21 09	
Herne Hill 4 d						20 46		20 35									21 16		21 05		
Loughborough Jn d						20 49		20 38									21 19		21 08		
Elephant & Castle d			21 00			20 54		20 43									21 24		21 13		
London Blackfriars 3 ⊖ d			21 04	21 08		21 00	21 24	20 48							21 38		21 30	21 54	21 18		
City Thameslink			21 06	21 10		21 02	21 26	20 50							21 40		21 32	21 56	21 20		
Farringdon 3 ⊖ d			21 10	21 14		21 06	21 30	20 54							21 44		21 36	22 00	21 24		
St Pancras International 15 ⊖ d		22 00																			
St Pancras International 15 ⊖ a			21 13	21 17		21 09	21 33	20 57							21 47		21 39	22 03	21 27		
d			21 14	21 18		21 10	21 34	20 58							21 48		21 40	22 04	21 28		
Kentish Town ⊖ d			21a20			21 14		21 02									21 44		21 32		
West Hampstead Thameslink ⊖ d						21 18	21 41	21 06									21 48	22 11	21 36		
Cricklewood d						21 21		21 09									21 51		21 39		
Hendon d						21 24		21 12									21 54		21 42		
Mill Hill Broadway d						21 27		21 15									21 57		21 45		
Elstree & Borehamwood d						21 32		21 20									22 02		21 50		
Radlett d						21 38		21 24									22 08		21 54		
St Albans City d				21 40		21 45	21 55	21a31							22 10		22 15	22 25	22a01		
Harpenden d				21 46		21 50	22 02								22 16		22 20	22 32			
Luton Airport Parkway 7 d				21 52		21 56	22 08								22 22		22 26	22 38			
Luton 10 d		22 24		21 55		22a00	22 11								22 25		22a30	22 41			
Leagrave d				21 58			22 14								22 28			22 44			
Harlington d				22 04			22 20								22 34			22 50			
Flitwick d				22 08			22 24								22 38			22 54			
Bedford 7 a		22 39		22 20			22 36								22 50			23 06			

Table 52

Mondays to Fridays

Brighton, Gatwick Airport and South London - City of London, St.Albans, Luton and Bedford

	SE 1	SN	SE 1	SE	SE	FC	FC 1	FC	SE 1	SN	SE 1	SN	SE	SN 1	SE	FC 1	SE 1	SN	SE 1
Brighton 10 d							21 11			21 14				21 34		21 37		21 44	
Preston Park d																21 41			
Hassocks 4 d							21 19									21 47			
Burgess Hill 4 d							21 23									21 51			
Wivelsfield 4 d																21 53			
Haywards Heath 3 d							21 32							21 46		22 02			
Balcombe d							21 37												
Three Bridges 4 d							21 42							21 56		22 12			
Gatwick Airport 10 d							21 46							22 02		22 16			
Redhill d																			
East Croydon d							22 02							22 17		22 32			
Sevenoaks 4 d	20 49		20 59	21 02	21 05				21 14		21 19		21 32		21 35		21 44		21 49
Bat & Ball d				21 05									21 35						
Otford 4 d				21 08									21 38						
Shoreham (Kent) d				21 11									21 41						
Eynsford d				21 15									21 45						
Swanley 4 d				21 20									21 50						
St Mary Cray 4 d				21 24									21 54						
Bickley d				21 28									21 58						
Bromley South d				21 31									22 01						
Shortlands 4 d				21 34									22 04						
Ravensbourne d				21 36									22 06						
Beckenham Hill d				21 38									22 08						
Bellingham d				21 40									22 10						
Catford d				21 43									22 13						
Crofton Park d				21 45									22 15						
Nunhead 4 d				21 48									22 18						
Peckham Rye 4 d		20 57		21 50								21 27	22 20						
Denmark Hill 4 d				21 53									22 23						
Sutton (Surrey) 4 d						21 10		21 12											
West Sutton d								21 15											
Sutton Common d								21 17											
St Helier d								21 20											
Morden South d								21 22											
South Merton d								21 24											
Wimbledon Chase d								21 26											
Wimbledon 5 ⊖ d								21 28											
Haydons Road d								21 38											
Tooting d								21 41											
Carshalton d						21 13													
Hackbridge d						21 15													
Mitcham Junction d						21 18													
Mitcham Eastfields d						21 21													
Streatham 4 d						21 25		21 46											
Tulse Hill 3 d		21 05				21 29		21 50				21 35							
London Bridge 4 ⊖ a	21 13		21 24		21 52				21 38		21 43				22 22		22 08		22 13
d	21 14		21 25		21 52				21 39		21 44				22 22		22 09		22 14
Herne Hill 4 d						21 35		21 54											
Loughborough Jn d						21 38		21 57											
Elephant & Castle d						21 43		22 02											
London Blackfriars 3 ⊖ d						21 48		22 08											
City Thameslink						21 50		22 10											
Farringdon 3 ⊖ d						21 54		22 14											
St Pancras International 15 ⊖ d																			
St Pancras International 15 ⊖ a						21 57		22 17											
d						21 58		22 18											
Kentish Town ⊖ d						22 02		22 22											
West Hampstead Thameslink ⊖ d						22 06		22 26											
Cricklewood d						22 09		22 29											
Hendon d						22 12		22 32											
Mill Hill Broadway d						22 15		22 35											
Elstree & Borehamwood d						22 20		22 40											
Radlett d						22 24		22 44											
St Albans City d						22a31		22 50											
Harpenden d								22 56											
Luton Airport Parkway 7 d								23 02											
Luton 10 d								23 05											
Leagrave d								23 08											
Harlington d								23 14											
Flitwick d								23 18											
Bedford 7 a								23 30											

Brighton, Gatwick Airport and South London - City of London, St.Albans, Luton and Bedford

		SN	SE 1	FC	SE	SE	FC 1	SE 1	SN	SE 1	EM ◇1	SN	SE	FC 1	FC 1	FC	SE 1	SN	FC	SE 1	FC	SN	SE 1
Brighton 10	d						22 07		22 14						22 33			22 44					
Preston Park	d						22 11								22 37								
Hassocks 4	d						22 17								22 43								
Burgess Hill 4	d						22 21								22 47								
Wivelsfield 4	d						22 23								22 49								
Haywards Heath 3	d						22 32								22 54								
Balcombe	d						22 37								23 00								
Three Bridges 4	d						22 42								23b12								
Gatwick Airport 10	d						22 46								23 16								
Redhill	d																						
East Croydon	d						23 02								23 32								
Sevenoaks 4	d		21 59		22 02	22 05		22 14		22 19			22 32				22 42			22 49			22 59
Bat & Ball	d				22 05								22 35										
Otford 4	d				22 08								22 38										
Shoreham (Kent)	d				22 11								22 41										
Eynsford	d				22 15								22 45										
Swanley 4	d				22 20								22 50										
St Mary Cray 4	d				22 24								22 54										
Bickley	d				22 28								22 58										
Bromley South	d				22 31								23 01										
Shortlands 4	d				22 34								23 04										
Ravensbourne	d				22 36								23 06										
Beckenham Hill	d				22 38								23 08										
Bellingham	d				22 40								23 10										
Catford	d				22 43								23 13										
Crofton Park	d				22 45								23 15										
Nunhead 4	d				22 48								23 18										
Peckham Rye 4	d	21 57			22 50							22 27	23 20									22 57	
Denmark Hill 4	d				22 53								23 23										
Sutton (Surrey) 4	d			22 12																			
West Sutton	d			22 15																			
Sutton Common	d			22 17																			
St Helier	d			22 20																			
Morden South	d			22 22																			
South Merton	d			22 24																			
Wimbledon Chase	d			22 26																			
Wimbledon 6 ⊖	d			22 30																			
Haydons Road	d			22 32																			
Tooting	d			22 35																			
Carshalton	d																						
Hackbridge	d																						
Mitcham Junction	d																						
Mitcham Eastfields	d																						
Streatham 4	d			22 40																			
Tulse Hill 3	d	22 05		22 43								22 35										23 05	
London Bridge 4 ⊖	a		22 24	22 55		22 52		22 38		22 43							23 08			23 13			23 24
	d		22 25			22 52		22 39		22 44						22 25	23 09			23 14	22 40		23 25
Herne Hill 4	d																						
Loughborough Jn	d																						
Elephant & Castle	d																						
London Blackfriars 3 ⊖	d															22 40					22 55		
Farringdon 3 ⊖	d															22 50					23 05		
St Pancras International 15 ⊖	d										22 25			22 32					22 46				
St Pancras International 15 ⊖	a															22 55					23 10		
	d																						
Kentish Town ⊖	d																		22 51				
West Hampstead Thameslink ⊖	d													22 40					22 55				
Cricklewood	d																		22 58				
Hendon	d																		23 01				
Mill Hill Broadway	d																		23 04				
Elstree & Borehamwood	d																		23 09				
Radlett	d																		23 14				
St Albans City	d													22 56					23 20				
Harpenden	d													23 02					23 26				
Luton Airport Parkway 7	d										22 48			23 08					23 32				
Luton 10	d													23 11					23 35				
Leagrave	d													23 14					23 38				
Harlington	d													23 20					23 44				
Flitwick	d													23 24					23 48				
Bedford 7	a										23 03			23 36					00 01				

b arr. 2305

Brighton, Gatwick Airport and South London - City of London, St.Albans, Luton and Bedford

		FC 1	FC	FC 1	SN	EM ◇1		FC	FC	SE 1	SN	FC 1	FC 1	FC	SN	FC		SN
Brighton 10	d			23 11	23 14								23 37		23 44			
Preston Park	d												23 41					
Hassocks 4	d			23 19									23 47					
Burgess Hill 4	d			23 23									23 51					
Wivelsfield 4	d												23 53					
Haywards Heath 3	d			23 28									23 59					
Balcombe	d												00 04					
Three Bridges 4	d			23 38									00 10					
Gatwick Airport 10	d			23 43									00 15					
Redhill	d												00 22					
East Croydon	d			00 04									00 36					
Sevenoaks 4	d									23 25								
Bat & Ball	d																	
Otford 4	d																	
Shoreham (Kent)	d																	
Eynsford	d																	
Swanley 4	d																	
St Mary Cray 4	d																	
Bickley	d																	
Bromley South	d																	
Shortlands 4	d																	
Ravensbourne	d																	
Beckenham Hill	d																	
Bellingham	d																	
Catford	d																	
Crofton Park	d																	
Nunhead 4	d																	
Peckham Rye 4	d										23 27							23 57
Denmark Hill 4	d																	
Sutton (Surrey) 4	d																	
West Sutton	d																	
Sutton Common	d																	
St Helier	d																	
Morden South	d																	
South Merton	d																	
Wimbledon Chase	d																	
Wimbledon 6 ⊖	d																	
Haydons Road	d																	
Tooting	d																	
Carshalton	d																	
Hackbridge	d																	
Mitcham Junction	d																	
Mitcham Eastfields	d																	
Streatham 4	d																	
Tulse Hill 3	d										23 35							00 07
London Bridge 4 ⊖	a									23 53								
	d		22 55						23 05	23 53				23 25				
Herne Hill 4	d																	
Loughborough Jn	d																	
Elephant & Castle	d																	
London Blackfriars 3 ⊖	d		23 10						23 20					23 40				
Farringdon 3 ⊖	d		23 20						23 30					23 50				
St Pancras International 15 ⊖	d	23 02				23 15		23 18				23 32				23 48		
St Pancras International 15 ⊖	a		23 25						23 35					23 55				
	d																	
Kentish Town ⊖	d							23 23								23 53		
West Hampstead Thameslink ⊖	d	23 10						23 27				23 40				23 57		
Cricklewood	d							23 30								23 59		
Hendon	d							23 33								00 03		
Mill Hill Broadway	d							23 36								00 06		
Elstree & Borehamwood	d							23 41								00 11		
Radlett	d							23 46								00 16		
St Albans City	d	23 26						23 52				23 56				00 22		
Harpenden	d	23 32						23 58				00 02				00 28		
Luton Airport Parkway 7	d	23 38						00 04				00 08				00 34		
Luton 10	d	23 41				23 46		00 07				00 11				00 37		
Leagrave	d	23 44						00 10				00 14				00 40		
Harlington	d	23 50						00 16				00 20				00 46		
Flitwick	d	23 54						00 20				00 24				00 50		
Bedford 7	a	00 06				00 09		00 32				00 36				01 02		

Table 52

Brighton, Gatwick Airport and South London - City of London, St.Albans, Luton and Bedford

		FC	FC 1	FC 1	EM ◇1	FC	FC 1	FC 1	FC	SN	FC 1	FC 1	SN	FC	EM ◇1	FC	FC 1	FC	FC	FC	FC	FC	FC
Brighton 10	d			23p11				23p37					00 10										
Preston Park	d							23p41															
Hassocks 4	d			23p19				23p47															
Burgess Hill 4	d			23p23				23p51															
Wivelsfield 4	d							23p53															
Haywards Heath 3	d			23p28				23p59															
Balcombe	d							00 04															
Three Bridges 4	d			23p38				00 10															
Gatwick Airport 10	d			23p43				00 15															
Redhill	d							00 22															
East Croydon	d			00 04				00 36															
Sevenoaks 4	d																						
Bat & Ball	d																						
Otford 4	d																						
Shoreham (Kent)	d																						
Eynsford	d																						
Swanley 4	d																						
St Mary Cray 4	d																						
Bickley	d																						
Bromley South	d																						
Shortlands 4	d																						
Ravensbourne	d																						
Beckenham Hill	d																						
Bellingham	d																						
Catford	d																						
Crofton Park	d																						
Nunhead 4	d																						
Peckham Rye 4	d									23p57													
Denmark Hill 4	d																						
Sutton (Surrey) 4	d																						
West Sutton	d																						
Sutton Common	d																						
St Helier	d																						
Morden South	d																						
South Merton	d																						
Wimbledon Chase	d																						
Wimbledon 6 ⊖	d																						
Haydons Road	d																						
Tooting	d																						
Carshalton	d																						
Hackbridge	d																						
Mitcham Junction	d																						
Mitcham Eastfields	d																						
Streatham 4	d																						
Tulse Hill 3	d									00 07													
London Bridge 4 ⊖	a																						
	d													23 55				00 25		01 00			
Herne Hill 4	d																						
Loughborough Jn	d																						
Elephant & Castle	d																						
London Blackfriars 3 ⊖	d													00 10				00 40		01 15			02 40
Farringdon 3 ⊖	d													00 20				00 50					
St Pancras International 15 ⊖	d	22p46	23p02		23p15	23p18	23p32		23p48			00 02			00 15	00 18	00 32		01 02		01 32	02 32	
St Pancras International 15 ⊖	a													00 25				00 55		01 30			02 55
	d										00 02												
Kentish Town ⊖	d	22p51				23p23			23p53							00 23	00 37		01 07		01 37	02 37	
West Hampstead Thameslink ⊖	d	22p55	23p10			23p27	23p40		23p57		00 10	00 10				00 27	00 41		01 11		01 41	02 41	
Cricklewood	d	22p58				23p30			23p59							00 30	00 44		01 14		01 44	02 44	
Hendon	d	23p01				23p33			00 03							00 33	00 47		01 17		01 47	02 47	
Mill Hill Broadway	d	23p04				23p36			00 06							00 36	00 50		01 20		01 50	02 50	
Elstree & Borehamwood	d	23p09				23p41			00 11							00 41	00 55		01 25		01 55	02 55	
Radlett	d	23p14				23p46			00 16							00 46	01 00		01 30		02 00	03 00	
St Albans City	d	23p20	23p26			23p52	23p56		00 22		00 26	00 26				00 52	01 06		01 36		02 06	03 06	
Harpenden	d	23p26	23p32			23p58	00 02		00 28		00 32	00 32				00 58	01 12		01 42		02 12	03 12	
Luton Airport Parkway 7	d	23p32	23p38			00 04	00 08		00 34		00 38	00 38			00 43	01 04	01 18		01 48		02 18	03 18	
Luton 10	d	23p35	23p41		23p46	00 07	00 11		00 37		00 41	00 41			00 47	01 07	01 21		01 51		02 21	03 21	
Leagrave	d	23p38	23p44			00 10	00 14		00 40		00 44	00 44				01 10	01 24		01 54		02 24	03 24	
Harlington	d	23p44	23p50			00 16	00 20		00 46		00 50	00 50				01 16	01 30		02 00		02 30	03 30	
Flitwick	d	23p48	23p54			00 20	00 24		00 50		00 54	00 54				01 20	01 34		02 04		02 34	03 34	
Bedford 7	a	00 01	00 06		00 09	00 32	00 36		01 02		01 06	01 06			01 08	01 32	01 46		02 16		02 46	03 46	

Table 52

Brighton, Gatwick Airport and South London - City of London, St.Albans, Luton and Bedford

		FC	FC	FC	FC	FC	FC 1	FC	FC	SE	SN	SE	SE	FC	FC	FC 1	SE	EM ◇1	SE 1	SN	FC 1	FC 1	SE
Brighton 10	d						05 24				05 44					06 04				06 14		06 24	
Preston Park	d						05 28															06 28	
Hassocks 4	d						05 34															06 34	
Burgess Hill 4	d						05 38									06 14						06 38	
Wivelsfield 4	d						05 40															06 40	
Haywards Heath 3	d						05 45									06 18						06 45	
Balcombe	d						05 51															06 51	
Three Bridges 4	d						05 56															06 56	
Gatwick Airport 10	d						06 01									06 31						07 01	
Redhill	d																						
East Croydon	d						06 17									06 47						07 17	
Sevenoaks 4	d									05 36			05 55				06 06		06 14				06 25
Bat & Ball	d												05 58										06 28
Otford 4	d												06 01										06 31
Shoreham (Kent)	d												06 04										06 34
Eynsford	d												06 08										06 38
Swanley 4	d												06 13										06 43
St Mary Cray 4	d												06 17										06 47
Bickley	d											05 51	06 21										06 51
Bromley South	d											05 54	06 24										06 54
Shortlands 4	d											05 57	06 27										06 57
Ravensbourne	d											05 59	06 29										06 59
Beckenham Hill	d											06 01	06 31										07 01
Bellingham	d											06 03	06 33										07 03
Catford	d											06 06	06 36										07 06
Crofton Park	d											06 08	06 38										07 08
Nunhead 4	d											06 11	06 41										07 11
Peckham Rye 4	d											06 13	06 43										07 13
Denmark Hill 4	d											06 17	06 47										07 17
Sutton (Surrey) 4	d																						
West Sutton	d																						
Sutton Common	d																						
St Helier	d																						
Morden South	d																						
South Merton	d																						
Wimbledon Chase	d																						
Wimbledon 6 ⊖	d																						
Haydons Road	d																						
Tooting	d																						
Carshalton	d																						
Hackbridge	d																						
Mitcham Junction	d																						
Mitcham Eastfields	d																						
Streatham 4	d																						
Tulse Hill 3	d													06 00									
London Bridge 4 ⊖	a									06 21							06 51		06 39				
	d	03 20			04 20				05 20	06 21							06 51		06 39				
Herne Hill 4	d													06 08									
Loughborough Jn	d													06 16									
Elephant & Castle	d													06 28									
London Blackfriars 3 ⊖	d	03 35			04 35				05 35					06a36									
Farringdon 3 ⊖	d								05 45														
St Pancras International 15 ⊖	d		03 52	04 32		05 02		05 32							06 02			06 10			06 20		
St Pancras International 15 ⊖	a	03 50			04 50				05 50														
	d																						
Kentish Town ⊖	d		03 57	04 37		05 07		05 37							06 07								
West Hampstead Thameslink ⊖	d		04 01	04 41		05 11		05 41							06 11						06 28		
Cricklewood	d		04 04	04 44		05 14		05 44							06 14								
Hendon	d		04 07	04 47		05 17		05 47							06 17								
Mill Hill Broadway	d		04 10	04 50		05 20		05 50							06 20								
Elstree & Borehamwood	d		04 15	04 55		05 25		05 55							06 25						06 38		
Radlett	d		04 20	05 00		05 30		06 00							06 30								
St Albans City	d		04 26	05 06		05 36		06 06							06 36						06 46		
Harpenden	d		04 32	05 12		05 42		06 12							06 42						06 52		
Luton Airport Parkway 7	d		04 38	05 18		05 48		06 18							06 48						06 58		
Luton 10	d		04 41	05 21		05 51		06 21							06 51			06 33			07 01		
Leagrave	d		04 44	05 24		05 54		06 24							06 54						07 04		
Harlington	d		04 50	05 30		06 00		06 30							07 00						07 10		
Flitwick	d		04 54	05 34		06 04		06 34							07 04						07 14		
Bedford 7	a		05 06	05 46		06 16		06 46							07 16			06 47			07 26		

Table 52

Saturdays

Brighton, Gatwick Airport and South London - City of London, St.Albans, Luton and Bedford

		FC	FC	FC	SE	FC ■	EM ◇■	FC	SE ■	SN	FC ■	SE	FC	EM ◇■	SN	SE ■	FC	EM ◇■	FC	FC ■	SE	FC ■	FC	SE ■	SN	FC	FC
Brighton ■	d					06 37				06 44										07 04		07 07			07 14		
Preston Park	d					06 41																07 11					
Hassocks ■	d					06 47																07 17					
Burgess Hill ■	d					06 51																07 21					
Wivelsfield ■	d					06 53																07 23					
Haywards Heath ■	d					07 02														07 18		07 32					
Balcombe	d																					07 37					
Three Bridges ■	d					07 12																07 42					
Gatwick Airport ■	d					07 16														07 31		07 46					
Redhill	d																										
East Croydon	d					07 32														07 47		08 02					
Sevenoaks ■	d				06 36				06 44			06 55				06 59					07 06			07 14			
Bat & Ball	d											06 58															
Otford ■	d											07 01															
Shoreham (Kent)	d											07 04															
Eynsford	d											07 08															
Swanley ■	d											07 13															
St Mary Cray ■	d											07 17															
Bickley	d											07 21															
Bromley South	d											07 24															
Shortlands ■	d											07 27															
Ravensbourne	d											07 29															
Beckenham Hill	d											07 31															
Bellingham	d											07 33															
Catford	d											07 36															
Crofton Park	d											07 38															
Nunhead ■	d											07 41															
Peckham Rye ■	d											07 43			06 57												
Denmark Hill ■	d											07 47															
Sutton (Surrey) ■	d												07 08				07 07										07 38
West Sutton	d																07 10										
Sutton Common	d																07 12										
St Helier	d																07 15										
Morden South	d																07 17										
South Merton	d																07 19										
Wimbledon Chase	d																07 21										
Wimbledon ■ ⊖	d							07 00									07b30										
Haydons Road	d							07 02									07 32										
Tooting	d							07 05									07 35										
Carshalton	d												07 11														07 41
Hackbridge	d												07 13														07 43
Mitcham Junction	d												07 16														07 46
Mitcham Eastfields	d												07 19														07 49
Streatham ■	d		06 49					07 10					07 23				07 40										07 53
Tulse Hill ■	d	06 30	06 57					07 17					07 27		07 05		07 47									07 20	07 57
London Bridge ■ ⊖	a				07 21			07 30	07 09							07 24	08a00				07 49			07 39			
	d				07 21				07 09							07 24					07 49			07 39			
Herne Hill ■	d	06 38	07a01										07a31										07 08			07 28	08a01
Loughborough Jn	d	06 46																					07 16			07 36	
Elephant & Castle	d	06 58																					07 28			07 48	
London Blackfriars ■ ⊖	d	07a06																					07a36			07a56	
Farringdon ■ ⊖	d																										
St Pancras International ■ ⊖	d			06 32			06 37				06 50			06 55				07 00	07 04								
St Pancras International ■ ⊖	a																										
	d																										
Kentish Town ⊖	d			06 37															07 09								
West Hampstead Thameslink ⊖	d			06 41							06 58								07 13								
Cricklewood	d			06 44															07 16								
Hendon	d			06 47															07 19								
Mill Hill Broadway	d			06 50															07 22								
Elstree & Borehamwood	d			06 55							07 08								07 27								
Radlett	d			07 00															07 32								
St Albans City	d			07 06							07 16								07 38								
Harpenden	d			07 12							07 22								07 44								
Luton Airport Parkway ■	d			07 18							07 28			07 16					07 50								
Luton ■	d			07a22			06 59				07 31							07 23	07a54								
Leagrave	d										07 34																
Harlington	d										07 40																
Flitwick	d										07 44																
Bedford ■	a										07 56							07 38									

Table 52

Saturdays

Brighton, Gatwick Airport and South London - City of London, St.Albans, Luton and Bedford

		FC ■	SN ■	SE	SN	SE ■	EM ◇■	FC ■		FC ■	SE	FC ■	FC	SN	FC	SE ■	SN	SE ■	FC	FC ■	SE	SN	SE ■	EM ◇■
Brighton ■	d		07 22					07 34				07 37					07 44							
Preston Park	d											07 41												
Hassocks ■	d											07 47												
Burgess Hill ■	d											07 51												
Wivelsfield ■	d											07 53												
Haywards Heath ■	d							07 48				08 02												
Balcombe	d																							
Three Bridges ■	d											08 12												
Gatwick Airport ■	d							08 01				08 16												
Redhill	d																							
East Croydon	d							08 17				08 32												
Sevenoaks ■	d			07 25		07 29					07 36					07 44		07 49			07 55		07 59	
Bat & Ball	d			07 28																	07 58			
Otford ■	d			07 31																	08 01			
Shoreham (Kent)	d			07 34																	08 04			
Eynsford	d			07 38																	08 08			
Swanley ■	d			07 43																	08 13			
St Mary Cray ■	d			07 47																	08 17			
Bickley	d			07 51																	08 21			
Bromley South	d			07 54																	08 24			
Shortlands ■	d			07 57																	08 27			
Ravensbourne	d			07 59																	08 29			
Beckenham Hill	d			08 01																	08 31			
Bellingham	d			08 03																	08 33			
Catford	d			08 06																	08 36			
Crofton Park	d			08 08																	08 38			
Nunhead ■	d			08 11																	08 41			
Peckham Rye ■	d			08 13	07 27									07 42							08 43	07 57		
Denmark Hill ■	d			08 17																	08 47			
Sutton (Surrey) ■	d																							
West Sutton	d																							
Sutton Common	d																							
St Helier	d																							
Morden South	d																							
South Merton	d																							
Wimbledon Chase	d																							
Wimbledon ■ ⊖	d																							
Haydons Road	d																							
Tooting	d																							
Carshalton	d																							
Hackbridge	d																							
Mitcham Junction	d																							
Mitcham Eastfields	d																							
Streatham ■	d																							
Tulse Hill ■	d				07 35									07 50					07 50			08 05		
London Bridge ■ ⊖	a					07 55					08 19					08 10		08 13					08 25	
	d					07 55					08 19					08 11		08 14					08 25	
Herne Hill ■	d												07 38						07 58					
Loughborough Jn	d												07 46						08 06					
Elephant & Castle	d												07 58						08 18					
London Blackfriars ■ ⊖	d												08a06						08a26					
Farringdon ■ ⊖	d																							
St Pancras International ■ ⊖	d	07 20					07 30			07 34					07 38					07 50				08 00
St Pancras International ■ ⊖	a																							
	d																							
Kentish Town ⊖	d														07 42									
West Hampstead Thameslink ⊖	d	07 28													07 46					07 58				
Cricklewood	d														07 49									
Hendon	d														07 52									
Mill Hill Broadway	d														07 55									
Elstree & Borehamwood	d	07 38													08 00					08 08				
Radlett	d														08 04									
St Albans City	d	07 45								07 55					08 10					08 15				
Harpenden	d	07 52								08 02					08 16					08 22				
Luton Airport Parkway ■	d	07 58					07 51			08 08					08 22					08 28				
Luton ■	d	08 01								08 11					08a26					08 31				08 23
Leagrave	d	08 04								08 14										08 34				
Harlington	d	08 10								08 20										08 40				
Flitwick	d	08 14								08 24										08 44				
Bedford ■	a	08 26					08 06			08 36										08 56				08 37

Table 52

Saturdays

Brighton, Gatwick Airport and South London - City of London, St.Albans, Luton and Bedford

		FC 1	FC 1	SE		FC 1	FC	SN	FC	SE 1	SE	SN	SE 1	SE	FC	FC	FC 1	SN 1	SE	SN	SE 1	EM ◇1	FC 1	FC 1	FC
Brighton 10	d	08 04				08 07						08 14						08 22					08 34		
Preston Park	d					08 11																			
Hassocks 4	d					08 17																			
Burgess Hill 4	d					08 21																			
Wivelsfield 4	d					08 23																			
Haywards Heath 5	d	08 18				08 32																	08 48		
Balcombe	d					08 37																			
Three Bridges 4	d					08 42																			
Gatwick Airport 10	d	08 31				08 46																	09 01		
Redhill	d																								
East Croydon	d	08 47				09 02																	09 17		
Sevenoaks 4	d			08 06						08 14			08 19						08 25		08 29				
Bat & Ball	d																		08 28						
Otford 4	d																		08 31						
Shoreham (Kent)	d																		08 34						
Eynsford	d																		08 38						
Swanley 4	d																		08 43						
St Mary Cray 4	d																		08 47						
Bickley	d																		08 51						
Bromley South	d																		08 54						
Shortlands 4	d																		08 57						
Ravensbourne	d																		08 59						
Beckenham Hill	d																		09 01						
Bellingham	d																		09 03						
Catford	d																		09 06						
Crofton Park	d																		09 08						
Nunhead 4	d																		09 11						
Peckham Rye 4	d							08 12											09 13	08 27					
Denmark Hill 4	d																		09 17						
Sutton (Surrey) 4	d															08 08									08 07
West Sutton	d																								08 10
Sutton Common	d																								08 12
St Helier	d																								08 15
Morden South	d																								08 17
South Merton	d																								08 19
Wimbledon Chase	d																								08 21
Wimbledon 6 ⊖	d																								08c30
Haydons Road	d																								08 32
Tooting	d																								08 35
Carshalton	d															08 11									
Hackbridge	d															08 13									
Mitcham Junction	d															08 16									
Mitcham Eastfields	d															08 19									
Streatham 4	d																								08 40
Tulse Hill 3	d							08 20							08 20					08 35					08 47
London Bridge 4 ⊖	a			08 49						08 40	08 13		08 43	08 18							08 55				09a00
	d			08 49						08 41	08 14		08 44	08 21							08 55				
Herne Hill 4	d						08 08								08 28										
Loughborough Jn	d						08 16								08 36										
Elephant & Castle	d						08 28								08 48										
London Blackfriars 3 ⊖	d						08a36								08a56										
Farringdon 3 ⊖	d																								
St Pancras International 15 ⊖	d		08 04						08 08								08 20					08 30		08 34	
St Pancras International 15 ⊖	a																								
	d																								
Kentish Town ⊖	d								08 12																
West Hampstead Thameslink ⊖	d								08 16								08 28								
Cricklewood	d								08 19																
Hendon	d								08 22																
Mill Hill Broadway	d								08 25																
Elstree & Borehamwood	d								08 30								08 38								
Radlett	d								08 34																
St Albans City	d		08 25						08 40								08 45							08 55	
Harpenden	d		08 32						08 46								08 52							09 02	
Luton Airport Parkway 7	d		08 38						08 52								08 58					08 51		09 08	
Luton 10	d		08 41						08a56								09 01							09 11	
Leagrave	d		08 44														09 04							09 14	
Harlington	d		08 50														09 10							09 20	
Flitwick	d		08 54														09 14							09 24	
Bedford 7	a		09 06														09 26					09 06		09 36	

Table 52

Saturdays

Brighton, Gatwick Airport and South London - City of London, St.Albans, Luton and Bedford

		SE	FC	FC 1	FC	SN	FC	FC	FC	SE 1	SE	SN	SE 1	SE	FC	FC 1	SE	SN	SE 1	EM ◇1	FC 1	FC 1	SE	FC 1	FC	FC	SN
Brighton 10	d			08 37								08 44									09 04			09 07			
Preston Park	d			08 41																				09 11			
Hassocks 4	d			08 47																				09 17			
Burgess Hill 4	d			08 51																				09 21			
Wivelsfield 4	d			08 53																				09 23			
Haywards Heath 5	d			09 02																	09 18			09 32			
Balcombe	d																							09 37			
Three Bridges 4	d			09 12																				09 42			
Gatwick Airport 10	d			09 16																	09 31			09 46			
Redhill	d																										
East Croydon	d			09 32																	09 47			10 02			
Sevenoaks 4	d	08 36								08 44			08 49				08 55		08 59				09 06				
Bat & Ball	d																08 58										
Otford 4	d																09 01										
Shoreham (Kent)	d																09 04										
Eynsford	d																09 08										
Swanley 4	d																09 13										
St Mary Cray 4	d																09 17										
Bickley	d																09 21										
Bromley South	d																09 24										
Shortlands 4	d																09 27										
Ravensbourne	d																09 29										
Beckenham Hill	d																09 31										
Bellingham	d																09 33										
Catford	d																09 36										
Crofton Park	d																09 38										
Nunhead 4	d																09 41										
Peckham Rye 4	d					08 42											09 43	08 57									09 12
Denmark Hill 4	d																09 47										
Sutton (Surrey) 4	d		08 38				08 38		08 37																09 08		
West Sutton	d								08 40																		
Sutton Common	d								08 42																		
St Helier	d								08 45																		
Morden South	d								08 47																		
South Merton	d								08 49																		
Wimbledon Chase	d								08 51																		
Wimbledon 6 ⊖	d								09e00																		
Haydons Road	d								09 02																		
Tooting	d								09 05																		
Carshalton	d		08 41				08 41																		09 11		
Hackbridge	d		08 43				08 43																		09 13		
Mitcham Junction	d		08 46				08 46																		09 16		
Mitcham Eastfields	d		08 49				08 49																		09 19		
Streatham 4	d		08 53				08 53		09 10																09 23		
Tulse Hill 3	d		08 57			08 50	08 57		09 17						08 50			09 05							09 27		09 20
London Bridge 4 ⊖	a	09 19							09a30	09 10	08 43		09 13	08 48					09 25				09 49				
	d	09 19								09 11	08 44		09 14	08 51					09 25				09 49				
Herne Hill 4	d				08 38		09a01								08 58										09a31	09 08	
Loughborough Jn	d				08 46										09 06											09 16	
Elephant & Castle	d				08 58										09 18											09 28	
London Blackfriars 3 ⊖	d				09a06										09a26											09a36	
Farringdon 3 ⊖	d																										
St Pancras International 15 ⊖	d							08 38								08 50				09 00		09 04					
St Pancras International 15 ⊖	a																										
	d																										
Kentish Town ⊖	d							08 42																			
West Hampstead Thameslink ⊖	d							08 46								08 58											
Cricklewood	d							08 49																			
Hendon	d							08 52																			
Mill Hill Broadway	d							08 55																			
Elstree & Borehamwood	d							09 00								09 08											
Radlett	d							09 04																			
St Albans City	d							09 10								09 15						09 25					
Harpenden	d							09 16								09 22						09 32					
Luton Airport Parkway 7	d							09 22								09 28				09 23		09 38					
Luton 10	d							09a26								09 31						09 41					
Leagrave	d															09 34						09 44					
Harlington	d															09 40						09 50					
Flitwick	d															09 44						09 54					
Bedford 7	a															09 56				09 37		10 06					

Table 52

Brighton, Gatwick Airport and South London - City of London, St.Albans, Luton and Bedford

Station		FC	SE 1	FC	SE	SN	SE 1	SE	FC	FC 1	SN 1	SE	SN	SE 1	EM ◇1	FC 1		FC 1	SE	FC 1	FC	SN	FC	SE 1	SE
Brighton 10	d					09 14					09 22					09 34				09 37					
Preston Park	d																			09 41					
Hassocks 4	d																			09 47					
Burgess Hill 4	d																			09 51					
Wivelsfield 4	d																			09 53					
Haywards Heath 3	d															09 48				10 02					
Balcombe	d																								
Three Bridges 4	d																			10 12					
Gatwick Airport 10	d															10 01				10 16					
Redhill	d																								
East Croydon	d															10 17				10 32					
Sevenoaks 4	d		09 14				09 19					09 25		09 29					09 36					09 44	
Bat & Ball	d											09 28													
Otford 4	d											09 31													
Shoreham (Kent)	d											09 34													
Eynsford	d											09 38													
Swanley 4	d											09 43													
St Mary Cray 4	d											09 47													
Bickley	d											09 51													
Bromley South	d											09 54													
Shortlands 4	d											09 57													
Ravensbourne	d											09 59													
Beckenham Hill	d											10 01													
Bellingham	d											10 03													
Catford	d											10 06													
Crofton Park	d											10 08													
Nunhead 4	d											10 11													
Peckham Rye 4	d											10 13	09 27									09 42			
Denmark Hill 4	d											10 17													
Sutton (Surrey) 4	d			09 07																					
West Sutton	d			09 10																					
Sutton Common	d			09 12																					
St Helier	d			09 15																					
Morden South	d			09 17																					
South Merton	d			09 19																					
Wimbledon Chase	d			09 21																					
Wimbledon 6 ⊖	d			09b30																					
Haydons Road	d			09 32																					
Tooting	d			09 35																					
Carshalton	d																								
Hackbridge	d																								
Mitcham Junction	d																								
Mitcham Eastfields	d																								
Streatham 4	d			09 40																					
Tulse Hill 3	d			09 47					09 20				09 35									09 50			
London Bridge 4 ⊖	a		09 40	10a00	09 13		09 43	09 18						09 55					10 19					10 10	09 43
	d		09 41		09 14		09 44	09 21						09 55					10 19					10 11	09 44
Herne Hill 4	d								09 28												09 38				
Loughborough Jn	d								09 36												09 46				
Elephant & Castle	d								09 48												09 58				
London Blackfriars 3 ⊖	d								09a56												10a06				
Farringdon 3 ⊖	d																								
St Pancras International 15 ⊖	d	09 08								09 20					09 30			09 34					09 38		
St Pancras International 15 ⊖	a																								
	d																								
Kentish Town ⊖	d	09 12																					09 42		
West Hampstead Thameslink ⊖	d	09 16								09 28													09 46		
Cricklewood	d	09 19																					09 49		
Hendon	d	09 22																					09 52		
Mill Hill Broadway	d	09 25																					09 55		
Elstree & Borehamwood	d	09 30								09 38													10 00		
Radlett	d	09 34																					10 04		
St Albans City	d	09 40								09 45								09 55					10 10		
Harpenden	d	09 46								09 52								10 02					10 16		
Luton Airport Parkway 7	d	09 52								09 58					09 51			10 08					10 22		
Luton 10	d	09a56								10 01								10 11					10a26		
Leagrave	d									10 04								10 14							
Harlington	d									10 10								10 20							
Flitwick	d									10 14								10 24							
Bedford 7	a									10 26					10 06			10 36							

Table 52

Brighton, Gatwick Airport and South London - City of London, St.Albans, Luton and Bedford

Station		SN	SE 1	SE	FC	FC	FC 1	SE	SN	SE 1	EM ◇1	FC 1	FC	FC 1	SE	FC 1	FC	SN	FC	SE 1	SE	SN	FC	SE 1	SE
Brighton 10	d	09 44										10 04				10 07						10 14			
Preston Park	d															10 11									
Hassocks 4	d															10 17									
Burgess Hill 4	d															10 21									
Wivelsfield 4	d															10 23									
Haywards Heath 3	d											10 18				10 32									
Balcombe	d															10 37									
Three Bridges 4	d															10 42									
Gatwick Airport 10	d											10 31				10 46									
Redhill	d																								
East Croydon	d											10 47				11 02									
Sevenoaks 4	d		09 49					09 55		09 59					10 06					10 14				10 19	
Bat & Ball	d							09 58																	
Otford 4	d							10 01																	
Shoreham (Kent)	d							10 04																	
Eynsford	d							10 08																	
Swanley 4	d							10 13																	
St Mary Cray 4	d							10 17																	
Bickley	d							10 21																	
Bromley South	d							10 24																	
Shortlands 4	d							10 27																	
Ravensbourne	d							10 29																	
Beckenham Hill	d							10 31																	
Bellingham	d							10 33																	
Catford	d							10 36																	
Crofton Park	d							10 38																	
Nunhead 4	d							10 41																	
Peckham Rye 4	d							10 43	09 57									10 12							
Denmark Hill 4	d							10 47																	
Sutton (Surrey) 4	d					09 38							09 37										10 08		
West Sutton	d												09 40												
Sutton Common	d												09 42												
St Helier	d												09 45												
Morden South	d												09 47												
South Merton	d												09 49												
Wimbledon Chase	d												09 51												
Wimbledon 6 ⊖	d												10c00												
Haydons Road	d												10 02												
Tooting	d												10 05												
Carshalton	d					09 41																	10 11		
Hackbridge	d					09 43																	10 13		
Mitcham Junction	d					09 46																	10 16		
Mitcham Eastfields	d					09 49																	10 19		
Streatham 4	d					09 53							10 10										10 23		
Tulse Hill 3	d				09 50	09 57			10 05				10 17					10 20					10 27		
London Bridge 4 ⊖	a		10 13	09 48						10 25			10a30		10 49					10 40	10 13			10 43	10 18
	d		10 14	09 51						10 25					10 49					10 41	10 14			10 44	10 21
Herne Hill 4	d				09 58	10a01											10 08						10a31		
Loughborough Jn	d				10 06												10 16								
Elephant & Castle	d				10 18												10 28								
London Blackfriars 3 ⊖	d				10a26												10a36								
Farringdon 3 ⊖	d																								
St Pancras International 15 ⊖	d						09 50				10 00			10 04					10 08						
St Pancras International 15 ⊖	a																								
	d																								
Kentish Town ⊖	d																		10 12						
West Hampstead Thameslink ⊖	d						09 58												10 16						
Cricklewood	d																		10 19						
Hendon	d																		10 22						
Mill Hill Broadway	d																		10 25						
Elstree & Borehamwood	d						10 08												10 30						
Radlett	d																		10 34						
St Albans City	d						10 15							10 25					10 40						
Harpenden	d						10 22							10 32					10 46						
Luton Airport Parkway 7	d						10 28							10 38					10 52						
Luton 10	d						10 31				10 23			10 41					10a56						
Leagrave	d						10 34							10 44											
Harlington	d						10 40							10 50											
Flitwick	d						10 44							10 54											
Bedford 7	a						10 56				10 37			11 06											

Brighton, Gatwick Airport and South London - City of London, St.Albans, Luton and Bedford

		FC	FC	FC ■	SN ■	FC	SE	FC	SN	SE ■	EM ◇■	FC	FC ■	FC ■	SE	FC ■	FC	SN	FC	SE ■	SE	SN	SE ■	SE	FC	FC ■	SE
Brighton ■	d				10 22								10 34			10 37						10 44					
Preston Park	d															10 41											
Hassocks ■	d															10 47											
Burgess Hill ■	d															10 51											
Wivelsfield ■	d															10 53											
Haywards Heath ■	d												10 48			11 02											
Balcombe	d																										
Three Bridges ■	d															11 12											
Gatwick Airport ■	d												11 01			11 16											
Redhill	d																										
East Croydon	d												11 17			11 32											
Sevenoaks ■	d						10 25			10 29					10 36					10 44			10 49				10 55
Bat & Ball	d						10 28																				10 58
Otford ■	d						10 31																				11 01
Shoreham (Kent)	d						10 34																				11 04
Eynsford	d						10 38																				11 08
Swanley ■	d						10 43																				11 13
St Mary Cray ■	d						10 47																				11 17
Bickley	d						10 51																				11 21
Bromley South	d						10 54																				11 24
Shortlands ■	d						10 57																				11 27
Ravensbourne	d						10 59																				11 29
Beckenham Hill	d						11 01																				11 31
Bellingham	d						11 03																				11 33
Catford	d						11 06																				11 36
Crofton Park	d						11 08																				11 38
Nunhead ■	d						11 11																				11 41
Peckham Rye ■	d						11 13		10 27									10 42									11 43
Denmark Hill ■	d						11 17																				11 47
Sutton (Surrey) ■	d	10 07				10 38		10 37				11 08															
West Sutton	d	10 10						10 40																			
Sutton Common	d	10 12						10 42																			
St Helier	d	10 15						10 45																			
Morden South	d	10 17						10 47																			
South Merton	d	10 19						10 49																			
Wimbledon Chase	d	10 21						10 51																			
Wimbledon ■ ⊖	d	10e30						11b00																			
Haydons Road	d	10 32						11 02																			
Tooting	d	10 35						11 05																			
Carshalton	d					10 41						11 11															
Hackbridge	d					10 43						11 13															
Mitcham Junction	d					10 46						11 16															
Mitcham Eastfields	d					10 49						11 19															
Streatham ■	d	10 40				10 53		11 10				11 23															
Tulse Hill ■	d	10 47	10 20			10 57		11 17	10 35			11 27						10 50							10 50		
London Bridge ■ ⊖	a	11a00						11a30		10 55					11 19					11 10	10 43		11 13	10 48			
	d									10 55					11 19					11 11	10 44		11 14	10 51			
Herne Hill ■	d		10 28			11a01						11a31					10 38								10 58		
Loughborough Jn	d		10 36														10 46								11 06		
Elephant & Castle	d		10 48														10 58								11 18		
London Blackfriars ■ ⊖	d		10a56														11a06								11a26		
Farringdon ■ ⊖	d																										
St Pancras International ■ ⊖	d			10 20							10 30			10 34					10 38							10 50	
St Pancras International ■ ⊖	a																										
	d																										
Kentish Town ⊖	d																		10 42								
West Hampstead Thameslink ⊖	d			10 28															10 46							10 58	
Cricklewood	d																		10 49								
Hendon	d																		10 52								
Mill Hill Broadway	d																		10 55								
Elstree & Borehamwood	d			10 38															11 00							11 08	
Radlett	d																		11 04								
St Albans City	d			10 45										10 55					11 10							11 15	
Harpenden	d			10 52										11 02					11 16							11 22	
Luton Airport Parkway ■	d			10 58							10 51			11 08					11 22							11 28	
Luton ■	d			11 01										11 11					11a26							11 31	
Leagrave	d			11 04										11 14												11 34	
Harlington	d			11 10										11 20												11 40	
Flitwick	d			11 14										11 24												11 44	
Bedford ■	a			11 26							11 06			11 36												11 56	

Brighton, Gatwick Airport and South London - City of London, St.Albans, Luton and Bedford

		SN	SE ■	EM ◇■		FC ■	FC ■	SE	FC ■	FC	SN	FC	SE ■	SE		SN	SE ■	SE	FC	FC ■	SN ■	SE	SN	SE ■
Brighton ■	d					11 04			11 07							11 14					11 22			
Preston Park	d								11 11															
Hassocks ■	d								11 17															
Burgess Hill ■	d								11 21															
Wivelsfield ■	d								11 23															
Haywards Heath ■	d					11 18			11 32															
Balcombe	d								11 37															
Three Bridges ■	d								11 42															
Gatwick Airport ■	d					11 31			11 46															
Redhill	d																							
East Croydon	d					11 47			12 02															
Sevenoaks ■	d		10 59					11 06					11 14				11 19					11 25		11 29
Bat & Ball	d																					11 28		
Otford ■	d																					11 31		
Shoreham (Kent)	d																					11 34		
Eynsford	d																					11 38		
Swanley ■	d																					11 43		
St Mary Cray ■	d																					11 47		
Bickley	d																					11 51		
Bromley South	d																					11 54		
Shortlands ■	d																					11 57		
Ravensbourne	d																					11 59		
Beckenham Hill	d																					12 01		
Bellingham	d																					12 03		
Catford	d																					12 06		
Crofton Park	d																					12 08		
Nunhead ■	d																					12 11		
Peckham Rye ■	d	10 57									11 12											12 13	11 27	
Denmark Hill ■	d																					12 17		
Sutton (Surrey) ■	d																							
West Sutton	d																							
Sutton Common	d																							
St Helier	d																							
Morden South	d																							
South Merton	d																							
Wimbledon Chase	d																							
Wimbledon ■ ⊖	d																							
Haydons Road	d																							
Tooting	d																							
Carshalton	d																							
Hackbridge	d																							
Mitcham Junction	d																							
Mitcham Eastfields	d																							
Streatham ■	d																							
Tulse Hill ■	d	11 05									11 20								11 20				11 35	
London Bridge ■ ⊖	a		11 25					11 49					11 40	11 13			11 43	11 18						11 55
	d		11 25					11 49					11 41	11 14			11 44	11 21						11 55
Herne Hill ■	d									11 08									11 28					
Loughborough Jn	d									11 16									11 36					
Elephant & Castle	d									11 28									11 48					
London Blackfriars ■ ⊖	d									11a36									11a56					
Farringdon ■ ⊖	d																							
St Pancras International ■ ⊖	d			11 00			11 04					11 08								11 20				
St Pancras International ■ ⊖	a																							
	d																							
Kentish Town ⊖	d											11 12												
West Hampstead Thameslink ⊖	d											11 16								11 28				
Cricklewood	d											11 19												
Hendon	d											11 22												
Mill Hill Broadway	d											11 25												
Elstree & Borehamwood	d											11 30								11 38				
Radlett	d											11 34												
St Albans City	d						11 25					11 40								11 45				
Harpenden	d						11 32					11 46								11 52				
Luton Airport Parkway ■	d						11 38					11 52								11 58				
Luton ■	d			11 23			11 41					11a56								12 01				
Leagrave	d						11 44													12 04				
Harlington	d						11 50													12 10				
Flitwick	d						11 54													12 14				
Bedford ■	a			11 37			12 06													12 26				

Brighton, Gatwick Airport and South London - City of London, St.Albans, Luton and Bedford

Station		FC	EM ◇■	FC ■	FC ■	SE	FC ■	FC	SN	FC	SE ■	FC	SE	SN	SE ■	SE	FC	FC ■	SE	SN	SE ■	FC	EM ◇■	FC ■	FC ■	SE
Brighton	d			11 34			11 37							11 44										12 04		
Preston Park	d						11 41																			
Hassocks	d						11 47																			
Burgess Hill	d						11 51																			
Wivelsfield	d						11 53																			
Haywards Heath	d			11 48			12 02																	12 18		
Balcombe	d																									
Three Bridges	d						12 12																			
Gatwick Airport	d			12 01			12 16																	12 31		
Redhill	d																							12 47		
East Croydon	d			12 17			12 32																			
Sevenoaks	d					11 36					11 44				11 49				11 55		11 59					12 06
Bat & Ball	d																		11 58							
Otford	d																		12 01							
Shoreham (Kent)	d																		12 04							
Eynsford	d																		12 08							
Swanley	d																		12 13							
St Mary Cray	d																		12 17							
Bickley	d																		12 21							
Bromley South	d																		12 24							
Shortlands	d																		12 27							
Ravensbourne	d																		12 29							
Beckenham Hill	d																		12 31							
Bellingham	d																		12 33							
Catford	d																		12 36							
Crofton Park	d																		12 38							
Nunhead	d																		12 41							
Peckham Rye	d								11 42										12 43	11 57						
Denmark Hill	d																		12 47							
Sutton (Surrey)	d	11 07										11 38										11 37				
West Sutton	d	11 10																				11 40				
Sutton Common	d	11 12																				11 42				
St Helier	d	11 15																				11 45				
Morden South	d	11 17																				11 47				
South Merton	d	11 19																				11 49				
Wimbledon Chase	d	11 21																				11 51				
Wimbledon	d	11c30																				12e00				
Haydons Road	d	11 32																				12 02				
Tooting	d	11 35																				12 05				
Carshalton	d											11 41														
Hackbridge	d											11 43														
Mitcham Junction	d											11 46														
Mitcham Eastfields	d											11 49														
Streatham	d	11 40										11 53										12 10				
Tulse Hill	d	11 47							11 50			11 57					11 50			12 05		12 17				
London Bridge	a	12a00				12 19					12 10		11 43		12 13	11 48					12 25	12a30				12 49
	d					12 19					12 11		11 44		12 14	11 51					12 25					12 49
Herne Hill	d							11 38				12a01					11 58									
Loughborough Jn	d							11 46									12 06									
Elephant & Castle	d							11 58									12 18									
London Blackfriars	d							12a06									12a26									
Farringdon	d																									
St Pancras International	d		11 30		11 34					11 38								11 50					12 00		12 04	
St Pancras International	a																									
	d																									
Kentish Town	d									11 42																
West Hampstead Thameslink	d									11 46								11 58								
Cricklewood	d									11 49																
Hendon	d									11 52																
Mill Hill Broadway	d									11 55																
Elstree & Borehamwood	d									12 00								12 08								
Radlett	d									12 04																
St Albans City	d				11 55					12 10								12 15							12 25	
Harpenden	d				12 02					12 16								12 22							12 32	
Luton Airport Parkway	d		11 51		12 08					12 22								12 28							12 38	
Luton	d				12 11					12a26								12 31					12 23		12 41	
Leagrave	d				12 14													12 34							12 44	
Harlington	d				12 20													12 40							12 50	
Flitwick	d				12 24													12 44							12 54	
Bedford	a		12 06		12 36													12 56					12 37		13 06	

Brighton, Gatwick Airport and South London - City of London, St.Albans, Luton and Bedford

Station		FC	FC ■	FC	SN	FC	SE ■	SE	SN	SE ■	SE	FC	FC ■	SN ■	SE	SN	FC	FC	SE ■	EM ◇■	FC ■	FC ■	SE	FC ■	FC	SN
Brighton	d		12 07						12 14					12 22							12 34			12 37		
Preston Park	d		12 11																					12 41		
Hassocks	d		12 17																					12 47		
Burgess Hill	d		12 21																					12 51		
Wivelsfield	d		12 23																					12 53		
Haywards Heath	d		12 32																		12 48			13 02		
Balcombe	d		12 37																							
Three Bridges	d		12 42																					13 12		
Gatwick Airport	d		12 46																		13 01			13 16		
Redhill	d																									
East Croydon	d		13 02																		13 17			13 32		
Sevenoaks	d						12 14			12 19					12 25				12 29				12 36			
Bat & Ball	d														12 28											
Otford	d														12 31											
Shoreham (Kent)	d														12 34											
Eynsford	d														12 38											
Swanley	d														12 43											
St Mary Cray	d														12 47											
Bickley	d														12 51											
Bromley South	d														12 54											
Shortlands	d														12 57											
Ravensbourne	d														12 59											
Beckenham Hill	d														13 01											
Bellingham	d														13 03											
Catford	d														13 06											
Crofton Park	d														13 08											
Nunhead	d														13 11											
Peckham Rye	d				12 12										13 13	12 27										12 42
Denmark Hill	d														13 17											
Sutton (Surrey)	d	12 08															12 07									
West Sutton	d																12 10									
Sutton Common	d																12 12									
St Helier	d																12 15									
Morden South	d																12 17									
South Merton	d																12 19									
Wimbledon Chase	d																12 21									
Wimbledon	d																12b30									
Haydons Road	d																12 32									
Tooting	d																12 35									
Carshalton	d	12 11																								
Hackbridge	d	12 13																								
Mitcham Junction	d	12 16																								
Mitcham Eastfields	d	12 19																								
Streatham	d	12 23															12 40									
Tulse Hill	d	12 27			12 20							12 20				12 35	12 47									12 50
London Bridge	a						12 40	12 13		12 43	12 18						13a00		12 55				13 19			
	d						12 41	12 14		12 44	12 21								12 55				13 19			
Herne Hill	d	12a31		12 08								12 28						12 38							12 38	
Loughborough Jn	d			12 16								12 36						12 46							12 46	
Elephant & Castle	d			12 28								12 48						12 58							12 58	
London Blackfriars	d			12a36								12a56						13a06							13a06	
Farringdon	d																									
St Pancras International	d					12 08							12 20							12 30		12 34				
St Pancras International	a																									
	d																									
Kentish Town	d					12 12																				
West Hampstead Thameslink	d					12 16							12 28													
Cricklewood	d					12 19																				
Hendon	d					12 22																				
Mill Hill Broadway	d					12 25																				
Elstree & Borehamwood	d					12 30							12 38													
Radlett	d					12 34																				
St Albans City	d					12 40							12 45									12 55				
Harpenden	d					12 46							12 52									13 02				
Luton Airport Parkway	d					12 52							12 58							12 51		13 08				
Luton	d					12a56							13 01									13 11				
Leagrave	d												13 04									13 14				
Harlington	d												13 10									13 20				
Flitwick	d												13 14									13 24				
Bedford	a												13 26							13 06		13 36				

Table 52

Saturdays

Brighton, Gatwick Airport and South London - City of London, St.Albans, Luton and Bedford

Station		FC		SE 1	SE	SN	SE 1	SE	FC	FC 1	FC	SE	SN	SE 1	EM ◇1	FC 1	FC 1	SE	FC 1	FC	SN	FC	FC	SE 1	SE
Brighton 10	d					12 44										13 04			13 07						
Preston Park	d																		13 11						
Hassocks 4	d																		13 17						
Burgess Hill 4	d																		13 21						
Wivelsfield 4	d																		13 23						
Haywards Heath 5	d															13 18			13 32						
Balcombe	d																		13 37						
Three Bridges 4	d																		13 42						
Gatwick Airport 10	d															13 31			13 46						
Redhill	d																								
East Croydon	d															13 47			14 02						
Sevenoaks 4	d			12 44			12 49					12 55		12 59				13 06						13 14	
Bat & Ball	d											12 58													
Otford 4	d											13 01													
Shoreham (Kent)	d											13 04													
Eynsford	d											13 08													
Swanley 4	d											13 13													
St Mary Cray 4	d											13 17													
Bickley	d											13 21													
Bromley South	d											13 24													
Shortlands 4	d											13 27													
Ravensbourne	d											13 29													
Beckenham Hill	d											13 31													
Bellingham	d											13 33													
Catford	d											13 36													
Crofton Park	d											13 38													
Nunhead 4	d											13 41													
Peckham Rye 4	d											13 43	12 57								13 12				
Denmark Hill 4	d											13 47													
Sutton (Surrey) 4	d										12 38												13 08		
West Sutton	d																								
Sutton Common	d																								
St Helier	d																								
Morden South	d																								
South Merton	d																								
Wimbledon Chase	d																								
Wimbledon 6 ⊖	d																								
Haydons Road	d																								
Tooting	d																								
Carshalton	d										12 41												13 11		
Hackbridge	d										12 43												13 13		
Mitcham Junction	d										12 46												13 16		
Mitcham Eastfields	d										12 49												13 19		
Streatham 4	d										12 53												13 23		
Tulse Hill 3	d								12 50		12 57		13 05								13 20		13 27		
London Bridge 4 ⊖	a			13 10	12 43		13 13	12 48						13 25				13 49						13 40	13 13
	d			13 11	12 44		13 14	12 51						13 25				13 49						13 41	13 14
Herne Hill 4	d								12 58		13a01									13 08			13a31		
Loughborough Jn	d								13 06											13 16					
Elephant & Castle	d								13 18											13 28					
London Blackfriars 5 ⊖	d								13a26											13a36					
Farringdon 5 ⊖	d																								
St Pancras International 15 ⊖	d	12 38								12 50					13 00		13 04					13 08			
St Pancras International 15 ⊖	a																								
	d																								
Kentish Town ⊖	d	12 42																				13 12			
West Hampstead Thameslink ⊖	d	12 46								12 58												13 16			
Cricklewood	d	12 49																				13 19			
Hendon	d	12 52																				13 22			
Mill Hill Broadway	d	12 55																				13 25			
Elstree & Borehamwood	d	13 00								13 08												13 30			
Radlett	d	13 04																				13 34			
St Albans City	d	13 10								13 15							13 25					13 40			
Harpenden	d	13 16								13 22							13 32					13 46			
Luton Airport Parkway 7	d	13 22								13 28							13 38					13 52			
Luton 10	d	13a26								13 31					13 23		13 41					13a56			
Leagrave	d									13 34							13 44								
Harlington	d									13 40							13 50								
Flitwick	d									13 44							13 54								
Bedford 7	a									13 56					13 37		14 06								

Table 52

Saturdays

Brighton, Gatwick Airport and South London - City of London, St.Albans, Luton and Bedford

Station		SN	SE 1	SE	FC	FC 1	SN 1	SE	SN	SE 1	FC	FC	EM ◇1	FC 1	FC 1	SE	FC 1	FC	SN	FC	SE 1	SE	SN	SE 1	SE
Brighton 10	d	13 14					13 22							13 34			13 37						13 44		
Preston Park	d																13 41								
Hassocks 4	d																13 47								
Burgess Hill 4	d																13 51								
Wivelsfield 4	d																13 53								
Haywards Heath 5	d													13 48			14 02								
Balcombe	d																								
Three Bridges 4	d																14 12								
Gatwick Airport 10	d													14 01			14 16								
Redhill	d																								
East Croydon	d													14 17			14 32								
Sevenoaks 4	d		13 19					13 25		13 29						13 36					13 44			13 49	
Bat & Ball	d							13 28																	
Otford 4	d							13 31																	
Shoreham (Kent)	d							13 34																	
Eynsford	d							13 38																	
Swanley 4	d							13 43																	
St Mary Cray 4	d							13 47																	
Bickley	d							13 51																	
Bromley South	d							13 54																	
Shortlands 4	d							13 57																	
Ravensbourne	d							13 59																	
Beckenham Hill	d							14 01																	
Bellingham	d							14 03																	
Catford	d							14 06																	
Crofton Park	d							14 08																	
Nunhead 4	d							14 11																	
Peckham Rye 4	d							14 13	13 27										13 42						
Denmark Hill 4	d							14 17																	
Sutton (Surrey) 4	d										13 07	13 38													
West Sutton	d										13 10														
Sutton Common	d										13 12														
St Helier	d										13 15														
Morden South	d										13 17														
South Merton	d										13 19														
Wimbledon Chase	d										13 21														
Wimbledon 6 ⊖	d										13e30														
Haydons Road	d										13 32														
Tooting	d										13 35														
Carshalton	d											13 41													
Hackbridge	d											13 43													
Mitcham Junction	d											13 46													
Mitcham Eastfields	d											13 49													
Streatham 4	d										13 40	13 53													
Tulse Hill 3	d				13 20				13 35		13 47	13 57							13 50						
London Bridge 4 ⊖	a		13 43	13 18						13 55	14a00	14a01				14 19					14 10	13 43		14 13	13 48
	d		13 44	13 21						13 55						14 19					14 11	13 44		14 14	13 51
Herne Hill 4	d				13 28													13 38							
Loughborough Jn	d				13 36													13 46							
Elephant & Castle	d				13 48													13 58							
London Blackfriars 5 ⊖	d				13a56													14a06							
Farringdon 5 ⊖	d																								
St Pancras International 15 ⊖	d					13 20							13 30		13 34					13 38					
St Pancras International 15 ⊖	a																								
	d																								
Kentish Town ⊖	d																			13 42					
West Hampstead Thameslink ⊖	d					13 28														13 46					
Cricklewood	d																			13 49					
Hendon	d																			13 52					
Mill Hill Broadway	d																			13 55					
Elstree & Borehamwood	d					13 38														14 00					
Radlett	d																			14 04					
St Albans City	d					13 45									13 55					14 10					
Harpenden	d					13 52									14 02					14 16					
Luton Airport Parkway 7	d					13 58							13 51		14 08					14 22					
Luton 10	d					14 01									14 11					14a26					
Leagrave	d					14 04									14 14										
Harlington	d					14 10									14 20										
Flitwick	d					14 14									14 24										
Bedford 7	a					14 26							14 06		14 36										

Table 52

Brighton, Gatwick Airport and South London - City of London, St.Albans, Luton and Bedford

		FC	FC ■	SE	SN	FC	SE ■	EM ◇■	FC ■	FC ■	SE	FC ■	FC	SN	FC	FC	SE ■	SE	SN	SE ■	SE	FC	FC ■	SN ■
		🚌					🛒	🍴					🚌							🛒		🚌		
Brighton	d								14 04			14 07							14 14					14 22
Preston Park	d											14 11												
Hassocks	d											14 17												
Burgess Hill	d											14 21												
Wivelsfield	d											14 23												
Haywards Heath	d								14 18			14 32												
Balcombe	d											14 37												
Three Bridges	d											14 42												
Gatwick Airport	d								14 31			14 46												
Redhill	d																							
East Croydon	d								14 47			15 02												
Sevenoaks	d			13 55			13 59				14 06						14 14			14 19				
Bat & Ball	d			13 58																				
Otford	d			14 01																				
Shoreham (Kent)	d			14 04																				
Eynsford	d			14 08																				
Swanley	d			14 13																				
St Mary Cray	d			14 17																				
Bickley	d			14 21																				
Bromley South	d			14 24																				
Shortlands	d			14 27																				
Ravensbourne	d			14 29																				
Beckenham Hill	d			14 31																				
Bellingham	d			14 33																				
Catford	d			14 36																				
Crofton Park	d			14 38																				
Nunhead	d			14 41																				
Peckham Rye	d			14 43	13 57									14 12										
Denmark Hill	d			14 47																				
Sutton (Surrey)	d					13 37									14 08									
West Sutton	d					13 40																		
Sutton Common	d					13 42																		
St Helier	d					13 45																		
Morden South	d					13 47																		
South Merton	d					13 49																		
Wimbledon Chase	d					13 51																		
Wimbledon ⊖	d					14b00																		
Haydons Road	d					14 02																		
Tooting	d					14 05																		
Carshalton	d														14 11									
Hackbridge	d														14 13									
Mitcham Junction	d														14 16									
Mitcham Eastfields	d														14 19									
Streatham	d					14 10									14 23									
Tulse Hill	d	13 50			14 05	14 17								14 20	14 27							14 20		
London Bridge ⊖	a					14a30	14 25				14 49						14 40	14 13		14 43	14 18			
	d						14 25				14 49						14 41	14 14		14 44	14 21			
Herne Hill	d	13 58											14 08		14a31							14 28		
Loughborough Jn	d	14 06											14 16									14 36		
Elephant & Castle	d	14 18											14 28									14 48		
London Blackfriars ⊖	d	14a26											14a36									14a56		
Farringdon ⊖	d																							
St Pancras International ⊖	d		13 50					14 00		14 04						14 08							14 20	
St Pancras International ⊖	a																							
	d																							
Kentish Town ⊖	d															14 12								
West Hampstead Thameslink ⊖	d		13 58													14 16							14 28	
Cricklewood	d															14 19								
Hendon	d															14 22								
Mill Hill Broadway	d															14 25								
Elstree & Borehamwood	d		14 08													14 30							14 38	
Radlett	d															14 34								
St Albans City	d		14 15							14 25						14 40							14 45	
Harpenden	d		14 22							14 32						14 46							14 52	
Luton Airport Parkway	d		14 28							14 38						14 52							14 58	
Luton	d		14 31					14 23		14 41						14a56							15 01	
Leagrave	d		14 34							14 44													15 04	
Harlington	d		14 40							14 50													15 10	
Flitwick	d		14 44							14 54													15 14	
Bedford	a		14 56					14 37		15 06													15 26	

Table 52

Brighton, Gatwick Airport and South London - City of London, St.Albans, Luton and Bedford

		SE	SN	SE ■	EM ◇■	FC ■	FC ■	SE	FC ■	FC		SN	FC	SE ■	SE	SN	SE ■	SE	FC	FC ■	FC	SE	SN	SE ■	EM ◇■
				🛒	🍴					🚌							🛒		🚌					🛒	🍴
Brighton	d					14 34			14 37							14 44									
Preston Park	d								14 41																
Hassocks	d								14 47																
Burgess Hill	d								14 51																
Wivelsfield	d								14 53																
Haywards Heath	d					14 48			15 02																
Balcombe	d																								
Three Bridges	d								15 12																
Gatwick Airport	d					15 01			15 16																
Redhill	d																								
East Croydon	d					15 17			15 32																
Sevenoaks	d	14 25		14 29				14 36						14 44			14 49					14 55		14 59	
Bat & Ball	d	14 28																				14 58			
Otford	d	14 31																				15 01			
Shoreham (Kent)	d	14 34																				15 04			
Eynsford	d	14 38																				15 08			
Swanley	d	14 43																				15 13			
St Mary Cray	d	14 47																				15 17			
Bickley	d	14 51																				15 21			
Bromley South	d	14 54																				15 24			
Shortlands	d	14 57																				15 27			
Ravensbourne	d	14 59																				15 29			
Beckenham Hill	d	15 01																				15 31			
Bellingham	d	15 03																				15 33			
Catford	d	15 06																				15 36			
Crofton Park	d	15 08																				15 38			
Nunhead	d	15 11																				15 41			
Peckham Rye	d	15 13	14 27									14 42										15 43	14 57		
Denmark Hill	d	15 17																				15 47			
Sutton (Surrey)	d																				14 07				
West Sutton	d																				14 10				
Sutton Common	d																				14 12				
St Helier	d																				14 15				
Morden South	d																				14 17				
South Merton	d																				14 19				
Wimbledon Chase	d																				14 21				
Wimbledon ⊖	d																				14c30				
Haydons Road	d																				14 32				
Tooting	d																				14 35				
Carshalton	d																								
Hackbridge	d																								
Mitcham Junction	d																								
Mitcham Eastfields	d																								
Streatham	d																				14 40				
Tulse Hill	d		14 35									14 50							14 50		14 47		15 05		
London Bridge ⊖	a			14 55				15 19						15 10	14 43		15 13	14 48			15a00			15 25	
	d			14 55				15 19						15 11	14 44		15 14	14 51						15 25	
Herne Hill	d									14 38									14 58						
Loughborough Jn	d									14 46									15 06						
Elephant & Castle	d									14 58									15 18						
London Blackfriars ⊖	d									15a06									15a26						
Farringdon ⊖	d																								
St Pancras International ⊖	d				14 30		14 34						14 38							14 50					15 00
St Pancras International ⊖	a																								
	d																								
Kentish Town ⊖	d												14 42												
West Hampstead Thameslink ⊖	d												14 46							14 58					
Cricklewood	d												14 49												
Hendon	d												14 52												
Mill Hill Broadway	d												14 55												
Elstree & Borehamwood	d												15 00							15 08					
Radlett	d												15 04												
St Albans City	d						14 55						15 10							15 15					
Harpenden	d						15 02						15 16							15 22					
Luton Airport Parkway	d				14 51		15 08						15 22							15 28					
Luton	d						15 11						15a26							15 31					15 23
Leagrave	d						15 14													15 34					
Harlington	d						15 20													15 40					
Flitwick	d						15 24													15 44					
Bedford	a				15 06		15 36													15 56					15 37

Table 52

Saturdays

Brighton, Gatwick Airport and South London - City of London, St.Albans, Luton and Bedford

Station		FC	FC	FC ■	FC ■	SE	FC ■	FC	SN	FC	SE ■	SE	SN	SE ■	SE	FC	FC ■	SN ■	SE	SN	SE ■	EM ◇■	FC ■	FC ■	SE
Brighton ■	d			15 04			15 07						15 14					15 22					15 34		
Preston Park	d						15 11																		
Hassocks ■	d						15 17																		
Burgess Hill ■	d						15 21																		
Wivelsfield ■	d						15 23																		
Haywards Heath ■	d			15 18			15 32																15 48		
Balcombe	d						15 37																		
Three Bridges ■	d						15 42																		
Gatwick Airport ■	d			15 31			15 46																16 01		
Redhill	d																								
East Croydon	d			15 47			16 02																16 17		
Sevenoaks ■	d					15 06					15 14			15 19					15 25		15 29				15 36
Bat & Ball	d																		15 28						
Otford ■	d																		15 31						
Shoreham (Kent)	d																		15 34						
Eynsford	d																		15 38						
Swanley ■	d																		15 43						
St Mary Cray ■	d																		15 47						
Bickley	d																		15 51						
Bromley South	d																		15 54						
Shortlands ■	d																		15 57						
Ravensbourne	d																		15 59						
Beckenham Hill	d																		16 01						
Bellingham	d																		16 03						
Catford	d																		16 06						
Crofton Park	d																		16 08						
Nunhead ■	d																		16 11						
Peckham Rye ■	d								15 12										16 13	15 27					
Denmark Hill ■	d																		16 17						
Sutton (Surrey) ■	d	14 38	14 37																						
West Sutton	d		14 40																						
Sutton Common	d		14 42																						
St Helier	d		14 45																						
Morden South	d		14 47																						
South Merton	d		14 49																						
Wimbledon Chase	d		14 51																						
Wimbledon ■ ⊖	d		15e00																						
Haydons Road	d		15 02																						
Tooting	d		15 05																						
Carshalton	d	14 41																							
Hackbridge	d	14 43																							
Mitcham Junction	d	14 46																							
Mitcham Eastfields	d	14 49																							
Streatham ■	d	14 53	15 10																						
Tulse Hill ■	d	14 57	15 17						15 20							15 20				15 35					
London Bridge ■ ⊖	a		15a30			15 49					15 40	15 13		15 43	15 18						15 55				16 19
	d					15 49					15 41	15 14		15 44	15 21						15 55				16 19
Herne Hill ■	d	15a01						15 08								15 28									
Loughborough Jn	d							15 16								15 36									
Elephant & Castle	d							15 28								15 48									
London Blackfriars ■ ⊖	d							15a36								15a56									
Farringdon ■ ⊖	d																								
St Pancras International ■ ⊖	d				15 04					15 08							15 20					15 30		15 34	
St Pancras International ■ ⊖	a																								
	d																								
Kentish Town ⊖	d									15 12															
West Hampstead Thameslink ⊖	d									15 16															
Cricklewood	d									15 19							15 28								
Hendon	d									15 22															
Mill Hill Broadway	d									15 25															
Elstree & Borehamwood	d									15 30															
Radlett	d									15 34							15 38								
St Albans City	d				15 25					15 40							15 45							15 55	
Harpenden	d				15 32					15 46							15 52							16 02	
Luton Airport Parkway ■	d				15 38					15 52							15 58							16 08	
Luton ■	d				15 41					15a56							16 01					15 51		16 11	
Leagrave	d				15 44												16 04							16 14	
Harlington	d				15 50												16 10							16 20	
Flitwick	d				15 54												16 14							16 24	
Bedford ■	a				16 06												16 26					16 06		16 36	

Table 52

Saturdays

Brighton, Gatwick Airport and South London - City of London, St.Albans, Luton and Bedford

Station		FC ■	FC	FC	SN	FC	FC	SE ■	SE	SN	SE ■	SE	FC	FC ■	SE	SN	SE ■	EM ◇■	FC	FC ■	FC ■	SE	FC ■	FC	FC	SN
Brighton ■	d	15 37								15 44										16 04			16 07			
Preston Park	d	15 41																					16 11			
Hassocks ■	d	15 47																					16 17			
Burgess Hill ■	d	15 51																					16 21			
Wivelsfield ■	d	15 53																					16 23			
Haywards Heath ■	d	16 02																		16 18			16 32			
Balcombe	d																						16 37			
Three Bridges ■	d	16 12																					16 42			
Gatwick Airport ■	d	16 16																		16 31			16 46			
Redhill	d																									
East Croydon	d	16 32																		16 47			17 02			
Sevenoaks ■	d							15 44			15 49				15 55		15 59					16 06				
Bat & Ball	d														15 58											
Otford ■	d														16 01											
Shoreham (Kent)	d														16 04											
Eynsford	d														16 08											
Swanley ■	d														16 13											
St Mary Cray ■	d														16 17											
Bickley	d														16 21											
Bromley South	d														16 24											
Shortlands ■	d														16 27											
Ravensbourne	d														16 29											
Beckenham Hill	d														16 31											
Bellingham	d														16 33											
Catford	d														16 36											
Crofton Park	d														16 38											
Nunhead ■	d														16 41											
Peckham Rye ■	d				15 42										16 43	15 57										16 12
Denmark Hill ■	d														16 47											
Sutton (Surrey) ■	d		15 08				15 07												15 37					15 38		
West Sutton	d						15 10												15 40							
Sutton Common	d						15 12												15 42							
St Helier	d						15 15												15 45							
Morden South	d						15 17												15 47							
South Merton	d						15 19												15 49							
Wimbledon Chase	d						15 21												15 51							
Wimbledon ■ ⊖	d						15b30												16c00							
Haydons Road	d						15 32												16 02							
Tooting	d						15 35												16 05							
Carshalton	d		15 11																					15 41		
Hackbridge	d		15 13																					15 43		
Mitcham Junction	d		15 16																					15 46		
Mitcham Eastfields	d		15 19																					15 49		
Streatham ■	d		15 23				15 40												16 10					15 53		
Tulse Hill ■	d		15 27		15 50		15 47						15 50			16 05			16 17					15 57		16 20
London Bridge ■ ⊖	a						16a00	16 10	15 43		16 13	15 48					16 25		16a30			16 49				
	d							16 11	15 44		16 14	15 51					16 25					16 49				
Herne Hill ■	d		15a31	15 38									15 58											16a01	16 08	
Loughborough Jn	d			15 46									16 06												16 16	
Elephant & Castle	d			15 58									16 18												16 28	
London Blackfriars ■ ⊖	d			16a06									16a26												16a36	
Farringdon ■ ⊖	d																									
St Pancras International ■ ⊖	d					15 38								15 50				16 00			16 04					
St Pancras International ■ ⊖	a																									
	d																									
Kentish Town ⊖	d					15 42																				
West Hampstead Thameslink ⊖	d					15 46								15 58												
Cricklewood	d					15 49																				
Hendon	d					15 52																				
Mill Hill Broadway	d					15 55																				
Elstree & Borehamwood	d					16 00								16 08												
Radlett	d					16 04																				
St Albans City	d					16 10								16 15							16 25					
Harpenden	d					16 16								16 22							16 32					
Luton Airport Parkway ■	d					16 22								16 28							16 38					
Luton ■	d					16a26								16 31				16 23			16 41					
Leagrave	d													16 34							16 44					
Harlington	d													16 40							16 50					
Flitwick	d													16 44							16 54					
Bedford ■	a													16 56				16 37			17 06					

Brighton, Gatwick Airport and South London - City of London, St.Albans, Luton and Bedford

		FC	SE ■	SE	SN	SE ■	SE	FC	FC	FC ■	SN ■	SE	SN	SE ■	EM ◇■	FC ■	FC	FC ■	SE	FC ■	FC	SN	FC	SE ■	SE
Brighton 10	d				16 14						16 22					16 34				16 37					
Preston Park	d																			16 41					
Hassocks 4	d																			16 47					
Burgess Hill 4	d																			16 51					
Wivelsfield 4	d																			16 53					
Haywards Heath 3	d															16 48				17 02					
Balcombe	d																								
Three Bridges 4	d																			17 12					
Gatwick Airport 10	d															17 01				17 16					
Redhill	d																								
East Croydon	d															17 17				17 32					
Sevenoaks 4	d		16 14			16 19						16 25		16 29					16 36					16 44	
Bat & Ball	d											16 28													
Otford 4	d											16 31													
Shoreham (Kent)	d											16 34													
Eynsford	d											16 38													
Swanley 4	d											16 43													
St Mary Cray 4	d											16 47													
Bickley	d											16 51													
Bromley South	d											16 54													
Shortlands 4	d											16 57													
Ravensbourne	d											16 59													
Beckenham Hill	d											17 01													
Bellingham	d											17 03													
Catford	d											17 06													
Crofton Park	d											17 08													
Nunhead 4	d											17 11													
Peckham Rye 4	d											17 13	16 27									16 42			
Denmark Hill 4	d											17 17													
Sutton (Surrey) 4	d								16 08								16 07								
West Sutton	d																16 10								
Sutton Common	d																16 12								
St Helier	d																16 15								
Morden South	d																16 17								
South Merton	d																16 19								
Wimbledon Chase	d																16 21								
Wimbledon 6 ⊖	d																16e30								
Haydons Road	d																16 32								
Tooting	d																16 35								
Carshalton	d								16 11																
Hackbridge	d								16 13																
Mitcham Junction	d								16 16																
Mitcham Eastfields	d								16 19																
Streatham 4	d								16 23								16 40								
Tulse Hill 3	d							16 20	16 27				16 35				16 47					16 50			
London Bridge 4 ⊖	a		16 40	16 13		16 43	16 18							16 55			17a00		17 19					17 10	16 43
	d		16 41	16 14		16 44	16 21							16 55					17 19					17 11	16 44
Herne Hill 4	d							16 28	16a31												16 38				
Loughborough Jn	d							16 36													16 46				
Elephant & Castle	d							16 48													16 58				
London Blackfriars 3 ⊖	d							16a57													17a06				
Farringdon 3 ⊖	d																								
St Pancras International 15 ⊖	d	16 08								16 20					16 30			16 34					16 38		
St Pancras International 15 ⊖	a																								
	d																								
Kentish Town ⊖	d	16 12																					16 42		
West Hampstead Thameslink ⊖	d	16 16								16 28													16 46		
Cricklewood	d	16 19																					16 49		
Hendon	d	16 22																					16 52		
Mill Hill Broadway	d	16 25																					16 55		
Elstree & Borehamwood	d	16 30								16 38													17 00		
Radlett	d	16 34																					17 04		
St Albans City	d	16 40								16 45								16 55					17 10		
Harpenden	d	16 46								16 52								17 02					17 16		
Luton Airport Parkway 7	d	16 52								16 58					16 51			17 08					17 22		
Luton 10	d	16a56								17 01					16 55			17 11					17a26		
Leagrave	d									17 04								17 14							
Harlington	d									17 10								17 20							
Flitwick	d									17 14								17 24							
Bedford 7	a									17 26					17 06			17 36							

Brighton, Gatwick Airport and South London - City of London, St.Albans, Luton and Bedford

		SN	SE ■	SE		FC	FC ■	SE	SN	SE ■	EM ◇■	FC ■	FC ■	SE	FC	FC ■	FC	SN	FC	SE ■	SE	SN	SE ■	SE	FC
Brighton 10	d	16 44										17 04				17 07						17 14			
Preston Park	d															17 11									
Hassocks 4	d															17 17									
Burgess Hill 4	d															17 21									
Wivelsfield 4	d															17 23									
Haywards Heath 3	d											17 18				17 32									
Balcombe	d															17 37									
Three Bridges 4	d															17 42									
Gatwick Airport 10	d											17 31				17 46									
Redhill	d																								
East Croydon	d											17 47				18 02									
Sevenoaks 4	d		16 49					16 55		16 59				17 06						17 14			17 19		
Bat & Ball	d							16 58																	
Otford 4	d							17 01																	
Shoreham (Kent)	d							17 04																	
Eynsford	d							17 08																	
Swanley 4	d							17 13																	
St Mary Cray 4	d							17 17																	
Bickley	d							17 21																	
Bromley South	d							17 24																	
Shortlands 4	d							17 27																	
Ravensbourne	d							17 29																	
Beckenham Hill	d							17 31																	
Bellingham	d							17 33																	
Catford	d							17 36																	
Crofton Park	d							17 38																	
Nunhead 4	d							17 41																	
Peckham Rye 4	d							17 43	16 57									17 12							
Denmark Hill 4	d							17 47																	
Sutton (Surrey) 4	d														16 38										16 37
West Sutton	d																								16 40
Sutton Common	d																								16 42
St Helier	d																								16 45
Morden South	d																								16 47
South Merton	d																								16 49
Wimbledon Chase	d																								16 51
Wimbledon 6 ⊖	d																								17b00
Haydons Road	d																								17 02
Tooting	d																								17 05
Carshalton	d														16 41										
Hackbridge	d														16 43										
Mitcham Junction	d														16 46										
Mitcham Eastfields	d														16 49										
Streatham 4	d														16 53										17 10
Tulse Hill 3	d					16 50			17 05						16 57			17 20							17 17
London Bridge 4 ⊖	a		17 13	16 48						17 25				17 49						17 40	17 13		17 43	17 18	17a30
	d		17 14	16 51						17 25				17 49						17 41	17 14		17 44	17 21	
Herne Hill 4	d					16 58									17a01		17 08								
Loughborough Jn	d					17 06											17 16								
Elephant & Castle	d					17 18											17 28								
London Blackfriars 3 ⊖	d					17a26											17a36								
Farringdon 3 ⊖	d																								
St Pancras International 15 ⊖	d						16 50				17 00		17 04						17 08						
St Pancras International 15 ⊖	a																								
	d																								
Kentish Town ⊖	d																		17 12						
West Hampstead Thameslink ⊖	d						16 58												17 16						
Cricklewood	d																		17 19						
Hendon	d																		17 22						
Mill Hill Broadway	d																		17 25						
Elstree & Borehamwood	d						17 08												17 30						
Radlett	d																		17 34						
St Albans City	d						17 15						17 25						17 40						
Harpenden	d						17 22						17 32						17 46						
Luton Airport Parkway 7	d						17 28						17 38						17 52						
Luton 10	d						17 31				17 23		17 41						17a56						
Leagrave	d						17 34						17 44												
Harlington	d						17 40						17 50												
Flitwick	d						17 44						17 54												
Bedford 7	a						17 56				17 37		18 06												

Table 52

Saturdays

Brighton, Gatwick Airport and South London - City of London, St.Albans, Luton and Bedford

		FC	FC 1	FC	SN 1	SE	SN	SE 1	EM ◇1	FC 1	FC 1	SE	FC 1	SN	FC	FC	FC	FC	SE 1	FC	SE	SN	SE 1	SE	FC	FC 1	SE	SN
Brighton 10	d				17 22					17 34			17 37									17 44						
Preston Park	d												17 41															
Hassocks 4	d												17 47															
Burgess Hill 4	d												17 51															
Wivelsfield 4	d												17 53															
Haywards Heath 3	d									17 48			18 02															
Balcombe	d																											
Three Bridges 4	d												18 12															
Gatwick Airport 10	d									18 01			18 16															
Redhill	d																											
East Croydon	d									18 17			18 32															
Sevenoaks 4	d					17 25		17 29				17 36							17 44				17 49				17 55	
Bat & Ball	d					17 28																					17 58	
Otford 4	d					17 31																					18 01	
Shoreham (Kent)	d					17 34																					18 04	
Eynsford	d					17 38																					18 08	
Swanley 4	d					17 43																					18 13	
St Mary Cray 4	d					17 47																					18 17	
Bickley	d					17 51																					18 21	
Bromley South	d					17 54																					18 24	
Shortlands 4	d					17 57																					18 27	
Ravensbourne	d					17 59																					18 29	
Beckenham Hill	d					18 01																					18 31	
Bellingham	d					18 03																					18 33	
Catford	d					18 06																					18 36	
Crofton Park	d					18 08																					18 38	
Nunhead 4	d					18 11																					18 41	
Peckham Rye 4	d					18 13	17 27							17 42													18 43	17 57
Denmark Hill 4	d					18 17																					18 47	
Sutton (Surrey) 4	d			17 08												17 07	17 38			17 37								
West Sutton	d															17 10				17 40								
Sutton Common	d															17 12				17 42								
St Helier	d															17 15				17 45								
Morden South	d															17 17				17 47								
South Merton	d															17 19				17 49								
Wimbledon Chase	d															17 21				17 51								
Wimbledon 6 ⊖	d															17c30				18e00								
Haydons Road	d															17 32				18 02								
Tooting	d															17 35				18 05								
Carshalton	d			17 11													17 41											
Hackbridge	d			17 13													17 43											
Mitcham Junction	d			17 16													17 46											
Mitcham Eastfields	d			17 19													17 49											
Streatham 4	d			17 23												17 40	17 53			18 10								
Tulse Hill 3	d	17 20		17 27			17 35							17 50		17 47	17 57			18 17					17 50			18 05
London Bridge 4 ⊖	a							17 55				18 19				18a00			18 10	18a30	17 43		18 13	17 48				
	d							17 55				18 19							18 11		17 44		18 14	17 51				
Herne Hill 4	d	17 28		17a31													18a01	17 38							17 58			
Loughborough Jn	d	17 36																17 46							18 06			
Elephant & Castle	d	17 48																17 58							18 18			
London Blackfriars 3 ⊖	d	17a56																18a06							18a26			
Farringdon 3 ⊖	d																											
St Pancras International 15 ⊖	d		17 20						17 30		17 34				17 38											17 50		
St Pancras International 15 ⊖	a																											
	d																											
Kentish Town ⊖	d														17 42													
West Hampstead Thameslink ⊖	d		17 28												17 46											17 58		
Cricklewood	d														17 49													
Hendon	d														17 52													
Mill Hill Broadway	d														17 55													
Elstree & Borehamwood	d		17 38												18 00											18 08		
Radlett	d														18 04													
St Albans City	d		17 45								17 55				18 10											18 15		
Harpenden	d		17 52								18 02				18 16											18 22		
Luton Airport Parkway 7	d		17 58						17 51		18 08				18 22											18 28		
Luton 10	d		18 01								18 11				18a26											18 31		
Leagrave	d		18 04								18 14															18 34		
Harlington	d		18 10								18 20															18 40		
Flitwick	d		18 14								18 24															18 44		
Bedford 7	a		18 26						18 06		18 36															18 56		

Table 52

Saturdays

Brighton, Gatwick Airport and South London - City of London, St.Albans, Luton and Bedford

		SE 1	EM ◇1	FC 1	FC 1	SE		FC 1	FC	SN	FC	SE 1	SE	SN	SE 1	FC		FC 1	SN 1	SE	SN	SE 1	EM ◇1	FC 1	FC 1
Brighton 10	d			18 04				18 07						18 14					18 22					18 34	
Preston Park	d							18 11																	
Hassocks 4	d							18 17																	
Burgess Hill 4	d							18 21																	
Wivelsfield 4	d							18 23																	
Haywards Heath 3	d			18 18				18 32																18 48	
Balcombe	d							18 37																	
Three Bridges 4	d							18 42																	
Gatwick Airport 10	d			18 31				18 46																19 01	
Redhill	d																								
East Croydon	d			18 47				19 02																19 17	
Sevenoaks 4	d	17 59				18 06						18 14			18 19					18 25		18 29			
Bat & Ball	d																			18 28					
Otford 4	d																			18 31					
Shoreham (Kent)	d																			18 34					
Eynsford	d																			18 38					
Swanley 4	d																			18 43					
St Mary Cray 4	d																			18 47					
Bickley	d																			18 51					
Bromley South	d																			18 54					
Shortlands 4	d																			18 57					
Ravensbourne	d																			18 59					
Beckenham Hill	d																			19 01					
Bellingham	d																			19 03					
Catford	d																			19 06					
Crofton Park	d																			19 08					
Nunhead 4	d																			19 11					
Peckham Rye 4	d									18 12										19 13	18 27				
Denmark Hill 4	d																			19 17					
Sutton (Surrey) 4	d																								
West Sutton	d																								
Sutton Common	d																								
St Helier	d																								
Morden South	d																								
South Merton	d																								
Wimbledon Chase	d																								
Wimbledon 6 ⊖	d																								
Haydons Road	d																								
Tooting	d																								
Carshalton	d																								
Hackbridge	d																								
Mitcham Junction	d																								
Mitcham Eastfields	d																								
Streatham 4	d																								
Tulse Hill 3	d									18 20						18 20					18 35				
London Bridge 4 ⊖	a	18 25				18 49						18 40	18 13		18 43							18 55			
	d	18 25				18 49						18 41	18 14		18 44							18 55			
Herne Hill 4	d								18 08							18 28									
Loughborough Jn	d								18 16							18 36									
Elephant & Castle	d								18 28							18 48									
London Blackfriars 3 ⊖	d								18a36							18a56									
Farringdon 3 ⊖	d																								
St Pancras International 15 ⊖	d		18 00		18 04						18 08							18 20					18 30		18 34
St Pancras International 15 ⊖	a																								
	d																								
Kentish Town ⊖	d										18 12														
West Hampstead Thameslink ⊖	d										18 16							18 28							
Cricklewood	d										18 19														
Hendon	d										18 22														
Mill Hill Broadway	d										18 25														
Elstree & Borehamwood	d										18 30							18 38							
Radlett	d										18 34														
St Albans City	d				18 25						18 40							18 45							18 55
Harpenden	d				18 32						18 46							18 52							19 02
Luton Airport Parkway 7	d				18 38						18 52							18 58					18 51		19 08
Luton 10	d		18 23		18 41						18a56							19 01							19 11
Leagrave	d				18 44													19 04							19 14
Harlington	d				18 50													19 10							19 20
Flitwick	d				18 54													19 14							19 24
Bedford 7	a		18 37		19 06													19 26					19 06		19 36

Table 52

Saturdays

Brighton, Gatwick Airport and South London - City of London, St.Albans, Luton and Bedford

		SE	FC ■	FC	SN	FC	SE ■	SE	SN	SE ■	FC	FC ■	SE	SN	SE ■	EM ◇■	FC ■	FC ■	SE	FC ■	FC	SN
Brighton	d		18 37						18 44								19 04			19 07		
Preston Park	d		18 41																	19 11		
Hassocks	d		18 47																	19 17		
Burgess Hill	d		18 51																	19 21		
Wivelsfield	d		18 53																	19 23		
Haywards Heath	d		19 02														19 18			19 32		
Balcombe	d																			19 37		
Three Bridges	d		19 12																	19 42		
Gatwick Airport	d		19 16														19 31			19 46		
Redhill	d																					
East Croydon	d		19 32														19 47			20 02		
Sevenoaks	d	18 36					18 44			18 49			18 55		18 59				19 06			
Bat & Ball	d												18 58									
Otford	d												19 01									
Shoreham (Kent)	d												19 04									
Eynsford	d												19 08									
Swanley	d												19 13									
St Mary Cray	d												19 17									
Bickley	d												19 21									
Bromley South	d												19 24									
Shortlands	d												19 27									
Ravensbourne	d												19 29									
Beckenham Hill	d												19 31									
Bellingham	d												19 33									
Catford	d												19 36									
Crofton Park	d												19 38									
Nunhead	d												19 41									
Peckham Rye	d				18 42								19 43	18 57								19 12
Denmark Hill	d												19 47									
Sutton (Surrey)	d																					
West Sutton	d																					
Sutton Common	d																					
St Helier	d																					
Morden South	d																					
South Merton	d																					
Wimbledon Chase	d																					
Wimbledon	d																					
Haydons Road	d																					
Tooting	d																					
Carshalton	d																					
Hackbridge	d																					
Mitcham Junction	d																					
Mitcham Eastfields	d																					
Streatham	d																					
Tulse Hill	d				18 50						18 50			19 05								19 20
London Bridge	a	19 21					19 10	18 43		19 13					19 24				19 52			
	d	19 21					19 11	18 44		19 14					19 25				19 52			
Herne Hill	d			18 38							18 58										19 08	
Loughborough Jn	d			18 46							19 06										19 16	
Elephant & Castle	d			18 58							19 18										19 28	
London Blackfriars	d			19a06							19a26										19a36	
Farringdon	d																					
St Pancras International	d					18 38						18 50				19 00		19 04				
St Pancras International	a																					
	d																					
Kentish Town	d					18 42																
West Hampstead Thameslink	d					18 46						18 58										
Cricklewood	d					18 49																
Hendon	d					18 52																
Mill Hill Broadway	d					18 55																
Elstree & Borehamwood	d					19 00						19 08										
Radlett	d					19 04																
St Albans City	d					19 10						19 15						19 25				
Harpenden	d					19 16						19 22						19 32				
Luton Airport Parkway	d					19 22						19 28				19 23		19 38				
Luton	d					19a26						19 31						19 41				
Leagrave	d											19 34						19 44				
Harlington	d											19 40						19 50				
Flitwick	d											19 44						19 54				
Bedford	a											19 56				19 37		20 06				

Table 52

Saturdays

Brighton, Gatwick Airport and South London - City of London, St.Albans, Luton and Bedford

		FC	SE	SN	SE ■	FC	FC ■	SN ■	SE	SN	SE ■	EM ◇■	FC ■	FC ■	SE	FC ■	FC	SN	SN	SE ■	FC	FC	SE
Brighton	d			19 14				19 22					19 34			19 37			19 44				
Preston Park	d															19 41							
Hassocks	d															19 47							
Burgess Hill	d															19 51							
Wivelsfield	d															19 53							
Haywards Heath	d												19 48			20 02							
Balcombe	d																						
Three Bridges	d															20 12							
Gatwick Airport	d												20 01			20 16							
Redhill	d																						
East Croydon	d												20 17			20 32							
Sevenoaks	d				19 19				19 25		19 29				19 36					19 49			19 55
Bat & Ball	d								19 28														19 58
Otford	d								19 31														20 01
Shoreham (Kent)	d								19 34														20 04
Eynsford	d								19 38														20 08
Swanley	d								19 43														20 13
St Mary Cray	d								19 47														20 17
Bickley	d								19 51														20 21
Bromley South	d								19 54														20 24
Shortlands	d								19 57														20 27
Ravensbourne	d								19 59														20 29
Beckenham Hill	d								20 01														20 31
Bellingham	d								20 03														20 33
Catford	d								20 06														20 36
Crofton Park	d								20 08														20 38
Nunhead	d								20 11														20 41
Peckham Rye	d								20 13	19 27								19 42					20 43
Denmark Hill	d								20 17														20 47
Sutton (Surrey)	d																						
West Sutton	d																						
Sutton Common	d																						
St Helier	d																						
Morden South	d																						
South Merton	d																						
Wimbledon Chase	d																						
Wimbledon	d																						
Haydons Road	d																						
Tooting	d																						
Carshalton	d																						
Hackbridge	d																						
Mitcham Junction	d																						
Mitcham Eastfields	d																						
Streatham	d																						
Tulse Hill	d					19 20				19 35								19 50				19 50	
London Bridge	a		19 13		19 43						19 54				20 22					20 13			
	d		19 14		19 44						19 55				20 22					20 14			
Herne Hill	d					19 28											19 38					19 58	
Loughborough Jn	d					19 36											19 46					20 06	
Elephant & Castle	d					19 48											19 58					20 18	
London Blackfriars	d					19a56											20a06					20a26	
Farringdon	d																						
St Pancras International	d	19 08					19 20					19 30		19 34							19 48		
St Pancras International	a																						
	d																						
Kentish Town	d	19 12																			19 53		
West Hampstead Thameslink	d	19 16					19 28							19 40							19 57		
Cricklewood	d	19 19																			20 00		
Hendon	d	19 22																			20 03		
Mill Hill Broadway	d	19 25																			20 06		
Elstree & Borehamwood	d	19 30					19 38														20 11		
Radlett	d	19 34																			20 16		
St Albans City	d	19 40					19 45							19 56							20 22		
Harpenden	d	19 46					19 52							20 02							20 28		
Luton Airport Parkway	d	19 52					19 58					19 51		20 08							20 34		
Luton	d	19a56					20 01							20 11							20 37		
Leagrave	d						20 04							20 14							20 40		
Harlington	d						20 10							20 20							20 46		
Flitwick	d						20 14							20 24							20 50		
Bedford	a						20 26					20 06		20 36							21 02		

Table 52

Saturdays

Brighton, Gatwick Airport and South London - City of London, St.Albans, Luton and Bedford

Station		SN	SE ■	EM ◇■	FC	FC ■	FC ■	SE	FC ■	SN	SE ■	FC	FC	SE	SN	SE ■	FC	EM ◇■	FC ■	FC ■	SE	FC ■	SN	SE ■
Brighton ■	d					20 04			20 07	20 14									20 34			20 37	20 44	
Preston Park	d								20 11													20 41		
Hassocks ■	d								20 17													20 47		
Burgess Hill ■	d								20 21													20 51		
Wivelsfield ■	d								20 23													20 53		
Haywards Heath ■	d					20 18			20 32										20 48			21 02		
Balcombe	d								20 37															
Three Bridges ■	d								20 42													21 12		
Gatwick Airport ■	d					20 31			20 46										21 01			21 16		
Redhill	d																							
East Croydon	d					20 47			21 02										21 17			21 32		
Sevenoaks ■	d		19 59					20 06			20 19			20 25		20 [illegible]					20 36			20 49
Bat & Ball	d													20 28										
Otford ■	d													20 31										
Shoreham (Kent)	d													20 34										
Eynsford	d													20 38										
Swanley ■	d													20 43										
St Mary Cray ■	d													20 47										
Bickley	d													20 51										
Bromley South	d													20 54										
Shortlands ■	d													20 57										
Ravensbourne	d													20 59										
Beckenham Hill	d													21 01										
Bellingham	d													21 03										
Catford	d													21 06										
Crofton Park	d													21 08										
Nunhead ■	d													21 11										
Peckham Rye ■	d	19 57												21 13	20 27									
Denmark Hill ■	d													21 17										
Sutton (Surrey) ■	d				19 37												20 07							
West Sutton	d				19 40												20 10							
Sutton Common	d				19 42												20 12							
St Helier	d				19 45												20 15							
Morden South	d				19 47												20 17							
South Merton	d				19 49												20 19							
Wimbledon Chase	d				19 51												20 21							
Wimbledon ■ ⊖	d				20b00												20c30							
Haydons Road	d				20 02												20 32							
Tooting	d				20 05												20 35							
Carshalton	d																							
Hackbridge	d																							
Mitcham Junction	d																							
Mitcham Eastfields	d																							
Streatham ■	d				20 10												20 40							
Tulse Hill ■	d	20 05			20 17								20 20		20 35		20 47							
London Bridge ■ ⊖	a		20 24		20a30			20 52			20 43					20 54	21a00				21 22			21 13
	d		20 25					20 52			20 44					20 55					21 22			21 14
Herne Hill ■	d												20 28											
Loughborough Jn	d												20 36											
Elephant & Castle	d												20 48											
London Blackfriars ■ ⊖	d												20a56											
Farringdon ■ ⊖	d																							
St Pancras International ■ ⊖	d			20 00			20 04					20 18						20 30		20 34				
St Pancras International ■ ⊖	a																							
	d																							
Kentish Town ⊖	d											20 23												
West Hampstead Thameslink ⊖	d						20 10					20 27								40				
Cricklewood	d											20 30												
Hendon	d											20 33												
Mill Hill Broadway	d											20 36												
Elstree & Borehamwood	d											20 41												
Radlett	d											20 46												
St Albans City	d						20 26					20 52								20 56				
Harpenden	d						20 32					[illegible]								21 02				
Luton Airport Parkway ■	d						20 38					21 04						20 51		21 08				
Luton ■	d			20 23			20 41					21 07								21 11				
Leagrave	d						20 44					21 10								21 14				
Harlington	d						20 50					21 16								21 20				
Flitwick	d						20 54					21 20								21 24				
Bedford ■	a			20 37			21 06					21 32						21 06		21 36				

Table 52

Saturdays

Brighton, Gatwick Airport and South London - City of London, St.Albans, Luton and Bedford

Station		FC	FC	SE	SN	SE ■	EM ◇■	FC ■	SE	FC ■	FC	SN	SE ■	FC	FC	SE	SN	SE ■	EM ◇■	FC ■	FC	SE	FC ■	SN	SE ■
Brighton ■	d									21 07		21 14											21 37	21 44	
Preston Park	d									21 11													21 41		
Hassocks ■	d									21 17													21 47		
Burgess Hill ■	d									21 21													21 51		
Wivelsfield ■	d									21 23													21 53		
Haywards Heath ■	d									21 32													22 02		
Balcombe	d									21 37															
Three Bridges ■	d									21 42													22 12		
Gatwick Airport ■	d									21 46													22 16		
Redhill	d																								
East Croydon	d									22 02													22 32		
Sevenoaks ■	d			20 55		20 59			21 06				21 19			21 25		21 29				21 36			21 49
Bat & Ball	d			20 58												21 28									
Otford ■	d			21 01												21 31									
Shoreham (Kent)	d			21 04												21 34									
Eynsford	d			21 08												21 38									
Swanley ■	d			21 13												21 43									
St Mary Cray ■	d			21 17												21 47									
Bickley	d			21 21												21 51									
Bromley South	d			21 24												21 54									
Shortlands ■	d			21 27												21 57									
Ravensbourne	d			21 29												21 59									
Beckenham Hill	d			21 31												22 01									
Bellingham	d			21 33												22 03									
Catford	d			21 36												22 06									
Crofton Park	d			21 38												22 08									
Nunhead ■	d			21 41												22 11									
Peckham Rye ■	d			21 43	20 57											22 13	21 27								
Denmark Hill ■	d			21 47												22 17									
Sutton (Surrey) ■	d										20 37										21 07				
West Sutton	d										20 40										21 10				
Sutton Common	d										20 42										21 12				
St Helier	d										20 45										21 15				
Morden South	d										20 47										21 17				
South Merton	d										20 49										21 19				
Wimbledon Chase	d										20 51										21 21				
Wimbledon ■ ⊖	d										21e00										21f30				
Haydons Road	d										21 02										21 32				
Tooting	d										21 05										21 35				
Carshalton	d																								
Hackbridge	d																								
Mitcham Junction	d																								
Mitcham Eastfields	d																								
Streatham ■	d										21 10										21 40				
Tulse Hill ■	d		20 50		21 05						21 17				21 20		21 35				21 47				
London Bridge ■ ⊖	a					21 24			21 52		21a30		21 43					21 54			22a00	22 22			22 13
	d					21 25			21 52				21 44					21 55				22 22			22 14
Herne Hill ■	d		20 58												21 28										
Loughborough Jn	d		21 06												21 36										
Elephant & Castle	d		21 18												21 48										
London Blackfriars ■ ⊖	d		21a26												21a56										
Farringdon ■ ⊖	d																								
St Pancras International ■ ⊖	d	20 48					21 00	21 04						21 18					21 30	21 34					
St Pancras International ■ ⊖	a																								
	d																								
Kentish Town ⊖	d	20 53												21 23											
West Hampstead Thameslink ⊖	d	20 57						21 10						21 27						21 40					
Cricklewood	d	21 00												21 30											
Hendon	d	21 03												21 33											
Mill Hill Broadway	d	21 06												21 36											
Elstree & Borehamwood	d	21 11												21 41											
Radlett	d	21 16												21 46											
St Albans City	d	21 22						21 26						21 52						21 56					
Harpenden	d	21 28						21 32						21 58						22 02					
Luton Airport Parkway ■	d	21 34						21 38						22 04					21 51	22 08					
Luton ■	d	21 37					21 23	21 41						22 07						22 11					
Leagrave	d	21 40						21 44						22 10						22 14					
Harlington	d	21 46						21 50						22 16						22 20					
Flitwick	d	21 50						21 54						22 20						22 24					
Bedford ■	a	22 02					21 38	22 06						22 32					22 09	22 36					

Table 52

Brighton, Gatwick Airport and South London - City of London, St.Albans, Luton and Bedford

Saturdays

		FC	FC	SE	SN	SE ■	FC	EM ◇■	FC ■	SE	FC ■	SN	SE ■	FC	FC	EM ◇■	EM ◇■	SE	SN	SE ■	FC ■	FC ■	SN	SE ■
																A	B							
Brighton ■	d										22 07	22 14										22 33	[illegible]	
Preston Park	d										22 11													
Hassocks ■	d										22 17													
Burgess Hill ■	d										22 21													
Wivelsfield ■	d										22 23													
Haywards Heath ■	d										22 32											22 54		
Balcombe	d										22 37											23 00		
Three Bridges ■	d										22 42											23b12		
Gatwick Airport ■	d										22 46											23 16		
Redhill	d																							
East Croydon	d										23 02											23 32		
Sevenoaks ■	d			21 55		21 59				22 06			22 19					22 25		22 29				22 49
Bat & Ball	d			21 58														22 28						
Otford ■	d			22 01														22 31						
Shoreham (Kent)	d			22 04														22 34						
Eynsford	d			22 08														22 38						
Swanley ■	d			22 13														22 43						
St Mary Cray ■	d			22 17														22 47						
Bickley	d			22 21														22 51						
Bromley South	d			22 24														22 54						
Shortlands ■	d			22 27														22 57						
Ravensbourne	d			22 29														[illegible]						
Beckenham Hill	d			22 31														[illegible]						
Bellingham	d			22 33														[illegible]						
Catford	d			22 36														23 06						
Crofton Park	d			22 38														23 08						
Nunhead ■	d			22 41														23 11						
Peckham Rye ■	d			22 43	21 57													23 13	22 27					
Denmark Hill ■	d			22 47														23 17						
Sutton (Surrey) ■	d						21 37																	
West Sutton	d						21 40																	
Sutton Common	d						21 42																	
St Helier	d						21 45																	
Morden South	d						21 47																	
South Merton	d						21 49																	
Wimbledon Chase	d						21 51																	
Wimbledon ■ ⊖	d						22c00																	
Haydons Road	d						22 02																	
Tooting	d						22 05																	
Carshalton	d																							
Hackbridge	d																							
Mitcham Junction	d																							
Mitcham Eastfields	d																							
Streatham ■	d						22 10																	
Tulse Hill ■	d		21 50				22 17								22 20									
London Bridge ■ ⊖	a				22 05	22 24	22a30			22 52			22 43						22 35	22 54				23 13
	d					22 25				22 52			22 44							22 55				23 14
Herne Hill ■	d		21 58												22 28									
Loughborough Jn	d		22 06												22 36									
Elephant & Castle	d		22 18												[illegible]									
London Blackfriars ■ ⊖	d		22a26												[illegible]									
Farringdon ■ ⊖	d																							
St Pancras International ■ ⊖	d	21 48							22 04					22 18							22 32			
St Pancras International ■ ⊖	a																							
	d							22 00								22 25	22 25							
Kentish Town ⊖	d	21 53												22 23										
West Hampstead Thameslink ⊖	d	21 57							22 10					22 27							22 40			
Cricklewood	d	[illegible]												22 30										
Hendon	d	22 03												22 33										
Mill Hill Broadway	d	22 06												[illegible]										
Elstree & Borehamwood	d	22 11												[illegible]										
Radlett	d	22 16												22 46										
St Albans City	d	22 22							22 26					22 52							22 56			
Harpenden	d	22 28							22 33					22 58							23 02			
Luton Airport Parkway ■	d	22 34							22 38					23 04							23 08			
Luton ■	d	22 37						22 24	22 41					23 07		[illegible]	22 48				23 11			
Leagrave	d	22 40							22 44					23 10							23 14			
Harlington	d	22 46							22 50					23 16							23 20			
Flitwick	d	22 50							22 54					23 20							23 24			
Bedford ■	a	23 02						22 41	23 06					23 32		23 02	23 03				23 36			

A not 11 December

B 29 May

b arr. 2305

Table 52

Brighton, Gatwick Airport and South London - City of London, St.Albans, Luton and Bedford

		[illegible]	[illegible]	[illegible]	[illegible]	■	FC ■	FC ■	SN	FC	SE ■	SN	FC ■	FC ■	SN	FC	SN
Brighton ■	d							23 11	23 14					23 37	23 44		
Preston Park	d													23 41			
Hassocks ■	d							23 19						23 47			
Burgess Hill ■	d							23 23						23 51			
Wivelsfield ■	d													23 53			
Haywards Heath ■	d							23 28						23 59			
Balcombe	d													00 04			
Three Bridges ■	d							23 38						00 10			
Gatwick Airport ■	d							23 43						00 15			
Redhill	d													00 22			
East Croydon	d							00 04						00 36			
Sevenoaks ■	d					22 59					23 25						
Bat & Ball	d																
Otford ■	d																
Shoreham (Kent)	d																
Eynsford	d																
Swanley ■	d																
St Mary Cray ■	d																
Bickley	d																
Bromley South ■	d																
Shortlands ■	d																
Ravensbourne	d																
Beckenham Hill	d																
Bellingham	d																
Catford	d																
Crofton Park	d																
Nunhead ■	d																
Peckham Rye ■	d				22 57							23 27					23 57
Denmark Hill ■	d																
Sutton (Surrey) ■	d		22 07														
West Sutton	d		22 10														
Sutton Common	d		22 12														
St Helier	d		22 15														
Morden South	d		22 17														
South Merton	d		22 19														
Wimbledon Chase	d		22 21														
Wimbledon ■ ⊖	d		22c30														
Haydons Road	d		22 32														
Tooting	d		22 35														
Carshalton	d																
Hackbridge	d																
Mitcham Junction	d																
Mitcham Eastfields	d																
Streatham ■	d		22 40														
Tulse Hill ■	d		22 47	22 50													
London Bridge ■ ⊖	a		23a00		23 05	23 24					23 53	23 35					00 07
	d					23 25					23 53						
Herne Hill ■	d			22 58													
Loughborough Jn	d			23 06													
Elephant & Castle	d			23 18													
London Blackfriars ■ ⊖	d			23a26													
Farringdon ■ ⊖	d																
St Pancras International ■ ⊖	d	22 48					23 02			23 18			23 32			23 48	
St Pancras International ■ ⊖	a																
	d																
Kentish Town ⊖	d	22 53								23 23						23 53	
West Hampstead Thameslink ⊖	d	22 57					23 10			23 27			23 40			23 57	
Cricklewood	d	23 00								23 30						00 01	
Hendon	d	23 03								23 33						00 03	
Mill Hill Broadway	d	23 06								23 36						00 06	
Elstree & Borehamwood	d	23 11								23 41						00 11	
Radlett	d	23 16								23 46						00 16	
St Albans City	d	23 22					23 26			23 52			23 56			00 22	
Harpenden	d	23 28					23 32			23 58			00 02			00 28	
Luton Airport Parkway ■	d	23 34					23 38			00 04			00 08			00 34	
Luton ■	d	23 37					23 41			00 07			00 11			00 37	
Leagrave	d	23 40					23 44			00 10			00 14			00 40	
Harlington	d	23 46					23 50			00 16			00 20			00 46	
Flitwick	d	23 50					23 54			00 20			00 24			00 50	
Bedford ■	a	00 02					00 06			00 32			00 36			01 02	

Table 52

Sundays

Brighton, Gatwick Airport and South London - City of London, St.Albans, Luton and Bedford

Station		FC A	FC ■ A	FC ■ A	FC A	FC ■ A	FC ■ A	FC A	SN A	FC ■	SN ■	FC	FC ■	FC	FC 🚌	FC	SN B 🚌	FC ■	FC	SN ■ C	FC ■	FC 🚌	FC ■ C
Brighton	d			23p11			23p37				00 10						03 50	05 44		06b16	06 13		06 45
Preston Park	d						23p41													06 19			
Hassocks	d			23p19			23p47											05 52		06 26			06 53
Burgess Hill	d			23p23			23p51											05 56		06 29	06 26		06 57
Wivelsfield	d						23p53													06 32			
Haywards Heath	d			23p28			23p59										04 25	06 01		06 37	06 31		07 02
Balcombe	d						00 04																
Three Bridges	d			23p38			00 10										04a45	06 10		06 46	06 40		07 12
Gatwick Airport	d			23p43			00 15											06 15		06a51	06 45		07 17
Redhill	d						00 22																
East Croydon 🚌	d			00 04			00 36											06 32			07 02		07 33
Sevenoaks	d																						
Bat & Ball	d																						
Otford	d																						
Shoreham (Kent)	d																						
Eynsford	d																						
Swanley	d																						
St Mary Cray	d																						
Bickley	d																						
Bromley South	d																						
Shortlands	d																						
Ravensbourne	d																						
Beckenham Hill	d																						
Bellingham	d																						
Catford	d																						
Crofton Park	d																						
Nunhead	d																						
Peckham Rye	d								22p57														
Denmark Hill	d																						
Sutton (Surrey)	d																						
West Sutton	d																						
Sutton Common	d																						
St Helier	d																						
Morden South	d																						
South Merton	d																						
Wimbledon Chase	d																						
Wimbledon ⊖ 🚌	d																						
Haydons Road	d																						
Tooting	d																						
Carshalton	d																						
Hackbridge	d																						
Mitcham Junction	d																						
Mitcham Eastfields	d																						
Streatham	d																						
Tulse Hill	d								00 07														
London Bridge ⊖	a																						
	d																						
Herne Hill	d														01 00							06 05	
Loughborough Jn	d																						
Elephant & Castle	d																						
London Blackfriars ⊖	d														01 15							06 20	
Farringdon ⊖	d																						
St Pancras International ⊖	d	22p48	23p02		23p18	23p32		23p48		00 02		00 18	00 32	01 02		01 32							
St Pancras International ⊖	a														01 30							06 35	
	d																		06 02				
Kentish Town ⊖	d	22p53			23p23			23p53				00 23	00 37	01 07		01 37			06 06				
West Hampstead Thameslink ⊖	d	22p57	23p10		23p27	23p40		23p57		00 10		00 27	00 41	01 11		01 41			06 10				
Cricklewood	d	23p00			23p30			00 01				00 30	00 44	01 14		01 44			06 13				
Hendon	d	23p03			23p33			00 03				00 33	00 47	01 17		01 47			06 16				
Mill Hill Broadway	d	23p06			23p36			00 06				00 36	00 50	01 20		01 50			06 19				
Elstree & Borehamwood	d	23p11			23p41			00 11				00 41	00 55	01 25		01 55			06 24				
Radlett	d	23p16			23p46			00 16				00 46	01 00	01 30		02 00			06 29				
St Albans City	d	23p22	23p26		23p52	23p56		00 22		00 26		00 52	01 06	01 36		02 06			06 36				
Harpenden	d	23p28	23p32		23p58	00 02		00 28		00 32		00 58	01 12	01 42		02 12			06 42				
Luton Airport Parkway	d	23p34	23p38		00 04	00 08		00 34		00 38		01 04	01 18	01 48		02 18			06 48				
Luton	d	23p37	23p41		00 07	00 11		00 37		00 41		01 07	01 21	01 51		02 21			06 51				
Leagrave	d	23p40	23p44		00 10	00 14		00 40		00 44		01 10	01 24	01 54		02 24			06 54				
Harlington	d	23p46	23p50		00 16	00 20		00 46		00 50		01 16	01 30	02 00		02 30			07 00				
Flitwick	d	23p50	23p54		00 20	00 24		00 50		00 54		01 20	01 34	02 04		02 34			07 04				
Bedford	a	00 02	00 06		00 32	00 36		01 02		01 06		01 32	01 46	02 16		02 46			07 16				

A not 23 May
B 23 May
C until 5 September
b arr. 0609

Table 52

Sundays

Brighton, Gatwick Airport and South London - City of London, St.Albans, Luton and Bedford

Station		SE	FC	SN	FC ■ A	FC ■ B	SE ■	SE	SE ■	FC	SN	SN	FC ■ A	FC ■ B	SE ■	SE	SE	FC	SN	SN	FC ■ A	FC ■ B	SE ■
Brighton	d				07 16	07 17							07 44	07 45							08 16	08 17	
Preston Park	d																						
Hassocks	d												07 52	07 53									
Burgess Hill	d				07 26	07 27							07 56	07 57							08 26	08 27	
Wivelsfield	d																						
Haywards Heath	d				07 31	07 32							08 01	08 02							08 31	08 32	
Balcombe	d																						
Three Bridges	d				07 40	07 42							08 10	08 12							08 40	08 42	
Gatwick Airport	d				07 45	07 47							08 15	08 17							08 45	08 47	
Redhill	d																						
East Croydon 🚌	d			07 14	08 02	08 03						07 44	08 32	08 33						08 14	09 02	09 03	
Sevenoaks	d						07 19		07 32						07 49		07 54						08 19
Bat & Ball	d																07 57						
Otford	d																08 00						
Shoreham (Kent)	d																08 03						
Eynsford	d																08 07						
Swanley	d																08 12						
St Mary Cray	d																08 16						
Bickley	d	06 50						07 20								07 50	08 20						
Bromley South	d	06 53						07 23								07 53	08 23						
Shortlands	d	06 56						07 26								07 55	08 26						
Ravensbourne	d	06 58						07 28								07 58	08 28						
Beckenham Hill	d	07 00						07 30								08 00	08 30						
Bellingham	d	07 02						07 32								08 02	08 32						
Catford	d	07 05						07 35								08 05	08 35						
Crofton Park	d	07 07						07 37								08 07	08 37						
Nunhead	d	07 10						07 40								08 10	08 40						
Peckham Rye	d	07 12		07 39				07 42			07 34	08 09				08 12	08 42		08 04	08 39			
Denmark Hill	d	07 16						07 46								08 16	08 46						
Sutton (Surrey)	d																						
West Sutton	d																						
Sutton Common	d																						
St Helier	d																						
Morden South	d																						
South Merton	d																						
Wimbledon Chase	d																						
Wimbledon ⊖ 🚌	d																						
Haydons Road	d																						
Tooting	d																						
Carshalton	d																						
Hackbridge	d																						
Mitcham Junction	d																						
Mitcham Eastfields	d																						
Streatham	d																						
Tulse Hill	d										07 42								08 12				
London Bridge ⊖	a						07 44		07 58						08 14								08 44
	d						07 45		07 59						08 15								08 45
Herne Hill	d																						
Loughborough Jn	d																						
Elephant & Castle	d																						
London Blackfriars ⊖	d																						
Farringdon ⊖	d																						
St Pancras International ⊖	d																						
St Pancras International ⊖	a																						
	d		07 02							07 32								08 02					
Kentish Town ⊖	d		07 06							07 36								08 06					
West Hampstead Thameslink ⊖	d		07 10							07 40								08 10					
Cricklewood	d		07 13							07 43								08 13					
Hendon	d		07 16							07 46								08 16					
Mill Hill Broadway	d		07 19							07 49								08 19					
Elstree & Borehamwood	d		07 24							07 54								08 24					
Radlett	d		07 29							07 59								08 29					
St Albans City	d		07 36							08 06								08 36					
Harpenden	d		07 42							08 12								08 42					
Luton Airport Parkway	d		07 48							08 18								08 48					
Luton	d		07 51							08 21								08 51					
Leagrave	d		07 54							08 24								08 54					
Harlington	d		08 00							08 30								09 00					
Flitwick	d		08 04							08 34								09 04					
Bedford	a		08 16							08 46								09 16					

A from 12 September
B until 5 September

Table 52

Sundays

Brighton, Gatwick Airport and South London - City of London, St.Albans, Luton and Bedford

		SE	SE	SE ■	FC	SN	SN	FC ■ A	FC ■ B	SE ■	SE	EM ◇■	SE ■	FC	SN	SN	FC ■ A	FC ■ B	SE ■	SE	SE	EM ◇■
Brighton	d							08 44	08 45								09 16	09 17				
Preston Park	d																					
Hassocks	d							08 52	08 53													
Burgess Hill	d							08 56	08 57								09 26	09 27				
Wivelsfield	d																					
Haywards Heath	d							09 01	09 02								09 31	09 32				
Balcombe	d																					
Three Bridges	d							09 10	09 12								09 40	09 42				
Gatwick Airport	d							09 15	09 17								09 45	09 47				
Redhill	d																					
East Croydon	d						08 44	09 32	09 33							09 14	10 02	10 03				
Sevenoaks	d	08 24	08 25	08 33						08 49	08 54		09 03						09 19	09 24	09 25	
Bat & Ball	d	08 27									08 57									09 27		
Otford	d	08 30									09 00									09 30		
Shoreham (Kent)	d	08 33									09 03									09 33		
Eynsford	d	08 37									09 07									09 37		
Swanley	d	08 42									09 12									09 42		
St Mary Cray	d	08 46									09 16									09 46		
Bickley	d	08 50									09 20									09 50		
Bromley South	d	08 53									09 23									09 53		
Shortlands	d	08 56									09 26									09 56		
Ravensbourne	d	08 58									09 28									09 58		
Beckenham Hill	d	09 00									09 30									10 00		
Bellingham	d	09 02									09 32									10 02		
Catford	d	09 05									09 35									10 05		
Crofton Park	d	09 07									09 37									10 07		
Nunhead	d	09 10									09 40									10 10		
Peckham Rye	d	09 12				08 34	09 09				09 42				09 04	09 39				10 12		
Denmark Hill	d	09 16									09 46									10 16		
Sutton (Surrey)	d																					
West Sutton	d																					
Sutton Common	d																					
St Helier	d																					
Morden South	d																					
South Merton	d																					
Wimbledon Chase	d																					
Wimbledon	d																					
Haydons Road	d																					
Tooting	d																					
Carshalton	d																					
Hackbridge	d																					
Mitcham Junction	d																					
Mitcham Eastfields	d																					
Streatham	d																					
Tulse Hill	d					08 42									09 12							
London Bridge	a		09 09	08 58						09 14			09 28						09 44		10 10	
	d		09 10	08 59						09 15			09 29						09 45		10 11	
Herne Hill	d																					
Loughborough Jn	d																					
Elephant & Castle	d																					
London Blackfriars	d																					
Farringdon	d																					
St Pancras International	d											09 00										09 30
St Pancras International	a																					
	d				08 32									09 02								
Kentish Town	d				08 36									09 06								
West Hampstead Thameslink	d				08 40									09 10								
Cricklewood	d				08 43									09 13								
Hendon	d				08 46									09 16								
Mill Hill Broadway	d				08 49									09 19								
Elstree & Borehamwood	d				08 54									09 24								
Radlett	d				08 59									09 29								
St Albans City	d				09 06									09 36								
Harpenden	d				09 12									09 42								
Luton Airport Parkway	d				09 18							09 28		09 48								
Luton	d				09 21									09 51								10 01
Leagrave	d				09 24									09 54								
Harlington	d				09 30									10 00								
Flitwick	d				09 34									10 04								
Bedford	a				09 46							09 52		10 16								10 21

A from 12 September

B until 5 September

Table 52

Sundays

Brighton, Gatwick Airport and South London - City of London, St.Albans, Luton and Bedford

		SE ■	FC ■	SN	FC	SN	FC ■ A	FC ■ B	SE ■	SE	EM ◇■	SE ■	FC ■	SN	FC	SN	FC ■ A	FC	FC ■ B	FC ■	SE ■	SE	SE	EM ◇■
Brighton	d						09 44	09 45									10 16		10 17					
Preston Park	d																							
Hassocks	d						09 52	09 53																
Burgess Hill	d						09 56	09 57									10 26		10 27					
Wivelsfield	d																							
Haywards Heath	d						10 01	10 02									10 31		10 32					
Balcombe	d																							
Three Bridges	d						10 10	10 12									10 40		10 42					
Gatwick Airport	d						10 15	10 17									10 45		10 47					
Redhill	d																							
East Croydon	d					09 44	10 32	10 33								10 14	11 02		11 03					
Sevenoaks	d	09 33							09 49	09 54		10 03									10 19	10 24	10 24	
Bat & Ball	d									09 57												10 27		
Otford	d									10 00												10 30		
Shoreham (Kent)	d									10 03												10 33		
Eynsford	d									10 07												10 37		
Swanley	d									10 12												10 42		
St Mary Cray	d									10 16												10 46		
Bickley	d									10 20												10 50		
Bromley South	d									10 23												10 53		
Shortlands	d									10 26												10 56		
Ravensbourne	d									10 28												10 58		
Beckenham Hill	d									10 30												11 00		
Bellingham	d									10 32												11 02		
Catford	d									10 35												11 05		
Crofton Park	d									10 37												11 07		
Nunhead	d									10 40												11 10		
Peckham Rye	d			09 34		10 09				10 42				10 04		10 39						11 12		
Denmark Hill	d									10 46												11 16		
Sutton (Surrey)	d																							
West Sutton	d																							
Sutton Common	d																							
St Helier	d																							
Morden South	d																							
South Merton	d																							
Wimbledon Chase	d																							
Wimbledon	d																							
Haydons Road	d																							
Tooting	d																							
Carshalton	d																							
Hackbridge	d																							
Mitcham Junction	d																							
Mitcham Eastfields	d																							
Streatham	d																							
Tulse Hill	d			09 42										10 12										
London Bridge	a	09 58							10 14			10 28									10 44		11 09	
	d	09 59							10 15			10 29									10 45		11 10	
Herne Hill	d																							
Loughborough Jn	d																							
Elephant & Castle	d																							
London Blackfriars	d																							
Farringdon	d																							
St Pancras International	d										10 00													10 30
St Pancras International	a																							
	d		09 32		09 36								10 02		10 06					10 17				
Kentish Town	d				09 40										10 10									
West Hampstead Thameslink	d		09 40		09 44								10 10		10 14					10 25				
Cricklewood	d				09 47										10 17									
Hendon	d				09 50										10 20									
Mill Hill Broadway	d				09 53										10 23									
Elstree & Borehamwood	d				09 58										10 28									
Radlett	d				10 02										10 32									
St Albans City	d		09 56		10 08								10 26		10 38					10 42				
Harpenden	d		10 02		10 14								10 32		10 44					10 48				
Luton Airport Parkway	d		10 08		10 20						10 29		10 38		10 50					10 54				
Luton	d		10 11		10a23								10 41		10a53					10 57				11 02
Leagrave	d		10 14										10 44							11 00				
Harlington	d		10 20										10 50							11 06				
Flitwick	d		10 24										10 54							11 10				
Bedford	a		10 36								10 50		11 06							11 22				11 26

A from 12 September

B until 5 September

Table 52

Sundays

Brighton, Gatwick Airport and South London - City of London, St.Albans, Luton and Bedford

		SE 1	FC 1	SN	FC	FC	SN	FC 1 A	FC 1 B	FC 1	SE 1	SE	FC	EM ◇1	FC	SE 1	FC 1	SN	FC	SN	FC 1 A	FC 1 B	FC 1	SE 1	FC
Brighton	d							10 44	10 45												11 16	11 17			
Preston Park	d																								
Hassocks	d							10 52	10 53																
Burgess Hill	d							10 56	10 57												11 26	11 27			
Wivelsfield	d																								
Haywards Heath	d							11 01	11 02												11 31	11 32			
Balcombe	d																								
Three Bridges	d							11 10	11 12												11 40	11 42			
Gatwick Airport	d							11 15	11 17												11 45	11 47			
Redhill	d																								
East Croydon	d						10 44	11 32	11 33											11 14	12 02	12 03			
Sevenoaks	d	10 33									10 49	10 54				11 03								11 19	
Bat & Ball	d											10 57													
Otford	d											11 00													
Shoreham (Kent)	d											11 03													
Eynsford	d											11 07													
Swanley	d											11 12													
St Mary Cray	d											11 16													
Bickley	d											11 20													
Bromley South	d											11 23													
Shortlands	d											11 26													
Ravensbourne	d											11 28													
Beckenham Hill	d											11 30													
Bellingham	d											11 32													
Catford	d											11 35													
Crofton Park	d											11 37													
Nunhead	d											11 40													
Peckham Rye	d			10 34			11 09					11 42						11 04		11 39					
Denmark Hill	d											11 46													
Sutton (Surrey)	d				10 16										10 46										
West Sutton	d				10 19										10 49										
Sutton Common	d				10 21										10 51										
St Helier	d				10 24										10 54										
Morden South	d				10 26										10 56										
South Merton	d				10 28										10 58										
Wimbledon Chase	d				10 30										11 00										
Wimbledon ⊖	d				10 33										11 03										
Haydons Road	d				10 35										11 05										
Tooting	d				10 38										11 08										
Carshalton	d																								
Hackbridge	d																								
Mitcham Junction	d																								
Mitcham Eastfields	d																								
Streatham	d				10 43										11 13										
Tulse Hill	d			10 42	10 47								10 55		11 17			11 12							
London Bridge ⊖	a	10 58			10a59						11 14				11a29	11 28								11 44	
	d	10 59									11 15					11 29								11 45	
Herne Hill	d												11 03												
Loughborough Jn	d												11 11												
Elephant & Castle	d												11 23												
London Blackfriars ⊖	d												11a31												
Farringdon ⊖	d																								
St Pancras International ⊖	d													11 00											
St Pancras International ⊖	a																								
	d		10 32			10 36				10 47							11 02		11 06				11 17		
Kentish Town ⊖	d					10 40													11 10						
West Hampstead Thameslink ⊖	d		10 40			10 44				10 55							11 10		11 14				11 25		
Cricklewood	d					10 47													11 17						
Hendon	d					10 50													11 20						
Mill Hill Broadway	d					10 53													11 23						
Elstree & Borehamwood	d					10 58													11 28						
Radlett	d					11 02													11 32						
St Albans City	d		10 56			11 08				11 12							11 26		11 38				11 42		
Harpenden	d		11 02			11 14				11 18							11 32		11 44				11 48		
Luton Airport Parkway	d		11 08			11 20				11 24				11 29			11 38		11 50				11 54		
Luton	d		11 11			11a23				11 27				11 32			11 41		11a53				11 57		
Leagrave	d		11 14							11 30							11 44						12 00		
Harlington	d		11 20							11 36							11 50						12 06		
Flitwick	d		11 24							11 40							11 54						12 10		
Bedford	a		11 36							11 52				11 55			12 06						12 22		

A from 12 September

B until 5 September

Table 52

Sundays

Brighton, Gatwick Airport and South London - City of London, St.Albans, Luton and Bedford

		SE	FC	SE	EM ◇1	SE 1	FC 1	SN	FC	SN	FC	FC 1 A	FC 1 B	FC 1	SE 1	SE	FC	EM ◇1	SE 1	FC 1	FC	SN	FC	SN	FC 1 A
Brighton	d											11 44	11 45												12 16
Preston Park	d																								
Hassocks	d											11 52	11 53												
Burgess Hill	d											11 56	11 57												12 26
Wivelsfield	d																								
Haywards Heath	d											12 01	12 02												12 31
Balcombe	d																								
Three Bridges	d											12 10	12 12												12 40
Gatwick Airport	d											12 15	12 17												12 45
Redhill	d																								
East Croydon	d									11 44		12 32	12 33											12 14	13 02
Sevenoaks	d	11 24		11 25		11 33									11 49	11 54			12 03						
Bat & Ball	d	11 27														11 57									
Otford	d	11 30														12 00									
Shoreham (Kent)	d	11 33														12 03									
Eynsford	d	11 37														12 07									
Swanley	d	11 42														12 12									
St Mary Cray	d	11 46														12 16									
Bickley	d	11 50														12 20									
Bromley South	d	11 53														12 23									
Shortlands	d	11 56														12 26									
Ravensbourne	d	11 58														12 28									
Beckenham Hill	d	12 00														12 30									
Bellingham	d	12 02														12 32									
Catford	d	12 05														12 35									
Crofton Park	d	12 07														12 37									
Nunhead	d	12 10														12 40									
Peckham Rye	d	12 12.						11 34		12 09						12 42						12 04		12 39	
Denmark Hill	d	12 16														12 46									
Sutton (Surrey)	d										11 16										11 46				
West Sutton	d										11 19										11 49				
Sutton Common	d										11 21										11 51				
St Helier	d										11 24										11 54				
Morden South	d										11 26										11 56				
South Merton	d										11 28										11 58				
Wimbledon Chase	d										11 30										12 00				
Wimbledon ⊖	d										11 33										12 03				
Haydons Road	d										11 35										1205				
Tooting	d										11 38										12 08				
Carshalton	d																								
Hackbridge	d																								
Mitcham Junction	d																								
Mitcham Eastfields	d																								
Streatham	d										11 43										12 13				
Tulse Hill	d		11 25					11 42			11 47						11 55				12 17	12 12			
London Bridge ⊖	a			12 09		11 58					11a59				12 14				12 28		12a29				
	d			12 10		11 59									12 15				12 29						
Herne Hill	d		11 33														12 03								
Loughborough Jn	d		11 41														12 11								
Elephant & Castle	d		11 53														12 23								
London Blackfriars ⊖	d		12a01														12a31								
Farringdon ⊖	d																								
St Pancras International ⊖	d				11 30													12 00							
St Pancras International ⊖	a																								
	d						11 32		11 36					11 47						12 02			12 06		
Kentish Town ⊖	d								11 40														12 10		
West Hampstead Thameslink ⊖	d						11 40		11 44					11 55						12 10			12 14		
Cricklewood	d								11 47														12 17		
Hendon	d								11 50														12 20		
Mill Hill Broadway	d								11 53														12 23		
Elstree & Borehamwood	d								11 58														12 28		
Radlett	d								12 02														12 32		
St Albans City	d						11 56		12 08					12 12						12 26			12 38		
Harpenden	d						12 02		12 14					12 18						12 32			12 44		
Luton Airport Parkway	d				11 58		12 08		12 20					12 24				12 29		12 38			12 50		
Luton	d				12 02		12 11		12a23					12 27				12 33		12 41			12a53		
Leagrave	d						12 14							12 30						12 44					
Harlington	d						12 20							12 36						12 50					
Flitwick	d						12 24							12 40						12 54					
Bedford	a				12 25		12 36							12 52				12 56		13 06					

A from 12 September

B until 5 September

Brighton, Gatwick Airport and South London - City of London, St.Albans, Luton and Bedford

		FC 1 A	FC 1	SE 1	SE	FC	FC	SE	EM ◇1	SE 1	FC 1	SN	FC	SN	FC 1 B	FC 1 A	FC	FC 1	SE 1	SE	FC	EM ◇1	SE 1	FC 1	SN
Brighton 10	d	12 17													12 44	12 45									
Preston Park	d																								
Hassocks 4	d														12 52	12 53									
Burgess Hill 4	d	12 27													12 56	12 57									
Wivelsfield 4	d																								
Haywards Heath 3	d	12 32													13 01	13 02									
Balcombe	d																								
Three Bridges 4	d	12 42													13 10	13 12									
Gatwick Airport 10	d	12 47													13 15	13 17									
Redhill	d																								
East Croydon	d	13 03												12 44	13 32	13 33									
Sevenoaks 4	d			12 19	12 24			12 25		12 33									12 49	12 54			13 03		
Bat & Ball	d				12 27															12 57					
Otford 4	d				12 30															13 00					
Shoreham (Kent)	d				12 33															13 03					
Eynsford	d				12 37															13 07					
Swanley 4	d				12 42															13 12					
St Mary Cray 4	d				12 46															13 16					
Bickley	d				12 50															13 20					
Bromley South	d				12 53															13 23					
Shortlands 4	d				12 56															13 26					
Ravensbourne	d				12 58															13 28					
Beckenham Hill	d				13 00															13 30					
Bellingham	d				13 02															13 32					
Catford	d				13 05															13 35					
Crofton Park	d				13 07															13 37					
Nunhead 4	d				13 10															13 40					
Peckham Rye 4	d				13 12							12 34		13 09					....	13 42					13 04
Denmark Hill 4	d				13 16															13 46					
Sutton (Surrey) 4	d						12 16																		
West Sutton	d						12 19																		
Sutton Common	d						12 21																		
St Helier	d						12 24																		
Morden South	d						12 26																		
South Merton	d						12 28																		
Wimbledon Chase	d						12 30																		
Wimbledon 6 ⊖	d						12 33																		
Haydons Road	d						12 35																		
Tooting	d						12 38																		
Carshalton	d																								
Hackbridge	d																								
Mitcham Junction	d																								
Mitcham Eastfields	d																								
Streatham 4	d						12 43																		
Tulse Hill 3	d					12 25	12 47					12 42									12 55				13 12
London Bridge 4 ⊖	a			12 44			12a59	13 09		12 58									13 14				13 28		
	d			12 45				13 10		12 59									13 15				13 29		
Herne Hill 4	d					12 33															13 03				
Loughborough Jn	d					12 41															13 11				
Elephant & Castle	d					12 53															13 23				
London Blackfriars 3 ⊖	d					13a01															13a31				
Farringdon 3 ⊖	d																								
St Pancras International 15 ⊖	d								12 30													13 00			
St Pancras International 15 ⊖	a																								
	d		12 17								12 32		12 36					12 47						13 02	
Kentish Town ⊖	d												12 40												
West Hampstead Thameslink ⊖	d		12 25								12 40		12 44					12 55						13 10	
Cricklewood	d												12 47												
Hendon	d												12 50												
Mill Hill Broadway	d												12 53												
Elstree & Borehamwood	d												12 58												
Radlett	d												13 02												
St Albans City	d		12 42								12 56		13 08					13 12						13 26	
Harpenden	d		12 48								13 02		13 14					13 18						13 32	
Luton Airport Parkway 7	d		12 54						12 59		13 08		13 20					13 24				13 29		13 38	
Luton 10	d		12 57						13 03		13 11		13a23					13 27				13 33		13 41	
Leagrave	d		13 00								13 14							13 30						13 44	
Harlington	d		13 06								13 20							13 36						13 50	
Flitwick	d		13 10								13 24							13 40						13 54	
Bedford 7	a		13 22						13 26		13 36							13 52				13 56		14 06	

A until 5 September

B from 12 September

Brighton, Gatwick Airport and South London - City of London, St.Albans, Luton and Bedford

		FC	FC	SN	FC 1 A	FC 1 B	FC 1	SE 1	SE	FC	SE	EM ◇1	FC	SE 1	FC 1	SN	FC	SN	FC 1 A	FC 1 B	FC 1	SE 1	FC	SE	FC
Brighton 10	d				13 16	13 17													13 44	13 45					
Preston Park	d																								
Hassocks 4	d																		13 52	13 53					
Burgess Hill 4	d				13 26	13 27													13 56	13 57					
Wivelsfield 4	d																								
Haywards Heath 3	d				13 31	13 32													14 01	14 02					
Balcombe	d																								
Three Bridges 4	d				13 40	13 42													14 10	14 12					
Gatwick Airport 10	d				13 45	13 47													14 15	14 17					
Redhill	d																								
East Croydon	d			13 14	14 02	14 03												13 44	14 32	14 33					
Sevenoaks 4	d							13 19	13 24		13 25			13 33								13 49		13 54	
Bat & Ball	d								13 27															13 57	
Otford 4	d								13 30															14 00	
Shoreham (Kent)	d								13 33															14 03	
Eynsford	d								13 37															14 07	
Swanley 4	d								13 42															14 12	
St Mary Cray 4	d								13 46															14 16	
Bickley	d								13 50															14 20	
Bromley South	d								13 53															14 23	
Shortlands 4	d								13 56															14 26	
Ravensbourne	d								13 58															14 28	
Beckenham Hill	d								14 00															14 30	
Bellingham	d								14 02															14 32	
Catford	d								14 05															14 35	
Crofton Park	d								14 07															14 37	
Nunhead 4	d								14 10															14 40	
Peckham Rye 4	d			13 39					14 12							13 34		14 09						14 42	
Denmark Hill 4	d								14 16															14 46	
Sutton (Surrey) 4	d		12 46										13 16												
West Sutton	d		12 49										13 19												
Sutton Common	d		12 51										13 21												
St Helier	d		12 54										13 24												
Morden South	d		12 56										13 26												
South Merton	d		12 58										13 28												
Wimbledon Chase	d		13 00										13 30												
Wimbledon 6 ⊖	d		13 03										13 33												
Haydons Road	d		13 05										13 35												
Tooting	d		13 08										13 38												
Carshalton	d																								
Hackbridge	d																								
Mitcham Junction	d																								
Mitcham Eastfields	d																								
Streatham 4	d		13 13										13 43												
Tulse Hill 3	d		13 17							13 25			13 47			13 42									13 55
London Bridge 4 ⊖	a		13a29					13 44			14 09		13a59	13 58								14 14			
	d							13 45			14 10			13 59								14 15			
Herne Hill 4	d									13 33															14 03
Loughborough Jn	d									13 41															14 11
Elephant & Castle	d									13 53															14 23
London Blackfriars 3 ⊖	d									14a01															14a31
Farringdon 3 ⊖	d																								
St Pancras International 15 ⊖	d											13 30													
St Pancras International 15 ⊖	a																								
	d	13 06					13 17								13 32		13 36				13 47				
Kentish Town ⊖	d	13 10															13 40								
West Hampstead Thameslink ⊖	d	13 14					13 25								13 40		13 44				13 55				
Cricklewood	d	13 17															13 47								
Hendon	d	13 20															13 50								
Mill Hill Broadway	d	13 23															13 53								
Elstree & Borehamwood	d	13 28															13 58								
Radlett	d	13 32															14 02								
St Albans City	d	13 38					13 42								13 56		14 08				14 12				
Harpenden	d	13 44					13 48								14 02		14 14				14 18				
Luton Airport Parkway 7	d	13 50					13 54					14 02			14 08		14 20				14 24				
Luton 10	d	13a53					13 57					14 06			14 11		14a23				14 27				
Leagrave	d						14 00								14 14						14 30				
Harlington	d						14 06								14 20						14 36				
Flitwick	d						14 10								14 24						14 40				
Bedford 7	a						14 22					14 21			14 36						14 52				

A from 12 September

B until 5 September

Table 52

Sundays

Brighton, Gatwick Airport and South London - City of London, St.Albans, Luton and Bedford

		EM ◇1	SE 1	FC 1	SN	FC	SN	FC 1	FC	FC 1	FC 1	SE 1	SE	SE	FC	EM ◇1	SE 1	FC 1	FC	SN	FC	SN	FC 1	FC 1	FC 1
								A		B													A	B	
Brighton 10	d							14 16		14 17													14 44	14 45	
Preston Park	d																								
Hassocks 4	d																						14 52	14 53	
Burgess Hill 4	d							14 26		14 27													14 56	14 57	
Wivelsfield 4	d																								
Haywards Heath 3	d							14 31		14 32													15 01	15 02	
Balcombe	d																								
Three Bridges 4	d							14 40		14 42													15 10	15 12	
Gatwick Airport 10	d							14 45		14 47													15 15	15 17	
Redhill	d																								
East Croydon	d						14 14	15 02		15 03												14 44	15 32	15 33	
Sevenoaks 4	d		14 03									14 19	14 24	14 24			14 33								
Bat & Ball	d												14 27												
Otford 4	d												14 30												
Shoreham (Kent)	d												14 33												
Eynsford	d												14 37												
Swanley 4	d												14 42												
St Mary Cray 4	d												14 46												
Bickley	d												14 50												
Bromley South	d												14 53												
Shortlands 4	d												14 56												
Ravensbourne	d												14 58												
Beckenham Hill	d												15 00												
Bellingham	d												15 02												
Catford	d												15 05												
Crofton Park	d												15 07												
Nunhead 4	d												15 10												
Peckham Rye 4	d				14 04		14 39						15 12							14 34		15 09			
Denmark Hill 4	d												15 16												
Sutton (Surrey) 4	d								13 46										14 16						
West Sutton	d								13 49										14 19						
Sutton Common	d								13 51										14 21						
St Helier	d								13 54										14 24						
Morden South	d								13 56										14 26						
South Merton	d								13 58										14 28						
Wimbledon Chase	d								14 00										14 30						
Wimbledon 6 ⊖	d								14 03										14 33						
Haydons Road	d								14 05										14 35						
Tooting	d								14 08										14 38						
Carshalton	d																								
Hackbridge	d																								
Mitcham Junction	d																								
Mitcham Eastfields	d																								
Streatham 4	d								14 13										14 43						
Tulse Hill 3	d				14 12				14 17						14 25				14 47	14 42					
London Bridge 4 ⊖	a		14 28						14a29			14 44		15 09			14 58		14a59						
	d		14 29									14 45		15 10			14 59								
Herne Hill 4	d														14 33										
Loughborough Jn	d														14 41										
Elephant & Castle	d														14 53										
London Blackfriars 3 ⊖	d														15a01										
Farringdon 3 ⊖	d																								
St Pancras International 15 ⊖	d	14 00														14 30									
St Pancras International 15 ⊖	a																								
	d			14 02		14 06					14 17							14 32			14 36				14 47
Kentish Town ⊖	d					14 10															14 40				
West Hampstead Thameslink ⊖	d			14 10		14 14					14 25							14 40			14 44				14 55
Cricklewood	d					14 17															14 47				
Hendon	d					14 20															14 50				
Mill Hill Broadway	d					14 23															14 53				
Elstree & Borehamwood	d					14 28															14 58				
Radlett	d					14 32															15 02				
St Albans City	d			14 26		14 38					14 42							14 56			15 08				15 12
Harpenden	d			14 32		14 44					14 48							15 02			15 14				15 18
Luton Airport Parkway 7	d	14 29		14 38		14 50					14 54							15 08			15 20				15 24
Luton 10	d			14 41		14a53					14 57					15 01		15 11			15a23				15 27
Leagrave	d			14 44							15 00							15 14							15 30
Harlington	d			14 50							15 06							15 20							15 36
Flitwick	d			14 54							15 10							15 24							15 40
Bedford 7	a	14 47		15 06							15 22					15 17		15 36							15 52

A from 12 September

B until 5 September

Table 52

Sundays

Brighton, Gatwick Airport and South London - City of London, St.Albans, Luton and Bedford

		SE 1	SE	FC	FC	EM ◇1	SE 1	FC 1	SN	FC	SN	FC 1	FC 1	FC 1	FC	SE 1	SE	FC	SE	EM ◇1	SE 1	FC 1	SN	FC	FC
												A	B												
Brighton 10	d											15 16	15 17												
Preston Park	d																								
Hassocks 4	d																								
Burgess Hill 4	d											15 26	15 27												
Wivelsfield 4	d																								
Haywards Heath 3	d											15 31	15 32												
Balcombe	d																								
Three Bridges 4	d											15 40	15 42												
Gatwick Airport 10	d											15 45	15 47												
Redhill	d																								
East Croydon	d										15 14	16 02	16 03												
Sevenoaks 4	d	14 49	14 54				15 03									15 19	15 24		15 25		15 33				
Bat & Ball	d		14 57														15 27								
Otford 4	d		15 00														15 30								
Shoreham (Kent)	d		15 03														15 33								
Eynsford	d		15 07														15 37								
Swanley 4	d		15 12														15 42								
St Mary Cray 4	d		15 16														15 46								
Bickley	d		15 20														15 50								
Bromley South	d		15 23														15 53								
Shortlands 4	d		15 26														15 56								
Ravensbourne	d		15 28														15 58								
Beckenham Hill	d		15 30														16 00								
Bellingham	d		15 32														16 02								
Catford	d		15 35														16 05								
Crofton Park	d		15 37														16 07								
Nunhead 4	d		15 40														16 10								
Peckham Rye 4	d		15 42						15 04		15 39						16 12						15 34		
Denmark Hill 4	d		15 46														16 16								
Sutton (Surrey) 4	d				14 46																				15 16
West Sutton	d				14 49																				15 19
Sutton Common	d				14 51																				15 21
St Helier	d				14 54																				15 24
Morden South	d				14 56																				15 26
South Merton	d				14 58																				15 28
Wimbledon Chase	d				15 00																				15 30
Wimbledon 6 ⊖	d				15 03																				15 33
Haydons Road	d				15 05																				15 35
Tooting	d				15 08																				15 38
Carshalton	d																								
Hackbridge	d																								
Mitcham Junction	d																								
Mitcham Eastfields	d																								
Streatham 4	d				15 13																				15 43
Tulse Hill 3	d			14 55	15 17				15 12									15 25					15 42		15 47
London Bridge 4 ⊖	a	15 14			15a29		15 28									15 44			16 09		15 58				15a59
	d	15 15					15 29									15 45			16 10		15 59				
Herne Hill 4	d			15 03														15 33							
Loughborough Jn	d			15 11														15 41							
Elephant & Castle	d			15 23														15 53							
London Blackfriars 3 ⊖	d			15a31														16a01							
Farringdon 3 ⊖	d																								
St Pancras International 15 ⊖	d					15 00														15 30					
St Pancras International 15 ⊖	a																								
	d							15 02		15 06				15 17								15 32		15 36	
Kentish Town ⊖	d									15 10														15 40	
West Hampstead Thameslink ⊖	d							15 10		15 14				15 25								15 40		15 44	
Cricklewood	d									15 17														15 47	
Hendon	d									15 20														15 50	
Mill Hill Broadway	d									15 23														15 53	
Elstree & Borehamwood	d									15 28														15 58	
Radlett	d									15 32														16 02	
St Albans City	d							15 26		15 38				15 42								15 56		16 08	
Harpenden	d							15 32		15 44				15 48								16 02		16 14	
Luton Airport Parkway 7	d					15 29		15 38		15 50				15 54								16 08		16 20	
Luton 10	d							15 41		15a53				15 57						16 01		16 11		16a23	
Leagrave	d							15 44						16 00								16 14			
Harlington	d							15 50						16 06								16 20			
Flitwick	d							15 54						16 10								16 24			
Bedford 7	a					15 47		16 06						16 22						16 17		16 36			

A from 12 September

B until 5 September

Table 52

Sundays

Brighton, Gatwick Airport and South London - City of London, St.Albans, Luton and Bedford

		SN	FC ■ A	FC ■ B	FC ■	SE ■	SE	FC	EM ◇■	SE ■	FC	FC ■	SN	FC	SN	FC ■ A	FC ■ B	FC ■	SE ■	SE	FC	FC	SE	EM ◇■	SE ■
Brighton	d		15 44	15 45												16 16	16 17								
Preston Park	d																								
Hassocks	d		15 52	15 53																					
Burgess Hill	d		15 56	15 57												16 26	16 27								
Wivelsfield	d																								
Haywards Heath	d		16 01	16 02												16 31	16 32								
Balcombe	d																								
Three Bridges	d		16 10	16 12												16 40	16 42								
Gatwick Airport	d		16 15	16 17												16 45	16 47								
Redhill	d																								
East Croydon	d	15 44	16 32	16 33											16 14	17 02	17 03								
Sevenoaks	d					15 49	15 54			16 03									16 19	16 24			16 25		16 33
Bat & Ball	d						15 57													16 27					
Otford	d						16 00													16 30					
Shoreham (Kent)	d						16 03													16 33					
Eynsford	d						16 07													16 37					
Swanley	d						16 12													16 42					
St Mary Cray	d						16 16													16 46					
Bickley	d						16 20													16 50					
Bromley South	d						16 23													16 53					
Shortlands	d						16 26													16 56					
Ravensbourne	d						16 28													16 58					
Beckenham Hill	d						16 30													17 00					
Bellingham	d						16 32													17 02					
Catford	d						16 35													17 05					
Crofton Park	d						16 37													17 07					
Nunhead	d						16 40													17 10					
Peckham Rye	d	16 09					16 42						16 04		16 39					17 12					
Denmark Hill	d						16 46													17 16					
Sutton (Surrey)	d										15 46										16 16				
West Sutton	d										15 49										16 19				
Sutton Common	d										15 51										16 21				
St Helier	d										15 54										16 24				
Morden South	d										15 56										16 26				
South Merton	d										15 58										16 28				
Wimbledon Chase	d										16 00										16 30				
Wimbledon	d										16 03										16 33				
Haydons Road	d										16 05										16 35				
Tooting	d										16 08										16 38				
Carshalton	d																								
Hackbridge	d																								
Mitcham Junction	d																								
Mitcham Eastfields	d																								
Streatham	d										16 13										16 43				
Tulse Hill	d							15 55			16 17		16 12								16 47	16 25			
London Bridge	a					16 14				16 28	16a29								16 44		16a59		17 09		16 58
	d					16 15				16 29									16 45				17 10		16 59
Herne Hill	d							16 03														16 33			
Loughborough Jn	d							16 11														16 41			
Elephant & Castle	d							16 23														16 53			
London Blackfriars	d							16a31														17a01			
Farringdon	d																								
St Pancras International	d								16 00															16 30	
St Pancras International	a																								
	d				15 47							16 02		16 06				16 17							
Kentish Town	d													16 10											
West Hampstead Thameslink	d				15 55							16 10		16 14				16 25							
Cricklewood	d													16 17											
Hendon	d													16 20											
Mill Hill Broadway	d													16 23											
Elstree & Borehamwood	d													16 28											
Radlett	d													16 32											
St Albans City	d				16 12							16 26		16 38				16 42							
Harpenden	d				16 18							16 32		16 44				16 48							
Luton Airport Parkway	d				16 24				16 29			16 38		16 50				16 54						16 52	
Luton	d				16 27							16 41		16a53				16 57							
Leagrave	d				16 30							16 44						17 00							
Harlington	d				16 36							16 50						17 06							
Flitwick	d				16 40							16 54						17 10							
Bedford	a				16 52				16 47			17 06						17 22						17 15	

A from 12 September

B until 5 September

Table 52

Sundays

Brighton, Gatwick Airport and South London - City of London, St.Albans, Luton and Bedford

		FC ■	SN	FC	SN	FC ■ A	FC	FC ■ B	FC ■	SE ■	SE	FC	EM ◇■	SE ■	FC ■	SN	FC	FC	SN	FC ■ A	FC ■ B	FC ■	SE ■	SE	SE
Brighton	d					16 44		16 45												17 16	17 17				
Preston Park	d																								
Hassocks	d					16 52		16 53																	
Burgess Hill	d					16 56		16 57												17 26	17 27				
Wivelsfield	d																								
Haywards Heath	d					17 01		17 02												17 31	17 32				
Balcombe	d																								
Three Bridges	d					17 10		17 12												17 40	17 42				
Gatwick Airport	d					17 15		17 17												17 45	17 47				
Redhill	d																								
East Croydon	d				16 44	17 32		17 33											17 14	18 02	18 03				
Sevenoaks	d									16 49	16 54			17 03									17 19	17 24	17 24
Bat & Ball	d										16 57													17 27	
Otford	d										17 00													17 30	
Shoreham (Kent)	d										17 03													17 33	
Eynsford	d										17 07													17 37	
Swanley	d										17 12													17 42	
St Mary Cray	d										17 16													17 46	
Bickley	d										17 20													17 50	
Bromley South	d										17 23													17 53	
Shortlands	d										17 26													17 56	
Ravensbourne	d										17 28													17 58	
Beckenham Hill	d										17 30													18 00	
Bellingham	d										17 32													18 02	
Catford	d										17 35													18 05	
Crofton Park	d										17 37													18 07	
Nunhead	d										17 40													18 10	
Peckham Rye	d		16 34		7 09						17 42					17 04			17 39					18 12	
Denmark Hill	d										17 46													18 16	
Sutton (Surrey)	d																16 46								
West Sutton	d																16 49								
Sutton Common	d																16 51								
St Helier	d																16 54								
Morden South	d																16 56								
South Merton	d																16 58								
Wimbledon Chase	d																17 00								
Wimbledon	d																17 03								
Haydons Road	d																17 05								
Tooting	d																17 08								
Carshalton	d																								
Hackbridge	d																								
Mitcham Junction	d																								
Mitcham Eastfields	d																								
Streatham	d																17 13								
Tulse Hill	d		16 42									16 55				17 12	17 17								
London Bridge	a									17 14				17 28			17a29						17 44		18 09
	d									17 15				17 29									17 45		18 10
Herne Hill	d											17 03													
Loughborough Jn	d											17 11													
Elephant & Castle	d											17 23													
London Blackfriars	d											17a31													
Farringdon	d																								
St Pancras International	d												17 00												
St Pancras International	a																								
	d	16 32		16 36					16 47						17 02			17 06				17 17			
Kentish Town	d			16 40														17 10							
West Hampstead Thameslink	d	16 40		16 44					16 55						17 10			17 14				17 25			
Cricklewood	d			16 47														17 17							
Hendon	d			16 50														17 20							
Mill Hill Broadway	d			16 53														17 23							
Elstree & Borehamwood	d			16 58														17 28							
Radlett	d			17 02														17 32							
St Albans City	d	16 56		17 08					17 12						17 26			17 38				17 42			
Harpenden	d	17 02		17 14					17 18						17 32			17 44				17 48			
Luton Airport Parkway	d	17 08		17 20					17 24				17 21		17 38			17 50				17 54			
Luton	d	17 11		17a23					17 27						17 41			17a53				17 57			
Leagrave	d	17 14							17 30						17 44							18 00			
Harlington	d	17 20							17 36						17 50							18 06			
Flitwick	d	17 24							17 40						17 54							18 10			
Bedford	a	17 36							17 52				17 45		18 06							18 22			

A from 12 September

B until 5 September

Table 52

Sundays

Brighton, Gatwick Airport and South London - City of London, St.Albans, Luton and Bedford

Station		FC	FC	EM ◇■	SE ■	FC ■	SN	FC	SN	FC ■ A	FC ■ B	FC ■		SE ■	SE	FC	EM ◇■	SE ■	FC ■	SN	FC	SN	FC	FC ■ A	FC ■ B
Brighton	d									17 44	17 45													18 16	18 17
Preston Park	d																								
Hassocks	d									17 52	17 53														
Burgess Hill	d									17 56	17 57													18 26	18 27
Wivelsfield	d																								
Haywards Heath	d									18 01	18 02													18 31	18 32
Balcombe	d																								
Three Bridges	d									18 10	18 12													18 40	18 42
Gatwick Airport	d									18 15	18 17													18 45	18 47
Redhill	d																								
East Croydon	d								17 44	18 32	18 33											18 14		19 02	19 03
Sevenoaks	d				17 33									17 49	17 54			18 03							
Bat & Ball	d														17 57										
Otford	d														18 00										
Shoreham (Kent)	d														18 03										
Eynsford	d														18 07										
Swanley	d														18 12										
St Mary Cray	d														18 16										
Bickley	d														18 20										
Bromley South	d														18 23										
Shortlands	d														18 26										
Ravensbourne	d														18 28										
Beckenham Hill	d														18 30										
Bellingham	d														18 32										
Catford	d														18 35										
Crofton Park	d														18 37										
Nunhead	d														18 40										
Peckham Rye	d						17 34		18 09						18 42					18 04		18 39			
Denmark Hill	d														18 46										
Sutton (Surrey)	d		17 16																						
West Sutton	d		17 19																				17 46		
Sutton Common	d		17 21																				17 49		
St Helier	d		17 24																				17 51		
Morden South	d		17 26																				17 54		
South Merton	d		17 28																				17 56		
Wimbledon Chase	d		17 30																				17 58		
Wimbledon	d		17 33																				18 00		
Haydons Road	d		17 35																				18 03		
Tooting	d		17 38																				18 05		
Carshalton	d																						18 08		
Hackbridge	d																								
Mitcham Junction	d																								
Mitcham Eastfields	d																								
Streatham	d		17 43																				18 13		
Tulse Hill	d	17 25	17 47				17 42									17 55				18 12			18 17		
London Bridge	a		17a59		17 58									18 14				18 28					18a29		
	d				17 59									18 15				18 29							
Herne Hill	d	17 33														18 03									
Loughborough Jn	d	17 41														18 11									
Elephant & Castle	d	17 53														18 23									
London Blackfriars	d	18a01														18a31									
Farringdon	d																								
St Pancras International	d			17 30													18 00								
St Pancras International	a																								
	d					17 32		17 36				17 47							18 02		18 06				
Kentish Town	d							17 40													18 10				
West Hampstead Thameslink	d					17 40		17 44				17 55							18 10		18 14				
Cricklewood	d							17 47													18 17				
Hendon	d							17 50													18 20				
Mill Hill Broadway	d							17 53													18 23				
Elstree & Borehamwood	d							17 58													18 28				
Radlett	d							18 02													18 32				
St Albans City	d					17 56		18 08				18 12							18 26		18 38				
Harpenden	d					18 02		18 14				18 18							18 32		18 44				
Luton Airport Parkway	d					18 08		18 20				18 24					18 21		18 38		18 50				
Luton	d			17 52		18 11		18a23				18 27							18 41		18a53				
Leagrave	d					18 14						18 30							18 44						
Harlington	d					18 20						18 36							18 50						
Flitwick	d					18 24						18 40							18 54						
Bedford	a			18 15		18 36						18 52					18 45		19 06						

A from 12 September

B until 5 September

Table 52

Sundays

Brighton, Gatwick Airport and South London - City of London, St.Albans, Luton and Bedford

Station		FC ■	SE ■	SE	SE	FC	EM ◇■	SE ■	FC	FC ■	SN	FC	SN	FC ■ A	FC ■ B	FC ■	SE ■	SE	FC	FC	EM ◇■	SE ■	FC ■	SN	FC
Brighton	d													18 44	18 45										
Preston Park	d																								
Hassocks	d													18 52	18 53										
Burgess Hill	d													18 56	18 57										
Wivelsfield	d																								
Haywards Heath	d													19 01	19 02										
Balcombe	d																								
Three Bridges	d													19 10	19 12										
Gatwick Airport	d													19 15	19 17										
Redhill	d																								
East Croydon	d												18 44	19 32	19 33										
Sevenoaks	d		18 19	18 24	18 24			18 33									18 49	18 54				19 03			
Bat & Ball	d			18 27														18 57							
Otford	d			18 30														19 00							
Shoreham (Kent)	d			18 33														19 03							
Eynsford	d			18 37														19 07							
Swanley	d			18 42														19 12							
St Mary Cray	d			18 46														19 16							
Bickley	d			18 50														19 20							
Bromley South	d			18 53														19 23							
Shortlands	d			18 56														19 26							
Ravensbourne	d			18 58														19 28							
Beckenham Hill	d			19 00														19 30							
Bellingham	d			19 02														19 32							
Catford	d			19 05														19 35							
Crofton Park	d			19 07														19 37							
Nunhead	d			19 10														19 40							
Peckham Rye	d			19 12							18 34		19 09					19 42						19 04	
Denmark Hill	d			19 16														19 46							
Sutton (Surrey)	d								18 16										18 46						
West Sutton	d								18 19										18 49						
Sutton Common	d								18 21										18 51						
St Helier	d								18 24										18 54						
Morden South	d								18 26										18 56						
South Merton	d								18 28										18 58						
Wimbledon Chase	d								18 30										19 00						
Wimbledon	d								18 33										19 03						
Haydons Road	d								18 35										19 05						
Tooting	d								18 38										19 08						
Carshalton	d																								
Hackbridge	d																								
Mitcham Junction	d																								
Mitcham Eastfields	d																								
Streatham	d								18 43										19 13						
Tulse Hill	d					18 25			18 47		18 42								19 17	18 55				19 12	
London Bridge	a		18 44		19 09			18 58	18a59								19 14		19a29			19 28			
	d		18 45		19 10			18 59									19 15					19 29			
Herne Hill	d					18 33														19 03					
Loughborough Jn	d					18 41														19 11					
Elephant & Castle	d					18 53														19 23					
London Blackfriars	d					19a01														19a31					
Farringdon	d																								
St Pancras International	d						18 30														19 00				
St Pancras International	a																								
	d	18 17								18 32		18 36				18 47							19 02		19 06
Kentish Town	d											18 40													19 10
West Hampstead Thameslink	d	18 25								18 40		18 44				18 55							19 10		19 14
Cricklewood	d											18 47													19 17
Hendon	d											18 50													19 20
Mill Hill Broadway	d											18 53													19 23
Elstree & Borehamwood	d											18 58													19 28
Radlett	d											19 02													19 32
St Albans City	d	18 42								18 56		19 08				19 12							19 26		19 38
Harpenden	d	18 48								19 02		19 14				19 18							19 32		19 44
Luton Airport Parkway	d	18 54								19 08		19 20				19 24					19 21		19 38		19 50
Luton	d	18 57					18 52			19 11		19a23				19 27							19 41		19a53
Leagrave	d	19 00								19 14						19 30							19 44		
Harlington	d	19 06								19 20						19 36							19 50		
Flitwick	d	19 10								19 24						19 40							19 54		
Bedford	a	19 22					19 15			19 36						19 52					19 45		20 06		

A from 12 September

B until 5 September

Table 52

Sundays

Brighton, Gatwick Airport and South London - City of London, St.Albans, Luton and Bedford

		SN	FC 1 A	FC 1 B	FC	FC	SE 1	SE	SE	FC	EM ◇1	SE 1	FC 1	SN		SN	FC 1 A	FC 1 B	FC	SE 1	SE	FC	EM ◇1	FC 1	FC
Brighton	d		19 16	19 17													19 44	19 45							
Preston Park	d																								
Hassocks	d																19 52	19 53							
Burgess Hill	d		19 26	19 27													19 56	19 57							
Wivelsfield	d																								
Haywards Heath	d		19 31	19 32													20 01	20 02							
Balcombe	d																								
Three Bridges	d		19 40	19 42													20 10	20 12							
Gatwick Airport	d		19 45	19 47													20 15	20 17							
Redhill	d																								
East Croydon	d	19 14	20 02	20 03												19 44	20 32	20 33							
Sevenoaks	d						19 19	19 24	19 24			19 33								19 49	19 54				
Bat & Ball	d							19 27													19 57				
Otford	d							19 30													20 00				
Shoreham (Kent)	d							19 33													20 03				
Eynsford	d							19 37													20 07				
Swanley	d							19 42													20 12				
St Mary Cray	d							19 46													20 16				
Bickley	d							19 50													20 20				
Bromley South	d							19 53													20 23				
Shortlands	d							19 56													20 26				
Ravensbourne	d							19 58													20 28				
Beckenham Hill	d							20 00													20 30				
Bellingham	d							20 02													20 32				
Catford	d							20 05													20 35				
Crofton Park	d							20 07													20 37				
Nunhead	d							20 10													20 40				
Peckham Rye	d	19 39						20 12						19 34		20 09					20 42				
Denmark Hill	d							20 16													20 46				
Sutton (Surrey)	d				19 16																				19 46
West Sutton	d				19 19																				19 49
Sutton Common	d				19 21																				19 51
St Helier	d				19 24																				19 54
Morden South	d				19 26																				19 56
South Merton	d				19 28																				19 58
Wimbledon Chase	d				19 30																				20 00
Wimbledon	d				19 33																				20 03
Haydons Road	d				19 35																				20 05
Tooting	d				19 38																				20 08
Carshalton	d																								
Hackbridge	d																								
Mitcham Junction	d																								
Mitcham Eastfields	d																								
Streatham	d				19 43																				20 13
Tulse Hill	d				19 47					19 25				19 42								19 55			20 17
London Bridge	a				19a59		19 44		20 09			19 58								20 14					20a29
	d						19 45		20 10			19 59								20 15					
Herne Hill	d									19 33												20 03			
Loughborough Jn	d									19 41												20 11			
Elephant & Castle	d									19 53												20 23			
London Blackfriars	d									20a01												20a31			
Farringdon	d																								
St Pancras International	d										19 30												20 00		
St Pancras International	a																								
	d					19 17							19 32						19 47					20 02	
Kentish Town	d					19 22													19 52						
West Hampstead Thameslink	d					19 26							19 40						19 56					20 10	
Cricklewood	d					19 29													19 59						
Hendon	d					19 32													20 02						
Mill Hill Broadway	d					19 35													20 05						
Elstree & Borehamwood	d					19 40													20 10						
Radlett	d					19 44													20 14						
St Albans City	d					19 50							19 56						20 20					20 26	
Harpenden	d					19 56							20 02						20 26					20 32	
Luton Airport Parkway	d					20 02							20 08						20 32				20 23	20 38	
Luton	d					20 05					19 52		20 11						20 35					20 41	
Leagrave	d					20 08							20 14						20 38					20 44	
Harlington	d					20 14							20 20						20 44					20 50	
Flitwick	d					20 18							20 24						20 48					20 54	
Bedford	a					20 30					20 15		20 36						21 00				20 47	21 06	

A from 12 September

B until 5 September

Table 52

Sundays

Brighton, Gatwick Airport and South London - City of London, St.Albans, Luton and Bedford

		SN	SN	FC 1 A	FC 1 B	FC	SE 1	SE	SE	FC	FC	EM ◇1	SE 1	FC 1	SN	SN	FC 1 A	FC 1 B	FC	SE 1		SE	FC	EM ◇1	FC 1
Brighton	d			20 16	20 17												20 44	20 45							
Preston Park	d																								
Hassocks	d																20 52	20 53							
Burgess Hill	d			20 26	20 27												20 56	20 57							
Wivelsfield	d																								
Haywards Heath	d			20 31	20 32												21 01	21 02							
Balcombe	d																								
Three Bridges	d			20 40	20 42												21 10	21 12							
Gatwick Airport	d			20 45	20 47												21 15	21 17							
Redhill	d																								
East Croydon	d		20 14	21 02	21 03											20 44	21 32	21 33							
Sevenoaks	d						20 19	20 24	20 24				20 33							20 49		20 54			
Bat & Ball	d							20 27														20 57			
Otford	d							20 30														21 00			
Shoreham (Kent)	d							20 33														21 03			
Eynsford	d							20 37														21 07			
Swanley	d							20 42														21 12			
St Mary Cray	d							20 46														21 16			
Bickley	d							20 50														21 20			
Bromley South	d							20 53														21 23			
Shortlands	d							20 56														21 26			
Ravensbourne	d							20 58														21 28			
Beckenham Hill	d							21 00														21 30			
Bellingham	d							21 02														21 32			
Catford	d							21 05														21 35			
Crofton Park	d							21 07														21 37			
Nunhead	d							21 10														21 40			
Peckham Rye	d	20 04	20 39					21 12							20 34	21 09						21 42			
Denmark Hill	d							21 16														21 46			
Sutton (Surrey)	d										20 16														
West Sutton	d										20 19														
Sutton Common	d										20 21														
St Helier	d										20 24														
Morden South	d										20 26														
South Merton	d										20 28														
Wimbledon Chase	d										20 30														
Wimbledon	d										20 33														
Haydons Road	d										20 35														
Tooting	d										20 38														
Carshalton	d																								
Hackbridge	d																								
Mitcham Junction	d																								
Mitcham Eastfields	d																								
Streatham	d										20 43														
Tulse Hill	d	20 12								20 25	20 47				20 42								20 55		
London Bridge	a						20 44		21 09		20a59		20 58							21 14					
	d						20 45		21 10				20 59							21 15					
Herne Hill	d									20 33													21 03		
Loughborough Jn	d									20 41													21 11		
Elephant & Castle	d									20 53													21 23		
London Blackfriars	d									21a01													21a31		
Farringdon	d																								
St Pancras International	d											20 30												21 00	
St Pancras International	a																								
	d					20 17								20 32					20 47						21 02
Kentish Town	d					20 22													20 52						
West Hampstead Thameslink	d					20 26								20 40					20 56						21 10
Cricklewood	d					20 29													20 59						
Hendon	d					20 32													21 02						
Mill Hill Broadway	d					20 35													21 05						
Elstree & Borehamwood	d					20 40													21 10						
Radlett	d					20 44													21 14						
St Albans City	d					20 50								20 56					21 20						21 26
Harpenden	d					20 56								21 02					21 26						21 32
Luton Airport Parkway	d					21 02								21 08					21 32					21 23	21 38
Luton	d					21 05						20 54		21 11					21 35						21 41
Leagrave	d					21 08								21 14					21 38						21 44
Harlington	d					21 14								21 20					21 44						21 50
Flitwick	d					21 18								21 24					21 48						21 54
Bedford	a					21 30						21 17		21 36					22 00					21 47	22 06

A from 12 September

B until 5 September

Table 52

Sundays

Brighton, Gatwick Airport and South London - City of London, St.Albans, Luton and Bedford

Station		SN	SN	FC ■ A	FC ■ B	FC	FC	SE ■	SE	SE	FC	EM ◇■	SE ■	FC ■	SN	SN	FC	FC ■ A	FC ■ B	FC	SE ■	SE	FC	FC	SN
Brighton	d			21 16	21 17													21 44	21 45						
Preston Park	d																								
Hassocks	d																	21 52	21 53						
Burgess Hill	d			21 26	21 27													21 56	21 57						
Wivelsfield	d																								
Haywards Heath	d			21 31	21 32													22 01	22 02						
Balcombe	d																								
Three Bridges	d			21 40	21 42													22 10	22 12						
Gatwick Airport	d			21 45	21 47													22 15	22 17						
Redhill	d																								
East Croydon	d		21 14	22 02	22 03											21 44		22 32	22 33						
Sevenoaks	d							21 19	21 24	21 24			21 33								21 49	21 54			
Bat & Ball	d								21 27													21 57			
Otford	d								21 30													22 00			
Shoreham (Kent)	d								21 33													22 03			
Eynsford	d								21 37													22 07			
Swanley	d								21 42													22 12			
St Mary Cray	d								21 46													22 16			
Bickley	d								21 50													22 20			
Bromley South	d								21 53													22 23			
Shortlands	d								21 56													22 26			
Ravensbourne	d								21 58													22 28			
Beckenham Hill	d								22 00													22 30			
Bellingham	d								22 02													22 32			
Catford	d								22 05													22 35			
Crofton Park	d								22 07													22 37			
Nunhead	d								22 10													22 40			
Peckham Rye	d	21 04	21 39						22 12						21 34	22 09						22 42			
Denmark Hill	d								22 16													22 46			22 04
Sutton (Surrey)	d						20 46										21 16								
West Sutton	d						20 49										21 19								
Sutton Common	d						20 51										21 21								
St Helier	d						20 54										21 24								
Morden South	d						20 56										21 26								
South Merton	d						20 58										21 28								
Wimbledon Chase	d						21 00										21 30								
Wimbledon ⊖	d						21 03										21 33								
Haydons Road	d						21 05										21 35								
Tooting	d						21 08										21 38								
Carshalton	d																								
Hackbridge	d																								
Mitcham Junction	d																								
Mitcham Eastfields	d																								
Streatham	d						21 13										21 43								
Tulse Hill	d	21 12					21 17				21 25				21 42		21 47						21 55		22 12
London Bridge ⊖	a						21a29	21 44		22 09			21 58				21a59				22 14				
	d							21 45		22 10			21 59								22 15				
Herne Hill	d										21 33												22 03		
Loughborough Jn	d										21 41												22 11		
Elephant & Castle	d										21 53												22 23		
London Blackfriars ⊖	d										22a01												22a31		
Farringdon ⊖	d																								
St Pancras International ⊖	d											21 30													
St Pancras International ⊖	a																								
	d					21 17								21 32						21 47				22 02	
Kentish Town ⊖	d					21 22														21 52				22 06	
West Hampstead Thameslink ⊖	d					21 26								21 40						21 56				22 10	
Cricklewood	d					21 29														21 59				22 13	
Hendon	d					21 32														22 02				22 16	
Mill Hill Broadway	d					21 35														22 05				22 19	
Elstree & Borehamwood	d					21 40														22 10				22 24	
Radlett	d					21 44														22 14				22 29	
St Albans City	d					21 50								21 56						22 20				22 36	
Harpenden	d					21 56								22 02						22 26				22 42	
Luton Airport Parkway	d					22 02								22 08						22 32				22 48	
Luton	d					22 05						21 54		22 11						22 35				22 51	
Leagrave	d					22 08								22 14						22 38				22 54	
Harlington	d					22 14								22 20						22 44				23 00	
Flitwick	d					22 18								22 24						22 48				23 04	
Bedford	a					22 30						22 17		22 36						23 00				23 16	

A from 12 September B until 5 September

Table 52

Sundays

Brighton, Gatwick Airport and South London - City of London, St.Albans, Luton and Bedford

Station		SN ■		SN	FC ■ A	FC ■ B	SE ■	SE	SE	EM ◇■	SE ■	FC		SN	SN	FC ■ A	FC ■ B	SE ■	SE	EM ◇■	FC	SN		SN ■	FC ■
Brighton	d	22 10			22 16	22 17										22 44	22 45							23 09	23 11
Preston Park	d																								
Hassocks	d															22 52	22 53								23 19
Burgess Hill	d				22 26	22 27										22 56	22 57								23 23
Wivelsfield	d																								
Haywards Heath	d				22 31	22 32										23 01	23 02								23 28
Balcombe	d																								
Three Bridges	d				22 40	22 42										23 10	23 12								23 38
Gatwick Airport	d				22 45	22 47										23 15	23 17								23 43
Redhill	d																								
East Croydon	d			22 14	23 02	23 03									22 44	23 32	23 33								00 04
Sevenoaks	d						22 19	22 24	22 25		22 33							22 49	22 54						
Bat & Ball	d							22 27											22 57						
Otford	d							22 30											23 00						
Shoreham (Kent)	d							22 33											23 03						
Eynsford	d							22 37											23 07						
Swanley	d							22 42											23 12						
St Mary Cray	d							22 46											23 16						
Bickley	d							22 50											23 20						
Bromley South	d							22 53											23 23						
Shortlands	d							22 56											23 26						
Ravensbourne	d							22 58											23 28						
Beckenham Hill	d							23 00											23 30						
Bellingham	d							23 02											23 32						
Catford	d							23 05											23 35						
Crofton Park	d							23 07											23 37						
Nunhead	d							23 10											23 40						
Peckham Rye	d			22 39				23 12						22 34	23 09				23 42			23 04			
Denmark Hill	d							23 16											23 46						
Sutton (Surrey)	d																								
West Sutton	d																								
Sutton Common	d																								
St Helier	d																								
Morden South	d																								
South Merton	d																								
Wimbledon Chase	d																								
Wimbledon ⊖	d																								
Haydons Road	d																								
Tooting	d																								
Carshalton	d																								
Hackbridge	d																								
Mitcham Junction	d																								
Mitcham Eastfields	d																								
Streatham	d																								
Tulse Hill	d													22 42								23 12			
London Bridge ⊖	a						22 44		23 09		22 58							23 14							
	d						22 45		23 10		22 59							23 15							
Herne Hill	d																								
Loughborough Jn	d																								
Elephant & Castle	d																								
London Blackfriars ⊖	d																								
Farringdon ⊖	d																								
St Pancras International ⊖	d									22 30										23 00					
St Pancras International ⊖	a																								
	d											22 32									23 02				
Kentish Town ⊖	d											22 36									23 06				
West Hampstead Thameslink ⊖	d											22 40									23 10				
Cricklewood	d											22 43									23 13				
Hendon	d											22 46									23 16				
Mill Hill Broadway	d											22 49									23 19				
Elstree & Borehamwood	d											22 54									23 24				
Radlett	d											22 59									23 29				
St Albans City	d											23 06									23 36				
Harpenden	d											23 12									23 42				
Luton Airport Parkway	d									22 53		23 18								23 28	23 48				
Luton	d											23 21									23 51				
Leagrave	d											23 24									23 55				
Harlington	d											23 30									00 01				
Flitwick	d											23 34									00 04				
Bedford	a									23 17		23 46								23 52	00 16				

A from 12 September B until 5 September

Table 52

Sundays

Brighton, Gatwick Airport and South London - City of London, St.Albans, Luton and Bedford

		SN 1	FC	SN	SN 1	FC 1
Brighton 10	d	23 15			23 39	23 44
Preston Park	d					
Hassocks 4	d					23 52
Burgess Hill 4	d					23 56
Wivelsfield 4	d					
Haywards Heath 5	d					00 01
Balcombe	d					
Three Bridges 4	d					00 10
Gatwick Airport 10	d					00 15
Redhill	d					00 22
East Croydon	d					00 36
Sevenoaks 4	d					
Bat & Ball	d					
Otford 4	d					
Shoreham (Kent)	d					
Eynsford	d					
Swanley 4	d					
St Mary Cray 4	d					
Bickley	d					
Bromley South	d					
Shortlands 4	d					
Ravensbourne	d					
Beckenham Hill	d					
Bellingham	d					
Catford	d					
Crofton Park	d					
Nunhead 4	d					
Peckham Rye 4	d			23 34		
Denmark Hill 4	d					
Sutton (Surrey) 4	d					
West Sutton	d					
Sutton Common	d					
St Helier	d					
Morden South	d					
South Merton	d					
Wimbledon Chase	d					
Wimbledon 6 ⊖	d					
Haydons Road	d					
Tooting	d					
Carshalton	d					
Hackbridge	d					
Mitcham Junction	d					
Mitcham Eastfields	d					
Streatham 4	d					
Tulse Hill 5	d			23 42		
London Bridge 4 ⊖	a					
	d					
Herne Hill 4	d					
Loughborough Jn	d					
Elephant & Castle	d					
London Blackfriars 5 ⊖	d					
Farringdon 3 ⊖	d					
St Pancras International 15 ⊖	d					
St Pancras International 15 ⊖	a					
	d		23 32			
Kentish Town ⊖	d		23 36			
West Hampstead Thameslink ⊖	d		23 40			
Cricklewood	d		23 43			
Hendon	d		23 46			
Mill Hill Broadway	d		23 49			
Elstree & Borehamwood	d		23 54			
Radlett	d		23 59			
St Albans City	d		00 06			
Harpenden	d		00 12			
Luton Airport Parkway 7	d		00 18			
Luton 10	d		00 21			
Leagrave	d		00 24			
Harlington	d		00 30			
Flitwick	d		00 34			
Bedford 7	a		00 46			

Table 52A

Mondays to Fridays

Luton - Dunstable

Bus Service

		FC	FC	FC	FC	FC	FC	FC	FC	FC	FC	FC	FC	FC	FC	FC	FC	FC	FC	FC	FC	FC	FC	FC	FC
Luton	d	05 57	06 15	06 40	07 10	07 32	07 53	08 06	08 27	08 47	09 08	09 27	09 34	09 52	10 04	10 22	10 34	10 52	11 04	11 22	11 34	11 52	12 04	12 22	12 34
Dunstable	a	06 20	06 50	07 10	07 45	08 05	08 25	08 45	09 00	09 25	09 40	09 55	10 10	10 25	10 40	10 55	11 10	11 25	11 40	11 55	12 10	12 29	12 40	12 55	13 10

		FC	FC	FC	FC	FC	FC	FC	FC	FC	FC	FC	FC	FC	FC	FC	FC	FC	FC	FC	FC	FC	FC	FC	FC
Luton	d	12 52	13 04	13 22	13 34	13 52	14 04	14 22	14 34	14 52	15 04	15 22	15 36	15 52	16 04	16 22	16 37	16 50	17 07	17 25	17 40	17 57	18 27	18 43	19 15
Dunstable	a	13 25	13 40	13 55	14 10	14 29	14 40	14 55	15 10	15 25	15 40	15 55	16 10	16 25	16 40	16 59	17 14	17 34	17 46	18 00	18 12	18 32	18 55	19 08	19 42

		FC	FC	FC	FC	FC	FC	FC	FC
Luton	d	19 30	20 02	20 32	21 00	21 17	21 45	22 15	22 45
Dunstable	a	19 54	20 32	21 02	21 20	21 41	22 09	22 37	23 08

Saturdays

		FC	FC	FC	FC	FC	FC	FC	FC	FC	FC	FC	FC	FC	FC	FC	FC	FC	FC	FC	FC	FC	FC	FC	FC
Luton	d	05 55	06 30	07 07	07 37	08 07	08 37	09 07	09 27	09 42	10 02	10 22	10 42	11 02	11 22	11 42	12 02	12 22	12 42	13 02	13 22	13 42	14 02	14 22	14 42
Dunstable	a	06 13	06 48	07 35	08 05	08 40	09 10	09 40	09 57	10 15	10 35	10 55	11 15	11 35	11 55	12 15	12 39	12 55	13 15	13 35	13 55	14 15	14 39	14 55	15 15

		FC	FC	FC	FC	FC	FC	FC	FC	FC	FC	FC	FC	FC	FC	FC
Luton	d	15 02	15 22	15 42	16 02	16 13	16 22	16 42	17 12	17 42	19 00	19 30	20 02	20 30	21 17	21 45
Dunstable	a	15 35	15 55	16 15	16 31	16 47	17 00	17 11	17 45	18 11	19 18	19 54	21 02	21 02	21 41	21 59

Sundays

		FC					FC					FC					FC					FC			
Luton	d	18 42					19 42					20 42					21 42					22 42			
Dunstable	a	19 04					20 04					21 04					22 04					23 06			

Table 52A

Mondays to Fridays

Dunstable - Luton

Bus Service

		FC	FC	FC	FC	FC	FC	FC	FC	FC	FC	FC	FC	FC	FC	FC	FC	FC	FC	FC	FC	FC	FC	FC	FC
Dunstable	d	05 15	05 45	05 50	06 00	06 05	06 25	06 40	06 50	07 15	07 30	07 36	07 53	08 00	08 08	08 10	08 18	08 28	08 30	08 49	09 00	09 05	09 17	09 30	09 35
Luton	a	05 40	06 04	06 04	06 15	06 30	06 40	07 06	07 04	07 32	08 04	07 53	08 12	08 36	08 27	08 46	08 37	08 47	09 06	09 08	09 34	09 27	09 34	10 04	09 52
		FC	FC	FC	FC	FC	FC	FC	FC	FC	FC	FC	FC	FC	FC	FC	FC	FC	FC	FC	FC	FC	FC	FC	FC
Dunstable	d	09 47	10 00	10 05	10 17	10 30	10 35	10 47	11 00	11 05	11 17	11 30	11 35	11 47	12 00	12 05	12 17	12 30	12 35	12 47	13 00	13 05	13 17	13 35	13 47
Luton	a	10 04	10 34	10 22	10 34	11 04	10 52	11 07	11 34	11 22	11 34	12 04	11 52	12 04	12 34	12 22	12 34	13 04	12 52	13 04	13 34	13 22	13 34	13 52	14 04
		FC FC	FC FC	FC FC	FC FC	FC FC	FC FC	FC FC	FC FC	FC FC	FC FC	FC FC	FC FC	FC FC	FC FC	FC FC	FC FC	FC FC	FC FC	FC FC	FC FC	FC FC	FC FC	FC FC	FC FC
Dunstable	d	14 00	14 05	14 17	14 30	14 35	14 47	15 00	15 05	15 19	15 35	15 40	15 47	16 05	16 10	16 20	16 33	16 40	16 50	17 08	17 10	17 20	17 23	17 40	17 40
Luton	a	14 34	14 22	14 34	15 04	14 52	15 04	15 34	15 22	15 36	15 52	16 15	16 04	16 22	16 47	16 37	16 50	17 17	17 07	17 25	17 47	17 59	17 40	17 57	18 17
Dunstable	d	18 10	18 20	18 45	19 15	20 15	20 45	21 45	23 08																
Luton	a	18 27	18 51	19 16	19 44	20 35	21 10	22 07	23 31																

Saturdays

		FC	FC	FC	FC	FC	FC	FC	FC	FC	FC	FC	FC	FC	FC	FC	FC	FC	FC	FC	FC	FC	FC	FC	FC
Dunstable	d	06 00	06 15	06 20	06 50	07 00	07 15	07 40	07 50	08 10	08 20	08 40	08 50	09 05	09 10	09 25	09 30	09 45	10 00	10 05	10 25	10 30	11 45	12 00	12 05
Luton	a	06 26	06 30	06 44	07 07	07 34	07 28	08 10	08 07	08 40	08 37	09 10	09 07	09 27	09 34	09 42	10 04	10 02	10 34	10 22	10 42	11 02	12 02	12 34	12 22
		FC	FC	FC	FC	FC	FC	FC	FC	FC	FC	FC	FC	FC	FC	FC	FC	FC	FC	FC	FC	FC	FC	FC	FC
Dunstable	d	12 25	12 30	12 45	13 00	13 05	13 25	13 30	13 45	14 00	14 05	14 25	14 30	14 45	15 00	15 05	15 25	15 30	15 45	16 00	16 05	16 25	16 40	16 55	17 10
Luton	a	12 42	13 04	13 02	13 34	13 22	13 42	14 04	14 02	14 34	14 22	14 42	15 04	15 02	15 34	15 22	15 42	16 04	16 02	16 34	16 22	16 42	17 14	17 12	17 44
		FC	FC	FC	FC	FC	FC	FC																	
Dunstable	d	17 23	17 40	18 00	18 45	19 15	20 45	23 08																	
Luton	a	17 40	18 10	18 33	19 16	19 44	21 10	23 31																	

Route Diagram for Table 53

DM-7/09(2)
Design BAJS

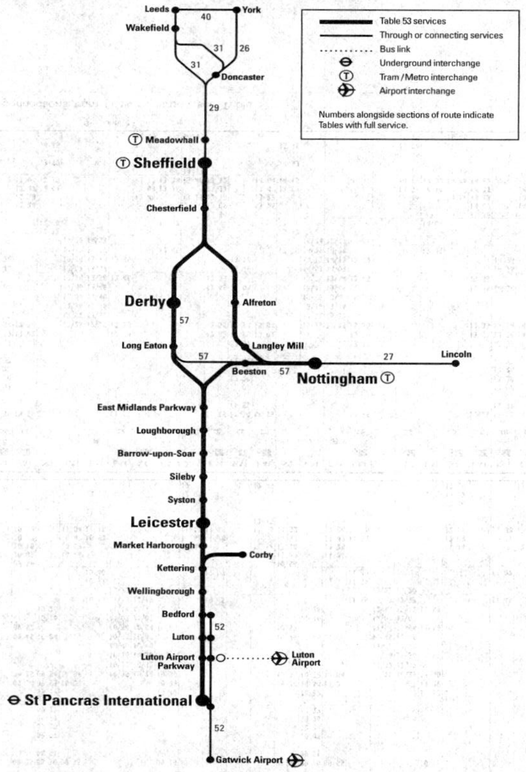

London - East Midlands - Sheffield

	EM	EM	EM MX	EM MX	EM MO	EM MO	EM MX	EM MX	EM	XC	NT	XC	EM	NT	EM	EM	XC	EM	NT	EM
	◇1	◇1	◇1	◇1	◇1	◇1	◇1	◇1	◇	◇1		◇1	◇1			◇	◇1	◇1		
	A	B																		
	☕	☕	☕	☕	☕	☕	☕	☕		🛒		🛒	☕				🛒	☕		
St Pancras International ⊖ d	21p30	21p30	22p00	22p25	22p30	23p00	23p15	00 15												
Luton Airport Parkway 7 ✈ d				22p48	22p53	23p28		00 43												
Luton 10 d	21p54	21p54	22p24				23p46	00 47												
Bedford 7 d	22p17	22p17	22p40	23p04	23p17	23p52	00 10	01 09												
Wellingborough d	22p30	22p30	22p53	23p17	23p31	00 06	00 23	01 34												
Kettering 4 a	22p37	22p37	23p00	23p25	23p37	00 12	00 39	01 44												
d	22p38	22p38	23p01	23p26	23p38	00 13	00 40	01 45												
Corby d																				
Market Harborough d	22p48	22p48	23p12	23p37	23p48	00 23	00 50													
Leicester a	23p07	23p07	23p29	23p53	00 07	00 42	01 03	02 09												
d	23p09	23p09	23p30	23p55	00 09	00 44	01 05								06 33					07 25
Syston d															06 41					07 32
Sileby d															06 46					07 36
Barrow Upon Soar d															06 51					07 40
Loughborough d	23p19	23p19	23p41	00 06	00 19	00 54	01 15								06 56					07 45
East Midlands Parkway ✈ d	23p27	23p32	23p50	00 14	00 27	01 02	01 23								07 06					07 54
Beeston a			00 04		00 40		01 36								07 16					08 06
Nottingham 8 🚊 a			00 12		00 48		01 44								07 27					08 15
d							01 51		05 20					06 23		06 40			07 13	
Lincoln a																				
Langley Mill d														06 38					07 29	
Alfreton d														06 46		07 02			07 37	
Long Eaton a	23p38	23p38																		
Derby 6 a	23p49	23p49		00 34		01 21	02 10													
d	23p51	23p51		00 35						05 56		06 34	06 20				07 13	07 20		
Chesterfield d	00 10	00 10		00 58					05 49	06 15	06 26	06 53	06 42	06 58		07 13	07 32	07 42	07 50	
Sheffield 7 🚊 a	00 24	00 24		01 13					06 15	06 37	06 46	07 06	07 13	07 18		07 31	07 48	08 00	08 08	
Doncaster 7 a										07 04							08 25			
Wakefield Kirkgate 4 a											07 27			07 57					08 57	
Wakefield Westgate 7 a												07 36								
Leeds 10 a											07 51	07 52		08 21					09 19	
York 8 a										07 27		08 23					08 47			

	XC	EM	XC	EM	EM	EM	NT	EM	EM	EM	XC	EM	XC	EM	EM	EM	NT	EM	EM	EM	XC	EM
	◇1	◇	◇1	◇1	◇1	◇1				◇1	◇1	◇	◇1	◇1	◇1	◇1				◇1	◇1	◇
								C	D									C	D			
	🛒		🛒	☕	☕	☕				☕	🛒		🛒	☕	☕	☕				☕	🛒	
St Pancras International ⊖ d				06 10	06 37	06 55				07 00				07 25	07 30	07 55				08 15		
Luton Airport Parkway 7 ✈ d						07 16									07 51							
Luton 10 d				06 33	06 59					07 23												
Bedford 7 d				06 48						07 38					08 07							
Wellingborough d				07 01						07 51					08 20							
Kettering 4 a				07 07	07 27					08 00					08 26							
d				07 08	07 28					08 01					08 27							
Corby d																						
Market Harborough d				07 18	07 38					08 12				08 21	08 37					09 12		
Leicester a				07 35	07 53	08 04				08 29				08 36	08 52	09 02				09 29		
d				07 36	07 57	08 06		08 25	08 25	08 30				08 38	08 54	09 04		09 25	09 25	09 30		
Syston d								08 32	08 32									09 32	09 32			
Sileby d								08 36	08 36									09 36	09 36			
Barrow Upon Soar d								08 40	08 40									09 40	09 40			
Loughborough d				07 47	08 07	08 17		08 45	08 45	08 41				08 48	09 04			09 45	09 45			
East Midlands Parkway ✈ d				07 54				08 54	08 54	08 50				08 56				09 54	09 54	09 46		
Beeston a						08 30		09 02	09 02						09 16			10 02	10 02			
Nottingham 8 🚊 a						08 40		09 13	09 13	09 03					09 26			10 13	10 13	09 59		
d		07 45					08 11	09 21	09 23			08 45					09 15	10 29	10 29			09 45
Lincoln a								10 17	10 18									11 31	11 30			
Langley Mill d							08 31										09 32					
Alfreton d		08 07					08 39					09 07					09 40					10 07
Long Eaton a				07 58										08 59								
Derby 6 a				08 11	08 24									09 14		09 26						
d	07 44		08 11	08 18	08 28						08 44		09 13	09 18		09 28					09 44	
Chesterfield d	08 03	08 18	08 32	08 38	08 47		08 51				09 03	09 18		09 37		09 47	09 52				10 03	10 18
Sheffield 7 🚊 a	08 17	08 38	08 46	08 55	09 04		09 15				09 17	09 38	09 46	09 52		10 04	10 15				10 17	10 38
Doncaster 7 a			09 20										10 15									
Wakefield Kirkgate 4 a							09 57										10 57					
Wakefield Westgate 7 a	08 48										09 46										10 46	
Leeds 10 a	09 03						10 18				10 02						11 18				11 02	
York 8 a	09 33		09 48								10 27		10 40								11 28	

A MO until 6 September
B MO from 13 September
C from 27 September
D until 24 September

For connections from Gatwick Airport see Table 52

London - East Midlands - Sheffield

	XC	EM	EM	EM	NT	EM	EM	EM	XC	EM	XC	EM	EM	EM	NT	EM	EM	EM	XC	EM	XC
	◇1	◇1	◇1	◇1				◇1	◇1	◇	◇1	◇1	◇1	◇1				◇1	◇1	◇	◇1
						A	B									A	B				
	🛒	☕	☕	☕				☕	🛒		🛒	☕	☕	☕				☕	🛒		🛒
St Pancras International ⊖ d		08 25	08 30	08 55				09 15				09 25	09 30	09 55				10 15			
Luton Airport Parkway 7 ✈ d			08 51										09 51								
Luton 10 d																					
Bedford 7 d			09 07										10 07								
Wellingborough d			09 20										10 20								
Kettering 4 a			09 27										10 26								
d			09 27										10 27								
Corby d																					
Market Harborough d			09 37					10 12					10 37					11 12			
Leicester a		09 34	09 53	10 02				10 29				10 34	10 54	11 02				11 29			
d		09 35	09 54	10 04		10 25	10 25	10 30				10 35	10 54	11 04		11 25	11 25	11 30			
Syston d						10 32	10 32									11 32	11 32				
Sileby d						10 36	10 36									11 36	11 36				
Barrow Upon Soar d						10 40	10 40									11 40	11 40				
Loughborough d		09 45	10 04			10 45	10 45					10 46	11 04			11 45	11 45				
East Midlands Parkway ✈ d		09 52				10 54	10 54	10 46				10 53				11 54	11 54	11 46			
Beeston a			10 16			11 02	11 02						11 16			12 02	12 02				
Nottingham 8 🚊 a			10 26			11 14	11 14	10 59					11 26			12 13	12 13	11 59			
d					10 15	11 15	11 17			10 45					11 15	12 27	12 27			11 45	
Lincoln a						12 22	12 21									13 22	13 20				
Langley Mill d					10 32										11 31						
Alfreton d					10 40					11 07					11 39					12 07	
Long Eaton a		09 56										10 56									
Derby 6 a		10 09		10 26								11 09		11 26							
d	10 11	10 18		10 28					10 44		11 11	11 18		11 28					11 44		12 11
Chesterfield d		10 37		10 47	10 52				11 03	11 18		11 37		11 47	11 52				12 03	12 18	
Sheffield 7 🚊 a	10 46	10 52		11 04	11 15				11 17	11 38	11 46	11 52		12 04	12 16				12 17	12 38	12 46
Doncaster 7 a	11 15										12 15										13 20
Wakefield Kirkgate 4 a					11 57										12 57						
Wakefield Westgate 7 a									11 46										12 46		
Leeds 10 a					12 18				12 01						13 18				13 02		
York 8 a	11 45								12 29		12 45								13 29		13 46

	EM	EM	EM	NT	EM	EM	EM	XC	EM	XC	EM	EM	EM	NT	EM	EM	EM	XC	EM	XC	EM	EM	EM
	◇1	◇1	◇1				◇1	◇1	◇	◇1	◇1	◇1	◇1				◇1	◇1	◇	◇1	◇1	◇1	◇1
					A	B									A	B							
	☕	☕	☕				☕	🛒		🛒	☕	☕	☕				☕	🛒		🛒	☕	☕	☕
St Pancras International ⊖ d	10 25	10 30	10 55				11 15				11 25	11 30	11 55				12 15				12 25	12 30	12 55
Luton Airport Parkway 7 ✈ d		10 51										11 51										12 51	
Luton 10 d																							
Bedford 7 d		11 07										12 07										13 07	
Wellingborough d		11 20										12 20										13 20	
Kettering 4 a		11 26										12 26										13 26	
d		11 27										12 27										13 27	
Corby d																							
Market Harborough d		11 37					12 12					12 37					13 12					13 37	
Leicester a	11 33	11 52	12 02				12 29				12 33	12 53	13 02				13 30				13 33	13 54	14 02
d	11 35	11 54	12 04		12 25	12 25	12 30				12 35	12 54	13 04		13 25	13 25	13 30				13 35	13 54	14 04
Syston d					12 32	12 32									13 32	13 32							
Sileby d					12 36	12 36									13 36	13 36							
Barrow Upon Soar d					12 40	12 40									13 40	13 40							
Loughborough d	11 45	12 04			12 46	12 46					12 45	13 04			13 45	13 45					13 45	14 04	
East Midlands Parkway ✈ d	11 53				12 58	12 58	12 46				12 53				13 54	13 54	13 45				13 53		
Beeston a		12 16			13 07	13 07						13 16			14 02	14 02						14 16	
Nottingham 8 🚊 a		12 26			13 14	13 14	12 59					13 26			14 13	14 13	13 59					14 26	
d				12 15	13 17	13 17			12 45					13 15	14 29	14 29			13 45				
Lincoln a					14 26	14 23									15 24	15 22							
Langley Mill d				12 32										13 32									
Alfreton d				12 40					13 07					13 40					14 07				
Long Eaton a	11 56										12 56										13 56		
Derby 6 a	12 11		12 26								13 09		13 26								14 09		14 26
d	12 18		12 28					12 44		13 11	13 18		13 28					13 44		14 11	14 18		14 28
Chesterfield d	12 37		12 47	12 52				13 03	13 18		13 37		13 47	13 52				14 03	14 19		14 37		14 47
Sheffield 7 🚊 a	12 52		13 04	13 15				13 17	13 38	13 46	13 52		14 04	14 15				14 17	14 38	14 46	14 52		15 04
Doncaster 7 a										14 17										15 16			
Wakefield Kirkgate 4 a				13 57										14 57									
Wakefield Westgate 7 a								13 46										14 46					
Leeds 10 a				14 18				14 02						15 18				15 04					
York 8 a								14 29		14 43								15 29		15 40			

A from 27 September
B until 24 September

For connections from Gatwick Airport see Table 52

London - East Midlands - Sheffield

Station		NT	EM A	EM B	EM ◇1	XC ◇1	EM ◇	XC ◇1	EM ◇1	EM ◇1	EM ◇1	EM A	EM B	EM ◇1	XC ◇1	EM ◇	XC ◇1	EM ◇1	EM ◇1	EM ◇1	EM A	EM B
St Pancras International ⊖	d				13 15				13 25	13 30	13 55			14 15				14 25	14 30	14 55		
Luton Airport Parkway 7 ✈	d									13 51									14 51			
Luton 10	d																					
Bedford 7	d									14 07									15 07			
Wellingborough	d									14 20									15 20			
Kettering 4	a									14 26									15 26			
	d									14 27									15 27			
Corby	d																					
Market Harborough	d				14 12					14 37				15 12					15 37			
Leicester	a				14 29				14 33	14 54	15 02			15 29				15 33	15 54	16 02		
	d		14 25	14 25	14 30				14 35	14 54	15 04	15 25	15 25	15 30				15 35	15 54	16 04	16 25	16 25
Syston	d		14 32	14 32								15 32	15 32								16 32	16 32
Sileby	d		14 36	14 36								15 36	15 36								16 36	16 36
Barrow Upon Soar	d		14 40	14 40								15 40	15 40								16 40	16 40
Loughborough	d		14 45	14 45					14 45	15 04		15 45	15 45					15 45	16 04		16 45	16 45
East Midlands Parkway ✈	d		14 54	14 54	14 46				14 53			15 54	15 54	15 46				15 53			16 54	16 54
Beeston	a		15 02	15 02						15 16		16 02	16 02						16 16		17 02	17 02
Nottingham 8	a		15 13	15 13	14 59					15 26		16 13	16 13	15 59					16 26		17 13	17 13
	d	14 15	15 25	15 27			14 45					16 13	16 14			15 45					17 17	17 17
Lincoln	a		16 27	16 25								17 15	17 14								18 27	18 26
Langley Mill	d	14 30																				
Alfreton	d	14 38					15 07									16 07						
Long Eaton	a								14 56									15 56				
Derby 6	a								15 13		15 26							16 09		16 26		
	d					14 44		15 11	15 15		15 30				15 44		16 11	16 17		16 28		
Chesterfield	d	14 52				15 03	15 20		15 34		15 49				16 03	16 18		16 36		16 47		
Sheffield 7	a	15 15				15 17	15 38	15 46	15 52		16 04				16 17	16 38	16 46	16 55		17 04		
Doncaster 7	a							16 15									17 15					
Wakefield Kirkgate 4	a	15 57																				
Wakefield Westgate 7	a					15 46									16 47							
Leeds 10	a	16 19				16 02									17 02							
York 8	a					16 29		16 39							17 30		17 40					

Station		EM ◇1	XC ◇1	EM ◇	XC ◇1	EM ◇1	EM ◇1	EM ◇1	NT	EM A	EM B	EM ◇1	XC ◇1	EM ◇	XC ◇1	EM ◇1	EM ◇1	EM ◇1	NT	EM	XC ◇1	EM ◇	XC ◇1
St Pancras International ⊖	d	15 15				15 25	15 30	15 55				16 15				16 25	16 30	16 55					
Luton Airport Parkway 7 ✈	d						15 51										16 51						
Luton 10	d																16 55						
Bedford 7	d						16 07										17 10						
Wellingborough	d						16 20										17 23						
Kettering 4	a						16 26										17 29						
	d						16 27										17 30						
Corby	d																						
Market Harborough	d	16 12					16 37					17 12					17 40						
Leicester	a	16 29				16 33	16 54	17 02				17 29				17 35	17 55	18 02					
	d	16 30				16 35	16 54	17 04		17 25	17 25	17 30				17 35	17 55	18 04		18 25			
Syston	d									17 32	17 32									18 32			
Sileby	d									17 36	17 36									18 36			
Barrow Upon Soar	d									17 40	17 40									18 40			
Loughborough	d					16 45	17 04			17 45	17 45					17 45	18 05			18 45			
East Midlands Parkway ✈	d	16 46				16 53				17 54	17 54	17 46				17 52				18 54			
Beeston	a						17 16			18 02	18 02						18 17			19 07			
Nottingham 8	a	16 59					17 26			18 13	18 13	17 59					18 30			19 15			
	d			16 45					17 15	18 14	18 15			17 45					18 15			18 45	
Lincoln	a									19 23	19 22												
Langley Mill	d								17 31					18 02					18 32				
Alfreton	d			17 07					17 39					18 09					18 40			19 07	
Long Eaton	a					16 56										18 00							
Derby 6	a					17 09		17 26								18 14		18 26					
	d		16 42		17 11	17 18		17 28					17 41		18 11	18 18		18 28			18 44		19 11
Chesterfield	d		17 03	17 18		17 37		17 47	17 52				18 02	18 21		18 42		18 50	18 52		19 03	19 18	19 30
Sheffield 7	a		17 19	17 34	17 44	17 52		18 04	18 15				18 19	18 38	18 49	19 01		19 04	19 15		19 19	19 39	19 47
Doncaster 7	a														19 17								20 20
Wakefield Kirkgate 4	a								18 58										19 58				
Wakefield Westgate 7	a		17 47		18 12								18 47								19 49		
Leeds 10	a		18 03		18 30				19 23				19 02						20 19		20 05		
York 8	a		18 31		18 58								19 30		19 44						20 31		20 46

A from 27 September
B until 24 September

For connections from Gatwick Airport see Table 52

London - East Midlands - Sheffield

Station		EM ◇1	EM ◇1	EM ◇1	EM ◇1	EM ◇1	NT	EM	EM ◇1	XC ◇1	EM ◇	XC ◇1	EM ◇1	EM ◇1	EM	XC ◇1	EM ◇1	EM ◇1	EM ◇1	EM ◇1	XC ◇1	NT	EM ◇1
St Pancras International ⊖	d		17 15	17 30	17 55	17 45			18 15				18 25	18 30			18 55	19 15	19 25	19 30			19 55
Luton Airport Parkway 7 ✈	d					18 10								18 54						19 51			
Luton 10	d		17 41										18 51										
Bedford 7	d			18 09										19 11						20 07			
Wellingborough	d			18 22		18 35			19 02					19 24						20 20			
Kettering 4	a			18 28		18 45			19 09					19 30					20 16				
	d	18 04		18 29		18 47			19 10					19 32					20 17				
Corby	d																						
Market Harborough	d		18 19	18 39		19 00							19 28				19 54	20 12	20 27	20 37			
Leicester	a	18 30	18 36	18 54	19 04	19 21			19 34				19 45	19 56			20 11	20 30	20 42	20 54			21 04
	d	18 32	18 37	18 56	19 04	19 25		19 25	19 36				19 46	19 57	20 25		20 13	20 30	20 43	20 54			21 04
Syston	d							19 32							20 32								
Sileby	d							19 36							20 36								
Barrow Upon Soar	d							19 40							20 40								
Loughborough	d	18 43		19 06		19 36		19 45	19 47				19 57		20 45		20 23		20 54	21 04			
East Midlands Parkway ✈	d	18 50	18 53	19 13		19 44		19 54	19 55					20 12	20 54		20 31	20 45	21 01				
Beeston	a		19 02	19 18				20 07						20 17	21 03					21 18			
Nottingham 8	a		19 10	19 27		19 58		20 20	20 08					20 28	21 15			21 07		21 29			
	d					20 07	19 15		20 15		19 40			20 29						21 43		20 45	
Lincoln	a													21 24									
Langley Mill	d						19 32		20 33											22 01			
Alfreton	d						19 40		20 41		20 01									22 09			
Long Eaton	a	18 55				20 22							20 06						21 05				
Derby 6	a	19 09			19 28	20 35							20 19				20 46		21 16			21 05	21 32
	d	19 18			19 28					19 42		20 11	20 21			20 44	20 48				21 13	21 06	21 34
Chesterfield	d	19 37			19 47		19 52		20 53	20 03	20 12		20 41			21 03	21 09			22 21	21 34	21 28	21 55
Sheffield 7	a	19 52			20 04		20 15		21 14	20 19	20 28	20 49	20 58			21 18	21 25			22 37	21 48	21 54	22 16
Doncaster 7	a											21 21									22 29		
Wakefield Kirkgate 4	a						20 57																
Wakefield Westgate 7	a								21 54	20 53						21 50				23 21			22 46
Leeds 10	a						21 22		22 12	21 10						22 04				23 38			23 05
York 8	a											21 45									22 54		

Station		NT	EM	EM ◇1	EM ◇1	EM ◇1	XC ◇1	EM ◇1	EM ◇1	EM ◇1	EM ◇1	EM ◇1	EM ◇1	EM ◇1
St Pancras International ⊖	d			20 15	20 25	20 30		20 55	21 00	21 25	21 30	22 00	22 25	23 15
Luton Airport Parkway 7 ✈	d					20 51					21 53		22 48	
Luton 10	d								21 23			22 24		23 46
Bedford 7	d					21 07			21 38		22 09	22 40	23 04	00 10
Wellingborough	d					21 20			21 51		22 22	22 53	23 17	00 23
Kettering 4	a					21 26			21 57		22 30	23 00	23 25	00 39
	d					21 27			21 58		22 31	23 01	23 26	00 40
Corby	d													
Market Harborough	d			21 11		21 37			22 08	22 23	22 42	23 12	23 37	00 50
Leicester	a			21 25	21 33	21 53		22 02	22 26	22 40	23 01	23 29	23 53	01 03
	d		21 25	21 26	21 35	21 54		22 04	22 28	22 41	23 02	23 30	23 55	01 05
Syston	d		21 32											
Sileby	d		21 36											
Barrow Upon Soar	d		21 40											
Loughborough	d		21 45		21 45	22 04			22 38	22 52	23 13	23 41	00 06	01 15
East Midlands Parkway ✈	d		21 54	21 43	21 53				22 46	23 01	23 24	23 50	00 14	01 23
Beeston	a		22 07			22 16						00 04		01 36
Nottingham 8	a		22 16	21 58		22 27				23 12		00 12		01 44
	d	21 11												01 51
Lincoln	a													
Langley Mill	d	21 31												
Alfreton	d	21 39												
Long Eaton	a				21 58						23 37			
Derby 6	a				22 10			22 26	22 59		23 50		00 34	02 10
	d						21 44	22 28					00 35	
Chesterfield	d	22 00					22 07	22 47					00 58	
Sheffield 7	a	22 19					22 24	23 04					01 13	
Doncaster 7	a													
Wakefield Kirkgate 4	a													
Wakefield Westgate 7	a						22 57							
Leeds 10	a						23 16							
York 8	a													

For connections from Gatwick Airport see Table 52

Table 53

London - East Midlands - Sheffield

Saturdays

	EM	EM	EM	EM	EM	XC	EM	XC	EM	EM	XC	EM	XC	NT	EM	EM	XC	EM	EM	EM	NT	EM	EM
	◇1	◇1	◇1	◇1	◇	◇1	◇1	◇1		◇	◇1	◇1	◇1			◇	◇1	◇1	◇1	◇1			
																						A	B
	☕	☕	☕	☕		🛒	☕	🛒			🛒	☕	🛒				🛒	☕	☕	☕			
St Pancras International ⊖ d	22p00	22p25	23p15	00 15														06 10	06 37	06 55			
Luton Airport Parkway ✈ d		22p48		00 43																07 16			
Luton d	22p24		23p46	00 47														06 33	06 59				
Bedford d	22p40	23p04	00 10	01 09														06 48					
Wellingborough d	22p53	23p17	00 23	01 34														07 01					
Kettering a	23p00	23p25	00 39	01 45														07 07	07 27				
Kettering d	23p01	23p26	00 40	01 45														07 08	07 28				
Corby d																							
Market Harborough d	23p12	23p37	00 50															07 18	07 38				
Leicester a	23p29	23p53	01 03	02 09														07 35	07 53	08 04			
Leicester d	23p30	23p55	01 05						06 36						07 25			07 36	07 55	08 06		08 25	08 25
Syston d									06 43						07 32							08 32	08 32
Sileby d									06 47						07 36							08 36	08 36
Barrow Upon Soar d									06 51						07 40							08 40	08 40
Loughborough d	23p41	00 06	01 15						06 56						07 46			07 47	08 05	08 18		08 45	08 45
East Midlands Parkway ✈ d	23p50	00 14	01 23						07 06						07 57				08 13			08 57	08 57
Beeston a	00 04		01 36						07 15						08 04					08 31		09 05	09 05
Nottingham a	00 12		01 44						07 24						08 13					08 42		09 14	09 14
Nottingham d			01 51		05 18					06 40				07 13		07 45					08 11	09 21	09 23
Lincoln a																						10 17	10 17
Langley Mill d														07 29							08 31		
Alfreton d										07 02				07 37		08 07					08 39		
Long Eaton a																		07 55					
Derby a		00 34	02 10															08 09	08 26				
Derby d		00 35				05 55	06 26	06 37			07 11	07 20	07 44				08 11	08 18	08 28				
Chesterfield d		00 58			05 49	06 31	06 45	06 56		07 13	07 30	07 42	08 03	07 50		08 18	08 30	08 37	08 47		08 51		
Sheffield a		01 13			06 15	06 44	07 09	07 09		07 31	07 48	07 59	08 17	08 08		08 38	08 46	08 52	09 07		09 15		
Doncaster a						07 16					08 23						09 21		09 53				
Wakefield Kirkgate a														08 57							09 57		
Wakefield Westgate a								07 36					08 46										
Leeds a								07 52					09 02	09 19							10 18		
York a						07 39		08 25			08 49		09 30				09 45		10 16				

	EM	XC	EM	XC	EM	EM	EM	NT	EM	EM	EM	XC	EM	XC	EM	EM	EM	NT	EM	EM	EM	XC
	◇1	◇1	◇	◇1	◇1	◇1	◇1				◇1	◇1	◇	◇1	◇1	◇1	◇1				◇1	◇1
									A	B									A	B		
	☕	🛒		🛒	☕	☕	☕				☕	🛒		🛒	☕	☕	☕				☕	🛒
St Pancras International ⊖ d	07 00					07 30	07 55				08 15				08 25	08 30	08 55				09 15	
Luton Airport Parkway ✈ d						07 51										08 51						
Luton d	07 23																					
Bedford d	07 38					08 07										09 07						
Wellingborough d	07 51					08 20										09 20						
Kettering a	08 00					08 27										09 26						
Kettering d	08 01					08 27										09 27						
Corby d																						
Market Harborough d	08 12					08 37					09 12					09 37					10 12	
Leicester a	08 29					08 53	09 02				09 29				09 33	09 52	10 02				10 29	
Leicester d	08 30				08 38	08 54	09 04		09 25	09 25	09 30				09 35	09 54	10 04		10 25	10 25	10 30	
Syston d									09 32	09 32									10 32	10 32		
Sileby d									09 36	09 36									10 36	10 36		
Barrow Upon Soar d									09 40	09 40									10 40	10 40		
Loughborough d	08 41				08 49	09 04			09 45	09 45					09 45	10 05			10 45	10 45		
East Midlands Parkway ✈ d	08 50				08 56				09 54	09 54	09 46				09 53				10 54	10 54	10 46	
Beeston a						09 16			10 02	10 02						10 16			11 02	11 02		
Nottingham a	09 03					09 26			10 13	10 13	09 59					10 26			11 13	11 13	10 59	
Nottingham d			08 45					09 15	10 29	10 29			09 45					10 15	11 15	11 17		
Lincoln a									11 31	11 30									12 22	12 21		
Langley Mill d								09 32										10 32				
Alfreton d			09 07					09 40					10 07					10 40				
Long Eaton a					09 00										09 56							
Derby a					09 14		09 26								10 09		10 26					
Derby d		08 44		09 11	09 18		09 28					09 44		10 11	10 18		10 28					10 44
Chesterfield d		09 03	09 18		09 37		09 47	09 52				10 03	10 18		10 37		10 49	10 52				11 03
Sheffield a		09 17	09 38	09 46	09 52		10 04	10 15				10 17	10 38	10 46	10 52		11 04	11 15				11 17
Doncaster a				10 18										11 16								
Wakefield Kirkgate a								10 57										11 57				
Wakefield Westgate a		09 46										10 46										11 46
Leeds a		10 02						11 18				11 02						12 18				12 02
York a		10 30		10 44								11 30		11 44								12 30

A from 2 October

B until 25 September

For connections from Gatwick Airport see Table 52

Table 53

London - East Midlands - Sheffield

	EM	XC	EM	EM	EM	NT	EM	EM	EM	XC	EM	XC	EM	EM	EM	NT	EM	EM	EM	XC
	◇	◇1	◇1	◇1	◇1				◇1	◇1	◇	◇1	◇1	◇1	◇1				◇1	◇1
							A	B									A	B		
		🛒	☕	☕	☕				☕	🛒		🛒	☕	☕	☕				☕	🛒
St Pancras International ⊖ d			09 25	09 30	09 55				10 15				10 25	10 30	10 55				11 15	
Luton Airport Parkway ✈ d				09 51										10 51						
Luton d																				
Bedford d				10 07										11 07						
Wellingborough d				10 20										11 20						
Kettering a				10 26										11 26						
Kettering d				10 27										11 27						
Corby d																				
Market Harborough d				10 37					11 12					11 37					12 12	
Leicester a			10 33	10 54	11 02				11 29				11 33	11 54	12 02				12 29	
Leicester d			10 35	10 54	11 04		11 25	11 25	11 30				11 35	11 54	12 04		12 25	12 25	12 30	
Syston d							11 32	11 32									12 32	12 32		
Sileby d							11 36	11 36									12 36	12 36		
Barrow Upon Soar d							11 40	11 40									12 40	12 40		
Loughborough d			10 45	11 04			11 45	11 45					11 45	12 04			12 45	12 45		
East Midlands Parkway ✈ d			10 53				11 54	11 54	11 46				11 53				12 54	12 54	12 46	
Beeston a				11 16			12 02	12 02						12 16			13 02	13 02		
Nottingham a				11 26			12 13	12 13	11 59					12 26			13 13	13 13	12 59	
Nottingham d	10 45					11 15	12 27	12 27			11 45					12 15	13 17	13 17		
Lincoln a							13 22	13 20									14 26	14 23		
Langley Mill d						11 31										12 32				
Alfreton d	11 07					11 39					12 07					12 40				
Long Eaton a			10 56										11 56							
Derby a			11 09		11 26								12 09		12 26					
Derby d		11 11	11 18		11 28					11 44		12 11	12 18		12 28					12 44
Chesterfield d	11 18		11 37		11 47	11 52				12 03	12 18		12 37		12 47	12 52				13 03
Sheffield a	11 38	11 46	11 52		12 04	12 16				12 16	12 38	12 46	12 52		13 04	13 15				13 17
Doncaster a		12 16										13 19								
Wakefield Kirkgate a						12 57										13 57				
Wakefield Westgate a										12 46										13 46
Leeds a						13 18				13 02						14 18				14 02
York a		12 44								13 32		13 44								14 30

	XC	EM	EM	EM	NT	EM	EM	EM	XC	EM	XC	EM	EM	EM	NT	EM	EM	EM	XC	EM	XC
	◇1	◇1	◇1	◇1				◇1	◇1	◇	◇1	◇1	◇1	◇1				◇1	◇1	◇	◇1
						A	B									A	B				
	🛒	☕	☕	☕				☕	🛒		🛒	☕	☕	☕				☕	🛒		🛒
St Pancras International ⊖ d		11 25	11 30	11 55				12 15				12 25	12 30	12 55				13 15			
Luton Airport Parkway ✈ d			11 51										12 51								
Luton d																					
Bedford d			12 07										13 07								
Wellingborough d			12 20										13 20								
Kettering a			12 26										13 26								
Kettering d			12 27										13 27								
Corby d																					
Market Harborough d			12 37					13 12					13 37					14 12			
Leicester a		12 33	12 54	13 02				13 29				13 33	13 52	14 02				14 29			
Leicester d		12 35	12 54	13 04		13 25	13 25	13 30				13 35	13 54	14 04		14 25	14 25	14 30			
Syston d						13 32	13 32									14 32	14 32				
Sileby d						13 36	13 36									14 36	14 36				
Barrow Upon Soar d						13 40	13 40									14 40	14 40				
Loughborough d		12 45	13 04			13 45	13 45					13 45	14 04			14 45	14 45				
East Midlands Parkway ✈ d		12 53				13 54	13 54	13 46				13 53				14 54	14 54	14 46			
Beeston a			13 16			14 02	14 02						14 16			15 02	15 02				
Nottingham a			13 27			14 13	14 13	13 59		13 36			14 26			15 13	15 13	14 59		14 36	
Nottingham d					13 15	14 29	14 29			13 45					14 15	15 25	15 27			14 45	
Lincoln a						15 23	15 22									16 25	16 25				
Langley Mill d					13 32										14 30						
Alfreton d					13 40					14 07					14 38					15 07	
Long Eaton a		12 56										13 56									
Derby a		13 09		13 26								14 09		14 26							
Derby d	13 11	13 18		13 28					13 44		14 11	14 18		14 28					14 44		15 11
Chesterfield d		13 37		13 47	13 52				14 03	14 18		14 37		14 47	14 52				15 03	15 18	
Sheffield a	13 46	13 52		14 04	14 15				14 17	14 38	14 46	14 52		15 04	15 15				15 17	15 38	15 46
Doncaster a	14 16										15 16										16 15
Wakefield Kirkgate a					14 57										15 57						
Wakefield Westgate a									14 46										15 46		
Leeds a					15 18				15 02						16 19				16 02		
York a	14 44								15 32		15 44								16 30		16 39

A from 2 October

B until 25 September

For connections from Gatwick Airport see Table 52

London - East Midlands - Sheffield

		EM	EM	NT	EM	EM	EM	XC	XC	EM	XC	EM	EM	EM	NT	EM	EM	EM	XC	XC	EM	XC
		◇1 ☕	◇1 ☕		A	B	◇1 ☕	◇1 C 🛒	◇1 D 🛒	◇	◇1 🛒	◇1 ☕	◇1 ☕	◇1 ☕		A	B	◇1 ☕	◇1 D 🛒	◇1 C 🛒	◇	◇1 🛒
St Pancras International ⊖	d	13 30	13 55				14 15					14 25	14 30	14 55				15 15				
Luton Airport Parkway 7 ✈	d	13 51											14 51									
Luton 10	d																					
Bedford 7	d	14 07											15 07									
Wellingborough	d	14 20											15 20									
Kettering 4	a	14 26											15 26									
	d	14 27											15 27									
Corby	d																					
Market Harborough	d	14 37					15 12						15 37					16 12				
Leicester	a	14 54	15 02				15 29					15 33	15 53	16 02				16 29				
	d	14 54	15 04		15 25	15 25	15 30					15 35	15 54	16 04		16 25	16 25	16 30				
Syston	d				15 32	15 32										16 32	16 32					
Sileby	d				15 36	15 36										16 36	16 36					
Barrow Upon Soar	d				15 40	15 40										16 40	16 40					
Loughborough	d	15 04			15 45	15 45						15 45	16 04			16 45	16 45					
East Midlands Parkway ✈	d				15 54	15 54	15 46					15 53				16 54	16 54	16 45				
Beeston	a	15 16			16 02	16 02							16 16			17 02	17 02					
Nottingham 8 🚊	a	15 26			16 13	16 13	16 01						16 26			17 13	17 13	16 59				
	d			15 15	16 13	16 14				15 45					16 15	17 17	17 17				16 45	
Lincoln	a				17 15	17 14										18 27	18 26					
Langley Mill	d			15 32											16 32							
Alfreton	d			15 40						16 07					16 40						17 07	
Long Eaton	a											15 56										
Derby 6	a											16 09		16 26								
	d		15 28					15 44	15 45		16 11	16 18		16 28					16 42	16 42		17 11
Chesterfield	d		15 47	15 51				16 03	16 03	16 18		16 37		16 47	16 54				17 02	17 01	17 18	
Sheffield 7 🚊	a		16 04	16 15				16 18	16 18	16 38	16 46	16 52		17 04	17 15				17 19	17 18	17 34	17 44
Doncaster 7	a										17 19											
Wakefield Kirkgate 4	a			16 57											17 57							
Wakefield Westgate 7	a							16 49	16 49										17 47	17 47		18 14
Leeds 10	a			17 18				17 04	17 04						18 18				18 02	18 02		18 32
York 8	a							17 29	17 29		17 44								18 31	18 31		18 59

		EM	EM	EM	NT	EM	EM	EM	XC	EM	XC	EM	EM	EM	NT	EM	EM	XC	EM	XC	EM	EM	EM
		◇1 ☕	◇1 ☕	◇1 ☕		A	B	◇1 ☕	◇1 🛒	◇	◇1 🛒	◇1 ☕	◇1 ☕	◇1 ☕			◇1 ☕	◇1 🛒	◇	◇1 🛒	◇1 ☕	◇1 ☕	◇1 ☕
St Pancras International ⊖	d	15 25	15 30	15 55				16 15				16 25	16 30	16 55			17 15				17 25	17 30	17 55
Luton Airport Parkway 7 ✈	d		15 51										16 51									17 51	
Luton 10	d																						
Bedford 7	d		16 07										17 07									18 07	
Wellingborough	d		16 20										17 20									18 20	
Kettering 4	a		16 26										17 26									18 26	
	d		16 27										17 27									18 27	
Corby	d																						
Market Harborough	d		16 37					17 12					17 37				18 12					18 37	
Leicester	a	16 33	16 54	17 02				17 29				17 33	17 52	18 02			18 29				18 33	18 52	19 02
	d	16 35	16 54	17 04		17 25	17 25	17 30				17 35	17 54	18 04		18 25	18 30				18 35	18 54	19 04
Syston	d					17 32	17 32									18 32							
Sileby	d					17 36	17 36									18 36							
Barrow Upon Soar	d					17 40	17 40									18 40							
Loughborough	d	16 45	17 04			17 45	17 45					17 45	18 04			18 45					18 45	19 04	
East Midlands Parkway ✈	d	16 52				17 54	17 54	17 46				17 53				18 54	18 46				18 53		
Beeston	a		17 16			18 02	18 02						18 16			19 02						19 16	
Nottingham 8 🚊	a		17 26			18 12	18 12	17 59					18 26			19 14	18 59					19 26	
	d				17 15	18 14	18 15			17 45					18 15				18 45			19 29	
Lincoln	a					19 23	19 22															20 26	
Langley Mill	d				17 31					18 03					18 32								
Alfreton	d				17 39					18 10					18 40				19 07				
Long Eaton	a	16 56										17 56									18 56		
Derby 6	a	17 09		17 26								18 09		18 26							19 09		19 26
	d	17 18		17 28					17 44		18 11	18 18		18 28				18 44		19 11	19 18		19 28
Chesterfield	d	17 37		17 47	17 52				18 03	18 22		18 39		18 47	18 52			19 03	19 18	19 30	19 37		19 47
Sheffield 7 🚊	a	17 52		18 04	18 15				18 18	18 39	18 47	18 59		19 04	19 15			19 18	19 39	19 51	19 52		20 06
Doncaster 7	a										19 18									20 16			
Wakefield Kirkgate 4	a				18 58										19 58								
Wakefield Westgate 7	a								18 46									19 46					
Leeds 10	a				19 23				19 01						20 19			20 02					
York 8	a								19 31		19 44							20 31		20 40			

A from 2 October
B until 25 September
C from 11 September
D until 4 September

For connections from Gatwick Airport see Table 52

London - East Midlands - Sheffield

		EM	EM	XC	EM	XC	EM	EM	EM	EM	EM	EM	EM	EM	XC	NT	XC	NT	EM	EM	EM	EM
			◇1 ☕	◇1 🛒	◇	◇1 🛒	◇1 ☕	◇1 ☕	◇1 ☕	A	B	◇1 ☕	◇1 ☕	◇1 ☕	◇1 🛒		◇1 🛒		◇1 ☕		◇1 ☕	◇1 ☕
St Pancras International ⊖	d		18 15				18 25	18 30	18 55			19 15	19 25	19 30					19 55		20 15	20 25
Luton Airport Parkway 7 ✈	d							18 51						19 51								
Luton 10	d																					
Bedford 7	d							19 07						20 07								
Wellingborough	d							19 20						20 20								
Kettering 4	a							19 26						20 26								
	d							19 27						20 27								
Corby	d																					
Market Harborough	d		19 12					19 37				20 12		20 37							21 12	
Leicester	a		19 29				19 33	19 52	20 02			20 29	20 33	20 52					21 04		21 29	21 33
	d	19 25	19 30				19 35	19 54	20 04	20 25	20 25	20 30	20 35	20 54					21 06	21 25	21 30	21 35
Syston	d	19 32								20 32	20 32									21 32		
Sileby	d	19 36								20 36	20 36									21 36		
Barrow Upon Soar	d	19 40								20 40	20 40									21 40		
Loughborough	d	19 45					19 45	20 04		20 45	20 45		20 45	21 04						21 45		21 45
East Midlands Parkway ✈	d	19 54	19 46				19 53			20 54	20 54	20 46	20 53							21 54	21 46	21 53
Beeston	a	20 05						20 16		21 05	21 05			21 16						22 06		
Nottingham 8 🚊	a	20 15	19 59					20 26		21 15	21 15	20 59		21 26						22 14	22 01	
	d	20 29	20 15		19 40						21 25					20 39		21 15				
Lincoln	a	21 24									22 40											
Langley Mill	d		20 33													21 02		21 31				
Alfreton	d		20 41		20 01											21 10		21 39				
Long Eaton	a						19 56						20 56									21 57
Derby 6	a						20 09		20 26				21 10						21 32			22 12
	d			19 44		20 11	20 18		20 28						20 44		21 11		21 34			
Chesterfield	d		20 53	20 03	20 11	20 30	20 37		20 47						21 03	21 22	21 30	21 50	21 56			
Sheffield 7 🚊	a		21 14	20 18	20 27	20 49	20 54		21 00						21 18	21 40	21 44	22 13	22 16			
Doncaster 7	a					21 25											22 19					
Wakefield Kirkgate 4	a																					
Wakefield Westgate 7	a		21 53	20 48											21 48				22 44			
Leeds 10	a		22 10	21 04											22 02				23 04			
York 8	a			21 58		21 48											22 43					

		EM	EM	XC	EM	EM	EM	EM	EM	EM	EM	EM	EM	EM	EM	EM	EM	EM	EM	EM	EM
		◇1 D ☕	◇1 C ☕	◇1 🛒	C 🚌	◇1 D ☕	◇1 C ☕	◇1 D ☕	◇1 C ☕	◇1 D ☕	◇1 C ☕	C 🚌	C 🚌	◇1 D ☕	◇1 C ☕	C 🚌	◇1 D ☕	◇1 E ☕	◇1 F ☕	E 🚌	◇1 G ☕
St Pancras International ⊖	d	20 30	20 30			20 55	20 55	21 00	21 00	21 25	21 25			21 30	21 30		22 00	22 00	22 00		22 25
Luton Airport Parkway 7 ✈	d	20 51	20 51											21 51	21 51						22 47
Luton 10	d							21 23	21 23								22 24	22 24	22 24		
Bedford 7	d	21 07	21 07					21 38	21 38					22 10	22 10		22 42	22 42	22 42		23 03
Wellingborough	d	21 20	21 20					21 51	21 51					22 22	22 22		22 55	22 55	22 55		23 15
Kettering 4	a	21 26	21 26					22 00	22 00					22 29	22 29		23 02	23 02	23 05		23 22
	d	21 27	21 27					22 01	22 01					22 30	22 30		23 03	23 03	23 06		23 23
Corby	d																				
Market Harborough	d	21 37	21 37					22 12	22 12	22 20	22 20			22 40	22 40		23 14	23 14	23 18		23 33
Leicester	a	21 52	21 52			22 02	22 02	22 29	22 29	22 36	22 36			22 54	22 54		23 31	23 31	23 34		23 48
	d	21 54	21 54		22 02	22 04	22 04	22 30	22 30	22 37	22 37	22 39	22 46	22 54	22 54	23 04	23 32	23 32	23 36	23 41	23 49
Syston	d																				
Sileby	d																				
Barrow Upon Soar	d																				
Loughborough	d	22 04			22a37			22 41		22 48		23 15	23a21	23 07		23a39	23 46			00a16	00 01
East Midlands Parkway ✈	d	22 12	22 14							22 55	22 59			23 14	23 18		23 54	23 57	00 01		00 08
Beeston	a	22 17	22 20														00 01	00 05	00 08		
Nottingham 8 🚊	a	22 27	22 30							23 06	23 11						00 11	00 15	00 17		
	d																				
Lincoln	a																				
Langley Mill	d																				
Alfreton	d																				
Long Eaton	a													23 18	23 22						
Derby 6	a			21 44		22 26	22 37	23 02	23 08			23 55		23 29	23 35						00 21
	d			21 45		22 28	22 39														
Chesterfield	d			22 08		22 47	22 58														
Sheffield 7 🚊	a			22 23		23 00	23 11														
Doncaster 7	a			22 47																	
Wakefield Kirkgate 4	a																				
Wakefield Westgate 7	a			23 09																	
Leeds 10	a			23 24																	
York 8	a																				

A from 11 September until 16 October
B until 4 September, from 23 October
C until 4 September
D from 11 September
E until 10 July
F from 17 July until 4 September
G from 11 September until 4 December

For connections from Gatwick Airport see Table 52

Table 53

London - East Midlands - Sheffield

Saturdays

		EM	EM	EM	EM
		◇1 A	◇1 B	◇1 C	A Bus
St Pancras International	d	22 25	22 25	22 25	
Luton Airport Parkway	d	22 47	22 47	22 48	
Luton	d				
Bedford	d	23 03	23 03	23 04	
Wellingborough	d	23 15	23 15	23 17	
Kettering	a	23 22	23 25	23 25	
	d	23 23	23 26	23 26	
Corby	d				
Market Harborough	d	23 33	23 37	23 37	
Leicester	a	23 48	23 52	23 53	
	d	23 56	23 57	23 55	23 58
Syston	d				
Sileby	d				
Barrow Upon Soar	d				
Loughborough	d			00 06	00a33
East Midlands Parkway	d	00 18	00 19	00 14	
Beeston	a				
Nottingham	a				
	d				
Lincoln	a				
Langley Mill	d				
Alfreton	d				
Long Eaton	a				
Derby	a	00 31	00 32	00 34	
	d			00 35	
Chesterfield	d			00 58	
Sheffield	a			01 13	
Doncaster	a				
Wakefield Kirkgate	a				
Wakefield Westgate	a				
Leeds	a				
York	a				

Sundays until 11 July

		EM	EM	EM	EM	XC	EM	NT	XC	EM	EM	EM	EM	NT	EM	XC	EM	EM	EM	EM	NT	EM	XC
		◇1	◇1	◇1 E	Bus	◇1	◇		◇1	◇	◇1	◇1	Bus		Bus	◇1	◇	◇1	◇1	Bus		Bus	◇1
St Pancras International	d	22p00	22p25	22p25								09 00						09 30	10 00				
Luton Airport Parkway	d		22p47	22p48								09 28							10 29				
Luton	d	22p24																10 01					
Bedford	d	22p42	23p03	23p04								09 52						10 21	10 50				
Wellingborough	d	22p55	23p15	23p17								10 06						10 37	11 04				
Kettering	a	23p02	23p22	23p25								10 14						10 43	11 12				
	d	23p03	23p23	23p26								10 15						10 44	11 13				
Corby	d																						
Market Harborough	d	23p14	23p33	23p37								10 26						10 54	11 24				
Leicester	a	23p31	23p48	23p53								10 46						11 13	11 44				
	d	23p32	23p56	23p55	09 19						10 10	10 48	10 56		11 23			11 16	11 46	11 54		12 26	
Syston	d																						
Sileby	d																						
Barrow Upon Soar	d																						
Loughborough	d			00 06	09 55								11a31		11a58					12a29		13a01	
East Midlands Parkway	d	23p57	00 18	00 14	10a20						10 31	11 10						11 38	12 07				
Beeston	a	00 05										11 18											
Nottingham	a	00 15										11 26							12 21				
	d						09 31	10 06		10 41				11 15			11 46				12 19		
Lincoln	a																						
Langley Mill	d							10 27						11 31							12 35		
Alfreton	d						09 55	10 35		11 03				11 39			12 08				12 43		
Long Eaton	a										10 35							11 43					
Derby	a		00 31	00 34							10 55							11 54					
	d			00 35		09 44			10 44		11 05					11 44		12 10					12 44
Chesterfield	d			00 58		10 03	10 08	10 54	11 03	11 15	11 25			11 51		12 03	12 19	12 30			12 54		13 03
Sheffield	a			01 13		10 16	10 33	11 15	11 17	11 35	11 42			12 15		12 18	12 36	12 46			13 15		13 17
Doncaster	a										12 06												
Wakefield Kirkgate	a							11 52						12 52							13 52		
Wakefield Westgate	a					10 44			11 44							12 44							13 44
Leeds	a					11 02		12 18	12 02					13 18		13 02					14 18		14 02
York	a					11 34			12 32		12 29					13 32							14 32

A until 10 July
B from 17 July until 4 September
C 29 May
E 30 May

For connections from Gatwick Airport see Table 52

Table 53

London - East Midlands - Sheffield

Sundays until 11 July

		EM	EM	EM	EM	XC	NT	EM	XC	EM	EM	EM	EM	XC	NT	XC	EM	EM	EM	XC	NT	XC	EM
		◇	◇1	◇1	Bus	◇1		Bus	◇1	◇	◇1	◇1	Bus	◇1		◇1	◇	◇1	◇1	◇1		◇1	◇1
St Pancras International	d		10 30	11 00							11 30	12 00						12 30	13 00				13 30
Luton Airport Parkway	d			11 29							11 58	12 29						12 59	13 29				14 02
Luton	d		11 02	11 32							12 02	12 33						13 03	13 33				14 06
Bedford	d		11 27	11 55							12 26	12 56						13 26	13 56				14 21
Wellingborough	d		11 39	12 09							12 40	13 10						13 40	14 10				14 35
Kettering	a		11 46	12 15							12 47	13 16						13 48	14 16				14 42
	d		11 46	12 16							12 48	13 17						13 49	14 17				14 43
Corby	d																						
Market Harborough	d		11 56	12 26							12 58	13 27						14 00	14 27				14 54
Leicester	a		12 16	12 45							13 17	13 46						14 20	14 46				15 16
	d		12 19	12 47	12 55			13 27			13 19	13 48	13 56					14 22	14 48				15 18
Syston	d																						
Sileby	d																						
Barrow Upon Soar	d																						
Loughborough	d				13a30			14a02					14a31					14 33	14 58				15 29
East Midlands Parkway	d		12 39	13 08							13 42	14 08						14 41	15 06				15 37
Beeston	a			13 14								14 17							15 12				
Nottingham	a			13 23								14 25							15 20				
	d	12 39					13 09			13 38					14 19		14 37				15 12		
Lincoln	a																						
Langley Mill	d	12 56					13 27			13 55					14 35		14 54				15 34		
Alfreton	d	13 04					13 35			14 03					14 43		15 02				15 44		
Long Eaton	a		12 44								13 47							14 45					15 43
Derby	a		12 55								14 00							15 00					15 56
	d		13 04			13 11			13 44		14 04			14 11		14 44		15 01		15 07		15 44	15 57
Chesterfield	d	13 17	13 24			13 30	13 51		14 03	14 18	14 24			14 30	14 54	15 03	15 13	15 22			15 53	16 03	16 18
Sheffield	a	13 33	13 43			13 43	14 15		14 17	14 36	14 42			14 46	15 15	15 17	15 31	15 41		15 47	16 15	16 18	16 33
Doncaster	a					14 13								15 13						16 15			
Wakefield Kirkgate	a						14 52								15 52						16 52		
Wakefield Westgate	a								14 44							15 44						16 44	
Leeds	a						15 18		15 02						16 18	16 02					17 18	17 02	
York	a					14 43			15 32					15 40		16 32				16 40		17 32	

		EM	EM	XC	NT	XC	EM	EM	EM	XC	NT	XC	EM	EM	EM	XC	EM	EM	EM	EM	NT	XC
		◇1	◇	◇1		◇1	◇1	◇1	◇	◇1		◇1	◇1	◇1	◇	◇1	◇1	◇1	◇1	◇1		◇1
St Pancras International	d	14 00					14 30	15 00					15 30	16 00			16 25	16 30	16 55	17 00		
Luton Airport Parkway	d	14 29						15 29						16 29						17 21		
Luton	d						15 01						16 01					16 52				
Bedford	d	14 47					15 17	15 47					16 17	16 47				17 15		17 45		
Wellingborough	d	15 00					15 31	16 01					16 31	17 00				17 28		17 58		
Kettering	a	15 07					15 38	16 08					16 38	17 07				17 35		18 05		
	d	15 08					15 39	16 09					16 39	17 08				17 36		18 06		
Corby	d																					
Market Harborough	d	15 18					15 50	16 20					16 50	17 18				17 46		18 16		
Leicester	a	15 37					16 17	16 41					17 11	17 37			17 47	18 07	18 21	18 35		
	d	15 39					16 19	16 43					17 12	17 39			17 49	18 09	18 22	18 37		
Syston	d																					
Sileby	d																					
Barrow Upon Soar	d																					
Loughborough	d	15 49					16 30	16 54					17 24	17 49				18 20		18 47		
East Midlands Parkway	d	15 57					16 38	17 02					17 32	17 57			18 05	18 28	18 36	18 55		
Beeston	a	16 05												18 06						19 00		
Nottingham	a	16 12						17 14						18 14					18 52	19 07		
	d		15 44		16 14				16 40		17 14				17 37						18 14	
Lincoln	a																					
Langley Mill	d				16 30				17 00		17 30				17 54						18 30	
Alfreton	d		16 06		16 38				17 08		17 38				18 02						18 38	
Long Eaton	a						16 42						17 36					18 31				
Derby	a						16 55						17 48				18 17	18 47				
	d			16 05		16 44	16 56			17 07		17 44	17 50			18 05	18 19					18 44
Chesterfield	d		16 23		16 50	17 03	17 17		17 22		17 49	18 04			18 17		18 40				18 50	19 05
Sheffield	a		16 39	16 48	17 15	17 17	17 32		17 40	17 48	18 15	18 19	18 29		18 34	18 46	18 57				19 15	19 20
Doncaster	a			17 13						18 13						19 13						
Wakefield Kirkgate	a				17 52						18 52										19 52	
Wakefield Westgate	a					17 45	18 06			18 33		18 47										19 48
Leeds	a				18 18	18 02	18 24			18 51	19 18	19 04									20 18	20 05
York	a			17 42		18 32				19 21		19 32				19 42						20 32

For connections from Gatwick Airport see Table 52

Table 53

London - East Midlands - Sheffield

Sundays until 11 July

		EM ◇	XC ◇1	EM ◇1	EM ◇1	EM ◇1	EM ◇1	NT	XC ◇1	EM ◇	XC ◇1	EM ◇1	EM ◇1	EM ◇1	EM ◇1	NT	XC ◇1	EM ◇1	EM ◇1	EM ◇1	EM ◇1	EM ◇1	XC ◇1
St Pancras International	d			17 25	17 30	17 55	18 00					18 25	18 30	18 55	19 00			19 25	19 30	19 55	20 00	20 25	
Luton Airport Parkway	d						18 21								19 21						20 23		
Luton	d				17 52								18 52						19 52				
Bedford	d				18 15		18 45						19 15		19 45				20 15		20 48		
Wellingborough	d				18 28		18 58						19 28		19 58				20 28		21 00		
Kettering	a				18 35		19 05						19 35		20 05				20 35		21 07		
	d				18 36		19 06						19 36		20 06				20 36		21 08		
Corby	d																						
Market Harborough	d				18 46		19 16						19 46		20 16				20 46		21 18		
Leicester	a			18 44	19 08	19 20	19 35					19 47	20 05	20 18	20 35			20 47	21 05	21 17	21 37	21 47	
	d			18 46	19 10	19 22	19 37					19 49	20 07	20 20	20 37			20 49	21 07	21 19	21 39	21 49	
Syston	d																						
Sileby	d																						
Barrow Upon Soar	d																						
Loughborough	d				19 21		19 47						20 17		20 47				21 17	21 30	21 49	22 01	
East Midlands Parkway	d			19 00	19 29	19 36	19 55					20 08	20 25	20 34	20 55			21 05	21 25	21 39	21 57	22 09	
Beeston	a						20 01								21 02						22 03		
Nottingham	a					19 51	20 08							20 48	21 12					21 52	22 11		
	d	18 37						19 19		19 38						20 13							
Lincoln	a																						
Langley Mill	d	18 54						19 35								20 29							
Alfreton	d	19 02						19 43		20 00						20 37							
Long Eaton	a				19 32								20 28						21 28				
Derby	a			19 14	19 47							20 20	20 45					21 17	21 40			22 21	
	d		19 04	19 16					19 41		20 05	20 22					20 44	21 19					21 44
Chesterfield	d	19 12		19 35				19 54	20 02	20 10		20 43				20 48	21 03	21 40					22 03
Sheffield	a	19 31	19 39	19 50				20 15	20 17	20 31	20 38	20 58				21 14	21 16	21 55					22 18
Doncaster	a		20 16								21 19												
Wakefield Kirkgate	a							20 52															
Wakefield Westgate	a								20 46			21 32					21 44						22 45
Leeds	a							21 16	21 03			21 49					22 01						23 04
York	a		20 44						21 32		21 42												

		NT	XC ◇1	EM ◇1	EM ◇1	EM ◇1	EM ◇1	EM ◇1
St Pancras International	d			20 30	21 00	21 30	22 30	23 00
Luton Airport Parkway	d				21 23		22 53	23 28
Luton	d			20 54		21 54		
Bedford	d			21 18	21 47	22 17	23 17	23 52
Wellingborough	d			21 31	22 00	22 30	23 31	00 06
Kettering	a			21 38	22 07	22 37	23 37	00 12
	d			21 39	22 08	22 38	23 38	00 13
Corby	d							
Market Harborough	d			21 50	22 18	22 48	23 48	00 23
Leicester	a			22 11	22 37	23 07	00 07	00 42
	d			22 13	22 39	23 09	00 09	00 44
Syston	d							
Sileby	d							
Barrow Upon Soar	d							
Loughborough	d				22 49	23 19	00 19	00 54
East Midlands Parkway	d			22 29	22 57	23 27	00 27	01 02
Beeston	a				23 10		00 40	
Nottingham	a				23 18		00 48	
	d	21 20						
Lincoln	a							
Langley Mill	d	21 41						
Alfreton	d	21 49						
Long Eaton	a					23 38		
Derby	a			22 43		23 49		01 21
	d		22 46	22 51		23 51		
Chesterfield	d	22 08	23 07	23 13		00 10		
Sheffield	a	22 32	23 22	23 28		00 24		
Doncaster	a							
Wakefield Kirkgate	a							
Wakefield Westgate	a			00 15				
Leeds	a		00 33	00 32				
York	a							

For connections from Gatwick Airport see Table 52

Table 53

London - East Midlands - Sheffield

Sundays 18 July to 05 September

		EM ◇1	EM ◇1	XC ◇1	EM ◇	NT	XC ◇1	EM ◇1	EM ◇1	EM ◇	NT	XC ◇1	EM ◇	EM ◇1	EM ◇1	NT	XC ◇1	EM ◇	EM ◇1	EM ◇1	XC ◇1	NT	XC ◇1
St Pancras International	d	22p00	22p25						09 00					09 30	10 00				10 30	11 00			
Luton Airport Parkway	d		22p47						09 28						10 29					11 29			
Luton	d	22p24												10 01					11 02	11 32			
Bedford	d	22p42	23p03						09 52					10 21	10 50				11 27	11 55			
Wellingborough	d	22p55	23p15						10 06					10 37	11 04				11 39	12 09			
Kettering	a	23p05	23p25						10 16					10 46	11 14				11 49	12 18			
	d	23p06	23p26						10 21					10 53	11 20				11 52	12 23			
Corby	d																						
Market Harborough	d	23p18	23p37						10 33					11 04	11 32				12 03	12 34			
Leicester	a	23p34	23p52						10 53					11 23	11 53				12 24	12 53			
	d	23p36	23p57					10 10	10 55					11 26	11 54				12 26	12 55			
Syston	d																						
Sileby	d																						
Barrow Upon Soar	d																						
Loughborough	d							10 21	11 06					11 36	12 05				12 36	13 05			
East Midlands Parkway	d	00 01	00 19						11 14					11 44	12 14				12 44	13 13			
Beeston	a	00 08							11 24											13 18			
Nottingham	a	00 17							11 34						12 30					13 26			
	d				09 31	10 06				10 41	11 15		11 46			12 19		12 39				13 09	
Lincoln	a																						
Langley Mill	d					10 27					11 31					12 35		12 56				13 27	
Alfreton	d				09 53	10 35				11 03	11 39		12 08			12 43		13 04				13 35	
Long Eaton	a							10 29						11 47					12 47				
Derby	a		00 32					10 46						11 58					12 58				
	d			09 44			10 44	10 48				11 44		12 10			12 44		13 00		13 11		13 44
Chesterfield	d			10 03	10 08	10 54	11 03	11 09		11 15	11 51	12 03	12 18	12 30		12 54	13 03	13 17	13 23		13 30	13 51	14 03
Sheffield	a			10 16	10 33	11 15	11 17	11 28		11 35	12 15	12 18	12 36	12 47		13 15	13 17	13 33	13 43		13 43	14 15	14 17
Doncaster	a							11 52													14 13		
Wakefield Kirkgate	a					11 52					12 52					13 52						14 52	
Wakefield Westgate	a			10 44			11 44					12 44					13 44						14 44
Leeds	a			11 02		12 18	12 02				13 18	13 02				14 18	14 02					15 18	15 02
York	a			11 34			12 32	12 15				13 32					14 32				14 43		15 32

		EM ◇	EM ◇1	EM ◇1	XC ◇1	NT	XC ◇1	EM ◇	EM ◇1	EM ◇1	XC ◇1	NT	XC ◇1	EM ◇1	EM ◇1	EM ◇	XC ◇1	NT	XC ◇1	EM ◇1	EM ◇1	EM ◇	XC ◇1
St Pancras International	d		11 30	12 00					12 30	13 00				13 30	14 00					14 30	15 00		
Luton Airport Parkway	d		11 58	12 29					12 59	13 29				14 02	14 29						15 29		
Luton	d		12 02	12 33					13 03	13 33				14 06						15 01			
Bedford	d		12 26	12 56					13 26	13 56				14 21	14 47					15 17	15 47		
Wellingborough	d		12 40	13 10					13 40	14 13				14 35	15 00					15 31	16 01		
Kettering	a		12 50	13 19					13 50	14 22				14 42	15 07					15 38	16 08		
	d		12 51	13 20					13 51	14 23				14 43	15 08					15 39	16 09		
Corby	d																						
Market Harborough	d		13 02	13 31					14 03	14 34				14 54	15 18					15 50	16 20		
Leicester	a		13 21	13 51					14 24	14 53				15 16	15 37					16 17	16 41		
	d		13 23	13 53					14 25	14 55				15 18	15 39					16 19	16 43		
Syston	d																						
Sileby	d																						
Barrow Upon Soar	d																						
Loughborough	d		13 34	14 03					14 36	15 05				15 29	15 49					16 30	16 54		
East Midlands Parkway	d		13 41	14 11					14 45	15 13				15 37	15 57					16 38	17 02		
Beeston	a			14 18						15 21					16 05								
Nottingham	a			14 29						15 29					16 12						17 14		
	d	13 38				14 19		14 37				15 14				15 44		16 14				16 40	
Lincoln	a																						
Langley Mill	d	13 55				14 35		14 54				15 36						16 30				17 00	
Alfreton	d	14 03				14 43		15 02				15 44				16 06		16 38				17 08	
Long Eaton	a		13 45						14 48					15 43						16 42			
Derby	a		13 56						15 01					15 56						16 55			
	d		14 01		14 11		14 44		15 02		15 07		15 44	15 57			16 05		16 44	16 56			17 07
Chesterfield	d	14 18	14 23		14 30	14 54	15 03	15 13	15 22			15 53	16 03	16 18		16 23		16 50	17 03	17 17		17 22	
Sheffield	a	14 36	14 38		14 46	15 15	15 17	15 31	15 41		15 47	16 15	16 18	16 33		16 39	16 48	17 15	17 17	17 32		17 40	17 48
Doncaster	a				15 13						16 15						17 13						18 13
Wakefield Kirkgate	a					15 52						16 52						17 52					
Wakefield Westgate	a						15 44						16 44						17 45	18 06			18 33
Leeds	a					16 18	16 02					17 18	17 02					18 18	18 02	18 24			18 51
York	a				15 40		16 32				16 40		17 32				17 42		18 32				19 21

For connections from Gatwick Airport see Table 52

Table 53

London - East Midlands - Sheffield

Sundays
18 July to 05 September

		NT	XC	EM	EM	EM	XC	EM	EM	EM	EM	NT	XC	EM	XC	EM	EM	EM	EM	NT	XC	EM
			◇1	◇1	◇1	◇	◇1	◇1	◇1	◇1	◇1		◇1	◇	◇1	◇1	◇1	◇1	◇1		◇1	◇
St Pancras International ⊖	d			15 30	16 00			16 25	16 30	16 55	17 00					17 25	17 30	17 55	18 00			
Luton Airport Parkway 7 ✈	d				16 29						17 21								18 21			
Luton 10	d			16 01					16 52								17 52					
Bedford 7	d			16 17	16 47				17 15		17 45						18 15		18 45			
Wellingborough	d			16 31	17 00				17 28		17 58						18 28		18 58			
Kettering 4	a			16 38	17 07				17 35		18 05						18 35		19 05			
	d			16 39	17 08				17 36		18 06						18 36		19 06			
Corby	d																					
Market Harborough	d			16 50	17 18				17 46		18 16						18 46		19 16			
Leicester	a			17 11	17 37			17 47	18 08	18 21	18 35					18 44	19 07	19 18	19 35			
	d			17 12	17 39			17 49	18 10	18 22	18 37					18 46	19 09	19 20	19 37			
Syston	d																					
Sileby	d																					
Barrow Upon Soar	d																					
Loughborough	d			17 24	17 49				18 20		18 47						19 21		19 47			
East Midlands Parkway ✈	d			17 32	17 57			18 05	18 28	18 36	18 55					19 00	19 29	19 35	19 55			
Beeston	a				18 06						19 02								20 01			
Nottingham 8	a				18 14					18 52	19 09							19 51	20 08			
	d	17 14				17 37						18 14		18 37						19 19		19 38
Lincoln	a																					
Langley Mill	d	17 30				17 54						18 30		18 54						19 35		
Alfreton	d	17 38				18 02						18 38		19 02						19 43		20 00
Long Eaton	a			17 36					18 31								19 32					
Derby 6	a			17 48				18 17	18 47							19 14	19 47					
	d		17 44	17 50			18 05	18 19					18 44		19 04	19 16					19 41	
Chesterfield	d	17 49	18 04			18 17		18 40				18 50	19 05	19 12		19 35				19 54	20 02	20 10
Sheffield 7	a	18 15	18 19	18 29		18 34	18 46	18 57				19 15	19 20	19 31	19 39	19 50				20 15	20 17	20 31
Doncaster 7	a						19 13								20 16							
Wakefield Kirkgate 4	a	18 52										19 52								20 52		
Wakefield Westgate 7	a		18 47										19 48								20 46	
Leeds 10	a	19 18	19 04									20 18	20 05							21 16	21 03	
York 8	a		19 32				19 42						20 32		20 44						21 32	

		XC	EM	EM	EM	EM	NT	XC	EM	EM	EM	EM	EM	XC	NT	XC	EM	EM	EM	EM	EM
		◇1	◇1	◇1	◇1	◇1		◇1	◇1	◇1	◇1	◇1	◇1	◇1		◇1	◇1	◇1	◇1	◇1	◇1
St Pancras International ⊖	d		18 25	18 30	18 55	19 00			19 25	19 30	19 55	20 00	20 25				20 30	21 00	21 30	22 30	23 00
Luton Airport Parkway 7 ✈	d					19 21						20 23						21 23		22 53	23 28
Luton 10	d			18 52						19 52							20 54		21 54		
Bedford 7	d			19 15		19 45				20 15		20 48					21 18	21 47	22 17	23 17	23 52
Wellingborough	d			19 28		19 58				20 28		21 00					21 31	22 00	22 30	23 31	00 06
Kettering 4	a			19 35		20 05				20 35		21 07					21 38	22 07	22 37	23 37	00 12
	d			19 36		20 06				20 36		21 08					21 39	22 08	22 38	23 38	00 13
Corby	d																				
Market Harborough	d			19 46		20 16				20 46		21 18					21 50	22 18	22 48	23 48	00 23
Leicester	a		19 47	20 05	20 17	20 35			20 47	21 05	21 17	21 37	21 47				22 11	22 37	23 07	00 07	00 42
	d		19 49	20 07	20 20	20 37			20 49	21 07	21 19	21 39	21 49				22 13	22 39	23 09	00 09	00 44
Syston	d																				
Sileby	d																				
Barrow Upon Soar	d																				
Loughborough	d			20 17		20 47				21 17	21 30	21 49	22 01					22 49	23 19	00 19	00 54
East Midlands Parkway ✈	d		20 08	20 25	20 34	20 55			21 05	21 25	21 39	21 57	22 09				22 29	22 57	23 27	00 27	01 02
Beeston	a					21 02						22 03						23 10		00 40	
Nottingham 8	a				20 48	21 12					21 52	22 11						23 18		00 48	
	d						20 13								21 20						
Lincoln	a																				
Langley Mill	d						20 29								21 41						
Alfreton	d						20 37								21 49						
Long Eaton	a			20 28						21 28									23 38		
Derby 6	a		20 20	20 45					21 17	21 40			22 21				22 43		23 49		01 21
	d	20 05	20 22					20 44	21 19					21 44		22 46	22 51		23 51		
Chesterfield	d		20 43				20 48	21 03	21 40					22 03	22 08	23 07	23 13		00 10		
Sheffield 7	a	20 38	20 58				21 14	21 16	21 55					22 18	22 32	23 22	23 28		00 24		
Doncaster 7	a	21 19																			
Wakefield Kirkgate 4	a																				
Wakefield Westgate 7	a		21 32					21 44						22 45			00 15				
Leeds 10	a		21 49					22 01						23 04		00 33	00 32				
York 8	a	21 42																			

For connections from Gatwick Airport see Table 52

Table 53

London - East Midlands - Sheffield

Sundays
from 12 September

		EM	EM	XC	EM	NT	XC	EM	EM	EM	NT	XC	EM	EM	EM	NT	XC	EM	EM	EM	XC	NT	XC	EM
		◇1	◇1	◇1	◇		◇1	◇1	◇1	◇		◇1	◇1	◇1	◇		◇1	◇	◇1	◇1	◇1		◇1	◇1
St Pancras International ⊖	d	22p00	22p25						09 00				09 30	10 00					10 30	11 00				11 30
Luton Airport Parkway 7 ✈	d		22p47						09 28					10 29						11 29				11 58
Luton 10	d	22p24											10 01						11 02	11 32				12 02
Bedford 7	d	22p42	23p03						09 52				10 21	10 50					11 27	11 55				12 26
Wellingborough	d	22p55	23p15						10 06				10 37	11 04					11 39	12 09				12 40
Kettering 4	a	23p02	23p22						10 14				10 43	11 12					11 46	12 15				12 47
	d	23p03	23p23						10 15				10 44	11 13					11 46	12 16				12 48
Corby	d																							
Market Harborough	d	23p14	23p33						10 26				10 54	11 24					11 56	12 26				12 58
Leicester	a	23p31	23p48						10 46				11 13	11 44					12 16	12 45				13 17
	d	23p32	23p49					10 10	10 48				11 16	11 46					12 19	12 47				13 19
Syston	d																							
Sileby	d																							
Barrow Upon Soar	d																							
Loughborough	d	23p46	00 01					10 21	10 59				11 26	11 57					12 29	12 57				13 30
East Midlands Parkway ✈	d	23p54	00 08						11 07				11 34	12 05					12 37	13 05				13 37
Beeston	a	00 01							11 13											13 10				
Nottingham 8	a	00 11							11 22					12 18						13 19				
	d				09 31	10 06				10 41	11 15				11 46	12 19		12 39				13 09		
Lincoln	a																							
Langley Mill	d					10 27					11 31					12 35		12 56				13 27		
Alfreton	d				09 53	10 35				11 03	11 39				12 08	12 43		13 04				13 35		
Long Eaton	a							10 29					11 37						12 40					13 41
Derby 6	a		00 21					10 46					11 49						12 51					13 52
	d			09 44			10 44	10 48				11 44	11 50				12 44		12 53		13 11		13 44	13 54
Chesterfield	d			10 03	10 08	10 54	11 03	11 09		11 15	11 51	12 03	12 10		12 18	12 54	13 03	13 17	13 12		13 30	13 51	14 03	14 13
Sheffield 7	a			10 16	10 33	11 15	11 17	11 28		11 35	12 15	12 18	12 28		12 36	13 15	13 17	10 33	13 33		13 43	14 15	14 17	14 28
Doncaster 7	a							11 52													14 13			
Wakefield Kirkgate 4	a					11 52					12 52					13 52						14 52		
Wakefield Westgate 7	a			10 44			11 44					12 44					13 44						14 44	
Leeds 10	a			11 02		12 18	12 02				13 18	13 02				14 18	14 02					15 18	15 02	
York 8	a			11 34			12 32	12 15				13 32					14 32				14 43		15 32	

		EM	EM	XC	NT	XC	EM	EM	EM	XC	NT	XC	EM	EM	EM	XC	NT	XC	EM	EM	EM
		◇1	◇	◇1		◇1	◇	◇1	◇1	◇1		◇1	◇1	◇1	◇	◇1		◇1	◇1	◇1	◇
St Pancras International ⊖	d	12 00						12 30	13 00				13 30	14 00					14 30	15 00	
Luton Airport Parkway 7 ✈	d	12 29						12 59	13 29				14 02	14 29						15 29	
Luton 10	d	12 33						13 03	13 33				14 06						15 01		
Bedford 7	d	12 56						13 26	13 56				14 21	14 47					15 17	15 47	
Wellingborough	d	13 10						13 40	14 10				14 35	15 00					15 31	16 01	
Kettering 4	a	13 16						13 48	14 16				14 42	15 07					15 38	16 08	
	d	13 17						13 49	14 17				14 43	15 08					15 39	16 09	
Corby	d																				
Market Harborough	d	13 27						14 00	14 27				14 54	15 18					15 53	16 20	
Leicester	a	13 46						14 20	14 46				15 16	15 37					16 17	16 41	
	d	13 48						14 22	14 48				15 18	15 39					16 19	16 43	
Syston	d																				
Sileby	d																				
Barrow Upon Soar	d																				
Loughborough	d	13 58						14 33	14 58				15 29	15 49					16 30	16 54	
East Midlands Parkway ✈	d	14 06						14 41	15 06				15 37	15 57					16 38	17 02	
Beeston	a	14 13							15 12					16 05							
Nottingham 8	a	14 22							15 21					16 12						17 14	
	d		13 38		14 19		14 37				15 14				15 44		16 14				16 41
Lincoln	a																				
Langley Mill	d		13 55		14 35		14 54				15 34						16 30				17 00
Alfreton	d		14 03		14 43		15 02				15 44				16 06		16 38				17 08
Long Eaton	a							14 45					15 43						16 42		
Derby 6	a							15 00					15 56						16 55		
	d			14 11		14 44		15 01		15 07		15 44	15 57			16 05		16 44	16 56		
Chesterfield	d		14 18	14 30	14 54	15 03	15 13	15 22			15 53	16 03	16 18		16 23		16 50	17 03	17 17		17 22
Sheffield 7	a		14 36	14 46	15 15	15 17	15 31	15 41		15 47	16 15	16 18	16 33		16 39	16 48	17 15	17 17	17 32		17 40
Doncaster 7	a			15 13						16 15						17 13					
Wakefield Kirkgate 4	a				15 52						16 52						17 52				
Wakefield Westgate 7	a					15 44						16 44						17 45	18 06		
Leeds 10	a				16 18	16 02					17 18	17 02					18 18	18 02	18 24		
York 8	a			15 40		16 32				16 40		17 32				17 42		18 32			

For connections from Gatwick Airport see Table 52

Table 53

London - East Midlands - Sheffield

Sundays from 12 September

		XC ◇1	NT	XC ◇1	EM ◇1	EM ◇1	EM ◇	XC ◇1	EM ◇1	EM ◇1	EM ◇1	EM ◇1	NT	XC ◇1	EM ◇ B	EM ◇ A	XC ◇1	EM ◇1	EM ◇1	EM ◇1	EM ◇1
St Pancras International ⊖	d				15 30	16 00			16 25	16 30	16 55	17 00						17 25	17 30	17 55	18 00
Luton Airport Parkway 7 ✈	d					16 29						17 21									18 21
Luton 10	d				16 01					16 52									17 52		
Bedford 7	d				16 17	16 47				17 15		17 45							18 15		18 45
Wellingborough	d				16 31	17 00				17 28		17 58							18 28		18 58
Kettering 4	a				16 38	17 07				17 35		18 05							18 35		19 05
	d				16 39	17 08				17 36		18 06							18 36		19 06
Corby	d																				
Market Harborough	d				16 50	17 18				17 46		18 16							18 46		19 16
Leicester	a				17 11	17 37			17 47	18 08	18 21	18 35						18 44	19 05	19 20	19 35
	d				17 12	17 39			17 49	18 10	18 22	18 37						18 46	19 07	19 21	19 37
Syston	d																				
Sileby	d																				
Barrow Upon Soar	d																				
Loughborough	d				17 24	17 49				18 20		18 47							19 17		19 47
East Midlands Parkway ✈	d				17 32	17 57			18 05	18 28	18 36	18 55						19 00	19 25	19 39	19 55
Beeston	a					18 06						19 01									20 01
Nottingham 8	a					18 14					18 52	19 07								19 51	20 08
	d		17 14				17 37						18 14		18 35	18 37					
Lincoln	a																				
Langley Mill	d		17 30				17 54						18 30		18 54	18 54					
Alfreton	d		17 38				18 02						18 38		19 02	19 02					
Long Eaton	a				17 36					18 31									19 30		
Derby 6	a				17 48				18 17	18 47								19 14	19 45		
	d	17 07		17 44	17 50			18 05	18 19					18 44			19 04	19 16			
Chesterfield	d		17 49	18 04			18 17		18 40				18 50	19 05	19 13	19 13		19 35			
Sheffield 7	a	17 48	18 15	18 19	18 29		18 34	18 46	18 57				19 15	19 20	19 31	19 31	19 39	19 50			
Doncaster 7	a	18 13						19 13									20 16				
Wakefield Kirkgate 4	a		18 52										19 52								
Wakefield Westgate 7	a	18 33		18 47										19 48							
Leeds 10	a	18 51	19 18	19 04									20 18	20 05							
York 8	a	19 21		19 32				19 42						20 32			20 44				

		NT	XC ◇1	EM ◇ A	EM ◇ B	XC ◇1	EM ◇1	EM ◇1	EM ◇1	EM ◇1	NT	XC ◇1	EM ◇1	EM ◇1	EM ◇1	EM ◇1	EM ◇1	XC ◇1	NT	XC ◇1	EM ◇1	EM ◇1	EM ◇1
St Pancras International ⊖	d						18 25	18 30	18 55	19 00			19 25	19 30	19 55	20 00	20 25				20 30	21 00	21 30
Luton Airport Parkway 7 ✈	d									19 21						20 23						21 23	
Luton 10	d							18 52						19 52							20 54		21 54
Bedford 7	d							19 15		19 45				20 15		20 48					21 18	21 47	22 17
Wellingborough	d							19 28		19 58				20 28		21 00					21 31	22 00	22 30
Kettering 4	a							19 35		20 05				20 35		21 07					21 38	22 07	22 37
	d							19 36		20 06				20 36		21 08					21 39	22 08	22 38
Corby	d																						
Market Harborough	d							19 46		20 16				20 46		21 18					21 50	22 18	22 48
Leicester	a						19 47	20 05	20 17	20 35			20 47	21 05	21 17	21 37	21 47				22 11	22 37	23 07
	d						19 49	20 07	20 20	20 37			20 49	21 07	21 19	21 39	21 49				22 13	22 39	23 09
Syston	d																						
Sileby	d																						
Barrow Upon Soar	d																						
Loughborough	d							20 17		20 47				21 17	21 30	21 49	22 01					22 49	23 19
East Midlands Parkway ✈	d						20 08	20 25	20 35	20 55			21 05	21 25	21 39	21 57	22 09				22 29	22 57	23 32
Beeston	a									21 02						22 03						23 10	
Nottingham 8	a								20 48	21 12					21 52	22 11						23 18	
	d	19 19		19 38	19 41						20 13								21 20				
Lincoln	a																						
Langley Mill	d	19 35									20 29								21 41				
Alfreton	d	19 43		20 00	20 03						20 37								21 49				
Long Eaton	a							20 28						21 28									23 38
Derby 6	a						20 20	20 45					21 17	21 40			22 21				22 43		23 49
	d		19 41			20 05	20 22					20 44	21 19					21 44		22 46	22 51		23 51
Chesterfield	d	19 54	20 02	20 10	20 13		20 43				20 48	21 03	21 40					22 03	22 08	23 07	23 13		00 10
Sheffield 7	a	20 15	20 17	20 31	20 31	20 38	20 58				21 14	21 16	21 55					22 18	22 32	23 22	23 28		00 24
Doncaster 7	a					21 19																	
Wakefield Kirkgate 4	a	20 52																					
Wakefield Westgate 7	a		20 46				21 32					21 44						22 45			00 15		
Leeds 10	a	21 16	21 03				21 49					22 01						23 04		00 33	00 32		
York 8	a		21 32			21 42																	

A from 24 October

B from 12 September until 17 October

For connections from Gatwick Airport see Table 52

Table 53

London - East Midlands - Sheffield

Sundays from 12 September

		EM ◇1	EM ◇1
St Pancras International ⊖	d	22 30	23 00
Luton Airport Parkway 7 ✈	d	22 53	23 28
Luton 10	d		
Bedford 7	d	23 17	23 52
Wellingborough	d	23 31	00 06
Kettering 4	a	23 37	00 12
	d	23 38	00 13
Corby	d		
Market Harborough	d	23 48	00 23
Leicester	a	00 07	00 42
	d	00 09	00 44
Syston	d		
Sileby	d		
Barrow Upon Soar	d		
Loughborough	d	00 19	00 54
East Midlands Parkway ✈	d	00 27	01 02
Beeston	a	00 40	
Nottingham 8	a	00 48	
	d		
Lincoln	a		
Langley Mill	d		
Alfreton	d		
Long Eaton	a		
Derby 6	a		01 21
	d		
Chesterfield	d		
Sheffield 7	a		
Doncaster 7	a		
Wakefield Kirkgate 4	a		
Wakefield Westgate 7	a		
Leeds 10	a		
York 8	a		

For connections from Gatwick Airport see Table 52

Sheffield - East Midlands - London

		EM MX	EM	EM	EM	EM MX	EM	EM	NT	EM	EM	EM	EM	EM	EM	NT	XC	EM	EM	EM MO	EM MSX	EM	EM	XC	NT
		◇■	◇	◇	◇	◇	◇■	◇■		◇■	◇■		◇■	◇■	◇■		◇■	◇■		◇■	◇■	◇■	◇■	◇■	
			A	B	C																				
York	d																								
Leeds	d																			05 25	05 25			06 00	06 05
Wakefield Westgate	d																			05 37	05 37			06 12	
Wakefield Kirkgate	d																							06 12	06 21
Doncaster	d																			05 57	05 57				
Sheffield	d	23p21	23p29	23p29	23p29	23p37			05 05				05 27		05 56	06 00	06 01			06 27	06 27		06 47	06 50	07 03
Chesterfield	d	23p45	23p43	23p43	23p43	00 02			05 20				05 39		06 09	06 16	06 27			06 39	06 39		06 59	07 04	07 20
Derby	a	00 11											06 01		06 30		06 46			07 03	07 03		07 19	07 25	
	d							04 55		05 17			06 03		06 32					07 05	07 05		07 20		
Long Eaton	d									05 27					06 42										
Alfreton	d		23p54	23p54	23p54											06 30									07 33
Langley Mill	d		00 03	00 02	00 02											06 37									07 40
Lincoln	d																								
Nottingham	a		00 30	00 30	00 33	00 41			06 12							07 08									08 02
	d										05 34	05 43		06 28				06 48				07 10			
Beeston	d													06 34				06 54				07 17			
East Midlands Parkway	d							05 06			05 45		06 16	06 40				07 01				07 25	07 34		
Loughborough	d							05 14			05 53	06 05	06 24		06 52				06 53				07 42		
Barrow Upon Soar	d											06 09							06 57						
Sileby	d											06 14							07 03						
Syston	d											06 20							07 08						
Leicester	a							05 24		05 42	06 05	06 28	06 36	06 54	07 04			07 15	07 19	07 34	07 34	07 41	07 53		
	d						04 40	05 26		05 44	06 07		06 38	06 57	07 06			07 16		07 35	07 35	07 42	07 55		
Market Harborough	d							05 41		05 58	06 22		06 53	07 12				07 31				07 58			
Corby	d																								
Kettering	a						05 00	05 50		06 07	06 32		07 03	07 21	07 28			07 40		07 57	07 57	08 08	08 15		
	d						05 01	05 51		06 09	06 33		07 05	07 22	07 29			07 41		07 59	07 59	08 09	08 17		
Wellingborough	d						05 19	05 59		06 17	06 41		07 13	07 30	07 38			07 49		08 07	08 07		08 25		
Bedford	d						05 32			06 32					07 55							08 29			
Luton	d							06 24						07 56				08 15							
Luton Airport Parkway	d						05 55				07 07		07 40		08 12										
St Pancras International	a						06 21	06 53		07 13	07 36		08 09	08 26	08 38			08 44		09 01	08 57	09 08	09 13		

		XC	EM	EM	EM	EM	EM	EM	EM	XC	EM	EM	XC	EM	EM	EM	EM	XC	NT	XC	EM	EM	EM	EM	EM
		◇■	◇■	◇■		◇■	◇■	◇■	◇■	◇■			◇■	◇■	◇■	◇	◇■	◇■		◇■	◇■			◇■	◇■
											D	E										D	E		
York	d									06 32			07 27					07 44		08 27					
Leeds	d	06 15						06 34		07 05								08 11	08 02						
Wakefield Westgate	d	06 27						06 46		07 18								08 23							
Wakefield Kirkgate	d																		08 23						
Doncaster	d	06 45											07 52							08 51					
Sheffield	d	07 18				07 27		07 32	07 41	07 53			08 20	08 27		08 38	08 47	08 54	09 05	09 23				09 27	
Chesterfield	d	07 30				07 39		07 45	07 55	08 06			08 32	08 39		08 53	08 59	09 06	09 22					09 39	
Derby	a	07 49				07 59			08 14	08 26			08 51	08 59			09 19	09 25		09 51				09 59	
	d		07 26			08 01			08 16					09 01			09 20							10 01	
Long Eaton	d		07 36						08 26								09 30								
Alfreton	d							07 58								09 03			09 33						
Langley Mill	d							08 06											09 40						
Lincoln	d										07 26	07 26										08 35	08 35		
Nottingham	a							08 21			08 32	08 30				09 30			10 00			09 32	09 30		
	d			07 50	07 31		08 02	08 28			08 32	08 32			09 02						09 28	09 32	09 32		10 02
Beeston	d				07 37		08 08				08 38	08 38			09 08							09 38	09 38		10 08
East Midlands Parkway	d			08 01	07 46			08 39	08 32		08 46	08 46					09 35				09 40	09 46	09 46		
Loughborough	d		07 47		07 55		08 22		08 40		08 55	08 55			09 20		09 42					09 55	09 55		10 20
Barrow Upon Soar	d				07 59						08 59	08 59										09 59	09 59		
Sileby	d				08 04						09 03	09 03										10 03	10 03		
Syston	d				08 09						09 08	09 08										10 08	10 08		
Leicester	a		07 59	08 17	08 21	08 23	08 32	08 57	08 52		09 22	09 22		09 23	08 32		09 54				09 58	10 21	10 21	10 23	10 33
	d		08 01	08 18		08 25	08 33	08 58	08 52					09 25	08 33		09 55				09 59			10 25	10 33
Market Harborough	d		08 16				08 47	09 13							08 47						10 14				10 47
Corby	d																								
Kettering	a		08 26				08 56								09 56										10 55
	d		08 28				08 56								09 26										10 56
Wellingborough	d		08 39				09 04								10 04										11 04
Bedford	d		09 02				09 18								10 18										11 18
Luton	d		09 19																						
Luton Airport Parkway	d						09 34								10 34										11 33
St Pancras International	a		09 47	09 30		09 37	10 00	10 19	10 05					10 31	11 01		11 05				11 18			11 34	12 02

A MO from 19 July until 6 September
B MO from 13 September
C MO until 12 July
D from 27 September
E until 24 September

For connections to Gatwick Airport see Table 52

Sheffield - East Midlands - London

		EM	EM	XC	NT	XC	EM	EM	EM	EM	EM	EM	EM	XC	NT	XC	EM	EM	EM	EM	EM	EM		EM	XC
		◇■	◇	◇■		◇■	◇■			◇■	◇	◇■	◇■	◇■		◇■	◇■			◇■	◇■	◇		◇■	◇■
								A	B									A	B						
York	d			08 45		09 27								09 44		10 34									10 44
Leeds	d			09 11	09 05									10 12	10 05										11 11
Wakefield Westgate	d			09 24										10 24											11 24
Wakefield Kirkgate	d				09 23										10 23										
Doncaster	d					09 56										10 58									
Sheffield	d	09 35	09 38	09 54	10 05	10 23				10 27	10 38		10 47	10 54	11 05	11 23				11 27		11 38		11 47	11 54
Chesterfield	d	09 47	09 53	10 06	10 22					10 39	10 52		10 59	11 06	11 22					11 39		11 53		11 59	12 06
Derby	a	10 16		10 26		10 51				10 59			11 19	11 25		11 51				11 59				12 19	12 26
	d	10 20								11 01			11 20							12 01				12 20	
Long Eaton	d	10 30											11 30											12 30	
Alfreton	d		10 04		10 33						11 03				11 33							12 03			
Langley Mill	d				10 40										11 40										
Lincoln	d							09 31	09 31									10 36	10 36						
Nottingham	a		10 30		11 00			10 32	10 30		11 30				12 02			11 32	11 29			12 30			
	d						10 28	10 32	10 32			11 02					11 28	11 32	11 32		12 02				
Beeston	d							10 38	10 38			11 08						11 38	11 38		12 08				
East Midlands Parkway	d	10 35					10 40	10 46	10 46				11 35				11 39	11 46	11 46					12 35	
Loughborough	d	10 42						10 55	10 55			11 20	11 42					11 55	11 55		12 20			12 42	
Barrow Upon Soar	d							10 59	10 59									11 59	11 59						
Sileby	d							11 03	11 03									12 03	12 03						
Syston	d							11 08	11 08									12 08	12 08						
Leicester	a	10 54					10 58	11 20	11 21	11 23		11 31	11 54				11 57	12 20	12 21	12 23	12 31			12 53	
	d	10 55					10 59			11 25		11 33	11 55				11 57			12 25	12 33			12 55	
Market Harborough	d						11 14					11 47					12 12				12 47				
Corby	d																								
Kettering	a											11 56									12 56				
	d											11 56									12 56				
Wellingborough	d											12 04									13 04				
Bedford	d											12 18									13 18				
Luton	d																								
Luton Airport Parkway	d											12 34									13 34				
St Pancras International	a	12 06					12 13			12 33		13 01	13 06				13 13			13 34	14 02			14 06	

		NT	XC	EM	EM	EM	EM	EM		EM	EM	XC	NT	XC	EM	EM	EM	EM		EM	EM	EM	XC	NT	XC
			◇■	◇■			◇■	◇■		◇■	◇	◇■		◇■	◇■			◇■		◇	◇■	◇■	◇■		◇■
					A	B										A	B								
York	d		11 27									11 45		12 27									12 45		13 26
Leeds	d	11 05										12 12	12 05										13 12	13 05	
Wakefield Westgate	d											12 24											13 24		
Wakefield Kirkgate	d	11 23											12 23											13 23	
Doncaster	d		11 54											12 55											13 55
Sheffield	d	12 05	12 23				12 27			12 35	12 38	12 54	13 05	13 23				13 27		13 38		13 47	13 54	14 05	14 23
Chesterfield	d	12 22					12 39			12 48	12 53	13 06	13 22					13 39		13 52		13 59	14 06	14 22	
Derby	a		12 51				12 59			13 15		13 25		13 51				13 59				14 19	14 25		14 51
	d						13 01			13 20								14 01				14 20			
Long Eaton	d									13 30												14 30			
Alfreton	d	12 33									13 03		13 33							14 03				14 33	
Langley Mill	d	12 40											13 40											14 40	
Lincoln	d				11 42	11 42										12 30	12 30								
Nottingham	a	13 00			12 32	12 30					13 30		14 00			13 32	13 30			14 31				15 00	
	d			12 28	12 32	12 32		13 02							13 28	13 32	13 32				14 02				
Beeston	d				12 38	12 38		13 08								13 38	13 38				14 08				
East Midlands Parkway	d			12 40	12 46	12 46				13 35					13 39	13 46	13 46					14 35			
Loughborough	d				12 55	12 55		13 20		13 42						13 55	13 55				14 20	14 42			
Barrow Upon Soar	d				12 59	12 59										13 59	13 59								
Sileby	d				13 03	13 03										14 03	14 03								
Syston	d				13 08	13 08										14 08	14 08								
Leicester	a			12 58	13 21	13 21	13 23	13 32		13 54					13 57	14 21	14 21	14 23			14 31	14 53			
	d			12 59			13 25	13 33		13 55					13 57			14 25			14 33	14 55			
Market Harborough	d			13 12				13 47							14 12						14 47				
Corby	d																								
Kettering	a							13 56													14 56				
	d							13 56													14 56				
Wellingborough	d							14 04													15 04				
Bedford	d							14 18													15 18				
Luton	d																								
Luton Airport Parkway	d							14 34													15 34				
St Pancras International	a			14 13			14 38	15 01		15 06					15 13			15 34			16 01	16 06			

A from 27 September
B until 24 September

For connections to Gatwick Airport see Table 52

Table 53

Sheffield - East Midlands - London

		EM	EM	EM	EM		EM	EM	XC	NT	XC	EM	EM	EM	EM	EM	EM	EM	XC	NT	XC	EM	EM	EM	EM	
		◇■		◇■	◇■		◇■	◇	◇■		◇■	◇■			◇■	◇■	◇	◇■	◇■		◇■	◇■			◇■	
													A	B									A	B		
		🍴		🍴	🍴		🍴		🛒		🛒	🍴			🍴	🍴		🍴	🛒		🛒	🍴			🍴	
York 8	d								13 44		14 32								14 44		15 29					
Leeds 10	d								14 12	14 05									15 12	15 05						
Wakefield Westgate 7	d								14 24										15 24							
Wakefield Kirkgate 4	d									14 23										15 23						
Doncaster 7	d										14 57										15 55					
Sheffield 7	d			14 27			14 35	14 38	14 54	15 05	15 23				15 27		15 38	15 47	15 54	16 05	16 23				16 27	
Chesterfield	d			14 39			14 47	14 53	15 06	15 22					15 39		15 53		16 06	16 22					16 39	
Derby 6	a			14 59			15 16		15 25		15 51				15 59			16 16	16 25		16 51				16 59	
	d			15 01			15 20								16 01			16 18							17 01	
Long Eaton	d						15 30											16 28								
Alfreton	d							15 07		15 33							16 03			16 33						
Langley Mill	d									15 40										16 40						
Lincoln	d		13 40										14 35	14 35									15 30	15 30		
Nottingham 8	a		14 32					15 28		16 00			15 32	15 29			16 33			17 00			16 32	16 30		
	d	14 28	14 32		15 02							15 28	15 32	15 30		16 02						16 28	16 32	16 32		
Beeston	d		14 38		15 08								15 38	15 36		16 08							16 38	16 38		
East Midlands Parkway	d	14 39	14 46				15 35					15 40	15 46	15 45				16 32				16 39	16 48	16 48		
Loughborough	d		14 55		15 20		15 42						15 55	15 53		16 20		16 40					16 57	16 57		
Barrow Upon Soar	d		14 59										15 59	15 58									17 01	17 01		
Sileby	d		15 08										16 03	16 02									17 05	17 05		
Syston	d												16 08	16 07									17 10	17 09		
Leicester	a	14 57	15 21	15 23	15 31		15 53					15 58	16 21	16 21	16 23	16 31		16 51				16 55	17 22	17 22	17 23	
	d	14 57		15 25	15 33		15 54					15 58			16 25	16 33		16 53				16 57			17 25	
Market Harborough	d	15 12			15 47							16 13				16 47						17 12				
Corby	d																									
Kettering 4	a				15 56											16 56		17 14								
	d				15 56											16 56		17 15								
Wellingborough	d				16 04											17 04										
Bedford 7	d				16 18											17 18										
Luton 10	d																					17 50			18 15	
Luton Airport Parkway 7	d				16 34											17 30										
St Pancras International	a	16 13		16 34	17 00		17 06					17 20			17 33	18 05		18 09				18 19			18 39	

		EM	EM	EM	XC	NT	XC	EM	EM	EM	EM		EM	EM	EM	XC	NT	XC	EM	EM	EM	EM	EM	EM	EM	XC
		◇■	◇■	◇	◇■		◇■	◇■			◇■		◇■	◇■	◇	◇■		◇■	◇■			◇■	◇■	◇■	◇	◇■
									A	B										A	B					
		🍴	🍴		🛒		🛒	🍴			🍴		🍴	🍴		🛒		🛒	🍴			🍴	🍴	🍴		🛒
York 8	d				15 44		16 25									16 44		17 34								17 44
Leeds 10	d				16 11	16 05										17 12	17 05									18 11
Wakefield Westgate 7	d				16 23											17 24										18 23
Wakefield Kirkgate 4	d					16 23											17 23									
Doncaster 7	d						16 53											17 58								
Sheffield 7	d		16 35	16 38	16 54	17 05	17 23				17 27			17 35	17 44	17 54	18 05	18 23				18 27		18 35	18 45	18 54
Chesterfield	d		16 50	16 56	17 06	17 22					17 39			17 50	18 02	18 07	18 22					18 39		18 47	19 01	19 06
Derby 6	a		17 16		17 26		17 51				17 59			18 16		18 26		18 51				18 59		19 14		19 26
	d		17 18								18 01			18 18								19 01		19 18		
Long Eaton	d		17 28											18 28										19 28		
Alfreton	d			17 07		17 33									18 12		18 33								19 11	
Langley Mill	d					17 40											18 40									
Lincoln	d								16 35	16 35										17 28	17 28					
Nottingham 8	a			17 31		18 00			17 32	17 30					18 34		19 00			18 32	18 31				19 38	
	d	17 02						17 28	17 32	17 32			18 02						18 28	18 32	18 32		19 02			
Beeston	d	17 08							17 38	17 38			18 08							18 38	18 38		09 08			
East Midlands Parkway	d		17 32					17 39	17 48	17 48				18 32					18 39	18 47	18 47			19 32		
Loughborough	d	17 20	17 40						17 57	17 57			18 20	18 40						18 55	18 55		19 20	19 40		
Barrow Upon Soar	d								18 01	18 01										19 00	19 00					
Sileby	d								18 05	18 05										19 04	19 04					
Syston	d								18 10	18 09										19 09	19 09					
Leicester	a	17 31	17 52					17 56	18 23	18 22	18 23		18 31	18 51					18 55	19 21	19 22	19 23	19 31	19 51		
	d	17 33	17 54					17 58			18 25		18 33	18 53					18 57			19 25	19 33	19 53		
Market Harborough	d	17 47						18 13					18 47						19 12				19 47			
Corby	d																									
Kettering 4	a	17 56	18 14										18 56										19 56			
	d	17 56	18 15										18 56										19 56			
Wellingborough	d	18 04											19 04										20 04			
Bedford 7	d	18 18											19 18										20 18			
Luton 10	d																									
Luton Airport Parkway 7	d	18 34											19 34										20 34			
St Pancras International	a	19 01	19 06					19 18			19 34		20 01	20 06					20 11			20 34	21 04	21 09		

A from 27 September

B until 24 September

For connections to Gatwick Airport see Table 52

Table 53

Sheffield - East Midlands - London

		NT	XC	EM	EM	EM		EM	EM	XC	NT	XC	EM	EM	EM	EM		EM	XC	XC	EM	EM	EM	EM	XC
			◇■	◇■				◇■	◇	◇■		◇■	◇■		◇■	◇■		◇	◇■	◇■	◇■		◇	◇■	◇■
					A	B																			
			🛒	🍴				🍴		🛒		🛒	🍴		🍴	🍴					🍴			🍴	
York 8	d		18 24							18 44		19 29							19 44	20 32					20 44
Leeds 10	d	18 05								19 11	19 05								20 11						21 11
Wakefield Westgate 7	d									19 23									20 23						21 23
Wakefield Kirkgate 4	d	18 23									19 24														
Doncaster 7	d		18 52									19 57								20 57					
Sheffield 7	d	19 05	19 23					19 27	19 38	19 54	20 05	20 23				20 39		20 41	20 54	21 27			21 39	21 42	22 00
Chesterfield	d	19 22						19 39	19 53	20 06	20 22					20 53		20 58	21 06	21 39			21 55	22 00	22 24
Derby 6	a		19 52					19 59		20 26		20 52				21 18			21 26	21 58				22 19	22 44
	d							20 01								21 20									
Long Eaton	d																								
Alfreton	d	19 33							20 04		20 33							21 09					22 05		
Langley Mill	d	19 40									20 40												22 12		
Lincoln	d				18 35	18 35																			
Nottingham 8	a	20 00			19 31	19 29			20 31		21 00							21 38					22 38		
	d			19 28	19 32	19 32							20 02	20 32	21 02						21 28	21 32			
Beeston	d				19 38	19 38							20 08	20 38	21 08							21 38			
East Midlands Parkway	d			19 39	19 46	19 46							20 16	20 46	21 15	21 33						21 46			
Loughborough	d				19 55	19 55							20 24	20 55	21 22	21 41					21 47	21 55			
Barrow Upon Soar	d				19 59	19 59								20 59								21 59			
Sileby	d				20 03	20 03								21 03								22 03			
Syston	d				20 08	20 08								21 08								22 08			
Leicester	a			19 57	20 20	20 20		20 23					20 34	21 22	21 32	21 52					21 58	22 21			
	d			19 57				20 25					20 36		21 33	21 55					22 00				
Market Harborough	d			20 12									20 50		21 47						22 14				
Corby	d																								
Kettering 4	a												20 59		21 56						22 23				
	d												20 59		21 57						22 24				
Wellingborough	d												21 07		22 05						22 32				
Bedford 7	d												21 25		22 19						22 47				
Luton 10	d														22 34						23 05				
Luton Airport Parkway 7	d												21 41		22 38										
St Pancras International	a			21 15				21 37					22 06		23 04	23 06					23 38				

		EM		EM	EM
				◇■	◇
				🍴	
York 8	d				
Leeds 10	d				
Wakefield Westgate 7	d				
Wakefield Kirkgate 4	d				
Doncaster 7	d				
Sheffield 7	d			23 21	23 37
Chesterfield	d			23 45	00 02
Derby 6	a			00 11	
	d				
Long Eaton	d				
Alfreton	d				
Langley Mill	d				
Lincoln	d				
Nottingham 8	a				00 41
	d	23 10			
Beeston	d	23 16			
East Midlands Parkway	d	23 25			
Loughborough	d	23 33			
Barrow Upon Soar	d				
Sileby	d				
Syston	d				
Leicester	a	23 58			
	d				
Market Harborough	d				
Corby	d				
Kettering 4	a				
	d				
Wellingborough	d				
Bedford 7	d				
Luton 10	d				
Luton Airport Parkway 7	d				
St Pancras International	a				

A from 27 September

B until 24 September

For connections to Gatwick Airport see Table 52

Sheffield - East Midlands - London

		EM	EM	EM	EM	EM	XC	NT	EM	EM	EM	EM	EM	XC	NT	XC	EM	EM	EM	EM	EM	EM	EM
		◇■ ☕	◇	◇■ ☕	◇■ ☕	◇■ ☕	◇■ A 🍴		◇■ ☕	◇■ ☕	◇■ ☕		◇■ ☕	◇■ 🍴		◇■ 🍴	◇■ ☕	◇■ ☕	◇■ ☕		◇■ ☕	◇■ ☕	◇■ ⊠
York	d																						
Leeds	d													06 00		06 15							
Wakefield Westgate	d													06 12		06 29							
Wakefield Kirkgate	d																						
Doncaster	d															06 47							
Sheffield	d	23p21	23p37			05 27	05 42	05 54					06 25	06 50	07 03	07 18					07 27		
Chesterfield	d	23p45	00 02			05 39	05 54	06 20					06 37	07 03	07 20	07 30					07 39		
Derby	a	00 11				05 59	06 40						06 59	07 24		07 49					07 59		
	d				05 25	06 01				06 18			07 01					07 18			08 01		08 18
Long Eaton	d				05 35					06 28								07 28					08 28
Alfreton	d							06 30							07 33								
Langley Mill	d							06 38							07 40								
Lincoln	d																					07 08	
Nottingham	a		00 41					07 04							08 02							07 58	
	d								06 02		06 28						07 02		07 28	07 31		08 02	
Beeston	d								06 08								07 08			07 37		08 08	
East Midlands Parkway	d				05 39					06 32	06 39							07 32	07 39	07 46			08 32
Loughborough	d				05 47				06 20	06 40		06 50					07 20	07 40		07 55		08 20	08 40
Barrow Upon Soar	d											06 57								07 59			
Sileby	d											07 05								08 03			
Syston	d											07 10								08 08			
Leicester	a				05 57	06 23			06 31	06 51	06 55	07 21	07 23				07 31	07 51	07 55	08 21	08 23	08 31	08 51
	d			04 40	05 59	06 25			06 33	06 53	06 57		07 25				07 33	07 53	07 57		08 25	08 33	08 53
Market Harborough	d				06 14				06 47		07 12						07 47		08 12			08 47	
Corby	d																						
Kettering	a			05 00	06 23				06 56	07 15							07 56					08 56	
	d			05 01	06 26				06 56	07 26							07 56					08 56	
Wellingborough	d			05 09	06 34				07 04	07 34							08 04					09 04	
Bedford	d			05 32	06 49				07 19	07 49							08 19					09 19	
Luton	d				07 04					08 05													
Luton Airport Parkway	d			05 55					07 35								08 35					09 35	
St Pancras International	a			06 21	07 31	07 34			08 00	08 31	08 19		08 34				09 01	09 06	09 19		09 34	10 00	10 06

		EM	XC	EM	EM	XC	EM	EM	EM	EM	EM	XC	XC	NT	XC	EM	EM	EM	EM	EM	EM	XC	NT
		◇■ ☕	◇■ 🍴	B	C	◇■ 🍴	◇■ ☕	◇■ ☕	◇	◇■ ☕	◇■ ☕	◇■ D 🍴	◇■ A 🍴		◇■ 🍴	B	C	◇■ ☕	◇	◇■ ☕	◇■ ☕	◇■ 🍴	
York	d		06 09			07 25						07 44	07 44		08 27							08 44	
Leeds	d	06 34	07 05					07 34				08 12	08 12	08 05								09 11	09 05
Wakefield Westgate	d	06 46	07 18					07 46				08 24	08 24									09 24	
Wakefield Kirkgate	d													08 23									09 23
Doncaster	d					07 52									08 53								
Sheffield	d	07 32	07 54			08 20	08 27	08 32	08 38		08 47	08 54	08 54	09 05	09 23			09 27	09 38		09 47	09 54	10 05
Chesterfield	d	07 45	08 06			08 32	08 39	08 45	08 53		08 59	09 06	09 08	09 22				09 39	09 53		09 59	10 06	10 22
Derby	a		08 26			08 51	08 59				09 19	09 25	09 28		09 51			09 59			10 19	10 25	
	d						09 01				09 20							10 01			10 20		
Long Eaton	d										09 30										10 30		
Alfreton	d	07 56						08 56	09 03					09 33					10 03				10 33
Langley Mill	d	08 04												09 40									10 40
Lincoln	d			07 26	07 26											08 35	08 35						
Nottingham	a	08 23		08 32	08 30			09 21	09 30					10 00		09 32	09 30		10 30				11 00
	d	08 28		08 32	08 32			09 28		09 02						09 32	09 32			10 02			
Beeston	d			08 38	08 38					09 08						09 38	09 38			10 08			
East Midlands Parkway	d	08 39		08 46	08 46			09 40			09 35					09 46	09 46				10 35		
Loughborough	d			08 55	08 55					09 20	09 42					09 55	09 55			10 20	10 42		
Barrow Upon Soar	d			08 59	08 59											09 59	09 59						
Sileby	d			09 03	09 03											10 03	10 03						
Syston	d			09 08	09 08											10 08	10 08						
Leicester	a	08 55		09 18	09 18		09 23	09 58		09 31	09 54					10 21	10 21	10 23		10 31	10 54		
	d	08 57					09 25	09 59		09 33	09 55							10 25		10 33	10 55		
Market Harborough	d	09 12						10 14		09 47										10 47			
Corby	d																						
Kettering	a									09 56										10 56			
	d									09 56										10 56			
Wellingborough	d									10 04										11 04			
Bedford	d									10 19										11 19			
Luton	d																						
Luton Airport Parkway	d									10 35										11 35			
St Pancras International	a	10 19					10 34	11 19		11 01	11 05							11 34		12 01	12 05		

A until 4 September
B from 2 October
C until 25 September
D from 11 September

For connections to Gatwick Airport see Table 52

Table 53

Saturdays

Sheffield - East Midlands - London

		XC	EM	EM	EM	EM	EM	EM	EM	XC	XC	EM	EM	EM	EM	EM	EM	EM	XC	NT	XC	EM
		◇■ 🍴	◇■ ☕	A	B	◇■ ☕	◇	◇■ ☕	◇■ ☕	◇■ 🍴	◇■ 🍴	◇■ ☕	A	B	◇■ ☕	◇	◇■ ☕	◇■ ☕	◇■ 🍴		◇■ 🍴	◇■ ☕
York	d	09 28								09 44	10 25								10 45		11 27	
Leeds	d									10 12									11 11	11 05		
Wakefield Westgate	d									10 24									11 24			
Wakefield Kirkgate	d																			11 23		
Doncaster	d	09 53									10 53										11 55	
Sheffield	d	10 23				10 27	10 38		10 47	10 54	11 23				11 27	11 38		11 47	11 54	12 05	12 23	
Chesterfield	d					10 39	10 53		10 59	11 06					11 39	11 53		11 59	12 07	12 22		
Derby	a	10 51				10 59			11 19	11 26	11 51				11 59			12 19	12 26		12 51	
	d					11 01			11 20						12 01			12 20				
Long Eaton	d								11 30									12 30				
Alfreton	d						11 03									12 03				12 33		
Langley Mill	d																			12 40		
Lincoln	d			09 31	09 31								10 36	10 36								
Nottingham	a			10 32	10 30		11 29						11 32	11 29		12 29				13 00		
	d		10 28	10 32	10 32			11 02				11 28	11 32	11 32			12 02					12 28
Beeston	d			10 38	10 38			11 08					11 38	11 38			12 08					
East Midlands Parkway	d		10 39	10 46	10 46				11 35			11 39	11 46	11 46				12 35				12 40
Loughborough	d			10 55	10 55			11 20	11 42				11 55	11 55			12 20	12 42				
Barrow Upon Soar	d			10 59	10 59								11 59	11 59								
Sileby	d			11 03	11 03								12 03	12 03								
Syston	d			11 08	11 08								12 08	12 08								
Leicester	a		10 57	11 20	11 20	11 23		11 31	11 54			11 57	12 19	12 19	12 23		12 31	12 54				12 58
	d		10 57			11 25		11 33	11 55			11 57			12 25		12 33	12 55				13 00
Market Harborough	d		11 12					11 47				12 12					12 47					13 15
Corby	d																					
Kettering	a							11 56									12 56					
	d							11 56									12 56					
Wellingborough	d							12 04									13 04					
Bedford	d							12 19									13 19					
Luton	d																					
Luton Airport Parkway	d							12 35									13 35					
St Pancras International	a		12 19			12 34		13 01	13 05			13 19			13 34		14 01	14 05				14 20

		EM	EM	EM	EM	EM	EM	XC	NT	XC	EM	EM	EM	EM	EM	EM	EM	XC	NT	XC	EM	EM	EM
		A	B	◇■ ☕	◇	◇■ ☕	◇■ ☕	◇■ 🍴		◇■ 🍴	◇■ ☕	A	B	◇■ ☕	◇	◇■ ☕	◇■ ☕	◇■ 🍴		◇■ 🍴	◇■ ☕	A	B
York	d							11 45		12 25								12 45		13 27			
Leeds	d							12 11	12 05									13 11	13 05				
Wakefield Westgate	d							12 24										13 23					
Wakefield Kirkgate	d								12 23										13 23				
Doncaster	d									12 52										13 54			
Sheffield	d			12 27	12 38		12 47	12 54	13 05	13 23				13 27	13 38		13 47	13 54	14 05	14 23			
Chesterfield	d			12 39	12 53		12 59	13 06	13 22					13 39	13 53		13 59	14 07	14 22				
Derby	a			12 59			13 19	13 25		13 51				13 59			14 19	14 26		14 51			
	d			13 01			13 20							14 01			14 20						
Long Eaton	d						13 30										14 30						
Alfreton	d				13 03				13 33						14 03				14 33				
Langley Mill	d								13 40										14 40				
Lincoln	d	11 42	11 42									12 30	12 30									13 40	13 40
Nottingham	a	12 32	12 30		13 30				14 00			13 32	13 30		14 29				15 00			14 32	14 30
	d	12 32	12 32			13 02					13 28	13 32	13 32			14 02					14 28	14 32	14 32
Beeston	d	12 38	12 38			13 08						13 38	13 38			14 08						14 38	14 38
East Midlands Parkway	d	12 46	12 46				13 35				13 39	13 46	13 46				14 35				14 39	14 46	14 46
Loughborough	d	12 55	12 55			13 20	13 42					13 55	13 55			14 20	14 42					14 55	14 55
Barrow Upon Soar	d	12 59	12 59									13 59	13 59									14 59	14 59
Sileby	d	13 03	13 03									14 03	14 03									15 03	15 03
Syston	d	13 08	13 08									14 08	14 08									15 08	15 08
Leicester	a	13 19	13 19	13 23		13 31	13 54				13 57	14 19	14 19	14 23		14 31	14 54				14 57	15 21	15 21
	d			13 25		13 33	13 55				13 57			14 25		14 33	14 55				14 57		
Market Harborough	d					13 47					14 12					14 47					15 12		
Corby	d																						
Kettering	a					13 56										14 56							
	d					13 56										14 56							
Wellingborough	d					14 04										15 04							
Bedford	d					14 19										15 19							
Luton	d																						
Luton Airport Parkway	d					14 35										15 35							
St Pancras International	a			14 34		15 01	15 05				15 19			15 34		16 01	16 05				16 19		

A from 2 October
B until 25 September

For connections to Gatwick Airport see Table 52

Table 53

Saturdays

Sheffield - East Midlands - London

		EM ◇1 ⊐	EM ◇	EM ◇1 ⊐	EM ◇1 ⊐	XC ◇1 ⊤	NT	XC ◇1 ⊤	EM ◇1 ⊐	EM A	EM B	EM ◇1 ⊐	EM ◇	EM ◇1 ⊐	EM ◇1 ⊐	XC ◇1 ⊤	NT	XC ◇1 ⊤	EM ◇1 ⊐	EM A	EM B	EM ◇1 ⊐
York 8	d					13 44		14 27								14 44		15 26				
Leeds 10	d					14 11	14 05									15 12	15 05					
Wakefield Westgate 7	d					14 24										15 24						
Wakefield Kirkgate 4	d						14 23										15 23					
Doncaster 7	d							14 56										15 55				
Sheffield 7	d	14 27	14 38		14 47	14 54	15 05	15 23				15 27	15 38		15 47	15 54	16 05	16 23				16 27
Chesterfield	d	14 39	14 53		14 59	15 06	15 22					15 39	15 53		15 59	16 07	16 22					16 39
Derby 6	a	14 59			15 19	15 26		15 51				15 59			16 19	16 26		16 51				16 59
	d	15 01			15 20							16 01			16 20							17 01
Long Eaton	d				15 30										16 30							
Alfreton	d		15 04				15 33						16 03				16 33					
Langley Mill	d						15 40										16 40					
Lincoln	d									14 35	14 35									15 30	15 30	
Nottingham 8	a		15 29				16 00			15 32	15 30		16 33				17 00			16 32	16 30	
	d			15 02					15 28	15 32	15 32			16 02					16 28	16 32	16 32	
Beeston	d			15 08						15 38	15 38			16 08						16 38	16 38	
East Midlands Parkway	d				15 35				15 39	15 46	15 46				16 35				16 39	16 48	16 48	
Loughborough	d			15 20	15 42					15 55	15 55			16 19	16 42					16 57	16 57	
Barrow Upon Soar	d									15 59	15 59									17 01	17 01	
Sileby	d									16 03	16 03									17 05	17 05	
Syston	d									16 08	16 08									17 10	17 10	
Leicester	a	15 23		15 31	15 54				15 57	16 21	16 21	16 23		16 31	16 54				16 57	17 22	17 22	17 23
	d	15 25		15 33	15 55				15 57			16 25		16 33	16 55				16 57			17 25
Market Harborough	d			15 47					16 12					16 47					17 12			
Corby	d																					
Kettering 4	a			15 56										16 56								
	d			15 56										16 56								
Wellingborough	d			16 04										17 04								
Bedford 7	d			16 19										17 19								
Luton 10	d																					
Luton Airport Parkway 7	d			16 35										17 35								
St Pancras International	a	16 34		17 01	17 05				17 19			17 34		18 01	18 06				18 19			18 34

		EM ◇1 ⊐	EM ◇1 ⊐	EM ◇	XC ◇1 ⊤	NT	XC ◇1 ⊤	EM ◇1 ⊐	EM A	EM B	EM ◇1 ⊐	EM ◇1 ⊐	EM ◇1 ⊐	XC ◇1 ⊤	NT	XC ◇1 ⊤	EM ◇1 ⊐	EM A	EM B	EM ◇1 ⊐	EM ◇1 ⊐	EM ◇	EM ◇1 ⊐	XC ◇1 ⊤	NT
York 8	d				15 45		16 25							16 45		17 25							17 49	17 45	
Leeds 10	d				16 12	16 05								17 12	17 05									18 11	18 05
Wakefield Westgate 7	d				16 24									17 24										18 24	
Wakefield Kirkgate 4	d					16 23									17 23										18 23
Doncaster 7	d						16 53									17 55							18 17		
Sheffield 7	d		16 35	16 38	16 54	17 05	17 23				17 27		17 35	17 54	18 05	18 23				18 27		18 38	18 47	18 54	19 05
Chesterfield	d		16 47	16 53	17 06	17 22					17 39		17 51	18 06	18 22					18 39		18 53		19 06	19 22
Derby 6	a		17 16		17 26		17 51				17 59		18 16	18 26		18 51				18 59			19 19	19 26	
	d		17 18								18 01		18 18							19 01			19 21		
Long Eaton	d		17 28										18 28										19 31		
Alfreton	d			17 04		17 33									18 33							19 03			19 33
Langley Mill	d					17 40									18 40										19 40
Lincoln	d								16 35	16 35								17 28	17 28						
Nottingham 8	a			17 29		18 00			17 32	17 30					19 00			18 32	18 31			19 33			20 00
	d	17 02						17 28	17 32	17 32		18 02					18 28	18 32	18 32		19 02				
Beeston	d	17 08							17 38	17 38		18 08						18 38	18 38		09 08				
East Midlands Parkway	d		17 32					17 39	17 48	17 48			18 32				18 39	18 47	18 47				19 35		
Loughborough	d	17 20	17 40						17 57	17 57		18 20	18 40					18 55	18 55		19 20		19 41		
Barrow Upon Soar	d								18 01	18 01								19 00	19 00						
Sileby	d								18 05	18 05								19 04	19 04						
Syston	d								18 10	18 10								19 09	19 09						
Leicester	a	17 31	17 51					17 55	18 22	18 22	18 23	18 31	18 51				18 55	19 22	19 22	19 23	19 31		19 54		
	d	17 33	17 53					17 57			18 25	18 33	18 53				18 57			19 25	19 33		19 55		
Market Harborough	d	17 47						18 12				18 47					19 12				19 47				
Corby	d																								
Kettering 4	a	17 56										18 56									19 56				
	d	17 56										18 56									19 56				
Wellingborough	d	18 04										19 04									20 04				
Bedford 7	d	18 19										19 18									20 18				
Luton 10	d																								
Luton Airport Parkway 7	d	18 35										19 30									20 34				
St Pancras International	a	18 59	19 08					19 19			19 34	20 02	20 05				20 18			20 34	21 01		21 06		

A from 2 October

B until 25 September

For connections to Gatwick Airport see Table 52

Table 53

Saturdays

Sheffield - East Midlands - London

		XC ◇1 ⊤	EM ◇1 ⊐	EM A	EM B	EM ◇1 ⊐	EM ◇	XC ◇1 ⊤	NT	XC ◇1 ⊤	EM ◇1 ⊐	EM ◇1 ⊐	EM	EM ◇1 ⊐	EM ◇	XC ◇1 ⊤	XC ◇1 ⊤	EM ◇1 ⊐	EM	EM ◇	XC ◇1 ⊤	EM ◇	EM C
York 8	d	18 25						18 44		19 25						19 44	20 23				20 44		
Leeds 10	d							19 11	19 05							20 11					21 11		
Wakefield Westgate 7	d							19 24								20 23					21 23		
Wakefield Kirkgate 4	d								19 24														
Doncaster 7	d	18 54								19 53													
Sheffield 7	d	19 24				19 27	19 38	19 54	20 05	20 23				20 27	20 41	20 54	21 23			21 38	21 54	22 35	
Chesterfield	d					19 39	19 53	20 06	20 22					20 39	20 59	21 06	21 35			21 54	22 06	22 51	
Derby 6	a	19 52				19 59		20 26		20 51				21 00		21 26	21 54				22 25		
	d					20 01								21 01									
Long Eaton	d																						
Alfreton	d						20 04		20 33						21 09					22 05			
Langley Mill	d								20 40											22 12			
Lincoln	d			18 35	18 35																		
Nottingham 8	a			19 31	19 29		20 31		21 00						21 33					22 33		23 31	
	d		19 28	19 32	19 32						20 02	20 43	20 32					21 18	21 32				23 11
Beeston	d			19 38	19 38						20 08	20 49	20 38						21 38				23 17
East Midlands Parkway	d		19 41	19 46	19 46						20 16	20 55	20 46	21 14					21 46				23 25
Loughborough	d			19 55	19 55						20 24	21 03	20 55	21 23				21 32	21 55				23 34
Barrow Upon Soar	d			19 59	19 59								20 59						21 59				
Sileby	d			20 03	20 03								21 03						22 03				
Syston	d			20 08	20 08								21 08						22 13				
Leicester	a		19 58	20 20	20 20	20 23					20 34	21 13	21 19	21 39				21 43	22 26				23 57
	d		20 00			20 25					20 36	21 15						21 45					
Market Harborough	d		20 15								20 50	21 29						21 59					
Corby	d																						
Kettering 4	a										20 59	21 38						22 14					
	d										20 59	21 38						22 15					
Wellingborough	d										21 07	21 47						22 22					
Bedford 7	d										21 22	22 02						22 37					
Luton 10	d											22 17											
Luton Airport Parkway 7	d										21 38	22 20						22 59					
St Pancras International	a		21 15			21 38					22 05	22 47						23 35					

		EM D	EM E	EM ◇1 F ⊐	EM ◇1 G ⊐
York 8	d				
Leeds 10	d				
Wakefield Westgate 7	d				
Wakefield Kirkgate 4	d				
Doncaster 7	d				
Sheffield 7	d			23 20	23 31
Chesterfield	d			23 33	23 44
Derby 6	a			23 53	00 04
	d				
Long Eaton	d				
Alfreton	d				
Langley Mill	d				
Lincoln	d				
Nottingham 8	a				
	d	23 11	23 11		
Beeston	d	23 17	23 17		
East Midlands Parkway	d	23 25	23 25		
Loughborough	d	23 34	23 33		
Barrow Upon Soar	d				
Sileby	d				
Syston	d				
Leicester	a	23 59	23 59		
	d				
Market Harborough	d				
Corby	d				
Kettering 4	a				
	d				
Wellingborough	d				
Bedford 7	d				
Luton 10	d				
Luton Airport Parkway 7	d				
St Pancras International	a				

A from 2 October

B until 25 September

C until 10 July

D from 17 July until 4 September

E from 11 September until 4 December

F from 11 September

G until 4 September

For connections to Gatwick Airport see Table 52

Sheffield - East Midlands - London

		EM	EM	EM	EM	EM	EM	XC	EM	EM		EM	NT	EM	EM	EM	EM	XC	EM	EM		EM	EM	NT	EM
		◇1	◇1	◇1		◇1		◇1	◇1			◇1			◇1		◇1	◇1		◇1			◇1		
		☕	☕	☕	🚌	☕	🚌	🍴	☕	🚌		☕		🚌	☕	🚌	☕	🍴	🚌	☕		🚌	☕		🚌
York 8	d																								
Leeds 10	d							08 10										09 00						09 05	
Wakefield Westgate 7	d							08 22										09 11							
Wakefield Kirkgate 4	d																							09 21	
Doncaster 7	d																	09 32							
Sheffield 7	d	23p31						08 54					09 00				09 08	09 57					10 04	10 07	
Chesterfield	d	23p44						09 07					09 17				09 23	10 09					10 17	10 23	
Derby 6	a	00 04						09 28									09 43	10 32					10 37		
	d		06 38			07 46						08 42					09 48						10 48		
Long Eaton	d											08 52					09 58						10 58		
Alfreton	d												09 28											10 33	
Langley Mill	d												09 35											10 41	
Lincoln	d																								
Nottingham 8	a												09 53											10 59	
	d			07 19					08 14						09 11					10 15					
Beeston	d								08 20											10 22					
East Midlands Parkway	d		06 55	07 29		07 59			08 28			08 58			09 23		10 03			10 30			11 03		
Loughborough	d				07 38		08 07			08 37				09 04		09 40			10 08			10 41			11 06
Barrow Upon Soar	d																								
Sileby	d																								
Syston	d																								
Leicester	a		07 18	07 52	08 13	08 22	08 42		08 50	09 12		09 21		09 39	09 47	10 15	10 23		10 43	10 51		11 16	11 24		11 41
	d		07 20	07 54		08 23			08 52			09 22			09 49		10 25			10 53			11 26		
Market Harborough	d		07 38	08 11		08 40			09 09			09 39			10 07		10 39			11 08			11 40		
Corby	d																								
Kettering 4	a		07 48	08 20		08 49			09 18			09 48			10 17		10 48			11 18			11 49		
	d		07 49	08 21		08 50			09 19			09 51			10 18		10 51			11 19			11 50		
Wellingborough	d		08 01	08 32		09 02			09 30			10 04			10 26		10 58			11 27			11 58		
Bedford 7	d		08 15	08 45		09 14			09 45			10 16			10 45		11 16			11 45			12 15		
Luton 10	d		08 34			09 39						10 41					11 38						12 40		
Luton Airport Parkway 7	d			09 11					10 10						11 10					12 09					
St Pancras International	a		09 16	09 50		10 20			10 49			11 20			11 49		12 20			12 50			13 20		

		EM	EM	XC	NT	EM	XC	NT	EM	EM	EM	EM	EM	NT	EM	XC		EM	EM	EM	NT	EM	XC	EM	EM
		◇1	◇	◇1		◇1	◇1				◇1		◇1		◇	◇1			◇1	◇1		◇	◇1	◇1	◇1
		☕		🍴		☕	🍴		🚌	🚌	☕	🚌	☕			🍴		🚌	☕	☕			🍴	☕	☕
York 8	d			09 28			10 28									11 28							12 28		
Leeds 10	d	09 44		10 00	10 02	10 15	11 00	10 57						11 29		12 00					12 29		13 00		
Wakefield Westgate 7	d	09 58		10 12		10 27	11 12									12 12							13 12		
Wakefield Kirkgate 4	d				10 18			11 13						11 46							12 46				
Doncaster 7	d			10 30			11 30									12 30							13 30		
Sheffield 7	d	10 26	10 49	10 57	11 03	10 57	11 57	12 00					12 19	12 31	12 49	12 57				13 20	13 31	13 49	13 57		14 07
Chesterfield	d	10 41	11 04	11 09	11 20	11 13	12 09	12 18					12 32	12 49	13 03	13 09				13 33	13 48	14 03	14 09		14 20
Derby 6	a			11 28		11 34	12 28						12 52			13 31				13 52			14 28		14 42
	d					11 41							12 55							13 54					14 49
Long Eaton	d												13 05							14 05					15 03
Alfreton	d		11 14		11 30			12 28						12 59	13 14						13 59	14 14			
Langley Mill	d				11 38			12 36						13 07							14 06				
Lincoln	d																								
Nottingham 8	a	11 11	11 38		11 54			12 53						13 25	13 39						14 22	14 40			
	d	11 18									12 14								13 13					14 30	
Beeston	d										12 21								13 20					14 36	
East Midlands Parkway	d	11 30				11 54					12 30		13 10						13 30	14 09				14 43	15 08
Loughborough	d								11 37	12 08		12 49						13 08		14 17				14 51	15 15
Barrow Upon Soar	d																								
Sileby	d																								
Syston	d																								
Leicester	a	11 50				12 20			12 12	12 43	12 52	13 24	13 32					13 43	13 51	14 27				15 02	15 26
	d	11 51				12 22					12 53		13 34						13 53	14 29				15 04	15 27
Market Harborough	d	12 06				12 37					13 08		13 48						14 08	14 43				15 18	
Corby	d																								
Kettering 4	a	12 16				12 47					13 18		13 57						14 18	14 52				15 27	
	d	12 17				12 48					13 19		13 58						14 19	14 53				15 28	
Wellingborough	d	12 25				12 56					13 27		14 06						14 29	15 00				15 35	
Bedford 7	d	12 44				13 15					13 46		14 23						14 54	15 25				15 55	
Luton 10	d					13 38							14 47							15 42					16 25
Luton Airport Parkway 7	d	13 08									14 10								15 11					16 14	
St Pancras International	a	13 50				14 20					14 44		15 22						15 45	16 15				16 45	16 55

For connections to Gatwick Airport see Table 52

Table 53

Sundays
until 11 July

Sheffield - East Midlands - London

		XC		XC	EM	EM	EM	EM	NT	XC	EM	EM		XC	NT	XC	EM	EM	EM	EM	EM	XC		NT	XC
		◇1		◇1	◇	◇1	◇1	◇1		◇1	◇1	◇		◇1		◇1	◇1	◇1	◇1	◇1	◇	◇1			◇1
		🍴		🍴		☕	☕	☕		🍴	☕			🍴		🍴	☕	☕	☕	☕		🍴			🍴
York 8	d			13 28						14 22				14 28		15 20						15 28			16 20
Leeds 10	d			14 00				14 05	14 05					15 00	15 05							16 00		16 05	
Wakefield Westgate 7	d			14 12				14 18						15 12								16 12			
Wakefield Kirkgate 4	d								14 21						15 22									16 22	
Doncaster 7	d									14 50						15 50									16 50
Sheffield 7	d	14 20		14 50	14 53			15 02	15 07	15 20	15 32	15 43		15 50	16 07	16 20				16 29	16 40	16 50		17 07	17 20
Chesterfield	d	14 32		15 02	15 07			15 15	15 24		15 44	15 57		16 02	16 23					16 43	16 56	17 02		17 23	
Derby 6	a	14 51		15 22				15 38		15 49	16 09			16 22		16 49				17 04		17 22			17 49
	d							15 38			16 14								16 47	17 09					
Long Eaton	d																		16 57						
Alfreton	d				15 18				15 34			16 08			16 33						17 07			17 33	
Langley Mill	d				15 25				15 42			16 15			16 41						17 14			17 41	
Lincoln	d																								
Nottingham 8	a				15 44				16 00			16 33			16 59						17 32			17 59	
	d					15 10	15 36										16 18	16 45							
Beeston	d					15 16											16 24								
East Midlands Parkway	d					15 23	15 46	15 52			16 25						16 31	16 55	17 01	17 21					
Loughborough	d					15 30		16 01									16 39		17 09						
Barrow Upon Soar	d																								
Sileby	d																								
Syston	d																								
Leicester	a					15 42	16 02	16 13			16 40						16 50	17 12	17 20	17 38					
	d					15 44	16 03	16 15			16 41						16 52	17 13	17 22	17 40					
Market Harborough	d					16 01		16 30									17 06		17 36						
Corby	d																								
Kettering 4	a					16 10		16 40									17 15		17 45						
	d					16 11		16 41									17 16		17 46						
Wellingborough	d					16 18		16 49									17 23		17 53						
Bedford 7	d					16 35		17 07									17 40		18 11						
Luton 10	d							17 25											18 29						
Luton Airport Parkway 7	d					16 53											17 59								
St Pancras International	a					17 27	17 31	17 59			18 05						18 29	18 34	18 59	19 04					

		EM	EM	EM	EM	EM	XC	NT	XC	EM	EM	EM	EM	XC	NT	XC	EM	EM		EM	XC	NT	XC	EM	EM
		◇1	◇1	◇1	◇1	◇	◇1		◇1	◇1	◇1	◇1	◇	◇1		◇1	◇1	◇1		◇	◇1		◇1	◇1	◇
		☕	☕	☕	☕		🍴		🍴	☕	☕	☕		🍴		🍴	☕	☕			🍴		🍴	☕	
York 8	d						16 28		17 21			17 40		17 28		18 20					18 28		19 20		
Leeds 10	d						17 00	17 05						18 00	18 05						19 00	19 04			
Wakefield Westgate 7	d						17 12							18 12							19 12				
Wakefield Kirkgate 4	d							17 21							18 22							19 21			
Doncaster 7	d								17 50			18 06				18 50							19 50		
Sheffield 7	d				17 29	17 39	17 50	18 07	18 20			18 32	18 41	18 50	19 07	19 20		19 31		19 40	19 50	20 06	20 20	20 24	20 40
Chesterfield	d				17 43	17 54	18 02	18 25				18 44	18 56	19 02	19 25			19 44		19 55	20 02	20 23		20 38	20 55
Derby 6	a				18 04		18 22		18 49			19 08		19 22		19 49		20 04			20 21		20 49	20 57	
	d			17 47	18 07							19 09						20 06						20 59	
Long Eaton	d			17 57								19 20						20 16							
Alfreton	d					18 04		18 36					19 06		19 36					20 06		20 34			21 06
Langley Mill	d					18 12		18 43					19 14		19 43					20 14		20 41			21 14
Lincoln	d																								
Nottingham 8	a					18 29		19 00					19 36		19 59					20 31		20 57			21 36
	d	17 20	17 34							18 10	18 44						19 46								
Beeston	d	17 26								18 19							19 52								
East Midlands Parkway	d	17 32	17 49	18 01	18 20					18 25	18 54	19 25					19 58	20 21						21 11	
Loughborough	d	17 40		18 09						18 33	19 02	19 32					20 06	20 30							
Barrow Upon Soar	d																								
Sileby	d																								
Syston	d																								
Leicester	a	17 50	18 06	18 19	18 39					18 43	19 13	19 44					20 16	20 42						21 28	
	d	17 52	18 08	18 21	18 40					18 45	19 15	19 45					20 18	20 44						21 30	
Market Harborough	d	18 06		18 35						19 05	19 31	20 03					20 32	20 59						21 45	
Corby	d																								
Kettering 4	a	18 15		18 44						19 14	19 40	20 12					20 41	21 09						21 55	
	d	18 16		18 45						19 15	19 41	20 13					20 42	21 10						21 56	
Wellingborough	d	18 23		18 52						19 22	19 48	20 21					20 49	21 18						22 04	
Bedford 7	d	18 40		19 10						19 40	20 07	20 40					21 08	21 37						22 24	
Luton 10	d			19 29							20 26						21 23	21 52						22 40	
Luton Airport Parkway 7	d	18 59								19 59		20 55													
St Pancras International	a	19 29	19 34	19 59	20 04					20 29	20 57	21 27					21 57	22 27						23 13	

For connections to Gatwick Airport see Table 52

Table 53

Sheffield - East Midlands - London

Sundays until 11 July

Station		XC ◇1	XC ◇1	EM ◇1	EM ◇	XC ◇1	EM ◇1	EM ◇
York	d	19 28	20 20			20 28		
Leeds	d	20 00				21 00		
Wakefield Westgate	d	20 12				21 12		
Wakefield Kirkgate	d							
Doncaster	d		20 50					
Sheffield	d	20 50	21 20		21 40	21 50	22 13	23 29
Chesterfield	d	21 02	21 32		21 54	22 02	22 27	23 43
Derby	a	21 22	21 51			22 22	23 04	
	d							
Long Eaton	d							
Alfreton	d				22 05			23 54
Langley Mill	d				22 12			00 02
Lincoln	d							
Nottingham	a				22 35			00 33
	d			21 13				
Beeston	d							
East Midlands Parkway	d			21 23				
Loughborough	d			21 31				
Barrow Upon Soar	d							
Sileby	d							
Syston	d							
Leicester	a			21 41				
	d			21 43				
Market Harborough	d			21 57				
Corby	d							
Kettering	a			22 06				
	d			22 07				
Wellingborough	d			22 14				
Bedford	d			22 32				
Luton	d			22 50				
Luton Airport Parkway	d							
St Pancras International	a			23 27				

Sundays 18 July to 05 September

Station		EM ◇1	EM ◇1	EM ◇1	EM ◇1	XC ◇1	EM ◇1	EM ◇1	NT	EM ◇1	EM ◇1	XC ◇1	NT	EM ◇1	EM ◇1	EM ◇1	EM ◇	XC ◇1	NT	EM ◇1	XC ◇1	NT	EM ◇1	EM ◇1
York	d																	09 28			10 28			
Leeds	d					08 10						09 00	09 05			09 44		10 00	10 02		11 00	10 57		
Wakefield Westgate	d					08 22						09 11				09 58		10 12		10 15	11 12			
Wakefield Kirkgate	d												09 21						10 18	10 27		11 13		
Doncaster	d											09 32						10 30			11 30			
Sheffield	d	23p31				08 54			09 00		09 17	09 57	10 07		10 17	10 26	10 49	10 57	11 03		11 57	12 00		12 24
Chesterfield	d	23p44				09 07			09 17		09 29	10 09	10 23		10 29	10 41	11 04	11 09	11 20	10 57	12 09	12 18		12 37
Derby	a	00 04				09 28					09 49	10 32			10 49			11 28		11 13	12 28			12 56
	d		06 41		07 42			08 47			09 51				10 51					11 34				12 58
Long Eaton	d							08 58			10 01				11 01					11 41				13 08
Alfreton	d								09 28				10 33				11 14		11 30			12 28		
Langley Mill	d								09 35				10 41						11 38			12 36		
Lincoln	d																							
Nottingham	a								09 53				10 59			11 11	11 38		11 54			12 53		
	d			07 15			08 15			09 15				10 14		11 18							12 03	
Beeston	d						08 21							10 21									12 10	
East Midlands Parkway	d		06 55	07 25	07 54		08 27	09 02		09 26	10 05			10 29	11 05	11 29							12 21	13 12
Loughborough	d						08 35	09 10		09 34	10 13			10 37	11 13	11 38				11 54			12 30	13 20
Barrow Upon Soar	d																							
Sileby	d																							
Syston	d																							
Leicester	a		07 18	07 48	08 18		08 46	09 21		09 47	10 24			10 50	11 24	11 50				12 20			12 43	13 31
	d		07 20	07 50	08 19		08 48	09 23		09 49	10 26			10 52	11 26	11 52				12 22			12 44	13 33
Market Harborough	d		07 38	08 07	08 36		09 05	09 39		10 07	10 40			11 07	11 40	12 07				12 37			13 05	13 50
Corby	d																							
Kettering	a		07 49	08 17	08 47		09 15	09 50		10 18	10 51			11 18	11 50	12 18							13 16	14 00
	d		07 50	08 18	08 48		09 16	09 51		10 19	10 52			11 19	11 51	12 19				12 47			13 17	14 01
Wellingborough	d		08 04	08 32	09 02		09 30	10 05		10 29	11 02			11 29	12 01	12 29				12 48			13 27	14 12
Bedford	d		08 17	08 45	09 14		09 45	10 17		10 45	11 17			11 45	12 17	12 46				12 56			13 46	14 32
Luton	d		08 37		09 39			10 41			11 39				12 40					13 15				14 49
Luton Airport Parkway	d			09 11			10 10			11 10				12 09		13 10				13 38			14 10	
St Pancras International	a		09 16	09 50	10 20		10 49	11 20		11 49	12 20			12 50	13 20	13 50				14 20			14 44	15 22

For connections to Gatwick Airport see Table 52

Table 53

Sheffield - East Midlands - London

Sundays 18 July to 05 September

Station		NT	EM ◇	XC ◇1	EM ◇1	EM ◇1	NT	EM ◇	XC ◇1	EM ◇1	EM ◇1	XC ◇1	XC ◇1	EM ◇	EM ◇1	EM ◇1	EM ◇1	NT	XC ◇1	EM ◇1	EM ◇	XC ◇1	NT
York	d			11 28					12 28				13 28						14 22			14 28	
Leeds	d	11 29		12 00			12 29		13 00				14 00				14 05	14 05				15 00	15 05
Wakefield Westgate	d			12 12					13 12				14 12				14 18					15 12	
Wakefield Kirkgate	d	11 46					12 46											14 21					15 22
Doncaster	d			12 30					13 30										14 50				
Sheffield	d	12 31	12 49	12 57		13 20	13 31	13 49	13 57		14 07	14 20	14 50	14 53			15 02	15 07	15 20	15 32	15 43	15 50	16 07
Chesterfield	d	12 49	13 03	13 09		13 33	13 48	14 03	14 09		14 20	14 32	15 02	15 07			15 15	15 24		15 44	15 57	16 02	16 23
Derby	a			13 31		13 52			14 28		14 42	14 51	15 22				15 37		15 49	16 09		16 22	
	d					13 54					14 49						15 37			16 14			
Long Eaton	d					14 04					15 02												
Alfreton	d	12 59	13 14				13 59	14 14						15 18				15 34			16 08		16 33
Langley Mill	d	13 07					14 06							15 25				15 42			16 15		16 41
Lincoln	d																						
Nottingham	a	13 25	13 39				14 22	14 40						15 44				16 00			16 33		16 59
	d				13 00					14 30					15 12	15 36							
Beeston	d				13 07					14 36					15 18								
East Midlands Parkway	d				13 20	14 08				14 43	15 07				15 25	15 46	15 51			16 25			
Loughborough	d				13 29	14 16				14 51	15 14				15 32		16 00						
Barrow Upon Soar	d																						
Sileby	d																						
Syston	d																						
Leicester	a				13 42	14 27				15 02	15 26				15 44	16 02	16 13			16 40			
	d				13 43	14 29				15 04	15 27				15 46	16 03	16 15			16 42			
Market Harborough	d				14 07	14 43				15 18					16 00		16 30						
Corby	d																						
Kettering	a				14 18	14 52				15 27					16 09		16 40						
	d				14 21	14 53				15 28					16 10		16 41						
Wellingborough	d				14 31	15 00				15 35					16 17		16 49						
Bedford	d				14 54	15 25				15 55					16 34		17 07						
Luton	d					15 42					16 25						17 25						
Luton Airport Parkway	d				15 11					16 14					16 53								
St Pancras International	a				15 45	16 15				16 45	16 55				17 27	17 31	17 59			18 04			

Station		XC ◇1	EM ◇1	EM ◇1	EM ◇1	EM ◇1	EM ◇	XC ◇1	NT	XC ◇1	EM ◇1	EM ◇1	EM ◇1	EM ◇1	EM ◇	XC ◇1	NT	XC ◇1	EM ◇1	EM ◇1	EM ◇1	EM ◇
York	d	15 20						15 28		16 20						16 28		17 21			17 40	
Leeds	d							16 00	16 05							17 00	17 05					
Wakefield Westgate	d							16 12								17 12						
Wakefield Kirkgate	d								16 22								17 21					
Doncaster	d	15 50								16 50								17 50			18 06	
Sheffield	d	16 20				16 29	16 40	16 50	17 07	17 20				17 27	17 39	17 50	18 07	18 20			18 32	18 41
Chesterfield	d					16 43	16 56	17 02	17 23					17 41	17 54	18 02	18 25				18 44	18 56
Derby	a	16 49				17 03		17 22		17 49				18 02		18 22		18 49			19 08	
	d				16 47	17 08							17 46	18 05							19 09	
Long Eaton	d				16 57								17 56								19 20	
Alfreton	d						17 07		17 33						18 04		18 36					19 06
Langley Mill	d						17 14		17 41						18 12		18 43					19 14
Lincoln	d																					
Nottingham	a						17 32		17 59						18 29		19 00					19 36
	d		16 18	16 45							17 19	17 34							18 10	18 44		
Beeston	d		16 24								17 25								18 17			
East Midlands Parkway	d		16 31	16 55	17 01	17 21					17 31	17 49	18 00	18 18					18 23	18 54	19 25	
Loughborough	d		16 39		17 09						17 39		18 08						18 31	19 02	19 32	
Barrow Upon Soar	d																					
Sileby	d																					
Syston	d																					
Leicester	a		16 50	17 12	17 20	17 38					17 50	18 06	18 19	18 37					18 42	19 13	19 44	
	d		16 52	17 13	17 22	17 40					17 52	18 08	18 21	18 38					18 44	19 15	19 45	
Market Harborough	d		17 06		17 36						18 06		18 35						19 05	19 31	20 03	
Corby	d																					
Kettering	a		17 15		17 45						18 15		18 44						19 14	19 40	20 12	
	d		17 16		17 46						18 16		18 45						19 15	19 41	20 13	
Wellingborough	d		17 23		17 53						18 23		18 52						19 22	19 48	20 21	
Bedford	d		17 40		18 11						18 40		19 10						19 40	20 07	20 40	
Luton	d				18 29								19 29							20 26		
Luton Airport Parkway	d		17 59								18 59								19 59		20 55	
St Pancras International	a		18 29	18 34	18 59	19 04					19 29	19 34	19 59	20 04					20 29	20 57	21 27	

For connections to Gatwick Airport see Table 52

Table 53

Sundays
18 July to 05 September

Sheffield - East Midlands - London

		XC	NT	XC	EM	EM	EM	XC	NT	XC	EM	EM	XC	XC	EM	EM	XC	EM	EM
		◇■		◇■	◇■	◇■	◇	◇■		◇■	◇■	◇	◇■	◇■	◇■	◇	◇■	◇■	◇
York	d	17 28		18 20				18 28		19 20			19 28	20 20			20 28		
Leeds	d	18 00	18 05					19 00	19 04				20 00				21 00		
Wakefield Westgate	d	18 12						19 12					20 12				21 12		
Wakefield Kirkgate	d		18 22						19 21										
Doncaster	d			18 50						19 50				20 50					
Sheffield	d	18 50	19 07	19 20		19 31	19 40	19 50	20 06	20 20	20 24	20 40	20 50	21 20		21 40	21 50	22 13	23 29
Chesterfield	d	19 02	19 25			19 44	19 55	20 02	20 23		20 38	20 55	21 02	21 32		21 54	22 02	22 27	23 43
Derby	a	19 22		19 49		20 04		20 21		20 49	20 57		21 22	21 51			22 22	23 05	
	d					20 05					20 59								
Long Eaton	d					20 16													
Alfreton	d		19 36				20 06		20 34			21 06				22 05			23 54
Langley Mill	d		19 43				20 14		20 41			21 14				22 12			00 03
Lincoln	d																		
Nottingham	a		19 59				20 31		20 57			21 36				22 35			00 30
	d				19 45										21 12				
Beeston	d				19 51														
East Midlands Parkway	d				19 57	20 21					21 11				21 22				
Loughborough	d				20 05	20 29									21 30				
Barrow Upon Soar	d																		
Sileby	d																		
Syston	d																		
Leicester	a				20 16	20 42					21 28				21 41				
	d				20 18	20 44					21 30				21 43				
Market Harborough	d				20 32	20 59					21 45				21 57				
Corby	d																		
Kettering	a				20 41	21 09					21 55				22 06				
	d				20 42	21 10					21 56				22 07				
Wellingborough	d				20 49	21 18					22 04				22 14				
Bedford	d				21 08	21 37					22 24				22 32				
Luton	d				21 23	21 52					22 40				22 50				
Luton Airport Parkway	d																		
St Pancras International	a				21 57	22 27					23 13				23 27				

Sundays
from 12 September

		EM	EM	EM	XC	EM	EM	NT	EM	EM	XC	NT	EM	EM	EM	XC	NT	EM	XC	NT	EM	EM	NT
		◇■	◇■	◇■	◇■	◇■	◇■		◇■	◇■	◇■		◇■	◇■	◇■	◇■		◇■	◇■		◇■	◇■	
											A												
York	d															09 28			10 28				
Leeds	d				08 10						09 00	09 05			09 44	10 00	10 02	10 20	11 00	10 57			11 29
Wakefield Westgate	d				08 22						09 11				09 58	10 12		10 32	11 12				
Wakefield Kirkgate	d											09 21					10 18			11 13			11 46
Doncaster	d										09 32					10 30			11 30				
Sheffield	d				08 54			09 00		09 17	09 57	10 07		10 17	10 26	10 57	11 03	11 06	11 57	12 00		12 24	12 31
Chesterfield	d				09 07			09 17		09 29	10 09	10 23		10 29	10 41	11 09	11 20	11 25	12 09	12 18		12 37	12 49
Derby	a				09 28					09 49	10 32			10 50		11 28		11 47	12 28			12 57	
	d	06 50		07 52			08 47			09 51				10 52				11 48				13 02	
Long Eaton	d						08 58			10 01				11 02								13 12	
Alfreton	d							09 28				10 33					11 30			12 28			12 59
Langley Mill	d							09 35				10 41					11 38			12 36			13 07
Lincoln	d																						
Nottingham	a							09 53				10 59			11 11		11 54			12 53			13 25
	d		07 28			08 19			09 15				10 15		11 18						12 15		
Beeston	d					08 25							10 22								12 22		
East Midlands Parkway	d	07 02	07 38	08 03		08 32	09 02		09 26	10 05			10 30	11 06	11 30			12 01			12 30	13 16	
Loughborough	d			08 11		08 39	09 10		09 34	10 13			10 38	11 14	11 38			12 09			12 38	13 24	
Barrow Upon Soar	d																						
Sileby	d																						
Syston	d																						
Leicester	a	07 18	07 52	08 22		08 50	09 21		09 47	10 23			10 51	11 24	11 51			12 21			12 52	13 34	
	d	07 20	07 54	08 23		08 52	09 22		09 49	10 25			10 53	11 26	11 53			12 23			12 53	13 36	
Market Harborough	d	07 38	08 11	08 40		09 09	09 39		10 07	10 39			11 08	11 40	12 08			12 38			13 08	13 50	
Corby	d																						
Kettering	a	07 48	08 20	08 49		09 18	09 48		10 17	10 48			11 18	11 49	12 18			12 48			13 18	13 59	
	d	07 49	08 21	08 50		09 19	09 51		10 18	10 51			11 19	11 50	12 19			12 49			13 19	14 00	
Wellingborough	d	08 01	08 32	09 02		09 30	10 04		10 26	10 59			11 27	11 58	12 27			12 57			13 27	14 07	
Bedford	d	08 15	08 45	09 14		09 45	10 16		10 45	11 16			11 45	12 15	12 46			13 15			13 46	14 25	
Luton	d	08 34		09 39			10 41			11 39				12 40				13 39				14 49	
Luton Airport Parkway	d		09 11			10 10			11 10				12 09		13 10						14 10		
St Pancras International	a	09 16	09 50	10 20		10 49	11 20		11 49	12 20			12 50	13 20	13 50			14 19			14 44	15 22	

A from 12 September until 17 October

For connections to Gatwick Airport see Table 52

Table 53

Sundays
from 12 September

Sheffield - East Midlands - London

		EM	XC	EM	EM	NT	EM	XC	EM	EM	XC	XC	EM	EM	EM	EM	NT	XC	EM	EM
		◇	◇■	◇■	◇■		◇	◇■	◇■	◇■	◇■	◇■	◇	◇■	◇■	◇■		◇■	◇■	◇
York	d		11 28					12 28				13 28						14 22		
Leeds	d		12 00			12 29		13 00				14 00				14 05	14 05			
Wakefield Westgate	d		12 12					13 12				14 12				14 18				
Wakefield Kirkgate	d					12 46											14 21			
Doncaster	d		12 30					13 30										14 50		
Sheffield	d	12 49	12 57		13 20	13 31	13 49	13 57		14 07	14 20	14 50	14 53			15 02	15 07	15 20	15 32	15 43
Chesterfield	d	13 03	13 09		13 33	13 48	14 03	14 09		14 20	14 32	15 02	15 07			15 15	15 24		15 44	15 57
Derby	a		13 31		13 52			14 28		14 42	14 51	15 22				15 38		15 49	16 09	
	d				13 54					14 49						15 38			16 14	
Long Eaton	d				14 05					15 03										
Alfreton	d	13 14				13 59	14 14						15 19				15 34			16 08
Langley Mill	d					14 06							15 26				15 42			16 15
Lincoln	d																			
Nottingham	a	13 39				14 22	14 38						15 44				16 00			16 33
	d			13 14					14 30					15 10	15 36					
Beeston	d			13 21					14 36					15 16						
East Midlands Parkway	d			13 30	14 09				14 43	15 08				15 23	15 46	15 52			16 25	
Loughborough	d			13 38	14 17				14 51	15 15				15 30		16 01				
Barrow Upon Soar	d																			
Sileby	d																			
Syston	d																			
Leicester	a			13 51	14 27				15 02	15 26				15 42	16 02	16 13			16 40	
	d			13 53	14 29				15 04	15 27				15 44	16 03	16 15			16 41	
Market Harborough	d			14 08	14 43				15 18					15 59		16 30				
Corby	d																			
Kettering	a			14 18	14 52				15 27					16 08		16 40				
	d			14 19	14 53				15 28					16 09		16 41				
Wellingborough	d			14 29	15 00				15 35					16 16		16 49				
Bedford	d			14 54	15 25				15 55					16 33		17 07				
Luton	d				15 42					16 25						17 25				
Luton Airport Parkway	d			15 11					16 14					16 53						
St Pancras International	a			15 45	16 15				16 45	16 55				17 27	17 31	17 59			18 04	

		XC	NT	XC	EM	EM	EM	EM	EM	EM	XC	NT	XC	EM	EM	EM	EM	EM	XC	NT	XC
		◇■		◇■	◇■	◇■	◇■	◇■	◇	◇	◇■		◇■	◇■	◇■	◇■	◇■	◇	◇■		◇■
									A	B											
York	d	14 28		15 20							15 28		16 20						16 28		17 21
Leeds	d	15 00	15 05								16 00	16 05							17 00	17 05	
Wakefield Westgate	d	15 12									16 12								17 12		
Wakefield Kirkgate	d		15 22									16 22								17 21	
Doncaster	d			15 50									16 50								17 50
Sheffield	d	15 50	16 07	16 20				16 29	16 40	16 40	16 50	17 07	17 20				17 29	17 39	17 50	18 07	18 20
Chesterfield	d	16 02	16 23					16 43	16 56	16 56	17 02	17 23					17 43	17 54	18 02	18 25	
Derby	a	16 22		16 49				17 04			17 22		17 49				18 04		18 22		18 49
	d						16 47	17 09								17 47	18 07				
Long Eaton	d						16 57									17 57					
Alfreton	d		16 33						17 07	17 08		17 33						18 04		18 36	
Langley Mill	d		16 41						17 14	17 16		17 41						18 12		18 43	
Lincoln	d																				
Nottingham	a		16 59						17 32	17 32		17 59						18 29		19 00	
	d				16 18	16 45								17 20	17 39						
Beeston	d				16 24									17 26							
East Midlands Parkway	d				16 31	16 55	17 01	17 21						17 32	17 50	18 01	18 20				
Loughborough	d				16 39		17 09							17 40		18 09					
Barrow Upon Soar	d																				
Sileby	d																				
Syston	d																				
Leicester	a				16 50	17 12	17 20	17 38						17 50	18 07	18 19	18 39				
	d				16 52	17 13	17 22	17 40						17 52	18 09	18 21	18 40				
Market Harborough	d				17 06		17 36							18 06		18 35					
Corby	d																				
Kettering	a				17 15		17 45							18 15		18 44					
	d				17 16		17 46							18 16		18 45					
Wellingborough	d				17 23		17 53							18 23		18 52					
Bedford	d				17 40		18 11							18 40		19 10					
Luton	d						18 29									19 29					
Luton Airport Parkway	d				17 59									18 59							
St Pancras International	a				18 29	18 34	18 59	19 04						19 29	19 34	19 59	20 04				

A from 24 October
B from 12 September until 17 October

For connections to Gatwick Airport see Table 52

Table 53

Sheffield - East Midlands - London

Sundays
from 12 September

		EM	EM	EM	EM	XC	NT	XC	EM	EM	EM	XC	NT	XC	EM	EM	XC	XC	EM	EM	XC	EM	EM
		◇■	◇■	◇■	◇	◇■		◇■	◇■	◇■	◇	◇■		◇■	◇■	◇	◇■	◇■	◇■	◇	◇■	◇■	◇
York	d			17 40		17 28		18 20				18 28		19 20			19 28	20 20			20 28		
Leeds	d					18 00	18 05					19 00	19 04				20 00				21 00		
Wakefield Westgate	d					18 12						19 12					20 12				21 12		
Wakefield Kirkgate	d						18 22						19 21										
Doncaster	d			18 06	18 41			18 50						19 50				20 50					
Sheffield	d			18 32	18 56	18 50	19 07	19 20		19 31	19 40	19 50	20 06	20 20	20 24	20 40	20 50	21 20		21 40	21 50	22 13	23 29
Chesterfield	d			18 44		19 02	19 25			19 44	19 55	20 02	20 23		20 38	20 55	21 02	21 32		21 54	22 02	22 27	23 43
Derby	a			19 08		19 22		19 49		20 04		20 21		20 49	20 57		21 22	21 51			22 22	23 04	
	d			19 09						20 06					20 59								
Long Eaton	d			19 20	19 06					20 16													
Alfreton	d				19 14		19 36				20 06		20 34			21 06				22 05			23 54
Langley Mill	d						19 43				20 14		20 41			21 13				22 12			00 02
Lincoln	d				19 36																		
Nottingham	a						19 59				20 31		20 57			21 36				22 35			00 30
	d	18 10	18 44						19 46										21 13				
Beeston	d	18 19							19 52														
East Midlands Parkway	d	18 25	18 54	19 25					19 53	20 21					21 11				21 23				
Loughborough	d	18 33	19 02	19 32					20 06	20 30									21 31				
Barrow Upon Soar	d																						
Sileby	d																						
Syston	d																						
Leicester	a	18 43	19 13	19 44					20 16	20 42					21 28				21 41				
	d	18 45	19 15	19 45					20 18	20 44					21 30				21 43				
Market Harborough	d	19 05	19 31	20 03					20 32	20 59					21 45				21 57				
Corby	d																						
Kettering	a	19 14	19 40	20 12					20 41	21 09					21 55				22 06				
	d	19 15	19 41	20 13					20 42	21 10					21 56				22 07				
Wellingborough	d	19 22	19 48	20 21					20 49	21 18					22 04				22 14				
Bedford	d	19 40	20 07	20 40					21 08	21 37					22 24				22 32				
Luton	d		20 26						21 23	21 52					22 40				22 50				
Luton Airport Parkway	d	19 59		20 55																			
St Pancras International	a	20 29	20 57	21 27					21 57	22 27					23 13				23 27				

Table 55

Nottingham - Mansfield - Worksop

Mondays to Fridays
until 24 September

		EM	EM	EM	EM	EM	EM	EM	EM	EM	EM	EM	EM	EM	EM	EM	EM	EM	EM	EM	EM	EM	EM
Nottingham	d	05 40	06 05	07 00	08 25	08 53	09 25	09 55	10 25	10 55	11 25	11 55	12 25	12 55	13 25	13 55	14 25	14 55	15 25	15 55	16 25	16 55	17 25
Bulwell	d	05 49	06 14	07 10	08 36	09 02		10 06		11 06		12 06		13 06		14 06		15 06		16 06		17 06	17 39
Hucknall	d	05 54	06 19	07 15	08 41	09 07	09 39	10 11	10 39	11 11	11 39	12 11	12 39	13 11	13 39	14 11	14 39	15 11	15 39	16 11	16 39	17 12	17 44
Newstead	d	05 59	06 24	07 21	08 46	09 12	09 44		10 44		11 44		12 44		13 44		14 44		15 44		16 44	17 17	17 49
Kirkby In Ashfield	d	06 05	06 30	07 31	08 52	09 18	09 49	10 19	10 49	11 19	11 49	12 19	12 49	13 19	13 49	14 19	14 49	15 19	15 49	16 19	16 49	17 23	17 55
Sutton Parkway	d	06 08	06 33	07 34	08 55	09 21	09 52	10 22	10 52	11 22	11 52	12 22	12 52	13 22	13 52	14 22	14 52	15 22	15 52	16 22	16 52	17 27	17 58
Mansfield	d	06 13	06 38	07 40	09 00	09 26	09 57	10 27	10 57	11 27	11 57	12 27	12 57	13 27	13 57	14 27	14 57	15 27	15 57	16 27	16 57	17 32	18 03
Mansfield Woodhouse	d	06 18	06 47	07 45	09 04	09a33	10 02	10a34	11 02	11a34	12 02	12a34	13 02	13a34	14 02	14a34	15 02	15a34	16 02	16a34	17 02	17a39	18 08
Shirebrook	d	06 24	06 54	07 51	09 11		10 08		11 08		12 08		13 08		14 08		15 08		16 08		17 08		18 14
Langwith - Whaley Thorns	d	06 28	06 58	07 55	09 15		10 12		11 12		12 12		13 12		14 12		15 12		16 12		17 12		18 18
Creswell (Derbys)	d	06 32	07 02	07 59	09 19		10 16		11 16		12 16		13 16		14 16		15 16		16 16		17 16		18 22
Whitwell	d	06 36	07 05	08 03	09 22		10 20		11 20		12 20		13 20		14 20		15 20		16 20		17 20		18 26
Worksop	a	06 48	07 20	08 18	09 35		10 34		11 34		12 34		13 34		14 34		15 34		16 34		17 34		18 37

		EM	EM	EM	EM	EM
Nottingham	d	17 55	18 55	19 55	20 55	22 05
Bulwell	d	18 11	19 05	20 05	21 05	22 19
Hucknall	d	18 16	19 10	20 16	21 16	22 24
Newstead	d	18 21	19 15	20 21	21 21	22 29
Kirkby In Ashfield	d	18 27	19 21	20 27	21 27	22 34
Sutton Parkway	d	18 30	19 24	20 30	21 30	22 37
Mansfield	d	18 35	19 29	20 35	21 35	22 42
Mansfield Woodhouse	d	18 39	19 33	20 39	21 40	22 47
Shirebrook	d	18 46	19 40	20 46	21 46	22 53
Langwith - Whaley Thorns	d	18 50	19 44	20 50	21 50	22 57
Creswell (Derbys)	d	18 54	19 48	20 54	21 54	23 01
Whitwell	d	18 57	19 51	20 57	21 58	23 05
Worksop	a	19 07	20 04	21 09	22 06	23 16

Mondays to Fridays
from 27 September

		EM	EM	EM	EM	EM	EM	EM	EM	EM	EM	EM	EM	EM	EM	EM	EM	EM	EM	EM	EM	EM	EM
Nottingham	d	05 40	06 05	07 00	08 25	08 53	09 25	09 55	10 25	10 55	11 25	11 55	12 25	12 55	13 25	13 55	14 25	14 55	15 25	15 55	16 25	16 55	17 25
Bulwell	d		06 14	07 10																		17 05	17 39
Hucknall	d	05 52	06 19	07 15	08 39	09 06	09 39	10 09	10 39	11 09	11 39	12 09	12 39	13 09	13 39	14 09	14 39	15 09	15 39	16 09	16 39	17 11	17 44
Newstead	d		06 24	07 21	08 44	09 11														16 14		17 16	17 49
Kirkby In Ashfield	d		06 30	07 31	08 52	09 18	09 49	10 19	10 49	11 19	11 49	12 19	12 49	13 19	13 49	14 19	14 49	15 19	15 49	16 20	16 49	17 22	17 55
Sutton Parkway	d	06 05	06 33	07 34	08 55	09 22	09 52		10 52		11 52		12 52		13 52		14 52		15 52		16 52	17 26	17 58
Mansfield	d	06 11	06 38	07 40	09 00	09 27	09 57	10 26	10 57	11 26	11 57	12 26	12 57	13 26	13 57	14 26	14 57	15 26	15 57	16 27	16 57	17 31	18 03
Mansfield Woodhouse	d	06 16	06 47	07 45	09 04	09a34	10 02	10a34	11 02	11a34	12 02	12a34	13 02	13a34	14 02	14a34	15 02	15a34	16 02	16a35	17 02	17a39	18 08
Shirebrook	d	06 23	06 54	07 51	09 11		10 08		11 08		12 08		13 08		14 08		15 08		16 08		17 08		18 14
Langwith - Whaley Thorns	d	06 27	06 58	07 55	09 15		10 12		11 12		12 12		13 12		14 12		15 12		16 12		17 12		18 18
Creswell (Derbys)	d	06 31	07 02	07 59	09 19		10 16		11 16		12 16		13 16		14 16		15 16		16 16		17 16		18 22
Whitwell	d	06 34	07 05	08 03	09 22		10 20		11 20		12 20		13 20		14 20		15 20		16 20		17 20		18 26
Worksop	a	06 48	07 20	08 18	09 35		10 36		11 36		12 36		13 36		14 36		15 36		16 36		17 36		18 39

		EM	EM	EM	EM	EM
Nottingham	d	17 55	18 55	19 55	20 55	22 05
Bulwell	d	18 06	19 05	20 05	21 05	22 19
Hucknall	d	18 16	19 10	20 16	21 16	22 24
Newstead	d	18 21	19 15	20 21	21 21	22 29
Kirkby In Ashfield	d	18 27	19 23	20 29	21 27	22 35
Sutton Parkway	d	18 30	19 26	20 32	21 30	22 38
Mansfield	d	18 35	19 31	20 37	21 35	22 43
Mansfield Woodhouse	d	18 39	19 36	20 42	21 40	22 48
Shirebrook	d	18 46	19 43	20 49	21 46	22 54
Langwith - Whaley Thorns	d	18 50	19 47	20 53	21 50	22 58
Creswell (Derbys)	d	18 54	19 51	20 57	21 54	23 02
Whitwell	d	18 57	19 54	21 00	21 58	23 06
Worksop	a	19 09	20 07	21 12	22 06	23 17

Saturdays
until 25 September

		EM	EM	EM	EM	EM	EM	EM	EM	EM	EM	EM	EM	EM	EM	EM	EM	EM	EM	EM	EM	EM	EM
Nottingham	d	05 40	06 05	06 59	08 25	08 53	09 25	09 55	10 25	10 55	11 25	11 55	12 25	12 55	13 25	13 55	14 25	14 55	15 25	15 55	16 25	16 55	17 25
Bulwell	d	05 49	06 14	07 09	08 36	09 02		10 06		11 06		12 06		13 06		14 06		15 06		16 06		17 06	17 39
Hucknall	d	05 54	06 19	07 14	08 41	09 07	09 39	10 11	10 39	11 11	11 39	12 11	12 39	13 11	13 39	14 11	14 39	15 11	15 39	16 11	16 39	17 12	17 44
Newstead	d	05 59	06 24	07 20	08 46	09 12	09 44		10 44		11 44		12 44		13 44		14 44		15 44		16 44	17 17	17 49
Kirkby In Ashfield	d	06 05	06 30	07b31	08 52	09 18	09 49	10 19	10 49	11 19	11 49	12 19	12 49	13 19	13 49	14 19	14 49	15 19	15 49	16 19	16 49	17 23	17 55
Sutton Parkway	d	06 08	06 33	07 34	08 55	09 21	09 52	10 22	10 52	11 22	11 52	12 22	12 52	13 22	13 52	14 22	14 52	15 22	15 52	16 22	16 52	17 27	17 58
Mansfield	d	06 13	06 38	07 40	09 00	09 26	09 57	10 27	10 57	11 27	11 57	12 27	12 57	13 27	13 57	14 27	14 57	15 27	15 57	16 27	16 57	17 32	18 03
Mansfield Woodhouse	d	06 18	06 47	07 45	09 04	09a33	10 02	10a34	11 02	11a34	12 02	12a34	13 02	13a34	14 02	14a34	15 02	15a34	16 02	16a34	17 02	17a39	18 08
Shirebrook	d	06 24	06 54	07 51	09 11		10 08		11 08		12 08		13 08		14 08		15 08		16 08		17 08		18 14
Langwith - Whaley Thorns	d	06 28	06 58	07 55	09 15		10 12		11 12		12 12		13 12		14 12		15 12		16 12		17 12		18 18
Creswell (Derbys)	d	06 32	07 02	07 59	09 19		10 16		11 16		12 16		13 16		14 16		15 16		16 16		17 16		18 22
Whitwell	d	06 36	07 05	08 03	09 22		10 20		11 20		12 20		13 20		14 20		15 20		16 20		17 20		18 26
Worksop	a	06 48	07 20	08 12	09 34		10 34		11 34		12 34		13 34		14 34		15 34		16 34		17 34		18 37

b arr. 0725

Table 55

Nottingham - Mansfield - Worksop

Saturdays
until 25 September

		EM	EM	EM	EM	EM	EM
Nottingham ⑧	d	17 55	18 55	19 55	20 55	22 05	23 05
Bulwell	d	18 11	19 05	20 05	21 05	22 19	23 18
Hucknall	d	18 16	19 10	20 16	21 16	22 24	23 23
Newstead	d	18 21	19 15	20 21	21 21	22 29	23 28
Kirkby In Ashfield	d	18 27	19 21	20 27	21 27	22 34	23 33
Sutton Parkway	d	18 30	19 24	20 30	21 30	22 37	23 36
Mansfield	d	18 35	19 29	20 35	21 35	22 42	23 41
Mansfield Woodhouse	d	18 39	19 33	20 39	21 40	22 47	23a46
Shirebrook	d	18 46	19 40	20 46	21 46	22 53	
Langwith - Whaley Thorns	d	18 50	19 44	20 50	21 50	22 57	
Creswell (Derbys)	d	18 54	19 48	20 54	21 54	23 01	
Whitwell	d	18 57	19 51	20 57	21 58	23 05	
Worksop	a	19 07	20 04	21 09	22 06	23 16	

Saturdays
from 02 October

		EM	EM	EM	EM	EM	EM	EM	EM	EM	EM	EM
Nottingham ⑧	d	05 40	06 05	06 59	08 25	08 50	09 25	09 55	10 25	10 55	11 25	11 55
Bulwell	d		06 14	07 09		08 59						
Hucknall	d	05 52	06 19	07 14	08 38	09 05	09 39	10 09	10 39	11 09	11 39	12 09
Newstead	d	05 57	06 24	07 20		09 10						
Kirkby In Ashfield	d	06 05	06 30	07b31	08 48	09 18	09 49	10 19	10 49	11 19	11 49	12 19
Sutton Parkway	d	06 08	06 33	07 34	08 51	09 22	09 52		10 52		11 52	
Mansfield	d	06 13	06 38	07 40	08 57	09 27	09 57	10 26	10 57	11 26	11 57	12 26
Mansfield Woodhouse	d	06 19	06 47	07 45	09 02	09a34	10 02	10a34	11 02	11a34	12 02	12a34
Shirebrook	d	06 25	06 54	07 51	09 09		10 08		11 08		12 08	
Langwith - Whaley Thorns	d	06 29	06 58	07 55	09 13		10 12		11 12		12 12	
Creswell (Derbys)	d	06 33	07 02	07 59	09 17		10 16		11 16		12 16	
Whitwell	d	06 37	07 05	08 03	09 20		10 20		11 20		12 20	
Worksop	a	06 50	07 20	08 12	09 33		10 36		11 36		12 36	

		EM	EM	EM	EM	EM	EM	EM	EM	EM	EM	EM
Nottingham ⑧	d	12 25	12 55	13 25	13 55	14 25	14 55	15 25	15 55	16 25	16 55	17 25
Bulwell	d										17 05	17 39
Hucknall	d	12 39	13 09	13 39	14 09	14 39	15 09	15 39	16 09	16 39	17 11	17 44
Newstead	d								16 14		17 16	17 49
Kirkby In Ashfield	d	12 49	13 19	13 49	14 19	14 49	15 19	15 49	16 20	16 49	17 22	17 55
Sutton Parkway	d	12 52		13 52		14 52		15 52		16 52	17 26	17 58
Mansfield	d	12 57	13 26	13 57	14 26	14 57	15 26	15 57	16 27	16 57	17 31	18 03
Mansfield Woodhouse	d	13 02	13a34	14 02	14a34	15 02	15a34	16 02	16a35	17 02	17a39	18 08
Shirebrook	d	13 08		14 08		15 08		16 08		17 08		18 14
Langwith - Whaley Thorns	d	13 12		14 12		15 12		16 12		17 12		18 18
Creswell (Derbys)	d	13 16		14 16		15 16		16 16		17 16		18 22
Whitwell	d	13 20		14 20		15 20		16 20		17 20		18 26
Worksop	a	13 36		14 36		15 36		16 36		17 36		18 39

		EM	EM	EM	EM	EM	EM
Nottingham ⑧	d	17 55	18 55	19 55	20 55	22 05	23 05
Bulwell	d	18 06	19 05	20 05	21 05	22 19	23 18
Hucknall	d	18 16	19 10	20 16	21 16	22 24	23 23
Newstead	d	18 21	19 15	20 21	21 21	22 29	23 28
Kirkby In Ashfield	d	18 27	19 23	20 29	21 27	22 35	23 33
Sutton Parkway	d	18 30	19 26	20 32	21 30	22 38	23 36
Mansfield	d	18 35	19 31	20 37	21 35	22 43	23 41
Mansfield Woodhouse	d	18 39	19 36	20 42	21 40	22 48	23a46
Shirebrook	d	18 46	19 43	20 49	21 46	22 54	
Langwith - Whaley Thorns	d	18 50	19 47	20 53	21 50	22 58	
Creswell (Derbys)	d	18 54	19 51	20 57	21 54	23 02	
Whitwell	d	18 57	19 54	21 00	21 58	23 06	
Worksop	a	19 09	20 07	21 12	22 06	23 17	

Sundays

		EM	EM	EM	EM	EM	EM	EM	EM	EM	EM A	EM B
Nottingham ⑧	d	07 53	08 25	09 25	11 25	13 25	14 25	16 25	17 25	19 25	20 26	20 25
Bulwell	d	08 03	08 34	09 34		13 34	14 35		17 36			
Hucknall	d	08 08	08 39	09 39	11 38	13 39	14 40	16 39	17 41	19 39	20 39	20 39
Newstead	d	08 13	08 44	09 44	11 43	13 44	14 45	16 44	17 46	19 44	20 44	20 44
Kirkby In Ashfield	d	08 18	08 50	09 50	11 48	13 50	14 51	16 49	17 51	19 50	20 49	20 49
Sutton Parkway	d	08 21	08 53	09 53	11 51	13 53	14 54	16 52	17 54	19 53	20 52	20 52
Mansfield	d	08 26	08 58	09 58	11 56	13 58	14 59	16 57	17 59	19 58	20 57	20 57
Mansfield Woodhouse	d	08a33	09 02	10 02	12a03	14a04	15 02	17a04	18 04	20a04	21a04	21a04
Shirebrook	d		09 09	10 09			15 09		18 10			
Langwith - Whaley Thorns	d		09 13	10 13			15 13		18 14			
Creswell (Derbys)	d		09 17	10 17			15 17		18 18			
Whitwell	d		09 20	10 20			15 20		18 22			
Worksop	a		09 32	10 30			15 32		18 36			

A until 5 September
B from 12 September
b arr. 0725

Table 55

Worksop - Mansfield - Nottingham

Mondays to Fridays
until 24 September

		EM	EM ◇	EM	EM	EM	EM	EM	EM	EM	EM	EM
Worksop	d	05 50		06 56		07 38	08 38		09 38		10 38	
Whitwell	d	05 59		07 05		07 47	08 47		09 47		10 47	
Creswell (Derbys)	d	06 02		07 08		07 50	08 50		09 50		10 50	
Langwith - Whaley Thorns	d	06 06		07 13		07 55	08 55		09 55		10 55	
Shirebrook	d	06 10		07 16		07 58	08 58		09 58		10 58	
Mansfield Woodhouse	d	06 17	07 07	07 25	07 39	08 06	09 06	09 37	10 07	10 37	11 07	11 37
Mansfield	d	06 22	07 11	07 29	07 43	08 10	09 10	09 40	10 10	10 40	11 10	11 40
Sutton Parkway	d	06 27	07 16	07 35	07 48	08 15	09 15	09 46	10 16	10 46	11 16	11 46
Kirkby In Ashfield	d	06 30	07 19	07 38	07 52	08 18	09 18	09 49	10 19	10 49	11 19	11 49
Newstead	d	06 35	07 26	07 43	07 57	08 23	09 23	09 54		10 54		11 54
Hucknall	d	06 39	07 31	07 48	08 02	08 28	09 27	09 58	10 26	10 58	11 26	11 58
Bulwell	d	06 43	07 35	07 53	08 06	08 32	09 31		10 30		11 30	
Nottingham ⑧	a	06 58	07 48	08 04	08 18	08 44	09 44	10 14	10 44	11 14	11 44	12 14

		EM	EM	EM	EM	EM	EM	EM	EM	EM	EM	EM
Worksop	d	11 38		12 38		13 38		14 38		15 38		16 42
Whitwell	d	11 47		12 47		13 47		14 47		15 47		16 51
Creswell (Derbys)	d	11 50		12 50		13 50		14 50		15 50		16 54
Langwith - Whaley Thorns	d	11 55		12 55		13 55		14 55		15 55		16 59
Shirebrook	d	11 58		12 58		13 58		14 58		15 58		17 02
Mansfield Woodhouse	d	12 07	12 37	13 07	13 37	14 07	14 37	15 07	15 37	16 07	16 37	17 10
Mansfield	d	12 10	12 40	13 10	13 40	14 10	14 40	15 10	15 40	16 10	16 40	17 14
Sutton Parkway	d	12 16	12 46	13 16	13 46	14 16	14 46	15 16	15 46	16 16	16 46	17 19
Kirkby In Ashfield	d	12 19	12 49	13 19	13 49	14 19	14 49	15 19	15 49	16 19	16 49	17 22
Newstead	d		12 54		13 54		14 54		15 54		16 54	
Hucknall	d	12 26	12 58	13 26	13 58	14 26	14 58	15 26	15 58	16 26	16 58	17 30
Bulwell	d	12 30		13 30		14 30		15 30		16 30		17 34
Nottingham ⑧	a	12 44	13 19	13 44	14 14	14 44	15 14	15 44	16 14	16 44	17 14	17 48

		EM	EM	EM	EM	EM	EM	EM
Worksop	d		17 45	18 41	19 21	20 15	21 20	22 20
Whitwell	d		17 54	18 50	19 30	20 24	21 29	22 29
Creswell (Derbys)	d		17 57	18 53	19 33	20 27	21 32	22 32
Langwith - Whaley Thorns	d		18 01	18 58	19 37	20 31	21 37	22 37
Shirebrook	d		18 07	19 01	19 41	20 35	21 40	22 40
Mansfield Woodhouse	d	17 43	18 14	19 09	19 48	20 43	21 48	22 48
Mansfield	d	17 46	18 18	19 13	19 52	20 50	21 53	22 52
Sutton Parkway	d	17 52	18 24	19 18	19 57	20 55	21 58	22 57
Kirkby In Ashfield	d	17 55	18 27	19 21	20 00	20 58	22 01	23 00
Newstead	d	17 59	18 31	19 26	20 05	21 03	22 06	23 05
Hucknall	d	18 04	18 36	19 30	20 09	21 07	22 10	23 09
Bulwell	d		18 40	19 34	20 14	21 14	22 14	23 13
Nottingham ⑧	a	18 20	18 51	19 47	20 36	21 26	22 28	23 26

Mondays to Fridays
from 27 September

		EM	EM ◇	EM	EM	EM	EM	EM	EM	EM	EM	EM
Worksop	d	05 47		06 56		07 33	08 34		09 38		10 38	
Whitwell	d	05 56		07 05		07 42	08 43		09 47		10 47	
Creswell (Derbys)	d	05 59		07 08		07 45	08 46		09 50		10 50	
Langwith - Whaley Thorns	d	06 03		07 13		07 50	08 51		09 55		10 55	
Shirebrook	d	06 07		07 16		07 53	08 54		09 58		10 58	
Mansfield Woodhouse	d	06 15	07 07	07 25	07 36	08 01	09 03	09 37	10 06	10 37	11 06	11 37
Mansfield	d	06 20	07 11	07 29	07 40	08 05	09 07	09 41	10 10	10 41	11 10	11 41
Sutton Parkway	d	06 25	07 16	07 35	07 45	08 11	09 12		10 15		11 15	
Kirkby In Ashfield	d	06 28	07 19	07 38	07 49	08 14	09 15	09 48	10 18	10 48	11 18	11 48
Newstead	d	06 34	07 26	07 43	07 55	08 20	09 21	09 54				
Hucknall	d	06 39	07 31	07 48	08 00	08 25	09 26	09 58	10 27	10 56	11 27	11 56
Bulwell	d	06 43	07 35	07 53	08 05	08 29	09 30					
Nottingham ⑧	a	06 58	07 48	08 04	08 18	08 44	09 44	10 15	10 44	11 14	11 44	12 14

		EM	EM	EM	EM	EM	EM	EM	EM	EM	EM	EM
Worksop	d	11 38		12 38		13 38		14 38		15 38		16 42
Whitwell	d	11 47		12 47		13 47		14 47		15 47		16 51
Creswell (Derbys)	d	11 50		12 50		13 50		14 50		15 50		16 54
Langwith - Whaley Thorns	d	11 55		12 55		13 55		14 55		15 55		16 59
Shirebrook	d	11 58		12 58		13 58		14 58		15 58		17 02
Mansfield Woodhouse	d	12 06	12 37	13 06	13 37	14 06	14 37	15 06	15 37	16 06	16 40	17 10
Mansfield	d	12 10	12 41	13 10	13 41	14 10	14 41	15 10	15 41	16 10	16 44	17 14
Sutton Parkway	d	12 15		13 15		14 15		15 15		16 15		17 19
Kirkby In Ashfield	d	12 18	12 48	13 18	13 48	14 18	14 48	15 18	15 48	16 18		17 22
Newstead	d											
Hucknall	d	12 27	12 56	13 27	13 56	14 27	14 56	15 27	15 56	16 27		17 30
Bulwell	d											17 34
Nottingham ⑧	a	12 44	13 19	13 44	14 14	14 44	15 14	15 44	16 14	16 44	17 14	17 48

		EM	EM	EM	EM	EM	EM	EM
Worksop	d		17 45	18 41	19 21	20 15	21 20	22 20
Whitwell	d		17 54	18 50	19 30	20 24	21 29	22 29
Creswell (Derbys)	d		17 57	18 53	19 33	20 27	21 32	22 32
Langwith - Whaley Thorns	d		18 01	18 58	19 37	20 31	21 37	22 37
Shirebrook	d		18 07	19 01	19 41	20 35	21 40	22 40
Mansfield Woodhouse	d	17 43	18 14	19 09	19 48	20 43	21 48	22 48
Mansfield	d	17 46	18 18	19 13	19 52	20 47	21 53	22 52
Sutton Parkway	d	17 52	18 24	19 18	19 57	20 52	21 58	22 57
Kirkby In Ashfield	d	17 55	18 27	19 21	20 00	20 55	22 01	23 00
Newstead	d	18 01	18 31	19 26	20 05	21 02	22 06	23 05
Hucknall	d	18 05	18 36	19 30	20 09	21 06	22 10	23 09
Bulwell	d		18 40	19 34	20 14	21 12	22 14	23 13
Nottingham ⑧	a	18 26	18 51	19 47	20 36	21 25	22 28	23 26

Saturdays
until 25 September

		EM	EM	EM	EM	EM	EM	EM	EM	EM	EM	EM
Worksop	d	05 50	06 56	07 38	08 38		09 38		10 38		11 38	
Whitwell	d	05 59	07 05	07 47	08 47		09 47		10 47		11 47	
Creswell (Derbys)	d	06 02	07 08	07 50	08 50		09 50		10 50		11 50	
Langwith - Whaley Thorns	d	06 06	07 13	07 55	08 55		09 55		10 55		11 55	
Shirebrook	d	06 10	07 16	07 58	08 58		09 58		10 58		11 58	
Mansfield Woodhouse	d	06 17	07 25	08 06	09 06	09 37	10 07	10 37	11 07	11 37	12 07	12 37
Mansfield	d	06 22	07 29	08 10	09 10	09 40	10 10	10 40	11 10	11 40	12 10	12 40
Sutton Parkway	d	06 27	07 35	08 15	09 15	09 46	10 16	10 46	11 16	11 46	12 16	12 46
Kirkby In Ashfield	d	06 30	07 38	08 18	09 18	09 49	10 19	10 49	11 19	11 49	12 19	12 49
Newstead	d	06 35	07 43	08 23	09 23	09 54		10 54		11 54		12 54
Hucknall	d	06 39	07 48	08 28	09 27	09 58	10 26	10 58	11 26	11 58	12 26	12 58
Bulwell	d	06 43	07 53	08 32	09 31		10 30		11 30		12 30	
Nottingham ⑧	a	06 58	08 05	08 44	09 44	10 15	10 44	11 14	11 44	12 14	12 44	13 15

		EM	EM	EM	EM	EM	EM	EM	EM	EM	EM	EM
Worksop	d	12 38		13 38		14 38		15 38		16 42		17 45
Whitwell	d	12 47		13 47		14 47		15 47		16 51		17 54
Creswell (Derbys)	d	12 50		13 50		14 50		15 50		16 54		17 57
Langwith - Whaley Thorns	d	12 55		13 55		14 55		15 55		16 59		18 01
Shirebrook	d	12 58		13 58		14 58		15 58		17 02		18 07
Mansfield Woodhouse	d	13 07	13 37	14 07	14 37	15 07	15 37	16 07	16 37	17 10	17 43	18 14
Mansfield	d	13 10	13 40	14 10	14 40	15 10	15 40	16 10	16 40	17 14	17 46	18 18
Sutton Parkway	d	13 16	13 46	14 16	14 46	15 16	15 46	16 16	16 46	17 19	17 52	18 24
Kirkby In Ashfield	d	13 19	13 49	14 19	14 49	15 19	15 49	16 19	16 49	17 22	17 55	18 27
Newstead	d		13 54		14 54		15 54		16 54		17 59	18 31
Hucknall	d	13 26	13 58	14 26	14 58	15 26	15 58	16 26	16 58	17 30	18 04	18 36
Bulwell	d	13 30		14 30		15 30		16 30		17 34		18 40
Nottingham ⑧	a	13 44	14 14	14 44	15 14	15 44	16 15	16 44	17 14	17 48	18 20	18 51

Table 55

Worksop - Mansfield - Nottingham

Saturdays
until 25 September

		EM	EM	EM	EM	EM
Worksop	d	18 41	19 21	20 15	21 19	22 20
Whitwell	d	18 50	19 30	20 24	21 28	22 29
Creswell (Derbys)	d	18 53	19 33	20 27	21 31	22 32
Langwith - Whaley Thorns	d	18 58	19 37	20 31	21 36	22 37
Shirebrook	d	19 01	19 41	20 35	21 39	22 40
Mansfield Woodhouse	d	19 09	19 48	20 43	21 47	22 48
Mansfield	d	19 13	19 52	20 50	21 52	22 52
Sutton Parkway	d	19 18	19 57	20 55	21 57	22 57
Kirkby In Ashfield	d	19 21	20 00	20 58	22 00	23 00
Newstead	d	19 26	20 05	21 03	22 05	23 05
Hucknall	d	19 30	20 09	21 07	22 09	23 09
Bulwell	d	19 34	20 14	21 14	22 13	23 13
Nottingham 8	a	19 47	20 32	21 26	22 25	23 26

Saturdays
from 02 October

		EM	EM	EM	EM	EM	EM	EM	EM	EM	EM	EM	EM	EM	EM	EM	EM	EM	EM	EM	EM	EM	EM
Worksop	d	05 47	06 56	07 33	08 38		09 38		10 38		11 38		12 38		13 38		14 38		15 38		16 42		17 45
Whitwell	d	05 56	07 05	07 42	08 47		09 47		10 47		11 47		12 47		13 47		14 47		15 47		16 51		17 54
Creswell (Derbys)	d	05 59	07 08	07 45	08 50		09 50		10 50		11 50		12 50		13 50		14 50		15 50		16 54		17 57
Langwith - Whaley Thorns	d	06 03	07 13	07 50	08 55		09 55		10 55		11 55		12 55		13 55		14 55		15 55		16 59		18 01
Shirebrook	d	06 07	07 16	07 53	08 58		09 58		10 58		11 58		12 58		13 58		14 58		15 58		17 02		18 07
Mansfield Woodhouse	d	06 15	07 25	08 01	09 06	09 37	10 06	10 37	11 06	11 37	12 06	12 37	13 06	13 37	14 06	14 37	15 06	15 37	16 06	16 40	17 10	17 43	18 14
Mansfield	d	06 20	07 29	08 05	09 10	09 41	10 10	10 41	11 10	11 41	12 10	12 41	13 10	13 41	14 10	14 41	15 10	15 41	16 10	16 44	17 14	17 46	18 18
Sutton Parkway	d	06 25	07 35	08 11	09 15		10 15		11 15		12 15		13 15		14 15		15 15		16 15		17 19	17 52	18 24
Kirkby In Ashfield	d	06 28	07 38	08 14	09 18	09 48	10 18	10 48	11 18	11 48	12 18	12 48	13 18	13 48	14 18	14 48	15 18	15 48	16 18		17 22	17 55	18 27
Newstead	d	06 34	07 43	08 20	09 23																	18 01	18 31
Hucknall	d	06 39	07 48	08 25	09 27	09 56	10 27	10 56	11 27	11 56	12 27	12 56	13 27	13 56	14 27	14 56	15 27	15 56	16 27		17 30	18 05	18 36
Bulwell	d	06 43	07 53	08 29	09 31																17 34		18 40
Nottingham 8	a	06 58	08 05	08 44	09 44	10 15	10 44	11 14	11 44	12 14	12 44	13 15	13 44	14 14	14 44	15 14	15 44	16 15	16 44	17 14	17 48	18 25	18 51

		EM	EM	EM	EM	EM
Worksop	d	18 41	19 21	20 15	21 19	22 20
Whitwell	d	18 50	19 30	20 24	21 28	22 29
Creswell (Derbys)	d	18 53	19 33	20 27	21 31	22 32
Langwith - Whaley Thorns	d	18 58	19 37	20 31	21 36	22 37
Shirebrook	d	19 01	19 41	20 35	21 39	22 40
Mansfield Woodhouse	d	19 09	19 48	20 43	21 47	22 48
Mansfield	d	19 13	19 52	20 47	21 52	22 52
Sutton Parkway	d	19 18	19 57	20 52	21 57	22 57
Kirkby In Ashfield	d	19 21	20 00	20 55	22 00	23 00
Newstead	d	19 26	20 05	21 02	22 05	23 05
Hucknall	d	19 30	20 09	21 06	22 09	23 09
Bulwell	d	19 34	20 14	21 12	22 13	23 13
Nottingham 8	a	19 47	20 32	21 25	22 25	23 26

Sundays

		EM A	EM B	EM	EM	EM	EM	EM	EM	EM	EM	EM
Worksop	d			09 38	10 38			15 38		18 40		
Whitwell	d			09 47	10 47			15 47		18 49		
Creswell (Derbys)	d			09 50	10 50			15 50		18 52		
Langwith - Whaley Thorns	d			09 55	10 55			15 55		18 57		
Shirebrook	d			09 58	10 58			15 58		19 00		
Mansfield Woodhouse	d	08 37	08 37	10 07	11 07	12 07	14 07	16 06	17 07	19 08	20 07	21 07
Mansfield	d	08 40	08 40	10 10	11 10	12 10	14 10	16 10	17 10	19 12	20 10	21 10
Sutton Parkway	d	08 46	08 46	10 16	11 16	12 16	14 16	16 15	17 16	19 17	20 16	21 16
Kirkby In Ashfield	d	08 49	08 49	10 19	11 19	12 19	14 19	16 18	17 19	19 20	20 19	21 19
Newstead	d	08 54	08 54	10 23	11 23	12 23	14 23	16 23	17 23	19 25	20 23	21 23
Hucknall	d	08 59	08 59	10 28	11 28	12 28	14 28	16 27	17 28	19 29	20 28	21 28
Bulwell	d	09 03		10 32		12 32		16 31				21 32
Nottingham 8	a	09 13	09 13	10 42	11 42	12 43	14 45	16 41	17 42	19 44	20 42	21 42

A from 12 September
B until 5 September

Table 56

Nottingham - Derby - Matlock

Mondays to Fridays
until 24 September

		EM MX	EM	XC	EM	EM	XC	EM	EM	XC	EM	EM	EM	XC	EM	EM	XC	EM	EM	XC	EM	EM	XC	EM	EM
		◇■ ☕		◇■ 🍽		◇■ ⊠🍽	■ A 🍽	◇■ ⊠🍽	◇■ ☕	◇■ 🍽	◇■ ☕			■	◇■ ☕	◇■ ☕	◇■ 🍽			■	◇■ ☕	◇■ ☕	◇■ 🍽		
Nottingham 8	d	01 51		06 00	06 18	06 28	06 37	06 48		06 56	07 10	07 18	07 31	07 37		08 02	08 08	08 15	08 32	08 37		09 02	09 11	09 18	09 32
Beeston	d			06 06	06 23	06a34	06 43	06a54		07 07	07a17	07 24	07a37	07 43		08a07		08 24	08a38	08 43		09a07		09 24	09a38
Attenborough	d			06 10	06 27					07 11		07 27						08 27						09 27	
Long Eaton	d			06 17	06 35					07 18		07 35		07 51	07 59			08 35		08 51	09 00			09 35	
Spondon	d			06 24	06 42							07 42						08 42		08 57					
Derby 6	a	02 10		06 30	06 49		07 01			07 31		07 48		08 02	08 11		08 32	08 49		09 02	09 14		09 31	09 48	
	d		05 38		06 50				07 20			07 50						08 50						09 50	
Duffield	d		05 45		06 57							07 57						08 57						09 57	
Belper	d		05 50		07 02				07 28			08 02						09 02						10 02	
Ambergate	d		05 56		07 08							08 08						09 08						10 08	
Whatstandwell	d		06 00		07 12							08 12						09 12						10 12	
Cromford	d		06 05		07 17							08 17						09 17						10 17	
Matlock Bath	d		06 08		07 21							08 20						09 20						10 20	
Matlock	a		06 12		07 24							08 24						09 24						10 24	

		XC	EM	EM	XC	EM	EM	XC	EM	EM	XC	EM	EM	XC	EM	EM	XC	EM	EM	XC	EM	EM	XC	EM	EM
		■	◇■ ☕	◇■ ☕	◇■ 🍽			■	◇■ ☕	◇■ ☕	◇■ 🍽			■	◇■ ☕	◇■ ☕	◇■ 🍽			■	◇■ ☕	◇■ ☕	◇■ 🍽		
Nottingham 8	d	09 37		10 02	10 11	10 18	10 32	10 37		11 02	11 08	11 18	11 32	11 37		12 02	12 08	12 18	12 32	12 37		13 02	13 11	13 18	13 32
Beeston	d	09 43		10a07		10 24	10a38	10 43		11a08		11 24	11a38	11 43		12a07		12 24	12a38	12 43		13a08		13 24	13a38
Attenborough	d					10 27						11 27						12 27						13 27	
Long Eaton	d	09 51	09 56			10 35		10 51	10 56			11 35		11 51	11 57			12 35		12 51	12 57			13 35	
Spondon	d																								
Derby 6	a	10 02	10 09		10 33	10 49		11 02	11 09		11 31	11 48		12 02	12 11		12 33	12 48		13 02	13 09		13 31	13 48	
	d					10 50						11 50						12 50						13 50	
Duffield	d					10 57						11 57						12 57						13 57	
Belper	d					11 02						12 02						13 02						14 02	
Ambergate	d					11 08						12 08						13 08						14 08	
Whatstandwell	d					11 12						12 12						13 12						14 12	
Cromford	d					11 17						12 17						13 17						14 17	
Matlock Bath	d					11 20						12 21						13 21						14 20	
Matlock	a					11 24						12 24						13 24						14 24	

		XC	EM		EM	XC	EM	XC	EM	EM	XC	EM	EM	XC	EM	EM	XC	EM	EM	XC	EM	EM	EM	XC	EM
		■	◇■ ☕		◇■ ☕	◇■ 🍽		■	◇■ ☕	◇■ ☕	◇■ 🍽			■	◇■ ☕	◇■ ☕	◇■ 🍽			■	◇■ ☕		◇■ ☕	◇■ 🍽	
Nottingham 8	d	13 37			14 02	14 08	14 18	14 37		15 02	15 11	15 18	15 30	15 37		16 02	16 08	16 18	16 32	16 37		16 50	17 02	17 08	17 18
Beeston	d	13 43			14a08		14 24	14 43		15a08		15 24	15a36	15 43		16a07		16 24	16 38	16 43		16 55	17a08		17 24
Attenborough	d						14 27					15 27						16 27	16 41			16 58			17 27
Long Eaton	d	13 51	13 57				14 35	14 51	14 57			15 35		15 51	15 57			16 35		16 51	16 57	17 07			17 35
Spondon	d																								17 42
Derby 6	a	14 02	14 09			14 31	14 47	15 02	15 13		15 31	15 48		16 02	16 09		16 31	16 48		17 02	17 09	17 23		17 31	17 49
	d						14 50					15 50						16 50							17 50
Duffield	d						14 57					15 57						16 57							17 57
Belper	d						15 02					16 02						17 02							18 02
Ambergate	d						15 08					16 08						17 08							18 08
Whatstandwell	d						15 12					16 12						17 12							18 12
Cromford	d						15 17					16 17						17 17							18 17
Matlock Bath	d						15 20					16 20						17 21							18 21
Matlock	a						15 28					16 24						17 24							18 24

		EM	XC	EM	EM	XC	EM	EM	XC	EM	EM	XC FO	XC FX	EM	EM	XC	EM	EM	EM	EM	EM	XC	NT	EM	EM
			■	◇■ ☕	◇■ ☕	◇■ 🍽			■	◇■ ☕	◇■ ☕	◇■ 🍽	◇■ 🍽			■	◇■ ☕	◇■ ☕	◇■ ☕			■		◇■ ☕	◇■ ☕
Nottingham 8	d	17 32	17 37		18 02	18 08	18 18	18 32	18 37		19 02	19 08	19 08	19 18	19 32	19 37	20 02		20 07	20 11	20 32	20 37	20 45	21 02	
Beeston	d	17 38	17 43		18a08		18 24	18a38	18 43		19a07			19 24	19a38	19 43	20a08			20 17	20a38	20 43		21a08	
Attenborough	d	17 41					18 27							19 27						20 20					
Long Eaton	d		17 51	18 01			18 37		18 51	18 56				19 35		19 53		20 07	20 23	20 28		20 51			21 06
Spondon	d		17 57																						
Derby 6	a		18 02	18 14		18 33	18 48		19 02	19 09		19 32	19 32	19 48		20 02		20 19	20 35	20 44		21 07	21 03		21 16
	d						18 50							19 50						20 36					
Duffield	d						18 57							19 57						21 03					
Belper	d						19 02							20 02						21 08					
Ambergate	d						19 08							20 08						21 14					
Whatstandwell	d						19 12							20 12						21 18					
Cromford	d						19 17							20 17						21 23					
Matlock Bath	d						19 21							20 20						21 27					
Matlock	a						19 24							20 24						21 30					

A 🍽 to Beeston

For connections from St Pancras International please refer to Table 53

Table 56

Nottingham - Derby - Matlock

Mondays to Fridays until 24 September

Station		EM	EM	XC	EM	EM	EM	EM	EM	EM
Nottingham	d	21 15	21 32	21 37			22 16	23 10	23 15	
Beeston	d	21 21	21a38	21 43			22 22	23a16	23 21	
Attenborough	d	21 25		21 46			22 25		23 24	
Long Eaton	d	21 33		21 53	21 59		22 33		23 33	23 38
Spondon	d			21 59						
Derby	a	21 50		22 04	22 10		22 49		23 48	23 50
	d					22 16				
Duffield	d					22 23				
Belper	d					22 28				
Ambergate	d					22 34				
Whatstandwell	d					22 38				
Cromford	d					22 43				
Matlock Bath	d					22 47				
Matlock	a					22 50				

Mondays to Fridays from 27 September

Station		EM MX	EM	XC	EM	EM	XC	EM	EM	XC	EM	EM	EM	XC	EM	XC	EM	EM	XC	EM	XC	EM	EM
Nottingham	d	01 51		06 00	06 18	06 28	06 37	06 48		06 56	07 10	07 18	07 31	07 37		08 08	08 15	08 32	08 37		09 11	09 18	09 32
Beeston	d			06 06	06 23	06a34	06 43	06a54		07 07	07a17	07 24	07a37	07 43			08 24	08a38	08 43			09 24	09a38
Attenborough	d			06 10	06 27					07 11		07 27					08 27					09 27	
Long Eaton	d			06 17	06 35					07 18		07 35		07 51	07 59		08 35		08 51	09 00		09 35	
Spondon	d			06 24	06 42							07 42					08 42		08 57				
Derby	a	02 10		06 30	06 49		07 01			07 31		07 48		08 02	08 11	08 32	08 49		09 02	09 14	09 31	09 48	
	d		05 38		06 50				07 20			07 50					08 50					09 50	
Duffield	d		05 45		06 57							07 57					08 57					09 57	
Belper	d		05 50		07 02				07a28			08 02					09 02					10 02	
Ambergate	d		05 57		07 08							08 09					09 09					10 09	
Whatstandwell	d		06 01		07 12							08 13					09 13					10 13	
Cromford	d		06 06		07 17							08 18					09 18					10 18	
Matlock Bath	d		06 09		07 21							08 21					09 21					10 21	
Matlock	a		06 14		07 25							08 25					09 26					10 26	

Station		XC	EM	XC	EM	EM	XC	EM	EM	XC	EM	XC	EM	XC	EM	EM	XC	EM	EM	XC	EM	EM	XC
Nottingham	d	09 37		10 11	10 18	10 32	10 37		11 02	11 08	11 32	11 37		12 08	12 18	12 32	12 37		13 02	13 11	13 18	13 32	13 37
Beeston	d	09 43			10 24	10a38	10 43		11a08		11a38	11 43			12 24	12a38	12 43		13a08		13 24	13a38	13 43
Attenborough	d				10 27										12 27						13 27		
Long Eaton	d	09 51	09 56		10 35		10 51	10 56				11 51	11 57		12 35		12 51	12 57			13 35		13 51
Spondon	d																						
Derby	a	10 02	10 09	10 33	10 49		11 02	11 09		11 31		12 02	12 11	12 33	12 48		13 02	13 09		13 31	13 48		14 02
	d				10 50										12 50						13 50		
Duffield	d				10 57										12 57						13 57		
Belper	d				11 02										13 02						14 02		
Ambergate	d				11 09										13 09						14 09		
Whatstandwell	d				11 13										13 13						14 13		
Cromford	d				11 18										13 18						14 18		
Matlock Bath	d				11 21										13 22						14 21		
Matlock	a				11 26										13 26						14 26		

Station		EM	EM	XC	XC	EM	EM	XC	EM	EM	XC	EM	EM	XC	EM	EM	XC	EM	EM	EM	XC	EM	EM
Nottingham	d		14 02	14 08	14 37		15 02	15 11	15 18	15 32	15 37		16 02	16 08	16 18	16 32	16 37		16 50	17 02	17 08	17 18	17 32
Beeston	d		14a08		14 43		15a08		15 24	15a38	15 43		16a07		16 24	16 38	16 43		16 55	17a08		17 24	17 38
Attenborough	d								15 27						16 27	16 41			16 58			17 27	17a41
Long Eaton	d	13 57			14 51	14 57			15 35		15 51	15 57			16 35		16 51	16 57	17 07			17 35	
Spondon	d																					17 42	
Derby	a	14 09		14 31	15 02	15 13		15 31	15 48		16 02	16 09		16 31	16 48		17 02	17 09	17 23		17 31	17 49	
	d								15 50						16 50							17 50	
Duffield	d								15 57						16 57							17 57	
Belper	d								16 02						17 02							18 02	
Ambergate	d								16 09						17 09							18 09	
Whatstandwell	d								16 13						17 13							18 13	
Cromford	d								16 18						17 18							18 18	
Matlock Bath	d								16 21						17 22							18 22	
Matlock	a								16 26						17 26							18 26	

For connections from St Pancras International please refer to Table 53

Table 56

Nottingham - Derby - Matlock

Mondays to Fridays from 27 September

Station		XC	EM	EM	XC	EM	EM	XC	EM	XC FO	XC FX	EM	EM	XC	EM	EM	EM	EM	EM	XC	NT	EM	EM	EM
Nottingham	d	17 37		18 02	18 08	18 18	18 32	18 37		19 08	19 08	19 18	19 32	19 37	20 02		20 07	20 11	20 32	20 37	20 45	21 02		21 15
Beeston	d	17 43		18a08		18 24	18a38	18 43				19 24	19a38	19 43	20a08			20 17	20a38	20 43		21a08		21 21
Attenborough	d					18 27						19 27		19 46				20 20						21 25
Long Eaton	d	17 51	18 01			18 37		18 51	18 56			19 35		19 53		20 07	20 23	20 28		20 51			21 06	21 33
Spondon	d	17 57																						
Derby	a	18 02	18 14		18 33	18 48		19 02	19 09	19 32	19 32	19 48		20 02		20 19	20 35	20 44		21 02	21 05		21 16	21 50
	d					18 50						19 50						20 56						
Duffield	d					18 57						19 57						21 03						
Belper	d					19 02						20 02						21 08						
Ambergate	d					19 09						20 09						21 15						
Whatstandwell	d					19 13						20 13						21 19						
Cromford	d					19 18						20 18						21 24						
Matlock Bath	d					19 22						20 21						21 28						
Matlock	a					19 26						20 26						21 32						

Station		EM	XC	EM	EM	EM	EM	EM	EM
Nottingham	d	21 32	21 37			22 16	23 10	23 15	
Beeston	d	21a38	21 43			22 22	23a16	23 21	
Attenborough	d		21 46			22 25		23 24	
Long Eaton	d		21 53	21 59		22 33		23 33	23 38
Spondon	d		21 59						
Derby	a		22 04	22 10		22 49		23 48	23 50
	d				22 16				
Duffield	d				22 23				
Belper	d				22 28				
Ambergate	d				22 34				
Whatstandwell	d				22 38				
Cromford	d				22 43				
Matlock Bath	d				22 47				
Matlock	a				22 50				

Saturdays until 25 September

Station		EM	EM	XC	EM	EM	XC	EM	XC	EM	EM	EM	XC	EM	EM	XC	EM	EM	XC	EM	EM	XC	EM
Nottingham	d	01 51		05 57	06 02	06 10	06 37		06 56	07 02	07 18	07 31	07 34		08 02	08 08	08 18	08 32	08 37		09 02	09 08	09 18
Beeston	d			06 03	06a08	06 17	06 43		07 03	07a08	07 24	07a37	07 41		08a08		08 24	08a38	08 43		09a08		09 24
Attenborough	d			06 06		06 20			07 06		07 27						08 27						09 27
Long Eaton	d			06 16		06 28			07 14		07 35		07 49	07 56			08 35		08 51	09 01			09 35
Spondon	d			06 23		06 40			07 24								08 42						
Derby	a	02 10		06 32		06 45	07 01		07 30		07 49		08 02	08 09		08 31	08 48		09 02	09 14		09 31	09 48
	d		05 40			06 48		07 20			07 50						08 50						09 50
Duffield	d		05 47			06 55					07 57						08 57						09 56
Belper	d		05 52			07 00		07a28			08 02						09 02						10 01
Ambergate	d		05 58			07 06					08 08						09 08						10 08
Whatstandwell	d		06 02			07 10					08 12						09 12						10 12
Cromford	d		06 07			07 15					08 17						09 17						10 17
Matlock Bath	d		06 11			07 19					08 20						09 21						10 20
Matlock	a		06 14			07 22					08 24						09 24						10 24

Station		EM	XC	EM	EM	XC	EM	EM	XC	EM	EM	XC	EM	EM	XC	EM	EM	XC	EM	EM	XC	EM	EM
Nottingham	d	09 32	09 37		10 02	10 08	10 18	10 32	10 37		11 02	11 11	11 18	11 32	11 37		12 02	12 08	12 18	12 32	12 37		13 02
Beeston	d	09a38	09 43		10a08		10 24	10a38	10 43		11a08		11 24	11a38	11 43		12a08		12 24	12a38	12 43		13a08
Attenborough	d						10 27						11 27						12 27				
Long Eaton	d		09 51	09 57			10 37		10 51	10 57			11 36		11 51	11 57			12 36		12 51	12 57	
Spondon	d																						
Derby	a		10 02	10 09		10 31	10 50		11 02	11 09		11 31	11 48		12 02	12 09		12 31	12 48		13 02	13 09	
	d						10 51						11 50						12 50				
Duffield	d						10 58						11 57						12 57				
Belper	d						11 03						12 02						13 02				
Ambergate	d						11 09						12 08						13 08				
Whatstandwell	d						11 13						12 12						13 12				
Cromford	d						11 18						12 17						13 17				
Matlock Bath	d						11 21						12 20						13 20				
Matlock	a						11 25						12 24						13 24				

For connections from St Pancras International please refer to Table 53

Table 56

Nottingham - Derby - Matlock

Saturdays until 25 September

Station		XC ◇1 🍴	EM	EM	XC 1	EM ◇1 ☕	EM A	EM ◇1 ☕	XC ◇1 🍴	EM	EM	XC 1	EM ◇1 ☕	EM ◇1 ☕	XC ◇1 🍴	EM	EM	XC 1	EM ◇1 ☕	EM ◇1 ☕	XC ◇1 🍴	EM	EM
Nottingham ■	d	13 08	13 18	13 32	13 37		13 52	14 02	14 08	14 18	14 32	14 37		15 02	15 08	15 18	15 32	15 37		16 02	16 08	16 18	16 32
Beeston	d		13 24	13a38	13 43		13 59	14a08		14 24	14a38	14 43		15a08		15 24	15a38	15 43		16a08		16 24	16 38
Attenborough	d		13 27							14 27						15 27						16 27	16a41
Long Eaton	d		13 36		13 51	13 57	14 08			14 36		14 51	14 57			15 36		15 51	15 57			16 36	
Spondon	d																						
Derby ■	a	13 31	13 48		14 02	14 09	14 22		14 32	14 48		15 02	15 09		15 31	15 48		16 02	16 09		16 31	16 48	
	d		13 50							14 50						15 50						16 50	
Duffield	d		13 57							14 57						15 57						16 57	
Belper	d		14 02							15 02						16 02						17 02	
Ambergate	d		14 08							15 08						16 08						17 08	
Whatstandwell	d		14 12							15 12						16 12						17 12	
Cromford	d		14 17							15 17						16 17						17 17	
Matlock Bath	d		14 20							15 20						16 20						17 20	
Matlock	a		14 24							15 24						16 24						17 24	

Station		XC 1	EM ◇1 ☕	EM ◇1 ☕	XC ◇1 🍴	EM	EM	XC 1	EM ◇1 ☕	EM ◇1 ☕	XC ◇1 🍴	EM	EM	XC 1	EM ◇1 ☕	EM ◇1 ☕	XC ◇1 🍴	EM	EM	XC 1	EM ◇1 ☕	EM ◇1 ☕	EM	EM	XC 1
Nottingham ■	d	16 37		17 02	17 08	17 18	17 32	17 37		18 02	18 08	18 19	18 32	18 37		19 02	19 08	19 18	19 32	19 37		20 02	20 09	20 32	20 36
Beeston	d	16 43		17a08		17 24	17 38	17 43		18a07		18 24	18a38	18 43		19a07		19 24	19a38	19 43		20a08	20 15	20a38	20 42
Attenborough	d					17 27	17a41					18 27						19 27		19 46			20 18		
Long Eaton	d	16 51	16 56			17 35		17 51	17 57			18 37		18 51	18 57			19 35		19 53	19 57		20 27		20 51
Spondon	d					17 42											19 27								
Derby ■	a	17 02	17 09		17 31	17 48		18 02	18 09		18 31	18 48		19 02	19 09		19 32	19 48		20 02	20 09		20 42		21 02
	d					17 50						18 50						19 50					20 50		
Duffield	d					17 57						18 57						19 57					20 57		
Belper	d					18 02						19 02						20 02					21 02		
Ambergate	d					18 08						19 08						20 08					21 08		
Whatstandwell	d					18 12						19 12						20 12					21 12		
Cromford	d					18 17						19 17						20 17					21 17		
Matlock Bath	d					18 20						19 20						20 20					21 20		
Matlock	a					18 24						19 24						20 24					21 24		

Station		EM ◇1 ☕	EM ◇1 ☕	EM	EM	EM	XC 1	EM ◇1 ☕	EM	EM	EM ◇1 B ☕	EM ◇1 C ☕	EM
Nottingham ■	d	20 43		21 08	21 32		21 37		22 15	23 11			23 15
Beeston	d	20a49		21 14	21a38		21 43		22 21	23a17			23 21
Attenborough	d			21 17			21 46		22 24				23 24
Long Eaton	d		20 57	21 26			21 53	21 57	22 32		23 19	23 23	23 32
Spondon	d						21 59						
Derby ■	a		21 10	21 41			22 04	22 12	22 48		23 29	23 35	23 47
	d					21 50							
Duffield	d					21 57							
Belper	d					22 02							
Ambergate	d					22 09							
Whatstandwell	d					22 13							
Cromford	d					22 18							
Matlock Bath	d					22 21							
Matlock	a					22 24							

Saturdays from 02 October

Station		EM ◇1 ☕	EM	XC ◇1 🍴	EM ◇1 ☕	EM	XC 1 🍴	EM ◇1 ☕	XC ◇1 🍴	EM ◇1 ☕	EM	EM	XC 1	EM ◇1 ☕	EM ◇1 ☕	XC ◇1 🍴	EM	EM	XC 1	EM ◇1 ☕	EM ◇1 ☕	XC ◇1 🍴	EM
Nottingham ■	d	01 51		05 57	06 02	06 10	06 37		06 56	07 02	07 18	07 31	07 34		08 02	08 08	08 18	08 32	08 37		09 02	09 08	09 18
Beeston	d			06 03	06a08	06 17	06 43		07 03	07a08	07 24	07a37	07 41		08a08		08 24	08a38	08 43		09a08		09 24
Attenborough	d			06 06		06 20			07 06		07 27						08 27						09 27
Long Eaton	d			06 16		06 28			07 14		07 35		07 49	07 56			08 35		08 51	09 01			09 35
Spondon	d			06 23		06 40			07 24								08 42						
Derby ■	a	02 10		06 32		06 45	07 01		07 30		07 49		08 02	08 09		08 31	08 48		09 02	09 14		09 31	09 48
	d		05 40			06 48		07 20			07 50						08 50						09 50
Duffield	d		05 47			06 55					07 57						08 57						09 56
Belper	d		05 52			07 00		07a28			08 02						09 02						10 01
Ambergate	d		05 58			07 07					08 09						09 09						10 09
Whatstandwell	d		06 02			07 11					08 13						09 13						10 13
Cromford	d		06 07			07 16					08 18						09 18						10 18
Matlock Bath	d		06 11			07 20					08 21						09 22						10 21
Matlock	a		06 15			07 24					08 26						09 26						10 26

A from 17 July until 4 September
B 11 September, 18 September, 25 September
C until 4 September

For connections from St Pancras International please refer to Table 53

Table 56

Nottingham - Derby - Matlock

Saturdays from 02 October

Station		EM	XC 1	EM ◇1 ☕	EM ◇1 ☕	XC ◇1 🍴	EM	EM	XC 1	EM ◇1 ☕	EM ◇1 ☕	XC ◇1 🍴	EM	EM	XC 1	EM ◇1 ☕	EM ◇1 ☕	XC ◇1 🍴	EM	EM	XC 1	EM ◇1 ☕	EM ◇1 ☕
Nottingham ■	d	09 32	09 37		10 02	10 08	10 18	10 32	10 37		11 02	11 11	11 18	11 32	11 37		12 02	12 08	12 18	12 32	12 37		13 02
Beeston	d	09a38	09 43		10a08		10 24	10a38	10 43		11a08		11 24	11a38	11 43		12a08		12 24	12a38	12 43		13a08
Attenborough	d						10 27						11 27						12 27				
Long Eaton	d		09 51	09 57			10 35		10 51	10 57			11 35		11 51	11 57			12 35		12 51	12 57	
Spondon	d																						
Derby ■	a		10 02	10 09		10 31	10 49		11 02	11 09		11 31	11 48		12 02	12 09		12 31	12 48		13 02	13 09	
	d						10 50						11 50						12 50				
Duffield	d						10 57						11 57						12 57				
Belper	d						11 02						12 02						13 02				
Ambergate	d						11 09						12 09						13 09				
Whatstandwell	d						11 13						12 13						13 13				
Cromford	d						11 18						12 18						13 18				
Matlock Bath	d						11 21						12 21						13 21				
Matlock	a						11 26						12 26						13 26				

Station		XC ◇1 🍴	EM	EM	XC 1	EM ◇1 ☕	EM ◇1 ☕	XC ◇1 🍴	EM	EM	XC 1	EM ◇1 ☕	EM ◇1 ☕	XC ◇1 🍴	EM	EM	XC 1	EM ◇1 ☕	EM ◇1 ☕	XC ◇1 🍴	EM	EM
Nottingham ■	d	13 08	13 18	13 32	13 37		14 02	14 08	14 18	14 32	14 37		15 02	15 08	15 18	15 32	15 37		16 02	16 08	16 18	16 32
Beeston	d		13 24	13a38	13 43		14a08		14 24	14a38	14 43		15a08		15 24	15a38	15 43		16a08		16 24	16 38
Attenborough	d		13 27						14 27						15 27						16 27	16a41
Long Eaton	d		13 35		13 51	13 57			14 35		14 51	14 57			15 35		15 51	15 57			16 35	
Spondon	d																					
Derby ■	a	13 31	13 48		14 02	14 09		14 32	14 48		15 02	15 09		15 31	15 48		16 02	16 09		16 31	16 48	
	d		13 50						14 50						15 50						16 50	
Duffield	d		13 57						14 57						15 57						16 57	
Belper	d		14 02						15 02						16 02						17 02	
Ambergate	d		14 09						15 09						16 09						17 09	
Whatstandwell	d		14 13						15 13						16 13						17 13	
Cromford	d		14 18						15 18						16 18						17 18	
Matlock Bath	d		14 21						15 21						16 21						17 21	
Matlock	a		14 26						15 26						16 26						17 26	

Station		XC 1	EM ◇1 ☕	EM ◇1 ☕	XC ◇1 🍴	EM	EM	XC 1	EM ◇1 ☕	EM ◇1 ☕	XC ◇1 🍴	EM	EM	XC 1	EM ◇1 ☕	EM ◇1 ☕	XC ◇1 🍴	EM	EM	XC 1	EM ◇1 ☕	EM ◇1 ☕	EM	EM	XC 1
Nottingham ■	d	16 37		17 02	17 08	17 18	17 32	17 37		18 02	18 08	18 18	18 32	18 37		19 02	19 08	19 18	19 32	19 37		20 02	20 09	20 32	20 36
Beeston	d	16 43		17a08		17 24	17 38	17 43		18a07		18 24	18a38	18 43		19a07		19 24	19a38	19 43		20a08	20 15	20a38	20 42
Attenborough	d					17 27	17a41					18 27						19 27		19 46			20 18		
Long Eaton	d	16 51	16 56			17 35		17 51	17 57			18 37		18 51	18 57			19 35		19 53	19 57		20 27		20 51
Spondon	d					17 42											19 27								
Derby ■	a	17 02	17 09		17 31	17 48		18 02	18 09		18 31	18 48		19 02	19 09		19 32	19 48		20 02	20 09		20 42		21 02
	d					17 50						18 50						19 50					20 50		
Duffield	d					17 57						18 57						19 57					20 57		
Belper	d					18 02						19 02						20 02					21 02		
Ambergate	d					18 09						19 09						20 09					21 09		
Whatstandwell	d					18 13						19 13						20 13					21 13		
Cromford	d					18 18						19 18						20 18					21 18		
Matlock Bath	d					18 21						19 21						20 21					21 21		
Matlock	a					18 26						19 26						20 26					21 26		

Station		EM ◇1 ☕	EM ◇1 ☕	EM	EM	EM	XC 1	EM ◇1 ☕	EM	EM A	EM ◇1 ☕	EM
Nottingham ■	d	20 43		21 08	21 32		21 37		22 15	23 11		23 15
Beeston	d	20a49		21 14	21a38		21 43		22 21	23a17		23 21
Attenborough	d			21 17			21 46		22 24			23 24
Long Eaton	d		20 57	21 26			21 53	21 57	22 32		23 19	23 32
Spondon	d						21 59					
Derby ■	a		21 10	21 41			22 04	22 12	22 48		23 29	23 47
	d					21 50						
Duffield	d					21 57						
Belper	d					22 02						
Ambergate	d					22 09						
Whatstandwell	d					22 13						
Cromford	d					22 18						
Matlock Bath	d					22 21						
Matlock	a					22 25						

A not 11 December

For connections from St Pancras International please refer to Table 53

Table 56

Nottingham - Derby - Matlock

Sundays until 11 July

		EM	EM	EM	EM	EM	EM	EM	EM	EM	EM	EM	EM	EM	EM	EM	EM	EM	EM	EM	EM	EM	EM
		◇1		◇1	◇1		◇1	◇1	◇1	◇1		◇1		◇1	◇1		◇1	◇1	◇1		◇1	◇1	◇1
		☕		☕	☕		☕	☕	☕	☕		☕		☕	☕		☕	☕	☕		☕	☕	☕
Nottingham	d	08 14	09 28	10 15		11 22		12 14		13 13	13 19		14 23	14 30		14 58	15 10		16 18	16 21		17 20	
Beeston	d	08a20	09 34	10a22		11 27		12a21		13a20	13 25		14 28	14a36		15 03	15a16		16a24	16 27		17a26	
Attenborough	d		09 37			11 30					13 28		14 32			15 06				16 30			
Long Eaton	d		09 45		10 35	11 37	11 44		12 45		13 35	13 48	14 40		14 46	15 14		15 44		16 37	16 43		17 37
Spondon	d																						
Derby	a		09 56		10 55	11 49	11 54		12 55		13 48	14 00	14 53		15 00	15 27		15 56		16 49	16 55		17 48
	d		09 58			11 54					13 50					15 31							
Duffield	d		10 05			12 01					13 57					15 38							
Belper	d		10 10			12 06					14 02					15 43							
Ambergate	d		10 16			12 12					14 08					15 49							
Whatstandwell	d		10 20			12 16					14 12					15 53							
Cromford	d		10 25			12 21					14 17					15 58							
Matlock Bath	d		10 29			12 24					14 20					16 02							
Matlock	a		10 32			12 27					14 23					16 06							

		EM	EM	EM	EM	XC	EM	EM	EM	XC	EM	EM	XC	EM	EM	EM
			◇1	◇1		◇1	◇1		◇1	◇1	◇1		◇1	◇1		◇1
			☕	☕		🛒	☕		☕	🛒	☕		🛒	☕		☕
Nottingham	d	17 23	18 10		18 23	19 10		19 23	19 46	20 10		20 22	21 08		21 25	
Beeston	d	17 29	18a19		18 29			19 28	19a52			20 28			21 31	
Attenborough	d	17 32			18 32			19 31				20 31			21 34	
Long Eaton	d	17 42		18 32	18 41		19 33	19 39			20 29	20 41		21 29	21 41	23 39
Spondon	d															
Derby	a	17 52		18 47	18 52	19 30	19 47	19 50		20 28	20 45	20 53	21 31	21 40	21 53	23 49
	d	17 58						19 52							21 56	
Duffield	d	18 05						19 59							22 04	
Belper	d	18 10						20 04							22 09	
Ambergate	d	18 16						20 10							22 15	
Whatstandwell	d	18 20						20 14							22 19	
Cromford	d	18 25						20 19							22 24	
Matlock Bath	d	18 28						20 23							22 27	
Matlock	a	18 31						20 26							22 30	

Sundays 18 July to 05 September

		EM	EM	EM	EM	XC	EM	EM	EM	EM	EM	XC	EM	EM	EM	EM	EM	EM	EM	EM	EM	EM	EM
		◇1		◇1	◇1	◇1		◇1	◇1	◇1	◇1	◇1		◇1		◇1	◇1		◇1	◇1	◇1		◇1
		☕		☕	☕	🛒		☕	☕	☕	☕	🛒		☕		☕	☕		☕	☕	☕		☕
Nottingham	d	08 15	09 28	10 14		11 10	11 22		12 03		13 00	13 05	13 19		14 23	14 30		14 58	15 12		16 18	16 21	
Beeston	d	08a21	09 34	10a21			11 27		12a10		13a07		13 25		14 28	14a36		15 03	15a18		16a24	16 27	
Attenborough	d		09 37				11 30						13 28		14 32			15 06				16 30	
Long Eaton	d		09 45		10 29		11 37	11 48		12 48			13 35	13 46	14 40		14 49	15 14		15 44		16 37	16 43
Spondon	d																						
Derby	a		09 56		10 46	11 34	11 49	11 58		12 58		13 30	13 47	13 56	14 53		15 01	15 27		15 56		16 49	16 55
	d		09 58				11 54						13 50					15 31					
Duffield	d		10 05				12 01						13 57					15 38					
Belper	d		10 10				12 06						14 02					15 43					
Ambergate	d		10 16				12 12						14 08					15 49					
Whatstandwell	d		10 20				12 16						14 12					15 53					
Cromford	d		10 25				12 21						14 17					15 58					
Matlock Bath	d		10 29				12 24						14 20					16 02					
Matlock	a		10 32				12 27						14 23					16 06					

		EM	EM	EM	EM	EM	EM	XC	EM	EM	EM	XC	EM	EM	XC	EM	EM	EM
		◇1	◇1		◇1	◇1		◇1	◇1		◇1	◇1	◇1		◇1	◇1		◇1
		☕	☕		☕	☕		🛒	☕		☕	🛒	☕		🛒	☕		☕
Nottingham	d	17 19		17 23	18 10		18 23	19 10		19 23	19 45	20 10		20 22	21 08		21 25	
Beeston	d	17a25		17 29	18a17		18 29			19 28	19a51			20 28			21 31	
Attenborough	d			17 32			18 32			19 31				20 31			21 34	
Long Eaton	d		17 37	17 42		18 32	18 41		19 33	19 39			20 29	20 41		21 29	21 41	23 39
Spondon	d																	
Derby	a		17 48	17 52		18 47	18 52	19 30	19 47	19 50		20 28	20 45	20 53	21 31	21 40	21 53	23 49
	d			17 58						19 52							21 56	
Duffield	d			18 05						19 59							22 04	
Belper	d			18 10						20 04							22 09	
Ambergate	d			18 16						20 10							22 15	
Whatstandwell	d			18 20						20 14							22 19	
Cromford	d			18 25						20 19							22 24	
Matlock Bath	d			18 28						20 23							22 27	
Matlock	a			18 31						20 26							22 30	

For connections from St Pancras International please refer to Table 53

Table 56

Nottingham - Derby - Matlock

Sundays from 12 September

		EM	EM	EM	EM	EM	EM	EM	EM	EM	EM	EM	EM	EM	EM	EM	EM	EM	EM	EM	EM	EM	EM
		◇1		◇1	◇1	◇1	◇1	◇1	◇1		◇1		◇1	◇1		◇1	◇1	◇1		◇1	◇1	◇1	
		☕		☕	☕	☕	☕	☕	☕		☕		☕	☕		☕	☕	☕		☕	☕	☕	
Nottingham	d	08 19	09 28	10 15			12 15		13 14	13 19		14 23	14 30		14 58	15 10		16 18	16 21		17 20		17 23
Beeston	d	08a25	09 34	10a22			12a22		13a21	13 25		14 28	14a36		15 03	15a16		16a24	16 27		17a26		17 29
Attenborough	d		09 37							13 28		14 32			15 06				16 30				17 32
Long Eaton	d		09 45		10 29	11 38		12 41		13 35	13 42	14 40		14 46	15 14		15 44		16 37	16 43		17 37	17 42
Spondon	d																						
Derby	a		09 56		10 46	11 49		12 51		13 48	13 52	14 53		15 00	15 27		15 56		16 49	16 55		17 48	17 52
	d		09 58							13 58					15 31								17 58
Duffield	d		10 05							14 06					15 38								18 05
Belper	d		10 10							14 11					15 43								18 10
Ambergate	d		10 16							14 17					15 49								18 16
Whatstandwell	d		10 20							14 21					15 53								18 20
Cromford	d		10 25							14 26					15 58								18 25
Matlock Bath	d		10 29							14 28					16 02								18 28
Matlock	a		10 32							14 32					16 06								18 31

		EM	EM	EM	XC	EM	EM	EM	XC	EM	EM	XC	EM	EM	EM
		◇1	◇1		◇1	◇1		◇1	◇1	◇1		◇1	◇1		◇1
		☕	☕		🛒	☕		☕	🛒	☕		🛒	☕		☕
Nottingham	d	18 10		18 23	19 10		19 23	19 46	20 10		20 22	21 08		21 25	
Beeston	d	18a19		18 29			19 28	19a52			20 28			21 31	
Attenborough	d			18 32			19 31				20 31			21 34	
Long Eaton	d		18 32	18 41		19 31	19 39			20 29	20 41		21 29	21 41	23 39
Spondon	d														
Derby	a		18 47	18 52	19 30	19 45	19 50		20 28	20 45	20 53	21 31	21 40	21 53	23 49
	d						19 52							21 56	
Duffield	d						19 59							22 04	
Belper	d						20 04							22 09	
Ambergate	d						20 10							22 15	
Whatstandwell	d						20 14							22 19	
Cromford	d						20 19							22 24	
Matlock Bath	d						20 23							22 27	
Matlock	a						20 26							22 30	

For connections from St Pancras International please refer to Table 53

Table 56

Matlock - Derby - Nottingham

Mondays to Fridays
until 24 September

		EM	EM	XC	EM	EM	EM	EM	EM	EM		EM	XC	EM	EM	XC	EM	EM	XC	EM		EM	EM	XC	EM
		MX	MX ◇1 ☕	MX 1	MO ◇1 ☕	◇1 ⊠☕		◇1 ⊠☕				◇1 ⊠☕	1	◇1 ☕		1			1	◇1 ⊠		◇1 ☕		1	
Matlock	d	22p55							06 21														07 36		
Matlock Bath	d	22p57							06 23														07 38		
Cromford	d	23p00							06 26														07 41		
Whatstandwell	d	23p05							06 31														07 46		
Ambergate	d	23p10							06 37														07 51		
Belper	d	23p17							06 43														07 58		
Duffield	d	23p21							06 47														08 02		
Derby	a	23p29							06 56														08 10		
	d	23p31		23p59		05 17	06 24	06 32				07 01	07 10	07 26	07 33	07 40		07 53	08 10	08 16			08 20	08 39	
Spondon	d						06 29						07 18			07 45							08 25		
Long Eaton	d	23p41				05a27	06 36	06a42					07 25	07a36	07 42	07 49		08 03	08 19	08a26			08 32		
Attenborough	d	23p48					06 44			07 13			07 31		07 52			08 13					08 39		
Beeston	d	23p51	00 05		00 41		06 47			07 16			07 35		07 55	07 58	08 06	08 16	08 27			08 31	08 42		09 02
Nottingham	a	00 02	00 12	00 18	00 48		06 57			07 27		07 29	07 41		08 05	08 08	08 15	08 26	08 33			08 40	08 50	09 05	09 13

		EM	XC	EM	EM	XC		EM	EM	XC	EM	EM	XC	EM	EM	XC		EM	EM	XC	EM	EM	XC	EM	EM
		◇1 ☕	1		◇1 ☕	◇1			◇1 ☕	1		◇1 ☕	◇1		◇1 ☕	1			◇1 ☕	◇1		◇1 ☕	1		◇1 ☕
Matlock	d			08 36							09 36							10 36						11 36	
Matlock Bath	d			08 38							09 38							10 38						11 38	
Cromford	d			08 41							09 41							10 41						11 41	
Whatstandwell	d			08 46							09 46							10 46						11 46	
Ambergate	d			08 51							09 51							10 51						11 51	
Belper	d			08 58							09 58							10 58						11 58	
Duffield	d			09 02							10 02							11 02						12 02	
Derby	a			09 10							10 10							11 10						12 10	
	d		09 10	09 24	09 20	09 39				10 10	10 24	10 20	10 40			11 10		11 24	11 20	11 39			12 10	12 24	12 20
Spondon	d																								
Long Eaton	d		09 19	09 33	09a30					10 19	10 33	10a30				11 19		11 33	11a30				12 19	12 33	12a30
Attenborough	d		09 26	09 40							10 40							11 40						12 40	
Beeston	d	09 17	09 29	09 43				10 02	10 17	10 27	10 43			11 02	11 17	11 27		11 43			12 02	12 17	12 27	12 43	
Nottingham	a	09 26	09 35	09 53		10 05		10 13	10 26	10 33	10 53		11 04	11 14	11 26	11 33		11 53		12 05	12 13	12 26	12 33	12 53	

		XC		EM	EM	XC	EM	EM	XC	EM	EM	XC		EM	EM	XC	EM	EM	XC	EM	EM	XC		EM	EM
		◇1			◇1 ☕	1		◇1 ☕	◇1		◇1 ☕	1			◇1 ☕	◇1		◇1 ☕	1		◇1 ☕	◇1			◇1 ☕
Matlock	d						12 36							13 36						14 36					
Matlock Bath	d						12 38							13 38						14 38					
Cromford	d						12 41							13 41						14 41					
Whatstandwell	d						12 46							13 46						14 46					
Ambergate	d						12 51							13 51						14 51					
Belper	d						12 58							13 58						14 58					
Duffield	d						13 02							14 02						15 02					
Derby	a						13 10							14 10						15 10					
	d	12 40				13 10	13 24	13 20	13 39			14 10		14 24	14 20	14 39			15 10	15 24	15 20	15 39			
Spondon	d																								
Long Eaton	d					13 19	13 33	13a30				14 19		14 33	14a30				15 19	15 33	15a30				
Attenborough	d						13 40							14 40						15 40					
Beeston	d			13 07	13 17	13 27	13 43			14 02	14 16	14 29		14 43			15 02	15 17	15 27	15 43				16 02	16 17
Nottingham	a	13 05		13 14	13 26	13 33	13 53		14 05	14 13	14 26	14 35		14 53		15 05	15 13	15 26	15 33	15 53		16 05		16 13	16 26

		XC	EM	EM	XC	EM	EM	XC		EM	EM	XC	EM	EM	EM	XC	EM	EM		XC	EM	EM	EM	XC	EM
		1		◇1 ☕	◇1		◇1 ☕	1			◇1 ☕	◇1			◇1 ☕	1		◇1 ☕		◇1	◇1 ☕		◇1 ☕	1	
Matlock	d		15 36							16 36							17 36								18 36
Matlock Bath	d		15 38							16 38							17 38								18 38
Cromford	d		15 41							16 41							17 41								18 41
Whatstandwell	d		15 46							16 46							17 46								18 46
Ambergate	d		15 51							16 51							17 51								18 51
Belper	d		15 58							16 58							17 58								18 58
Duffield	d		16 02							17 02							18 02								19 02
Derby	a		16 10							17 10							18 10								19 10
	d	16 10	16 24	16 18	16 39			17 10		17 24	17 18	17 39		17 47		18 10	18 24	18 18		18 39				19 10	19 24
Spondon	d									17 29				17 53											
Long Eaton	d	16 19	16 33	16a28				17 19		17 36	17a28			18 01		18 19	18 33	18a28						19 19	19 33
Attenborough	d		16 40							17 43				18 09			18 40								19 40
Beeston	d	16 27	16 43			17 02	17 17	17 27		17 46			18 02	18 12	18 18	18 27	18 43				19 03	19 07	19 19	19 27	19 43
Nottingham	a	16 33	16 54		17 05	17 13	17 26	17 33		17 54		18 05	18 13	18 22	18 30	18 33	18 54			19 05	19 10	19 15	19 27	19 35	19 53

		EM	XC	EM		EM	XC	EM	XC	EM	EM	EM	XC	EM		EM	EM	XC	EM	XC					
		◇1 ☕	◇1			◇1 ☕	1		◇1		◇1 ☕		◇1				◇1 ☕	◇1		1					
Matlock	d							19 36				20 36		21 36					22 55						
Matlock Bath	d							19 38				20 38		21 38					22 57						
Cromford	d							19 41				20 41		21 41					23 00						
Whatstandwell	d							19 46				20 46		21 46					23 05						
Ambergate	d							19 51				20 51		21 31					23 10						
Belper	d							19 58				20 58		21 58					23 17						
Duffield	d							20 02				21 02		22 02					23 21						
Derby	a							20 10				21 10		22 11					23 29						
	d	19 18	19 39				20 10	20 24	20 40			21 24	21 40					22 59	23 31	23 59					
Spondon	d												21 45					23 04							
Long Eaton	d	19a28					20 19	20 33	20 49			21 33	21 52					23 11	23 41						
Attenborough	d							20 40				21 40	21 58					23 17	23 48						
Beeston	d			20 07		20 18	20 27	20 43	20 59	21 03	21 19	21 43	22 02			22 07	22 17	23 20	23 51						
Nottingham	a		20 03	20 20		20 28	20 35	20 53	21 06	21 15	21 29	21 54	22 08			22 16	22 27	23 27	00 02	00 18					

For connections to St Pancras International please refer to Table 53

Table 56

Matlock - Derby - Nottingham

Mondays to Fridays
from 27 September

		EM	EM	XC	EM	EM	EM	EM	EM	EM		EM	XC	EM	EM	XC	EM	EM	XC	EM		EM	EM	XC	EM
		MX	MX ◇1 ☕	MX 1	MO ◇1 ☕	◇1 ⊠☕		◇1 ⊠☕				◇1 ⊠☕	1	◇1 ☕		1			1	◇1 ⊠		◇1 ☕		1	
Matlock	d	22p55							06 20														07 35		
Matlock Bath	d	22p57							06 22														07 37		
Cromford	d	23p00							06 25														07 40		
Whatstandwell	d	23p05							06 30														07 45		
Ambergate	d	23p10							06 36														07 50		
Belper	d	23p17							06 43														07 58		
Duffield	d	23p21							06 47														08 02		
Derby	a	23p29							06 56														08 10		
	d	23p31		23p59		05 17	06 24	06 32				07 01	07 10	07 26	07 33	07 40		07 53	08 10	08 16			08 20	08 39	
Spondon	d						06 29						07 18			07 45							08 25		
Long Eaton	d	23p41				05a27	06 36	06a42					07 25	07a36	07 42	07 49		08 03	08 19	08a26			08 32		
Attenborough	d	23p48					06 44			07 13			07 31		07 52			08 13					08 39		
Beeston	d	23p51	00 05		00 41		06 47			07 16			07 35		07 55	07 58	08 06	08 16	08 27			08 31	08 42		09 02
Nottingham	a	00 02	00 12	00 18	00 48		06 57			07 27		07 29	07 41		08 05	08 08	08 15	08 26	08 33			08 40	08 50	09 05	09 13

		EM	XC	EM	EM	XC		EM	EM	XC	EM	EM	XC	EM	EM	XC		EM	EM	XC	EM	EM	XC	EM	EM
		◇1 ☕	1		◇1 ☕	◇1			◇1 ☕	1		◇1 ☕	◇1		◇1 ☕	1			◇1 ☕	◇1		◇1 ☕	1		◇1 ☕
Matlock	d			08 35							09 35							10 35						11 35	
Matlock Bath	d			08 37							09 37							10 37						11 37	
Cromford	d			08 40							09 40							10 40						11 40	
Whatstandwell	d			08 45							09 45							10 45						11 45	
Ambergate	d			08 50							09 50							10 50						11 50	
Belper	d			08 58							09 58							10 58						11 58	
Duffield	d			09 02							10 02							11 02						12 02	
Derby	a			09 10							10 10							11 10						12 10	
	d		09 10	09 24	09 20	09 39				10 10	10 24	10 20	10 40			11 10		11 24	11 20	11 39			12 10	12 24	12 20
Spondon	d																								
Long Eaton	d		09 19	09 33	09a30					10 19	10 33	10a30				11 19		11 33	11a30				12 19	12 33	12a30
Attenborough	d		09 26	09 40							10 40							11 40						12 40	
Beeston	d	09 17	09 29	09 43				10 02	10 17	10 27	10 43			11 02	11 17	11 27		11 43			12 02	12 17	12 27	12 43	
Nottingham	a	09 26	09 35	09 53		10 05		10 13	10 26	10 33	10 53		11 04	11 14	11 26	11 33		11 53		12 05	12 13	12 26	12 33	12 53	

		XC		EM	EM	XC	EM	EM	XC	EM	EM	XC		EM	EM	XC	EM	EM	XC	EM	EM	XC		EM	EM
		◇1			◇1 ☕	1		◇1 ☕	◇1		◇1 ☕	1			◇1 ☕	◇1		◇1 ☕	1		◇1 ☕	◇1			◇1 ☕
Matlock	d						12 35							13 35						14 35					
Matlock Bath	d						12 37							13 37						14 37					
Cromford	d						12 40							13 40						14 40					
Whatstandwell	d						12 45							13 45						14 45					
Ambergate	d						12 50							13 50						14 50					
Belper	d						12 58							13 58						14 58					
Duffield	d						13 02							14 02						15 02					
Derby	a						13 10							14 10						15 10					
	d	12 40				13 10	13 24	13 20	13 39			14 10		14 24	14 20	14 39			15 10	15 24	15 20	15 39			
Spondon	d																								
Long Eaton	d					13 19	13 33	13a30				14 19		14 33	14a30				15 19	15 33	15a30				
Attenborough	d						13 40							14 40						15 40					
Beeston	d			13 07	13 17	13 27	13 43			14 02	14 16	14 29		14 43			15 02	15 17	15 27	15 43				16 02	16 17
Nottingham	a	13 05		13 14	13 26	13 33	13 53		14 05	14 13	14 26	14 35		14 53		15 05	15 13	15 26	15 33	15 53		16 05		16 13	16 26

		XC	EM	EM	XC	EM	EM	XC		EM	EM	XC	EM	EM	EM	XC	EM	EM		XC	EM	EM	EM	XC	EM
		1		◇1 ☕	◇1		◇1 ☕	1			◇1 ☕	◇1			◇1 ☕	1		◇1 ☕		◇1	◇1 ☕		◇1 ☕	1	
Matlock	d		15 35							16 35							17 35								18 35
Matlock Bath	d		15 37							16 37							17 37								18 37
Cromford	d		15 40							16 40							17 40								18 40
Whatstandwell	d		15 45							16 45							17 45								18 45
Ambergate	d		15 50							16 50							17 50								18 50
Belper	d		15 58							16 58							17 58								18 58
Duffield	d		16 02							17 02							18 02								19 02
Derby	a		16 10							17 10							18 10								19 10
	d	16 10	16 24	16 18	16 39			17 10		17 24	17 18	17 39		17 47		18 10	18 24	18 18		18 39				19 10	19 24
Spondon	d									17 29				17 53											
Long Eaton	d	16 19	16 33	16a28				17 19		17 36	17a28			18 01		18 19	18 33	18a28						19 19	19 33
Attenborough	d		16 40							17 43				18 09			18 40								19 40
Beeston	d	16 27	16 43			17 02	17 17	17 27		17 46			18 02	18 12	18 18	18 27	18 43				19 03	19 07	19 19	19 27	19 43
Nottingham	a	16 33	16 54		17 05	17 13	17 26	17 33		17 54		18 05	18 13	18 22	18 30	18 33	18 54			19 05	19 10	19 15	19 27	19 35	19 53

		EM	XC	EM		EM	XC	EM	XC	EM	EM	EM	XC	EM		EM	EM	XC	EM	XC					
		◇1 ☕	◇1			◇1 ☕	1		◇1		◇1 ☕		◇1				◇1 ☕	◇1		1					
Matlock	d							19 35				20 35		21 35					22 55						
Matlock Bath	d							19 37				20 37		21 37					22 57						
Cromford	d							19 40				20 40		21 40					23 00						
Whatstandwell	d							19 45				20 45		21 45					23 05						
Ambergate	d							19 50				20 50		21 50					23 10						
Belper	d							19 58				20 58		21 58					23 17						
Duffield	d							20 02				21 02		22 02					23 21						
Derby	a							20 10				21 10		22 11					23 29						
	d	19 18	19 39				20 10	20 24	20 40			21 24	21 40					22 59	23 31	23 59					
Spondon	d												21 45					23 04							
Long Eaton	d	19a28					20 19	20 33	20 49			21 33	21 52					23 11	23 41						
Attenborough	d							20 40				21 40	21 58					23 17	23 48						
Beeston	d			20 07		20 18	20 27	20 43	20 59	21 03	21 19	21 43	22 02			22 07	22 17	23 20	23 51						
Nottingham	a		20 03	20 20		20 28	20 35	20 53	21 06	21 15	21 29	21 54	22 08			22 16	22 27	23 27	00 02	00 18					

For connections to St Pancras International please refer to Table 53

Table 56

Saturdays until 25 September

Matlock - Derby - Nottingham

		EM	EM ◇1 ☕	XC 1	EM ◇1 ☕	EM ◇1 ☕	EM	EM	EM	XC 1		EM ◇1 ☕	EM	XC 1	EM	EM A	XC 1	EM ◇1 ⊠	EM ◇1 ☕	EM		XC 1	EM	EM ◇1 ☕	XC 1
Matlock	d	22p55						06 21												07 36					
Matlock Bath	d	22p57						06 23												07 38					
Cromford	d	23p00						06 26												07 41					
Whatstandwell	d	23p05						06 31												07 46					
Ambergate	d	23p10						06 37												07 51					
Belper	d	23p17						06 43												07 58					
Duffield	d	23p21						06 47												08 02					
Derby	a	23p29						06 55												08 10					
	d	23p31		23p59	05 25	06 18	06 24			07 10		07 18	07 33	07 39		07 53	08 09	08 18		08 24		08 39			09 10
Spondon	d						06 29			07 15				07 44						08 29					
Long Eaton	d	23p41			05a35	06a28	06 35			07 22		07a28	07 42	07 52		08 03	08 19	08a28		08 36					09 19
Attenborough	d	23p48					06 43		07 12	07 28			07 51							08 43					09 26
Beeston	d	23p51	00 05				06 46		07 15	07 32			07 54	07 59	08 04	08 12	08 27		08 31	08 46			09 05	09 17	09 29
Nottingham	a	00 02	00 12	00 18			06 57		07 24	07 38			08 05	08 08	08 13	08 19	08 34		08 42	08 53		09 05	09 14	09 26	09 35

		EM	EM ◇1 ☕	XC ◇1	EM	EM ◇1 ☕		XC 1	EM	EM ◇1 ☕	XC ◇1	EM	EM ◇1 ☕	XC 1	EM	EM ◇1 ☕		XC ◇1	EM	EM ◇1 ☕	XC 1	EM	EM ◇1 ☕	XC ◇1	EM
Matlock	d	08 36							09 36						10 36							11 36			
Matlock Bath	d	08 38							09 38						10 38							11 38			
Cromford	d	08 41							09 41						10 41							11 41			
Whatstandwell	d	08 46							09 46						10 46							11 46			
Ambergate	d	08 51							09 51						10 51							11 51			
Belper	d	08 58							09 58						10 58							11 58			
Duffield	d	09 02							10 02						11 02							12 02			
Derby	a	09 10							10 10						11 10							12 10			
	d	09 24	09 20	09 39				10 09	10 24	10 20	10 39			11 09	11 24	11 20		11 39			12 09	12 24	12 20	12 39	
Spondon	d																								
Long Eaton	d	09 33	09a30					10 19	10 33	10a30				11 19	11 33	11a30					12 19	12 33	12a30		
Attenborough	d	09 40							10 40						11 40							12 40			
Beeston	d	09 43			10 02	10 17		10 27	10 43			11 02	11 17	11 27	11 43				12 02	12 16	12 27	12 43			13 02
Nottingham	a	09 53		10 05	10 13	10 26		10 33	10 53		11 05	11 13	11 26	11 33	11 53			12 05	12 13	12 26	12 33	12 53		13 05	13 13

		EM ◇1 ☕		XC 1	EM	EM ◇1 ☕	XC ◇1	EM	EM ◇1 ☕	XC 1	EM	EM ◇1 ☕		XC ◇1	EM	EM ◇1 ☕	XC 1	EM	EM ◇1 ☕	XC ◇1	EM	EM ◇1 ☕		XC 1	EM
Matlock	d				12 36						13 36							14 36							15 36
Matlock Bath	d				12 38						13 38							14 38							15 38
Cromford	d				12 41						13 41							14 41							15 41
Whatstandwell	d				12 46						13 46							14 46							15 46
Ambergate	d				12 51						13 51							14 51							15 51
Belper	d				12 58						13 58							14 58							15 58
Duffield	d				13 02						14 02							15 02							16 02
Derby	a				13 10						14 10							15 10							16 12
	d			13 09	13 24	13 20	13 39			14 10	14 24	14 20		14 39			15 09	15 24	15 20	15 39				16 09	16 24
Spondon	d																								
Long Eaton	d			13 19	13 33	13a30				14 19	14 33	14a30					15 19	15 33	15a30					16 19	16 33
Attenborough	d				13 40						14 40							15 40							16 40
Beeston	d	13 16		13 29	13 43			14 02	14 17	14 27	14 43				15 02	15 17	15 27	15 43			16 02	16 17		16 27	16 43
Nottingham	a	13 27		13 35	13 53		14 06	14 13	14 26	14 33	14 53			15 05	15 13	15 26	15 33	15 53		16 05	16 13	16 26		16 33	16 53

		EM ◇1 ☕	XC ◇1	EM	EM ◇1 ☕	XC 1	EM	EM ◇1 ☕		XC ◇1	EM	EM ◇1 ☕	XC 1	EM	EM ◇1 ☕	XC ◇1	EM	EM ◇1 ☕		XC 1	EM	EM ◇1 ☕	XC ◇1	EM	EM ◇1 ☕
Matlock	d						16 36							17 36							18 36				
Matlock Bath	d						16 38							17 38							18 38				
Cromford	d						16 41							17 41							18 41				
Whatstandwell	d						16 46							17 46							18 46				
Ambergate	d						16 51							17 51							18 51				
Belper	d						16 58							17 58							18 58				
Duffield	d						17 02							18 02							19 02				
Derby	a						17 10							18 10							19 12				
	d	16 20	16 39			17 09	17 24	17 18		17 39			18 09	18 24	18 18	18 39				19 09	19 24	19 21	19 39		
Spondon	d						17 29																		
Long Eaton	d	16a30				17 19	17 36	17a28					18 19	18 33	18a28					19 19	19 33	19a31			
Attenborough	d						17 43							18 40							19 40				
Beeston	d			17 02	17 17	17 27	17 46				18 02	18 16	18 27	18 43			19 02	19 17		19 27	19 43			20 05	20 16
Nottingham	a		17 05	17 13	17 26	17 33	17 53			18 05	18 12	18 26	18 33	18 53		19 05	19 14	19 26		19 33	19 53		20 05	20 15	20 26

A from 17 July until 4 September

For connections to St Pancras International please refer to Table 53

Table 56

Saturdays until 25 September

Matlock - Derby - Nottingham

		XC 1	EM	XC ◇1			EM	EM ◇1 ☕	EM	XC ◇1	EM	EM	EM ◇1 B ☕	EM ◇1 A ☕		XC ◇1	EM
Matlock	d		19 36						20 36		21 38						22 55
Matlock Bath	d		19 38						20 38		21 40						22 57
Cromford	d		19 41						20 41		21 43						23 00
Whatstandwell	d		19 46						20 46		21 48						23 05
Ambergate	d		19 51						20 51		21 54						23 11
Belper	d		19 58						20 58		22 00						23 17
Duffield	d		20 02						21 02		22 04						23 21
Derby	a		20 10						21 10		22 12						23 29
	d	20 09	20 24	20 39					21 24	21 40						23 00	23 31
Spondon	d									21 45						23 05	
Long Eaton	d	20 19	20 33	20 49					21 33	21 52						23 12	23 41
Attenborough	d		20 40						21 40	21 58						23 18	23 48
Beeston	d	20 27	20 43	20 57			21 05	21 17	21 43	22 02		22 06	22 18	22 21		23 22	23 52
Nottingham	a	20 35	20 53	21 04			21 15	21 26	21 53	22 08		22 14	22 27	22 30		23 28	23 57

Saturdays from 02 October

		EM	EM ◇1 ☕	XC 1	EM ◇1 ☕	EM ◇1 ☕	EM	EM	EM	XC 1		EM ◇1 ☕	EM	XC 1	EM	XC 1	EM ◇1 ⊠	EM ◇1 ☕	EM	XC 1		EM	EM ◇1 ☕	XC 1	EM
Matlock	d	22p55						06 20											07 35						08 35
Matlock Bath	d	22p57						06 22											07 37						08 37
Cromford	d	23p00						06 25											07 40						08 40
Whatstandwell	d	23p05						06 30											07 45						08 45
Ambergate	d	23p10						06 36											07 50						08 50
Belper	d	23p17						06 43											07 58						08 58
Duffield	d	23p21						06 47											08 02						09 02
Derby	a	23p29						06 55											08 10						09 10
	d	23p31		23p59	05 25	06 18	06 24			07 10		07 18	07 33	07 39		08 09	08 18		08 24	08 39				09 10	09 24
Spondon	d						06 29			07 15				07 44					08 29						
Long Eaton	d	23p41			05a35	06a28	06 35			07 22		07a28	07 42	07 52		08 19	08a28		08 36					09 19	09 33
Attenborough	d	23p48					06 43		07 12	07 28			07 51						08 43					09 26	09 40
Beeston	d	23p51	00 05				06 46		07 15	07 32			07 54	07 59	08 04	08 27		08 31	08 46			09 05	09 17	09 29	09 43
Nottingham	a	00 02	00 12	00 18			06 57		07 24	07 38			08 05	08 08	08 13	08 34		08 42	08 53	09 05		09 14	09 26	09 35	09 53

		EM ◇1 ☕	XC ◇1	EM	EM ◇1 ☕	XC 1		EM	EM ◇1 ☕	XC ◇1	EM	EM ◇1 ☕	XC 1	EM	EM ◇1 ☕	XC ◇1		EM	EM ◇1 ☕	XC 1	EM	EM ◇1 ☕	XC ◇1	EM	EM ◇1 ☕
Matlock	d							09 35						10 35							11 35				
Matlock Bath	d							09 37						10 37							11 37				
Cromford	d							09 40						10 40							11 40				
Whatstandwell	d							09 45						10 45							11 45				
Ambergate	d							09 50						10 50							11 50				
Belper	d							09 58						10 58							11 58				
Duffield	d							10 02						11 02							12 02				
Derby	a							10 10						11 10							12 10				
	d	09 20	09 39			10 09		10 24	10 20	10 39			11 09	11 24	11 20	11 39				12 09	12 24	12 20	12 39		
Spondon	d																								
Long Eaton	d	09a30				10 19		10 33	10a30				11 19	11 33	11a30					12 19	12 33	12a30			
Attenborough	d							10 40						11 40							12 40				
Beeston	d			10 02	10 17	10 27		10 43			11 02	11 17	11 27	11 43				12 02	12 16	12 27	12 43			13 02	13 16
Nottingham	a		10 05	10 13	10 26	10 33		10 53		11 05	11 13	11 26	11 33	11 53		12 05		12 13	12 26	12 33	12 53		13 05	13 13	13 27

		XC 1		EM	EM ◇1 ☕	XC ◇1	EM	EM ◇1 ☕	XC 1	EM	EM ◇1 ☕	XC ◇1		EM	EM ◇1 ☕	XC 1	EM	EM ◇1 ☕	XC ◇1	EM	EM ◇1 ☕	XC 1		EM	EM ◇1 ☕
Matlock	d			12 35						13 35							14 35							15 35	
Matlock Bath	d			12 37						13 37							14 37							15 37	
Cromford	d			12 40						13 40							14 40							15 40	
Whatstandwell	d			12 45						13 45							14 45							15 45	
Ambergate	d			12 50						13 50							14 50							15 50	
Belper	d			12 58						13 58							14 58							15 58	
Duffield	d			13 02						14 02							15 02							16 02	
Derby	a			13 10						14 10							15 10							16 12	
	d	13 09		13 24	13 20	13 39			14 10	14 24	14 20	14 39				15 09	15 24	15 20	15 39			16 09		16 24	16 20
Spondon	d																								
Long Eaton	d	13 19		13 33	13a30				14 19	14 33	14a30					15 19	15 33	15a30				16 19		16 33	16a30
Attenborough	d			13 40						14 40							15 40							16 40	
Beeston	d	13 29		13 43			14 02	14 17	14 27	14 43				15 02	15 17	15 27	15 43			16 02	16 17	16 27		16 43	
Nottingham	a	13 35		13 53		14 06	14 13	14 26	14 33	14 53		15 05		15 13	15 26	15 33	15 53		16 05	16 13	16 26	16 33		16 53	

A until 4 September

B 11 September, 18 September, 25 September

For connections to St Pancras International please refer to Table 53

Table 56

Matlock - Derby - Nottingham

Saturdays from 02 October

		XC ◇1	EM	EM ◇1 ☕	XC 1	EM	EM ◇1 ☕	XC ◇1	EM	EM ◇1 ☕	XC 1	EM	EM ◇1 ☕	XC ◇1	EM	EM ◇1 ☕	XC 1	EM	EM ◇1 ☕	XC ◇1	EM	EM ◇1 ☕	XC 1
Matlock	d					16 35						17 35						18 35					
Matlock Bath	d					16 37						17 37						18 37					
Cromford	d					16 40						17 40						18 40					
Whatstandwell	d					16 45						17 45						18 45					
Ambergate	d					16 50						17 50						18 50					
Belper	d					16 58						17 58						18 58					
Duffield	d					17 02						18 02						19 02					
Derby 6	a					17 10						18 10						19 12					
	d	16 39			17 09	17 24	17 18	17 39			18 09	18 24	18 18	18 39			19 09	19 24	19 21	19 39			20 09
Spondon	d					17 29																	
Long Eaton	d				17 19	17 36	17a28				18 19	18 33	18a28				19 19	19 33	19a31				20 19
Attenborough	d					17 43						18 40						19 40					
Beeston	d		17 02	17 17	17 27	17 46			18 02	18 16	18 27	18 43			19 02	19 17	19 27	19 43			20 05	20 16	20 27
Nottingham 8	a	17 05	17 13	17 26	17 33	17 53		18 05	18 12	18 26	18 33	18 54		19 05	19 14	19 26	19 33	19 53		20 05	20 15	20 26	20 35

		EM	XC ◇1	EM	EM ◇1 ☕	EM	XC ◇1	EM	EM	EM ◇1 ☕	XC ◇1	EM
Matlock	d	19 35				20 35		21 37				22 55
Matlock Bath	d	19 37				20 37		21 39				22 57
Cromford	d	19 40				20 40		21 42				23 00
Whatstandwell	d	19 45				20 45		21 47				23 05
Ambergate	d	19 50				20 50		21 53				23 11
Belper	d	19 58				20 58		22 00				23 17
Duffield	d	20 02				21 02		22 04				23 21
Derby 6	a	20 10				21 10		22 12				23 29
	d	20 24	20 39			21 24	21 40				23 00	23 31
Spondon	d						21 45				23 05	
Long Eaton	d	20 33	20 49			21 33	21 52				23 12	23 41
Attenborough	d	20 40				21 40	21 58				23 18	23 48
Beeston	d	20 43	20 57	21 05	21 17	21 43	22 02		22 06	22 18	23 22	23 52
Nottingham 8	a	20 53	21 04	21 15	21 26	21 53	22 08		22 14	22 27	23 28	23 57

Sundays until 11 July

		EM ◇1 ☕	EM	EM ◇1 ☕	EM	EM ◇1 ☕	EM ◇1 ☕	EM ◇1 ☕	EM	XC ◇1	EM ◇1 ☕	EM ◇1 ☕	EM	XC ◇1	EM ◇1 ☕	EM ◇1 ☕	XC ◇1	EM ◇1 ☕	EM ◇1 ☕	EM	XC ◇1	EM ◇1 ☕	EM
Matlock	d								10 42				12 38							14 39			
Matlock Bath	d								10 44				12 40							14 41			
Cromford	d								10 47				12 43							14 44			
Whatstandwell	d								10 52				12 48							14 49			
Ambergate	d								10 57				12 53							14 53			
Belper	d								11 04				13 00							15 00			
Duffield	d								11 08				13 04							15 04			
Derby 6	a								11 16				13 12							15 12			
	d		08 18	08 42	09 18	09 48	10 48		11 19	12 38	12 55		13 25	13 41	13 54		14 41	14 49		15 15	15 44		16 30
Spondon	d																						
Long Eaton	d		08 28	08a52	09 28	09a58	10a58		11 29		13a05		13 35		14a05			15a03		15 25			16 39
Attenborough	d		08 35		09 34				11 36				13 42							15 32			16 46
Beeston	d	00 06	08 39		09 37			11 19	11 39			13 15	13 45			14 18			15 13	15 35		16 06	16 49
Nottingham 8	a	00 15	08 48		09 44			11 26	11 46	13 02		13 23	13 53	14 02		14 25	15 07		15 20	15 40	16 08	16 12	16 56

		XC ◇1	EM ◇1 ☕	EM	XC ◇1	EM ◇1 ☕	EM ◇1 ☕	EM	XC ◇1	EM ◇1 ☕	EM ◇1 ☕	EM	XC ◇1	EM ◇1 ☕	EM ◇1 ☕	EM	XC ◇1	EM ◇1 ☕	EM	EM ◇1 ☕	EM	EM	EM ◇1 ☕
Matlock	d			16 38								18 39							20 39			22 44	
Matlock Bath	d			16 40								18 41							20 41			22 46	
Cromford	d			16 43								18 44							20 44			22 49	
Whatstandwell	d			16 48								18 49							20 49			22 54	
Ambergate	d			16 53								18 54							20 53			22 59	
Belper	d			17 00								19 01							21 00			23 07	
Duffield	d			17 04								19 05							21 04			23 11	
Derby 6	a			17 12								19 13							21 12			23 20	
	d	16 41	16 47	17 21	17 43	17 47		18 21	18 41		19 09	19 21	19 37		20 06	20 29	20 37		21 21		22 30		
Spondon	d																						
Long Eaton	d		16a57	17 31		17a57		18 30			19a20	19 31			20a16	20 38			21 31		22 40		
Attenborough	d			17 38				18 38				19 38				20 47			21 38		22 46		
Beeston	d			17 41			18 06	18 41		19 01		19 41		20 02		20 50		21 03	21 41	22 04	22 49		23 11
Nottingham 8	a	17 03		17 47	18 02		18 14	18 48	19 04	19 07		19 47	19 56	20 08		20 56	21 01	21 12	21 47	22 11	22 57		23 18

For connections to St Pancras International please refer to Table 53

Table 56

Matlock - Derby - Nottingham

Sundays 18 July to 05 September

		EM ◇1 ☕	EM	EM ◇1 ☕	EM	EM ◇1 ☕	EM ◇1 ☕	EM ◇1 ☕	EM	XC ◇1	EM ◇1 ☕	EM ◇1 ☕	EM	XC ◇1	EM ◇1 ☕	EM ◇1 ☕	XC ◇1	EM ◇1 ☕	EM ◇1 ☕	EM	XC ◇1	EM ◇1 ☕	EM
Matlock	d								10 42				12 38							14 39			
Matlock Bath	d								10 44				12 40							14 41			
Cromford	d								10 47				12 43							14 44			
Whatstandwell	d								10 52				12 48							14 49			
Ambergate	d								10 57				12 53							14 53			
Belper	d								11 04				13 00							15 00			
Duffield	d								11 08				13 04							15 04			
Derby 6	a								11 16				13 12							15 12			
	d		08 18	08 47	09 18	09 51	10 51		11 19	12 38	12 58		13 25	13 41	13 54		14 41	14 49		15 15	15 44		16 29
Spondon	d																						
Long Eaton	d		08 28	08a58	09 28	10a01	11a01		11 29		13a08		13 35		14a04			15a02		15 25			16 38
Attenborough	d		08 35		09 34				11 36				13 42							15 32			16 45
Beeston	d	00 09	08 39		09 37			11 25	11 39			13 19	13 45			14 19			15 22	15 35		16 06	16 48
Nottingham 8	a	00 17	08 48		09 44			11 34	11 46	13 02		13 26	13 53	14 02		14 29	15 07		15 29	15 40	16 08	16 12	16 55

		XC ◇1	EM ◇1 ☕	EM	XC ◇1	EM ◇1 ☕	EM ◇1 ☕	EM	XC ◇1	EM ◇1 ☕	EM ◇1 ☕	EM	XC ◇1	EM ◇1 ☕	EM ◇1 ☕	EM	XC ◇1	EM ◇1 ☕	EM	EM ◇1 ☕	EM	EM	EM ◇1 ☕
Matlock	d			16 38								18 39							20 39			22 44	
Matlock Bath	d			16 40								18 41							20 41			22 46	
Cromford	d			16 43								18 44							20 44			22 49	
Whatstandwell	d			16 48								18 49							20 49			22 54	
Ambergate	d			16 53								18 54							20 53			22 59	
Belper	d			17 00								19 01							21 00			23 07	
Duffield	d			17 04								19 05							21 04			23 11	
Derby 6	a			17 12								19 13							21 12			23 20	
	d	16 41	16 47	17 21	17 42	17 46		18 21	18 41		19 09	19 21	19 37		20 05	20 29	20 37		21 21		22 30		
Spondon	d																						
Long Eaton	d		16a57	17 31		17a56		18 30			19a20	19 31			20a16	20 38			21 31		22 40		
Attenborough	d			17 38				18 38				19 38				20 47			21 38		22 46		
Beeston	d			17 41			18 06	18 41		19 03		19 41		20 02		20 50		21 03	21 41	22 04	22 49		23 11
Nottingham 8	a	17 03		17 47	18 02		18 14	18 48	19 04	19 09		19 47	19 56	20 08		20 56	21 01	21 12	21 47	22 11	22 57		23 18

Sundays from 12 September

		EM ◇1 ☕	EM ◇1 ☕	EM	EM ◇1 ☕	EM ◇1 ☕	EM ◇1 ☕	EM	XC ◇1	EM ◇1 ☕	EM ◇1 ☕	EM	XC ◇1	EM ◇1 ☕	EM ◇1 ☕	XC ◇1	EM ◇1 ☕	EM ◇1 ☕	EM	XC ◇1	EM ◇1 ☕	EM	XC ◇1
Matlock	d							10 42				12 38							14 39				
Matlock Bath	d							10 44				12 40							14 41				
Cromford	d							10 47				12 43							14 44				
Whatstandwell	d							10 52				12 48							14 49				
Ambergate	d							10 57				12 53							14 53				
Belper	d							11 04				13 00							15 00				
Duffield	d							11 08				13 04							15 04				
Derby 6	a							11 16				13 12							15 12				
	d		08 47	09 18	09 51	10 52		11 19	12 38	13 02		13 25	13 41	13 54		14 41	14 49		15 15	15 44		16 30	16 41
Spondon	d																						
Long Eaton	d		08a58	09 28	10a01	11a02		11 29		13a12		13 35		14a05			15a03		15 25			16 39	
Attenborough	d			09 34				11 36				13 42							15 32			16 46	
Beeston	d	00 02		09 37			11 14	11 39			13 11	13 45			14 14			15 13	15 35		16 06	16 49	
Nottingham 8	a	00 11		09 44			11 22	11 46	13 02		13 19	13 53	14 04		14 22	15 07		15 21	15 40	16 08	16 12	16 56	17 03

		EM ◇1 ☕	EM	XC ◇1	EM ◇1 ☕	EM ◇1 ☕	EM	XC ◇1	EM ◇1 ☕	EM ◇1 ☕	EM	XC ◇1	EM ◇1 ☕	EM ◇1 ☕	EM	XC ◇1	EM ◇1 ☕	EM	EM ◇1 ☕	EM	EM	EM ◇1 ☕
Matlock	d		16 38								18 39							20 39			22 44	
Matlock Bath	d		16 40								18 41							20 41			22 46	
Cromford	d		16 43								18 44							20 44			22 49	
Whatstandwell	d		16 48								18 49							20 49			22 54	
Ambergate	d		16 53								18 54							20 53			22 59	
Belper	d		17 00								19 01							21 00			23 07	
Duffield	d		17 04								19 05							21 04			23 11	
Derby 6	a		17 12								19 13							21 12			23 20	
	d	16 47	17 21	17 43	17 47		18 21	18 41		19 09	19 21	19 37		20 06	20 29	20 37		21 21		22 30		
Spondon	d																					
Long Eaton	d	16a57	17 31		17a57		18 30			19a20	19 31			20a16	20 38			21 31		22 40		
Attenborough	d		17 38				18 38				19 38				20 47			21 38		22 46		
Beeston	d		17 41			18 06	18 41		19 02		19 41		20 02		20 50		21 03	21 41	22 04	22 49		23 11
Nottingham 8	a		17 47	18 02		18 14	18 48	19 04	19 07		19 47	19 56	20 08		20 56	21 01	21 12	21 47	22 11	22 57		23 18

Table 57

Nottingham, Derby and Leicester - Birmingham - Cardiff and Bristol

		XC MO	AW	GW	XC	GW	GW	XC	GW	XC	GW	AW	XC	XC	XC	XC	XC	XC	XC	XC	GW
Nottingham	d														06 00				06 37		
Beeston	d														06 06				06 43		
Attenborough	d														06 10						
Long Eaton	d														06 17						
Derby	a														06 30				07 01		
	d												06 10		06 36	06 48			07 06		
Willington	d																				
Burton-on-Trent	d												06 20		06 48	06 58			07 18		
Tamworth	d												06 31		07 00	07 09			07 30		
Wilnecote	d														07 04						
Leicester	d	23p19												06 16				06 43		07 10	
South Wigston	d	23p25												06 22				06 49			
Narborough	d	23p29												06 27				06 54			
Hinckley	d	23p38												06 35				07 02			
Nuneaton	d	23p46												06 42				07 10		07 30	
Coleshill Parkway	d	00 02												06 59				07 26		07 46	
Water Orton	d																	07 30			
Birmingham New Street	a	00 14											06 52	07 15	07 24	07 27	07 31	07 44	07 55	08 00	
	d				05 00			05 42		06 42			07 12		07 30		07 42				
Worcester Shrub Hill	d								06 47												
Ashchurch for Tewkesbury	d							06 34	07 03												
Cheltenham Spa	d		05 37	05 53	06 03	06 23	06 30	06 43	07 13	07 22	07 29	07 45	07 52		08 16		08 25				08 31
Gloucester	a		05 48	06 03	06 16	06 34	06 40	06 53	07 24		07 39	07 57			08 27						08 40
Bristol Parkway	a					07 23			08 19	07 56			08 25				08 56				
Bristol Temple Meads	a					07 40			08 36	08 08			08 40				09 14				
Newport (South Wales)	a		06 41		07 09			07 52				08 50			09 12						
Cardiff Central	a		07 00		07 26			08 08				09 07			09 30						

		AW	XC	XC	XC	XC	XC	XC	XC	GW	GW	XC	XC	XC	XC	XC	XC	XC	GW	AW	XC	XC	XC
Nottingham	d				06 56				07 37					08 08				08 37					09 11
Beeston	d				07 07				07 43									08 43					
Attenborough	d				07 11																		
Long Eaton	d				07 18				07 51									08 51					
Derby	a				07 31				08 02					08 32				09 02					09 31
	d		07 26		07 36	07 50			08 06			08 28		08 36	08 53			09 06			09 28		09 36
Willington	d				07 43																		
Burton-on-Trent	d		07 37		07 49	08 00			08 18			08 38		08 49				09 17			09 38		09 49
Tamworth	d		07 49		08 01	08 11			08 30			08 49		09 01				09 30					10 01
Wilnecote	d				08 05				08 34									09 33					
Leicester	d			07 24				07 49					08 16			08 49						09 16	
South Wigston	d							07 55															
Narborough	d			07 33				08 00					08 25									09 25	
Hinckley	d			07 42				08 08					08 34									09 34	
Nuneaton	d			07 50				08 17					08 41			09 10						09 42	
Coleshill Parkway	d			08 05				08 32					08 57			09 25						09 57	
Water Orton	d			08 09																		10 01	
Birmingham New Street	a		08 09	08 19	08 24	08 29		08 45	08 54			09 09	09 15	09 24	09 27	09 38		09 54			10 07	10 14	10 24
	d		08 12		08 30		08 42					09 12		09 30			09 42				10 12		10 30
Worcester Shrub Hill	d									08 57													
Ashchurch for Tewkesbury	d									09 21													
Cheltenham Spa	d	08 45	08 52		09 11		09 25			09 31	09 40	09 52		10 11			10 25		10 31	10 45	10 52		11 11
Gloucester	a	08 57			09 22					09 42	09 51			10 22					10 40	10 57			11 22
Bristol Parkway	a		09 24				09 56			10 22		10 26					10 56				11 26		
Bristol Temple Meads	a		09 39				10 08			10 38		10 41					11 12				11 38		
Newport (South Wales)	a	09 50			10 09									11 11						11 50			12 09
Cardiff Central	a	10 07			10 25									11 27						12 07			12 27

Table 57

Nottingham, Derby and Leicester - Birmingham - Cardiff and Bristol

		XC	XC	XC	XC	GW	GW	AW	XC	XC	XC	XC	XC	XC	XC	GW	XC	XC	XC	XC	XC	XC
Nottingham	d				09 37						10 11				10 37				11 08			
Beeston	d				09 43										10 43							
Attenborough	d																					
Long Eaton	d				09 51										10 51							
Derby	a				10 02						10 33				11 02				11 31			
	d	09 53			10 06				10 28		10 37	10 53			11 06		11 28		11 36	11 53		
Willington	d																					
Burton-on-Trent	d				10 18						10 49				11 17				11 49			
Tamworth	d				10 30				10 48		11 01				11 30				12 01			
Wilnecote	d				10 34										11 33							
Leicester	d		09 49							10 16			10 49					11 16			11 49	
South Wigston	d									10 22												
Narborough	d									10 27								11 25				
Hinckley	d									10 35								11 34				
Nuneaton	d		10 10							10 42			11 10					11 42			12 10	
Coleshill Parkway	d		10 25							10 59			11 25					11 57			12 25	
Water Orton	d																	12 01				
Birmingham New Street	a	10 27	10 38		10 54				11 09	11 14	11 24	11 27	11 38		11 54		12 07	12 14	12 24	12 27	12 39	
	d			10 42					11 12		11 30			11 42			12 12		12 30			12 42
Worcester Shrub Hill	d					11 06																
Ashchurch for Tewkesbury	d					11 21																
Cheltenham Spa	d			11 25		11 31	11 40	11 45	11 52		12 11			12 25		12 31	12 52		13 11			13 25
Gloucester	a					11 42	11 51	11 57			12 22					12 40			13 22			
Bristol Parkway	a			11 56		12 22			12 28					12 56			13 24					13 57
Bristol Temple Meads	a			12 08		12 35			12 41					13 10			13 39					14 09
Newport (South Wales)	a							12 50			13 11								14 09			
Cardiff Central	a							13 07			13 29								14 27			

		XC	GW	GW	AW	XC	XC	XC	XC	XC	XC	XC	GW	AW	XC	XC	XC	XC	XC	XC	XC	GW	GW
Nottingham	d	11 37						12 08				12 37					13 11				13 37		
Beeston	d	11 43										12 43									13 43		
Attenborough	d																						
Long Eaton	d	11 51										12 51									13 51		
Derby	a	12 02						12 33				13 02					13 31				14 02		
	d	12 06				12 28		12 37	12 53			13 06			13 28		13 36	13 53			14 06		
Willington	d											13 14											
Burton-on-Trent	d	12 18						12 49				13 20			13 38		13 49				14 18		
Tamworth	d	12 30				12 48		13 01				13 32					14 01				14 30		
Wilnecote	d	12 34																			14 34		
Leicester	d						12 16			12 49						13 16				13 49			
South Wigston	d						12 22																
Narborough	d						12 27									13 25							
Hinckley	d						12 35									13 34							
Nuneaton	d						12 42			13 10						13 42				14 10			
Coleshill Parkway	d						12 59			13 25						13 57				14 25			
Water Orton	d															14 01							
Birmingham New Street	a	12 54				13 09	13 14	13 24	13 27	13 39		13 54			14 07	14 14	14 24	14 27		14 44	14 54		
	d					13 12		13 30			13 42				14 12		14 30		14 42				
Worcester Shrub Hill	d		13 06																			15 06	
Ashchurch for Tewkesbury	d		13 21																			15 21	
Cheltenham Spa	d		13 31	13 40	13 45	13 56		14 11			14 25		14 31	14 45	14 52		15 11		15 25			15 31	15 40
Gloucester	a		13 42	13 51	13 57			14 22					14 40	14 56			15 22					15 42	15 51
Bristol Parkway	a		14 22			14 27					14 56				15 24				15 56			16 22	
Bristol Temple Meads	a		14 38			14 41					15 10				15 40				16 08			16 38	
Newport (South Wales)	a				14 50			15 12						15 50			16 10						
Cardiff Central	a				15 07			15 29						16 10			16 29						

Table 57

Mondays to Fridays

Nottingham, Derby and Leicester - Birmingham - Cardiff and Bristol

Station		XC	XC	XC	XC	XC	XC	XC	GW	AW	XC	XC	XC	XC	XC	XC	XC	GW	GW	AW	XC	XC
		◇1 🛒	1	◇1 🛒	◇1 🛒	◇1 🛒	◇1 🛒	1	◇1 🍴		◇1 🛒	1	◇1 🛒	◇1 🛒	◇1 🛒	◇1 🛒	1				◇1 🛒	1
Nottingham 8	d			14 08				14 37					15 11				15 37					
Beeston	d							14 43									15 43					
Attenborough	d																					
Long Eaton	d							14 51									15 51					
Derby 6	a			14 31				15 02					15 31				16 02					
	d	14 28		14 36	14 53			15 06			15 28		15 36	15 53			16 06				16 28	
Willington	d							15 14														
Burton-on-Trent	d			14 49				15 20			15 38		15 49				16 18					
Tamworth	d	14 48		15 01				15 31					16 01				16 30				16 48	
Wilnecote	d																16 34					
Leicester	d		14 16				14 49					15 16			15 49							16 16
South Wigston	d		14 22																			16 22
Narborough	d		14 27									15 25										16 27
Hinckley	d		14 35									15 34										16 35
Nuneaton	d		14 42				15 10					15 42			16 10							16 42
Coleshill Parkway	d		14 59				15 25					15 57			16 25							16 59
Water Orton	d											16 01										
Birmingham New Street 12	a	15 07	15 14	15 24	15 27		15 44	15 54			16 08	16 14	16 24	16 27	16 39		16 54				17 09	17 14
	d	15 12		15 30		15 42					16 12		16 30			16 42					17 12	
Worcester Shrub Hill 7	d																		17 06			
Ashchurch for Tewkesbury	d												17 05						17 21			
Cheltenham Spa	d	15 52		16 11		16 25			16 31	16 45	16 52		17 15			17 25		17 30	17 40	17 45	17 52	
Gloucester 7	a			16 22					16 40	16 56			17 26					17 39	17 50	17 57		
Bristol Parkway 7	a	16 26				16 56					17 24					17 58		18 20			18 27	
Bristol Temple Meads 10	a	16 41				17 11					17 40					18 10		18 37			18 40	
Newport (South Wales)	a			17 11						17 50			18 10							18 51		
Cardiff Central 7	a			17 28						18 10			18 27							19 09		

Station		XC	XC	XC	XC	XC	GW	AW	XC	XC	XC	XC	XC	XC	XC	GW	AW	XC	XC	GW	XC	XC	XC
		◇1 🛒	◇1 🛒	◇1 🛒	◇1 🛒	1	◇1 🍴		◇1 🛒	1	◇1 🛒	◇1 🛒	◇1 A 🛒	◇1 🛒	1			◇1 🛒	1		◇1 🛒	◇1 🛒	◇1 🛒
Nottingham 8	d	16 08				16 37					17 08				17 37						18 08		
Beeston	d					16 43									17 43								
Attenborough	d																						
Long Eaton	d					16 51									17 51								
Derby 6	a	16 31				17 02					17 31				18 02						18 33		
	d	16 36	16 53			17 06			17 28		17 36	17 53			18 05			18 28			18 37	18 53	
Willington	d					17 14									18 14								
Burton-on-Trent	d	16 49				17 20			17 38		17 49				18 20						18 49		
Tamworth	d	17 01				17 31					18 04				18 32			18 48			19 01		
Wilnecote	d														18 36								
Leicester	d			16 49						17 16				17 49					18 16				18 49
South Wigston	d									17 22				17 55					18 25				
Narborough	d									17 27				18 01					18 30				
Hinckley	d									17 35				18 09					18 38				
Nuneaton	d			17 10						17 42				18 17					18 46				19 10
Coleshill Parkway	d			17 25						17 59				18 33					19 02				19 25
Water Orton	d																						
Birmingham New Street 12	a	17 25	17 28	17 38		17 54			18 07	18 14	18 25	18 28		18 45	18 57			19 08	19 14		19 24	19 28	19 39
	d	17 30			17 42				18 12		18 30		18 42					19 12			19 30		
Worcester Shrub Hill 7	d															19 07							
Ashchurch for Tewkesbury	d	18 09														19 21							
Cheltenham Spa	d	18 18			18 25		18 34	18 45	18 52		19 15		19 25			19 31	19 45	19 52		20 00	20 11		
Gloucester 7	a	18 30					18 45	18 56			19 27					19 42	19 56			20 10	20 22		
Bristol Parkway 7	a				18 55				19 27				19 56			20 22		20 27					
Bristol Temple Meads 10	a				19 07				19 39				20 13			20 38		20 41					
Newport (South Wales)	a	19 16						19 50			20 12		20 47				20 51				21 08		
Cardiff Central 7	a	19 33						20 12			20 31		21 02				21 10				21 27		

Table 57

Mondays to Fridays

Nottingham, Derby and Leicester - Birmingham - Cardiff and Bristol

Station		XC	XC	GW	XC	XC	GW	XC FO	XC FX	XC	XC	XC	XC	XC	XC	XC	XC	XC	XC	XC	GW	GW	GW	XC FO
		◇1 🛒	1	1	◇1 🛒	1		◇1 🛒	◇1 🛒	◇1	◇1	◇1 🛒	1	◇1 🛒	1	◇1 🛒	◇1 🛒	1	1			◇1 🍴	◇1
Nottingham 8	d		18 37					19 08	19 08				19 37					20 37					
Beeston	d		18 43										19 43					20 43					
Attenborough	d												19 46										
Long Eaton	d		18 51										19 53					20 51					
Derby 6	a		19 02					19 32	19 32				20 02					21 02					
	d		19 06		19 28			19 37	19 36	19 54			20 05	20 28		20 54		21 06					21 28
Willington	d																	21 14					
Burton-on-Trent	d		19 17		19 38			19 49	19 49				20 17					21 20					21 38
Tamworth	d		19 29					20 01	20 01				20 29	20 48				21 33					21 49
Wilnecote	d		19 32										20 33					21 37					
Leicester	d					19 16						19 49			20 16		20 49		21 16				
South Wigston	d					19 22									20 22				21 22				
Narborough	d					19 27									20 27				21 27				
Hinckley	d					19 35									20 35				21 35				
Nuneaton	d					19 42						20 10			20 42		21 10		21 42				
Coleshill Parkway	d					19 59						20 25			20 59		21 25		21 59				
Water Orton	d																						
Birmingham New Street 12	a		19 54		20 09	20 15		20 24	20 24	20 27		20 43	20 57	21 07	21 15	21 35	21 39	21 58	22 11				22 07
	d	19 42			20 12			20 30	20 30		20 42			21 12									22 12
Worcester Shrub Hill 7	d																				21 31		
Ashchurch for Tewkesbury	d																				21 52		
Cheltenham Spa	d	20 25		20 48	20 52		21 00	21 11	21 11		21 27			21 52						22 00	22 05	22 31	22 52
Gloucester 7	a			20 58			21 11	21 22	21 22					22 02						22 11	22 17	22 41	
Bristol Parkway 7	a	20 56			21 25		21 52				21 57			22 52									23 53
Bristol Temple Meads 10	a	21 08			21 38		22 10				22 14			23 04								00 15	00 16
Newport (South Wales)	a							22 15	22 15														
Cardiff Central 7	a							22 31	22 35														

Station		XC FX	AW FO	AW FX	XC	XC	GW	LM FO	XC	XC	XC	XC
		◇1			◇1 🛒	◇1			1	1	◇1	◇1 🛒
Nottingham 8	d								21 37			
Beeston	d								21 43			
Attenborough	d								21 46			
Long Eaton	d								21 53			
Derby 6	a								22 04			
	d	21 28				22 00			22 10		22 45	
Willington	d											
Burton-on-Trent	d	21 38							22 21		22 55	
Tamworth	d	21 49							22 33		23 06	
Wilnecote	d								22 37			
Leicester	d				21 49					22 27		22 49
South Wigston	d									22 33		
Narborough	d									22 38		
Hinckley	d									22 46		
Nuneaton	d				22 10					22 54		23 10
Coleshill Parkway	d				22 25					23 10		23 25
Water Orton	d											
Birmingham New Street 12	a	22 07			22 45	22 54			23 02	23 23	23 34	23 39
	d	22 12						23 00				
Worcester Shrub Hill 7	d						22 32	23 46				
Ashchurch for Tewkesbury	d						22 51	00 01				
Cheltenham Spa	d	22 52	23 00	23 00			23 05	00 09				
Gloucester 7	a		23 12	23 12			23 18	00 20				
Bristol Parkway 7	a	23 54										
Bristol Temple Meads 10	a	00 17										
Newport (South Wales)	a		00 07	00 07								
Cardiff Central 7	a		00 35	00 36								

Nottingham, Derby and Leicester - Birmingham - Cardiff and Bristol

Station		GW	XC	LM	GW	XC	XC	GW	GW	XC	XC	GW	AW	XC	XC	XC	XC	XC	XC	XC	AW	XC
		◇1	◇1			◇1	◇1			◇1	1	◇1		◇1	◇1	◇1	◇1	1	1	◇1		◇1
		🍴				✕	✕			✕		🍴		✕	✕	✕	✕		✕	✕		✕
Nottingham 8 ⇌	d														05 57				06 37			
Beeston	d														06 03				06 43			
Attenborough	d														06 06							
Long Eaton	d														06 16							
Derby 6	a														06 32				07 01			
	d		21p28											06 10	06 36	06 47			07 06			07 25
Willington	d																					
Burton-on-Trent	d		21p38											06 20	06 48	06 57			07 18			07 36
Tamworth	d		21p49											06 31	07 00	07 08			07 30			07 48
Wilnecote	d														07 04							
Leicester	d										05 49							06 49		07 16		
South Wigston	d										05 55							06 55				
Narborough	d										06 00							07 00				
Hinckley	d										06 08							07 08				
Nuneaton	d										06 15							07 15		07 36		
Coleshill Parkway	d										06 31							07 31		07 52		
Water Orton	d																	07 36				
Birmingham New Street 12	a		22p07								06 43			06 50	07 24	07 27	07 31	07 47	07 55	08 04		08 08
	d		22p12	23p00		05 00	05 42			06 42				07 12	07 30	07 33	07 42					08 12
Worcester Shrub Hill 7	d			23p46					06 47													
Ashchurch for Tewkesbury	d			00 01			06 33		07 03													
Cheltenham Spa	d	22p31	22p52	00 09	05 30	06 04	06 43	06 48	07 13	07 25		07 30	07 45	07 52	08 11		08 25				08 45	08 52
Gloucester 7	a	22p41		00 20	05 40	06 13	06 54	06 58	07 24			07 40	07 57		08 22						08 57	
Bristol Parkway 7	a		23p53					07 39	08 19	07 56				08 24			08 56					09 24
Bristol Temple Meads 10	a	00 15	00 16					07 54	08 36	08 08				08 38			09 08					09 38
Newport (South Wales)	a					07 06	07 52						08 50		09 07						09 50	
Cardiff Central 7	a					07 22	08 08						09 10		09 23						10 07	

Station		GW	XC	XC	XC	XC	XC	XC	GW	XC	XC	GW	XC	XC	XC	XC	XC	XC	AW	XC	XC	XC	GW	XC
		◇1	◇1	◇1	◇1	◇1	◇1	1		◇1	1		◇1	◇1	◇1	◇1	◇1	1		◇1	◇1	1	◇1	◇1
						B	A									B	A			B	A			
		🍴	✕	✕	✕	✕	✕			✕			✕	✕	✕	✕	✕			✕	✕		🍴	✕
Nottingham 8 ⇌	d		06 56					07 34					08 08					08 37						09 08
Beeston	d		07 03					07 41										08 43						
Attenborough	d		07 06																					
Long Eaton	d		07 14					07 49										08 51						
Derby 6	a		07 30	07 49				08 02		08 26			08 31	08 51				09 02		09 25	09 28			09 31
	d		07 36	07 50				08 03		08 28			08 35	08 53				09 06		09 28	09 30			09 36
Willington	d		07 43																					
Burton-on-Trent	d		07 49	08 00				08 18		08 38			08 48					09 18		09 38	09 41			09 48
Tamworth	d		08 01	08 11				08 30		08 50			09 00					09 29						10 00
Wilnecote	d		08 05					08 34										09 34						
Leicester	d																							
South Wigston	d										08 22													
Narborough	d										08 27											09 25		
Hinckley	d										08 35											09 34		
Nuneaton	d				08 10						08 43				09 10							09 42		
Coleshill Parkway	d				08 25						09 01				09 25							09 57		
Water Orton	d																					10 02		
Birmingham New Street 12	a		08 24	08 29	08 38			08 54		09 07	09 14		09 24	09 29	09 38			09 54		10 07	10 08	10 14		10 24
	d		08 30			08 42	08 42			09 12			09 30			09 42	09 42			10 12	10 12			10 30
Worcester Shrub Hill 7	d								09 08															
Ashchurch for Tewkesbury	d								09 25															
Cheltenham Spa	d	08 59	09 11			09 25	09 26		09 35	09 52		10 01	10 11			10 25	10 26		10 45	10 52	10 53		11 00	11 12
Gloucester 7	a	09 09	09 22						09 44			10 11	10 22						10 56				11 10	11 23
Bristol Parkway 7	a					09 56	09 58		10 24	10 29						10 57	10 58			11 24	11 25			
Bristol Temple Meads 10	a					10 08	10 11		10 39	10 42						11 10	11 11			11 38	11 39			
Newport (South Wales)	a		10 05										11 05						11 50					12 06
Cardiff Central 7	a		10 21										11 24						12 07					12 22

A until 4 September

B from 11 September

Table 57 Saturdays

Nottingham, Derby and Leicester - Birmingham - Cardiff and Bristol

Station		XC	XC	XC	GW	XC	AW	XC	XC	GW	XC	XC	XC	XC	XC	XC	XC	GW	XC	XC	XC	GW	XC
		◇1	◇1	◇1		1		◇1	1		◇1	◇1	◇1	◇1	1	◇1	1	◇1	◇1	◇1	◇1		◇1
		✕	✕	✕	✕			✕			✕	✕	✕	✕		✕		🍴	✕	✕	✕	✕	✕
Nottingham 8 ⇌	d					09 37					10 08				10 37				11 11				
Beeston	d					09 43									10 43								
Attenborough	d																						
Long Eaton	d					09 51									10 51								
Derby 6	a					10 02					10 31				11 02				11 31				
	d	09 53				10 06		10 28			10 36	10 53			11 06	11 28			11 36	11 53			
Willington	d																						
Burton-on-Trent	d					10 18					10 48				11 17	11 38			11 48				
Tamworth	d					10 30		10 48			11 00				11 29				12 00				
Wilnecote	d					10 34									11 33								
Leicester	d		09 49						10 16				10 49				11 16				11 49		
South Wigston	d								10 22														
Narborough	d								10 27								11 25						
Hinckley	d								10 35								11 34						
Nuneaton	d		10 10						10 43				11 10				11 42				12 10		
Coleshill Parkway	d		10 25						10 59				11 25				11 57				12 25		
Water Orton	d																12 01						
Birmingham New Street 12	a	10 27	10 38			10 54		11 07	11 14		11 24	11 27	11 38		11 54	12 07	12 14		12 24	12 27	12 38		
	d			10 42				11 12			11 30			11 42		12 12			12 30				12 42
Worcester Shrub Hill 7	d				11 06																	12 54	
Ashchurch for Tewkesbury	d				11 21																	13 10	
Cheltenham Spa	d			11 25	11 31		11 45	11 52		12 01	12 11			12 25		12 52		13 00	13 11			13 20	13 26
Gloucester 7	a				11 44		11 57			12 11	12 22							13 10	13 22			13 32	
Bristol Parkway 7	a			11 56	12 24			12 29						12 56		13 24						14 20	13 58
Bristol Temple Meads 10	a			12 08	12 39			12 42						13 08		13 38						14 40	14 10
Newport (South Wales)	a						12 50				13 06								14 05				
Cardiff Central 7	a						13 07				13 22								14 21				

Station		XC	AW	XC	XC	GW	XC	XC	XC	XC	XC	AW	XC	XC	GW	XC	XC	XC	XC	GW	XC	XC	XC	GW
		1		◇1	1		◇1	◇1	◇1	◇1	1		◇1	1	◇1	◇1	◇1	◇1	◇1		1	◇1	1	
				✕			✕	✕	✕	✕			✕		🍴	✕	✕	✕	✕	✕		✕		
Nottingham 8 ⇌	d	11 37					12 08				12 37					13 08					13 37			
Beeston	d	11 43									12 43										13 43			
Attenborough	d																							
Long Eaton	d	11 51									12 51										13 51			
Derby 6	a	12 02					12 31				13 02					13 31					14 02			
	d	12 06		12 29			12 36	12 53			13 06		13 28			13 36	13 53				14 06	14 29		
Willington	d										13 14													
Burton-on-Trent	d	12 18					12 48				13 20		13 38			13 48					14 18			
Tamworth	d	12 30		12 49			13 00				13 32					14 00					14 30	14 48		
Wilnecote	d	12 34																			14 34			
Leicester	d				12 16				12 49					13 16				13 49					14 16	
South Wigston	d				12 22																		14 22	
Narborough	d				12 27									13 25									14 27	
Hinckley	d				12 35									13 34									14 35	
Nuneaton	d				12 43				13 10					13 42				14 10					14 43	
Coleshill Parkway	d				12 59				13 25					13 57				14 25					14 59	
Water Orton	d													14 01										
Birmingham New Street 12	a	12 54		13 09	13 14		13 24	13 27	13 38		13 54		14 07	14 14		14 24	14 27	14 38			14 54	15 08	15 14	
	d			13 12			13 30			13 42			14 12			14 30			14 42			15 12		
Worcester Shrub Hill 7	d																			15 06				
Ashchurch for Tewkesbury	d																			15 21				
Cheltenham Spa	d		13 45	13 52		14 01	14 11			14 25		14 45	14 52		15 00	15 11			15 25	15 31		15 52		16 01
Gloucester 7	a		13 57			14 11	14 22					14 56			15 10	15 22				15 42				16 11
Bristol Parkway 7	a			14 26						14 57			15 24						15 56	16 22		16 29		
Bristol Temple Meads 10	a			14 41						15 10			15 38						16 08	16 38		16 42		
Newport (South Wales)	a		14 50				15 06					15 50				16 06								
Cardiff Central 7	a		15 09				15 22					16 07				16 22								

Table 57

Saturdays

Nottingham, Derby and Leicester - Birmingham - Cardiff and Bristol

		XC ◇■ 🍴	XC ◇■ 🍴	XC ◇■ 🍴	XC ◇■ A 🍴	XC ◇■ B 🍴	XC ■	AW	XC ◇■ 🍴	XC ■	GW ◇■ ⊑	XC ◇■ 🍴	XC ◇■ 🍴	XC ◇■ 🍴	XC ◇■ 🍴	XC ■	GW	AW	XC ◇■ A 🍴	XC ◇■ B 🍴	XC ■	GW
Nottingham ■	d	14 08					14 37					15 08				15 37						
Beeston	d						14 43									15 43						
Attenborough	d																					
Long Eaton	d						14 51									15 51						
Derby ■	a	14 32					15 02					15 31				16 02						
	d	14 36	14 53				15 06		15 28			15 36	15 53			16 06			16 28	16 28		
Willington	d						15 13															
Burton-on-Trent	d	14 48					15 20		15 38			15 48				16 18						
Tamworth	d	15 00					15 32					16 00				16 30			16 48	16 48		
Wilnecote	d															16 34						
Leicester	d			14 49						15 16				15 49							16 16	
South Wigston	d																				16 22	
Narborough	d									15 25											16 27	
Hinckley	d									15 34											16 35	
Nuneaton	d			15 10						15 42				16 10							16 43	
Coleshill Parkway	d			15 25						15 57				16 25							16 59	
Water Orton	d									16 01												
Birmingham New Street ■	a	15 24	15 27	15 38			15 54		16 07	16 14		16 24	16 27	16 38		16 54			17 07	17 07	17 14	
	d	15 30			15 42	15 42			16 12			16 30			16 42				17 12	17 12		
Worcester Shrub Hill ■	d																17 08					
Ashchurch for Tewkesbury	d																17 21					
Cheltenham Spa	d	16 11			16 25	16 25		16 45	16 52		17 00	17 11			17 25		17 31	17 45	17 52	17 52		18 01
Gloucester ■	a	16 22						16 56			17 10	17 22					17 44	17 56				18 11
Bristol Parkway ■	a				16 56	16 56			17 24						17 56		18 24		18 29	18 29		
Bristol Temple Meads ■	a				17 10	17 08			17 38						18 08		18 39		18 43	18 42		
Newport (South Wales)	a	17 06						17 50				18 05						18 50				
Cardiff Central ■	a	17 24						18 10				18 21						19 10				

		XC ◇■ 🍴	XC ◇■ 🍴	XC ◇■ 🍴	XC ◇■ B 🍴	XC ◇■ A 🍴	XC ■	AW	XC ◇■ 🍴	XC ■	GW ◇■ ⊑	XC ◇■ 🍴	XC ◇■ 🍴	XC ◇■ 🍴	XC ◇■ 🍴	XC ■	AW	GW	XC ◇■ 🍴	XC ■	GW	XC ◇■ 🍴	XC ◇■ 🍴	XC ◇■ 🍴
Nottingham ■	d	16 08					16 37					17 08				17 37						18 08		
Beeston	d						16 43									17 43								
Attenborough	d																							
Long Eaton	d						16 51									17 51								
Derby ■	a	16 31					17 02					17 31				18 02						18 31		
	d	16 36	16 53				17 06		17 28			17 36	17 53			18 05			18 28			18 36	18 53	
Willington	d						17 13									18 14								
Burton-on-Trent	d	16 48					17 20		17 38			17 48				18 20						18 48		
Tamworth	d	17 00					17 32					18 00				18 33			18 48			19 00		
Wilnecote	d															18 36								
Leicester	d			16 49						17 16				17 49						18 16				18 49
South Wigston	d									17 22										18 22				
Narborough	d									17 27										18 27				
Hinckley	d									17 35										18 35				
Nuneaton	d			17 10						17 43				18 10						18 43				19 10
Coleshill Parkway	d			17 25						17 59				18 25						18 59				19 25
Water Orton	d																							
Birmingham New Street ■	a	17 24	17 27	17 38			17 54		18 07	18 14		18 24	18 27	18 38		18 57			19 07	19 14		19 24	19 27	19 38
	d	17 30			17 42	17 42			18 12			18 30			18 42				19 12			19 30		
Worcester Shrub Hill ■	d																	19 07						
Ashchurch for Tewkesbury	d	18 08																19 21						
Cheltenham Spa	d	18 18			18 25	18 25		18 45	18 52		19 00	19 11			19 25		19 45	19 31	19 52		20 01	20 11		
Gloucester ■	a	18 29						18 56			19 10	19 22					19 56	19 42			20 11	20 22		
Bristol Parkway ■	a				18 55	18 55			19 27						19 56			20 22	20 29					
Bristol Temple Meads ■	a				19 07	19 08			19 41						20 08			20 39	20 42					
Newport (South Wales)	a	19 12						19 50				20 05			20 55		20 50					21 10		
Cardiff Central ■	a	19 29						20 11				20 21			21 11		21 09					21 28		

A until 4 September

B from 11 September

Table 57

Saturdays

Nottingham, Derby and Leicester - Birmingham - Cardiff and Bristol

		XC ◇■ 🍴	XC ■	XC ◇■ 🍴	XC ■	GW	XC ◇■ 🍴	XC ◇■ 🍴	XC ◇■ 🍴	GW	XC ◇■ 🍴	XC ■	XC ◇■ 🍴	XC ■	XC ◇■ 🍴	XC ◇■ 🍴	XC ■	XC ◇■ 🍴	XC ■	GW	XC ◇■ 🍴	XC ◇■ 🍴	XC ■	XC ◇■ 🍴
Nottingham ■	d		18 37				19 08					19 37					20 36						21 37	
Beeston	d		18 43									19 43					20 42						21 43	
Attenborough	d											19 46											21 46	
Long Eaton	d		18 51									19 53					20 51						21 53	
Derby ■	a		19 02				19 32					20 02					21 02						22 04	
	d		19 06	19 28			19 36	19 54				20 05	20 28		20 53		21 06	21 28				21 57	22 10	22 27
Willington	d																21 14							
Burton-on-Trent	d		19 18	19 38			19 48					20 17					21 20	21 38				22 07	22 21	22 37
Tamworth	d		19 30				20 00					20 29	20 49				21 33	21 49				22 18	22 33	22 48
Wilnecote	d		19 33									20 33					21 37						22 37	
Leicester	d				19 16				19 49					20 16		20 49			21 16		21 49			
South Wigston	d				19 22									20 22					21 22					
Narborough	d				19 27									20 27					21 27					
Hinckley	d				19 35									20 35					21 35					
Nuneaton	d				19 43				20 10					20 43		21 10			21 43		22 10			
Coleshill Parkway	d				19 59				20 25					20 59		21 25			21 59		22 25			
Water Orton	d																							
Birmingham New Street ■	a		19 54	20 07	20 15		20 24	20 27	20 38			20 56	21 07	21 14	21 27	21 38	21 55	22 07	22 14		22 38	22 45	23 02	23 06
	d	19 42		20 12			20 30				20 42		21 12											
Worcester Shrub Hill ■	d																			21 31				
Ashchurch for Tewkesbury	d																			21 51				
Cheltenham Spa	d	20 25		20 52		21 02	21 11			21 19	21 25		21 52							22 01				
Gloucester ■	a					21 12	21 22			21 29			22 02							22 10				
Bristol Parkway ■	a	20 56		21 23		21 53					21 58		22 33											
Bristol Temple Meads ■	a	21 08		21 35		22 05					22 12		22 46											
Newport (South Wales)	a						22 21																	
Cardiff Central ■	a						22 44																	

		XC ■
Nottingham ■	d	
Beeston	d	
Attenborough	d	
Long Eaton	d	
Derby ■	a	
	d	
Willington	d	
Burton-on-Trent	d	
Tamworth	d	
Wilnecote	d	
Leicester	d	22 16
South Wigston	d	22 22
Narborough	d	22 27
Hinckley	d	22 35
Nuneaton	d	22 43
Coleshill Parkway	d	22 59
Water Orton	d	
Birmingham New Street ■	a	23 15
	d	
Worcester Shrub Hill ■	d	
Ashchurch for Tewkesbury	d	
Cheltenham Spa	d	
Gloucester ■	a	
Bristol Parkway ■	a	
Bristol Temple Meads ■	a	
Newport (South Wales)	a	
Cardiff Central ■	a	

Table 57

Nottingham, Derby and Leicester - Birmingham - Cardiff and Bristol

Sundays until 11 July

		GW	GW	GW	GW	XC	XC	GW	AW	XC	XC	XC	XC	GW	XC	XC	XC	XC	AW	XC	XC	GW	XC	XC	XC
				◇1		◇1	◇1			◇1	◇1	◇1	◇1	◇1	◇1	1	◇1	◇1		◇1	◇1		1	◇1	◇1
				🍽		🛒	🛒			🛒	🛒	🛒	🛒	🍽	🛒		🛒	🛒		🛒	🛒			🛒	🛒
Nottingham [8]	d												11 10				12 10							13 05	
Beeston	d																								
Attenborough	d																								
Long Eaton	d																								
Derby [6]	a												11 34				12 30							13 30	
	d					09 28	10 33					11 30	11 36		12 30		12 36				13 32			13 36	13 52
Willington	d																								
Burton-on-Trent	d											11 41	11 48				12 48				13 43			13 48	
Tamworth	d												12 00		12 48		13 00							14 00	
Wilnecote	d																								
Leicester	d										11 19					12 19		12 49					13 19		
South Wigston	d															12 24									
Narborough	d										11 28					12 29							13 28		
Hinckley	d										11 36					12 38							13 36		
Nuneaton	d										11 44					12 46		13 09					13 44		
Coleshill Parkway	d										11 59					13 01		13 25					13 59		
Water Orton	d																								
Birmingham New Street [12]	a					10 21	11 31				12 15	12 16	12 26		13 07	13 15	13 21	13 39			14 10		14 16	14 22	14 27
	d					10 28				12 12			12 30		13 12		13 30			13 42	14 12			14 30	
Worcester Shrub Hill [7]	d																					14 36			
Ashchurch for Tewkesbury	d					11 52																14 51			
Cheltenham Spa	d	09 30	10 05	11 46	12 00	12 06		12 24	12 40	12 52			13 11	13 46	13 52		14 12		14 18	14 25	14 52	15 01		15 10	
Gloucester [7]	a	09 40	10 15	11 56	12 10			12 34	12 50				13 21	13 57			14 22		14 29			15 10		15 21	
Bristol Parkway [7]	a		10 55		12 51	12 37				13 23					14 23					14 56	15 25	15 49			
Bristol Temple Meads [10]	a		11 08		13 09	12 50				13 35					14 39					15 08	15 38	16 06			
Newport (South Wales)	a								13 51				14 10				15 08		15 30					16 06	
Cardiff Central [7]	a								14 11				14 30				15 29		15 53					16 26	

		XC	XC	GW	XC	XC	XC	XC	XC	AW	XC	GW	XC	XC	XC	XC	XC	GW	XC	GW	XC	XC	XC	XC	XC
		◇1	◇1	◇1	◇1	1	◇1	◇1	◇1		◇1		◇1	1	◇1	◇1	◇1		◇1	◇1	◇1	1	◇1	◇1	◇1
		🛒	🛒	🍽	🛒		🛒	🛒	🛒		🛒		🛒		🛒	🛒	🛒		🛒	🍽	🛒		🛒	🛒	🛒
Nottingham [8]	d						14 10								15 05								16 05		
Beeston	d																								
Attenborough	d																								
Long Eaton	d																								
Derby [6]	a						14 28								15 31								16 28		
	d				14 30		14 35	14 53					15 23		15 35	15 51					16 23		16 35	16 51	
Willington	d																								
Burton-on-Trent	d						14 48						15 35		15 48								16 48		
Tamworth	d				14 49		15 00								16 00						16 43		17 00		
Wilnecote	d														16 04										
Leicester	d	13 49				14 19			14 49					15 19			15 49					16 19			16 48
South Wigston	d					14 24																16 24			
Narborough	d					14 29								15 28								16 29			
Hinckley	d					14 38								15 36								16 38			
Nuneaton	d	14 09				14 46			15 09					15 44			16 09					16 46			17 09
Coleshill Parkway	d	14 25				15 01			15 25					15 59			16 25					17 01			17 25
Water Orton	d																								
Birmingham New Street [12]	a	14 37			15 07	15 15	15 21	15 27	15 39				16 00	16 15	16 23	16 27	16 39				17 02	17 15	17 21	17 27	17 37
	d		14 42		15 12		15 30				15 42		16 12		16 30				16 42		17 12		17 30		
Worcester Shrub Hill [7]	d																	16 40							
Ashchurch for Tewkesbury	d																	16 58							
Cheltenham Spa	d		15 25	15 46	15 52		16 11			16 18	16 25	16 33	16 52		17 11			17 08	17 25	17 46	17 52		18 11		
Gloucester [7]	a			15 57			16 21			16 27		16 43			17 21			17 16		17 57			18 21		
Bristol Parkway [7]	a		15 57		16 23						16 57		17 23					17 57	18 01		18 23				
Bristol Temple Meads [10]	a		16 10		16 35						17 09		17 35					18 10	18 13		18 37				
Newport (South Wales)	a						17 06			17 39					18 06								19 06		
Cardiff Central [7]	a						17 26			17 59					18 28								19 26		

		XC	AW	XC	GW	XC	XC	XC	XC	XC	GW	XC	XC	XC	XC	XC	AW	XC	XC	XC	XC	XC	XC	GW	XC
		◇1		◇1		1	◇1	◇1	◇1	◇1	◇1	◇1	1	◇1	◇1	◇1		◇1	◇1	1	◇1	◇1	◇1		◇1
		🛒		🛒			🛒	🛒	🛒	🛒	🍽	🛒		🛒	🛒	🛒		🛒	🛒		🛒	🛒	🛒		🛒
Nottingham [8]	d						17 10							18 05							19 10				
Beeston	d																								
Attenborough	d																								
Long Eaton	d																								
Derby [6]	a						17 28							18 31							19 30				
	d			17 25			17 36	17 51				18 23		18 35	18 51						19 34	19 51			
Willington	d																								
Burton-on-Trent	d			17 35			17 48							18 48							19 48				
Tamworth	d						18 00					18 43		19 00							20 00				
Wilnecote	d																				20 04				
Leicester	d					17 16			17 48				18 16			18 49				19 19			19 49		
South Wigston	d					17 22														19 24					
Narborough	d					17 27							18 25							19 29					
Hinckley	d					17 36							18 33							19 38					
Nuneaton	d					17 43			18 09				18 41			19 09				19 45			20 09		
Coleshill Parkway	d					17 59			18 25				18 57			19 25				20 01			20 25		
Water Orton	d																								
Birmingham New Street [12]	a			18 00		18 15	18 21	18 27	18 39			19 02	19 15	19 21	19 27	19 37				20 15	20 23	20 27	20 39		
	d	17 42		18 12			18 30			18 42		19 12		19 30				19 42	20 12						20 42
Worcester Shrub Hill [7]	d				18 40																			20 37	
Ashchurch for Tewkesbury	d				18 55																			20 53	
Cheltenham Spa	d	18 25	18 35	18 52	19 06		19 13			19 25	19 46	19 52		20 11			20 18	20 25	20 52					21 03	21 25
Gloucester [7]	a		18 46		19 16		19 24				19 57			20 21			20 29							21 13	
Bristol Parkway [7]	a	18 57		19 23	19 56					20 02		20 23						20 57	21 23					21 53	21 59
Bristol Temple Meads [10]	a	19 09		19 35	20 10					20 14		20 35						21 09	21 35					22 07	22 11
Newport (South Wales)	a		19 48				20 09							21 06			21 31								
Cardiff Central [7]	a		20 06				20 29							21 26			21 49								

Table 57

Nottingham, Derby and Leicester - Birmingham - Cardiff and Bristol

Sundays until 11 July

		XC	GW	XC	XC	XC	XC	GW	XC	XC		XC	XC	XC	XC	XC	XC
		1		◇1	◇1	◇1	◇1		◇1	◇1		1	◇1	◇1	◇1	◇1	1
				🛒	🛒	🛒	🛒		🛒	🛒			🛒	🛒	🛒	🛒	
Nottingham [8]	d				20 10								21 08				
Beeston	d																
Attenborough	d																
Long Eaton	d																
Derby [6]	a				20 28								21 31				
	d			20 23	20 35	20 51				21 23			21 35	21 53		22 23	
Willington	d																
Burton-on-Trent	d				20 48					21 35			21 48	22 04		22 35	
Tamworth	d			20 43	21 00					21 46			22 00	22 14		22 46	
Wilnecote	d												22 04				
Leicester	d	20 08					20 49					21 19			21 49		23 19
South Wigston	d	20 15										21 25					23 25
Narborough	d	20 20										21 29					23 29
Hinckley	d	20 29										21 38					23 38
Nuneaton	d	20 36					21 09					21 46			22 09		23 46
Coleshill Parkway	d	20 52					21 25					22 01			22 25		00 02
Water Orton	d																
Birmingham New Street [12]	a	21 06		21 02	21 18	21 24	21 37			22 04		22 18	22 23	22 33	22 38	23 04	00 14
	d			21 12					21 42	22 12							
Worcester Shrub Hill [7]	d																
Ashchurch for Tewkesbury	d																
Cheltenham Spa	d		21 46	21 52				22 01	22 25	22 52							
Gloucester [7]	a		21 56	22 01				22 12									
Bristol Parkway [7]	a			22 35					23 00	23 23							
Bristol Temple Meads [10]	a			22 47					23 13	23 35							
Newport (South Wales)	a																
Cardiff Central [7]	a																

Sundays 18 July to 05 September

		GW	GW	AW	GW	XC	XC	XC	GW	GW		XC	XC	XC	GW	XC	XC	XC	XC	AW	XC	XC	XC	GW	XC
					◇1	◇1	◇1	◇1				◇1	◇1	◇1	◇1	◇1	1	◇1	◇1		◇1	◇1	1		◇1
				🚌	🍽	🛒	🛒	🛒				🛒	🛒	🛒	🍽	🛒		🛒	🛒		🛒	🛒			🛒
Nottingham [8]	d													11 10				12 10							13 05
Beeston	d																								
Attenborough	d																								
Long Eaton	d																								
Derby [6]	a													11 34				12 30							13 30
	d					09 28	10 33	11 30						11 36		12 30		12 36				13 32			13 36
Willington	d																								
Burton-on-Trent	d							11 41						11 48				12 48				13 43			13 48
Tamworth	d													12 00		12 48		13 00							14 00
Wilnecote	d																								
Leicester	d												11 19				12 19		12 49				13 19		
South Wigston	d																12 24								
Narborough	d												11 28				12 29						13 28		
Hinckley	d												11 36				12 38						13 36		
Nuneaton	d												11 44				12 46		13 09				13 44		
Coleshill Parkway	d												11 59				13 01		13 25				13 59		
Water Orton	d																								
Birmingham New Street [12]	a					10 21	11 31	12 07					12 15	12 26		13 07	13 15	13 21	13 39			14 10	14 16		14 22
	d					10 28						12 12		12 30		13 12		13 30			13 42	14 12			14 30
Worcester Shrub Hill [7]	d																							14 36	
Ashchurch for Tewkesbury	d					11 15																		14 51	
Cheltenham Spa	d	09 24	10 05	11 22	11 46	11 52			12 00	12 24		12 52		13 11	13 46	13 52		14 12		14 18	14 25	14 52		15 01	15 11
Gloucester [7]	a	09 34	10 15	11 42	11 56				12 10	12 34				13 21	13 57			14 22		14 29				15 10	15 21
Bristol Parkway [7]	a		10 55			12 23			12 51			13 23				14 23					14 56	15 25		15 49	
Bristol Temple Meads [10]	a		11 08			12 37			13 09			13 35				14 39					15 08	15 38		16 09	
Newport (South Wales)	a			13 32														15 03		15 29					16 06
Cardiff Central [7]	a			14 02														15 28		15 52					16 26

Table 57

Sundays
18 July to 05 September

Nottingham, Derby and Leicester - Birmingham - Cardiff and Bristol

		XC	XC	XC	GW	XC	XC	XC	XC	XC	AW	XC	GW	XC	XC	GW	XC	XC	XC	XC	GW	XC	XC	XC	XC
		◇1 ✕	◇1 ✕	◇1 ✕	◇1 ⊡	◇1 ✕	1	◇1 ✕	◇1 ✕	◇1 ✕		◇1 ✕		◇1 ✕	1		◇1 ✕	◇1 ✕	◇1 ✕	◇1 ✕	◇1 ⊡	◇1 ✕	1	◇1 ✕	◇1 ✕
Nottingham	d							14 10										15 05						16 05	
Beeston	d																								
Attenborough	d																								
Long Eaton	d																								
Derby	a							14 28										15 31						16 28	
	d	13 52				14 30		14 35	14 53					15 23			15 51	15 35				16 23		16 35	16 51
Willington	d																								
Burton-on-Trent	d							14 48						15 35				15 48						16 48	
Tamworth	d					14 49		15 00										16 00				16 43		17 00	
Wilnecote	d																	16 04							
Leicester	d		13 49				14 19			14 49					15 19				15 49				16 19		
South Wigston	d						14 24																16 24		
Narborough	d						14 29								15 28								16 29		
Hinckley	d						14 38								15 36								16 38		
Nuneaton	d		14 09				14 46			15 09					15 44				16 09				16 46		
Coleshill Parkway	d		14 25				15 01			15 25					15 59				16 25				17 01		
Water Orton	d																								
Birmingham New Street	a	14 27	14 37			15 07	15 15	15 21	15 27	15 39				16 00	16 15		16 27	16 23	16 39			17 02	17 15	17 21	17 27
	d			14 42		15 12		15 30				15 42		16 12				16 30		16 42		17 12		17 30	
Worcester Shrub Hill	d															16 40									
Ashchurch for Tewkesbury	d															16 58									
Cheltenham Spa	d			15 25	15 46	15 52		16 11			16 18	16 25	16 33	16 52		17 08		17 11		17 25	17 46	17 52		18 11	
Gloucester	a				15 57			16 21			16 27		16 43			17 16		17 21			17 57			18 21	
Bristol Parkway	a			16 00		16 23						16 57		17 23		17 57				18 01		18 23			
Bristol Temple Meads	a			16 11		16 35						17 09		17 35		18 10				18 13		18 37			
Newport (South Wales)	a							17 02			17 28							18 02						19 02	
Cardiff Central	a							17 26			17 51							18 28						19 26	

		XC	XC	AW	XC	XC	GW	XC	XC	XC	XC	GW	XC	XC	XC	XC	XC	AW	XC	XC	XC	XC	XC	XC	GW
		◇1 ✕	◇1 ✕		◇1 ✕	1		◇1 ✕	◇1 ✕	◇1 ✕	◇1 ✕	◇1 ⊡	◇1 ✕	1	◇1 ✕	◇1 ✕	◇1 ✕		◇1 ✕	◇1 ✕	1	◇1 ✕	◇1 ✕	◇1 ✕	
Nottingham	d							17 10							18 05							19 10			
Beeston	d																								
Attenborough	d																								
Long Eaton	d																								
Derby	a							17 28							18 31							19 30			
	d				17 25			17 36	17 51				18 23		18 35	18 51						19 34	19 51		
Willington	d																								
Burton-on-Trent	d				17 35			17 48							18 48							19 48			
Tamworth	d							18 00					18 43		19 00							20 00			
Wilnecote	d																					20 04			
Leicester	d	16 48				17 16				17 49				18 16			18 49				19 19			19 50	
South Wigston	d					17 22															19 24				
Narborough	d					17 27								18 25							19 29				
Hinckley	d					17 36								18 33							19 38				
Nuneaton	d	17 09				17 43				18 09				18 41			19 09				19 45			20 10	
Coleshill Parkway	d	17 25				17 59				18 25				18 57			19 25				20 01			20 26	
Water Orton	d																								
Birmingham New Street	a	17 37			18 00	18 15		18 21	18 27	18 39			19 02	19 15	19 21	19 27	19 37				20 15	20 23	20 27	20 40	
	d		17 42		18 12			18 30			18 42		19 12		19 30				19 42	20 12					
Worcester Shrub Hill	d						18 40																		20 37
Ashchurch for Tewkesbury	d						18 55																		20 53
Cheltenham Spa	d		18 25	18 35	18 52		19 06	19 13			19 25	19 46	19 52		20 11			20 18	20 25	20 52					21 03
Gloucester	a			18 46			19 16	19 24				19 57			20 21			20 29							21 13
Bristol Parkway	a		18 57		19 23		19 56				20 02		20 23						20 57	21 23					21 53
Bristol Temple Meads	a		19 09		19 35		20 10				20 14		20 35						21 09	21 35					22 07
Newport (South Wales)	a			19 48				20 05							21 05			21 27							
Cardiff Central	a			20 09				20 29							21 29			21 48							

		XC	XC	GW	XC	XC	XC	XC	GW	XC	XC	XC	XC	XC	XC	XC	XC
		◇1 ✕	1		◇1 ✕	◇1 ✕	◇1 ✕	◇1 ✕		◇1 ✕	◇1 ✕	1	◇1 ✕	◇1 ✕	◇1 ✕	◇1 ✕	1
Nottingham	d					20 10							21 08				
Beeston	d																
Attenborough	d																
Long Eaton	d																
Derby	a					20 28							21 31				
	d				20 23	20 35	20 51				21 23		21 35	21 53		22 23	
Willington	d																
Burton-on-Trent	d					20 48					21 35		21 48	22 04		22 35	
Tamworth	d				20 43	21 00					21 46		22 00	22 14		22 46	
Wilnecote	d												22 04				
Leicester	d		20 08					20 49				21 19			21 49		23 19
South Wigston	d		20 15									21 25					23 25
Narborough	d		20 20									21 29					23 29
Hinckley	d		20 29									21 38					23 38
Nuneaton	d		20 36					21 09				21 46			22 09		23 46
Coleshill Parkway	d		20 52					21 25				22 01			22 25		00 02
Water Orton	d																
Birmingham New Street	a		21 06		21 02	21 18	21 24	21 37			22 04	22 18	22 23	22 33	22 38	23 04	00 14
	d	20 42			21 12					21 42	22 12						
Worcester Shrub Hill	d																
Ashchurch for Tewkesbury	d																
Cheltenham Spa	d	21 25		21 46	21 52				22 01	22 25	22 52						
Gloucester	a			21 56	22 01				22 12								
Bristol Parkway	a	21 59			22 35					23 00	23 23						
Bristol Temple Meads	a	22 11			22 47					23 13	23 35						
Newport (South Wales)	a																
Cardiff Central	a																

Table 57

Sundays
12 September to 17 October

Nottingham, Derby and Leicester - Birmingham - Cardiff and Bristol

		GW	XC	GW	XC	XC	GW	XC	GW	XC	AW	GW	XC	XC	XC	GW	XC	XC	XC	XC	AW	XC	XC	XC	GW
			◇1 ✕		◇1 ✕	◇1 ✕	◇1 ⊡	◇1 ✕		◇1 ✕			◇1 ✕	◇1 ✕	◇1 ✕	◇1 ⊡	◇1 ✕	1	◇1 ✕	◇1 ✕		◇1 ✕	◇1 ✕	1	
Nottingham	d														11 10				12 10						
Beeston	d																								
Attenborough	d																								
Long Eaton	d																								
Derby	a														11 34				12 30						
	d				09 28			10 33					11 30		11 36		12 30		12 36				13 32		
Willington	d																								
Burton-on-Trent	d												11 41		11 48				12 48				13 43		
Tamworth	d				09 47										12 00		12 48		13 00						
Wilnecote	d																								
Leicester	d													11 19				12 19		12 49				13 19	
South Wigston	d																	12 24							
Narborough	d													11 28				12 29						13 28	
Hinckley	d													11 36				12 38						13 36	
Nuneaton	d													11 44				12 46		13 09				13 44	
Coleshill Parkway	d													11 59				13 01		13 25				13 59	
Water Orton	d																								
Birmingham New Street	a				10 09			11 08					12 07	12 15	12 26		13 07	13 15	13 21	13 39			14 10	14 16	
	d		09 12		10 12	10 30		11 12		11 30			12 12		12 30		13 12		13 30			13 42	14 12		
Worcester Shrub Hill	d																								14 36
Ashchurch for Tewkesbury	d																								14 51
Cheltenham Spa	d	09 24	09 52	10 05	10 57	11 11	11 20	11 52	12 00	12 11	12 18	12 24	12 52		13 11	13 46	13 52		14 12		14 18	14 25	14 52		15 01
Gloucester	a	09 34		10 15		11 23	11 30		12 10	12 21	12 28	12 34			13 21	13 58			14 22		14 29				15 10
Bristol Parkway	a		10 23	10 55	11 28			12 23	12 51				13 23				14 23					14 56	15 25		15 49
Bristol Temple Meads	a		10 35	11 08	11 41			12 36	13 09				13 35				14 39					15 08	15 38		16 09
Newport (South Wales)	a					12 06				13 06	13 32				14 10				15 07		15 31				
Cardiff Central	a					12 26				13 26	13 52				14 30				15 28		15 51				

		XC	XC	XC	XC	GW	XC	XC	XC	XC	XC	AW	XC	GW	XC	XC	XC	XC	XC	GW	XC	GW	XC	XC	XC
		◇1 ✕	◇1 ✕	◇1 ✕	◇1 ✕	◇1 ⊡	◇1 ✕	1	◇1 ✕	◇1 ✕	◇1 ✕		◇1 ✕		◇1 ✕	1	◇1 ✕	◇1 ✕	◇1 ✕		◇1 ✕	◇1 ⊡	◇1 ✕	1	◇1 ✕
Nottingham	d	13 05							14 10									15 05							16 05
Beeston	d																								
Attenborough	d																								
Long Eaton	d																								
Derby	a	13 30							14 28									15 31							16 28
	d	13 36	13 52				14 30		14 35	14 53					15 23		15 51	15 35					16 23		16 35
Willington	d																								
Burton-on-Trent	d	13 48							14 48						15 35			15 48							16 48
Tamworth	d	14 00					14 49		15 00									16 00					16 43		17 00
Wilnecote	d																	16 04							
Leicester	d			13 49				14 19			14 49					15 19			15 49					16 19	
South Wigston	d							14 24																16 24	
Narborough	d							14 29								15 28								16 29	
Hinckley	d							14 38								15 36								16 38	
Nuneaton	d			14 09				14 46			15 09					15 44			16 09					16 46	
Coleshill Parkway	d			14 25				15 01			15 25					15 59			16 25					17 01	
Water Orton	d																								
Birmingham New Street	a	14 22	14 27	14 37			15 07	15 15	15 21	15 27	15 39				16 00	16 15	16 27	16 23	16 39				17 02	17 15	17 21
	d	14 30			14 42		15 12		15 30				15 42		16 12			16 30			16 42		17 12		17 30
Worcester Shrub Hill	d																			16 40					
Ashchurch for Tewkesbury	d																			16 58					
Cheltenham Spa	d	15 10			15 25	15 46	15 52		16 11			16 18	16 25	16 33	16 52			17 11		17 08	17 25	17 46	17 52		18 11
Gloucester	a	15 21				15 57			16 21			16 27		16 43				17 21		17 16		17 57			18 21
Bristol Parkway	a				16 00		16 23						16 57		17 23					17 57	18 01		18 23		
Bristol Temple Meads	a				16 11		16 35						17 09		17 35					18 10	18 13		18 37		
Newport (South Wales)	a	16 06							17 06			17 35						18 06							19 02
Cardiff Central	a	16 26							17 26			17 55						18 28							19 26

		XC	XC	XC	AW	XC	XC	XC	XC	XC	GW	XC	XC	XC	XC	XC	XC	GW	AW	XC	XC	XC	XC	XC
		◇1 ✕	◇1 ✕	◇1 ✕		◇1 ✕	1	◇1 ✕	◇1 ✕	◇1 ✕		◇1 ✕	◇1 ✕	1	◇1 ✕	◇1 ✕	◇1 ✕	◇1 ⊡		◇1 ✕	◇1 ✕	1	◇1 ✕	◇1 ✕
Nottingham	d							17 10							18 05								19 10	
Beeston	d																							
Attenborough	d																							
Long Eaton	d																							
Derby	a							17 28							18 31								19 30	
	d	16 51				17 25		17 36	17 51				18 23		18 35	18 51							19 34	19 51
Willington	d																							
Burton-on-Trent	d					17 35		17 48							18 48								19 48	
Tamworth	d							18 00					18 43		19 00								20 00	
Wilnecote	d																						20 04	
Leicester	d		16 48				17 16			17 48				18 16			18 49					19 19		
South Wigston	d						17 22															19 24		
Narborough	d						17 27							18 25								19 29		
Hinckley	d						17 36							18 33								19 38		
Nuneaton	d		17 09				17 43			18 09				18 41			19 09					19 45		
Coleshill Parkway	d		17 25				17 59			18 25				18 57			19 25					20 01		
Water Orton	d																							
Birmingham New Street	a	17 27	17 37			18 00	18 15	18 21	18 27	18 39			19 02	19 15	19 21	19 27	19 37					20 15	20 23	20 27
	d			17 42		18 12		18 30				18 42	19 12		19 30					19 42	20 12			
Worcester Shrub Hill	d										18 40													
Ashchurch for Tewkesbury	d										18 55													
Cheltenham Spa	d			18 25	18 35	18 52		19 13			19 06	19 25	19 52		20 11			20 05	20 18	20 25	20 52			
Gloucester	a				18 46			19 24			19 16				20 21			20 15	20 29					
Bristol Parkway	a			18 57		19 23					19 56	20 02	20 23							20 57	21 23			
Bristol Temple Meads	a			19 09		19 35					20 10	20 14	20 35							21 09	21 35			
Newport (South Wales)	a				19 53			20 09							21 06				21 31					
Cardiff Central	a				20 11			20 29							21 26				21 49					

Table 57

Nottingham, Derby and Leicester - Birmingham - Cardiff and Bristol

Sundays
12 September to 17 October

		XC	GW	XC	XC	GW	XC	XC	XC	XC	GW	XC	XC	XC	XC	XC	XC	XC	XC
		◇■		◇■	■		◇■	◇■	◇■	◇■		◇■	◇■	■	◇■	◇■	◇■	◇■	■
Nottingham ■ ⇌	d							20 10							21 08				
Beeston	d																		
Attenborough	d																		
Long Eaton	d																		
Derby ■	a							20 28							21 31				
	d						20 23	20 35	20 51				21 23		21 35	21 53		22 23	
Willington	d																		
Burton-on-Trent	d							20 48					21 35		21 48	22 04		22 35	
Tamworth	d						20 43	21 00					21 46		22 00	22 14		22 46	
Wilnecote	d														22 04				
Leicester	d	19 49			20 08					20 49				21 19			21 49		23 19
South Wigston	d				20 15									21 25					23 25
Narborough	d				20 20									21 29					23 29
Hinckley	d				20 29									21 38					23 38
Nuneaton	d	20 09			20 36					21 09				21 46			22 09		23 46
Coleshill Parkway	d	20 25			20 52					21 25				22 01			22 25		00 02
Water Orton	d																		
Birmingham New Street ■	a	20 39			21 06		21 02	21 18	21 24	21 37			22 04	22 18	22 23	22 33	22 38	23 04	00 14
	d			20 42			21 12					21 42	22 12						
Worcester Shrub Hill ■	d		20 37																
Ashchurch for Tewkesbury	d		20 53																
Cheltenham Spa	d		21 03	21 25		21 46	21 52				22 01	22 25	22 52						
Gloucester ■	a		21 13			21 56	22 01				22 12								
Bristol Parkway ■	a		21 53	21 59			22 35					23 00	23 23						
Bristol Temple Meads ■	a		22 07	22 11			22 47					23 13	23 35						
Newport (South Wales)	a																		
Cardiff Central ■	a																		

Sundays
from 24 October

		GW	XC	GW	XC	XC	GW	GW	XC	AW	GW	XC	XC	GW	XC	XC	XC	XC	AW	XC	XC	XC	GW	XC	XC
			◇■		◇■	◇■	◇■		◇■			◇■	◇■	◇■	◇■	◇■	■	◇■		◇■	■	◇■		◇■	◇■
Nottingham ■ ⇌	d														11 10							12 10		13 05	
Beeston	d																								
Attenborough	d																								
Long Eaton	d																								
Derby ■	a														11 34							12 30		13 30	
	d				09 28							11 30			11 36	12 30				13 32		12 36		13 36	13 52
Willington	d																								
Burton-on-Trent	d											11 41			11 48					13 43		12 48		13 48	
Tamworth	d				09 47										12 00	12 48						13 00		14 00	
Wilnecote	d																								
Leicester	d												11 19				12 19	12 49			13 19				
South Wigston	d																12 24								
Narborough	d												11 28				12 29				13 28				
Hinckley	d												11 36				12 38				13 36				
Nuneaton	d												11 44				12 46	13 09			13 44				
Coleshill Parkway	d												11 59				13 01	13 25			13 59				
Water Orton	d																								
Birmingham New Street ■	a				10 09							12 07	12 15		12 26	13 07	13 15	13 39		14 10	14 16	13 21		14 22	14 27
	d		09 12		10 12	10 30			11 30			12 12			12 30	13 12				14 12		13 30		14 30	
Worcester Shrub Hill ■	d																						14 36		
Ashchurch for Tewkesbury	d																						14 51		
Cheltenham Spa	d	09 24	09 52	10 05	10 55	11 11	11 20	12 00	12 11	12 18	12 24	12 52		13 46	13 11	13 52			14 18	14 52		14 12	15 01	15 10	
Gloucester ■	a	09 34	10 01	10 16	11 04	11 23	11 30	12 10	12 21	12 28	12 34	13 01		13 58	13 21	14 02			14 29			14 22	15 10	15 21	
Bristol Parkway ■	a		11 15		12 19							14 25				15 11				15 25			15 49		
Bristol Temple Meads ■	a		11 40		12 41							14 40				15 26				15 38			16 09		
Newport (South Wales)	a					12 06			13 09	13 32					14 10				15 31			15 07		16 06	
Cardiff Central ■	a					12 26			13 29	13 52					14 30				15 51			15 28		16 26	

Table 57

Nottingham, Derby and Leicester - Birmingham - Cardiff and Bristol

Sundays
from 24 October

		XC	XC	GW	XC	XC	XC	XC	XC	AW	XC	GW	XC	XC	GW	XC	XC	XC	XC	GW	XC	XC	XC	XC	XC
		◇■	◇■	◇■	◇■	■	◇■	◇■	◇■		◇■		◇■	■		◇■	◇■	◇■	◇■	◇■	◇■	◇■	■	◇■	◇■
Nottingham ■ ⇌	d						14 10									15 05						16 05			
Beeston	d																								
Attenborough	d																								
Long Eaton	d																								
Derby ■	a						14 28									15 31						16 28			
	d				14 30		14 35	14 53					15 23			15 35	15 51				16 23	16 35		16 51	
Willington	d																								
Burton-on-Trent	d						14 48						15 35			15 48						16 48			
Tamworth	d				14 49		15 00									16 00					16 43	17 00			
Wilnecote	d															16 04									
Leicester	d	13 49				14 19			14 49					15 19				15 49					16 19		16 48
South Wigston	d					14 24																	16 24		
Narborough	d					14 29								15 28									16 29		
Hinckley	d					14 38								15 36									16 38		
Nuneaton	d	14 09				14 46			15 09					15 44				16 09					16 46		17 09
Coleshill Parkway	d	14 25				15 01			15 25					15 59				16 25					17 01		17 25
Water Orton	d																								
Birmingham New Street ■	a	14 37			15 07	15 15	15 21	15 27	15 39				16 00	16 15		16 23	16 27	16 39			17 02	17 21	17 15	17 27	17 37
	d		14 42		15 12		15 30				15 42		16 12			16 30			16 42		17 12	17 30			
Worcester Shrub Hill ■	d														16 40										
Ashchurch for Tewkesbury	d														16 58										
Cheltenham Spa	d		15 25	15 46	15 52		16 11			16 18	16 25	16 33	16 52		17 08	17 11			17 25	17 46	17 52	18 11			
Gloucester ■	a			15 57			16 21			16 27		16 43			17 16	17 21				17 57		18 21			
Bristol Parkway ■	a		16 00		16 23						16 57		17 23		17 57				18 01		18 23				
Bristol Temple Meads ■	a		16 11		16 35						17 09		17 35		18 10				18 13		18 37				
Newport (South Wales)	a						17 06			17 35						18 06						19 02			
Cardiff Central ■	a						17 26			17 55						18 28						19 26			

		XC	AW	XC	XC	GW	XC	XC	XC	XC	XC	XC	XC	XC	XC	GW	AW	XC	XC	XC	XC	XC	XC	GW	XC
		◇■		◇■	■		◇■	◇■	◇■	◇■	◇■	■	◇■	◇■	◇■	◇■		◇■	◇■	■	◇■	◇■	◇■		◇■
Nottingham ■ ⇌	d						17 10						18 05								19 10				
Beeston	d																								
Attenborough	d																								
Long Eaton	d																								
Derby ■	a						17 28						18 31								19 30				
	d			17 25			17 36	17 51			18 23		18 35	18 51							19 34	19 51			
Willington	d																								
Burton-on-Trent	d			17 35			17 48						18 48								19 48				
Tamworth	d						18 00				18 43		19 00								20 00				
Wilnecote	d																				20 04				
Leicester	d				17 16				17 48			18 16			18 49					19 19			19 49		
South Wigston	d				17 22															19 24					
Narborough	d				17 27							18 25								19 29					
Hinckley	d				17 36							18 33								19 38					
Nuneaton	d				17 43				18 09			18 41			19 09					19 45			20 09		
Coleshill Parkway	d				17 59				18 25			18 57			19 25					20 01			20 25		
Water Orton	d																								
Birmingham New Street ■	a			18 00	18 15		18 21	18 27	18 39		19 02	19 15	19 21	19 27	19 37					20 15	20 23	20 27	20 39		
	d	17 42		18 12			18 30			18 42	19 12		19 30					19 42	20 12						20 42
Worcester Shrub Hill ■	d					18 40																		20 37	
Ashchurch for Tewkesbury	d					18 55																		20 53	
Cheltenham Spa	d	18 25	18 35	18 52		19 06	19 13			19 25	19 52		20 11			20 05	20 18	20 25	20 52					21 03	21 25
Gloucester ■	a		18 46			19 16	19 24						20 21			20 15	20 29							21 13	
Bristol Parkway ■	a	18 57		19 23		19 56				20 02	20 23							20 57	21 23					21 53	21 59
Bristol Temple Meads ■	a	19 09		19 35		20 10				20 14	20 35							21 09	21 35					22 07	22 11
Newport (South Wales)	a		19 53				20 09						21 06				21 31								
Cardiff Central ■	a		20 11				20 29						21 26				21 49								

		XC	GW	XC	XC	XC	XC	GW	XC	XC	XC	XC	XC	XC	XC
		■		◇■	◇■	◇■	◇■		◇■	■	◇■	◇■	◇■	◇■	■
Nottingham ■ ⇌	d				20 10						21 08				
Beeston	d														
Attenborough	d														
Long Eaton	d														
Derby ■	a				20 28						21 31				
	d			20 23	20 35	20 51			21 23		21 35	21 53		22 23	
Willington	d														
Burton-on-Trent	d				20 48				21 35		21 48	22 04		22 35	
Tamworth	d			20 43	21 00				21 46		22 00	22 14		22 46	
Wilnecote	d										22 04				
Leicester	d	20 08					20 49			21 19			21 49		23 19
South Wigston	d	20 15								21 25					23 25
Narborough	d	20 20								21 29					23 29
Hinckley	d	20 29								21 38					23 38
Nuneaton	d	20 36					21 09			21 46			22 09		23 46
Coleshill Parkway	d	20 52					21 25			22 01			22 25		00 02
Water Orton	d														
Birmingham New Street ■	a	21 06		21 02	21 18	21 24	21 37		22 04	22 18	22 23	22 33	22 38	23 04	00 14
	d			21 12					22 12						
Worcester Shrub Hill ■	d														
Ashchurch for Tewkesbury	d														
Cheltenham Spa	d		21 46	21 52				22 01	22 52						
Gloucester ■	a		21 56	22 01				22 12							
Bristol Parkway ■	a			22 35					23 59						
Bristol Temple Meads ■	a			22 47					00 14						
Newport (South Wales)	a														
Cardiff Central ■	a														

Bristol and Cardiff - Birmingham - Leicester, Derby and Nottingham

		XC MX 1	XC MX ◇1	XC MX ◇1	AW MX	XC ◇1	XC 1	XC ◇1 🍴	GW	XC 1		XC ◇1 🍴	XC ◇1 🍴	XC 1	XC 1	XC ◇1 🍴	XC 1	XC ◇1 🍴	XC ◇1 🍴	XC 1		XC 1	XC ◇1 🍴	XC ◇1 🍴	GW
Cardiff Central 7	d		21p50		23p19																				
Newport (South Wales)	d		22p05		23p40																				
Bristol Temple Meads 10	d			22p00																			06 27		
Bristol Parkway 7	d			22p15																			06 40		
Gloucester 7	d		22p47		00 41				06 01															07 10	07 15
Cheltenham Spa	d		22p59	23p27	00a54				06 12														07 12	07 21	07 25
Ashchurch for Tewkesbury	d								06 20															07 29	07 34
Worcester Shrub Hill 7	a								06 40																07 54
Birmingham New Street 12	a		00 04	00 10																			07 56	08 16	
	d	23p09				05 22	05 52	06 00		06 19		06 22	06 30	06 49	06 52	07 03	07 19	07 22	07 30	07 49		07 52	08 03	08 22	
Water Orton	d																								
Coleshill Parkway	d						06 05					06 35			07 05			07 35				08 05		08 35	
Nuneaton	d					05 50	06 22					06 52			07 22			07 51				08 22		08 51	
Hinckley	d						06 29								07 29			07 58				08 29			
Narborough	d						06 37								07 37			08 06				08 37			
South Wigston	d						06 42								07 42			08 10				08 42			
Leicester	a					06 10	06 50					07 15			07 48			08 15				08 48		09 15	
Wilnecote	d	23p24								06 35							07 34								
Tamworth	d	23p28								06 39				07 07		07 19	07 38			08 07			08 19		
Burton-on-Trent	d	23p39								06 50				07 19		07 29	07 50			08 19			08 29		
Willington	d	23p45															07 56								
Derby 6	a	23p55						06 32		07 04			07 11	07 34		07 42	08 05		08 11	08 34			08 42		
	d	23p59								07 10				07 40			08 10			08 39					
Long Eaton	d									07 25				07 49			08 19								
Attenborough	d									07 31															
Beeston	d									07 35				07 58			08 27								
Nottingham 6	a	00 18								07 41				08 08			08 33			09 05					

		AW	XC ◇1 🍴	XC 1	XC ◇1 🍴	XC ◇1		GW ◇1 🛒	XC 1	XC ◇1 🍴	AW	XC ◇1 🍴	XC 1	XC ◇1 🍴	XC ◇1 🍴	XC ◇1		GW	XC 1	XC ◇1 🍴	XC ◇1 🍴	XC 1	XC ◇1 🍴	XC ◇1 🍴	GW
Cardiff Central 7	d	06 12				06 40					07 12				07 00	07 45									
Newport (South Wales)	d	06 28				06 55					07 27				07 15	08 02									
Bristol Temple Meads 10	d				07 00					07 30					08 00					08 30				09 00	08 41
Bristol Parkway 7	d				07 10					07 40					08 10					08 40				09 10	08 52
Gloucester 7	d	07 21				07 46		07 51			08 21					08 46		08 53							09 38
Cheltenham Spa	d	07a34			07 42	07 57		08a01		08 12	08a34				08 42	08 58		09a03		09 12				09 42	09 48
Ashchurch for Tewkesbury	d					08 05																			09 56
Worcester Shrub Hill 7	a																								10 14
Birmingham New Street 12	a				08 26	08 45				08 56					09 26	09 45				09 56				10 26	
	d		08 30	08 19		08 49			08 52	09 03		09 30	09 19	09 22		09 49			09 52	10 03	10 30	10 19	10 22		
Water Orton	d								09 03																
Coleshill Parkway	d								09 07					09 35					10 07				10 35		
Nuneaton	d								09 22					09 52					10 23				10 52		
Hinckley	d								09 30										10 30						
Narborough	d								09 39										10 38						
South Wigston	d																		10 43						
Leicester	a								09 49					10 15					10 50				11 15		
Wilnecote	d												09 35												
Tamworth	d			08 37		09 07							09 39			10 07				10 19		10 36			
Burton-on-Trent	d			08 49		09 19				09 26			09 50			10 19						10 48			
Willington	d			08 56																		10 54			
Derby 6	a		09 11	09 05		09 34				09 39		10 08	10 05			10 36				10 39	11 08	11 05			
	d			09 10		09 39							10 10			10 40						11 10			
Long Eaton	d			09 19									10 19									11 19			
Attenborough	d			09 26																					
Beeston	d			09 29									10 27									11 27			
Nottingham 6	a			09 35		10 05							10 33			11 04						11 33			

Table 57 Mondays to Fridays

Bristol and Cardiff - Birmingham - Leicester, Derby and Nottingham

		XC ◇1		GW ◇1 🛒	XC 1	XC ◇1 🍴	AW	XC ◇1 🍴	XC 1	XC ◇1 🍴	XC ◇1 🍴	XC ◇1		GW	XC 1	XC ◇1 🍴	AW	XC ◇1 🍴	XC 1	XC ◇1 🍴	XC ◇1 🍴	GW ◇		XC ◇1	GW ◇1 🛒
Cardiff Central 7	d	08 45					09 12					09 45					10 12							10 45	
Newport (South Wales)	d	09 02					09 27					10 00					10 27							11 00	
Bristol Temple Meads 10	d					09 30					10 00					10 30					11 00	10 41			
Bristol Parkway 7	d					09 40					10 10					10 40					11 10	10 52			
Gloucester 7	d	09 46		09 51			10 21					10 46		10 53			11 21					11 36		11 46	11 51
Cheltenham Spa	d	09 57		10a01		10 12	10a34				10 42	10 57		11a03		11 12	11a34				11 42	11 48		11 57	12a01
Ashchurch for Tewkesbury	d																					11 56			
Worcester Shrub Hill 7	a																					12 14			
Birmingham New Street 12	a	10 45				10 56					11 26	11 45				11 58					12 26			12 45	
	d	10 49			10 52	11 03		11 30	11 19	11 22		11 49			11 52	12 03		12 30	12 19	12 22				12 49	
Water Orton	d				11 03																				
Coleshill Parkway	d				11 07					11 35					12 07					12 35					
Nuneaton	d				11 23					11 52					12 23					12 52					
Hinckley	d				11 30										12 30										
Narborough	d				11 39										12 38										
South Wigston	d														12 43										
Leicester	a				11 48					12 15					12 49					13 15					
Wilnecote	d								11 35																
Tamworth	d	11 07							11 39			12 07				12 19			12 38					13 07	
Burton-on-Trent	d	11 19				11 26			11 50			12 19							12 49					13 19	
Willington	d																		12 54						
Derby 6	a	11 34				11 39		12 08	12 05			12 36				12 41		13 09	13 05					13 35	
	d	11 39							12 10			12 40							13 10					13 39	
Long Eaton	d								12 19										13 19						
Attenborough	d																								
Beeston	d								12 27										13 27						
Nottingham 6	a	12 05							12 33			13 05							13 33					14 05	

		XC 1	XC ◇1 🍴	XC ◇1 🍴	XC 1	XC ◇1 🍴	XC ◇1 🍴	XC ◇1		GW	XC 1	XC ◇1 🍴	AW	XC ◇1 🍴	XC 1	XC ◇1 🍴	XC ◇1 🍴	GW ◇		XC ◇1	GW ◇1 🛒	XC 1	XC ◇1 🍴	AW	XC ◇1 🍴
Cardiff Central 7	d							11 45					12 12							12 45				13 12	
Newport (South Wales)	d							12 00					12 28							13 01				13 28	
Bristol Temple Meads 10	d		11 30				12 00					12 30					13 00	12 41					13 30		
Bristol Parkway 7	d		11 40				12 10					12 40					13 10	12 52					13 40		
Gloucester 7	d							12 46		12 53			13 22					13 38		13 46	13 51			14 21	
Cheltenham Spa	d		12 12				12 42	12 57		13a03		13 12	13a34				13 42	13 48		13 57	14a01		14 12	14a34	
Ashchurch for Tewkesbury	d							13 05										13 56							
Worcester Shrub Hill 7	a																	14 14							
Birmingham New Street 12	a		12 56				13 26	13 45				13 56					14 26			14 45			14 56		
	d	12 52	13 03	13 30	13 19	13 22		13 49			13 52	14 03		14 30	14 19	14 22				14 49		14 52	15 03		15 30
Water Orton	d	13 03																				15 03			
Coleshill Parkway	d	13 07				13 35					14 07					14 35						15 07			
Nuneaton	d	13 23				13 52					14 23					14 52						15 23			
Hinckley	d	13 30									14 30											15 30			
Narborough	d	13 39									14 38											15 39			
South Wigston	d										14 43														
Leicester	a	13 50				14 15					14 50					15 15						15 50			
Wilnecote	d				13 35										14 35										
Tamworth	d				13 39			14 07				14 19			14 39					15 07					
Burton-on-Trent	d		13 28		13 50			14 19							14 50					15 19			15 26		
Willington	d																								
Derby 6	a		13 40	14 08	14 05			14 34				14 39		15 08	15 05					15 34			15 39		16 08
	d				14 10			14 39							15 10					15 39					
Long Eaton	d				14 19										15 19										
Attenborough	d																								
Beeston	d				14 29										15 27										
Nottingham 6	a				14 35			15 05							15 33					16 05					

Bristol and Cardiff - Birmingham - Leicester, Derby and Nottingham

		XC	XC	XC	XC	GW	XC	XC	XC	XC	XC	XC	XC	GW	XC	GW	XC	XC	AW	XC	XC	XC	XC
		[1]	◇[1] 🛒	◇[1] 🛒	◇[1]		[1]	◇[1] 🛒	[1]	◇[1] 🛒	[1]	◇[1] 🛒	◇[1] 🛒	◇	◇[1]	◇[1] 🍽	[1]	◇[1] 🛒		[1]	◇[1] 🛒	[1]	◇[1] 🛒
Cardiff Central [7]	d				13 45										14 45				15 12				
Newport (South Wales)	d				14 00										15 01				15 28				
Bristol Temple Meads [10]	d			14 00				14 30					15 00	14 41				15 30					
Bristol Parkway [7]	d			14 10				14 40					15 10	14 52				15 40					
Gloucester [7]	d				14 46	14 53								15 37	15 46	15 51			16 22				
Cheltenham Spa	d			14 42	14 57	15a03		15 12					15 42	15 48	15 57	16a01		16 12	16a34				
Ashchurch for Tewkesbury	d													15 56									
Worcester Shrub Hill [7]	a													16 21									
Birmingham New Street [12]	a			15 26	15 45			15 56					16 26		16 45			16 58					
	d	15 19	15 22		15 49		15 52	16 03	16 09	16 30	16 19	16 22			16 49		16 52	17 03		17 09	17 30	17 19	17 22
Water Orton	d								16 19											17 23			
Coleshill Parkway	d		15 35				16 07		16 23			16 35					17 05			17 27			17 35
Nuneaton	d		15 52				16 23		16 39			16 52					17 22			17 44			17 52
Hinckley	d						16 30		16 46								17 29			17 51			
Narborough	d						16 39		16 55								17 37						
South Wigston	d						16 43													18 03			
Leicester	a		16 15				16 50		17 06			17 15					17 50			18 09			18 15
Wilnecote	d	15 35									16 35											17 34	
Tamworth	d	15 39			16 07			16 19			16 39				17 07							17 39	
Burton-on-Trent	d	15 50			16 19						16 50				17 19			17 26				17 51	
Willington	d																						
Derby [6]	a	16 05			16 34			16 40		17 08	17 05				17 34			17 40			18 08	18 05	
	d	16 10			16 39						17 10				17 39							18 10	
Long Eaton	d	16 19									17 19											18 19	
Attenborough	d																						
Beeston	d	16 27									17 27											18 27	
Nottingham [8] 🚊	a	16 33			17 05						17 33				18 05							18 33	

		XC	XC	XC	GW	XC	XC	AW	XC	XC	XC	XC	GW	XC	GW	XC	XC	AW	XC	XC	XC	XC	XC	GW
		◇[1] 🛒	[1]	◇[1]		[1]	◇[1] 🛒		◇[1] 🛒	[1]	◇[1] 🛒	◇[1] 🛒		◇[1]	◇[1] 🍽	[1]	◇[1] 🛒		◇[1] 🛒	[1]	◇[1] 🛒	◇[1] 🛒	◇[1]	
Cardiff Central [7]	d			15 45				16 05						16 45				17 12					17 45	
Newport (South Wales)	d			16 00				16 21						17 00				17 28					18 00	
Bristol Temple Meads [10]	d	16 00					16 30					17 00	16 41				17 30					18 00		
Bristol Parkway [7]	d	16 10					16 40					17 10	16 52				17 40					18 10		
Gloucester [7]	d			16 46	16 53			17 22					17 38	17 46	17 51			18 22					18 46	18 53
Cheltenham Spa	d	16 42		16 57	17a03		17 12	17a34				17 42	17 48	17 57	18a01		18 12	18a34				18 42	18 57	19a03
Ashchurch for Tewkesbury	d												17 56											
Worcester Shrub Hill [7]	a												18 19											
Birmingham New Street [12]	a	17 26		17 45			17 56					18 26		18 45			18 55					19 26	19 45	
	d		17 39	17 49		17 52	18 03		18 30	18 19	18 22			18 49		18 52	19 03		19 30	19 19	19 22		19 49	
Water Orton	d		17 50			18 03																		
Coleshill Parkway	d					18 07					18 35					19 07					19 35			
Nuneaton	d					18 23					18 52					19 23					19 52			
Hinckley	d					18 30										19 30								
Narborough	d					18 39										19 38								
South Wigston	d					18 44										19 43								
Leicester	a					18 50					19 15					19 50					20 15			
Wilnecote	d									18 35										19 35				
Tamworth	d		18 00	18 07			18 19			18 39				19 07						19 39			20 07	
Burton-on-Trent	d		18 12	18 19						18 50				19 19			19 26			19 50			20 19	
Willington	d		18 18																					
Derby [6]	a		18 31	18 35			18 42		19 08	19 05				19 34			19 39		20 08	20 05			20 34	
	d			18 39						19 10				19 39						20 10			20 40	
Long Eaton	d									19 19										20 19			20 49	
Attenborough	d																							
Beeston	d									19 27										20 27			20 59	
Nottingham [8] 🚊	a			19 05						19 35				20 03						20 35			21 06	

Bristol and Cardiff - Birmingham - Leicester, Derby and Nottingham

		XC	XC	AW	XC	XC	XC	GW	XC	GW	XC	XC	GW	XC	GW	XC	XC	XC	GW	GW	GW	XC	XC
		[1]	◇[1] 🛒		◇[1]	◇[1] 🛒	◇[1] 🛒		◇[1]	◇[1] 🍽	[1]	◇[1] 🛒		◇[1]	◇[1] 🍽	◇[1]	◇[1]	◇[1]		◇	◇[1] 🍽	[1]	[1]
Cardiff Central [7]	d			18 12					18 45							19 50							
Newport (South Wales)	d			18 27					19 01							20 05							
Bristol Temple Meads [10]	d		18 30				19 00	18 41				19 30	19 41	20 00				20 30		20 41			
Bristol Parkway [7]	d		18 40				19 10	18 52				19 40	19 52	20 10				20 40		20 52			
Gloucester [7]	d			19 21				19 38	19 46	19 51			20 36	20 46	20 51	20 58			21 18	21 35	21 53		
Cheltenham Spa	d		19 12	19a34			19 42	19 48	19 57	20a01		20 12	20a48	20 56	21a01	21 09		21 17	21a29	21 46	22a02		
Ashchurch for Tewkesbury	d							19 56	20 05											21 54			
Worcester Shrub Hill [7]	a							20 15												22 13			
Birmingham New Street [12]	a		19 56				20 28		20 45			20 52		21 46		21 53		22 09					
	d	19 52	20 03		20 30	20 22			20 49		20 52	21 03					22 02					22 22	23 09
Water Orton	d	20 03																					
Coleshill Parkway	d	20 07				20 35					21 05											22 37	
Nuneaton	d	20 23				20 52					21 22											22 54	
Hinckley	d	20 30									21 29											23 01	
Narborough	d	20 39									21 37											23 09	
South Wigston	d	20 44									21 42											23 14	
Leicester	a	20 50				21 15					21 58											23 20	
Wilnecote	d								21 04														23 24
Tamworth	d		20 19						21 09			21 19					22 28						23 28
Burton-on-Trent	d								21 21			21 30					22 40						23 39
Willington	d																						23 45
Derby [6]	a		20 42		21 11				21 36			21 44					22 54						23 55
	d								21 40								22 59						23 59
Long Eaton	d								21 52								23 11						
Attenborough	d								21 58								23 17						
Beeston	d								22 02								23 20						
Nottingham [8] 🚊	a								22 08								23 27						00 18

		XC	AW	XC	GW	XC	AW FX	AW FO
		◇[1]		◇[1]		◇[1]		
Cardiff Central [7]	d	21 05	21 12	21 50			23 19	23 20
Newport (South Wales)	d	21 20	21 27	22 05			23 40	23 40
Bristol Temple Meads [10]	d					22 00		
Bristol Parkway [7]	d					22 15		
Gloucester [7]	d	22 06	22 24	22 47	22 54		00 41	00 40
Cheltenham Spa	d	22 17	22a36	22 59	23a03	23 27	00a54	00a53
Ashchurch for Tewkesbury	d	22 25						
Worcester Shrub Hill [7]	a							
Birmingham New Street [12]	a	23 27		00 04		00 10		
	d							
Water Orton	d							
Coleshill Parkway	d							
Nuneaton	d							
Hinckley	d							
Narborough	d							
South Wigston	d							
Leicester	a							
Wilnecote	d							
Tamworth	d							
Burton-on-Trent	d							
Willington	d							
Derby [6]	a							
	d							
Long Eaton	d							
Attenborough	d							
Beeston	d							
Nottingham [8] 🚊	a							

Table 57

Bristol and Cardiff - Birmingham - Leicester, Derby and Nottingham

		XC ■	XC ◇■	XC ◇■	AW	XC ◇■ 🍴	GW	XC ■	XC ◇■ 🍴	XC ■	XC ◇■ 🍴	XC ◇■ 🍴	XC ■	XC ■	XC ◇■ 🍴	XC ■	XC ◇■ 🍴	XC ◇■ 🍴	XC ■	XC ■	XC ◇■ 🍴	XC ◇■ 🍴	GW	AW
Cardiff Central 7	d		21p50		23p20																			06 12
Newport (South Wales)	d		22p05		23p40																			06 28
Bristol Temple Meads 10	d			22p00																	06 27			
Bristol Parkway 7	d			22p15																	06 40			
Gloucester 7	d		22p47		00 40		05 50															07 06	07 15	07 21
Cheltenham Spa	d		22p59	23p27	00a53		06 00														07 12	07 18	07 25	07a34
Ashchurch for Tewkesbury	d						06 09															07 25	07 34	
Worcester Shrub Hill 7	a						06 33																07 52	
Birmingham New Street 12	a		00 04	00 10																	07 56	08 08		
	d	23p09				05 22		05 52	05 55	06 19	06 22	06 30	06 49	06 52	07 03	07 19	07 22	07 30	07 49	07 52	08 03	08 22		
Water Orton	d													07 02										
Coleshill Parkway	d					05 35		06 05			06 35			07 06			07 35			08 05		08 35		
Nuneaton	d					05 52		06 22			06 52			07 22			07 52			08 22		08 52		
Hinckley	d							06 29						07 29						08 29				
Narborough	d							06 37						07 37						08 37				
South Wigston	d							06 42						07 42						08 42				
Leicester	a					06 13		06 50			07 13			07 48			08 13			08 48		09 13		
Wilnecote	d	23p24								06 35						07 34								
Tamworth	d	23p28							06 12	06 39		06 46	07 07		07 19	07 38		07 46	08 07		08 19			
Burton-on-Trent	d	23p39							06 22	06 50		06 56	07 19		07 29	07 50		07 56	08 22		08 29			
Willington	d	23p45														07 55								
Derby 6	a	23p55							06 35	07 06		07 09	07 37		07 42	08 05		08 09	08 34		08 42			
	d	23p59								07 10			07 39			08 09			08 39					
Long Eaton	d									07 22			07 52			08 19								
Attenborough	d									07 28														
Beeston	d									07 32			07 59			08 27								
Nottingham 8	a	00 18								07 38			08 08			08 34			09 05					

		XC ◇■ 🍴	XC ■	XC ◇■ B 🍴	XC ◇■	XC ■	XC ◇■ 🍴	GW	AW	XC ■	XC ◇■ 🍴	XC ◇■ 🍴	XC ◇■ B 🍴	XC ◇■	XC ■	XC ◇■ 🍴	XC ◇■ 🍴	XC ■	XC ◇■ 🍴	XC ◇■	GW	XC ◇■	XC ■
Cardiff Central 7	d				06 40				07 12				07 00	07 45								08 45	
Newport (South Wales)	d				06 55				07 27				07 15	08 00								09 02	
Bristol Temple Meads 10	d			07 00			07 30						08 00			08 30				09 00	08 41		
Bristol Parkway 7	d			07 10			07 40						08 10			08 40				09 10	08 52		
Gloucester 7	d				07 46			08 10	08 22					08 46							09 38	09 46	
Cheltenham Spa	d			07 42	07 57		08 12	08a24	08a32				08 42	08 57		09 12				09 42	09 48	09 57	
Ashchurch for Tewkesbury	d				08 04																09 56		
Worcester Shrub Hill 7	a																				10 14		
Birmingham New Street 12	a			08 26	08 45		08 56						09 26	09 45		09 56				10 26		10 45	
	d	08 30	08 19		08 49	08 52	09 03			09 19	09 30	09 22		09 49	09 52	10 03	10 30	10 19	10 22			10 49	10 52
Water Orton	d					09 03																	11 03
Coleshill Parkway	d					09 07						09 35			10 07				10 35				11 07
Nuneaton	d					09 23						09 52			10 23				10 52				11 23
Hinckley	d					09 30									10 30								11 30
Narborough	d					09 39									10 39								11 39
South Wigston	d														10 43								
Leicester	a					09 48						10 13			10 50				11 13				11 48
Wilnecote	d									09 35													
Tamworth	d		08 36		09 07					09 39				10 07		10 19		10 36				11 07	
Burton-on-Trent	d		08 48		09 19		09 26			09 52				10 20				10 48				11 19	
Willington	d		08 55															10 54					
Derby 6	a	09 08	09 05		09 34		09 41			10 06	10 09			10 34		10 41	11 09	11 05				11 34	
	d		09 10		09 39					10 09				10 39				11 09				11 39	
Long Eaton	d		09 19							10 19								11 19					
Attenborough	d		09 26																				
Beeston	d		09 29							10 27								11 27					
Nottingham 8	a		09 35		10 05					10 33				11 05				11 33				12 05	

Table 57

Saturdays

Bristol and Cardiff - Birmingham - Leicester, Derby and Nottingham

		XC ◇■ 🍴	GW ◇■ 🛒	AW	XC ◇■ 🍴	XC ■	XC ◇■ 🍴	XC ◇■ 🍴	XC ◇■	XC ■	XC ◇■ 🍴	GW	AW	XC ◇■ 🍴	XC ■	XC ◇■ 🍴	XC ◇■ 🍴	GW ◇	XC ◇■	XC ■	XC ◇■ 🍴	GW ◇■ 🛒
Cardiff Central 7	d			09 12					09 45				10 12						10 45			
Newport (South Wales)	d			09 26					10 00				10 27						11 00			
Bristol Temple Meads 10	d	09 30						10 00			10 30						11 00	10 41			11 30	
Bristol Parkway 7	d	09 40						10 10			10 40						11 10	10 52			11 40	
Gloucester 7	d		10 11	10 21					10 46			11 11	11 22					11 38	11 46			12 11
Cheltenham Spa	d	10 12	10a22	10a34				10 42	10 57		11 12	11a22	11a34				11 42	11 48	11 57		12 12	12a22
Ashchurch for Tewkesbury	d																	11 56				
Worcester Shrub Hill 7	a																	12 15				
Birmingham New Street 12	a	10 56						11 26	11 45		11 56						12 26		12 45		12 56	
	d	11 03			11 30	11 19	11 22		11 49	11 52	12 03			12 30	12 19	12 22			12 49	12 52	13 03	
Water Orton	d																			13 03		
Coleshill Parkway	d						11 35			12 07						12 35				13 07		
Nuneaton	d						11 52			12 23						12 52				13 23		
Hinckley	d									12 30										13 30		
Narborough	d									12 39										13 39		
South Wigston	d									12 43												
Leicester	a						12 13			12 50						13 13				13 48		
Wilnecote	d					11 34																
Tamworth	d					11 39			12 07		12 19				12 38				13 07			
Burton-on-Trent	d	11 26				11 51			12 19						12 51				13 19		13 26	
Willington	d														12 56							
Derby 6	a	11 41			12 09	12 05			12 35		12 41			13 09	13 05				13 34		13 41	
	d	11 44			12 11	12 09			12 39		12 44			13 11	13 09				13 39		13 44	
Long Eaton	d					12 19									13 19							
Attenborough	d																					
Beeston	d					12 27									13 29							
Nottingham 8	a					12 33			13 05						13 35				14 06			

		XC ◇■ 🍴	XC ■	XC ◇■ 🍴	XC ◇■ 🍴	XC ◇■	XC ■	XC ◇■ 🍴	GW	AW	XC ◇■ 🍴	XC ■	XC ◇■ 🍴	XC ◇■ 🍴	GW ◇	XC ◇■	XC ■	XC ◇■ B 🍴	XC ◇■ C 🍴	GW ◇■ 🛒	AW	XC ◇■ 🍴	XC ■
Cardiff Central 7	d					11 45				12 12						12 45					13 12		
Newport (South Wales)	d					12 00				12 27						13 01					13 27		
Bristol Temple Meads 10	d				12 00			12 30						13 00	12 41			13 30	13 30				
Bristol Parkway 7	d				12 10			12 40						13 10	12 52			13 40	13 40				
Gloucester 7	d					12 46			13 11	13 22					13 38	13 46				14 11	14 21		
Cheltenham Spa	d				12 42	12 57		13 12	13a22	13a35				13 42	13 48	13 57		14 12	14 13	14a22	14a34		
Ashchurch for Tewkesbury	d					13 05									13 56								
Worcester Shrub Hill 7	a														14 15								
Birmingham New Street 12	a				13 26	13 45		13 56						14 26		14 45		14 56	14 56				
	d	13 30	13 19	13 22		13 49	13 52	14 03			14 30	14 19	14 22			14 49	14 52	15 03	15 03			15 30	15 19
Water Orton	d																15 03						
Coleshill Parkway	d			13 35			14 07						14 35				15 07						
Nuneaton	d			13 52			14 23						14 52				15 23						
Hinckley	d						14 30										15 30						
Narborough	d						14 39										15 39						
South Wigston	d						14 43																
Leicester	a			14 13			14 50						15 13				15 48						
Wilnecote	d		13 35									14 34											15 35
Tamworth	d		13 39			14 07		14 19				14 38				15 07							15 39
Burton-on-Trent	d		13 51			14 19						14 50				15 19		15 26	15 26				15 50
Willington	d																						
Derby 6	a	14 09	14 05			14 35		14 41			15 08	15 05				15 34		15 41	15 43			16 08	16 05
	d		14 10			14 39						15 09				15 39							16 09
Long Eaton	d		14 19									15 19											16 19
Attenborough	d																						
Beeston	d		14 27									15 27											16 27
Nottingham 8	a		14 33			15 05						15 33				16 05							16 33

B from 11 September

C until 4 September

Table 57

Bristol and Cardiff - Birmingham - Leicester, Derby and Nottingham

		XC ◇1 ✠	XC ◇1 ✠	XC ◇1	XC 1	XC ◇1 B ✠	XC ◇1 C ✠	GW	XC ◇1 ✠	XC 1	XC ◇1 ✠	XC ◇1 ✠	GW ◇	XC ◇1	XC 1	XC ◇1 ✠	GW ◇1 ☕	AW	XC ◇1 ✠	XC 1	XC ◇1 ✠	XC ◇1 ✠
Cardiff Central 7	d			13 45										14 45				15 12				
Newport (South Wales)	d			14 00										15 01				15 27				
Bristol Temple Meads 10	d		14 00			14 30	14 30					15 00	14 41			15 30						16 00
Bristol Parkway 7	d		14 10			14 40	14 40					15 10	14 52			15 40						16 10
Gloucester 7	d			14 46				15 14					1538	15 46			16 11	16 21				
Cheltenham Spa	d		14 42	14 57		15 12	15 12	15a25				15 42	15 48	15 57		16 12	16a22	16a34				16 42
Ashchurch for Tewkesbury	d												15 56									
Worcester Shrub Hill 7	a												16 14									
Birmingham New Street 12	a		15 26	15 45		15 54	15 55					16 26		16 45		16 56						17 26
	d	15 22		15 49	15 52	16 03	16 03		16 30	16 19	16 22			16 49	16 52	17 03			17 30	17 19	17 22	
Water Orton	d														17 03							
Coleshill Parkway	d	15 35			16 07						16 35				17 07						17 35	
Nuneaton	d	15 52			16 23						16 52				17 23						17 52	
Hinckley	d				16 30										17 30							
Narborough	d				16 39										17 39							
South Wigston	d				16 43																	
Leicester	a	16 13			16 50						17 13				17 48						18 13	
Wilnecote	d									16 35										17 34		
Tamworth	d			16 07		16 17	16 17			16 39				17 07						17 39		
Burton-on-Trent	d			16 19						16 50				17 19		17 26				17 51		
Willington	d																					
Derby 6	a			16 34		16 40	16 40		17 08	17 05				17 34		17 41			18 08	18 05		
	d			16 39						17 09				17 39						18 09		
Long Eaton	d									17 19										18 19		
Attenborough	d																					
Beeston	d									17 27										18 27		
Nottingham 8	a			17 05						17 33				18 05						18 33		

		XC ◇1	XC 1	XC ◇1 ✠	GW	AW	XC ◇1 ✠	XC 1	XC ◇1 ✠	XC ◇1 ✠	GW	XC ◇1 ✠	XC 1	XC ◇1 ✠	GW ◇1 ☕	AW	XC ◇1 ✠	XC 1	XC ◇1 ✠	XC ◇1 ✠	XC ◇1	XC 1	XC ◇1 C ✠
Cardiff Central 7	d	15 45				16 12						16 45				17 12					17 45		
Newport (South Wales)	d	16 00				16 27						17 01				17 27					18 00		
Bristol Temple Meads 10	d			16 30						17 00	16 41			17 30						18 00			18 30
Bristol Parkway 7	d			16 40						17 10	16 52			17 40						18 10			18 40
Gloucester 7	d	16 46			17 14	17 21					17 38	17 46			18 11	18 23					18 46		
Cheltenham Spa	d	16 57		17 12	17a25	17a34				17 42	17 48	17 57		18 12	18a22	18a33				18 42	18 57		19 12
Ashchurch for Tewkesbury	d										17 56												
Worcester Shrub Hill 7	a										18 15												
Birmingham New Street 12	a	17 45		17 56						18 26		18 45		18 56						19 26	19 45		19 56
	d	17 49	17 52	18 03			18 30	18 19	18 22			18 49	18 52	19 03			19 30	19 19	19 22		19 49	19 52	20 03
Water Orton	d																					20 03	
Coleshill Parkway	d		18 05						18 35				19 05						19 35			20 07	
Nuneaton	d		18 22						18 52				19 22						19 52			20 23	
Hinckley	d		18 29										19 29									20 30	
Narborough	d		18 37										19 37									20 39	
South Wigston	d		18 42										19 42									20 43	
Leicester	a		18 48						19 13				19 48						20 13			20 49	
Wilnecote	d							18 35										19 35					
Tamworth	d	18 07		18 19				18 39				19 07						19 39			20 07		20 19
Burton-on-Trent	d	18 19						18 50				19 19		19 26				19 50			20 19		
Willington	d	18 26																					
Derby 6	a	18 35		18 41			19 08	19 05				19 35		19 41			20 08	20 05			20 34		20 42
	d	18 39						19 09				19 39						20 09			20 39		
Long Eaton	d							19 19										20 19			20 49		
Attenborough	d																						
Beeston	d							19 27										20 27			20 57		
Nottingham 8	a	19 05						19 33				20 05						20 35			21 04		

B until 4 September

C from 11 September

Table 57

Bristol and Cardiff - Birmingham - Leicester, Derby and Nottingham

		XC ◇1 A ✠	GW	AW	XC ◇1 ✠	XC ◇1 ✠	XC ◇1 ✠	GW	XC ◇1	XC ◇1 ✠	XC ◇1 A ✠	XC 1	XC ◇1 E ✠	GW ◇1 ☕	XC ◇1 ✠	GW	GW	XC ◇1	XC ◇1 ✠	GW 1 C	GW 1 F
Cardiff Central 7	d			18 12					18 45									20 00			
Newport (South Wales)	d			18 27					19 01									20 15			
Bristol Temple Meads 10	d	18 30					19 00	18 41		19 30			19 30		20 00	19 41			20 30	20 41	20 41
Bristol Parkway 7	d	18 40					19 10	18 52		19 40			19 40		20 10	19 52			20 40	20 52	20 52
Gloucester 7	d		19 14	19 21				19 38	19 46					20 11		20 38	20 55	21 07	21 14	21 38	21 38
Cheltenham Spa	d	19 12	19a25	19a34			19 42	19 48	19 57	20 12			20 12	20a22	20 42	20a46	21a05	21 18	21 25	21a47	21 49
Ashchurch for Tewkesbury	d							19 56										21 25			21 57
Worcester Shrub Hill 7	a							20 15													22 17
Birmingham New Street 12	a	19 56					20 26		20 40	20 50			20 53		21 38			22 07	22 11		
	d	20 03			20 30	20 22			20 49		21 03	20 52	21 03					22 10			
Water Orton	d																				
Coleshill Parkway	d					20 35						21 05									
Nuneaton	d					20 52						21 22									
Hinckley	d											21 29									
Narborough	d											21 37									
South Wigston	d											21 42									
Leicester	a					21 13						21 49									
Wilnecote	d								21 04												
Tamworth	d	20 19							21 08		21 20		21 19					22 28			
Burton-on-Trent	d								21 20		21 30		21 30					22 39			
Willington	d																	22 45			
Derby 6	a	20 41			21 09				21 35		21 45		21 44					22 55			
	d								21 40									23 00			
Long Eaton	d								21 52									23 12			
Attenborough	d								21 58									23 18			
Beeston	d								22 02									23 22			
Nottingham 8	a								22 08									23 28			

		GW C 🚌	XC 1	XC ◇1	GW ◇1 ☕	XC ◇1
Cardiff Central 7	d			20 50		
Newport (South Wales)	d			21 05		
Bristol Temple Meads 10	d					
Bristol Parkway 7	d					
Gloucester 7	d			21 49	22 11	
Cheltenham Spa	d	21 54		22 00	22a20	
Ashchurch for Tewkesbury	d	22 16				
Worcester Shrub Hill 7	a	22 41				
Birmingham New Street 12	a			22 42		
	d		22 22			22 49
Water Orton	d					
Coleshill Parkway	d		22 35			
Nuneaton	d		22 52			
Hinckley	d		22 59			
Narborough	d		23 07			
South Wigston	d		23 12			
Leicester	a		23 18			
Wilnecote	d					23 04
Tamworth	d					23 08
Burton-on-Trent	d					23 20
Willington	d					
Derby 6	a					23 33
	d					
Long Eaton	d					
Attenborough	d					
Beeston	d					
Nottingham 8	a					

A until 4 September

C from 17 July until 4 September

D until 10 July

E from 11 September

F until 10 July, from 11 September

Table 57

Bristol and Cardiff - Birmingham - Leicester, Derby and Nottingham

		XC ◇1 🛒	XC 1	XC ◇1 🛒	XC ◇1 🛒	XC 1	XC ◇1 🛒	XC ◇1 🛒	GW	GW ◇1 ☕		GW	AW	XC ◇1	XC 1	XC ◇1 🛒	XC ◇1 🛒	XC ◇1	XC 1	XC ◇1 🛒		XC ◇1 🛒	XC ◇1 🛒	XC ◇1	GW ◇1 ☕
Cardiff Central [7]	d												10 23											11 45	
Newport (South Wales)	d												10 38											11 59	
Bristol Temple Meads [10]	d				08 45			09 30	09 41													11 30			
Bristol Parkway [7]	d				08 55			09 40	09 54													11 40			
Gloucester [7]	d							10 12	10 37	10 46		11 40	11 45									12c25		12 47	12 52
Cheltenham Spa	d				09 27			10 21	10a48	10a56		11a50	11a57									12 35		12 58	13a03
Ashchurch for Tewkesbury	d				09 38			10 32																	
Worcester Shrub Hill [7]	a																								
Birmingham New Street [12]	a				10 40			11 36														13 11		13 41	
	d	09 30	09 52	10 30		10 52	11 22	12 03						11 49	11 52	12 22	12 30	12 49	12 52	13 03		13 30	13 22	13 49	
Water Orton	d																								
Coleshill Parkway	d		10 05			11 05	11 35								12 05	12 35			13 05				13 35		
Nuneaton	d		10 22			11 22	11 52								12 22	12 52			13 22				13 52		
Hinckley	d		10 29			11 29									12 29				13 29						
Narborough	d		10 37			11 37									12 37				13 37						
South Wigston	d		10 42												12 42										
Leicester	a		10 51			11 49	12 13								12 57	13 13			13 52				14 12		
Wilnecote	d																								
Tamworth	d							12 19						12 07				13 07						14 07	
Burton-on-Trent	d	10 30		11 26										12 19				13 19		13 26				14 19	
Willington	d																								
Derby [6]	a	10 42		11 42				12 42						12 34			13 09	13 38		13 44		14 09		14 34	
	d													12 38				13 41						14 41	
Long Eaton	d																								
Attenborough	d																								
Beeston	d																								
Nottingham [8]	a													13 02				14 02						15 07	

		XC ◇1 🛒	XC 1	XC ◇1 🛒	XC ◇1 🛒	XC ◇1 🛒		GW	AW	XC ◇1	XC ◇1 🛒	XC 1	XC ◇1 🛒	XC ◇1 🛒	XC ◇1 🛒	GW ◇1 ☕		XC ◇1	XC ◇1 🛒	GW	XC 1	XC ◇1 🛒	XC ◇1 🛒	XC ◇1 🛒	AW
Cardiff Central [7]	d								12 23									13 45							14 23
Newport (South Wales)	d								12 38									13 59							14 38
Bristol Temple Meads [10]	d	12 30				13 00		12 41			13 30				14 00				14 30					15 00	
Bristol Parkway [7]	d	12 40				13 10		12 52			13 40				14 10				14 40					15 10	
Gloucester [7]	d							13 35	13 38	13 51						14 39		14 47		15 24					15 38
Cheltenham Spa	d	13 12				13 42		13 48	13a49	14 02	14 12				14 42	14a49		14 58	15 12	15a33				15 42	15a49
Ashchurch for Tewkesbury	d							13 57																	
Worcester Shrub Hill [7]	a							14 24																	
Birmingham New Street [12]	a	13 50				14 26				14 45	14 50				15 27			15 41	15 50					16 26	
	d	14 03	13 52	14 30	14 22					14 49	15 03	14 52	15 30	15 22				15 49	16 03		15 52	16 30	16 22		
Water Orton	d																								
Coleshill Parkway	d		14 05		14 35							15 05		15 35							16 05		16 35		
Nuneaton	d		14 22		14 52							15 22		15 52							16 22		16 52		
Hinckley	d		14 28									15 29									16 29				
Narborough	d		14 37									15 37									16 37				
South Wigston	d		14 42																		16 42				
Leicester	a		14 54		15 12							15 49		16 12							16 48		17 17		
Wilnecote	d									15 04															
Tamworth	d	14 19								15 09								16 07	16 19						
Burton-on-Trent	d									15 21	15 26							16 19							
Willington	d																								
Derby [6]	a	14 42		15 04						15 34	15 42		16 02					16 34	16 42			17 04			
	d									15 44	15 44							16 41							
Long Eaton	d																								
Attenborough	d																								
Beeston	d																								
Nottingham [8]	a									16 08								17 03							

Table 57

Bristol and Cardiff - Birmingham - Leicester, Derby and Nottingham

		XC ◇1		GW	XC ◇1 🛒	XC 1	XC ◇1 🛒	XC ◇1 🛒	XC ◇1 🛒	GW ◇1 ☕	XC ◇1	XC ◇1 🛒		XC 1	XC ◇1 🛒	XC ◇1 🛒	XC ◇1 🛒	GW	AW	XC ◇1	XC ◇1 🛒	XC 1		XC ◇1 🛒	XC ◇1 🛒
Cardiff Central [7]	d	14 45									15 45								16 22	16 45					
Newport (South Wales)	d	14 59									15 59								16 37	16 59					
Bristol Temple Meads [10]	d			14 41	15 30				16 00			16 30					17 00	16 41			17 30				
Bristol Parkway [7]	d			14 53	15 40				16 10			16 40					17 10	16 52			17 40				
Gloucester [7]	d	15 47		15 52						16 39	16 47							17 35	17 38	17 47					
Cheltenham Spa	d	15 58		16 03	16 11				16 42	16a49	16 58	17 11					17 42	17 46	17a51	17 58	18 11				
Ashchurch for Tewkesbury	d			16 11														17 54							
Worcester Shrub Hill [7]	a			16 34														18 14							
Birmingham New Street [12]	a	16 41			16 50				17 26		17 41	17 49					18 27			18 41	18 51				
	d	16 49			17 03	16 52	17 30	17 22			17 49	18 03		17 52	18 30	18 22				18 49	19 03	18 52		19 30	19 22
Water Orton	d																								
Coleshill Parkway	d					17 05		17 35						18 05		18 35						19 05			19 35
Nuneaton	d					17 22		17 52						18 22		18 52						19 22			19 52
Hinckley	d					17 29								18 29								19 29			
Narborough	d					17 37								18 37								19 37			
South Wigston	d					17 42								18 42								19 42			
Leicester	a					17 51		18 13						18 50		19 13						19 53			20 12
Wilnecote	d																			19 04					
Tamworth	d	17 07									18 07	18 19								19 09					
Burton-on-Trent	d	17 19			17 29						18 19									19 21	19 26				
Willington	d																								
Derby [6]	a	17 35			17 42		18 05				18 34	18 42			19 02					19 33	19 40			20 02	
	d	17 43									18 41									19 37					
Long Eaton	d																								
Attenborough	d																								
Beeston	d																								
Nottingham [8]	a	18 02									19 04									19 56					

		XC ◇1 🛒	GW ◇1 ☕	XC ◇1	XC ◇1 🛒	XC 1	XC ◇1 🛒	XC ◇1 🛒		GW	AW	XC ◇1	XC ◇1 🛒	XC 1	XC ◇1 🛒	GW ◇1 ☕	XC ◇1	XC ◇1 🛒		GW	GW	XC 1	XC ◇1	XC ◇1 🛒	GW ◇1 ☕
Cardiff Central [7]	d			17 45							18 23	18 45					19 45						20 45		
Newport (South Wales)	d			17 59							18 38	18 59					20 00						20 59		
Bristol Temple Meads [10]	d	18 00			18 30			19 00		18 41			19 30		20 00			20 30			20 41			22 10	
Bristol Parkway [7]	d	18 10			18 40			19 10		18 52			19 40		20 10			20 40			20 52			22 20	
Gloucester [7]	d		18 42	18 47						19 38	19 42	19 50				20 42	20 50			21 25	21 38		21 47		22 47
Cheltenham Spa	d	18 42	18a51	18 58	19 12			19 42		19 48	19a52	20 00	20 12		20 42	20a50	21 00	21 11		21a34	21a46		21 58	22 52	22a58
Ashchurch for Tewkesbury	d									19 57															
Worcester Shrub Hill [7]	a									20 18															
Birmingham New Street [12]	a	19 26		19 41	19 50			20 26				20 42	20 50		21 20		21 45	21 51					22 41	23 39	
	d			19 49	20 03	19 52	20 22						21 03	20 52				22 03				21 52			
Water Orton	d																								
Coleshill Parkway	d					20 05	20 35							21 05								22 05			
Nuneaton	d					20 22	20 51							21 22								22 26			
Hinckley	d					20 29								21 29								22 33			
Narborough	d					20 37								21 37								22 42			
South Wigston	d					20 42								21 42								22 46			
Leicester	a					20 52	21 11							21 53								22 53			
Wilnecote	d																								
Tamworth	d			20 07	20 19								21 19					22 19							
Burton-on-Trent	d			20 19									21 29												
Willington	d																								
Derby [6]	a			20 34	20 42								21 42					22 45							
	d			20 37																					
Long Eaton	d																								
Attenborough	d																								
Beeston	d																								
Nottingham [8]	a			21 01																					

		GW
Cardiff Central [7]	d	
Newport (South Wales)	d	
Bristol Temple Meads [10]	d	
Bristol Parkway [7]	d	
Gloucester [7]	d	23 56
Cheltenham Spa	d	00a05
Ashchurch for Tewkesbury	d	
Worcester Shrub Hill [7]	a	
Birmingham New Street [12]	a	
	d	
Water Orton	d	
Coleshill Parkway	d	
Nuneaton	d	
Hinckley	d	
Narborough	d	
South Wigston	d	
Leicester	a	
Wilnecote	d	
Tamworth	d	
Burton-on-Trent	d	
Willington	d	
Derby [6]	a	
	d	
Long Eaton	d	
Attenborough	d	
Beeston	d	
Nottingham [8]	a	

Table 57

Bristol and Cardiff - Birmingham - Leicester, Derby and Nottingham

Sundays 18 July to 05 September

		XC	XC	XC	XC	XC	XC	XC	GW	GW		GW	AW	XC	XC	XC	XC	XC	XC	XC		XC	XC	XC	GW
		◇1 🛒	1	◇1 🛒	◇1 🛒	1	◇1 🛒	◇1 🛒		◇1 ☕			🚌	◇1	1	◇1 🛒	◇1 🛒	◇1	1	◇1 🛒		◇1 🛒	◇1 🛒	◇1	◇1 ☕
Cardiff Central 7	d												09 17											11 25	
Newport (South Wales)	d												09 47											11 43	
Bristol Temple Meads 10	d				08 45			09 30	09 41													11 30			
Bristol Parkway 7	d				08 55			09 40	09 54													11 40			
Gloucester 7	d							10 12	10 37	10 46		11 40	11 37									12 25		12 46	12 52
Cheltenham Spa	d				09 30			10 24	10a48	10a55		11a50	11a57									12 35		12 58	13a03
Ashchurch for Tewkesbury	d				09 53			10 47																	
Worcester Shrub Hill 7	a																								
Birmingham New Street 12	a				10 36			11 36														13 11		13 41	
	d	09 30	09 52	10 30		10 52	11 22	12 03						11 49	11 52	12 22	12 30	12 49	12 52	13 03		13 30	13 22	13 49	
Water Orton	d																								
Coleshill Parkway	d		10 05			11 05	11 35								12 05	12 35			13 05				13 35		
Nuneaton	d		10 22			11 22	11 52								12 22	12 52			13 22				13 52		
Hinckley	d		10 29			11 29									12 29				13 29						
Narborough	d		10 37			11 37									12 37				13 37						
South Wigston	d		10 42												12 42										
Leicester	a		10 58			11 47	12 12								12 48	13 13			13 47				14 12		
Wilnecote	d																								
Tamworth	d							12 19						12 07				13 07						14 07	
Burton-on-Trent	d	10 30		11 26										12 19				13 19		13 26				14 19	
Willington	d																								
Derby 6	a	10 42		11 42				12 42						12 34			13 09	13 38		13 44		14 09		14 34	
	d													12 38				13 41						14 41	
Long Eaton	d																								
Attenborough	d																								
Beeston	d																								
Nottingham 6	a													13 02				14 02						15 07	

		XC	XC	XC	XC	XC		GW	AW	XC	XC	XC	XC	XC	XC	GW		XC	XC	GW	XC	XC	XC	XC	AW
		◇1 🛒	1	◇1 🛒	◇1 🛒	◇1 🛒				◇1	◇1 🛒	1	◇1 🛒	◇1 🛒	◇1 🛒	◇1 ☕		◇1	◇1 🛒		1	◇1 🛒	◇1 🛒	◇1 🛒	
Cardiff Central 7	d																								14 23
Newport (South Wales)	d																								14 41
Bristol Temple Meads 10	d	12 30				13 00		12 41			13 30				14 00				14 30					15 00	
Bristol Parkway 7	d	12 40				13 10		12 52			13 40				14 10				14 40					15 10	
Gloucester 7	d							13 35	13 44	13 51						14 39		14 47		15 24					15 38
Cheltenham Spa	d	13 12				13 42		13 48	13a55	14 02	14 12				14 42	14a49		14 58	15 12	15a33				15 42	15a48
Ashchurch for Tewkesbury	d							13 57																	
Worcester Shrub Hill 7	a							14 24																	
Birmingham New Street 12	a	13 50				14 26				14 45	14 50				15 27			15 41	15 50					16 26	
	d	14 03	13 52	14 30	14 22					14 49	15 03	14 52	15 30	15 22				15 49	16 03		15 52	16 30	16 22		
Water Orton	d																								
Coleshill Parkway	d		14 05		14 35							15 05		15 35							16 05		16 35		
Nuneaton	d		14 22		14 52							15 22		15 52							16 22		16 52		
Hinckley	d		14 28									15 29									16 29				
Narborough	d		14 37									15 37									16 37				
South Wigston	d		14 42																		16 42				
Leicester	a		14 48		15 12							15 48		16 12							16 48		17 15		
Wilnecote	d									15 04															
Tamworth	d	14 19								15 09								16 07	16 19						
Burton-on-Trent	d									15 21	15 26							16 19							
Willington	d																								
Derby 6	a	14 42		15 04						15 34	15 42		16 02					16 34	16 42			17 04			
	d									15 44								16 41							
Long Eaton	d																								
Attenborough	d																								
Beeston	d																								
Nottingham 6	a									16 08								17 03							

Table 57

Bristol and Cardiff - Birmingham - Leicester, Derby and Nottingham

Sundays 18 July to 05 September

		XC		GW	XC	XC	XC	XC	XC	GW	XC	XC		XC	XC	XC	XC	GW	AW	XC	XC	XC		XC	XC
		◇1			◇1 🛒	1	◇1 🛒	◇1 🛒	◇1 🛒	◇1 ☕	◇1	◇1 🛒		1	◇1 🛒	◇1 🛒	◇1 🛒			◇1	◇1 🛒	1		◇1 🛒	◇1 🛒
Cardiff Central 7	d	14 45									15 45								16 23	16 45					
Newport (South Wales)	d	15 03									16 03								16 41	17 04					
Bristol Temple Meads 10	d			14 41	15 30				16 00			16 30					17 00	16 41			17 30				
Bristol Parkway 7	d			14 53	15 40				16 10			16 40					17 10	16 52			17 40				
Gloucester 7	d	15 47		15 52						16 39	16 47							17 35	17 38	17 47					
Cheltenham Spa	d	15 58		16 03	16 11				16 42	16a49	16 58	17 11					17 42	17 46	17a50	17 58	18 11				
Ashchurch for Tewkesbury	d			16 11														17 54							
Worcester Shrub Hill 7	a			16 34														18 14							
Birmingham New Street 12	a	16 41			16 50				17 26		17 41	17 49					18 27			18 41	18 51				
	d	16 49			17 03	16 52	17 30	17 22			17 49	18 03		17 52	18 30	18 22				18 49	19 03	18 52		19 30	19 22
Water Orton	d																								
Coleshill Parkway	d					17 05		17 35						18 05		18 35						19 05			19 35
Nuneaton	d					17 22		17 52						18 22		18 52						19 22			19 52
Hinckley	d					17 29								18 29								19 29			
Narborough	d					17 37								18 37								19 37			
South Wigston	d					17 42								18 42								19 42			
Leicester	a					17 52		18 12						18 48		19 12						19 50			20 12
Wilnecote	d																			19 04					
Tamworth	d	17 07									18 07	18 19								19 09					
Burton-on-Trent	d	17 19			17 29						18 19									19 21	19 26				
Willington	d																								
Derby 6	a	17 35			17 42		18 05				18 34	18 42			19 02					19 33	19 40			20 02	
	d	17 42									18 41									19 37					
Long Eaton	d																								
Attenborough	d																								
Beeston	d																								
Nottingham 6	a	18 02									19 04									19 56					

		XC	GW	XC	XC	XC	XC	XC		GW	AW	XC	XC	XC	XC	GW	XC	XC		GW	GW	XC	XC	XC	GW
		◇1 🛒	◇1 ☕	◇1	◇1 🛒	1	◇1 🛒	◇1 🛒				◇1	◇1 🛒	1	◇1 🛒	◇1 ☕	◇1	◇1 🛒				1	◇1	◇1 🛒	◇1 ☕
Cardiff Central 7	d			17 45							18 29	18 45					19 45						20 45		
Newport (South Wales)	d			18 03							18 48	19 03					20 04						21 03		
Bristol Temple Meads 10	d	18 00			18 30			19 00		18 41			19 30		20 00			20 30			20 41			22 10	
Bristol Parkway 7	d	18 10			18 40			19 10		18 52			19 40		20 10			20 40			20 52			22 20	
Gloucester 7	d		18 42	18 47						19 38	19 42	19 50				20 42	20 50			21 25	21 38		21 47		22 47
Cheltenham Spa	d	18 42	18a51	18 58	19 12			19 42		19 48	19a52	20 00	20 12		20 42	20a50	21 00	21 11		21a34	21a46		21 58	22 52	22a58
Ashchurch for Tewkesbury	d									19 57															
Worcester Shrub Hill 7	a									20 18															
Birmingham New Street 12	a	19 26		19 41	19 50			20 26				20 42	20 50		21 20		21 45	21 51					22 41	23 39	
	d			19 49	20 03	19 52	20 22						21 03	20 52				22 03				21 52			
Water Orton	d																								
Coleshill Parkway	d					20 05	20 35							21 05								22 05			
Nuneaton	d					20 22	20 51							21 22								22 26			
Hinckley	d					20 29								21 29								22 33			
Narborough	d					20 37								21 37								22 42			
South Wigston	d					20 42								21 42								22 46			
Leicester	a					20 50	21 12							21 52								22 53			
Wilnecote	d																								
Tamworth	d			20 07	20 19								21 19					22 19							
Burton-on-Trent	d			20 19									21 29												
Willington	d																								
Derby 6	a			20 34	20 42								21 42					22 45							
	d			20 37																					
Long Eaton	d																								
Attenborough	d																								
Beeston	d																								
Nottingham 6	a			21 01																					

		GW
Cardiff Central 7	d	
Newport (South Wales)	d	
Bristol Temple Meads 10	d	
Bristol Parkway 7	d	
Gloucester 7	d	23 56
Cheltenham Spa	d	00a05
Ashchurch for Tewkesbury	d	
Worcester Shrub Hill 7	a	
Birmingham New Street 12	a	
	d	
Water Orton	d	
Coleshill Parkway	d	
Nuneaton	d	
Hinckley	d	
Narborough	d	
South Wigston	d	
Leicester	a	
Wilnecote	d	
Tamworth	d	
Burton-on-Trent	d	
Willington	d	
Derby 6	a	
	d	
Long Eaton	d	
Attenborough	d	
Beeston	d	
Nottingham 6	a	

Table 57

Sundays

12 September to 17 October

Bristol and Cardiff - Birmingham - Leicester, Derby and Nottingham

		XC	XC	XC	XC	GW	GW	XC	XC	XC		XC	GW	AW	XC	XC	XC	XC	XC	XC		XC	XC	XC	GW
		◇■ ⊥	■	◇■ ⊥	◇■ ⊥		◇■ ⊡	■	◇■ ⊥	◇■		◇■ ⊥			■	◇■ ⊥	◇■ ⊥	◇■	◇■ ⊥	■		◇■ ⊥	◇■ ⊥	◇■	◇■ ⊡
Cardiff Central ■	d													10 23				10 45						11 45	
Newport (South Wales)	d													10 38				10 59						11 59	
Bristol Temple Meads ■	d				09 15	09 41						10 30							11 30						
Bristol Parkway ■	d				09 25	09 54						10 40							11 40						
Gloucester ■	d				10 01	10 37	10 46						11 40	11 45				11 52						12 47	12 52
Cheltenham Spa	d				10 12	10a48	10a55					11 12	11a49	11a57				12 03	12 12					12 58	13a03
Ashchurch for Tewkesbury	d																								
Worcester Shrub Hill ■	a																								
Birmingham New Street ■	a				10 50							11 50						12 45	12 50					13 41	
	d	09 03	09 52	10 03	11 03			10 52	11 22	11 49		12 03			11 52	12 22	12 30	12 49	13 03	12 52		13 22	13 30	13 49	
Water Orton	d																								
Coleshill Parkway	d		10 05					11 05	11 35						12 05	12 35				13 05		13 35			
Nuneaton	d		10 22					11 22	11 52						12 22	12 52				13 22		13 52			
Hinckley	d		10 29					11 29							12 29					13 29					
Narborough	d		10 37					11 37							12 37					13 37					
South Wigston	d		10 42												12 42										
Leicester	a		10 50					11 49	12 12						12 50	13 13				13 50		14 17			
Wilnecote	d																								
Tamworth	d	09 19		10 19						12 07		12 19						13 07						14 07	
Burton-on-Trent	d	09 29		10 29	11 26					12 19								13 19	13 26					14 19	
Willington	d																								
Derby ■	a	09 42		10 42	11 42					12 34		12 42					13 09	13 38	13 44				14 09	14 34	
	d									12 38								13 41						14 41	
Long Eaton	d																								
Attenborough	d																								
Beeston	d																								
Nottingham ■	a									13 02								14 04						15 07	

		XC	XC	XC	XC	XC		GW	AW	XC	XC	XC	XC	XC	XC	GW		XC	XC	GW	XC	XC	XC	XC	AW
		◇■ ⊥	■	◇■ ⊥	◇■ ⊥	◇■ ⊥				◇■	◇■ ⊥	■	◇■ ⊥	◇■ ⊥	◇■ ⊥	◇■ ⊡		◇■	◇■ ⊥		■	◇■ ⊥	◇■ ⊥	◇■ ⊥	
Cardiff Central ■	d								12 23	12 45								13 45							14 23
Newport (South Wales)	d								12 38	12 59								13 59							14 38
Bristol Temple Meads ■	d	12 30				13 00		12 41			13 30				14 00				14 30					15 00	
Bristol Parkway ■	d	12 40				13 10		12 52			13 40				14 10				14 40					15 10	
Gloucester ■	d							13 35	13 44	13 51						14 39		14 47		15 24					15 38
Cheltenham Spa	d	13 12				13 42		13 48	13a55	14 02	14 12				14 42	14a48		14 58	15 12	15a33				15 42	15a49
Ashchurch for Tewkesbury	d							13 57																	
Worcester Shrub Hill ■	a							14 24																	
Birmingham New Street ■	a	13 50				14 26				14 45	14 50				15 27			15 41	15 50					16 26	
	d	14 03	13 52	14 30	14 22					14 49	15 03	14 52	15 30	15 22				15 49	16 03		15 52	16 30	16 22		
Water Orton	d																								
Coleshill Parkway	d		14 05		14 35							15 05		15 35							16 05		16 35		
Nuneaton	d		14 22		14 52							15 22		15 52							16 22		16 52		
Hinckley	d		14 28									15 29									16 29				
Narborough	d		14 37									15 37									16 37				
South Wigston	d		14 42																		16 42				
Leicester	a		14 50		15 12							15 49		16 12							16 48		17 15		
Wilnecote	d									15 04															
Tamworth	d	14 19								15 09								16 07	16 19						
Burton-on-Trent	d									15 21	15 26							16 19							
Willington	d																								
Derby ■	a	14 42		15 04						15 34	15 42		16 02					16 34	16 42			17 04			
	d									15 44								16 41							
Long Eaton	d																								
Attenborough	d																								
Beeston	d																								
Nottingham ■	a									16 08								17 03							

Table 57

Sundays

12 September to 17 October

Bristol and Cardiff - Birmingham - Leicester, Derby and Nottingham

		XC		GW	XC	XC	XC	XC	XC	GW	XC	XC		XC	XC	XC	XC	GW	AW	XC	XC	XC		XC	XC
		◇■			◇■ ⊥	■	◇■ ⊥	◇■ ⊥	◇■ ⊥	◇■ ⊡	◇■	◇■ ⊥		■	◇■ ⊥	◇■ ⊥	◇■ ⊥			◇■	◇■ ⊥	■		◇■ ⊥	◇■ ⊥
Cardiff Central ■	d	14 45									15 45								16 22	16 45					
Newport (South Wales)	d	14 59									15 59								16 37	16 59					
Bristol Temple Meads ■	d			14 41	15 30				16 00			16 30					17 00	16 41			17 30				
Bristol Parkway ■	d			14 53	15 40				16 10			16 40					17 10	16 52			17 40				
Gloucester ■	d	15 47		15 52						16 35	16 47							17 35	17 38	17 47					
Cheltenham Spa	d	15 58		16 03	16 11				16 42	16a46	16 58	17 11					17 42	17 46	17a51	17 58	18 11				
Ashchurch for Tewkesbury	d			16 11														17 54							
Worcester Shrub Hill ■	a			16 34														18 14							
Birmingham New Street ■	a	16 41			16 50				17 26		17 41	17 49					18 27			18 41	18 51				
	d	16 49			17 03	16 52	17 30	17 22			17 49	18 03		17 52	18 30	18 22				18 49	19 03	18 52		19 30	19 22
Water Orton	d																								
Coleshill Parkway	d					17 05		17 35						18 05		18 35						19 05			19 35
Nuneaton	d					17 22		17 52						18 22		18 52						19 22			19 52
Hinckley	d					17 29								18 29								19 29			
Narborough	d					17 37								18 37								19 37			
South Wigston	d					17 42								18 42								19 42			
Leicester	a					17 50		18 12						18 48		19 12						19 50			20 12
Wilnecote	d																			19 04					
Tamworth	d	17 07									18 07	18 19								19 09					
Burton-on-Trent	d	17 19			17 29						18 19									19 21	19 26				
Willington	d																								
Derby ■	a	17 35			17 42		18 05				18 34	18 42			19 02					19 33	19 40			20 02	
	d	17 43									18 41	18 44								19 37					
Long Eaton	d																								
Attenborough	d																								
Beeston	d																								
Nottingham ■	a	18 02									19 04									19 56					

		XC	GW	XC	XC	XC	XC	XC		GW	AW	XC	XC	XC	XC	GW	XC	XC		GW	GW	XC	XC	GW	XC
		◇■ ⊥	◇■ ⊡	◇■	◇■ ⊥	■	◇■ ⊥	◇■ ⊥				◇■	◇■ ⊥	■	◇■ ⊥	◇■ ⊡	◇■	◇■ ⊥				■	◇■	◇■ ⊡	◇■ ⊥
Cardiff Central ■	d			17 45							18 23	18 45					19 45						20 45		
Newport (South Wales)	d			17 59							18 38	18 59					20 00						20 59		
Bristol Temple Meads ■	d	18 00			18 30			19 00		18 41			19 30		20 00			20 30			20 41				22 10
Bristol Parkway ■	d	18 10			18 40			19 10		18 52			19 40		20 10			20 40			20 52				22 20
Gloucester ■	d		18 37	18 47						19 38	19 42	19 50				20 38	20 50			21 25	21 38		21 47	22 36	
Cheltenham Spa	d	18 42	18a47	18 58	19 12			19 42		19 48	19a52	20 00	20 12		20 42	20a48	21 00	21 11		21a34	21a46		21 58	22a45	22 52
Ashchurch for Tewkesbury	d									19 57															
Worcester Shrub Hill ■	a									20 18															
Birmingham New Street ■	a	19 26		19 41	19 50			20 26				20 42	20 50		21 20		21 45	21 51					22 41		23 39
	d			19 49	20 03	19 52	20 22						21 03	20 52				22 03				21 52			
Water Orton	d																								
Coleshill Parkway	d					20 05	20 35							21 05								22 05			
Nuneaton	d					20 22	20 51							21 22								22 26			
Hinckley	d					20 29								21 29								22 33			
Narborough	d					20 37								21 37								22 42			
South Wigston	d					20 42								21 42								22 46			
Leicester	a					20 50	21 12							21 52								22 53			
Wilnecote	d																								
Tamworth	d			20 07	20 19								21 19					22 19							
Burton-on-Trent	d			20 19									21 29												
Willington	d																								
Derby ■	a			20 34	20 42								21 42					22 45							
	d			20 37																					
Long Eaton	d																								
Attenborough	d																								
Beeston	d																								
Nottingham ■	a			21 01																					

		GW
Cardiff Central ■	d	
Newport (South Wales)	d	
Bristol Temple Meads ■	d	
Bristol Parkway ■	d	
Gloucester ■	d	23 56
Cheltenham Spa	d	00a05
Ashchurch for Tewkesbury	d	
Worcester Shrub Hill ■	a	
Birmingham New Street ■	a	
	d	
Water Orton	d	
Coleshill Parkway	d	
Nuneaton	d	
Hinckley	d	
Narborough	d	
South Wigston	d	
Leicester	a	
Wilnecote	d	
Tamworth	d	
Burton-on-Trent	d	
Willington	d	
Derby ■	a	
	d	
Long Eaton	d	
Attenborough	d	
Beeston	d	
Nottingham ■	a	

Table 57

Sundays from 24 October

Bristol and Cardiff - Birmingham - Leicester, Derby and Nottingham

		XC	XC	XC	GW	XC	XC	XC	XC	XC		GW	AW	XC	XC	XC	XC	XC	XC	XC		XC	XC	GW	XC
		◇1 🛒	1	◇1 🛒	◇1 ☕	1	◇1 🛒	◇1 🛒	◇1	◇1 🛒				1	◇1 🛒	◇1 🛒	◇1	◇1 🛒	1	◇1 🛒		◇1 🛒	◇1	◇1 ☕	◇1 🛒
Cardiff Central 7	d												10 23				10 45						11 45		
Newport (South Wales)	d												10 38				10 59						11 59		
Bristol Temple Meads 10	d									09 30								10 30							11 30
Bristol Parkway 7	d									09 43								10 43							11 43
Gloucester 7	d				10 46					10 58		11 40	11 45				11 52	12 00					12 47	12 52	13 00
Cheltenham Spa	d				10a55					11 12		11a49	11a57				12 03	12 12					12 58	13a03	13 12
Ashchurch for Tewkesbury	d																								
Worcester Shrub Hill 7	a																								
Birmingham New Street 12	a									11 50							12 45	12 50					13 41		13 50
	d	09 03	09 52	10 03		10 52	11 03	11 22	11 49	12 03				11 52	12 22	12 30	12 49	13 03	12 52	13 22		13 30	13 49		14 03
Water Orton	d																								
Coleshill Parkway	d		10 05			11 05		11 35						12 05	12 35				13 05	13 35					
Nuneaton	d		10 22			11 22		11 52						12 22	12 52				13 22	13 52					
Hinckley	d		10 29			11 29								12 29					13 29						
Narborough	d		10 37			11 37								12 37					13 37						
South Wigston	d		10 42											12 42											
Leicester	a		10 50			11 49		12 12						12 50	13 13				13 50	14 12					
Wilnecote	d																								
Tamworth	d	09 19		10 19					12 07	12 19							13 07						14 07		14 19
Burton-on-Trent	d	09 29		10 29			11 26		12 19								13 19	13 26					14 19		
Willington	d																								
Derby 6	a	09 42		10 42			11 42		12 34	12 42						13 09	13 38	13 44				14 09	14 34		14 42
	d								12 38								13 41						14 41		
Long Eaton	d																								
Attenborough	d																								
Beeston	d																								
Nottingham 8	a								13 02								14 04						15 07		

		GW	AW	XC	XC	XC		XC	XC	XC	GW	XC	XC	XC	XC	GW		XC	XC	XC	XC	AW	XC	GW	XC
				1	◇1 🛒	◇1 🛒		◇1	1	◇1 🛒	◇1 ☕	◇1 🛒	◇1 🛒	◇1	◇1 🛒			1	◇1 🛒	◇1 🛒	◇1 🛒		◇1		◇1 🛒
Cardiff Central 7	d		12 23					12 45						13 45								14 23	14 45		
Newport (South Wales)	d		12 38					12 59						13 59								14 38	14 59		
Bristol Temple Meads 10	d									12 30					13 30						15 00			14 41	15 30
Bristol Parkway 7	d									12 43					13 43						15 10			14 53	15 40
Gloucester 7	d	13 37	13 44					13 51		14 01	14 39			14 47	14 57	15 24						15 38	15 47	15 52	
Cheltenham Spa	d	13 49	13a55					14 02		14 12	14a48			14 58	15 12	15a33					15 42	15a49	15 58	16 03	16 11
Ashchurch for Tewkesbury	d	13 57																						16 11	
Worcester Shrub Hill 7	a	14 24																						16 34	
Birmingham New Street 12	a							14 45		14 53				15 41	15 50						16 26		16 41		16 50
	d			13 52	14 30	14 22		14 49	14 52	15 03		15 30	15 22	15 49	16 03			15 52	16 30	16 22			16 49		17 03
Water Orton	d																								
Coleshill Parkway	d			14 05		14 35			15 05				15 35					16 05		16 35					
Nuneaton	d			14 22		14 52			15 22				15 52					16 22		16 52					
Hinckley	d			14 28					15 29									16 29							
Narborough	d			14 37					15 37									16 37							
South Wigston	d			14 42														16 42							
Leicester	a			14 50		15 12			15 49				16 12					16 48		17 15					
Wilnecote	d							15 04																	
Tamworth	d							15 09						16 07	16 19								17 07		
Burton-on-Trent	d							15 21		15 26				16 19									17 19		17 29
Willington	d																								
Derby 6	a				15 04			15 34		15 42		16 02		16 34	16 42				17 04				17 35		17 42
	d							15 44						16 41									17 43		
Long Eaton	d																								
Attenborough	d																								
Beeston	d																								
Nottingham 8	a							16 08						17 03									18 02		

Table 57

Sundays from 24 October

Bristol and Cardiff - Birmingham - Leicester, Derby and Nottingham

		XC		XC	XC	XC	GW	XC	XC	XC	XC	XC		XC	GW	AW	XC	XC	XC	XC	XC	XC		GW	XC
		1		◇1 🛒	◇1 🛒	◇1 🛒	◇1 ☕	◇1	◇1 🛒	1	◇1 🛒	◇1 🛒		◇1 🛒			◇1	◇1 🛒	1	◇1 🛒	◇1 🛒	◇1 🛒		◇1 ☕	◇1
Cardiff Central 7	d							15 45								16 22	16 45								17 45
Newport (South Wales)	d							15 59								16 37	16 59								17 59
Bristol Temple Meads 10	d					16 00			16 30					17 00	16 41			17 30				18 00			
Bristol Parkway 7	d					16 10			16 40					17 10	16 52			17 40				18 10			
Gloucester 7	d						16 35	16 47							17 35	17 38	17 47							18 37	18 47
Cheltenham Spa	d					16 42	16a46	16 58	17 11					17 42	17 46	17a51	17 58	18 11				18 42		18a47	18 58
Ashchurch for Tewkesbury	d														17 54										
Worcester Shrub Hill 7	a														18 14										
Birmingham New Street 12	a					17 26		17 41	17 49					18 27			18 41	18 51				19 26			19 41
	d	16 52		17 30	17 22			17 49	18 03	17 52	18 30	18 22					18 49	19 03	18 52	19 30	19 22				19 49
Water Orton	d																								
Coleshill Parkway	d	17 05			17 35					18 05		18 35							19 05		19 35				
Nuneaton	d	17 22			17 52					18 22		18 52							19 22		19 52				
Hinckley	d	17 29								18 29									19 29						
Narborough	d	17 37								18 37									19 37						
South Wigston	d	17 42								18 42									19 42						
Leicester	a	17 50			18 12					18 48		19 12							19 50		20 12				
Wilnecote	d																19 04								
Tamworth	d							18 07	18 19								19 09								20 07
Burton-on-Trent	d							18 19									19 21	19 26							20 19
Willington	d																								
Derby 6	a			18 05				18 34	18 42		19 02						19 33	19 40		20 02					20 34
	d							18 41									19 37								20 37
Long Eaton	d																								
Attenborough	d																								
Beeston	d																								
Nottingham 8	a							19 04									19 56								21 01

		XC	XC	XC	XC	GW	AW	XC		XC	XC	XC	GW	XC	XC	GW	GW	XC		XC	GW	XC	GW		
		◇1 🛒	1	◇1 🛒	◇1 🛒			◇1		◇1 🛒	1	◇1 🛒	◇1 ☕	◇1	◇1 🛒			1		◇1	◇1 ☕	◇1 🛒			
Cardiff Central 7	d						18 23	18 45						19 45						20 45					
Newport (South Wales)	d						18 38	18 59						20 00						20 59					
Bristol Temple Meads 10	d	18 30			19 00	18 41				19 30		20 00			20 30		20 41					21 39			
Bristol Parkway 7	d	18 40			19 10	18 52				19 40		20 10			20 40		20 52					21 52			
Gloucester 7	d					19 38	19 42	19 50					20 38	20 50		21 25	21 38			21 47	22 36		23 56		
Cheltenham Spa	d	19 12			19 42	19 48	19a52	20 00		20 12		20 42	20a48	21 00	21 11	21a34	21a46			21 58	22a45	22 52	00a05		
Ashchurch for Tewkesbury	d					19 57																			
Worcester Shrub Hill 7	a					20 18																			
Birmingham New Street 12	a	19 50			20 26			20 42		20 50		21 20		21 45	21 51					22 41		23 39			
	d	20 03	19 52	20 22						21 03	20 52				22 03			21 52							
Water Orton	d																								
Coleshill Parkway	d		20 05	20 35							21 05							22 05							
Nuneaton	d		20 22	20 51							21 22							22 26							
Hinckley	d		20 29								21 29							22 33							
Narborough	d		20 37								21 37							22 42							
South Wigston	d		20 42								21 42							22 46							
Leicester	a		20 50	21 12							21 52							22 53							
Wilnecote	d																								
Tamworth	d	20 19								21 19					22 19										
Burton-on-Trent	d									21 29															
Willington	d																								
Derby 6	a	20 42								21 42					22 45										
	d																								
Long Eaton	d																								
Attenborough	d																								
Beeston	d																								
Nottingham 8	a																								

Network Diagram for Tables 59, 60, 61, 62, 64, 66

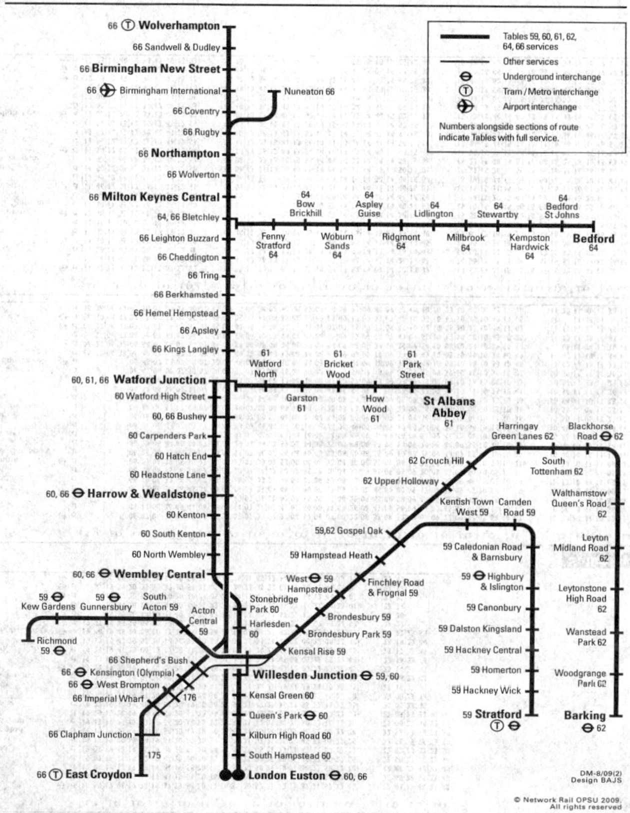

Stratford - Highbury and Islington, West Hampstead, Willesden Junction and Richmond.

		LO MO	LO MO	LO MO	LO MO	LO	LO	LO	LO	LO	LO	LO	LO	LO	LO	LO	LO	LO	LO	LO	LO	LO	LO	LO	LO
Stratford ⊖	d	23p00		23p30				06 09	06 19	06 29	06 39	06 49	06 59	07 09	07 19	07 29	07 37	07 49	07 59	08 09	08 19		08 29	08 39	08 49
Hackney Wick	d	23p10		23p40				06 12	06 22	06 32	06 42	06 52	07 02	07 12	07 22	07 32	07 40	07 52	08 02	08 12	08 22		08 32	08 42	08 52
Homerton	d	23p17		23p47				06 15	06 25	06 35	06 45	06 55	07 05	07 15	07 25	07 35	07 43	07 55	08 05	08 15	08 25		08 35	08 45	08 55
Hackney Central	d	23p25		23p55				06 17	06 27	06 37	06 47	06 57	07 07	07 17	07 27	07 37	07 45	07 57	08 07	08 17	08 27		08 37	08 47	08 57
Dalston Kingsland	d	23p33		00 03				06 19	06 29	06 39	06 49	06 59	07 09	07 19	07 29	07 39	07 47	07 59	08 09	08 19	08 29		08 39	08 49	08 59
Canonbury	d	23p41		00 11				06 22	06 32	06 42	06 52	07 02	07 12	07 22	07 32	07 42	07 50	08 02	08 12	08 22	08 32		08 42	08 52	09 02
Highbury & Islington ⊖	d	23p46		00 16				06 25	06 35	06 45	06 55	07 05	07 15	07 25	07 35	07 45	07 53	08 05	08 15	08 25	08 35		08 45	08 55	09 05
Caledonian Rd & Barnsbury	d							06 27	06 37	06 47	06 57	07 07	07 17	07 27	07 37	07 47	07 55	08 07	08 17	08 27	08 37		08 47	08 57	09 07
Camden Road	d	23p59		00 30				06 33	06 42	06 50	07 00	07 10	07 20	07 30	07 40	07 50	07 59	08 10	08 20	08 30	08 40		08 50	09 00	09 10
Kentish Town West	d	00 08		00 38				06 35	06 44	06 52	07 02	07 12	07 22	07 32	07 42	07 52	08 01	08 12	08 22	08 32	08 42		08 52	09 02	09 12
Gospel Oak	d		23p25		23p50			06 40	06 48	06 56	07 06	07 16	07 26	07 36	07 46	07 56	08 05	08 16	08 26	08 36	08 46		08 56	09 06	09 16
Hampstead Heath	d	00a14	23p30	00a44	23p55			06 42	06 50	06 58	07 08	07 18	07 28	07 38	07 48	07 58	08 07	08 18	08 28	08 38	08 48		08 58	09 08	09 18
Finchley Road & Frognal	d		23p40		00 05			06 44	06 52	07 00	07 10	07 20	07 30	07 40	07 50	08 00	08 09	08 20	08 30	08 40	08 50		09 00	09 10	09 20
West Hampstead ⊖	d		23p45		00 10			06 46	06 54	07 02	07 12	07 22	07 32	07 42	07 52	08 02	08 11	08 22	08 32	08 42	08 52		09 02	09 12	09 22
Brondesbury	d		23p50		00 15			06 48	06 56	07 04	07 14	07 24	07 34	07 44	07 54	08 04	08 13	08 24	08 34	08 44	08 54		09 04	09 14	09 24
Brondesbury Park	d		23p53		00 18			06 49	06 57	07 05	07 15	07 25	07 35	07 45	07 55	08 05	08 14	08 25	08 35	08 45	08 55		09 05	09 15	09 25
Kensal Rise	d		23p57		00 22			06 51	06 59	07 07	07 17	07 27	07 37	07 47	07 57	08 07	08 16	08 27	08 37	08 47	08 57		09 07	09 17	09 27
Willesden Jn. High Level ⊖	a		00 08		00 34			06 54	07 02	07 11	07 20	07 31	07 40	07 51	08 00	08 11	08 19	08 31	08 40	08 51	09 01		09 10	09 21	09 31
	d		00 09			06 19	06 32	06 55	07 03	07 12	07 22	07 32	07 42	07 52	08 02	08 12	08 20	08 32	08 42	08 52	09 02	08 25	09 12	09 22	09 32
Acton Central	d		00 21			06 24	06 37	07 00		07 17		07 37		07 57		08 17		08 37		08 57		08 30	09 17		09 37
South Acton	d		00 24			06 28	06 41	07 04		07 21		07 41		08 01		08 21		08 41		09 01		08 34	09 21		09 41
Gunnersbury ⊖	d		00a30			06 30	06 43	07 07		07 24		07 44		08 04		08 24		08 44		09 04		08 36	09 24		09 47
Kew Gardens ⊖	d					06 33	06 46	07 09		07 26		07 46		08 06		08 26		08 46		09 06		08 39	09 26		09 50
Richmond ⊖	a					06 39	06 51	07 18		07 34		07 54		08 14		08 34		08 54		09 14		08 45	09 34		09 53

		LO	LO	LO	LO	LO	LO	LO	LO	LO	LO	LO	LO	LO	LO	LO	LO	LO	LO	LO	LO	LO	LO	LO	LO
Stratford ⊖	d	08 59	09 09	09 22	09 37	09 52	10 07	10 22	10 37	10 52	11 07	11 22	11 37	11 52	12 07	12 22	12 37	12 52	13 07	13 22	13 37	13 52	14 07	14 22	14 37
Hackney Wick	d	09 02	09 12	09 26	09 41	09 56	10 11	10 26	10 41	10 56	11 11	11 26	11 41	11 56	12 11	12 26	12 41	12 56	13 11	13 26	13 41	13 56	14 11	14 26	14 41
Homerton	d	09 05	09 15	09 28	09 43	09 58	10 13	10 28	10 43	10 58	11 13	11 28	11 43	11 58	12 13	12 28	12 43	12 58	13 13	13 28	13 43	13 58	14 13	14 28	14 43
Hackney Central	d	09 07	09 17	09 30	09 45	10 00	10 15	10 30	10 45	11 00	11 15	11 30	11 45	12 01	12 15	12 30	12 45	13 00	13 15	13 31	13 45	14 00	14 15	14 30	14 45
Dalston Kingsland	d	09 09	09 19	09 33	09 48	10 03	10 18	10 33	10 48	11 03	11 18	11 33	11 48	12 03	12 18	12 33	12 48	13 03	13 18	13 33	13 48	14 03	14 18	14 33	14 48
Canonbury	d	09 12	09 22	09 35	09 50	10 05	10 20	10 35	10 50	11 05	11 20	11 35	11 50	12 06	12 20	12 35	12 50	13 05	13 20	13 36	13 50	14 05	14 20	14 35	14 50
Highbury & Islington ⊖	d	09 15	09 25	09 38	09 53	10 08	10 23	10 38	10 53	11 08	11 23	11 38	11 53	12 09	12 23	12 38	12 53	13 08	13 23	13 39	13 53	14 08	14 23	14 38	14 53
Caledonian Rd & Barnsbury	d	09 17	09 27	09 40	09 55	10 10	10 25	10 40	10 55	11 10	11 25	11 40	11 55	12 10	12 25	12 40	12 55	13 10	13 25	13 41	13 55	14 10	14 25	14 40	14 55
Camden Road	d	09 20	09 30	09 44	09 59	10 14	10 29	10 44	10 59	11 14	11 29	11 44	11 59	12 14	12 29	12 44	12 59	13 14	13 29	13 44	13 59	14 14	14 29	14 44	14 59
Kentish Town West	d	09 22	09 32	09 46	10 01	10 16	10 31	10 46	11 01	11 16	11 31	11 46	12 01	12 16	12 31	12 46	13 01	13 16	13 31	13 46	14 01	14 16	14 31	14 46	15 01
Gospel Oak	d	09 26	09 36	09 49	10 04	10 19	10 34	10 49	11 04	11 19	11 34	11 49	12 04	12 19	12 34	12 49	13 05	13 19	13 34	13 49	14 04	14 19	14 34	14 49	15 04
Hampstead Heath	d	09 28	09 38	09 50	10 06	10 21	10 36	10 50	11 06	11 20	11 36	11 50	12 06	12 20	12 36	12 50	13 07	13 20	13 36	13 51	14 06	14 20	14 36	14 50	15 06
Finchley Road & Frognal	d	09 30	09 40	09 53	10 08	10 23	10 38	10 53	11 08	11 23	11 38	11 53	12 08	12 23	12 38	12 53	13 09	13 23	13 38	13 53	14 08	14 23	14 38	14 53	15 08
West Hampstead ⊖	d	09 32	09 42	09 54	10 10	10 25	10 40	10 54	11 10	11 24	11 40	11 54	12 10	12 24	12 40	12 54	13 11	13 24	13 40	13 55	14 10	14 24	14 40	14 54	15 10
Brondesbury	d	09 34	09 44	09 56	10 11	10 26	10 41	10 56	11 11	11 26	11 41	11 56	12 11	12 26	12 41	12 56	13 12	13 26	13 41	13 56	14 11	14 26	14 41	14 56	15 11
Brondesbury Park	d	09 35	09 45	09 57	10 13	10 28	10 43	10 57	11 13	11 27	11 43	11 57	12 13	12 27	12 43	12 57	13 14	13 27	13 43	13 58	14 13	14 27	14 43	14 57	15 13
Kensal Rise	d	09 37	09 47	09 59	10 15	10 30	10 45	10 59	11 15	11 29	11 45	11 59	12 15	12 29	12 45	12 59	13 16	13 29	13 45	14 00	14 15	14 29	14 45	14 59	15 15
Willesden Jn. High Level ⊖	a	09 41	09 51	10 02	10 18	10 33	10 48	11 02	11 18	11 32	11 48	12 02	12 18	12 33	12 48	13 02	13 19	13 32	13 48	14 03	14 18	14 32	14 48	15 02	15 18
	d	09 42	09 52	10 03	10 19	10 34	10 49	11 03	11 19	11 33	11 49	12 03	12 19	12 33	12 49	13 03	13 19	13 33	13 49	14 04	14 19	14 33	14 49	15 03	15 19
Acton Central	d		09 57	10 08	10 24	10 39	10 54	11 08	11 24	11 38	11 54	12 08	12 24	12 38	12 54	13 08	13 24	13 38	13 54	14 09	14 24	14 38	14 54	15 08	15 24
South Acton	d		10 01	10 12	10 28	10 43	10 58	11 12	11 28	11 42	11 58	12 12	12 28	12 42	12 58	13 12	13 29	13 42	13 58	14 13	14 28	14 42	14 58	15 12	15 28
Gunnersbury ⊖	d		10 04	10 15	10 32	10 45	11 02	11 15	11 32	11 45	12 02	12 15	12 32	12 45	13 02	13 15	13 32	13 45	14 02	14 15	14 32	14 45	15 02	15 15	15 32
Kew Gardens ⊖	d		10 06	10 17	10 35	10 48	11 05	11 17	11 35	11 47	12 05	12 17	12 35	12 47	13 05	13 17	13 35	13 47	14 05	14 18	14 35	14 47	15 05	15 17	15 35
Richmond ⊖	a		10 14	10 23	10 40	10 54	11 10	11 23	11 40	11 53	12 10	12 23	12 40	12 54	13 10	13 23	13 40	13 53	14 10	14 24	14 40	14 53	15 10	15 23	15 39

		LO	LO	LO	LO	LO	LO	LO	LO	LO	LO	LO	LO	LO	LO	LO	LO	LO	LO	LO	LO	LO	LO	LO
Stratford ⊖	d	14 52	15 07	15 22	15 37	15 52	16 09	16 19	16 29	16 39	16 49	16 59	17 09	17 19	17 29	17 39		17 49	17 59	18 09	18 19	18 29	18 39	18 49
Hackney Wick	d	14 56	15 11	15 26	15 41	15 56	16 12	16 22	16 32	16 42	16 52	17 02	17 12	17 22	17 32	17 42		17 52	18 02	18 12	18 22	18 32	18 42	18 52
Homerton	d	14 58	15 13	15 28	15 43	15 58	16 15	16 25	16 35	16 45	16 55	17 05	17 15	17 25	17 35	17 45		17 55	18 05	18 15	18 25	18 35	18 45	18 55
Hackney Central	d	15 00	15 15	15 30	15 46	16 00	16 17	16 27	16 37	16 47	16 57	17 07	17 17	17 27	17 37	17 47		17 57	18 07	18 17	18 27	18 37	18 47	18 57
Dalston Kingsland	d	15 03	15 18	15 34	15 48	16 03	16 19	16 31	16 39	16 49	16 59	17 09	17 19	17 29	17 39	17 49		17 59	18 09	18 19	18 29	18 39	18 49	18 59
Canonbury	d	15 05	15 20	15 36	15 51	16 05	16 22	16 34	16 42	16 52	17 02	17 12	17 22	17 32	17 42	17 52		18 02	18 12	18 22	18 32	18 42	18 52	19 02
Highbury & Islington ⊖	d	15 08	15 23	15 39	15 54	16 08	16 25	16 37	16 45	16 55	17 05	17 15	17 25	17 35	17 45	17 55		18 05	18 15	18 25	18 35	18 45	18 55	19 05
Caledonian Rd & Barnsbury	d	15 10	15 25	15 41	15 55	16 10	16 27	16 39	16 47	16 57	17 07	17 17	17 27	17 37	17 47	17 57		18 07	18 17	18 27	18 37	18 47	18 57	19 07
Camden Road	d	15 14	15 29	15 45	15 59	16 14	16 30	16 42	16 50	17 00	17 10	17 20	17 30	17 40	17 50	18 00		18 10	18 20	18 30	18 40	18 50	19 00	19 10
Kentish Town West	d	15 16	15 31	15 47	16 01	16 16	16 32	16 43	16 52	17 02	17 12	17 22	17 32	17 42	17 52	18 02		18 12	18 22	18 32	18 42	18 52	19 02	19 12
Gospel Oak	d	15 19	15 34	15 50	16 04	16 19	16 36	16 47	16 56	17 06	17 16	17 26	17 37	17 46	17 56	18 06		18 16	18 26	18 36	18 46	18 56	19 06	19 16
Hampstead Heath	d	15 20	15 35	15 51	16 06	16 20	16 38	16 49	16 58	17 08	17 18	17 28	17 39	17 48	17 58	18 08		18 18	18 28	18 38	18 48	18 58	19 08	19 18
Finchley Road & Frognal	d	15 23	15 38	15 54	16 08	16 23	16 40	16 51	17 00	17 10	17 20	17 30	17 41	17 50	18 00	18 10		18 20	18 30	18 40	18 50	19 00	19 10	19 20
West Hampstead ⊖	d	15 24	15 39	15 55	16 10	16 24	16 42	16 53	17 02	17 12	17 22	17 32	17 43	17 52	18 02	18 12		18 22	18 32	18 42	18 52	19 02	19 12	19 22
Brondesbury	d	15 26	15 41	15 57	16 11	16 26	16 44	16 55	17 04	17 14	17 24	17 34	17 45	17 54	18 04	18 14		18 24	18 34	18 44	18 54	19 04	19 14	19 24
Brondesbury Park	d	15 27	15 42	15 58	16 13	16 27	16 45	16 56	17 05	17 15	17 25	17 35	17 46	17 55	18 05	18 15		18 25	18 35	18 45	18 55	19 05	19 15	19 25
Kensal Rise	d	15 29	15 44	16 00	16 15	16 29	16 47	16 58	17 07	17 17	17 27	17 37	17 48	17 57	18 07	18 17		18 27	18 37	18 47	18 57	19 07	19 17	19 27
Willesden Jn. High Level ⊖	a	15 32	15 47	16 03	16 19	16 32	16 51	17 02	17 11	17 21	17 31	17 40	17 52	18 01	18 11	18 21		18 31	18 41	18 51	19 01	19 11	19 21	19 31
	d	15 33	15 48	16 04	16 19	16 33	16 52	17 03	17 12	17 22	17 32	17 42	17 53	18 02	18 12	18 22	18 27	18 32	18 42	18 52	19 02	19 12	19 22	19 32
Acton Central	d	15 38	15 53	16 09	16 24	16 38	16 57		17 17		17 37		17 58		18 17		18 32	18 37		18 57		19 17		19 37
South Acton	d	15 42	15 57	16 13	16 28	16 42	17 01		17 21		17 41		18 02		18 21		18 36	18 41		19 01		19 21		19 41
Gunnersbury ⊖	d	15 45	16 00	16 16	16 32	16 45	17 04		17 24		17 44		18 04		18 24		18 38	18 44		19 04		19 24		19 44
Kew Gardens ⊖	d	15 47	16 02	16 18	16 36	16 47	17 09		17 30		17 47		18 07		18 30		18 41	18 47		19 06		19 29		19 46
Richmond ⊖	a	15 53	16 08	16 25	16 41	16 53	17 14		17 34		17 54		18 15		18 34		18 47	18 54		19 14		19 34		19 54

Table 59

Stratford - Highbury and Islington West Hampstead, Willesden Junction and Richmond.

			LO	LO	LO	LO	LO	LO	LO	LO	LO	LO	LO	LO	LO	LO	LO
Stratford 7	⊖	d	18 59	19 06	19 22	19 37	19 52	20 12	20 32	20 52	21 12	21 32	21 52	22 12	22 42	23 12	23 42
Hackney Wick		d	19 02	19 10	19 26	19 41	19 56	20 16	20 36	20 56	21 16	21 36	21 56	22 16	22 45	23 15	23 45
Homerton		d	19 05	19 12	19 29	19 44	19 58	20 18	20 38	20 58	21 18	21 38	21 58	22 18	22 48	23 18	23 48
Hackney Central		d	19 07	19 15	19 32	19 46	20 00	20 20	20 41	21 00	21 20	21 40	22 00	22 20	22 50	23 20	23 50
Dalston Kingsland		d	19 09	19 17	19 35	19 48	20 05	20 24	20 43	21 05	21 23	21 43	22 03	22 23	22 52	23 22	23 52
Canonbury		d	19 12	19 20	19 38	19 51	20 09	20 27	20 46	21 07	21 25	21 45	22 05	22 25	22 55	23 25	23 55
Highbury & Islington	⊖	d	19 15	19 23	19 41	19 54	20 12	20 30	20 49	21 10	21 28	21 48	22 08	22 28	22 58	23 28	23 57
Caledonian Rd & Barnsbury		d	19 17	19 25	19 43	19 56	20 14	20 32	20 50	21 12	21 30	21 50	22 10	22 30	23 00	23 30	23 59
Camden Road		d	19 20	19 28	19 46	19 59	20 17	20 35	20 53	21 15	21 33	21 53	22 13	22 33	23 03	23 33	00a04
Kentish Town West		d	19 22	19 30	19 48	20 01	20 19	20 36	20 55	21 17	21 35	21 55	22 15	22 35	23 05	23 35	
Gospel Oak		d	19 26	19 33	19 51	20 04	20 22	20 39	20 58	21 20	21 38	21 58	22 18	22 38	23 08	23 38	
Hampstead Heath		d	19 28	19 34	19 53	20 05	20 24	20 41	20 59	21 22	21 39	21 59	22 19	22 39	23 10	23 40	
Finchley Road & Frognal		d	19 30	19 36	19 56	20 08	20 26	20 43	21 02	21 24	21 42	22 02	22 22	22 43	23 13	23 43	
West Hampstead	⊖	d	19 32	19 38	19 57	20 09	20 28	20 45	21 03	21 26	21 43	22 03	22 23	22 43	23 14	23 44	
Brondesbury		d	19 33	19 39	19 59	20 11	20 29	20 46	21 05	21 27	21 45	22 05	22 25	22 46	23 16	23 46	
Brondesbury Park		d	19 35	19 41	20 00	20 12	20 31	20 48	21 06	21 29	21 46	22 06	22 26	22 46	23 17	23 47	
Kensal Rise		d	19 37	19 43	20 02	20 14	20 33	20 50	21 08	21 31	21 48	22 08	22 28	22 48	23 19	23 49	
Willesden Jn. High Level	⊖	a	19 40	19 45	20 06	20 17	20 35	20 54	21 12	21 35	21 52	22 12	22 32	22 52	23 22	23 54	
		d	19 41	19 45	20 06	20 18	20 37	20 54	21 12	21 35	21 52	22 12	22 32	22 52	23 23		
Acton Central		d		19 50	20 14	20 23	20 42	20 59	21 17	21 40	21 57	22 17	22 37	22 57	23 28		
South Acton		d		19 54	20 16	20 27	20 46	21 03	21 21	21 44	22 01	22 21	22 41	23 01	23 32		
Gunnersbury	⊖	d		19 57	20 18	20 30	20 48	21 05	21 24	21 46	22 04	22 24	22 44	23 05	23 35		
Kew Gardens	⊖	d		19 59	20 21	20 32	20 51	21 08	21 26	21 49	22 06	22 26	22 46	23 06	23 37		
Richmond	⊖	a		20 09	20 24	20 36	20 54	21 14	21 36	21 55	22 14	22 32	22 53	23 13	23 43		

Saturdays

			LO	LO	LO	LO	LO	LO	LO	LO	LO	LO	LO	LO	LO	LO	LO	LO	LO	LO	LO	LO	LO	LO	LO
Stratford 7	⊖	d			06 07	06 22	06 37	06 52	07 07	07 22	07 37	07 52	08 07	08 22	08 37	08 52	09 07	09 22	09 37	09 52	10 07	10 22	10 37	10 52	11 07
Hackney Wick		d			06 11	06 26	06 41	06 56	07 11	07 26	07 41	07 56	08 11	08 26	08 41	08 56	09 11	09 26	09 41	09 56	10 11	10 26	10 41	10 56	11 11
Homerton		d			06 13	06 28	06 43	06 58	07 13	07 28	07 43	07 58	08 13	08 28	08 43	08 58	09 13	09 28	09 43	09 58	10 13	10 28	10 43	10 58	11 13
Hackney Central		d			06 15	06 30	06 45	07 00	07 15	07 31	07 45	08 00	08 15	08 30	08 45	09 00	09 15	09 30	09 45	10 00	10 15	10 30	10 45	11 00	11 15
Dalston Kingsland		d			06 18	06 33	06 48	07 03	07 18	07 33	07 48	08 03	08 18	08 33	08 48	09 03	09 18	09 33	09 48	10 03	10 18	10 33	10 48	11 03	11 18
Canonbury		d			06 20	06 35	06 50	07 05	07 20	07 36	07 50	08 05	08 20	08 35	08 50	09 05	09 20	09 35	09 50	10 05	10 20	10 35	10 50	11 05	11 20
Highbury & Islington	⊖	d			06 23	06 38	06 53	07 08	07 23	07 39	07 53	08 08	08 23	08 38	08 53	09 08	09 23	09 38	09 53	10 08	10 23	10 38	10 53	11 08	11 23
Caledonian Rd & Barnsbury		d			06 25	06 40	06 55	07 10	07 25	07 40	07 55	08 10	08 25	08 40	08 55	09 10	09 25	09 40	09 55	10 10	10 25	10 40	10 55	11 10	11 25
Camden Road		d			06 29	06 44	06 59	07 14	07 29	07 44	07 59	08 14	08 29	08 44	08 59	09 14	09 29	09 44	09 59	10 14	10 29	10 44	10 59	11 14	11 29
Kentish Town West		d			06 31	06 46	07 01	07 16	07 31	07 46	08 01	08 16	08 31	08 46	09 01	09 16	09 31	09 46	10 01	10 16	10 31	10 46	11 01	11 16	11 31
Gospel Oak		d			06 34	06 49	07 04	07 19	07 34	07 49	08 04	08 19	08 34	08 49	09 04	09 19	09 34	09 49	10 04	10 19	10 34	10 49	11 04	11 19	11 34
Hampstead Heath		d			06 36	06 50	07 06	07 21	07 36	07 50	08 06	08 21	08 36	08 50	09 06	09 21	09 36	09 50	10 06	10 21	10 36	10 50	11 06	11 21	11 36
Finchley Road & Frognal		d			06 38	06 53	07 08	07 23	07 38	07 53	08 08	08 23	08 38	08 53	09 08	09 23	09 38	09 53	10 08	10 23	10 38	10 53	11 08	11 23	11 38
West Hampstead	⊖	d			06 40	06 54	07 10	07 25	07 40	07 54	08 10	08 25	08 40	08 54	09 10	09 25	09 40	09 54	10 10	10 25	10 40	10 54	11 10	11 25	11 40
Brondesbury		d			06 41	06 56	07 11	07 26	07 41	07 56	08 11	08 26	08 41	08 56	09 11	09 26	09 41	09 56	10 11	10 26	10 41	10 56	11 11	11 26	11 41
Brondesbury Park		d			06 43	06 57	07 13	07 28	07 43	07 57	08 13	08 28	08 43	08 57	09 13	09 28	09 43	09 57	10 13	10 28	10 43	10 57	11 13	11 28	11 43
Kensal Rise		d			06 45	06 59	07 15	07 30	07 45	07 59	08 15	08 30	08 45	08 59	09 15	09 30	09 45	09 59	10 15	10 30	10 45	10 59	11 15	11 30	11 45
Willesden Jn. High Level	⊖	a			06 48	07 02	07 18	07 33	07 48	08 03	08 18	08 33	08 48	09 02	09 18	09 33	09 48	10 02	10 18	10 33	10 48	11 02	11 18	11 33	11 48
		d	06 17	06 33	06 49	07 03	07 19	07 34	07 49	08 03	08 19	08 34	08 49	09 03	09 19	09 34	09 49	10 03	10 19	10 34	10 49	11 03	11 19	11 34	11 49
Acton Central		d	06 22	06 38	06 54	07 08	07 24	07 39	07 54	08 08	08 24	08 39	08 54	09 08	09 24	09 39	09 54	10 08	10 24	10 39	10 54	11 08	11 24	11 39	11 54
South Acton		d	06 26	06 42	06 58	07 12	07 28	07 43	07 58	08 12	08 28	08 43	08 58	09 12	09 28	09 43	09 58	10 12	10 28	10 43	10 58	11 12	11 28	11 43	11 58
Gunnersbury	⊖	d	06 27	06 45	07 02	07 15	07 32	07 45	08 02	08 15	08 32	08 45	09 02	09 15	09 32	09 45	10 02	10 15	10 32	10 45	11 02	11 15	11 32	11 45	12 02
Kew Gardens	⊖	d	06 30	06 47	07 05	07 17	07 35	07 48	08 05	08 17	08 35	08 48	09 05	09 17	09 35	09 48	10 05	10 17	10 35	10 48	11 05	11 17	11 35	11 48	12 05
Richmond	⊖	a	06 36	06 53	07 10	07 23	07 40	07 53	08 10	08 24	08 40	08 53	09 10	09 23	09 40	09 53	10 10	10 23	10 40	10 53	11 10	11 23	11 40	11 53	12 10

			LO	LO	LO	LO	LO	LO	LO	LO	LO	LO	LO	LO	LO	LO	LO	LO	LO	LO	LO	LO	LO	LO
Stratford 7	⊖	d	11 22	11 37	11 52	12 07	12 22	12 37	12 52	13 07	13 22	13 37	13 52	14 07	14 22	14 37	14 52	15 07	15 22	15 37	15 52	16 07	16 22	16 37
Hackney Wick		d	11 26	11 41	11 56	12 11	12 26	12 41	12 56	13 11	13 26	13 41	13 56	14 11	14 26	14 41	14 56	15 11	15 26	15 41	15 56	16 11	16 26	16 41
Homerton		d	11 28	11 43	11 58	12 13	12 28	12 43	12 58	13 13	13 28	13 43	13 58	14 13	14 28	14 43	14 58	15 13	15 28	15 43	15 58	16 13	16 28	16 43
Hackney Central		d	11 30	11 45	12 00	12 15	12 30	12 45	13 00	13 15	13 30	13 45	14 00	14 15	14 30	14 45	15 00	15 15	15 30	15 45	16 00	16 15	16 30	16 45
Dalston Kingsland		d	11 33	11 48	12 03	12 18	12 33	12 48	13 03	13 18	13 33	13 48	14 03	14 18	14 33	14 48	15 03	15 18	15 33	15 48	16 03	16 18	16 33	16 48
Canonbury		d	11 35	11 50	12 05	12 20	12 35	12 50	13 05	13 20	13 35	13 50	14 05	14 20	14 35	14 50	15 05	15 20	15 35	15 50	16 05	16 20	16 35	16 50
Highbury & Islington	⊖	d	11 38	11 53	12 08	12 23	12 38	12 53	13 08	13 23	13 38	13 53	14 08	14 23	14 38	14 53	15 08	15 23	15 38	15 53	16 08	16 23	16 38	16 53
Caledonian Rd & Barnsbury		d	11 40	11 55	12 10	12 25	12 40	12 55	13 10	13 25	13 40	13 55	14 10	14 25	14 40	14 55	15 10	15 25	15 40	15 55	16 10	16 25	16 40	16 55
Camden Road		d	11 44	11 59	12 14	12 29	12 44	12 59	13 14	13 29	13 44	13 59	14 14	14 29	14 44	14 59	15 14	15 29	15 44	15 59	16 14	16 29	16 44	16 59
Kentish Town West		d	11 46	12 01	12 16	12 31	12 46	13 01	13 16	13 31	13 46	14 01	14 16	14 31	14 46	15 01	15 16	15 31	15 46	16 01	16 16	16 31	16 46	17 01
Gospel Oak		d	11 49	12 04	12 19	12 34	12 49	13 04	13 19	13 34	13 49	14 04	14 19	14 34	14 49	15 04	15 19	15 34	15 49	16 04	16 19	16 34	16 49	17 04
Hampstead Heath		d	11 50	12 06	12 21	12 36	12 50	13 06	13 21	13 36	13 50	14 06	14 21	14 36	14 50	15 06	15 21	15 36	15 50	16 06	16 21	16 36	16 50	17 06
Finchley Road & Frognal		d	11 53	12 08	12 23	12 38	12 53	13 08	13 23	13 38	13 53	14 08	14 23	14 38	14 53	15 08	15 23	15 38	15 53	16 08	16 23	16 38	16 53	17 08
West Hampstead	⊖	d	11 54	12 10	12 25	12 40	12 54	13 10	13 25	13 40	13 54	14 10	14 25	14 40	14 54	15 10	15 25	15 40	15 54	16 10	16 25	16 40	16 54	17 10
Brondesbury		d	11 56	12 11	12 26	12 41	12 56	13 11	13 26	13 41	13 56	14 11	14 26	14 41	14 56	15 11	15 26	15 41	15 56	16 11	16 26	16 41	16 56	17 11
Brondesbury Park		d	11 57	12 13	12 28	12 43	12 57	13 13	13 28	13 43	13 57	14 13	14 28	14 43	14 57	15 13	15 28	15 43	15 57	16 13	16 28	16 43	16 57	17 13
Kensal Rise		d	11 59	12 15	12 30	12 45	12 59	13 15	13 30	13 45	13 59	14 15	14 30	14 45	14 59	15 15	15 30	15 45	15 59	16 15	16 30	16 45	16 59	17 15
Willesden Jn. High Level	⊖	a	12 02	12 18	12 33	12 48	13 02	13 18	13 33	13 48	14 02	14 18	14 33	14 48	15 02	15 18	15 33	15 48	16 02	16 18	16 33	16 48	17 02	17 18
		d	12 03	12 19	12 34	12 49	13 03	13 19	13 34	13 49	14 03	14 19	14 34	14 49	15 03	15 19	15 34	15 49	16 03	16 19	16 34	16 49	17 03	17 19
Acton Central		d	12 08	12 24	12 39	12 54	13 08	13 24	13 39	13 54	14 08	14 24	14 39	14 54	15 08	15 24	15 39	15 54	16 08	16 24	16 39	16 54	17 08	17 24
South Acton		d	12 12	12 28	12 43	12 58	13 12	13 28	13 43	13 58	14 12	14 28	14 43	14 58	15 12	15 28	15 43	15 58	16 12	16 28	16 43	16 58	17 12	17 28
Gunnersbury	⊖	d	12 15	12 32	12 45	13 02	13 15	13 32	13 45	14 02	14 15	14 32	14 45	15 02	15 15	15 32	15 45	16 02	16 15	16 32	16 45	17 02	17 15	17 32
Kew Gardens	⊖	d	12 17	12 35	12 48	13 05	13 17	13 35	13 48	14 05	14 17	14 35	14 48	15 05	15 17	15 35	15 48	16 05	16 17	16 35	16 48	17 05	17 17	17 35
Richmond	⊖	a	12 23	12 40	12 53	13 10	13 23	13 40	13 53	14 10	14 23	14 40	14 53	15 10	15 23	15 40	15 53	16 10	16 23	16 40	16 53	17 10	17 23	17 40

Table 59

Stratford - Highbury and Islington West Hampstead, Willesden Junction and Richmond.

			LO	LO	LO	LO	LO	LO	LO	LO	LO	LO	LO	LO	LO	LO	LO	LO	LO	LO	LO	LO	LO
Stratford 7	⊖	d	16 52	17 07	17 22	17 37	17 52	18 07	18 22	18 37	18 52	19 07	19 22	19 37	19 52	20 12	20 32	20 52	21 12	21 32	21 52	22 12	22 42
Hackney Wick		d	16 56	17 11	17 26	17 41	17 56	18 11	18 26	18 40	18 56	19 11	19 26	19 41	19 56	20 16	20 36	20 56	21 16	21 36	21 56	22 16	22 46
Homerton		d	16 58	17 13	17 28	17 43	17 58	18 13	18 28	18 43	18 58	19 13	19 28	19 43	19 58	20 18	20 38	20 58	21 18	21 38	21 58	22 18	22 48
Hackney Central		d	17 00	17 15	17 30	17 45	18 00	18 15	18 30	18 45	19 00	19 15	19 30	19 45	20 00	20 20	20 40	21 00	21 20	21 40	22 00	22 20	22 50
Dalston Kingsland		d	17 03	17 18	17 33	17 48	18 03	18 18	18 33	18 47	19 03	19 18	19 33	19 48	20 03	20 23	20 43	21 03	21 23	21 43	22 03	22 23	22 53
Canonbury		d	17 05	17 20	17 35	17 50	18 05	18 20	18 35	18 50	19 05	19 20	19 35	19 50	20 05	20 25	20 45	21 05	21 25	21 45	22 05	22 25	22 55
Highbury & Islington	⊖	d	17 08	17 23	17 38	17 53	18 08	18 23	18 38	18 53	19 08	19 23	19 38	19 53	20 08	20 28	20 48	21 08	21 28	21 48	22 08	22 28	22 58
Caledonian Rd & Barnsbury		d	17 10	17 25	17 40	17 55	18 10	18 25	18 40	18 55	19 10	19 25	19 40	19 55	20 10	20 30	20 50	21 10	21 30	21 50	22 10	22 30	23 00
Camden Road		d	17 14	17 29	17 44	17 59	18 14	18 29	18 44	18 58	19 14	19 29	19 44	19 59	20 14	20 34	20 54	21 14	21 34	21 54	22 14	22 34	23 04
Kentish Town West		d	17 16	17 31	17 46	18 01	18 16	18 31	18 46	19 00	19 16	19 31	19 46	20 01	20 16	20 36	20 56	21 16	21 36	21 56	22 16	22 36	23 06
Gospel Oak		d	17 19	17 34	17 49	18 04	18 19	18 34	18 49	19 03	19 19	19 34	19 49	20 04	20 19	20 39	20 59	21 19	21 39	21 59	22 19	22 39	23 09
Hampstead Heath		d	17 21	17 36	17 50	18 06	18 21	18 36	18 51	19 05	19 21	19 36	19 51	20 06	20 20	20 40	21 00	21 20	21 40	22 00	22 20	22 40	23 11
Finchley Road & Frognal		d	17 23	17 38	17 53	18 08	18 23	18 38	18 53	19 08	19 23	19 38	19 53	20 08	20 23	20 43	21 03	21 23	21 43	22 03	22 23	22 43	23 13
West Hampstead	⊖	d	17 25	17 40	17 54	18 10	18 25	18 40	18 55	19 09	19 25	19 40	19 55	20 10	20 24	20 44	21 04	21 24	21 44	22 04	22 24	22 44	23 15
Brondesbury		d	17 26	17 41	17 56	18 11	18 26	18 41	18 56	19 11	19 26	19 41	19 56	20 11	20 26	20 46	21 06	21 26	21 46	22 06	22 26	22 46	23 16
Brondesbury Park		d	17 28	17 43	17 57	18 13	18 28	18 43	18 58	19 12	19 28	19 43	19 58	20 13	20 27	20 47	21 07	21 27	21 47	22 07	22 27	22 47	23 18
Kensal Rise		d	17 30	17 45	17 59	18 15	18 30	18 45	19 00	19 14	19 30	19 45	20 00	20 15	20 29	20 49	21 09	21 29	21 49	22 09	22 29	22 49	23 20
Willesden Jn. High Level	⊖	a	17 33	17 48	18 02	18 18	18 33	18 48	19 04	19 17	19 33	19 48	20 03	20 18	20 32	20 52	21 13	21 33	21 52	22 12	22 33	22 52	23 23
		d	17 34	17 49	18 03	18 19	18 34	18 49	19 04	19 18	19 34	19 49	20 05	20 19	20 33	20 53	21 13	21 33	21 53	22 13	22 33	22 53	23 24
Acton Central		d	17 39	17 54	18 08	18 24	18 39	18 54	19 09	19 23	19 39	19 54	20 13	20 24	20 38	20 58	21 18	21 38	21 58	22 18	22 38	22 58	23 29
South Acton		d	17 43	17 58	18 12	18 28	18 43	18 58	19 13	19 27	19 43	19 58	20 17	20 28	20 42	21 02	21 22	21 42	22 02	22 22	22 42	23 02	23 33
Gunnersbury	⊖	d	17 45	18 02	18 15	18 32	18 45	19 00	19 15	19 32	19 45	20 02	20 22	20 32	20 44	21 04	21 24	21 44	22 04	22 24	22 44	23 04	23 35
Kew Gardens	⊖	d	17 48	18 05	18 17	18 35	18 48	19 03	19 18	19 35	19 48	20 05	20 25	20 34	20 47	21 07	21 27	21 47	22 07	22 27	22 47	23 07	23 38
Richmond	⊖	a	17 53	18 10	18 23	18 41	18 53	19 08	19 21	19 40	19 53	20 10	20 30	20 40	20 53	21 13	21 36	21 53	22 12	22 32	22 53	23 13	23 43

			LO	LO
Stratford 7	⊖	d	23 12	23 42
Hackney Wick		d	23 16	23 46
Homerton		d	23 18	23 48
Hackney Central		d	23 20	23 50
Dalston Kingsland		d	23 23	23 53
Canonbury		d	23 25	23 55
Highbury & Islington	⊖	d	23 28	23 58
Caledonian Rd & Barnsbury		d	23 30	23 59
Camden Road		d	23 34	00a05
Kentish Town West		d	23 36	
Gospel Oak		d	23 39	
Hampstead Heath		d	23 41	
Finchley Road & Frognal		d	23 43	
West Hampstead	⊖	d	23 45	
Brondesbury		d	23 46	
Brondesbury Park		d	23 48	
Kensal Rise		d	23 50	
Willesden Jn. High Level	⊖	a	23 53	
		d		
Acton Central		d		
South Acton		d		
Gunnersbury	⊖	d		
Kew Gardens	⊖	d		
Richmond	⊖	a		

Sundays

			LO 🚌	LO	LO 🚌	LO 🚌	LO 🚌	LO 🚌	LO 🚌	LO 🚌	LO 🚌	LO 🚌	LO 🚌	LO 🚌	LO 🚌	LO 🚌	LO 🚌	LO 🚌	LO 🚌	LO 🚌	LO 🚌	LO 🚌	LO 🚌	LO 🚌	LO 🚌
Stratford 7	⊖	d					08 00		08 30		09 00		09 30		10 00		10 30		11 00		11 30		12 00		12 30
Hackney Wick		d					08 10		08 40		09 10		09 40		10 10		10 40		11 10		11 40		12 10		12 40
Homerton		d					08 17		08 47		09 17		09 47		10 17		10 47		11 17		11 47		12 17		12 47
Hackney Central		d					08 25		08 55		09 25		09 55		10 25		10 55		11 25		11 55		12 25		12 55
Dalston Kingsland		d					08 33		09 03		09 33		10 03		10 33		11 03		11 33		12 03		12 33		13 03
Canonbury		d					08 41		09 11		09 41		10 11		10 41		11 11		11 41		12 11		12 41		13 11
Highbury & Islington	⊖	d					08 46		09 16		09 46		10 16		10 46		11 16		11 46		12 16		12 46		13 16
Caledonian Rd & Barnsbury		d																							
Camden Road		d					09 00		09 30		10 00		10 30		11 00		11 30		12 00		12 30		13 00		13 30
Kentish Town West		d					09 08		09 38		10 08		10 38		11 08		11 38		12 08		12 38		13 08		13 38
Gospel Oak		d			08 25	08 55	09 11	09 25	09 41	09 55	10 11	10 25	10 41	10 55	11 11	11 25	11 41	11 55	12 11	12 25	12 41	12 55	13 11	13 25	13 41
Hampstead Heath		d			08 30	09 00	09a14	09 30	09a44	10 00	10a14	10 30	10a44	11 00	11a14	11 30	11a44	12 00	12a14	12 30	12a44	13 00	13a14	13 30	13a44
Finchley Road & Frognal		d			08 40	09 10		09 40		10 10		10 40		11 10		11 40		12 10		12 40		13 10		13 40	
West Hampstead	⊖	d			08 45	09 15		09 45		10 15		10 45		11 15		11 45		12 15		12 45		13 15		13 45	
Brondesbury		d			08 50	09 20		09 50		10 20		10 50		11 20		11 50		12 20		12 50		13 20		13 50	
Brondesbury Park		d			08 53	09 23		09 53		10 23		10 53		11 23		11 53		12 23		12 53		13 23		13 53	
Kensal Rise		d			08 57	09 27		09 57		10 27		10 57		11 27		11 57		12 27		12 57		13 27		13 57	
Willesden Jn. High Level	⊖	a			09 08	09 38		10 08		10 38		11 08		11 38		12 08		12 38		13 08		13 38		14 08	
		d	08 39	09 01	09 09	09 39		10 09		10 39		11 09		11 39		12 09		12 39		13 09		13 39		14 09	
Acton Central		d	08 51	09 06	09 21	09 51		10 21		10 51		11 21		11 51		12 21		12 51		13 21		13 51		14 21	
South Acton		d	08 54	09 10	09 24	09 54		10 24		10 54		11 24		11 54		12 24		12 54		13 24		13 54		14 24	
Gunnersbury	⊖	d	09a00	09 13	09a30	10a00		10a30		11a00		11a30		12a00		12a30		13a00		13a30		14a00		14a30	
Kew Gardens	⊖	d		09 16																					
Richmond	⊖	a		09 23																					

Table 59

Sundays

Stratford - Highbury and Islington, West Hampstead, Willesden Junction and Richmond.

Station		LO	LO	LO	LO	LO	LO	LO	LO	LO	LO	LO	LO	LO	LO	LO	LO	LO	LO	LO	LO	LO	LO
Stratford 7 ⊖	d		13 00		13 30		14 00		14 30		15 00		15 30		16 00		16 30		17 00		17 30		18 00
Hackney Wick	d		13 10		13 40		14 10		14 40		15 10		15 40		16 10		16 40		17 10		17 40		18 10
Homerton	d		13 17		13 47		14 17		14 47		15 17		15 47		16 17		16 47		17 17		17 47		18 17
Hackney Central	d		13 25		13 55		14 25		14 55		15 25		15 55		16 25		16 55		17 25		17 55		18 25
Dalston Kingsland	d		13 33		14 03		14 33		15 03		15 33		16 03		16 33		17 03		17 33		18 03		18 33
Canonbury	d		13 41		14 11		14 41		15 11		15 41		16 11		16 41		17 11		17 41		18 11		18 41
Highbury & Islington ⊖	d		13 46		14 16		14 46		15 16		15 46		16 16		16 46		17 16		17 46		18 16		18 46
Caledonian Rd & Barnsbury	d																						
Camden Road	d		14 00		14 30		15 00		15 30		16 00		16 30		17 00		17 30		18 00		18 30		19 00
Kentish Town West	d		14 08		14 38		15 08		15 38		16 08		16 38		17 08		17 38		18 08		18 38		19 08
Gospel Oak	d	13 55	14 11	14 25	14 41	14 55	15 11	15 25	15 41	15 55	16 11	16 25	16 41	16 55	17 11	17 25	17 41	17 55	18 11	18 25	18 41	18 55	19 11
Hampstead Heath	d	14 00	14a14	14 30	14a44	15 00	15a14	15 30	15a44	16 00	16a14	16 30	16a44	17 00	17a14	17 30	17a44	18 00	18a14	18 30	18a44	19 00	19a14
Finchley Road & Frognal	d	14 10		14 40		15 10		15 40		16 10		16 40		17 10		17 40		18 10		18 40		19 10	
West Hampstead ⊖	d	14 15		14 45		15 15		15 45		16 15		16 45		17 15		17 45		18 15		18 45		19 15	
Brondesbury	d	14 20		14 50		15 20		15 50		16 20		16 50		17 20		17 50		18 20		18 50		19 20	
Brondesbury Park	d	14 23		14 53		15 23		15 53		16 23		16 53		17 23		17 53		18 23		18 53		19 23	
Kensal Rise	d	14 27		14 57		15 27		15 57		16 27		16 57		17 27		17 57		18 27		18 57		19 27	
Willesden Jn. High Level ⊖	a	14 38		15 08		15 38		16 08		16 38		17 08		17 38		18 08		18 38		19 08		19 38	
	d	14 39		15 09		15 39		16 09		16 39		17 09		17 39		18 09		18 39		19 09		19 39	
Acton Central	d	14 51		15 21		15 51		16 21		16 51		17 21		17 51		18 21		18 51		19 21		19 51	
South Acton	d	14 54		15 24		15 54		16 24		16 54		17 24		17 54		18 24		18 54		19 24		19 54	
Gunnersbury ⊖	d	15a00		15a30		16a00		16a30		17a00		17a30		18a00		18a30		19a00		19a30		20a00	
Kew Gardens ⊖	d																						
Richmond ⊖	a																						

Station		LO	LO	LO	LO	LO	LO	LO	LO	LO	LO	LO	LO	LO	LO	LO	LO	LO	LO	LO	LO	LO
Stratford 7 ⊖	d		18 30		19 00		19 30		20 00		20 30		21 00		21 30		22 00		22 30		23 00	23 30
Hackney Wick	d		18 40		19 10		19 40		20 10		20 40		21 10		21 40		22 10		22 40		23 10	23 40
Homerton	d		18 47		19 17		19 47		20 17		20 47		21 17		21 47		22 17		22 47		23 17	23 47
Hackney Central	d		18 55		19 25		19 55		20 25		20 55		21 25		21 55		22 25		22 55		23 25	23 55
Dalston Kingsland	d		19 03		19 33		20 03		20 33		21 03		21 33		22 03		22 33		23 03		23 33	00 03
Canonbury	d		19 11		19 41		20 11		20 41		21 11		21 41		22 11		22 41		23 11		23 41	00 11
Highbury & Islington ⊖	d		19 16		19 46		20 16		20 46		21 16		21 46		22 16		22 46		23 16		23 46	00 16
Caledonian Rd & Barnsbury	d																					
Camden Road	d		19 30		20 00		20 30		21 00		21 30		22 00		22 30		23 00		23 30		23 59	00 30
Kentish Town West	d		19 38		20 08		20 38		21 08		21 38		22 08		22 38		23 08		23 38		00 08	00 38
Gospel Oak	d	19 25	19 41	19 55	20 11	20 25	20 41	20 55	21 11	21 25	21 41	21 55	22 11	22 25	22 41	22 55	23 11	23 25	23 41	23 50	00 11	00 41
Hampstead Heath	d	19 30	19a44	20 00	20a14	20 30	20a44	21 00	21a14	21 30	21a44	22 00	22a14	22 30	22a44	23 00	23a14	23 30	23a44	23 55	00a14	00a44
Finchley Road & Frognal	d	19 40		20 10		20 40		21 10		21 40		22 10		22 40		23 10		23 40		00 05		
West Hampstead ⊖	d	19 45		20 15		20 45		21 15		21 45		22 15		22 45		23 15		23 45		00 10		
Brondesbury	d	19 50		20 20		20 50		21 20		21 50		22 20		22 50		23 20		23 50		00 15		
Brondesbury Park	d	19 53		20 23		20 53		21 23		21 53		22 23		22 53		23 23		23 53		00 18		
Kensal Rise	d	19 57		20 27		20 57		21 27		21 57		22 27		22 57		23 27		23 57		00 22		
Willesden Jn. High Level ⊖	a	20 08		20 38		21 08		21 38		22 08		22 38		23 08		23 38		00 08		00 34		
	d	20 09		20 39		21 09		21 39		22 09		22 39		23 09		23 39		00 09				
Acton Central	d	20 21		20 51		21 21		21 51		22 21		22 51		23 21		23 51		00 21				
South Acton	d	20 24		20 54		21 24		21 54		22 24		22 54		23 24		23 54		00 24				
Gunnersbury ⊖	d	20a30		21a00		21a30		22a00		22a30		23a00		23a30		23a59		00a30				
Kew Gardens ⊖	d																					
Richmond ⊖	a																					

Table 59

Mondays to Fridays

Richmond - Willesden Junction, West Hampstead, Highbury and Islington and Stratford

Station		LO MO	LO MO	LO MO	LO	LO	LO	LO	LO	LO	LO	LO	LO	LO	LO	LO	LO	LO	LO	LO	LO	LO	LO	LO	LO
Richmond ⊖	d						06 04		06 21		06 41		07 04		07 25		07 42	07 49		08 04		08 25		08 42	
Kew Gardens ⊖	d						06 07		06 24		06 44		07 07		07 28		07 45	07 52		08 07		08 28		08 45	
Gunnersbury ⊖	d	23p00					06 10		06 27		06 47		07 10		07 31		07 48	07 55		08 10		08 31		08 48	
South Acton	d	23p06					06 12		06 29		06 49		07 12		07 33		07 50	07 57		08 12		08 33		08 50	
Acton Central	d	23p09					06 15		06 34		06 54		07 15		07 36		07 53	08 00		08 15		08 36		08 55	
Willesden Jn. High Level ⊖	a	23p22					06 20	06 30	06 39	06 50	06 59	07 10	07 20	07 30	07 41	07 50	07 58	08 08	08 10	08 21	08 30	08 43	08 50	09 00	09 10
	d	23p23			05 57	06 11	06 21	06 31	06 41	06 51	07 01	07 11	07 21	07 31	07 41	07 55	08 01		08 11	08 21	08 31	08 43	08 51	09 01	09 11
Kensal Rise	d	23p35			06 03	06 16	06 24	06 34	06 44	06 54	07 04	07 14	07 24	07 34	07 44	07 57	08 04		08 14	08 24	08 34	08 45	08 54	09 04	09 14
Brondesbury Park	d	23p39			06 05	06 18	06 26	06 36	06 46	06 56	07 06	07 16	07 26	07 36	07 46	07 59	08 06		08 16	08 26	08 36	08 47	08 56	09 06	09 16
Brondesbury	d	23p42			06 07	06 20	06 28	06 38	06 48	06 58	07 08	07 18	07 28	07 38	07 48	08 01	08 08		08 18	08 28	08 38	08 49	08 58	09 08	09 18
West Hampstead ⊖	d	23p47			06 09	06 22	06 30	06 40	06 50	07 00	07 10	07 20	07 30	07 40	07 50	08 04	08 10		08 20	08 30	08 40	08 51	09 00	09 10	09 20
Finchley Road & Frognal	d	23p51			06 10	06 24	06 31	06 41	06 51	07 01	07 11	07 21	07 31	07 41	07 51	08 05	08 11		08 21	08 31	08 41	08 52	09 01	09 11	09 21
Hampstead Heath	d	00 01	23p15	23p45	06 13	06 27	06 34	06 44	06 54	07 04	07 14	07 24	07 34	07 44	07 54	08 08	08 14		08 24	08 34	08 44	08 55	09 04	09 14	09 24
Gospel Oak	d	00a05			06 15	06 29	06 37	06 47	06 57	07 07	07 17	07 27	07 37	07 47	07 57	08 11	08 17		08 27	08 37	08 47	08 58	09 07	09 17	09 27
Kentish Town West	d		23p21	23p51	06 17	06 31	06 39	06 49	06 59	07 09	07 19	07 29	07 39	07 49	07 59	08 13	08 19		08 29	08 39	08 49	09 00	09 09	09 19	09 29
Camden Road	d		23p26	23p56	06 22	06 33	06 41	06 51	07 01	07 11	07 21	07 31	07 41	07 51	08 01	08 15	08 22		08 31	08 41	08 51	09 02	09 11	09 21	09 31
Caledonian Rd & Barnsbury	d				06 25	06 36	06 43	06 55	07 04	07 14	07 23	07 34	07 43	07 54	08 03	08 19	08 24		08 34	08 43	08 54	09 04	09 15	09 23	09 34
Highbury & Islington ⊖	d		23p40	00 10	06 27	06 39	06 47	06 58	07 07	07 17	07 27	07 37	07 47	07 57	08 07	08 22	08 28		08 37	08 47	08 57	09 08	09 18	09 27	09 37
Canonbury ⊖	d		23p45	00 15	06 29	06 41	06 49	06 59	07 09	07 19	07 29	07 39	07 49	07 59	08 09	08 23	08 30		08 39	08 49	08 59	09 10	09 19	09 29	09 39
Dalston Kingsland	d		23p53	00 23	06 32	06 44	06 52	07 03	07 12	07 22	07 32	07 42	07 52	08 02	08 12	08 27	08 33		08 42	08 52	09 02	09 13	09 23	09 32	09 42
Hackney Central	d		00 01	00 31	06 34	06 46	06 54	07 04	07 14	07 24	07 34	07 44	07 54	08 04	08 14	08 28	08 35		08 44	08 54	09 04	09 15	09 24	09 34	09 44
Homerton	d		00 09	00 39	06 36	06 48	06 56	07 06	07 16	07 26	07 36	07 46	07 56	08 06	08 16	08 30	08 37		08 46	08 56	09 06	09 17	09 26	09 36	09 46
Hackney Wick	d		00 16	00 46	06 39	06 51	06 58	07 08	07 18	07 28	07 38	07 48	07 58	08 08	08 18	08 32	08 39		08 48	08 58	09 08	09 19	09 28	09 38	09 48
Stratford 7 ⊖	a		00 26	00 56	06 46	06 58	07 09	07 17	07 26	07 36	07 46	07 56	08 06	08 16	08 27	08 41	08 48		08 56	09 09	09 16	09 28	09 36	09 47	09 59

Station		LO	LO	LO	LO	LO	LO	LO	LO	LO	LO	LO	LO	LO	LO	LO	LO	LO	LO	LO	LO	LO	LO	LO	LO
Richmond ⊖	d	09 04	09 22	09 41	09 57	10 11	10 27	10 41	10 57	11 11	11 27	11 41	11 57	12 11	12 27	12 41	12 57	13 11	13 27	13 41	13 57	14 11	14 27	14 41	14 57
Kew Gardens ⊖	d	09 07	09 25	09 44	10 00	10 14	10 30	10 44	11 00	11 14	11 30	11 44	12 00	12 14	12 30	12 44	13 00	13 14	13 30	13 44	14 00	14 14	14 30	14 44	15 00
Gunnersbury ⊖	d	09 10	09 28	09 47	10 03	10 17	10 33	10 47	11 03	11 17	11 33	11 47	12 03	12 17	12 33	12 47	13 03	13 17	13 33	13 47	14 03	14 17	14 33	14 47	15 03
South Acton	d	09 12	09 30	09 49	10 05	10 19	10 35	10 49	11 05	11 19	11 35	11 49	12 05	12 19	12 35	12 49	13 05	13 19	13 35	13 49	14 05	14 19	14 35	14 49	15 05
Acton Central	d	09 15	09 35	09 53	10 08	10 23	10 38	10 53	11 08	11 23	11 38	11 53	12 08	12 23	12 38	12 53	13 08	13 23	13 38	13 53	14 08	14 23	14 38	14 53	15 08
Willesden Jn. High Level ⊖	a	09 23	09 40	09 59	10 13	10 29	10 43	10 59	11 13	11 29	11 43	11 59	12 13	12 30	12 43	12 58	13 13	13 29	13 43	13 59	14 13	14 29	14 44	14 59	15 13
	d	09 25	09 41	10 00	10 14	10 30	10 44	11 00	11 14	11 30	11 44	12 00	12 14	12 30	12 44	13 00	13 14	13 30	13 44	14 00	14 14	14 30	14 45	15 00	15 14
Kensal Rise	d	09 28	09 44	10 03	10 17	10 33	10 47	11 03	11 17	11 33	11 47	12 03	12 17	12 33	12 47	13 03	13 17	13 33	13 47	14 03	14 17	14 33	14 47	15 03	15 17
Brondesbury Park	d	09 30	09 46	10 05	10 19	10 35	10 49	11 05	11 19	11 35	11 49	12 05	12 19	12 35	12 49	13 05	13 19	13 35	13 49	14 05	14 19	14 35	14 49	15 05	15 19
Brondesbury	d	09 32	09 48	10 07	10 21	10 37	10 51	11 07	11 21	11 37	11 51	12 07	12 21	12 37	12 51	13 07	13 21	13 37	13 51	14 07	14 21	14 37	14 51	15 07	15 21
West Hampstead ⊖	d	09 34	09 50	10 08	10 22	10 38	10 52	11 08	11 22	11 38	11 52	12 08	12 22	12 38	12 52	13 08	13 22	13 38	13 52	14 08	14 22	14 38	14 53	15 08	15 22
Finchley Road & Frognal	d	09 35	09 51	10 10	10 24	10 40	10 54	11 10	11 24	11 40	11 54	12 10	12 24	12 40	12 54	13 10	13 24	13 40	13 54	14 10	14 24	14 40	14 54	15 10	15 24
Hampstead Heath	d	09 38	09 54	10 13	10 27	10 43	10 57	11 13	11 27	11 43	11 57	12 13	12 27	12 43	12 57	13 13	13 27	13 43	13 57	14 13	14 27	14 43	14 57	15 13	15 27
Gospel Oak	d	09 41	09 57	10 15	10 29	10 45	10 59	11 15	11 29	11 45	11 59	12 15	12 29	12 45	12 59	13 15	13 29	13 45	13 59	14 15	14 29	14 45	14 59	15 15	15 29
Kentish Town West	d	09 43	09 59	10 17	10 31	10 47	11 01	11 17	11 31	11 47	12 01	12 17	12 31	12 47	13 01	13 17	13 31	13 47	14 01	14 17	14 31	14 47	15 01	15 17	15 31
Camden Road	d	09 45	10 01	10 19	10 33	10 49	11 03	11 19	11 33	11 49	12 03	12 19	12 33	12 49	13 03	13 19	13 33	13 49	14 03	14 19	14 33	14 49	15 03	15 19	15 33
Caledonian Rd & Barnsbury	d	09 47	10 03	10 21	10 36	10 51	11 05	11 21	11 36	11 51	12 05	12 21	12 35	12 51	13 05	13 21	13 35	13 51	14 05	14 21	14 35	14 51	15 05	15 21	15 35
Highbury & Islington ⊖	d	09 51	10 07	10 25	10 39	10 55	11 09	11 25	11 39	11 55	12 09	12 25	12 39	12 55	13 09	13 25	13 39	13 55	14 09	14 25	14 39	14 55	15 09	15 25	15 39
Canonbury ⊖	d	09 53	10 09	10 27	10 41	10 57	11 11	11 27	11 41	11 57	12 11	12 27	12 41	12 57	13 11	13 27	13 41	13 57	14 11	14 27	14 41	14 57	15 11	15 27	15 41
Dalston Kingsland	d	09 56	10 12	10 30	10 44	11 00	11 14	11 30	11 44	12 00	12 14	12 30	12 44	13 00	13 14	13 30	13 44	14 00	14 14	14 30	14 44	15 00	15 14	15 30	15 44
Hackney Central	d	09 58	10 14	10 32	10 46	11 02	11 16	11 32	11 46	12 02	12 16	12 32	12 46	13 02	13 16	13 32	13 46	14 02	14 16	14 32	14 46	15 02	15 16	15 32	15 46
Homerton	d	10 00	10 16	10 34	10 48	11 04	11 18	11 34	11 48	12 04	12 18	12 34	12 48	13 04	13 18	13 34	13 48	14 04	14 18	14 34	14 48	15 04	15 18	15 34	15 48
Hackney Wick	d	10 02	10 18	10 37	10 51	11 07	11 21	11 37	11 51	12 07	12 21	12 37	12 51	13 07	13 21	13 37	13 51	14 07	14 21	14 37	14 51	15 07	15 21	15 37	15 51
Stratford 7 ⊖	a	10 10	10 27	10 44	10 58	11 14	11 28	11 44	11 58	12 14	12 28	12 44	12 58	13 15	13 28	13 44	13 59	14 14	14 28	14 44	14 58	15 14	15 28	15 44	15 58

Station		LO	LO	LO	LO	LO	LO	LO	LO	LO	LO	LO	LO	LO	LO	LO	LO	LO	LO	LO	LO	LO	LO	LO
Richmond ⊖	d	15 11	15 27		15 41	15 57		16 11	16 22		16 43		17 03		17 24		17 36	17 43		18 02		18 22	18 45	
Kew Gardens ⊖	d	15 14	15 30		15 44	16 00		16 14	16 25		16 46		17 06		17 27		17 39	17 46		18 05		18 25	18 48	
Gunnersbury ⊖	d	15 17	15 33		15 47	16 03		16 17	16 28		16 49		17 09		17 30		17 42	17 49		18 08		18 28	18 51	
South Acton	d	15 19	15 35		15 49	16 05		16 19	16 30		16 51		17 11		17 32		17 44	17 51		18 10		18 30	18 53	
Acton Central	d	15 23	15 38		15 53	16 08		16 22	16 35		16 54		17 14		17 37		17 47	17 54		18 15		18 35	18 56	
Willesden Jn. High Level ⊖	a	15 29	15 43	15 57	16 00	16 14	16 27	16 32	16 40	16 51	16 59	17 10	17 19	17 30	17 42	17 50	17 58	17 59	18 10	18 20	18 30	18 40	19 00	19 10
	d	15 30	15 44	15 57	16 02	16 15	16 28	16 34	16 41	16 53	17 01	17 11	17 21	17 31	17 43	17 51		18 01	18 11	18 21	18 31	18 41	19 01	19 11
Kensal Rise	d	15 33	15 47	16 00	16 05	16 18	16 31	16 37	16 44	16 56	17 04	17 14	17 24	17 34	17 46	17 54		18 04	18 14	18 24	18 34	18 44	19 04	19 14
Brondesbury Park	d	15 35	15 49	16 02	16 07	16 20	16 33	16 39	16 46	16 58	17 06	17 16	17 26	17 36	17 48	17 56		18 06	18 16	18 26	18 36	18 46	19 06	19 16
Brondesbury	d	15 37	15 51	16 04	16 09	16 22	16 35	16 41	16 48	17 00	17 08	17 18	17 28	17 38	17 50	17 58		18 08	18 18	18 28	18 38	18 48	19 08	19 18
West Hampstead ⊖	d	15 38	15 52	16 05	16 10	16 23	16 36	16 42	16 50	17 02	17 10	17 20	17 30	17 40	17 52	18 00		18 10	18 20	18 30	18 40	18 50	19 10	19 20
Finchley Road & Frognal	d	15 40	15 54	16 07	16 12	16 25	16 38	16 44	16 51	17 03	17 11	17 21	17 31	17 41	17 53	18 01		18 11	18 21	18 31	18 41	18 51	19 11	19 21
Hampstead Heath	d	15 43	15 57	16 10	16 15	16 28	16 41	16 47	16 54	17 06	17 14	17 24	17 34	17 44	17 56	18 04		18 14	18 24	18 34	18 44	18 54	19 14	19 24
Gospel Oak	d	15 45	15 59	16 12	16 17	16 30	16 43	16 49	16 57	17 09	17 17	17 27	17 37	17 47	17 59	18 07		18 17	18 27	18 37	18 47	18 57	19 16	19 27
Kentish Town West	d	15 47	16 01	16 14	16 19	16 32	16 45	16 51	16 59	17 11	17 19	17 29	17 39	17 49	18 01	18 09		18 19	18 29	18 39	18 49	18 59	19 19	19 29
Camden Road	d	15 49	16 03	16 16	16 21	16 34	16 47	16 53	17 01	17 13	17 21	17 31	17 44	17 51	18 03	18 11		18 21	18 31	18 41	18 51	19 01	19 21	19 31
Caledonian Rd & Barnsbury	d	15 51	16 05	16 19	16 24	16 37	16 50	16 56	17 03	17 16	17 23	17 34	17 46	17 54	18 06	18 14		18 23	18 34	18 44	18 54	19 03	19 23	19 34
Highbury & Islington ⊖	d	15 55	16 09	16 22	16 27	16 40	16 53	16 59	17 07	17 19	17 27	17 37	17 50	17 57	18 09	18 17		18 27	18 37	18 47	18 57	19 07	19 27	19 37
Canonbury ⊖	d	15 57	16 11	16 24	16 29	16 42	16 55	17 01	17 09	17 21	17 29	17 39	17 52	17 59	18 11	18 19		18 29	18 39	18 49	18 59	19 09	19 29	19 39
Dalston Kingsland	d	16 00	16 14	16 27	16 32	16 45	16 58	17 04	17 12	17 24	17 32	17 42	17 55	18 02	18 14	18 22		18 32	18 42	18 52	19 02	19 12	19 32	19 42
Hackney Central	d	16 02	16 16	16 29	16 34	16 47	17 00	17 06	17 14	17 26	17 34	17 44	17 57	18 04	18 16	18 24		18 34	18 44	18 54	19 04	19 14	19 34	19 44
Homerton	d	16 04	16 18	16 31	16 36	16 49	17 02	17 08	17 16	17 28	17 36	17 46	17 59	18 06	18 18	18 26		18 36	18 46	18 56	19 06	19 16	19 36	19 46
Hackney Wick	d	16 07	16 21	16 33	16 38	16 52	17 04	17 10	17 18	17 30	17 38	17 48	18 01	18 08	18 20	18 28		18 38	18 48	18 58	19 08	19 18	19 38	19 48
Stratford 7 ⊖	a	16 14	16 28	16 38	16 44	16 57	17 09	17 15	17 27	17 36	17 48	17 56	18 11	18 16	18 26	18 36		18 48	18 56	19 07	19 16	19 27	19 49	19 56

Table 59

Richmond - Willesden Junction, West Hampstead, Highbury and Islington and Stratford

Mondays to Fridays

		LO	LO	LO	LO	LO	LO	LO	LO	LO	LO	LO		LO	LO
Richmond	⊖ d	19 01	19 25	19 41	19 58	20 15	20 35	20 55	21 15	21 35	21 55	22 15		22 47	23 15
Kew Gardens	⊖ d	19 04	19 28	19 44	20 02	20 18	20 38	20 58	21 18	21 38	21 58	22 18		22 50	23 18
Gunnersbury	⊖ d	19 07	19 31	19 47	20 05	20 21	20 41	21 01	21 21	21 41	22 01	22 21		22 53	23 21
South Acton	d	19 09	19 33	19 49	20 07	20 23	20 43	21 03	21 23	21 43	22 03	22 23		22 55	23 23
Acton Central	d	19 15	19 36	19 53	20 10	20 26	20 46	21 06	21 26	21 46	22 06	22 26		22 58	23 26
Willesden Jn. High Level	⊖ a	19 20	19 41	20 00	20 15	20 32	20 52	21 12	21 31	21 52	22 12	22 32		23 03	23 35
	d	19 21	19 41	20 01	20 16	20 32	20 52	21 12	21 32	21 52	22 12	22 32		23 04	
Kensal Rise	d	19 24	19 44	20 03	20 19	20 35	20 55	21 15	21 35	21 55	22 15	22 35		23 07	
Brondesbury Park	d	19 26	19 46	20 05	20 21	20 37	20 57	21 17	21 37	21 57	22 17	22 37		23 09	
Brondesbury	d	19 28	19 48	20 07	20 23	20 39	20 59	21 19	21 39	21 59	22 19	22 39		23 11	
West Hampstead	⊖ d	19 30	19 50	20 08	20 24	20 40	21 00	21 20	21 40	22 00	22 20	22 40		23 12	
Finchley Road & Frognal	d	19 31	19 51	20 10	20 26	20 42	21 02	21 22	21 42	22 02	22 22	22 42		23 14	
Hampstead Heath	d	19 34	19 54	20 13	20 29	20 45	21 05	21 25	21 45	22 05	22 25	22 45		23 17	
Gospel Oak	d	19 37	19 57	20 15	20 31	20 47	21 07	21 27	21 47	22 07	22 27	22 47		23 19	
Kentish Town West	d	19 39	19 59	20 17	20 33	20 49	21 09	21 29	21 49	22 09	22 29	22 49		23 21	
Camden Road	d	19 41	20 01	20 19	20 35	20 51	21 11	21 31	21 51	22 11	22 31	22 51		23 23	
Caledonian Rd & Barnsbury	d	19 43	20 04	20 22	20 37	20 53	21 15	21 35	21 54	22 15	22 35	22 55		23 26	
Highbury & Islington	⊖ d	19 47	20 07	20 25	20 41	20 57	21 18	21 38	21 57	22 18	22 38	22 58		23 29	
Canonbury	⊖ d	19 49	20 09	20 27	20 43	20 59	21 19	21 39	21 59	22 19	22 39	22 59		23 31	
Dalston Kingsland	d	19 52	20 12	20 30	20 46	21 02	21 23	21 43	22 02	22 23	22 43	23 03		23 34	
Hackney Central	d	19 54	20 14	20 32	20 48	21 04	21 24	21 44	22 04	22 24	22 44	23 04		23 36	
Homerton	d	19 56	20 16	20 34	20 50	21 06	21 26	21 46	22 06	22 26	22 46	23 06		23 38	
Hackney Wick	d	19 58	20 18	20 37	20 53	21 09	21 29	21 49	22 09	22 29	22 49	23 09		23 41	
Stratford	⊖ a	20 06	20 30	20 42	21 01	21 17	21 37	21 57	22 17	22 37	2 57	23 17		23 48	

Table 59

Saturdays

Richmond - Willesden Junction, West Hampstead Highbury and Islington and Stratford

		LO	LO	LO	LO	LO	LO	LO	LO	LO	LO	LO	LO	LO	LO	LO	LO	LO	LO	LO	LO	LO	LO	LO	LO
Richmond	⊖ d			06 14	06 27	06 41	06 57	07 11	07 27	07 41	07 57	08 11	08 27	08 41	08 57	09 11	09 27	09 41	09 57	10 11	10 27	10 41	10 57	11 11	11 27
Kew Gardens	⊖ d			06 17	06 30	06 44	07 00	07 14	07 30	07 44	08 00	08 14	08 30	08 44	09 00	09 14	09 30	09 44	10 00	10 14	10 30	10 44	11 00	11 14	11 30
Gunnersbury	⊖ d			06 20	06 33	06 47	07 03	07 17	07 33	07 47	08 03	08 17	08 33	08 47	09 03	09 17	09 33	09 47	10 03	10 17	10 33	10 47	11 03	11 17	11 33
South Acton	d			06 22	06 35	06 49	07 05	07 19	07 35	07 49	08 05	08 19	08 35	08 49	09 05	09 19	09 35	09 49	10 05	10 19	10 35	10 49	11 05	11 19	11 35
Acton Central	d			06 25	06 38	06 53	07 08	07 23	07 38	07 53	08 08	08 23	08 38	08 53	09 08	09 23	09 38	09 53	10 08	10 23	10 38	10 53	11 08	11 23	11 38
Willesden Jn. High Level	⊖ a			06 30	06 43	06 58	07 13	07 29	07 43	07 58	08 13	08 29	08 43	08 58	09 13	09 29	09 43	09 58	10 13	10 28	10 43	10 59	11 13	11 29	11 43
	d	05 59	06 11	06 31	06 44	06 59	07 14	07 29	07 44	07 59	08 14	08 29	08 44	08 59	09 14	09 29	09 44	09 59	10 14	10 29	10 44	10 59	11 14	11 29	11 44
Kensal Rise	d	06 04	06 16	06 34	06 47	07 02	07 17	07 32	07 47	08 02	08 17	08 32	08 47	09 02	09 17	09 32	09 47	10 02	10 17	10 32	10 47	11 02	11 17	11 32	11 47
Brondesbury Park	d	06 06	06 18	06 36	06 49	07 04	07 19	07 34	07 49	08 04	08 19	08 34	08 49	09 04	09 19	09 34	09 49	10 04	10 19	10 34	10 49	11 04	11 19	11 34	11 49
Brondesbury	d	06 08	06 20	06 38	06 51	07 06	07 21	07 36	07 51	08 06	08 21	08 36	08 51	09 06	09 21	09 36	09 51	10 06	10 21	10 36	10 51	11 06	11 21	11 36	11 51
West Hampstead	⊖ d	06 09	06 21	06 39	06 52	07 07	07 22	07 37	07 52	08 07	08 22	08 37	08 52	09 07	09 22	09 37	09 52	10 07	10 22	10 37	10 52	11 07	11 22	11 37	11 52
Finchley Road & Frognal	d	06 11	06 24	06 41	06 54	07 09	07 24	07 39	07 54	08 09	08 24	08 39	08 54	09 09	09 24	09 39	09 54	10 09	10 24	10 39	10 54	11 09	11 24	11 39	11 54
Hampstead Heath	d	06 14	06 27	06 44	06 57	07 12	07 27	07 42	07 57	08 12	08 27	08 42	08 57	09 12	09 27	09 42	09 57	10 12	10 27	10 42	10 57	11 12	11 27	11 42	11 57
Gospel Oak	d	06 16	06 29	06 46	06 59	07 14	07 29	07 44	07 59	08 14	08 29	08 44	08 59	09 14	09 29	09 44	09 59	10 14	10 29	10 44	10 59	11 14	11 29	11 44	11 59
Kentish Town West	d	06 18	06 31	06 48	07 01	07 16	07 31	07 46	08 01	08 16	08 31	08 46	09 01	09 16	09 31	09 46	10 01	10 16	10 31	10 46	11 01	11 16	11 31	11 46	12 01
Camden Road	d	06 20	06 34	06 50	07 03	07 18	07 33	07 48	08 03	08 18	08 33	08 48	09 03	09 18	09 33	09 48	10 03	10 18	10 33	10 48	11 03	11 18	11 33	11 48	12 03
Caledonian Rd & Barnsbury	d	06 23	06 37	06 53	07 06	07 21	07 35	07 50	08 05	08 20	08 35	08 50	09 05	09 20	09 35	09 50	10 05	10 20	10 35	10 50	11 05	11 20	11 35	11 50	12 05
Highbury & Islington	⊖ d	06 25	06 40	06 56	07 09	07 24	07 39	07 54	08 09	08 24	08 39	08 54	09 09	09 24	09 39	09 54	10 09	10 24	10 39	10 54	11 09	11 24	11 39	11 54	12 09
Canonbury	⊖ d	06 27	06 42	06 58	07 11	07 26	07 41	07 56	08 11	08 26	08 41	08 56	09 11	09 26	09 41	09 56	10 11	10 26	10 41	10 56	11 11	11 26	11 41	11 56	12 11
Dalston Kingsland	d	06 30	06 45	07 01	07 14	07 29	07 44	07 59	08 14	08 29	08 44	08 59	09 14	09 29	09 44	09 59	10 14	10 29	10 44	10 59	11 14	11 29	11 44	11 59	12 14
Hackney Central	d	06 32	06 47	07 03	07 16	07 31	07 46	08 01	08 16	08 31	08 46	09 01	09 16	09 31	09 46	10 01	10 16	10 31	10 46	11 01	11 16	11 31	11 46	12 01	12 16
Homerton	d	06 34	06 49	07 05	07 18	07 33	07 48	08 03	08 18	08 33	08 48	09 03	09 18	09 33	09 48	10 03	10 18	10 33	10 48	11 03	11 18	11 33	11 48	12 03	12 18
Hackney Wick	d	06 37	06 52	07 07	07 20	07 36	07 51	08 06	08 21	08 36	08 51	09 06	09 21	09 36	09 51	10 06	10 21	10 36	10 51	11 06	11 21	11 36	11 51	12 06	12 21
Stratford	⊖ a	06 42	06 59	07 12	07 28	07 43	07 58	08 14	08 28	08 43	08 58	09 14	09 28	09 43	09 58	10 14	10 28	10 43	10 58	11 13	11 28	11 43	11 59	12 13	12 28

		LO	LO	LO	LO	LO	LO	LO	LO	LO	LO	LO	LO	LO	LO	LO	LO	LO	LO	LO	LO	LO	LO	LO	LO
Richmond	⊖ d	11 41	11 57	12 11	12 27	12 41	12 57	13 11	13 27	13 41	13 57	14 11	14 27	14 41	14 57	15 11	15 27	15 41	15 57	16 11	16 27	16 41	16 57	17 11	17 27
Kew Gardens	⊖ d	11 44	12 00	12 14	12 30	12 44	13 00	13 14	13 30	13 44	14 00	14 14	14 30	14 44	15 00	15 14	15 30	15 44	16 00	16 14	16 30	16 44	17 00	17 14	17 30
Gunnersbury	⊖ d	11 47	12 03	12 17	12 33	12 47	13 03	13 17	13 33	13 47	14 03	14 17	14 33	14 47	15 03	15 17	15 33	15 47	16 03	16 17	16 33	16 47	17 03	17 17	17 33
South Acton	d	11 49	12 05	12 19	12 35	12 49	13 05	13 19	13 35	13 49	14 05	14 19	14 35	14 49	15 05	15 19	15 35	15 49	16 05	16 19	16 35	16 49	17 05	17 19	17 35
Acton Central	d	11 53	12 08	12 23	12 38	12 53	13 08	13 23	13 38	13 53	14 08	14 23	14 38	14 53	15 08	15 23	15 38	15 53	16 08	16 23	16 38	16 53	17 08	17 23	17 38
Willesden Jn. High Level	⊖ a	11 59	12 13	12 29	12 43	12 58	13 13	13 29	13 43	13 58	14 13	14 28	14 43	14 58	15 13	15 29	15 43	15 59	16 13	16 29	16 43	16 58	17 13	17 29	17 43
	d	11 59	12 14	12 29	12 44	12 59	13 14	13 29	13 44	13 59	14 14	14 29	14 44	14 59	15 14	15 29	15 44	15 59	16 14	16 29	16 44	16 59	17 14	17 29	17 44
Kensal Rise	d	12 02	12 17	12 32	12 47	13 02	13 17	13 32	13 47	14 02	14 17	14 32	14 47	15 02	15 17	15 32	15 47	16 02	16 17	16 32	16 47	17 02	17 17	17 32	17 47
Brondesbury Park	d	12 04	12 19	12 34	12 49	13 04	13 19	13 34	13 49	14 04	14 19	14 34	14 49	15 04	15 19	15 34	15 49	16 04	16 19	16 34	16 49	17 04	17 19	17 34	17 49
Brondesbury	d	12 06	12 21	12 36	12 51	13 06	13 21	13 36	13 51	14 06	14 21	14 36	14 51	15 06	15 21	15 36	15 51	16 06	16 21	16 36	16 51	17 06	17 21	17 36	17 51
West Hampstead	⊖ d	12 07	12 22	12 37	12 52	13 07	13 22	13 37	13 52	14 07	14 22	14 37	14 52	15 07	15 22	15 37	15 52	16 07	16 22	16 37	16 52	17 07	17 22	17 37	17 52
Finchley Road & Frognal	d	12 09	12 24	12 39	12 54	13 09	13 24	13 39	13 54	14 09	14 24	14 39	14 54	15 09	15 24	15 39	15 54	16 09	16 24	16 39	16 54	17 09	17 24	17 39	17 54
Hampstead Heath	d	12 12	12 27	12 42	12 57	13 12	13 27	13 42	13 57	14 12	14 27	14 42	14 57	15 12	15 27	15 42	15 57	16 12	16 27	16 42	16 57	17 12	17 27	17 42	17 57
Gospel Oak	d	12 14	12 29	12 44	12 59	13 14	13 29	13 44	13 59	14 14	14 29	14 44	14 59	15 14	15 29	15 44	15 59	16 14	16 29	16 44	16 59	17 14	17 29	17 44	17 59
Kentish Town West	d	12 16	12 31	12 46	13 01	13 16	13 31	13 46	14 01	14 16	14 31	14 46	15 01	15 16	15 31	15 46	16 01	16 16	16 31	16 46	17 01	17 16	17 31	17 46	18 01
Camden Road	d	12 18	12 33	12 48	13 03	13 18	13 33	13 48	14 03	14 18	14 33	14 48	15 03	15 18	15 33	15 48	16 03	16 18	16 33	16 48	17 03	17 18	17 33	17 48	18 03
Caledonian Rd & Barnsbury	d	12 20	12 35	12 50	13 05	13 20	13 35	13 50	14 05	14 21	14 35	14 50	15 05	15 21	15 35	15 52	16 05	16 20	16 35	16 50	17 05	17 21	17 36	17 50	18 05
Highbury & Islington	⊖ d	12 24	12 39	12 54	13 09	13 24	13 39	13 54	14 09	14 24	14 39	14 54	15 09	15 24	15 39	15 55	16 08	16 24	16 39	16 55	17 09	17 24	17 39	17 54	18 09
Canonbury	⊖ d	12 26	12 41	12 56	13 11	13 26	13 41	13 56	14 11	14 26	14 41	14 56	15 11	15 26	15 41	15 57	16 11	16 26	16 41	16 56	17 11	17 26	17 41	17 56	18 11
Dalston Kingsland	d	12 29	12 44	12 59	13 14	13 29	13 44	13 59	14 14	14 29	14 44	14 59	15 14	15 29	15 44	16 00	16 14	16 29	16 44	16 59	17 14	17 29	17 44	17 59	18 14
Hackney Central	d	12 31	12 46	13 01	13 16	13 31	13 46	14 01	14 16	14 31	14 46	15 01	15 16	15 31	15 46	16 02	16 16	16 32	16 46	17 01	17 16	17 31	17 46	18 01	18 16
Homerton	d	12 33	12 48	13 03	13 18	13 33	13 48	14 03	14 18	14 33	14 48	15 03	15 18	15 33	15 48	16 04	16 18	16 34	16 48	17 03	17 18	17 33	17 48	18 03	18 18
Hackney Wick	d	12 36	12 51	13 06	13 21	13 36	13 51	14 06	14 21	14 36	14 51	15 06	15 21	15 36	15 51	16 07	16 21	16 37	16 51	17 06	17 21	17 36	17 51	18 06	18 21
Stratford	⊖ a	12 43	12 58	13 13	13 28	13 43	13 58	14 13	14 28	14 43	14 58	15 13	15 28	15 43	15 58	16 14	16 28	16 44	16 58	17 14	17 28	17 43	17 58	18 13	18 28

		LO	LO	LO	LO		LO	LO	LO	LO	LO	LO	LO	LO	LO	LO	LO		LO	LO	LO	LO			
Richmond	⊖ d	17 41	17 57	18 11	18 26		18 41	18 56	19 16	19 26	19 40	19 56	20 16	20 36	20 56	21 16	21 36		21 56	22 16	22 47	23 16			
Kew Gardens	⊖ d	17 44	18 00	18 14	18 29		18 44	18 59	19 19	19 29	19 43	19 59	20 19	20 39	20 59	21 19	21 39		21 59	22 19	22 50	23 19			
Gunnersbury	⊖ d	17 47	18 03	18 17	18 32		18 47	19 02	19 22	19 32	19 46	20 02	20 22	20 42	21 02	21 22	21 42		22 02	22 22	22 53	23 22			
South Acton	d	17 49	18 05	18 19	18 34		18 49	19 04	19 24	19 34	19 48	20 04	20 24	20 44	21 04	21 24	21 44		22 04	22 24	22 55	23 24			
Acton Central	d	17 53	18 08	18 23	18 38		18 52	19 07	19 27	19 37	19 51	20 07	20 27	20 47	21 07	21 27	21 47		22 07	22 27	22 58	23 27			
Willesden Jn. High Level	⊖ a	17 58	18 13	18 29	18 43		18 57	19 12	19 32	19 42	19 59	20 12	20 32	20 52	21 12	21 32	21 52		22 12	22 32	23 03	23 35			
	d	17 59	18 14	18 29	18 44		18 58	19 13	19 33	19 43	20 00	20 13	20 33	20 53	21 13	21 33	21 53		22 13	22 33	23 04				
Kensal Rise	d	18 02	18 17	18 32	18 47		19 01	19 16	19 36	19 46	20 03	20 16	20 36	20 56	21 16	21 36	21 56		22 16	22 36	23 09				
Brondesbury Park	d	18 04	18 19	18 34	18 49		19 03	19 18	19 38	19 48	20 05	20 18	20 38	20 58	21 18	21 38	21 58		22 18	22 38	23 11				
Brondesbury	d	18 06	18 21	18 36	18 51		19 05	19 20	19 40	19 50	20 07	20 20	20 40	21 00	21 20	21 40	22 00		22 20	22 40	23 13				
West Hampstead	⊖ d	18 07	18 22	18 37	18 52		19 06	19 21	19 41	19 51	20 08	20 21	20 41	21 01	21 21	21 41	22 01		22 21	22 41	23 14				
Finchley Road & Frognal	d	18 09	18 24	18 39	18 54		19 08	19 23	19 43	19 53	20 10	20 23	20 43	21 03	21 23	21 43	22 03		22 23	22 43	23 16				
Hampstead Heath	d	18 12	18 27	18 42	18 57		19 11	19 26	19 46	19 56	20 13	20 26	20 46	21 06	21 26	21 46	22 06		22 26	22 46	23 19				
Gospel Oak	d	18 14	18 29	18 44	18 59		19 13	19 28	19 48	19 58	20 15	20 28	20 48	21 08	21 28	21 48	22 08		22 28	22 48	23 21				
Kentish Town West	d	18 16	18 31	18 46	19 01		19 15	19 30	19 50	20 00	20 17	20 30	20 50	21 10	21 30	21 50	22 10		22 30	22 50	23 23				
Camden Road	d	18 18	18 33	18 48	19 03		19 17	19 32	19 52	20 02	20 19	20 32	20 52	21 12	21 32	21 52	22 11		22 32	22 52	23 25				
Caledonian Rd & Barnsbury	d	18 20	18 35	18 50	19 05		19 19	19 34	19 55	20 05	20 21	20 34	20 54	21 14	21 34	21 54	22 14		22 34	22 54	23 28				
Highbury & Islington	⊖ d	18 24	18 39	18 54	19 09		19 23	19 37	19 57	20 07	20 24	20 37	20 57	21 17	21 37	21 57	22 17		22 37	22 56	23 31				
Canonbury	⊖ d	18 26	18 41	18 56	19 11		19 24	19 39	19 59	20 09	20 26	20 39	20 59	21 19	21 39	21 59	22 19		22 39	22 59	23 33				
Dalston Kingsland	d	18 29	18 44	18 59	19 14		19 28	19 42	20 02	20 12	20 29	20 42	21 02	21 22	21 42	22 02	22 22		22 42	23 02	23 36				
Hackney Central	d	18 31	18 46	19 01	19 16		19 29	19 44	20 04	20 14	20 31	20 44	21 04	21 24	21 44	22 04	22 24		22 44	23 04	23 38				
Homerton	d	18 33	18 48	19 03	19 18		19 31	19 46	20 06	20 16	20 33	20 46	21 06	21 26	21 46	22 06	22 26		22 46	23 06	23 40				
Hackney Wick	d	18 36	18 51	19 06	19 21		19 34	19 49	20 09	20 19	20 35	20 49	21 09	21 29	21 49	22 09	22 29		22 49	23 09	23 42				
Stratford	⊖ a	18 43	18 59	19 13	19 28		19 44	19 59	20 16	20 26	20 42	20 59	21 19	21 39	21 59	22 17	22 37		22 57	23 18	23 49				

Table 59

Sundays

Richmond - Willesden Junction, West Hampstead Highbury and Islington and Stratford

Station		LO	LO	LO	LO	LO	LO	LO	LO	LO	LO	LO
Richmond ⊖	d											
Kew Gardens ⊖	d											
Gunnersbury ⊖	d					08 30		09 00		09 30		10 00
South Acton	d					08 36		09 06		09 36		10 06
Acton Central	d					08 39		09 09		09 39		10 09
Willesden Jn. High Level ⊖	a					08 52		09 22		09 52		10 22
	d			08 23		08 53		09 23		09 53		10 23
Kensal Rise	d			08 35		09 05		09 35		10 05		10 35
Brondesbury Park	d			08 39		09 09		09 39		10 09		10 39
Brondesbury	d			08 42		09 12		09 42		10 12		10 42
West Hampstead ⊖	d			08 47		09 17		09 47		10 17		10 47
Finchley Road & Frognal	d			08 51		09 21		09 51		10 21		10 51
Hampstead Heath	d	08 15	08 45	09 01	09 15	09 31	09 45	10 01	10 15	10 31	10 45	11 01
Gospel Oak	d			09a05		09a35		10a05		10a35		11a05
Kentish Town West	d	08 21	08 51		09 21		09 51		10 21		10 51	
Camden Road	d	08 26	08 56		09 26		09 56		10 26		10 56	
Caledonian Rd & Barnsbury	d											
Highbury & Islington ⊖	d	08 40	09 10		09 40		10 10		10 40		11 10	
Canonbury ⊖	d	08 45	09 15		09 45		10 15		10 45		11 15	
Dalston Kingsland	d	08 53	09 23		09 53		10 23		10 53		11 23	
Hackney Central	d	09 01	09 31		10 01		10 31		11 01		11 31	
Homerton	d	09 09	09 39		10 09		10 39		11 09		11 39	
Hackney Wick	d	09 16	09 46		10 16		10 46		11 16		11 46	
Stratford [7] ⊖	a	09 26	09 56		10 26		10 56		11 26		11 56	

Station		LO	LO	LO	LO	LO	LO	LO	LO	LO	LO	LO	LO
Richmond ⊖	d												
Kew Gardens ⊖	d												
Gunnersbury ⊖	d		10 30		11 00		11 30		12 00		12 30		13 00
South Acton	d		10 36		11 06		11 36		12 06		12 36		13 06
Acton Central	d		10 39		11 09		11 39		12 09		12 39		13 09
Willesden Jn. High Level ⊖	a		10 52		11 22		11 52		12 22		12 52		13 22
	d		10 53		11 23		11 53		12 23		12 53		13 23
Kensal Rise	d		11 05		11 35		12 05		12 35		13 05		13 35
Brondesbury Park	d		11 09		11 39		12 09		12 39		13 09		13 39
Brondesbury	d		11 12		11 42		12 12		12 42		13 12		13 42
West Hampstead ⊖	d		11 17		11 47		12 17		12 47		13 17		13 47
Finchley Road & Frognal	d		11 21		11 51		12 21		12 51		13 21		13 51
Hampstead Heath	d	11 15	11 31	11 45	12 01	12 15	12 31	12 45	13 01	13 15	13 31	13 45	14 01
Gospel Oak	d		11a35		12a05		12a35		13a05		13a35		14a05
Kentish Town West	d	11 21		11 51		12 21		12 51		13 21		13 51	
Camden Road	d	11 26		11 56		12 26		12 56		13 26		13 56	
Caledonian Rd & Barnsbury	d												
Highbury & Islington ⊖	d	11 40		12 10		12 40		13 10		13 40		14 10	
Canonbury ⊖	d	11 45		12 15		12 45		13 15		13 45		14 15	
Dalston Kingsland	d	11 53		12 23		12 53		13 23		13 53		14 23	
Hackney Central	d	12 01		12 31		13 01		13 31		14 01		14 31	
Homerton	d	12 09		12 39		13 09		13 39		14 09		14 39	
Hackney Wick	d	12 16		12 46		13 16		13 46		14 16		14 46	
Stratford [7] ⊖	a	12 26		12 56		13 26		13 56		14 26		14 56	

Station		LO	LO	LO	LO	LO	LO	LO	LO	LO	LO
Richmond ⊖	d										
Kew Gardens ⊖	d										
Gunnersbury ⊖	d		13 30		14 00		14 30		15 00		15 30
South Acton	d		13 36		14 06		14 36		15 06		15 36
Acton Central	d		13 39		14 09		14 39		15 09		15 39
Willesden Jn. High Level ⊖	a		13 52		14 22		14 52		15 22		15 52
	d		13 53		14 23		14 53		15 23		15 53
Kensal Rise	d		14 05		14 35		15 05		15 35		16 05
Brondesbury Park	d		14 09		14 39		15 09		15 39		16 09
Brondesbury	d		14 12		14 42		15 12		15 42		16 12
West Hampstead ⊖	d		14 17		14 47		15 17		15 47		16 17
Finchley Road & Frognal	d		14 21		14 51		15 21		15 51		16 21
Hampstead Heath	d	14 15	14 31	14 45	15 01	15 15	15 31	15 45	16 01	16 15	16 31
Gospel Oak	d		14a35		15a05		15a35		16a05		16a35
Kentish Town West	d	14 21		14 51		15 21		15 51		16 21	
Camden Road	d	14 26		14 56		15 26		15 56		16 26	
Caledonian Rd & Barnsbury	d										
Highbury & Islington ⊖	d	14 40		15 10		15 40		16 10		16 40	
Canonbury ⊖	d	14 45		15 15		15 45		16 15		16 45	
Dalston Kingsland	d	14 53		15 23		15 53		16 23		16 53	
Hackney Central	d	15 01		15 31		16 01		16 31		17 01	
Homerton	d	15 09		15 39		16 09		16 39		17 09	
Hackney Wick	d	15 16		15 46		16 16		16 46		17 16	
Stratford [7] ⊖	a	15 26		15 56		16 26		16 56		17 26	

Station		LO	LO	LO	LO	LO	LO	LO	LO	LO	LO	LO	LO
Richmond ⊖	d												
Kew Gardens ⊖	d												
Gunnersbury ⊖	d		16 00		16 30		17 00		17 30		18 00		18 30
South Acton	d		16 06		16 36		17 06		17 36		18 06		18 36
Acton Central	d		16 09		16 39		17 09		17 39		18 09		18 39
Willesden Jn. High Level ⊖	a		16 22		16 52		17 22		17 52		18 22		18 52
	d		16 23		16 53		17 23		17 53		18 23		18 53
Kensal Rise	d		16 35		17 05		17 35		18 05		18 35		19 05
Brondesbury Park	d		16 39		17 09		17 39		18 09		18 39		19 09
Brondesbury	d		16 42		17 12		17 42		18 12		18 42		19 12
West Hampstead ⊖	d		16 47		17 17		17 47		18 17		18 47		19 17
Finchley Road & Frognal	d		16 51		17 21		17 51		18 21		18 51		19 21
Hampstead Heath	d	16 45	17 01	17 15	17 31	17 45	18 01	18 15	18 31	18 45	19 01	19 15	19 31
Gospel Oak	d		17a05		17a35		18a05		18a35		19a05		19a35
Kentish Town West	d	16 51		17 21		17 51		18 21		18 51		19 21	
Camden Road	d	16 56		17 26		17 56		18 26		18 56		19 26	
Caledonian Rd & Barnsbury	d												
Highbury & Islington ⊖	d	17 10		17 40		18 10		18 40		19 10		19 40	
Canonbury ⊖	d	17 15		17 45		18 15		18 45		19 15		19 45	
Dalston Kingsland	d	17 23		17 53		18 23		18 53		19 23		19 53	
Hackney Central	d	17 31		18 01		18 31		19 01		19 31		20 01	
Homerton	d	17 39		18 09		18 39		19 09		19 39		20 09	
Hackney Wick	d	17 46		18 16		18 46		19 16		19 46		20 16	
Stratford [7] ⊖	a	17 56		18 26		18 56		19 26		19 56		20 26	

Station		LO	LO	LO	LO	LO	LO	LO	LO	LO
Richmond ⊖	d									
Kew Gardens ⊖	d									
Gunnersbury ⊖	d		19 00		19 30		20 00		20 30	
South Acton	d		19 06		19 36		20 06		20 36	
Acton Central	d		19 09		19 39		20 09		20 39	
Willesden Jn. High Level ⊖	a		19 22		19 52		20 22		20 52	
	d		19 23		19 53		20 23		20 53	
Kensal Rise	d		19 35		20 05		20 35		21 05	
Brondesbury Park	d		19 39		20 09		20 39		21 09	
Brondesbury	d		19 42		20 12		20 42		21 12	
West Hampstead ⊖	d		19 47		20 17		20 47		21 17	
Finchley Road & Frognal	d		19 51		20 21		20 51		21 21	
Hampstead Heath	d	19 45	20 01	20 15	20 31	20 45	21 01	21 15	21 31	21 45
Gospel Oak	d		20a05		20a35		21a05		21a35	
Kentish Town West	d	19 51		20 21		20 51		21 21		21 51
Camden Road	d	19 56		20 26		20 56		21 26		21 56
Caledonian Rd & Barnsbury	d									
Highbury & Islington ⊖	d	20 10		20 40		21 10		21 40		22 10
Canonbury ⊖	d	20 15		20 45		21 15		21 45		22 15
Dalston Kingsland	d	20 23		20 53		21 23		21 53		22 23
Hackney Central	d	20 31		21 01		21 31		22 01		22 31
Homerton	d	20 39		21 09		21 39		22 09		22 39
Hackney Wick	d	20 46		21 16		21 46		22 16		22 46
Stratford [7] ⊖	a	20 56		21 26		21 56		22 26		22 56

Station		LO	LO	LO	LO	LO	LO	LO	LO	LO
Richmond ⊖	d									
Kew Gardens ⊖	d									
Gunnersbury ⊖	d	21 00		21 30		22 00		22 30		23 00
South Acton	d	21 06		21 36		22 06		22 36		23 06
Acton Central	d	21 09		21 39		22 09		22 39		23 09
Willesden Jn. High Level ⊖	a	21 22		21 52		22 22		22 52		23 22
	d	21 23		21 53		22 23		22 53		23 23
Kensal Rise	d	21 35		22 05		22 35		23 05		23 35
Brondesbury Park	d	21 39		22 09		22 39		23 09		23 39
Brondesbury	d	21 42		22 12		22 42		23 12		23 42
West Hampstead ⊖	d	21 47		22 17		22 47		23 17		23 47
Finchley Road & Frognal	d	21 51		22 21		22 51		23 21		23 51
Hampstead Heath	d	22 01	22 15	22 31	22 45	23 01	23 15	23 31	23 45	00 01
Gospel Oak	d	22a05		22a35		23a05		23a35		00a05
Kentish Town West	d		22 21		22 51		23 21		23 51	
Camden Road	d		22 26		22 56		23 26		23 56	
Caledonian Rd & Barnsbury	d									
Highbury & Islington ⊖	d		22 40		23 10		23 40		00 10	
Canonbury ⊖	d		22 45		23 15		23 45		00 15	
Dalston Kingsland	d		22 53		23 23		23 53		00 23	
Hackney Central	d		23 01		23 31		00 01		00 31	
Homerton	d		23 09		23 39		00 09		00 39	
Hackney Wick	d		23 16		23 46		00 16		00 46	
Stratford [7] ⊖	a		23 26		23 56		00 26		00 56	

Table 60

Mondays to Fridays

London, Queen's Park and Harrow & Wealdstone - Watford Junction

Station		LO	LO MX	LO MO	LO MX	LO	LO	LO	LO	LO
London Euston [15] ⊖	d	23p17	23p37	23p47	23p57	05 27	05 57	06 17	06 37	06 57
South Hampstead	d	23p23	23p43	23p53	00 03	05 33	06 03	06 23	06 43	07 03
Kilburn High Road	d	23p24	23p44	23p54	00 04	05 34	06 04	06 24	06 44	07 04
Queen's Park (London) ⊖	d	23p26	23p46	23p56	00 06	05 36	06 06	06 26	06 46	07 06
Kensal Green	d	23p28	23p48	23p58	00 08	05 38	06 08	06 28	06 48	07 08
Willesden Jn Low Level	d	23p31	23p51	00 01	00 11	05 41	06 11	06 31	06 51	07 11
Harlesden	d	23p33	23p53	00 03	00 13	05 43	06 13	06 33	06 53	07 13
Stonebridge Park	d	23p35	23p55	00 05	00 15	05 45	06 15	06 35	06 55	07 15
Wembley Central	d	23p38	23p58	00 08	00 18	05 48	06 18	06 38	06 58	07 18
North Wembley	d	23p40	23p59	00 10	00 20	05 50	06 20	06 40	07 00	07 20
South Kenton	d	23p42	00 02	00 12	00 22	05 52	06 22	06 42	07 02	07 22
Kenton	d	23p44	00 04	00 14	00 24	05 54	06 24	06 44	07 04	07 24
Harrow & Wealdstone	d	23p46	00 06	00 16	00 26	05 56	06 26	06 46	07 06	07 26
Headstone Lane	d	23p49	00 09	00 19	00 29	05 59	06 29	06 49	07 09	07 29
Hatch End	d	23p51	00 11	00 21	00 31	06 01	06 31	06 51	07 11	07 31
Carpenders Park	d	23p54	00 14	00 24	00 34	06 04	06 34	06 54	07 14	07 34
Bushey	d	23p57	00 17	00 27	00 37	06 07	06 37	06 57	07 17	07 37
Watford High Street	d	23p59	00 20	00 30	00 40	06 10	06 40	07 00	07 20	07 40
Watford Junction	a	00 04	00 24	00 34	00 44	06 14	06 44	07 05	07 24	07 44

Station		LO	LO	LO	LO	LO	LO	LO	LO	LO	LO	LO	LO	LO
London Euston [15] ⊖	d	07 17	07 37	07 57	08 17	08 37	08 57	09 17	09 37	09 57	10 17	10 37	10 57	11 17
South Hampstead	d	07 23	07 43	08 03	08 23	08 43	09 03	09 23	09 43	10 03	10 23	10 43	11 03	11 23
Kilburn High Road	d	07 24	07 44	08 04	08 24	08 44	09 04	09 24	09 44	10 04	10 24	10 44	11 04	11 24
Queen's Park (London) ⊖	d	07 26	07 46	08 06	08 26	08 46	09 06	09 26	09 46	10 06	10 26	10 46	11 06	11 26
Kensal Green	d	07 28	07 48	08 08	08 28	08 48	09 08	09 28	09 48	10 08	10 28	10 48	11 08	11 28
Willesden Jn Low Level	d	07 31	07 51	08 11	08 31	08 51	09 11	09 31	09 51	10 11	10 31	10 51	11 11	11 31
Harlesden	d	07 33	07 53	08 13	08 33	08 53	09 13	09 33	09 53	10 13	10 33	10 53	11 13	11 33
Stonebridge Park	d	07 35	07 55	08 15	08 35	08 55	09 15	09 35	09 55	10 15	10 35	10 55	11 15	11 35
Wembley Central	d	07 38	07 58	08 18	08 38	08 58	09 18	09 38	09 58	10 18	10 38	10 58	11 18	11 38
North Wembley	d	07 40	08 00	08 20	08 40	09 00	09 20	09 40	10 00	10 20	10 40	11 00	11 20	11 40
South Kenton	d	07 42	08 02	08 22	08 42	09 02	09 22	09 42	10 02	10 22	10 42	11 02	11 22	11 42
Kenton	d	07 44	08 04	08 24	08 44	09 04	09 24	09 44	10 04	10 24	10 44	11 04	11 24	11 44
Harrow & Wealdstone	d	07 46	08 06	08 26	08 46	09 06	09 26	09 46	10 06	10 26	10 46	11 06	11 26	11 46
Headstone Lane	d	07 49	08 09	08 29	08 49	09 09	09 29	09 49	10 09	10 29	10 49	11 09	11 29	11 49
Hatch End	d	07 51	08 11	08 31	08 51	09 11	09 31	09 51	10 11	10 31	10 51	11 11	11 31	11 51
Carpenders Park	d	07 54	08 14	08 34	08 54	09 14	09 34	09 54	10 14	10 34	10 54	11 14	11 34	11 54
Bushey	d	07 57	08 17	08 37	08 57	09 17	09 37	09 57	10 17	10 37	10 57	11 17	11 37	11 57
Watford High Street	d	08 00	08 20	08 40	09 00	09 20	09 40	10 00	10 20	10 40	11 00	11 20	11 40	12 00
Watford Junction	a	08 04	08 24	08 44	09 04	09 24	09 44	10 04	10 24	10 45	11 04	11 24	11 44	12 04

Station		LO	LO	LO	LO	LO	LO	LO	LO	LO	LO	LO	LO	LO	LO
London Euston [15] ⊖	d	11 37	11 57	12 17	12 37	12 57	13 17	13 37	13 57	14 17	14 37	14 57	15 17	15 37	15 57
South Hampstead	d	11 43	12 03	12 23	12 43	13 03	13 23	13 43	14 03	14 23	14 43	15 03	15 23	15 43	16 03
Kilburn High Road	d	11 44	12 04	12 24	12 44	13 04	13 24	13 44	14 04	14 24	14 44	15 04	15 24	15 44	16 04
Queen's Park (London) ⊖	d	11 46	12 06	12 26	12 46	13 06	13 26	13 46	14 06	14 26	14 46	15 06	15 26	15 46	16 06
Kensal Green	d	11 48	12 08	12 28	12 48	13 08	13 28	13 48	14 08	14 28	14 48	15 08	15 28	15 48	16 08
Willesden Jn Low Level	d	11 51	12 11	12 31	12 51	13 11	13 31	13 51	14 11	14 31	14 51	15 11	15 31	15 51	16 11
Harlesden	d	11 53	12 13	12 33	12 53	13 13	13 33	13 53	14 13	14 33	14 53	15 13	15 33	15 53	16 13
Stonebridge Park	d	11 55	12 15	12 35	12 55	13 15	13 35	13 55	14 15	14 35	14 55	15 15	15 35	15 55	16 15
Wembley Central	d	11 58	12 18	12 38	12 58	13 18	13 38	13 58	14 18	14 38	14 58	15 18	15 38	15 58	16 18
North Wembley	d	12 00	12 20	12 40	13 00	13 20	13 40	14 00	14 20	14 40	15 00	15 20	15 40	16 00	16 20
South Kenton	d	12 02	12 22	12 42	13 02	13 22	13 42	14 02	14 22	14 42	15 02	15 22	15 42	16 02	16 22
Kenton	d	12 04	12 24	12 44	13 04	13 24	13 44	14 04	14 24	14 44	15 04	15 24	15 44	16 04	16 24
Harrow & Wealdstone	d	12 06	12 26	12 46	13 06	13 26	13 46	14 06	14 26	14 46	15 06	15 26	15 46	16 06	16 26
Headstone Lane	d	12 09	12 29	12 49	13 09	13 29	13 49	14 09	14 29	14 49	15 09	15 29	15 49	16 09	16 29
Hatch End	d	12 11	12 31	12 51	13 11	13 31	13 51	14 11	14 31	14 51	15 11	15 31	15 51	16 11	16 31
Carpenders Park	d	12 14	12 34	12 54	13 14	13 34	13 54	14 14	14 34	14 54	15 14	15 34	15 54	16 14	16 34
Bushey	d	12 17	12 37	12 57	13 17	13 37	13 57	14 17	14 37	14 57	15 17	15 37	15 57	16 17	16 37
Watford High Street	d	12 20	12 40	13 00	13 20	13 40	14 00	14 20	14 40	15 00	15 20	15 40	16 00	16 20	16 40
Watford Junction	a	12 24	12 44	13 04	13 24	13 44	14 04	14 24	14 44	15 04	15 24	15 44	16 04	16 24	16 44

Station		LO	LO	LO	LO	LO	LO	LO	LO
London Euston [15] ⊖	d	16 17	16 37	16 57	17 17	17 37	17 57	18 17	18 37
South Hampstead	d	16 23	16 43	17 03	17 23	17 43	18 03	18 23	18 43
Kilburn High Road	d	16 24	16 44	17 04	17 24	17 44	18 04	18 24	18 44
Queen's Park (London) ⊖	d	16 27	16 47	17 07	17 27	17 47	18 07	18 27	18 47
Kensal Green	d	16 29	16 49	17 09	17 29	17 49	18 09	18 29	18 49
Willesden Jn Low Level	d	16 32	16 52	17 12	17 32	17 52	18 12	18 32	18 52
Harlesden	d	16 34	16 54	17 14	17 34	17 54	18 14	18 34	18 54
Stonebridge Park	d	16 36	16 56	17 16	17 36	17 56	18 16	18 36	18 56
Wembley Central	d	16 39	16 59	17 19	17 39	17 59	18 19	18 39	18 59
North Wembley	d	16 41	17 01	17 21	17 41	18 01	18 21	18 41	19 01
South Kenton	d	16 43	17 03	17 23	17 43	18 03	18 23	18 43	19 03
Kenton	d	16 45	17 05	17 25	17 45	18 05	18 25	18 45	19 05
Harrow & Wealdstone	d	16 48	17 08	17 28	17 48	18 08	18 28	18 48	19 08
Headstone Lane	d	16 51	17 11	17 31	17 51	18 11	18 31	18 51	19 11
Hatch End	d	16 53	17 13	17 33	17 53	18 13	18 33	18 53	19 13
Carpenders Park	d	16 56	17 16	17 36	17 56	18 16	18 36	18 56	19 16
Bushey	d	16 59	17 19	17 39	17 59	18 19	18 39	18 59	19 19
Watford High Street	d	17 01	17 21	17 41	18 01	18 21	18 41	19 01	19 21
Watford Junction	a	17 08	17 28	17 48	18 08	18 28	18 48	19 08	19 28

Station		LO	LO	LO	LO	LO	LO	LO	LO	LO	LO	LO	LO	LO	LO	LO	LO
London Euston [15] ⊖	d	18 57	19 17	19 37	19 57	20 17	20 37	20 57	21 17	21 37	21 57	22 17	22 37	22 57	23 17	23 37	23 57
South Hampstead	d	19 03	19 23	19 43	20 03	20 23	20 43	21 03	21 23	21 43	22 03	22 23	22 43	23 03	23 23	23 43	00 03
Kilburn High Road	d	19 04	19 24	19 44	20 04	20 24	20 44	21 04	21 24	21 44	22 04	22 24	22 44	23 04	23 24	23 44	00 04
Queen's Park (London) ⊖	d	19 07	19 26	19 46	20 06	20 26	20 46	21 06	21 26	21 46	22 06	22 26	22 46	23 06	23 26	23 46	00 06
Kensal Green	d	19 09	19 28	19 48	20 09	20 28	20 48	21 08	21 28	21 48	22 08	22 28	22 48	23 08	23 28	23 48	00 08
Willesden Jn Low Level	d	19 12	19 31	19 51	20 13	20 31	20 51	21 11	21 31	21 51	22 11	22 31	22 51	23 11	23 31	23 51	00 11
Harlesden	d	19 14	19 33	19 53	20 15	20 33	20 53	21 13	21 33	21 53	22 13	22 33	22 53	23 13	23 33	23 53	00 13
Stonebridge Park	d	19 16	19 35	19 55	20 17	20 35	20 55	21 15	21 35	21 55	22 15	22 35	22 55	23 15	23 35	23 55	00 15
Wembley Central	d	19 19	19 38	19 58	20 20	20 38	20 58	21 18	21 38	21 58	22 18	22 38	22 58	23 18	23 38	23 58	00 18
North Wembley	d	19 21	19 40	20 00	20 22	20 40	21 00	21 20	21 40	22 00	22 20	22 40	23 00	23 20	23 40	23 59	00 20
South Kenton	d	19 23	19 42	20 02	20 24	20 42	21 02	21 22	21 42	22 02	22 22	22 42	23 02	23 22	23 42	00 02	00 22
Kenton	d	19 25	19 44	20 04	20 26	20 44	21 04	21 24	21 44	22 04	22 24	22 44	23 04	23 24	23 44	00 04	00 24
Harrow & Wealdstone	d	19 28	19 46	20 06	20 28	20 46	21 06	21 26	21 46	22 06	22 26	22 46	23 06	23 26	23 46	00 06	00 26
Headstone Lane	d	19 31	19 49	20 09	20 31	20 49	21 09	21 29	21 49	22 09	22 29	22 49	23 09	23 29	23 49	00 09	00 29
Hatch End	d	19 33	19 51	20 11	20 33	20 51	21 11	21 31	21 51	22 11	22 31	22 51	23 11	23 31	23 51	00 11	00 31
Carpenders Park	d	19 36	19 54	20 14	20 36	20 54	21 14	21 34	21 54	22 14	22 34	22 54	23 14	23 34	23 54	00 14	00 34
Bushey	d	19 39	19 57	20 17	20 39	20 57	21 17	21 37	21 57	22 17	22 37	22 57	23 17	23 37	23 57	00 17	00 37
Watford High Street	d	19 41	20 00	20 20	20 42	21 00	21 20	21 40	22 00	22 20	22 40	23 00	23 20	23 40	23 59	00 20	00 40
Watford Junction	a	19 48	20 04	20 24	20 46	21 04	21 24	21 44	22 04	22 25	22 44	23 04	23 24	23 44	00 04	00 24	00 44

Saturdays

Station		LO	LO	LO	LO	LO	LO	LO	LO	LO
London Euston [15] ⊖	d	23p17	23p37	23p57	05 27	05 57	06 17	06 37	06 57	07 17
South Hampstead	d	23p23	23p43	00 03	05 33	06 03	06 23	06 43	07 03	07 23
Kilburn High Road	d	23p24	23p44	00 04	05 34	06 04	06 24	06 44	07 04	07 24
Queen's Park (London) ⊖	d	23p26	23p46	00 06	05 36	06 06	06 26	06 46	07 06	07 26
Kensal Green	d	23p28	23p48	00 08	05 38	06 08	06 28	06 48	07 08	07 28
Willesden Jn Low Level	d	23p31	23p51	00 11	05 41	06 11	06 31	06 51	07 11	07 31
Harlesden	d	23p33	23p53	00 13	05 43	06 13	06 33	06 53	07 13	07 33
Stonebridge Park	d	23p35	23p55	00 15	05 45	06 15	06 35	06 55	07 15	07 35
Wembley Central	d	23p38	23p58	00 18	05 48	06 18	06 38	06 58	07 18	07 38
North Wembley	d	23p40	23p59	00 20	05 50	06 20	06 40	07 00	07 20	07 40
South Kenton	d	23p42	00 02	00 22	05 52	06 22	06 42	07 02	07 22	07 42
Kenton	d	23p44	00 04	00 24	05 54	06 24	06 44	07 04	07 24	07 44
Harrow & Wealdstone	d	23p46	00 06	00 26	05 56	06 26	06 46	07 06	07 26	07 46
Headstone Lane	d	23p49	00 09	00 29	05 59	06 29	06 49	07 09	07 29	07 49
Hatch End	d	23p51	00 11	00 31	06 01	06 31	06 51	07 11	07 31	07 51
Carpenders Park	d	23p54	00 14	00 34	06 04	06 34	06 54	07 14	07 34	07 54
Bushey	d	23p57	00 17	00 37	06 07	06 37	06 57	07 17	07 37	07 57
Watford High Street	d	23p59	00 20	00 40	06 10	06 40	07 00	07 20	07 40	08 00
Watford Junction	a	00 04	00 24	00 44	06 14	06 44	07 05	07 24	07 44	08 04

Station		LO	LO	LO	LO	LO	LO	LO	LO	LO	LO	LO	LO	LO
London Euston [15] ⊖	d	07 37	07 57	08 17	08 37	08 57	09 17	09 37	09 57	10 17	10 37	10 57	11 17	11 37
South Hampstead	d	07 43	08 03	08 23	08 43	09 03	09 23	09 43	10 03	10 23	10 43	11 03	11 23	11 43
Kilburn High Road	d	07 44	08 04	08 24	08 44	09 04	09 24	09 44	10 04	10 24	10 44	11 04	11 24	11 44
Queen's Park (London) ⊖	d	07 46	08 06	08 26	08 46	09 06	09 26	09 46	10 06	10 26	10 46	11 06	11 26	11 46
Kensal Green	d	07 48	08 08	08 28	08 48	09 08	09 28	09 48	10 08	10 28	10 48	11 08	11 28	11 48
Willesden Jn Low Level	d	07 51	08 11	08 31	08 51	09 11	09 31	09 51	10 11	10 31	10 51	11 11	11 31	11 51
Harlesden	d	07 53	08 13	08 33	08 53	09 13	09 33	09 53	10 13	10 33	10 53	11 13	11 33	11 53
Stonebridge Park	d	07 55	08 15	08 35	08 55	09 15	09 35	09 55	10 15	10 35	10 55	11 15	11 35	11 55
Wembley Central	d	07 58	08 18	08 38	08 58	09 18	09 38	09 58	10 18	10 38	10 58	11 18	11 38	11 58
North Wembley	d	08 00	08 20	08 40	09 00	09 20	09 40	10 00	10 20	10 40	11 00	11 20	11 40	12 00
South Kenton	d	08 02	08 22	08 42	09 02	09 22	09 42	10 02	10 22	10 42	11 02	11 22	11 42	12 02
Kenton	d	08 04	08 24	08 44	09 04	09 24	09 44	10 04	10 24	10 44	11 04	11 24	11 44	12 04
Harrow & Wealdstone	d	08 06	08 26	08 46	09 06	09 26	09 46	10 06	10 26	10 46	11 06	11 26	11 46	12 06
Headstone Lane	d	08 09	08 29	08 49	09 09	09 29	09 49	10 09	10 29	10 49	11 09	11 29	11 49	12 09
Hatch End	d	08 11	08 31	08 51	09 11	09 31	09 51	10 11	10 31	10 51	11 11	11 31	11 51	12 11
Carpenders Park	d	08 14	08 34	08 54	09 14	09 34	09 54	10 14	10 34	10 54	11 14	11 34	11 54	12 14
Bushey	d	08 17	08 37	08 57	09 17	09 37	09 57	10 17	10 37	10 57	11 17	11 37	11 57	12 17
Watford High Street	d	08 20	08 40	09 00	09 20	09 40	10 00	10 20	10 40	11 00	11 20	11 40	12 00	12 20
Watford Junction	a	08 24	08 44	09 04	09 24	09 44	10 04	10 24	10 44	11 04	11 24	11 44	12 04	12 24

Stations Queen's Park to Harrow & Wealdstone inclusive are also served by London Underground Bakerloo Line Services

London, Queen's Park and Harrow & Wealdstone - Watford Junction

		LO	LO	LO	LO	LO	LO	LO	LO	LO	LO	LO	LO	LO	LO	LO	LO	LO	LO	LO	LO	LO	LO
London Euston 15	⊖ d	11 57	12 17	12 37	12 57	13 17	13 37	13 57	14 17	14 37	14 57	15 17	15 37	15 57	16 17	16 37	16 57	17 17	17 37	17 57	18 17	18 37	18 57
South Hampstead	d	12 03	12 23	12 43	13 03	13 23	13 43	14 03	14 23	14 43	15 03	15 23	15 43	16 03	16 23	16 43	17 03	17 23	17 43	18 03	18 23	18 43	19 03
Kilburn High Road	d	12 04	12 24	12 44	13 04	13 24	13 44	14 04	14 24	14 44	15 04	15 24	15 44	16 04	16 24	16 44	17 04	17 24	17 44	18 04	18 24	18 44	19 04
Queen's Park (London)	⊖ d	12 06	12 26	12 46	13 06	13 26	13 46	14 06	14 26	14 46	15 06	15 26	15 46	16 06	16 26	16 46	17 06	17 26	17 46	18 06	18 26	18 46	19 06
Kensal Green	d	12 08	12 28	12 48	13 08	13 28	13 48	14 08	14 28	14 48	15 08	15 28	15 48	16 08	16 28	16 48	17 08	17 28	17 48	18 08	18 28	18 48	19 08
Willesden Jn Low Level	d	12 11	12 31	12 51	13 11	13 31	13 51	14 11	14 31	14 51	15 11	15 31	15 51	16 11	16 31	16 51	17 11	17 31	17 51	18 11	18 31	18 51	19 11
Harlesden	d	12 13	12 33	12 53	13 13	13 33	13 53	14 13	14 33	14 53	15 13	15 33	15 53	16 13	16 33	16 53	17 13	17 33	17 53	18 13	18 33	18 53	19 13
Stonebridge Park	d	12 15	12 35	12 55	13 15	13 35	13 55	14 15	14 35	14 55	15 15	15 35	15 55	16 15	16 35	16 55	17 15	17 35	17 55	18 15	18 35	18 55	19 15
Wembley Central	d	12 18	12 38	12 58	13 18	13 38	13 58	14 18	14 38	14 58	15 18	15 38	15 58	16 18	16 38	16 58	17 18	17 38	17 58	18 18	18 38	18 58	19 18
North Wembley	d	12 20	12 40	13 00	13 20	13 40	14 00	14 20	14 40	15 00	15 20	15 40	16 00	16 20	16 40	17 00	17 20	17 40	18 00	18 20	18 40	19 00	19 20
South Kenton	d	12 22	12 42	13 02	13 22	13 42	14 02	14 22	14 42	15 02	15 22	15 42	16 02	16 22	16 42	17 02	17 22	17 42	18 02	18 22	18 42	19 02	19 22
Kenton	d	12 24	12 44	13 04	13 24	13 44	14 04	14 24	14 44	15 04	15 24	15 44	16 04	16 24	16 44	17 04	17 24	17 44	18 04	18 24	18 44	19 04	19 24
Harrow & Wealdstone	d	12 26	12 46	13 06	13 26	13 46	14 06	14 26	14 46	15 06	15 26	15 46	16 06	16 26	16 46	17 06	17 26	17 46	18 06	18 26	18 46	19 06	19 26
Headstone Lane	d	12 29	12 49	13 09	13 29	13 49	14 09	14 29	14 49	15 09	15 29	15 49	16 09	16 29	16 49	17 09	17 29	17 49	18 09	18 29	18 49	19 09	19 29
Hatch End	d	12 31	12 51	13 11	13 31	13 51	14 11	14 31	14 51	15 11	15 31	15 51	16 11	16 31	16 51	17 11	17 31	17 51	18 11	18 31	18 51	19 11	19 31
Carpenders Park	d	12 34	12 54	13 14	13 34	13 54	14 14	14 34	14 54	15 14	15 34	15 54	16 14	16 34	16 54	17 14	17 34	17 54	18 14	18 34	18 54	19 14	19 34
Bushey	d	12 37	12 57	13 17	13 37	13 57	14 17	14 37	14 57	15 17	15 37	15 57	16 17	16 37	16 57	17 17	17 37	17 57	18 17	18 37	18 57	19 17	19 37
Watford High Street	d	12 40	13 00	13 20	13 40	14 00	14 20	14 40	15 00	15 20	15 40	16 00	16 20	16 40	17 00	17 20	17 40	18 00	18 20	18 40	19 00	19 20	19 40
Watford Junction	a	12 44	13 04	13 24	13 44	14 04	14 24	14 44	15 04	15 24	15 44	16 04	16 24	16 44	17 04	17 24	17 44	18 04	18 24	18 44	19 04	19 24	19 44

		LO	LO	LO	LO	LO	LO	LO	LO	LO	LO	LO	LO	LO	LO	LO
London Euston 15	⊖ d	19 17	19 37	19 57	20 17	20 37	20 57	21 17	21 37	21 57	22 17	22 37	22 57	23 17	23 37	23 57
South Hampstead	d	19 23	19 43	20 03	20 23	20 43	21 03	21 23	21 43	22 03	22 23	22 43	23 03	23 23	23 43	00 03
Kilburn High Road	d	19 24	19 44	20 04	20 24	20 44	21 04	21 24	21 44	22 04	22 24	22 44	23 04	23 24	23 44	00 04
Queen's Park (London)	⊖ d	19 26	19 46	20 06	20 26	20 46	21 06	21 26	21 46	22 06	22 26	22 46	23 06	23 26	23 46	00 06
Kensal Green	d	19 28	19 48	20 08	20 28	20 48	21 08	21 28	21 48	22 08	22 28	22 48	23 08	23 28	23 48	00 08
Willesden Jn Low Level	d	19 31	19 51	20 11	20 31	20 51	21 11	21 31	21 51	22 11	22 31	22 51	23 11	23 31	23 51	00 11
Harlesden	d	19 33	19 53	20 13	20 33	20 53	21 13	21 33	21 53	22 13	22 33	22 53	23 13	23 33	23 53	00 13
Stonebridge Park	d	19 35	19 55	20 15	20 35	20 55	21 15	21 35	21 55	22 15	22 35	22 55	23 15	23 35	23 55	00 15
Wembley Central	d	19 38	19 58	20 18	20 38	20 58	21 18	21 38	21 58	22 18	22 38	22 58	23 18	23 38	23 58	00 18
North Wembley	d	19 40	20 00	20 20	20 40	21 00	21 20	21 40	22 00	22 20	22 40	23 00	23 20	23 40	23 59	00 20
South Kenton	d	19 42	20 02	20 22	20 42	21 02	21 22	21 42	22 02	22 22	22 42	23 02	23 22	23 42	00 02	00 22
Kenton	d	19 44	20 04	20 24	20 44	21 04	21 24	21 44	22 04	22 24	22 44	23 04	23 24	23 44	00 04	00 24
Harrow & Wealdstone	d	19 46	20 06	20 26	20 46	21 06	21 26	21 46	22 06	22 26	22 46	23 06	23 26	23 46	00 06	00 26
Headstone Lane	d	19 49	20 09	20 29	20 49	21 09	21 29	21 49	22 09	22 29	22 49	23 09	23 29	23 49	00 09	00 29
Hatch End	d	19 51	20 11	20 31	20 51	21 11	21 31	21 51	22 11	22 31	22 51	23 11	23 31	23 51	00 11	00 31
Carpenders Park	d	19 54	20 14	20 34	20 54	21 14	21 34	21 54	22 14	22 34	22 54	23 14	23 34	23 54	00 14	00 34
Bushey	d	19 57	20 17	20 37	20 57	21 17	21 37	21 57	22 17	22 37	22 57	23 17	23 37	23 57	00 17	00 37
Watford High Street	d	20 00	20 20	20 40	21 00	21 20	21 40	22 00	22 20	22 40	23 00	23 20	23 40	23 59	00 20	00 40
Watford Junction	a	20 04	20 24	20 44	21 04	21 24	21 44	22 06	22 24	22 44	23 04	23 24	23 44	00 04	00 24	00 44

Sundays

		LO	LO	LO	LO	LO	LO	LO	LO	LO	LO	LO	LO	LO	LO	LO	LO	LO	LO	LO	LO	LO	LO
London Euston 15	⊖ d	23p17	23p37	23p57	06 47	07 17	07 47	08 17	08 47	09 17	09 47	10 17	10 47	11 17	11 47	12 17	12 47	13 17	13 47	14 17	14 47	15 17	15 47
South Hampstead	d	23p23	23p43	00 03	06 53	07 23	07 53	08 23	08 53	09 23	09 53	10 23	10 53	11 23	11 53	12 23	12 53	13 23	13 53	14 23	14 53	15 23	15 53
Kilburn High Road	d	23p24	23p44	00 04	06 54	07 24	07 54	08 24	08 54	09 24	09 54	10 24	10 54	11 24	11 54	12 24	12 54	13 24	13 54	14 24	14 54	15 24	15 54
Queen's Park (London)	⊖ d	23p26	23p46	00 06	06 56	07 26	07 56	08 26	08 56	09 26	09 56	10 26	10 56	11 26	11 56	12 26	12 56	13 26	13 56	14 26	14 56	15 26	15 56
Kensal Green	d	23p28	23p48	00 08	06 58	07 28	07 58	08 28	08 58	09 28	09 58	10 28	10 58	11 28	11 58	12 28	12 58	13 28	13 58	14 28	14 58	15 28	15 58
Willesden Jn Low Level	d	23p31	23p51	00 11	07 01	07 31	08 01	08 31	09 01	09 31	10 01	10 31	11 01	11 31	12 01	12 31	13 01	13 31	14 01	14 31	15 01	15 31	16 01
Harlesden	d	23p33	23p53	00 13	07 03	07 33	08 03	08 33	09 03	09 33	10 03	10 33	11 03	11 33	12 03	12 33	13 03	13 33	14 03	14 33	15 03	15 33	16 03
Stonebridge Park	d	23p35	23p55	00 15	07 05	07 35	08 05	08 35	09 05	09 35	10 05	10 35	11 05	11 35	12 05	12 35	13 05	13 35	14 05	14 35	15 05	15 35	16 05
Wembley Central	d	23p38	23p58	00 18	07 08	07 38	08 08	08 38	09 08	09 38	10 08	10 38	11 08	11 38	12 08	12 38	13 08	13 38	14 08	14 38	15 08	15 38	16 08
North Wembley	d	23p40	23p59	00 20	07 10	07 40	08 10	08 40	09 10	09 40	10 10	10 40	11 10	11 40	12 10	12 40	13 10	13 40	14 10	14 40	15 10	15 40	16 10
South Kenton	d	23p42	00 02	00 22	07 12	07 42	08 12	08 42	09 12	09 42	10 12	10 42	11 12	11 42	12 12	12 42	13 12	13 42	14 12	14 42	15 12	15 42	16 12
Kenton	d	23p44	00 04	00 24	07 14	07 44	08 14	08 44	09 14	09 44	10 14	10 44	11 14	11 44	12 14	12 44	13 14	13 44	14 14	14 44	15 14	15 44	16 14
Harrow & Wealdstone	d	23p46	00 06	00 26	07 16	07 46	08 16	08 46	09 16	09 46	10 16	10 46	11 16	11 46	12 16	12 46	13 16	13 46	14 16	14 46	15 16	15 46	16 16
Headstone Lane	d	23p49	00 09	00 29	07 19	07 49	08 19	08 49	09 19	09 49	10 19	10 49	11 19	11 49	12 19	12 49	13 19	13 49	14 19	14 49	15 19	15 49	16 19
Hatch End	d	23p51	00 11	00 31	07 21	07 51	08 21	08 51	09 21	09 51	10 21	10 51	11 21	11 51	12 21	12 51	13 21	13 51	14 21	14 51	15 21	15 51	16 21
Carpenders Park	d	23p54	00 14	00 34	07 24	07 54	08 24	08 54	09 24	09 54	10 24	10 54	11 24	11 54	12 24	12 54	13 24	13 54	14 24	14 54	15 24	15 54	16 24
Bushey	d	23p57	00 17	00 37	07 27	07 57	08 27	08 57	09 27	09 57	10 27	10 57	11 27	11 57	12 27	12 57	13 27	13 57	14 27	14 57	15 27	15 57	16 27
Watford High Street	d	23p59	00 20	00 40	07 30	08 00	08 30	09 00	09 30	10 00	10 30	11 00	11 30	12 00	12 30	13 00	13 30	14 00	14 30	15 00	15 30	16 00	16 30
Watford Junction	a	00 04	00 24	00 44	07 34	08 04	08 34	09 04	09 34	10 04	10 34	11 04	11 34	12 04	12 34	13 04	13 34	14 04	14 34	15 04	15 34	16 04	16 34

		LO	LO	LO	LO	LO	LO	LO	LO	LO	LO	LO	LO	LO	LO	LO	LO
London Euston 15	⊖ d	16 17	16 47	17 17	17 47	18 17	18 47	19 17	19 47	20 17	20 47	21 17	21 47	22 17	22 47	23 17	23 47
South Hampstead	d	16 23	16 53	17 23	17 53	18 23	18 53	19 23	19 53	20 23	20 53	21 23	21 53	22 23	22 53	23 23	23 53
Kilburn High Road	d	16 24	16 54	17 24	17 54	18 24	18 54	19 24	19 54	20 24	20 54	21 24	21 54	22 24	22 54	23 24	23 54
Queen's Park (London)	⊖ d	16 26	16 56	17 26	17 56	18 26	18 56	19 26	19 56	20 26	20 56	21 26	21 56	22 26	22 56	23 26	23 56
Kensal Green	d	16 28	16 58	17 28	17 58	18 28	18 58	19 28	19 58	20 28	20 58	21 28	21 58	22 28	22 58	23 28	23 58
Willesden Jn Low Level	d	16 31	17 01	17 31	18 01	18 31	19 01	19 31	20 01	20 31	21 01	21 31	22 01	22 31	23 01	23 31	00 01
Harlesden	d	16 33	17 03	17 33	18 03	18 33	19 03	19 33	20 03	20 33	21 03	21 33	22 03	22 33	23 03	23 33	00 03
Stonebridge Park	d	16 35	17 05	17 35	18 05	18 35	19 05	19 35	20 05	20 35	21 05	21 35	22 05	22 35	23 05	23 35	00 05
Wembley Central	d	16 38	17 08	17 38	18 08	18 38	19 08	19 38	20 08	20 38	21 08	21 38	22 08	22 38	23 08	23 38	00 08
North Wembley	d	16 40	17 10	17 40	18 10	18 40	19 10	19 40	20 10	20 40	21 10	21 40	22 10	22 40	23 10	23 40	00 10
South Kenton	d	16 42	17 12	17 42	18 12	18 42	19 12	19 42	20 12	20 42	21 12	21 42	22 12	22 42	23 12	23 42	00 12
Kenton	d	16 44	17 14	17 44	18 14	18 44	19 14	19 44	20 14	20 44	21 14	21 44	22 14	22 44	23 14	23 44	00 14
Harrow & Wealdstone	d	16 46	17 16	17 46	18 16	18 46	19 16	19 46	20 16	20 46	21 16	21 46	22 16	22 46	23 16	23 46	00 16
Headstone Lane	d	16 49	17 19	17 49	18 19	18 49	19 19	19 49	20 19	20 49	21 19	21 49	22 19	22 49	23 19	23 49	00 19
Hatch End	d	16 51	17 21	17 51	18 21	18 51	19 21	19 51	20 21	20 51	21 21	21 51	22 21	22 51	23 21	23 51	00 21
Carpenders Park	d	16 54	17 24	17 54	18 24	18 54	19 24	19 54	20 24	20 54	21 24	21 54	22 24	22 54	23 24	23 54	00 24
Bushey	d	16 57	17 27	17 57	18 27	18 57	19 27	19 57	20 27	20 57	21 27	21 57	22 27	22 57	23 27	23 57	00 27
Watford High Street	d	17 00	17 30	18 00	18 30	19 00	19 30	20 00	20 30	21 00	21 30	22 00	22 30	23 00	23 30	23 59	00 30
Watford Junction	a	17 04	17 34	18 04	18 34	19 04	19 34	20 04	20 34	21 04	21 34	22 04	22 34	23 04	23 34	00 04	00 34

Stations Queen's Park to Harrow & Wealdstone inclusive are also served by London Underground Bakerloo Line Services

Watford Junction - Harrow & Wealdstone, Queen's Park and London

		LO MO	LO	LO	LO	LO	LO	LO	LO	LO	LO	LO	LO	LO	LO	LO	LO	LO	LO	LO	LO	LO	LO	LO
Watford Junction	d	23p21	05 05	05 21	05 41	06 01	06 20	06 40	07 00	07 20	07 40	08 00	08 20	08 40	09 00	09 21	09 41	10 01	10 21	10 41	11 01	11 21	11 41	12 01
Watford High Street	d	23p24	05 08	05 24	05 44	06 04	06 23	06 43	07 03	07 23	07 43	08 03	08 23	08 43	09 03	09 24	09 44	10 04	10 24	10 44	11 04	11 24	11 44	12 04
Bushey	d	23p26	05 10	05 26	05 46	06 06	06 25	06 45	07 05	07 25	07 45	08 05	08 25	08 45	09 05	09 26	09 46	10 06	10 26	10 46	11 06	11 26	11 46	12 06
Carpenders Park	d	23p29	05 13	05 29	05 49	06 09	06 28	06 48	07 08	07 28	07 48	08 08	08 28	08 48	09 08	09 29	09 49	10 09	10 29	10 49	11 09	11 29	11 49	12 09
Hatch End	d	23p32	05 16	05 32	05 52	06 12	06 31	06 51	07 11	07 31	07 51	08 11	08 31	08 51	09 11	09 32	09 52	10 12	10 32	10 52	11 12	11 32	11 52	12 12
Headstone Lane	d	23p34	05 18	05 34	05 54	06 14	06 33	06 53	07 13	07 33	07 53	08 13	08 33	08 53	09 13	09 34	09 54	10 14	10 34	10 54	11 14	11 34	11 54	12 14
Harrow & Wealdstone	d	23p37	05 21	05 37	05 57	06 17	06 36	06 56	07 16	07 36	07 56	08 16	08 36	08 56	09 16	09 37	09 57	10 17	10 37	10 57	11 17	11 37	11 57	12 17
Kenton	d	23p39	05 23	05 39	05 59	06 19	06 39	06 59	07 19	07 39	07 59	08 19	08 39	08 59	09 19	09 39	09 59	10 19	10 39	10 59	11 19	11 39	11 59	12 19
South Kenton	d	23p41	05 25	05 41	06 01	06 21	06 41	07 01	07 21	07 41	08 01	08 21	08 41	09 01	09 21	09 41	10 01	10 21	10 41	11 01	11 21	11 41	12 01	12 21
North Wembley	d	23p43	05 27	05 43	06 03	06 23	06 43	07 03	07 23	07 43	08 03	08 23	08 43	09 03	09 23	09 43	10 03	10 23	10 43	11 03	11 23	11 43	12 03	12 23
Wembley Central	d	23p45	05 29	05 45	06 05	06 25	06 45	07 05	07 25	07 45	08 05	08 25	08 45	09 05	09 25	09 45	10 05	10 25	10 45	11 05	11 25	11 45	12 05	12 25
Stonebridge Park	d	23p48	05 32	05 48	06 08	06 28	06 48	07 08	07 28	07 48	08 08	08 28	08 48	09 08	09 28	09 48	10 08	10 28	10 48	11 08	11 28	11 48	12 08	12 28
Harlesden	d	23p50	05 34	05 50	06 10	06 30	06 50	07 10	07 30	07 50	08 10	08 30	08 50	09 10	09 30	09 50	10 10	10 30	10 50	11 10	11 30	11 50	12 10	12 30
Willesden Jn Low Level	d	23p52	05 36	05 52	06 12	06 32	06 53	07 13	07 33	07 53	08 13	08 33	08 53	09 13	09 33	09 52	10 12	10 32	10 52	11 12	11 32	11 52	12 12	12 32
Kensal Green	d	23p55	05 39	05 55	06 15	06 35	06 55	07 15	07 35	07 55	08 15	08 35	08 55	09 15	09 35	09 55	10 15	10 35	10 55	11 15	11 35	11 55	12 15	12 35
Queen's Park (London)	⊖ d	23p57	05 41	05 57	06 17	06 37	06 58	07 18	07 40	07 58	08 18	08 38	08 58	09 18	09 38	09 57	10 17	10 37	10 57	11 17	11 37	11 57	12 17	12 37
Kilburn High Road	d	23p59	05 43	05 59	06 19	06 39	07 00	07 20	07 42	08 00	08 20	08 40	09 00	09 20	09 40	09 59	10 19	10 39	10 59	11 19	11 39	11 59	12 19	12 39
South Hampstead	d	00 01	05 45	06 01	06 21	06 41	07 02	07 22	07 44	08 02	08 22	08 42	09 02	09 22	09 42	10 01	10 21	10 41	11 01	11 21	11 41	12 01	12 21	12 41
London Euston 15	⊖ a	00 08	05 52	06 13	06 32	06 51	07 13	07 32	07 52	08 12	08 32	08 53	09 12	09 32	09 52	10 11	10 30	10 50	11 11	11 30	11 50	12 11	12 30	12 50

		LO	LO	LO	LO	LO	LO	LO	LO	LO	LO	LO	LO	LO	LO	LO	LO	LO	LO	LO	LO	LO	LO
Watford Junction	d	12 21	12 41	13 01	13 21	13 41	14 01	14 21	14 41	15 01	15 21	15 41	16 01	16 21	16 41	17 01	17 21	17 41	18 01	18 21	18 41	19 01	19 21
Watford High Street	d	12 24	12 44	13 04	13 24	13 44	14 04	14 24	14 44	15 04	15 24	15 44	16 04	16 24	16 44	17 04	17 24	17 44	18 04	18 24	18 44	19 04	19 24
Bushey	d	12 26	12 46	13 06	13 26	13 46	14 06	14 26	14 46	15 06	15 26	15 46	16 06	16 26	16 46	17 06	17 26	17 46	18 06	18 26	18 46	19 06	19 26
Carpenders Park	d	12 29	12 49	13 09	13 29	13 49	14 09	14 29	14 49	15 09	15 29	15 49	16 09	16 29	16 49	17 09	17 29	17 49	18 09	18 29	18 49	19 09	19 29
Hatch End	d	12 32	12 52	13 12	13 32	13 52	14 12	14 32	14 52	15 12	15 32	15 52	16 12	16 32	16 52	17 12	17 32	17 52	18 12	18 32	18 52	19 12	19 32
Headstone Lane	d	12 34	12 54	13 14	13 34	13 54	14 14	14 34	14 54	15 14	15 34	15 54	16 14	16 34	16 54	17 14	17 34	17 54	18 14	18 34	18 54	19 14	19 34
Harrow & Wealdstone	d	12 37	12 57	13 17	13 37	13 57	14 17	14 37	14 57	15 17	15 37	15 57	16 17	16 37	16 57	17 17	17 37	17 57	18 17	18 37	18 57	19 17	19 37
Kenton	d	12 39	12 59	13 19	13 39	13 59	14 19	14 39	14 59	15 19	15 39	15 59	16 19	16 39	16 59	17 19	17 39	17 59	18 19	18 39	18 59	19 19	19 39
South Kenton	d	12 41	13 01	13 21	13 41	14 01	14 21	14 41	15 01	15 21	15 41	16 01	16 21	16 41	17 01	17 21	17 41	18 01	18 21	18 41	19 01	19 21	19 41
North Wembley	d	12 43	13 03	13 23	13 43	14 03	14 23	14 43	15 03	15 23	15 43	16 03	16 23	16 43	17 03	17 23	17 43	18 03	18 23	18 43	19 03	19 23	19 43
Wembley Central	d	12 45	13 05	13 25	13 45	14 05	14 25	14 45	15 05	15 25	15 45	16 05	16 25	16 45	17 05	17 25	17 45	18 05	18 25	18 45	19 05	19 25	19 45
Stonebridge Park	d	12 48	13 08	13 28	13 48	14 08	14 28	14 48	15 08	15 28	15 48	16 08	16 28	16 48	17 08	17 28	17 48	18 08	18 28	18 48	19 08	19 28	19 48
Harlesden	d	12 50	13 10	13 30	13 50	14 10	14 30	14 50	15 10	15 30	15 50	16 10	16 30	16 50	17 10	17 30	17 50	18 10	18 30	18 50	19 10	19 30	19 50
Willesden Jn Low Level	d	12 52	13 12	13 32	13 52	14 12	14 32	14 52	15 12	15 32	15 52	16 12	16 32	16 52	17 12	17 32	17 52	18 12	18 32	18 52	19 12	19 32	19 52
Kensal Green	d	12 55	13 15	13 35	13 55	14 15	14 35	14 55	15 15	15 35	15 55	16 15	16 35	16 55	17 15	17 35	17 55	18 15	18 35	18 55	19 15	19 35	19 55
Queen's Park (London)	⊖ d	12 57	13 17	13 37	13 57	14 17	14 37	14 57	15 17	15 37	15 57	16 17	16 37	16 57	17 17	17 37	17 57	18 17	18 37	18 57	19 17	19 37	19 57
Kilburn High Road	d	12 59	13 19	13 39	13 59	14 19	14 39	14 59	15 19	15 39	15 59	16 19	16 39	16 59	17 19	17 39	17 59	18 19	18 39	18 59	19 19	19 39	19 59
South Hampstead	d	13 01	13 21	13 41	14 01	14 21	14 41	15 01	15 21	15 41	16 01	16 21	16 41	17 01	17 21	17 41	18 01	18 21	18 41	19 01	19 21	19 41	20 01
London Euston 15	⊖ a	13 11	13 30	13 50	14 11	14 30	14 50	15 11	15 30	15 50	16 11	16 30	16 49	17 11	17 30	17 53	18 15	18 30	18 50	19 11	19 30	19 51	20 10

		LO	LO	LO	LO	LO	LO	LO	LO	LO	LO	LO
Watford Junction	d	19 41	20 01	20 21	20 41	21 01	21 21	21 41	22 01	22 21	22 41	23 01
Watford High Street	d	19 44	20 04	20 24	20 44	21 04	21 24	21 44	22 04	22 24	22 44	23 04
Bushey	d	19 46	20 06	20 26	20 46	21 06	21 26	21 46	22 06	22 26	22 46	23 06
Carpenders Park	d	19 49	20 09	20 29	20 49	21 09	21 29	21 49	22 09	22 29	22 49	23 09
Hatch End	d	19 52	20 12	20 32	20 52	21 12	21 32	21 52	22 12	22 32	22 52	23 12
Headstone Lane	d	19 54	20 14	20 34	20 54	21 14	21 34	21 54	22 14	22 34	22 54	23 14
Harrow & Wealdstone	d	19 57	20 17	20 37	20 57	21 17	21 37	21 57	22 17	22 37	22 57	23 17
Kenton	d	19 59	20 19	20 39	20 59	21 19	21 39	21 59	22 19	22 39	22 59	23 19
South Kenton	d	20 01	20 21	20 41	21 01	21 21	21 41	22 01	22 21	22 41	23 01	23 21
North Wembley	d	20 03	20 23	20 43	21 03	21 23	21 43	22 03	22 23	22 43	23 03	23 23
Wembley Central	d	20 05	20 25	20 45	21 05	21 25	21 45	22 05	22 25	22 45	23 05	23 25
Stonebridge Park	d	20 08	20 28	20 48	21 08	21 28	21 48	22 08	22 28	22 48	23 08	23 28
Harlesden	d	20 10	20 30	20 50	21 10	21 30	21 50	22 10	22 30	22 50	23 10	23 30
Willesden Jn Low Level	d	20 12	20 32	20 52	21 12	21 32	21 52	22 12	22 32	22 52	23 12	23 32
Kensal Green	d	20 15	20 35	20 55	21 15	21 35	21 55	22 15	22 35	22 55	23 15	23 35
Queen's Park (London)	⊖ d	20 17	20 37	20 57	21 17	21 37	21 57	22 17	22 37	22 57	23 17	23 37
Kilburn High Road	d	20 19	20 39	20 59	21 19	21 39	21 59	22 19	22 39	22 59	23 19	23 39
South Hampstead	d	20 21	20 41	21 01	21 21	21 41	22 01	22 21	22 41	23 01	23 21	23 41
London Euston 15	⊖ a	20 30	20 51	21 11	21 30	21 51	22 11	22 30	22 50	23 10	23 30	23 50

Saturdays

		LO	LO	LO	LO	LO	LO	LO	LO	LO	LO	LO	LO	LO	LO	LO	LO	LO	LO	LO	LO	LO	LO
Watford Junction	d	05 05	05 21	05 41	06 01	06 21	06 41	07 01	07 21	07 41	08 01	08 21	08 41	09 01	09 21	09 41	10 01	10 21	10 41	11 01	11 21	11 41	12 01
Watford High Street	d	05 08	05 24	05 44	06 04	06 24	06 44	07 04	07 24	07 44	08 04	08 24	08 44	09 04	09 24	09 44	10 04	10 24	10 44	11 04	11 24	11 44	12 04
Bushey	d	05 10	05 26	05 46	06 06	06 26	06 46	07 06	07 26	07 46	08 06	08 26	08 46	09 06	09 26	09 46	10 06	10 26	10 46	11 06	11 26	11 46	12 06
Carpenders Park	d	05 13	05 29	05 49	06 09	06 29	06 49	07 09	07 29	07 49	08 09	08 29	08 49	09 09	09 29	09 49	10 09	10 29	10 49	11 09	11 29	11 49	12 09
Hatch End	d	05 16	05 32	05 52	06 12	06 32	06 52	07 12	07 32	07 52	08 12	08 32	08 52	09 12	09 32	09 52	10 12	10 32	10 52	11 12	11 32	11 52	12 12
Headstone Lane	d	05 18	05 34	05 54	06 14	06 34	06 54	07 14	07 34	07 54	08 14	08 34	08 54	09 14	09 34	09 54	10 14	10 34	10 54	11 14	11 34	11 54	12 14
Harrow & Wealdstone	d	05 21	05 37	05 57	06 17	06 37	06 57	07 17	07 37	07 57	08 17	08 37	08 57	09 17	09 37	09 57	10 17	10 37	10 57	11 17	11 37	11 57	12 17
Kenton	d	05 23	05 39	05 59	06 19	06 39	06 59	07 19	07 39	07 59	08 19	08 39	08 59	09 19	09 39	09 59	10 19	10 39	10 59	11 19	11 39	11 59	12 19
South Kenton	d	05 25	05 41	06 01	06 21	06 41	07 01	07 21	07 41	08 01	08 21	08 41	09 01	09 21	09 41	10 01	10 21	10 41	11 01	11 21	11 41	12 01	12 21
North Wembley	d	05 27	05 43	06 03	06 23	06 43	07 03	07 23	07 43	08 03	08 23	08 43	09 03	09 23	09 43	10 03	10 23	10 43	11 03	11 23	11 43	12 03	12 23
Wembley Central	d	05 29	05 45	06 05	06 25	06 45	07 05	07 25	07 45	08 05	08 25	08 45	09 05	09 25	09 45	10 05	10 25	10 45	11 05	11 25	11 45	12 05	12 25
Stonebridge Park	d	05 32	05 48	06 08	06 28	06 48	07 08	07 28	07 48	08 08	08 28	08 48	09 08	09 28	09 48	10 08	10 28	10 48	11 08	11 28	11 48	12 08	12 28
Harlesden	d	05 34	05 50	06 10	06 30	06 50	07 10	07 30	07 50	08 10	08 30	08 50	09 10	09 30	09 50	10 10	10 30	10 50	11 10	11 30	11 50	12 10	12 30
Willesden Jn Low Level	d	05 36	05 52	06 12	06 32	06 52	07 12	07 32	07 52	08 12	08 32	08 52	09 12	09 32	09 52	10 12	10 32	10 52	11 12	11 32	11 52	12 12	12 32
Kensal Green	d	05 39	05 55	06 15	06 35	06 55	07 15	07 35	07 55	08 15	08 35	08 55	09 15	09 35	09 55	10 15	10 35	10 55	11 15	11 35	11 55	12 15	12 35
Queen's Park (London)	⊖ d	05 41	05 57	06 17	06 37	06 57	07 17	07 37	07 57	08 17	08 37	08 57	09 17	09 37	09 57	10 17	10 37	10 57	11 17	11 37	11 57	12 17	12 37
Kilburn High Road	d	05 43	05 59	06 19	06 39	06 59	07 19	07 39	07 59	08 19	08 39	08 59	09 19	09 39	09 59	10 19	10 39	10 59	11 19	11 39	11 59	12 19	12 39
South Hampstead	d	05 45	06 01	06 21	06 41	07 01	07 21	07 41	08 01	08 21	08 41	09 01	09 21	09 41	10 01	10 21	10 41	11 01	11 21	11 41	12 01	12 21	12 41
London Euston 15	⊖ a	05 54	06 10	06 30	06 50	07 10	07 30	07 51	08 12	08 30	08 51	09 11	09 30	09 51	10 11	10 30	10 51	11 11	11 30	11 51	12 11	12 30	12 49

Stations Harrow & Wealdstone to Queen's Park inclusive are also served by London Underground Bakerloo Line Services

Table 60

Saturdays

Watford Junction - Harrow & Wealdstone, Queen's Park and London

		LO	LO	LO	LO	LO	LO	LO	LO	LO	LO	LO	LO	LO	LO
Watford Junction	d	12 21	12 41	13 01	13 21	13 41	14 01	14 21	14 41	15 01	15 21	15 41	16 01	16 21	16 41
Watford High Street	d	12 24	12 44	13 04	13 24	13 44	14 04	14 24	14 44	15 04	15 24	15 44	16 04	16 24	16 44
Bushey	d	12 26	12 46	13 06	13 26	13 46	14 06	14 26	14 46	15 06	15 26	15 46	16 06	16 26	16 46
Carpenders Park	d	12 29	12 49	13 09	13 29	13 49	14 09	14 29	14 49	15 09	15 29	15 49	16 09	16 29	16 49
Hatch End	d	12 32	12 52	13 12	13 32	13 52	14 12	14 32	14 52	15 12	15 32	15 52	16 12	16 32	16 52
Headstone Lane	d	12 34	12 54	13 14	13 34	13 54	14 14	14 34	14 54	15 14	15 34	15 54	16 14	16 34	16 54
Harrow & Wealdstone	d	12 37	12 57	13 17	13 37	13 57	14 17	14 37	14 57	15 17	15 37	15 57	16 17	16 37	16 57
Kenton	d	12 39	12 59	13 19	13 39	13 59	14 19	14 39	14 59	15 19	15 39	15 59	16 19	16 39	16 59
South Kenton	d	12 41	13 01	13 21	13 41	14 01	14 21	14 41	15 01	15 21	15 41	16 01	16 21	16 41	17 01
North Wembley	d	12 43	13 03	13 23	13 43	14 03	14 23	14 43	15 03	15 23	15 43	16 03	16 23	16 43	17 03
Wembley Central	d	12 45	13 05	13 25	13 45	14 05	14 25	14 45	15 05	15 25	15 45	16 05	16 25	16 45	17 05
Stonebridge Park	d	12 48	13 08	13 28	13 48	14 08	14 28	14 48	15 08	15 28	15 48	16 08	16 28	16 48	17 08
Harlesden	d	12 50	13 10	13 30	13 50	14 10	14 30	14 50	15 10	15 30	15 50	16 10	16 30	16 50	17 10
Willesden Jn Low Level	d	12 52	13 12	13 32	13 52	14 12	14 32	14 52	15 12	15 32	15 52	16 12	16 32	16 52	17 12
Kensal Green	d	12 55	13 15	13 35	13 55	14 15	14 35	14 55	15 15	15 35	15 55	16 15	16 35	16 55	17 15
Queen's Park (London) ⊖	d	12 57	13 17	13 37	13 57	14 17	14 37	14 57	15 17	15 37	15 57	16 17	16 37	16 57	17 17
Kilburn High Road	d	12 59	13 19	13 39	13 59	14 19	14 39	14 59	15 19	15 39	15 59	16 19	16 39	16 59	17 19
South Hampstead	d	13 01	13 21	13 41	14 01	14 21	14 41	15 01	15 21	15 41	16 01	16 21	16 41	17 01	17 21
London Euston 15 ⊖	a	13 13	13 31	13 50	14 11	14 30	14 51	15 11	15 30	15 51	16 11	16 30	16 51	17 11	17 30

		LO	LO	LO	LO	LO	LO	LO	LO
Watford Junction	d	17 01	17 21	17 41	18 01	18 21	18 41	19 01	19 21
Watford High Street	d	17 04	17 24	17 44	18 04	18 24	18 44	19 04	19 24
Bushey	d	17 06	17 26	17 46	18 06	18 26	18 46	19 06	19 26
Carpenders Park	d	17 09	17 29	17 49	18 09	18 29	18 49	19 09	19 29
Hatch End	d	17 12	17 32	17 52	18 12	18 32	18 52	19 12	19 32
Headstone Lane	d	17 14	17 34	17 54	18 14	18 34	18 54	19 14	19 34
Harrow & Wealdstone	d	17 17	17 37	17 57	18 17	18 37	18 57	19 17	19 37
Kenton	d	17 19	17 39	17 59	18 19	18 39	18 59	19 19	19 39
South Kenton	d	17 21	17 41	18 01	18 21	18 41	19 01	19 21	19 41
North Wembley	d	17 23	17 43	18 03	18 23	18 43	19 03	19 23	19 43
Wembley Central	d	17 25	17 45	18 05	18 25	18 45	19 05	19 25	19 45
Stonebridge Park	d	17 28	17 48	18 08	18 28	18 48	19 08	19 28	19 48
Harlesden	d	17 30	17 50	18 10	18 30	18 50	19 10	19 30	19 50
Willesden Jn Low Level	d	17 32	17 52	18 12	18 32	18 52	19 12	19 32	19 52
Kensal Green	d	17 35	17 55	18 15	18 35	18 55	19 15	19 35	19 55
Queen's Park (London) ⊖	d	17 37	17 57	18 17	18 37	18 57	19 17	19 37	19 57
Kilburn High Road	d	17 39	17 59	18 19	18 39	18 59	19 19	19 39	19 59
South Hampstead	d	17 41	18 01	18 21	18 41	19 01	19 21	19 41	20 01
London Euston 15 ⊖	a	17 51	18 11	18 30	18 51	19 11	19 30	19 51	20 11

		LO	LO	LO	LO	LO	LO	LO	LO	LO	LO
Watford Junction	d	19 41	20 01	20 21	20 41	21 01	21 21	21 41	22 01	22 21	22 41
Watford High Street	d	19 44	20 04	20 24	20 44	21 04	21 24	21 44	22 04	22 24	22 44
Bushey	d	19 46	20 06	20 26	20 46	21 06	21 26	21 46	22 06	22 26	22 46
Carpenders Park	d	19 49	20 09	20 29	20 49	21 09	21 29	21 49	22 09	22 29	22 49
Hatch End	d	19 52	20 12	20 32	20 52	21 12	21 32	21 52	22 12	22 32	22 52
Headstone Lane	d	19 54	20 14	20 34	20 54	21 14	21 34	21 54	22 14	22 34	22 54
Harrow & Wealdstone	d	19 57	20 17	20 37	20 57	21 17	21 37	21 57	22 17	22 37	22 57
Kenton	d	19 59	20 19	20 39	20 59	21 19	21 39	21 59	22 19	22 39	22 59
South Kenton	d	20 01	20 21	20 41	21 01	21 21	21 41	22 01	22 21	22 41	23 01
North Wembley	d	20 03	20 23	20 43	21 03	21 23	21 43	22 03	22 23	22 43	23 03
Wembley Central	d	20 05	20 25	20 45	21 05	21 25	21 45	22 05	22 25	22 45	23 05
Stonebridge Park	d	20 08	20 28	20 48	21 08	21 28	21 48	22 08	22 28	22 48	23 08
Harlesden	d	20 10	20 30	20 50	21 10	21 30	21 50	22 10	22 30	22 50	23 10
Willesden Jn Low Level	d	20 12	20 32	20 52	21 12	21 32	21 52	22 12	22 32	22 52	23 12
Kensal Green	d	20 15	20 35	20 55	21 15	21 35	21 55	22 15	22 35	22 55	23 15
Queen's Park (London) ⊖	d	20 17	20 37	20 57	21 17	21 37	21 57	22 17	22 37	22 57	23 17
Kilburn High Road	d	20 19	20 39	20 59	21 19	21 39	21 59	22 19	22 39	22 59	23 19
South Hampstead	d	20 21	20 41	21 01	21 21	21 41	22 01	22 21	22 41	23 01	23 21
London Euston 15 ⊖	a	20 30	20 50	21 14	21 30	21 50	22 10	22 30	22 51	23 10	23 32

Sundays

		LO	LO	LO	LO	LO	LO	LO	LO	LO
Watford Junction	d	06 51	07 21	07 51	08 21	08 51	09 21	09 51	10 21	10 51
Watford High Street	d	06 54	07 24	07 54	08 24	08 54	09 24	09 54	10 24	10 54
Bushey	d	06 56	07 26	07 56	08 26	08 56	09 26	09 56	10 26	10 56
Carpenders Park	d	06 59	07 29	07 59	08 29	08 59	09 29	09 59	10 29	10 59
Hatch End	d	07 02	07 32	08 02	08 32	09 02	09 32	10 02	10 32	11 02
Headstone Lane	d	07 04	07 34	08 04	08 34	09 04	09 34	10 04	10 34	11 04
Harrow & Wealdstone	d	07 07	07 37	08 07	08 37	09 07	09 37	10 07	10 37	11 07
Kenton	d	07 09	07 39	08 09	08 39	09 09	09 39	10 09	10 39	11 09
South Kenton	d	07 11	07 41	08 11	08 41	09 11	09 41	10 11	10 41	11 11
North Wembley	d	07 13	07 43	08 13	08 43	09 13	09 43	10 13	10 43	11 13
Wembley Central	d	07 15	07 45	08 15	08 45	09 15	09 45	10 15	10 45	11 15
Stonebridge Park	d	07 18	07 48	08 18	08 48	09 18	09 48	10 18	10 48	11 18
Harlesden	d	07 20	07 50	08 20	08 50	09 20	09 50	10 20	10 50	11 20
Willesden Jn Low Level	d	07 22	07 52	08 22	08 52	09 22	09 52	10 22	10 52	11 22
Kensal Green	d	07 25	07 55	08 25	08 55	09 25	09 55	10 25	10 55	11 25
Queen's Park (London) ⊖	d	07 27	07 57	08 27	08 57	09 27	09 57	10 27	10 57	11 27
Kilburn High Road	d	07 29	07 59	08 29	08 59	09 29	09 59	10 29	10 59	11 29
South Hampstead	d	07 31	08 01	08 31	09 01	09 31	10 01	10 31	11 01	11 31
London Euston 15 ⊖	a	07 38	08 08	08 38	09 08	09 38	10 08	10 38	11 08	11 39

		LO	LO	LO	LO	LO	LO	LO	LO	LO	LO	LO	LO	LO
Watford Junction	d	11 21	11 51	12 21	12 51	13 21	13 51	14 21	14 51	15 21	15 51	16 21	16 51	17 21
Watford High Street	d	11 24	11 54	12 24	12 54	13 24	13 54	14 24	14 54	15 24	15 54	16 24	16 54	17 24
Bushey	d	11 26	11 56	12 26	12 56	13 26	13 56	14 26	14 56	15 26	15 56	16 26	16 56	17 26
Carpenders Park	d	11 29	11 59	12 29	12 59	13 29	13 59	14 29	14 59	15 29	15 59	16 29	16 59	17 29
Hatch End	d	11 32	12 02	12 32	13 02	13 32	14 02	14 32	15 02	15 32	16 02	16 32	17 02	17 32
Headstone Lane	d	11 34	12 04	12 34	13 04	13 34	14 04	14 34	15 04	15 34	16 04	16 34	17 04	17 34
Harrow & Wealdstone	d	11 37	12 07	12 37	13 07	13 37	14 07	14 37	15 07	15 37	16 07	16 37	17 07	17 37
Kenton	d	11 39	12 09	12 39	13 09	13 39	14 09	14 39	15 09	15 39	16 09	16 39	17 09	17 39
South Kenton	d	11 41	12 11	12 41	13 11	13 41	14 11	14 41	15 11	15 41	16 11	16 41	17 11	17 41
North Wembley	d	11 43	12 13	12 43	13 13	13 43	14 13	14 43	15 13	15 43	16 13	16 43	17 13	17 43
Wembley Central	d	11 45	12 15	12 45	13 15	13 45	14 15	14 45	15 15	15 45	16 15	16 45	17 15	17 45
Stonebridge Park	d	11 48	12 18	12 48	13 18	13 48	14 18	14 48	15 18	15 48	16 18	16 48	17 18	17 48
Harlesden	d	11 50	12 20	12 50	13 20	13 50	14 20	14 50	15 20	15 50	16 20	16 50	17 20	17 50
Willesden Jn Low Level	d	11 52	12 22	12 52	13 22	13 52	14 22	14 52	15 22	15 52	16 22	16 52	17 22	17 52
Kensal Green	d	11 55	12 25	12 55	13 25	13 55	14 25	14 55	15 25	15 55	16 25	16 55	17 25	17 55
Queen's Park (London) ⊖	d	11 57	12 27	12 57	13 27	13 57	14 27	14 57	15 27	15 57	16 27	16 57	17 27	17 57
Kilburn High Road	d	11 59	12 29	12 59	13 29	13 59	14 29	14 59	15 29	15 59	16 29	16 59	17 29	17 59
South Hampstead	d	12 01	12 31	13 01	13 31	14 01	14 31	15 01	15 31	16 01	16 31	17 01	17 31	18 01
London Euston 15 ⊖	a	12 09	12 40	13 08	13 40	14 08	14 40	15 08	15 40	16 08	16 40	17 08	17 40	18 08

		LO	LO	LO	LO	LO	LO	LO	LO	LO	LO	LO	LO
Watford Junction	d	17 51	18 21	18 51	19 21	19 51	20 21	20 51	21 21	21 51	22 21	22 51	23 21
Watford High Street	d	17 54	18 24	18 54	19 24	19 54	20 24	20 54	21 24	21 54	22 24	22 54	23 24
Bushey	d	17 56	18 26	18 56	19 26	19 56	20 26	20 56	21 26	21 56	22 26	22 56	23 26
Carpenders Park	d	17 59	18 29	18 59	19 29	19 59	20 29	20 59	21 29	21 59	22 29	22 59	23 29
Hatch End	d	18 02	18 32	19 02	19 32	20 02	20 32	21 02	21 32	22 02	22 32	23 02	23 32
Headstone Lane	d	18 04	18 34	19 04	19 34	20 04	20 34	21 04	21 34	22 04	22 34	23 04	23 34
Harrow & Wealdstone	d	18 07	18 37	19 07	19 37	20 07	20 37	21 07	21 37	22 07	22 37	23 07	23 37
Kenton	d	18 09	18 39	19 09	19 39	20 09	20 39	21 09	21 39	22 09	22 39	23 09	23 39
South Kenton	d	18 11	18 41	19 11	19 41	20 11	20 41	21 11	21 41	22 11	22 41	23 11	23 41
North Wembley	d	18 13	18 43	19 13	19 43	20 13	20 43	21 13	21 43	22 13	22 43	23 13	23 43
Wembley Central	d	18 15	18 45	19 15	19 45	20 15	20 45	21 15	21 45	22 15	22 45	23 15	23 45
Stonebridge Park	d	18 18	18 48	19 18	19 48	20 18	20 48	21 18	21 48	22 18	22 48	23 18	23 48
Harlesden	d	18 20	18 50	19 20	19 50	20 20	20 50	21 20	21 50	22 20	22 50	23 20	23 50
Willesden Jn Low Level	d	18 22	18 52	19 22	19 52	20 22	20 52	21 22	21 52	22 22	22 52	23 22	23 52
Kensal Green	d	18 25	18 55	19 25	19 55	20 25	20 55	21 25	21 55	22 25	22 55	23 25	23 55
Queen's Park (London) ⊖	d	18 27	18 57	19 27	19 57	20 27	20 57	21 27	21 57	22 27	22 57	23 27	23 57
Kilburn High Road	d	18 29	18 59	19 29	19 59	20 29	20 59	21 29	21 59	22 29	22 59	23 29	23 59
South Hampstead	d	18 31	19 01	19 31	20 01	20 31	21 01	21 31	22 01	22 31	23 01	23 31	00 01
London Euston 15 ⊖	a	18 40	19 08	19 40	20 08	20 40	21 08	21 38	22 08	22 38	23 08	23 38	00 08

Table 61

Watford Junction - St. Albans

Mondays to Fridays
until 22 October

		LM 1	LM 1	LM 1	LM 1	LM 1	LM 1	LM 1	LM 1	LM 1
Watford Junction	d	05 57	06 39	07 21	08 04	09 01	09 46	10 31	11 16	12 01
Watford North	d	05 59	06 41	07 23	08 06	09 03	09 48	10 33	11 18	12 03
Garston (Hertfordshire)	d	06 02	06 44	07 26	08 09	09 06	09 51	10 36	11 21	12 06
Bricket Wood	d	06 05	06 47	07 29	08 12	09 09	09 54	10 39	11 24	12 09
How Wood	d	06 07	06 49	07 31	08 14	09 11	09 56	10 41	11 26	12 11
Park Street	d	06 09	06 51	07 33	08 16	09 13	09 58	10 43	11 28	12 13
St Albans Abbey	a	06 13	06 55	07 37	08 20	09 17	10 02	10 47	11 32	12 17

		LM 1	LM 1	LM 1	LM 1	LM 1	LM 1	LM 1	LM 1	LM 1	LM 1	LM 1	LM 1
Watford Junction	d	12 46	13 31	14 16	15 01	15 46	16 31	17 21	18 10	18 55	19 38	20 31	21 31
Watford North	d	12 48	13 33	14 18	15 03	15 48	16 33	17 23	18 12	18 57	19 40	20 33	21 33
Garston (Hertfordshire)	d	12 51	13 36	14 21	15 06	15 51	16 36	17 26	18 15	19 00	19 43	20 36	21 36
Bricket Wood	d	12 54	13 39	14 24	15 09	15 54	16 39	17 29	18 18	19 03	19 46	20 39	21 39
How Wood	d	12 56	13 41	14 26	15 11	15 56	16 41	17 31	18 20	19 05	19 48	20 41	21 41
Park Street	d	12 58	13 43	14 28	15 13	15 58	16 43	17 33	18 22	19 07	19 50	20 43	21 43
St Albans Abbey	a	13 02	13 47	14 32	15 17	16 02	16 47	17 37	18 26	19 11	19 54	20 47	21 47

Mondays to Fridays
from 25 October

		LM 1	LM 1	LM 1	LM 1	LM 1	LM 1	LM 1	LM 1	LM 1
Watford Junction	d	05 46	06 32	07 18	08 04	08 53	09 39	10 25	11 25	12 25
Watford North	d	05 48	06 34	07 20	08 06	08 55	09 41	10 27	11 27	12 27
Garston (Hertfordshire)	d	05 51	06 37	07 23	08 09	08 58	09 44	10 30	11 30	12 30
Bricket Wood	d	05 54	06 40	07 26	08 12	09 01	09 47	10 33	11 33	12 33
How Wood	d	05 56	06 42	07 28	08 14	09 03	09 49	10 35	11 35	12 35
Park Street	d	05 58	06 44	07 30	08 16	09 05	09 51	10 37	11 37	12 37
St Albans Abbey	a	06 04	06 50	07 36	08 22	09 11	09 57	10 43	11 43	12 43

		LM 1	LM 1	LM 1	LM 1	LM 1	LM 1	LM 1	LM 1	LM 1	LM 1	LM 1
Watford Junction	d	13 25	14 15	15 01	15 48	16 35	17 21	18 08	18 54	19 40	20 30	21 31
Watford North	d	13 27	14 17	15 03	15 50	16 37	17 23	18 10	18 56	19 42	20 32	21 33
Garston (Hertfordshire)	d	13 30	14 20	15 06	15 53	16 40	17 26	18 13	18 59	19 45	20 35	21 36
Bricket Wood	d	13 33	14 23	15 09	15 56	16 43	17 29	18 16	19 02	19 48	20 38	21 39
How Wood	d	13 35	14 25	15 11	15 58	16 45	17 31	18 18	19 04	19 50	20 40	21 41
Park Street	d	13 37	14 27	15 13	16 00	16 47	17 33	18 20	19 06	19 52	20 42	21 43
St Albans Abbey	a	13 43	14 33	15 19	16 06	16 53	17 39	18 26	19 12	19 58	20 48	21 49

Saturdays
until 23 October

		LM 1	LM 1	LM 1	LM 1	LM 1	LM 1	LM 1	LM 1	LM 1
Watford Junction	d	06 01	06 45	07 31	08 15	09 01	09 46	10 31	11 16	12 01
Watford North	d	06 03	06 47	07 33	08 17	09 03	09 48	10 33	11 18	12 03
Garston (Hertfordshire)	d	06 06	06 50	07 36	08 20	09 06	09 51	10 36	11 21	12 06
Bricket Wood	d	06 09	06 53	07 39	08 23	09 09	09 54	10 39	11 24	12 09
How Wood	d	06 11	06 55	07 41	08 25	09 11	09 56	10 41	11 26	12 11
Park Street	d	06 13	06 57	07 43	08 27	09 13	09 58	10 43	11 28	12 13
St Albans Abbey	a	06 17	07 01	07 47	08 31	09 17	10 02	10 47	11 32	12 17

		LM 1	LM 1	LM 1	LM 1	LM 1	LM 1	LM 1	LM 1	LM 1	LM 1	LM 1	LM 1
Watford Junction	d	12 46	13 31	14 16	15 01	15 46	16 31	17 16	18 01	18 46	19 31	20 31	21 31
Watford North	d	12 48	13 33	14 18	15 03	15 48	16 33	17 18	18 03	18 48	19 33	20 33	21 33
Garston (Hertfordshire)	d	12 51	13 36	14 21	15 06	15 51	16 36	17 21	18 06	18 51	19 36	20 36	21 36
Bricket Wood	d	12 54	13 39	14 24	15 09	15 54	16 39	17 24	18 09	18 54	19 39	20 39	21 39
How Wood	d	12 56	13 41	14 26	15 11	15 56	16 41	17 26	18 11	18 56	19 41	20 41	21 41
Park Street	d	12 58	13 43	14 28	15 13	15 58	16 43	17 28	18 13	18 58	19 43	20 43	21 43
St Albans Abbey	a	13 02	13 47	14 32	15 17	16 02	16 47	17 32	18 17	19 02	19 47	20 47	21 47

Saturdays
from 30 October

		LM 1	LM 1	LM 1	LM 1	LM 1	LM 1	LM 1	LM 1	LM 1
Watford Junction	d	05 49	06 35	07 21	08 07	08 53	09 39	10 25	11 25	12 25
Watford North	d	05 51	06 37	07 23	08 09	08 55	09 41	10 27	11 27	12 27
Garston (Hertfordshire)	d	05 54	06 40	07 26	08 12	08 58	09 44	10 30	11 30	12 30
Bricket Wood	d	05 57	06 43	07 29	08 15	09 01	09 47	10 33	11 33	12 33
How Wood	d	05 59	06 45	07 31	08 17	09 03	09 49	10 35	11 35	12 35
Park Street	d	06 01	06 47	07 33	08 19	09 05	09 51	10 37	11 37	12 37
St Albans Abbey	a	06 07	06 53	07 39	08 25	09 11	09 57	10 43	11 43	12 43

		LM 1	LM 1	LM 1	LM 1	LM 1	LM 1	LM 1	LM 1	LM 1	LM 1	LM 1
Watford Junction	d	13 25	14 15	15 01	15 48	16 35	17 21	18 08	18 54	19 40	20 30	21 31
Watford North	d	13 27	14 17	15 03	15 50	16 37	17 23	18 10	18 56	19 42	20 32	21 33
Garston (Hertfordshire)	d	13 30	14 20	15 06	15 53	16 40	17 26	18 13	18 59	19 45	20 35	21 36
Bricket Wood	d	13 33	14 23	15 09	15 56	16 43	17 29	18 16	19 02	19 48	20 38	21 39
How Wood	d	13 35	14 25	15 11	15 58	16 45	17 31	18 18	19 04	19 50	20 40	21 41
Park Street	d	13 37	14 27	15 13	16 00	16 47	17 33	18 20	19 06	19 52	20 42	21 43
St Albans Abbey	a	13 43	14 33	15 19	16 06	16 53	17 39	18 26	19 12	19 58	20 48	21 49

Sundays
until 24 October

		LM 1	LM 1	LM 1	LM 1	LM 1	LM 1	LM 1	LM 1	LM 1	LM 1	LM 1	LM 1	LM 1	LM 1	LM 1
Watford Junction	d	08 07	09 07	10 20	11 20	12 07	13 07	14 07	15 07	16 07	17 07	18 07	19 07	20 07	21 02	22 04
Watford North	d	08 09	09 09	10 22	11 22	12 09	13 09	14 09	15 09	16 09	17 09	18 09	19 09	20 09	21 04	22 06
Garston (Hertfordshire)	d	08 12	09 12	10 25	11 25	12 12	13 12	14 12	15 12	16 12	17 12	18 12	19 12	20 12	21 07	22 09
Bricket Wood	d	08 15	09 15	10 28	11 28	12 15	13 15	14 15	15 15	16 15	17 15	18 15	19 15	20 15	21 10	22 12
How Wood	d	08 17	09 17	10 30	11 30	12 17	13 17	14 17	15 17	16 17	17 17	18 17	19 17	20 17	21 12	22 14
Park Street	d	08 19	09 19	10 32	11 32	12 19	13 19	14 19	15 19	16 19	17 19	18 19	19 19	20 19	21 14	22 16
St Albans Abbey	a	08 23	09 23	10 36	11 36	12 23	13 23	14 23	15 23	16 23	17 23	18 23	19 23	20 23	21 18	22 20

Sundays
from 31 October

		LM 1	LM 1	LM 1	LM 1	LM 1	LM 1	LM 1	LM 1	LM 1	LM 1	LM 1	LM 1	LM 1	LM 1	LM 1
Watford Junction	d	08 07	09 07	10 20	11 20	12 07	13 07	14 07	15 07	16 07	17 07	18 07	19 07	20 07	21 02	22 04
Watford North	d	08 09	09 09	10 22	11 22	12 09	13 09	14 09	15 09	16 09	17 09	18 09	19 09	20 09	21 04	22 06
Garston (Hertfordshire)	d	08 12	09 12	10 25	11 25	12 12	13 12	14 12	15 12	16 12	17 12	18 12	19 12	20 12	21 07	22 09
Bricket Wood	d	08 15	09 15	10 28	11 28	12 15	13 15	14 15	15 15	16 15	17 15	18 15	19 15	20 15	21 10	22 12
How Wood	d	08 17	09 17	10 30	11 30	12 17	13 17	14 17	15 17	16 17	17 17	18 17	19 17	20 17	21 12	22 14
Park Street	d	08 19	09 19	10 32	11 32	12 19	13 19	14 19	15 19	16 19	17 19	18 19	19 19	20 19	21 14	22 16
St Albans Abbey	a	08 25	09 25	10 38	11 38	12 25	13 25	14 25	15 25	16 25	17 25	18 25	19 25	20 25	21 20	22 22

For connections from London Euston please refer to Table 66

Table 61

Mondays to Fridays
until 22 October

St. Albans - Watford Junction

		LM ■	LM ■	LM ■	LM ■	LM ■	LM ■	LM ■	LM ■	LM ■	LM ■	LM ■	LM ■	LM ■	LM ■	LM ■	LM ■	LM ■	LM ■	LM ■	LM ■	LM ■
St Albans Abbey	d	06 18	07 00	07 42	08 25	09 22	10 07	10 52	11 37	12 22	13 07	13 52	14 37	15 22	16 07	16 52	17 42	18 32	19 16	20 00	20 52	21 52
Park Street	d	06 21	07 03	07 45	08 28	09 25	10 10	10 55	11 40	12 25	13 10	13 55	14 40	15 25	16 10	16 55	17 45	18 35	19 19	20 03	20 55	21 55
How Wood	d	06 23	07 05	07 47	08 30	09 27	10 12	10 57	11 42	12 27	13 12	13 57	14 42	15 27	16 12	16 57	17 47	18 37	19 21	20 05	20 57	21 57
Bricket Wood	d	06 26	07 08	07 50	08 33	09 30	10 15	11 00	11 45	12 30	13 15	14 00	14 45	15 30	16 15	17 00	17 50	18 40	19 24	20 08	21 00	22 00
Garston (Hertfordshire)	d	06 29	07 11	07 53	08 36	09 33	10 18	11 03	11 48	12 33	13 18	14 03	14 48	15 33	16 18	17 03	17 53	18 43	19 27	20 11	21 03	22 03
Watford North	d	06 31	07 13	07 55	08 38	09 35	10 20	11 05	11 50	12 35	13 20	14 05	14 50	15 35	16 20	17 05	17 55	18 45	19 29	20 13	21 05	22 05
Watford Junction	a	06 34	07 16	07 58	08 41	09 38	10 23	11 08	11 53	12 38	13 23	14 08	14 53	15 38	16 24	17 08	17 58	18 48	19 32	20 16	21 08	22 08

Mondays to Fridays
from 25 October

		LM ■	LM ■	LM ■	LM ■	LM ■	LM ■	LM ■	LM ■	LM ■	LM ■	LM ■	LM ■	LM ■	LM ■	LM ■	LM ■	LM ■	LM ■	LM ■	LM ■
St Albans Abbey	d	06 09	06 55	07 41	08 27	09 16	10 02	10 48	11 48	12 48	13 48	14 38	15 24	16 11	16 58	17 44	18 31	19 17	20 03	20 53	21 54
Park Street	d	06 12	06 58	07 44	08 30	09 19	10 05	10 51	11 51	12 51	13 51	14 41	15 27	16 14	17 01	17 47	18 34	19 20	20 06	20 56	21 57
How Wood	d	06 14	07 00	07 46	08 32	09 21	10 07	10 53	11 53	12 53	13 53	14 43	15 29	16 16	17 03	17 49	18 36	19 22	20 08	20 58	21 59
Bricket Wood	d	06 17	07 03	07 49	08 35	09 24	10 10	10 56	11 56	12 56	13 56	14 46	15 32	16 19	17 06	17 52	18 39	19 25	20 11	21 01	22 02
Garston (Hertfordshire)	d	06 20	07 06	07 52	08 38	09 27	10 13	10 59	11 59	12 59	13 59	14 49	15 35	16 22	17 09	17 55	18 42	19 28	20 14	21 04	22 05
Watford North	d	06 22	07 08	07 54	08 40	09 29	10 15	11 01	12 01	13 01	14 01	14 51	15 37	16 24	17 11	17 57	18 44	19 30	20 16	21 06	22 07
Watford Junction	a	06 27	07 13	07 59	08 45	09 34	10 20	11 06	12 06	13 06	14 06	14 56	15 42	16 29	17 16	18 02	18 49	19 35	20 21	21 10	22 12

Saturdays
until 23 October

		LM ■	LM ■	LM ■	LM ■	LM ■	LM ■	LM ■	LM ■	LM ■	LM ■	LM ■	LM ■	LM ■	LM ■	LM ■	LM ■	LM ■	LM ■	LM ■	LM ■	LM ■
St Albans Abbey	d	06 22	07 06	07 52	08 36	09 22	10 07	10 52	11 37	12 22	13 07	13 52	14 37	15 22	16 07	16 52	17 37	18 22	19 07	19 52	20 52	21 52
Park Street	d	06 25	07 09	07 55	08 39	09 25	10 10	10 55	11 40	12 25	13 10	13 55	14 40	15 25	16 10	16 55	17 40	18 25	19 10	19 55	20 55	21 55
How Wood	d	06 27	07 11	07 57	08 41	09 27	10 12	10 57	11 42	12 27	13 12	13 57	14 42	15 27	16 12	16 57	17 42	18 27	19 12	19 57	20 57	21 57
Bricket Wood	d	06 30	07 14	08 00	08 44	09 30	10 15	11 00	11 45	12 30	13 15	14 00	14 45	15 30	16 15	17 00	17 45	18 30	19 15	20 00	21 00	22 00
Garston (Hertfordshire)	d	06 33	07 17	08 03	08 47	09 33	10 18	11 03	11 48	12 33	13 18	14 03	14 48	15 33	16 18	17 03	17 48	18 33	19 18	20 03	21 03	22 03
Watford North	d	06 35	07 19	08 05	08 49	09 35	10 20	11 05	11 50	12 35	13 20	14 05	14 50	15 35	16 20	17 05	17 50	18 35	19 20	20 05	21 05	22 05
Watford Junction	a	06 38	07 22	08 08	08 52	09 38	10 23	11 08	11 53	12 38	13 23	14 08	14 53	15 38	16 23	17 08	17 53	18 38	19 23	20 08	21 08	22 08

Saturdays
from 30 October

		LM ■	LM ■	LM ■	LM ■	LM ■	LM ■	LM ■	LM ■	LM ■	LM ■	LM ■	LM ■	LM ■	LM ■	LM ■	LM ■	LM ■	LM ■	LM ■	LM ■
St Albans Abbey	d	06 12	06 58	07 44	08 30	09 16	10 02	10 48	11 48	12 48	13 48	14 38	15 24	16 11	16 58	17 44	18 31	19 17	20 03	20 53	21 54
Park Street	d	06 15	07 01	07 47	08 33	09 19	10 05	10 51	11 51	12 51	13 51	14 41	15 27	16 14	17 01	17 47	18 34	19 20	20 06	20 56	21 57
How Wood	d	06 17	07 03	07 49	08 35	09 21	10 07	10 53	11 53	12 53	13 53	14 43	15 29	16 16	17 03	17 49	18 36	19 22	20 08	20 58	21 59
Bricket Wood	d	06 20	07 06	07 52	08 38	09 24	10 10	10 56	11 56	12 56	13 56	14 46	15 32	16 19	17 06	17 52	18 39	19 25	20 11	21 01	22 02
Garston (Hertfordshire)	d	06 23	07 09	07 55	08 41	09 27	10 13	10 59	11 59	12 59	13 59	14 49	15 35	16 22	17 09	17 55	18 42	19 28	20 14	21 04	22 05
Watford North	d	06 25	07 11	07 57	08 43	09 29	10 15	11 01	12 01	13 01	14 01	14 51	15 37	16 24	17 11	17 57	18 44	19 30	20 16	21 06	22 07
Watford Junction	a	06 30	07 16	08 02	08 48	09 34	10 20	11 06	12 06	13 06	14 06	14 56	15 42	16 29	17 16	18 02	18 49	19 35	20 21	21 10	22 12

Sundays
until 24 October

		LM ■	LM ■	LM ■	LM ■	LM ■	LM ■	LM ■	LM ■	LM ■	LM ■	LM ■	LM ■	LM ■	LM ■	LM ■
St Albans Abbey	d	08 28	09 28	10 42	11 42	12 28	13 28	14 28	15 28	16 28	17 28	18 28	19 28	20 28	21 23	22 25
Park Street	d	08 31	09 31	10 45	11 45	12 31	13 31	14 31	15 31	16 31	17 31	18 31	19 31	20 31	21 26	22 28
How Wood	d	08 33	09 33	10 47	11 47	12 33	13 33	14 33	15 33	16 33	17 33	18 33	19 33	20 33	21 28	22 30
Bricket Wood	d	08 36	09 36	10 50	11 50	12 36	13 36	14 36	15 36	16 36	17 36	18 36	19 36	20 36	21 31	22 33
Garston (Hertfordshire)	d	08 39	09 39	10 53	11 53	12 39	13 39	14 39	15 39	16 39	17 39	18 39	19 39	20 39	21 34	22 36
Watford North	d	08 41	09 41	10 55	11 55	12 41	13 41	14 41	15 41	16 41	17 41	18 41	19 41	20 41	21 36	22 38
Watford Junction	a	08 44	09 44	10 58	11 58	12 44	13 44	14 44	15 44	16 44	17 44	18 44	19 44	20 44	21 39	22 41

Sundays
from 31 October

		LM ■	LM ■	LM ■	LM ■	LM ■	LM ■	LM ■	LM ■	LM ■	LM ■	LM ■	LM ■	LM ■	LM ■	LM ■
St Albans Abbey	d	08 30	09 30	10 43	11 43	12 30	13 30	14 30	15 30	16 30	17 30	18 30	19 30	20 30	21 25	22 27
Park Street	d	08 33	09 33	10 46	11 46	12 33	13 33	14 33	15 33	16 33	17 33	18 33	19 33	20 33	21 28	22 30
How Wood	d	08 35	09 35	10 48	11 48	12 35	13 35	14 35	15 35	16 35	17 35	18 35	19 35	20 35	21 30	22 32
Bricket Wood	d	08 38	09 38	10 51	11 51	12 38	13 38	14 38	15 38	16 38	17 38	18 38	19 38	20 38	21 33	22 35
Garston (Hertfordshire)	d	08 41	09 41	10 54	11 54	12 41	13 41	14 41	15 41	16 41	17 41	18 41	19 41	20 41	21 36	22 38
Watford North	d	08 43	09 43	10 56	11 56	12 43	13 43	14 43	15 43	16 43	17 43	18 43	19 43	20 43	21 38	22 40
Watford Junction	a	08 48	09 48	11 00	12 01	12 47	13 47	14 47	15 47	16 47	17 47	18 47	19 47	20 48	21 43	22 45

Table 62

Mondays to Fridays

Gospel Oak-Barking

		LO	LO	LO	LO	LO	LO	LO	LO	LO	LO	LO	LO	LO	LO	LO	LO	LO	LO	LO	LO	LO	LO
Gospel Oak	d	06 35	06 51	07 05	07 20	07 35	07 50	08 05	08 20	08 35	08 50	09 05	09 20	09 35	09 50	10 05	10 20	10 35	11 05	11 35	12 05	12 35	13 05
Upper Holloway	d	06 39	06 54	07 09	07 24	07 39	07 54	08 09	08 24	08 39	08 54	09 09	09 24	09 39	09 54	10 09	10 24	10 39	11 09	11 39	12 09	12 39	13 09
Crouch Hill	d	06 42	06 57	07 12	07 27	07 42	07 57	08 12	08 27	08 42	08 57	09 12	09 27	09 42	09 57	10 12	10 27	10 42	11 12	11 42	12 12	12 42	13 12
Harringay Green Lanes	d	06 45	07 00	07 15	07 30	07 45	08 00	08 15	08 30	08 45	09 00	09 15	09 30	09 45	10 00	10 15	10 30	10 45	11 15	11 45	12 15	12 45	13 15
South Tottenham	d	06 48	07 03	07 18	07 33	07 48	08 03	08 18	08 33	08 48	09 03	09 18	09 33	09 48	10 03	10 18	10 33	10 48	11 18	11 48	12 18	12 48	13 18
Blackhorse Road ⊖	d	06 51	07 07	07 21	07 36	07 51	08 06	08 21	08 36	08 51	09 06	09 21	09 36	09 51	10 06	10 21	10 36	10 51	11 21	11 51	12 21	12 51	13 21
Walthamstow Queen's Road	d	06 54	07 09	07 24	07 39	07 54	08 09	08 24	08 39	08 54	09 09	09 24	09 39	09 54	10 09	10 24	10 39	10 54	11 24	11 54	12 24	12 54	13 24
Leyton Midland Road	d	06 57	07 12	07 27	07 42	07 57	08 12	08 27	08 42	08 57	09 12	09 27	09 42	09 57	10 12	10 27	10 42	10 57	11 27	11 57	12 27	12 57	13 27
Leytonstone High Road	d	07 00	07 15	07 30	07 45	08 00	08 15	08 30	08 45	09 00	09 15	09 30	09 45	10 00	10 15	10 30	10 45	11 00	11 30	12 00	12 30	13 00	13 30
Wanstead Park	d	07 03	07 18	07 33	07 48	08 03	08 18	08 33	08 48	09 03	09 18	09 33	09 48	10 03	10 18	10 33	10 48	11 03	11 33	12 03	12 33	13 03	13 33
Woodgrange Park	d	07 05	07 20	07 35	07 50	08 05	08 20	08 35	08 50	09 05	09 20	09 35	09 50	10 05	10 20	10 35	10 50	11 05	11 35	12 05	12 35	13 05	13 35
Barking ⊖	a	07 11	07 27	07 41	07 56	08 11	08 26	08 41	08 56	09 11	09 26	09 41	09 56	10 11	10 26	10 41	10 56	11 11	11 41	12 11	12 41	13 11	13 41

		LO	LO	LO	LO	LO	LO	LO	LO	LO	LO	LO	LO	LO	LO	LO	LO	LO	LO	LO	LO	LO	LO
Gospel Oak	d	13 35	14 05	14 35	15 05	15 35	16 05	16 20	16 35	16 50	17 05	17 20	17 35	17 50	18 05	18 20	18 35	18 50	19 05	19 35	20 05	20 35	21 05
Upper Holloway	d	13 39	14 09	14 39	15 09	15 39	16 09	16 24	16 39	16 54	17 09	17 24	17 39	17 54	18 09	18 24	18 39	18 54	19 09	19 39	20 09	20 39	21 09
Crouch Hill	d	13 42	14 12	14 42	15 12	15 42	16 12	16 27	16 42	16 57	17 12	17 27	17 42	17 57	18 12	18 27	18 42	18 57	19 12	19 42	20 12	20 42	21 12
Harringay Green Lanes	d	13 45	14 15	14 45	15 15	15 45	16 15	16 30	16 45	17 00	17 15	17 30	17 45	18 00	18 15	18 30	18 45	19 00	19 15	19 45	20 15	20 45	21 15
South Tottenham	d	13 48	14 18	14 48	15 18	15 48	16 18	16 33	16 48	17 03	17 18	17 33	17 48	18 03	18 18	18 33	18 48	19 03	19 18	19 48	20 19	20 48	21 18
Blackhorse Road ⊖	d	13 51	14 21	14 51	15 21	15 51	16 21	16 36	16 51	17 06	17 21	17 36	17 51	18 06	18 21	18 36	18 51	19 06	19 21	19 51	20 22	20 51	21 21
Walthamstow Queen's Road	d	13 54	14 24	14 54	15 24	15 54	16 24	16 39	16 54	17 09	17 24	17 39	17 54	18 09	18 24	18 39	18 54	19 09	19 24	19 54	20 25	20 54	21 24
Leyton Midland Road	d	13 57	14 27	14 57	15 27	15 57	16 27	16 42	16 57	17 12	17 27	17 42	17 57	18 12	18 27	18 42	18 57	19 12	19 27	19 57	20 28	20 57	21 27
Leytonstone High Road	d	14 00	14 30	15 00	15 30	16 00	16 30	16 45	17 00	17 15	17 30	17 45	18 00	18 15	18 30	18 45	19 00	19 15	19 30	20 00	20 31	21 00	21 30
Wanstead Park	d	14 03	14 33	15 03	15 33	16 03	16 33	16 48	17 03	17 18	17 33	17 48	18 03	18 18	18 33	18 48	19 03	19 18	19 33	20 03	20 34	21 03	21 33
Woodgrange Park	d	14 05	14 35	15 05	15 35	16 05	16 35	16 50	17 05	17 20	17 35	17 50	18 05	18 20	18 35	18 50	19 05	19 20	19 35	20 05	20 36	21 05	21 35
Barking ⊖	a	14 11	14 41	15 11	15 41	16 11	16 41	16 56	17 11	17 26	17 41	17 56	18 11	18 26	18 41	18 56	19 11	19 26	19 41	20 11	20 42	21 11	21 41

		LO	LO	LO	LO
Gospel Oak	d	21 35	22 05	22 35	23 05
Upper Holloway	d	21 39	22 09	22 39	23 09
Crouch Hill	d	21 42	22 12	22 42	23 12
Harringay Green Lanes	d	21 45	22 15	22 45	23 15
South Tottenham	d	21 48	22 18	22 48	23 18
Blackhorse Road ⊖	d	21 51	22 21	22 51	23 21
Walthamstow Queen's Road	d	21 54	22 24	22 54	23 24
Leyton Midland Road	d	21 57	22 27	22 57	23 27
Leytonstone High Road	d	22 00	22 30	23 00	23 30
Wanstead Park	d	22 03	22 33	23 03	23 33
Woodgrange Park	d	22 05	22 35	23 05	23 35
Barking ⊖	a	22 11	22 41	23 11	23 41

Saturdays

		LO	LO	LO	LO	LO	LO	LO	LO	LO	LO	LO	LO	LO	LO	LO	LO	LO	LO	LO	LO	LO	LO
Gospel Oak	d	06 25	06 55	07 10	07 25	07 40	07 55	08 10	08 25	08 40	08 55	09 10	09 25	09 40	09 55	10 10	10 25	10 40	11 10	11 40	12 10	12 40	13 10
Upper Holloway	d	06 29	06 59	07 14	07 29	07 44	07 59	08 14	08 29	08 44	08 59	09 14	09 29	09 44	09 59	10 14	10 29	10 44	11 14	11 44	12 14	12 44	13 14
Crouch Hill	d	06 32	07 02	07 17	07 32	07 47	08 02	08 17	08 32	08 47	09 02	09 17	09 32	09 47	10 02	10 17	10 32	10 47	11 17	11 47	12 17	12 47	13 17
Harringay Green Lanes	d	06 35	07 05	07 20	07 35	07 50	08 05	08 20	08 35	08 50	09 05	09 20	09 35	09 50	10 05	10 20	10 35	10 50	11 20	11 50	12 20	12 50	13 20
South Tottenham	d	06 38	07 08	07 23	07 38	07 53	08 08	08 23	08 38	08 53	09 08	09 23	09 38	09 53	10 08	10 23	10 38	10 53	11 23	11 53	12 23	12 53	13 23
Blackhorse Road ⊖	d	06 41	07 11	07 26	07 41	07 56	08 11	08 26	08 41	08 56	09 11	09 26	09 41	09 56	10 11	10 26	10 41	10 56	11 26	11 56	12 26	12 56	13 26
Walthamstow Queen's Road	d	06 44	07 14	07 29	07 44	07 59	08 14	08 29	08 44	08 59	09 14	09 29	09 44	09 59	10 14	10 29	10 44	10 59	11 29	11 59	12 29	12 59	13 29
Leyton Midland Road	d	06 47	07 17	07 32	07 47	08 02	08 17	08 32	08 47	09 02	09 17	09 32	09 47	10 02	10 17	10 32	10 47	11 02	11 32	12 02	12 32	13 02	13 32
Leytonstone High Road	d	06 50	07 20	07 35	07 50	08 05	08 20	08 35	08 50	09 05	09 20	09 35	09 50	10 05	10 20	10 35	10 50	11 05	11 35	12 05	12 35	13 05	13 35
Wanstead Park	d	06 53	07 23	07 38	07 53	08 08	08 23	08 38	08 53	09 08	09 23	09 38	09 53	10 08	10 23	10 38	10 53	11 08	11 38	12 08	12 38	13 08	13 38
Woodgrange Park	d	06 55	07 25	07 40	07 55	08 10	08 25	08 40	08 55	09 10	09 25	09 40	09 55	10 10	10 25	10 40	10 55	11 10	11 40	12 10	12 40	13 10	13 40
Barking ⊖	a	06 59	07 29	07 44	07 59	08 14	08 29	08 44	08 59	09 14	09 29	09 44	09 59	10 14	10 29	10 44	10 59	11 14	11 44	12 14	12 44	13 14	13 44

		LO	LO	LO	LO	LO	LO	LO	LO	LO	LO	LO	LO	LO	LO	LO	LO	LO	LO	LO	LO	LO	LO
Gospel Oak	d	13 40	14 10	14 40	15 10	15 40	15 55	16 10	16 25	16 40	16 55	17 10	17 25	17 40	17 55	18 10	18 25	18 40	18 55	19 10	19 40	20 10	20 40
Upper Holloway	d	13 44	14 14	14 44	15 14	15 44	15 59	16 14	16 29	16 44	16 59	17 14	17 29	17 44	17 59	18 14	18 29	18 44	18 59	19 14	19 44	20 14	20 44
Crouch Hill	d	13 47	14 17	14 47	15 17	15 47	16 02	16 17	16 32	16 47	17 02	17 17	17 32	17 47	18 02	18 17	18 32	18 47	19 02	19 17	19 47	20 17	20 47
Harringay Green Lanes	d	13 50	14 20	14 50	15 20	15 50	16 05	16 20	16 35	16 50	17 05	17 20	17 35	17 50	18 05	18 20	18 35	18 50	19 05	19 20	19 50	20 20	20 50
South Tottenham	d	13 53	14 23	14 53	15 23	15 53	16 08	16 23	16 38	16 53	17 08	17 23	17 38	17 53	18 08	18 23	18 38	18 53	19 08	19 23	19 53	20 23	20 53
Blackhorse Road ⊖	d	13 56	14 26	14 56	15 26	15 56	16 11	16 26	16 41	16 56	17 11	17 26	17 41	17 56	18 11	18 26	18 41	18 56	19 11	19 26	19 56	20 26	20 56
Walthamstow Queen's Road	d	13 59	14 29	14 59	15 29	15 59	16 14	16 29	16 44	16 59	17 14	17 29	17 44	17 59	18 14	18 29	18 44	18 59	19 14	19 29	19 59	20 29	20 59
Leyton Midland Road	d	14 02	14 32	15 02	15 32	16 02	16 17	16 32	16 47	17 02	17 17	17 32	17 47	18 02	18 17	18 32	18 47	19 02	19 17	19 32	20 02	20 32	21 02
Leytonstone High Road	d	14 05	14 35	15 05	15 35	16 05	16 20	16 35	16 50	17 05	17 20	17 35	17 50	18 05	18 20	18 35	18 50	19 05	19 20	19 35	20 05	20 35	21 05
Wanstead Park	d	14 08	14 38	15 08	15 38	16 08	16 23	16 38	16 53	17 08	17 23	17 38	17 53	18 08	18 23	18 38	18 53	19 08	19 23	19 38	20 08	20 38	21 08
Woodgrange Park	d	14 10	14 40	15 10	15 40	16 10	16 25	16 40	16 55	17 10	17 25	17 40	17 55	18 10	18 25	18 40	18 55	19 10	19 25	19 40	20 10	20 40	21 10
Barking ⊖	a	14 14	14 44	15 14	15 44	16 14	16 29	16 44	16 59	17 14	17 29	17 46	17 59	18 14	18 29	18 44	18 59	19 14	19 29	19 44	20 14	20 44	21 14

		LO	LO	LO	LO	LO
Gospel Oak	d	21 10	21 40	22 10	22 40	23 10
Upper Holloway	d	21 14	21 44	22 14	22 44	23 14
Crouch Hill	d	21 17	21 47	22 17	22 47	23 17
Harringay Green Lanes	d	21 20	21 50	22 20	22 50	23 20
South Tottenham	d	21 23	21 53	22 23	22 53	23 23
Blackhorse Road ⊖	d	21 26	21 56	22 26	22 56	23 26
Walthamstow Queen's Road	d	21 29	21 59	22 29	22 59	23 29
Leyton Midland Road	d	21 32	22 02	22 32	23 02	23 32
Leytonstone High Road	d	21 35	22 05	22 35	23 05	23 35
Wanstead Park	d	21 38	22 08	22 38	23 08	23 38
Woodgrange Park	d	21 40	22 10	22 40	23 10	23 40
Barking ⊖	a	21 44	22 14	22 44	23 14	23 44

Table 62

Sundays

Gospel Oak-Barking

		LO	LO	LO	LO	LO	LO	LO	LO	LO	LO	LO	LO	LO	LO	LO	LO	LO	LO	LO	LO	LO	LO
Gospel Oak	d	08 50	09 20	09 50	10 20	10 50	11 20	11 50	12 20	12 50	13 20	13 50	14 20	14 50	15 20	15 50	16 20	16 50	17 20	17 50	18 20	18 50	19 20
Upper Holloway	d	08 54	09 24	09 54	10 24	10 54	11 24	11 54	12 24	12 54	13 24	13 54	14 24	14 54	15 24	15 54	16 24	16 54	17 24	17 54	18 24	18 54	19 24
Crouch Hill	d	08 57	09 27	09 57	10 27	10 57	11 27	11 57	12 27	12 57	13 27	13 57	14 27	14 57	15 27	15 57	16 27	16 57	17 27	17 57	18 27	18 57	19 27
Harringay Green Lanes	d	09 00	09 30	10 00	10 30	11 00	11 30	12 00	12 30	13 00	13 30	14 00	14 30	15 00	15 30	16 00	16 30	17 00	17 30	18 00	18 30	19 00	19 30
South Tottenham	d	09 03	09 33	10 03	10 33	11 03	11 33	12 03	12 33	13 03	13 33	14 03	14 33	15 03	15 33	16 03	16 33	17 03	17 33	18 03	18 33	19 03	19 33
Blackhorse Road ⊖	d	09 06	09 36	10 06	10 36	11 06	11 36	12 06	12 36	13 06	13 36	14 06	14 36	15 06	15 36	16 06	16 36	17 06	17 36	18 06	18 36	19 06	19 36
Walthamstow Queen's Road	d	09 09	09 39	10 09	10 39	11 09	11 39	12 09	12 39	13 09	13 39	14 09	14 39	15 09	15 39	16 09	16 39	17 09	17 39	18 09	18 39	19 09	19 39
Leyton Midland Road	d	09 12	09 42	10 12	10 42	11 12	11 42	12 12	12 42	13 12	13 42	14 12	14 42	15 12	15 42	16 12	16 42	17 12	17 42	18 12	18 42	19 12	19 42
Leytonstone High Road	d	09 15	09 45	10 15	10 45	11 15	11 45	12 15	12 45	13 15	13 45	14 15	14 45	15 15	15 45	16 15	16 45	17 15	17 45	18 15	18 45	19 15	19 45
Wanstead Park	d	09 18	09 48	10 18	10 48	11 18	11 48	12 18	12 48	13 18	13 48	14 18	14 48	15 18	15 48	16 18	16 48	17 18	17 48	18 18	18 48	19 18	19 48
Woodgrange Park	d	09 20	09 50	10 20	10 50	11 20	11 50	12 20	12 50	13 20	13 50	14 20	14 50	15 20	15 50	16 20	16 50	17 20	17 50	18 20	18 50	19 20	19 50
Barking ⊖	a	09 24	09 54	10 24	10 54	11 24	11 54	12 24	12 54	13 24	13 54	14 24	14 54	15 24	15 54	16 24	16 54	17 24	17 54	18 24	18 54	19 24	19 54

		LO	LO	LO	LO	LO	LO	LO	LO
Gospel Oak	d	19 50	20 20	20 50	21 20	21 50	22 20	22 50	23 20
Upper Holloway	d	19 54	20 24	20 54	21 24	21 54	22 24	22 54	23 24
Crouch Hill	d	19 57	20 27	20 57	21 27	21 57	22 27	22 57	23 27
Harringay Green Lanes	d	20 00	20 30	21 00	21 30	22 00	22 30	23 00	23 30
South Tottenham	d	20 03	20 33	21 03	21 33	22 03	22 33	23 03	23 33
Blackhorse Road ⊖	d	20 06	20 36	21 06	21 36	22 06	22 36	23 06	23 36
Walthamstow Queen's Road	d	20 09	20 39	21 09	21 39	22 09	22 39	23 09	23 39
Leyton Midland Road	d	20 12	20 42	21 12	21 42	22 12	22 42	23 12	23 42
Leytonstone High Road	d	20 15	20 45	21 15	21 45	22 15	22 45	23 15	23 45
Wanstead Park	d	20 18	20 48	21 18	21 48	22 18	22 48	23 18	23 48
Woodgrange Park	d	20 20	20 50	21 20	21 50	22 20	22 50	23 20	23 50
Barking ⊖	a	20 24	20 54	21 24	21 54	22 24	22 54	23 24	23 54

Table 62

Mondays to Fridays

Barking-Gospel Oak

		LO	LO	LO	LO	LO	LO	LO	LO	LO	LO	LO	LO	LO	LO	LO	LO	LO	LO	LO	LO	LO	LO
Barking ⊖	d	06 24	06 47	07 02	07 17	07 32	07 47	08 02	08 17	08 32	08 47	09 02	09 17	09 32	09 47	10 17	10 47	11 17	11 47	12 17	12 47	13 17	13 47
Woodgrange Park	d	06 27	06 50	07 05	07 20	07 35	07 50	08 05	08 20	08 35	08 50	09 05	09 20	09 35	09 50	10 20	10 50	11 20	11 50	12 20	12 50	13 20	13 50
Wanstead Park	d	06 30	06 53	07 08	07 23	07 38	07 53	08 08	08 23	08 38	08 53	09 08	09 23	09 38	09 53	10 23	10 53	11 23	11 53	12 23	12 53	13 23	13 53
Leytonstone High Road	d	06 34	06 57	07 12	07 27	07 42	07 57	08 12	08 27	08 42	08 57	09 12	09 27	09 42	09 57	10 27	10 57	11 27	11 57	12 27	12 57	13 27	13 57
Leyton Midland Road	d	06 36	06 59	07 14	07 29	07 44	07 59	08 14	08 29	08 44	08 59	09 14	09 29	09 44	09 59	10 29	10 59	11 29	11 59	12 29	12 59	13 29	13 59
Walthamstow Queen's Road	d	06 39	07 02	07 17	07 32	07 47	08 02	08 17	08 32	08 47	09 02	09 17	09 32	09 47	10 02	10 32	11 02	11 32	12 02	12 32	13 02	13 32	14 02
Blackhorse Road ⊖	d	06 42	07 05	07 20	07 35	07 50	08 05	08 20	08 35	08 50	09 05	09 20	09 35	09 50	10 05	10 35	11 05	11 35	12 05	12 35	13 05	13 35	14 05
South Tottenham	d	06 46	07 09	07 24	07 39	07 54	08 09	08 24	08 39	08 54	09 09	09 24	09 39	09 54	10 09	10 39	11 09	11 39	12 09	12 39	13 09	13 39	14 09
Harringay Green Lanes	d	06 49	07 12	07 27	07 42	07 57	08 12	08 27	08 42	08 57	09 12	09 27	09 42	09 57	10 12	10 42	11 12	11 42	12 12	12 42	13 12	13 42	14 12
Crouch Hill	d	06 52	07 15	07 30	07 45	08 00	08 15	08 30	08 45	09 00	09 15	09 30	09 45	10 00	10 15	10 45	11 15	11 45	12 15	12 45	13 15	13 45	14 15
Upper Holloway	d	06 54	07 17	07 32	07 47	08 02	08 17	08 32	08 47	09 02	09 17	09 32	09 47	10 02	10 17	10 47	11 17	11 47	12 17	12 47	13 17	13 47	14 17
Gospel Oak	a	06 59	07 23	07 38	07 53	08 08	08 23	08 38	08 53	09 08	09 23	09 38	09 53	10 08	10 26	10 53	11 23	11 53	12 23	12 53	13 23	13 53	14 23

		LO	LO	LO	LO	LO	LO	LO	LO	LO	LO	LO	LO	LO	LO	LO	LO	LO	LO	LO	LO	LO	LO
Barking ⊖	d	14 17	14 47	15 17	15 32	15 47	16 05	16 17	16 32	16 47	17 02	17 17	17 32	17 47	18 02	18 17	18 32	18 47	19 02	19 17	19 47	20 17	20 47
Woodgrange Park	d	14 20	14 50	15 20	15 35	15 50	16 08	16 20	16 35	16 50	17 05	17 20	17 35	17 50	18 05	18 20	18 35	18 50	19 05	19 20	19 50	20 20	20 50
Wanstead Park	d	14 23	14 53	15 23	15 38	15 53	16 11	16 23	16 38	16 53	17 08	17 23	17 38	17 53	18 08	18 23	18 38	18 53	19 08	19 23	19 53	20 23	20 53
Leytonstone High Road	d	14 27	14 57	15 27	15 42	15 57	16 15	16 27	16 42	16 57	17 12	17 27	17 42	17 57	18 12	18 27	18 42	18 57	19 12	19 27	19 57	20 27	20 57
Leyton Midland Road	d	14 29	14 59	15 29	15 44	15 59	16 17	16 29	16 44	16 59	17 14	17 29	17 44	17 59	18 14	18 29	18 44	18 59	19 14	19 29	19 59	20 29	20 59
Walthamstow Queen's Road	d	14 32	15 02	15 32	15 47	16 02	16 20	16 32	16 47	17 02	17 17	17 32	17 47	18 02	18 17	18 32	18 47	19 02	19 17	19 32	20 02	20 32	21 02
Blackhorse Road ⊖	d	14 35	15 05	15 35	15 50	16 05	16 23	16 35	16 50	17 05	17 20	17 35	17 50	18 05	18 20	18 35	18 50	19 05	19 20	19 35	20 05	20 35	21 05
South Tottenham	d	14 39	15 09	15 39	15 54	16 09	16 27	16 39	16 54	17 09	17 24	17 39	17 54	18 09	18 24	18 39	18 54	19 09	19 24	19 39	20 09	20 39	21 09
Harringay Green Lanes	d	14 42	15 12	15 42	15 57	16 12	16 30	16 42	16 57	17 12	17 27	17 42	17 57	18 12	18 27	18 42	18 57	19 12	19 27	19 42	20 12	20 42	21 12
Crouch Hill	d	14 45	15 15	15 45	16 00	16 15	16 33	16 45	17 00	17 15	17 30	17 45	18 00	18 15	18 30	18 45	19 00	19 15	19 30	19 45	20 15	20 45	21 15
Upper Holloway	d	14 47	15 17	15 47	16 02	16 17	16 35	16 47	17 02	17 17	17 32	17 47	18 02	18 17	18 32	18 47	19 02	19 17	19 32	19 47	20 17	20 47	21 17
Gospel Oak	a	14 53	15 23	15 53	16 08	16 23	16 40	16 53	17 08	17 23	17 38	17 53	18 08	18 23	18 38	18 53	19 08	19 26	19 38	19 53	20 23	20 53	21 23

		LO	LO	LO	LO	LO
Barking ⊖	d	21 17	21 47	22 17	22 47	23 17
Woodgrange Park	d	21 20	21 50	22 20	22 50	23 20
Wanstead Park	d	21 23	21 53	22 23	22 53	23 23
Leytonstone High Road	d	21 27	21 57	22 27	22 57	23 27
Leyton Midland Road	d	21 29	21 59	22 29	22 59	23 29
Walthamstow Queen's Road	d	21 32	22 02	22 32	23 02	23 32
Blackhorse Road ⊖	d	21 35	22 05	22 35	23 05	23 35
South Tottenham	d	21 39	22 09	22 39	23 09	23 39
Harringay Green Lanes	d	21 42	22 12	22 42	23 12	23 42
Crouch Hill	d	21 45	22 15	22 45	23 15	23 45
Upper Holloway	d	21 47	22 17	22 47	23 17	23 47
Gospel Oak	a	21 53	22 23	22 53	23 25	23 53

Saturdays

		LO	LO	LO	LO	LO	LO	LO	LO	LO	LO	LO	LO	LO	LO	LO	LO	LO	LO	LO	LO	LO	LO
Barking ⊖	d	06 39	06 54	07 09	07 24	07 39	07 54	08 09	08 24	08 39	08 54	09 09	09 24	09 39	09 54	10 09	10 39	11 09	11 39	12 09	12 39	13 09	13 39
Woodgrange Park	d	06 42	06 57	07 12	07 27	07 42	07 57	08 12	08 27	08 42	08 57	09 12	09 27	09 42	09 57	10 12	10 42	11 12	11 42	12 12	12 42	13 12	13 42
Wanstead Park	d	06 45	07 00	07 15	07 30	07 45	08 00	08 15	08 30	08 45	09 00	09 15	09 30	09 45	10 00	10 15	10 45	11 15	11 45	12 15	12 45	13 15	13 45
Leytonstone High Road	d	06 49	07 04	07 19	07 34	07 49	08 04	08 19	08 34	08 49	09 04	09 19	09 34	09 49	10 04	10 19	10 49	11 19	11 49	12 19	12 49	13 19	13 49
Leyton Midland Road	d	06 51	07 06	07 21	07 36	07 51	08 06	08 21	08 36	08 51	09 06	09 21	09 36	09 51	10 06	10 21	10 51	11 21	11 51	12 21	12 51	13 21	13 51
Walthamstow Queen's Road	d	06 54	07 09	07 24	07 39	07 54	08 09	08 24	08 39	08 54	09 09	09 24	09 39	09 54	10 09	10 24	10 54	11 24	11 54	12 24	12 54	13 24	13 54
Blackhorse Road ⊖	d	06 57	07 12	07 27	07 42	07 57	08 12	08 27	08 42	08 57	09 12	09 27	09 42	09 57	10 12	10 27	10 57	11 27	11 57	12 27	12 57	13 27	13 57
South Tottenham	d	07 01	07 16	07 31	07 46	08 01	08 16	08 31	08 46	09 01	09 16	09 31	09 46	10 01	10 16	10 31	11 01	11 31	12 01	12 31	13 01	13 31	14 01
Harringay Green Lanes	d	07 04	07 19	07 34	07 49	08 04	08 19	08 34	08 49	09 04	09 19	09 34	09 49	10 04	10 19	10 34	11 04	11 34	12 04	12 34	13 04	13 34	14 04
Crouch Hill	d	07 07	07 22	07 37	07 52	08 07	08 22	08 37	08 52	09 07	09 22	09 37	09 52	10 07	10 22	10 37	11 07	11 37	12 07	12 37	13 07	13 37	14 07
Upper Holloway	d	07 09	07 24	07 39	07 54	08 09	08 24	08 39	08 54	09 09	09 24	09 39	09 54	10 09	10 24	10 39	11 09	11 39	12 09	12 39	13 09	13 39	14 09
Gospel Oak	a	07 14	07 29	07 44	07 59	08 14	08 29	08 44	08 59	09 14	09 29	09 44	09 59	10 14	10 29	10 44	11 14	11 44	12 14	12 44	13 14	13 44	14 14

		LO	LO	LO	LO	LO	LO	LO	LO	LO	LO	LO	LO	LO	LO	LO	LO	LO	LO	LO	LO	LO	LO
Barking ⊖	d	14 09	14 39	15 09	15 24	15 39	15 54	16 09	16 24	16 39	16 54	17 09	17 24	17 39	17 54	18 09	18 24	18 39	18 54	19 09	19 39	20 09	20 39
Woodgrange Park	d	14 12	14 42	15 12	15 27	15 42	15 57	16 12	16 27	16 42	16 57	17 12	17 27	17 42	17 57	18 12	18 27	18 42	18 57	19 12	19 42	20 12	20 42
Wanstead Park	d	14 15	14 45	15 15	15 30	15 45	16 00	16 15	16 30	16 45	17 00	17 15	17 30	17 45	18 00	18 15	18 30	18 45	19 00	19 15	19 45	20 15	20 45
Leytonstone High Road	d	14 19	14 49	15 19	15 34	15 49	16 04	16 19	16 34	16 49	17 04	17 19	17 34	17 49	18 04	18 19	18 34	18 49	19 04	19 19	19 49	20 19	20 49
Leyton Midland Road	d	14 21	14 51	15 21	15 36	15 51	16 06	16 21	16 36	16 51	17 06	17 21	17 36	17 51	18 06	18 21	18 36	18 51	19 06	19 21	19 51	20 21	20 51
Walthamstow Queen's Road	d	14 24	14 54	15 24	15 39	15 54	16 09	16 24	16 39	16 54	17 09	17 24	17 39	17 54	18 09	18 24	18 39	18 54	19 09	19 24	19 54	20 24	20 54
Blackhorse Road ⊖	d	14 27	14 57	15 27	15 42	15 57	16 12	16 27	16 42	16 57	17 12	17 27	17 42	17 57	18 12	18 27	18 42	18 57	19 12	19 27	19 57	20 27	20 57
South Tottenham	d	14 31	15 01	15 31	15 46	16 01	16 16	16 31	16 46	17 01	17 16	17 31	17 46	18 01	18 16	18 31	18 46	19 01	19 16	19 31	20 01	20 31	21 01
Harringay Green Lanes	d	14 34	15 04	15 34	15 49	16 04	16 19	16 34	16 49	17 04	17 19	17 34	17 49	18 04	18 19	18 34	18 49	19 04	19 19	19 34	20 04	20 34	21 04
Crouch Hill	d	14 37	15 07	15 37	15 52	16 07	16 22	16 37	16 52	17 07	17 22	17 37	17 52	18 07	18 22	18 37	18 52	19 07	19 22	19 37	20 07	20 37	21 07
Upper Holloway	d	14 39	15 09	15 39	15 54	16 09	16 24	16 39	16 54	17 09	17 24	17 39	17 54	18 09	18 24	18 39	18 54	19 09	19 24	19 39	20 09	20 39	21 09
Gospel Oak	a	14 44	15 14	15 44	15 59	16 14	16 29	16 44	16 59	17 14	17 29	17 44	17 59	18 14	18 29	18 44	18 59	19 14	19 29	19 44	20 14	20 44	21 14

		LO	LO	LO	LO	LO
Barking ⊖	d	21 09	21 39	22 09	22 39	23 09
Woodgrange Park	d	21 12	21 42	22 12	22 42	23 12
Wanstead Park	d	21 15	21 45	22 15	22 45	23 15
Leytonstone High Road	d	21 19	21 49	22 19	22 49	23 19
Leyton Midland Road	d	21 21	21 51	22 21	22 51	23 21
Walthamstow Queen's Road	d	21 24	21 54	22 24	22 54	23 24
Blackhorse Road ⊖	d	21 27	21 57	22 27	22 57	23 27
South Tottenham	d	21 31	22 01	22 31	23 01	23 31
Harringay Green Lanes	d	21 34	22 04	22 34	23 04	23 34
Crouch Hill	d	21 37	22 07	22 37	23 07	23 37
Upper Holloway	d	21 39	22 09	22 39	23 09	23 39
Gospel Oak	a	21 44	22 14	22 44	23 14	23 44

Table 62

Sundays

Barking-Gospel Oak

		LO	LO	LO	LO	LO	LO	LO	LO	LO	LO	LO	LO	LO	LO	LO	LO	LO	LO	LO	LO	LO	LO
Barking ⊖	d	09 05	09 35	10 05	10 35	11 05	11 35	12 05	12 35	13 05	13 35	14 05	14 35	15 05	15 35	16 05	16 35	17 05	17 35	18 05	18 35	19 05	19 35
Woodgrange Park	d	09 08	09 38	10 08	10 38	11 08	11 38	12 08	12 38	13 08	13 38	14 08	14 38	15 08	15 38	16 08	16 38	17 08	17 38	18 08	18 38	19 08	19 38
Wanstead Park	d	09 11	09 41	10 11	10 41	11 11	11 41	12 11	12 41	13 11	13 41	14 11	14 41	15 11	15 41	16 11	16 41	17 11	17 41	18 11	18 41	19 11	19 41
Leytonstone High Road	d	09 15	09 45	10 15	10 45	11 15	11 45	12 15	12 45	13 15	13 45	14 15	14 45	15 15	15 45	16 15	16 45	17 15	17 45	18 15	18 45	19 15	19 45
Leyton Midland Road	d	09 17	09 47	10 17	10 47	11 17	11 47	12 17	12 47	13 17	13 47	14 17	14 47	15 17	15 47	16 17	16 47	17 17	17 47	18 17	18 47	19 17	19 47
Walthamstow Queen's Road	d	09 20	09 50	10 20	10 50	11 20	11 50	12 20	12 50	13 20	13 50	14 20	14 50	15 20	15 50	16 20	16 50	17 20	17 50	18 20	18 50	19 20	19 50
Blackhorse Road ⊖	d	09 23	09 53	10 23	10 53	11 23	11 53	12 23	12 53	13 23	13 53	14 23	14 53	15 23	15 53	16 23	16 53	17 23	17 53	18 23	18 53	19 23	19 53
South Tottenham	d	09 27	09 57	10 27	10 57	11 27	11 57	12 27	12 57	13 27	13 57	14 27	14 57	15 27	15 57	16 27	16 57	17 27	17 57	18 27	18 57	19 27	19 57
Harringay Green Lanes	d	09 30	10 00	10 30	11 00	11 30	12 00	12 30	13 00	13 30	14 00	14 30	15 00	15 30	16 00	16 30	17 00	17 30	18 00	18 30	19 00	19 30	20 00
Crouch Hill	d	09 33	10 03	10 33	11 03	11 33	12 03	12 33	13 03	13 33	14 03	14 33	15 03	15 33	16 03	16 33	17 03	17 33	18 03	18 33	19 03	19 33	20 03
Upper Holloway	d	09 35	10 05	10 35	11 05	11 35	12 05	12 35	13 05	13 35	14 05	14 35	15 05	15 35	16 05	16 35	17 05	17 35	18 05	18 35	19 05	19 35	20 05
Gospel Oak	a	09 40	10 10	10 40	11 10	11 40	12 10	12 40	13 10	13 40	14 10	14 40	15 10	15 40	16 10	16 40	17 10	17 40	18 10	18 40	19 10	19 40	20 10

		LO	LO	LO	LO	LO	LO	LO
Barking ⊖	d	20 05	20 35	21 05	21 35	22 05	22 35	23 05
Woodgrange Park	d	20 08	20 38	21 08	21 38	22 08	22 38	23 08
Wanstead Park	d	20 11	20 41	21 11	21 41	22 11	22 41	23 11
Leytonstone High Road	d	20 15	20 45	21 15	21 45	22 15	22 45	23 15
Leyton Midland Road	d	20 17	20 47	21 17	21 47	22 17	22 47	23 17
Walthamstow Queen's Road	d	20 20	20 50	21 20	21 50	22 20	22 50	23 20
Blackhorse Road ⊖	d	20 23	20 53	21 23	21 53	22 23	22 53	23 23
South Tottenham	d	20 27	20 57	21 27	21 57	22 27	22 57	23 27
Harringay Green Lanes	d	20 30	21 00	21 30	22 00	22 30	23 00	23 30
Crouch Hill	d	20 33	21 03	21 33	22 03	22 33	23 03	23 33
Upper Holloway	d	20 35	21 05	21 35	22 05	22 35	23 05	23 35
Gospel Oak	a	20 40	21 10	21 40	22 10	22 40	23 10	23 40

Table 64

Mondays to Fridays

Bletchley - Bedford

		LM	LM	LM	LM	LM	LM	LM	LM	LM	LM	LM	LM	LM	LM	LM	LM
Bletchley	d	05 41	06 37	07 32	08 39	10 01	11 01	12 01	13 01	14 01	15 01	15 47	16 47	17 31	18 31	20 01	21 01
Fenny Stratford	d	05 44	06 40	07 35	08 42	10 04	11 04	12 04	13 04	14 04	15 04	15 50	16 50	17 34	18 34	20 04	21 04
Bow Brickhill	d	05 48	06 44	07 39	08 46	10 08	11 08	12 08	13 08	14 08	15 08	15 54	16 54	17 38	18 38	20 08	21 08
Woburn Sands	d	05 52	06 48	07 43	08 50	10 12	11 12	12 12	13 12	14 12	15 12	15 58	16 58	17 42	18 42	20 12	21 12
Aspley Guise	d	05 55	06 51	07 46	08 53	10 15	11 15	12 15	13 15	14 15	15 15	16 01	17 01	17 45	18 45	20 15	21 15
Ridgmont	d	05 58	06 54	07 49	08 56	10 18	11 18	12 18	13 18	14 18	15 18	16 04	17 04	17 48	18 48	20 18	21 18
Lidlington	d	06 02	06 58	07 53	09 00	10 22	11 22	12 22	13 22	14 22	15 22	16 08	17 08	17 52	18 52	20 22	21 22
Millbrook (Bedfordshire)	d	06 05	07 01	07 56	09 03	10 25	11 25	12 25	13 25	14 25	15 25	16 11	17 11	17 55	18 55	20 25	21 25
Stewartby	d	06 09	07 05	08 00	09 07	10 29	11 29	12 29	13 29	14 29	15 29	16 15	17 15	17 59	18 59	20 29	21 29
Kempston Hardwick	d	06 12	07 08	08 03	09 10	10 32	11 32	12 32	13 32	14 32	15 32	16 18	17 18	18 02	19 02	20 32	21 32
Bedford St Johns	d	06 19	07 15	08 10	09 17	10 39	11 39	12 39	13 39	14 39	15 39	16 25	17 25	18 09	19 09	20 39	21 39
Bedford 7	a	06 25	07 21	08 16	09 23	10 45	11 45	12 45	13 45	14 45	15 45	16 31	17 31	18 15	19 15	20 45	21 45

Saturdays

		LM	LM	LM	LM	LM	LM	LM	LM	LM	LM	LM	LM	LM	LM	LM	LM
Bletchley	d	05 41	06 37	07 32	08 39	10 01	11 01	12 01	13 01	14 01	15 01	15 47	16 47	17 31	18 31	20 01	21 01
Fenny Stratford	d	05 44	06 40	07 35	08 42	10 04	11 04	12 04	13 04	14 04	15 04	15 50	16 50	17 34	18 34	20 04	21 04
Bow Brickhill	d	05 48	06 44	07 39	08 46	10 08	11 08	12 08	13 08	14 08	15 08	15 54	16 54	17 38	18 38	20 08	21 08
Woburn Sands	d	05 52	06 48	07 43	08 50	10 12	11 12	12 12	13 12	14 12	15 12	15 58	16 58	17 42	18 42	20 12	21 12
Aspley Guise	d	05 55	06 51	07 46	08 53	10 15	11 15	12 15	13 15	14 15	15 15	16 01	17 01	17 45	18 45	20 15	21 15
Ridgmont	d	05 58	06 54	07 49	08 56	10 18	11 18	12 18	13 18	14 18	15 18	16 04	17 04	17 48	18 48	20 18	21 18
Lidlington	d	06 02	06 58	07 53	09 00	10 22	11 22	12 22	13 22	14 22	15 22	16 08	17 08	17 52	18 52	20 22	21 22
Millbrook (Bedfordshire)	d	06 05	07 01	07 56	09 03	10 25	11 25	12 25	13 25	14 25	15 25	16 11	17 11	17 55	18 55	20 25	21 25
Stewartby	d	06 09	07 05	08 00	09 07	10 29	11 29	12 29	13 29	14 29	15 29	16 15	17 15	17 59	18 59	20 29	21 29
Kempston Hardwick	d	06 12	07 08	08 03	09 10	10 32	11 32	12 32	13 32	14 32	15 32	16 18	17 18	18 02	19 02	20 32	21 32
Bedford St Johns	d	06 19	07 15	08 10	09 17	10 39	11 39	12 39	13 39	14 39	15 39	16 25	17 25	18 09	19 09	20 39	21 39
Bedford 7	a	06 25	07 21	08 16	09 23	10 45	11 45	12 45	13 45	14 45	15 45	16 31	17 31	18 15	19 15	20 45	21 45

No Sunday Service

For connections from Milton Keynes Central please refer to Table 66

Table 64

Mondays to Fridays

Bedford - Bletchley

		LM	LM	LM	LM	LM	LM	LM	LM	LM	LM	LM	LM	LM	LM	LM	LM
Bedford ■	d	06 31	07 31	08 31	09 33	10 55	11 55	12 55	13 55	14 55	15 55	16 37	17 37	18 25	19 35	20 55	21 56
Bedford St Johns	d	06 34	07 34	08 34	09 36	10 58	11 58	12 58	13 58	14 58	15 58	16 40	17 40	18 28	19 38	20 58	21 59
Kempston Hardwick	d	06 41	07 41	08 41	09 43	11 05	12 05	13 05	14 05	15 05	16 05	16 47	17 47	18 35	19 45	21 05	22 06
Stewartby	d	06 44	07 44	08 44	09 46	11 08	12 08	13 08	14 08	15 08	16 08	16 50	17 50	18 38	19 48	21 08	22 09
Millbrook (Bedfordshire)	d	06 48	07 48	08 48	09 50	11 12	12 12	13 12	14 12	15 12	16 12	16 54	17 54	18 42	19 52	21 12	22 13
Lidlington	d	06 51	07 51	08 51	09 53	11 15	12 15	13 15	14 15	15 15	16 15	16 57	17 57	18 45	19 55	21 15	22 16
Ridgmont	d	06 56	07 56	08 56	09 58	11 20	12 20	13 20	14 20	15 20	16 20	17 02	18 02	18 50	20 00	21 20	22 21
Aspley Guise	d	06 59	07 59	08 59	10 01	11 23	12 23	13 23	14 23	15 23	16 23	17 05	18 05	18 53	20 03	21 23	22 24
Woburn Sands	d	07 02	08 02	09 02	10 04	11 26	12 26	13 26	14 26	15 26	16 26	17 08	18 08	18 56	20 06	21 26	22 27
Bow Brickhill	d	07 06	08 06	09 06	10 08	11 30	12 30	13 30	14 30	15 30	16 30	17 12	18 12	19 00	20 10	21 30	22 31
Fenny Stratford	d	07 09	08 09	09 09	10 11	11 33	12 33	13 33	14 33	15 33	16 33	17 15	18 15	19 03	20 13	21 33	22 34
Bletchley	a	07 14	08 14	09 14	10 16	11 38	12 38	13 38	14 38	15 38	16 38	17 20	18 20	19 08	20 18	21 38	22 39

Saturdays

		LM	LM	LM	LM	LM	LM	LM	LM	LM	LM	LM	LM	LM	LM	LM
Bedford ■	d	06 31	07 31	08 31	09 33	10 55	11 55	13 55	14 55	15 55	16 37	17 37	18 25	19 35	20 55	21 56
Bedford St Johns	d	06 34	07 34	08 34	09 36	10 58	11 58	13 58	14 58	15 58	16 40	17 40	18 28	19 38	20 58	21 59
Kempston Hardwick	d	06 41	07 41	08 41	09 43	11 05	12 05	14 05	15 05	16 05	16 47	17 47	18 35	19 45	21 05	22 06
Stewartby	d	06 44	07 44	08 44	09 46	11 08	12 08	14 08	15 08	16 08	16 50	17 50	18 38	19 48	21 08	22 09
Millbrook (Bedfordshire)	d	06 48	07 48	08 48	09 50	11 12	12 12	14 12	15 12	16 12	16 54	17 54	18 42	19 52	21 12	22 13
Lidlington	d	06 51	07 51	08 51	09 53	11 15	12 15	14 15	15 15	16 15	16 57	17 57	18 45	19 55	21 15	22 16
Ridgmont	d	06 56	07 56	08 56	09 58	11 20	12 20	14 20	15 20	16 20	17 02	18 02	18 50	20 00	21 20	22 21
Aspley Guise	d	06 59	07 59	08 59	10 01	11 23	12 23	14 23	15 23	16 23	17 05	18 05	18 53	20 03	21 23	22 24
Woburn Sands	d	07 02	08 02	09 02	10 04	11 26	12 26	14 26	15 26	16 26	17 08	18 08	18 56	20 06	21 26	22 27
Bow Brickhill	d	07 06	08 06	09 06	10 08	11 30	12 30	14 30	15 30	16 30	17 12	18 12	19 00	20 10	21 30	22 31
Fenny Stratford	d	07 09	08 09	09 09	10 11	11 33	12 33	14 33	15 33	16 33	17 15	18 15	19 03	20 13	21 33	22 34
Bletchley	a	07 14	08 14	09 14	10 16	11 38	12 38	14 38	15 38	16 38	17 20	18 20	19 08	20 18	21 38	22 39

Route Diagram for Table 65

London-Scotland
See Tables 400-404 for Sleeper trains.

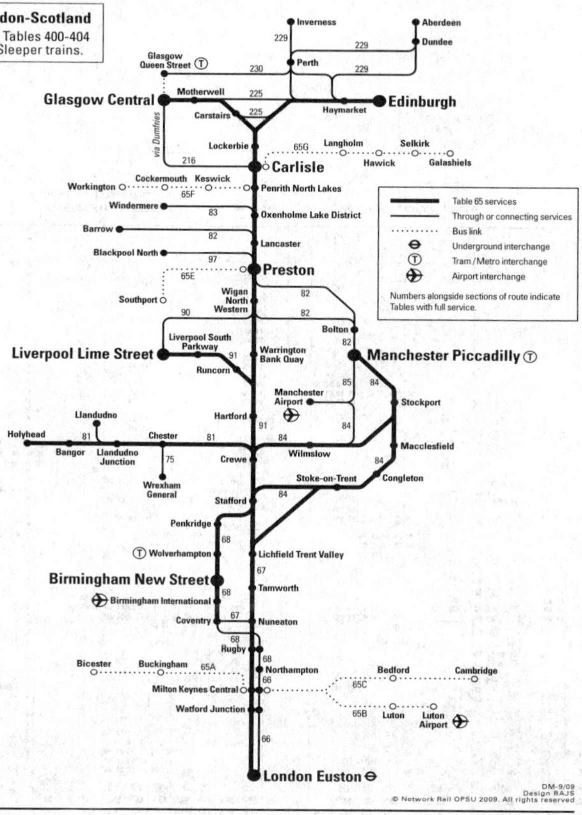

DM-9/09
Design BAJS

London and West Midlands - North West England and Scotland

				TP	NT	TP		VT	TP	LM	VT	VT	TP		XC	LM		AW	LM	XC		NT	TP	VT	VT
				◇1		◇1		◇1	◇1	1	1	◇1	◇1		◇1	◇1		◇	◇1	◇1			◇1	◇1	◇1
																								A	B
						⌶		⊠	⌶			⊠	⌶		⌶			⌶		☕				☕	⊠
London Euston 15 ⊖	d																								
Watford Junction	d																								
Milton Keynes Central	d																								
Rugby	d																								
Nuneaton	d																								
Tamworth Low Level	d																								
Lichfield Trent Valley	d																								
Coventry	d																								
Birmingham International ✈	d																								
Birmingham New Street 12	d											05 30			05 57				06 01	06 20				06 17	06 17
Wolverhampton 7	d											05 48			06 16				06 19	06 40				06 35	06 34
Penkridge	d																		06 29						
Stafford	a											06 01			06 29				06 35	06 53					
	d											06 02			06 30				06 36	06 54					
Stoke-on-Trent	a														06 50					07 12					
Congleton	a														07 02										
Macclesfield	a														07 11					07 30					
Crewe 10	a											06 21							06 56					07 06	07 07
	d							05 57		06 02	06 12	06 24				06 32		06 54	06 57					07 07	07 09
Chester	a											06 44						07 14							
Wrexham General	a																								
Llandudno	a																								
Bangor (Gwynedd)	a											07 49						08 36							
Holyhead	a											08 23						09 19							
Wilmslow	a										06 27														
Stockport	a										06 37				07 27					07 45					
Manchester Piccadilly 10	a										06 49				07 37					08 00					
Hartford	a									06 14						06 46			07 09						
Warrington Bank Quay	a							06 13																07 25	07 26
	d							06 14																07 25	07 27
Runcorn	a									06 27						06 59			07 23						
Liverpool South Parkway 7 ✈	a									06 36						07 08			07 32						
Liverpool Lime Street 10	a									06 49						07 22			07 42						
	d																					06 57			
Manchester Airport ✈	d			04 00					05 45				06 18												
Manchester Piccadilly 10	d			04 15		05 46			06 03				06 33												
Bolton	d			04s29					06 19				06 50												
Wigan North Western	a			04 44		06 15		06 24														07 30		07 36	07 37
	d			04 44		06 15		06 25														07 31		07 36	07 38
Preston 8	a			05s04		06 35		06 37	06 42				07 11									07 56		07 50	07 51
Blackpool North	a			05 33		07 06																			
Preston 8	d				05 22			06 40	06 44				07 14										07 20	07 51	07 53
Lancaster 6	a				05 42			06 54	06 59				07 30										07 36	08 07	08 08
	d				05 42			06 54	07 00				07 30										07 36	08 08	08 08
Barrow-in-Furness	a				06 47																		08 39		
Oxenholme Lake District	a							07 08	07 15															08 20	08 21
	d							07 10	07 15															08 21	08 22
Windermere	a																								
Penrith North Lakes	d							07 35					08 07												
Carlisle 8	a				09 21			07 50	07 55				08 24											09 01	09 01
	d							07 51	07 56				08 25											09 02	09 01
Lockerbie	d							08 10	08 16																
Carstairs	a																								
Motherwell	a																								
Glasgow Central 15	a							09 14					09 45												
Haymarket	a								09s16															10 15	10 15
Edinburgh 10	a								09 22															10 20	10 20
Perth	a																								
Dundee	a																								
Aberdeen	a																								
Inverness	a																								

A from 19 July until 3 September

B until 16 July and from 6 September

OVERNIGHT SLEEPERS. For sleeper trains, operated by First ScotRail, please refer to Tables 400 - 404

London and West Midlands - North West England and Scotland

		TP		AW	VT	VT	VT	LM	XC	LM	TP	NT		NT	VT	VT	XC	VT	TP	AW	LM	VT		VT	VT
		◇1			◇1	◇1	◇1	◇1	◇1	◇1	◇1				◇1	◇1	◇1	◇1	◇1		◇1	◇1		◇1	◇1
		⌶			⊠	⊠	⊠		⌶		⌶				⊠	⊠	⌶	⊠	⌶			⊠		⊠	⊠
London Euston 15 ⊖	d				05 27	05 39	06 17									06 36		06 55				07 07		07 10	07 20
Watford Junction	d				05u45	06u02										06u51									
Milton Keynes Central	d				06 10	06 22	06 47											07 27						07 41	07 50
Rugby	d					06 45																			
Nuneaton	d				06 39																				
Tamworth Low Level	d																								
Lichfield Trent Valley	d																								
Coventry	d																								
Birmingham International ✈	d																				07 17				
Birmingham New Street 12	d							06 36	06 57	07 01					07 19		07 31				07 36				
Wolverhampton 7	d							06 51	07 16	07 19					07 36		07 49				07 53				
Penkridge	d									07 30											08 03				
Stafford	a				07 03			07 05	07 29	07 36											08 09	08 22			
	d				07 03			07 05	07 30	07 36											08 09	08 23			
Stoke-on-Trent	a						07 45										08 18	08 24							08 48
Congleton	a																								
Macclesfield	a						08 01										08 35	08 41							
Crewe 10	a				07 22	07 30		07 29	07 50	07 56					08 07	08 10					08 30			08 47	
	d			07 23	07 24	07 32		07 33	07 52	07 58					08 09	08 11				08 23	08 31			08 49	
Chester	a			07 46																08 46				09 12	
Wrexham General	a																								
Llandudno	a																								
Bangor (Gwynedd)	a																								
Holyhead	a																								
Wilmslow	a								08 08							08 27									
Stockport	a						08 16		08 20							08 37	08 49	08 55							09 16
Manchester Piccadilly 10	a						08 28		08 34							08 49	08 59	09 07							09 28
Hartford	a							07 46		08 09															
Warrington Bank Quay	a					07 49									08 26										
	d					07 49									08 27										
Runcorn	a				07 42			07 59		08 22											08 50	08 55			
Liverpool South Parkway 7 ✈	a							08 08		08 31											08 59				
Liverpool Lime Street 10	a				08 01			08 21		08 44											09 10	09 15			
	d											07 57													
Manchester Airport ✈	d	07 00									07 25								07 58						
Manchester Piccadilly 10	d	07 15									07 45								08 15						
Bolton	d	07 31									07 59								08 32						
Wigan North Western	a					08 00						08 30			08 37										
	d					08 00						08 31			08 38										
Preston 8	a	07 57				08 13					08 22	08 56			08 51				08 58						
Blackpool North	a	08 29																	09 25						
Preston 8	d					08 15					08 24			08 38	08 53										
Lancaster 6	a					08 29					08 39			08 58	09 08										
	d					08 30					08 40			08 58	09 08										
Barrow-in-Furness	a													10 03											
Oxenholme Lake District	a					08 43					08 54														
	d					08 43					08 54														
Windermere	a																								
Penrith North Lakes	d										09 20				09 45										
Carlisle 8	a					09 21					09 34			12 39	09 59										
	d					09 22					09 36				10 01										
Lockerbie	d										09 55														
Carstairs	a																								
Motherwell	a																								
Glasgow Central 15	a					10 36									11 16										
Haymarket	a										10s56														
Edinburgh 10	a										11 04														
Perth	a																								
Dundee	a																								
Aberdeen	a																								
Inverness	a																								

OVERNIGHT SLEEPERS. For sleeper trains, operated by First ScotRail, please refer to Tables 400 - 404

Table 65

London and West Midlands - North West England and Scotland

Station		XC	LM	TP	VT	NT	VT	VT	XC	VT	TP	TP	AW	LM	VT	VT	VT	XC	LM	TP	TP	LM	VT	NT
																				A				
London Euston	d				07 30			07 35		08 00					08 07	08 10	08 20						08 30	
Watford Junction	d																							
Milton Keynes Central	d							08 06								08 41	08 50							
Rugby	d																							
Nuneaton	d																							
Tamworth Low Level	d																							
Lichfield Trent Valley	d																							
Coventry	d	07 27																08 27						
Birmingham International	d	07 38																08 38						
Birmingham New Street	d	07b57	08 01				08 20		08 31					08 36				08c57	09 01			10 01		
Wolverhampton	d	08 15	08 19				08 37		08 49					08 53				09 15	09 19			10 19		
Penkridge	d		08 29											09 03										
Stafford	a	08 29	08 35						09 00					09 09	09 22			09 29	09 34			10 34		
	d	08 30	08 36						09 01					09 09	09 23			09 30	09 35			10 35		
Stoke-on-Trent	a	08 54							09 19	09 24							09 48	09 54						
Congleton	a																							
Macclesfield	a	09 11								09 41								10 11						
Crewe	a		08 56				09 07	09 10						09 30		09 47			09 56			10 56		
	d		08 58				09 09	09 11					09 23	09 31		09 49			09 57			10 57		
Chester	a												09 46			10 09								
Wrexham General	a																							
Llandudno	a																							
Bangor (Gwynedd)	a															11 27								
Holyhead	a																							
Wilmslow	a							09 27																
Stockport	a	09 27						09 36	09 49	09 55							10 16	10 27						
Manchester Piccadilly	a	09 39						09 49	09 59	10 07							10 28	10 39						
Hartford	a		09 11																10 10			11 11		
Warrington Bank Quay	a				09 14		09 26																10 14	
	d				09 14		09 27																10 14	
Runcorn	a		09 22											09 50	09 55				10 22			11 21		
Liverpool South Parkway	a		09 31											09 59					10 31			11 30		
Liverpool Lime Street	a		09 43											10 10	10 15				10 44			11 43		
	d					08 57																		09 57
Manchester Airport	d			08 25							09 00									09 29				
Manchester Piccadilly	d			08 46							09 16									09 46				
Bolton	d			09 07							09 33									10 07				
Wigan North Western	a				09 25	09 30	09 37																10 25	10 30
	d				09 25	09 31	09 38																10 25	10 31
Preston	a			09 33	09 38	09 54	09 51				09 55									10 33			10 38	10 54
Blackpool North	a			10 05		10 21														11 05				11 21
Preston	d				09 41		09 53				09 58	10 07								>	10 45		10 41	
Lancaster	a				09 54		10 09				10 13	10 22									11 01		10 54	
	d				09 55		10 10				10 14	10 23									11 14		10 55	
Barrow-in-Furness	a											11 17												
Oxenholme Lake District	a						10 24														11 17		11 08	
	d						10 25														11 18		11 08	
Windermere	a																				11 39			
Penrith North Lakes	d				10 31																			
Carlisle	a				10 46		11 02				11 06												11 46	
	d				10 47		11 04				11 07												11 47	
Lockerbie	d										11 27													
Carstairs	a																							
Motherwell	a																							
Glasgow Central	a				12 01						12 28												13 01	
Haymarket	a						12 17																	
Edinburgh	a						12 22																	
Perth	a																							
Dundee	a																							
Aberdeen	a																							
Inverness	a																							

A Through portion to Windermere
b arr. 0748
c arr. 0848

OVERNIGHT SLEEPERS. For sleeper trains, operated by First ScotRail, please refer to Tables 400 - 404

Table 65

London and West Midlands - North West England and Scotland

Station		VT	VT	XC	TP	AW	LM	XC	VT	VT	VT	VT	VT	VT	TP	VT	NT	VT	VT	VT	XC
									A									A	B		
London Euston	d		08 40						08 43	09 00	09 07	09 10	09 10	09 20		09 30				09 40	
Watford Junction	d																				
Milton Keynes Central	d								09 13			09u40	09 41	09 50							
Rugby	d																				
Nuneaton	d																				
Tamworth Low Level	d																				
Lichfield Trent Valley	d																				
Coventry	d							09 27	09 43												
Birmingham International	d							09 38	09 54												
Birmingham New Street	d	09 20		09 31			09 36	09b57	10c19										10 20		10 31
Wolverhampton	d	09 37		09 49			09 53	10 15	10 38										10 37		10 49
Penkridge	d						10 03														
Stafford	a			10 00			10 09	10 29			10 22										11 00
	d			10 01			10 09	10 30			10 23										11 01
Stoke-on-Trent	a			10 19				10 54		10 24				10 48							11 19
Congleton	a																				
Macclesfield	a							11 11		10 41											
Crewe	a	10 07	10 10				10 30		11 07			10 47	10 47						11 07	11 10	
	d	10 09	10 11			10 23	10 31		11 09			10 49	10 49						11 09	11 11	
Chester	a					10 46						11 09	11 09								
Wrexham General	a																				
Llandudno	a																				
Bangor (Gwynedd)	a												12 16								
Holyhead	a												12 50								
Wilmslow	a		10 27																	11 27	
Stockport	a		10 36	10 49				11 27		10 55				11 16						11 36	11 49
Manchester Piccadilly	a		10 49	10 59				11 39		11 07				11 28						11 49	11 59
Hartford	a																				
Warrington Bank Quay	a	10 26							11 26							11 14			11 26		
	d	10 27							11 27							11 14			11 27		
Runcorn	a						10 50				10 55										
Liverpool South Parkway	a						10 59														
Liverpool Lime Street	a						11 10				11 15										
	d																10 57				
Manchester Airport	d				10 00										10 29						
Manchester Piccadilly	d				10 16										10 46						
Bolton	d				10 33										11 07			←			
Wigan North Western	a	10 37							11 37							11 25	11 30	11 37	11 37		
	d	10 38							11 38							11 25	11 31	11 38	11 38		
Preston	a	10 51			10 55				→						11 33	11 38	11 54	11 51	11 51		
Blackpool North	a														12 05		12 21				
Preston	d	10 53			10 58											11 41		11 52	11 53		
Lancaster	a	11 08			11 13											11 54		12 07	12 08		
	d	11 08			11 14											11 55		12 07	12 08		
Barrow-in-Furness	a																				
Oxenholme Lake District	a				11 28													12 22	12 22		
	d				11 28													12 24	12 24		
Windermere	a																				
Penrith North Lakes	d	11 45			11 53											12 30					
Carlisle	a	12 00			12 10											12 45		13 01	13 01		
	d	12 02			12 11											12 47		13 03	13 03		
Lockerbie	d																				
Carstairs	a																				
Motherwell	a																				
Glasgow Central	a	13 17														14 01					
Haymarket	a				13s34													14 16	14 16		
Edinburgh	a				13 39													14 22	14 22		
Perth	a																				
Dundee	a																				
Aberdeen	a																				
Inverness	a																				

A from 19 July until 3 September
B until 16 July and from 6 September
b arr. 0948
c arr. 1008

OVERNIGHT SLEEPERS. For sleeper trains, operated by First ScotRail, please refer to Tables 400 - 404

London and West Midlands - North West England and Scotland

		VT	TP	AW	LM	VT	VT	VT	XC	LM	TP	VT	NT	VT	VT	XC	VT	TP	AW	LM	VT	VT	VT
		◇1	◇1		◇1	◇1	◇1	◇1	◇1	◇1	◇1	◇1		◇1	◇1	◇1	◇1	◇1		◇1	◇1	◇1	◇1
			A																				
		🛒	⌶			🛒	🛒	🛒	⌶		⌶	🛒		🛒	🛒	⌶	🛒	⌶			🛒	🛒	🛒
London Euston [15] ⊖	d	10 00				10 07	10 10	10 20				10 30			10 40		11 00				11 07	11 10	11 20
Watford Junction	d																						
Milton Keynes Central	d						10 41	10 50														11 41	11 50
Rugby	d																						
Nuneaton	d																						
Tamworth Low Level	d																						
Lichfield Trent Valley	d																						
Coventry	d								10 27														
Birmingham International ✈	d								10 38														
Birmingham New Street [12]	d				10 36				10b57	11 01				11 20		11 31				11 36			
Wolverhampton [7]	d				10 53				11 15	11 19				11 37		11 49				11 53			
Penkridge	d				11 03															12 03			
Stafford	a				11 09	11 22			11 28	11 34						12 00				12 09	12 22		
	d				11 09	11 23			11 30	11 35						12 01				12 09	12 23		
Stoke-on-Trent	a	11 24						11 48	11 54							12 19	12 24						12 48
Congleton	a																						
Macclesfield	a	11 41							12 11								12 41						
Crewe [10]	a				11 30		11 47			11 56				12 07	12 10					12 30		12 47	
	d			11 23	11 31		11 49			11 57				12 09	12 11				12 23	12 31		12 49	
Chester	a			11 46			12 12												12 46			13 12	
Wrexham General	a																						
Llandudno	a																						
Bangor (Gwynedd)	a																						
Holyhead	a																						
Wilmslow	a														12 27								
Stockport	a	11 55						12 16	12 27						12 36	12 49	12 55						13 16
Manchester Piccadilly [10]	a	12 07						12 28	12 39						12 49	12 59	13 07						13 28
Hartford	a									12 10													
Warrington Bank Quay	a											12 15		12 26									
	d											12 15		12 27									
Runcorn	a				11 50	11 55				12 23										12 50	12 55		
Liverpool South Parkway [7] ✈	a				11 59					12 32										12 59			
Liverpool Lime Street [10]	a				12 10	12 15				12 44										13 10	13 15		
	d												11 57										
Manchester Airport ✈	d		11 00								11 29							12 00					
Manchester Piccadilly [10]	d		11 16								11 46							12 16					
Bolton	d		11 33								12 07							12 33					
Wigan North Western	a											12 26	12 30	12 37									
	d											12 26	12 31	12 38									
Preston [8]	a		11 55								12 33	12 39	12 54	12 51				12 55					
Blackpool North	a										13 05		13 21										
Preston [8]	d		11 58									12 42		12 53				12 58					
Lancaster [6]	a		12 13									13 00		13 08				13 13					
	d		12 14											13 08				13 14					
Barrow-in-Furness	a		13 10																				
Oxenholme Lake District	a													13 22				13 28					
	d													13 24				13 28					
Windermere	a																						
Penrith North Lakes	d																	13 53					
Carlisle [8]	a													14 01				14 10					
	d													14 03				14 11					
Lockerbie	d																	14 30					
Carstairs	a																						
Motherwell	a																						
Glasgow Central [15]	a													15 17									
Haymarket	a																	15s38					
Edinburgh [10]	a																	15 43					
Perth	a																						
Dundee	a																						
Aberdeen	a																						
Inverness	a																						

A ⌶ to Preston

b arr. 1048

OVERNIGHT SLEEPERS. For sleeper trains, operated by First ScotRail, please refer to Tables 400 - 404

London and West Midlands - North West England and Scotland

		XC	LM	TP	TP	VT	NT	VT	VT	XC	VT	TP	TP	AW	LM	VT	VT	VT	XC	LM	TP	VT	NT
		◇1	◇1	◇1	◇1	1		◇1	◇1	◇1	◇1	◇1	◇1		◇1	◇1	◇1	◇1	◇1	◇1	◇1	◇1	
												A											
		⌶		⌶		⊠		🛒	🛒	⌶	🛒	⌶				🛒	🛒	🛒	⌶		⌶	🛒	
London Euston [15] ⊖	d					11 30			11 40		12 00					12 07	12 10	12 20				12 30	
Watford Junction	d																						
Milton Keynes Central	d																12 41	12 50					
Rugby	d																						
Nuneaton	d																						
Tamworth Low Level	d																						
Lichfield Trent Valley	d																						
Coventry	d	11 27																	12 27				
Birmingham International ✈	d	11 38																	12 38				
Birmingham New Street [12]	d	11b57	12 01					12 20		12 31					12 36				12c57	13 01			
Wolverhampton [7]	d	12 15	12 19					12 37		12 49					12 53				13 15	13 19			
Penkridge	d														13 03								
Stafford	a	12 29	12 34							13 00					13 09	13 22			13 29	13 34			
	d	12 30	12 35							13 01					13 09	13 23			13 30	13 35			
Stoke-on-Trent	a	12 54								13 19	13 24							13 48	13 54				
Congleton	a																						
Macclesfield	a	13 11									13 41								14 11				
Crewe [10]	a		12 56					13 07	13 10						13 30		13 47			13 56			
	d		12 57					13 09	13 11					13 23	13 31		13 49			13 57			
Chester	a													13 46			14 12						
Wrexham General	a																						
Llandudno	a																						
Bangor (Gwynedd)	a																						
Holyhead	a																						
Wilmslow	a								13 27														
Stockport	a	13 27							13 36	13 49	13 55							14 16	14 27				
Manchester Piccadilly [10]	a	13 39							13 49	13 59	14 07							14 28	14 39				
Hartford	a		13 11																	14 11			
Warrington Bank Quay	a					13 14		13 26														14 14	
	d					13 14		13 27														14 14	
Runcorn	a		13 21												13 50	13 55				14 21			
Liverpool South Parkway [7] ✈	a		13 30												13 59					14 30			
Liverpool Lime Street [10]	a		13 43												14 10	14 15				14 43			
	d						12 57																13 57
Manchester Airport ✈	d			12 29								13 00									13 29		
Manchester Piccadilly [10]	d			12 46								13 16									13 46		
Bolton	d			13 07								13 33									14 07		
Wigan North Western	a					13 25	13 30	13 37														14 25	14 30
	d					13 25	13 31	13 38														14 25	14 31
Preston [8]	a			13 33		13 38	13 54	13 51				13 55									14 33	14 38	14 54
Blackpool North	a			14 05			14 21					>									15 05		15 21
Preston [8]	d				13 04	13 41		13 53				13 58	14 04									14 41	
Lancaster [6]	a				13 19	13 54		14 08				14 13	14 19									15 00	
	d				13 20	13 55		14 08				14 14	14 20										
Barrow-in-Furness	a												15 15										
Oxenholme Lake District	a				13 36	14 08																	
	d				13 37	14 08																	
Windermere	a				13 56																		
Penrith North Lakes	d							14 45															
Carlisle [8]	a					14 46		15 00				15 06											
	d					14 47		15 02				15 07											
Lockerbie	d											15 27											
Carstairs	a																						
Motherwell	a																						
Glasgow Central [15]	a					16 01						16 30											
Haymarket	a							16 17															
Edinburgh [10]	a							16 22															
Perth	a																						
Dundee	a																						
Aberdeen	a																						
Inverness	a																						

A Through portion to Barrow-in-Furness

b arr. 1148

c arr. 1248

OVERNIGHT SLEEPERS. For sleeper trains, operated by First ScotRail, please refer to Tables 400 - 404

Table 65

London and West Midlands - North West England and Scotland

Station		VT		VT	XC	VT	TP	AW	LM	VT	VT	VT		XC	LM	TP	TP	VT	NT	VT	TP	VT FO		VT	XC
																A	B				C				
London Euston	d			12 40		13 00				13 07	13 10	13 20						13 30				13 33		13 40	
Watford Junction	d																								
Milton Keynes Central	d										13 41	13 50													
Rugby	d																								
Nuneaton	d																								
Tamworth Low Level	d																								
Lichfield Trent Valley	d																								
Coventry	d													13 27											
Birmingham International	d													13 38											
Birmingham New Street	d	13 20			13 31				13 36					13b57	14 01					14 20					14 31
Wolverhampton	d	13 37			13 49				13 53					14 15	14 19					14 37					14 49
Penkridge	d								14 03																
Stafford	a				14 00				14 09	14 22				14 29	14 34										15 00
	d				14 01				14 09	14 23				14 30	14 35										15 01
Stoke-on-Trent	a				14 19	14 24						14 48		14 54											15 19
Congleton	a																								
Macclesfield	a					14 41								15 11											
Crewe	a	14 07		14 10					14 30		14 47				14 56					15 07		15 16		15 10	
	d	14 09		14 11				14 23	14 31		14 49				14 57					15 09		15 19		15 11	
Chester	a							14 46			15 12														
Wrexham General	a																								
Llandudno	a																								
Bangor (Gwynedd)	a																								
Holyhead	a																								
Wilmslow	a			14 27																				15 27	
Stockport	a			14 36	14 49	14 55						15 16		15 27										15 36	15 49
Manchester Piccadilly	a			14 49	14 59	15 07						15 28		15 39										15 49	15 59
Hartford	a														15 11										
Warrington Bank Quay	a	14 26																15 14		15 26		15 39			
	d	14 27																15 14		15 27		15 40			
Runcorn	a								14 50	14 55					15 21										
Liverpool South Parkway	a								14 59						15 30										
Liverpool Lime Street	a								15 10	15 15					15 43										
	d																		14 57						
Manchester Airport	d						14 00									14 29	14 29				15 00				
Manchester Piccadilly	d						14 16									14 46	14 46				15 16				
Bolton	d						14 33									15 07	15 07				15 33				
Wigan North Western	a	14 37																15 25	15 30	15 37		15 50			
	d	14 38																15 25	15 31	15 38		15 51			
Preston	a	14 51					14 55									15 33	15 33	15 38	15 54	15 51	15 55	16 07			
Blackpool North	a															16 05	16 11		16 21						
Preston	d	14 53					14 58											15 41		15 53	15 58	16 10			
Lancaster	a	15 08					15 13													16 08	16 13	16 29			
	d	15 09					15 14													16 08	16 14				
Barrow-in-Furness	a																				17 18				
Oxenholme Lake District	a	15 22					15 28											16 04							
	d	15 24					15 28											16 06							
Windermere	a																								
Penrith North Lakes	d						15 53											16 31		16 45					
Carlisle	a	16 01					16 10											16 46		17 00					
	d	16 03					16 11											16 47		17 02					
Lockerbie	d						16 30																		
Carstairs	a																								
Motherwell	a																								
Glasgow Central	a	17 13																18 01							
Haymarket	a						17s30													18 14					
Edinburgh	a						17 39													18 22					
Perth	a																								
Dundee	a																								
Aberdeen	a																								
Inverness	a																								

A Fridays excepted 2 July to 3 September
B FO from 2 July until 3 September
C to Preston
b arr. 1348

OVERNIGHT SLEEPERS. For sleeper trains, operated by First ScotRail, please refer to Tables 400 - 404

Table 65

London and West Midlands - North West England and Scotland

Station		LM	AW	LM	XC	VT	VT	VT	VT	VT	TP	VT FO	VT FX	NT	VT	VT	VT	XC	VT	TP	TP	AW	LM	VT
						A									A	B				C				
London Euston	d					13 43	14 00	14 07	14 10	14 20		14 30	14 30				14 40		15 00					15 07
Watford Junction	d																							
Milton Keynes Central	d					14 13			14 41	14 50														
Rugby	d																							
Nuneaton	d																							
Tamworth Low Level	d																							
Lichfield Trent Valley	d																							
Coventry	d				14 27	14 43																		
Birmingham International	d				14 38	14 54																		
Birmingham New Street	d	15 01		14 36	14b57	15c20										15 20		15 31					15 36	
Wolverhampton	d	15 19		14 53	15 15	15 37										15 37		15 50					15 53	
Penkridge	d			15 03																			16 03	
Stafford	a	15 34		15 09	15 29			15 22															16 09	16 22
	d	15 35		15 09	15 30			15 23															16 09	16 23
Stoke-on-Trent	a				15 54		15 24			15 48								16 18	16 24					
Congleton	a																							
Macclesfield	a				16 11		15 41												16 41					
Crewe	a	15 56		15 30		16 07			15 47							16 07	16 11						16 30	
	d	15 57	15 23	15 31		16 09			15 49							16 09	16 12					16 23	16 31	
Chester	a		15 46						16 12													16 46		
Wrexham General	a																							
Llandudno	a																							
Bangor (Gwynedd)	a																							
Holyhead	a																							
Wilmslow	a																16 27							
Stockport	a				16 27		15 55			16 16							16 36	16 47	16 54					
Manchester Piccadilly	a				16 39		16 07			16 28							16 49	16 59	17 07					
Hartford	a	16 10																						
Warrington Bank Quay	a					16 26						16 16	16 16			16 26								
	d					16 27						16 17	16 17			16 27								
Runcorn	a	16 22		15 50				15 55															16 50	16 55
Liverpool South Parkway	a	16 31		15 59																			16 59	
Liverpool Lime Street	a	16 45		16 10				16 15															17 10	17 15
	d													15 57										
Manchester Airport	d										15 29									16 00				
Manchester Piccadilly	d										15 46									16 16				
Bolton	d										16 07				←					16 33				
Wigan North Western	a					16 37						16 28	16 28	16 29	16 37	16 37								
	d					16 38						16 29	16 29	16 31	16 38	16 38								
Preston	a					→					16 35	16 42	16 42	16 56	16 51	16 51				16 55				
Blackpool North	a										17 07			17 24						>				
Preston	d											16 43	16 44		16 53	16 53				17 00	17 04			
Lancaster	a											17 00	17 00		17 09	17 09				17 15	17 23			
	d											17 00			17 10	17 10				17 16	17 25			
Barrow-in-Furness	a																							
Oxenholme Lake District	a											17 15			17 24	17 24				17 30	17 43			
	d											17 16			17 25	17 25				17 30	17 49			
Windermere	a																				18 08			
Penrith North Lakes	d											17 42			17 51	17 51								
Carlisle	a											18 00			18 06	18 06				18 10				
	d											18 00			18 07	18 07				18 11				
Lockerbie	d																			18 30				
Carstairs	a																							
Motherwell	a																							
Glasgow Central	a											19 14			19 19	19 19								
Haymarket	a																			19s31				
Edinburgh	a																			19 39				
Perth	a																							
Dundee	a																							
Aberdeen	a																							
Inverness	a																							

A from 19 July until 3 September
B until 16 July and from 6 September
C Through portion to Windermere
b arr. 1448
c arr. 1508

OVERNIGHT SLEEPERS. For sleeper trains, operated by First ScotRail, please refer to Tables 400 - 404

London and West Midlands - North West England and Scotland

		VT	VT	XC	LM	TP	VT	NT	VT	VT	XC	VT	TP	TP	AW	LM	VT	VT	VT	XC	LM	VT	TP
		◇1	◇1	◇1	◇1	◇1	◇1		■ 1	◇1	◇1	◇1	◇1	◇1		◇1	◇1	◇1	◇1	◇1	◇1	◇1	◇1
													A										
		🛒	🛒	🍴		🍴	⊠		🛒	🛒	🍴	🛒	🍴				🛒	🛒	🛒	🍴		🛒	
London Euston 15 ⊖	d	15 10	15 20				15 30			15 40		16 00					16 07	16 10	16 20			16 30	
Watford Junction	d																						
Milton Keynes Central	d	15 41	15 50															16u41	16u50				
Rugby	d																						
Nuneaton	d																						
Tamworth Low Level	d																						
Lichfield Trent Valley	d																						
Coventry	d			15 27																16 27			
Birmingham International ✈	d			15 38																16 39			
Birmingham New Street 12	d			15b57	16 01				16 20		16 31					16 36				16c57	17 01		
Wolverhampton 7	d			16 15	16 19				16 37		16 49					16 53				17 15	17 19		
Penkridge	d															17 03					17 29		
Stafford	a			16 29	16 34						17 00					17 09	17 22			17 29	17 35		
	d			16 30	16 35						17 01					17 09	17 23			17 30	17 36		
Stoke-on-Trent	a		16 48	16 54							17 19	17 24							17 48	17 54			
Congleton	a																						
Macclesfield	a			17 11								17 41								18 11			
Crewe 10	a	16 47			16 56				17 07	17 10						17 30		17 47			17 56		
	d	16 49			16 57				17 09	17 11					17 23	17 31		17 49			18 01		
Chester	a	17 12													17 46			18 08					
Wrexham General	a																						
Llandudno	a																						
Bangor (Gwynedd)	a																	19 21					
Holyhead	a																						
Wilmslow	a									17 27													
Stockport	a		17 16	17 27						17 36	17 49	17 55							18 16	18 27			
Manchester Piccadilly 10	a		17 28	17 39						17 49	17 59	18 07							18 28	18 39			
Hartford	a				17 11																18 13		
Warrington Bank Quay	a						17 14		17 26														
	d						17 14		17 27														
Runcorn	a				17 21											17 50	17 55				18 23		
Liverpool South Parkway 7 ✈	a				17 30											17 59					18 32		
Liverpool Lime Street 10	a				17 43											18 10	18 15				18 44		
	d							16 57															
Manchester Airport ✈	d					16 29							17 00										
Manchester Piccadilly 10	d					16 46							17 15										
Bolton	d					17 06							17 32										
Wigan North Western	a						17 25	17 30	17 37														
	d						17 25	17 31	17 38														
Preston 8	a					17 30	17 38	17 54	17 51				17 55									18 30	
Blackpool North	a					18 02		18 24					>										
Preston 8	d						17 41		17 53				18 00	18 08								18 32	
Lancaster 6	a						17 54		18 08				18 15	18 23									
	d						17 55		18 08				18 16	18 24									18 29
Barrow-in-Furness	a													19 30									
Oxenholme Lake District	a						18 08		18 22				18 30										18 45
	d						18 08		18 23				18 30										18 46
Windermere	a																						19 08
Penrith North Lakes	d								18 49				18 55										
Carlisle 8	a						18 47		19 04				19 12										
	d						18 47		19 04				19 13										
Lockerbie	d																						
Carstairs	a																						
Motherwell	a												20s15										
Glasgow Central 15	a						19 58						20 33									20 39	
Haymarket	a								20 16														
Edinburgh 10	a								20 22														
Perth	a																						
Dundee	a																						
Aberdeen	a																						
Inverness	a																						

A Through portion to Barrow-in-Furness

b arr. 1548

c arr. 1648

OVERNIGHT SLEEPERS. For sleeper trains, operated by First ScotRail, please refer to Tables 400 - 404

London and West Midlands - North West England and Scotland

		TP	VT	NT	TP	TP	VT	VT	XC	AW	LM	VT	NT	VT	VT	VT	VT	XC	LM	TP	VT	VT	VT	VT	XC
		◇1	■ 1		◇1	◇1	◇1	◇1	◇1		◇1	◇1		◇1	◇1	◇1	◇1	◇1	◇1	◇1	◇1	◇1	◇1	◇1	◇1
					A																				
			🛒		🍴		🛒	🛒	🍴			⊠		⊠	⊠	⊠	⊠	🍴		🍴	⊠	⊠	🛒	⊠	🍴
London Euston 15 ⊖	d						16 33	16 40				16 57		17 00	17 07	17 10	17 20				17 30	17 33		17 40	
Watford Junction	d																								
Milton Keynes Central	d															17u41	17u50								
Rugby	d						17 22															18 23			
Nuneaton	d															18 12									
Tamworth Low Level	d											18 00													
Lichfield Trent Valley	d											18 08													
Coventry	d																	17 27							
Birmingham International ✈	d																	17 38							
Birmingham New Street 12	d		17 20						17 31		17 36							17b57	18 01				18 20		18 31
Wolverhampton 7	d		17 37						17 50		17 54							18 15	18 19				18 37		18 49
Penkridge	d										18 04								18 29						
Stafford	a						17 52		18 01		18 10				18 24			18 29	18 35			18 52			
	d						17 56		18 02		18 10				18 25			18 30	18 35			18 56			
Stoke-on-Trent	a								18 20					18 24			18 49	18 54							19 18
Congleton	a																								
Macclesfield	a													18 41				19 11							
Crewe 10	a		18 07				18 15	18 10			18 31				18 43	18 53			19 00			19 15	19 07	19 10	
	d		18 09				18 17	18 11		18 23	18 33				18 45	18 56			19 02			19 17	19 09	19 11	
Chester	a									18 46						19 15									
Wrexham General	a																								
Llandudno	a																								
Bangor (Gwynedd)	a															20 27									
Holyhead	a															20 59									
Wilmslow	a							18 27																19 27	
Stockport	a							18 37	18 49					18 55			19 16	19 27						19 36	19 47
Manchester Piccadilly 10	a							18 49	18 59					19 07			19 28	19 39						19 49	20 00
Hartford	a										18 45														
Warrington Bank Quay	a		18 26				18 34					18 49									19 14		19 26		
	d		18 27				18 35					18 50									19 14		19 27		
Runcorn	a										18 58				19 02				19 22			19 34			
Liverpool South Parkway 7 ✈	a										19 07								19 31						
Liverpool Lime Street 10	a										19 18				19 23				19 44			19 52			
	d			17 44									18 01												
Manchester Airport ✈	d				18 00															18 29					
Manchester Piccadilly 10	d				18 16															18 46					
Bolton	d				18 33															19 07					
Wigan North Western	a		18 37	18 30			18 45					19 00	18 49								19 25		19 37		
	d		18 38	18 31			18 46					19 01	18 49								19 25		19 38		
Preston 8	a		18 51	18 54	18 55		18 59					19 14	18 54							19 33	19 38		19 51		
Blackpool North	a			19 23	>								19 15							20 05					
Preston 8	d		18 53		19 00	19 04						19 15									19 41		19 53		
Lancaster 6	a		19 08		19 15	19 20						19 30									19 54		20 08		
	d		19 09		19 16	19 20						19 30									19 55		20 08		
Barrow-in-Furness	a					20 24																			
Oxenholme Lake District	a		19 23		19 30							19 43									20 08				
	d		19 24		19 32							19 45									20 08				
Windermere	a																								
Penrith North Lakes	d				19 57							20 10											20 45		
Carlisle 8	a		20 02		20 14							20 25									20 46		21 00		
	d		20 03		20 15							20 25									20 47		21 02		
Lockerbie	d											20 44													
Carstairs	a																								
Motherwell	a											21 26													
Glasgow Central 15	a		21 17									21 47									22 01				
Haymarket	a				21s31																		22 14		
Edinburgh 10	a				21 39																		22 22		
Perth	a																								
Dundee	a																								
Aberdeen	a																								
Inverness	a																								

A Through portion to Barrow-in-Furness

b arr. 1748

OVERNIGHT SLEEPERS. For sleeper trains, operated by First ScotRail, please refer to Tables 400 - 404

London and West Midlands - North West England and Scotland

		TP	AW	LM	NT	VT	VT	VT	VT	VT	XC	LM	TP	VT	VT	VT	VT	XC	TP	AW	LM	XC	VT
		◇1		◇1		◇1	◇1	◇1	◇1	◇1	◇1	◇1	◇1	◇1	◇1	◇1	◇1	◇1	◇1		◇1	◇1	◇1
									A														
						⊠	⊠	⊠	⊠	⊠	⌶			⊠	⊠	⊡	⊠	⌶				⌶	⊠
London Euston 15 ⊖	d					17 57	18 00	18 07	18 10	18 20				18 30	18 33		18 40						18 43
Watford Junction	d																						
Milton Keynes Central	d								18u41	18u50													19 13
Rugby	d														19 23								
Nuneaton	d								19 13														
Tamworth Low Level	d					19 00																	
Lichfield Trent Valley	d					19 08																	
Coventry	d										18b27											19 27	19 42
Birmingham International ✈	d										18 38											19 38	19 53
Birmingham New Street 12	d			18 36							18c57	19 01				19 20		19 31			19 36	19e57	20f20
Wolverhampton 7	d			18 53							19 15	19 19				19 37		19 49			19 53	20 16	20 36
Penkridge	d			19 03								19 29									20 03		
Stafford	a			19 09				19 23			19 27	19 36			19 52			20 00			20 09	20 29	20 50
	d			19 09				19 24			19 29	19 36			19 56			20 01			20 09	20 30	20 52
Stoke-on-Trent	a						19 24			19 48	19 54							20 19				20 54	
Congleton	a																						
Macclesfield	a						19 41				20 11											21 11	
Crewe 10	a			19 30				19 42	19 53			20 01			20 15	20 07	20 10				20 30		21 15
	d		19 23	19 31				19 44	19 56						20 17	20 09	20 11			20 23	20 31		
Chester	a		19 46						20 15											20 46			
Wrexham General	a								20 38														
Llandudno	a																						
Bangor (Gwynedd)	a								21 25														
Holyhead	a								21 59														
Wilmslow	a																20 27						
Stockport	a						19 55			20 16	20 27						20 36	20 48				21 27	
Manchester Piccadilly 10	a						20 07			20 28	20 39						20 49	20 58				21 40	
Hartford	a			19 47																	20 45		
Warrington Bank Quay	a					19 49								20 14		20 26							
	d					19 50								20 14		20 27							
Runcorn	a			19 57				20 01							20 34						20 56		
Liverpool South Parkway 7 ✈	a			20 06																	21 05		
Liverpool Lime Street 10	a			20 18				20 21							20 53						21 16		
	d				19 23																		
Manchester Airport ✈	d	19 00											19 29						20 00				
Manchester Piccadilly 10	d	19 16											19 46						20 16				
Bolton	d	19 33											20 07						20 33				
Wigan North Western	a				19 54	20 00								20 25		20 37							
	d				19 55	20 01								20 25		20 38							
Preston 8	a	19 55			20 18	20 14							20 33	20 38		20 51			20 57				
Blackpool North	a				20 44								21 06										
Preston 8	d	19 58				20 15								20 41		20 53			20 59				
Lancaster 6	a	20 13				20 30								20 54		21 08			21 14				
	d	20 14				20 30								20 55		21 08			21 15				
Barrow-in-Furness	a	21 18																	22 18				
Oxenholme Lake District	a													21 08		21 22							
	d													21 09		21 24							
Windermere	a																						
Penrith North Lakes	d													21 34									
Carlisle 8	a					21 17								21 49		22 01							
	d					21 18								21 51		22 03							
Lockerbie	d					21 37																	
Carstairs	a																						
Motherwell	a					22 21																	
Glasgow Central 15	a					22 39								23 04		23 17							
Haymarket	a																						
Edinburgh 10	a																						
Perth	a																						
Dundee	a																						
Aberdeen	a																						
Inverness	a																						

A Through portion to Wrexham

b arr. 1822
c arr. 1848
e arr. 1948
f arr. 2008

OVERNIGHT SLEEPERS. For sleeper trains, operated by First ScotRail, please refer to Tables 400 - 404

London and West Midlands - North West England and Scotland

		VT	VT	VT	VT	VT	NT	TP	VT	VT	AW	NT	VT	XC	VT	AW	LM	VT	VT	XC	TP	NT	VT	VT
		FO								FO														
		■	■	■	■	■			■	■														
			1	1	1	1		◇1	1		◇		◇1	◇1	◇1		◇1	◇1	◇1	◇1	◇1		◇1	◇1
																				A				
		⊡	⊡	⊡	⊡	⊡			⊡	⊡	⌶		⊡		⊡			⊡	⊡	⌶			⊡	⊡
London Euston 15 ⊖	d	18 46	19 00	19 07	19 10	19 20			19 30				19 40		20 00			20 07	20 10				20 30	20 40
Watford Junction	d																							
Milton Keynes Central	d				19u40	19u50													20 41					
Rugby	d																							
Nuneaton	d			20 03														21 03						
Tamworth Low Level	d	20s04											20 43										21 34	
Lichfield Trent Valley	d	20s12											20 50										21 42	
Coventry	d																			20 27				
Birmingham International ✈	d																			20 38				
Birmingham New Street 12	d													20 31			20 36			20b58				
Wolverhampton 7	d													20 49			20 53			21 17				
Penkridge	d																21 03							
Stafford	a	20s35		20 26									21 02				21 09	21 27		21 31				
	d	20s36		20 27									21 04				21 09	21 27		21 32				
Stoke-on-Trent	a		20 24			20 48								21 18	21 23					21 54				
Congleton	a																							
Macclesfield	a		20 41												21 40					22 11				
Crewe 10	a	21s01			20 48								21 21				21 30		21 48					22 12
	d	21s03			20 50						21 00		21 23			21 23	21 31		21 50					22 13
Chester	a				21 10						21 21					21 46			22 12					
Wrexham General	a																							
Llandudno	a																							
Bangor (Gwynedd)	a				22 22						22 47													
Holyhead	a				22 56						23 21													
Wilmslow	a												21 38											22 29
Stockport	a		20 55			21 16								21 47	21 55					22 25				22 38
Manchester Piccadilly 10	a		21 07			21 28							21 57	22 00	22 07					22 35				22 48
Hartford	a																21 43							
Warrington Bank Quay	a	21s23							21 15														22 22	
	d	21s24							21 15														22 23	
Runcorn	a			21 01													21 54	21 59						
Liverpool South Parkway 7 ✈	a																22 05							
Liverpool Lime Street 10	a			21 21													22 15	22 20						
	d						20 25															21 42		
Manchester Airport ✈	d							20 29													21 29			
Manchester Piccadilly 10	d							20 46													21 46			
Bolton	d							21 07		←											22 07			
Wigan North Western	a	21s34					20 57		21 26	21s34												22 28	22 33	
	d	21s36					20 57		21 26	21s36												22 28	22 34	
Preston 8	a	→					21 22	21 33	21 39	21 51											22 33	22 55	22 53	
Blackpool North	a						21 53	22 06													23 02	23 22		
Preston 8	d								21 41			21 51												
Lancaster 6	a								21 55			22 11												
	d								21 56			22 11												
Barrow-in-Furness	a											23 16												
Oxenholme Lake District	a								22 09															
	d								22 09															
Windermere	a																							
Penrith North Lakes	d								22 35															
Carlisle 8	a								22 50															
	d								22 51															
Lockerbie	d																							
Carstairs	a																							
Motherwell	a																							
Glasgow Central 15	a								00 09															
Haymarket	a																							
Edinburgh 10	a																							
Perth	a																							
Dundee	a																							
Aberdeen	a																							
Inverness	a																							

A ⌶ to Birmingham International

b arr. 2048

OVERNIGHT SLEEPERS. For sleeper trains, operated by First ScotRail, please refer to Tables 400 - 404

London and West Midlands - North West England and Scotland

		VT	VT	TP	AW	LM	VT	XC	TP	VT	AW	SR	VT	XC	XC MTO	LM	NT	AW	VT	LM	SR FX	SR FO
		◇1	◇1	◇1		◇1	◇1	◇1	◇1	◇1		B	◇1	◇1 A	◇1	◇1		◇	◇1	◇1	B	B
		⊡	⊡				⊡			⊡		⊡	⊡					✕	⊡		⊡	⊡
London Euston 15 ⊖	d	21 00					21 07			21 10		21 15	21 40						22 00		23 50	23 50
Watford Junction	d									21u25		21u33									00u10	00u10
Milton Keynes Central	d	21 31					21 38												22 31			
Rugby	d									22 04									22 54			
Nuneaton	d						22 07												23 05			
Tamworth Low Level	d																		23s17			
Lichfield Trent Valley	d																		23s24			
Coventry	d							21 27														
Birmingham International ✈	d							21 38														
Birmingham New Street 12	d		21 20			21 36		21b57						22 28	22 28	22 36		22 55		23 09		
Wolverhampton 7	d		21 42			21 53		22 16						22 46	22 46	22 57		23 13		23 36		
Penkridge	d					22 03										23 07				23 46		
Stafford	a		21 54			22 09		22 29		22 34				22 58	22 58	23 13		23 30	23s38	23 52		
	d		21 55			22 09		22 30		22 35				22 59	22 59	23 13		23 30	23s39	23 53		
Stoke-on-Trent	a	22 28						22 53					23 06	23 20	23 20							
Congleton	a																					
Macclesfield	a	22 44						23 11					23 23									
Crewe 10	a		22 17			22 30	22 46			22 53						23 43		23 55	00s03	00 16		
	d		22 18		22 23	22 31	22 48			22 54	23 23	23u54						23 57	00s05			
Chester	a				22 45						23 44							00 18				
Wrexham General	a																					
Llandudno	a																					
Bangor (Gwynedd)	a																	01 45				
Holyhead	a																	02 15				
Wilmslow	a																					
Stockport	a	22 58						23 25					23 37						00s26			
Manchester Piccadilly 10	a	23 11						23 37					23 48	00 12	00 32				00 35			
Hartford	a					22 43																
Warrington Bank Quay	a		22 36							23 12												
	d		22 36							23 12												
Runcorn	a					22 56	23 07															
Liverpool South Parkway 7 ✈	a					23 07																
Liverpool Lime Street 10	a					23 23	23 31															
	d																23 02					
Manchester Airport ✈	d			22 00					22 29													
Manchester Piccadilly 10	d			22 16					22 46													
Bolton	d			22 33					23 07													
Wigan North Western	a		22 46	22 48						23 23							23 48					
	d		22 46	22 51						23 23							23 48					
Preston 8	a		23 02	23 09					23 33	23 41							00 13					
Blackpool North	a								00 02													
Preston 8	d			23 13								00u52										
Lancaster 6	a			23 28																		
	d			23 29																		
Barrow-in-Furness	a			00 32																		
Oxenholme Lake District	a																					
	d																					
Windermere	a																					
Penrith North Lakes	d																					
Carlisle 8	a																				05s11	05s18
	d																					
Lockerbie	d																					
Carstairs	a																				06s22	06s25
Motherwell	a																				07s01	06s59
Glasgow Central 15	a																				07 19	07 21
Haymarket	a																					
Edinburgh 10	a																				07 17	07 15
Perth	a											05s40										
Dundee	a											06s08										
Aberdeen	a											07 35										
Inverness	a											08 31										

A WThFO

b arr. 2148

OVERNIGHT SLEEPERS. For sleeper trains, operated by First ScotRail, please refer to Tables 400 - 404

London and West Midlands - North West England and Scotland

		TP	TP	NT	TP	TP	VT	VT	TP	AW	XC	LM	LM	XC
		◇1	◇1		◇1	◇1	◇1	◇1	◇1		◇1	◇1	◇1	◇1
							⊡	⊡	✕		✕			✕
London Euston 15 ⊖	d													
Watford Junction	d													
Milton Keynes Central	d													
Rugby	d													
Nuneaton	d													
Tamworth Low Level	d													
Lichfield Trent Valley	d													
Coventry	d													
Birmingham International ✈	d													
Birmingham New Street 12	d							05 30			05 57		06 01	06 31
Wolverhampton 7	d							05 48			06 16		06 18	06 49
Penkridge	d												06 29	
Stafford	a							06 00			06 29		06 35	07 00
	d							06 01			06 30		06 36	07 01
Stoke-on-Trent	a										06 50			07 18
Congleton	a										07 02			
Macclesfield	a										07 11			07 36
Crewe 10	a							06 20					06 56	
	d			00 44			05 57	06 23		06 27		06 32	06 57	
Chester	a							06 43						
Wrexham General	a													
Llandudno	a													
Bangor (Gwynedd)	a							07 49						
Holyhead	a							08 23						
Wilmslow	a									06 44				
Stockport	a									06 54	07 27			07 49
Manchester Piccadilly 10	a									07 09	07 38			07 59
Hartford	a											06 46	07 10	
Warrington Bank Quay	a						06 13							
	d						06 14							
Runcorn	a											06 59	07 20	
Liverpool South Parkway 7 ✈	a											07 08	07 30	
Liverpool Lime Street 10	a											07 22	07 42	
	d													
Manchester Airport ✈	d	00 01		01 20	04 00	05 29			06 18					
Manchester Piccadilly 10	d	00 16		01a36	04 15	05 46			06 33					
Bolton	d	00s32			04s29	06 02			06 50					
Wigan North Western	a						06 24							
	d						06 25							
Preston 8	a	01s03			05s04	06 35	06 37		07 11					
Blackpool North	a	01 30			05 33	07 06								
Preston 8	d						06 40		07 14					
Lancaster 6	a						06 54		07 30					
	d		05 46				06 54		07 30					
Barrow-in-Furness	a													
Oxenholme Lake District	a		06 21				07 08							
	d		06 21				07 10							
Windermere	a		06 41											
Penrith North Lakes	d						07 37		08 07					
Carlisle 8	a						07 50		08 24					
	d						07 51		08 25					
Lockerbie	d						08 10							
Carstairs	a													
Motherwell	a													
Glasgow Central 15	a						09 13		09 45					
Haymarket	a													
Edinburgh 10	a													
Perth	a													
Dundee	a													
Aberdeen	a													
Inverness	a													

OVERNIGHT SLEEPERS. For sleeper trains, operated by First ScotRail, please refer to Tables 400 - 404

London and West Midlands - North West England and Scotland

		NT	NT	AW	TP	VT	VT	TP	AW	LM	XC	TP	VT	LM	NT	NT	VT	VT	XC	VT	TP	AW	LM
				◇	◇1	◇1	◇1	◇1		◇1	◇1	◇1	◇1	◇1			◇1	◇1	◇1	◇1	◇1		◇1
						A	B																
				🛒		☕	☕	🛒			🛒	🛒	☕				☕	☕	🛒	☕	🛒		
London Euston 15 ⊖	d												06 05					06 36		06 55			
Watford Junction	d												06u20					06u51					
Milton Keynes Central	d												06 41							07 27			
Rugby	d												07 03										
Nuneaton	d																						
Tamworth Low Level	d																						
Lichfield Trent Valley	d																						
Coventry	d																						
Birmingham International ✈	d																						
Birmingham New Street 12	d					06 20	06 20			06 36	06 57			07 01			07 20		07 31				07 36
Wolverhampton 7	d					06 36	06 37			06 54	07 14			07 18			07 37		07 49				07 53
Penkridge	d													07 30									08 03
Stafford	a									07 08	07 29		07 34	07 36					08 00				08 09
	d									07 08	07 29		07 35	07 38					08 01				08 09
Stoke-on-Trent	a																		08 19	08 24			
Congleton	a																						
Macclesfield	a																		08 36	08 41			
Crewe 10	a					07 07	07 07			07 33	07 50		07 53	07 58			08 07	08 10					08 30
	d			07 03		07 08	07 09		07 23	07 35	07 53		07 55	08 00			08 09	08 11				08 23	08 31
Chester	a			07 23					07 46													08 46	
Wrexham General	a																						
Llandudno	a																						
Bangor (Gwynedd)	a			08 36																			
Holyhead	a			09 19																			
Wilmslow	a										08 09							08 27					
Stockport	a										08 20							08 37	08 49	08 55			
Manchester Piccadilly 10	a										08 35							08 49	08 59	09 07			
Hartford	a									07 48				08 11									
Warrington Bank Quay	a					07 26	07 26						08 11				08 27						
	d					07 26	07 27						08 12				08 28						
Runcorn	a									08 02				08 24									08 50
Liverpool South Parkway 7 ✈	a									08 11				08 33									08 59
Liverpool Lime Street 10	a									08 24				08 46									09 12
	d		06 57												07 57								
Manchester Airport ✈	d							07 00				07 25									07 58		
Manchester Piccadilly 10	d							07 15				07 45									08 15		
Bolton	d	07 01						07 31				07 59									08 32		
Wigan North Western	a	07 19	07 30			07 37	07 37						08 22		08 30		08 38						
	d		07 31			07 37	07 38						08 23		08 31		08 39						
Preston 8	a		07 54			07 50	07 51	07 57				08 22	08 36		08 54		08 52				08 58		
Blackpool North	a		08 21					08 29							09 21						09 25		
Preston 8	d				07 20	07 52	07 53					08 24	08 37			08 42	08 54						
Lancaster 6	a				07 36	08 08	08 08					08 39	08 52			09 02	09 09						
	d				07 36	08 09	08 09					08 40	08 52			09 02	09 09						
Barrow-in-Furness	a				08 39											10 07							
Oxenholme Lake District	a					08 22	08 22					08 54	09 05										
	d					08 23	08 23					08 54	09 06										
Windermere	a																						
Penrith North Lakes	d											09 20	09 32				09 46						
Carlisle 8	a					09 01	09 01					09 34	09 47				10 01						
	d					09 02	09 02					09 36	09 48				10 04						
Lockerbie	d											09 55											
Carstairs	a																						
Motherwell	a																						
Glasgow Central 15	a												11 03				11 17						
Haymarket	a					10 16	10 16					11s04											
Edinburgh 10	a					10 22	10 22					11 10											
Perth	a																						
Dundee	a																						
Aberdeen	a																						
Inverness	a																						

A from 17 July until 4 September
B until 10 July and from 11 September

OVERNIGHT SLEEPERS. For sleeper trains, operated by First ScotRail, please refer to Tables 400 - 404

London and West Midlands - North West England and Scotland

		VT	XC	LM	VT	TP	XC	VT	VT	VT	VT	NT	AW	LM	VT	VT	XC	LM	VT	XC
		◇1	◇1	◇1	◇1	◇1	◇1	◇1	◇1	◇1	◇1			◇1	◇1	◇1	◇1	◇1	◇1	◇1
						A														
		☕	🛒		☕	🛒	☕	☕	☕	☕	☕				☕	☕	🛒		☕	☕
London Euston 15 ⊖	d	07 07						07 20	07 30	07 35	08 00				08 07	08 10				
Watford Junction	d																			
Milton Keynes Central	d							07 50		08 06						08 41				
Rugby	d																			
Nuneaton	d																			
Tamworth Low Level	d																			
Lichfield Trent Valley	d																			
Coventry	d		07 27														08 27			
Birmingham International ✈	d		07 40														08 38			
Birmingham New Street 12	d		07b57	08 01	08 20		08 31							08 36			08e57	09 01	09 20	09 31
Wolverhampton 7	d		08 15	08 19	08 37		08 49							08 53			09 15	09 19	09 37	09 49
Penkridge	d			08 29										09 03						
Stafford	a	08 22	08 29	08 35			09 00							09 09	09 22		09 29	09 34		10 00
	d	08 23	08 30	08 36			09 01							09 09	09 23		09 30	09 35		10 01
Stoke-on-Trent	a		08 54				09 19	08 48			09 24						09 54			10 19
Congleton	a																			
Macclesfield	a		09 11								09 41						10 11			
Crewe 10	a	08 41		08 56	09 07					09 10				09 30		09 48		09 56	10 07	
	d	08 43		08 58	09 09					09 11			09 23	09 31		09 50		09 57	10 09	
Chester	a												09 46			10 12				
Wrexham General	a																			
Llandudno	a																			
Bangor (Gwynedd)	a																			
Holyhead	a																			
Wilmslow	a									09 27										
Stockport	a		09 27				09 49	09 16		09 36	09 55						10 27			10 49
Manchester Piccadilly 10	a		09 39				09 59	09 28		09 49	10 07						10 39			10 59
Hartford	a			09 11														10 10		
Warrington Bank Quay	a				09 26				09 14										10 26	
	d				09 27				09 14										10 27	
Runcorn	a	09 00		09 21										09 50	09 55			10 22		
Liverpool South Parkway 7 ✈	a			09 30										09 59				10 31		
Liverpool Lime Street 10	a	09 21		09 43										10 10	10 15			10 44		
	d											08 57								
Manchester Airport ✈	d					08 25														
Manchester Piccadilly 10	d					08 46														
Bolton	d					09 07														
Wigan North Western	a				09 37				09 25			09 30							10 37	
	d				09 38				09 25			09 31							10 38	
Preston 8	a				→	09 30			09 38			09 54							→	
Blackpool North	a											10 21								
Preston 8	d					09 32			09 41											
Lancaster 6	a					09 47			09 54											
	d					09 48			09 55											
Barrow-in-Furness	a																			
Oxenholme Lake District	a					10 04														
	d					10 05														
Windermere	a					10 26														
Penrith North Lakes	d								10 31											
Carlisle 8	a								10 46											
	d								10 47											
Lockerbie	d																			
Carstairs	a																			
Motherwell	a																			
Glasgow Central 15	a								12 01											
Haymarket	a																			
Edinburgh 10	a																			
Perth	a																			
Dundee	a																			
Aberdeen	a																			
Inverness	a																			

A 🛒 to Preston
b arr. 0751
c arr. 0748
e arr. 0848
f arr. 0847

OVERNIGHT SLEEPERS. For sleeper trains, operated by First ScotRail, please refer to Tables 400 - 404

London and West Midlands - North West England and Scotland

		VT ◇1 ☕	TP ◇1	VT ◇1 ☕	TP ◇1 🍴	TP ◇1 🍴	VT ◇1 ☕	VT ◇1 ☕		NT	LM ◇1	AW	LM ◇1	XC ◇1 🍴	VT ◇1 A ☕	VT ◇1 ☕	VT ◇1 ☕	VT ◇1 ☕		VT ◇1 ☕	TP ◇1	VT ◇1 ☕	TP ◇1 🍴	TP ◇1 🍴	VT ◇1 ☕
London Euston ⊖	d	08 20					08 30	08 40							08 43	08 50	09 00	09 07		09 20					09 30
Watford Junction	d															09 05									
Milton Keynes Central	d	08 50													09 13	09 25				09 50					
Rugby	d																								
Nuneaton	d																								
Tamworth Low Level	d																								
Lichfield Trent Valley	d																								
Coventry	d													09 27	09 42										
Birmingham International ✈	d													09 39	09 53										
Birmingham New Street	d										10 01		09 36	09b57	10c20										
Wolverhampton	d										10 19		09 53	10 15	10 37										
Penkridge	d												10 03												
Stafford	a										10 35		10 09	10 29				10 22							
	d										10 35		10 09	10 30				10 23							
Stoke-on-Trent	a	09 48												10 54			10 24			10 48					
Congleton	a																								
Macclesfield	a													11 11			10 41								
Crewe	a							10 10			10 56		10 30		11 07	10 34									
	d							10 11			10 57	10 23	10 31		11 10	10 45									
Chester	a											10 46				11 12									
Wrexham General	a																								
Llandudno	a																								
Bangor (Gwynedd)	a															12 22									
Holyhead	a															12 58									
Wilmslow	a							10 27																	
Stockport	a	10 16						10 36						11 27			10 55			11 16					
Manchester Piccadilly	a	10 28						10 49						11 39			11 07			11 28					
Hartford	a										11 11														
Warrington Bank Quay	a						10 14								11 27										11 14
	d						10 14								11 28										11 14
Runcorn	a										11 21		10 50					10 55							
Liverpool South Parkway ✈	a										11 30		10 59												
Liverpool Lime Street	a										11 43		11 10					11 15							
	d									09 57															
Manchester Airport ✈	d				09 00	09 29																	10 00	10 29	
Manchester Piccadilly	d				09 16	09 46																	10 16	10 46	
Bolton	d			←	09 33	10 07																←	10 33	11 07	
Wigan North Western	a			09 37			10 25			10 30					11 38							10 37			11 25
	d			09 38			10 25			10 31					11 39							10 38			11 25
Preston	a			09 51	09 55	10 33	10 38			10 54					→							10 51	10 55	11 33	11 38
Blackpool North	a					11 05				11 21														12 05	
Preston	d		09 45	09 53	09 58		10 41														10 45	10 53	10 58		11 41
Lancaster	a		10 00	10 08	10 13		10 54														11 00	11 08	11 13		11 54
	d		10 01	10 08	10 14		10 55														11 01	11 08	11 14		11 55
Barrow-in-Furness	a		11 03																						
Oxenholme Lake District	a			10 22			11 08														11 17		11 28		
	d			10 24			11 08														11 18		11 28		
Windermere	a																				11 39				
Penrith North Lakes	d				10 53																	11 45	11 53		12 30
Carlisle	a			11 01	11 10		11 46															12 00	12 10		12 45
	d			11 03	11 11		11 47															12 03	12 11		12 47
Lockerbie	d				11 30																		12 30		
Carstairs	a																								
Motherwell	a																								
Glasgow Central	a				12 32		13 01															13 17			14 01
Haymarket	a			12 16																			13s34		
Edinburgh	a			12 22																			13 39		
Perth	a																								
Dundee	a																								
Aberdeen	a																								
Inverness	a																								

A from 17 July until 4 September

b arr. 0948

c arr. 1008

OVERNIGHT SLEEPERS. For sleeper trains, operated by First ScotRail, please refer to Tables 400 - 404

London and West Midlands - North West England and Scotland

		NT	VT ◇1 A ☕	VT ◇1 B ☕		VT ◇1 ☕	XC ◇1 ☕	VT ◇1 ☕	TP ◇1 C 🍴	AW	LM ◇1	VT ◇1 ☕	VT ◇1 ☕	VT ◇1 ☕		XC ◇1 🍴	LM ◇1	TP ◇1 🍴	VT ◇1 ☕	NT	VT ◇1 ☕	VT ◇1 ☕	XC ◇1 ☕	VT ◇1 ☕	
London Euston ⊖	d					09 40		10 00				10 07	10 10	10 20					10 30			10 40		11 00	
Watford Junction	d																								
Milton Keynes Central	d												10 41	10 50											
Rugby	d																								
Nuneaton	d																								
Tamworth Low Level	d																								
Lichfield Trent Valley	d																								
Coventry	d															10 27									
Birmingham International ✈	d															10 38									
Birmingham New Street	d		10 20				10 31				10 36					10b57	11 01				11 20		11 31		
Wolverhampton	d		10 37				10 49				10 53					11 15	11 19				11 37		11 49		
Penkridge	d										11 03														
Stafford	a						11 00				11 09	11 22				11 29	11 35						12 00		
	d						11 01				11 09	11 23				11 30	11 35						12 01		
Stoke-on-Trent	a						11 19	11 24						11 48		11 54							12 19	12 24	
Congleton	a																								
Macclesfield	a							11 41								12 11								12 41	
Crewe	a		11 07			11 10					11 30		11 48				11 56				12 07	12 10			
	d		11 09			11 11				11 23	11 31		11 50				11 57				12 09	12 11			
Chester	a									11 46			12 12												
Wrexham General	a																								
Llandudno	a																								
Bangor (Gwynedd)	a																								
Holyhead	a																								
Wilmslow	a					11 27																12 27			
Stockport	a					11 36	11 49	11 55						12 16		12 27						12 36	12 49	12 55	
Manchester Piccadilly	a					11 49	11 59	12 07						12 28		12 39						12 49	12 59	13 07	
Hartford	a																12 10								
Warrington Bank Quay	a		11 26																12 14		12 26				
	d		11 27																12 14		12 27				
Runcorn	a										11 50	11 55					12 22								
Liverpool South Parkway ✈	a										11 59						12 31								
Liverpool Lime Street	a										12 10	12 15					12 44								
	d	10 57																		11 57					
Manchester Airport ✈	d								11 00									11 29							
Manchester Piccadilly	d								11 16									11 46							
Bolton	d			←					11 33									12 07							
Wigan North Western	a	11 30	11 37	11 38															12 25	12 30	12 37				
	d	11 31	11 38	11 39															12 25	12 31	12 38				
Preston	a	11 54	11 51	11 52					11 55									12 33	12 38	12 54	12 51				
Blackpool North	a	12 21																13 05		13 21					
Preston	d		11 53	11 53					11 58										12 41		12 53				
Lancaster	a		12 08	12 08					12 13										12 54		13 08				
	d		12 08	12 08					12 14										12 55		13 08				
Barrow-in-Furness	a								13 10																
Oxenholme Lake District	a		12 22	12 22															13 08		13 22				
	d		12 24	12 24															13 09		13 24				
Windermere	a																								
Penrith North Lakes	d																								
Carlisle	a		13 01	13 01															13 46		14 01				
	d		13 03	13 03															13 47		14 03				
Lockerbie	d																								
Carstairs	a																								
Motherwell	a																								
Glasgow Central	a																		15 01		15 17				
Haymarket	a		14 16	14 16																					
Edinburgh	a		14 22	14 22																					
Perth	a																								
Dundee	a																								
Aberdeen	a																								
Inverness	a																								

A until 10 July and from 11 September
B from 17 July until 4 September

C 🍴 to Preston

b arr. 1048

OVERNIGHT SLEEPERS. For sleeper trains, operated by First ScotRail, please refer to Tables 400 - 404

London and West Midlands - North West England and Scotland

		TP	AW	LM	VT	VT	VT	XC	LM	TP	VT	NT	TP	VT	VT	XC	VT	TP	AW	LM	VT	VT
		◇1		◇1	◇1	◇1	◇1	◇1	◇1	◇1	◇1		◇1	◇1	◇1	◇1	◇1	◇1		◇1	◇1	◇1
London Euston ⊖	d				11 07	11 10	11 20				11 30				11 40		12 00				12 07	12 10
Watford Junction	d																					
Milton Keynes Central	d					11 41	11 50															12 41
Rugby	d																					
Nuneaton	d																					
Tamworth Low Level	d																					
Lichfield Trent Valley	d																					
Coventry	d							11 27														
Birmingham International ✈	d							11 38														
Birmingham New Street	d			11 36				11b57	12 01					12 20		12 31				12 36		
Wolverhampton	d			11 53				12 15	12 19					12 37		12 49				12 53		
Penkridge	d			12 03																13 03		
Stafford	a			12 09	12 22			12 29	12 35							13 00				13 09	13 22	
	d			12 09	12 23			12 30	12 35							13 01				13 09	13 23	
Stoke-on-Trent	a						12 48	12 54								13 19	13 24					
Congleton	a																					
Macclesfield	a							13 11									13 41					
Crewe	a			12 30		12 47			12 56					13 07	13 10					13 30		13 47
	d		12 23	12 31		12 49			12 57					13 09	13 11				13 23	13 31		13 49
Chester	a		12 46			13 12													13 46			14 12
Wrexham General	a																					
Llandudno	a																					
Bangor (Gwynedd)	a																					
Holyhead	a																					
Wilmslow	a														13 27							
Stockport	a						13 16	13 27							13 36	13 49	13 55					
Manchester Piccadilly	a						13 28	13 39							13 49	13 59	14 07					
Hartford	a								13 11													
Warrington Bank Quay	a										13 14			13 26								
	d										13 14			13 27								
Runcorn	a			12 50	12 55				13 21											13 50	13 55	
Liverpool South Parkway ✈	a			12 59					13 30											13 59		
Liverpool Lime Street	a			13 10	13 15				13 43											14 10	14 15	
	d											12 57										
Manchester Airport ✈	d	12 00								12 29								13 00				
Manchester Piccadilly	d	12 16								12 46								13 16				
Bolton	d	12 33								13 07								13 33				
Wigan North Western	a										13 25	13 30		13 37								
	d										13 25	13 31		13 38								
Preston	a	12 55								13 33	13 38	13 54		13 51				13 55				
Blackpool North	a									14 05		14 21										
Preston	d	12 58									13 41		13 04	13 53				13 58				
Lancaster	a	13 13									13 54		13 19	14 08				14 13				
	d	13 14									13 55		13 20	14 08				14 14				
Barrow-in-Furness	a																					
Oxenholme Lake District	a	13 28											13 36					14 28				
	d	13 28											13 37					14 28				
Windermere	a												13 56									
Penrith North Lakes	d	13 53									14 08			14 45				14 53				
Carlisle	a	14 10									14 46			15 00				15 12				
	d	14 11									14 47			15 02				15 14				
Lockerbie	d	14 30																15 33				
Carstairs	a																					
Motherwell	a																	16s23				
Glasgow Central	a										16 01							16 42				
Haymarket	a	15s34												16 15								
Edinburgh	a	15 40												16 22								
Perth	a																					
Dundee	a																					
Aberdeen	a																					
Inverness	a																					

OVERNIGHT SLEEPERS. For sleeper trains, operated by First ScotRail, please refer to Tables 400 - 404

London and West Midlands - North West England and Scotland

		VT	XC	LM	TP	VT	NT	TP	VT	VT	XC	VT	TP	AW	LM	VT	VT	VT	XC	LM	TP	VT	NT
		◇1	◇1	◇1	◇1	◇1		◇1	◇1	◇1	◇1	◇1	◇1		◇1	◇1	◇1	◇1	◇1	◇1	◇1	◇1	
London Euston ⊖	d	12 20				12 30				12 40		13 00				13 07	13 10	13 20				13 30	
Watford Junction	d																						
Milton Keynes Central	d	12 50															13 41	13 50					
Rugby	d																						
Nuneaton	d																						
Tamworth Low Level	d																						
Lichfield Trent Valley	d																						
Coventry	d		12 27																13 27				
Birmingham International ✈	d		12 38																13 38				
Birmingham New Street	d		12b57	13 01					13 20		13 31				13 36				13c57	14 01			
Wolverhampton	d		13 15	13 19					13 37		13 49				13 53				14 15	14 19			
Penkridge	d														14 03								
Stafford	a		13 29	13 35							14 00				14 09	14 22			14 29	14 35			
	d		13 30	13 35							14 01				14 09	14 23			14 30	14 35			
Stoke-on-Trent	a	13 48	13 54								14 19	14 24						14 48	14 54				
Congleton	a																						
Macclesfield	a		14 11									14 41							15 11				
Crewe	a			13 56					14 07	14 10					14 30		14 48			14 56			
	d			13 57					14 09	14 11				14 23	14 31		14 50			14 57			
Chester	a													14 46			15 12						
Wrexham General	a																						
Llandudno	a																						
Bangor (Gwynedd)	a																						
Holyhead	a																						
Wilmslow	a									14 27													
Stockport	a	14 16	14 27							14 36	14 49	14 55						15 16	15 27				
Manchester Piccadilly	a	14 28	14 39							14 49	14 59	15 07						15 28	15 39				
Hartford	a			14 11																15 11			
Warrington Bank Quay	a					14 14			14 26													15 14	
	d					14 14			14 27													15 14	
Runcorn	a			14 21											14 50	14 55				15 21			
Liverpool South Parkway ✈	a			14 30											14 59					15 30			
Liverpool Lime Street	a			14 43											15 10	15 15				15 43			
	d						13 57																14 57
Manchester Airport ✈	d				13 29								14 00								14 29		
Manchester Piccadilly	d				13 46								14 16								14 46		
Bolton	d				14 07								14 33								15 07		
Wigan North Western	a					14 25	14 30		14 37													15 25	15 30
	d					14 25	14 31		14 38													15 25	15 31
Preston	a				14 33	14 38	14 54		14 51				14 55								15 33	15 38	15 54
Blackpool North	a				15 05		15 21														16 05		16 21
Preston	d					14 41		14 47	14 53				14 58									15 41	
Lancaster	a					14 54		15 02	15 08				15 13									15 54	
	d					14 55		15 03	15 09				15 14									15 56	
Barrow-in-Furness	a							15 58															
Oxenholme Lake District	a								15 22				15 28									16 08	
	d								15 24				15 28									16 09	
Windermere	a																						
Penrith North Lakes	d					15 30							15 53										
Carlisle	a					15 45			16 01				16 10									16 46	
	d					15 47			16 03				16 11									16 47	
Lockerbie	d												16 30										
Carstairs	a																						
Motherwell	a																						
Glasgow Central	a					17 01			17 17													18 01	
Haymarket	a												17s30										
Edinburgh	a												17 39										
Perth	a																						
Dundee	a																						
Aberdeen	a																						
Inverness	a																						

b arr. 1248

c arr. 1348

OVERNIGHT SLEEPERS. For sleeper trains, operated by First ScotRail, please refer to Tables 400 - 404

Table 65

Saturdays
until 16 October

London and West Midlands - North West England and Scotland

		VT	VT	XC	TP	LM	AW	LM	XC	VT	VT	VT	VT	VT	TP	VT	NT	VT	VT	VT	XC	VT
		◇1	◇1	◇1	◇1	◇1		◇1	◇1	◇1	◇1	◇1	◇1	◇1	◇1	◇1		◇1	◇1	◇1	◇1	◇1
					A					B								B	C			
London Euston 15 ⊖	d		13 40							13 43	14 00	14 07	14 10	14 20		14 30				14 40		15 00
Watford Junction	d																					
Milton Keynes Central	d									14 13			14 41	14 50								
Rugby	d																					
Nuneaton	d																					
Tamworth Low Level	d																					
Lichfield Trent Valley	d																					
Coventry	d								14 27	14 43												
Birmingham International ✈	d								14 38	14 54												
Birmingham New Street 12	d	14 20		14 31		15 01		14 36	14b57	15c20									15 20		15 31	
Wolverhampton 7	d	14 37		14 49		15 19		14 53	15 15	15 37									15 37		15 49	
Penkridge	d							15 03														
Stafford	a			15 00		15 35		15 09	15 29			15 22									16 00	
	d			15 01		15 35		15 09	15 30			15 23									16 01	
Stoke-on-Trent	a			15 19					15 54		15 24			15 48							16 19	16 24
Congleton	a																					
Macclesfield	a								16 11		15 41											16 41
Crewe 10	a	15 07	15 10			15 56		15 30		16 08			15 47						16 08	16 11		
	d	15 09	15 11			15 57	15 23	15 31		16 09			15 49						16 09	16 12		
Chester	a						15 46						16 10									
Wrexham General	a																					
Llandudno	a																					
Bangor (Gwynedd)	a												17 17									
Holyhead	a												17 51									
Wilmslow	a		15 27																	16 27		
Stockport	a		15 36	15 49					16 27		15 55			16 16						16 36	16 49	16 54
Manchester Piccadilly 10	a		15 49	15 59					16 39		16 07			16 28						16 49	16 59	17 07
Hartford	a					16 10																
Warrington Bank Quay	a	15 26								16 26						16 14			16 26			
	d	15 27								16 27						16 14			16 27			
Runcorn	a					16 23		15 50				15 55										
Liverpool South Parkway 7 ✈	a					16 32		15 59														
Liverpool Lime Street 10	a					16 44		16 10				16 15										
	d																15 57					
Manchester Airport ✈	d				15 00										15 29							
Manchester Piccadilly 10	d				15 16										15 46							
Bolton	d				15 33										16 07			←				
Wigan North Western	a	15 37								16 37						16 25	16 30	16 37	16 37			
	d	15 38								16 38						16 25	16 31	16 38	16 38			
Preston 8	a	15 51			15 55					→					16 33	16 38	16 54	16 51	16 51			
Blackpool North	a														17 07		17 21					
Preston 8	d	15 53			15 58											16 41		16 53	16 53			
Lancaster 6	a	16 08			16 13											16 54		17 09	17 09			
	d	16 09			16 14											16 55		17 10	17 10			
Barrow-in-Furness	a				17 18																	
Oxenholme Lake District	a																	17 24	17 24			
	d																	17 25	17 25			
Windermere	a																					
Penrith North Lakes	d	16 45														17 30						
Carlisle 8	a	17 00														17 45		18 03	18 03			
	d	17 03														17 47		18 04	18 04			
Lockerbie	d																					
Carstairs	a																					
Motherwell	a																					
Glasgow Central 15	a															19 01		19 17	19 17			
Haymarket	a	18 14																				
Edinburgh 10	a	18 22																				
Perth	a																					
Dundee	a																					
Aberdeen	a																					
Inverness	a																					

A to Preston
B from 17 July until 4 September
C until 10 July and from 11 September
b arr. 1448
c arr. 1508

OVERNIGHT SLEEPERS. For sleeper trains, operated by First ScotRail, please refer to Tables 400 - 404

Table 65

Saturdays
until 16 October

London and West Midlands - North West England and Scotland

		TP	AW	LM	VT	VT	VT	XC	LM	TP	TP	VT	NT	VT	VT	XC	VT	TP	NT	AW	LM	VT	VT
		◇1		◇1	◇1	◇1	◇1	◇1	◇1	◇1	◇1	◇1		◇1	◇1	◇1	◇1	◇1			◇1	◇1	◇1
																		A					
London Euston 15 ⊖	d				15 07	15 10	15 20					15 30			15 40		16 00					16 07	16 10
Watford Junction	d																						
Milton Keynes Central	d					15 41	15 50																16 41
Rugby	d																						
Nuneaton	d																						
Tamworth Low Level	d																						
Lichfield Trent Valley	d																						
Coventry	d							15 27															
Birmingham International ✈	d							15 38															
Birmingham New Street 12	d			15 36				15b57	16 01					16 20		16 31					16 36		
Wolverhampton 7	d			15 53				16 15	16 19					16 37		16 49					16 53		
Penkridge	d			16 03																	17 03		
Stafford	a			16 09	16 22			16 29	16 35							17 00					17 09	17 22	
	d			16 09	16 23			16 30	16 35							17 01					17 09	17 23	
Stoke-on-Trent	a						16 48	16 54								17 19	17 24						
Congleton	a																						
Macclesfield	a							17 11									17 41						
Crewe 10	a			16 30		16 47			16 56					17 07	17 10						17 30		17 47
	d		16 23	16 31		16 49			16 57					17 09	17 11					17 23	17 31		17 49
Chester	a		16 46			17 12														17 46			18 09
Wrexham General	a																						
Llandudno	a																						
Bangor (Gwynedd)	a																						19 21
Holyhead	a																						19 55
Wilmslow	a														17 27								
Stockport	a						17 16	17 27							17 36	17 49	17 55						
Manchester Piccadilly 10	a						17 28	17 39							17 49	17 59	18 07						
Hartford	a								17 11														
Warrington Bank Quay	a											17 14		17 26									
	d											17 14		17 27									
Runcorn	a			16 50	16 55				17 21												17 50	17 55	
Liverpool South Parkway 7 ✈	a			16 59					17 30												17 59		
Liverpool Lime Street 10	a			17 10	17 15				17 43												18 10	18 15	
	d												16 57						17 27				
Manchester Airport ✈	d	16 00								16 29								17 00					
Manchester Piccadilly 10	d	16 16								16 46								17 15					
Bolton	d	16 33								17 06								17 32					
Wigan North Western	a											17 25	17 30	17 37					18 05				
	d											17 25	17 31	17 38					18 05				
Preston 8	a	16 55								17 30		17 38	17 54	17 51				17 55	18 31				
Blackpool North	a									18 02			18 24										
Preston 8	d	17 00									17 04	17 41		17 53				17 58					
Lancaster 6	a	17 15									17 20	17 54		18 08				18 13					
	d	17 16									17 21	17 55		18 08				18 14					
Barrow-in-Furness	a																	19 18					
Oxenholme Lake District	a	17 30									17 38	18 08		18 22									
	d	17 30									17 38	18 08		18 23									
Windermere	a										18 00												
Penrith North Lakes	d													18 49									
Carlisle 8	a	18 10										18 46		19 04									
	d	18 11										18 47		19 04									
Lockerbie	d	18 30																					
Carstairs	a																						
Motherwell	a																						
Glasgow Central 15	a											20 01											
Haymarket	a	19s31												20 19									
Edinburgh 10	a	19 39												20 24									
Perth	a																						
Dundee	a																						
Aberdeen	a																						
Inverness	a																						

A to Bolton
b arr. 1548

OVERNIGHT SLEEPERS. For sleeper trains, operated by First ScotRail, please refer to Tables 400 - 404

Table 65

Saturdays
until 16 October

London and West Midlands - North West England and Scotland

		VT	XC	VT	LM	VT	TP	VT	VT	XC	VT	TP	NT	AW	LM	VT	VT	VT	XC	LM	TP	TP
		◇1	◇1	◇1	◇1	◇1	◇1	◇1	◇1	◇1	◇1	◇1			◇1	◇1	◇1	◇1	◇1	◇1	◇1	◇1
London Euston 15 ⊖	d	16 20		16 30		16 33			16 40		17 00					17 07	17 10	17 20				
Watford Junction	d																					
Milton Keynes Central	d	16 50															17 41	17 50				
Rugby	d																					
Nuneaton	d															18 03						
Tamworth Low Level	d					17 38																
Lichfield Trent Valley	d					17 45																
Coventry	d		16 27																17 27			
Birmingham International ✈	d		16 38																17 38			
Birmingham New Street 12	d		16b57		17 01			17 20		17 31					17 36				17c57	18 01		
Wolverhampton 7	d		17 15		17 19			17 37		17 49					17 53				18 15	18 19		
Penkridge	d				17 29										18 03					18 29		
Stafford	a		17 29		17 35	17 59				18 00					18 09	18 26			18 29	18 35		
	d		17 30		17 36	17 59				18 01					18 09	18 27			18 30	18 35		
Stoke-on-Trent	a	17 48	17 54							18 19	18 24							18 48	18 54			
Congleton	a																					
Macclesfield	a		18 11								18 41								19 11			
Crewe 10	a				17 56			18 07	18 10						18 30		18 48			18 56		
	d				18 00			18 09	18 11					18 23	18 33		18 50			18 59		
Chester	a													18 46			19 10					
Wrexham General	a																					
Llandudno	a																					
Bangor (Gwynedd)	a																20 22					
Holyhead	a																20 56					
Wilmslow	a								18 27													
Stockport	a	18 16	18 27						18 36	18 49	18 55							19 16	19 27			
Manchester Piccadilly 10	a	18 28	18 39						18 49	18 59	19 07							19 28	19 40			
Hartford	a				18 13										18 43					19 12		
Warrington Bank Quay	a			18 14				18 26														
	d			18 14				18 27														
Runcorn	a				18 23	18 31									18 52	18 59				19 22		
Liverpool South Parkway 7 ✈	a				18 32										19 02					19 31		
Liverpool Lime Street 10	a				18 44	18 53									19 14	19 17				19 44		
	d												17 44									
Manchester Airport ✈	d						17 29					18 00									18 29	
Manchester Piccadilly 10	d						17 46					18 16									18 46	
Bolton	d						18 07					18 33									19 07	
Wigan North Western	a			18 25				18 37					18 30									
	d			18 25				18 38					18 31									
Preston 8	a			18 38			18 38	18 51				18 55	18 54								19 33	
Blackpool North	a						19 09						19 21								20 05	
Preston 8	d			18 41				18 53				19 00										19 04
Lancaster 6	a			18 54				19 08				19 15										19 20
	d			18 55				19 08				19 16										19 20
Barrow-in-Furness	a																					20 24
Oxenholme Lake District	a			19 08				19 22				19 30										
	d			19 09				19 24				19 30										
Windermere	a																					
Penrith North Lakes	d			19 34								19 55										
Carlisle 8	a			19 49				20 01				20 12										
	d			19 51				20 03				20 13										
Lockerbie	d											20 32										
Carstairs	a																					
Motherwell	a																					
Glasgow Central 15	a			21 01				21 17				21 32										
Haymarket	a																					
Edinburgh 10	a																					
Perth	a																					
Dundee	a																					
Aberdeen	a																					
Inverness	a																					

b arr. 1648 c arr. 1748

OVERNIGHT SLEEPERS. For sleeper trains, operated by First ScotRail, please refer to Tables 400 - 404

Table 65

Saturdays
until 16 October

London and West Midlands - North West England and Scotland

		VT	TP	VT	VT	XC	VT	LM	VT	AW	VT	VT	XC	LM	NT	TP	VT	VT	TP	VT	VT	XC	VT
		◇1	◇1	◇1	◇1	◇1	◇1	◇1	◇1		◇1	◇1	◇1	◇1		◇1	◇1	◇1	◇1	◇1	◇1	◇1	◇1
London Euston 15 ⊖	d	17 30			17 40		18 00		18 07		18 10	18 20					18 30	18 33			18 40		19 00
Watford Junction	d																						
Milton Keynes Central	d										18 41	18 50											
Rugby	d																						
Nuneaton	d																						
Tamworth Low Level	d																	19 38					
Lichfield Trent Valley	d																	19 46					
Coventry	d												18 27										
Birmingham International ✈	d												18 38										
Birmingham New Street 12	d			18 20		18 31		18 36					18b57	19 01						19 20		19 31	
Wolverhampton 7	d			18 37		18 49		18 53					19 15	19 19						19 37		19 49	
Penkridge	d							19 03						19 29									
Stafford	a					19 00		19 09	19 22				19 29	19 35				19 58				20 00	
	d					19 01		19 09	19 23				19 30	19 36				19 59				20 01	
Stoke-on-Trent	a					19 19	19 24					19 48	19 54									20 19	20 24
Congleton	a																						
Macclesfield	a						19 41						20 11									20 36	20 41
Crewe 10	a			19 07	19 10			19 30			19 48			19 58						20 07	20 10		
	d			19 09	19 11					19 23	19 50			19 58						20 09	20 11		
Chester	a									19 46	20 12												
Wrexham General	a																						
Llandudno	a																						
Bangor (Gwynedd)	a																						
Holyhead	a																						
Wilmslow	a				19 27																20 27		
Stockport	a				19 36	19 49	19 55					20 16	20 27								20 36	20 49	20 55
Manchester Piccadilly 10	a				19 49	19 59	20 07					20 28	20 39								20 49	20 59	21 07
Hartford	a													20 11									
Warrington Bank Quay	a	19 14		19 26													20 14			20 26			
	d	19 14		19 27													20 14			20 27			
Runcorn	a								19 55					20 24				20 32					
Liverpool South Parkway 7 ✈	a													20 33									
Liverpool Lime Street 10	a								20 15					20 46				20 52					
	d														19 23								
Manchester Airport ✈	d		19 00													19 29			20 00				
Manchester Piccadilly 10	d		19 16													19 46			20 16				
Bolton	d		19 33													20 07			20 33				
Wigan North Western	a	19 25		19 37											19 54		20 25			20 37			
	d	19 25		19 38											19 55		20 25			20 38			
Preston 8	a	19 38	19 58	19 59											20 18	20 33	20 38		20 57	20 59			
Blackpool North	a														20 44	21 06							
Preston 8	d	19 41	20 02														20 41		21 02				
Lancaster 6	a	19 54	20 17														20 54		21 17				
	d	19 55	20 18														20 55		21 18				
Barrow-in-Furness	a		21 20																22 20				
Oxenholme Lake District	a	20 08															21 08						
	d	20 08															21 09						
Windermere	a																						
Penrith North Lakes	d	20 34															21 34						
Carlisle 8	a	20 49															21 49						
	d	20 50															21 50						
Lockerbie	d																						
Carstairs	a																						
Motherwell	a																22s44						
Glasgow Central 15	a	22 01															23 04						
Haymarket	a																						
Edinburgh 10	a																						
Perth	a																						
Dundee	a																						
Aberdeen	a																						
Inverness	a																						

b arr. 1848

OVERNIGHT SLEEPERS. For sleeper trains, operated by First ScotRail, please refer to Tables 400 - 404

Table 65

London and West Midlands - North West England and Scotland

		AW	VT	VT	XC	NT		TP	AW	VT	LM	VT	VT	XC	LM	XC	TP	AW	XC	XC	NT	XC	VT	VT	VT
			◇1	◇1	◇1			◇1	◇	◇1	◇1	◇1	◇1	◇1	◇1	◇1	◇1		◇1	◇1			◇1	◇1	◇1
																A			B	C		B 🚌		D	B
London Euston 15 ⊖	d		19 07	19 20						19 30		19 40											20 11	20 20	20 20
Watford Junction	d																								
Milton Keynes Central	d			19 50																				21 05	21 05
Rugby	d																						21 18		
Nuneaton	d		20 03																					21 33	21 33
Tamworth Low Level	d																								
Lichfield Trent Valley	d																								
Coventry	d				19 27											20 27									
Birmingham International ✈	d				19 38											20 39									
Birmingham New Street 12	d				19b57						20 01		20 20	20 31	20 36	20c57			21e01	21e03					
Wolverhampton 7	d				20 16						20 20		20 37	20 49	20 53	21 17			21 18	21 19					
Penkridge	d										20 29				21 03										
Stafford	a		20 26		20 29						20 36		20 49	21 00	21 09	21 29			21 31	21 32			21 48		21 57
	d		20 27		20 30						20 36		20 50	21 01	21 09	21 30			21 31	21 32		21 40	21 49		21 58
Stoke-on-Trent	a			20 48	20 54									21 20		21 54				21 50		22 10		22 05	
Congleton	a																								
Macclesfield	a				21 11									21 38		22 11				22 10		23 10		22 21	
Crewe 10	a		20 45							21 01	20 57	21 18	21 09		21 30				21 58				22 13		
	d	20 23	20 47						21 00	21 03	21 05	21 19						21 23	22 03				22 14		
Chester	a	20 46							21 21									21 46							
Wrexham General	a																								
Llandudno	a																								
Bangor (Gwynedd)	a								22 42																
Holyhead	a								23 15																
Wilmslow	a											21 34							22 20						22 38
Stockport	a			21 16	21 27							21 44		21 53		22 27			22 36	22 24				22 35	22 51
Manchester Piccadilly 10 ⇌	a			21 28	21 39							21 53		22 04		22 39			22 48	22 39				22 51	23 04
Hartford	a										21 19														
Warrington Bank Quay	a									21 19															
	d									21 20															
Runcorn	a		21 05								21 29												22 32		
Liverpool South Parkway 7 ✈	a										21 38														
Liverpool Lime Street 10	a		21 25								21 50												22 54		
	d					20 25															21 42				
Manchester Airport ✈	d							20 29									21 29								
Manchester Piccadilly 10 ⇌	d							20 46									21 46								
Bolton	d							21 07									22 07								
Wigan North Western	a					20 57				21 32											22 28				
	d					20 57				21 32											22 28				
Preston 8	a					21 22		21 33		21 48							22 33				22 55				
Blackpool North	a					21 53		22 06									23 02				23 22				
Preston 8	d																								
Lancaster 6	a																								
	d																								
Barrow-in-Furness	a																								
Oxenholme Lake District	a																								
	d																								
Windermere	a																								
Penrith North Lakes	d																								
Carlisle 8	a																								
	d																								
Lockerbie	d																								
Carstairs	a																								
Motherwell	a																								
Glasgow Central 15	a																								
Haymarket	a																								
Edinburgh 10	a																								
Perth	a																								
Dundee	a																								
Aberdeen	a																								
Inverness	a																								

A from 11 September until 16 October
B until 10 July
C from 17 July until 4 September
D from 17 July until 16 October
b arr. 1948
c arr. 2048
e arr. 2050

OVERNIGHT SLEEPERS. For sleeper trains, operated by First ScotRail, please refer to Tables 400 - 404

Table 65

London and West Midlands - North West England and Scotland

		VT	LM	NT	TP		XC	XC	AW	VT	VT	TP	NT	XC	XC	XC	XC	LM	AW
			◇1		◇1		◇1	◇1		◇1	◇1	◇1			◇1	◇1		◇1	
		A 🚌					B	A						A 🚌	B	A	A 🚌		
London Euston 15 ⊖	d									20 30	21 00								
Watford Junction	d									20u45									
Milton Keynes Central	d										21 45								
Rugby	d									21 36									
Nuneaton	d																		
Tamworth Low Level	d									21 53									
Lichfield Trent Valley	d									22 00									
Coventry	d						21 27	21 27											
Birmingham International ✈	d						21 38	21 38											
Birmingham New Street 12	d		21 36				21b57	21b57							22 31	22 31		22 36	
Wolverhampton 7	d		21 53				22 16	22 16							22 49	22 49		22 56	
Penkridge	d		22 03															23 06	
Stafford	a		22 09				22 29	22 29			22 32				23 02	23 02		23 13	
	d	22 10	22 09				22 30	22 30			22 34			22 40	23 03	23 03	23 10	23 13	
Stoke-on-Trent	a	22 40					22 50							23 10	23 20		23 40		
Congleton	a																		
Macclesfield	a	23 30					23 07							00 10	23 38		00 40		
Crewe 10	a		22 34							22 38	22 59							23 37	
	d								22 23	22 40	23 00								23 21
Chester	a								22 45										23 42
Wrexham General	a																		
Llandudno	a																		
Bangor (Gwynedd)	a																		
Holyhead	a																		
Wilmslow	a							23 11			23 16					23 42			
Stockport	a	23 59					23 21	23 21			23 25				23 53	23 53			
Manchester Piccadilly 10 ⇌	a						23 32	23 32			23 38				00 10	00 10			
Hartford	a																		
Warrington Bank Quay	a									22 57									
	d									22 57									
Runcorn	a																		
Liverpool South Parkway 7 ✈	a																		
Liverpool Lime Street 10	a																		
	d												23 02						
Manchester Airport ✈	d				22 00							22 29							
Manchester Piccadilly 10 ⇌	d				22 16							22 46							
Bolton	d				22 33							23 07							
Wigan North Western	a									23 08			23 48						
	d									23 08			23 48						
Preston 8	a				22 54					23 22		23 33	00 13						
Blackpool North	a											00 02							
Preston 8	d			21 59	22 55														
Lancaster 6	a			22 19	23 11														
	d			22 19	23 11														
Barrow-in-Furness	a			23 24	00 15														
Oxenholme Lake District	a																		
	d																		
Windermere	a																		
Penrith North Lakes	d																		
Carlisle 8	a																		
	d																		
Lockerbie	d																		
Carstairs	a																		
Motherwell	a																		
Glasgow Central 15	a																		
Haymarket	a																		
Edinburgh 10	a																		
Perth	a																		
Dundee	a																		
Aberdeen	a																		
Inverness	a																		

A until 10 July
B from 17 July until 16 October
b arr. 2148

OVERNIGHT SLEEPERS. For sleeper trains, operated by First ScotRail, please refer to Tables 400 - 404

Table 65

Saturdays
from 23 October

London and West Midlands - North West England and Scotland

		TP	TP	TP	TP	VT	VT	TP	AW	XC	LM	LM	XC	NT
		◇■	◇■	◇■	◇■	◇■	◇■	◇■		◇■	◇■	◇■	◇■	
London Euston	d													
Watford Junction	d													
Milton Keynes Central	d													
Rugby	d													
Nuneaton	d													
Tamworth Low Level	d													
Lichfield Trent Valley	d													
Coventry	d													
Birmingham International	d													
Birmingham New Street	d						05 30			05 57		06 01	06 31	
Wolverhampton	d						05 48			06 16		06 18	06 49	
Penkridge	d											06 29		
Stafford	a						06 00			06 29		06 35	07 00	
	d						06 01			06 30		06 36	07 01	
Stoke-on-Trent	a									06 50			07 18	
Congleton	a									07 02				
Macclesfield	a									07 11			07 36	
Crewe	a						06 20					06 56		
	d					05 57	06 23		06 27		06 32	06 57		
Chester	a						06 43							
Wrexham General	a													
Llandudno	a													
Bangor (Gwynedd)	a						07 49							
Holyhead	a						08 23							
Wilmslow	a								06 44					
Stockport	a								06 54	07 27			07 49	
Manchester Piccadilly	a								07 09	07 38			07 59	
Hartford	a										06 46	07 10		
Warrington Bank Quay	a					06 13								
	d					06 14								
Runcorn	a										06 59	07 20		
Liverpool South Parkway	a										07 08	07 30		
Liverpool Lime Street	a										07 22	07 42		
	d													
Manchester Airport	d	00 01		04 00	05 29			06 18						
Manchester Piccadilly	d	00 16		04 15	05 46			06 33						
Bolton	d	00s32		04s29	06 02			06 50						07 01
Wigan North Western	a					06 24								07 19
	d					06 25								
Preston	a	01s03		05s04	06 35	06 37		07 11						
Blackpool North	a	01 30		05 33	07 06									
Preston	d					06 40		07 14						
Lancaster	a					06 54		07 30						
	d		05 46			06 54		07 30						
Barrow-in-Furness	a													
Oxenholme Lake District	a		06 21			07 08								
	d		06 21			07 10								
Windermere	a		06 41											
Penrith North Lakes	d					07 37		08 07						
Carlisle	a					07 50		08 24						
	d					07 51		08 25						
Lockerbie	d					08 10								
Carstairs	a													
Motherwell	a													
Glasgow Central	a					09 13		09 45						
Haymarket	a													
Edinburgh	a													
Perth	a													
Dundee	a													
Aberdeen	a													
Inverness	a													

OVERNIGHT SLEEPERS. For sleeper trains, operated by First ScotRail, please refer to Tables 400 - 404

Table 65

Saturdays
from 23 October

London and West Midlands - North West England and Scotland

		NT	AW	TP	VT	TP	AW	LM	XC	TP	VT	LM	NT	NT	VT	VT	XC	VT	TP	AW	LM	VT	XC
			◇	◇■	◇■	◇■		◇■	◇■	◇■	◇■	◇■			◇■	◇■	◇■	◇■	◇■		◇■	◇■	◇■
London Euston	d										06 05					06 36		06 55				07 07	
Watford Junction	d										06u20					06u51							
Milton Keynes Central	d										06 41							07 27					
Rugby	d										07 03												
Nuneaton	d																						
Tamworth Low Level	d																						
Lichfield Trent Valley	d																						
Coventry	d																						07 27
Birmingham International	d																						07 40
Birmingham New Street	d				06 20			06 36	06 57			07 01			07 20		07 31				07 36		07b57
Wolverhampton	d				06 37			06 54	07 14			07 18			07 37		07 49				07 53		08 15
Penkridge	d											07 30									08 03		
Stafford	a							07 08	07 29		07 34	07 36					08 00				08 09	08 22	08 29
	d							07 08	07 29		07 35	07 38					08 01				08 09	08 23	08 30
Stoke-on-Trent	a																08 19	08 24					08 54
Congleton	a																						
Macclesfield	a																08 36	08 41					09 11
Crewe	a				07 07			07 33	07 50		07 53	07 58			08 07	08 10					08 30	08 41	
	d		07 03		07 09		07 23	07 35	07 53		07 55	08 00			08 09	08 11				08 23	08 31	08 43	
Chester	a		07 23				07 46													08 46			
Wrexham General	a																						
Llandudno	a																						
Bangor (Gwynedd)	a		08 36																				
Holyhead	a		09 19																				
Wilmslow	a								08 09							08 27							
Stockport	a								08 20							08 37	08 49	08 55					09 27
Manchester Piccadilly	a								08 35							08 49	08 59	09 07					09 39
Hartford	a							07 48				08 11											
Warrington Bank Quay	a				07 26						08 11				08 27								
	d				07 27						08 12				08 28								
Runcorn	a							08 02				08 24									08 50	09 00	
Liverpool South Parkway	a							08 11				08 33									08 59		
Liverpool Lime Street	a							08 24				08 46									09 12	09 21	
	d	06 57											07 57										
Manchester Airport	d					07 00				07 25									07 58				
Manchester Piccadilly	d					07 15				07 45									08 15				
Bolton	d					07 31				07 59									08 32				
Wigan North Western	a	07 30			07 37						08 22		08 30		08 38								
	d	07 31			07 38						08 23		08 31		08 39								
Preston	a	07 54			07 51	07 57				08 22	08 36		08 54		08 52				08 58				
Blackpool North	a	08 21				08 29							09 21						09 25				
Preston	d			07 20	07 53					08 24	08 37			08 42	08 54								
Lancaster	a			07 36	08 08					08 39	08 52			09 02	09 09								
	d			07 36	08 09					08 40	08 52			09 02	09 09								
Barrow-in-Furness	a			08 39										10 07									
Oxenholme Lake District	a				08 22					08 54	09 05												
	d				08 23					08 54	09 06												
Windermere	a																						
Penrith North Lakes	d									09 20	09 32				09 46								
Carlisle	a				09 01					09 34	09 47				10 01								
	d				09 02					09 36	09 48				10 04								
Lockerbie	d									09 55													
Carstairs	a																						
Motherwell	a																						
Glasgow Central	a										11 03				11 17								
Haymarket	a				10 16					11s04													
Edinburgh	a				10 22					11 10													
Perth	a																						
Dundee	a																						
Aberdeen	a																						
Inverness	a																						

b arr. 0751

OVERNIGHT SLEEPERS. For sleeper trains, operated by First ScotRail, please refer to Tables 400 - 404

Table 65

Saturdays
from 23 October

London and West Midlands - North West England and Scotland

		LM	VT	TP	XC	VT	VT	VT	VT	NT	AW	LM	VT	VT	XC	LM	VT	XC	VT	TP
		◇1	◇1	◇1	◇1	◇1	◇1	◇1	◇1			◇1	◇1	◇1	◇1	◇1	◇1	◇1	◇1	◇1
				A																
			☕	✕	☕	☕	☕	☕	☕				☕	☕	✕		☕	☕	☕	
London Euston ⊖	d					07 20	07 30	07 35	08 00				08 07	08 10					08 20	
Watford Junction	d																			
Milton Keynes Central	d					07 50		08 06						08 41					08 50	
Rugby	d																			
Nuneaton	d																			
Tamworth Low Level	d																			
Lichfield Trent Valley	d																			
Coventry	d														08 27					
Birmingham International ✈	d														08 38					
Birmingham New Street	d	08 01	08 20		08 31							08 36			08c57	09 01	09 20	09 31		
Wolverhampton	d	08 19	08 37		08 49							08 53			09 15	09 19	09 37	09 49		
Penkridge	d	08 29										09 03								
Stafford	a	08 35			09 00							09 09	09 22		09 29	09 34		10 00		
	d	08 36			09 01							09 09	09 23		09 30	09 35		10 01		
Stoke-on-Trent	a				09 19	08 48			09 24						09 54			10 19	09 48	
Congleton	a																			
Macclesfield	a								09 41						10 11					
Crewe	a	08 56	09 07					09 10				09 30		09 48		09 56	10 07			
	d	08 58	09 09					09 11			09 23	09 31		09 50		09 57	10 09			
Chester	a										09 46			10 12						
Wrexham General	a																			
Llandudno	a																			
Bangor (Gwynedd)	a																			
Holyhead	a																			
Wilmslow	a							09 27												
Stockport	a				09 49	09 16		09 36	09 55						10 27			10 49	10 16	
Manchester Piccadilly	a				09 59	09 28		09 49	10 07						10 39			10 59	10 28	
Hartford	a	09 11														10 10				
Warrington Bank Quay	a		09 26				09 14										10 26			
	d		09 27				09 14										10 27			
Runcorn	a	09 21										09 50	09 55			10 22				
Liverpool South Parkway ✈	a	09 30										09 59				10 31				
Liverpool Lime Street	a	09 43										10 10	10 15			10 44				
	d									08 57										
Manchester Airport ✈	d			08 25																
Manchester Piccadilly	d			08 46																
Bolton	d			09 07																
Wigan North Western	a		09 37				09 25			09 30							10 37			
	d		09 38				09 25			09 31							10 38			
Preston	a		↦	09 30			09 38			09 54							↦			
Blackpool North	a									10 21										
Preston	d			09 32			09 41													09 45
Lancaster	a			09 47			09 54													10 00
	d			09 48			09 55													10 01
Barrow-in-Furness	a																			11 03
Oxenholme Lake District	a			10 04																
	d			10 05																
Windermere	a			10 26																
Penrith North Lakes	d						10 31													
Carlisle	a						10 46													
	d						10 47													
Lockerbie	d																			
Carstairs	a																			
Motherwell	a																			
Glasgow Central	a						12 01													
Haymarket	a																			
Edinburgh	a																			
Perth	a																			
Dundee	a																			
Aberdeen	a																			
Inverness	a																			

A ✕ to Bolton
b arr. 0748
c arr. 0848
e arr. 0847

OVERNIGHT SLEEPERS. For sleeper trains, operated by First ScotRail, please refer to Tables 400 - 404

Table 65

Saturdays
from 23 October

London and West Midlands - North West England and Scotland

		VT	TP	TP	VT	VT	NT	AW	LM	VT	VT	VT	VT	XC	LM	TP	VT	TP	TP	VT	NT	VT	VT
		◇1	◇1	◇1	◇1	◇1			◇1	◇1	◇1	◇1	◇1	◇1	◇1	◇1	◇1	◇1	◇1	◇1		◇1	◇1
		☕	✕	✕	☕	☕				☕	☕	☕	☕	✕			☕	✕	✕	☕		☕	☕
London Euston ⊖	d				08 30	08 40				08 50	09 00	09 07	09 20							09 30			09 40
Watford Junction	d									09 05													
Milton Keynes Central	d									09 25			09 50										
Rugby	d																						
Nuneaton	d																						
Tamworth Low Level	d																						
Lichfield Trent Valley	d																						
Coventry	d													09 27									
Birmingham International ✈	d													09 39									
Birmingham New Street	d								09 36					09b57	10 01							10 20	
Wolverhampton	d								09 53					10 15	10 19							10 37	
Penkridge	d								10 03														
Stafford	a								10 09			10 22		10 29	10 35								
	d								10 09			10 23		10 30	10 35								
Stoke-on-Trent	a										10 24		10 48	10 54									
Congleton	a																						
Macclesfield	a										10 41			11 11									
Crewe	a					10 10			10 30	10 34					10 56							11 07	11 10
	d					10 11		10 23	10 31	10 45					10 57							11 09	11 11
Chester	a							10 46		11 12													
Wrexham General	a																						
Llandudno	a																						
Bangor (Gwynedd)	a									12 22													
Holyhead	a									12 58													
Wilmslow	a					10 27																	11 27
Stockport	a					10 36					10 55		11 16	11 27									11 36
Manchester Piccadilly	a					10 49					11 07		11 28	11 39									11 49
Hartford	a														11 11								
Warrington Bank Quay	a				10 14															11 14		11 26	
	d				10 14															11 14		11 27	
Runcorn	a								10 50			10 55			11 21								
Liverpool South Parkway ✈	a								10 59						11 30								
Liverpool Lime Street	a								11 10			11 15			11 43								
	d						09 57														10 57		
Manchester Airport ✈	d		09 00	09 29														10 00	10 29				
Manchester Piccadilly	d		09 16	09 46														10 16	10 46				
Bolton	d	←	09 33	10 07													←	10 33	11 07				
Wigan North Western	a	09 37			10 25		10 30										10 37			11 25	11 30	11 37	
	d	09 38			10 25		10 31										10 38			11 25	11 31	11 38	
Preston	a	09 51	09 55	10 33	10 38		10 54										10 51	10 55	11 33	11 38	11 54	11 51	
Blackpool North	a			11 05			11 21												12 05		12 21		
Preston	d	09 53	09 58		10 41											10 45	10 53	10 58		11 41		11 53	
Lancaster	a	10 08	10 13		10 54											11 00	11 08	11 13		11 54		12 08	
	d	10 08	10 14		10 55											11 01	11 08	11 14		11 55		12 08	
Barrow-in-Furness	a																						
Oxenholme Lake District	a	10 22			11 08											11 17		11 28				12 22	
	d	10 24			11 08											11 18		11 28				12 24	
Windermere	a															11 39							
Penrith North Lakes	d		10 53														11 45	11 53		12 30			
Carlisle	a	11 01	11 10		11 46												12 00	12 10		12 45		13 01	
	d	11 03	11 11		11 47												12 03	12 11		12 47		13 03	
Lockerbie	d		11 30															12 30					
Carstairs	a																						
Motherwell	a																						
Glasgow Central	a		12 32		13 01												13 17			14 01			
Haymarket	a	12 16																13s34				14 16	
Edinburgh	a	12 22																13 39				14 22	
Perth	a																						
Dundee	a																						
Aberdeen	a																						
Inverness	a																						

b arr. 0948

OVERNIGHT SLEEPERS. For sleeper trains, operated by First ScotRail, please refer to Tables 400 - 404

Table 65

Saturdays from 23 October

London and West Midlands - North West England and Scotland

		XC	VT	TP	AW	LM	VT	VT	VT	XC	LM	TP	VT	NT	VT	VT	XC	VT	TP	AW	LM	VT
				A																		
London Euston	d		10 00				10 07	10 10	10 20				10 30			10 40		11 00				11 07
Watford Junction	d																					
Milton Keynes Central	d							10 41	10 50													
Rugby	d																					
Nuneaton	d																					
Tamworth Low Level	d																					
Lichfield Trent Valley	d																					
Coventry	d									10 27												
Birmingham International	d									10 38												
Birmingham New Street	d	10 31				10 36				10b57	11 01				11 20		11 31				11 36	
Wolverhampton	d	10 49				10 53				11 15	11 19				11 37		11 49				11 53	
Penkridge	d					11 03															12 03	
Stafford	a	11 00				11 09	11 22			11 29	11 35						12 00				12 09	12 22
	d	11 01				11 09	11 23			11 30	11 35						12 01				12 09	12 23
Stoke-on-Trent	a	11 19	11 24						11 48	11 54							12 19	12 24				
Congleton	a																					
Macclesfield	a		11 41							12 11								12 41				
Crewe	a					11 30		11 48			11 56				12 07	12 10					12 30	
	d				11 23	11 31		11 50			11 57				12 09	12 11				12 23	12 31	
Chester	a				11 46			12 12												12 46		
Wrexham General	a																					
Llandudno	a																					
Bangor (Gwynedd)	a																					
Holyhead	a																					
Wilmslow	a															12 27						
Stockport	a	11 49	11 55						12 16	12 27						12 36	12 49	12 55				
Manchester Piccadilly	a	11 59	12 07						12 28	12 39						12 49	12 59	13 07				
Hartford	a										12 10											
Warrington Bank Quay	a												12 14		12 26							
	d												12 14		12 27							
Runcorn	a					11 50	11 55				12 22										12 50	12 55
Liverpool South Parkway	a					11 59					12 31										12 59	
Liverpool Lime Street	a					12 10	12 15				12 44										13 10	13 15
	d													11 57								
Manchester Airport	d			11 00								11 29							12 00			
Manchester Piccadilly	d			11 16								11 46							12 16			
Bolton	d			11 33								12 07							12 33			
Wigan North Western	a												12 25	12 30	12 37							
	d												12 25	12 31	12 38							
Preston	a			11 55								12 33	12 38	12 54	12 51				12 55			
Blackpool North	a											13 05		13 21								
Preston	d			11 58									12 41		12 53				12 58			
Lancaster	a			12 13									12 54		13 08				13 13			
	d			12 14									12 55		13 08				13 14			
Barrow-in-Furness	a			13 10																		
Oxenholme Lake District	a												13 08		13 22				13 28			
	d												13 09		13 24				13 28			
Windermere	a																					
Penrith North Lakes	d																		13 53			
Carlisle	a												13 46		14 01				14 10			
	d												13 47		14 03				14 11			
Lockerbie	d																		14 30			
Carstairs	a																					
Motherwell	a																					
Glasgow Central	a												15 01		15 17							
Haymarket	a																		15s34			
Edinburgh	a																		15 40			
Perth	a																					
Dundee	a																					
Aberdeen	a																					
Inverness	a																					

A to Bolton

b arr. 1048

OVERNIGHT SLEEPERS. For sleeper trains, operated by First ScotRail, please refer to Tables 400 - 404

Table 65

Saturdays from 23 October

London and West Midlands - North West England and Scotland

		VT	VT	XC	LM	VT	TP	NT	TP	VT	VT	VT	XC	VT	TP	AW	LM	VT	VT	VT	XC	LM	VT	TP
London Euston	d	11 10	11 20							11 30		11 40		12 00				12 07	12 10	12 20			12 30	
Watford Junction	d																							
Milton Keynes Central	d	11 41	11 50																12 41	12 50				
Rugby	d																							
Nuneaton	d																							
Tamworth Low Level	d																							
Lichfield Trent Valley	d																							
Coventry	d			11 27																	12 27			
Birmingham International	d			11 38																	12 38			
Birmingham New Street	d			11b57	12 01	12 20					12 20		12 31				12 36				12c57	13 01		
Wolverhampton	d			12 15	12 19	12 37					12 37		12 49				12 53				13 15	13 19		
Penkridge	d																13 03							
Stafford	a			12 29	12 35								13 00				13 09	13 22			13 29	13 35		
	d			12 30	12 35								13 01				13 09	13 23			13 30	13 35		
Stoke-on-Trent	a		12 48	12 54									13 19	13 24						13 48	13 54			
Congleton	a																							
Macclesfield	a			13 11										13 41							14 11			
Crewe	a	12 47			12 56	13 07					13 07	13 10					13 30		13 47			13 56	14 01	
	d	12 49			12 57	13 09					13 09	13 11				13 23	13 31		13 49			13 57	14 03	
Chester	a	13 12														13 46			14 12					
Wrexham General	a																							
Llandudno	a																							
Bangor (Gwynedd)	a																							
Holyhead	a																							
Wilmslow	a											13 27												
Stockport	a		13 16	13 27								13 36	13 49	13 55						14 16	14 27			
Manchester Piccadilly	a		13 28	13 39								13 49	13 59	14 07						14 28	14 39			
Hartford	a				13 11																	14 11		
Warrington Bank Quay	a					13 26				13 14	13 26												14 19	
	d									13 14	13 27													
Runcorn	a				13 21												13 50	13 55				14 21		
Liverpool South Parkway	a				13 30												13 59					14 30		
Liverpool Lime Street	a				13 43												14 10	14 15				14 43		
	d							12 57																
Manchester Airport	d						12 29								13 00									13 29
Manchester Piccadilly	d						12 46								13 16									13 46
Bolton	d						13 07								13 33									14 07
Wigan North Western	a							13 30		13 25	13 37													
	d							13 31		13 25	13 38													
Preston	a						13 33	13 54		13 38	13 51				13 55									14 33
Blackpool North	a						14 05	14 21																15 05
Preston	d								13 04	13 41	13 53				13 58									
Lancaster	a								13 19	13 54	14 08				14 13									
	d								13 20	13 55	14 08				14 14									
Barrow-in-Furness	a																							
Oxenholme Lake District	a								13 36						14 28									
	d								13 37						14 28									
Windermere	a								13 56															
Penrith North Lakes	d									14 08	14 45				14 53									
Carlisle	a									14 46	15 00				15 12									
	d									14 47	15 02				15 14									
Lockerbie	d														15 33									
Carstairs	a																							
Motherwell	a														16s23									
Glasgow Central	a									16 01					16 42									
Haymarket	a										16 15													
Edinburgh	a										16 22													
Perth	a																							
Dundee	a																							
Aberdeen	a																							
Inverness	a																							

b arr. 1148

c arr. 1248

OVERNIGHT SLEEPERS. For sleeper trains, operated by First ScotRail, please refer to Tables 400 - 404

Table 65

Saturdays from 23 October

London and West Midlands - North West England and Scotland

		VT ◇1	NT	TP ◇1	VT ◇1	VT ◇1			XC ◇1	VT ◇1	TP ◇1	AW	LM ◇1	VT ◇1	VT ◇1	VT ◇1		XC ◇1		LM ◇1	TP ◇1	VT ◇1	NT	VT ◇1	VT ◇1
London Euston	d	12 30				12 40				13 00				13 07	13 10	13 20						13 30			13 40
Watford Junction	d																								
Milton Keynes Central	d														13 41	13 50									
Rugby	d																								
Nuneaton	d																								
Tamworth Low Level	d																								
Lichfield Trent Valley	d																								
Coventry	d																	13 27							
Birmingham International	d																	13 38							
Birmingham New Street	d				13 20				13 31				13 36					13b57		14 01				14 20	
Wolverhampton	d				13 37				13 49				13 53					14 15		14 19				14 37	
Penkridge	d												14 03												
Stafford	a								14 00				14 09	14 22				14 29		14 35					
	d								14 01				14 09	14 23				14 30		14 35					
Stoke-on-Trent	a								14 19	14 24						14 48		14 54							
Congleton	a																								
Macclesfield	a									14 41								15 11							
Crewe	a				14 07	14 10							14 30		14 48					14 56				15 07	15 10
	d				14 09	14 11						14 23	14 31		14 50					14 57				15 09	15 11
Chester	a											14 46			15 12										
Wrexham General	a																								
Llandudno	a																								
Bangor (Gwynedd)	a																								
Holyhead	a																								
Wilmslow	a					14 27																			15 27
Stockport	a					14 36			14 49	14 55						15 16		15 27							15 36
Manchester Piccadilly	a					14 49			14 59	15 07						15 28		15 39							15 49
Hartford	a																			15 11					
Warrington Bank Quay	a	14 14			14 26																	15 14		15 26	
	d	14 14			14 27																	15 14		15 27	
Runcorn	a												14 50	14 55						15 21					
Liverpool South Parkway	a												14 59							15 30					
Liverpool Lime Street	a												15 10	15 15						15 43					
	d		13 57																				14 57		
Manchester Airport	d										14 00										14 29				
Manchester Piccadilly	d										14 16										14 46				
Bolton	d										14 33										15 07				
Wigan North Western	a	14 25	14 30		14 37																	15 25	15 30	15 37	
	d	14 25	14 31		14 38																	15 25	15 31	15 38	
Preston	a	14 38	14 54		14 51						14 55										15 33	15 38	15 54	15 51	
Blackpool North	a		15 21																		16 05		16 21		
Preston	d	14 41		14 47	14 53						14 58											15 41		15 53	
Lancaster	a	14 54		15 02	15 08						15 13											15 54		16 08	
	d	14 55		15 03	15 09						15 14											15 56		16 09	
Barrow-in-Furness	a			15 58																					
Oxenholme Lake District	a				15 22						15 28											16 08			
	d				15 24						15 28											16 09			
Windermere	a																								
Penrith North Lakes	d	15 30									15 53													16 45	
Carlisle	a	15 45			16 01						16 10											16 46		17 00	
	d	15 47			16 03						16 11											16 47		17 03	
Lockerbie	d										16 30														
Carstairs	a																								
Motherwell	a																								
Glasgow Central	a	17 01			17 17																	18 01			
Haymarket	a										17s30													18 14	
Edinburgh	a										17 39													18 22	
Perth	a																								
Dundee	a																								
Aberdeen	a																								
Inverness	a																								

b arr. 1348

OVERNIGHT SLEEPERS. For sleeper trains, operated by First ScotRail, please refer to Tables 400 - 404

Table 65

Saturdays from 23 October

London and West Midlands - North West England and Scotland

		XC ◇1		VT ◇1	TP ◇1 A	AW	LM ◇1	VT ◇1	VT ◇1	VT ◇1	XC ◇1	LM ◇1			TP ◇1	VT ◇1	NT	VT ◇1	VT ◇1		XC ◇1	VT ◇1		TP ◇1	AW
London Euston	d			14 00				14 07	14 10	14 20						14 30			14 40			15 00			
Watford Junction	d																								
Milton Keynes Central	d								14 41	14 50															
Rugby	d																								
Nuneaton	d																								
Tamworth Low Level	d																								
Lichfield Trent Valley	d																								
Coventry	d										14 27														
Birmingham International	d										14 38														
Birmingham New Street	d	14 31					14 36				14b57	15 01						15 20			15 31				
Wolverhampton	d	14 49					14 53				15 15	15 19						15 37			15 49				
Penkridge	d						15 03																		
Stafford	a	15 00					15 09	15 22			15 29	15 35									16 00				
	d	15 01					15 09	15 23			15 30	15 35									16 01				
Stoke-on-Trent	a	15 19		15 24						15 48	15 54										16 19	16 24			
Congleton	a																								
Macclesfield	a			15 41							16 11											16 41			
Crewe	a						15 30		15 47			15 56						16 08	16 11						
	d					15 23	15 31		15 49			15 57						16 09	16 12						16 23
Chester	a					15 46			16 10																16 46
Wrexham General	a																								
Llandudno	a																								
Bangor (Gwynedd)	a								17 17																
Holyhead	a								17 51																
Wilmslow	a																		16 27						
Stockport	a	15 49		15 55						16 16	16 27								16 36		16 49	16 54			
Manchester Piccadilly	a	15 59		16 07						16 28	16 39								16 49		16 59	17 07			
Hartford	a											16 10													
Warrington Bank Quay	a															16 14		16 26							
	d															16 14		16 27							
Runcorn	a						15 50	15 55				16 23													
Liverpool South Parkway	a						15 59					16 32													
Liverpool Lime Street	a						16 10	16 15				16 44													
	d																15 57								
Manchester Airport	d				15 00										15 29									16 00	
Manchester Piccadilly	d				15 16										15 46									16 16	
Bolton	d				15 33										16 07									16 33	
Wigan North Western	a															16 25	16 30	16 37							
	d															16 25	16 31	16 38							
Preston	a				15 55										16 33	16 38	16 54	16 51						16 55	
Blackpool North	a														17 07		17 21								
Preston	d				15 58											16 41		16 53						17 00	
Lancaster	a				16 13											16 54		17 09						17 15	
	d				16 14											16 55		17 10						17 16	
Barrow-in-Furness	a				17 18																				
Oxenholme Lake District	a																	17 24						17 30	
	d																	17 25						17 30	
Windermere	a																								
Penrith North Lakes	d															17 30									
Carlisle	a															17 45		18 03						18 10	
	d															17 47		18 04						18 11	
Lockerbie	d																							18 30	
Carstairs	a																								
Motherwell	a																								
Glasgow Central	a															19 01		19 17							
Haymarket	a																							19s31	
Edinburgh	a																							19 39	
Perth	a																								
Dundee	a																								
Aberdeen	a																								
Inverness	a																								

A to Bolton

b arr. 1448

OVERNIGHT SLEEPERS. For sleeper trains, operated by First ScotRail, please refer to Tables 400 - 404

Table 65

London and West Midlands - North West England and Scotland

		LM	VT	VT	VT	XC	LM	TP	TP	VT	NT	VT	VT	XC	VT	TP	NT	AW	LM	VT
		◇1	◇1	◇1	◇1	◇1	◇1	◇1	◇1	◇1		◇1	◇1	◇1	◇1	◇1			◇1	◇1
			⊡	⊡	⊡	⫪		⫪		⊡		⊡	⊡	⊡	⊡	A ⫪				⊡
London Euston 15 ⊖	d		15 07	15 10	15 20					15 30			15 40		16 00					16 07
Watford Junction	d																			
Milton Keynes Central	d			15 41	15 50															
Rugby	d																			
Nuneaton	d																			
Tamworth Low Level	d																			
Lichfield Trent Valley	d																			
Coventry	d					15 27														
Birmingham International ✈	d					15 38														
Birmingham New Street 12	d	15 36				15b57	16 01					16 20		16 31					16 36	
Wolverhampton 7	d	15 53				16 15	16 19					16 37		16 49					16 53	
Penkridge	d	16 03																	17 03	
Stafford	a	16 09	16 22			16 29	16 35							17 00					17 09	17 22
	d	16 09	16 23			16 30	16 35							17 01					17 09	17 23
Stoke-on-Trent	a				16 48	16 54								17 19	17 24					
Congleton	a																			
Macclesfield	a					17 11									17 41					
Crewe 10	a	16 30		16 47			16 56					17 07	17 10						17 30	
	d	16 31		16 49			16 57					17 09	17 11					17 23	17 31	
Chester	a			17 12														17 46		
Wrexham General	a																			
Llandudno	a																			
Bangor (Gwynedd)	a																			
Holyhead	a																			
Wilmslow	a												17 27							
Stockport	a				17 16	17 27							17 36	17 49	17 55					
Manchester Piccadilly 10	a				17 28	17 39							17 49	17 59	18 07					
Hartford	a						17 11													
Warrington Bank Quay	a									17 14		17 26								
	d									17 14		17 27								
Runcorn	a	16 50	16 55				17 21												17 50	17 55
Liverpool South Parkway 7 ✈	a	16 59					17 30												17 59	
Liverpool Lime Street 10	a	17 10	17 15				17 43												18 10	18 15
	d										16 57						17 27			
Manchester Airport ✈	d							16 29								17 00				
Manchester Piccadilly 10	d							16 46								17 15				
Bolton	d							17 06								17 32				
Wigan North Western	a									17 25	17 30	17 37					18 05			
	d									17 25	17 31	17 38					18 05			
Preston 8	a							17 30		17 38	17 54	17 51				17 55	18 31			
Blackpool North	a							18 02			18 24									
Preston 8	d								17 04	17 41		17 53				17 58				
Lancaster 6	a								17 20	17 54		18 08				18 13				
	d								17 21	17 55		18 08				18 14				
Barrow-in-Furness	a															19 18				
Oxenholme Lake District	a								17 38	18 08		18 22								
	d								17 38	18 08		18 23								
Windermere	a								18 00											
Penrith North Lakes	d											18 49								
Carlisle 8	a									18 46		19 04								
	d									18 47		19 04								
Lockerbie	d																			
Carstairs	a																			
Motherwell	a																			
Glasgow Central 15	a									20 01										
Haymarket	a											20 19								
Edinburgh 10	a											20 24								
Perth	a																			
Dundee	a																			
Aberdeen	a																			
Inverness	a																			

A ⫪ to Bolton

b arr. 1548

OVERNIGHT SLEEPERS. For sleeper trains, operated by First ScotRail, please refer to Tables 400 - 404

Table 65

London and West Midlands - North West England and Scotland

		VT	VT	XC	VT	LM	VT	TP	VT	VT	XC	VT	TP	AW	LM	VT	VT	VT	XC	LM	NT
		◇1	◇1	◇1	◇1	◇1	◇1	◇1	◇1	◇1	◇1	◇1	◇1		◇1	◇1	◇1	◇1	◇1	◇1	
		⊡	⊡	⫪	⊡		⊡	⫪	⊡	⊡	⫪	⊡	⫪			⊡	⊡	⊡	⫪		
London Euston 15 ⊖	d	16 10	16 20		16 30		16 33			16 40		17 00				17 07	17 10	17 20			
Watford Junction	d																				
Milton Keynes Central	d	16 41	16 50														17 41	17 50			
Rugby	d																				
Nuneaton	d															18 03					
Tamworth Low Level	d						17 38														
Lichfield Trent Valley	d						17 45														
Coventry	d			16 27															17 27		
Birmingham International ✈	d			16 38															17 38		
Birmingham New Street 12	d			16b57		17 01			17 20		17 31				17 36				17c57	18 01	
Wolverhampton 7	d			17 15		17 19			17 37		17 49				17 53				18 15	18 19	
Penkridge	d					17 29									18 03					18 29	
Stafford	a			17 29		17 35	17 59				18 00				18 09	18 26			18 29	18 35	
	d			17 30		17 36	17 59				18 01				18 09	18 27			18 30	18 35	
Stoke-on-Trent	a		17 48	17 54							18 19	18 24						18 48	18 54		
Congleton	a																				
Macclesfield	a			18 11								18 41							19 11		
Crewe 10	a	17 47				17 56			18 07	18 10					18 30		18 48			18 56	
	d	17 49				18 00			18 09	18 11				18 23	18 33		18 50			18 59	
Chester	a	18 09												18 46			19 10				
Wrexham General	a																				
Llandudno	a																				
Bangor (Gwynedd)	a	19 21															20 22				
Holyhead	a	19 55															20 56				
Wilmslow	a									18 27											
Stockport	a		18 16	18 27						18 36	18 49	18 55						19 16	19 27		
Manchester Piccadilly 10	a		18 28	18 39						18 49	18 59	19 07						19 28	19 40		
Hartford	a					18 13									18 43					19 12	
Warrington Bank Quay	a				18 14				18 26												
	d				18 14				18 27												
Runcorn	a					18 23	18 31								18 52	18 59				19 22	
Liverpool South Parkway 7 ✈	a					18 32									19 02					19 31	
Liverpool Lime Street 10	a					18 44	18 53								19 14	19 17				19 44	
	d																				17 44
Manchester Airport ✈	d							17 29					18 00								
Manchester Piccadilly 10	d							17 46					18 16								
Bolton	d							18 07					18 33								
Wigan North Western	a				18 25				18 37												18 30
	d				18 25				18 38												18 31
Preston 8	a				18 38			18 38	18 51				18 55								18 54
Blackpool North	a							19 09													19 21
Preston 8	d				18 41				18 53				19 00								
Lancaster 6	a				18 54				19 08				19 15								
	d				18 55				19 08				19 16								
Barrow-in-Furness	a																				
Oxenholme Lake District	a				19 08				19 22				19 30								
	d				19 09				19 24				19 30								
Windermere	a																				
Penrith North Lakes	d				19 34								19 55								
Carlisle 8	a				19 49				20 01				20 12								
	d				19 51				20 03				20 13								
Lockerbie	d												20 32								
Carstairs	a																				
Motherwell	a																				
Glasgow Central 15	a				21 01				21 17				21 32								
Haymarket	a																				
Edinburgh 10	a																				
Perth	a																				
Dundee	a																				
Aberdeen	a																				
Inverness	a																				

b arr. 1648

c arr. 1748

OVERNIGHT SLEEPERS. For sleeper trains, operated by First ScotRail, please refer to Tables 400 - 404

Table 65

London and West Midlands - North West England and Scotland

		NT	TP	TP	VT	VT	TP	VT	VT	XC	VT	LM	VT	AW	VT	VT	XC	LM	NT	TP	VT
			◇■	◇■	◇■	◇■	◇■	◇■	◇■	◇■	◇■	◇■	◇■		◇■	◇■	◇■	◇■		◇■	◇■
London Euston ⊖	d				17 30				17 40		18 00		18 07		18 10	18 20					18 30
Watford Junction	d																				
Milton Keynes Central	d														18 41	18 50					
Rugby	d																				
Nuneaton	d																				
Tamworth Low Level	d																				
Lichfield Trent Valley	d																				
Coventry	d																18 27				
Birmingham International ✈	d																18 38				
Birmingham New Street	d							18 20		18 31		18 36					18b57	19 01			
Wolverhampton	d							18 37		18 49		18 53					19 15	19 19			
Penkridge	d											19 03						19 29			
Stafford	a									19 00		19 09	19 22				19 29	19 35			
	d									19 01		19 09	19 23				19 30	19 36			
Stoke-on-Trent	a									19 19	19 24					19 48	19 54				
Congleton	a																				
Macclesfield	a										19 41						20 11				
Crewe	a							19 07	19 10			19 30			19 48			19 58			
	d							19 09	19 11					19 23	19 50			19 58			
Chester	a													19 46	20 12						
Wrexham General	a																				
Llandudno	a																				
Bangor (Gwynedd)	a																				
Holyhead	a																				
Wilmslow	a								19 27												
Stockport	a								19 36	19 49	19 55					20 16	20 27				
Manchester Piccadilly	a								19 49	19 59	20 07					20 28	20 39				
Hartford	a																	20 11			
Warrington Bank Quay	a				19 14			19 26													20 14
	d				19 14			19 27													20 14
Runcorn	a												19 55					20 24			
Liverpool South Parkway ✈	a																	20 33			
Liverpool Lime Street	a												20 15					20 46			
	d	18 01																	19 23		
Manchester Airport ✈	d		18 29				19 00													19 29	
Manchester Piccadilly	d		18 46				19 16													19 46	
Bolton	d		19 07				19 33													20 07	
Wigan North Western	a	18 49			19 25			19 37											19 54		20 25
	d	18 49			19 25			19 38											19 55		20 25
Preston	a	19 15	19 33		19 38		19 58	19 59											20 18	20 33	20 38
Blackpool North	a		20 05																20 44	21 06	
Preston	d			19 04	19 41	19 58	20 02														20 41
Lancaster	a			19 20	19 54	20 11	20 17														20 54
	d			19 20	19 55	20 12	20 18														20 55
Barrow-in-Furness	a			20 24			21 20														
Oxenholme Lake District	a				20 08	20 25															21 08
	d				20 08	20 25															21 09
Windermere	a																				
Penrith North Lakes	d				20 34	20 51															21 34
Carlisle	a				20 49	21 06															21 49
	d				20 50	21 07															21 50
Lockerbie	d																				
Carstairs	a																				
Motherwell	a																				22s44
Glasgow Central	a				22 01	22 26															23 04
Haymarket	a																				
Edinburgh	a																				
Perth	a																				
Dundee	a																				
Aberdeen	a																				
Inverness	a																				

b arr. 1848

OVERNIGHT SLEEPERS. For sleeper trains, operated by First ScotRail, please refer to Tables 400 - 404

Table 65

London and West Midlands - North West England and Scotland

		VT	TP	VT	VT	XC	VT	AW	VT	VT	XC	NT	TP	AW	VT	LM	VT	VT	XC	LM	XC	AW	VT
		◇■	◇■	◇■	◇■	◇■	◇■		◇■	◇■	◇■		◇■	◇	◇■	◇■	◇■	◇■	◇■	◇■	◇■		◇■
London Euston ⊖	d	18 33			18 40		19 00		19 07	19 20					19 30		19 40						20 11
Watford Junction	d																						
Milton Keynes Central	d									19 50													
Rugby	d																						21 18
Nuneaton	d								20 03														
Tamworth Low Level	d	19 38																					
Lichfield Trent Valley	d	19 46																					
Coventry	d										19 27										20 27		
Birmingham International ✈	d										19 38										20 39		
Birmingham New Street	d			19 20		19 31					19b57					20 01		20 20	20 31	20 36	20c57		
Wolverhampton	d			19 37		19 49					20 16					20 20		20 37	20 49	20 53	21 17		
Penkridge	d															20 29				21 03			
Stafford	a	19 58				20 00			20 26		20 29					20 36		20 49	21 00	21 09	21 29		21 48
	d	19 59				20 01			20 27		20 30					20 36		20 50	21 01	21 09	21 30		21 49
Stoke-on-Trent	a					20 19	20 24			20 48	20 54								21 20		21 54		
Congleton	a																						
Macclesfield	a					20 36	20 41				21 11								21 38		22 11		
Crewe	a			20 07	20 10				20 45						21 01	20 57	21 18	21 09		21 30			22 13
	d			20 09	20 11			20 23	20 47					21 00	21 03	21 05	21 19					21 23	22 14
Chester	a							20 46						21 21								21 46	
Wrexham General	a																						
Llandudno	a																						
Bangor (Gwynedd)	a													22 42									
Holyhead	a													23 15									
Wilmslow	a				20 27												21 34						
Stockport	a				20 36	20 49	20 55			21 16	21 27						21 44		21 53		22 27		
Manchester Piccadilly	a				20 49	20 59	21 07			21 28	21 39						21 53		22 04		22 39		
Hartford	a															21 19							
Warrington Bank Quay	a			20 26											21 19								
	d			20 27											21 20								
Runcorn	a	20 32							21 05							21 29							22 32
Liverpool South Parkway ✈	a															21 38							
Liverpool Lime Street	a	20 52							21 25							21 50							22 54
	d											20 25											
Manchester Airport ✈	d		20 00										20 29										
Manchester Piccadilly	d		20 16										20 46										
Bolton	d		20 33										21 07										
Wigan North Western	a			20 37								20 57			21 32								
	d			20 38								20 57			21 32								
Preston	a		20 57	20 59								21 22	21 33		21 48								
Blackpool North	a											21 53	22 06										
Preston	d		21 02																				
Lancaster	a		21 17																				
	d		21 18																				
Barrow-in-Furness	a		22 20																				
Oxenholme Lake District	a																						
	d																						
Windermere	a																						
Penrith North Lakes	d																						
Carlisle	a																						
	d																						
Lockerbie	d																						
Carstairs	a																						
Motherwell	a																						
Glasgow Central	a																						
Haymarket	a																						
Edinburgh	a																						
Perth	a																						
Dundee	a																						
Aberdeen	a																						
Inverness	a																						

b arr. 1948
c arr. 2048

OVERNIGHT SLEEPERS. For sleeper trains, operated by First ScotRail, please refer to Tables 400 - 404

Table 65

Saturdays
from 23 October

London and West Midlands - North West England and Scotland

		NT	VT	VT	TP	LM	XC	TP	AW	VT	TP	XC	LM	AW
			◇1	◇1	◇1	◇1	◇1	◇1		◇1	◇1	◇1	◇1	
London Euston 15 ⊖	d		20 20	20 30						21 00				
Watford Junction	d			20 45										
Milton Keynes Central	d		21 05							21 45				
Rugby	d			21 36										
Nuneaton	d		21 33											
Tamworth Low Level	d			21 53										
Lichfield Trent Valley	d			22 00										
Coventry	d						21 27							
Birmingham International ✈	d						21 38							
Birmingham New Street 12	d					21 36	21b57					22 31	22 36	
Wolverhampton 7	d					21 53	22 16					22 49	22 56	
Penkridge	d					22 03							23 06	
Stafford	a					22 09	22 29			22 32		23 02	23 13	
	d					22 09	22 30			22 34		23 03	23 13	
Stoke-on-Trent	a		22 05				22 50					23 20		
Congleton	a													
Macclesfield	a		22 21				23 07					23 38		
Crewe 10	a			22 38		22 34				22 59			23 37	
	d								22 23	23 00				23 21
Chester	a								22 45					23 42
Wrexham General	a													
Llandudno	a													
Bangor (Gwynedd)	a													
Holyhead	a													
Wilmslow	a									23 16				
Stockport	a		22 35				23 21			23 25		23 53		
Manchester Piccadilly 10	a		22 51				23 32			23 38		00 10		
Hartford	a													
Warrington Bank Quay	a													
	d													
Runcorn	a													
Liverpool South Parkway 7 ✈	a													
Liverpool Lime Street 10	a													
	d													
Manchester Airport ✈	d				21 29			22 00			22 29			
Manchester Piccadilly 10	d				21 46			22 16			22 46			
Bolton	d				22 07			22 33			23 07			
Wigan North Western	a													
	d													
Preston 8	a				22 33			22 54			23 33			
Blackpool North	a				23 02						00 02			
Preston 8	d	21 59						22 55						
Lancaster 6	a	22 19						23 11						
	d	22 19						23 11						
Barrow-in-Furness	a	23 24						00 15						
Oxenholme Lake District	a													
	d													
Windermere	a													
Penrith North Lakes	d													
Carlisle 8	a													
	d													
Lockerbie	d													
Carstairs	a													
Motherwell	a													
Glasgow Central 15	a													
Haymarket	a													
Edinburgh 10	a													
Perth	a													
Dundee	a													
Aberdeen	a													
Inverness	a													

b arr. 2148

OVERNIGHT SLEEPERS. For sleeper trains, operated by First ScotRail, please refer to Tables 400 - 404

Table 65

Sundays
until 11 July

London and West Midlands - North West England and Scotland

		TP	TP	TP	AW	TP	NT	TP	AW	VT	XC	TP	XC	AW	NT	TP
				◇1	◇	◇1		◇1	◇	◇1	◇1	◇1				◇1
London Euston 15 ⊖	d															
Watford Junction	d															
Milton Keynes Central	d															
Rugby	d															
Nuneaton	d															
Tamworth Low Level	d															
Lichfield Trent Valley	d															
Coventry	d															
Birmingham International ✈	d															
Birmingham New Street 12	d									08 45	09 01					
Wolverhampton 7	d									09 04	09 19					
Penkridge	d															
Stafford	a									09 17	09 33					
	d									09 18	09 34		09 45			
Stoke-on-Trent	a												10 20			
Congleton	a															
Macclesfield	a												11 10			
Crewe 10	a									09 38	09 54					
	d				08 27				09 27	09 39	09 56			09 57		
Chester	a				08 50				09 45					10 22		
Wrexham General	a															
Llandudno	a															
Bangor (Gwynedd)	a				10 11				11 04							
Holyhead	a				10 48				11 48							
Wilmslow	a										10 12					
Stockport	a										10 22					
Manchester Piccadilly 10	a										10 39					
Hartford	a															
Warrington Bank Quay	a									09 57						
	d									09 57						
Runcorn	a															
Liverpool South Parkway 7 ✈	a															
Liverpool Lime Street 10	a															
	d						08 31								09 31	
Manchester Airport ✈	d	00 10	05 30	07 55		08 29		09 00				09 30				
Manchester Piccadilly 10	d	00 35	05 55	08 11		08 46		09 16				09 46				
Bolton	d	01s00	06s20	08 30		09 05		09 33				10 05				
Wigan North Western	a						09 13			10 08					10 13	
	d						09 14			10 08					10 14	
Preston 8	a	01s35	06s55	08 56		09 33	09 37	09 57		10 25		10 32			10 39	
Blackpool North	a	02 15	07 35	09 25		10 00	10 07					11 00			11 09	
Preston 8	d							10 00								10 06
Lancaster 6	a							10 16								10 22
	d							10 16								10 23
Barrow-in-Furness	a															
Oxenholme Lake District	a							10 30								10 39
	d							10 30								10 40
Windermere	a															10 58
Penrith North Lakes	d							10 55								
Carlisle 8	a							11 12								
	d							11 13								
Lockerbie	d							11 32								
Carstairs	a															
Motherwell	a															
Glasgow Central 15	a															
Haymarket	a							12s32								
Edinburgh 10	a							12 39								
Perth	a															
Dundee	a															
Aberdeen	a															
Inverness	a															

OVERNIGHT SLEEPERS. For sleeper trains, operated by First ScotRail, please refer to Tables 400 - 404

Table 65

Sundays
until 11 July

London and West Midlands - North West England and Scotland

		VT	TP	VT	VT	VT	VT	LM	XC	TP	VT	NT	VT	XC	AW	VT	TP	AW	VT	LM	XC	TP	LM	XC	AW
		◇1	◇1	◇1	◇1	◇1	◇1	◇1	◇1	◇1	◇1		◇1			◇1	◇1	◇	◇1	◇1	◇1	◇1			
London Euston 15 ⊖	d			08 10		08 15	08 20						08 45						09 15						
Watford Junction	d																								
Milton Keynes Central	d			08 56			09 05						09 32												
Rugby	d												10 08												
Nuneaton	d					09 42													10 45						
Tamworth Low Level	d																								
Lichfield Trent Valley	d																								
Coventry	d																				10b28				
Birmingham International ✈	d																				10 40				
Birmingham New Street 12	d	09 20						09 42	10 00							10 20				10 42	11c01				
Wolverhampton 7	d	09 37						09 59	10 18							10 37				10 58	11 19				
Penkridge	d							10 10												11 08					
Stafford	a					10 08	10 13	10 17	10 32										11 11	11 14	11 32				
	d					10 08	10 14	10 17	10 33					10 45					11 11	11 14	11 33		11 41	11 45	
Stoke-on-Trent	a													11 20									12 17	12 20	
Congleton	a																								
Macclesfield	a													12 10										13 10	
Crewe 10	a	10 06		10 15		10 28		10 37					10 55			11 08			11 30	11 38			13 07		
	d	10 08		10 17	10 21	10 30		10 39			10 42		10 57		10 57	11 10		11 27	11 32	11 39					11 57
Chester	a										11 02				11 22			11 48							12 20
Wrexham General	a																								
Llandudno	a																								
Bangor (Gwynedd)	a										12 09							13 10							
Holyhead	a										12 43							13 45							
Wilmslow	a			10 31			10 46		11 06												12 07				
Stockport	a			10 41			10 56		11 16												12 20				
Manchester Piccadilly 10	a			10 55			11 10		11 32												12 40				
Hartford	a							10 50												11 51					
Warrington Bank Quay	a	10 26			10 37								11 13			11 27									
	d	10 26			10 37								11 14			11 28									
Runcorn	a					10 47		11 00											11 49	12 02					
Liverpool South Parkway 7 ✈	a							11 10												12 12					
Liverpool Lime Street 10	a					11 09		11 21											12 10	12 22					
	d											10 31													
Manchester Airport ✈	d		10 00							10 29							11 00					11 30			
Manchester Piccadilly 10	d		10 16							10 46							11 16					11 46			
Bolton	d		10 33							11 05							11 33					12 05			
Wigan North Western	a	10 37			10 48							11 13	11 24			11 38									
	d	10 37			10 48							11 14	11 25			11 39									
Preston 8	a	10 51	10 57		11 04					11 32		11 37	11 38			11 52	11 57					12 32			
Blackpool North	a									12 00		12 07										13 00			
Preston 8	d	10 52	11 00		11 06								11 39			11 54	11 58								
Lancaster 6	a	11 07	11 15		11 22								11 54			12 09	12 13								
	d	11 08	11 16										11 54			12 09	12 14								
Barrow-in-Furness	a																13 17								
Oxenholme Lake District	a	11 22	11 30										12 07			12 23									
	d	11 23	11 30										12 08			12 25									
Windermere	a																								
Penrith North Lakes	d		11 55										12 34												
Carlisle 8	a	12 01	12 12										12 49			13 02									
	d	12 02	12 13										12 49			13 04									
Lockerbie	d		12 32																						
Carstairs	a																								
Motherwell	a																								
Glasgow Central 15	a	13 19	13 36										14 01												
Haymarket	a															14 14									
Edinburgh 10	a															14 22									
Perth	a																								
Dundee	a																								
Aberdeen	a																								
Inverness	a																								

b arr. 1022

c arr. 1050

OVERNIGHT SLEEPERS. For sleeper trains, operated by First ScotRail, please refer to Tables 400 - 404

Table 65

Sundays
until 11 July

London and West Midlands - North West England and Scotland

		NT	VT	VT	TP	AW	VT	LM	VT	XC	TP	XC	NT	AW	VT	VT	VT	VT	TP	AW	LM	VT	NT	VT	XC
			◇1	◇1	◇1	◇	◇1	◇1	◇1	◇1	◇1				◇1	◇1	◇1	◇1	◇1	◇	◇1	◇1		◇1	◇1
London Euston 15 ⊖	d		09 45				10 15		10 20						10 45		11 15	11 20				12 02		12 15	
Watford Junction	d																								
Milton Keynes Central	d		10 33						11 07						11 32		12 04	12 09						12 48	
Rugby	d		11 08												12 08										
Nuneaton	d						11 46																		
Tamworth Low Level	d																								
Lichfield Trent Valley	d																								
Coventry	d									11b28															12e28
Birmingham International ✈	d									11 40															12 40
Birmingham New Street 12	d			11 20				11 42		12c01						12 20					12 35				13f01
Wolverhampton 7	d			11 37				11 58		12 20						12 37					12 52				13 19
Penkridge	d							12 08													13 03				
Stafford	a						12 11	12 14	12 16	12 33							12 54	13 00			13 10	13 23			13 33
	d						12 12	12 14	12 18	12 34		12 45					12 55	13 02			13 10	13 24			13 34
Stoke-on-Trent	a											13 20												13 50	13 56
Congleton	a																								
Macclesfield	a											14 10													14 14
Crewe 10	a		11 56	12 07			12 31	12 38							12 57	13 07	13 15	13 20			13 30	13 42			
	d		11 58	12 09		12 27	12 33	12 39						12 57	12 59	13 09	13 17	13 21		13 27	13 31	13 44			
Chester	a					12 48								13 18						13 47					
Wrexham General	a																								
Llandudno	a																								
Bangor (Gwynedd)	a					14 18														15 12					
Holyhead	a					14 55														15 55					
Wilmslow	a								12 50	13 08								13 35							
Stockport	a								12 59	13 19								13 45						14 18	14 28
Manchester Piccadilly 10	a								13 12	13 40								13 59						14 30	14 40
Hartford	a							12 51													13 43				
Warrington Bank Quay	a		12 15	12 26											13 16	13 26									
	d		12 15	12 27											13 16	13 27									
Runcorn	a						12 50	13 02									13 34				13 54	14 01			
Liverpool South Parkway 7 ✈	a							13 12													14 04				
Liverpool Lime Street 10	a						13 11	13 22									13 57				14 14	14 23			
	d	11 31											12 31										13 31		
Manchester Airport ✈	d				12 00						12 30								13 00						
Manchester Piccadilly 10	d				12 16						12 46								13 16						
Bolton	d				12 33						13 05								13 33						
Wigan North Western	a	12 13	12 26	12 37									13 13		13 27	13 37							14 13		
	d	12 14	12 26	12 38									13 14		13 27	13 38							14 14		
Preston 8	a	12 37	12 39	12 51	12 57						13 32		13 37		13 40	13 51			13 57				14 37		
Blackpool North	a	13 07									14 01		14 09										15 07		
Preston 8	d		12 41	12 53	12 58										13 42	13 53			14 00						
Lancaster 6	a		12 55	13 08	13 13										13 56	14 08			14 15						
	d		12 56	13 08	13 14										13 57	14 08			14 16						
Barrow-in-Furness	a																								
Oxenholme Lake District	a		13 09	13 22	13 28										14 10				14 30						
	d		13 09	13 24	13 28										14 10				14 30						
Windermere	a																								
Penrith North Lakes	d		13 35		13 53										14 36	14 45			14 55						
Carlisle 8	a		13 50	14 01	14 10										14 51	15 00			15 12						
	d		13 51	14 03	14 11										14 52	15 02			15 17						
Lockerbie	d				14 30																				
Carstairs	a																								
Motherwell	a																								
Glasgow Central 15	a		15 04	15 16											16 05				16 35						
Haymarket	a				15s28											16 14									
Edinburgh 10	a				15 36											16 22									
Perth	a																								
Dundee	a																								
Aberdeen	a																								
Inverness	a																								

b arr. 1122

c arr. 1150

e arr. 1222

f arr. 1250

OVERNIGHT SLEEPERS. For sleeper trains, operated by First ScotRail, please refer to Tables 400 - 404

Table 65

Sundays until 11 July

London and West Midlands - North West England and Scotland

		TP ◇1	AW	TP ◇1	VT ◇1	VT ◇1	VT ◇1	XC ◇1		VT ◇1	TP ◇1	AW ◇	LM ◇1	VT ◇1	VT ◇1	XC ◇1	TP ◇1	VT ◇1	NT	AW	VT ◇1	VT ◇1	XC ◇1	VT ◇1	TP ◇1
London Euston 15 ⊖	d				12 25		12 35			12 55				13 02	13 15			13 25				13 35		13 55	
Watford Junction	d																								
Milton Keynes Central	d														13 48										
Rugby	d																								
Nuneaton	d																								
Tamworth Low Level	d																								
Lichfield Trent Valley	d																								
Coventry	d															13 26									
Birmingham International ✈	d															13 38									
Birmingham New Street 12	d					13 20		13 31					13 35			14b01					14 20		14 31		
Wolverhampton 7	d					13 37		13 49					13 52			14 19					14 37		14 49		
Penkridge	d												14 03												
Stafford	a												14 10	14 20		14 33									
	d												14 10	14 22		14 34									
Stoke-on-Trent	a							14 19		14 26					14 50	14 56							15 19	15 25	
Congleton	a																								
Macclesfield	a									14 42						15 14								15 42	
Crewe 10	a					14 09	14 12						14 30	14 40							15 09	15 12			
	d		13 57			14 11	14 13					14 27	14 31	14 42						14 57	15 11	15 13			
Chester	a		14 20									14 47								15 20					
Wrexham General	a																								
Llandudno	a																								
Bangor (Gwynedd)	a											16 18													
Holyhead	a											16 55													
Wilmslow	a						14 29															15 29			
Stockport	a						14 38			14 56					15 18	15 28						15 38		15 56	
Manchester Piccadilly 10	a						14 51	14 57		15 09					15 30	15 40						15 51	15 59	16 09	
Hartford	a												14 43												
Warrington Bank Quay	a				14 16	14 28												15 16			15 28				
	d				14 16	14 29												15 16			15 29				
Runcorn	a												14 54	14 59											
Liverpool South Parkway 7 ✈	a												15 04												
Liverpool Lime Street 10	a												15 14	15 21											
	d																		14 31						
Manchester Airport ✈	d	13 30									14 00						14 30								15 00
Manchester Piccadilly 10	d	13 46									14 16						14 46								15 16
Bolton	d	14 05									14 33						15 05								15 33
Wigan North Western	a				14 27	14 39												15 27	15 13		15 39				
	d				14 27	14 40												15 27	15 14		15 40				
Preston 8	a	14 32			14 40	14 52					14 57						15 32	15 40	15 37		15 53				15 57
Blackpool North	a	15 00															16 00		16 07						
Preston 8	d			14 05	14 42	14 55					15 00							15 42			15 55				16 00
Lancaster 6	a			14 21	14 56	15 10					15 15							15 56			16 10				16 15
	d			14 21	14 58	15 11					15 16							15 58			16 10				16 16
Barrow-in-Furness	a			15 25																					17 19
Oxenholme Lake District	a					15 24					15 30							16 10							
	d					15 25					15 30							16 11							
Windermere	a																								
Penrith North Lakes	d				15 32						15 55										16 47				
Carlisle 8	a				15 47	16 03					16 12							16 48			17 02				
	d				15 48	16 05					16 13							16 49			17 04				
Lockerbie	d										16 32														
Carstairs	a																								
Motherwell	a																								
Glasgow Central 15	a				17 00	17 18												18 02							
Haymarket	a										17s30										18 13				
Edinburgh 10	a										17 39										18 22				
Perth	a																								
Dundee	a																								
Aberdeen	a																								
Inverness	a																								

b arr. 1348

OVERNIGHT SLEEPERS. For sleeper trains, operated by First ScotRail, please refer to Tables 400 - 404

Table 65

Sundays until 11 July

London and West Midlands - North West England and Scotland

		AW ◇	LM ◇1	VT ◇1	NT	VT ◇1	XC ◇1	TP ◇1	VT ◇1	AW	VT ◇1	VT ◇1	XC ◇1	VT ◇1		TP ◇1	AW ◇	LM ◇1	VT ◇1	VT ◇1	VT ◇1	XC ◇1	TP ◇1	TP ◇1	NT
London Euston 15 ⊖	d			14 02		14 15			14 25			14 35		14 55					15 02	15 05	15 15				
Watford Junction	d																								
Milton Keynes Central	d					14 48														15 39	15 48				
Rugby	d																								
Nuneaton	d																								
Tamworth Low Level	d																								
Lichfield Trent Valley	d																								
Coventry	d						14 26															15 26			
Birmingham International ✈	d						14 38															15 38			
Birmingham New Street 12	d		14 35				15b01				15 20		15 31					15 35				16c01			
Wolverhampton 7	d		14 52				15 19				15 37		15 49					15 52				16 19			
Penkridge	d		15 03															16 03							
Stafford	a		15 10	15 24			15 33											16 10	16 20			16 35			
	d		15 10	15 25			15 34											16 10	16 21			16 36			
Stoke-on-Trent	a					15 50	15 56						16 19	16 24							16 50	16 56			
Congleton	a																								
Macclesfield	a						16 14							16 42								17 14			
Crewe 10	a		15 30	15 43							16 09	16 12						16 32		16 50					
	d	15 27	15 31	15 45						15 57	16 11	16 13					16 27	16 34		16 52					
Chester	a	15 47								16 20							16 47			17 14					
Wrexham General	a																								
Llandudno	a																								
Bangor (Gwynedd)	a	17 12															18 18								
Holyhead	a	17 55															18 55								
Wilmslow	a											16 29													
Stockport	a					16 18	16 28					16 38		16 56							17 18	17 28			
Manchester Piccadilly 10	a					16 30	16 40					16 51	16 59	17 09							17 30	17 40			
Hartford	a		15 43															16 45							
Warrington Bank Quay	a								16 16		16 28														
	d								16 16		16 29														
Runcorn	a		15 54	16 02														16 56	16 59						
Liverpool South Parkway 7 ✈	a		16 04															17 06							
Liverpool Lime Street 10	a		16 14	16 23														17 17	17 23						
	d				15 31																				16 31
Manchester Airport ✈	d							15 30								16 00							16 30		
Manchester Piccadilly 10	d							15 46								16 16							16 46		
Bolton	d							16 05								16 33							17 05		
Wigan North Western	a				16 13				16 27		16 39														17 13
	d				16 14				16 27		16 40														17 14
Preston 8	a				16 37			16 32	16 40		16 53					16 57							17 32		17 37
Blackpool North	a				17 07			17 00															18 00		18 07
Preston 8	d								16 42		16 55					17 00								17 04	
Lancaster 6	a								16 56		17 10					17 15								17 22	
	d								16 57		17 10					17 16								17 22	
Barrow-in-Furness	a																								
Oxenholme Lake District	a										17 24					17 30								17 39	
	d										17 25					17 30								17 39	
Windermere	a																							17 59	
Penrith North Lakes	d								17 32							17 55									
Carlisle 8	a								17 47		18 03					18 12									
	d								17 48		18 05					18 13									
Lockerbie	d																								
Carstairs	a																								
Motherwell	a																								
Glasgow Central 15	a								19 00		19 18														
Haymarket	a																								
Edinburgh 10	a															19 37									
Perth	a																								
Dundee	a																								
Aberdeen	a																								
Inverness	a																								

b arr. 1448

c arr. 1548

OVERNIGHT SLEEPERS. For sleeper trains, operated by First ScotRail, please refer to Tables 400 - 404

Table 65

London and West Midlands - North West England and Scotland

		VT	VT	VT	VT	XC	VT	TP	AW	TP	LM	VT	VT	VT	XC	TP	TP	TP	VT	NT	VT	VT	XC	VT
		◇1	◇1	◇1	◇1	◇1	◇1	◇1		◇1	◇1	◇1	◇1	◇1	◇1	◇1	◇1	◇1	◇1		◇1	◇1	◇1	◇1
			A	B				B		B						A	A							
		🛒	🛒	🛒	🛒	🍴	🛒	🍴				🛒	🛒	🛒	🍴	🍴			🛒		🛒	🛒	🍴	🛒
London Euston 15 ⊖	d	15 25			15 35		15 55					16 02	16 05	16 15					16 25			16 35		16 55
Watford Junction	d																							
Milton Keynes Central	d												16 39	16 48										
Rugby	d																							
Nuneaton	d																							
Tamworth Low Level	d																							
Lichfield Trent Valley	d																							
Coventry	d														16 26									
Birmingham International ✈	d														16 38									
Birmingham New Street 12	d		16 20	16 20		16 31					16 35				17b01						17 20		17 31	
Wolverhampton 7	d		16u37	16u37		16 49					16 52				17 19						17u37		17 49	
Penkridge	d										17 03													
Stafford	a										17 10	17 24			17 35									
	d										17 10	17 25			17 36									
Stoke-on-Trent	a					17 19	17 25							17 50	17 56								18 19	18 25
Congleton	a																							
Macclesfield	a						17 42								18 14									18 42
Crewe 10	a		17 07	17 09	17 12						17 30		17 50								18 09	18 12		
	d		17 08	17 11	17 13				17 27		17 31		17 52								18 11	18 13		
Chester	a								17 48				18 14											
Wrexham General	a																							
Llandudno	a																							
Bangor (Gwynedd)	a																							
Holyhead	a																							
Wilmslow	a				17 29																	18 29		
Stockport	a				17 38		17 56							18 18	18 28							18 38		18 56
Manchester Piccadilly 10	a				17 51	17 56	18 09							18 30	18 40							18 51	18 56	19 09
Hartford	a										17 43													
Warrington Bank Quay	a	17 16	17 26	17 28															18 16		18 28			
	d	17 16	17 26	17 29															18 17		18 29			
Runcorn	a										17 54	17 57												
Liverpool South Parkway 7 ✈	a										18 04													
Liverpool Lime Street 10	a										18 14	18 20												
	d																			17 31				
Manchester Airport ✈	d							17 00								17 00		17 30						
Manchester Piccadilly 10	d							17 16								17 16		17 46						
Bolton	d							17 33								17 33		18 05						
Wigan North Western	a	17 27	17 37	17 39															18 27	18 13	18 39			
	d	17 27	17 37	17 40															18 28	18 14	18 40			
Preston 8	a	17 40	17 51	17 53				17 57								17 57		18 32	18 40	18 37	18 53			
Blackpool North	a																	19 00		19 07				
Preston 8	d	17 42	17 52	17 55				18 00		18 06						18 08	18 12		18 42		18 55			
Lancaster 6	a	17 56	18 07	18 10				18 15		18 22						18 23	18 28		18 56		19 10			
	d	17 57	18 08	18 10				18 16		18 22						18 24	18 28		18 58		19 10			
Barrow-in-Furness	a									19 26							19 32							
Oxenholme Lake District	a	18 10	18 22	18 24				18 30								18 38			19 10		19 24			
	d	18 10	18 23	18 25				18 30								18 38			19 11		19 26			
Windermere	a																							
Penrith North Lakes	d		18 48	18 51				18 55								19 03			19 36					
Carlisle 8	a	18 48	19 03	19 06				19 12								19 20			19 51		20 03			
	d	18 49	19 04	19 06				19 21								19 21			19 53		20 05			
Lockerbie	d							19 40								19 40								
Carstairs	a																							
Motherwell	a							20s27								20s27								
Glasgow Central 15	a	20 02						20 45								20 45			21 08		21 18			
Haymarket	a																							
Edinburgh 10	a		20 23	20 25																				
Perth	a																							
Dundee	a																							
Aberdeen	a																							
Inverness	a																							

A From 4 July **B** until 27 June **b** arr. 1648

OVERNIGHT SLEEPERS. For sleeper trains, operated by First ScotRail, please refer to Tables 400 - 404

Table 65

Sundays
until 11 July

London and West Midlands - North West England and Scotland

		TP	AW	LM	VT	VT	NT	VT	TP	VT	VT	VT	XC	VT	TP	AW	NT	LM	VT	VT	VT	XC	TP	VT	VT
		◇1	◇	◇1	◇1	◇1		◇1	◇1	◇1	◇1	◇1	◇1	◇1	◇1			◇1	◇1	◇1	◇1	◇1	◇1	◇1	■ 1
		🍴			🛒	🛒		🛒		🛒	🛒	🛒	🍴	🛒					🛒	🛒	🛒	🍴		🛒	🛒
London Euston 15 ⊖	d				17 02	17 05		17 15		17 25		17 35		17 55					18 02	18 05	18 15			18 25	
Watford Junction	d																								
Milton Keynes Central	d					17 39		17 48												18 39	18 48				
Rugby	d																								
Nuneaton	d					18 10																			
Tamworth Low Level	d																								
Lichfield Trent Valley	d																								
Coventry	d																					18 26			
Birmingham International ✈	d																					18 38			
Birmingham New Street 12	d			17 35							18 20		18 31					18 35				19b01			19 20
Wolverhampton 7	d			17 52							18 37		18 49					18 52				19 19			19 37
Penkridge	d			18 03														19 03							
Stafford	a			18 10	18 24													19 10	19 24			19 37			
	d			18 10	18 25													19 10	19 25			19 38			
Stoke-on-Trent	a							18 50					19 19	19 25							19 50	19 56			
Congleton	a																								
Macclesfield	a													19 42								20 14			
Crewe 10	a			18 30		18 53					19 09	19 12						19 30		19 50					20 09
	d		18 27	18 31		18 56					19 11	19 13				19 27		19 31		19 52					20 11
Chester	a		18 47			19 14										19 48				20 11					
Wrexham General	a																								
Llandudno	a																								
Bangor (Gwynedd)	a		20 08			20 26														21 23					
Holyhead	a		20 44			20 59														21 57					
Wilmslow	a											19 29													
Stockport	a							19 18				19 38		19 56							20 18	20 28			
Manchester Piccadilly 10	a							19 30				19 51	19 58	20 09							20 30	20 40			
Hartford	a			18 43														19 43							
Warrington Bank Quay	a									19 16	19 28													20 16	20 28
	d									19 16	19 29													20 16	20 29
Runcorn	a			18 54	18 57													19 54	19 58						
Liverpool South Parkway 7 ✈	a			19 04														20 04							
Liverpool Lime Street 10	a			19 14	19 20													20 14	20 20						
	d						18 31										19 31								
Manchester Airport ✈	d	18 00							18 30						19 00								19 30		
Manchester Piccadilly 10	d	18 16							18 46						19 16								19 46		
Bolton	d	18 33							19 05						19 33								20 05		
Wigan North Western	a						19 13			19 27	19 39						20 13							20 27	20 39
	d						19 14			19 27	19 40						20 14							20 27	20 40
Preston 8	a	18 57					19 37		19 32	19 40	19 53				19 57		20 37						20 32	20 40	20 53
Blackpool North	a						20 07		20 00								21 07						21 00		
Preston 8	d	19 00								19 42	19 55				20 00									20 42	20 55
Lancaster 6	a	19 15								19 56	20 10				20 15									20 56	21 10
	d	19 16								19 57	20 10				20 16									20 57	21 10
Barrow-in-Furness	a														21 19										
Oxenholme Lake District	a	19 30								20 10														21 10	21 24
	d	19 30								20 10														21 11	21 26
Windermere	a																								
Penrith North Lakes	d	19 55								20 36	20 47													21 36	
Carlisle 8	a	20 12								20 51	21 02													21 51	22 03
	d	20 13								20 52	21 04													21 52	22 05
Lockerbie	d	20 32																							22 23
Carstairs	a																								
Motherwell	a																							22 48	23 07
Glasgow Central 15	a									22 07														23 09	23 22
Haymarket	a	21s30									22 15														
Edinburgh 10	a	21 39									22 23														
Perth	a																								
Dundee	a																								
Aberdeen	a																								
Inverness	a																								

b arr. 1848

OVERNIGHT SLEEPERS. For sleeper trains, operated by First ScotRail, please refer to Tables 400 - 404

Table 65

Sundays until 11 July

London and West Midlands - North West England and Scotland

		VT		XC	VT	AW	LM	VT	VT	VT	XC	VT	NT	TP	VT	VT	XC	VT	AW	VT	VT	VT	XC	TP	NT
London Euston	d	18 35			18 55			19 02	19 05	19 15					19 25	19 35		19 55		20 02	20 05	20 15			
Watford Junction	d																								
Milton Keynes Central	d								19 39	19 48											20 38	20 48			
Rugby	d																								
Nuneaton	d							20 01												21 01					
Tamworth Low Level	d																								
Lichfield Trent Valley	d																								
Coventry	d										19 26												20 26		
Birmingham International	d										19 38												20 38		
Birmingham New Street	d			19 31			19 35				20b01	20 20					20 31						21c01		
Wolverhampton	d			19 49			19 52				20 19	20 38					20 49						21 19		
Penkridge	d						20 03																		
Stafford	a						20 10	20 25			20 37	20 51									21 32		21 37		
	d						20 10	20 30			20 38	20 52									21 33		21 38		
Stoke-on-Trent	a			20 19	20 25					20 50	20 56						21 19	21 25				21 50	21 56		
Congleton	a																								
Macclesfield	a				20 42						21 15							21 42					22 14		
Crewe	a	20 12					20 30	20 48	20 53			21 10				21 13				21 44	21 53				
	d	20 13				20 27	20 31	20 50	20 55							21 14			21 27	21 46	21 55				
Chester	a					20 48			21 14										21 46						
Wrexham General	a																								
Llandudno	a																								
Bangor (Gwynedd)	a								22 22										23 10						
Holyhead	a								22 56										23 52						
Wilmslow	a	20 29														21 30									
Stockport	a	20 38			20 56					21 18	21 28					21 39		21 56				22 18	22 28		
Manchester Piccadilly	a	20 51		21 00	21 09					21 30	21 40					21 52	21 56	22 09				22 30	22 40		
Hartford	a						20 43																		
Warrington Bank Quay	a														21 16										
	d														21 16										
Runcorn	a						20 54	21 07												22 03	22 12				
Liverpool South Parkway	a						21 04																		
Liverpool Lime Street	a						21 14	21 28												22 24	22 33				
	d												20 31												21 31
Manchester Airport	d													20 30										21 30	
Manchester Piccadilly	d													20 46										21 46	
Bolton	d													21 05										22 05	
Wigan North Western	a												21 13		21 27										22 13
	d												21 14		21 27										22 14
Preston	a												21 37	21 32	21 40									22 29	22 37
Blackpool North	a												22 07	22 00										22 55	23 07
Preston	d														21 42										
Lancaster	a														21 56										
	d														21 57										
Barrow-in-Furness	a																								
Oxenholme Lake District	a														22 10										
	d														22 11										
Windermere	a																								
Penrith North Lakes	d														22 36										
Carlisle	a														22 51										
	d														22 53										
Lockerbie	d																								
Carstairs	a																								
Motherwell	a																								
Glasgow Central	a														00 02										
Haymarket	a																								
Edinburgh	a																								
Perth	a																								
Dundee	a																								
Aberdeen	a																								
Inverness	a																								

b arr. 1948 c arr. 2048

OVERNIGHT SLEEPERS. For sleeper trains, operated by First ScotRail, please refer to Tables 400 - 404

Table 65

Sundays until 11 July

London and West Midlands - North West England and Scotland

		SR	AW	VT	VT	VT	LM	XC	AW	VT	AW	VT	VT	AW	VT	NT	SR
London Euston	d	20 07		20 25		20 35				20 50		21 21	21 24		21 50		22 32
Watford Junction	d																
Milton Keynes Central	d									21 39			22 13		22 38		
Rugby	d									22 01					23 18		
Nuneaton	d											22 54			23 29		
Tamworth Low Level	d			21 32													
Lichfield Trent Valley	d			21 39													
Coventry	d							21 26									
Birmingham International	d							21 38						22 40			
Birmingham New Street	d				21 20		21 35	22b01						22 55			
Wolverhampton	d				21 37		21 58	22 19						23 15			
Penkridge	d						22 08										
Stafford	a				21 56	22 03	22 16	22 37				23 19		23 30	23s53		
	d				21 57	22 04	22 16	22 38				23 19		23 31	23s54		
Stoke-on-Trent	a							22 55					23 29				
Congleton	a																
Macclesfield	a							23 12					23 45				
Crewe	a			22 10	22 15	22 22	22 39			22 49		23 38		23 55	00s12		
	d		21 57	22 13	22 17	22 23			22 29	22 51	23 38	23 41		00 10	00s13		
Chester	a		22 18						22 50		23 59			00 30			
Wrexham General	a																
Llandudno	a																
Bangor (Gwynedd)	a								00 12					01 40			
Holyhead	a								00 49					02 15			
Wilmslow	a					22 38											
Stockport	a					22 48		23 27					23 59		00s40		
Manchester Piccadilly	a					23 00		23 41					00 13		00 53		
Hartford	a																
Warrington Bank Quay	a			22 29	22 34					23 08							
	d			22 30	22 35					23 08							
Runcorn	a											00 02					
Liverpool South Parkway	a																
Liverpool Lime Street	a											00 29					
	d															22 31	
Manchester Airport	d																
Manchester Piccadilly	d																
Bolton	d																
Wigan North Western	a			22 40	22 45					23 19						23 13	
	d			22 41	22 46					23 19						23 14	
Preston	a			22 58	23 05					23 41						23 35	
Blackpool North	a															00 05	
Preston	d																
Lancaster	a																
	d																
Barrow-in-Furness	a																
Oxenholme Lake District	a																
	d																
Windermere	a																
Penrith North Lakes	d																
Carlisle	a																
	d																
Lockerbie	d																
Carstairs	a																06s42
Motherwell	a																06s59
Glasgow Central	a																07 19
Haymarket	a																
Edinburgh	a	03s13															
Perth	a	05s39															
Dundee	a	06s08															
Aberdeen	a	07 35															
Inverness	a	08 30															

b arr. 2148

OVERNIGHT SLEEPERS. For sleeper trains, operated by First ScotRail, please refer to Tables 400 - 404

London and West Midlands - North West England and Scotland

					TP	TP	TP	AW		TP	NT		TP	AW	AW	VT	XC	TP	AW	NT		TP	VT	VT	VT
							◇1	◇		◇1			◇1	◇		◇1	◇1	◇1				◇1	◇1	◇1	◇1
					🚌	🚌							🛒			🍴	🛒						🍴	🍴	🍴
London Euston 15 ⊖	d																							08 10	
Watford Junction	d																								
Milton Keynes Central	d																							08 56	
Rugby	d																								
Nuneaton	d																								
Tamworth Low Level	d																								
Lichfield Trent Valley	d																								
Coventry	d																								
Birmingham International ✈	d																								
Birmingham New Street 12	d															08 45	09 01						09 20		
Wolverhampton 7 🚊	d															09 04	09 19						09 37		
Penkridge	d																								
Stafford	a															09 17	09 33								
	d															09 18	09 34								
Stoke-on-Trent	a																								
Congleton	a																								
Macclesfield	a																								
Crewe 10	a															09 38	09 54						10 06	10 15	
	d							08 27						09 27	09 28	09 39	09 56		09 57				10 08	10 17	10 21
Chester	a							08 50						09 45					10 22						
Wrexham General	a																								
Llandudno	a																								
Bangor (Gwynedd)	a							10 11						11 04											
Holyhead	a							10 48						11 48											
Wilmslow	a														09 46		10 12							10 31	
Stockport	a																10 22							10 41	
Manchester Piccadilly 10 🚊	a														10 12		10 39							10 55	
Hartford	a																								
Warrington Bank Quay	a															09 57							10 26		10 37
	d															09 57							10 26		10 37
Runcorn	a																								
Liverpool South Parkway 7 ✈	a																								
Liverpool Lime Street 10	a																								
	d										08 31									09 31					
Manchester Airport ✈	d				00 10	05 30	07 55			08 29			09 00					09 30							
Manchester Piccadilly 10 🚊	d				00 35	05 55	08 11			08 46			09 16					09 46							
Bolton	d				01s00	06s20	08 30			09 05			09 33					10 05							
Wigan North Western	a										09 13					10 08				10 13			10 37		10 48
	d										09 14					10 08				10 14			10 37		10 48
Preston 8	a				01s35	06s55	08 56			09 33	09 37		09 57			10 25		10 32		10 39			10 51		11 04
Blackpool North	a				02 15	07 35	09 25			10 00	10 07							11 00		11 09					
Preston 8	d												10 00									10 06	10 52		11 06
Lancaster 6	a												10 16									10 22	11 07		11 22
	d												10 16									10 23	11 08		
Barrow-in-Furness	a																								
Oxenholme Lake District	a												10 30									10 39	11 22		
	d												10 30									10 40	11 23		
Windermere	a																					10 58			
Penrith North Lakes	d												10 55												
Carlisle 8	a												11 12										12 01		
	d												11 13										12 02		
Lockerbie	d												11 32												
Carstairs	a																								
Motherwell	a																								
Glasgow Central 15	a																						13 19		
Haymarket	a												12s32												
Edinburgh 10	a												12 39												
Perth	a																								
Dundee	a																								
Aberdeen	a																								
Inverness	a																								

OVERNIGHT SLEEPERS. For sleeper trains, operated by First ScotRail, please refer to Tables 400 - 404

London and West Midlands - North West England and Scotland

		VT	VT	LM	XC	TP	NT	VT	VT	AW	VT	TP	AW	VT	VT	LM	NT	XC	TP	LM	AW	VT	VT	TP	AW
		◇1	◇1	◇1	◇1	◇1		◇1	◇1		◇1	◇1	◇	◇1	◇1	◇1		◇1	◇1	1		◇1	◇1	◇1	◇
		🍴	🍴		🛒			🍴	🍴		🍴			🍴	🍴			🛒				🍴	🍴	🛒	🛒
London Euston 15 ⊖	d	08 15	08 20						08 45					09 15	09 20							09 45			
Watford Junction	d																								
Milton Keynes Central	d		09 05						09 32						10 07							10 33			
Rugby	d								10 08													11 08			
Nuneaton	d	09 42												10 45											
Tamworth Low Level	d																								
Lichfield Trent Valley	d																								
Coventry	d																	10b28							
Birmingham International ✈	d																	10 40							
Birmingham New Street 12	d			09 42	10 00						10 20					10 42		11c01					11 20		
Wolverhampton 7 🚊	d			09 59	10 18						10 37					10 59		11 19					11 37		
Penkridge	d			10 10												11 10									
Stafford	a	10 08		10 17	10 31									11 11		11 17		11 32							
	d	10 08		10 17	10 32									11 11		11 17		11 33		11 44					
Stoke-on-Trent	a		10 19		10 51										11 22			11 52		12 02					
Congleton	a																								
Macclesfield	a		10 36		11 08										11 39			12 10							
Crewe 10	a	10 28		10 37					10 55		11 08			11 30		11 37				12 26		11 56	12 07		
	d	10 30		10 38				10 42	10 57	10 57	11 10		11 27	11 32		11 38					11 57	11 58	12 09		12 27
Chester	a							11 02		11 22			11 48								12 20				12 48
Wrexham General	a																								
Llandudno	a																								
Bangor (Gwynedd)	a							12 09					13 10												14 18
Holyhead	a							12 43					13 45												14 55
Wilmslow	a																								
Stockport	a		10 51		11 22										11 55			12 28							
Manchester Piccadilly 10 🚊	a		11 04		11 32										12 09			12 40							
Hartford	a			10 50												11 50									
Warrington Bank Quay	a								11 13		11 27											12 15	12 26		
	d								11 14		11 28											12 15	12 27		
Runcorn	a	10 47		11 00										11 49		12 01									
Liverpool South Parkway 7 ✈	a			11 10												12 11									
Liverpool Lime Street 10	a	11 09		11 20										12 10		12 21									
	d						10 31										11 31								
Manchester Airport ✈	d					10 29						11 00							11 30					12 00	
Manchester Piccadilly 10 🚊	d					10 46						11 16							11 46					12 16	
Bolton	d					11 05						11 33							12 05					12 33	
Wigan North Western	a						11 13		11 24		11 38						12 13					12 26	12 37		
	d						11 14		11 25		11 39						12 14					12 26	12 38		
Preston 8	a					11 32	11 37		11 38		11 52	11 57					12 37		12 32			12 39	12 51	12 57	
Blackpool North	a					12 00	12 07										13 07		13 00						
Preston 8	d								11 39		11 54	11 58										12 41	12 53	12 58	
Lancaster 6	a								11 54		12 09	12 13										12 55	13 08	13 13	
	d								11 54		12 09	12 14										12 56	13 08	13 14	
Barrow-in-Furness	a											13 17													
Oxenholme Lake District	a								12 07		12 23											13 09	13 22	13 28	
	d								12 08		12 25											13 09	13 24	13 28	
Windermere	a																								
Penrith North Lakes	d								12 34													13 35		13 53	
Carlisle 8	a								12 49		13 02											13 50	14 01	14 10	
	d								12 49		13 04											13 51	14 03	14 11	
Lockerbie	d																							14 30	
Carstairs	a																								
Motherwell	a																								
Glasgow Central 15	a								14 01													15 04	15 16		
Haymarket	a										14 14													15s28	
Edinburgh 10	a										14 22													15 36	
Perth	a																								
Dundee	a																								
Aberdeen	a																								
Inverness	a																								

b arr. 1022

c arr. 1050

OVERNIGHT SLEEPERS. For sleeper trains, operated by First ScotRail, please refer to Tables 400 - 404

Table 65

Sundays

18 July to 05 September

London and West Midlands - North West England and Scotland

		VT	NT	VT	LM	XC	TP	AW	VT	VT	VT	VT		TP	AW	LM	VT	VT	XC	TP	AW	TP	NT	VT	VT
		◇1		◇1	◇1	◇1	◇1		◇1	◇1	◇1	◇1		◇1	◇	◇1	◇1	◇1	◇1	◇1		◇1		◇1	◇1
		🍴		🍴		🛒			🍴	🍴	🍴	🍴		🛒	🛒		🍴	🍴	🛒					🍴	🍴
London Euston [15] ⊖	d	10 15		10 20					10 45		11 15	11 20					12 02	12 15						12 25	
Watford Junction	d																								
Milton Keynes Central	d			11 07					11 32		12 04	12 09						12 48							
Rugby	d								12 08																
Nuneaton	d	11 46																							
Tamworth Low Level	d																								
Lichfield Trent Valley	d																								
Coventry	d					11b28													12e28						
Birmingham International ✈	d					11 40													12 40						
Birmingham New Street [12]	d				11 42	12c01				12 20						12 35			13f01						13 20
Wolverhampton [7]	d				11 59	12 20				12 37						12 52			13 19						13 37
Penkridge	d				12 10											13 03									
Stafford	a	12 11			12 16	12 33					12 54					13 10	13 23		13 33						
	d	12 12			12 16	12 34					12 55					13 10	13 24		13 34						
Stoke-on-Trent	a			12 23		12 51						13 07						13 50	13 56						
Congleton	a																								
Macclesfield	a			12 40		13 09						13 24							14 14						
Crewe [10]	a	12 31			12 37				12 57	13 07	13 15					13 30	13 42								14 09
	d	12 33			12 38			12 57	12 59	13 09	13 17				13 27	13 31	13 44				13 57				14 11
Chester	a							13 18							13 47						14 20				
Wrexham General	a																								
Llandudno	a																								
Bangor (Gwynedd)	a														15 12										
Holyhead	a														15 55										
Wilmslow	a																								
Stockport	a			12 54		13 28						13 38						14 18	14 28						
Manchester Piccadilly [10]	a			13 08		13 40						13 52						14 30	14 40						
Hartford	a				12 50											13 43									
Warrington Bank Quay	a								13 16	13 26														14 16	14 28
	d								13 16	13 27														14 16	14 29
Runcorn	a	12 50			13 01						13 34					13 54	14 01								
Liverpool South Parkway [7] ✈	a				13 11											14 04									
Liverpool Lime Street [10]	a	13 11			13 21						13 57					14 14	14 23								
	d		12 31																				13 31		
Manchester Airport ✈	d						12 30							13 00						13 30					
Manchester Piccadilly [10]	d						12 46							13 16						13 46					
Bolton	d						13 05							13 33						14 05					
Wigan North Western	a		13 13						13 27	13 37													14 13	14 27	14 39
	d		13 14						13 27	13 38													14 14	14 27	14 40
Preston [8]	a		13 37				13 32		13 40	13 51				13 57						14 32			14 37	14 40	14 52
Blackpool North	a		14 09				14 01													15 00			15 07		
Preston [8]	d								13 42	13 53				14 00								14 05		14 42	14 55
Lancaster [6]	a								13 56	14 08				14 15								14 21		14 56	15 10
	d								13 57	14 08				14 16								14 21		14 58	15 11
Barrow-in-Furness	a																					15 25			
Oxenholme Lake District	a								14 10					14 30											15 24
	d								14 10					14 30											15 25
Windermere	a																								
Penrith North Lakes	d								14 36	14 45				14 55										15 32	
Carlisle [8]	a								14 51	15 00				15 12										15 47	16 03
	d								14 52	15 02				15 17										15 48	16 05
Lockerbie	d																								
Carstairs	a																								
Motherwell	a																								
Glasgow Central [15]	a								16 05					16 35										17 00	17 18
Haymarket	a									16 14															
Edinburgh [10]	a									16 22															
Perth	a																								
Dundee	a																								
Aberdeen	a																								
Inverness	a																								

b arr. 1122
c arr. 1150
e arr. 1222
f arr. 1250

OVERNIGHT SLEEPERS. For sleeper trains, operated by First ScotRail, please refer to Tables 400 - 404

Table 65

Sundays

18 July to 05 September

London and West Midlands - North West England and Scotland

		VT	XC	VT	TP	AW	LM	VT	NT	VT	XC	TP	VT	AW	VT	VT	XC	VT		TP	AW	LM	VT	VT	XC
		◇1	◇1	◇1	◇1	◇	◇1	◇1		◇1	◇1	◇1	◇1		◇1	◇1	◇1	◇1		◇1	◇	◇1	◇1	◇1	◇1
		🍴	🛒	🍴	🛒	🛒		🍴		🍴	🛒		🍴		🍴	🍴	🛒	🍴			🛒		🍴	🍴	🛒
London Euston [15] ⊖	d	12 35		12 55				13 02		13 15			13 25			13 35		13 55					14 02	14 15	
Watford Junction	d																								
Milton Keynes Central	d									13 48														14 48	
Rugby	d																								
Nuneaton	d																								
Tamworth Low Level	d																								
Lichfield Trent Valley	d																								
Coventry	d										13 26														14 26
Birmingham International ✈	d										13 38														14 38
Birmingham New Street [12]	d		13 31				13 35				14b01				14 20		14 31					14 35			15c01
Wolverhampton [7]	d		13 49				13 52				14 19				14 37		14 49					14 52			15 19
Penkridge	d						14 03															15 03			
Stafford	a						14 10	14 20			14 33											15 10	15 24		15 33
	d						14 10	14 22			14 34											15 10	15 25		15 34
Stoke-on-Trent	a		14 19	14 26						14 50	14 56						15 19	15 25						15 50	15 56
Congleton	a																								
Macclesfield	a			14 42							15 14							15 42							16 14
Crewe [10]	a	14 12					14 30	14 40							15 09	15 12						15 30	15 43		
	d	14 13				14 27	14 31	14 42						14 57	15 11	15 13					15 27	15 31	15 45		
Chester	a					14 47								15 20							15 47				
Wrexham General	a																								
Llandudno	a																								
Bangor (Gwynedd)	a					16 18															17 12				
Holyhead	a					16 55															17 55				
Wilmslow	a	14 29														15 29									
Stockport	a	14 38		14 56						15 18	15 28					15 38		15 56						16 18	16 28
Manchester Piccadilly [10]	a	14 51	14 57	15 09						15 30	15 40					15 51	15 59	16 09						16 30	16 40
Hartford	a						14 43															15 43			
Warrington Bank Quay	a												15 16		15 28										
	d												15 16		15 29										
Runcorn	a						14 54	14 59														15 54	16 02		
Liverpool South Parkway [7] ✈	a						15 04															16 04			
Liverpool Lime Street [10]	a						15 14	15 21														16 14	16 23		
	d								14 31																
Manchester Airport ✈	d				14 00							14 30								15 00					
Manchester Piccadilly [10]	d				14 16							14 46								15 16					
Bolton	d				14 33							15 05								15 33					
Wigan North Western	a								15 13				15 27		15 39										
	d								15 14				15 27		15 40										
Preston [8]	a				14 57				15 37			15 32	15 40		15 53					15 57					
Blackpool North	a								16 07			16 00													
Preston [8]	d				15 00								15 42		15 55					16 00					
Lancaster [6]	a				15 15								15 56		16 10					16 15					
	d				15 16								15 58		16 10					16 16					
Barrow-in-Furness	a																			17 19					
Oxenholme Lake District	a				15 30								16 10												
	d				15 30								16 11												
Windermere	a																								
Penrith North Lakes	d				15 55										16 47										
Carlisle [8]	a				16 12								16 48		17 02										
	d				16 13								16 49		17 04										
Lockerbie	d				16 32																				
Carstairs	a																								
Motherwell	a																								
Glasgow Central [15]	a												18 02												
Haymarket	a				17s30										18 13										
Edinburgh [10]	a				17 39										18 22										
Perth	a																								
Dundee	a																								
Aberdeen	a																								
Inverness	a																								

b arr. 1348
c arr. 1448

OVERNIGHT SLEEPERS. For sleeper trains, operated by First ScotRail, please refer to Tables 400 - 404

Table 65

Sundays
18 July to 05 September

London and West Midlands - North West England and Scotland

		TP	VT	AW	NT	VT	VT	XC	VT	TP	AW	LM	VT	VT	VT	XC	TP	TP	NT	VT	VT	VT	XC	VT
		◇1	◇1			◇1	◇1	◇1	◇1	◇1	◇	◇1	◇1	◇1	◇1	◇1	◇1	◇1		◇1	◇1	◇1	◇1	◇1
			⊡			⊡	⊡	⊼	⊡	⊼	⊼		⊡	⊡	⊡	⊼				⊡	⊡	⊡	⊼	⊡
London Euston 15 ⊖	d		14 25				14 35		14 55				15 02	15 05	15 15					15 25		15 35		15 55
Watford Junction	d																							
Milton Keynes Central	d													15 39	15 48									
Rugby	d																							
Nuneaton	d																							
Tamworth Low Level	d																							
Lichfield Trent Valley	d																							
Coventry	d															15 26								
Birmingham International ✈	d															15 38								
Birmingham New Street 12	d					15 20		15 31				15 35				16b01					16 20		16 31	
Wolverhampton 7	d					15 37		15 49				15 52				16 19					16u37		16 49	
Penkridge	d											16 03												
Stafford	a											16 10	16 20			16 35								
	d											16 10	16 21			16 36								
Stoke-on-Trent	a							16 19	16 24						16 50	16 56							17 19	17 25
Congleton	a																							
Macclesfield	a								16 42							17 14								17 42
Crewe 10	a					16 09	16 12					16 32		16 50							17 07	17 12		
	d			15 57		16 11	16 13				16 27	16 34		16 52							17 08	17 13		
Chester	a			16 20							16 47			17 14										
Wrexham General	a																							
Llandudno	a																							
Bangor (Gwynedd)	a										18 18													
Holyhead	a										18 55													
Wilmslow	a						16 29															17 29		
Stockport	a						16 38		16 56						17 18	17 28						17 38		17 56
Manchester Piccadilly 10	a						16 51	16 59	17 09						17 30	17 40						17 51	17 56	18 09
Hartford	a											16 45												
Warrington Bank Quay	a		16 16			16 28														17 16	17 26			
	d		16 16			16 29														17 16	17 26			
Runcorn	a											16 56	16 59											
Liverpool South Parkway 7 ✈	a											17 06												
Liverpool Lime Street 10	a											17 17	17 23											
	d				15 31														16 31					
Manchester Airport ✈	d	15 30								16 00							16 30							
Manchester Piccadilly 10	d	15 46								16 16							16 46							
Bolton	d	16 05								16 33							17 05							
Wigan North Western	a		16 27		16 13	16 39													17 13	17 27	17 37			
	d		16 27		16 14	16 40													17 14	17 27	17 37			
Preston 8	a	16 32	16 40		16 37	16 53				16 57							17 32		17 37	17 40	17 51			
Blackpool North	a	17 00			17 07												18 00		18 07					
Preston 8	d		16 42			16 55				17 00								17 04		17 42	17 52			
Lancaster 6	a		16 56			17 10				17 15								17 22		17 56	18 07			
	d		16 57			17 10				17 16								17 22		17 57	18 08			
Barrow-in-Furness	a																							
Oxenholme Lake District	a					17 24				17 30								17 39		18 10	18 22			
	d					17 25				17 30								17 39		18 10	18 23			
Windermere	a																	17 59						
Penrith North Lakes	d		17 32							17 55											18 48			
Carlisle 8	a		17 47			18 03				18 12										18 48	19 03			
	d		17 48			18 05				18 13										18 49	19 04			
Lockerbie	d																							
Carstairs	a																							
Motherwell	a																							
Glasgow Central 15	a		19 00			19 18														20 02				
Haymarket	a																							
Edinburgh 10	a									19 37											20 23			
Perth	a																							
Dundee	a																							
Aberdeen	a																							
Inverness	a																							

b arr. 1548

OVERNIGHT SLEEPERS. For sleeper trains, operated by First ScotRail, please refer to Tables 400 - 404

Table 65

Sundays
18 July to 05 September

London and West Midlands - North West England and Scotland

		TP	AW	LM	VT	VT	VT	XC	TP	TP	NT	VT	VT	VT	XC	VT	TP	AW	LM	VT	VT	VT	TP	VT
		◇1		◇1	◇1	◇1	◇1	◇1	◇1	◇1		◇1	◇1	◇1	◇1	◇1	◇1	◇	◇1	◇1	◇1	◇1	◇1	◇1
		⊼			⊡	⊡	⊡	⊼				⊡	⊡	⊡	⊼	⊡	⊼			⊡	⊡	⊡		⊡
London Euston 15 ⊖	d				16 02	16 05	16 15					16 25		16 35		16 55				17 02	17 05	17 15		17 25
Watford Junction	d																							
Milton Keynes Central	d					16 39	16 48														17 39	17 48		
Rugby	d																				18 10			
Nuneaton	d																							
Tamworth Low Level	d																							
Lichfield Trent Valley	d																							
Coventry	d							16 26																
Birmingham International ✈	d							16 38																
Birmingham New Street 12	d			16 35				17b01					17 20		17 31				17 35					
Wolverhampton 7	d			16 52				17 19					17u37		17 49				17 52					
Penkridge	d			17 03															18 03					
Stafford	a			17 10	17 24			17 35											18 10	18 24				
	d			17 10	17 25			17 36											18 10	18 25				
Stoke-on-Trent	a						17 50	17 56							18 19	18 25						18 50		
Congleton	a																							
Macclesfield	a							18 14								18 42								
Crewe 10	a			17 30		17 50							18 09	18 12					18 30		18 53			
	d		17 27	17 31		17 52							18 11	18 13				18 27	18 31		18 56			
Chester	a		17 48			18 14												18 47			19 14			
Wrexham General	a																							
Llandudno	a																							
Bangor (Gwynedd)	a																	20 08			20 26			
Holyhead	a																	20 44			20 59			
Wilmslow	a													18 29										
Stockport	a						18 18	18 28						18 38		18 56						19 18		
Manchester Piccadilly 10	a						18 30	18 40						18 51	18 56	19 09						19 30		
Hartford	a			17 43															18 43					
Warrington Bank Quay	a											18 16	18 28											19 16
	d											18 17	18 29											19 16
Runcorn	a			17 54	17 57														18 54	18 57				
Liverpool South Parkway 7 ✈	a			18 04															19 04					
Liverpool Lime Street 10	a			18 14	18 20														19 14	19 20				
	d										17 31													
Manchester Airport ✈	d	17 00							17 30								18 00						18 30	
Manchester Piccadilly 10	d	17 16							17 46								18 16						18 46	
Bolton	d	17 33							18 05								18 33						19 05	
Wigan North Western	a										18 13	18 27	18 39											19 27
	d										18 14	18 28	18 40											19 27
Preston 8	a	17 57							18 32		18 37	18 40	18 53				18 57						19 32	19 40
Blackpool North	a								19 00		19 07												20 00	
Preston 8	d	18 08								18 12		18 42	18 55				19 00							19 42
Lancaster 6	a	18 23								18 28		18 56	19 10				19 15							19 56
	d	18 24								18 28		18 58	19 10				19 16							19 57
Barrow-in-Furness	a									19 32														
Oxenholme Lake District	a	18 38										19 10	19 24				19 30							20 10
	d	18 38										19 11	19 26				19 30							20 10
Windermere	a																							
Penrith North Lakes	d	19 03										19 36					19 55							20 36
Carlisle 8	a	19 20										19 51	20 03				20 12							20 51
	d	19 21										19 53	20 05				20 13							20 52
Lockerbie	d	19 40															20 32							
Carstairs	a																							
Motherwell	a	20s27																						
Glasgow Central 15	a	20 45										21 08	21 18											22 07
Haymarket	a																21s30							
Edinburgh 10	a																21 39							
Perth	a																							
Dundee	a																							
Aberdeen	a																							
Inverness	a																							

b arr. 1648

OVERNIGHT SLEEPERS. For sleeper trains, operated by First ScotRail, please refer to Tables 400 - 404

Table 65

London and West Midlands - North West England and Scotland

Sundays

18 July to 05 September

		NT	VT	VT	XC	VT	TP	AW	LM	VT	VT	VT	XC	TP	NT	VT	VT	VT	XC	VT	AW	LM	VT	VT	VT
			◇1	◇1	◇1	◇1	◇1		◇1	◇1	◇1	◇1	◇1	◇1		◇1	1	◇1	◇1	◇1		◇1	◇1	◇1	◇1
London Euston 15 ⊖	d			17 35		17 55				18 02	18 05	18 15				18 25		18 35		18 55			19 02	19 05	19 15
Watford Junction	d																								
Milton Keynes Central	d										18 39	18 48												19 39	19 48
Rugby	d																								
Nuneaton	d																						20 01		
Tamworth Low Level	d																								
Lichfield Trent Valley	d																								
Coventry	d												18 26												
Birmingham International ✈	d												18 38												
Birmingham New Street 12	d		18 20		18 31				18 35				19b01				19 20		19 31			19 35			
Wolverhampton 7	d		18 37		18 49				18 52				19 19				19 37		19 49			19 52			
Penkridge	d								19 03													20 03			
Stafford	a								19 10	19 24			19 37									20 10	20 25		
	d								19 10	19 25			19 38									20 10	20 30		
Stoke-on-Trent	a				19 19	19 25						19 50	19 56						20 19	20 25					20 50
Congleton	a																								
Macclesfield	a					19 42							20 14							20 42					
Crewe 10	a		19 09	19 12					19 30		19 50						20 09	20 12				20 30	20 48	20 53	
	d		19 11	19 13				19 27	19 31		19 52						20 11	20 13			20 27	20 31	20 50	20 55	
Chester	a							19 48			20 11										20 48			21 14	
Wrexham General	a																								
Llandudno	a																								
Bangor (Gwynedd)	a										21 23													22 22	
Holyhead	a										21 57													22 56	
Wilmslow	a			19 29														20 29							
Stockport	a			19 38		19 56						20 18	20 28					20 38		20 56					21 18
Manchester Piccadilly 10	a			19 51	19 58	20 09						20 30	20 40					20 51	21 00	21 09					21 30
Hartford	a								19 43													20 43			
Warrington Bank Quay	a		19 28													20 16	20 28								
	d		19 29													20 16	20 29								
Runcorn	a								19 54	19 58												20 54	21 07		
Liverpool South Parkway 7 ✈	a								20 04													21 04			
Liverpool Lime Street 10	a								20 14	20 20												21 14	21 28		
	d	18 31													19 31										
Manchester Airport ✈	d						19 00							19 30											
Manchester Piccadilly 10	d						19 16							19 46											
Bolton	d						19 33							20 05											
Wigan North Western	a	19 13	19 39												20 13	20 27	20 39								
	d	19 14	19 40												20 14	20 27	20 40								
Preston 8	a	19 37	19 53				19 57							20 32	20 37	20 40	20 53								
Blackpool North	a	20 07												21 00	21 07										
Preston 8	d		19 55				20 00									20 42	20 55								
Lancaster 6	a		20 10				20 15									20 56	21 10								
	d		20 10				20 16									20 57	21 10								
Barrow-in-Furness	a						21 19																		
Oxenholme Lake District	a															21 10	21 24								
	d															21 11	21 26								
Windermere	a																								
Penrith North Lakes	d		20 47													21 36									
Carlisle 8	a		21 02													21 51	22 03								
	d		21 04													21 52	22 05								
Lockerbie	d																22 23								
Carstairs	a																								
Motherwell	a															22 48	23 07								
Glasgow Central 15	a															23 09	23 22								
Haymarket	a		22 15																						
Edinburgh 10	a		22 23																						
Perth	a																								
Dundee	a																								
Aberdeen	a																								
Inverness	a																								

b arr. 1848

OVERNIGHT SLEEPERS. For sleeper trains, operated by First ScotRail, please refer to Tables 400 - 404

Table 65

London and West Midlands - North West England and Scotland

Sundays

18 July to 05 September

		XC	NT	VT	TP	VT	VT	XC	VT	AW	VT	VT	NT	SR	VT	XC	TP	AW	VT	VT	VT	LM	XC	NT	AW	VT
		◇1		◇1	◇1	◇1	◇1	◇1	◇1	◇	◇1	◇1			◇1	◇1	◇1		◇1	◇1	◇1	◇1	◇1		◇	◇1
London Euston 15 ⊖	d					19 25	19 35		19 55		20 02	20 05		20 07	20 15				20 25		20 35					20 50
Watford Junction	d																									
Milton Keynes Central	d											20 38			20 48											21 39
Rugby	d																									22 01
Nuneaton	d										21 01															
Tamworth Low Level	d																		21 32							
Lichfield Trent Valley	d																		21 39							
Coventry	d	19 26														20 26							21 26			
Birmingham International ✈	d	19 38														20 38							21 38			
Birmingham New Street 12	d	20b01		20 20				20 31								21c01				21 20		21 35	22e01			
Wolverhampton 7	d	20 19		20 38				20 49								21 19				21 37		21 58	22 19			
Penkridge	d																					22 08				
Stafford	a	20 37		20 51								21 32				21 37				21 56	22 03	22 16	22 37			
	d	20 38		20 52								21 33				21 38				21 57	22 04	22 16	22 38			
Stoke-on-Trent	a	20 56						21 19	21 25						21 50	21 56							22 55			
Congleton	a																									
Macclesfield	a	21 15							21 42							22 14							23 12			
Crewe 10	a			21 10			21 13				21 44	21 53							22 10	22 15	22 22	22 39				22 49
	d						21 14			21 27	21 46	21 55						21 57	22 13	22 17	22 23				22 29	22 51
Chester	a									21 46								22 18							22 50	
Wrexham General	a																									
Llandudno	a																									
Bangor (Gwynedd)	a									23 10															00 12	
Holyhead	a									23 52															00 49	
Wilmslow	a						21 30														22 38					
Stockport	a	21 28					21 39		21 56						22 18	22 28					22 48		23 27			
Manchester Piccadilly 10	a	21 40					21 52	21 56	22 09						22 30	22 40					23 00		23 41			
Hartford	a																									
Warrington Bank Quay	a					21 16													22 29	22 34						23 08
	d					21 16													22 30	22 35						23 08
Runcorn	a										22 03	22 12														
Liverpool South Parkway 7 ✈	a																									
Liverpool Lime Street 10	a										22 24	22 33														
	d		20 31										21 31											22 31		
Manchester Airport ✈	d				20 30												21 30									
Manchester Piccadilly 10	d				20 46												21 46									
Bolton	d				21 05												22 05									
Wigan North Western	a		21 13			21 27							22 13						22 40	22 45				23 13		23 19
	d		21 14			21 27							22 14						22 41	22 46				23 14		23 19
Preston 8	a		21 37		21 32	21 40							22 37				22 29		22 58	23 05				23 35		23 41
Blackpool North	a		22 07		22 00								23 07				22 55							00 05		
Preston 8	d					21 42																				
Lancaster 6	a					21 56																				
	d					21 57																				
Barrow-in-Furness	a																									
Oxenholme Lake District	a					22 10																				
	d					22 11																				
Windermere	a																									
Penrith North Lakes	d					22 36																				
Carlisle 8	a					22 51																				
	d					22 53																				
Lockerbie	d																									
Carstairs	a																									
Motherwell	a																									
Glasgow Central 15	a					00 02																				
Haymarket	a																									
Edinburgh 10	a													03s13												
Perth	a													05s39												
Dundee	a													06s08												
Aberdeen	a													07 35												
Inverness	a													08 30												

b arr. 1948

c arr. 2048

e arr. 2148

OVERNIGHT SLEEPERS. For sleeper trains, operated by First ScotRail, please refer to Tables 400 - 404

Table 65

Sundays
18 July to 05 September

London and West Midlands - North West England and Scotland

		AW	VT	VT	AW	VT	SR
			◇1	◇1	◇	◇1	
London Euston 15 ⊖	d		21 21	21 24		21 50	22 32
Watford Junction	d						
Milton Keynes Central	d			22 13		22 38	
Rugby	d					23 18	
Nuneaton	d		22 54			23 29	
Tamworth Low Level	d						
Lichfield Trent Valley	d						
Coventry	d						
Birmingham International ✈	d				22 40		
Birmingham New Street 12	d				22 55		
Wolverhampton 7	d				23 15		
Penkridge	d						
Stafford	a		23 19		23 30	23s53	
	d		23 19		23 31	23s54	
Stoke-on-Trent	a			23 29			
Congleton	a						
Macclesfield	a			23 45			
Crewe 10	a		23 38		23 55	00s12	
	d	23 38	23 41		00 10	00s13	
Chester	a	23 59			00 30		
Wrexham General	a						
Llandudno	a						
Bangor (Gwynedd)	a				01 40		
Holyhead	a				02 15		
Wilmslow	a						
Stockport	a			23 59		00s40	
Manchester Piccadilly 10	a			00 13		00 53	
Hartford	a						
Warrington Bank Quay	a						
	d						
Runcorn	a		00 02				
Liverpool South Parkway 7 ✈	a						
Liverpool Lime Street 10	a		00 29				
	d						
Manchester Airport ✈	d						
Manchester Piccadilly 10	d						
Bolton	d						
Wigan North Western	a						
	d						
Preston 8	a						
Blackpool North	a						
Preston 8	d						
Lancaster 6	a						
	d						
Barrow-in-Furness	a						
Oxenholme Lake District	a						
	d						
Windermere	a						
Penrith North Lakes	d						
Carlisle 8	a						
	d						
Lockerbie	d						
Carstairs	a						06s42
Motherwell	a						06s59
Glasgow Central 15	a						07 19
Haymarket	a						
Edinburgh 10	a						07 17
Perth	a						
Dundee	a						
Aberdeen	a						
Inverness	a						

OVERNIGHT SLEEPERS. For sleeper trains, operated by First ScotRail, please refer to Tables 400 - 404

Table 65

Sundays
12 September to 17 October

London and West Midlands - North West England and Scotland

		TP	TP	TP	NT	TP	TP	AW	AW	VT	XC	TP	AW	VT	VT	NT	TP	VT	VT	VT
				◇1		◇1	◇1	◇		◇1	◇1	◇1		◇1	◇1		◇1	◇1	◇1	◇1
London Euston 15 ⊖	d														08 10				08 15	08 20
Watford Junction	d																			
Milton Keynes Central	d														08 56					09 05
Rugby	d																			
Nuneaton	d																		09 42	
Tamworth Low Level	d																			
Lichfield Trent Valley	d																			
Coventry	d																			
Birmingham International ✈	d																			
Birmingham New Street 12	d									08 45	09 01			09 20						
Wolverhampton 7	d									09 04	09 19			09 37						
Penkridge	d																			
Stafford	a									09 17	09 33								10 08	
	d									09 18	09 34								10 08	
Stoke-on-Trent	a																			10 19
Congleton	a																			
Macclesfield	a																			10 36
Crewe 10	a									09 38	09 54			10 06	10 15				10 28	
	d							09 24	09 28	09 39	09 56		10 07	10 08	10 17			10 21	10 30	
Chester	a							09 45					10 30							
Wrexham General	a																			
Llandudno	a																			
Bangor (Gwynedd)	a							11 04												
Holyhead	a							11 44												
Wilmslow	a								09 46		10 12				10 31					
Stockport	a										10 21				10 41					10 51
Manchester Piccadilly 10	a								10 13		10 34				10 54					11 04
Hartford	a																			
Warrington Bank Quay	a									09 57				10 26				10 37		
	d									09 57				10 26				10 37		
Runcorn	a																		10 47	
Liverpool South Parkway 7 ✈	a																			
Liverpool Lime Street 10	a																		11 09	
	d				08 31											09 31				
Manchester Airport ✈	d	00 10	05 30	07 30		08 47	09 00					09 30					10 00			
Manchester Piccadilly 10	d	00 35	05 55	07 46		09 03	09 16					09 46					10 16			
Bolton	d	01s00	06s20	08 06		09 23	09 33					10 05					10 32			
Wigan North Western	a				09 13					10 08				10 37		10 13		10 48		
	d				09 14					10 08				10 37		10 14		10 48		
Preston 8	a	01s35	06s55	08 31	09 37	09 50	09 57			10 25		10 32		10 51		10 39	10 55	11 04		
Blackpool North	a	02 15	07 35	08 58	10 07	10 17						11 00				11 09				
Preston 8	d						10 00							10 52			11 00	11 06		
Lancaster 6	a						10 15							11 07			11 15	11 22		
	d						10 16							11 08			11 16			
Barrow-in-Furness	a																			
Oxenholme Lake District	a						10 30							11 22			11 30			
	d						10 30							11 23			11 30			
Windermere	a																			
Penrith North Lakes	d						10 55										11 56			
Carlisle 8	a						11 12							12 01			12 12			
	d						11 13							12 02			12 13			
Lockerbie	d						11 32										12 30			
Carstairs	a																			
Motherwell	a																			
Glasgow Central 15	a													13 19			13 34			
Haymarket	a						12s32													
Edinburgh 10	a						12 39													
Perth	a																			
Dundee	a																			
Aberdeen	a																			
Inverness	a																			

OVERNIGHT SLEEPERS. For sleeper trains, operated by First ScotRail, please refer to Tables 400 - 404

Table 65

London and West Midlands - North West England and Scotland

Sundays
12 September to 17 October

		LM	XC	TP	VT	TP	NT	VT	AW	VT	AW	VT	VT	LM	XC	TP	NT	LM	AW	VT	VT	TP	AW	VT	VT
London Euston ⊖	d							08 45				09 15	09 20							09 45				10 15	10 20
Watford Junction	d																								
Milton Keynes Central	d							09 32					10 07							10 33					11 07
Rugby	d							10 08												11 08					
Nuneaton	d											10 45												11 46	
Tamworth Low Level	d																								
Lichfield Trent Valley	d																								
Coventry	d														10b28										
Birmingham International ✈	d														10 40										
Birmingham New Street	d	09 42	10 00							10 20				10 42	11c01						11 20				
Wolverhampton	d	09 59	10 18							10 37				10 59	11 19						11 37				
Penkridge	d	10 10												11 10											
Stafford	a	10 17	10 32									11 11		11 17	11 32									12 11	
	d	10 17	10 33									11 11		11 17	11 33			11 44						12 12	
Stoke-on-Trent	a		10 51										11 22		11 51			12 02							12 23
Congleton	a																								
Macclesfield	a		11 08										11 39		12 09										12 40
Crewe	a	10 37						10 55		11 08		11 30		11 37				12 26		11 56	12 07			12 31	
	d	10 38			10 42			10 57	11 05	11 10	11 27	11 32		11 38					11 57	11 58	12 09		12 27	12 33	
Chester	a				11 02				11 26		11 48								12 20				12 48		
Wrexham General	a																								
Llandudno	a																								
Bangor (Gwynedd)	a				12 09						13 10												14 18		
Holyhead	a				12 43						13 45												14 55		
Wilmslow	a																								
Stockport	a		11 22										11 53		12 22										12 54
Manchester Piccadilly	a		11 34										12 06		12 34										13 09
Hartford	a	10 50												11 50											
Warrington Bank Quay	a							11 13		11 27										12 15	12 26				
	d							11 14		11 28										12 15	12 27				
Runcorn	a	11 00										11 49		12 01										12 50	
Liverpool South Parkway ✈	a	11 10												12 11											
Liverpool Lime Street	a	11 20										12 10		12 21										13 11	
	d						10 31										11 31								
Manchester Airport ✈	d			10 25												11 30						11 58			
Manchester Piccadilly	d			10 43												11 46						12 16			
Bolton	d			11 05												12 05						12 33			
Wigan North Western	a						11 13	11 24		11 38							12 13			12 26	12 37				
	d						11 14	11 25		11 39							12 14			12 26	12 38				
Preston	a			11 32			11 37	11 38		11 52						12 32	12 37			12 39	12 51	12 57			
Blackpool North	a			12 00			12 07									13 00	13 07								
Preston	d					11 18		11 39		11 54										12 41	12 53	12 58			
Lancaster	a					11 33		11 54		12 09										12 55	13 08	13 13			
	d					11 34		11 54		12 09										12 56	13 08	13 14			
Barrow-in-Furness	a					12 37																			
Oxenholme Lake District	a							12 07		12 23										13 09	13 22	13 28			
	d							12 08		12 25										13 09	13 24	13 28			
Windermere	a																								
Penrith North Lakes	d							12 34												13 35		13 53			
Carlisle	a							12 49		13 02										13 50	14 01	14 10			
	d							12 49		13 04										13 51	14 03	14 11			
Lockerbie	d																					14 30			
Carstairs	a																								
Motherwell	a																								
Glasgow Central	a							14 01												15 04	15 16				
Haymarket	a									14 14												15s28			
Edinburgh	a									14 22												15 36			
Perth	a																								
Dundee	a																								
Aberdeen	a																								
Inverness	a																								

b arr. 1022
c arr. 1050

OVERNIGHT SLEEPERS. For sleeper trains, operated by First ScotRail, please refer to Tables 400 - 404

Table 65

London and West Midlands - North West England and Scotland

Sundays
12 September to 17 October

		LM	NT	XC	TP	AW	VT	TP	VT	VT	VT	TP	NT	AW	LM	VT	VT	XC	TP	VT	AW	VT		VT	XC
London Euston ⊖	d						10 45			11 15	11 20					12 02	12 15			12 25				12 35	
Watford Junction	d																								
Milton Keynes Central	d						11 32			12 04	12 09						12 48								
Rugby	d						12 08																		
Nuneaton	d																								
Tamworth Low Level	d																								
Lichfield Trent Valley	d																								
Coventry	d			11b28														12e28							
Birmingham International ✈	d			11 40														12 40							
Birmingham New Street	d	11 42		12c01					12 20						12 35			13f01				13 20			13 31
Wolverhampton	d	11 59		12 20					12 37						12 52			13 19				13 37			13 49
Penkridge	d	12 10													13 03										
Stafford	a	12 16		12 33						12 54					13 10	13 23		13 33							
	d	12 16		12 34						12 55					13 10	13 24		13 34							
Stoke-on-Trent	a			12 51							13 07						13 50	13 56							14 19
Congleton	a																								
Macclesfield	a			13 09							13 24							14 14							
Crewe	a	12 37					12 57		13 07	13 15					13 30	13 42						14 09		14 12	
	d	12 38				12 54	12 59		13 09	13 17				13 27	13 31	13 44					13 57	14 11		14 13	
Chester	a					13 15								13 47							14 18				
Wrexham General	a																								
Llandudno	a																								
Bangor (Gwynedd)	a													15 12											
Holyhead	a													15 55											
Wilmslow	a																							14 29	
Stockport	a			13 28							13 38						14 18	14 28						14 38	
Manchester Piccadilly	a			13 40							13 52						14 30	14 40						14 51	14 57
Hartford	a	12 50													13 43										
Warrington Bank Quay	a						13 16		13 26											14 16		14 28			
	d						13 16		13 27											14 16		14 29			
Runcorn	a	13 01								13 34					13 54	14 01									
Liverpool South Parkway ✈	a	13 11													14 04										
Liverpool Lime Street	a	13 21								13 57					14 14	14 23									
	d		12 31										13 31												
Manchester Airport ✈	d				12 30							12 58							13 30						
Manchester Piccadilly	d				12 46							13 16							13 46						
Bolton	d				13 05							13 33							14 05						
Wigan North Western	a		13 13				13 27		13 37				14 13							14 27		14 39			
	d		13 14				13 27		13 38				14 14							14 27		14 40			
Preston	a		13 37		13 32		13 40		13 51			13 57	14 37						14 32	14 40		14 52			
Blackpool North	a		14 09		14 01								15 07						15 00						
Preston	d						13 42	13 47	13 53			14 00								14 42		14 55			
Lancaster	a						13 56	14 03	14 08			14 15								14 56		15 10			
	d						13 57	14 03	14 08			14 16								14 58		15 11			
Barrow-in-Furness	a							15 07																	
Oxenholme Lake District	a						14 10					14 30										15 24			
	d						14 10					14 30										15 25			
Windermere	a																								
Penrith North Lakes	d						14 36		14 45			14 55								15 32					
Carlisle	a						14 51		15 00			15 12								15 47		16 03			
	d						14 52		15 02			15 17								15 48		16 05			
Lockerbie	d																								
Carstairs	a																								
Motherwell	a																								
Glasgow Central	a						16 05					16 35								17 00		17 18			
Haymarket	a								16 14																
Edinburgh	a								16 22																
Perth	a																								
Dundee	a																								
Aberdeen	a																								
Inverness	a																								

b arr. 1122
c arr. 1150
e arr. 1222
f arr. 1250

OVERNIGHT SLEEPERS. For sleeper trains, operated by First ScotRail, please refer to Tables 400 - 404

Table 65

London and West Midlands - North West England and Scotland

		VT	TP	AW	LM	VT	VT	XC	NT	TP	VT	AW	VT	VT	XC	VT	TP	AW		LM	VT	VT	XC	TP	VT
		◇1	◇1	◇	◇1	◇1	◇1	◇1		◇1	◇1		◇1	◇1	◇1	◇1	◇1	◇		◇1	◇1	◇1	◇1	◇1	◇1
		R	T	T		R	R	T			R		R	R	T	R		T			R	R	T		R
London Euston 15 ⊖	d	12 55				13 02	13 15				13 25			13 35		13 55					14 02	14 15			14 25
Watford Junction	d																								
Milton Keynes Central	d						13 48															14 48			
Rugby	d																								
Nuneaton	d																								
Tamworth Low Level	d																								
Lichfield Trent Valley	d																								
Coventry	d							13 26															14 26		
Birmingham International ✈	d							13 38															14 38		
Birmingham New Street 12	d				13 35			14b01					14 20		14 31					14 35			15c01		
Wolverhampton 7	d				13 52			14 19					14 37		14 49					14 52			15 19		
Penkridge	d				14 03															15 03					
Stafford	a				14 10	14 20		14 33												15 10	15 24		15 33		
	d				14 10	14 22		14 34												15 10	15 25		15 34		
Stoke-on-Trent	a	14 26					14 50	14 56							15 19	15 25						15 50	15 56		
Congleton	a																								
Macclesfield	a	14 42						15 14								15 42							16 14		
Crewe 10	a				14 30	14 40							15 09	15 12						15 30	15 43				
	d			14 27	14 31	14 42						14 57	15 11	15 13				15 27		15 31	15 45				
Chester	a			14 47								15 18						15 47							
Wrexham General	a																								
Llandudno	a																								
Bangor (Gwynedd)	a			16 18														17 12							
Holyhead	a			16 54														17 55							
Wilmslow	a													15 29											
Stockport	a	14 56					15 18	15 28						15 38		15 56						16 18	16 28		
Manchester Piccadilly 10	a	15 09					15 30	15 40						15 51	16 00	16 09						16 30	16 40		
Hartford	a				14 43															15 43					
Warrington Bank Quay	a										15 16		15 28												16 16
	d										15 16		15 29												16 16
Runcorn	a				14 54	14 59														15 54	16 02				
Liverpool South Parkway 7 ✈	a				15 04															16 04					
Liverpool Lime Street 10	a				15 14	15 21														16 14	16 23				
	d								14 31										15 31						
Manchester Airport ✈	d		13 58							14 30							15 00							15 30	
Manchester Piccadilly 10	d		14 16							14 46							15 16							15 46	
Bolton	d		14 33							15 05							15 33							16 05	
Wigan North Western	a								15 13		15 27		15 39						16 13						16 27
	d								15 14		15 27		15 40						16 14						16 27
Preston 8	a		14 57						15 37	15 32	15 40		15 53				15 57		16 37					16 32	16 40
Blackpool North	a								16 07	16 00									17 07					17 00	
Preston 8	d		15 00								15 42		15 55				16 00								16 42
Lancaster 6	a		15 15								15 56		16 10				16 15								16 56
	d		15 16								15 58		16 10				16 16								16 57
Barrow-in-Furness	a																17 19								
Oxenholme Lake District	a		15 30								16 10														
	d		15 30								16 11														
Windermere	a																								
Penrith North Lakes	d		15 55										16 47												17 32
Carlisle 8	a		16 12								16 48		17 02												17 47
	d		16 13								16 49		17 04												17 48
Lockerbie	d		16 32																						
Carstairs	a																								
Motherwell	a																								
Glasgow Central 15	a										18 02														19 00
Haymarket	a		17s30										18 13												
Edinburgh 10	a		17 39										18 22												
Perth	a																								
Dundee	a																								
Aberdeen	a																								
Inverness	a																								

b arr. 1348   c arr. 1448

OVERNIGHT SLEEPERS. For sleeper trains, operated by First ScotRail, please refer to Tables 400 - 404

Table 65

London and West Midlands - North West England and Scotland

		AW	VT	VT		XC	VT	TP	AW	LM	VT	VT	VT	XC	NT	TP	VT	VT	VT	XC	VT	TP	AW	LM	NT
			◇1	◇1		◇1	◇1	◇1	◇	◇1	◇1	◇1	◇1	◇1		◇1	◇1	◇1	◇1	◇1	◇1	◇1	◇	◇1	
		A																							
			R	R		T	R	T	T		R	R	R	T			R	R	R	T	R	T			
London Euston 15 ⊖	d			14 35			14 55				15 02	15 05	15 15				15 25		15 35		15 55				
Watford Junction	d																								
Milton Keynes Central	d											15 39	15 48												
Rugby	d																								
Nuneaton	d																								
Tamworth Low Level	d																								
Lichfield Trent Valley	d																								
Coventry	d													15 26											
Birmingham International ✈	d													15 38											
Birmingham New Street 12	d		15 20			15 31				15 35				16b01				16 20		16 31				16 35	
Wolverhampton 7	d		15 37			15 49				15 52				16 19				16u37		16 49				16 52	
Penkridge	d									16 03														17 03	
Stafford	a									16 10	16 20			16 35										17 10	
	d									16 10	16 21			16 36										17 10	
Stoke-on-Trent	a					16 19	16 24						16 50	16 56						17 19	17 25				
Congleton	a																								
Macclesfield	a						16 42							17 14							17 42				
Crewe 10	a		16 09	16 12						16 32		16 50						17 07	17 12					17 30	
	d	15\57	16 11	16 13					16 27	16 34		16 52						17 08	17 13				17 27	17 31	
Chester	a	16\20							16 47			17 14											17 47		
Wrexham General	a																								
Llandudno	a																								
Bangor (Gwynedd)	a								18 18														19 12		
Holyhead	a								18 55														19 55		
Wilmslow	a			16 29															17 29						
Stockport	a			16 38			16 56						17 18	17 28					17 38		17 56				
Manchester Piccadilly 10	a			16 51		16 59	17 09						17 30	17 40					17 51	17 56	18 09				
Hartford	a									16 45														17 43	
Warrington Bank Quay	a		16 28														17 16	17 26							
	d		16 29														17 16	17 26							
Runcorn	a									16 56	16 59													17 54	
Liverpool South Parkway 7 ✈	a									17 06														18 04	
Liverpool Lime Street 10	a									17 17	17 23													18 14	
	d														16 31										17 31
Manchester Airport ✈	d							16 00								16 30						17 00			
Manchester Piccadilly 10	d							16 16								16 46						17 16			
Bolton	d							16 33								17 05						17 33			
Wigan North Western	a		16 39												17 13		17 27	17 37							18 13
	d		16 40												17 14		17 27	17 37							18 14
Preston 8	a		16 53					16 57							17 37	17 32	17 40	17 51				17 57			18 37
Blackpool North	a														18 07	18 00									19 07
Preston 8	d		16 55					17 00									17 42	17 52				18 00			
Lancaster 6	a		17 10					17 15									17 56	18 07				18 15			
	d		17 10					17 16									17 57	18 08				18 16			
Barrow-in-Furness	a																								
Oxenholme Lake District	a		17 24					17 30									18 10	18 22				18 30			
	d		17 25					17 30									18 10	18 23				18 30			
Windermere	a																								
Penrith North Lakes	d							17 55										18 48				18 55			
Carlisle 8	a		18 03					18 12									18 48	19 03				19 12			
	d		18 05					18 13									18 49	19 04				19 21			
Lockerbie	d																					19 40			
Carstairs	a																								
Motherwell	a																					20s27			
Glasgow Central 15	a		19 18														20 02					20 45			
Haymarket	a																								
Edinburgh 10	a							19 37										20 23							
Perth	a																								
Dundee	a																								
Aberdeen	a																								
Inverness	a																								

A 12 September   b arr. 1548

OVERNIGHT SLEEPERS. For sleeper trains, operated by First ScotRail, please refer to Tables 400 - 404

Table 65

Sundays

12 September to 17 October

London and West Midlands - North West England and Scotland

		VT	VT	VT	XC	TP	TP	VT	VT	VT		XC	VT	TP	AW	LM	VT	VT	VT	TP	NT	VT	VT	VT	XC
		◇1 ⊐	◇1 ⊐	◇1 ⊐	◇1 ⌶	◇1	◇1	◇1 ⊐	◇1 ⊐	◇1 ⊐		◇1 ⌶	◇1 ⊐	◇1 ⌶	◇	◇1	◇1 ⊐	◇1 ⊐	◇1 ⊐	◇1		◇1 ⊐	◇1 ⊐	◇1 ⊐	◇1 ⌶
London Euston 15 ⊖	d	16 02	16 05	16 15				16 25		16 35			16 55				17 02	17 05	17 15			17 25		17 35	
Watford Junction	d																								
Milton Keynes Central	d		16 39	16 48														17 39	17 48						
Rugby	d																								
Nuneaton	d																	18 10							
Tamworth Low Level	d																								
Lichfield Trent Valley	d																								
Coventry	d				16 26																				
Birmingham International ✈	d				16 38																				
Birmingham New Street 12	d				17b01				17 20			17 31				17 35							18 20		18 31
Wolverhampton 7	d				17 19				17u37			17 49				17 52							18 37		18 49
Penkridge	d															18 03									
Stafford	a	17 24			17 35											18 10	18 24								
	d	17 25			17 36											18 10	18 25								
Stoke-on-Trent	a			17 50	17 56							18 19	18 25						18 50						19 19
Congleton	a																								
Macclesfield	a				18 14								18 42												
Crewe 10	a		17 50						18 09	18 12						18 30		18 53					19 09	19 12	
	d		17 52						18 11	18 13					18 27	18 31		18 56					19 11	19 13	
Chester	a		18 14												18 47			19 14							
Wrexham General	a																								
Llandudno	a																								
Bangor (Gwynedd)	a														20 08			20 26							
Holyhead	a														20 44			20 59							
Wilmslow	a									18 29														19 29	
Stockport	a			18 18	18 28					18 38			18 56						19 18					19 38	
Manchester Piccadilly 10	a			18 30	18 40					18 51		18 56	19 09						19 30					19 51	19 58
Hartford	a															18 43									
Warrington Bank Quay	a							18 16	18 28													19 16	19 28		
	d							18 17	18 29													19 16	19 29		
Runcorn	a	17 57														18 54	18 57								
Liverpool South Parkway 7 ✈	a															19 04									
Liverpool Lime Street 10	a	18 20														19 14	19 20								
	d																				18 31				
Manchester Airport ✈	d					17 30								18 00						18 30					
Manchester Piccadilly 10	d					17 46								18 16						18 46					
Bolton	d					18 05								18 33						19 05					
Wigan North Western	a							18 27	18 39												19 13	19 27	19 39		
	d							18 28	18 40												19 14	19 27	19 40		
Preston 8	a					18 32		18 40	18 53					18 57						19 32	19 37	19 40	19 53		
Blackpool North	a					19 00														20 00	20 07				
Preston 8	d						18 06	18 42	18 55					19 00								19 42	19 55		
Lancaster 6	a						18 22	18 56	19 10					19 15								19 56	20 10		
	d						18 22	18 58	19 10					19 16								19 57	20 10		
Barrow-in-Furness	a						19 26																		
Oxenholme Lake District	a							19 10	19 24					19 30								20 10			
	d							19 11	19 26					19 30								20 10			
Windermere	a																								
Penrith North Lakes	d							19 36						19 55								20 36	20 47		
Carlisle 8	a							19 51	20 03					20 12								20 51	21 02		
	d							19 53	20 05					20 13								20 52	21 04		
Lockerbie	d													20 32											
Carstairs	a																								
Motherwell	a																								
Glasgow Central 15	a							21 08	21 18													22 07			
Haymarket	a													21s30									22 15		
Edinburgh 10	a													21 39									22 23		
Perth	a																								
Dundee	a																								
Aberdeen	a																								
Inverness	a																								

b arr. 1648

OVERNIGHT SLEEPERS. For sleeper trains, operated by First ScotRail, please refer to Tables 400 - 404

Table 65

Sundays

12 September to 17 October

London and West Midlands - North West England and Scotland

		VT	TP	AW	LM	VT	NT	VT	VT	XC	TP	VT	VT	VT	XC	VT	NT	AW	LM	VT	VT	VT	XC	VT	TP
		◇1 ⊐	◇1		◇1	◇1 ⊐		◇1 ⊐	◇1 ⊐	◇1 ⌶	◇1	◇1 ⊐	■ 1 ⊐	◇1 ⊐	◇1 ⌶	◇1 ⊐			◇1	◇1 ⊐	◇1 ⊐	◇1 ⊐	◇1 ⌶	◇1 ⊐	◇1
London Euston 15 ⊖	d	17 55				18 02		18 05	18 15			18 25		18 35		18 55				19 02	19 05	19 15			
Watford Junction	d																								
Milton Keynes Central	d							18 39	18 48												19 39	19 48			
Rugby	d																								
Nuneaton	d																			20 01					
Tamworth Low Level	d																								
Lichfield Trent Valley	d																								
Coventry	d									18 26													19 26		
Birmingham International ✈	d									18 38													19 38		
Birmingham New Street 12	d				18 35					19b01			19 20		19 31				19 35				20c01	20 20	
Wolverhampton 7	d				18 52					19 19			19 37		19 49				19 52				20 19	20 38	
Penkridge	d				19 03														20 03						
Stafford	a				19 10	19 24				19 37									20 10	20 25			20 37	20 51	
	d				19 10	19 25				19 38									20 10	20 30			20 38	20 52	
Stoke-on-Trent	a	19 25							19 50	19 56					20 19	20 25						20 50	20 56		
Congleton	a																								
Macclesfield	a	19 42								20 14						20 42							21 15		
Crewe 10	a				19 30			19 50					20 09	20 12					20 30	20 48	20 53			21 10	
	d			19 27	19 31			19 52					20 11	20 13				20 27	20 31	20 50	20 55				
Chester	a			19 48				20 11										20 48			21 14				
Wrexham General	a																								
Llandudno	a																								
Bangor (Gwynedd)	a							21 23													22 22				
Holyhead	a							21 57													22 56				
Wilmslow	a													20 29											
Stockport	a	19 56							20 18	20 28				20 38		20 56						21 18	21 28		
Manchester Piccadilly 10	a	20 09							20 30	20 40				20 51	21 00	21 09						21 30	21 40		
Hartford	a				19 43														20 43						
Warrington Bank Quay	a											20 16	20 28												
	d											20 16	20 29												
Runcorn	a				19 54	19 58													20 54	21 07					
Liverpool South Parkway 7 ✈	a				20 04														21 04						
Liverpool Lime Street 10	a				20 14	20 20													21 14	21 28					
	d						19 31										20 31								
Manchester Airport ✈	d		19 00								19 30														20 30
Manchester Piccadilly 10	d		19 16								19 46														20 46
Bolton	d		19 33								20 05														21 05
Wigan North Western	a						20 13					20 27	20 39				21 13								
	d						20 14					20 27	20 40				21 14								
Preston 8	a		19 57				20 37				20 32	20 40	20 53				21 37								21 32
Blackpool North	a						21 07				21 00						22 07								22 00
Preston 8	d		20 00									20 42	20 55												
Lancaster 6	a		20 15									20 56	21 10												
	d		20 16									20 57	21 10												
Barrow-in-Furness	a		21 19																						
Oxenholme Lake District	a											21 10	21 24												
	d											21 11	21 26												
Windermere	a																								
Penrith North Lakes	d											21 36													
Carlisle 8	a											21 51	22 03												
	d											21 52	22 05												
Lockerbie	d												22 23												
Carstairs	a																								
Motherwell	a											22 48	23 07												
Glasgow Central 15	a											23 09	23 22												
Haymarket	a																								
Edinburgh 10	a																								
Perth	a																								
Dundee	a																								
Aberdeen	a																								
Inverness	a																								

b arr. 1848

c arr. 1948

OVERNIGHT SLEEPERS. For sleeper trains, operated by First ScotRail, please refer to Tables 400 - 404

Table 65

London and West Midlands - North West England and Scotland

		VT		VT	XC	VT	AW	VT	VT	VT	XC	TP	NT	AW	VT	VT	VT	LM	XC	AW	VT	AW	NT	SR	VT
		◇1		◇1	◇1	◇1	◇	◇1	◇1	◇1	◇1	◇1			◇1	◇1	◇1	◇1	◇1	◇	◇1			B	◇1
London Euston 15 ⊖	d	19 25		19 35		19 55		20 02	20 05	20 15					20 25		20 35				20 50			20 55	21 21
Watford Junction	d																							21u17	
Milton Keynes Central	d								20 38	20 48											21 39				
Rugby	d																				22 01				
Nuneaton	d							21 01																	22 54
Tamworth Low Level	d														21 32										
Lichfield Trent Valley	d														21 39										
Coventry	d										20 26								21 26						
Birmingham International ✈	d										20 38								21 38						
Birmingham New Street 12	d				20 31						21b01					21 20		21 35	22c01						
Wolverhampton 7	d				20 49						21 19					21 37		21 58	22 19						
Penkridge	d																	22 08							
Stafford	a								21 32		21 37					21 56	22 03	22 16	22 37						23 19
	d								21 33		21 38					21 57	22 04	22 16	22 38						23 19
Stoke-on-Trent	a				21 19	21 25				21 50	21 56								22 55						
Congleton	a																								
Macclesfield	a					21 42					22 14								23 12						
Crewe 10	a			21 13				21 44	21 53						22 10	22 15	22 22	22 39			22 49				23 38
	d			21 14			21 27	21 46	21 55					22 00	22 13	22 17	22 23			22 29	22 51	23 38		23u39	23 41
Chester	a						21 46							22 21						22 50		23 59			
Wrexham General	a																								
Llandudno	a																								
Bangor (Gwynedd)	a						23 10													00 12					
Holyhead	a						23 52													00 49					
Wilmslow	a			21 30													22 38								
Stockport	a			21 39		21 56				22 18	22 28						22 48		23 27						
Manchester Piccadilly 10	a			21 52	21 56	22 09				22 30	22 40						23 00		23 41						
Hartford	a																								
Warrington Bank Quay	a	21 16													22 29	22 34					23 08				
	d	21 16													22 30	22 35					23 08				
Runcorn	a							22 03	22 12																00 04
Liverpool South Parkway 7 ✈	a																								
Liverpool Lime Street 10	a							22 24	22 33																00 31
	d												21 31										22 31		
Manchester Airport ✈	d											21 30													
Manchester Piccadilly 10	d											21 46													
Bolton	d											22 05													
Wigan North Western	a	21 27											22 13		22 40	22 45					23 19		23 13		
	d	21 27											22 14		22 41	22 46					23 19		23 14		
Preston 8	a	21 40										22 29	22 37		22 58	23 05					23 41		23 35		
Blackpool North	a											22 55	23 07										00 05		
Preston 8	d	21 42																						00u30	
Lancaster 6	a	21 56																							
	d	21 57																							
Barrow-in-Furness	a																								
Oxenholme Lake District	a	22 10																							
	d	22 11																							
Windermere	a																								
Penrith North Lakes	d	22 36																							
Carlisle 8	a	22 51																							
	d	22 53																							
Lockerbie	d																								
Carstairs	a																								
Motherwell	a																								
Glasgow Central 15	a	00 02																							
Haymarket	a																								
Edinburgh 10	a																								
Perth	a																							05s39	
Dundee	a																							06s08	
Aberdeen	a																							07 35	
Inverness	a																							08 31	

b arr. 2048

c arr. 2148

OVERNIGHT SLEEPERS. For sleeper trains, operated by First ScotRail, please refer to Tables 400 - 404

Table 65

Sundays
12 September to 17 October

London and West Midlands - North West England and Scotland

		VT		AW	VT	SR
		◇1		◇	◇1	B
London Euston 15 ⊖	d	21 24			21 50	23 27
Watford Junction	d					23u47
Milton Keynes Central	d	22 13			22 38	
Rugby	d				23 18	
Nuneaton	d				23 29	
Tamworth Low Level	d					
Lichfield Trent Valley	d					
Coventry	d					
Birmingham International ✈	d			22 40		
Birmingham New Street 12	d			22 55		
Wolverhampton 7	d			23 13		
Penkridge	d					
Stafford	a			23 30	23s53	
	d			23 31	23s54	
Stoke-on-Trent	a	23 29				
Congleton	a					
Macclesfield	a	23 45				
Crewe 10	a			23 55	00s12	
	d			00 10	00s13	
Chester	a			00 31		
Wrexham General	a					
Llandudno	a					
Bangor (Gwynedd)	a			01 40		
Holyhead	a			02 15		
Wilmslow	a					
Stockport	a	23 59			00s40	
Manchester Piccadilly 10	a	00 13			00 53	
Hartford	a					
Warrington Bank Quay	a					
	d					
Runcorn	a					
Liverpool South Parkway 7 ✈	a					
Liverpool Lime Street 10	a					
	d					
Manchester Airport ✈	d					
Manchester Piccadilly 10	d					
Bolton	d					
Wigan North Western	a					
	d					
Preston 8	a					
Blackpool North	a					
Preston 8	d					
Lancaster 6	a					
	d					
Barrow-in-Furness	a					
Oxenholme Lake District	a					
	d					
Windermere	a					
Penrith North Lakes	d					
Carlisle 8	a					05s04
	d					
Lockerbie	d					
Carstairs	a					06s22
Motherwell	a					07s01
Glasgow Central 15	a					07 19
Haymarket	a					
Edinburgh 10	a					07 17
Perth	a					
Dundee	a					
Aberdeen	a					
Inverness	a					

OVERNIGHT SLEEPERS. For sleeper trains, operated by First ScotRail, please refer to Tables 400 - 404

Table 65

Sundays
from 24 October

London and West Midlands - North West England and Scotland

		TP	TP	TP	NT	TP	TP	NT	AW	AW	VT	XC	TP	TP	AW	VT	TP		VT	TP	VT	VT
		bus	bus	◇1		◇1	◇1		◇		◇1	◇1	◇1	◇1		bus	◇1		bus	◇1	◇1	◇1
London Euston 15 ⊖	d																					
Watford Junction	d																					
Milton Keynes Central	d																					
Rugby	d																					
Nuneaton	d																					
Tamworth Low Level	d																					
Lichfield Trent Valley	d																					
Coventry	d																					
Birmingham International ✈	d																					
Birmingham New Street 12	d										08 45	09 01										09 20
Wolverhampton 7	d										09 04	09 19										09 37
Penkridge	d																					
Stafford	a										09 18	09 33										
	d										09 19	09 34										
Stoke-on-Trent	a																					
Congleton	a																					
Macclesfield	a																					
Crewe 10	a										09 37	09 54										10 06
	d								09 24	09 28	09 38	09 56			10 07							10 08
Chester	a								09 45						10 30							
Wrexham General	a																					
Llandudno	a																					
Bangor (Gwynedd)	a								11 04													
Holyhead	a								11 44													
Wilmslow	a									09 46		10 12										
Stockport	a											10 21										
Manchester Piccadilly 10	a									10 13		10 34										
Hartford	a																					
Warrington Bank Quay	a										09 56											
	d															10 10			10 15			
Runcorn	a																					
Liverpool South Parkway 7 ✈	a																					
Liverpool Lime Street 10	a																					
	d				08 31			09 31										10 31				
Manchester Airport ✈	d	00 10	05 30	07 30		08 47	09 00						09 30	10 00			10 25					
Manchester Piccadilly 10	d	00 35	05 55	07 46		09 03	09 16						09 46	10 16			10 43					
Bolton	d	01s00	06s20	08 06		09 23	09 33						10 05	10 32			11 05					
Wigan North Western	a				09 13			10 13										11 13				
	d				09 14			10 14										11 14				
Preston 8	a	01s35	06s55	08 31	09 39	09 50	09 57	10 39					10 32	10 55		11 10	11 32	11 39	11 40			11 44
Blackpool North	a	02 15	07 35	08 58	10 07	10 17		11 09					11 00				12 00	12 07				
Preston 8	d						10 00							11 00						11 18	11 39	11 53
Lancaster 6	a						10 15							11 15						11 33	11 53	12 08
	d						10 16							11 16						11 34	11 54	12 08
Barrow-in-Furness	a																			12 37		
Oxenholme Lake District	a						10 30							11 30							12 07	12 22
	d						10 30							11 30							12 07	12 24
Windermere	a																					
Penrith North Lakes	d						10 55							11 56							12 33	
Carlisle 8	a						11 12							12 12							12 48	13 02
	d						11 13							12 13							12 49	13 04
Lockerbie	d						11 32							12 30								
Carstairs	a																					
Motherwell	a																					
Glasgow Central 15	a													13 34							14 01	
Haymarket	a						12s32															14 14
Edinburgh 10	a						12 39															14 22
Perth	a																					
Dundee	a																					
Aberdeen	a																					
Inverness	a																					

OVERNIGHT SLEEPERS. For sleeper trains, operated by First ScotRail, please refer to Tables 400 - 404

Table 65

Sundays
from 24 October

London and West Midlands - North West England and Scotland

		VT	VT	VT	LM	XC	NT	VT	AW	TP	VT	VT	VT	AW	VT	VT	NT	LM	XC	LM	AW	TP	VT	TP	VT
		◇1	◇1	◇1	◇1	◇1		◇1		◇1	◇1	◇1	◇1	◇	◇1	◇1		◇1	◇1	1		◇1	bus	◇1	◇1
London Euston 15 ⊖	d	08 10	08 15	08 20									08 45		09 15	09 20									
Watford Junction	d																								
Milton Keynes Central	d	08 56		09 05									09 32			10 07									
Rugby	d												10 08												
Nuneaton	d		09 42												10 45										
Tamworth Low Level	d																								
Lichfield Trent Valley	d																								
Coventry	d																		10b28						
Birmingham International ✈	d																		10 40						
Birmingham New Street 12	d				09 42	10 00						10 20						10 42	11c01						
Wolverhampton 7	d				09 59	10 18						10 37						10 59	11 19						
Penkridge	d				10 10													11 10							
Stafford	a		10 08		10 17	10 32									11 11			11 17	11 32						
	d		10 08		10 17	10 33									11 11			11 17	11 33	11 44					
Stoke-on-Trent	a			10 19		10 51										11 22			11 51	12 02					
Congleton	a																								
Macclesfield	a			10 36		11 08										11 39			12 09						
Crewe 10	a	10 15	10 28		10 37							11 07	10 55		11 30			11 37		12 26					
	d	10 17	10 30		10 38			10 42	11 05			11 14	11 17	11 27	11 32			11 38			11 57				
Chester	a							11 02	11 26					11 48							12 20				
Wrexham General	a																								
Llandudno	a																								
Bangor (Gwynedd)	a							12 09						13 10											
Holyhead	a							12 43						13 45											
Wilmslow	a	10 31																							
Stockport	a	10 41		10 51		11 22										11 53			12 22						
Manchester Piccadilly 10	a	10 54		11 04		11 34										12 06			12 34						
Hartford	a				10 50													11 50							
Warrington Bank Quay	a												11 33												
	d																						11 45		
Runcorn	a		10 47		11 00										11 49			12 01							
Liverpool South Parkway 7 ✈	a				11 10													12 11							
Liverpool Lime Street 10	a		11 09		11 20										12 10			12 21							
	d						11 31										12 31								
Manchester Airport ✈	d									11 30												11 58		12 30	
Manchester Piccadilly 10	d									11 46												12 16		12 46	
Bolton	d									12 05												12 33		13 05	
Wigan North Western	a						12 13										13 13								
	d						12 14										13 14								
Preston 8	a						12 39			12 32		12 45					13 39					12 57	13 10	13 32	
Blackpool North	a						13 07			13 00							14 07							14 01	
Preston 8	d										12 39	12 53										12 58			13 37
Lancaster 6	a										12 53	13 08										13 13			13 51
	d										12 54	13 08										13 14			13 52
Barrow-in-Furness	a																								
Oxenholme Lake District	a										13 07	13 22										13 28			14 05
	d										13 07	13 24										13 28			14 05
Windermere	a																								
Penrith North Lakes	d										13 33											13 53			14 31
Carlisle 8	a										13 48	14 01										14 10			14 46
	d										13 49	14 03										14 11			14 47
Lockerbie	d																					14 30			
Carstairs	a																								
Motherwell	a																								
Glasgow Central 15	a										15 04	15 16													16 06
Haymarket	a																					15s28			
Edinburgh 10	a																					15 36			
Perth	a																								
Dundee	a																								
Aberdeen	a																								
Inverness	a																								

b arr. 1022

c arr. 1050

OVERNIGHT SLEEPERS. For sleeper trains, operated by First ScotRail, please refer to Tables 400 - 404

Table 65

Sundays from 24 October

London and West Midlands - North West England and Scotland

	TP		VT	VT	AW	VT	VT	LM	XC	AW	TP	NT	VT	TP	VT	VT	VT	VT	VT	AW	LM		VT	VT
	◇1		◇1	◇1	◇	◇1	◇1	◇1	◇1		◇1		🚌	◇1	◇1	◇1	◇1	◇1	◇1	◇	◇1		◇1	◇1
			🍴	🍴	🛒	🍴	🍴		🛒		🛒				🍴	🍴	🍴	🍴	🍴	🛒			🍴	🍴
London Euston 15 ⊖ d				09 45		10 15	10 20										10 45	11 15	11 20				12 02	12 15
Watford Junction d																								
Milton Keynes Central d				10 33			11 07										11 32	12 04	12 09					12 48
Rugby d				11 08													12 08							
Nuneaton d						11 46																		
Tamworth Low Level d																								
Lichfield Trent Valley d																								
Coventry d									11b28															
Birmingham International ✈ d									11 40															
Birmingham New Street 12 d			11 20					11 42	12c01							12 20					12 35			
Wolverhampton 7 ⇌ d			11 37					11 59	12 20							12 37					12 52			
Penkridge d								12 10													13 03			
Stafford a						12 11		12 16	12 33									12 54			13 10		13 23	
d						12 12		12 16	12 34									12 55			13 10		13 24	
Stoke-on-Trent a							12 23		12 51										13 07					13 50
Congleton a																								
Macclesfield a							12 40		13 09										13 24					
Crewe 10 a			12 07	11 56		12 31		12 37								13 07	12 59	13 15			13 30		13 42	
d			12 14	12 17	12 27	12 33		12 38		12 54						13 14	13 17	13 17		13 27	13 31		13 44	
Chester a					12 48					13 15										13 47				
Wrexham General a																								
Llandudno a																								
Bangor (Gwynedd) a					14 18															15 12				
Holyhead a					14 55															15 55				
Wilmslow a																								
Stockport a							12 54		13 28										13 38					14 18
Manchester Piccadilly 10 ⇌ a							13 09		13 40										13 52					14 30
Hartford a								12 50													13 43			
Warrington Bank Quay a				12 33													13 38							
d													12 45											
Runcorn a						12 50		13 01										13 34			13 54		14 01	
Liverpool South Parkway 7 ✈ a								13 11													14 04			
Liverpool Lime Street 10 a						13 11		13 21										13 57			14 14		14 23	
d												13 31												
Manchester Airport ✈ d											12 58			13 30										
Manchester Piccadilly 10 ⇌ d											13 16			13 46										
Bolton d											13 33			14 05										
Wigan North Western a												14 13												
d												14 14												
Preston 8 a			13 42								13 57	14 39	14 10	14 32		14 42								
Blackpool North a												15 07		15 00										
Preston 8 d	13 47		13 53								14 00				14 42	14 55								
Lancaster 6 a	14 03		14 08								14 15				14 56	15 10								
d	14 03		14 08								14 16				14 58	15 10								
Barrow-in-Furness a	15 07																							
Oxenholme Lake District a											14 30					15 24								
d											14 30					15 25								
Windermere a																								
Penrith North Lakes d			14 45								14 55				15 32									
Carlisle 8 a			15 00								15 12				15 47	16 03								
d			15 02								15 17				15 48	16 05								
Lockerbie d																								
Carstairs a																								
Motherwell a																								
Glasgow Central 15 a											16 35				17 00	17 18								
Haymarket a			16 14																					
Edinburgh 10 a			16 22																					
Perth a																								
Dundee a																								
Aberdeen a																								
Inverness a																								

b arr. 1122 c arr. 1150

OVERNIGHT SLEEPERS. For sleeper trains, operated by First ScotRail, please refer to Tables 400 - 404

Table 65

Sundays from 24 October

London and West Midlands - North West England and Scotland

	XC	AW	VT	XC	VT	TP	VT	SR	AW	LM	VT	VT	XC	TP	VT	AW	VT		VT	XC	VT	TP	AW	LM
	◇1		◇1	◇1	◇1	◇1	🚌		◇	◇1	◇1	◇1	◇1	◇1	◇1		◇1		◇1	◇1	◇1	◇1	◇	◇1
	🛒		🍴	🛒	🍴	🛒			🛒		🍴	🍴	🛒		🍴		🍴		🍴	🛒	🍴		🛒	
London Euston 15 ⊖ d			12 35		12 55						13 02	13 15			13 25				13 35		13 55			
Watford Junction d																								
Milton Keynes Central d												13 48												
Rugby d																								
Nuneaton d																								
Tamworth Low Level d																								
Lichfield Trent Valley d																								
Coventry d	12b28												13 26											
Birmingham International ✈ d	12 40												13 38											
Birmingham New Street 12 d	13c01			13 31						13 35			14e01				14 20			14 31				14 35
Wolverhampton 7 ⇌ d	13 19			13 49						13 52			14 19				14 37			14 49				14 52
Penkridge d										14 03														15 03
Stafford a	13 33									14 10	14 20		14 33											15 10
d	13 34									14 10	14 22		14 34											15 10
Stoke-on-Trent a	13 56			14 19	14 26							14 50	14 56							15 19	15 25			
Congleton a																								
Macclesfield a	14 14				14 42								15 14								15 42			
Crewe 10 a			14 12							14 30	14 40						15 09		15 12					15 30
d		13 57	14 13						14 27	14 31	14 42					14 57	15 11		15 13				15 27	15 31
Chester a		14 18							14 47							15 18							15 47	
Wrexham General a																								
Llandudno a																								
Bangor (Gwynedd) a									16 18														17 12	
Holyhead a									16 54														17 55	
Wilmslow a			14 29																15 29					
Stockport a	14 28		14 38		14 56							15 18	15 28						15 38		15 56			
Manchester Piccadilly 10 ⇌ a	14 40		14 51	14 57	15 09							15 30	15 40						15 51	16 00	16 09			
Hartford a										14 43														15 43
Warrington Bank Quay a															15 16		15 28							
d							13 50								15 16		15 29							
Runcorn a										14 54	14 59													15 54
Liverpool South Parkway 7 ✈ a										15 04														16 04
Liverpool Lime Street 10 a										15 14	15 21													16 14
d								14 31																
Manchester Airport ✈ d						13 58								14 30								15 00		
Manchester Piccadilly 10 ⇌ d						14 16								14 46								15 16		
Bolton d						14 33								15 05								15 33		
Wigan North Western a								15 13							15 27		15 39							
d								15 14							15 27		15 40							
Preston 8 a						14 57	15 15	15 37						15 32	15 40		15 53					15 57		
Blackpool North a								16 07						16 00										
Preston 8 d						15 00									15 42		15 55					16 00		
Lancaster 6 a						15 15									15 56		16 10					16 15		
d						15 16									15 58		16 10					16 16		
Barrow-in-Furness a																						17 19		
Oxenholme Lake District a						15 30									16 10									
d						15 30									16 11									
Windermere a																								
Penrith North Lakes d						15 55											16 47							
Carlisle 8 a						16 12									16 48		17 02							
d						16 13									16 49		17 04							
Lockerbie d						16 32																		
Carstairs a																								
Motherwell a																								
Glasgow Central 15 a															18 02									
Haymarket a						17s30											18 13							
Edinburgh 10 a						17 39											18 22							
Perth a																								
Dundee a																								
Aberdeen a																								
Inverness a																								

b arr. 1222 c arr. 1250 e arr. 1348

OVERNIGHT SLEEPERS. For sleeper trains, operated by First ScotRail, please refer to Tables 400 - 404

Table 65

Sundays
from 24 October

London and West Midlands - North West England and Scotland

Station		VT	VT	XC	NT	TP	VT	VT	VT	XC	VT	TP	AW	LM	VT	VT	VT	XC	TP	VT	VT	VT	XC	
		◇1	◇1	◇1		◇1	◇1	◇1	◇1	◇1	◇1	◇1	◇	◇1	◇1	◇1	◇1	◇1	◇1	◇1	◇1	◇1	◇1	
		☕	☕	🛒			☕	☕	☕	🛒	☕	🛒	🛒		☕	☕	☕	🛒		☕	☕	☕	🛒	
London Euston 15 ⊖	d	14 02	14 15				14 25		14 35		14 55				15 02	15 05	15 15			15 25		15 35		
Watford Junction	d																							
Milton Keynes Central	d		14 48													15 39	15 48							
Rugby	d																							
Nuneaton	d																							
Tamworth Low Level	d																							
Lichfield Trent Valley	d																							
Coventry	d			14 26														15 26						
Birmingham International ✈	d			14 38														15 38						
Birmingham New Street 12	d			15b01				15 20		15 31				15 35				16c01			16 20		16 31	
Wolverhampton 7	d			15 19				15 37		15 49				15 52				16 19			16u37		16 49	
Penkridge	d													16 03										
Stafford	a	15 24		15 33										16 10	16 20			16 35						
	d	15 25		15 34										16 10	16 21			16 36						
Stoke-on-Trent	a		15 50	15 56						16 19	16 24						16 50	16 56					17 19	
Congleton	a																							
Macclesfield	a			16 14							16 42							17 14						
Crewe 10	a	15 43						16 09	16 12					16 32		16 50					17 07	17 12		
	d	15 45						16 11	16 13				16 27	16 34		16 52					17 08	17 13		
Chester	a												16 47			17 14								
Wrexham General	a																							
Llandudno	a																							
Bangor (Gwynedd)	a												18 18											
Holyhead	a												18 55											
Wilmslow	a								16 29													17 29		
Stockport	a		16 18	16 28					16 38		16 56						17 18	17 28				17 38		
Manchester Piccadilly 10	a		16 30	16 40					16 51	16 59	17 09						17 30	17 40				17 51	17 56	
Hartford	a													16 45										
Warrington Bank Quay	a						16 16	16 28												17 16	17 26			
	d						16 16	16 29												17 16	17 26			
Runcorn	a	16 02												16 56	16 59									
Liverpool South Parkway 7 ✈	a													17 06										
Liverpool Lime Street 10	a	16 23												17 17	17 23									
	d				15 31																			16 31
Manchester Airport ✈	d					15 30						16 00							16 30					
Manchester Piccadilly 10	d					15 46						16 16							16 46					
Bolton	d					16 05						16 33							17 05					
Wigan North Western	a				16 13		16 27	16 39												17 27	17 37			17 13
	d				16 14		16 27	16 40												17 27	17 37			17 14
Preston 8	a				16 37	16 32	16 40	16 53				16 57							17 32	17 40	17 51			17 37
Blackpool North	a				17 07	17 00													18 00					18 07
Preston 8	d						16 42	16 55				17 00								17 42	17 52			
Lancaster 6	a						16 56	17 10				17 15								17 56	18 07			
	d						16 57	17 10				17 16								17 57	18 08			
Barrow-in-Furness	a																							
Oxenholme Lake District	a							17 24				17 30								18 10	18 22			
	d							17 25				17 30								18 10	18 23			
Windermere	a																							
Penrith North Lakes	d						17 32					17 55									18 48			
Carlisle 8	a						17 47	18 03				18 12								18 48	19 03			
	d						17 48	18 05				18 13								18 49	19 04			
Lockerbie	d																							
Carstairs	a																							
Motherwell	a																							
Glasgow Central 15	a						19 00	19 18												20 02				
Haymarket	a																							
Edinburgh 10	a											19 37									20 23			
Perth	a																							
Dundee	a																							
Aberdeen	a																							
Inverness	a																							

b arr. 1448

c arr. 1548

OVERNIGHT SLEEPERS. For sleeper trains, operated by First ScotRail, please refer to Tables 400 - 404

Table 65

Sundays
from 24 October

London and West Midlands - North West England and Scotland

Station		VT	TP	AW	LM	VT	VT	VT	XC	TP	NT	TP	VT	VT	VT	XC	VT	TP	AW	LM	VT	VT	VT	TP
		◇1	◇1	◇	◇1	◇1	◇1	◇1	◇1	◇1		◇1	◇1	◇1	◇1	◇1	◇1	◇1	◇	◇1	◇1	◇1	◇1	◇1
		☕	🛒			☕	☕	☕	🛒				☕	☕	☕	🛒	☕	🛒			☕	☕	☕	
London Euston 15 ⊖	d	15 55				16 02	16 05	16 15					16 25		16 35		16 55				17 02	17 05	17 15	
Watford Junction	d																							
Milton Keynes Central	d						16 39	16 48														17 39	17 48	
Rugby	d																							
Nuneaton	d																					18 10		
Tamworth Low Level	d																							
Lichfield Trent Valley	d																							
Coventry	d								16 26															
Birmingham International ✈	d								16 38															
Birmingham New Street 12	d				16 35				17b01					17 20		17 31				17 35				
Wolverhampton 7	d				16 52				17 19					17u37		17 49				17 52				
Penkridge	d				17 03															18 03				
Stafford	a				17 10	17 24			17 35											18 10	18 24			
	d				17 10	17 25			17 36											18 10	18 25			
Stoke-on-Trent	a	17 25						17 50	17 56							18 19	18 25						18 50	
Congleton	a																							
Macclesfield	a	17 42							18 14								18 42							
Crewe 10	a				17 30		17 50							18 09	18 12					18 30		18 53		
	d			17 27	17 31		17 52							18 11	18 13				18 27	18 31		18 56		
Chester	a			17 47			18 14												18 47			19 14		
Wrexham General	a																							
Llandudno	a																							
Bangor (Gwynedd)	a			19 12															20 08			20 26		
Holyhead	a			19 55															20 44			20 59		
Wilmslow	a														18 29									
Stockport	a	17 56						18 18	18 28						18 38		18 56						19 18	
Manchester Piccadilly 10	a	18 09						18 30	18 40						18 51	18 56	19 09						19 30	
Hartford	a				17 43															18 43				
Warrington Bank Quay	a												18 16	18 28										
	d												18 17	18 29										
Runcorn	a				17 54	17 57														18 54	18 57			
Liverpool South Parkway 7 ✈	a				18 04															19 04				
Liverpool Lime Street 10	a				18 14	18 20														19 14	19 20			
	d										17 31													
Manchester Airport ✈	d		17 00							17 30								18 00						18 30
Manchester Piccadilly 10	d		17 16							17 46								18 16						18 46
Bolton	d		17 33							18 05								18 33						19 05
Wigan North Western	a										18 13		18 27	18 39										
	d										18 14		18 28	18 40										
Preston 8	a		17 57							18 32	18 37		18 40	18 53				18 57						19 32
Blackpool North	a									19 00	19 07													20 00
Preston 8	d		18 00									18 06	18 42	18 55				19 00						
Lancaster 6	a		18 15									18 22	18 56	19 10				19 15						
	d		18 16									18 22	18 58	19 10				19 16						
Barrow-in-Furness	a											19 26												
Oxenholme Lake District	a		18 30										19 10	19 24				19 30						
	d		18 30										19 11	19 26				19 30						
Windermere	a																							
Penrith North Lakes	d		18 55										19 36					19 55						
Carlisle 8	a		19 12										19 51	20 03				20 12						
	d		19 21										19 53	20 05				20 13						
Lockerbie	d		19 40															20 32						
Carstairs	a																							
Motherwell	a		20s27																					
Glasgow Central 15	a		20 45										21 08	21 18										
Haymarket	a																	21s30						
Edinburgh 10	a																	21 39						
Perth	a																							
Dundee	a																							
Aberdeen	a																							
Inverness	a																							

b arr. 1648

OVERNIGHT SLEEPERS. For sleeper trains, operated by First ScotRail, please refer to Tables 400 - 404

Table 65

Sundays
from 24 October

London and West Midlands - North West England and Scotland

		VT	VT	VT	XC	VT	NT	TP	AW	LM	VT	VT	VT	XC	TP	VT	NT	VT	VT	XC	VT	AW	LM	VT	VT
		◇1	◇1	◇1	◇1	◇1		◇1		◇1	◇1	◇1	◇1	◇1	◇1	◇1		1	◇1	◇1	◇1		◇1	◇1	◇1
London Euston 15 ⊖	d	17 25		17 35		17 55					18 02	18 05	18 15			18 25			18 35		18 55			19 02	19 05
Watford Junction	d																								
Milton Keynes Central	d											18 39	18 48												19 39
Rugby	d																								
Nuneaton	d																							20 01	
Tamworth Low Level	d																								
Lichfield Trent Valley	d																								
Coventry	d													18 26											
Birmingham International ✈	d													18 38											
Birmingham New Street 12	d		18 20		18 31					18 35				19b01				19 20		19 31			19 35		
Wolverhampton 7	d		18 37		18 49					18 52				19 19				19 37		19 49			19 52		
Penkridge	d									19 03													20 03		
Stafford	a									19 10	19 24			19 37									20 10	20 25	
	d									19 10	19 25			19 38									20 10	20 30	
Stoke-on-Trent	a				19 19	19 25							19 50	19 56						20 19	20 25				
Congleton	a																								
Macclesfield	a					19 42								20 14							20 42				
Crewe 10	a		19 09	19 12						19 30		19 50						20 09	20 12				20 30	20 48	20 53
	d		19 11	19 13					19 27	19 31		19 52						20 11	20 13			20 27	20 31	20 50	20 55
Chester	a								19 48			20 11										20 48			21 14
Wrexham General	a																								
Llandudno	a																								
Bangor (Gwynedd)	a											21 23													22 22
Holyhead	a											21 57													22 56
Wilmslow	a			19 29															20 29						
Stockport	a			19 38		19 56							20 18	20 28					20 38		20 56				
Manchester Piccadilly 10	a			19 51	19 58	20 09							20 30	20 40					20 51	21 00	21 09				
Hartford	a									19 43													20 43		
Warrington Bank Quay	a	19 16	19 28													20 16		20 28							
	d	19 16	19 29													20 16		20 29							
Runcorn	a									19 54	19 58												20 54	21 07	
Liverpool South Parkway 7 ✈	a									20 04													21 04		
Liverpool Lime Street 10	a									20 14	20 20												21 14	21 28	
	d						18 31										19 31								
Manchester Airport ✈	d							19 00							19 30										
Manchester Piccadilly 10	d							19 16							19 46										
Bolton	d							19 33							20 05										
Wigan North Western	a	19 27	19 39				19 13									20 27	20 13	20 39							
	d	19 27	19 40				19 14									20 27	20 14	20 40							
Preston 8	a	19 40	19 53				19 37	19 57							20 32	20 40	20 37	20 53							
Blackpool North	a						20 07								21 00		21 07								
Preston 8	d	19 42	19 55					20 00								20 42		20 55							
Lancaster 6	a	19 56	20 10					20 15								20 56		21 10							
	d	19 57	20 10					20 16								20 57		21 10							
Barrow-in-Furness	a							21 19																	
Oxenholme Lake District	a	20 10														21 10		21 24							
	d	20 10														21 11		21 26							
Windermere	a																								
Penrith North Lakes	d	20 36	20 47													21 36									
Carlisle 8	a	20 51	21 02													21 51		22 03							
	d	20 52	21 04													21 52		22 05							
Lockerbie	d																	22 23							
Carstairs	a																								
Motherwell	a															22 48		23 07							
Glasgow Central 15	a	22 07														23 09		23 22							
Haymarket	a		22 15																						
Edinburgh 10	a		22 23																						
Perth	a																								
Dundee	a																								
Aberdeen	a																								
Inverness	a																								

b arr. 1848

OVERNIGHT SLEEPERS. For sleeper trains, operated by First ScotRail, please refer to Tables 400 - 404

Table 65

Sundays
from 24 October

London and West Midlands - North West England and Scotland

		VT		XC	VT	TP	VT	VT	XC	VT	AW	VT	NT	VT	VT	XC	TP	AW	VT	VT	VT	LM	NT	XC	AW
		◇1		◇1	◇1	◇1	◇1	◇1	◇1	◇1	◇	◇1		◇1	◇1	◇1	◇1		◇1	◇1	◇1	◇1		◇1	◇
London Euston 15 ⊖	d	19 15					19 25	19 35		19 55		20 02		20 05	20 15				20 25		20 35				
Watford Junction	d																								
Milton Keynes Central	d	19 48												20 38	20 48										
Rugby	d																								
Nuneaton	d											21 01													
Tamworth Low Level	d																		21 32						
Lichfield Trent Valley	d																		21 39						
Coventry	d			19 26												20 26								21 26	
Birmingham International ✈	d			19 38												20 38								21 38	
Birmingham New Street 12	d			20b01	20 20				20 31							21c01				21 20		21 35		22e01	
Wolverhampton 7	d			20 19	20 38				20 49							21 19				21 37		21 58		22 19	
Penkridge	d																					22 08			
Stafford	a			20 37	20 51									21 32		21 37				21 56	22 03	22 16		22 37	
	d			20 38	20 52									21 33		21 38				21 57	22 04	22 16		22 38	
Stoke-on-Trent	a	20 50		20 56					21 19	21 25					21 50	21 56								22 55	
Congleton	a																								
Macclesfield	a			21 15						21 42						22 14								23 12	
Crewe 10	a				21 10			21 13				21 44		21 53					22 10	22 15	22 22	22 39			
	d							21 14			21 27	21 46		21 55				22 00	22 13	22 17	22 23				22 29
Chester	a										21 46							22 21							22 50
Wrexham General	a																								
Llandudno	a																								
Bangor (Gwynedd)	a										23 10														00 12
Holyhead	a										23 52														00 49
Wilmslow	a							21 30													22 38				
Stockport	a	21 18		21 28				21 39		21 56					22 18	22 28					22 48			23 27	
Manchester Piccadilly 10	a	21 30		21 40				21 52	21 56	22 09					22 30	22 40					23 00			23 41	
Hartford	a																								
Warrington Bank Quay	a						21 16												22 29	22 34					
	d						21 16												22 30	22 35					
Runcorn	a											22 03		22 12											
Liverpool South Parkway 7 ✈	a																								
Liverpool Lime Street 10	a											22 24		22 33											
	d		20 31										21 31										22 31		
Manchester Airport ✈	d					20 30											21 30								
Manchester Piccadilly 10	d					20 46											21 46								
Bolton	d					21 05											22 05								
Wigan North Western	a		21 13				21 27						22 13						22 40	22 45			23 13		
	d		21 14				21 27						22 14						22 41	22 46			23 14		
Preston 8	a		21 37			21 32	21 40						22 37				22 29		22 58	23 05			23 35		
Blackpool North	a		22 07			22 00							23 07				22 55						00 05		
Preston 8	d						21 42																		
Lancaster 6	a						21 56																		
	d						21 57																		
Barrow-in-Furness	a																								
Oxenholme Lake District	a						22 10																		
	d						22 11																		
Windermere	a																								
Penrith North Lakes	d						22 36																		
Carlisle 8	a						22 51																		
	d						22 53																		
Lockerbie	d																								
Carstairs	a																								
Motherwell	a																								
Glasgow Central 15	a						00 02																		
Haymarket	a																								
Edinburgh 10	a																								
Perth	a																								
Dundee	a																								
Aberdeen	a																								
Inverness	a																								

b arr. 1948 c arr. 2048 e arr. 2148

OVERNIGHT SLEEPERS. For sleeper trains, operated by First ScotRail, please refer to Tables 400 - 404

Table 65

Sundays from 24 October

London and West Midlands - North West England and Scotland

		VT	AW	SR	VT	VT	AW	VT		SR
				🛏						🛏
		◇1			◇1	◇1	◇	◇1		
		☕		🛏 ☕	☕	☕		☕		🛏 ☕
London Euston 15 ⊖	d	20 50		20 55	21 21	21 24		21 50		23 27
Watford Junction	d			21u17						23u47
Milton Keynes Central	d	21 39				22 13		22 38		
Rugby	d	22 01						23 18		
Nuneaton	d				22 54			23 29		
Tamworth Low Level	d									
Lichfield Trent Valley	d									
Coventry	d									
Birmingham International ✈	d						22 40			
Birmingham New Street 12	d						22 55			
Wolverhampton 7 🚌	d						23 13			
Penkridge	d									
Stafford	a				23 19		23 30	23s53		
	d				23 19		23 31	23s54		
Stoke-on-Trent	a					23 29				
Congleton	a									
Macclesfield	a					23 45				
Crewe 10	a	22 49			23 38		23 55	00s12		
	d	22 51	23 38	23u39	23 41		00 10	00s13		
Chester	a		23 59				00 31			
Wrexham General	a									
Llandudno	a									
Bangor (Gwynedd)	a						01 40			
Holyhead	a						02 15			
Wilmslow	a									
Stockport	a					23 59		00s40		
Manchester Piccadilly 10 🚌	a					00 13		00 53		
Hartford	a									
Warrington Bank Quay	a	23 08								
	d	23 08								
Runcorn	a				00 04					
Liverpool South Parkway 7 ✈	a									
Liverpool Lime Street 10	a				00 31					
	d									
Manchester Airport ✈	d									
Manchester Piccadilly 10 🚌	d									
Bolton	d									
Wigan North Western	a	23 19								
	d	23 19								
Preston 8	a	23 41								
Blackpool North	a									
Preston 8	d			00u30						
Lancaster 6	a									
	d									
Barrow-in-Furness	a									
Oxenholme Lake District	a									
	d									
Windermere	a									
Penrith North Lakes	d									
Carlisle 8	a									05s04
	d									
Lockerbie	d									
Carstairs	a									06s22
Motherwell	a									07s01
Glasgow Central 15	a									07 19
Haymarket	a									
Edinburgh 10	a									07 17
Perth	a			05s39						
Dundee	a			06s08						
Aberdeen	a			07 35						
Inverness	a			08 31						

OVERNIGHT SLEEPERS. For sleeper trains, operated by First ScotRail, please refer to Tables 400 - 404

Table 65

Mondays to Fridays

Scotland and North West England - West Midlands and London

		TP	AW MX	AW MO	TP	XC	VT	TP	VT	XC	VT	TP	LM	VT	VT	XC	VT	VT	VT
		◇1			◇1	◇1	◇1	◇1	◇1	◇1	◇1	◇1	◇1	◇1	◇1	◇1	◇1	◇1 A	◇1
						🛒	⊠		⊠	🛒	⊠	🛒		⊠	⊠	🛒	⊠	⊠	⊠
Inverness	d																		
Aberdeen	d																		
Dundee	d																		
Perth	d																		
Edinburgh 10	d																		
Haymarket	d																		
Glasgow Central 15	d																		
Motherwell	d																		
Carstairs	d																		
Lockerbie	d																		
Carlisle 8	a																		
	d																		
Penrith North Lakes	d																		
Windermere	d																		
Oxenholme Lake District	a																		
	d																		
Barrow-in-Furness	d				04 35														
Lancaster 6	a				05 28														
	d																	05 35	
Preston 8	a																	05 52	
Blackpool North	d	03 36										05 44							
Preston 8	d	04u01						05 16			05 30	06 09						06 00	
Wigan North Western	a										05 44							06 11	
	d										05 45							06 11	
Blackrod	d																		
Lostock	d											06 30							
Bolton	a	04u30						05 42				06 34							
Manchester Piccadilly 10 🚌	a	04 48						06 01				06 56							
Manchester Airport ✈	a	05 07						06 18				07 17							
Liverpool Lime Street 10	a																		
	d								05 27						06 05				
Liverpool South Parkway ✈	d																		
Runcorn	d								05 43						06 21				
Warrington Bank Quay	a										05 55							06 22	
	d										05 56							06 22	
Hartford	d																		
Manchester Piccadilly 10 🚌	d					05 00	05 05							05 55		06 00	06 10		
Stockport	d						05 13							06 03		06 08	06 18		
Wilmslow	d													06 11					
Holyhead	d																		04 50
Bangor (Gwynedd)	d																		05 16
Llandudno Junction	d																		05 34
Wrexham General	d																		
Chester	d		04 23	04 23															06b26
Crewe 10	a		04 44	04 44		05 44	05 34		06 00					06 27		06 32		06 42	06 46
	d		05 00	05 00		05 47	05 36		06 02				06 20	06 29		06 38		>	06 52
Macclesfield	d																06 31		
Congleton	d																		
Stoke-on-Trent	d					06 07				←							06 48		
Stafford	a		05 24	05 24		06 24	05 53		06 20	06 24			06 40		06 52	06 57			
	d		05 24	05 25		06 25	05 55		06 21	06 25			06 41		06 53	06 58			
Penkridge	a					→							06 46						
Wolverhampton 7 🚌	a		05 38	05 39						06 39			06 57			07 12			
Birmingham New Street 12	a		05 58	05 58						06 58			07 18			07 31			
Birmingham International ✈	a									07 13									
Coventry	a									07 24									
Lichfield Trent Valley	a										06 40				07 07				
Tamworth Low Level	a										06 46				07 14				
Nuneaton	a						06 17							07 06					07 32
Rugby	a						06 30		06 52		07 06						07 28		
Milton Keynes Central	a						06 51		07 12										
Watford Junction	a																		
London Euston 15 ⊖	a						07 28		07 50		07 57			08 07	08 22		08 22		08 33

A Through portion to London Euston

OVERNIGHT SLEEPERS. For sleeper trains, operated by First ScotRail, please refer to Tables 400 - 404

Scotland and North West England - West Midlands and London

		LM ◇1		VT ◇1 ⊠	TP ◇1 A ⊼	VT ◇1 ⊠	LM 1	VT ◇1 ⊠	VT ◇1 ⊠	LM 1	VT ◇1 ⊠	VT ◇1 ⊠	VT ◇1 ⊠	TP ◇1 ⊼	XC ◇1 ⊼	LM 1	VT ◇1 ⊠	VT ◇1 B ⊠	VT ◇1 ⊠	XC ◇1 ⊼	NT	LM 1	VT ◇1 ⊠	VT ◇1 ⊠	LM 1	VT ◇1 ⊠
Inverness	d																									
Aberdeen	d																									
Dundee	d																									
Perth	d																									
Edinburgh 10	d																									
Haymarket	d																									
Glasgow Central 15	d												04 28													
Motherwell	d																									
Carstairs	d																									
Lockerbie	d																									
Carlisle 8	a												05 42													
	d												05 43													
Penrith North Lakes	d												05 57													
Windermere	d																									
Oxenholme Lake District	a												06 20													
	d												06 20													
Barrow-in-Furness	d				05 31																					
Lancaster 6	a				06 23								06 35													
	d				06 26								06 35						06 58							
Preston 8	a				06 45								06 53						07 15							
Blackpool North	d													06 34												
Preston 8	d			06 16	06 47								06 56	07 03					07 17							
Wigan North Western	a			06 27									07 06						07 28							
	d			06 27									07 08						07 28							
Blackrod	d													07 21												
Lostock	d													07 29												
Bolton	a				07 08									07 34												
Manchester Piccadilly 10	a				07 27									07 56												
Manchester Airport	a				07 47									08 17												
Liverpool Lime Street 10	a																									
	d						06 30					07 00				07 04						07 34		07 48		
Liverpool South Parkway	d						06 40									07 14						07 44				
Runcorn	d						06 48					07 15				07 22						07 52		08 04		
Warrington Bank Quay	a			06 38									07 17						07 39							
	d			06 38									07 18						07 39							
Hartford	d						07 02									07 36						08 04				
Manchester Piccadilly 10	d					06 27		06 35	06 43		07 00				07 06		07 15			07 26			07 35			07 55
Stockport	d					06 35		06 43	06 51		07 07				07 16		07 23			07 35			07 43			08 04
Wilmslow	d								06 59																	08 11
Holyhead	d																	05 51								
Bangor (Gwynedd)	d																	06 18								
Llandudno Junction	d																	06 36								
Wrexham General	d																	07 00								
Chester	d																	07 35								
Crewe 10	a			06 58			07 14		07 15							07 48		07 54	07 58			08 19				08 27
	d	06 47		07 01			07 16		07 17							07 49		07 57	08 01			08 22				08 29
Macclesfield	d					06 48		06 55												07 49			07 56			
Congleton	d																									
Stoke-on-Trent	d					07 06		07 12		←					07 44		07 50			08 07			08 12		←	
Stafford	a	07 10				07 27	07 40		07 34	07 40						08 10				08 24		08 42		08 35	08 42	
	d	07 12				07 28	07 41		07 35	07 41						08 10				08 25		08 43		08 36	08 43	
Penkridge	a	07 17					→			07 46						08 16						→			08 48	
Wolverhampton 7	a	07 28		07 31		07 43				07 57					08 13	08 26			08 31	08 39					08 58	
Birmingham New Street 12	a	07 48		07 55		08 05				08 17					08 31	08 47			08 55	08 58					09 18	
Birmingham International	a					08 19														09 13						
Coventry	a					08 30														09 24						
Lichfield Trent Valley	a																									
Tamworth Low Level	a																									
Nuneaton	a																						08 44			
Rugby	a							07 55										08 45								
Milton Keynes Central	a																08s46									
Watford Junction	a					09s15																	09s31			
London Euston 15 ⊖	a					09 34		08 46	08 52		08 58	09 01	09 05				09 23	09 38					09 52	09 56		10 04

A ⊼ from Preston

B Through portion from Wrexham General to London Euston

OVERNIGHT SLEEPERS. For sleeper trains, operated by First ScotRail, please refer to Tables 400 - 404

Scotland and North West England - West Midlands and London

		XC ◇1 ⊼	NT	LM 1	VT ◇1 ⊠		TP ◇1 A ⊼	VT ◇1 ⊠	TP ◇1 ⊼	VT ◇1 ⊠	VT ◇1 ⊠	NT		XC ◇1 ⊼	LM 1	VT ◇1 ⊠	VT ◇1 ⊠	LM 1	VT ◇1 ⊠	XC ◇1 ⊼	LM 1	VT ◇1 ⊠			TP ◇1 A ⊼
Inverness	d																								
Aberdeen	d																								
Dundee	d																								
Perth	d																								
Edinburgh 10	d								05 36																
Haymarket	d								05u40																
Glasgow Central 15	d							05 40			05 50														
Motherwell	d										06 04														
Carstairs	d																								
Lockerbie	d																								
Carlisle 8	a							06 46	06 58		07 02														
	d							06 49	06 58		07 04														
Penrith North Lakes	d										07 19														
Windermere	d																								
Oxenholme Lake District	a							07 22			07 42														
	d							07 24			07 42														
Barrow-in-Furness	d						06 19					07 00													07 28
Lancaster 6	a						07 21	07 37	07 47		07 56	08 03													08 26
	d						07 22	07 38	07 47		07 57	08 04													08 27
Preston 8	a						07 41	07 56	08 07		08 15	08 29													08 45
Blackpool North	d		07 02																						
Preston 8	d		07 30				07 47	07 58	08 12		08 17														08 47
Wigan North Western	a		07 50					08 09			08 28														
	d		07 50					08 09			08 28														
Blackrod	d																								
Lostock	d																								
Bolton	a						08 08		08 34																09 08
Manchester Piccadilly 10	a						08 27		08 56																09 27
Manchester Airport	a						08 47		09 19																09 47
Liverpool Lime Street 10	a		08 35																						
	d			08 04											08 34		08 48				09 04				
Liverpool South Parkway	d			08 15											08 44						09 15				
Runcorn	d			08 24											08 52		09 04				09 25				
Warrington Bank Quay	a							08 20			08 39														
	d							08 20			08 39														
Hartford	d														09 06										
Manchester Piccadilly 10	d	08 07			08 15									08 27		08 35			08 55	09 07		09 15			
Stockport	d	08 16			08 23									08 35		08 42			09 04	09 16		09 23			
Wilmslow	d																		09 11						
Holyhead	d									06 55															
Bangor (Gwynedd)	d									07 22															
Llandudno Junction	d									07 40															
Wrexham General	d																								
Chester	d									08 35															
Crewe 10	a			08 47						08 54	08 58				09 20				09 27		09 44				
	d			08 49						08 56	09 01				09 22				09 29		09 49				
Macclesfield	d													08 49		08 55									
Congleton	d																								
Stoke-on-Trent	d	08 44			08 50									09 07		09 12		←		09 44		09 50			
Stafford	a	09 02		09 09										09 24	09 42		09 35	09 42		10 02	10 09				
	d	09 03		09 10										09 25	09 43		09 36	09 43		10 03	10 10				
Penkridge	a			09 15											→						10 15				
Wolverhampton 7	a	09 15		09 27							09 31			09 39				09 56		10 15	10 27				
Birmingham New Street 12	a	09 39		09 47							09 55			09 58				10 17		10 39	10 47				
Birmingham International	a													10 13											
Coventry	a													10 24											
Lichfield Trent Valley	a																								
Tamworth Low Level	a																								
Nuneaton	a																								
Rugby	a																								
Milton Keynes Central	a				09 46					10 01												10 46			
Watford Junction	a																								
London Euston 15 ⊖	a				10 23			10 12		10 38						10 42	10 55		11 04			11 23			

A ⊼ from Preston

OVERNIGHT SLEEPERS. For sleeper trains, operated by First ScotRail, please refer to Tables 400 - 404

Table 65

Mondays to Fridays

Scotland and North West England - West Midlands and London

		VT	NT	TP	TP	VT	VT	XC	LM	VT	VT	LM	VT	XC	LM	VT	TP	VT	VT	NT	TP
		◇■		◇■	◇■	◇■	◇■	◇■	■	◇■	◇■	■	◇■	◇■	■	◇■	◇■	◇■	◇■		◇■
				A	B																
		⊠		⊥	⊥	⊠	⊠	⊥		⊠	⊠		⊠	⊥		⊏	⊥	⊠	⊠		⊥
Inverness	d																				
Aberdeen	d																				
Dundee	d																				
Perth	d																				
Edinburgh	d						06 52														07 42
Haymarket	d						06 56														07u46
Glasgow Central	d	06 30															07 10	07 37			
Motherwell	d	06u45																07u52			
Carstairs	d																				
Lockerbie	d	07 26															08 06				
Carlisle	a	07 43					08 06										08 29	08 46			08 59
	d	07 46					08 08										08 31	08 49			09 00
Penrith North Lakes	d	08 00					08 23										08 45				
Windermere	d																				
Oxenholme Lake District	a	08 22															09 09	09 22			
	d	08 23															09 11	09 23			
Barrow-in-Furness	d																				
Lancaster	a	08 37					08 56										09 26	09 37			
	d	08 38					08 57										09 26	09 38			
Preston	a	08 56					09 15										09 45	09 56			10 04
Blackpool North	d			08 43	08 45															09 37	
Preston	d	08 58	09 04	09 10	09 10		09 17										09 47	09 58		10 04	10 12
Wigan North Western	a	09 09	09 24				09 28											10 09		10 24	
	d	09 09	09 24				09 28											10 09		10 24	
Blackrod	d																				
Lostock	d																				
Bolton	a			09 34	09 34												10 08				10 34
Manchester Piccadilly	a			09 56	09 56												10 27				10 56
Manchester Airport	a			10 17	10 17												10 47				11 17
Liverpool Lime Street	a		10 02																	11 02	
	d								09 34		09 48				10 04						
Liverpool South Parkway	d								09 44						10 15						
Runcorn	d								09 52		10 04				10 25						
Warrington Bank Quay	a	09 20					09 39											10 20			
	d	09 20					09 39											10 20			
Hartford	d								10 04												
Manchester Piccadilly	d							09 27		09 35			09 55	10 07		10 15					
Stockport	d							09 35		09 42			10 04	10 16		10 23					
Wilmslow	d												10 11								
Holyhead	d																		08 55		
Bangor (Gwynedd)	d																		09 22		
Llandudno Junction	d																		09 40		
Wrexham General	d																				
Chester	d					09 35													10 35		
Crewe	a					09 54	09 58		10 19				10 27		10 45				10 54		
	d					09 56	10 01		10 22				10 29		10 49				10 56		
Macclesfield	d							09 49		09 55											
Congleton	d																				
Stoke-on-Trent	d							10 07		10 11		←		10 44		10 50					
Stafford	a							10 24	10 42		10 35	10 42			11 09						
	d							10 25	10 43		10 36	10 43			11 10						
Penkridge	a								→						11 15						
Wolverhampton	a						10 31	10 39				10 56		11 16	11 27						
Birmingham New Street	a						10 55	10 58				11 18		11 39	11 47						
Birmingham International	a							11 13													
Coventry	a							11 24													
Lichfield Trent Valley	a																				
Tamworth Low Level	a																				
Nuneaton	a																				
Rugby	a																				
Milton Keynes Central	a					11 01										11 46			12 01		
Watford Junction	a																				
London Euston	a	11 12				11 38				11 42	11 56		12 04			12 23		12 12	12 38		

A FO from 2 July until 3 September

B Does not apply Fridays 2 July to 3 September

OVERNIGHT SLEEPERS. For sleeper trains, operated by First ScotRail, please refer to Tables 400 - 404

Table 65

Mondays to Fridays

Scotland and North West England - West Midlands and London

		VT	XC	LM	VT	VT	LM	VT	XC	LM	VT	VT	TP	VT	NT	TP	VT	VT	XC
		◇■	◇■	■	◇■	◇■	■	◇■	◇■	■	◇■	◇■	◇■	◇■		◇■	◇■	◇■	◇■
													B						
		⊠	⊥		⊏	⊏		⊏	⊥		⊏	⊠	⊥	⊠		⊥	⊏	⊏	⊥
Inverness	d																		
Aberdeen	d																		
Dundee	d																		
Perth	d																		
Edinburgh	d																	08 52	
Haymarket	d																	08 57	
Glasgow Central	d	08 00												08 40					
Motherwell	d																		
Carstairs	d																		
Lockerbie	d																		
Carlisle	a	09 08												09 47				10 05	
	d	09 09												09 49				10 07	
Penrith North Lakes	d													10 03					
Windermere	d																		
Oxenholme Lake District	a																	10 41	
	d																	10 42	
Barrow-in-Furness	d												09 22						
Lancaster	a	09 56											10 25	10 37				10 56	
	d	09 57											10 26	10 38				10 57	
Preston	a	10 15											10 45	10 56				11 15	
Blackpool North	d														10 37	10 45			
Preston	d	10 17										10 38	10 47	10 58	11 04	11 10		11 17	
Wigan North Western	a	10 28										10 49		11 09	11 24			11 28	
	d	10 28										10 49		11 09	11 24			11 28	
Blackrod	d																		
Lostock	d																		
Bolton	a												11 08			11 34			
Manchester Piccadilly	a												11 27			11 56			
Manchester Airport	a												11 50			12 17			
Liverpool Lime Street	a														12 02				
	d			10 34		10 48				11 04									
Liverpool South Parkway	d			10 44						11 15									
Runcorn	d			10 52		11 04				11 25									
Warrington Bank Quay	a	10 39										11 00		11 20				11 39	
	d	10 39										11 00		11 20				11 39	
Hartford	d			11 04															
Manchester Piccadilly	d		10 27		10 35			10 55	11 07		11 15								11 27
Stockport	d		10 35		10 42			11 04	11 16		11 23								11 35
Wilmslow	d							11 11											
Holyhead	d																		
Bangor (Gwynedd)	d																		
Llandudno Junction	d																		
Wrexham General	d																		
Chester	d																11 35		
Crewe	a	10 58		11 19				11 27		11 45							11 54	11 58	
	d	11 01		11 22				11 29		11 49							11 56	12 01	
Macclesfield	d		10 49		10 55														11 49
Congleton	d																		
Stoke-on-Trent	d		11 07		11 11		←		11 44		11 50								12 07
Stafford	a		11 24	11 43		11 37	11 43		12 02	12 09									12 24
	d		11 25	11 43		11 38	11 43		12 03	12 10									12 25
Penkridge	a			→						12 15									
Wolverhampton	a	11 31	11 39				11 57		12 15	12 27								12 31	12 39
Birmingham New Street	a	11 55	11 58				12 17		12 39	12 47								12 55	12 58
Birmingham International	a		12 13																13 13
Coventry	a		12 24																13 24
Lichfield Trent Valley	a																		
Tamworth Low Level	a																		
Nuneaton	a																		
Rugby	a																		
Milton Keynes Central	a										12 46						13 01		
Watford Junction	a																		
London Euston	a				12 42	12 58		13 04			13 23	12 58		13 12			13 38		

B ⊥ from Preston

OVERNIGHT SLEEPERS. For sleeper trains, operated by First ScotRail, please refer to Tables 400 - 404

Scotland and North West England - West Midlands and London

		LM	VT	VT	LM	VT	XC	LM	VT	NT	TP	VT	TP	NT	TP	VT	VT	XC	LM	VT	VT	LM
		1	◇1	◇1	1	◇1	◇1	1	◇1		◇1	◇1	◇1		◇1	◇1	◇1	◇1	1	◇1	◇1	1
			☕	☕		☕	🍴		☕		A 🍴	⊠			🍴	☕	☕	🍴		☕	☕	
Inverness	d																					
Aberdeen	d																					
Dundee	d																					
Perth	d																					
Edinburgh 10	d																					
Haymarket	d																					
Glasgow Central 15	d											09 40					10 00					
Motherwell	d																					
Carstairs	d																					
Lockerbie	d																					
Carlisle 8	a											10 47					11 08					
	d											10 49					11 09					
Penrith North Lakes	d																11 24					
Windermere	d										10 49											
Oxenholme Lake District	a										11 08	11 22										
	d										11 09	11 23										
Barrow-in-Furness	d												11 25									
Lancaster 6	a										11 26	11 37	12 18									
	d										11 26	11 38	12 18									
Preston 8	a										11 45	11 56	12 37				12 15					
Blackpool North	d													11 37	11 45							
Preston 8	d									11 23	11 47	11 58		12 04	12 10		12 17					
Wigan North Western	a											12 09		12 24			12 28					
	d											12 09		12 24			12 28					
Blackrod	d																					
Lostock	d									11 50												
Bolton	a									11 55	12 08				12 34							
Manchester Piccadilly 10	a									12 18	12 27				12 56							
Manchester Airport ✈	a										12 47				13 17							
Liverpool Lime Street 10	a													13 02								
	d	11 34		11 48				12 04											12 34		12 48	
Liverpool South Parkway ✈	d	11 44						12 15											12 44			
Runcorn	d	11 52		12 04				12 25											12 52		13 04	
Warrington Bank Quay	a											12 20					12 39					
	d											12 20					12 39					
Hartford	d	12 04																	13 06			
Manchester Piccadilly 10	d		11 35			11 55	12 07		12 15	12 21								12 27		12 35		
Stockport	d		11 42			12 04	12 16		12 23	12 35								12 35		12 42		
Wilmslow	d					12 11																
Holyhead	d																					
Bangor (Gwynedd)	d																					
Llandudno Junction	d																					
Wrexham General	d																					
Chester	d															12 35						
Crewe 10	a	12 19				12 27		12 45								12 54	12 58		13 20			
	d	12 22				12 29		12 49								12 56	13 01		13 22			
Macclesfield	d		11 55															12 49		12 55		
Congleton	d																					
Stoke-on-Trent	d		12 11		←		12 44		12 50									13 07		13 11		←
Stafford	a	12 42		12 35	12 42			13 09										13 24	13 42		13 35	13 42
	d	12 43		12 36	12 43			13 10										13 25	13 43		13 36	13 43
Penkridge	a	→						13 15											→			
Wolverhampton 7	a				12 56		13 13	13 27									13 31	13 39				13 56
Birmingham New Street 12	a				13 17		13 31	13 47									13 55	13 58				14 17
Birmingham International ✈	a																	14 13				
Coventry	a																	14 24				
Lichfield Trent Valley	a																					
Tamworth Low Level	a																					
Nuneaton	a																					
Rugby	a																					
Milton Keynes Central	a								13 46							14 01						
Watford Junction	a																					
London Euston 15 ⊖	a		13 42	13 56		14 04			14 23			14 12				14 38				14 42	14 56	

A 🍴 from Preston

OVERNIGHT SLEEPERS. For sleeper trains, operated by First ScotRail, please refer to Tables 400 - 404

Scotland and North West England - West Midlands and London

		VT	XC	LM	VT	TP	TP	VT	VT	NT	TP	VT	XC	VT	LM	VT	VT	LM	VT	XC	LM	VT
		◇1	◇1	1	◇1	◇1	◇1	◇1	◇1		◇1	◇1	◇1	◇1	1	◇1	◇1	1	◇1	◇1	1	◇1
		☕	🍴		☕	C 🍴	🍴	⊠	☕		🍴	A ☕	🍴	B ☕		☕	☕		☕	🍴		☕
Inverness	d																					
Aberdeen	d																					
Dundee	d																					
Perth	d																					
Edinburgh 10	d					09 53						10 52		10 52								
Haymarket	d					09u57						10 57		10 57								
Glasgow Central 15	d						10 10	10 40														
Motherwell	d																					
Carstairs	d																					
Lockerbie	d					11 00																
Carlisle 8	a					11 22	11 27	11 47				12 05		12 05								
	d					>	11 31	11 49				12 07		12 07								
Penrith North Lakes	d						11 45															
Windermere	d																					
Oxenholme Lake District	a						12 10	12 22				12 41		12 41								
	d						12 10	12 23				12 43		12 43								
Barrow-in-Furness	d																					
Lancaster 6	a						12 26	12 37				12 56		12 56								
	d						12 26	12 38				12 57		12 57								
Preston 8	a						12 45	12 56				13 15		13 15								
Blackpool North	d									12 37	12 45											
Preston 8	d						12 47	12 58		13 04	13 10	13 17		13 17								
Wigan North Western	a							13 09		13 24		13 28		13 28								
	d							13 09		13 24		13 28		13 28								
Blackrod	d																					
Lostock	d																					
Bolton	a						13 08				13 34											
Manchester Piccadilly 10	a						13 27				13 56											
Manchester Airport ✈	a						13 47				14 17											
Liverpool Lime Street 10	a									14 02												
	d			13 04											13 34		13 48				14 04	
Liverpool South Parkway ✈	d			13 15											13 44						14 15	
Runcorn	d			13 25											13 52		14 04				14 25	
Warrington Bank Quay	a							13 20				13 39		13 39								
	d							13 20				13 39		13 39								
Hartford	d														14 04							
Manchester Piccadilly 10	d	12 55	13 07		13 15								13 27			13 35			13 55	14 07		14 15
Stockport	d	13 04	13 16		13 23								13 35			13 42			14 04	14 16		14 23
Wilmslow	d	13 11																	14 11			
Holyhead	d																					
Bangor (Gwynedd)	d								12 24													
Llandudno Junction	d								12 42													
Wrexham General	d																					
Chester	d								13 35													
Crewe 10	a	13 27		13 45					13 54			13 58		13 58	14 19				14 27		14 45	
	d	13 29		13 49					13 56			14 01		14 01	14 22				14 29		14 49	
Macclesfield	d												13 49			13 55						
Congleton	d																					
Stoke-on-Trent	d		13 44		13 50								14 07			14 11		←		14 44		14 50
Stafford	a			14 09									14 24		14 46		14 35	14 46		15 02	15 09	
	d			14 10									14 25		14 46		14 36	14 46		15 03	15 10	
Penkridge	a			14 15											→						15 15	
Wolverhampton 7	a		14 13	14 27								14 31	14 39	14 33				14 59		15 15	15 27	
Birmingham New Street 12	a		14 31	14 47								14 55	14 58	15 05				15 20		15 39	15 47	
Birmingham International ✈	a												15 13	15 19								
Coventry	a												15 24	15 30								
Lichfield Trent Valley	a																					
Tamworth Low Level	a																					
Nuneaton	a																					
Rugby	a																					
Milton Keynes Central	a				14 46				15 01													15 46
Watford Junction	a													16s15								
London Euston 15 ⊖	a	15 04			15 23			15 12	15 38					16 34		15 42	15 56		16 04			16 23

A until 16 July and from 6 September

B from 19 July until 3 September

C Through portion to Manchester Airport

OVERNIGHT SLEEPERS. For sleeper trains, operated by First ScotRail, please refer to Tables 400 - 404

Table 65

Mondays to Fridays

Scotland and North West England - West Midlands and London

		TP			VT	VT	NT	TP	NT	VT	VT	TP		XC	LM	VT	VT	LM	VT	XC	LM	VT			TP
		◇1			◇1	◇1		◇1		◇1	◇1	◇1		◇1	1	◇1	◇1	1	◇1	◇1	1	◇1			◇1
		A																							
		⊼			⊠	⊏		⊼		⊏	⊏			⊼		⊏	⊏		⊏	⊼		⊏			⊼
Inverness	d																								
Aberdeen	d																								
Dundee	d																								
Perth	d																								
Edinburgh 10	d																								12 08
Haymarket	d																								12u12
Glasgow Central 15	d				11 40						12 00														
Motherwell	d																								
Carstairs	d																								
Lockerbie	d																								13 06
Carlisle 8	a				12 46						13 08														13 28
	d				12 49						13 09														13 29
Penrith North Lakes	d				13 03																				
Windermere	d	12 51																							
Oxenholme Lake District	a	13 07																							14 10
	d	13 09																							14 10
Barrow-in-Furness	d								14 16			13 25													
Lancaster 6	a	13 26							15 20		13 56	14 18													14 25
	d	13 26				13 39					13 58	14 18													14 26
Preston 8	a	13 45			13 50	13 56					14 15	14 37													14 45
Blackpool North	d						13 37	13 45																	
Preston 8	d	13 47			13 53	13 59	14 04	14 10			14 17														14 47
Wigan North Western	a					14 09	14 24				14 28														
	d					14 10	14 24				14 28														
Blackrod	d																								
Lostock	d																								
Bolton	a	14 08						14 34																	15 08
Manchester Piccadilly 10	a	14 27						14 56																	15 27
Manchester Airport ✈	a	14 47						15 17																	15 47
Liverpool Lime Street 10	a						15 02																		
	d														14 34		14 48				15 04				
Liverpool South Parkway ✈	d														14 44						15 15				
Runcorn	d														14 52		15 04				15 25				
Warrington Bank Quay	a					14 20					14 39														
	d					14 21					14 39														
Hartford	d														15 04										
Manchester Piccadilly 10	d													14 27		14 35			14 55	15 07		15 15			
Stockport	d													14 35		14 42			15 04	15 16		15 23			
Wilmslow	d																		15 11						
Holyhead	d																								
Bangor (Gwynedd)	d																								
Llandudno Junction	d																								
Wrexham General	d																								
Chester	d									14 35															
Crewe 10	a									14 54	14 58				15 19				15 27		15 45				
	d									14 56	15 01				15 22				15 29		15 49				
Macclesfield	d													14 49		14 55									
Congleton	d																								
Stoke-on-Trent	d													15 07		15 11		←		15 44		15 50			
Stafford	a													15 24	15 42		15 35	15 42		16 02	16 09				
	d													15 25	15 43		15 36	15 43		16 03	16 10				
Penkridge	a														→						16 15				
Wolverhampton 7	a										15 31			15 39				15 56		16 15	16 26				
Birmingham New Street 12	a										15 55			15 58				16 17		16 39	16 47				
Birmingham International ✈	a													16 13											
Coventry	a													16 24											
Lichfield Trent Valley	a																								
Tamworth Low Level	a																								
Nuneaton	a																								
Rugby	a																								
Milton Keynes Central	a									16 01												16 46			
Watford Junction	a																								
London Euston 15 ⊖	a				16 03	16 11				16 38						16 42	16 56		17 04			17 23			

A ⊼ from Preston

OVERNIGHT SLEEPERS. For sleeper trains, operated by First ScotRail, please refer to Tables 400 - 404

Table 65

Mondays to Fridays

Scotland and North West England - West Midlands and London

		VT	VT	NT	TP	VT	VT	XC		LM	VT	VT	LM	VT	XC	LM	VT			TP		VT	VT	TP	NT
		◇1	◇1		◇1	◇1	◇1	◇1		1	◇1	◇1	1	◇1	◇1	1	◇1			◇1		◇1	◇1	◇1	
		⊠	⊏		⊼	⊏	⊏	⊼			⊏	⊏		⊏	⊼		⊏			⊼		⊠	⊏		
Inverness	d																								
Aberdeen	d																								
Dundee	d																								
Perth	d																								
Edinburgh 10	d						12 52																		
Haymarket	d						12 57																		
Glasgow Central 15	d	12 40																		12 54		13 40			
Motherwell	d																								
Carstairs	d																								
Lockerbie	d																			13 56					
Carlisle 8	a	13 47					14 05													14 18		14 46			
	d	13 49					14 07													14 20		14 49			
Penrith North Lakes	d						14 22													14 34					
Windermere	d																								
Oxenholme Lake District	a	14 22																		14 58		15 22			
	d	14 24																		14 58		15 24			
Barrow-in-Furness	d																								
Lancaster 6	a	14 37					14 56													15 13					
	d	14 38					14 57													15 13			15 39		
Preston 8	a	14 56					15 15													15 34		15 50	15 56		
Blackpool North	d			14 37	14 45																				15 37
Preston 8	d	14 58		15 04	15 10		15 17													15 47		15 53	15 59		16 04
Wigan North Western	a	15 09		15 24			15 28																16 09		16 24
	d	15 09		15 24			15 28																16 10		16 24
Blackrod	d																								
Lostock	d																								
Bolton	a				15 34															16 08					
Manchester Piccadilly 10	a				15 56															16 27					
Manchester Airport ✈	a				16 17															16 47					
Liverpool Lime Street 10	a			16 02																					17 05
	d									15 34		15 48				16 04									
Liverpool South Parkway ✈	d									15 44						16 15									
Runcorn	d									15 52		16 04				16 25									
Warrington Bank Quay	a	15 20					15 39																16 20		
	d	15 20					15 39																16 21		
Hartford	d									16 04															
Manchester Piccadilly 10	d							15 27			15 35			15 55	16 07		16 15								
Stockport	d							15 35			15 42			16 04	16 16		16 23								
Wilmslow	d													16 11											
Holyhead	d		13 58																						
Bangor (Gwynedd)	d		14 25																						
Llandudno Junction	d		14 43																						
Wrexham General	d																								
Chester	d		15b35			15 35																			
Crewe 10	a		15 54			15 54	15 58			16 19				16 27		16 45									
	d		15 57			15 57	16 01			16 22				16 29		16 49									
Macclesfield	d							15 49			15 55														
Congleton	d																								
Stoke-on-Trent	d							16 07			16 11		←		16 44		16 50								
Stafford	a							16 24		16 46		16 35	16 46		17 02	17 10									
	d							16 25		16 46		16 36	16 46		17 03	17 10									
Penkridge	a									→						17 15									
Wolverhampton 7	a						16 32	16 39					16 59		17 15	17 27									
Birmingham New Street 12	a						16 55	16 58					17 20		17 39	17 47									
Birmingham International ✈	a							17 13																	
Coventry	a							17 24																	
Lichfield Trent Valley	a																								
Tamworth Low Level	a																								
Nuneaton	a																								
Rugby	a																								
Milton Keynes Central	a		17 01			17s01											17 46								
Watford Junction	a																								
London Euston 15 ⊖	a	17 12	17 38			17 38					17 42	17 56		18 02			18 23					18 01	18 09		

b arr. 1528

OVERNIGHT SLEEPERS. For sleeper trains, operated by First ScotRail, please refer to Tables 400 - 404

Table 65

Mondays to Fridays

Scotland and North West England - West Midlands and London

		TP	VT	VT	XC	LM	VT	VT	LM	VT	XC	LM	TP	TP	VT	VT	NT	TP	VT	VT	VT
		◇1	◇1	◇1	◇1	1	◇1	◇1	1	◇1	◇1	1	◇1	◇1	◇1	◇1		◇1	◇1	■ 1	■ 1
													C							A	B
		⊼	🍽	🍽	⊼		🍽	🍽		🍽	⊼			⊼	⊠	⊠		⊼	⊠	🍽	🍽
Inverness	d																				
Aberdeen	d																				
Dundee	d																				
Perth	d																				
Edinburgh 10	d													14 08						14 52	14 52
Haymarket	d													14u12						14 56	14 56
Glasgow Central 15	d			14 00												14 40					
Motherwell	d																				
Carstairs	d																				
Lockerbie	d													15 06							
Carlisle 8	a			15 08										15 28		15 47				16 05	16 05
	d			15 09										15 30		15 49				16 06	16 06
Penrith North Lakes	d																			16 21	16 21
Windermere	d																				
Oxenholme Lake District	a			15 44										16 08		16 22					
	d			15 44										16 08		16 24					
Barrow-in-Furness	d												15 25								
Lancaster 6	a												16 18	16 23		16 37				16 56	16 56
	d												16 18	16 23		16 38				16 56	16 56
Preston 8	a			16 15									16 37	16 42		16 56				17 14	17 14
Blackpool North	d	15 45															16 35	16 40			
Preston 8	d	16 10		16 17									>	16 47		16 58	17 04	17 09		17 17	17 17
Wigan North Western	a			16 28												17 09	17 24			17 28	17 27
	d			16 28												17 09	17 24			17 28	17 28
Blackrod	d																				
Lostock	d																				
Bolton	a	16 34												17 08				17 34			
Manchester Piccadilly 10	a	16 56												17 27				17 56			
Manchester Airport ✈	a	17 17												17 48				18 17			
Liverpool Lime Street 10	a																18 02				
	d					16 34		16 48				17 04									
Liverpool South Parkway ✈	d					16 44						17 15									
Runcorn	d					16 52		17 04				17 25									
Warrington Bank Quay	a			16 39												17 20				17 39	17 38
	d			16 39												17 20				17 39	17 39
Hartford	d					17 06															
Manchester Piccadilly 10	d				16 27		16 35			16 55	17 06				17 15						
Stockport	d				16 35		16 42			17 04					17 23						
Wilmslow	d									17 11											
Holyhead	d																				
Bangor (Gwynedd)	d																				
Llandudno Junction	d																				
Wrexham General	d																				
Chester	d		16 35																17 35		
Crewe 10	a		16 54	16 58		17 19				17 27		17 47							17 54	17 58	17 58
	d		16 56	17 01		17 22				17 29		17 49							17 56	18 01	18 01
Macclesfield	d				16 49		16 56				17 27										
Congleton	d																				
Stoke-on-Trent	d				17 07		17 12		←		17 44				17 50						
Stafford	a				17 24	17 42		17 35	17 42		18 03	18 09									
	d				17 25	17 43		17 36	17 43		18 04	18 10									
Penkridge	a					→						18 15									
Wolverhampton 7	a			17 31	17 39				17 56		18 15	18 27								18 31	18 33
Birmingham New Street 12	a			17 55	17 58				18 17		18 38	18 48								18 55	19 05
Birmingham International ✈	a				18 13																19 19
Coventry	a				18 24																19 30
Lichfield Trent Valley	a																				
Tamworth Low Level	a																				
Nuneaton	a																				
Rugby	a																				
Milton Keynes Central	a		18 01					18 23							18 47				19 02		
Watford Junction	a									18s48											20s15
London Euston 15 ⊖	a		18 38				18 42	18 59		19 08					19 23	19 13			19 38		20 34

A until 16 July and from 6 September
B from 19 July until 3 September
C Through portion to Manchester Airport

OVERNIGHT SLEEPERS. For sleeper trains, operated by First ScotRail, please refer to Tables 400 - 404

Table 65

Mondays to Fridays

Scotland and North West England - West Midlands and London

		TP	XC	LM	VT	VT	LM	VT	VT	NT	TP	XC	LM	VT	TP	VT	XC	LM	VT	NT	VT	VT
		◇1	◇1	1	◇1	◇1	1	◇1	◇1		◇1	◇1	1	◇1	◇1	◇1	◇1	1	◇1		◇1	◇1
											A						B					
		⊼	⊼		⊠	⊠		⊠	⊠		⊼	⊼		🍽	⊼	⊠	⊼		⊠		⊠	⊠
Inverness	d																					
Aberdeen	d																					
Dundee	d																					
Perth	d																					
Edinburgh 10	d														16 11							
Haymarket	d														16u15							
Glasgow Central 15	d													16 00								
Motherwell	d																					
Carstairs	d																					
Lockerbie	d														17 10							
Carlisle 8	a													17 08	17 32							
	d													17 09	17 33							
Penrith North Lakes	d														17 48							
Windermere	d										17 06											
Oxenholme Lake District	a										17 25			17 44								
	d										17 30			17 44								
Barrow-in-Furness	d																					
Lancaster 6	a										17 47				18 26							
	d								17 36		17 48				18 26							
Preston 8	a								17 54		18 06			18 15	18 45							
Blackpool North	d	17 20								17 37										18 37		
Preston 8	d	17 47							17 56	18 04	18 08			18 17	18 47					19 04		
Wigan North Western	a								18 07	18 24				18 28						19 24		
	d								18 08	18 24				18 28						19 24		
Blackrod	d																					
Lostock	d										18 30											
Bolton	a	18 08									18 34				19 08							
Manchester Piccadilly 10	a	18 27									18 56				19 27							
Manchester Airport ✈	a	18 47									19 17				19 47							
Liverpool Lime Street 10	a									19 03										20 02		
	d			17 34		17 48							18 04					18 34			18 48	
Liverpool South Parkway ✈	d			17 44									18 15					18 44				
Runcorn	d			17 52		18 04							18 24					18 52			19 04	
Warrington Bank Quay	a								18 19					18 39								
	d								18 19					18 39								
Hartford	d			18 06														19 04				
Manchester Piccadilly 10	d		17 27		17 35			17 55				18 05				18 15	18 27		18 35			18 55
Stockport	d		17 35		17 43			18 04				18 13				18 23	18 35		18 42			19 04
Wilmslow	d		17 44					18 11														19 11
Holyhead	d																					
Bangor (Gwynedd)	d																					
Llandudno Junction	d																					
Wrexham General	d																					
Chester	d																					
Crewe 10	a		18 05	18 20				18 27					18 47	18 59				19 16			19 21	19 27
	d		18 07	18 22				18 29					18 49	19 01				19 18			19 23	19 29
Macclesfield	d				17 55							18 26							18 55			
Congleton	d																18 54					
Stoke-on-Trent	d				18 12		←					18 44				18 50	19 07		19 12			
Stafford	a		18 27	18 42		18 35	18 42						19 09				19 24	19 41			19 41	
	d		18 28	18 43		18 36	18 43						19 10				19 25	19 42			19 42	
Penkridge	a			→									19 15					19 47				
Wolverhampton 7	a		18 39				18 56					19 13	19 27	19 31			19 39	19 57				
Birmingham New Street 12	a		18 58				19 17					19 31	19 47	19 55			19 58	20 18				
Birmingham International ✈	a		19 13														20 13					
Coventry	a		19 24														20 24					
Lichfield Trent Valley	a																					
Tamworth Low Level	a																					
Nuneaton	a																					
Rugby	a																					
Milton Keynes Central	a							19 31								19 46						20 32
Watford Junction	a					19s42															20s46	
London Euston 15 ⊖	a				19 42	20 02		20 06	20 11							20 23			20 42		21 05	21 06

A ⊼ from Preston
B ⊼ to Wolverhampton

OVERNIGHT SLEEPERS. For sleeper trains, operated by First ScotRail, please refer to Tables 400 - 404

Scotland and North West England - West Midlands and London

		VT	TP	TP	XC	LM	NT	VT	VT	VT	TP		XC	LM	VT	VT		VT	NT	XC	LM	VT	TP	TP	VT
		◇1	◇1	◇1	◇1	1		◇1	◇1	1	◇1		◇1	1	◇1	◇1		◇1		◇1	1	◇1	◇1	◇1	◇1
					A								A												
Inverness	d																								
Aberdeen	d																								
Dundee	d																								
Perth	d																								
Edinburgh	d									16 52														18 12	
Haymarket	d									16 57														18u16	
Glasgow Central	d	16 40									17 06											17 40			
Motherwell	d	16u54																							
Carstairs	d																								
Lockerbie	d										18 06											18 33		19 12	
Carlisle	a	17 49								18 05	18 28											18 52		19 34	
	d	17 51								18 07	18 29											18 54		19 34	
Penrith North Lakes	d	18 05									18 44											19 09		19 48	
Windermere	d			18 15																					
Oxenholme Lake District	a	18 27		18 34						18 41	19 08											19 32		20 12	
	d	18 29		18 36						18 42	19 08											19 32		20 12	
Barrow-in-Furness	d						18 03																		
Lancaster	a	18 43		18 52			19 04			18 56	19 26											19 47		20 26	
	d	18 44		18 52			19 05			18 57	19 26											19 47		20 26	
Preston	a	19 02		19 11			19 30			19 15	19 45											20 05		20 45	
Blackpool North	d		18 45																19 37				19 45		
Preston	d	19 05	19 10	19 16						19 17	19 47							19 58	20 04			20 08	20 10	20 47	
Wigan North Western	a	19 16								19 28								20 09	20 24			20 19			
	d	19 16								19 28								20 09	20 24			20 19			
Blackrod	d																								
Lostock	d																								
Bolton	a		19 34	19 42							20 08												20 34	21 08	
Manchester Piccadilly	a		19 56	20 01							20 27												20 56	21 27	
Manchester Airport	a		20 17	20 24							20 47												21 17	21 47	
Liverpool Lime Street	a																		21 02						
	d					19 11								19 34	19 48						20 04				
Liverpool South Parkway	d					19 21								19 44							20 15				
Runcorn	d					19 29								19 52	20 04						20 24				
Warrington Bank Quay	a	19 27								19 39								20 20				20 30			
	d	19 27								19 39								20 20				20 31			
Hartford	d													20 04											
Manchester Piccadilly	d				19 07			19 15					19 27			19 55				20 07					20 15
Stockport	d				19 16			19 23					19 35			20 04				20 16					20 23
Wilmslow	d															20 11									
Holyhead	d																								
Bangor (Gwynedd)	d																								
Llandudno Junction	d																								
Wrexham General	d																								
Chester	d								19 35																
Crewe	a					19 53			19 54	19 59				20 16	20 21	20 27		20 39			20 45	20 50			
	d					19 55			19 56	20 01				20 18	20 23	20 29		20 41			20 47	20 53			
Macclesfield	d							19 36					19 49												20 36
Congleton	d																								
Stoke-on-Trent	d				19 44			19 52					20 07							20 44					20 53
Stafford	a				20 03	20 15							20 25	20 38		20 47					21 08	21 12			
	d				20 04	20 16							20 26	20 42		20 48					21 10	21 14			
Penkridge	a													20 47							21 15				
Wolverhampton	a				20 16	20 29				20 33			20 40	20 57						21 13	21 26	21 29			
Birmingham New Street	a				20 33	20 47				20 55			21 00	21 18						21 31	21 47	21 50			
Birmingham International	a												21 13												
Coventry	a												21 24												
Lichfield Trent Valley	a																								
Tamworth Low Level	a																								
Nuneaton	a														21 02										
Rugby	a																	21 27							
Milton Keynes Central	a	20 45						20 48	21 03							21 35		21 47							21 50
Watford Junction	a														21s48										22s11
London Euston	a	21 24						21 25	21 42						22 09	22 12		22 22							22 33

A to Wolverhampton

OVERNIGHT SLEEPERS. For sleeper trains, operated by First ScotRail, please refer to Tables 400 - 404

Table 65

Mondays to Fridays

Scotland and North West England - West Midlands and London

		VT	NT	XC	LM	TP	VT	VT	VT	VT	TP	XC	LM	TP	VT FX	VT FO	TP FO	NT	NT	XC	TP	NT	TP	SR FO	SR FX
		◇1		◇1	1	◇1	◇1	◇1	◇1	◇1	◇1	◇1	1	◇1	◇1	◇1	◇1			◇1	◇1		◇1		
Inverness	d																								
Aberdeen	d																								
Dundee	d																								
Perth	d																								
Edinburgh	d									18 52							20 11							23 40	23 40
Haymarket	d									18 57							20u15								
Glasgow Central	d	18 40													20 10	20 10								23 40	23 40
Motherwell	d																							23u56	23u57
Carstairs	d														20 36									00u16	00c35
Lockerbie	d														21 05	21 05	21 12								
Carlisle	a	19 47								20 06					21 25	21 25	21 34							01u39	01u39
	d	19 49								20 08					21 26	21 26	21 36							01u42	01u44
Penrith North Lakes	d														21 41	21 42									
Windermere	d																						22 45		
Oxenholme Lake District	a	20 22								20 42					22 04	22 04	22 11						23 04		
	d	20 24								20 42					22 05	22 06	22 12						23 06		
Barrow-in-Furness	d										20 07								21 43						
Lancaster	a	20 37								20 57	21 10				22 19	22 19	22 26		22 44			23 05	23 23		
	d	20 38								20 57	21 10				22 20	22 21	22 26		22 45			23 07	23 24		
Preston	a	20 56								21 15	21 29				22 37	22 38	22 45		23 10			23 28	23 45		
Blackpool North	d		19 37			20 45								21 45				22 14			22 45		00a16		
Preston	d	20 58	21 04			21 10				21 17	21 31			22 10	22 40	22 40	22 47	22 43			23 10				
Wigan North Western	a	21 09	21 23							21 28	21 47				22 51	22 51		23 02							
	d	21 09	21 23							21 28	21 48				22 52	22 52		23 02							
Blackrod	d																								
Lostock	d																								
Bolton	a					21 34								22 34			23 06				23 34				
Manchester Piccadilly	a					21 56					22 30			22 56			23 30				23 53				
Manchester Airport	a					22 17					22 47			23 17							00 22				
Liverpool Lime Street	a		22 16															23 54							
	d				20 34			20 48					21 34												
Liverpool South Parkway	d				20 44								21 44												
Runcorn	d				20 52			21 04					21 52												
Warrington Bank Quay	a	21 20								21 39					23 02	23 02									
	d	21 20								21 39					23 03	23 03									
Hartford	d				21 04								22 04												
Manchester Piccadilly	d			20 27			21 15					21 28								22 07					
Stockport	d			20 35			21 23					21 36								22 16					
Wilmslow	d																								
Holyhead	d																								
Bangor (Gwynedd)	d								20 20																
Llandudno Junction	d								20 38																
Wrexham General	d																								
Chester	d								21b35																
Crewe	a				21 16			21 22	21 54	21 59			22 18		23 26	23 26									
	d				21 18			21 24	21 56	22 01			22 28												
Macclesfield	d			20 49			21 36					21 50								22 29					
Congleton	d																								
Stoke-on-Trent	d			21 08			21 53					22 08								22 47					
Stafford	a			21 25	21 38			21 43				22 25	22 40							23 06					
	d			21 26	21 41			21 44				22 26	22 41							23 07					
Penkridge	a				21 46								22 47												
Wolverhampton	a			21 39	21 57				22 27	22 32		22 39	22 57							23 19					
Birmingham New Street	a			22 00	22 17				22 50	22 55		22 58	23 18							23 38					
Birmingham International	a																								
Coventry	a																								
Lichfield Trent Valley	a							21 57																	
Tamworth Low Level	a							22 04																	
Nuneaton	a							22 16																	
Rugby	a							22 30																	
Milton Keynes Central	a	22 39					22 52	22 57																	
Watford Junction	a	23s14					23s25	23s31																06s27	06s19
London Euston	a	23 38					23 48	23 58																06 50	06 40

b arr. 2128

c stops to pick up only, arr. 0016

OVERNIGHT SLEEPERS. For sleeper trains, operated by First ScotRail, please refer to Tables 400 - 404

Table 65

Scotland and North West England - West Midlands and London

Mondays to Fridays

		SR FX	SR FO
		B	B
Inverness	d	20 46	20 46
Aberdeen	d	21 40	21 40
Dundee	d	23u06	23u06
Perth	d	23u21	23u21
Edinburgh 10	d		
Haymarket	d		
Glasgow Central 15	d		
Motherwell	d		
Carstairs	d		
Lockerbie	d		
Carlisle 8	a		
	d		
Penrith North Lakes	d		
Windermere	d		
Oxenholme Lake District	a		
	d		
Barrow-in-Furness	d		
Lancaster 6	a		
	d		
Preston 8	a		
Blackpool North	d		
Preston 8	d	04s42	04s42
Wigan North Western	a		
	d		
Blackrod	d		
Lostock	d		
Bolton	a		
Manchester Piccadilly 10	a		
Manchester Airport	a		
Liverpool Lime Street 10	a		
	d		
Liverpool South Parkway	d		
Runcorn	d		
Warrington Bank Quay	a		
	d		
Hartford	d		
Manchester Piccadilly 10	d		
Stockport	d		
Wilmslow	d		
Holyhead	d		
Bangor (Gwynedd)	d		
Llandudno Junction	d		
Wrexham General	d		
Chester	d		
Crewe 10	a		
	d	05s40	05s40
Macclesfield	d		
Congleton	d		
Stoke-on-Trent	d		
Stafford	a		
	d		
Penkridge	a		
Wolverhampton 7	a		
Birmingham New Street 12	a		
Birmingham International	a		
Coventry	a		
Lichfield Trent Valley	a		
Tamworth Low Level	a		
Nuneaton	a		
Rugby	a		
Milton Keynes Central	a		
Watford Junction	a		
London Euston 15	a	07 56	07 56

b arr. 0100

OVERNIGHT SLEEPERS. For sleeper trains, operated by First ScotRail, please refer to Tables 400 - 404

Table 65

Scotland and North West England - West Midlands and London

Saturdays until 16 October

		AW	TP	XC	TP	VT	XC	VT	LM	VT	VT	TP	XC	VT	VT	LM	VT	TP	LM
			◇1	◇1	◇1	◇1	◇1	◇1	◇1	◇1	◇1	◇1	◇1	◇1	◇1	◇1	◇1	◇1	1
Inverness	d																		
Aberdeen	d																		
Dundee	d																		
Perth	d																		
Edinburgh 10	d																		
Haymarket	d																		
Glasgow Central 15	d																		
Motherwell	d																		
Carstairs	d																		
Lockerbie	d																		
Carlisle 8	a																		
	d																		
Penrith North Lakes	d																		
Windermere	d																		
Oxenholme Lake District	a																		
	d																		
Barrow-in-Furness	d		04 35															05 31	
Lancaster 6	a		05 28															06 23	
	d										05 40							06 26	
Preston 8	a										05 55							06 45	
Blackpool North	d											05 44							
Preston 8	d				05 16						05 58	06 09					06 17	06 47	
Wigan North Western	a										06 09						06 28		
	d										06 09						06 28		
Blackrod	d																		
Lostock	d											06 30							
Bolton	a				05 42							06 34						07 08	
Manchester Piccadilly 10	a				06 01							06 56						07 27	
Manchester Airport	a				06 18							07 17						07 47	
Liverpool Lime Street 10	a																		
	d							05 47											06 32
Liverpool South Parkway	d																		06 42
Runcorn	d							06 03											06 50
Warrington Bank Quay	a										06 20						06 39		
	d										06 20						06 39		
Hartford	d																		07 02
Manchester Piccadilly 10	d			05 11		05 25				05 55			06 00	06 10	06 35				
Stockport	d					05 34				06 03			06 08	06 18	06 43				
Wilmslow	d					05 41				06 11									
Holyhead	d																		
Bangor (Gwynedd)	d																		
Llandudno Junction	d																		
Wrexham General	d																		
Chester	d	04 23																	
Crewe 10	a	04 44		05 41		05 57				06 27							06 58		07 14
	d	05 00		05 47		06 00			06 20	06 29						06 47	07 01		07 16
Macclesfield	d												06 21	06 31	06 55				
Congleton	d																		
Stoke-on-Trent	d			06 08			←						06 39	06 48	07 12				
Stafford	a	05 24		06 25		06 17	06 25	06 34	06 41				06 57			07 10			07 40
	d	05 24		06 26		06 19	06 26	06 35	06 41				06 58			07 12			07 41
Penkridge	a			→					06 47							07 17			→
Wolverhampton 7	a	05 38					06 39		06 57				07 12			07 28	07 32		
Birmingham New Street 12	a	05 55					06 57		07 17				07 31			07 47	07 55		
Birmingham International	a						07 13												
Coventry	a						07 24												
Lichfield Trent Valley	a													07 11					
Tamworth Low Level	a													07 18					
Nuneaton	a							06 57											
Rugby	a					06 49									07 52				
Milton Keynes Central	a					07 11				07 31	07 37								
Watford Junction	a					07s32		07s44											
London Euston 15	a					07 52		08 05		08 09	08 14			08 28	08 46				

OVERNIGHT SLEEPERS. For sleeper trains, operated by First ScotRail, please refer to Tables 400 - 404

Table 65

Saturdays until 16 October

Scotland and North West England - West Midlands and London

		VT	LM	VT	VT	TP	XC	XC	VT	VT	LM	VT	VT	XC	NT	LM	VT	VT	LM	VT	XC	XC
		◇1	1	◇1	◇1	◇1	◇1	◇1	◇1	◇1	1	◇1	◇1	◇1		1	◇1	◇1	1	◇1	◇1	◇1
							A	B													A	B
		🍴		🍴	🍴	🛒	🛒	🛒	🍴	🍴		🍴	🍴	🛒			🍴	🍴		🍴	🛒	🛒
Inverness	d																					
Aberdeen	d																					
Dundee	d																					
Perth	d																					
Edinburgh 10	d																					
Haymarket	d																					
Glasgow Central 15	d				04 26																	
Motherwell	d																					
Carstairs	d																					
Lockerbie	d																					
Carlisle 8	a				05 43																	
	d				05 44																	
Penrith North Lakes	d				05 59																	
Windermere	d																					
Oxenholme Lake District	a				06 21																	
	d				06 22																	
Barrow-in-Furness	d																					
Lancaster 6	a				06 36																	
	d				06 37								06 58									
Preston 8	a				06 55								07 15									
Blackpool North	d					06 34									07 02							
Preston 8	d				06 58	07 03							07 17		07 30							
Wigan North Western	a				07 09								07 28		07 50							
	d				07 10								07 28		07 50							
Blackrod	d					07 21																
Lostock	d					07 29																
Bolton	a					07 34																
Manchester Piccadilly 10	a					07 56																
Manchester Airport ✈	a					08 17																
Liverpool Lime Street 10	a														08 34							
	d	06 45									07 04	07 19				07 34		07 48				
Liverpool South Parkway ✈	d										07 14					07 44						
Runcorn	d	07 01									07 22	07 36				07 52		08 04				
Warrington Bank Quay	a				07 20								07 39									
	d				07 20								07 39									
Hartford	d										07 36					08 04						
Manchester Piccadilly 10	d			06 55			07 00	07 07	07 15					07 27			07 35			07 55	07 58	08 07
Stockport	d			07 04			07 09	07 16	07 23					07 35			07 43			08 04	08 08	08 16
Wilmslow	d			07 11																08 11		
Holyhead	d																					
Bangor (Gwynedd)	d																					
Llandudno Junction	d																					
Wrexham General	d																					
Chester	d									07 17												
Crewe 10	a	07 18		07 27						07 36	07 47	07 52	07 58			08 19				08 27		
	d	07 20		07 29						07 39	07 49	07 55	08 01			08 22				08 29		
Macclesfield	d						07 25							07 49			07 56				08 25	
Congleton	d																					
Stoke-on-Trent	d		←				07 44	07 44	07 50					08 07			08 12		←		08 44	08 44
Stafford	a	07 38	07 40				08 03	08 02			08 10	08 14		08 25		08 42		08 35	08 42		09 03	09 02
	d	07 39	07 41				08 03	08 03			08 10	08 16		08 26		08 43		08 36	08 43		09 04	09 03
Penkridge	a		07 46								08 16					→			08 48			
Wolverhampton 7	a		07 57				08 16	08 16			08 28		08 31	08 39					08 58		09 17	09 15
Birmingham New Street 12	a		08 17				08 38	08 38			08 47		08 55	08 58					09 18		09 39	09 39
Birmingham International ✈	a													09 13								
Coventry	a													09 24								
Lichfield Trent Valley	a											08 30										
Tamworth Low Level	a											08 36										
Nuneaton	a																	08 58				
Rugby	a																					
Milton Keynes Central	a								08 46													
Watford Junction	a																					
London Euston 15 ⊖	a	08 59		09 04	09 12				09 23	09 30		09 46					09 42	10 00		10 04		

A until 4 September

B from 11 September until 16 October

OVERNIGHT SLEEPERS. For sleeper trains, operated by First ScotRail, please refer to Tables 400 - 404

Table 65

Saturdays until 16 October

Scotland and North West England - West Midlands and London

		LM	VT	TP	VT	VT	TP	VT	XC	LM	VT	VT	LM	VT	XC	LM	VT	TP	VT	VT
		1	◇1	◇1	◇1	◇1	◇1	◇1	◇1	1	◇1	◇1	1	◇1	◇1	1	◇1	◇1	◇1	◇1
				A														A		
			🍴	🛒	🍴	🍴	🛒	🍴	🛒		🍴	🍴		🍴	🛒		🍴	🛒	🍴	🍴
Inverness	d																			
Aberdeen	d																			
Dundee	d																			
Perth	d																			
Edinburgh 10	d																			
Haymarket	d																			
Glasgow Central 15	d				05 40			05 50											06 30	
Motherwell	d							06 05											06u45	
Carstairs	d																			
Lockerbie	d																		07 25	
Carlisle 8	a				06 47			07 02											07 43	
	d				06 49			07 03											07 46	
Penrith North Lakes	d							07 18											08 00	
Windermere	d																			
Oxenholme Lake District	a				07 22			07 41											08 22	
	d				07 24			07 42											08 23	
Barrow-in-Furness	d			06 19														07 28		
Lancaster 6	a			07 21	07 37			07 56										08 26	08 37	
	d			07 22	07 38			07 57										08 27	08 38	
Preston 8	a			07 41	07 56			08 15										08 45	08 56	
Blackpool North	d						07 44													
Preston 8	d			07 47	07 58		08 12	08 17										08 47	08 58	
Wigan North Western	a				08 09			08 28											09 09	
	d				08 09			08 28											09 09	
Blackrod	d																			
Lostock	d																			
Bolton	a			08 08			08 34											09 08		
Manchester Piccadilly 10	a			08 27			08 56											09 27		
Manchester Airport ✈	a			08 47			09 19											09 47		
Liverpool Lime Street 10	a																			
	d	08 04								08 34		08 48				09 04				
Liverpool South Parkway ✈	d	08 15								08 44						09 15				
Runcorn	d	08 24								08 52		09 04				09 24				
Warrington Bank Quay	a				08 20			08 39											09 20	
	d				08 20			08 39											09 20	
Hartford	d									09 06										
Manchester Piccadilly 10	d		08 15						08 27		08 35			08 55	09 07		09 15			
Stockport	d		08 23						08 35		08 42			09 04	09 16		09 23			
Wilmslow	d													09 11						
Holyhead	d					06 53														07 55
Bangor (Gwynedd)	d					07 20														08 22
Llandudno Junction	d					07 38														08 40
Wrexham General	d																			
Chester	d					08b35														09 35
Crewe 10	a	08 47				08 54		08 58		09 20				09 27		09 44				09 54
	d	08 49				08 56		09 01		09 22				09 29		09 49				09 56
Macclesfield	d								08 49		08 55									
Congleton	d																			
Stoke-on-Trent	d		08 50						09 07		09 13		←		09 44		09 50			
Stafford	a	09 09							09 25	09 42		09 35	09 42		10 02	10 10				
	d	09 10							09 26	09 43		09 36	09 43		10 03	10 10				
Penkridge	a	09 15								→						10 16				
Wolverhampton 7	a	09 27						09 31	09 39				09 56		10 15	10 27				
Birmingham New Street 12	a	09 47						09 55	09 58				10 17		10 39	10 47				
Birmingham International ✈	a								10 13											
Coventry	a								10 24											
Lichfield Trent Valley	a																			
Tamworth Low Level	a																			
Nuneaton	a											09 58								
Rugby	a																			
Milton Keynes Central	a		09 46			10 01											10 46			11 01
Watford Junction	a																			
London Euston 15 ⊖	a		10 23		10 12	10 37					10 42	11 01		11 04			11 23		11 12	11 38

A 🛒 from Preston

b arr. 0828

OVERNIGHT SLEEPERS. For sleeper trains, operated by First ScotRail, please refer to Tables 400 - 404

Table 65

Saturdays until 16 October

Scotland and North West England - West Midlands and London

		NT	TP ◇1 ⊼	VT ◇1 ⌂	XC ◇1 ⊼	LM 1	VT ◇1 ⌂	VT ◇1 ⌂	LM 1	VT ◇1 ⌂	XC ◇1 ⊼	LM 1	VT ◇1 ⌂	TP ◇1 ⊼	VT ◇1 ⌂	VT ◇1 ⌂	NT	TP ◇1 ⊼	VT ◇1 ⌂	TP ◇1
Inverness	d																			
Aberdeen	d																			
Dundee	d																			
Perth	d																			
Edinburgh 10	d			06 52																
Haymarket	d			06 56																
Glasgow Central 15	d													07 10	07 35				08 00	
Motherwell	d														07u51					
Carstairs	d																			
Lockerbie	d													08 06						
Carlisle 8	a			08 05										08 29	08 47				09 08	
	d			08 07										08 31	08 49				09 09	
Penrith North Lakes	d			08 22										08 45						
Windermere	d																			09 38
Oxenholme Lake District	a													09 09	09 22					09 57
	d													09 11	09 23					09 58
Barrow-in-Furness	d																			
Lancaster 6	a			08 56										09 26	09 37				09 56	10 16
	d			08 57										09 26	09 38				09 57	10 16
Preston 8	a			09 15										09 45	09 56				10 15	10 35
Blackpool North	d	08 38	08 45														09 37	09 45		
Preston 8	d	09 04	09 10	09 17										09 47	09 58		10 04	10 10	10 17	
Wigan North Western	a	09 24		09 28											10 09		10 24		10 28	
	d	09 24		09 28											10 09		10 24		10 28	
Blackrod	d																			
Lostock	d																			
Bolton	a		09 34											10 08				10 34		
Manchester Piccadilly 10	a		09 56											10 27				10 56		
Manchester Airport ✈	a		10 17											10 47				11 17		
Liverpool Lime Street 10	a	10 02															11 02			
	d					09 34		09 48				10 04								
Liverpool South Parkway ✈	d					09 44						10 15								
Runcorn	d					09 52		10 04				10 25								
Warrington Bank Quay	a			09 39											10 20				10 39	
	d			09 39											10 20				10 39	
Hartford	d					10 04														
Manchester Piccadilly 10	d				09 27		09 35			09 55	10 07		10 15							
Stockport	d				09 35		09 42			10 04	10 16		10 23							
Wilmslow	d									10 11										
Holyhead	d															08 55				
Bangor (Gwynedd)	d															09 22				
Llandudno Junction	d															09 40				
Wrexham General	d																			
Chester	d															10c35				
Crewe 10	a			09 58		10 19				10 27		10 45				10 54			10 58	
	d			10 01		10 22				10 29		10 49				10 56			11 01	
Macclesfield	d				09 49		09 55													
Congleton	d																			
Stoke-on-Trent	d				10 07		10 12		⟵		10 44		10 50							
Stafford	a				10 25	10 42		10 35	10 42		11 02	11 09								
	d				10 26	10 43		10 36	10 43		11 03	11 10								
Penkridge	a					⟶						11 15								
Wolverhampton 7	a			10 31	10 39				10 56		11 16	11 27							11 31	
Birmingham New Street 12	a			10 55	10 58				11 17		11 39	11 47							11 55	
Birmingham International ✈	a				11 13															
Coventry	a				11 24															
Lichfield Trent Valley	a																			
Tamworth Low Level	a																			
Nuneaton	a																			
Rugby	a																			
Milton Keynes Central	a												11 46			12 01				
Watford Junction	a																			
London Euston 15 ⊖	a						11 42	11 56		12 04			12 23		12 12	12 38				

b arr. 1007   c arr. 1028

OVERNIGHT SLEEPERS. For sleeper trains, operated by First ScotRail, please refer to Tables 400 - 404

Table 65

Saturdays until 16 October

Scotland and North West England - West Midlands and London

		XC ◇1 ⊼	LM 1	VT ◇1 ⌂	VT ◇1 ⌂	LM 1	VT ◇1 ⌂	XC ◇1 ⊼	LM 1	VT ◇1 ⌂	TP ◇1 A ⊼	VT ◇1 ⌂	NT	TP ◇1 ⊼	VT ◇1 ⌂	VT ◇1 ⌂	XC ◇1 ⊼	LM 1	VT ◇1 ⌂	VT ◇1 ⌂	LM 1
Inverness	d																				
Aberdeen	d																				
Dundee	d																				
Perth	d																				
Edinburgh 10	d															08 52					
Haymarket	d															08 57					
Glasgow Central 15	d											08 40									
Motherwell	d																				
Carstairs	d																				
Lockerbie	d																				
Carlisle 8	a											09 46				10 05					
	d											09 49				10 07					
Penrith North Lakes	d											10 03									
Windermere	d																				
Oxenholme Lake District	a															10 41					
	d															10 42					
Barrow-in-Furness	d										09 22										
Lancaster 6	a										10 25	10 37				10 56					
	d										10 26	10 38				10 57					
Preston 8	a										10 45	10 56				11 15					
Blackpool North	d												10 37	10 45							
Preston 8	d										10 47	10 58	11 04	11 10		11 17					
Wigan North Western	a											11 09	11 24			11 28					
	d											11 09	11 24			11 28					
Blackrod	d																				
Lostock	d																				
Bolton	a										11 08			11 34							
Manchester Piccadilly 10	a										11 27			11 56							
Manchester Airport ✈	a										11 47			12 17							
Liverpool Lime Street 10	a												12 02								
	d		10 34		10 48				11 04									11 34		11 48	
Liverpool South Parkway ✈	d		10 44						11 15									11 44			
Runcorn	d		10 52		11 04				11 25									11 52		12 04	
Warrington Bank Quay	a											11 20				11 39					
	d											11 20				11 39					
Hartford	d		11 04															12 04			
Manchester Piccadilly 10	d	10 27		10 35			10 55	11 07		11 15							11 27		11 35		
Stockport	d	10 35		10 42			11 04	11 16		11 23							11 35		11 42		
Wilmslow	d						11 11														
Holyhead	d																				
Bangor (Gwynedd)	d																				
Llandudno Junction	d																				
Wrexham General	d																				
Chester	d														11 35						
Crewe 10	a		11 19				11 27		11 45						11 54	11 58		12 19			
	d		11 22				11 29		11 49						11 56	12 01		12 22			
Macclesfield	d	10 49		10 55													11 49		11 55		
Congleton	d																				
Stoke-on-Trent	d	11 07		11 12		⟵		11 44		11 50							12 07		12 12		⟵
Stafford	a	11 25	11 42		11 35	11 42		12 02	12 09								12 24	12 42		12 35	12 42
	d	11 26	11 43		11 36	11 43		12 03	12 10								12 25	12 43		12 36	12 43
Penkridge	a		⟶						12 15									⟶			
Wolverhampton 7	a	11 39				11 56		12 16	12 27							12 31	12 39				12 56
Birmingham New Street 12	a	11 58				12 17		12 39	12 47							12 55	12 58				13 17
Birmingham International ✈	a	12 13															13 13				
Coventry	a	12 24															13 24				
Lichfield Trent Valley	a																				
Tamworth Low Level	a																				
Nuneaton	a																				
Rugby	a																				
Milton Keynes Central	a									12 46					13 01						
Watford Junction	a																				
London Euston 15 ⊖	a			12 42	12 56		13 04			13 23		13 12			13 38				13 42	13 56	

A ⊼ from Preston

OVERNIGHT SLEEPERS. For sleeper trains, operated by First ScotRail, please refer to Tables 400 - 404

Table 65

Saturdays until 16 October

Scotland and North West England - West Midlands and London

		VT	XC	LM	VT	TP A	VT	NT	TP	TP	VT	VT	XC	LM	VT	VT	LM	VT	XC	LM	VT
Inverness	d																				
Aberdeen	d																				
Dundee	d																				
Perth	d																				
Edinburgh	d								09 22												
Haymarket	d								09u26												
Glasgow Central	d						09 40					10 00									
Motherwell	d																				
Carstairs	d																				
Lockerbie	d								10 22												
Carlisle	a						10 47		10 43			11 08									
	d						10 49		10 53			11 09									
Penrith North Lakes	d								11 07			11 24									
Windermere	d					10 49															
Oxenholme Lake District	a					11 08	11 22		11 31												
	d					11 09	11 23		11 31												
Barrow-in-Furness	d									11 25											
Lancaster	a					11 26	11 37		11 46	12 18											
	d					11 26	11 38		11 46	12 18											
Preston	a					11 45	11 56		12 05	12 37		12 15									
Blackpool North	d							11 37													
Preston	d					11 47	11 58	12 04	12 10			12 17									
Wigan North Western	a						12 09	12 24				12 28									
	d						12 09	12 24				12 28									
Blackrod	d																				
Lostock	d																				
Bolton	a					12 08			12 34												
Manchester Piccadilly	a					12 27			12 56												
Manchester Airport	a					12 47			13 17												
Liverpool Lime Street	a							13 02													
	d			12 04										12 34		12 48				13 04	
Liverpool South Parkway	d			12 15										12 44						13 15	
Runcorn	d			12 25										12 52		13 04				13 25	
Warrington Bank Quay	a						12 20					12 39									
	d						12 20					12 39									
Hartford	d													13 06							
Manchester Piccadilly	d	11 55	12 07		12 15								12 27		12 35			12 55	13 07		13 15
Stockport	d	12 04	12 16		12 23								12 35		12 42			13 04	13 16		13 23
Wilmslow	d	12 11																13 11			
Holyhead	d																				
Bangor (Gwynedd)	d																				
Llandudno Junction	d																				
Wrexham General	d																				
Chester	d										12 35										
Crewe	a	12 27		12 45							12 54	12 58		13 20				13 27		13 45	
	d	12 29		12 49							12 57	13 01		13 22				13 29		13 49	
Macclesfield	d												12 49		12 55						
Congleton	d																				
Stoke-on-Trent	d		12 44		12 50								13 07		13 12		←		13 44		13 50
Stafford	a		13 02	13 09									13 25	13 42		13 35	13 42		14 02	14 09	
	d		13 03	13 10									13 26	13 43		13 36	13 43		14 03	14 10	
Penkridge	a			13 15										→						14 15	
Wolverhampton	a		13 15	13 27								13 31	13 39				13 56		14 16	14 27	
Birmingham New Street	a		13 39	13 47								13 55	13 58				14 17		14 39	14 47	
Birmingham International	a												14 13								
Coventry	a												14 24								
Lichfield Trent Valley	a																				
Tamworth Low Level	a																				
Nuneaton	a																				
Rugby	a																				
Milton Keynes Central	a				13 46						14 01										14 46
Watford Junction	a																				
London Euston	a	14 04			14 23		14 12				14 38				14 42	14 56		15 04			15 23

A ⚲ from Preston

OVERNIGHT SLEEPERS. For sleeper trains, operated by First ScotRail, please refer to Tables 400 - 404

Table 65

Saturdays until 16 October

Scotland and North West England - West Midlands and London

		TP	VT	VT A	NT	TP	VT B	VT C	XC	VT D	LM	VT	VT	LM	VT	XC	LM	VT	TP E	VT
Inverness	d																			
Aberdeen	d																			
Dundee	d																			
Perth	d																			
Edinburgh	d							10 52		10 52										
Haymarket	d							10 57		10 57										
Glasgow Central	d	10 10	10 40																	11 40
Motherwell	d																			
Carstairs	d																			
Lockerbie	d																			
Carlisle	a	11 27	11 46					12 05		12 05										12 46
	d	11 28	11 49					12 07		12 07										12 49
Penrith North Lakes	d	11 42																		13 03
Windermere	d																		12 51	
Oxenholme Lake District	a	12 06	12 22					12 41		12 41									13 07	
	d	12 07	12 23					12 43		12 43									13 09	
Barrow-in-Furness	d																			
Lancaster	a	12 22	12 37					12 56		12 56									13 26	13 37
	d	12 23	12 38					12 57		12 57									13 26	13 38
Preston	a	12 41	12 56					13 15		13 15									13 45	13 56
Blackpool North	d				12 37	12 45														
Preston	d	12 47	12 58		13 04	13 10		13 17		13 17									13 47	13 58
Wigan North Western	a		13 09		13 24			13 28		13 28										14 09
	d		13 09		13 24			13 28		13 28										14 09
Blackrod	d																			
Lostock	d																			
Bolton	a	13 08				13 34													14 08	
Manchester Piccadilly	a	13 27				13 56													14 27	
Manchester Airport	a	13 47				14 17													14 47	
Liverpool Lime Street	a				14 02															
	d										13 34		13 48				14 04			
Liverpool South Parkway	d										13 44						14 15			
Runcorn	d										13 52		14 04				14 25			
Warrington Bank Quay	a		13 20					13 39		13 39										14 20
	d		13 20					13 39		13 39										14 20
Hartford	d										14 04									
Manchester Piccadilly	d								13 27			13 35			13 55	14 07		14 15		
Stockport	d								13 35			13 42			14 04	14 16		14 23		
Wilmslow	d														14 11					
Holyhead	d			11 55																
Bangor (Gwynedd)	d			12 21																
Llandudno Junction	d			12 39																
Wrexham General	d																			
Chester	d			13b35			13 35													
Crewe	a			13 54			13 54	13 58		13 59	14 19				14 27		14 45			
	d			13 56			13 56	14 01		14 01	14 22				14 29		14 49			
Macclesfield	d								13 49			13 55								
Congleton	d																			
Stoke-on-Trent	d								14 07			14 12		←		14 44		14 50		
Stafford	a								14 25		14 46		14 35	14 46		15 02	15 09			
	d								14 26		14 46		14 36	14 46		15 03	15 10			
Penkridge	a										→						15 15			
Wolverhampton	a							14 31	14 39	14 32				14 59		15 16	15 27			
Birmingham New Street	a							14 55	14 58	15 05				15 18		15 39	15 47			
Birmingham International	a								15 13	15 19										
Coventry	a								15 24	15 30										
Lichfield Trent Valley	a																			
Tamworth Low Level	a																			
Nuneaton	a																			
Rugby	a																			
Milton Keynes Central	a			15 01			15 01											15 46		
Watford Junction	a									16s15										
London Euston	a		15 12	15 38			15 38			16 34		15 42	15 56		16 04			16 23		16 12

A until 4 September
B from 11 September
C until 10 July and from 11 September
D from 17 July until 4 September
E ⚲ from Preston
b arr. 1324

OVERNIGHT SLEEPERS. For sleeper trains, operated by First ScotRail, please refer to Tables 400 - 404

Scotland and North West England - West Midlands and London

		NT	TP	VT	VT	TP	XC	LM	VT	VT	LM	VT	XC	VT	TP	VT	NT	TP	VT	LM	VT
			◇1	◇1	◇1	◇1	◇1	1	◇1	◇1	1	◇1	◇1	◇1	◇1	◇1		◇1	◇1	1	◇1
Inverness	d																				
Aberdeen	d																				
Dundee	d																				
Perth	d																				
Edinburgh 10	d														12 08						
Haymarket	d														12u12						
Glasgow Central 15	d				12 00											12 40					
Motherwell	d																				
Carstairs	d																				
Lockerbie	d														13 06						
Carlisle 8	a				13 08										13 28	13 47					
	d				13 09										13 29	13 49					
Penrith North Lakes	d																				
Windermere	d																				
Oxenholme Lake District	a														14 05	14 22					
	d														14 06	14 24					
Barrow-in-Furness	d					13 25															
Lancaster 6	a				13 56	14 18									14 22	14 37					
	d				13 58	14 18									14 22	14 38					
Preston 8	a				14 15	14 37									14 41	14 56					
Blackpool North	d	13 37	13 45														14 37	14 45			
Preston 8	d	14 04	14 10		14 17										14 47	14 58	15 04	15 10			
Wigan North Western	a	14 24			14 28											15 09	15 24				
	d	14 24			14 28											15 09	15 24				
Blackrod	d																				
Lostock	d																				
Bolton	a		14 34												15 08			15 34			
Manchester Piccadilly 10	a		14 56												15 27			15 56			
Manchester Airport	a		15 17												15 47			16 17			
Liverpool Lime Street 10	a	15 02															16 02				
	d							14 34		14 48										15 04	
Liverpool South Parkway	d							14 44												15 15	
Runcorn	d							14 52		15 04										15 25	
Warrington Bank Quay	a				14 39											15 20					
	d				14 39											15 20					
Hartford	d							15 04													
Manchester Piccadilly 10	d						14 27		14 35			14 55	15 07	15 15							
Stockport	d						14 35		14 42			15 04	15 16	15 23							
Wilmslow	d											15 11									
Holyhead	d																				
Bangor (Gwynedd)	d																				
Llandudno Junction	d																				
Wrexham General	d																				
Chester	d			14 35																	15 35
Crewe 10	a			14 54	14 58			15 19				15 27								15 45	15 54
	d			14 56	15 01			15 22				15 29							15 35	15 49	15 56
Macclesfield	d						14 49		14 55												
Congleton	d																				
Stoke-on-Trent	d						15 07		15 12		←		15 44	15 50							
Stafford	a						15 25	15 42		15 35	15 42		16 02							16 09	
	d						15 26	15 43		15 36	15 43		16 03							16 10	
Penkridge	a							→												16 15	
Wolverhampton 7	a				15 31		15 39				15 56		16 16							16 27	
Birmingham New Street 12	a				15 55		15 58				16 17		16 39							16 47	
Birmingham International	a						16 13														
Coventry	a						16 24														
Lichfield Trent Valley	a																				
Tamworth Low Level	a																				
Nuneaton	a																				
Rugby	a																				
Milton Keynes Central	a			16 01										16 46							17 01
Watford Junction	a																				
London Euston 15 ⊖	a			16 38					16 42	16 56		17 04		17 23		17 12			17 12		17 38

OVERNIGHT SLEEPERS. For sleeper trains, operated by First ScotRail, please refer to Tables 400 - 404

Scotland and North West England - West Midlands and London

		VT	XC	LM	VT	VT	LM	VT	XC	LM	VT	NT	TP	VT	VT	NT	TP	VT	TP	XC	LM	VT
		◇1	◇1	1	◇1	◇1	1	◇1	◇1	1	◇1		◇1	◇1	◇1		◇1	◇1	◇1	◇1	1	◇1
Inverness	d																					
Aberdeen	d																					
Dundee	d																					
Perth	d																					
Edinburgh 10	d	12 52																	14 08			
Haymarket	d	12 57																	14u12			
Glasgow Central 15	d												12 54	13 40				14 00				
Motherwell	d																					
Carstairs	d																					
Lockerbie	d												13 56						15 06			
Carlisle 8	a	14 05											14 18	14 46				15 09	15 28			
	d	14 07											14 30	14 49				15 11	15 30			
Penrith North Lakes	d	14 22											14 44						15 44			
Windermere	d																					
Oxenholme Lake District	a												15 08	15 22				15 45	16 08			
	d												15 09	15 23				15 46	16 08			
Barrow-in-Furness	d																					
Lancaster 6	a	14 56											15 26	15 37					16 25			
	d	14 57											15 26	15 38					16 26			
Preston 8	a	15 15											15 45	15 56				16 15	16 45			
Blackpool North	d															15 37	15 45					
Preston 8	d	15 17										15 23	15 47	15 58		16 04	16 10	16 17	16 47			
Wigan North Western	a	15 28												16 09		16 24		16 28				
	d	15 28												16 09		16 24		16 28				
Blackrod	d																					
Lostock	d											15 50										
Bolton	a											15 55	16 08				16 34		17 08			
Manchester Piccadilly 10	a											16 18	16 27				16 56		17 27			
Manchester Airport	a												16 47				17 17		17 48			
Liverpool Lime Street 10	a															17 05						
	d			15 34		15 48				16 04											16 34	
Liverpool South Parkway	d			15 44						16 15											16 44	
Runcorn	d			15 52		16 04				16 25											16 52	
Warrington Bank Quay	a	15 39												16 20				16 39				
	d	15 39												16 20				16 39				
Hartford	d			16 04																	17 06	
Manchester Piccadilly 10	d		15 27		15 35			15 55	16 07		16 15	16 21								16 27		16 35
Stockport	d		15 35		15 42			16 04	16 16		16 23	16 35								16 35		16 42
Wilmslow	d							16 11														
Holyhead	d														14 36							
Bangor (Gwynedd)	d														15 06							
Llandudno Junction	d														15 25							
Wrexham General	d																					
Chester	d														16 20							
Crewe 10	a	15 58		16 19				16 27		16 45					16 43			16 58			17 20	
	d	16 01		16 22				16 29		16 49					16 56			17 01			17 22	
Macclesfield	d		15 49		15 55															16 49		16 56
Congleton	d																					
Stoke-on-Trent	d		16 07		16 12		←		16 44		16 50									17 07		17 13
Stafford	a		16 24	16 46		16 35	16 46		17 02	17 09										17 25	17 42	
	d		16 25	16 46		16 36	16 46		17 03	17 10										17 26	17 43	
Penkridge	a			→						17 15											→	
Wolverhampton 7	a	16 31	16 39				16 59		17 16	17 27								17 31		17 39		
Birmingham New Street 12	a	16 55	16 58				17 18		17 39	17 47								17 55		17 58		
Birmingham International	a		17 13																	18 13		
Coventry	a		17 24																	18 24		
Lichfield Trent Valley	a																					
Tamworth Low Level	a																					
Nuneaton	a																					
Rugby	a																					
Milton Keynes Central	a										17 46				18 01							
Watford Junction	a																					
London Euston 15 ⊖	a				17 42	17 55		18 04			18 23			18 12	18 37							18 42

OVERNIGHT SLEEPERS. For sleeper trains, operated by First ScotRail, please refer to Tables 400 - 404

Table 65

Saturdays
until 16 October

Scotland and North West England - West Midlands and London

		VT	LM	VT	VT	NT	TP	XC	LM	VT	VT	XC	VT	TP	LM	VT	VT	LM	VT	XC	LM	VT
										A			B									
Inverness	d																					
Aberdeen	d																					
Dundee	d																					
Perth	d																					
Edinburgh	d									14 52			14 52									
Haymarket	d									14 57			14 57									
Glasgow Central	d				14 40																	
Motherwell	d																					
Carstairs	d																					
Lockerbie	d																					
Carlisle	a				15 46					16 05			16 05									
	d				15 49					16 07			16 07									
Penrith North Lakes	d									16 22			16 22									
Windermere	d																					
Oxenholme Lake District	a				16 22																	
	d				16 24																	
Barrow-in-Furness	d													16 17								
Lancaster	a				16 37					16 56			16 56	17 15								
	d				16 38					16 57			16 57	17 15								
Preston	a				16 56					17 15			17 15	17 34								
Blackpool North	d					16 35	16 40															
Preston	d				16 58	17 04	17 09			17 17			17 17									
Wigan North Western	a				17 09	17 24				17 28			17 28									
	d				17 09	17 24				17 28			17 28									
Blackrod	d																					
Lostock	d																					
Bolton	a						17 34															
Manchester Piccadilly	a						17 56															
Manchester Airport	a						18 17															
Liverpool Lime Street	a					18 02																
	d	16 48							17 04						17 34		17 48				18 04	
Liverpool South Parkway	d								17 15						17 44						18 15	
Runcorn	d	17 04							17 25						17 52		18 04				18 24	
Warrington Bank Quay	a				17 20					17 39			17 39									
	d				17 20					17 39			17 39									
Hartford	d														18 06							
Manchester Piccadilly	d			16 55				17 06			17 15	17 27				17 35			17 55	18 05		18 15
Stockport	d			17 04							17 23	17 36				17 43			18 04	18 13		18 23
Wilmslow	d			17 11															18 11			
Holyhead	d																					
Bangor (Gwynedd)	d																					
Llandudno Junction	d																					
Wrexham General	d																					
Chester	d																					
Crewe	a			17 27					17 47	17 59			17 59		18 20				18 27		18 46	
	d			17 29					17 49	18 01			18 01		18 22				18 29		18 49	
Macclesfield	d							17 26								17 55				18 26		
Congleton	d											17 54										
Stoke-on-Trent	d		←					17 43			17 50	18 08				18 13		←		18 44		18 50
Stafford	a	17 35	17 42					18 03	18 09			18 26			18 42		18 34	18 42		19 02	19 09	
	d	17 36	17 43					18 04	18 10			18 27			18 43		18 36	18 43		19 03	19 10	
Penkridge	a								18 15						→						19 15	
Wolverhampton	a		17 56					18 16	18 27	18 31		18 40	18 32					18 56		19 16	19 27	
Birmingham New Street	a		18 17					18 38	18 47	18 55		18 58	19 05					19 17		19 33	19 47	
Birmingham International	a											19 13	19 19									
Coventry	a											19 24	19 30									
Lichfield Trent Valley	a																					
Tamworth Low Level	a																					
Nuneaton	a																					
Rugby	a												19 42									
Milton Keynes Central	a										18 46		20 05									19 46
Watford Junction	a												20s34									
London Euston	a	18 56		19 04	19 12						19 23		20 56			19 42	19 56		20 04			20 25

A until 10 July and from 11 September

B from 17 July until 4 September

OVERNIGHT SLEEPERS. For sleeper trains, operated by First ScotRail, please refer to Tables 400 - 404

Table 65

Saturdays
until 16 October

Scotland and North West England - West Midlands and London

		NT	TP	VT	NT	TP	VT	TP	TP	XC	LM	VT	VT	LM	VT	VT	NT	TP	XC	NT	LM	VT	TP	XC
						A																		
Inverness	d																							
Aberdeen	d																							
Dundee	d																							
Perth	d																							
Edinburgh	d								16 11													16 52		
Haymarket	d								16u15													16 57		
Glasgow Central	d			15 40			16 00									16 40							17 06	
Motherwell	d															16u54								
Carstairs	d																							
Lockerbie	d								17 10														18 06	
Carlisle	a			16 46			17 08		17 32							17 49						18 05	18 28	
	d			16 49			17 09		17 33							17 52						18 07	18 29	
Penrith North Lakes	d			17 03					17 48														18 44	
Windermere	d					17 06																		
Oxenholme Lake District	a					17 25	17 44									18 25						18 41	19 08	
	d					17 30	17 44									18 26						18 42	19 08	
Barrow-in-Furness	d							17 21												18 03				
Lancaster	a			17 37		17 47		18 17	18 26							18 40				19 04		18 56	19 26	
	d			17 38		17 48		18 17	18 26							18 41				19 05		18 57	19 26	
Preston	a			17 56		18 06	18 15	18 36	18 45							18 59				19 30		19 15	19 45	
Blackpool North	d		17 20		17 37												18 37	18 45						
Preston	d	17 23	17 47	17 58	18 04	18 08	18 17		18 47							19 01	19 04	19 10				19 17	19 47	
Wigan North Western	a			18 09	18 24		18 28									19 12	19 24					19 28		
	d			18 09	18 24		18 28									19 12	19 24					19 28		
Blackrod	d																							
Lostock	d	17 50				18 30																		
Bolton	a	17 55	18 08			18 34			19 08									19 34					20 08	
Manchester Piccadilly	a	18 18	18 27			18 56			19 27									19 56					20 27	
Manchester Airport	a		18 47			19 17			19 50									20 17					20 47	
Liverpool Lime Street	a				19 02												20 02							
	d										18 34		18 48								19 04			
Liverpool South Parkway	d										18 44										19 14			
Runcorn	d										18 52		19 04								19 23			
Warrington Bank Quay	a			18 20			18 39									19 23						19 39		
	d			18 20			18 39									19 23						19 39		
Hartford	d										19 04													
Manchester Piccadilly	d	18 21								18 27		18 35			18 55				19 07					19 27
Stockport	d	18 35								18 35		18 42			19 04				19 16					19 35
Wilmslow	d														19 11									
Holyhead	d																							
Bangor (Gwynedd)	d																							
Llandudno Junction	d																							
Wrexham General	d																							
Chester	d																							
Crewe	a						18 59				19 19				19 27						19 49	19 59		
	d						19 01				19 22				19 29						19 51	20 01		
Macclesfield	d											18 55												19 49
Congleton	d									18 54														
Stoke-on-Trent	d									19 07		19 12		←					19 44					20 07
Stafford	a									19 25	19 42		19 35	19 42					20 02		20 11			20 25
	d									19 25	19 43		19 36	19 43					20 03		20 12			20 26
Penkridge	a										→			19 48										
Wolverhampton	a						19 31			19 39				19 59					20 16		20 28	20 31		20 39
Birmingham New Street	a						19 55			19 58				20 17					20 33		20 47	20 55		20 58
Birmingham International	a									20 13														21 13
Coventry	a									20 24														21 24
Lichfield Trent Valley	a																							
Tamworth Low Level	a																							
Nuneaton	a																							
Rugby	a																							
Milton Keynes Central	a															20 41								
Watford Junction	a															21s15								
London Euston	a			20 15								20 58	21 15		21 18	21 38								

A from Preston

OVERNIGHT SLEEPERS. For sleeper trains, operated by First ScotRail, please refer to Tables 400 - 404

Table 65

Scotland and North West England - West Midlands and London

		LM	VT	NT	VT	LM		VT	TP	XC	VT	TP	TP
		1	◇1		◇1	1		◇1	◇1	◇1	◇1	◇1	◇1
			☕		☕			☕		🛒	☕	🛒	
Inverness	d												
Aberdeen	d												
Dundee	d												
Perth	d												
Edinburgh 10	d											18 12	
Haymarket	d											18u16	
Glasgow Central 15	d							17 40			18 00		
Motherwell	d												
Carstairs	d												
Lockerbie	d							18 32				19 12	
Carlisle 8	a							18 50			19 08	19 34	
	d							18 52			19 09	19 34	
Penrith North Lakes	d							19 06				19 48	
Windermere	d												
Oxenholme Lake District	a							19 28				20 12	
	d							19 29				20 12	
Barrow-in-Furness	d												19 32
Lancaster 6	a							19 43			19 55	20 26	20 33
	d							19 44			19 56	20 26	20 34
Preston 8	a							20 02			20 15	20 45	20 54
Blackpool North	d			19 37					19 45				
Preston 8	d			20 04				20 04	20 10		20 17	20 47	
Wigan North Western	a			20 24				20 15			20 28		
	d			20 24				20 15			20 28		
Blackrod	d												
Lostock	d												
Bolton	a								20 34			21 08	
Manchester Piccadilly 10 ⇌	a								20 56			21 27	
Manchester Airport ✈	a								21 17			21 47	
Liverpool Lime Street 10	a			21 02									
	d	19 34			19 48								
Liverpool South Parkway ✈	d	19 44											
Runcorn	d	19 52			20 04								
Warrington Bank Quay	a							20 26			20 39		
	d							20 26			20 39		
Hartford	d	20 04											
Manchester Piccadilly 10 ⇌	d		19 35							20 07			
Stockport	d		19 42							20 16			
Wilmslow	d												
Holyhead	d												
Bangor (Gwynedd)	d												
Llandudno Junction	d												
Wrexham General	d												
Chester	d												
Crewe 10	a	20 16						20 45			20 59		
	d	20 22						20 47			21 01		
Macclesfield	d		19 55										
Congleton	d												
Stoke-on-Trent	d		20 12			←				20 44			
Stafford	a	20 42			20 35	20 42				21 02			
	d	20 43			20 36	20 43				21 03			
Penkridge	a	→				20 48							
Wolverhampton 7 ⇌	a					20 57				21 15	21 31		
Birmingham New Street 12	a					21 17				21 32	21 54		
Birmingham International ✈	a												
Coventry	a												
Lichfield Trent Valley	a												
Tamworth Low Level	a												
Nuneaton	a												
Rugby	a												
Milton Keynes Central	a		21 10					21 50					
Watford Junction	a												
London Euston 15 ⊖	a		22 01		22 14			22 45					

		XC	LM	VT	NT	XC	VT	TP	XC	VT	XC	XC	LM
		◇1	1	◇1		◇1	◇1	◇1		◇1	◇1	◇1	1
									A		B	A	
		🛒		☕		🛒	☕		🚌	☕	🛒	🛒	
Inverness	d												
Aberdeen	d												
Dundee	d												
Perth	d												
Edinburgh 10	d									18 52			
Haymarket	d									18 57			
Glasgow Central 15	d						18 40						
Motherwell	d												
Carstairs	d												
Lockerbie	d												
Carlisle 8	a						19 46			20 05			
	d						19 48			20 07			
Penrith North Lakes	d						20 02			20 22			
Windermere	d												
Oxenholme Lake District	a						20 24			20 45			
	d						20 25			20 45			
Barrow-in-Furness	d												
Lancaster 6	a						20 39			20 59			
	d						20 40			21 00			
Preston 8	a						20 58			21 18			
Blackpool North	d				20 37			20 42					
Preston 8	d				21 04		21 00	21 10		21 20			
Wigan North Western	a				21 23		21 11			21 31			
	d				21 23		21 11			21 31			
Blackrod	d												
Lostock	d												
Bolton	a							21 34					
Manchester Piccadilly 10 ⇌	a							21 56					
Manchester Airport ✈	a							22 17					
Liverpool Lime Street 10	a				22 14								
	d		20 34										21 34
Liverpool South Parkway ✈	d		20 44										21 44
Runcorn	d		20 52										21 52
Warrington Bank Quay	a						21 22			21 42			
	d						21 22			21 42			
Hartford	d		21 03										22 04
Manchester Piccadilly 10 ⇌	d	20 27		20 35		21 07					21 28	21 28	
Stockport	d	20 35		20 43							21 36	21 36	
Wilmslow	d											21 45	
Holyhead	d												
Bangor (Gwynedd)	d												
Llandudno Junction	d												
Wrexham General	d												
Chester	d												
Crewe 10	a		21 16				21 41			22 02		22 05	22 21
	d		21 17				21 43			22 04		22 09	22 23
Macclesfield	d	20 49		20 56							21 50		
Congleton	d												
Stoke-on-Trent	d	21 07		21 13		21 45			21 50		22 08		
Stafford	a	21 26	21 42			22 02	22 07		22 20	22 28	22 33	22 32	22 47
	d	21 27	21 42			22 03	22 08			22 29	22 34	22 34	22 47
Penkridge	a		21 48										22 53
Wolverhampton 7 ⇌	a	21 39	21 58			22 14	22 22			22 40	22 50	22 50	23 03
Birmingham New Street 12	a	21 58	22 20			22 32	22 46			22 59	23 17	23 17	23 21
Birmingham International ✈	a												
Coventry	a												
Lichfield Trent Valley	a												
Tamworth Low Level	a												
Nuneaton	a												
Rugby	a												
Milton Keynes Central	a			22 12									
Watford Junction	a			22s42									
London Euston 15 ⊖	a			23 04									

A until 10 July

B from 17 July until 16 October

OVERNIGHT SLEEPERS. For sleeper trains, operated by First ScotRail, please refer to Tables 400 - 404

Table 65

Scotland and North West England - West Midlands and London

		TP		NT	TP		NT			TP
		◇1			◇1					◇1
Inverness	d									
Aberdeen	d									
Dundee	d									
Perth	d									
Edinburgh 10	d									
Haymarket	d									
Glasgow Central 15	d									
Motherwell	d									
Carstairs	d									
Lockerbie	d									
Carlisle 8	a									
	d									
Penrith North Lakes	d									
Windermere	d	21 40								
Oxenholme Lake District	a	21 59								
	d	22 01								
Barrow-in-Furness	d			21 43						
Lancaster 6	a	22 17		22 44						
	d	22 17		22 45						
Preston 8	a	22 38		23 10						
Blackpool North	d				21 45		22 14			22 45
Preston 8	d				22 10		22 43			23 10
Wigan North Western	a						23 02			
	d						23 03			
Blackrod	d									
Lostock	d									
Bolton	a				22 34					23 34
Manchester Piccadilly 10 ⇌	a				22 56					23 53
Manchester Airport ✈	a				23 17					00 22
Liverpool Lime Street 10	a						23 54			
	d									
Liverpool South Parkway ✈	d									
Runcorn	d									
Warrington Bank Quay	a									
	d									
Hartford	d									
Manchester Piccadilly 10 ⇌	d									
Stockport	d									
Wilmslow	d									
Holyhead	d									
Bangor (Gwynedd)	d									
Llandudno Junction	d									
Wrexham General	d									
Chester	d									
Crewe 10	a									
	d									
Macclesfield	d									
Congleton	d									
Stoke-on-Trent	d									
Stafford	a									
	d									
Penkridge	a									
Wolverhampton 7 ⇌	a									
Birmingham New Street 12	a									
Birmingham International ✈	a									
Coventry	a									
Lichfield Trent Valley	a									
Tamworth Low Level	a									
Nuneaton	a									
Rugby	a									
Milton Keynes Central	a									
Watford Junction	a									
London Euston 15 ⊖	a									

OVERNIGHT SLEEPERS. For sleeper trains, operated by First ScotRail, please refer to Tables 400 - 404

Table 65

Saturdays from 23 October

Scotland and North West England - West Midlands and London

		TP	AW	TP	XC	TP	VT	XC	VT	LM	VT	VT	TP	XC	VT	VT	LM	VT	TP	LM
		◇1		◇1	◇1	◇1	◇1	◇1	◇1	◇1	◇1	◇1	◇1	◇1	◇1	◇1	◇1	◇1	◇1	1
					✕		⊡	✕	⊡		⊡	⊡		✕	⊡	⊡		⊡		
Inverness	d																			
Aberdeen	d																			
Dundee	d																			
Perth	d																			
Edinburgh 10	d																			
Haymarket	d																			
Glasgow Central 15	d																			
Motherwell	d																			
Carstairs	d																			
Lockerbie	d																			
Carlisle 8	a																			
	d																			
Penrith North Lakes	d																			
Windermere	d																			
Oxenholme Lake District	a																			
	d																			
Barrow-in-Furness	d			04 35															05 31	
Lancaster 6	a			05 28															06 23	
	d											05 40							06 26	
Preston 8	a											05 55							06 45	
Blackpool North	d	03 36											05 44							
Preston 8	d	04u01				05 16						05 58	06 09					06 17	06 47	
Wigan North Western	a											06 09						06 28		
	d											06 09						06 28		
Blackrod	d																			
Lostock	d												06 30							
Bolton	a	04u30				05 42							06 34						07 08	
Manchester Piccadilly 10	a	04 48				06 01							06 56						07 27	
Manchester Airport	a	05 07				06 18							07 17						07 47	
Liverpool Lime Street 10	a																			
	d								05 47											06 32
Liverpool South Parkway	d																			06 42
Runcorn	d								06 03											06 50
Warrington Bank Quay	a											06 20						06 39		
	d											06 20						06 39		
Hartford	d																			07 02
Manchester Piccadilly 10	d				05 11		05 25				05 55			06 00	06 10	06 35				
Stockport	d						05 34				06 03			06 08	06 18	06 43				
Wilmslow	d						05 41				06 11									
Holyhead	d																			
Bangor (Gwynedd)	d																			
Llandudno Junction	d																			
Wrexham General	d																			
Chester	d		04 23																	
Crewe 10	a		04 44		05 41		05 57				06 27							06 58		07 14
	d		05 00		05 47		06 00			06 20	06 29						06 47	07 01		07 16
Macclesfield	d													06 21	06 31	06 55				
Congleton	d																			
Stoke-on-Trent	d				06 08			←						06 39	06 48	07 12				
Stafford	a		05 24		06 25		06 17	06 25	06 34	06 41				06 57			07 10			07 40
	d		05 24		06 26		06 19	06 26	06 35	06 41				06 58			07 12			07 41
Penkridge	a				→					06 47							07 17			→
Wolverhampton 7	a		05 38					06 39		06 57				07 12			07 28	07 32		
Birmingham New Street 12	a		05 55					06 57		07 17				07 31			07 47	07 55		
Birmingham International	a							07 13												
Coventry	a							07 24												
Lichfield Trent Valley	a														07 11					
Tamworth Low Level	a														07 18					
Nuneaton	a								06 57											
Rugby	a						06 49									07 52				
Milton Keynes Central	a						07 11				07 31	07 37								
Watford Junction	a						07s32		07s44											
London Euston 15	a						07 52		08 05		08 09	08 14			08 28	08 46				

OVERNIGHT SLEEPERS. For sleeper trains, operated by First ScotRail, please refer to Tables 400 - 404

Table 65

Saturdays from 23 October

Scotland and North West England - West Midlands and London

		VT	LM	VT	VT	TP	XC	VT	VT	LM	VT	VT	XC	LM	VT	NT	VT	LM	VT	XC	LM	VT	TP
		◇1	1	◇1	◇1	◇1	◇1	◇1	◇1	1	◇1	◇1	◇1	1	◇1		◇1	1	◇1	◇1	1	◇1	◇1
																							A
		⊡		⊡	⊡	✕	✕	⊡	⊡		⊡	⊡	✕		⊡		⊡		⊡	✕		⊡	✕
Inverness	d																						
Aberdeen	d																						
Dundee	d																						
Perth	d																						
Edinburgh 10	d																						
Haymarket	d																						
Glasgow Central 15	d				04 26																		
Motherwell	d																						
Carstairs	d																						
Lockerbie	d																						
Carlisle 8	a				05 43																		
	d				05 44																		
Penrith North Lakes	d				05 59																		
Windermere	d																						
Oxenholme Lake District	a				06 21																		
	d				06 22																		
Barrow-in-Furness	d																						06 19
Lancaster 6	a				06 36																		07 21
	d				06 37							06 58											07 22
Preston 8	a				06 55							07 15											07 41
Blackpool North	d					06 34										07 02							
Preston 8	d				06 58	07 03						07 17				07 30							07 47
Wigan North Western	a				07 09							07 28				07 50							
	d				07 10							07 28				07 50							
Blackrod	d					07 21																	
Lostock	d					07 29																	
Bolton	a					07 34																	08 08
Manchester Piccadilly 10	a					07 56																	08 27
Manchester Airport	a					08 17																	08 47
Liverpool Lime Street 10	a															08 34							
	d	06 45								07 04	07 19			07 34			07 48				08 04		
Liverpool South Parkway	d									07 14				07 44							08 15		
Runcorn	d	07 01								07 22	07 36			07 52			08 04				08 24		
Warrington Bank Quay	a				07 20							07 39											
	d				07 20							07 39											
Hartford	d									07 36				08 04									
Manchester Piccadilly 10	d			06 55			07 07	07 15					07 27		07 35				07 55	08 07		08 15	
Stockport	d			07 04			07 16	07 23					07 35		07 43				08 04	08 16		08 23	
Wilmslow	d			07 11															08 11				
Holyhead	d																						
Bangor (Gwynedd)	d																						
Llandudno Junction	d																						
Wrexham General	d																						
Chester	d								07 17														
Crewe 10	a	07 18		07 27					07 36	07 47	07 52	07 58		08 19					08 27		08 47		
	d	07 20		07 29					07 39	07 49	07 55	08 01		08 22					08 29		08 49		
Macclesfield	d												07 49		07 56								
Congleton	d																						
Stoke-on-Trent	d		←				07 44	07 50					08 07		08 12			←		08 44		08 50	
Stafford	a	07 38	07 40				08 02			08 10	08 14		08 25	08 42			08 35	08 42		09 02	09 09		
	d	07 39	07 41				08 03			08 10	08 16		08 26	08 43			08 36	08 43		09 03	09 10		
Penkridge	a		07 46							08 16				→				08 48			09 15		
Wolverhampton 7	a		07 57				08 16			08 28		08 31	08 39					08 58		09 15	09 27		
Birmingham New Street 12	a		08 17				08 38			08 47		08 55	08 58					09 18		09 39	09 47		
Birmingham International	a												09 13										
Coventry	a												09 24										
Lichfield Trent Valley	a										08 30												
Tamworth Low Level	a										08 36												
Nuneaton	a																08 58						
Rugby	a																						
Milton Keynes Central	a							08 46														09 46	
Watford Junction	a																						
London Euston 15	a	08 59		09 04	09 12			09 23	09 30		09 46				09 42		10 00		10 04			10 23	

A ✕ from Preston

OVERNIGHT SLEEPERS. For sleeper trains, operated by First ScotRail, please refer to Tables 400 - 404

Table 65

Saturdays
from 23 October

Scotland and North West England - West Midlands and London

		VT	VT	TP	VT	XC	LM	VT	VT	LM	VT	XC	LM	VT	TP	VT	VT	NT	TP	VT	XC
		◇1	◇1	◇1	◇1	◇1	1	◇1	◇1	1	◇1	◇1	1	◇1	◇1 A	◇1	◇1		◇1	◇1	◇1
Inverness	d																				
Aberdeen	d																				
Dundee	d																				
Perth	d																				
Edinburgh	d																			06 52	
Haymarket	d																			06 56	
Glasgow Central	d	05 40			05 50											06 30					
Motherwell	d				06 05											06u45					
Carstairs	d																				
Lockerbie	d															07 25					
Carlisle	a	06 47			07 02											07 43				08 05	
	d	06 49			07 03											07 46				08 07	
Penrith North Lakes	d				07 18											08 00				08 22	
Windermere	d																				
Oxenholme Lake District	a	07 22			07 41											08 22					
	d	07 24			07 42											08 23					
Barrow-in-Furness	d														07 28						
Lancaster	a	07 37			07 56										08 26	08 37				08 56	
	d	07 38			07 57										08 27	08 38				08 57	
Preston	a	07 56			08 15										08 45	08 56				09 15	
Blackpool North	d			07 44														08 38	08 45		
Preston	d	07 58		08 12	08 17										08 47	08 58		09 04	09 10	09 17	
Wigan North Western	a	08 09			08 28											09 09		09 24		09 28	
	d	08 09			08 28											09 09		09 24		09 28	
Blackrod	d																				
Lostock	d																				
Bolton	a			08 34											09 08				09 34		
Manchester Piccadilly	a			08 56											09 27				09 56		
Manchester Airport	a			09 19											09 47				10 17		
Liverpool Lime Street	a																	10 02			
	d						08 34		08 48				09 04								
Liverpool South Parkway	d						08 44						09 15								
Runcorn	d						08 52		09 04				09 24								
Warrington Bank Quay	a	08 20			08 39											09 20				09 39	
	d	08 20			08 39											09 20				09 39	
Hartford	d						09 06														
Manchester Piccadilly	d					08 27		08 35			08 55	09 07		09 15							09 27
Stockport	d					08 35		08 42			09 04	09 16		09 23							09 35
Wilmslow	d										09 11										
Holyhead	d		06 53														07 55				
Bangor (Gwynedd)	d		07 20														08 22				
Llandudno Junction	d		07 38														08 40				
Wrexham General	d																				
Chester	d		08b35														09 35				
Crewe	a		08 54		08 58		09 20				09 27		09 44				09 54			09 58	
	d		08 56		09 01		09 22				09 29		09 49				09 56			10 01	
Macclesfield	d					08 49		08 55													09 49
Congleton	d																				
Stoke-on-Trent	d					09 07		09 13		←		09 44		09 50							10 07
Stafford	a					09 25	09 42		09 35	09 42		10 02	10 10								10 25
	d					09 26	09 43		09 36	09 43		10 03	10 10								10 26
Penkridge	a						→						10 16								
Wolverhampton	a				09 31	09 39				09 56		10 15	10 27							10 31	10 39
Birmingham New Street	a				09 55	09 58				10 17		10 39	10 47							10 55	10 58
Birmingham International	a					10 13															11 13
Coventry	a					10 24															11 24
Lichfield Trent Valley	a																				
Tamworth Low Level	a																				
Nuneaton	a								09 58												
Rugby	a																				
Milton Keynes Central	a		10 01											10 46			11 01				
Watford Junction	a																				
London Euston	a	10 12	10 37					10 42	11 01		11 04			11 23		11 12	11 38				

A from Preston

b arr. 0828

OVERNIGHT SLEEPERS. For sleeper trains, operated by First ScotRail, please refer to Tables 400 - 404

Table 65

Saturdays
from 23 October

Scotland and North West England - West Midlands and London

		LM	VT	VT	LM	VT	XC	LM	VT	NT	TP	VT	VT	NT	TP	VT	TP	XC	LM	VT	VT
		1	◇1	◇1	1	◇1	◇1	1	◇1		◇1	◇1	◇1		◇1	◇1	◇1	◇1	1	◇1	◇1
Inverness	d																				
Aberdeen	d																				
Dundee	d																				
Perth	d																				
Edinburgh	d																				
Haymarket	d																				
Glasgow Central	d										07 10	07 35				08 00					
Motherwell	d											07u51									
Carstairs	d																				
Lockerbie	d										08 06										
Carlisle	a										08 29	08 47				09 08					
	d										08 31	08 49				09 09					
Penrith North Lakes	d										08 45										
Windermere	d																09 38				
Oxenholme Lake District	a										09 09	09 22					09 57				
	d										09 11	09 23					09 58				
Barrow-in-Furness	d																				
Lancaster	a										09 26	09 37				09 56	10 16				
	d										09 26	09 38				09 57	10 16				
Preston	a										09 45	09 56				10 15	10 35				
Blackpool North	d													09 37	09 45						
Preston	d									09 23	09 47	09 58		10 04	10 10	10 17					
Wigan North Western	a											10 09		10 24		10 28					
	d											10 09		10 24		10 28					
Blackrod	d																				
Lostock	d									09 50											
Bolton	a									09 55	10 08				10 34						
Manchester Piccadilly	a									10 18	10 27				10 56						
Manchester Airport	a										10 47				11 17						
Liverpool Lime Street	a													11 02							
	d	09 34		09 48				10 04											10 34		10 48
Liverpool South Parkway	d	09 44						10 15											10 44		
Runcorn	d	09 52		10 04				10 25											10 52		11 04
Warrington Bank Quay	a											10 20				10 39					
	d											10 20				10 39					
Hartford	d	10 04																	11 04		
Manchester Piccadilly	d		09 35			09 55	10 07		10 15	10 21								10 27		10 35	
Stockport	d		09 42			10 04	10 16		10 23	10 35								10 35		10 42	
Wilmslow	d					10 11															
Holyhead	d												08 55								
Bangor (Gwynedd)	d												09 22								
Llandudno Junction	d												09 40								
Wrexham General	d																				
Chester	d												10c35								
Crewe	a	10 19				10 27		10 45					10 54			10 58			11 19		
	d	10 22				10 29		10 49					10 56			11 01			11 22		
Macclesfield	d		09 55															10 49		10 55	
Congleton	d																				
Stoke-on-Trent	d		10 12		←		10 44		10 50									11 07		11 12	
Stafford	a	10 42		10 35	10 42		11 02	11 09										11 25	11 42		11 35
	d	10 43		10 36	10 43		11 03	11 10										11 26	11 43		11 36
Penkridge	a	→						11 15											→		
Wolverhampton	a				10 56		11 16	11 27								11 31		11 39			
Birmingham New Street	a				11 17		11 39	11 47								11 55		11 58			
Birmingham International	a																	12 13			
Coventry	a																	12 24			
Lichfield Trent Valley	a																				
Tamworth Low Level	a																				
Nuneaton	a																				
Rugby	a																				
Milton Keynes Central	a								11 46				12 01								
Watford Junction	a																				
London Euston	a		11 42	11 56		12 04			12 23			12 12	12 38							12 42	12 56

b arr. 1007

c arr. 1028

OVERNIGHT SLEEPERS. For sleeper trains, operated by First ScotRail, please refer to Tables 400 - 404

Table 65

Saturdays
from 23 October

Scotland and North West England - West Midlands and London

		LM	VT	XC	LM	VT	TP	VT	NT	TP	VT	VT	XC	LM	VT	VT	LM	VT	XC	LM	VT
		1	◇1	◇1	1	◇1	◇1	◇1		◇1	◇1	◇1	◇1	1	◇1	◇1	1	◇1	◇1	1	◇1
							A														
			☕	🛒		☕	🛒	☕		🛒	☕	☕	🛒		☕	☕		☕	🛒		☕
Inverness	d																				
Aberdeen	d																				
Dundee	d																				
Perth	d																				
Edinburgh 10	d											08 52									
Haymarket	d											08 57									
Glasgow Central 15	d							08 40													
Motherwell	d																				
Carstairs	d																				
Lockerbie	d																				
Carlisle 8	a							09 46				10 05									
	d							09 49				10 07									
Penrith North Lakes	d							10 03													
Windermere	d																				
Oxenholme Lake District	a											10 41									
	d											10 42									
Barrow-in-Furness	d						09 22														
Lancaster 6	a						10 25	10 37				10 56									
	d						10 26	10 38				10 57									
Preston 8	a						10 45	10 56				11 15									
Blackpool North	d								10 37	10 45											
Preston 8	d						10 47	10 58	11 04	11 10		11 17									
Wigan North Western	a							11 09	11 24			11 28									
	d							11 09	11 24			11 28									
Blackrod	d																				
Lostock	d																				
Bolton	a						11 08			11 34											
Manchester Piccadilly 10	a						11 27			11 56											
Manchester Airport	a						11 47			12 17											
Liverpool Lime Street 10	a								12 02												
	d				11 04									11 34		11 48				12 04	
Liverpool South Parkway	d				11 15									11 44						12 15	
Runcorn	d				11 25									11 52		12 04				12 25	
Warrington Bank Quay	a							11 20				11 39									
	d							11 20				11 39									
Hartford	d													12 04							
Manchester Piccadilly 10	d		10 55	11 07		11 15							11 27		11 35			11 55	12 07		12 15
Stockport	d		11 04	11 16		11 23							11 35		11 42			12 04	12 16		12 23
Wilmslow	d		11 11															12 11			
Holyhead	d																				
Bangor (Gwynedd)	d																				
Llandudno Junction	d																				
Wrexham General	d																				
Chester	d										11 35										
Crewe 10	a		11 27		11 45						11 54	11 58		12 19				12 27		12 45	
	d		11 29		11 49						11 56	12 01		12 22				12 29		12 49	
Macclesfield	d												11 49		11 55						
Congleton	d																				
Stoke-on-Trent	d	←		11 44		11 50							12 07		12 12		←		12 44		12 50
Stafford	a	11 42		12 02	12 09								12 24	12 42		12 35	12 42		13 02	13 09	
	d	11 43		12 03	12 10								12 25	12 43		12 36	12 43		13 03	13 10	
Penkridge	a				12 15									→						13 15	
Wolverhampton 7	a	11 56		12 16	12 27							12 31	12 39				12 56		13 15	13 27	
Birmingham New Street 12	a	12 17		12 39	12 47							12 55	12 58				13 17		13 39	13 47	
Birmingham International	a												13 13								
Coventry	a												13 24								
Lichfield Trent Valley	a																				
Tamworth Low Level	a																				
Nuneaton	a																				
Rugby	a																				
Milton Keynes Central	a					12 46					13 01										13 46
Watford Junction	a																				
London Euston 15 ⊖	a		13 04			13 23		13 12			13 38				13 42	13 56		14 04			14 23

A 🛒 from Preston

OVERNIGHT SLEEPERS. For sleeper trains, operated by First ScotRail, please refer to Tables 400 - 404

Table 65

Saturdays
from 23 October

Scotland and North West England - West Midlands and London

		TP	VT	NT	TP	TP	VT	VT	XC	LM	VT	VT	LM	VT	XC	LM	VT	NT	TP	VT	NT	TP
		◇1	◇1		◇1	◇1	◇1	◇1	◇1	1	◇1	◇1	1	◇1	◇1	1	◇1		◇1	◇1		◇1
		A																				
		🛒	☕		🛒		☕	☕	🛒		☕	☕		☕	🛒		☕		🛒	☕		🛒
Inverness	d																					
Aberdeen	d																					
Dundee	d																					
Perth	d																					
Edinburgh 10	d				09 22																	
Haymarket	d				09u26																	
Glasgow Central 15	d		09 40					10 00											10 10	10 40		
Motherwell	d																					
Carstairs	d																					
Lockerbie	d				10 22																	
Carlisle 8	a		10 47		10 43			11 08											11 27	11 46		
	d		10 49		10 53			11 09											11 28	11 49		
Penrith North Lakes	d				11 07			11 24											11 42			
Windermere	d	10 49																				
Oxenholme Lake District	a	11 08	11 22		11 31														12 06	12 22		
	d	11 09	11 23		11 31														12 07	12 23		
Barrow-in-Furness	d					11 25																
Lancaster 6	a	11 26	11 37		11 46	12 18													12 22	12 37		
	d	11 26	11 38		11 46	12 18													12 23	12 38		
Preston 8	a	11 45	11 56		12 05	12 37		12 15											12 41	12 56		
Blackpool North	d			11 37																	12 37	12 45
Preston 8	d	11 47	11 58	12 04	12 10			12 17										12 23	12 47	12 58	13 04	13 10
Wigan North Western	a		12 09	12 24				12 28												13 09	13 24	
	d		12 09	12 24				12 28												13 09	13 24	
Blackrod	d																					
Lostock	d																	12 50				
Bolton	a	12 08			12 34													12 55	13 08			13 34
Manchester Piccadilly 10	a	12 27			12 56													13 18	13 27			13 56
Manchester Airport	a	12 47			13 17														13 47			14 17
Liverpool Lime Street 10	a			13 02																	14 02	
	d									12 34		12 48				13 04						
Liverpool South Parkway	d									12 44						13 15						
Runcorn	d									12 52		13 04				13 25						
Warrington Bank Quay	a		12 20					12 39												13 20		
	d		12 20					12 39												13 20		
Hartford	d									13 06												
Manchester Piccadilly 10	d								12 27		12 35			12 55	13 07		13 15	13 21				
Stockport	d								12 35		12 42			13 04	13 16		13 23	13 35				
Wilmslow	d													13 11								
Holyhead	d																					
Bangor (Gwynedd)	d																					
Llandudno Junction	d																					
Wrexham General	d																					
Chester	d						12 35															
Crewe 10	a						12 54	12 58		13 20				13 27		13 45						
	d						12 57	13 01		13 22				13 29		13 49						
Macclesfield	d								12 49		12 55											
Congleton	d																					
Stoke-on-Trent	d								13 07		13 12		←		13 44		13 50					
Stafford	a								13 25	13 42		13 35	13 42		14 02	14 09						
	d								13 26	13 43		13 36	13 43		14 03	14 10						
Penkridge	a									→						14 15						
Wolverhampton 7	a							13 31	13 39				13 56		14 16	14 27						
Birmingham New Street 12	a							13 55	13 58				14 17		14 39	14 47						
Birmingham International	a								14 13													
Coventry	a								14 24													
Lichfield Trent Valley	a																					
Tamworth Low Level	a																					
Nuneaton	a																					
Rugby	a																					
Milton Keynes Central	a						14 01										14 46					
Watford Junction	a																					
London Euston 15 ⊖	a		14 12				14 38				14 42	14 56		15 04			15 23			15 12		

A 🛒 from Preston

OVERNIGHT SLEEPERS. For sleeper trains, operated by First ScotRail, please refer to Tables 400 - 404

Table 65

Scotland and North West England - West Midlands and London

		VT	VT	XC	LM	VT	VT	LM	VT	XC	VT	LM	VT	VT	VT	TP	VT	NT	TP	VT	TP
		◇1	◇1	◇1	1	◇1	◇1	1	◇1	◇1	◇1	1	◇1	◇1	◇1	◇1 A	◇1		◇1	◇1	◇1
Inverness	d																				
Aberdeen	d																				
Dundee	d																				
Perth	d																				
Edinburgh 10	d		10 52												10 52						
Haymarket	d		10 57												10 57						
Glasgow Central 15	d																11 40			12 00	
Motherwell	d																				
Carstairs	d																				
Lockerbie	d																				
Carlisle 8	a		12 05												12 05		12 46			13 08	
	d		12 07												12 07		12 49			13 09	
Penrith North Lakes	d																13 03				
Windermere	d															12 51					
Oxenholme Lake District	a		12 41												12 41	13 07					
	d		12 43												12 43	13 09					
Barrow-in-Furness	d																				13 25
Lancaster 6	a		12 56												12 56	13 26	13 37			13 56	14 18
	d		12 57												12 57	13 26	13 38			13 58	14 18
Preston 8	a		13 15												13 15	13 45	13 56			14 15	14 37
Blackpool North	d																	13 37	13 45		
Preston 8	d		13 17												13 17	13 47	13 58	14 04	14 10	14 17	
Wigan North Western	a		13 28														14 09	14 24		14 28	
	d		13 28														14 09	14 24		14 28	
Blackrod	d																				
Lostock	d																				
Bolton	a															14 08			14 34		
Manchester Piccadilly 10	a															14 27			14 56		
Manchester Airport	a															14 47			15 17		
Liverpool Lime Street 10	a																	15 02			
	d				13 34		13 48					14 04									
Liverpool South Parkway	d				13 44							14 15									
Runcorn	d				13 52		14 04					14 25									
Warrington Bank Quay	a		13 39														14 20			14 39	
	d		13 39								14 14						14 20			14 39	
Hartford	d				14 04																
Manchester Piccadilly 10	d			13 27		13 35			13 55	14 07			14 15								
Stockport	d			13 35		13 42			14 04	14 16			14 23								
Wilmslow	d								14 11												
Holyhead	d																				
Bangor (Gwynedd)	d																				
Llandudno Junction	d																				
Wrexham General	d																				
Chester	d	13 35												14 35							
Crewe 10	a	13 54	13 59		14 19				14 27		14 33	14 45		14 54	14 52					14 58	
	d	13 56	14 01		14 22				14 29		14 35	14 49		14 56	15 01					15 01	
Macclesfield	d			13 49		13 55															
Congleton	d																				
Stoke-on-Trent	d			14 07		14 12		←		14 44			14 50								
Stafford	a			14 25	14 46		14 35	14 46		15 02		15 09									
	d			14 26	14 46		14 36	14 46		15 03		15 10									
Penkridge	a				→							15 15									
Wolverhampton 7	a		14 31	14 39				14 59		15 16		15 27			15 31					15 31	
Birmingham New Street 12	a		14 55	14 58				15 18		15 39		15 47			15 55					15 55	
Birmingham International	a			15 13																	
Coventry	a			15 24																	
Lichfield Trent Valley	a																				
Tamworth Low Level	a																				
Nuneaton	a																				
Rugby	a																				
Milton Keynes Central	a	15 01											15 46	16 01							
Watford Junction	a																				
London Euston 15	a	15 38				15 42	15 56		16 04		16 14		16 23	16 38			16 12				

A from Preston

OVERNIGHT SLEEPERS. For sleeper trains, operated by First ScotRail, please refer to Tables 400 - 404

Table 65

Scotland and North West England - West Midlands and London

		XC	LM	VT	VT	LM	VT	XC	VT	TP	VT	NT	TP	VT	LM	VT	VT	VT	XC	LM	VT
		◇1	1	◇1	◇1	1	◇1	◇1	◇1	◇1	◇1		◇1	◇1	1	◇1	◇1	◇1	◇1	1	◇1
Inverness	d																				
Aberdeen	d																				
Dundee	d																				
Perth	d																				
Edinburgh 10	d									12 08								12 52			
Haymarket	d									12u12								12 57			
Glasgow Central 15	d										12 40										
Motherwell	d																				
Carstairs	d																				
Lockerbie	d									13 06											
Carlisle 8	a									13 28	13 47							14 05			
	d									13 29	13 49							14 07			
Penrith North Lakes	d																	14 22			
Windermere	d																				
Oxenholme Lake District	a									14 05	14 22										
	d									14 06	14 24										
Barrow-in-Furness	d																				
Lancaster 6	a									14 22	14 37							14 56			
	d									14 22	14 38							14 57			
Preston 8	a									14 41	14 56							15 15			
Blackpool North	d											14 37	14 45								
Preston 8	d									14 47	14 58	15 04	15 10					15 17			
Wigan North Western	a										15 09	15 24						15 28			
	d										15 09	15 24						15 28			
Blackrod	d																				
Lostock	d																				
Bolton	a									15 08			15 34								
Manchester Piccadilly 10	a									15 27			15 56								
Manchester Airport	a									15 47			16 17								
Liverpool Lime Street 10	a											16 02									
	d		14 34		14 48										15 04					15 34	
Liverpool South Parkway	d		14 44												15 15					15 44	
Runcorn	d		14 52		15 04										15 25					15 52	
Warrington Bank Quay	a										15 20							15 39			
	d										15 20						15 39	15 39			
Hartford	d		15 04																	16 04	
Manchester Piccadilly 10	d	14 27		14 35			14 55	15 07	15 15										15 27		15 35
Stockport	d	14 35		14 42			15 04	15 16	15 23										15 35		15 42
Wilmslow	d						15 11														
Holyhead	d																				
Bangor (Gwynedd)	d																				
Llandudno Junction	d																				
Wrexham General	d																				
Chester	d															15 35					
Crewe 10	a		15 19				15 27								15 45	15 54	15 58	15 58		16 19	
	d		15 22				15 29							15 35	15 49	15 56	16 00	16 01		16 22	
Macclesfield	d	14 49		14 55															15 49		15 55
Congleton	d																				
Stoke-on-Trent	d	15 07		15 12		←		15 44	15 50										16 07		16 12
Stafford	a	15 25	15 42		15 35	15 42		16 02							16 09				16 24	16 46	
	d	15 26	15 43		15 36	15 43		16 03							16 10				16 25	16 46	
Penkridge	a		→												16 15					→	
Wolverhampton 7	a	15 39				15 56		16 16							16 27		16 32	16 31	16 39		
Birmingham New Street 12	a	15 58				16 17		16 39							16 47		16 55	16 55	16 58		
Birmingham International	a	16 13																	17 13		
Coventry	a	16 24																	17 24		
Lichfield Trent Valley	a																				
Tamworth Low Level	a																				
Nuneaton	a																				
Rugby	a																				
Milton Keynes Central	a								16 46							17 01					
Watford Junction	a																				
London Euston 15	a			16 42	16 56		17 04		17 23		17 12			17 12		17 38					17 42

OVERNIGHT SLEEPERS. For sleeper trains, operated by First ScotRail, please refer to Tables 400 - 404

Table 65

Saturdays
from 23 October

Scotland and North West England - West Midlands and London

		VT	LM	VT	XC	LM	VT	TP	VT	VT	NT	TP	VT	TP	XC	LM	VT	VT	LM	VT	VT
Inverness	d																				
Aberdeen	d																				
Dundee	d																				
Perth	d																				
Edinburgh	d													14 08							
Haymarket	d													14u12							
Glasgow Central	d							12 54	13 40				14 00								14 40
Motherwell	d																				
Carstairs	d																				
Lockerbie	d							13 56						15 06							
Carlisle	a							14 18	14 46				15 09	15 28							15 46
	d							14 30	14 49				15 11	15 30							15 49
Penrith North Lakes	d							14 44						15 44							
Windermere	d																				
Oxenholme Lake District	a							15 08	15 22				15 45	16 08							16 22
	d							15 09	15 23				15 46	16 08							16 24
Barrow-in-Furness	d																				
Lancaster	a							15 26	15 37					16 25							16 37
	d							15 26	15 38					16 26							16 38
Preston	a							15 45	15 56				16 15	16 45							16 56
Blackpool North	d										15 37	15 45									
Preston	d							15 47	15 58		16 04	16 10	16 17	16 47							16 58
Wigan North Western	a								16 09		16 24		16 28								17 09
	d								16 09		16 24		16 28								17 09
Blackrod	d																				
Lostock	d																				
Bolton	a							16 08				16 34		17 08							
Manchester Piccadilly	a							16 27				16 56		17 27							
Manchester Airport	a							16 47				17 17		17 48							
Liverpool Lime Street	a										17 05										
	d	15 48				16 04										16 34		16 48			
Liverpool South Parkway	d					16 15										16 44					
Runcorn	d	16 04				16 25										16 52		17 04			
Warrington Bank Quay	a								16 20				16 39								17 20
	d								16 20				16 39								17 20
Hartford	d															17 06					
Manchester Piccadilly	d			15 55	16 07		16 15								16 27		16 35			16 55	
Stockport	d			16 04	16 16		16 23								16 35		16 42			17 04	
Wilmslow	d			16 11																17 11	
Holyhead	d									14 36											
Bangor (Gwynedd)	d									15 06											
Llandudno Junction	d									15 25											
Wrexham General	d																				
Chester	d									16 20											
Crewe	a			16 27		16 45				16 43			16 58			17 20				17 27	
	d			16 29		16 49				16 56			17 01			17 22				17 29	
Macclesfield	d														16 49		16 56				
Congleton	d																				
Stoke-on-Trent	d		←		16 44		16 50								17 07		17 13		←		
Stafford	a	16 35	16 46		17 02	17 09									17 25	17 42		17 35	17 42		
	d	16 36	16 46		17 03	17 10									17 26	17 43		17 36	17 43		
Penkridge	a					17 15										→					
Wolverhampton	a		16 59		17 16	17 27							17 31		17 39				17 56		
Birmingham New Street	a		17 18		17 39	17 47							17 55		17 58				18 17		
Birmingham International	a														18 13						
Coventry	a														18 24						
Lichfield Trent Valley	a																				
Tamworth Low Level	a																				
Nuneaton	a																				
Rugby	a																				
Milton Keynes Central	a						17 46			18 01											
Watford Junction	a																				
London Euston	a	17 55		18 04			18 23		18 12	18 37							18 42	18 56		19 04	19 12

OVERNIGHT SLEEPERS. For sleeper trains, operated by First ScotRail, please refer to Tables 400 - 404

Table 65

Saturdays
from 23 October

Scotland and North West England - West Midlands and London

		NT	TP	XC	VT	LM	VT	TP	VT	VT	XC	LM	VT	VT	LM	VT	XC	VT	LM	VT	TP
Inverness	d																				
Aberdeen	d																				
Dundee	d																				
Perth	d																				
Edinburgh	d						14 52														
Haymarket	d						14 57														
Glasgow Central	d								15 40												
Motherwell	d																				
Carstairs	d																				
Lockerbie	d																				
Carlisle	a						16 05		16 46												
	d						16 07		16 49												
Penrith North Lakes	d						16 22		17 03												
Windermere	d																				
Oxenholme Lake District	a																				
	d																				
Barrow-in-Furness	d							16 17													
Lancaster	a						16 56	17 15	17 37												
	d						16 57	17 15	17 38												
Preston	a						17 15	17 34	17 56												
Blackpool North	d	16 35	16 40																		17 20
Preston	d	17 04	17 09				17 17														17 47
Wigan North Western	a	17 24					17 28														
	d	17 24					17 28														
Blackrod	d																				
Lostock	d																				
Bolton	a		17 34																		18 08
Manchester Piccadilly	a		17 56																		18 27
Manchester Airport	a		18 17																		18 47
Liverpool Lime Street	a	18 02																			
	d					17 04						17 34		17 48					18 04		
Liverpool South Parkway	d					17 15						17 44							18 15		
Runcorn	d					17 25						17 52		18 04					18 24		
Warrington Bank Quay	a						17 39														
	d				17 14		17 39											18 14			
Hartford	d											18 06									
Manchester Piccadilly	d			17 06						17 15	17 27		17 35			17 55	18 05			18 15	
Stockport	d									17 23	17 36		17 43			18 04	18 13			18 23	
Wilmslow	d															18 11					
Holyhead	d																				
Bangor (Gwynedd)	d																				
Llandudno Junction	d																				
Wrexham General	d																				
Chester	d																				
Crewe	a				17 33	17 47	17 59					18 20				18 27		18 33	18 46		
	d				17 35	17 49	18 01					18 22				18 29		18 35	18 49		
Macclesfield	d			17 26									17 55				18 26				
Congleton	d										17 54										
Stoke-on-Trent	d			17 44						17 50	18 08		18 13		←		18 44			18 50	
Stafford	a			18 03		18 09					18 26	18 42		18 34	18 42		19 02		19 09		
	d			18 04		18 10					18 27	18 43		18 36	18 43		19 03		19 10		
Penkridge	a					18 15						→							19 15		
Wolverhampton	a			18 16		18 27	18 31				18 40				18 56		19 16		19 27		
Birmingham New Street	a			18 38		18 47	18 55				18 58				19 17		19 33		19 47		
Birmingham International	a										19 13										
Coventry	a										19 24										
Lichfield Trent Valley	a																				
Tamworth Low Level	a																				
Nuneaton	a																				
Rugby	a																				
Milton Keynes Central	a									18 46										19 46	
Watford Junction	a																				
London Euston	a				19 12					19 23			19 42	19 56		20 04		20 15		20 25	

OVERNIGHT SLEEPERS. For sleeper trains, operated by First ScotRail, please refer to Tables 400 - 404

Table 65

Saturdays from 23 October

Scotland and North West England - West Midlands and London

		VT	NT	TP	VT	TP	TP	XC	LM	VT		VT	LM	VT	VT	NT	TP	VT	XC	LM	NT	VT	TP	XC	LM
		◇1 ☕		◇1 A 🛒	◇1 ☕	◇1	◇1 🛒	◇1 🛒	1	◇1 ☕		◇1 ☕	1	◇1 ☕	◇1 ☕		◇1	◇1 ☕	◇1 🛒	1		◇1 ☕	◇1 🛒	◇1 🛒	1
Inverness	d																								
Aberdeen	d																								
Dundee	d																								
Perth	d																								
Edinburgh 10	d						16 11															16 52			
Haymarket	d						16u15															16 57			
Glasgow Central 15	d	15 40			16 00										16 40								17 06		
Motherwell	d														16u54										
Carstairs	d																								
Lockerbie	d						17 10																18 06		
Carlisle 8	a	16 46			17 08		17 32								17 49							18 05	18 28		
	d	16 49			17 09		17 33								17 52							18 07	18 29		
Penrith North Lakes	d	17 03					17 48																18 44		
Windermere	d			17 06																					
Oxenholme Lake District	a			17 25	17 44										18 25							18 41	19 08		
	d			17 30	17 44										18 26							18 42	19 08		
Barrow-in-Furness	d					17 21															18 03				
Lancaster 6	a	17 37		17 47		18 17	18 26								18 40						19 04	18 56	19 26		
	d	17 38		17 48		18 17	18 26								18 41						19 05	18 57	19 26		
Preston 8	a	17 56		18 06	18 15	18 36	18 45								18 59						19 30	19 15	19 45		
Blackpool North	d		17 37													18 37	18 45								
Preston 8	d	17 58	18 04	18 08	18 17		18 47								19 01	19 04	19 10					19 17	19 47		
Wigan North Western	a	18 09	18 24		18 28										19 12	19 24						19 28			
	d	18 09	18 24		18 28										19 12	19 24						19 28			
Blackrod	d																								
Lostock	d			18 30																					
Bolton	a			18 34			19 08										19 34						20 08		
Manchester Piccadilly 10	a			18 56			19 27										19 56						20 27		
Manchester Airport	a			19 17			19 50										20 17						20 47		
Liverpool Lime Street 10	a		19 02													20 02									
	d								18 34			18 48								19 04					19 34
Liverpool South Parkway	d								18 44											19 14					19 44
Runcorn	d								18 52			19 04								19 23					19 52
Warrington Bank Quay	a	18 20			18 39										19 23							19 39			
	d	18 20			18 39										19 23			19 17				19 39			
Hartford	d								19 04																20 04
Manchester Piccadilly 10	d							18 27		18 35				18 55					19 07					19 27	
Stockport	d							18 35		18 42				19 04					19 16					19 35	
Wilmslow	d													19 11											
Holyhead	d																								
Bangor (Gwynedd)	d																								
Llandudno Junction	d																								
Wrexham General	d																								
Chester	d																								
Crewe 10	a				18 59				19 19					19 27				19 36		19 49		19 59			20 16
	d				19 01				19 22					19 29				19 38		19 51		20 01			20 22
Macclesfield	d									18 55														19 49	
Congleton	d							18 54																	
Stoke-on-Trent	d							19 07		19 12			←						19 44					20 07	
Stafford	a							19 25	19 42			19 35	19 42					19 58	20 02	20 11				20 25	20 42
	d							19 25	19 43			19 36	19 43						20 03	20 12				20 26	20 43
Penkridge	a								→				19 48												→
Wolverhampton 7	a				19 31			19 39					19 59						20 16	20 28		20 31		20 39	
Birmingham New Street 12	a				19 55			19 58					20 17						20 33	20 47		20 55		20 58	
Birmingham International	a							20 13																21 13	
Coventry	a							20 24																21 24	
Lichfield Trent Valley	a																								
Tamworth Low Level	a																								
Nuneaton	a																								
Rugby	a																								
Milton Keynes Central	a														20 41										
Watford Junction	a														21s15										
London Euston 15 ⊖	a	20 15								20 58		21 15		21 18	21 38										

A 🛒 from Preston

OVERNIGHT SLEEPERS. For sleeper trains, operated by First ScotRail, please refer to Tables 400 - 404

Table 65

Saturdays from 23 October

Scotland and North West England - West Midlands and London

		VT	NT	VT	LM	VT		TP	XC	VT	VT	TP	TP	XC	LM	VT	NT	XC	VT	TP	VT	VT	XC	LM	TP
		◇1 ☕		◇1 ☕	1	◇1 ☕		◇1	◇1 🛒	◇1 ☕	◇1 ☕	◇1 🛒	◇1	◇1 🛒	1	◇1 ☕		◇1 🛒	◇1 ☕	◇1	◇1 ☕	◇1 ☕	◇1 🛒	1	◇1
Inverness	d																								
Aberdeen	d																								
Dundee	d																								
Perth	d																								
Edinburgh 10	d											18 12										18 52			
Haymarket	d											18u16										18 57			
Glasgow Central 15	d					17 40					18 00								18 40						
Motherwell	d																								
Carstairs	d																								
Lockerbie	d					18 32						19 12													
Carlisle 8	a					18 50					19 08	19 34							19 46			20 05			
	d					18 52					19 09	19 34							19 48			20 07			
Penrith North Lakes	d					19 06						19 48							20 02			20 22			
Windermere	d																								21 40
Oxenholme Lake District	a					19 28						20 12							20 24			20 45			21 59
	d					19 29						20 12							20 25			20 45			22 01
Barrow-in-Furness	d												19 32												
Lancaster 6	a					19 43					19 55	20 26	20 33						20 39			20 59			22 17
	d					19 44					19 56	20 26	20 34						20 40			21 00			22 17
Preston 8	a					20 02					20 15	20 45	20 54						20 58			21 18			22 38
Blackpool North	d		19 37					19 45									20 37			20 42					
Preston 8	d		20 04			20 04		20 10			20 17	20 47					21 04		21 00	21 10		21 20			
Wigan North Western	a		20 24			20 15					20 28						21 23		21 11			21 31			
	d		20 24			20 15					20 28						21 23		21 11			21 31			
Blackrod	d																								
Lostock	d																								
Bolton	a							20 34				21 08								21 34					
Manchester Piccadilly 10	a							20 56				21 27								21 56					
Manchester Airport	a							21 17				21 47								22 17					
Liverpool Lime Street 10	a		21 02														22 14								
	d			19 48											20 34									21 34	
Liverpool South Parkway	d														20 44									21 44	
Runcorn	d			20 04											20 52									21 52	
Warrington Bank Quay	a					20 26					20 39								21 22			21 42			
	d					20 26				20 26	20 39								21 22		21 42	21 42			
Hartford	d														21 03									22 04	
Manchester Piccadilly 10	d	19 35							20 07					20 27		20 35		21 07					21 28		
Stockport	d	19 42							20 16					20 35		20 43							21 36		
Wilmslow	d																								
Holyhead	d																								
Bangor (Gwynedd)	d																								
Llandudno Junction	d																								
Wrexham General	d																								
Chester	d																								
Crewe 10	a					20 45				20 45	20 59				21 16				21 41		22 01	22 02		22 21	
	d					20 47				20 47	21 01				21 17				21 43		22 03	22 04		22 23	
Macclesfield	d	19 55												20 49		20 56							21 50		
Congleton	d																								
Stoke-on-Trent	d	20 12			←				20 44					21 07		21 13		21 45					22 08		
Stafford	a			20 35	20 42				21 02					21 26	21 42			22 02	22 07		22 27	22 28	22 33	22 47	
	d			20 36	20 43				21 03					21 27	21 42			22 03	22 08		22 28	22 29	22 34	22 47	
Penkridge	a				20 48										21 48									22 53	
Wolverhampton 7	a				20 57				21 15		21 31			21 39	21 58			22 14	22 22		22 42	22 40	22 50	23 03	
Birmingham New Street 12	a				21 17				21 32		21 54			21 58	22 20			22 32	22 46		23 01	22 59	23 17	23 21	
Birmingham International	a																								
Coventry	a																								
Lichfield Trent Valley	a																								
Tamworth Low Level	a																								
Nuneaton	a																								
Rugby	a																								
Milton Keynes Central	a	21 10				21 50				21 50						22 12									
Watford Junction	a															22s42									
London Euston 15 ⊖	a	22 01		22 14		22 45				22 45						23 04									

OVERNIGHT SLEEPERS. For sleeper trains, operated by First ScotRail, please refer to Tables 400 - 404

Table 65

Saturdays
from 23 October

Scotland and North West England - West Midlands and London

		NT	TP	TP
			◇■	◇■
Inverness	d			
Aberdeen	d			
Dundee	d			
Perth	d			
Edinburgh	d			
Haymarket	d			
Glasgow Central	d			
Motherwell	d			
Carstairs	d			
Lockerbie	d			
Carlisle	a			
	d			
Penrith North Lakes	d			
Windermere	d			
Oxenholme Lake District	a			
	d			
Barrow-in-Furness	d	21 43		
Lancaster	a	22 44		
	d	22 45		
Preston	a	23 10		
Blackpool North	d		21 45	22 45
Preston	d		22 10	23 10
Wigan North Western	a			
	d			
Blackrod	d			
Lostock	d			
Bolton	a		22 34	23 34
Manchester Piccadilly	a		22 56	23 53
Manchester Airport	a		23 17	00 22
Liverpool Lime Street	a			
	d			
Liverpool South Parkway	d			
Runcorn	d			
Warrington Bank Quay	a			
	d			
Hartford	d			
Manchester Piccadilly	d			
Stockport	d			
Wilmslow	d			
Holyhead	d			
Bangor (Gwynedd)	d			
Llandudno Junction	d			
Wrexham General	d			
Chester	d			
Crewe	a			
	d			
Macclesfield	d			
Congleton	d			
Stoke-on-Trent	d			
Stafford	a			
	d			
Penkridge	a			
Wolverhampton	a			
Birmingham New Street	a			
Birmingham International	a			
Coventry	a			
Lichfield Trent Valley	a			
Tamworth Low Level	a			
Nuneaton	a			
Rugby	a			
Milton Keynes Central	a			
Watford Junction	a			
London Euston	a			

OVERNIGHT SLEEPERS. For sleeper trains, operated by First ScotRail, please refer to Tables 400 - 404

Table 65

Sundays
until 11 July

Scotland and North West England - West Midlands and London

		TP	TP	TP	VT	XC	VT	VT	XC		VT	VT	TP	VT	XC	XC	LM	VT	LM	NT	XC	VT	TP	LM
				◇■	◇■		◇■	◇■	◇■		◇■	◇■	◇■	◇■		◇■		◇■	◇■			◇■	◇■	
Inverness	d																							
Aberdeen	d																							
Dundee	d																							
Perth	d																							
Edinburgh	d																							
Haymarket	d																							
Glasgow Central	d																							
Motherwell	d																							
Carstairs	d																							
Lockerbie	d																							
Carlisle	a																							
	d																							
Penrith North Lakes	d																							
Windermere	d																							
Oxenholme Lake District	a																							
	d																							
Barrow-in-Furness	d																							
Lancaster	a																							
	d																							
Preston	a																							
Blackpool North	d	03 20	05 20	07 48									08 44							08 50			09 44	
Preston	d	04u00	06u00	08 14								09 00	09 10							09 15		10 00	10 10	
Wigan North Western	a											09 10								09 35		10 10		
	d											09 11								09 36		10 11		
Blackrod	d																							
Lostock	d																							
Bolton	a	04u35	06u35	08 37									09 34										10 34	
Manchester Piccadilly	a	05u00	07u00	08 59									09 57										10 57	
Manchester Airport	a	05 25	07 25	09 19									10 17										11 18	
Liverpool Lime Street	a																			10 24				
	d						08 15				08 38							09 38						
Liverpool South Parkway	d																							
Runcorn	d						08 35				08 54							09 54						
Warrington Bank Quay	a											09 21										10 21		
	d											09 22										10 22		
Hartford	d																							
Manchester Piccadilly	d				08 05			08 20	08 27					09 20		09 27								
Stockport	d				08 14			08 29	08 36					09 28		09 36								
Wilmslow	d				08 22			08 38	08 43					09 36		09 44								
Holyhead	d																							
Bangor (Gwynedd)	d																							
Llandudno Junction	d																							
Wrexham General	d																							
Chester	d																							
Crewe	a				08 39		08 52		09 02		09 11	09 41						10 12				10 41		
	d				08 43		08 53		09 05		09 13	09 43					09 53	10 14	10 20			10 43		10 45
Macclesfield	d					07 50									08 47						09 43			
Congleton	d																							
Stoke-on-Trent	d					08 45									09 42		10 41				10 38			11 33
Stafford	a				09 00	09 15		09 15	09 25		09 31			10 09	10 12	10 22	11 17	10 32	10 41		11 08			12 09
	d				09 02			09 17	09 26		09 32			10 11		10 26		10 33	10 42					
Penkridge	a																		10 48					
Wolverhampton	a								09 40							10 40			11 00					
Birmingham New Street	a								09 58							10 58			11 17					
Birmingham International	a								10 13							11 13								
Coventry	a								10 24							11 24								
Lichfield Trent Valley	a																							
Tamworth Low Level	a																							
Nuneaton	a										09 54							10 55						
Rugby	a											10 31										11 31		
Milton Keynes Central	a						10 17					11 06		11 16				11 49				12 05		
Watford Junction	a				10s34			10s51			11s16	11s42												
London Euston	a				10 56		11 06	11 12			11 39	12 04		12 09				12 37				12 44		

OVERNIGHT SLEEPERS. For sleeper trains, operated by First ScotRail, please refer to Tables 400 - 404

Table 65

Scotland and North West England - West Midlands and London

Sundays until 11 July

		VT	VT	TP	XC	VT	NT	VT	VT	TP	VT	XC	VT	VT	XC	LM	NT	VT	VT	LM	VT	VT	TP	VT	VT
		◇1	◇1	◇1	◇1	◇1		◇1	◇1	◇1	◇1		◇1	◇1	◇1	1		◇1	◇1	1	◇1	◇1	◇1	◇1	◇1
		⊏P	⊏P		⊶	⊏P		⊏P	⊏P		⊏P	🚌	⊏P	⊏P	⊶			⊏P	⊏P		⊏P	⊏P		⊏P	⊏P
Inverness	d																								
Aberdeen	d																								
Dundee	d																								
Perth	d																								
Edinburgh [10]	d																								
Haymarket	d																								
Glasgow Central [15]	d																					09 37			
Motherwell	d																								
Carstairs	d																								
Lockerbie	d																								
Carlisle [8]	a																					10 44			
	d																					10 46			
Penrith North Lakes	d																					11 00			
Windermere	d																								
Oxenholme Lake District	a																					11 22			
	d																					11 23			
Barrow-in-Furness	d			09 15																					
Lancaster [8]	a			10 17																		11 37			
	d			10 21																		11 38			
Preston [8]	a			10 40																		11 56			
Blackpool North	d						09 50			10 44							10 50						11 44		
Preston [8]	d		10 17	10 47			10 15		10 58	11 10				11 17			11 15					11 58	12 10		
Wigan North Western	a		10 28				10 36		11 09					11 28			11 36					12 09			
	d		10 28				10 36		11 09					11 28			11 36					12 09			
Blackrod	d																								
Lostock	d																								
Bolton	a			11 08						11 34													12 34		
Manchester Piccadilly [10]	a			11 27						11 57													12 57		
Manchester Airport ✈	a			11 47						12 17													13 17		
Liverpool Lime Street [10]	a						11 24										12 24								
	d							10 38								11 34			11 48						
Liverpool South Parkway ✈	d															11 44									
Runcorn	d							10 54								11 52			12 04						
Warrington Bank Quay	a		10 39						11 20					11 39								12 20			
	d		10 39						11 20					11 39								12 20			
Hartford	d															12 04									
Manchester Piccadilly [10]	d	10 20			10 24	10 35					11 08				11 27			11 35			11 55			12 15	
Stockport	d	10 29			10 33	10 45					11 18				11 36			11 44			12 05			12 24	
Wilmslow	d	10 37			10 43	10 53					11 26				11 44			11 53			12 12			12 32	
Holyhead	d																								10 55
Bangor (Gwynedd)	d																								11 22
Llandudno Junction	d																								11 40
Wrexham General	d																								
Chester	d												11 28												12 33
Crewe [10]	a	10 53	11 00					11 12					11 47	11 59		12 19					12 28				12 52
	d	10 55	11 03					11 14					11 49	12 01		12 22					12 30				12 54
Macclesfield	d											10 49													
Congleton	d																								
Stoke-on-Trent	d											11 44								←					
Stafford	a				11 18	11 27		11 32			11 59	12 14			12 24	12 41		12 27	12 35	12 41				13 05	
	d				11 24	11 28		11 33			12 01				12 25	12 42		12 28	12 36	12 42				13 07	
Penkridge	a															→				12 48					
Wolverhampton [7]	a		11 33		11 40									12 32	12 40					12 59					
Birmingham New Street [12]	a		11 56		11 58									12 55	12 58					13 16					
Birmingham International ✈	a				12 13										13 13										
Coventry	a				12 24										13 24										
Lichfield Trent Valley	a																								
Tamworth Low Level	a																								
Nuneaton	a							12 04					12 30												
Rugby	a																								
Milton Keynes Central	a					12 24					12 51		13 03											14 01	14 04
Watford Junction	a	12s34						12s54																	
London Euston [15] ⊖	a	12 56				13 04		13 15	13 24		13 32		13 44					13 51	14 06		14 12	14 17		14 41	14 45

OVERNIGHT SLEEPERS. For sleeper trains, operated by First ScotRail, please refer to Tables 400 - 404

Table 65

Scotland and North West England - West Midlands and London

Sundays until 11 July

		XC	NT	VT	TP	XC	LM	VT	VT	LM	VT	VT	NT	TP	XC	VT	VT	VT	TP	XC	LM	VT	NT	VT	LM
				◇1	◇1	◇1	1	◇1	◇1	1	◇1	◇1		◇1	◇1	◇1	◇1	◇1	◇1	◇1	1	◇1		◇1	1
		🚌		⊏P		⊶		⊏P	⊏P		⊏P	⊏P			⊶	⊏P	⊏P	⊏P	⊶	⊶		⊏P		⊏P	
Inverness	d																								
Aberdeen	d																								
Dundee	d																								
Perth	d																								
Edinburgh [10]	d																	10 52	11 10						
Haymarket	d																	10 57	11u14						
Glasgow Central [15]	d											10 32													
Motherwell	d											10u49													
Carstairs	d																								
Lockerbie	d																		12 08						
Carlisle [8]	a											11 44						12 05	12 30						
	d											11 46						12 07	12 32						
Penrith North Lakes	d											12 00							12 46						
Windermere	d																								
Oxenholme Lake District	a											12 22						12 41	13 10						
	d											12 24						12 43	13 10						
Barrow-in-Furness	d				11 23																				
Lancaster [8]	a				12 26							12 37						12 56	13 26						
	d			12 00	12 26							12 38						12 57	13 26						
Preston [8]	a			12 15	12 45							12 56						13 15	13 45						
Blackpool North	d		11 50										12 50	12 44									13 50		
Preston [8]	d		12 15	12 17	12 47							12 58	13 15	13 10				13 17	13 47				14 15		
Wigan North Western	a		12 35	12 28								13 09	13 35					13 28					14 35		
	d		12 36	12 28								13 09	13 36					13 28					14 36		
Blackrod	d																								
Lostock	d																								
Bolton	a				13 08									13 34					14 08						
Manchester Piccadilly [10]	a				13 27									13 57					14 27						
Manchester Airport ✈	a				13 47									14 17					14 47						
Liverpool Lime Street [10]	a		13 24										14 24										15 24		
	d						12 34		12 48												13 34	13 10		13 48	
Liverpool South Parkway ✈	d						12 44														13 44				
Runcorn	d						12 52		13 04												13 52			14 04	
Warrington Bank Quay	a			12 39								13 20						13 39							
	d			12 39								13 20						13 39							
Hartford	d						13 03														14 03	13 34			
Manchester Piccadilly [10]	d					12 26		12 35			12 55				13 07	13 15				13 27		13 57			
Stockport	d							12 45			13 05					13 22				13 36		14 17			
Wilmslow	d					12 43		12 53			13 12														
Holyhead	d																11 50								
Bangor (Gwynedd)	d																12 17								
Llandudno Junction	d																12 35								
Wrexham General	d																								
Chester	d																13b30								
Crewe [10]	a			12 59			13 19				13 28						13 49	13 59			14 18				
	d			13 01			13 22				13 30						13 51	14 01			14 22				
Macclesfield	d	11 50																		13 49		13 55			
Congleton	d																								
Stoke-on-Trent	d	12 45								←					13 43	13 50				14 07		14 12			←
Stafford	a	13 15				13 25	13 42	13 27	13 35	13 42										14 24	14 42			14 35	14 42
	d					13 26	13 43	13 29	13 36	13 43										14 25	14 43			14 36	14 43
Penkridge	a						→			13 48											→				14 48
Wolverhampton [7]	a			13 31		13 40				13 58					14 13			14 32		14 40					14 58
Birmingham New Street [12]	a			13 55		13 58				14 15					14 31			14 55		14 58					15 15
Birmingham International ✈	a					14 13														15 13					
Coventry	a					14 24														15 24					
Lichfield Trent Valley	a																								
Tamworth Low Level	a																								
Nuneaton	a																14 31								
Rugby	a																								
Milton Keynes Central	a															14 49	15 04								
Watford Junction	a																								
London Euston [15] ⊖	a							14 52	15 03		15 11	15 14				15 30	15 45					15 48		16 03	

b arr. 1323

OVERNIGHT SLEEPERS. For sleeper trains, operated by First ScotRail, please refer to Tables 400 - 404

Table 65

Scotland and North West England - West Midlands and London

		VT	VT	TP	XC	VT	VT	VT		TP	XC	LM	VT	VT	LM	VT	VT	TP	NT	XC	VT	VT	VT	TP	XC
		◇1	◇1	◇1	◇1	◇1	◇1	◇1		◇1	◇1	1	◇1	◇1	1	◇1	◇1	◇1		◇1	◇1	◇1	◇1	◇1	◇1
Inverness	d																								
Aberdeen	d																								
Dundee	d																								
Perth	d																								
Edinburgh 10	d																					12 52	13 09	
Haymarket	d																					12 56	13u13	
Glasgow Central 15	d		11 32					11 52									12 42							
Motherwell	d																								
Carstairs	d																								
Lockerbie	d																							14 08	
Carlisle 8	a		12 47					13 09									13 51						14 05	14 30	
	d		12 49					13 10									13 54						14 07	14 32	
Penrith North Lakes	d																						14 22	14 46	
Windermere	d																								
Oxenholme Lake District	a		13 22														14 27							15 10	
	d		13 23														14 28							15 10	
Barrow-in-Furness	d									13 23															
Lancaster 6	a		13 37					13 56		14 26							14 42						14 56	15 25	
	d		13 38					13 58		14 26							14 43						14 57	15 25	
Preston 8	a		13 56					14 15		14 45							15 01						15 15	15 45	
Blackpool North	d			13 44														14 44	14 50						
Preston 8	d		13 58	14 10				14 17		14 47							15 03	15 10	15 15				15 17	15 47	
Wigan North Western	a		14 09					14 28									15 14		15 35				15 28		
	d		14 09					14 28									15 14		15 36				15 28		
Blackrod	d																								
Lostock	d																								
Bolton	a			14 34						15 08								15 34						16 08	
Manchester Piccadilly 10	a			14 57						15 27								15 57						16 27	
Manchester Airport ✈	a			15 17						15 47								16 17						16 47	
Liverpool Lime Street 10	a																		16 24						
	d											14 34		14 48											
Liverpool South Parkway ✈	d											14 44													
Runcorn	d											14 52		15 04											
Warrington Bank Quay	a		14 20					14 39									15 25						15 39		
	d		14 20					14 39									15 25						15 39		
Hartford	d											15 03													
Manchester Piccadilly 10	d	13 55			14 07	14 15					14 27		14 35			14 55				15 07	15 15				15 27
Stockport	d	14 04				14 22					14 36		14 42			15 04					15 22				15 36
Wilmslow	d	14 11														15 11									
Holyhead	d						12 50															13 55			
Bangor (Gwynedd)	d						13 18															14 22			
Llandudno Junction	d						13 36															14 40			
Wrexham General	d																								
Chester	d						14b33															15 33			
Crewe 10	a	14 27					14 54	14 59				15 20				15 27						15 54	15 59		
	d	14 29					14 56	15 01				15 22				15 29						15 56	16 01		
Macclesfield	d										14 49		14 55												15 49
Congleton	d																								
Stoke-on-Trent	d				14 43	14 50					15 07		15 12		←					15 43	15 50				16 07
Stafford	a										15 24	15 42		15 35	15 42										16 24
	d										15 25	15 43		15 36	15 43										16 25
Penkridge	a											→			15 48										
Wolverhampton 7	a				15 13			15 31			15 40				15 58					16 13			16 32		16 40
Birmingham New Street 12	a				15 31			15 55			15 58				16 15					16 31			16 56		16 58
Birmingham International ✈	a										16 13														17 13
Coventry	a										16 24														17 24
Lichfield Trent Valley	a																								
Tamworth Low Level	a																								
Nuneaton	a																								
Rugby	a																								
Milton Keynes Central	a					15 49	16 04														16 49	17 03			
Watford Junction	a																								
London Euston 15 ⊖	a	16 11	16 14			16 30	16 44						16 48	17 03		17 11	17 23				17 30	17 44			

b arr. 1426

OVERNIGHT SLEEPERS. For sleeper trains, operated by First ScotRail, please refer to Tables 400 - 404

Table 65

Scotland and North West England - West Midlands and London

		LM	VT	VT		LM	VT	VT	TP	XC	VT	VT	NT	VT	TP		XC	LM	VT	VT	LM	VT	VT	TP	NT
		1	◇1	◇1		1	◇1	◇1	◇1	◇1	◇1	◇1		◇1	◇1		◇1	1	◇1	◇1	1	◇1	◇1	◇1	
Inverness	d																								
Aberdeen	d																								
Dundee	d																								
Perth	d																								
Edinburgh 10	d																								
Haymarket	d																								
Glasgow Central 15	d							13 34						13 55									14 35		
Motherwell	d																								
Carstairs	d																								
Lockerbie	d																								
Carlisle 8	a							14 46						15 08									15 47		
	d							14 49						15 09									15 49		
Penrith North Lakes	d																								
Windermere	d																								
Oxenholme Lake District	a							15 22						15 44									16 22		
	d							15 23						15 44									16 23		
Barrow-in-Furness	d														15 23										
Lancaster 6	a							15 37							16 26								16 37		
	d							15 38							16 26								16 38		
Preston 8	a							15 56						16 13	16 45								16 56		
Blackpool North	d								15 44				15 50											16 44	16 50
Preston 8	d							15 58	16 10				16 15	16 15	16 47								16 58	17 10	17 15
Wigan North Western	a							16 09					16 35	16 26									17 09		17 35
	d							16 09					16 36	16 26									17 09		17 36
Blackrod	d																								
Lostock	d																								
Bolton	a								16 34						17 08									17 34	
Manchester Piccadilly 10	a								16 57						17 27									17 57	
Manchester Airport ✈	a								17 17						17 47									18 17	
Liverpool Lime Street 10	a												17 24												18 24
	d	15 34		15 48								16 18						16 34		16 48					
Liverpool South Parkway ✈	d	15 44																16 44							
Runcorn	d	15 52		16 04								16 34						16 52		17 04					
Warrington Bank Quay	a							16 20						16 37									17 20		
	d							16 20						16 37									17 20		
Hartford	d	16 03																17 03							
Manchester Piccadilly 10	d		15 35				15 55			16 07	16 15						16 27		16 35			16 55			
Stockport	d		15 42				16 04				16 23						16 36		16 42			17 04			
Wilmslow	d						16 11															17 11			
Holyhead	d																								
Bangor (Gwynedd)	d																								
Llandudno Junction	d																								
Wrexham General	d																								
Chester	d																								
Crewe 10	a	16 18					16 27					16 50		16 57				17 18				17 27			
	d	16 22					16 29					16 53		16 59				17 22				17 29			
Macclesfield	d		15 55														16 49		16 55						
Congleton	d																								
Stoke-on-Trent	d		16 12			←				16 43	16 50						17 08		17 12		←				
Stafford	a	16 42		16 36		16 42											17 25	17 42		17 35	17 42				
	d	16 43		16 37		16 43											17 26	17 43		17 36	17 43				
Penkridge	a	→				16 48												→			17 48				
Wolverhampton 7	a					16 58				17 13				17 31			17 40				17 58				
Birmingham New Street 12	a					17 15				17 31				17 55			17 58				18 15				
Birmingham International ✈	a																18 13								
Coventry	a																18 24								
Lichfield Trent Valley	a											17 25													
Tamworth Low Level	a																								
Nuneaton	a																								
Rugby	a																								
Milton Keynes Central	a										17 49	18 02													
Watford Junction	a																								
London Euston 15 ⊖	a		17 48	18 04			18 11	18 14			18 30	18 42							18 48	19 03		19 11	19 14		

OVERNIGHT SLEEPERS. For sleeper trains, operated by First ScotRail, please refer to Tables 400 - 404

Scotland and North West England - West Midlands and London

		XC	VT	VT	VT	TP	TP	TP	XC	LM		VT	VT	LM	VT	VT	TP	XC	VT	VT		VT	TP		XC
		◇1	◇1	◇1	◇1	◇1	◇1	◇1	◇1	1		◇1	◇1	1	◇1	◇1	◇1	◇1	◇1	◇1		◇1	◇1		◇1
Inverness	d																								
Aberdeen	d																								
Dundee	d																								
Perth	d																								
Edinburgh 10	d				14 52																		16 10		
Haymarket	d				14 57																		16u14		
Glasgow Central 15	d						15 06									15 36						15 56			
Motherwell	d																								
Carstairs	d																								
Lockerbie	d						16 06																17 08		
Carlisle 8	a				16 05		16 28									16 46						17 08	17 30		
	d				16 07		16 30									16 49						17 09	17 32		
Penrith North Lakes	d				16 22		16 44									17 03							17 46		
Windermere	d							16 58																	
Oxenholme Lake District	a						17 08	17 15														17 44	18 10		
	d						17 08	17 16														17 44	18 10		
Barrow-in-Furness	d					16 25																			
Lancaster 6	a				16 56	17 17	17 23	17 31								17 37							18 26		
	d				16 57	17 17	17 23	17 32								17 38							18 26		
Preston 8	a				17 15	17 37	17 42	17 50								17 56						18 15	18 45		
Blackpool North	d																17 40				17 50				
Preston 8	d				17 17		17 47									17 58	18b10				18 14	18 17	18 47		
Wigan North Western	a				17 28											18 09					18 15	18 28			
	d				17 28											18 09					18 36	18 28			
Blackrod	d																								
Lostock	d																								
Bolton	a						18 08										18 34						19 08		
Manchester Piccadilly 10	a						18 27										18 57						19 27		
Manchester Airport ✈	a						18 47										19 17						19 47		
Liverpool Lime Street 10	a																				19 24				
	d									17 34			17 48												
Liverpool South Parkway ✈	d									17 44															
Runcorn	d									17 52			18 04												
Warrington Bank Quay	a				17 39											18 20						18 39			
	d				17 39											18 20						18 39			
Hartford	d									18 03															
Manchester Piccadilly 10	d	17 07	17 15						17 27			17 35			17 55			18 07	18 15						18 27
Stockport	d		17 22						17 36			17 42			18 04				18 22						18 36
Wilmslow	d														18 11										
Holyhead	d																								
Bangor (Gwynedd)	d																								
Llandudno Junction	d																								
Wrexham General	d																								
Chester	d			17 35																18 35					
Crewe 10	a			17 53	17 59					18 20					18 27					18 53		18 59			
	d			17 55	18 01					18 22					18 29					18 55		19 01			
Macclesfield	d								17 49			17 55													18 49
Congleton	d																								
Stoke-on-Trent	d	17 43	17 50						18 08			18 12		←				18 43	18 50						19 07
Stafford	a								18 25	18 42			18 35	18 42											19 24
	d								18 26	18 43			18 36	18 43											19 25
Penkridge	a									→				18 48											
Wolverhampton 7	a	18 13			18 32				18 40					18 58				19 13				19 31			19 40
Birmingham New Street 12	a	18 31			18 56				18 58					19 15				19 31				19 55			19 58
Birmingham International ✈	a								19 13																20 13
Coventry	a								19 24																20 24
Lichfield Trent Valley	a																								
Tamworth Low Level	a																								
Nuneaton	a																								
Rugby	a																								
Milton Keynes Central	a		18 49	19 03															19 49	20 03					
Watford Junction	a																								
London Euston 15 ⊖	a		19 30	19 44								19 48	20 03		20 11	20 15			20 30	20 44					

b arr. 1804

OVERNIGHT SLEEPERS. For sleeper trains, operated by First ScotRail, please refer to Tables 400 - 404

Scotland and North West England - West Midlands and London

		LM	VT	VT	LM	VT	NT	VT	TP	XC	VT	TP	TP	VT	XC	LM	NT	VT	VT	VT	TP	TP	NT	XC	AW
		1	◇1	◇1	1	◇1		◇1	◇1	◇1	◇1	◇1	◇1	◇1	◇1	1		◇1	◇1	◇1	◇1	◇1		◇1	◇
Inverness	d																								
Aberdeen	d																								
Dundee	d																								
Perth	d																								
Edinburgh 10	d										16 52											18 10			
Haymarket	d										16 56											18u14			
Glasgow Central 15	d							16 38					17 06							17 36					
Motherwell	d							16 54																	
Carstairs	d																								
Lockerbie	d																			18 32		19 08			
Carlisle 8	a							17 49			18 05		18 26							18 50		19 30			
	d							17 51			18 07		18 28							18 52		19 32			
Penrith North Lakes	d							18 05					18 42							19 06		19 46			
Windermere	d																								
Oxenholme Lake District	a							18 27			18 41		19 06							19 28		20 10			
	d							18 28			18 42		19 07							19 29		20 10			
Barrow-in-Furness	d											18 15											20 02		
Lancaster 6	a							18 42			18 56	19 17	19 21							19 43		20 26	21 09		
	d							18 43			18 57	19 17	19 22							19 44		20 26			
Preston 8	a							19 01			19 15	19 37	19 41							20 02		20 45			
Blackpool North	d						18 50		18 44								19 50				19 44				
Preston 8	d						19 14	19 03	19 10		19 17		19 47				20 14			20 04	20 10	20 47			
Wigan North Western	a						19 15	19 14			19 28						20 15			20 15					
	d						19 36	19 14			19 28						20 36			20 15					
Blackrod	d																								
Lostock	d																								
Bolton	a								19 34				20 08								20 34	21 08			
Manchester Piccadilly 10	a								19 57				20 27								20 57	21 27			
Manchester Airport ✈	a								20 17				20 47								21 17	21 47			
Liverpool Lime Street 10	a						20 24										21 24								
	d	18 34		18 48												19 34			19 48						
Liverpool South Parkway ✈	d	18 44														19 44									
Runcorn	d	18 52		19 04												19 52			20 04						
Warrington Bank Quay	a							19 25			19 39									20 26					
	d							19 25			19 39									20 26					
Hartford	d	19 03														20 03									
Manchester Piccadilly 10	d		18 35			18 55				19 07				19 15	19 27			19 35						20 07	
Stockport	d		18 42			19 04								19 22	19 36			19 42						20 16	
Wilmslow	d					19 11																			
Holyhead	d																								18 25
Bangor (Gwynedd)	d																								19 04
Llandudno Junction	d																								19 24
Wrexham General	d																								
Chester	d																								20b27
Crewe 10	a	19 20				19 27					19 59					20 16			20 22	20 45					20 48
	d	19 22				19 29					20 01					20 18			20 24	20 47					20 54
Macclesfield	d		18 55												19 49			19 55						20 29	
Congleton	d																								
Stoke-on-Trent	d		19 12		←					19 43				19 50	20 07			20 12						20 47	
Stafford	a	19 42		19 35	19 42										20 24	20 37			20 41					21 08	21 16
	d	19 43		19 36	19 43										20 25	20 38			20 43					21 09	21 16
Penkridge	a	→			19 48											20 44									
Wolverhampton 7	a				19 58					20 13	20 31				20 39	20 55								21 21	21 34
Birmingham New Street 12	a				20 15					20 31	20 55				21 00	21 15								21 39	21 52
Birmingham International ✈	a														21 13										22 09
Coventry	a														21 23										
Lichfield Trent Valley	a																								
Tamworth Low Level	a																								
Nuneaton	a																								
Rugby	a																								
Milton Keynes Central	a													20 47					21 36	21 55					
Watford Junction	a																			22s31					
London Euston 15 ⊖	a		20 48	21 04		21 14		21 21						21 32				22 04	22 29	22 53					

b arr. 2019

OVERNIGHT SLEEPERS. For sleeper trains, operated by First ScotRail, please refer to Tables 400 - 404

Table 65

Sundays until 11 July

Scotland and North West England - West Midlands and London

		VT	LM	VT	VT	VT	TP	XC	NT	VT	TP	TP	VT	LM	XC	TP	SR	SR
		◇1	1	◇1	◇1	◇1	◇1	◇1		◇1	◇1	◇1	◇1	1	◇1	◇1	B	B
Inverness	d																	20 25
Aberdeen	d																	21 40
Dundee	d																	23u06
Perth	d																	23u01
Edinburgh	d									18 52		19 57					23 26	
Haymarket	d									18 57		20u01						
Glasgow Central	d					18 30							20 05				21 39	
Motherwell	d																22u01	
Carstairs	d																22u22	
Lockerbie	d												21 02					
Carlisle	a					19 43				20 05		21 14	21 21					
	d					19 44				20 07		21 15	21 24					
Penrith North Lakes	d									20 22			21 39					
Windermere	d										20 40							
Oxenholme Lake District	a					20 19					20 59		22 02					
	d					20 19					21 01		22 03					
Barrow-in-Furness	d																	
Lancaster	a					20 34				20 56	21 18	22 02	22 17					
	d					20 34				20 57	21 23	22 03	22 18					
Preston	a					20 52				21 15		22 23	22 35					
Blackpool North	d						20 44		20 50							23 03		
Preston	d					20 55	21 10		21 14	21 17		22 29	22 38			23 29		
Wigan North Western	a					21 06			21 15	21 28			22 49					
	d					21 07			21 36	21 28			22 50					
Blackrod	d															23 49		
Lostock	d															23 56		
Bolton	a						21 34					22 50				00 02		
Manchester Piccadilly	a						21 57					23 14				00 18		
Manchester Airport	a						22 17					23 30				00 32		
Liverpool Lime Street	a								22 24									
	d		20 34		20 48									21 34				
Liverpool South Parkway	d		20 44											21 44				
Runcorn	d		20 52		21 04									21 52				
Warrington Bank Quay	a					21 18				21 39			23 00					
	d					21 18				21 39			23 01					
Hartford	d		21 03											22 03				
Manchester Piccadilly	d	20 20		20 55				21 07							22 07			
Stockport	d	20 27		21 03				21 16							22 16			
Wilmslow	d																	
Holyhead	d																	
Bangor (Gwynedd)	d																	
Llandudno Junction	d																	
Wrexham General	d																	
Chester	d																	
Crewe	a		21 16		21 21	21 38				21 59			23 20	22 18				
	d		21 17		21 23	21 40				22 01				22 22				
Macclesfield	d	20 40		21 15				21 29							22 29			
Congleton	d																	
Stoke-on-Trent	d	20 57		21 33				21 47							22 47			
Stafford	a		21 37		21 42	22 01		22 06						22 41	23 04			
	d		21 38		21 44	22 02		22 06						22 44	23 05			
Penkridge	a		21 44											22 50				
Wolverhampton	a		21 55			22 16		22 20		22 31				23 00	23 18			
Birmingham New Street	a		22 15			22 40		22 40		22 57				23 17	23 36			
Birmingham International	a																	
Coventry	a																	
Lichfield Trent Valley	a				21 58													
Tamworth Low Level	a				22 04													
Nuneaton	a				22 15													
Rugby	a				22 28													
Milton Keynes Central	a	22 03		22 50	23 04													
Watford Junction	a			23s31	23s36													
London Euston	a	22 56		23 53	23 57												07 06	08 30

OVERNIGHT SLEEPERS. For sleeper trains, operated by First ScotRail, please refer to Tables 400 - 404

Table 65

Sundays 18 July to 05 September

Scotland and North West England - West Midlands and London

		TP	TP	TP	VT	VT	VT	XC	VT	VT	TP	VT	NT	XC	LM	VT	LM	LM	VT	TP	NT	VT	VT	TP
				◇1	◇1	◇1	◇1	◇1	◇1	◇1	◇1	◇1		◇1		◇1	◇1	1	◇1	◇1		◇1	◇1	◇1
Inverness	d																							
Aberdeen	d																							
Dundee	d																							
Perth	d																							
Edinburgh	d																							
Haymarket	d																							
Glasgow Central	d																							
Motherwell	d																							
Carstairs	d																							
Lockerbie	d																							
Carlisle	a																							
	d																							
Penrith North Lakes	d																							
Windermere	d																							
Oxenholme Lake District	a																							
	d																							
Barrow-in-Furness	d																							09 15
Lancaster	a																							10 17
	d																							10 21
Preston	a																							10 40
Blackpool North	d	03 20	05 20	07 48							08 44		08 50							09 44	09 50			
Preston	d	04u00	06u00	08 14						09 00	09 10		09 15						10 00	10 10	10 15		10 17	10 47
Wigan North Western	a									09 10			09 35						10 10		10 36		10 28	
	d									09 11			09 36						10 11		10 36		10 28	
Blackrod	d																							
Lostock	d																							
Bolton	a	04u35	06u35	08 37							09 34									10 34				11 08
Manchester Piccadilly	a	05u00	07u00	08 59							09 57									10 57				11 27
Manchester Airport	a	05 25	07 25	09 19							10 17									11 18				11 47
Liverpool Lime Street	a												10 24								11 24			
	d						08 15		08 38							09 38								
Liverpool South Parkway	d																							
Runcorn	d						08 35		08 54							09 54								
Warrington Bank Quay	a									09 21									10 21				10 39	
	d									09 22									10 22				10 39	
Hartford	d																							
Manchester Piccadilly	d				08 05	08 20		08 27				09 20		09 27								10 20		
Stockport	d				08 14	08 28		08 36				09 27		09 36								10 29		
Wilmslow	d				08 22			08 43														10 37		
Holyhead	d																							
Bangor (Gwynedd)	d																							
Llandudno Junction	d																							
Wrexham General	d																							
Chester	d																							
Crewe	a				08 39		08 52	09 02	09 11	09 41						10 12			10 41			10 53	11 00	
	d				08 43		08 53	09 05	09 13	09 43					09 53	10 14	10 20	10 37	10 43			10 55	11 03	
Macclesfield	d					08 42						09 40		09 49										
Congleton	d																							
Stoke-on-Trent	d					08 59						09 57		10 07	10 41			10 58						
Stafford	a				09 00			09 25	09 31					10 26	11 17	10 32	10 41	11 17						
	d				09 02			09 26	09 32					10 27		10 33	10 42							
Penkridge	a																10 48							
Wolverhampton	a							09 40						10 42			11 00						11 33	
Birmingham New Street	a							09 58						10 59			11 17						11 56	
Birmingham International	a							10 13						11 13										
Coventry	a							10 24						11 24										
Lichfield Trent Valley	a																							
Tamworth Low Level	a																							
Nuneaton	a								09 54							10 55								
Rugby	a									10 31									11 31					
Milton Keynes Central	a						10 17			11 06		11 12				11 49			12 05					
Watford Junction	a				10s34	10s39			11s16	11s42												12s34		
London Euston	a				10 56	11 00	11 06		11 39	12 04		12 07				12 37			12 44			12 56		

OVERNIGHT SLEEPERS. For sleeper trains, operated by First ScotRail, please refer to Tables 400 - 404

Table 65

Sundays

18 July to 05 September

Scotland and North West England - West Midlands and London

		XC	VT	VT	VT	TP	NT	VT	VT	VT	XC	LM	VT	VT	LM	VT	VT	TP	VT	NT	VT	VT	TP	XC	LM
		◇1	◇1	◇1	◇1	◇1		◇1	◇1	◇1	◇1	1	◇1	◇1	1	◇1	◇1	◇1	◇1		◇1	◇1	◇1	◇1	1
		⊼	☕	☕	☕			☕	☕	☕	⊼		☕	☕		☕	☕		☕		☕	☕		⊼	
Inverness	d																								
Aberdeen	d																								
Dundee	d																								
Perth	d																								
Edinburgh 10	d																								
Haymarket	d																								
Glasgow Central 15	d																09 37								
Motherwell	d																								
Carstairs	d																								
Lockerbie	d																								
Carlisle 8	a																10 44								
	d																10 46								
Penrith North Lakes	d																11 00								
Windermere	d																								
Oxenholme Lake District	a																11 22								
	d																11 23								
Barrow-in-Furness	d																						11 23		
Lancaster 6	a																11 37						12 26		
	d																11 38					12 00	12 26		
Preston 8	a																11 56					12 15	12 45		
Blackpool North	d					10 44	10 50											11 44		11 50					
Preston 8	d				10 58	11 10	11 15			11 17							11 58	12 10		12 15		12 17	12 47		
Wigan North Western	a				11 09		11 35			11 28							12 09			12 35		12 28			
	d				11 09		11 36			11 28							12 09			12 36		12 28			
Blackrod	d																								
Lostock	d																								
Bolton	a					11 34												12 34					13 08		
Manchester Piccadilly 10	a					11 57												12 57					13 27		
Manchester Airport ✈	a					12 17												13 17					13 47		
Liverpool Lime Street 10	a						12 24													13 24					
	d			10 38								11 34		11 48											12 34
Liverpool South Parkway ✈	d											11 44													12 44
Runcorn	d			10 54								11 52		12 04											12 52
Warrington Bank Quay	a				11 20					11 39							12 20					12 39			
	d				11 20					11 39							12 20					12 39			
Hartford	d											12 04													13 03
Manchester Piccadilly 10	d	10 24	10 35					11 15			11 27		11 35			11 55			12 15					12 26	
Stockport	d	10 34	10 43					11 23			11 36		11 43			12 05			12 23					12 36	
Wilmslow	d															12 12									
Holyhead	d																				10 55				
Bangor (Gwynedd)	d																				11 22				
Llandudno Junction	d																				11 40				
Wrexham General	d																								
Chester	d								11 28												12 33				
Crewe 10	a			11 12					11 47	11 59		12 19				12 28					12 52	12 59			13 19
	d			11 14					11 49	12 01		12 22				12 30					12 54	13 01			13 22
Macclesfield	d	10 47	10 56								11 49		11 56											12 49	
Congleton	d																								
Stoke-on-Trent	d	11 07	11 13					11 51			12 07		12 13		←				12 51					13 07	
Stafford	a	11 27		11 32							12 24	12 41		12 35	12 41									13 24	13 42
	d	11 28		11 33							12 25	12 42		12 36	12 42									13 25	13 43
Penkridge	a											→			12 48										→
Wolverhampton 7	a	11 42								12 32	12 40				12 59							13 31		13 40	
Birmingham New Street 12	a	12 00								12 55	12 58				13 16							13 55		13 58	
Birmingham International ✈	a	12 13									13 13													14 13	
Coventry	a	12 24									13 24													14 24	
Lichfield Trent Valley	a																								
Tamworth Low Level	a																								
Nuneaton	a			12 04					12 30																
Rugby	a																								
Milton Keynes Central	a		12 19					12 50	13 03										13 50		14 04				
Watford Junction	a			12s54																					
London Euston 15 ⊖	a		13 00	13 15	13 23			13 31	13 44				13 49	14 06		14 12	14 17		14 30		14 45				

OVERNIGHT SLEEPERS. For sleeper trains, operated by First ScotRail, please refer to Tables 400 - 404

Table 65

Sundays

18 July to 05 September

Scotland and North West England - West Midlands and London

		VT		VT	LM	VT	VT	TP	XC	VT	VT	VT	NT	TP	XC	LM	VT	VT	LM	VT	VT	TP	NT	XC	VT
		◇1		◇1	1	◇1	◇1	◇1	◇1	◇1	◇1	◇1		◇1	◇1	1	◇1	◇1	1	◇1	◇1	◇1		◇1	◇1
		☕		☕		☕	☕		⊼	☕	☕	☕		⊼	⊼		☕	☕		☕	☕			⊼	☕
Inverness	d																								
Aberdeen	d																								
Dundee	d																								
Perth	d																								
Edinburgh 10	d											10 52		11 10											
Haymarket	d											10 57		11u14											
Glasgow Central 15	d						10 32														11 32				
Motherwell	d						10u49																		
Carstairs	d																								
Lockerbie	d													12 08											
Carlisle 8	a						11 44					12 05		12 30							12 47				
	d						11 46					12 07		12 32							12 49				
Penrith North Lakes	d						12 00							12 46											
Windermere	d																								
Oxenholme Lake District	a						12 22					12 41		13 10							13 22				
	d						12 24					12 43		13 10							13 23				
Barrow-in-Furness	d																								
Lancaster 6	a						12 37					12 56		13 26							13 37				
	d						12 38					12 57		13 26							13 38				
Preston 8	a						12 56					13 15		13 45							13 56				
Blackpool North	d							12 44					12 50									13 44	13 50		
Preston 8	d						12 58	13 10				13 17	13 15	13 47							13 58	14 10	14 15		
Wigan North Western	a						13 09					13 28	13 35								14 09		14 35		
	d						13 09					13 28	13 36								14 09		14 36		
Blackrod	d																								
Lostock	d																								
Bolton	a							13 34						14 08								14 34			
Manchester Piccadilly 10	a							13 57						14 27								14 57			
Manchester Airport ✈	a							14 17						14 47								15 17			
Liverpool Lime Street 10	a												14 24										15 24		
	d			12 48												13 34		13 48							
Liverpool South Parkway ✈	d															13 44									
Runcorn	d			13 04												13 52		14 04							
Warrington Bank Quay	a						13 20					13 39									14 20				
	d						13 20					13 39									14 20				
Hartford	d															14 03									
Manchester Piccadilly 10	d	12 35				12 55			13 07	13 15					13 27		13 35			13 55				14 07	14 15
Stockport	d	12 44				13 05				13 22					13 36		13 42			14 04					14 22
Wilmslow	d					13 12														14 11					
Holyhead	d										11 50														
Bangor (Gwynedd)	d										12 17														
Llandudno Junction	d										12 35														
Wrexham General	d																								
Chester	d										13b30														
Crewe 10	a					13 28					13 49	13 59				14 18				14 27					
	d					13 30					13 51	14 01				14 22				14 29					
Macclesfield	d	12 57													13 49		13 55								
Congleton	d																								
Stoke-on-Trent	d	13 14			←				13 43	13 50					14 07		14 12		←					14 43	14 50
Stafford	a			13 35	13 42										14 24	14 42		14 35	14 42						
	d			13 36	13 43										14 25	14 43		14 36	14 43						
Penkridge	a				13 48											→			14 48						
Wolverhampton 7	a				13 58				14 13			14 32			14 40				14 58					15 13	
Birmingham New Street 12	a				14 15				14 31			14 55			14 58				15 15					15 31	
Birmingham International ✈	a														15 13										
Coventry	a														15 24										
Lichfield Trent Valley	a																								
Tamworth Low Level	a																								
Nuneaton	a										14 31														
Rugby	a																								
Milton Keynes Central	a									14 49	15 04														15 49
Watford Junction	a																								
London Euston 15 ⊖	a	14 50		15 03		15 11	15 14			15 30	15 45						15 48	16 03		16 11	16 14				16 30

barr. 1323

OVERNIGHT SLEEPERS. For sleeper trains, operated by First ScotRail, please refer to Tables 400 - 404

Table 65

Sundays

18 July to 05 September

Scotland and North West England - West Midlands and London

Station		VT ◇1	VT ◇1	TP ◇1	XC ◇1	LM 1	VT ◇1	VT ◇1	LM 1	VT ◇1	VT ◇1	TP ◇1	NT	XC ◇1	VT ◇1	VT ◇1	VT ◇1	TP ◇1	XC ◇1	LM 1	VT ◇1	VT ◇1	LM 1	VT ◇1
Inverness	d																							
Aberdeen	d																							
Dundee	d																							
Perth	d																							
Edinburgh 10	d																12 52	13 09						
Haymarket	d																12 56	13u13						
Glasgow Central 15	d		11 52								12 42													
Motherwell	d																							
Carstairs	d																							
Lockerbie	d																	14 08						
Carlisle 8	a		13 09								13 51						14 05	14 30						
	d		13 10								13 54						14 07	14 32						
Penrith North Lakes	d																14 22	14 46						
Windermere	d																							
Oxenholme Lake District	a										14 27							15 10						
	d										14 28							15 10						
Barrow-in-Furness	d			13 23																				
Lancaster 6	a		13 56	14 26							14 42						14 56	15 25						
	d		13 58	14 26							14 43						14 57	15 25						
Preston 8	a		14 15	14 45							15 01						15 15	15 45						
Blackpool North	d											14 44	14 50											
Preston 8	d		14 17	14 47							15 03	15 10	15 15				15 17	15 47						
Wigan North Western	a		14 28								15 14		15 35				15 28							
	d		14 28								15 14		15 36				15 28							
Blackrod	d																							
Lostock	d																							
Bolton	a			15 08								15 34						16 08						
Manchester Piccadilly 10	a			15 27								15 57						16 27						
Manchester Airport ✈	a			15 47								16 17						16 47						
Liverpool Lime Street 10	a												16 24											
	d					14 34		14 48												15 34		15 48		
Liverpool South Parkway ✈	d					14 44														15 44				
Runcorn	d					14 52		15 04												15 52		16 04		
Warrington Bank Quay	a		14 39								15 25						15 39							
	d		14 39								15 25						15 39							
Hartford	d					15 03														16 03				
Manchester Piccadilly 10	d				14 27		14 35			14 55				15 07	15 15				15 27		15 35			15 55
Stockport	d				14 36		14 42			15 04					15 22				15 36		15 42			16 04
Wilmslow	d									15 11														16 11
Holyhead	d	12 50														13 55								
Bangor (Gwynedd)	d	13 18														14 22								
Llandudno Junction	d	13 36														14 40								
Wrexham General	d																							
Chester	d	14b33														15 33								
Crewe 10	a	14 54	14 59			15 20				15 27						15 54	15 59			16 18				16 27
	d	14 56	15 01			15 22				15 29						15 56	16 01			16 22				16 29
Macclesfield	d				14 49		14 55												15 49		15 55			
Congleton	d																							
Stoke-on-Trent	d				15 07		15 12		←					15 43	15 50				16 07		16 12		←	
Stafford	a				15 24	15 42		15 35	15 42										16 24	16 42		16 36	16 42	
	d				15 25	15 43		15 36	15 43										16 25	16 43		16 37	16 43	
Penkridge	a					→			15 48											→			16 48	
Wolverhampton 7	a		15 31		15 40				15 58					16 13			16 32		16 40				16 58	
Birmingham New Street 12	a		15 55		15 58				16 15					16 31			16 56		16 58				17 15	
Birmingham International ✈	a				16 13														17 13					
Coventry	a				16 24														17 24					
Lichfield Trent Valley	a																							
Tamworth Low Level	a																							
Nuneaton	a																							
Rugby	a																							
Milton Keynes Central	a	16 04													16 49	17 03								
Watford Junction	a																							
London Euston 15 ⊖	a	16 44					16 48	17 03		17 11	17 23				17 30	17 44					17 48	18 04		18 11

b arr. 1426

OVERNIGHT SLEEPERS. For sleeper trains, operated by First ScotRail, please refer to Tables 400 - 404

Table 65

Sundays

18 July to 05 September

Scotland and North West England - West Midlands and London

Station		VT ◇1	TP ◇1	XC ◇1	NT	VT ◇1	VT ◇1	VT ◇1	TP ◇1	NT	XC ◇1	LM 1	VT ◇1	VT ◇1	LM 1	VT ◇1	VT ◇1	TP ◇1	XC ◇1	VT ◇1	VT ◇1	VT ◇1	TP ◇1	NT
Inverness	d																							
Aberdeen	d																							
Dundee	d																							
Perth	d																							
Edinburgh 10	d																					14 52		
Haymarket	d																					14 57		
Glasgow Central 15	d	13 34						13 55									14 35							
Motherwell	d																							
Carstairs	d																							
Lockerbie	d																							
Carlisle 8	a	14 46						15 08									15 47					16 05		
	d	14 49						15 09		15 35							15 49					16 07		
Penrith North Lakes	d																					16 22		
Windermere	d																							
Oxenholme Lake District	a	15 22						15 44									16 22							
	d	15 23						15 44									16 23							
Barrow-in-Furness	d								15 23														16 25	
Lancaster 6	a	15 37							16 26								16 37					16 56	17 17	
	d	15 38							16 26								16 38					16 57	17 17	
Preston 8	a	15 56						16 13	16 45	18 50							16 56					17 15	17 37	
Blackpool North	d		15 44		15 50													16 44						16 50
Preston 8	d	15 58	16 10		16 15			16 15	16 47								16 58	17 10				17 17		17 15
Wigan North Western	a	16 09			16 35			16 26									17 09					17 28		17 35
	d	16 09			16 36			16 26									17 09					17 28		17 36
Blackrod	d																							
Lostock	d																							
Bolton	a		16 34						17 08									17 34						
Manchester Piccadilly 10	a		16 57						17 27									17 57						
Manchester Airport ✈	a		17 17						17 47									18 17						
Liverpool Lime Street 10	a				17 24																			18 24
	d						16 18					16 34		16 48										
Liverpool South Parkway ✈	d											16 44												
Runcorn	d						16 34					16 52		17 04										
Warrington Bank Quay	a	16 20						16 37									17 20					17 39		
	d	16 20						16 37									17 20					17 39		
Hartford	d											17 03												
Manchester Piccadilly 10	d			16 07		16 15					16 27		16 35			16 55			17 07	17 15				
Stockport	d					16 23					16 36		16 42			17 04				17 22				
Wilmslow	d															17 11								
Holyhead	d																							
Bangor (Gwynedd)	d																							
Llandudno Junction	d																							
Wrexham General	d																							
Chester	d																				17 35			
Crewe 10	a						16 50	16 57				17 18				17 27					17 53	17 59		
	d						16 53	16 59				17 22				17 29					17 55	18 01		
Macclesfield	d										16 49		16 55											
Congleton	d																							
Stoke-on-Trent	d			16 43		16 50					17 08		17 12		←				17 43	17 50				
Stafford	a										17 25	17 42		17 35	17 42									
	d										17 26	17 43		17 36	17 43									
Penkridge	a											→			17 48									
Wolverhampton 7	a			17 13				17 31			17 40				17 58				18 13			18 32		
Birmingham New Street 12	a			17 31				17 55			17 58				18 15				18 31			18 56		
Birmingham International ✈	a										18 13													
Coventry	a										18 24													
Lichfield Trent Valley	a						17 25																	
Tamworth Low Level	a																							
Nuneaton	a																							
Rugby	a																							
Milton Keynes Central	a					17 49	18 02													18 49	19 03			
Watford Junction	a																							
London Euston 15 ⊖	a	18 14				18 30	18 42						18 48	19 03		19 11	19 14			19 30	19 44			

OVERNIGHT SLEEPERS. For sleeper trains, operated by First ScotRail, please refer to Tables 400 - 404

Table 65

Sundays

18 July to 05 September

Scotland and North West England - West Midlands and London

		TP	TP	XC	LM	VT	VT	LM	VT	VT	TP	NT	XC	VT	VT	VT	TP	XC	LM	VT	VT	LM	VT
		◇1	◇1	◇1	1	◇1	◇1	1	◇1	◇1	◇1		◇1	◇1	◇1	◇1	◇1	◇1	1	◇1	◇1	1	◇1
		🛒		🛒		☕	☕		☕	☕			🛒	☕	☕	☕	🛒	🛒		☕	☕		☕
Inverness	d																						
Aberdeen	d																						
Dundee	d																						
Perth	d																						
Edinburgh 10	d																16 10						
Haymarket	d																16u14						
Glasgow Central 15	d	15 06								15 36						15 56							
Motherwell	d																						
Carstairs	d																						
Lockerbie	d	16 06															17 08						
Carlisle 8	a	16 28								16 46						17 08	17 30						
	d	16 30								16 49						17 09	17 32						
Penrith North Lakes	d	16 44								17 03							17 46						
Windermere	d		16 58																				
Oxenholme Lake District	a	17 08	17 15													17 44	18 10						
	d	17 08	17 16													17 44	18 10						
Barrow-in-Furness	d																						
Lancaster 6	a	17 23	17 31							17 37							18 26						
	d	17 23	17 32							17 38							18 26						
Preston 8	a	17 42	17 50							17 56						18 15	18 45						
Blackpool North	d										17 40	17 50											
Preston 8	d	17 47								17 58	18b10	18 14				18 17	18 47						
Wigan North Western	a									18 09		18 15				18 28							
	d									18 09		18 36				18 28							
Blackrod	d																						
Lostock	d																						
Bolton	a	18 08									18 34						19 08						
Manchester Piccadilly 10	a	18 27									18 57						19 27						
Manchester Airport	a	18 47									19 17						19 47						
Liverpool Lime Street 10	a											19 24											
	d				17 34		17 48												18 34		18 48		
Liverpool South Parkway	d				17 44														18 44				
Runcorn	d				17 52		18 04												18 52		19 04		
Warrington Bank Quay	a									18 20						18 39							
	d									18 20						18 39							
Hartford	d				18 03														19 03				
Manchester Piccadilly 10	d			17 27		17 35			17 55				18 07	18 15				18 27		18 35			18 55
Stockport	d			17 36		17 42			18 04					18 22				18 36		18 42			19 04
Wilmslow	d								18 11														19 11
Holyhead	d																						
Bangor (Gwynedd)	d																						
Llandudno Junction	d																						
Wrexham General	d																						
Chester	d														18 35								
Crewe 10	a				18 20				18 27						18 53	18 59			19 20				19 27
	d				18 22				18 29						18 55	19 01			19 22				19 29
Macclesfield	d			17 49		17 55												18 49		18 55			
Congleton	d																						
Stoke-on-Trent	d			18 08		18 12		←					18 43	18 50				19 07		19 12		←	
Stafford	a			18 25	18 42		18 35	18 42										19 24	19 42		19 35	19 42	
	d			18 26	18 43		18 36	18 43										19 25	19 43		19 36	19 43	
Penkridge	a				→			18 48											→			19 48	
Wolverhampton 7	a			18 40				18 58					19 13			19 31		19 40				19 58	
Birmingham New Street 12	a			18 58				19 15					19 31			19 55		19 58				20 15	
Birmingham International	a			19 13														20 13					
Coventry	a			19 24														20 24					
Lichfield Trent Valley	a																						
Tamworth Low Level	a																						
Nuneaton	a																						
Rugby	a																						
Milton Keynes Central	a													19 49	20 03								
Watford Junction	a																						
London Euston 15	a					19 48	20 03		20 11	20 15				20 30	20 44					20 48	21 04		21 14

b arr. 1804

OVERNIGHT SLEEPERS. For sleeper trains, operated by First ScotRail, please refer to Tables 400 - 404

Table 65

Sundays

18 July to 05 September

Scotland and North West England - West Midlands and London

		VT	TP	XC	VT	TP	NT	TP	VT	XC	LM	VT	VT	VT	TP	TP	NT	XC	AW	VT	LM	VT	VT	VT
		◇1	◇1	◇1	◇1	◇1		◇1	◇1	◇1	1	◇1	◇1	◇1	◇1	◇1		◇1	◇	◇1	1	◇1	◇1	◇1
		☕		🛒	☕			🛒	☕	🛒		☕	☕	☕		🛒		🛒		☕		☕	☕	☕
Inverness	d																							
Aberdeen	d																							
Dundee	d																							
Perth	d																							
Edinburgh 10	d				16 52											18 10								
Haymarket	d				16 56											18u14								
Glasgow Central 15	d	16 38						17 06						17 36										18 30
Motherwell	d	16 54																						
Carstairs	d																							
Lockerbie	d													18 32		19 08								
Carlisle 8	a	17 49			18 05			18 26						18 50		19 30								19 43
	d	17 51			18 07			18 28						18 52		19 32								19 44
Penrith North Lakes	d	18 05						18 42						19 06		19 46								
Windermere	d																							
Oxenholme Lake District	a	18 27			18 41			19 06						19 28		20 10								20 19
	d	18 28			18 42			19 07						19 29		20 10								20 19
Barrow-in-Furness	d					18 15																		
Lancaster 6	a	18 42			18 56	19 17		19 21						19 43		20 26								20 34
	d	18 43			18 57	19 17		19 22						19 44		20 26								20 34
Preston 8	a	19 01			19 15	19 37		19 41						20 02		20 45								20 52
Blackpool North	d		18 44				18 50								19 44		19 50							
Preston 8	d	19 03	19 10		19 17		19 14	19 47						20 04	20 10	20 47	20 14							20 55
Wigan North Western	a	19 14			19 28		19 15							20 15			20 15							21 06
	d	19 14			19 28		19 36							20 15			20 36							21 07
Blackrod	d																							
Lostock	d																							
Bolton	a		19 34					20 08							20 34	21 08								
Manchester Piccadilly 10	a		19 57					20 27							20 57	21 27								
Manchester Airport	a		20 17					20 47							21 17	21 47								
Liverpool Lime Street 10	a						20 24										21 24							
	d										19 34		19 48								20 34		20 48	
Liverpool South Parkway	d										19 44										20 44			
Runcorn	d										19 52		20 04								20 52		21 04	
Warrington Bank Quay	a	19 25			19 39									20 26										21 18
	d	19 25			19 39									20 26										21 18
Hartford	d										20 03										21 03			
Manchester Piccadilly 10	d			19 07					19 15	19 27		19 35						20 07		20 20		20 55		
Stockport	d								19 22	19 36		19 42						20 16		20 27		21 03		
Wilmslow	d																							
Holyhead	d																		18 25					
Bangor (Gwynedd)	d																		19 04					
Llandudno Junction	d																		19 24					
Wrexham General	d																							
Chester	d																		20b27					
Crewe 10	a				19 59						20 16		20 22	20 45					20 48		21 16		21 21	21 38
	d				20 01						20 18		20 24	20 47					20 54		21 17		21 23	21 40
Macclesfield	d									19 49		19 55						20 29		20 40		21 15		
Congleton	d																							
Stoke-on-Trent	d			19 43					19 50	20 07		20 12						20 47		20 57		21 33		
Stafford	a									20 24	20 37		20 41					21 08	21 16		21 37		21 42	22 01
	d									20 25	20 38		20 43					21 09	21 16		21 38		21 44	22 02
Penkridge	a										20 44										21 44			
Wolverhampton 7	a			20 13	20 31					20 39	20 55							21 21	21 34		21 55			22 16
Birmingham New Street 12	a			20 31	20 55					21 00	21 15							21 39	21 52		22 15			22 40
Birmingham International	a									21 13									22 09					
Coventry	a									21 23														
Lichfield Trent Valley	a																						21 58	
Tamworth Low Level	a																						22 04	
Nuneaton	a																						22 15	
Rugby	a																						22 28	
Milton Keynes Central	a								20 47				21 36	21 55						22 03		22 50	23 04	
Watford Junction	a													22s31								23s31	23s36	
London Euston 15	a	21 21							21 32			22 04	22 29	22 53						22 56		23 53	23 57	

b arr. 2019

OVERNIGHT SLEEPERS. For sleeper trains, operated by First ScotRail, please refer to Tables 400 - 404

Table 65

Sundays

18 July to 05 September

Scotland and North West England - West Midlands and London

		TP	NT	XC	VT	TP	TP	VT	LM	XC	TP	SR	SR
		◇1		◇1	◇1	◇1	◇1	◇1	1	◇1	◇1	B	B
Inverness	d												20 25
Aberdeen	d												21 40
Dundee	d												23u06
Perth	d												23u01
Edinburgh 10	d				18 52		19 57					23 26	
Haymarket	d				18 57		20u01						
Glasgow Central 15	d							20 05				21 39	
Motherwell	d											22u01	
Carstairs	d											22u22	
Lockerbie	d							21 02					
Carlisle 8	a				20 05		21 14	21 21					
	d				20 07		21 15	21 24					
Penrith North Lakes	d				20 22			21 39					
Windermere	d					20 40							
Oxenholme Lake District	a					20 59		22 02					
	d					21 01		22 03					
Barrow-in-Furness	d												
Lancaster 6	a				20 56	21 18	22 02	22 17					
	d				20 57	21 23	22 03	22 18					
Preston 8	a				21 15		22 23	22 35					
Blackpool North	d	20 44	20 50								23 03		
Preston 8	d	21 10	21 15		21 17		22 29	22 38			23 29		
Wigan North Western	a		21 15		21 28			22 49					
	d		21 36		21 28			22 50					
Blackrod	d										23 49		
Lostock	d										23 56		
Bolton	a	21 34					22 50				00 02		
Manchester Piccadilly 10	a	21 57					23 14				00 18		
Manchester Airport ✈	a	22 17					23 30				00 32		
Liverpool Lime Street 10	a		22 24										
	d								21 34				
Liverpool South Parkway ✈	d								21 44				
Runcorn	d								21 52				
Warrington Bank Quay	a				21 39			23 00					
	d				21 39			23 01					
Hartford	d								22 03				
Manchester Piccadilly 10	d			21 07						22 07			
Stockport	d			21 16						22 16			
Wilmslow	d												
Holyhead	d												
Bangor (Gwynedd)	d												
Llandudno Junction	d												
Wrexham General	d												
Chester	d												
Crewe 10	a				21 59			23 20	22 18				
	d				22 01				22 22				
Macclesfield	d			21 29						22 29			
Congleton	d												
Stoke-on-Trent	d			21 47						22 47			
Stafford	a			22 06					22 41	23 04			
	d			22 06					22 44	23 05			
Penkridge	a								22 50				
Wolverhampton 7	a			22 20	22 31				23 00	23 18			
Birmingham New Street 12	a			22 40	22 57				23 17	23 36			
Birmingham International ✈	a												
Coventry	a												
Lichfield Trent Valley	a												
Tamworth Low Level	a												
Nuneaton	a												
Rugby	a												
Milton Keynes Central	a												
Watford Junction	a												
London Euston 15 ⊖	a											07 06	08 30

OVERNIGHT SLEEPERS. For sleeper trains, operated by First ScotRail, please refer to Tables 400 - 404

Table 65

Sundays

12 September to 17 October

Scotland and North West England - West Midlands and London

		TP	TP	VT	TP	VT	VT	XC	VT	VT	TP	NT	VT	TP	XC	LM	VT	LM	LM	VT	TP	NT	VT	VT
				◇1	◇1	◇1	◇1	◇1	◇1	◇1	◇1		◇1	◇1	◇1		◇1	◇1	1	◇1	◇1		◇1	◇1
Inverness	d																							
Aberdeen	d																							
Dundee	d																							
Perth	d																							
Edinburgh 10	d																							
Haymarket	d																							
Glasgow Central 15	d																							
Motherwell	d																							
Carstairs	d																							
Lockerbie	d																							
Carlisle 8	a																							
	d																							
Penrith North Lakes	d																							
Windermere	d																							
Oxenholme Lake District	a																							
	d																							
Barrow-in-Furness	d													09 25										
Lancaster 6	a													10 17										
	d													10 21										
Preston 8	a													10 40										
Blackpool North	d	03 20	05 20		08 14						08 44	08 50									09 44	09 50		
Preston 8	d	04u00	06u00		08 42					09 00	09 10	09 15								10 00	10 10	10 15		10 17
Wigan North Western	a									09 10		09 35								10 10		10 36		10 28
	d									09 11		09 36								10 11		10 36		10 28
Blackrod	d																							
Lostock	d																							
Bolton	a	04u35	06u35		09 05						09 34										10 34			
Manchester Piccadilly 10	a	05u00	07u00		09 28						09 57										10 57			
Manchester Airport ✈	a	05 25	07 25		09 53						10 17										11 18			
Liverpool Lime Street 10	a											10 24										11 24		
	d						08 15		08 38								09 38							
Liverpool South Parkway ✈	d																							
Runcorn	d						08 35		08 54								09 54							
Warrington Bank Quay	a									09 21										10 21				10 39
	d									09 22										10 22				10 39
Hartford	d																							
Manchester Piccadilly 10	d			08 05		08 20		08 26					09 20		09 27								10 20	
Stockport	d			08 14		08 28		08 35					09 27		09 36								10 29	
Wilmslow	d			08 22				08 41															10 36	
Holyhead	d																							
Bangor (Gwynedd)	d																							
Llandudno Junction	d																							
Wrexham General	d																							
Chester	d																							
Crewe 10	a			08 39			08 52	09 01	09 11	09 41							10 12			10 41			10 52	11 00
	d			08 43			08 53	09 05	09 13	09 43						09 53	10 14	10 20	10 37	10 43			10 55	11 03
Macclesfield	d					08 42							09 40		09 49									
Congleton	d																							
Stoke-on-Trent	d					08 59							09 57		10 07	10 41			10 58					
Stafford	a			09 00				09 25	09 31						10 26	11 17	10 32	10 41	11 17					
	d			09 02				09 26	09 32						10 27		10 33	10 42						
Penkridge	a																	10 48						
Wolverhampton 7	a							09 40							10 42			11 00						
Birmingham New Street 12	a							09 58							10 59			11 17						11 33
Birmingham International ✈	a							10 13							11 13									11 56
Coventry	a							10 24							11 24									
Lichfield Trent Valley	a																							
Tamworth Low Level	a																							
Nuneaton	a								09 54								10 55							
Rugby	a									10 31										11 31				
Milton Keynes Central	a						10 17			11 06			11 12				11 49			12 05				
Watford Junction	a			10s34		10s39			11s16	11s42													12s34	
London Euston 15 ⊖	a			10 56		11 00	11 06		11 39	12 04			12 07				12 37			12 44			12 56	

OVERNIGHT SLEEPERS. For sleeper trains, operated by First ScotRail, please refer to Tables 400 - 404

Table 65

Sundays

12 September to 17 October

Scotland and North West England - West Midlands and London

		XC	VT	VT	VT	TP	NT	VT	VT	VT	XC	LM	VT	VT	LM	VT	VT	TP	NT	VT	VT	VT	TP	XC	LM
		◇1	◇1	◇1	◇1	◇1		◇1	◇1	◇1	◇1	1	◇1	◇1	1	◇1	◇1	◇1		◇1	◇1	◇1	◇1	◇1	1
Inverness	d																								
Aberdeen	d																								
Dundee	d																								
Perth	d																								
Edinburgh 10	d																								
Haymarket	d																								
Glasgow Central 15	d																09 37								
Motherwell	d																								
Carstairs	d																								
Lockerbie	d																								
Carlisle 8	a																10 44								
	d																10 46								
Penrith North Lakes	d																11 00								
Windermere	d																								
Oxenholme Lake District	a																11 22								
	d																11 23								
Barrow-in-Furness	d																						11 23		
Lancaster 6	a																11 37						12 26		
	d																11 38					12 00	12 26		
Preston 8	a																11 56					12 15	12 45		
Blackpool North	d					10 44	10 50											11 44	11 50						
Preston 8	d				10 58	11 10	11 15			11 17							11 58	12 10	12 15			12 17	12 47		
Wigan North Western	a				11 09		11 35			11 28							12 09		12 35			12 28			
	d				11 09		11 36			11 28							12 09		12 36			12 28			
Blackrod	d																								
Lostock	d																								
Bolton	a					11 34												12 34					13 08		
Manchester Piccadilly 10	a					11 57												12 56					13 27		
Manchester Airport	a					12 17												13 17					13 47		
Liverpool Lime Street 10	a						12 24												13 24						
	d			10 38								11 34		11 48											12 34
Liverpool South Parkway	d											11 44													12 44
Runcorn	d			10 54								11 52		12 04											12 52
Warrington Bank Quay	a				11 20					11 39							12 20					12 39			
	d				11 20					11 39							12 20					12 39			
Hartford	d											12 04													13 03
Manchester Piccadilly 10	d	10 27	10 35					11 15			11 27		11 35			11 55				12 15				12 26	
Stockport	d	10 36	10 42					11 23			11 36		11 43			12 05				12 23				12 35	
Wilmslow	d															12 12									
Holyhead	d																				10 55				
Bangor (Gwynedd)	d																				11 22				
Llandudno Junction	d																				11 40				
Wrexham General	d																								
Chester	d								11 28												12 33				
Crewe 10	a			11 12					11 47	11 59		12 19				12 28					12 52	12 59			13 19
	d			11 14					11 49	12 01		12 22				12 30					12 54	13 01			13 22
Macclesfield	d	10 49	10 55								11 49		11 56											12 49	
Congleton	d																								
Stoke-on-Trent	d	11 07	11 12					11 51			12 07		12 13		←					12 51				13 07	
Stafford	a	11 26		11 32							12 24	12 41		12 35	12 41									13 24	13 42
	d	11 27		11 33							12 25	12 42		12 36	12 42									13 25	13 43
Penkridge	a											→			12 48										→
Wolverhampton 7	a	11 41								12 32	12 40				12 59							13 31		13 40	
Birmingham New Street 12	a	12 00								12 55	12 58				13 16							13 55		13 58	
Birmingham International	a	12 13									13 13													14 13	
Coventry	a	12 24									13 24													14 24	
Lichfield Trent Valley	a																								
Tamworth Low Level	a																								
Nuneaton	a			12 04					12 30																
Rugby	a																								
Milton Keynes Central	a		12 19					12 50	13 03											13 50	14 04				
Watford Junction	a			12s54																					
London Euston 15	a		12 59	13 15	13 23			13 31	13 44				13 49	14 06		14 12	14 17			14 30	14 45				

OVERNIGHT SLEEPERS. For sleeper trains, operated by First ScotRail, please refer to Tables 400 - 404

Table 65

Sundays

12 September to 17 October

Scotland and North West England - West Midlands and London

		VT			VT	LM	VT	VT	TP	XC	VT	VT	NT	VT	TP	XC	LM	VT	VT	LM	VT	VT		TP	XC
		◇1			◇1	1	◇1	◇1	◇1	◇1	◇1	◇1		◇1	◇1	◇1	1	◇1	◇1	1	◇1	◇1		◇1	◇1
Inverness	d																								
Aberdeen	d																								
Dundee	d																								
Perth	d																								
Edinburgh 10	d													10 52	11 10										
Haymarket	d													10 57	11u14										
Glasgow Central 15	d							10 32														11 32			
Motherwell	d							10u49																	
Carstairs	d																								
Lockerbie	d														12 08										
Carlisle 8	a							11 44						12 05	12 30							12 47			
	d							11 46						12 07	12 32							12 49			
Penrith North Lakes	d							12 00							12 46										
Windermere	d																								
Oxenholme Lake District	a							12 22						12 41	13 10							13 22			
	d							12 24						12 43	13 10							13 23			
Barrow-in-Furness	d																								
Lancaster 6	a							12 37						12 56	13 26							13 37			
	d							12 38						12 57	13 26							13 38			
Preston 8	a							12 56						13 15	13 45							13 56			
Blackpool North	d								12 44				12 50											13 44	
Preston 8	d							12 58	13 10				13 15	13 17	13 47							13 58		14 10	
Wigan North Western	a							13 09					13 35	13 28								14 09			
	d							13 09					13 36	13 28								14 09			
Blackrod	d																								
Lostock	d																								
Bolton	a								13 34						14 08									14 34	
Manchester Piccadilly 10	a								13 57						14 27									14 57	
Manchester Airport	a								14 17						14 47									15 17	
Liverpool Lime Street 10	a												14 24												
	d				12 48												13 34		13 48						
Liverpool South Parkway	d																13 44								
Runcorn	d				13 04												13 52		14 04						
Warrington Bank Quay	a							13 20						13 39								14 20			
	d							13 20						13 39								14 20			
Hartford	d																14 03								
Manchester Piccadilly 10	d	12 35					12 55			13 07	13 15					13 27		13 35			13 55				14 07
Stockport	d	12 44					13 05				13 22					13 36		13 42			14 04				
Wilmslow	d						13 12														14 11				
Holyhead	d											11 50													
Bangor (Gwynedd)	d											12 17													
Llandudno Junction	d											12 35													
Wrexham General	d																								
Chester	d											13b30													
Crewe 10	a						13 28					13 49		13 59			14 18				14 27				
	d						13 30					13 51		14 01			14 22				14 29				
Macclesfield	d	12 57														13 49		13 55							
Congleton	d																								
Stoke-on-Trent	d	13 14				←				13 43	13 50					14 07		14 12		←					14 43
Stafford	a				13 35	13 42										14 24	14 42		14 35	14 42					
	d				13 36	13 43										14 25	14 43		14 36	14 43					
Penkridge	a					13 48											→			14 48					
Wolverhampton 7	a					13 58				14 13				14 32		14 40				14 58					15 13
Birmingham New Street 12	a					14 15				14 31				14 55		14 58				15 15					15 31
Birmingham International	a															15 13									
Coventry	a															15 24									
Lichfield Trent Valley	a																								
Tamworth Low Level	a																								
Nuneaton	a											14 31													
Rugby	a																								
Milton Keynes Central	a										14 49	15 04													
Watford Junction	a																								
London Euston 15	a	14 50			15 03		15 11	15 14			15 30	15 45						15 48	16 03		16 11	16 14			

b arr. 1323

OVERNIGHT SLEEPERS. For sleeper trains, operated by First ScotRail, please refer to Tables 400 - 404

Table 65

Sundays

12 September to 17 October

Scotland and North West England - West Midlands and London

		VT	NT	VT	VT	TP	XC	LM	VT	VT	LM	VT	VT	TP	XC	VT	VT	VT	NT	TP	XC	LM	VT	VT	LM
		◇1		◇1	◇1	◇1	◇1	1	◇1	◇1	1	◇1	◇1	◇1	◇1	◇1	◇1	◇1		◇1	◇1	1	◇1	◇1	1
Inverness	d																								
Aberdeen	d																								
Dundee	d																								
Perth	d																								
Edinburgh 10	d																	12 52		13 09					
Haymarket	d																	12 56		13u13					
Glasgow Central 15	d				11 52								12 42												
Motherwell	d																								
Carstairs	d																								
Lockerbie	d																			14 08					
Carlisle 8	a				13 09								13 51					14 05		14 30					
	d				13 10								13 54					14 07		14 32					
Penrith North Lakes	d																	14 22		14 46					
Windermere	d																								
Oxenholme Lake District	a												14 27							15 10					
	d												14 28							15 10					
Barrow-in-Furness	d					13 23																			
Lancaster 6	a				13 56	14 26							14 42					14 56		15 25					
	d				13 58	14 26							14 43					14 57		15 25					
Preston 8	a				14 15	14 45							15 01					15 15		15 45					
Blackpool North	d		13 50											14 44					14 50						
Preston 8	d		14 15		14 17	14 47							15 03	15 10				15 17	15 15	15 47					
Wigan North Western	a		14 35		14 28								15 14					15 28	15 35						
	d		14 36		14 28								15 14					15 28	15 36						
Blackrod	d																								
Lostock	d																								
Bolton	a					15 08								15 34						16 08					
Manchester Piccadilly 10	a					15 27								15 57						16 27					
Manchester Airport	a					15 47								16 17						16 47					
Liverpool Lime Street 10	a		15 24																16 24						
	d							14 34		14 48												15 34		15 48	
Liverpool South Parkway	d							14 44														15 44			
Runcorn	d							14 52		15 04												15 52		16 04	
Warrington Bank Quay	a				14 39								15 25					15 39							
	d				14 39								15 25					15 39							
Hartford	d							15 03														16 03			
Manchester Piccadilly 10	d	14 15					14 27		14 35			14 55			15 07	15 15					15 27		15 35		
Stockport	d	14 22					14 36		14 42			15 04				15 22					15 36		15 42		
Wilmslow	d											15 11													
Holyhead	d			12 50													13 55								
Bangor (Gwynedd)	d			13 18													14 22								
Llandudno Junction	d			13 36													14 40								
Wrexham General	d																								
Chester	d			14b33													15 33								
Crewe 10	a			14 54	14 59			15 20				15 27					15 54	15 59				16 18			
	d			14 56	15 01			15 22				15 29					15 56	16 01				16 22			
Macclesfield	d						14 49		14 55												15 49		15 55		
Congleton	d																								
Stoke-on-Trent	d	14 50					15 07		15 12		←				15 43	15 50					16 07		16 12		←
Stafford	a						15 24	15 42		15 35	15 42										16 24	16 42		16 36	16 42
	d						15 25	15 43		15 36	15 43										16 25	16 43		16 37	16 43
Penkridge	a							→			15 48											→			16 48
Wolverhampton 7	a				15 31		15 40				15 58				16 13			16 32			16 40				16 58
Birmingham New Street 12	a				15 55		15 58				16 15				16 31			16 56			16 58				17 15
Birmingham International	a						16 13														17 13				
Coventry	a						16 24														17 24				
Lichfield Trent Valley	a																								
Tamworth Low Level	a																								
Nuneaton	a																								
Rugby	a																								
Milton Keynes Central	a	15 49		16 04												16 49	17 03								
Watford Junction	a																								
London Euston 15 ⊖	a	16 30		16 44					16 48	17 03		17 11	17 23			17 30	17 44						17 48	18 04	

b arr. 1426

OVERNIGHT SLEEPERS. For sleeper trains, operated by First ScotRail, please refer to Tables 400 - 404

Table 65

Sundays

12 September to 17 October

Scotland and North West England - West Midlands and London

		VT	VT	TP	NT	XC	VT	VT	VT	TP	XC	LM	VT	VT		LM	VT	VT	TP	XC	VT	VT	VT	TP	NT
		◇1	◇1	◇1		◇1	◇1	◇1	◇1	◇1	◇1	1	◇1	◇1		1	◇1	◇1	◇1	◇1	◇1	◇1	◇1	◇1	
Inverness	d																								
Aberdeen	d																								
Dundee	d																								
Perth	d																								
Edinburgh 10	d																						14 52		
Haymarket	d																						14 57		
Glasgow Central 15	d		13 34						13 55									14 35						15 06	
Motherwell	d																								
Carstairs	d																								
Lockerbie	d																							16 06	
Carlisle 8	a		14 46						15 08									15 47					16 05	16 28	
	d		14 49						15 09									15 49					16 07	16 30	
Penrith North Lakes	d																						16 22	16 44	
Windermere	d																								
Oxenholme Lake District	a		15 22						15 44									16 22						17 08	
	d		15 23						15 44									16 23						17 08	
Barrow-in-Furness	d									15 23															
Lancaster 6	a		15 37							16 26								16 37					16 56	17 23	
	d		15 38							16 26								16 38					16 57	17 23	
Preston 8	a		15 56						16 13	16 45								16 56					17 15	17 42	
Blackpool North	d			15 44	15 50														16 44						16 50
Preston 8	d		15 58	16 10	16 15				16 15	16 47								16 58	17 10				17 17	17 47	17 15
Wigan North Western	a		16 09		16 35				16 26									17 09					17 28		17 35
	d		16 09		16 36				16 26									17 09					17 28		17 36
Blackrod	d																								
Lostock	d																								
Bolton	a			16 34						17 08									17 34					18 08	
Manchester Piccadilly 10	a			16 57						17 27									17 57					18 27	
Manchester Airport	a			17 17						17 47									18 17					18 47	
Liverpool Lime Street 10	a				17 24																				18 24
	d							16 18				16 34		16 48											
Liverpool South Parkway	d											16 44													
Runcorn	d							16 34				16 52		17 04											
Warrington Bank Quay	a		16 20						16 37									17 20					17 39		
	d		16 20						16 37									17 20					17 39		
Hartford	d											17 03													
Manchester Piccadilly 10	d	15 55				16 07	16 15				16 27		16 35				16 55			17 07	17 15				
Stockport	d	16 04					16 23				16 36		16 42				17 04				17 22				
Wilmslow	d	16 11															17 11								
Holyhead	d																								
Bangor (Gwynedd)	d																								
Llandudno Junction	d																								
Wrexham General	d																								
Chester	d																					17 35			
Crewe 10	a	16 27						16 50	16 57			17 18					17 27					17 53	17 59		
	d	16 29						16 53	16 59			17 22					17 29					17 55	18 01		
Macclesfield	d										16 49		16 55												
Congleton	d																								
Stoke-on-Trent	d					16 43	16 50				17 08		17 12			←				17 43	17 50				
Stafford	a										17 25	17 42		17 35		17 42									
	d										17 26	17 43		17 36		17 43									
Penkridge	a											→				17 48									
Wolverhampton 7	a					17 13			17 31		17 40					17 58				18 13			18 32		
Birmingham New Street 12	a					17 31			17 55		17 58					18 15				18 31			18 56		
Birmingham International	a										18 13														
Coventry	a										18 24														
Lichfield Trent Valley	a							17 25																	
Tamworth Low Level	a																								
Nuneaton	a																								
Rugby	a																								
Milton Keynes Central	a						17 49	18 02													18 49	19 03			
Watford Junction	a																								
London Euston 15 ⊖	a	18 11	18 14				18 30	18 42					18 48	19 03			19 11	19 14			19 30	19 44			

OVERNIGHT SLEEPERS. For sleeper trains, operated by First ScotRail, please refer to Tables 400 - 404

Table 65

12 September to 17 October

Scotland and North West England - West Midlands and London

		XC	LM	VT	VT	LM	VT	VT	TP	XC	NT	VT	VT	VT	TP		XC	LM	VT	VT		LM	VT	VT	TP
		◇1	1	◇1	◇1	1	◇1	◇1	◇1	◇1		◇1	◇1	◇1	◇1		◇1	1	◇1	◇1		1	◇1	◇1	◇1
		⊼		⊞	⊞		⊞	⊞		⊼		⊞	⊞	⊞	⊼		⊼		⊞	⊞			⊞	⊞	
Inverness	d																								
Aberdeen	d																								
Dundee	d																								
Perth	d																								
Edinburgh 10	d														16 10										
Haymarket	d														16u14										
Glasgow Central 15	d							15 36						15 56										16 38	
Motherwell	d																							16 54	
Carstairs	d																								
Lockerbie	d														17 08										
Carlisle 8	a							16 46						17 08	17 30									17 49	
	d							16 49						17 09	17 32									17 51	
Penrith North Lakes	d							17 03							17 46									18 05	
Windermere	d																								
Oxenholme Lake District	a													17 44	18 10									18 27	
	d													17 44	18 10									18 28	
Barrow-in-Furness	d																								
Lancaster 6	a							17 37							18 26									18 42	
	d							17 38							18 26									18 43	
Preston 8	a							17 56						18 15	18 45									19 01	
Blackpool North	d								17 44		17 50														18 44
Preston 8	d							17 58	18 10		18 14			18 17	18 47									19 03	19 10
Wigan North Western	a							18 09			18 15			18 28										19 14	
	d							18 09			18 36			18 28										19 14	
Blackrod	d																								
Lostock	d																								
Bolton	a								18 34						19 08										19 34
Manchester Piccadilly 10	a								18 57						19 27										19 57
Manchester Airport ✈	a								19 17						19 47										20 17
Liverpool Lime Street 10	a										19 24														
	d		17 34		17 48													18 34		18 48					
Liverpool South Parkway ✈	d		17 44															18 44							
Runcorn	d		17 52		18 04													18 52		19 04					
Warrington Bank Quay	a							18 20						18 39										19 25	
	d							18 20						18 39										19 25	
Hartford	d		18 03															19 03							
Manchester Piccadilly 10	d	17 27		17 35			17 55			18 07		18 15					18 27		18 35				18 55		
Stockport	d	17 36		17 42			18 04					18 22					18 36		18 42				19 04		
Wilmslow	d						18 11																19 11		
Holyhead	d																								
Bangor (Gwynedd)	d																								
Llandudno Junction	d																								
Wrexham General	d																								
Chester	d												18 35												
Crewe 10	a		18 20				18 27						18 53	18 59				19 20					19 27		
	d		18 22				18 29						18 55	19 01				19 22					19 29		
Macclesfield	d	17 49		17 55													18 49		18 55						
Congleton	d																								
Stoke-on-Trent	d	18 08		18 12		←				18 43		18 50					19 07		19 12			←			
Stafford	a	18 25	18 42		18 35	18 42											19 24	19 42		19 35		19 42			
	d	18 26	18 43		18 36	18 43											19 25	19 43		19 36		19 43			
Penkridge	a		→			18 48												→				19 48			
Wolverhampton 7	a	18 40				18 58				19 13				19 31			19 40					19 58			
Birmingham New Street 12	a	18 58				19 15				19 31				19 55			19 58					20 15			
Birmingham International ✈	a	19 13															20 13								
Coventry	a	19 24															20 24								
Lichfield Trent Valley	a																								
Tamworth Low Level	a																								
Nuneaton	a																								
Rugby	a																								
Milton Keynes Central	a											19 49	20 03												
Watford Junction	a																								
London Euston 15 ⊖	a			19 48	20 03		20 11	20 15				20 30	20 44						20 48	21 04			21 14	21 21	

OVERNIGHT SLEEPERS. For sleeper trains, operated by First ScotRail, please refer to Tables 400 - 404

Table 65

Sundays

12 September to 17 October

Scotland and North West England - West Midlands and London

		XC	NT	VT	TP	TP	VT	XC	LM	VT	VT	VT	TP	NT	TP	XC		AW	VT	LM	VT	VT	VT	TP	XC
		◇1		◇1	◇1	◇1	◇1	◇1	1	◇1	◇1	◇1	◇1		◇1	◇1		◇	◇1	1	◇1	◇1	◇1	◇1	◇1
		⊼		⊞		⊼	⊞	⊼		⊞	⊞	⊞			⊼	⊼			⊞		⊞	⊞	⊞		⊼
Inverness	d																								
Aberdeen	d																								
Dundee	d																								
Perth	d																								
Edinburgh 10	d			16 52											18 10										
Haymarket	d			16 56											18u14										
Glasgow Central 15	d					17 06						17 36											18 30		
Motherwell	d																								
Carstairs	d																								
Lockerbie	d											18 32			19 08										
Carlisle 8	a			18 05		18 26						18 50			19 30								19 43		
	d			18 07		18 28						18 52			19 32								19 44		
Penrith North Lakes	d					18 42						19 06			19 46										
Windermere	d																								
Oxenholme Lake District	a			18 41		19 06						19 28			20 10								20 19		
	d			18 42		19 07						19 29			20 10								20 19		
Barrow-in-Furness	d				18 15																				
Lancaster 6	a			18 56	19 17	19 21						19 43			20 26								20 34		
	d			18 57	19 17	19 22						19 44			20 26								20 34		
Preston 8	a			19 15	19 37	19 41						20 02			20 45								20 52		
Blackpool North	d		18 50										19 44	19 50										20 44	
Preston 8	d		19 14	19 17		19 47						20 04	20 10	20 14	20 47								20 55	21 10	
Wigan North Western	a		19 15	19 28								20 15		20 15									21 06		
	d		19 36	19 28								20 15		20 36									21 07		
Blackrod	d																								
Lostock	d																								
Bolton	a					20 08							20 34		21 08									21 34	
Manchester Piccadilly 10	a					20 27							20 57		21 27									21 57	
Manchester Airport ✈	a					20 47							21 17		21 47									22 17	
Liverpool Lime Street 10	a		20 24											21 24											
	d								19 34		19 48									20 34		20 48			
Liverpool South Parkway ✈	d								19 44											20 44					
Runcorn	d								19 52		20 04									20 52		21 04			
Warrington Bank Quay	a			19 39								20 26											21 18		
	d			19 39								20 26											21 18		
Hartford	d								20 03											21 03					
Manchester Piccadilly 10	d	19 07					19 15	19 27		19 35						20 07			20 20		20 55				21 07
Stockport	d						19 22	19 36		19 42						20 16			20 27		21 03				21 16
Wilmslow	d																								
Holyhead	d																	18 25							
Bangor (Gwynedd)	d																	19 04							
Llandudno Junction	d																	19 24							
Wrexham General	d																								
Chester	d																	20b27							
Crewe 10	a			19 59					20 16		20 22	20 45						20 48		21 16		21 21	21 38		
	d			20 01					20 18		20 24	20 47						20 54		21 17		21 23	21 40		
Macclesfield	d							19 49		19 55						20 29			20 40		21 15				21 29
Congleton	d																								
Stoke-on-Trent	d	19 43					19 50	20 07		20 12						20 47			20 57		21 33				21 47
Stafford	a							20 24	20 37		20 41					21 08		21 16		21 37		21 42	22 01		22 06
	d							20 25	20 38		20 43					21 09		21 16		21 38		21 44	22 02		22 06
Penkridge	a								20 44											21 44					
Wolverhampton 7	a	20 13		20 31				20 39	20 55							21 21		21 34		21 55			22 16		22 20
Birmingham New Street 12	a	20 31		20 55				21 00	21 15							21 39		21 52		22 15			22 40		22 40
Birmingham International ✈	a							21 13										22 09							
Coventry	a							21 23																	
Lichfield Trent Valley	a																					21 58			
Tamworth Low Level	a																					22 04			
Nuneaton	a																					22 15			
Rugby	a																					22 28			
Milton Keynes Central	a						20 47				21 36	21 55							22 03		22 50	23 04			
Watford Junction	a											22s31									23s31	23s36			
London Euston 15 ⊖	a						21 32			22 04	22 29	22 53							22 56		23 53	23 57			

b arr. 2019

OVERNIGHT SLEEPERS. For sleeper trains, operated by First ScotRail, please refer to Tables 400 - 404

Table 65

Sundays
12 September to 17 October

Scotland and North West England - West Midlands and London

		VT	NT	TP	TP	VT	LM	XC	TP	SR	SR
		◇1		◇1	◇1	◇1	1	◇1	◇1	R	R
Inverness	d										20 25
Aberdeen	d										21 40
Dundee	d										23u06
Perth	d										23u00
Edinburgh 10	d	18 52			19 57					23 15	
Haymarket	d	18 57			20u01						
Glasgow Central 15	d					20 05				23 15	
Motherwell	d									23u30	
Carstairs	d									23u46	
Lockerbie	d					21 02					
Carlisle 8	a	20 05			21 14	21 21				01u08	
	d	20 07			21 15	21 24					
Penrith North Lakes	d	20 22				21 39					
Windermere	d			20 40							
Oxenholme Lake District	a			20 59		22 02					
	d			21 01		22 03					
Barrow-in-Furness	d										
Lancaster 6	a	20 56		21 18	22 02	22 17					
	d	20 57		21 23	22 03	22 18					
Preston 8	a	21 15			22 23	22 35					04s41
Blackpool North	d		20 50						23 03		
Preston 8	d	21 17	21 14		22 29	22 38			23 29		
Wigan North Western	a	21 28	21 15			22 49					
	d	21 28	21 36			22 50					
Blackrod	d								23 49		
Lostock	d								23 56		
Bolton	a				22 50				00 02		
Manchester Piccadilly 10	a				23 14				00 18		
Manchester Airport	a				23 30				00 32		
Liverpool Lime Street 10	a		22 24								
	d						21 34				
Liverpool South Parkway	d						21 44				
Runcorn	d						21 52				
Warrington Bank Quay	a	21 39				23 00					
	d	21 39				23 01					
Hartford	d						22 03				
Manchester Piccadilly 10	d							22 07			
Stockport	d							22 16			
Wilmslow	d										
Holyhead	d										
Bangor (Gwynedd)	d										
Llandudno Junction	d										
Wrexham General	d										
Chester	d										
Crewe 10	a	21 59				23 20	22 18				05s37
	d	22 01					22 22				
Macclesfield	d							22 29			
Congleton	d										
Stoke-on-Trent	d							22 47			
Stafford	a						22 41	23 04			
	d						22 44	23 05			
Penkridge	a						22 50				
Wolverhampton 7	a	22 31					23 00	23 18			
Birmingham New Street 12	a	22 57					23 17	23 36			
Birmingham International	a										
Coventry	a										
Lichfield Trent Valley	a										
Tamworth Low Level	a										
Nuneaton	a										
Rugby	a										
Milton Keynes Central	a										
Watford Junction	a									06s23	
London Euston 15	a									06 46	07 56

b arr. 0047

OVERNIGHT SLEEPERS. For sleeper trains, operated by First ScotRail, please refer to Tables 400 - 404

Table 65

Sundays
from 24 October

Scotland and North West England - West Midlands and London

		TP	TP	VT	VT	TP	VT	VT	XC	VT	VT	TP	NT	TP	VT	VT	VT	VT	XC	NT	TP	LM	VT	LM
					◇1	◇1	◇1	◇1	◇1	◇1		◇1		◇1		◇1	◇1	◇1	◇1		◇1		◇1	◇1
Inverness	d																							
Aberdeen	d																							
Dundee	d																							
Perth	d																							
Edinburgh 10	d																							
Haymarket	d																							
Glasgow Central 15	d															09 37								
Motherwell	d																							
Carstairs	d																							
Lockerbie	d																							
Carlisle 8	a															10 44								
	d															10 46								
Penrith North Lakes	d															11 00								
Windermere	d																							
Oxenholme Lake District	a															11 22								
	d															11 23								
Barrow-in-Furness	d													09 25										
Lancaster 6	a													10 17		11 37								
	d													10 21		11 38								
Preston 8	a													10 40		11 56								
Blackpool North	d	03 20	05 20			08 14						08 44	08 50							09 50	09 44			
Preston 8	d	04u00	06u00	08 05		08 42					09 05	09 10	09 15		09 30					10 15	10 10			
Wigan North Western	a												09 38							10 38				
	d												09 39							10 39				
Blackrod	d																							
Lostock	d																							
Bolton	a	04u35	06u35			09 05						09 34									10 34			
Manchester Piccadilly 10	a	05u00	07u00			09 28						09 57									10 57			
Manchester Airport	a	05 25	07 25			09 53						10 17									11 18			
Liverpool Lime Street 10	a												10 26							11 26				
	d							08 15		08 38													09 38	
Liverpool South Parkway	d																							
Runcorn	d							08 35		08 54													09 54	
Warrington Bank Quay	a														11 00									
	d																							
Hartford	d																							
Manchester Piccadilly 10	d				08 05		08 20		08 26									09 20	09 27					
Stockport	d				08 14		08 28		08 35									09 27	09 36					
Wilmslow	d				08 22				08 41															
Holyhead	d																							
Bangor (Gwynedd)	d																							
Llandudno Junction	d																							
Wrexham General	d																							
Chester	d																							
Crewe 10	a			09 30	08 39			08 52	09 01	09 11	10 30												10 12	
	d				08 43			08 53	09 05	09 13							09 43					09 53	10 14	10 20
Macclesfield	d						08 42											09 40	09 49					
Congleton	d																							
Stoke-on-Trent	d						08 59											09 57	10 07			10 41		
Stafford	a				09 00				09 25	09 31									10 26			11 17	10 32	10 41
	d				09 02				09 26	09 32									10 27				10 33	10 42
Penkridge	a																							10 48
Wolverhampton 7	a								09 40										10 42					11 00
Birmingham New Street 12	a								09 58										10 59					11 17
Birmingham International	a								10 13										11 13					
Coventry	a								10 24										11 24					
Lichfield Trent Valley	a																							
Tamworth Low Level	a																							
Nuneaton	a									09 54													10 55	
Rugby	a																10 31							
Milton Keynes Central	a							10 17									11 06	11 12					11 49	
Watford Junction	a				10s34		10s39			11s16							11s42							
London Euston 15	a				10 56		11 00	11 06		11 39							12 04	12 07					12 37	

OVERNIGHT SLEEPERS. For sleeper trains, operated by First ScotRail, please refer to Tables 400 - 404

Table 65

Sundays
from 24 October

Scotland and North West England - West Midlands and London

		VT	LM	VT	VT	TP	NT	VT	XC	VT	VT	VT	VT	XC	VT	VT	NT	LM	VT	TP	VT	LM	VT	VT	VT
		🚌	1	◇1 🍴	◇1 🍴	◇1		◇1 🍴	◇1 🛒	◇1 🍴	◇1 🍴	◇1 🍴	◇1 🍴	◇1 🛒	◇1 🍴	🚌		1	◇1 🍴	◇1	◇1 🍴	1	◇1 🍴	🚌	◇1 🍴
Inverness	d																								
Aberdeen	d																								
Dundee	d																								
Perth	d																								
Edinburgh	d																								
Haymarket	d																								
Glasgow Central	d																								
Motherwell	d																								
Carstairs	d																								
Lockerbie	d																								
Carlisle	a																								
	d																								
Penrith North Lakes	d																								
Windermere	d																								
Oxenholme Lake District	a																								
	d																								
Barrow-in-Furness	d																								
Lancaster	a																								
	d																								
Preston	a																								
Blackpool North	d					10 44	10 47										11 47			11 44					
Preston	d	10 30				11 10	11 12									11 30	12 12			12 10				12 10	
Wigan North Western	a						11 35										12 35								
	d						11 36										12 36								
Blackrod	d																								
Lostock	d																								
Bolton	a					11 34														12 34					
Manchester Piccadilly	a					11 57														12 56					
Manchester Airport	a					12 17														13 17					
Liverpool Lime Street	a						12 24										13 24								
	d										10 38							11 34			11 48				
Liverpool South Parkway	d																	11 44							
Runcorn	d										10 54							11 52			12 04				
Warrington Bank Quay	a	12 00														13 00								13 40	
	d											11 14													12 15
Hartford	d																	12 04							
Manchester Piccadilly	d				10 20				10 27	10 35			11 15	11 27					11 35				11 55		
Stockport	d				10 29				10 36	10 42			11 23	11 36					11 43				12 05		
Wilmslow	d				10 36																		12 12		
Holyhead	d																								
Bangor (Gwynedd)	d																								
Llandudno Junction	d																								
Wrexham General	d																								
Chester	d														11 28										
Crewe	a				10 52						11 12	11 33			11 47			12 19					12 28		12 33
	d		10 37	10 43	10 55			11 03			11 14	11 35			11 49			12 22					12 30		12 35
Macclesfield	d								10 49	10 55				11 49					11 56						
Congleton	d																								
Stoke-on-Trent	d		10 58						11 07	11 12			11 51	12 07					12 13			←			
Stafford	a		11 17						11 26		11 32			12 24				12 41			12 35	12 41			
	d								11 27		11 33			12 25				12 42			12 36	12 42			
Penkridge	a																	→				12 48			
Wolverhampton	a							11 32	11 41					12 40								12 59			
Birmingham New Street	a							11 56	12 00					12 58								13 16			
Birmingham International	a								12 13					13 13											
Coventry	a								12 24					13 24											
Lichfield Trent Valley	a																								
Tamworth Low Level	a																								
Nuneaton	a										12 04				12 30										
Rugby	a			11 31																					
Milton Keynes Central	a			12 05						12 19			12 50		13 03										
Watford Junction	a				12s34						12s54														
London Euston	a			12 44	12 56					12 59	13 15	13 23	13 31		13 44				13 49		14 06		14 12		14 17

OVERNIGHT SLEEPERS. For sleeper trains, operated by First ScotRail, please refer to Tables 400 - 404

Table 65

Sundays
from 24 October

Scotland and North West England - West Midlands and London

		VT		VT		VT	XC	LM	VT	VT	LM	VT		XC	VT	VT	VT	VT	TP	VT	TP	VT	NT	XC	LM
		◇1 🍴		◇1 🍴		◇1 🍴	◇1 🛒	1	◇1 🍴	◇1 🍴	1	◇1 🍴		◇1 🛒	◇1 🍴	◇1 🍴	◇1 🍴	◇1 🍴	◇1	◇1 🍴	◇1	🚌		◇1 🛒	1
Inverness	d																								
Aberdeen	d																								
Dundee	d																								
Perth	d																								
Edinburgh	d																								
Haymarket	d																								
Glasgow Central	d																			10 32					
Motherwell	d																			10u49					
Carstairs	d																								
Lockerbie	d																								
Carlisle	a																			11 44					
	d																			11 46					
Penrith North Lakes	d																			12 00					
Windermere	d																								
Oxenholme Lake District	a																			12 22					
	d																			12 24					
Barrow-in-Furness	d																		11 23						
Lancaster	a																		12 26	12 37					
	d																	12 10	12 26	12 38					
Preston	a																	12 27	12 45	12 56					
Blackpool North	d																				12 44		12 47		
Preston	d																	12 30	12 47		13 10	13 25	13 12		
Wigan North Western	a																						13 35		
	d																						13 36		
Blackrod	d																								
Lostock	d																								
Bolton	a																		13 08		13 34				
Manchester Piccadilly	a																		13 27		13 57				
Manchester Airport	a																		13 47		14 17				
Liverpool Lime Street	a																						14 24		
	d							12 34		12 48															13 34
Liverpool South Parkway	d							12 44																	13 44
Runcorn	d							12 52		13 04															13 52
Warrington Bank Quay	a																					14 55			
	d														13 14										
Hartford	d							13 03																	14 03
Manchester Piccadilly	d	12 15					12 26		12 35			12 55		13 07		13 15								13 27	
Stockport	d	12 23					12 35		12 44			13 05				13 22								13 36	
Wilmslow	d											13 12													
Holyhead	d			10 55													11 50								
Bangor (Gwynedd)	d			11 22													12 17								
Llandudno Junction	d			11 40													12 35								
Wrexham General	d																								
Chester	d			12 33													13b30								
Crewe	a			12 52				13 19				13 28			13 33		13 49	13 48							14 18
	d			12 54		13 01		13 22				13 30			13 35		13 51	14 01							14 22
Macclesfield	d						12 49		12 57															13 49	
Congleton	d																								
Stoke-on-Trent	d	12 51					13 07		13 14		←			13 43		13 50								14 07	
Stafford	a						13 24	13 42		13 35	13 42													14 24	14 42
	d						13 25	13 43		13 36	13 43													14 25	14 43
Penkridge	a							→			13 48														→
Wolverhampton	a					13 31	13 40				13 58			14 13				14 32						14 40	
Birmingham New Street	a					13 55	13 58				14 15			14 31				14 55						14 58	
Birmingham International	a						14 13																	15 13	
Coventry	a						14 24																	15 24	
Lichfield Trent Valley	a																								
Tamworth Low Level	a																								
Nuneaton	a																14 31								
Rugby	a																								
Milton Keynes Central	a	13 50		14 04												14 49	15 04								
Watford Junction	a																								
London Euston	a	14 30		14 45					14 50	15 03		15 11			15 14	15 30	15 45								

b arr. 1323

OVERNIGHT SLEEPERS. For sleeper trains, operated by First ScotRail, please refer to Tables 400 - 404

Table 65

Sundays
from 24 October

Scotland and North West England - West Midlands and London

		VT ◇1	VT ◇1	LM 1	VT ◇1	XC ◇1	VT ◇1	VT ◇1		VT ◇1	VT ◇1	TP ◇1	VT ◇1	TP ◇1	NT	VT	TP ◇1	XC ◇1	LM 1	VT ◇1	VT ◇1	LM 1	VT ◇1	VT ◇1	TP ◇1
Inverness	d																								
Aberdeen	d																								
Dundee	d																								
Perth	d																								
Edinburgh 10	d										10 52	11 10													
Haymarket	d										10 57	11u14													
Glasgow Central 15	d												11 32											12 42	
Motherwell	d																								
Carstairs	d																								
Lockerbie	d											12 08													
Carlisle 8	a										12 05	12 30	12 47											13 51	
	d										12 07	12 32	12 49											13 54	
Penrith North Lakes	d											12 46													
Windermere	d																								
Oxenholme Lake District	a										12 41	13 10	13 22											14 27	
	d										12 43	13 10	13 23											14 28	
Barrow-in-Furness	d																13 23								
Lancaster 6	a										12 56	13 26	13 37				14 26							14 42	
	d										12 57	13 26	13 38				14 26							14 43	
Preston 8	a										13 15	13 45	13 56				14 45							15 01	
Blackpool North	d													13 44	13 47										14 44
Preston 8	d										13 30	13 47		14 10	14 12	14 10	14 47							15 03	15 10
Wigan North Western	a														14 35	14 55								15 14	
	d														14 36									15 14	
Blackrod	d																								
Lostock	d																								
Bolton	a											14 08		14 34			15 08								15 34
Manchester Piccadilly 10	a											14 27		14 57			15 27								15 57
Manchester Airport	a											14 47		15 17			15 47								16 17
Liverpool Lime Street 10	a														15 24										
	d		13 48																14 34		14 48				
Liverpool South Parkway	d																		14 44						
Runcorn	d		14 04																14 52		15 04				
Warrington Bank Quay	a																							15 25	
	d						14 14																	15 25	
Hartford	d																		15 03						
Manchester Piccadilly 10	d	13 35			13 55	14 07		14 15										14 27		14 35			14 55		
Stockport	d	13 42			14 04			14 22										14 36		14 42			15 04		
Wilmslow	d				14 11																		15 11		
Holyhead	d									12 50															
Bangor (Gwynedd)	d									13 18															
Llandudno Junction	d									13 36															
Wrexham General	d																								
Chester	d									14b33															
Crewe 10	a				14 27		14 33			14 54	14 52								15 20				15 27		
	d				14 29		14 35			14 56	15 01								15 22				15 29		
Macclesfield	d	13 55																14 49		14 55					
Congleton	d																								
Stoke-on-Trent	d	14 12		←		14 43		14 50										15 07		15 12		←			
Stafford	a		14 35	14 42														15 24	15 42		15 35	15 42			
	d		14 36	14 43														15 25	15 43		15 36	15 43			
Penkridge	a			14 48															→			15 48			
Wolverhampton 7	a			14 58		15 13					15 31							15 40				15 58			
Birmingham New Street 12	a			15 15		15 31					15 54							15 58				16 15			
Birmingham International	a																	16 13							
Coventry	a																	16 24							
Lichfield Trent Valley	a																								
Tamworth Low Level	a																								
Nuneaton	a																								
Rugby	a																								
Milton Keynes Central	a							15 49		16 04															
Watford Junction	a																								
London Euston 15	a	15 48	16 03		16 11		16 14	16 30		16 44										16 48	17 03		17 11	17 23	

b arr. 1426

OVERNIGHT SLEEPERS. For sleeper trains, operated by First ScotRail, please refer to Tables 400 - 404

Table 65

Sundays
from 24 October

Scotland and North West England - West Midlands and London

		XC ◇1	VT ◇1	VT ◇1	NT	VT ◇1	TP ◇1	XC ◇1	LM 1	VT ◇1	VT ◇1	LM 1	VT ◇1	VT ◇1	TP ◇1	NT	XC ◇1	VT ◇1	VT ◇1	VT ◇1	TP ◇1	XC ◇1	LM 1	VT ◇1
Inverness	d																							
Aberdeen	d																							
Dundee	d																							
Perth	d																							
Edinburgh 10	d					12 52	13 09																	
Haymarket	d					12 56	13u13																	
Glasgow Central 15	d													13 34						13 55				
Motherwell	d																							
Carstairs	d																							
Lockerbie	d						14 08																	
Carlisle 8	a					14 05	14 30							14 46						15 08				
	d					14 07	14 32							14 49						15 09				
Penrith North Lakes	d					14 22	14 46																	
Windermere	d																							
Oxenholme Lake District	a						15 10							15 22						15 44				
	d						15 10							15 23						15 44				
Barrow-in-Furness	d																				15 23			
Lancaster 6	a					14 56	15 25							15 37							16 26			
	d					14 57	15 25							15 38							16 26			
Preston 8	a					15 15	15 45							15 56						16 13	16 45			
Blackpool North	d				14 50										15 44	15 50								
Preston 8	d				15 15	15 17	15 47							15 58	16 10	16 15				16 15	16 47			
Wigan North Western	a				15 35	15 28								16 09		16 35				16 26				
	d				15 36	15 28								16 09		16 36				16 26				
Blackrod	d																							
Lostock	d																							
Bolton	a						16 08								16 34						17 08			
Manchester Piccadilly 10	a						16 27								16 57						17 27			
Manchester Airport	a						16 47								17 17						17 47			
Liverpool Lime Street 10	a				16 24											17 24								
	d								15 34		15 48								16 18				16 34	
Liverpool South Parkway	d								15 44														16 44	
Runcorn	d								15 52		16 04								16 34				16 52	
Warrington Bank Quay	a					15 39								16 20						16 37				
	d					15 39								16 20						16 37				
Hartford	d								16 03														17 03	
Manchester Piccadilly 10	d	15 07	15 15					15 27		15 35			15 55				16 07	16 15				16 27		16 35
Stockport	d		15 22					15 36		15 42			16 04					16 23				16 36		16 42
Wilmslow	d												16 11											
Holyhead	d			13 55																				
Bangor (Gwynedd)	d			14 22																				
Llandudno Junction	d			14 40																				
Wrexham General	d																							
Chester	d			15 33																				
Crewe 10	a			15 54		15 59			16 18				16 27						16 50	16 57			17 18	
	d			15 56		16 01			16 22				16 29						16 53	16 59			17 22	
Macclesfield	d							15 49		15 55												16 49		16 55
Congleton	d																							
Stoke-on-Trent	d	15 43	15 50					16 07		16 12		←					16 43	16 50				17 08		17 12
Stafford	a							16 24	16 42		16 36	16 42										17 25	17 42	
	d							16 25	16 43		16 37	16 43										17 26	17 43	
Penkridge	a								→			16 48											→	
Wolverhampton 7	a	16 13				16 32		16 40				16 58					17 13			17 31		17 40		
Birmingham New Street 12	a	16 31				16 56		16 58				17 15					17 31			17 55		17 58		
Birmingham International	a							17 13														18 13		
Coventry	a							17 24														18 24		
Lichfield Trent Valley	a																		17 25					
Tamworth Low Level	a																							
Nuneaton	a																							
Rugby	a																							
Milton Keynes Central	a		16 49	17 03														17 49	18 02					
Watford Junction	a																							
London Euston 15	a		17 30	17 44						17 48	18 04		18 11	18 14				18 30	18 42					18 48

OVERNIGHT SLEEPERS. For sleeper trains, operated by First ScotRail, please refer to Tables 400 - 404

Table 65

Sundays from 24 October

Scotland and North West England - West Midlands and London

		VT	LM	VT	VT	TP	XC	VT	VT	VT		TP	XC	LM	VT	VT	LM	VT	VT	TP		XC	VT	VT	VT
		◇1	1	◇1	◇1	◇1	◇1	◇1	◇1	◇1		◇1	◇1	1	◇1	◇1	1	◇1	◇1	◇1		◇1	◇1	◇1	◇1
Inverness	d																								
Aberdeen	d																								
Dundee	d																								
Perth	d																								
Edinburgh	d									14 52															
Haymarket	d									14 57															
Glasgow Central	d				14 35							15 06							15 36						15 56
Motherwell	d																								
Carstairs	d																								
Lockerbie	d											16 06													
Carlisle	a				15 47					16 05		16 28							16 46						17 08
	d				15 49					16 07		16 30							16 49						17 09
Penrith North Lakes	d									16 22		16 44							17 03						
Windermere	d																								
Oxenholme Lake District	a				16 22							17 08													17 44
	d				16 23							17 08													17 44
Barrow-in-Furness	d																								
Lancaster	a				16 37					16 56		17 23							17 37						
	d				16 38					16 57		17 23							17 38						
Preston	a				16 56					17 15		17 42							17 56						18 15
Blackpool North	d					16 44					16 50									17 44	17 50				
Preston	d				16 58	17 10				17 17	17 15	17 47							17 58	18 10	18 15				18 17
Wigan North Western	a				17 09					17 28	17 35								18 09		18 35				18 28
	d				17 09					17 28	17 36								18 09		18 36				18 28
Blackrod	d																								
Lostock	d																								
Bolton	a					17 34						18 08								18 34					
Manchester Piccadilly	a					17 57						18 27								18 57					
Manchester Airport	a					18 17						18 47								19 17					
Liverpool Lime Street	a										18 24										19 24				
	d	16 48												17 34		17 48									
Liverpool South Parkway	d													17 44											
Runcorn	d	17 04												17 52		18 04									
Warrington Bank Quay	a				17 20					17 39									18 20						18 39
	d				17 20					17 39									18 20						18 39
Hartford	d													18 03											
Manchester Piccadilly	d			16 55			17 07	17 15					17 27		17 35			17 55				18 07	18 15		
Stockport	d			17 04				17 22					17 36		17 42			18 04					18 22		
Wilmslow	d			17 11														18 11							
Holyhead	d																								
Bangor (Gwynedd)	d																								
Llandudno Junction	d																								
Wrexham General	d																								
Chester	d								17 35															18 35	
Crewe	a			17 27					17 53	17 59				18 20				18 27						18 53	18 59
	d			17 29					17 55	18 01				18 22				18 29						18 55	19 01
Macclesfield	d												17 49		17 55										
Congleton	d																								
Stoke-on-Trent	d		←				17 43	17 50					18 08		18 12		←					18 43	18 50		
Stafford	a	17 35	17 42										18 25	18 42		18 35	18 42								
	d	17 36	17 43										18 26	18 43		18 36	18 43								
Penkridge	a		17 48											↦			18 48								
Wolverhampton	a		17 58				18 13			18 32			18 40				18 58					19 13			19 31
Birmingham New Street	a		18 15				18 31			18 56			18 58				19 15					19 31			19 55
Birmingham International	a												19 13												
Coventry	a												19 24												
Lichfield Trent Valley	a																								
Tamworth Low Level	a																								
Nuneaton	a																								
Rugby	a																								
Milton Keynes Central	a							18 49	19 03														19 49	20 03	
Watford Junction	a																								
London Euston	a	19 03		19 11	19 14			19 30	19 44						19 48	20 03		20 11	20 15				20 30	20 44	

OVERNIGHT SLEEPERS. For sleeper trains, operated by First ScotRail, please refer to Tables 400 - 404

Table 65

Sundays from 24 October

Scotland and North West England - West Midlands and London

		TP	XC	LM	VT	VT		LM	VT	VT	TP	NT	XC	VT	TP	TP	VT	XC	LM	VT	VT	VT	TP	TP	NT
		◇1	◇1	1	◇1	◇1		1	◇1	◇1	◇1		◇1	◇1	◇1	◇1	◇1	◇1	1	◇1	◇1	◇1	◇1	◇1	
Inverness	d																								
Aberdeen	d																								
Dundee	d																								
Perth	d																								
Edinburgh	d	16 10												16 52										18 10	
Haymarket	d	16u14												16 56										18u14	
Glasgow Central	d									16 38						17 06						17 36			
Motherwell	d									16 54															
Carstairs	d																								
Lockerbie	d	17 08																				18 32		19 08	
Carlisle	a	17 30								17 49				18 05		18 26						18 50		19 30	
	d	17 32								17 51				18 07		18 28						18 52		19 32	
Penrith North Lakes	d	17 46								18 05						18 42						19 06		19 46	
Windermere	d																								
Oxenholme Lake District	a	18 10								18 27				18 41		19 06						19 28		20 10	
	d	18 10								18 28				18 42		19 07						19 29		20 10	
Barrow-in-Furness	d														18 15										
Lancaster	a	18 26								18 42				18 56	19 17	19 21						19 43		20 26	
	d	18 26								18 43				18 57	19 17	19 22						19 44		20 26	
Preston	a	18 45								19 01				19 15	19 37	19 41						20 02		20 45	
Blackpool North	d										18 44	18 50											19 44		19 50
Preston	d	18 47								19 03	19 10	19 15		19 17		19 47						20 04	20 10	20 47	20 15
Wigan North Western	a									19 14		19 35		19 28								20 15			20 35
	d									19 14		19 36		19 28								20 15			20 36
Blackrod	d																								
Lostock	d																								
Bolton	a	19 08									19 34					20 08							20 34	21 08	
Manchester Piccadilly	a	19 27									19 57					20 27							20 57	21 27	
Manchester Airport	a	19 47									20 17					20 47							21 17	21 47	
Liverpool Lime Street	a											20 24													21 24
	d			18 34		18 48													19 34		19 48				
Liverpool South Parkway	d			18 44															19 44						
Runcorn	d			18 52		19 04													19 52		20 04				
Warrington Bank Quay	a									19 25				19 39								20 26			
	d									19 25				19 39								20 26			
Hartford	d			19 03															20 03						
Manchester Piccadilly	d		18 27		18 35				18 55				19 07				19 15	19 27		19 35					
Stockport	d		18 36		18 42				19 04								19 22	19 36		19 42					
Wilmslow	d								19 11																
Holyhead	d																								
Bangor (Gwynedd)	d																								
Llandudno Junction	d																								
Wrexham General	d																								
Chester	d																								
Crewe	a			19 20					19 27					19 59					20 16		20 22	20 45			
	d			19 22					19 29					20 01					20 18		20 24	20 47			
Macclesfield	d		18 49		18 55													19 49		19 55					
Congleton	d																								
Stoke-on-Trent	d		19 07		19 12			←					19 43				19 50	20 07		20 12					
Stafford	a		19 24	19 42		19 35		19 42										20 24	20 37		20 41				
	d		19 25	19 43		19 36		19 43										20 25	20 38		20 43				
Penkridge	a			↦				19 48											20 44						
Wolverhampton	a		19 40					19 58					20 13	20 31				20 39	20 55						
Birmingham New Street	a		19 58					20 15					20 31	20 55				21 00	21 15						
Birmingham International	a		20 13															21 13							
Coventry	a		20 24															21 23							
Lichfield Trent Valley	a																								
Tamworth Low Level	a																								
Nuneaton	a																								
Rugby	a																								
Milton Keynes Central	a																20 47				21 36	21 55			
Watford Junction	a																					22s31			
London Euston	a				20 48	21 04			21 14	21 21							21 32			22 04	22 29	22 53			

OVERNIGHT SLEEPERS. For sleeper trains, operated by First ScotRail, please refer to Tables 400 - 404

Table 65

Sundays
from 24 October

Scotland and North West England - West Midlands and London

		XC		AW	VT	LM	VT	VT	VT	TP	XC	VT	NT	TP	NT	TP	VT	LM	XC	TP	SR	SR
		◇1		◇	◇1	1	◇1	◇1	◇1	◇1	◇1	◇1		◇1		◇1	◇1	1	◇1	◇1	B	B
Inverness	d																					20 25
Aberdeen	d																					21 40
Dundee	d																					23u06
Perth	d																					23u00
Edinburgh 10	d											18 52				19 57					23 15	
Haymarket	d											18 57				20u01						
Glasgow Central 15	d								18 30								20 05				23 15	
Motherwell	d																				23u30	
Carstairs	d																				23u46	
Lockerbie	d																21 02					
Carlisle 8	a								19 43			20 05				21 14	21 21				01u08	
	d								19 44			20 07				21 15	21 24					
Penrith North Lakes	d											20 22					21 39					
Windermere	d													20 40								
Oxenholme Lake District	a								20 19					20 59			22 02					
	d								20 19					21 01			22 03					
Barrow-in-Furness	d																					
Lancaster 6	a								20 34			20 56		21 18		22 02	22 17					
	d								20 34			20 57		21 23		22 03	22 18					
Preston 8	a								20 52			21 15				22 23	22 35					04s41
Blackpool North	d									20 44			20 50		21 50					23 03		
Preston 8	d								20 55	21 10		21 17	21 15		22 15	22 29	22 38			23 29		
Wigan North Western	a								21 06			21 28	21 35		22 35		22 49					
	d								21 07			21 28	21 36		22 36		22 50					
Blackrod	d																			23 49		
Lostock	d																			23 56		
Bolton	a									21 34						22 50				00 02		
Manchester Piccadilly 10	a									21 57						23 14				00 18		
Manchester Airport ✈	a									22 17						23 30				00 32		
Liverpool Lime Street 10	a												22 24		23 24							
	d					20 34		20 48										21 34				
Liverpool South Parkway ✈	d					20 44												21 44				
Runcorn	d					20 52		21 04										21 52				
Warrington Bank Quay	a								21 18			21 39					23 00					
	d								21 18			21 39					23 01					
Hartford	d					21 03												22 03				
Manchester Piccadilly 10	d	20 07			20 20		20 55				21 07								22 07			
Stockport	d	20 16			20 27		21 03				21 16								22 16			
Wilmslow	d																					
Holyhead	d			18 25																		
Bangor (Gwynedd)	d			19 04																		
Llandudno Junction	d			19 24																		
Wrexham General	d																					
Chester	d			20b27																		
Crewe 10	a			20 48		21 16		21 21	21 38			21 59					23 20	22 18				05s37
	d			20 54		21 17		21 23	21 40			22 01						22 22				
Macclesfield	d	20 29			20 40		21 15				21 29								22 29			
Congleton	d																					
Stoke-on-Trent	d	20 48			20 57		21 33				21 47								22 47			
Stafford	a	21 08		21 16		21 37		21 42	22 01		22 06							22 41	23 04			
	d	21 09		21 16		21 38		21 44	22 02		22 06							22 44	23 05			
Penkridge	a					21 44												22 50				
Wolverhampton 7	a	21 22		21 34		21 55			22 16		22 20	22 31						23 00	23 18			
Birmingham New Street 12	a	21 39		21 52		22 15			22 40		22 40	22 57						23 17	23 36			
Birmingham International ✈	a			22 09																		
Coventry	a																					
Lichfield Trent Valley	a							21 58														
Tamworth Low Level	a							22 04														
Nuneaton	a							22 15														
Rugby	a							22 28														
Milton Keynes Central	a				22 03		22 50	23 04														
Watford Junction	a						23s31	23s36													06s23	
London Euston 15 ⊖	a				22 56		23 53	23 57													06 46	07 56

b arr. 2019 c arr. 0047

Table 65A

Mondays to Fridays

Milton Keynes Central - Buckingham and Bicester

Bus Service

		VT	VT	VT	VT	VT	VT	VT	VT	VT	VT	VT	VT	VT	VT	VT	VT	VT	VT	VT	VT	VT	VT	VT	VT
Milton Keynes Central	d	05.45	06.15	06.45	07.15	07.35	08.05	08.45	09.15	09.45	10.15	10.45	11.15	11.45	12.15	12.45	13.15	13.45	14.15	14.45	15.15	15.45	16.15	16.45	17.15
Buckingham Tesco	d	06.05	06.35	07.05	07.35	07.55	08.25	09.05	09.35	10.05	10.35	11.05	11.35	12.05	12.35	13.05	13.35	14.05	14.35	15.05	15.35	16.05	16.35	17.05	17.35
Bicester Bure Place	a	06.25	06.55	07.25	07.55	08.15	08.45	09.25	09.55	10.25	10.55	11.25	11.55	12.25	12.55	13.25	13.55	14.25	14.55	15.25	15.55	16.25	16.55	17.25	17.55

		VT	VT	VT	VT	VT
Milton Keynes Central	d	17.45	18.15	18.45	19.45	20.45
Buckingham Tesco	d	18.05	18.35	19.05	20.05	21.05
Bicester Bure Place	a	08.25	18.55	19.25	20.25	21.25

Saturdays

		VT	VT	VT	VT	VT	VT	VT	VT	VT	VT	VT	VT	VT	VT	VT	VT	VT	VT	VT	VT	VT	VT	VT	VT
Milton Keynes Central	d	05.50	06.20	06.50	07.20	07.45	18.15	08.45	09.15	09.45	10.15	10.45	11.15	11.45	12.15	12.45	13.15	13.45	14.15	14.45	15.15	15.45	16.15	16.45	17.15
Buckingham Tesco	d	06.10	06.40	07.10	07.40	08.05	08.35	09.05	09.35	10.05	10.35	11.05	11.35	12.05	12.35	13.05	13.35	14.05	14.35	15.05	15.35	16.05	16.35	17.05	17.35
Bicester Bure Place	a	06.30	07.00	07.30	08.00	08.25	08.55	09.25	09.55	10.25	10.55	11.25	11.55	12.25	12.55	13.25	13.55	14.25	14.55	15.25	15.55	16.25	16.55	17.25	17.55

		VT	VT	VT	VT	VT
Milton Keynes Central	d	17.45	18.15	18.45	19.45	20.45
Buckingham Tesco	d	18.05	18.35	19.05	20.05	21.05
Bicester Bure Place	a	18.25	18.55	19.25	20.25	21.25

Sundays

		VT	VT	VT	VT	VT	VT	VT	VT	VT	VT	VT	VT	VT	VT	VT	VT	VT	VT	VT	VT	VT	VT	VT	VT
Milton Keynes Central	d	06.45	07.45	08.45	09.45	10.15	10.45	11.15	11.45	12.15	12.45	13.15	13.45	14.15	14.45	15.15	15.45	16.15	16.45	17.15	17.45	18.15	18.45	19.45	20.40
Buckingham Tesco	d	07.05	08.05	09.05	10.05	10.35	11.05	11.35	12.05	12.35	13.05	13.35	14.05	14.35	15.05	15.35	16.05	16.35	17.05	17.35	18.05	18.35	19.05	20.05	21.00
Bicester Bure Place	a	07.25	08.25	09.25	10.25	10.55	11.25	11.55	12.25	12.55	13.25	13.55	14.25	14.55	15.25	15.55	16.25	16.55	17.25	17.55	18.25	18.55	19.25	20.25	21.20

		VT
Milton Keynes Central	d	21.35
Buckingham Tesco	d	21.55
Bicester Bure Place	a	22.15

This is the X5 service operated by Stagecoach East

Sunday service operates on Bank Holidays. Please check with local operator before travelling

Table 65A

Mondays to Fridays

Bicester and Buckingham - Milton Keynes Central

Bus Service

		VT	VT	VT	VT	VT	VT	VT	VT	VT	VT	VT	VT	VT	VT	VT	VT	VT	VT	VT	VT	VT	VT	VT	VT
Bicester Bure Place	d	07.35	08.05	08.35	09.05	09.35	10.05	10.35	11.05	11.35	12.05	12.35	13.05	13.35	14.05	14.35	15.05	15.35	16.05	16.35	17.05	17.35	18.05	18.35	19.05
Buckingham Tesco	d	07.55	08.25	08.55	09.25	09.55	10.25	10.55	11.25	11.55	12.25	12.55	13.25	13.55	14.25	14.55	15.25	15.55	16.25	16.55	17.25	17.55	18.25	18.55	19.25
Milton Keynes Central	a	08.15	08.45	09.15	09.45	10.15	10.45	11.15	11.45	12.15	12.45	13.15	13.45	14.15	14.45	15.15	15.45	16.15	16.45	17.15	17.45	18.15	18.45	19.15	19.45

		VT	VT	VT	VT	VT
Bicester Bure Place	d	19.30	20.00	20.30	21.30	22.30
Buckingham Tesco	d	19.50	20.20	20.50	21.50	22.50
Milton Keynes Central	a	20.10	20.40	21.10	22.10	23.10

Saturdays

		VT	VT	VT	VT	VT	VT	VT	VT	VT	VT	VT	VT	VT	VT	VT	VT	VT	VT	VT	VT	VT	VT	VT	VT
Bicester Bure Place	d	07.35	08.05	08.35	09.05	09.35	10.05	10.35	11.05	11.35	12.05	12.35	13.05	13.35	14.05	14.35	15.05	15.35	16.05	16.35	17.05	17.35	18.05	18.35	19.05
Buckingham Tesco	d	07.55	08.25	08.55	09.25	09.55	10.25	10.55	11.25	11.55	12.25	12.55	13.25	13.55	14.25	14.55	15.25	15.55	16.25	16.55	17.25	17.55	18.25	18.55	19.25
Milton Keynes Central	a	08.15	08.45	09.15	09.45	10.15	10.45	11.15	11.45	12.15	12.45	13.15	13.45	14.15	14.45	15.15	15.45	16.15	16.45	17.15	17.45	18.15	18.45	19.15	19.45

		VT	VT	VT	VT	VT
Bicester Bure Place	d	19.30	20.00	20.30	21.30	22.30
Buckingham Tesco	d	19.50	20.20	20.50	21.50	22.50
Milton Keynes Central	a	20.10	20.40	21.10	22.10	23.10

Sundays

		VT	VT	VT	VT	VT	VT	VT	VT	VT	VT	VT	VT	VT	VT	VT	VT	VT	VT	VT	VT	VT	VT	VT	VT
Bicester Bure Place	d	08.35	09.35	10.35	11.35	12.05	12.35	13.05	13.35	14.05	14.35	15.05	15.35	16.05	16.35	17.05	17.35	18.05	18.35	19.05	19.30	20.00	20.30	21.30	22.30
Buckingham Tesco	d	08.55	09.55	10.55	11.55	12.25	12.55	13.25	13.55	14.25	14.55	15.25	15.55	16.25	16.55	17.25	17.55	18.25	18.55	19.25	19.50	20.20	20.50	21.50	22.50
Milton Keynes Central	a	09.15	10.15	11.15	12.15	12.45	13.15	13.45	14.15	14.45	15.15	15.45	16.15	16.45	17.15	17.45	18.15	18.45	19.15	19.45	20.10	20.40	21.10	22.10	23.10

Table 65B

Mondays to Fridays

Milton Keynes Central - London Luton Airport

Bus Service

		VT	VT	VT	VT	VT	VT	VT	VT	VT	VT	VT	VT	VT	VT	VT	VT	VT
Milton Keynes Central	d	06.40	07.50	08.55	09.55	10.55	11.55	12.55	13.55	14.55	15.55	16.55	17.25	17.55	18.55	19.55	20.55	21.55
Milton Keynes The Point	d	06.45	07.55	09.00	10.00	11.00	12.00	13.00	14.00	15.00	16.00	17.00	17.30	18.00	19.00	20.00	21.00	22.00
Luton	d	07.25	08.40	09.40	10.40	11.40	12.40	13.40	14.40	15.40	16.40	17.40	18.10	18.40	19.40	20.40	21.40	22.40
London Luton Airport	a	07.35	08.55	09.50	10.50	11.50	12.50	13.50	14.50	15.50	16.50	17.50	18.20	18.50	19.50	20.50	21.50	22.50

Saturdays

		VT	VT	VT	VT	VT	VT	VT	VT	VT	VT	VT	VT	VT	VT	VT
Milton Keynes Central	d	06.40	07.50	08.55	09.55	10.55	11.55	12.55	13.55	14.55	15.55	16.55	17.55	18.55	19.55	20.55
Milton Keynes The Point	d	06.45	07.55	09.00	10.00	11.00	12.00	13.00	14.00	15.00	16.00	17.00	18.00	19.00	20.00	21.00
Luton	d	07.25	08.40	09.40	10.40	11.40	12.40	13.40	14.40	15.40	16.40	17.40	18.40	19.40	20.40	21.40
London Luton Airport	a	07.35	08.55	09.50	10.50	11.50	12.50	13.50	14.50	15.50	16.50	17.50	18.50	19.50	20.50	21.50

Sundays

		VT	VT	VT	VT	VT	VT	VT	VT	VT	VT	VT	VT	VT
Milton Keynes Central	d	09.20	10.20	11.20	12.20	13.20	14.20	15.20	16.20	17.20	18.20	19.20	20.20	21.20
Milton Keynes The Point	d	09.25	10.25	11.25	12.25	13.25	14.25	15.25	16.25	17.25	18.25	19.25	20.25	21.25
Luton	d	10.05	11.05	12.05	13.05	14.05	15.05	16.05	17.05	18.05	19.05	20.05	21.05	22.05
London Luton Airport	a	10.15	11.15	12.15	13.15	14.15	15.15	16.15	17.15	18.15	19.15	20.15	21.15	22.15

Sunday service operates on Bank Holidays. Please check with local operator before travelling

Table 65B

Mondays to Fridays

London Luton Airport - Milton Keynes Central

Bus Service

		VT	VT	VT	VT	VT	VT	VT	VT	VT	VT	VT	VT	VT	VT	VT	VT
London Luton Airport	d	05.50	06.50	07.50	09.05	10.05	11.05	12.05	13.05	14.05	15.05	16.05	17.05	18.05	19.05	20.05	21.05
Luton	d	06.00	07.00	08.00	09.15	10.15	11.15	12.15	13.15	14.15	15.15	16.15	17.15	18.15	19.15	20.15	21.15
Luton Galaxy Centre	d	06.02	07.02	08.02	09.17	10.17	11.17	12.17	13.17	14.17	15.17	16.17	17.17	18.17	19.17	20.17	21.17
Milton Keynes The Point	d	06.40	07.45	08.48	09.55	10.55	11.55	12.55	13.55	14.55	15.55	16.55	17.55	18.55	19.55		
Milton Keynes Central	d	06.45	07.50	09.00	10.00	11.00	12.00	13.00	14.00	15.00	16.00	17.00	18.00	19.00	20.00	20.55	21.55

Saturdays

		VT	VT	VT	VT	VT	VT	VT	VT	VT	VT	VT	VT	VT	VT	VT
London Luton Airport	d	05.50	06.50	07.50	09.05	10.05	11.05	12.05	13.05	14.05	15.05	16.05	17.05	18.05	19.05	20.05
Luton	d	06.00	07.00	08.00	09.15	10.15	11.15	12.15	13.15	14.15	15.15	16.15	17.15	18.15	19.15	20.15
Luton Galaxy Centre	d	06.02	07.02	08.02	09.17	10.17	11.17	12.17	13.17	14.17	15.17	16.17	17.17	18.17	19.17	20.17
Milton Keynes The Point	d		07.45	08.55	09.55	10.55	11.55	12.55	13.55	14.55	15.55	16.55	17.55	18.55		
Milton Keynes Central	d	06.40	07.50	09.00	10.00	11.00	123.00	13.00	14.00	15.00	16.00	17.00	18.00	19.00	19.50	20.50

Sundays

		VT	VT	VT	VT	VT	VT	VT	VT	VT	VT	VT	VT	VT
London Luton Airport	d	08.20	09.20	10.20	11.20	12.20	13.20	14.20	15.20	16.20	17.20	18.20	19.20	20.20
Luton	d	08.30	09.30	10.30	11.30	12.30	13.30	14.30	15.30	16.30	17.30	18.30	19.30	20.30
Luton Galaxy Centre	d	08.32	09.32	10.32	11.32	12.32	13.32	14.32	15.32	16.32	17.32	18.32	19.32	20.32
Milton Keynes The Point	d	09.10	10.10	11.10	12.10	13.10	14.10	15.10	16.10	17.10	18.10	19.10	20.10	21.10
Milton Keynes Central	d	09.15	10.15	11.15	12.15	13.15	14.15	15.15	16.15	17.15	18.15	19.15	20.15	21.15

Table 65C

Mondays to Fridays

Milton Keynes Central - Bedford and Cambridge

Bus Service

		VT	VT	VT	VT	VT	VT	VT	VT	VT	VT	VT	VT	VT	VT	VT	VT	VT	VT	VT	VT	VT	VT	VT	VT
Milton Keynes Central	d	07.00	07.45	08.15	08.45	09.15	09.45	10.15	10.45	11.15	11.45	12.15	12.45	13.15	13.45	14.15	14.45	15.15	15.45	16.15	16.45	17.15	17.45	18.15	18.45
Bedford Bus Station	a	08.10	08.40	09.05	09.35	10.05	10.35	11.05	11.35	12.05	12.35	13.05	13.35	14.05	14.35	15.05	15.35	16.05	16.35	17.05	17.35	18.10	18.40	19.10	19.40
St Neots Cross Keys	a	08.47	09.47	09.47	10.17	10.47	11.17	11.47	12.17	12.47	13.17	13.47	14.17	14.47	15.17	15.47	16.17	16.47	17.17	17.47	18.17	18.47	19.15		19.40
Cambridge Parkside	a	09.25	09.55	10.25	10.55	11.25	11.55	12.25	12.55	13.25	13.55	14.25	14.55	15.25	15.55	16.25	16.55	17.25	17.55	18.25	18.55	19.25	19.48		20.48

		VT	VT	VT	VT	VT	VT	VT
Milton Keynes Central	d	19.15	19.45	20.10	20.40	21.10	22.10	23.10
Bedford Bus Station	a	20.05	20.30	20.50	21.20	21.50	22.50	23.50
St Neots Cross Keys	a		21.10		22.00			
Cambridge Parkside	a		21.43		22.33			

Saturdays

		VT	VT	VT	VT	VT	VT	VT	VT	VT	VT	VT	VT	VT	VT	VT	VT	VT	VT	VT	VT	VT	VT	VT	VT
Milton Keynes Central	d	07.15	07.50	08.15	08.45	09.15	09.45	10.15	10.45	11.15	11.45	12.15	12.45	13.15	13.45	14.15	14.45	15.15	15.45	16.15	16.45	17.15	17.45	18.15	18.45
Bedford Bus Station	a	08.05	08.40	09.05	09.35	10.05	10.35	11.05	11.35	12.05	12.35	13.05	13.35	14.05	14.35	15.05	15.35	16.05	16.35	17.05	17.35	18.10	18.40	19.10	19.40
St Neots Cross Keys	a	08.47	09.17	09.47	10.17	10.47	11.17	11.47	12.17	12.47	13.17	13.47	14.17	14.47	15.17	15.47	16.17	16.47	17.17	17.47	18.17	18.47	19.15		20.15
Cambridge Parkside	a	09.25	09.55	10.25	10.55	11.25	11.55	12.25	12.55	13.25	13.55	14.25	14.55	15.25	15.55	16.25	16.55	17.25	17.55	18.25	18.55	19.25	19.48		20.48

		VT	VT	VT	VT	VT	VT	VT
Milton Keynes Central	d	19.15	19.45	20.10	2040	21.10	22.10	23.10
Bedford Bus Station	a	20.05	20.30	20.50	21.20	21.50	22.50	23.50
St Neots Cross Keys	a		21.10		22.00			
Cambridge Parkside	a		21.43		22.33			

Sundays

		VT	VT	VT	VT	VT	VT	VT	VT	VT	VT	VT	VT	VT	VT	VT	VT	VT	VT	VT	VT	VT	VT	VT	VT
Milton Keynes Central	d	09.15	10.15	11.15	12.15	12.45	13.15	13.45	14.15	14.45	15.15	15.45	16.15	16.45	17.15	17.45	18.15	18.45	19.15	19.45	20.10	20.40	21.10	22.10	23.10
Bedford Bus Station	a	10.05	11.05	12.05	13.05	13.35	14.05	14.35	15.05	15.35	16.05	16.35	17.05	17.356	18.05	18.35	19.05	19.35	20.00	20.30	20.50	21.20	21.50	22.50	23.50
St Neots Cross Keys	a	10.47	11.47	12.47	13.47	14.17	14.47	15.17	15.47	16.17	16.45	17.15	17.45	18.15	18.45	19.15		20.15		21.10		22.00			
Cambridge Parkside	a	11.25	12.25	13.25	14.25	14.55	15.25	15.55	16.25	16.55	17.18	17.48	18.18	18.48	19.18	19.48		20.48		21.43		22.33			

Sunday service operates on Bank Holidays. Please check with local operator before travelling

Table 65C

Cambridge and Bedford - Milton Keynes Central

Bus Service

		VT	VT	VT	VT	VT	VT	VT	VT	VT	VT	VT	VT	VT	VT	VT	VT	VT	VT	VT	VT	VT	VT	VT	VT
Cambridge Parkside	d					05.30		06.30	07.00	07.30	08.10	08.40	09.10	09.40	10.10	10.40	11.10	11.40	12.10	12.40	13.10	13.40	14.10	14.40	15.10
St Neots Sq (Bus)	d					06.05		07.05	07.35	08.05	08.45	09.15	09.45	10.15	10.45	11.15	11.45	12.15	12.45	13.15	13.45	14.15	14.45	15.15	15.45
Bedford Bus Station	d	05.00	05.30	06.00	06.30	06.45	07.15	07.45	08.15	09.00	09.30	10.00	10.30	11.00	11.30	12.00	12.30	13.00	13.30	14.00	14.30	15.00	15.30	16.00	16.30
Milton Keynes Central	a	05.45	06.15	06.45	07.15	07.35	08.05	08.45	09.15	09.45	10.15	10.45	11.15	11.45	12.15	12.45	13.15	13.45	14.15	14.45	15.15	15.45	16.15	16.45	17.15

		VT	VT	VT	VT	VT	VT	VT
Cambridge Parkside	d	15.40	16.10	16.40	17.10	17.40	.18.10	18.40
St Neots Sq (Bus)	d	16.15	16.45	17.15	17.45	18.15	18.45	19.15
Bedford Bus Station	d	17.00	17.30	18.00	18.30	19.00	19.30	20.00
Milton Keynes Central	a	17.45	18.15	18.45	19.10	19.45	20.10	20.45

Saturdays

		VT	VT	VT	VT	VT	VT	VT	VT	VT	VT	VT	VT	VT	VT	VT	VT	VT	VT	VT	VT	VT	VT	VT	VT
Cambridge Parkside	d							06.40	07.10	07.40	08.10	08.40	09.10	09.40	10.10	10.40	11.10	11.40	12.10	12.40	13.10	13.40	14.10	14.40	15.10
St Neots Sq (Bus)	d							07.15	07.45	08.51	08.45	09.15	09.45	10.15	10.45	11.15	11.45	12.15	12.45	13.15	13.45	14.15	14.45	15.15	15.45
Bedford Bus Station	d	05.05	05.35	06.05	06.35	07.00	07.30	08.00	08.30	09.00	09.30	10.00	10.30	11.00	11.30	12.00	12.30	13.00	13.30	14.00	14.30	15.00	15.30	16.00	16.30
Milton Keynes Central	a	05.50	06.20	06.50	07.20	07.45	08.15	08.45	09.15	09.45	10.15	10.45	11.15	11.45	12.15	12.45	13.15	13.45	14.15	14.45	15.15	15.45	16.15	16.45	17.15

		VT	VT	VT	VT	VT	VT	VT
Cambridge Parkside	d	15.40	16.10	16.40	17.10	17.40	.18.10	18.40
St Neots Sq (Bus)	d	16.15	16.45	17.15	17.45	18.15	18.45	19.15
Bedford Bus Station	d	17.00	17.30	18.00	18.30	19.00	19.30	20.00
Milton Keynes Central	a	17.45	18.15	18.45	19.10	19.45	20.10	20.45

Sundays

		VT	VT	VT	VT	VT	VT	VT	VT	VT	VT	VT	VT	VT	VT	VT	VT	VT	VT	VT	VT	VT	VT	VT	VT
Cambridge Parkside	d					08.10		09.10		10.10		11.10	11.40	12.10	12.40	13.10	13.40	14.10	14.40	15.10	15.40	16.10	16.40	17.10	17.40
St Neots Sq (Bus)	d					08.45		09.45		10.45		11.45	12.15	12.45	13.15	13.45	14.15	14.45	15.15	15.45	16.15	16.45	17.15	17.45	18.15
Bedford Bus Station	d	06.00	07.00	08.00	09.00	09.30	10.00	10.30	11.00	11.30	12.00	12.30	13.00	13.30	14.00	14.30	15.00	15.30	16.00	16.30	17.00	17.30	18.00	18.30	19.00
Milton Keynes Central	a	06.45	07.45	08.45	09.45	10.15	10.45	11.15	11.45	12.15	12.45	13.15	13.45	14.15	14.45	15.15	15.45	16.15	16.45	17.15	17.45	18.15	18.45	19.10	19.40

		VT
Cambridge Parkside	d	18.40
St Neots Sq (Bus)	d	19.15
Bedford Bus Station	d	20.00
Milton Keynes Central	a	20.40

Table 65E

Preston - Southport

Bus Service

		VT	VT	VT	VT	VT	VT	VT	VT	VT	VT	VT	VT	VT	VT	VT	VT	VT	VT	VT	VT	VT	VT	VT	VT
Preston	d	05.04	05.36	06.058	06.25	06.55	07.25	08.09	08.39	09.09	09.39	10.09	10.39	11.09	11.39	12.09	12.39	13.09	13.39	14.09	14.39	15.09	15.39	16.19	16.49
Southport (Lord Street)	a	05.33	06.05	06.35	06.55	07.25	07.58	08.46	09.16	09.45	10.16	10.46	11.16	11.46	12.16	12.46	.13.16	13.46	14.16	14.46	15.16	15.46	16.16	16.56	17.26

		VT	VT
Preston	d	17.19	18.24
Southport (Lord Street)	a	17.56	19.01

Saturdays

		VT	VT	VT	VT	VT	VT	VT	VT	VT	VT	VT	VT	VT	VT	VT	VT	VT	VT	VT	VT	VT	VT
Preston	d	06.13	07.05	08.09	08.39	09.09	09.39	10.09	10.39	11.09	11.39	12.09	12.39	13.09	13.39	14.09	14.39	15.09	15.39	16.09	16.39	17.19	18.19
Southport (Lord Street)	a	06.45	07.38	08.46	09.16	09.46	10.16	.10.46	11.16	11.46	12.16	12.46	13.16	13.46	14.16	14.46	15.16	15.46	16.16	16.46	17.16	17.56	19.24

Sundays

		VT	VT	VT	VT	VT	VT	VT	VT	VT	VT	VT
Preston	d	06.33	08.09	09.09	10.09	11.09	12.09	13.09	14.09	15.09	16.09	18.09
Southport (Lord Street)	a	07.02	08.46	09.46	10.46	11.46	.12.46	13.46	14.46	15.56	16.56	18.46

This is the X2 service operated jointly by Stagecoach in Lancashire and Stagecoach in Merseyside

Sunday service operates on Bank Holidays. Please check with local operator before travelling

Table 65E

Mondays to Fridays

Southport - Preston

Bus Service

		VT	VT	VT	VT	VT	VT	VT	VT	VT	VT	VT	VT	VT	VT	VT	VT	VT	VT	VT	VT	VT	VT	VT	VT
Southport (Lord Street)	d	06.55	07.21	07.41	08.38	09.08	09.38	10.08	10.38	11.08	11.38	12.08	12.38	13.08	13.38	14.08	14.38	15.08	15.38	16.08	16.43	17.30	18.00	18.20	18.50
Preston	a	07.31	08.06	08.41	09.20	09.50	10.20	10.50	11.20	11.50	12.20	12.08	12.38	13.08	13.38	14.08	14.38	15.08	15.38	16.08	16.43	18.11	18.41	18.52	19.22

		VT	VT	VT	VT
Southport (Lord Street)	d	19.20	19.50	20.20	21.20
Preston	a	19.52	20.22	20.52	21.52

Saturdays

		VT	VT	VT	VT	VT	VT	VT	VT	VT	VT	VT	VT	VT	VT	VT	VT	VT	VT	VT	VT	VT	VT	VT	VT
Southport (Lord Street)	d	08.08	08.38	09.08	09.38	10.08	10.38	11.08	11.38	12.08	12.38	13.08	13.38	14.08	14.38	15.08	15.38	16.08	16.38	17.03	17.41	18.20	18.50	19.20	19.50
Preston	a	08.50	09.20	09.50	10.20	10.50	11.20	11.50	12.20	12.50	13.20	13.50	14.20	14.50	15.20	15.50	16.20	16.50	17.20	17.45	18.23.	19.02	19.32	20.02	20.32

		VT	VT
Southport (Lord Street)	d	20.20	21.20
Preston	a	20.52	21.52

Sundays

		VT	VT	VT	VT	VT	VT	VT	VT	VT	VT	VT
Southport (Lord Street)	d	09.06	11.05	12.05	13.05	14.05	15.05	16.05	17.05	18.05	19.05	21.05
Preston	a	09.45	11.45	12.45	13.45	14.45	15.45	16.45	17.45	18.45	19.45	21.45

Table 65F

Mondays to Fridays

Penrith - Keswick, Cockermouth and Workington

Bus Service

		VT	VT	VT	VT	VT	VT	VT	VT	VT	VT	VT	VT	VT	VT	VT	VT
Penrith North Lakes	d	07.22	08.22	09.22	10.22	11.22	12.22	13.22	14.22	15.22	16.22	17.22	18.30	19.30	20.35	21.40	22.45
Keswick (Bus Station)	a	07.53	09.00	10.00	11.00	12.00	13.00	14.00	15.00	16.00	17.00	18.00	19.00	0.00	21.05	22.10	23.15
Cockermouth (Main Street)	a	08.32	09.39	10.39	11.39	12.39	13.39	14.39	15.39	16.39	17.39	18.39	19.39	20.39	21.40	22.40	23.45
Workington (Bus Station)	a	08.57	10.04	11.04	12.04	13.04	14.04	15.04	16.04	17.04	18.04	19.04	20.04	20.58	21.58	22.58	00.03

Saturdays

		VT	VT	VT	VT	VT	VT	VT	VT	VT	VT	VT	VT	VT	VT	VT	VT
Penrith North Lakes	d	07.22	08.22	09.22	10.22	11.22	12.22	13.22	14.22	15.22	16.22	17.22	18.30	19.30	20.35	21.40	22.45
Keswick (Bus Station)	a	07.53	09.00	10.00	11.00	12.00	13.00	14.00	15.00	16.00	17.00	18.00	19.00	20.00	21.05	22.10	23.15
Cockermouth (Main Street)	a	08.32	09.39	10.39	11.39	12.39	13.39	14.39	15.39	16.39	17.39	18.39	19.39	20.39	21.40	22.40	23.45
Workington (Bus Station)	a	08.57	10.04	11.04	12.04	13.04	14.04	15.04	16.04	17.04	18.04	19.04	20.04	20.58	21.58	22.58	00.03

Sundays

		VT	VT	VT	VT	VT	VT	VT	VT
Penrith North Lakes	d	22.45	08.45	09.20	11.20	13.20	15.20	17.20	19.20
Keswick (Bus Station)	a	23.15	09.22	09.55	11.55	13.55	15.55	17.55	19.55
Cockermouth (Main Street)	a	23.45		10.31	12.31	14.31	16.31	18.31	20.31
Workington (Bus Station)	a	00.03		10.52	12.52	14.52	16.52	18.52	20.52

This is an amalgamation of the X4/X5/X50 services operated by Stagecaoch in Cumbria

Sunday service operates on Bank Holidays. Please check with local operator before travelling

Table 65F

Workington, Cockermouth and Keswick - Penrith

Bus Service

		VT	VT	VT	VT	VT	VT	VT	VT	VT	VT	VT	VT	VT	VT	VT	VT	VT
Workington (Bus Station)	d	05.20	06.20	06.55	07.55	09.20	10.20	11.20	12.20	13.20	14.20	15.20	16.20	17.20		18.20	19.15	21.15
Cockermouth (Main Street)	d	05.41	06.41	07.16	08.16	09.41	10.41	11.41	12.41	13.41	14.41	15.41	16.41	17.41		18.41	19.37	21.37
Keswick (Bus Station)	d	06.25	07.25	07.55	08.55	10.20	11.20	12.20	13.20	14.20	15.20	16.20	17.20	18.20	18.40	19.20	20.10	22.06
Penrith North Lakes	a	06.50	07.59	08.36	09.36	11.01	12.01	13.01	14.01	15.01	16.01	17.01	18.01	19.01	19.15	19.55	20.45	22.33

Saturdays

		VT	VT	VT	VT	VT	VT	VT	VT	VT	VT	VT	VT	VT	VT	VT	VT	VT
Workington (Bus Station)	d	05.20	06.20	06.55	07.55	09.20	10.20	11.20	12.20	13.20	14.20	15.20	16.20	17.20		18.20	19.15	21.15
Cockermouth (Main Street)	d	05.41	06.41	07.16	08.16	09.41	10.41	11.41	12.41	13.41	14.41	15.41	16.41	17.41		18.41	19.37	21.37
Keswick (Bus Station)	d	06.25	07.25	07.55	08.55	10.20	11.20	12.20	13.20	14.20	15.20	16.20	17.20	18.20	18.40	19.20	20.10	22.06
Penrith North Lakes	a	06.50	07.59	08.36	09.36	11.01	12.01	13.01	14.01	15.01	16.01	17.01	18.01	19.01	19.15	19.55	20.45	22.33

Sundays

		VT	VT	VT	VT	VT	VT	VT
Workington (Bus Station)	d	07.15	09.15	11.15	13.15	15.15	17.15	
Cockermouth (Main Street)	d	07.36	09.36	11.36	13.36	15.36	17.36	
Keswick (Bus Station)	d	08.15	10.15	12.15	14.15	16.15	18.12	18.40
Penrith North Lakes	a	08.50	10.50	12.50	14.50	16.50	18.47	19.15

Table 65G

Carlisle - Scottish Border Towns

Bus Service

		VT	VT	VT	VT	VT	VT	VT	VT	VT	VT	VT	VT FO
Carlisle	d	09.10	10.10	11.10	12.10	13.10	14.10	15.10	16.10	17.10	18.50	20.50	22.50
Langholm	a	09.57	10.57	11.57	12.57	13.57	14.57	15.57	16.57	17.57	19.37	21.37	23.32
Hawick	a	10.32	11.32	12.32	13.32	14.32	15.32	16.32	17.32	18.32	20.12	22.12	00.07
Selkirk	a	10.55	11.55	12.55	13.55	14.55	15.55	16.55	17.55	18.55	20.35	22.35	00.30
Galashiels	d	11.15	12.15	13.15	14.15	15.15	16.15	17.15	18.15	19.15	20.50	22.50	00.45

Saturdays

		VT	VT	VT	VT	VT	VT	VT	VT	VT	VT	VT	VT	VT
Carlisle	d	22.50	09.10	10.10	11.10	12.10	13.10	14.10	15.10	16.10	17.10	18.50	20.50	22.50
Langholm	a	23.32	09.57	10.57	11.57	12.57	13.57	14.57	15.57	16.57	17.57	19.37	21.37	23.32
Hawick	a	00.07	10.32	11.32	12.32	13.32	14.32	15.32	16.32	17.32	18.32	20.12	22.12	00.07
Selkirk	a	00.30	10.55	11.55	12.55	13.55	14.55	15.55	16.55	17.55	18.55	20.35	22.35	00.30
Galashiels	d	00.45	11.15	12.15	13.15	14.15	15.15	16.15	17.15	18.15	19.15	20.50	22.50	00.45

Sundays

		VT	VT	VT	VT
Carlisle	d	22.50	14.05	18.05	21.20
Langholm	a	23.32	14.50	18.50	22.05
Hawick	a	00.07	15.25	19.25	22.40
Selkirk	a	00.30	15.45	19.45	23.00
Galashiels	d	00.45	16.00	20.00	23.15

Table 65G

Mondays to Fridays

Scottish Border Towns - Carlisle

Bus Service

		VT	VT	VT	VT	VT	VT	VT	VT	VT	VT	VT	VT FO
		🚌	🚌	🚌	🚌	🚌	🚌	🚌	🚌	🚌	🚌	🚌	🚌
Galashiels	d	06.20	07.15	08.10	09.25	10.25	11.25	12.25	13.25	14.25	16.30	17.35	19.25
Selkirk	d	06.35	07.30	08.25	09.40	10.40	11.40	12.40	13.40	14.40	16.45	17.50	19.40
Hawick	d	06.55	07.50	08.45	10.00	11.00	12.00	13.00	14.00	15.00	17.05	18.10	19.58
Langholm	d	07.35	08.30	09.25	10.40	11.40	12.40	13.40	14.40	15.40	17.45	18.50	20.38
Selkirk	a	08.27	09.17	10.12	11.27	12.27	13.27	14.27	15.27	16.27	18.32	19.37	21.25

Saturdays

		VT	VT	VT	VT	VT	VT	VT	VT	VT	VT
		🚌	🚌	🚌	🚌	🚌	🚌	🚌	🚌	🚌	🚌
Galashiels	d	06.20	07.15	08.10	09.25	10.25	11.25	12.25	13.25	14.25	19.25
Selkirk	d	06.35	07.30	08.25	09.40	10.40	11.40	12.40	13.40	14.40	19.40
Hawick	d	06.55	07.50	08.45	10.00	11.00	12.00	13.00	14.00	15.00	19.58
Langholm	d	07.35	08.30	09.25	10.40	11.40	12.40	13.40	14.40	15.40	20.38
Selkirk	a	08.27	09.17	10.12	11.27	12.27	13.27	14.27	15.27	16.27	21.25

Sundays

		VT	VT	VT	VT
		🚌	🚌	🚌	🚌
Galashiels	d	09.30	11.30	15.30	17.30
Selkirk	d	09.45	11.45	15.45	17.45
Hawick	d	10.05	12.05	16.05	18.05
Langholm	d	10.38	12.38	16.38	18.38
Selkirk	a	11.27	13.27	17.27	19.27

Table 66

Mondays to Fridays

London - Watford Junction, Milton Keynes, Northampton and West Midlands

		LM MX	VT MO	VT MO	VT MX	LM MX	LM MO	VT MO	LM MX	VT MX	LM MO	LM MX	LM	LM MO	LM MX	LM	SN	LM	VT	LM	VT	VT	SN
		◇1	◇1	◇1	◇1	◇1	◇1	◇1	◇1	◇1	◇1	1	◇1	◇1	◇1	1	1	◇1	◇1	◇1	◇1	◇1	1
			☕	☕	☕			☕		☕									⊠		⊠	⊠	
London Euston 15	⊖ d	21p46	21p55	22p25	22p30	22p54	22p58	23p25	23p24	23p30	23p34	23p34	00 04	00 34	00 34	01 34			05 27	05 30	05 39	06 17	
East Croydon	d																						
Clapham Junction 10	d																05 03						
Imperial Wharf	d																05 07						05 39
West Brompton	⊖ d																05 10						05 41
Kensington (Olympia)	⊖ d																05 14						05 44
Shepherd's Bush	d																05 17						05 47
Wembley Central	⊖ d												00 16	00 44	00 46	01 45							06s02
Harrow & Wealdstone	⊖ d						23p10				23p46	23p46		00 48	00 51	01 50	05 33			05 43			06 07
Bushey	d											23p51			00 56								
Watford Junction	a		22b09	22b39	22b45	23p09	23p17	23b39	23p40		23p53	23p54	00 23	00 55	00 59	01 56	05 40		05u44	05 50	06u01		06 14
	d		22b09	22b39	22b45	23p10	23p17	23b40	23p41		23p53	23p54	00 23	00 59	00 59	01 57			05u45	05 50	06u02		06 14
Kings Langley	d					23p14	23p22				23p58	23p59		01 04	01 04					05 55			
Apsley	d					23p18	23p25				00 01	00 02		01 07	01 07					05 58			
Hemel Hempstead	d					23p21	23p28		23p48		00 04	00 05	00 31	01 10	01 10	02 04				06 01			06 22
Berkhamsted	d					23p26	23p33		23p53		00 09	00 09	00 35	01 15	01 15	02 09				06 06			06 26
Tring	d					23p33	23p38				00 14	00 14	00 40	01 20	01 20	02 14				06 13			06 33
Cheddington	d						23p43				00 19	00 19		01 25	01 25					06 18			
Leighton Buzzard	d	22p19				23p40	23p50		00 06		00 26	00 25	00 50	01 32	01 32	02 24				06 23			06 42
Bletchley	d					23p47	23p57		00 13		00 33	00 32	00 58	01 39	01 39	02 31		05 17		06 31			06 49
Milton Keynes Central 10	a	22p32	22p42	23p11	23p28	23p55	00 06	00 11	00 22	00 26	00 42	00 40	01 06	01 48	01 48	02 40		05 21	06 09	06 36	06 22	06 47	06 55
	d	22p32	22p44	23p12	23p29	23p55	00 06	00 12	00 22	00 26	00 42		01 07	01 48	01 48			05 21	06 10	06 37	06 22		
Wolverton	d	22p36				23p59	00 10		00 26		00 46		01 10	01 52	01 52			05 25		06 40			
Northampton	a	22p51				00 12	00 24		00 40		01 00		01 25	02 06	02 06			05 39		06 54			
Rugby	a	23p16	23p21	23p47	23p59			00s47		01s00								06 02		07 16	06 44		
Nuneaton	a																	06 16	06 38				
Coventry	a	23p29	23p33	23p59	00 11			00s58		01s13										07 28			
Birmingham International	✈ a	23p47	23p51	00 10	00 22			01s09		01s24										07 45			
Birmingham New Street 12	a	00 04	00 04	00 23	00 33			01s22		01s36										08 03			
Sandwell & Dudley	a																						
Wolverhampton 7	a		00 27	00 55	01 03			01 54		02 07													

		LM	SN	VT	VT	LM	VT	VT	LM	VT	LM	VT	LM	SN	LM	VT	VT	VT	LM	LM	LM	VT	LM
		1	1	◇1	◇1	1	◇1	◇1	1	◇1	◇1	◇1	◇1	1	1	◇1	◇1	◇1	1	1	◇1	◇1	◇1
				⊠	⊠		⊠	⊠		⊠		⊠				⊠	⊠	⊠				⊠	
London Euston 15	⊖ d	06 04		06 23	06 43	06 24	06 36	06 55	06 34	07 10	06 53	07 20	07 13		07 04	07 23	07 35	07 43	07 24	07 34	07 47	08 10	07 54
East Croydon	d																						
Clapham Junction 10	d		05 55																				
Imperial Wharf	d		06 00											06 42									
West Brompton	⊖ d		06 03											06 45									
Kensington (Olympia)	⊖ d		06 07											06 49									
Shepherd's Bush	d		06 10											06 52									
Wembley Central	⊖ d		06 23											07s07									
Harrow & Wealdstone	⊖ d	06 16	06 28						06 47					07 12	07 16					07 46			
Bushey	d																						
Watford Junction	a	06 23	06 35	06u37		06 40	06u50		06 53		07 09			07 19	07 24	07u37			07 41	07 53	08 01		08 11
	d	06 23		06u37		06 41			06 54		07 10			07 19	07 24	07u37			07 42	07 53	08 02		08 11
Kings Langley	d	06 28							06 58						07 29					07 58			
Apsley	d	06 31							07 02						07 32					08 01			
Hemel Hempstead	d	06 34				06 48			07 05		07 17			07 27	07 35				07 50	08 04			08 19
Berkhamsted	d	06 39				06 53			07 09		07 22			07 32	07 40				07 54	08 09			08 23
Tring	d	06a46				07 00			07 16					07 39	07a47				08 01	08a16			
Cheddington	d					07 05			07 21										08 06				
Leighton Buzzard	d					07 10			07 26		07 35		07 42	07 51					08 12				08 36
Bletchley	d					07 17			07 34		07 43		07 50	07 58					08 19				08 44
Milton Keynes Central 10	a				07 13	07 23		07 25	07 39	07 40	07 49	07 50	07 54	08 03			08 05	08 13	08 25		08 25	08 40	08 49
	d				07 13	07 23					07 49		07 55					08 13			08 31		08 50
Wolverton	d					07 27					07 53		07 59										08 53
Northampton	a					07 42					08 06		08 13								08 44		09 08
Rugby	a					08 03					08 37										09 03		09 37
Nuneaton	a					08 17															09 16		
Coventry	a			07 22	07 42						08 49					08 22		08 42					09 49
Birmingham International	✈ a			07 33	07 54						09 04					08 33		08 53					10 04
Birmingham New Street 12	a			07 45	08 08						09 16					08 45		09 08					10 16
Sandwell & Dudley	a			07 57												08 57							
Wolverhampton 7	a			08 11												09 11							

b previous night, stops to pick up only

London - Watford Junction, Milton Keynes, Northampton and West Midlands

Station		VT ◇1 ⊠		LM ◇1	SN 1	LM 1	VT ◇1 ⊠	LM 1	LM 1	VT ◇1 A ⊠	VT ◇1 B ⊠	LM ◇1		VT ◇1 ⊠	VT ◇1 ⊠	LM ◇1	VT ◇1 ⊠	LM ◇1	SN 1	LM 1	VT ◇1 ⊠	VT ◇1 ⊠		LM 1	LM 1
London Euston	d	08 20		08 13		08 05	08 23	08 24	08 34	08 43	08 43	08 46		09 10	09 10	08 54	09 20	09 13		09 05	09 23	09 43		09 24	09 34
East Croydon	d																		08 07						
Clapham Junction	d																								
Imperial Wharf	d				07 44														08 44						
West Brompton	d				07 47														08 47						
Kensington (Olympia)	d				07 50														08 50						
Shepherd's Bush	d				07 53														08 53						
Wembley Central	d				08s08														09s08						
Harrow & Wealdstone	d				08 13	08 21		08 36	08 46										09 13	09 17					09 47
Bushey	d					08 26			08 51											09 22					09 52
Watford Junction	a				08 20	08 29	08u37	08 43	08 54			09 00				09 10			09 20	09 25	09u37			09 40	09 55
	d				08 20	08 29	08u37	08 44	08 55			09 01				09 11			09 20	09 26	09u37			09 41	09 56
Kings Langley	d					08 34			08 59											09 30					10 00
Apsley	d					08 38			09 03											09 34					10 04
Hemel Hempstead	d				08 28	08 40		08 52	09 06							09 18			09 28	09 37				09 48	10 07
Berkhamsted	d				08 32	08 45		08 57	09 10							09 23			09 32	09 41				09 53	10 11
Tring	d				08 39	08a52		09 04	09a17										09 39	09a48				10 00	10a19
Cheddington	d							09 09																10 05	
Leighton Buzzard	d			08 42	08 48			09 14								09 36		09 42	09 48					10 10	
Bletchley	d			08 50	08 55			09 21								09 43		09 50	09 55					10 17	
Milton Keynes Central	a	08 50		08 54	09 01			09 27		09 13	09 13	09 24		09u40	09 40	09 49	09 50	09 54	10 01			10 13		10 23	
	d			08 55						09 13	09 13	09 25				09 49		09 55				10 13			
Wolverton	d			08 59												09 53		09 59							
Northampton	a			09 13								09 40				10 06		10 13							
Rugby	a											10 04				10 37									
Nuneaton	a											10 16													
Coventry	a						09 22			09 42	09 42					10 49					10 22	10 42			
Birmingham International	a						09 33			09 53	09 53					11 04					10 33	10 53			
Birmingham New Street	a						09 45			10 08	10 08					11 17					10 45	11 08			
Sandwell & Dudley	a						09 57														10 57				
Wolverhampton	a						10 11				10 36										11 11				

Station		LM ◇1	VT ◇1 🍴	VT ◇1 🍴	LM ◇1	LM ◇1	SN 1	LM 1		VT ◇1 🍴	VT ◇1 🍴	LM 1	LM 1	LM 1	VT ◇1 🍴	LM ◇1	VT ◇1 🍴	LM ◇1		SN 1	LM 1	VT ◇1 🍴	VT ◇1 B 🍴	VT ◇1 A 🍴	LM 1
London Euston	d	09 46	10 10	10 20	09 54	10 13		10 05		10 23	10 43	10 24	10 34	10 46	11 10	10 54	11 20	11 13			11 04	11 23	11 43	11 43	11 24
East Croydon	d						09 08													10 10					
Clapham Junction	d																								
Imperial Wharf	d						09 44													10 44					
West Brompton	d						09 47													10 47					
Kensington (Olympia)	d						09 50													10 50					
Shepherd's Bush	d						09 53													10 53					
Wembley Central	d						10s08													11s08					
Harrow & Wealdstone	d						10 13	10 17					10 47							11 13	11 17				
Bushey	d							10 22					10 52								11 22				
Watford Junction	a	10 00			10 10		10 20	10 25		10u37		10 40	10 55	11 00		11 10				11 20	11 25	11u37			11 40
	d	10 01			10 11		10 20	10 26		10u37		10 41	10 56	11 01		11 11				11 20	11 26	11u37			11 41
Kings Langley	d							10 30					11 00								11 30				
Apsley	d							10 34					11 04								11 34				
Hemel Hempstead	d				10 18		10 28	10 37				10 48	11 07			11 18				11 28	11 37				11 48
Berkhamsted	d				10 23		10 32	10 41				10 53	11 11			11 23				11 32	11 41				11 53
Tring	d						10 39	10a48				11 00	11a18							11 39	11a48				12 00
Cheddington	d											11 05													12 05
Leighton Buzzard	d				10 38	10 43	10 48					11 10				11 36		11 42		11 48					12 10
Bletchley	d				10 46	10 52	10 57					11 17				11 43		11 50		11 55					12 17
Milton Keynes Central	a	10 25	10 40	10 50	10 51	10 56	11 02				11 13	11 23		11 25	11 40	11 49	11 50	11 54		12 01			12 13	12 13	12 23
	d	10 25	10 41	10 50	10 52	10 57					11 13			11 25	11 41	11 49	11 50	11 55					12 13	12 13	
Wolverton	d				10 55	11 01										11 53		11 59							
Northampton	a	10 41			11 09	11 14								11 41		12 06		12 13							
Rugby	a	11 04			11 37									12 03		12 37									
Nuneaton	a	11 16												12 16											
Coventry	a				11 49					11 22	11 42					12 49						12 22	12 43	12 42	
Birmingham International	a				12 04					11 33	11 53					13 04						12 33	12 54	12 53	
Birmingham New Street	a				12 17					11 45	12 08					13 17						12 45	13 08	13 08	
Sandwell & Dudley	a									11 57												12 57			
Wolverhampton	a									12 11												13 11			

A until 16 July, from 6 September

B from 19 July until 3 September

London - Watford Junction, Milton Keynes, Northampton and West Midlands

Station		LM 1	LM ◇1	VT ◇1 🍴		LM ◇1	VT ◇1 🍴	LM ◇1	SN 1	LM 1	VT ◇1 🍴	VT ◇1 🍴	LM 1	LM 1		LM ◇1	VT ◇1 🍴	LM ◇1	VT ◇1 🍴	LM ◇1	SN 1	LM 1	VT ◇1 🍴	VT ◇1 A 🍴	
London Euston	d	11 34	11 46	12 10		11 54	12 20	12 13		12 04	12 23	12 43	12 24	12 34		12 46	13 10	12 54	13 20	13 13		13 04	13 23	13 43	
East Croydon	d								11 11												12 10				
Clapham Junction	d																								
Imperial Wharf	d								11 44												12 44				
West Brompton	d								11 47												12 47				
Kensington (Olympia)	d								11 50												12 50				
Shepherd's Bush	d								11 53												12 53				
Wembley Central	d								12s08												13s08				
Harrow & Wealdstone	d	11 46							12 13	12 17				12 46							13 13	13 17			
Bushey	d	11 51								12 22				12 51								13 22			
Watford Junction	a	11 54	12 00			12 10			12 20	12 25	12u37		12 40	12 54		13 00		13 10			13 20	13 25	13u37		
	d	11 55	12 01			12 11			12 20	12 26	12u37		12 41	12 55		13 01		13 11			13 20	13 26	13u37		
Kings Langley	d	11 59								12 30				12 59								13 30			
Apsley	d	12 03								12 34				13 03								13 34			
Hemel Hempstead	d	12 06				12 18			12 28	12 37			12 48	13 06				13 18			13 28	13 37			
Berkhamsted	d	12 10				12 23			12 32	12 41			12 53	13 10				13 23			13 32	13 41			
Tring	d	12a17							12 39	12a48			13 00	13a17							13 39	13a48			
Cheddington	d												13 05												
Leighton Buzzard	d					12 36		12 42	12 48				13 10					13 36		13 42	13 48				
Bletchley	d					12 43		12 50	12 55				13 18					13 43		13 50	13 55				
Milton Keynes Central	a		12 24	12 40		12 49	12 50	12 54	13 01			13 13	13 23			13 25	13 40	13 49	13 50	13 54	14 01			14 13	
	d		12 25			12 49		12 55				13 13				13 25		13 49		13 55				14 13	
Wolverton	d					12 53		12 59										13 53		13 59					
Northampton	a		12 40			13 06		13 13								13 41		14 08		14 13					
Rugby	a		13 04			13 37										14 03		14 37							
Nuneaton	a		13 16													14 16									
Coventry	a					13 49					13 22	13 42						14 49					14 22	14 42	
Birmingham International	a					14 04					13 33	13 53						15 04					14 33	14 53	
Birmingham New Street	a					14 16					13 45	14 08						15 16					14 45	15 08	
Sandwell & Dudley	a										13 57												14 57		
Wolverhampton	a										14 11												15 11		

Station		VT ◇1 B 🍴	LM 1	LM 1	LM 1	VT ◇1 🍴	LM ◇1	VT ◇1 🍴	LM ◇1	SN 1		LM 1	VT ◇1 🍴	LM 1	LM 1	VT ◇1 🍴	LM ◇1	VT ◇1 🍴	LM ◇1	VT ◇1 🍴		LM ◇1	SN 1	LM 1	VT ◇1 B 🍴
London Euston	d	13 43	13 24	13 34	13 46	14 10	13 54	14 20	14 13			14 04	14 23	14 24	14 34	14 43	14 46	15 10	14 54	15 20		15 13		15 04	15 23
East Croydon	d									13 10													14 10		
Clapham Junction	d																								
Imperial Wharf	d									13 44													14 44		
West Brompton	d									13 47													14 47		
Kensington (Olympia)	d									13 50													14 50		
Shepherd's Bush	d									13 53													14 53		
Wembley Central	d									14s08													15s08		
Harrow & Wealdstone	d			13 46						14 13		14 17			14 46								15 13	15 17	
Bushey	d			13 51								14 22			14 51									15 22	
Watford Junction	a		13 40	13 54	14 00		14 10			14 20		14 25	14u37	14 40	14 54		15 00		15 10				15 20	15 25	15u37
	d		13 41	13 55	14 01		14 11			14 20		14 25	14u37	14 41	14 55		15 01		15 11				15 20	15 26	15u37
Kings Langley	d			13 59								14 30			14 59									15 30	
Apsley	d			14 03								14 33			15 03									15 34	
Hemel Hempstead	d		13 48	14 06			14 18			14 28		14 36		14 48	15 06				15 18				15 28	15 37	
Berkhamsted	d		13 53	14 10			14 23			14 32		14 41		14 53	15 10				15 23				15 32	15 41	
Tring	d		14 00	14a17						14 39		14a48		15 00	15a17								15 39	15a48	
Cheddington	d		14 05											15 05											
Leighton Buzzard	d		14 10				14 37		14 42	14 48				15 10					15 36			15 42	15 48		
Bletchley	d		14 18				14 44		14 50	14 55				15 18					15 43			15 50	15 55		
Milton Keynes Central	a	14 13	14 23		14 25	14 40	14 50	14 50	14 55	15 01				15 23		15 13	15 23	15 40	15 49	15 50		15 54	16 01		
	d	14 13			14 25		14 50		14 55							15 13	15 23		15 49			15 55			
Wolverton	d						14 54		14 59										15 53			15 59			
Northampton	a				14 42		15 08		15 13								15 41		16 06			16 13			
Rugby	a				15 04		15 37										16 03		16 37						
Nuneaton	a				15 16												16 16								
Coventry	a	14 43					15 49						15 22			15 42			16 49						16 22
Birmingham International	a	14 54					16 04						15 33			15 53			17 04						16 33
Birmingham New Street	a	15 08					16 17						15 45			16 08			17 16						16 45
Sandwell & Dudley	a												15 57												16 57
Wolverhampton	a	15 37											16 11												17 11

A until 16 July, from 6 September

B from 19 July until 3 September

London - Watford Junction, Milton Keynes, Northampton and West Midlands

		VT ◇1 A 🍴	VT ◇1 🍴	LM 1	LM 1	LM ◇1	VT ◇1 🍴	LM ◇1	VT ◇1 🍴	LM ◇1	SN 1	LM 1	VT ◇1 🍴	VT ◇1 🍴	LM 1	LM 1	LM ◇1	LM 1	VT ◇1 ⊠	VT ◇1 ⊠	LM ◇1	SN 1	LM 1
London Euston 15 ⊖	d	15 23	15 43	15 24	15 34	15 46	16 10	15 54	16 20	16 13		16 04	16 23	16 43	16 24	16 34	16 48	16 54	17 10	17 20	17 13		17 05
East Croydon	d										15 10											16 10	
Clapham Junction 10	d																						
Imperial Wharf	d										15 44											16 44	
West Brompton ⊖	d										15 47											16 47	
Kensington (Olympia) ⊖	d										15 50											16 50	
Shepherd's Bush	d										15 53											16 53	
Wembley Central ⊖	d										16s08											17s08	
Harrow & Wealdstone ⊖	d				15 46						16 13	16 17				16 46		17 06				17 13	17 18
Bushey	d				15 51							16 22				16 51		17 11					
Watford Junction	a	15u37		15 40	15 54	16 00		16 10			16 20	16 25	16u37		16 41	16 54		17 14				17 20	17 25
	d	15u37		15 41	15 55	16 01		16 11			16 20	16 26	16u37		16 42	16 55		17 14				17 21	17 26
Kings Langley	d				15 59							16 30				16 59							17 30
Apsley	d				16 03							16 34				17 03		17 20					
Hemel Hempstead	d			15 48	16 06			16 18			16 28	16 37			16 49	17 06		17 23				17 28	17 35
Berkhamsted	d			15 53	16 10			16 23			16 32	16 41			16 54	17 10		17 28				17 33	17 40
Tring	d			16 00	16a17						16 39	16a48			17 01	17a19		17a36				17 38	17 47
Cheddington	d			16 05											17 06								17 52
Leighton Buzzard	d			16 10				16 36		16 42	16 48				17 11		17 20				17 42	17 47	
Bletchley	d			16 17				16 43		16 50	16 56				17 18							17 54	18 01
Milton Keynes Central 10	a		16 13	16 23		16 25	16u40	16 49	16u50	16 54	17 00			17u13	17 25		17 30		17u40	17u50	17 52	17 59	18 05
	d		16 13			16 25		16 49		16 54				17u13			17 31		17u41		17 52		
Wolverton	d							16 53		16 58							17 35				17 56		
Northampton	a					16 41		17 06		17 13							17 49				18 11		
Rugby	a					17 03		17 37													18 37		
Nuneaton	a					17 16													18 11				
Coventry	a	16 22	16 42					17 49					17 22	17 42							18 49		
Birmingham International ✈	a	16 33	16 53					18 04					17 33	17 53							19 04		
Birmingham New Street 12	a	16 45	17 08					18 17					17 45	18 08							19 17		
Sandwell & Dudley	a	16 57											17 57										
Wolverhampton 7	a	17 11											18 11										

		LM 1	VT ◇1 ⊠	VT ◇1 ⊠	LM 1	LM ◇1	LM 1	LM 1	LM 1	VT ◇1 ⊠	LM ◇1	VT ◇1 ⊠	LM ◇1	SN 1	LM ◇1	LM 1	VT ◇1 ⊠	VT ◇1 ⊠	LM 1	LM ◇1	LM 1	LM 1
London Euston 15 ⊖	d	17 14	17 23	17 43	17 24	17 46	17 34	17 40	17 45	18 10	17 51	18 20	18 13		18 05	18 12	18 23	18 43	18 21	18 29	18 34	18 40
East Croydon	d													17 10								
Clapham Junction 10	d																					
Imperial Wharf	d													17 44								
West Brompton ⊖	d													17 47								
Kensington (Olympia) ⊖	d													17 50								
Shepherd's Bush	d													17 53								
Wembley Central ⊖	d													18s08								
Harrow & Wealdstone ⊖	d	17 27						17 52			18 03			18 13	18 18				18 34		18 46	
Bushey	d	17 32						17 56								18 25					18 51	18 55
Watford Junction	a	17 35	17u37		17 42		17 52	18 01	18 05		18 10			18 20	18 25	18 30	18u37		18 40	18 45	18 54	18 58
	d	17 36	17u37		17 43		17 53		18 05		18 11			18 20	18 25	18 30	18u37		18 40	18 45	18 54	18 59
Kings Langley	d						17 57								18 30				18 45			19 03
Apsley	d	17 42					18 01								18 33					18 52		19 07
Hemel Hempstead	d				17 50		18 04				18 18			18 28		18 39			18 50		19 01	19 10
Berkhamsted	d				17 55				18 14		18 22			18 32		18 43				18 58		19 14
Tring	d	17a52					18 13		18a23					18 38	18 44	18a53			18 58		19 10	19a25
Cheddington	d						18 18								18 49					19 08	19 15	
Leighton Buzzard	d				18 08	18 19	18 24						18 42	18 50	18 55				19 06		19 23	
Bletchley	d				18 15		18 32				18 39			18 59	19 04					19 18	19a30	
Milton Keynes Central 10	a			18u13	18 21	18 30	18 38			18u40	18 44	18u50	18 52	19 03	19 08			19 13	19 19	19 23		
	d			18u13	18 21	18 32				18u41	18 45		18 53		19 09			19 13		19 23		
Wolverton	d					18 36					18 48		18 57		19 12					19 27		
Northampton	a				18 37	18 50					19 03		19 10		19 26					19 39		
Rugby	a				19 03								19 37							20 03		
Nuneaton	a									19 12										20 18		
Coventry	a		18 22	18 42									19 49				19 22	19 42				
Birmingham International ✈	a		18 33	18 53									20 04				19 33	19 53				
Birmingham New Street 12	a		18 45	19 08									20 16				19 45	20 08				
Sandwell & Dudley	a		18 57														19 58					
Wolverhampton 7	a		19 11														20 12	20 36				

A until 16 July, from 6 September

Table 66

Mondays to Fridays

London - Watford Junction, Milton Keynes, Northampton and West Midlands

		LM ◇1	VT ▪ 1 🍴	VT ▪ 1 🍴	LM ◇1	LM 1	SN 1	LM 1	VT ▪ 1 🍴	VT ◇1 🍴	LM 1	LM 1	LM ◇1	VT ◇1 🍴	LM ◇1	LM ◇1	SN 1	LM 1	VT ◇1 🍴	VT ◇1 🍴	LM 1	LM 1	VT ◇1 🍴
London Euston 15 ⊖	d	18 49	19 10	19 20	19 13	18 54		19 04	19 23	19 43	19 24	19 34	19 46	20 10	19 54	20 13		20 04	20 23	20 43	20 24	20 34	21 00
East Croydon	d						18 10										19 10						
Clapham Junction 10	d																						
Imperial Wharf	d						18 44										19 44						
West Brompton ⊖	d						18 47										19 47						
Kensington (Olympia) ⊖	d						18 50										19 50						
Shepherd's Bush	d						18 53										19 53						
Wembley Central ⊖	d						19s08										20s08						
Harrow & Wealdstone ⊖	d					19 07	19 13	19 18				19 46					20 13	20 17				20 46	
Bushey	d							19 23				19 51						20 22				20 51	
Watford Junction	a					19 15	19 20	19 26	19u37		19 40	19 54			20 10		20 20	20 25	20u37		20 40	20 54	
	d					19 16	19 21	19 26	19u37		19 41	19 55			20 11		20 20	20 26	20u37		20 41	20 55	
Kings Langley	d							19 31				19 59						20 30				20 59	
Apsley	d							19 34				20 03						20 34				21 03	
Hemel Hempstead	d					19 23	19 28	19 37			19 48	20 06			20 18		20 28	20 37			20 48	21 06	
Berkhamsted	d					19 29	19 33	19 42			19 54	20 10			20 23		20 32	20 41			20 53	21 10	
Tring	d					19 36	19 40	19a49			20 01	20a17					20 39	20a48			21 00	21a17	
Cheddington	d										20 06										21 05		
Leighton Buzzard	d	19 19			19 42	19 47	19 52				20 11		20 20		20 36	20 42	20 48				21 10		
Bletchley	d	19 25				19 56	20 01				20 19				20 43	20 50	20 55				21 18		
Milton Keynes Central 10	a	19 30	19u40	19u50	19 55	20 02	20 06			20 13	20 25		20 30	20 40	20 49	20 54	21 01			21 13	21 23		21 30
	d	19 31			19 56					20 13			20 31		20 49	20 55				21 13			
Wolverton	d	19 35			20 00								20 35		20 53	20 59							
Northampton	a	19 49			20 13								20 49		21 06	21 13							
Rugby	a	20 16													21 37								
Nuneaton	a																						
Coventry	a	20 28							20 22	20 42					21 49				21 22	21 42			
Birmingham International ✈	a	20 45							20 33	20 53					22 04				21 33	21 53			
Birmingham New Street 12	a	21 01							20 45	21 06					22 16				21 46	22 06			
Sandwell & Dudley	a								20 58	21 23									21 58	22 23			
Wolverhampton 7	a								21 12	21 38									22 12	22 38			

		LM ◇1	VT ◇1 🍴	VT ◇1 🍴	LM ◇1	LM ◇1	SN 1	VT ◇1 🍴	LM 1	SR ▪ 🍴	LM 1	LM 1	VT ◇1 🍴	VT ◇1 🍴	LM ◇1	LM ◇1	LM 1	LM ◇1	VT ◇1 🍴	LM 1	LM ◇1	SN 1
London Euston 15 ⊖	d	20 46	21 03	21 07	20 54	21 13		21 10	21 04	21 15	21 24	21 34	21 43	22 00	21 46	21 54	22 04	22 24	22 30	22 34	22 54	
East Croydon	d																					
Clapham Junction 10	d																					
Imperial Wharf	d						20 44															22 44
West Brompton ⊖	d						20 47															22 47
Kensington (Olympia) ⊖	d						20 50															22 50
Shepherd's Bush	d						20 53															22 53
Wembley Central ⊖	d						21s08															
Harrow & Wealdstone ⊖	d						21 13		21 17			21 46					22 19			22 48		23 16
Bushey	d								21 22			21 51								22 53		
Watford Junction	a				21 10		21 20	21u24	21 25	21u33	21 40	21 53	21u57			22 10	22 25	22 40	22u45	22 56	23 09	23 23
	d				21 11		21 20	21u25	21 26		21 41	21 54	21u58			22 11	22 26	22 41	22u45	22 56	23 10	
Kings Langley	d								21 30			21 58					22 30			23 01	23 14	
Apsley	d								21 34			22 02					22 33			23 04	23 18	
Hemel Hempstead	d				21 18		21 28		21 36		21 48	22 05				22 18	22 36	22 48		23 07	23 21	
Berkhamsted	d				21 23		21 32		21 41		21 53	22 10				22 23	22 40	22 53		23 12	23 26	
Tring	d						21 39		21 48			22 16				22 30	22 45			23 17	23 33	
Cheddington	d								21 53			22 22								23 22		
Leighton Buzzard	d	21 20			21 36	21 45	21 50		21 57		22 06	22 26			22 19	22 41	22 54	23 07		23 29	23 40	
Bletchley	d				21 43	21 53	21 58		22a04		22 15	22 33				22 48	23 03	23 16		23 36	23 47	
Milton Keynes Central 10	a	21 31	21 33	21 37	21 49	21 57	22 05				22 21	22 38	22 17	22 30	22 32	22 57	23 11	23 22	23 28	23 46	23 55	
	d	21 32	21 34	21 38	21 49	21 58							22 17	22 31	22 32	22 57		23 31	23 29		23 55	
Wolverton	d	21 36			21 53	22 02									22 36	23 01		23 34			23 59	
Northampton	a	21 50			22 06	22 16									22 51	23 16		23 51			00 12	
Rugby	a	22 16	21 55			22 38		22 02						22 52	23 16				23 59			
Nuneaton	a			22 06										23 04								
Coventry	a	22 29	22 07			22 50							22 46		23 29				00 11			
Birmingham International ✈	a	22 45	22 18			23 06							23 00		23 47				00 22			
Birmingham New Street 12	a	23 03	22 29			23 19							23 16		00 04				00 33			
Sandwell & Dudley	a		22 41										23 33									
Wolverhampton 7	a		22 56										23 47						01 03			

London - Watford Junction, Milton Keynes, Northampton and West Midlands

		LM	VT	VT	LM
			FX	FO	
		◇1	◇1	◇1	1
			🛒	🛒	
London Euston 15 ⊖	d	23 24	23 30	23 30	23 34
East Croydon 🚊	d				
Clapham Junction 10	d				
Imperial Wharf	d				
West Brompton ⊖	d				
Kensington (Olympia) ⊖	d				
Shepherd's Bush	d				
Wembley Central ⊖	d				
Harrow & Wealdstone ⊖	d				23 46
Bushey	d				23 51
Watford Junction	a	23 40			23 54
	d	23 41			23 54
Kings Langley	d				23 59
Apsley	d				00 02
Hemel Hempstead	d	23 48			00 05
Berkhamsted	d	23 53			00 09
Tring	d				00 14
Cheddington	d				00 19
Leighton Buzzard	d	00 06			00 25
Bletchley	d	00 13			00 32
Milton Keynes Central 10	a	00 22	00 26	00 26	00 40
	d	00 22	00 26	00 26	
Wolverton	d	00 26			
Northampton	a	00 40			
Rugby	a		01s00	01s05	
Nuneaton	a				
Coventry	a		01s13	01s18	
Birmingham International ✈	a		01s24	01s29	
Birmingham New Street 12	a		01s36	01s41	
Sandwell & Dudley	a				
Wolverhampton 7 🚊	a		02 07	02 10	

Saturdays

		LM	VT	LM	LM	VT	LM	LM	LM	LM	SN	LM	LM	SN	VT	VT	LM	SN	VT	VT	ZZ	VT	SN
		◇1	◇1	◇1	◇1	◇1	1	◇1	◇1	1	1	◇1	◇1	1	◇1	◇1	◇1	1	◇1	◇1	1	◇1	1
			🛒			🛒									🛒	🛒			🛒	🛒		🛒	
London Euston 15 ⊖	d	21p46	22p30	22p54	23p24	23p30	23p34	00 04	00 34	01 34			05 34		06 05	06 23	06 24		06 36	06 55	07 13	07 20	
East Croydon 🚊	d																						06 10
Clapham Junction 10	d																						
Imperial Wharf	d										05 12			05 42				06 15					06 44
West Brompton ⊖	d										05 15			05 45				06 18					06 47
Kensington (Olympia) ⊖	d										05 19			05 49				06 22					06 50
Shepherd's Bush	d										05 22			05 52				06 25					06 53
Wembley Central ⊖	d								00 45	01 45				06s07				06 38					07s07
Harrow & Wealdstone ⊖	d						23p46	00 16	00 50	01 50	05 40		05 46	06 12				06 43					07 12
Bushey	d						23p51		00 55														
Watford Junction	a		22b45	23p09	23p40		23p54	00 23	00 58	01 56	05 47		05 53	06 19	06u19	06u37	06 40	06 50	06u50				07 19
	d		22b45	23p10	23p41		23p54	00 23	00 58	01 57			05 53	06 19	06u20	06u37	06 41						07 19
Kings Langley	d			23p14			23p59		01 03				05 58										
Apsley	d			23p18			00 02		01 06				06 01										
Hemel Hempstead	d			23p21	23p48		00 05	00 31	01 09	02 04			06 04	06 27			06 48						07 27
Berkhamsted	d			23p26	23p53		00 09	00 35	01 14	02 09			06 09	06 31			06 53						07 32
Tring	d			23p33			00 14	00 40	01 21	02 16			06 14	06 37			07 00						07 39
Cheddington	d						00 19		01 26				06 19				07 05						
Leighton Buzzard	d	22p19		23p40	00 06		00 25	00 50	01 31	02 24			06 25	06 47			07 10						07 48
Bletchley	d			23p47	00 13		00 32	00 58	01 38	02 31		05 17	06 34	06 55			07 17						07 55
Milton Keynes Central 10	a	22p32	23p28	23p55	00 22	00 26	00 40	01 06	01 45	02 37		05 21	06 39	07 00	06 39		07 23			07 25	07 48	07 50	08 00
	d	22p32	23p29	23p55	00 22	00 26		01 07	01 45			05 21	06 40		06 41		07 23				08 00		
Wolverton	d	22p36		23p59	00 26			01 10	01 49			05 25	06 43				07 27						
Northampton	a	22p51		00 12	00 40			01 25	02 05			05 37	06 57				07 40						
Rugby	a	23p16	23p59			01s05						06 01			07 02		08 04				08 25		
Nuneaton	a											06 16					08 16						
Coventry	a	23p29	00 11			01s18										07 22							
Birmingham International ✈	a	23p47	00 22			01s29										07 33							
Birmingham New Street 12	a	00 04	00 33			01s41										07 45							
Sandwell & Dudley	a															07 57							
Wolverhampton 7 🚊	a		01 03			02 10										08 11							

b previous night, stops to pick up only

London - Watford Junction, Milton Keynes, Northampton and West Midlands

		VT	LM	VT	VT	LM	LM	LM	VT	LM	ZZ	VT	SN	LM	VT	VT	VT	LM	LM	LM	VT	LM	VT
		◇1	◇1	◇1	◇1	1	1	◇1	◇1	◇1	1	◇1	1	1	◇1	◇1	◇1	◇1	1	1	◇1	◇1	◇1
																A	B						
		🛒		🛒	🛒				🛒			🛒			🛒	🛒	🛒				🛒		🛒
London Euston 15 ⊖	d	07 35	07 04	07 23	07 43	07 24	07 34	07 46	08 10	07 54	08 12	08 20		08 04	08 23	08 43	08 43	08 46	08 24	08 34	08 50	08 54	09 20
East Croydon 🚊	d												07 10										
Clapham Junction 10	d																						
Imperial Wharf	d												07 44										
West Brompton ⊖	d												07 47										
Kensington (Olympia) ⊖	d												07 50										
Shepherd's Bush	d												07 53										
Wembley Central ⊖	d												08s07										
Harrow & Wealdstone ⊖	d		07 16				07 46						08 12	08 16						08 46			
Bushey	d													08 21						08 51			
Watford Junction	a		07 23	07u37		07 40	07 53	08 00		08 10			08 19	08 24	08u37				08 40	08 54	09 04	09 10	
	d		07 23	07u37		07 41	07 53	08 01		08 11			08 19	08 25	08u37				08 41	08 55	09 05	09 11	
Kings Langley	d		07 28				07 58							08 29						08 59			
Apsley	d		07 31				08 01							08 33						09 03			
Hemel Hempstead	d		07 34			07 48	08 04			08 18			08 27	08 36					08 48	09 06		09 18	
Berkhamsted	d		07 39			07 53	08 09			08 23			08 31	08 40					08 53	09 10		09 23	
Tring	d		07 46			08 00	08a16						08 37	08a47					09 00	09a17			
Cheddington	d		07 51			08 05													09 05				
Leighton Buzzard	d		07 56			08 10				08 36			08 47						09 10			09 36	
Bletchley	d		08 03			08 18				08 43			08 55						09 17			09 43	
Milton Keynes Central 10	a	08 05	08 09		08 13	08 23		08 24	08 40	08 49	08 47	08 50	09 00			09 13	09 13	09 21	09 23		09 24	09 49	09 50
	d		08 09		08 13			08 25		08 49	09 00					09 13	09 13	09 23				09 49	
Wolverton	d		08 13							08 53												09 53	
Northampton	a		08 29					08 41		09 09								09 39				10 09	
Rugby	a							09 04			09 26							10 04					
Nuneaton	a							09 16										10 16					
Coventry	a			08 22	08 42										09 22	09 42	09 42						
Birmingham International ✈	a			08 33	08 53										09 33	09 53	09 53						
Birmingham New Street 12	a			08 45	09 08										09 45	10 08	10 08						
Sandwell & Dudley	a			08 57											09 57								
Wolverhampton 7 🚊	a			09 11											10 11		10 37						

		LM	SN	LM	VT	VT	VT	LM	LM	LM	VT	LM	VT	LM	SN	LM	VT	VT	LM	LM	LM	VT
		◇1	1	1	◇1	◇1	◇1	1	1	1	◇1	◇1	◇1	◇1	1	1	◇1	◇1	1	1	◇1	◇1
					B	A																
					🛒	🛒	🛒				🛒		🛒				🛒	🛒				🛒
London Euston 15 ⊖	d	09 13		09 04	09 23	09 23	09 43	09 24	09 34	09 46	10 10	09 54	10 20	10 13		10 04	10 23	10 43	10 24	10 34	10 46	11 10
East Croydon 🚊	d		08 10												09 10							
Clapham Junction 10	d																					
Imperial Wharf	d		08 44												09 44							
West Brompton ⊖	d		08 47												09 47							
Kensington (Olympia) ⊖	d		08 50												09 50							
Shepherd's Bush	d		08 53												09 53							
Wembley Central ⊖	d		09s07												10s07							
Harrow & Wealdstone ⊖	d		09 12	09 16					09 46						10 12	10 16				10 46		
Bushey	d			09 21					09 51							10 21				10 51		
Watford Junction	a		09 19	09 24	09u37	09u37		09 40	09 54	10 00		10 10			10 19	10 24	10u37		10 40	10 54	11 00	
	d		09 19	09 25	09u37	09u37		09 41	09 55	10 01		10 11			10 19	10 25	10u37		10 41	10 55	11 01	
Kings Langley	d			09 29					09 59							10 29				10 59		
Apsley	d			09 33					10 03							10 33				11 03		
Hemel Hempstead	d		09 27	09 36				09 48	10 06			10 18			10 27	10 36			10 48	11 06		
Berkhamsted	d		09 33	09 40				09 53	10 10			10 23			10 31	10 40			10 53	11 10		
Tring	d		09 38	09a47				10 00	10a17						10 37	10a47			11 00	11a17		
Cheddington	d							10 05											11 05			
Leighton Buzzard	d	09 42	09 47					10 10				10 36		10 42	10 47				11 10			
Bletchley	d	09 50	09 55					10 17				10 43		10 50	10 55				11 17			
Milton Keynes Central 10	a	09 54	10 00				10 13	10 23		10 23	10 40	10 49	10 50	10 54	11 00			11 13	11 23		11 24	11 40
	d	09 54					10 13			10 24		10 49		10 54				11 13			11 25	
Wolverton	d	09 58										10 53		10 58								
Northampton	a	10 13								10 40		11 09		11 13							11 41	
Rugby	a									11 04											12 04	
Nuneaton	a									11 16											12 16	
Coventry	a				10 23	10 22	10 42										11 22	11 42				
Birmingham International ✈	a				10 33	10 33	10 53										11 33	11 53				
Birmingham New Street 12	a				10 45	10 45	11 08										11 45	12 08				
Sandwell & Dudley	a				10 57	10 57											11 57					
Wolverhampton 7 🚊	a				11 11	11 11											12 11					

A until 10 July, from 11 September

B from 17 July until 4 September

London - Watford Junction, Milton Keynes, Northampton and West Midlands

		LM	VT	LM	SN	LM	VT	VT	LM	LM	LM	VT	LM	VT	LM	SN	LM	VT	VT	LM	LM	LM	VT
		◇1	◇1 ☕	◇1	1	1	◇1 ☕	◇1 ☕	1	1	◇1	◇1 ☕	◇1	◇1 ☕	◇1	1	1	◇1 ☕	◇1 ☕	1	1	◇1	◇1 ☕
London Euston 15 ⊖	d	10 54	11 20	11 13		11 04	11 23	11 43	11 24	11 34	11 46	12 10	11 54	12 20	12 13		12 04	12 23	12 43	12 24	12 34	12 46	13 10
East Croydon	d				10 10											11 10							
Clapham Junction 10	d																						
Imperial Wharf	d				10 44											11 44							
West Brompton ⊖	d				10 47											11 47							
Kensington (Olympia) ⊖	d				10 50											11 50							
Shepherd's Bush	d				10 53											11 53							
Wembley Central ⊖	d				11s08											12s07							
Harrow & Wealdstone ⊖	d				11 13	11 16				11 46						12 13	12 16				12 46		
Bushey	d					11 21				11 51							12 21				12 51		
Watford Junction	a	11 10			11 20	11 24	11u37		11 40	11 54	12 00		12 10			12 20	12 24	12u37		12 40	12 54	13 00	
	d	11 11			11 20	11 25	11u37		11 41	11 55	12 01		12 11			12 20	12 25	12u37		12 41	12 55	13 01	
Kings Langley	d					11 29				11 59							12 29				12 59		
Apsley	d					11 33				12 03							12 33				13 03		
Hemel Hempstead	d	11 18			11 28	11 36			11 48	12 06			12 18			12 28	12 36			12 48	13 06		
Berkhamsted	d	11 23			11 33	11 40			11 53	12 10			12 23			12 32	12 40			12 53	13 10		
Tring	d				11 38	11a47			12 00	12a17						12 37	12a47			13 00	13a17		
Cheddington	d								12 05											13 05			
Leighton Buzzard	d	11 36		11 42	11 47				12 10				12 36		12 42	12 47				13 10			
Bletchley	d	11 43		11 50	11 55				12 17				12 43		12 50	12 55				13 17			
Milton Keynes Central 10	a	11 49	11 50	11 54	12 00			12 13	12 23		12 24	12 40	12 49	12 50	12 54	13 00			13 13	13 23		13 24	13 40
	d	11 49		11 54				12 13			12 25		12 49		12 54				13 13			13 25	
Wolverton	d	11 53		11 58									12 53		12 58								
Northampton	a	12 09		12 13							12 41		13 09		13 13							13 41	
Rugby	a										13 04											14 04	
Nuneaton	a										13 16											14 16	
Coventry	a						12 22	12 42										13 22	13 42				
Birmingham International ✈	a						12 33	12 53										13 33	13 53				
Birmingham New Street 12	a						12 45	13 08										13 45	14 08				
Sandwell & Dudley	a						12 57											13 57					
Wolverhampton 7	a						13 11											14 11					

		LM	VT	LM	SN	LM	VT	VT	VT	LM	LM	LM	VT	LM	VT	LM	SN	LM	VT	VT	LM	LM
		◇1	◇1 ☕	◇1	1	1	◇1 ☕	◇1 A ☕	◇1 B ☕	1	1	◇1	◇1 ☕	◇1	◇1 ☕	◇1	1	1	◇1 ☕	◇1 ☕	1	1
London Euston 15 ⊖	d	12 54	13 20	13 13		13 04	13 23	13 43	13 43	13 24	13 34	13 46	14 10	13 54	14 20	14 13		14 04	14 23	14 43	14 24	14 34
East Croydon	d				12 10												13 10					
Clapham Junction 10	d																					
Imperial Wharf	d				12 44												13 44					
West Brompton ⊖	d				12 47												13 47					
Kensington (Olympia) ⊖	d				12 50												13 50					
Shepherd's Bush	d				12 53												13 53					
Wembley Central ⊖	d				13s07												14s08					
Harrow & Wealdstone ⊖	d				13 12	13 16					13 46						14 13	14 16				14 46
Bushey	d					13 21					13 51							14 21				14 51
Watford Junction	a	13 10			13 19	13 24	13u37			13 40	13 54	14 00		14 10			14 20	14 24	14u37		14 40	14 54
	d	13 11			13 19	13 25	13u37			13 41	13 55	14 01		14 11			14 20	14 25	14u37		14 41	14 55
Kings Langley	d					13 29					13 59							14 29				14 59
Apsley	d					13 33					14 03							14 33				15 03
Hemel Hempstead	d	13 18			13 27	13 36				13 48	14 06			14 18			14 28	14 36			14 48	15 06
Berkhamsted	d	13 23			13 32	13 40				13 53	14 10			14 23			14 32	14 40			14 53	15 10
Tring	d				13 37	13a47				14 00	14a17						14 37	14a47			15 00	15a17
Cheddington	d									14 05											15 05	
Leighton Buzzard	d	13 36		13 42	13 47					14 10				14 36		14 42	14 47				15 10	
Bletchley	d	13 43		13 50	13 55					14 17				14 43		14 50	14 55				15 17	
Milton Keynes Central 10	a	13 49	13 50	13 54	14 00			14 13	14 13	14 23		14 24	14 40	14 49	14 50	14 54	15 00			15 13	15 23	
	d	13 49		13 54				14 13	14 13			14 25		14 49		14 54				15 13		
Wolverton	d	13 53		13 58										14 53		14 58						
Northampton	a	14 09		14 13								14 41		15 09		15 13						
Rugby	a											15 04										
Nuneaton	a											15 16										
Coventry	a						14 22	14 42	14 43										15 22	15 42		
Birmingham International ✈	a						14 33	14 53	14 54										15 33	15 53		
Birmingham New Street 12	a						14 45	15 08	15 08										15 45	16 08		
Sandwell & Dudley	a						14 57												15 57			
Wolverhampton 7	a						15 11		15 37										16 11			

A until 10 July, from 11 September **B** from 17 July until 4 September

London - Watford Junction, Milton Keynes, Northampton and West Midlands

		LM	VT	LM	VT	LM	SN	LM	VT	VT	LM	LM	LM	VT	LM	VT	LM	SN	LM	VT	LM	LM	VT
		◇1	◇1 ☕	◇1	◇1 ☕	◇1	1	1	◇1 ☕	◇1 ☕	1	1	◇1	◇1 ☕	◇1	◇1 ☕	◇1	1	1	◇1 ☕	1	1	◇1 ☕
London Euston 15 ⊖	d	14 46	15 10	14 54	15 20	15 13		15 04	15 23	15 43	15 24	15 34	15 46	16 10	15 54	16 20	16 13		16 04	16 23	16 24	16 34	16 43
East Croydon	d						14 10											15 10					
Clapham Junction 10	d																						
Imperial Wharf	d						14 44											15 44					
West Brompton ⊖	d						14 47											15 47					
Kensington (Olympia) ⊖	d						14 50											15 50					
Shepherd's Bush	d						14 53											15 53					
Wembley Central ⊖	d						15s07											16s07					
Harrow & Wealdstone ⊖	d						15 12	15 16				15 46						16 12	16 16			16 46	
Bushey	d							15 21				15 51							16 21			16 51	
Watford Junction	a	15 00		15 10			15 19	15 24	15u37		15 40	15 54	16 00		16 10			16 19	16 24	16u37	16 41	16 54	
	d	15 01		15 11			15 19	15 25	15u37		15 41	15 55	16 01		16 11			16 19	16 25	16u37	16 42	16 55	
Kings Langley	d							15 29				15 59							16 29			16 59	
Apsley	d							15 33				16 03							16 33			17 03	
Hemel Hempstead	d			15 18			15 27	15 36			15 48	16 06			16 18			16 27	16 36		16 49	17 06	
Berkhamsted	d			15 23			15 32	15 40			15 53	16 10			16 23			16 32	16 40		16 54	17 10	
Tring	d						15 37	15a47			16 00	16a17						16 37	16a47		17 01	17a19	
Cheddington	d										16 05										17 06		
Leighton Buzzard	d			15 36		15 42	15 47				16 10				16 36		16 42	16 47			17 11		
Bletchley	d			15 43		15 50	15 55				16 17				16 43		16 50	16 55			17 18		
Milton Keynes Central 10	a	15 24	15 40	15 49	15 50	15 54	16 00			16 13	16 23		16 24	16 40	16 49	16 50	16 54	17 00			17 25		17 13
	d	15 25		15 49		15 54				16 13			16 25		16 49		16 54						17 13
Wolverton	d			15 53		15 58									16 53		16 58						
Northampton	a	15 41		16 09		16 13							16 41		17 09		17 13						
Rugby	a	16 04											17 04										
Nuneaton	a	16 16											17 16										
Coventry	a								16 22	16 42										17 22			17 42
Birmingham International ✈	a								16 33	16 53										17 33			17 53
Birmingham New Street 12	a								16 45	17 08										17 45			18 08
Sandwell & Dudley	a								16 57											17 57			
Wolverhampton 7	a								17 11											18 11			

		LM	VT	LM	VT	LM	SN	LM	VT	VT	VT	LM	LM	LM	VT	LM	VT	LM	SN	LM	VT	VT	LM
		◇1	◇1 ☕	◇1	◇1 ☕	◇1	1	1	◇1 ☕	◇1 A ☕	◇1 B ☕	1	1	◇1	◇1 ☕	◇1	◇1 ☕	◇1	1	1	◇1 ☕	◇1 ☕	1
London Euston 15 ⊖	d	16 46	17 10	16 54	17 20	17 13		17 04	17 23	17 43	17 43	17 24	17 34	17 46	18 10	17 54	18 20	18 13		18 04	18 23	18 43	18 24
East Croydon	d						16 10												17 10				
Clapham Junction 10	d																						
Imperial Wharf	d						16 44												17 44				
West Brompton ⊖	d						16 47												17 47				
Kensington (Olympia) ⊖	d						16 50												17 50				
Shepherd's Bush	d						16 53												17 53				
Wembley Central ⊖	d						17s07												18s07				
Harrow & Wealdstone ⊖	d						17 12	17 16					17 46						18 12	18 16			
Bushey	d							17 21					17 51							18 21			
Watford Junction	a	17 00		17 10			17 19	17 24	17u37			17 41	17 54	18 00		18 10			18 19	18 24	18u37		18 40
	d	17 01		17 11			17 19	17 25	17u37			17 42	17 55	18 01		18 11			18 19	18 25	18u37		18 41
Kings Langley	d							17 29					17 59							18 29			
Apsley	d							17 33					18 03							18 33			
Hemel Hempstead	d			17 18			17 27	17 36				17 49	18 06			18 18			18 27	18 36			18 48
Berkhamsted	d			17 23			17 32	17 40				17 54	18 10			18 23			18 32	18 40			18 53
Tring	d						17 37	17a49				18 01	18a17						18 37	18a47			19 00
Cheddington	d											18 06											19 05
Leighton Buzzard	d			17 36		17 42	17 47					18 11				18 36		18 42	18 47				19 10
Bletchley	d			17 43		17 50	17 55					18 18				18 43		18 50	18 55				19 17
Milton Keynes Central 10	a	17 24	17 40	17 49	17 50	17 54	18 00			18 13	18 13	18 24		18 24	18 40	18 49	18 50	18 54	19 00			19 13	19 23
	d	17 25		17 49		17 54				18 13	18 13			18 25		18 49		18 54				19 13	
Wolverton	d			17 53		17 58										18 53		18 58					
Northampton	a	17 41		18 09		18 13								18 40		19 09		19 13					
Rugby	a	18 04																					
Nuneaton	a	18 16																					
Coventry	a								18 22	18 42	18 43										19 22	19 42	
Birmingham International ✈	a								18 33	18 53	18 54										19 33	19 53	
Birmingham New Street 12	a								18 45	19 08	19 08										19 45	20 08	
Sandwell & Dudley	a								18 57												19 58		
Wolverhampton 7	a								19 11												20 12		

A until 10 July, from 11 September **B** from 17 July until 4 September

Table 66

London - Watford Junction, Milton Keynes, Northampton and West Midlands

		VT ◇1 ☕	LM 1	LM ◇1	LM ◇1	SN 1	LM 1	VT ◇1 ☕	LM ◇1	LM 1	VT ◇1 ☕	LM 1	VT ◇1 ☕	LM ◇1	SN 1	LM 1	VT ◇1 ☕	VT ◇1 ☕	VT ◇1 A ☕	VT ◇1 B ☕	LM ◇1	LM 1
London Euston 15 ⊖	d	18 35	18 34	18 46	18 54		19 04	19 20	19 13	19 14	19 23	19 30	19 43	19 44		20 02	20 20	20 23	20 30	20 30	20 34	20 40
East Croydon	d					18 10									19 10							
Clapham Junction 10	d																					
Imperial Wharf	d					18 44									19 42							
West Brompton ⊖	d					18 47									19 45							
Kensington (Olympia) ⊖	d					18 50									19 48							
Shepherd's Bush	d					18 53									19 50							
Wembley Central ⊖	d					19 08																
Harrow & Wealdstone ⊖	d		18 46			19 13	19 16					19 42			20 08							20 52
Bushey	d		18 51				19 21					19 47										
Watford Junction	a	18u50	18 54	19 00	19 10	19 21	19 24			19 30	19u37	19 50		19 59	20 15	20 18		20u38	20u45	20u44	20 50	20 59
	d	18u51	18 55	19 01	19 11		19 25			19 31	19u37	19 51		20 00		20 19		20u38	20u46	20u45	20 51	20 59
Kings Langley	d		18 59				19 29					19 55		20 04								21 04
Apsley	d		19 03				19 33					19 59		20 08								21 07
Hemel Hempstead	d		19 06		19 18					19 38		20 02		20 11		20 26					20 58	
Berkhamsted	d		19 10		19 23		19 39					20 06		20 16		20 31					21 03	
Tring	d		19a17				19a45			19 48		20 12		20 21								21 18
Cheddington	d									19 53				20 26							21 11	
Leighton Buzzard	d				19 36				19 42	19 58		20 22		20 31		20 42					21 16	
Bletchley	d				19 43				19 50	20 06		20a28		20 39		20 49					21 24	21 31
Milton Keynes Central 10	a			19 26	19 48			19 50	19 54	20 11			20 20	20 43		20 54	21 03				21 32	21 40
	d			19 27	19 48				19 54				20 20	20 47			21 05				21 33	
Wolverton	d				19 52				19 58					20 50							21 36	
Northampton	a			19 41	20 06				20 13					21 04							21 59	
Rugby	a	19 51																	21 35	21 34		
Nuneaton	a																21 32					
Coventry	a	20 02									20 22		20 49					21 35				
Birmingham International ✈	a	20 13									20 33		21 00					21 53				
Birmingham New Street 12	a	20 25									20 45		21 11					22 05				
Sandwell & Dudley	a	20 53									20 58							22 24				
Wolverhampton 7	a	21 08									21 12		21 38					22 38				

		SN 1	VT ◇1 ☕	VT ◇1 ☕	LM ◇1	LM ◇1	VT ◇1 ☕	LM ◇1	SN 1	LM ◇1	SN 1	LM ◇1	LM ◇1
London Euston 15 ⊖	d		21 00	21 03	21 07	21 28	21 43	21 54		22 34		23 04	23 48
East Croydon	d												
Clapham Junction 10	d												
Imperial Wharf	d	20 29							21 51		22 44		
West Brompton ⊖	d	20 32							21 54		22 47		
Kensington (Olympia) ⊖	d	20 36							21 57		22 50		
Shepherd's Bush	d	20 39							22 00		22 53		
Wembley Central ⊖	d												
Harrow & Wealdstone ⊖	d	21 02						22 06	22 20		23 12	23 16	00 01
Bushey	d												
Watford Junction	a	21 09		21u18	21 24	21 44	21u57	22 13	22 27	22 50	23 19	23 23	00 07
	d			21u18	21 24	21 45	21u58	22 13		22 51		23 23	00 07
Kings Langley	d							22 18				23 28	00 12
Apsley	d							22 21				23 31	00 15
Hemel Hempstead	d				21 32	21 52		22 24		22 58		23 34	00 18
Berkhamsted	d				21 37	21 57		22 29		23 03		23 39	00 23
Tring	d							22 34				23 44	00 30
Cheddington	d							22 41				23 51	00 35
Leighton Buzzard	d				21 50	22 08		22 46		23 14		23 56	00 40
Bletchley	d				21 57	22 15		22 53		23 21		00 03	00 47
Milton Keynes Central 10	a		21 43	21 50	22 06	22 24	22 29	23 02		23 30		00 12	00 56
	d			21 50	22 06	22 25	22 30	23 02		23 30		00 12	00 56
Wolverton	d				22 10	22 28		23 06		23 34		00 16	01 00
Northampton	a				22 29	22 47		23 20		23 52		00 30	01 18
Rugby	a			22 11			22 51						
Nuneaton	a												
Coventry	a			22 22			23 02						
Birmingham International ✈	a			22 33			23 13						
Birmingham New Street 12	a			22 45			23 25						
Sandwell & Dudley	a			22 56			23 37						
Wolverhampton 7	a			23 10			23 51						

A from 23 October

B until 16 October

Table 66

London - Watford Junction, Milton Keynes, Northampton and West Midlands

		LM ◇1 A	LM ◇1 A	LM ◇1	LM 🚌	LM 🚌	LM ◇1	LM ◇1	LM ◇1	VT ◇1 ☕	VT ◇1 ☕	LM ◇1	SN 1	VT ◇1 ☕	VT ◇1 ☕	LM ◇1	VT ◇1 B ☕	LM ◇1	SN 1	VT ◇1 ☕	VT ◇1 ☕	LM ◇1	VT ◇1 ☕
London Euston 15 ⊖	d	23p04	23p48	00 15			06 53	07 23	07 50	08 10	08 20	08 23		08 45	08 50	08 53	09 20	09 23		09 45	09 50	09 53	10 20
East Croydon	d																						
Clapham Junction 10	d																						
Imperial Wharf	d												08 19						09 19				
West Brompton ⊖	d												08 22						09 22				
Kensington (Olympia) ⊖	d												08 26						09 26				
Shepherd's Bush	d												08 29						09 29				
Wembley Central ⊖	d			00 24																			
Harrow & Wealdstone ⊖	d	23p16	00 01	00 29			07 05	07 35	08 02			08 35	08 48			09 05		09 35	09 48			10 05	
Bushey	d																						
Watford Junction	a	23p23	00 07	00 35			07 12	07 42	08 08			08 42	08 56		09u04	09 12		09 42	09 58		10u04	10 12	
	d	23p23	00 07	00 35	02 50	02 55	07 12	07 42	08 08			08 42			09u04	09 12		09 42			10u04	10 12	
Kings Langley	d	23p28	00 12	00 40		03 11		07 47				08 47						09 47					
Apsley	d	23p31	00 15	00 44		03 22		07 50				08 50						09 50					
Hemel Hempstead	d	23p34	00 18	00 46	03 16	03 28	07 20	07 53	08 15			08 53				09 20		09 53				10 20	
Berkhamsted	d	23p39	00 23	00 51		03 39	07 24	07 58	08 20			08 58				09 24		09 58				10 24	
Tring	d	23p44	00 30	00 56		03 55	07 29		08 25							09 29						10 29	
Cheddington	d	23p51	00 35	01 01		04 16	07 34		08 30							09 34						10 34	
Leighton Buzzard	d	23p56	00 40	01 06	03 53	04 37	07 41	08 11	08 37			09 11				09 41		10 11				10 41	
Bletchley	d	00 03	00 47	01 13	04 19	05 03	07 49	08 14	08 44			09 18				09 49		10 18				10 49	
Milton Keynes Central 10	a	00 12	00 56	01 21	04 34	05 18	07 57	08 27	08 50	08 55	09 05	09 27		09 31	09 38	09 57	10 06	10 27		10 32	10 38	10 57	11 06
	d	00 12	00 56	01 21			07 58	08 27	08 51			09 27		09 32	09 39	09 58		10 27		10 33	10 39	10 58	
Wolverton	d	00 16	01 00	01 25			08 01	08 31	08 54			09 31				10 01		10 31				11 01	
Northampton	a	00 30	01 18	01 38			08 16	08 45	09 09			09 45				10 16		10 45				11 16	
Rugby	a													10 06	10 12					11 06	11 12		
Nuneaton	a																						
Coventry	a														10 23						11 23		
Birmingham International ✈	a														10 34						11 34		
Birmingham New Street 12	a														10 47						11 47		
Sandwell & Dudley	a														10 59						11 59		
Wolverhampton 7	a														11 13						12 13		

		LM ◇1	SN 1	VT ◇1 ☕	VT ◇1 ☕	LM ◇1	VT ◇1 ☕	VT ◇1 ☕	LM ◇1	SN 1	VT ◇1 ☕	VT ◇1 ☕	LM ◇1	VT ◇1 ☕	LM 1	SN 1	VT ◇1 ☕	LM ◇1	LM ◇1	VT ◇1 ☕	LM 1	VT ◇1 ☕	LM 1
London Euston 15 ⊖	d	10 23		10 45	10 50	10 53	11 15	11 20	11 23		11 45	12 15	11 53	12 18	12 14		12 38	12 34	12 50	13 15	12 54	13 18	13 14
East Croydon	d																						
Clapham Junction 10	d																						
Imperial Wharf	d		10 19							11 19						12 09							
West Brompton ⊖	d		10 22							11 22						12 12							
Kensington (Olympia) ⊖	d		10 26							11 26						12 16							
Shepherd's Bush	d		10 29							11 29						12 19							
Wembley Central ⊖	d																						
Harrow & Wealdstone ⊖	d	10 35	10 48			11 05			11 35	11 48			12 05		12 26	12 36					13 06		13 26
Bushey	d														12 31								13 31
Watford Junction	a	10 42	10 56		11u04	11 12			11 42	11 56	12u01		12 12	12u32	12 34	12 44		12 50	13 06		13 13	13u32	13 34
	d	10 42			11u04	11 12			11 42		12u01		12 12	12u32	12 35			12 51	13 06		13 13	13u32	13 35
Kings Langley	d	10 47							11 47						12 39								13 39
Apsley	d	10 50							11 50						12 43								13 43
Hemel Hempstead	d	10 53				11 20			11 53				12 20		12 46			12 58			13 21		13 46
Berkhamsted	d	10 58				11 24			11 58				12 24		12 50			13 03			13 25		13 50
Tring	d					11 29							12 29		12a57						13 30		13a57
Cheddington	d					11 34							12 34								13 35		
Leighton Buzzard	d	11 11				11 41			12 12				12 41					13 16	13 27		13 42		
Bletchley	d	11 18				11 49			12 19				12 49					13 23			13 50		
Milton Keynes Central 10	a	11 27		11 31	11 36	11 57	12 02	12 08	12 27		12 26	12 48	12 57				13 11	13 29	13 36	13 48	13 56		
	d	11 27		11 32	11 37	11 58			12 27		12 27		12 58				13 11	13 29	13 37	13 48			
Wolverton	d	11 31				12 01			12 31				13 01					13 33					
Northampton	a	11 45				12 16			12 45				13 16					13 46	13 51				
Rugby	a			12 06	12 10						12 46								14 17				
Nuneaton	a																		14 29				
Coventry	a				12 21						12 56			13 20			13 40					14 20	
Birmingham International ✈	a				12 34						13 07			13 31			13 51					14 31	
Birmingham New Street 12	a				12 47						13 22			13 44			14 06					14 44	
Sandwell & Dudley	a				12 59									13 56								14 56	
Wolverhampton 7	a				13 13									14 10								15 10	

A not 23 May

B from 18 July

Table 66

London - Watford Junction, Milton Keynes, Northampton and West Midlands

		SN	VT	LM	LM	VT	LM	VT	LM	SN	VT	LM	LM	VT	VT	LM	VT	LM	SN	VT	LM	LM
		1	◇1 🍴	◇1	◇1	◇1 🍴	1	◇1 🍴	1	1	◇1 🍴	◇1	◇1	◇1 🍴	◇1 🍴	1	◇1 🍴	1	1	◇1 🍴	◇1	◇1
London Euston 15 ⊖	d		13 38	13 34	13 50	14 15	13 54	14 18	14 14		14 38	14 34	14 50	15 05	15 15	14 54	15 18	15 14		15 38	15 34	15 50
East Croydon	d																					
Clapham Junction 10	d																					
Imperial Wharf	d	13 09								14 09									15 09			
West Brompton ⊖	d	13 12								14 12									15 12			
Kensington (Olympia) ⊖	d	13 16								14 16									15 16			
Shepherd's Bush	d	13 19								14 19									15 19			
Wembley Central ⊖	d																					
Harrow & Wealdstone ⊖	d	13 36					14 06		14 26	14 36						15 06		15 26	15 36			
Bushey	d								14 31									15 31				
Watford Junction	a	13 44		13 50	14 05		14 13	14u32	14 34	14 44		14 50	15 06			15 13	15u32	15 34	15 44		15 50	16 05
	d			13 51	14 06		14 13	14u32	14 35			14 51	15 06			15 13	15u32	15 35			15 51	16 06
Kings Langley	d								14 39									15 39				
Apsley	d								14 43									15 43				
Hemel Hempstead	d			13 58			14 21		14 46			14 58				15 21		15 46			15 58	
Berkhamsted	d			14 03			14 25		14 50			15 03				15 25		15 50			16 03	
Tring	d						14 30		14a57							15 30		15a57				
Cheddington	d						14 35									15 35						
Leighton Buzzard	d			14 16	14 26		14 42					15 16	15 26			15 42					16 16	16 26
Bletchley	d			14 23			14 50					15 23				15 50					16 23	
Milton Keynes Central 10	a		14 11	14 29	14 36	14 48	14 56				15 11	15 29	15 36	15 38	15 48	15 56				16 11	16 29	16 36
	d		14 11	14 29	14 36						15 11	15 29	15 36	15 39						16 11	16 29	16 36
Wolverton	d			14 33								15 33									16 33	
Northampton	a			14 46	14 52							15 46	15 51								16 46	16 52
Rugby	a				15 19								16 17									17 19
Nuneaton	a												16 29									
Coventry	a		14 40					15 20			15 40						16 20			16 40		
Birmingham International ✈	a		14 51					15 31			15 51						16 31			16 51		
Birmingham New Street 12	a		15 06					15 44			16 06						16 44			17 06		
Sandwell & Dudley	a							15 56									16 56					
Wolverhampton 7	a							16 10									17 10					

		VT	VT	LM	VT	LM	SN	VT	LM	LM	VT	VT	LM	VT	LM	SN	VT	LM	LM	VT	VT	LM	VT
		◇1 🍴	◇1 🍴	1	◇1 🍴	1	1	◇1 🍴	◇1	◇1	◇1 🍴	◇1 🍴	1	◇1 🍴	1	1	◇1 🍴	◇1	◇1	◇1 🍴	◇1 🍴	1	◇1 🍴
London Euston 15 ⊖	d	16 05	16 15	15 54	16 18	16 14		16 38	16 34	16 50	17 05	17 15	16 54	17 18	17 14		17 38	17 34	17 50	18 05	18 15	17 54	18 18
East Croydon	d																						
Clapham Junction 10	d																						
Imperial Wharf	d						16 09									17 09							
West Brompton ⊖	d						16 12									17 12							
Kensington (Olympia) ⊖	d						16 16									17 16							
Shepherd's Bush	d						16 19									17 19							
Wembley Central ⊖	d																						
Harrow & Wealdstone ⊖	d			16 06		16 26	16 36						17 06		17 26	17 36						18 06	
Bushey	d					16 31									17 31								
Watford Junction	a			16 13	16u32	16 34	16 44		16 50	17 06			17 13	17u32	17 34	17 44		17 50	18 05			18 13	18u32
	d			16 13	16u32	16 35			16 51	17 06			17 13	17u32	17 35			17 51	18 06			18 13	18u32
Kings Langley	d					16 39									17 39								
Apsley	d					16 43									17 43								
Hemel Hempstead	d			16 21		16 46			16 58				17 21		17 46			17 58				18 21	
Berkhamsted	d			16 25		16 50			17 03				17 25		17 50			18 03				18 25	
Tring	d			16 30		16a57							17 30		17a57							18 30	
Cheddington	d			16 35									17 35									18 35	
Leighton Buzzard	d			16 42					17 16	17 26			17 42					18 16	18 26			18 42	
Bletchley	d			16 50					17 23				17 50					18 23				18 50	
Milton Keynes Central 10	a	16 38	16 48	16 56				17 11	17 29	17 36	17 38	17 48	17 56				18 11	18 29	18 36	18 38	18 48	18 56	
	d							17 11	17 29	17 36	17 39						18 11	18 29	18 36				
Wolverton	d								17 33									18 33					
Northampton	a								17 46	17 51								18 46	18 52				
Rugby	a									18 17									19 19				
Nuneaton	a									18 29	18 09												
Coventry	a				17 20			17 40						18 20			18 40						19 20
Birmingham International ✈	a				17 31			17 51						18 31			18 51						19 31
Birmingham New Street 12	a				17 44			18 06						18 44			19 06						19 44
Sandwell & Dudley	a				17 56									18 56									19 56
Wolverhampton 7	a				18 10									19 10									20 10

Table 66

Sundays

London - Watford Junction, Milton Keynes, Northampton and West Midlands

		LM	SN	VT	LM	LM	VT	VT	LM	VT	LM	SN	VT	LM	LM	VT	VT	LM	VT	LM	SN	VT
		1	1	◇1 🍴	◇1	◇1	◇1 🍴	◇1 🍴	1	◇1 🍴	1	1	◇1 🍴	◇1	◇1	◇1 🍴	◇1 🍴	1	◇1 🍴	1	1	◇1 🍴
London Euston 15 ⊖	d	18 14		18 38	18 34	18 50	19 05	19 15	18 54	19 18	19 14		19 38	19 34	19 50	20 05	20 15	19 54	20 18	20 14		20 38
East Croydon	d																					
Clapham Junction 10	d																					
Imperial Wharf	d		18 09									19 09									20 09	
West Brompton ⊖	d		18 12									19 12									20 12	
Kensington (Olympia) ⊖	d		18 16									19 16									20 16	
Shepherd's Bush	d		18 19									19 19									20 19	
Wembley Central ⊖	d																					
Harrow & Wealdstone ⊖	d	18 26	18 36						19 06		19 26	19 36						20 06		20 26	20 36	
Bushey	d	18 31									19 31									20 31		
Watford Junction	a	18 34	18 44		18 50	19 06			19 13	19u32	19 34	19 44		19 50	20 05			20 13	20u32	20 34	20 44	
	d	18 35			18 51	19 06			19 13	19u32	19 35			19 51	20 06			20 13	20u32	20 35		
Kings Langley	d	18 39									19 39									20 39		
Apsley	d	18 43									19 43									20 43		
Hemel Hempstead	d	18 46			18 58				19 21		19 46			19 58				20 21		20 46		
Berkhamsted	d	18 50			19 03				19 25		19 50			20 03				20 25		20 50		
Tring	d	18a57							19 30		19a57							20 30		20a57		
Cheddington	d								19 35									20 35				
Leighton Buzzard	d				19 16	19 26			19 42					20 16	20 26			20 42				
Bletchley	d				19 23				19 50					20 23				20 50				
Milton Keynes Central 10	a			19 11	19 28	19 36	19 38	19 48	19 56				20 11	20 29	20 36	20 38	20 48	20 56				21 16
	d			19 11	19 28	19 36	19 39						20 11	20 29	20 36	20 38						21 16
Wolverton	d				19 33									20 33								
Northampton	a				19 46	19 51								20 46	20 52							
Rugby	a					20 17									21 19							
Nuneaton	a					20 29																
Coventry	a			19 40						20 20			20 40						21 20			21 46
Birmingham International ✈	a			19 51						20 31			20 51						21 31			21 57
Birmingham New Street 12	a			20 06						20 44			21 04						21 44			22 09
Sandwell & Dudley	a									20 56			21 15						21 56			22 24
Wolverhampton 7	a									21 10			21 31						22 10			22 38

		LM	VT	VT	LM	VT	LM	SN	VT	VT	LM	VT	LM	SN	LM	VT	LM
		◇1	◇1 🍴	◇1 🍴	◇1	◇1 🍴	◇1	1	◇1 🍴	◇1 🍴	◇1	◇1 🍴	◇1	1	◇1	◇1 🍴	◇1
London Euston 15 ⊖	d	20 34	20 50	20 54	21 02	21 24	21 28		21 50	21 55	21 58	22 25	22 28		22 58	23 25	23 34
East Croydon	d																
Clapham Junction 10	d																
Imperial Wharf	d							21 19						22 19			
West Brompton ⊖	d							21 22						22 22			
Kensington (Olympia) ⊖	d							21 26						22 26			
Shepherd's Bush	d							21 29						22 29			
Wembley Central ⊖	d																
Harrow & Wealdstone ⊖	d						21 40	21 49			22 10		22 40	22 48	23 10		23 46
Bushey	d																
Watford Junction	a	20 50		21u11	21 17		21 47	21 56		22u09	22 17	22u39	22 47	22 56	23 17	23u39	23 53
	d	20 52		21u11	21 18		21 47			22u09	22 17	22u39	22 47		23 17	23u40	23 53
Kings Langley	d						21 52						22 52		23 22		23 58
Apsley	d						21 55						22 55		23 25		00 01
Hemel Hempstead	d	20 59			21 25		21 58				22 25		22 58		23 28		00 04
Berkhamsted	d	21 04			21 30		22 03				22 29		23 03		23 33		00 09
Tring	d				21 34						22 34				23 38		00 14
Cheddington	d				21 40						22 39				23 43		00 19
Leighton Buzzard	d	21 17			21 46		22 16				22 46		23 16		23 50		00 26
Bletchley	d	21 24			21 53		22 23				22 54		23 23		23 57		00 33
Milton Keynes Central 10	a	21 30	21 38	21 44	22 01	22 12	22 32		22 36	22 42	23 02	23 11	23 32		00 06	00 11	00 42
	d	21 30	21 39	21 45	22 02		22 32		22 38	22 44	23 03	23 12	23 32		00 06	00 12	00 42
Wolverton	d	21 34			22 05		22 36				23 06		23 36		00 10		00 46
Northampton	a	21 47			22 19		22 50				23 21		23 50		00 24		01 00
Rugby	a		21 59	22 05					23 17	23 21		23 47				00s47	
Nuneaton	a								23 28								
Coventry	a			22 16						23 33		23 59				00s58	
Birmingham International ✈	a			22 27						23 51		00 10				01s09	
Birmingham New Street 12	a			22 39						00 04		00 23				01s22	
Sandwell & Dudley	a			22 52													
Wolverhampton 7	a			23 06						00 27		00 55				01 54	

A from 12 September

West Midlands, Northampton, Milton Keynes and Watford Junction - London

Station		SN	SN	SN	VT	LM	LM	LM	VT	LM	LM	LM	VT	VT	LM	LM	LM	LM	LM	LM	SN	LM	LM
		MX	MO	MX	MX			MO	MO	TO			MO	MX									
						A	B				C	D			E	F	E	F	E	F		E	F
Wolverhampton	d				21p45				22p05				22p37	22p45									
Sandwell & Dudley	d				21p56				22p15				22p47	22p55									
Birmingham New Street	d				22p10	21p33	21p33		22e30				23p00	23f10									
Birmingham International	d				22p20	21p45	21p45		22p40				23p10	23p20									
Coventry	d				22p31	22p01	22p01		22p51				23p21	23p31									
Nuneaton	d																						
Rugby	d				22p43	22p13	22p13		23p04				23p35	23p44									
Northampton	d					22c55	22c55	22p55		23p30	23p46	23p46	23b54	00s07			04 15	04 15	04 48	04 48		05 05	05 05
Wolverton	d					23p07	23p07	23p11		23p44	23p58	23p58					04 27	04 27	05 00	05 00		05 17	05 17
Milton Keynes Central	a				23b06	23p12	23p12	23p14	23p38	23p50	00 03	00 03	00s12	00s23			04 30	04 30	05 03	05 03		05 20	05 20
	d	22p11			23b07	23p13	23p13	23p15	23p39	23p50	00 04	00 04	00s14	00s24	03 30	03 30	04 31	04 31	05 04	05 04		05 21	05 21
Bletchley	d	22p15				23p18	23p18	23p20		23p55	00 09	00 09			03 35	03 35	04 36	04 36	05 09	05 09		05 26	05 26
Leighton Buzzard	d	22p22				23p24	23p24	23p26		00 02	00 15	00 15			03 41	03 41	04 42	04 42	05 15	05 15		05 32	05 32
Cheddington	d					23p29	23p29	23p31		00 08	00 24	00 24							05 20	05 20			
Tring	d	22p34				23p38	23p38	23p40		00 14	00 29	00 29			03 53	03 53	04 54	04 54	05 29	05 29			
Berkhamsted	d	22p39				23p43	23p43	23p45		00 18	00 34	00 34			03 58	03 58	04 59	04 59	05 34	05 34		05 47	05 47
Hemel Hempstead	d	22p43				23p47	23p47	23p49		00 22	00 38	00 38			04 02	04 02	05 03	05 03	05 38	05 38		05 52	05 52
Apsley	d					23p50	23p50												05 41	05 41			
Kings Langley	d					23p53	23p53												05 45	05 45			
Watford Junction	a	22p52			23b37	23p58	23p58	23p56	00s13	00 29	00 45	00 45	00s42	00s52	04 09	04 09	05 10	05 10	05 49	05 49		05 59	05 59
	d	22p53	23p17	23p29	23b38	23p58	23p58	23p57	00s14	00 30	00 46	00 46	00s43	00s53	04 10	04 10	05 11	05 11	05 50	05 50	05 54	05 59	05 59
Bushey	d					00 01	00 01																
Harrow & Wealdstone	d	23p00	23p23	23p35		00 06	00 06	00 03		00 36	00 52	00 52			04 16	04 16	05 17	05 17	05 56	05 56	06 00		
Wembley Central	d									00 40	00 56	00 56			04 20	04 20	05 21	05 21			06 05		
Shepherd's Bush	a	23p21	23p45	23p53																	06 19		
Kensington (Olympia)	a	23p23	23p47	23p56																	06 21		
West Brompton	a	23p26	23p50	23p59																	06 24		
Imperial Wharf	a	23p28	23p53	00 02																	06 27		
Clapham Junction	a																						
East Croydon	a	00 01	00 22																				
London Euston	a				00 05	00 20	00 21	00 17	00 35	00 53	01 08	01 09	01 06	01 13	04 34	04 35	05 35	05 36	06 10	06 13		06 19	06 22

Station		LM	LM	SR	LM	LM	LM	VT	LM	SN	LM	VT	LM	LM	LM	VT	VT	LM	VT	SN	VT	LM	LM
				MX																			
		E	F																				
Wolverhampton	d							05 00				05 24				06 04			05 45				
Sandwell & Dudley	d											05 34				06 15			05 56				
Birmingham New Street	d							05 29				05g50				06h30			06 10			05 53	
Birmingham International	d							05 39				06 00				06 39			06 20			06 05	
Coventry	d							05 50				06 11				06 51			06 31			06 21	
Nuneaton	d																06 18						
Rugby	d					05 20		06 03									06 32	06 08			06 53	06 33	
Northampton	d					05 45					06 17							06 37				07i00	
Wolverton	d					05 57					06 29							06 49				07 12	
Milton Keynes Central	a					06 01		06 22			06 33	06 38					06 51	06 53	06 59		07 12	07 15	
	d				05 54	06 02	06 20	06 23			06 34	06 38			06 48		06 52	06 55	06 59	07 01	07 14	07 16	
Bletchley	d	05 38	05 38		05 59	06 07	06 25				06 39		06 34		06 53			07 00		07 05			07 12
Leighton Buzzard	d	05 44	05 44		06 05	06 14	06 32				06 46		06 41		06 59			07 07		07 13		07 25	
Cheddington	d	05 50	05 50				06 38								07 05								
Tring	d	05 56	05 56				06 43		06 24				06 52	07 00	07 11					07 22			07 28
Berkhamsted	d	06 01	06 01		06 17		06 47		06 28				06 56	07 04	07 16					07 26			07 32
Hemel Hempstead	d	06 05	06 05		06 22		06 52		06 33				07 01	07 09	07 20					07 31			07 37
Apsley	d	06 08	06 08						06 36				07 04		07 24								
Kings Langley	d	06 12	06 12						06 39				07 07		07 27								
Watford Junction	a	06 16	06 16	06 19	06 29	06 32	06 59	06s43	06 44		07 04		07 12	07 19	07 31	07s36				07 38			07 44
	d	06 17	06 17	06 20	06 29	06 33	06 59	06s44	06 44	06 53	07 05		07 12	07 19	07 32	07s37				07 38			07 44
Bushey	d								06 47				07 15	07 22	07 34								
Harrow & Wealdstone	d	06 23	06 23				07 05		06 52	06 59			07 20		07 40					07 45			
Wembley Central	d									07 04										07u49			
Shepherd's Bush	a									07 19										08 04			
Kensington (Olympia)	a									07 21										08 06			
West Brompton	a									07 24										08 09			
Imperial Wharf	a									07 27										08 12			
Clapham Junction	a																						
East Croydon	a																			09 04			
London Euston	a	06 37	06 40	06 40	06 49	06 50	07 20	07 02	07 07		07 22	07 13	07 34	07 40	07 54	07 53	07 28	07 43	07 34		07 50	08 02	08 04

A MX until 3 September
B MX from 7 September
C WThFO until 3 September
D WThFO from 8 September
E until 3 September
F from 6 September
b previous night, stops to set down only
c previous night, arr. 2234
e previous night, arr. 2224
f previous night, arr. 2304
g arr. 0543
h arr. 0624
i arr. 0654

West Midlands, Northampton, Milton Keynes and Watford Junction - London

Station		LM	LM	LM	VT	LM	LM	LM	LM	LM	LM	LM	SN	LM	VT	LM	VT	LM	LM	LM	VT	LM
Wolverhampton	d				06 27												07 45					
Sandwell & Dudley	d				06 37												07 56					
Birmingham New Street	d				06 50												08 10					
Birmingham International	d				07 00												08 20					
Coventry	d				07 11												08 31					
Nuneaton	d																			08 02	08 46	
Rugby	d								07 02											08 18		
Northampton	d			07 13					07b32	07 39				08 25						08c47		
Wolverton	d			07 25						07 51				08 37								
Milton Keynes Central	a			07 29	07s40				07 46	07 54				08 41						08 59		
	d		07 21	07 30	07s41				07 46	07 55	07 59		08 13	08 41	08s47				08 47	09 00		
Bletchley	d		07 26			07 39			07 51		08 04		08 17	08 46					08 52			
Leighton Buzzard	d		07 33	07 39		07 46			07 58	08 06	08 11		08 24	08 53					08 58			
Cheddington	d		07 38						08 04										09 04			
Tring	d		07 45					08 04	08 10			08 25	08 34			08 48		09 01	09 10			09 26
Berkhamsted	d		07 49			07 59			08 15			08 29	08 39			08 53		09 05	09 15			09 30
Hemel Hempstead	d		07 54			08 03			08 19		08 28	08 34	08 43			08 57		09 10	09 19			09 35
Apsley	d		07 57					08 13				08 37						09 13				09 38
Kings Langley	d		08 00					08 16				08 40						09 16				09 41
Watford Junction	a		08 05			08 10		08 20	08 26		08 35	08 45	08 51			09 04	09s15	09 20	09 26	09 27	09s31	09 46
	d	07 55	08 05			08 11	08 15	08 21	08 27		08 36	08 46	08 51			09 04	09s16	09 21	09 27	09 28	09s32	09 46
Bushey	d	07 58					08 18					08 48				09 07		09 23				09 49
Harrow & Wealdstone	d	08 03				08 17	08 23	08 28	08 33			08 54	08 58			09 12		09 28	09 33			09 54
Wembley Central	d												09u05									
Shepherd's Bush	a												09 18									
Kensington (Olympia)	a												09 20									
West Brompton	a												09 23									
Imperial Wharf	a												09 26									
Clapham Junction	a																					
East Croydon	a												09 57									
London Euston	a	08 18	08 24	08 16	08 16	08 33	08 37	08 42	08 49	08 39	08 55	09 08		09 27	09 23	09 27	09 34	09 42	09 47	09 44	09 52	10 08

Station		SN	VT	LM	VT	LM	VT	LM	LM	VT	LM	LM	SN	VT	LM	VT	LM	VT	LM	LM	VT	LM	LM
Wolverhampton	d				08 45											09 45							
Sandwell & Dudley	d				08 56											09 56							
Birmingham New Street	d		08 30	07 53	09 10									09 30	08 53	10 10							
Birmingham International	d		08 39	08 05	09 20									09 39	09 05	10 20							
Coventry	d		08 51	08 21	09 31									09 51	09 21	10 31							
Nuneaton	d										09 03											10 02	
Rugby	d			08 33							09 20				09 33							10 19	
Northampton	d			09e05		09 25					09f50				10g05		10 25					10h50	
Wolverton	d			09 17		09 37									10 17		10 37						
Milton Keynes Central	a		09 18	09 20		09 41					10 05			10 18	10 20		10 41					11 04	
	d	09 13	09 19	09 21		09 41	09 47		09 47	10 02	10 05		10 13	10 19	10 21		10 41	10 47		10 47	11 02	11 04	
Bletchley	d	09 17		09 26		09 46			09 52				10 17		10 26		10 46			10 52			
Leighton Buzzard	d	09 24		09 32		09 53			09 58				10 24		10 32		10 53			10 58			
Cheddington	d								10 04											11 04			
Tring	d	09 34						09 56	10 10			10 26	10 34						10 56	11 10			11 26
Berkhamsted	d	09 39		09 45				10 00	10 15			10 30	10 39		10 45				11 00	11 15			11 30
Hemel Hempstead	d	09 43		09 50				10 05	10 19			10 35	10 43		10 50				11 05	11 19			11 35
Apsley	d							10 08				10 38							11 08				11 38
Kings Langley	d							10 11				10 41							11 11				11 41
Watford Junction	a	09 51		09 57	10s15			10 16	10 26		10 30	10 46	10 51		10 57	11s15			11 16	11 26		11 29	11 46
	d	09 51		09 57	10s16			10 16	10 27		10 30	10 46	10 51		10 57	11s16			11 16	11 27		11 29	11 46
Bushey	d							10 19				10 49							11 19				11 49
Harrow & Wealdstone	d	09 58						10 24				10 54	10 59						11 24				11 54
Wembley Central	d	10u05											11u04										
Shepherd's Bush	a	10 21											11 19										
Kensington (Olympia)	a	10 23											11 21										
West Brompton	a	10 26											11 23										
Imperial Wharf	a	10 29											11 26										
Clapham Junction	a																						
East Croydon	a	10 57											11 57										
London Euston	a		09 54	10 20	10 34	10 27	10 23	10 38	10 46	10 38	10 49	11 08		10 54	11 18	11 34	11 27	11 23	11 38	11 46	11 38	11 49	12 08

b arr. 0724
c arr. 0841
e arr. 0856
f arr. 0942
g arr. 0954
h arr. 1042

Table 66

Mondays to Fridays

West Midlands, Northampton, Milton Keynes and Watford Junction - London

Station		SN ■	VT ◇■ A ☕	VT ◇■ B ☕	LM ◇■	VT ◇■ ☕	LM ◇■	VT ◇■ ☕	LM ■	LM ■	VT ◇■ ⊠	LM ◇■	LM ■	SN ■	VT ◇■ ☕	LM ◇■	VT ◇■ ☕	LM ◇■	VT ◇■ ☕	LM ■	LM ■	VT ◇■ ☕
Wolverhampton 7	d					10 45											11 45					
Sandwell & Dudley	d					10 56											11 56					
Birmingham New Street 12	d		10 30	10 30	09 53	11 10									11 30	10 53	12 10					
Birmingham International ✈	d		10 39	10 39	10 05	11 20									11 39	11 05	12 20					
Coventry	d		10 51	10 52	10 21	11 31									11 52	11 21	12 31					
Nuneaton	d											11 02										
Rugby	d				10 33							11 19				11 33						
Northampton	d				11b05		11 25					11c50				12e05		12 25				
Wolverton	d				11 17		11 37									12 17		12 37				
Milton Keynes Central 10	a		11 18	11 18	11 20		11 41					12 04			12 18	12 20		12 41				
	d	11 13	11 19	11 19	11 21		11 41	11 47		11 47	12 02	12 04		12 13	12 19	12 21		12 41	12 46		12 47	13 02
Bletchley	d	11 17			11 26		11 46			11 52				12 17		12 26		12 46			12 52	
Leighton Buzzard	d	11 24			11 32		11 53			11 58				12 24		12 32		12 53			12 58	
Cheddington	d									12 04											13 04	
Tring	d	11 34							11 56	12 10			12 26	12 34						12 56	13 10	
Berkhamsted	d	11 39			11 45				12 00	12 15			12 30	12 39		12 45				13 00	13 15	
Hemel Hempstead	d	11 43			11 50				12 05	12 19			12 35	12 43		12 50				13 05	13 19	
Apsley	d								12 08				12 38							13 08		
Kings Langley	d								12 11				12 41							13 11		
Watford Junction	a	11 51			11 57	12s15			12 16	12 26		12 29	12 46	12 51		12 57	13s15			13 16	13 26	
	d	11 51			11 57	12s16			12 16	12 27		12 29	12 46	12 51		12 57	13s16			13 16	13 27	
Bushey	d								12 19				12 49							13 19		
Harrow & Wealdstone ⊖	d	11 59							12 24				12 54	12 59						13 24		
Wembley Central ⊖	d	12u04												13u04								
Shepherd's Bush	a	12 19												13 19								
Kensington (Olympia) ⊖	a	12 21												13 21								
West Brompton ⊖	a	12 24												13 24								
Imperial Wharf	a	12 27												13 27								
Clapham Junction 10	a																					
East Croydon	a	12 57												13 57								
London Euston 15 ⊖	a		11 54	11 54	12 18	12 34	12 27	12 23	12 38	12 46	12 38	12 49	13 08		12 54	13 18	13 34	13 27	13 23	13 38	13 46	13 38

Station		LM ◇■	LM ■	SN ■	VT ◇■ ☕	LM ◇■	LM ◇■	VT ◇■ ☕	LM ■	VT ◇■ ☕	LM ■	VT ◇■ ☕	LM ◇■	LM ■	SN ■	VT ◇■ A ☕	VT ◇■ B ☕	LM ◇■	VT ◇■ ☕	LM ◇■	VT ◇■ ☕	LM ■	LM ■
Wolverhampton 7	d									12 45									13 45				
Sandwell & Dudley	d									12 56									13 56				
Birmingham New Street 12	d				12 30	11 53				13 10						13 30	13 30	12 53	14 10				
Birmingham International ✈	d				12 39	12 07				13 20						13 39	13 39	13 05	14 20				
Coventry	d				12 52	12 23				13 31						13 51	13 52	13 21	14 31				
Nuneaton	d	12 02											13 02										
Rugby	d	12 19				12 34							13h24					13 33					
Northampton	d	12f50				13g05	13 25						13 50					14i05		14 25			
Wolverton	d					13 17	13 37											14 17		14 37			
Milton Keynes Central 10	a	13 04			13 18	13 20	13 41						14 04			14 18	14 19	14 20		14 41			
	d	13 04		13 13	13 19	13 21	13 41	13 47			13 47	14 02	14 04		14 13	14 19	14 19	14 21		14 41	14 47		14 47
Bletchley	d			13 17		13 26	13 46				13 52				14 17			14 26		14 46			14 52
Leighton Buzzard	d			13 24		13 32	13 53				13 58				14 24			14 32		14 53			14 58
Cheddington	d										14 04												15 05
Tring	d		13 26	13 34					13 56		14 10			14 26	14 34							14 56	15 11
Berkhamsted	d		13 30	13 39		13 45			14 00		14 15			14 30	14 39			14 45				15 00	15 15
Hemel Hempstead	d		13 35	13 43		13 50			14 05		14 19			14 35	14 43			14 50				15 05	15 20
Apsley	d		13 38						14 08					14 38								15 08	
Kings Langley	d		13 41						14 11					14 41								15 11	
Watford Junction	a	13 29	13 46	13 51		13 57			14 16	14s17	14 26		14 29	14 46	14 51			14 57	15s15			15 16	15 27
	d	13 29	13 46	13 51		13 57			14 16	14s18	14 27		14 29	14 46	14 51			14 57	15s16			15 16	15 27
Bushey	d		13 49						14 19					14 49								15 19	
Harrow & Wealdstone ⊖	d		13 54	13 59					14 24					14 54	14 59							15 24	
Wembley Central ⊖	d			14u04											15u04								
Shepherd's Bush	a			14 19											15 22								
Kensington (Olympia) ⊖	a			14 21											15 24								
West Brompton ⊖	a			14 24											15 26								
Imperial Wharf	a			14 27											15 29								
Clapham Junction 10	a																						
East Croydon	a			14 57											15 57								
London Euston 15 ⊖	a	13 49	14 08		13 54	14 18	14 27	14 23	14 38	14 34	14 46	14 38	14 49	15 08		14 52	14 53	15 17	15 34	15 27	15 23	15 38	15 46

A until 16 July, from 6 September
B from 19 July until 3 September
b arr. 1054
c arr. 1142
e arr. 1154
f arr. 1243
g arr. 1254
h arr. 1317
i arr. 1354

Table 66

Mondays to Fridays

West Midlands, Northampton, Milton Keynes and Watford Junction - London

Station		VT ◇■ ☕	LM ◇■	LM ■	SN ■	VT ◇■ A ☕	VT ◇■ B ☕	LM ◇■	VT ◇■ ☕	LM ◇■	VT ◇■ ☕	LM ■	LM ■	VT ◇■ ☕	LM ◇■	LM ■	SN ■	VT ◇■ ☕	LM ◇■	VT ◇■ ☕	LM ◇■	VT ◇■ ☕	LM ■
Wolverhampton 7	d								~~14e45~~											15 45			
Sandwell & Dudley	d								~~14 56~~											15 56			
Birmingham New Street 12	d					14 30	14 30	13 53	15 10									15 30	14 53	16 10			
Birmingham International ✈	d					14 39	14 39	14 07	15 20									15 39	15 05	16 20			
Coventry	d					14 52	14 51	14 23	15 31									15 51	15 21	16 31			
Nuneaton	d		14 02												15 02								
Rugby	d		14 19					14 34							15 19				15 33				
Northampton	d		14b50					15c05		15 25					15f50				16g05		16 25		
Wolverton	d							15 17		15 37									16 17		16 37		
Milton Keynes Central 10	a		15 04			15 18	15 18	15 20		15 41					16 04			16 18	16 20		16 41		
	d	15 02	15 04		15 13	15 19	15 19	15 21		15 41	15 47		15 47	16 02	16 04		16 13	16 19	16 21		16 41	16 47	
Bletchley	d				15 17			15 26		15 46			15 52				16 17		16 26		16 46		
Leighton Buzzard	d				15 24			15 32		15 53			15 58				16 24		16 32		16 53		
Cheddington	d												16 04										
Tring	d			15 26	15 34							15 56	16 10			16 26	16 34						16 56
Berkhamsted	d			15 30	15 39			15 45				16 00	16 15			16 30	16 39		16 45				17 00
Hemel Hempstead	d			15 35	15 43			15 50				16 05	16 19			16 35	16 43		16 50				17 05
Apsley	d			15 38								16 08				16 38							17 08
Kings Langley	d			15 41								16 11				16 41							17 11
Watford Junction	a		15 29	15 46	15 51			15 57	16s15			16 16	16 26		16 29	16 46	16 51		16 57	17s15			17 16
	d		15 29	15 46	15 51			15 57	16s16			16 16	16 27		16 29	16 46	16 51		16 57	17s16			17 16
Bushey	d			15 49								16 19				16 49							17 19
Harrow & Wealdstone ⊖	d			15 54	15 59							16 24				16 54	16 59						17 24
Wembley Central ⊖	d				16u05												17u05						
Shepherd's Bush	a				16 19												17 19						
Kensington (Olympia) ⊖	a				16 21												17 21						
West Brompton ⊖	a				16 24												17 24						
Imperial Wharf	a				16 27												17 27						
Clapham Junction 10	a																						
East Croydon	a				16 59												17 59						
London Euston 15 ⊖	a	15 38	15 49	16 08		15 54	15 54	16 18	16 34	16 27	16 23	16 38	16 46	16 38	16 49	17 08		16 54	17 19	17 34	17 27	17 23	17 38

Station		LM ■	VT ◇■ ☕	VT ◇■ ☕	LM ◇■	LM ■	SN ■	VT ◇■ ☕	LM ◇■	VT ◇■ ☕	LM ◇■	VT ◇■ ☕	LM ■	LM ■	VT ◇■ ☕	LM ◇■	LM ■	VT ◇■ ☕	SN ■	VT ◇■ ⊠	LM ◇■	VT ◇■ B ⊠
Wolverhampton 7	d									16 45												17 45
Sandwell & Dudley	d									16 56												17 56
Birmingham New Street 12	d							16 30	15 53	17 10										17 30	16 53	18 10
Birmingham International ✈	d							16 39	16 05	17 20										17 39	17 05	18 20
Coventry	d							16 51	16 21	17 31										17 51	17 21	18 31
Nuneaton	d				16 02											17 02						
Rugby	d				16 19				16 33							17 19					17 33	
Northampton	d				16h50				17i05		17 25					17j50					18k05	
Wolverton	d								17 17		17 37										18 17	
Milton Keynes Central 10	a				17 04			17 18	17 20		17 41					18 04				18 18	18 20	
	d	16 47	17 02	17s02	17 04		17 13	17 19	17 21		17 41	17 47		17 47	18 02	18 04			18 13	18 19	18 21	
Bletchley	d	16 52					17 17		17 26		17 46			17 52					18 17		18 26	
Leighton Buzzard	d	16 58					17 24		17 32		17 53			17 58					18 24		18 32	
Cheddington	d	17 04												18 04								
Tring	d	17 10				17 26	17 34						17 59	18 10			18 27		18 34			
Berkhamsted	d	17 15				17 30	17 39		17 45				18 03	18 15			18 31		18 39		18 45	
Hemel Hempstead	d	17 19				17 35	17 43		17 50				18 07	18 19			18 36		18 43		18 50	
Apsley	d					17 38							18 10				18 39					
Kings Langley	d					17 41							18 13				18 42					
Watford Junction	a	17 26			17 29	17 46	17 51		17 57	18s15			18 18	18 26		18 29	18 46	18s48	18 51		18 57	19s16
	d	17 27			17 29	17 46	17 51		17 57	18s16			18 18	18 27		18 29	18 47	18s49	18 51		18 57	19s17
Bushey	d					17 49							18 21				18 49					
Harrow & Wealdstone ⊖	d					17 54	17 59						18 26				18 54		18 59			
Wembley Central ⊖	d						18u05												19u05			
Shepherd's Bush	a						18 19												19 18			
Kensington (Olympia) ⊖	a						18 21												19 20			
West Brompton ⊖	a						18 24												19 23			
Imperial Wharf	a						18 27												19 25			
Clapham Junction 10	a																					
East Croydon	a						19 02															
London Euston 15 ⊖	a	17 49	17 38	17 38	17 49	18 10		17 54	18 20	18 34	18 27	18 23	18 40	18 46	18 38	18 49	19 09	19 08		18 54	19 18	19 34

A from 19 July until 3 September
B until 16 July, from 6 September
b arr. 1442
c arr. 1454
e arr. 1433
f arr. 1542
g arr. 1554
h arr. 1644
i arr. 1654
j arr. 1742
k arr. 1754

Table 66

Mondays to Fridays

West Midlands, Northampton, Milton Keynes and Watford Junction - London

		VT	VT	LM	VT	LM	LM	VT	VT	LM	VT	LM	SN	VT	LM	VT	VT	VT	LM	VT	LM	LM	LM
		◇1 A ⊠	◇1 ☕	◇1	◇1 ⊠	1	1	◇1 B ⊠	◇1 A ⊠	◇1	◇1 ⊠	1	1	◇1 ⊠	◇1	R 1 A ☕	◇1 B ⊠	◇1 ⊠	◇1	◇1 ⊠	1	1	◇1
Wolverhampton 7	d	17 45														18 45	18 45						
Sandwell & Dudley	d	17 56														18 56	18 56						
Birmingham New Street 12	d	18 10		17 13										18 30	17 53	19 10	19 10						
Birmingham International	d	18 20		17 27										18 39	18 05	19 20	19 20						
Coventry	d	18 31		17 43										18 51	18 21	19 31	19 31						
Nuneaton	d									18 02													19 02
Rugby	d			17 55						18 19					18 33								19 21
Northampton	d			18b25						18c50					19e05				19 25				19g50
Wolverton	d			18 37											19 17				19 37				
Milton Keynes Central 10	a			18 41						19 04				19 18	19 20				19 41				20 04
	d		18 24	18 41	18 48		18 47	19 02	19 03	19 04			19 15	19 19	19 21			19 32	19 41	19 47		19 47	20 04
Bletchley	d			18 46			18 52						19 19		19 26				19 46			19 52	
Leighton Buzzard	d			18 53			18 58						19 26		19 32				19 53			19 58	
Cheddington	d						19 06															20 04	
Tring	d					19 00	19 12					19 29	19 36								19 56	20 10	
Berkhamsted	d					19 04	19 17					19 33	19 41		19 45						20 00	20 15	
Hemel Hempstead	d					19 09	19 21					19 38	19 45		19 50						20 05	20 19	
Apsley	d					19 12						19 41									20 08		
Kings Langley	d					19 15						19 44									20 11		
Watford Junction	a	19s16				19 20	19 28			19 30		19 49	19 54		19 59	20s15	20s15				20 16	20 26	20 29
	d	19s17				19 20	19 29			19 30	19s43	19 49	19 54		19 59	20s16	20s16				20 16	20 27	20 29
Bushey	d					19 23						19 52									20 19		
Harrow & Wealdstone ⊖	d					19 28						19 57	20 01								20 24		
Wembley Central ⊖	d												20u06										
Shepherd's Bush	a												20 21										
Kensington (Olympia) ⊖	a												20 23										
West Brompton ⊖	a												20 25										
Imperial Wharf	a												20 28										
Clapham Junction 10	a																						
East Croydon	a																						
London Euston 15 ⊖	a	19 34	18 59	19 29	19 23	19 42	19 48	19 38	19 38	19 50	20 02	20 11		19 54	20 20	20 34	20 34	20 06	20 27	20 23	20 38	20 49	20 49

		LM	VT	SN	VT	LM	VT	LM	VT	LM	VT	LM	VT	VT	LM	VT	SN	LM	VT	VT	LM	VT
		1	◇1 ⊠	1	◇1 ☕	◇1	◇1 ⊠	◇1	◇1 ⊠	1	◇1 ☕	1	◇1 ☕	◇1 ☕	1	◇1 ☕	1	◇1	◇1 ☕	◇1 ☕	◇1	◇1 ☕
Wolverhampton 7	d												19 45									
Sandwell & Dudley	d												19 56									
Birmingham New Street 12	d				19 30	18 53							20 10					19 53				
Birmingham International	d				19 39	19 05							20 20					20 05				
Coventry	d				19 51	19 21							20 31					20 21				
Nuneaton	d															21 03						
Rugby	d					19 33												20 33		21 28		
Northampton	d					20h05		20 25										21i05			21 32	
Wolverton	d					20 17		20 38										21 17			21 44	
Milton Keynes Central 10	a				20 18	20 20		20 41					20 58					21 20		21 47	21 47	
	d			20 13	20 19	20 21	20 33	20 42	20 46	20 47	20 49		20 59	21 04			21 13	21 21	21 36	21 49	21 48	21 52
Bletchley	d			20 17		20 26		20 47		20 52							21 17	21 26			21 53	
Leighton Buzzard	d			20 24		20 32		20 54		20 59							21 24	21 32			21 59	
Cheddington	d									21 06											22 05	
Tring	d	20 26		20 34						21 12		20 56			21 26		21 34				22 11	
Berkhamsted	d	20 30		20 39		20 45				21 17		21 00			21 30		21 39	21 45			22 16	
Hemel Hempstead	d	20 35		20 43		20 50				21 21		21 05			21 35		21 43	21 50			22 20	
Apsley	d	20 38										21 08			21 38							
Kings Langley	d	20 41										21 11			21 41							
Watford Junction	a	20 46	20s46	20 51		20 57				21 28		21 16	21s19		21 46	21s48	21 51	21 57			22 30	22s11
	d	20 46	20s47	20 51		20 57				21 29		21 16	21s20		21 46	21s49	21 51	21 57			22 31	22s12
Bushey	d	20 49										21 19			21 49							
Harrow & Wealdstone ⊖	d	20 54		20 59								21 24			21 54		21 59					
Wembley Central ⊖	d			21u04																		
Shepherd's Bush	a			21 22													22 23					
Kensington (Olympia) ⊖	a			21 24													22 25					
West Brompton ⊖	a			21 27													22 27					
Imperial Wharf	a			21 29													22 30					
Clapham Junction 10	a																					
East Croydon	a																					
London Euston 15 ⊖	a	21 09	21 05		20 54	21 18	21 06	21 29	21 24	21 48	21 25	21 38	21 38	21 42	22 08	22 09		22 20	22 12	22 22	22 52	22 33

A from 19 July until 3 September
B until 16 July, from 6 September
b arr. 1817
c arr. 1842
e arr. 1854
f arr. 1833
g arr. 1944
h arr. 1955
i arr. 2054

Table 66

Mondays to Fridays

West Midlands, Northampton, Milton Keynes and Watford Junction - London

		VT	SN	LM	SN	LM	VT	VT	SN	VT	VT	LM	LM	LM MO	LM	LM	VT
		◇1 ☕	1	1	1	◇1	◇1 ⊠	◇1 ☕	1	◇1 ☕	◇1 ☕	◇1 A	◇1 B	◇1	◇1 C	◇1 D	◇1 ☕
Wolverhampton 7	d	20 47									21 45						22 45
Sandwell & Dudley	d	20 57									21 56						22 55
Birmingham New Street 12	d	21 10				20 53					22 10	21 33	21 33				23e10
Birmingham International	d	21 20				21 05					22 20	21 45	21 45				23 20
Coventry	d	21 31				21 21					22 31	22 01	22 01				23 31
Nuneaton	d									22 17							
Rugby	d					21 33				22 33	22 43	22 13	22 13				23 44
Northampton	d					22b05						22c55	22c55	23 30	23 46	23 46	00s07
Wolverton	d					22 18						23 07	23 07	23 44	23 58	23 58	
Milton Keynes Central 10	a	21 58				22 22				22 57	23s06	23 12	23 12	23 50	00 03	00 03	00s23
	d	21 59		22 02	22 11	22 22	22 41	22 53		22 59	23s07	23 13	23 13	23 50	00 04	00 04	00s24
Bletchley	d			22 09	22 15	22 27						23 18	23 18	23 55	00 09	00 09	
Leighton Buzzard	d			22 16	22 22	22 34						23 24	23 24	00 02	00 15	00 15	
Cheddington	d			22 22								23 29	23 29	00 08	00 24	00 24	
Tring	d			22 27	22 34							23 38	23 38	00 14	00 29	00 29	
Berkhamsted	d			22 32	22 39	22 49						23 43	23 43	00 18	00 34	00 34	
Hemel Hempstead	d			22 36	22 43	22 53						23 47	23 47	00 22	00 38	00 38	
Apsley	d			22 39								23 50	23 50				
Kings Langley	d			22 43								23 53	23 53				
Watford Junction	a	22s20		22 47	22 52	23 00	23s14	23s25		23s31	23s37	23 58	23 58	00 29	00 45	00 45	00s52
	d	22s21	22 27	22 48	22 53	23 01	23s15	23s26	23 29	23s32	23s38	23 58	23 58	00 30	00 46	00 46	00s53
Bushey	d			22 51								00 01	00 01				
Harrow & Wealdstone ⊖	d		22 33	22 56	23 00				23 35			00 06	00 06	00 36	00 52	00 52	
Wembley Central ⊖	d													00 40	00 56	00 56	
Shepherd's Bush	a		22 49		23 21				23 53								
Kensington (Olympia) ⊖	a		22 51		23 23				23 56								
West Brompton ⊖	a		22 54		23 26				23 59								
Imperial Wharf	a		22 56		23 28				00 02								
Clapham Junction 10	a																
East Croydon	a				00 01												
London Euston 15 ⊖	a	22 43		23 11		23 25	23 38	23 48		23 58	00 05	00 20	00 21	00 53	01 08	01 09	01 13

Saturdays

		SN	SN	VT	LM	LM	LM	LM	VT	LM	LM	SN	LM	LM	LM	SN	LM	LM	VT	VT	VT	VT
		1	1	◇1 ☕	◇1 E	◇1 F	◇1 E	◇1 F	◇1 ☕	1	1	1	◇1	1	1	1	◇1	1	◇1 ☕	◇1 ☕	◇1 ☕	◇1 ☕
Wolverhampton 7	d			21p45					22p45										05 45		06 06	
Sandwell & Dudley	d			21p56					22p55										05 56		06 17	
Birmingham New Street 12	d			22p10	21p33	21p33			23h10										06 10		06 30	
Birmingham International	d			22p20	21p45	21p45			23p20										06 20		06 40	
Coventry	d			22p31	22p01	22p01			23p31										06 31		06 51	
Nuneaton	d																					06 59
Rugby	d			22p43	22p13	22p13			23p44											06 51		
Northampton	d				22g55	22g55	23p46	23p46	00s07				05 16				06 05					
Wolverton	d				23p07	23p07	23p58	23p58					05 28				06 17					
Milton Keynes Central 10	a			23f06	23p12	23p12	00 03	00 03	00s23				05 32				06 20		06 58	07 11		
	d	22p11		23f07	23p13	23p13	00 04	00 04	00s24	03 40	04 35		05 32		06 47		06 21		06 59	07 12		
Bletchley	d	22p15			23p18	23p18	00 09	00 09		03 45	04 40		05 37	06 10	06 52		06 26	06 40				
Leighton Buzzard	d	22p22			23p24	23p24	00 15	00 15		03 51	04 46		05 44	06 16	06 58		06 32	06 46				
Cheddington	d				23p29	23p29	00 24	00 24					05 50		07 04							
Tring	d	22p34			23p38	23p38	00 29	00 29		04 03	04 58		05 56	06 26	07 10			06 56				
Berkhamsted	d	22p39			23p43	23p43	00 34	00 34		04 08	05 03		06 00	06 31	07 15		06 45	07 01				
Hemel Hempstead	d	22p43			23p47	23p47	00 38	00 38		04 12	05 07		06 05	06 35	07 19		06 50	07 05				
Apsley	d				23p50	23p50							06 08	06 38				07 08				
Kings Langley	d				23p53	23p53							06 11	06 42				07 12				
Watford Junction	a	22p52		23f37	23p58	23p58	00 45	00 45	00s52	04 19	05 14		06 16	06 46	07 26		06 59	07 16	07s19	07s32	07s36	07s44
	d	22p53	23p29	23f38	23p58	23p58	00 46	00 46	00s53	04 20	05 15	05 52	06 16	06 47	07 27	06 55	07 00	07 17	07s20	07s33	07s37	07s45
Bushey	d				00 01	00 01							06 19	06 50				07 20				
Harrow & Wealdstone ⊖	d	23p00	23p35		00 06	00 06	00 52	00 52		04 26	05 21	05 58	06 24	06 55		07 01		07 25				
Wembley Central ⊖	d						00 56	00 56		04 34	05 25					07 06						
Shepherd's Bush	a	23p21	23p53									06 20				07 20						
Kensington (Olympia) ⊖	a	23p23	23p56									06 22				07 22						
West Brompton ⊖	a	23p26	23p59									06 25				07 25						
Imperial Wharf	a	23p28	00 02									06 28				07 28						
Clapham Junction 10	a																					
East Croydon	a	00 01										06 57				07 57						
London Euston 15 ⊖	a			00 05	00 20	00 21	01 08	01 09	01 13	04 46	05 41		06 38	07 11	07 46		07 20	07 39	07 38	07 52	07 55	08 05

A until 3 September
B from 6 September
C MX until 3 September
D MX from 7 September
E until 4 September
F from 11 September
b arr. 2154
c arr. 2234
e arr. 2304
f previous night, stops to set down only
g previous night, arr. 2234
h previous night, arr. 2304

Table 66

West Midlands, Northampton, Milton Keynes and Watford Junction - London

	LM 1	SN 1	LM ◇1	VT ◇1 ☕	VT ◇1 ☕	VT ◇1 ☕	LM 1	LM 1	LM ◇1	LM 1	SN 1	VT ◇1 A ☕	VT ◇1 B ☕	LM ◇1	LM ◇1	VT ◇1 ☕	LM 1	VT ◇1 ☕	LM 1	LM ◇1	LM 1	SN 1
Wolverhampton 7 d				06 45								07 04	07 04					07 44				
Sandwell & Dudley d				06 56								07 15	07 15					07 56				
Birmingham New Street 12 d				07 10								07b30	07b30					08 10				
Birmingham International ✈ d				07 20								07 40	07 40					08 20				
Coventry d				07 31								07 52	07 52					08 31				
Nuneaton d																				08 04		
Rugby d																				08 20		
Northampton d			07 05						07 33					08 05	08 25					08c50		
Wolverton d			07 17						07 45					08 17	08 37							
Milton Keynes Central 10 a			07 20						07 49			08 18	08 19	08 20	08 41					09 04		
d		07 13	07 21		07 32	07 38	07 44		07 49		08 13	08 19	08 20	08 21	08 41	08 47			08 47	09 04		09 13
Bletchley d	07 10	07 17	07 26				07 49		07 54		08 17			08 26	08 46				08 52			09 17
Leighton Buzzard d	07 16	07 24	07 32				07 55		08 03		08 24			08 32	08 53				08 58			09 24
Cheddington d							08 01												09 04			
Tring d	07 26	07 34					08 07	07 56		08 26	08 34						08 56		09 10		09 26	09 34
Berkhamsted d	07 31	07 39	07 45				08 12	08 00		08 30	08 39			08 45			09 00		09 15		09 30	09 39
Hemel Hempstead d	07 35	07 43	07 50				08 16	08 05		08 35	08 43			08 50			09 05		09 19		09 35	09 43
Apsley d	07 38							08 08		08 38							09 08				09 38	
Kings Langley d	07 42							08 11		08 41							09 11				09 41	
Watford Junction a	07 46	07 51	07 57	08s15			08 23	08 16	08 20	08 46	08 51			08 59			09 16	09s17	09 26	09 33	09 46	09 51
d	07 47	07 52	07 57	08s16			08 24	08 16	08 20	08 46	08 52			08 59			09 16	09s18	09 27	09 34	09 46	09 52
Bushey d	07 50							08 19		08 49							09 19				09 49	
Harrow & Wealdstone ⊖ d	07 55	07 59						08 24		08 54	08 59						09 24				09 54	09 59
Wembley Central ⊖ d		08u04									09u04											10u04
Shepherd's Bush a		08 20									09 20											10 20
Kensington (Olympia) ⊖ a		08 22									09 22											10 22
West Brompton ⊖ a		08 25									09 25											10 25
Imperial Wharf a		08 28									09 28											10 28
Clapham Junction 10 a																						
East Croydon a		08 57									09 57											10 57
London Euston 15 ⊖ a	08 09		08 19	08 34	08 09	08 14	08 44	08 41	08 38	09 08		08 54	08 54	09 18	09 27	09 23	09 38	09 35	09 46	09 50	10 08	

	VT ◇1 ☕	LM ◇1	VT ◇1 ☕	LM ◇1	VT ◇1 ☕	LM 1	LM 1	VT ◇1 ☕	LM ◇1	LM 1	SN 1	VT ◇1 ☕	LM ◇1	VT ◇1 ☕	LM ◇1	VT ◇1 ☕	LM 1	LM 1	VT ◇1 ☕	LM ◇1	LM 1
Wolverhampton 7 d	08 06		08 45											09 45							
Sandwell & Dudley d			08 56											09 56							
Birmingham New Street 12 d	08e30		09 10									09 30		10 10							
Birmingham International ✈ d	08 39		09 20									09 39		10 20							
Coventry d	08 51		09 31									09 51		10 31							
Nuneaton d									09 04											10 02	
Rugby d									09 20											10 18	
Northampton d		09 05		09 25					09f50				10 05		10 25					10g50	
Wolverton d		09 17		09 37									10 17		10 37						
Milton Keynes Central 10 a	09 18	09 20		09 41					10 04			10 18	10 20		10 41					11 04	
d	09 19	09 21		09 41	09 47		09 47	10 02	10 04		10 13	10 19	10 21		10 41	10 47		10 47	11 02	11 04	
Bletchley d		09 26		09 46			09 52				10 17		10 26		10 46			10 52			
Leighton Buzzard d		09 32		09 53			09 58				10 24		10 32		10 53			10 58			
Cheddington d							10 04											11 04			
Tring d						09 56	10 10			10 26	10 34						10 56	11 10			11 26
Berkhamsted d		09 45				10 00	10 15			10 30	10 39		10 45				11 00	11 15			11 30
Hemel Hempstead d		09 50				10 05	10 19			10 35	10 43		10 50				11 05	11 19			11 35
Apsley d						10 08				10 38							11 08				11 38
Kings Langley d						10 11				10 41							11 11				11 41
Watford Junction a		09 57	10s15			10 16	10 26		10 29	10 46	10 51		10 57	11s15			11 16	11 26		11 29	11 46
d		09 57	10s16			10 16	10 27		10 29	10 46	10 52		10 57	11s16			11 16	11 27		11 29	11 46
Bushey d						10 19				10 49							11 19				11 49
Harrow & Wealdstone ⊖ d						10 24				10 54	10 59						11 24				11 54
Wembley Central ⊖ d											11u04										
Shepherd's Bush a											11 20										
Kensington (Olympia) ⊖ a											11 22										
West Brompton ⊖ a											11 25										
Imperial Wharf a											11 28										
Clapham Junction 10 a																					
East Croydon a											11 57										
London Euston 15 ⊖ a	09 55	10 19	10 34	10 27	10 23	10 38	10 46	10 37	10 49	11 08		10 54	11 19	11 34	11 27	11 23	11 38	11 46	11 38	11 49	12 08

A until 10 July, from 11 September
B from 17 July until 4 September
b arr. 0724
c arr. 0840
e arr. 0824
f arr. 0941
g arr. 1038

Table 66

West Midlands, Northampton, Milton Keynes and Watford Junction - London

	SN 1	VT ◇1 A ☕	VT ◇1 B ☕	LM ◇1	VT ◇1 ☕	LM ◇1	VT ◇1 ☕	LM 1	LM 1	VT ◇1 ☕	LM ◇1	LM 1	SN 1	VT ◇1 ☕	LM ◇1	VT ◇1 B ☕	VT ◇1 A ☕	LM ◇1	VT ◇1 ☕	LM 1	LM 1	VT ◇1 ☕
Wolverhampton 7 d					10 45											11 45	11 45					
Sandwell & Dudley d					10 56											11 56	11 56					
Birmingham New Street 12 d		10 30	10 30		11 10									11 30		12 10	12 10					
Birmingham International ✈ d		10 40	10 39		11 20									11 39		12 20	12 20					
Coventry d		10 51	10 51		11 31									11 51		12 31	12 29					
Nuneaton d											11 03											
Rugby d											11 19											
Northampton d				11 05		11 25					11b50				12 05			12 25				
Wolverton d				11 17		11 37									12 17			12 37				
Milton Keynes Central 10 a		11 18	11 18	11 20		11 41					12 04			12 18	12 20			12 41				
d	11 13	11 19	11 19	11 21		11 41	11 47		11 47	12 02	12 04		12 13	12 19	12 21			12 41	12 47		12 47	13 02
Bletchley d	11 17			11 26		11 46			11 52				12 17		12 26			12 46			12 52	
Leighton Buzzard d	11 24			11 32		11 53			11 58				12 24		12 32			12 53			12 58	
Cheddington d									12 04												13 04	
Tring d	11 34							11 56	12 10			12 26	12 34							12 56	13 10	
Berkhamsted d	11 39			11 45				12 00	12 15			12 30	12 39		12 45					13 00	13 15	
Hemel Hempstead d	11 43			11 50				12 05	12 19			12 35	12 43		12 50					13 05	13 19	
Apsley d								12 08				12 38								13 08		
Kings Langley d								12 11				12 41								13 11		
Watford Junction a	11 51			11 57	12s15			12 16	12 26		12 29	12 46	12 51		12 57	13s15	13s15			13 16	13 26	
d	11 52			11 57	12s16			12 16	12 27		12 29	12 46	12 52		12 57	13s16	13s16			13 16	13 27	
Bushey d								12 19				12 49								13 19		
Harrow & Wealdstone ⊖ d	11 59							12 24				12 54	12 59							13 24		
Wembley Central ⊖ d	12u04												13u04									
Shepherd's Bush a	12 20												13 20									
Kensington (Olympia) ⊖ a	12 22												13 22									
West Brompton ⊖ a	12 25												13 25									
Imperial Wharf a	12 28												13 28									
Clapham Junction 10 a																						
East Croydon a	12 57												13 57									
London Euston 15 ⊖ a		11 54	11 54	12 18	12 34	12 27	12 23	12 38	12 46	12 38	12 49	13 08		12 54	13 18	13 34	13 34	13 27	13 23	13 38	13 46	13 38

	LM ◇1	LM 1	SN 1	VT ◇1 ☕	LM ◇1	VT ◇1 ☕	LM ◇1	VT ◇1 ☕	LM 1	LM 1	VT ◇1 ☕	LM ◇1	LM 1	SN 1	VT ◇1 ☕	LM ◇1	VT ◇1 ☕	LM ◇1	VT ◇1 ☕	LM 1	LM 1
Wolverhampton 7 d						12 45											13 45				
Sandwell & Dudley d						12 56											13 56				
Birmingham New Street 12 d				12 30		13 10									13 30		14 10				
Birmingham International ✈ d				12 39		13 20									13 39		14 20				
Coventry d				12 51		13 31									13 51		14 31				
Nuneaton d	12 02											13 03									
Rugby d	12 18											13 19									
Northampton d	12c50				13 05		13 25					13e50				14 05		14 25			
Wolverton d					13 17		13 37									14 17		14 37			
Milton Keynes Central 10 a	13 04			13 18	13 20		13 41					14 04			14 18	14 20		14 41			
d	13 04		13 13	13 19	13 21		13 41	13 47		13 47	14 02	14 04		14 13	14 19	14 21		14 41	14 47		14 47
Bletchley d			13 17		13 26		13 46			13 52				14 17		14 26		14 46			14 52
Leighton Buzzard d			13 24		13 32		13 53			13 58				14 24		14 32		14 53			14 58
Cheddington d										14 04											15 04
Tring d		13 26	13 34						13 56	14 10			14 26	14 34						14 56	15 10
Berkhamsted d		13 30	13 39		13 45				14 00	14 15			14 30	14 39		14 45				15 00	15 15
Hemel Hempstead d		13 35	13 43		13 50				14 05	14 19			14 35	14 43		14 50				15 05	15 19
Apsley d		13 38							14 08				14 38							15 08	
Kings Langley d		13 41							14 11				14 41							15 11	
Watford Junction a	13 29	13 46	13 51		13 57	14s15			14 16	14 26		14 29	14 46	14 51		14 57	15s15			15 16	15 28
d	13 29	13 46	13 52		13 57	14s16			14 16	14 27		14 29	14 46	14 52		14 57	15s16			15 16	15 29
Bushey d		13 49							14 19				14 49							15 19	
Harrow & Wealdstone ⊖ d		13 54	13 59						14 24				14 54	14 59						15 24	
Wembley Central ⊖ d			14u04											15u04							
Shepherd's Bush a			14 20											15 20							
Kensington (Olympia) ⊖ a			14 22											15 22							
West Brompton ⊖ a			14 25											15 25							
Imperial Wharf a			14 28											15 28							
Clapham Junction 10 a																					
East Croydon a			14 57											15 57							
London Euston 15 ⊖ a	13 49	14 08		13 54	14 18	14 34	14 27	14 23	14 38	14 46	14 38	14 49	15 08		14 54	15 18	15 34	15 27	15 23	15 38	15 46

A from 17 July until 4 September
B until 10 July, from 11 September
b arr. 1140
c arr. 1238
e arr. 1340

West Midlands, Northampton, Milton Keynes and Watford Junction - London

	VT ◇1 ☕	LM ◇1	LM 1	SN 1	VT ◇1 ☕	LM ◇1	VT ◇1 ☕	LM ◇1	VT ◇1 ☕	LM 1	LM 1	VT ◇1 ☕	LM ◇1	LM 1	SN 1	VT ◇1 ☕	LM ◇1	VT ◇1 ☒	LM ◇1	VT ◇1 ☕	LM 1	LM 1
Wolverhampton 7 d							~~14c45~~											15 45				
Sandwell & Dudley d							~~14 56~~											15 56				
Birmingham New Street 12 d					14 30		15 10									15 30		16 10				
Birmingham International ✈ d					14 39		15 20									15 39		16 20				
Coventry d					14 51		15 31									15 51		16 31				
Nuneaton d		14 02											15 02									
Rugby d		14 18											15 19									
Northampton d		14b50				15 05		15 25					15e50				16 05		16 25			
Wolverton d						15 17		15 37									16 17		16 37			
Milton Keynes Central 10 a		15 04			15 18	15 20		15 41					16 04			16 18	16 20		16 41			
d	15 02	15 04		15 13	15 19	15 21		15 41	15 47		15 47	16 02	16 04		16 13	16 19	16 21		16 41	16 47		16 47
Bletchley d				15 17		15 26		15 46			15 52				16 17		16 26		16 46			16 52
Leighton Buzzard d				15 24		15 32		15 53			15 58				16 24		16 32		16 53			16 58
Cheddington d											16 04											17 04
Tring d			15 26	15 34						15 56	16 10			16 26	16 34						16 56	17 10
Berkhamsted d			15 30	15 39		15 45				16 00	16 15			16 30	16 39		16 45				17 00	17 15
Hemel Hempstead d			15 35	15 43		15 50				16 05	16 19			16 35	16 43		16 50				17 05	17 19
Apsley d			15 38							16 08				16 38							17 08	
Kings Langley d			15 41							16 11				16 41							17 11	
Watford Junction a		15 29	15 46	15 51		15 57	16s15			16 16	16 28		16 29	16 46	16 51		16 57	17s15			17 16	17 28
d		15 29	15 46	15 52		15 57	16s16			16 16	16 29		16 29	16 46	16 52		16 57	17s16			17 16	17 29
Bushey d			15 49							16 19				16 49							17 19	
Harrow & Wealdstone ⊖ d			15 54	15 59						16 24				16 54	16 59						17 24	
Wembley Central ⊖ d				16u04											17u04							
Shepherd's Bush a				16 20											17 20							
Kensington (Olympia) ⊖ a				16 22											17 22							
West Brompton ⊖ a				16 25											17 25							
Imperial Wharf a				16 28											17 28							
Clapham Junction 10 a																						
East Croydon a				16 57											17 57							
London Euston 15 ⊖ a	15 38	15 49	16 08		15 54	16 18	16 34	16 27	16 23	16 38	16 46	16 38	16 49	17 08		16 54	17 18	17 34	17 27	17 23	17 38	17 46

	VT ◇1 ☕	LM ◇1	LM 1	SN 1	VT ◇1 ☕	LM ◇1	VT ◇1 ☕	LM ◇1	VT ◇1 ☕	LM 1	LM 1	VT ◇1 ☕	LM ◇1	LM 1	SN 1	VT ◇1 ☕	LM ◇1	VT ◇1 ☕	VT ◇1 ☕	LM 1	LM ◇1	SN 1
Wolverhampton 7 d							16 45											17 45				
Sandwell & Dudley d							16 56											17 56				
Birmingham New Street 12 d					16 30		17 10									17 30		18 10				
Birmingham International ✈ d					16 39		17 20									17 39		18 20				
Coventry d					16 51		17 31									17 51		18 31				
Nuneaton d		16 02											17 03									
Rugby d		16 18											17 19									
Northampton d		16f50				17 05		17 25					17g50				18 05				18 31	
Wolverton d						17 17		17 37									18 17				18 43	
Milton Keynes Central 10 a		17 04			17 18	17 20		17 41					18 04			18 18	18 20				18 46	
d	17 02	17 04		17 13	17 19	17 21		17 41	17 47		17 47	18 02	18 04		18 13	18 19	18 21		18 47		18 47	
Bletchley d				17 17		17 26		17 46			17 52				18 17		18 26				18 52	
Leighton Buzzard d				17 24		17 32		17 53			17 58				18 24		18 32				18 58	
Cheddington d											18 04										19 04	
Tring d			17 26	17 34						17 56	18 10			18 26	18 34					18 56	19 10	
Berkhamsted d			17 30	17 39		17 45				18 00	18 15			18 30	18 39		18 45			19 00	19 15	
Hemel Hempstead d			17 35	17 43		17 50				18 05	18 19			18 35	18 43		18 50			19 05	19 19	
Apsley d			17 38							18 08				18 38						19 08		
Kings Langley d			17 41							18 11				18 41						19 11		
Watford Junction a		17 29	17 46	17 51		17 57	18s15			18 16	18 28		18 29	18 46	18 51		18 57	19s15		19 15	19 26	
d		17 29	17 46	17 52		17 57	18s16			18 16	18 29		18 29	18 46	18 52		18 57	19s16		19 16	19 27	19 31
Bushey d			17 49							18 19				18 49						19 19		
Harrow & Wealdstone ⊖ d			17 54	17 59						18 24				18 54	18 59					19 24		19 38
Wembley Central ⊖ d				18u04											19u04							19 43
Shepherd's Bush a				18 20											19 20							19 57
Kensington (Olympia) ⊖ a				18 22											19 22							19 59
West Brompton ⊖ a				18 25											19 25							20 02
Imperial Wharf a				18 28											19 28							20 05
Clapham Junction 10 a																						
East Croydon a				18 57											19 57							
London Euston 15 ⊖ a	17 38	17 49	18 08		17 52	18 18	18 34	18 27	18 23	18 38	18 46	18 37	18 49	19 08		18 54	19 18	19 34	19 23	19 38	19 46	

b arr. 1438
c arr. 1432
e arr. 1539
f arr. 1638
g arr. 1740

West Midlands, Northampton, Milton Keynes and Watford Junction - London

	LM ◇1	LM 1	SN 1	VT ◇1 ☕	LM ◇1	VT ◇1 ☕	LM 1	LM ◇1	VT ◇1 ☕	SN 1	LM ◇1	VT ◇1 ☕	LM ◇1	LM 1	VT ◇1 ☕	VT ◇1 ☕	SN 1	LM ◇1	LM ◇1	VT ◇1 ☕	VT ◇1 A ☕
Wolverhampton 7 d									~~18c45~~						19 45						
Sandwell & Dudley d									~~18 56~~						19 56						
Birmingham New Street 12 d				18 30					19 10						20 10						
Birmingham International ✈ d				18 39					19 20						20 20						
Coventry d				18 51					19 31						20 31						
Nuneaton d	18 02																				
Rugby d	18 18								19 44						20 43						
Northampton d	18b50				19 05			19 31			20 00		20 30					21 00	21 14		
Wolverton d					19 17			19 43			20 12							21 12			
Milton Keynes Central 10 a	19 04			19 18	19 20			19 46	20 05		20 15		20 46		21 04			21 15	21 32		21 50
d	19 04		19 13	19 19	19 21	19 47		19 47	20 07		20 16	20 43	20 47	20 50	21 05	21 11		21 16	21 33	21 52	21 52
Bletchley d			19 17		19 26			19 52			20 21			20 55					21 38		
Leighton Buzzard d			19 24		19 32			19 58			20 27		20 56						21 44		
Cheddington d								20 05					21 03						21 49		
Tring d		19 24	19 34				19 56	20 10					21 08	21 13					21 56		
Berkhamsted d		19 28	19 39		19 45		20 00	20 15						21 18				21 38	22 01		
Hemel Hempstead d		19 33	19 43		19 50		20 05	20 19					21 15	21 22				21 43	22 05		
Apsley d		19 36					20 08						21 18						22 08		
Kings Langley d		19 39					20 12						21 22						22 12		
Watford Junction a	19 36	19 44	19 50		19 57		20 18	20 26	20s34		20 50	21s15	21 26	21 30	21s34			21 50	22 16		
d	19 36	19 44	19 51		20 00		20 19	20 27	20s35	20 43	20 51	21s16	21 27	21 31	21s35		21 43	21 50	22 17		
Bushey d		19 47																			
Harrow & Wealdstone ⊖ d		19 52	19 58				20 25			20 50				21 37			21 50				
Wembley Central ⊖ d																					
Shepherd's Bush a			20 20							21 08							22 08				
Kensington (Olympia) ⊖ a			20 22							21 10							22 10				
West Brompton ⊖ a			20 25							21 13							22 13				
Imperial Wharf a			20 28							21 16							22 16				
Clapham Junction 10 a																					
East Croydon a			20 59																		
London Euston 15 ⊖ a	19 54	20 06		19 54	20 19	20 25	20 39	20 46	20 56		21 09	21 38	21 46	21 52	21 57	22 01		22 11	22 36	22 45	22 45

	VT ◇1 ☕	VT ◇1 ☕	SN 1	LM ◇1	VT ◇1 ☕	SN 1	LM ◇1	LM ◇1
Wolverhampton 7 d	20 45				21 07			
Sandwell & Dudley d	20 56				21 17			
Birmingham New Street 12 d	21 10				21 30			
Birmingham International ✈ d	21 20				21 40			
Coventry d	21 31				21 51			
Nuneaton d								
Rugby d	21 43				22 03			
Northampton d				22 05			22 55	23 30
Wolverton d				22 16			23 07	23 42
Milton Keynes Central 10 a	22 04			22 23	22s37		23 10	23 45
d	22 05	22 13		22 24	22s38		23 11	23 46
Bletchley d				22 29			23 16	23 51
Leighton Buzzard d				22 34			23 22	23 57
Cheddington d				22 39			23 27	
Tring d				22 45			23 36	
Berkhamsted d				22 51			23 41	
Hemel Hempstead d				22 54			23 45	
Apsley d				22 57			23 48	
Kings Langley d				23 02			23 52	
Watford Junction a	22s34	22s42		23 06	23s11		23 56	00 18
d	22s35	22s43	22 48	23 07	23s12	23 25	23 57	00 18
Bushey d								
Harrow & Wealdstone ⊖ d			22 55	23 13		23 31	00 03	
Wembley Central ⊖ d								
Shepherd's Bush a			23 13			23 48		
Kensington (Olympia) ⊖ a			23 15			23 51		
West Brompton ⊖ a			23 18			23 54		
Imperial Wharf a			23 21			23 57		
Clapham Junction 10 a								
East Croydon a								
London Euston 15 ⊖ a	22 55	23 04		23 27	23 33		00 17	00 42

b arr. 1838

Table 66

Sundays

West Midlands, Northampton, Milton Keynes and Watford Junction - London

Station		LM ◇1 A	LM ◇1 A	LM 1	LM 1	LM 1	LM ◇1	LM (bus)	SN 1	LM ◇1	LM ◇1	VT ◇1	SN 1	LM ◇1	VT ◇1	VT ◇1	VT ◇1 B	VT ◇1 C	LM ◇1 B	LM ◇1 C	VT ◇1 B	VT ◇1 C	VT ◇1
Wolverhampton 7	d											08 05									09 05	09 05	
Sandwell & Dudley	d											08 15									09 15	09 15	
Birmingham New Street 12	d											08b30									09c30	09c30	
Birmingham International	d											08 40									09 40	09 40	
Coventry	d											08 51									09 51	09 51	
Nuneaton	d																						09 55
Rugby	d											09 04									10 04	10 04	
Northampton	d	22p55	23p30				07 53	06 20		08 23	08 53			09 30					10 07	10 11			
Wolverton	d	23p07	23p42				08 07	08 22		08 37	09 07			09 44					10 20	10 24			
Milton Keynes Central 10	a	23p10	23p45				08 10	08 30		08 40	09 10	09 37		09 47					10 24	10 28	10 37	10 37	
	d	23p11	23p46	06 42	07 11	07 41	08 11			08 41	09 11	09 39		09 48	10 18				10 24	10 28	10 39	10 39	
Bletchley	d	23p16	23p51	06 47	07 16	07 46	08 16			08 46	09 16			09 53					10 29	10 33			
Leighton Buzzard	d	23p22	23p57	06 53	07 22	07 52	08 22			08 52	09 22			09 59					10 36	10 40			
Cheddington	d	23p27			07 27		08 27				09 27								10 45	10 45			
Tring	d	23p36			07 36		08 36				09 36								10 50	10 50			
Berkhamsted	d	23p41		07 08	07 41	08 07	08 41			09 07	09 41			10 14					10 54	10 54			
Hemel Hempstead	d	23p45		07 13	07 45	08 12	08 45			09 12	09 45			10 19					10 59	10 59			
Apsley	d	23p48		07 16		08 15				09 15				10 22									
Kings Langley	d	23p52		07 19		08 18				09 18				10 25									
Watford Junction	a	23p56	00 18	07 24	07 52	08 23	08 52			09 23	09 52	10s07		10 30					11 06	11 07	11s11	11s11	11s16
	d	23p57	00 18	07 24	07 53	08 23	08 53		09 17	09 23	09 53	10s08	10 17	10 30		10s35	10s40	10s52	11 06	11 07	11s12	11s12	11s17
Bushey	d																						
Harrow & Wealdstone	d	00 03		07 30	07 59	08 29	08 59		09 23	09 29	09 59		10 23	10 36					11 12	11 14			
Wembley Central	d																						
Shepherd's Bush	a								09 45				10 45										
Kensington (Olympia)	a								09 47				10 47										
West Brompton	a								09 50				10 50										
Imperial Wharf	a								09 53				10 53										
Clapham Junction 10	a																						
East Croydon	a																						
London Euston 15	a	00 17	00 42	07 44	08 13	08 43	09 13			09 43	10 13	10 28		10 50	11 06	10 56	11 00	11 12	11 26	11 30	11 32	11 34	11 39

Station		SN 1	LM ◇1	VT ◇1	VT ◇1 B	VT ◇1 C	LM ◇1	VT ◇1	LM ◇1	VT ◇1	VT ◇1	SN 1	LM 1	VT ◇1	LM 1	VT ◇1	VT ◇1 D	VT ◇1 E	VT ◇1 C	VT ◇1	LM ◇1	VT ◇1	VT ◇1 B
Wolverhampton 7	d							10 05												11 05		11 45	
Sandwell & Dudley	d							10 15												11 15		11 57	
Birmingham New Street 12	d							10e30												11 30		12 10	
Birmingham International	d							10 40												11 40		12 20	
Coventry	d							10 51												11 51		12 31	
Nuneaton	d									10 56						12 05							
Rugby	d			10 33				11 04			11 33									12 07			
Northampton	d		10 37				11 07		11 25												12 25		
Wolverton	d		10 51				11 21		11 37												12 37		
Milton Keynes Central 10	a		10 54	11 06			11 24	11 37	11 41	11 49	12 05									12 27	12 40		
	d		10 55	11 08	11 14	11 18	11 25	11 39	11 42	11 51	12 06				12 11		12 20	12 20	12 25	12 28	12 41		12 52
Bletchley	d		11 00				11 30		11 47				11 53		12 16						12 46		
Leighton Buzzard	d		11 06				11 36		11 54				11 59		12 22						12 52		
Cheddington	d						11 41						12 04		12 30								
Tring	d						11 50						12 14		12 35								
Berkhamsted	d		11 21				11 55		12 06				12 18		12 40						13 05		
Hemel Hempstead	d		11 26				11 59		12 11				12 23		12 44						13 10		
Apsley	d		11 29										12 26										
Kings Langley	d		11 32										12 29										
Watford Junction	a		11 37	11s42			12 06	12s07	12 18				12 34		12 51						13 17	13s18	
	d	11 17	11 37	11s43			12 07	12s08	12 18			12 22	12 34	12s35	12 52	12s55					13 17	13s19	
Bushey	d												12 37										
Harrow & Wealdstone	d	11 23	11 43				12 13		12 24			12 29	12 42		12 58						13 23		
Wembley Central	d																						
Shepherd's Bush	a	11 45										12 45											
Kensington (Olympia)	a	11 47										12 47											
West Brompton	a	11 50										12 50											
Imperial Wharf	a	11 53										12 53											
Clapham Junction 10	a																						
East Croydon	a																						
London Euston 15	a		11 57	12 04	12 07	12 09	12 27	12 27	12 37	12 37	12 44		12 56	12 56	13 11	13 15	12 59	13 00	13 04	13 06	13 37	13 39	13 31

A not 23 May
B from 18 July
C until 11 July
D from 12 September
E from 18 July until 5 September
b arr. 0824
c arr. 0924
e arr. 1024

Table 66

Sundays

West Midlands, Northampton, Milton Keynes and Watford Junction - London

Station		VT ◇1 A	VT ◇1	SN 1	LM ◇1	LM 1	LM 1	VT ◇1	VT ◇1	LM ◇1	VT ◇1 B	VT ◇1 A	VT ◇1	SN 1	LM ◇1	LM 1	LM 1	VT ◇1	VT ◇1	LM ◇1	VT ◇1	VT ◇1
Wolverhampton 7	d								12 45										13 45			
Sandwell & Dudley	d								12 55										13 56			
Birmingham New Street 12	d							12 30	13 10									13 30	14 10			
Birmingham International	d							12 39	13 20									13 39	14 20			
Coventry	d							12 51	13 31									13 51	14 31			
Nuneaton	d		12 31												12 58							14 32
Rugby	d				12 26										13 17							
Northampton	d				12 50					13 25					13b50					14 25		
Wolverton	d									13 37										14 37		
Milton Keynes Central 10	a		13 03		13 04			13 18		13 40					14 04			14 18		14 40		15 04
	d	12 53	13 04		13 05		13 11	13 19		13 41	13 52	14 02	14 05		14 05		14 11	14 20		14 41	14 51	15 05
Bletchley	d						13 16			13 46							14 16			14 46		
Leighton Buzzard	d				13 18		13 22			13 52					14 15		14 22			14 52		
Cheddington	d						13 30										14 30					
Tring	d					13 15	13 35									14 15	14 35					
Berkhamsted	d					13 19	13 40			14 05						14 19	14 40			15 05		
Hemel Hempstead	d					13 24	13 44			14 10						14 24	14 44			15 10		
Apsley	d					13 27										14 27						
Kings Langley	d					13 30										14 30						
Watford Junction	a				13 33	13 35	13 51		14s16	14 17					14 33	14 35	14 51		15s16	15 17		
	d			13 22	13 33	13 35	13 52		14s17	14 17				14 22	14 34	14 35	14 52		15s17	15 17		
Bushey	d					13 38										14 38						
Harrow & Wealdstone	d			13 28		13 43	13 58			14 23				14 28		14 43	14 58			15 23		
Wembley Central	d																					
Shepherd's Bush	a			13 45										14 45								
Kensington (Olympia)	a			13 47										14 47								
West Brompton	a			13 50										14 50								
Imperial Wharf	a			13 53										14 53								
Clapham Junction 10	a																					
East Croydon	a																					
London Euston 15	a	13 32	13 44		13 53	13 57	14 11	13 59	14 36	14 37	14 30	14 41	14 45		14 53	14 57	15 11	14 58	15 36	15 37	15 30	15 45

Station		SN 1	LM ◇1	LM 1	LM 1	VT ◇1	VT ◇1	LM ◇1	VT ◇1	VT ◇1	SN 1	LM ◇1	LM 1	LM 1	VT ◇1	VT ◇1	LM ◇1	VT ◇1	VT ◇1	SN 1	LM ◇1	LM 1	LM 1
Wolverhampton 7	d						14 45									15 45							
Sandwell & Dudley	d						14 56									15 56							
Birmingham New Street 12	d					14 30	15 10								15 30	16 10							
Birmingham International	d					14 39	15 20								15 39	16 20							
Coventry	d					14 51	15 31								15 51	16 31							
Nuneaton	d											14 58											
Rugby	d		14 26									15 17									16 25		
Northampton	d		14 50					15 25				15c50					16 25				16 50		
Wolverton	d							15 37									16 37						
Milton Keynes Central 10	a		15 04			15 18		15 40				16 04			16 18		16 40				17 04		
	d		15 05		15 11	15 19		15 41	15 51	16 05		16 05		16 11	16 19		16 41	16 51	17 04		17 05		17 11
Bletchley	d				15 16			15 46						16 16			16 46						17 16
Leighton Buzzard	d		15 17		15 22			15 52				16 17		16 22			16 52				17 17		17 22
Cheddington	d				15 30									16 30									17 30
Tring	d			15 15	15 35								16 15	16 35								17 15	17 35
Berkhamsted	d			15 19	15 40			16 05					16 19	16 40			17 05					17 19	17 40
Hemel Hempstead	d			15 24	15 44			16 10					16 24	16 44			17 10					17 24	17 44
Apsley	d			15 27									16 27									17 27	
Kings Langley	d			15 30									16 30									17 30	
Watford Junction	a		15 33	15 35	15 51		16s16	16 17				16 33	16 35	16 51		17s16	17 17				17 33	17 35	17 51
	d	15 22	15 33	15 35	15 52		16s17	16 17			16 22	16 33	16 35	16 52		17s17	17 17			17 22	17 33	17 35	17 52
Bushey	d			15 38									16 38									17 38	
Harrow & Wealdstone	d	15 28		15 43	15 58			16 23			16 28		16 43	16 58			17 23			17 28		17 43	17 58
Wembley Central	d																						
Shepherd's Bush	a	15 45									16 45									17 45			
Kensington (Olympia)	a	15 47									16 47									17 47			
West Brompton	a	15 50									16 50									17 50			
Imperial Wharf	a	15 53									16 53									17 53			
Clapham Junction 10	a																						
East Croydon	a																						
London Euston 15	a		15 53	15 57	16 11	15 59	16 36	16 37	16 30	16 44		16 53	16 57	17 11	16 59	17 36	17 37	17 30	17 44		17 53	17 57	18 11

A until 11 July
B from 18 July
b arr. 1339
c arr. 1539

Table 66

Sundays

West Midlands, Northampton, Milton Keynes and Watford Junction - London

		VT	VT	LM		VT	VT	SN	LM	LM	LM	VT	VT	LM		VT	VT	SN	LM	LM	LM	VT	VT	LM
		◇1	◇1	◇1		◇1	◇1	1	◇1	1	1	◇1	◇1	◇1		◇1	◇1	1	◇1	1	1	◇1	◇1	◇1
		🍴	🍴			🍴	🍴					🍴	🍴			🍴	🍴					🍴	🍴	
Wolverhampton 7	d		16 45										17 45										18 45	
Sandwell & Dudley	d		16 56										17 56										18 56	
Birmingham New Street 12	d	16 30	17 10									17 30	18 10									18 30	19 10	
Birmingham International	d	16 39	17 20									17 40	18 20									18 39	19 20	
Coventry	d	16 51	17 31									17 51	18 31									18 51	19 31	
Nuneaton	d								16 58															
Rugby	d								17 18										18 24					
Northampton	d			17 25					17b50					18 25					18 50					19 25
Wolverton	d			17 37										18 37										19 37
Milton Keynes Central 10	a	17 18		17 40					18 04			18 18		18 40					19 04			19 18		19 40
	d	17 19		17 41		17 51	18 03		18 05		18 11	18 19		18 41		18 51	19 04		19 05		19 11	19 19		19 41
Bletchley	d			17 46							18 16			18 46							19 16			19 46
Leighton Buzzard	d			17 52					18 17		18 22			18 52					19 17		19 22			19 52
Cheddington	d										18 30										19 30			
Tring	d									18 15	18 35									19 15	19 35			
Berkhamsted	d			18 05						18 19	18 40			19 05						19 19	19 40			20 05
Hemel Hempstead	d			18 10						18 24	18 44			19 10						19 24	19 44			20 10
Apsley	d									18 27										19 27				
Kings Langley	d									18 30										19 30				
Watford Junction	a		18s16	18 17					18 35	18 35	18 51		19s16	19 17					19 33	19 35	19 51		20s16	20 17
	d		18s17	18 17				18 22	18 35	18 35	18 52		19s17	19 17				19 22	19 33	19 35	19 52		20s17	20 17
Bushey	d									18 38										19 38				
Harrow & Wealdstone ⊖	d			18 23				18 28		18 43	18 58			19 23				19 28		19 43	19 58			20 23
Wembley Central ⊖	d																							
Shepherd's Bush	a							18 45										19 45						
Kensington (Olympia) ⊖	a							18 47										19 47						
West Brompton ⊖	a							18 50										19 50						
Imperial Wharf	a							18 53										19 53						
Clapham Junction 10	a																							
East Croydon	a																							
London Euston 15 ⊖	a	17 59	18 36	18 37		18 30	18 42		18 53	18 57	19 11	18 59	19 36	19 37		19 30	19 44		19 53	19 57	20 11	19 59	20 36	20 37

		VT	VT	SN	LM	LM	LM	VT	SN	LM		VT	VT	LM	LM	VT	VT	SN	LM	VT		VT	LM	VT	SN
		◇1	◇1	1	◇1	1	1	◇1	1	◇1		◇1	◇1	◇1	1	◇1	◇1	1	◇1	◇1		◇1	◇1	◇1	1
		🍴	🍴					🍴				🍴	🍴			🍴	🍴			🍴		🍴		🍴	
Wolverhampton 7	d											19 45												21 05	
Sandwell & Dudley	d											19 56												21 17	
Birmingham New Street 12	d							19 30				20 10				20 30								21 30	
Birmingham International	d							19 39				20 20				20 40								21 40	
Coventry	d							19 51				20 31				20 51								21 51	
Nuneaton	d				18 58																		20 58		
Rugby	d				19 18									20 20		21 05							21 17	22 04	
Northampton	d				19c50					20 25				20 45					21 25				21e53		
Wolverton	d				20 02					20 37				21 02					21 39				22 07		
Milton Keynes Central 10	a				20 06			20 18		20 40			20 47	21 05		21 26			21 44				22 10	22 37	
	d	19 51	20 04		20 06		20 11	20 19		20 41			20 49	21 05	21 16	21 28	21 37		21 44	21 57		22 04	22 11	22 39	
Bletchley	d						20 16			20 46					21 21				21 49				22 16		
Leighton Buzzard	d				20 16		20 22			20 52				21 17	21 27				21 56				22 22		
Cheddington	d						20 27								21 32								22 27		
Tring	d					20 15	20 36								21 41								22 36		
Berkhamsted	d					20 19	20 41			21 10					21 46				22 11				22 41		
Hemel Hempstead	d					20 24	20 45			21 14					21 50				22 15				22 45		
Apsley	d					20 27				21 17									22 18						
Kings Langley	d					20 30				21 21									22 22						
Watford Junction	a				20 33	20 35	20 52			21 25		21s30		21 36	21 58	22s03			22 26	22s31			22 52	23s08	
	d			20 22	20 33	20 35	20 53		21 17	21 26		21s31		21 36	21 59	22s04		22 17	22 27	22s32			22 53	23s09	23 17
Bushey	d					20 38																			
Harrow & Wealdstone ⊖	d			20 28		20 43	20 59		21 23	21 32					22 05			22 23	22 33				22 59		23 23
Wembley Central ⊖	d																								
Shepherd's Bush	a			20 45					21 45									22 45							23 45
Kensington (Olympia) ⊖	a			20 47					21 47									22 47							23 47
West Brompton ⊖	a			20 50					21 50									22 50							23 50
Imperial Wharf	a			20 53					21 53									22 53							23 53
Clapham Junction 10	a																								
East Croydon	a																								00 22
London Euston 15 ⊖	a	20 30	20 44		20 53	20 58	21 15	20 59		21 46		21 54	21 32	21 57	22 18	22 24	22 29		22 47	22 53		22 56	23 13	23 28	

b arr. 1739 c arr. 1939 e arr. 2139

Table 66

Sundays

West Midlands, Northampton, Milton Keynes and Watford Junction - London

		LM	VT	VT	LM	VT		VT
		◇1	◇1	◇1	◇1	◇1		◇1
			🍴	🍴		🍴		🍴
Wolverhampton 7	d					22 05		22 37
Sandwell & Dudley	d					22 15		22 47
Birmingham New Street 12	d					22b30		23 00
Birmingham International	d					22 40		23 10
Coventry	d					22 51		23 21
Nuneaton	d			22 16				
Rugby	d			22 30		23 04		23 35
Northampton	d	22 25			22 55			23s54
Wolverton	d	22 38			23 11			
Milton Keynes Central 10	a	22 41		23 04	23 14	23 38		00s12
	d	22 42	22 52	23 06	23 15	23 39		00s14
Bletchley	d	22 47			23 20			
Leighton Buzzard	d	22 53			23 26			
Cheddington	d				23 31			
Tring	d				23 40			
Berkhamsted	d	23 08			23 45			
Hemel Hempstead	d	23 13			23 49			
Apsley	d	23 16						
Kings Langley	d	23 19						
Watford Junction	a	23 24	23s31	23s36	23 56	00s13		00s42
	d	23 24	23s32	23s37	23 57	00s14		00s43
Bushey	d							
Harrow & Wealdstone ⊖	d	23 30			00 03			
Wembley Central ⊖	d							
Shepherd's Bush	a							
Kensington (Olympia) ⊖	a							
West Brompton ⊖	a							
Imperial Wharf	a							
Clapham Junction 10	a							
East Croydon	a							
London Euston 15 ⊖	a	23 46	23 53	23 57	00 17	00 35		01 06

b arr. 2224

Network Diagram for Tables 67, 68, 69, 70

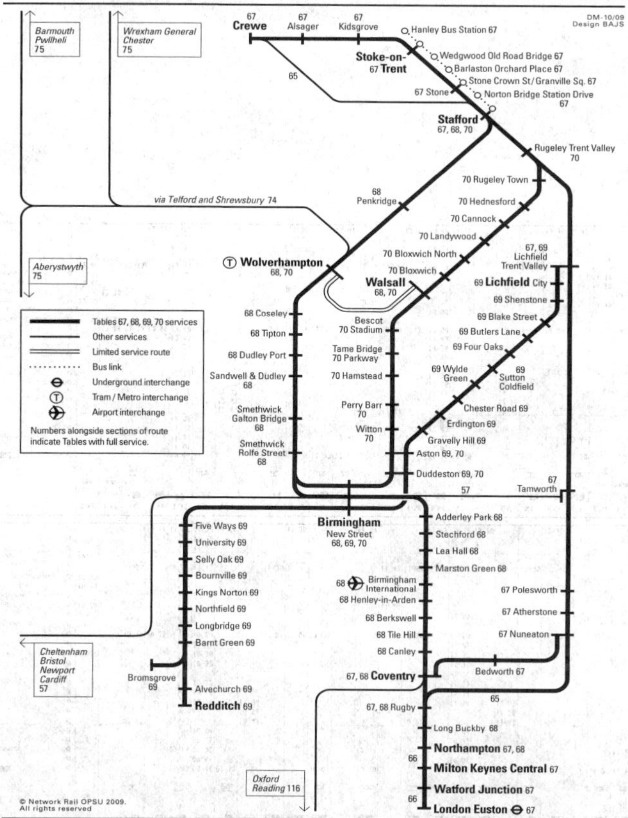

London - Stoke-on-Trent and Crewe Coventry - Nuneaton

		VT	LM	VT	VT	XC	LM	XC	LM	LM		VT	LM	VT	LM	XC	LM	VT	LM	LM		LM	VT	LM	LM
		MX	MX	MO																					
		◇1	◇1	◇1	◇1	◇1	◇1	◇1	◇1			◇1	◇1	◇1		◇1	◇1	◇1	◇1			◇1	◇1		
		⊟		⊟	⊠	Ŧ		⊟				⊠		⊠	bus	Ŧ		⊠					⊠	bus	bus
London Euston 15 ⊖	d	22p00		21p50								05 27		05 39				06 36					07 10		
Watford Junction	d											05u45		06u02				06u51							
Milton Keynes Central	d	22p31		22p38					05 21			06 10		06 22									07 41		
Northampton	d								05 42										06 41						
Rugby	d	22p54		23p18					06 05					06 45					07 00						
Coventry	d									06 12										07 06					
Bedworth	d									06 23										07 17					
Nuneaton	a	23p04		23p28					06 16	06 30		06 38							07 12	07 27					
	d	23p05		23p29					06 17			06 39							07 12						
Atherstone	d								06 23										07 18						
Polesworth	d																		07 23						
Tamworth	d	23b17							06 31										07 29						
Lichfield Trent Valley	d	23b24							06 37										07 35						
Rugeley Trent Valley	d								06 44										07 42						
Stafford	d	23b39	23p53	23b54	06 02	06 30	06 36	06 54	06 58			07 03	07 05			07 30	07 36		07 54			08 09			08 15
Norton Bridge Station Drv	d																								08 40
Stone	d								07 15										08 05						
Stone Crown Street	d														07 05									08 10	
Stone Granville Square	a																								08 59
Barlaston Orchard Place	d														07 15									08 20	
Wedgwood Old Road Bridge	d														07 17									08 22	
Stoke-on-Trent	d					06a51		07a13	07 26						07 38				08 13					08 44	
Hanley Bus Station	a														07 45									08 51	
Kidsgrove	d								07 34										08 21						
Alsager	d								07 39										08 26						
Crewe	a	00s03	00 16	00s12	06 21		06 56		07 49			07 22	07 29	07 30		07 50	07 56	08 10	08 38			08 30	08 47		

		VT	XC	LM	LM	VT		LM	XC	LM	VT	VT	LM	XC	LM	LM		VT	LM	XC	LM	LM	VT	VT
		◇1	◇1	◇1	1	◇1			◇1	◇1	◇1	◇1		◇1	◇1	◇1		◇1		◇1		◇1	◇1	◇1
		⊠	Ŧ			⊠			Ŧ		⊠	⊠	bus	Ŧ				⊠		Ŧ	bus		⊠	⊠
London Euston 15 ⊖	d	07 07			06 24	07 35					08 07	08 10				07 47		08 40					09 07	09 10
Watford Junction	d				06 41											08 02								
Milton Keynes Central	d				07 23	08 06						08 41				08c31								09u40
Northampton	d				07 45											08 45								
Rugby	d				08 03											09 03								
Coventry	d		07 27					08 04						08 27					09 06					
Bedworth	d							08 15											09 17					
Nuneaton	a				08 17			08 23								09 16			09 25					
	d				08 17											09 16								
Atherstone	d				08 23											09 22								
Polesworth	d																							
Tamworth	d				08 31											09 30								
Lichfield Trent Valley	d				08 37											09 36								
Rugeley Trent Valley	d				08 43											09 42								
Stafford	d	08a23	08 30	08 36	08 54				09 01	09 09	09a23			09 30	09 35	09 54				10 01	10 05	10 09	10a23	
Norton Bridge Station Drv	d																				10 31			
Stone	d				09 05											10 05								
Stone Crown Street	d												09 20											
Stone Granville Square	a																				10 52			
Barlaston Orchard Place	d												09 30											
Wedgwood Old Road Bridge	d												09 32											
Stoke-on-Trent	d		08a55		09 13				09a20				09 48	09a55		10 13				10a20				
Hanley Bus Station	a												09 55											
Kidsgrove	d				09 21											10 21								
Alsager	d				09 26											10 26								
Crewe	a			08 56	09 38	09 10				09 30		09 47			09 56	10 38		10 10				10 30		10 47

b previous night, stops to set down only

c arr. 0825

Table 67

London - Stoke-on-Trent and Crewe Coventry - Nuneaton

Mondays to Fridays

		LM		XC	LM	VT	LM	VT	LM	XC	LM	VT		VT	LM	XC	LM	LM	VT	LM	XC	LM		VT	VT
				◇1	◇1	◇1	◇1	◇1		◇1	◇1	◇1		◇1		◇1	◇1	◇1	◇1		◇1	◇1		◇1	◇1
						A																			
		🚌		🛒		☒		☒		🛒		☕		☕	🚌	🛒			☕		🛒			☕	☕
London Euston ⊖	d					08 43	08 46	09 40				10 07		10 10				09 46	10 40					11 07	11 10
Watford Junction	d						09 01											10 01							
Milton Keynes Central	d					09 13	09 25							10 41				10 25							11 41
Northampton	d						09 45											10 45							
Rugby	d						10 04											11 04							
Coventry	d			09 27		09 43			10 45							10 27				11 45					
Bedworth	d								10 56											11 56					
Nuneaton	a						10 16		11 04									11 16		12 03					
	d						10 16											11 16							
Atherstone	d						10 22											11 22							
Polesworth	d																								
Tamworth	d						10 30											11 31							
Lichfield Trent Valley	d						10 36											11 37							
Rugeley Trent Valley	d						10 42											11 43							
Stafford	d			10 30	10 35		10 54			11 01	11 09	11a23				11 30	11 35	11 54			12 01	12 09		12a23	
Norton Bridge Station Drv	d																								
Stone	d						11 05											12 05							
Stone Crown Street	d	10 20													11 20										
Stone Granville Square	a																								
Barlaston Orchard Place	d	10 30													11 30										
Wedgwood Old Road Bridge	d	10 32													11 32										
Stoke-on-Trent	d	10 48		10a55			11 13			11a20					11 48	11a55		12 13			12a20				
Hanley Bus Station	a	10 55													11 55										
Kidsgrove	d						11 21											12 21							
Alsager	d						11 26											12 26							
Crewe	a				10 56	11 07	11 38	11 10			11 30			11 47			11 56	12 38	12 10			12 30			12 47

		LM	LM	XC	LM	LM	VT	LM		XC	LM	VT	VT	LM	XC	LM	LM	VT		LM	XC	LM	VT	LM	LM
				◇1	◇1	1	◇1			◇1	◇1	◇1	◇1		◇1	◇1	◇1	◇1			◇1	◇1	◇1		
		🚌	🚌	🛒			☕			🛒		☕	☕	🚌	🛒			☕			🛒		☕	🚌	🚌
London Euston ⊖	d					10 46	11 40					12 07	12 10				11 46	12 40					13 10		
Watford Junction	d					11 01											12 01								
Milton Keynes Central	d					11 25							12 41				12 25						13 41		
Northampton	d					11 45											12 45								
Rugby	d					12 03											13 04								
Coventry	d			11 27				12 45							12 27					13 45					
Bedworth	d							12 56												13 56					
Nuneaton	a					12 16		13 03									13 16			14 03					
	d					12 16											13 16								
Atherstone	d					12 22											13 22								
Polesworth	d																								
Tamworth	d					12 31											13 30								
Lichfield Trent Valley	d					12 37											13 36								
Rugeley Trent Valley	d					12 43											13 42								
Stafford	d		12 25	12 30	12 35	12 54				13 01	13 09	13a23			13 30	13 35	13 54				14 01	14 09			14 20
Norton Bridge Station Drv	d		12 51																						14 46
Stone	d					13 05											14 05								
Stone Crown Street	d	12 20												13 20										14 20	
Stone Granville Square	a		13 30																						14 59
Barlaston Orchard Place	d	12 30												13 30										14 30	
Wedgwood Old Road Bridge	d	12 32												13 32										14 32	
Stoke-on-Trent	d	12 48		12a55		13 13				13a20				13 48	13a55		14 13				14a20			14 48	
Hanley Bus Station	a	12 55												13 55										14 55	
Kidsgrove	d					13 21											14 21								
Alsager	d					13 26											14 26								
Crewe	a				12 56	13 38	13 10				13 30		13 47			13 56	14 38	14 10				14 30	14 47		

A from 19 July until 3 September

Table 67

London - Stoke-on-Trent and Crewe Coventry - Nuneaton

Mondays to Fridays

		VT	XC	LM		LM	VT	VT FO	LM	XC	LM	VT	VT	LM		XC	LM	VT	LM	VT	LM	LM	VT	VT	
		◇1	◇1	◇1		◇1	◇1	◇		◇1	◇1	◇1	◇1			◇1	◇1	◇1	1	◇1		◇1	◇1	◇1	
																		A							
		☕	🛒				☕	☕		🛒		☕	☕	🚌		🛒		☕		☕			☕	☕	
London Euston ⊖	d	13 07				12 46	13 40	13 33				14 07	14 10					13 43	13 46	14 40			15 07	15 10	
Watford Junction	d					13 01													14 01						
Milton Keynes Central	d					13 25							14 41					14 13	14 25					15 41	
Northampton	d					13 45													14 45						
Rugby	d					14 03													15 04						
Coventry	d		13 27						14 45							14 27		14 43			15 45				
Bedworth	d								14 56												15 56				
Nuneaton	a					14 16			15 03										15 16		16 03				
	d					14 16													15 16						
Atherstone	d					14 22													15 22						
Polesworth	d																								
Tamworth	d					14 30													15 30						
Lichfield Trent Valley	d					14 36													15 36						
Rugeley Trent Valley	d					14 43													15 43						
Stafford	d	14a23	14 30	14 35		14 54				15 01	15 09	15a23				15 30	15 35		15 54			16 09	16a23		
Norton Bridge Station Drv	d																								
Stone	d					15 05													16 05						
Stone Crown Street	d													15 20											
Stone Granville Square	a																								
Barlaston Orchard Place	d													15 30											
Wedgwood Old Road Bridge	d													15 32											
Stoke-on-Trent	d		14a55			15 13				15a20				15 48		15a55			16 13						
Hanley Bus Station	a													15 55											
Kidsgrove	d					15 21													16 21						
Alsager	d					15 26													16 26						
Crewe	a			14 56		15 39	15 10	15 16			15 30		15 47				15 56	16 07	16 38	16 11		16 30		16 47	

		LM	XC	LM	VT	LM	LM	LM	XC	LM		VT	VT	LM	XC	LM	VT	LM	VT	XC		LM	LM	LM	VT
			◇1	◇1	◇1		◇1		◇1	◇1		◇1	◇1		◇1	◇1	◇1		◇1	◇1		◇1		◇1	◇1
		🚌	🛒		☕	🚌			🛒			☕	☕	🚌	🛒		☕	🚌	☕	🛒					☒
London Euston ⊖	d				15 40		14 46					16 07	16 10				16 40		16 33			15 46			17 07
Watford Junction	d						15 01															16 01			
Milton Keynes Central	d						15 23						16u41									16 25			
Northampton	d						15 45															16 45			
Rugby	d						16 03												17 22			17 03			
Coventry	d		15 27					16 45							16 27								17 45		
Bedworth	d							16 56															17 56		
Nuneaton	a						16 16	17 03														17 16	18 03		
	d						16 16															17 16			
Atherstone	d						16 22															17 22			
Polesworth	d																								
Tamworth	d						16 30															17 30			
Lichfield Trent Valley	d						16 36															17 36			
Rugeley Trent Valley	d						16 43															17 43			
Stafford	d		16 30	16 35		16 35	16 54		17 01	17 09		17a23			17 30	17 36		17 40	17 56	18 02		18b20		18 10	18 25
Norton Bridge Station Drv	d					17a01												18a08							
Stone	d						17 05															18 31			
Stone Crown Street	d	16 20												17 20											
Stone Granville Square	a																								
Barlaston Orchard Place	d	16 30												17 30											
Wedgwood Old Road Bridge	d	16 32												17 32											
Stoke-on-Trent	d	16 48	16a55				17 13		17a20					17 48	17a55					18a21		18 41			
Hanley Bus Station	a	16 55												17 55											
Kidsgrove	d						17 21															18 49			
Alsager	d						17 26															18 54			
Crewe	a			16 56	17 10		17 38			17 30			17 47			17 56	18 10		18 15			19 05		18 31	18 43

A from 19 July until 3 September

b arr. 1801

Table 67

Mondays to Fridays

London - Stoke-on-Trent and Crewe Coventry - Nuneaton

		VT	LM	XC	LM	VT	VT	LM	LM	LM	VT	VT	XC	LM	VT	VT	XC	LM	VT	VT	XC	VT FO	VT
		◇1	🚌	◇1	◇1	◇1	◇1		🚌	◇1	◇1	◇1	◇1	◇1	◇1	◇1	◇1	◇1	1	1	◇1		◇1
		⊠		🛒		⊠	⊠				⊠	⊠	🛒		⊠	⊠	🛒		☕	☕	🛒	☕	⊠
London Euston 15 ⊖	d	17 10				17 40	17 33				18 07	18 10			18 40	18 33			19 07	19 10		18 46	18 43
Watford Junction	d																						
Milton Keynes Central	d	17u41										18u41								19u40			19 13
Northampton	d																						
Rugby	d						18 23									19 23							
Coventry	d			17 27				18 45					18 27								19 27		19 42
Bedworth	d							18 56															
Nuneaton	a	18 11						19 03				19 12							20 02				
	d	18 12										19 13							20 03				
Atherstone	d																						
Polesworth	d																						
Tamworth	d																						
Lichfield Trent Valley	d																					20s04	
Rugeley Trent Valley	d																					20s12	
Stafford	d			18 30	18 35		18 56			19 09	19 24		19 29	19 36		19 56	20 01	20 09	20a27		20 30	20s36	20 52
Norton Bridge Station Drv	d																						
Stone	d																						
Stone Crown Street	d		18 20						18 45														
Stone Granville Square	a																						
Barlaston Orchard Place	d		18 30						18 53														
Wedgwood Old Road Bridge	d		18 32						18 55														
Stoke-on-Trent	d		18 48	18a55					19 06				19a55				20a20				20a55		
Hanley Bus Station	a		18 55						19 13														
Kidsgrove	d																						
Alsager	d																						
Crewe	a	18 53			19 00	19 10	19 15			19 30	19 42	19 53		20 01	20 10	20 15		20 30		20 48		21s01	21 15

		LM	LM	VT	LM	VT	VT	XC	VT	LM	LM	VT	LM	VT	XC	VT	XC	LM	VT	LM
			◇1	◇1	◇1	◇1	◇1	◇1	◇1			◇1	◇1	◇1	◇1	◇1	◇1	◇1	◇1	◇1
				☕		☕	☕		☕			☕		☕		☕			☕	
London Euston 15 ⊖	d		18 29	19 40		20 07	20 10		20 40					21 07		21 10			22 00	
Watford Junction	d		18 45													21u25				
Milton Keynes Central	d		19 23				20 41							21 38					22 31	
Northampton	d		19c45																	
Rugby	d		20 03													22 04			22 54	
Coventry	d	19 45						20 27		20 45	21 44				21 27					
Bedworth	d	19 56								20 56	21 55									
Nuneaton	a	20 03	20 18			21 02				21 03	22 02			22 06					23 04	
	d		20 18			21 03								22 07					23 05	
Atherstone	d		20 24																	
Polesworth	d																			
Tamworth	d		20 32	20 43																
Lichfield Trent Valley	d		20 38	20 50															23s17	
Rugeley Trent Valley	d		20 44																23s24	
Stafford	d			21 04	21 09	21a27		21 32				21 55	22 09		22 30	22 35	22 59	23 13	23s39	23 53
Norton Bridge Station Drv	d																			
Stone	d																			
Stone Crown Street	d																			
Stone Granville Square	a																			
Barlaston Orchard Place	d																			
Wedgwood Old Road Bridge	d																			
Stoke-on-Trent	d		21 05					21a55							22a55		23a21			
Hanley Bus Station	a																			
Kidsgrove	d		21 14																	
Alsager	d		21 18																	
Crewe	a		21 27	21 21	21 30		21 48		22 12			22 17	22 30	22 46		22 53		23 43	00s03	00 16

c arr. 1939

Table 67

Saturdays

London - Stoke-on-Trent and Crewe Coventry - Nuneaton

		VT	LM	VT	XC	LM	LM	LM	XC	LM	LM	XC	VT	LM	VT	LM	LM	XC	LM	LM	VT	LM	XC
		◇1	◇1	◇1	◇1	◇1	◇1		◇1	◇1	🚌	◇1	◇1	◇1	◇1	◇1		◇1	◇1	🚌	◇1	🚌	◇1
		☕		☕	🛒				🛒			🛒	☕		☕			🛒			☕		🛒
London Euston 15 ⊖	d	22p00											06 05		06 36						07 07		
Watford Junction	d												06u20		06u51								
Milton Keynes Central	d	22p31					05 21						06 41										
Northampton	d						05 42									06 38							
Rugby	d	22p54					06 05						07 03			06 56							
Coventry	d							06 16									07 16						07 27
Bedworth	d							06 27									07 27						
Nuneaton	a	23p04					06 16	06 34								07 09	07 35						
	d	23p05					06 17									07 10							
Atherstone	d						06 23									07 16							
Polesworth	d															07 21							
Tamworth	d	23b17					06 31									07 28							
Lichfield Trent Valley	d	23b24					06 37									07 34							
Rugeley Trent Valley	d						06 44									07 41							
Stafford	d	23b39	23p53	06 01	06 30	06 36	06 54		07 01	07 08		07 29	07 35	07 38		07 54		08 01	08 09	08 15	08 23		08 30
Norton Bridge Station Drv	d																			08 40			
Stone	d						07 05									08 05							
Stone Crown Street	d										07 20											08 20	
Stone Granville Square	a																			08 59			
Barlaston Orchard Place	d										07 28											08 28	
Wedgwood Old Road Bridge	d										07 30											08 30	
Stoke-on-Trent	d				06a51		07 13		07a19		07 41					08 13		08a20				08 41	08a55
Hanley Bus Station	a										07 47											08 47	
Kidsgrove	d						07 21									08 21							
Alsager	d						07 26									08 26							
Crewe	a	00s03	00 16	06 20		06 56	07 36			07 33		07 50	07 53	07 58	08 10	08 37			08 30		08 41		

		LM	LM	VT	LM	XC	LM	VT	VT	LM	XC	LM	LM	VT	LM	XC	LM	LM	VT	VT	LM
		◇1	◇1	◇1		◇1	◇1	◇1	◇1	🚌	◇1	◇1	◇1	◇1		◇1	🚌	◇1	◇1	◇1	🚌
				☕		☕		☕	☕		🛒			☕		☕			☕	☕	
London Euston 15 ⊖	d		06 24	07 35				08 07	08 10				07 46	08 40					08 50	09 07	
Watford Junction	d		06 41										08 01						09 05		
Milton Keynes Central	d		07 23	08 06					08 41				08 25						09 25		
Northampton	d		07c45										08 45								
Rugby	d		08 04										09 04								
Coventry	d				08 45						08 27				09 45						
Bedworth	d				08 56										09 56						
Nuneaton	a		08 16		09 03								09 16		10 03						
	d		08 17										09 16								
Atherstone	d		08 22										09 22								
Polesworth	d																				
Tamworth	d		08 31										09 31								
Lichfield Trent Valley	d		08 37										09 37								
Rugeley Trent Valley	d		08 43										09 43								
Stafford	d	08 36	08 54			09 01	09 09	09a23			09 30	09 35	09 54			10 01	10 05	10 09		10a23	
Norton Bridge Station Drv	d																10 31				
Stone	d		09 05										10 05								
Stone Crown Street	d									09 20											10 20
Stone Granville Square	a																10 52				
Barlaston Orchard Place	d									09 28											10 28
Wedgwood Old Road Bridge	d									09 30											10 30
Stoke-on-Trent	d		09 13			09a20				09 41	09a55		10 13			10a20					10 41
Hanley Bus Station	a									09 47											10 47
Kidsgrove	d		09 21										10 21								
Alsager	d		09 26										10 26								
Crewe	a	08 56	09 38	09 10			09 30		09 48			09 56	10 38	10 10				10 30	10 34		

b previous night, stops to set down only
c arr. 0740
e arr. 0748

Table 67

Saturdays

London - Stoke-on-Trent and Crewe Coventry - Nuneaton

		XC		LM	VT	LM	VT	LM	XC	LM	VT	VT		LM	XC	LM	LM	VT	LM	XC	LM	VT		VT	LM
					A																				
London Euston ⊖	d				08 43	08 46	09 40				10 07	10 10					09 46	10 40				11 07		11 10	
Watford Junction	d																10 01								
Milton Keynes Central	d				09 13	09 23						10 41					10 24							11 41	
Northampton	d					09b45											10 45								
Rugby	d					10 04											11 04								
Coventry	d	09 27			09 42			10 45							10 27				11 45						
Bedworth	d							10 56											11 56						
Nuneaton	a					10 16		11 04									11 16		12 03						
	d					10 16											11 16								
Atherstone	d					10 22											11 22								
Polesworth	d																								
Tamworth	d					10 31											11 31								
Lichfield Trent Valley	d					10 37											11 37								
Rugeley Trent Valley	d					10 43											11 43								
Stafford	d	10 30		10 35		10 54			11 01	11 09	11a23				11 30	11 35	11 54			12 01	12 09	12a23			
Norton Bridge Station Drv	d																								
Stone	d					11 05											12 05								
Stone Crown Street	d													11 20											12 20
Stone Granville Square	a																								
Barlaston Orchard Place	d													11 28											12 28
Wedgwood Old Road Bridge	d													11 30											12 30
Stoke-on-Trent	d	10a55				11 13			11a20					11 41	11a55		12 13			12a20					12 41
Hanley Bus Station	a													11 47											12 47
Kidsgrove	d					11 21											12 21								
Alsager	d					11 26											12 26								
Crewe	a			10 56	11 07	11 38	11 10			11 30		11 48				11 56	12 38	12 10			12 30			12 47	

		LM	XC	LM	LM	VT	LM	XC		LM	VT	VT	LM	XC	LM	LM		VT		LM	XC	LM	VT	LM	LM
London Euston ⊖	d				10 46	11 40					12 07	12 10				11 46		12 40					13 10		
Watford Junction	d				11 01											12 01									
Milton Keynes Central	d				11 25							12 41				12 25							13 41		
Northampton	d				11 45											12 45									
Rugby	d				12 04											13 04									
Coventry	d		11 27				12 45							12 27						13 45					
Bedworth	d						12 56													13 56					
Nuneaton	a				12 16		13 03									13 16				14 03					
	d				12 16											13 16									
Atherstone	d				12 22											13 22									
Polesworth	d																								
Tamworth	d				12 31											13 31									
Lichfield Trent Valley	d				12 37											13 37									
Rugeley Trent Valley	d				12 43											13 43									
Stafford	d	12 25	12 30	12 35	12 54			13 01		13 09	13a23			13 30	13 35	13 54					14 01	14 09			14 20
Norton Bridge Station Drv	d	12 51																							14 46
Stone	d				13 05											14 05									
Stone Crown Street	d												13 20											14 20	
Stone Granville Square	a	13 30																							14 59
Barlaston Orchard Place	d												13 28											14 28	
Wedgwood Old Road Bridge	d												13 30											14 30	
Stoke-on-Trent	d		12a55		13 13			13a20					13 41	13a55		14 13					14a20			14 41	
Hanley Bus Station	a												13 47											14 47	
Kidsgrove	d				13 21											14 21									
Alsager	d				13 26											14 26									
Crewe	a			12 56	13 38	13 10				13 30		13 47			13 56	14 38		14 10				14 30	14 48		

A from 17 July until 4 September

b arr. 0939

Table 67

Saturdays

London - Stoke-on-Trent and Crewe Coventry - Nuneaton

		VT	XC	LM		LM		VT	LM	XC	LM	VT	VT	LM		XC	LM	LM		VT	VT	LM	XC	LM	
																				B					
London Euston ⊖	d	13 07				12 46		13 40				14 07	14 10					13 46		13 43	14 40				
Watford Junction	d					13 01												14 01							
Milton Keynes Central	d					13 25							14 41					14 25		14 13					
Northampton	d					13 45												14 45							
Rugby	d					14 04												15 04							
Coventry	d		13 27						14 45							14 27				14 43		15 45			
Bedworth	d								14 56													15 56			
Nuneaton	a					14 16			15 03									15 16				16 03			
	d					14 16												15 16							
Atherstone	d					14 22												15 22							
Polesworth	d																								
Tamworth	d					14 31												15 31							
Lichfield Trent Valley	d					14 37												15 37							
Rugeley Trent Valley	d					14 43												15 43							
Stafford	d	14a23	14 30	14 35		14 54				15 01	15 09	15a23				15 30	15 35	15 54					16 01	16 09	
Norton Bridge Station Drv	d																								
Stone	d					15 05												16 05							
Stone Crown Street	d													15 20											
Stone Granville Square	a																								
Barlaston Orchard Place	d													15 28											
Wedgwood Old Road Bridge	d													15 30											
Stoke-on-Trent	d		14a55			15 13				15a20				15 41		15a55		16 13					16a20		
Hanley Bus Station	a													15 47											
Kidsgrove	d					15 21												16 21							
Alsager	d					15 26												16 26							
Crewe	a			14 56		15 38		15 10			15 30		15 47				15 56	16 38		16 08	16 11			16 30	

		VT	VT	LM	XC	LM		VT	LM	LM		LM	LM	XC	LM	VT	VT	LM	XC	LM			VT	LM	VT
London Euston ⊖	d	15 07	15 10					15 40		14 46			15 46			16 07	16 10						16 40		16 33
Watford Junction	d									15 01			16 01												
Milton Keynes Central	d		15 41							15 25			16 25				16 41								
Northampton	d									15 45			16 45												
Rugby	d									16 04			17 04												
Coventry	d				15 27							16 45							16 27						
Bedworth	d											16 56													
Nuneaton	a									16 16		17 03	17 16												
	d									16 16			17 16												
Atherstone	d									16 22			17 22												
Polesworth	d																								
Tamworth	d									16 31			17 31												17 38
Lichfield Trent Valley	d									16 37			17 37												17 45
Rugeley Trent Valley	d									16 43			17 43												
Stafford	d	16a23			16 30	16 35			16 35	16 54			18b20	17 01	17 09	17a23			17 30	17 36				17 40	17a59
Norton Bridge Station Drv	d								17a01															18a08	
Stone	d									17 05			18 31												
Stone Crown Street	d			16 20														17 20							
Stone Granville Square	a																								
Barlaston Orchard Place	d			16 28														17 28							
Wedgwood Old Road Bridge	d			16 30														17 30							
Stoke-on-Trent	d			16 41	16a55					17 13			18 41	17a20				17 41	17a55						
Hanley Bus Station	a			16 47														17 47							
Kidsgrove	d									17 21			18 50												
Alsager	d									17 26			18 54												
Crewe	a		16 47			16 56		17 10		17 38			19 05		17 30		17 47			17 56			18 10		

A from 23 October

B from 17 July until 4 September

b arr. 1804

Table 67

Saturdays

London - Stoke-on-Trent and Crewe Coventry - Nuneaton

		XC	LM	VT	VT	XC	LM	LM	VT	LM	LM	LM	XC	LM	VT	VT	XC	LM	VT	LM
		◇1	◇1	◇1	◇1	◇1		◇1	◇1		◇1		◇1	◇1	◇1	◇1	◇1	◇1	◇1	◇1
		✕		⊏	⊏	✕			⊏	🚌			⊏		⊏	⊏	✕		⊏	
London Euston 15 ⊖	d			17 07	17 10				17 40		16 46				18 07	18 10			18 40	
Watford Junction	d										17 01									
Milton Keynes Central	d				17 41						17 25					18 41				
Northampton	d										17 45									18 45
Rugby	d										18 04									19 03
Coventry	d					17 27	17 45					18 45					18 27			
Bedworth	d						17 56					18 56								
Nuneaton	a			18 02			18 03				18 16	19 03								19 16
	d			18 03							18 16									19 16
Atherstone	d										18 22									19 22
Polesworth	d																			
Tamworth	d										18 31									19 30
Lichfield Trent Valley	d										18 37									19 36
Rugeley Trent Valley	d										18 43									19 43
Stafford	d	18 00	18 09	18a27		18 30		18 35			18 54		19 01	19 09	19a23		19 30	19 36		19 53
Norton Bridge Station Drv	d																			
Stone	d										19 05									20 05
Stone Crown Street	d									18 45										
Stone Granville Square	a																			
Barlaston Orchard Place	d									18 53										
Wedgwood Old Road Bridge	d									18 55										
Stoke-on-Trent	d	18 20				18 55				19 06	19 13		19a20				19a55			20 13
Hanley Bus Station	a									19 12										
Kidsgrove	d										19 21									20 21
Alsager	d										19 26									20 25
Crewe	a		18 30		18 48			18 56	19 10		19 36			19 30		19 48		19 58	20 10	20 35

		VT	XC	VT	XC	LM	VT	VT	VT	LM	LM	XC	LM	XC	XC	XC	VT	XC	VT	VT	LM	LM
		◇1	◇1	◇1	◇1	◇1	◇1	◇1	◇1	◇1		◇1	◇1	◇1	◇1	◇1	◇1		◇1	◇1		◇1
														B	D	E	F	D		D		
		⊏	⊏	⊏	✕		⊏	⊏	⊏			⊏		✕	✕	✕	⊏	🚌	⊏	⊏		
London Euston 15 ⊖	d	18 33		19 07			19 30		19 40								20 20		20 11	20 20		
Watford Junction	d																					
Milton Keynes Central	d																21 05			21 05		
Northampton	d									19 45												
Rugby	d									20 03									21 18			
Coventry	d				19 27						20 15			20 27							21 45	
Bedworth	d										20 26										21 56	
Nuneaton	a			20 02						20 16	20 34						21 32			21 32	22 03	
	d			20 03						20 16							21 33			21 33		
Atherstone	d									20 22												
Polesworth	d																					
Tamworth	d	19 38								20 30												
Lichfield Trent Valley	d	19 46								20 36												
Rugeley Trent Valley	d									20 43												
Stafford	d	19a59	20 01	20 27	20 30	20a36		20 50		20 55		21 01	21 09	21 30	21 31	21 32		21 40	21 49	21a58		22 09
Norton Bridge Station Drv	d																					
Stone	d									21 08												
Stone Crown Street	d																					
Stone Granville Square	a																					
Barlaston Orchard Place	d																					
Wedgwood Old Road Bridge	d																					
Stoke-on-Trent	d		20a20		20a55					21 16		21a21		21a55		21a51	22a05	22a10				
Hanley Bus Station	a																					
Kidsgrove	d									21 24												
Alsager	d									21 28												
Crewe	a			20 45		20 57	21 01	21 09	21 18	21 38			21 30		21 58				22 13			22 34

A until 4 September
B from 11 September
D until 10 July
E from 17 July until 4 September
F from 17 July

Table 67

Saturdays

London - Stoke-on-Trent and Crewe Coventry - Nuneaton

		VT	VT	VT	XC	XC	VT	XC	XC	XC	LM
		◇1	◇1		◇1	◇1	◇1		◇1		◇1
		A	B	C	D	C		C	D	C	
		⊏	⊏	🚌	✕	✕	⊏	🚌	✕	🚌	
London Euston 15 ⊖	d	20 30	20 30				21 00				
Watford Junction	d	20u45	20u46								
Milton Keynes Central	d						21 45				
Northampton	d										
Rugby	d	21 36	21 36								
Coventry	d				21 27	21 27					
Bedworth	d										
Nuneaton	a										
	d										
Atherstone	d										
Polesworth	d										
Tamworth	d	21 53	21 54								
Lichfield Trent Valley	d	22 00	22 01								
Rugeley Trent Valley	d										
Stafford	d			22 10	22 30	22a30	22 34	22 40	23 03	23 10	23 13
Norton Bridge Station Drv	d										
Stone	d										
Stone Crown Street	d										
Stone Granville Square	a										
Barlaston Orchard Place	d										
Wedgwood Old Road Bridge	d										
Stoke-on-Trent	d			22a40	22a51			23a10	23a21	23a40	
Hanley Bus Station	a										
Kidsgrove	d										
Alsager	d										
Crewe	a	22 38	22 38				22 59				23 37

Sundays
until 11 July

		VT	XC	VT	XC	VT	VT	LM	VT	XC	VT	LM	VT	XC	LM	XC	VT	LM	LM	VT	VT	XC	XC
		◇1	◇1	◇1		◇1	◇1	◇1	◇1		◇1	◇1	◇1	◇1			◇1		◇1	◇1	◇1	◇1	
		⊏	✕	⊏	🚌	⊏	⊏		⊏	🚌	⊏		⊏	✕	🚌	🚌	⊏			⊏	⊏	✕	🚌
London Euston 15 ⊖	d			08 10		08 15	08 20		08 45		09 15		09 45				10 15			10 20	10 45		
Watford Junction	d																						
Milton Keynes Central	d			08 56			09 05		09 32				10 33							11 07	11 32		
Northampton	d																						
Rugby	d								10 08				11 08								12 08		
Coventry	d													10 28				11 55				11 28	
Bedworth	d																	12 06					
Nuneaton	a					09 41					10 44						11 44	12 13					
	d					09 42					10 45						11 46						
Atherstone	d																						
Polesworth	d																						
Tamworth	d																						
Lichfield Trent Valley	d																						
Rugeley Trent Valley	d																						
Stafford	d	09 18	09 34		09 45	10 08	10a14	10 17		10 45	11 11	11 14		11a33	11 41	11 45	12 12		12 14	12a18		12a34	12 45
Norton Bridge Station Drv	d																						
Stone	d																						
Stone Crown Street	d																						
Stone Granville Square	a														12 01								
Barlaston Orchard Place	d																						
Wedgwood Old Road Bridge	d																						
Stoke-on-Trent	d				10a20					11a20					12 20	12a20							13a20
Hanley Bus Station	a																						
Kidsgrove	d														12 38								
Alsager	d														12 52								
Crewe	a	09 38	09 54	10 15		10 28		10 37	10 55		11 30	11 38	11 56		13 07		12 31		12 38		12 57		

A until 16 October
B from 23 October
C until 10 July
D from 17 July

Table 67

Sundays until 11 July

London - Stoke-on-Trent and Crewe Coventry - Nuneaton

Station		VT ◇1 🍴	LM ◇1	VT ◇1 🍴	LM ◇1	VT ◇1 🍴	XC ◇1 🛒	VT ◇1 🍴	LM	LM ◇1	VT ◇1 🍴	XC ◇1 🛒
London Euston 15 ⊖	d	11 15		11 20		12 02		12 35			13 02	
Watford Junction	d											
Milton Keynes Central	d	12 04		12 09								
Northampton	d		11 36									
Rugby	d		12 02									
Coventry	d						12 28		13 46			13 26
Bedworth	d								13 57			
Nuneaton	a		12 13						14 04			
	d		12 16									
Atherstone	d		12 21									
Polesworth	d											
Tamworth	d		12 30									
Lichfield Trent Valley	d		12 36									
Rugeley Trent Valley	d		12 42									
Stafford	d	12 55	12 57	13 02	13 10	13 24	13 34			14 10	14 22	14 34
Norton Bridge Station Drv	d											
Stone	d		13 10									
Stone Crown Street	d											
Stone Granville Square	a											
Barlaston Orchard Place	d											
Wedgwood Old Road Bridge	d											
Stoke-on-Trent	d		13 18				13a57					14a57
Hanley Bus Station	a											
Kidsgrove	d		13 26									
Alsager	d		13 30									
Crewe	a	13 15	13 41	13 20	13 30	13 42		14 12		14 30	14 40	

Station		VT ◇1 🍴	LM ◇1	LM ◇1	VT ◇1 🍴	XC ◇1 🛒	VT ◇1 🍴	LM	LM	LM ◇1	VT ◇1 🍴	VT ◇1 🍴
London Euston 15 ⊖	d	13 35		12 50	14 02		14 35				15 02	15 05
Watford Junction	d			13 06								
Milton Keynes Central	d			13 37								15 39
Northampton	d			13 56								
Rugby	d			14 17								
Coventry	d					14 26		14 46	15 46			
Bedworth	d							14 57	15 57			
Nuneaton	a			14 29				15 04	16 04			
	d			14 30								
Atherstone	d			14 37								
Polesworth	d											
Tamworth	d			14 45								
Lichfield Trent Valley	d			14 51								
Rugeley Trent Valley	d			14 58								
Stafford	d		15 10	15 16	15 25	15 34				16 10	16a21	
Norton Bridge Station Drv	d											
Stone	d			15 32								
Stone Crown Street	d											
Stone Granville Square	a											
Barlaston Orchard Place	d											
Wedgwood Old Road Bridge	d											
Stoke-on-Trent	d			15 41		15a57						
Hanley Bus Station	a											
Kidsgrove	d			15 52								
Alsager	d			15 58								
Crewe	a	15 12	15 30	16 07	15 43		16 12			16 32		16 50

Station		XC ◇1 🛒	VT ◇1 🍴	LM ◇1	VT ◇1 🍴	LM ◇1	VT ◇1 🍴	XC ◇1 🛒	VT ◇1 🍴	LM	LM	LM ◇1
London Euston 15 ⊖	d		15 35		16 05	14 50	16 02		16 35			
Watford Junction	d					15 06						
Milton Keynes Central	d				16 39	15 36						
Northampton	d					15 56						
Rugby	d					16 17						
Coventry	d	15 26						16 26		16 46	17 46	
Bedworth	d									16 57	17 57	
Nuneaton	a					16 29				17 04	18 04	
	d					16 30						
Atherstone	d					16 37						
Polesworth	d											
Tamworth	d					16 45						
Lichfield Trent Valley	d					16 51						
Rugeley Trent Valley	d					16 58						
Stafford	d	16 36		17 10		17c20	17a25	17 36				18 10
Norton Bridge Station Drv	d											
Stone	d					17 30						
Stone Crown Street	d											
Stone Granville Square	a											
Barlaston Orchard Place	d											
Wedgwood Old Road Bridge	d											
Stoke-on-Trent	d	16a57				17 42		17a57				
Hanley Bus Station	a											
Kidsgrove	d					17 50						
Alsager	d					17 54						
Crewe	a		17 12	17 30	17 50	18 06			18 12			18 30

Station		VT ◇1 🍴	VT ◇1 🍴	XC ◇1 🛒	VT ◇1 🍴	LM ◇1	VT ◇1 🍴	LM ◇1	VT ◇1 🍴	XC ◇1 🛒	VT ◇1 🍴	LM ◇1
London Euston 15 ⊖	d	17 02	17 05		17 35		18 05	16 50	18 02		18 35	
Watford Junction	d							17 06				
Milton Keynes Central	d		17 39				18 39	17 36				
Northampton	d							17 56				
Rugby	d							18 17				
Coventry	d			17 26						18 26		
Bedworth	d											
Nuneaton	a		18 09					18 29				
	d		18 10					18 30				
Atherstone	d							18 37				
Polesworth	d											
Tamworth	d							18 45				
Lichfield Trent Valley	d							18 51				
Rugeley Trent Valley	d							18 58				
Stafford	d	18a25		18 36		19 10		19 16	19a25	19 38		20 10
Norton Bridge Station Drv	d											
Stone	d							19 32				
Stone Crown Street	d											
Stone Granville Square	a											
Barlaston Orchard Place	d											
Wedgwood Old Road Bridge	d											
Stoke-on-Trent	d			18a56				19 41		19a57		
Hanley Bus Station	a											
Kidsgrove	d							19 52				
Alsager	d							19 59				
Crewe	a		18 53		19 12	19 30	19 50	20 08			20 12	20 30

Station		VT ◇1 🍴	VT ◇1 🍴	XC ◇1 🛒	LM	VT ◇1 🍴	LM ◇1	VT ◇1 🍴	VT ◇1 🍴	VT ◇1 🍴	XC ◇1 🛒
London Euston 15 ⊖	d	19 02	19 05				18 50	19 35	20 02	20 05	
Watford Junction	d						19 06				
Milton Keynes Central	d		19 39				19 36			20 38	
Northampton	d						19 56				
Rugby	d						20 17				
Coventry	d			19 26	19 46						20 26
Bedworth	d				19 57						
Nuneaton	a	20 00			20 04		20 29		21 00		
	d	20 01					20 30		21 01		
Atherstone	d						20 37				
Polesworth	d										
Tamworth	d						20 45				
Lichfield Trent Valley	d						20 51				
Rugeley Trent Valley	d						20 58				
Stafford	d	20 30		20 38		20 52	21 16			21 33	21 38
Norton Bridge Station Drv	d										
Stone	d						21 32				
Stone Crown Street	d										
Stone Granville Square	a										
Barlaston Orchard Place	d										
Wedgwood Old Road Bridge	d										
Stoke-on-Trent	d			20a57			21 43				21a57
Hanley Bus Station	a										
Kidsgrove	d						21 54				
Alsager	d						22 01				
Crewe	a	20 48	20 53			21 10	22 12	21 13	21 44	21 53	

Station		VT ◇1 🍴	LM	VT ◇1 🍴	VT ◇1 🍴	LM ◇1	VT ◇1 🍴	XC ◇1 🛒	VT ◇1 🍴	VT ◇1 🍴
London Euston 15 ⊖	d	20 25			20 35		20 50		21 21	21 50
Watford Junction	d									
Milton Keynes Central	d						21 39			22 38
Northampton	d									
Rugby	d						22 01			23 18
Coventry	d		21 35					21 26		
Bedworth	d		21 46							
Nuneaton	a		21 53						22 53	23 28
	d								22 54	23 29
Atherstone	d									
Polesworth	d									
Tamworth	d	21 32								
Lichfield Trent Valley	d	21 39								
Rugeley Trent Valley	d									
Stafford	d			21 57	22 04	22 16		22 38	23 19	23s54
Norton Bridge Station Drv	d									
Stone	d									
Stone Crown Street	d									
Stone Granville Square	a									
Barlaston Orchard Place	d									
Wedgwood Old Road Bridge	d									
Stoke-on-Trent	d							22a57		
Hanley Bus Station	a									
Kidsgrove	d									
Alsager	d									
Crewe	a	22 10		22 15	22 22	22 39	22 49		23 38	00s12

b arr. 1222 c arr. 1714

Table 67

Sundays from 18 July

London - Stoke-on-Trent and Crewe Coventry - Nuneaton

Station		VT ◇1 A 🍴	VT ◇1 B 🍴	XC ◇1 🛒	VT ◇1 🍴	VT ◇1 🍴	LM ◇1	VT ◇1 🍴	XC ◇1 C 🛒	XC ◇1 D 🛒	VT ◇1 🍴	LM ◇1
London Euston 15 ⊖	d				08 10	08 15		08 45			09 15	
Watford Junction	d											
Milton Keynes Central	d				08 56			09 32				
Northampton	d											
Rugby	d							10 08				
Coventry	d											
Bedworth	d											
Nuneaton	a					09 41					10 44	
	d					09 42					10 45	
Atherstone	d											
Polesworth	d											
Tamworth	d											
Lichfield Trent Valley	d											
Rugeley Trent Valley	d											
Stafford	d	09 18	09 19	09 34		10 08	10 17		10 32	10 33	11 11	11 17
Norton Bridge Station Drv	d											
Stone	d											
Stone Crown Street	d											
Stone Granville Square	a											
Barlaston Orchard Place	d											
Wedgwood Old Road Bridge	d											
Stoke-on-Trent	d								10a52	10a52		
Hanley Bus Station	a											
Kidsgrove	d											
Alsager	d											
Crewe	a	09 38	09 37	09 54	10 15	10 28	10 37	10 55			11 30	11 37

Station		VT ◇1 🍴	XC ◇1 D 🛒	XC ◇1 C 🛒	LM 1	VT ◇1 🍴	LM	LM ◇1	VT ◇1 A 🍴	VT ◇1 B 🍴	XC ◇1 🛒	VT ◇1 🍴
London Euston 15 ⊖	d	09 45				10 15			10 45	10 45		11 15
Watford Junction	d											
Milton Keynes Central	d	10 33							11 32	11 32		12 04
Northampton	d											
Rugby	d	11 08							12 08	12 08		
Coventry	d		10 28	10 28			11 55				11 28	
Bedworth	d						12 06					
Nuneaton	a					11 44	12 13					
	d					11 46						
Atherstone	d											
Polesworth	d											
Tamworth	d											
Lichfield Trent Valley	d											
Rugeley Trent Valley	d											
Stafford	d		11 33	11 33	11 44	12 12		12 16			12 34	12 55
Norton Bridge Station Drv	d											
Stone	d				11 55							
Stone Crown Street	d											
Stone Granville Square	a											
Barlaston Orchard Place	d											
Wedgwood Old Road Bridge	d											
Stoke-on-Trent	d		11a52	11a54	12 03						12a53	
Hanley Bus Station	a											
Kidsgrove	d				12 11							
Alsager	d				12 15							
Crewe	a	11 56			12 26	12 31		12 37	12 57	12 59		13 15

Station		LM ◇1	LM ◇1	VT ◇1 🍴	XC ◇1 🛒	VT ◇1 🍴	LM	LM ◇1	VT ◇1 🍴	XC ◇1 🛒	VT ◇1 🍴	LM ◇1
London Euston 15 ⊖	d			12 02		12 35			13 02		13 35	
Watford Junction	d											
Milton Keynes Central	d											
Northampton	d	11 36										
Rugby	d	12 02										
Coventry	d				12 28		13 46			13 26		
Bedworth	d						13 57					
Nuneaton	a	12 13					14 04					
	d	12 16										
Atherstone	d	12 21										
Polesworth	d											
Tamworth	d	12 30										
Lichfield Trent Valley	d	12 36										
Rugeley Trent Valley	d	12 42										
Stafford	d	13e00	13 10	13 24	13 34			14 10	14 22	14 34		15 10
Norton Bridge Station Drv	d											
Stone	d	13 12										
Stone Crown Street	d											
Stone Granville Square	a											
Barlaston Orchard Place	d											
Wedgwood Old Road Bridge	d											
Stoke-on-Trent	d	13 20			13a57					14a57		
Hanley Bus Station	a											
Kidsgrove	d	13 28										
Alsager	d	13 32										
Crewe	a	13 43	13 30	13 42		14 12		14 30	14 40		15 12	15 30

Station		LM ◇1	VT ◇1 🍴	XC ◇1 🛒	VT ◇1 🍴	LM	LM	LM ◇1	VT ◇1 🍴	VT ◇1 🍴	XC ◇1 🛒	VT ◇1 🍴
London Euston 15 ⊖	d	12 50	14 02		14 35				15 02	15 05		15 35
Watford Junction	d	13 06										
Milton Keynes Central	d	13 37								15 39		
Northampton	d	13 56										
Rugby	d	14 17										
Coventry	d			14 26		14 46	15 46				15 26	
Bedworth	d					14 57	15 57					
Nuneaton	a	14 29				15 04	16 04					
	d	14 30										
Atherstone	d	14 37										
Polesworth	d											
Tamworth	d	14 45										
Lichfield Trent Valley	d	14 51										
Rugeley Trent Valley	d	14 58										
Stafford	d	15 16	15 25	15 34				16 10	16a21		16 36	
Norton Bridge Station Drv	d											
Stone	d	15 32										
Stone Crown Street	d											
Stone Granville Square	a											
Barlaston Orchard Place	d											
Wedgwood Old Road Bridge	d											
Stoke-on-Trent	d	15 41		15a57							16a57	
Hanley Bus Station	a											
Kidsgrove	d	15 52										
Alsager	d	15 58										
Crewe	a	16 07	15 43		16 12			16 32		16 50		17 12

A from 18 July until 17 October
B from 24 October
C from 18 July until 5 September
D from 12 September
e arr. 1253

Table 67

London - Stoke-on-Trent and Crewe Coventry - Nuneaton

Sundays
from 18 July

		LM		VT	LM	VT	XC	VT	LM	LM	LM	VT	XC	VT	VT	LM	VT	LM	VT	XC	VT	LM		VT	VT
		◇1		◇1 ⊏	◇1	◇1 ⊏	◇1 Ⲏ	◇1 ⊏			◇1	◇1 ⊏	◇1 Ⲏ	◇1 ⊏	◇1 ⊏	◇1	◇1 ⊏	◇1	◇1 ⊏	◇1 Ⲏ	◇1 ⊏	◇1		◇1 ⊏	◇1 ⊏
London Euston 15 ⊖	d			16 05	14 50	16 02		16 35				17 02		17 05	17 35		18 05	16 50	18 02		18 35			19 02	19 05
Watford Junction	d				15 06													17 06							
Milton Keynes Central	d			16 39	15 36									17 39			18 39	17 36							19 39
Northampton	d				15 56													17 56							
Rugby	d				16 17													18 17							
Coventry	d						16 26		16 46	17 46			17 26							18 26					
Bedworth	d								16 57	17 57															
Nuneaton	a				16 29				17 04	18 04				18 09				18 29						20 00	
	d				16 30									18 10				18 30						20 01	
Atherstone	d				16 37													18 37							
Polesworth	d																								
Tamworth	d				16 45													18 45							
Lichfield Trent Valley	d				16 51													18 51							
Rugeley Trent Valley	d				16 58													18 58							
Stafford	d	17 10			17b20	17a25	17 36				18 10	18a25	18 36			19 10		19 16	19 25	19 38		20 10		20 30	
Norton Bridge Station Drv	d																								
Stone	d				17 30													19 32							
Stone Crown Street	d																								
Stone Granville Square	a																								
Barlaston Orchard Place	d																								
Wedgwood Old Road Bridge	d																								
Stoke-on-Trent	d				17 42		17a57						18a56					19 41		19a57					
Hanley Bus Station	a																								
Kidsgrove	d				17 50													19 52							
Alsager	d				17 54													19 59							
Crewe	a	17 30		17 50	18 06			18 12			18 30			18 53	19 12	19 30	19 50	20 08			20 12	20 30		20 48	20 53

		XC	LM	VT	LM	VT	VT	VT		XC	VT	LM	VT	VT	LM	VT		XC		VT			VT		
		◇1 Ⲏ		◇1 ⊏	◇1	◇1 ⊏	◇1 ⊏	◇1 ⊏		◇1 Ⲏ	◇1 ⊏		◇1 ⊏	◇1 ⊏	◇1	◇1 ⊏		◇1 Ⲏ		◇1 ⊏			◇1 ⊏		
London Euston 15 ⊖	d				18 50	19 35	20 02	20 05			20 25			20 35		20 50				21 21			21 50		
Watford Junction	d				19 06																				
Milton Keynes Central	d				19 36			20 38								21 39							22 38		
Northampton	d				19 56																				
Rugby	d				20 17											22 01							23 18		
Coventry	d	19 26	19 46							20 26		21 35						21 26							
Bedworth	d		19 57									21 46													
Nuneaton	a		20 04		20 29		21 00					21 53								22 53			23 28		
	d				20 30		21 01													22 54			23 29		
Atherstone	d				20 37																				
Polesworth	d																								
Tamworth	d				20 45						21 32														
Lichfield Trent Valley	d				20 51						21 39														
Rugeley Trent Valley	d				20 58																				
Stafford	d	20 38		20 52	21 16			21 33		21 38			21 57	22 04	22 16			22 38		23 19			23s54		
Norton Bridge Station Drv	d																								
Stone	d				21 32																				
Stone Crown Street	d																								
Stone Granville Square	a																								
Barlaston Orchard Place	d																								
Wedgwood Old Road Bridge	d																								
Stoke-on-Trent	d	20a57			21 43					21a57								22a57							
Hanley Bus Station	a																								
Kidsgrove	d				21 54																				
Alsager	d				22 01																				
Crewe	a			21 10	22 12	21 13	21 44	21 53			22 10		22 15	22 22	22 39	22 49				23 38			00s12		

b arr. 1714

Table 67

Crewe and Stoke-on-Trent - London Nuneaton - Coventry

Mondays to Fridays

		AW MX	AW MO	VT		XC	VT	LM	LM	LM		VT	LM	VT	LM	XC	LM	VT	VT	LM		VT	LM	LM	LM
				◇1 ☒		◇1 Ⲏ	◇1 ☒	1	◇1			◇1 ☒	🚌	◇1 ☒	◇1	◇1 Ⲏ	◇1	◇1 ☒	◇1 ☒	1		◇1 ☒	◇1		1
Crewe	d	05b00	05b00	05 36		05 47	06 02		06 20			06 29			06 35	06 38	06 47	06 52		07 16		07 17	07 33		07 49
Alsager	d														06 44								07 41		
Kidsgrove	d														06 48								07 46		
Hanley Bus Station	d												06 50												
Stoke-on-Trent	d					06 07							06 56		06 58				07 06				07 54		
Wedgwood Old Road Bridge	d												07 08												
Barlaston Orchard Place	d												07 11												
Stone Granville Square	d												07a25												
Stone	d														07 06								08 02		
Norton Bridge Station Drv	d																								
Stafford	d	05 24	05 25	05 55		06 25	06 21		06 41					06 53	07c22	06a58	07a12		07 28	07a41		07 35	08g21		08a10
Rugeley Trent Valley	d							06 00							07 33								08 33		
Lichfield Trent Valley	d							06 07						07 08	07 40								08 40		
Tamworth	d							06 14						07 15	07 47								08 47		
Polesworth	d																								
Atherstone	d							06 23							07 56								08 56		
Nuneaton	a			06 17				06 29				07 06			08 02			07 32					09 02		
	d			06 18				06 30		06 37		07 07			08 02			07 34					09 03	07 37	
Bedworth	d									06 44														07 44	
Coventry	a					07a24				06a56									08 30					07a57	
Rugby	a			06 30			06 52	06 47							08 18								09 18		
Northampton	a														08 41								09 42		
Milton Keynes Central	a			06 51			07 12								08 59								10 05		
Watford Junction	a														09 27				09s15				10 30		
London Euston 15 ⊖	a			07 28			07 50					08 07		08 22	09 44			08 33	09 34			08 52	10 49		

		LM	LM	VT	XC	LM		VT	VT	LM	VT	XC	LM	LM	LM	VT		XC	LM	VT	LM	VT	XC	LM	LM
		🚌	🚌	◇1 ☒	◇1 Ⲏ			◇1 ☒	◇1 ☒	1	◇1 ☒	◇1 Ⲏ		◇1	1	◇1 ☒		◇1 Ⲏ	🚌	◇1 ☒	1	◇1 ☒	◇1 Ⲏ	🚌	◇1
Crewe	d			07 57						08 22	08 29			08 33	08 49	08 56					09 22	09 29			09 33
Alsager	d													08 41											09 41
Kidsgrove	d													08 46											09 47
Hanley Bus Station	d		07 50																09 00						
Stoke-on-Trent	d		08 01		08 07			08 12				08 44		08 54				09 07	09 11				09 44		09 55
Wedgwood Old Road Bridge	d		08 10																09 20						
Barlaston Orchard Place	d		08 11																09 21						
Stone Granville Square	d		08a25																09a30					08 59	
Stone	d													09 02											10 03
Norton Bridge Station Drv	d	07 49																						09 40	
Stafford	d	08a14			08 25				08 36	08a43		09 03		09h21	09 10			09 25		09 36	09a43		10a03	10a04	10i21
Rugeley Trent Valley	d													09 33											10 32
Lichfield Trent Valley	d													09 40											10 39
Tamworth	d													09 47											10 46
Polesworth	d																								
Atherstone	d													09 56											10 55
Nuneaton	a							08 44						10 02											11 01
	d					08 28		08 46					09 30	10 02											11 02
Bedworth	d					08 35							09 37												
Coventry	a				09a24	08a47							09A56					10A24							
Rugby	a			08 45										10 18											11 17
Northampton	a													10 42											11 42
Milton Keynes Central	a													11 04		10 01									12 04
Watford Junction	a							09s31						11 29											12 29
London Euston 15 ⊖	a			09 38				09 52	09 56		10 04			11 49		10 38				10 55		11 04			12 49

c arr. 0716

g arr. 0812

h arr. 0912

i arr. 1013

Crewe and Stoke-on-Trent - London Nuneaton - Coventry

		LM ■		VT ◇■ ⊠	XC ◇■ ⊤	LM 🚌	VT ◇■ ⊠	LM ■	VT ◇■ ⊠	LM	LM ◇■	LM ■		VT ◇■ ⊠	XC ◇■ ⊤	LM 🚌	VT ◇■ ⊏	LM ■	VT ◇■ ⊏	XC ◇■ ⊤	LM	LM ◇■		LM ■	LM 🚌
Crewe	d	09 49		09 56				10 22	10 29		10 33	10 49		10 56				11 22	11 29			11 33		11 49	
Alsager	d										10 41											11 41			
Kidsgrove	d										10 46											11 47			
Hanley Bus Station	d					10 00										11 00									
Stoke-on-Trent	d				10 07	10 11					10 54				11 07	11 11				11 44		11 55			
Wedgwood Old Road Bridge	d					10 20										11 20									
Barlaston Orchard Place	d					10 21										11 21									
Stone Granville Square	d					10a30										11a30									11 35
Stone	d										11 02											12 03			
Norton Bridge Station Drv	d																								11 59
Stafford	d	10a10			10 25		10 36	10a43			11b21	11a10			11 25		11 38	11a43		12a03		12c21		12a10	12a24
Rugeley Trent Valley	d										11 32											12 32			
Lichfield Trent Valley	d										11 39											12 39			
Tamworth	d										11 46											12 46			
Polesworth	d																								
Atherstone	d										11 55											12 55			
Nuneaton	a										12 01											13 01			
	d									11 10	12 02										12 10	13 02			
Bedworth	d									11 17											12 17				
Coventry	a				11 24					11 34					12 24						12 34				
Rugby	a										12 17											13 17			
Northampton	a										12 43											13 48			
Milton Keynes Central	a			11 01							13 04			12 01								14 04			
Watford Junction	a										13 29											14 29			
London Euston ⊖	a			11 38			11 56		12 04		13 49			12 38			12 58		13 04			14 49			

		VT ◇■ ⊏	XC ◇■ ⊤	LM 🚌	VT ◇■ ⊏	LM ■	VT ◇■ ⊏	LM		LM ◇■	LM ■	VT ◇■ ⊏	XC ◇■ ⊤	LM 🚌	VT ◇■ ⊏	LM ■	VT ◇■ ⊏	LM		LM ◇■	LM ■	LM 🚌	VT ◇■ ⊏	VT ◇■ A ⊏	XC ◇■ ⊤
Crewe	d	11 56				12 22	12 29			12 33	12 49	12 56				13 22	13 29			13 33	13 49		13 56	14 01	
Alsager	d									12 41										13 41					
Kidsgrove	d									12 46										13 46					
Hanley Bus Station	d			12 00										13 00											
Stoke-on-Trent	d		12 07	12 11						12 54			13 07	13 11						13 54					14 07
Wedgwood Old Road Bridge	d			12 20										13 20											
Barlaston Orchard Place	d			12 21										13 21											
Stone Granville Square	d			12a30										13a30								13 30			
Stone	d									13 02										14 02					
Norton Bridge Station Drv	d																					13 52			
Stafford	d		12 25		12 36	12a43				13e21	13a10		13 25		13 36	13a43				14f21	14a10	14a18			14 25
Rugeley Trent Valley	d									13 32										14 32					
Lichfield Trent Valley	d									13 39										14 39					
Tamworth	d									13 46										14 46					
Polesworth	d																								
Atherstone	d									13 55										14 55					
Nuneaton	a									14 01										15 01					
	d							13 10		14 02								14 10		15 02					
Bedworth	d							13 17										14 17							
Coventry	a		13 24					13 38					14 24					14 34						15 30	15 24
Rugby	a									14 17										15 17					
Northampton	a									14 42										15 42					
Milton Keynes Central	a	13 01								15 04		14 01								16 04			15 01		
Watford Junction	a									15 29										16 29				16s15	
London Euston ⊖	a	13 38			13 56		14 04			15 49		14 38			14 56		15 04			16 49			15 38	16 34	

A from 19 July until 3 September
b arr. 1112
c arr. 1213
e arr. 1312
f arr. 1412

Table 67 Mondays to Fridays

Crewe and Stoke-on-Trent - London Nuneaton - Coventry

		LM 🚌	VT ◇■ ⊏	LM ■		VT ◇■ ⊏	XC ◇■ ⊤	LM	LM ◇■	LM ■	VT ◇■ ⊏	XC ◇■ ⊤	LM 🚌	VT ◇■ ⊏		LM ■	VT ◇■ ⊏	XC ◇■ ⊤	LM	LM ◇■	LM ■	VT ◇■ ⊏	VT ◇■ ⊏	XC ◇■ ⊤
Crewe	d			14 22		14 29			14 33	14 49	14 56					15 22	15 29			15 33	15 49	15 57	15 57	
Alsager	d								14 41											15 41				
Kidsgrove	d								14 46											15 46				
Hanley Bus Station	d	14 00											15 00											
Stoke-on-Trent	d	14 11					14 44		14 54			15 07	15 11					15 44		15 54				16 07
Wedgwood Old Road Bridge	d	14 20											15 20											
Barlaston Orchard Place	d	14 21											15 21											
Stone Granville Square	d	14a30											15a30											
Stone	d								15 02											16 02				
Norton Bridge Station Drv	d																							
Stafford	d		14 36	14a46			15a03		15b21	15 10		15 25		15 36		15a43		16a03		16c21	16a10			16 25
Rugeley Trent Valley	d								15 32											16 32				
Lichfield Trent Valley	d								15 39											16 39				
Tamworth	d								15 46											16 46				
Polesworth	d																							
Atherstone	d								15 55											16 55				
Nuneaton	a								16 01											17 01				
	d							15 10	16 02										16 10	17 02				
Bedworth	d							15 17											16 17					
Coventry	a							15 34				16 24							16 34					17 24
Rugby	a								16 17											17 17				
Northampton	a								16 44											17 42				
Milton Keynes Central	a								17 04		16 01									18 04		17 01	17s01	
Watford Junction	a								17 29											18 29				
London Euston ⊖	a		15 56			16 04			17 49		16 38			16 56			17 04			18 49		17 38	17 38	

		LM 🚌	LM 🚌	VT ◇■ ⊏	LM ■	VT ◇■ ⊏	XC ◇■ ⊤	LM	LM ◇■	LM ■		VT ◇■ ⊏	XC ◇■ ⊤	LM 🚌	VT ◇■ ⊏	LM 🚌	LM ■	VT ◇■ ⊏	XC ◇■ ⊤	LM		LM ◇■	LM ■	VT ◇■ A ⊠	VT ◇■ B ⊠
Crewe	d				16 22	16 29			16 33	16 49		16 56					17 22	17 29				17 33	17 49	17 56	17 56
Alsager	d								16 41													17 41			
Kidsgrove	d								16 46													17 46			
Hanley Bus Station	d		16 00											17 00											
Stoke-on-Trent	d		16 11				16 44		16 54				17 07	17 11					17 44			17 54			
Wedgwood Old Road Bridge	d		16 20											17 20											
Barlaston Orchard Place	d		16 21											17 21											
Stone Granville Square	d	15 45	16a30											17a30											
Stone	d								17 02													18 02			
Norton Bridge Station Drv	d	16 09														17 15									
Stafford	d	16a34		16 36	16 46		17 03		17e21	17 10			17 25		17 36	17a39	17 43		18 04			18f21	18 10		
Rugeley Trent Valley	d								17 32													18 33			
Lichfield Trent Valley	d								17 39													18 40			
Tamworth	d								17 46													18 47			
Polesworth	d																								
Atherstone	d								17 55													18 56			
Nuneaton	a								18 01													19 02			
	d							17 10	18 02											18 10		19 02			
Bedworth	d							17 17												18 17					
Coventry	a							17 38					18 24							18 34					
Rugby	a								18 17													19 18			
Northampton	a								18 42													19 44			
Milton Keynes Central	a								19 04			18 01			18 23							20 04		19 01	19 02
Watford Junction	a								19 30									18s48				20 29			
London Euston ⊖	a			17 56		18 02			19 50			18 38			18 59			19 08				20 49		19 38	19 38

A until 16 July, from 6 September
B from 19 July until 3 September
b arr. 1512
c arr. 1612
e arr. 1713
f arr. 1812

Crewe and Stoke-on-Trent - London Nuneaton - Coventry

		VT	LM	XC	VT	LM	VT	LM	LM	LM	XC	LM	VT	VT	XC	LM	VT	XC	LM	LM	VT	VT	VT
		A									B							B					
Crewe	d	18 01		18 07		18 22	18 29		18 33	18 49		19 18	19 23	19 29		19 55	19 56			20 18	20 23	20 29	20 41
Alsager	d								18 41														
Kidsgrove	d								18 46														
Hanley Bus Station	d		18 00																				
Stoke-on-Trent	d		18 11						18 54		19 07				19 44			20 07					
Wedgwood Old Road Bridge	d		18 20																				
Barlaston Orchard Place	d		18 21																				
Stone Granville Square	d		18a30																				
Stone	d								19 02														
Norton Bridge Station Drv	d																						
Stafford	d			18 28	18 36	18a43			19b21	19a10	19 25	19a42	19 42		20a04	20a16		20 26		20a42		20 48	
Rugeley Trent Valley	d								19 33														
Lichfield Trent Valley	d								19 40														
Tamworth	d								19 47														
Polesworth	d																						
Atherstone	d								19 56														
Nuneaton	a								20 02												21 02		
	d							19 10	20 02										20 10		21 03		
Bedworth	d							19 17											20 17				
Coventry	a	19 30		19 24				19 38			20 24							21 24	20 34				
Rugby	a								20 18														21 27
Northampton	a								20 43														
Milton Keynes Central	a						19 31							20 32			21 03					21 35	21 47
Watford Junction	a	20s15			19s42								20s46								21s48		
London Euston	a	20 34			20 02		20 06						21 05	21 06			21 42				22 09	22 12	22 22

		LM	VT	XC	LM	LM	VT	XC	LM	LM	XC
Crewe	d	20 47	20 53			21 18	21 24			22 20	
Alsager	d										
Kidsgrove	d										
Hanley Bus Station	d										
Stoke-on-Trent	d			21 08				22 08			22 47
Wedgwood Old Road Bridge	d										
Barlaston Orchard Place	d										
Stone Granville Square	d										
Stone	d										
Norton Bridge Station Drv	d										
Stafford	d	21a10	21a14	21 26		21a41	21 44	22a26		22a40	23a07
Rugeley Trent Valley	d										
Lichfield Trent Valley	d						21 58				
Tamworth	d						22 05				
Polesworth	d										
Atherstone	d										
Nuneaton	a						22 16				
	d				21 10		22 17		22 20		
Bedworth	d				21 17				22 27		
Coventry	a				21 34				22 39		
Rugby	a						22 30				
Northampton	a										
Milton Keynes Central	a						22 57				
Watford Junction	a						23s31				
London Euston	a						23 58				

A from 19 July until 3 September

B to Stafford

b arr. 1912

Crewe and Stoke-on-Trent - London Nuneaton - Coventry

		AW	SR	XC	VT	LM	VT	LM	VT	XC	LM	LM	LM	VT	VT	XC	XC	LM	LM	VT	LM	LM	VT
																A	B						
Crewe	d	05b00	05c40	05 47	06 00			06 20	06 29		06 38	06 47	07 16	07 20	07 29				07 38	07 39	07 49		07 55
Alsager	d										06 47								07 46				
Kidsgrove	d										06 51								07 51				
Hanley Bus Station	d																	07 50					
Stoke-on-Trent	d			06 08						06 39	07 00					07 44	07 44	07 56	07 59				
Wedgwood Old Road Bridge	d																	08 05					
Barlaston Orchard Place	d																	08 06					
Stone Granville Square	d																	08a12					
Stone	d										07 08								08 07				
Norton Bridge Station Drv	d																					07 49	
Stafford	d	05 24		06 26	06 19		06 35	06a41		06a58	07 26	07a12	07a41	07 39		08 03	08 04		08 23		08a10	08a14	08 16
Rugeley Trent Valley	d										07 34								08 33				
Lichfield Trent Valley	d										07 41								08 40				08 31
Tamworth	d										07 48								08 47 →				08 37
Polesworth	d																						
Atherstone	d										07 57												
Nuneaton	a						06 57				08 03												
	d					06 47	06 59				08 04												
Bedworth	d					06 54																	
Coventry	a			07 24		07 06																	
Rugby	a				06 49						08 19												
Northampton	a										08 40												
Milton Keynes Central	a				07 11				07 31		09 04												
Watford Junction	a				07s32		07s44				09 33												
London Euston	a		07 56		07 52		08 05		08 09		09 50			08 59	09 04					09 30			09 46

		XC	LM	VT	LM	LM	VT	XC	XC	LM	LM	LM	VT	XC	LM	VT	LM	VT	XC	LM	LM	LM	LM
								A	B														
Crewe	d					08 22	08 29			08 33	08 49		08 56				09 22	09 29				09 33	09 49
Alsager	d									08 41												09 41	
Kidsgrove	d									08 46												09 46	
Hanley Bus Station	d											08 50											
Stoke-on-Trent	d	08 07						08 44	08 44	08 54		08 56		09 07					09 44			09 54	
Wedgwood Old Road Bridge	d											09 05											
Barlaston Orchard Place	d											09 06											
Stone Granville Square	d											09a12								08 59			
Stone	d									09 02												10 02	
Norton Bridge Station Drv	d																			09 40			
Stafford	d	08 26		08 36		08a43		09 03	09 04	09f21	09a10			09 26		09 36	09a43		10a03	10a04		10g21	10a10
Rugeley Trent Valley	d									09 32												10 32	
Lichfield Trent Valley	d				←					09 39												10 39	
Tamworth	d				08 47					09 46												10 46	
Polesworth	d																						
Atherstone	d				08 56					09 55												10 55	
Nuneaton	a			08 58	09 02					10 01						09 58						11 01	
	d		08 14	08 59	09 04					10 02					09 15	09 59					10 15	11 03	
Bedworth	d		08 21												09 22						10 22		
Coventry	a	09 24	08 33											10 24	09 34						10 34		
Rugby	a				09 20					10 17												11 19	
Northampton	a				09 41					10 38												11 40	
Milton Keynes Central	a				10 04					11 04			10 01									12 04	
Watford Junction	a				10 29					11 29												12 29	
London Euston	a			10 00	10 49		10 04			11 49			10 37			11 01		11 04				12 49	

A from 11 September

B until 4 September

f arr. 0912

g arr. 1013

Table 67

Saturdays

Crewe and Stoke-on-Trent - London Nuneaton - Coventry

		LM		VT	XC	VT	LM	VT	XC	LM	LM	LM		LM	VT	XC	VT	LM	VT	XC	LM	LM		LM	LM
				◇1	◇1	◇1	1	◇1	◇1		◇1	1			◇1	◇1	◇1	1	◇1	◇1		◇1		1	
		🚌		☕	🛒	☕		☕	🛒					🚌	☕	🛒	☕		☕	🛒					🚌
Crewe	d			09 56			10 22	10 29			10 33	10 49			10 56			11 22	11 29			11 33		11 49	
Alsager	d										10 41											11 41			
Kidsgrove	d										10 46											11 46			
Hanley Bus Station	d	09 50												10 50											
Stoke-on-Trent	d	09 56			10 07				10 44		10 54			10 56		11 07				11 44		11 54			
Wedgwood Old Road Bridge	d	10 05												11 05											
Barlaston Orchard Place	d	10 06												11 06											
Stone Granville Square	d	10a12												11a12											11 35
Stone	d										11 02											12 02			
Norton Bridge Station Drv	d																								11 59
Stafford	d				10 26	10 36	10a43		11 03		11b21	11a10				11 26	11 36	11a43		12a03		12c21		12a10	12a24
Rugeley Trent Valley	d										11 32											12 32			
Lichfield Trent Valley	d										11 39											12 39			
Tamworth	d										11 46											12 46			
Polesworth	d																								
Atherstone	d										11 55											12 55			
Nuneaton	a										12 01											13 01			
	d									11 15	12 02										12 15	13 03			
Bedworth	d									11 22											12 22				
Coventry	a				11 24					11 34						12 24					12 34				
Rugby	a										12 17											13 19			
Northampton	a										12 38											13 40			
Milton Keynes Central	a			11 01							13 04				12 01							14 04			
Watford Junction	a										13 29											14 29			
London Euston [15] ⊖	a			11 38		11 56		12 04			13 49				12 38		12 56		13 04			14 49			

		LM	VT	XC	VT	LM	VT	XC		LM	LM	LM	LM	VT	XC	VT	LM	VT		XC	LM	LM	LM	LM	LM
			◇1	◇1	◇1	1	◇1	◇1			◇1	1		◇1	◇1	◇1	1	◇1		◇1		◇1	1		
		🚌	☕	🛒	☕		☕	🛒					🚌	☕	🛒	☕		☕		🛒				🚌	🚌
Crewe	d		11 56			12 22	12 29				12 33	12 49		12 57			13 22	13 29				13 33	13 49		
Alsager	d										12 41											13 41			
Kidsgrove	d										12 46											13 46			
Hanley Bus Station	d	11 50											12 50												13 50
Stoke-on-Trent	d	11 56		12 07				12 44			12 54		12 56		13 07					13 44		13 54			13 56
Wedgwood Old Road Bridge	d	12 05											13 05												14 05
Barlaston Orchard Place	d	12 06											13 06												14 06
Stone Granville Square	d	12a12											13a12											13 30	14a12
Stone	d										13 02											14 02			
Norton Bridge Station Drv	d																							13 52	
Stafford	d			12 25	12 36	12a43		13 03			13e21	13a10			13 26	13 36	13a43			14a03		14f21	14a10	14a18	
Rugeley Trent Valley	d										13 32											14 32			
Lichfield Trent Valley	d										13 39											14 39			
Tamworth	d										13 46											14 46			
Polesworth	d																								
Atherstone	d										13 55											14 55			
Nuneaton	a										14 01											15 01			
	d									13 15	14 02										14 15	15 02			
Bedworth	d									13 22											14 22				
Coventry	a			13 24						13 34					14 24						14 34				
Rugby	a										14 17											15 17			
Northampton	a										14 38											15 39			
Milton Keynes Central	a		13 01								15 04			14 01								16 04			
Watford Junction	a										15 29											16 29			
London Euston [15] ⊖	a		13 38		13 56		14 04				15 49			14 38		14 56		15 04				16 49			

b arr. 1112
c arr. 1212
e arr. 1312
f arr. 1412

Table 67

Saturdays

Crewe and Stoke-on-Trent - London Nuneaton - Coventry

		VT	VT	XC		VT	LM	VT	XC	LM	LM		LM	LM		VT	XC	VT	LM	VT	XC	LM	LM	VT	
		◇1	◇1 A	◇1		◇1	1	◇1	◇1		◇1		1			◇1	◇1	◇1	1	◇1	◇1		◇1	◇1	
		☕	☕	🛒		☕		☕	🛒					🚌		☕	🛒	☕		☕	🛒			☕	
Crewe	d	13 56	14 01				14 22	14 29			14 33		14 49			14 56			15 22	15 29			15 33	15 35	
Alsager	d										14 41												15 41		
Kidsgrove	d										14 46												15 46		
Hanley Bus Station	d													14 50											
Stoke-on-Trent	d			14 07					14 44		14 54			14 56			15 07				15 44		15 54		
Wedgwood Old Road Bridge	d													15 05											
Barlaston Orchard Place	d													15 06											
Stone Granville Square	d													15a12											
Stone	d										15 02												16 02		
Norton Bridge Station Drv	d																								
Stafford	d			14 26		14 36	14a46		15a03		15b21		15a10				15 26	15 36	15a43		16a03		16c21		
Rugeley Trent Valley	d										15 32												16 32		
Lichfield Trent Valley	d										15 39												16 39		
Tamworth	d										15 46												16 46		
Polesworth	d																								
Atherstone	d										15 55												16 55		
Nuneaton	a										16 01												17 01		
	d									15 15	16 02											16 15	17 03		
Bedworth	d									15 22												16 22			
Coventry	a		15 30	15 24						15 34							16 24					16 34			
Rugby	a										16 17												17 19		
Northampton	a										16 38												17 40		
Milton Keynes Central	a	15 01									17 04					16 01							18 04		
Watford Junction	a		16s15								17 29												18 29		
London Euston [15] ⊖	a	15 38	16 34			15 56		16 04			17 49					16 38		16 56		17 04			18 49	17 12	

		LM	LM	VT	XC	LM	VT	LM	VT	XC		LM	LM	LM	VT	LM	XC	VT	LM	LM		VT	XC	XC	LM
		1		◇1	◇1		◇1	1	◇1	◇1			◇1	1	◇1		◇1	◇1		1		◇1	◇1 C	◇1 B	
			🚌	☕	🛒	🚌	☕		☕	🛒					☕	🚌	🛒	☕	🚌			☕	🛒	🛒	
Crewe	d	15 49		15 56				16 22	16 29				16 33	16 49	16 56					17 22		17 29			
Alsager	d												16 41												
Kidsgrove	d												16 46												
Hanley Bus Station	d		15 50													16 50									
Stoke-on-Trent	d		15 56		16 07					16 44			16 54			16 56	17 07						17 43	17 44	
Wedgwood Old Road Bridge	d		16 05													17 05									
Barlaston Orchard Place	d		16 06													17 06									
Stone Granville Square	d		16a12			15 45										17a12									
Stone	d												17 02												
Norton Bridge Station Drv	d					16 09													17 15						
Stafford	d	16a10			16 25	16a34	16 36	16a46		17a03			17e21	17a10			17 26	17 36	17a39	17a43			18a04	18a04	
Rugeley Trent Valley	d												17 32												
Lichfield Trent Valley	d												17 39												
Tamworth	d												17 46												
Polesworth	d																								
Atherstone	d												17 55												
Nuneaton	a												18 01												
	d											17 15	18 02												18 15
Bedworth	d											17 22													18 22
Coventry	a				17 24							17 34					18 24								18 34
Rugby	a												18 17												
Northampton	a												18 38												
Milton Keynes Central	a			17 01									19 04		18 01										
Watford Junction	a												19 36												
London Euston [15] ⊖	a			17 38			17 55		18 04				19 54		18 37			18 56				19 04			

A from 17 July until 4 September
C until 16 October
b arr. 1512
c arr. 1612
e arr. 1712

Table 67

Saturdays

Crewe and Stoke-on-Trent - London Nuneaton - Coventry

		LM ◇1	LM 1	LM 🚌	VT ◇1 B ☕	XC ◇1 ⌶	VT ◇1 ☕	LM 1	VT ◇1 ☕	XC ◇1 ⌶	LM	LM ◇1	LM 1	XC ◇1 ⌶	VT ◇1 ☕	LM 1	VT ◇1 ☕	VT ◇1 A ☕	XC ◇1 ⌶	LM 1	XC ◇1 ⌶
Crewe	d	17 33	17 49		18 01			18 22	18 29			18 33	18 49			19 22	19 29	19 38		19 51	
Alsager	d	17 41										18 41									
Kidsgrove	d	17 46										18 46									
Hanley Bus Station	d			17 50																	
Stoke-on-Trent	d	17 54		17 56		18 08				18 44		18 54		19 07					19 44		20 07
Wedgwood Old Road Bridge	d			18 05																	
Barlaston Orchard Place	d			18 06																	
Stone Granville Square	d			18a12																	
Stone	d	18 02										19 02									
Norton Bridge Station Drv	d																				
Stafford	d	18b21	18a10			18 27	18 36	18a43		19a03		19c21	19a10	19 25	19 36	19a43		19a58	20a03	20a12	20 26
Rugeley Trent Valley	d	18 32										19 32									
Lichfield Trent Valley	d	18 39										19 39									
Tamworth	d	18 46										19 46									
Polesworth	d																				
Atherstone	d	18 55										19 55									
Nuneaton	a	19 01										20 01									
	d	19 02									19 46	20 02									
Bedworth	d										19 53										
Coventry	a				19 30	19 24					20 05			20 24							21 24
Rugby	a	19 18			19 42							20 17									
Northampton	a	19 38										20 38									
Milton Keynes Central	a				20 05																
Watford Junction	a				20s34																
London Euston 15 ⊖	a				20 56		19 56		20 04						21 15		21 18				

		VT ◇1 ☕	LM 1	XC ◇1 ⌶	VT ◇1 ☕	XC ◇1 ⌶	LM 1	LM	XC ◇1 ⌶	VT ◇1 ☕	XC C 🚌	VT ◇1 ☕	XC ◇1 C ⌶	XC ◇1 D ⌶	LM	LM 1
Crewe	d		20 22		20 47		21 17			21 43		22 04	22 09			22 23
Alsager	d															
Kidsgrove	d															
Hanley Bus Station	d															
Stoke-on-Trent	d			20 44		21 07			21 45		21 50			22 08		
Wedgwood Old Road Bridge	d															
Barlaston Orchard Place	d															
Stone Granville Square	d															
Stone	d															
Norton Bridge Station Drv	d															
Stafford	d	20 36	20a43	21a03		21a27	21a42		22a03	22a08	22a20	22a29	22 34	22 34		22a47
Rugeley Trent Valley	d															
Lichfield Trent Valley	d															
Tamworth	d															
Polesworth	d															
Atherstone	d															
Nuneaton	a															
	d							21 15							22 15	
Bedworth	d							21 22							22 22	
Coventry	a							21 34							22 34	
Rugby	a															
Northampton	a															
Milton Keynes Central	a				21 50											
Watford Junction	a															
London Euston 15 ⊖	a	22 14			22 45											

A from 23 October
B from 17 July until 4 September
C until 10 July
D from 17 July
b arr. 1812
c arr. 1912

Table 67

Sundays
until 11 July

Crewe and Stoke-on-Trent - London Nuneaton - Coventry

		VT ◇1 ☕	XC 🚌	VT ◇1 ☕	VT ◇1 ☕	XC ◇1 A ⌶	VT ◇1 ☕	VT ◇1 ☕	VT ◇1 ☕	XC 🚌	XC ◇1	XC 🚌	LM 🚌	VT ◇1 ☕	LM ◇1	VT ◇1 ☕	LM 🚌	VT ◇1 ☕	XC ◇1	VT ◇1 ☕	VT ◇1 ☕	VT ◇1 ☕	VT ◇1 ☕
Crewe	d	08 43		08 53		09 05	09 13	09 43					09 53	10 14	10 20	10 43	10 45	10 55			11 14	11 49	
Alsager	d												10 10				11 02						
Kidsgrove	d												10 24				11 16						
Hanley Bus Station	d																						
Stoke-on-Trent	d		08 45							09 42		10 38	10 41				11 33						
Wedgwood Old Road Bridge	d																						
Barlaston Orchard Place	d																						
Stone Granville Square	d												10 57				11 49						
Stone	d																						
Norton Bridge Station Drv	d																						
Stafford	d	09 02	09a15		09 17	09 26	09 32		10 11	10a12	10 26	11a08	11a17	10 33	10a42		12a09		11 24	11 28	11 33		12 01
Rugeley Trent Valley	d																						
Lichfield Trent Valley	d																						
Tamworth	d																						
Polesworth	d																						
Atherstone	d																						
Nuneaton	a						09 54							10 55							12 04	12 30	
	d						09 55							10 56							12 05	12 31	
Bedworth	d																						
Coventry	a					10 24					11 24								12 24				
Rugby	a							10 31								11 31							
Northampton	a																						
Milton Keynes Central	a			10 17				11 06	11 16					11 49		12 05				12 24		13 03	12 51
Watford Junction	a	10s34			10s51		11s16	11s42										12s34			12s54		
London Euston 15 ⊖	a	10 56		11 06	11 12		11 39	12 04	12 09					12 37		12 44		12 56		13 04	13 15	13 44	13 32

		XC 🚌	LM	LM ◇1	XC ◇1	VT ◇1 ☕	VT ◇1 ☕	LM 1	VT ◇1 ☕	VT ◇1 ☕	VT ◇1 ☕	XC 🚌	XC ◇1	VT ◇1 ☕	VT ◇1 ☕	LM 1	VT ◇1 ☕	LM ◇1	XC ◇1 A ⌶	LM	VT ◇1 ☕	VT ◇1 ☕	LM 1
Crewe	d			11 58				12 22	12 30	12 54						13 22	13 30	13 38			13 51		14 22
Alsager	d																	13 46					
Kidsgrove	d																	13 51					
Hanley Bus Station	d																						
Stoke-on-Trent	d	11 44										12 45						13 59	14 07				
Wedgwood Old Road Bridge	d																						
Barlaston Orchard Place	d																						
Stone Granville Square	d																						
Stone	d																	14 07					
Norton Bridge Station Drv	d																						
Stafford	d	12a14		12 18	12 25	12 28	12 36	12a42			13 07	13a15	13 26	13 29	13 36	13a43		14 17	14 25			14 36	14a43
Rugeley Trent Valley	d			12 28														14 29					
Lichfield Trent Valley	d			12 35														14 36					
Tamworth	d			12 42														14 43					
Polesworth	d																						
Atherstone	d			12 51														14 52					
Nuneaton	a			12 58														14 58			14 31		
	d		12 30	12 58														14 58		14 11	14 32		
Bedworth	d		12 36																	14 17			
Coventry	a		12 54		13 24								14 24						15 24	14 34			
Rugby	a			13 17														15 17					
Northampton	a			13 39														15 39					
Milton Keynes Central	a			14 04						14 04	14 01							16 04			15 04		
Watford Junction	a			14 33														16 33					
London Euston 15 ⊖	a			14 53		13 51	14 06		14 12	14 45	14 41			14 52	15 03		15 11	16 53			15 45	16 03	

		VT ◇1 ☕	VT ◇1 ☕	XC ◇1 A ⌶	LM	VT ◇1 ☕	LM 1	VT ◇1 ☕	LM	LM ◇1	VT ◇1 ☕	XC ◇1 A ⌶	VT ◇1 ☕	LM 1	VT ◇1 ☕	VT ◇1 ☕	XC ◇1 A ⌶	LM	VT ◇1 ☕	LM 1	VT ◇1 ☕	LM
Crewe	d	14 29	14 56				15 22	15 29		15 38	15 56			16 22	16 29	16 53				17 22	17 29	
Alsager	d									15 46												
Kidsgrove	d									15 52												
Hanley Bus Station	d																					
Stoke-on-Trent	d			15 07						15 59		16 07					17 08					
Wedgwood Old Road Bridge	d																					
Barlaston Orchard Place	d																					
Stone Granville Square	d																					
Stone	d									16 08												
Norton Bridge Station Drv	d																					
Stafford	d			15 25		15 36	15a43			16 18		16 25	16 37	16a43			17 26		17 36	17a43		
Rugeley Trent Valley	d									16 28												
Lichfield Trent Valley	d									16 35						17 26						
Tamworth	d									16 42												
Polesworth	d																					
Atherstone	d									16 51												
Nuneaton	a									16 58												
	d				15 11				16 11	16 58								17 11				18 11
Bedworth	d				15 17				16 17									17 17				18 17
Coventry	a			16 24	15 34				16 34			17 24					18 24	17 34				18 34
Rugby	a									17 18												
Northampton	a									17 39												
Milton Keynes Central	a		16 04							18 04	17 03					18 02						
Watford Junction	a									18 35												
London Euston 15 ⊖	a	16 11	16 44			17 03		17 11		18 53	17 44		18 04		18 11	18 42			19 03		19 11	

A ⌶ to Stafford

Crewe and Stoke-on-Trent - London Nuneaton - Coventry

		LM	VT	XC	VT	LM	VT	VT		XC	VT	LM	VT	LM	LM	XC	LM	VT		VT	XC	AW	LM	LM	VT
		◇1	◇1	◇1	◇1	1	◇1	◇1		◇1	◇1	1	◇1		◇1	◇1	1	◇1		◇1	◇1	◇	1		◇1
				A						A						A									
			🍴	🛒	🍴		🍴	🍴		🛒	🍴		🍴			🛒		🍴		🍴	🛒				🍴
Crewe	d	17 38	17 55			18 22	18 29	18 55				19 22	19 29		19 36		20 18	20 24		20 47		20b54	21 17		21 23
Alsager	d	17 46													19 44										
Kidsgrove	d	17 51													19 50										
Hanley Bus Station	d																								
Stoke-on-Trent	d	17 59		18 08						19 07					19 57	20 07					20 47				
Wedgwood Old Road Bridge	d																								
Barlaston Orchard Place	d																								
Stone Granville Square	d																								
Stone	d	18 07													20 06										
Norton Bridge Station Drv	d																								
Stafford	d	18 18		18 26	18 36	18a43				19 25	19 36	19a43			20 16	20 25	20a38	20 43			21a09	21 16	21a38		21 44
Rugeley Trent Valley	d	18 27													20 28										
Lichfield Trent Valley	d	18 35													20 35										21 59
Tamworth	d	18 42													20 42										22 05
Polesworth	d																								
Atherstone	d	18 51													20 51										
Nuneaton	a	18 58													20 58										22 15
	d	18 58												20 11	20 58									22 00	22 16
Bedworth	d													20 17										22 06	
Coventry	a			19 24						20 24				20 34		21 23								22 21	
Rugby	a	19 18													21 16										22 28
Northampton	a	19 39													21 39										
Milton Keynes Central	a	20 06	19 03					20 03							22 10			21 36		21 55					23 04
Watford Junction	a	20 33													22 52					22s31					23s36
London Euston ⊖	a	20 53	19 44		20 03		20 11	20 44			21 04		21 14		23 13			22 29		22 53					23 57

		VT	XC	LM		XC
		◇1	◇1	1		◇1
		🍴	🛒			🛒
Crewe	d	21 40		22 22		
Alsager	d					
Kidsgrove	d					
Hanley Bus Station	d					
Stoke-on-Trent	d		21 47			22 47
Wedgwood Old Road Bridge	d					
Barlaston Orchard Place	d					
Stone Granville Square	d					
Stone	d					
Norton Bridge Station Drv	d					
Stafford	d	22a02	22a06	22a44		23a05
Rugeley Trent Valley	d					
Lichfield Trent Valley	d					
Tamworth	d					
Polesworth	d					
Atherstone	d					
Nuneaton	a					
	d					
Bedworth	d					
Coventry	a					
Rugby	a					
Northampton	a					
Milton Keynes Central	a					
Watford Junction	a					
London Euston ⊖	a					

A 🛒 to Stafford

Crewe and Stoke-on-Trent - London Nuneaton - Coventry

		VT	VT	XC	VT	VT	XC	LM	VT	LM		LM	VT	VT	XC	XC	VT		LM	VT		XC	LM	VT	LM
		◇1	◇1	◇1	◇1	◇1	◇1		◇1	◇1		1	◇1	◇1	◇1	◇1	◇1		◇1	◇1		◇1		◇1	1
				A			A								B	C						A			
		🍴	🍴	🛒	🍴	🍴	🛒	🚌	🍴				🍴	🍴	🛒	🛒	🍴			🍴		🛒		🍴	
Crewe	d	08 43	08 53	09 05	09 13	09 43		09 53	10 14	10 20		10 37	10 43	10 55			11 14		11 38	11 49					12 22
Alsager	d							10 10				10 46							11 46						
Kidsgrove	d							10 24				10 50							11 52						
Hanley Bus Station	d																								
Stoke-on-Trent	d						10 07	10 41				10 58			11 07	11 07			11 59			12 07			
Wedgwood Old Road Bridge	d																								
Barlaston Orchard Place	d																								
Stone Granville Square	d							10 57																	
Stone	d											11 06							12 08						
Norton Bridge Station Drv	d																								
Stafford	d	09 02		09 26	09 32		10 27	11a17	10 33	10a42		11a17			11 28	11 27	11 33		12 18			12 25		12 36	12a42
Rugeley Trent Valley	d																		12 28						
Lichfield Trent Valley	d																		12 35						
Tamworth	d																		12 42						
Polesworth	d																								
Atherstone	d																		12 51						
Nuneaton	a				09 54				10 55								12 04		12 58	12 30					
	d				09 55				10 56								12 05		12 58	12 31			12 30		
Bedworth	d																						12 36		
Coventry	a			10 24			11 24								12 24	12 24						13 24	12 54		
Rugby	a					10 31							11 31						13 17						
Northampton	a																		13 39						
Milton Keynes Central	a		10 17			11 06			11 49				12 05						14 04	13 03					
Watford Junction	a	10s34			11s16	11s42								12s34			12s54		14 33						
London Euston ⊖	a	10 56	11 06		11 39	12 04			12 37				12 44	12 56			13 15		14 53	13 44				14 06	

		VT		VT	XC	VT		LM	VT		LM	XC	LM	VT	VT	LM		VT		VT	XC	LM	VT	LM	VT
		◇1		◇1	◇1	◇1		1	◇1		◇1	◇1		◇1	◇1	1		◇1		◇1	◇1		◇1	1	◇1
					A							A									A				
		🍴		🍴	🛒	🍴			🍴			🛒		🍴	🍴			🍴		🍴	🛒		🍴		🍴
Crewe	d	12 30		12 54				13 22	13 30		13 38			13 51		14 22		14 29		14 56				15 22	15 29
Alsager	d										13 46														
Kidsgrove	d										13 51														
Hanley Bus Station	d																								
Stoke-on-Trent	d				13 07						13 59	14 07									15 07				
Wedgwood Old Road Bridge	d																								
Barlaston Orchard Place	d																								
Stone Granville Square	d																								
Stone	d										14 07														
Norton Bridge Station Drv	d																								
Stafford	d				13 25	13 36		13a43			14 17	14 25			14 36	14a43					15 25		15 36	15a43	
Rugeley Trent Valley	d										14 29														
Lichfield Trent Valley	d										14 36														
Tamworth	d										14 43														
Polesworth	d																								
Atherstone	d										14 52														
Nuneaton	a										14 58			14 31											
	d										14 58		14 11	14 32								15 11			
Bedworth	d												14 17									15 17			
Coventry	a				14 24							15 24	14 34								16 24	15 34			
Rugby	a										15 17														
Northampton	a										15 39														
Milton Keynes Central	a			14 04							16 04			15 04						16 04					
Watford Junction	a										16 33														
London Euston ⊖	a	14 12		14 45		15 03			15 11		16 53			15 45	16 03			16 11		16 44			17 03		17 11

A 🛒 to Stafford

B from 18 July until 5 September. 🛒 to Stafford

C from 12 September. 🛒 to Stafford

Table 67

Crewe and Stoke-on-Trent - London Nuneaton - Coventry

		LM		LM ◇1	VT ◇1 ☕	XC ◇1 A 🛒	VT ◇1 ☕	LM 1	VT ◇1 ☕	VT ◇1 ☕	XC ◇1 A 🛒	LM		VT ◇1 ☕	LM 1	VT ◇1 ☕	LM	LM ◇1	VT ◇1 ☕	XC ◇1 A 🛒	VT ◇1 ☕	LM 1		VT ◇1 ☕	VT ◇1 ☕
Crewe	d			15 38	15 56			16 22	16 29	16 53					17 22	17 29		17 38	17 55			18 22		18 29	18 55
Alsager	d			15 46														17 46							
Kidsgrove	d			15 52														17 51							
Hanley Bus Station	d																								
Stoke-on-Trent	d			15 59		16 07					17 08							17 59		18 08					
Wedgwood Old Road Bridge	d																								
Barlaston Orchard Place	d																								
Stone Granville Square	d																								
Stone	d			16 08														18 07							
Norton Bridge Station Drv	d																								
Stafford	d			16 18		16 25	16 37	16a43			17 26			17 36	17a43			18 18		18 26	18 36	18a43			
Rugeley Trent Valley	d			16 28														18 27							
Lichfield Trent Valley	d			16 35						17 26								18 35							
Tamworth	d			16 42														18 42							
Polesworth	d																								
Atherstone	d			16 51														18 51							
Nuneaton	a			16 58														18 58							
	d	16 11		16 58								17 11					18 11	18 58							
Bedworth	d	16 17										17 17					18 17								
Coventry	a	16 34				17 24					18 24	17 34					18 34			19 24					
Rugby	a			17 18														19 18							
Northampton	a			17 39														19 39							
Milton Keynes Central	a			18 04	17 03					18 02								20 06	19 03						20 03
Watford Junction	a			18 35														20 33							
London Euston 15	⊖ a			18 53	17 44		18 04		18 11	18 42				19 03		19 11		20 53	19 44		20 03			20 11	20 44

		XC ◇1 A 🛒	VT ◇1 ☕	LM 1	VT ◇1 ☕	LM	LM ◇1	XC ◇1 A 🛒		LM 1	VT ◇1 ☕	VT ◇1 ☕	XC ◇1 B 🛒	XC ◇1 C 🛒	AW ◇	LM 1	LM	VT ◇1 ☕		VT ◇1 ☕	XC ◇1 🛒	LM 1	XC ◇1 🛒		
Crewe	d			19 22	19 29		19 36			20 18	20 24	20 47			20b54	21 17		21 23		21 40		22 22			
Alsager	d						19 44																		
Kidsgrove	d						19 50																		
Hanley Bus Station	d																								
Stoke-on-Trent	d	19 07					19 57	20 07					20 48	20 47							21 47		22 47		
Wedgwood Old Road Bridge	d																								
Barlaston Orchard Place	d																								
Stone Granville Square	d																								
Stone	d						20 06																		
Norton Bridge Station Drv	d																								
Stafford	d	19 25	19 36	19a43			20 16	20 25		20a38	20 43		21a09	21a09	21a38	21 38		21 44		22a02	22a06	22a44	23a05		
Rugeley Trent Valley	d						20 28																		
Lichfield Trent Valley	d						20 35											21 59							
Tamworth	d						20 42											22 05							
Polesworth	d																								
Atherstone	d						20 51																		
Nuneaton	a						20 58											22 15							
	d					20 11	20 58										22 00	22 16							
Bedworth	d					20 17											22 06								
Coventry	a	20 24				20 34		21 23									22 21								
Rugby	a						21 16											22 28							
Northampton	a						21 39																		
Milton Keynes Central	a						22 10				21 36	21 55						23 04							
Watford Junction	a						22 52					22s31						23s36							
London Euston 15	⊖ a		21 04		21 14		23 13				22 29	22 53						23 57							

A 🛒 to Stafford
B from 24 October
C from 18 July until 17 October

Table 68

Northampton - Coventry - Birmingham - Wolverhampton - Stafford

		AW MX	LM MX ◇1	VT MO ◇1 ☕	VT MO ◇1 ☕	LM MO 1	VT MX ◇1 ☕	VT MO ◇1 ☕	VT MX ◇1 ☕	VT ◇1 ⊠		LM	XC ◇1 🛒	LM ◇1	LM	LM ◇1	LM ◇1	VT ◇1 A ⊠	VT ◇1 B ☕	XC ◇1 ☕		AW ◇ 🛒	LM	LM ◇1	LM
London Euston 15	⊖ d		21p46	21p55	22p25		22p30	23p25	23p30																
Northampton	d		22p56			23p32										05 17	05 42								
Long Buckby	d		23p06			23p42										05 27									
Rugby	d		23p16	23p22	23p49	23p52	00 01	00s49	01s02							05 37	06 05								
Coventry	a		23p29	23p33	23p59	00 06	00 11	00s58	01s13							05 49									
	d		23p29	23p34	00 01		00 11	01s00	01s14							05 49									
Canley	d		23p32																						
Tile Hill	d		23p36													05 54									
Berkswell	d		23p39																						
Hampton-in-Arden	d		23p44													06 00									
Birmingham International	✈ a		23p47	23p51	00 10		00 22	01s09	01s24							06 04									
	d		23p47	23p52	00 11		00 22	01s11	01s25							06 04							06 17		
Marston Green	d		23p50													06 07									
Lea Hall	d		23p54																				06 22		
Stechford	d		23p56																				06 25		
Adderley Park	d																						06 28		
Birmingham New Street 12	a		00 04	00 04	00 23		00 33	01s22	01s36							06 16							06 33		06 28
	d	23p32		00 08	00 26		00 36	01s25	01s39	05 30		05 51	05 57	06 01	06 06			06 17	06 17	06 20		06 24		06 36	06 38
Smethwick Rolfe Street	d														06 12										06 44
Smethwick Galton Bridge 7	d													06 08	06 14							06 30			06 46
Sandwell & Dudley	d											05 59			06 17										06 49
Dudley Port	d														06 20										06 52
Tipton	d														06 22										06 54
Coseley	d														06 25										06 57
Wolverhampton 7	a	00 02		00 27	00 55		01 03	01 54	02 07	05 47		06 09	06 14	06 19	06 31			06 34	06 34	06 38		06 42		06 51	07 03
	d	00 02								05 48		06 13	06 16	06 19				06 34	06 35	06 40		06 42		06 51	
Penkridge	d													06 29											
Stafford	a									06 01			06 29	06 35			06 58			06 53				07 05	

		LM 1	XC ◇1 🛒	LM ◇1	LM ◇1	LM		LM ◇1	VT ◇1 ⊠	AW ◇ 🛒	VT ◇1 ⊠	LM ◇1	LM	XC ◇1 🛒	LM ◇1	LM		VT ◇1 ⊠	XC ◇1 🛒	LM ◇1	LM ◇1	LM	VT ◇1 ⊠	LM	LM ◇1
London Euston 15	⊖ d										06 03							06 23			05 30		06 43		
Northampton	d			05 56				06 17				06 41									06 56				07 17
Long Buckby	d			06 06				06 27													07 06				07 27
Rugby	d			06 16				06 37			06 51	07 00									07 16				07 37
Coventry	a			06 28				06 49			07 02							07 22	07 22		07 28		07 42		07 49
	d	06 10		06 29				06 49			07 02					07 07		07 22	07 27		07 29		07 42		07 49
Canley	d	06 13		06 32												07 09					07 32				
Tile Hill	d	06 17		06 36				06 54								07 13					07 36				07 54
Berkswell	d	06 20		06 39												07 16					07 39				
Hampton-in-Arden	d	06 24						07 00								07 20									08 00
Birmingham International	✈ a	06 27		06 45				07 04			07 13					07 23		07 33	07 37		07 45		07 54		08 04
	d	06 28		06 45				07 04		07 09	07 13				07 17	07 24		07 33	07 38		07 45		07 55		08 04
Marston Green	d	06 31		06 48				07 07								07 27					07 48				08 07
Lea Hall	d			06 51											07 22						07 51				
Stechford	d			06 54											07 25						07 54				
Adderley Park	d														07 28						07 57				
Birmingham New Street 12	a	06 39		07 01				07 16		07 19	07 27				07 32	07 36		07 45	07 48	07 57	08 03		08 08		08 16
	d		06 57		07 01	07 08			07 19	07 22			07 27	07 31	07 36	07 38		07 49	07 57	08 01		08 05		08 08	
Smethwick Rolfe Street	d					07 14										07 44								08 14	
Smethwick Galton Bridge 7	d				07 08	07 16				07 28						07 46				08 08				08 16	
Sandwell & Dudley	d					07 19										07 49		07 58				08 13		08 19	
Dudley Port	d					07 22										07 52								08 22	
Tipton	d					07 24										07 54								08 24	
Coseley	d					07 27									07 46	07 57								08 27	
Wolverhampton 7	a		07 14		07 19	07 33			07 35	07 39			07 45	07 48	07 53	08 03		08 11	08 14	08 19		08 24		08 33	
	d		07 16		07 19				07 36	07 41			07 46	07 49	07 53				08 15	08 19		08 25			
Penkridge	d				07 30										08 03					08 29					
Stafford	a		07 29		07 36							07 53			08 09				08 29	08 35					

A until 16 July, from 6 September
B from 19 July until 3 September

Northampton - Coventry - Birmingham - Wolverhampton - Stafford

Station		VT		AW	VT	LM	XC	LM	LM	LM	LM	VT		XC	LM	LM	LM	VT	LM	LM	VT	AW		VT	VT
		◇1 ⊠		◇ ⊥	◇1 ⊠	1	◇1 ⊥		◇1		1	◇1 ⊠		◇1 ⊥	◇1	◇1		◇1 ⊠		◇1	◇1 ⊠	◇ ⊥		◇1 A ⊠	◇1 B ⊠
London Euston ⊖	d				07 03	06 24						07 23						07 43		06 53				08 03	08 03
Northampton	d					07 45									07 56					08b17					
Long Buckby	d														08 06					08 27					
Rugby	d				07 51	08 03									08 16					08 37				08 51	08 52
Coventry	a				08 02							08 22		08 23	08 28			08 42		08 49				09 02	09 03
	d				08 02						08 11	08 22		08 27	08 29			08 42		08 49				09 02	09 03
Canley	d										08 14				08 32										
Tile Hill	d										08 18				08 36					08 54					
Berkswell	d										08 21				08 39										
Hampton-in-Arden	d										08 25									09 00					
Birmingham International ✈	a				08 12						08 28	08 33		08 37	08 45			08 53		09 04				09 12	09 13
	d			08 09	08 13			08 17			08 29	08 33		08 38	08 45			08 53		09 04		09 09		09 14	09 14
Marston Green	d							08 20			08 32				08 48					09 07					
Lea Hall	d							08 23							08 51										
Stechford	d							08 26							08 54										
Adderley Park	d							08 29																	
Birmingham New Street	a			08 19	08 27		08 26	08 33		08 36	08 42	08 45		08 48	09 01			09 08		09 16		09 20		09 27	09 27
	d	08 20		08 24			08 31		08 36	08 38		08 49		08 57		09 01	09 05		09 08		09 20	09 24			
Smethwick Rolfe Street	d									08 44									09 14						
Smethwick Galton Bridge	d			08 30						08 46						09 08			09 16			09 30			
Sandwell & Dudley	d									08 49		08 58					09 13		09 19						
Dudley Port	d									08 52									09 22						
Tipton	d									08 54									09 24						
Coseley	d								08 46	08 57									09 27						
Wolverhampton	a	08 37		08 42			08 48		08 53	09 03		09 11		09 14		09 19	09 24		09 33		09 37	09 43			
	d	08 37		08 43			08 49		08 53					09 15		09 19	09 25				09 37	09 43			
Penkridge	d								09 03																
Stafford	a					08 53	09 00		09 09					09 29		09 34									

Station		LM	XC	LM	LM	LM	LM	VT		XC	LM	LM	LM	VT	LM	VT	LM	VT		AW	AW	VT	LM	XC	LM
		◇1	◇1 ⊥		◇1		1	◇1 ⊠		◇1 ⊥	◇1	◇1		◇1 A ⊠		◇1 B ⊠	◇1	◇1 A ⊐		C	◇ D ⊥	◇1 ⊠	◇1	◇1 ⊥	
London Euston ⊖	d	07 47						08 23						08 43		08 43	07 54					09 03	08 46		
Northampton	d	08 45									08 56						09c17						09 45		
Long Buckby	d										09 06						09 27								
Rugby	d	09 03									09 16						09 37					09 51	10 04		
Coventry	a							09 22		09 22	09 28			09 42		09 42	09 49					10 02			
	d						09 11	09 22		09 27	09 29			09 42		09 43	09 49					10 02			
Canley	d						09 14				09 32														
Tile Hill	d						09 18				09 36						09 54								
Berkswell	d						09 21				09 39														
Hampton-in-Arden	d						09 25										10 00								
Birmingham International ✈	a						09 28	09 33		09 37	09 45			09 53		09 53	10 04					10 13			
	d			09 17			09 29	09 33		09 38	09 45			09 54		09 54	10 04			10 09	10 09	10 13			10 17
Marston Green	d						09 32				09 48						10 07								
Lea Hall	d			09 22							09 51														10 22
Stechford	d			09 25							09 54														10 25
Adderley Park	d			09 28																					10 28
Birmingham New Street	a		09 26	09 33			09 42	09 45		09 48	10 01			10 08		10 08	10 16			10 19	10 19	10 27		10 26	10 33
	d		09 31		09 36	09 38		09 49		09 57		10 01	10 05		10 08	10 19		10 20		10 24	10 24			10 31	
Smethwick Rolfe Street	d					09 44									10 14										
Smethwick Galton Bridge	d					09 46						10 08			10 16					10 30	10 30				
Sandwell & Dudley	d					09 49		09 58					10 13		10 19										
Dudley Port	d					09 52									10 22										
Tipton	d					09 54									10 24										
Coseley	d				09 46	09 57									10 27										
Wolverhampton	a		09 48		09 53	10 03		10 11		10 14		10 19	10 24		10 33	10 36		10 37		10 42	10 42			10 48	
	d		09 49		09 53					10 15		10 19	10 25			10 38		10 37		10 43	10 43			10 49	
Penkridge	d				10 03																				
Stafford	a	09 53	10 00		10 09					10 29		10 34											10 53	11 00	

A until 16 July, from 6 September
B from 19 July until 3 September
C until 3 September
D from 6 September
b arr. 0806
c arr. 0908

Northampton - Coventry - Birmingham - Wolverhampton - Stafford

Station		LM	LM	LM		VT	XC	LM	LM	LM	LM	VT	LM	VT		AW	VT	LM	XC	LM	LM	LM	LM	VT	
		◇1		1		◇1 ⊠	◇1 ⊥	◇1	◇1			◇1 ⊠	◇1	◇1 ⊐		◇ ⊥	◇1 ⊐	◇1	◇1 ⊥		◇1		1	◇1 ⊐	
London Euston ⊖	d					09 23						09 43	08 54				10 03	09 46						10 23	
Northampton	d							09 56					10b17					10 45							
Long Buckby	d							10 06					10 27												
Rugby	d							10 16					10 37				10 51	11 04							
Coventry	a					10 22	10 22	10 28				10 42	10 49				11 02							11 22	
	d			10 11		10 22	10 27	10 29				10 42	10 49				11 02						11 11	11 22	
Canley	d			10 14				10 32															11 14		
Tile Hill	d			10 18				10 36					10 54										11 18		
Berkswell	d			10 21				10 39															11 21		
Hampton-in-Arden	d			10 25									11 00										11 25		
Birmingham International ✈	a			10 28		10 33	10 37	10 45				10 53	11 04				11 13						11 28	11 33	
	d			10 29		10 33	10 38	10 45				10 54	11 04			11 09	11 13			11 17			11 29	11 33	
Marston Green	d			10 32				10 48					11 07										11 32		
Lea Hall	d							10 51												11 22					
Stechford	d							10 54												11 25					
Adderley Park	d																			11 28					
Birmingham New Street	a		10 28	10 42		10 45	10 48	11 01			10 58	11 08	11 17			11 20	11 27		11 26	11 33		11 28	11 42	11 45	
	d	10 36	10 38			10 49	10 57		11 01	11 05	11 08			11 20		11 24			11 31		11 36	11 38		11 49	
Smethwick Rolfe Street	d		10 44								11 14											11 44			
Smethwick Galton Bridge	d		10 46						11 08		11 16					11 30						11 46			
Sandwell & Dudley	d		10 49			10 58				11 13	11 19											11 49		11 58	
Dudley Port	d		10 52								11 22											11 52			
Tipton	d		10 54								11 24											11 54			
Coseley	d	10 46	10 57								11 27										11 46	11 57			
Wolverhampton	a	10 53	11 03			11 11	11 14		11 19	11 24	11 33			11 37		11 42			11 48		11 53	12 03		12 11	
	d	10 53					11 15		11 19	11 25				11 37		11 43			11 49		11 53				
Penkridge	d	11 03																			12 03				
Stafford	a	11 09					11 28		11 34									11 53	12 00		12 09				

Station		XC	LM	LM	LM	LM	VT	LM	VT	AW		VT	LM	XC	LM	LM	LM	LM	VT	XC		LM	LM	LM	LM
		◇1 ⊥	◇1	◇1			◇1 ⊐	◇1	◇1 ⊐	◇ ⊥		◇1 ⊐	1	◇1 ⊥		◇1		1	◇1 ⊐	◇1 ⊥		◇1	◇1		
London Euston ⊖	d						10 43	09 54				11 03	10 46						11 23						
Northampton	d		10 56					11c17					11 45									11 56			
Long Buckby	d		11 06					11 27														12 06			
Rugby	d		11 16					11 37				11 51	12 03									12 16			
Coventry	a	11 22	11 28				11 42	11 49				12 02							12 22	12 24		12 28			
	d	11 27	11 29				11 42	11 49				12 02						12 11	12 22	12 27		12 29			
Canley	d		11 32															12 14				12 32			
Tile Hill	d		11 36					11 54										12 18				12 36			
Berkswell	d		11 39															12 21				12 39			
Hampton-in-Arden	d							12 00										12 25							
Birmingham International ✈	a	11 37	11 45				11 53	12 04				12 13						12 28	12 33	12 37		12 45			
	d	11 38	11 45				11 53	12 04		12 09		12 13			12 17			12 29	12 33	12 38		12 45			
Marston Green	d		11 48					12 07										12 32				12 48			
Lea Hall	d		11 51												12 22							12 51			
Stechford	d		11 54												12 25							12 54			
Adderley Park	d														12 28										
Birmingham New Street	a	11 48	12 01			11 58	12 08	12 17		12 20		12 27		12 26	12 33		12 28	12 42	12 45	12 48		13 01			12 58
	d	11 57		12 01	12 05	12 08			12 20	12 24				12 31		12 36	12 38		12 49	12 57			13 01	13 05	13 08
Smethwick Rolfe Street	d					12 14											12 44								13 14
Smethwick Galton Bridge	d			12 08		12 16				12 30							12 46						13 08		13 16
Sandwell & Dudley	d				12 13	12 19											12 49		12 58					13 13	13 19
Dudley Port	d					12 22											12 52								13 22
Tipton	d					12 24											12 54								13 24
Coseley	d					12 27										12 46	12 57								13 27
Wolverhampton	a	12 14		12 19	12 24	12 33			12 37	12 42				12 48		12 53	13 03		13 11	13 14			13 19	13 24	13 33
	d	12 15		12 19	12 25				12 37	12 43				12 49		12 53				13 15			13 19	13 25	
Penkridge	d															13 03									
Stafford	a	12 29		12 34									12 53	13 00		13 09				13 29			13 34		

b arr. 1006
c arr. 1109

Table 68

Mondays to Fridays

Northampton - Coventry - Birmingham - Wolverhampton - Stafford

		VT	VT	LM	VT	AW		VT	LM	XC	LM	LM	LM	VT	XC	LM		LM	LM	LM	VT	LM	VT	AW	VT
		◇1 A	◇1 B	◇1	◇1	◇		◇1	◇1	◇1		◇1	1	◇1	◇1	◇1		◇1			◇1	◇1	◇1	◇	◇1
London Euston ⊖	d	11 43	11 43	10 54				12 03	11 46					12 23							12 43	11 54			13 03
Northampton	d			12b17					12 45							12 56						13c17			
Long Buckby	d			12 27												13 06						13 27			
Rugby	d			12 37				12 51	13 04							13 16						13 37			13 51
Coventry	a	12 42	12 43	12 49				13 02						13 22	13 22	13 28					13 42	13 49			14 02
	d	12 42	12 43	12 49				13 02					13 11	13 22	13 27	13 29					13 42	13 49			14 02
Canley	d												13 14			13 32									
Tile Hill	d			12 54									13 18			13 36						13 54			
Berkswell	d												13 21			13 39									
Hampton-in-Arden	d			13 00									13 25									14 00			
Birmingham International ✈	a	12 53	12 54	13 04				13 13					13 28	13 33	13 37	13 45					13 53	14 04			14 13
	d	12 53	12 54	13 04		13 09		13 13			13 17		13 29	13 33	13 38	13 45					13 53	14 04		14 09	14 13
Marston Green	d			13 07									13 32			13 48						14 07			
Lea Hall	d										13 22					13 51									
Stechford	d										13 25					13 54									
Adderley Park	d										13 28														
Birmingham New Street 12	a	13 08	13 08	13 17		13 20		13 27		13 26	13 33		13 42	13 45	13 48	14 01				13 58	14 08	14 16		14 19	14 27
	d				13 20	13 24				13 31		13 36		13 49	13 57			14 01	14 05	14 08			14 20	14 24	
Smethwick Rolfe Street	d																			14 14					
Smethwick Galton Bridge 7	d					13 30												14 08		14 16				14 30	
Sandwell & Dudley	d													13 58					14 13	14 19					
Dudley Port	d																			14 22					
Tipton	d																			14 24					
Coseley	d											13 46								14 27					
Wolverhampton 7	a				13 37	13 42				13 48		13 53		14 11	14 14			14 19	14 24	14 33			14 37	14 42	
	d				13 37	13 43				13 49		13 53			14 15			14 19	14 25				14 37	14 43	
Penkridge	d											14 03													
Stafford	a								13 53	14 00		14 09			14 29			14 34							

		LM		XC	LM	LM	LM	LM	VT	XC	LM	LM		LM	LM	VT	VT	LM	VT	AW	VT	LM		XC	LM
		◇1		◇1		◇1		1	◇1	◇1	◇1	◇1				◇1 A	◇1 B	◇1	◇1 A	◇	◇1	1		◇1	
London Euston ⊖	d	12 46							13 23							13 43	13 43	12 54			14 03	13 46			
Northampton	d	13 45									13 56							14e17				14 45			
Long Buckby	d										14 06							14 27							
Rugby	d	14 03									14 16							14 37			14 51	15 04			
Coventry	a								14 22	14 22	14 28					14 42	14 43	14 49			15 02				
	d							14 11	14 22	14 27	14 29					14 42	14 43	14 49			15 02				
Canley	d							14 14			14 32														
Tile Hill	d							14 18			14 36							14 54							
Berkswell	d							14 21			14 39														
Hampton-in-Arden	d							14 25										15 00							
Birmingham International ✈	a							14 28	14 33	14 37	14 45					14 53	14 54	15 04			15 13				
	d				14 17			14 29	14 33	14 38	14 45					14 53	14 54	15 04		15 09	15 13				15 17
Marston Green	d							14 32			14 48							15 07							
Lea Hall	d				14 22						14 51														15 22
Stechford	d				14 25						14 54														15 25
Adderley Park	d				14 28																				15 28
Birmingham New Street 12	a			14 26	14 33		14 28	14 42	14 45	14 48	15 01				14 58	15 08	15 08	15 16		15 19	15 27			15 26	15 32
	d			14 31		14 36	14 38		14 49	14 57		15 01		15 05	15 08		15 20		15 20	15 26				15 31	
Smethwick Rolfe Street	d						14 44								15 14										
Smethwick Galton Bridge 7	d						14 46					15 08			15 16					15 32					
Sandwell & Dudley	d						14 49		14 58					15 13	15 19										
Dudley Port	d						14 52								15 22										
Tipton	d						14 54								15 24										
Coseley	d					14 46	14 57								15 27										
Wolverhampton 7	a			14 48		14 53	15 03		15 11	15 14		15 19		15 24	15 33		15 37		15 37	15 44				15 49	
	d			14 49		14 53				15 15		15 19		15 25			15 37		15 37	15 44				15 50	
Penkridge	d					15 03																			
Stafford	a	14 53		15 00		15 09				15 29		15 34										15 53			

A until 16 July, from 6 September
B from 19 July until 3 September
b arr. 1206
c arr. 1306
e arr. 1408

Table 68

Mondays to Fridays

Northampton - Coventry - Birmingham - Wolverhampton - Stafford

		LM	LM	LM	VT	XC	LM	LM		LM	LM	VT	LM	VT	AW	VT	LM	XC		LM	LM	LM	LM	VT	VT
		◇1		1	◇1	◇1	◇1	◇1				◇1	◇1	1	◇	◇1	◇1	◇1			◇1		1	◇1 A	◇1 B
London Euston ⊖	d				14 23							14 43	13 54			15 03	14 46							15 23	15 23
Northampton	d						14 56						15b17				15 45								
Long Buckby	d						15 06						15 27												
Rugby	d						15 16						15 37			15 51	16 03								
Coventry	a				15 22	15 24	15 28					15 42	15 49			16 02								16 22	16 22
	d			15 11	15 22	15 27	15 29					15 42	15 49			16 02							16 11	16 22	16 22
Canley	d			15 14			15 32																16 14		
Tile Hill	d			15 18			15 36						15 54										16 18		
Berkswell	d			15 21			15 39																16 21		
Hampton-in-Arden	d			15 25									16 00										16 25		
Birmingham International ✈	a			15 28	15 33	15 37	15 45					15 53	16 04			16 13							16 28	16 33	16 33
	d			15 29	15 33	15 38	15 45					15 53	16 04		16 09	16 13				16 17			16 29	16 33	16 33
Marston Green	d			15 32			15 48						16 07										16 32		
Lea Hall	d						15 51													16 22					
Stechford	d						15 54													16 25					
Adderley Park	d																			16 28					
Birmingham New Street 12	a		15 28	15 42	15 45	15 48	16 01				15 58	16 08	16 17		16 20	16 27		16 26		16 33		16 30	16 42	16 45	16 45
	d	15 36	15 38		15 49	15 57		16 01		16 05	16 08			16 20	16 24			16 31			16 36	16 38		16 49	16 49
Smethwick Rolfe Street	d		15 44								16 14											16 44			
Smethwick Galton Bridge 7	d		15 46					16 08			16 16				16 30							16 46			
Sandwell & Dudley	d		15 49		15 58					16 13	16 19											16 49		16 58	16 58
Dudley Port	d		15 52								16 22											16 53			
Tipton	d		15 54								16 24											16 55			
Coseley	d	15 46	15 57								16 27										16 46	16 58			
Wolverhampton 7	a	15 53	16 03		16 11	16 14		16 19		16 24	16 33			16 37	16 42			16 48			16 53	17 04		17 11	17 11
	d	15 53				16 15		16 19		16 25				16 37	16 43			16 49			16 53				
Penkridge	d	16 03																			17 03				
Stafford	a	16 09				16 29		16 34									16 53	17 00			17 09				

		XC	LM	LM		LM	LM	VT	LM	VT	AW	VT	LM	XC		LM	LM	LM	LM	LM	VT	XC	LM	LM
		◇1	◇1	◇1				◇1	◇1	1	◇	◇1	◇1	◇1			◇1		1		◇1	◇1	◇1	◇1
London Euston ⊖	d							15 43	14 54			16 03	15 46								16 23			
Northampton	d			15 56					16c17				16 45										16 56	
Long Buckby	d			16 06					16 27														17 06	
Rugby	d			16 16					16 37			16 51	17 03										17 16	
Coventry	a	16 22		16 28				16 42	16 49			17 02									17 22	17 23	17 28	
	d	16 27		16 29				16 42	16 49			17 02							17 11		17 22	17 27	17 29	
Canley	d			16 32															17 14				17 32	
Tile Hill	d			16 36					16 54										17 18				17 36	
Berkswell	d			16 39															17 21				17 39	
Hampton-in-Arden	d								17 00										17 25					
Birmingham International ✈	a	16 37		16 45				16 53	17 04			17 13							17 28		17 33	17 37	17 45	
	d	16 39		16 45				16 53	17 04		17 09	17 13				17 17			17 29		17 33	17 38	17 45	
Marston Green	d			16 48					17 07										17 32				17 48	
Lea Hall	d			16 51												17 22							17 51	
Stechford	d			16 54												17 25							17 54	
Adderley Park	d															17 28								
Birmingham New Street 12	a	16 48		17 02			16 59	17 08	17 16		17 19	17 27		17 26		17 33		17 28	17 42		17 45	17 48	18 01	
	d	16 57	17 01			17 05	17 08			17 20	17 26			17 31			17 36	17 38		17 46	17 49	17 57		18 01
Smethwick Rolfe Street	d						17 14											17 44						
Smethwick Galton Bridge 7	d		17 08				17 16				17 32							17 46						18 08
Sandwell & Dudley	d					17 13	17 19											17 49			17 58			
Dudley Port	d						17 22											17 52		17 56				
Tipton	d						17 24											17 54		17 58				
Coseley	d						17 27										17 47	17 57						
Wolverhampton 7	a	17 14	17 19			17 24	17 33			17 37	17 44			17 49			17 54	18 03		18 06	18 11	18 14		18 19
	d	17 15	17 19			17 25				17 37	17 44			17 50			17 54			18 07		18 15		18 19
Penkridge	d		17 29														18 04							18 29
Stafford	a	17 29	17 35										18 01	18 01			18 10					18 29		18 35

A from 19 July until 3 September
B until 16 July, from 6 September
b arr. 1508
c arr. 1606

Northampton - Coventry - Birmingham - Wolverhampton - Stafford

		LM	LM	VT	LM	VT	AW	VT	XC	LM		LM	LM	LM	VT	XC	LM	LM	LM	LM		VT	LM	VT	AW
				◇1 ☕	◇1	◇1 ☕	◇ 🛒	◇1 ⊠	◇1 🛒			◇1		1	◇1 ⊠	◇1 🛒	◇1	◇1				◇1 ⊠	◇1	◇1 ☕	◇ 🛒
London Euston 15 ⊖	d			16 43	15 54			17 03							17 23							17 43	17 13		
Northampton	d				17b17												17 56						18c17		
Long Buckby	d				17 27												18 06						18 27		
Rugby	d				17 37			17 51									18 16						18 37		
Coventry	a			17 42	17 49			18 02							18 22	18 22	18 28					18 42	18 49		
	d			17 42	17 49			18 02						18 11	18 22	18 27	18 29					18 42	18 49		
Canley	d													18 14			18 32								
Tile Hill	d				17 54									18 18			18 36						18 54		
Berkswell	d													18 21			18 39								
Hampton-in-Arden	d				18 00									18 25									19 00		
Birmingham International ✈	a			17 53	18 04			18 13						18 28	18 33	18 37	18 45					18 53	19 04		
	d			17 53	18 04		18 09	18 13		18 17				18 29	18 33	18 38	18 45					18 53	19 04		19 09
Marston Green	d				18 07									18 32			18 48						19 07		
Lea Hall	d									18 22							18 51								
Stechford	d									18 25							18 54								
Adderley Park	d									18 28															
Birmingham New Street 12	a		17 58	18 08	18 17		18 20	18 27	18 26	18 33			18 28	18 42	18 45	18 48	19 01			18 58		19 08	19 17		19 20
	d	18 05	18 08			18 20	18 24		18 31			18 36	18 38		18 49	18 57		19 01	19 05	19 08				19 20	19 24
Smethwick Rolfe Street	d		18 14										18 44							19 14					
Smethwick Galton Bridge 7	d		18 16				18 30						18 46					19 08		19 16					19 30
Sandwell & Dudley	d	18 13	18 19										18 49		18 58				19 13	19 19					
Dudley Port	d		18 22										18 52							19 22					
Tipton	d		18 24										18 54							19 24					
Coseley	d		18 27									18 46	18 57							19 27					
Wolverhampton 7 ⛴	a	18 24	18 33			18 37	18 42		18 48			18 53	19 03		19 11	19 14		19 19	19 24	19 33				19 37	19 42
	d	18 25				18 37	18 43		18 49			18 53				19 15		19 19	19 25					19 37	19 43
Penkridge	d											19 03						19 29							
Stafford	a											19 09				19 27		19 36							

		VT	LM	XC	LM	LM		LM	LM	VT	XC	LM	LM	LM	VT	LM	AW	VT	LM	XC	LM	LM	LM	LM	VT
		◇1 ⊠	1	◇1 🛒		◇1			1	◇1 ⊠	◇1 🛒	◇1			◇1 ⊠	◇1	◇	■ 1 ☕	◇1	◇1		◇1		1	■ 1 ☕
London Euston 15 ⊖	d	18 03	17 24							18 23					18 43	18 13		19 03	18 29						19 23
Northampton	d		18 41									18 56				19e17			19f45						
Long Buckby	d		18 51									19 06				19 27									
Rugby	d	18 51	19a03									19 16				19 37		19 51	20 03						
Coventry	a	19 02								19 22	19 22	19 28			19 42	19 49		20 02							20 22
	d	19 02							19 11	19 22	19 27	19 29			19 42	19 49		20 02						20 11	20 22
Canley	d								19 14			19 32												20 14	
Tile Hill	d								19 18			19 36				19 54								20 18	
Berkswell	d								19 21			19 39												20 21	
Hampton-in-Arden	d								19 25							20 00								20 25	
Birmingham International ✈	a	19 13							19 28	19 33	19 37	19 45			19 53	20 04		20 13						20 28	20 33
	d	19 13			19 17				19 29	19 33	19 38	19 45			19 53	20 04	20 09	20 13			20 17			20 29	20 33
Marston Green	d								19 32			19 48				20 07								20 32	
Lea Hall	d				19 22							19 51									20 22				
Stechford	d				19 25							19 54									20 25				
Adderley Park	d				19 28																20 28				
Birmingham New Street 12	a	19 27		19 26	19 33			19 28	19 42	19 45	19 48	20 01			20 08	20 16	20 20	20 27		20 28	20 33			20 42	20 45
	d			19 31		19 36		19 38		19 50	19 57		20 05	20 08	20 20		20 24			20 31		20 36	20 38		20 50
Smethwick Rolfe Street	d							19 44						20 14									20 44		
Smethwick Galton Bridge 7	d							19 46						20 16			20 30						20 46		
Sandwell & Dudley	d							19 49		19 59			20 13	20 19									20 49		20 59
Dudley Port	d							19 52						20 22									20 52		
Tipton	d							19 54						20 24									20 54		
Coseley	d					19 46		19 57						20 27								20 46	20 57		
Wolverhampton 7 ⛴	a			19 48		19 53		20 03		20 12	20 14		20 24	20 33	20 36		20 42			20 48		20 53	21 04		21 12
	d			19 49		19 53					20 16		20 25		20 36		20 43			20 49		20 53			
Penkridge	d					20 03																21 03			
Stafford	a			20 00		20 09					20 29				20 50							21 09			

b arr. 1706
c arr. 1811
e arr. 1910
f arr. 1939

Northampton - Coventry - Birmingham - Wolverhampton - Stafford

		XC		LM	LM	LM	VT	LM	VT	AW	VT	VT	LM		LM	LM	LM	VT	XC	LM	LM	VT	LM	LM	XC
		◇1 A 🛒		◇1			◇1 ☕	◇1	◇1 ☕	◇ 🛒	◇1 B ☕	◇1 C ☕			◇1		1	◇1 ☕	◇1	◇1		◇1 ☕	◇1		◇1
London Euston 15 ⊖	d			18 49			19 43				20 03	20 03						20 23				20 43	19 54		
Northampton	d			19b56				20 17												20 56			21c17		
Long Buckby	d			20 06				20 27												21 06			21 27		
Rugby	d			20 16				20 37			20 51	20 52								21 16			21 37		
Coventry	a	20 22		20 28			20 42	20 49			21 02	21 03						21 22	21 22	21 28		21 42	21 49		
	d	20 27		20 29			20 42	20 49			21 02	21 03					21 11	21 22	21 27	21 29		21 42	21 49		
Canley	d			20 32													21 14			21 32					
Tile Hill	d			20 36				20 54									21 18			21 36			21 54		
Berkswell	d			20 39													21 21			21 39					
Hampton-in-Arden	d							21 00									21 25						22 00		
Birmingham International ✈	a	20 37		20 45			20 53	21 04			21 13	21 13					21 28	21 33	21 37	21 44		21 53	22 04		
	d	20 38		20 45			20 53	21 04		21 09	21 13	21 13	21 17				21 29	21 33	21 38	21 45		21 53	22 04		
Marston Green	d			20 48				21 07									21 32			21 48			22 07		
Lea Hall	d			20 51									21 22							21 51					
Stechford	d			20 54									21 25							21 54					
Adderley Park	d												21 28												
Birmingham New Street 12	a	20 48		21 01			21 06	21 16		21 19	21 25	21 25	21 33				21 42	21 46	21 48	22 01		22 06	22 16		
	d	20 58			21 05	21 08	21 13		21 20	21 24	21 28	21 28			21 36	21 38		21 50	21 57		22 08	22 13		22 21	22 28
Smethwick Rolfe Street	d					21 14										21 44					22 14				
Smethwick Galton Bridge 7	d					21 16				21 30						21 46					22 16				
Sandwell & Dudley	d				21 13	21 19	21 24									21 49		21 59			22 19	22 24		22 29	
Dudley Port	d					21 22										21 52					22 22				
Tipton	d					21 24										21 54					22 24				
Coseley	d					21 27									21 46	21 57					22 27				
Wolverhampton 7 ⛴	a	21 15			21 24	21 33	21 38		21 41	21 42	21 56	21 56			21 53	22 03		22 12	22 14		22 33	22 38		22 41	22 45
	d	21 17			21 25				21 42						21 53				22 16					22 43	22 46
Penkridge	d														22 03										
Stafford	a	21 31							21 54						22 09				22 29						22 58

		VT	LM	LM	LM	LM	XC	AW		LM	LM	VT	LM	AW	XC	LM	VT	VT FX		VT FO
		◇1 ☕	◇1			1	◇1	◇ 🛒		◇1	◇1	◇1 ☕	◇1		◇1	◇1	◇1 ☕	◇1 ☕		◇1 ☕
London Euston 15 ⊖	d	21 03								20 46		21 43	21 13			21 46	22 30	23 30		23 30
Northampton	d									21e56			22 17			22 56				
Long Buckby	d									22 06			22 27			23 06				
Rugby	d	21 57								22 16			22 39			23 16	00 01	01s02		01s07
Coventry	a	22 07					22 22			22 29		22 46	22 50		23 25	23 29	00 11	01s13		01s18
	d	22 07				22 11	22 24			22 29		22 46	22 50		23 27	23 29	00 11	01s14		01s19
Canley	d					22 14				22 32						23 32				
Tile Hill	d					22 18				22 36			22 55			23 36				
Berkswell	d					22 21				22 39						23 39				
Hampton-in-Arden	d					22 25							23 02			23 44				
Birmingham International ✈	a	22 18				22 28	22 33			22 45		23 00	23 06		23 36	23 47	00 22	01s24		01s29
	d	22 18		22 22		22 29	22 34			22 45		23 01	23 06		23 37	23 47	00 22	01s25		01s30
Marston Green	d					22 32				22 48			23 09			23 50				
Lea Hall	d			22 27						22 51						23 54				
Stechford	d			22 30						22 54						23 56				
Adderley Park	d			22 33																
Birmingham New Street 12	a	22 29		22 38		22 42	22 45			23 03		23 16	23 19		23 49	00 04	00 33	01s36		01s41
	d	22 32	22 36		22 38			22 55			23 09	23 20		23 32			00 36	01s39		01s44
Smethwick Rolfe Street	d				22 44						23 15									
Smethwick Galton Bridge 7	d		22 43		22 46						23 17									
Sandwell & Dudley	d	22 42			22 49						23 20	23 34								
Dudley Port	d				22 52						23 24									
Tipton	d				22 54						23 26									
Coseley	d		22 50		22 57						23 29									
Wolverhampton 7 ⛴	a	22 56	22 57		23 03			23 11			23 35	23 47		00 02			01 03	02 07		02 10
	d		22 57					23 13			23 36			00 02						
Penkridge	d		23 07								23 46									
Stafford	a		23 13					23 30			23 52									

A 🛒 to Birmingham International
B until 16 July, from 6 September
C from 19 July until 3 September
b arr. 1949
c arr. 2106
e arr. 2150

Northampton - Coventry - Birmingham - Wolverhampton - Stafford

Station		AW	LM ◇1	VT ◇1	VT ◇1	VT ◇1	LM ◇1	XC ◇1	LM ◇1	LM	VT ◇1 A	VT ◇1 B	AW ◇	XC ◇1	LM	LM ◇1	LM	LM 1	XC ◇1	LM ◇1	LM ◇1	LM	LM
London Euston 15 ⊖	d		21p46	22p30	23p30																		
Northampton	d		22p56				05 42													05 56			
Long Buckby	d		23p06																	06 06			
Rugby	d		23p16	00 01	01s07		06 05													06 16			
Coventry	a		23p29	00 11	01s18															06 28			
	d		23p29	00 11	01s19													06 10		06 29			
Canley	d		23p32															06 13		06 32			
Tile Hill	d		23p36															06 17		06 36			
Berkswell	d		23p39															06 20		06 39			
Hampton-in-Arden	d		23p44															06 24					
Birmingham International ✈	a		23p47	00 22	01s29													06 27		06 45			
	d		23p47	00 22	01s30										06 17			06 28		06 45			
Marston Green	d		23p50															06 31		06 48			
Lea Hall	d		23p54												06 21					06 51			
Stechford	d		23p56												06 24					06 54			
Adderley Park	d														06 27								
Birmingham New Street 12	a		00 04	00 33	01s41										06 32		06 28	06 39		07 01			06 58
	d	23p32		00 36	01s44	05 30		05 57	06 01	06 08	06 20	06 20	06 24	06 31		06 36	06 38		06 57		07 01	07 05	07 08
Smethwick Rolfe Street	d									06 14							06 44						07 14
Smethwick Galton Bridge 7	d								06 07	06 16			06 30				06 46				07 07		07 16
Sandwell & Dudley	d									06 19							06 49					07 13	07 19
Dudley Port	d									06 22							06 52						07 22
Tipton	d									06 24							06 54						07 24
Coseley	d									06 27							06 57						07 27
Wolverhampton 7	a	00 02		01 03	02 10	05 47		06 14	06 18	06 33	06 37	06 36	06 42	06 48		06 54	07 03		07 14		07 18	07 24	07 33
	d	00 02				05 48		06 16	06 18		06 37	06 36	06 42	06 49		06 54			07 14		07 18	07 25	
Penkridge	d								06 29												07 30		
Stafford	a					06 00	06 54	06 29	06 35					07 00		07 08			07 29		07 36		

Station		LM ◇1	LM ◇1	VT ◇1	AW ◇	XC ◇1	LM	LM ◇1	LM	LM 1	VT ◇1	XC ◇1	LM ◇1	LM ◇1	LM	LM	LM ◇1	VT ◇1	AW ◇	VT ◇1	LM ◇1	XC ◇1	LM
London Euston 15 ⊖	d										06 23									07 03	06 24		
Northampton	d	06 17	06 38										06 56				07 17				07b45		
Long Buckby	d	06 27											07 06				07 27						
Rugby	d	06 37	06 56										07 16				07 37			07 51	08 04		
Coventry	a	06 49									07 22	07 24	07 28				07 49			08 02			
	d	06 49								07 10	07 22	07 27	07 29				07 49			08 02			
Canley	d									07 13			07 32										
Tile Hill	d	06 54								07 17			07 36				07 54						
Berkswell	d									07 20			07 39										
Hampton-in-Arden	d	07 00								07 24							08 00						
Birmingham International ✈	a	07 04								07 27	07 33	07 39	07 45				08 04			08 13			
	d	07 04			07 09		07 17			07 28	07 33	07 40	07 45				08 04		08 09	08 13			08 17
Marston Green	d	07 07								07 31			07 48				08 07						
Lea Hall	d						07 21						07 51										08 21
Stechford	d						07 24						07 54										08 24
Adderley Park	d						07 27																08 27
Birmingham New Street 12	a	07 16			07 20		07 32			07 42	07 45	07 51	08 01			07 58	08 16		08 20	08 27		08 26	08 32
	d			07 20	07 24	07 31		07 36	07 38		07 49	07 57		08 01	08 05	08 08		08 20	08 24			08 31	
Smethwick Rolfe Street	d								07 44							08 14							
Smethwick Galton Bridge 7	d				07 30				07 46					08 08		08 16			08 30				
Sandwell & Dudley	d								07 49		07 58				08 13	08 19							
Dudley Port	d								07 52							08 22							
Tipton	d								07 54							08 24							
Coseley	d							07 46	07 57							08 27							
Wolverhampton 7	a			07 37	07 42	07 48		07 53	08 03		08 11	08 14		08 19	08 24	08 33		08 37	08 42			08 48	
	d			07 37	07 42	07 49		07 53				08 15		08 19	08 25			08 37	08 43			08 49	
Penkridge	d							08 03						08 29									
Stafford	a		07 53			08 00		08 09				08 29		08 35							08 53	09 00	

A until 10 July, from 11 September

B from 17 July until 4 September

b arr. 0740

Northampton - Coventry - Birmingham - Wolverhampton - Stafford

Station		LM ◇1	LM	LM 1	VT ◇1	XC ◇1	LM ◇1	LM ◇1	LM	LM	VT ◇1	LM ◇1	VT ◇1	AW ◇	VT ◇1	LM ◇1	XC ◇1	LM	LM ◇1	LM	LM 1	VT ◇1
London Euston 15 ⊖	d				07 23						07 43				08 03	07 46						08 23
Northampton	d						07 56					08 17				08 45						
Long Buckby	d						08 06					08 27										
Rugby	d						08 16					08 37			08 51	09 04						
Coventry	a				08 22	08 22	08 28				08 42	08 49			09 02							09 22
	d			08 11	08 22	08 27	08 29				08 42	08 49			09 02						09 11	09 23
Canley	d			08 14			08 32														09 14	
Tile Hill	d			08 18			08 36					08 54									09 18	
Berkswell	d			08 21			08 39														09 21	
Hampton-in-Arden	d			08 25								09 00									09 25	
Birmingham International ✈	a			08 28	08 33	08 37	08 45				08 53	09 04			09 13						09 28	09 33
	d			08 29	08 33	08 38	08 45				08 53	09 04		09 09	09 13			09 17			09 29	09 34
Marston Green	d			08 32			08 48					09 07									09 32	
Lea Hall	d						08 51											09 21				
Stechford	d						08 54											09 24				
Adderley Park	d																	09 27				
Birmingham New Street 12	a		08 28	08 42	08 45	08 48	09 01			08 58	09 08	09 16		09 20	09 27		09 26	09 32		09 29	09 42	09 45
	d	08 36	08 38		08 49	08 57		09 01	09 05	09 08			09 20	09 24			09 31		09 36	09 38		09 49
Smethwick Rolfe Street	d		08 44							09 14										09 44		
Smethwick Galton Bridge 7	d		08 46					09 08		09 16				09 30						09 46		
Sandwell & Dudley	d		08 49		08 58				09 13	09 19										09 49		09 58
Dudley Port	d		08 52							09 22										09 52		
Tipton	d		08 55							09 24										09 54		
Coseley	d	08 46	08 57							09 27									09 46	09 57		
Wolverhampton 7	a	08 53	09 03		09 11	09 14		09 19	09 24	09 33			09 37	09 42			09 48		09 53	10 03		10 11
	d	08 53				09 15		09 19	09 25				09 37	09 43			09 49		09 53			
Penkridge	d	09 03																	10 03			
Stafford	a	09 09				09 29		09 34								09 53	10 00		10 09			

Station		XC ◇1	LM ◇1	LM ◇1	LM	LM	VT ◇1 A	VT ◇1 B	LM ◇1	VT ◇1 A	AW ◇	VT ◇1	LM ◇1	XC ◇1	LM	LM ◇1	LM	LM 1	VT ◇1 A	VT ◇1 B	XC ◇1	LM ◇1	LM ◇1
London Euston 15 ⊖	d						08 43	08 43				09 03	08 46						09 23	09 23			
Northampton	d		08 56						09 17				09b45									09 56	
Long Buckby	d		09 06						09 27													10 06	
Rugby	d		09 16						09 37			09 52	10 04									10 16	
Coventry	a	09 22	09 28				09 42	09 42	09 49			10 03							10 22	10 23	10 22	10 28	
	d	09 27	09 29				09 42	09 42	09 49			10 03						10 11	10 22	10 23	10 27	10 29	
Canley	d		09 32															10 14				10 32	
Tile Hill	d		09 36						09 54									10 18				10 36	
Berkswell	d		09 39															10 21				10 39	
Hampton-in-Arden	d								10 00									10 25					
Birmingham International ✈	a	09 37	09 45				09 53	09 53	10 04			10 14						10 28	10 33	10 33	10 37	10 45	
	d	09 39	09 45				09 53	09 53	10 04		10 09	10 14			10 17			10 29	10 33	10 33	10 38	10 45	
Marston Green	d		09 48						10 07									10 32				10 48	
Lea Hall	d		09 51												10 21							10 51	
Stechford	d		09 54												10 24							10 54	
Adderley Park	d														10 27								
Birmingham New Street 12	a	09 48	10 01			09 58	10 08	10 08	10 16		10 19	10 27		10 26	10 32		10 29	10 42	10 45	10 45	10 48	11 01	
	d	09 57		10 01	10 05	10 08		10 20		10 20	10 24			10 31		10 36	10 38		10 49	10 49	10 57		11 01
Smethwick Rolfe Street	d					10 14											10 44						
Smethwick Galton Bridge 7	d			10 08		10 16					10 30						10 46						11 08
Sandwell & Dudley	d				10 13	10 19											10 49		10 58	10 58			
Dudley Port	d					10 22											10 52						
Tipton	d					10 24											10 54						
Coseley	d					10 27										10 46	10 57						
Wolverhampton 7	a	10 14		10 19	10 24	10 33		10 37		10 37	10 42			10 48		10 53	11 03		11 11	11 11	11 14		11 19
	d	10 15		10 19	10 25			10 37		10 37	10 43			10 49		10 53					11 15		11 19
Penkridge	d															11 03							
Stafford	a	10 29		10 35									10 53	11 00		11 09					11 29		11 35

A until 10 July, from 11 September

B from 17 July until 4 September

b arr. 0939

Northampton - Coventry - Birmingham - Wolverhampton - Stafford

	LM	LM	VT ◇1	LM ◇1	VT ◇1	AW ◇	VT ◇1	LM 1	XC ◇1	LM	LM ◇1	LM	LM 1	VT ◇1	XC ◇1	LM ◇1	LM ◇1	LM	LM	VT ◇1	LM ◇1
London Euston 15 ⊖ d			09 43				10 03	09 46						10 23						10 43	
Northampton d				10 17				10 45								10 56					11 17
Long Buckby d				10 27												11 06					11 27
Rugby d				10 37			10 51	11 04								11 16					11 37
Coventry a			10 42	10 49			11 02							11 22	11 22	11 28				11 42	11 49
Coventry d			10 42	10 49			11 02						11 11	11 22	11 27	11 29				11 42	11 49
Canley d													11 14			11 32					
Tile Hill d				10 54									11 18			11 36					11 54
Berkswell d													11 21			11 39					
Hampton-in-Arden d				11 00									11 25								12 00
Birmingham International ✈ a			10 53	11 04			11 13						11 28	11 33	11 37	11 45				11 53	12 04
Birmingham International d			10 53	11 04		11 09	11 13			11 17			11 29	11 33	11 38	11 45				11 53	12 04
Marston Green d				11 07									11 32			11 48					12 07
Lea Hall d										11 21						11 51					
Stechford d										11 24						11 54					
Adderley Park d										11 27											
Birmingham New Street 12 a		10 58	11 08	11 16		11 20	11 27		11 26	11 32		11 28	11 42	11 45	11 48	12 01			11 58	12 08	12 16
Birmingham New Street d	11 05	11 08			11 20	11 24			11 31		11 36	11 38		11 49	11 57		12 01	12 05	12 08		
Smethwick Rolfe Street d		11 14										11 44							12 14		
Smethwick Galton Bridge 7 d		11 16				11 30						11 46					12 08		12 16		
Sandwell & Dudley d	11 13	11 19										11 49		11 58				12 13	12 19		
Dudley Port d		11 22										11 52							12 22		
Tipton d		11 24										11 54							12 24		
Coseley d		11 27									11 46	11 57							12 27		
Wolverhampton 7 a	11 24	11 33			11 37	11 42			11 48		11 53	12 03		12 11	12 14		12 19	12 24	12 33		
Wolverhampton d	11 25				11 37	11 43			11 49		11 53				12 15		12 19	12 25			
Penkridge d											12 03										
Stafford a								11 53	12 00		12 09				12 29		12 35				

	VT ◇1	VT ◇1 A	AW ◇	VT ◇1	LM ◇1	XC ◇1 B	XC ◇1 C	LM	LM ◇1	LM	LM 1	VT ◇1	XC ◇1	LM ◇1	LM ◇1	LM	LM	VT ◇1	LM ◇1	VT ◇1	VT ◇1 A	AW ◇
London Euston 15 ⊖ d				11 03	10 46							11 23						11 43				
Northampton d					11 45									11 56					12 17			
Long Buckby d														12 06					12 27			
Rugby d				11 51	12 04									12 16					12 37			
Coventry a				12 02								12 22	12 22	12 28				12 42	12 49			
Coventry d				12 02							12 11	12 22	12 27	12 29				12 42	12 49			
Canley d											12 14			12 32								
Tile Hill d											12 18			12 36					12 54			
Berkswell d											12 21			12 39								
Hampton-in-Arden d											12 25								13 00			
Birmingham International ✈ a				12 13							12 28	12 33	12 37	12 45				12 53	13 04			
Birmingham International d			12 09	12 13				12 17			12 29	12 33	12 38	12 45				12 53	13 04			13 09
Marston Green d											12 32			12 48					13 07			
Lea Hall d								12 21						12 51								
Stechford d								12 24						12 54								
Adderley Park d								12 27														
Birmingham New Street 12 a			12 20	12 27		12 26	12 26	12 32		12 28	12 42	12 45	12 48	13 01			12 58	13 08	13 16			13 20
Birmingham New Street d	12 20	12 20	12 24			12 31	12 31		12 36	12 38		12 49	12 57		13 01	13 05	13 08			13 20	13 20	13 23
Smethwick Rolfe Street d										12 44							13 14					
Smethwick Galton Bridge 7 d			12 30							12 46					13 08		13 16					13 29
Sandwell & Dudley d										12 49		12 58				13 13	13 19					
Dudley Port d										12 52							13 22					
Tipton d										12 54							13 24					
Coseley d									12 46	12 57							13 27					
Wolverhampton 7 a	12 37	12 37	12 42			12 48	12 48		12 53	13 03		13 11	13 14		13 19	13 24	13 33			13 37	13 37	13 42
Wolverhampton d	12 37	12 37	12 43			12 49	12 49		12 53				13 15		13 19	13 25				13 37	13 37	13 43
Penkridge d									13 03													
Stafford a					12 53	13 00	13 00		13 09				13 29		13 35							

A from 23 October B until 4 September C from 11 September

Table 68 — Saturdays

Northampton - Coventry - Birmingham - Wolverhampton - Stafford

	VT ◇1	LM ◇1	XC ◇1	LM	LM ◇1	LM	LM 1	VT ◇1	XC ◇1	LM ◇1	LM ◇1	LM	LM	VT ◇1	LM ◇1	VT ◇1	AW ◇	VT ◇1	LM ◇1	XC ◇1	LM	LM ◇1
London Euston 15 ⊖ d	12 03	11 46						12 23						12 43				13 03	12 46			
Northampton d		12 45								12 56					13 17				13 45			
Long Buckby d										13 06					13 27							
Rugby d	12 51	13 04								13 16					13 37			13 51	14 04			
Coventry a	13 02							13 22	13 22	13 28				13 42	13 49			14 02				
Coventry d	13 02						13 11	13 22	13 27	13 29				13 42	13 49			14 02				
Canley d							13 14			13 32												
Tile Hill d							13 18			13 36					13 54							
Berkswell d							13 21			13 39												
Hampton-in-Arden d							13 25								14 00							
Birmingham International ✈ a	13 13						13 28	13 33	13 37	13 45				13 53	14 04			14 13				
Birmingham International d	13 13			13 17			13 29	13 33	13 38	13 45				13 53	14 04		14 09	14 13			14 17	
Marston Green d							13 32			13 48					14 07							
Lea Hall d				13 21						13 51											14 21	
Stechford d				13 24						13 54											14 24	
Adderley Park d				13 27																	14 27	
Birmingham New Street 12 a	13 27		13 26	13 32		13 28	13 42	13 45	13 48	14 01			13 58	14 08	14 16		14 19	14 27		14 26	14 32	
Birmingham New Street d			13 31		13 36	13 38		13 49	13 57		14 01	14 05	14 08			14 20	14 24			14 31		14 36
Smethwick Rolfe Street d						13 44							14 14									
Smethwick Galton Bridge 7 d						13 46					14 08		14 16				14 30					
Sandwell & Dudley d						13 49		13 58				14 13	14 19									
Dudley Port d						13 52							14 22									
Tipton d						13 54							14 24									
Coseley d					13 46	13 57							14 27									14 46
Wolverhampton 7 a			13 48		13 53	14 03		14 11	14 14		14 19	14 24	14 33			14 37	14 42			14 48		14 53
Wolverhampton d			13 49		13 53				14 15		14 19	14 25				14 37	14 43			14 49		14 53
Penkridge d					14 03																	15 03
Stafford a		13 53	14 00		14 09				14 29		14 35								14 53	15 00		15 09

	EM	LM 1	VT ◇1	XC ◇1	LM ◇1	LM ◇1	LM	LM	VT ◇1 A	VT ◇1 B	LM ◇1	VT ◇1 A	VT ◇1 C	AW ◇	VT ◇1 A	VT ◇1 B	LM ◇1	XC ◇1	LM	LM ◇1	LM
London Euston 15 ⊖ d			13 23						13 43	13 43					14 03	14 03	13 46				
Northampton d					13 56						14 17						14 45				
Long Buckby d					14 06						14 27										
Rugby d					14 16						14 37				14 51	14 52	15 04				
Coventry a			14 22	14 22	14 28				14 42	14 43	14 49				15 02	15 03					
Coventry d		14 11	14 22	14 27	14 29				14 42	14 43	14 49				15 02	15 03					
Canley d		14 14			14 32																
Tile Hill d		14 18			14 36						14 54										
Berkswell d		14 21			14 39																
Hampton-in-Arden d		14 25									15 00										
Birmingham International ✈ a		14 28	14 33	14 37	14 45				14 53	14 54	15 04				15 13	15 13					
Birmingham International d		14 29	14 33	14 38	14 45				14 53	14 54	15 04			15 09	15 13	15 13			15 17		
Marston Green d		14 32			14 48						15 07										
Lea Hall d					14 51														15 21		
Stechford d					14 54														15 24		
Adderley Park d																			15 27		
Birmingham New Street 12 a	14 28	14 42	14 45	14 48	15 01			14 58	15 08	15 08	15 16			15 20	15 27	15 27		15 26	15 32		15 28
Birmingham New Street d	14 38		14 49	14 57		15 01	15 05	15 08		15 20		15 20	15 20	15 24				15 31		15 36	15 38
Smethwick Rolfe Street d	14 44							15 14													15 44
Smethwick Galton Bridge 7 d	14 46					15 08		15 16						15 30							15 46
Sandwell & Dudley d	14 49		14 58				15 13	15 19													15 49
Dudley Port d	14 52							15 22													15 52
Tipton d	14 54							15 24													15 54
Coseley d	14 57							15 27												15 46	15 57
Wolverhampton 7 a	15 03		15 11	15 14		15 19	15 24	15 33		15 37		15 37	15 37	15 42				15 48		15 53	16 03
Wolverhampton d				15 15		15 19	15 25			15 37		15 37	15 37	15 43				15 49		15 53	
Penkridge d																				16 03	
Stafford a				15 29		15 35											15 53	16 00		16 09	

A until 10 July, from 11 September B from 17 July until 4 September C from 23 October

Table 68

Saturdays

Northampton - Coventry - Birmingham - Wolverhampton - Stafford

		LM	VT	XC	LM	LM	LM	LM	VT	LM	VT	VT	AW	VT	LM	XC	LM	LM	LM	LM	VT	XC	LM
		1	◇1	◇1	◇1	◇1			◇1	◇1	◇1	◇1	■	◇1	◇1	◇1		◇1		1	◇1	◇1	◇1
											A												
			⊡	⊼					⊡		⊡	⊡	⊼	⊡		⊡					⊡	⊼	
London Euston 15 ⊖	d		14 23						14 43					15 03	14 46						15 23		
Northampton	d				14 56					15 17					15 45								15 56
Long Buckby	d				15 06					15 27													16 06
Rugby	d				15 16					15 37				15 51	16 04								16 16
Coventry	a		15 22	15 22	15 28				15 42	15 49				16 02							16 22	16 22	16 28
	d	15 11	15 22	15 27	15 29				15 42	15 49				16 02						16 11	16 22	16 27	16 29
Canley	d	15 14			15 32															16 14			16 32
Tile Hill	d	15 18			15 36					15 54										16 18			16 36
Berkswell	d	15 21			15 39															16 21			16 39
Hampton-in-Arden	d	15 25								16 00										16 25			
Birmingham International ✈	a	15 28	15 33	15 37	15 45				15 53	16 04				16 13						16 28	16 33	16 37	16 45
	d	15 29	15 33	15 38	15 45				15 53	16 04			16 09	16 13			16 17			16 29	16 33	16 38	16 45
Marston Green	d	15 32			15 48					16 07										16 32			16 48
Lea Hall	d				15 51												16 21						16 51
Stechford	d				15 54												16 24						16 54
Adderley Park	d																16 27						
Birmingham New Street 12	a	15 42	15 45	15 48	16 01			15 58	16 08	16 16			16 20	16 27		16 26	16 32		16 28	16 42	16 45	16 48	17 01
	d		15 49	15 57		16 01	16 05	16 08			16 20	16 20	16 24			16 31		16 36	16 38		16 49	16 57	
Smethwick Rolfe Street	d							16 14											16 44				
Smethwick Galton Bridge 7	d					16 08		16 16					16 30						16 46				
Sandwell & Dudley	d		15 58				16 13	16 19											16 49		16 58		
Dudley Port	d							16 22											16 52				
Tipton	d							16 24											16 54				
Coseley	d							16 27										16 46	16 57				
Wolverhampton 7 ⇌	a		16 11	16 14		16 19	16 24	16 33			16 36	16 37	16 42			16 48		16 53	17 04		17 11	17 14	
	d			16 15		16 19	16 25				16 37	16 37	16 43			16 49		16 53				17 15	
Penkridge	d																	17 03					
Stafford	a			16 29		16 35									16 53	17 00		17 09				17 29	

		LM	LM	LM	VT	LM	VT	VT	AW	VT	LM	XC	XC	LM	LM	LM	LM	VT	XC	LM	LM	LM
		◇1			◇1	◇1	◇1	◇1	◇	◇1	◇1	◇1	◇1		◇1		1	◇1	◇1	◇1	◇1	
							A					B	C									
					⊡		⊡	⊡	⊼	⊡		⊼	⊼					⊡	⊼			
London Euston 15 ⊖	d				15 43					16 03	15 46							16 23				
Northampton	d					16 17					16 45									16 56		
Long Buckby	d					16 27														17 06		
Rugby	d					16 37				16 51	17 04									17 16		
Coventry	a				16 42	16 49				17 02								17 22	17 22	17 28		
	d				16 42	16 49				17 02							17 11	17 22	17 27	17 29		
Canley	d																17 14			17 32		
Tile Hill	d					16 54											17 18			17 36		
Berkswell	d																17 21			17 39		
Hampton-in-Arden	d					17 00											17 25					
Birmingham International ✈	a				16 53	17 04				17 13							17 28	17 33	17 37	17 45		
	d				16 53	17 04			17 09	17 13				17 17			17 29	17 33	17 38	17 45		
Marston Green	d					17 07											17 32			17 48		
Lea Hall	d													17 21						17 51		
Stechford	d													17 24						17 54		
Adderley Park	d													17 27								
Birmingham New Street 12	a			16 58	17 08	17 16			17 20	17 27		17 26	17 26	17 32		17 28	17 42	17 45	17 48	18 01		
	d	17 01	17 05	17 08			17 20	17 20	17 24			17 31	17 31		17 36	17 38		17 49	17 57		18 01	18 05
Smethwick Rolfe Street	d			17 14												17 44						
Smethwick Galton Bridge 7	d	17 08		17 16					17 31							17 46					18 08	
Sandwell & Dudley	d		17 13	17 19												17 49		17 58				18 13
Dudley Port	d			17 22												17 52						
Tipton	d			17 24												17 54						
Coseley	d			17 27											17 46	17 57						
Wolverhampton 7 ⇌	a	17 19	17 24	17 33			17 37	17 37	17 42			17 47	17 48		17 53	18 03		18 11	18 14		18 19	18 24
	d	17 19	17 25				17 37	17 37	17 43			17 48	17 49		17 53				18 15		18 19	18 25
Penkridge	d	17 29													18 03						18 29	
Stafford	a	17 35									18 04	18 01	18 00		18 09				18 29		18 35	

A from 23 October B until 4 September C from 11 September

Table 68

Saturdays

Northampton - Coventry - Birmingham - Wolverhampton - Stafford

		LM	VT	LM	VT	VT	AW	VT	LM	XC	LM	LM	LM	LM	VT	XC	LM	LM	LM	LM	VT	VT	LM
			◇1	◇1	◇1	◇1	◇	◇1	◇1	◇1		◇1		1	◇1	◇1	◇1	◇1			◇1	◇1	◇1
					A																B	C	
			⊡		⊡	⊡	⊼	⊡		⊡					⊡	⊼					⊡	⊡	
London Euston 15 ⊖	d		16 43					17 03	16 46						17 23						17 43	17 43	
Northampton	d			17 17					17 45								17 56						18 17
Long Buckby	d			17 27													18 06						18 27
Rugby	d			17 37				17 51	18 04								18 16						18 37
Coventry	a		17 42	17 49				18 02							18 22	18 22	18 28				18 42	18 43	18 49
	d		17 42	17 49				18 02						18 11	18 22	18 27	18 29				18 42	18 43	18 49
Canley	d													18 14			18 32						
Tile Hill	d			17 54										18 18			18 36						18 54
Berkswell	d													18 21			18 39						
Hampton-in-Arden	d			18 00										18 25									19 00
Birmingham International ✈	a		17 53	18 04				18 13						18 28	18 33	18 37	18 45				18 53	18 54	19 04
	d		17 53	18 04			18 09	18 13			18 17			18 29	18 33	18 38	18 45				18 53	18 54	19 04
Marston Green	d			18 07										18 32			18 48						19 07
Lea Hall	d										18 21						18 51						
Stechford	d										18 24						18 54						
Adderley Park	d										18 27												
Birmingham New Street 12	a	17 58	18 08	18 16			18 20	18 27		18 26	18 32		18 28	18 42	18 45	18 48	19 01			18 58	19 08	19 08	19 16
	d	18 08			18 20	18 20	18 24			18 31		18 36	18 38		18 49	18 57		19 01	19 05	19 08			
Smethwick Rolfe Street	d	18 14											18 44							19 14			
Smethwick Galton Bridge 7	d	18 16					18 30						18 46					19 08		19 16			
Sandwell & Dudley	d	18 19											18 49		18 58				19 13	19 19			
Dudley Port	d	18 22											18 52							19 22			
Tipton	d	18 24											18 54							19 24			
Coseley	d	18 27										18 46	18 57							19 27			
Wolverhampton 7 ⇌	a	18 33			18 36	18 37	18 42			18 48		18 53	19 03		19 11	19 14		19 19	19 24	19 33			
	d				18 37	18 37	18 43			18 49		18 53				19 15		19 19	19 25				
Penkridge	d											19 03						19 29					
Stafford	a								18 53	19 00		19 09				19 29		19 35					

		VT	VT	AW	XC	LM	LM	VT	LM	LM	VT	XC	LM	LM	LM	VT	LM	LM	VT	AW	XC	LM	LM
		◇1	◇1	◇	◇1			◇1	◇1	1	◇1	◇1	◇1	◇1		◇1		◇1	◇1	◇	◇1		◇1
		A																					
		⊡	⊡	⊼	⊡			⊡			⊡	⊼				⊡			⊡		⊡		
London Euston 15 ⊖	d							18 03			18 23					18 43							
Northampton	d								18 45				18 56					19 17					
Long Buckby	d												19 06					19 27					
Rugby	d							18 51	19 03				19 16					19 37					
Coventry	a							19 02			19 22	19 22	19 28			19 42		19 49					
	d							19 02		19 11	19 22	19 27	19 29			19 42		19 49					
Canley	d									19 14			19 32										
Tile Hill	d									19 18			19 36					19 54					
Berkswell	d									19 21			19 39										
Hampton-in-Arden	d									19 25								20 00					
Birmingham International ✈	a							19 13		19 28	19 33	19 37	19 45			19 53		20 04					
	d			19 09		19 17		19 13		19 29	19 33	19 38	19 45			19 53		20 04		20 09		20 17	
Marston Green	d									19 32			19 48					20 07					
Lea Hall	d					19 21							19 51									20 21	
Stechford	d					19 24							19 54									20 24	
Adderley Park	d					19 27																20 27	
Birmingham New Street 12	a			19 20	19 26	19 32	19 28	19 25		19 42	19 45	19 48	20 01			20 08		20 16		20 20	20 26	20 32	
	d	19 20	19 20	19 24	19 31		19 38	19 42			19 50	19 57		20 01	20 05		20 08		20 20	20 24	20 31		20 36
Smethwick Rolfe Street	d						19 44										20 14						
Smethwick Galton Bridge 7	d			19 30			19 46							20 08			20 16			20 30			
Sandwell & Dudley	d						19 49	19 54			19 59				20 13		20 19						
Dudley Port	d						19 52										20 22						
Tipton	d						19 54										20 24						
Coseley	d						19 57										20 27						20 46
Wolverhampton 7 ⇌	a	19 37	19 37	19 42	19 48		20 03	20 08			20 12	20 14		20 20	20 28		20 33		20 37	20 42	20 48		20 53
	d	19 37	19 37	19 43	19 49							20 16		20 20	20 29				20 37	20 43	20 49		20 53
Penkridge	d													20 29									21 03
Stafford	a				20 00				19 53			20 29		20 36					20 49		21 00		21 09

A from 23 October B until 10 July, from 11 September C from 17 July until 4 September

Northampton - Coventry - Birmingham - Wolverhampton - Stafford

Saturdays

	LM	VT	LM	LM	VT	XC A	XC B	XC C	LM	XC D	LM	LM	VT	AW	LM	LM	LM	LM	LM	XC	LM
London Euston ⊖ d		18 35			19 23								19 43								
Northampton d			19 45						19 56						20 17						20 56
Long Buckby d									20 06						20 27						21 06
Rugby d		19 51	20 03						20 16						20 43						21 17
Coventry a		20 02			20 22	20 22	20 22		20 28				20 49		20 54					21 22	21 29
d		20 02		20 11	20 22	20 27	20 27		20 29				20 49		20 54				21 11	21 27	21 29
Canley d				20 14					20 32						20 57				21 14		21 32
Tile Hill d				20 18					20 36						21 01				21 18		21 36
Berkswell d				20 21					20 39						21 04				21 21		21 39
Hampton-in-Arden d				20 25											21 09				21 25		
Birmingham International ✈ a		20 13		20 28	20 33	20 37	20 37		20 45				21 00		21 12				21 28	21 37	21 45
d		20 13		20 29	20 33	20 39	20 39		20 45				21 00	21 09	21 12	21 17			21 29	21 38	21 45
Marston Green d				20 32					20 48						21 15				21 32		21 48
Lea Hall d									20 51							21 21					21 52
Stechford d									20 54							21 24					21 54
Adderley Park d																21 27					
Birmingham New Street a		20 25		20 42	20 45	20 48	20 48	20 50	21 01	20 50			21 11	21 19	21 25	21 32			21 42	21 48	22 01
d	20 38	20 42			20 50	20 57	21 03	21 01		21 03	21 05	21 08	21 15	21 24			21 36	21 38		21 57	
Smethwick Rolfe Street d	20 44											21 14						21 44			
Smethwick Galton Bridge d	20 46											21 16		21 30				21 46			
Sandwell & Dudley d	20 49	20 54			20 59						21 13	21 19						21 49			
Dudley Port d	20 52											21 22						21 52			
Tipton d	20 54											21 24						21 54			
Coseley d	20 57											21 27					21 46	21 57			
Wolverhampton a	21 03	21 08			21 12	21 15		21 17		21 18	21 24	21 33	21 38	21 42			21 53	22 03		22 14	
d						21 17		21 18		21 19	21 25			21 42			21 53			22 16	
Penkridge d																	22 03				
Stafford a			20 55			21 29		21 31		21 32							22 09			22 29	

	LM	LM	VT	LM	XC	XC	LM	LM	LM	LM	VT	XC	AW	LM	LM	LM	VT	AW	LM
London Euston ⊖ d			20 23								21 03						21 43		
Northampton d				21 17										21 56		22 17			22 56
Long Buckby d				21 27										22 06		22 27			23 06
Rugby d				21 37							22 12			22 16		22 37	22 53		23 16
Coventry a			21 35	21 49	21 55						22 22	22 22		22 28		22 49	23 02		23 28
d			21 35	21 49	21 56					22 11	22 23	22 27		22 29		22 49	23 03		23 29
Canley d										22 14				22 32					23 32
Tile Hill d				21 54						22 18				22 36		22 54			23 36
Berkswell d										22 21				22 39					23 39
Hampton-in-Arden d				22 00						22 25						23 00			23 44
Birmingham International ✈ a			21 53	22 04	22 12					22 28	22 33	22 37		22 45		23 04	23 13		23 47
d			21 53	22 04	22 13		22 21			22 29	22 34	22 39		22 45		23 04	23 14		23 47
Marston Green d				22 07						22 32				22 48		23 07			23 50
Lea Hall d							22 25							22 51					23 54
Stechford d							22 28							22 54					23 56
Adderley Park d							22 31												
Birmingham New Street a			22 05	22 16	22 25		22 36			22 42	22 45	22 48		23 01		23 16	23 25		00 04
d	22 05	22 08	22 16			22 31		22 36	22 38		22 48		22 55		23 08		23 29	23 35	
Smethwick Rolfe Street d		22 14							22 44						23 14				
Smethwick Galton Bridge d		22 16						22 42	22 46						23 16				
Sandwell & Dudley d	22 13	22 19	22 25						22 49		22 57				23 19		23 38		
Dudley Port d		22 22							22 52						23 22				
Tipton d		22 24							22 54						23 24				
Coseley d		22 27						22 48	22 57						23 27				
Wolverhampton a	22 24	22 33	22 38			22 48		22 55	23 03		23 10		23 12		23 33		23 51	23 53	
d	22 25					22 49		22 56					23 13					23 54	
Penkridge d								23 06											
Stafford a						23 02		23 13											

A from 11 September
B until 4 September
C until 10 July
D from 17 July until 4 September

Northampton - Coventry - Birmingham - Wolverhampton - Stafford

Sundays

	LM A	VT B	VT C	XC	LM	LM	LM	VT	LM	LM	XC D	XC E	AW F	VT	LM	LM	LM	LM G	LM H	VT	XC	AW F
London Euston ⊖ d																				08 50		
Northampton d	22p56															09 30						
Long Buckby d	23p06															09 40						
Rugby d	23p16															09 50				10 14		
Coventry a	23p28															10 03				10 23	10 22	
d	23p29				08 37				09 07							10 04	10 08			10 24	10 28	
Canley d	23p32				08 40				09 10								10 11					
Tile Hill d	23p36				08 44				09 14								10 15					
Berkswell d	23p39				08 47				09 17								10 18					
Hampton-in-Arden d	23p44				08 51				09 21								10 22					
Birmingham International ✈ a	23p47				08 54				09 24							10 13	10 26			10 34	10 38	
d	23p47				08 55		09 03		09 25				09 51			10 13	10 26			10 35	10 40	10 48
Marston Green d	23p50				08 58		09 06		09 28							10 16	10 29					
Lea Hall d	23p54						09 09									10 20						
Stechford d	23p56						09 12									10 22						
Adderley Park d							09 15									10 26						
Birmingham New Street a	00 04				09 06		09 20		09 36				10 02			10 30	10 38			10 47	10 50	10 58
d		08 45	08 45	09 01		09 09		09 20		09 42	10 00	10 00	10 05	10 20	10 23			10 42	10 42	10 51	11 01	11 05
Smethwick Rolfe Street d						09 15									10 29							
Smethwick Galton Bridge d						09 17									10 31							
Sandwell & Dudley d						09 19									10 33					11 00		
Dudley Port d						09 22									10 36							
Tipton d						09 24									10 38							
Coseley d						09 27									10 41							
Wolverhampton a		09 02	09 02	09 18		09 32		09 37		09 59	10 17	10 17	10 21	10 37	10 46			10 57	10 59	11 13	11 18	11 26
d		09 04	09 04	09 19				09 37		09 59	10 18	10 18	10 22	10 37				10 58	10 59		11 19	11 27
Penkridge d										10 10								11 08	11 10			
Stafford a		09 18	09 17	09 33						10 17	10 32	10 31						11 14	11 17		11 32	

	LM	LM	VT	WS G	LM	LM G	LM H	VT	XC	LM	LM	LM	VT	AW F	LM	LM	VT	XC	LM	LM	VT C	AW F
London Euston ⊖ d								09 50									10 50					
Northampton d	10 00									11 00	11 36								12 00			
Long Buckby d	10 10									11 10	11 46								12 10			
Rugby d	10 20							11 14		11 20	12 02						12 12		12 21			
Coventry a	10 32							11 23	11 22	11 32							12 21	12 22	12 32			
d	10 34				11 08			11 24	11 28	11 34						12 08	12 24	12 28	12 34			
Canley d	10 37									11 37									12 37			
Tile Hill d	10 41									11 41									12 41			
Berkswell d	10 44									11 44									12 44			
Hampton-in-Arden d	10 48									11 48									12 48			
Birmingham International ✈ a	10 51				11 18			11 34	11 38	11 51						12 17	12 34	12 38	12 51			
d	10 52				11 18			11 35	11 40	11 52				12 08		12 18	12 35	12 40	12 52			13 05
Marston Green d	10 55				11 21					11 55						12 21			12 55			
Lea Hall d					11 24											12 24						
Stechford d					11 27											12 27						
Adderley Park d					11 30											12 30						
Birmingham New Street a	11 03			11 32	11 36			11 47	11 50	12 03				12 18		12 36	12 47	12 50	13 03			13 15
d		11 09	11 20	11 33		11 42	11 42	11 51	12 01			12 09	12 20	12 24	12 35		12 51	13 01		13 09	13 20	13 24
Smethwick Rolfe Street d		11 15										12 15								13 15		
Smethwick Galton Bridge d		11 17										12 17								13 17		
Sandwell & Dudley d		11 19						12 00				12 19					13 00			13 19		
Dudley Port d		11 22										12 22								13 22		
Tipton d		11 24										12 24								13 24		
Coseley d		11 27										12 27								13 27		
Wolverhampton a		11 31	11 37	12u03		11 57	11 59	12 13	12 19			12 32	12 37	12 42	12 52		13 13	13 18		13 32	13 37	13 41
d			11 37	12u03		11 58	11 59		12 20				12 37	12 42	12 52			13 19			13 37	13 42
Penkridge d						12 08	12 10								13 03							
Stafford a						12 14	12 16		12 33		12 53				13 10			13 33				

A not 23 May
B from 24 October
C until 17 October
D until 11 July, from 12 September
E from 18 July until 5 September
F until 5 September
G until 11 July
H from 18 July

Northampton - Coventry - Birmingham - Wolverhampton - Stafford

		VT	XC	LM	LM	VT	XC	LM	VT	LM	VT	AW	VT	XC	XC	LM	LM	VT	XC	LM	LM	VT
		◇1	◇1	◇1	1	◇1	◇1	◇1	◇1		◇1	◇	◇1	◇1	◇1	◇1	1	◇1	◇1	◇1	◇1	◇1
												A		B	C							
		☕	🍴			☕	🍴		☕		☕	🍴	☕	🍴	🍴			☕	🍴			☕
London Euston 15 ⊖	d	11 45				12 18			12 38				12 58					13 18			12 50	13 38
Northampton	d							12 53												13 51	13 56	
Long Buckby	d							13 03												14 01	14 06	
Rugby	d	12 48						13 15					13 49							14 15	14 17	
Coventry	a	12 56				13 20	13 22	13 28	13 40				14 00					14 20	14 22	14 28		14 40
	d	12 57			13 10	13 21	13 26	13 29	13 40				14 00				14 10	14 20	14 26	14 29		14 40
Canley	d							13 32												14 32		
Tile Hill	d				13 15			13 36									14 15			14 36		
Berkswell	d							13 39												14 39		
Hampton-in-Arden	d							13 43												14 43		
Birmingham International ✈	a	13 07			13 22	13 31	13 37	13 46	13 51				14 11				14 22	14 31	14 35	14 46		14 51
	d	13 08			13 22	13 32	13 38	13 47	13 51			14 07	14 11				14 22	14 31	14 38	14 47		14 51
Marston Green	d				13 25			13 50									14 25			14 50		
Lea Hall	d				13 29												14 29					
Stechford	d				13 31												14 31					
Adderley Park	d				13 35												14 35					
Birmingham New Street 12	a	13 22			13 40	13 44	13 48	13 58	14 06			14 18	14 25	14 26			14 40	14 44	14 48	14 58		15 06
	d		13 31	13 35		13 48	14 01			14 09	14 20	14 24		14 31	14 31	14 35		14 48	15 01			
Smethwick Rolfe Street	d									14 15												
Smethwick Galton Bridge 7	d									14 17												
Sandwell & Dudley	d					13 57				14 19								14 57				
Dudley Port	d									14 22												
Tipton	d									14 24												
Coseley	d									14 27												
Wolverhampton 7	a		13 48	13 52		14 10	14 18			14 32	14 37	14 42		14 48	14 48	14 52		15 10	15 18			
	d		13 49	13 52			14 19				14 37	14 43		14 49	14 49	14 52			15 19			
Penkridge	d			14 03												15 03						
Stafford	a			14 10			14 33									15 10			15 33		15 14	

		LM	VT	AW	VT	XC	XC	LM	LM	VT	XC	LM	LM	VT	LM	VT	AW	VT	XC	LM	LM	VT	XC
			◇1	◇	◇1	◇1	◇1	◇1	1	◇1	◇1	◇1	◇1	◇1		◇1	◇	◇1	◇1	◇1	1	◇1	◇1
				A		B	C										A						
			☕	🍴	☕	🍴	🍴			☕	🍴			☕		☕	🍴	☕	🍴			☕	🍴
London Euston 15 ⊖	d				13 58					14 18			13 50	14 38				14 58				15 18	
Northampton	d											14 53	14b58										
Long Buckby	d											15 03	15 08										
Rugby	d				14 49							15 15	15a19					15 49					
Coventry	a				15 00					15 20	15 22	15 28		15 40				16 00				16 20	16 22
	d				15 00				15 10	15 20	15 26	15 29		15 40				16 00			16 10	16 20	16 26
Canley	d											15 32											
Tile Hill	d								15 15			15 36									16 15		
Berkswell	d											15 39											
Hampton-in-Arden	d											15 43											
Birmingham International ✈	a				15 11				15 22	15 31	15 35	15 46		15 51				16 11			16 22	16 31	16 35
	d			15 07	15 11				15 22	15 31	15 38	15 47		15 51			16 07	16 11			16 22	16 31	16 38
Marston Green	d								15 25			15 50									16 25		
Lea Hall	d								15 29												16 29		
Stechford	d								15 31												16 31		
Adderley Park	d								15 35												16 35		
Birmingham New Street 12	a			15 18	15 25	15 27			15 40	15 44	15 48	15 58		16 06			16 18	16 25	16 26		16 41	16 44	16 48
	d	15 09	15 20	15 24		15 31	15 31	15 35		15 48	16 01				16 09	16 20	16 24		16 31	16 35		16 48	17 01
Smethwick Rolfe Street	d	15 15													16 15								
Smethwick Galton Bridge 7	d	15 17													16 17								
Sandwell & Dudley	d	15 19								15 57					16 19							16 57	
Dudley Port	d	15 22													16 22								
Tipton	d	15 24													16 24								
Coseley	d	15 27													16 27								
Wolverhampton 7	a	15 32	15 37	15 42		15 48	15 48	15 52		16 10	16 18				16 32	16u37	16 42		16 48	16 52		17 10	17 18
	d		15 37	15 43		15 49	15 49	15 52			16 19					16u37	16 43		16 49	16 52			17 19
Penkridge	d							16 03												17 03			
Stafford	a							16 10			16 35									17 10			17 35

A until 5 September
B until 17 October
C from 24 October
b arr. 1452

Northampton - Coventry - Birmingham - Wolverhampton - Stafford

		LM	LM	VT	LM	VT	AW	VT	XC	LM	LM	VT	XC	LM	LM	WS	VT	LM	VT	AW	VT	XC	LM
		◇1	◇1	◇1		◇1	◇	◇1	◇1	◇1	1	◇1	◇1	◇1	◇1	◇1	◇1		◇1	◇	◇1	◇1	◇1
							A									B				A			
				☕		☕	🍴	☕	🍴			☕	🍴			☕	☕		☕	🍴	☕	🍴	
London Euston 15 ⊖	d		14 50	15 38				15 58				16 18			15 50		16 38				16 58		
Northampton	d	15 51	15 56											16 53	16b58								
Long Buckby	d	16 01	16 06											17 03	17 08								
Rugby	d	16 15	16 17					16 49						17 15	17a19						17 49		
Coventry	a	16 28		16 40				17 00				17 20		17 28			17 40				18 00		
	d	16 29		16 40				17 00			17 10	17 20	17 26	17 29			17 40				18 00		
Canley	d	16 32												17 32									
Tile Hill	d	16 36									17 15			17 36									
Berkswell	d	16 39												17 39									
Hampton-in-Arden	d	16 43												17 43									
Birmingham International ✈	a	16 46		16 51				17 11			17 22	17 31	17 35	17 46			17 51				18 11		
	d	16 47		16 51			17 07	17 11			17 22	17 31	17 38	17 47			17 51			18 07	18 11		
Marston Green	d	16 50									17 25			17 50									
Lea Hall	d										17 29												
Stechford	d										17 31												
Adderley Park	d										17 35												
Birmingham New Street 12	a	16 58		17 06			17 18	17 25	17 26		17 41	17 44	17 48	17 58		18 04	18 06			18 18	18 25	18 27	
	d				17 09	17 20	17 24		17 31	17 35		17 48	18 01			18 04		18 09	18 20	18 24		18 31	18 35
Smethwick Rolfe Street	d				17 15													18 15					
Smethwick Galton Bridge 7	d				17 17											18 13		18 17					
Sandwell & Dudley	d				17 19							17 57						18 19					
Dudley Port	d				17 22													18 22					
Tipton	d				17 24													18 24					
Coseley	d				17 27													18 27					
Wolverhampton 7	a				17 32	17u37	17 42		17 48	17 52		18 10	18 18			18u26		18 32	18 37	18 42		18 48	18 52
	d					17u37	17 43		17 49	17 52			18 19			18u26			18 37	18 43		18 49	18 52
Penkridge	d									18 03													19 03
Stafford	a		17 14							18 10			18 35										19 10

		LM	VT	XC	LM	LM	VT	LM	VT	AW	XC	LM	VT	LM	VT	XC	LM	LM	VT	LM	XC	VT	AW
		1	◇1	◇1	◇1	◇1	◇1		1	◇	◇1	◇1	◇1	1	◇1	◇1	◇1	◇1	◇1		◇1	◇1	◇
										A													A
			☕	🍴			☕		☕	🍴	🍴		☕		☕	🍴			☕		🍴	☕	
London Euston 15 ⊖	d		17 18			16 50	17 38						17 58		18 18			17 50	18 38				
Northampton	d				17 51	17 56											18 53	18c58					
Long Buckby	d				18 01	18 06											19 03	19 08					
Rugby	d				18 15	18 17							18 49				19 15	19a19					
Coventry	a		18 20	18 22	18 28		18 40						19 00		19 20	19 22	19 28		19 40		19 53		
	d	18 10	18 20	18 26	18 29		18 40						19 01	19 10	19 20	19 26	19 29		19 40		19 54		
Canley	d				18 32												19 32						
Tile Hill	d	18 15			18 36									19 15			19 36						
Berkswell	d				18 39												19 39						
Hampton-in-Arden	d				18 43												19 43						
Birmingham International ✈	a	18 22	18 31	18 35	18 46		18 51						19 11	19 22	19 31	19 35	19 46		19 51		20 03		
	d	18 22	18 31	18 38	18 47		18 51			19 07			19 12	19 22	19 31	19 38	19 47		19 51		20 04		20 07
Marston Green	d	18 25			18 50									19 25			19 50						
Lea Hall	d	18 29												19 29									
Stechford	d	18 31												19 31									
Adderley Park	d	18 35												19 35									
Birmingham New Street 12	a	18 41	18 44	18 48	18 58		19 06			19 18	19 26		19 24	19 40	19 44	19 48	19 58		20 06		20 15		20 18
	d		18 48	19 01				19 09	19 20	19 24	19 31	19 35	19 39		19 48	20 01				20 09		20 20	20 24
Smethwick Rolfe Street	d							19 15												20 15			
Smethwick Galton Bridge 7	d							19 17												20 17			
Sandwell & Dudley	d		18 57					19 19							19 57					20 19			
Dudley Port	d							19 22												20 22			
Tipton	d							19 24												20 24			
Coseley	d							19 27												20 27			
Wolverhampton 7	a		19 10	19 18				19 32	19 37	19 42	19 48	19 52	19 58		20 10	20 18				20 32		20 37	20 42
	d			19 19					19 37	19 43	19 49	19 52				20 19						20 38	20 43
Penkridge	d											20 03											
Stafford	a			19 37		19 14						20 10				20 37						20 51	

A until 5 September
B from 18 July until 5 September
b arr. 1652
c arr. 1852

Table 68

Sundays

Northampton - Coventry - Birmingham - Wolverhampton - Stafford

Station		XC	WS	VT	LM	VT	XC	LM	LM	VT	LM	XC	VT	AW	VT	LM	LM	VT	XC	LM	LM	LM	VT
		◇1 ⊥	◇1 A ☕	◇1 ☕	1	◇1 ☕	◇1 ⊥	◇1	◇1	◇1 ☕		◇1 ⊥	◇1 ☕	◇ B	◇1 ☕	◇1	1	◇1 ☕	◇1 ⊥	◇1	◇1		◇1 ☕
London Euston 15 ⊖	d			18 58		19 18			18 50	19 38					19 58			20 18			19 50		20 38
Northampton	d							19 51	19 56											20 53	20b58		
Long Buckby	d							20 01	20 06											21 03	21 08		
Rugby	d			19 49				20 15	20 17						20 49					21 15	21a19		
Coventry	a			20 00		20 20	20 22	20 28		20 40		20 53			21 00			21 20	21 22	21 27			21 46
	d			20 01	20 10	20 20	20 26	20 29		20 40		20 54			21 01		21 10	21 20	21 26	21 29			21 46
Canley	d							20 32												21 32			
Tile Hill	d				20 15			20 36									21 15			21 36			
Berkswell	d							20 39												21 39			
Hampton-in-Arden	d							20 43												21 43			
Birmingham International ✈	a			20 11	20 22	20 31	20 35	20 46		20 51		21 03			21 11		21 22	21 31	21 35	21 46			21 57
	d			20 12	20 22	20 31	20 38	20 47		20 51		21 04		21 07	21 12		21 22	21 31	21 38	21 47			21 57
Marston Green	d				20 25			20 50									21 25			21 50			
Lea Hall	d				20 29												21 29						
Stechford	d				20 31												21 31						
Adderley Park	d				20 35												21 35						
Birmingham New Street 12	a	20 26		20 24	20 41	20 44	20 48	20 58		21 04		21 15		21 18	21 24		21 40	21 44	21 48	21 58			22 09
	d	20 31		20 38		20 48	21 01			21 07	21 09		21 20	21 24	21 28	21 35		21 48	22 01			22 09	22 16
Smethwick Rolfe Street	d										21 15											22 15	
Smethwick Galton Bridge 7	d		20 41								21 17											22 17	
Sandwell & Dudley	d			20 47		20 57				21 16	21 19				21 37			21 57				22 19	22 25
Dudley Port	d										21 22											22 22	
Tipton	d										21 24											22 24	
Coseley	d										21 27											22 27	
Wolverhampton 7 ⇌	a	20 48	20u53	20 58		21 10	21 18			21 31	21 33		21 37	21 42	21 50	21 57		22 10	22 18			22 32	22 38
	d	20 49	20u53				21 19						21 37	21 43		21 58			22 19				
Penkridge	d															22 08							
Stafford	a						21 37		21 14				21 56			22 16			22 37				

Station		XC	AW	LM	VT	XC	AW	AW	LM	LM	XC	AW	LM	LM	VT	VT	LM	VT
		◇1 ⊥	B	1	◇1 ☕	◇1 ⊥	◇ C	◇ D	◇1		◇1 ⊥	B	1	◇1	◇1 ☕	◇1 ☕	1	◇1 ☕
London Euston 15 ⊖	d				20 54										21 55	22 25		23 25
Northampton	d								21 53					22 53			23 32	
Long Buckby	d								22 03					23 03			23 42	
Rugby	d				22 07				22 15					23 15	23 22	23 49	23 52	00s49
Coventry	a	21 53			22 16	22 22			22 27		22 53			23 27	23 33	23 59	00 06	00s58
	d	21 54		22 08	22 16	22 23			22 29		22 54		23 08	23 29	23 34	00 01		01s00
Canley	d								22 32					23 32				
Tile Hill	d								22 36					23 36				
Berkswell	d								22 39					23 39				
Hampton-in-Arden	d								22 43					23 43				
Birmingham International ✈	a	22 03		22 17	22 27	22 32			22 46		23 03		23 17	23 46	23 51	00 10		01s09
	d	22 04	22 11	22 18	22 27	22 33	22 40	22 40	22 47		23 04	23 08	23 18	23 47	23 52	00 11		01s11
Marston Green	d			22 21					22 50				23 21	23 50				
Lea Hall	d			22 24									23 24					
Stechford	d			22 27									23 27					
Adderley Park	d			22 30									23 30					
Birmingham New Street 12	a	22 15	22 21	22 36	22 39	22 42	22 50	22 50	22 58		23 14	23 19	23 36	23 58	00 04	00 23		01s22
	d		22 24		22 44		22 55	22 55		23 09		23 24			00 08	00 26		01s25
Smethwick Rolfe Street	d									23 15								
Smethwick Galton Bridge 7	d									23 17								
Sandwell & Dudley	d				22 53					23 19								
Dudley Port	d									23 22								
Tipton	d									23 24								
Coseley	d									23 27								
Wolverhampton 7 ⇌	a		22 41		23 06		23 11	23 13		23 32		23 40			00 27	00 55		01 54
	d		22 42				23 13	23 15				23 46						
Penkridge	d																	
Stafford	a						23 30	23 30										

A from 18 July until 5 September
B until 5 September
C from 25 July
D until 18 July
b arr. 2052

Table 68

Mondays to Fridays

Stafford - Wolverhampton - Birmingham - Coventry - Northampton

Station		LM	LM	VT MX	VT MO	VT MO	VT MX	LM MX	LM	VT	VT	LM	VT	LM	AW MX	AW MO	XC	VT	LM	VT	LM	LM	AW
		◇1 A	◇1 B	◇1 ☕	◇1 ☕	◇1 ☕	◇1 ☕	1	1	◇1 ⊠	◇1 ⊠	◇1	◇1 ⊠	◇1			◇1 ⊥	◇1 ⊠	1	◇1 ⊠	1	◇1	
Stafford	d														05 24	05 25							
Penkridge	d																						
Wolverhampton 7 ⇌	a														05 38	05 39							05 58
	d			21p45	22p05	22p37	22p45			05 00	05 24				05 40	05 40		05 45		06 04			06 00
Coseley	d																						
Tipton	d																						
Dudley Port	d																						
Sandwell & Dudley	d			21p56	22p15	22p47	22p55				05 34							05 56		06 15			
Smethwick Galton Bridge 7	d																						06 11
Smethwick Rolfe Street	d																						
Birmingham New Street 12	a			22p05	22p24	22p56	23p04			05 26	05 43				05 58	05 58		06 05		06 24			06 17
	d	21p33	21p33	22p10	22p30	23p00	23p10	23p53		05 29	05 50			05 53			06 03	06 10	06 13	06 30		06 33	06 36
Adderley Park	d																						
Stechford	d																		06 20				
Lea Hall	d																		06 23				
Marston Green	d	21p41	21p41					00 01						06 01					06 26			06 41	
Birmingham International ✈	a	21p45	21p45	22p19	22p39	23p09	23p19	00 04		05 37	05 59			06 05			06 13	06 19	06 29	06 38		06 45	06 50
	d	21p45	21p45	22p20	22p40	23p10	23p20	00 05		05 39	06 00			06 05			06 14	06 20	06 29	06 39		06 45	
Hampton-in-Arden	d	21p48	21p48																06 32			06 48	
Berkswell	d													06 11					06 37				
Tile Hill	d	21p55	21p55											06 14					06 40			06 55	
Canley	d													06 17					06 44				
Coventry	a	22p00	22p00	22p30	22p50	23p20	23p30	00 15		05 49	06 10			06 20			06 24	06 30	06 47	06 49		07 00	
	d	22p01	22p01	22p31	22p51	23p21	23p31			05 50	06 11			06 21			06 25	06 31		06 51		07 01	
Rugby	d	22p13	22p13	22p43	23p04	23p35	23p44		05 20	06 03		06 08	06 20	06 33							07 02	07 13	
Long Buckby	d	22p23	22p23						05 30			06 18		06 43							07 12	07 23	
Northampton	a	22p34	22p34			23b53	00s05		05 41			06 33	06 39	06 54							07 24	07 34	
London Euston 15 ⊖	a	00 20	00 21	00 05	00 35	01 06	01 13		06 50	07 02	07 13	07 43	07 30	08 02				07 34		07 53	08 49		

Station		LM	LM	VT	XC	VT	LM	LM	LM	VT	VT	LM	AW	XC	LM	LM	LM	LM	VT	LM	VT	LM	XC	LM
				◇1 ⊠	◇1 ⊥	◇1 ⊠	1		◇1	◇1 ⊠	◇1 ⊠	◇1		◇1 ⊥	◇1			◇1	◇1 ⊠	◇1	◇1 ⊠		■ 1 ⊥	
Stafford	d				06 25				06 41					06 58	07c22			07 12						
Penkridge	d								06 47									07 18						
Wolverhampton 7 ⇌	a		06 16		06 39				06 57				07 08	07 12				07 28						
	d		06 17	06 27	06 41	06 45		06 49	06 57	07 04			07 10	07 15			07 19	07 28			07 31	07 36		07 39
Coseley	d		06 22					06 54	07 03								07 24							07 44
Tipton	d		06 25					06 57									07 26							07 47
Dudley Port	d		06 27					06 59									07 28							07 49
Sandwell & Dudley	d		06 31	06 37		06 56		07 03		07 15							07 32					07 46		
Smethwick Galton Bridge 7	d		06 34					07 06					07 21				07 34	07 40						07 53
Smethwick Rolfe Street	d		06 36					07 09									07 36							07 55
Birmingham New Street 12	a		06 43	06 46	06 58	07 05		07 14	07 18	07 24			07 27	07 31			07 44	07 48			07 55	07 55	07 55	08 03
	d	06 39		06 50	07 03	07 10	07 13			07 30		07 33	07 36	07 42		07 39			07 50	07 53			08 03	
Adderley Park	d	06 44														07 44								
Stechford	d	06 47					07 20									07 47								
Lea Hall	d	06 50					07 23									07 50								
Marston Green	d						07 26					07 41								08 01				
Birmingham International ✈	a	06 55		06 59	07 13	07 19	07 29					07 45	07 50			07 55			07 59	08 05			08 13	
	d			07 00	07 14	07 20	07 29				07 41	07 45							08 00	08 05			08 14	
Hampton-in-Arden	d											07 48												
Berkswell	d						07 35													08 11				
Tile Hill	d						07 38					07 55								08 14				
Canley	d											07 58								08 17				
Coventry	a			07 10	07 24	07 30	07 43				07 51	08 02							08 10	08 20			08 24	
	d			07 11	07 25	07 31					07 52	08 03							08 11	08 21			08 25	
Rugby	d											08 15			08 18				08 23	08 33				
Long Buckby	d											08 25								08 43				
Northampton	a											08 37			08 41					08 56				
London Euston 15 ⊖	a			08 16		08 30				08 42	08 49				09 44				09 13	10 20				

A MX until 3 September
B MX from 7 September
b previous night, stops to set down only
c arr. 0716

Table 68

Stafford - Wolverhampton - Birmingham - Coventry - Northampton

Mondays to Fridays

		VT ◇■ ⊠	LM ■	LM	LM ■	LM	VT ◇■ ⊠	LM ◇■	AW ◇ 🛒	LM ◇■	XC ◇■ 🛒	LM	LM	LM ■	VT ◇■ ⊠	LM ◇■	VT ◇■ ⊠	LM	XC ◇■ 🛒	VT ◇■ ⊠	LM ■	LM
Stafford	d	07 28			07 41					08b21				08 10					08 25			
Penkridge	d				07 47									08 16								
Wolverhampton ■	a	07 43			07 57	08 02			08 08		08 13			08 26			08 31	08 36	08 39			
	d	07 45		07 49	07 57	08 03			08 09		08 15		08 19	08 28			08 32	08 36	08 41	08 45		08 49
Coseley	d			07 54	08 03								08 24									08 54
Tipton	d			07 57									08 26									08 56
Dudley Port	d			07 59									08 28									08 58
Sandwell & Dudley	d	07 56		08 02									08 32					08 46		08 56		09 02
Smethwick Galton Bridge ■	d			08 05					08 21				08 34	08 40								09 04
Smethwick Rolfe Street	d			08 07									08 36									09 06
Birmingham New Street ■	a	08 05		08 14	08 17	08 20			08 27		08 31		08 44	08 47			08 55	08 55	08 58	09 06		09 14
	d	08 10	08 13	08 17			08 30	08 33	08 36		08 42	08 39			08 50	08 53			09 03	09 10	09 13	09 17
Adderley Park	d											08 44										
Stechford	d		08 20									08 47									09 20	
Lea Hall	d		08 23									08 50									09 23	
Marston Green	d		08 26					08 41								09 01					09 26	
Birmingham International ✈	a	08 19	08 29				08 38	08 45	08 50			08 55			08 59	09 05			09 13	09 19	09 29	
	d	08 20	08 29				08 39	08 45							09 00	09 05			09 14	09 20	09 29	
Hampton-in-Arden	d		08 32					08 48													09 32	
Berkswell	d		08 37													09 11					09 37	
Tile Hill	d		08 40					08 55								09 14					09 40	
Canley	d		08 44													09 17					09 44	
Coventry	a	08 30	08 47				08 49	09 00							09 10	09 20			09 24	09 30	09 47	
	d	08 31					08 51	09 01							09 11	09 21			09 25	09 31		
Rugby	d							09 13		09 20					09 23	09 33						
Long Buckby	d							09 23								09 43						
Northampton	a							09 34		09 42						09 54						
London Euston ■ ⊖	a	09 34					09 54			10 49					10 14	11 18				10 34		

		LM ■	VT ◇■ ⊠	LM ◇■	AW ◇ 🛒	LM ◇■	LM	XC ◇■ 🛒	LM	LM ■	VT ◇■ A ⊠	VT ◇■ B ⊠	LM ◇■	VT ◇■ ⊠	LM	XC ◇■ 🛒	VT ◇■ ⊠	LM ■	LM	LM ■	VT ◇■ A ⊓	VT ◇■ B ⊓	LM ◇■
Stafford	d	08 43				09c21		09 03		09 10						09 25				09 43			
Penkridge	d	08 48								09 16													
Wolverhampton ■	a	08 58			09 08			09 15		09 27				09 31	09 36	09 39				09 56			
	d	08 58			09 10			09 16	09 19	09 28				09 32	09 36	09 41	09 45		09 49	09 57			
Coseley	d	09 04							09 24										09 54	10 03			
Tipton	d								09 26										09 56				
Dudley Port	d								09 28										09 58				
Sandwell & Dudley	d								09 32						09 46		09 56		10 02				
Smethwick Galton Bridge ■	d				09 21				09 34	09 40									10 04				
Smethwick Rolfe Street	d								09 36										10 06				
Birmingham New Street ■	a	09 18			09 27			09 39	09 44	09 47				09 55	09 56	09 58	10 05		10 14	10 17			
	d		09 30	09 33	09 36		09 39	09 42	09 47		09 50	09 50	09 53			10 03	10 10	10 13	10 17		10 30	10 30	10 33
Adderley Park	d						09 44																
Stechford	d						09 47											10 20					
Lea Hall	d						09 50											10 23					
Marston Green	d			09 41									10 01					10 26					10 41
Birmingham International ✈	a		09 38	09 45	09 50		09 55				09 59	09 59	10 05			10 13	10 19	10 29			10 38	10 38	10 45
	d		09 39	09 46							10 00	10 00	10 05			10 14	10 20	10 29			10 39	10 39	10 45
Hampton-in-Arden	d			09 49														10 32					10 48
Berkswell	d												10 11					10 37					
Tile Hill	d			09 56									10 14					10 40					10 55
Canley	d												10 17					10 44					
Coventry	a		09 49	10 01							10 10	10 10	10 20			10 24	10 30	10 47			10 49	10 50	11 00
	d		09 51	10 02							10 11	10 11	10 21			10 25	10 31				10 51	10 52	11 01
Rugby	d			10 14		10 19					10 24	10 24	10 33										11 13
Long Buckby	d			10 24									10 43										11 23
Northampton	a			10 35		10 42							10 54										11 35
London Euston ■ ⊖	a		10 54			11 49					11 14	11 14	12 18				11 34				11 54	11 54	

A until 16 July, from 6 September
B from 19 July until 3 September
b arr. 0812
c arr. 0912

Table 68

Stafford - Wolverhampton - Birmingham - Coventry - Northampton

Mondays to Fridays

		AW ◇ 🛒	LM ◇■	LM	XC ◇■ 🛒	LM	LM ■	VT ◇■ ⊓	LM ◇■	VT ◇■ ⊠	LM	XC ◇■ 🛒	VT ◇■ ⊓	LM ■	LM	LM ■	VT ◇■ ⊓	LM ◇■	AW ◇ 🛒	LM ◇■	LM	XC ◇■ 🛒
Stafford	d		10b21		10 03		10 10					10 25				10 43				11c21		
Penkridge	d						10 16															
Wolverhampton ■	a	10 08			10 15		10 27			10 31	10 36	10 39				10 56			11 09			11 16
	d	10 09			10 17	10 19	10 28			10 32	10 36	10 41	10 45		10 49	10 57			11 09			11 17
Coseley	d					10 24									10 54	11 03						
Tipton	d					10 26									10 56							
Dudley Port	d					10 28									10 58							
Sandwell & Dudley	d					10 32					10 46		10 56		11 02							
Smethwick Galton Bridge ■	d	10 20				10 34	10 40								11 04				11 20			
Smethwick Rolfe Street	d					10 36									11 06							
Birmingham New Street ■	a	10 26			10 39	10 44	10 47			10 55	10 55	10 58	11 05		11 14	11 18			11 26			11 39
	d	10 36		10 39	10 42	10 47		10 50	10 53			11 03	11 10	11 13	11 17		11 30	11 33	11 36		11 39	11 42
Adderley Park	d			10 44																	11 44	
Stechford	d			10 47										11 20							11 47	
Lea Hall	d			10 50										11 23							11 50	
Marston Green	d								11 01					11 26				11 41				
Birmingham International ✈	a	10 50		10 55				10 59	11 05			11 13	11 19	11 29			11 38	11 45	11 50		11 55	
	d							11 00	11 05			11 14	11 20	11 29			11 39	11 46				
Hampton-in-Arden	d													11 32				11 49				
Berkswell	d								11 11					11 37								
Tile Hill	d								11 14					11 40				11 56				
Canley	d								11 17					11 44								
Coventry	a							11 10	11 20			11 24	11 30	11 47			11 50	12 01				
	d							11 11	11 21			11 25	11 31				11 52	12 02				
Rugby	d		11 19					11 24	11 33									12 14		12 19		
Long Buckby	d								11 43									12 24				
Northampton	a		11 42						11 54									12 35		12 43		
London Euston ■ ⊖	a		12 49					12 14	13 18				12 34				12 54			13 49		

		LM	LM ■	VT ◇■ ⊓	LM ◇■	VT ◇■ ⊠	LM	XC ◇■ 🛒	VT ◇■ ⊓	LM ■ A	LM ■ B	LM	LM ■	VT ◇■ ⊓	LM ◇■	AW ◇ 🛒	LM ◇■	LM	XC ◇■ 🛒	LM	LM ■	VT ◇■ ⊠	LM ◇■
Stafford	d		11 10					11 25					11 43				12e21		12 03		12 10		
Penkridge	d		11 16																		12 16		
Wolverhampton ■	a		11 27			11 31	11 36	11 39					11 57			12 08			12 15		12 27		
	d	11 19	11 28			11 32	11 36	11 41	11 45			11 49	11 57			12 09			12 17	12 19	12 28		
Coseley	d	11 24										11 54	12 03							12 24			
Tipton	d	11 26										11 56								12 26			
Dudley Port	d	11 28										11 58								12 28			
Sandwell & Dudley	d	11 32					11 46		11 56			12 02								12 32			
Smethwick Galton Bridge ■	d	11 34	11 40									12 04				12 20				12 34	12 40		
Smethwick Rolfe Street	d	11 36										12 06								12 36			
Birmingham New Street ■	a	11 44	11 47			11 55	11 55	11 58	12 05			12 14	12 17			12 26			12 39	12 44	12 47		
	d	11 47		11 50	11 53			12 03	12 10	12 13	12 13	12 17		12 30	12 33	12 36		12 39	12 42	12 47		12 50	12 53
Adderley Park	d																	12 44					
Stechford	d									12 20	12 20							12 47					
Lea Hall	d									12 23	12 23							12 50					
Marston Green	d				12 01					12 26	12 26				12 41								13 01
Birmingham International ✈	a			11 59	12 07			12 13	12 19	12 29	12 29			12 38	12 45	12 50		12 55				12 59	13 05
	d			12 00	12 07			12 14	12 20	12 29	12 29			12 39	12 45							13 00	13 05
Hampton-in-Arden	d									12 32	12 32				12 48								
Berkswell	d				12 13					12 37	12 37												13 11
Tile Hill	d				12 16					12 40	12 40				12 55								13 14
Canley	d				12 19					12 44	12 44												13 17
Coventry	a			12 10	12 22			12 24	12 30	12 47	12 48			12 50	13 00							13 10	13 20
	d			12 11	12 23			12 25	12 31					12 52	13 01							13 11	13 21
Rugby	d			12 24	12 34										13 13		13f24					13 24	13 33
Long Buckby	d				12 44										13 23								13 43
Northampton	a				12 54										13 34		13 48						13 54
London Euston ■ ⊖	a			13 14	14 18				13 34					13 54			14 49					14 14	15 17

A until 16 July, from 6 September
B from 19 July until 3 September
b arr. 1013
c arr. 1112
e arr. 1213
f arr. 1317

Stafford - Wolverhampton - Birmingham - Coventry - Northampton

		VT	LM	XC	VT	LM	LM	LM	VT	VT	LM	AW	LM	XC	LM	LM	LM	VT	LM	VT	LM	XC	VT
		◇■ 🍴		◇■ ✕	◇■ 🍴	■		■	◇■ A 🍴	◇■ B 🍴	◇■	◇ ✕	◇■	◇■ ✕			■	◇■ 🍴	◇■	◇■ 🍴		◇■ ✕	◇■ 🍴
Stafford	d			12 25				12 43					13b21				13 10					13 25	
Penkridge	d																13 16						
Wolverhampton ■	a	12 31	12 36	12 39				12 56				13 08		13 13			13 27			13 31	13 36	13 39	
	d	12 32	12 36	12 41	12 45		12 49	12 57				13 09		13 14		13 19	13 28			13 32	13 36	13 41	13 45
Coseley	d						12 54	13 03								13 24							
Tipton	d						12 56									13 26							
Dudley Port	d						12 58									13 28							
Sandwell & Dudley	d		12 46		12 56		13 02									13 32					13 46		13 56
Smethwick Galton Bridge ■	d						13 04					13 20				13 34	13 40						
Smethwick Rolfe Street	d						13 06									13 36							
Birmingham New Street ■	a	12 55	12 55	12 58	13 05		13 14	13 17				13 27		13 31		13 44	13 47			13 55	13 55	13 58	14 05
	d			13 03	13 10	13 13	13 17		13 30	13 30	13 33	13 36		13 42	13 39	13 47		13 50	13 53			14 03	14 10
Adderley Park	d														13 44								
Stechford	d					13 20									13 47								
Lea Hall	d					13 23									13 50								
Marston Green	d					13 26					13 41								14 01				
Birmingham International ✈	a			13 13	13 19	13 29			13 38	13 38	13 45	13 51			13 55			13 59	14 07			14 13	14 19
	d			13 14	13 20	13 29			13 39	13 39	13 45							14 00	14 07			14 14	14 20
Hampton-in-Arden	d					13 32					13 48												
Berkswell	d					13 37													14 13				
Tile Hill	d					13 40					13 55								14 16				
Canley	d					13 44													14 19				
Coventry	a			13 24	13 30	13 47			13 49	13 50	14 00							14 10	14 22			14 24	14 30
	d			13 25	13 31				13 51	13 52	14 01							14 11	14 23			14 25	14 31
Rugby	d										14 13		14 19					14 24	14 34				
Long Buckby	d										14 23								14 44				
Northampton	a										14 35		14 42						14 54				
London Euston ■ ⊖	a				14 34				14 52	14 53			15 49					15 14	16 18				15 34

		LM	LM	LM	LM	VT	VT	LM	AW	LM	XC	LM	LM	LM	VT	LM	VT	LM	XC	VT	VT	LM
		■ A	■ B		■	◇■ A 🍴	◇■ B 🍴	◇■	◇ ✕	◇■	◇■ ✕			■	◇■ 🍴	◇■	◇■ A 🍴		◇■ ✕	◇■ B 🍴	◇■ A 🍴	■
Stafford	d				13 43					14c21				14 10					14 25			
Penkridge	d													14 16								
Wolverhampton ■	a				13 56				14 08		14 13			14 27			14 31	14 36	14 39	14 33		
	d			13 49	13 57				14 09		14 15		14 19	14 28			14 32	14 36	14 41	14 45	14 45	
Coseley	d			13 54	14 03								14 24									
Tipton	d			13 56									14 26									
Dudley Port	d			13 58									14 28									
Sandwell & Dudley	d			14 02									14 32					14 46		14 56	14 56	
Smethwick Galton Bridge ■	d			14 04					14 20				14 34	14 40								
Smethwick Rolfe Street	d			14 06									14 36									
Birmingham New Street ■	a			14 14	14 17				14 26		14 31		14 44	14 47			14 55	14 55	14 58	15 05	15 05	
	d	14 13	14 13	14 17		14 30	14 30	14 33	14 36		14 42	14 39	14 47		14 50	14 53			15 03	15 10	15 10	15 13
Adderley Park	d											14 44										
Stechford	d	14 20	14 20									14 47										15 20
Lea Hall	d	14 23	14 23									14 50										15 23
Marston Green	d	14 26	14 26					14 41								15 01						15 26
Birmingham International ✈	a	14 29	14 29			14 38	14 38	14 45	14 50			14 55			14 59	15 05			15 13	15 19	15 19	15 29
	d	14 29	14 29			14 39	14 39	14 45							15 00	15 05			15 14	15 20	15 20	15 29
Hampton-in-Arden	d	14 32	14 32					14 48														15 32
Berkswell	d	14 37	14 37													15 11						15 37
Tile Hill	d	14 40	14 40					14 55								15 14						15 40
Canley	d	14 44	14 44													15 17						15 44
Coventry	a	14 47	14 48			14 49	14 50	15 00							15 10	15 20			15 24	15 30	15 30	15 47
	d					14 51	14 52	15 01							15 11	15 21			15 25	15 31	15 31	
Rugby	d							15 13		15 19					15 24	15 33						
Long Buckby	d							15 23								15 43						
Northampton	a							15 34		15 42						15 54						
London Euston ■ ⊖	a					15 54	15 54			16 49					16 14	17 19				16 34	16 34	

A until 16 July, from 6 September
B from 19 July until 3 September
b arr. 1312
c arr. 1412

Stafford - Wolverhampton - Birmingham - Coventry - Northampton

		LM	LM	VT	LM	AW	LM	LM	XC	LM	LM	VT	LM	VT	LM	XC	VT	LM	LM	LM	VT	LM	AW
			■	◇■ 🍴	◇■	◇ ✕	◇■		◇■ ✕		■	◇■ 🍴	◇■	◇■ 🍴		◇■ ✕	◇■ 🍴	■		■	◇■ 🍴	◇■	◇ ✕
Stafford	d		14 46				15b21		15 03		15 10					15 25				15 43			
Penkridge	d										15 16												
Wolverhampton ■	a		14 59			15 08			15 15		15 27			15 31	15 36	15 39				15 56			16 08
	d	14 49	14 59			15 09			15 17	15 19	15 28			15 32	15 36	15 41	15 45		15 49	15 57			16 09
Coseley	d	14 54	15 05							15 24									15 54	16 03			
Tipton	d	14 56								15 26									15 56				
Dudley Port	d	14 58								15 28									15 58				
Sandwell & Dudley	d	15 02								15 32					15 46		15 56		16 02				
Smethwick Galton Bridge ■	d	15 04				15 20				15 34	15 40								16 04				16 20
Smethwick Rolfe Street	d	15 06								15 36									16 06				
Birmingham New Street ■	a	15 14	15 20			15 26			15 39	15 44	15 47			15 55	15 55	15 58	16 05		16 14	16 17			16 26
	d	15 17		15 30	15 33	15 36		15 39	15 42	15 47		15 50	15 53			16 03	16 10	16 13	16 17		16 30	16 33	16 36
Adderley Park	d							15 44															
Stechford	d							15 47										16 20					
Lea Hall	d							15 50										16 23					
Marston Green	d				15 41								16 01					16 26				16 41	
Birmingham International ✈	a			15 38	15 45	15 50		15 55				15 59	16 05			16 13	16 19	16 29			16 38	16 45	16 50
	d			15 39	15 45							16 00	16 05			16 14	16 20	16 29			16 39	16 45	
Hampton-in-Arden	d				15 48													16 32				16 48	
Berkswell	d												16 11					16 37					
Tile Hill	d				15 55								16 14					16 40				16 55	
Canley	d												16 17					16 44					
Coventry	a			15 49	16 00							16 10	16 20			16 24	16 30	16 47			16 49	17 00	
	d			15 51	16 01							16 11	16 21			16 25	16 31				16 51	17 01	
Rugby	d				16 13		16 19					16 24	16 33									17 13	
Long Buckby	d				16 23								16 43									17 23	
Northampton	a				16 34		16 44						16 54									17 34	
London Euston ■ ⊖	a			16 54			17 49					17 14	18 20				17 34				17 54		

		LM	LM	XC	LM	LM	VT	LM	VT	LM	XC	VT	LM	LM	LM	LM	VT	LM	AW	LM	LM	XC
		◇■		◇■ ✕		■	◇■ 🍴	◇■	◇■ 🍴		◇■ ✕	◇■ 🍴	◇■		■	■	◇■ ⊠	◇■	◇ ✕	◇■		◇■ ✕
Stafford	d	16c21		16 03		16 10					16 25					16 46				17e21		17 03
Penkridge	d					16 16																
Wolverhampton ■	a			16 15		16 26			16 32	16 36	16 39					16 59			17 10			17 15
	d			16 17	16 19	16 28			16 32	16 36	16 41	16 45		16 49		16 59			17 10			17 16
Coseley	d				16 24									16 54		17 05						
Tipton	d				16 26									16 56								
Dudley Port	d				16 28									16 58								
Sandwell & Dudley	d				16 32					16 46		16 56		17 02								
Smethwick Galton Bridge ■	d				16 34	16 40								17 04					17 21			
Smethwick Rolfe Street	d				16 36									17 06								
Birmingham New Street ■	a			16 39	16 44	16 47			16 55	16 55	16 58	17 05		17 14		17 20			17 27			17 39
	d		16 39	16 42	16 47		16 50	16 53			17 03	17 10	17 13	17 17	17 16		17 30	17 33	17 36		17 39	17 42
Adderley Park	d		16 44												17 21						17 44	
Stechford	d		16 47										17 20								17 47	
Lea Hall	d		16 50												17 25						17 50	
Marston Green	d							17 01							17 28			17 41				
Birmingham International ✈	a		16 55				16 59	17 05			17 13	17 19	17 27		17 32		17 38	17 45	17 50		17 55	
	d						17 00	17 05			17 14	17 20	17 27		17 33		17 39	17 45				
Hampton-in-Arden	d														17 36			17 48				
Berkswell	d							17 11							17 40							
Tile Hill	d							17 14					17 35					17 55				
Canley	d							17 17					17 39									
Coventry	a						17 10	17 20			17 24	17 30	17 43		17 47		17 49	18 00				
	d						17 11	17 21			17 25	17 31	17 43				17 51	18 01				
Rugby	d	17 19					17 24	17 33					17 55					18 13		18 19		
Long Buckby	d							17 43					18 05					18 23				
Northampton	a	17 42						17 54					18 17					18 34		18 42		
London Euston ■ ⊖	a	18 49					18 14	19 18				18 34	19 29				18 54			19 50		

b arr. 1512
c arr. 1612
e arr. 1713

Table 68

Stafford - Wolverhampton - Birmingham - Coventry - Northampton

		LM	LM 1	VT ◇1 ⊠	LM ◇1	VT ◇1 ⊡	LM	XC ◇1 ⚲	VT ◇1 A ⊠	VT ◇1 B ⊠	LM 1	LM	LM 1	VT ◇1 ⊠	LM ◇1	AW ◇ ⚲	XC ◇1 ⚲	LM ◇1	LM	LM	LM 1	VT ◇1 ⊠	LM ◇1	VT R 1 A ⊡
Stafford	d		17 10					17 25					17 43				18 04	18b21			18 10			
Penkridge	d		17 16																		18 16			
Wolverhampton 7	a		17 27			17 31	17 36	17 39					17 56			18 08	18 15				18 27			18 31
	d	17 19	17 28			17 32	17 36	17 41	17 45	17 45		17 49	17 57			18 09	18 16			18 19	18 28			18 31
Coseley	d	17 24										17 54	18 03							18 24				
Tipton	d	17 26										17 56								18 26				
Dudley Port	d	17 28										17 58								18 28				
Sandwell & Dudley	d	17 32					17 46		17 56	17 56		18 02								18 32				
Smethwick Galton Bridge 7	d	17 34	17 40									18 04				18 20				18 34	18 40			
Smethwick Rolfe Street	d	17 36										18 06								18 36				
Birmingham New Street 12	a	17 44	17 47			17 55	17 55	17 58	18 05	18 05		18 14	18 17			18 26	18 38			18 44	18 48			18 55
	d	17 47		17 50	17 53			18 03	18 10	18 10	18 13	18 17		18 30	18 33	18 36	18 42		18 39			18 50	18 53	
Adderley Park	d																		18 44					
Stechford	d										18 20								18 47					
Lea Hall	d										18 23								18 50					
Marston Green	d				18 01						18 26				18 41								19 01	
Birmingham International ✈	a			17 59	18 05			18 13	18 19	18 19	18 29			18 38	18 45	18 50			18 55			18 59	19 05	
	d			18 00	18 05			18 14	18 20	18 20	18 29			18 39	18 45							19 00	19 05	
Hampton-in-Arden	d										18 32				18 48									
Berkswell	d				18 11						18 37												19 11	
Tile Hill	d				18 14						18 40				18 55								19 14	
Canley	d				18 17						18 44												19 17	
Coventry	a			18 10	18 20			18 24	18 30	18 30	18 47			18 49	19 00							19 10	19 20	
	d			18 11	18 21			18 25	18 31	18 31				18 51	19 01							19 11	19 21	
Rugby	d			18 24	18 33										19 13			19 21				19 24	19 33	
Long Buckby	d				18 43										19 23								19 43	
Northampton	a				18 54										19 34			19 44					19 55	
London Euston 15 ⊖	a			19 14	20 20				19 34	19 34				19 54				20 49				20 14	21 18	

		LM	XC ◇1 ⚲	VT R 1 B ⊡	VT ◇1 A ⊠	LM 1	LM	LM 1	VT ◇1 ⊡	LM ◇1	AW ◇ ⚲	LM ◇1	XC ◇1 ⚲	LM	LM	LM 1	VT ◇1 ⊡	LM ◇1	VT ◇1 ⊡	LM	XC ◇1 C ⚲	VT ◇1 ⊡	LM 1
Stafford	d		18 28					18 43				19c21				19 10					19 25		
Penkridge	d															19 16							
Wolverhampton 7	a	18 36	18 39	18 33				18 56			19 08		19 13			19 27			19 31	19 36	19 39		
	d	18 36	18 41	18 45	18 45		18 49	18 57			19 09		19 15		19 19	19 28			19 32	19 36	19 41	19 45	
Coseley	d						18 54	19 03							19 24								
Tipton	d						18 56								19 26								
Dudley Port	d						18 58								19 28								
Sandwell & Dudley	d	18 46		18 56	18 56		19 02								19 32					19 46		19 56	
Smethwick Galton Bridge 7	d						19 04				19 20				19 34	19 40							
Smethwick Rolfe Street	d						19 06								19 36								
Birmingham New Street 12	a	18 55	18 58	19 05	19 05		19 14	19 17			19 26		19 31		19 44	19 47			19 55	19 55	19 58	20 05	
	d		19 03	19 10	19 10	19 13			19 30	19 33	19 36		19 42	19 39	19 47		19 50	19 53			20 03	20 10	20 13
Adderley Park	d													19 44									
Stechford	d					19 20								19 47									20 20
Lea Hall	d					19 23								19 50									20 23
Marston Green	d					19 26				19 41								20 01					20 26
Birmingham International ✈	a		19 13	19 19	19 19	19 29			19 38	19 45	19 50			19 55			19 59	20 05			20 13	20 19	20 29
	d		19 14	19 20	19 20	19 29			19 39	19 45							20 00	20 05			20 14	20 20	20 29
Hampton-in-Arden	d					19 32				19 48													20 32
Berkswell	d					19 37												20 11					20 37
Tile Hill	d					19 40				19 55								20 14					20 40
Canley	d					19 44												20 17					20 44
Coventry	a		19 24	19 30	19 30	19 47			19 49	20 00							20 10	20 20			20 24	20 30	20 47
	d		19 25	19 31	19 31				19 51	20 01							20 11	20 21			20 25	20 31	
Rugby	d									20 13		20 19					20 23	20 33					
Long Buckby	d									20 23								20 43					
Northampton	a									20 34		20 43						20 54					
London Euston 15 ⊖	a			20 34	20 34				20 54								21 14	22 20				21 38	

A until 16 July, from 6 September
B from 19 July until 3 September
C ⚲ to Wolverhampton
b arr. 1812
c arr. 1912

Table 68

Stafford - Wolverhampton - Birmingham - Coventry - Northampton

		LM	LM 1	LM ◇1	AW ◇ ⚲	XC ◇1 A ⚲	LM	LM	LM 1	VT ◇1 ⊡	LM ◇1	VT R 1 ⊡	LM	XC ◇1 A ⚲	VT ◇1 ⊡	LM 1	LM	LM 1	XC ◇1	LM ◇1 B	LM ◇1 C	LM
Stafford	d		19 42			20 04			20 16					20 26				20 42				
Penkridge	d		19 47															20 47				
Wolverhampton 7	a		19 57		20 10	20 16			20 29			20 33	20 36	20 40				20 57	21 13			
	d	19 49	19 57		20 10	20 17		20 19	20 29			20 34	20 36	20 43	20 47		20 49	20 57	21 15			
Coseley	d	19 54	20 03					20 24									20 54	21 03				
Tipton	d	19 56						20 26									20 56					
Dudley Port	d	19 58						20 28									20 58					
Sandwell & Dudley	d	20 02						20 32					20 46		20 57		21 02					
Smethwick Galton Bridge 7	d	20 04			20 21			20 34	20 41								21 04					
Smethwick Rolfe Street	d	20 06						20 36									21 06					
Birmingham New Street 12	a	20 15	20 18		20 27	20 33		20 44	20 47			20 55	20 57	21 00	21 06		21 14	21 18	21 31			
	d			20 33	20 36	20 42	20 39			20 50	20 53			21 03	21 10	21 13				21 33	21 33	21 39
Adderley Park	d						20 44															21 44
Stechford	d						20 47									21 20						21 47
Lea Hall	d						20 50									21 23						21 50
Marston Green	d			20 41							21 01					21 26				21 41	21 41	
Birmingham International ✈	a			20 45	20 50		20 55			20 59	21 05			21 13	21 19	21 29				21 45	21 45	21 55
	d			20 45						21 00	21 05			21 14	21 20	21 29				21 45	21 45	
Hampton-in-Arden	d			20 48												21 32				21 48	21 48	
Berkswell	d										21 11					21 37						
Tile Hill	d			20 55							21 14					21 40				21 55	21 55	
Canley	d										21 17					21 44						
Coventry	a			21 00						21 10	21 20			21 24	21 30	21 53				22 00	22 00	
	d			21 01						21 11	21 21			21 25	21 31					22 01	22 01	
Rugby	d			21 13						21 23	21 33									22 13	22 13	
Long Buckby	d			21 23							21 43									22 23	22 23	
Northampton	a			21 34							21 54									22 34	22 34	
London Euston 15 ⊖	a									22 12	23 25				22 43					00 20	00 21	

		LM	LM 1	VT ◇1 ⊡	LM ◇1	LM	XC ◇1	XC ◇1 ⚲	VT ◇1 ⊡	LM 1	LM	LM 1	AW ◇ ⚲	LM 1	LM	VT ◇1 ⊡	LM ◇1	VT ◇1 ⊡	LM	XC ◇1	VT ◇1 ⊡	LM 1	LM
Stafford	d		21 10	21 14			21 26					21 41								22 26			
Penkridge	d		21 16									21 47											
Wolverhampton 7	a		21 26	21 29		21 36	21 39					21 57	22 10			22 27		22 32	22 36	22 39			
	d	21 19	21 28	21 32		21 36	21 41		21 45		21 49	21 57	22 13		22 19	22 28		22 32	22 36	22 41	22 45		22 49
Coseley	d	21 24									21 54	22 03			22 24								22 54
Tipton	d	21 26									21 56				22 26								22 56
Dudley Port	d	21 28									21 58				22 28								22 58
Sandwell & Dudley	d	21 32				21 46			21 56		22 02				22 32				22 46		22 55		23 02
Smethwick Galton Bridge 7	d	21 34	21 40								22 04		22 24		22 34								23 04
Smethwick Rolfe Street	d	21 36									22 06				22 36								23 06
Birmingham New Street 12	a	21 44	21 47	21 50		21 55	22 00		22 05		22 14	22 17	22 30		22 44	22 50		22 55	22 55	22 58	23 04		23 14
	d				21 53			22 03	22 10	22 13				22 33			22 53				23 10	23 13	
Adderley Park	d																					23 18	
Stechford	d									22 20												23 21	
Lea Hall	d									22 23												23 24	
Marston Green	d				22 01					22 26				22 41			23 01					23 27	
Birmingham International ✈	a				22 05			22 13	22 19	22 29				22 45			23 05				23 19	23 30	
	d				22 05			22 14	22 20	22 29				22 45			23 05				23 20	23 30	
Hampton-in-Arden	d									22 32				22 48								23 33	
Berkswell	d				22 11					22 37							23 11					23 38	
Tile Hill	d				22 14					22 40				22 55			23 14					23 41	
Canley	d				22 17					22 44							23 17					23 45	
Coventry	a				22 20			22 24	22 30	22 47				23 00			23 20				23 30	23 48	
	d				22 21			22 25	22 31								23 21				23 31		
Rugby	d				22 33				22 43								23 33				23 44		
Long Buckby	d				22 43												23 43						
Northampton	a				22 55												23 54				00s05		
London Euston 15 ⊖	a								00 05												01 13		

A ⚲ to Wolverhampton
B until 3 September
C from 6 September

Table 68

Mondays to Fridays

Stafford - Wolverhampton - Birmingham - Coventry - Northampton

Station		LM	AW	XC	LM
Stafford	d	22 41		23 07	
Penkridge	d	22 47			
Wolverhampton	a	22 57	22 55	23 19	
	d	22 57	22 55	23 21	
Coseley	d	23 03			
Tipton	d				
Dudley Port	d				
Sandwell & Dudley	d				
Smethwick Galton Bridge	d				
Smethwick Rolfe Street	d				
Birmingham New Street	a	23 18	23 26	23 38	
	d				23 53
Adderley Park	d				
Stechford	d				
Lea Hall	d				
Marston Green	d				00 01
Birmingham International	a				00 04
	d				00 05
Hampton-in-Arden	d				
Berkswell	d				
Tile Hill	d				
Canley	d				
Coventry	a				00 15
	d				
Rugby	d				
Long Buckby	d				
Northampton	a				
London Euston	a				

Saturdays

Station		LM A	LM B	VT	VT	LM	VT	AW	XC	VT	LM	VT	LM	AW	LM	LM	VT	LM	XC	VT	LM	LM	LM
Stafford	d							05 24											06 26				06 41
Penkridge	d																						06 47
Wolverhampton	a							05 38						06 01					06 39				06 57
	d			21p45	22p45			05 40		05 45		06 06		06 03		06 19	06 27		06 41	06 45		06 49	06 57
Coseley	d															06 24						06 54	07 03
Tipton	d															06 26						06 56	
Dudley Port	d															06 28						06 58	
Sandwell & Dudley	d			21p56	22p55					05 56		06 17				06 32	06 37			06 56		07 02	
Smethwick Galton Bridge	d													06 14		06 34						07 04	
Smethwick Rolfe Street	d															06 36						07 06	
Birmingham New Street	a			22p05	23p04			05 55		06 05		06 26		06 20		06 44	06 47		06 57	07 05		07 14	07 17
	d	21p33	21p33	22p10	23p10	23p53	05 50		06 03	06 10	06 13	06 30	06 33	06 36	06 39		06 50	06 53	07 03	07 10	07 13	07 17	
Adderley Park	d														06 44								
Stechford	d										06 20				06 47						07 20		
Lea Hall	d										06 23				06 50						07 23		
Marston Green	d	21p41	21p41			00 01					06 26		06 41					07 01			07 26		
Birmingham International	a	21p45	21p45	22p19	23p19	00 04	05 59		06 13	06 19	06 29	06 39	06 45	06 50	06 54		06 59	07 05	07 13	07 19	07 29		
	d	21p45	21p45	22p20	23p20	00 05	06 00		06 14	06 20	06 29	06 40	06 45				07 00	07 05	07 15	07 20	07 29		
Hampton-in-Arden	d	21p48	21p48								06 32		06 48								07 32		
Berkswell	d										06 37							07 11			07 37		
Tile Hill	d	21p55	21p55								06 40		06 55					07 14			07 40		
Canley	d										06 44							07 17			07 44		
Coventry	a	22p00	22p00	22p30	23p30	00 15	06 10		06 24	06 30	06 47	06 50	07 00				07 10	07 20	07 24	07 30	07 47		
	d	22p01	22p01	22p31	23p31		06 10		06 25	06 31		06 51	07 01				07 11	07 21	07 25	07 31			
Rugby	d	22p13	22p13	22p43	23p44		06 24						07 13				07 23	07 33					
Long Buckby	d	22p23	22p23										07 23					07 43					
Northampton	a	22p34	22p34		00s05								07 34					07 54					
London Euston	a	00 20	00 21	00 05	01 13		07 16			07 38		07 55					08 14			08 34			

A until 4 September

B from 11 September

Table 68

Saturdays

Stafford - Wolverhampton - Birmingham - Coventry - Northampton

Station		VT	LM	AW	XC	LM	LM	LM	LM	VT	LM	VT	LM	XC	VT	LM	LM	LM	VT	LM	AW	XC A	XC B
Stafford	d				06 58	07 26			07 12									07 41				08 03	08 04
Penkridge	d								07 18									07 47					
Wolverhampton	a			07 08	07 12				07 28			07 32	07 36					07 57			08 08	08 16	08 17
	d	07 04		07 10	07 15			07 19	07 28			07 32	07 36		07 44		07 49	07 57	08 06		08 09	08 18	08 18
Coseley	d							07 24									07 54	08 03					
Tipton	d							07 26									07 56						
Dudley Port	d							07 28									07 58						
Sandwell & Dudley	d	07 15						07 32					07 46		07 56		08 02						
Smethwick Galton Bridge	d			07 21				07 34	07 40								08 04				08 21		
Smethwick Rolfe Street	d							07 36									08 06						
Birmingham New Street	a	07 24		07 27	07 31			07 44	07 47			07 55	07 55	07 55	08 05		08 14	08 17	08 24		08 27	08 38	08 38
	d	07 30	07 33	07 36	07 42		07 39	07 47		07 50	07 53			08 03	08 10	08 13	08 17		08 30	08 33	08 36	08 42	08 42
Adderley Park	d						07 44																
Stechford	d						07 47									08 20							
Lea Hall	d						07 50									08 23							
Marston Green	d		07 41								08 01					08 26				08 41			
Birmingham International	a	07 39	07 45	07 50			07 54			07 59	08 05			08 13	08 19	08 29			08 38	08 45	08 51		
	d	07 40	07 45							08 00	08 05			08 14	08 20	08 29			08 39	08 45			
Hampton-in-Arden	d		07 48													08 32				08 48			
Berkswell	d										08 11					08 37							
Tile Hill	d		07 55								08 14					08 40				08 55			
Canley	d										08 17					08 44							
Coventry	a	07 50	08 00							08 10	08 20			08 24	08 30	08 47			08 49	09 00			
	d	07 52	08 01							08 11	08 21			08 25	08 31				08 51	09 01			
Rugby	d		08 13			08 20				08 23	08 33									09 13			
Long Buckby	d		08 23								08 43									09 23			
Northampton	a		08 34			08 40					08 54									09 34			
London Euston	a	08 54				09 50				09 14					09 35				09 55				

Station		LM	LM	LM	LM	VT	LM	VT	LM	XC	VT	LM	LM	LM	VT	LM	AW	LM	LM	XC A	XC B	LM	LM	VT
Stafford	d	08 23			08 10					08 26				08 43				09b21		09 03	09 04		09 10	
Penkridge	d				08 16									08 48									09 16	
Wolverhampton	a				08 28			08 31	08 36	08 39				08 58			09 08			09 15	09 17		09 27	
	d			08 19	08 28			08 32	08 36	08 41	08 45		08 49	08 59			09 10			09 17	09 18	09 19	09 28	
Coseley	d			08 24									08 54	09 04								09 24		
Tipton	d			08 26									08 56									09 26		
Dudley Port	d			08 28									08 58									09 28		
Sandwell & Dudley	d			08 32					08 46		08 56		09 02									09 32		
Smethwick Galton Bridge	d			08 34	08 40								09 04				09 22					09 34	09 40	
Smethwick Rolfe Street	d			08 36									09 06									09 36		
Birmingham New Street	a			08 44	08 47			08 55	08 55	08 58	09 05		09 14	09 18			09 28			09 39	09 39	09 44	09 47	
	d		08 39			08 50	08 53			09 03	09 10	09 13	09 17		09 30	09 33	09 36		09 39	09 42	09 42			09 50
Adderley Park	d		08 44																09 44					
Stechford	d		08 47									09 20							09 47					
Lea Hall	d		08 50									09 23							09 50					
Marston Green	d						09 01					09 26				09 41								
Birmingham International	a		08 54			08 59	09 05			09 13	09 19	09 29			09 38	09 45	09 51		09 54					09 59
	d					09 00	09 05			09 14	09 20	09 29			09 39	09 46								10 00
Hampton-in-Arden	d											09 32				09 49								
Berkswell	d						09 11					09 37												
Tile Hill	d						09 14					09 40				09 56								
Canley	d						09 17					09 44												
Coventry	a					09 10	09 20			09 24	09 30	09 47			09 49	10 01								10 10
	d					09 11	09 21			09 25	09 31				09 51	10 02								10 11
Rugby	d	09 20				09 23	09 33									10 14		10 18						10 23
Long Buckby	d						09 43									10 24								
Northampton	a	09 41					09 54									10 35		10 38						
London Euston	a	10 49				10 14					10 34				10 54			11 49						11 14

A from 11 September

B until 4 September

b arr. 0912

Table 68

Saturdays

Stafford - Wolverhampton - Birmingham - Coventry - Northampton

	LM	VT	LM	XC	VT	LM	LM	LM	VT A	VT B	LM	AW	LM	LM	XC	LM	LM	VT	LM	VT	LM	XC
Stafford d				09 26				09 43					10b21		10 03		10 10					10 26
Penkridge d																	10 16					
Wolverhampton a		09 31	09 36	09 39				09 56				10 08			10 15		10 27			10 31	10 36	10 39
d		09 32	09 36	09 41	09 45		09 49	09 57				10 09			10 17	10 19	10 28			10 32	10 36	10 41
Coseley d							09 54	10 03								10 24						
Tipton d							09 56									10 26						
Dudley Port d							09 58									10 28						
Sandwell & Dudley d			09 46		09 56		10 02									10 32					10 46	
Smethwick Galton Bridge d							10 04					10 20				10 34	10 40					
Smethwick Rolfe Street d							10 06									10 36						
Birmingham New Street a		09 55	09 55	09 58	10 05		10 14	10 17				10 26			10 39	10 44	10 47			10 55	10 55	10 58
d	09 53			10 03	10 10	10 13	10 17		10 30	10 30	10 33	10 36		10 39	10 42	10 47		10 50	10 53			11 03
Adderley Park d														10 44								
Stechford d						10 20								10 47								
Lea Hall d						10 23								10 50								
Marston Green d	10 01					10 26					10 41								11 01			
Birmingham International a	10 05			10 13	10 19	10 29			10 38	10 39	10 45	10 50		10 54				10 59	11 05			11 13
d	10 05			10 14	10 20	10 29			10 39	10 40	10 45							11 00	11 05			11 14
Hampton-in-Arden d						10 32					10 48											
Berkswell d	10 11					10 37													11 11			
Tile Hill d	10 14					10 40					10 55								11 14			
Canley d	10 17					10 44													11 17			
Coventry a	10 20			10 24	10 30	10 47			10 49	10 50	11 00							11 10	11 20			11 24
d	10 21			10 25	10 31				10 51	10 51	11 01							11 11	11 21			11 25
Rugby d	10 33										11 13		11 19					11 23	11 33			
Long Buckby d	10 43										11 23								11 43			
Northampton a	10 54										11 34		11 40						11 54			
London Euston a					11 34				11 54	11 54			12 49					12 14				

	VT	LM	LM	LM	VT	LM	AW	LM	LM	XC	LM	LM	VT	LM	VT	LM	XC	VT B	VT A	LM	LM
Stafford d				10 43				11c21		11 03		11 10					11 26				
Penkridge d												11 16									
Wolverhampton a				10 56			11 08			11 16		11 27			11 31	11 36	11 39				
d	10 45		10 49	10 57			11 10			11 17	11 19	11 28			11 32	11 36	11 41	11 45	11 45		11 49
Coseley d			10 54	11 03							11 24										11 54
Tipton d			10 56								11 26										11 56
Dudley Port d			10 58								11 28										11 58
Sandwell & Dudley d	10 56		11 02								11 32					11 46		11 56	11 56		12 02
Smethwick Galton Bridge d			11 04				11 21				11 34	11 40									12 04
Smethwick Rolfe Street d			11 06								11 36										12 06
Birmingham New Street a	11 05		11 14	11 17			11 27			11 39	11 44	11 47			11 55	11 55	11 58	12 05	12 05		12 14
d	11 10	11 13	11 17		11 30	11 33	11 37		11 39	11 42	11 47		11 50	11 53			12 03	12 10	12 10	12 13	12 17
Adderley Park d									11 44												
Stechford d		11 20							11 47											12 20	
Lea Hall d		11 23							11 50											12 23	
Marston Green d		11 26				11 41								12 01						12 26	
Birmingham International a	11 19	11 29			11 38	11 45	11 51		11 54				11 59	12 05			12 13	12 19	12 19	12 29	
d	11 20	11 29			11 39	11 46							12 00	12 05			12 14	12 20	12 20	12 29	
Hampton-in-Arden d		11 32				11 49														12 32	
Berkswell d		11 37												12 11						12 37	
Tile Hill d		11 40				11 56								12 14						12 40	
Canley d		11 44												12 17						12 44	
Coventry a	11 30	11 48			11 49	12 01							12 10	12 20			12 24	12 29	12 30	12 47	
d	11 31				11 51	12 02							12 11	12 21			12 25	12 29	12 31		
Rugby d						12 14		12 18					12 23	12 33							
Long Buckby d						12 24								12 43							
Northampton a						12 35		12 38						12 54							
London Euston a	12 34				12 54			13 49					13 14					13 34	13 34		

A until 10 July, from 11 September
B from 17 July until 4 September
b arr. 1013
c arr. 1112

Table 68

Saturdays

Stafford - Wolverhampton - Birmingham - Coventry - Northampton

	LM	VT	LM	AW	LM	LM	XC	LM	LM	VT	LM	VT	LM	XC	VT	LM	LM	LM	VT	LM	AW	LM
Stafford d	11 43				12b21		12 03		12 10					12 25				12 43				13c21
Penkridge d									12 16													
Wolverhampton a	11 56			12 08			12 16		12 27			12 31	12 36	12 39				12 56			13 08	
d	11 57			12 09			12 17	12 19	12 28			12 32	12 36	12 41	12 45		12 49	12 57			13 09	
Coseley d	12 03							12 24									12 54	13 03				
Tipton d								12 26									12 56					
Dudley Port d								12 28									12 58					
Sandwell & Dudley d								12 32					12 46		12 56		13 02					
Smethwick Galton Bridge d				12 20				12 34	12 40								13 04				13 20	
Smethwick Rolfe Street d								12 36									13 06					
Birmingham New Street a	12 17			12 26			12 39	12 44	12 47			12 55	12 55	12 58	13 05		13 14	13 17			13 26	
d		12 30	12 33	12 36		12 39	12 42	12 47		12 50	12 53			13 03	13 10	13 13	13 17		13 30	13 33	13 36	
Adderley Park d						12 44																
Stechford d						12 47										13 20						
Lea Hall d						12 50										13 23						
Marston Green d			12 41								13 01					13 26				13 41		
Birmingham International a		12 38	12 45	12 50		12 54				12 59	13 05			13 13	13 19	13 29			13 38	13 45	13 51	
d		12 39	12 45							13 00	13 05			13 15	13 20	13 29			13 39	13 45		
Hampton-in-Arden d			12 48													13 32				13 48		
Berkswell d											13 11					13 37						
Tile Hill d			12 55								13 14					13 40				13 55		
Canley d											13 17					13 44						
Coventry a		12 49	13 00							13 10	13 20			13 24	13 30	13 47			13 49	14 00		
d		12 51	13 01							13 11	13 21			13 25	13 31				13 51	14 01		
Rugby d			13 13		13 19					13 23	13 33									14 13		14 18
Long Buckby d			13 23								13 43									14 23		
Northampton a			13 34		13 40						13 54									14 34		14 38
London Euston a		13 54			14 49					14 14					14 34				14 54			15 49

	LM	XC	LM	LM	VT	LM	VT	LM	XC	VT	LM	LM	LM	VT	LM	AW	LM	LM	XC	LM	LM	VT
Stafford d		13 03		13 10					13 26				13 43				14e21		14 03		14 10	
Penkridge d				13 16																	14 16	
Wolverhampton a		13 15		13 27			13 31	13 36	13 39				13 56			14 08			14 16		14 27	
d		13 16	13 19	13 28			13 32	13 36	13 41	13 45		13 49	13 57			14 09			14 17	14 19	14 28	
Coseley d			13 24									13 54	14 03							14 24		
Tipton d			13 26									13 56								14 26		
Dudley Port d			13 28									13 58								14 28		
Sandwell & Dudley d			13 32					13 46		13 56		14 02								14 32		
Smethwick Galton Bridge d			13 34	13 40								14 04				14 20				14 34	14 40	
Smethwick Rolfe Street d			13 36									14 06								14 36		
Birmingham New Street a		13 39	13 44	13 47			13 55	13 55	13 58	14 05		14 14	14 17			14 26			14 39	14 44	14 47	
d	13 39	13 42	13 47		13 50	13 53			14 03	14 10	14 13	14 17		14 30	14 33	14 36		14 39	14 42	14 47		14 50
Adderley Park d	13 44																	14 44				
Stechford d	13 47										14 20							14 47				
Lea Hall d	13 50										14 23							14 50				
Marston Green d						14 01					14 26				14 41							
Birmingham International a	13 54				13 59	14 05			14 13	14 19	14 29			14 38	14 45	14 50		14 54				14 59
d					14 00	14 05			14 14	14 20	14 29			14 39	14 45							15 00
Hampton-in-Arden d											14 32				14 48							
Berkswell d						14 11					14 37											
Tile Hill d						14 14					14 40				14 55							
Canley d						14 17					14 44											
Coventry a					14 10	14 20			14 24	14 30	14 47			14 49	15 00							15 10
d					14 11	14 21			14 25	14 31				14 51	15 01							15 11
Rugby d					14 23	14 33									15 13		15 19					15 23
Long Buckby d						14 43									15 23							
Northampton a						14 54									15 34		15 39					
London Euston a					15 14					15 34				15 54			16 49					16 14

b arr. 1212
c arr. 1312
e arr. 1412

Table 68

Stafford - Wolverhampton - Birmingham - Coventry - Northampton

		LM ◇1	VT ◇1 A	LM	XC ◇1	VT ◇1 B	VT ◇1 A	LM 1	LM	LM 1	VT ◇1	LM ◇1	AW ◇	LM ◇1	LM	XC ◇1	LM	LM 1	VT ◇1 A	VT ◇1 B	LM ◇1	VT ◇1
Stafford	d				14 26					14 46				15b21		15 03		15 10				
Penkridge	d																	15 16				
Wolverhampton 7	a		14 31	14 36	14 39	14 32				14 59			15 08			15 16		15 27				15 31
	d		14 32	14 36	14 41	14 45	14 45		14 49	14 59			15 09			15 17	15 19	15 28				15 32
Coseley	d								14 54	15 05							15 24					
Tipton	d								14 56								15 26					
Dudley Port	d								14 58								15 28					
Sandwell & Dudley	d			14 46		14 56	14 56		15 02								15 32					
Smethwick Galton Bridge 7	d								15 04				15 20				15 34	15 40				
Smethwick Rolfe Street	d								15 06								15 36					
Birmingham New Street 12	a		14 55	14 55	14 58	15 05	15 05		15 14	15 18			15 26			15 39	15 44	15 47				15 55
	d	14 53			15 03	15 10	15 10	15 13	15 17		15 30	15 33	15 36		15 39	15 42	15 47		15 50	15 50	15 53	
Adderley Park	d														15 44							
Stechford	d							15 20							15 47							
Lea Hall	d							15 23							15 50							
Marston Green	d	15 01						15 26				15 41									16 01	
Birmingham International	a	15 05			15 13	15 19	15 19	15 29			15 38	15 45	15 50		15 54				15 59	15 59	16 05	
	d	15 05			15 14	15 20	15 20	15 29			15 39	15 45							16 00	16 00	16 05	
Hampton-in-Arden	d							15 32				15 48										
Berkswell	d	15 11						15 37													16 11	
Tile Hill	d	15 14						15 40				15 55									16 14	
Canley	d	15 17						15 44													16 17	
Coventry	a	15 20			15 24	15 30	15 30	15 47			15 49	16 00							16 10	16 10	16 20	
	d	15 21			15 25	15 31	15 31				15 51	16 01							16 11	16 11	16 21	
Rugby	d	15 33										16 13		16 18					16 23	16 23	16 33	
Long Buckby	d	15 43										16 23									16 43	
Northampton	a	15 54										16 34		16 38							16 54	
London Euston 15 ⊖	a					16 34	16 34				16 54			17 49					17 14	17 14		

		VT ◇1 C	LM	XC ◇1	VT ◇1 ⊠	LM 1	LM	LM 1	VT ◇1	LM ◇1	AW ◇	LM ◇1	LM	XC ◇1	LM	LM 1	VT ◇1	LM ◇1	VT ◇1	VT ◇1 C	LM	XC ◇1	VT ◇1
Stafford	d			15 26				15 43				16c21		16 03		16 10						16 25	
Penkridge	d															16 16							
Wolverhampton 7	a	15 31	15 36	15 39				15 56			16 08			16 16		16 27			16 31	16 32	16 36	16 39	
	d	15 32	15 36	15 41	15 45		15 49	15 57			16 09			16 17	16 19	16 28			16 32	16 32	16 36	16 41	16 45
Coseley	d						15 54	16 03							16 24								
Tipton	d						15 56								16 26								
Dudley Port	d						15 58								16 28								
Sandwell & Dudley	d		15 46		15 56		16 02								16 32						16 46		16 56
Smethwick Galton Bridge 7	d						16 04				16 20				16 34	16 40							
Smethwick Rolfe Street	d						16 06								16 36								
Birmingham New Street 12	a	15 55	15 55	15 58	16 05		16 14	16 17			16 26			16 39	16 44	16 47			16 55	16 55	16 55	16 58	17 05
	d			16 03	16 10	16 13	16 17		16 30	16 33	16 36		16 39	16 42	16 47		16 50	16 53				17 03	17 10
Adderley Park	d												16 44										
Stechford	d					16 20							16 47										
Lea Hall	d					16 23							16 50										
Marston Green	d					16 26				16 41								17 01					
Birmingham International	a			16 13	16 19	16 29			16 38	16 45	16 50		16 54				16 59	17 05				17 13	17 19
	d			16 14	16 20	16 29			16 39	16 45							17 00	17 05				17 14	17 20
Hampton-in-Arden	d					16 32				16 48													
Berkswell	d					16 37												17 11					
Tile Hill	d					16 40				16 55								17 14					
Canley	d					16 44												17 17					
Coventry	a			16 24	16 30	16 47			16 49	17 00							17 10	17 20				17 24	17 30
	d			16 25	16 31				16 51	17 01							17 11	17 21				17 25	17 31
Rugby	d									17 13		17 19					17 23	17 33					
Long Buckby	d									17 23								17 43					
Northampton	a									17 34		17 40						17 54					
London Euston 15 ⊖	a				17 34				17 52			18 49					18 14						18 34

A until 10 July, from 11 September
B from 17 July until 4 September
C from 23 October
b arr. 1512
c arr. 1612

Table 68

Stafford - Wolverhampton - Birmingham - Coventry - Northampton

		LM 1	LM	LM 1	VT ◇1	LM ◇1	AW ◇	LM ◇1	LM	XC ◇1	LM	LM 1	VT ◇1	LM ◇1	VT ◇1	LM	XC ◇1	VT ◇1	LM 1	LM	LM 1	VT ◇1
Stafford	d			16 46				17b21		17 03		17 10					17 26				17 43	
Penkridge	d											17 16										
Wolverhampton 7	a			16 59			17 08			17 16		17 27			17 31	17 36	17 39				17 56	
	d		16 49	16 59			17 09			17 17	17 19	17 28			17 32	17 36	17 41	17 45		17 49	17 57	
Coseley	d		16 54	17 05							17 24									17 54	18 03	
Tipton	d		16 56								17 26									17 56		
Dudley Port	d		16 58								17 28									17 58		
Sandwell & Dudley	d		17 02								17 32					17 46		17 56		18 02		
Smethwick Galton Bridge 7	d		17 04				17 20				17 34	17 40								18 04		
Smethwick Rolfe Street	d		17 06								17 36									18 06		
Birmingham New Street 12	a		17 14	17 18			17 26			17 39	17 44	17 47			17 55	17 55	17 58	18 05		18 14	18 17	
	d	17 13	17 17		17 30	17 33	17 36		17 39	17 42	17 47		17 50	17 53			18 03	18 10	18 13	18 17		18 30
Adderley Park	d	17 17							17 44													
Stechford	d	17 21							17 47										18 20			
Lea Hall	d	17 23							17 50										18 23			
Marston Green	d	17 26				17 41								18 01					18 26			
Birmingham International	a	17 29			17 38	17 45	17 50		17 54				17 59	18 05			18 13	18 19	18 29			18 38
	d	17 30			17 39	17 45							18 00	18 05			18 14	18 20	18 29			18 39
Hampton-in-Arden	d	17 33				17 48													18 32			
Berkswell	d	17 38												18 11					18 37			
Tile Hill	d	17 41				17 55								18 14					18 40			
Canley	d	17 44												18 17					18 44			
Coventry	a	17 47			17 49	18 00							18 10	18 20			18 24	18 30	18 47			18 49
	d				17 51	18 01							18 11	18 21			18 25	18 31				18 51
Rugby	d					18 13		18 18					18 23	18 33								
Long Buckby	d					18 23								18 43								
Northampton	a					18 34		18 38						18 54								
London Euston 15 ⊖	a				18 54			19 54					19 14					19 34				19 54

		LM ◇1	AW ◇	XC ◇1	LM ◇1	LM	LM	LM 1	VT ◇1	LM ◇1	VT ◇1 A	LM	XC ◇1	VT ◇1 B	VT ◇1 A	LM 1	LM	LM 1	LM ◇1	AW ◇	XC ◇1	LM ◇1	LM
Stafford	d			18 04	18c21			18 10					18 27					18 43			19 03	19e21	
Penkridge	d							18 16															
Wolverhampton 7	a		18 08	18 16				18 27			18 31	18 36	18 40	18 32				18 56		19 08	19 16		
	d		18 09	18 17			18 19	18 28			18 32	18 36	18 41	18 45	18 45		18 49	18 57		19 09	19 17		
Coseley	d						18 24										18 54	19 03					
Tipton	d						18 26										18 56						
Dudley Port	d						18 28										18 58						
Sandwell & Dudley	d						18 32					18 46		18 56	18 56		19 02						
Smethwick Galton Bridge 7	d		18 20				18 34	18 40									19 04			19 20			
Smethwick Rolfe Street	d						18 36										19 06						
Birmingham New Street 12	a		18 26	18 38			18 44	18 47			18 55	18 55	18 58	19 05	19 05		19 14	19 17		19 26	19 33		
	d	18 33	18 36	18 42		18 39	18 47		18 50	18 53			19 03	19 10	19 10	19 13			19 33	19 36	19 42		19 39
Adderley Park	d					18 44																	19 44
Stechford	d					18 47										19 20							19 47
Lea Hall	d					18 50										19 23							19 50
Marston Green	d	18 41								19 01						19 26			19 41				
Birmingham International	a	18 45	18 50			18 54			18 59	19 05			19 13	19 19	19 19	19 29			19 45	19 50			19 54
	d	18 45							19 00	19 05			19 14	19 20	19 20	19 29			19 45				
Hampton-in-Arden	d	18 48														19 32			19 48				
Berkswell	d									19 11						19 37							
Tile Hill	d	18 55								19 14						19 40			19 55				
Canley	d									19 17						19 44							
Coventry	a	19 00							19 10	19 20			19 24	19 30	19 30	19 47			20 00				
	d	19 01							19 11	19 21			19 25	19 31	19 31				20 01				
Rugby	d	19 13			19 18				19 23	19 33				19 44	19 44				20 13			20 18	
Long Buckby	d	19 23								19 43									20 23				
Northampton	a	19 34			19 38					19 54									20 34			20 38	
London Euston 15 ⊖	a								20 16					20 56	20 56								

A until 10 July, from 11 September
B from 17 July until 4 September
b arr. 1712
c arr. 1812
e arr. 1912

Table 68

Saturdays

Stafford - Wolverhampton - Birmingham - Coventry - Northampton

		LM	LM ■	LM ◇■	VT ◇■ ☕	LM		XC ◇■ 🛒	VT ◇■ ☕	LM ■	LM	LM ■	LM ◇■	AW ◇ 🛒	XC ◇■ 🛒	LM		LM ■	LM ◇■	VT ◇■ ☕	LM	XC ◇■ 🛒	VT ◇■ ☕	LM ■	LM
Stafford	d		19 10					19 25				19 43			20 03			20 12				20 26			
Penkridge	d		19 16									19 49													
Wolverhampton ■	a		19 27		19 31	19 36		19 39				19 59		20 10	20 16			20 28		20 31	20 36	20 39			
	d	19 19	19 28		19 32	19 36		19 41	19 45		19 49	19 59		20 10	20 17			20 28		20 32	20 36	20 41	20 45		20 49
Coseley	d	19 24									19 54	20 04													20 54
Tipton	d	19 26									19 56														20 56
Dudley Port	d	19 28									19 58														20 58
Sandwell & Dudley	d	19 32				19 46			19 56		20 02										20 46		20 56		21 02
Smethwick Galton Bridge ■	d	19 34	19 40								20 04			20 21				20 40							21 04
Smethwick Rolfe Street	d	19 36									20 06														21 06
Birmingham New Street ■	a	19 44	19 47		19 55	19 55		19 58	20 05		20 16	20 17		20 27	20 33			20 47		20 55	20 57	20 58	21 05		21 14
	d	19 47		19 53				20 03	20 10	20 13			20 33	20 36	20 42	20 39			20 53			21 03	21 10	21 13	
Adderley Park	d															20 44									
Stechford	d									20 20						20 47								21 20	
Lea Hall	d									20 23						20 50								21 23	
Marston Green	d			20 01						20 26			20 41						21 01					21 26	
Birmingham International ✈	a			20 05				20 13	20 19	20 29			20 45	20 50		20 54			21 05			21 13	21 19	21 29	
	d			20 05				20 14	20 20	20 29			20 45						21 05			21 14	21 20	21 29	
Hampton-in-Arden	d									20 32			20 48											21 32	
Berkswell	d			20 11						20 37									21 11					21 37	
Tile Hill	d			20 14						20 40			20 55						21 14					21 40	
Canley	d			20 17						20 44									21 17					21 44	
Coventry	a			20 20				20 24	20 30	20 47			21 00						21 20			21 24	21 30	21 47	
	d			20 21				20 25	20 31				21 01						21 21			21 25	21 31		
Rugby	d			20 33					20 43				21 13						21 33				21 43		
Long Buckby	d			20 43									21 23						21 43						
Northampton	a			20 54									21 34						21 54						
London Euston ■ ⊖	a								21 57														22 55		

		LM ■		VT ◇■ ☕	XC ◇■ 🛒	LM ◇■	LM	LM	LM ◇■	VT ◇■ ☕	LM	XC ◇■ 🛒		LM ■	LM	LM ■	AW	XC ◇■ 🛒	LM ■	LM	VT ◇■ ☕	LM ◇■		LM	VT ◇■ ☕
Stafford	d	20 43			21 03							21 27				21 42		22 03			22 08				22 29
Penkridge	d	20 49														21 48									
Wolverhampton ■	a	20 57			21 15					21 31	21 36	21 39				21 58	22 10	22 14			22 22			22 36	22 40
	d	20 57		21 07	21 16			21 19		21 33	21 36	21 41			21 49	21 58	22 10	22 16		22 19	22 23			22 36	22 41
Coseley	d	21 03						21 24							21 54	22 04				22 24					
Tipton	d							21 26							21 56					22 26					
Dudley Port	d							21 28							21 58					22 28					
Sandwell & Dudley	d			21 17				21 32			21 46				22 02					22 32				22 46	
Smethwick Galton Bridge ■	d							21 34							22 04		22 21			22 34					
Smethwick Rolfe Street	d							21 36							22 06					22 36					
Birmingham New Street ■	a	21 17		21 26	21 32			21 44		21 54	21 55	21 58			22 14	22 20	22 32	22 32		22 44	22 46			22 55	22 59
	d			21 30		21 33	21 39		21 53					22 13					22 33			22 53			
Adderley Park	d						21 44																		
Stechford	d						21 47							22 20											
Lea Hall	d						21 50							22 23											
Marston Green	d					21 41			22 01					22 26					22 41			23 01			
Birmingham International ✈	a			21 39		21 45	21 54		22 05					22 29					22 45			23 05			
	d			21 40		21 45			22 05					22 29					22 45			23 05			
Hampton-in-Arden	d					21 48								22 32					22 48						
Berkswell	d								22 11					22 37								23 11			
Tile Hill	d					21 55			22 14					22 40					22 55			23 14			
Canley	d								22 17					22 44								23 17			
Coventry	a			21 50		22 00			22 20					22 47					23 00			23 20			
	d			21 51		22 01			22 21													23 21			
Rugby	d			22 03		22 13			22 33													23 33			
Long Buckby	d					22 23			22 43													23 43			
Northampton	a					22 34			22 54													23 57			
London Euston ■ ⊖	a			23 33																					

Table 68

Saturdays

Stafford - Wolverhampton - Birmingham - Coventry - Northampton

		VT ◇■ A ☕	LM ■	LM	XC ◇■ 🛒	LM ■	AW ◇
Stafford	d	22 28			22 34	22 47	
Penkridge	d					22 53	
Wolverhampton ■	a	22 42			22 50	23 03	23 08
	d	22 42		22 49	22 53	23 03	23 09
Coseley	d			22 54		23 09	
Tipton	d			22 56			
Dudley Port	d			22 58			
Sandwell & Dudley	d			23 02			
Smethwick Galton Bridge ■	d			23 04			
Smethwick Rolfe Street	d			23 06			
Birmingham New Street ■	a	23 01		23 14	23 17	23 21	23 29
	d		23 13				
Adderley Park	d		23 18				
Stechford	d		23 21				
Lea Hall	d		23 24				
Marston Green	d		23 27				
Birmingham International ✈	a		23 30				
	d		23 30				
Hampton-in-Arden	d		23 33				
Berkswell	d		23 38				
Tile Hill	d		23 41				
Canley	d		23 45				
Coventry	a		23 48				
	d						
Rugby	d						
Long Buckby	d						
Northampton	a						
London Euston ■ ⊖	a						

Sundays

		VT ◇■ ☕	LM ■	LM ■	LM	XC ◇■ 🛒	LM ◇■	AW B	VT ◇■ C ☕	VT ◇■ D ☕		LM ■	LM	XC ◇■ E ☕🛒	LM ◇■	AW B	VT ◇■ ☕	LM ■	LM	XC ◇■ F ☕🛒		XC ◇■ G ☕🛒	LM ◇■	AW ◇ B	LM ◇■
Stafford	d													09 26						10 26		10 27			10 42
Penkridge	d																								10 49
Wolverhampton ■	a							08 59						09 40		09 57				10 40		10 42		10 57	11 00
	d	08 05			08 22			09 00	09 05	09 05			09 22	09 41		09 59	10 05		10 22	10 41		10 43		10 58	11 01
Coseley	d				08 27								09 27						10 27						
Tipton	d				08 29								09 29						10 29						
Dudley Port	d				08 31								09 31						10 31						
Sandwell & Dudley	d	08 15			08 35				09 15	09 15			09 35				10 15		10 35						
Smethwick Galton Bridge ■	d				08 37								09 37						10 37						
Smethwick Rolfe Street	d				08 39								09 39						10 39						
Birmingham New Street ■	a	08 24			08 46			09 15	09 24	09 24			09 46	09 58		10 14	10 24		10 46	10 58		10 59		11 13	11 17
	d	08 30	08 34	08 38		09 03	09 14	09 20	09 30	09 30		09 34		10 03	10 14	10 20	10 30	10 34		11 03		11 03	11 14	11 20	
Adderley Park	d			08 42								09 38						10 38							
Stechford	d			08 46								09 42						10 42							
Lea Hall	d			08 48								09 44						10 44							
Marston Green	d		08 42	08 52			09 22					09 48			10 22			10 48					11 22		
Birmingham International ✈	a	08 39	08 45	08 55		09 13	09 25	09 31	09 39	09 39		09 51		10 13	10 25	10 32	10 39	10 52		11 13		11 13	11 25	11 32	
	d	08 40	08 45			09 14	09 25		09 40	09 40		09 51		10 14	10 25		10 40	10 52		11 14		11 14	11 25		
Hampton-in-Arden	d						09 28								10 28								11 28		
Berkswell	d		08 51				09 33								10 33								11 33		
Tile Hill	d		08 54				09 36								10 36								11 36		
Canley	d		08 57				09 40								10 40								11 40		
Coventry	a	08 50	09 00			09 24	09 44		09 50	09 50		10 01		10 24	10 44		10 50	11 03		11 24		11 24	11 44		
	d	08 51				09 25	09 44		09 51	09 51				10 25	10 44		10 51			11 25		11 25	11 44		
Rugby	d	09 04					09 56		10 04	10 04					10 56		11 04						11 56		
Long Buckby	d						10 06								11 06								12 06		
Northampton	a						10 17								11 17								12 17		
London Euston ■ ⊖	a	10 28							11 32	11 34							12 27								

A from 23 October
B until 5 September
C from 18 July
D until 11 July
E ☕ from Birmingham New Street 🛒 to Wolverhampton
F until 11 July. ☕ from Birmingham New Street 🛒 to Wolverhampton
G from 18 July. ☕ from Birmingham New Street 🛒 t
Wolverhampton

Table 68

Sundays

Stafford - Wolverhampton - Birmingham - Coventry - Northampton

Station		VT ◇1	LM 1	LM	VT ◇1	VT ◇1	XC ◇1 A	XC ◇1 B	XC ◇1 C	VT ◇1	LM ◇1	LM ◇1	WS ◇1 D	WS ◇1 E	LM ◇1	VT ◇1	LM 1	AW D	AW E	LM	VT ◇1	VT ◇1 F	XC ◇1 G
Stafford	d						11b24	11 28	11 27						12 18								12 25
Penkridge	d																						
Wolverhampton 7	a					11 33	11 40	11 42	11 41				12s07	12s10				12 17	12 17			12 32	12 40
	d	11 05		11 22		11 33	11 41	11 43	11 42	11 45			12s08	12s14				12 18	12 18	12 22		12 33	12 41
Coseley	d			11 27																12 27			
Tipton	d			11 29																12 29			
Dudley Port	d			11 31																12 31			
Sandwell & Dudley	d	11 15		11 35						11 57										12 35			
Smethwick Galton Bridge 7	d			11 37									12 18							12 37			
Smethwick Rolfe Street	d			11 39																12 39			
Birmingham New Street 12	a	11 26		11 49		11 56	11 58	12 00	12 00	12 06			12 26	12 55				12 33	12 33	12 46		12 55	12 58
	d	11 30	11 34		11 50		12 03	12 03	12 03	12 10		12 14	12 27	12 56		12 30	12 34	12 38	12 39		12 50		13 03
Adderley Park	d		11 38														12 38						
Stechford	d		11 42														12 42						
Lea Hall	d		11 44														12 44						
Marston Green	d		11 48									12 22					12 48						
Birmingham International	a	11 39	11 51		11 59		12 13	12 13	12 13	12 19		12 25				12 38	12 51	12 56	12 56		12 59		13 13
	d	11 40	11 51		12 00		12 14	12 14	12 14	12 20		12 25				12 39	12 51				13 00		13 14
Hampton-in-Arden	d											12 28											
Berkswell	d											12 33											
Tile Hill	d											12 36					12 58						
Canley	d											12 40											
Coventry	a	11 50	12 01		12 10		12 24	12 24	12 24	12 30		12 44				12 49	13 04				13 10		13 24
	d	11 51			12 11		12 25	12 25	12 25	12 31		12 44				12 51					13 11		13 25
Rugby	d	12 07			12 25						12 26	12 56			13 17						13 25		
Long Buckby	d										12 37	13 06			13 28								
Northampton	a										12 48	13 17			13 39								
London Euston 15	a	13 06			13 19					13 39	13 53				14 53	13 59					14 19		

Station		VT ◇1	LM ◇1	LM 1	VT ◇1	LM 1	AW ◇ H	LM	VT ◇1	VT ◇1	XC ◇1 I	XC ◇1 A	VT ◇1	LM ◇1	LM ◇1	LM 1	LM ◇1	VT ◇1	LM 1	AW ◇ H	XC ◇1	LM
Stafford	d			12 42							13 25	13 26				13 43	14 17					
Penkridge	d			12 49												13 49						
Wolverhampton 7	a			12 59			13 08			13 31	13 40	13 40				13 58				14 08	14 13	
	d	12 45		12 59			13 09	13 22		13 32	13 41	13 41	13 45			13 58				14 09	14 15	14 22
Coseley	d							13 27														14 27
Tipton	d							13 29														14 29
Dudley Port	d							13 31														14 31
Sandwell & Dudley	d	12 55						13 35					13 56									14 35
Smethwick Galton Bridge 7	d							13 37														14 37
Smethwick Rolfe Street	d							13 39														14 39
Birmingham New Street 12	a	13 06		13 16			13 24	13 46		13 55	13 58	13 58	14 05			14 15				14 24	14 31	14 46
	d	13 10	13 14		13 30	13 36	13 37		13 50		14 03	14 03	14 10		14 14			14 30	14 34	14 37	14 42	
Adderley Park	d					13 40													14 38			
Stechford	d					13 44													14 42			
Lea Hall	d					13 46													14 44			
Marston Green	d		13 22			13 50									14 22				14 48			
Birmingham International	a	13 19	13 25		13 38	13 53	13 54		13 59		14 13	14 13	14 19		14 25			14 38	14 51	14 56		
	d	13 20	13 25		13 39	13 53			14 01		14 14	14 14	14 20		14 25			14 39	14 51			
Hampton-in-Arden	d		13 28												14 28							
Berkswell	d		13 33												14 33							
Tile Hill	d		13 36			14 00									14 36				14 58			
Canley	d		13 40												14 40							
Coventry	a	13 30	13 44		13 49	14 06			14 11		14 24	14 24	14 30		14 44			14 49	15 04			
	d	13 31	13 44		13 51				14 11		14 25	14 25	14 31		14 44			14 51				
Rugby	d		13 56						14 26					14 26	14 56		15 17					
Long Buckby	d		14 06											14 37	15 06		15 28					
Northampton	a		14 17											14 48	15 17		15 39					
London Euston 15	a	14 36			14 58				15 19				15 36	15 53			16 53	15 59				

A until 11 July. from Birmingham New Street to Wolverhampton
B from 18 July until 5 September. from Birmingham New Street to Wolverhampton
C from 12 September. from Birmingham New Street to Wolverhampton
D from 18 July until 5 September
E until 11 July
F until 17 October
G from Birmingham New Street to Wolverhampton
H until 5 September
I from 18 July. from Birmingham New Street to Wolverhampton
b arr. 1118

Table 68

Sundays

Stafford - Wolverhampton - Birmingham - Coventry - Northampton

Station		VT ◇1	VT ◇1 A	VT ◇1 B	WS ◇1 C	XC ◇1 D	VT ◇1	WS ◇1 E	LM ◇1	LM 1	VT ◇1	LM 1	AW ◇ F	XC ◇1	LM	VT ◇1	VT ◇1 A	VT ◇1 B	XC ◇1 D	VT ◇1	LM ◇1	LM ◇1	LM 1
Stafford	d					14 25				14 43									15 25				15 43
Penkridge	d									14 49													15 49
Wolverhampton 7	a		14 32	14 32	14s35	14 40		14s49		14 58			15 08	15 13			15 31	15 31	15 40				15 58
	d		14 32	14 33	14s35	14 41	14 45	14s51		14 58			15 09	15 15	15 22		15 32	15 32	15 41	15 45			15 58
Coseley	d														15 27								
Tipton	d														15 29								
Dudley Port	d														15 31								
Sandwell & Dudley	d						14 56								15 35					15 56			
Smethwick Galton Bridge 7	d							15 03							15 37								
Smethwick Rolfe Street	d														15 39								
Birmingham New Street 12	a		14 55	14 55	15 10	14 58	15 05	15 11		15 15			15 24	15 31	15 46		15 54	15 55	15 58	16 05			16 15
	d	14 50			15 13	15 03	15 10	15 13	15 14		15 30	15 34	15 39	15 42		15 50			16 04	16 10		16 14	
Adderley Park	d											15 38											
Stechford	d											15 42											
Lea Hall	d											15 44											
Marston Green	d								15 22			15 48										16 22	
Birmingham International	a	14 59				15 13	15 19		15 25		15 38	15 51	15 57			15 59			16 13	16 19		16 25	
	d	15 01				15 14	15 20		15 25		15 39	15 51				16 01			16 14	16 20		16 25	
Hampton-in-Arden	d								15 28													16 28	
Berkswell	d								15 33													16 33	
Tile Hill	d								15 36			15 58										16 36	
Canley	d								15 40													16 40	
Coventry	a	15 11				15 24	15 30		15 44		15 49	16 04				16 11			16 24	16 30		16 44	
	d	15 11				15 25	15 31		15 44		15 51					16 11			16 25	16 31		16 44	
Rugby	d	15 26							15 56							16 24					16 25	16 56	
Long Buckby	d								16 06												16 37	17 06	
Northampton	a								16 17												16 48	17 17	
London Euston 15	a	16 19					16 36				16 59					17 19				17 36	17 53		

Station		LM ◇1	VT ◇1	LM 1	AW ◇ F	XC ◇1	LM	VT ◇1	VT ◇1	XC ◇1 D	VT ◇1	LM ◇1	LM 1	VT ◇1	XC ◇1	LM 1	AW ◇ F	LM	VT ◇1	VT ◇1	XC ◇1 D	VT ◇1
Stafford	d	16 18								16 25			16 43								17 26	
Penkridge	d												16 49									
Wolverhampton 7	a				16 10	16 13			16 32	16 40			16 58		17 13		17 17			17 31	17 40	
	d				16 10	16 15	16 22		16 33	16 41	16 45		16 58		17 15		17 19	17 22		17 32	17 41	17 45
Coseley	d						16 27											17 27				
Tipton	d						16 29											17 29				
Dudley Port	d						16 31											17 31				
Sandwell & Dudley	d						16 35				16 56							17 35				17 56
Smethwick Galton Bridge 7	d						16 37											17 37				
Smethwick Rolfe Street	d						16 39											17 39				
Birmingham New Street 12	a				16 26	16 31	16 46		16 56	16 58	17 05		17 15		17 31		17 35	17 46		17 55	17 58	18 05
	d		16 30	16 34	16 36	16 42		16 50		17 03	17 10	17 14		17 30	17 42	17 34	17 38		17 50		18 03	18 10
Adderley Park	d			16 38												17 38						
Stechford	d			16 42												17 42						
Lea Hall	d			16 44												17 44						
Marston Green	d			16 48								17 22				17 48						
Birmingham International	a		16 38	16 51	16 56			16 59		17 13	17 19	17 25		17 39		17 51	17 56		17 59		18 13	18 19
	d		16 39	16 51				17 01		17 14	17 20	17 25		17 40		17 51			18 01		18 14	18 20
Hampton-in-Arden	d											17 28										
Berkswell	d											17 33										
Tile Hill	d			16 58								17 36				17 58						
Canley	d											17 40										
Coventry	a		16 49	17 05				17 11		17 24	17 30	17 44		17 50		18 05			18 11		18 24	18 30
	d		16 51					17 11		17 25	17 31	17 44		17 51					18 11		18 25	18 31
Rugby	d	17 18						17 26				17 56							18 26			
Long Buckby	d	17 28										18 06										
Northampton	a	17 39										18 17										
London Euston 15	a	18 53	17 59					18 19			18 36			18 59					19 19			19 36

A from 24 October
B until 17 October
C until 11 July
D from Birmingham New Street to Wolverhampton
E from 18 July until 5 September
F until 5 September

Table 68

Sundays

Stafford - Wolverhampton - Birmingham - Coventry - Northampton

		LM	LM	LM	LM	VT	LM	AW	XC	LM		VT	VT	WS	XC	VT	WS	LM	LM	VT		LM	AW	XC	LM
								A						B	C		D						A		
Stafford	d			17 43	18 18										18 26				18 43						
Penkridge	d			17 49															18 49						
Wolverhampton	a			17 58				18 10	18 13				18 32	18s35	18 40		18s35		18 58				19 08	19 13	
	d			17 58				18 10	18 15	18 22			18 33	18s37	18 41	18 45	18s53		18 58				19 09	19 15	19 22
Coseley	d									18 27															19 27
Tipton	d									18 29															19 29
Dudley Port	d									18 31															19 31
Sandwell & Dudley	d									18 35						18 56									19 35
Smethwick Galton Bridge	d									18 37							19 03								19 37
Smethwick Rolfe Street	d									18 39															19 39
Birmingham New Street	a			18 15				18 28	18 31	18 46			18 56	19 10	18 58	19 05	19 11		19 15				19 24	19 31	19 46
	d		18 14			18 30	18 34	18 37	18 42			18 50		19 13	19 03	19 10	19 13	19 14		19 30		19 34	19 37	19 42	
Adderley Park	d						18 38															19 38			
Stechford	d						18 42															19 42			
Lea Hall	d						18 44															19 44			
Marston Green	d		18 22				18 48											19 22				19 48			
Birmingham International	a		18 25			18 38	18 51	18 56				18 59			19 13	19 19		19 25		19 38		19 51	19 56		
	d		18 25			18 39	18 51					19 01			19 14	19 20		19 25		19 39		19 51			
Hampton-in-Arden	d		18 28															19 28							
Berkswell	d		18 33															19 33							
Tile Hill	d		18 36				18 58											19 36				19 58			
Canley	d		18 40															19 40							
Coventry	a		18 44			18 49	19 05					19 11			19 24	19 30		19 44		19 49		20 05			
	d		18 44			18 51						19 11			19 25	19 31		19 44		19 51					
Rugby	d	18 24	18 56		19 18							19 26						19 56							
Long Buckby	d	18 37	19 06		19 28													20 06							
Northampton	a	18 48	19 17		19 39													20 17							
London Euston	a	19 53			20 53	19 59						20 19				20 36				20 59					

		VT	XC	VT	LM	LM		LM	VT	LM	LM	AW	XC	LM	VT	XC		LM	LM	VT	LM	AW	XC	XC	LM
			C									A				C						A	E	F	
Stafford	d		19 25					19 43		20 16						20 25			20 38				21 09	21 09	
Penkridge	d							19 49											20 45						
Wolverhampton	a	19 31	19 40					19 58				20 08	20 13		20 31	20 39			20 55			21 11	21 21	21 22	
	d	19 32	19 41	19 45				19 58				20 09	20 15	20 22	20 32	20 41			20 58	21 05		21 12	21 22	21 23	21 25
Coseley	d													20 27											21 30
Tipton	d													20 29											21 32
Dudley Port	d													20 31											21 34
Sandwell & Dudley	d			19 56										20 35						21 17					21 38
Smethwick Galton Bridge	d													20 37											21 40
Smethwick Rolfe Street	d													20 39											21 42
Birmingham New Street	a	19 55	19 58	20 05				20 15				20 24	20 31	20 47	20 55	21 00			21 15	21 26		21 29	21 39	21 39	21 49
	d		20 03	20 10		20 14			20 30		20 34	20 39	20 42			21 03		21 14		21 30	21 34	21 37	21 42		
Adderley Park	d										20 38										21 38				
Stechford	d										20 42										21 42				
Lea Hall	d										20 44										21 44				
Marston Green	d					20 22					20 48							21 22			21 48				
Birmingham International	a		20 13	20 19		20 25			20 39		20 51	20 58				21 13		21 25		21 39	21 51	21 56			
	d		20 14	20 20		20 25			20 40		20 51					21 14		21 25		21 40	21 51				
Hampton-in-Arden	d					20 28												21 28							
Berkswell	d					20 33												21 33							
Tile Hill	d					20 36					20 58							21 36							
Canley	d					20 40												21 40							
Coventry	a		20 24	20 30		20 44			20 50		21 04					21 23		21 44		21 50	22 01				
	d		20 25	20 31		20 44			20 51							21 24		21 44		21 51					
Rugby	d				20 20	20 56			21 05	21 17								21 56		22 04					
Long Buckby	d				20 32	21 06				21 28								22 06							
Northampton	a				20 43	21 17				21 39								22 17							
London Euston	a			21 54	21 57				22 24	23 13										23 28					

A until 5 September
B until 11 July
C from Birmingham New Street to Wolverhampton
D from 18 July until 5 September
E until 17 October
F from 24 October

Table 68

Sundays

Stafford - Wolverhampton - Birmingham - Coventry - Northampton

		AW		LM	LM	VT	LM	AW	VT	XC	LM	VT		VT	LM	LM	XC
								A									
Stafford	d	21 16			21 38				22 02	22 06						22 44	23 05
Penkridge	d				21 45											22 51	
Wolverhampton	a	21 34			21 55			22 08	22 16	22 20		22 31				23 00	23 18
	d	21 35			21 58	22 05		22 09	22 16	22 22	22 25	22 32		22 37		23 00	23 19
Coseley	d										22 30						
Tipton	d										22 32						
Dudley Port	d										22 34						
Sandwell & Dudley	d					22 15					22 38			22 47			
Smethwick Galton Bridge	d										22 40						
Smethwick Rolfe Street	d										22 42						
Birmingham New Street	a	21 52			22 15	22 24		22 28	22 40	22 40	22 49	22 57		22 56		23 17	23 36
	d	21 55		22 14		22 30	22 34	22 41						23 00	23 14		
Adderley Park	d						22 38								23 19		
Stechford	d						22 42								23 22		
Lea Hall	d						22 45								23 25		
Marston Green	d			22 22			22 48								23 28		
Birmingham International	a	22 09		22 25		22 39	22 51	22 55						23 09	23 31		
	d			22 25		22 40	22 52							23 10	23 32		
Hampton-in-Arden	d			22 28											23 35		
Berkswell	d			22 33											23 40		
Tile Hill	d			22 36											23 43		
Canley	d			22 40											23 46		
Coventry	a			22 44		22 50	23 01							23 20	23 50		
	d			22 44		22 51								23 21			
Rugby	d			22 56		23 04								23 35			
Long Buckby	d			23 06													
Northampton	a			23 17										23s53			
London Euston	a					00 35								01 06			

A until 5 September

Lichfield - Birmingham - Longbridge and Redditch

		LM	LM	LM	LM	LM	LM	LM	LM	LM	LM	LM	LM	XC ◇1	LM	LM	LM	LM	LM	LM	LM	XC ◇1	LM
Lichfield Trent Valley	d																						
Lichfield City	d							06 12		06 25			06 45		06 54		07 14		07 24		07 44		07 57
Shenstone	d							06 17					06 50				07 19				07 49		
Blake Street	d					06 04		06 21		06 33			06 53		07 02		07 23		07 32		07 53		08 05
Butlers Lane	d					06 06		06 23		06 35			06 55		07 04		07 25		07 34		07 55		08 07
Four Oaks	d					06 09	06 18	06 26		06 38	06 48		06 58		07 07	07 18	07 28		07 37	07 48	07 58		08 10
Sutton Coldfield	d					06 12	06 21	06 30		06 41	06 51		07 02		07 11	07 21	07 32		07 41	07 51	08 02		08 13
Wylde Green	d					06 15	06 24	06 32		06 44	06 54		07 04		07 13	07 24	07 34		07 43	07 54	08 04		08 16
Chester Road	d					06 17	06 26	06 35		06 46	06 56		07 06		07 16	07 26	07 37		07 46	07 56	08 07		08 18
Erdington	d					06 18	06 28	06 36		06 47	06 58		07 08		07 17	07 28	07 38		07 47	07 58	08 08		08 20
Gravelly Hill	d					06 21	06 30	06 39		06 50	07 00		07 10		07 20	07 30	07 41		07 50	08 00	08 11		08 22
Aston	d					06 24	06 34	06 42		06 53	07 04		07 14		07 23	07 34	07 44		07 53	08 04	08 14		08 25
Duddeston	d					06 27	06 36	06 45			07 06					07 36	07 47			08 06	08 17		
Birmingham New Street	a					06 31	06 41	06 49		07 00	07 12		07 20		07 30	07 41	07 51		08 01	08 12	08 21		08 31
	d	05 54	06 04	06 14	06 24	06 34	06 44	06 54	06 59	07 04	07 14	07 20	07 24	07 30	07 34	07 44	07 54	07 59	08 04	08 14	08 24	08 30	08 34
Five Ways	d	05 57	06 07	06 17	06 27	06 37	06 47	06 57		07 07	07 17		07 27		07 37	07 47	07 57		08 07	08 17	08 27		08 37
University	d	06 01	06 11	06 21	06 31	06 41	06 51	07 01	07a05	07 11	07 21	07a27	07 31	07a36	07 41	07 51	08 01	08 06	08 11	08 21	08 31	08a36	08 41
Selly Oak	d	06 03	06 13	06 23	06 33	06 43	06 53	07 03		07 13	07 23		07 33		07 43	07 53	08 03		08 13	08 23	08 33		08 43
Bournville	d	06 05	06 15	06 25	06 35	06 45	06 55	07 05		07 15	07 25		07 35		07 45	07 55	08 05		08 15	08 25	08 35		08 45
Kings Norton	d	06 07	06 17	06 27	06 37	06 47	06 57	07 07		07 17	07 27		07 37		07 47	07 57	08 07		08 17	08 27	08 37		08 47
Northfield	d	06 10	06 20	06 30	06 40	06 50	07 00	07 10		07 20	07 30		07 40		07 50	08 00	08 10		08 20	08 30	08 40		08 50
Longbridge	d	06a14	06a24	06 34	06a44	06a54	07 04	07a14		07a24	07 34		07a44		07a54	08 04	08a14		08a24	08 34	08a44		08a54
Barnt Green	d			06 39			07 09				07 39	07 43				08 09				08 39			
Alvechurch	d			06 43			07 13				07 43					08 13				08 43			
Redditch	a			06 53			07 23				07 53					08 23				08 53			
Bromsgrove	a								07 22			07 48						08 21					

		LM	LM	LM	LM	LM	LM	LM	XC ◇1	LM	LM	LM	LM	LM	LM	LM	XC ◇1	LM	LM	LM	LM	LM	LM
Lichfield Trent Valley	d																						
Lichfield City	d		08 10		08 15	08 26		08 45		08 55			09 14	09 25		09 44		09 55			10 14	10 25	
Shenstone	d				08 20			08 50					09 19			09 49					10 19		
Blake Street	d				08 24	08 33		08 54		09 03			09 23	09 33		09 53		10 03			10 23	10 33	
Butlers Lane	d				08 26	08 35		08 56		09 05			09 25	09 35		09 55		10 05			10 25	10 35	
Four Oaks	d	08 15	08 20		08 29	08 38	08 48	08 59		09 08	09 18		09 28	09 38	09 48	09 58		10 08	10 18		10 28	10 38	10 48
Sutton Coldfield	d	08 18	08 23		08 32	08 42	08 51	09 02		09 11	09 21		09 31	09 41	09 51	10 01		10 11	10 21		10 31	10 41	10 51
Wylde Green	d	08 21	08 26		08 35	08 44	08 54	09 05		09 14	09 24		09 34	09 44	09 54	10 04		10 14	10 24		10 34	10 44	10 54
Chester Road	d	08 23	08 28		08 37	08 47	08 56	09 07		09 16	09 26		09 36	09 46	09 56	10 06		10 16	10 26		10 36	10 46	10 56
Erdington	d	08 25	08 29		08 38	08 48	08 58	09 09		09 18	09 28		09 38	09 48	09 58	10 08		10 18	10 28		10 38	10 48	10 58
Gravelly Hill	d		08 32		08 41	08 51	09 00	09 11		09 20	09 30		09 40	09 50	10 00	10 10		10 20	10 30		10 40	10 50	11 00
Aston	d		08 35		08 44	08 54	09 04	09 14		09 24	09 34		09 44	09 54	10 04	10 14		10 24	10 34		10 44	10 54	11 04
Duddeston	d		08 37		08 47	08 57	09 06				09 36				10 06				10 36				11 06
Birmingham New Street	a	08 36	08 42		08 51	09 01	09 12	09 22		09 31	09 41		09 51	10 01	10 11	10 22		10 31	10 41		10 51	11 01	11 12
	d		08 44	08 49	08 54	09 04	09 14	09 24	09 30	09 34	09 44	09 49	09 54	10 04	10 14	10 24	10 30	10 34	10 44	10 49	10 54	11 04	11 14
Five Ways	d		08 47		08 57	09 07	09 17	09 27		09 37	09 47		09 57	10 07	10 17	10 27		10 37	10 47		10 57	11 07	11 17
University	d		08 51	08 55	09 01	09 11	09 21	09 31	09a36	09 41	09 51	09 55	10 01	10 11	10 21	10 31	10a36	10 41	10 51	10 55	11 01	11 11	11 21
Selly Oak	d		08 53		09 03	09 13	09 23	09 33		09 43	09 53		10 03	10 13	10 23	10 33		10 43	10 53		11 03	11 13	11 23
Bournville	d		08 55		09 05	09 15	09 25	09 35		09 45	09 55		10 05	10 15	10 25	10 35		10 45	10 55		11 05	11 15	11 25
Kings Norton	d		08 57		09 07	09 17	09 27	09 37		09 47	09 57		10 07	10 17	10 27	10 37		10 47	10 57		11 07	11 17	11 27
Northfield	d		09 00		09 10	09 20	09 30	09 40		09 50	10 00		10 10	10 20	10 30	10 40		10 50	11 00		11 10	11 20	11 30
Longbridge	d		09 06		09a14	09a24	09 34	09a44		09a54	10 06		10a14	10a24	10 34	10a44		10a54	11 06		11a14	11a24	11 34
Barnt Green	d		09 10				09 39				10 10				10 39				11 10				11 39
Alvechurch	d		09 15				09 43				10 15				10 43				11 15				11 43
Redditch	a		09 23				09 53				10 23				10 53				11 23				11 53
Bromsgrove	a			09 10								10 11								11 10			

		LM	XC ◇1	LM	LM	LM	LM	LM	LM	LM	XC ◇1	LM	LM	LM	LM	LM	LM	LM	XC ◇1	LM	LM	LM
Lichfield Trent Valley	d																					
Lichfield City	d	10 44		10 55			11 14	11 25		11 44		11 55			12 14	12 25		12 44		12 55		
Shenstone	d	10 49					11 19			11 49					12 19			12 49				
Blake Street	d	10 53		11 03			11 23	11 33		11 53		12 03			12 23	12 33		12 53		13 03		
Butlers Lane	d	10 55		11 05			11 25	11 35		11 55		12 05			12 25	12 35		12 55		13 05		
Four Oaks	d	10 58		11 08	11 18		11 28	11 38	11 48	11 58		12 08	12 18		12 28	12 38	12 48	12 58		13 08	13 18	
Sutton Coldfield	d	11 01		11 11	11 21		11 31	11 41	11 51	12 01		12 11	12 21		12 31	12 41	12 51	13 01		13 11	13 21	
Wylde Green	d	11 04		11 14	11 24		11 34	11 44	11 54	12 04		12 14	12 24		12 34	12 44	12 54	13 04		13 14	13 24	
Chester Road	d	11 06		11 16	11 26		11 36	11 46	11 56	12 06		12 16	12 26		12 36	12 46	12 56	13 06		13 16	13 26	
Erdington	d	11 08		11 18	11 28		11 38	11 48	11 58	12 08		12 18	12 28		12 38	12 48	12 58	13 08		13 18	13 28	
Gravelly Hill	d	11 10		11 20	11 30		11 40	11 50	12 00	12 10		12 20	12 30		12 40	12 50	13 00	13 10		13 20	13 30	
Aston	d	11 14		11 24	11 34		11 44	11 54	12 04	12 14		12 24	12 34		12 44	12 54	13 04	13 14		13 24	13 34	
Duddeston	d				11 36				12 06				12 36				13 06				13 36	
Birmingham New Street	a	11 22		11 31	11 41		11 51	12 01	12 11	12 22		12 31	12 42		12 51	13 01	13 11	13 22		13 31	13 42	
	d	11 24	11 30	11 34	11 44	11 49	11 54	12 04	12 14	12 24	12 30	12 34	12 44	12 49	12 54	13 04	13 14	13 24	13 30	13 34	13 44	13 49
Five Ways	d	11 27		11 37	11 47		11 57	12 07	12 17	12 27		12 37	12 47		12 57	13 07	13 17	13 27		13 37	13 47	
University	d	11 31	11a36	11 41	11 51	11 55	12 01	12 11	12 21	12 31	12a36	12 41	12 51	12 55	13 01	13 11	13 21	13 31	13a36	13 41	13 51	13 55
Selly Oak	d	11 33		11 43	11 53		12 03	12 13	12 23	12 33		12 43	12 53		13 03	13 13	13 23	13 33		13 43	13 53	
Bournville	d	11 35		11 45	11 55		12 05	12 15	12 25	12 35		12 45	12 55		13 05	13 15	13 25	13 35		13 45	13 55	
Kings Norton	d	11 37		11 47	11 57		12 07	12 17	12 27	12 37		12 47	12 57		13 07	13 17	13 27	13 37		13 47	13 57	
Northfield	d	11 40		11 50	12 00		12 10	12 20	12 30	12 40		12 50	13 00		13 10	13 20	13 30	13 40		13 50	14 00	
Longbridge	d	11a44		11a54	12 06		12a14	12a24	12 34	12a44		12a54	13 06		13a14	13a24	13 34	13a44		13a54	14 06	
Barnt Green	d				12 10				12 39				13 10				13 39				14 10	
Alvechurch	d				12 15				12 43				13 15				13 43				14 15	
Redditch	a				12 23				12 53				13 23				13 53				14 23	
Bromsgrove	a					12 10								13 11								14 12

Lichfield - Birmingham - Longbridge and Redditch

		LM	LM	LM	LM	XC ◇1	LM	LM	LM	LM	LM	LM	LM	XC ◇1	LM	LM	LM	LM	LM	LM	LM	LM	XC ◇1
Lichfield Trent Valley	d																						
Lichfield City	d	13 14	13 25		13 44		13 55			14 14	14 25		14 44		14 55			15 14	15 25			15 44	
Shenstone	d	13 19			13 49					14 19			14 49					15 19				15 49	
Blake Street	d	13 23	13 33		13 53		14 03			14 23	14 33		14 53		15 03			15 23	15 33			15 53	
Butlers Lane	d	13 25	13 35		13 55		14 05			14 25	14 35		14 55		15 05			15 25	15 35			15 55	
Four Oaks	d	13 28	13 38	13 48	13 58		14 08	14 18		14 28	14 38	14 48	14 58		15 08	15 18		15 28	15 38	15 48		15 58	
Sutton Coldfield	d	13 31	13 41	13 51	14 01		14 11	14 21		14 31	14 41	14 51	15 01		15 11	15 21		15 31	15 41	15 51		16 01	
Wylde Green	d	13 34	13 44	13 54	14 04		14 14	14 24		14 34	14 44	14 54	15 04		15 14	15 24		15 34	15 44	15 54		16 04	
Chester Road	d	13 36	13 46	13 56	14 06		14 16	14 26		14 36	14 46	14 56	15 06		15 16	15 26		15 36	15 46	15 56		16 06	
Erdington	d	13 38	13 48	13 58	14 08		14 18	14 28		14 38	14 48	14 58	15 08		15 18	15 28		15 38	15 48	15 58		16 08	
Gravelly Hill	d	13 40	13 50	14 00	14 10		14 20	14 30		14 40	14 50	15 00	15 10		15 20	15 30		15 40	15 50	16 00		16 10	
Aston	d	13 44	13 54	14 04	14 14		14 24	14 34		14 44	14 54	15 04	15 14		15 24	15 34		15 44	15 54	16 04		16 14	
Duddeston	d			14 06				14 36				15 06				15 36				16 06			
Birmingham New Street	a	13 51	14 01	14 11	14 22		14 31	14 41		14 51	15 01	15 11	15 22		15 31	15 41		15 51	16 01	16 11		16 22	
	d	13 54	14 04	14 14	14 24	14 30	14 34	14 44	14 49	14 54	15 04	15 14	15 24	15 30	15 34	15 44	15 49	15 54	16 04	16 14	16 20	16 24	16 30
Five Ways	d	13 57	14 07	14 17	14 27		14 37	14 47		14 57	15 07	15 17	15 27		15 37	15 47		15 57	16 07	16 17		16 27	
University	d	14 01	14 11	14 21	14 31	14a36	14 41	14 51	14 55	15 01	15 11	15 21	15 31	15a36	15 41	15 51	15 55	16 01	16 11	16 21	16 26	16 31	16a36
Selly Oak	d	14 03	14 13	14 23	14 33		14 43	14 53		15 03	15 13	15 23	15 33		15 43	15 53		16 04	16 14	16 24		16 34	
Bournville	d	14 05	14 15	14 25	14 35		14 45	14 55		15 05	15 15	15 25	15 35		15 45	15 55		16 06	16 16	16 26		16 36	
Kings Norton	d	14 07	14 17	14 27	14 37		14 47	14 57		15 07	15 17	15 27	15 37		15 47	15 57		16 09	16 19	16 29		16 39	
Northfield	d	14 10	14 20	14 30	14 40		14 50	15 00		15 10	15 20	15 30	15 40		15 50	16 00		16 11	16 21	16 31		16 41	
Longbridge	d	14a14	14a24	14 34	14a44		14a54	15 06		15a14	15a24	15 34	15a44		15a54	16 06		16a15	16a25	16 37		16a45	
Barnt Green	d			14 39				15 10				15 39				16 10				16 41			
Alvechurch	d			14 43				15 15				15 43				16 15				16 45			
Redditch	a			14 53				15 23				15 53				16 23				16 54			
Bromsgrove	a								15 10								16 11				16 41		

		LM	LM	LM	LM	LM	LM	LM	LM	XC ◇1	LM	LM	LM	LM	LM	LM	LM	LM	LM	XC ◇1	LM	LM
Lichfield Trent Valley	d																					
Lichfield City	d	15 54			16 14	16 25			16 44		16 55	17 05				17 24			17 44		17 55	
Shenstone	d	15 59			16 19				16 49							17 29			17 49			
Blake Street	d	16 03			16 23	16 33			16 53		17 03	17 13				17 33			17 53		18 03	
Butlers Lane	d	16 05			16 25	16 35			16 55		17 05	17 15				17 35			17 55		18 05	
Four Oaks	d	16 08	16 18		16 28	16 38	16 48		16 58		17 08	17 18		17 28		17 38	17 48		17 58		18 08	18 18
Sutton Coldfield	d	16 11	16 21		16 31	16 41	16 51		17 01		17 11	17 21		17 31		17 41	17 51		18 01		18 11	18 21
Wylde Green	d	16 14	16 24		16 34	16 44	16 54		17 04		17 14	17 24		17 34		17 44	17 54		18 04		18 14	18 24
Chester Road	d	16 16	16 26		16 36	16 46	16 56		17 06		17 16	17 26		17 36		17 46	17 56		18 06		18 16	18 26
Erdington	d	16 18	16 28		16 38	16 48	16 58		17 08		17 18	17 28		17 38		17 48	17 58		18 08		18 18	18 28
Gravelly Hill	d	16 20	16 30		16 40	16 50	17 00		17 10		17 20	17 30		17 40		17 50	18 00		18 10		18 20	18 30
Aston	d	16 24	16 34		16 44	16 54	17 04		17 14		17 24	17 34		17 44		17 54	18 04		18 14		18 24	18 34
Duddeston	d		16 36				17 06					17 36					18 06					18 36
Birmingham New Street	a	16 31	16 42		16 51	17 01	17 11		17 22		17 31	17 41		17 51		18 01	18 11		18 22		18 31	18 41
	d	16 34	16 44	16 49	16 54	17 04	17 14	17 19	17 24	17 30	17 34	17 44	17 49	17 54	17 59	18 04	18 14	18 19	18 24	18 30	18 34	18 44
Five Ways	d	16 37	16 47		16 57	17 07	17 17		17 27		17 37	17 47		17 57		18 07	18 17		18 27		18 37	18 47
University	d	16 41	16 51	16 55	17 01	17 11	17 21	17 25	17 31	17 36	17 41	17 51	17a55	18 01	18 05	18 11	18 21		18 31	18a36	18 41	18 51
Selly Oak	d	16 44	16 54		17 04	17 14	17 24		17 34		17 44	17 54		18 04		18 14	18 24		18 34		18 44	18 54
Bournville	d	16 46	16 56		17 06	17 16	17 26		17 36		17 46	17 56		18 06		18 16	18 26		18 36		18 46	18 56
Kings Norton	d	16 49	16 59		17 09	17 19	17 29		17 39		17 49	17 59		18 09		18 19	18 29		18 39		18 49	18 59
Northfield	d	16 51	17 01		17 11	17 21	17 31		17 41		17 51	18 01		18 11		18 21	18 31		18 41		18 51	19 01
Longbridge	d	16a55	17 06		17a15	17a25	17 34		17a45		17a55	18 06		18a15		18a25	18 34		18a45		18a55	19 04
Barnt Green	d		17 10				17 39					18 10					18 39					19 09
Alvechurch	d		17 15				17 43					18 15					18 43					19 13
Redditch	a		17 23				17 53					18 23					18 53					19 23
Bromsgrove	a			17 10				17 45		17 51					18 20			18 45		18 49		

		LM	LM	LM	LM	LM	XC ◇1	LM	LM	LM	LM	LM	LM	LM	XC ◇1	LM	LM	LM	LM	LM	LM	LM	LM
Lichfield Trent Valley	d																						
Lichfield City	d	18 14	18 25			18 44		18 55			19 14	19 25		19 44		20 04			20 34		21 04		
Shenstone	d	18 19				18 49					19 19			19 49		20 09			20 39		21 09		
Blake Street	d	18 23	18 33			18 53		19 03			19 23	19 33		19 53		20 13			20 43		21 13		
Butlers Lane	d	18 25	18 35			18 55		19 05			19 25	19 35		19 55		20 15			20 45		21 15		
Four Oaks	d	18 28	18 38	18 48		18 58		19 08	19 18		19 28	19 38	19 50	19 58		20 18			20 48		21 18		
Sutton Coldfield	d	18 31	18 41	18 51		19 01		19 11	19 21		19 31	19 41	19 53	20 01		20 21			20 51		21 21		
Wylde Green	d	18 34	18 44	18 54		19 04		19 14	19 24		19 34	19 44	19 56	20 04		20 24			20 54		21 24		
Chester Road	d	18 36	18 46	18 56		19 06		19 16	19 26		19 36	19 46	19 58	20 06		20 26			20 56		21 26		
Erdington	d	18 38	18 48	18 58		19 08		19 18	19 28		19 38	19 48	20 00	20 08		20 28			20 58		21 28		
Gravelly Hill	d	18 40	18 50	19 00		19 10		19 20	19 30		19 40	19 50	20 02	20 10		20 30			21 00		21 30		
Aston	d	18 44	18 54	19 04		19 14		19 24	19 34		19 44	19 54	20 06	20 14		20 34			21 04		21 34		
Duddeston	d			19 06					19 36			19 56				20 36			21 06		21 36		
Birmingham New Street	a	18 51	19 01	19 11		19 22	19 24	19 31	19 41		19 51	20 03	20 13	20 22	20 24	20 41			21 12		21 42		
	d	18 54	19 04	19 14	19 19	19 24	19 30	19 34	19 44	19 49	19 54		20 14	20 24	20 30	20 44	20 54	20 59	21 14	21 24	21 44	21 54	22 00
Five Ways	d	18 57	19 07	19 17		19 27		19 37	19 47		19 57		20 17	20 27		20 47	20 57		21 17	21 27	21 47	21 57	
University	d	19 01	19 11	19 21	19 25	19 31	19 36	19 41	19 51	19 55	20 01		20 21	20 31	20 36	20 51	21 01	21 06	21 21	21 31	21 51	22 01	22 06
Selly Oak	d	19 03	19 13	19 23		19 33		19 43	19 53		20 03		20 23	20 33		20 53	21 03		21 23	21 33	21 53	22 03	
Bournville	d	19 05	19 15	19 25		19 35		19 45	19 55		20 05		20 25	20 35		20 55	21 05		21 25	21 35	21 55	22 05	
Kings Norton	d	19 07	19 17	19 27		19 37		19 47	19 57		20 07		20 27	20 37		20 57	21 07		21 27	21 37	21 57	22 07	
Northfield	d	19 10	19 20	19 30		19 40		19 50	20 00		20 10		20 30	20 40		21 00	21 10		21 30	21 40	22 00	22 10	
Longbridge	d	19a14	19a24	19 36		19a44		19a54	20 06		20a14		20 34	20a44		21 04	21a14		21 34	21a44	22 04	22a14	
Barnt Green	d			19 40					20 10				20 39			21 09			21 39		22 09		
Alvechurch	d			19 44					20 14				20 43			21 13			21 43		22 13		
Redditch	a			19 53					20 23				20 53			21 23			21 53		22 23		
Bromsgrove	a				19 40					20 09								21 22					22 22

Lichfield - Birmingham - Longbridge and Redditch

		LM	LM	LM	LM	LM	LM	LM	LM
Lichfield Trent Valley	d								
Lichfield City	d	21 34		22 04			22 34	23 00	
Shenstone	d	21 39		22 09			22 39	23 05	
Blake Street	d	21 43		22 13			22 43	23 09	23 36
Butlers Lane	d	21 45		22 15			22 45	23 11	23 38
Four Oaks	d	21 48		22 18			22 48	23 14	23 41
Sutton Coldfield	d	21 51		22 21			22 51	23 17	23 44
Wylde Green	d	21 54		22 24			22 54	23 20	
Chester Road	d	21 56		22 26			22 56		
Erdington	d	21 58		22 28			22 58		
Gravelly Hill	d	22 00		22 30			23 00		
Aston	d	22 04		22 34			23 04		
Duddeston	d	22 06		22 36			23 06		
Birmingham New Street 12	a	22 12		22 42			23 12	23 31	23 59
	d	22 14	22 24	22 44	22 54	23 00	23 14	23 34	
Five Ways	d	22 17	22 27	22 47	22 57		23 17	23 37	
University	d	22 21	22 31	22 51	23 01	23 06	23 21	23 41	
Selly Oak	d	22 23	22 33	22 53	23 03		23 23	23 43	
Bournville	d	22 25	22 35	22 55	23 05		23 25	23 45	
Kings Norton	d	22 27	22 37	22 57	23 07		23 27	23 47	
Northfield	d	22 30	22 40	23 00	23 10		23 30	23 50	
Longbridge	d	22 34	22a44	23 04	23a14		23 34	23a54	
Barnt Green	d	22 39		23 09			23 39		
Alvechurch	d	22 43		23 13			23 43		
Redditch	a	22 53		23 23			23 53		
Bromsgrove	a					23 20			

Saturdays

		XC ◇1	LM	LM	LM	LM	LM	LM	LM	LM	LM	LM
Lichfield Trent Valley	d											
Lichfield City	d										06 25	06 38
Shenstone	d										06 30	
Blake Street	d						06 03				06 34	
Butlers Lane	d						06 05				06 36	
Four Oaks	d						06 08				06 39	06 48
Sutton Coldfield	d						06 12				06 42	06 51
Wylde Green	d						06 14				06 45	06 54
Chester Road	d						06 17				06 47	06 56
Erdington	d						06 18				06 48	06 58
Gravelly Hill	d						06 21				06 51	07 00
Aston	d						06 24				06 54	07 04
Duddeston	d						06 27				06 57	07 06
Birmingham New Street 12	a						06 31				07 01	07 12
	d	05 42	05 54	06 04	06 14	06 24	06 34	06 44	06 49	06 54	07 04	07 14
Five Ways	d		05 57	06 07	06 17	06 27	06 37	06 47		06 57	07 07	07 17
University	d		06 01	06 11	06 21	06 31	06 41	06 51	06 57	07 01	07 11	07 21
Selly Oak	d		06 03	06 13	06 23	06 33	06 43	06 53		07 03	07 13	07 23
Bournville	d		06 05	06 15	06 25	06 35	06 45	06 55		07 05	07 15	07 25
Kings Norton	d		06 07	06 17	06 27	06 37	06 47	06 57		07 07	07 17	07 27
Northfield	d		06 10	06 20	06 30	06 40	06 50	07 00		07 10	07 20	07 30
Longbridge	d		06a14	06a24	06 34	06a44	06a54	07 06		07a14	07a24	07 34
Barnt Green	d				06 39			07 10				07 39
Alvechurch	d				06 43			07 15				07 43
Redditch	a				06 53			07 23				07 53
Bromsgrove	a	06 03							07 11			

		LM	XC ◇1	LM	LM	LM	LM	LM	LM	LM	XC ◇1	LM
Lichfield Trent Valley	d											
Lichfield City	d			06 55	07 08			07 25		07 44		07 55
Shenstone	d			07 00				07 30		07 49		
Blake Street	d			07 04				07 34		07 53		08 03
Butlers Lane	d			07 06				07 36		07 55		08 05
Four Oaks	d			07 09	07 18			07 39	07 48	07 58		08 08
Sutton Coldfield	d			07 12	07 21			07 42	07 51	08 01		08 11
Wylde Green	d			07 15	07 24			07 45	07 54	08 04		08 14
Chester Road	d			07 17	07 26			07 47	07 56	08 06		08 16
Erdington	d			07 18	07 28			07 48	07 58	08 08		08 18
Gravelly Hill	d			07 21	07 30			07 51	08 00	08 10		08 20
Aston	d			07 24	07 34			07 54	08 04	08 14		08 24
Duddeston	d			07 27	07 36				08 06			
Birmingham New Street 12	a		07 24	07 31	07 42			08 01	08 11	08 21	08 24	08 32
	d	07 24	07 30	07 34	07 44	07 49	07 54	08 04	08 14	08 24	08 30	08 34
Five Ways	d	07 27		07 37	07 47		07 57	08 07	08 17	08 27		08 37
University	d	07 31	07 36	07 41	07 51	07 57	08 01	08 11	08 21	08 31	08 36	08 41
Selly Oak	d	07 33		07 43	07 53		08 03	08 13	08 23	08 33		08 43
Bournville	d	07 35		07 45	07 55		08 05	08 15	08 25	08 35		08 45
Kings Norton	d	07 37		07 47	07 57		08 07	08 17	08 27	08 37		08 47
Northfield	d	07 40		07 50	08 00		08 10	08 20	08 30	08 40		08 50
Longbridge	d	07a44		07a54	08 06		08a14	08a24	08 34	08a44		08a54
Barnt Green	d				08 10				08 39			
Alvechurch	d				08 15				08 43			
Redditch	a				08 23				08 53			
Bromsgrove	a					08 11						

		LM	LM	LM	LM	LM	LM	XC ◇1	LM	LM	LM	LM
Lichfield Trent Valley	d											
Lichfield City	d			08 14	08 25		08 44		08 55			09 14
Shenstone	d			08 19			08 49					09 19
Blake Street	d			08 23	08 33		08 53		09 03			09 23
Butlers Lane	d			08 25	08 35		08 55		09 05			09 25
Four Oaks	d	08 18		08 28	08 38	08 48	08 58		09 08	09 18		09 28
Sutton Coldfield	d	08 21		08 31	08 41	08 51	09 01		09 11	09 21		09 31
Wylde Green	d	08 24		08 34	08 44	08 54	09 04		09 14	09 24		09 34
Chester Road	d	08 26		08 36	08 46	08 56	09 06		09 16	09 26		09 36
Erdington	d	08 28		08 38	08 48	08 58	09 08		09 18	09 28		09 38
Gravelly Hill	d	08 30		08 40	08 50	09 00	09 10		09 20	09 30		09 40
Aston	d	08 34		08 44	08 54	09 04	09 14		09 24	09 34		09 44
Duddeston	d	08 36				09 06				09 36		
Birmingham New Street 12	a	08 41		08 51	09 01	09 11	09 22	09 24	09 32	09 41		09 51
	d	08 44	08 49	08 54	09 04	09 14	09 24	09 30	09 34	09 44	09 49	09 54
Five Ways	d	08 47		08 57	09 07	09 17	09 27		09 37	09 47		09 57
University	d	08 51	08 57	09 01	09 11	09 21	09 31	09 36	09 41	09 51	09 57	10 01
Selly Oak	d	08 53		09 03	09 13	09 23	09 33		09 43	09 53		10 03
Bournville	d	08 55		09 05	09 15	09 25	09 35		09 45	09 55		10 05
Kings Norton	d	08 57		09 07	09 17	09 27	09 37		09 47	09 57		10 07
Northfield	d	09 00		09 10	09 20	09 30	09 40		09 50	10 00		10 10
Longbridge	d	09 06		09a14	09a24	09 34	09a44		09a54	10 06		10a14
Barnt Green	d	09 10				09 39				10 10		
Alvechurch	d	09 15				09 43				10 15		
Redditch	a	09 23				09 53				10 23		
Bromsgrove	a		09 11								10 11	

		LM	LM	LM	XC ◇1	LM	LM	LM	LM	LM	LM	LM
Lichfield Trent Valley	d											
Lichfield City	d	09 25		09 44		09 55			10 14	10 25		10 44
Shenstone	d			09 49					10 19			10 49
Blake Street	d	09 33		09 53		10 03			10 23	10 33		10 53
Butlers Lane	d	09 35		09 55		10 05			10 25	10 35		10 55
Four Oaks	d	09 38	09 48	09 58		10 08	10 18		10 28	10 38	10 48	10 58
Sutton Coldfield	d	09 41	09 51	10 01		10 11	10 21		10 31	10 41	10 51	11 01
Wylde Green	d	09 44	09 54	10 04		10 14	10 24		10 34	10 44	10 54	11 04
Chester Road	d	09 46	09 56	10 06		10 16	10 26		10 36	10 46	10 56	11 06
Erdington	d	09 48	09 58	10 08		10 18	10 28		10 38	10 48	10 58	11 08
Gravelly Hill	d	09 50	10 00	10 10		10 20	10 30		10 40	10 50	11 00	11 10
Aston	d	09 54	10 04	10 14		10 24	10 34		10 44	10 54	11 04	11 14
Duddeston	d		10 06				10 36				11 06	
Birmingham New Street 12	a	10 01	10 11	10 21	10 24	10 31	10 41		10 51	11 01	11 11	11 21
	d	10 04	10 14	10 24	10 30	10 34	10 44	10 49	10 54	11 04	11 14	11 24
Five Ways	d	10 07	10 17	10 27		10 37	10 47		10 57	11 07	11 17	11 27
University	d	10 11	10 21	10 31	10 36	10 41	10 51	10 57	11 01	11 11	11 21	11 31
Selly Oak	d	10 13	10 23	10 33		10 43	10 53		11 03	11 13	11 23	11 33
Bournville	d	10 15	10 25	10 35		10 45	10 55		11 05	11 15	11 25	11 35
Kings Norton	d	10 17	10 27	10 37		10 47	10 57		11 07	11 17	11 27	11 37
Northfield	d	10 20	10 30	10 40		10 50	11 00		11 10	11 20	11 30	11 40
Longbridge	d	10a24	10 34	10a44		10a54	11 06		11a14	11a24	11 34	11a44
Barnt Green	d		10 39				11 10				11 39	
Alvechurch	d		10 43				11 15				11 43	
Redditch	a		10 53				11 23				11 53	
Bromsgrove	a							11 11				

Lichfield - Birmingham - Longbridge and Redditch

		XC ◇1	LM	LM	LM	LM	LM	LM	LM	XC ◇1	LM	LM
Lichfield Trent Valley	d											
Lichfield City	d		10 55			11 14	11 25		11 44		11 55	
Shenstone	d					11 19			11 49			
Blake Street	d		11 03			11 23	11 33		11 53		12 03	
Butlers Lane	d		11 05			11 25	11 35		11 55		12 05	
Four Oaks	d		11 08	11 18		11 28	11 38	11 48	11 58		12 08	12 18
Sutton Coldfield	d		11 11	11 21		11 31	11 41	11 51	12 01		12 11	12 21
Wylde Green	d		11 14	11 24		11 34	11 44	11 54	12 04		12 14	12 24
Chester Road	d		11 16	11 26		11 36	11 46	11 56	12 06		12 16	12 26
Erdington	d		11 18	11 28		11 38	11 48	11 58	12 08		12 18	12 28
Gravelly Hill	d		11 20	11 30		11 40	11 50	12 00	12 10		12 20	12 30
Aston	d		11 24	11 34		11 44	11 54	12 04	12 14		12 24	12 34
Duddeston	d			11 36				12 06				12 36
Birmingham New Street 12	a	11 24	11 31	11 41		11 51	12 01	12 11	12 21	12 24	12 31	12 41
	d	11 30	11 34	11 44	11 49	11 54	12 04	12 14	12 24	12 30	12 34	12 44
Five Ways	d		11 37	11 47		11 57	12 07	12 17	12 27		12 37	12 47
University	d	11 36	11 41	11 51	11 57	12 01	12 11	12 21	12 31	12 36	12 41	12 51
Selly Oak	d		11 43	11 53		12 03	12 13	12 23	12 33		12 43	12 53
Bournville	d		11 45	11 55		12 05	12 15	12 25	12 35		12 45	12 55
Kings Norton	d		11 47	11 57		12 07	12 17	12 27	12 37		12 47	12 57
Northfield	d		11 50	12 00		12 10	12 20	12 30	12 40		12 50	13 00
Longbridge	d		11a54	12 06		12a14	12a24	12 34	12a44		12a54	13 06
Barnt Green	d			12 10				12 39				13 10
Alvechurch	d			12 15				12 43				13 15
Redditch	a			12 23				12 53				13 23
Bromsgrove	a				12 11							

		LM	LM	LM	LM	LM	XC ◇1	LM	LM	LM	LM
Lichfield Trent Valley	d										
Lichfield City	d		12 14	12 25		12 44		12 55			13 14
Shenstone	d		12 19			12 49					13 19
Blake Street	d		12 23	12 33		12 53		13 03			13 23
Butlers Lane	d		12 25	12 35		12 55		13 05			13 25
Four Oaks	d		12 28	12 38	12 48	12 58		13 08	13 18		13 28
Sutton Coldfield	d		12 31	12 41	12 51	13 01		13 11	13 21		13 31
Wylde Green	d		12 34	12 44	12 54	13 04		13 14	13 24		13 34
Chester Road	d		12 36	12 46	12 56	13 06		13 16	13 26		13 36
Erdington	d		12 38	12 48	12 58	13 08		13 18	13 28		13 38
Gravelly Hill	d		12 40	12 50	13 00	13 10		13 20	13 30		13 40
Aston	d		12 44	12 54	13 04	13 14		13 24	13 34		13 44
Duddeston	d				13 06				13 36		
Birmingham New Street 12	a		12 51	13 01	13 11	13 21	13 24	13 31	13 41		13 51
	d	12 49	12 54	13 04	13 14	13 24	13 30	13 34	13 44	13 49	13 54
Five Ways	d		12 57	13 07	13 17	13 27		13 37	13 47		13 57
University	d	12 57	13 01	13 11	13 21	13 31	13 36	13 41	13 51	13 57	14 01
Selly Oak	d		13 03	13 13	13 23	13 33		13 43	13 53		14 03
Bournville	d		13 05	13 15	13 25	13 35		13 45	13 55		14 05
Kings Norton	d		13 07	13 17	13 27	13 37		13 47	13 57		14 07
Northfield	d		13 10	13 20	13 30	13 40		13 50	14 00		14 10
Longbridge	d		13a14	13a24	13 34	13a44		13a54	14 06		14a14
Barnt Green	d				13 39				14 10		
Alvechurch	d				13 43				14 15		
Redditch	a				13 53				14 23		
Bromsgrove	a	13 11								14 11	

		LM	LM	LM	XC ◇1	LM	LM	LM	LM	LM	LM	LM
Lichfield Trent Valley	d											
Lichfield City	d	13 25		13 44		13 55			14 14	14 25		14 44
Shenstone	d			13 49					14 19			14 49
Blake Street	d	13 33		13 53		14 03			14 23	14 33		14 53
Butlers Lane	d	13 35		13 55		14 05			14 25	14 35		14 55
Four Oaks	d	13 38	13 48	13 58		14 08	14 18		14 28	14 38	14 48	14 58
Sutton Coldfield	d	13 41	13 51	14 01		14 11	14 21		14 31	14 41	14 51	15 01
Wylde Green	d	13 44	13 54	14 04		14 14	14 24		14 34	14 44	14 54	15 04
Chester Road	d	13 46	13 56	14 06		14 16	14 26		14 36	14 46	14 56	15 06
Erdington	d	13 48	13 58	14 08		14 18	14 28		14 38	14 48	14 58	15 08
Gravelly Hill	d	13 50	14 00	14 10		14 20	14 30		14 40	14 50	15 00	15 10
Aston	d	13 54	14 04	14 14		14 24	14 34		14 44	14 54	15 04	15 14
Duddeston	d		14 06				14 36				15 06	
Birmingham New Street 12	a	14 01	14 11	14 21	14 24	14 31	14 41		14 51	15 01	15 11	15 21
	d	14 04	14 14	14 24	14 30	14 34	14 44	14 49	14 54	15 04	15 14	15 24
Five Ways	d	14 07	14 17	14 27		14 37	14 47		14 57	15 07	15 17	15 27
University	d	14 11	14 21	14 31	14 36	14 41	14 51	14 57	15 01	15 11	15 21	15 31
Selly Oak	d	14 13	14 23	14 33		14 43	14 53		15 03	15 13	15 23	15 33
Bournville	d	14 15	14 25	14 35		14 45	14 55		15 05	15 15	15 25	15 35
Kings Norton	d	14 17	14 27	14 37		14 47	14 57		15 07	15 17	15 27	15 37
Northfield	d	14 20	14 30	14 40		14 50	15 00		15 10	15 20	15 30	15 40
Longbridge	d	14a24	14 34	14a44		14a54	15 06		15a14	15a24	15 34	15a44
Barnt Green	d		14 39				15 10				15 39	
Alvechurch	d		14 43				15 15				15 43	
Redditch	a		14 53				15 23				15 53	
Bromsgrove	a							15 11				

		XC ◇1	LM	LM	LM	LM	LM	LM	LM	LM	XC ◇1	LM
Lichfield Trent Valley	d											
Lichfield City	d		14 55			15 14	15 25			15 44		15 55
Shenstone	d					15 19				15 49		
Blake Street	d		15 03			15 23	15 33			15 53		16 03
Butlers Lane	d		15 05			15 25	15 35			15 55		16 05
Four Oaks	d		15 08	15 18		15 28	15 38	15 48		15 58		16 08
Sutton Coldfield	d		15 11	15 21		15 31	15 41	15 51		16 01		16 11
Wylde Green	d		15 14	15 24		15 34	15 44	15 54		16 04		16 14
Chester Road	d		15 16	15 26		15 36	15 46	15 56		16 06		16 16
Erdington	d		15 18	15 28		15 38	15 48	15 58		16 08		16 18
Gravelly Hill	d		15 20	15 30		15 40	15 50	16 00		16 10		16 20
Aston	d		15 24	15 34		15 44	15 54	16 04		16 14		16 24
Duddeston	d			15 36				16 06				
Birmingham New Street 12	a	15 24	15 31	15 41		15 51	16 01	16 11		16 21	16 24	16 31
	d	15 30	15 34	15 44	15 49	15 54	16 04	16 14	16 19	16 24	16 30	16 34
Five Ways	d		15 37	15 47		15 57	16 07	16 17		16 27		16 37
University	d	15 36	15 41	15 51	15 57	16 01	16 11	16 21		16 31	16 36	16 41
Selly Oak	d		15 43	15 53		16 04	16 14	16 24		16 34		16 44
Bournville	d		15 45	15 55		16 06	16 16	16 26		16 36		16 46
Kings Norton	d		15 47	15 57		16 09	16 19	16 29		16 39		16 49
Northfield	d		15 50	16 00		16 11	16 21	16 31		16 41		16 51
Longbridge	d		15a54	16 06		16a15	16a25	16 37		16a45		16a55
Barnt Green	d			16 10				16 41				
Alvechurch	d			16 15				16 45				
Redditch	a			16 23				16 54				
Bromsgrove	a				16 11				16 43			

		LM	LM	LM	LM	LM	LM	LM	XC ◇1	LM	LM	LM
Lichfield Trent Valley	d											
Lichfield City	d			16 14	16 25			16 44		16 55		
Shenstone	d			16 19				16 49				
Blake Street	d			16 23	16 33			16 53		17 03		
Butlers Lane	d			16 25	16 35			16 55		17 05		
Four Oaks	d	16 18		16 28	16 38	16 48		16 58		17 08	17 18	
Sutton Coldfield	d	16 21		16 31	16 41	16 51		17 01		17 11	17 21	
Wylde Green	d	16 24		16 34	16 44	16 54		17 04		17 14	17 24	
Chester Road	d	16 26		16 36	16 46	16 56		17 06		17 16	17 26	
Erdington	d	16 28		16 38	16 48	16 58		17 08		17 18	17 28	
Gravelly Hill	d	16 30		16 40	16 50	17 00		17 10		17 20	17 30	
Aston	d	16 34		16 44	16 54	17 04		17 14		17 24	17 34	
Duddeston	d	16 36				17 06					17 36	
Birmingham New Street 12	a	16 41		16 51	17 01	17 11		17 21	17 24	17 31	17 41	
	d	16 44	16 49	16 54	17 04	17 14	17 19	17 24	17 30	17 34	17 44	17 49
Five Ways	d	16 47		16 57	17 07	17 17		17 27		17 37	17 47	
University	d	16 51	16 57	17 01	17 11	17 21		17 31	17 36	17 41	17 51	17 57
Selly Oak	d	16 54		17 04	17 14	17 24		17 34		17 44	17 54	
Bournville	d	16 56		17 06	17 16	17 26		17 36		17 46	17 56	
Kings Norton	d	16 59		17 09	17 19	17 29		17 39		17 49	17 59	
Northfield	d	17 01		17 11	17 21	17 31		17 41		17 51	18 01	
Longbridge	d	17 06		17a15	17a25	17 36		17a45		17a55	18 06	
Barnt Green	d	17 10				17 40					18 10	
Alvechurch	d	17 15				17 45					18 15	
Redditch	a	17 23				17 53					18 23	
Bromsgrove	a		17 11				17 41		17 49			18 10

		LM	LM	LM	LM	XC ◇1	LM	LM	LM	LM	LM	LM
Lichfield Trent Valley	d											
Lichfield City	d	17 14	17 25		17 44		17 55			18 14	18 25	
Shenstone	d	17 19			17 49					18 19		
Blake Street	d	17 23	17 33		17 53		18 03			18 23	18 33	
Butlers Lane	d	17 25	17 35		17 55		18 05			18 25	18 35	
Four Oaks	d	17 28	17 38	17 48	17 58		18 08	18 18		18 28	18 38	18 48
Sutton Coldfield	d	17 31	17 41	17 51	18 01		18 11	18 21		18 31	18 41	18 51
Wylde Green	d	17 34	17 44	17 54	18 04		18 14	18 24		18 34	18 44	18 54
Chester Road	d	17 36	17 46	17 56	18 06		18 16	18 26		18 36	18 46	18 56
Erdington	d	17 38	17 48	17 58	18 08		18 18	18 28		18 38	18 48	18 58
Gravelly Hill	d	17 40	17 50	18 00	18 10		18 20	18 30		18 40	18 50	19 00
Aston	d	17 44	17 54	18 04	18 14		18 24	18 34		18 44	18 54	19 04
Duddeston	d			18 06				18 36				19 06
Birmingham New Street 12	a	17 51	18 01	18 11	18 21	18 24	18 31	18 41		18 51	19 01	19 11
	d	17 54	18 04	18 14	18 24	18 30	18 34	18 44	18 49	18 54	19 04	19 14
Five Ways	d	17 57	18 07	18 17	18 27		18 37	18 47		18 57	19 07	19 17
University	d	18 01	18 11	18 21	18 31	18 36	18 41	18 51	18 57	19 01	19 11	19 21
Selly Oak	d	18 04	18 14	18 24	18 34		18 44	18 54		19 03	19 13	19 23
Bournville	d	18 06	18 16	18 26	18 36		18 46	18 56		19 05	19 15	19 25
Kings Norton	d	18 09	18 19	18 29	18 39		18 49	18 59		19 07	19 17	19 27
Northfield	d	18 11	18 21	18 31	18 41		18 51	19 01		19 10	19 20	19 30
Longbridge	d	18a15	18a25	18 34	18a45		18a55	19 06		19a14	19a24	19 36
Barnt Green	d			18 39				19 10				19 40
Alvechurch	d			18 43				19 15				19 45
Redditch	a			18 53				19 23				19 53
Bromsgrove	a								19 10			

Saturdays

Lichfield - Birmingham - Longbridge and Redditch

		LM	LM	XC ◇1 ⊼	LM	LM	LM	LM	LM	LM	XC ◇1 ⊼	LM	LM	LM	LM	LM	LM	LM	LM	LM	LM	LM	LM
Lichfield Trent Valley	d																						
Lichfield City	d		18 44		18 55		19 14	19 25		19 44		20 04			20 34		21 04		21 34		22 04		22 34
Shenstone	d		18 49				19 19			19 49		20 09			20 39		21 09		21 39		22 09		22 39
Blake Street	d		18 53		19 03		19 23	19 33		19 53		20 13			20 43		21 13		21 43		22 13		22 43
Butlers Lane	d		18 55		19 05		19 25	19 35		19 55		20 15			20 45		21 15		21 45		22 15		22 45
Four Oaks	d		18 58		19 08	19 18	19 28	19 38	19 50	19 58		20 18			20 48		21 18		21 48		22 18		22 48
Sutton Coldfield	d		19 01		19 11	19 21	19 31	19 41	19 53	20 01		20 21			20 51		21 21		21 51		22 21		22 51
Wylde Green	d		19 04		19 14	19 24	19 34	19 44	19 56	20 04		20 24			20 54		21 24		21 54		22 24		22 54
Chester Road	d		19 06		19 16	19 26	19 36	19 46	19 58	20 06		20 26			20 56		21 26		21 56		22 26		22 56
Erdington	d		19 08		19 18	19 28	19 38	19 48	20 00	20 08		20 28			20 58		21 28		21 58		22 28		22 58
Gravelly Hill	d		19 10		19 20	19 30	19 40	19 50	20 02	20 10		20 30			21 00		21 30		22 00		22 30		23 00
Aston	d		19 14		19 24	19 34	19 44	19 54	20 06	20 14		20 34			21 04		21 34		22 04		22 34		23 04
Duddeston	d					19 36		19 56				20 36			21 06		21 36		22 06		22 36		23 06
Birmingham New Street ■	a		19 21	19 24	19 31	19 41	19 51	20 03	20 13	20 21	20 24	20 41			21 12		21 42		22 11		22 42		23 12
	d	19 19	19 24	19 30	19 34	19 44	19 54		20 14	20 24	20 30	20 44	20 54	20 59	21 14	21 24	21 44	21 54	22 14	22 24	22 44	22 54	23 14
Five Ways	d		19 27		19 37	19 47	19 57		20 17	20 27		20 47	20 57		21 17	21 27	21 47	21 57	22 17	22 27	22 47	22 57	23 17
University	d	19 27	19 31	19 36	19 41	19 51	20 01		20 21	20 31	20 36	20 51	21 01	21 05	21 21	21 31	21 51	22 01	22 21	22 31	22 51	23 01	23 21
Selly Oak	d		19 33		19 43	19 53	20 03		20 23	20 33		20 53	21 03		21 23	21 33	21 53	22 03	22 23	22 33	22 53	23 03	23 23
Bournville	d		19 35		19 45	19 55	20 05		20 25	20 35		20 55	21 05		21 25	21 35	21 55	22 05	22 25	22 35	22 55	23 05	23 25
Kings Norton	d		19 37		19 47	19 57	20 07		20 27	20 37		20 57	21 07		21 27	21 37	21 57	22 07	22 27	22 37	22 57	23 07	23 27
Northfield	d		19 40		19 50	20 00	20 10		20 30	20 40		21 00	21 10		21 30	21 40	22 00	22 10	22 30	22 40	23 00	23 10	23 30
Longbridge	d		19a44		19a54	20 04	20a14		20 34	20a44		21 04	21a14		21 34	21a44	22 04	22a14	22 34	22a44	23 04	23a14	23 34
Barnt Green	d					20 09			20 39			21 09			21 39		22 09		22 39		23 09		23 39
Alvechurch	d					20 13			20 43			21 13			21 43		22 13		22 43		23 13		23 43
Redditch	a					20 23			20 53			21 23			21 53		22 23		22 53		23 23		23 53
Bromsgrove	a	19 41												21 21									

		LM	LM
Lichfield Trent Valley	d		
Lichfield City	d	23 00	
Shenstone	d	23 05	
Blake Street	d	23 09	23 36
Butlers Lane	d	23 11	23 38
Four Oaks	d	23 14	23 41
Sutton Coldfield	d	23 17	23 44
Wylde Green	d	23 20	
Chester Road	d		
Erdington	d		
Gravelly Hill	d		
Aston	d		
Duddeston	d		
Birmingham New Street ■	a	23 31	23 59
	d	23 34	
Five Ways	d	23 37	
University	d	23 41	
Selly Oak	d	23 44	
Bournville	d	23 46	
Kings Norton	d	23 48	
Northfield	d	23 51	
Longbridge	d	23a54	
Barnt Green	d		
Alvechurch	d		
Redditch	a		
Bromsgrove	a		

Sundays

		LM	LM	LM	LM	LM	LM	LM	XC ◇1 A ⊼	LM	LM	LM	LM	LM	XC ◇1 A ⊼	LM	LM	LM	LM	LM	LM	LM	LM
Lichfield Trent Valley	d																						
Lichfield City	d			09 35	10 05	10 35	11 05	11 35		12 05	12 35		13 05	13 35		14 05	14 35	15 05		15 35	16 05	16 35	17 05
Shenstone	d			09 40	10 10	10 40	11 10	11 40		12 10	12 40		13 10	13 40		14 10	14 40	15 10		15 40	16 10	16 40	17 10
Blake Street	d			09 44	10 14	10 44	11 14	11 44		12 14	12 44		13 14	13 44		14 14	14 44	15 14		15 44	16 14	16 44	17 14
Butlers Lane	d			09 46	10 16	10 46	11 16	11 46		12 16	12 46		13 16	13 46		14 16	14 46	15 16		15 46	16 16	16 46	17 16
Four Oaks	d		09 19	09 49	10 19	10 49	11 19	11 49		12 19	12 49		13 19	13 49		14 19	14 49	15 19		15 49	16 19	16 49	17 19
Sutton Coldfield	d		09 22	09 52	10 22	10 52	11 22	11 52		12 22	12 52		13 22	13 52		14 22	14 52	15 22		15 52	16 22	16 52	17 22
Wylde Green	d		09 25	09 55	10 25	10 55	11 25	11 55		12 25	12 55		13 25	13 55		14 25	14 55	15 25		15 55	16 25	16 55	17 25
Chester Road	d		09 27	09 57	10 27	10 57	11 27	11 57		12 27	12 57		13 27	13 57		14 27	14 57	15 27		15 57	16 27	16 57	17 27
Erdington	d		09 29	09 59	10 29	10 59	11 29	11 59		12 29	12 59		13 29	13 59		14 29	14 59	15 29		15 59	16 29	16 59	17 29
Gravelly Hill	d		09 31	10 01	10 31	11 01	11 31	12 01		12 31	13 01		13 31	14 01		14 31	15 01	15 31		16 01	16 31	17 01	17 31
Aston	d		09 35	10 05	10 35	11 05	11 35	12 05		12 35	13 05		13 35	14 05		14 35	15 05	15 35		16 05	16 35	17 05	17 35
Duddeston	d		09 37	10 07	10 37	11 07	11 37	12 07		12 38	13 07		13 37	14 07		14 37	15 07	15 37		16 07	16 37	17 07	17 37
Birmingham New Street ■	a		09 42	10 12	10 42	11 12	11 42	12 12	12 26	12 42	13 12		13 42	14 13	14 22	14 42	15 12	15 42		16 12	16 42	17 12	17 42
	d	09 15	09 45	10 15	10 45	11 15	11 45	12 15	12 30	12 45	13 15	13 24	13 45	14 15	14 30	14 45	15 15	15 45	16 00	16 15	16 45	17 15	17 45
Five Ways	d	09 19	09 49	10 19	10 49	11 19	11 49	12 19		12 49	13 19		13 49	14 19		14 49	15 19	15 49		16 19	16 49	17 19	17 49
University	d	09 23	09 53	10 23	10 53	11 23	11 53	12 23	12 36	12 53	13 23		13 53	14 23	14 36	14 53	15 23	15 53		16 23	16 53	17 23	17 53
Selly Oak	d	09 25	09 55	10 25	10 55	11 25	11 55	12 25		12 55	13 25		13 55	14 25		14 55	15 25	15 55		16 25	16 55	17 25	17 55
Bournville	d	09 27	09 57	10 27	10 57	11 27	11 57	12 27		12 57	13 27		13 57	14 27		14 57	15 27	15 57		16 27	16 57	17 27	17 57
Kings Norton	d	09 30	10 00	10 30	11 00	11 30	12 00	12 30		13 00	13 30		14 00	14 30		15 00	15 30	16 00		16 30	17 00	17 30	18 00
Northfield	d	09 33	10 03	10 33	11 03	11 33	12 03	12 33		13 03	13 33		14 03	14 33		15 03	15 33	16 03		16 33	17 03	17 33	18 03
Longbridge	d	09 36	10 06	10 36	11 06	11 36	12 06	12 36		13 06	13 36		14 06	14 36		15 06	15 36	16 06		16 36	17 06	17 36	18 06
Barnt Green	d	09 40	10 10	10 40	11 10	11 40	12 10	12 40		13 10	13 40		14 10	14 40		15 10	15 40	16 10		16 40	17 10	17 40	18 10
Alvechurch	d	09 45	10 15	10 45	11 15	11 45	12 15	12 45		13 15	13 45		14 15	14 45		15 15	15 45	16 15		16 45	17 15	17 45	18 15
Redditch	a	09 53	10 23	10 53	11 23	11 53	12 23	12 53		13 23	13 53		14 23	14 53		15 23	15 53	16 23		16 53	17 23	17 53	18 23
Bromsgrove	a											13 41							16 20				

A from 18 July until 5 September

Sundays

Lichfield - Birmingham - Longbridge and Redditch

		LM	LM	LM	LM	LM	LM	LM	LM	LM	LM	LM	LM	LM	LM	LM
Lichfield Trent Valley	d															
Lichfield City	d		17 35	18 05		18 35	19 05	19 35	20 05		20 35	21 05	21 35	22 05	22 35	23 05
Shenstone	d		17 40	18 10		18 40	19 10	19 40	20 10		20 40	21 10	21 40	22 10	22 40	23 10
Blake Street	d		17 44	18 14		18 44	19 14	19 44	20 14		20 44	21 14	21 44	22 14	22 44	23 14
Butlers Lane	d		17 46	18 16		18 46	19 16	19 46	20 16		20 46	21 16	21 46	22 16	22 46	23 16
Four Oaks	d		17 49	18 19		18 49	19 19	19 49	20 19		20 49	21 19	21 49	22 19	22 49	23 19
Sutton Coldfield	d		17 52	18 22		18 52	19 22	19 52	20 22		20 52	21 22	21 52	22 22	22 52	23 22
Wylde Green	d		17 55	18 25		18 55	19 25	19 55	20 25		20 55	21 25	21 55	22 25	22 55	23 25
Chester Road	d		17 57	18 27		18 57	19 27	19 57	20 27		20 57	21 27	21 57	22 27	22 57	
Erdington	d		17 59	18 29		18 59	19 29	19 59	20 29		20 59	21 29	21 59	22 29	22 59	
Gravelly Hill	d		18 01	18 31		19 01	19 31	20 01	20 31		21 01	21 31	22 01	22 31	23 01	
Aston	d		18 05	18 35		19 05	19 35	20 05	20 35		21 05	21 35	22 05	22 35	23 05	
Duddeston	d		18 07	18 37		19 07	19 37	20 07	20 37		21 07	21 37	22 07	22 37	23 07	
Birmingham New Street ■	a		18 12	18 42		19 12	19 42	20 12	20 42		21 12	21 42	22 12	22 42	23 12	23 39
	d	18 00	18 15	18 45	19 00	19 15	19 45	20 15	20 45	21 00	21 15	21 45	22 15	22 45	23 15	
Five Ways	d		18 19	18 49		19 19	19 49	20 19	20 49		21 19	21 49	22 19	22 49	23 19	
University	d		18 23	18 53		19 23	19 53	20 23	20 53		21 23	21 53	22 23	22 53	23 23	
Selly Oak	d		18 25	18 55		19 25	19 55	20 25	20 55		21 25	21 55	22 25	22 55	23 25	
Bournville	d		18 27	18 57		19 27	19 57	20 27	20 57		21 27	21 57	22 27	22 57	23 27	
Kings Norton	d		18 30	19 00		19 30	20 00	20 30	21 00		21 30	22 00	22 30	23 00	23 30	
Northfield	d		18 33	19 03		19 33	20 03	20 33	21 03		21 33	22 03	22 33	23 03	23 33	
Longbridge	d		18 36	19 06		19 36	20 06	20 36	21 06		21 36	22 06	22 36	23 06	23 36	
Barnt Green	d		18 40	19 10		19 40	20 10	20 40	21 10		21 40	22 10	22 40	23 10	23 40	
Alvechurch	d		18 45	19 15		19 45	20 15	20 45	21 15		21 45	22 15	22 45	23 15	23 45	
Redditch	a		18 53	19 23		19 53	20 23	20 53	21 23		21 53	22 23	22 53	23 23	23 53	
Bromsgrove	a	18 20			19 21					21 21						

Redditch and Longbridge - Birmingham - Lichfield

		LM	LM	LM	LM	LM	LM	LM	LM	LM		LM	LM	LM	LM	LM	LM	LM	LM	LM		XC ◇1	LM	LM	LM
Bromsgrove	d					06 21			06 44						07 25							07 49			
Redditch	d							06 27					06 57					07 27						07 57	
Alvechurch	d							06 32					07 02					07 32						08 02	
Barnt Green	d							06 38					07 08					07 38						08 08	
Longbridge	d			06 13	06 23		06 33	06 43		06 53		07 03	07 13	07 23		07 33		07 43		07 53			08 03	08 13	
Northfield	d			06 15	06 25		06 35	06 45		06 55		07 05	07 15	07 25		07 35		07 45		07 55			08 05	08 15	
Kings Norton	d			06 17	06 27		06 37	06 47		06 57		07 07	07 17	07 27		07 37		07 47		07 57			08 07	08 17	
Bournville	d			06 20	06 30		06 40	06 50		07 00		07 10	07 20	07 30		07 40		07 50		08 00			08 10	08 20	
Selly Oak	d			06 22	06 32		06 42	06 52		07 02		07 12	07 22	07 32		07 42		07 52		08 02			08 12	08 22	
University	d			06 24	06 34	06 39	06 44	06 54	06 59	07 04		07 14	07 24	07 34		07 44		07 54	08 00	08 04		08 09	08 14	08 24	08 30
Five Ways	d			06 27	06 37		06 47	06 57		07 07		07 17	07 27	07 37		07 47		07 57		08 07			08 17	08 27	
Birmingham New Street	a			06 34	06 42	06 45	06 52	07 02	07 07	07 14		07 22	07 34	07 42	07 45	07 52		08 03	08 09	08 12		08 16	08 22	08 34	08 37
	d	06 02	06 25	06 35	06 45		06 55	07 05		07 15		07 25	07 35	07 45		07 58	07 55	08 05		08 15		08 22	08 25	08 35	
Duddeston	d	06 06	06 29				06 59					07 29				08 02							08 29		
Aston	d	06 09	06 32	06 41	06 51		07 02	07 11		07 21		07 32	07 41	07 51		08 05		08 11		08 21			08 32	08 41	
Gravelly Hill	d	06 12	06 35	06 45	06 54		07 05	07 14		07 24		07 35	07 44	07 54		08 08		08 14		08 24			08 35	08 44	
Erdington	d	06 15	06 38	06 46	06 56		07 08	07 16		07 26		07 38	07 46	07 56		08 10		08 16		08 26			08 37	08 46	
Chester Road	d	06 17	06 40	06 48	06 58		07 10	07 18		07 28		07 40	07 48	07 58		08 12		08 18		08 28			08 39	08 48	
Wylde Green	d	06 19	06 42	06 50	07 00		07 12	07 21		07 30		07 42	07 50	08 00		08 14		08 20		08 30			08 41	08 50	
Sutton Coldfield	d	06 22	06 45	06 54	07 04		07 15	07 24		07 34		07 45	07 53	08 03		08 17	08 07	08 24		08 34			08 44	08 54	
Four Oaks	d	06 25	06 48	06 58	07a11		07 18	07 28		07a41		07 48		08a09		08 21	08 11	08 28		08a41			08 48	08 58	
Butlers Lane	d	06 27	06 50	07 00			07 20	07 30				07 50						08 30					08 50	09 00	
Blake Street	d	06 30	06 53	07 02			07 23	07 32				07 53				08 24		08 32					08 52	09 02	
Shenstone	d	06 34	06 57				07 27					07 57				08 28		08 36					08 56		
Lichfield City	d	06a40	07 02	07 12			07 32	07 42				08 02	08a08			08 33	08a22	08 42					09a02	09 11	
Lichfield Trent Valley	a																								

		LM	XC ◇1	LM	LM	LM		LM	LM	LM	LM	LM	XC ◇1	LM	LM	LM		LM	LM	LM	LM	XC ◇1	LM	LM	LM
Bromsgrove	d		08 24			08 41					09 09							09 54							10 42
Redditch	d				08 27					08 57					09 27					09 57				10 27	
Alvechurch	d				08 32					09 02					09 32					10 02				10 32	
Barnt Green	d				08 38					09 08					09 38					10 08				10 38	
Longbridge	d	08 23		08 33	08 43			08 53	09 03	09 13		09 23		09 33	09 43	09 53			10 03	10 13	10 23		10 33	10 43	
Northfield	d	08 25		08 35	08 45			08 55	09 05	09 15		09 25		09 35	09 45	09 55			10 05	10 15	10 25		10 35	10 45	
Kings Norton	d	08 27		08 37	08 47			08 57	09 07	09 17		09 27		09 37	09 47	09 57			10 07	10 17	10 27		10 37	10 47	
Bournville	d	08 30		08 40	08 50			09 00	09 10	09 20		09 30		09 40	09 50	10 00			10 10	10 20	10 30		10 40	10 50	
Selly Oak	d	08 32		08 42	08 52			09 02	09 12	09 22		09 32		09 42	09 52	10 02			10 12	10 22	10 32		10 42	10 52	
University	d	08 34	08 39	08 44	08 54	09 00		09 04	09 14	09 24	09 30	09 34	09 39	09 44	09 54	10 04		10 09	10 14	10 24	10 34	10 39	10 44	10 54	10 59
Five Ways	d	08 37		08 47	08 57			09 07	09 17	09 27		09 37		09 47	09 57	10 07			10 17	10 27	10 37		10 47	10 57	
Birmingham New Street	a	08 42	08 45	08 53	09 03	09 07		09 12	09 21	09 33	09 42	09 42	09 45	09 53	10 03	10 12		10 24	10 22	10 34	10 42	10 45	10 53	11 02	11 13
	d	08 45	08 49	08 55	09 05			09 15	09 25	09 35		09 45	09 49	09 55	10 05	10 15			10 25	10 35	10 45	10 49	10 55	11 05	
Duddeston	d			08 59					09 29					09 59					10 29				10 59		
Aston	d	08 51		09 02	09 11			09 21	09 32	09 41		09 51		10 02	10 11	10 21			10 32	10 41	10 51		11 02	11 11	
Gravelly Hill	d	08 54		09 05	09 14			09 24	09 35	09 44		09 54		10 05	10 14	10 24			10 35	10 44	10 54		11 05	11 14	
Erdington	d	08 56		09 08	09 16			09 26	09 38	09 46		09 56		10 08	10 16	10 26			10 38	10 46	10 56		11 08	11 16	
Chester Road	d	08 58		09 09	09 18			09 28	09 40	09 48		09 58		10 10	10 18	10 28			10 40	10 48	10 58		11 10	11 18	
Wylde Green	d	09 00		09 11	09 20			09 30	09 42	09 50		10 00		10 12	10 20	10 30			10 42	10 50	11 00		11 12	11 20	
Sutton Coldfield	d	09 04		09 14	09 24			09 34	09 45	09 54		10 04		10 15	10 24	10 34			10 45	10 54	11 04		11 15	11 24	
Four Oaks	d	09a11		09 18	09 28			09a41	09 48	09 58		10a11		10 18	10 28	10a41			10 48	10 58	11a11		11 18	11 28	
Butlers Lane	d			09 20	09 30				09 50	10 00				10 20	10 30				10 50	11 00			11 20	11 30	
Blake Street	d			09 22	09 32				09 53	10 02				10 23	10 32				10 53	11 02			11 23	11 32	
Shenstone	d			09 26					09 57					10 27					10 57				11 27		
Lichfield City	d			09a34	09 41				10a02	10 11				10a32	10 41				11a02	11 11			11a32	11 41	
Lichfield Trent Valley	a																								

		LM		LM	LM	LM	XC ◇1	LM	LM	LM	LM	LM		LM	LM	XC ◇1	LM	LM	LM	LM	LM	LM		LM	XC ◇1
Bromsgrove	d									11 42									12 42						
Redditch	d				10 57				11 27					11 57				12 27				12 57			
Alvechurch	d				11 02				11 32					12 02				12 32				13 02			
Barnt Green	d				11 08				11 38					12 08				12 38				13 08			
Longbridge	d	10 53		11 03	11 13	11 23		11 33	11 43		11 53	12 03		12 13	12 23		12 33	12 43		12 53	13 03	13 13		13 23	
Northfield	d	10 55		11 05	11 15	11 25		11 35	11 45		11 55	12 05		12 15	12 25		12 35	12 45		12 55	13 05	13 15		13 25	
Kings Norton	d	10 57		11 07	11 17	11 27		11 37	11 47		11 57	12 07		12 17	12 27		12 37	12 47		12 57	13 07	13 17		13 27	
Bournville	d	11 00		11 10	11 20	11 30		11 40	11 50		12 00	12 10		12 20	12 30		12 40	12 50		13 00	13 10	13 20		13 30	
Selly Oak	d	11 02		11 12	11 22	11 32		11 42	11 52		12 02	12 12		12 22	12 32		12 42	12 52		13 02	13 12	13 22		13 32	
University	d	11 04		11 14	11 24	11 34	11 39	11 44	11 54	11 59	12 04	12 14		12 24	12 34	12 39	12 44	12 54	12 59	13 04	13 14	13 24		13 34	13 39
Five Ways	d	11 07		11 17	11 27	11 37		11 47	11 57		12 07	12 17		12 27	12 37		12 47	12 57		13 07	13 17	13 27		13 37	
Birmingham New Street	a	11 12		11 22	11 33	11 42	11 45	11 53	12 03	12 13	12 12	12 22		12 34	12 42	12 45	12 53	13 03	13 13	13 12	13 22	13 33		13 42	13 45
	d	11 15		11 25	11 35	11 45	11 49	11 55	12 05		12 15	12 25		12 35	12 45	12 49	12 55	13 05		13 15	13 25	13 35		13 45	13 49
Duddeston	d			11 29				11 59				12 29					12 59				13 29				
Aston	d	11 21		11 32	11 41	11 51		12 02	12 11		12 21	12 32		12 41	12 51		13 02	13 11		13 21	13 32	13 41		13 51	
Gravelly Hill	d	11 24		11 35	11 44	11 54		12 05	12 14		12 24	12 35		12 44	12 54		13 05	13 14		13 24	13 35	13 44		13 54	
Erdington	d	11 26		11 38	11 46	11 56		12 08	12 16		12 26	12 38		12 46	12 56		13 08	13 16		13 26	13 38	13 46		13 56	
Chester Road	d	11 28		11 40	11 48	11 58		12 10	12 18		12 28	12 40		12 48	12 58		13 10	13 18		13 28	13 40	13 48		13 58	
Wylde Green	d	11 30		11 42	11 50	12 00		12 12	12 20		12 30	12 42		12 50	13 00		13 12	13 20		13 30	13 42	13 50		14 00	
Sutton Coldfield	d	11 34		11 45	11 54	12 04		12 15	12 24		12 34	12 45		12 54	13 04		13 15	13 24		13 34	13 45	13 54		14 04	
Four Oaks	d	11a41		11 48	11 58	12a11		12 18	12 28		12a41	12 48		12 58	13a11		13 18	13 28		13a41	13 48	13 58		14a11	
Butlers Lane	d			11 50	12 00			12 20	12 30			12 50		13 00			13 20	13 30			13 50	14 00			
Blake Street	d			11 53	12 02			12 23	12 32			12 53		13 02			13 23	13 32			13 53	14 02			
Shenstone	d			11 57				12 27				12 57					13 27				13 57				
Lichfield City	d			12a02	12 11			12a32	12 41			13a02		13 11			13a32	13 41			14a02	14 11			
Lichfield Trent Valley	a																								

Table 69 — Mondays to Fridays

Redditch and Longbridge - Birmingham - Lichfield

		LM	LM	LM	LM	LM	LM	LM		XC ◇1	LM	LM	LM	LM	LM	LM	LM	XC ◇1		LM	LM	LM	LM	LM	LM
Bromsgrove	d			13 42									14 42									15 42			
Redditch	d		13 27				13 57					14 27				14 57					15 27				15 57
Alvechurch	d		13 32				14 02					14 32				15 02					15 32				16 02
Barnt Green	d		13 38				14 08					14 38				15 08					15 38				16 08
Longbridge	d	13 33	13 43		13 53	14 03	14 13	14 23			14 33	14 43		14 53	15 03	15 13	15 23			15 33	15 43		15 53	16 03	16 13
Northfield	d	13 35	13 45		13 55	14 05	14 15	14 25			14 35	14 45		14 55	15 05	15 15	15 25			15 35	15 45		15 55	16 05	16 15
Kings Norton	d	13 37	13 47		13 57	14 07	14 17	14 27			14 37	14 47		14 57	15 07	15 17	15 27			15 37	15 47		15 57	16 07	16 17
Bournville	d	13 40	13 50		14 00	14 10	14 20	14 30			14 40	14 50		15 00	15 10	15 20	15 30			15 40	15 50		16 00	16 10	16 20
Selly Oak	d	13 42	13 52		14 02	14 12	14 22	14 32			14 42	14 52		15 02	15 12	15 22	15 32			15 42	15 52		16 02	16 12	16 22
University	d	13 44	13 54	13 59	14 04	14 14	14 24	14 34		14 39	14 44	14 54	14 59	15 04	15 14	15 24	15 34	15 39		15 44	15 54	15 59	16 04	16 14	16 24
Five Ways	d	13 47	13 57		14 07	14 17	14 27	14 37			14 47	14 57		15 07	15 17	15 27	15 37			15 47	15 57		16 07	16 17	16 27
Birmingham New Street	a	13 53	14 03	14 13	14 12	14 22	14 33	14 42		14 45	14 53	15 03	15 13	15 12	15 22	15 33	15 42	15 45		15 53	16 03	16 13	16 12	16 22	16 34
	d	13 55	14 05		14 15	14 25	14 35	14 45		14 49	14 55	15 05		15 15	15 25	15 35	15 45	15 49		15 55	16 05		16 15	16 25	16 35
Duddeston	d	13 59				14 29					14 59				15 29					15 59				16 29	
Aston	d	14 02	14 11		14 21	14 32	14 41	14 51			15 02	15 11		15 21	15 32	15 41	15 51			16 02	16 11		16 21	16 32	16 41
Gravelly Hill	d	14 05	14 14		14 24	14 35	14 44	14 54			15 05	15 14		15 24	15 35	15 44	15 54			16 05	16 14		16 24	16 35	16 44
Erdington	d	14 08	14 16		14 26	14 38	14 46	14 56			15 08	15 16		15 26	15 38	15 46	15 56			16 08	16 16		16 26	16 38	16 46
Chester Road	d	14 10	14 18		14 28	14 40	14 48	14 58			15 10	15 18		15 28	15 40	15 48	15 58			16 10	16 18		16 28	16 39	16 48
Wylde Green	d	14 12	14 20		14 30	14 42	14 50	15 00			15 12	15 20		15 30	15 42	15 50	16 00			16 12	16 20		16 30	16 41	16 50
Sutton Coldfield	d	14 15	14 24		14 34	14 45	14 54	15 04			15 15	15 24		15 34	15 45	15 54	16 04			16 15	16 24		16 34	16 44	16 54
Four Oaks	d	14 18	14 28		14a41	14 48	14 58	15a11			15 18	15 28		15a41	15 48	15 58	16a11			16 18	16 28		16a41	16 48	16 58
Butlers Lane	d	14 20	14 30			14 50	15 00				15 20	15 30			15 50	16 00				16 20	16 30			16 50	17 00
Blake Street	d	14 23	14 32			14 53	15 02				15 23	15 32			15 53	16 02				16 23	16 32			16 52	17 02
Shenstone	d	14 27				14 57					15 27				15 57					16 27				16 56	
Lichfield City	d	14a32	14 41			15a02	15 11				15a32	15 41			16a02	16 11				16a32	16 41			17a02	17 11
Lichfield Trent Valley	a																								

		LM	XC ◇1	LM		LM	LM	LM	LM	LM	LM	XC ◇1	LM	LM		LM	LM	LM	LM	LM	XC ◇1	LM	LM	LM	
Bromsgrove	d						16 42									17 43								18 42	
Redditch	d					16 27				16 57				17 27					17 57				18 27		
Alvechurch	d					16 32				17 02				17 32					18 02				18 32		
Barnt Green	d					16 38	16 49			17 08				17 38					18 08				18 38	18 49	
Longbridge	d	16 23		16 33		16 43		16 53	17 03	17 13	17 23		17 33	17 43			17 53	18 03	18 13	18 23		18 33	18 43		
Northfield	d	16 25		16 35		16 45		16 55	17 05	17 15	17 25		17 35	17 45			17 55	18 05	18 15	18 25		18 35	18 45		
Kings Norton	d	16 27		16 37		16 47		16 57	17 07	17 17	17 27		17 37	17 47			17 57	18 07	18 17	18 27		18 37	18 47		
Bournville	d	16 30		16 40		16 50		17 00	17 10	17 20	17 30		17 40	17 50			18 00	18 10	18 20	18 30		18 40	18 50		
Selly Oak	d	16 32		16 42		16 52		17 02	17 12	17 22	17 32		17 42	17 52			18 02	18 12	18 22	18 32		18 42	18 52		
University	d	16 34	16 39	16 44		16 54	16 59	17 04	17 14	17 24	17 34	17 39	17 44	17 54		17 59	18 04	18 14	18 24	18 34	18 39	18 44	18 54	18 59	
Five Ways	d	16 37		16 47		16 57		17 07	17 17	17 27	17 37		17 47	17 57			18 07	18 17	18 27	18 37		18 47	18 57		
Birmingham New Street	a	16 42	16 45	16 53		17 03	17 13	17 12	17 23	17 33	17 42	17 45	17 53	18 03		18 13	18 12	18 23	18 33	18 42	18 45	18 53	19 03	19 12	
	d	16 45	16 49	16 55		17 05		17 15	17 25	17 35	17 45	17 49	17 55	18 05			18 15	18 25	18 35	18 45	18 49	18 55	19 05		
Duddeston	d			16 59					17 29				17 59					18 29				18 59			
Aston	d	16 51		17 02		17 11		17 21	17 32	17 41	17 51		18 02	18 11			18 21	18 32	18 41	18 51		19 02	19 11		
Gravelly Hill	d	16 54		17 05		17 14		17 24	17 35	17 44	17 54		18 05	18 14			18 24	18 35	18 44	18 54		19 05	19 14		
Erdington	d	16 56		17 08		17 16		17 26	17 38	17 46	17 56		18 08	18 16			18 26	18 38	18 46	18 56		19 08	19 16		
Chester Road	d	16 58		17 10		17 18		17 28	17 40	17 48	17 58		18 10	18 18			18 28	18 40	18 48	18 58		19 10	19 18		
Wylde Green	d	17 00		17 12		17 20		17 30	17 42	17 50	18 00		18 12	18 20			18 30	18 42	18 50	19 00		19 12	19 20		
Sutton Coldfield	d	17 04		17 15		17 24		17 34	17 45	17 54	18 04		18 15	18 24			18 34	18 45	18 54	19 04		19 15	19 24		
Four Oaks	d	17a11		17 18		17 28		17a41	17 48	17 58	18a11		18 18	18 28			18a41	18 48	18 58	19a11		19 18	19 28		
Butlers Lane	d			17 20		17 30			17 50	18 00			18 20	18 30				18 50	19 00			19 20	19 30		
Blake Street	d			17 23		17 32			17 53	18 02			18 23	18 32				18 53	19 02			19 23	19 32		
Shenstone	d			17 27		17 36			17 57	18 06			18 27					18 57				19 27			
Lichfield City	d			17 32		17 42			18 02	18 12			18a32	18 41				19a02	19 11			19a32	19 41		
Lichfield Trent Valley	a																								

		LM	LM	LM	LM	XC ◇1	LM	LM	LM	LM		LM	LM	XC ◇1	LM	LM	LM	LM	LM	LM		XC ◇1	LM	LM	LM
Bromsgrove	d									19 46								20 59							
Redditch	d			18 57				19 27					19 57			20 27			20 57				21 27		21 57
Alvechurch	d			19 02				19 32					20 02			20 32			21 02				21 32		22 02
Barnt Green	d			19 08				19 38					20 08			20 38			21 08				21 38		22 08
Longbridge	d	18 53	19 03	19 13	19 23		19 33	19 43	19 53			20 03	20 13		20 30	20 43	21 00		21 13	21 30			21 43	22 00	22 13
Northfield	d	18 55	19 05	19 15	19 26		19 35	19 45	19 55			20 05	20 15		20 32	20 45	21 02		21 15	21 32			21 45	22 02	22 15
Kings Norton	d	18 57	19 07	19 17	19 27		19 37	19 47	19 57			20 07	20 17		20 34	20 47	21 04		21 17	21 34			21 47	22 04	22 17
Bournville	d	19 00	19 10	19 20	19 30		19 40	19 50	20 00			20 10	20 20		20 37	20 50	21 07		21 20	21 37			21 50	22 07	22 20
Selly Oak	d	19 02	19 12	19 22	19 32		19 42	19 52	20 02			20 12	20 22		20 39	20 52	21 09		21 22	21 39			21 52	22 09	22 22
University	d	19 04	19 14	19 24	19 34	19 39	19 44	19 54	20 04	20 09		20 14	20 24	20 39	20 42	20 54	21 12	21 16	21 24	21 42		21 47	21 54	22 12	22 24
Five Ways	d	19 07	19 17	19 27	19 37		19 47	19 57	20 07			20 17	20 27		20 45	20 57	21 15		21 27	21 45			21 57	22 15	22 27
Birmingham New Street	a	19 12	19 23	19 33	19 43	19 45	19 53	20 03	20 13	20 20		20 23	20 34	20 45	20 50	21 02	21 20	21 23	21 33	21 50		21 53	22 03	22 20	22 33
	d	19 15		19 35		19 49		20 05					20 35	20 49		21 05			21 35				22 05		22 35
Duddeston	d			19 39				20 09					20 39			21 09			21 39				22 09		22 39
Aston	d	19 21		19 42				20 12					20 42			21 12			21 42				22 12		22 42
Gravelly Hill	d	19 24		19 45				20 15					20 45			21 15			21 45				22 15		22 45
Erdington	d	19 26		19 48				20 18					20 48			21 18			21 48				22 18		22 48
Chester Road	d	19 28		19 50				20 20					20 50			21 20			21 50				22 20		22 50
Wylde Green	d	19 30		19 52				20 22					20 52			21 22			21 52				22 22		22 52
Sutton Coldfield	d	19 34		19 55				20 25					20 55			21 25			21 55				22 25		22 55
Four Oaks	d	19a41		19 58				20 28					20 58			21 28			21 58				22 28		22 58
Butlers Lane	d			20 00				20 30					21 00			21 30			22 00				22 30		23 00
Blake Street	d			20 03				20 33					21 03			21 33			22 03				22 33		23 03
Shenstone	d			20 07				20 37					21 07			21 37			22 07				22 37		23 07
Lichfield City	d			20 12				20 42					21 12			21 42			22 12				22 42		23 12
Lichfield Trent Valley	a																								

Table 69

Mondays to Fridays

Redditch and Longbridge - Birmingham - Lichfield

		LM	LM	LM	LM	LM	LM
Bromsgrove	d	22 29					
Redditch	d			22 27		22 57	
Alvechurch	d			22 32		23 02	
Barnt Green	d			22 38		23 08	
Longbridge	d		22 30	22 43	22 52	23 13	23 30
Northfield	d		22 32	22 45	22 54	23 15	23 32
Kings Norton	d		22 34	22 47	22 56	23 17	23 34
Bournville	d		22 37	22 50	22 59	23 20	23 37
Selly Oak	d		22 39	22 52	23 01	23 22	23 39
University	d	22 45	22 42	22 54	23 03	23 24	23 41
Five Ways	d		22 45	22 57	23 06	23 27	23 44
Birmingham New Street 12	a	22 52	22 49	23 03	23 12	23 34	23 50
	d		22 55		23 15		
Duddeston	d		22 59		23 19		
Aston	d		23 02		23 22		
Gravelly Hill	d		23 05		23 25		
Erdington	d		23 08		23 28		
Chester Road	d		23 10		23 30		
Wylde Green	d		23 12		23 32		
Sutton Coldfield	d		23 15		23 35		
Four Oaks	d		23 18		23 38		
Butlers Lane	d		23 20		23 40		
Blake Street	d		23a24		23 43		
Shenstone	d				23 47		
Lichfield City	d				23 52		
Lichfield Trent Valley	a						

Saturdays

		LM	LM	LM	LM	LM	LM	LM	LM	LM	LM	LM	LM	LM	XC	LM	LM	LM	LM	LM	XC	LM	LM
															1						◇1		
Bromsgrove	d								06 51						07 44		07 50						
Redditch	d						06 27				06 57			07 27					07 57				08 27
Alvechurch	d						06 32				07 02			07 32					08 02				08 32
Barnt Green	d						06 38				07 08			07 38					08 08				08 38
Longbridge	d			06 13	06 23	06 33	06 43	06 53		07 03	07 13	07 23	07 33	07 43		07 53		08 03	08 13	08 23		08 33	08 43
Northfield	d			06 15	06 25	06 35	06 45	06 55		07 05	07 15	07 25	07 35	07 45		07 55		08 05	08 15	08 25		08 35	08 45
Kings Norton	d			06 17	06 27	06 37	06 47	06 57		07 07	07 17	07 27	07 37	07 47		07 57		08 07	08 17	08 27		08 37	08 47
Bournville	d			06 20	06 30	06 40	06 50	07 00		07 10	07 20	07 30	07 40	07 49		08 00		08 10	08 20	08 30		08 40	08 50
Selly Oak	d			06 22	06 32	06 42	06 52	07 02		07 12	07 22	07 32	07 42	07 52		08 02		08 12	08 22	08 32		08 42	08 52
University	d			06 24	06 34	06 44	06 54	07 04	07 09	07 14	07 24	07 34	07 44	07 54	08 00	08 04	08 09	08 14	08 24	08 34	08 39	08 44	08 54
Five Ways	d			06 27	06 37	06 47	06 57	07 07		07 17	07 27	07 37	07 47	07 57		08 07		08 17	08 27	08 37		08 47	08 57
Birmingham New Street 12	a			06 34	06 44	06 52	07 02	07 12	07 16	07 22	07 34	07 42	07 52	08 03	08 08	08 12	08 16	08 22	08 34	08 42	08 45	08 53	09 03
	d	05 57	06 25	06 35		06 55	07 05	07 15		07 25	07 35	07 45	07 55	08 05	08 22	08 15		08 25	08 35	08 45	08 49	08 55	09 05
Duddeston	d	06 01	06 29			06 59				07 29			07 59					08 29				08 59	
Aston	d	06 04	06 32			07 02	07 11	07 21		07 32	07 41	07 51	08 02	08 11		08 21		08 32	08 41	08 51		09 02	09 11
Gravelly Hill	d	06 07	06 35			07 05	07 14	07 24		07 35	07 44	07 54	08 05	08 14		08 24		08 35	08 44	08 54		09 05	09 14
Erdington	d	06 10	06 38	06 45		07 08	07 16	07 26		07 38	07 46	07 56	08 08	08 16		08 26		08 38	08 46	08 56		09 08	09 16
Chester Road	d	06 12	06 40	06 47		07 10	07 18	07 28		07 40	07 48	07 58	08 10	08 18		08 28		08 40	08 48	08 58		09 10	09 18
Wylde Green	d	06 14	06 42	06 49		07 12	07 20	07 30		07 42	07 50	08 00	08 12	08 20		08 30		08 42	08 50	09 00		09 12	09 20
Sutton Coldfield	d	06 17	06 45	06 52		07 15	07 24	07 34		07 45	07 54	08 04	08 15	08 24		08 34		08 45	08 54	09 04		09 15	09 24
Four Oaks	d	06 20	06 48	06 56		07 18	07 28	07a41		07 48	07 58	08a11	08 18	08 28		08a41		08 48	08 58	09a11		09 18	09 28
Butlers Lane	d	06 22	06 50	06 58		07 20	07 30			07 50	08 00		08 20	08 30				08 50	09 00			09 20	09 30
Blake Street	d	06 24	06 53	07 00		07 23	07 32			07 53	08 02		08 23	08 32				08 53	09 02			09 23	09 32
Shenstone	d	06 28	06 57			07 27				07 57			08 27	08 36				08 57				09 27	
Lichfield City	d	06a34	07a02	07 09		07a32	07 41			08a02	08 11		08a32	08 42				09a02	09 11			09a32	09 41
Lichfield Trent Valley	a																						

		LM	LM	LM	LM	LM	XC	LM	LM	LM	LM	LM	LM	LM	LM	XC	LM	LM	LM	LM	LM	LM	LM
							◇1									◇1							
Bromsgrove	d	08 40								09 40				10 14					10 42				11 13
Redditch	d				08 57				09 27				09 57					10 27				10 57	
Alvechurch	d				09 02				09 32				10 02					10 32				11 02	
Barnt Green	d				09 08				09 38				10 08					10 38				11 08	
Longbridge	d		08 53	09 03	09 13	09 23		09 33	09 43		09 53	10 03	10 13		10 23		10 33	10 43		10 53	11 03	11 13	
Northfield	d		08 55	09 05	09 15	09 25		09 35	09 45		09 55	10 05	10 15		10 25		10 35	10 45		10 55	11 05	11 15	
Kings Norton	d		08 57	09 07	09 17	09 27		09 37	09 47		09 57	10 07	10 17		10 27		10 37	10 47		10 57	11 07	11 17	
Bournville	d		09 00	09 10	09 20	09 30		09 40	09 50		10 00	10 10	10 20		10 30		10 40	10 50		11 00	11 10	11 20	
Selly Oak	d		09 02	09 12	09 22	09 32		09 42	09 52		10 02	10 12	10 22		10 32		10 42	10 52		11 02	11 12	11 22	
University	d	08 59	09 04	09 14	09 24	09 34	09 39	09 44	09 54	09 59	10 04	10 14	10 24		10 34	10 39	10 44	10 54	10 59	11 04	11 14	11 24	
Five Ways	d		09 07	09 17	09 27	09 37		09 47	09 57		10 07	10 17	10 27		10 37		10 47	10 57		11 07	11 17	11 27	
Birmingham New Street 12	a	09 11	09 12	09 22	09 33	09 42	09 45	09 53	10 03	10 11	10 12	10 22	10 34	10 41	10 42	10 45	10 53	11 02	11 11	11 12	11 22	11 33	11 38
	d		09 15	09 25	09 35	09 45	09 49	09 55	10 05		10 15	10 25	10 35		10 45	10 49	10 55	11 05		11 15	11 25	11 35	
Duddeston	d			09 29				09 59				10 29					10 59				11 29		
Aston	d		09 21	09 32	09 41	09 51		10 02	10 11		10 21	10 32	10 41		10 51		11 02	11 11		11 21	11 32	11 41	
Gravelly Hill	d		09 24	09 35	09 44	09 54		10 05	10 14		10 24	10 35	10 44		10 54		11 05	11 14		11 24	11 35	11 44	
Erdington	d		09 26	09 38	09 46	09 56		10 08	10 16		10 26	10 38	10 46		10 56		11 08	11 16		11 26	11 38	11 46	
Chester Road	d		09 28	09 40	09 48	09 58		10 10	10 18		10 28	10 40	10 48		10 58		11 10	11 18		11 28	11 40	11 48	
Wylde Green	d		09 30	09 42	09 50	10 00		10 12	10 20		10 30	10 42	10 50		11 00		11 12	11 20		11 30	11 42	11 50	
Sutton Coldfield	d		09 34	09 45	09 54	10 04		10 15	10 24		10 34	10 45	10 54		11 04		11 15	11 24		11 34	11 45	11 54	
Four Oaks	d		09a41	09 48	09 58	10a11		10 18	10 28		10a41	10 48	10 58		11a11		11 18	11 28		11a41	11 48	11 58	
Butlers Lane	d			09 50	10 00			10 20	10 30			10 50	11 00				11 20	11 30			11 50	12 00	
Blake Street	d			09 53	10 02			10 23	10 32			10 53	11 02				11 23	11 32			11 53	12 02	
Shenstone	d			09 57				10 27				10 57					11 27				11 57		
Lichfield City	d			10a02	10 11			10a32	10 41			11a02	11 11				11a32	11 41			12a02	12 11	
Lichfield Trent Valley	a																						

Table 69

Saturdays

Redditch and Longbridge - Birmingham - Lichfield

		LM	XC	LM	LM	LM	LM	LM	LM	LM	XC	LM	LM	LM	LM	LM	LM	LM	XC	LM	LM	LM
			◇1								◇1								◇1			
Bromsgrove	d					11 42								12 42								13 42
Redditch	d				11 27				11 57				12 27				12 57				13 27	
Alvechurch	d				11 32				12 02				12 32				13 02				13 32	
Barnt Green	d				11 38				12 08				12 38				13 08				13 38	
Longbridge	d	11 23		11 33	11 43		11 53	12 03	12 13	12 23		12 33	12 43		12 53	13 03	13 13	13 23		13 33	13 43	
Northfield	d	11 25		11 35	11 45		11 55	12 05	12 15	12 25		12 35	12 45		12 55	13 05	13 15	13 25		13 35	13 45	
Kings Norton	d	11 27		11 37	11 47		11 57	12 07	12 17	12 27		12 37	12 47		12 57	13 07	13 17	13 27		13 37	13 47	
Bournville	d	11 30		11 40	11 50		12 00	12 10	12 20	12 30		12 40	12 50		13 00	13 10	13 20	13 30		13 40	13 50	
Selly Oak	d	11 32		11 42	11 52		12 02	12 12	12 22	12 32		12 42	12 52		13 02	13 12	13 22	13 32		13 42	13 52	
University	d	11 34	11 39	11 44	11 54	11 59	12 04	12 14	12 24	12 34	12 39	12 44	12 54	12 59	13 04	13 14	13 24	13 34	13 39	13 44	13 54	13 59
Five Ways	d	11 37		11 47	11 57		12 07	12 17	12 27	12 37		12 47	12 57		13 07	13 17	13 27	13 37		13 47	13 57	
Birmingham New Street 12	a	11 42	11 45	11 53	12 03	12 11	12 12	12 22	12 33	12 42	12 45	12 53	13 03	13 11	13 12	13 22	13 33	13 42	13 45	13 53	14 03	14 11
	d	11 45	11 49	11 55	12 05		12 15	12 25	12 35	12 45	12 49	12 55	13 05		13 15	13 25	13 35	13 45	13 49	13 55	14 05	
Duddeston	d			11 59				12 29				12 59				13 29				13 59		
Aston	d	11 51		12 02	12 11		12 21	12 32	12 41	12 51		13 02	13 11		13 21	13 32	13 41	13 51		14 02	14 11	
Gravelly Hill	d	11 54		12 05	12 14		12 24	12 35	12 44	12 54		13 05	13 14		13 24	13 35	13 44	13 54		14 05	14 14	
Erdington	d	11 56		12 08	12 16		12 26	12 38	12 46	12 56		13 08	13 16		13 26	13 38	13 46	13 56		14 08	14 16	
Chester Road	d	11 58		12 10	12 18		12 28	12 40	12 48	12 58		13 10	13 18		13 28	13 40	13 48	13 58		14 10	14 18	
Wylde Green	d	12 00		12 12	12 20		12 30	12 42	12 50	13 00		13 12	13 20		13 30	13 42	13 50	14 00		14 12	14 20	
Sutton Coldfield	d	12 04		12 15	12 24		12 34	12 45	12 54	13 04		13 15	13 24		13 34	13 45	13 54	14 04		14 15	14 24	
Four Oaks	d	12a11		12 18	12 28		12a41	12 48	12 58	13a11		13 18	13 28		13a41	13 48	13 58	14a11		14 18	14 28	
Butlers Lane	d			12 20	12 30			12 50	13 00			13 20	13 30			13 50	14 00			14 20	14 30	
Blake Street	d			12 23	12 32			12 53	13 02			13 23	13 32			13 53	14 02			14 23	14 32	
Shenstone	d			12 27				12 57				13 27				13 57				14 27		
Lichfield City	d			12a32	12 41			13a02	13 11			13a32	13 41			14a02	14 11			14a32	14 41	
Lichfield Trent Valley	a																					

		LM	LM	LM	LM	XC	LM	LM	LM	LM	LM	LM	LM	XC	LM	LM	LM	LM	LM	LM	LM	LM	XC
						◇1								◇1									◇1
Bromsgrove	d								14 42								15 42					16 13	
Redditch	d			13 57				14 27				14 57				15 27				15 57			
Alvechurch	d			14 02				14 32				15 02				15 32				16 02			
Barnt Green	d			14 08				14 38				15 08				15 38				16 08			
Longbridge	d	13 53	14 03	14 13	14 23		14 33	14 43		14 53	15 03	15 13	15 23		15 33	15 43		15 53	16 03	16 13	16 23		
Northfield	d	13 55	14 05	14 15	14 25		14 35	14 45		14 55	15 05	15 15	15 25		15 35	15 45		15 55	16 05	16 15	16 25		
Kings Norton	d	13 57	14 07	14 17	14 27		14 37	14 47		14 57	15 07	15 17	15 27		15 37	15 47		15 57	16 07	16 17	16 27		
Bournville	d	14 00	14 10	14 20	14 30		14 40	14 50		15 00	15 10	15 20	15 30		15 40	15 50		16 00	16 10	16 20	16 30		
Selly Oak	d	14 02	14 12	14 22	14 32		14 42	14 52		15 02	15 12	15 22	15 32		15 42	15 52		16 02	16 12	16 22	16 32		
University	d	14 04	14 14	14 24	14 34	14 39	14 44	14 54	14 59	15 04	15 14	15 24	15 34	15 39	15 44	15 54	15 59	16 04	16 14	16 24	16 34		16 39
Five Ways	d	14 07	14 17	14 27	14 37		14 47	14 57		15 07	15 17	15 27	15 37		15 47	15 57		16 07	16 17	16 27	16 37		
Birmingham New Street 12	a	14 12	14 22	14 33	14 42	14 45	14 53	15 03	15 11	15 12	15 22	15 33	15 42	15 45	15 53	16 03	16 11	16 12	16 22	16 34	16 42	16 45	16 45
	d	14 15	14 25	14 35	14 45	14 49	14 55	15 05		15 15	15 25	15 35	15 45	15 49	15 55	16 05		16 15	16 25	16 35	16 45		16 49
Duddeston	d		14 29				14 59				15 29				15 59				16 29				
Aston	d	14 21	14 32	14 41	14 51		15 02	15 11		15 21	15 32	15 41	15 51		16 02	16 11		16 21	16 32	16 41	16 51		
Gravelly Hill	d	14 24	14 35	14 44	14 54		15 05	15 14		15 24	15 35	15 44	15 54		16 05	16 14		16 24	16 35	16 44	16 54		
Erdington	d	14 26	14 38	14 46	14 56		15 08	15 16		15 26	15 38	15 46	15 56		16 08	16 16		16 26	16 38	16 46	16 56		
Chester Road	d	14 28	14 40	14 48	14 58		15 10	15 18		15 28	15 40	15 48	15 58		16 10	16 18		16 28	16 40	16 48	16 58		
Wylde Green	d	14 30	14 42	14 50	15 00		15 12	15 20		15 30	15 42	15 50	16 00		16 12	16 20		16 30	16 42	16 50	17 00		
Sutton Coldfield	d	14 34	14 45	14 54	15 04		15 15	15 24		15 34	15 45	15 54	16 04		16 15	16 24		16 34	16 45	16 54	17 04		
Four Oaks	d	14a41	14 48	14 58	15a11		15 18	15 28		15a41	15 48	15 58	16a11		16 18	16 28		16a41	16 48	16 58	17a11		
Butlers Lane	d		14 50	15 00			15 20	15 30			15 50	16 00			16 20	16 30			16 50	17 00			
Blake Street	d		14 53	15 02			15 23	15 32			15 53	16 02			16 23	16 32			16 53	17 02			
Shenstone	d		14 57				15 27				15 57				16 27				16 57				
Lichfield City	d		15a02	15 11			15a32	15 41			16a02	16 11			16a32	16 41			17a02	17 11			
Lichfield Trent Valley	a																						

		LM	LM	LM	LM	LM	LM	LM	XC	LM	LM	LM	LM	LM	LM	LM	XC	LM	LM	LM	LM	LM
									◇1								◇1					
Bromsgrove	d			16 42								17 42								18 44		
Redditch	d		16 27				16 57				17 27				17 57				18 27			
Alvechurch	d		16 32				17 02				17 32				18 02				18 32			
Barnt Green	d		16 38				17 08				17 38				18 08				18 38			
Longbridge	d	16 33	16 43		16 53	17 03	17 13	17 23		17 33	17 43		17 53	18 03	18 13	18 23		18 33	18 43		18 53	19 03
Northfield	d	16 35	16 45		16 55	17 05	17 15	17 25		17 35	17 45		17 55	18 05	18 15	18 25		18 35	18 45		18 55	19 05
Kings Norton	d	16 37	16 47		16 57	17 07	17 17	17 27		17 37	17 47		17 57	18 07	18 17	18 27		18 37	18 47		18 57	19 07
Bournville	d	16 40	16 50		17 00	17 10	17 20	17 30		17 40	17 50		18 00	18 10	18 20	18 30		18 40	18 50		19 00	19 10
Selly Oak	d	16 42	16 52		17 02	17 12	17 22	17 32		17 42	17 52		18 02	18 12	18 22	18 32		18 42	18 52		19 02	19 12
University	d	16 44	16 54	16 59	17 04	17 14	17 24	17 34	17 39	17 44	17 54	17 59	18 04	18 14	18 24	18 34	18 39	18 44	18 54	18 59	19 04	19 14
Five Ways	d	16 47	16 57		17 07	17 17	17 27	17 37		17 47	17 57		18 07	18 17	18 27	18 37		18 47	18 57		19 07	19 17
Birmingham New Street 12	a	16 53	17 03	17 11	17 12	17 23	17 33	17 42	17 45	17 53	18 03	18 11	18 12	18 23	18 33	18 42	18 45	18 53	19 03	19 12	19 12	19 23
	d	16 55	17 05		17 15	17 25	17 35	17 45	17 49	17 55	18 05		18 15	18 25	18 35	18 45	18 49	18 55	19 05		19 15	
Duddeston	d	16 59				17 29				17 59				18 29				18 59				
Aston	d	17 02	17 11		17 21	17 32	17 41	17 51		18 02	18 11		18 21	18 32	18 41	18 51		19 02	19 11		19 21	
Gravelly Hill	d	17 05	17 14		17 24	17 35	17 44	17 54		18 05	18 14		18 24	18 35	18 44	18 54		19 05	19 14		19 24	
Erdington	d	17 08	17 16		17 26	17 38	17 46	17 56		18 08	18 16		18 26	18 38	18 46	18 56		19 08	19 16		19 26	
Chester Road	d	17 10	17 18		17 28	17 40	17 48	17 58		18 10	18 18		18 28	18 40	18 48	18 58		19 10	19 18		19 28	
Wylde Green	d	17 12	17 20		17 30	17 42	17 50	18 00		18 12	18 20		18 30	18 42	18 50	19 00		19 12	19 20		19 30	
Sutton Coldfield	d	17 15	17 24		17 34	17 45	17 54	18 04		18 15	18 24		18 34	18 45	18 54	19 04		19 15	19 24		19 34	
Four Oaks	d	17 18	17 28		17a41	17 48	17 58	18a11		18 18	18 28		18a41	18 48	18 58	19a11		19 18	19 28		19a41	
Butlers Lane	d	17 20	17 30			17 50	18 00			18 20	18 30			18 50	19 00			19 20	19 30			
Blake Street	d	17 23	17 32			17 53	18 02			18 23	18 32			18 53	19 02			19 23	19 32			
Shenstone	d	17 27				17 57				18 27				18 57				19 27				
Lichfield City	d	17a32	17 41			18a02	18 11			18a32	18 41			19a02	19 11			19a32	19 41			
Lichfield Trent Valley	a																					

Table 69

Saturdays

Redditch and Longbridge - Birmingham - Lichfield

		LM	LM	XC ◇1	LM	LM	LM	LM	LM	XC ◇1	LM	LM	LM	LM	LM	LM	LM	XC ◇1	LM	LM	XC ◇1	LM	LM
Bromsgrove	d													21 00				21 44					
Redditch	d	18 57				19 27			19 57			20 27			20 57		21 27			21 57			22 27
Alvechurch	d	19 02				19 32			20 02			20 32			21 02		21 32			22 02			22 32
Barnt Green	d	19 08				19 38			20 08			20 38			21 08		21 38			22 08			22 38
Longbridge	d	19 13	19 23		19 33	19 43	19 53	20 03	20 13		20 30	20 43	21 00		21 13	21 30	21 43		22 00	22 13		22 30	22 43
Northfield	d	19 15	19 25		19 35	19 45	19 55	20 05	20 15		20 32	20 45	21 02		21 15	21 32	21 45		22 02	22 15		22 32	22 45
Kings Norton	d	19 17	19 27		19 37	19 47	19 57	20 07	20 17		20 34	20 47	21 04		21 17	21 34	21 47		22 04	22 17		22 34	22 47
Bournville	d	19 20	19 30		19 40	19 50	20 00	20 10	20 20		20 37	20 50	21 07		21 20	21 37	21 50		22 07	22 20		22 37	22 50
Selly Oak	d	19 22	19 32		19 42	19 52	20 02	20 12	20 22		20 39	20 52	21 09		21 22	21 39	21 52		22 09	22 22		22 39	22 52
University	d	19 24	19 34	19 39	19 44	19 54	20 04	20 14	20 24	20 34	20 42	20 54	21 12	21 16	21 24	21 42	21 54	22 01	22 12	22 24	22 36	22 42	22 54
Five Ways	d	19 27	19 37		19 47	19 57	20 07	20 17	20 27		20 45	20 57	21 15		21 27	21 45	21 57		22 15	22 27		22 45	22 57
Birmingham New Street 12	a	19 33	19 43	19 45	19 53	20 03	20 13	20 23	20 34	20 40	20 50	21 03	21 20	21 22	21 33	21 50	22 03	22 07	22 20	22 33	22 42	22 49	23 03
	d	19 35		19 49		20 05			20 35	20 49		21 05			21 35		22 05	22 10		22 35		22 55	
Duddeston	d	19 39				20 09			20 39			21 09			21 39		22 09			22 39		22 59	
Aston	d	19 42				20 12			20 42			21 12			21 42		22 12			22 42		23 02	
Gravelly Hill	d	19 45				20 15			20 45			21 15			21 45		22 15			22 45		23 05	
Erdington	d	19 48				20 18			20 48			21 18			21 48		22 18			22 48		23 08	
Chester Road	d	19 50				20 20			20 50			21 20			21 50		22 20			22 50		23 10	
Wylde Green	d	19 52				20 22			20 52			21 22			21 52		22 22			22 52		23 12	
Sutton Coldfield	d	19 55				20 25			20 55			21 25			21 55		22 25			22 55		23 15	
Four Oaks	d	19 58				20 28			20 58			21 28			21 58		22 28			22 58		23 18	
Butlers Lane	d	20 00				20 30			21 00			21 30			22 00		22 30			23 00		23 20	
Blake Street	d	20 03				20 32			21 03			21 33			22 03		22 33			23 03		23a24	
Shenstone	d	20 07				20 37			21 07			21 37			22 07		22 37			23 07			
Lichfield City	d	20 12				20 42			21 12			21 42			22 12		22 42			23 12			
Lichfield Trent Valley	a																						

		LM	LM	LM
Bromsgrove	d			
Redditch	d		22 57	
Alvechurch	d		23 02	
Barnt Green	d		23 08	
Longbridge	d	22 52	23 13	23 30
Northfield	d	22 54	23 15	23 32
Kings Norton	d	22 56	23 17	23 34
Bournville	d	22 59	23 20	23 37
Selly Oak	d	23 01	23 22	23 39
University	d	23 03	23 24	23 41
Five Ways	d	23 06	23 27	23 44
Birmingham New Street 12	a	23 12	23 33	23 50
	d	23 15		
Duddeston	d	23 19		
Aston	d	23 22		
Gravelly Hill	d	23 25		
Erdington	d	23 28		
Chester Road	d	23 30		
Wylde Green	d	23 32		
Sutton Coldfield	d	23 35		
Four Oaks	d	23 38		
Butlers Lane	d	23 40		
Blake Street	d	23 43		
Shenstone	d	23 47		
Lichfield City	d	23a52		
Lichfield Trent Valley	a			

Sundays

		LM	LM	LM	LM	LM	LM	LM	LM	XC ◇1 A	LM	LM	XC ◇1	LM	LM	XC ◇1	LM	LM	LM	XC ◇1	LM	LM	XC ◇1
Bromsgrove	d																		15 09				
Redditch	d			09 27	09 57	10 27	10 57	11 27	11 57		12 27	12 57		13 27	13 57		14 27	14 57			15 27	15 57	
Alvechurch	d			09 32	10 02	10 32	11 02	11 32	12 02		12 32	13 02		13 32	14 02		14 32	15 02			15 32	16 02	
Barnt Green	d			09 38	10 08	10 38	11 08	11 38	12 08		12 38	13 08		13 39	14 08		14 38	15 08			15 38	16 08	
Longbridge	d			09 43	10 13	10 43	11 13	11 43	12 13		12 43	13 13		13 43	14 13		14 43	15 13			15 43	16 13	
Northfield	d			09 45	10 15	10 45	11 15	11 45	12 15		12 45	13 15		13 45	14 15		14 45	15 15			15 45	16 15	
Kings Norton	d			09 48	10 18	10 48	11 18	11 48	12 18		12 48	13 18		13 48	14 18		14 48	15 18			15 48	16 18	
Bournville	d			09 51	10 21	10 51	11 21	11 51	12 21		12 51	13 21		13 51	14 21		14 51	15 21			15 51	16 21	
Selly Oak	d			09 53	10 23	10 53	11 23	11 53	12 23		12 53	13 23		13 53	14 23		14 53	15 23			15 53	16 23	
University	d			09 56	10 26	10 56	11 26	11 56	12 26	12 39	12 56	13 26	13 35	13 56	14 26	14 38	14 56	15 26		15 35	15 56	16 26	16 35
Five Ways	d			10 00	10 30	11 00	11 30	12 00	12 30		13 00	13 30		14 00	14 30		15 00	15 30			16 00	16 30	
Birmingham New Street 12	a			10 03	10 33	11 03	11 33	12 03	12 33	12 45	13 03	13 33	13 41	14 03	14 33	14 45	15 03	15 33	15 37	15 41	16 03	16 33	16 41
	d	09 06	09 36	10 06	10 36	11 06	11 36	12 06	12 36	12 49	13 06	13 36	13 49	14 06	14 36	14 49	15 06	15 36		15 49	16 06	16 36	16 49
Duddeston	d	09 10	09 40	10 10	10 40	11 10	11 40	12 10	12 40		13 10	13 40		14 10	14 40		15 10	15 40			16 10	16 40	
Aston	d	09 13	09 43	10 13	10 43	11 13	11 43	12 13	12 43		13 13	13 43		14 13	14 43		15 13	15 43			16 13	16 43	
Gravelly Hill	d	09 16	09 46	10 16	10 46	11 16	11 46	12 16	12 46		13 16	13 46		14 16	14 46		15 16	15 46			16 16	16 46	
Erdington	d	09 19	09 49	10 19	10 49	11 19	11 49	12 19	12 49		13 19	13 49		14 19	14 49		15 19	15 49			16 19	16 49	
Chester Road	d	09 21	09 51	10 21	10 51	11 21	11 51	12 21	12 51		13 21	13 51		14 21	14 51		15 21	15 51			16 21	16 51	
Wylde Green	d	09 23	09 53	10 23	10 53	11 23	11 53	12 23	12 53		13 23	13 53		14 23	14 53		15 23	15 53			16 23	16 53	
Sutton Coldfield	d	09 26	09 56	10 26	10 56	11 26	11 56	12 26	12 56		13 26	13 56		14 26	14 56		15 26	15 56			16 26	16 56	
Four Oaks	d	09 29	09 59	10 29	10 59	11 29	11 59	12 29	12 59		13 29	13 59		14 29	14 59		15 29	15 59			16 29	16 59	
Butlers Lane	d	09 31	10 01	10 31	11 01	11 31	12 01	12 31	13 01		13 31	14 01		14 31	15 01		15 31	16 01			16 31	17 01	
Blake Street	d	09 34	10 04	10 34	11 04	11 34	12 04	12 34	13 04		13 34	14 04		14 34	15 04		15 34	16 04			16 34	17 04	
Shenstone	d	09 38	10 08	10 38	11 08	11 38	12 08	12 38	13 08		13 38	14 08		14 38	15 08		15 38	16 08			16 38	17 08	
Lichfield City	d	09 43	10 13	10 43	11 13	11 43	12 13	12 43	13 13		13 43	14 13		14 43	15 13		15 43	16 13			16 43	17 13	
Lichfield Trent Valley	a																						

A from 12 September

Table 69

Sundays

Redditch and Longbridge - Birmingham - Lichfield

		LM	LM	LM	XC ◇1	LM	LM	LM	XC ◇1	LM	LM	XC ◇1	LM	LM	LM	XC ◇1	LM	LM	LM A	LM B	XC ◇1	LM	LM
Bromsgrove	d		16 51				17 52								20 10				21 08	21 11			
Redditch	d	16 27		16 57		17 27		17 57		18 27	18 57		19 27	19 57			20 27	20 57				21 27	21 57
Alvechurch	d	16 32		17 02		17 32		18 02		18 32	19 02		19 32	20 02			20 32	21 02				21 32	22 02
Barnt Green	d	16 38		17 08		17 38		18 08		18 38	19 08		19 38	20 08			20 38	21 08				21 38	22 08
Longbridge	d	16 43		17 13		17 43		18 13		18 43	19 13		19 43	20 13			20 43	21 13				21 43	22 13
Northfield	d	16 45		17 15		17 45		18 15		18 45	19 15		19 45	20 15			20 45	21 15				21 45	22 15
Kings Norton	d	16 48		17 18		17 48		18 18		18 48	19 18		19 48	20 18			20 48	21 18				21 48	22 18
Bournville	d	16 51		17 21		17 51		18 21		18 51	19 21		19 51	20 21			20 51	21 21				21 51	22 21
Selly Oak	d	16 53		17 23		17 53		18 23		18 53	19 23		19 53	20 23			20 53	21 23				21 53	22 23
University	d	16 56		17 26	17 35	17 56		18 26	18 35	18 56	19 26	19 35	19 56	20 26		20 36	20 56	21 26			21 39	21 56	22 26
Five Ways	d	17 00		17 30		18 00		18 30		19 00	19 30		20 00	20 30			21 00	21 30				22 00	22 30
Birmingham New Street 12	a	17 03	17 17	17 33	17 41	18 03	18 13	18 33	18 41	19 03	19 33	19 41	20 03	20 33	20 36	20 42	21 03	21 33	21 42	21 42	21 45	22 03	22 33
	d	17 06		17 36	17 49	18 06		18 36	18 49	19 06	19 36	19 49	20 06	20 36			21 06	21 36				22 06	22 36
Duddeston	d	17 10		17 40		18 10		18 40		19 10	19 40		20 10	20 40			21 10	21 40				22 10	22 40
Aston	d	17 13		17 43		18 13		18 43		19 13	19 43		20 13	20 43			21 13	21 43				22 13	22 43
Gravelly Hill	d	17 16		17 46		18 16		18 46		19 16	19 46		20 16	20 46			21 16	21 46				22 16	22 46
Erdington	d	17 19		17 49		18 19		18 49		19 19	19 49		20 19	20 49			21 19	21 49				22 19	22 49
Chester Road	d	17 21		17 51		18 21		18 51		19 21	19 51		20 21	20 51			21 21	21 51				22 21	22 51
Wylde Green	d	17 23		17 53		18 23		18 53		19 23	19 53		20 23	20 53			21 23	21 53				22 23	22 53
Sutton Coldfield	d	17 26		17 56		18 26		18 56		19 26	19 56		20 26	20 56			21 26	21 56				22 26	22 56
Four Oaks	d	17 29		17 59		18 29		18 59		19 29	19 59		20 29	20 59			21 29	21 59				22 29	22 59
Butlers Lane	d	17 31		18 01		18 31		19 01		19 31	20 01		20 31	21 01			21 31	22 01				22 31	23 01
Blake Street	d	17 34		18 04		18 34		19 04		19 34	20 04		20 34	21 04			21 34	22 04				22 34	23 04
Shenstone	d	17 38		18 08		18 38		19 08		19 38	20 08		20 38	21 08			21 38	22 08				22 38	23 08
Lichfield City	d	17 43		18 13		18 43		19 13		19 43	20 13		20 43	21 13			21 43	22 13				22 43	23 13
Lichfield Trent Valley	a																						

		XC ◇1	LM	LM
Bromsgrove	d			
Redditch	d		22 27	22 57
Alvechurch	d		22 32	23 02
Barnt Green	d		22 38	23 08
Longbridge	d		22 43	23 13
Northfield	d		22 45	23 15
Kings Norton	d		22 48	23 18
Bournville	d		22 51	23 21
Selly Oak	d		22 53	23 23
University	d	22 35	22 56	23 26
Five Ways	d		23 00	23 30
Birmingham New Street 12	a	22 41	23 03	23 33
	d		23 06	
Duddeston	d		23 10	
Aston	d		23 13	
Gravelly Hill	d		23 16	
Erdington	d		23 19	
Chester Road	d		23 21	
Wylde Green	d		23 23	
Sutton Coldfield	d		23 26	
Four Oaks	d		23 29	
Butlers Lane	d		23 31	
Blake Street	d		23 34	
Shenstone	d		23 38	
Lichfield City	d		23 43	
Lichfield Trent Valley	a			

A from 18 July
B until 11 July

Table 70

Mondays to Fridays

Birmingham - Walsall and Rugeley

		LM A 🚌	LM MX	LM A 🚌	LM	LM	LM	LM 1	LM	LM	LM	LM	LM	LM	LM	LM	LM	LM	LM	LM	LM	LM	LM
Wolverhampton 7 ⇌	d												07 49				08 49		09 19		09 49		10 19
Birmingham New Street 12	d	22p50	23p18	23p12	05 33	05 56	06 27	06 47	07 17	07 39	07 47	08 07	08 17	08 39	08 47	09 07	09 17	09 39	09 47	10 07	10 17	10 39	10 47
Duddeston	d		23p23	23p22		06 00	06 32	06 52	07 22		07 52		08 22		08 52		09 22		09 52		10 22		10 52
Aston	d		23p26	23p27		06 03	06 35	06 55	07 25		07 55		08 25		08 55		09 25		09 55		10 25		10 55
Witton	d		23p28	23p34		06 05	06 37	06 57	07 27		07 57		08 27		08 57		09 27		09 57		10 27		10 57
Perry Barr	d		23p31	23p42		06 07	06 39	06 59	07 29		07 59		08 29		08 59		09 29		09 59		10 29		10 59
Hamstead	d		23p34	23p51	05 41	06 10	06 42	07 01	07 32		08 02		08 31		09 01		09 31		10 01		10 31		11 01
Tame Bridge Parkway	d	23p16	23p39	00 02	05 45	06 15	06 47	07 05	07 37	07 50	08 07	08 20	08 35	08 50	09 05	09 20	09 35	09 50	10 05	10 20	10 35	10 50	11 05
Bescot Stadium	d		23p41	00 11	05 48	06 18	06 50	07 08	07 40		08 10		08 38		09 08		09 38		10 08		10 38		11 08
Walsall	a	23p31	23p47	00 19	05 55	06 23	06 55	07 14	07 44	07 59	08 14	08 29	08 44	08 59	09 14	09 29	09 44	09 59	10 14	10 29	10 46	10 59	11 14
	d	23p32	23p47			06 24	06 56		07 45	08 00		08 30		09 00		09 30		10 00		10 30		11 00	
Bloxwich	d	23p41	23p54			06 31	07 03		07 52	08 07				09 07				10 07				11 07	
Bloxwich North	d	23p47	23p57			06 33	07 05		07 54	08 09				09 09				10 09				11 09	
Landywood	d	23p58	00 01			06 37	07 09		07 58	08 13				09 13				10 13				11 13	
Cannock	d	00 10	00 06			06 42	07 14		08 03	08 18		08 44		09 18		09 44		10 18		10 44		11 18	
Hednesford	d	00 18	00a12			06 47	07 19		08a09	08 23		08 49		09 23		09 49		10 23		10 49		11 23	
Rugeley Town	d	00 29				06 55	07 27			08 31		08 57		09 31		09 57		10 31		10 57		11 31	
Rugeley Trent Valley	a	00 34				07 00	07 32			08 36		09 04		09 36		10 04		10 36		11 04		11 36	

		LM	LM	LM	LM	LM	LM	LM	LM	LM	LM	LM	LM	LM	LM	LM	LM	LM	LM	LM	LM	LM	LM
Wolverhampton 7 ⇌	d		10 49		11 19		11 49		12 19		12 49		13 19		13 49		14 19		14 49		15 19		15 49
Birmingham New Street 12	d	11 07	11 17	11 39	11 47	12 07	12 17	12 39	12 47	13 07	13 17	13 39	13 47	14 07	14 17	14 39	14 47	15 07	15 17	15 39	15 47	16 07	16 17
Duddeston	d		11 22		11 52		12 22		12 52		13 22		13 52		14 22		14 52		15 22		15 52		16 22
Aston	d		11 25		11 55		12 25		12 55		13 25		13 55		14 25		14 55		15 25		15 55		16 25
Witton	d		11 27		11 57		12 27		12 57		13 27		13 57		14 27		14 57		15 27		15 57		16 27
Perry Barr	d		11 29		11 59		12 29		12 59		13 29		13 59		14 29		14 59		15 29		15 59		16 29
Hamstead	d		11 31		12 01		12 31		13 01		13 31		14 01		14 31		15 01		15 31		16 01		16 31
Tame Bridge Parkway	d	11 20	11 35	11 50	12 05	12 20	12 35	12 50	13 05	13 20	13 35	13 50	14 05	14 20	14 35	14 50	15 05	15 20	15 35	15 50	16 05	16 20	16 35
Bescot Stadium	d		11 38		12 08		12 38		13 08		13 38		14 08		14 38		15 08		15 38		16 08		16 38
Walsall	a	11 29	11 44	11 59	12 14	12 29	12 46	12 59	13 14	13 29	13 44	13 59	14 14	14 29	14 44	14 59	15 14	15 29	15 46	15 59	16 14	16 29	16 44
	d	11 30		12 00		12 30		13 00		13 33		14 00		14 33		15 00		15 30		16 00		16 31	
Bloxwich	d			12 07				13 07				14 07				15 07				16 07		16 38	
Bloxwich North	d			12 09				13 09				14 09				15 09				16 09		16 40	
Landywood	d			12 13				13 13				14 13				15 13				16 13		16 45	
Cannock	d	11 44		12 18		12 44		13 18		13 48		14 18		14 48		15 18		15 44		16 18		16 49	
Hednesford	d	11 49		12 23		12 49		13 23		13a59		14 23		14a59		15 23		15 49		16 23		16 54	
Rugeley Town	d	11 57		12 31		12 57		13 31				14 31				15 31		15 57		16 31		17 02	
Rugeley Trent Valley	a	12 04		12 36		13 04		13 36				14 36				15 36		16 04		16 36		17 08	

		LM	LM	LM	LM	LM	LM	LM	LM	LM	LM	LM	LM	LM	LM	LM	LM	LM	LM	LM
Wolverhampton 7 ⇌	d		16 19		16 49		17 19		17 49		18 19		19 19							
Birmingham New Street 12	d	16 39	16 47	17 07	17 17	17 42	17 47	18 12	18 17	18 39	18 47	19 17	19 47	20 17	20 47	21 17	21 47	22 17	22 47	23 18
Duddeston	d		16 52		17 22		17 52		18 22		18 52	19 22	19 52		20 52		21 52		22 52	23 23
Aston	d		16 55		17 25		17 55		18 25		18 55	19 25	19 55		20 55		21 55		22 55	23 26
Witton	d		16 57		17 27		17 57		18 27		18 57	19 27	19 57		20 57		21 57		22 57	23 28
Perry Barr	d		16 59		17 29		17 59		18 29		18 59	19 29	19 59		20 59		21 59		22 59	23 31
Hamstead	d		17 01		17 31		18 01		18 31		19 01	19 32	20 01		21 01		22 01		23 01	23 34
Tame Bridge Parkway	d	16 50	17 05	17 20	17 35	17 54	18 05	18 24	18 35	18 50	19 05	19 37	20 05	20 30	21 05	21 30	22 05	22 30	23 05	23 39
Bescot Stadium	d		17 08		17 38		18 08		18 38		19 08	19 40	20 08		21 08		22 08		23 08	23 41
Walsall	a	16 59	17 14	17 29	17 44	18 01	18 14	18 31	18 44	18 59	19 15	19 45	20 14	20 38	21 14	21 38	22 14	22 38	23 14	23 47
	d	17 00		17 30		18 02		18 31		19 00		19 46		20 39		21 39		22 39		23 47
Bloxwich	d	17 07		17 37		18 09		18 38		19 07		19 53		20 46		21 46		22 46		23 54
Bloxwich North	d	17 09		17 39		18 11		18 40		19 09		19 56		20 49		21 49		22 49		23 57
Landywood	d	17 13		17 43		18 15		18 44		19 13		20 00		20 53		21 53		22 53		00 01
Cannock	d	17 18		17 48		18 20		18 48		19 18		20 05		20 57		21 57		22 57		00 06
Hednesford	d	17 23		17 53		18 25		18 53		19 23		20 10		21 02		22 02		23 02		00a12
Rugeley Town	d	17 31		18 01		18 33		19 01		19 31		20 18		21 10		22 10		23 10		
Rugeley Trent Valley	a	17 36		18 06		18 38		19 08		19 36		20 22		21 15		22 15		23 15		

Saturdays

		LM	LM	LM	LM	LM	LM	LM	LM	LM	LM	LM	LM	LM	LM	LM	LM	LM	LM	LM	LM	LM	LM	LM	LM
Wolverhampton 7 ⇌	d					06 49		07 19		07 49		08 19		08 49		09 19		09 49		10 19		10 49		11 19	
Birmingham New Street 12	d	23p18	06 02	06 27	07 00	07 17	07 39	07 47	08 07	08 17	08 39	08 47	09 07	09 17	09 39	09 47	10 07	10 17	10 39	10 47	11 07	11 17	11 39	11 47	12 07
Duddeston	d	23p23	06 06	06 32		07 22		07 52		08 22		08 52		09 22		09 52		10 22		10 52		11 22		11 52	
Aston	d	23p26	06 09	06 35	07 06	07 25		07 55		08 25		08 55		09 25		09 55		10 25		10 55		11 25		11 55	
Witton	d	23p28	06 11	06 37		07 27		07 57		08 27		08 57		09 27		09 57		10 27		10 57		11 27		11 57	
Perry Barr	d	23p31	06 13	06 40	07 09	07 29		07 59		08 29		08 59		09 29		09 59		10 29		10 59		11 29		11 59	
Hamstead	d	23p34	06 16	06 43	07 12	07 31		08 01		08 31		09 01		09 31		10 01		10 31		11 01		11 31		12 01	
Tame Bridge Parkway	d	23p39	06 21	06 48	07 17	07 35	07 50	08 05	08 20	08 35	08 50	09 05	09 20	09 35	09 50	10 05	10 20	10 35	10 50	11 05	11 20	11 35	11 50	12 05	12 20
Bescot Stadium	d	23p41	06 24	06 50		07 38		08 08		08 38		09 08		09 38		10 08		10 38		11 08		11 38		12 08	
Walsall	a	23p47	06 29	06 56	07 25	07 44	07 59	08 14	08 29	08 44	08 59	09 14	09 29	09 44	09 59	10 14	10 29	10 44	10 59	11 14	11 29	11 44	11 59	12 14	12 29
	d	23p47	06 30	06 57	07 26		07 57		08 30		09 00		09 30		10 00		10 30		11 00		11 30		12 00		12 30
Bloxwich	d	23p54	06 37	07 04	07 33		08 04				09 07				10 07				11 07				12 07		
Bloxwich North	d	23p57	06 39	07 06	07 35		08 06				09 09				10 09				11 09				12 09		
Landywood	d	00 01	06 43	07 10	07 39		08 10				09 13				10 13				11 13				12 13		
Cannock	d	00 06	06 48	07 15	07 44		08 15		08 44		09 18		09 44		10 18		10 44		11 18		11 44		12 18		12 44
Hednesford	d	00a12	06a53	07 20	07 49		08 20		08 49		09 23		09 49		10 23		10 49		11 23		11 49		12 23		12 49
Rugeley Town	d			07 28	07 57		08 28		08 57		09 31		09 57		10 31		10 57		11 31		11 57		12 31		12 57
Rugeley Trent Valley	a			07 32	08 04		08 35		09 04		09 36		10 04		10 36		11 04		11 36		12 04		12 36		13 04

A MO from 19 July until 6 September

For connections to Stafford please refer to Table 67

Table 70

Saturdays

Birmingham - Walsall and Rugeley

		LM	LM	LM	LM	LM	LM	LM	LM	LM	LM	LM	LM	LM	LM	LM	LM	LM	LM	LM	LM	LM	LM	LM
Wolverhampton 7 ⇌	d	11 49		12 19		12 49		13 19		13 49		14 19		14 49		15 19		15 49		16 19		16 49		17 19
Birmingham New Street 12	d	12 17	12 39	12 47	13 07	13 17	13 39	13 47	14 07	14 17	14 39	14 47	15 07	15 17	15 39	15 47	16 07	16 17	16 39	16 47	17 07	17 17	17 39	17 47
Duddeston	d	12 22		12 52		13 22		13 52		14 22		14 52		15 22		15 52		16 22		16 52		17 22		17 52
Aston	d	12 25		12 55		13 25		13 55		14 25		14 55		15 25		15 55		16 25		16 55		17 25		17 55
Witton	d	12 27		12 57		13 27		13 57		14 27		14 57		15 27		15 57		16 27		16 57		17 27		17 57
Perry Barr	d	12 29		12 59		13 29		13 59		14 29		14 59		15 29		15 59		16 29		16 59		17 29		17 59
Hamstead	d	12 31		13 01		13 31		14 01		14 31		15 01		15 31		16 01		16 31		17 01		17 31		18 01
Tame Bridge Parkway	d	12 35	12 50	13 05	13 20	13 35	13 50	14 05	14 20	14 35	14 50	15 05	15 20	15 35	15 50	16 05	16 20	16 35	16 50	17 05	17 20	17 35	17 50	18 05
Bescot Stadium	d	12 38		13 08		13 38		14 08		14 38		15 08		15 38		16 08		16 38		17 08		17 38		18 08
Walsall	a	12 44	12 59	13 14	13 29	13 44	13 59	14 14	14 29	14 44	14 59	15 14	15 29	15 46	15 59	16 14	16 29	16 44	16 59	17 14	17 29	17 44	17 59	18 14
	d		13 00		13 30		14 00		14 30		15 00		15 30		16 00		16 30		17 00		17 30		18 00	
Bloxwich	d		13 07				14 07				15 07				16 07				17 07		17 37		18 07	
Bloxwich North	d		13 09				14 09				15 09				16 09				17 09		17 39		18 09	
Landywood	d		13 13				14 13				15 13				16 13				17 13		17 43		18 13	
Cannock	d		13 18		13 44		14 18		14 44		15 18		15 44		16 18		16 44		17 18		17 48		18 18	
Hednesford	d		13 23		13 49		14 23		14 49		15 23		15 49		16 23		16 49		17 23		17 53		18 23	
Rugeley Town	d		13 31		13 57		14 31		14 57		15 31		15 57		16 31		16 57		17 31		18 01		18 31	
Rugeley Trent Valley	a		13 36		14 04		14 36		15 04		15 36		16 04		16 36		17 04		17 36		18 06		18 36	

		LM	LM	LM	LM	LM	LM	LM	LM	LM	LM	LM	LM	LM
Wolverhampton 7 ⇌	d		17 49		18 19		19 19							
Birmingham New Street 12	d	18 07	18 17	18 39	18 47	19 17	19 47	20 17	20 47	21 17	21 47	22 17	22 47	23 18
Duddeston	d		18 22		18 52	19 22	19 52		20 52		21 52		22 52	23 23
Aston	d		18 25		18 55	19 25	19 55		20 55		21 55		22 55	23 26
Witton	d		18 27		18 57	19 27	19 57		20 57		21 57		22 57	23 28
Perry Barr	d		18 29		18 59	19 29	19 59		20 59		21 59		22 59	23 31
Hamstead	d		18 31		19 01	19 32	20 01		21 01		22 01		23 01	23 34
Tame Bridge Parkway	d	18 20	18 35	18 50	19 05	19 37	20 05	20 31	21 05	21 31	22 05	22 31	23 05	23 39
Bescot Stadium	d		18 38		19 08	19 40	20 08		21 08		22 08		23 08	23 41
Walsall	a	18 29	18 44	18 59	19 14	19 45	20 14	20 38	21 14	21 38	22 14	22 38	23 14	23 47
	d	18 30		19 00		19 46		20 39		21 39		22 39		23 47
Bloxwich	d	18 37		19 07		19 53		20 46		21 46		22 46		23 54
Bloxwich North	d	18 39		19 09		19 56		20 49		21 49		22 49		23 57
Landywood	d	18 43		19 13		20 00		20 53		21 53		22 53		00 01
Cannock	d	18 48		19 18		20 05		20 57		21 57		22 57		00 06
Hednesford	d	18 53		19 23		20 10		21 02		22 02		23 02		00a12
Rugeley Town	d	19 01		19 31		20 18		21 10		22 10		23 10		
Rugeley Trent Valley	a	19 06		19 36		20 22		21 15		22 15		23 15		

Sundays
until 11 July

		LM	LM	LM	LM	LM	LM	LM	LM	LM	LM	LM	LM	LM	LM	LM	LM	LM	LM	LM	LM	LM	LM
Wolverhampton 7 ⇌	d																						
Birmingham New Street 12	d	23p18	09 23	09 33	10 12	10 33	11 12	11 36	12 12	12 33	13 12	13 33	14 12	14 33	15 12	15 33	16 12	16 33	17 12	17 33	18 12	18 33	19 12
Duddeston	d	23p23																					
Aston	d	23p26																					
Witton	d	23p28																					
Perry Barr	d	23p31																					
Hamstead	d	23p34	09 35		10 24		11 24		12 24		13 24		14 24		15 24		16 24		17 24		18 24		19 24
Tame Bridge Parkway	d	23p39	09 40	09 48	10 29	10 48	11 29	11 53	12 29	12 48	13 29	13 48	14 29	14 48	15 29	15 48	16 29	16 48	17 29	17 48	18 29	18 48	19 29
Bescot Stadium	d	23p41	09 43		10 32		11 32		12 32		13 32		14 32		15 32		16 32		17 32		18 32		19 32
Walsall	a	23p47	09 47	09 55	10 36	10 55	11 36	12 00	12 36	12 55	13 36	13 55	14 36	14 55	15 36	15 55	16 36	16 55	17 36	17 55	18 36	18 55	19 36
	d	23p47		09 56		10 56		12 01		12 56		13 56		14 56		15 56		16 56		17 56		18 56	
Bloxwich	d	23p54		10 03		11 03		12 08		13 03		14 03		15 03		16 03		17 03		18 03		19 03	
Bloxwich North	d	23p57		10 05		11 05		12 10		13 05		14 05		15 05		16 05		17 05		18 05		19 05	
Landywood	d	00 01		10 10		11 10		12 15		13 10		14 10		15 10		16 10		17 10		18 10		19 10	
Cannock	d	00 06		10 14		11 14		12 19		13 14		14 14		15 14		16 14		17 14		18 14		19 14	
Hednesford	d	00a12		10 19		11 19		12 24		13 19		14 19		15 19		16 19		17 19		18 19		19 19	
Rugeley Town	d			10 27		11 27		12 32		13 27		14 27		15 27		16 27		17 27		18 27		19 27	
Rugeley Trent Valley	a			10 32		11 32		12 37		13 32		14 32		15 32		16 32		17 32		18 32		19 32	

		LM	LM	LM	LM	LM	LM	LM	LM
Wolverhampton 7 ⇌	d								
Birmingham New Street 12	d	19 33	20 12	20 27	21 12	21 33	22 12	22 33	23 12
Duddeston	d								
Aston	d								
Witton	d								
Perry Barr	d								
Hamstead	d		20 24		21 24		22 24		23 24
Tame Bridge Parkway	d	19 48	20 29	20 42	21 29	21 48	22 29	22 48	23 29
Bescot Stadium	d		20 32		21 32		22 32		23 32
Walsall	a	19 55	20 36	20 49	21 37	21 55	22 36	22 55	23 36
	d	19 56		20 56		21 56		22 56	
Bloxwich	d	20 03		21 03		22 03		23 03	
Bloxwich North	d	20 05		21 05		22 05		23 05	
Landywood	d	20 10		21 10		22 10		23 10	
Cannock	d	20 14		21 14		22 14		23 14	
Hednesford	d	20 19		21 19		22 19		23 19	
Rugeley Town	d	20 27		21 27		22 27		23 27	
Rugeley Trent Valley	a	20 32		21 32		22 32		23 32	

For connections to Stafford please refer to Table 67

Table 70

Birmingham - Walsall and Rugeley

Sundays

18 July to 05 September

		LM	LM	LM	LM	LM	LM	LM	LM	LM	LM	LM	LM	LM	LM	LM	LM	LM	LM	LM	LM	LM	LM
			🚌	🚌	🚌	🚌	🚌	🚌	🚌	🚌	🚌	🚌	🚌	🚌	🚌	🚌	🚌	🚌	🚌	🚌	🚌	🚌	🚌
Wolverhampton 7	d																						
Birmingham New Street 12	d	23p18	08 12	08 50	09 12	09 50	10 12	10 50	11 12	11 50	12 12	12 50	13 12	13 50	14 12	14 50	15 12	15 50	16 12	16 50	17 12	17 50	18 12
Duddeston	d	23p23	08 22		09 22		10 22		11 22		12 22		13 22		14 22		15 22		16 22		17 22		18 22
Aston	d	23p26	08 27		09 27		10 27		11 27		12 27		13 27		14 27		15 27		16 27		17 27		18 27
Witton	d	23p28	08 34		09 34		10 34		11 34		12 34		13 34		14 34		15 34		16 34		17 34		18 34
Perry Barr	d	23p31	08 42		09 42		10 42		11 42		12 42		13 42		14 42		15 42		16 42		17 42		18 42
Hamstead	d	23p34	08 51		09 51		10 51		11 51		12 51		13 51		14 51		15 51		16 51		17 51		18 51
Tame Bridge Parkway	d	23p39	09 02	09 16	10 02	10 16	11 02	11 16	12 02	12 16	13 02	13 16	14 02	14 16	15 02	15 16	16 02	16 16	17 02	17 16	18 02	18 16	19 02
Bescot Stadium	d	23p41	09 11		10 11		11 11		12 11		13 11		14 11		15 11		16 11		17 11		18 11		19 11
Walsall	a	23p47	09 19	09 31	10 19	10 31	11 19	11 31	12 19	12 31	13 19	13 31	14 19	14 31	15 19	15 31	16 19	16 31	17 19	17 31	18 19	18 31	19 19
	d	23p47		09 32		10 32		11 32		12 32		13 32		14 32		15 32		16 32		17 32		18 32	
Bloxwich	d	23p54		09 41		10 41		11 41		12 41		13 41		14 41		15 41		16 41		17 41		18 41	
Bloxwich North	d	23p57		09 47		10 47		11 47		12 47		13 47		14 47		15 47		16 47		17 47		18 47	
Landywood	d	00 01		09 58		10 58		11 58		12 58		13 58		14 58		15 58		16 58		17 58		18 58	
Cannock	d	00 06		10 10		11 10		12 10		13 10		14 10		15 10		16 10		17 10		18 10		19 10	
Hednesford	d	00a12		10 18		11 18		12 18		13 18		14 18		15 18		16 18		17 18		18 18		19 18	
Rugeley Town	d			10 29		11 29		12 29		13 29		14 29		15 29		16 29		17 29		18 29		19 29	
Rugeley Trent Valley	a			10 34		11 34		12 34		13 34		14 34		15 34		16 34		17 34		18 34		19 34	

		LM	LM	LM	LM	LM	LM	LM	LM	LM	LM
		🚌	🚌	🚌	🚌	🚌	🚌	🚌	🚌	🚌	🚌
Wolverhampton 7	d										
Birmingham New Street 12	d	18 50	19 12	19 50	20 12	20 50	21 12	21 50	22 12	22 50	23 12
Duddeston	d		19 22		20 22		21 22		22 22		23 22
Aston	d		19 27		20 27		21 27		22 27		23 27
Witton	d		19 34		20 34		21 34		22 34		23 34
Perry Barr	d		19 42		20 42		21 42		22 42		23 42
Hamstead	d		19 51		20 51		21 51		22 51		23 51
Tame Bridge Parkway	d	19 16	20 02	20 16	21 02	21 16	22 02	22 16	23 02	23 16	00 02
Bescot Stadium	d		20 11		21 11		22 11		23 11		00 11
Walsall	a	19 31	20 19	20 31	21 19	21 31	22 19	22 31	23 19	23 31	00 19
	d	19 32		20 32		21 32		22 32		23 32	
Bloxwich	d	19 41		20 41		21 41		22 41		23 41	
Bloxwich North	d	19 47		20 47		21 47		22 47		23 47	
Landywood	d	19 58		20 58		21 58		22 58		23 58	
Cannock	d	20 10		21 10		22 10		23 10		00 10	
Hednesford	d	20 18		21 18		22 18		23 18		00 18	
Rugeley Town	d	20 29		21 29		22 29		23 29		00 29	
Rugeley Trent Valley	a	20 34		21 34		22 34		23 34		00 34	

Sundays

from 12 September

		LM	LM	LM	LM	LM	LM	LM	LM	LM	LM	LM	LM	LM	LM	LM	LM	LM	LM	LM	LM	LM	LM
Wolverhampton 7	d																						
Birmingham New Street 12	d	23p18	09 17	09 40	10 17	10 40	11 17	11 40	12 17	12 40	13 17	13 40	14 17	14 40	15 17	15 40	16 17	16 40	17 17	17 40	18 17	18 40	19 17
Duddeston	d	23p23	09 21		10 21		11 21		12 21		13 21		14 21		15 21		16 21		17 21		18 21		19 21
Aston	d	23p26	09 24		10 24		11 24		12 24		13 24		14 24		15 24		16 24		17 24		18 24		19 24
Witton	d	23p28	09 26		10 26		11 26		12 26		13 26		14 26		15 26		16 26		17 26		18 26		19 26
Perry Barr	d	23p31	09 29		10 29		11 29		12 29		13 29		14 29		15 29		16 29		17 29		18 29		19 29
Hamstead	d	23p34	09 32		10 32		11 32		12 32		13 32		14 32		15 32		16 32		17 32		18 32		19 32
Tame Bridge Parkway	d	23p39	09 37	09 52	10 37	10 52	11 37	11 52	12 37	12 52	13 37	13 52	14 37	14 52	15 37	15 52	16 37	16 52	17 37	17 52	18 37	18 52	19 37
Bescot Stadium	d	23p41	09 39		10 39		11 39		12 39		13 39		14 39		15 39		16 39		17 39		18 39		19 39
Walsall	a	23p47	09 44	10 00	10 44	11 00	11 44	12 00	12 44	13 00	13 44	14 00	14 44	15 00	15 44	16 00	16 44	17 00	17 44	18 00	18 44	19 00	19 44
	d	23p47		10 01		11 01		12 01		13 01		14 01		15 01		16 01		17 01		18 01		19 01	
Bloxwich	d	23p54		10 08		11 08		12 08		13 08		14 08		15 08		16 08		17 08		18 08		19 08	
Bloxwich North	d	23p57		10 10		11 10		12 10		13 10		14 10		15 10		16 10		17 10		18 10		19 10	
Landywood	d	00 01		10 15		11 15		12 15		13 15		14 15		15 15		16 15		17 15		18 15		19 15	
Cannock	d	00 06		10 19		11 19		12 19		13 19		14 19		15 19		16 19		17 19		18 19		19 19	
Hednesford	d	00a12		10 24		11 24		12 24		13 24		14 24		15 24		16 24		17 24		18 24		19 24	
Rugeley Town	d			10 32		11 32		12 32		13 32		14 32		15 32		16 32		17 32		18 32		19 32	
Rugeley Trent Valley	a			10 37		11 37		12 37		13 37		14 37		15 37		16 37		17 37		18 37		19 37	

		LM	LM	LM	LM	LM	LM	LM	LM
Wolverhampton 7	d								
Birmingham New Street 12	d	19 40	20 17	20 40	21 17	21 40	22 17	22 40	23 17
Duddeston	d		20 21		21 21		22 21		23 21
Aston	d		20 24		21 24		22 24		23 24
Witton	d		20 26		21 26		22 26		23 26
Perry Barr	d		20 29		21 29		22 29		23 29
Hamstead	d		20 32		21 32		22 32		23 32
Tame Bridge Parkway	d	19 52	20 37	20 52	21 37	21 52	22 37	22 52	23 37
Bescot Stadium	d		20 39		21 39		22 39		23 39
Walsall	a	20 00	20 44	21 00	21 46	22 00	22 44	23 00	23 44
	d	20 01		21 01		22 01		23 01	
Bloxwich	d	20 08		21 08		22 08		23 08	
Bloxwich North	d	20 10		21 10		22 10		23 10	
Landywood	d	20 15		21 15		22 15		23 15	
Cannock	d	20 19		21 19		22 19		23 19	
Hednesford	d	20 24		21 24		22 24		23 24	
Rugeley Town	d	20 32		21 32		22 32		23 32	
Rugeley Trent Valley	a	20 37		21 37		22 37		23 37	

For connections to Stafford please refer to Table 67

Table 70

Rugeley and Walsall - Birmingham

Mondays to Fridays

		LM MX	LM	LM	LM	LM	LM ◇1	LM	LM	LM	LM	LM	LM	LM	LM	LM	LM	LM	LM	LM	LM	LM	LM
Rugeley Trent Valley	d				06 21	06 39		07 04		07 40				08 42		09 06		09 42		10 06		10 42	
Rugeley Town	d				06 25	06 43		07 08		07 44				08 46		09 10		09 46		10 10		10 46	
Hednesford	d			06 07	06 33	06 51		07 16	07 39	07 52		08 17		08 54		09 18		09 54		10 18		10 54	
Cannock	d			06 11	06 37	06 55		07 20	07 43	07 56		08 21		08 58		09 22		09 58		10 22		10 58	
Landywood	d			06 14	06 40	06 58		07 23		07 59		08 24				09 25				10 25			
Bloxwich North	d			06 19	06 45	07 03		07 27		08 04		08 29				09 30				10 30			
Bloxwich	d			06 21	06 47	07 05		07 29		08 06		08 31				09 32				10 32			
Walsall	a			06 28	06 54	07 12		07 37	07 57	08 13		08 38		09 12		09 39		10 12		10 39		11 12	
	d	23p40	06 01	06 29	07 00	07 13	07 30	07 37	08 00	08 14	08 30	08 39	09 01	09 13	09 30	09 40	10 01	10 13	10 31	10 40	11 01	11 13	11 31
Bescot Stadium	d	23p44	06 04	06 34	07 04		07 34		08 04		08 34		09 04		09 34		10 04		10 34		11 04		11 34
Tame Bridge Parkway	d	23p47	06 07	06 37	07 07	07 19	07 37	07 43	08 07	08 20	08 37	08 46	09 07	09 19	09 37	09 46	10 07	10 19	10 37	10 46	11 07	11 19	11 37
Hamstead	d	23p51	06 11	06 41	07 12		07 41		08 11		08 41		09 11		09 41		10 11		10 41		11 11		11 41
Perry Barr	d	23p55	06 14	06 44	07 15		07 44		08 14		08 44		09 14		09 44		10 14		10 44		11 14		11 44
Witton	d	23p57	06 16	06 46	07 17		07 47		08 17		08 47		09 16		09 47		10 16		10 46		11 16		11 46
Aston	d	00 01	06 18	06 49	07 20		07 50		08 20		08 50		09 19		09 50		10 19		10 49		11 19		11 49
Duddeston	d	00 04	06 21	06 52	07 23		07 53		08 23		08 53		09 21		09 53		10 21		10 51		11 21		11 51
Birmingham New Street 12	a	00 09	06 28	06 57	07 28	07 36	07 57	08 00	08 29	08 37	08 57	09 02	09 28	09 36	09 57	10 03	10 28	10 36	10 58	11 03	11 28	11 36	11 58
Wolverhampton 7	a		07 03				08 19										11 03		11 33		12 03		12 33

		LM	LM	LM	LM	LM	LM	LM	LM	LM	LM	LM	LM	LM	LM	LM	LM	LM	LM	LM	LM	LM	LM
Rugeley Trent Valley	d	11 06		11 42		12 06	12 42		13 06		13 42				14 42				15 42		16 06		16 42
Rugeley Town	d	11 10		11 46		12 10	12 46		13 10		13 46				14 46				15 46		16 10		16 46
Hednesford	d	11 18		11 54		12 18	12 54		13 18		13 54		14 18		14 54		15 18		15 54		16 18		16 54
Cannock	d	11 22		11 58		12 22	12 58		13 22		13 58		14 22		14 58		15 22		15 58		16 22		16 58
Landywood	d	11 25				12 25			13 25				14 25				15 25				16 25		
Bloxwich North	d	11 30				12 30			13 30				14 30				15 30				16 30		
Bloxwich	d	11 32				12 32			13 32				14 32				15 32				16 32		
Walsall	a	11 39		12 12		12 39	13 12		13 39		14 12		14 39		15 12		15 39		16 12		16 39		17 12
	d	11 40	12 01	12 13	12 31	12 40	13 13	13 31	13 40	14 01	14 13	14 31	14 40	15 01	15 13	15 31	15 40	16 01	16 13	16 31	16 40	17 01	17 13
Bescot Stadium	d		12 04		12 34			13 34		14 04		14 34		15 04		15 34		16 04		16 34		17 04	
Tame Bridge Parkway	d	11 46	12 07	12 19	12 37	12 46	13 19	13 37	13 46	14 07	14 19	14 37	14 46	15 07	15 19	15 37	15 46	16 07	16 19	16 37	16 46	17 07	17 19
Hamstead	d		12 11		12 41			13 41		14 11		14 41		15 11		15 41		16 11		16 41		17 11	
Perry Barr	d		12 14		12 44			13 44		14 14		14 44		15 14		15 44		16 14		16 44		17 14	
Witton	d		12 16		12 46			13 46		14 16		14 46		15 16		15 46		16 16		16 46		17 16	
Aston	d		12 19		12 49			13 49		14 19		14 49		15 19		15 49		16 19		16 49		17 19	
Duddeston	d		12 21		12 51			13 51		14 21		14 51		15 21		15 51		16 21		16 51		17 21	
Birmingham New Street 12	a	12 03	12 28	12 36	12 58	13 03	13 36	13 58	14 03	14 28	14 36	14 58	15 03	15 28	15 36	15 58	16 03	16 30	16 36	16 59	17 03	17 28	17 36
Wolverhampton 7	a		13 03		13 33			14 33		15 03		15 33		16 03		16 33		17 04		17 33		18 03	

		LM	LM	LM	LM	LM	LM	LM	LM	LM	LM	LM	LM	LM	LM	LM	LM	LM	LM
Rugeley Trent Valley	d		17 13		17 42		18 12		18 46		19 10	19 42		20 35		21 40		22 33	
Rugeley Town	d		17 17		17 46		18 16		18 50		19 14	19 46		20 39		21 44		22 37	
Hednesford	d		17 25		17 54		18 24		18 58		19 21	19 54		20 47		21 52		22 45	
Cannock	d		17 29		17 58		18 28		19 02		19 25	19 58		20 51		21 56		22 49	
Landywood	d		17 32				18 31				19 29	20 01		20 54		21 59		22 53	
Bloxwich North	d		17 37				18 36				19 33	20 06		20 59		22 04		22 58	
Bloxwich	d		17 39				18 38				19 35	20 08		21 01		22 06		23 00	
Walsall	a		17 46		18 12		18 45		19 16		19 43	20 15		21 08		22 16		23 07	
	d	17 31	17 47	18 01	18 13	18 31	18 46	19 01	19 18	19 36	19 43	20 16	20 40	21 10	21 40	22 17	22 40	23 10	23 40
Bescot Stadium	d	17 34		18 04		18 34		19 04	19 23		19 48		20 44		21 44		22 44		23 44
Tame Bridge Parkway	d	17 37	17 53	18 07	18 19	18 37	18 52	19 07	19 26		19 51	20 22	20 47	21 16	21 47	22 23	22 47	23 16	23 47
Hamstead	d	17 41		18 11		18 41		19 11	19 30		19 55		20 51		21 51		22 51		23 51
Perry Barr	d	17 44		18 14		18 44		19 14	19 33		19 58		20 55		21 55		22 55		23 55
Witton	d	17 46		18 16		18 46		19 16	19 36		20 01		20 57		21 57		22 57		23 57
Aston	d	17 49		18 19		18 49		19 19	19 39		20 03		21 00		22 00		23 00		00 01
Duddeston	d	17 51		18 21		18 51		19 21	19 42		20 06		21 03		22 03		23 03		00 04
Birmingham New Street 12	a	17 58	18 10	18 28	18 36	18 58	19 09	19 28	19 46		20 11	20 39	21 09	21 35	22 09	22 40	23 09	23 33	00 09
Wolverhampton 7	a	18 33		19 03		19 33		20 03		19 50									

Saturdays

		LM	LM	LM	LM	LM	LM	LM	LM	LM	LM	LM	LM	LM	LM	LM	LM	LM	LM	LM	LM	LM	LM
Rugeley Trent Valley	d				06 26				07 39		08 06		08 42		09 06		09 42		10 06		10 42		11 06
Rugeley Town	d				06 30				07 43		08 10		08 46		09 10		09 46		10 10		10 46		11 10
Hednesford	d				06 38	06 58			07 51		08 18		08 54		09 18		09 54		10 18		10 54		11 18
Cannock	d				06 42	07 02			07 55		08 22		08 58		09 22		09 58		10 22		10 58		11 22
Landywood	d				06 45	07 05			07 58		08 25				09 25				10 25				11 25
Bloxwich North	d				06 50	07 10			08 03		08 30				09 30				10 30				11 30
Bloxwich	d				06 52	07 12			08 05		08 32				09 32				10 32				11 32
Walsall	a				06 59	07 19			08 12		08 39		09 12		09 39		10 12		10 39		11 12		11 39
	d	23p40	06 01	06 31	07 00	07 20	07 31	08 01	08 13	08 31	08 40	09 01	09 13	09 31	09 40	10 01	10 13	10 31	10 40	11 01	11 13	11 31	11 40
Bescot Stadium	d	23p44	06 04	06 34	07 04		07 34	08 04		08 34		09 04		09 34		10 04		10 34		11 04		11 34	
Tame Bridge Parkway	d	23p47	06 07	06 37	07 07	07 26	07 37	08 07	08 19	08 37	08 46	09 07	09 19	09 37	09 46	10 07	10 19	10 37	10 46	11 07	11 19	11 37	11 46
Hamstead	d	23p51	06 11	06 41	07 12		07 41	08 11		08 41		09 11		09 41		10 11		10 41		11 11		11 41	
Perry Barr	d	23p55	06 14	06 44	07 15		07 44	08 14		08 44		09 14		09 44		10 14		10 44		11 14		11 44	
Witton	d	23p57	06 16	06 46	07 17		07 46	08 16		08 46		09 16		09 46		10 16		10 46		11 16		11 46	
Aston	d	00 01	06 18	06 48	07 20		07 48	08 18		08 48		09 19		09 49		10 19		10 49		11 19		11 49	
Duddeston	d	00 04	06 21	06 51	07 23		07 51	08 21		08 51		09 21		09 51		10 21		10 51		11 21		11 51	
Birmingham New Street 12	a	00 09	06 28	06 58	07 28	07 48	07 58	08 28	08 36	08 58	09 03	09 29	09 36	09 58	10 03	10 29	10 36	10 58	11 03	11 28	11 36	11 58	12 03
Wolverhampton 7	a		07 03	07 33			08 33	09 03		09 33		10 03		10 33		11 03		11 33		12 03		12 33	

For connections from Stafford please refer to Table 67

Table 70

Saturdays

Rugeley and Walsall - Birmingham

		LM	LM	LM	LM	LM	LM	LM	LM	LM	LM	LM	LM	LM	LM	LM	LM	LM	LM	LM	LM	LM	LM
Rugeley Trent Valley	d		11 42		12 06		12 42		13 06		13 42		14 06		14 42		15 06		15 42		16 06		16 42
Rugeley Town	d		11 46		12 10		12 46		13 10		13 46		14 10		14 46		15 10		15 46		16 10		16 46
Hednesford	d		11 54		12 18		12 54		13 18		13 54		14 18		14 54		15 18		15 54		16 18		16 54
Cannock	d		11 58		12 22		12 58		13 22		13 58		14 22		14 58		15 22		15 58		16 22		16 58
Landywood	d				12 25				13 25				14 25				15 25				16 25		
Bloxwich North	d				12 30				13 30				14 30				15 30				16 30		
Bloxwich	d				12 32				13 32				14 32				15 32				16 32		
Walsall	a		12 12		12 39		13 12		13 39		14 12		14 39		15 12		15 39		16 12		16 39		17 12
	d	12 01	12 13	12 31	12 40	13 01	13 13	13 31	13 40	14 01	14 13	14 31	14 40	15 01	15 13	15 31	15 40	16 01	16 13	16 31	16 40	17 01	17 13
Bescot Stadium	d	12 04		12 34		13 04		13 34		14 04		14 34		15 04		15 34		16 04		16 34		17 04	
Tame Bridge Parkway	d	12 07	12 19	12 37	12 46	13 07	13 19	13 37	13 46	14 07	14 19	14 37	14 46	15 07	15 19	15 37	15 46	16 07	16 19	16 37	16 46	17 07	17 19
Hamstead	d	12 11		12 41		13 11		13 41		14 11		14 41		15 11		15 41		16 11		16 41		17 11	
Perry Barr	d	12 14		12 44		13 14		13 44		14 14		14 44		15 14		15 44		16 14		16 44		17 14	
Witton	d	12 16		12 46		13 16		13 46		14 16		14 46		15 16		15 46		16 16		16 46		17 16	
Aston	d	12 19		12 49		13 19		13 49		14 19		14 49		15 19		15 49		16 19		16 49		17 19	
Duddeston	d	12 21		12 51		13 21		13 51		14 21		14 51		15 21		15 51		16 21		16 51		17 21	
Birmingham New Street 12	a	12 28	12 36	12 58	13 03	13 28	13 36	13 58	14 03	14 28	14 36	14 58	15 03	15 28	15 36	15 58	16 03	16 28	16 36	16 58	17 03	17 28	17 36
Wolverhampton 7	a	13 03		13 33		14 03		14 33		15 03		15 33		16 03		16 33		17 04		17 33		18 03	

		LM	LM	LM	LM	LM	LM	LM	LM	LM	LM	LM	LM	LM	LM	LM	LM	LM
Rugeley Trent Valley	d		17 06		17 42		18 12		18 45	19 10	19 42		20 35		21 35		22 35	
Rugeley Town	d		17 10		17 46		18 16		18 49	19 14	19 46		20 39		21 39		22 39	
Hednesford	d		17 18		17 54		18 24		18 57	19 21	19 54		20 47		21 47		22 47	
Cannock	d		17 22		17 58		18 28		19 01	19 25	19 58		20 51		21 51		22 51	
Landywood	d		17 25				18 31			19 29	20 01		20 54		21 54		22 54	
Bloxwich North	d		17 30				18 36			19 33	20 06		20 59		21 59		22 59	
Bloxwich	d		17 32				18 38			19 35	20 08		21 01		22 01		23 01	
Walsall	a		17 39		18 12		18 45		19 15	19 43	20 15		21 08		22 08		23 08	
	d	17 31	17 40	18 01	18 13	18 31	18 46	19 01	19 18	19 43	20 16	20 40	21 10	21 40	22 10	22 40	23 10	23 40
Bescot Stadium	d	17 34		18 04		18 34		19 04	19 23	19 48		20 44		21 44		22 44		23 44
Tame Bridge Parkway	d	17 37	17 46	18 07	18 19	18 37	18 52	19 07	19 26	19 51	20 22	20 47	21 16	21 47	22 16	22 47	23 16	23 47
Hamstead	d	17 41		18 11		18 41		19 11	19 30	19 55		20 51		21 51		22 51		23 51
Perry Barr	d	17 44		18 14		18 44		19 14	19 33	19 58		20 55		21 55		22 55		23 55
Witton	d	17 46		18 16		18 46		19 16	19 36	20 01		20 57		21 57		22 57		23 57
Aston	d	17 49		18 19		18 49		19 19	19 39	20 03		21 00		22 00		23 00		00 01
Duddeston	d	17 51		18 21		18 51		19 21	19 42	20 06		21 03		22 03		23 03		00 04
Birmingham New Street 12	a	17 58	18 03	18 28	18 36	18 58	19 09	19 28	19 46	20 11	20 39	21 09	21 33	22 09	22 33	23 09	23 34	00 09
Wolverhampton 7	a	18 33		19 03		19 33		20 03										

Sundays
until 11 July

		LM	LM	LM	LM	LM	LM	LM	LM	LM	LM	LM	LM	LM	LM	LM	LM	LM	LM	LM	LM	LM	LM
Rugeley Trent Valley	d			09 45		10 45		11 45		12 45		13 45		14 45		15 45		16 45		17 45		18 45	
Rugeley Town	d			09 49		10 49		11 49		12 49		13 49		14 49		15 49		16 49		17 49		18 49	
Hednesford	d			09 57		10 57		11 57		12 57		13 57		14 57		15 57		16 57		17 57		18 57	
Cannock	d			10 01		11 01		12 01		13 01		14 01		15 01		16 01		17 01		18 01		19 01	
Landywood	d			10 04		11 04		12 04		13 04		14 04		15 04		16 04		17 04		18 04		19 04	
Bloxwich North	d			10 09		11 09		12 09		13 09		14 09		15 09		16 09		17 09		18 09		19 09	
Bloxwich	d			10 11		11 11		12 11		13 11		14 11		15 11		16 11		17 11		18 11		19 11	
Walsall	a			10 18		11 18		12 18		13 18		14 18		15 18		16 18		17 18		18 18		19 18	
	d	23p40	09 57	10 20	10 57	11 20	11 57	12 20	12 57	13 20	13 57	14 20	14 57	15 20	15 57	16 20	16 57	17 20	17 57	18 20	18 57	19 20	19 57
Bescot Stadium	d	23p44	10 01		11 01		12 01		13 01		14 01		15 01		16 01		17 01		18 01		19 01		20 01
Tame Bridge Parkway	d	23p47	10 04	10 26	11 04	11 26	12 04	12 26	13 04	13 26	14 04	14 26	15 04	15 26	16 04	16 26	17 04	17 26	18 04	18 26	19 04	19 26	20 04
Hamstead	d	23p51	10 08		11 08		12 08		13 08		14 08		15 08		16 08		17 08		18 08		19 08		20 08
Perry Barr	d	23p55																					
Witton	d	23p57																					
Aston	d	00 01																					
Duddeston	d	00 04																					
Birmingham New Street 12	a	00 09	10 21	10 43	11 21	11 43	12 21	12 43	13 21	13 43	14 21	14 43	15 21	15 43	16 21	16 43	17 21	17 43	18 21	18 43	19 21	19 43	20 21
Wolverhampton 7	a																						

		LM	LM	LM	LM	LM	LM	LM
Rugeley Trent Valley	d	19 45		20 45		21 48		22 48
Rugeley Town	d	19 49		20 49		21 52		22 52
Hednesford	d	19 57		20 57		22 00		23 00
Cannock	d	20 01		21 01		22 04		23 04
Landywood	d	20 04		21 04		22 07		23 07
Bloxwich North	d	20 09		21 09		22 12		23 12
Bloxwich	d	20 11		21 11		22 14		23 14
Walsall	a	20 18		21 18		22 21		23 21
	d	20 20	20 57	21 20	21 57	22 23	22 57	23 23
Bescot Stadium	d		21 01		22 01		23 01	
Tame Bridge Parkway	d	20 26	21 04	21 26	22 04	22 29	23 04	23 29
Hamstead	d		21 08		22 08		23 08	
Perry Barr	d							
Witton	d							
Aston	d							
Duddeston	d							
Birmingham New Street 12	a	20 43	21 21	21 43	22 21	22 46	23 21	23 46
Wolverhampton 7	a							

For connections from Stafford please refer to Table 67

Table 70

Sundays
18 July to 05 September

Rugeley and Walsall - Birmingham

		LM	LM (bus)	LM (bus)	LM (bus)	LM (bus)	LM (bus)	LM (bus)	LM (bus)	LM (bus)	LM (bus)	LM (bus)	LM (bus)	LM (bus)	LM (bus)	LM (bus)	LM (bus)	LM (bus)	LM (bus)	LM (bus)	LM (bus)	LM (bus)	LM (bus)
Rugeley Trent Valley	d			08 48		09 48		10 48		11 48		12 48		13 48		14 48		15 48		16 48		17 48	
Rugeley Town	d			08 54		09 54		10 54		11 54		12 54		13 54		14 54		15 54		16 54		17 54	
Hednesford	d			09 05		10 05		11 05		12 05		13 05		14 05		15 05		16 05		17 05		18 05	
Cannock	d			09 13		10 13		11 13		12 13		13 13		14 13		15 13		16 13		17 13		18 13	
Landywood	d			09 25		10 25		11 25		12 25		13 25		14 25		15 25		16 25		17 25		18 25	
Bloxwich North	d			09 36		10 36		11 36		12 36		13 36		14 36		15 36		16 36		17 36		18 36	
Bloxwich	d			09 42		10 42		11 42		12 42		13 42		14 42		15 42		16 42		17 42		18 42	
Walsall	a			09 50		10 50		11 50		12 50		13 50		14 50		15 50		16 50		17 50		18 50	
	d	23p40	09 25	09 55	10 25	10 55	11 25	11 55	12 25	12 55	13 25	13 55	14 25	14 55	15 25	15 55	16 25	16 55	17 25	17 55	18 25	18 55	19 25
Bescot Stadium	d	23p44	09 34		10 34		11 34		12 34		13 34		14 34		15 34		16 34		17 34		18 34		19 34
Tame Bridge Parkway	d	23p47	09 43	10 11	10 43	11 11	11 43	12 11	12 43	13 11	13 43	14 11	14 43	15 11	15 43	16 11	16 43	17 11	17 43	18 11	18 43	19 11	19 43
Hamstead	d	23p51	09 53		10 53		11 53		12 53		13 53		14 53		15 53		16 53		17 53		18 53		19 53
Perry Barr	d	23p55	10 03		11 03		12 03		13 03		14 03		15 03		16 03		17 03		18 03		19 03		20 03
Witton	d	23p57	10 10		11 10		12 10		13 10		14 10		15 10		16 10		17 10		18 10		19 10		20 10
Aston	d	00 01	10 14		11 14		12 14		13 14		14 14		15 14		16 14		17 14		18 14		19 14		20 14
Duddeston	d	00 04	10 19		11 19		12 19		13 19		14 19		15 19		16 19		17 19		18 19		19 19		20 19
Birmingham New Street 12	a	00 09	10 28	10 36	11 28	11 36	12 28	12 36	13 28	13 36	14 28	14 36	15 28	15 36	16 28	16 36	17 28	17 36	18 28	18 36	19 28	19 36	20 28
Wolverhampton 7	a																						

		LM (bus)	LM (bus)	LM (bus)	LM (bus)	LM (bus)	LM (bus)	LM (bus)
Rugeley Trent Valley	d	18 48		19 48		20 48		22 00
Rugeley Town	d	18 54		19 54		20 54		22 06
Hednesford	d	19 05		20 05		21 05		22 17
Cannock	d	19 13		20 13		21 13		22 25
Landywood	d	19 25		20 25		21 25		22 37
Bloxwich North	d	19 36		20 36		21 36		22 48
Bloxwich	d	19 42		20 42		21 42		22 54
Walsall	a	19 50		20 50		21 50		23 02
	d	19 55	20 25	20 55	21 25	21 55	22 25	23 03
Bescot Stadium	d		20 34		21 34		22 34	
Tame Bridge Parkway	d	20 11	20 43	21 11	21 43	22 11	22 43	23 19
Hamstead	d		20 53		21 53		22 53	
Perry Barr	d		21 03		22 03		23 03	
Witton	d		21 10		22 10		23 10	
Aston	d		21 14		22 14		23 14	
Duddeston	d		21 19		22 19		23 19	
Birmingham New Street 12	a	20 36	21 28	21 36	22 28	22 36	23 28	23 44
Wolverhampton 7	a							

Sundays
from 12 September

		LM	LM	LM	LM	LM	LM	LM	LM	LM	LM	LM	LM	LM	LM	LM	LM	LM	LM	LM	LM	LM	LM
Rugeley Trent Valley	d			09 48		10 48		11 48		12 48		13 48		14 48		15 48		16 48		17 48		18 48	
Rugeley Town	d			09 52		10 52		11 52		12 52		13 52		14 52		15 52		16 52		17 52		18 52	
Hednesford	d			10 00		11 00		12 00		13 00		14 00		15 00		16 00		17 00		18 00		19 00	
Cannock	d			10 04		11 04		12 04		13 04		14 04		15 04		16 04		17 04		18 04		19 04	
Landywood	d			10 07		11 07		12 07		13 07		14 07		15 07		16 07		17 07		18 07		19 07	
Bloxwich North	d			10 12		11 12		12 12		13 12		14 12		15 12		16 12		17 12		18 12		19 12	
Bloxwich	d			10 14		11 14		12 14		13 14		14 14		15 14		16 14		17 14		18 14		19 14	
Walsall	a			10 21		11 21		12 21		13 21		14 21		15 21		16 21		17 21		18 21		19 21	
	d	23p40	10 00	10 23	11 00	11 23	12 00	12 23	13 00	13 23	14 00	14 23	15 00	15 23	16 00	16 23	17 00	17 23	18 00	18 23	19 00	19 23	20 00
Bescot Stadium	d	23p44	10 04		11 04		12 04		13 04		14 04		15 04		16 04		17 04		18 04		19 04		20 04
Tame Bridge Parkway	d	23p47	10 07	10 29	11 07	11 29	12 07	12 29	13 07	13 29	14 07	14 29	15 07	15 29	16 07	16 29	17 07	17 29	18 07	18 29	19 07	19 29	20 07
Hamstead	d	23p51	10 11		11 11		12 11		13 11		14 11		15 11		16 11		17 11		18 11		19 11		20 11
Perry Barr	d	23p55	10 14		11 14		12 14		13 14		14 14		15 14		16 14		17 14		18 14		19 14		20 14
Witton	d	23p57	10 17		11 17		12 17		13 17		14 17		15 17		16 17		17 17		18 17		19 17		20 17
Aston	d	00 01	10 20		11 20		12 20		13 20		14 20		15 20		16 20		17 20		18 20		19 20		20 20
Duddeston	d	00 04	10 23		11 23		12 23		13 23		14 23		15 23		16 23		17 23		18 23		19 23		20 23
Birmingham New Street 12	a	00 09	10 27	10 46	11 27	11 46	12 27	12 46	13 27	13 46	14 27	14 46	15 30	15 46	16 30	16 46	17 30	17 46	18 28	18 46	19 27	19 47	20 27
Wolverhampton 7	a																						

		LM	LM	LM	LM	LM	LM	LM
Rugeley Trent Valley	d	19 48		20 48		21 48		22 48
Rugeley Town	d	19 52		20 52		21 52		22 52
Hednesford	d	20 00		21 00		22 00		23 00
Cannock	d	20 04		21 04		22 04		23 04
Landywood	d	20 07		21 07		22 07		23 07
Bloxwich North	d	20 12		21 12		22 12		23 12
Bloxwich	d	20 14		21 14		22 14		23 14
Walsall	a	20 21		21 21		22 21		23 21
	d	20 23	21 00	21 23	22 00	22 23	23 00	23 23
Bescot Stadium	d		21 04		22 04		23 04	
Tame Bridge Parkway	d	20 29	21 07	21 29	22 07	22 29	23 07	23 29
Hamstead	d		21 11		22 11		23 11	
Perry Barr	d		21 14		22 14		23 14	
Witton	d		21 17		22 17		23 17	
Aston	d		21 20		22 20		23 20	
Duddeston	d		21 23		22 23		23 23	
Birmingham New Street 12	a	20 46	21 27	21 46	22 27	22 48	23 27	23 46
Wolverhampton 7	a							

Network Diagram for Tables 71, 72

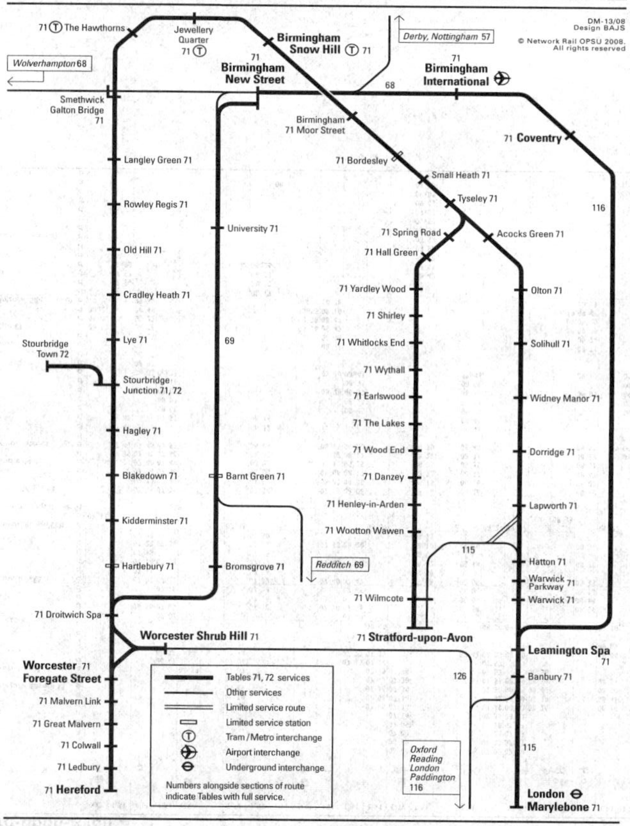

Table 71

Mondays to Fridays

until 01 October

Hereford, Worcester and Stourbridge - Birmingham - Leamington Spa, Marylebone and Stratford-upon-Avon

		CH MX	GW	CH	CH	LM	LM	XC	CH	LM		LM	LM	CH	CH	XC	CH	CH	WS	XC	LM	CH	LM	LM	GW
			◇1		◇			◇1								◇1		◇	◇1	◇1		◇			◇1 Ø
Hereford 7	d																								05 34
Ledbury	a																								05 50
	d																								05 50
Colwall	d																								05 58
Great Malvern	a																								06 03
	d		05 17			05 50																			06 03
Malvern Link	d		05 20			05 53																			06 07
Worcester Foregate Street 7	a		05 30			06 01																			06 18
	d		05 31			06 02																			06 18
Worcester Shrub Hill 7	a		05 35																						06 21
	d									06 28														06 15	
Droitwich Spa	d					06 12				06 35														06 23	
Bromsgrove	d					06 21				06 44															
Barnt Green	d																								
University	d					06 39				06 59															
Hartlebury	d																							06 30	
Kidderminster	d																	06 10				06 30		06 36	
Blakedown	d																							06 41	
Hagley	d																							06 44	
Stourbridge Junction 2	d																	06 18			06 24	06 39		06 49	
Lye	d																				06 28			06 53	
Cradley Heath	d																	06 24			06 31	06 44		06 56	
Old Hill	d																				06 35			07 00	
Rowley Regis	d																	06 30			06 39	06 50		07 04	
Langley Green	d																				06 42			07 07	
Birmingham New Street 12	a					06 45				07 07															
	d							06 03								06 33				07 03					
Birmingham International ✈	d							06 14												07 14					
Coventry	d							06 25												07 25					
Smethwick Galton Bridge 7	d																	06 35			06 46	06 56		07 11	
The Hawthorns	d																	06 38			06 48	06 58		07 13	
Jewellery Quarter	d																				06 52			07 17	
Birmingham Snow Hill	a																	06 46			06 55	07 04		07 21	
	d	23p30			05 43		05 55		06 15			06 36	06 43					06 50			07 02	07 14	07 19	07 23	
Birmingham Moor Street	d	23p33			05 46		05 58		06 18			06 39	06 46					06 53			07 05	07 17	07 22	07 26	
Bordesley	d																								
Small Heath	d						06 02					06 43	06 50								07 09			07 30	
Tyseley	d	23p38					06 04					06 45	06 52								07 11			07 32	
Acocks Green	d	23p40					06 07					06 48									07 14		07 27		
Olton	d	23p43					06 10					06 51									07 17		07 30		
Solihull	d	23p47			05 56		06 13		06 28			06 55						07 03			07 20	07 28	07 34		
Widney Manor	d	23p50					06 17					06 58									07 23		07 37		
Dorridge	d	23p54			06 01		06 21		06 33			07a03						07 08			07 27	07 34	07a42		
Lapworth	d	23p58					06 25														07 31				
Hatton	d	00 04															07 03				07 37				
Warwick Parkway	d	00 08		05 40	06 12				06 44								07 09	07 19				07 47			
Warwick	d	00 11			06 15												07 13				07 43	07 50			
Leamington Spa 8	a	00 14		05 45	06 20			06 36	06 49							06 58	07 17	07 24		07 37	07 49	07 54			
	d	00 15		05 45	06 20			06 38	06 49					06 55	06 55	07 00	07 18	07 24	07 29	07 38		07 54			
Banbury	d	00a38		06 03	06 38			06a57	07 07						07 18	07a22	07 36	07 42	07 48	07a55		08 12			
London Marylebone 10 ⊖	a			07 18	07 53				08 17						08 40		08 51	08 54	08 57			09 27			
Spring Road	d												06 55											07 35	
Hall Green	d												06 58											07 38	
Yardley Wood	d												07 01											07 41	
Shirley	d												07 05											07 44	
Whitlocks End	d												07 07											07 47	
Wythall	d												07 10											07 50	
Earlswood (West Midlands)	d												07 12											07 52	
The Lakes	d												07x15											07x55	
Wood End	d												07x17											07x57	
Danzey	d												07x20											08x01	
Henley-in-Arden	d												07 25											08 07	
Wootton Wawen	d												07x27											08x10	
Wilmcote	d						06 42						07 33	07 21										08 15	
Stratford-upon-Avon	a						06 48						07 40	07 30										08 21	

Table 71

Mondays to Fridays
until 01 October

Hereford, Worcester and Stourbridge - Birmingham - Leamington Spa, Marylebone and Stratford-upon-Avon

		XC	LM	CH	LM	GW	LM	LM	CH	XC	CH	LM	LM	GW	LM	LM	LM	LM	GW	XC	CH	LM	LM
		◇1 🛒		◇ 🛒		1			◇	2 1 🛒	◇ 🛒			◇1 Ø						◇1 🛒	◇ 🛒		
Hereford 7	d													06 43			07 08	07 34					
Ledbury	a													06 59			07 23	07 51					
	d													07 00			07 24	07 51					
Colwall	d													07 09			07 30	07 57					
Great Malvern	a													07 14			07 35	08 02					
	d						06 48						07 05	07 14			07 39	08 03	08 26			08 38	
Malvern Link	d						06 50						07 08	07 18			07 42	08 06	08 29			08 41	
Worcester Foregate Street 7	a						06 59						07 16	07 30			07 50	08 15	08 42			08 50	
	d					06 51	06 59						07 17	07 30		07 33	07 51	08 19	08 54			08 51	
Worcester Shrub Hill 7	a					06 53	07 02						07 19	07 34			07 53		08 56				
	d				06 47		07 06					07 15	07 24				07 57						
Droitwich Spa	d				06 55		07 14					07 23	07 32			07 42	08 05	08 30				09 00	
Bromsgrove	d						07 25											08 41				09 09	
Barnt Green	d																						
University	d												08 00				08 30	09 00				09 30	
Hartlebury	d				07 02							07 30											
Kidderminster	d			06 56	07 09			07 18			07 30	07 36				07 54					08 09		
Blakedown	d				07 14			07 24				07 41				08 00					08 14		
Hagley	d				07 18			07 28				07 45				08 04					08 18		
Stourbridge Junction 2	d			07 07	07 22			07 32			07 40	07 49			07 55	08 09					08 23		
Lye	d			07 11				07 36							07 59								
Cradley Heath	d			07 14	07 28			07 39			07 45	07 55			08 02	08 14					08 28		
Old Hill	d			07 18				07 43							08 06								
Rowley Regis	d			07 22	07 34			07 47			07 53	08 00			08 10	08 20					08 34		
Langley Green	d			07 25				07 50							08 13								
Birmingham New Street 12	a						07 45						08 09				08 37	09 07				09 42	
	d	07 33								08 03										08 33			
Birmingham International ✈	d									08 14													
Coventry	d									08 25													
Smethwick Galton Bridge 7	d			07 29	07 39			07 54			07 59	08 06			08 16	08 26					08 40		
The Hawthorns 🚋	d			07 32	07 42			07 56			08 02	08 08			08 19	08 28					08 42		
Jewellery Quarter 🚋	d			07 36	07 46			08 00			08 06	08 12			08 23	08 32					08 47		
Birmingham Snow Hill 🚋	a			07 40	07 49			08 03			08 11	08 15			08 26	08 35					08 51		
	d		07 39	07 45	07 50			08 05			08 12	08 17			08 27	08 37					08 52		08 57
Birmingham Moor Street	d		07 42	07 48	07 53			08 08			08 15	08 20			08 30	08 40					08 55		09 00
Bordesley	d																						
Small Heath	d		07 46					08 12								08 44							
Tyseley	d		07 48		07 57			08 14								08 46							
Acocks Green	d				08 00							08 25				08 49							09 05
Olton	d				08 03							08 28				08 52							09 08
Solihull	d			07 58	08 07						08 25	08 32				08 56					09 05		09 12
Widney Manor	d				08 10							08 35				08 59							09 15
Dorridge	d			08 03	08a16						08 30	08a41				09a04					09 10		09a22
Lapworth	d			08 07																			
Hatton	d			08 13																			
Warwick Parkway	d			08 19							08 41										09 21		
Warwick	d			08 23							08 44										09 24		
Leamington Spa 8	a	08 03		08 26						08 36	08 49									08 59	09 29		
	d	08 04		08 27					08 30	08 38	08 49									09 00	09 29		
Banbury	d	08a21		08 45						08a55	09 10									09a19	09 47		
London Marylebone 10 ⊖	a			09 59							10 28										10 59		
Spring Road	d		07 51					08 17							08 36								
Hall Green	d		07 54					08 20							08 39								
Yardley Wood	d		07 57					08 23							08 42								
Shirley	d		08a00					08a26							08 45								
Whitlocks End	d														08 48								
Wythall	d														08 50								
Earlswood (West Midlands)	d														08 53								
The Lakes	d														08x55								
Wood End	d														08x57								
Danzey	d														09x00								
Henley-in-Arden	d														09 05								
Wootton Wawen	d														09x08								
Wilmcote	d								08 56						09 13								
Stratford-upon-Avon	a								09 05						09 21								

Table 71

Mondays to Fridays
until 01 October

Hereford, Worcester and Stourbridge - Birmingham - Leamington Spa, Marylebone and Stratford-upon-Avon

		XC	WS	CH	LM	LM	LM	XC	CH	LM	LM	GW	LM	XC	CH	CH	LM	LM	LM	LM	GW	XC
		◇1 🛒	◇1 🍴	◇				◇1 🛒	◇			◇1 🛒		◇1 🛒	◇ 🛒	◇					◇1 🛒	◇1 🛒
Hereford 7	d												08 49									
Ledbury	a												09 05									
	d												09 08									
Colwall	d												09 14									
Great Malvern	a												09 19									
	d											08 58	09 19								09 54	
Malvern Link	d											09 00	09 22								09 56	
Worcester Foregate Street 7	a											09 09	09 31								10 05	
	d										09 06	09 09	09 31								10 05	
Worcester Shrub Hill 7	a											09 12	09 34								10 08	
	d												09 37							09 47		
Droitwich Spa	d										09 15		09 45							09 55		
Bromsgrove	d												09 54									
Barnt Green	d																					
University	d												10 09									
Hartlebury	d																					
Kidderminster	d						08 57				09 26						09 36		09 56	10 06		
Blakedown	d						09 02				09 31						09 41			10 11		
Hagley	d						09 05				09 35						09 45			10 15		
Stourbridge Junction 2	d				08 45	08 54	09 09			09 25	09 39						09 49	09 55	10 09	10 19		
Lye	d					08 58				09 29								09 59				
Cradley Heath	d				08 51	09 01	09 15			09 32	09 44						09 54	10 02	10 14	10 24		
Old Hill	d					09 05				09 36								10 06				
Rowley Regis	d				08 57	09 09	09 21			09 39	09 50						10 00	10 10	10 20	10 30		
Langley Green	d					09 12				09 42								10 13				
Birmingham New Street 12	a												10 24									
	d	09 03						09 33						10 03								10 33
Birmingham International ✈	d	09 14												10 14								
Coventry	d	09 25												10 25								
Smethwick Galton Bridge 7	d				09 02	09 15	09 26			09 46	09 56						10 06	10 16	10 26	10 36		
The Hawthorns 🚋	d				09 05	09 17	09 29			09 48	09 58						10 08	10 18	10 28	10 38		
Jewellery Quarter 🚋	d				09 09	09 21	09 33			09 52	10 02						10 12	10 22	10 32	10 42		
Birmingham Snow Hill 🚋	a				09 14	09 25	09 36			09 55	10 05						10 15	10 25	10 35	10 45		
	d			09 12	09 17	09 27	09 37		09 52	09 57	10 07					10 12	10 17	10 27	10 37	10 47		
Birmingham Moor Street	d			09 15	09 20	09 30	09 40		09 55	10 00	10 10					10 15	10 20	10 30	10 40	10 50		
Bordesley	d																					
Small Heath	d						09 44				10 14								10 44			
Tyseley	d						09 46				10 16								10 46			
Acocks Green	d				09 25		09 49			10 05							10 25		10 49			
Olton	d				09 28		09 52			10 08							10 28		10 52			
Solihull	d			09 25	09 32		09 56		10 05	10 12						10 25	10 32		10 56			
Widney Manor	d				09 35		09 59			10 15							10 35		10 59			
Dorridge	d			09 30	09a41		10a04		10 10	10a22						10 30	10a41		11a04			
Lapworth	d			09 34												10 34						
Hatton	d			09 40												10 40						
Warwick Parkway	d			09 45					10 21							10 45						
Warwick	d			09 49					10 24							10 49						
Leamington Spa 8	a	09 36		09 53				09 58	10 29					10 36		10 53						10 58
	d	09 38	09 46	09 54				10 00	10 29					10 38	10 49	10 54						11 00
Banbury	d	09a55	10 04	10 12				10a19	10 47					10a55		11 12						11a19
London Marylebone 10 ⊖	a		11 15	11 32					12 02							12 31						
Spring Road	d					09 36					10 19							10 36		10 56		
Hall Green	d					09 39					10 22							10 39		10 59		
Yardley Wood	d					09 42					10 25							10 42		11 02		
Shirley	d					09 45					10a28							10 45		11a05		
Whitlocks End	d					09 48												10 48				
Wythall	d					09 50												10 50				
Earlswood (West Midlands)	d					09 53												10 53				
The Lakes	d					09x55												10x55				
Wood End	d					09x57												10x57				
Danzey	d					10x00												11x00				
Henley-in-Arden	d					10 05												11 05				
Wootton Wawen	d					10x08												11x08				
Wilmcote	d					10 13												11 13				
Stratford-upon-Avon	a					10 21										11 16		11 22				

Table 71

Mondays to Fridays

until 01 October

Hereford, Worcester and Stourbridge - Birmingham - Leamington Spa, Marylebone and Stratford-upon-Avon

		CH	LM	LM	XC	CH	LM	LM	LM	LM	LM	GW	XC	CH	CH	LM	LM	XC	GW	CH	CH	LM	LM
		◇			◇1 ⊥	◇						■	◇1 ⊥					◇1 ⊥	◇1 ⊥	◇ ⊥	◇		
Hereford 7	d							09 40															10 40
Ledbury	a							09 57															10 56
	d							09 58															10 59
Colwall	d							10 04															11 05
Great Malvern	a							10 09															11 10
	d							10 10				10 51											11 10
Malvern Link	d							10 13				10 53											11 13
Worcester Foregate Street 7	a							10 22				11 02											11 22
	d						10 16	10 23				11 02							12 06			11 16	11 23
Worcester Shrub Hill 7	a											11 06							12 08				
	d										10 47												
Droitwich Spa	d						10 25	10 33			10 55											11 25	11 33
Bromsgrove	d							10 42															11 42
Barnt Green	d																						
University	d							10 59															11 59
Hartlebury	d																						
Kidderminster	d			10 26			10 36			10 56	11 06						11 26					11 36	
Blakedown	d						10 41				11 11											11 41	
Hagley	d						10 44				11 14											11 44	
Stourbridge Junction 2	d		10 25	10 39			10 49		10 55	11 09	11 19					11 25	11 39					11 49	
Lye	d		10 29						10 59							11 29							
Cradley Heath	d		10 32	10 44			10 54		11 02	11 14	11 24					11 32	11 44					11 54	
Old Hill	d		10 36						11 06							11 36							
Rowley Regis	d		10 40	10 50			11 00		11 10	11 20	11 30					11 40	11 50					12 00	
Langley Green	d		10 43						11 13							11 43							
Birmingham New Street 12	a							11 13															12 13
	d				11 03								11 33					12 03					
Birmingham International ✈	d				11 14													12 14					
Coventry	d				11 25													12 25					
Smethwick Galton Bridge 7	d		10 46	10 56			11 06		11 16	11 26	11 36					11 46	11 56					12 06	
The Hawthorns	d		10 48	10 58			11 08		11 18	11 28	11 38					11 48	11 58					12 08	
Jewellery Quarter	d		10 52	11 02			11 12		11 22	11 32	11 42					11 52	12 02					12 12	
Birmingham Snow Hill	a		10 55	11 05			11 15		11 25	11 35	11 45					11 55	12 05					12 15	
	d	10 52	10 57	11 07		11 12	11 17		11 27	11 37	11 47				11 52	11 57	12 07				12 12	12 17	
Birmingham Moor Street	d	10 55	11 00	11 10		11 15	11 20		11 30	11 40	11 50				11 55	12 00	12 10				12 15	12 20	
Bordesley	d																						
Small Heath	d			11 14						11 44							12 14						
Tyseley	d			11 16						11 46							12 16						
Acocks Green	d		11 05				11 25			11 49						12 05						12 25	
Olton	d		11 08				11 28			11 52						12 08						12 28	
Solihull	d	11 05	11 12			11 25	11 32			11 56					12 05	12 12					12 25	12 32	
Widney Manor	d		11 15				11 35			11 59						12 15						12 35	
Dorridge	d	11 10	11a21			11 30	11a41			12a04					12 10	12a22					12 30	12a41	
Lapworth	d																				12 34		
Hatton	d													11 57							12 40		
Warwick Parkway	d	11 21				11 41									12 21						12 45		
Warwick	d	11 24				11 45								12 04	12 24						12 49		
Leamington Spa 8	a	11 29			11 36	11 51							11 59	12 09	12 29			12 36			12 53		
	d	11 29			11 38	11 52							12 00	12 09	12 29			12 38		12 38	12 54		
Banbury	d	11 47			11a55	12 09							12a19	12 28	12 47			12a55			13 12		
London Marylebone 10 ⊖	a	12 59				13 29								13 55	13 59						14 31		
Spring Road	d			11 19					11 36		11 56						12 19						
Hall Green	d			11 22					11 39		11 59						12 22						
Yardley Wood	d			11 25					11 42		12 02						12 25						
Shirley	d			11a28					11 45		12a05						12a28						
Whitlocks End	d								11 48														
Wythall	d								11 50														
Earlswood (West Midlands)	d								11 53														
The Lakes	d								11x55														
Wood End	d								11x57														
Danzey	d								12x00														
Henley-in-Arden	d								12 05														
Wootton Wawen	d								12x08														
Wilmcote	d								12 13														
Stratford-upon-Avon	a								12 21											13 11			

Table 71

Mondays to Fridays

until 01 October

Hereford, Worcester and Stourbridge - Birmingham - Leamington Spa, Marylebone and Stratford-upon-Avon

		LM	LM	LM	XC	CH	LM	LM	XC	WS	CH	LM	LM	LM	LM	LM	GW	LM	XC	CH	LM	LM	XC
					◇1 ⊥	◇			◇1 ⊥	◇1 ⊏	◇								◇1 ⊥	◇			◇1 ⊥
Hereford 7	d												11 40					12 39					
Ledbury	a												11 57					12 55					
	d												11 57					13 00					
Colwall	d												12 04					13 06					
Great Malvern	a												12 09					13 11					
	d			11 34									12 11				12 51	13 11					
Malvern Link	d			11 36									12 14				12 53	13 14					
Worcester Foregate Street 7	a			11 45									12 23				13 02	13 23					
	d			11 46								12 16	12 23			12 46	13 02	13 23					
Worcester Shrub Hill 7	a																13 06						
	d																						
Droitwich Spa	d			11 55								12 25	12 33			12 55		13 33					
Bromsgrove	d												12 42					13 42					
Barnt Green	d																						
University	d												12 59					13 59					
Hartlebury	d																						
Kidderminster	d		11 56	12 06				12 26				12 36			12 56	13 06							
Blakedown	d			12 11								12 41				13 11							
Hagley	d			12 14								12 44				13 14							
Stourbridge Junction 2	d	11 55	12 09	12 19			12 25	12 39				12 49		12 55	13 09	13 19					13 25	13 39	
Lye	d	11 59					12 29							12 59							13 29		
Cradley Heath	d	12 02	12 14	12 24			12 32	12 44				12 54		13 02	13 14	13 24					13 32	13 44	
Old Hill	d	12 06					12 36							13 06							13 36		
Rowley Regis	d	12 10	12 20	12 30			12 40	12 50				13 00		13 10	13 20	13 30					13 40	13 50	
Langley Green	d	12 13					12 43							13 13							13 43		
Birmingham New Street 12	a												13 13					14 13					
	d				12 33				13 03										13 33				14 03
Birmingham International ✈	d								13 14														14 14
Coventry	d								13 25														14 25
Smethwick Galton Bridge 7	d	12 16	12 26	12 36			12 46	12 56				13 06		13 16	13 26	13 36					13 46	13 56	
The Hawthorns	d	12 18	12 28	12 38			12 48	12 58				13 08		13 18	13 28	13 38					13 48	13 58	
Jewellery Quarter	d	12 22	12 32	12 42			12 52	13 02				13 12		13 22	13 32	13 42					13 52	14 02	
Birmingham Snow Hill	a	12 25	12 35	12 45			12 55	13 05				13 15		13 25	13 35	13 45					13 55	14 05	
	d	12 27	12 37	12 47		12 52	12 57	13 07			13 12	13 17		13 27	13 37	13 47				13 52	13 57	14 07	
Birmingham Moor Street	d	12 30	12 40	12 50		12 55	13 00	13 10			13 15	13 20		13 30	13 40	13 50				13 55	14 00	14 10	
Bordesley	d																						
Small Heath	d		12 44					13 14							13 44							14 14	
Tyseley	d		12 46					13 16							13 46							14 16	
Acocks Green	d		12 49				13 05					13 25			13 49						14 05		
Olton	d		12 52				13 08					13 28			13 52						14 08		
Solihull	d		12 56			13 05	13 12				13 25	13 32			13 56					14 05	14 12		
Widney Manor	d		12 59				13 15					13 35			13 59						14 15		
Dorridge	d		13a04			13 10	13a21				13 30	13a41			14a04					14 10	14a22		
Lapworth	d																						
Hatton	d																						
Warwick Parkway	d					13 21					13 41									14 21			
Warwick	d					13 24					13 45									14 24			
Leamington Spa 8	a				12 58	13 29			13 36		13 51								13 59	14 29			14 36
	d				13 00	13 29			13 38	13 46	13 52								14 00	14 29			14 38
Banbury	d				13a19	13 47			13a55	14 04	14 09								14a19	14 47			14a55
London Marylebone 10 ⊖	a					14 59				15 15	15 29									16 02			
Spring Road	d	12 36		12 56				13 19						13 36		13 56						14 19	
Hall Green	d	12 39		12 59				13 22						13 39		13 59						14 22	
Yardley Wood	d	12 42		13 02				13 25						13 42		14 02						14 25	
Shirley	d	12 45		13a05				13a28						13 45		14a05						14a28	
Whitlocks End	d	12 48												13 48									
Wythall	d	12 50												13 50									
Earlswood (West Midlands)	d	12 53												13 53									
The Lakes	d	12x55												13x55									
Wood End	d	12x57												13x57									
Danzey	d	13x00												14x00									
Henley-in-Arden	d	13 05												14 05									
Wootton Wawen	d	13x08												14x08									
Wilmcote	d	13 13												14 13									
Stratford-upon-Avon	a	13 21												14 21									

Table 71

Mondays to Fridays
until 01 October

Hereford, Worcester and Stourbridge - Birmingham - Leamington Spa, Marylebone and Stratford-upon-Avon

Station		CH ◇	LM	LM	LM	LM	GW ◇1	XC ◇1	CH ◇	LM	LM	CH ◇	XC ◇1	CH ◇	LM	LM	LM	LM	LM	GW ◇1	GW	XC ◇1	CH ◇
Hereford 7	d						13 11									13 41							
Ledbury	a						13 27									13 58							
	d						13 30									13 59							
Colwall	d						13 37									14 05							
Great Malvern	a						13 43									14 10							
	d						13 47								14 00	14 11				14 34	14 51		
Malvern Link	d						13 51								14 02	14 14				14 37	14 53		
Worcester Foregate Street 7	a						14 01								14 10	14 23				14 51	15 02		
	d						14 02								14 16	14 23				14 52	15 02		
Worcester Shrub Hill 7	a						14 06													14 56	15 06		
	d		13 17			13 47													14 47				
Droitwich Spa	d		13 25			13 55									14 25	14 33			14 55				
Bromsgrove	d															14 42							
Barnt Green	d																						
University	d															14 59							
Hartlebury	d																						
Kidderminster	d		13 36		13 56	14 06					14 26				14 36			14 56	15 06				
Blakedown	d		13 41			14 11									14 41				15 11				
Hagley	d		13 44			14 14									14 44				15 14				
Stourbridge Junction 2	d		13 49	13 55	14 09	14 19				14 25	14 39				14 49		14 55	15 09	15 19				
Lye	d			13 59						14 29							14 59						
Cradley Heath	d		13 54	14 02	14 14	14 24				14 32	14 44				14 54		15 02	15 14	15 24				
Old Hill	d			14 06						14 36							15 06						
Rowley Regis	d		14 00	14 10	14 20	14 30				14 40	14 50				15 00		15 10	15 20	15 30				
Langley Green	d			14 13						14 43							15 13						
Birmingham New Street 12	a															15 13							
	d							14 33					15 03									15 33	
Birmingham International ✈	d												15 14										
Coventry	d												15 25										
Smethwick Galton Bridge 7	d		14 06	14 16	14 26	14 36				14 46	14 56				15 06		15 16	15 26	15 36				
The Hawthorns	d		14 08	14 18	14 28	14 38				14 48	14 58				15 08		15 18	15 28	15 38				
Jewellery Quarter	d		14 12	14 22	14 32	14 42				14 52	15 02				15 12		15 22	15 32	15 42				
Birmingham Snow Hill	a		14 15	14 25	14 35	14 45				14 55	15 05				15 15		15 25	15 35	15 45				
	d	14 12	14 17	14 27	14 37	14 47			14 52	14 57	15 07			15 12	15 17		15 26	15 37	15 47				15 52
Birmingham Moor Street	d	14 15	14 20	14 30	14 40	14 50			14 55	15 00	15 10			15 15	15 20		15 29	15 40	15 50				15 55
Bordesley	d																						
Small Heath	d				14 44						15 14							15 44					
Tyseley	d				14 46						15 16							15 46					
Acocks Green	d		14 25		14 49					15 05					15 25			15 49					
Olton	d		14 28		14 52					15 08					15 28			15 52					
Solihull	d	14 25	14 32		14 56				15 05	15 12				15 25	15 32			15 56					16 05
Widney Manor	d		14 35		14 59					15 15					15 35			15 59					
Dorridge	d	14 30	14a41		15a04				15 10	15a21				15 30	15a41			16a04					16 10
Lapworth	d	14 34																					
Hatton	d	14 40																					
Warwick Parkway	d	14 45							15 21					15 41									16 21
Warwick	d	14 49							15 24					15 44									16 24
Leamington Spa 8	a	14 53						14 58	15 29			15 33	15 36	15 49								15 58	16 29
	d	14 54						15 00	15 29			15 33	15 38	15 49								16 00	16 29
Banbury	d	15 12						15a19	15 47				15a55	16 07								16a19	16 47
London Marylebone 15 ⊖	a	16 32							17 02					17 31									18 04
Spring Road	d			14 36		14 56					15 19						15 35		15 56				
Hall Green	d			14 39		14 59					15 22						15 38		15 59				
Yardley Wood	d			14 42		15 02					15 25						15 41		16 02				
Shirley	d			14 45		15a05					15a28						15 44		16a05				
Whitlocks End	d			14 48													15 47						
Wythall	d			14 50													15 49						
Earlswood (West Midlands)	d			14 53													15 52						
The Lakes	d			14x55													15x54						
Wood End	d			14x57													15x56						
Danzey	d			15x00													15x59						
Henley-in-Arden	d			15 05													16 04						
Wootton Wawen	d			15x08													16x07						
Wilmcote	d			15 13								16 00					16 12						
Stratford-upon-Avon	a			15 21								16 12					16 21						

Table 71

Mondays to Fridays
until 01 October

Hereford, Worcester and Stourbridge - Birmingham - Leamington Spa, Marylebone and Stratford-upon-Avon

Station		LM	LM	XC ◇1	CH	LM	LM	LM	LM	LM	GW ◇1	XC ◇1	CH	LM	LM	XC ◇1	WS ◇1	CH ◇	LM	LM	LM	LM	XC ◇1
Hereford 7	d						14 40				15 11									15 40			
Ledbury	a						14 56				15 27									15 57			
	d						14 59				15 27									16 00			
Colwall	d						15 05				15 35									16 06			
Great Malvern	a						15 10				15 40									16 11			
	d						15 10			15 29	15 40									16 11			
Malvern Link	d						15 13			15 31	15 44									16 14			
Worcester Foregate Street 7	a						15 22			15 39	15 57									16 23			
	d					15 16	15 23			15 40	16 02								16 07	16 23			
Worcester Shrub Hill 7	a									15 42	16 06												
	d									15 47											16 17		
Droitwich Spa	d					15 25	15 33			15 55									16 16	16 33	16 25		
Bromsgrove	d						15 42													16 42			
Barnt Green	d																			16 49			
University	d						15 59													16 59			
Hartlebury	d																		16 23				
Kidderminster	d		15 26			15 36			15 56	16 06					16 23				16 30		16 37		
Blakedown	d		15 31			15 41				16 11					16 28				16 35		16 43		
Hagley	d		15 34			15 44				16 14					16 31				16 39		16 47		
Stourbridge Junction 2	d	15 25	15 39			15 49		15 55	16 09	16 19				16 25	16 35				16 44		16 51	16 55	
Lye	d	15 29						15 59						16 29								16 59	
Cradley Heath	d	15 32	15 44			15 54		16 02	16 14	16 24				16 32	16 41				16 50		16 57	17 02	
Old Hill	d	15 36						16 06						16 36								17 06	
Rowley Regis	d	15 40	15 50			16 00		16 10	16 20	16 30				16 40	16 47				16 55		17 03	17 10	
Langley Green	d	15 43						16 13						16 43								17 13	
Birmingham New Street 12	a						16 13													17 13			
	d			16 03								16 33				17 03							17 33
Birmingham International ✈	d			16 14												17 14							
Coventry	d			16 25												17 25							
Smethwick Galton Bridge 7	d	15 46	15 56			16 06		16 16	16 26	16 36				16 46	16 52				17 01		17 08	17 16	
The Hawthorns	d	15 48	15 58			16 08		16 18	16 28	16 38				16 48	16 55				17 03		17 11	17 19	
Jewellery Quarter	d	15 52	16 02			16 12		16 22	16 32	16 42				16 52	16 59				17 07		17 15	17 22	
Birmingham Snow Hill	a	15 55	16 05			16 15		16 25	16 35	16 45				16 55	17 02				17 10		17 18	17 25	
	d	15 57	16 07		16 12	16 17		16 27	16 37	16 47			16 52	16 57	17 03			17 10	17 14		17 22	17 27	
Birmingham Moor Street	d	16 00	16 10		16 15	16 20		16 30	16 40	16 50			16 55	17 00	17 06			17 13	17 17		17 25	17 30	
Bordesley	d																						
Small Heath	d		16 14						16 44	16 54									17 21				
Tyseley	d		16 16					16 34	16 46	16 56				17 04					17 23			17 34	
Acocks Green	d	16 05				16 25			16 49					17 07							17 30		
Olton	d	16 08				16 28			16 52					17 10							17 33		
Solihull	d	16 12			16 25	16 32			16 56				17 05	17 14				17 23			17 37		
Widney Manor	d	16 15				16 35			16 59					17 17				17 26			17 40		
Dorridge	d	16a22			16 30	16a41			17a04				17 10	17a22				17 30			17a46		
Lapworth	d				16 34													17 34					
Hatton	d				16 40													17 40					
Warwick Parkway	d				16 45								17 20					17 45					
Warwick	d				16 49								17 23					17 49					
Leamington Spa 8	a			16 36	16 53							16 58	17 28			17 37	17 45	17 53					17 59
	d			16 38	16 54							17 00	17 28			17 38	17 46	17 54					18 00
Banbury	d			16a55	17 12							17a19	17 46			17a55	18 04	18 12					18a19
London Marylebone 15 ⊖	a				18 33								19 08				19 15	19 35					
Spring Road	d		16 19					16 37		16 59					17 12				17 26			17 37	
Hall Green	d		16 22					16 40		17 02					17 15				17 29			17 40	
Yardley Wood	d		16 25					16 43		17 05					17 18				17 32			17 43	
Shirley	d		16a28					16 46		17a08					17 21				17a35			17 46	
Whitlocks End	d							16 49							17 24							17 49	
Wythall	d							16 51							17 26							17 51	
Earlswood (West Midlands)	d							16 54														17 54	
The Lakes	d							16x56														17x56	
Wood End	d							16x58														17x58	
Danzey	d							17x01														18x01	
Henley-in-Arden	d							17 06							17 36							18 06	
Wootton Wawen	d							17x09														18x09	
Wilmcote	d							17 14														18 14	
Stratford-upon-Avon	a							17 22							17 50							18 22	

Table 71

Mondays to Fridays
until 01 October

Hereford, Worcester and Stourbridge - Birmingham - Leamington Spa, Marylebone and Stratford-upon-Avon

		CH	LM	LM	LM	GW	CH	CH	XC ◇1 ⌶	LM	LM	CH ◇	LM	GW ◇1 ⌶	LM	LM	LM	XC ◇1 ⌶	LM	LM	LM	XC ◇1 ⌶
Hereford 7	d														16 40						17 40	
Ledbury	a														16 56						17 56	
	d														16 59						18 01	
Colwall	d														17 05						18 08	
Great Malvern	a														17 10						18 12	
	d													17 00	17 10	17 41					18 13	
Malvern Link	d													17 02	17 13	17 44					18 16	
Worcester Foregate Street 7	a													17 17	17 23	17 52					18 24	
	d			16 34	16 47	17 02							17 16	17 20	17 24	17 53				17 56	18 25	
Worcester Shrub Hill 7	a			16 36		17 04								17 23		17 55						
	d			16 40																		
Droitwich Spa	d			16 48	16 56								17 25		17 33					18 05	18 34	
Bromsgrove	d														17 43						18 42	
Barnt Green	d																				18 49	
University	d														17 59						18 59	
Hartlebury	d												17 32									
Kidderminster	d		16 53	16 59	17 06						17 27		17 38						18 00	18 17		
Blakedown	d			17 04	17 11						17 32		17 43						18 05			
Hagley	d			17 08	17 15						17 35		17 46						18 09			
Stourbridge Junction 2	d		17 06	17 13	17 19					17 25	17 39		17 50				17 55		18 13	18 26		
Lye	d									17 29							17 59			18 29		
Cradley Heath	d		17 12	17 19	17 24					17 32	17 45		17 56				18 02		18 19	18 32		
Old Hill	d									17 36							18 06			18 36		
Rowley Regis	d		17 17	17 24	17 30					17 40	17 51		18 02				18 10		18 25	18 40		
Langley Green	d									17 43							18 13			18 43		
Birmingham New Street 12	a														18 13						19 12	
	d								18 03									18 33				19 03
Birmingham International ✈	d								18 14													19 14
Coventry	d								18 25													19 25
Smethwick Galton Bridge 7	d		17 23	17 30	17 36					17 46	17 56		18 08				18 16		18 30	18 46		
The Hawthorns	d		17 25	17 32	17 38					17 48	17 58		18 10				18 19		18 33	18 49		
Jewellery Quarter	d		17 29	17 36	17 42					17 52	18 02		18 14				18 23		18 37	18 52		
Birmingham Snow Hill	a		17 32	17 39	17 45					17 55	18 05		18 17				18 26		18 41	18 55		
	d		17 35	17 42	17 47			17 52		17 57	18 07	18 12	18 22				18 27		18 45	18 57		
Birmingham Moor Street	d		17 38	17 45	17 50			17 55		18 00	18 10	18 15	18 25				18 30		18 48	19 00		
Bordesley	d																					
Small Heath	d		17 42	17 49	17 54					18 04	18 14						18 34		18 52	19 04		
Tyseley	d		17 45	17 51	17 56					18 06	18 16						18 36		18 54	19 06		
Acocks Green	d		17 48	17 54						18 09			18 30						18 57			
Olton	d		17 50	17 57						18 12			18 33						19 00			
Solihull	d		17 54	18 01				18 05		18 16		18 25	18 37						19 04			
Widney Manor	d		17 58	18 04						18 19			18 40						19 07			
Dorridge	d		18 02	18a09				18 12		18 23		18 30	18a45						19 11			
Lapworth	d		18 06							18 27		18 34							19 15			
Hatton	d		18 12							18 33		18 40							19 21			
Warwick Parkway	d		18 16					18 23		18 38		18 45										
Warwick	d	18 04	18 19					18 26		18 41		18 49							19 27			
Leamington Spa 8	a	18 08	18 24				18 27	18 30	18 36	18 47		18 53						18 58	19 32			19 37
	d	18 08					18 28	18 30	18 38			18 54						19 00				19 38
Banbury	d	18 26						18 48	18a55			19 12						19a19				19a55
London Marylebone 10 ⊖	a	19 39						20 06				20 37										
Spring Road	d				17 59						18 19						18 39			19 09		
Hall Green	d				18 02						18 22						18 42			19 12		
Yardley Wood	d				18 05						18 25						18 45			19 15		
Shirley	d				18 09						18a28						18 48			19a18		
Whitlocks End	d				18 11												18 51					
Wythall	d				18 14												18 53					
Earlswood (West Midlands)	d				18 16												18 56					
The Lakes	d				18x19												18x58					
Wood End	d				18x21												19x00					
Danzey	d				18x25												19x03					
Henley-in-Arden	d				18 30												19 08					
Wootton Wawen	d				18x33												19x10					
Wilmcote	d				18 38		18 58										19 16					
Stratford-upon-Avon	a				18 45		19 06										19 22					

Table 71

Mondays to Fridays
until 01 October

Hereford, Worcester and Stourbridge - Birmingham - Leamington Spa, Marylebone and Stratford-upon-Avon

		CH	LM	LM	LM	LM	GW ◇1 🍽	GW	LM	GW 1	XC ◇1 ⌶	XC ◇1	CH ◇	LM	LM	LM	XC ◇1	CH ◇	XC ◇1	CH ◇	LM	LM	GW
Hereford 7	d								18 48							19 50							
Ledbury	a								19 03							20 07							
	d								19 04							20 18							
Colwall	d								19 10							20 24							
Great Malvern	a								19 15							20 29							
	d							18 51	19 15							20 29							21 15
Malvern Link	d							18 53	19 18							20 32							21 18
Worcester Foregate Street 7	a							19 03	19 27							20 41							21 27
	d					18 46	18 49	19 03	19 27	19 27					19 46	20 42							21 27
Worcester Shrub Hill 7	a						18 52	19 06		19 29													21 30
	d				18 37																	20 52	
Droitwich Spa	d				18 45	18 55			19 36						19 55	20 49						21 00	
Bromsgrove	d								19 46							20 59							
Barnt Green	d																						
University	d								20 09							21 16							
Hartlebury	d					19 02																	
Kidderminster	d		18 38		18 55	19 10									20 10							21 10	
Blakedown	d		18 43		19 00	19 15									20 15							21 15	
Hagley	d		18 46		19 04	19 19									20 19							21 19	
Stourbridge Junction 2	d		18 50		19 09	19 25								19 55	20 25						20 55	21 25	
Lye	d		18 54			19 29								19 59	20 29						20 59	21 29	
Cradley Heath	d		18 57		19 15	19 32								20 02	20 32						21 02	21 32	
Old Hill	d		19 01			19 36								20 06	20 36						21 06	21 36	
Rowley Regis	d		19 05		19 21	19 40								20 10	20 40						21 10	21 40	
Langley Green	d		19 08			19 43								20 13	20 43						21 13	21 43	
Birmingham New Street 12	a								20 20							21 23							
	d										19 33	20 03					20 33		21 03				
Birmingham International ✈	d											20 14							21 14				
Coventry	d											20 25							21 25				
Smethwick Galton Bridge 7	d		19 11		19 26	19 46								20 16	20 46						21 16	21 46	
The Hawthorns	d		19 14		19 29	19 48								20 18	20 48						21 18	21 48	
Jewellery Quarter	d		19 18		19 33	19 52								20 22	20 52						21 22	21 52	
Birmingham Snow Hill	a		19 21		19 36	19 55								20 25	20 55						21 25	21 55	
	d	19 12	19 22	19 27	19 37	19 57							20 12	20 27	20 57					21 15	21 27	21 57	
Birmingham Moor Street	d	19 15	19 25	19 30	19a39	20 00							20 15	20 30	21 00					21 18	21 30	22 00	
Bordesley	d																						
Small Heath	d			19 34		20 04								20 34	21 04						21 34	22 04	
Tyseley	d			19 36		20 06								20 36	21 06						21 36	22 06	
Acocks Green	d		19 30			20 09									21 09							22 09	
Olton	d		19 33			20 12									21 12							22 12	
Solihull	d	19 25	19 37			20 16							20 25		21 16					21 27		22 16	
Widney Manor	d	19 28	19 40			20 19							20 28		21 19							22 19	
Dorridge	d	19 32	19a47			20a24							20 32		21a24					21 33		22a24	
Lapworth	d	19 36											20 36							21 37			
Hatton	d	19 42											20 42							21 42			
Warwick Parkway	d	19 47											20 47							21 47			
Warwick	d	19 50											20 50							21 51			
Leamington Spa 8	a	19 54									20 04	20 36	20 54				20 58	21 06	21 36	21 54			
	d	19 54									20 05	20 38	20 54				21 00	21 07	21 38	21 55			
Banbury	d	20 12									20a22	20a55	21 12				21a19		21a55	22 15			
London Marylebone 10 ⊖	a	21 32											22 32							23 34			
Spring Road	d			19 39										20 39							21 39		
Hall Green	d			19 42										20 42							21 42		
Yardley Wood	d			19 45										20 45							21 45		
Shirley	d			19 48										20 48							21a48		
Whitlocks End	d			19 51										20 51									
Wythall	d			19 53										20 53									
Earlswood (West Midlands)	d			19 56										20 56									
The Lakes	d			19x58										20x58									
Wood End	d			20x00										21x00									
Danzey	d			20x03										21x03									
Henley-in-Arden	d			20 08										21 08									
Wootton Wawen	d			20x10										21x10									
Wilmcote	d			20 16										21 16				21 34					
Stratford-upon-Avon	a			20 23										21 23				21 45					

Table 71

Mondays to Fridays
until 01 October

Hereford, Worcester and Stourbridge - Birmingham - Leamington Spa, Marylebone and Stratford-upon-Avon

		LM	LM	CH		XC	CH	LM	LM	LM	LM	CH	CH
						◇1							
						🍴							
Hereford [7]	d	20 52	21 28								22 55		
Ledbury	a	21 09	21 44								23 11		
	d	21 13	21 45								23 13		
Colwall	d	21 20	21 51								23 19		
Great Malvern	a	21 24	21 56								23 24		
	d	21 25	21 57								23 24		
Malvern Link	d	21 28	22 00								23 27		
Worcester Foregate Street [7]	a	21 36	22 09								23 34		
	d	21 37	22 10							22 17	23 34		
Worcester Shrub Hill [7]	a	21 39								22 19	23 39		
	d								21 52	22 27			
Droitwich Spa	d		22 19						22 00	22 35			
Bromsgrove	d		22 29										
Barnt Green	d												
University	d		22 45										
Hartlebury	d												
Kidderminster	d								22 10	22 45			
Blakedown	d								22 15				
Hagley	d								22 19				
Stourbridge Junction [2]	d							21 55	22 25	22 55			
Lye	d							21 59	22 29	22 59			
Cradley Heath	d							22 02	22 32	23 02			
Old Hill	d							22 06	22 36	23 06			
Rowley Regis	d							22 10	22 40	23 10			
Langley Green	d							22 13	22 43	23 13			
Birmingham New Street [12]	a		22 52										
	d					22 03							
Birmingham International ✈	d					22 14							
Coventry	d					22 25							
Smethwick Galton Bridge [7]	d							22 16	22 46	23 16			
The Hawthorns 🚊	d							22 18	22 48	23 18			
Jewellery Quarter 🚊	d							22 22	22 52	23 22			
Birmingham Snow Hill 🚊	a							22 25	22 55	23 24			
	d						22 15	22 27	22 57	23 25			23 30
Birmingham Moor Street	d						22 18	22 30	23 00	23 28			23 33
Bordesley	d												
Small Heath	d							22 34	23 04	23 32			
Tyseley	d						22 23	22 36	23 06	23 34			23 38
Acocks Green	d						22 25		23 09				23 40
Olton	d						22 28		23 12				23 43
Solihull	d						22 32		23 16				23 47
Widney Manor	d						22 35		23 19				23 50
Dorridge	d						22 39		23a24				23 54
Lapworth	d						22 43						23 58
Hatton	d						22 49						00 04
Warwick Parkway	d						22 53						00 08
Warwick	d						22 56					23 21	00 11
Leamington Spa [8]	a					22 37	23 00					23 24	00 14
	d			22 25		22 38	23 01					23 25	00 15
Banbury	d					22a55	23a23					23a44	00a38
London Marylebone [10] ⊖	a												
Spring Road	d							22 39		23 37			
Hall Green	d							22 42		23 40			
Yardley Wood	d							22 45		23 43			
Shirley	d							22a48		23a46			
Whitlocks End	d												
Wythall	d												
Earlswood (West Midlands)	d												
The Lakes	d												
Wood End	d												
Danzey	d												
Henley-in-Arden	d												
Wootton Wawen	d												
Wilmcote	d												
Stratford-upon-Avon	a			22 55									

Table 71

Mondays to Fridays
from 04 October

Hereford, Worcester and Stourbridge - Birmingham - Leamington Spa, Marylebone and Stratford-upon-Avon

		CH MX	GW	CH	CH	LM	LM	XC	CH	LM		LM	LM	CH	CH	XC	CH	CH	XC	LM		CH	LM	LM	GW
			◇1		◇			◇1								◇1		◇	◇1			◇			◇1
			🍽	🍴	🍴			🍴	🍴							🍴		🍴	🍴			🍴			Ø
Hereford [7]	d																								05 34
Ledbury	a																								05 50
	d																								05 50
Colwall	d																								05 58
Great Malvern	a																								06 03
	d		05 17			05 50																			06 03
Malvern Link	d		05 20			05 53																			06 07
Worcester Foregate Street [7]	a		05 30			06 01																			06 18
	d		05 31			06 02																			06 18
Worcester Shrub Hill [7]	a		05 35																						06 21
	d									06 28														06 15	
Droitwich Spa	d					06 12				06 35														06 23	
Bromsgrove	d					06 21				06 44															
Barnt Green	d																								
University	d					06 39				06 59															
Hartlebury	d																							06 30	
Kidderminster	d																	06 10				06 30		06 36	
Blakedown	d																							06 41	
Hagley	d																							06 44	
Stourbridge Junction [2]	d																	06 18		06 24		06 39		06 49	
Lye	d																			06 28				06 53	
Cradley Heath	d																	06 24		06 31		06 44		06 56	
Old Hill	d																			06 35				07 00	
Rowley Regis	d																	06 30		06 39		06 50		07 04	
Langley Green	d																			06 42				07 07	
Birmingham New Street [12]	a					06 45				07 07															
	d							06 03								06 33			07 03						
Birmingham International ✈	d							06 14											07 14						
Coventry	d							06 25											07 25						
Smethwick Galton Bridge [7]	d																	06 35		06 46		06 56		07 11	
The Hawthorns 🚊	d																	06 38		06 48		06 58		07 13	
Jewellery Quarter 🚊	d																			06 52				07 17	
Birmingham Snow Hill 🚊	a																	06 46		06 55		07 04		07 21	
	d	23p30			05 43		05 55		06 15			06 36	06 43					06 50		07 02		07 14	07 19	07 23	
Birmingham Moor Street	d	23p33			05 46		05 58		06 18			06 39	06 46					06 53		07 05		07 17	07 22	07 26	
Bordesley	d																								
Small Heath	d						06 02					06 43	06 50							07 09				07 30	
Tyseley	d	23p38					06 04					06 45	06 52							07 11				07 32	
Acocks Green	d	23p40					06 07					06 48								07 14			07 27		
Olton	d	23p43					06 10					06 51								07 17			07 30		
Solihull	d	23p47			05 56		06 13		06 28			06 55						07 03		07 20		07 28	07 34		
Widney Manor	d	23p50					06 17					06 58								07 23			07 37		
Dorridge	d	23p54			06 01		06 21		06 33			07a03						07 08		07 27		07 34	07a42		
Lapworth	d	23p58					06 25													07 31					
Hatton	d	00 04															07 03			07 37					
Warwick Parkway	d	00 08		05 40	06 12				06 44								07 09	07 19				07 47			
Warwick	d	00 11			06 15												07 13			07 43		07 50			
Leamington Spa [8]	a	00 14		05 45	06 20			06 36	06 49							06 58	07 17	07 24	07 37	07 49		07 54			
	d	00 15		05 45	06 20			06 38	06 49					06 55	06 55	07 00	07 18	07 24	07 38			07 54			
Banbury	d	00a41		06 03	06 38			06a57	07 07						07 18	07a22	07 36	07 42	07a55			08 12			
London Marylebone [10] ⊖	a			07 21	07 56				08 20						08 43		08 54	08 57				09 30			
Spring Road	d												06 55											07 35	
Hall Green	d												06 58											07 38	
Yardley Wood	d												07 01											07 41	
Shirley	d												07 05											07 44	
Whitlocks End	d												07 07											07 47	
Wythall	d												07 10											07 50	
Earlswood (West Midlands)	d												07 12											07 52	
The Lakes	d												07x15											07x55	
Wood End	d												07x17											07x57	
Danzey	d												07x20											08x01	
Henley-in-Arden	d												07 25											08 07	
Wootton Wawen	d												07x27											08x10	
Wilmcote	d						06 42						07 33	07 21										08 15	
Stratford-upon-Avon	a						06 48						07 40	07 33										08 21	

Table 71

Mondays to Fridays
from 04 October

Hereford, Worcester and Stourbridge - Birmingham - Leamington Spa, Marylebone and Stratford-upon-Avon

Station		XC	LM	CH	LM	GW	LM	LM	CH	XC	CH	LM	LM	GW	LM	LM	LM	LM	GW	XC	CH	LM	LM
		◇1		◇		1			◇	1	◇			◇1						◇1	◇		
Hereford	d													06 43			07 08	07 34					
Ledbury	a													06 59			07 23	07 51					
	d													07 00			07 24	07 51					
Colwall	d													07 09			07 30	07 57					
Great Malvern	a													07 14			07 35	08 02					
	d						06 48						07 05	07 14			07 39	08 03	08 26			08 38	
Malvern Link	d						06 50						07 08	07 18			07 42	08 06	08 29			08 41	
Worcester Foregate Street	a						06 59						07 16	07 30			07 50	08 15	08 42			08 50	
	d					06 51	06 59						07 17	07 30		07 33	07 51	08 19	08 54			08 51	
Worcester Shrub Hill	a					06 53	07 02						07 19	07 34			07 53		08 56				
	d				06 47		07 06					07 15	07 24				07 57						
Droitwich Spa	d				06 55		07 14					07 23	07 32			07 42	08 05	08 30				09 00	
Bromsgrove	d						07 25											08 41				09 09	
Barnt Green	d																						
University	d												08 00				08 30	09 00				09 30	
Hartlebury	d				07 02							07 30											
Kidderminster	d			06 56	07 09			07 18			07 30	07 36				07 54					08 09		
Blakedown	d				07 14			07 24				07 41				08 00					08 14		
Hagley	d				07 18			07 28				07 45				08 04					08 18		
Stourbridge Junction	d			07 07	07 22			07 32			07 40	07 49			07 55	08 09					08 23		
Lye	d			07 11				07 36							07 59								
Cradley Heath	d			07 14	07 28			07 39			07 45	07 55			08 02	08 14					08 28		
Old Hill	d			07 18				07 43							08 06								
Rowley Regis	d			07 22	07 34			07 47			07 53	08 00			08 10	08 20					08 34		
Langley Green	d			07 25				07 50							08 13								
Birmingham New Street	a						07 45						08 09				08 37	09 07				09 42	
	d	07 33								08 03										08 33			
Birmingham International	d									08 14													
Coventry	d									08 25													
Smethwick Galton Bridge	d			07 29	07 39			07 54			07 59	08 06			08 16	08 26					08 40		
The Hawthorns	d			07 32	07 42			07 56			08 02	08 08			08 19	08 28					08 42		
Jewellery Quarter	d			07 36	07 46			08 00			08 06	08 12			08 23	08 32					08 47		
Birmingham Snow Hill	a			07 40	07 49			08 03			08 11	08 15			08 26	08 35					08 51		
	d		07 39	07 45	07 50			08 05			08 12	08 17			08 27	08 37					08 52		08 57
Birmingham Moor Street	d		07 42	07 48	07 53			08 08			08 15	08 20			08 30	08 40					08 55		09 00
Bordesley	d																						
Small Heath	d		07 46					08 12								08 44							
Tyseley	d		07 48		07 57			08 14								08 46							
Acocks Green	d				08 00							08 25				08 49							09 05
Olton	d				08 03							08 28				08 52							09 08
Solihull	d			07 58	08 07						08 25	08 32				08 56					09 05		09 12
Widney Manor	d				08 10							08 35				08 59							09 15
Dorridge	d			08 03	08a16						08 30	08a41				09a04					09 10		09a22
Lapworth	d			08 07																			
Hatton	d			08 13																			
Warwick Parkway	d			08 19							08 41										09 21		
Warwick	d			08 23							08 44										09 24		
Leamington Spa	a	08 03		08 26						08 36	08 49									08 59	09 29		
	d	08 04		08 27					08 30	08 38	08 49									09 00	09 29		
Banbury	d	08a21		08 45						08a55	09 10									09a19	09 47		
London Marylebone ⊖	a			09 59							10 31										11 02		
Spring Road	d		07 51					08 17							08 36								
Hall Green	d		07 54					08 20							08 39								
Yardley Wood	d		07 57					08 23							08 42								
Shirley	d		08a00					08a26							08 45								
Whitlocks End	d														08 48								
Wythall	d														08 50								
Earlswood (West Midlands)	d														08 53								
The Lakes	d														08x55								
Wood End	d														08x57								
Danzey	d														09x00								
Henley-in-Arden	d														09 05								
Wootton Wawen	d														09x08								
Wilmcote	d								08 56						09 13								
Stratford-upon-Avon	a								09 08						09 21								

Table 71

Mondays to Fridays
from 04 October

Hereford, Worcester and Stourbridge - Birmingham - Leamington Spa, Marylebone and Stratford-upon-Avon

Station		XC	WS	CH	LM	LM	LM	XC	CH	LM	LM	GW	LM	XC	CH	CH	LM	LM	LM	LM	GW	XC
		◇1	◇1	◇				◇1	◇			◇1		◇1	◇	◇					◇1	◇1
Hereford	d												08 49									
Ledbury	a												09 05									
	d												09 08									
Colwall	d												09 14									
Great Malvern	a												09 19									
	d											08 58	09 19								09 54	
Malvern Link	d											09 00	09 22								09 56	
Worcester Foregate Street	a											09 09	09 31								10 05	
	d										09 06	09 09	09 31								10 05	
Worcester Shrub Hill	a											09 12	09 34								10 08	
	d												09 37							09 47		
Droitwich Spa	d										09 15		09 45							09 55		
Bromsgrove	d												09 54									
Barnt Green	d																					
University	d												10 09									
Hartlebury	d																					
Kidderminster	d						08 57				09 26						09 36		09 56	10 06		
Blakedown	d						09 02				09 31						09 41			10 11		
Hagley	d						09 05				09 35						09 45			10 15		
Stourbridge Junction	d				08 45	08 54	09 09			09 25	09 39						09 49	09 55	10 09	10 19		
Lye	d					08 58				09 29								09 59				
Cradley Heath	d				08 51	09 01	09 15			09 32	09 44						09 54	10 02	10 14	10 24		
Old Hill	d					09 05				09 36								10 06				
Rowley Regis	d				08 57	09 09	09 21			09 39	09 50						10 00	10 10	10 20	10 30		
Langley Green	d					09 12				09 42								10 13				
Birmingham New Street	a												10 24									
	d	09 03						09 33						10 03								10 33
Birmingham International	d	09 14												10 14								
Coventry	d	09 25												10 25								
Smethwick Galton Bridge	d				09 02	09 15	09 26			09 46	09 56						10 06	10 16	10 26	10 36		
The Hawthorns	d				09 05	09 17	09 29			09 48	09 58						10 08	10 18	10 28	10 38		
Jewellery Quarter	d				09 09	09 21	09 33			09 52	10 02						10 12	10 22	10 32	10 42		
Birmingham Snow Hill	a				09 14	09 25	09 36			09 55	10 05						10 15	10 25	10 35	10 45		
	d			09 12	09 17	09 27	09 37		09 52	09 57	10 07					10 12	10 17	10 27	10 37	10 47		
Birmingham Moor Street	d			09 15	09 20	09 30	09 40		09 55	10 00	10 10					10 15	10 20	10 30	10 40	10 50		
Bordesley	d																					
Small Heath	d						09 44				10 14								10 44			
Tyseley	d						09 46				10 16								10 46			
Acocks Green	d				09 25		09 49			10 05							10 25		10 49			
Olton	d				09 28		09 52			10 08							10 28		10 52			
Solihull	d			09 25	09 32		09 56		10 05	10 12						10 25	10 32		10 56			
Widney Manor	d				09 35		09 59			10 15							10 35		10 59			
Dorridge	d			09 30	09a41		10a04		10 10	10a22						10 30	10a41		11a04			
Lapworth	d			09 34												10 34						
Hatton	d			09 40												10 40						
Warwick Parkway	d			09 45					10 21							10 45						
Warwick	d			09 49					10 24							10 49						
Leamington Spa	a	09 36		09 53				09 58	10 29					10 36		10 53						10 58
	d	09 38	09 46	09 54				10 00	10 29					10 38	10 49	10 54						11 00
Banbury	d	09a55	10 04	10 12				10a19	10 47					10a55		11 12						11a19
London Marylebone ⊖	a		11 15	11 35					12 05							12 34						
Spring Road	d					09 36					10 19							10 36		10 56		
Hall Green	d					09 39					10 22							10 39		10 59		
Yardley Wood	d					09 42					10 25							10 42		11 02		
Shirley	d					09 45					10a28							10 45		11a05		
Whitlocks End	d					09 48												10 48				
Wythall	d					09 50												10 50				
Earlswood (West Midlands)	d					09 53												10 53				
The Lakes	d					09x55												10x55				
Wood End	d					09x57												10x57				
Danzey	d					10x00												11x00				
Henley-in-Arden	d					10 05												11 05				
Wootton Wawen	d					10x08												11x08				
Wilmcote	d					10 13												11 13				
Stratford-upon-Avon	a					10 21									11 18			11 22				

Table 71

Mondays to Fridays
from 04 October

Hereford, Worcester and Stourbridge - Birmingham - Leamington Spa, Marylebone and Stratford-upon-Avon

		CH	LM	LM	XC	CH	LM	LM	LM	LM	LM	GW	XC	CH	CH	LM	LM	XC	GW	CH	CH	LM	LM
		◇			◇1 🛒	◇						■	◇1 🛒					◇1 🛒	◇1 🛒	◇ 🛒	◇		
Hereford 7	d							09 40															10 40
Ledbury	a							09 57															10 56
	d							09 58															10 59
Colwall	d							10 04															11 05
Great Malvern	a							10 09															11 10
	d							10 10				10 51											11 10
Malvern Link	d							10 13				10 53											11 13
Worcester Foregate Street 7	a							10 22				11 02											11 22
	d						10 16	10 23				11 02							12 06			11 16	11 23
Worcester Shrub Hill 7	a											11 06							12 08				
	d										10 47												
Droitwich Spa	d						10 25	10 33			10 55											11 25	11 33
Bromsgrove	d							10 42															11 42
Barnt Green	d																						
University	d							10 59															11 59
Hartlebury	d																						
Kidderminster	d			10 26			10 36			10 56	11 06						11 26					11 36	
Blakedown	d						10 41				11 11											11 41	
Hagley	d						10 44				11 14											11 44	
Stourbridge Junction 2	d		10 25	10 39			10 49		10 55	11 09	11 19					11 25	11 39					11 49	
Lye	d		10 29						10 59							11 29							
Cradley Heath	d		10 32	10 44			10 54		11 02	11 14	11 24					11 32	11 44					11 54	
Old Hill	d		10 36						11 06							11 36							
Rowley Regis	d		10 40	10 50			11 00		11 10	11 20	11 30					11 40	11 50					12 00	
Langley Green	d		10 43						11 13							11 43							
Birmingham New Street 12	a							11 13															12 13
	d				11 03								11 33					12 03					
Birmingham International ✈	d				11 14													12 14					
Coventry	d				11 25													12 25					
Smethwick Galton Bridge 7	d		10 46	10 56			11 06		11 16	11 26	11 36					11 46	11 56					12 06	
The Hawthorns 🚊	d		10 48	10 58			11 08		11 18	11 28	11 38					11 48	11 58					12 08	
Jewellery Quarter 🚊	d		10 52	11 02			11 12		11 22	11 32	11 42					11 52	12 02					12 12	
Birmingham Snow Hill 🚊	a		10 55	11 05			11 15		11 25	11 35	11 45					11 55	12 05					12 15	
	d	10 52	10 57	11 07		11 12	11 17		11 27	11 37	11 47				11 52	11 57	12 07				12 12	12 17	
Birmingham Moor Street	d	10 55	11 00	11 10		11 15	11 20		11 30	11 40	11 50				11 55	12 00	12 10				12 15	12 20	
Bordesley	d																						
Small Heath	d			11 14						11 44							12 14						
Tyseley	d			11 16						11 46							12 16						
Acocks Green	d		11 05				11 25			11 49						12 05						12 25	
Olton	d		11 08				11 28			11 52						12 08						12 28	
Solihull	d	11 05	11 12			11 25	11 32			11 56					12 05	12 12					12 25	12 32	
Widney Manor	d		11 15				11 35			11 59						12 15						12 35	
Dorridge	d	11 10	11a21			11 30	11a41			12a04					12 10	12a22					12 30	12a41	
Lapworth	d																				12 34		
Hatton	d													11 57							12 40		
Warwick Parkway	d	11 21				11 41									12 21						12 45		
Warwick	d	11 24				11 45								12 04	12 24						12 49		
Leamington Spa 8	a	11 29			11 36	11 51							11 59	12 09	12 29			12 36			12 53		
	d	11 29			11 38	11 52							12 00	12 09	12 29			12 38		12 38	12 54		
Banbury	d	11 47			11a55	12 09							12a19	12 28	12 47			12a55			13 12		
London Marylebone 10 ⊖	a	13 02				13 32								13 58	14 02						14 34		
Spring Road	d			11 19					11 36		11 56						12 19						
Hall Green	d			11 22					11 39		11 59						12 22						
Yardley Wood	d			11 25					11 42		12 02						12 25						
Shirley	d			11a28					11 45		12a05						12a28						
Whitlocks End	d								11 48														
Wythall	d								11 50														
Earlswood (West Midlands)	d								11 53														
The Lakes	d								11x55														
Wood End	d								11x57														
Danzey	d								12x00														
Henley-in-Arden	d								12 05														
Wootton Wawen	d								12x08														
Wilmcote	d								12 13														
Stratford-upon-Avon	a								12 21											13 14			

Table 71

Mondays to Fridays
from 04 October

Hereford, Worcester and Stourbridge - Birmingham - Leamington Spa, Marylebone and Stratford-upon-Avon

		LM	LM	LM	XC	CH	LM	LM	XC	CH	LM	LM	LM	LM	LM	GW	LM	XC	CH	LM	LM	XC
					◇1 🛒	◇			◇1 🛒	◇								◇1 🛒	◇			◇1 🛒
Hereford 7	d											11 40					12 39					
Ledbury	a											11 57					12 55					
	d											11 57					13 00					
Colwall	d											12 04					13 06					
Great Malvern	a											12 09					13 11					
	d			11 34								12 11				12 51	13 11					
Malvern Link	d			11 36								12 14				12 53	13 14					
Worcester Foregate Street 7	a			11 45								12 23				13 02	13 23					
	d			11 46							12 16	12 23			12 46	13 02	13 23					
Worcester Shrub Hill 7	a															13 06						
	d																					
Droitwich Spa	d			11 55							12 25	12 33			12 55		13 33					
Bromsgrove	d											12 42					13 42					
Barnt Green	d																					
University	d											12 59					13 59					
Hartlebury	d																					
Kidderminster	d		11 56	12 06				12 26			12 36			12 56	13 06							
Blakedown	d			12 11							12 41				13 11							
Hagley	d			12 14							12 44				13 14							
Stourbridge Junction 2	d	11 55	12 09	12 19			12 25	12 39			12 49		12 55	13 09	13 19					13 25	13 39	
Lye	d	11 59					12 29						12 59							13 29		
Cradley Heath	d	12 02	12 14	12 24			12 32	12 44			12 54		13 02	13 14	13 24					13 32	13 44	
Old Hill	d	12 06					12 36						13 06							13 36		
Rowley Regis	d	12 10	12 20	12 30			12 40	12 50			13 00		13 10	13 20	13 30					13 40	13 50	
Langley Green	d	12 13					12 43						13 13							13 43		
Birmingham New Street 12	a											13 13					14 13					
	d				12 33				13 03									13 33				14 03
Birmingham International ✈	d								13 14													14 14
Coventry	d								13 25													14 25
Smethwick Galton Bridge 7	d	12 16	12 26	12 36			12 46	12 56			13 06		13 16	13 26	13 36					13 46	13 56	
The Hawthorns 🚊	d	12 18	12 28	12 38			12 48	12 58			13 08		13 18	13 28	13 38					13 48	13 58	
Jewellery Quarter 🚊	d	12 22	12 32	12 42			12 52	13 02			13 12		13 22	13 32	13 42					13 52	14 02	
Birmingham Snow Hill 🚊	a	12 25	12 35	12 45			12 55	13 05			13 15		13 25	13 35	13 45					13 55	14 05	
	d	12 27	12 37	12 47		12 52	12 57	13 07		13 12	13 17		13 27	13 37	13 47				13 52	13 57	14 07	
Birmingham Moor Street	d	12 30	12 40	12 50		12 55	13 00	13 10		13 15	13 20		13 30	13 40	13 50				13 55	14 00	14 10	
Bordesley	d																					
Small Heath	d		12 44					13 14						13 44							14 14	
Tyseley	d		12 46					13 16						13 46							14 16	
Acocks Green	d		12 49				13 05				13 25			13 49						14 05		
Olton	d		12 52				13 08				13 28			13 52						14 08		
Solihull	d		12 56			13 05	13 12			13 25	13 32			13 56					14 05	14 12		
Widney Manor	d		12 59				13 15				13 35			13 59						14 15		
Dorridge	d		13a04			13 10	13a21			13 30	13a41			14a04					14 10	14a22		
Lapworth	d																					
Hatton	d																					
Warwick Parkway	d					13 21				13 41									14 21			
Warwick	d					13 24				13 45									14 24			
Leamington Spa 8	a				12 58	13 29			13 36	13 51								13 59	14 29			14 36
	d				13 00	13 29			13 38	13 52								14 00	14 29			14 38
Banbury	d				13a19	13 47			13a55	14 09								14a19	14 47			14a55
London Marylebone 10 ⊖	a					15 02				15 32									16 05			
Spring Road	d	12 36		12 56				13 19					13 36		13 56						14 19	
Hall Green	d	12 39		12 59				13 22					13 39		13 59						14 22	
Yardley Wood	d	12 42		13 02				13 25					13 42		14 02						14 25	
Shirley	d	12 45		13a05				13a28					13 45		14a05						14a28	
Whitlocks End	d	12 48											13 48									
Wythall	d	12 50											13 50									
Earlswood (West Midlands)	d	12 53											13 53									
The Lakes	d	12x55											13x55									
Wood End	d	12x57											13x57									
Danzey	d	13x00											14x00									
Henley-in-Arden	d	13 05											14 05									
Wootton Wawen	d	13x08											14x08									
Wilmcote	d	13 13											14 13									
Stratford-upon-Avon	a	13 21											14 21									

Table 71

Mondays to Fridays
from 04 October

Hereford, Worcester and Stourbridge - Birmingham - Leamington Spa, Marylebone and Stratford-upon-Avon

		CH	LM	LM	LM	LM	GW	XC	CH	LM	LM	CH	XC	CH	LM	LM	LM	LM	LM	GW	GW	XC	CH
		◇					◇1 ☕	◇1 ✕	◇			◇	◇1 ✕	◇						◇1 ☕		◇1 ✕	◇
Hereford [7]	d						13 11									13 41							
Ledbury	a						13 27									13 58							
	d						13 30									13 59							
Colwall	d						13 37									14 05							
Great Malvern	a						13 43									14 10							
	d						13 47								14 00	14 11				14 34	14 51		
Malvern Link	d						13 51								14 02	14 14				14 37	14 53		
Worcester Foregate Street [7]	a						14 01								14 10	14 23				14 51	15 02		
	d						14 02								14 16	14 23				14 52	15 02		
Worcester Shrub Hill [7]	a						14 06													14 56	15 06		
	d		13 17			13 47													14 47				
Droitwich Spa	d		13 25			13 55									14 25	14 33			14 55				
Bromsgrove	d															14 42							
Barnt Green	d																						
University	d															14 59							
Hartlebury	d																						
Kidderminster	d		13 36		13 56	14 06					14 26				14 36			14 56	15 06				
Blakedown	d		13 41			14 11									14 41				15 11				
Hagley	d		13 44			14 14									14 44				15 14				
Stourbridge Junction [2]	d		13 49	13 55	14 09	14 19				14 25	14 39				14 49		14 55	15 09	15 19				
Lye	d			13 59						14 29							14 59						
Cradley Heath	d		13 54	14 02	14 14	14 24				14 32	14 44				14 54		15 02	15 14	15 24				
Old Hill	d			14 06						14 36							15 06						
Rowley Regis	d		14 00	14 10	14 20	14 30				14 40	14 50				15 00		15 10	15 20	15 30				
Langley Green	d			14 13						14 43							15 13						
Birmingham New Street [12]	a															15 13							
	d							14 33					15 03									15 33	
Birmingham International ✈	d												15 14										
Coventry	d												15 25										
Smethwick Galton Bridge [7]	d		14 06	14 16	14 26	14 36				14 46	14 56				15 06		15 16	15 26	15 36				
The Hawthorns 🚋	d		14 08	14 18	14 28	14 38				14 48	14 58				15 08		15 18	15 28	15 38				
Jewellery Quarter 🚋	d		14 12	14 22	14 32	14 42				14 52	15 02				15 12		15 22	15 32	15 42				
Birmingham Snow Hill 🚋	a		14 15	14 25	14 35	14 45				14 55	15 05				15 15		15 25	15 35	15 45				
	d	14 12	14 17	14 27	14 37	14 47			14 52	14 57	15 07			15 12	15 17		15 26	15 37	15 47				15 52
Birmingham Moor Street	d	14 15	14 20	14 30	14 40	14 50			14 55	15 00	15 10			15 15	15 20		15 29	15 40	15 50				15 55
Bordesley	d																						
Small Heath	d				14 44						15 14							15 44					
Tyseley	d				14 46						15 16							15 46					
Acocks Green	d		14 25		14 49					15 05					15 25			15 49					
Olton	d		14 28		14 52					15 08					15 28			15 52					
Solihull	d	14 25	14 32		14 56				15 05	15 12				15 25	15 32			15 56					16 05
Widney Manor	d		14 35		14 59					15 15					15 35			15 59					
Dorridge	d	14 30	14a41		15a04				15 10	15a21				15 30	15a41			16a04					16 10
Lapworth	d	14 34																					
Hatton	d	14 40																					
Warwick Parkway	d	14 45							15 21					15 41									16 21
Warwick	d	14 49							15 24					15 44									16 24
Leamington Spa [8]	a	14 53						14 58	15 29				15 36	15 49								15 58	16 29
	d	14 54						15 00	15 29			15 33	15 38	15 49								16 00	16 29
Banbury	d	15 12						15a19	15 47				15a55	16 07								16a19	16 47
London Marylebone [10] ⊖	a	16 35							17 05					17 34									18 07
Spring Road	d			14 36		14 56					15 19						15 35		15 56				
Hall Green	d			14 39		14 59					15 22						15 38		15 59				
Yardley Wood	d			14 42		15 02					15 25						15 41		16 02				
Shirley	d			14 45		15a05					15a28						15 44		16a05				
Whitlocks End	d			14 48													15 47						
Wythall	d			14 50													15 49						
Earlswood (West Midlands)	d			14 53													15 52						
The Lakes	d			14x55													15x54						
Wood End	d			14x57													15x56						
Danzey	d			15x00													15x59						
Henley-in-Arden	d			15 05													16 04						
Wootton Wawen	d			15x08													16x07						
Wilmcote	d			15 13								16 00					16 12						
Stratford-upon-Avon	a			15 21								16 15					16 21						

Table 71

Mondays to Fridays
from 04 October

Hereford, Worcester and Stourbridge - Birmingham - Leamington Spa, Marylebone and Stratford-upon-Avon

		LM	LM	XC	CH	LM	LM	LM	LM	LM	GW	XC	CH	LM	LM	XC	WS	CH	LM	LM	LM	LM	XC
				◇1 ✕							◇1 ☕	◇1 ✕				◇1 ✕	◇1 ☕	◇					◇1 ✕
Hereford [7]	d						14 40				15 11									15 40			
Ledbury	a						14 56				15 27									15 57			
	d						14 59				15 27									16 00			
Colwall	d						15 05				15 35									16 06			
Great Malvern	a						15 10				15 40									16 11			
	d						15 10			15 29	15 40									16 11			
Malvern Link	d						15 13			15 31	15 44									16 14			
Worcester Foregate Street [7]	a						15 22			15 39	15 57									16 23			
	d					15 16	15 23			15 40	16 02								16 07	16 23			
Worcester Shrub Hill [7]	a									15 42	16 06												
	d									15 47											16 17		
Droitwich Spa	d					15 25	15 33			15 55									16 16	16 33	16 25		
Bromsgrove	d						15 42													16 42			
Barnt Green	d																			16 49			
University	d						15 59													16 59			
Hartlebury	d																		16 23				
Kidderminster	d		15 26			15 36			15 56	16 06					16 23				16 30		16 37		
Blakedown	d		15 31			15 41				16 11					16 28				16 35		16 43		
Hagley	d		15 34			15 44				16 14					16 31				16 39		16 47		
Stourbridge Junction [2]	d	15 25	15 39			15 49		15 55	16 09	16 19				16 25	16 35				16 44		16 51	16 55	
Lye	d	15 29						15 59						16 29								16 59	
Cradley Heath	d	15 32	15 44			15 54		16 02	16 14	16 24				16 32	16 41				16 50		16 57	17 02	
Old Hill	d	15 36						16 06						16 36								17 06	
Rowley Regis	d	15 40	15 50			16 00		16 10	16 20	16 30				16 40	16 47				16 55		17 03	17 10	
Langley Green	d	15 43						16 13						16 43								17 13	
Birmingham New Street [12]	a						16 13													17 13			
	d			16 03								16 33				17 03							17 33
Birmingham International ✈	d			16 14												17 14							
Coventry	d			16 25												17 25							
Smethwick Galton Bridge [7]	d	15 46	15 56			16 06		16 16	16 26	16 36				16 46	16 52				17 01		17 08	17 16	
The Hawthorns 🚋	d	15 48	15 58			16 08		16 18	16 28	16 38				16 48	16 55				17 03		17 11	17 19	
Jewellery Quarter 🚋	d	15 52	16 02			16 12		16 22	16 32	16 42				16 52	16 59				17 07		17 15	17 22	
Birmingham Snow Hill 🚋	a	15 55	16 05			16 15		16 25	16 35	16 45				16 55	17 02				17 10		17 18	17 25	
	d	15 57	16 07		16 12	16 17		16 27	16 37	16 47			16 52	16 57	17 03			17 10	17 14		17 22	17 27	
Birmingham Moor Street	d	16 00	16 10		16 15	16 20		16 30	16 40	16 50			16 55	17 00	17 06			17 13	17 17		17 25	17 30	
Bordesley	d																						
Small Heath	d		16 14						16 44	16 54									17 21				
Tyseley	d		16 16					16 34	16 46	16 56				17 04					17 23			17 34	
Acocks Green	d	16 05				16 25			16 49					17 07							17 30		
Olton	d	16 08				16 28			16 52					17 10							17 33		
Solihull	d	16 12			16 25	16 32			16 56				17 05	17 14				17 23			17 37		
Widney Manor	d	16 15				16 35			16 59					17 17				17 26			17 40		
Dorridge	d	16a22			16 30	16a41			17a04				17 10	17a22				17 30			17a46		
Lapworth	d				16 34													17 34					
Hatton	d				16 40													17 40					
Warwick Parkway	d				16 45								17 20					17 45					
Warwick	d				16 49								17 23					17 49					
Leamington Spa [8]	a			16 36	16 53							16 58	17 28			17 37	17 45	17 53					17 59
	d			16 38	16 54							17 00	17 28			17 38	17 46	17 54					18 00
Banbury	d			16a55	17 12							17a19	17 46			17a55	18 04	18 12					18a19
London Marylebone [10] ⊖	a				18 36								19 11				19 15	19 38					
Spring Road	d		16 19					16 37		16 59					17 12				17 26			17 37	
Hall Green	d		16 22					16 40		17 02					17 15				17 29			17 40	
Yardley Wood	d		16 25					16 43		17 05					17 18				17 32			17 43	
Shirley	d		16a28					16 46		17a08					17 21				17a35			17 46	
Whitlocks End	d							16 49							17 24							17 49	
Wythall	d							16 51							17 26							17 51	
Earlswood (West Midlands)	d							16 54														17 54	
The Lakes	d							16x56														17x56	
Wood End	d							16x58														17x58	
Danzey	d							17x01														18x01	
Henley-in-Arden	d							17 06							17 36							18 06	
Wootton Wawen	d							17x09														18x09	
Wilmcote	d							17 14														18 14	
Stratford-upon-Avon	a							17 22							17 50							18 22	

Hereford, Worcester and Stourbridge - Birmingham - Leamington Spa, Marylebone and Stratford-upon-Avon

		CH		LM	LM	LM	GW	CH	CH	XC	LM	LM		CH	LM	GW	LM	LM	LM	XC	LM	LM		LM	XC
										◇1				◇		◇1				◇1					◇1
Hereford 7	d																16 40							17 40	
Ledbury	a																16 56							17 56	
	d																16 59							18 01	
Colwall	d																17 05							18 08	
Great Malvern	a																17 10							18 12	
	d															17 00	17 10	17 41						18 13	
Malvern Link	d															17 02	17 13	17 44						18 16	
Worcester Foregate Street 7	a															17 17	17 23	17 52						18 24	
	d				16 34	16 47	17 02								17 16	17 20	17 24	17 53				17 56		18 25	
Worcester Shrub Hill 7	a				16 36		17 04									17 23		17 55							
	d				16 40		17a06									17a24									
Droitwich Spa	d				16 48	16 56									17 25		17 33					18 05		18 34	
Bromsgrove	d																17 43							18 42	
Barnt Green	d																							18 49	
University	d																17 59							18 59	
Hartlebury	d														17 32										
Kidderminster	d			16 53	16 59	17 06						17 27			17 38						18 00	18 17			
Blakedown	d				17 04	17 11						17 32			17 43						18 05				
Hagley	d				17 08	17 15						17 35			17 46						18 09				
Stourbridge Junction 2	d			17 06	17 13	17 19					17 25	17 39			17 50				17 55		18 13	18 26			
Lye	d										17 29								17 59			18 29			
Cradley Heath	d			17 12	17 19	17 24					17 32	17 45			17 56				18 02		18 19	18 32			
Old Hill	d										17 36								18 06			18 36			
Rowley Regis	d			17 17	17 24	17 30					17 40	17 51			18 02				18 10		18 25	18 40			
Langley Green	d										17 43								18 13			18 43			
Birmingham New Street 12	a																18 13							19 12	
	d									18 03										18 33					19 03
Birmingham International ✈	d									18 14															19 14
Coventry	d									18 25															19 25
Smethwick Galton Bridge 7	d			17 23	17 30	17 36					17 46	17 56			18 08				18 16		18 30	18 46			
The Hawthorns	d			17 25	17 32	17 38					17 48	17 58			18 10				18 19		18 33	18 49			
Jewellery Quarter	d			17 29	17 36	17 42					17 52	18 02			18 14				18 23		18 37	18 52			
Birmingham Snow Hill	a			17 32	17 39	17 45					17 55	18 05			18 17				18 26		18 41	18 55			
	d			17 35	17 42	17 47			17 52		17 57	18 07		18 12	18 22				18 27		18 45	18 57			
Birmingham Moor Street	d			17 38	17 45	17 50			17 55		18 00	18 10		18 15	18 25				18 30		18 48	19 00			
Bordesley	d																								
Small Heath	d			17 42	17 49	17 54					18 04	18 14							18 34		18 52	19 04			
Tyseley	d			17 45	17 51	17 56					18 06	18 16							18 36		18 54	19 06			
Acocks Green	d			17 48	17 54						18 09				18 30						18 57				
Olton	d			17 50	17 57						18 12				18 33						19 00				
Solihull	d			17 54	18 01				18 05		18 16			18 25	18 37						19 04				
Widney Manor	d			17 58	18 04						18 19				18 40						19 07				
Dorridge	d			18 02	18a09				18 12		18 23			18 30	18a45						19 11				
Lapworth	d			18 06							18 27			18 34							19 15				
Hatton	d			18 12							18 33			18 40							19 21				
Warwick Parkway	d			18 16					18 23		18 38			18 45											
Warwick	d	18 04		18 19					18 26		18 41			18 49							19 27				
Leamington Spa 8	a	18 08		18 24				18 27	18 30	18 36	18 47			18 53						18 58	19 32				19 37
	d	18 08						18 28	18 30	18 38				18 54						19 00					19 38
Banbury	d	18 26							18 48	18a55				19 12						19a19					19a55
London Marylebone 10 ⊖	a	19 42							20 09					20 40											
Spring Road	d					17 59						18 19							18 39			19 09			
Hall Green	d					18 02						18 22							18 42			19 12			
Yardley Wood	d					18 05						18 25							18 45			19 15			
Shirley	d					18 09						18a28							18 48			19a18			
Whitlocks End	d					18 11													18 51						
Wythall	d					18 14													18 53						
Earlswood (West Midlands)	d					18 16													18 56						
The Lakes	d					18x19													18x58						
Wood End	d					18x21													19x00						
Danzey	d					18x25													19x03						
Henley-in-Arden	d					18 30													19 08						
Wootton Wawen	d					18x33													19x10						
Wilmcote	d					18 38		18 58											19 16						
Stratford-upon-Avon	a					18 45		19 09											19 22						

Table 71

Mondays to Fridays
from 04 October

Hereford, Worcester and Stourbridge - Birmingham - Leamington Spa, Marylebone and Stratford-upon-Avon

		CH	LM	LM	LM	LM	GW	GW		LM	GW	XC	XC	CH	LM	LM	LM	XC		CH	XC	CH	LM	LM	GW
							◇1				1	◇1	◇1	◇				◇1		◇	◇1	◇			
Hereford 7	d									18 48							19 50								
Ledbury	a									19 03							20 07								
	d									19 04							20 18								
Colwall	d									19 10							20 24								
Great Malvern	a									19 15							20 29								
	d							18 51		19 15							20 29								21 15
Malvern Link	d							18 53		19 18							20 32								21 18
Worcester Foregate Street 7	a							19 03		19 27							20 41								21 27
	d					18 46	18 49	19 03		19 27	19 27					19 46	20 42								21 27
Worcester Shrub Hill 7	a						18 52	19 06			19 29														21 30
	d				18 37																			20 52	
Droitwich Spa	d				18 45	18 55				19 36						19 55	20 49							21 00	
Bromsgrove	d									19 46							20 59								
Barnt Green	d																								
University	d									20 09							21 16								
Hartlebury	d					19 02																			
Kidderminster	d		18 38		18 55	19 10										20 10								21 10	
Blakedown	d		18 43		19 00	19 15										20 15								21 15	
Hagley	d		18 46		19 04	19 19										20 19								21 19	
Stourbridge Junction 2	d		18 50		19 09	19 25									19 55	20 25							20 55	21 25	
Lye	d		18 54			19 29									19 59	20 29							20 59	21 29	
Cradley Heath	d		18 57		19 15	19 32									20 02	20 32							21 02	21 32	
Old Hill	d		19 01			19 36									20 06	20 36							21 06	21 36	
Rowley Regis	d		19 05		19 21	19 40									20 10	20 40							21 10	21 40	
Langley Green	d		19 08			19 43									20 13	20 43							21 13	21 43	
Birmingham New Street 12	a									20 20							21 23								
	d											19 33	20 03					20 33			21 03				
Birmingham International ✈	d												20 14								21 14				
Coventry	d												20 25								21 25				
Smethwick Galton Bridge 7	d		19 11		19 26	19 46									20 16	20 46							21 16	21 46	
The Hawthorns	d		19 14		19 29	19 48									20 18	20 48							21 18	21 48	
Jewellery Quarter	d		19 18		19 33	19 52									20 22	20 52							21 22	21 52	
Birmingham Snow Hill	a		19 21		19 36	19 55									20 25	20 55							21 25	21 55	
	d	19 12	19 22	19 27	19 37	19 57								20 12	20 27	20 57						21 15	21 27	21 57	
Birmingham Moor Street	d	19 15	19 25	19 30	19a39	20 00								20 15	20 30	21 00						21 18	21 30	22 00	
Bordesley	d																								
Small Heath	d			19 34		20 04									20 34	21 04							21 34	22 04	
Tyseley	d			19 36		20 06									20 36	21 06							21 36	22 06	
Acocks Green	d		19 30			20 09										21 09								22 09	
Olton	d		19 33			20 12										21 12								22 12	
Solihull	d	19 25	19 37			20 16								20 25		21 16						21 27		22 16	
Widney Manor	d	19 28	19 40			20 19								20 28		21 19								22 19	
Dorridge	d	19 32	19a47			20a24								20 32		21a24						21 33		22a24	
Lapworth	d	19 36												20 36								21 37			
Hatton	d	19 42												20 42								21 42			
Warwick Parkway	d	19 47												20 47								21 47			
Warwick	d	19 50												20 50								21 51			
Leamington Spa 8	a	19 54										20 04	20 36	20 54				20 58			21 36	21 54			
	d	19 54										20 05	20 38	20 54				21 00		21 07	21 38	21 55			
Banbury	d	20 12										20a22	20a55	21 12				21a19			21a55	22 15			
London Marylebone 10 ⊖	a	21 35												22 35								23 37			
Spring Road	d			19 39											20 39								21 39		
Hall Green	d			19 42											20 42								21 42		
Yardley Wood	d			19 45											20 45								21 45		
Shirley	d			19 48											20 48								21a48		
Whitlocks End	d			19 51											20 51										
Wythall	d			19 53											20 53										
Earlswood (West Midlands)	d			19 56											20 56										
The Lakes	d			19x58											20x58										
Wood End	d			20x00											21x00										
Danzey	d			20x03											21x03										
Henley-in-Arden	d			20 08											21 08										
Wootton Wawen	d			20x10											21x10										
Wilmcote	d			20 16											21 16					21 34					
Stratford-upon-Avon	a			20 23											21 23					21 48					

Table 71

Mondays to Fridays
from 04 October

Hereford, Worcester and Stourbridge - Birmingham - Leamington Spa, Marylebone and Stratford-upon-Avon

Station		LM	LM	CH	XC	CH	LM	LM	LM	LM	CH	CH
					◇■							
Hereford	d	20 52	21 28							22 55		
Ledbury	a	21 09	21 44							23 11		
	d	21 13	21 45							23 13		
Colwall	d	21 20	21 51							23 19		
Great Malvern	a	21 24	21 56							23 24		
	d	21 25	21 57							23 24		
Malvern Link	d	21 28	22 00							23 27		
Worcester Foregate Street	a	21 36	22 09							23 34		
	d	21 37	22 10						22 17	23 34		
Worcester Shrub Hill	a	21 39							22 19	23 39		
	d							21 52	22 27			
Droitwich Spa	d		22 19					22 00	22 35			
Bromsgrove	d		22 29									
Barnt Green	d											
University	d		22 45									
Hartlebury	d											
Kidderminster	d							22 10	22 45			
Blakedown	d							22 15				
Hagley	d							22 19				
Stourbridge Junction	d						21 55	22 25	22 55			
Lye	d						21 59	22 29	22 59			
Cradley Heath	d						22 02	22 32	23 02			
Old Hill	d						22 06	22 36	23 06			
Rowley Regis	d						22 10	22 40	23 10			
Langley Green	d						22 13	22 43	23 13			
Birmingham New Street	a		22 52									
	d				22 03							
Birmingham International	d				22 14							
Coventry	d				22 25							
Smethwick Galton Bridge	d						22 16	22 46	23 16			
The Hawthorns	d						22 18	22 48	23 18			
Jewellery Quarter	d						22 22	22 52	23 22			
Birmingham Snow Hill	a						22 25	22 55	23 24			
	d					22 15	22 27	22 57	23 25			23 30
Birmingham Moor Street	d					22 18	22 30	23 00	23 28			23 33
Bordesley	d											
Small Heath	d						22 34	23 04	23 32			
Tyseley	d					22 23	22 36	23 06	23 34			23 38
Acocks Green	d					22 25		23 09				23 40
Olton	d					22 28		23 12				23 43
Solihull	d					22 32		23 16				23 47
Widney Manor	d					22 35		23 19				23 50
Dorridge	d					22 39		23a24				23 54
Lapworth	d					22 43						23 58
Hatton	d					22 49						00 04
Warwick Parkway	d					22 53						00 08
Warwick	d					22 56					23 21	00 11
Leamington Spa	a				22 37	23 00					23 24	00 14
	d			22 25	22 38	23 01					23 25	00 15
Banbury	d				22a55	23a26					23a44	00a41
London Marylebone	a											
Spring Road	d						22 39		23 37			
Hall Green	d						22 42		23 40			
Yardley Wood	d						22 45		23 43			
Shirley	d						22a48		23a46			
Whitlocks End	d											
Wythall	d											
Earlswood (West Midlands)	d											
The Lakes	d											
Wood End	d											
Danzey	d											
Henley-in-Arden	d											
Wootton Wawen	d											
Wilmcote	d											
Stratford-upon-Avon	a			22 58								

Table 71

Saturdays
until 02 October

Hereford, Worcester and Stourbridge - Birmingham - Leamington Spa, Marylebone and Stratford-upon-Avon

Station		CH	XC	CH	XC	CH	LM	GW	LM	XC	CH	LM	LM	GW	XC	LM	LM	CH	CH	LM	CH	XC	CH
			◇■	◇	◇■	◇		◇■		◇■	◇			◇■	◇■			◇				■	◇
Hereford	d																						
Ledbury	a																						
	d																						
Colwall	d																						
Great Malvern	a																						
	d							05 39	06 21					06 35									
Malvern Link	d							05 42	06 24					06 39									
Worcester Foregate Street	a							05 51	06 31					06 48									
	d							05 52	06 33					06 50									
Worcester Shrub Hill	a							05 55						06 53									
	d						05 44						06 25			07 33				07 01			
Droitwich Spa	d						05 52		06 42				06 33			07 40				07 09			
Bromsgrove	d								06 51							07 50							
Barnt Green	d																						
University	d								07 09							08 09							
Hartlebury	d												06 40							07 16			
Kidderminster	d						06 02				06 37		06 46						07 14	07 22			
Blakedown	d						06 07						06 51							07 27			
Hagley	d						06 11						06 54							07 30			
Stourbridge Junction	d						06 15				06 45		07 02						07 22	07 35			
Lye	d						06 19						07 06							07 39			
Cradley Heath	d						06 22				06 50		07 09						07 27	07 42			
Old Hill	d						06 26						07 13							07 46			
Rowley Regis	d						06 30				06 56		07 17						07 33	07 50			
Langley Green	d						06 33						07 20							07 53			
Birmingham New Street	a								07 16							08 16							
	d		06 03		06 33					07 03					07 33							08 03	
Birmingham International	d		06 14							07 15												08 14	
Coventry	d		06 25							07 25												08 25	
Smethwick Galton Bridge	d						06 36				07 02		07 23						07 39	07 56			
The Hawthorns	d						06 38				07 04		07 25						07 41	07 58			
Jewellery Quarter	d						06 42						07 29							08 02			
Birmingham Snow Hill	a						06 45				07 10		07 32						07 48	08 05			
	d	23p30		06 12		06 36	06 51				07 12	07 20	07 37				07 47		07 52	08 07			08 12
Birmingham Moor Street	d	23p33		06 15		06 39	06 54				07 15	07 23	07 40				07 50		07 55	08 10			08 15
Bordesley	d																						
Small Heath	d						06 58					07 27								08 14			
Tyseley	d	23p38					07 00					07 29								08 16			
Acocks Green	d	23p40					07 03						07 45										
Olton	d	23p43					07 06						07 48										
Solihull	d	23p47		06 25		06 49	07 10				07 25		07 52						08 05				08 25
Widney Manor	d	23p50					07 13						07 55										08 28
Dorridge	d	23p54		06 31		06 54	07a18				07 31		08a01						08 11				08 32
Lapworth	d	23p58									07 35												08 36
Hatton	d	00 04									07 41							07 57					08 42
Warwick Parkway	d	00 08		06 41		07 05					07 45								08 22				08 46
Warwick	d	00 11		06 45		07 08					07 48							08 04	08 25				08 49
Leamington Spa	a	00 14	06 36	06 49	06 58	07 12				07 36	07 52				07 58			08 08	08 30			08 36	08 51
	d	00 15	06 38	06 49	07 00	07 13				07 38	07 53				08 00			08 09	08 30		08 30	08 38	08 53
Banbury	d	00a38	06a55	07 07	07a19	07 33				07a55	08 13				08a19			08 29	08 49			08a55	09 13
London Marylebone	a			08 29		08 49					09 30							09 55	10 01				10 34
Spring Road	d											07 32					07 56			08 19			
Hall Green	d											07 35					07 59			08 22			
Yardley Wood	d											07 38					08 02			08 25			
Shirley	d											07 41					08 11			08a28			
Whitlocks End	d											07 44					08 14						
Wythall	d											07 46					08 16						
Earlswood (West Midlands)	d											07 49					08 19						
The Lakes	d											07x51					08x21						
Wood End	d											07x53					08x23						
Danzey	d											07x56					08x26						
Henley-in-Arden	d											08 01					08 31						
Wootton Wawen	d											08x04					08x34						
Wilmcote	d											08 09					08 40				08 57		
Stratford-upon-Avon	a											08 17					08 46				09 09		

Table 71

Saturdays until 02 October

Hereford, Worcester and Stourbridge - Birmingham - Leamington Spa, Marylebone and Stratford-upon-Avon

		LM	LM	LM	LM	GW	LM	XC	CH	LM	LM	XC	WS	CH	LM	LM	LM	XC	LM	CH	LM	GW	LM
						◇1		◇1	◇			◇1	◇1	◇				◇1		◇		◇1	
Hereford 7	d					07 10	07 40																
Ledbury	a					07 28	07 57																
	d					07 30	07 58																
Colwall	d					07 38	08 04																
Great Malvern	a					07 42	08 09																
	d				07 32	07 43	08 10															08 43	
Malvern Link	d				07 35	07 46	08 13															08 46	
Worcester Foregate Street 7	a				07 43	07 57	08 22															08 57	
	d				07 46	07 57	08 22														08 56	08 57	
Worcester Shrub Hill 7	a					08 01																09 01	
	d														08 15								
Droitwich Spa	d				07 55		08 31								08 23						09 05		
Bromsgrove	d						08 40																
Barnt Green	d																						
University	d						08 59																
Hartlebury	d														08 30								
Kidderminster	d		07 46		08 06				08 13						08 36					09 03	09 16		09 26
Blakedown	d		07 51		08 11										08 41					09 08			09 31
Hagley	d		07 54		08 14										08 44					09 12			09 34
Stourbridge Junction 2	d		07 59	08 05	08 19				08 26		08 35				08 49	08 55	09 09			09 15	09 25		09 39
Lye	d			08 09							08 39					08 59					09 29		
Cradley Heath	d		08 04	08 12	08 24				08 32		08 42				08 54	09 02	09 14			09 21	09 32		09 44
Old Hill	d			08 16							08 46					09 06					09 36		
Rowley Regis	d		08 10	08 20	08 30				08 37		08 50				09 00	09 10	09 20			09 27	09 40		09 50
Langley Green	d			08 23							08 53					09 13					09 43		
Birmingham New Street 12	a						09 11																
	d							08 33				09 03						09 33					
Birmingham International ✈	d											09 14											
Coventry	d											09 25											
Smethwick Galton Bridge 7	d		08 16	08 26	08 36				08 43		08 56				09 06	09 16	09 26			09 33	09 46		09 56
The Hawthorns	d		08 18	08 28	08 38				08 45		08 58				09 08	09 18	09 28			09 35	09 48		09 58
Jewellery Quarter	d		08 22	08 32	08 42						09 02				09 12	09 22	09 32				09 52		10 02
Birmingham Snow Hill	a		08 25	08 35	08 45				08 51		09 05				09 15	09 25	09 35			09 42	09 55		10 05
	d	08 17	08 27	08 37	08 47				08 52	08 57	09 07			09 12	09 17	09 27	09 37		09 47	09 52	09 57		10 07
Birmingham Moor Street	d	08 20	08 30	08 40	08 50				08 55	09 00	09 10			09 15	09 20	09 30	09 40		09 50	09 55	10 00		10 10
Bordesley	d																						
Small Heath	d			08 44							09 14						09 44						10 14
Tyseley	d			08 46							09 16						09 46						10 16
Acocks Green	d	08 25		08 49						09 05					09 25		09 49				10 05		
Olton	d	08 28		08 52						09 08					09 28		09 52				10 08		
Solihull	d	08 32		08 56					09 05	09 12				09 25	09 32		09 56			10 05	10 12		
Widney Manor	d	08 35		08 59						09 15					09 35		09 59				10 15		
Dorridge	d	08a41		09a04					09 11	09a21				09 31	09a41		10a04			10 11	10a22		
Lapworth	d													09 35									
Hatton	d																						
Warwick Parkway	d								09 22					09 44						10 22			
Warwick	d								09 25					09 47						10 25			
Leamington Spa 8	a							08 58	09 29			09 36	09 49	09 52				09 58		10 29			
	d							09 00	09 30			09 38	09 49	09 53				10 00		10 30			
Banbury	d							09a19	09 49			09a55	10 08	10 13				10a19		10 49			
London Marylebone 10 ⊖	a								11 02				11 15	11 32						11 59			
Spring Road	d		08 36		08 56						09 19					09 36			09 56				10 19
Hall Green	d		08 39		08 59						09 22					09 39			09 59				10 22
Yardley Wood	d		08 42		09 02						09 25					09 42			10 02				10 25
Shirley	d		08 45		09 07						09a28					09 45			10 07				10a28
Whitlocks End	d				09 10														10 10				
Wythall	d		08 49		09 12											09 49			10 12				
Earlswood (West Midlands)	d				09 15														10 15				
The Lakes	d				09x17														10x17				
Wood End	d				09x19														10x19				
Danzey	d				09x22														10x22				
Henley-in-Arden	d		08 59		09 27											09 59			10 27				
Wootton Wawen	d				09x29														10x29				
Wilmcote	d				09 35														10 35				
Stratford-upon-Avon	a		09 11		09 42											10 11			10 42				

Table 71

Saturdays until 02 October

Hereford, Worcester and Stourbridge - Birmingham - Leamington Spa, Marylebone and Stratford-upon-Avon

		LM	XC	CH	WS	CH	LM	LM	LM	LM	LM	GW	XC	CH	LM	LM	XC	CH	LM	LM	LM	LM
			◇1	◇	◇1	◇						◇1	◇1	◇			◇1	◇				
Hereford 7	d							08 40												09 36	10 40	
Ledbury	a							08 57												09 52	10 56	
	d							08 58												09 58	10 58	
Colwall	d							09 04												10 04	11 04	
Great Malvern	a							09 09												10 09	11 09	
	d						09 00	09 10				09 43								10 10	11 10	
Malvern Link	d						09 03	09 13				09 46								10 13	11 13	
Worcester Foregate Street 7	a						09 11	09 22				09 55								10 22	11 22	
	d						09 16	09 22				09 57							10 16	10 22	11 22	
Worcester Shrub Hill 7	a											09 59										
	d	09 56									09 47											
Droitwich Spa	d	10 04					09 25	09 31			09 55								10 25	10 33	11 33	
Bromsgrove	d	10 14						09 40												10 42	11 42	
Barnt Green	d																					
University	d							09 59												10 59	11 59	
Hartlebury	d																					
Kidderminster	d						09 36			09 56	10 06					10 26			10 36			
Blakedown	d						09 41				10 11								10 41			
Hagley	d						09 44				10 14								10 44			
Stourbridge Junction 2	d						09 49		09 55	10 09	10 19				10 25	10 39			10 49			10 55
Lye	d								09 59						10 29							10 59
Cradley Heath	d						09 54		10 02	10 14	10 24				10 32	10 44			10 54			11 02
Old Hill	d								10 06						10 36							11 06
Rowley Regis	d						10 00		10 10	10 20	10 30				10 40	10 50			11 00			11 10
Langley Green	d								10 13						10 43							11 13
Birmingham New Street 12	a	10 41						10 11												11 11	12 11	
	d		10 03										10 33				11 03					
Birmingham International ✈	d		10 14														11 14					
Coventry	d		10 25														11 25					
Smethwick Galton Bridge 7	d						10 06		10 16	10 26	10 36				10 46	10 56			11 06			11 16
The Hawthorns	d						10 08		10 18	10 28	10 38				10 48	10 58			11 08			11 18
Jewellery Quarter	d						10 12		10 22	10 32	10 42				10 52	11 02			11 12			11 22
Birmingham Snow Hill	a						10 15		10 25	10 35	10 45				10 55	11 05			11 15			11 25
	d					10 12	10 17		10 27	10 37	10 47			10 52	10 57	11 07		11 12	11 17			11 27
Birmingham Moor Street	d					10 15	10 20		10 30	10 40	10 50			10 55	11 00	11 10		11 15	11 20			11 30
Bordesley	d																					
Small Heath	d									10 44						11 14						
Tyseley	d									10 46						11 16						
Acocks Green	d						10 25			10 49					11 05				11 25			
Olton	d						10 28			10 52					11 08				11 28			
Solihull	d					10 25	10 32			10 56				11 05	11 12			11 25	11 32			
Widney Manor	d						10 35			10 59					11 15				11 35			
Dorridge	d					10 31	10a41			11a04				11 11	11a22			11 31	11a41			
Lapworth	d					10 35																
Hatton	d					10 41																
Warwick Parkway	d					10 45								11 22				11 41				
Warwick	d					10 48								11 25				11 45				
Leamington Spa 8	a		10 36			10 52							10 58	11 29			11 36	11 49				
	d		10 38	10 38	10 49	10 53							11 00	11 30			11 38	11 49				
Banbury	d		10a55		11 08	11 13							11a19	11 49			11a55	12 07				
London Marylebone 10 ⊖	a				12 15	12 30								13 01				13 26				
Spring Road	d								10 36		10 56					11 19						11 36
Hall Green	d								10 39		10 59					11 22						11 39
Yardley Wood	d								10 42		11 02					11 25						11 42
Shirley	d								10 45		11 12					11a28						11 45
Whitlocks End	d										11 15											
Wythall	d								10 49		11 17											11 49
Earlswood (West Midlands)	d										11 20											
The Lakes	d										11x22											
Wood End	d										11x24											
Danzey	d										11x27											
Henley-in-Arden	d								10 59		11 32											11 59
Wootton Wawen	d										11x34											
Wilmcote	d										11 40											
Stratford-upon-Avon	a			11 11					11 15		11 47											12 11

Table 71

Saturdays
until 02 October

Hereford, Worcester and Stourbridge - Birmingham - Leamington Spa, Marylebone and Stratford-upon-Avon

		LM	LM	XC ◇1	CH	LM	LM	XC ◇1	CH ◇	CH	GW	LM	LM	LM	LM	XC ◇1	GW	CH	LM	LM	XC ◇1	WS ◇1	CH ◇	LM
Hereford 7	d																							
Ledbury	a																							
	d																							
Colwall	d																							
Great Malvern	a																							
	d										10 51				11 35									
Malvern Link	d										10 53				11 37									
Worcester Foregate Street 7	a										11 02				11 45									
	d										11 02				11 46		12 40							12 16
Worcester Shrub Hill 7	a										11 06						12 42							
	d		10 47									11 17												
Droitwich Spa	d		10 55									11 25			11 55									12 25
Bromsgrove	d																							
Barnt Green	d																							
University	d																							
Hartlebury	d																							
Kidderminster	d	10 56	11 06				11 26					11 36		11 56	12 06					12 26				12 36
Blakedown	d		11 11									11 41			12 11									12 41
Hagley	d		11 14									11 44			12 14									12 44
Stourbridge Junction 2	d	11 09	11 19			11 25	11 39					11 49	11 55	12 09	12 19				12 25	12 39				12 49
Lye	d					11 29							11 59						12 29					
Cradley Heath	d	11 14	11 24			11 32	11 44					11 54	12 02	12 14	12 24				12 32	12 44				12 54
Old Hill	d					11 36							12 06						12 36					
Rowley Regis	d	11 20	11 30			11 40	11 50					12 00	12 10	12 20	12 30				12 40	12 50				13 00
Langley Green	d					11 43							12 13						12 43					
Birmingham New Street 12	a																							
	d			11 33				12 03								12 33					13 03			
Birmingham International ✈	d							12 14													13 15			
Coventry	d							12 25													13 25			
Smethwick Galton Bridge 7	d	11 26	11 36			11 46	11 56					12 06	12 16	12 26	12 36				12 46	12 56				13 06
The Hawthorns	d	11 28	11 38			11 48	11 58					12 08	12 18	12 28	12 38				12 48	12 58				13 08
Jewellery Quarter	d	11 32	11 42			11 52	12 02					12 12	12 22	12 32	12 42				12 52	13 02				13 12
Birmingham Snow Hill	a	11 35	11 45			11 55	12 05					12 15	12 25	12 35	12 45				12 55	13 05				13 15
	d	11 37	11 47		11 52	11 57	12 07			12 12		12 17	12 27	12 37	12 47			12 52	12 57	13 07			13 12	13 17
Birmingham Moor Street	d	11 40	11 50		11 55	12 00	12 10			12 15		12 20	12 30	12 40	12 50			12 55	13 00	13 10			13 15	13 20
Bordesley	d																							
Small Heath	d	11 44					12 14							12 44						13 14				
Tyseley	d	11 46					12 16							12 46						13 16				
Acocks Green	d	11 49				12 05						12 25		12 49					13 05					13 25
Olton	d	11 52				12 08						12 28		12 52					13 08					13 28
Solihull	d	11 56			12 05	12 12				12 25		12 32		12 56				13 05	13 12				13 25	13 32
Widney Manor	d	11 59				12 15						12 35		12 59					13 15					13 35
Dorridge	d	12a04			12 11	12a22				12 31		12a41		13a04				13 11	13a21				13 31	13a41
Lapworth	d									12 35														
Hatton	d									12 41														
Warwick Parkway	d				12 22					12 45								13 22					13 41	
Warwick	d				12 25					12 48								13 25					13 45	
Leamington Spa 8	a			11 58	12 29			12 36	12 36	12 51						13 00		13 29			13 36	13 49	13 52	
	d			12 00	12 30			12 38	12 38	12 53						13 02		13 30			13 38	13 49	13 53	
Banbury	d			12a19	12 49			12a55		13 13						13a21		13 49			13a55	14 08	14 13	
London Marylebone 10 ⊖	a				14 02					14 32								15 01				15 15	15 31	
Spring Road	d		11 56				12 19						12 36		12 56					13 19				
Hall Green	d		11 59				12 22						12 39		12 59					13 22				
Yardley Wood	d		12 02				12 25						12 42		13 02					13 25				
Shirley	d		12 07				12a28						12 45		13 10					13a28				
Whitlocks End	d		12 10												13 13									
Wythall	d		12 12										12 49		13 15									
Earlswood (West Midlands)	d		12 15												13 18									
The Lakes	d		12x17												13x20									
Wood End	d		12x19												13x22									
Danzey	d		12x22												13x25									
Henley-in-Arden	d		12 27										12 59		13 30									
Wootton Wawen	d		12x29												13x32									
Wilmcote	d		12 35						13 03						13 38									
Stratford-upon-Avon	a		12 42						13 13				13 17		13 45									

Table 71

Saturdays
until 02 October

Hereford, Worcester and Stourbridge - Birmingham - Leamington Spa, Marylebone and Stratford-upon-Avon

		LM	LM	LM	LM	GW ◇1	LM	XC ◇1	CH ◇	LM	LM	XC ◇1	CH	LM	LM	LM	LM	XC ◇1	CH ◇	LM	LM	CH
Hereford 7	d	11 40				12 13	12 40															
Ledbury	a	11 57				12 30	12 57															
	d	11 58				12 31	12 58															
Colwall	d	12 04				12 39	13 04															
Great Malvern	a	12 09				12 43	13 09															
	d	12 10				12 43	13 10										13 35					
Malvern Link	d	12 13				12 46	13 13										13 37					
Worcester Foregate Street 7	a	12 22				12 57	13 22										13 45					
	d	12 22			12 46	12 57	13 22										13 46					
Worcester Shrub Hill 7	a					13 02																
	d													13 17								
Droitwich Spa	d	12 33			12 55		13 33							13 25			13 55					
Bromsgrove	d	12 42					13 42															
Barnt Green	d																					
University	d	12 59					13 59															
Hartlebury	d																					
Kidderminster	d			12 56	13 06						13 26			13 36		13 56	14 06				14 26	
Blakedown	d				13 11									13 41			14 11					
Hagley	d				13 14									13 44			14 14					
Stourbridge Junction 2	d		12 55	13 09	13 19					13 25	13 39			13 49	13 55	14 09	14 19			14 25	14 39	
Lye	d		12 59							13 29					13 59					14 29		
Cradley Heath	d		13 02	13 14	13 24					13 32	13 44			13 54	14 02	14 14	14 24			14 32	14 44	
Old Hill	d		13 06							13 36					14 06					14 36		
Rowley Regis	d		13 10	13 20	13 30					13 40	13 50			14 00	14 10	14 20	14 30			14 40	14 50	
Langley Green	d		13 13							13 43					14 13					14 43		
Birmingham New Street 12	a	13 11					14 11															
	d							13 33				14 03						14 33				
Birmingham International ✈	d											14 14										
Coventry	d											14 25										
Smethwick Galton Bridge 7	d		13 16	13 26	13 36					13 46	13 56			14 06	14 16	14 26	14 36			14 46	14 56	
The Hawthorns	d		13 18	13 28	13 38					13 48	13 58			14 08	14 18	14 28	14 38			14 48	14 58	
Jewellery Quarter	d		13 22	13 32	13 42					13 52	14 02			14 12	14 22	14 32	14 42			14 52	15 02	
Birmingham Snow Hill	a		13 25	13 35	13 45					13 55	14 05			14 15	14 25	14 35	14 45			14 55	15 05	
	d		13 27	13 37	13 47				13 52	13 57	14 07		14 12	14 17	14 27	14 37	14 47		14 52	14 57	15 07	
Birmingham Moor Street	d		13 30	13 40	13 50				13 55	14 00	14 10		14 15	14 20	14 30	14 40	14 50		14 55	15 00	15 10	
Bordesley	d																					
Small Heath	d			13 44							14 14					14 44					15 14	
Tyseley	d			13 46							14 16					14 46					15 16	
Acocks Green	d			13 49						14 05				14 25		14 49				15 05		
Olton	d			13 52						14 08				14 28		14 52				15 08		
Solihull	d			13 56					14 05	14 12			14 25	14 32		14 56			15 05	15 12		
Widney Manor	d			13 59						14 15				14 35		14 59				15 15		
Dorridge	d			14a04					14 11	14a22			14 31	14a41		15a04			15 11	15a21		
Lapworth	d												14 35									
Hatton	d												14 41									
Warwick Parkway	d								14 22				14 45						15 22			
Warwick	d								14 25				14 48						15 25			
Leamington Spa 8	a							13 58	14 29			14 36	14 51					14 58	15 29			15 33
	d							14 00	14 30			14 38	14 53					15 00	15 30			15 34
Banbury	d							14a19	14 49			14a55	15 13					15a20	15 49			
London Marylebone 10 ⊖	a								16 01				16 37						16 59			
Spring Road	d		13 36		13 56						14 19				14 36		14 56				15 19	
Hall Green	d		13 39		13 59						14 22				14 39		14 59				15 22	
Yardley Wood	d		13 42		14 02						14 25				14 42		15 02				15 25	
Shirley	d		13 45		14 07						14a28				14 45		15 10				15a28	
Whitlocks End	d				14 10												15 13					
Wythall	d		13 49		14 12										14 49		15 15					
Earlswood (West Midlands)	d				14 15												15 18					
The Lakes	d				14x17												15x20					
Wood End	d				14x19												15x22					
Danzey	d				14x22												15x25					
Henley-in-Arden	d		13 59		14 27										14 59		15 30					
Wootton Wawen	d				14x29												15x32					
Wilmcote	d				14 35												15 38					16 00
Stratford-upon-Avon	a		14 11		14 42										15 11		15 45					16 12

Table 71

Saturdays until 02 October

Hereford, Worcester and Stourbridge - Birmingham - Leamington Spa, Marylebone and Stratford-upon-Avon

		XC	CH	LM	LM	LM	LM	LM	GW	XC	GW	CH	LM	LM	LM	XC	WS	CH	LM	LM	LM	LM	LM	GW
		◇1							◇1	◇1		◇				◇1	◇1							◇1
Hereford [7]	d				13 40															14 40				15 10
Ledbury	a				13 57															14 56				15 27
	d				13 58															14 57				15 29
Colwall	d				14 04															15 03				15 36
Great Malvern	a				14 09															15 08				15 41
	d				14 10				14 32		14 51									15 10			15 30	15 42
Malvern Link	d				14 13				14 35		14 53									15 13			15 32	15 45
Worcester Foregate Street [7]	a				14 22				14 55		15 02									15 22			15 40	15 55
	d			14 16	14 22				14 57		15 02								15 16	15 22			15 46	15 56
Worcester Shrub Hill [7]	a										15 06													15 59
	d							14 43							15 54									
Droitwich Spa	d			14 25	14 33			14 55							16 03				15 25	15 33			15 55	
Bromsgrove	d				14 42										16 13					15 42				
Barnt Green	d																							
University	d				14 59															15 59				
Hartlebury	d																							
Kidderminster	d			14 36			14 56	15 06						15 26					15 36			15 56	16 06	
Blakedown	d			14 41				15 11						15 31					15 41				16 11	
Hagley	d			14 44				15 14						15 34					15 44				16 14	
Stourbridge Junction [2]	d			14 49		14 55	15 09	15 19					15 25	15 39					15 49		15 55	16 09	16 19	
Lye	d					14 59							15 29								15 59			
Cradley Heath	d			14 54		15 02	15 14	15 24					15 32	15 44					15 54		16 02	16 14	16 24	
Old Hill	d					15 06							15 36								16 06			
Rowley Regis	d			15 00		15 10	15 20	15 30					15 40	15 50					16 00		16 10	16 20	16 30	
Langley Green	d					15 13							15 43								16 13			
Birmingham New Street [12]	a				15 11										16 45					16 11				
	d	15 03								15 33						16 03								
Birmingham International ✈	d	15 14														16 14								
Coventry	d	15 25														16 25								
Smethwick Galton Bridge [7]	d			15 06		15 16	15 26	15 36					15 46	15 56					16 06		16 16	16 26	16 36	
The Hawthorns	d			15 08		15 18	15 28	15 38					15 48	15 58					16 08		16 18	16 28	16 38	
Jewellery Quarter	d			15 12		15 22	15 32	15 42					15 52	16 02					16 12		16 22	16 32	16 42	
Birmingham Snow Hill	a			15 15		15 25	15 35	15 45					15 55	16 05					16 15		16 25	16 35	16 45	
	d		15 12	15 17		15 27	15 37	15 47				15 52	15 57	16 07				16 12	16 17		16 27	16 37	16 47	
Birmingham Moor Street	d		15 15	15 20		15 30	15 40	15 50				15 55	16 00	16 10				16 15	16 20		16 30	16 40	16 50	
Bordesley	d																							
Small Heath	d						15 44							16 14								16 44	16 54	
Tyseley	d						15 46							16 16							16 34	16 46	16 56	
Acocks Green	d			15 25			15 49						16 05						16 25			16 49		
Olton	d			15 28			15 52						16 08						16 28			16 52		
Solihull	d		15 25	15 32			15 56					16 05	16 12					16 25	16 32			16 56		
Widney Manor	d			15 35			15 59						16 15						16 35			16 59		
Dorridge	d		15 31	15a41			16a04					16 11	16a21					16 31	16a41			17a04		
Lapworth	d																	16 35						
Hatton	d																	16 41						
Warwick Parkway	d		15 41									16 22						16 45						
Warwick	d		15 45									16 25						16 48						
Leamington Spa [8]	a	15 36	15 49							16 00		16 29				16 36	16 49	16 52						
	d	15 38	15 49							16 02		16 30				16 38	16 49	16 53						
Banbury	d	15a55	16 07							16a20		16 49				16a55	17 08	17 13						
London Marylebone [10] ⊖	a		17 29									18 01					18 15	18 32						
Spring Road	d					15 36		15 56						16 19							16 37		16 59	
Hall Green	d					15 39		15 59						16 22							16 40		17 02	
Yardley Wood	d					15 42		16 02						16 25							16 43		17 05	
Shirley	d					15 45		16 07						16a28							16 46		17 10	
Whitlocks End	d							16 10															17 13	
Wythall	d					15 49		16 12													16 50		17 15	
Earlswood (West Midlands)	d							16 15															17 18	
The Lakes	d							16x17															17x20	
Wood End	d							16x19															17x22	
Danzey	d							16x22															17x25	
Henley-in-Arden	d					15 59		16 27													17 00		17 30	
Wootton Wawen	d							16x29															17x32	
Wilmcote	d							16 35															17 38	
Stratford-upon-Avon	a					16 15		16 42													17 12		17 45	

Table 71

Saturdays until 02 October

Hereford, Worcester and Stourbridge - Birmingham - Leamington Spa, Marylebone and Stratford-upon-Avon

		XC	CH	LM	LM	XC	CH	LM	LM	LM	LM	LM	GW	GW	LM	XC	CH	CH	LM	LM	XC	CH	CH
		◇1	◇			◇1							◇1 A			◇1					◇1		◇
Hereford [7]	d								15 40						16 40								
Ledbury	a								15 57						16 57								
	d								15 58						16 58								
Colwall	d								16 04						17 04								
Great Malvern	a								16 09						17 09								
	d								16 10				16 32	16 51	17 10								
Malvern Link	d								16 13				16 35	16 53	17 13								
Worcester Foregate Street [7]	a								16 22				16 56	17 04	17 22								
	d							16 15	16 22				16 57	17 04	17 22								
Worcester Shrub Hill [7]	a												17 00	17 07									
	d											16 47											
Droitwich Spa	d							16 24	16 33			16 55			17 33								
Bromsgrove	d								16 42						17 42								
Barnt Green	d																						
University	d								16 59						17 59								
Hartlebury	d							16 31															
Kidderminster	d				16 26			16 37			16 56	17 06								17 26			
Blakedown	d				16 31			16 42				17 11								17 31			
Hagley	d				16 34			16 45				17 14								17 34			
Stourbridge Junction [2]	d			16 25	16 39			16 49		16 55	17 09	17 19							17 25	17 39			
Lye	d			16 29						16 59									17 29				
Cradley Heath	d			16 32	16 44			16 54		17 02	17 14	17 24							17 32	17 44			
Old Hill	d			16 36						17 06									17 36				
Rowley Regis	d			16 40	16 50			17 00		17 10	17 20	17 30							17 40	17 50			
Langley Green	d			16 43						17 13									17 43				
Birmingham New Street [12]	a								17 11						18 11								
	d	16 33				17 03										17 33					18 03		
Birmingham International ✈	d					17 14															18 14		
Coventry	d					17 25															18 25		
Smethwick Galton Bridge [7]	d			16 46	16 56			17 06		17 16	17 26	17 36							17 46	17 56			
The Hawthorns	d			16 48	16 58			17 08		17 18	17 28	17 38							17 48	17 58			
Jewellery Quarter	d			16 52	17 02			17 12		17 22	17 32	17 42							17 52	18 02			
Birmingham Snow Hill	a			16 55	17 05			17 16		17 25	17 35	17 45							17 55	18 05			
	d		16 52	16 57	17 07		17 12	17 17		17 27	17 37	17 47						17 52	17 57	18 07			18 12
Birmingham Moor Street	d		16 55	17 00	17 10		17 15	17 20		17 30	17 40	17 50						17 55	18 00	18 10			18 15
Bordesley	d																						
Small Heath	d				17 14						17 44	17 54								18 14			
Tyseley	d			17 04	17 16					17 34	17 46	17 56								18 16			
Acocks Green	d			17 07				17 25			17 49								18 05				
Olton	d			17 10				17 28			17 52								18 08				
Solihull	d		17 05	17 14			17 25	17 32			17 56							18 05	18 12				18 25
Widney Manor	d			17 17				17 35			17 59								18 15				18 28
Dorridge	d		17 11	17a22			17 31	17a41			18a04							18 11	18a22				18 32
Lapworth	d						17 35																18 36
Hatton	d						17 41																18 42
Warwick Parkway	d		17 22				17 45											18 22					18 46
Warwick	d		17 25				17 48										18 02	18 25					18 49
Leamington Spa [8]	a	16 59	17 29			17 36	17 52									17 58	18 05	18 29			18 36	18 37	18 53
	d	17 00	17 30			17 38	17 53									18 00	18 06	18 30			18 38	18 38	18 53
Banbury	d	17a19	17 49			17a55	18 13									18a19	18 24	18 49			18a55		19 13
London Marylebone [10] ⊖	a		19 02				19 30										19 37	20 02					20 37
Spring Road	d				17 19					17 37		17 59								18 19			
Hall Green	d				17 22					17 40		18 02								18 22			
Yardley Wood	d				17 25					17 43		18 05								18 25			
Shirley	d				17a28					17 46		18 08								18a28			
Whitlocks End	d											18 11											
Wythall	d									17 50		18 13											
Earlswood (West Midlands)	d											18 16											
The Lakes	d											18x18											
Wood End	d											18x20											
Danzey	d											18x23											
Henley-in-Arden	d									18 00		18 28											
Wootton Wawen	d											18x30											
Wilmcote	d											18 36										19 04	
Stratford-upon-Avon	a									18 12		18 43										19 15	

A until 4 September

Table 71

Saturdays
until 02 October

Hereford, Worcester and Stourbridge - Birmingham - Leamington Spa, Marylebone and Stratford-upon-Avon

		LM	LM	LM	GW ◇1 ✕	XC ◇1 ✕	LM	XC ◇1 ✕	WS ◇1	CH ◇	LM	LM	GW ◇1 ✕	LM	LM	XC ◇1 ✕	GW	XC ◇1 ✕	GW ◇1	CH	CH ◇	LM	LM
Hereford 7	d											17 40											19 11
Ledbury	a											17 56											19 27
	d											17 58											19 28
Colwall	d											18 04											19 34
Great Malvern	a											18 09											19 39
	d				17 43						18 00	18 10	18 29				18 51						19 39
Malvern Link	d				17 46						18 02	18 13	18 31				18 53						19 42
Worcester Foregate Street 7	a				17 57						18 10	18 22	18 41				19 03						19 51
	d			17 48	17 57						18 11	18 25	18 42		18 51		19 03		20 02				19 51
Worcester Shrub Hill 7	a				18 00						18 13		18 45				19 06		20 05				
	d	17 15									18 17												
Droitwich Spa	d	17 23		17 57							18 25	18 35			19 00								20 00
Bromsgrove	d											18 44											
Barnt Green	d																						
University	d											18 59											
Hartlebury	d	17 30													19 07								
Kidderminster	d	17 36		18 07							18 36				19 13							19 40	20 10
Blakedown	d	17 41		18 12							18 41				19 18							19 45	20 15
Hagley	d	17 44		18 16							18 44				19 21							19 49	20 19
Stourbridge Junction 2	d	17 49	17 55	18 20			18 27				18 49			18 55	19 25							19 55	20 25
Lye	d		17 59				18 30							18 59	19 29							19 59	20 29
Cradley Heath	d	17 54	18 02	18 25			18 33				18 54			19 02	19 32							20 02	20 32
Old Hill	d		18 06				18 37							19 06	19 36							20 06	20 36
Rowley Regis	d	18 00	18 10	18 31			18 41				19 00			19 10	19 40							20 10	20 40
Langley Green	d		18 13				18 44							19 13	19 43							20 13	20 43
Birmingham New Street 12	a											19 12											
	d					18 33		19 03								19 33		20 03					
Birmingham International ✈	d							19 14										20 14					
Coventry	d							19 25										20 25					
Smethwick Galton Bridge 7	d	18 06	18 16	18 37			18 47				19 06			19 16	19 46							20 16	20 46
The Hawthorns	d	18 08	18 18	18 39			18 50				19 08			19 18	19 48							20 18	20 48
Jewellery Quarter	d	18 12	18 22	18 43			18 53				19 12			19 22	19 52							20 22	20 52
Birmingham Snow Hill	a	18 15	18 25	18 46			18 56				19 15			19 25	19 55							20 25	20 55
	d	18 17	18 27	18 47			18 57			19 10	19 17			19 27	19 57						20 10	20 27	20 57
Birmingham Moor Street	d	18 20	18 30	18 50			19 00			19 13	19 20			19 30	20 00						20 13	20 30	21 00
Bordesley	d																						
Small Heath	d	18 24		18 54			19 04				19 24			19 34	20 04							20 34	21 04
Tyseley	d	18 26		18 56			19 06				19 26			19 36	20 06							20 36	21 06
Acocks Green	d	18 29		18 59							19 29				20 09								21 09
Olton	d	18 32		19 02							19 32				20 12								21 12
Solihull	d	18 36		19 06						19 23	19 36				20 16						20 23		21 16
Widney Manor	d	18 39		19 09						19 26	19 39				20 19						20 26		21 19
Dorridge	d	18a44		19a14						19 30	19a44				20a24						20 30		21a24
Lapworth	d									19 34											20 34		
Hatton	d									19 40											20 40		
Warwick Parkway	d									19 44											20 44		
Warwick	d									19 47											20 47		
Leamington Spa 8	a					18 58		19 36	19 46	19 51						20 01		20 36		20 37	20 51		
	d					19 00		19 38	19 47	19 52						20 03		20 38		20 38	20 52		
Banbury	d					19a19		19a55	20 05	20 13						20a21		20a55			21 15		
London Marylebone 10 ⊖	a								21 15	21 37											22 40		
Spring Road	d		18 36				19 09							19 39								20 39	
Hall Green	d		18 39				19 12							19 42								20 42	
Yardley Wood	d		18 42				19 15							19 45								20 45	
Shirley	d		18 45				19a18							19 48								20 48	
Whitlocks End	d		18 48											19 51								20 51	
Wythall	d		18 50											19 53								20 53	
Earlswood (West Midlands)	d		18 53											19 56								20 56	
The Lakes	d		18x55											19x58								20x58	
Wood End	d		18x57											20x00								21x00	
Danzey	d		19x00											20x03								21x03	
Henley-in-Arden	d		19 05											20 08								21 08	
Wootton Wawen	d		19x07											20x10								21x10	
Wilmcote	d		19 13											20 16								21 16	
Stratford-upon-Avon	a		19 21											20 23						21 10		21 23	

Table 71

Saturdays
until 02 October

Hereford, Worcester and Stourbridge - Birmingham - Leamington Spa, Marylebone and Stratford-upon-Avon

		LM	XC ◇1 ✕	XC ◇1 ✕	CH ◇	LM	LM	GW	CH	LM	LM	LM	LM	LM	GW 1	LM
Hereford 7	d	20 00										21 33				22 43
Ledbury	a	20 15										21 48				23 00
	d	20 16										21 49				23 02
Colwall	d	20 22										21 55				23 09
Great Malvern	a	20 27										22 00				23 13
	d	20 28						21 15			21 30	22 00			22 40	23 14
Malvern Link	d	20 31						21 17			21 32	22 03			22 43	23 16
Worcester Foregate Street 7	a	20 39						21 27			21 41	22 17			22 50	23 24
	d	20 42						21 27			21 42	22 18			22 51	23 25
Worcester Shrub Hill 7	a							21 30			21 44	22 20			22 53	23 31
	d						20 52				21 52			22 47		
Droitwich Spa	d	20 51					21 00				22 00			22 55		
Bromsgrove	d	21 00														
Barnt Green	d															
University	d	21 16														
Hartlebury	d															
Kidderminster	d						21 10				22 10			23 05		
Blakedown	d						21 15				22 15			23 10		
Hagley	d						21 19				22 19			23 14		
Stourbridge Junction 2	d					20 55	21 25			21 55	22 25		22 55	23 18		
Lye	d					20 59	21 29			21 59	22 29		22 59			
Cradley Heath	d					21 02	21 32			22 02	22 32		23 02			
Old Hill	d					21 06	21 36			22 06	22 36		23 06			
Rowley Regis	d					21 10	21 40			22 10	22 40		23 10			
Langley Green	d					21 13	21 43			22 13	22 43		23 13			
Birmingham New Street 12	a	21 22														
	d		20 33	21 03												
Birmingham International ✈	d			21 14												
Coventry	d			21 25												
Smethwick Galton Bridge 7	d					21 16	21 46			22 16	22 46		23 16			
The Hawthorns	d					21 18	21 48			22 18	22 48		23 18			
Jewellery Quarter	d					21 22	21 52			22 22	22 52		23 22			
Birmingham Snow Hill	a					21 25	21 55			22 25	22 55		23 25	23 36		
	d				21 15	21 27	21 57		22 15	22 27	22 57		23 27	23 37		
Birmingham Moor Street	d				21 18	21 30	22 00		22 18	22 30	23 00		23 30	23 40		
Bordesley	d															
Small Heath	d					21 34	22 04			22 34	23 04		23 34	23 44		
Tyseley	d					21 36	22 06		22 23	22 36	23 06		23 36	23 46		
Acocks Green	d						22 09		22 25		23 09			23 49		
Olton	d						22 12		22 28		23 12			23 52		
Solihull	d				21 27		22 16		22 32		23 16			23 56		
Widney Manor	d				21 30		22 19		22 35		23 19			23 59		
Dorridge	d				21 34		22a24		22 39		23a24			00 03		
Lapworth	d				21 38				22 43					00 07		
Hatton	d				21 43				22 49					00 13		
Warwick Parkway	d				21 48				22 53					00 18		
Warwick	d				21 51				22 56					00 21		
Leamington Spa 8	a		20 58	21 36	21 54				23 00					00 26		
	d		21 00	21 38	21 55				23 01							
Banbury	d		21a20	21a55	22 15				23a23							
London Marylebone 10 ⊖	a				23 40											
Spring Road	d					21 39				22 39			23 39			
Hall Green	d					21 42				22 42			23 42			
Yardley Wood	d					21 45				22 45			23 45			
Shirley	d					21a48				22a48			23a48			
Whitlocks End	d															
Wythall	d															
Earlswood (West Midlands)	d															
The Lakes	d															
Wood End	d															
Danzey	d															
Henley-in-Arden	d															
Wootton Wawen	d															
Wilmcote	d															
Stratford-upon-Avon	a															

Table 71

Saturdays from 09 October

Hereford, Worcester and Stourbridge - Birmingham - Leamington Spa, Marylebone and Stratford-upon-Avon

		CH	XC	CH	XC	CH	LM	GW	LM	XC	CH	LM	LM	GW	XC	LM	LM	CH	CH	LM	CH	XC	CH
			◇1	◇	◇1	◇		◇1		◇1	◇			◇1	◇1			◇		A		◇1	◇
Hereford 7	d																						
Ledbury	a																						
	d																						
Colwall	d																						
Great Malvern	a																						
	d							05 39	06 21					06 35									
Malvern Link	d							05 42	06 24					06 39									
Worcester Foregate Street 7	a							05 51	06 31					06 48									
	d							05 52	06 33					06 50									
Worcester Shrub Hill 7	a							05 55						06 53									
	d						05 44						06 25			07 33				07 01			
Droitwich Spa	d						05 52		06 42				06 33			07 40				07 09			
Bromsgrove	d								06 51							07 50							
Barnt Green	d																						
University	d								07 09							08 09							
Hartlebury	d												06 40							07 16			
Kidderminster	d						06 02				06 37		06 46						07 14	07 22			
Blakedown	d						06 07						06 51							07 27			
Hagley	d						06 11						06 54							07 30			
Stourbridge Junction 2	d						06 15				06 45		07 02						07 22	07 35			
Lye	d						06 19						07 06							07 39			
Cradley Heath	d						06 22				06 50		07 09						07 27	07 42			
Old Hill	d						06 26						07 13							07 46			
Rowley Regis	d						06 30				06 56		07 17						07 33	07 50			
Langley Green	d						06 33						07 20							07 53			
Birmingham New Street 12	a								07 16							08 16							
	d		06 03		06 33					07 03					07 33							08 03	
Birmingham International ✈	d		06 14							07 15												08 14	
Coventry	d		06 25							07 25												08 25	
Smethwick Galton Bridge 7	d						06 36				07 02		07 23						07 39	07 56			
The Hawthorns	d						06 38				07 04		07 25						07 41	07 58			
Jewellery Quarter	d						06 42						07 29							08 02			
Birmingham Snow Hill	a						06 45				07 10		07 32						07 48	08 05			
	d	23p30		06 12		06 36	06 51				07 12	07 20	07 37				07 47		07 52	08 07			08 12
Birmingham Moor Street	d	23p33		06 15		06 39	06 54				07 15	07 23	07 40				07 50		07 55	08 10			08 15
Bordesley	d																						
Small Heath	d						06 58					07 27								08 14			
Tyseley	d	23p38					07 00					07 29								08 16			
Acocks Green	d	23p40					07 03						07 45										
Olton	d	23p43					07 06						07 48										
Solihull	d	23p47		06 25		06 49	07 10				07 25		07 52						08 05				08 25
Widney Manor	d	23p50					07 13						07 55										08 28
Dorridge	d	23p54		06 31		06 54	07a18				07 31		08a01						08 11				08 32
Lapworth	d	23p58									07 35												08 36
Hatton	d	00 04									07 41							07 57					08 42
Warwick Parkway	d	00 08		06 41		07 05					07 45								08 22				08 46
Warwick	d	00 11		06 45		07 08					07 48							08 04	08 25				08 49
Leamington Spa 8	a	00 14	06 36	06 49	06 58	07 12				07 36	07 52				07 58			08 08	08 30			08 36	08 51
	d	00 15	06 38	06 49	07 00	07 13				07 38	07 53				08 00			08 09	08 30		08 30	08 38	08 53
Banbury	d	00a41	06a55	07 07	07a19	07 33				07a55	08 13				08a19			08 29	08 49			08a55	09 13
London Marylebone 15 ⊖	a			08 32		08 52					09 33							09 58	10 04				10 37
Spring Road	d											07 32					07 56			08 19			
Hall Green	d											07 35					07 59			08 22			
Yardley Wood	d											07 38					08 02			08 25			
Shirley	d											07 41					08b11			08a28			
Whitlocks End	d											07 44					08 14						
Wythall	d											07 46					08 16						
Earlswood (West Midlands)	d											07 49					08 19						
The Lakes	d											07x51					08x21						
Wood End	d											07x53					08x23						
Danzey	d											07x56					08x26						
Henley-in-Arden	d											08 01					08 31						
Wootton Wawen	d											08x04					08x34						
Wilmcote	d											08 09					08 40				08 57		
Stratford-upon-Avon	a											08 17					08 46				09 12		

A 9 October, 16 October, 23 October

b arr. 0805

Table 71

Saturdays from 09 October

Hereford, Worcester and Stourbridge - Birmingham - Leamington Spa, Marylebone and Stratford-upon-Avon

		LM	LM	LM	LM	GW	LM	XC	CH	LM	LM	XC	WS	CH	LM	LM	LM	XC	LM	CH	LM	GW	LM
						◇1		◇1	◇		A	◇1	◇1	◇				◇1		◇		◇1	A
Hereford 7	d					07 10	07 40																
Ledbury	a					07 28	07 57																
	d					07 30	07 58																
Colwall	d					07 38	08 04																
Great Malvern	a					07 42	08 09																
	d				07 32	07 43	08 10															08 43	
Malvern Link	d				07 35	07 46	08 13															08 46	
Worcester Foregate Street 7	a				07 43	07 57	08 22															08 57	
	d				07 46	07 57	08 22														08 56	08 57	
Worcester Shrub Hill 7	a					08 01																09 01	
	d														08 15								
Droitwich Spa	d				07 55		08 31								08 23						09 05		
Bromsgrove	d						08 40																
Barnt Green	d																						
University	d						08 59																
Hartlebury	d														08 30								
Kidderminster	d		07 46		08 06				08 13						08 36					09 03	09 16		09 26
Blakedown	d		07 51		08 11										08 41					09 08			09 31
Hagley	d		07 54		08 14										08 44					09 12			09 34
Stourbridge Junction 2	d		07 59	08 05	08 19				08 26		08 35				08 49	08 55	09 09			09 15	09 25		09 39
Lye	d			08 09							08 39					08 59					09 29		
Cradley Heath	d		08 04	08 12	08 24				08 32		08 42				08 54	09 02	09 14			09 21	09 32		09 44
Old Hill	d			08 16							08 46					09 06					09 36		
Rowley Regis	d		08 10	08 20	08 30				08 37		08 50				09 00	09 10	09 20			09 27	09 40		09 50
Langley Green	d			08 23							08 53					09 13					09 43		
Birmingham New Street 12	a						09 11																
	d							08 33				09 03						09 33					
Birmingham International ✈	d											09 14											
Coventry	d											09 25											
Smethwick Galton Bridge 7	d		08 16	08 26	08 36				08 43		08 56				09 06	09 16	09 26			09 33	09 46		09 56
The Hawthorns	d		08 18	08 28	08 38				08 45		08 58				09 08	09 18	09 28			09 35	09 48		09 58
Jewellery Quarter	d		08 22	08 32	08 42						09 02				09 12	09 22	09 32				09 52		10 02
Birmingham Snow Hill	a		08 25	08 35	08 45				08 51		09 05				09 15	09 25	09 35			09 42	09 55		10 05
	d	08 17	08 27	08 37	08 47				08 52	08 57	09 07			09 12	09 17	09 27	09 37		09 47	09 52	09 57		10 07
Birmingham Moor Street	d	08 20	08 30	08 40	08 50				08 55	09 00	09 10			09 15	09 20	09 30	09 40		09 50	09 55	10 00		10 10
Bordesley	d																						
Small Heath	d			08 44							09 14						09 44						10 14
Tyseley	d			08 46							09 16						09 46						10 16
Acocks Green	d	08 25		08 49						09 05					09 25		09 49				10 05		
Olton	d	08 28		08 52						09 08					09 28		09 52				10 08		
Solihull	d	08 32		08 56					09 05	09 12				09 25	09 32		09 56			10 05	10 12		
Widney Manor	d	08 35		08 59						09 15					09 35		09 59				10 15		
Dorridge	d	08a41		09a04					09 11	09a21				09 31	09a41		10a04			10 11	10a22		
Lapworth	d													09 35									
Hatton	d																						
Warwick Parkway	d								09 22					09 44						10 22			
Warwick	d								09 25					09 47						10 25			
Leamington Spa 8	a							08 58	09 29			09 36	09 49	09 52				09 58		10 29			
	d							09 00	09 30			09 38	09 49	09 53				10 00		10 30			
Banbury	d							09a19	09 49			09a55	10 08	10 13				10a19		10 49			
London Marylebone 15 ⊖	a								11 05				11 15	11 35						12 02			
Spring Road	d		08 36		08 56						09 19					09 36			09 56				10 19
Hall Green	d		08 39		08 59						09 22					09 39			09 59				10 22
Yardley Wood	d		08 42		09 02						09 25					09 42			10 02				10 25
Shirley	d		08 45		09 07						09a28					09 45			10 07				10a28
Whitlocks End	d				09 10														10 10				
Wythall	d		08 49		09 12											09 49			10 12				
Earlswood (West Midlands)	d				09 15														10 15				
The Lakes	d				09x17														10x17				
Wood End	d				09x19														10x19				
Danzey	d				09x22														10x22				
Henley-in-Arden	d		08 59		09 27											09 59			10 27				
Wootton Wawen	d				09x29														10x29				
Wilmcote	d				09 35														10 35				
Stratford-upon-Avon	a		09 11		09 42											10 11			10 42				

A 9 October, 16 October, 23 October

Table 71

Saturdays
from 09 October

Hereford, Worcester and Stourbridge - Birmingham - Leamington Spa, Marylebone and Stratford-upon-Avon

		LM		XC	CH	WS	CH	LM	LM	LM	LM	LM		GW	XC	CH	LM	LM	XC	CH	LM	LM		LM	LM
				◇1	◇	◇1	◇							◇1	◇1	◇		A	◇1	◇					
Hereford 7	d								08 40													09 36		10 40	
Ledbury	a								08 57													09 52		10 56	
	d								08 58													09 58		10 58	
Colwall	d								09 04													10 04		11 04	
Great Malvern	a								09 09													10 09		11 09	
	d							09 00	09 10					09 43								10 10		11 10	
Malvern Link	d							09 03	09 13					09 46								10 13		11 13	
Worcester Foregate Street 7	a							09 11	09 22					09 55								10 22		11 22	
	d							09 16	09 22					09 57							10 16	10 22		11 22	
Worcester Shrub Hill 7	a													09 59											
	d	09 56										09 47													
Droitwich Spa	d	10 04						09 25	09 31			09 55									10 25	10 33		11 33	
Bromsgrove	d	10 14							09 40													10 42		11 42	
Barnt Green	d																								
University	d								09 59													10 59		11 59	
Hartlebury	d																								
Kidderminster	d							09 36			09 56	10 06						10 26			10 36				
Blakedown	d							09 41				10 11									10 41				
Hagley	d							09 44				10 14									10 44				
Stourbridge Junction 2	d							09 49		09 55	10 09	10 19					10 25	10 39			10 49				10 55
Lye	d									09 59							10 29								10 59
Cradley Heath	d							09 54		10 02	10 14	10 24					10 32	10 44			10 54				11 02
Old Hill	d									10 06							10 36								11 06
Rowley Regis	d							10 00		10 10	10 20	10 30					10 40	10 50			11 00				11 10
Langley Green	d									10 13							10 43								11 13
Birmingham New Street 12	a	10 41							10 11													11 11		12 11	
	d			10 03											10 33				11 03						
Birmingham International ✈	d			10 14															11 14						
Coventry	d			10 25															11 25						
Smethwick Galton Bridge 7	d							10 06		10 16	10 26	10 36					10 46	10 56			11 06				11 16
The Hawthorns	d							10 08		10 18	10 28	10 38					10 48	10 58			11 08				11 18
Jewellery Quarter	d							10 12		10 22	10 32	10 42					10 52	11 02			11 12				11 22
Birmingham Snow Hill	a							10 15		10 25	10 35	10 45					10 55	11 05			11 15				11 25
	d						10 12	10 17		10 27	10 37	10 47				10 52	10 57	11 07		11 12	11 17				11 27
Birmingham Moor Street	d						10 15	10 20		10 30	10 40	10 50				10 55	11 00	11 10		11 15	11 20				11 30
Bordesley	d																								
Small Heath	d										10 44							11 14							
Tyseley	d										10 46							11 16							
Acocks Green	d							10 25			10 49						11 05				11 25				
Olton	d							10 28			10 52						11 08				11 28				
Solihull	d						10 25	10 32			10 56					11 05	11 12			11 25	11 32				
Widney Manor	d							10 35			10 59						11 15				11 35				
Dorridge	d						10 31	10a41			11a04					11 11	11a22			11 31	11a41				
Lapworth	d						10 35																		
Hatton	d						10 41																		
Warwick Parkway	d						10 45									11 22				11 41					
Warwick	d						10 48									11 25				11 45					
Leamington Spa 8	a			10 36			10 52								10 58	11 29			11 36	11 49					
	d			10 38	10 38	10 49	10 53								11 00	11 30			11 38	11 49					
Banbury	d			10a55		11 08	11 13								11a19	11 49			11a55	12 07					
London Marylebone 10 ⊖	a					12 15	12 33									13 04				13 29					
Spring Road	d									10 36		10 56						11 19							11 36
Hall Green	d									10 39		10 59						11 22							11 39
Yardley Wood	d									10 42		11 02						11 25							11 42
Shirley	d									10 45		11 12						11a28							11 45
Whitlocks End	d											11 15													
Wythall	d									10 49		11 17													11 49
Earlswood (West Midlands)	d											11 20													
The Lakes	d											11x22													
Wood End	d											11x24													
Danzey	d											11x27													
Henley-in-Arden	d									10 59		11 32													11 59
Wootton Wawen	d											11x34													
Wilmcote	d											11 40													
Stratford-upon-Avon	a				11 14					11 15		11 47													12 11

A 9 October, 16 October, 23 October

Table 71

Saturdays
from 09 October

Hereford, Worcester and Stourbridge - Birmingham - Leamington Spa, Marylebone and Stratford-upon-Avon

		LM	LM	XC	CH	LM	LM	XC		CH	CH	LM	LM	LM	LM	XC	GW	CH		LM	LM	XC	WS	CH	LM
				◇1			A	◇1		◇						◇1					A	◇1	◇1	◇	
Hereford 7	d																								
Ledbury	a																								
	d																								
Colwall	d																								
Great Malvern	a																								
	d														11 35										
Malvern Link	d														11 37										
Worcester Foregate Street 7	a														11 45										
	d														11 46		12 40								12 16
Worcester Shrub Hill 7	a																12 42								
	d		10 47									11 17													
Droitwich Spa	d		10 55									11 25			11 55										12 25
Bromsgrove	d																								
Barnt Green	d																								
University	d																								
Hartlebury	d																								
Kidderminster	d	10 56	11 06				11 26					11 36		11 56	12 06						12 26				12 36
Blakedown	d		11 11									11 41			12 11										12 41
Hagley	d		11 14									11 44			12 14										12 44
Stourbridge Junction 2	d	11 09	11 19			11 25	11 39					11 49	11 55	12 09	12 19					12 25	12 39				12 49
Lye	d					11 29							11 59							12 29					
Cradley Heath	d	11 14	11 24			11 32	11 44					11 54	12 02	12 14	12 24					12 32	12 44				12 54
Old Hill	d					11 36							12 06							12 36					
Rowley Regis	d	11 20	11 30			11 40	11 50					12 00	12 10	12 20	12 30					12 40	12 50				13 00
Langley Green	d					11 43							12 13							12 43					
Birmingham New Street 12	a																								
	d			11 33				12 03								12 33						13 03			
Birmingham International ✈	d							12 14														13 15			
Coventry	d							12 25														13 25			
Smethwick Galton Bridge 7	d	11 26	11 36			11 46	11 56					12 06	12 16	12 26	12 36					12 46	12 56				13 06
The Hawthorns	d	11 28	11 38			11 48	11 58					12 08	12 18	12 28	12 38					12 48	12 58				13 08
Jewellery Quarter	d	11 32	11 42			11 52	12 02					12 12	12 22	12 32	12 42					12 52	13 02				13 12
Birmingham Snow Hill	a	11 35	11 45			11 55	12 05					12 15	12 25	12 35	12 45					12 55	13 05				13 15
	d	11 37	11 47		11 52	11 57	12 07				12 12	12 17	12 27	12 37	12 47			12 52		12 57	13 07			13 12	13 17
Birmingham Moor Street	d	11 40	11 50		11 55	12 00	12 10				12 15	12 20	12 30	12 40	12 50			12 55		13 00	13 10			13 15	13 20
Bordesley	d																								
Small Heath	d	11 44					12 14							12 44							13 14				
Tyseley	d	11 46					12 16							12 46							13 16				
Acocks Green	d	11 49				12 05						12 25		12 49						13 05					13 25
Olton	d	11 52				12 08						12 28		12 52						13 08					13 28
Solihull	d	11 56			12 05	12 12					12 25	12 32		12 56				13 05		13 12				13 25	13 32
Widney Manor	d	11 59				12 15						12 35		12 59						13 15					13 35
Dorridge	d	12a04			12 11	12a22					12 31	12a41		13a04				13 11		13a21				13 31	13a41
Lapworth	d										12 35														
Hatton	d										12 41														
Warwick Parkway	d				12 22						12 45							13 22						13 41	
Warwick	d				12 25						12 48							13 25						13 45	
Leamington Spa 8	a			11 58	12 29			12 36			12 51					13 00		13 29				13 36		13 52	
	d			12 00	12 30			12 38		12 38	12 53					13 02		13 30				13 38	13 49	13 53	
Banbury	d			12a19	12 49			12a55			13 13					13a21		13 49				13a55	14 08	14 13	
London Marylebone 10 ⊖	a				14 05						14 35							15 04					15 15	15 34	
Spring Road	d		11 56				12 19						12 36		12 56						13 19				
Hall Green	d		11 59				12 22						12 39		12 59						13 22				
Yardley Wood	d		12 02				12 25						12 42		13 02						13 25				
Shirley	d		12 07				12a28						12 45		13 10						13a28				
Whitlocks End	d		12 10												13 13										
Wythall	d		12 12										12 49		13 15										
Earlswood (West Midlands)	d		12 15												13 18										
The Lakes	d		12x17												13x20										
Wood End	d		12x19												13x22										
Danzey	d		12x22												13x25										
Henley-in-Arden	d		12 27										12 59		13 30										
Wootton Wawen	d		12x29												13x32										
Wilmcote	d		12 35								13 03				13 38										
Stratford-upon-Avon	a		12 42								13 16			13 17		13 45									

A 9 October, 16 October, 23 October

Table 71

Saturdays
from 09 October

Hereford, Worcester and Stourbridge - Birmingham - Leamington Spa, Marylebone and Stratford-upon-Avon

Station		LM	LM	LM	LM	GW	LM	XC	CH	LM	LM	XC	CH	LM	LM	LM	LM	XC	CH	LM	LM	CH
						◇1		◇1	◇		A	◇1						◇1	◇		A	
Hereford	d	11 40				12 13	12 40															
Ledbury	a	11 57				12 30	12 57															
	d	11 58				12 31	12 58															
Colwall	d	12 04				12 39	13 04															
Great Malvern	a	12 09				12 43	13 09															
	d	12 10				12 43	13 10										13 35					
Malvern Link	d	12 13				12 46	13 13										13 37					
Worcester Foregate Street	a	12 22				12 57	13 22										13 45					
	d	12 22			12 46	12 57	13 22										13 46					
Worcester Shrub Hill	a					13 02																
	d													13 17								
Droitwich Spa	d	12 33			12 55		13 33							13 25			13 55					
Bromsgrove	d	12 42					13 42															
Barnt Green	d																					
University	d	12 59					13 59															
Hartlebury	d																					
Kidderminster	d			12 56	13 06						13 26			13 36		13 56	14 06				14 26	
Blakedown	d				13 11									13 41			14 11					
Hagley	d				13 14									13 44			14 14					
Stourbridge Junction	d		12 55	13 09	13 19					13 25	13 39			13 49	13 55	14 09	14 19			14 25	14 39	
Lye	d		12 59							13 29					13 59					14 29		
Cradley Heath	d		13 02	13 14	13 24					13 32	13 44			13 54	14 02	14 14	14 24			14 32	14 44	
Old Hill	d		13 06							13 36					14 06					14 36		
Rowley Regis	d		13 10	13 20	13 30					13 40	13 50			14 00	14 10	14 20	14 30			14 40	14 50	
Langley Green	d		13 13							13 43					14 13					14 43		
Birmingham New Street	a	13 11					14 11															
	d							13 33				14 03						14 33				
Birmingham International	d											14 14										
Coventry	d											14 25										
Smethwick Galton Bridge	d		13 16	13 26	13 36					13 46	13 56			14 06	14 16	14 26	14 36			14 46	14 56	
The Hawthorns	d		13 18	13 28	13 38					13 48	13 58			14 08	14 18	14 28	14 38			14 48	14 58	
Jewellery Quarter	d		13 22	13 32	13 42					13 52	14 02			14 12	14 22	14 32	14 42			14 52	15 02	
Birmingham Snow Hill	a		13 25	13 35	13 45					13 55	14 05			14 15	14 25	14 35	14 45			14 55	15 05	
	d		13 27	13 37	13 47				13 52	13 57	14 07		14 12	14 17	14 27	14 37	14 47		14 52	14 57	15 07	
Birmingham Moor Street	d		13 30	13 40	13 50				13 55	14 00	14 10		14 15	14 20	14 30	14 40	14 50		14 55	15 00	15 10	
Bordesley	d																					
Small Heath	d			13 44							14 14					14 44					15 14	
Tyseley	d			13 46							14 16					14 46					15 16	
Acocks Green	d			13 49						14 05				14 25		14 49				15 05		
Olton	d			13 52						14 08				14 28		14 52				15 08		
Solihull	d			13 56					14 05	14 12			14 25	14 32		14 56			15 05	15 12		
Widney Manor	d			13 59						14 15				14 35		14 59				15 15		
Dorridge	d			14a04					14 11	14a22			14 31	14a41		15a04			15 11	15a21		
Lapworth	d												14 35									
Hatton	d												14 41									
Warwick Parkway	d								14 22				14 45						15 22			
Warwick	d								14 25				14 48						15 25			
Leamington Spa	a							13 58	14 29			14 36	14 51					14 58	15 29			
	d							14 00	14 30			14 38	14 53					15 00	15 30			15 34
Banbury	d							14a19	14 49			14a55	15 13					15a20	15 49			
London Marylebone	a								16 04				16 40						17 02			
Spring Road	d		13 36		13 56						14 19				14 36		14 56				15 19	
Hall Green	d		13 39		13 59						14 22				14 39		14 59				15 22	
Yardley Wood	d		13 42		14 02						14 25				14 42		15 02				15 25	
Shirley	d		13 45		14 07						14a28				14 45		15 10				15a28	
Whitlocks End	d				14 10												15 13					
Wythall	d		13 49		14 12										14 49		15 15					
Earlswood (West Midlands)	d				14 15												15 18					
The Lakes	d				14x17												15x20					
Wood End	d				14x19												15x22					
Danzey	d				14x22												15x25					
Henley-in-Arden	d		13 59		14 27										14 59		15 30					
Wootton Wawen	d				14x29												15x32					
Wilmcote	d				14 35												15 38					16 00
Stratford-upon-Avon	a		14 11		14 42										15 11		15 45					16 15

A 9 October, 16 October, 23 October

Table 71

Saturdays
from 09 October

Hereford, Worcester and Stourbridge - Birmingham - Leamington Spa, Marylebone and Stratford-upon-Avon

Station		XC	CH	LM	LM	LM	LM	LM	GW	XC	CH	LM	LM	LM	XC	WS	CH	LM	LM	LM	LM	LM	GW
		◇1							◇1	◇1	◇		A		◇1	◇1							◇1
Hereford	d				13 40														14 40				15 10
Ledbury	a				13 57														14 56				15 27
	d				13 58														14 57				15 29
Colwall	d				14 04														15 03				15 36
Great Malvern	a				14 09														15 08				15 41
	d				14 10				14 32										15 10			15 30	15 42
Malvern Link	d				14 13				14 35										15 13			15 32	15 45
Worcester Foregate Street	a				14 22				14 55										15 22			15 40	15 55
	d			14 16	14 22				14 57									15 16	15 22			15 46	15 56
Worcester Shrub Hill	a								14 59														15 59
	d							14 43						15 54									
Droitwich Spa	d			14 25	14 33			14 55						16 03				15 25	15 33			15 55	
Bromsgrove	d				14 42									16 13					15 42				
Barnt Green	d																						
University	d				14 59														15 59				
Hartlebury	d																						
Kidderminster	d			14 36			14 56	15 06					15 26					15 36			15 56	16 06	
Blakedown	d			14 41				15 11					15 31					15 41				16 11	
Hagley	d			14 44				15 14					15 34					15 44				16 14	
Stourbridge Junction	d			14 49		14 55	15 09	15 19				15 25	15 39					15 49		15 55	16 09	16 19	
Lye	d					14 59						15 29								15 59			
Cradley Heath	d			14 54		15 02	15 14	15 24				15 32	15 44					15 54		16 02	16 14	16 24	
Old Hill	d					15 06						15 36								16 06			
Rowley Regis	d			15 00		15 10	15 20	15 30				15 40	15 50					16 00		16 10	16 20	16 30	
Langley Green	d					15 13						15 43								16 13			
Birmingham New Street	a				15 11									16 45					16 11				
	d	15 03								15 33					16 03								
Birmingham International	d	15 14													16 14								
Coventry	d	15 25													16 25								
Smethwick Galton Bridge	d			15 06		15 16	15 26	15 36				15 46	15 56					16 06		16 16	16 26	16 36	
The Hawthorns	d			15 08		15 18	15 28	15 38				15 48	15 58					16 08		16 18	16 28	16 38	
Jewellery Quarter	d			15 12		15 22	15 32	15 42				15 52	16 02					16 12		16 22	16 32	16 42	
Birmingham Snow Hill	a			15 15		15 25	15 35	15 45				15 55	16 05					16 15		16 25	16 35	16 45	
	d		15 12	15 17		15 27	15 37	15 47			15 52	15 57	16 07				16 12	16 17		16 27	16 37	16 47	
Birmingham Moor Street	d		15 15	15 20		15 30	15 40	15 50			15 55	16 00	16 10				16 15	16 20		16 30	16 40	16 50	
Bordesley	d																						
Small Heath	d						15 44						16 14								16 44	16 54	
Tyseley	d						15 46						16 16							16 34	16 46	16 56	
Acocks Green	d			15 25			15 49					16 05						16 25			16 49		
Olton	d			15 28			15 52					16 08						16 28			16 52		
Solihull	d		15 25	15 32			15 56				16 05	16 12					16 25	16 32			16 56		
Widney Manor	d			15 35			15 59					16 15						16 35			16 59		
Dorridge	d		15 31	15a41			16a04				16 11	16a21					16 31	16a41			17a04		
Lapworth	d																16 35						
Hatton	d																16 41						
Warwick Parkway	d		15 41								16 22						16 45						
Warwick	d		15 45								16 25						16 48						
Leamington Spa	a	15 36	15 49							16 00	16 29				16 36		16 52						
	d	15 38	15 49							16 02	16 30				16 38	16 49	16 53						
Banbury	d	15a55	16 07							16a20	16 49				16a55	17 08	17 13						
London Marylebone	a		17 32								18 04					18 15	18 35						
Spring Road	d					15 36		15 56					16 19							16 37		16 59	
Hall Green	d					15 39		15 59					16 22							16 40		17 02	
Yardley Wood	d					15 42		16 02					16 25							16 43		17 05	
Shirley	d					15 45		16 07					16a28							16 46		17 10	
Whitlocks End	d							16 10														17 13	
Wythall	d					15 49		16 12												16 50		17 15	
Earlswood (West Midlands)	d							16 15														17 18	
The Lakes	d							16x17														17x20	
Wood End	d							16x19														17x22	
Danzey	d							16x22														17x25	
Henley-in-Arden	d					15 59		16 27												17 00		17 30	
Wootton Wawen	d							16x29														17x32	
Wilmcote	d							16 35														17 38	
Stratford-upon-Avon	a					16 15		16 42												17 12		17 45	

A 9 October, 16 October, 23 October

Table 71

Saturdays
from 09 October

Hereford, Worcester and Stourbridge - Birmingham - Leamington Spa, Marylebone and Stratford-upon-Avon

		XC	CH	LM	LM	XC	CH	LM	LM	LM	LM	LM	GW	LM	XC	CH	CH	LM	LM	XC	CH	CH	LM
		◇1 ☕	◇		A	◇1 ☕									◇1 ☕				A	◇1 ☕		◇	
Hereford 7	d								15 40					16 40									
Ledbury	a								15 57					16 57									
	d								15 58					16 58									
Colwall	d								16 04					17 04									
Great Malvern	a								16 09					17 09									
	d								16 10				16 51	17 10									
Malvern Link	d								16 13				16 53	17 13									
Worcester Foregate Street 7	a								16 22				17 04	17 22									
	d							16 15	16 22				17 04	17 22									
Worcester Shrub Hill 7	a												17 07										
	d											16 47											17 15
Droitwich Spa	d							16 24	16 33			16 55		17 33									17 23
Bromsgrove	d								16 42					17 42									
Barnt Green	d																						
University	d								16 59					17 59									
Hartlebury	d							16 31															17 30
Kidderminster	d				16 26			16 37			16 56	17 06							17 26				17 36
Blakedown	d				16 31			16 42				17 11							17 31				17 41
Hagley	d				16 34			16 45				17 14							17 34				17 44
Stourbridge Junction 2	d			16 25	16 39			16 49		16 55	17 09	17 19						17 25	17 39				17 49
Lye	d			16 29						16 59								17 29					
Cradley Heath	d			16 32	16 44			16 54		17 02	17 14	17 24						17 32	17 44				17 54
Old Hill	d			16 36						17 06								17 36					
Rowley Regis	d			16 40	16 50			17 00		17 10	17 20	17 30						17 40	17 50				18 00
Langley Green	d			16 43						17 13								17 43					
Birmingham New Street 12	a								17 11					18 11									
	d	16 33				17 03									17 33					18 03			
Birmingham International ✈	d					17 14														18 14			
Coventry	d					17 25														18 25			
Smethwick Galton Bridge 7	d			16 46	16 56			17 06		17 16	17 26	17 36						17 46	17 56				18 06
The Hawthorns 🚋	d			16 48	16 58			17 08		17 18	17 28	17 38						17 48	17 58				18 08
Jewellery Quarter 🚋	d			16 52	17 02			17 12		17 22	17 32	17 42						17 52	18 02				18 12
Birmingham Snow Hill 🚋	a			16 55	17 05			17 16		17 25	17 35	17 45						17 55	18 05				18 15
	d		16 52	16 57	17 07		17 12	17 17		17 27	17 37	17 47					17 52	17 57	18 07			18 12	18 17
Birmingham Moor Street	d		16 55	17 00	17 10		17 15	17 20		17 30	17 40	17 50					17 55	18 00	18 10			18 15	18 20
Bordesley	d																						
Small Heath	d				17 14						17 44	17 54							18 14				18 24
Tyseley	d			17 04	17 16					17 34	17 46	17 56							18 16				18 26
Acocks Green	d			17 07				17 25			17 49							18 05					18 29
Olton	d			17 10				17 28			17 52							18 08					18 32
Solihull	d		17 05	17 14			17 25	17 32			17 56						18 05	18 12				18 25	18 36
Widney Manor	d			17 17				17 35			17 59							18 15				18 28	18 39
Dorridge	d		17 11	17a22			17 31	17a41			18a04						18 11	18a22				18 32	18a44
Lapworth	d						17 35															18 36	
Hatton	d						17 41															18 42	
Warwick Parkway	d		17 22				17 45										18 22					18 46	
Warwick	d		17 25				17 48									18 02	18 25					18 49	
Leamington Spa 8	a	16 59	17 29			17 36	17 52								17 58	18 05	18 29			18 36	18 37	18 53	
	d	17 00	17 30			17 38	17 53								18 00	18 06	18 30			18 38	18 38	18 53	
Banbury	d	17a19	17 49			17a55	18 13								18a19	18 24	18 49			18a55		19 13	
London Marylebone 10 ⊖	a		19 05				19 33									19 40	20 05					20 40	
Spring Road	d				17 19					17 37		17 59							18 19				
Hall Green	d				17 22					17 40		18 02							18 22				
Yardley Wood	d				17 25					17 43		18 05							18 25				
Shirley	d				17a28					17 46		18 08							18a28				
Whitlocks End	d											18 11											
Wythall	d									17 50		18 13											
Earlswood (West Midlands)	d											18 16											
The Lakes	d											18x18											
Wood End	d											18x20											
Danzey	d											18x23											
Henley-in-Arden	d									18 00		18 28											
Wootton Wawen	d											18x30											
Wilmcote	d											18 36									19 04		
Stratford-upon-Avon	a									18 12		18 43									19 18		

A 9 October, 16 October, 23 October

Table 71

Saturdays
from 09 October

Hereford, Worcester and Stourbridge - Birmingham - Leamington Spa, Marylebone and Stratford-upon-Avon

		LM	LM	GW	XC	LM	LM	XC	WS	CH	LM	LM	GW	LM	LM	XC	XC	GW	CH	CH	LM	LM
				◇1 ☕	◇1 ☕	A	B	◇1 ☕	◇1 🍴	◇			◇1 ☕			◇1 ☕	◇1 ☕	◇1		◇		
Hereford 7	d											17 40										19 11
Ledbury	a											17 56										19 27
	d											17 58										19 28
Colwall	d											18 04										19 34
Great Malvern	a											18 09										19 39
	d			17 43							18 00	18 10	18 29									19 39
Malvern Link	d			17 46							18 02	18 13	18 31									19 42
Worcester Foregate Street 7	a			17 57							18 10	18 22	18 41									19 51
	d		17 48	17 57							18 11	18 25	18 42		18 51			20 02				19 51
Worcester Shrub Hill 7	a			18 00							18 13		18 45					20 05				
	d										18 17											
Droitwich Spa	d		17 57								18 25	18 35			19 00							20 00
Bromsgrove	d											18 44										
Barnt Green	d																					
University	d											18 59										
Hartlebury	d														19 07							
Kidderminster	d		18 07								18 36				19 13						19 40	20 10
Blakedown	d		18 12								18 41				19 18						19 45	20 15
Hagley	d		18 16								18 44				19 21						19 49	20 19
Stourbridge Junction 2	d	17 55	18 20			18 27	18 27				18 49			18 55	19 25						19 55	20 25
Lye	d	17 59				18 30	18 30							18 59	19 29						19 59	20 29
Cradley Heath	d	18 02	18 25			18 33	18 33				18 54			19 02	19 32						20 02	20 32
Old Hill	d	18 06				18 37	18 37							19 06	19 36						20 06	20 36
Rowley Regis	d	18 10	18 31			18 41	18 41				19 00			19 10	19 40						20 10	20 40
Langley Green	d	18 13				18 44	18 44							19 13	19 43						20 13	20 43
Birmingham New Street 12	a											19 12										
	d				18 33			19 03								19 33	20 03					
Birmingham International ✈	d							19 14									20 14					
Coventry	d							19 25									20 25					
Smethwick Galton Bridge 7	d	18 16	18 37			18 47	18 47				19 06			19 16	19 46						20 16	20 46
The Hawthorns 🚋	d	18 18	18 39			18 50	18 50				19 08			19 18	19 48						20 18	20 48
Jewellery Quarter 🚋	d	18 22	18 43			18 53	18 53				19 12			19 22	19 52						20 22	20 52
Birmingham Snow Hill 🚋	a	18 25	18 46			18 56	18 56				19 15			19 25	19 55						20 25	20 55
	d	18 27	18 47			18 57	18 57			19 10	19 17			19 27	19 57					20 10	20 27	20 57
Birmingham Moor Street	d	18 30	18 50			19 00	19 00			19 13	19 20			19 30	20 00					20 13	20 30	21 00
Bordesley	d																					
Small Heath	d		18 54			19 04	19 04				19 24			19 34	20 04						20 34	21 04
Tyseley	d		18 56			19 06	19 06				19 26			19 36	20 06						20 36	21 06
Acocks Green	d		18 59								19 29				20 09							21 09
Olton	d		19 02								19 32				20 12							21 12
Solihull	d		19 06							19 23	19 36				20 16					20 23		21 16
Widney Manor	d		19 09							19 26	19 39				20 19					20 26		21 19
Dorridge	d		19a14							19 30	19a44				20a24					20 30		21a24
Lapworth	d									19 34										20 34		
Hatton	d									19 40										20 40		
Warwick Parkway	d									19 44										20 44		
Warwick	d									19 47										20 47		
Leamington Spa 8	a				18 58			19 36		19 51						20 01	20 36			20 51		
	d				19 00			19 38	19 47	19 52						20 03	20 38		20 38	20 52		
Banbury	d				19a19			19a55	20 05	20 13						20a21	20a55			21 15		
London Marylebone 10 ⊖	a								21 15	21 40										22 43		
Spring Road	d	18 36				19 09	19 09							19 39							20 39	
Hall Green	d	18 39				19 12	19 12							19 42							20 42	
Yardley Wood	d	18 42				19 15	19 15							19 45							20 45	
Shirley	d	18 45				19a18	19 18							19 48							20 48	
Whitlocks End	d	18 48					19a21							19 51							20 51	
Wythall	d	18 50												19 53							20 53	
Earlswood (West Midlands)	d	18 53												19 56							20 56	
The Lakes	d	18x55												19x58							20x58	
Wood End	d	18x57												20x00							21x00	
Danzey	d	19x00												20x03							21x03	
Henley-in-Arden	d	19 05												20 08							21 08	
Wootton Wawen	d	19x07												20x10							21x10	
Wilmcote	d	19 13												20 16							21 16	
Stratford-upon-Avon	a	19 21												20 23					21 13		21 23	

A 9 October, 16 October, 23 October

B from 30 October

Saturdays
from 09 October

Hereford, Worcester and Stourbridge - Birmingham - Leamington Spa, Marylebone and Stratford-upon-Avon

		LM	XC	XC	CH	LM	LM	GW	CH	LM	LM	LM	LM	LM	GW	LM
			◇■	◇■	◇	A				A			A		■	
Hereford ■	d	20 00										21 33				22 43
Ledbury	a	20 15										21 48				23 00
	d	20 16										21 49				23 02
Colwall	d	20 22										21 55				23 09
Great Malvern	a	20 27										22 00				23 13
	d	20 28						21 15			21 30	22 00			22 40	23 14
Malvern Link	d	20 31						21 17			21 32	22 03			22 43	23 16
Worcester Foregate Street ■	a	20 39						21 27			21 41	22 17			22 50	23 24
	d	20 42						21 27			21 42	22 18			22 51	23 25
Worcester Shrub Hill ■	a							21 30			21 44	22 20			22 53	23 31
	d						20 52				21 52			22 47		
Droitwich Spa	d	20 51					21 00				22 00			22 55		
Bromsgrove	d	21 00														
Barnt Green	d															
University	d	21 16														
Hartlebury	d															
Kidderminster	d						21 10				22 10			23 05		
Blakedown	d						21 15				22 15			23 10		
Hagley	d						21 19				22 19			23 14		
Stourbridge Junction ■	d					20 55	21 25			21 55	22 25		22 55	23 18		
Lye	d					20 59	21 29			21 59	22 29		22 59			
Cradley Heath	d					21 02	21 32			22 02	22 32		23 02			
Old Hill	d					21 06	21 36			22 06	22 36		23 06			
Rowley Regis	d					21 10	21 40			22 10	22 40		23 10			
Langley Green	d					21 13	21 43			22 13	22 43		23 13			
Birmingham New Street ■	a	21 22														
	d		20 33	21 03												
Birmingham International ✈	d			21 14												
Coventry	d			21 25												
Smethwick Galton Bridge ■	d					21 16	21 46			22 16	22 46		23 16			
The Hawthorns	d					21 18	21 48			22 18	22 48		23 18			
Jewellery Quarter	d					21 22	21 52			22 22	22 52		23 22			
Birmingham Snow Hill	a					21 25	21 55			22 25	22 55		23 25	23 36		
	d				21 15	21 27	21 57		22 15	22 27	22 57		23 27	23 37		
Birmingham Moor Street	d				21 18	21 30	22 00		22 18	22 30	23 00		23 30	23 40		
Bordesley	d															
Small Heath	d					21 34	22 04			22 34	23 04		23 34	23 44		
Tyseley	d					21 36	22 06		22 23	22 36	23 06		23 36	23 46		
Acocks Green	d						22 09		22 25		23 09			23 49		
Olton	d						22 12		22 28		23 12			23 52		
Solihull	d				21 27		22 16		22 32		23 16			23 56		
Widney Manor	d				21 30		22 19		22 35		23 19			23 59		
Dorridge	d				21 34		22a24		22 39		23a24			00 03		
Lapworth	d				21 38				22 43					00 07		
Hatton	d				21 43				22 49					00 13		
Warwick Parkway	d				21 48				22 53					00 18		
Warwick	d				21 51				22 56					00 21		
Leamington Spa ■	a		20 58	21 36	21 54				23 00					00 26		
	d		21 00	21 38	21 55				23 01							
Banbury	d		21a20	21a55	22 15				23a26							
London Marylebone ■ ⊖	a				23 43											
Spring Road	d					21 39				22 39			23 39			
Hall Green	d					21 42				22 42			23 42			
Yardley Wood	d					21 45				22 45			23 45			
Shirley	d					21a48				22a48			23a48			
Whitlocks End	d															
Wythall	d															
Earlswood (West Midlands)	d															
The Lakes	d															
Wood End	d															
Danzey	d															
Henley-in-Arden	d															
Wootton Wawen	d															
Wilmcote	d															
Stratford-upon-Avon	a															

A 9 October, 16 October, 23 October

Sundays
until 26 September

Hereford, Worcester and Stourbridge - Birmingham - Leamington Spa, Marylebone and Stratford-upon-Avon

		LM	CH	XC	CH	CH	XC	CH	CH	LM	CH	XC	CH	XC	CH	LM	XC	CH	WS	XC
			◇	◇■	◇		◇■	◇	◇		◇	◇■ C	◇	◇■			◇■ C		◇■ E	◇■
Hereford ■	d																			
Ledbury	a																			
	d																			
Colwall	d																			
Great Malvern	a																			
	d																			
Malvern Link	d																			
Worcester Foregate Street ■	a																			
	d																			
Worcester Shrub Hill ■	a																			
	d	22p47																		
Droitwich Spa	d	22p55																		
Bromsgrove	d																			
Barnt Green	d																			
University	d																			
Hartlebury	d																			
Kidderminster	d	23p05								10 08										
Blakedown	d	23p10								10 13										
Hagley	d	23p14								10 17										
Stourbridge Junction ■	d	23p18								10 22						11 22				
Lye	d									10 25						11 25				
Cradley Heath	d									10 29						11 29				
Old Hill	d									10 33						11 33				
Rowley Regis	d									10 36						11 36				
Langley Green	d									10 39						11 39				
Birmingham New Street ■	a																			
	d			09 03			10 03					11 03		11 33			12 03		12 27	12 33
Birmingham International ✈	d			09 14			10 14					11 14					12 14			
Coventry	d			09 25			10 25					11 25					12 25			
Smethwick Galton Bridge ■	d									10 43						11 43				
The Hawthorns	d									10 45						11 45				
Jewellery Quarter	d									10 49						11 49				
Birmingham Snow Hill	a	23p36								10 52						11 52				
	d	23p37	08 40		09 10	09 40		10 10	10 40	10 53			11 10		11 40	11 53		12 10		
Birmingham Moor Street	d	23p40	08 43		09 13	09 43		10 13	10 43	10 56			11 13		11 43	11 56		12 13		
Bordesley	d																			
Small Heath	d	23p44																		
Tyseley	d	23p46																		
Acocks Green	d	23p49								11 02						12 02				
Olton	d	23p52								11 04						12 04				
Solihull	d	23p56	08 52		09 22	09 52		10 22	10 52	11 08			11 22		11 52	12 08		12 22		
Widney Manor	d	23p59								11 11						12 11				
Dorridge	d	00 03	08 58		09 28	09 58		10 28	10 58	11a16			11 28		11 58	12a16		12 28		
Lapworth	d	00 07							11 02											
Hatton	d	00 13							11 07											
Warwick Parkway	d	00 18	09 09		09 38	10 09		10 38	11 12				11 38		12 09			12 38		
Warwick	d	00 21	09 12		09 41			10 41					11 41					12 41		
Leamington Spa ■	a	00 26	09 16	09 36	09 46	10 15	10 36	10 46	11 16			11 36	11 46	11 59	12 15		12 36	12 46	12 56	12 59
	d		09 17	09 38	09 47	10 16	10 38	10 47	11 18		11 20	11 38	11 47	12 00	12 16		12 38	12 47	12 56	13 00
Banbury	d		09 36	09a55	10 06	10 35	10a55	11 06	11 37			11a55	12 06	12a19	12 35		12a55	13 06	13 15	13a19
London Marylebone ■ ⊖	a		10 51		11 23	11 58		12 22	13 01				13 22		13 58			14 22	14 37	
Spring Road	d																			
Hall Green	d																			
Yardley Wood	d																			
Shirley	d																			
Whitlocks End	d																			
Wythall	d																			
Earlswood (West Midlands)	d																			
The Lakes	d																			
Wood End	d																			
Danzey	d																			
Henley-in-Arden	d																			
Wootton Wawen	d																			
Wilmcote	d										11 43									
Stratford-upon-Avon	a										11 59									

C until 26 September

E from 18 July until 5 September

Table 71

Sundays
until 26 September

Hereford, Worcester and Stourbridge - Birmingham - Leamington Spa, Marylebone and Stratford-upon-Avon

		CH	LM	CH	WS	XC		XC	CH	XC	CH	LM	XC	CH	XC	LM	CH	LM	CH	XC	WS	WS	CH	XC	LM
				◇	◇1	◇1		◇1	◇	◇1			◇1	◇	◇1				◇	◇1	◇1	◇1	◇	◇1	
					A	A		B													A	C			
					☕	☕		☕		🛒			☕		🛒					☕	☕	☕		🛒	
Hereford [7]	d																								15 30
Ledbury	a																								15 47
	d																								15 51
Colwall	d																								15 58
Great Malvern	a																								16 02
	d															14 35									16 03
Malvern Link	d															14 37									16 05
Worcester Foregate Street [7]	a															14 45									16 14
	d															14 45									16 15
Worcester Shrub Hill [7]	a															14 48									16 18
	d															14 51									16 33
Droitwich Spa	d															14 59									16 41
Bromsgrove	d															15 09									16 51
Barnt Green	d																								
University	d																								
Hartlebury	d																								
Kidderminster	d																								
Blakedown	d																								
Hagley	d																								
Stourbridge Junction [2]	d		12 22									13 22						14 22							
Lye	d		12 25									13 25						14 25							
Cradley Heath	d		12 29									13 29						14 29							
Old Hill	d		12 33									13 33						14 33							
Rowley Regis	d		12 36									13 36						14 36							
Langley Green	d		12 39									13 39						14 39							
Birmingham New Street [12]	a															15 37									17 17
	d				12 56	13 03		13 03		13 33			14 03		14 33					15 03	15 13	15 13		15 33	
Birmingham International ✈	d					13 14		13 14					14 14							15 14					
Coventry	d					13 25		13 25					14 25							15 25					
Smethwick Galton Bridge [7]	d		12 43									13 43						14 43							
The Hawthorns	d		12 45									13 45						14 45							
Jewellery Quarter	d		12 49									13 49						14 49							
Birmingham Snow Hill	a		12 52									13 52						14 52							
	d	12 40	12 53						13 10		13 40	13 53		14 10			14 40	14 53					15 10		
Birmingham Moor Street	d	12 43	12 56						13 13		13 43	13 56		14 13			14 43	14 56					15 13		
Bordesley	d																								
Small Heath	d																								
Tyseley	d																								
Acocks Green	d		13 04									14 02						15 02							
Olton	d		13 06									14 04						15 04							
Solihull	d	12 52	13 10						13 22		13 52	14 08		14 22			14 52	15 08					15 22		
Widney Manor	d		13 13									14 11						15 11							
Dorridge	d	12 58	13a18						13 28		13 58	14a17		14 28			14 58	15a17					15 28		
Lapworth	d										14 02														
Hatton	d										14 07														
Warwick Parkway	d	13 09							13 38		14 12			14 38			15 09						15 40		
Warwick	d								13 41					14 41									15 44		
Leamington Spa [8]	a	13 15			13 33	13 37		13 36	13 46		14 17		14 36	14 46			15 15			15 36	15 42	15 42	15 48	15 59	
	d	13 16		13 20	13 33	13 38		13 38	13 47	14 00	14 18		14 38	14 47	15 00		15 16		15 20	15 38	15 43	15 43	15 49	16 00	
Banbury	d	13 35			13 52	13a56		13a55	14 06	14a19	14 37		14a55	15 06	15a19		15 35			15a55	16 03	16 03	16 08	16a19	
London Marylebone [10] ⊖	a	15 00			15 14				15 23		16 02			16 22			16 58				17 10	17 10	17 23		
Spring Road	d																								
Hall Green	d																								
Yardley Wood	d																								
Shirley	d																								
Whitlocks End	d																								
Wythall	d																								
Earlswood (West Midlands)	d																								
The Lakes	d																								
Wood End	d																								
Danzey	d																								
Henley-in-Arden	d																								
Wootton Wawen	d																								
Wilmcote	d			13 43															15 43						
Stratford-upon-Avon	a			13 54															15 54						

A until 11 July
B from 18 July until 26 September
C from 18 July until 5 September

Table 71

Sundays
until 26 September

Hereford, Worcester and Stourbridge - Birmingham - Leamington Spa, Marylebone and Stratford-upon-Avon

		CH		LM	XC	CH	XC	CH	LM	LM	CH	XC		CH	XC	CH	LM	XC	CH	XC	GW	GW		CH	CH
					◇1		◇1				◇	◇1			◇1			◇1	◇	◇1	◇1	◇1			◇
																					A	B			
					☕		🛒					☕			🛒			☕		🛒	🛒	🛒			
Hereford [7]	d																				18 30	18 30			
Ledbury	a																				18 46	18 47			
	d																				18 48	18 48			
Colwall	d																				18 55	18 55			
Great Malvern	a																				19 00	19 00			
	d									17 17											19 08	19 11			
Malvern Link	d									17 20											19 12	19 14			
Worcester Foregate Street [7]	a									17 28											19 23	19 23			
	d									17 28											19 25	19 25			
Worcester Shrub Hill [7]	a									17 31											19 27	19 27			
	d									17 34															
Droitwich Spa	d									17 42															
Bromsgrove	d									17 52															
Barnt Green	d																								
University	d																								
Hartlebury	d																								
Kidderminster	d																								
Blakedown	d																								
Hagley	d																								
Stourbridge Junction [2]	d			15 22					16 22								17 22								
Lye	d			15 25					16 25								17 25								
Cradley Heath	d			15 29					16 29								17 29								
Old Hill	d			15 33					16 33								17 33								
Rowley Regis	d			15 36					16 36								17 36								
Langley Green	d			15 39					16 39								17 39								
Birmingham New Street [12]	a									18 13															
	d				16 04		16 33					17 03			17 33			18 03		18 33					
Birmingham International ✈	d				16 14							17 14						18 14							
Coventry	d				16 25							17 25						18 25							
Smethwick Galton Bridge [7]	d			15 43					16 43								17 43								
The Hawthorns	d			15 45					16 45								17 45								
Jewellery Quarter	d			15 49					16 49								17 49								
Birmingham Snow Hill	a			15 52					16 52								17 53								
	d	15 40		15 53		16 10		16 40	16 53					17 10		17 40	17 53		18 10					18 40	
Birmingham Moor Street	d	15 43		15 56		16 13		16 43	16 56					17 13		17 43	17 56		18 13					18 43	
Bordesley	d																								
Small Heath	d																								
Tyseley	d																								
Acocks Green	d			16 02					17 02								18 02								
Olton	d			16 04					17 04								18 04								
Solihull	d	15 52		16 08		16 22		16 52	17 08					17 22		17 52	18 08		18 22					18 52	
Widney Manor	d			16 11					17 11								18 11								
Dorridge	d	15 58		16a16		16 28		16 58	17a17					17 28		17 58	18a17		18 28					18 58	
Lapworth	d	16 02														18 02									
Hatton	d	16 07														18 07									
Warwick Parkway	d	16 12				16 38		17 09						17 38		18 12			18 38					19 09	
Warwick	d					16 41								17 41					18 41						
Leamington Spa [8]	a	16 17			16 36	16 46	16 59	17 15				17 36		17 46	17 59	18 17		18 36	18 46	18 59				19 15	
	d	16 18			16 38	16 47	17 00	17 16			17 20	17 38		17 47	18 00	18 18		18 38	18 47	19 00				19 16	19 20
Banbury	d	16 37			16a55	17 06	17a19	17 35				17a55		18 06	18a19	18 37		18a55	19 06	19a19				19 35	
London Marylebone [10] ⊖	a	18 02				18 21		18 59						19 22		20 02			20 21					20 58	
Spring Road	d																								
Hall Green	d																								
Yardley Wood	d																								
Shirley	d																								
Whitlocks End	d																								
Wythall	d																								
Earlswood (West Midlands)	d																								
The Lakes	d																								
Wood End	d																								
Danzey	d																								
Henley-in-Arden	d																								
Wootton Wawen	d																								
Wilmcote	d										17 43														19 43
Stratford-upon-Avon	a										17 54														19 54

A until 5 September
B 12 September, 19 September, 26 September

Table 71

Sundays until 26 September

Hereford, Worcester and Stourbridge - Birmingham - Leamington Spa, Marylebone and Stratford-upon-Avon

		XC ◇1	WS ◇1 A	WS ◇1 B	XC ◇1	CH ◇	LM	XC ◇1	GW ◇1 C	GW ◇1 D	LM E	LM A	CH ◇	XC ◇1	GW ◇1	XC ◇1	CH ◇	LM	LM
Hereford 7	d										20 05	20 09							22 40
Ledbury	a										20 20	20 23							22 56
	d										20 21	20 24							22 56
Colwall	d										20 27	20 30							23 03
Great Malvern	a										20 32	20 35							23 07
	d								20 10	20 08	20 32	20 35			20 55			22 02	23 08
Malvern Link	d								20 11	20 11	20 35	20 38			20 59			22 05	23 10
Worcester Foregate Street 7	a								20 23	20 24	20 43	20 46			21 08			22 13	23 19
	d								20 24	20 25	20 44	20 47			21 10			22 17	23 22
Worcester Shrub Hill 7	a								20 27	20 27	20 46	20 49			21 12			22 19	23 24
	d						19 53				20 51	20 54						22 26	
Droitwich Spa	d						20 01				20 59	21 02						22 34	
Bromsgrove	d						20 10				21 08	21 11							
Barnt Green	d																		
University	d																		
Hartlebury	d																		
Kidderminster	d																	22 44	
Blakedown	d																		
Hagley	d																	22 51	
Stourbridge Junction 2	d																	22 55	
Lye	d																		
Cradley Heath	d																	23 01	
Old Hill	d																		
Rowley Regis	d																	23 06	
Langley Green	d																		
Birmingham New Street 12	a						20 36				21 42	21 42							
	d	19 03	19 13	19 13	19 33			20 03						20 33		21 03			
Birmingham International ✈	d	19 14						20 14								21 14			
Coventry	d	19 25						20 25								21 24			
Smethwick Galton Bridge 7	d																	23 11	
The Hawthorns 🚋	d																	23 14	
Jewellery Quarter 🚋	d																	23 17	
Birmingham Snow Hill 🚋	a																	23 21	
	d					19 10							20 15				21 15		
Birmingham Moor Street	d					19 13							20 18				21 18		
Bordesley	d																		
Small Heath	d																		
Tyseley	d																		
Acocks Green	d																		
Olton	d																		
Solihull	d					19 21							20 28				21 28		
Widney Manor	d					19 24							20 31				21 31		
Dorridge	d					19 28							20 35				21 35		
Lapworth	d					19 32													
Hatton	d					19 39													
Warwick Parkway	d					19 43							20 46				21 46		
Warwick	d					19 46							20 49				21 49		
Leamington Spa 8	a	19 36	19 42	19 42	19 59	19 50		20 36					20 53	20 59		21 34	21 53		
	d	19 38	19 43	19 43	20 00	19 50		20 38					20 54	21 00			21 54		
Banbury	d	19a55	20 01	20 01	20a19	20 10		20a5					21 13	21a19			22 15		
London Marylebone 10 ⊖	a		21 06	21 06		21 53							22 52				23 54		
Spring Road	d																		
Hall Green	d																		
Yardley Wood	d																		
Shirley	d																		
Whitlocks End	d																		
Wythall	d																		
Earlswood (West Midlands)	d																		
The Lakes	d																		
Wood End	d																		
Danzey	d																		
Henley-in-Arden	d																		
Wootton Wawen	d																		
Wilmcote	d																		
Stratford-upon-Avon	a																		

A until 11 July
B from 18 July until 5 September
C 12 September, 19 September, 26 September
D until 5 September
E from 18 July until 26 September

Table 71

Sundays from 03 October

Hereford, Worcester and Stourbridge - Birmingham - Leamington Spa, Marylebone and Stratford-upon-Avon

		LM	CH ◇	XC ◇1	CH ◇	CH	XC ◇1	CH ◇	CH ◇	LM	CH ◇	XC ◇1	CH ◇	XC ◇1	CH	LM	XC ◇1	CH	XC ◇1	CH	LM	CH ◇	XC ◇1
Hereford 7	d																						
Ledbury	a																						
	d																						
Colwall	d																						
Great Malvern	a																						
	d																						
Malvern Link	d																						
Worcester Foregate Street 7	a																						
	d																						
Worcester Shrub Hill 7	a																						
	d	22p47																					
Droitwich Spa	d	22p55																					
Bromsgrove	d																						
Barnt Green	d																						
University	d																						
Hartlebury	d																						
Kidderminster	d	23p05								10 08													
Blakedown	d	23p10								10 13													
Hagley	d	23p14								10 17													
Stourbridge Junction 2	d	23p18								10 22						11 22					12 22		
Lye	d									10 25						11 25					12 25		
Cradley Heath	d									10 29						11 29					12 29		
Old Hill	d									10 33						11 33					12 33		
Rowley Regis	d									10 36						11 36					12 36		
Langley Green	d									10 39						11 39					12 39		
Birmingham New Street 12	a																						
	d			09 03			10 03					11 03		11 33			12 03		12 33				13 03
Birmingham International ✈	d			09 14			10 14					11 14					12 14						13 14
Coventry	d			09 25			10 25					11 25					12 25						13 25
Smethwick Galton Bridge 7	d									10 43						11 43					12 43		
The Hawthorns 🚋	d									10 45						11 45					12 45		
Jewellery Quarter 🚋	d									10 49						11 49					12 49		
Birmingham Snow Hill 🚋	a	23p36								10 52						11 52					12 52		
	d	23p37	08 40		09 10	09 40		10 10	10 40	10 53			11 10		11 40	11 53		12 10		12 40	12 53		
Birmingham Moor Street	d	23p40	08 43		09 13	09 43		10 13	10 43	10 56			11 13		11 43	11 56		12 13		12 43	12 56		
Bordesley	d																						
Small Heath	d	23p44																					
Tyseley	d	23p46																					
Acocks Green	d	23p49								11 02						12 02					13 04		
Olton	d	23p52								11 04						12 04					13 06		
Solihull	d	23p56	08 52		09 22	09 52		10 22	10 52	11 08			11 22		11 52	12 08		12 22		12 52	13 10		
Widney Manor	d	23p59								11 11						12 11					13 13		
Dorridge	d	00 03	08 58		09 28	09 58		10 28	10 58	11a16			11 28		11 58	12a16		12 28		12 58	13a18		
Lapworth	d	00 07							11 02														
Hatton	d	00 13							11 07														
Warwick Parkway	d	00 18	09 09		09 38	10 09		10 38	11 12				11 38		12 09			12 38		13 09			
Warwick	d	00 21	09 12		09 41			10 41					11 41					12 41					
Leamington Spa 8	a	00 26	09 16	09 36	09 46	10 15	10 36	10 46	11 16			11 36	11 46	11 59	12 15		12 36	12 46	12 59	13 15			13 36
	d		09 17	09 38	09 47	10 16	10 38	10 47	11 18		11 20	11 38	11 47	12 00	12 16		12 38	12 47	13 00	13 16		13 20	13 38
Banbury	d		09 36	09a55	10 06	10 35	10a55	11 06	11 37			11a55	12 06	12a19	12 35		12a55	13 06	13a19	13 35			13a55
London Marylebone 10 ⊖	a		10 54		11 26	12 01		12 25	13 04				13 25		14 01			14 25		15 03			
Spring Road	d																						
Hall Green	d																						
Yardley Wood	d																						
Shirley	d																						
Whitlocks End	d																						
Wythall	d																						
Earlswood (West Midlands)	d																						
The Lakes	d																						
Wood End	d																						
Danzey	d																						
Henley-in-Arden	d																						
Wootton Wawen	d																						
Wilmcote	d										11 43											13 43	
Stratford-upon-Avon	a										12 02											13 57	

Table 71

Sundays from 03 October

Hereford, Worcester and Stourbridge - Birmingham - Leamington Spa, Marylebone and Stratford-upon-Avon

		CH ◇	XC ◇1	CH	LM	XC ◇1		CH ◇	XC ◇1	LM	CH	LM	CH ◇	XC ◇1	XC ◇1	LM		CH	LM	XC ◇1	CH	XC ◇1	CH	LM	LM
Hereford 7	d															15 30									
Ledbury	a															15 47									
	d															15 51									
Colwall	d															15 58									
Great Malvern	a															16 02									
	d									14 35						16 03									17 17
Malvern Link	d									14 37						16 05									17 20
Worcester Foregate Street 7	a									14 45						16 14									17 28
	d									14 45						16 15									17 28
Worcester Shrub Hill 7	a									14 48						16 18									17 31
	d									14 51						16 33									17 34
Droitwich Spa	d									14 59						16 41									17 42
Bromsgrove	d									15 09						16 51									17 52
Barnt Green	d																								
University	d																								
Hartlebury	d																								
Kidderminster	d																								
Blakedown	d																								
Hagley	d																								
Stourbridge Junction 2	d				13 22							14 22							15 22					16 22	
Lye	d				13 25							14 25							15 25					16 25	
Cradley Heath	d				13 29							14 29							15 29					16 29	
Old Hill	d				13 33							14 33							15 33					16 33	
Rowley Regis	d				13 36							14 36							15 36					16 36	
Langley Green	d				13 39							14 39							15 39					16 39	
Birmingham New Street 12	a									15 37						17 17									18 13
	d		13 33			14 03			14 33					15 03	15 33					16 04		16 33			
Birmingham International ✈	d					14 14								15 14						16 14					
Coventry	d					14 25								15 25						16 25					
Smethwick Galton Bridge 7	d				13 43							14 43							15 43					16 43	
The Hawthorns	d				13 45							14 45							15 45					16 45	
Jewellery Quarter	d				13 49							14 49							15 49					16 49	
Birmingham Snow Hill	a				13 52							14 52							15 52					16 52	
	d	13 10		13 40	13 53			14 10			14 40	14 53						15 40	15 53		16 10		16 40	16 53	
Birmingham Moor Street	d	13 13		13 43	13 56			14 13			14 43	14 56						15 43	15 56		16 13		16 43	16 56	
Bordesley	d																								
Small Heath	d																								
Tyseley	d																								
Acocks Green	d				14 02							15 02							16 02					17 02	
Olton	d				14 04							15 04							16 04					17 04	
Solihull	d	13 22		13 52	14 08			14 22			14 52	15 08						15 52	16 08		16 22		16 52	17 08	
Widney Manor	d				14 11							15 11							16 11					17 11	
Dorridge	d	13 28		13 58	14a17			14 28			14 58	15a17						15 58	16a16		16 28		16 58	17a17	
Lapworth	d			14 02														16 02							
Hatton	d			14 07														16 07							
Warwick Parkway	d	13 38		14 12				14 38			15 09							16 12			16 38		17 09		
Warwick	d	13 41						14 41													16 41				
Leamington Spa 8	a	13 46	13 59	14 17		14 36		14 46	14 59		15 15			15 36	15 59			16 17		16 36	16 46	16 59	17 15		
	d	13 47	14 00	14 18		14 38		14 47	15 00		15 16		15 20	15 38	16 00			16 18		16 38	16 47	17 00	17 16		
Banbury	d	14 06	14a19	14 37		14a55		15 06	15a19		15 35			15a55	16a19			16 37		16a55	17 06	17a19	17 35		
London Marylebone 10 ⊖	a	15 26		16 05				16 25			17 01							18 05			18 24		19 02		
Spring Road	d																								
Hall Green	d																								
Yardley Wood	d																								
Shirley	d																								
Whitlocks End	d																								
Wythall	d																								
Earlswood (West Midlands)	d																								
The Lakes	d																								
Wood End	d																								
Danzey	d																								
Henley-in-Arden	d																								
Wootton Wawen	d																								
Wilmcote	d												15 43												
Stratford-upon-Avon	a												15 57												

Table 71

Sundays from 03 October

Hereford, Worcester and Stourbridge - Birmingham - Leamington Spa, Marylebone and Stratford-upon-Avon

		CH ◇		XC ◇1	CH	XC ◇1	CH	LM	XC ◇1	CH ◇	XC ◇1	GW ◇1		CH	CH ◇	XC ◇1	XC ◇1	LM	XC ◇1	GW ◇1	LM	CH ◇		XC ◇1	GW ◇1
Hereford 7	d											18 30									20 05				
Ledbury	a											18 47									20 20				
	d											18 48									20 21				
Colwall	d											18 55									20 27				
Great Malvern	a											19 00									20 32				
	d											19 11								20 10	20 32				20 55
Malvern Link	d											19 14								20 11	20 35				20 59
Worcester Foregate Street 7	a											19 23								20 23	20 43				21 08
	d											19 25								20 24	20 44				21 10
Worcester Shrub Hill 7	a											19 27								20 27	20 46				21 12
	d																	19 53			20 51				
Droitwich Spa	d																	20 01			20 59				
Bromsgrove	d																	20 10			21 08				
Barnt Green	d																								
University	d																								
Hartlebury	d																								
Kidderminster	d																								
Blakedown	d																								
Hagley	d																								
Stourbridge Junction 2	d							17 22																	
Lye	d							17 25																	
Cradley Heath	d							17 29																	
Old Hill	d							17 33																	
Rowley Regis	d							17 36																	
Langley Green	d							17 39																	
Birmingham New Street 12	a																	20 36			21 42				
	d			17 03		17 33			18 03		18 33					19 03	19 33		20 03					20 33	
Birmingham International ✈	d			17 14					18 14							19 14			20 14						
Coventry	d			17 25					18 25							19 25			20 25						
Smethwick Galton Bridge 7	d							17 43																	
The Hawthorns	d							17 45																	
Jewellery Quarter	d							17 49																	
Birmingham Snow Hill	a							17 53																	
	d				17 10		17 40	17 53		18 10				18 40								20 15			
Birmingham Moor Street	d				17 13		17 43	17 56		18 13				18 43								20 18			
Bordesley	d																								
Small Heath	d																								
Tyseley	d																								
Acocks Green	d							18 02																	
Olton	d							18 04																	
Solihull	d				17 22		17 52	18 08		18 22				18 52								20 28			
Widney Manor	d							18 11														20 31			
Dorridge	d				17 28		17 58	18a17		18 28				18 58								20 35			
Lapworth	d						18 02																		
Hatton	d						18 07																		
Warwick Parkway	d				17 38		18 12			18 38				19 09								20 46			
Warwick	d				17 41					18 41												20 49			
Leamington Spa 8	a			17 36	17 46	17 59	18 17		18 36	18 46	18 59			19 15			19 59		20 36			20 53		20 59	
	d	17 20		17 38	17 47	18 00	18 18		18 38	18 47	19 00			19 16	19 20	19 38	20 00		20 38			20 54		21 00	
Banbury	d			17a55	18 06	18a19	18 37		18a55	19 06	19a19			19 35		19a55	20a19		20a55			21 13		21a19	
London Marylebone 10 ⊖	a				19 25		20 05			20 24				21 01								22 55			
Spring Road	d																								
Hall Green	d																								
Yardley Wood	d																								
Shirley	d																								
Whitlocks End	d																								
Wythall	d																								
Earlswood (West Midlands)	d																								
The Lakes	d																								
Wood End	d																								
Danzey	d																								
Henley-in-Arden	d																								
Wootton Wawen	d																								
Wilmcote	d	17 43													19 43										
Stratford-upon-Avon	a	17 57													19 57										

Table 71

Sundays
from 03 October

Hereford, Worcester and Stourbridge - Birmingham - Leamington Spa, Marylebone and Stratford-upon-Avon

		XC	CH	LM	LM
		◇1	◇		
Hereford	d				22 40
Ledbury	a				22 56
	d				22 56
Colwall	d				23 03
Great Malvern	a				23 07
	d			22 02	23 08
Malvern Link	d			22 05	23 10
Worcester Foregate Street	a			22 13	23 19
	d			22 17	23 22
Worcester Shrub Hill	a			22 19	23 24
	d			22 26	
Droitwich Spa	d			22 34	
Bromsgrove	d				
Barnt Green	d				
University	d				
Hartlebury	d				
Kidderminster	d			22 44	
Blakedown	d				
Hagley	d			22 51	
Stourbridge Junction	d			22 55	
Lye	d				
Cradley Heath	d			23 01	
Old Hill	d				
Rowley Regis	d			23 06	
Langley Green	d				
Birmingham New Street	a				
	d	21 03			
Birmingham International	d	21 14			
Coventry	d	21 24			
Smethwick Galton Bridge	d			23 11	
The Hawthorns	d			23 14	
Jewellery Quarter	d			23 17	
Birmingham Snow Hill	a			23 21	
	d		21 15		
Birmingham Moor Street	d		21 18		
Bordesley	d				
Small Heath	d				
Tyseley	d				
Acocks Green	d				
Olton	d				
Solihull	d		21 28		
Widney Manor	d		21 31		
Dorridge	d		21 35		
Lapworth	d				
Hatton	d				
Warwick Parkway	d		21 46		
Warwick	d		21 49		
Leamington Spa	a	21 34	21 53		
	d				
Banbury	d		22 15		
London Marylebone	a		23 57		
Spring Road	d				
Hall Green	d				
Yardley Wood	d				
Shirley	d				
Whitlocks End	d				
Wythall	d				
Earlswood (West Midlands)	d				
The Lakes	d				
Wood End	d				
Danzey	d				
Henley-in-Arden	d				
Wootton Wawen	d				
Wilmcote	d				
Stratford-upon-Avon	a				

Table 71

Mondays to Fridays
until 01 October

Stratford-upon-Avon, Marylebone and Leamington Spa - Birmingham - Stourbridge, Worcester and Hereford

		CH	LM	GW	LM	LM	LM	LM	LM	GW	LM	LM	CH	LM	LM	LM	LM	LM	XC	CH	CH	XC
		MX ◇		1															◇1			◇1
Stratford-upon-Avon	d												06 10	06 29			06 52			06 46		
Wilmcote	d												06 14	06 34			06 57					
Wootton Wawen	d													06x39			07x02					
Henley-in-Arden	d													06 43			07 06					
Danzey	d													06x47			07x11					
Wood End	d													06x51			07x15					
The Lakes	d													06x53			07x18					
Earlswood (West Midlands)	d													06 55			07 20					
Wythall	d													06 58			07 23					
Whitlocks End	d													07 00			07 26					
Shirley	d							06 31	06 52					07 03			07 29					
Yardley Wood	d							06 34	06 55					07 06			07 32					
Hall Green	d							06 37	06 58					07 09			07 36					
Spring Road	d							06 39	07 00					07 11			07 38					
London Marylebone	d	22p20																				
Banbury	d	23p31																	06 54		07 02	07 26
Leamington Spa	a	23p48											06 45						07 10	07 17	07 22	07 42
	d	23p48				05 47						06 29						07 08	07 12		07 22	07 43
Warwick	d	23p53				05 51						06 33						07 12			07 26	
Warwick Parkway	d	23p56				05 55						06 37						07 16			07 30	
Hatton	d					06 00						06 42						07 21			07 34	
Lapworth	d					06 06						06 48						07 28				
Dorridge	d	00 07			05 54	06 11						06 53			07 09			07 34			07 43	
Widney Manor	d				05 59	06 14						06 56			07 14			07 37			07 47	
Solihull	d	00 13			06 02	06 18						07 00			07 17			07 41			07 51	
Olton	d				06 06	06 21						07 03			07 21			07 44			07 55	
Acocks Green	d				06 08	06 24						07 06			07 23			07 47				
Tyseley	d				06 11	06 27		06 42	07 03			07 09		07 14	07 26		07 41	07 50				
Small Heath	d				06 14	06 29		06 44	07 05			07 11		07 17	07 29		07 43	07 53				
Bordesley	d																					
Birmingham Moor Street	d	00 23			06 18	06 33		06 48	07 09			07 15		07 21	07 33		07 47	07 57			08 04	
Birmingham Snow Hill	a	00 32			06 20	06 37		06 51	07 12			07 19		07 24	07 35		07 52	07 59			08 11	
	d				06 22			06 53	07 13			07 23			07 37		07 53	08 03				
Jewellery Quarter	d				06 24			06 55	07 15			07 25			07 39		07 55	08 05				
The Hawthorns	d				06 29			07 00	07 20			07 30			07 44		08 00	08 10				
Smethwick Galton Bridge	d				06 31			07 03	07 23			07 33			07 47		08 03	08 13				
Coventry	a																		07 22			
Birmingham International	a																		07 37			
Birmingham New Street	a																		07 48			08 16
	d						06 59				07 20					07 59						
Langley Green	d				06 34			07 06				07 36			07 50			08 16				
Rowley Regis	d				06 38			07 09	07 28			07 39			07 53		08 08	08 19				
Old Hill	d				06 41			07 12				07 42			07 56			08 22				
Cradley Heath	d				06 44			07 16	07 33			07 46			08 00		08 13	08 26				
Lye	d				06 47			07 19				07 49			08 03			08 29				
Stourbridge Junction	d				06 51			07 23	07a39			07 53			08a07		08 19	08 33				
Hagley	d				06 54			07 26				07 56					08 23	08 36				
Blakedown	d				06 57			07 29				07 59					08 26	08 39				
Kidderminster	d				07 02			07 34				08 04					08 31	08a45				
Hartlebury	d							07 39				08 09					08 36					
University	d						07 05				07 27					08 06						
Barnt Green	d										07 43											
Bromsgrove	d						07 23				07 48					08 21						
Droitwich Spa	d				07 13		07 33	07 46			07 58	08 17				08 31	08 44					
Worcester Shrub Hill	a			06 32						07 54	08 05	08 25										
	d		06 00	06 32						07 55	08 09	08 29										
Worcester Foregate Street	a		06 02	06 38	07 22		07 41	07 57		07 58	08 11	08 31				08 39	08 59					
	d		06 03				07 42			07 58	08 12					08 41						
Malvern Link	d		06 12				07 52			08 07	08 20					08 51						
Great Malvern	a		06 15				07 54			08 12	08 23					08 53						
	d		06 15				08 01									08 54						
Colwall	d		06 20				08 06									08 59						
Ledbury	a		06 27				08 13									09 07						
	d		06 29				08 14									09 10						
Hereford	a		06 50				08 34									09 30						

Table 71

Mondays to Fridays
until 01 October

Stratford-upon-Avon, Marylebone and Leamington Spa - Birmingham - Stourbridge, Worcester and Hereford

		LM	LM	LM	LM	LM	LM	CH	XC	LM	CH	XC	LM	LM	CH	WS	XC	GW	LM	GW	LM	LM	LM	CH
									◇1		◇	◇1			◇	◇1	◇1	1						◇
Stratford-upon-Avon	d	07 23						07 36					08 27											
Wilmcote	d							07 40					08 32											
Wootton Wawen	d												08x37											
Henley-in-Arden	d	07 34											08 41											
Danzey	d												08x45											
Wood End	d												08x49											
The Lakes	d												08x51											
Earlswood (West Midlands)	d	07 43											08 54											
Wythall	d	07 45											08 56											
Whitlocks End	d	07 48											08 59											
Shirley	d	07 51		08 09						08 38			09 02									09 22		
Yardley Wood	d	07 54		08 12						08 41			09 05									09 25		
Hall Green	d	07 58		08 15						08 44			09 08									09 28		
Spring Road	d	08 00		08 17						08 46			09 10									09 30		
London Marylebone 10 ⊖	d										06 50				07 15	07 33								07 50
Banbury	d								07 55		08 05	08 27			08 34	08 37	08 54							08 58
Leamington Spa 8	a							08 11	08 11		08 23	08 43			08 51	08 54	09 10							09 15
	d				07 47		08 00		08 12		08 24	08 44			08 52		09 12							09 15
Warwick	d				07 51		08 04				08 28				08 57									09 19
Warwick Parkway	d				07 55		08 08				08 32				09 00									09 22
Hatton	d				08 00		08 13								09 07									
Lapworth	d				08 06		08 19								09 12									
Dorridge	d		07 56		08 11	08 20	08 25				08 43			09 09	09 16								09 28	09 33
Widney Manor	d		08 01		08 14	08 24	08 28							09 13									09 32	
Solihull	d		08 04		08 18	08 28	08 32				08 48			09 16	09 21								09 36	09 39
Olton	d		08 08		08 21	08 32	08 36							09 20									09 39	
Acocks Green	d		08 11		08 24	08 35	08 38							09 22									09 42	
Tyseley	d		08 14	08 20	08 27	08 38	08 41			08 49												09 33		09 47
Small Heath	d			08 23	08 29		08 44			08 51												09 35		
Bordesley	d																							
Birmingham Moor Street	d	08 07	08 19	08 27	08 33	08 42	08 48			08 55	09 00		09 17	09 29	09 33							09 39	09 48	09 51
Birmingham Snow Hill ⇌	a	08 11	08 21	08 29	08 37	08 47	08 51			08 58	09 07		09 20	09 31	09 41							09 42	09 51	10 01
	d	08 13	08 23	08 33			08 53			09 03			09 23	09 33								09 43	09 53	
Jewellery Quarter ⇌	d	08 15	08 25	08 35			08 55			09 05			09 25	09 35								09 45	09 55	
The Hawthorns ⇌	d	08 20	08 30	08 40			09 00			09 10			09 30	09 40								09 50	10 00	
Smethwick Galton Bridge 7	d	08 23	08 33	08 43			09 03			09 13			09 33	09 43								09 53	10 03	
Coventry	a								08 23								09 22							
Birmingham International ✈	a								08 37								09 37							
Birmingham New Street 12	a								08 48			09 18					09 48							
	d																		08 49		09 49			
Langley Green	d			08 46						09 16				09 46										
Rowley Regis	d	08 28	08 38	08 49			09 08			09 19			09 38	09 49								09 58	10 08	
Old Hill	d			08 52						09 22				09 52										
Cradley Heath	d	08 33	08 43	08 56			09 13			09 26			09 43	09 56								10 03	10 13	
Lye	d			08 59						09 29				09 59										
Stourbridge Junction 2	d	08a39	08a49	09 03			09a19			09 33			09a49	10 03								10 09	10a19	
Hagley	d																					10 12		
Blakedown	d																					10 15		
Kidderminster	d			09a12						09a42				10a13								10 20		
Hartlebury	d																							
University	d																		08 55		09 55			
Barnt Green	d																							
Bromsgrove	d																		09 11		10 11			
Droitwich Spa	d																		09 21		10 23	10 31		
Worcester Shrub Hill 7	a																	09 16		10 14				
	d																	09 16		10 15				
Worcester Foregate Street 7	a																	09 19	09 29	10 17	10 31	10 40		
	d																	09 19	09 30	10 18	10 32	10 41		
Malvern Link	d																	09 28	09 40	10 27	10 42	10 51		
Great Malvern	a																	09 31	09 42	10 31	10 45	10 54		
	d																		09 43		10 45			
Colwall	d																		09 48		10 50			
Ledbury	a																		09 56		10 58			
	d																		10 00		11 00			
Hereford 7	a																		10 19		11 20			

Table 71

Mondays to Fridays
until 01 October

Stratford-upon-Avon, Marylebone and Leamington Spa - Birmingham - Stourbridge, Worcester and Hereford

		XC	LM	LM	LM	CH	CH	XC	GW	LM	GW	LM	LM	CH	XC	CH	LM	LM	LM	CH	XC	XC
		◇1				◇	◇	◇1	◇1		◇1			◇	◇1	◇				◇	◇1	◇1
Stratford-upon-Avon	d			09 27			09 36											10 27				
Wilmcote	d			09 32			09 40											10 32				
Wootton Wawen	d			09x37														10x37				
Henley-in-Arden	d			09 41														10 41				
Danzey	d			09x45														10x45				
Wood End	d			09x49														10x49				
The Lakes	d			09x51														10x51				
Earlswood (West Midlands)	d			09 54														10 54				
Wythall	d			09 56														10 56				
Whitlocks End	d			09 59														10 59				
Shirley	d		09 42	10 02								10 22					10 42	11 02				
Yardley Wood	d		09 45	10 05								10 25					10 45	11 05				
Hall Green	d		09 48	10 08								10 28					10 48	11 08				
Spring Road	d		09 50	10 10								10 30					10 50	11 10				
London Marylebone 10 ⊖	d					08 20								08 50		09 17				09 20		
Banbury	d	09 26				09 35		09 54						09 57	10 25	10 29				10 35	10 54	11 25
Leamington Spa 8	a	09 42				09 53	10 09	10 10						10 15	10 44	10 49				10 54	11 10	11 41
	d	09 43				09 54		10 12						10 15	10 45	10 49				10 54	11 12	11 43
Warwick	d					09 58								10 19		10a53				10 59		
Warwick Parkway	d					10 02								10 22						11 02		
Hatton	d					10 07																
Lapworth	d					10 12																
Dorridge	d				10 09	10 17							10 28	10 33					11 09	11 13		
Widney Manor	d				10 13								10 32						11 13			
Solihull	d				10 17	10 23							10 36	10 39					11 17	11 19		
Olton	d				10 20								10 39						11 20			
Acocks Green	d				10 23								10 42						11 23			
Tyseley	d											10 33										
Small Heath	d											10 35										
Bordesley	d																					
Birmingham Moor Street	d		09 57	10 17	10 29	10 34						10 39	10 48	10 51			10 57	11 17	11 29	11 31		
Birmingham Snow Hill ⇌	a		10 01	10 20	10 32	10 41						10 42	10 51	11 01			11 01	11 20	11 32	11 41		
	d		10 03	10 23	10 33							10 43	10 53				11 03	11 23	11 33			
Jewellery Quarter ⇌	d		10 05	10 25	10 35							10 45	10 55				11 05	11 25	11 35			
The Hawthorns ⇌	d		10 10	10 30	10 40							10 50	11 00				11 10	11 30	11 40			
Smethwick Galton Bridge 7	d		10 13	10 33	10 43							10 53	11 03				11 13	11 33	11 43			
Coventry	a							10 22													11 22	
Birmingham International ✈	a							10 37													11 37	
Birmingham New Street 12	a	10 18						10 48							11 18						11 48	12 18
	d									10 49												
Langley Green	d		10 16		10 46												11 16		11 46			
Rowley Regis	d		10 19	10 38	10 49							10 58	11 08				11 19	11 38	11 49			
Old Hill	d		10 22		10 52												11 22		11 52			
Cradley Heath	d		10 26	10 43	10 56							11 03	11 13				11 26	11 43	11 56			
Lye	d		10 29		10 59												11 29		11 59			
Stourbridge Junction 2	d		10 33	10a49	11 03							11 09	11a19				11 33	11a49	12 03			
Hagley	d											11 12										
Blakedown	d											11 15										
Kidderminster	d		10a43		11a13							11 20					11a43		12a13			
Hartlebury	d																					
University	d									10 55												
Barnt Green	d																					
Bromsgrove	d									11 11												
Droitwich Spa	d									11 22		11 31										
Worcester Shrub Hill 7	a											11 39										
	d								10 52		11 36											
Worcester Foregate Street 7	a								10 55	11 31	11 39											
	d								10 56	11 32												
Malvern Link	d								11 05	11 42												
Great Malvern	a								11 09	11 44												
	d								11 09	11 45												
Colwall	d								11 15	11 50												
Ledbury	a								11 23	11 58												
	d								11 24	12 00												
Hereford 7	a								11 44	12 22												

Stratford-upon-Avon, Marylebone and Leamington Spa - Birmingham - Stourbridge, Worcester and Hereford

		GW	LM	LM	LM	CH	LM	GW	LM	LM	LM	CH	CH	XC	CH	CH	LM	XC	LM	LM	LM	LM	LM	WS	CH
		◇				🛒		◇■1 🍴				◇ 🛒		◇■1 🛒	🛒	◇ 🛒		◇■1 🛒						◇■1 🍴	🛒
Stratford-upon-Avon	d									11 27			11 40								12 27				
Wilmcote	d									11 32											12 32				
Wootton Wawen	d									11x37											12x37				
Henley-in-Arden	d									11 41											12 41				
Danzey	d									11x45											12x45				
Wood End	d									11x49											12x49				
The Lakes	d									11x51											12x51				
Earlswood (West Midlands)	d									11 54											12 54				
Wythall	d									11 56											12 56				
Whitlocks End	d									11 59											12 59				
Shirley	d			11 22			11 42			12 02							12 22			12 42	13 02				
Yardley Wood	d			11 25			11 45			12 05							12 25			12 45	13 05				
Hall Green	d			11 28			11 48			12 08							12 28			12 48	13 08				
Spring Road	d			11 30			11 50			12 10							12 30			12 50	13 10				
London Marylebone 10 ⊖	d					09 50						10 20			10 50	10 54								11 20	11 24
Banbury	d					10 57						11 35		11 56	11 59	12 17		12 27						12 30	12 38
Leamington Spa 8	a					11 15						11 54	12 09	12 12	12 16	12 37		12 44						12 47	12 55
	d					11 15						11 54		12 13	12 16	12 38		12 45							12 56
Warwick	d					11 19						11 59			12 20	12 42									13 00
Warwick Parkway	d					11 22						12 02			12 23										13 04
Hatton	d											12 07				12a49									
Lapworth	d											12 13													
Dorridge	d				11 28	11 33			11 46		12 09	12 17			12 33				12 28				13 09		13 15
Widney Manor	d				11 32				11 50		12 13								12 32				13 13		
Solihull	d				11 36	11 39			11 54		12 17	12 23			12 39				12 36				13 17		13 20
Olton	d				11 39				11 57		12 20								12 39				13 20		
Acocks Green	d				11 42				12 00		12 23								12 42				13 23		
Tyseley	d			11 33					12 03								12 33								
Small Heath	d			11 35					12 05								12 35								
Bordesley	d																								
Birmingham Moor Street	d			11 39	11 48	11 49	11 57		12 09	12 17	12 29	12 35			12 49		12 39		12 48	12 57	13 17		13 29		13 32
Birmingham Snow Hill 🚊	a			11 42	11 51	12 02	12 00		12 12	12 20	12 32	12 42			13 02		12 42		12 51	13 01	13 20		13 32		13 41
	d			11 43	11 53		12 03		12 13	12 23	12 33						12 43		12 53	13 03	13 23		13 33		
Jewellery Quarter 🚊	d			11 45	11 55		12 05		12 15	12 25	12 35						12 45		12 55	13 05	13 25		13 35		
The Hawthorns 🚊	d			11 50	12 00		12 10		12 20	12 30	12 40						12 50		13 00	13 10	13 30		13 40		
Smethwick Galton Bridge 7	d			11 53	12 03		12 13		12 23	12 33	12 43						12 53		13 03	13 13	13 33		13 43		
Coventry	a													12 24											
Birmingham International ✈	a													12 37											
Birmingham New Street 12	a													12 48				13 18							
	d		11 49											12 57				12 57				12 49			
Langley Green	d						12 16				12 46									13 16			13 46		
Rowley Regis	d			11 58	12 08		12 19		12 28	12 38	12 49						12 58		13 08	13 19	13 38		13 49		
Old Hill	d						12 22				12 52									13 22			13 52		
Cradley Heath	d			12 03	12 13		12 26		12 33	12 43	12 56						13 03		13 13	13 26	13 43		13 56		
Lye	d						12 29				12 59									13 29			13 59		
Stourbridge Junction 7	d			12 09	12a19		12 33		12 39	12a49	13 03						13 09		13a19	13a33	13a50		14 03		
Hagley	d			12 12					12 42								13 12								
Blakedown	d			12 15					12 45								13 15								
Kidderminster	d			12 20			12a43		12 50		13a13						13 20						14a13		
Hartlebury	d																								
University	d		11 55																			12 55			
Barnt Green	d																								
Bromsgrove	d		12 11																			13 11			
Droitwich Spa	d		12 21	12 31					13 01								13 31					13 22			
Worcester Shrub Hill 7	a																13 39								
	d	12 15						12 50																	
Worcester Foregate Street 7	a	12 17	12 30	12 40				12 54	13 10													13 30			
	d	12 18	12 31					12 54	13 11													13 31			
Malvern Link	d	12 27	12 40					13 03	13 20													13 41			
Great Malvern	a	12 33	12 42					13 07	13 24													13 43			
	d		12 43					13 09														13 44			
Colwall	d		12 48					13 15														13 49			
Ledbury	a		12 56					13 23														13 57			
	d		12 58					13 28														14 00			
Hereford 7	a		13 18					13 45														14 22			

Table 71

Mondays to Fridays
until 01 October

Stratford-upon-Avon, Marylebone and Leamington Spa - Birmingham - Stourbridge, Worcester and Hereford

		XC	GW	GW	LM		LM	LM	CH	XC	LM	LM	LM	LM	CH		XC	LM	LM	LM	CH	XC	LM	GW	LM
		◇■1 🛒	◇■1 🍴	◇					◇ 🛒	◇■1 🛒							◇■1 🛒				◇	◇■1 🛒		◇■1 🛒	
Stratford-upon-Avon	d												13 27												
Wilmcote	d												13 32												
Wootton Wawen	d												13x37												
Henley-in-Arden	d												13 41												
Danzey	d												13x45												
Wood End	d												13x49												
The Lakes	d												13x51												
Earlswood (West Midlands)	d												13 54												
Wythall	d												13 56												
Whitlocks End	d												13 59												
Shirley	d						13 22				13 42		14 02						14 22				14 42		
Yardley Wood	d						13 25				13 45		14 05						14 25				14 45		
Hall Green	d						13 28				13 48		14 08						14 28				14 48		
Spring Road	d						13 30				13 50		14 10						14 30				14 50		
London Marylebone 10 ⊖	d								11 50						12 20						12 50				
Banbury	d	12 54							12 57	13 25					13 35		13 54				13 57	14 28			
Leamington Spa 8	a	13 10							13 15	13 42					13 54		14 10				14 14	14 44			
	d	13 12							13 15	13 43					13 54		14 12				14 15	14 45			
Warwick	d								13 19						13 59						14 19				
Warwick Parkway	d								13 22						14 02						14 22				
Hatton	d														14 07										
Lapworth	d														14 13										
Dorridge	d							13 28	13 33			13 46		14 09	14 17					14 28	14 33				14 46
Widney Manor	d							13 32				13 50		14 13						14 32					14 50
Solihull	d							13 36	13 39			13 54		14 17	14 23					14 36	14 39				14 54
Olton	d							13 39				13 57		14 20						14 39					14 57
Acocks Green	d							13 42				14 00		14 23						14 42					15 00
Tyseley	d						13 33		13 47			14 03			14 28				14 33						15 03
Small Heath	d						13 35					14 05							14 35						15 05
Bordesley	d																								
Birmingham Moor Street	d						13 39	13 48	13 51		13 57	14 09	14 17	14 29	14 35				14 39	14 48	14 51		14 57		15 09
Birmingham Snow Hill 🚊	a						13 42	13 51	14 01		14 01	14 12	14 20	14 32	14 42				14 42	14 51	15 02		15 01		15 12
	d						13 43	13 53			14 03	14 13	14 23	14 33					14 43	14 53			15 03		15 13
Jewellery Quarter 🚊	d						13 45	13 55			14 05	14 15	14 25	14 35					14 45	14 55			15 05		15 15
The Hawthorns 🚊	d						13 50	14 00			14 10	14 20	14 30	14 40					14 50	15 00			15 10		15 20
Smethwick Galton Bridge 7	d						13 53	14 03			14 13	14 23	14 33	14 43					14 53	15 03			15 13		15 23
Coventry	a	13 22															14 22								
Birmingham International ✈	a	13 37															14 37								
Birmingham New Street 12	a	13 48								14 18							14 48					15 18			
	d	12 57			13 49													14 49							
Langley Green	d										14 16			14 46									15 16		
Rowley Regis	d						13 58	14 08			14 19	14 28	14 38	14 49					14 58	15 08			15 19		15 28
Old Hill	d										14 22			14 52									15 22		
Cradley Heath	d						14 03	14 13			14 26	14 33	14 43	14 56					15 03	15 13			15 26		15 33
Lye	d										14 29			14 59									15 29		
Stourbridge Junction 7	d						14 09	14a19			14 33	14 39	14a49	15 03					15 09	15a19			15 33		15 39
Hagley	d						14 12					14 42							15 12				15 37		15 43
Blakedown	d						14 15					14 45							15 15						15 46
Kidderminster	d						14 20				14a43	14 50		15a13					15 20				15a44		15 51
Hartlebury	d																								
University	d				13 55													14 55							
Barnt Green	d																								
Bromsgrove	d				14 13													15 11							
Droitwich Spa	d				14 23		14 31					15 01						15 21	15 31						16 01
Worcester Shrub Hill 7	a						14 39																		16 11
	d		13 40	14 15			14 43																	15 44	
Worcester Foregate Street 7	a		13 43	14 18	14 31		14 45					15 10						15 31	15 40					15 47	
	d		13 44	14 18	14 32		14 46											15 32						15 48	
Malvern Link	d		13 53	14 27	14 42		14 54											15 42						15 57	
Great Malvern	a		13 57	14 37	14 45		14 58											15 44						16 00	
	d				14 45													15 45							
Colwall	d				14 50													15 50							
Ledbury	a				14 57													15 58							
	d				14 58													16 01							
Hereford 7	a				15 19													16 22							

Table 71

Mondays to Fridays

until 01 October

Stratford-upon-Avon, Marylebone and Leamington Spa - Birmingham - Stourbridge, Worcester and Hereford

		LM	LM	CH	CH	XC	CH	XC	LM	LM	LM		LM	GW	LM	LM	LM	LM	CH	XC	LM	LM	LM	CH	XC
					◇	◇1	◇	◇1						◇						◇1				◇	◇1
						🛒		🛒												🛒					🛒
Stratford-upon-Avon	d	14 27			14 36												15 27								
Wilmcote	d	14 32			14 40												15 32								
Wootton Wawen	d	14x37															15x37								
Henley-in-Arden	d	14 41															15 41								
Danzey	d	14x45															15x45								
Wood End	d	14x49															15x49								
The Lakes	d	14x51															15x51								
Earlswood (West Midlands)	d	14 54															15 54								
Wythall	d	14 56															15 56								
Whitlocks End	d	14 59															15 59								
Shirley	d	15 02								15 22			15 42				16 02					16 21			
Yardley Wood	d	15 05								15 25			15 45				16 05					16 24			
Hall Green	d	15 08								15 28			15 48				16 08					16 27			
Spring Road	d	15 10								15 30			15 50				16 10					16 29			
London Marylebone [10] ⊖	d			13 20			13 50												14 20					14 50	
Banbury	d			14 35		14 56	14 59	15 25											15 35	15 54				15 57	16 30
Leamington Spa [8]	a			14 54	15 08	15 13	15 17	15 42											15 54	16 10				16 15	16 48
	d			14 54	15 09	15 14	15 17	15 43											15 54	16 12				16 15	16 49
Warwick	d			14 59			15 21												15 59					16 19	
Warwick Parkway	d			15 02			15 24												16 02					16 22	
Hatton	d																		16 07						
Lapworth	d																		16 13						
Dorridge	d		15 09	15 13			15 34				15 28					15 46		16 09	16 17				16 27	16 33	
Widney Manor	d		15 13								15 32					15 50		16 13					16 31		
Solihull	d		15 17	15 19			15 40				15 36					15 54		16 17	16 23				16 35	16 39	
Olton	d		15 20								15 39					15 57		16 20					16 38		
Acocks Green	d		15 23								15 42					16 00		16 23					16 41		
Tyseley	d			15 27						15 33						16 03						16 32	16 44		
Small Heath	d									15 35						16 05						16 34			
Bordesley	d																								
Birmingham Moor Street	d	15 17	15 29	15 33			15 51			15 39	15 48		15 57			16 09	16 17	16 29	16 35			16 38	16 49	16 51	
Birmingham Snow Hill ⇌	a	15 20	15 32	15 41			16 01			15 42	15 51		16 01			16 12	16 21	16 32	16 42			16 41	16 51	17 01	
	d	15 23	15 33							15 43	15 53		16 03			16 13	16 23	16 33				16 43	16 53		
Jewellery Quarter ⇌	d	15 25	15 35							15 45	15 55		16 05			16 15	16 25	16 35				16 46	16 55		
The Hawthorns ⇌	d	15 30	15 40							15 50	16 00		16 10			16 20	16 30	16 40				16 51	17 00		
Smethwick Galton Bridge [7]	d	15 33	15 43							15 53	16 03		16 13			16 23	16 33	16 43				16 54	17 03		
Coventry	a					15 24														16 22					
Birmingham International ✈	a					15 37														16 37					
Birmingham New Street [12]	a					15 48		16 18												16 48					17 18
	d								15 49						16 20						16 49				
Langley Green	d		15 46										16 16					16 46							
Rowley Regis	d	15 38	15 49							15 58	16 08		16 19			16 28	16 38	16 49				16 59	17 08		
Old Hill	d		15 52										16 22					16 52							
Cradley Heath	d	15 43	15 56							16 03	16 13		16 26			16 33	16 43	16 56				17 05	17 13		
Lye	d		15 59										16 29					16 59							
Stourbridge Junction [2]	d	15a49	16 03							16 09	16a19		16 33			16 39	16a49	17 03				17 11	17a19		
Hagley	d		16 06							16 12						16 42		17 06				17 15			
Blakedown	d									16 15						16 45		17 09				17 19			
Kidderminster	d		16a14							16 20			16a43			16 50		17a15				17 24			
Hartlebury	d																					17 29			
University	d								15 55						16 26						16 55				
Barnt Green	d																								
Bromsgrove	d								16 11						16 42						17 11				
Droitwich Spa	d								16 21	16 31					16 52	17 01					17 22	17 37			
Worcester Shrub Hill [7]	a														16 59						17 29				
	d													16 40	17 07						17 33				
Worcester Foregate Street [7]	a								16 31	16 40				16 42	17 09	17 10					17 35	17 47			
	d								16 32						17 10						17 36				
Malvern Link	d								16 42						17 19						17 45				
Great Malvern	a								16 44						17 22						17 47				
	d								16 45												17 48				
Colwall	d								16 50												17 53				
Ledbury	a								16 58												18 01				
	d								17 00												18 03				
Hereford [7]	a								17 20												18 23				

Table 71

Mondays to Fridays

until 01 October

Stratford-upon-Avon, Marylebone and Leamington Spa - Birmingham - Stourbridge, Worcester and Hereford

		LM	LM	LM	LM	GW	LM	LM	CH	XC	LM	XC	LM	LM	LM	CH	LM	LM	WS	CH	CH	XC	LM	GW	LM
										◇1		◇1							◇1			◇1		1	
										🛒		🛒				🛒			🍽	🛒		🛒			
Stratford-upon-Avon	d				16 23												17 27				17 40				17 58
Wilmcote	d				16 28												17 32								
Wootton Wawen	d				16x33												17x37								
Henley-in-Arden	d				16 38												17 41								18 08
Danzey	d				16x43												17x45								
Wood End	d				16x47												17x49								
The Lakes	d				16x49												17x51								
Earlswood (West Midlands)	d				16 52												17 54								
Wythall	d				16 55												17 56								
Whitlocks End	d				16 58												17 59								
Shirley	d	16 42			17 01						17 21				17 44		18 02								18 22
Yardley Wood	d	16 45			17 04						17 24				17 47		18 05								18 25
Hall Green	d	16 48			17 07						17 27				17 50		18 08								18 28
Spring Road	d	16 50			17 09						17 29				17 52		18 10								18 30
London Marylebone [10] ⊖	d								15 20							16 00			16 30	16 33					
Banbury	d								16 36	16 55		17 28				17 03			17 33	17 40		17 55			
Leamington Spa [8]	a								16 54	17 12		17 44				17 22			17 50	17 57	18 08	18 11			
	d								16 54	17 13		17 45				17 22				17 58	18 08	18 12			
Warwick	d								16 59							17 27				18 02					
Warwick Parkway	d								17 03							17 30				18 05					
Hatton	d																			18 10					
Lapworth	d								17 10											18 15					
Dorridge	d			16 46				17 09	17 15					17 27		17 43		18 02		18 19					
Widney Manor	d			16 50				17 13						17 31				18 06							
Solihull	d			16 54				17 17	17 21					17 35		17 48		18 10		18 24					
Olton	d			16 57				17 20						17 38				18 13							
Acocks Green	d			17 00				17 23						17 41				18 16							
Tyseley	d	16 53		17 03							17 32			17 44				18 19							18 33
Small Heath	d			17 05							17 34			17 46				18 21							18 35
Bordesley	d																								
Birmingham Moor Street	d	16 57		17 09	17 16			17 29	17 33		17 38			17 50	17 59	17 59	18 17	18 25		18 34					18 39
Birmingham Snow Hill ⇌	a	17 01		17 12	17 19			17 32	17 41		17 41			17 53	18 01	18 12	18 20	18 29		18 42					18 42
	d	17 03		17 13	17 20			17 33			17 43			17 53	18 03		18 23								18 43
Jewellery Quarter ⇌	d	17 05		17 16	17 23			17 36			17 45			17 56	18 05		18 25								18 45
The Hawthorns ⇌	d	17 10		17 21	17 27			17 41			17 50			18 01	18 10		18 30								18 50
Smethwick Galton Bridge [7]	d	17 13		17 24	17 30			17 44			17 53			18 04	18 13		18 33								18 53
Coventry	a									17 23												18 22			
Birmingham International ✈	a									17 37												18 37			
Birmingham New Street [12]	a									17 48		18 18										18 48			
	d		17 19				17 49						17 59										18 19		
Langley Green	d	17 16			17 33						17 56				18 16		18 36								
Rowley Regis	d	17 19		17 30	17 37			17 50			17 59			18 09	18 19		18 39								18 58
Old Hill	d	17 22			17 40						18 02				18 22		18 42								
Cradley Heath	d	17 26		17 35	17 43			17 55			18 06			18 15	18 26		18 46								19 04
Lye	d	17 29			17 46						18 09				18 29		18 49								
Stourbridge Junction [2]	d	17 33		17 42	17a51			18 03			18 13			18 21	18 33		18 54								19 09
Hagley	d	17 37		17 46				18 07			18 17			18 25	18 37		18 58								19 13
Blakedown	d	17 40		17 49				18 10			18 20			18 28	18 40		19 01								19 16
Kidderminster	d	17a45		17 54				18 15			18a26			18 33	18a45		19a06								19 21
Hartlebury	d							18 20						18 38											
University	d		17 25				17 55						18 05												
Barnt Green	d																								
Bromsgrove	d		17 45										18 22										18 46		
Droitwich Spa	d		17 55	18 05			18 19	18 28					18 40	18 46									18 56		19 31
Worcester Shrub Hill [7]	a		18 04	18 18			18 28						18 48	18 58									19 11		
	d		18 09			18 19	18 32						18 54											19 12	
Worcester Foregate Street [7]	a		18 11			18 22	18 34	18 38					18 56											19 17	19 41
	d		18 12			18 22	18 35						18 57												
Malvern Link	d		18 21			18 30	18 45						19 06												
Great Malvern	a		18 24			18 36	18 47						19 09												
	d		18 24				18 48																		
Colwall	d		18 28				18 53																		
Ledbury	a		18 36				19 01																		
	d		18 37				19 06																		
Hereford [7]	a		18 57				19 26																		

Table 71

Mondays to Fridays
until 01 October

Stratford-upon-Avon, Marylebone and Leamington Spa - Birmingham - Stourbridge, Worcester and Hereford

		LM		LM	CH	LM	XC	GW	LM	GW	LM	LM		CH	XC	LM	LM	GW	LM	CH	CH	LM		XC	WS
					◇ 🛒		◇1 🛒	◇1 🍽							◇1 🛒			◇1 🍽		◇ 🛒				◇1 🛒	◇1 🍽
Stratford-upon-Avon	d					18 25						18 50										19 26			
Wilmcote	d					18 30						18 55										19 31			
Wootton Wawen	d					18x35						19x00										19x36			
Henley-in-Arden	d					18 39						19 04										19 40			
Danzey	d					18x43																19x44			
Wood End	d					18x47																19x48			
The Lakes	d					18x49																19x50			
Earlswood (West Midlands)	d					18 52																19 53			
Wythall	d					18 54																19 55			
Whitlocks End	d					18 57																19 58			
Shirley	d			18 39		19 00						19 17				19 27						20 01			
Yardley Wood	d			18 42		19 03						19 20				19 30						20 04			
Hall Green	d			18 45		19 06						19 23				19 33						20 07			
Spring Road	d			18 47		19 08						19 25				19 35						20 09			
London Marylebone [10] ⊖	d				17 00									17 30						18 00	17 38				18 30
Banbury	d				18 03		18 27							18 41	18 55					19 05	19b09			19 31	19 34
Leamington Spa [8]	a				18 23		18 44							18 59	19 10					19 22	19 27			19 47	19 53
	d				18 23		18 45							19 00	19 12					19 22	19 28			19 48	
Warwick	d													19 04							19 32				
Warwick Parkway	d				18 29									19 08						19 28	19a41				
Hatton	d													19 13											
Lapworth	d													19 18											
Dorridge	d	18 23			18 40						18 58			19 23					19 30	19 39					
Widney Manor	d	18 27									19 02								19 34						
Solihull	d	18 31			18 45						19 06			19 28					19 38	19 44					
Olton	d	18 34									19 09								19 41						
Acocks Green	d	18 37									19 12								19 44						
Tyseley	d	18 40		18 50							19 15					19 38			19 47						
Small Heath	d	18 42									19 17					19 40			19 49						
Bordesley	d																								
Birmingham Moor Street	d	18 46		18 55	18 56	19 15					19 21	19 32		19 38		19 44			19 53	19 57		20 16			
Birmingham Snow Hill 🚊	a	18 49		18 57	19 01	19 18					19 24	19 35		19 48		19 47			19 56	20 01		20 19			
	d			18 59	19 10						19 27	19 39							19 58	20 10		20 20			
Jewellery Quarter 🚊	d			19 01							19 29	19 41							20 00			20 22			
The Hawthorns 🚊	d			19 06	19 16						19 34	19 46							20 05	20 16		20 27			
Smethwick Galton Bridge [7]	d			19 09	19 19						19 37	19 49							20 08	20 19		20 30			
Coventry	a														19 22										
Birmingham International ✈	a														19 37									20 18	
Birmingham New Street [12]	a						19 18								19 48										
	d								19 19								19 49								
Langley Green	d			19 12							19 40								20 11			20 33			
Rowley Regis	d			19 15	19 24						19 43	19 54							20 14	20 24		20 36			
Old Hill	d			19 18							19 46								20 17			20 39			
Cradley Heath	d			19 22	19 29						19 50	20 00							20 21	20 29		20 43			
Lye	d			19 25							19 53								20 24			20 46			
Stourbridge Junction [2]	d			19a29	19 36						19 57	20a06							20 28	20 36		20a51			
Hagley	d										20 00								20 31						
Blakedown	d										20 03								20 34						
Kidderminster	d				19a48						20 08								20 39	20a50					
Hartlebury	d																								
University	d								19 25								19 55								
Barnt Green	d																								
Bromsgrove	d								19 40								20 09								
Droitwich Spa	d								19 50		20 19						20 25		20 50						
Worcester Shrub Hill [7]	a								20 01		20 27						20 34		20 59						
	d							19 45	20 12	20 20								20 41							
Worcester Foregate Street [7]	a							19 48	20 14	20 22								20 45							
	d							19 49	20 15	20 25								20 45							
Malvern Link	d							19 58	20 24	20 34								20 54							
Great Malvern	a							20 02	20 26	20 38								20 58							
	d							20 02	20 27									20 58							
Colwall	d							20 08	20 33									21 04							
Ledbury	a							20 16	20 40									21 12							
	d							20 17	20 40									21 14							
Hereford [7]	a							20 34	21 00									21 31							

Table 71

Mondays to Fridays
until 01 October

Stratford-upon-Avon, Marylebone and Leamington Spa - Birmingham - Stourbridge, Worcester and Hereford

		CH	XC	LM	GW	LM	CH	CH		LM	XC	CH	XC	CH	GW	LM	LM	CH		XC	LM	CH	XC	LM FO	LM FX
			◇1 🛒		◇1 🍽		◇ 🛒	◇			◇1 🛒		◇1		◇1					◇1		◇	◇1		
Stratford-upon-Avon	d							19 48		20 26															
Wilmcote	d							19 53		20 31															
Wootton Wawen	d									20x36															
Henley-in-Arden	d									20 40															
Danzey	d									20x44															
Wood End	d									20x48															
The Lakes	d									20x50															
Earlswood (West Midlands)	d									20 53															
Wythall	d									20 55															
Whitlocks End	d									20 58															
Shirley	d									21 01											21 57				
Yardley Wood	d									21 04											22 00				
Hall Green	d									21 07											22 03				
Spring Road	d									21 09											22 05				
London Marylebone [10] ⊖	d	18 33					19 00					19 30						20 00				20 30			
Banbury	d	19 40	19 54				20 03				20 28	20 38	20 54					21 07		21 41		21 47	21 54		
Leamington Spa [8]	a	19 58	20 10				20 23	20 23			20 45	20 55	21 10					21 25		21 59		22 04	22 10		
	d	19 59	20 12				20 23				20 46	20 56	21 12	22 25				21 26		22 00		22 05	22 12		
Warwick	d	20 03										21 00		22 29								22 10			
Warwick Parkway	d	20 07					20 29					21 04						21 31				22 14			
Hatton	d	20 12										21 09										22 19			
Lapworth	d	20 17										21 14										22 24			
Dorridge	d	20 23				20 29	20 40					21 19					21 31	21 42				22 29			
Widney Manor	d					20 33											21 35					22 32			
Solihull	d	20 29				20 36	20 45					21 25					21 38	21 47				22 36			
Olton	d					20 40											21 42					22 40			
Acocks Green	d					20 42											21 44					22 43			
Tyseley	d					20 45	20 55										21 47				22 08				
Small Heath	d					20 48											21 50				22 10				
Bordesley	d																								
Birmingham Moor Street	d	20 38				20 52	20 57			21 16		21 37					21 54	21 59			22 14	22 50			
Birmingham Snow Hill 🚊	a	20 48				20 54	21 03			21 19		21 47					21 56	22 04			22 17	22 58			
	d					20 55	21 05			21 20							21 57	22 10			22 20				
Jewellery Quarter 🚊	d					20 58				21 22							22 00				22 22				
The Hawthorns 🚊	d					21 02	21 11			21 27							22 04	22 16			22 27				
Smethwick Galton Bridge [7]	d					21 05	21 14			21 30							22 07	22 19			22 30				
Coventry	a		20 22										21 22										22 22		
Birmingham International ✈	a		20 37										21 37										22 33		
Birmingham New Street [12]	a		20 48								21 22		21 48							22 30			22 45		
	d			20 59												22 00								23 00	23 00
Langley Green	d					21 08				21 33							22 10				22 33				
Rowley Regis	d					21 11	21 20			21 36							22 13	22 24			22 36				
Old Hill	d					21 14				21 39							22 16				22 39				
Cradley Heath	d					21 17	21 25			21 43							22 19	22 29			22 43				
Lye	d					21 20				21 46							22 22				22 46				
Stourbridge Junction [2]	d					21 24	21 33			21a50							22 26	22 36			22a50				
Hagley	d					21 28											22 30								
Blakedown	d					21 31											22 33								
Kidderminster	d					21 36	21a49										22 38	22a50							
Hartlebury	d																								
University	d			21 06												22 06								23 06	23 06
Barnt Green	d																								
Bromsgrove	d			21 23												22 23								23 20	23 20
Droitwich Spa	d			21 33		21 47										22 34	22 49							23 30	23 30
Worcester Shrub Hill [7]	a					21 57										22 48	22 57							23 39	23 39
	d				21 49	22 03									22 40		23 05								
Worcester Foregate Street [7]	a			21 41	21 52	22 05									22 44		23 07								
	d			21 42	21 53										22 44		23 08								
Malvern Link	d			21 52	22 04										22 53		23 16								
Great Malvern	a			21 54	22 08										22 57		23 19								
	d			21 55	22 19																				
Colwall	d			22 00	22 25																				
Ledbury	a			22 08	22 33																				
	d			22 10	22 35																				
Hereford [7]	a			22 30	22 52																				

Table 71

Mondays to Fridays
until 01 October

Stratford-upon-Avon, Marylebone and Leamington Spa - Birmingham - Stourbridge, Worcester and Hereford

		LM	CH	LM	CH	XC	CH	CH	CH FO	CH FO
			◇		◇	◇1		◇		◇
Stratford-upon-Avon	d						23 00			
Wilmcote	d									
Wootton Wawen	d									
Henley-in-Arden	d									
Danzey	d									
Wood End	d									
The Lakes	d									
Earlswood (West Midlands)	d									
Wythall	d									
Whitlocks End	d									
Shirley	d			22 57						
Yardley Wood	d			23 00						
Hall Green	d			23 03						
Spring Road	d			23 05						
London Marylebone 10 ⊖	d		21 00		21 33			22 20	23 10	23 54
Banbury	d		22 10		22 43	22 53		23 31	00 33	01 19
Leamington Spa 8	a		22 28		23 00	23 12	23 24	23 48	00 51	01 39
	d		22 30		23 00	23 13		23 48	00 52	
Warwick	d				23 05			23 53	00 56	
Warwick Parkway	d		22 35		23 07			23 56	01a06	
Hatton	d									
Lapworth	d									
Dorridge	d	22 32	22 46		23 18			00 07		
Widney Manor	d	22 36								
Solihull	d	22 40	22 51		23 24			00 13		
Olton	d	22 43								
Acocks Green	d	22 46								
Tyseley	d	22 49		23 08						
Small Heath	d	22 51		23 10						
Bordesley	d									
Birmingham Moor Street	d	22 55	23 00	23 14	23 34			00 23		
Birmingham Snow Hill	a	22 58	23 05	23 17	23 45			00 32		
	d	22 59	23 22							
Jewellery Quarter	d	23 01	23 24							
The Hawthorns	d	23 06	23 29							
Smethwick Galton Bridge 7	d	23 09	23 32							
Coventry	a					23 25				
Birmingham International ✈	a					23 36				
Birmingham New Street 12	a					23 49				
	d									
Langley Green	d	23 12	23 35							
Rowley Regis	d	23 15	23 38							
Old Hill	d	23 18	23 41							
Cradley Heath	d	23 22	23 44							
Lye	d	23 25	23 47							
Stourbridge Junction 2	d	23 29	23 52							
Hagley	d	23 32								
Blakedown	d	23 35								
Kidderminster	d	23 40								
Hartlebury	d									
University	d									
Barnt Green	d									
Bromsgrove	d									
Droitwich Spa	d	23 51								
Worcester Shrub Hill 7	a	23 59								
	d									
Worcester Foregate Street 7	a									
	d									
Malvern Link	d									
Great Malvern	a									
	d									
Colwall	d									
Ledbury	a									
	d									
Hereford 7	a									

Table 71

Mondays to Fridays
from 04 October

Stratford-upon-Avon, Marylebone and Leamington Spa - Birmingham - Stourbridge, Worcester and Hereford

		CH MO	CH MX	LM	GW	LM	LM	LM	LM	LM	GW	LM	LM	CH	LM	LM	LM	LM	LM	XC	CH	CH	XC
		◇	◇		1															◇1 ⚲			◇1 ⚲
Stratford-upon-Avon	d													06 10	06 29			06 52			06 46		
Wilmcote	d													06 14	06 34			06 57					
Wootton Wawen	d														06x39			07x02					
Henley-in-Arden	d														06 43			07 06					
Danzey	d														06x47			07x11					
Wood End	d														06x51			07x15					
The Lakes	d														06x53			07x18					
Earlswood (West Midlands)	d														06 55			07 20					
Wythall	d														06 58			07 23					
Whitlocks End	d														07 00			07 26					
Shirley	d								06 31	06 52					07 03			07 29					
Yardley Wood	d								06 34	06 55					07 06			07 32					
Hall Green	d								06 37	06 58					07 09			07 36					
Spring Road	d								06 39	07 00					07 11			07 38					
London Marylebone 10 ⊖	d	22p00	22p20																				
Banbury	d	23p06	23p31																	06 54		07 02	07 26
Leamington Spa 8	a	23p23	23p48											06 48						07 10	07 17	07 22	07 42
	d	23p24	23p48				05 47						06 29						07 08	07 12		07 22	07 43
Warwick	d	23p28	23p53				05 51						06 33						07 12			07 26	
Warwick Parkway	d	23p32	23p56				05 55						06 37						07 16			07 30	
Hatton	d						06 00						06 42						07 21			07 34	
Lapworth	d						06 06						06 48						07 28				
Dorridge	d	23p43	00 07			05 54	06 11						06 53			07 09			07 34			07 43	
Widney Manor	d					05 59	06 14						06 56			07 14			07 37			07 47	
Solihull	d	23p48	00 13			06 02	06 18						07 00			07 17			07 41			07 51	
Olton	d					06 06	06 21						07 03			07 21			07 44			07 55	
Acocks Green	d					06 08	06 24						07 06			07 23			07 47				
Tyseley	d					06 11	06 27		06 42	07 03			07 09		07 14	07 26		07 41	07 50				
Small Heath	d					06 14	06 29		06 44	07 05			07 11		07 17	07 29		07 43	07 53				
Bordesley	d																						
Birmingham Moor Street	d	23p59	00 23			06 18	06 33		06 48	07 09			07 15		07 21	07 33		07 47	07 57			08 04	
Birmingham Snow Hill	a	00 11	00 35			06 20	06 37		06 51	07 12			07 19		07 24	07 35		07 52	07 59			08 14	
	d					06 22			06 53	07 13			07 23			07 37		07 53	08 03				
Jewellery Quarter	d					06 24			06 55	07 15			07 25			07 39		07 55	08 05				
The Hawthorns	d					06 29			07 00	07 20			07 30			07 44		08 00	08 10				
Smethwick Galton Bridge 7	d					06 31			07 03	07 23			07 33			07 47		08 03	08 13				
Coventry	a																			07 22			
Birmingham International ✈	a																			07 37			
Birmingham New Street 12	a																			07 48			08 16
	d							06 59				07 20					07 59						
Langley Green	d					06 34			07 06				07 36			07 50			08 16				
Rowley Regis	d					06 38			07 09	07 28			07 39			07 53		08 08	08 19				
Old Hill	d					06 41			07 12				07 42			07 56			08 22				
Cradley Heath	d					06 44			07 16	07 33			07 46			08 00		08 13	08 26				
Lye	d					06 47			07 19				07 49			08 03			08 29				
Stourbridge Junction 2	d					06 51			07 23	07a39			07 53			08a07		08 19	08 33				
Hagley	d					06 54			07 26				07 56					08 23	08 36				
Blakedown	d					06 57			07 29				07 59					08 26	08 39				
Kidderminster	d					07 02			07 34				08 04					08 31	08a45				
Hartlebury	d								07 39				08 09					08 36					
University	d							07 05				07 27					08 06						
Barnt Green	d											07 43											
Bromsgrove	d							07 23				07 48					08 21						
Droitwich Spa	d					07 13		07 33	07 46			07 58	08 17				08 31	08 44					
Worcester Shrub Hill 7	a											08 05	08 25										
	d			06 00	06 32						07 55	08 09	08 29										
Worcester Foregate Street 7	a			06 02	06 38	07 22		07 41	07 57		07 58	08 11	08 31				08 39	08 59					
	d			06 03				07 42			07 58	08 12					08 41						
Malvern Link	d			06 12				07 52			08 07	08 20					08 51						
Great Malvern	a			06 15				07 54			08 12	08 23					08 53						
	d			06 15				08 01									08 54						
Colwall	d			06 20				08 06									08 59						
Ledbury	a			06 27				08 13									09 07						
	d			06 29				08 14									09 10						
Hereford 7	a			06 50				08 34									09 30						

Table 71

Mondays to Fridays
from 04 October

Stratford-upon-Avon, Marylebone and Leamington Spa - Birmingham - Stourbridge, Worcester and Hereford

Station		LM	LM	LM	LM	LM	LM	XC ◇1	CH	LM	CH ◇	XC ◇1	LM	LM	CH ◇	XC ◇1	GW 1	LM	GW	LM	LM	LM	CH ◇
Stratford-upon-Avon	d	07 23							07 36				08 27										
Wilmcote	d								07 40				08 32										
Wootton Wawen	d												08x37										
Henley-in-Arden	d	07 34											08 41										
Danzey	d												08x45										
Wood End	d												08x49										
The Lakes	d												08x51										
Earlswood (West Midlands)	d	07 43											08 54										
Wythall	d	07 45											08 56										
Whitlocks End	d	07 48											08 59										
Shirley	d	07 51		08 09						08 38			09 02								09 22		
Yardley Wood	d	07 54		08 12						08 41			09 05								09 25		
Hall Green	d	07 58		08 15						08 44			09 08								09 28		
Spring Road	d	08 00		08 17						08 46			09 10								09 30		
London Marylebone 10 ⊖	d										06 50				07 15								07 50
Banbury	d							07 55			08 05	08 27			08 34	08 54							08 58
Leamington Spa 8	a							08 11	08 14		08 23	08 43			08 51	09 10							09 15
	d				07 47		08 00	08 12			08 24	08 44			08 52	09 12							09 15
Warwick	d				07 51		08 04				08 28				08 57								09 19
Warwick Parkway	d				07 55		08 08				08 32				09 00								09 22
Hatton	d				08 00		08 13								09 07								
Lapworth	d				08 06		08 19								09 12								
Dorridge	d		07 56		08 11	08 20	08 25				08 43			09 09	09 16							09 28	09 33
Widney Manor	d		08 01		08 14	08 24	08 28							09 13								09 32	
Solihull	d		08 04		08 18	08 28	08 32				08 48			09 16	09 21							09 36	09 39
Olton	d		08 08		08 21	08 32	08 36							09 20								09 39	
Acocks Green	d		08 11		08 24	08 35	08 38							09 22								09 42	
Tyseley	d		08 14	08 20	08 27	08 38	08 41			08 49											09 33		09 47
Small Heath	d			08 23	08 29		08 44			08 51											09 35		
Bordesley	d																						
Birmingham Moor Street	d	08 07	08 19	08 27	08 33	08 42	08 48			08 55	09 00		09 17	09 29	09 33						09 39	09 48	09 51
Birmingham Snow Hill ⇌	a	08 11	08 21	08 29	08 37	08 47	08 51			08 58	09 10		09 20	09 31	09 44						09 42	09 51	10 04
	d	08 13	08 23	08 33			08 53			09 03			09 23	09 33							09 43	09 53	
Jewellery Quarter ⇌	d	08 15	08 25	08 35			08 55			09 05			09 25	09 35							09 45	09 55	
The Hawthorns ⇌	d	08 20	08 30	08 40			09 00			09 10			09 30	09 40							09 50	10 00	
Smethwick Galton Bridge 7	d	08 23	08 33	08 43			09 03			09 13			09 33	09 43							09 53	10 03	
Coventry	a							08 23								09 22							
Birmingham International ✈	a							08 37								09 37							
Birmingham New Street 12	a							08 48				09 18				09 48							
	d																	08 49		09 49			
Langley Green	d			08 46						09 16				09 46									
Rowley Regis	d	08 28	08 38	08 49			09 08			09 19			09 38	09 49							09 58	10 08	
Old Hill	d			08 52						09 22				09 52									
Cradley Heath	d	08 33	08 43	08 56			09 13			09 26			09 43	09 56							10 03	10 13	
Lye	d			08 59						09 29				09 59									
Stourbridge Junction 2	d	08a39	08a49	09 03			09a19			09 33			09a49	10 03							10 09	10a19	
Hagley	d																				10 12		
Blakedown	d																				10 15		
Kidderminster	d			09a12						09a42				10a13							10 20		
Hartlebury	d																						
University	d																	08 55		09 55			
Barnt Green	d																						
Bromsgrove	d																	09 11		10 11			
Droitwich Spa	d																	09 21		10 23	10 31		
Worcester Shrub Hill 7	a																						
	d																09 16		10 15				
Worcester Foregate Street 7	a																09 19	09 29	10 17	10 31	10 40		
	d																09 19	09 30	10 18	10 32	10 41		
Malvern Link	d																09 28	09 40	10 27	10 42	10 51		
Great Malvern	a																09 31	09 42	10 31	10 45	10 54		
	d																	09 43		10 45			
Colwall	d																	09 48		10 50			
Ledbury	a																	09 56		10 58			
	d																	10 00		11 00			
Hereford 7	a																	10 19		11 20			

Table 71

Mondays to Fridays
from 04 October

Stratford-upon-Avon, Marylebone and Leamington Spa - Birmingham - Stourbridge, Worcester and Hereford

Station		XC ◇1	LM	LM	LM	CH ◇	CH ◇	XC ◇1	GW ◇1	LM	GW ◇1	LM	LM	CH ◇	XC ◇1	CH ◇	LM	LM	LM	CH ◇	XC ◇1	XC ◇1
Stratford-upon-Avon	d			09 27			09 36											10 27				
Wilmcote	d			09 32			09 40											10 32				
Wootton Wawen	d			09x37														10x37				
Henley-in-Arden	d			09 41														10 41				
Danzey	d			09x45														10x45				
Wood End	d			09x49														10x49				
The Lakes	d			09x51														10x51				
Earlswood (West Midlands)	d			09 54														10 54				
Wythall	d			09 56														10 56				
Whitlocks End	d			09 59														10 59				
Shirley	d		09 42	10 02								10 22					10 42	11 02				
Yardley Wood	d		09 45	10 05								10 25					10 45	11 05				
Hall Green	d		09 48	10 08								10 28					10 48	11 08				
Spring Road	d		09 50	10 10								10 30					10 50	11 10				
London Marylebone 10 ⊖	d					08 20								08 50		09 17				09 20		
Banbury	d	09 26				09 35		09 54						09 57	10 25	10 29				10 35	10 54	11 25
Leamington Spa 8	a	09 42				09 53	10 09	10 10						10 15	10 44	10 49				10 54	11 10	11 41
	d	09 43				09 54		10 12						10 15	10 45	10 49				10 54	11 12	11 43
Warwick	d					09 58								10 19		10 53				10 59		
Warwick Parkway	d					10 02								10 22						11 02		
Hatton	d					10 07																
Lapworth	d					10 12																
Dorridge	d				10 09	10 17							10 28	10 33					11 09	11 13		
Widney Manor	d				10 13								10 32						11 13			
Solihull	d				10 17	10 23							10 36	10 39					11 17	11 19		
Olton	d				10 20								10 39						11 20			
Acocks Green	d				10 23								10 42						11 23			
Tyseley	d											10 33										
Small Heath	d											10 35										
Bordesley	d																					
Birmingham Moor Street	d		09 57	10 17	10 29	10 34						10 39	10 48	10 51			10 57	11 17	11 29	11 31		
Birmingham Snow Hill ⇌	a		10 01	10 20	10 32	10 44						10 42	10 51	11 04			11 01	11 20	11 32	11 44		
	d		10 03	10 23	10 33							10 43	10 53				11 03	11 23	11 33			
Jewellery Quarter ⇌	d		10 05	10 25	10 35							10 45	10 55				11 05	11 25	11 35			
The Hawthorns ⇌	d		10 10	10 30	10 40							10 50	11 00				11 10	11 30	11 40			
Smethwick Galton Bridge 7	d		10 13	10 33	10 43							10 53	11 03				11 13	11 33	11 43			
Coventry	a							10 22													11 22	
Birmingham International ✈	a							10 37													11 37	
Birmingham New Street 12	a	10 18						10 48							11 18						11 48	12 18
	d																					
Langley Green	d		10 16		10 46												11 16		11 46			
Rowley Regis	d		10 19	10 38	10 49							10 58	11 08				11 19	11 38	11 49			
Old Hill	d		10 22		10 52												11 22		11 52			
Cradley Heath	d		10 26	10 43	10 56							11 03	11 13				11 26	11 43	11 56			
Lye	d		10 29		10 59												11 29		11 59			
Stourbridge Junction 2	d		10 33	10a49	11 03							11 09	11a19				11 33	11a49	12 03			
Hagley	d											11 12										
Blakedown	d											11 15										
Kidderminster	d		10a43		11a13							11 20					11a43		12a13			
Hartlebury	d																					
University	d									10 55												
Barnt Green	d																					
Bromsgrove	d									11 11												
Droitwich Spa	d									11 22		11 31										
Worcester Shrub Hill 7	a											11 39										
	d								10 52		11 36											
Worcester Foregate Street 7	a								10 55	11 31	11 39											
	d								10 56	11 32												
Malvern Link	d								11 05	11 42												
Great Malvern	a								11 09	11 44												
	d								11 09	11 45												
Colwall	d								11 15	11 50												
Ledbury	a								11 23	11 58												
	d								11 24	12 00												
Hereford 7	a								11 44	12 22												

Table 71

Mondays to Fridays

from 04 October

Stratford-upon-Avon, Marylebone and Leamington Spa - Birmingham - Stourbridge, Worcester and Hereford

		GW ◇	LM	LM	LM	LM	GW ◇■	LM	LM	LM	CH ◇	CH	XC ◇■	CH ◇	LM	XC ◇■	LM	LM	LM	LM	LM	CH	XC ◇■
Stratford-upon-Avon	d								11 27			11 40							12 27				
Wilmcote	d								11 32										12 32				
Wootton Wawen	d								11x37										12x37				
Henley-in-Arden	d								11 41										12 41				
Danzey	d								11x45										12x45				
Wood End	d								11x49										12x49				
The Lakes	d								11x51										12x51				
Earlswood (West Midlands)	d								11 54										12 54				
Wythall	d								11 56										12 56				
Whitlocks End	d								11 59										12 59				
Shirley	d			11 22		11 42			12 02						12 22			12 42	13 02				
Yardley Wood	d			11 25		11 45			12 05						12 25			12 45	13 05				
Hall Green	d			11 28		11 48			12 08						12 28			12 48	13 08				
Spring Road	d			11 30		11 50			12 10						12 30			12 50	13 10				
London Marylebone ■ ⊖	d										10 20			10 54								11 24	
Banbury	d										11 35		11 56	12 17		12 27						12 38	12 54
Leamington Spa ■	a										11 54	12 09	12 12	12 37		12 44						12 55	13 10
	d										11 54		12 13	12 38		12 45						12 56	13 12
Warwick	d										11 59			12 42								13 00	
Warwick Parkway	d										12 02											13 04	
Hatton	d										12 07			12 49									
Lapworth	d										12 13												
Dorridge	d				11 28			11 46		12 09	12 17						12 28				13 09	13 15	
Widney Manor	d				11 32			11 50		12 13							12 32				13 13		
Solihull	d				11 36			11 54		12 17	12 23						12 36				13 17	13 20	
Olton	d				11 39			11 57		12 20							12 39				13 20		
Acocks Green	d				11 42			12 00		12 23							12 42				13 23		
Tyseley	d			11 33				12 03							12 33								
Small Heath	d			11 35				12 05							12 35								
Bordesley	d																						
Birmingham Moor Street	d			11 39	11 48	11 57		12 09	12 17	12 29	12 35				12 39		12 48	12 57	13 17		13 29	13 32	
Birmingham Snow Hill	a			11 42	11 51	12 00		12 12	12 20	12 32	12 45				12 42		12 51	13 01	13 20		13 32	13 44	
	d			11 43	11 53	12 03		12 13	12 23	12 33					12 43		12 53	13 03	13 23		13 33		
Jewellery Quarter	d			11 45	11 55	12 05		12 15	12 25	12 35					12 45		12 55	13 05	13 25		13 35		
The Hawthorns	d			11 50	12 00	12 10		12 20	12 30	12 40					12 50		13 00	13 10	13 30		13 40		
Smethwick Galton Bridge ■	d			11 53	12 03	12 13		12 23	12 33	12 43					12 53		13 03	13 13	13 33		13 43		
Coventry	a												12 24										13 22
Birmingham International ✈	a												12 37										13 37
Birmingham New Street ■	a												12 48			13 18							13 48
	d		11 49																	12 49			
Langley Green	d					12 16				12 46								13 16			13 46		
Rowley Regis	d			11 58	12 08	12 19		12 28	12 38	12 49					12 58		13 08	13 19	13 38		13 49		
Old Hill	d					12 22				12 52								13 22			13 52		
Cradley Heath	d			12 03	12 13	12 26		12 33	12 43	12 56					13 03		13 13	13 26	13 43		13 56		
Lye	d					12 29				12 59								13 29			13 59		
Stourbridge Junction ■	d			12 09	12a19	12 33		12 39	12a49	13 03					13 09		13a19	13a33	13a50		14 03		
Hagley	d			12 12				12 42							13 12								
Blakedown	d			12 15				12 45							13 15								
Kidderminster	d			12 20		12a43		12 50		13a13					13 20						14a13		
Hartlebury	d																						
University	d		11 55																	12 55			
Barnt Green	d																						
Bromsgrove	d		12 11																	13 11			
Droitwich Spa	d		12 21	12 31				13 01							13 31					13 22			
Worcester Shrub Hill ■	a														13 39								
	d	12 15					12 50																
Worcester Foregate Street ■	a	12 17	12 30	12 40			12 54	13 10												13 30			
	d	12 18	12 31				12 54	13 11												13 31			
Malvern Link	d	12 27	12 40				13 03	13 20												13 41			
Great Malvern	a	12 33	12 42				13 07	13 24												13 43			
	d		12 43				13 09													13 44			
Colwall	d		12 48				13 15													13 49			
Ledbury	a		12 56				13 23													13 57			
	d		12 58				13 28													14 00			
Hereford ■	a		13 18				13 45													14 22			

Table 71

Mondays to Fridays

from 04 October

Stratford-upon-Avon, Marylebone and Leamington Spa - Birmingham - Stourbridge, Worcester and Hereford

		GW ◇■	GW ◇	LM	LM	LM	CH ◇	XC ◇■	LM	LM	LM	LM	CH	XC ◇■	LM	LM	LM	CH ◇	XC ◇■	LM	GW ◇■	LM
Stratford-upon-Avon	d										13 27											
Wilmcote	d										13 32											
Wootton Wawen	d										13x37											
Henley-in-Arden	d										13 41											
Danzey	d										13x45											
Wood End	d										13x49											
The Lakes	d										13x51											
Earlswood (West Midlands)	d										13 54											
Wythall	d										13 56											
Whitlocks End	d										13 59											
Shirley	d				13 22				13 42		14 02					14 22				14 42		
Yardley Wood	d				13 25				13 45		14 05					14 25				14 45		
Hall Green	d				13 28				13 48		14 08					14 28				14 48		
Spring Road	d				13 30				13 50		14 10					14 30				14 50		
London Marylebone ■ ⊖	d						11 50						12 20					12 50				
Banbury	d						12 57	13 25					13 35	13 54				13 57	14 28			
Leamington Spa ■	a						13 15	13 42					13 54	14 10				14 14	14 44			
	d						13 15	13 43					13 54	14 12				14 15	14 45			
Warwick	d						13 19						13 59					14 19				
Warwick Parkway	d						13 22						14 02					14 22				
Hatton	d												14 07									
Lapworth	d												14 13									
Dorridge	d					13 28	13 33			13 46		14 09	14 17				14 28	14 33				14 46
Widney Manor	d					13 32				13 50		14 13					14 32					14 50
Solihull	d					13 36	13 39			13 54		14 17	14 23				14 36	14 39				14 54
Olton	d					13 39				13 57		14 20					14 39					14 57
Acocks Green	d					13 42				14 00		14 23					14 42					15 00
Tyseley	d				13 33		13 47			14 03			14 28			14 33						15 03
Small Heath	d				13 35					14 05						14 35						15 05
Bordesley	d																					
Birmingham Moor Street	d				13 39	13 48	13 51		13 57	14 09	14 17	14 29	14 35			14 39	14 48	14 51		14 57		15 09
Birmingham Snow Hill	a				13 42	13 51	14 04		14 01	14 12	14 20	14 32	14 45			14 42	14 51	15 05		15 01		15 12
	d				13 43	13 53			14 03	14 13	14 23	14 33				14 43	14 53			15 03		15 13
Jewellery Quarter	d				13 45	13 55			14 05	14 15	14 25	14 35				14 45	14 55			15 05		15 15
The Hawthorns	d				13 50	14 00			14 10	14 20	14 30	14 40				14 50	15 00			15 10		15 20
Smethwick Galton Bridge ■	d				13 53	14 03			14 13	14 23	14 33	14 43				14 53	15 03			15 13		15 23
Coventry	a													14 22								
Birmingham International ✈	a													14 37								
Birmingham New Street ■	a							14 18						14 48					15 18			
	d			13 49											14 49							
Langley Green	d								14 16			14 46								15 16		
Rowley Regis	d				13 58	14 08			14 19	14 28	14 38	14 49				14 58	15 08			15 19		15 28
Old Hill	d								14 22			14 52								15 22		
Cradley Heath	d				14 03	14 13			14 26	14 33	14 43	14 56				15 03	15 13			15 26		15 33
Lye	d								14 29			14 59								15 29		
Stourbridge Junction ■	d				14 09	14a19			14 33	14 39	14a49	15 03				15 09	15a19			15 33		15 39
Hagley	d				14 12					14 42						15 12				15 37		15 43
Blakedown	d				14 15					14 45						15 15						15 46
Kidderminster	d				14 20				14a43	14 50		15a13				15 20				15a44		15 51
Hartlebury	d																					
University	d			13 55											14 55							
Barnt Green	d																					
Bromsgrove	d			14 13											15 11							
Droitwich Spa	d			14 23	14 31					15 01					15 21	15 31						16 01
Worcester Shrub Hill ■	a				14 39																	16 11
	d	13 40	14 15		14 43																15 44	
Worcester Foregate Street ■	a	13 43	14 18	14 31	14 45					15 10					15 31	15 40					15 47	
	d	13 44	14 18	14 32	14 46										15 32						15 48	
Malvern Link	d	13 53	14 27	14 42	14 54										15 42						15 57	
Great Malvern	a	13 57	14 37	14 45	14 58										15 44						16 00	
	d			14 45											15 45							
Colwall	d			14 50											15 50							
Ledbury	a			14 57											15 58							
	d			14 58											16 01							
Hereford ■	a			15 19											16 22							

Table 71

Mondays to Fridays
from 04 October

Stratford-upon-Avon, Marylebone and Leamington Spa - Birmingham - Stourbridge, Worcester and Hereford

		LM	LM	CH	CH	XC	XC	LM	LM	LM		LM	GW	LM	LM	LM	LM	CH	XC	LM		LM	LM	CH	XC
					◇	◇1 🚲	◇1 🚲						◇						◇1 🚲					◇	◇1 🚲
Stratford-upon-Avon	d	14 27			14 36											15 27									
Wilmcote	d	14 32			14 40											15 32									
Wootton Wawen	d	14x37														15x37									
Henley-in-Arden	d	14 41														15 41									
Danzey	d	14x45														15x45									
Wood End	d	14x49														15x49									
The Lakes	d	14x51														15x51									
Earlswood (West Midlands)	d	14 54														15 54									
Wythall	d	14 56														15 56									
Whitlocks End	d	14 59														15 59									
Shirley	d	15 02							15 22			15 42				16 02						16 21			
Yardley Wood	d	15 05							15 25			15 45				16 05						16 24			
Hall Green	d	15 08							15 28			15 48				16 08						16 27			
Spring Road	d	15 10							15 30			15 50				16 10						16 29			
London Marylebone 10 ⊖	d			13 20														14 20						14 50	
Banbury	d			14 35		14 56	15 25											15 35	15 54					15 57	16 30
Leamington Spa 8	a			14 54	15 08	15 13	15 42											15 54	16 10					16 15	16 48
	d			14 54		15 14	15 43											15 54	16 12					16 15	16 49
Warwick	d			14 59														15 59						16 19	
Warwick Parkway	d			15 02														16 02						16 22	
Hatton	d																	16 07							
Lapworth	d																	16 13							
Dorridge	d		15 09	15 13						15 28					15 46		16 09	16 17					16 27	16 33	
Widney Manor	d		15 13							15 32					15 50		16 13						16 31		
Solihull	d		15 17	15 19						15 36					15 54		16 17	16 23					16 35	16 39	
Olton	d		15 20							15 39					15 57		16 20						16 38		
Acocks Green	d		15 23							15 42					16 00		16 23						16 41		
Tyseley	d			15 27					15 33						16 03							16 32	16 44		
Small Heath	d								15 35						16 05							16 34			
Bordesley	d																								
Birmingham Moor Street	d	15 17	15 29	15 33					15 39	15 48		15 57			16 09	16 17	16 29	16 35				16 38	16 49	16 51	
Birmingham Snow Hill 🚊	a	15 20	15 32	15 44					15 42	15 51		16 01			16 12	16 21	16 32	16 45				16 41	16 51	17 04	
	d	15 23	15 33						15 43	15 53		16 03			16 13	16 23	16 33					16 43	16 53		
Jewellery Quarter 🚊	d	15 25	15 35						15 45	15 55		16 05			16 15	16 25	16 35					16 46	16 55		
The Hawthorns 🚊	d	15 30	15 40						15 50	16 00		16 10			16 20	16 30	16 40					16 51	17 00		
Smethwick Galton Bridge 7	d	15 33	15 43						15 53	16 03		16 13			16 23	16 33	16 43					16 54	17 03		
Coventry	a					15 24													16 22						
Birmingham International ✈	a					15 37													16 37						
Birmingham New Street 12	a					15 48	16 18												16 48						17 18
	d							15 49						16 20						16 49					
Langley Green	d		15 46									16 16					16 46								
Rowley Regis	d	15 38	15 49						15 58	16 08		16 19			16 28	16 38	16 49					16 59	17 08		
Old Hill	d		15 52									16 22					16 52								
Cradley Heath	d	15 43	15 56						16 03	16 13		16 26			16 33	16 43	16 56					17 05	17 13		
Lye	d		15 59									16 29					16 59								
Stourbridge Junction 2	d	15a49	16 03						16 09	16a19		16 33			16 39	16a49	17 03					17 11	17a19		
Hagley	d		16 06						16 12						16 42		17 06					17 15			
Blakedown	d								16 15						16 45		17 09					17 19			
Kidderminster	d		16a14						16 20			16a43			16 50		17a15					17 24			
Hartlebury	d																					17 29			
University	d							15 55						16 26						16 55					
Barnt Green	d																								
Bromsgrove	d							16 11						16 42						17 11					
Droitwich Spa	d							16 21	16 31					16 52	17 01					17 22		17 37			
Worcester Shrub Hill 7	a													16 59						17 29					
	d												16 40	17 07						17 33					
Worcester Foregate Street 7	a							16 31	16 40				16 42	17 09	17 10					17 35		17 47			
	d							16 32						17 10						17 36					
Malvern Link	d							16 42						17 19						17 45					
Great Malvern	a							16 44						17 22						17 47					
	d							16 45												17 48					
Colwall	d							16 50												17 53					
Ledbury	a							16 58												18 01					
	d							17 00												18 03					
Hereford 7	a							17 20												18 23					

Table 71

Mondays to Fridays
from 04 October

Stratford-upon-Avon, Marylebone and Leamington Spa - Birmingham - Stourbridge, Worcester and Hereford

		LM	LM	LM	LM	GW		LM	LM	CH	XC	LM	XC	LM	LM	LM		LM	LM	CH	CH	XC	LM	GW	LM
											◇1 🚲		◇1 🚲							🚲		◇1 🚲		1	
Stratford-upon-Avon	d				16 23													17 27			17 40				17 58
Wilmcote	d				16 28													17 32							
Wootton Wawen	d				16x33													17x37							
Henley-in-Arden	d				16 38													17 41							18 08
Danzey	d				16x43													17x45							
Wood End	d				16x47													17x49							
The Lakes	d				16x49													17x51							
Earlswood (West Midlands)	d				16 52													17 54							
Wythall	d				16 55													17 56							
Whitlocks End	d				16 58													17 59							
Shirley	d	16 42			17 01							17 21				17 44		18 02							18 22
Yardley Wood	d	16 45			17 04							17 24				17 47		18 05							18 25
Hall Green	d	16 48			17 07							17 27				17 50		18 08							18 28
Spring Road	d	16 50			17 09							17 29				17 52		18 10							18 30
London Marylebone 10 ⊖	d									15 20										16 33					
Banbury	d									16 36	16 55		17 28							17 40		17 55			
Leamington Spa 8	a									16 54	17 12		17 44							17 57	18 08	18 11			
	d									16 54	17 13		17 45							17 58		18 12			
Warwick	d									16 59										18 02					
Warwick Parkway	d									17 03										18 05					
Hatton	d																			18 10					
Lapworth	d									17 10										18 15					
Dorridge	d			16 46					17 09	17 15					17 27				18 02	18 19					
Widney Manor	d			16 50					17 13						17 31				18 06						
Solihull	d			16 54					17 17	17 21					17 35				18 10	18 24					
Olton	d			16 57					17 20						17 38				18 13						
Acocks Green	d			17 00					17 23						17 41				18 16						
Tyseley	d	16 53		17 03								17 32			17 44				18 19						18 33
Small Heath	d			17 05								17 34			17 46				18 21						18 35
Bordesley	d																								
Birmingham Moor Street	d	16 57		17 09	17 16				17 29	17 33		17 38			17 50	17 59		18 17	18 25	18 34					18 39
Birmingham Snow Hill 🚊	a	17 01		17 12	17 19				17 32	17 44		17 41			17 53	18 01		18 20	18 29	18 45					18 42
	d	17 03		17 13	17 20				17 33			17 43			17 53	18 03		18 23							18 43
Jewellery Quarter 🚊	d	17 05		17 16	17 23				17 36			17 45			17 56	18 05		18 25							18 45
The Hawthorns 🚊	d	17 10		17 21	17 27				17 41			17 50			18 01	18 10		18 30							18 50
Smethwick Galton Bridge 7	d	17 13		17 24	17 30				17 44			17 53			18 04	18 13		18 33							18 53
Coventry	a										17 23											18 22			
Birmingham International ✈	a										17 37											18 37			
Birmingham New Street 12	a										17 48		18 18									18 48			
	d		17 19					17 49						17 59									18 19		
Langley Green	d	17 16			17 33							17 56				18 16		18 36							
Rowley Regis	d	17 19		17 30	17 37				17 50			17 59			18 09	18 19		18 39							18 58
Old Hill	d	17 22			17 40							18 02				18 22		18 42							
Cradley Heath	d	17 26		17 35	17 43				17 55			18 06			18 15	18 26		18 46							19 04
Lye	d	17 29			17 46							18 09				18 29		18 49							
Stourbridge Junction 2	d	17 33		17 42	17a51				18 03			18 13			18 21	18 33		18 54							19 09
Hagley	d	17 37		17 46					18 07			18 17			18 25	18 37		18 58							19 13
Blakedown	d	17 40		17 49					18 10			18 20			18 28	18 40		19 01							19 16
Kidderminster	d	17a45		17 54					18 15			18a26			18 33	18a45		19a06							19 21
Hartlebury	d								18 20						18 38										
University	d		17 25					17 55						18 05											
Barnt Green	d																								
Bromsgrove	d		17 45											18 22									18 46		
Droitwich Spa	d		17 55	18 05				18 19	18 28					18 40	18 46								18 56		19 31
Worcester Shrub Hill 7	a		18 04	18 18				18 28						18 48	18 58								19 11		
	d		18 09			18 19		18 32						18 54										19 12	
Worcester Foregate Street 7	a		18 11			18 22		18 34	18 38					18 56										19 17	19 41
	d		18 12			18 22		18 35						18 57											
Malvern Link	d		18 21			18 30		18 45						19 06											
Great Malvern	a		18 24			18 36		18 47						19 09											
	d		18 24					18 48																	
Colwall	d		18 28					18 53																	
Ledbury	a		18 36					19 01																	
	d		18 37					19 06																	
Hereford 7	a		18 57					19 26																	

Table 71

Mondays to Fridays
from 04 October

Stratford-upon-Avon, Marylebone and Leamington Spa - Birmingham - Stourbridge, Worcester and Hereford

		LM	LM	CH	LM	XC	GW	LM	GW	LM	LM	CH	XC	LM	LM	GW	LM	CH	CH	LM	XC	WS
				◇		◇1	◇1						◇1			◇1		◇			◇1	◇1
				⊥		⊥	⊐						⊥			⊐		⊥			⊥	⊐
Stratford-upon-Avon	d				18 25						18 50									19 26		
Wilmcote	d				18 30						18 55									19 31		
Wootton Wawen	d				18x35						19x00									19x36		
Henley-in-Arden	d				18 39						19 04									19 40		
Danzey	d				18x43															19x44		
Wood End	d				18x47															19x48		
The Lakes	d				18x49															19x50		
Earlswood (West Midlands)	d				18 52															19 53		
Wythall	d				18 54															19 55		
Whitlocks End	d				18 57															19 58		
Shirley	d		18 39		19 00						19 17			19 27						20 01		
Yardley Wood	d		18 42		19 03						19 20			19 30						20 04		
Hall Green	d		18 45		19 06						19 23			19 33						20 07		
Spring Road	d		18 47		19 08						19 25			19 35						20 09		
London Marylebone 10 ⊖	d			17 00								17 30						18 00	17 38			18 30
Banbury	d			18 03		18 27						18 41	18 55					19 05	19 09		19 31	19 34
Leamington Spa 8	a			18 23		18 44						18 59	19 10					19 22	19 27		19 47	19 53
	d			18 23		18 45						19 00	19 12					19 22	19 28		19 48	
Warwick	d											19 04							19 32			
Warwick Parkway	d			18 29								19 08						19 28	19a44			
Hatton	d											19 13										
Lapworth	d											19 18										
Dorridge	d	18 23		18 40						18 58		19 23					19 30	19 39				
Widney Manor	d	18 27								19 02							19 34					
Solihull	d	18 31		18 45						19 06		19 28					19 38	19 44				
Olton	d	18 34								19 09							19 41					
Acocks Green	d	18 37								19 12							19 44					
Tyseley	d	18 40	18 50							19 15				19 38			19 47					
Small Heath	d	18 42								19 17				19 40			19 49					
Bordesley	d																					
Birmingham Moor Street	d	18 46	18 55	18 56	19 15					19 21	19 32	19 38		19 44			19 53	19 57		20 16		
Birmingham Snow Hill ⇌	a	18 49	18 57	19 01	19 18					19 24	19 35	19 51		19 47			19 56	20 01		20 19		
	d		18 59	19 10						19 27	19 39						19 58	20 10		20 20		
Jewellery Quarter ⇌	d		19 01							19 29	19 41						20 00			20 22		
The Hawthorns ⇌	d		19 06	19 16						19 34	19 46						20 05	20 16		20 27		
Smethwick Galton Bridge 7	d		19 09	19 19						19 37	19 49						20 08	20 19		20 30		
Coventry	a												19 22									
Birmingham International ✈	a												19 37									
Birmingham New Street 12	a					19 18							19 48								20 18	
	d							19 19							19 49							
Langley Green	d		19 12							19 40							20 11			20 33		
Rowley Regis	d		19 15	19 24						19 43	19 54						20 14	20 24		20 36		
Old Hill	d		19 18							19 46							20 17			20 39		
Cradley Heath	d		19 22	19 29						19 50	20 00						20 21	20 29		20 43		
Lye	d		19 25							19 53							20 24			20 46		
Stourbridge Junction 2	d		19a29	19 36						19 57	20a06						20 28	20 36		20a51		
Hagley	d									20 00							20 31					
Blakedown	d									20 03							20 34					
Kidderminster	d			19a51						20 08							20 39	20a53				
Hartlebury	d																					
University	d							19 25							19 55							
Barnt Green	d																					
Bromsgrove	d							19 40							20 09							
Droitwich Spa	d							19 50		20 19					20 25		20 50					
Worcester Shrub Hill 7	a							20 01		20 27					20 34		20 59					
	d						19 45	20 12	20 20							20 41						
Worcester Foregate Street 7	a						19 48	20 14	20 22							20 45						
	d						19 49	20 15	20 25							20 45						
Malvern Link	d						19 58	20 24	20 34							20 54						
Great Malvern	a						20 02	20 26	20 38							20 58						
	d						20 02	20 27								20 58						
Colwall	d						20 08	20 33								21 04						
Ledbury	a						20 16	20 40								21 12						
	d						20 17	20 40								21 14						
Hereford 7	a						20 34	21 00								21 31						

Table 71

Mondays to Fridays
from 04 October

Stratford-upon-Avon, Marylebone and Leamington Spa - Birmingham - Stourbridge, Worcester and Hereford

		CH	XC	LM	GW	LM	CH	CH	LM	XC	CH	XC	CH	GW	LM	LM	CH	XC	LM	CH	XC	LM FO	LM FX
			◇1		◇1		◇	◇		◇1		◇1		◇1				◇1		◇	◇1		
			⊥		⊐		⊥			⊥													
Stratford-upon-Avon	d							19 48	20 26														
Wilmcote	d							19 53	20 31														
Wootton Wawen	d								20x36														
Henley-in-Arden	d								20 40														
Danzey	d								20x44														
Wood End	d								20x48														
The Lakes	d								20x50														
Earlswood (West Midlands)	d								20 53														
Wythall	d								20 55														
Whitlocks End	d								20 58														
Shirley	d								21 01										21 57				
Yardley Wood	d								21 04										22 00				
Hall Green	d								21 07										22 03				
Spring Road	d								21 09										22 05				
London Marylebone 10 ⊖	d	18 33					19 00				19 30						20 00			20 30			
Banbury	d	19 40	19 54				20 03			20 28	20 38	20 54					21 07	21 41		21 47	21 54		
Leamington Spa 8	a	19 58	20 10				20 23	20 23		20 45	20 55	21 10					21 25	21 59		22 04	22 10		
	d	19 59	20 12				20 23	20 24		20 46	20 56	21 12	22 25				21 26	22 00		22 05	22 12		
Warwick	d	20 03									21 00		22 29							22 10			
Warwick Parkway	d	20 07					20 29				21 04						21 31			22 14			
Hatton	d	20 12									21 09									22 19			
Lapworth	d	20 17									21 14									22 24			
Dorridge	d	20 23				20 29	20 40				21 19					21 31	21 42			22 29			
Widney Manor	d					20 33										21 35				22 32			
Solihull	d	20 29				20 36	20 45				21 25					21 38	21 47			22 36			
Olton	d					20 40										21 42				22 40			
Acocks Green	d					20 42										21 44				22 43			
Tyseley	d					20 45	20 55									21 47			22 08				
Small Heath	d					20 48										21 50			22 10				
Bordesley	d																						
Birmingham Moor Street	d	20 38				20 52	20 57		21 16		21 37					21 54	21 59		22 14	22 50			
Birmingham Snow Hill ⇌	a					20 54	21 03		21 19							21 56	22 04		22 17				
	d					20 55	21 05		21 20							21 57	22 10		22 20				
Jewellery Quarter ⇌	d					20 58			21 22							22 00			22 22				
The Hawthorns ⇌	d					21 02	21 11		21 27							22 04	22 16		22 27				
Smethwick Galton Bridge 7	d					21 05	21 14		21 30							22 07	22 19		22 30				
Coventry	a		20 22									21 22									22 22		
Birmingham International ✈	a		20 37									21 37									22 33		
Birmingham New Street 12	a		20 48							21 22		21 48						22 30			22 45		
	d			20 59											22 00							23 00	23 00
Langley Green	d					21 08			21 33							22 10			22 33				
Rowley Regis	d					21 11	21 20		21 36							22 13	22 24		22 36				
Old Hill	d					21 14			21 39							22 16			22 39				
Cradley Heath	d					21 17	21 25		21 43							22 19	22 29		22 43				
Lye	d					21 20			21 46							22 22			22 46				
Stourbridge Junction 2	d					21 24	21 33		21a50							22 26	22 36		22a50				
Hagley	d					21 28										22 30							
Blakedown	d					21 31										22 33							
Kidderminster	d					21 36	21a52									22 38	22a53						
Hartlebury	d																						
University	d			21 06											22 06							23 06	23 06
Barnt Green	d																						
Bromsgrove	d			21 23											22 23							23 20	23 20
Droitwich Spa	d			21 33		21 47									22 34	22 49						23 30	23 30
Worcester Shrub Hill 7	a					21 57									22 48	22 57						23 39	23 39
	d				21 49	22 03								22 40		23 05							
Worcester Foregate Street 7	a			21 41	21 52	22 05								22 44		23 07							
	d			21 42	21 53									22 44		23 08							
Malvern Link	d			21 52	22 04									22 53		23 16							
Great Malvern	a			21 54	22 08									22 57		23 19							
	d			21 55	22 19																		
Colwall	d			22 00	22 25																		
Ledbury	a			22 08	22 33																		
	d			22 10	22 35																		
Hereford 7	a			22 30	22 52																		

Table 71

Mondays to Fridays
from 04 October

Stratford-upon-Avon, Marylebone and Leamington Spa - Birmingham - Stourbridge, Worcester and Hereford

		LM	LM	CH	XC	CH	CH	CH FO	CH FO
				◇	◇1		◇		◇
Stratford-upon-Avon	d					23 00			
Wilmcote	d								
Wootton Wawen	d								
Henley-in-Arden	d								
Danzey	d								
Wood End	d								
The Lakes	d								
Earlswood (West Midlands)	d								
Wythall	d								
Whitlocks End	d								
Shirley	d		22 57						
Yardley Wood	d		23 00						
Hall Green	d		23 03						
Spring Road	d		23 05						
London Marylebone 10 ⊖	d			21 33			22 20	23 10	23 54
Banbury	d			22 43	22 53		23 31	00 33	01 19
Leamington Spa 8	a			23 00	23 12	23 24	23 48	00 51	01 42
	d			23 00	23 13	23 25	23 48	00 52	
Warwick	d			23 05			23 53	00 56	
Warwick Parkway	d			23 07			23 56	01a09	
Hatton	d								
Lapworth	d								
Dorridge	d	22 32		23 18			00 07		
Widney Manor	d	22 36							
Solihull	d	22 40		23 24			00 13		
Olton	d	22 43							
Acocks Green	d	22 46							
Tyseley	d	22 49	23 08						
Small Heath	d	22 51	23 10						
Bordesley	d								
Birmingham Moor Street	d	22 55	23 14	23 34			00 23		
Birmingham Snow Hill ⇌	a	22 58	23 17	23 48			00 35		
	d	22 59							
Jewellery Quarter ⇌	d	23 01							
The Hawthorns ⇌	d	23 06							
Smethwick Galton Bridge 7	d	23 09							
Coventry	a				23 25				
Birmingham International ✈	a				23 36				
Birmingham New Street 12	a				23 49				
	d								
Langley Green	d	23 12							
Rowley Regis	d	23 15							
Old Hill	d	23 18							
Cradley Heath	d	23 22							
Lye	d	23 25							
Stourbridge Junction 2	d	23 29							
Hagley	d	23 32							
Blakedown	d	23 35							
Kidderminster	d	23 40							
Hartlebury	d								
University	d								
Barnt Green	d								
Bromsgrove	d								
Droitwich Spa	d	23 51							
Worcester Shrub Hill 7	a	23 59							
	d								
Worcester Foregate Street 7	a								
	d								
Malvern Link	d								
Great Malvern	a								
	d								
Colwall	d								
Ledbury	a								
	d								
Hereford 7	a								

Table 71

Saturdays
until 02 October

Stratford-upon-Avon, Marylebone and Leamington Spa - Birmingham - Stourbridge, Worcester and Hereford

		CH	CH	CH	LM	LM	LM	LM	LM	XC	LM	XC	LM	GW	LM	LM	CH	LM	LM	LM	GW	LM	CH	XC
		◇		◇						◇1 🍴		◇1 🍴		◇1			◇				◇1 🍴		◇	◇1 🍴
Stratford-upon-Avon	d															07 02			07 45				07 35	
Wilmcote	d															07 07			07 50					
Wootton Wawen	d															07x12			07x55					
Henley-in-Arden	d															07 16			07 59					
Danzey	d															07x20			08x04					
Wood End	d															07x24			08x08					
The Lakes	d															07x26			08x10					
Earlswood (West Midlands)	d															07 28			08 13					
Wythall	d															07 31			08 15					
Whitlocks End	d															07 33			08 18					
Shirley	d										07 05					07 36			08 21					
Yardley Wood	d										07 08					07 39			08 24					
Hall Green	d										07 11					07 42			08 27					
Spring Road	d										07 13					07 44			08 29					
London Marylebone 10 ⊖	d	22p20	23p10	23p54																				
Banbury	d	23p31	00 33	01 19						06 56		07 33					07 02							07 54
Leamington Spa 8	a	23p48	00 51	01 39						07 12		07 50					07 21						08 08	08 10
	d	23p48	00 52						06 26	07 14		07 51					07 21					07 56	08 09	08 12
Warwick	d	23p53	00 56						06 30								07 25					08 00		
Warwick Parkway	d	23p56	01a06						06 34								07 29					08 04		
Hatton	d								06 39													08 09		
Lapworth	d								06 45													08 15		
Dorridge	d	00 07							06 50						07 25		07 40	08 05				08 21		
Widney Manor	d								06 53						07 29			08 09				08 24		
Solihull	d	00 13							06 57						07 33		07 46	08 13				08 28		
Olton	d								07 00						07 36			08 16				08 31		
Acocks Green	d								07 03						07 39			08 19				08 34		
Tyseley	d								07 06		07 16				07 42	07 47		08 22	08 32			08 37		
Small Heath	d								07 08		07 19				07 44	07 50			08 34			08 39		
Bordesley	d																							
Birmingham Moor Street	d	00 23				06 31		07 01	07 12		07 23				07 48	07 54	07 59	08 27	08 38			08 43		
Birmingham Snow Hill ⇌	a	00 32				06 33		07 03	07 15		07 25				07 51	07 57	08 08	08 29	08 42			08 47		
	d					06 35		07 05			07 28				07 53	08 03		08 30	08 43			08 53		
Jewellery Quarter ⇌	d					06 37		07 07			07 30				07 55	08 05		08 33	08 45			08 55		
The Hawthorns ⇌	d					06 42		07 12			07 35				08 00	08 10		08 37	08 50			09 00		
Smethwick Galton Bridge 7	d					06 45		07 15			07 38				08 03	08 13		08 40	08 53			09 03		
Coventry	a									07 24														08 22
Birmingham International ✈	a									07 39														08 37
Birmingham New Street 12	a									07 51		08 17												08 48
	d						06 49						07 49							08 49				
Langley Green	d					06 48		07 18			07 41					08 16		08 43						
Rowley Regis	d					06 51		07 21			07 44				08 08	08 19		08 47	08 58			09 08		
Old Hill	d					06 54		07 24			07 47					08 22		08 50						
Cradley Heath	d					06 57		07 27			07 51				08 12	08 26		08 53	09 02			09 13		
Lye	d					07 00		07 30			07 54					08 29		08 56						
Stourbridge Junction 2	d					07 04		07 35			07a58				08 18	08a33		09a00	09a08			09 19		
Hagley	d					07 08		07 38							08 21							09 22		
Blakedown	d					07 11		07 41							08 24							09 25		
Kidderminster	d					07 16		07 46							08 29							09 30		
Hartlebury	d					07 21																		
University	d						06 57						07 57							08 57				
Barnt Green	d																							
Bromsgrove	d						07 11						08 11							09 11				
Droitwich Spa	d					07 28	07 21	07 57					08 21		08 40					09 21		09 41		
Worcester Shrub Hill 7	a					07 39		08 07														09 49		
	d				06 30			08 11						08 45							09 44			
Worcester Foregate Street 7	a				06 32		07 29	08 13					08 29	08 47	08 49					09 29	09 46			
	d				06 33		07 30	08 14					08 30	08 48						09 30	09 48			
Malvern Link	d				06 42		07 39	08 23					08 40	08 57						09 40	09 57			
Great Malvern	a				06 44		07 41	08 26					08 42	09 04						09 42	10 04			
	d				06 45		07 42						08 43							09 43				
Colwall	d				06 50		07 47						08 48							09 48				
Ledbury	a				06 57		07 55						08 56							09 56				
	d				06 58		08 00						09 00							10 00				
Hereford 7	a				07 14		08 21						09 20							10 21				

Table 71

Saturdays until 02 October

Stratford-upon-Avon, Marylebone and Leamington Spa - Birmingham - Stourbridge, Worcester and Hereford

		LM	CH	XC	LM	LM	XC	LM	GW	LM	LM	CH	XC	LM	LM	GW	LM	LM	LM	WS	CH	XC	LM
			◇	◇1			◇1					◇	◇1			◇1				◇1	◇	◇1	
Stratford-upon-Avon	d					08 27				08 59								09 27					09 59
Wilmcote	d					08 32												09 32					
Wootton Wawen	d					08x37												09x37					
Henley-in-Arden	d					08 41				09 09								09 41					10 09
Danzey	d					08x45												09x45					
Wood End	d					08x49												09x49					
The Lakes	d					08x51												09x51					
Earlswood (West Midlands)	d					08 54												09 54					
Wythall	d					08 56				09 20								09 56					10 20
Whitlocks End	d					08 59												09 59					
Shirley	d	08 38				09 02				09 24				09 42				10 02					10 24
Yardley Wood	d	08 41				09 05				09 27				09 45				10 05					10 27
Hall Green	d	08 44				09 08				09 30				09 48				10 08					10 30
Spring Road	d	08 46				09 10				09 32				09 50				10 10					10 32
London Marylebone 10 ⊖	d		06 24									07 24								08 14	08 18		
Banbury	d		08 01	08 35			08 54					08 58	09 25							09 29	09 39	09 54	
Leamington Spa 8	a		08 20	08 54			09 10					09 16	09 41							09 48	09 57	10 10	
	d		08 21	08 55			09 12					09 17	09 43								09 58	10 12	
Warwick	d		08 24									09 21									10 02		
Warwick Parkway	d		08 28									09 25									10 06		
Hatton	d		08 33																				
Lapworth	d		08 38																				
Dorridge	d		08 42		08 46			09 09			09 28	09 36					09 46		10 09		10 17		
Widney Manor	d		08 47		08 50			09 13			09 32						09 50		10 13				
Solihull	d		08 50		08 54			09 17			09 36	09 42					09 54		10 17		10 23		
Olton	d				08 57			09 20			09 39						09 57		10 20				
Acocks Green	d				09 00			09 23			09 42						10 00		10 23				
Tyseley	d	08 49			09 03					09 35							10 03						10 35
Small Heath	d	08 51			09 05					09 37							10 05						10 37
Bordesley	d																						
Birmingham Moor Street	d	08 55	09 00		09 09	09 17		09 29		09 41	09 48	09 52		09 58			10 09	10 17	10 29		10 34		10 41
Birmingham Snow Hill ⇌	a	08 58	09 08		09 12	09 20		09 32		09 44	09 51	10 02		10 00			10 12	10 20	10 32		10 41		10 44
	d	09 03			09 13	09 23		09 33		09 45	09 53			10 03			10 13	10 23	10 33				10 45
Jewellery Quarter ⇌	d	09 05			09 15	09 25		09 35		09 47	09 55			10 05			10 15	10 25	10 35				10 47
The Hawthorns ⇌	d	09 10			09 20	09 30		09 40		09 52	10 00			10 10			10 20	10 30	10 40				10 52
Smethwick Galton Bridge 7	d	09 13			09 23	09 33		09 43		09 55	10 03			10 13			10 23	10 33	10 43				10 55
Coventry	a						09 22															10 22	
Birmingham International ✈	a						09 37															10 37	
Birmingham New Street 12	a			09 19			09 48						10 17									10 48	
	d														09 49								
Langley Green	d	09 16						09 46						10 16					10 46				
Rowley Regis	d	09 19			09 28	09 38		09 49		10 00	10 08			10 19			10 28	10 38	10 49				11 00
Old Hill	d	09 22						09 52						10 22					10 52				
Cradley Heath	d	09 26			09 33	09 43		09 56		10 04	10 13			10 26			10 33	10 43	10 56				11 04
Lye	d	09 29						09 59						10 29					10 59				
Stourbridge Junction 2	d	09 33			09 39	09a49		10 03		10 10	10a19			10 33			10 39	10a49	11 03				11 10
Hagley	d				09 42					10 13							10 42						11 13
Blakedown	d				09 45					10 16							10 45						11 16
Kidderminster	d	09a42			09 50			10a12		10 21				10a42			10 50		11a12				11 21
Hartlebury	d																						
University	d														09 57								
Barnt Green	d																						
Bromsgrove	d														10 11								
Droitwich Spa	d				10 01					10 32					10 21		11 01						11 32
Worcester Shrub Hill 7	a									10 40													11 40
	d								10 15							10 45							
Worcester Foregate Street 7	a				10 10				10 17						10 29	10 48	11 10						
	d								10 18						10 30	10 48	11 11						
Malvern Link	d								10 27						10 40	10 57	11 19						
Great Malvern	a								10 31						10 42	11 04	11 22						
	d														10 43	11 07							
Colwall	d														10 48	11 14							
Ledbury	a														10 56	11 21							
	d														11 00	11 23							
Hereford 7	a														11 20	11 42							

Table 71

Saturdays until 02 October

Stratford-upon-Avon, Marylebone and Leamington Spa - Birmingham - Stourbridge, Worcester and Hereford

		LM	CH	CH	XC	LM	LM	LM	LM	LM	CH	XC	GW	LM	LM	LM	CH	XC	LM	GW	LM	LM
			◇	◇	◇1						◇	◇1	◇				◇	◇1		◇1		
Stratford-upon-Avon	d							10 27							10 59							11 27
Wilmcote	d							10 32														11 32
Wootton Wawen	d							10x37														11x37
Henley-in-Arden	d							10 41							11 09							11 41
Danzey	d							10x45														11x45
Wood End	d							10x49														11x49
The Lakes	d							10x51														11x51
Earlswood (West Midlands)	d							10 54														11 54
Wythall	d							10 56							11 20							11 56
Whitlocks End	d							10 59														11 59
Shirley	d					10 42		11 02							11 24				11 42			12 02
Yardley Wood	d					10 45		11 05							11 27				11 45			12 05
Hall Green	d					10 48		11 08							11 30				11 48			12 08
Spring Road	d					10 50		11 10							11 32				11 50			12 10
London Marylebone 10 ⊖	d		08 45	09 12							09 15						09 45					
Banbury	d		09 58	10 20	10 25						10 38	10 54					10 58	11 25				
Leamington Spa 8	a		10 17	10 37	10 41						10 57	11 10					11 16	11 41				
	d		10 17	10 38	10 43						10 58	11 12					11 17	11 43				
Warwick	d		10 21	10 42							11 02						11 21					
Warwick Parkway	d		10 25								11 05						11 25					
Hatton	d		10 30																			
Lapworth	d		10 35																			
Dorridge	d	10 28	10 40					10 46		11 09	11 17					11 28	11 36				11 46	
Widney Manor	d	10 32						10 50		11 13						11 32					11 50	
Solihull	d	10 36	10 45					10 54		11 17	11 23					11 36	11 42				11 54	
Olton	d	10 39						10 57		11 20						11 39					11 57	
Acocks Green	d	10 42						11 00		11 23						11 42					12 00	
Tyseley	d							11 03							11 35						12 03	
Small Heath	d							11 05							11 37						12 05	
Bordesley	d																					
Birmingham Moor Street	d	10 48	10 55			10 58		11 09	11 17	11 29	11 34				11 41	11 48	11 52		11 57		12 09	12 17
Birmingham Snow Hill ⇌	a	10 51	11 04			11 01		11 12	11 20	11 32	11 41				11 44	11 51	12 01		12 01		12 12	12 20
	d	10 53				11 03		11 13	11 23	11 33					11 45	11 53			12 03		12 13	12 23
Jewellery Quarter ⇌	d	10 55				11 05		11 15	11 25	11 35					11 47	11 55			12 05		12 15	12 25
The Hawthorns ⇌	d	11 00				11 10		11 20	11 30	11 40					11 52	12 00			12 10		12 20	12 30
Smethwick Galton Bridge 7	d	11 03				11 13		11 23	11 33	11 43					11 55	12 03			12 13		12 23	12 33
Coventry	a											11 22										
Birmingham International ✈	a											11 37										
Birmingham New Street 12	a				11 17							11 48						12 17				
	d						10 49							11 49								
Langley Green	d					11 16				11 46									12 16			
Rowley Regis	d	11 08				11 19		11 28	11 38	11 49					12 00	12 08			12 19		12 28	12 38
Old Hill	d					11 22				11 52									12 22			
Cradley Heath	d	11 13				11 26		11 33	11 43	11 56					12 04	12 13			12 26		12 33	12 43
Lye	d					11 29				11 59									12 29			
Stourbridge Junction 2	d	11a19				11 33		11 39	11a49	12 03					12 10	12a19			12 33		12 39	12a49
Hagley	d							11 42							12 13						12 42	
Blakedown	d							11 45							12 16						12 45	
Kidderminster	d					11a43		11 50		12a12					12 21				12a42		12 50	
Hartlebury	d																					
University	d						10 57							11 57								
Barnt Green	d																					
Bromsgrove	d						11 11							12 11								
Droitwich Spa	d						11 21	12 01						12 21	12 32						13 01	
Worcester Shrub Hill 7	a																					
	d												12 16							12 45		
Worcester Foregate Street 7	a						11 29	12 10					12 17	12 29	12 41					12 48	13 10	
	d						11 30							12 30						12 48	13 11	
Malvern Link	d						11 40							12 40						12 57	13 19	
Great Malvern	a						11 42							12 42						13 04	13 22	
	d						11 43							12 43						13 07		
Colwall	d						11 48							12 49						13 14		
Ledbury	a						11 56							12 57						13 21		
	d						12 00							13 00						13 23		
Hereford 7	a						12 21							13 20						13 42		

Stratford-upon-Avon, Marylebone and Leamington Spa - Birmingham - Stourbridge, Worcester and Hereford

Station		LM	CH	CH	XC	LM	LM	CH		XC	LM	LM	GW	LM	LM	LM	CH	XC		GW	LM	LM	LM	CH	XC
			◇		◇1 🍴			◇		◇1 🍴			◇1 🍴					◇1 🍴		◇				◇	◇1 🍴
Stratford-upon-Avon	d			11 36		11 59									12 27							12 59			
Wilmcote	d			11 41											12 32										
Wootton Wawen	d														12x37										
Henley-in-Arden	d					12 09									12 41							13 09			
Danzey	d														12x45										
Wood End	d														12x49										
The Lakes	d														12x51										
Earlswood (West Midlands)	d														12 54										
Wythall	d					12 20									12 56							13 20			
Whitlocks End	d														12 59										
Shirley	d					12 24					12 42				13 02							13 24			
Yardley Wood	d					12 27					12 45				13 05							13 27			
Hall Green	d					12 30					12 48				13 08							13 30			
Spring Road	d					12 32					12 50				13 10							13 32			
London Marylebone 10 ⊖	d		10 18					10 50									11 20							11 50	
Banbury	d		11 35		11 54			11 58		12 25							12 35	12 54						12 58	13 25
Leamington Spa 8	a		11 54	12 08	12 10			12 16		12 43							12 53	13 10						13 17	13 41
	d		11 54		12 12			12 17		12 45							12 54	13 12						13 17	13 43
Warwick	d		11 59					12 21									12 59							13 21	
Warwick Parkway	d		12 02					12 25									13 02							13 25	
Hatton	d		12 07																						
Lapworth	d		12 13																						
Dorridge	d	12 09	12 17				12 28	12 36						12 46		13 09	13 13						13 28	13 36	
Widney Manor	d	12 13					12 32							12 50		13 13							13 32		
Solihull	d	12 17	12 23				12 36	12 42						12 54		13 17	13 20						13 36	13 42	
Olton	d	12 20					12 39							12 57		13 20							13 39		
Acocks Green	d	12 23					12 42							13 00		13 23							13 42		
Tyseley	d		12 28			12 35								13 03			13 27					13 35			
Small Heath	d					12 37								13 05								13 37			
Bordesley	d																					13 40			
Birmingham Moor Street	d	12 29	12 35			12 41	12 48	12 53			12 57			13 09	13 17	13 29	13 32					13 43	13 48	13 53	
Birmingham Snow Hill 🚊	a	12 32	12 42			12 44	12 51	13 01			13 01			13 12	13 20	13 32	13 41					13 45	13 51	14 01	
	d	12 33				12 45	12 53				13 03			13 13	13 23	13 33						13 45	13 53		
Jewellery Quarter 🚊	d	12 35				12 47	12 55				13 05			13 15	13 25	13 35						13 47	13 55		
The Hawthorns 🚊	d	12 40				12 52	13 00				13 10			13 20	13 30	13 40						13 52	14 00		
Smethwick Galton Bridge 7	d	12 43				12 55	13 03				13 13			13 23	13 33	13 43						13 55	14 03		
Coventry	a				12 22													13 22							
Birmingham International ✈	a				12 37													13 37							
Birmingham New Street 12	a				12 48					13 17								13 48							14 17
	d				12 57					13 30		12 49						13 57			13 49				14 30
Langley Green	d	12 46									13 16					13 46									
Rowley Regis	d	12 49				13 00	13 08				13 19			13 28	13 38	13 49						14 00	14 08		
Old Hill	d	12 52									13 22					13 52									
Cradley Heath	d	12 56				13 04	13 13				13 26			13 33	13 43	13 56						14 04	14 13		
Lye	d	12 59									13 29					13 59									
Stourbridge Junction 8	d	13 03				13 10	13a19				13 33			13 39	13a49	14 03						14 10	14a19		
Hagley	d					13 13								13 42								14 13			
Blakedown	d					13 16								13 45								14 16			
Kidderminster	d	13a12				13 21					13a42			13 50		14a12						14 21			
Hartlebury	d																								
University	d											12 57									13 57				
Barnt Green	d																								
Bromsgrove	d											13 11									14 11				
Droitwich Spa	d					13 32						13 21		14 01							14 21	14 32			
Worcester Shrub Hill 7	a					13 40																14 41			
	d												13 45							14 15		14 46			
Worcester Foregate Street 7	a											13 29	13 47	14 10						14 18	14 29	14 48			
	d											13 30	13 48							14 18	14 30	14 49			
Malvern Link	d											13 40	13 57							14 27	14 40	14 57			
Great Malvern	a											13 42	14 04							14 31	14 42	15 00			
	d											13 43									14 43				
Colwall	d											13 48									14 48				
Ledbury	a											13 56									14 56				
	d											14 00									14 58				
Hereford 7	a											14 21									15 18				

Stratford-upon-Avon, Marylebone and Leamington Spa - Birmingham - Stourbridge, Worcester and Hereford

Station		LM	LM	LM	LM	CH	WS	XC	LM	LM	CH	XC	LM	LM		GW	LM	LM	LM	CH	CH	XC	GW	LM
							◇1 🍽	◇1 🍴			◇	◇1 🍴				◇1 🍴						◇1 🍴	◇	
Stratford-upon-Avon	d			13 27					13 59									14 27			14 36			14 59
Wilmcote	d			13 32														14 32			14 41			
Wootton Wawen	d			13x37														14x37						
Henley-in-Arden	d			13 41					14 09									14 41						15 09
Danzey	d			13x45														14x45						
Wood End	d			13x49														14x49						
The Lakes	d			13x51														14x51						
Earlswood (West Midlands)	d			13 54														14 54						
Wythall	d			13 56					14 20									14 56						15 20
Whitlocks End	d			13 59														14 59						
Shirley	d	13 42		14 02					14 24				14 42					15 02						15 24
Yardley Wood	d	13 45		14 05					14 27				14 45					15 05						15 27
Hall Green	d	13 48		14 08					14 30				14 48					15 08						15 30
Spring Road	d	13 50		14 10					14 32				14 50					15 10						15 32
London Marylebone 10 ⊖	d					12 20	12 24				12 50									13 20				
Banbury	d					13 32	13 37	13 54			13 58	14 25								14 35		14 54		
Leamington Spa 8	a					13 50	13 55	14 10			14 17	14 44								14 54	15 08	15 10		
	d					13 51		14 12			14 17	14 45								14 54	15 09	15 12		
Warwick	d					13 58					14 21									14 59				
Warwick Parkway	d					14 02					14 25									15 02				
Hatton	d					14 07																		
Lapworth	d					14 13																		
Dorridge	d		13 46		14 09	14 17				14 28	14 36						14 46		15 09	15 13				
Widney Manor	d		13 50		14 13					14 32							14 50		15 13					
Solihull	d		13 54		14 17	14 23				14 36	14 42						14 54		15 17	15 20				
Olton	d		13 57		14 20					14 39							14 57		15 20					
Acocks Green	d		14 00		14 23					14 42							15 00		15 23					
Tyseley	d		14 03						14 35		14 47						15 03			15 27				15 35
Small Heath	d		14 05						14 37								15 05							15 37
Bordesley	d																							
Birmingham Moor Street	d	13 57	14 09	14 17	14 29	14 34			14 41	14 48	14 53		14 57				15 09	15 17	15 29	15 33				15 41
Birmingham Snow Hill 🚊	a	14 01	14 12	14 20	14 32	14 42			14 44	14 51	15 01		15 01				15 12	15 20	15 32	15 41				15 44
	d	14 03	14 13	14 23	14 33				14 45	14 53			15 03				15 13	15 23	15 33					15 45
Jewellery Quarter 🚊	d	14 05	14 15	14 25	14 35				14 47	14 55			15 05				15 15	15 25	15 35					15 47
The Hawthorns 🚊	d	14 10	14 20	14 30	14 40				14 52	15 00			15 10				15 20	15 30	15 40					15 52
Smethwick Galton Bridge 7	d	14 13	14 23	14 33	14 43				14 55	15 03			15 13				15 23	15 33	15 43					15 55
Coventry	a							14 22														15 22		
Birmingham International ✈	a							14 37														15 37		
Birmingham New Street 12	a							14 48				15 17										15 48		
	d													14 49										
Langley Green	d	14 16			14 46								15 16						15 46					
Rowley Regis	d	14 19	14 28	14 38	14 49				15 00	15 08			15 19				15 28	15 38	15 49					16 00
Old Hill	d	14 22			14 52								15 22						15 52					
Cradley Heath	d	14 26	14 33	14 43	14 56				15 04	15 13			15 26				15 33	15 43	15 56					16 04
Lye	d	14 29			14 59								15 29						15 59					
Stourbridge Junction 8	d	14 33	14 39	14a49	15 03				15 10	15a19			15 33				15 39	15a49	16 03					16 10
Hagley	d		14 42						15 13								15 42							16 13
Blakedown	d		14 45						15 16								15 45							16 16
Kidderminster	d	14a42	14 50		15a12				15 21				15a42				15 50		16a12					16 21
Hartlebury	d																							
University	d													14 57										
Barnt Green	d																							
Bromsgrove	d													15 11										
Droitwich Spa	d		15 01						15 32					15 21			16 01							16 32
Worcester Shrub Hill 7	a								15 40							15 43							16 14	16 40
	d															15 45							16 15	
Worcester Foregate Street 7	a		15 10											15 29		15 47	16 10						16 17	
	d													15 30		15 48							16 18	
Malvern Link	d													15 40		15 57							16 26	
Great Malvern	a													15 42		16 04							16 31	
	d													15 43										
Colwall	d													15 48										
Ledbury	a													15 56										
	d													15 58										
Hereford 7	a													16 19										

Table 71

Saturdays
until 02 October

Stratford-upon-Avon, Marylebone and Leamington Spa - Birmingham - Stourbridge, Worcester and Hereford

		LM	CH ◇	XC ◇1	LM	LM	GW ◇1	LM	LM	LM		CH ◇	XC ◇1	LM	LM	LM	CH ◇	XC ◇1	LM	GW ◇1		LM	LM	LM	LM
Stratford-upon-Avon	d								15 27						15 59									16 27	
Wilmcote	d								15 32															16 32	
Wootton Wawen	d								15x37															16x37	
Henley-in-Arden	d								15 41						16 09									16 41	
Danzey	d								15x45															16x45	
Wood End	d								15x49															16x49	
The Lakes	d								15x51															16x51	
Earlswood (West Midlands)	d								15 54															16 54	
Wythall	d								15 56						16 20									16 56	
Whitlocks End	d								15 59															16 59	
Shirley	d				15 42				16 02						16 24				16 42					17 02	
Yardley Wood	d				15 45				16 05						16 27				16 45					17 05	
Hall Green	d				15 48				16 08						16 30				16 48					17 08	
Spring Road	d				15 50				16 10						16 32				16 50					17 10	
London Marylebone 10 ⊖	d		13 50									14 20					14 50								
Banbury	d		14 58	15 25								15 35	15 54				15 58	16 25							
Leamington Spa 8	a		15 17	15 41								15 54	16 10				16 16	16 47							
	d		15 17	15 43								15 54	16 12				16 17	16 48							
Warwick	d		15 21									15 59					16 21								
Warwick Parkway	d		15 25									16 02					16 25								
Hatton	d											16 07													
Lapworth	d											16 13													
Dorridge	d	15 28	15 36					15 46		16 09		16 17				16 27	16 36						16 46		17 09
Widney Manor	d	15 32						15 50		16 13						16 31							16 50		17 13
Solihull	d	15 36	15 42					15 54		16 17		16 23				16 35	16 42						16 54		17 17
Olton	d	15 39						15 57		16 20						16 38							16 57		17 20
Acocks Green	d	15 42						16 00		16 23						16 41							17 00		17 23
Tyseley	d							16 03							16 35	16 44	16 48		16 53				17 03		
Small Heath	d							16 05							16 37								17 05		
Bordesley	d																								
Birmingham Moor Street	d	15 48	15 53		15 57			16 09	16 17	16 29		16 34			16 41	16 49	16 53		16 58				17 09	17 17	17 29
Birmingham Snow Hill	a	15 51	16 01		16 01			16 12	16 20	16 32		16 41			16 44	16 51	17 02		17 02				17 12	17 20	17 32
	d	15 53			16 03			16 13	16 23	16 33					16 45	16 53			17 03				17 13	17 23	17 33
Jewellery Quarter	d	15 55			16 05			16 15	16 25	16 35					16 47	16 55			17 05				17 15	17 25	17 35
The Hawthorns	d	16 00			16 10			16 20	16 30	16 40					16 52	17 00			17 10				17 20	17 30	17 40
Smethwick Galton Bridge 7	d	16 03			16 13			16 23	16 33	16 43					16 55	17 03			17 13				17 23	17 33	17 43
Coventry	a												16 22												
Birmingham International ✈	a												16 37												
Birmingham New Street 12	a			16 17									16 48					17 17							
	d					15 49								16 49								17 19			
Langley Green	d				16 16					16 46									17 16						17 46
Rowley Regis	d	16 08			16 19			16 28	16 38	16 49					17 00	17 08			17 19				17 28	17 38	17 49
Old Hill	d				16 22					16 52									17 22						17 52
Cradley Heath	d	16 13			16 26			16 33	16 43	16 56					17 04	17 13			17 26				17 33	17 43	17 56
Lye	d				16 29					16 59									17 29						17 59
Stourbridge Junction 2	d	16a19			16 33			16 39	16a49	17 03					17 10	17a19			17 33				17 39	17a49	18 03
Hagley	d							16 42		17 06					17 13								17 42		18 06
Blakedown	d							16 45		17 09					17 16								17 45		18 09
Kidderminster	d				16a42			16 50		17a15					17 21				17a42				17 50		18a15
Hartlebury	d														17 26								17 55		
University	d					15 57								16 57											
Barnt Green	d																								
Bromsgrove	d					16 11								17 11								17 42			
Droitwich Spa	d					16 21		17 01						17 21	17 34							17 52	18 03		
Worcester Shrub Hill 7	a																					18 06	18 12		
	d						16 45													17 45					
Worcester Foregate Street 7	a					16 29	16 48	17 10						17 29	17 43					17 47					
	d					16 30	16 48	17 11						17 30						17 48					
Malvern Link	d					16 40	16 57	17 20						17 39						17 57					
Great Malvern	a					16 42	17 04	17 23						17 41						18 04					
	d					16 43								17 42											
Colwall	d					16 48								17 47											
Ledbury	a					16 56								17 55											
	d					17 00								18 00											
Hereford 7	a					17 20								18 21											

Table 71

Saturdays
until 02 October

Stratford-upon-Avon, Marylebone and Leamington Spa - Birmingham - Stourbridge, Worcester and Hereford

		CH	XC ◇1	GW	LM	LM		LM	CH	XC ◇1	LM	LM	GW ◇1	LM	LM	CH		LM	XC ◇1	LM	GW ◇1	LM	CH	LM	XC ◇1
Stratford-upon-Avon	d					16 59								17 27						17 59				18 19	
Wilmcote	d													17 32										18 24	
Wootton Wawen	d													17x37										18x29	
Henley-in-Arden	d					17 09								17 41						18 09				18 33	
Danzey	d													17x45										18x37	
Wood End	d													17x49										18x41	
The Lakes	d													17x51										18x43	
Earlswood (West Midlands)	d													17 54										18 46	
Wythall	d					17 20								17 56						18 20				18 48	
Whitlocks End	d													17 59										18 51	
Shirley	d					17 24					17 42			18 02						18 23				18 54	
Yardley Wood	d					17 27					17 45			18 05						18 26				18 57	
Hall Green	d					17 30					17 48			18 08						18 29				19 00	
Spring Road	d					17 32					17 50			18 10						18 31				19 02	
London Marylebone 10 ⊖	d	15 20							15 50							16 20							16 50		
Banbury	d	16 35	16 54						16 58	17 25						17 35			17 54				17 58		18 25
Leamington Spa 8	a	16 53	17 10						17 16	17 41						17 54			18 10				18 17		18 44
	d	16 54	17 12						17 17	17 43						17 54			18 12				18 17		18 45
Warwick	d	16 59							17 21							17 59							18 21		
Warwick Parkway	d	17 02							17 25							18 02							18 25		
Hatton	d	17 07														18 07									
Lapworth	d	17 13														18 13									
Dorridge	d	17 17						17 28	17 36			17 46			18 09	18 17						18 28	18 36		
Widney Manor	d							17 32				17 50			18 13							18 32			
Solihull	d	17 23						17 36	17 42			17 54			18 17	18 23						18 36	18 42		
Olton	d							17 39				17 57			18 20							18 39			
Acocks Green	d							17 42				18 00			18 23							18 42			
Tyseley	d					17 35		17 45				18 03								18 34		18 45		19 05	
Small Heath	d					17 37						18 05								18 37		18 47		19 07	
Bordesley	d																								
Birmingham Moor Street	d	17 34				17 41		17 50	17 53		17 57	18 09		18 17	18 29	18 34				18 41		18 51	18 55	19 11	
Birmingham Snow Hill	a					17 44		17 52				18 12		18 20	18 32							18 54			
	d					17 45		17 53				18 13		18 23	18 33							18 58			
Jewellery Quarter	d					17 47		17 55				18 15		18 25	18 35							19 00			
The Hawthorns	d					17 52		18 00				18 20		18 30	18 40							19 05			
Smethwick Galton Bridge 7	d					17 55		18 03				18 23		18 33	18 43							19 08			
Coventry	a		17 22																18 22						
Birmingham International ✈	a		17 37																18 37						
Birmingham New Street 12	a		17 48							18 17									18 48						19 17
	d				17 49													18 49							
Langley Green	d							18 06				18 26			18 46							19 11			
Rowley Regis	d					18 00		18 09				18 29		18 38	18 49							19 14			
Old Hill	d							18 12				18 32			18 52							19 17			
Cradley Heath	d					18 05		18 16				18 36		18 43	18 56							19 21			
Lye	d							18 19				18 39			18 59							19 24			
Stourbridge Junction 2	d					18 11		18a23				18a43		18 49	19 03							19 28			
Hagley	d					18 14								18 52	19 06							19 31			
Blakedown	d					18 17								18 55	19 09							19 34			
Kidderminster	d					18 22								19 00	19a15							19 39			
Hartlebury	d					18 27								19 05											
University	d				17 57													18 57							
Barnt Green	d																								
Bromsgrove	d				18 11													19 11							
Droitwich Spa	d				18 19	18 35								19 13				19 21				19 50			
Worcester Shrub Hill 7	a				18 27													19 28				19 58			
	d			18 19	18 31								18 51					19 33			19 43				
Worcester Foregate Street 7	a			18 21	18 33	18 44							18 54	19 22				19 35			19 45				
	d			18 22	18 34								18 55	19 23				19 36							
Malvern Link	d			18 30	18 44								19 04	19 32				19 45							
Great Malvern	a			18 36	18 46								19 07	19 35				19 50							
	d				18 47								19 08												
Colwall	d				18 52								19 14												
Ledbury	a				18 59								19 21												
	d				19 00								19 29												
Hereford 7	a				19 20								19 45												

Table 71

Saturdays
until 02 October

Stratford-upon-Avon, Marylebone and Leamington Spa - Birmingham - Stourbridge, Worcester and Hereford

		LM		GW	LM	CH	WS	LM	XC	GW	LM	CH	XC		LM	CH	XC	CH	LM	CH	CH	LM	XC	CH	WS
							◇[1] ⊏		◇[1] ⊥	◇[1] ⊏		◇	◇[1] ⊥				◇[1] ⊥	◇		◇			◇[1] ⊥		◇[1] ⊏
Stratford-upon-Avon	d							18 50							19 26			19 48				20 26			
Wilmcote	d							18 55							19 31			19 53				20 31			
Wootton Wawen	d							19x00							19x36							20x36			
Henley-in-Arden	d							19 04							19 40							20 40			
Danzey	d							19x08							19x44							20x44			
Wood End	d							19x12							19x48							20x48			
The Lakes	d							19x14							19x50							20x50			
Earlswood (West Midlands)	d							19 16							19 53							20 53			
Wythall	d							19 19							19 55							20 55			
Whitlocks End	d							19 21							19 58							20 58			
Shirley	d							19 25							20 01							21 01			
Yardley Wood	d							19 28							20 04							21 04			
Hall Green	d							19 31							20 07							21 07			
Spring Road	d							19 33							20 09							21 09			
London Marylebone [10] ⊖	d					17 20	17 24					17 50				18 20				18 50	18 53			19 20	19 24
Banbury	d					18 32	18 37		18 54			19 03	19 25			19 35	19 54			20 03	20 19		20 30	20 32	20 37
Leamington Spa [8]	a					18 50	18 55		19 10			19 22	19 41			19 53	20 10	20 21		20 22	20 37		20 46	20 50	20 55
	d					18 51			19 12			19 23	19 43			19 54	20 12			20 23	20 38		20 47	20 51	
Warwick	d					18 58						19 27				19 59				20 27	20 42			20 58	
Warwick Parkway	d					19 02						19 30				20 02				20 30				21 02	
Hatton	d					19 07										20 07					20 49			21 07	
Lapworth	d					19 13										20 13								21 13	
Dorridge	d				19 00	19 17					19 28	19 42				20 17			20 28	20 42				21 17	
Widney Manor	d				19 04						19 32								20 32						
Solihull	d				19 08	19 23					19 36	19 48				20 23			20 36	20 47				21 23	
Olton	d				19 11						19 39								20 39						
Acocks Green	d				19 14						19 42								20 42						
Tyseley	d				19 17			19 36			19 45								20 45						
Small Heath	d				19 19			19 38			19 47								20 47						
Bordesley	d																								
Birmingham Moor Street	d				19 23	19 34		19 42			19 51	19 59			20 16	20 35			20 51	20 58		21 16		21 34	
Birmingham Snow Hill ⇌	a				19 26	19 41		19 46			19 54	20 06			20 19	20 42			20 54	21 06		21 19		21 41	
	d				19 28						19 55				20 20				20 55			21 20			
Jewellery Quarter ⇌	d				19 30						19 57				20 22				20 57			21 22			
The Hawthorns ⇌	d				19 35						20 02				20 27				21 02			21 27			
Smethwick Galton Bridge [7]	d				19 38						20 05				20 30				21 05			21 30			
Coventry	a								19 22								20 22								
Birmingham International ✈	a								19 37								20 37								
Birmingham New Street [12]	a								19 48				20 18				20 48						21 16		
	d	19 19							19 57																
Langley Green	d				19 41						20 08				20 33				21 08			21 33			
Rowley Regis	d				19 44						20 11				20 36				21 11			21 36			
Old Hill	d				19 47						20 14				20 39				21 14			21 39			
Cradley Heath	d				19 51						20 18				20 43				21 18			21 43			
Lye	d				19 54						20 21				20 46				21 21			21 46			
Stourbridge Junction [2]	d				19 58						20 25				20a50				21 25			21a50			
Hagley	d				20 01						20 28								21 28						
Blakedown	d				20 04						20 31								21 31						
Kidderminster	d				20 09						20 36								21 36						
Hartlebury	d																								
University	d	19 27																							
Barnt Green	d																								
Bromsgrove	d	19 42																							
Droitwich Spa	d	19 57			20 20						20 47								21 47						
Worcester Shrub Hill [7]	a				20 30						20 55								21 55						
	d			20 20						20 48	20 59														
Worcester Foregate Street [7]	a	20 05		20 22						20 50	21 01														
	d	20 06		20 25						20 52	21 02														
Malvern Link	d	20 16		20 34						21 01	21 11														
Great Malvern	a	20 18		20 38						21 04	21 14														
	d	20 25								21 05															
Colwall	d	20 30								21 11															
Ledbury	a	20 38								21 18															
	d	20 39								21 20															
Hereford [7]	a	21 03								21 36															

Table 71

Saturdays
until 02 October

Stratford-upon-Avon, Marylebone and Leamington Spa - Birmingham - Stourbridge, Worcester and Hereford

		XC	LM	GW	LM	LM	CH	XC		XC	LM	CH	XC	LM	CH
		◇[1] ⊥		◇[1] ⊥			◇	◇[1] ⊥		◇[1] ⊥		◇	◇[1] ⊥		◇
Stratford-upon-Avon	d														
Wilmcote	d														
Wootton Wawen	d														
Henley-in-Arden	d														
Danzey	d														
Wood End	d														
The Lakes	d														
Earlswood (West Midlands)	d														
Wythall	d														
Whitlocks End	d														
Shirley	d					21 57								23 00	
Yardley Wood	d					22 00								23 03	
Hall Green	d					22 03								23 06	
Spring Road	d					22 05								23 08	
London Marylebone [10] ⊖	d						20 00					20 50			22 00
Banbury	d	20 54					21 19	21 25		21 54		22 07	22 25		23 06
Leamington Spa [8]	a	21 10					21 37	21 44		22 10		22 27	22 41		23 23
	d	21 12					21 38	21 45		22 12		22 27	22 43		23 24
Warwick	d						21 42					22 31			23 28
Warwick Parkway	d						21 46					22 35			23 32
Hatton	d														
Lapworth	d														
Dorridge	d				21 28		21 58				22 32	22 46			23 43
Widney Manor	d				21 32						22 36				23 46
Solihull	d				21 36		22 03				22 40	22 52			23 50
Olton	d				21 39						22 43				
Acocks Green	d				21 42						22 46				
Tyseley	d				21 45	22 08					22 49			23 11	
Small Heath	d				21 47	22 10					22 51			23 13	
Bordesley	d														
Birmingham Moor Street	d				21 51	22 14	22 16				22 55	23 03		23 17	23 59
Birmingham Snow Hill ⇌	a				21 54	22 17	22 26				22 58	23 10		23 20	00 10
	d				21 55	22 20					22 59			23 23	
Jewellery Quarter ⇌	d				21 57	22 22					23 01			23 25	
The Hawthorns ⇌	d				22 02	22 27					23 06			23 30	
Smethwick Galton Bridge [7]	d				22 05	22 30					23 09			23 33	
Coventry	a	21 22						21 55		22 22					
Birmingham International ✈	a	21 37						22 12		22 37					
Birmingham New Street [12]	a	21 48						22 25		22 48			23 09		
	d		20 59												
Langley Green	d				22 08	22 33					23 12			23 36	
Rowley Regis	d				22 11	22 36					23 15			23 39	
Old Hill	d				22 14	22 39					23 18			23 42	
Cradley Heath	d				22 18	22 43					23 22			23 46	
Lye	d				22 21	22 46					23 25			23 49	
Stourbridge Junction [2]	d				22 25	22a50					23 29			23a52	
Hagley	d				22 28						23 32				
Blakedown	d				22 31						23 35				
Kidderminster	d				22 36						23 40				
Hartlebury	d														
University	d		21 05												
Barnt Green	d														
Bromsgrove	d		21 21												
Droitwich Spa	d		21 31		22 47						23 51				
Worcester Shrub Hill [7]	a				22 55						23 59				
	d			22 08	22 59										
Worcester Foregate Street [7]	a		21 39	22 11	23 01										
	d		21 42	22 11	23 02										
Malvern Link	d		21 52	22 20	23 10										
Great Malvern	a		21 54	22 27	23 13										
	d		22 00												
Colwall	d		22 05												
Ledbury	a		22 13												
	d		22 14												
Hereford [7]	a		22 34												

Table 71

Saturdays
from 09 October

Stratford-upon-Avon, Marylebone and Leamington Spa - Birmingham - Stourbridge, Worcester and Hereford

		CH ◇	CH	CH ◇	LM	LM	LM	LM	LM	XC ◇1 ✠		LM A	XC ◇1 ✠	LM	GW ◇1	LM	LM	LM	LM	LM		GW ◇1 ✠	LM	CH ◇	XC ◇1 ✠
Stratford-upon-Avon	d																07 02		07 45					07 35	
Wilmcote	d																07 07		07 50						
Wootton Wawen	d																07x12		07x55						
Henley-in-Arden	d																07 16		07 59						
Danzey	d																07x20		08x04						
Wood End	d																07x24		08x08						
The Lakes	d																07x26		08x10						
Earlswood (West Midlands)	d																07 28		08 13						
Wythall	d																07 31		08 15						
Whitlocks End	d																07 33		08 18						
Shirley	d											07 05					07 36		08 21						
Yardley Wood	d											07 08					07 39		08 24						
Hall Green	d											07 11					07 42		08 27						
Spring Road	d											07 13					07 44		08 29						
London Marylebone 10 ⊖	d	22p20	23p10	23p54																					
Banbury	d	23p31	00 33	01 19						06 56			07 33												07 54
Leamington Spa 8	a	23p48	00 51	01 42						07 12			07 50											08 08	08 10
	d	23p48	00 52						06 26	07 14			07 51										07 56		08 12
Warwick	d	23p53	00 56						06 30														08 00		
Warwick Parkway	d	23p56	01a09						06 34														08 04		
Hatton	d								06 39														08 09		
Lapworth	d								06 45														08 15		
Dorridge	d	00 07							06 50							07 25		08 05					08 21		
Widney Manor	d								06 53							07 29		08 09					08 24		
Solihull	d	00 13							06 57							07 33		08 13					08 28		
Olton	d								07 00							07 36		08 16					08 31		
Acocks Green	d								07 03							07 39		08 19					08 34		
Tyseley	d								07 06			07 16				07 42	07 47	08 22	08 32				08 37		
Small Heath	d								07 08			07 19				07 44	07 50		08 34				08 39		
Bordesley	d																								
Birmingham Moor Street	d	00 23				06 31		07 01	07 12			07 23				07 48	07 54	08 27	08 38				08 43		
Birmingham Snow Hill ⇌	a	00 35				06 33		07 03	07 15			07 25				07 51	07 57	08 29	08 42				08 47		
	d					06 35		07 05				07 28				07 53	08 03	08 30	08 43				08 53		
Jewellery Quarter ⇌	d					06 37		07 07				07 30				07 55	08 05	08 33	08 45				08 55		
The Hawthorns ⇌	d					06 42		07 12				07 35				08 00	08 10	08 37	08 50				09 00		
Smethwick Galton Bridge 7	d					06 45		07 15				07 38				08 03	08 13	08 40	08 53				09 03		
Coventry	a									07 24															08 22
Birmingham International ✈	a									07 39															08 37
Birmingham New Street 12	a									07 51			08 17												08 48
	d						06 49							07 49						08 49					
Langley Green	d					06 48		07 18				07 41					08 16	08 43							
Rowley Regis	d					06 51		07 21				07 44				08 08	08 19	08 47	08 58				09 08		
Old Hill	d					06 54		07 24				07 47					08 22	08 50							
Cradley Heath	d					06 57		07 27				07 51				08 12	08 26	08 53	09 02				09 13		
Lye	d					07 00		07 30				07 54					08 29	08 56							
Stourbridge Junction 2	d					07 04		07 35				07a58				08 18	08a33	09a00	09a08				09 19		
Hagley	d					07 08		07 38								08 21							09 22		
Blakedown	d					07 11		07 41								08 24							09 25		
Kidderminster	d					07 16		07 46								08 29							09 30		
Hartlebury	d					07 21																			
University	d						06 57							07 57						08 57					
Barnt Green	d																								
Bromsgrove	d						07 11							08 11						09 11					
Droitwich Spa	d					07 28	07 21	07 57						08 21		08 40				09 21			09 41		
Worcester Shrub Hill 7	a					07 39		08 07															09 49		
	d				06 30			08 11							08 45							09 44			
Worcester Foregate Street 7	a				06 32		07 29	08 13						08 29	08 47	08 49				09 29		09 46			
	d				06 33		07 30	08 14						08 30	08 48					09 30		09 48			
Malvern Link	d				06 42		07 39	08 23						08 40	08 57					09 40		09 57			
Great Malvern	a				06 44		07 41	08 26						08 42	09 04					09 42		10 04			
	d				06 45		07 42							08 43						09 43					
Colwall	d				06 50		07 47							08 48						09 48					
Ledbury	a				06 57		07 55							08 56						09 56					
	d				06 58		08 00							09 00						10 00					
Hereford 7	a				07 14		08 21							09 20						10 21					

A 9 October, 16 October, 23 October

Table 71

Saturdays
from 09 October

Stratford-upon-Avon, Marylebone and Leamington Spa - Birmingham - Stourbridge, Worcester and Hereford

		LM A	LM B	CH ◇	XC ◇1 ✠	LM		LM	XC ◇1 ✠	LM	GW	LM	LM	CH ◇	XC ◇1 ✠	LM B		LM	GW ◇1	LM	LM	LM	CH ◇	CH	XC ◇1 ✠
Stratford-upon-Avon	d							08 27				08 59									09 27			09 36	
Wilmcote	d							08 32													09 32			09 41	
Wootton Wawen	d							08x37													09x37				
Henley-in-Arden	d							08 41				09 09									09 41				
Danzey	d							08x45													09x45				
Wood End	d							08x49													09x49				
The Lakes	d							08x51													09x51				
Earlswood (West Midlands)	d							08 54													09 54				
Wythall	d							08 56				09 20									09 56				
Whitlocks End	d	08 35						08 59													09 59				
Shirley	d	08 38	08 38					09 02				09 24				09 42					10 02				
Yardley Wood	d	08 41	08 41					09 05				09 27				09 45					10 05				
Hall Green	d	08 44	08 44					09 08				09 30				09 48					10 08				
Spring Road	d	08 46	08 46					09 10				09 32				09 50					10 10				
London Marylebone 10 ⊖	d			06 24										07 24									08 18		
Banbury	d			08 01	08 35				08 54					08 58	09 25								09 39		09 54
Leamington Spa 8	a			08 20	08 54				09 10					09 16	09 41								09 57	10 08	10 10
	d			08 21	08 55				09 12					09 17	09 43								09 58	10 09	10 12
Warwick	d			08 24										09 21									10 02		
Warwick Parkway	d			08 28										09 25									10 06		
Hatton	d			08 33																					
Lapworth	d			08 38																					
Dorridge	d			08 42		08 46				09 09			09 28	09 36						09 46		10 09	10 17		
Widney Manor	d			08 47		08 50				09 13			09 32							09 50		10 13			
Solihull	d			08 50		08 54				09 17			09 36	09 42						09 54		10 17	10 23		
Olton	d					08 57				09 20			09 39							09 57		10 20			
Acocks Green	d					09 00				09 23			09 42							10 00		10 23			
Tyseley	d	08 49	08 49			09 03						09 35								10 03					
Small Heath	d	08 51	08 51			09 05						09 37								10 05					
Bordesley	d																								
Birmingham Moor Street	d	08 55	08 55	09 00		09 09		09 17		09 29		09 41	09 48	09 52		09 58				10 09	10 17	10 29	10 34		
Birmingham Snow Hill ⇌	a	08 58	08 58	09 11		09 12		09 20		09 32		09 44	09 51	10 05		10 00				10 12	10 20	10 32	10 44		
	d	09 03	09 03			09 13		09 23		09 33		09 45	09 53			10 03				10 13	10 23	10 33			
Jewellery Quarter ⇌	d	09 05	09 05			09 15		09 25		09 35		09 47	09 55			10 05				10 15	10 25	10 35			
The Hawthorns ⇌	d	09 10	09 10			09 20		09 30		09 40		09 52	10 00			10 10				10 20	10 30	10 40			
Smethwick Galton Bridge 7	d	09 13	09 13			09 23		09 33		09 43		09 55	10 03			10 13				10 23	10 33	10 43			
Coventry	a								09 22																10 22
Birmingham International ✈	a								09 37																10 37
Birmingham New Street 12	a				09 19				09 48						10 17										10 48
	d																	09 49							
Langley Green	d	09 16	09 16							09 46						10 16						10 46			
Rowley Regis	d	09 19	09 19			09 28		09 38		09 49		10 00	10 08			10 19				10 28	10 38	10 49			
Old Hill	d	09 22	09 22							09 52						10 22						10 52			
Cradley Heath	d	09 26	09 26			09 33		09 43		09 56		10 04	10 13			10 26				10 33	10 43	10 56			
Lye	d	09 29	09 29							09 59						10 29						10 59			
Stourbridge Junction 2	d	09 33	09 33			09 39		09a49		10 03		10 10	10a19			10 33				10 39	10a49	11 03			
Hagley	d					09 42						10 13								10 42					
Blakedown	d					09 45						10 16								10 45					
Kidderminster	d	09a42	09a42			09 50				10a12		10 21				10a42				10 50		11a12			
Hartlebury	d																								
University	d																	09 57							
Barnt Green	d																								
Bromsgrove	d																	10 11							
Droitwich Spa	d					10 01						10 32						10 21		11 01					
Worcester Shrub Hill 7	a											10 40													
	d										10 15								10 45						
Worcester Foregate Street 7	a					10 10					10 17							10 29	10 48	11 10					
	d										10 18							10 30	10 48	11 11					
Malvern Link	d										10 27							10 40	10 57	11 19					
Great Malvern	a										10 31							10 42	11 04	11 22					
	d																	10 43	11 07						
Colwall	d																	10 48	11 14						
Ledbury	a																	10 56	11 21						
	d																	11 00	11 23						
Hereford 7	a																	11 20	11 42						

A from 30 October

B 9 October, 16 October, 23 October

Table 71

Saturdays
from 09 October

Stratford-upon-Avon, Marylebone and Leamington Spa - Birmingham - Stourbridge, Worcester and Hereford

		LM	LM	CH	CH	XC	LM	LM	LM	LM	LM	CH	XC	GW	LM	LM	LM	CH	XC	LM	LM	GW
				◇	◇	◇[1]	A					◇	◇[1]	◇				◇	◇[1]	B	A	◇[1]
						⊥							⊥						⊥			⊏⊐
Stratford-upon-Avon	d	09 59								10 27						10 59						
Wilmcote	d									10 32												
Wootton Wawen	d									10x37												
Henley-in-Arden	d	10 09								10 41						11 09						
Danzey	d									10x45												
Wood End	d									10x49												
The Lakes	d									10x51												
Earlswood (West Midlands)	d									10 54												
Wythall	d	10 20								10 56						11 20						
Whitlocks End	d									10 59										11 39		
Shirley	d	10 24					10 42			11 02						11 24				11 42	11 42	
Yardley Wood	d	10 27					10 45			11 05						11 27				11 45	11 45	
Hall Green	d	10 30					10 48			11 08						11 30				11 48	11 48	
Spring Road	d	10 32					10 50			11 10						11 32				11 50	11 50	
London Marylebone [10] ⊖	d			08 45	09 12							09 15						09 45				
Banbury	d			09 58	10 20	10 25						10 38	10 54					10 58	11 25			
Leamington Spa [8]	a			10 17	10 37	10 41						10 57	11 10					11 16	11 41			
	d			10 17	10 38	10 43						10 58	11 12					11 17	11 43			
Warwick	d			10 21	10 42							11 02						11 21				
Warwick Parkway	d			10 25								11 05						11 25				
Hatton	d			10 30																		
Lapworth	d			10 35																		
Dorridge	d		10 28	10 40					10 46		11 09	11 17					11 28	11 36				
Widney Manor	d		10 32						10 50		11 13						11 32					
Solihull	d		10 36	10 45					10 54		11 17	11 23					11 36	11 42				
Olton	d		10 39						10 57		11 20						11 39					
Acocks Green	d		10 42						11 00		11 23						11 42					
Tyseley	d	10 35							11 03							11 35						
Small Heath	d	10 37							11 05							11 37						
Bordesley	d																					
Birmingham Moor Street	d	10 41	10 48	10 55			10 58		11 09	11 17	11 29	11 34				11 41	11 48	11 52		11 57	11 57	
Birmingham Snow Hill 🚊	a	10 44	10 51	11 07			11 01		11 12	11 20	11 32	11 44				11 44	11 51	12 04		12 01	12 01	
	d	10 45	10 53				11 03		11 13	11 23	11 33					11 45	11 53			12 03	12 03	
Jewellery Quarter 🚊	d	10 47	10 55				11 05		11 15	11 25	11 35					11 47	11 55			12 05	12 05	
The Hawthorns 🚊	d	10 52	11 00				11 10		11 20	11 30	11 40					11 52	12 00			12 10	12 10	
Smethwick Galton Bridge [7]	d	10 55	11 03				11 13		11 23	11 33	11 43					11 55	12 03			12 13	12 13	
Coventry	a												11 22									
Birmingham International ✈	a												11 37									
Birmingham New Street [12]	a					11 17							11 48						12 17			
	d							10 49							11 49							
Langley Green	d						11 16				11 46									12 16	12 16	
Rowley Regis	d	11 00	11 08				11 19		11 28	11 38	11 49					12 00	12 08			12 19	12 19	
Old Hill	d						11 22				11 52									12 22	12 22	
Cradley Heath	d	11 04	11 13				11 26		11 33	11 43	11 56					12 04	12 13			12 26	12 26	
Lye	d						11 29				11 59									12 29	12 29	
Stourbridge Junction [2]	d	11 10	11a19				11 33		11 39	11a49	12 03					12 10	12a19			12 33	12 33	
Hagley	d	11 13							11 42							12 13						
Blakedown	d	11 16							11 45							12 16						
Kidderminster	d	11 21					11a43		11 50		12a12					12 21				12a42	12a42	
Hartlebury	d																					
University	d							10 57							11 57							
Barnt Green	d																					
Bromsgrove	d							11 11							12 11							
Droitwich Spa	d	11 32						11 21	12 01						12 21	12 32						
Worcester Shrub Hill [7]	a	11 40																				
	d													12 16								12 45
Worcester Foregate Street [7]	a							11 29	12 10					12 17	12 29	12 41						12 48
	d							11 30							12 30							12 48
Malvern Link	d							11 40							12 40							12 57
Great Malvern	a							11 42							12 42							13 04
	d							11 43							12 43							13 07
Colwall	d							11 48							12 49							13 14
Ledbury	a							11 56							12 57							13 21
	d							12 00							13 00							13 23
Hereford [7]	a							12 21							13 20							13 42

A 9 October, 16 October, 23 October

B from 30 October

Table 71

Saturdays
from 09 October

Stratford-upon-Avon, Marylebone and Leamington Spa - Birmingham - Stourbridge, Worcester and Hereford

		LM	LM	LM	CH	CH	XC	LM	LM	CH	XC	LM	LM	GW	LM	LM	LM	CH	XC	GW	LM	LM	LM
					◇		◇[1]			◇	◇[1]	A		◇[1]					◇[1]	◇			
							⊥				⊥			⊥					⊥				
Stratford-upon-Avon	d		11 27			11 36		11 59								12 27						12 59	
Wilmcote	d		11 32			11 41										12 32							
Wootton Wawen	d		11x37													12x37							
Henley-in-Arden	d		11 41					12 09								12 41						13 09	
Danzey	d		11x45													12x45							
Wood End	d		11x49													12x49							
The Lakes	d		11x51													12x51							
Earlswood (West Midlands)	d		11 54													12 54							
Wythall	d		11 56					12 20								12 56						13 20	
Whitlocks End	d		11 59													12 59							
Shirley	d		12 02					12 24				12 42				13 02						13 24	
Yardley Wood	d		12 05					12 27				12 45				13 05						13 27	
Hall Green	d		12 08					12 30				12 48				13 08						13 30	
Spring Road	d		12 10					12 32				12 50				13 10						13 32	
London Marylebone [10] ⊖	d				10 18					10 50								11 20					
Banbury	d				11 35		11 54			11 58	12 25							12 35	12 54				
Leamington Spa [8]	a				11 54	12 08	12 10			12 16	12 43							12 53	13 10				
	d				11 54	12 09	12 12			12 17	12 45							12 54	13 12				
Warwick	d				11 59					12 21								12 59					
Warwick Parkway	d				12 02					12 25								13 02					
Hatton	d				12 07																		
Lapworth	d				12 13																		
Dorridge	d	11 46		12 09	12 17				12 28	12 36					12 46		13 09	13 13					13 28
Widney Manor	d	11 50		12 13					12 32						12 50		13 13						13 32
Solihull	d	11 54		12 17	12 23				12 36	12 42					12 54		13 17	13 20					13 36
Olton	d	11 57		12 20					12 39						12 57		13 20						13 39
Acocks Green	d	12 00		12 23					12 42						13 00		13 23						13 42
Tyseley	d	12 03			12 28			12 35							13 03			13 27				13 35	
Small Heath	d	12 05						12 37							13 05							13 37	
Bordesley	d																					13 40	
Birmingham Moor Street	d	12 09	12 17	12 29	12 35			12 41	12 48	12 53		12 57			13 09	13 17	13 29	13 32				13 43	13 48
Birmingham Snow Hill 🚊	a	12 12	12 20	12 32	12 45			12 44	12 51	13 04		13 01			13 12	13 20	13 32	13 44				13 45	13 51
	d	12 13	12 23	12 33				12 45	12 53			13 03			13 13	13 23	13 33					13 45	13 53
Jewellery Quarter 🚊	d	12 15	12 25	12 35				12 47	12 55			13 05			13 15	13 25	13 35					13 47	13 55
The Hawthorns 🚊	d	12 20	12 30	12 40				12 52	13 00			13 10			13 20	13 30	13 40					13 52	14 00
Smethwick Galton Bridge [7]	d	12 23	12 33	12 43				12 55	13 03			13 13			13 23	13 33	13 43					13 55	14 03
Coventry	a						12 22												13 22				
Birmingham International ✈	a						12 37												13 37				
Birmingham New Street [12]	a						12 48				13 17								13 48				
	d												12 49								13 49		
Langley Green	d			12 46								13 16					13 46						
Rowley Regis	d	12 28	12 38	12 49				13 00	13 08			13 19			13 28	13 38	13 49					14 00	14 08
Old Hill	d			12 52								13 22					13 52						
Cradley Heath	d	12 33	12 43	12 56				13 04	13 13			13 26			13 33	13 43	13 56					14 04	14 13
Lye	d			12 59								13 29					13 59						
Stourbridge Junction [2]	d	12 39	12a49	13 03				13 10	13a19			13 33			13 39	13a49	14 03					14 10	14a19
Hagley	d	12 42						13 13							13 42							14 13	
Blakedown	d	12 45						13 16							13 45							14 16	
Kidderminster	d	12 50		13a12				13 21				13a42			13 50		14a12					14 21	
Hartlebury	d																						
University	d												12 57								13 57		
Barnt Green	d																						
Bromsgrove	d												13 11								14 11		
Droitwich Spa	d	13 01						13 32					13 21		14 01						14 21	14 32	
Worcester Shrub Hill [7]	a							13 40														14 41	
	d													13 45						14 15		14 46	
Worcester Foregate Street [7]	a	13 10											13 29	13 47	14 10					14 18	14 29	14 48	
	d	13 11											13 30	13 48						14 18	14 30	14 49	
Malvern Link	d	13 19											13 40	13 57						14 27	14 40	14 57	
Great Malvern	a	13 22											13 42	14 04						14 31	14 42	15 00	
	d												13 43								14 43		
Colwall	d												13 48								14 48		
Ledbury	a												13 56								14 56		
	d												14 00								14 58		
Hereford [7]	a												14 21								15 18		

A 9 October, 16 October, 23 October

Table 71

Saturdays from 09 October

Stratford-upon-Avon, Marylebone and Leamington Spa - Birmingham - Stourbridge, Worcester and Hereford

		CH ◇	XC ◇1 🛒	LM A	LM B	LM	LM	LM	CH	XC ◇1 🛒	LM	LM	CH ◇	XC ◇1 🛒	LM A	LM B	LM	GW ◇1 🛒	LM	LM	LM	CH
Stratford-upon-Avon	d						13 27				13 59									14 27		
Wilmcote	d						13 32													14 32		
Wootton Wawen	d						13x37													14x37		
Henley-in-Arden	d						13 41				14 09									14 41		
Danzey	d						13x45													14x45		
Wood End	d						13x49													14x49		
The Lakes	d						13x51													14x51		
Earlswood (West Midlands)	d						13 54													14 54		
Wythall	d						13 56				14 20									14 56		
Whitlocks End	d			13 39			13 59								14 39					14 59		
Shirley	d			13 42	13 42		14 02				14 24				14 42	14 42				15 02		
Yardley Wood	d			13 45	13 45		14 05				14 27				14 45	14 45				15 05		
Hall Green	d			13 48	13 48		14 08				14 30				14 48	14 48				15 08		
Spring Road	d			13 50	13 50		14 10				14 32				14 50	14 50				15 10		
London Marylebone 10 ⊖	d	11 50							12 20				12 50									13 20
Banbury	d	12 58	13 25						13 32	13 54			13 58	14 25								14 35
Leamington Spa 8	a	13 17	13 41						13 50	14 10			14 17	14 44								14 54
	d	13 17	13 43						13 51	14 12			14 17	14 45								14 54
Warwick	d	13 21							13 58				14 21									14 59
Warwick Parkway	d	13 25							14 02				14 25									15 02
Hatton	d								14 07													
Lapworth	d								14 13													
Dorridge	d	13 36				13 46		14 09	14 17			14 28	14 36						14 46		15 09	15 13
Widney Manor	d					13 50		14 13				14 32							14 50		15 13	
Solihull	d	13 42				13 54		14 17	14 23			14 36	14 42						14 54		15 17	15 20
Olton	d					13 57		14 20				14 39							14 57		15 20	
Acocks Green	d					14 00		14 23				14 42							15 00		15 23	
Tyseley	d					14 03					14 35		14 47						15 03			15 27
Small Heath	d					14 05					14 37								15 05			
Bordesley	d																					
Birmingham Moor Street	d	13 53		13 57	13 57	14 09	14 17	14 29	14 34		14 41	14 48	14 53		14 57	14 57			15 09	15 17	15 29	15 33
Birmingham Snow Hill 🚊	a	14 04		14 01	14 01	14 12	14 20	14 32	14 45		14 44	14 51	15 04		15 01	15 01			15 12	15 20	15 32	15 44
	d			14 03	14 03	14 13	14 23	14 33			14 45	14 53			15 03	15 03			15 13	15 23	15 33	
Jewellery Quarter 🚊	d			14 05	14 05	14 15	14 25	14 35			14 47	14 55			15 05	15 05			15 15	15 25	15 35	
The Hawthorns 🚊	d			14 10	14 10	14 20	14 30	14 40			14 52	15 00			15 10	15 10			15 20	15 30	15 40	
Smethwick Galton Bridge 7	d			14 13	14 13	14 23	14 33	14 43			14 55	15 03			15 13	15 13			15 23	15 33	15 43	
Coventry	a									14 22												
Birmingham International ✈	a									14 37												
Birmingham New Street 12	a		14 17							14 48				15 17								
	d																14 49					
Langley Green	d			14 16	14 16			14 46							15 16	15 16					15 46	
Rowley Regis	d			14 19	14 19	14 28	14 38	14 49			15 00	15 08			15 19	15 19			15 28	15 38	15 49	
Old Hill	d			14 22	14 22			14 52							15 22	15 22					15 52	
Cradley Heath	d			14 26	14 26	14 33	14 43	14 56			15 04	15 13			15 26	15 26			15 33	15 43	15 56	
Lye	d			14 29	14 29			14 59							15 29	15 29					15 59	
Stourbridge Junction 2	d			14 33	14 33	14 39	14a49	15 03			15 10	15a19			15 33	15 33			15 39	15a49	16 03	
Hagley	d					14 42					15 13								15 42			
Blakedown	d					14 45					15 16								15 45			
Kidderminster	d			14a42	14a42	14 50		15a12			15 21				15a42	15a42			15 50		16a12	
Hartlebury	d																					
University	d																14 57					
Barnt Green	d																					
Bromsgrove	d																15 11					
Droitwich Spa	d					15 01					15 32						15 21		16 01			
Worcester Shrub Hill 7	a										15 40											
	d																	15 45				
Worcester Foregate Street 7	a					15 10											15 29	15 47	16 10			
	d																15 30	15 48				
Malvern Link	d																15 40	15 57				
Great Malvern	a																15 42	16 04				
	d																15 43					
Colwall	d																15 48					
Ledbury	a																15 56					
	d																15 58					
Hereford 7	a																16 19					

A from 30 October

B 9 October, 16 October, 23 October

Table 71

Saturdays from 09 October

Stratford-upon-Avon, Marylebone and Leamington Spa - Birmingham - Stourbridge, Worcester and Hereford

		CH	XC ◇1 🛒	GW ◇	LM	LM	CH ◇	XC ◇1 🛒	LM A	LM B	LM	GW ◇1 🛒	LM	LM	LM	CH ◇	XC ◇1 🛒	LM	LM	LM	CH ◇	XC ◇1 🛒	LM A
Stratford-upon-Avon	d	14 36			14 59									15 27					15 59				
Wilmcote	d	14 41												15 32									
Wootton Wawen	d													15x37									
Henley-in-Arden	d				15 09									15 41					16 09				
Danzey	d													15x45									
Wood End	d													15x49									
The Lakes	d													15x51									
Earlswood (West Midlands)	d													15 54									
Wythall	d				15 20									15 56					16 20				
Whitlocks End	d								15 39					15 59									16 39
Shirley	d				15 24				15 42	15 42				16 02					16 24				16 42
Yardley Wood	d				15 27				15 45	15 45				16 05					16 27				16 45
Hall Green	d				15 30				15 48	15 48				16 08					16 30				16 48
Spring Road	d				15 32				15 50	15 50				16 10					16 32				16 50
London Marylebone 10 ⊖	d						13 50									14 20					14 50		
Banbury	d		14 54				14 58	15 25								15 35	15 54				15 58	16 25	
Leamington Spa 8	a	15 08	15 10				15 17	15 41								15 54	16 10				16 16	16 47	
	d		15 12				15 17	15 43								15 54	16 12				16 17	16 48	
Warwick	d						15 21									15 59					16 21		
Warwick Parkway	d						15 25									16 02					16 25		
Hatton	d															16 07							
Lapworth	d															16 13							
Dorridge	d					15 28	15 36						15 46		16 09	16 17				16 27	16 36		
Widney Manor	d					15 32							15 50		16 13					16 31			
Solihull	d					15 36	15 42						15 54		16 17	16 23				16 35	16 42		
Olton	d					15 39							15 57		16 20					16 38			
Acocks Green	d					15 42							16 00		16 23					16 41			
Tyseley	d				15 35								16 03						16 35	16 44	16 48		16 53
Small Heath	d				15 37								16 05						16 37				
Bordesley	d																						
Birmingham Moor Street	d				15 41	15 48	15 53		15 57	15 57			16 09	16 17	16 29	16 34			16 41	16 49	16 53		16 58
Birmingham Snow Hill 🚊	a				15 44	15 51	16 04		16 01	16 01			16 12	16 20	16 32	16 44			16 44	16 51	17 05		17 02
	d				15 45	15 53			16 03	16 03			16 13	16 23	16 33				16 45	16 53			17 03
Jewellery Quarter 🚊	d				15 47	15 55			16 05	16 05			16 15	16 25	16 35				16 47	16 55			17 05
The Hawthorns 🚊	d				15 52	16 00			16 10	16 10			16 20	16 30	16 40				16 52	17 00			17 10
Smethwick Galton Bridge 7	d				15 55	16 03			16 13	16 13			16 23	16 33	16 43				16 55	17 03			17 13
Coventry	a		15 22														16 22						
Birmingham International ✈	a		15 37														16 37						
Birmingham New Street 12	a		15 48					16 17									16 48					17 17	
	d										15 49							16 49					
Langley Green	d								16 16	16 16					16 46								17 16
Rowley Regis	d				16 00	16 08			16 19	16 19			16 28	16 38	16 49				17 00	17 08			17 19
Old Hill	d								16 22	16 22					16 52								17 22
Cradley Heath	d				16 04	16 13			16 26	16 26			16 33	16 43	16 56				17 04	17 13			17 26
Lye	d								16 29	16 29					16 59								17 29
Stourbridge Junction 2	d				16 10	16a19			16 33	16 33			16 39	16a49	17 03				17 10	17a19			17 33
Hagley	d				16 13								16 42		17 06				17 13				
Blakedown	d				16 16								16 45		17 09				17 16				
Kidderminster	d				16 21				16a42	16a42			16 50		17a15				17 21				17a42
Hartlebury	d																		17 26				
University	d										15 57							16 57					
Barnt Green	d																						
Bromsgrove	d										16 11							17 11					
Droitwich Spa	d				16 32						16 21		17 01					17 21	17 34				
Worcester Shrub Hill 7	a				16 40																		
	d			16 15								16 45											
Worcester Foregate Street 7	a			16 17							16 29	16 48	17 10					17 29	17 43				
	d			16 18							16 30	16 48	17 11					17 30					
Malvern Link	d			16 26							16 40	16 57	17 20					17 39					
Great Malvern	a			16 31							16 42	17 04	17 23					17 41					
	d										16 43							17 42					
Colwall	d										16 48							17 47					
Ledbury	a										16 56							17 55					
	d										17 00							18 00					
Hereford 7	a										17 20							18 21					

A from 30 October

B 9 October, 16 October, 23 October

Stratford-upon-Avon, Marylebone and Leamington Spa - Birmingham - Stourbridge, Worcester and Hereford

		LM	GW	LM	LM	LM	LM	CH	XC	GW	LM	LM	LM	CH	XC	LM	LM	LM	GW	LM	LM	CH	CH
			◇1						◇1						◇1				◇1				
		A														A	B						
Stratford-upon-Avon	d					16 27						16 59								17 27			17 40
Wilmcote	d					16 32														17 32			
Wootton Wawen	d					16x37														17x37			
Henley-in-Arden	d					16 41						17 09								17 41			
Danzey	d					16x45														17x45			
Wood End	d					16x49														17x49			
The Lakes	d					16x51														17x51			
Earlswood (West Midlands)	d					16 54														17 54			
Wythall	d					16 56						17 20								17 56			
Whitlocks End	d					16 59											17 39			17 59			
Shirley	d	16 42				17 02						17 24				17 42	17 42			18 02			
Yardley Wood	d	16 45				17 05						17 27				17 45	17 46			18 05			
Hall Green	d	16 48				17 08						17 30				17 48	17 49			18 08			
Spring Road	d	16 50				17 10						17 32				17 50	17 51			18 10			
London Marylebone ⊖	d							15 20						15 50								16 20	
Banbury	d							16 35	16 54					16 58	17 25							17 35	
Leamington Spa	a							16 53	17 10					17 16	17 41							17 54	18 05
	d							16 54	17 12					17 17	17 43							17 54	
Warwick	d							16 59						17 21								17 59	
Warwick Parkway	d							17 02						17 25								18 02	
Hatton	d							17 07														18 07	
Lapworth	d							17 13														18 13	
Dorridge	d				16 46		17 09	17 17					17 28	17 36				17 46			18 09	18 17	
Widney Manor	d				16 50		17 13						17 32					17 50			18 13		
Solihull	d				16 54		17 17	17 23					17 36	17 42				17 54			18 17	18 23	
Olton	d				16 57		17 20						17 39					17 57			18 20		
Acocks Green	d				17 00		17 23						17 42					18 00			18 23		
Tyseley	d	16 53			17 03							17 35	17 45					18 03					
Small Heath	d				17 05							17 37						18 05					
Bordesley	d																						
Birmingham Moor Street	d	16 58			17 09	17 17	17 29	17 34				17 41	17 50	17 53		17 57	18 01	18 09		18 17	18 29	18 34	
Birmingham Snow Hill	a	17 02			17 12	17 20	17 32	17 44				17 44	17 52	18 05		18 01	18 04	18 12		18 20	18 32	18 44	
	d	17 03			17 13	17 23	17 33					17 45	17 53					18 13		18 23	18 33		
Jewellery Quarter	d	17 05			17 15	17 25	17 35					17 47	17 55					18 15		18 25	18 35		
The Hawthorns	d	17 10			17 20	17 30	17 40					17 52	18 00					18 20		18 30	18 40		
Smethwick Galton Bridge	d	17 13			17 23	17 33	17 43					17 55	18 03					18 23		18 33	18 43		
Coventry	a								17 22														
Birmingham International ✈	a								17 37														
Birmingham New Street	a								17 48						18 17								
	d			17 19							17 49												
Langley Green	d	17 16					17 46						18 06					18 26			18 46		
Rowley Regis	d	17 19			17 28	17 38	17 49					18 00	18 09					18 29		18 38	18 49		
Old Hill	d	17 22					17 52						18 12					18 32			18 52		
Cradley Heath	d	17 26			17 33	17 43	17 56					18 05	18 16					18 36		18 43	18 56		
Lye	d	17 29					17 59						18 19					18 39			18 59		
Stourbridge Junction	d	17 33			17 39	17a49	18 03					18 11	18a23					18a43		18 49	19 03		
Hagley	d				17 42		18 06					18 14								18 52	19 06		
Blakedown	d				17 45		18 09					18 17								18 55	19 09		
Kidderminster	d	17a42			17 50		18a15					18 22								19 00	19a15		
Hartlebury	d				17 55							18 27								19 05			
University	d										17 57												
Barnt Green	d																						
Bromsgrove	d			17 42							18 11												
Droitwich Spa	d			17 52	18 03						18 19	18 35								19 13			
Worcester Shrub Hill	a			18 06	18 12						18 27												
	d		17 45							18 19	18 31								18 51				
Worcester Foregate Street	a		17 47							18 21	18 33	18 44							18 54	19 22			
	d		17 48							18 22	18 34								18 55	19 23			
Malvern Link	d		17 57							18 30	18 44								19 04	19 32			
Great Malvern	a		18 04							18 36	18 46								19 07	19 35			
	d										18 47								19 08				
Colwall	d										18 52								19 14				
Ledbury	a										18 59								19 21				
	d										19 00								19 29				
Hereford	a										19 20								19 45				

A 9 October, 16 October, 23 October

B from 30 October

Stratford-upon-Avon, Marylebone and Leamington Spa - Birmingham - Stourbridge, Worcester and Hereford

		XC	LM	GW	LM	CH	LM	XC	LM	GW	LM	CH	LM	XC	GW	LM	CH	XC	LM	CH	XC	CH
		◇1		◇1				◇1						◇1	◇1		◇	◇1			◇1	◇
Stratford-upon-Avon	d		17 59				18 19						18 50						19 26			19 48
Wilmcote	d						18 24						18 55						19 31			19 53
Wootton Wawen	d						18x29						19x00						19x36			
Henley-in-Arden	d		18 09				18 33						19 04						19 40			
Danzey	d						18x37						19x08						19x44			
Wood End	d						18x41						19x12						19x48			
The Lakes	d						18x43						19x14						19x50			
Earlswood (West Midlands)	d						18 46						19 16						19 53			
Wythall	d		18 20				18 48						19 19						19 55			
Whitlocks End	d						18 51						19 21						19 58			
Shirley	d		18 23				18 54						19 25						20 01			
Yardley Wood	d		18 26				18 57						19 28						20 04			
Hall Green	d		18 29				19 00						19 31						20 07			
Spring Road	d		18 31				19 02						19 33						20 09			
London Marylebone ⊖	d					16 50						17 20					17 50			18 20		
Banbury	d	17 54				17 58		18 25				18 32		18 54			19 03	19 25		19 35	19 54	
Leamington Spa	a	18 10				18 17		18 44				18 50		19 10			19 22	19 41		19 53	20 10	20 21
	d	18 12				18 17		18 45				18 51		19 12			19 23	19 43		19 54	20 12	
Warwick	d					18 21						18 58					19 27			19 59		
Warwick Parkway	d					18 25						19 02					19 30			20 02		
Hatton	d											19 07								20 07		
Lapworth	d											19 13								20 13		
Dorridge	d				18 28	18 36					19 00	19 17				19 28	19 42			20 17		
Widney Manor	d				18 32						19 04					19 32						
Solihull	d				18 36	18 42					19 08	19 23				19 36	19 48			20 23		
Olton	d				18 39						19 11					19 39						
Acocks Green	d				18 42						19 14					19 42						
Tyseley	d		18 34		18 45		19 05				19 17		19 36			19 45						
Small Heath	d		18 37		18 47		19 07				19 19		19 38			19 47						
Bordesley	d																					
Birmingham Moor Street	d		18 41		18 51	18 55	19 11				19 23	19 34	19 42			19 51	19 59		20 16	20 35		
Birmingham Snow Hill	a		18 44		18 54	19 07	19 15				19 26	19 44	19 46			19 54	20 09		20 19	20 45		
	d				18 58						19 28					19 55			20 20			
Jewellery Quarter	d				19 00						19 30					19 57			20 22			
The Hawthorns	d				19 05						19 35					20 02			20 27			
Smethwick Galton Bridge	d				19 08						19 38					20 05			20 30			
Coventry	a	18 22												19 22							20 22	
Birmingham International ✈	a	18 37												19 37							20 37	
Birmingham New Street	a	18 48						19 17						19 48				20 18			20 48	
	d								19 19													
Langley Green	d				19 11						19 41					20 08			20 33			
Rowley Regis	d				19 14						19 44					20 11			20 36			
Old Hill	d				19 17						19 47					20 14			20 39			
Cradley Heath	d				19 21						19 51					20 18			20 43			
Lye	d				19 24						19 54					20 21			20 46			
Stourbridge Junction	d				19 28						19 58					20 25			20a50			
Hagley	d				19 31						20 01					20 28						
Blakedown	d				19 34						20 04					20 31						
Kidderminster	d				19 39						20 09					20 36						
Hartlebury	d																					
University	d								19 27													
Barnt Green	d																					
Bromsgrove	d								19 42													
Droitwich Spa	d				19 50				19 57		20 20					20 47						
Worcester Shrub Hill	a				19 58						20 30					20 55						
	d			19 43						20 20					20 48	20 59						
Worcester Foregate Street	a			19 45					20 05	20 22					20 50	21 01						
	d								20 06	20 25					20 52	21 02						
Malvern Link	d								20 16	20 34					21 01	21 11						
Great Malvern	a								20 18	20 38					21 04	21 14						
	d								20 25						21 05							
Colwall	d								20 30						21 11							
Ledbury	a								20 38						21 18							
	d								20 39						21 20							
Hereford	a								21 03						21 36							

Table 71

Saturdays from 09 October

Stratford-upon-Avon, Marylebone and Leamington Spa - Birmingham - Stourbridge, Worcester and Hereford

Station		LM	CH ◇	CH	LM	XC ◇1	CH	XC ◇1	LM	GW ◇1	LM	LM A	LM B	CH ◇	XC ◇1	XC ◇1	LM	CH ◇	XC ◇1	LM A	LM B	CH ◇
Stratford-upon-Avon	d				20 26																	
Wilmcote	d				20 31																	
Wootton Wawen	d				20x36																	
Henley-in-Arden	d				20 40																	
Danzey	d				20x44																	
Wood End	d				20x48																	
The Lakes	d				20x50																	
Earlswood (West Midlands)	d				20 53																	
Wythall	d				20 55																	
Whitlocks End	d				20 58							21 54								22 57		
Shirley	d				21 01							21 57	21 57							23 00	23 00	
Yardley Wood	d				21 04							22 00	22 00							23 03	23 03	
Hall Green	d				21 07							22 03	22 03							23 06	23 06	
Spring Road	d				21 09							22 05	22 05							23 08	23 08	
London Marylebone 10 ⊖	d		18 50	18 53			19 20							20 00				20 50				22 00
Banbury	d		20 03	20 19		20 30	20 32	20 54						21 19	21 25	21 54		22 07	22 25			23 06
Leamington Spa 8	a		20 22	20 37		20 46	20 50	21 10						21 37	21 44	22 10		22 27	22 41			23 23
	d		20 23	20 38		20 47	20 51	21 12						21 38	21 45	22 12		22 27	22 43			23 24
Warwick	d		20 27	20 42			20 58							21 42				22 31				23 28
Warwick Parkway	d		20 30				21 02							21 46				22 35				23 32
Hatton	d			20 49			21 07															
Lapworth	d						21 13															
Dorridge	d	20 28	20 42				21 17				21 28			21 58			22 32	22 46				23 43
Widney Manor	d	20 32									21 32						22 36					23 46
Solihull	d	20 36	20 47				21 23				21 36			22 03			22 40	22 52				23 50
Olton	d	20 39									21 39						22 43					
Acocks Green	d	20 42									21 42						22 46					
Tyseley	d	20 45									21 45	22 08	22 08				22 49			23 11	23 11	
Small Heath	d	20 47									21 47	22 10	22 10				22 51			23 13	23 13	
Bordesley	d																					
Birmingham Moor Street	d	20 51	20 58		21 16		21 34				21 51	22 14	22 14	22 16			22 55	23 03		23 17	23 17	23 59
Birmingham Snow Hill ⛴	a	20 54	21 09		21 19		21 44				21 54	22 17	22 17	22 29			22 58	23 13		23 20	23 20	00 13
	d	20 55			21 20						21 55	22 20	22 20				22 59			23 23	23 23	
Jewellery Quarter ⛴	d	20 57			21 22						21 57	22 22	22 22				23 01			23 25	23 25	
The Hawthorns ⛴	d	21 02			21 27						22 02	22 27	22 27				23 06			23 30	23 30	
Smethwick Galton Bridge 7	d	21 05			21 30						22 05	22 30	22 30				23 09			23 33	23 33	
Coventry	a							21 22							21 55	22 22						
Birmingham International ✈	a							21 37							22 12	22 37						
Birmingham New Street 12	a					21 16		21 48							22 25	22 48			23 09			
	d								20 59													
Langley Green	d	21 08			21 33						22 08	22 33	22 33				23 12			23 36	23 36	
Rowley Regis	d	21 11			21 36						22 11	22 36	22 36				23 15			23 39	23 39	
Old Hill	d	21 14			21 39						22 14	22 39	22 39				23 18			23 42	23 42	
Cradley Heath	d	21 18			21 43						22 18	22 43	22 43				23 22			23 46	23 46	
Lye	d	21 21			21 46						22 21	22 46	22 46				23 25			23 49	23 49	
Stourbridge Junction 2	d	21 25			21a50						22 25	22a50	22a50				23 29			23a52	23a52	
Hagley	d	21 28									22 28						23 32					
Blakedown	d	21 31									22 31						23 35					
Kidderminster	d	21 36									22 36						23 40					
Hartlebury	d																					
University	d								21 05													
Barnt Green	d																					
Bromsgrove	d								21 21													
Droitwich Spa	d	21 47							21 31		22 47						23 51					
Worcester Shrub Hill 7	a	21 55									22 55						23 59					
	d									22 08	22 59											
Worcester Foregate Street 7	a								21 39	22 11	23 01											
	d								21 42	22 11	23 02											
Malvern Link	d								21 52	22 20	23 10											
Great Malvern	a								21 54	22 27	23 13											
	d								22 00													
Colwall	d								22 05													
Ledbury	a								22 13													
	d								22 14													
Hereford 7	a								22 34													

A from 30 October

B 9 October, 16 October, 23 October

Table 71

Sundays until 26 September

Stratford-upon-Avon, Marylebone and Leamington Spa - Birmingham - Stourbridge, Worcester and Hereford

Station		CH ◇	CH ◇	XC ◇1	CH ◇	WS ◇1	LM	CH ◇	GW ◇1	XC ◇1	LM	CH ◇	XC ◇1	GW ◇1 C	GW ◇1 D	LM	CH ◇	CH ◇	CH	XC ◇1	GW ◇1 D	GW ◇1 C	LM
Stratford-upon-Avon	d				10 00													12 00					
Wilmcote	d				10 04													12 04					
Wootton Wawen	d																						
Henley-in-Arden	d																						
Danzey	d																						
Wood End	d																						
The Lakes	d																						
Earlswood (West Midlands)	d																						
Wythall	d																						
Whitlocks End	d																						
Shirley	d																						
Yardley Wood	d																						
Hall Green	d																						
Spring Road	d																						
London Marylebone 10 ⊖	d	22p00	08 10			09 33		09 15				10 15					10 50		11 20				
Banbury	d	23p06	09 27	09 54		10 37		10 41		10 54		11 38	11 54				12 02		12 41	12 54			
Leamington Spa 8	a	23p23	09 46	10 11	10 28	10 55		11 00		11 11		11 57	12 11				12 21	12 28	12 59	13 11			
	d	23p24	09 46	10 12				11 01		11 12		11 58	12 12				12 22		13 01	13 12			
Warwick	d	23p28	09 51					11 05				12 02							13 05				
Warwick Parkway	d	23p32	09 54					11 09				12 06					12 27		13 09				
Hatton	d		09 59									12 11											
Lapworth	d		10 05									12 16											
Dorridge	d	23p43	10 09				10 25	11 20			11 25	12 20				12 25	12 39		13 20				
Widney Manor	d	23p46					10 29				11 29					12 29							
Solihull	d	23p50	10 15				10 32	11 26			11 32	12 26				12 32	12 44		13 26				
Olton	d						10 36				11 36					12 36							
Acocks Green	d						10 38				11 38					12 38							
Tyseley	d																						
Small Heath	d																						
Bordesley	d																						
Birmingham Moor Street	d	23p59	10 26				10 45	11 36			11 45	12 36				12 45	12 56		13 39				
Birmingham Snow Hill ⛴	a	00 10					10 47				11 47					12 47							
	d						10 48				11 48					12 48							
Jewellery Quarter ⛴	d						10 51				11 51					12 51							
The Hawthorns ⛴	d						10 55				11 55					12 55							
Smethwick Galton Bridge 7	d						10 58				11 58					12 58							
Coventry	a			10 22						11 22			12 22							13 22			
Birmingham International ✈	a			10 38						11 38			12 38							13 37			
Birmingham New Street 12	a			10 50						11 50			12 50							13 48			
	d																						13 24
Langley Green	d						11 01				12 01					13 01							
Rowley Regis	d						11 04				12 04					13 04							
Old Hill	d						11 07				12 07					13 07							
Cradley Heath	d						11 10				12 10					13 10							
Lye	d						11 13				12 13					13 13							
Stourbridge Junction 2	d						11a17				12a17					13a17							
Hagley	d																						
Blakedown	d																						
Kidderminster	d																						
Hartlebury	d																						
University	d																						
Barnt Green	d																						
Bromsgrove	d																						13 42
Droitwich Spa	d																						13 52
Worcester Shrub Hill 7	a																						13 59
	d								10 37					12 04	12 04						13 12	13 12	14 21
Worcester Foregate Street 7	a								10 39					12 07	12 07						13 14	13 14	14 23
	d								10 41					12 08	12 08						13 16	13 16	14 24
Malvern Link	d								10 50					12 17	12 17						13 25	13 25	14 32
Great Malvern	a								10 54					12 20	12 20						13 28	13 28	14 35
	d													12 22	12 22						13 29	13 29	14 36
Colwall	d													12 28	12 28						13 35	13 35	14 41
Ledbury	a													12 35	12 35						13 42	13 42	14 48
	d													12 37	12 37						13 48	13 48	14 49
Hereford 7	a													12 54	12 58						14 04	14 05	15 10

C 12 September, 19 September, 26 September

D until 5 September

Stratford-upon-Avon, Marylebone and Leamington Spa - Birmingham - Stourbridge, Worcester and Hereford

		LM	CH	XC	CH	XC	LM	CH	CH	XC	CH	XC	GW	LM	CH	XC	CH	XC	LM	LM	CH	CH	XC
			◇	◇1		◇1		◇		◇1		◇1	◇1		◇	◇1	◇	◇1			◇	◇	◇1
Stratford-upon-Avon	d								14 00													16 00	
Wilmcote	d								14 04													16 04	
Wootton Wawen	d																						
Henley-in-Arden	d																						
Danzey	d																						
Wood End	d																						
The Lakes	d																						
Earlswood (West Midlands)	d																						
Wythall	d																						
Whitlocks End	d																						
Shirley	d																						
Yardley Wood	d																						
Hall Green	d																						
Spring Road	d																						
London Marylebone 10 ⊖	d		11 50		12 20			12 50			13 20				13 50		14 20				14 50		
Banbury	d		13 05	13 35	13 41	13 54		14 02		14 25	14 41	14 54			15 05	15 25	15 40	15 54			16 02		16 25
Leamington Spa 8	a		13 25	13 51	13 59	14 11		14 21	14 28	14 41	15 00	15 11			15 25	15 41	15 58	16 11			16 21	16 28	16 41
	d		13 25	13 53	14 00	14 12		14 22	14 29	14 43	15 01	15 12			15 25	15 43	15 59	16 12			16 22	16 29	16 43
Warwick	d				14 04						15 05						16 03						
Warwick Parkway	d		13 31		14 08			14 27			15 09				15 31		16 06				16 27		
Hatton	d																16 11						
Lapworth	d				14 16												16 16						
Dorridge	d	13 25	13 42		14 21		14 25	14 39			15 20			15 25	15 42		16 21			16 25	16 39		
Widney Manor	d	13 29					14 29							15 29						16 29			
Solihull	d	13 32	13 48		14 26		14 32	14 44			15 26			15 32	15 48		16 26			16 32	16 44		
Olton	d	13 36					14 36							15 36						16 36			
Acocks Green	d	13 38					14 38							15 38						16 38			
Tyseley	d																						
Small Heath	d																						
Bordesley	d																						
Birmingham Moor Street	d	13 45	13 59		14 38		14 45	14 55			15 37			15 45	15 58		16 36			16 45	16 55		
Birmingham Snow Hill	a	13 48	14 08		14 47		14 47	15 03			15 49			15 48	16 06		16 49			16 48	17 03		
	d	13 48					14 48							15 48						16 48			
Jewellery Quarter	d	13 51					14 51							15 51						16 51			
The Hawthorns	d	13 55					14 55							15 55						16 55			
Smethwick Galton Bridge 7	d	13 58					14 58							15 58						16 58			
Coventry	a					14 22						15 22						16 22					
Birmingham International ✈	a					14 35						15 35						16 35					
Birmingham New Street 12	a			14 19		14 48				15 10		15 48				16 09		16 48					17 09
	d																		16 00				
Langley Green	d	14 01					15 01							16 01						17 01			
Rowley Regis	d	14 04					15 04							16 04						17 04			
Old Hill	d	14 07					15 07							16 07						17 07			
Cradley Heath	d	14 10					15 10							16 10						17 10			
Lye	d	14 13					15 13							16 13						17 13			
Stourbridge Junction 2	d	14a18					15a17							16a18						17a18			
Hagley	d																						
Blakedown	d																						
Kidderminster	d																						
Hartlebury	d																						
University	d																						
Barnt Green	d																						
Bromsgrove	d																		16 21				
Droitwich Spa	d																		16 30				
Worcester Shrub Hill 7	a																		16 38				
	d												15 10						16 45				
Worcester Foregate Street 7	a												15 13						16 47				
	d												15 14						16 48				
Malvern Link	d												15 23						16 57				
Great Malvern	a												15 26						17 01				
	d												15 28										
Colwall	d												15 34										
Ledbury	a												15 41										
	d												15 48										
Hereford 7	a												16 07										

Stratford-upon-Avon, Marylebone and Leamington Spa - Birmingham - Stourbridge, Worcester and Hereford

		CH	XC	LM	CH	WS	XC	CH	XC	CH	LM	CH	XC	CH	XC	CH	LM	XC	WS	CH	XC	CH	CH
			◇1			◇1 B	◇1		◇1			◇	◇1		◇1			◇1	◇1 B		◇1	◇	
Stratford-upon-Avon	d											18 00										19 57	
Wilmcote	d											18 04										20 01	
Wootton Wawen	d																						
Henley-in-Arden	d																						
Danzey	d																						
Wood End	d																						
The Lakes	d																						
Earlswood (West Midlands)	d																						
Wythall	d																						
Whitlocks End	d																						
Shirley	d																						
Yardley Wood	d																						
Hall Green	d																						
Spring Road	d																						
London Marylebone 10 ⊖	d	15 20			15 57	16 11		16 22		16 57				17 20		17 57			18 33	18 20			18 57
Banbury	d	16 41	16 54		17 07	17 16	17 25	17 43	17 54	18 09			18 25	18 41	18 54	19 09		19 25	19 43	19 46	19 54		20 09
Leamington Spa 8	a	17 00	17 11		17 25	17 34	17 41	18 02	18 11	18 28		18 28	18 41	19 00	19 11	19 28		19 41	20 01	20 05	20 11	20 25	20 28
	d	17 01	17 12		17 25		17 43	18 03	18 12	18 29			18 43	19 01	19 12	19 29		19 43		20 05	20 12		20 29
Warwick	d	17 05						18 07						19 05						20 09			
Warwick Parkway	d	17 09			17 31			18 10		18 34				19 09		19 34				20 13			20 34
Hatton	d							18 15															
Lapworth	d							18 20												20 21			
Dorridge	d	17 20		17 25	17 42			18 24		18 46				19 20		19 46				20 26			20 46
Widney Manor	d			17 29				18 28						19 24						20 29			
Solihull	d	17 26		17 32	17 48			18 31		18 51				19 27		19 51				20 33			20 51
Olton	d			17 36																			
Acocks Green	d			17 38																			
Tyseley	d																						
Small Heath	d																						
Bordesley	d																						
Birmingham Moor Street	d	17 39		17 45	17 58			18 42		19 02				19 38		20 02				20 43			21 02
Birmingham Snow Hill	a	17 46		17 48	18 07			18 49		19 10				19 46		20 10				20 53			21 10
	d			17 48																			
Jewellery Quarter	d			17 51																			
The Hawthorns	d			17 55																			
Smethwick Galton Bridge 7	d			17 58																			
Coventry	a		17 22						18 22						19 22			19 53			20 22		
Birmingham International ✈	a		17 35						18 35						19 35			20 03			20 35		
Birmingham New Street 12	a		17 48				18 09		18 48				19 09		19 48			20 15			20 48		
	d										18 00						19 00						
Langley Green	d			18 01																			
Rowley Regis	d			18 04																			
Old Hill	d			18 07																			
Cradley Heath	d			18 10																			
Lye	d			18 13																			
Stourbridge Junction 2	d			18a19																			
Hagley	d																						
Blakedown	d																						
Kidderminster	d																						
Hartlebury	d																						
University	d																						
Barnt Green	d																						
Bromsgrove	d										18 21						19 21						
Droitwich Spa	d										18 30						19 31						
Worcester Shrub Hill 7	a										18 38						19 41						
	d										18 43												
Worcester Foregate Street 7	a										18 45												
	d										18 46												
Malvern Link	d										18 55												
Great Malvern	a										18 58												
	d										18 58												
Colwall	d										19 03												
Ledbury	a										19 10												
	d										19 10												
Hereford 7	a										19 31												

B until 5 September

Table 71

Sundays
until 26 September

Stratford-upon-Avon, Marylebone and Leamington Spa - Birmingham - Stourbridge, Worcester and Hereford

		XC	CH	XC	CH	LM	XC	CH	XC	CH	XC	CH
		◇1	◇	◇1			◇1	◇	◇1	◇	◇1	◇
		✠		✠			✠		✠		✠	
Stratford-upon-Avon	d											
Wilmcote	d											
Wootton Wawen	d											
Henley-in-Arden	d											
Danzey	d											
Wood End	d											
The Lakes	d											
Earlswood (West Midlands)	d											
Wythall	d											
Whitlocks End	d											
Shirley	d											
Yardley Wood	d											
Hall Green	d											
Spring Road	d											
London Marylebone 10 ⊖	d		19 22		19 57			20 20		20 50		22 00
Banbury	d	20 25	20 44	20 54	21 09		21 25	21 41	21 54	22 11	22 25	23 06
Leamington Spa 8	a	20 41	21 02	21 11	21 28		21 41	22 01	22 11	22 30	22 41	23 23
	d	20 43	21 03	21 12	21 29		21 43	22 01	22 12	22 31	22 43	23 24
Warwick	d		21 08					22 05		22 35		23 28
Warwick Parkway	d		21 11		21 34			22 09		22 39		23 32
Hatton	d									22 43		
Lapworth	d									22 48		
Dorridge	d		21 22		21 46			22 20		22 53		23 43
Widney Manor	d		21 26							22 56		
Solihull	d		21 29		21 51			22 26		23 00		23 48
Olton	d											
Acocks Green	d											
Tyseley	d											
Small Heath	d											
Bordesley	d											
Birmingham Moor Street	d		21 41		22 02			22 38		23 11		23 59
Birmingham Snow Hill ⇌	a		21 48		22 10			22 45		23 18		00 08
	d											
Jewellery Quarter ⇌	d											
The Hawthorns ⇌	d											
Smethwick Galton Bridge 7	d											
Coventry	a	20 53		21 22			21 53		22 22		22 53	
Birmingham International ✈	a	21 03		21 35			22 03		22 32		23 03	
Birmingham New Street 12	a	21 15		21 48			22 15		22 42		23 14	
	d					21 00						
Langley Green	d											
Rowley Regis	d											
Old Hill	d											
Cradley Heath	d											
Lye	d											
Stourbridge Junction 2	d											
Hagley	d											
Blakedown	d											
Kidderminster	d											
Hartlebury	d											
University	d											
Barnt Green	d											
Bromsgrove	d					21 21						
Droitwich Spa	d					21 31						
Worcester Shrub Hill 7	a					21 38						
	d					21 42						
Worcester Foregate Street 7	a					21 44						
	d					21 45						
Malvern Link	d					21 54						
Great Malvern	a					21 57						
	d					21 57						
Colwall	d					22 02						
Ledbury	a					22 09						
	d					22 10						
Hereford 7	a					22 30						

Table 71

Sundays
from 03 October

Stratford-upon-Avon, Marylebone and Leamington Spa - Birmingham - Stourbridge, Worcester and Hereford

		CH	XC	CH	LM	CH	GW	XC	LM	CH	XC	GW	LM	CH	CH	CH	XC	GW	LM	LM	CH
		◇	◇1	◇		◇	◇1	◇1		◇	◇1	◇1		◇	◇		◇1	◇1			◇
			✠				✠	✠			✠	⊡					✠	⊡			
Stratford-upon-Avon	d			10 00											12 00						
Wilmcote	d			10 04											12 04						
Wootton Wawen	d																				
Henley-in-Arden	d																				
Danzey	d																				
Wood End	d																				
The Lakes	d																				
Earlswood (West Midlands)	d																				
Wythall	d																				
Whitlocks End	d																				
Shirley	d																				
Yardley Wood	d																				
Hall Green	d																				
Spring Road	d																				
London Marylebone 10 ⊖	d	08 10				09 15				10 15				10 50		11 20					11 50
Banbury	d	09 27	09 54			10 41		10 54		11 38	11 54			12 02		12 41	12 54				13 05
Leamington Spa 8	a	09 46	10 11	10 28		11 00		11 11		11 57	12 11			12 21	12 28	12 59	13 11				13 25
	d	09 46		10 29		11 01		11 12		11 58	12 12			12 22		13 01	13 12				13 25
Warwick	d	09 51				11 05				12 02						13 05					
Warwick Parkway	d	09 54				11 09				12 06				12 27		13 09					13 31
Hatton	d	09 59								12 11											
Lapworth	d	10 05								12 16											
Dorridge	d	10 09			10 25	11 20			11 25	12 20			12 25	12 39		13 20				13 25	13 42
Widney Manor	d				10 29				11 29				12 29							13 29	
Solihull	d	10 15			10 32	11 26			11 32	12 26			12 32	12 44		13 26				13 32	13 48
Olton	d				10 36				11 36				12 36							13 36	
Acocks Green	d				10 38				11 38				12 38							13 38	
Tyseley	d																				
Small Heath	d																				
Bordesley	d																				
Birmingham Moor Street	d	10 26			10 45	11 36			11 45	12 36			12 45	12 56		13 39				13 45	13 59
Birmingham Snow Hill ⇌	a	10 42			10 47	11 48			11 47	12 47			12 47	13 06		13 49				13 48	14 11
	d				10 48				11 48				12 48							13 48	
Jewellery Quarter ⇌	d				10 51				11 51				12 51							13 51	
The Hawthorns ⇌	d				10 55				11 55				12 55							13 55	
Smethwick Galton Bridge 7	d				10 58				11 58				12 58							13 58	
Coventry	a		10 22					11 22			12 22						13 22				
Birmingham International ✈	a		10 38					11 38			12 38						13 37				
Birmingham New Street 12	a		10 50					11 50			12 50						13 48				
	d																		13 24		
Langley Green	d				11 01				12 01				13 01							14 01	
Rowley Regis	d				11 04				12 04				13 04							14 04	
Old Hill	d				11 07				12 07				13 07							14 07	
Cradley Heath	d				11 10				12 10				13 10							14 10	
Lye	d				11 13				12 13				13 13							14 13	
Stourbridge Junction 2	d				11a17				12a17				13a17							14a18	
Hagley	d																				
Blakedown	d																				
Kidderminster	d																				
Hartlebury	d																				
University	d																				
Barnt Green	d																				
Bromsgrove	d																		13 42		
Droitwich Spa	d																		13 52		
Worcester Shrub Hill 7	a																		13 59		
	d						10 37					12 04						13 12	14 21		
Worcester Foregate Street 7	a						10 39					12 07						13 14	14 23		
	d						10 41					12 08						13 16	14 24		
Malvern Link	d						10 50					12 17						13 25	14 32		
Great Malvern	a						10 54					12 20						13 28	14 35		
	d											12 22						13 29	14 36		
Colwall	d											12 28						13 35	14 41		
Ledbury	a											12 35						13 42	14 48		
	d											12 37						13 48	14 49		
Hereford 7	a											12 54						14 05	15 10		

Table 71

Sundays from 03 October

Stratford-upon-Avon, Marylebone and Leamington Spa - Birmingham - Stourbridge, Worcester and Hereford

		XC	CH	XC	LM	CH	CH	XC	CH	XC	GW	LM	CH	XC	CH	XC	LM	LM	CH	CH	XC	CH	LM
		◇1		◇1		◇		◇1		◇1	◇1		◇	◇1	◇	◇1			◇	◇	◇1		
Stratford-upon-Avon	d						14 00													16 00			
Wilmcote	d						14 04													16 04			
Wootton Wawen	d																						
Henley-in-Arden	d																						
Danzey	d																						
Wood End	d																						
The Lakes	d																						
Earlswood (West Midlands)	d																						
Wythall	d																						
Whitlocks End	d																						
Shirley	d																						
Yardley Wood	d																						
Hall Green	d																						
Spring Road	d																						
London Marylebone ⊖	d		12 20			12 50			13 20				13 50		14 20				14 50			15 20	
Banbury	d	13 35	13 41	13 54		14 02		14 25	14 41	14 54			15 05	15 25	15 40	15 54			16 02		16 25	16 41	
Leamington Spa	a	13 51	13 59	14 11		14 21	14 28	14 41	15 00	15 11			15 25	15 41	15 58	16 11			16 21	16 28	16 41	17 00	
	d	13 53	14 00	14 12		14 22	14 29	14 43	15 01	15 12			15 25	15 43	15 59	16 12			16 22	16 29	16 43	17 01	
Warwick	d		14 04						15 05						16 03							17 05	
Warwick Parkway	d		14 08			14 27			15 09				15 31		16 06				16 27			17 09	
Hatton	d														16 11								
Lapworth	d		14 16												16 16								
Dorridge	d		14 21		14 25	14 39			15 20			15 25	15 42		16 21			16 25	16 39			17 20	17 25
Widney Manor	d				14 29							15 29						16 29					17 29
Solihull	d		14 26		14 32	14 44			15 26			15 32	15 48		16 26			16 32	16 44			17 26	17 32
Olton	d				14 36							15 36						16 36					17 36
Acocks Green	d				14 38							15 38						16 38					17 38
Tyseley	d																						
Small Heath	d																						
Bordesley	d																						
Birmingham Moor Street	d		14 38		14 45	14 55			15 37			15 45	15 58		16 36			16 45	16 55			17 39	17 45
Birmingham Snow Hill	a		14 50		14 47	15 06			15 52			15 48	16 09		16 52			16 48	17 06			17 49	17 48
	d				14 48							15 48						16 48					17 48
Jewellery Quarter	d				14 51							15 51						16 51					17 51
The Hawthorns	d				14 55							15 55						16 55					17 55
Smethwick Galton Bridge	d				14 58							15 58						16 58					17 58
Coventry	a			14 22						15 22						16 22							
Birmingham International	a			14 35						15 35						16 35							
Birmingham New Street	a	14 19		14 48				15 10		15 48				16 09		16 48					17 09		
	d																16 00						
Langley Green	d				15 01							16 01						17 01					18 01
Rowley Regis	d				15 04							16 04						17 04					18 04
Old Hill	d				15 07							16 07						17 07					18 07
Cradley Heath	d				15 10							16 10						17 10					18 10
Lye	d				15 13							16 13						17 13					18 13
Stourbridge Junction	d				15a17							16a18						17a18					18a19
Hagley	d																						
Blakedown	d																						
Kidderminster	d																						
Hartlebury	d																						
University	d																						
Barnt Green	d																						
Bromsgrove	d																16 21						
Droitwich Spa	d																16 30						
Worcester Shrub Hill	a																16 38						
	d										15 10						16 45						
Worcester Foregate Street	a										15 13						16 47						
	d										15 14						16 48						
Malvern Link	d										15 23						16 57						
Great Malvern	a										15 26						17 01						
	d										15 28												
Colwall	d										15 34												
Ledbury	a										15 41												
	d										15 48												
Hereford	a										16 07												

Table 71

Sundays from 03 October

Stratford-upon-Avon, Marylebone and Leamington Spa - Birmingham - Stourbridge, Worcester and Hereford

		CH	XC	CH	XC	CH	LM	CH	XC	CH	XC	CH	LM	XC	CH	XC	CH	CH	XC	CH	XC	CH
			◇1		◇1			◇	◇1		◇1			◇1		◇1	◇		◇1	◇	◇1	
Stratford-upon-Avon	d							18 00									19 57					
Wilmcote	d							18 04									20 01					
Wootton Wawen	d																					
Henley-in-Arden	d																					
Danzey	d																					
Wood End	d																					
The Lakes	d																					
Earlswood (West Midlands)	d																					
Wythall	d																					
Whitlocks End	d																					
Shirley	d																					
Yardley Wood	d																					
Hall Green	d																					
Spring Road	d																					
London Marylebone ⊖	d	15 57		16 22		16 57				17 20		17 57			18 20			18 57		19 22		19 57
Banbury	d	17 07	17 25	17 43	17 54	18 09			18 25	18 41	18 54	19 09		19 25	19 46	19 54		20 09	20 25	20 44	20 54	21 09
Leamington Spa	a	17 25	17 41	18 02	18 11	18 28		18 28	18 41	19 00	19 11	19 28		19 41	20 05	20 11	20 25	20 28	20 41	21 02	21 11	21 28
	d	17 25	17 43	18 03	18 12	18 29			18 43	19 01	19 12	19 29		19 43	20 05	20 12		20 29	20 43	21 03	21 12	21 29
Warwick	d			18 07						19 05					20 09					21 08		
Warwick Parkway	d	17 31		18 10		18 34				19 09		19 34			20 13			20 34		21 11		21 34
Hatton	d			18 15																		
Lapworth	d			18 20											20 21							
Dorridge	d	17 42		18 24		18 46				19 20		19 46			20 26			20 46		21 22		21 46
Widney Manor	d			18 28						19 24					20 29					21 26		
Solihull	d	17 48		18 31		18 51				19 27		19 51			20 33			20 51		21 29		21 51
Olton	d																					
Acocks Green	d																					
Tyseley	d																					
Small Heath	d																					
Bordesley	d																					
Birmingham Moor Street	d	17 58		18 42		19 02				19 38		20 02			20 43			21 02		21 41		22 02
Birmingham Snow Hill	a	18 10		18 52		19 13				19 49		20 13			20 56			21 13		21 51		22 13
	d																					
Jewellery Quarter	d																					
The Hawthorns	d																					
Smethwick Galton Bridge	d																					
Coventry	a				18 22						19 22			19 53		20 22			20 53		21 22	
Birmingham International	a				18 35						19 35			20 03		20 35			21 03		21 35	
Birmingham New Street	a		18 09		18 48				19 09		19 48			20 15		20 48			21 15		21 48	
	d						18 00															
Langley Green	d																					
Rowley Regis	d																					
Old Hill	d																					
Cradley Heath	d																					
Lye	d																					
Stourbridge Junction	d																					
Hagley	d																					
Blakedown	d																					
Kidderminster	d																					
Hartlebury	d																					
University	d																					
Barnt Green	d																					
Bromsgrove	d						18 21						19 21									
Droitwich Spa	d						18 30						19 31									
Worcester Shrub Hill	a						18 38						19 41									
	d						18 43															
Worcester Foregate Street	a						18 45															
	d						18 46															
Malvern Link	d						18 55															
Great Malvern	a						18 58															
	d						18 58															
Colwall	d						19 03															
Ledbury	a						19 10															
	d						19 10															
Hereford	a						19 31															

Table 71

Sundays from 03 October

Stratford-upon-Avon, Marylebone and Leamington Spa - Birmingham - Stourbridge, Worcester and Hereford

		LM	XC ◇■ 🍴	CH ◇	XC ◇■ 🍴	CH ◇	XC ◇■ 🍴	CH ◇
Stratford-upon-Avon	d							
Wilmcote	d							
Wootton Wawen	d							
Henley-in-Arden	d							
Danzey	d							
Wood End	d							
The Lakes	d							
Earlswood (West Midlands)	d							
Wythall	d							
Whitlocks End	d							
Shirley	d							
Yardley Wood	d							
Hall Green	d							
Spring Road	d							
London Marylebone ■ ⊖	d			20 20		20 50		22 00
Banbury	d		21 25	21 41	21 54	22 11	22 25	23 06
Leamington Spa ■	a		21 41	22 01	22 11	22 30	22 41	23 23
	d		21 43	22 01	22 12	22 31	22 43	23 24
Warwick	d			22 05		22 35		23 28
Warwick Parkway	d			22 09		22 39		23 32
Hatton	d					22 43		
Lapworth	d					22 48		
Dorridge	d			22 20		22 53		23 43
Widney Manor	d					22 56		
Solihull	d			22 26		23 00		23 48
Olton	d							
Acocks Green	d							
Tyseley	d							
Small Heath	d							
Bordesley	d							
Birmingham Moor Street	d			22 38		23 11		23 59
Birmingham Snow Hill	a			22 48		23 21		00 11
	d							
Jewellery Quarter	d							
The Hawthorns	d							
Smethwick Galton Bridge ■	d							
Coventry	a		21 53		22 22		22 53	
Birmingham International ✈	a		22 03		22 32		23 03	
Birmingham New Street ■	a		22 15		22 42		23 14	
	d	21 00						
Langley Green	d							
Rowley Regis	d							
Old Hill	d							
Cradley Heath	d							
Lye	d							
Stourbridge Junction ■	d							
Hagley	d							
Blakedown	d							
Kidderminster	d							
Hartlebury	d							
University	d							
Barnt Green	d							
Bromsgrove	d	21 21						
Droitwich Spa	d	21 31						
Worcester Shrub Hill ■	a	21 38						
	d	21 42						
Worcester Foregate Street ■	a	21 44						
	d	21 45						
Malvern Link	d	21 54						
Great Malvern	a	21 57						
	d	21 57						
Colwall	d	22 02						
Ledbury	a	22 09						
	d	22 10						
Hereford ■	a	22 30						

Table 72

Mondays to Saturdays

Stourbridge Junction - Stourbridge Town

		LM SX	LM	LM SX	LM	LM SX	LM SX	LM	LM SX	LM		LM	LM	LM	LM	LM	LM	LM	LM	LM		LM	LM	LM	LM
Stourbridge Junction ■	d	05 47	05 58	06 08	06 19	06 29	06 39	06 49	06 59	07 09		07 19	07 29	07 39	07 49	07 59	08 09	08 19	08 29	08 39		08 49	08 59	09 09	09 19
Stourbridge Town	a	05 50	06 01	06 11	06 22	06 32	06 42	06 52	07 02	07 12		07 22	07 32	07 42	07 52	08 02	08 12	08 22	08 32	08 42		08 52	09 02	09 12	09 22

		LM	LM	LM	LM	LM		LM	LM	LM	LM	LM	LM	LM	LM	LM		LM	LM	LM	LM	LM	LM	LM	LM
Stourbridge Junction ■	d	09 29	09 39	09 49	09 59	10 09		10 19	10 29	10 39	10 49	10 59	11 09	11 19	11 29	11 39		11 49	11 59	12 09	12 19	12 29	12 39	12 49	12 59
Stourbridge Town	a	09 32	09 42	09 52	10 02	10 12		10 22	10 32	10 42	10 52	11 02	11 12	11 22	11 32	11 42		11 52	12 02	12 12	12 22	12 32	12 42	12 52	13 02

		LM		LM	LM	LM	LM	LM	LM	LM	LM	LM		LM	LM	LM	LM	LM	LM	LM	LM	LM		LM	LM
Stourbridge Junction ■	d	13 09		13 19	13 29	13 39	13 49	13 59	14 39	14 49	14 59	15 09		15 19	15 29	15 39	15 49	15 59	16 09	16 19	16 29	16 39		16 49	16 59
Stourbridge Town	a	13 12		13 22	13 32	13 42	13 52	14 02	14 42	14 52	15 02	15 12		15 22	15 32	15 42	15 52	16 02	16 12	16 22	16 32	16 42		16 52	17 02

		LM	LM	LM	LM	LM	LM	LM		LM	LM	LM	LM	LM	LM	LM	LM	LM		LM	LM	LM	LM	LM	LM
Stourbridge Junction ■	d	17 09	17 19	17 29	17 39	17 49	17 59	18 09		18 19	18 29	18 39	18 49	18 59	19 09	19 19	19 29	19 39		19 49	19 59	20 09	20 19	20 29	20 39
Stourbridge Town	a	17 12	17 22	17 32	17 42	17 52	18 02	18 12		18 22	18 32	18 42	18 52	19 02	19 12	19 22	19 32	19 42		19 52	20 02	20 12	20 22	20 32	20 42

		LM	LM	LM		LM	LM	LM	LM	LM	LM	LM	LM	LM		LM	LM	LM	LM	LM					
Stourbridge Junction ■	d	20 49	20 59	21 09		21 19	21 29	21 39	21 49	21 59	22 09	22 19	22 29	22 39		22 50	23 00	23 15	23 30	23 54					
Stourbridge Town	a	20 52	21 02	21 12		21 22	21 32	21 42	21 52	22 02	22 12	22 22	22 32	22 42		22 53	23 03	23 18	23 33	23 57					

Sundays

		LM	LM	LM	LM	LM	LM	LM	LM	LM		LM	LM	LM	LM	LM	LM	LM	LM	LM		LM	LM	LM	LM
Stourbridge Junction ■	d	09 43	10 00	10 11	10 21	10 41	10 54	11 11	11 21	11 41		11 54	12 11	12 21	12 41	12 54	13 11	13 21	13 41	13 54		14 11	14 21	14 41	14 54
Stourbridge Town	a	09 46	10 03	10 14	10 24	10 44	10 57	11 14	11 24	11 44		11 57	12 14	12 24	12 44	12 57	13 14	13 24	13 44	13 57		14 14	14 24	14 44	14 57

		LM	LM	LM	LM	LM		LM	LM	LM	LM	LM	LM	LM	LM	LM		LM	LM	LM	LM	LM			
Stourbridge Junction ■	d	15 11	15 21	15 41	15 54	16 11		16 21	16 41	16 54	17 11	17 21	17 41	17 54	18 11	18 21		18 41	18 54	19 11	19 21	19 47			
Stourbridge Town	a	15 14	15 24	15 44	15 57	16 14		16 24	16 44	16 57	17 14	17 24	17 44	17 57	18 14	18 24		18 44	18 57	19 14	19 24	19 50			

Table 72

Stourbridge Town - Stourbridge Junction

		LM	LM	LM	LM	LM	LM	LM	LM	LM		LM	LM	LM	LM	LM	LM	LM	LM	LM		LM	LM	LM	LM
		MX	SX	SX	SO	SX	SX	SX	SO	SX			SX												
Stourbridge Town	d	23p59	05 52	06 03	06 10	06 13	06 24	06 34	06 40	06 44	.....	06 54	07 04	07 14	07 24	07 34	07 44	07 54	08 04	08 14	.....	08 24	08 34	08 44	08 54
Stourbridge Junction ■	a	00 02	05 55	06 06	06 13	06 16	06 27	06 37	06 43	06 47		06 57	07 07	07 17	07 27	07 37	07 47	07 57	08 07	08 17		08 27	08 37	08 47	08 57

		LM	LM	LM	LM	LM		LM	LM	LM	LM	LM	LM	LM	LM	LM		LM	LM	LM	LM	LM	LM	LM	LM
Stourbridge Town	d	09 04	09 14	09 24	09 34	09 44	.....	09 54	10 04	10 14	10 24	10 34	10 44	10 54	11 04	11 14	.....	11 24	11 34	11 44	11 54	12 04	12 14	12 24	12 34
Stourbridge Junction ■	a	09 07	09 17	09 27	09 37	09 47		09 57	10 07	10 17	10 27	10 37	10 47	10 57	11 07	11 17		11 27	11 37	11 47	11 57	12 07	12 17	12 27	12 37

		LM		LM	LM	LM	LM	LM	LM	LM	LM	LM		LM	LM	LM	LM	LM	LM	LM	LM	LM		LM	LM
Stourbridge Town	d	12 44	.....	12 54	13 04	13 14	13 24	13 34	13 44	13 54	14 04	14 44	.....	14 54	15 04	15 14	15 24	15 34	15 44	15 54	16 04	16 14	.....	16 24	16 34
Stourbridge Junction ■	a	12 47		12 57	13 07	13 17	13 27	13 37	13 47	13 57	14 07	14 47		14 57	15 07	15 17	15 27	15 37	15 47	15 57	16 07	16 17		16 27	16 37

		LM	LM	LM	LM	LM	LM	LM		LM	LM	LM	LM	LM	LM	LM	LM	LM		LM	LM	LM	LM	LM	LM
Stourbridge Town	d	16 44	16 54	17 04	17 14	17 24	17 34	17 44	.....	17 54	18 04	18 14	18 24	18 34	18 44	18 54	19 04	19 14	.....	19 24	19 34	19 44	19 54	20 04	20 14
Stourbridge Junction ■	a	16 47	16 57	17 07	17 17	17 27	17 37	17 47		17 57	18 07	18 17	18 27	18 37	18 47	18 57	19 07	19 17		19 27	19 37	19 47	19 57	20 07	20 17

		LM	LM	LM		LM	LM	LM	LM	LM	LM	LM	LM	LM		LM	LM	LM	LM	LM	LM	LM	LM		
Stourbridge Town	d	20 24	20 34	20 44	.....	20 54	21 04	21 14	21 24	21 34	21 44	21 54	22 04	22 14	.....	22 24	22 34	22 44	22 55	23 05	23 20	23 35	23 59	.....	.....
Stourbridge Junction ■	a	20 27	20 37	20 47		20 57	21 07	21 17	21 27	21 37	21 47	21 57	22 07	22 17		22 27	22 37	22 47	22 58	23 08	23 23	23 38	00 02		

Sundays

		LM	LM	LM	LM	LM	LM	LM	LM	LM		LM	LM	LM	LM	LM	LM	LM	LM	LM		LM	LM	LM	LM
		A																							
Stourbridge Town	d	23p59	09 49	10 05	10 16	10 36	10 46	11 00	11 16	11 36	.....	11 46	12 00	12 16	12 36	12 46	13 00	13 16	13 36	13 46	.....	14 00	14 16	14 36	14 46
Stourbridge Junction ■	a	00 02	09 52	10 08	10 19	10 39	10 49	11 03	11 19	11 39		11 49	12 03	12 19	12 39	12 49	13 03	13 19	13 39	13 49		14 03	14 19	14 39	14 49

		LM	LM	LM	LM	LM		LM	LM	LM	LM	LM	LM	LM	LM	LM		LM	LM	LM	LM	LM	LM		
Stourbridge Town	d	15 00	15 16	15 36	15 46	16 00	.....	16 16	16 36	16 46	17 00	17 16	17 36	17 46	18 00	18 16	.....	18 36	18 46	19 00	19 16	19 36	19 55	.....	.....
Stourbridge Junction ■	a	15 03	15 19	15 39	15 49	16 03		16 19	16 39	16 49	17 03	17 19	17 39	17 49	18 03	18 19		18 39	18 49	19 03	19 19	19 39	19 58		

A not 23 May

Network Diagram for Tables 74, 75

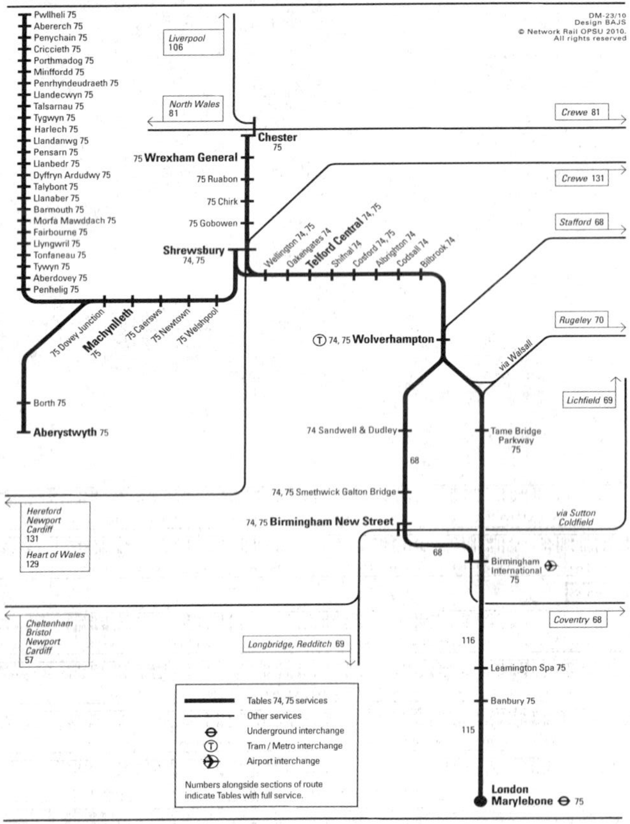

Table 74

Birmingham - Shrewsbury

Mondays to Fridays

		AW	AW	AW	AW	LM	AW	LM	AW	LM	LM	AW	LM	AW	LM	AW	LM	AW	LM	AW	LM	AW
			MX	MX																		
		A			B 🚌		◇ 🛒		◇ 🛒			◇ 🛒		◇ 🛒		◇ 🛒		◇ 🛒		◇ 🛒		◇ 🛒
Birmingham New Street	d	23p24	23p32			05 51	06 24		07 22	07 27	08 05	08 24	09 05	09 24	10 05	10 24	11 05	11 24	12 05	12 24	13 05	13 24
Smethwick Galton Bridge	d						06 30		07 28			08 30		09 30		10 30		11 30		12 30		13 30
Sandwell & Dudley	d					05 59					08 13		09 13		10 13		11 13		12 13		13 13	
Wolverhampton 7	d	23p46	00 02	00 20	23p46	06 13	06 42	06 48	07 41	07 46	08 25	08 43	09 25	09 43	10 25	10 43	11 25	11 43	12 25	12 43	13 25	13 43
Bilbrook	d	23p52	00 08		23p56	06 19		06 54		07 51	08 31		09 31		10 31		11 31		12 31		13 31	
Codsall	d	23p54	00 11		00 01	06 21		06 57		07 54	08 33		09 33		10 33		11 33		12 33		13 33	
Albrighton	d	23p59	00 15		00 16	06 26		07 01		07 58	08 38		09 38		10 38		11 38		12 38		13 38	
Cosford	d	00 02	00 19		00 25	06 29		07 05		08 02	08 41		09 41		10 41		11 41		12 41		13 41	
Shifnal	d	00 07	00 24		00 35	06 34		07 10		08 06	08 46		09 46		10 46		11 46		12 46		13 46	
Telford Central	d	00 13	00 29	00 36	00 45	06 40	06 59	07 16	07 58	08 13	08 52	08 59	09 52	10 00	10 52	10 59	11 52	11 59	12 52	12 59	13 52	13 59
Oakengates	d	00 15	00 31		00 55	06 42		07 18		08 16	08 54		09 54		10 54		11 54		12 54		13 54	
Wellington (Shropshire)	d	00 20	00 36	00 43	01 10	06 47	07 05	07 24	08 04	08 22	08 59	09 06	09 59	10 06	10 59	11 06	11 59	12 06	12 59	13 06	13 59	14 06
Shrewsbury	a	00 35	00 49	01 02	01 35	07 00	07 18	07 38	08 18	08 37	09 15	09 19	10 15	10 19	11 15	11 19	12 15	12 19	13 15	13 19	14 15	14 19

		LM	AW	LM	AW	LM	AW	LM	AW	LM	LM	AW	LM	AW	LM	AW	WS	LM	LM	AW
			◇ 🛒		◇ 🛒		◇ 🛒		◇ 🛒			◇ 🛒		◇ 🛒		◇	◇ 1 🍽			
Birmingham New Street	d	14 05	14 24	15 05	15 26	16 05	16 24	17 05	17 26	17 46	18 05	18 24	19 05	19 24	20 05	20 24		21 05	22 21	23 32
Smethwick Galton Bridge	d		14 30		15 32		16 30		17 32			18 30		19 30		20 30				
Sandwell & Dudley	d	14 13		15 13		16 13		17 13			18 13		19 13		20 13			21 13	22 29	
Wolverhampton 7	d	14 25	14 43	15 25	15 44	16 25	16 43	17 25	17 44	18 07	18 25	18 43	19 25	19 43	20 25	20 43	21u04	21 25	22 43	00 02
Bilbrook	d	14 31		15 31		16 31		17 31		18 13	18 31		19 31		20 31			21 31	22 49	00 08
Codsall	d	14 33		15 33		16 33		17 33		18 15	18 33		19 33		20 33			21 33	22 51	00 11
Albrighton	d	14 38		15 38		16 38		17 38		18 20	18 38		19 38		20 38			21 38	22 56	00 15
Cosford	d	14 41		15 41		16 41		17 41		18 23	18 41		19 41		20 41		21 15	21 41	22 59	00 19
Shifnal	d	14 46		15 46		16 46		17 46		18 28	18 46		19 46		20 46			21 46	23 04	00 24
Telford Central	d	14 52	14 59	15 52	16 01	16 52	16 59	17 52	18 01	18 33	18 52	18 59	19 52	19 59	20 52	20 59	21 24	21 52	23 10	00 29
Oakengates	d	14 54		15 54		16 54		17 54		18 35	18 54		19 54		20 54			21 54	23 12	00 31
Wellington (Shropshire)	d	14 59	15 06	15 59	16 07	16 59	17 06	17 59	18 07	18 41	18 59	19 06	19 59	20 06	20 59	21 06	21 30	21 59	23 17	00 36
Shrewsbury	a	15 15	15 19	16 15	16 20	17 15	17 19	18 15	18 20	18 56	19 15	19 19	20 15	20 19	21 15	21 19	21 46	22 14	23 30	00 49

Saturdays

		AW	AW	AW	LM	AW	LM	AW	LM	AW	LM	AW	LM	AW	LM	AW	LM	AW	LM	AW	LM
				◇ 🛒		◇ 🛒		◇ 🛒		◇ 🛒		◇ 🛒		◇ 🛒		◇ 🛒		◇ 🛒		◇ 🛒	
Birmingham New Street	d	23p32		06 24	07 05	07 24	08 05	08 24	09 05	09 24	10 05	10 24	11 05	11 24	12 05	12 24	13 05	13 23	14 05	14 24	15 05
Smethwick Galton Bridge	d			06 30		07 30		08 30		09 30		10 30		11 30		12 30		13 29		14 30	
Sandwell & Dudley	d				07 13		08 13		09 13		10 13		11 13		12 13		13 13		14 13		15 13
Wolverhampton 7	d	00 02	00 20	06 42	07 25	07 42	08 25	08 43	09 25	09 43	10 25	10 43	11 25	11 43	12 25	12 43	13 25	13 43	14 25	14 43	15 25
Bilbrook	d	00 08			07 31		08 31		09 31		10 31		11 31		12 31		13 31		14 31		15 31
Codsall	d	00 11			07 33		08 33		09 33		10 33		11 33		12 33		13 33		14 33		15 33
Albrighton	d	00 15			07 38		08 38		09 38		10 38		11 38		12 38		13 38		14 38		15 38
Cosford	d	00 19			07 41		08 41		09 41		10 41		11 41		12 41		13 41		14 41		15 41
Shifnal	d	00 24			07 46		08 46		09 46		10 46		11 46		12 46		13 46		14 46		15 46
Telford Central	d	00 29	00 36	06 59	07 52	07 59	08 52	08 59	09 52	09 59	10 52	10 59	11 52	11 59	12 52	12 59	13 52	13 59	14 52	14 59	15 52
Oakengates	d	00 31			07 54		08 54		09 54		10 54		11 54		12 54		13 54		14 54		15 54
Wellington (Shropshire)	d	00 36	00 43	07 05	07 59	08 05	08 59	09 06	09 59	10 06	10 59	11 06	11 59	12 06	12 59	13 06	13 59	14 06	14 59	15 06	15 59
Shrewsbury	a	00 49	00 59	07 18	08 15	08 18	09 15	09 19	10 15	10 19	11 15	11 19	12 15	12 19	13 15	13 19	14 15	14 19	15 15	15 19	16 15

		AW	LM	AW	LM	AW	LM	AW	LM	AW	LM	AW	LM	AW	LM	AW	AW
		◇ 🛒		■ 🛒		◇ 🛒		◇ 🛒		◇ 🛒		◇		◇ 🛒			
Birmingham New Street	d	15 24	16 05	16 24	17 05	17 24	18 05	18 24	19 05	19 24	20 05	20 24	21 05	21 24	22 05	22 55	23 35
Smethwick Galton Bridge	d	15 30		16 30		17 31		18 30		19 30		20 30		21 30			
Sandwell & Dudley	d		16 13		17 13		18 13		19 13		20 13		21 13		22 13		
Wolverhampton 7	d	15 43	16 25	16 43	17 25	17 43	18 25	18 43	19 25	19 43	20 29	20 43	21 25	21 42	22 25	23 13	23 54
Bilbrook	d		16 31		17 31		18 31		19 31		20 35		21 31		22 31		00 01
Codsall	d		16 33		17 33		18 33		19 33		20 37		21 33		22 33		00 03
Albrighton	d		16 38		17 38		18 38		19 38		20 42		21 38		22 38		00 08
Cosford	d		16 41		17 41		18 41		19 41		20 45		21 41		22 41		00 11
Shifnal	d		16 46		17 46		18 46		19 46		20 50		21 46		22 46		00 16
Telford Central	d	15 59	16 52	16 59	17 52	17 59	18 52	18 59	19 52	19 59	20 56	21 02	21 52	21 59	22 52	23 29	00 22
Oakengates	d		16 54		17 54		18 54		19 54		20 58		21 54		22 54		00 24
Wellington (Shropshire)	d	16 06	16 59	17 06	17 59	18 06	18 59	19 06	19 59	20 06	21 03	21 09	21 59	22 05	22 59	23 36	00 29
Shrewsbury	a	16 19	17 15	17 19	18 15	18 19	19 15	19 19	20 15	20 19	21 19	21 23	22 14	22 22	23 15	23 49	00 42

A MO until 6 September
B MO from 13 September

Table 74

Birmingham - Shrewsbury

Sundays until 05 September

		AW	AW	AW	AW	WS	AW	AW	AW	AW	AW	AW	WS	AW	AW	AW	WS	WS	AW	AW	AW
					◇ 🛒	◇ 1 B 🍽	◇ 🛒	◇ 🛒	◇ 🛒	◇ 🛒	◇ 🛒	◇ 🛒	◇ 1 C 🍽	◇ 🛒	◇ 🛒	◇	◇ 1 C 🍽	◇ 1 B 🍽	◇		
Birmingham New Street	d	23p35		10 05	11 05	11 33	12 24	13 24	14 24	15 24	16 24	17 24		18 24	19 24	20 24			21 24	22 24	23 24
Smethwick Galton Bridge	d												18 13				20 41				
Sandwell & Dudley	d																				
Wolverhampton 7	d	23p54	00 20	10 22	11 27	12u03	12 42	13 42	14 43	15 43	16 43	17 43	18u26	18 43	19 43	20 43	20u53	21u01	21 43	22 42	23 46
Bilbrook	d	00 01		10 28	11 33			13 48		15 49		17 49			19 49				21 49	22 48	23 52
Codsall	d	00 03		10 31	11 35			13 50		15 51		17 51			19 51				21 51	22 50	23 54
Albrighton	d	00 08		10 35	11 40			13 55		15 56		17 56			19 56				21 56	22 55	23 59
Cosford	d	00 11		10 39	11 43	12 15		13 58		15 59		17 59	18 38		19 59		21 04	21 12	21 59	22 58	00 02
Shifnal	d	00 16		10 44	11 48			14 03		16 04		18 04			20 04				22 04	23 03	00 07
Telford Central	d	00 22	00 36	10 49	11 54	12 23	12 59	14 09	14 59	16 09	16 59	18 09	18 46	18 59	20 09	20 59	21 12	21 21	22 10	23 09	00 13
Oakengates	d	00 24		10 51	11 56			14 11		16 11		18 11			20 11				22 12	23 11	00 15
Wellington (Shropshire)	d	00 29	00 43	10 57	12 01	12 29	13 05	14 15	15 06	16 17	17 06	18 16	18 52	19 06	20 17	21 06	21 18	21 27	22 17	23 16	00 20
Shrewsbury	a	00 42	00 59	11 10	12 15	12 45	13 18	14 29	15 19	16 30	17 19	18 30	19 06	19 19	20 30	21 19	21 32	21 40	22 30	23 32	00 35

Sundays from 12 September

		AW	AW	AW	AW	AW	AW	AW	AW	AW	AW	AW	AW	AW	AW	AW	AW
				🚌	🚌	🚌	🚌	🚌	🚌	🚌	🚌	🚌	🚌	🚌	🚌	🚌	🚌
Birmingham New Street	d	23p35															
Smethwick Galton Bridge	d																
Sandwell & Dudley	d																
Wolverhampton 7	d	23p54	00 20	09 21	10 17	12 05	12 31	14 06	14 33	16 06	16 31	18 07	18 35	20 06	20 33	21 44	23 46
Bilbrook	d	00 01		09 31	10 27		12 41		14 43		16 41		18 45		20 43	21 54	23 56
Codsall	d	00 03		09 36	10 32		12 46		14 48		16 46		18 50		20 48	21 59	00 01
Albrighton	d	00 08		09 51	10 47		13 01		15 03		17 01		19 05		21 03	22 14	00 16
Cosford	d	00 11		10 00	10 56		13 10		15 12		17 10		19 14		21 12	22 23	00 25
Shifnal	d	00 16		10 10	11 06		13 20		15 22		17 20		19 24		21 22	22 33	00 35
Telford Central	d	00 22	00 36	10 20	11 16	12 35	13 30	14 36	15 32	16 36	17 30	18 37	19 34	20 36	21 32	22 43	00 45
Oakengates	d	00 24		10 30	11 26		13 40		15 42		17 40		19 44		21 42	22 53	00 55
Wellington (Shropshire)	d	00 29	00 43	10 45	11 41	12 50	13 55	14 51	15 57	16 51	17 55	18 52	19 59	20 51	21 57	23 08	01 10
Shrewsbury	a	00 42	00 59	11 10	12 06	13 15	14 20	15 16	16 22	17 16	18 20	19 17	20 24	21 16	22 22	23 33	01 35

B until 11 July
C from 18 July until 5 September

Table 74

Shrewsbury - Birmingham

Mondays to Fridays

		AW	AW MX	AW	LM	LM	AW	LM	LM	AW	LM	WS	AW	LM	AW	LM	AW	LM	AW	LM
		A 🚌	◇ ⊼							◇ ⊼		◇1 🍽	◇ ⊼		◇ ⊼		◇ ⊼		◇ ⊼	
Shrewsbury	d	22p38	23p26	05 21	05 28	05 58	06 31	06 55	07 14	07 31	07 47	08 07	08 31	08 47	09 31	09 47	10 32	10 47	11 31	11 47
Wellington (Shropshire)	d	23p02	23p40	05 35	05 41	06 12	06 45	07 09	07 28	07 45	08 01	08 21	08 45	09 01	09 45	10 01	10 46	11 01	11 45	12 01
Oakengates	d	23p11	23p44		05 46	06 16			07 32		08 05			09 05		10 05		11 05		12 05
Telford Central	d	23p20	23p47	05 41	05 49	06 19	06 51	07 15	07 35	07 51	08 08	08 27	08 51	09 08	09 51	10 08	10 52	11 08	11 51	12 08
Shifnal	d	23p30	23p52		05 54	06 24			07 40		08 13			09 13		10 13		11 13		12 13
Cosford	d	23p40	23p57		05 59	06 29			07 45		08 18	08 36		09 18		10 18		11 18		12 18
Albrighton	d	23p50	00 01		06 02	06 33			07 48		08 22			09 22		10 22		11 22		12 22
Codsall	d	00 05	00 06		06 07	06 38			07 54		08 27			09 27		10 27		11 27		12 27
Bilbrook	d	00 10	00 08		06 09	06 40			07 56		08 29			09 29		10 29		11 29		12 29
Wolverhampton 7	a	00 20	00 20	05 58	06 16	06 47	07 08	07 34	08 02	08 08	08 36	08 47	09 08	09 36	10 08	10 36	11 09	11 36	12 08	12 36
Sandwell & Dudley	a				06 31	07 03		07 45			08 46			09 46		10 46		11 46		12 46
Smethwick Galton Bridge	a			06 11	06 34	07 06	07 21			08 20			09 21		10 20		11 20		12 20	
Birmingham New Street 12	a			06 17	06 43	07 14	07 27	07 55	08 20	08 27	08 55		09 27	09 56	10 26	10 55	11 26	11 55	12 26	12 55

		AW	LM	AW	LM	AW	LM	AW	LM	WS	AW	LM	AW	LM	AW	LM	AW	LM	LM	AW	LM	AW	AW
		◇ ⊼		◇ ⊼		◇ ⊼		◇ ⊼		◇1 🍽	◇ ⊼		◇ ⊼		◇ ⊼		◇ ⊼			◇ ⊼		◇ ⊼	◇ ⊼
Shrewsbury	d	12 31	12 47	13 31	13 47	14 31	14 47	15 31	15 47	16 07	16 33	16 47	17 31	17 47	18 31	18 47	19 33	19 47	20 47	21 33	21 47	22 18	23 26
Wellington (Shropshire)	d	12 45	13 01	13 45	14 01	14 45	15 01	15 45	16 01	16 21	16 47	17 01	17 45	18 01	18 45	19 01	19 47	20 01	21 01	21 47	22 01	22 32	23 40
Oakengates	d		13 05		14 05		15 05		16 05			17 05		18 05		19 05		20 05	21 05		22 05		23 44
Telford Central	d	12 51	13 08	13 51	14 08	14 51	15 08	15 51	16 08	16 27	16 53	17 08	17 51	18 08	18 51	19 08	19 53	20 08	21 08	21 53	22 08	22 38	23 47
Shifnal	d		13 13		14 13		15 13		16 13			17 13		18 13		19 13		20 13	21 13		22 13		23 52
Cosford	d		13 18		14 18		15 18		16 18	16 36		17 18		18 18		19 18		20 18	21 18		22 18		23 57
Albrighton	d		13 22		14 22		15 22		16 22			17 22		18 22		19 22		20 22	21 22		22 22		00 01
Codsall	d		13 27		14 27		15 27		16 27			17 27		18 27		19 27		20 27	21 27		22 27		00 06
Bilbrook	d		13 29		14 29		15 29		16 29			17 29		18 29		19 29		20 29	21 29		22 29		00 08
Wolverhampton 7	a	13 08	13 36	14 08	14 36	15 08	15 36	16 08	16 36	16s47	17 10	17 36	18 08	18 36	19 08	19 36	20 10	20 36	21 36	22 10	22 36	22 55	00 20
Sandwell & Dudley	a		13 46		14 46		15 46		16 46			17 46		18 46		19 46		20 46	21 46		22 46		
Smethwick Galton Bridge	a	13 20		14 20		15 20		16 20			17 21		18 20		19 20		20 21			22 24			
Birmingham New Street 12	a	13 27	13 55	14 26	14 55	15 26	15 55	16 26	16 55		17 27	17 55	18 26	18 55	19 26	19 55	20 27	20 57	21 55	22 30	22 55	23 26	

Saturdays

		AW	AW	AW	LM	AW	LM	WS	AW	LM	WS	AW	LM	AW	LM	AW	LM	WS	AW	LM	AW	LM	AW
		◇ ⊼						◇1 🍽			◇1 🍽	◇ ⊼		◇ ⊼		◇ ⊼		◇1 🍽			◇ ⊼		◇ ⊼
Shrewsbury	d	23p26	05 24	06 31	06 47	07 31	07 47	08 07	08 31	08 47	09 07	09 31	09 47	10 31	10 47	11f31	11 47	12 07	12 31	12 47	13 31	13 47	14 31
Wellington (Shropshire)	d	23p40	05 38	06 45	07 01	07 45	08 01	08 21	08 45	09 01	09 21	09 45	10 01	10 45	11 01	11 45	12 01	12 21	12 45	13 01	13 45	14 01	14 45
Oakengates	d	23p44			07 05		08 05			09 05			10 05		11 05		12 05			13 05		14 05	
Telford Central	d	23p47	05 44	06 51	07 08	07 51	08 08	08 27	08 51	09 08	09 27	09 51	10 08	10 51	11 08	11 51	12 08	12 27	12 51	13 08	13 51	14 08	14 51
Shifnal	d	23p52			07 13		08 13			09 13			10 13		11 13		12 13			13 13		14 13	
Cosford	d	23p57			07 18		08 18	08 36		09 18	09 35		10 18		11 18		12 18	12 36		13 18		14 18	
Albrighton	d	00 01			07 22		08 22			09 22			10 22		11 22		12 22			13 22		14 22	
Codsall	d	00 06			07 27		08 27			09 27			10 27		11 27		12 27			13 27		14 27	
Bilbrook	d	00 08			07 29		08 29			09 29			10 29		11 29		12 29			13 29		14 29	
Wolverhampton 7	a	00 20	06 01	07 08	07 36	08 08	08 36	08s47	09 08	09 36	09s48	10 08	10 36	11 08	11 36	12 08	12 36	12s47	13 08	13 36	14 08	14 36	15 08
Sandwell & Dudley	a				07 46		08 46			09 46			10 46		11 46		12 46			13 46		14 46	
Smethwick Galton Bridge	a		06 14	07 21		08 20			09 22			10 20		11 21		12 20			13 20		14 20		15 20
Birmingham New Street 12	a		06 20	07 27	07 55	08 27	08 55		09 28	09 55		10 26	10 55	11 27	11 55	12 26	12 55		13 26	13 55	14 26	14 55	15 26

		LM	WS	AW	LM	AW	LM	AW	LM	WS	AW	LM	AW	LM	LM	AW	LM	AW	AW
			◇1 🍽	◇ ⊼		◇ ⊼		◇ ⊼		◇1 🍽	◇ ⊼		◇ ⊼					◇	◇
Shrewsbury	d	14 47	15 07	15 31	15 47	16 31	16 47	17 31	17 47	18 07	18 31	18 47	19 33	19 47	20 47	21 33	21 47	22 31	23 26
Wellington (Shropshire)	d	15 01	15 21	15 45	16 01	16 45	17 01	17 45	18 01	18 21	18 45	19 01	19 47	20 01	21 01	21 47	22 01	22 45	23 40
Oakengates	d	15 05			16 05		17 05		18 05			19 05		20 05	21 05		22 05		23 44
Telford Central	d	15 08	15 27	15 51	16 08	16 51	17 08	17 51	18 08	18 27	18 51	19 08	19 53	20 08	21 08	21 53	22 08	22 51	23 47
Shifnal	d	15 13			16 13		17 13		18 13			19 13		20 13	21 13		22 13		23 52
Cosford	d	15 18	15 36		16 18		17 18		18 18	18 36		19 18		20 18	21 18		22 18		23 57
Albrighton	d	15 22			16 22		17 22		18 22			19 22		20 22	21 22		22 22		00 01
Codsall	d	15 27			16 27		17 27		18 27			19 27		20 27	21 27		22 27		00 07
Bilbrook	d	15 29			16 29		17 29		18 29			19 29		20 29	21 29		22 29		00 09
Wolverhampton 7	a	15 36	15s47	16 08	16 36	17 08	17 36	18 08	18 36	18s49	19 08	19 36	20 10	20 36	21 36	22 10	22 36	23 08	00 18
Sandwell & Dudley	a	15 46			16 46		17 46		18 46			19 46		20 46	21 46		22 45		
Smethwick Galton Bridge	a			16 20		17 20		18 20			19 20		20 21			22 21			
Birmingham New Street 12	a	15 55		16 26	16 55	17 26	17 55	18 26	18 55		19 26	19 55	20 27	20 57	21 55	22 32	22 55	23 29	

A MO from 13 September

Table 74

Shrewsbury - Birmingham

Sundays until 05 September

		AW	AW	AW	AW	WS	WS	AW	AW	AW	WS	WS	AW	AW	AW	AW	WS	WS	AW	AW	AW	AW	AW
		◇			◇	◇1 B 🍽	◇1 C 🍽		◇ ⊼	◇ ⊼	◇1 C 🍽	◇1 B 🍽	◇ ⊼	◇ ⊼	◇ ⊼	◇ ⊼	◇1 C 🍽	◇1 B 🍽	◇	◇ ⊼	◇	◇ ⊼	◇
Shrewsbury	d	23p26	08 10	09 09	10 09	11 28	11 31	11 40	12 20	13 31	13 55	14 09	14 20	15 33	16 29	17 33	17 55	17 55	18 20	19 31	20 23	21 31	22 23
Wellington (Shropshire)	d	23p40	08 24	09 23	10 23	11 41	11 44	11 54	12 34	13 45	14 09	14 23	14 34	15 47	16 43	17 47	18 09	18 09	18 34	19 45	20 37	21 45	22 37
Oakengates	d	23p44	08 28	09 27	10 27				12 38				14 38		16 47				18 38		20 41		22 42
Telford Central	d	23p47	08 31	09 30	10 30	11 47	11 50	12 00	12 41	13 51	14 15	14 29	14 41	15 53	16 50	17 53	18 15	18 15	18 41	19 51	20 44	21 51	22 45
Shifnal	d	23p52	08 36	09 35	10 35				12 46				14 46		16 55				18 46		20 49		22 50
Cosford	d	23p57	08 41	09 40	10 40	11 56	11 59		12 51		14 24	14 38	14 51		17 00		18 24	18 24	18 51		20 54		22 55
Albrighton	d	00 01	08 44	09 43	10 43				12 54				14 54		17 03				18 54		20 57		22 58
Codsall	d	00 07	08 50	09 48	10 48				12 59				14 59		17 08				18 59		21 02		23 04
Bilbrook	d	00 09	08 52	09 50	10 50				13 01				15 01		17 10				19 01		21 04		23 06
Wolverhampton 7	a	00 18	08 59	09 57	10 57	12s07	12s10	12 17	13 08	14 08	14s35	14s49	15 08	16 10	17 17	18 10	18s35	18s35	19 08	20 08	21 11	22 08	23 17
Sandwell & Dudley	a																						
Smethwick Galton Bridge	a					12 18						15 03						19 03					
Birmingham New Street 12	a		09 15	10 14	11 13	12 26	12 55	12 33	13 24	14 24	15 10	15 11	15 24	16 26	17 35	18 28	19 10	19 11	19 24	20 24	21 29	22 28	

Sundays from 12 September

		AW	AW	AW	AW	AW	AW	AW	AW	AW	AW	AW	AW	AW	AW	AW	AW	AW
		◇	🚌	🚌	🚌	🚌	🚌	🚌	🚌	🚌	🚌	🚌	🚌	🚌	🚌	🚌	🚌	🚌
Shrewsbury	d	23p26	07 15	09 09	10 20	11 35	12 28	13 35	14 28	15 35	16 28	17 35	18 28	19 35	20 38	21 35	22 38	
Wellington (Shropshire)	d	23p40	07 40	09 34	10 45	11 59	12 52	13 59	14 52	15 59	16 52	17 59	18 52	19 59	21 02	21 59	23 02	
Oakengates	d	23p44	07 50	09 44	10 55		13 01		15 01		17 01		19 01		21 11		23 11	
Telford Central	d	23p47	08 00	09 54	11 05	12 14	13 10	14 14	15 10	16 14	17 10	18 14	19 10	20 14	21 20	22 14	23 20	
Shifnal	d	23p52	08 10	10 04	11 15		13 20		15 20		17 20		19 20		21 30		23 30	
Cosford	d	23p57	08 20	10 14	11 25		13 30		15 30		17 30		19 30		21 40		23 40	
Albrighton	d	00 01	08 25	10 19	11 30		13 40		15 40		17 40		19 40		21 50		23 50	
Codsall	d	00 07	08 35	10 29	11 40		13 55		15 55		17 55		19 55		22 05		00 05	
Bilbrook	d	00 09	08 40	10 34	11 45		14 00		16 00		18 00		20 00		22 10		00 10	
Wolverhampton 7	a	00 18	09 00	10 54	12 05	12 44	14 10	14 44	16 10	16 44	18 10	18 44	20 10	20 44	22 20	22 44	00 20	
Sandwell & Dudley	a																	
Smethwick Galton Bridge	a																	
Birmingham New Street 12	a																	

B from 18 July until 5 September

C until 11 July

Table 75

Birmingham and Shrewsbury - Chester, Aberystwyth, Barmouth and Pwllheli

		AW MX	AW	AW	AW	AW	AW	AW	VT	AW	AW	AW	AW	AW	AW	AW	AW	AW	AW	WS	AW	AW	AW	AW	AW
				◇				◇	◇1	◇		◇	◇	◇	◇	◇	A	◇ B	◇	◇1	◇	◇	◇ A	◇ B	◇
										🛒		🛒		🛒	🛒	🛒			🛒	🍽	🛒	🛒			🛒
London Marylebone 10 ⊖	d																			07 33					
Banbury	d																			08 37					
Leamington Spa 8	d																			08 56					
Birmingham International ✈	d													07 09		08 09			09 09			10 09			11 09
Birmingham New Street 12	d											06 24		07 22		08 24			09 24			10 24			11 24
Tame Bridge Parkway	d																			09 42					
Smethwick Galton Bridge	d											06 30		07 28		08 30			09 30			10 30			11 30
Wolverhampton 7 ⛴	d											06 42		07 41		08 43			09 43	09u59		10 43			11 43
Cosford	d																			10 10					
Telford Central	d											06 59		07 58		08 59			10 00	10 19		10 59			11 59
Wellington (Shropshire)	d											07 05		08 04		09 06			10 06			11 06			12 06
Shrewsbury	a											07 18		08 18		09 19			10 19	10 40		11 19			12 19
Cardiff Central 7	d									05 10					07 20						09 20				
Shrewsbury	d	23p37			05 20	06 10				07 24		07 27		08 24	09 24	09 27			10 23	10 41	11 24	11 27			12 22
Gobowen	d	23p57			05 39	06 30				07 43				08 43	09 43				10 42	11 02	11 43				12 42
Chirk	d	00 03			05 45	06 35				07 48				08 49	09 48				10 48		11 48				12 47
Ruabon	d	00 09			05 51	06 42				07 54				08 55	09 54				10 54		11 54				12 54
Wrexham General	a	00 14			05 57	06 49				08 01				09 02	10 01				11 00	11 19	12 01				13 00
	d	00 15			06 04				07 00	08 02				09 03	10 02				11 01		12 02				13 00
Chester	a	00 35			06 25				07 16	08 20				09 20	10 20				11 19		12 19				13 19
Welshpool	d											07 49				09 49						11 49			
Newtown (Powys)	d											08 04				10 05						12 05			
Caersws	d											08 13				10 14						12 14			
Machynlleth 4	a											08 46				10 46						12 46			
	d		04 35	05 15			06 35	06 49			08 07	08 48	09 03			10 48	11§00	11§00				12 48	12§56	12§56	
Dovey Junction 4	d		04 42	05 22			06 42	06 56			08 14	08 55	09 10			10 55	11§07	11§07				12 55	13§03	13§03	
Borth	d		04 53				06 53				08 25	09 06				11 06	§	§				13 06	§	§	
Aberystwyth	a		05 12				07 10				08 44	09 25				11 25	§	§				13 25	§	§	
Penhelig	d			05x30				07x04					09x18				11x15	11x15					13x11	13x11	
Aberdovey	d			05 34				07 08					09 22				11§20	11§20					13§15	13§15	
Tywyn	a			05 40				07 14					09 28				11§26	11§26					13§21	13§21	
	d			05 41				07 15					09 29				11§26	11§32					13§23	13§25	
Tonfanau	d			05x44				07x19					09x32				11x30	11x36					13x26	13x28	
Llwyngwril	d			05x51				07x25					09x39				11x36	11x42					13x33	13x35	
Fairbourne	d			05 59				07 33					09 47				11§45	11§51					13§41	13§43	
Morfa Mawddach	d			06x00				07x35					09 48				11x46	11x52					13x42	13x44	
Barmouth	a			06 07				07 41					09 55				11§53	11§59					13§49	13§51	
	d			06 11				07 47					09 57				11§56	12§01					13§52	13§54	
Llanaber	d			06x14				07x50					10x00				11x59	12x04					13x55	13x57	
Talybont	d							07x54					10x04				12x03	12x08					13x59	14x01	
Dyffryn Ardudwy	d							07x57					10x07				12x06	12x11					14x02	14x04	
Llanbedr	d							08x01					10x11				12x10	12x15					14x06	14x08	
Pensarn	d							08x03					10x13				12x12	12x17					14x08	14x10	
Llandanwg	d							08x05					10x15				12x14	12x19					14x10	14x12	
Harlech	a			06 32				08 09					10 21				12§20	12§25					14§16	14§18	
	d			06 32				08 21					10 24				12§26	12§28					14§31	14§31	
Tygwyn	d							08x24					10x27				12x29	12x31					14x34	14x34	
Talsarnau	d							08x27					10x30				12x32	12x34					14x37	14x37	
Llandecwyn	d							08x30					10x33				12x35	12x37					14x40	14x40	
Penrhyndeudraeth	d							08 34					10 37				12§39	12§41					14§44	14§44	
Minffordd	d							08 37					10 40				12§42	12§44					14§47	14§47	
Porthmadog	a			06 48				08 43					10 45				12§47	12§49					14§52	14§52	
	d			06 50				08 43					10 46				12§48	12§50					14§53	14§53	
Criccieth	d							08 51					10 54				12§56	12§58					15§01	15§01	
Penychain	d			07x02				08x56					10x59				13x01	13x03					15x06	15x06	
Abererch	d							08x59					11x02				13x04	13x06					15x09	15x09	
Pwllheli	a			07 10				09 06					11 09				13§14	13§16					15§18	15§18	

For connections from London Euston please refer to Table 66

For connections from Manchester Piccadilly and Crewe please refer to Table 131

Table 75

Birmingham and Shrewsbury - Chester, Aberystwyth, Barmouth and Pwllheli

		AW	AW	AW	AW	WS	AW	AW	AW	AW	AW		AW	AW	AW FO	AW	AW	AW	WS	AW	AW	AW	AW		WS
		◇	◇	◇	◇	◇1	◇	◇	◇ A	◇ B	◇		■	◇		◇	■	◇	◇1	◇	◇	◇	◇		◇1
		🛒	🛒		🛒	🍽	🛒	🛒			🛒		🛒	🛒		🛒	🛒	🛒	🍽		🛒		🛒		🍽
London Marylebone 10 ⊖	d					11 20													16 30						19 30
Banbury	d					12 30													17 33						19 34
Leamington Spa 8	d					12 49													17 50						19 53
Birmingham International ✈	d		12 09		13 09			14 09			15 09			16 09		17 09		18 09			19 09		20 09		
Birmingham New Street 12	d		12 24		13 24			14 24			15 26			16 24		17 26		18 24			19 24		20 24		
Tame Bridge Parkway	d																		18 40						20 40
Smethwick Galton Bridge	d		12 30		13 30			14 30			15 32			16 30		17 32		18 30			19 30		20 30		
Wolverhampton 7 ⛴	d		12 43		13 43			14 43			15 44			16 43		17 44		18 43	18u57		19 43		20 43		21u02
Cosford	d					14 10													19 08						21 13
Telford Central	d		12 59		13 59	14 19		14 59			16 01			16 59		18 01		18 59	19 16		19 59		20 59		21 22
Wellington (Shropshire)	d		13 06		14 06			15 06			16 07			17 06		18 07		19 06	19 22		20 06		21 06		21 28
Shrewsbury	a		13 19		14 19	14 36		15 19			16 20			17 19		18 20		19 19	19 34		20 19		21 19		21 44
Cardiff Central 7	d	11 20					13 20						15 20				17 20					19 34			
Shrewsbury	d	13 24	13 27		14 22	14 38	15 24	15 27			16 24		17 24	17 27		18 24	19 24	19 30	19 39		20 24	21 39	21 42		21 51
Gobowen	d	13 43			14 42	14 59	15 43				16 43		17 43			18 43	19 43		20 03		20 43	21 58			22 16
Chirk	d	13 48			14 47		15 48				16 49		17 48			18 49	19 48		20 08		20 49	22 03			22 21
Ruabon	d	13 54			14 54		15 54				16 55		17 54			18 55	19 54		20 15		20 55	22 09			22 28
Wrexham General	a	14 01			15 00	15 16	16 01				17 01		18 01			19 01	20 01		20 23		21 01	22 15			22 36
	d	14 02			15 00		16 02				17 02		18 02			19 02	20 02				21 02	22 15			
Chester	a	14 20			15 20		16 20				17 22		18 20			19 20	20 24				21 19	22 34			
Welshpool	d		13 49					15 49						17 49				19 52					22 04		
Newtown (Powys)	d		14 04					16 05						18 04				20 07					22 20		
Caersws	d		14 13					16 14						18 13				20 16					22 29		
Machynlleth 4	a		14 46					16 46						18 46				20 47					22 59		
	d		14 48	14 56				16 48	17§00	17§06				18 48	19 00			20 49		21 17			23 07		
Dovey Junction 4	d		14 55	15 03				16 55	17§07	17§12				18 55	19 07			20 56		21 24			23 14		
Borth	d		15 06					17 06	§	§				19 06				21 07					23 25		
Aberystwyth	a		15 25					17 25	§	§				19 25				21 26					23 44		
Penhelig	d			15x11					17x15	17x21					19x15					21x32					
Aberdovey	d			15 15					17§19	17§25					19 20					21 36					
Tywyn	a			15 21					17§25	17§31					19 26					21 42					
	d			15 26					17§27	17§31					19 26					21 43					
Tonfanau	d			15x29					17x30	17x35					19x30					21x46					
Llwyngwril	d			15x36					17x37	17x41					19x36					21x53					
Fairbourne	d			15 44					17§45	17§49					19 44					22 01					
Morfa Mawddach	d			15x45					17x46	17x51					19x46					22x02					
Barmouth	a			15 52					17§53	17§57					19 56					22 09					
	d			15 56					17§57	18§00										22 10					
Llanaber	d			15x59					18x00	18x03										22x13					
Talybont	d			16x02					18x03	18x06										22x17					
Dyffryn Ardudwy	d			16x05					18x06	18x09										22x20					
Llanbedr	d			16x09					18x10	18x13										22x24					
Pensarn	d			16x11					18x12	18x15										22x26					
Llandanwg	d			16x13					18x14	18x17										22x28					
Harlech	a			16 20					18§21	18§24										22 34					
	d			16 22					18§26	18§26										22 37					
Tygwyn	d			16x26					18x29	18x30										22x40					
Talsarnau	d			16x28					18x32	18x32										22x43					
Llandecwyn	d			16x31					18x35	18x35										22x46					
Penrhyndeudraeth	d			16 35					18§39	18§39										22 50					
Minffordd	d			16 39					18§42	18§43										22 53					
Porthmadog	a			16 44					18§47	18§48										22 59					
	d			16 44					18§48	18§48										22 59					
Criccieth	d			16 52					18§56	18§56										23 07					
Penychain	d			16x57					19x01	19x01										23x12					
Abererch	d			17x00					19x04	19x04										23x15					

A from 6 September

B until 3 September

For connections from London Euston please refer to Table 66

For connections from Manchester Piccadilly and Crewe please refer to Table 131

Table 75

Birmingham and Shrewsbury - Chester, Aberystwyth, Barmouth and Pwllheli

Station		AW ◇ H	AW ◇
London Marylebone 10 ⊖	d		
Banbury	d		
Leamington Spa 8	d		
Birmingham International ✈	d	21 09	
Birmingham New Street 12	d	21 24	
Tame Bridge Parkway	d		
Smethwick Galton Bridge	d	21 30	
Wolverhampton 7 ⛴	d	21 43	
Cosford	d		
Telford Central	d	21 59	
Wellington (Shropshire)	d	22 07	
Shrewsbury	a	22 19	
Cardiff Central 7	d		
Shrewsbury	d	22 23	
Gobowen	d	22 43	
Chirk	d	22 48	
Ruabon	d	22 54	
Wrexham General	a	23 00	
	d	23 01	
Chester	a	23 18	
Welshpool	d		
Newtown (Powys)	d		
Caersws	d		
Machynlleth 4	a		
	d		14 56
Dovey Junction 4	d		15 03
Borth	d		
Aberystwyth	a		
Penhelig	d		15x11
Aberdovey	d		15 15
Tywyn	a		15 21
	d		15 26
Tonfanau	d		15x29
Llwyngwril	d		15x36
Fairbourne	d		15 44
Morfa Mawddach	d		15x45
Barmouth	a		15 52
	d		15 56
Llanaber	d		15x59
Talybont	d		16x02
Dyffryn Ardudwy	d		16x05
Llanbedr	d		16x09
Pensarn	d		16x11
Llandanwg	d		16x13
Harlech	a		16 20
	d		16 22
Tygwyn	d		16x26
Talsarnau	d		16x28
Llandecwyn	d		16x31
Penrhyndeudraeth	d		16 35
Minffordd	d		16 39
Porthmadog	a		16 44
	d		16 44
Criccieth	d		16 52
Penychain	d		16x57
Abererch	d		17x00

Table 75

Birmingham and Shrewsbury - Chester, Aberystwyth, Barmouth and Pwllheli

Station		AW	AW	AW ◇	AW	AW	AW ◇ H	AW	AW ◇	AW ◇ H	AW ◇	AW ◇ H	AW ◇ H
London Marylebone 10 ⊖	d												
Banbury	d												
Leamington Spa 8	d												
Birmingham International ✈	d											07 09	
Birmingham New Street 12	d									06 24		07 24	
Tame Bridge Parkway	d												
Smethwick Galton Bridge	d									06 30		07 30	
Wolverhampton 7 ⛴	d									06 42		07 42	
Cosford	d												
Telford Central	d									06 59		07 59	
Wellington (Shropshire)	d									07 05		08 05	
Shrewsbury	a									07 18		08 18	
Cardiff Central 7	d						05 20						07 20
Shrewsbury	d	23p37			05 20	06 10	07 24			07 27		08 24	09 24
Gobowen	d	23p57			05 39	06 30	07 43					08 43	09 43
Chirk	d	00 03			05 45	06 35	07 48					08 49	09 48
Ruabon	d	00 09			05 51	06 42	07 54					08 55	09 54
Wrexham General	a	00 14			05 57	06 48	08 00					09 01	10 01
	d	00 15			05 58	06 49	08 01					09 02	10 02
Chester	a	00 35			06 16	07 07	08 19					09 19	10 19
Welshpool	d									07 49			
Newtown (Powys)	d									08 04			
Caersws	d									08 13			
Machynlleth 4	a									08 46			
	d		04 35	05 15				06 35	06 49	08 48	09 03		
Dovey Junction 4	d		04 42	05 22				06 42	06 56	08 55	09 10		
Borth	d		04 53					06 53		09 06			
Aberystwyth	a		05 12					07 10		09 25			
Penhelig	d			05x30					07x04		09x18		
Aberdovey	d			05 34					07 08		09 22		
Tywyn	a			05 40					07 14		09 28		
	d			05 41					07 15		09 29		
Tonfanau	d			05x44					07x19		09x32		
Llwyngwril	d			05x51					07x25		09x39		
Fairbourne	d			05 59					07 33		09 47		
Morfa Mawddach	d			06x00					07x35		09 48		
Barmouth	a			06 07					07 41		09 55		
	d			06 11					07 47		09 57		
Llanaber	d			06x14					07x50		10x00		
Talybont	d								07x54		10x04		
Dyffryn Ardudwy	d								07x57		10x07		
Llanbedr	d								08x01		10x11		
Pensarn	d								08x03		10x13		
Llandanwg	d								08x05		10x15		
Harlech	a			06 32					08 09		10 21		
	d			06 32					08 21		10 24		
Tygwyn	d								08x24		10x27		
Talsarnau	d								08x27		10x30		
Llandecwyn	d								08x30		10x33		
Penrhyndeudraeth	d								08 34		10 37		
Minffordd	d								08 37		10 40		
Porthmadog	a			06 48					08 43		10 45		
	d			06 50					08 43		10 46		
Criccieth	d								08 51		10 54		
Penychain	d			07x02					08x56		10x59		
Abererch	d								08x59		11x02		
Pwllheli	a			07 10					09 06		11 09		

Station		AW ◇ H	AW ◇	AW ◇ H	AW ◇ H	AW ◇ H	AW ◇	WS ◇ 1 ⊡	AW ◇ H	AW ◇ H	AW ◇ H	AW ◇	AW ◇ H
London Marylebone 10 ⊖	d							08 14					
Banbury	d							09 30					
Leamington Spa 8	d							09 49					
Birmingham International ✈	d	08 09		09 09		10 09			11 09		12 09		13 09
Birmingham New Street 12	d	08 24		09 24		10 24			11 24		12 24		13 23
Tame Bridge Parkway	d							10 44					
Smethwick Galton Bridge	d	08 30		09 30		10 30			11 30		12 30		13 29
Wolverhampton 7 ⛴	d	08 43		09 43		10 43		10u59	11 43		12 43		13 43
Cosford	d							10 10					
Telford Central	d	08 59		09 59		10 59		10 19	11 59		12 59		13 59
Wellington (Shropshire)	d	09 06		10 06		11 06			12 06		13 06		14 06
Shrewsbury	a	09 19		10 19		11 19		10 40	12 19		13 19		14 19
Cardiff Central 7	d				09 20					11 20			
Shrewsbury	d	09 27		10 22	11 24	11 27		10 41	12 22	13 24	13 27		14 22
Gobowen	d			10 42	11 43			11 02	12 42	13 43			14 42
Chirk	d			10 47	11 48				12 47	13 48			14 47
Ruabon	d			10 54	11 54				12 54	13 54			14 54
Wrexham General	a			11 00	12 01			11 19	13 00	14 01			15 00
	d			11 00	12 02				13 00	14 02			15 00
Chester	a			11 19	12 19				13 19	14 20			15 21
Welshpool	d	09 49				11 49					13 49		
Newtown (Powys)	d	10 05				12 05					14 05		
Caersws	d	10 14				12 14					14 14		
Machynlleth 4	a	10 46				12 46					14 45		
	d	10 48	11 00			12 49	12 56				14 48	14 56	
Dovey Junction 4	d	10 55	11 07			12 55	13 03				14 55	15 03	
Borth	d	11 06				13 06					15 06		
Aberystwyth	a	11 25				13 25					15 25		
Penhelig	d		11x15				13x11					15x11	
Aberdovey	d		11 20				13 15					15 15	
Tywyn	a		11 26				13 21					15 21	
	d		11 26				13 23					15 26	
Tonfanau	d		11x30				13x26					15x29	
Llwyngwril	d		11x36				13x33					15x36	
Fairbourne	d		11 45				13 41					15 44	
Morfa Mawddach	d		11x46				13x42					15x45	
Barmouth	a		11 53				13 49					15 52	
	d		11 56				13 52					15 56	
Llanaber	d		11x59				13x55					15x59	
Talybont	d		12x03				13x59					16x02	
Dyffryn Ardudwy	d		12x06				14x02					16x05	
Llanbedr	d		12x10				14x06					16x09	
Pensarn	d		12x12				14x08					16x11	
Llandanwg	d		12x14				14x10					16x13	
Harlech	a		12 20				14 16					16 20	
	d		12 26				14 31					16 22	
Tygwyn	d		12x29				14x34					16x26	
Talsarnau	d		12x32				14x37					16x28	
Llandecwyn	d		12x35				14x40					16x31	
Penrhyndeudraeth	d		12 39				14 44					16 35	
Minffordd	d		12 42				14 47					16 39	
Porthmadog	a		12 47				14 52					16 44	
	d		12 48				14 53					16 44	
Criccieth	d		12 56				15 01					16 52	
Penychain	d		13x01				15x06					16x57	
Abererch	d		13x04				15x09					17x00	
Pwllheli	a		13 14				15 18					17 09	

For connections from London Euston please refer to Table 66

For connections from Manchester Piccadilly and Crewe please refer to Table 131

Table 75

Saturdays

Birmingham and Shrewsbury - Chester, Aberystwyth, Barmouth and Pwllheli

		AW	AW	AW	WS	AW	AW	AW	AW	AW	AW	AW	AW	AW	WS	AW	AW	AW	WS	AW
		◇ ✠	◇ ✠	◇	◇1 ⊡	◇ ✠	◇ ✠	◇ ✠	◇ ✠		◇ ✠	◇ ✠	◇	◇ ✠	◇1 ⊡	◇	◇	◇ ✠	◇1 ⊡	
London Marylebone 10 ⊖	d				12 24										17 24				19 24	
Banbury	d				13 37										18 37				20 37	
Leamington Spa 8	d				13 55										18 55				20 55	
Birmingham International ✈	d		14 09			15 09		16 09	17 09			18 09		19 09			20 09	21 09		
Birmingham New Street 12	d		14 24			15 24		16 24	17 24			18 24		19 24			20 24	21 24		
Tame Bridge Parkway	d				14 41										19 43				21 40	
Smethwick Galton Bridge	d		14 30			15 30		16 30	17 31			18 30		19 30			20 30	21 30		
Wolverhampton 7	d		14 43		14u55	15 43		16 43	17 43			18 43		19 43	20u00		20 43	21 42	22u00	
Cosford	d				15 06										20 11				22 11	
Telford Central	d		14 59		15 15	15 59		16 59	17 59			18 59		19 59	20 20		21 02	21 59	22 20	
Wellington (Shropshire)	d		15 06		15 21	16 06		17 06	18 06			19 06		20 06	20 27		21 09	22 05	22 26	
Shrewsbury	a		15 19		15 34	16 19		17 19	18 19			19 19		20 19	20 40		21 23	22 22	22 39	
Cardiff Central 7	d	13 20					15 20				17 20					19 34				
Shrewsbury	d	15 24	15 27		15 38	16 22	17 24	17 27	18 22		19 24	19 30		20 24	20 44	21 37	21 42	22 24	22 43	23 33
Gobowen	d	15 43			16 02	16 42	17 43		18 42		19 44			20 43	21 05	21 56		22 43	23 05	23 52
Chirk	d	15 48			16 07	16 47	17 48		18 47		19 49			20 49	21 10	22 01		22 49	23 10	23 58
Ruabon	d	15 54			16 14	16 54	17 54		18 54		19 55			20 55	21 17	22 07		22 55	23 17	00 04
Wrexham General	a	16 01			16 23	17 01	18 01		19 01		20 01			21 01	21 26	22 13		23 01	23 25	00 10
	d	16 02				17 02	18 01		19 02	19 46	20 02			21 02		22 13		23 02		00 14
Chester	a	16 21				17 20	18 20		19 20	20 04	20 20			21 19		22 31		23 19		00 31
Welshpool	d		15 49					17 49				19 52					22 04			
Newtown (Powys)	d		16 05					18 05				20 07					22 20			
Caersws	d		16 14					18 14				20 16					22 29			
Machynlleth 4	a		16 46					18 46				20 47					22 59			
	d		16 48	17 00				18 48				20 49	21 17				23 04			
Dovey Junction 4	d		16 55	17 07				18 55				20 56	21 24				23 11			
Borth	d		17 06					19 06				21 07					23 21			
Aberystwyth	a		17 25					19 25				21 26					23 41			
Penhelig	d			17x15									21x32							
Aberdovey	d			17 19									21 36							
Tywyn	a			17 25									21 42							
	d			17 27									21 43							
Tonfanau	d			17x30									21x46							
Llwyngwril	d			17x37									21x53							
Fairbourne	d			17 45									22 01							
Morfa Mawddach	d			17x46									22x02							
Barmouth	a			17 53									22 09							
	d			17 57									22 10							
Llanaber	d			18x00									22x13							
Talybont	d			18x03									22x17							
Dyffryn Ardudwy	d			18x06									22x20							
Llanbedr	d			18x10									22x24							
Pensarn	d			18x12									22x26							
Llandanwg	d			18x14									22x28							
Harlech	a			18 21									22 34							
	d			18 26									22 37							
Tygwyn	d			18x29									22x40							
Talsarnau	d			18x32									22x43							
Llandecwyn	d			18x35									22x46							
Penrhyndeudraeth	d			18 39									22 50							
Minffordd	d			18 42									22 53							
Porthmadog	a			18 47									22 59							
	d			18 48									22 59							
Criccieth	d			18 56									23 07							
Penychain	d			19x01									23x12							
Abererch	d			19x04									23x15							
Pwllheli	a			19 13									23 22							

For connections from London Euston please refer to Table 66

For connections from Manchester Piccadilly and Crewe please refer to Table 131

Table 75

Sundays
until 05 September

Birmingham and Shrewsbury - Chester, Aberystwyth, Barmouth and Pwllheli

		AW	AW	AW	AW	AW	AW	AW	AW	WS	WS	AW	AW	AW	AW	AW	AW	AW	AW	AW	AW	WS	AW	AW	AW
		A		◇	◇	✠			◇ ✠	◇1 B ⊡	◇1 C ⊡	◇ ✠	◇	◇ ✠	◇ ✠	◇ ✠	◇ ✠	◇	■ B	■ C	◇ ✠	◇1 B ⊡	◇ ✠	■ B	■ C
London Marylebone 10 ⊖	d									09 33	09 33											16 11			
Banbury	d									10 37	10 37											17 16			
Leamington Spa 8	d									10 56	10 56											17 34			
Birmingham International ✈	d								10 48			12 08		13 05	14 07	15 07	16 07				17 07		18 07		
Birmingham New Street 12	d								11 05			12 24		13 24	14 24	15 24	16 24				17 24		18 24		
Tame Bridge Parkway	d										11 46														
Smethwick Galton Bridge	d									11 40												18 13			
Wolverhampton 7	d								11 27	11u50	12u03	12 42		13 42	12 42	15 43	16 43				17 43	18u26	18 43		
Cosford	d								11 43	12 01	12 15			13 58		15 59					17 59	18 38			
Telford Central	d								11 54	12 10	12 23	12 59		14 09	14 59	16 09	16 59				18 09	18 46	18 59		
Wellington (Shropshire)	d								12 01	12 16	12 29	13 05		14 15	15 06	16 17	17 06				18 16	18 52	19 06		
Shrewsbury	a								12 05	12 31	12 45	13 18		14 29	15 19	16 30	17 19				18 30	19 06	19 19		
Cardiff Central 7	d																		15 16	15 22				17 16	17 22
Shrewsbury	d	23p33		08 45		10 16			12 17	12 36	12 49	13 27		14 31	15 27	16 32	17 27		17 30	17 30	18 31	19 10	19 27	19 32	19 32
Gobowen	d	23p52				10 35			12 37	12 57	13 10			14 50		16 51			17 49	17 49	18 51	19 31		19 52	19 51
Chirk	d	23p58				10 41			12 42	13 02	13 15			14 56		16 57			17 55	17 55	18 56	19 36		19 58	19 57
Ruabon	d	00 04				10 47			12 49	13 08	13 22			15 02		17 03			18 01	18 01	19 03	19 43		20 04	20 03
Wrexham General	a	00 10				10 53			12 55	13 17	13 30			15 08		17 09			18 07	18 07	19 09	19 51		20 10	20 09
	d	00 14				10 54			12 56					15 09		17 10			18 08	18 08	19 09			20 11	20 10
Chester	a	00 31				11 12			13 20					15 30		17 30			18 25	18 25	19 30			20 31	20 31
Welshpool	d			09 07								13 49			15 49		17 49						19 49		
Newtown (Powys)	d			09 23								14 04			16 04		18 04						20 04		
Caersws	d			09 32								14 13			16 13		18 13						20 13		
Machynlleth 4	a			10 02								14 46			16 46		18 46						20 46		
	d		08 50	10 05	10 10		10 50	12 35				14 48	15 00		16 48		18 48	18 55					20 48		
Dovey Junction 4	d		08 57	10 12	10 17		10 57	12 42				14 55	15 07		16 55		18 55	19 02					20 55		
Borth	d		09 08	10 22			11 08	12 53				15 06			17 06		19 06						21 06		
Aberystwyth	a		09 25	10 36			11 25	13 10				15 25			17 25		19 25						21 25		
Penhelig	d				10x25								15x15					19x10							
Aberdovey	d				10 30								15 20					19 14							
Tywyn	a				10 36								15 26					19 20							
	d				10 36								15 31					19 21							
Tonfanau	d				10x40								15x34					19x24							
Llwyngwril	d				10x47								15x41					19x31							
Fairbourne	d				10 55								15 49					19 39							
Morfa Mawddach	d				10x56								15x51					19x41							
Barmouth	a				11 03								15 58					19 48							
	d				11 05								15 59					19 49							
Llanaber	d				11x08								16x02					19x53							
Talybont	d				11x12								16x06					19x56							
Dyffryn Ardudwy	d				11x15								16x10					20x00							
Llanbedr	d				11x19								16x14					20x04							
Pensarn	d				11x22								16x16					20x07							
Llandanwg	d				11x24								16x18					20x09							
Harlech	a				11 30								16 25					20 15							
	d				11 33								16 25					20 18							
Tygwyn	d				11x36								16x29					20x21							
Talsarnau	d				11x39								16x32					20x24							
Llandecwyn	d				11x42								16x36					20x27							
Penrhyndeudraeth	d				11 46								16 39					20 31							
Minffordd	d				11 50								16 42					20 35							
Porthmadog	a				11 55								16 47					20 40							
	d				11 58								16 48					20 41							
Criccieth	d				12 05								16 55					20 48							
Penychain	d				12x11								17x01					20x54							
Abererch	d				12x14								17x04					20x57							
Pwllheli	a				12 24								17 14					21 07							

A not 23 May
B from 18 July until 5 September
C until 11 July

For connections from London Euston please refer to Table 66

For connections from Manchester Piccadilly and Crewe please refer to Table 131

Table 75

Sundays
until 05 September

Birmingham and Shrewsbury - Chester, Aberystwyth, Barmouth and Pwllheli

		WS	AW	AW	WS	WS	AW
		◇■	◇	◇	◇■	◇■	
		A			B	A	
London Marylebone ■ ⊖	d	16 19		AW	18 33	18 33	
Banbury	d	17 29			19 43	19 43	
Leamington Spa ■	d	17 47			20 01	20 01	
Birmingham International ✈	d		19 07	20 07			
Birmingham New Street ■	d		19 24	20 24			
Tame Bridge Parkway	d	18 32				20 47	
Smethwick Galton Bridge	d				20 41		
Wolverhampton ■	d	18u54	19 43	20 43	20u53	21u01	
Cosford	d	19 05	19 59		21 04	21 12	
Telford Central	d	19 14	20 09	20 59	21 12	21 21	
Wellington (Shropshire)	d	19 20	20 17	21 06	21 18	21 27	
Shrewsbury	a	19 33	20 30	21 19	21 32	21 40	
Cardiff Central ■	d						
Shrewsbury	d	19 50	20 34	21 30	21 35	21 43	
Gobowen	d	20 11	20 53		21 56	22 04	
Chirk	d	20 16	20 59		22 01	22 09	
Ruabon	d	20 23	21 05		22 08	22 16	
Wrexham General	a	20 31	21 11		22 17	22 25	
	d		21 13				22 35
Chester	a		21 31				22 53
Welshpool	d			21 52			
Newtown (Powys)	d			22 07			
Caersws	d			22 16			
Machynlleth ■	a			22 47			
	d			22 49			
Dovey Junction ■	d			22 56			
Borth	d			23 07			
Aberystwyth	a			23 26			
Penhelig	d						
Aberdovey	d						
Tywyn	a						
	d						
Tonfanau	d						
Llwyngwril	d						
Fairbourne	d						
Morfa Mawddach	d						
Barmouth	a						
	d						
Llanaber	d						
Talybont	d						
Dyffryn Ardudwy	d						
Llanbedr	d						
Pensarn	d						
Llandanwg	d						
Harlech	a						
	d						
Tygwyn	d						
Talsarnau	d						
Llandecwyn	d						
Penrhyndeudraeth	d						
Minffordd	d						
Porthmadog	a						
	d						
Criccieth	d						
Penychain	d						
Abererch	d						
Pwllheli	a						

A until 11 July

B from 18 July until 5 September

For connections from London Euston please refer to Table 66

For connections from Manchester Piccadilly and Crewe please refer to Table 131

Table 75

Sundays
from 12 September

Birmingham and Shrewsbury - Chester, Aberystwyth, Barmouth and Pwllheli

		AW	AW	AW	AW	AW	AW	AW	AW	AW	AW	AW	AW
						◇	◇	◇	◇	◇	◇	◇	■
London Marylebone ■ ⊖	d												
Banbury	d												
Leamington Spa ■	d												
Birmingham International ✈	d												
Birmingham New Street ■	d												
Tame Bridge Parkway	d												
Smethwick Galton Bridge	d												
Wolverhampton ■	d												
Cosford	d												
Telford Central	d												
Wellington (Shropshire)	d												
Shrewsbury	a												
Cardiff Central ■	d												15 22
Shrewsbury	d	23p33		10 16		11 27	12 18	13 27	14 31	15 27	16 32	17 27	17 30
Gobowen	d	23p52		10 35			12 37		14 50		16 51		17 49
Chirk	d	23p58		10 41			12 43		14 56		16 57		17 55
Ruabon	d	00 04		10 47			12 49		15 02		17 03		18 01
Wrexham General	a	00 10		10 53			12 55		15 08		17 09		18 07
	d	00 14		10 54			12 56		15 09		17 10		18 09
Chester	a	00 31		11 12			13 20		15 30		17 30		18 27
Welshpool	d					11 49		13 49		15 49		17 49	
Newtown (Powys)	d					12 05		14 04		16 04		18 04	
Caersws	d					12 14		14 13		16 13		18 13	
Machynlleth ■	a					12 46		14 46		16 46		18 46	
	d		08 50		10 50	12 48		14 48		16 48		18 48	
Dovey Junction ■	d		08 57		10 57	12 55		14 55		16 55		18 55	
Borth	d		09 08		11 08	13 06		15 06		17 06		19 06	
Aberystwyth	a		09 25		11 25	13 23		15 25		17 25		19 25	
Penhelig	d												
Aberdovey	d												
Tywyn	a												
	d												
Tonfanau	d												
Llwyngwril	d												
Fairbourne	d												
Morfa Mawddach	d												
Barmouth	a												
	d												
Llanaber	d												
Talybont	d												
Dyffryn Ardudwy	d												
Llanbedr	d												
Pensarn	d												
Llandanwg	d												
Harlech	a												
	d												
Tygwyn	d												
Talsarnau	d												
Llandecwyn	d												
Penrhyndeudraeth	d												
Minffordd	d												
Porthmadog	a												
	d												
Criccieth	d												
Penychain	d												
Abererch	d												
Pwllheli	a												

For connections from London Euston please refer to Table 66

For connections from Manchester Piccadilly and Crewe please refer to Table 131

Table 75

Sundays
from 12 September

Birmingham and Shrewsbury - Chester, Aberystwyth, Barmouth and Pwllheli

		AW	AW	AW	AW	AW	AW	AW
			■					
		◇		◇	◇	◇	◇	
		H			H	H		
London Marylebone 10 ⊖	d							
Banbury	d							
Leamington Spa 8	d							
Birmingham International ✈	d							
Birmingham New Street 12	d							
Tame Bridge Parkway	d							
Smethwick Galton Bridge	d							
Wolverhampton 7	d							
Cosford	d							
Telford Central	d							
Wellington (Shropshire)	d							
Shrewsbury	a							
Cardiff Central 7	d		17 14					
Shrewsbury	d	18 31	19 15		19 28	20 34	21 30	
Gobowen	d	18 51	19 34			20 53		
Chirk	d	18 56	19 40			20 59		
Ruabon	d	19 03	19 46			21 05		
Wrexham General	a	19 09	19 52			21 11		
	d	19 09	20 10			21 13		22 35
Chester	a	19 30	20 31			21 31		22 53
Welshpool	d				19 50		21 52	
Newtown (Powys)	d				20 05		22 07	
Caersws	d				20 14		22 16	
Machynlleth 4	a				20 47		22 47	
	d			18 55	20 49		22 49	
Dovey Junction 4	d			19 02	20 56		22 56	
Borth	d				21 07		23 07	
Aberystwyth	a				21 26		23 26	
Penhelig	d			19x10				
Aberdovey	d			19 14				
Tywyn	a			19 20				
	d			19 21				
Tonfanau	d			19x24				
Llwyngwril	d			19x31				
Fairbourne	d			19 39				
Morfa Mawddach	d			19x41				
Barmouth	a			19 48				
	d			19 49				
Llanaber	d			19x53				
Talybont	d			19x56				
Dyffryn Ardudwy	d			20x00				
Llanbedr	d			20x04				
Pensarn	d			20x07				
Llandanwg	d			20x09				
Harlech	a			20 15				
	d			20 18				
Tygwyn	d			20x21				
Talsarnau	d			20x24				
Llandecwyn	d			20x27				
Penrhyndeudraeth	d			20 31				
Minffordd	d			20 35				
Porthmadog	a			20 40				
	d			20 41				
Criccieth	d			20 48				
Penychain	d			20x54				
Abererch	d			20x57				
Pwllheli	a			21 07				

For connections from London Euston please refer to Table 66

For connections from Manchester Piccadilly and Crewe please refer to Table 131

Table 75

Mondays to Fridays

Pwllheli, Barmouth, Aberystwyth and Chester - Shrewsbury and Birmingham

		AW MX	WS	AW	AW	AW	AW	AW	WS	AW	AW	AW	AW	AW	AW	AW	AW	WS	AW	AW	AW	AW	AW
																						■	
			◇1	◇	◇		◇	◇	◇1	◇	◇	◇	◇		◇	◇	◇	◇1	A	◇ B	◇		◇ B
			ꝑ		H		H		ꝑ	H	H	H			H	H	H	ꝑ			H	H	H
Pwllheli	d												06 25	07 25					09§36	09§36			
Abererch	d												06x28	07x28					09x39	09x39			
Penychain	d												06x31	07x31					09x42	09x42			
Criccieth	d												06 39	07 39					09§50	09§50			
Porthmadog	a												06 47	07 47					09§58	09§58			
	d												06 52	07 49					10§00	10§00			
Minffordd	d												06 56	07 53					10§04	10§04			
Penrhyndeudraeth	d												07 00	07 57					10§08	10§08			
Llandecwyn	d												07x02	07x59					10x10	10x10			
Talsarnau	d												07x04	08x02					10x12	10x12			
Tygwyn	d												07x07	08x04					10x15	10x15			
Harlech	a												07 12	08 09					10§20	10§20			
	d												07 16	08 30					10§25	10§25			
Llandanwg	d												07x20	08x34					10x29	10x29			
Pensarn	d												07x21	08x35					10x30	10x30			
Llanbedr	d												07x24	08x38					10x33	10x33			
Dyffryn Ardudwy	d												07x28	08x42					10x37	10x37			
Talybont	d												07x31	08x45					10x40	10x40			
Llanaber	d												07x35	08x49					10x44	10x44			
Barmouth	a												07 40	08 54					10§49	10§49			
	d							06 46					07 49	09 00					10§52	11§04			
Morfa Mawddach	d							06x50					07x53	09x04					10x56	11x08			
Fairbourne	d							06 54					07 57	09 08					11§00	11§12			
Llwyngwril	d							07x00					08x03	09x14					11x06	11x18			
Tonfanau	d							07x07					08x10	09x21					11x13	11x25			
Tywyn	a							07 11					08 14	09 25					11§17	11§30			
	d							07 16					08 18	09 30					11§27	11§31			
Aberdovey	d							07 22					08 24	09 36					11§33	11§37			
Penhelig	d							07x25					08x26	09x38					11x36	11x40			
Aberystwyth	d	23p53			05 14							07 30					09 30						11§30
Borth	d	00 06			05 27							07 43					09 43						11§43
Dovey Junction 4	d	00 17			05 38			07 37				07 54	08 38	09 50			09 54		11§48	11§52			11§54
Machynlleth 4	a	00 24			05 45			07 44				08 03	08 48	09 57			10 03		11§57	12§01			12§03
	d				05 47							08 07					10 07						12§07
Caersws	d				06 15							08 37					10 37						12§37
Newtown (Powys)	d				06 25							08 46					10 46						12§46
Welshpool	d				06 41							09 01					11 01						13§01
Chester	d			05 15		05 45	06 20			07 22	08 22				09 30	10 22					11 22	12 22	
Wrexham General	a			05 31		06 03	06 38			07 38	08 38				09 46	10 38					11 38	12 38	
	d		05 10	05 31			06 38		07 23	07 44	08 38				09 46	10 38		11 27			11 45	12 40	
Ruabon	d			05 38			06 45		07 31	07 51	08 45				09 53	10 45					11 53	12 47	
Chirk	d			05 44			06 51		07 38	07 57	08 51				09 59	10 51		11 39			11 59	12 53	
Gobowen	d		05 25	05 50			06 57		07 43	08 03	08 57				10 05	10 57		11 44			12 05	12 59	
Shrewsbury	a		05 50	06 10	07 11		07 17		08 05	08 23	09 17	09 25			10 27	11 17	11 25	12 05			12 27	13 19	13§25
Cardiff Central 7	a			08 17			09 22				11 14					13 20						15 20	
Shrewsbury	d		05 52		07 31				08 07	08 31		09 31			10 32		11 31	12 07			12 31		13§31
Wellington (Shropshire)	d				07 45				08 21	08 45		09 45			10 46		11 45	12 21			12 45		13§45
Telford Central	d		06 09		07 51				08 27	08 51		09 51			10 52		11 51	12 27			12 51		13§51
Cosford	d		06 17						08 36									12 36					
Wolverhampton 7	a				08 08				08s47	09 08		10 08			11 09		12 08	12s47			13 08		14§08
Smethwick Galton Bridge	a				08 20					09 21		10 20			11 20		12 20				13 20		14§20
Tame Bridge Parkway	d		06 41						09 02									13 02					
Birmingham New Street 12	a				08 27					09 27		10 26			11 26		12 26				13 27		14§26
Birmingham International ✈	a				08 50					09 50		10 50			11 50		12 50				13 51		14§50
Leamington Spa 8	a		07 29						09 45									13 45					
Banbury	a		07 47						10 04									14 04					
London Marylebone 10 ⊖	a		08 57						11 15									15 15					

A from 6 September

B until 3 September

For connections to Crewe and Manchester Piccadilly please refer to Table 131

For connections to London Euston please refer to Table 66

Pwllheli, Barmouth, Aberystwyth and Chester - Shrewsbury and Birmingham

		AW	AW	AW	AW	AW		AW	AW	WS	AW	AW	AW	AW	AW	AW		AW	AW	AW	AW	AW	AW	AW	VT
		◇ A	◇ A	◇ B	◇	◇		◇	◇	◇1	◇	◇	◇	◇ A	B	◇		◇	◇ B	◇ A	A	B	◇	◇	◇1
Pwllheli	d		11§38	11§38					13 42					15§34	15§34						17§38	17§38			
Abererch	d		11x41	11x41					13x45					15x37	15x37						17x41	17x41			
Penychain	d		11x44	11x44					13x48					15x40	15x40						17x44	17x44			
Criccieth	d		11§52	11§52					13 56					15§48	15§48						17§52	17§52			
Porthmadog	a		12§00	12§00					14 04					15§56	15§56						18§00	18§00			
	d		12§02	12§02					14 06					15§58	15§58						18§02	18§02			
Minffordd	d		12§06	12§06					14 10					16§02	16§02						18§06	18§06			
Penrhyndeudraeth	d		12§10	12§10					14 14					16§06	16§06						18§10	18§10			
Llandecwyn	d		12x12	12x12					14x16					16x08	16x08						18x12	18x12			
Talsarnau	d		12x14	12x14					14x18					16x10	16x10						18x14	18x14			
Tygwyn	d		12x17	12x17					14x21					16x13	16x13						18x17	18x17			
Harlech	a		12§22	12§22					14 26					16§18	16§18						18§22	18§22			
	d		12§25	12§29					14 30					16§23	16§23						18§24	18§27			
Llandanwg	d		12x29	12x33					14x34					16x28	16x28						18x29	18x32			
Pensarn	d		12x30	12x34					14x35					16x29	16x29						18x31	18x34			
Llanbedr	d		12x33	12x37					14x38					16x31	16x31						18x32	18x35			
Dyffryn Ardudwy	d		12x37	12x41					14x42					16x35	16x35						18x36	18x39			
Talybont	d		12x40	12x44					14x45					16x38	16x38						18x39	18x42			
Llanaber	d		12x44	12x48					14x49					16x43	16x43						18x44	18x47			
Barmouth	a		12§49	12§53					14 54					16§48	16§48						18§49	18§52			
	d		12§53	12§56					14 57					16§53	16§53						18§51	18§54			
Morfa Mawddach	d		12x57	13x00					15x01					16x57	16x57						18x55	18x58			
Fairbourne	d		13§01	13§04					15 05					17§01	17§01						18§59	19§02			
Llwyngwril	d		13x07	13x10					15x11					17x07	17x07						19x05	19x08			
Tonfanau	d		13x14	13x17					15x18					17x14	17x14						19x12	19x15			
Tywyn	a		13§18	13§21					15 22					17§18	17§19						19§17	19§20			
	d		13§24	13§24					15 24					17§28	17§32						19§27	19§27			
Aberdovey	d		13§30	13§30					15 30					17§34	17§38						19§33	19§33			
Penhelig	d		13x32	13x32					15x32					17x36	17x41						19x36	19x36			
Aberystwyth	d	11§30						13 30					15 30						17§30	17§30				19 30	
Borth	d	11§43						13 43					15 43						17§43	17§43				19 43	
Dovey Junction 4	d	11§54	13§44	13§44				13 54	15 44				15 54	17§48	17§52				17§54	17§54	19§48	19§48		19 54	
Machynlleth 4	a	12§03	13§53	13§53				14 03	15 51				16 03	17§58	18§01				18§03	18§03	19§57	19§57		20 03	
	d	12§07						14 07					16 07						18§07	18§07				20 07	
Caersws	d	12§37						14 37					16 37						18§37	18§37				20 40	
Newtown (Powys)	d	12§46						14 46					16 46						18§46	18§46				20 49	
Welshpool	d	13§01						15 01					17 01						19§01	19§01				21 04	
Chester	d				13 22	14 22					15 22	16 22				17 22		18 20					19 27		20 22
Wrexham General	a				13 38	14 38					15 38	16 38				17 38		18 36					19 43		20 38
	d				13 44	14 38				15 25	15 44	16 38				17 44		18 36					19 43		
Ruabon	d				13 51	14 45					15 51	16 45				17 51		18 43					19 50		
Chirk	d				13 57	14 51				15 38	15 58	16 51				17 57		18 49					19 56		
Gobowen	d				14 03	14 57				15 43	16 03	16 57				18 03		18 55					20 02		
Shrewsbury	a	13§25			14 27	15 17		15 25		16 05	16 28	17 17	17 25			18 24		19 15	19§25	19§25			20 25	21 28	
Cardiff Central 7	a					17 17						19 21						21 19							
Shrewsbury	d	13§31			14 31			15 31		16 07	16 33		17 31			18 31			19§33	19§33				21 33	
Wellington (Shropshire)	d	13§45			14 45			15 45		16 21	16 47		17 45			18 45			19§47	19§47				21 47	
Telford Central	d	13§51			14 51			15 51		16 27	16 53		17 51			18 51			19§53	19§53				21 53	
Cosford	d									16 36															
Wolverhampton 7	a	14§08			15 08			16 08		16s47	17 10		18 08			19 08			20§10	20§10				22 10	
Smethwick Galton Bridge	a	14§20			15 20			16 20			17 21		18 20			19 20			20§21	20§21				22 24	
Tame Bridge Parkway	d									17 02															
Birmingham New Street 12	a	14§26			15 26			16 26			17 27		18 26			19 26			20§27	20§27				22 30	
Birmingham International	a	14§50			15 50			16 50			17 50		18 50			19 50			20§50	20§50					
Leamington Spa 8	a									17 45															
Banbury	a									18 04															
London Marylebone 10	a									19 15															

A from 6 September

B until 3 September

For connections to Crewe and Manchester Piccadilly please refer to Table 131

For connections to London Euston please refer to Table 66

Pwllheli, Barmouth, Aberystwyth and Chester - Shrewsbury and Birmingham

		AW		AW	AW	AW	AW FO	AW	AW
				◇		◇		◇	
Pwllheli	d					20 00			
Abererch	d					20x03			
Penychain	d					20x06			
Criccieth	d					20 14			
Porthmadog	a					20 22			
	d					20 24			
Minffordd	d					20 28			
Penrhyndeudraeth	d					20 32			
Llandecwyn	d					20x34			
Talsarnau	d					20x36			
Tygwyn	d					20x39			
Harlech	a					20 44			
	d					20 46			
Llandanwg	d					20x50			
Pensarn	d					20x52			
Llanbedr	d					20x54			
Dyffryn Ardudwy	d					20x58			
Talybont	d					21x01			
Llanaber	d					21x06			
Barmouth	a					21 11			
	d					21 13	22 12		
Morfa Mawddach	d					21x17	22x16		
Fairbourne	d					21 21	22 20		
Llwyngwril	d					21x27	22x26		
Tonfanau	d					21x34	22x33		
Tywyn	a					21 39	22 37		
	d					21 46	22 39		
Aberdovey	d					21 52	22 45		
Penhelig	d					21x54	22x47		
Aberystwyth	d				21 36				23 53
Borth	d				21 49				00 06
Dovey Junction 4	d				22 00	22 06	22 59		00 17
Machynlleth 4	a				22 07	22 16	23 06		00 24
	d								
Caersws	d								
Newtown (Powys)	d								
Welshpool	d								
Chester	d			21 21				22 28	
Wrexham General	a			21 37				22 44	
	d	20 49		21 37				22 44	
Ruabon	d	20 57		21 44				22 51	
Chirk	d	21 03		21 50				22 57	
Gobowen	d	21 08		21 56				23 03	
Shrewsbury	a	21 28		22 16				23 23	
Cardiff Central 7	a								
Shrewsbury	d			22 18				23 26	
Wellington (Shropshire)	d			22 32				23 40	
Telford Central	d			22 38				23 47	
Cosford	d							23 57	
Wolverhampton 7	a			22 55				00 20	
Smethwick Galton Bridge	a								
Tame Bridge Parkway	d								
Birmingham New Street 12	a			23 26					
Birmingham International	a								
Leamington Spa 8	a								
Banbury	a								
London Marylebone 10	a								

For connections to Crewe and Manchester Piccadilly please refer to Table 131

For connections to London Euston please refer to Table 66

Table 75

Pwllheli, Barmouth, Aberystwyth and Chester - Shrewsbury and Birmingham

		AW	AW	AW	AW	AW	WS	AW	WS	AW	AW	AW	AW	AW	AW	AW	AW	WS	AW	AW	AW	AW	AW
			◇ [trolley]		◇ [trolley]	◇	◇■1 [restaurant]		◇■1 [restaurant]	◇ [trolley]	◇ [trolley]	◇	◇	◇ [trolley]	◇ [trolley]	◇ [trolley]	◇	◇■1 [restaurant]		◇ [trolley]	◇ [trolley]	◇	◇ [trolley]
Pwllheli	d											06 25	07 25				09 36					11 38	
Abererch	d											06x28	07x28				09x39					11x41	
Penychain	d											06x31	07x31				09x42					11x44	
Criccieth	d											06 39	07 39				09 50					11 52	
Porthmadog	a											06 47	07 47				09 58					12 00	
	d											06 52	07 49				10 00					12 02	
Minffordd	d											06 56	07 53				10 04					12 06	
Penrhyndeudraeth	d											07 00	07 57				10 08					12 10	
Llandecwyn	d											07x02	07x59				10x10					12x12	
Talsarnau	d											07x04	08x02				10x12					12x14	
Tygwyn	d											07x07	08x04				10x15					12x17	
Harlech	a											07 12	08 09				10 20					12 22	
	d											07 16	08 30				10 25					12 25	
Llandanwg	d											07x20	08x34				10x29					12x29	
Pensarn	d											07x21	08x35				10x30					12x30	
Llanbedr	d											07x24	08x38				10x33					12x33	
Dyffryn Ardudwy	d											07x28	08x42				10x37					12x37	
Talybont	d											07x31	08x45				10x40					12x40	
Llanaber	d											07x35	08x49				10x44					12x44	
Barmouth	a											07 40	08 54				10 49					12 49	
	d					06 46						07 49	09 00				10 52					12 53	
Morfa Mawddach	d					06x50						07x53	09x04				10x56					12x57	
Fairbourne	d					06 54						07 57	09 08				11 00					13 01	
Llwyngwril	d					07x00						08x03	09x14				11x06					13x07	
Tonfanau	d					07x07						08x10	09x21				11x13					13x14	
Tywyn	a					07 11						08 14	09 25				11 17					13 18	
	d					07 16						08 18	09 30				11 27					13 24	
Aberdovey	d					07 22						08 24	09 36				11 33					13 30	
Penhelig	d					07x25						08x26	09x38				11x36					13x32	
Aberystwyth	d	23p53	05 14								07 30					09 30					11 30		
Borth	d	00 06	05 27								07 43					09 43					11 43		
Dovey Junction ■4	d	00 17	05 38			07 37					07 54	08 38	09 50			09 54	11 48				11 54	13 44	
Machynlleth ■4	a	00 24	05 45			07 44					08 03	08 48	09 57			10 03	11 57				12 03	13 53	
	d		05 47								08 07					10 07					12 07		
Caersws	d		06 15								08 37					10 37					12 37		
Newtown (Powys)	d		06 25								08 46					10 46					12 46		
Welshpool	d		06 41								09 01					11 01					13 01		
Chester	d			05 37	06 12			07 22		08 22				09 30	10 22				11 22	12 22			13 22
Wrexham General	a			05 55	06 28			07 38		08 38				09 46	10 38				11 38	12 38			13 38
	d				06 38		07 23	07 44	08 17	08 38				09 46	10 38			11 23	11 44	12 38			13 44
Ruabon	d				06 45		07 31	07 51	08 25	08 45				09 53	10 45			11 31	11 51	12 45			13 51
Chirk	d				06 51		07 38	07 57	08 32	08 51				09 59	10 51			11 38	11 57	12 51			13 57
Gobowen	d				06 57		07 43	08 03	08 37	08 57				10 05	10 57			11 43	12 03	12 57			14 03
Shrewsbury	a		07 11		07 17		08 06	08 23	09 00	09 17	09 25			10 27	11 17	11 25		12 06	12 27	13 17	13 25		14 27
Cardiff Central ■7	a				09 22					11 20					13 20					15 21			
Shrewsbury	d		07 31				08 07	08 31	09 07		09 31			10 31		11 31		12 07	12 31		13 31		14 31
Wellington (Shropshire)	d		07 45				08 21	08 45	09 21		09 45			10 45		11 45		12 21	12 45		13 45		14 45
Telford Central	d		07 51				08 27	08 51	09 27		09 51			10 51		11 51		12 27	12 51		13 51		14 51
Cosford	d						08 36		09 35									12 36					
Wolverhampton ■7	a		08 08				08s47	09 08	09s48		10 08			11 08		12 08		12s47	13 08		14 08		15 08
Smethwick Galton Bridge	a		08 20					09 22			10 20			11 21		12 20			13 20		14 20		15 20
Tame Bridge Parkway	d						09 01		10 02									13 01					
Birmingham New Street ■12	a		08 27					09 28			10 26			11 27		12 26			13 26		14 26		15 26
Birmingham International	a		08 51					09 51			10 50			11 51		12 50			13 51		14 50		15 50
Leamington Spa ■8	a						09 49		10 49									13 49					
Banbury	a						10 07		11 07									14 07					
London Marylebone ■10	a						11 15		12 15									15 15					

For connections to Crewe and Manchester Piccadilly please refer to Table 131

For connections to London Euston please refer to Table 66

Table 75

Pwllheli, Barmouth, Aberystwyth and Chester - Shrewsbury and Birmingham

		WS	AW	AW	AW	AW	AW	AW	AW	WS	AW	AW	AW	AW	AW	AW	AW	AW	AW	AW	AW	AW
		◇■1 [restaurant]	■ [trolley]	◇ [trolley]	◇	◇ [trolley]	◇ [trolley]	◇ [trolley]	◇	◇■1 [restaurant]	◇ [trolley]	◇ [trolley]	◇ [trolley]	◇	◇ [trolley]		◇ A	◇		◇	◇	
Pwllheli	d				13 42				15 34					17 38						20 00		
Abererch	d				13x45				15x37					17x41						20x03		
Penychain	d				13x48				15x40					17x44						20x06		
Criccieth	d				13 56				15 48					17 52						20 14		
Porthmadog	a				14 04				15 56					18 00						20 22		
	d				14 06				15 58					18 02						20 24		
Minffordd	d				14 10				16 02					18 06						20 28		
Penrhyndeudraeth	d				14 14				16 06					18 10						20 32		
Llandecwyn	d				14x16				16x08					18x12						20x34		
Talsarnau	d				14x18				16x10					18x14						20x36		
Tygwyn	d				14x21				16x13					18x17						20x39		
Harlech	a				14 26				16 18					18 22						20 44		
	d				14 30				16 23					18 24						20 46		
Llandanwg	d				14x34				16x28					18x29						20x50		
Pensarn	d				14x35				16x29					18x31						20x52		
Llanbedr	d				14x38				16x31					18x32						20x54		
Dyffryn Ardudwy	d				14x42				16x35					18x36						20x58		
Talybont	d				14x45				16x38					18x39						21x01		
Llanaber	d				14x49				16x43					18x44						21x06		
Barmouth	a				14 54				16 48					18 49						21 11		
	d				14 57				16 53					18 51						21 13		
Morfa Mawddach	d				15x01				16x57					18x55						21x17		
Fairbourne	d				15 05				17 01					18 59						21 21		
Llwyngwril	d				15x11				17x07					19x05						21x27		
Tonfanau	d				15x18				17x14					19x12						21x34		
Tywyn	a				15 22				17 18					19 17						21 39		
	d				15 24				17 28					19 27						21 46		
Aberdovey	d				15 30				17 34					19 33						21 52		
Penhelig	d				15x32				17x36					19x36						21x54		
Aberystwyth	d			13 30				15 30					17 30				19 30		21 36			23 46
Borth	d			13 43				15 43					17 43				19 43		21 49			23 59
Dovey Junction ■4	d			13 54	15 44			15 54	17 48				17 54	19 48			19 54		22 00	22 06		00 10
Machynlleth ■4	a			14 03	15 51			16 03	17 58				18 03	19 57			20 03		22 07	22 16		00 17
	d			14 07				16 07					18 07				20 07					
Caersws	d			14 37				16 37					18 37				20 38					
Newtown (Powys)	d			14 46				16 46					18 46				20 48					
Welshpool	d			15 01				17 01					19 01				21 04					
Chester	d		14 22			15 22	16 22				17 22	18 22			19 27	20 27		21 22			22 28	
Wrexham General	a		14 38			15 38	16 38				17 38	18 38			19 43	20 43		21 38			22 44	
	d	14 18	14 38			15 44	16 38			17 23	17 44	18 38			19 43	20 43		21 39			22 44	
Ruabon	d	14 26	14 45			15 51	16 45			17 31	17 51	18 45			19 50	20 51		21 47			22 51	
Chirk	d	14 32	14 51			15 57	16 51			17 38	17 57	18 52			19 56	20 57		21 54			22 57	
Gobowen	d	14 37	14 57			16 03	16 57			17 43	18 03	18 57			20 02	21 02		22 01			23 03	
Shrewsbury	a	15 00	15 17	15 25		16 27	17 17	17 25		18 06	18 23	19 18	19 25		20 25	21 22	21 28	22 23			23 23	
Cardiff Central ■7	a		17 17				19 21					21 21										
Shrewsbury	d	15 07		15 31		16 31		17 31		18 07	18 31		19 33				21 33	22 31			23 26	
Wellington (Shropshire)	d	15 21		15 45		16 45		17 45		18 21	18 45		19 47				21 47	22 45			23 40	
Telford Central	d	15 27		15 51		16 51		17 51		18 27	18 51		19 53				21 53	22 51			23 47	
Cosford	d	15 36								18 36											23 57	
Wolverhampton ■7	a	15s47		16 08		17 08		18 08		18s49	19 08		20 10				22 10	23 08			00 18	
Smethwick Galton Bridge	a			16 20		17 20		18 20			19 20		20 21				22 21					
Tame Bridge Parkway	d	16 01								19 02												
Birmingham New Street ■12	a			16 26		17 26		18 26			19 26		20 27				22 32	23 29				
Birmingham International	a			16 50		17 50		18 50			19 50		20 50									
Leamington Spa ■8	a	16 49								19 46												
Banbury	a	17 07								20 05												
London Marylebone ■10	a	18 15								21 15												

A

For connections to Crewe and Manchester Piccadilly please refer to Table 131

For connections to London Euston please refer to Table 66

Table 75

Sundays
until 05 September

Pwllheli, Barmouth, Aberystwyth and Chester - Shrewsbury and Birmingham

		AW ◇ A	AW A	AW	AW ◇	AW ◇ ⊥	WS ◇1 C ⊡	WS ◇1 D ⊡	AW ◇ ⊥	AW D	AW C	AW ◇ ⊥	AW ◇	WS ◇1 D ⊡	WS ◇1 C ⊡	AW ◇ ⊥	AW ◇ ⊥	AW ◇	AW ◇ ⊥	AW ◇ ⊥	WS ◇1 D ⊡	WS ◇1 C ⊡	AW ◇
Pwllheli	d												11 28					13 48					
Abererch	d												11x32					13x51					
Penychain	d												11x35					13x54					
Criccieth	d												11 41					14 02					
Porthmadog	a												11 51					14 10					
	d												11 57					14 12					
Minffordd	d												12 02					14 16					
Penrhyndeudraeth	d												12 06					14 20					
Llandecwyn	d												12x09					14x22					
Talsarnau	d												12x11					14x24					
Tygwyn	d												12x13					14x27					
Harlech	a												12 18					14 32					
	d												12 19					14 34					
Llandanwg	d												12x25					14x38					
Pensarn	d												12x28					14x40					
Llanbedr	d												12x30					14x42					
Dyffryn Ardudwy	d												12x34					14x46					
Talybont	d												12x37					14x49					
Llanaber	d												12x42					14x54					
Barmouth	a												12 46					14 59					
	d												12 48					15 01					
Morfa Mawddach	d												12x53					15x05					
Fairbourne	d												12 56					15 09					
Llwyngwril	d												13x04					15x15					
Tonfanau	d												13x11					15x22					
Tywyn	a												13 16					15 27					
	d												13 16					15 28					
Aberdovey	d												13 22					15 35					
Penhelig	d												13x26					15x37					
Aberystwyth	d		23p46			09 30						11 30					13 30			15 30			
Borth	d		23p59			09 43						11 43					13 43			15 43			
Dovey Junction 4	d		00⌇10			09 54						11 54	13 36				13 54	15 49		15 54			
Machynlleth 4	a		00⌇17			10 03						12 03	13 45				14 03	15 56		16 03			
	d					10 07						12 07					14 07			16 07			
Caersws	d					10 35						12 37					14 37			16 37			
Newtown (Powys)	d					10 45						12 46					14 46			16 46			
Welshpool	d					11 01						13 01					15 01			17 01			
Chester	d	22p28		08 08	09 11				11 22	12⌇21	12⌇21					13 22			15 31				17 22
Wrexham General	a	22p44		08 26	09 27				11 38	12⌇38	12⌇38					13 38			15 47				17 38
	d	22p44			09 28		10⌇44	10⌇47	11 39	12⌇38	12⌇38			13⌇11	13⌇11	13 39			15 48		17⌇02	17⌇02	17 39
Ruabon	d	22p51			09 35		10⌇52	10⌇55	11 46	12⌇45	12⌇45			13⌇19	13⌇19	13 46			15 55		17⌇10	17⌇10	17 46
Chirk	d	22p57			09 41		10⌇59	11⌇02	11 52	12⌇52	12⌇52			13⌇26	13⌇26	13 52			16 01		17⌇17	17⌇17	17 52
Gobowen	d	23p03			09 47		11⌇04	11⌇07	11 58	12⌇57	12⌇57			13⌇31	13⌇31	13 58			16 07		17⌇22	17⌇22	17 58
Shrewsbury	a	23p23			10 07	11 25	11⌇27	11⌇30	12 18	13⌇18	13⌇18	13 25		13⌇54	13⌇54	14 18	15 25		16 27	17 27	17⌇45	17⌇45	18 18
Cardiff Central 7	a									15⌇28	15⌇37												
Shrewsbury	d	23p26			10 09	11 40	11⌇28	11⌇31	12 20			13 31		13⌇55	14⌇09	14 20	15 33		16 29	17 33	17⌇55	17⌇55	18 20
Wellington (Shropshire)	d	23p40			10 23	11 54	11⌇41	11⌇44	12 34			13 45		14⌇09	14⌇23	14 34	15 47		16 43	17 47	18⌇09	18⌇09	18 34
Telford Central	d	23p47			10 30	12 00	11⌇47	11⌇50	12 41			13 51		14⌇15	14⌇29	14 41	15 53		16 50	17 53	18⌇15	18⌇15	18 41
Cosford	d	23p57			10 40		11⌇56	11⌇59	12 51					14⌇24	14⌇38	14 51			17 00		18⌇24	18⌇24	18 51
Wolverhampton 7	a	00⌇18			10 57	12 17	12s07	12s10	13 08			14 08		14s35	14s49	15 08	16 10		17 17	18 10	18s35	18s35	19 08
Smethwick Galton Bridge	a						12⌇18								15⌇03							19⌇03	
Tame Bridge Parkway	d							12⌇33						14⌇51							18⌇51		
Birmingham New Street 12	a				11 13	12 33	12⌇26	12⌇55	13 24			14 24		15⌇10	15⌇11	15 24	16 26		17 35	18 28	19⌇10	19⌇11	19 24
Birmingham International	a				11 32	12 56			13 54			14 56				15 57	16 56		17 56	18 56			19 56
Leamington Spa 8	a						12⌇56	13⌇33						15⌇42	15⌇42						19⌇42	19⌇42	
Banbury	a						13⌇14	13⌇51						16⌇03	16⌇03						20⌇01	20⌇01	
London Marylebone 10	a						14⌇37	15⌇14						17⌇10	17⌇10						21⌇06	21⌇06	

A not 23 May
C from 18 July until 5 September
D until 11 July

For connections to Crewe and Manchester Piccadilly please refer to Table 131

For connections to London Euston please refer to Table 66

Table 75

Sundays
until 05 September

Pwllheli, Barmouth, Aberystwyth and Chester - Shrewsbury and Birmingham

		AW ■ A ⊥	AW ■ B ⊥	AW ◇ ⊥	AW ◇	AW ◇	AW ◇ ⊥	AW ◇	AW	AW	AW
Pwllheli	d				17 36						
Abererch	d				17x40						
Penychain	d				17x44						
Criccieth	d				17 50						
Porthmadog	a				17 59						
	d				18 00						
Minffordd	d				18 05						
Penrhyndeudraeth	d				18 09						
Llandecwyn	d				18x12						
Talsarnau	d				18x14						
Tygwyn	d				18x16						
Harlech	a				18 21						
	d				18 22						
Llandanwg	d				18x28						
Pensarn	d				18x30						
Llanbedr	d				18x32						
Dyffryn Ardudwy	d				18x36						
Talybont	d				18x39						
Llanaber	d				18x45						
Barmouth	a				18 48						
	d				18 50						
Morfa Mawddach	d				18x55						
Fairbourne	d				18 57						
Llwyngwril	d				19x05						
Tonfanau	d				19x12						
Tywyn	a				19 17						
	d				19 22						
Aberdovey	d				19 28						
Penhelig	d				19x32						
Aberystwyth	d			17 30			19 30		21 30		23 30
Borth	d			17 43			19 43		21 43		23 43
Dovey Junction 4	d			17 54	19 42		19 54		21 54		23 54
Machynlleth 4	a			18 03	19 55		20 03		22 04		00 04
	d			18 07			20 07				
Caersws	d			18 37			20 37				
Newtown (Powys)	d			18 46			20 46				
Welshpool	d			19 01			21 01				
Chester	d	18⌇24	18⌇24			19 26		21 24		22 04	
Wrexham General	a	18⌇40	18⌇40			19 42		21 41		22 22	
	d	18⌇41	18⌇41			19 42		21 43			
Ruabon	d	18⌇47	18⌇48			19 49		21 50			
Chirk	d	18⌇54	18⌇54			19 55		21 56			
Gobowen	d	18⌇59	19⌇00			20 01		22 01			
Shrewsbury	a	19⌇20	19⌇20	19 25		20 21	21 25	22 22			
Cardiff Central 7	a	21⌇36	21⌇38								
Shrewsbury	d			19 31		20 23	21 31	22 23			
Wellington (Shropshire)	d			19 45		20 37	21 45	22 37			
Telford Central	d			19 51		20 44	21 51	22 45			
Cosford	d					20 54		22 55			
Wolverhampton 7	a			20 08		21 11	22 08	23 17			
Smethwick Galton Bridge	a										
Tame Bridge Parkway	d										
Birmingham New Street 12	a			20 24		21 29	22 28				
Birmingham International	a			20 58		21 56	22 55				
Leamington Spa 8	a										
Banbury	a										
London Marylebone 10	a										

A until 11 July
B from 18 July until 5 September

For connections to Crewe and Manchester Piccadilly please refer to Table 131

For connections to London Euston please refer to Table 66

Table 75

Sundays
from 12 September

Pwllheli, Barmouth, Aberystwyth and Chester - Shrewsbury and Birmingham

		AW	AW	AW	AW	AW	AW	AW	AW	AW		AW	AW	AW	AW	AW	AW	AW	AW	AW		AW	AW	AW	AW
		◇			◇	◇ H	◇ H		◇ H	◇ H		◇ H	◇	◇ H	◇	◇	■ H	◇ H	◇	◇		◇			
Pwllheli	d												13 48												
Abererch	d												13x51												
Penychain	d												13x54												
Criccieth	d												14 02												
Porthmadog	a												14 10												
	d												14 12												
Minffordd	d												14 16												
Penrhyndeudraeth	d												14 20												
Llandecwyn	d												14x22												
Talsarnau	d												14x24												
Tygwyn	d												14x27												
Harlech	a												14 32												
	d												14 34												
Llandanwg	d												14x38												
Pensarn	d												14x40												
Llanbedr	d												14x42												
Dyffryn Ardudwy	d												14x46												
Talybont	d												14x49												
Llanaber	d												14x54												
Barmouth	a												14 59												
	d												15 01												
Morfa Mawddach	d												15x05												
Fairbourne	d												15 09												
Llwyngwril	d												15x15												
Tonfanau	d												15x22												
Tywyn	a												15 27												
	d												15 28												
Aberdovey	d												15 35												
Penhelig	d												15x37												
Aberystwyth	d		23p46			09 30			11 30			13 30			15 30			17 30		19 30			21 30		23 30
Borth	d		23p59			09 43			11 43			13 43			15 43			17 43		19 43			21 43		23 43
Dovey Junction 4	d		00 10			09 54			11 54			13 54	15 49		15 54			17 54		19 54			21 54		23 54
Machynlleth 4	a		00 17			10 03			12 03			14 03	15 56		16 03			18 03		20 03			22 04		00 04
	d					10 07			12 07			14 07			16 07			18 07		20 08					
Caersws	d					10 35			12 37			14 37			16 37			18 37		20 38					
Newtown (Powys)	d					10 45			12 46			14 46			16 46			18 46		20 47					
Welshpool	d					11 01			13 01			15 01			17 01			19 01		21 02					
Chester	d	22p28		08 08	09 11		11 22	12 21		13 22				15 31		17 22	18 24		19 25			21 24		22 04	
Wrexham General	a	22p44		08 26	09 27		11 38	12 38		13 38				15 47		17 38	18 40		19 41			21 41		22 22	
	d	22p44			09 27		11 39	12 38		13 39				15 48		17 39	18 41		19 42			21 43			
Ruabon	d	22p51			09 34		11 46	12 45		13 46				15 55		17 46	18 48		19 49			21 50			
Chirk	d	22p57			09 40		11 52	12 52		13 52				16 01		17 52	18 54		19 55			21 56			
Gobowen	d	23p03			09 46		11 58	12 57		13 58				16 07		17 58	19 00		20 01			22 02			
Shrewsbury	a	23p23			10 06	11 25	12 18	13 18	13 25	14 18		15 25		16 27	17 33	18 18	19 20	19 26	20 21	21 26		22 22			
Cardiff Central 7	a							15 27									21 36								
Shrewsbury	d	23p26																							
Wellington (Shropshire)	d	23p40																							
Telford Central	d	23p47																							
Cosford	d	23p57																							
Wolverhampton 7	a	00 18																							
Smethwick Galton Bridge	a																								
Tame Bridge Parkway	d																								
Birmingham New Street 12	a																								
Birmingham International ✈	a																								
Leamington Spa 8	a																								
Banbury	a																								
London Marylebone 10 ⊖	a																								

Network Diagram for Tables 78, 79, 84, 85, 86

DM-22/08
Design BAJS

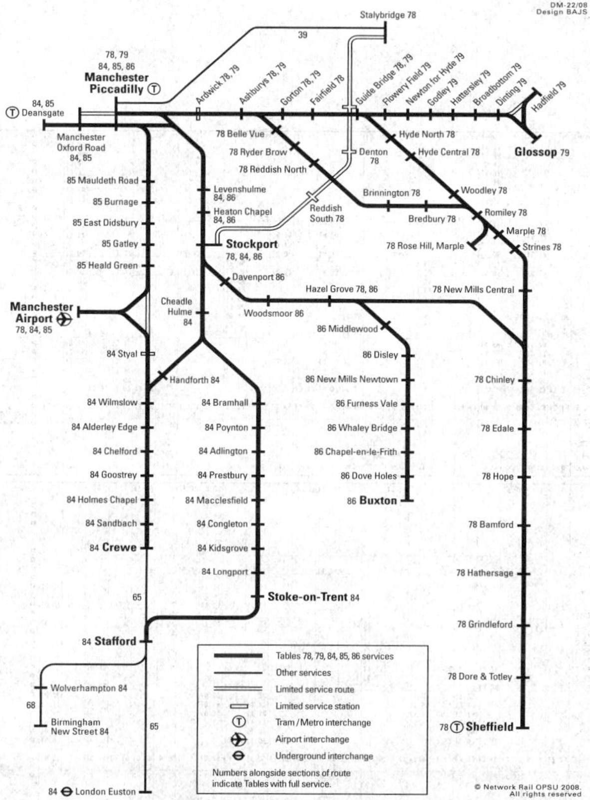

Manchester Airport and Manchester - Romiley, Marple, Chinley and Sheffield

	TP MO ◇1	TP MX ◇1	TP ◇1	NT	NT	NT	NT	NT	NT	NT	NT	NT	NT A	NT B	NT	TP ◇1	NT A	NT B	NT	NT	EM ◇	NT
Manchester Airport 85 ✈ d	22p55	23p52	05 15													06 55						
Manchester Piccadilly a	23p09	00 09	05 33													07 13						
d	23p20	00 15	05 44	05 50	06 16	06 24	06 30		06 41	06 46	06 57	07 03	07 06	07 06	07 18	07 20			07 23	07 39	07 42	07 48
Ardwick d																						
Ashburys d					06 20				06 45	06 50		07 07	07 10	07 10	07 22				07 27			07 52
Belle Vue d									06 47				07 12	07 12					07 29			
Ryder Brow d									06 49				07 14	07 14					07 31			
Reddish North d									06 52				07 17	07 17					07 34			
Brinnington d									06 55				07 20	07 20					07 37			
Bredbury d									06 58				07 23	07 23					07 40			
Gorton d					06 22					06 52		07 09			07 24							07 54
Fairfield d						06 31														07 46		
Guide Bridge a					06 26	06 34				06 56		07 13			07 28					07 49		07 58
d						06 34														07 49		
Hyde North d						06 38														07 53		
Hyde Central d						06 40														07 55		
Woodley d						06 43		←												07 58		
Romiley d						06 47	06 44	06 47	07 02		07 09		07 26	07 26					07 43	08 02		
Rose Hill Marple a						→		06 53												08 08		
Marple d							06 47		07 05		07 13		07 30	07 30					07a48			
Strines d																						
New Mills Central a							06 55		07 12		07 20		07 35	07 35								
d													07 39	07 39								
Stockport 86 d	23p28		05 52	06 00												07 28					07 54	
Hazel Grove 86 d				06 07																		
Chinley d				06 18									07 47	07 47								
Edale d				06 26									07 55	07 55								
Hope (Derbyshire) d				06 32									08 01	08 01								
Bamford d				06 35									08 04	08 04								
Hathersage d				06 39									08 10	08 09								
Grindleford d				06 42									08 11	08 11			←	←				
Dore & Totley d				06 51									08 22	08 22		08 03	08 22	08 22			08 28	
Sheffield 7 a	00 15	01 06	06 49	07 01									→	→		08 10	08 32	08 32			08 34	

	NT	NT	NT	NT	NT	NT	TP ◇1	NT	NT	EM ◇	NT	NT	NT	NT	NT	NT	NT	TP ◇1	NT	EM ◇	NT	NT
Manchester Airport 85 ✈ d							07 54											08 55				
Manchester Piccadilly a							08 13											09 13				
d	07 52	08 04	08 07	08 12	08 15		08 20	08 29	08 37	08 43	08 45	08 48	09 00	09 05		09 15	09 18	09 20	09 36	09 43	09 45	09 48
Ardwick d																						
Ashburys d		08 08	08 11					08 33				08 52		09 09		09 19	09 23					09 52
Belle Vue d		08 10															09 26					
Ryder Brow d		08 12															09 28					
Reddish North d		08 15									08 52			09 14							09 52	
Brinnington d		08 18									08 56			09 17							09 56	
Bredbury d		08 21									08 59			09 20							09 59	
Gorton d			08 13					08 35				08 54				09 21						09 54
Fairfield d				08 20									09 07						09 43			
Guide Bridge a			08 17	08 23				08 39				08 58	09 10			09 25			09 46			09 58
d				08 23									09 11						09 46			
Hyde North d				08 28									09 17						09 50			
Hyde Central d				08 30									09 20						09 52			
Woodley d				08 33		←							09 23		←				09 55			
Romiley d	08 05	08 24		08 37	08 29	08 37					09 02		09 26	09 23	09 26		09 35		09 59		10 02	
Rose Hill Marple a		08 30		→		08 45							→		09 33				10 05			
Marple d	08 08				08a33				08 52		09 06			09a28			09a40				10 06	
Strines d									08 56												10 10	
New Mills Central a	08 15								09 01		09 11										10 15	
d											09 11											
Stockport 86 d							08 28			08 54								09 28		09 54		
Hazel Grove 86 d																						
Chinley d											09 19											
Edale d											09 28											
Hope (Derbyshire) d											09 34											
Bamford d											09 37											
Hathersage d											09 40											
Grindleford d											09 44											
Dore & Totley d											09 53											
Sheffield 7 a							09 08			09 35	10 03							10 08		10 33		

A FO from 2 July until 3 September

B Does not apply Fridays 2 July to 3 September

Table 78

Mondays to Fridays
until 03 September

Manchester Airport and Manchester - Romiley, Marple, Chinley and Sheffield

	NT	NT	NT	TP ◇1	NT	EM ◇	NT	NT	NT	NT	TP ◇1	NT	NT	EM ◇	NT	NT	NT	NT	TP ◇1	NT	NT
Manchester Airport 85 ✈ d				09 55							10 55								11 55		
Manchester Piccadilly a				10 13							11 13								12 13		
d	10 03	10 15	10 18	10 20	10 36	10 43	10 45	10 48	11 03	11 18	11 20	11 23	11 36	11 43	11 45	11 48	12 03	12 18	12 20	12 23	12 36
Ardwick d																					
Ashburys d	10 07	10 19						10 52	11 07	11 22						11 52	12 07	12 22			
Belle Vue d	10 09								11 09								12 09				
Ryder Brow d	10 11								11 11								12 11				
Reddish North d	10 14						10 52		11 14						11 52		12 14				
Brinnington d	10 17						10 56		11 17						11 56		12 17				
Bredbury d	10 20						10 59		11 20						11 59		12 20				
Gorton d		10 21						10 54		11 24						11 54		12 24			
Fairfield d					10 43								11 43								12 43
Guide Bridge a		10 25			10 46			10 58		11 28			11 46			11 58		12 28			12 46
d					10 46								11 46								12 46
Hyde North d					10 50								11 50								12 50
Hyde Central d					10 52								11 52								12 52
Woodley d					10 55								11 55								12 55
Romiley d	10 23		10 30		10 59		11 02		11 23			11 37	11 59		12 02		12 23			12 37	12 59
Rose Hill Marple a					11 05								12 05								13 05
Marple d	10 27		10a35				11 06		11 27			11a43			12 06		12 27			12a43	
Strines d															12 10						
New Mills Central a	10 34						11 11		11 34						12 15		12 34				
d							11 11														
Stockport 86 d				10 28		10 54					11 28			11 54					12 28		
Hazel Grove 86 d																					
Chinley d							11 19														
Edale d							11 28														
Hope (Derbyshire) d							11 34														
Bamford d							11 37														
Hathersage d							11 40														
Grindleford d							11 44														
Dore & Totley d							11 53														
Sheffield 7 a				11 08		11 34	12 03				12 08			12 34					13 08		

	EM ◇	NT	NT	NT	NT	TP ◇1	NT	NT	EM ◇	NT	NT	NT	NT	TP ◇1	NT	NT	EM ◇	NT	NT	NT	NT	TP ◇1
Manchester Airport 85 ✈ d						12 55								13 55								14 55
Manchester Piccadilly a						13 13								14 13								15 13
d	12 43	12 45	12 48	13 03	13 18	13 20	13 23	13 36	13 43	13 45	13 48	14 03	14 18	14 20	14 23	14 36	14 43	14 45	14 48	15 03	15 18	15 20
Ardwick d																						
Ashburys d			12 52	13 07	13 22						13 52	14 07	14 22						14 52	15 07	15 22	
Belle Vue d				13 09								14 09								15 09		
Ryder Brow d				13 11								14 11								15 11		
Reddish North d		12 52		13 14						13 52		14 14						14 52		15 14		
Brinnington d		12 56		13 17						13 56		14 17						14 56		15 17		
Bredbury d		12 59		13 20						13 59		14 20						14 59		15 20		
Gorton d			12 54		13 24						13 54		14 24						14 54		15 24	
Fairfield d								13 43								14 43						
Guide Bridge a			12 58		13 28			13 46			13 58		14 28			14 46			14 58		15 28	
d								13 46								14 46						
Hyde North d								13 50								14 50						
Hyde Central d								13 52								14 52						
Woodley d								13 55								14 55						
Romiley d		13 02		13 23			13 37	13 59		14 02		14 23			14 37	14 59		15 02		15 23		
Rose Hill Marple a								14 05								15 05						
Marple d		13 06		13 27			13a43			14 06		14 27			14a43			15 06		15 27		
Strines d										14 10												
New Mills Central a		13 11		13 34						14 15		14 34						15 11		15 34		
d		13 11																15 11				
Stockport 86 d	12 54					13 28			13 54					14 28			14 54					15 28
Hazel Grove 86 d																						
Chinley d		13 19																15 19				
Edale d		13 28																15 28				
Hope (Derbyshire) d		13 34																15 34				
Bamford d		13 37																15 37				
Hathersage d		13 40																15 40				
Grindleford d		13 44																15 44				
Dore & Totley d		13 53																15 53				
Sheffield 7 a	13 34	14 03				14 08			14 35					15 08			15 34	16 03				16 08

Table 78

Mondays to Fridays until 03 September

Manchester Airport and Manchester - Romiley, Marple, Chinley and Sheffield

		NT	NT	EM ◇	NT	NT	NT	NT	NT	TP ◇1	NT	NT	EM ◇	NT	NT	NT	NT	NT	NT	TP ◇1	NT	NT	NT
Manchester Airport 85 ✈	d									15 55										16 55			
Manchester Piccadilly 10	a									16 13										17 13			
	d	15 23	15 36	15 43	15 45	15 48	16 03	16 06	16 15	16 20	16 23	16 36	16 43	16 45	16 48	16 59	17 03	17 15	17 18	17 20		17 21	17 32
Ardwick	d																17 07						
Ashburys	d					15 52	16 07		16 19			16 40		16 49	16 52	17 03	17 09	17 19					17 36
Belle Vue	d						16 09							16 51			17 12						17 38
Ryder Brow	d						16 11							16 53			17 14						17 40
Reddish North	d				15 52		16 14				16 30			16 56			17 16						17 43
Brinnington	d				15 56		16 17				16 34			16 59			17 20						17 46
Bredbury	d				15 59		16 20				16 37			17 02			17 23		17 30				17 49
Gorton	d					15 54			16 21			16 42				17 05		17 21					
Fairfield	d		15 43					16 13							16 56								
Guide Bridge	a		15 46			15 58		16 16	16 25			16 46			16 59	17 10		17 25				17 30	
	d		15 46					16 16							16 59							17 30	
Hyde North	d		15 50					16 20							17 03							17 34	
Hyde Central	d		15 52					16 22							17 05							17 36	
Woodley	d		15 55					16 25							17 08							17 39	
Romiley	d	15 37	15 59		16 02		16 23	16 29			16 40			17 05	17 13		17 27		17 33			17 43	17 53
Rose Hill Marple	a		16 05					16 36							17 20							17 49	
Marple	d	15a43			16 06		16 27				16a44			17 09			17a31		17 37				17 57
Strines	d				16 10														17 41				18 01
New Mills Central	a				16 13		16 34							17 16					17 45				18 04
	d				16 13														17 45				
Stockport 86	d			15 54						16 28			16 54							17 28			
Hazel Grove 86	d																						
Chinley	d				16 21								17 09						17 51	17 43			
Edale	d				16 30														18 00				
Hope (Derbyshire)	d				16 36														18 06				
Bamford	d				16 39														18 09				
Hathersage	d				16 42														18 13				
Grindleford	d				16 46														18 16		←		
Dore & Totley	d				16 54								17 30						18 26	18 06	18 26		
Sheffield 7	a			16 34	17 03					17 08			17 37						→	18 15	18 36		

		NT	EM ◇	NT	NT	NT	NT	NT	TP ◇1	NT	NT	EM ◇	NT	NT	NT	NT	TP ◇1	NT	EM ◇	NT	NT	TP FO ◇1	TP FX ◇1	NT	EM ◇
Manchester Airport 85 ✈	d								17 55								18 55					19 55	19 55		
Manchester Piccadilly 10	a								18 13								19 13					20 13	20 13		
	d	17 37	17 43	17 48	17 59	18 03	18 06	18 15	18 20	18 22	18 36	18 43	18 45	18 48	19 00	19 18	19 18	19 23	19 43	19 45	19 48	20 20	20 20	20 36	20 43
Ardwick	d						18 09																		
Ashburys	d	17 41		17 52	18 03	18 07	18 11	18 19						18 52	19 04	19 22				19 49	19 52				
Belle Vue	d					18 09									19 06					19 51					
Ryder Brow	d					18 11									19 08					19 53					
Reddish North	d			17 57		18 14							18 52		19 11					19 56					
Brinnington	d			18 00		18 17							18 56		19 14					19 59					
Bredbury	d			18 04		18 20							18 59		19 17					20 02					
Gorton	d	17 43			18 05			18 21						18 54		19 24					19 54				
Fairfield	d						18 15				18 43													20 43	
Guide Bridge	a	17 47			18 09		18 18	18 25			18 46			18 58		19 28					19 58			20 46	
	d						18 18				18 46													20 46	
Hyde North	d						18 22				18 50													20 50	
Hyde Central	d						18 25				18 52													20 52	
Woodley	d						18 28				18 55													20 55	
Romiley	d			18 07		18 23	18 31			18 35	18 59		19 02		19 20			19 38		20 05				20 59	
Rose Hill Marple	a						18 37				19 05													21 05	
Marple	d			18 11		18a28				18 39			19 06		19a25			19a43		20 09					
Strines	d			18 15						18 43										20 13					
New Mills Central	a			18 19						18 48			19 11							20 18					
	d			18 19									19 11												
Stockport 86	d		17 54						18 28			18 54					19 26		19 54			20 28	20 28		20 54
Hazel Grove 86	d																								
Chinley	d		18 09	18a27									19 19												
Edale	d												19 28												
Hope (Derbyshire)	d												19 34												
Bamford	d												19 37												
Hathersage	d												19 40												
Grindleford	d												19 44												
Dore & Totley	d		18 34						19 04				19 53				20 02					21 04	21 04		
Sheffield 7	a		18 41						19 10			19 33	20 03				20 08		20 36			21 10	21 14		21 35

Table 78

Mondays to Fridays until 03 September

Manchester Airport and Manchester - Romiley, Marple, Chinley and Sheffield

		NT	NT	TP ◇1	NT	NT	TP ◇1	EM ◇	NT	NT	NT	NT	TP ◇1
Manchester Airport 85 ✈	d			20 47			21 47						23 52
Manchester Piccadilly 10	a			21 13			22 13						00 09
	d	20 45	20 48	21 20	21 45	21 48	22 20	22 28	22 45	22 48	23 24	23 27	00 15
Ardwick	d												
Ashburys	d		20 52		21 49	21 52			22 49	22 52	23 28	23 31	
Belle Vue	d				21 51				22 51		23 30		
Ryder Brow	d				21 53				22 53		23 32		
Reddish North	d	20 52			21 56				22 56		23 35		
Brinnington	d	20 56			21 59				22 59		23 38		
Bredbury	d	20 59			22 02				23 02		23 41		
Gorton	d		20 54			21 54				22 54		23 33	
Fairfield	d												
Guide Bridge	a		20 58			21 58				22 58		23 37	
	d												
Hyde North	d												
Hyde Central	d												
Woodley	d												
Romiley	d	21 02			22 05				23 05		23 44		
Rose Hill Marple	a												
Marple	d	21 06			22 09				23 09		23 48		
Strines	d				22 13				23 13		23 52		
New Mills Central	a	21 11			22 18				23 18		23 57		
	d	21 11											
Stockport 86	d			21 28			22 28	22 37					
Hazel Grove 86	d												
Chinley	d	21 19						22 53					
Edale	d	21 28						23 02					
Hope (Derbyshire)	d	21 34						23 08					
Bamford	d	21 37						23 11					
Hathersage	d	21 40						23 15					
Grindleford	d	21 44						23 19					
Dore & Totley	d	21 53						23 28					
Sheffield 7	a	22 03		22 08			23 13	23 35					01 06

Mondays to Fridays from 06 September

		TP MO ◇1	TP MX ◇1	TP ◇1	NT	NT	NT	NT	NT	NT	NT	NT	NT	NT	NT	TP ◇1	NT	NT	NT	EM ◇	NT	NT	NT
Manchester Airport 85 ✈	d	22p55	23p52	05 15												06 55							
Manchester Piccadilly 10	a	23p09	00 09	05 33												07 13							
	d	23p20	00 15	05 44	05 50	06 13	06 24	06 30		06 41	06 46	06 57	07 03	07 06	07 18	07 20		07 23	07 39	07 42	07 47	07 52	08 04
Ardwick	d																						
Ashburys	d					06 17				06 45			07 07	07 10	07 22			07 27					08 08
Belle Vue	d									06 47				07 12				07 29					08 10
Ryder Brow	d									06 49				07 14				07 31					08 12
Reddish North	d									06 52				07 17				07 34					08 15
Brinnington	d									06 55				07 20				07 37					08 18
Bredbury	d									06 58				07 23				07 40					08 21
Gorton	d					06 19							07 09		07 24								
Fairfield	d						06 31												07 46				
Guide Bridge	a					06 23	06 34				06 54		07 13		07 28				07 49		07 55		
	d						06 34												07 49				
Hyde North	d						06 38												07 53				
Hyde Central	d						06 40												07 55				
Woodley	d						06 43		←										07 58				
Romiley	d						06 47	06 44	06 47	07 02		07 09		07 26				07 43	08 02			08 05	08 24
Rose Hill Marple	a						→		06 53										08 08				08 30
Marple	d							06 47		07 05		07 13		07 30				07a48				08 08	
Strines	d																						
New Mills Central	a							06 55		07 12		07 20		07 35								08 15	
	d													07 39									
Stockport 86	d	23p28		05 52	06 00											07 28				07 54			
Hazel Grove 86	d				06 07																		
Chinley	d				06 18									07 47									
Edale	d				06 26									07 55									
Hope (Derbyshire)	d				06 32									08 01									
Bamford	d				06 35									08 04									
Hathersage	d				06 39									08 09									
Grindleford	d				06 42									08 11			←						
Dore & Totley	d				06 51									08 22		08 03	08 22			08 28			
Sheffield 7	a	00 15	01 06	06 49	07 01									→		08 10	08 32			08 34			

Manchester Airport and Manchester - Romiley, Marple, Chinley and Sheffield

		NT	NT	NT	NT	TP	NT	NT	EM	NT	NT	NT	NT	NT	NT	NT	TP	NT	EM	NT	NT	NT	NT
						◇1 🛒			◇								◇1 🛒		◇				
Manchester Airport 85 ✈	d					07 54											08 55						
Manchester Piccadilly 10	a					08 13											09 13						
	d	08 07	08 12	08 15		08 20	08 29	08 37	08 43	08 45	08 48	09 00	09 05		09 15	09 18	09 20	09 36	09 43	09 45	09 48	10 03	10 15
Ardwick	d																						
Ashburys	d	08 11									08 52		09 09		09 19	09 23					09 52	10 07	10 19
Belle Vue	d															09 26						10 09	
Ryder Brow	d															09 28						10 11	
Reddish North	d									08 52			09 14							09 52		10 14	
Brinnington	d									08 56			09 17							09 56		10 17	
Bredbury	d									08 59			09 20							09 59		10 20	
Gorton	d	08 13									08 54				09 21						09 54		10 21
Fairfield	d		08 20									09 07						09 43					
Guide Bridge	a	08 17	08 23				08 37				08 58	09 10			09 25			09 46			09 58		10 25
	d		08 23									09 11						09 46					
Hyde North	d		08 28									09 17						09 50					
Hyde Central	d		08 30									09 20						09 52					
Woodley	d		08 33		←							09 23		←				09 55					
Romiley	d		08 37	08 29	08 37					09 02		09 26	09 23	09 26		09 35		09 59		10 02		10 23	
Rose Hill Marple	a		→		08 45							→		09 33				10 05					
Marple	d			08a33				08 52		09 06			09a28			09a40				10 06		10 27	
Strines	d							08 56												10 10			
New Mills Central	a							09 01		09 11										10 15		10 34	
	d									09 11													
Stockport 86	d					08 28			08 54								09 28		09 54				
Hazel Grove 86	d																						
Chinley	d									09 19													
Edale	d									09 28													
Hope (Derbyshire)	d									09 34													
Bamford	d									09 37													
Hathersage	d									09 40													
Grindleford	d									09 44													
Dore & Totley	d									09 53													
Sheffield 7	a					09 08			09 35	10 03							10 08		10 33				

		NT	TP	NT	EM	NT	NT	NT	NT	TP	NT	NT	EM	NT	NT	NT	NT	TP	NT	NT	EM	NT
			◇1 🛒		◇					◇1 🛒			◇					◇1 🛒			◇	
Manchester Airport 85 ✈	d		09 55							10 55								11 55				
Manchester Piccadilly 10	a		10 13							11 13								12 13				
	d	10 18	10 20	10 36	10 43	10 45	10 48	11 03	11 18	11 20	11 23	11 36	11 43	11 45	11 48	12 03	12 18	12 20	12 23	12 36	12 43	12 45
Ardwick	d																					
Ashburys	d						10 52	11 07	11 22						11 52	12 07	12 22					
Belle Vue	d							11 09								12 09						
Ryder Brow	d							11 11								12 11						
Reddish North	d					10 52		11 14						11 52		12 14						12 52
Brinnington	d					10 56		11 17						11 56		12 17						12 56
Bredbury	d					10 59		11 20						11 59		12 20						12 59
Gorton	d						10 54		11 24						11 54		12 24					
Fairfield	d			10 43								11 43								12 43		
Guide Bridge	a			10 46			10 58		11 28			11 46			11 58		12 28			12 46		
	d			10 46								11 46								12 46		
Hyde North	d			10 50								11 50								12 50		
Hyde Central	d			10 52								11 52								12 52		
Woodley	d			10 55								11 55								12 55		
Romiley	d	10 30		10 59		11 02		11 23			11 37	11 59		12 02		12 23			12 37	12 59		13 02
Rose Hill Marple	a			11 05								12 05								13 05		
Marple	d	10a35				11 06		11 27			11a43			12 06		12 27			12a43			13 06
Strines	d													12 10								
New Mills Central	a					11 11		11 34						12 15		12 34						13 11
	d					11 11																13 11
Stockport 86	d		10 28		10 54					11 28			11 54					12 28			12 54	
Hazel Grove 86	d																					
Chinley	d					11 19																13 19
Edale	d					11 28																13 28
Hope (Derbyshire)	d					11 34																13 34
Bamford	d					11 37																13 37
Hathersage	d					11 40																13 40
Grindleford	d					11 44																13 44
Dore & Totley	d					11 53																13 53
Sheffield 7	a		11 08		11 34	12 03				12 08			12 34					13 08			13 34	14 03

Table 78

Mondays to Fridays
from 06 September

Manchester Airport and Manchester - Romiley, Marple, Chinley and Sheffield

		NT	NT	NT	TP	NT	NT	EM	NT	NT	NT	NT	TP	NT	NT	EM	NT	NT	NT	NT	TP	NT	NT
					◇1 🛒			◇					◇1 🛒			◇					◇1 🛒		
Manchester Airport 85 ✈	d				12 55								13 55								14 55		
Manchester Piccadilly 10	a				13 13								14 13								15 13		
	d	12 48	13 03	13 18	13 20	13 23	13 36	13 43	13 45	13 48	14 03	14 18	14 20	14 23	14 36	14 43	14 45	14 48	15 03	15 18	15 20	15 23	15 36
Ardwick	d																						
Ashburys	d	12 52	13 07	13 22						13 52	14 07	14 22						14 52	15 07	15 22			
Belle Vue	d		13 09								14 09								15 09				
Ryder Brow	d		13 11								14 11								15 11				
Reddish North	d		13 14						13 52		14 14						14 52		15 14				
Brinnington	d		13 17						13 56		14 17						14 56		15 17				
Bredbury	d		13 20						13 59		14 20						14 59		15 20				
Gorton	d	12 54		13 24						13 54		14 24						14 54		15 24			
Fairfield	d						13 43								14 43								15 43
Guide Bridge	a	12 58		13 28			13 46			13 58		14 28			14 46			14 58		15 28			15 46
	d						13 46								14 46								15 46
Hyde North	d						13 50								14 50								15 50
Hyde Central	d						13 52								14 52								15 52
Woodley	d						13 55								14 55								15 55
Romiley	d		13 23			13 37	13 59		14 02		14 23			14 37	14 59		15 02		15 23			15 37	15 59
Rose Hill Marple	a						14 05								15 05								16 05
Marple	d		13 27			13a43			14 06		14 27			14a43			15 06		15 27			15a43	
Strines	d								14 10														
New Mills Central	a		13 34						14 15		14 34						15 11		15 34				
	d																15 11						
Stockport 86	d				13 28			13 54					14 28			14 54					15 28		
Hazel Grove 86	d																						
Chinley	d																15 19						
Edale	d																15 28						
Hope (Derbyshire)	d																15 34						
Bamford	d																15 37						
Hathersage	d																15 40						
Grindleford	d																15 44						
Dore & Totley	d																15 53						
Sheffield 7	a				14 08			14 35					15 08			15 34	16 03				16 08		

		EM	NT	NT	NT	NT	NT	TP	NT	NT	EM	NT	NT	NT	NT	NT	NT	TP	NT	NT	NT	NT	EM
		◇						◇1 🛒			◇							◇1 🛒					◇
Manchester Airport 85 ✈	d							15 55										16 55					
Manchester Piccadilly 10	a							16 13										17 13					
	d	15 43	15 45	15 48	16 03	16 06	16 15	16 20	16 23	16 36	16 43	16 45	16 48	16 59	17 03	17 15	17 18	17 20		17 21	17 32	17 37	17 43
Ardwick	d														17 07								
Ashburys	d			15 52	16 07		16 19			16 40		16 49	16 52	17 03	17 09	17 19					17 36	17 41	
Belle Vue	d				16 09							16 51			17 12						17 38		
Ryder Brow	d				16 11							16 53			17 14						17 40		
Reddish North	d		15 52		16 14				16 30			16 56			17 16						17 43		
Brinnington	d		15 56		16 17				16 34			16 59			17 20						17 46		
Bredbury	d		15 59		16 20				16 37			17 02			17 23		17 30				17 49		
Gorton	d			15 54			16 21			16 42				17 05		17 21						17 43	
Fairfield	d					16 13							16 56										
Guide Bridge	a			15 58		16 16	16 25			16 46			16 59	17 10		17 25				17 30		17 47	
	d					16 16							16 59							17 30			
Hyde North	d					16 20							17 03							17 34			
Hyde Central	d					16 22							17 05							17 36			
Woodley	d					16 25							17 08							17 39			
Romiley	d		16 02		16 23	16 29			16 40			17 05	17 13		17 27		17 33			17 43	17 53		
Rose Hill Marple	a					16 36							17 20							17 49			
Marple	d		16 06		16 27				16a44			17 09			17a31		17 37				17 57		
Strines	d		16 10														17 41				18 01		
New Mills Central	a		16 13		16 34							17 16					17 45				18 04		
	d		16 13														17 45						
Stockport 86	d	15 54						16 28			16 54							17 28					17 54
Hazel Grove 86	d																						
Chinley	d		16 21								17 09						17 51	17 43					18 09
Edale	d		16 30														18 00						
Hope (Derbyshire)	d		16 36														18 06						
Bamford	d		16 39														18 09						
Hathersage	d		16 42														18 13						
Grindleford	d		16 46														18 16		←				
Dore & Totley	d		16 54								17 30						18 26	18 06	18 26				18 34
Sheffield 7	a	16 34	17 03					17 08			17 37						→	18 15	18 36				18 41

Manchester Airport and Manchester - Romiley, Marple, Chinley and Sheffield

		NT	NT	NT	NT	NT	TP	NT	NT	EM	NT	NT	NT	NT	TP	NT	EM	NT	NT	TP FO	TP FX	NT	EM	NT	NT
							◇1			◇					◇1		◇			◇1	◇1		◇		
Manchester Airport 85 ✈	d						17 55								18 55					19 55	19 55				
Manchester Piccadilly 10	a						18 13								19 13					20 13	20 13				
	d	17 48	17 59	18 03	18 06	18 15	18 20	18 22	18 36	18 43	18 45	18 48	19 00	19 18	19 18	19 23	19 43	19 45	19 48	20 20	20 20	20 36	20 43	20 45	20 48
Ardwick	d				18 09																				
Ashburys	d	17 52	18 03	18 07	18 11	18 19						18 52	19 04	19 22				19 49	19 52						20 52
Belle Vue	d			18 09									19 06					19 51							
Ryder Brow	d			18 11									19 08					19 53							
Reddish North	d	17 57		18 14							18 52		19 11					19 56						20 52	
Brinnington	d	18 00		18 17							18 56		19 14					19 59						20 56	
Bredbury	d	18 04		18 20							18 59		19 17					20 02						20 59	
Gorton	d		18 05			18 21						18 54		19 24					19 54						20 54
Fairfield	d				18 15				18 43													20 43			
Guide Bridge	a		18 09		18 18	18 25			18 46			18 58		19 28					19 58			20 46			20 58
	d				18 18				18 46													20 46			
Hyde North	d				18 22				18 50													20 50			
Hyde Central	d				18 25				18 52													20 52			
Woodley	d				18 28				18 55													20 55			
Romiley	d	18 07		18 23	18 31			18 35	18 59		19 02		19 20			19 38		20 05				20 59		21 02	
Rose Hill Marple	a				18 37				19 05													21 05			
Marple	d	18 11		18a28				18 39			19 06		19a25			19a43		20 09						21 06	
Strines	d	18 15						18 43										20 13							
New Mills Central	a	18 19						18 48			19 11							20 18						21 11	
	d	18 19									19 11													21 11	
Stockport 86	d						18 28			18 54					19 26		19 54			20 28	20 28		20 54		
Hazel Grove 86	d																								
Chinley	d	18a27									19 19													21 19	
Edale	d										19 28													21 28	
Hope (Derbyshire)	d										19 34													21 34	
Bamford	d										19 37													21 37	
Hathersage	d										19 40													21 40	
Grindleford	d										19 44													21 44	
Dore & Totley	d						19 04				19 53				20 02					21 04	21 04			21 53	
Sheffield 7	a						19 10			19 33	20 03				20 08		20 36			21 10	21 14		21 35	22 03	

		TP	NT	NT	TP	EM	NT	NT	NT	NT	TP
		◇1			◇1	◇					◇1
Manchester Airport 85 ✈	d	20 47			21 47						23 52
Manchester Piccadilly 10	a	21 13			22 13						00 09
	d	21 20	21 45	21 48	22 20	22 28	22 45	22 48	23 24	23 27	00 15
Ardwick	d										
Ashburys	d		21 49	21 52			22 49	22 52	23 28	23 31	
Belle Vue	d		21 51				22 51		23 30		
Ryder Brow	d		21 53				22 53		23 32		
Reddish North	d		21 56				22 56		23 35		
Brinnington	d		21 59				22 59		23 38		
Bredbury	d		22 02				23 02		23 41		
Gorton	d			21 54				22 54		23 33	
Fairfield	d										
Guide Bridge	a			21 58				22 58		23 37	
	d										
Hyde North	d										
Hyde Central	d										
Woodley	d										
Romiley	d		22 05				23 05		23 44		
Rose Hill Marple	a										
Marple	d		22 09				23 09		23 48		
Strines	d		22 13				23 13		23 52		
New Mills Central	a		22 18				23 18		23 57		
	d										
Stockport 86	d	21 28			22 28	22 37					
Hazel Grove 86	d										
Chinley	d					22 53					
Edale	d					23 02					
Hope (Derbyshire)	d					23 08					
Bamford	d					23 11					
Hathersage	d					23 15					
Grindleford	d					23 19					
Dore & Totley	d					23 28					
Sheffield 7	a	22 08			23 13	23 35					01 06

Manchester Airport and Manchester - Romiley, Marple, Chinley and Sheffield

		TP	TP	NT	NT	NT	NT	NT	NT	TP	NT	EM	NT	NT	NT	NT	TP	NT	NT	EM	NT	NT	NT	NT
		◇1	◇1							◇1		◇					◇1			◇				
Manchester Airport 85 ✈	d	23p52	05 15							06 55							07 54							
Manchester Piccadilly 10	a	00 09	05 33							07 13							08 13							
	d	00 15	05 44	05 50	06 16	06 35	06 48	07 03	07 18	07 20	07 39	07 42	07 44	07 48	08 03	08 15	08 20	08 23	08 36	08 43	08 45	08 48	09 03	09 18
Ardwick	d																							
Ashburys	d				06 20	06 39	06 52	07 07	07 22					07 52	08 07	08 19						08 52	09 07	09 22
Belle Vue	d					06 41		07 09							08 09								09 09	
Ryder Brow	d					06 43		07 11							08 11								09 11	
Reddish North	d					06 46		07 14					07 52		08 14						08 52		09 14	
Brinnington	d					06 49		07 17					07 56		08 17						08 56		09 17	
Bredbury	d					06 52		07 20					07 59		08 20						08 59		09 20	
Gorton	d				06 22		06 54		07 24					07 54		08 21						08 54		09 24
Fairfield	d										07 46								08 43					
Guide Bridge	a				06 26		06 58		07 28		07 49			07 58		08 25			08 46			08 58		09 28
	d										07 49								08 46					
Hyde North	d										07 53								08 50					
Hyde Central	d										07 55								08 52					
Woodley	d										07 58								08 55					
Romiley	d					06 55		07 23			08 02		08 02		08 23			08 37	08 59		09 02		09 23	
Rose Hill Marple	a										08 10								09 05					
Marple	d					06 59		07a28					08 06		08a28			08a43			09 06		09a28	
Strines	d																				09 10			
New Mills Central	a					07 04							08 11								09 13			
	d					07 04							08 11								09 13			
Stockport 86	d		05 52	06 00						07 28		07 54					08 28			08 54				
Hazel Grove 86	d			06 07																				
Chinley	d			06 18		07 12							08 19								09 21			
Edale	d			06 26		07 21							08 28								09 30			
Hope (Derbyshire)	d			06 32		07 27							08 34								09 36			
Bamford	d			06 35		07 30							08 37								09 39			
Hathersage	d			06 39		07 33							08 40								09 42			
Grindleford	d			06 42		07 37							08 44								09 46			
Dore & Totley	d			06 51		07 47				08 03		08 28	08 53								09 54			
Sheffield 7	a	01 06	06 49	07 01		07 57				08 10		08 34	09 03				09 08			09 34	10 03			

		TP	NT	NT	EM	NT	NT	NT	NT	TP	NT	NT	EM	NT	NT	NT	NT	TP	NT	NT	EM	NT	NT
		◇1			◇					◇1			◇					◇1			◇		
Manchester Airport 85 ✈	d	08 55								09 55								10 55					
Manchester Piccadilly 10	a	09 13								10 13								11 13					
	d	09 20	09 23	09 36	09 43	09 45	09 48	10 03	10 18	10 20	10 23	10 36	10 43	10 45	10 48	11 03	11 18	11 20	11 23	11 36	11 43	11 45	11 48
Ardwick	d																						
Ashburys	d						09 52	10 07	10 22						10 52	11 07	11 22						11 52
Belle Vue	d							10 09								11 09							
Ryder Brow	d							10 11								11 11							
Reddish North	d					09 52		10 14						10 52		11 14						11 52	
Brinnington	d					09 56		10 17						10 56		11 17						11 56	
Bredbury	d					09 59		10 20						10 59		11 20						11 59	
Gorton	d						09 54		10 24						10 54		11 24						11 54
Fairfield	d			09 43								10 43								11 43			
Guide Bridge	a			09 46			09 58		10 28			10 46			10 58		11 28			11 46			11 58
	d			09 46								10 46								11 46			
Hyde North	d			09 50								10 50								11 50			
Hyde Central	d			09 52								10 52								11 52			
Woodley	d			09 55								10 55								11 55			
Romiley	d		09 37	09 59		10 02		10 23			10 37	10 59		11 02		11 23			11 37	11 59		12 02	
Rose Hill Marple	a			10 05								11 05								12 05			
Marple	d		09a43			10 06		10a28			10a43			11 06		11a28			11a43			12 06	
Strines	d					10 10																12 10	
New Mills Central	a					10 13								11 11								12 13	
	d					10 13								11 11								12 13	
Stockport 86	d	09 28			09 54					10 28			10 54					11 28			11 54		
Hazel Grove 86	d																						
Chinley	d					10 21								11 19								12 21	
Edale	d					10 30								11 28								12 30	
Hope (Derbyshire)	d					10 36								11 34								12 36	
Bamford	d					10 39								11 37								12 39	
Hathersage	d					10 42								11 40								12 42	
Grindleford	d					10 46								11 44								12 46	
Dore & Totley	d					10 54								11 53								12 54	
Sheffield 7	a	10 08			10 34	11 03				11 08			11 34	12 03				12 08			12 34	13 03	

Table 78

Manchester Airport and Manchester - Romiley, Marple, Chinley and Sheffield

		NT		NT	TP	NT	NT	EM	NT	NT	NT	NT		TP	NT	NT	EM	NT	NT	NT	NT	TP		NT	NT
					◇1			◇						◇1			◇					◇1			
Manchester Airport 85 ✈	d				11 55									12 55								13 55			
Manchester Piccadilly 10	a				12 13									13 13								14 13			
	d	12 03		12 18	12 20	12 23	12 36	12 43	12 45	12 48	13 03	13 18		13 20	13 23	13 36	13 43	13 45	13 48	14 03	14 18	14 20		14 23	14 36
Ardwick	d																								
Ashburys	d	12 07		12 22						12 52	13 07	13 22							13 52	14 07	14 22				
Belle Vue	d	12 09									13 09									14 09					
Ryder Brow	d	12 11									13 11									14 11					
Reddish North	d	12 14							12 52		13 14							13 52		14 14					
Brinnington	d	12 17							12 56		13 17							13 56		14 17					
Bredbury	d	12 20							12 59		13 20							13 59		14 20					
Gorton	d			12 24						12 54		13 24							13 54		14 24				
Fairfield	d						12 43									13 43									14 43
Guide Bridge	a			12 28			12 46			12 58		13 28				13 46			13 58		14 28				14 46
	d						12 46									13 46									14 46
Hyde North	d						12 50									13 50									14 50
Hyde Central	d						12 52									13 52									14 52
Woodley	d						12 55									13 55									14 55
Romiley	d	12 23				12 37	12 59		13 02		13 23				13 37	13 59		14 02		14 23				14 37	14 59
Rose Hill Marple	a						13 05									14 05									15 05
Marple	d	12a28				12a43			13 06		13a28				13a43			14 06		14a28				14a43	
Strines	d																	14 10							
New Mills Central	a								13 11									14 13							
	d								13 11									14 13							
Stockport 86	d				12 28			12 54						13 28			13 54					14 28			
Hazel Grove 86	d																								
Chinley	d								13 19									14 21							
Edale	d								13 28									14 30							
Hope (Derbyshire)	d								13 34									14 36							
Bamford	d								13 37									14 39							
Hathersage	d								13 40									14 42							
Grindleford	d								13 44									14 46							
Dore & Totley	d								13 53									14 54							
Sheffield 7	a				13 08			13 34	14 03					14 08			14 34	15 03				15 08			

		EM	NT	NT	NT	NT	TP	NT		NT	EM	NT	NT	NT	NT	TP	NT	NT	EM	NT	NT	NT	NT	TP	NT
		◇					◇1				◇					◇1			◇					◇1	
Manchester Airport 85 ✈	d						14 55									15 55								16 55	
Manchester Piccadilly 10	a						15 13									16 13								17 13	
	d	14 43	14 45	14 48	15 03	15 18	15 20	15 23		15 36	15 43	15 45	15 48	16 02	16 18	16 20	16 23	16 36	16 43	16 45	16 48	17 02	17 18	17 20	17 23
Ardwick	d																								
Ashburys	d			14 52	15 07	15 22							15 52	16 06	16 22						16 52	17 06	17 22		
Belle Vue	d				15 09									16 08								17 08			
Ryder Brow	d				15 11									16 10								17 10			
Reddish North	d		14 52		15 14							15 52		16 13						16 52		17 13			
Brinnington	d		14 56		15 17							15 56		16 16						16 56		17 16			
Bredbury	d		14 59		15 20							15 59		16 19						16 59		17 19			
Gorton	d			14 54		15 24							15 54		16 24						16 54		17 24		
Fairfield	d									15 43								16 43							
Guide Bridge	a			14 58		15 28				15 46			15 58		16 28			16 46			16 58		17 28		
	d									15 46								16 46							
Hyde North	d									15 50								16 50							
Hyde Central	d									15 52								16 52							
Woodley	d									15 55								16 55							
Romiley	d		15 02		15 23			15 37		15 59		16 02		16 22			16 37	16 59		17 02		17 22			17 37
Rose Hill Marple	a									16 05								17 05							
Marple	d		15 06		15a28			15a43				16 06		16a27			16a43			17 06		17a27			17a43
Strines	d											16 10													
New Mills Central	a		15 11									16 13								17 11					
	d		15 11									16 13								17 11					
Stockport 86	d	14 54					15 28				15 54					16 28			16 54					17 28	
Hazel Grove 86	d																								
Chinley	d		15 19									16 21								17 19				17 43	
Edale	d		15 28									16 30								17 28					
Hope (Derbyshire)	d		15 34									16 36								17 34					
Bamford	d		15 37									16 39								17 37					
Hathersage	d		15 40									16 42								17 40					
Grindleford	d		15 44									16 46								17 44					
Dore & Totley	d		15 53									16 54								17 52				18 06	
Sheffield 7	a	15 34	16 03				16 08				16 35	17 03				17 08			17 37	18 01				18 15	

Table 78

Manchester Airport and Manchester - Romiley, Marple, Chinley and Sheffield

		NT	EM	NT		NT	NT	NT	TP	NT	NT	EM	NT	NT	TP	NT	EM	NT	NT	TP	NT	EM	NT	NT	TP
			◇						◇1			◇			◇1		◇			◇1		◇			◇1
Manchester Airport 85 ✈	d								17 55						18 55					19 55					20 47
Manchester Piccadilly 10	a								18 13			18 41			19 13					20 13					21 13
	d	17 36	17 43	17 45		17 48	18 03	18 18	18 20	18 23	18 36	18 43	18 45	18 48	19 18	19 23	19 43	19 45	19 48	20 20	20 36	20 43	20 45	20 48	21 20
Ardwick	d																								
Ashburys	d					17 52	18 07	18 22						18 52		19 28		19 49	19 52					20 52	
Belle Vue	d						18 09									19 31		19 51							
Ryder Brow	d						18 11									19 33		19 53							
Reddish North	d			17 52			18 14						18 52			19 35		19 56					20 52		
Brinnington	d			17 56			18 17						18 56			19 39		19 59					20 56		
Bredbury	d			17 59			18 20						18 59			19 42		20 02					20 59		
Gorton	d					17 54		18 24						18 54					19 54					20 54	
Fairfield	d	17 43									18 43										20 43				
Guide Bridge	a	17 46				17 58		18 28			18 46			18 58					19 58		20 46			20 58	
	d	17 46									18 46										20 46				
Hyde North	d	17 50									18 50										20 50				
Hyde Central	d	17 52									18 52										20 52				
Woodley	d	17 55									18 55										20 55				
Romiley	d	17 59		18 02			18 23			18 37	18 59		19 02			19 45		20 05			20 59		21 02		
Rose Hill Marple	a	18 05									19 05										21 05				
Marple	d			18 06			18a28			18a43			19 06			19a49		20 09					21 06		
Strines	d			18 10														20 13							
New Mills Central	a			18 13									19 11					20 18					21 11		
	d			18 13									19 11										21 11		
Stockport 86	d		17 54						18 28			18 54			19 26		19 54			20 28		20 54			21 28
Hazel Grove 86	d																								
Chinley	d		18 08	18 21									19 19										21 19		
Edale	d			18 30									19 28										21 28		
Hope (Derbyshire)	d			18 36									19 34										21 34		
Bamford	d			18 39									19 37										21 37		
Hathersage	d			18 42									19 40										21 40		
Grindleford	d			18 46									19 44										21 44		
Dore & Totley	d			18 54					19 04				19 53		20 02					21 04			21 53		
Sheffield 7	a		18 35	19 03					19 10			19 35	20 03		20 08		20 35			21 14		21 34	22 03		22 08

		EM	NT	NT	TP	NT	NT	NT	NT
		◇			◇1				
Manchester Airport 85 ✈	d				21 47				
Manchester Piccadilly 10	a				22 13				
	d	21 43	21 45	21 48	22 20	22 45	22 48	23 24	23 27
Ardwick	d								
Ashburys	d		21 49	21 52		22 49	22 52	23 28	23 31
Belle Vue	d		21 51			22 51		23 30	
Ryder Brow	d		21 53			22 53		23 32	
Reddish North	d		21 56			22 56		23 35	
Brinnington	d		21 59			22 59		23 38	
Bredbury	d		22 02			23 02		23 41	
Gorton	d			21 54			22 54		23 33
Fairfield	d								
Guide Bridge	a			21 58			22 58		23 37
	d								
Hyde North	d								
Hyde Central	d								
Woodley	d								
Romiley	d		22 05			23 05		23 44	
Rose Hill Marple	a								
Marple	d		22 09			23 09		23 48	
Strines	d		22 13			23 13		23 52	
New Mills Central	a		22 18			23 18		23 57	
	d								
Stockport 86	d	21 52			22 28				
Hazel Grove 86	d								
Chinley	d				22 45				
Edale	d				22 53				
Hope (Derbyshire)	d				22 58				
Bamford	d				23 01				
Hathersage	d				23 04				
Grindleford	d				23 08				
Dore & Totley	d				23 15				
Sheffield 7	a	22 31			23 24				

Table 78

Sundays
until 11 July

Manchester Airport and Manchester - Romiley, Marple, Chinley and Sheffield

		NT	NT	TP	NT	NT	NT	NT	NT	NT	TP	NT	NT	NT	NT	TP	EM	NT	NT	TP	EM	NT	NT
				◇■							◇■					◇■	◇			◇■	◇		
Manchester Airport 85 ✈	d			08 39							10 44									12 55			
Manchester Piccadilly 10	a			08 54							10 58									13 09			
	d	07 45	08 22	08 58	09 18	09 45	09 48	10 18	10 45	10 48	11 18	11 18	11 45	11 48	12 18	12 18	12 44	12 48	13 18	13 20	13 44	13 45	13 48
Ardwick	d																						
Ashburys	d				09 22		09 52	10 22		10 52		11 22		11 52	12 22			12 52	13 22				13 52
Belle Vue	d																						
Ryder Brow	d																						
Reddish North	d	07 52	08 29			09 52			10 52				11 52									13 52	
Brinnington	d	07 56	08 33			09 56			10 56				11 56									13 56	
Bredbury	d	07 59	08 36			09 59			10 59				11 59									13 59	
Gorton	d				09 24		09 54	10 24		10 54		11 24		11 54	12 24			12 54	13 24				13 54
Fairfield	d																						
Guide Bridge	a				09 28		09 58	10 28		10 58		11 28		11 58	12 28			12 58	13 28				13 58
	d																						
Hyde North	d																						
Hyde Central	d																						
Woodley	d																						
Romiley	d	08 02	08 39			10 02			11 02				12 02									14 02	
Rose Hill Marple	a																						
Marple	d	08 06	08 43			10 06			11 06				12 06									14 06	
Strines	d	08 10	08 47			10 10			11 10				12 10									14 10	
New Mills Central	a	08 14	08 51			10 14			11 14				12 14									14 14	
	d	08 14	08 51			10 14			11 14				12 14									14 14	
Stockport 86	d			09 06							11 27					12 28	12 54			13 28	13 54		
Hazel Grove 86	d																						
Chinley	d	08 23	09 00			10 23			11 23				12 23									14 23	
Edale	d	08 32	09 09			10 32			11 32				12 32									14 32	
Hope (Derbyshire)	d	08 38	09 15			10 38			11 38				12 38									14 38	
Bamford	d	08 41	09 18			10 41			11 41				12 41									14 41	
Hathersage	d	08 45	09 22			10 45			11 45				12 45									14 45	
Grindleford	d	08 48	09 25			10 48			11 48				12 48									14 48	
Dore & Totley	d	08 57	09 34			10 57			11 57				12 57									14 57	
Sheffield 7	a	09 06	09 42	09 45		11 06			12 06		12 08		13 06			13 08	13 37			14 08	14 39	15 06	

		NT	TP	EM	NT	NT	NT	TP	EM	NT	NT	NT	TP	EM	NT	NT	NT	TP	EM	NT	NT	NT	TP
			◇■	◇				◇■	◇				◇■	◇				◇■	◇				◇■
Manchester Airport 85 ✈	d		13 55					14 55					15 55					16 55					17 55
Manchester Piccadilly 10	a		14 09					15 09					16 09										18 09
	d	14 18	14 20	14 44	14 45	14 48	15 18	15 20	15 44	15 45	15 48	16 18	16 20	16 44	16 45	16 48	17 18	17 20	17 44	17 45	17 48	18 18	18 20
Ardwick	d																						
Ashburys	d	14 22				14 52	15 22				15 52	16 22				16 52	17 22				17 52	18 22	
Belle Vue	d																						
Ryder Brow	d																						
Reddish North	d				14 52					15 52					16 52					17 52			
Brinnington	d				14 56					15 56					16 56					17 56			
Bredbury	d				14 59					15 59					16 59					17 59			
Gorton	d	14 24				14 54	15 24				15 54	16 24				16 54	17 24				17 54	18 24	
Fairfield	d																						
Guide Bridge	a	14 28				14 58	15 28				15 58	16 28				16 58	17 28				17 58	18 28	
	d																						
Hyde North	d																						
Hyde Central	d																						
Woodley	d																						
Romiley	d				15 02					16 02					17 02					18 02			
Rose Hill Marple	a																						
Marple	d				15 06					16 06					17 06					18 06			
Strines	d				15 10					16 10					17 10					18 10			
New Mills Central	a				15 14					16 14					17 14					18 14			
	d				15 14					16 14					17 14					18 14			
Stockport 86	d		14 28	14 54				15 28	15 54				16 28	16 54				17 28	17 54				18 28
Hazel Grove 86	d																						
Chinley	d				15 23					16 23					17 23					18 23			
Edale	d				15 32					16 32					17 32					18 32			
Hope (Derbyshire)	d				15 38					16 38					17 38					18 38			
Bamford	d				15 41					16 41					17 41					18 41			
Hathersage	d				15 45					16 45					17 45					18 45			
Grindleford	d				15 48					16 48					17 48					18 48			
Dore & Totley	d				15 57					16 57					17 57					18 57			
Sheffield 7	a		15 08	15 33	16 06			16 08	16 36	17 06			17 08	17 36	18 06			18 08	18 37	19 06			19 08

Manchester Airport and Manchester - Romiley, Marple, Chinley and Sheffield

		EM	NT	NT	TP	EM	NT	NT	TP	EM	NT	TP	EM	TP	NT	TP
		◇			◇■	◇			◇■	◇		◇■	◇	◇■		◇■
Manchester Airport 85 ✈	d				18 55				19 55			20 55		21 55		22 55
Manchester Piccadilly 10	a				19 09				20 09	20 41		21 09		22 09		23 09
	d	18 44	18 48	19 18	19 20	19 44	19 45	19 48	20 18	20 44	20 48	21 20	22 11	22 15	22 20	23 20
Ardwick	d															
Ashburys	d		18 52	19 22				19 52			20 52					
Belle Vue	d															
Ryder Brow	d															
Reddish North	d						19 52								22 27	
Brinnington	d						19 56								22 31	
Bredbury	d						19 59								22 34	
Gorton	d		18 54	19 24				19 54			20 54					
Fairfield	d															
Guide Bridge	a		18 58	19 28				19 58			20 58					
	d															
Hyde North	d															
Hyde Central	d															
Woodley	d															
Romiley	d						20 02								22 37	
Rose Hill Marple	a															
Marple	d						20 06								22 40	
Strines	d						20 10								22 44	
New Mills Central	a						20 14								22 49	
	d						20 14									
Stockport 86	d	18 54			19 28	19 54			20 27	20 54		21 28	22b28	22 23		23 28
Hazel Grove 86	d															
Chinley	d						20 23						22 43			
Edale	d						20 32						22 52			
Hope (Derbyshire)	d						20 38						22 57			
Bamford	d						20 41						23 00			
Hathersage	d						20 45						23 04			
Grindleford	d						20 48						23 08			
Dore & Totley	d						20 57						23 17			
Sheffield 7	a	19 34			20 08	20 34	21 06		21 08	21 36		22 11	23 25	23 04		00 15

Sundays
18 July to 05 September

		NT	NT	TP	NT	NT	NT	NT	NT	NT	TP	NT	NT	NT	NT	TP	EM	NT	NT	TP	NT	EM	NT
				◇■							◇■					◇■	◇			◇■		◇	
Manchester Airport 85 ✈	d			08 39							10 44									12 55			
Manchester Piccadilly 10	a			08 54							10 58									13 09			
	d	07 45	08 22	08 58	09 18	09 37	09 48	10 18	10 38	10 48	11 18	11 18	11 31	11 48	12 18	12 18	12 44	12 48	13 18	13 20	13 38	13 44	13 48
Ardwick	d																						
Ashburys	d				09 22		09 52	10 22		10 52		11 22		11 52	12 22			12 52	13 22				13 52
Belle Vue	d																						
Ryder Brow	d																						
Reddish North	d	07 52	08 29			09 45			10 45				11 40								13 45		
Brinnington	d	07 56	08 33			09 49			10 49				11 43								13 49		
Bredbury	d	07 59	08 36			09 52			10 52				11 46								13 52		
Gorton	d				09 24		09 54	10 24		10 54		11 24		11 54	12 24			12 54	13 24				13 54
Fairfield	d																						
Guide Bridge	a				09 28		09 58	10 28		10 58		11 28		11 58	12 28			12 58	13 28				13 58
	d																						
Hyde North	d																						
Hyde Central	d																						
Woodley	d																						
Romiley	d	08 02	08 39			09 55			10 55				11 50								13 55		
Rose Hill Marple	a																						
Marple	d	08 06	08 43			09 59			10 59				11 54								13 59		
Strines	d	08 10	08 47			10 03			11 03				11 58								14 03		
New Mills Central	a	08 14	08 51			10 07			11 07				12 01								14 07		
	d	08 14	08 51			10 14			11 14				12 14								14 14		
Stockport 86	d			09 06							11 27					12 28	12 54			13 28		13 54	
Hazel Grove 86	d																						
Chinley	d	08 23	09 00			10 23			11 23				12 23								14 23		
Edale	d	08 32	09 09			10 32			11 32				12 32								14 32		
Hope (Derbyshire)	d	08 38	09 15			10 38			11 38				12 38								14 38		
Bamford	d	08 41	09 18			10 41			11 41				12 41								14 41		
Hathersage	d	08 45	09 22			10 45			11 45				12 45								14 45		
Grindleford	d	08 48	09 25			10 48			11 48				12 48								14 48		
Dore & Totley	d	08 57	09 34			10 57			11 57				12 57								14 57		
Sheffield 7	a	09 06	09 42	09 45		11 06			12 06		12 08		13 06			13 08	13 37			14 08	15 06	14 42	

b arr. 2220

Table 78

Sundays

18 July to 05 September

Manchester Airport and Manchester - Romiley, Marple, Chinley and Sheffield

	NT	TP ◇1	NT	EM ◇	NT	NT	TP ◇1	NT	EM ◇	NT	NT	TP ◇1	NT	EM ◇	NT	NT	TP ◇1	NT	EM ◇	NT	NT	TP ◇1
Manchester Airport 85 ✈ d		13 55					14 55					15 55					16 55					17 55
Manchester Piccadilly 10 a		14 09					15 09					16 09					17 09					18 09
d	14 18	14 20	14 38	14 44	14 48	15 18	15 20	15 38	15 44	15 48	16 18	16 20	16 38	16 44	16 48	17 18	17 20	17 38	17 44	17 48	18 18	18 20
Ardwick d																						
Ashburys d	14 22				14 52	15 22				15 52	16 22				16 52	17 22				17 52	18 22	
Belle Vue d																						
Ryder Brow d																						
Reddish North d			14 45					15 45					16 45					17 45				
Brinnington d			14 49					15 49					16 49					17 49				
Bredbury d			14 52					15 52					16 52					17 52				
Gorton d	14 24				14 54	15 24				15 54	16 24				16 54	17 24				17 54	18 24	
Fairfield d																						
Guide Bridge a	14 28				14 58	15 28				15 58	16 28				16 58	17 28				17 58	18 28	
d																						
Hyde North d																						
Hyde Central d																						
Woodley d																						
Romiley d			14 55					15 55					16 55					17 55				
Rose Hill Marple a																						
Marple d			14 59					15 59					16 59					17 59				
Strines d			15 03					16 03					17 03					18 03				
New Mills Central a			15 07					16 07					17 07					18 07				
d			15 14					16 14					17 14					18 14				
Stockport 86 d		14 28		14 54			15 28		15 54			16 28		16 54			17 28		17 54			18 28
Hazel Grove 86 d																						
Chinley d			15 23					16 23					17 23					18 23				
Edale d			15 32					16 32					17 32					18 32				
Hope (Derbyshire) d			15 38					16 38					17 38					18 38				
Bamford d			15 41					16 41					17 41					18 41				
Hathersage d			15 45					16 45					17 45					18 45				
Grindleford d			15 48					16 48					17 48					18 48				
Dore & Totley d			15 57					16 57					17 57					18 57				
Sheffield 7 a		15 08	16 06	15 33			16 08	17 06	16 36			17 08	18 06	17 36			18 08	19 06	18 37			19 08

	EM ◇	NT	NT	TP ◇1	NT	EM ◇	NT	TP ◇1	EM ◇	NT	TP ◇1	EM ◇	TP ◇1	NT	TP ◇1
Manchester Airport 85 ✈ d				18 55				19 55			20 55		21 55		22 55
Manchester Piccadilly 10 a				19 09				20 09			21 09		22 09		23 09
d	18 44	18 48	19 18	19 20	19 37	19 44	19 48	20 18	20 44	20 48	21 20	22 11	22 15	22 20	23 20
Ardwick d															
Ashburys d		18 52	19 22				19 52			20 52					
Belle Vue d															
Ryder Brow d															
Reddish North d					19 44									22 27	
Brinnington d					19 48									22 31	
Bredbury d					19 51									22 34	
Gorton d		18 54	19 24				19 54			20 54					
Fairfield d															
Guide Bridge a		18 58	19 28				19 58			20 58					
d															
Hyde North d															
Hyde Central d															
Woodley d															
Romiley d					19 54									22 37	
Rose Hill Marple a															
Marple d					19 58									22 40	
Strines d					20 02									22 44	
New Mills Central a					20 06									22 49	
d					20 14										
Stockport 86 d	18 54			19 28		19 54		20 27	20 54		21 28	22b28	22 23		23 28
Hazel Grove 86 d															
Chinley d					20 23							22 43			
Edale d					20 32							22 52			
Hope (Derbyshire) d					20 38							22 57			
Bamford d					20 41							23 00			
Hathersage d					20 45							23 04			
Grindleford d					20 48							23 08			
Dore & Totley d					20 57							23 17			
Sheffield 7 a	19 34			20 08	21 06	20 34		21 08	21 36		22 11	23 25	23 04		00 15

b arr. 2220

Table 78

Sundays

from 12 September

Manchester Airport and Manchester - Romiley, Marple, Chinley and Sheffield

	NT	TP ◇1	NT A	NT	NT	NT	NT	NT A	NT	TP ◇1	NT	NT	NT	NT	TP ◇1	EM ◇	NT	NT	TP ◇1	EM ◇	NT	NT
Manchester Airport 85 ✈ d		08 39								10 44									12 55			
Manchester Piccadilly 10 a		08 54								10 58									13 09			
d	07 45	08 58	09 00	09 18	09 22	09 32	10 18	10 45	10 48	11 18	11 18	11 45	11 48	12 18	12 18	12 44	12 48	13 18	13 20	13 44	13 45	13 48
Ardwick d																						
Ashburys d				09 22		09 36	10 22		10 52		11 22		11 52	12 22			12 52	13 22				13 52
Belle Vue d																						
Ryder Brow d																						
Reddish North d	07 52				09 29			10 52				11 52									13 52	
Brinnington d	07 56				09 33			10 56				11 56									13 56	
Bredbury d	07 59				09 36			10 59				11 59									13 59	
Gorton d				09 24		09 38	10 24		10 54		11 24		11 54	12 24			12 54	13 24				13 54
Fairfield d																						
Guide Bridge a				09 28		09 42	10 28		10 58		11 28		11 58	12 28			12 58	13 28				13 58
d																						
Hyde North d																						
Hyde Central d																						
Woodley d																						
Romiley d	08 02				09 39			11 02				12 02									14 02	
Rose Hill Marple a																						
Marple d	08 06				09 43			11 06				12 06									14 06	
Strines d	08 10				09 47			11 10				12 10									14 10	
New Mills Central a	08 14		09 20		09 51			11 14				12 14									14 14	
d	08 14		09 21		09 51			11 14				12 14									14 14	
Stockport 86 d		09 06								11 27					12 28	12 55			13 28	13 54		
Hazel Grove 86 d																						
Chinley d	08 23		09 28		09 59			11 23				12 23									14 23	
Edale d	08 32		09 37		10 08			11 32				12 32									14 32	
Hope (Derbyshire) d	08 38		09 43		10 14			11 38				12 38									14 38	
Bamford d	08 41		09 46		10 17			11 41				12 41									14 41	
Hathersage d	08 45		09 50		10 20			11 45				12 45									14 45	
Grindleford d	08 48		09 53		10 24			11 48				12 48									14 48	
Dore & Totley d	08 57		10 02		10 34			11 57				12 57									14 57	
Sheffield 7 a	09 06	09 45	10 10		10 43			12 06		12 08		13 06			13 08	13 37			14 08	14 39	15 06	

	NT	TP ◇1	EM ◇	NT A	NT	NT	TP ◇1	EM ◇	NT	NT	NT	TP ◇1	EM ◇	NT A	NT	NT	TP ◇1	EM ◇	NT	NT	NT	TP ◇1
Manchester Airport 85 ✈ d		13 55					14 55					15 55					16 55					17 55
Manchester Piccadilly 10 a		14 09					15 09					16 09					17 09					18 09
d	14 18	14 20	14 44	14 45	14 48	15 18	15 20	15 44	15 45	15 48	16 18	16 20	16 44	16 45	16 48	17 18	17 20	17 44	17 45	17 48	18 18	18 20
Ardwick d																						
Ashburys d	14 22				14 52	15 22				15 52	16 22				16 52	17 22				17 52	18 22	
Belle Vue d																						
Ryder Brow d																						
Reddish North d				14 52					15 52					16 52					17 52			
Brinnington d				14 56					15 56					16 56					17 56			
Bredbury d				14 59					15 59					16 59					17 59			
Gorton d	14 24				14 54	15 24				15 54	16 24				16 54	17 24				17 54	18 24	
Fairfield d																						
Guide Bridge a	14 28				14 58	15 28				15 58	16 28				16 58	17 28				17 58	18 28	
d																						
Hyde North d																						
Hyde Central d																						
Woodley d																						
Romiley d				15 02					16 02					17 02					18 02			
Rose Hill Marple a																						
Marple d				15 06					16 06					17 06					18 06			
Strines d				15 10					16 10					17 10					18 10			
New Mills Central a				15 14					16 14					17 14					18 14			
d				15 14					16 14					17 14					18 14			
Stockport 86 d		14 28	14 54				15 28	15 54				16 28	16 54				17 28	17 54				18 28
Hazel Grove 86 d																						
Chinley d				15 23					16 23					17 23					18 23			
Edale d				15 32					16 32					17 32					18 32			
Hope (Derbyshire) d				15 38					16 38					17 38					18 38			
Bamford d				15 41					16 41					17 41					18 41			
Hathersage d				15 45					16 45					17 45					18 45			
Grindleford d				15 48					16 48					17 48					18 48			
Dore & Totley d				15 57					16 57					17 57					18 57			
Sheffield 7 a		15 08	15 37	16 06			16 08	16 36	17 06			17 08	17 36	18 06			18 08	18 37	19 06			19 08

A 12 September

Table 78

Sundays
from 12 September

Manchester Airport and Manchester - Romiley, Marple, Chinley and Sheffield

		EM	NT	NT	TP	EM	NT	NT	TP	EM	NT	TP	EM		TP	NT	TP
		◇			◇1	◇			◇1	◇		◇1	◇		◇1		◇1
Manchester Airport 85	d				18 55				19 55			20 55			21 55		22 55
Manchester Piccadilly 10	a				19 09				20 09			21 09			22 09		23 09
	d	18 44	18 48	19 18	19 20	19 44	19 45	19 48	20 18	20 44	20 48	21 20	22 11		22 15	22 20	23 20
Ardwick	d																
Ashburys	d		18 52	19 22				19 52			20 52						
Belle Vue	d																
Ryder Brow	d																
Reddish North	d						19 52									22 27	
Brinnington	d						19 56									22 31	
Bredbury	d						19 59									22 34	
Gorton	d		18 54	19 24				19 54			20 54						
Fairfield	d																
Guide Bridge	a		18 58	19 28				19 58			20 58						
	d																
Hyde North	d																
Hyde Central	d																
Woodley	d																
Romiley	d						20 02									22 37	
Rose Hill Marple	a																
Marple	d						20 06									22 40	
Strines	d						20 10									22 44	
New Mills Central	a						20 14									22 49	
	d						20 14										
Stockport 86	d	18 54			19 28	19 54			20 27	20 54		21 28	22b28		22 23		23 28
Hazel Grove 86	d																
Chinley	d						20 23						22 43				
Edale	d						20 32						22 51				
Hope (Derbyshire)	d						20 38						22 57				
Bamford	d						20 41						23 00				
Hathersage	d						20 45						23 03				
Grindleford	d						20 48						23 07				
Dore & Totley	d						20 57						23 17				
Sheffield 7	a	19 34			20 08	20 34	21 06		21 08	21 36		22 11	23 25		23 04		00 15

b arr. 2220

Table 78

Mondays to Fridays
until 03 September

Sheffield, Chinley, Marple and Romiley - Manchester and Manchester Airport

		NT MX	NT MX	TP	TP MO	NT	NT	TP FO	TP FX	NT		NT	NT	EM	NT	NT	NT	NT	TP	NT		NT	NT	NT	NT
				◇1	◇1			◇1	◇1					◇					◇1						
Sheffield 7	d	22p47		03 45	05 11			06 11	06 11					06 20					07 09						
Dore & Totley	d	22p54												06 27					07 14						
Grindleford	d	23p01												06 35											
Hathersage	d	23p05												06 39											
Bamford	d	23p08												06 43											
Hope (Derbyshire)	d	23p12												06 47											
Edale	d	23p19												06 55											
Chinley	d	23p27												07 03											
Hazel Grove 86	a																								
Stockport 86	a	23p47			05 53			06 53	06 53					07 22					07 53						
New Mills Central	d		23p30				06 13					06 36			07 01			07 23					07 39		
Strines	d		23p33				06 16					06 39			07 04			07 26					07 42		
Marple	d		23p36				06 19					06 42			07 07			07 29					07 45		07 59
Rose Hill Marple	d									06 32							07 16					07 41			
Romiley	d		23p40				06 23			06 37		06 46			07 12		07 21	07 33				07 46	07 49		08 03
Woodley	d									06 40							07 24					07 49			
Hyde Central	d									06 43							07 27					07 52			
Hyde North	d									06 46							07 30					07 55			
Guide Bridge	d					06 27				06 50			06 57			07 27	07 34			07 47		07 59		08 10	
Fairfield	d									06 53							07 37					08 02			
Gorton	d					06 30							07 00			07 30				07 50				08 13	
Bredbury	d		23p43				06 26					06 49			07 15			07 36					07 52		08 06
Brinnington	d		23p45				06 28					06 52			07 17			07 39					07 55		08 09
Reddish North	d		23p48				06 31					06 55			07 20			07 43					07 58		08 12
Ryder Brow	d		23p51				06 34					06 58			07 24			07 45							08 15
Belle Vue	d		23p52				06 36					07 00			07 26			07 47							08 16
Ashburys	d		23p55			06 33	06 39					07 03	07 06		07 29	07 33		07 50		07 53				08 16	08 20
Ardwick	d															07 36									08 22
Manchester Piccadilly 10	a	00 02	00 03	04 40	06 05	06 42	06 47	07 02	07 02	07 03		07 12	07 15	07 34	07 36	07 43	07 47	07 56	08 02	08 03		08 12	08 09	08 25	08 30
Manchester Airport 85	a			05 00	06 29			07 29	07 29										08 26						

		NT	EM	NT	NT	NT	NT	TP	NT	NT	NT	NT	NT	NT FO A	EM	NT	NT	TP	NT	NT	NT	NT	EM	NT
			◇					◇1							◇			◇1					◇	
Sheffield 7	d	07 12	07 35					08 05							08 42			09 11				09 14	09 42	
Dore & Totley	d	07 19	07 42					08 10														09 21		
Grindleford	d	07 29																				09 29		
Hathersage	d	07 32																				09 32		
Bamford	d	07 36																				09 36		
Hope (Derbyshire)	d	07 39																				09 39		
Edale	d	07 47																				09 47		
Chinley	d	07 55	08 03					08 32														09 55		
Hazel Grove 86	a		08 16																					
Stockport 86	a		08 24					08 53						09d22	09 25			09 53					10 25	
New Mills Central	d	08 02				08 24							09 04									10 01		
Strines	d	08 05											09 07									10 04		
Marple	d	08 09				08 29				08 48			09 10				09 35			09 52		10 07		
Rose Hill Marple	d				08 15		08 35					08 59									09 55			
Romiley	d	08 13			08 20	08 33	08 40			08 51		09 04	09 14				09 38			09 56	10 00	10 11		
Woodley	d				08 23							09 07									10 03			
Hyde Central	d				08 26							09 10									10 06			
Hyde North	d				08 29							09 13									10 09			
Guide Bridge	d			08 27	08 33				08 49		09 12	09 17		09a42		09 28			09 58		10 13			10 28
Fairfield	d				08 36							09 20									10 16			
Gorton	d			08 31					08 52		09 15					09 31			10 01					10 31
Bredbury	d					08 36	08 43			08 54			09 17				09 41					10 14		
Brinnington	d					08 39	08 45			08 57			09 19				09 44					10 16		
Reddish North	d					08 43	08 48			09 00			09 22				09 47					10 19		
Ryder Brow	d									09 03										10 03				
Belle Vue	d									09 04										10 05				
Ashburys	d			08 34		08 48			08 56	09 07	09 18					09 34			10 04	10 07				10 34
Ardwick	d						08 54																	
Manchester Piccadilly 10	a	08 33	08 36	08 43	08 47	08 55	09 00	09 02	09 04	09 15	09 27	09 30	09 34		09 36	09 42	09 57	10 02	10 12	10 15	10 26	10 32	10 36	10 42
Manchester Airport 85	a							09 33										10 26						

A To Stalybridge arr. 09.49. Also stops at Reddish South 09x26 and Denton 09x31

Table 78

Sheffield, Chinley, Marple and Romiley - Manchester and Manchester Airport

	NT		NT	TP ◇1	NT	NT	NT	EM ◇	NT	NT	NT		TP FX ◇1	TP FO ◇1	NT	NT	NT	EM ◇	NT	NT	NT		TP ◇1	
Sheffield 7 d				10 11			10 14	10 42					11 11	11 11				11 42					12 11	
Dore & Totley d							10 21																	
Grindleford d							10 29																	
Hathersage d							10 32																	
Bamford d							10 36																	
Hope (Derbyshire) d							10 39																	
Edale d							10 47																	
Chinley d							10 55																	
Hazel Grove 86 a																								
Stockport 86 a				10 53				11 25					11 53	11 53				12 25					12 53	
New Mills Central d			10 30				11 01				11 30						12 01				12 30			
Strines d																	12 04							
Marple d			10 35			10 52	11 07				11 35					11 52	12 07				12 35			
Rose Hill Marple d	10 30									11 30										12 30				
Romiley d	10 35		10 38			10 56	11 11			11 35	11 38					11 56	12 11			12 35	12 38			
Woodley d	10 38									11 38										12 38				
Hyde Central d	10 41									11 41										12 41				
Hyde North d	10 44									11 44										12 44				
Guide Bridge d	10 48				10 58				11 28	11 48					11 58				12 28	12 48				
Fairfield d	10 51									11 51										12 51				
Gorton d					11 01				11 31						12 01				12 31					
Bredbury d			10 41				11 14				11 41						12 14				12 41			
Brinnington d			10 44				11 16				11 44						12 16				12 44			
Reddish North d			10 47				11 19				11 47						12 19				12 47			
Ryder Brow d						11 03										12 03								
Belle Vue d						11 05										12 05								
Ashburys d					11 04	11 07			11 34						12 04	12 07			12 34					
Ardwick d																								
Manchester Piccadilly 10 a	11 02		10 57	11 02	11 12	11 15	11 32	11 36	11 42	12 02	11 57		12 02	12 02	12 12	12 15	12 32	12 36	12 42	13 02	12 57		13 02	
Manchester Airport 85 a				11 26									12 26	12 26									13 26	

	NT	NT	NT	EM ◇	NT	NT	NT		TP ◇1		NT	NT	NT	EM ◇	NT	NT	NT		TP ◇1	NT	NT	NT	EM ◇	NT
Sheffield 7 d			12 14	12 42					13 11					13 42					14 11			14 14	14 42	
Dore & Totley d			12 21																			14 21		
Grindleford d			12 29																			14 29		
Hathersage d			12 32																			14 32		
Bamford d			12 36																			14 36		
Hope (Derbyshire) d			12 39																			14 39		
Edale d			12 47																			14 47		
Chinley d			12 55																			14 55		
Hazel Grove 86 a																								
Stockport 86 a				13 25					13 53					14 25					14 53				15 25	
New Mills Central d			13 01				13 30						14 01				14 30					15 01		
Strines d													14 04											
Marple d		12 52	13 07				13 35					13 52	14 07				14 35				14 52	15 07		
Rose Hill Marple d						13 30										14 30								
Romiley d		12 56	13 11			13 35	13 38					13 56	14 11			14 35	14 38				14 56	15 11		
Woodley d						13 38										14 38								
Hyde Central d						13 41										14 41								
Hyde North d						13 44										14 44								
Guide Bridge d	12 58				13 28	13 48					13 58				14 28	14 48				14 58				15 28
Fairfield d						13 51										14 51								
Gorton d	13 01				13 31						14 01				14 31					15 01				15 31
Bredbury d			13 14				13 41						14 14				14 41					15 14		
Brinnington d			13 16				13 44						14 16				14 44					15 16		
Reddish North d			13 19				13 47						14 19				14 47					15 19		
Ryder Brow d		13 03										14 03									15 03			
Belle Vue d		13 05										14 05									15 05			
Ashburys d	13 04	13 07			13 34						14 04	14 07			14 34					15 04	15 07			15 34
Ardwick d																								
Manchester Piccadilly 10 a	13 12	13 15	13 32	13 36	13 42	14 02	13 57		14 02		14 12	14 15	14 32	14 36	14 42	15 02	14 57		15 02	15 12	15 15	15 32	15 36	15 42
Manchester Airport 85 a									14 26										15 26					

Table 78

Sheffield, Chinley, Marple and Romiley - Manchester and Manchester Airport

	NT	NT	TP ◇1		NT	NT	NT	EM ◇	NT	NT	TP ◇1	NT	NT		NT	NT	NT	EM ◇	NT	NT	NT	NT	TP ◇1	
Sheffield 7 d			15 11					15 42			16 10					16 14		16 42					17 11	
Dore & Totley d																16 21								
Grindleford d																16 29								
Hathersage d																16 32								
Bamford d																16 36								
Hope (Derbyshire) d																16 39								
Edale d																16 47								
Chinley d																16 55								
Hazel Grove 86 a																								
Stockport 86 a			15 53					16 25			16 53							17 25					17 53	
New Mills Central d		15 30					16 01						16 37			17 01				17 23				
Strines d							16 04																	
Marple d		15 35				15 52	16 07						16 42		16 52	17 06				17 27				
Rose Hill Marple d	15 30									16 26									17 10			17 36		
Romiley d	15 35	15 38				15 56	16 11			16 31			16 45		16 56	17 10			17 15	17 32		17 41		
Woodley d	15 38												16 49						17 18					
Hyde Central d	15 41												16 52						17 21					
Hyde North d	15 44												16 54						17 24					
Guide Bridge d	15 48				15 58				16 28			16 49	16 58				17 15		17 28		17 42			
Fairfield d	15 51																		17 31					
Gorton d					16 01				16 31			16 52					17 18				17 45			
Bredbury d		15 41					16 14			16 34						17 13						17 44		
Brinnington d		15 44					16 16			16 37												17 46		
Reddish North d		15 47					16 19			16 40												17 49		
Ryder Brow d						16 03				16 42					17 03									
Belle Vue d						16 05				16 44					17 05									
Ashburys d					16 04	16 07			16 34	16 47		16 55	17 03		17 07		17 24				17 48	17 55		
Ardwick d																								
Manchester Piccadilly 10 a	16 02	15 57	16 02		16 12	16 15	16 32	16 36	16 42	16 56	17 02	17 05	17 10		17 15	17 29	17 33	17 37	17 42	17 48	17 57	18 01	18 02	
Manchester Airport 85 a			16 26								17 32												18 26	

	NT	NT	NT	NT	EM ◇	NT	NT	TP FX ◇1	TP FO ◇1 A		TP FO ◇1 B	NT	NT	NT	NT	EM ◇	NT	TP ◇1	NT		NT	NT	NT	EM ◇
Sheffield 7 d			17 14		17 40			18 10	18 10		18 10					18 42		19 11					19 14	19 42
Dore & Totley d			17 21																				19 21	
Grindleford d			17 29																				19 29	
Hathersage d			17 32																				19 32	
Bamford d			17 36																				19 36	
Hope (Derbyshire) d			17 39																				19 39	
Edale d			17 47																				19 47	
Chinley d			17 55					18 34	18 34		18 34				18 54								19 55	
Hazel Grove 86 a																								
Stockport 86 a					18 25			18 53	18 53		18 53					19 25		19 53						20 25
New Mills Central d			18 01												19 01								20 01	
Strines d			18 04												19 04									
Marple d		17 52	18 07				18 35								19 07						19 37		20 07	
Rose Hill Marple d						18 11							18 44						19 30					
Romiley d		17 56	18 11			18 16	18 38						18 49		19 11				19 35		19 40		20 11	
Woodley d						18 19													19 38					
Hyde Central d						18 22													19 41					
Hyde North d						18 25													19 44					
Guide Bridge d	17 58			18 17		18 29						18 46		19 01			19 28		19 48			19 58		
Fairfield d						18 32													19 51					
Gorton d	18 01			18 20								18 49		19 04			19 31					20 01		
Bredbury d			18 14				18 41						18 52		19 14						19 43		20 14	
Brinnington d							18 44						18 54		19 16						19 46		20 16	
Reddish North d							18 47						18 58		19 19						19 49		20 19	
Ryder Brow d		18 03											19 00								19 51			
Belle Vue d		18 05											19 02								19 53			
Ashburys d	18 04	18 07		18 23								18 54	19 05	19 08			19 34				19 56	20 04		
Ardwick d																								
Manchester Piccadilly 10 a	18 12	18 15	18 31	18 34	18 36	18 41	18 57	19 02	19 02		19 02	19 03	19 12	19 15	19 32	19 36	19 42	20 02	20 02		20 05	20 12	20 32	20 36
Manchester Airport 85 a								19 28	19 28		19 33							20 37						

A until 25 June

B from 2 July until 3 September

Table 78

Mondays to Fridays
until 03 September

Sheffield, Chinley, Marple and Romiley - Manchester and Manchester Airport

		NT		TP	NT	NT		EM	NT	NT	NT	TP	NT	NT	NT	NT
				◇1 ⊼				◇				◇1				
Sheffield 7	d			20 11				20 32		20 35		22 11			22 47	
Dore & Totley	d									20 43					22 54	
Grindleford	d									20 50					23 01	
Hathersage	d									20 53					23 05	
Bamford	d									20 57					23 08	
Hope (Derbyshire)	d									21 00					23 12	
Edale	d									21 08					23 19	
Chinley	d									21 16					23 27	
Hazel Grove 86	a															
Stockport 86	a			20 53				21 20				22 53			23 47	
New Mills Central	d				20 30					21b30			22 30			23 30
Strines	d				20 33								22 33			23 33
Marple	d				20 36					21 36			22 36			23 36
Rose Hill Marple	d								21 12							
Romiley	d				20 40				21 17	21 40			22 40			23 40
Woodley	d								21 20							
Hyde Central	d								21 23							
Hyde North	d								21 26							
Guide Bridge	d	20 28				20 58			21 30		21 58			22 58		
Fairfield	d								21 33							
Gorton	d	20 31				21 01					22 01			23 01		
Bredbury	d				20 43					21 43			22 43			23 43
Brinnington	d				20 45					21 45			22 45			23 45
Reddish North	d				20 48					21 48			22 48			23 48
Ryder Brow	d				20 51					21 51			22 51			23 51
Belle Vue	d				20 52					21 52			22 52			23 52
Ashburys	d	20 34			20 55	21 04				21 55	22 04		22 55	23 04		23 55
Ardwick	d															
Manchester Piccadilly 10	a	20 42		21 02	21 03	21 12		21 32	21 42	22 05	22 12	23 02	23 03	23 12	00 02	00 03
Manchester Airport 85 ✈	a			21 36								23 26				

Mondays to Fridays
from 06 September

		NT MX	NT MX	TP	TP MO	NT	NT		TP	NT		NT	NT	EM	NT	NT	NT	NT	TP	NT		NT	NT	NT	NT
				◇1	◇1				◇1					◇					◇1 ⊼						
Sheffield 7	d	22p47		03 45	05 11				06 11					06 20					07 09						
Dore & Totley	d	22p54												06 27					07 14						
Grindleford	d	23p01												06 35											
Hathersage	d	23p05												06 39											
Bamford	d	23p08												06 43											
Hope (Derbyshire)	d	23p12												06 47											
Edale	d	23p19												06 55											
Chinley	d	23p27												07 03											
Hazel Grove 86	a																								
Stockport 86	a	23p47			05 53				06 53					07 22					07 53						
New Mills Central	d		23p30				06 10					06 33			06 58			07 20					07 36		
Strines	d		23p33				06 13					06 36			07 01			07 23					07 39		
Marple	d		23p36				06 16					06 39			07 04			07 26					07 42		07 59
Rose Hill Marple	d									06 30							07 16					07 41			
Romiley	d		23p40				06 20			06 37		06 43			07 09		07 21	07 30				07 46	07 49		08 03
Woodley	d									06 40							07 24					07 49			
Hyde Central	d									06 43							07 27					07 52			
Hyde North	d									06 46							07 30					07 55			
Guide Bridge	d					06 27				06 50			06 57			07 27	07 34			07 47		07 59		08 10	
Fairfield	d									06 53							07 37					08 02			
Gorton	d					06 30							07 00			07 30				07 50				08 13	
Bredbury	d		23p43				06 23					06 46			07 12			07 33					07 52		08 06
Brinnington	d		23p45				06 25					06 49			07 14			07 36					07 55		08 09
Reddish North	d		23p48				06 28					06 52			07 17			07 40					07 58		08 12
Ryder Brow	d		23p51				06 31					06 55			07 21			07 42							08 15
Belle Vue	d		23p52				06 33					06 57			07 23			07 44							08 16
Ashburys	d		23p55			06 33	06 39					07 03	07 06		07 29	07 33		07 50		07 53				08 16	08 20
Ardwick	d															07 36									08 22
Manchester Piccadilly 10	a	00 02	00 03	04 40	06 05	06 42	06 47		07 02	07 03		07 12	07 15	07 34	07 36	07 43	07 47	07 56	08 02	08 03		08 12	08 09	08 25	08 30
Manchester Airport 85 ✈	a			05 00	06 29				07 29										08 26						

b arr. 2122

Table 78

Mondays to Fridays
from 06 September

Sheffield, Chinley, Marple and Romiley - Manchester and Manchester Airport

		NT	EM	NT	NT	NT		NT	TP	NT	NT	NT	NT	NT	NT FO A	EM	NT		NT	TP	NT	NT	NT	NT	EM	NT
			◇						◇1 ⊼							◇				◇1 ⊼					◇	
Sheffield 7	d	07 12	07 35						08 05							08 42				09 11				09 14	09 42	
Dore & Totley	d	07 19	07 42						08 10															09 21		
Grindleford	d	07 29																						09 29		
Hathersage	d	07 32																						09 32		
Bamford	d	07 36																						09 36		
Hope (Derbyshire)	d	07 39																						09 39		
Edale	d	07 47																						09 47		
Chinley	d	07 55	08 03						08 32															09 55		
Hazel Grove 86	a		08 16																							
Stockport 86	a		08 24						08 53						09d22	09 25				09 53					10 25	
New Mills Central	d	08 02				08 24								09 04										10 01		
Strines	d	08 05												09 07										10 04		
Marple	d	08 09				08 29					08 48			09 10					09 35			09 52		10 07		
Rose Hill Marple	d				08 15			08 35					08 59										09 55			
Romiley	d	08 13			08 20	08 33		08 40			08 51		09 04	09 14					09 38			09 56	10 00	10 11		
Woodley	d				08 23								09 07										10 03			
Hyde Central	d				08 26								09 10										10 06			
Hyde North	d				08 29								09 13										10 09			
Guide Bridge	d			08 27	08 33					08 49		09 12	09 17		09a42		09 28				09 58		10 13			10 28
Fairfield	d				08 36								09 20										10 16			
Gorton	d			08 31						08 52		09 15					09 31				10 01					10 31
Bredbury	d					08 36		08 43			08 54			09 17					09 41					10 14		
Brinnington	d					08 39		08 45			08 57			09 19					09 44					10 16		
Reddish North	d					08 43		08 48			09 00			09 22					09 47					10 19		
Ryder Brow	d										09 03											10 03				
Belle Vue	d										09 04											10 05				
Ashburys	d			08 34		08 48				08 56	09 07	09 18					09 34				10 04	10 07				10 34
Ardwick	d							08 54																		
Manchester Piccadilly 10	a	08 33	08 36	08 43	08 47	08 55		09 00	09 02	09 04	09 15	09 27	09 30	09 34		09 36	09 42		09 57	10 02	10 12	10 15	10 26	10 32	10 36	10 40
Manchester Airport 85 ✈	a								09 33											10 26						

		NT		NT	TP	NT	NT	NT	EM	NT	NT	NT		TP		NT	NT	NT	EM	NT	NT	NT		TP	NT
					◇1 ⊼				◇					◇1 ⊼					◇					◇1 ⊼	
Sheffield 7	d				10 11			10 14	10 42					11 11					11 42					12 11	
Dore & Totley	d							10 21																	
Grindleford	d							10 29																	
Hathersage	d							10 32																	
Bamford	d							10 36																	
Hope (Derbyshire)	d							10 39																	
Edale	d							10 47																	
Chinley	d							10 55																	
Hazel Grove 86	a																								
Stockport 86	a				10 53				11 25					11 53					12 25					12 53	
New Mills Central	d			10 30				11 01				11 30						12 01				12 30			
Strines	d																	12 04							
Marple	d			10 35			10 52	11 07				11 35					11 52	12 07				12 35			
Rose Hill Marple	d	10 30									11 30										12 30				
Romiley	d	10 35		10 38			10 56	11 11			11 35	11 38					11 56	12 11			12 35	12 38			
Woodley	d	10 38									11 38										12 38				
Hyde Central	d	10 41									11 41										12 41				
Hyde North	d	10 44									11 44										12 44				
Guide Bridge	d	10 48				10 58				11 28	11 48					11 58				12 28	12 48				12 58
Fairfield	d	10 51									11 51										12 51				
Gorton	d					11 01				11 31						12 01				12 31					13 01
Bredbury	d			10 41				11 14				11 41						12 14				12 41			
Brinnington	d			10 44				11 16				11 44						12 16				12 44			
Reddish North	d			10 47				11 19				11 47						12 19				12 47			
Ryder Brow	d						11 03										12 03								
Belle Vue	d						11 05										12 05								
Ashburys	d					11 04	11 07			11 34						12 04	12 07			12 34					13 04
Ardwick	d																								
Manchester Piccadilly 10	a	11 02		10 57	11 02	11 10	11 15	11 32	11 36	11 42	12 02	11 57		12 02		12 12	12 15	12 32	12 36	12 42	13 02	12 57		13 02	13 12
Manchester Airport 85 ✈	a				11 26									12 26										13 26	

A To Stalybridge arr. 09.49. Also stops at Reddish South 09x26 and Denton 09x31

Table 78

Mondays to Fridays
from 06 September

Sheffield, Chinley, Marple and Romiley - Manchester and Manchester Airport

	NT	NT	EM	NT	NT	NT	TP FX		TP FO	NT	NT	NT	EM	NT	NT	NT	TP		NT	NT	NT	EM	NT	NT
			◇				◇1 🛒		◇1 🛒				◇				◇1 🛒					◇		
Sheffield 7 d		12 14	12 42				13 11		13 11				13 42				14 11				14 14	14 42		
Dore & Totley d		12 21																			14 21			
Grindleford d		12 29																			14 29			
Hathersage d		12 32																			14 32			
Bamford d		12 36																			14 36			
Hope (Derbyshire) d		12 39																			14 39			
Edale d		12 47																			14 47			
Chinley d		12 55																			14 55			
Hazel Grove 86 a																								
Stockport 86 a			13 25				13 53		13 53				14 25				14 53					15 25		
New Mills Central d		13 01				13 30						14 01				14 30					15 01			
Strines d												14 04												
Marple d	12 52	13 07				13 35					13 52	14 07				14 35				14 52	15 07			
Rose Hill Marple d					13 30										14 30									15 30
Romiley d	12 56	13 11			13 35	13 38					13 56	14 11			14 35	14 38				14 56	15 11			15 35
Woodley d					13 38										14 38									15 38
Hyde Central d					13 41										14 41									15 41
Hyde North d					13 44										14 44									15 44
Guide Bridge d				13 28	13 48					13 58				14 28	14 48				14 58				15 28	15 48
Fairfield d					13 51										14 51									15 51
Gorton d				13 31						14 01				14 31					15 01				15 31	
Bredbury d		13 14				13 41						14 14				14 41					15 14			
Brinnington d		13 16				13 44						14 16				14 44					15 16			
Reddish North d		13 19				13 47						14 19				14 47					15 19			
Ryder Brow d	13 03										14 03									15 03				
Belle Vue d	13 05										14 05									15 05				
Ashburys d	13 07			13 34						14 04	14 07			14 34					15 04	15 07			15 34	
Ardwick d																								
Manchester Piccadilly 10 a	13 15	13 32	13 36	13 42	14 02	13 57	14 02		14 02	14 12	14 15	14 32	14 36	14 42	15 02	14 57	15 02		15 12	15 15	15 32	15 36	15 42	16 02
Manchester Airport 85 ✈ a							14 26		14 26								15 26							

	NT	TP	NT		NT	NT	EM	NT	NT	TP	NT	NT	NT		NT	NT	EM	NT	NT	NT	NT	TP	NT
		◇1 🛒					◇			◇1 🛒							◇					◇1 🛒	
Sheffield 7 d		15 11					15 42			16 10					16 14		16 42					17 11	
Dore & Totley d															16 21								
Grindleford d															16 29								
Hathersage d															16 32								
Bamford d															16 36								
Hope (Derbyshire) d															16 39								
Edale d															16 47								
Chinley d															16 55								
Hazel Grove 86 a																							
Stockport 86 a		15 53					16 25			16 53							17 25					17 53	
New Mills Central d	15 30					16 01						16 37			17 01				17 23				
Strines d						16 04																	
Marple d	15 35				15 52	16 07						16 42	16 52		17 06				17 27				
Rose Hill Marple d									16 26									17 10			17 36		
Romiley d	15 38				15 56	16 11			16 31			16 45	16 56		17 10			17 15	17 32		17 41		
Woodley d												16 49						17 18					
Hyde Central d												16 52						17 21					
Hyde North d												16 54						17 24					
Guide Bridge d			15 58					16 28			16 49	16 58				17 17		17 28		17 42			18 00
Fairfield d																		17 31					
Gorton d			16 01					16 31			16 52					17 20				17 45			
Bredbury d	15 41					16 14			16 34						17 13						17 44		
Brinnington d	15 44					16 16			16 37												17 46		
Reddish North d	15 47					16 19			16 40												17 49		
Ryder Brow d					16 03				16 42				17 03										
Belle Vue d					16 05				16 44				17 05										
Ashburys d			16 04		16 07			16 34	16 47		16 55	17 03	17 07			17 24				17 48	17 55		
Ardwick d																							
Manchester Piccadilly 10 a	15 57	16 02	16 12		16 15	16 32	16 36	16 42	16 56	17 02	17 05	17 10	17 15		17 29	17 33	17 37	17 42	17 48	17 57	18 01	18 02	18 12
Manchester Airport 85 ✈ a		16 26								17 32												18 26	

Table 78

Mondays to Fridays
from 06 September

Sheffield, Chinley, Marple and Romiley - Manchester and Manchester Airport

	NT	NT	NT	EM	NT	NT		TP	NT		NT	NT	NT	EM	NT	TP	NT	NT	NT		NT	EM	NT
				◇				◇1 🛒						◇		◇1 🛒						◇	
Sheffield 7 d		17 14		17 40				18 10						18 42		19 11					19 14	19 42	
Dore & Totley d		17 21																			19 21		
Grindleford d		17 29																			19 29		
Hathersage d		17 32																			19 32		
Bamford d		17 36																			19 36		
Hope (Derbyshire) d		17 39																			19 39		
Edale d		17 47																			19 47		
Chinley d		17 55						18 34					18 54								19 55		
Hazel Grove 86 a																							
Stockport 86 a				18 25				18 53						19 25		19 53						20 25	
New Mills Central d		18 01											19 01								20 01		
Strines d		18 04											19 04										
Marple d	17 52	18 07				18 35							19 07					19 37			20 07		
Rose Hill Marple d					18 11						18 44						19 30						
Romiley d	17 56	18 11			18 16	18 38					18 49		19 11				19 35	19 40			20 11		
Woodley d					18 19												19 38						
Hyde Central d					18 22												19 41						
Hyde North d					18 25												19 44						
Guide Bridge d			18 17		18 29				18 46			19 01			19 28		19 48		19 58				20 28
Fairfield d					18 32												19 51						
Gorton d			18 20						18 49			19 04			19 31				20 01				20 31
Bredbury d		18 14				18 41					18 52		19 14					19 43			20 14		
Brinnington d						18 44					18 54		19 16					19 46			20 16		
Reddish North d						18 47					18 58		19 19					19 49			20 19		
Ryder Brow d	18 03										19 00							19 51					
Belle Vue d	18 05										19 02							19 53					
Ashburys d	18 07		18 23						18 54		19 05	19 08			19 34			19 56	20 04				20 34
Ardwick d																							
Manchester Piccadilly 10 a	18 15	18 31	18 34	18 36	18 41	18 57		19 02	19 03		19 12	19 15	19 32	19 36	19 42	20 02	20 02	20 05	20 12		20 32	20 36	20 42
Manchester Airport 85 ✈ a								19 28								20 37							

	TP	NT	NT	EM	NT		NT	NT	TP	NT	NT	NT	NT
	◇1 🛒			◇					◇1				
Sheffield 7 d	20 11			20 32			20 35		22 11			22 47	
Dore & Totley d							20 43					22 54	
Grindleford d							20 50					23 01	
Hathersage d							20 53					23 05	
Bamford d							20 57					23 08	
Hope (Derbyshire) d							21 00					23 12	
Edale d							21 08					23 19	
Chinley d							21 16					23 27	
Hazel Grove 86 a													
Stockport 86 a	20 53			21 20					22 53			23 47	
New Mills Central d		20 30					21c30			22 30			23 30
Strines d		20 33								22 33			23 33
Marple d		20 36					21 36			22 36			23 36
Rose Hill Marple d					21 12								
Romiley d		20 40			21 17		21 40			22 40			23 40
Woodley d					21 20								
Hyde Central d					21 23								
Hyde North d					21 26								
Guide Bridge d			20 58		21 30			21 58			22 58		
Fairfield d					21 33								
Gorton d			21 01					22 01			23 01		
Bredbury d		20 43					21 43			22 43			23 43
Brinnington d		20 45					21 45			22 45			23 45
Reddish North d		20 48					21 48			22 48			23 48
Ryder Brow d		20 51					21 51			22 51			23 51
Belle Vue d		20 52					21 52			22 52			23 52
Ashburys d		20 55	21 04				21 55	22 04		22 55	23 04		23 55
Ardwick d													
Manchester Piccadilly 10 a	21 02	21 03	21 12	21 32	21 42		22 05	22 12	23 02	23 03	23 12	00 02	00 03
Manchester Airport 85 ✈ a	21 36								23 26				

c arr. 2122

Sheffield, Chinley, Marple and Romiley - Manchester and Manchester Airport

		NT	NT	TP ◇1	TP ◇1	TP ◇1	NT	EM ◇	NT A	NT B		NT A	NT B	NT	NT	TP ◇1	NT	NT	EM ◇	NT		NT	NT	TP ◇1	NT
Sheffield 7	d	22p47		03 45	05 11	06 11		06 20								07 09		07 12	07 35					08 05	
Dore & Totley	d	22p54						06 27								07 14		07 19	07 42					08 10	
Grindleford	d	23p01						06 35										07 29							
Hathersage	d	23p05						06 39										07 32							
Bamford	d	23p08						06 43										07 36							
Hope (Derbyshire)	d	23p12						06 47										07 39							
Edale	d	23p19						06 55										07 47							
Chinley	d	23p27						07 03										07 55	08 03					08 32	
Hazel Grove 86	a																		08 16						
Stockport 86	a	23p47			05 53	06 53		07 22								07 53			08 24					08 53	
New Mills Central	d		23p30						06 58	07 01								08 01							
Strines	d		23p33						07 01	07 04								08 04							
Marple	d		23p36						07 04	07 07					07 35			08 07					08 35		
Rose Hill Marple	d													07 30								08 30			
Romiley	d		23p40						07 09	07 12				07 35	07 38			08 12				08 35	08 38		
Woodley	d													07 38								08 38			
Hyde Central	d													07 41								08 41			
Hyde North	d													07 44								08 44			
Guide Bridge	d						06 57					07 28	07 28	07 48			07 58			08 28		08 48			08 58
Fairfield	d													07 51								08 51			
Gorton	d						07 00					07 31	07 31				08 01			08 31					09 01
Bredbury	d		23p43						07 12	07 15					07 41			08 15					08 41		
Brinnington	d		23p45						07 14	07 17					07 44			08 16					08 44		
Reddish North	d		23p48						07 17	07 20					07 47			08 19					08 47		
Ryder Brow	d		23p51						07 21	07 24															
Belle Vue	d		23p52						07 23	07 26															
Ashburys	d		23p55				07 03		07 29	07 29		07 34	07 34				08 04			08 34					09 04
Ardwick	d																								
Manchester Piccadilly 10	a	00 02	00 03	04 40	06 05	07 02	07 12	07 34	07 36	07 36		07 42	07 43	08 02	07 59	08 02	08 12	08 32	08 36	08 42		09 02	08 57	09 02	09 12
Manchester Airport 85 ✈	a			05 00	06 29	07 29										08 26								09 26	

		NT	NT	EM ◇	NT	NT		NT	TP ◇1	NT	NT	NT	EM ◇	NT	NT	NT		TP ◇1	NT	NT	NT	EM ◇	NT	NT	NT
Sheffield 7	d		08 14	08 42					09 11			09 14	09 42					10 11			10 14	10 42			
Dore & Totley	d		08 21									09 21									10 21				
Grindleford	d		08 29									09 29									10 29				
Hathersage	d		08 32									09 32									10 32				
Bamford	d		08 36									09 36									10 36				
Hope (Derbyshire)	d		08 39									09 39									10 39				
Edale	d		08 47									09 47									10 47				
Chinley	d		08 55									09 55									10 55				
Hazel Grove 86	a																								
Stockport 86	a			09 25					09 53				10 25					10 53				11 25			
New Mills Central	d		09 01									10 01									11 01				
Strines	d		09 04									10 04													
Marple	d	08 52	09 07					09 35			09 52	10 07				10 35				10 52	11 07				11 35
Rose Hill Marple	d					09 30									10 30									11 30	
Romiley	d	08 56	09 11			09 35		09 38			09 56	10 11			10 35	10 38				10 56	11 11			11 35	11 38
Woodley	d					09 38									10 38									11 38	
Hyde Central	d					09 41									10 41									11 41	
Hyde North	d					09 44									10 44									11 44	
Guide Bridge	d				09 28	09 48				09 58				10 28	10 48				10 58				11 28	11 48	
Fairfield	d					09 51									10 51									11 51	
Gorton	d				09 31					10 01				10 31					11 01				11 31		
Bredbury	d		09 14					09 41				10 14				10 41					11 14				11 41
Brinnington	d		09 16					09 44				10 16				10 44					11 16				11 44
Reddish North	d		09 19					09 47				10 19				10 47					11 19				11 47
Ryder Brow	d	09 03									10 03									11 03					
Belle Vue	d	09 05									10 05									11 05					
Ashburys	d	09 07			09 34					10 04	10 07			10 34					11 04	11 07			11 34		
Ardwick	d																								
Manchester Piccadilly 10	a	09 15	09 32	09 36	09 42	10 02		09 57	10 02	10 12	10 15	10 32	10 36	10 42	11 02	10 57		11 02	11 12	11 15	11 32	11 36	11 42	12 02	11 57
Manchester Airport 85 ✈	a								10 26									11 26							

A from 11 September

B until 4 September

Sheffield, Chinley, Marple and Romiley - Manchester and Manchester Airport

		TP ◇1		NT	NT	NT	EM ◇	NT	NT	NT	TP ◇1	NT		NT	NT	EM ◇	NT	NT	NT	TP ◇1	NT	NT		NT	EM ◇
Sheffield 7	d	11 11				11 14	11 42				12 11				12 14	12 42				13 11				13 14	13 42
Dore & Totley	d					11 21									12 21									13 21	
Grindleford	d					11 29									12 29									13 29	
Hathersage	d					11 32									12 32									13 32	
Bamford	d					11 36									12 36									13 36	
Hope (Derbyshire)	d					11 39									12 39									13 39	
Edale	d					11 47									12 47									13 47	
Chinley	d					11 55									12 55									13 55	
Hazel Grove 86	a																								
Stockport 86	a	11 53					12 25				12 53					13 25				13 53					14 25
New Mills Central	d					12 01									13 01									14 01	
Strines	d					12 04																		14 04	
Marple	d				11 52	12 07				12 35				12 52	13 07				13 35			13 52		14 07	
Rose Hill Marple	d								12 30									13 30							
Romiley	d				11 56	12 11			12 35	12 38				12 56	13 11			13 35	13 38			13 56		14 11	
Woodley	d								12 38									13 38							
Hyde Central	d								12 41									13 41							
Hyde North	d								12 44									13 44							
Guide Bridge	d			11 58				12 28	12 48			12 58					13 28	13 48			13 58				
Fairfield	d								12 51									13 51							
Gorton	d			12 01				12 31				13 01					13 31				14 01				
Bredbury	d					12 14				12 41					13 14				13 41					14 14	
Brinnington	d					12 16				12 44					13 16				13 44					14 16	
Reddish North	d					12 19				12 47					13 19				13 47					14 19	
Ryder Brow	d				12 03									13 03								14 03			
Belle Vue	d				12 05									13 05								14 05			
Ashburys	d			12 04	12 07			12 34				13 04		13 07			13 34				14 04	14 07			
Ardwick	d																								
Manchester Piccadilly 10	a	12 02		12 12	12 15	12 32	12 36	12 42	13 02	12 57	13 02	13 12		13 15	13 32	13 36	13 42	14 02	13 57	14 02	14 12	14 15		14 32	14 36
Manchester Airport 85 ✈	a	12 26									13 33									14 26					

		NT	NT	NT	TP ◇1	NT	NT	NT		EM ◇	NT	NT	NT	TP ◇1	NT	NT	NT	EM ◇		NT	NT	NT	TP ◇1	NT	NT
Sheffield 7	d				14 11			14 14		14 42				15 11			15 14	15 42					16 10		
Dore & Totley	d							14 21									15 21								
Grindleford	d							14 29									15 29								
Hathersage	d							14 32									15 32								
Bamford	d							14 36									15 36								
Hope (Derbyshire)	d							14 39									15 39								
Edale	d							14 47									15 47								
Chinley	d							14 55									15 55								
Hazel Grove 86	a																								
Stockport 86	a				14 53					15 25				15 53				16 25					16 53		
New Mills Central	d							15 01									16 01								
Strines	d																16 04								
Marple	d			14 35			14 52	15 07					15 35			15 52	16 07					16 34			16 52
Rose Hill Marple	d		14 30									15 30									16 30				
Romiley	d		14 35	14 38			14 56	15 11				15 35	15 38			15 56	16 11				16 35	16 38			16 56
Woodley	d		14 38									15 38									16 38				
Hyde Central	d		14 41									15 41									16 41				
Hyde North	d		14 44									15 44									16 44				
Guide Bridge	d	14 28	14 48			14 58					15 28	15 48			15 58					16 28	16 48			16 58	
Fairfield	d		14 51									15 51									16 51				
Gorton	d	14 31				15 01					15 31				16 01					16 31				17 01	
Bredbury	d			14 41				15 14					15 41				16 14					16 41			
Brinnington	d			14 44				15 16					15 44				16 16					16 43			
Reddish North	d			14 47				15 19					15 47				16 19					16 46			
Ryder Brow	d						15 03									16 03									17 03
Belle Vue	d						15 05									16 05									17 05
Ashburys	d	14 34				15 04	15 07				15 34				16 04	16 07				16 34				17 04	17 07
Ardwick	d																								
Manchester Piccadilly 10	a	14 42	15 02	14 57	15 02	15 12	15 15	15 32		15 36	15 42	16 02	15 57	16 02	16 12	16 15	16 33	16 36		16 42	17 02	16 56	17 02	17 12	17 15
Manchester Airport 85 ✈	a				15 26									16 26									17 32		

Table 78

Saturdays

Sheffield, Chinley, Marple and Romiley - Manchester and Manchester Airport

		NT	EM ◇	NT	NT	NT	TP ◇1 ⊼	NT	NT	NT	EM ◇	NT	NT	NT	TP ◇1 ⊼	NT	NT	NT	EM ◇	NT	TP ◇1 ⊼	NT
Sheffield 7 ⇌	d	16 14	16 42				17 11			17 14	17 40				18 10			18 14	18 42		19 11	
Dore & Totley	d	16 21								17 21								18 21				
Grindleford	d	16 29								17 29								18 28				
Hathersage	d	16 32								17 32								18 32				
Bamford	d	16 36								17 36								18 35				
Hope (Derbyshire)	d	16 39								17 39								18 39				
Edale	d	16 47								17 47								18 46				
Chinley	d	16 55								17 55					18 34			18 54				
Hazel Grove 86	a																					
Stockport 86	a		17 25				17 53				18 25				18 53				19 25		19 53	
New Mills Central	d	17 01								18 01								19 01				
Strines	d									18 04								19 04				
Marple	d	17 07				17 34			17 52	18 07				18 35			18 52	19 07				
Rose Hill Marple	d				17 30								18 30									19 30
Romiley	d	17 11			17 35	17 38			17 56	18 11			18 35	18 38			18 56	19 11				19 35
Woodley	d				17 38								18 38									19 38
Hyde Central	d				17 41								18 41									19 41
Hyde North	d				17 44								18 44									19 44
Guide Bridge	d			17 28	17 48			17 58				18 28	18 48			18 58				19 28		19 48
Fairfield	d				17 51								18 51									19 51
Gorton	d			17 31				18 01				18 31				19 01				19 31		
Bredbury	d	17 14				17 41				18 14				18 41				19 14				
Brinnington	d	17 16				17 43				18 16				18 44				19 16				
Reddish North	d	17 19				17 46				18 19				18 47				19 19				
Ryder Brow	d								18 03								19 03					
Belle Vue	d								18 05								19 05					
Ashburys	d			17 34				18 04	18 07			18 34				19 04	19 07			19 34		
Ardwick	d																					
Manchester Piccadilly 10 ⇌	a	17 32	17 37	17 42	18 02	17 56	18 02	18 12	18 15	18 32	18 36	18 42	19 02	18 57	19 02	19 12	19 15	19 32	19 36	19 42	20 02	20 02
Manchester Airport 85 ✈	a						18 26								19 28						20 36	

		NT	NT	NT	EM ◇	TP ◇1 ⊼	NT	NT	EM ◇	NT	NT	NT	NT	NT	NT	NT
Sheffield 7 ⇌	d			19 14	19 42	20 11			20 31		20 35				22 24	
Dore & Totley	d			19 21							20 42				22 31	
Grindleford	d			19 29							20 50				22 38	
Hathersage	d			19 32							20 53				22 41	
Bamford	d			19 36							20 57				22 45	
Hope (Derbyshire)	d			19 39							21 00				22 48	
Edale	d			19 47							21 08				22 56	
Chinley	d			19 55							21 16				23 04	
Hazel Grove 86	a															
Stockport 86	a				20 25	20 53			21 20						23 21	
New Mills Central	d			20 01			20 30				21c30		22 30			23 30
Strines	d						20 33						22 33			23 33
Marple	d		19 56	20 07			20 36				21 36		22 36			23 36
Rose Hill Marple	d									21 12						
Romiley	d		19 59	20 11			20 40			21 17	21 40		22 40			23 40
Woodley	d									21 20						
Hyde Central	d									21 23						
Hyde North	d									21 26						
Guide Bridge	d	19 58						20 58		21 30		21 58		22 58		
Fairfield	d									21 33						
Gorton	d	20 01						21 01				22 01		23 01		
Bredbury	d		20 02	20 14			20 43				21 43		22 43			23 43
Brinnington	d		20 05	20 16			20 45				21 45		22 45			23 45
Reddish North	d		20 08	20 19			20 48				21 48		22 48			23 48
Ryder Brow	d		20 10				20 51				21 51		22 51			23 51
Belle Vue	d		20 12				20 52				21 52		22 52			23 52
Ashburys	d	20 04	20 15				20 55	21 04			21 55	22 04	22 55	23 04		23 55
Ardwick	d															
Manchester Piccadilly 10 ⇌	a	20 12	20 22	20 32	20 37	21 02	21 03	21 12	21 32	21 42	22 05	22 12	23 03	23 12	23 43	00 03
Manchester Airport 85 ✈	a					21 36										

c arr. 2122

Table 78

Sundays until 11 July

Sheffield, Chinley, Marple and Romiley - Manchester and Manchester Airport

		NT A	TP ◇1	TP ◇1	NT	NT	TP ◇1	NT	NT	EM ◇	NT	TP ◇1	NT	NT	EM ◇	NT	TP ◇1	NT	NT	EM ◇	NT	TP ◇1	NT
Sheffield 7 ⇌	d		07 50	09 10	09 20		10 10	10 20		10 41		11 10		11 14	11 38		12 10		12 13	12 41		13 10	
Dore & Totley	d				09 27			10 27		10 48				11 21					12 21				
Grindleford	d				09 34			10 34						11 29					12 28				
Hathersage	d				09 38			10 38						11 32					12 32				
Bamford	d				09 41			10 41						11 36					12 35				
Hope (Derbyshire)	d				09 45			10 45						11 39					12 39				
Edale	d				09 52			10 52						11 47					12 46				
Chinley	d				10 00			11 00						11 55					12 54				
Hazel Grove 86	a																						
Stockport 86	a		08 31	09 53			10 53			11 25		11 53			12 25		12 53			13 25		13 53	
New Mills Central	d	23p30			10 07			11 07						12 01					13 01				
Strines	d	23p33			10 10			11 10						12 04					13 04				
Marple	d	23p36			10 13			11 13						12 07					13 07				
Rose Hill Marple	d	⌇																					
Romiley	d	23p40			10 17			11 17						12 11					13 11				
Woodley	d	⌇																					
Hyde Central	d	⌇																					
Hyde North	d	⌇																					
Guide Bridge	d	⌇				10 28			10 58		11 28		11 58			12 28		12 58			13 28		13 58
Fairfield	d	⌇																					
Gorton	d	⌇				10 31			11 01		11 31		12 01			12 31		13 01			13 31		14 01
Bredbury	d	23p43			10 20			11 20						12 14					13 14				
Brinnington	d	23p45			10 22			11 22						12 16					13 16				
Reddish North	d	23p48			10 25			11 25						12 19					13 19				
Ryder Brow	d	23p51																					
Belle Vue	d	23p52																					
Ashburys	d	23p55				10 34			11 04		11 34		12 04			12 34		13 04			13 34		14 04
Ardwick	d	⌇																					
Manchester Piccadilly 10 ⇌	a	00 03	08 42	10 06	10 37	10 42	11 06	11 38	11 13	11 37	11 42	12 06	12 12	12 31	12 37	12 42	13 06	13 12	13 31	13 37	13 42	14 06	14 12
Manchester Airport 85 ✈	a		09 07									12 29					13 29					14 29	

		NT	EM ◇	NT	TP ◇1	NT	EM ◇	NT	TP ◇1	NT	NT	EM ◇	NT	TP ◇1	NT	NT	EM ◇	NT	TP ◇1	NT	NT	EM ◇	NT
Sheffield 7 ⇌	d	13 13	13 38		14 11		14 39		15 11		15 14	15 38		16 11		16 15	16 44		17 11		17 14	17 44	
Dore & Totley	d	13 20									15 21					16 22					17 21		
Grindleford	d	13 28									15 29					16 30					17 29		
Hathersage	d	13 31									15 32					16 33					17 32		
Bamford	d	13 35									15 36					16 37					17 36		
Hope (Derbyshire)	d	13 38									15 39					16 40					17 39		
Edale	d	13 46									15 47					16 48					17 47		
Chinley	d	13 54									15 55					16 56					17 55		
Hazel Grove 86	a																						
Stockport 86	a		14 25		14 53		15 25		15 53			16 25		16 53			17 26		17 53			18 25	
New Mills Central	d	14 00									16 01					17 02					18 01		
Strines	d	14 03									16 04					17 05					18 04		
Marple	d	14 07									16 07					17 08					18 07		
Rose Hill Marple	d																						
Romiley	d	14 10									16 11					17 12					18 11		
Woodley	d																						
Hyde Central	d																						
Hyde North	d																						
Guide Bridge	d			14 28		14 58		15 28		15 58			16 28		16 58			17 28		17 58			18 28
Fairfield	d																						
Gorton	d			14 31		15 01		15 31		16 01			16 31		17 01			17 31		18 01			18 31
Bredbury	d	14 13									16 14					17 15					18 14		
Brinnington	d	14 16									16 16					17 17					18 16		
Reddish North	d	14 19									16 19					17 20					18 19		
Ryder Brow	d																						
Belle Vue	d																						
Ashburys	d			14 34		15 04		15 34		16 04			16 34		17 04			17 34		18 04			18 34
Ardwick	d																						
Manchester Piccadilly 10 ⇌	a	14 31	14 37	14 42	15 06	15 12	15 37	15 42	16 06	16 12	16 31	16 37	16 42	17 06	17 12	17 32	17 37	17 42	18 06	18 12	18 31	18 37	18 42
Manchester Airport 85 ✈	a				15 29				16 29					17 29					18 29				

A not 23 May

Table 78

Sundays
until 11 July

Sheffield, Chinley, Marple and Romiley - Manchester and Manchester Airport

		TP	NT	NT	EM	NT	TP	NT	NT	EM	NT	TP	NT	EM	TP	NT	NT	NT
		◇1			◇		◇1			◇		◇1		◇	◇1			
Sheffield 7	d	18 11		18 15	18 37		19 11		19 14	19 35		20 11		20 35	21 11		22 17	
Dore & Totley	d			18 22					19 21								22 24	
Grindleford	d			18 30					19 29								22 32	
Hathersage	d			18 33					19 32								22 35	
Bamford	d			18 37					19 36								22 39	
Hope (Derbyshire)	d			18 40					19 39								22 42	
Edale	d			18 48					19 47								22 50	
Chinley	d			18 56					19 55								22 58	
Hazel Grove 86	a																	
Stockport 86	a	18 53			19 25		19 53			20 25		20 53		21 24	21 53		23 16	
New Mills Central	d			19 02					20 01									23 01
Strines	d			19 05					20 04									23 04
Marple	d			19 08					20 07									23 07
Rose Hill Marple	d																	
Romiley	d			19 12					20 11									23 11
Woodley	d																	
Hyde Central	d																	
Hyde North	d																	
Guide Bridge	d		18 58			19 28		19 58			20 28		20 58			21 58		
Fairfield	d																	
Gorton	d		19 01			19 31		20 01			20 31		21 01			22 01		
Bredbury	d			19 15					20 14									23 14
Brinnington	d			19 17					20 16									23 16
Reddish North	d			19 20					20 19									23 19
Ryder Brow	d																	
Belle Vue	d																	
Ashburys	d		19 04			19 34		20 04			20 34		21 04			22 04		
Ardwick	d																	
Manchester Piccadilly 10	a	19 06	19 12	19 36	19 37	19 42	20 06	20 12	20 32	20 38	20 42	21 06	21 12	21 36	22 06	22 12	23 29	23 31
Manchester Airport 85 ✈	a	19 29					20 29					21 29			22 29			

Sundays
18 July to 05 September

		NT	TP	TP	NT	NT	TP	NT	NT	EM	NT	TP	NT	NT	EM	NT	TP	NT	NT	EM	NT	TP	NT
			◇1	◇1			◇1			◇		◇1			◇		◇1			◇		◇1	
Sheffield 7	d		07 50	09 10	09 20		10 10	10 20		10 41		11 10		11 14	11 38		12 10		12 13	12 41		13 10	
Dore & Totley	d				09 27			10 27		10 48				11 21					12 21				
Grindleford	d				09 34			10 34						11 29					12 28				
Hathersage	d				09 38			10 38						11 32					12 32				
Bamford	d				09 41			10 41						11 36					12 35				
Hope (Derbyshire)	d				09 45			10 45						11 39					12 39				
Edale	d				09 52			10 52						11 47					12 46				
Chinley	d				10 00			11 00						11 55					12 54				
Hazel Grove 86	a																						
Stockport 86	a		08 31	09 53			10 53			11 25		11 53			12 25		12 53			13 25		13 53	
New Mills Central	d	23p30			10 07			11 07						12 01					13 01				
Strines	d	23p33			10 10			11 10						12 04					13 04				
Marple	d	23p36			10 13			11 13						12 07					13 07				
Rose Hill Marple	d																						
Romiley	d	23p40			10 17			11 17						12 11					13 11				
Woodley	d																						
Hyde Central	d																						
Hyde North	d																						
Guide Bridge	d					10 28			10 58		11 28		11 58			12 28		12 58			13 28		13 58
Fairfield	d																						
Gorton	d					10 31			11 01		11 31		12 01			12 31		13 01			13 31		14 01
Bredbury	d	23p43			10 20			11 20						12 14					13 14				
Brinnington	d	23p45			10 22			11 22						12 16					13 16				
Reddish North	d	23p48			10 25			11 25						12 19					13 19				
Ryder Brow	d	23p51																					
Belle Vue	d	23p52																					
Ashburys	d	23p55				10 34			11 04		11 34		12 04			12 34		13 04			13 34		14 04
Ardwick	d																						
Manchester Piccadilly 10	a	00 03	08 42	10 06	10 37	10 42	11 07	11 38	11 13	11 37	11 42	12 06	12 12	12 31	12 37	12 42	13 06	13 12	13 31	13 37	13 42	14 06	14 12
Manchester Airport 85 ✈	a		09 07									12 29					13 29					14 29	

Table 78

Sundays
18 July to 05 September

Sheffield, Chinley, Marple and Romiley - Manchester and Manchester Airport

		NT	EM	NT	TP	NT	EM	NT	TP	NT	NT	EM	NT	TP	NT	NT	EM	NT	TP	NT	NT	EM	NT
			◇		◇1		◇		◇1			◇		◇1			◇		◇1			◇	
Sheffield 7	d	13 13	13 38		14 11		14 39		15 11		15 14	15 38		16 11		16 15	16 44		17 11		17 14	17 44	
Dore & Totley	d	13 20									15 21					16 22					17 21		
Grindleford	d	13 28									15 29					16 30					17 29		
Hathersage	d	13 31									15 32					16 33					17 32		
Bamford	d	13 35									15 36					16 37					17 36		
Hope (Derbyshire)	d	13 38									15 39					16 40					17 39		
Edale	d	13 46									15 47					16 48					17 47		
Chinley	d	13 54									15 55					16 56					17 55		
Hazel Grove 86	a																						
Stockport 86	a		14 25		14 53		15 25		15 53			16 25		16 53			17 26		17 53			18 25	
New Mills Central	d	14 00									16 01					17 02					18 01		
Strines	d	14 03									16 04					17 05					18 04		
Marple	d	14 07									16 07					17 08					18 07		
Rose Hill Marple	d																						
Romiley	d	14 10									16 11					17 12					18 11		
Woodley	d																						
Hyde Central	d																						
Hyde North	d																						
Guide Bridge	d			14 28		14 58		15 28		15 58			16 28		16 58			17 28		17 58			18 28
Fairfield	d																						
Gorton	d			14 31		15 01		15 31		16 01			16 31		17 01			17 31		18 01			18 31
Bredbury	d	14 13									16 14					17 15					18 14		
Brinnington	d	14 16									16 16					17 17					18 16		
Reddish North	d	14 19									16 19					17 20					18 19		
Ryder Brow	d																						
Belle Vue	d																						
Ashburys	d			14 34		15 04		15 34		16 04			16 34		17 04			17 34		18 04			18 34
Ardwick	d																						
Manchester Piccadilly 10	a	14 31	14 37	14 42	15 06	15 12	15 37	15 42	16 06	16 12	16 31	16 37	16 42	17 06	17 12	17 32	17 37	17 42	18 06	18 12	18 31	18 37	18 42
Manchester Airport 85 ✈	a				15 29				16 29					17 29					18 29				

		TP	NT	NT	EM	NT	TP	NT	NT	EM	NT	TP	NT	EM	TP	NT	NT	NT
		◇1			◇		◇1			◇		◇1		◇	◇1			
Sheffield 7	d	18 11		18 15	18 37		19 11		19 14	19 35		20 11		20 35	21 11		22 17	
Dore & Totley	d			18 22					19 21								22 24	
Grindleford	d			18 30					19 29								22 32	
Hathersage	d			18 33					19 32								22 35	
Bamford	d			18 37					19 36								22 39	
Hope (Derbyshire)	d			18 40					19 39								22 42	
Edale	d			18 48					19 47								22 50	
Chinley	d			18 56					19 55								22 58	
Hazel Grove 86	a																	
Stockport 86	a	18 53			19 25		19 53			20 25		20 53		21 24	21 53		23 16	
New Mills Central	d			19 02					20 01									23 01
Strines	d			19 05					20 04									23 04
Marple	d			19 08					20 07									23 07
Rose Hill Marple	d																	
Romiley	d			19 12					20 11									23 11
Woodley	d																	
Hyde Central	d																	
Hyde North	d																	
Guide Bridge	d		18 58			19 28		19 58			20 28		20 58			21 58		
Fairfield	d																	
Gorton	d		19 01			19 31		20 01			20 31		21 01			22 01		
Bredbury	d			19 15					20 14									23 14
Brinnington	d			19 17					20 16									23 16
Reddish North	d			19 20					20 19									23 19
Ryder Brow	d																	
Belle Vue	d																	
Ashburys	d		19 04			19 34		20 04			20 34		21 04			22 04		
Ardwick	d																	
Manchester Piccadilly 10	a	19 06	19 12	19 36	19 37	19 42	20 06	20 12	20 32	20 38	20 42	21 06	21 12	21 36	22 06	22 12	23 29	23 31
Manchester Airport 85 ✈	a	19 29					20 29					21 29			22 29			

Table 78

Sundays
from 12 September

Sheffield, Chinley, Marple and Romiley - Manchester and Manchester Airport

	NT	TP ◇1	TP ◇1	NT	NT	TP ◇1	NT A	NT	EM ◇	NT	NT	NT	EM ◇	NT	TP ◇1	NT	NT A	EM ◇	NT	TP ◇1	NT	NT
Sheffield 7 d		07 50	09 10	09 20		10 10	10 20		10 41			11 14	11 38		12 10		12 13	12 41		13 10		13 13
Dore & Totley d				09 27			10 27		10 48			11 21					12 21					13 20
Grindleford d				09 34			10 34					11 29					12 28					13 28
Hathersage d				09 38			10 38					11 32					12 32					13 31
Bamford d				09 41			10 41					11 36					12 35					13 35
Hope (Derbyshire) d				09 45			10 45					11 39					12 39					13 38
Edale d				09 52			10 52					11 47					12 46					13 46
Chinley d				10 00			11 00					11 55					12 54					13 54
Hazel Grove 86 a																						
Stockport 86 a		08 31	09 53						11 25				12 25		12 53			13 25		13 53		
New Mills Central d	23p30			10 07			11 07					12 01					13 01					14 00
Strines d	23p33			10 10			11 10					12 04					13 04					14 03
Marple d	23p36			10 13			11 13					12 07					13 07					14 07
Rose Hill Marple d																						
Romiley d	23p40			10 17			11 17					12 11					13 11					14 10
Woodley d																						
Hyde Central d																						
Hyde North d																						
Guide Bridge d					10 28			10 58		11 28	11 58			12 28		12 58			13 28		13 58	
Fairfield d																						
Gorton d					10 31			11 01		11 31	12 01			12 31		13 01			13 31		14 01	
Bredbury d	23p43			10 20			11 20					12 14					13 14					14 13
Brinnington d	23p45			10 22			11 22					12 16					13 16					14 16
Reddish North d	23p48			10 25			11 25					12 19					13 19					14 19
Ryder Brow d	23p51																					
Belle Vue d	23p52																					
Ashburys d	23p55				10 34			11 04		11 34	12 04			12 34		13 04			13 34		14 04	
Ardwick d																						
Manchester Piccadilly 10 a	00 03	08 42	10 04	10 37	10 42	11 06	11 37	11 12	11 37	11 42	12 12	12 31	12 37	12 42	13 02	13 12	13 31	13 37	13 42	14 06	14 12	14 31
Manchester Airport 85 a		09 07													13 29					14 29		

	NT	TP ◇1	NT	EM ◇	NT	TP ◇1	NT	NT	EM ◇	NT	TP ◇1	NT	NT A	EM ◇	NT	TP ◇1	NT	NT	EM ◇	NT	TP ◇1	NT	NT A
Sheffield 7 d		14 11		14 39		15 11		15 14	15 38		16 11		16 15	16 44		17 11		17 14	17 44		18 11		18 15
Dore & Totley d								15 21					16 22					17 21					18 22
Grindleford d								15 29					16 30					17 29					18 30
Hathersage d								15 32					16 33					17 32					18 33
Bamford d								15 36					16 37					17 36					18 37
Hope (Derbyshire) d								15 39					16 40					17 39					18 40
Edale d								15 47					16 48					17 47					18 48
Chinley d								15 55					16 56					17 55					18 56
Hazel Grove 86 a																							
Stockport 86 a		14 53		15 25		15 53			16 25		16 53			17 26		17 53			18 25		18 53		
New Mills Central d								16 01					17 02					18 01					19 02
Strines d								16 04					17 05					18 04					19 05
Marple d								16 07					17 08					18 07					19 08
Rose Hill Marple d																							
Romiley d								16 11					17 12					18 11					19 12
Woodley d																							
Hyde Central d																							
Hyde North d																							
Guide Bridge d	14 28		14 58		15 28		15 58			16 28		16 58			17 28		17 58			18 28		18 58	
Fairfield d																							
Gorton d	14 31		15 01		15 31		16 01			16 31		17 01			17 31		18 01			18 31		19 01	
Bredbury d								16 14					17 15					18 14					19 15
Brinnington d								16 16					17 17					18 16					19 17
Reddish North d								16 19					17 20					18 19					19 20
Ryder Brow d																							
Belle Vue d																							
Ashburys d	14 34		15 04		15 34		16 04			16 34		17 04			17 34		18 04			18 34		19 04	
Ardwick d																							
Manchester Piccadilly 10 a	14 42	15 06	15 12	15 37	15 42	16 06	16 12	16 31	16 37	16 42	17 06	17 12	17 32	17 37	17 42	18 06	18 12	18 31	18 37	18 42	19 06	19 12	19 36
Manchester Airport 85 a		15 29				16 29					17 29					18 29					19 29		

A 12 September

Table 78

Sundays
from 12 September

Sheffield, Chinley, Marple and Romiley - Manchester and Manchester Airport

	EM ◇	NT	TP ◇1	NT	NT	EM ◇	NT	TP ◇1	NT	EM ◇	TP ◇1	NT	NT	NT
Sheffield 7 d	18 37		19 11		19 14	19 35		20 11		20 35	21 11		22 17	
Dore & Totley d					19 21								22 24	
Grindleford d					19 29								22 32	
Hathersage d					19 32								22 35	
Bamford d					19 36								22 39	
Hope (Derbyshire) d					19 39								22 42	
Edale d					19 47								22 50	
Chinley d					19 55								22 58	
Hazel Grove 86 a														
Stockport 86 a	19 25		19 53			20 25		20 53		21 24	21 53		23 16	
New Mills Central d					20 01									23 01
Strines d					20 04									23 04
Marple d					20 07									23 07
Rose Hill Marple d														
Romiley d					20 11									23 11
Woodley d														
Hyde Central d														
Hyde North d														
Guide Bridge d		19 28		19 58			20 28		20 58			21 58		
Fairfield d														
Gorton d		19 31		20 01			20 31		21 01			22 01		
Bredbury d					20 14									23 14
Brinnington d					20 16									23 16
Reddish North d					20 19									23 19
Ryder Brow d														
Belle Vue d														
Ashburys d		19 34		20 04			20 34		21 04			22 04		
Ardwick d														
Manchester Piccadilly 10 a	19 37	19 42	20 06	20 12	20 32	20 38	20 42	21 06	21 12	21 36	22 06	22 12	23 29	23 31
Manchester Airport 85 a			20 29					21 29			22 29			

Table 79

Manchester - Glossop and Hadfield

Mondays to Fridays

until 03 September

		NT	NT	NT	NT	NT	NT	NT	NT	NT	NT	NT	NT	NT	NT	NT	NT	NT	NT	NT	NT	NT	NT
Manchester Piccadilly 10 78	d	06 16	06 46	07 03	07 18	07 48	08 07	08 29	08 48	09 15	09 48	10 15	10 48	11 18	11 48	12 18	12 48	13 18	13 48	14 18	14 48	15 18	15 48
Ardwick 78	d																						
Ashburys 78	d	06 20	06 50	07 07	07 22	07 52	08 11	08 33	08 52	09 19	09 52	10 19	10 52	11 22	11 52	12 22	12 52	13 22	13 52	14 22	14 52	15 22	15 52
Gorton 78	d	06 22	06 52	07 09	07 24	07 54	08 13	08 35	08 54	09 21	09 54	10 21	10 54	11 24	11 54	12 24	12 54	13 24	13 54	14 24	14 54	15 24	15 54
Guide Bridge 78	d	06 26	06 56	07 13	07 28	07 58	08 17	08 39	08 58	09 25	09 58	10 25	10 58	11 28	11 58	12 28	12 58	13 28	13 58	14 28	14 58	15 28	15 58
Flowery Field	d	06 29	06 59	07 16	07 31	08 01	08 20	08 42	09 01	09 28	10 01	10 28	11 01	11 31	12 01	12 31	13 01	13 31	14 01	14 31	15 01	15 31	16 01
Newton for Hyde	d	06 31	07 01	07 18	07 33	08 03	08 22	08 44	09 03	09 30	10 03	10 30	11 03	11 33	12 03	12 33	13 03	13 33	14 03	14 33	15 03	15 33	16 03
Godley	d	06 33	07 03	07 20	07 35	08 05	08 24	08 46	09 05	09 32	10 05	10 32	11 05	11 35	12 05	12 35	13 05	13 35	14 05	14 35	15 05	15 35	16 05
Hattersley	d	06 35	07 05	07 22	07 37	08 07	08 26	08 48	09 07	09 34	10 07	10 34	11 07	11 37	12 07	12 37	13 07	13 37	14 07	14 37	15 07	15 37	16 07
Broadbottom	d	06 37	07 07	07 24	07 39	08 09	08 28	08 50	09 09	09 36	10 09	10 36	11 09	11 39	12 09	12 39	13 09	13 39	14 09	14 39	15 09	15 39	16 09
Dinting 3	d	06 45	07 15	07 35	07 45	08 14	08 34	08 56	09 16	09 46	10 16	10 46	11 16	11 46	12 16	12 46	13 16	13 46	14 16	14 46	15 16	15 46	16 16
Glossop	a	06 48							09 19	09 49	10 19	10 49	11 19	11 49	12 19	12 49	13 19	13 49	14 19	14 49	15 19	15 49	16 19
	d	06 51							09 22	09 52	10 22	10 52	11 22	11 52	12 22	12 52	13 22	13 52	14 22	14 52	15 22	15 52	16 22
Hadfield	a	06 59	07 17	07 37	07 47	08 17	08 38	08 58	09 29	09 59	10 29	10 59	11 29	11 59	12 29	12 59	13 29	13 59	14 29	14 59	15 29	15 59	16 29

		NT	NT	NT	NT	NT	NT	NT	NT	NT	NT	NT	NT	NT	NT
Manchester Piccadilly 10 78	d	16 15	16 36	16 59	17 15	17 37	17 59	18 15	18 48	19 18	19 48	20 48	21 48	22 48	23 27
Ardwick 78	d														
Ashburys 78	d	16 19	16 40	17 03	17 19	17 41	18 03	18 19	18 52	19 22	19 52	20 52	21 52	22 52	23 31
Gorton 78	d	16 21	16 42	17 05	17 21	17 43	18 05	18 21	18 54	19 24	19 54	20 54	21 54	22 54	23 33
Guide Bridge 78	d	16 25	16 46	17 10	17 25	17 47	18 10	18 25	18 58	19 28	19 58	20 58	21 58	22 58	23 37
Flowery Field	d	16 28	16 49	17 13	17 28	17 50	18 13	18 28	19 01	19 31	20 01	21 01	22 01	23 01	23 40
Newton for Hyde	d	16 30	16 51	17 15	17 30	17 52	18 15	18 30	19 03	19 33	20 03	21 03	22 03	23 03	23 42
Godley	d	16 32	16 53	17 17	17 32	17 54	18 17	18 32	19 05	19 35	20 05	21 05	22 05	23 05	23 44
Hattersley	d	16 34	16 55	17 19	17 34	17 56	18 19	18 34	19 07	19 37	20 07	21 07	22 07	23 07	23 46
Broadbottom	d	16 36	16 57	17 21	17 36	17 59	18 21	18 36	19 09	19 39	20 09	21 09	22 09	23 09	23 48
Dinting 3	d	16 42	17 03	17 27	17 42	18 05	18 27	18 42	19 16	19 46	20 16	21 16	22 16	23 16	23 54
Glossop	a	16 45	17 06	17 31	17 45	18 08	18 30	18 45	19 19	19 49	20 19	21 19	22 19	23 19	
	d	16 48	17 09	17 33	17 48	18 11	18 33	18 48	19 22	19 52	20 22	21 22	22 22	23 22	
Hadfield	a	16 54	17 15	17 40	17 54	18 17	18 39	18 54	19 29	19 59	20 29	21 29	22 29	23 29	23 56

Mondays to Fridays

from 06 September

		NT	NT	NT	NT	NT	NT	NT	NT	NT	NT	NT	NT	NT	NT	NT	NT	NT	NT	NT	NT	NT	NT
Manchester Piccadilly 10 78	d	06 13	06 46	07 03	07 18	07 47	08 07	08 29	08 48	09 15	09 48	10 15	10 48	11 18	11 48	12 18	12 48	13 18	13 48	14 18	14 48	15 18	15 48
Ardwick 78	d																						
Ashburys 78	d	06 17		07 07	07 22		08 11		08 52	09 19	09 52	10 19	10 52	11 22	11 52	12 22	12 52	13 22	13 52	14 22	14 52	15 22	15 52
Gorton 78	d	06 19		07 09	07 24		08 13		08 54	09 21	09 54	10 21	10 54	11 24	11 54	12 24	12 54	13 24	13 54	14 24	14 54	15 24	15 54
Guide Bridge 78	d	06 23	06 54	07 13	07 28	07 55	08 17	08 37	08 58	09 25	09 58	10 25	10 58	11 28	11 58	12 28	12 58	13 28	13 58	14 28	14 58	15 28	15 58
Flowery Field	d	06 26	06 57	07 16	07 31	07 58	08 20		09 01	09 28	10 01	10 28	11 01	11 31	12 01	12 31	13 01	13 31	14 01	14 31	15 01	15 31	16 01
Newton for Hyde	d	06 28	06 59	07 18	07 33	08 00	08 22		09 03	09 30	10 03	10 30	11 03	11 33	12 03	12 33	13 03	13 33	14 03	14 33	15 03	15 33	16 03
Godley	d	06 30		07 20	07 35	08 02	08 24		09 05	09 32	10 05	10 32	11 05	11 35	12 05	12 35	13 05	13 35	14 05	14 35	15 05	15 35	16 05
Hattersley	d	06 32	07 02	07 22	07 37	08 04	08 26		09 07	09 34	10 07	10 34	11 07	11 37	12 07	12 37	13 07	13 37	14 07	14 37	15 07	15 37	16 07
Broadbottom	d	06 34	07 04	07 24	07 39	08 06	08 28		09 09	09 36	10 09	10 36	11 09	11 39	12 09	12 39	13 09	13 39	14 09	14 39	15 09	15 39	16 09
Dinting 3	d	06 44	07 10	07 30	07 50	08 11	08 34	08 48	09 16	09 46	10 16	10 46	11 16	11 46	12 16	12 46	13 16	13 46	14 16	14 46	15 16	15 46	16 16
Glossop	a															12 49	13 19	13 49	14 19	14 49	15 19	15 49	16 19
	d															12 54	13 24	13 54	14 24	14 54	15 24	15 54	16 22
Hadfield	a	06 47	07 12	07 32	07 52	08 14	08 36	08 51	09 19	09 49	10 19	10 49	11 19	11 49	12 19	13 01	13 31	14 01	14 31	15 01	15 31	16 01	16 29

		NT	NT	NT	NT	NT	NT	NT	NT	NT	NT	NT	NT	NT	NT
Manchester Piccadilly 10 78	d	16 15	16 36	16 59	17 15	17 37	17 59	18 15	18 48	19 18	19 48	20 48	21 48	22 48	23 27
Ardwick 78	d														
Ashburys 78	d	16 19	16 40	17 03	17 19	17 41	18 03	18 19	18 52	19 22	19 52	20 52	21 52	22 52	23 31
Gorton 78	d	16 21	16 42	17 05	17 21	17 43	18 05	18 21	18 54	19 24	19 54	20 54	21 54	22 54	23 33
Guide Bridge 78	d	16 25	16 46	17 10	17 25	17 47	18 10	18 25	18 58	19 28	19 58	20 58	21 58	22 58	23 37
Flowery Field	d	16 28	16 49	17 13	17 28	17 50	18 13	18 28	19 01	19 31	20 01	21 01	22 01	23 01	23 40
Newton for Hyde	d	16 30	16 51	17 15	17 30	17 52	18 15	18 30	19 03	19 33	20 03	21 03	22 03	23 03	23 42
Godley	d	16 32	16 53	17 17	17 32	17 54	18 17	18 32	19 05	19 35	20 05	21 05	22 05	23 05	23 44
Hattersley	d	16 34	16 55	17 19	17 34	17 56	18 19	18 34	19 07	19 37	20 07	21 07	22 07	23 07	23 46
Broadbottom	d	16 36	16 57	17 21	17 36	17 58	18 21	18 36	19 09	19 39	20 09	21 09	22 09	23 09	23 48
Dinting 3	d	16 42	17 03	17 27	17 42	18 05	18 28	18 42	19 16	19 46	20 16	21 16	22 16	23 16	23 54
Glossop	a	16 45	17 06	17 30	17 45	18 08	18 31	18 45	19 19	19 49	20 19	21 19	22 19	23 19	
	d	16 48	17 09	17 33	17 48	18 11	18 34	18 48	19 22	19 52	20 22	21 22	22 22	23 22	
Hadfield	a	16 54	17 15	17 39	17 54	18 18	18 40	18 54	19 29	19 59	20 29	21 29	22 29	23 29	23 56

Saturdays

		NT	NT	NT	NT	NT	NT	NT	NT	NT	NT	NT	NT	NT	NT	NT	NT	NT	NT	NT	NT	NT	NT
Manchester Piccadilly 10 78	d	06 16	06 48	07 18	07 48	08 15	08 48	09 18	09 48	10 18	10 48	11 18	11 48	12 18	12 48	13 18	13 48	14 18	14 48	15 18	15 48	16 18	16 48
Ardwick 78	d																						
Ashburys 78	d	06 20	06 52	07 22	07 52	08 19	08 52	09 22	09 52	10 22	10 52	11 22	11 52	12 22	12 52	13 22	13 52	14 22	14 52	15 22	15 52	16 22	16 52
Gorton 78	d	06 22	06 54	07 24	07 54	08 21	08 54	09 24	09 54	10 24	10 54	11 24	11 54	12 24	12 54	13 24	13 54	14 24	14 54	15 24	15 54	16 24	16 54
Guide Bridge 78	d	06 26	06 58	07 28	07 58	08 25	08 58	09 28	09 58	10 28	10 58	11 28	11 58	12 28	12 58	13 28	13 58	14 28	14 58	15 28	15 58	16 28	16 58
Flowery Field	d	06 29	07 01	07 31	08 01	08 28	09 01	09 31	10 01	10 31	11 01	11 31	12 01	12 31	13 01	13 31	14 01	14 31	15 01	15 31	16 01	16 31	17 01
Newton for Hyde	d	06 31	07 03	07 33	08 03	08 30	09 03	09 33	10 03	10 33	11 03	11 33	12 03	12 33	13 03	13 33	14 03	14 33	15 03	15 33	16 03	16 33	17 03
Godley	d	06 33	07 05	07 35	08 05	08 32	09 05	09 35	10 05	10 35	11 05	11 35	12 05	12 35	13 05	13 35	14 05	14 35	15 05	15 35	16 05	16 35	17 05
Hattersley	d	06 35	07 07	07 37	08 07	08 34	09 07	09 37	10 07	10 37	11 07	11 37	12 07	12 37	13 07	13 37	14 07	14 37	15 07	15 37	16 07	16 37	17 07
Broadbottom	d	06 37	07 09	07 39	08 09	08 36	09 09	09 39	10 09	10 39	11 09	11 39	12 09	12 39	13 09	13 39	14 09	14 39	15 09	15 39	16 09	16 39	17 09
Dinting 3	d	06 45	07 16	07 46	08 16	08 46	09 16	09 46	10 16	10 46	11 16	11 46	12 16	12 46	13 16	13 46	14 16	14 46	15 16	15 46	16 16	16 46	17 16
Glossop	a	06 48	07 19	07 49	08 19	08 49	09 19	09 49	10 19	10 49	11 19	11 49	12 19	12 49	13 19	13 49	14 19	14 49	15 19	15 49	16 19	16 49	17 19
	d	06 51	07 22	07 52	08 22	08 52	09 22	09 52	10 22	10 52	11 22	11 52	12 22	12 52	13 22	13 52	14 22	14 52	15 22	15 52	16 22	16 52	17 22
Hadfield	a	06 59	07 29	07 59	08 29	08 59	09 29	09 59	10 29	10 59	11 29	11 59	12 29	12 59	13 29	13 59	14 29	14 59	15 29	15 59	16 29	16 59	17 29

Table 79

Saturdays

Manchester - Glossop and Hadfield

		NT	NT	NT	NT	NT	NT	NT	NT	NT
Manchester Piccadilly 10 78	d	17 18	17 48	18 18	18 48	19 48	20 48	21 48	22 48	23 27
Ardwick 78	d									
Ashburys 78	d	17 22	17 52	18 22	18 52	19 52	20 52	21 52	22 52	23 31
Gorton 78	d	17 24	17 54	18 24	18 54	19 54	20 54	21 54	22 54	23 33
Guide Bridge 78	d	17 28	17 58	18 28	18 58	19 58	20 58	21 58	22 58	23 37
Flowery Field	d	17 31	18 01	18 31	19 01	20 01	21 01	22 01	23 01	23 40
Newton for Hyde	d	17 33	18 03	18 33	19 03	20 03	21 03	22 03	23 03	23 42
Godley	d	17 35	18 05	18 35	19 05	20 05	21 05	22 05	23 05	23 44
Hattersley	d	17 37	18 07	18 37	19 07	20 07	21 07	22 07	23 07	23 46
Broadbottom	d	17 39	18 09	18 39	19 09	20 09	21 09	22 09	23 09	23 48
Dinting 3	d	17 46	18 16	18 46	19 16	20 16	21 16	22 16	23 16	23 54
Glossop	a	17 49	18 19	18 49	19 19	20 19	21 19	22 19	23 19	
	d	17 52	18 22	18 52	19 22	20 22	21 22	22 22	23 22	
Hadfield	a	17 59	18 29	18 59	19 29	20 29	21 29	22 29	23 29	23 56

Sundays

		NT	NT A	NT B	NT	NT	NT	NT	NT	NT	NT	NT	NT	NT	NT	NT	NT	NT	NT	NT	NT	NT	NT
Manchester Piccadilly 10 78	d	09 18	09 32	09 48	10 18	10 48	11 18	11 48	12 18	12 48	13 18	13 48	14 18	14 48	15 18	15 48	16 18	16 48	17 18	17 48	18 18	18 48	19 18
Ardwick 78	d																						
Ashburys 78	d	09 22	09 36	09 52	10 22	10 52	11 22	11 52	12 22	12 52	13 22	13 52	14 22	14 52	15 22	15 52	16 22	16 52	17 22	17 52	18 22	18 52	19 22
Gorton 78	d	09 24	09 38	09 54	10 24	10 54	11 24	11 54	12 24	12 54	13 24	13 54	14 24	14 54	15 24	15 54	16 24	16 54	17 24	17 54	18 24	18 54	19 24
Guide Bridge 78	d	09 28	09b58	09 58	10 28	10 58	11 28	11 58	12 28	12 58	13 28	13 58	14 28	14 58	15 28	15 58	16 28	16 58	17 28	17 58	18 28	18 58	19 28
Flowery Field	d	09 31	10 01	10 01	10 31	11 01	11 31	12 01	12 31	13 01	13 31	14 01	14 31	15 01	15 31	16 01	16 31	17 01	17 31	18 01	18 31	19 01	19 31
Newton for Hyde	d	09 33	10 03	10 03	10 33	11 03	11 33	12 03	12 33	13 03	13 33	14 03	14 33	15 03	15 33	16 03	16 33	17 03	17 33	18 03	18 33	19 03	19 33
Godley	d	09 35	10 05	10 05	10 35	11 05	11 35	12 05	12 35	13 05	13 35	14 05	14 35	15 05	15 35	16 05	16 35	17 05	17 35	18 05	18 35	19 05	19 35
Hattersley	d	09 37	10 07	10 07	10 37	11 07	11 37	12 07	12 37	13 07	13 37	14 07	14 37	15 07	15 37	16 07	16 37	17 07	17 37	18 07	18 37	19 07	19 37
Broadbottom	d	09 39	10 09	10 09	10 39	11 09	11 39	12 09	12 39	13 09	13 39	14 09	14 39	15 09	15 39	16 09	16 39	17 09	17 39	18 09	18 39	19 09	19 39
Dinting 3	d	09 46	10 16	10 16	10 46	11 16	11 46	12 16	12 46	13 16	13 46	14 16	14 46	15 16	15 46	16 16	16 46	17 16	17 46	18 16	18 46	19 16	19 46
Glossop	a	09 49	10 19	10 19	10 49	11 19	11 49	12 19	12 49	13 19	13 49	14 19	14 49	15 19	15 49	16 19	16 49	17 19	17 49	18 19	18 49	19 19	19 49
	d	09 52	10 22	10 22	10 52	11 22	11 52	12 22	12 52	13 22	13 52	14 22	14 52	15 22	15 52	16 22	16 52	17 22	17 52	18 22	18 52	19 22	19 52
Hadfield	a	09 58	10 28	10 28	10 58	11 28	11 58	12 28	12 58	13 28	13 58	14 28	14 58	15 28	15 58	16 28	16 58	17 28	17 58	18 28	18 58	19 28	19 58

		NT	NT
Manchester Piccadilly 10 78	d	19 48	20 48
Ardwick 78	d		
Ashburys 78	d	19 52	20 52
Gorton 78	d	19 54	20 54
Guide Bridge 78	d	19 58	20 58
Flowery Field	d	20 01	21 01
Newton for Hyde	d	20 03	21 03
Godley	d	20 05	21 05
Hattersley	d	20 07	21 07
Broadbottom	d	20 09	21 09
Dinting 3	d	20 16	21 16
Glossop	a	20 19	21 19
	d	20 22	21 22
Hadfield	a	20 28	21 28

A from 12 September

B until 5 September

b arr. 0942

Table 79

Hadfield and Glossop - Manchester

Mondays to Fridays
until 03 September

	NT	NT	NT	NT	NT	NT	NT	NT	NT	NT	NT	NT	NT	NT	NT	NT	NT	NT	NT	NT	NT	NT
Hadfield d	06 00	06 30	07 00	07 20	07 40	07 58	08 21	08 41	09 01	09 31	10 01	10 31	11 01	11 31	12 01	12 31	13 01	13 31	14 01	14 31	15 01	15 31
Glossop a	06 05	06 35	07 05	07 25	07 45	08 03	08 26	08 46	09 06	09 36	10 06	10 36	11 06	11 36	12 06	12 36	13 06	13 36	14 06	14 36	15 06	15 36
d	06 08	06 38	07 08	07 28	07 48	08 06	08 29	08 49	09 09	09 39	10 09	10 39	11 09	11 39	12 09	12 39	13 09	13 39	14 09	14 39	15 09	15 39
Dinting 3 d	06 11	06 41	07 11	07 31	07 51	08 09	08 32	08 52	09 12	09 42	10 12	10 42	11 12	11 42	12 12	12 42	13 12	13 42	14 12	14 42	15 12	15 42
Broadbottom d	06 15	06 45	07 15	07 35	07 56	08 13	08 37	08 57	09 16	09 46	10 16	10 46	11 16	11 46	12 16	12 46	13 16	13 46	14 16	14 46	15 16	15 46
Hattersley d	06 18	06 48	07 18	07 38	07 59	08 16	08 40	08 59	09 19	09 49	10 19	10 49	11 19	11 49	12 19	12 49	13 19	13 49	14 19	14 49	15 19	15 49
Godley d	06 20	06 50	07 20	07 40	08 01	08 18	08 42	09 02	09 21	09 51	10 21	10 51	11 21	11 51	12 21	12 51	13 21	13 51	14 21	14 51	15 21	15 51
Newton for Hyde d	06 22	06 52	07 22	07 42	08 03	08 21	08 44	09 04	09 23	09 53	10 23	10 53	11 23	11 53	12 23	12 53	13 23	13 53	14 23	14 53	15 23	15 53
Flowery Field d	06 24	06 54	07 24	07 44	08 06	08 23	08 46	09 07	09 25	09 55	10 25	10 55	11 25	11 55	12 25	12 55	13 25	13 55	14 25	14 55	15 25	15 55
Guide Bridge 78 a	06 27	06 57	07 27	07 47	08 10	08 26	08 49	09 11	09 28	09 58	10 28	10 58	11 28	11 58	12 28	12 58	13 28	13 58	14 28	14 58	15 28	15 58
Gorton 78 a	06 30	07 00	07 30	07 50	08 13	08 30	08 52	09 15	09 31	10 01	10 31	11 01	11 31	12 01	12 31	13 01	13 31	14 01	14 31	15 01	15 31	16 01
Ashburys 78 a	06 33	07 06	07 33	07 53	08 16	08 34	08 56	09 18	09 34	10 04	10 34	11 04	11 34	12 04	12 34	13 04	13 34	14 04	14 34	15 04	15 34	16 04
Ardwick 78 a			07 35																			
Manchester Piccadilly 10 78 a	06 42	07 15	07 43	08 03	08 25	08 43	09 04	09 27	09 42	10 12	10 42	11 12	11 42	12 12	12 42	13 12	13 42	14 12	14 42	15 12	15 42	16 12

	NT	NT	NT	NT	NT	NT	NT	NT	NT	NT	NT	NT	NT	NT
Hadfield d	16 01	16 31	16 57	17 22	17 44	17 59	18 28	18 43	19 01	19 31	20 01	20 31	21 31	22 31
Glossop a	16 06								19 06	19 36	20 06	20 36	21 36	22 36
d	16 09								19 09	19 39	20 09	20 39	21 39	22 39
Dinting 3 d	16 12	16 33	16 59	17 24	17 46	18 01	18 30	18 45	19 12	19 42	20 12	20 42	21 42	22 42
Broadbottom d	16 16	16 37	17 03	17 28	17 50	18 05	18 34	18 49	19 16	19 46	20 16	20 46	21 46	22 46
Hattersley d	16 19	16 40	17 06	17 31		18 08	18 37	18 52	19 19	19 49	20 19	20 49	21 49	22 49
Godley d	16 21	16 42	17 08	17 33		18 10	18 39	18 54	19 21	19 51	20 21	20 51	21 51	22 51
Newton for Hyde d	16 23	16 44	17 10	17 36	17 54	18 12	18 41	18 56	19 23	19 53	20 23	20 53	21 53	22 53
Flowery Field d	16 25	16 46	17 12	17 38		18 14	18 43	18 58	19 25	19 55	20 25	20 55	21 55	22 55
Guide Bridge 78 a	16 28	16 49	17 15	17 42	17 58	18 17	18 46	19 01	19 28	19 58	20 28	20 58	21 58	22 58
Gorton 78 a	16 31	16 52	17 18	17 45	18 01	18 20	18 49	19 04	19 31	20 01	20 31	21 01	22 01	23 01
Ashburys 78 a	16 34	16 55	17 24	17 48	18 04	18 23	18 54	19 08	19 34	20 04	20 34	21 04	22 04	23 04
Ardwick 78 a														
Manchester Piccadilly 10 78 a	16 42	17 05	17 33	17 57	18 12	18 34	19 03	19 15	19 42	20 12	20 42	21 12	22 12	23 12

Mondays to Fridays
from 06 September

	NT	NT	NT	NT	NT	NT	NT	NT	NT	NT	NT	NT	NT	NT	NT	NT	NT	NT	NT	NT	NT	NT
Hadfield d	05 55	06 25	06 55	07 15	07 35	07 55	08 17	08 39	08 55	09 24	09 54	10 24	10 54	11 24	11 54	12 24	13 05	13 35	14 05	14 35	15 05	15 35
Glossop a	06 00	06 30	07 00	07 20	07 40	08 00	08 22	08 44	09 00	09 29	09 59	10 29	10 59	11 29	11 59	12 29						
d	06 03	06 33	07 03	07 23	07 43	08 03	08 25	08 50	09 03	09 34	10 04	10 34	11 04	11 34	12 04	12 34						
Dinting 3 d	06 06	06 36	07 06	07 26	07 46	08 06	08 28	08 54	09 07	09 37	10 07	10 37	11 07	11 37	12 07	12 37	13 07	13 37	14 07	14 37	15 07	15 37
Broadbottom d	06 10	06 40	07 10	07 30	07 51	08 10	08 32	08 58	09 11	09 41	10 11	10 41	11 11	11 41	12 11	12 41	13 11	13 41	14 11	14 41	15 11	15 41
Hattersley d	06 13	06 43	07 13	07 33	07 54	08 13	08 35	09 00	09 14	09 44	10 14	10 44	11 14	11 44	12 14	12 44	13 14	13 44	14 14	14 44	15 14	15 44
Godley d	06 15	06 45	07 15	07 35	07 56	08 15	08 37	09 02	09 16	09 46	10 16	10 46	11 16	11 46	12 16	12 46	13 16	13 46	14 16	14 46	15 16	15 46
Newton for Hyde d	06 17	06 47	07 17	07 37	07 58	08 18	08 39	09 04	09 19	09 48	10 18	10 48	11 18	11 48	12 18	12 48	13 18	13 48	14 18	14 48	15 18	15 48
Flowery Field d	06 19	06 49	07 20	07 39	08 01	08 20	08 41	09 06	09 21	09 50	10 20	10 50	11 20	11 50	12 20	12 50	13 20	13 50	14 20	14 50	15 20	15 50
Guide Bridge 78 a	06 27	06 57	07 27	07 47	08 10	08 26	08 49	09 11	09 28	09 58	10 28	10 58	11 28	11 58	12 28	12 58	13 28	13 58	14 28	14 58	15 28	15 58
Gorton 78 a	06 30	07 00	07 30	07 50	08 13	08 30	08 52	09 15	09 31	10 01	10 31	11 01	11 31	12 01	12 31	13 01	13 31	14 01	14 31	15 01	15 31	16 01
Ashburys 78 a	06 33	07 06	07 33	07 53	08 16	08 34	08 56	09 18	09 34	10 04	10 34	11 04	11 34	12 04	12 34	13 04	13 34	14 04	14 34	15 04	15 34	16 04
Ardwick 78 a			07 36																			
Manchester Piccadilly 10 78 a	06 42	07 15	07 43	08 03	08 25	08 43	09 04	09 27	09 42	10 12	10 40	11 10	11 42	12 12	12 42	13 12	13 42	14 12	14 42	15 12	15 42	16 12

	NT	NT	NT	NT	NT	NT	NT	NT	NT	NT	NT	NT	NT	NT
Hadfield d	16 05	16 31	16 57	17 18	17 44	17 56	18 22	18 43	19 01	19 31	20 01	20 31	21 31	22 31
Glossop a									19 06	19 36	20 06	20 36	21 36	22 36
d									19 09	19 39	20 09	20 39	21 39	22 39
Dinting 3 d	16 07	16 33	16 59	17 20	17 46	17 59	18 24	18 45	19 12	19 42	20 12	20 42	21 42	22 42
Broadbottom d	16 11	16 37	17 03	17 24	17 50	18 03	18 28	18 49	19 16	19 46	20 16	20 46	21 46	22 46
Hattersley d	16 14	16 40	17 06	17 27		18 05	18 31	18 52	19 19	19 49	20 19	20 49	21 49	22 49
Godley d	16 16	16 42	17 08	17 29		18 07	18 33	18 54	19 21	19 51	20 21	20 51	21 51	22 51
Newton for Hyde d	16 18	16 44	17 10	17 32	17 54	18 09	18 35	18 56	19 23	19 53	20 23	20 53	21 53	22 53
Flowery Field d	16 20	16 46	17 12	17 34		18 11	18 37	18 58	19 25	19 55	20 25	20 55	21 55	22 55
Guide Bridge 78 a	16 28	16 49	17 17	17 42	18 00	18 17	18 46	19 01	19 28	19 58	20 28	20 58	21 58	22 58
Gorton 78 a	16 31	16 52	17 20	17 45		18 20	18 49	19 04	19 31	20 01	20 31	21 01	22 01	23 01
Ashburys 78 a	16 34	16 55	17 24	17 48		18 23	18 54	19 08	19 34	20 04	20 34	21 04	22 04	23 04
Ardwick 78 a														
Manchester Piccadilly 10 78 a	16 42	17 05	17 33	17 57	18 12	18 34	19 03	19 15	19 42	20 12	20 42	21 12	22 12	23 12

Saturdays

	NT	NT A	NT B	NT	NT	NT	NT	NT	NT	NT	NT	NT	NT	NT	NT	NT	NT	NT	NT	NT	NT	NT
Hadfield d	06 30	07 01	07 01	07 31	08 01	08 31	09 01	09 31	10 01	10 31	11 01	11 31	12 01	12 31	13 01	13 31	14 01	14 31	15 01	15 31	16 01	16 31
Glossop a	06 35	07 06	07 06	07 36	08 06	08 36	09 06	09 36	10 06	10 36	11 06	11 36	12 06	12 36	13 06	13 36	14 06	14 36	15 06	15 36	16 06	16 36
d	06 38	07 09	07 09	07 39	08 09	08 39	09 09	09 39	10 09	10 39	11 09	11 39	12 09	12 39	13 09	13 39	14 09	14 39	15 09	15 39	16 09	16 39
Dinting 3 d	06 41	07 12	07 12	07 42	08 12	08 42	09 12	09 42	10 12	10 42	11 12	11 42	12 12	12 42	13 12	13 42	14 12	14 42	15 12	15 42	16 12	16 42
Broadbottom d	06 45	07 16	07 16	07 46	08 16	08 46	09 16	09 46	10 16	10 46	11 16	11 46	12 16	12 46	13 16	13 46	14 16	14 46	15 16	15 46	16 16	16 46
Hattersley d	06 48	07 19	07 19	07 49	08 19	08 49	09 19	09 49	10 19	10 49	11 19	11 49	12 19	12 49	13 19	13 49	14 19	14 49	15 19	15 49	16 19	16 49
Godley d	06 50	07 21	07 21	07 51	08 21	08 51	09 21	09 51	10 21	10 51	11 21	11 51	12 21	12 51	13 21	13 51	14 21	14 51	15 21	15 51	16 21	16 51
Newton for Hyde d	06 52	07 23	07 23	07 53	08 23	08 53	09 23	09 53	10 23	10 53	11 23	11 53	12 23	12 53	13 23	13 53	14 23	14 53	15 23	15 53	16 23	16 53
Flowery Field d	06 54	07 25	07 25	07 55	08 25	08 55	09 25	09 55	10 25	10 55	11 25	11 55	12 25	12 55	13 25	13 55	14 25	14 55	15 25	15 55	16 25	16 55
Guide Bridge 78 a	06 57	07 28	07 28	07 58	08 28	08 58	09 28	09 58	10 28	10 58	11 28	11 58	12 28	12 58	13 28	13 58	14 28	14 58	15 28	15 58	16 28	16 58
Gorton 78 a	07 00	07 31	07 31	08 01	08 31	09 01	09 31	10 01	10 31	11 01	11 31	12 01	12 31	13 01	13 31	14 01	14 31	15 01	15 31	16 01	16 31	17 01
Ashburys 78 a	07 03	07 34	07 34	08 04	08 34	09 04	09 34	10 04	10 34	11 04	11 34	12 04	12 34	13 04	13 34	14 04	14 34	15 04	15 34	16 04	16 34	17 04
Ardwick 78 a																						
Manchester Piccadilly 10 78 a	07 12	07 42	07 43	08 12	08 42	09 12	09 42	10 12	10 42	11 12	11 42	12 12	12 42	13 12	13 42	14 12	14 42	15 12	15 42	16 12	16 42	17 12

A from 11 September B until 4 September

Table 79

Hadfield and Glossop - Manchester

Saturdays

	NT	NT	NT	NT	NT	NT	NT	NT	NT
Hadfield d	17 01	17 31	18 01	18 31	19 01	19 31	20 31	21 31	22 31
Glossop a	17 06	17 36	18 06	18 36	19 06	19 36	20 36	21 36	22 36
d	17 09	17 39	18 09	18 39	19 09	19 39	20 39	21 39	22 39
Dinting 3 d	17 12	17 42	18 12	18 42	19 12	19 42	20 42	21 42	22 42
Broadbottom d	17 16	17 46	18 16	18 46	19 16	19 46	20 46	21 46	22 46
Hattersley d	17 19	17 49	18 19	18 49	19 19	19 49	20 49	21 49	22 49
Godley d	17 21	17 51	18 21	18 51	19 21	19 51	20 51	21 51	22 51
Newton for Hyde d	17 23	17 53	18 23	18 53	19 23	19 53	20 53	21 53	22 53
Flowery Field d	17 25	17 55	18 25	18 55	19 25	19 55	20 55	21 55	22 55
Guide Bridge 78 a	17 28	17 58	18 28	18 58	19 28	19 58	20 58	21 58	22 58
Gorton 78 a	17 31	18 01	18 31	19 01	19 31	20 01	21 01	22 01	23 01
Ashburys 78 a	17 34	18 04	18 34	19 04	19 34	20 04	21 04	22 04	23 04
Ardwick 78 a									
Manchester Piccadilly 10 78 a	17 42	18 12	18 42	19 12	19 42	20 12	21 12	22 12	23 12

Sundays

	NT	NT A	NT B	NT	NT	NT	NT	NT	NT	NT	NT	NT	NT	NT	NT	NT	NT	NT	NT	NT	NT	NT
Hadfield d	10 01	10 31	10 31	11 01	11 31	12 01	12 31	13 01	13 31	14 01	14 31	15 01	15 31	16 01	16 31	17 01	17 31	18 01	18 31	19 01	19 31	20 01
Glossop a	10 06	10 36	10 36	11 06	11 36	12 06	12 36	13 06	13 36	14 06	14 36	15 06	15 36	16 06	16 36	17 06	17 36	18 06	18 36	19 06	19 36	20 06
d	10 09	10 39	10 39	11 09	11 39	12 09	12 39	13 09	13 39	14 09	14 39	15 09	15 39	16 09	16 39	17 09	17 39	18 09	18 39	19 09	19 39	20 09
Dinting 3 d	10 12	10 42	10 42	11 12	11 42	12 12	12 42	13 12	13 42	14 12	14 42	15 12	15 42	16 12	16 42	17 12	17 42	18 12	18 42	19 12	19 42	20 12
Broadbottom d	10 16	10 46	10 46	11 16	11 46	12 16	12 46	13 16	13 46	14 16	14 46	15 16	15 46	16 16	16 46	17 16	17 46	18 16	18 46	19 16	19 46	20 16
Hattersley d	10 19	10 49	10 49	11 19	11 49	12 19	12 49	13 19	13 49	14 19	14 49	15 19	15 49	16 19	16 49	17 19	17 49	18 19	18 49	19 19	19 49	20 19
Godley d	10 21	10 51	10 51	11 21	11 51	12 21	12 51	13 21	13 51	14 21	14 51	15 21	15 51	16 21	16 51	17 21	17 51	18 21	18 51	19 21	19 51	20 21
Newton for Hyde d	10 23	10 53	10 53	11 23	11 53	12 23	12 53	13 23	13 53	14 23	14 53	15 23	15 53	16 23	16 53	17 23	17 53	18 23	18 53	19 23	19 53	20 23
Flowery Field d	10 25	10 55	10 55	11 25	11 55	12 25	12 55	13 25	13 55	14 25	14 55	15 25	15 55	16 25	16 55	17 25	17 55	18 25	18 55	19 25	19 55	20 25
Guide Bridge 78 a	10 28	10 58	10 58	11 28	11 58	12 28	12 58	13 28	13 58	14 28	14 58	15 28	15 58	16 28	16 58	17 28	17 58	18 28	18 58	19 28	19 58	20 28
Gorton 78 a	10 31	11 01	11 01	11 31	12 01	12 31	13 01	13 31	14 01	14 31	15 01	15 31	16 01	16 31	17 01	17 31	18 01	18 31	19 01	19 31	20 01	20 31
Ashburys 78 a	10 34	11 04	11 04	11 34	12 04	12 34	13 04	13 34	14 04	14 34	15 04	15 34	16 04	16 34	17 04	17 34	18 04	18 34	19 04	19 34	20 04	20 34
Ardwick 78 a																						
Manchester Piccadilly 10 78 a	10 42	11 12	11 13	11 42	12 12	12 42	13 12	13 42	14 12	14 42	15 12	15 42	16 12	16 42	17 12	17 42	18 12	18 42	19 12	19 42	20 12	20 42

	NT	NT
Hadfield d	20 31	21 31
Glossop a	20 36	21 36
d	20 39	21 39
Dinting 3 d	20 42	21 42
Broadbottom d	20 46	21 46
Hattersley d	20 49	21 49
Godley d	20 51	21 51
Newton for Hyde d	20 53	21 53
Flowery Field d	20 55	21 55
Guide Bridge 78 a	20 58	21 58
Gorton 78 a	21 01	22 01
Ashburys 78 a	21 04	22 04
Ardwick 78 a		
Manchester Piccadilly 10 78 a	21 12	22 12

A from 12 September B until 5 September

Network Diagram for Tables 81, 102

DM-35/08
Design BAJS

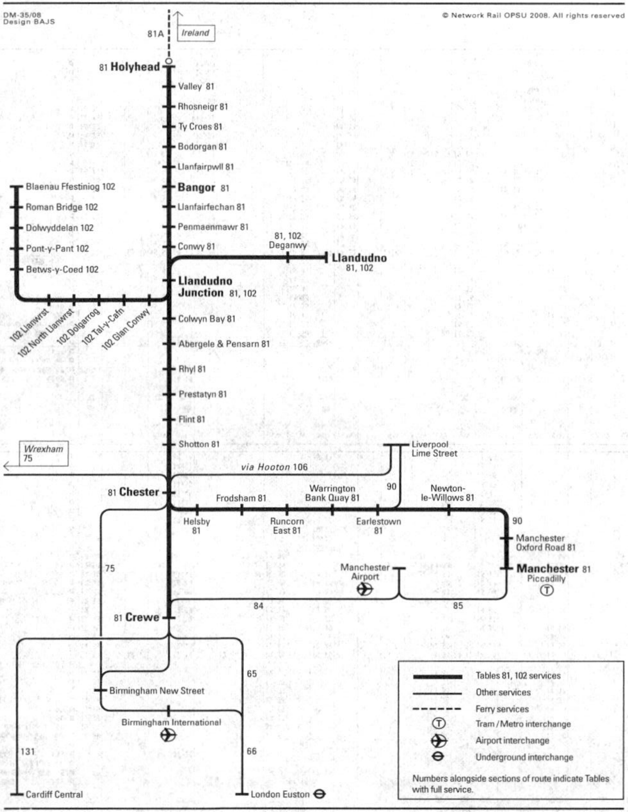

Table 81

Crewe and Manchester - Chester and North Wales

Mondays to Fridays
until 03 September

Station		AW	AW	AW	VT	AW	AW	AW	AW	AW	AW
					◇ 1	◇	◇			◇	◇
					⊠	⊤	⊤			⊤	⊤
London Euston [15] ⊖65	d										
Birmingham New Street [12] 65	d				05 30						
Manchester Airport 84,85 ✈	d					05 33					
Cardiff Central [7] 131	d										05 10
Crewe [10]	d				06 24		06 54	07 23			
Manchester Piccadilly [10] ⇌	d					05 50				06 50	
Manchester Oxford Road 90	d					05 53				06 53	
Newton-le-Willows 90	d					06 12				07 12	
Earlestown [8] 90	d					06 15				07 15	
Warrington Bank Quay 90	d					06 26				07 22	
Runcorn East	d					06 33				07 29	
Frodsham	d					06 37				07 34	
Helsby	d					06 41				07 38	
Liverpool Lime Street [10] 106	d										
Chester	a				06 44	06 53	07 14	07 46		07 50	08 20
	d				06 44	06 55	07 26			07 55	08 26
Shotton	d					07 04				08 04	
Flint	d				06 57	07 10	07 39			08 10	08 39
Prestatyn	d				07 10	07 23	07 52			08 23	08 52
Rhyl	d				07 16	07 29	07 58			08 29	08 58
Abergele & Pensarn	d					07 35				08 35	
Colwyn Bay	d				07 27	07 43	08 09			08 43	09 09
Llandudno Junction	a				07 33	07 48	08 14			08 48	09 14
	d	06 51	07 31	06 13	07 33	07 50	08 15		08 25	08 50	09 15
Deganwy	d	06x54	07x34	06x16		07x54			08x28	08x54	
Llandudno	a	07 01	07 41	06 23		08 06			08 35	09 06	
Conwy	d						08x17				
Penmaenmawr	d						08x23				
Llanfairfechan	d						08x27				
Bangor (Gwynedd)	a				07 49		08 36				09 31
	d				07 50		08 38				09 32
Llanfairpwll	d						08x44				
Bodorgan	d						08 54				
Ty Croes	d						08 58				
Rhosneigr	d						09 01				
Valley	d						09x07				
Holyhead	a				08 23		09 19				10 05

Station		AW	AW	AW	VT	AW	AW	AW	AW	AW	VT	AW	AW	AW	AW	VT	VT	AW	AW	AW
				◇	◇ 1	◇	◇			◇	◇ 1	◇			◇	◇ 1	◇ 1	◇		
				⊤	⊠		⊤			⊤	⊠	⊤			⊤	⊠	⊠	⊤		
London Euston [15] ⊖65	d				07 10						08 10					09 10	09 10			
Birmingham New Street [12] 65	d						07 22											09 24		
Manchester Airport 84,85 ✈	d																			
Cardiff Central [7] 131	d											07 20								
Crewe [10]	d	08 23			08 49			09 23			09 49		10 23			10 49	10 49		11 23	
Manchester Piccadilly [10] ⇌	d			07 50						08 50					09 50					
Manchester Oxford Road 90	d			07 53						08 53					09 53					
Newton-le-Willows 90	d			08 12						09 12					10 12					
Earlestown [8] 90	d			08 15						09 15					10 15					
Warrington Bank Quay 90	d			08 24						09 26					10 26					
Runcorn East	d			08 31						09 33					10 33					
Frodsham	d			08 35						09 37					10 37					
Helsby	d			08 39						09 41					10 41					
Liverpool Lime Street [10] 106	d																			
Chester	a	08 46		08 51	09 12		09 20	09 46		09 53	10 09	10 20	10 46		10 53	11 09	11 09	11 19	11 46	
	d			08 55			09 25			09 55	10 16	10 26			10 55		11 16	11 26		
Shotton	d			09 04						10 04					11 04					
Flint	d			09 10			09 39			10 10	10 29	10 39			11 10			11 39		
Prestatyn	d			09 23			09 52			10 23	10 42	10 52			11 23			11 52		
Rhyl	d			09 29			09 58			10 29	10 48	10 58			11 29		11 43	11 58		
Abergele & Pensarn	d			09 35						10 35					11 35					
Colwyn Bay	d			09 43			10 09			10 43	10 59	11 09			11 43		11 54	12 09		
Llandudno Junction	a			09 48			10 14			10 48	11 04	11 14			11 48		12 00	12 14		
	d		09 26	09 50		10 00	10 15		10 26	10 50	11 06	11 15		11 26	11 50		12 01	12 15		12 26
Deganwy	d		09x29	09x54		10x03			10x29	10x54				11x29	11x54					12x29
Llandudno	a		09 36	10 06		10 08			10 36	11 06				11 36	12 06					12 36
Conwy	d						10x17					11x17						12x17		
Penmaenmawr	d						10x23					11x23						12x23		
Llanfairfechan	d						10x27					11x27						12x27		
Bangor (Gwynedd)	a						10 36				11 27	11 38					12 16	12 36		
	d						10 38					11 40					12 17	12 38		
Llanfairpwll	d						10x44											12x44		
Bodorgan	d						10x54											12x54		
Ty Croes	d						10x58											12x58		
Rhosneigr	d						11x01											13x01		
Valley	d						11x07											13x07		
Holyhead	a						11 19					12 13					12 50	13 19		

Crewe and Manchester - Chester and North Wales

	AW	VT	AW	AW	AW	AW	AW	VT	AW	AW	AW	AW	VT	AW	AW	AW	VT	AW
	◇ ⊥	◇1 ⊐	◇	◇ ⊥			◇ ⊥	◇1 ⊐	◇ ⊥			◇ ⊥	◇1 ⊐	◇ ⊥		◇ ⊥	◇1 ⊐	◇
London Euston 15 ⊖65 d		10 10						11 10					12 10				13 10	
Birmingham New Street 12 65 d									11 24									
Manchester Airport 84,85 ✈ d																		
Cardiff Central 7 131 d				09 20										11 20				
Crewe 10 d		11 49			12 23			12 49		13 23			13 49		14 23		14 49	
Manchester Piccadilly 10 ⇌ d	10 50						11 50					12 50				13 50		
Manchester Oxford Road 90 d	10 53						11 53					12 53				13 53		
Newton-le-Willows 90 d	11 12						12 12					13 12				14 12		
Earlestown 8 90 d	11 15						12 15					13 15				14 15		
Warrington Bank Quay 90 d	11 26						12 26					13 26				14 26		
Runcorn East d	11 33						12 33					13 33				14 33		
Frodsham d	11 37						12 37					13 37				14 37		
Helsby d	11 41						12 41					13 41				14 41		
Liverpool Lime Street 10 106 d																		
Chester a	11 53	12 12		12 19	12 46		12 53	13 12	13 19	13 46		13 53	14 12	14 20	14 46	14 53	15 12	
d	11 55			12 26			12 55		13 25			13 55		14 25		14 55		
Shotton d	12 04						13 04					14 04				15 04		
Flint d	12 10			12 39			13 10		13 39			14 10		14 38		15 10		
Prestatyn d	12 23			12 52			13 23		13 52			14 23		14 51		15 23		
Rhyl d	12 29			12 58			13 29		13 58			14 29		14 57		15 29		
Abergele & Pensarn d	12 35						13 35					14 35				15 35		
Colwyn Bay d	12 43			13 09			13 43		14 09			14 43		15 08		15 43		
Llandudno Junction a	12 48			13 14			13 48		14 14			14 48		15 13		15 48		
d	12 50		13 00	13 15		13 26	13 50		14 15		14 26	14 50		15 15		15 50		16 04
Deganwy d	12x54		13x03			13x29	13x54				14x29	14x54				15x54		16x07
Llandudno a	13 06		13 09			13 36	14 06				14 36	15 06				16 06		16 13
Conwy d									14x17									
Penmaenmawr d									14x23									
Llanfairfechan d									14x27									
Bangor (Gwynedd) a				13 31					14 36					15 31				
d				13 32					14 38					15 32				
Llanfairpwll d				13x39										15x39				
Bodorgan d				13x49										15x49				
Ty Croes d				13x53										15x53				
Rhosneigr d				13x56										15x56				
Valley d				14x01										16x01				
Holyhead a				14 14					15 11					16 14				

	AW	AW	AW	VT	AW	AW	AW	VT	AW	AW	AW	AW	AW	VT	AW	AW	AW	AW
	◇ ⊥		◇ ⊥	◇1 ⊐	◇ ⊥		◇ ⊥	◇1 ⊐	◇ ⊥			◇	◇ ⊥	◇1 ⊐	■ ⊥			
London Euston 15 ⊖65 d				14 10				15 10						16 10				
Birmingham New Street 12 65 d	13 24								15 26									
Manchester Airport 84,85 ✈ d																		
Cardiff Central 7 131 d					13 20										15 20			
Crewe 10 d		15 23		15 49		16 23		16 49		17 23				17 49			18 23	
Manchester Piccadilly 10 ⇌ d			14 50				15 50						16 50			17 19		
Manchester Oxford Road 90 d			14 53				15 53						16 53			17 22		
Newton-le-Willows 90 d			15 12				16 12						17 12			17 40		
Earlestown 8 90 d			15 15				16 15						17 15			17 44		
Warrington Bank Quay 90 d			15 26				16 26						17 26			17 53		
Runcorn East d			15 33				16 33						17 33			18 00		
Frodsham d			15 37				16 37						17 37			18 05		
Helsby d			15 41				16 41						17 41			18 09		
Liverpool Lime Street 10 106 d																		
Chester a	15 20	15 46	15 53	16 12	16 20	16 46	16 54	17 12	17 22	17 46			17 53	18 08	18 20	18 23	18 46	
d	15 25		15 55		16 26		16 55		17 25				17 55	18 10	18 27			
Shotton d			16 04				17 04		17 35				18 04					
Flint d	15 39		16 10		16 39		17 10		17 41				18 10	18 23	18 40			
Prestatyn d	15 52		16 23		16 52		17 23		17 54				18 23	18 36	18 53			
Rhyl d	15 58		16 29		16 58		17 29		18 00				18 29	18 42	18 59			
Abergele & Pensarn d			16 35				17 35		18 06				18 35					
Colwyn Bay d	16 09		16 43		17 09		17 43		18 14				18 43	18 53	19 10			
Llandudno Junction a	16 14		16 48		17 14		17 49		18 19				18 48	18 58	19 15			
d	16 15		16 50		17 15		17 50		18 21		18 26	18 41	18 50	19 00	19 16			19 26
Deganwy d			16x54				17x54				18x29	18x44	18x54					19x29
Llandudno a			17 06				18 06				18 36	18 49	19 06					19 36
Conwy d	16x17				17x17				18x23									
Penmaenmawr d	16x23				17x23				18x29									
Llanfairfechan d	16x27				17x27				18x33									
Bangor (Gwynedd) a	16 36				17 36				18 42					19 21	19 33			
d	16 38				17 38				18 43						19 34			
Llanfairpwll d					17x44										19x41			
Bodorgan d					17x54										19x51			
Ty Croes d					17x58										19x55			
Rhosneigr d					18x01										19x58			
Valley d					18x07										20x04			
Holyhead a	17 11				18 19				19 16						20 14			

Crewe and Manchester - Chester and North Wales

	AW	AW	VT	AW	AW	AW	AW	VT	AW	AW	AW	AW	VT	AW	AW	AW	AW	VT	AW
	◇ ⊥		◇1 ⊠		◇ ⊥			◇1 ⊠	■ ⊥			◇	■ 1 ⊐	◇ ⊥	◇ ⊥			◇1 ⊐	◇
London Euston 15 ⊖65 d			17 10					18 10					19 10					20 10	
Birmingham New Street 12 65 d					17 26									19 24					
Manchester Airport 84,85 ✈ d																	20 32		
Cardiff Central 7 131 d		16 15							17 20										19 34
Crewe 10 d		18 43	18 56			19 23		19 56		20 23			20 50		21 00	21 23		21 50	
Manchester Piccadilly 10 ⇌ d	17 50						18 50				19 50						20 50		
Manchester Oxford Road 90 d	17 53						18 53				19 53						20 53		
Newton-le-Willows 90 d	18 12						19 12				20 12						21 12		
Earlestown 8 90 d	18 15						19 16				20 15						21 15		
Warrington Bank Quay 90 d	18 24						19 26				20 26						21 24		
Runcorn East d	18 31						19 33				20 33						21 33		
Frodsham d	18 36						19 37				20 37						21 37		
Helsby d	18 40						19 41				20 41						21 41		
Liverpool Lime Street 10 106 d																			
Chester a	18 53	19 06	19 15		19 20	19 46	19 53	20 15	20 24	20 46	20 53		21 10	21 19	21 21	21 46	21 53	22 12	22 34
d	18 55	19 07	19 21		19 31			20 26	20 35				21 17		21 30				22 56
Shotton d	19 04				19 40				20 44						21 39				23 05
Flint d	19 10	19 21	19 35		19 46				20 50				21 30		21 45				23 11
Prestatyn d	19 23		19 48		19 59				21 03				21 43		21 59				23 24
Rhyl d	19 29	19 39	19 54		20 05			20 53	21 09				21 50		22 05				23 30
Abergele & Pensarn d	19 35				20 11										22 11				23 36
Colwyn Bay d	19 43		20 05		20 19			21 04	21 20				22 01		22 19				23 44
Llandudno Junction a	19 48	19 52	20 10		20 24			21 09	21 25				22 06		22 24				23 49
d	19 50	19 53	20 12	20 24	20 26			21 10	21 26			21 32	22 07		22 26				23 51
Deganwy d	19x54			20x27								21x35							
Llandudno a	20 06			20 34								21 42							
Conwy d					20x28										22x28				23x54
Penmaenmawr d					20x34										22x34				23x58
Llanfairfechan d					20x38										22x38				00x04
Bangor (Gwynedd) a		20 09	20 27		20 47			21 25	21 42				22 22		22 47				00 12
d		20 11	20 28		20 48			21 27	21 43				22 24		22 48				00 13
Llanfairpwll d									21x50										00x20
Bodorgan d									22x00										00x30
Ty Croes d									22x04										00x34
Rhosneigr d									22x07										00x37
Valley d									22x12										00x42
Holyhead a		20 49	20 59		21 21			21 59	22 24				22 56		23 21				00 53

	AW	AW	AW	AW	AW	AW	AW
						◇ ⊥	◇
London Euston 15 ⊖65 d							
Birmingham New Street 12 65 d						22 55	
Manchester Airport 84,85 ✈ d		21 32					
Cardiff Central 7 131 d							20 53
Crewe 10 d	22 23			23 23		23 57	00e02
Manchester Piccadilly 10 ⇌ d		21 50	22 12		23 14		
Manchester Oxford Road 90 d		21 53	22c29		23 17		
Newton-le-Willows 90 d		22 12	22 47		23 36		
Earlestown 8 90 d		22 15	22 50		23 39		
Warrington Bank Quay 90 d		22 24	22 59		23 48		
Runcorn East d		22 31	23 06		23 55		
Frodsham d		22 35	23 10		23 59		
Helsby d		22 39	23 14		00 03		
Liverpool Lime Street 10 106 d							
Chester a	22 45	22 51	23 26	23 44	00 15	00 18	00 27
d						00 40	
Shotton d							
Flint d						00 53	
Prestatyn d						01 06	
Rhyl d						01 12	
Abergele & Pensarn d							
Colwyn Bay d						01 23	
Llandudno Junction a						01 28	
d						01 29	
Deganwy d							
Llandudno a							
Conwy d							
Penmaenmawr d							
Llanfairfechan d							
Bangor (Gwynedd) a						01 45	
d						01 45	
Llanfairpwll d							
Bodorgan d							
Ty Croes d							
Rhosneigr d							
Valley d							
Holyhead a						02 15	

c arr. 2214

e arr. 2353

Table 81

Crewe and Manchester - Chester and North Wales

Mondays to Fridays
from 06 September

Station		AW	AW	AW	VT	AW	AW	AW	AW	AW	AW	AW
					◇■1 ⊠	◇ ⊥	◇ ⊥			◇ ⊥	◇ ⊥	
London Euston ⊖65	d											
Birmingham New Street 65	d				05 30							
Manchester Airport 84,85 ✈	d					05 33						
Cardiff Central 131	d										05 10	
Crewe	d				06 24		06 54	07 23				08 23
Manchester Piccadilly ⇌	d					05 50				06 50		
Manchester Oxford Road 90	d					05 53				06 53		
Newton-le-Willows 90	d					06 12				07 12		
Earlestown 90	d					06 15				07 15		
Warrington Bank Quay 90	d					06 26				07 22		
Runcorn East	d					06 33				07 29		
Frodsham	d					06 37				07 34		
Helsby	d					06 41				07 38		
Liverpool Lime Street 106	d											
Chester	a				06 44	06 53	07 14	07 46		07 50	08 20	08 46
	d				06 44	06 55	07 26			07 55	08 26	
Shotton	d					07 04				08 04		
Flint	d				06 57	07 10	07 39			08 10	08 39	
Prestatyn	d				07 10	07 23	07 52			08 23	08 52	
Rhyl	d				07 16	07 29	07 58			08 29	08 58	
Abergele & Pensarn	d					07 35				08 35		
Colwyn Bay	d				07 27	07 43	08 09			08 43	09 09	
Llandudno Junction	a				07 33	07 48	08 14			08 48	09 14	
	d	06 13	06 51	07 31	07 33	07 50	08 15		08 25	08 50	09 15	
Deganwy	d	06x16	06x54	07x34		07x54			08x28	08x54		
Llandudno	a	06 23	07 01	07 41		08 06			08 35	09 06		
Conwy	d						08x17					
Penmaenmawr	d						08x23					
Llanfairfechan	d						08x27					
Bangor (Gwynedd)	a				07 49		08 36				09 31	
	d				07 50		08 38				09 32	
Llanfairpwll	d						08x44					
Bodorgan	d						08 54					
Ty Croes	d						08 58					
Rhosneigr	d						09 01					
Valley	d						09x07					
Holyhead	a				08 23		09 19				10 05	

Station		AW	AW	VT	AW	AW	AW	AW	AW	VT	AW	AW	AW	AW	VT	VT	AW	AW	AW	AW
			◇ ⊥	◇■1 ⊠	◇	◇ ⊥			◇ ⊥	◇■1 ⊠	◇ ⊥			◇ ⊥	◇■1 ⊠	◇■1 ⊠	◇ ⊥			◇ ⊥
London Euston ⊖65	d			07 10						08 10					09 10	09 10				
Birmingham New Street 65	d					07 22											09 24			
Manchester Airport 84,85 ✈	d																			
Cardiff Central 131	d										07 20									
Crewe	d			08 49			09 23			09 49		10 23			10 49	10 49		11 23		
Manchester Piccadilly ⇌	d		07 50						08 50					09 50						10 50
Manchester Oxford Road 90	d		07 53						08 53					09 53						10 53
Newton-le-Willows 90	d		08 12						09 12					10 12						11 12
Earlestown 90	d		08 15						09 15					10 15						11 15
Warrington Bank Quay 90	d		08 24						09 26					10 26						11 26
Runcorn East	d		08 31						09 33					10 33						11 33
Frodsham	d		08 35						09 37					10 37						11 37
Helsby	d		08 39						09 41					10 41						11 41
Liverpool Lime Street 106	d																			
Chester	a		08 51	09 12		09 20	09 46		09 53	10 09	10 20	10 46		10 53	11 09	11 09	11 19	11 46		11 53
	d		08 55			09 25			09 55	10 16	10 26			10 55		11 16	11 26			11 55
Shotton	d		09 04						10 04					11 04						12 04
Flint	d		09 10			09 39			10 10	10 29	10 39			11 10			11 39			12 10
Prestatyn	d		09 23			09 52			10 23	10 42	10 52			11 23			11 52			12 23
Rhyl	d		09 29			09 58			10 29	10 48	10 58			11 29		11 43	11 58			12 29
Abergele & Pensarn	d		09 35						10 35					11 35						12 35
Colwyn Bay	d		09 43			10 09			10 43	10 59	11 09			11 43		11 54	12 09			12 43
Llandudno Junction	a		09 48			10 14			10 48	11 04	11 14			11 48		12 00	12 14			12 48
	d	09 26	09 50		10 00	10 15		10 26	10 50	11 06	11 15		11 26	11 50		12 01	12 15		12 26	12 50
Deganwy	d	09x29	09x54		10x03			10x29	10x54				11x29	11x54					12x29	12x54
Llandudno	a	09 36	10 06		10 08			10 36	11 06				11 36	12 06					12 36	13 06
Conwy	d					10x17					11x17						12x17			
Penmaenmawr	d					10x23					11x23						12x23			
Llanfairfechan	d					10x27					11x27						12x27			
Bangor (Gwynedd)	a					10 36				11 27	11 38					12 16	12 36			
	d					10 38					11 40					12 17	12 38			
Llanfairpwll	d					10x44											12x44			
Bodorgan	d					10x54											12x54			
Ty Croes	d					10x58											12x58			
Rhosneigr	d					11x01											13x01			
Valley	d					11x07											13x07			
Holyhead	a					11 19					12 13					12 50	13 19			

Table 81

Crewe and Manchester - Chester and North Wales

Mondays to Fridays
from 06 September

Station		VT	AW	AW	AW	AW	AW	VT	AW	AW	AW	AW	VT	AW	AW	AW	VT	AW	AW
		◇■1 ⊏	◇	◇ ⊥			◇ ⊥	◇■1 ⊏	◇ ⊥			◇ ⊥	◇■1 ⊏	◇ ⊥		◇ ⊥	◇■1 ⊏	◇	◇ ⊥
London Euston ⊖65	d	10 10						11 10					12 10				13 10		
Birmingham New Street 65	d								11 24										13 24
Manchester Airport 84,85 ✈	d																		
Cardiff Central 131	d			09 20										11 20					
Crewe	d	11 49			12 23			12 49		13 23			13 49		14 23		14 49		
Manchester Piccadilly ⇌	d						11 50					12 50				13 50			
Manchester Oxford Road 90	d						11 53					12 53				13 53			
Newton-le-Willows 90	d						12 12					13 12				14 12			
Earlestown 90	d						12 15					13 15				14 15			
Warrington Bank Quay 90	d						12 26					13 26				14 26			
Runcorn East	d						12 33					13 33				14 33			
Frodsham	d						12 37					13 37				14 37			
Helsby	d						12 41					13 41				14 41			
Liverpool Lime Street 106	d																		
Chester	a	12 12		12 19	12 46		12 53	13 12	13 19	13 46		13 53	14 12	14 20	14 46	14 53	15 12		15 20
	d			12 26			12 55		13 25			13 55		14 25		14 55			15 25
Shotton	d						13 04					14 04				15 04			
Flint	d			12 39			13 10		13 39			14 10		14 38		15 10			15 39
Prestatyn	d			12 52			13 23		13 52			14 23		14 51		15 23			15 52
Rhyl	d			12 58			13 29		13 58			14 29		14 57		15 29			15 58
Abergele & Pensarn	d						13 35					14 35				15 35			
Colwyn Bay	d			13 09			13 43		14 09			14 43		15 08		15 43			16 09
Llandudno Junction	a			13 14			13 48		14 14			14 48		15 13		15 48			16 14
	d		13 00	13 15		13 26	13 50		14 15		14 26	14 50		15 15		15 50		16 04	16 15
Deganwy	d		13x03			13x29	13x54				14x29	14x54				15x54		16x07	
Llandudno	a		13 09			13 36	14 06				14 36	15 06				16 06		16 13	
Conwy	d								14x17										16x17
Penmaenmawr	d								14x23										16x23
Llanfairfechan	d								14x27										16x27
Bangor (Gwynedd)	a			13 31					14 36					15 31					16 36
	d			13 32					14 38					15 32					16 38
Llanfairpwll	d			13x39										15x39					
Bodorgan	d			13x49										15x49					
Ty Croes	d			13x53										15x53					
Rhosneigr	d			13x56										15x56					
Valley	d			14x01										16x01					
Holyhead	a			14 14					15 11					16 14					17 11

Station		AW	AW	VT	AW	AW	AW	VT	AW	AW	AW	AW	AW	VT	AW	AW	AW	AW	AW
			◇ ⊥	◇■1 ⊏	◇ ⊥		◇ ⊥	◇■1 ⊏	◇ ⊥			◇	◇ ⊥	◇■1 ⊏	■ ⊥				◇ ⊥
London Euston ⊖65	d			14 10				15 10						16 10					
Birmingham New Street 65	d								15 26										
Manchester Airport 84,85 ✈	d																		
Cardiff Central 131	d				13 20										15 20				
Crewe	d	15 23		15 49		16 23		16 49		17 23				17 49			18 23		
Manchester Piccadilly ⇌	d		14 50				15 50						16 50			17 19			17 50
Manchester Oxford Road 90	d		14 53				15 53						16 53			17 22			17 53
Newton-le-Willows 90	d		15 12				16 12						17 12			17 40			18 12
Earlestown 90	d		15 15				16 15						17 15			17 44			18 15
Warrington Bank Quay 90	d		15 26				16 26						17 26			17 53			18 24
Runcorn East	d		15 33				16 33						17 33			18 00			18 31
Frodsham	d		15 37				16 37						17 37			18 05			18 36
Helsby	d		15 41				16 41						17 41			18 09			18 40
Liverpool Lime Street 106	d																		
Chester	a	15 46	15 53	16 12	16 20	16 46	16 54	17 12	17 22	17 46			17 53	18 08	18 20	18 23	18 46		18 53
	d		15 55		16 26		16 55		17 25				17 55	18 10	18 27				18 55
Shotton	d		16 04				17 04		17 35				18 04						19 04
Flint	d		16 10		16 39		17 10		17 41				18 10	18 23	18 40				19 10
Prestatyn	d		16 23		16 52		17 23		17 54				18 23	18 36	18 53				19 23
Rhyl	d		16 29		16 58		17 29		18 00				18 29	18 42	18 59				19 29
Abergele & Pensarn	d		16 35				17 35		18 06				18 35						19 35
Colwyn Bay	d		16 43		17 09		17 43		18 14				18 43	18 53	19 10				19 43
Llandudno Junction	a		16 48		17 14		17 49		18 19				18 48	18 58	19 15				19 48
	d		16 50		17 15		17 50		18 21		18 26	18 41	18 50	19 00	19 16			19 26	19 50
Deganwy	d		16x54				17x54				18x29	18x44	18x54					19x29	19x54
Llandudno	a		17 06				18 06				18 36	18 49	19 06					19 36	20 06
Conwy	d				17x17				18x23										
Penmaenmawr	d				17x23				18x29										
Llanfairfechan	d				17x27				18x33										
Bangor (Gwynedd)	a				17 36				18 42					19 21	19 33				
	d				17 38				18 43						19 34				
Llanfairpwll	d				17x44										19x41				
Bodorgan	d				17x54										19x51				
Ty Croes	d				17x58										19x55				
Rhosneigr	d				18x01										19x58				
Valley	d				18x07										20x04				
Holyhead	a				18 19				19 16						20 14				

Crewe and Manchester - Chester and North Wales

	AW	VT	AW	AW	AW	AW	VT	AW	AW	AW	AW	VT	AW	AW	AW	AW	VT	AW	AW
		◇1 ⊠		◇ ⊼			◇1 ⊠	⊼			◇	1 ⊏	◇ ⊼	◇ ⊼			◇1 ⊏	◇	
London Euston 15 ⊖65 d		17 10					18 10					19 10					20 10		
Birmingham New Street 12 65 d				17 26									19 24						
Manchester Airport 84,85 ✈ d																20 32			
Cardiff Central 7 131 d	16 15							17 20										19 34	
Crewe 10 d	18 43	18 56			19 23		19 56		20 23			20 50		21 00	21 23		21 50		22 23
Manchester Piccadilly 10 ⇌ d						18 50				19 50						20 50			
Manchester Oxford Road 90 d						18 53				19 53						20 53			
Newton-le-Willows 90 d						19 12				20 12						21 12			
Earlestown 8 90 d						19 16				20 15						21 15			
Warrington Bank Quay 90 d						19 26				20 26						21 24			
Runcorn East d						19 33				20 33						21 33			
Frodsham d						19 37				20 37						21 37			
Helsby d						19 41				20 41						21 41			
Liverpool Lime Street 10 106 d																			
Chester a	19 06	19 15		19 20	19 46	19 53	20 15	20 24	20 46	20 53		21 10	21 19	21 21	21 46	21 53	22 12	22 34	22 45
d	19 07	19 21		19 31			20 26	20 35				21 17		21 30				22 56	
Shotton d				19 40				20 44						21 39				23 05	
Flint d	19 21	19 35		19 46				20 50				21 30		21 45				23 11	
Prestatyn d		19 48		19 59				21 03				21 43		21 59				23 24	
Rhyl d	19 39	19 54		20 05			20 53	21 09				21 50		22 05				23 30	
Abergele & Pensarn d				20 11										22 11				23 36	
Colwyn Bay d		20 05		20 19			21 04	21 20				22 01		22 19				23 44	
Llandudno Junction a	19 52	20 10		20 24			21 09	21 25				22 06		22 24				23 49	
d	19 53	20 12	20 24	20 26			21 10	21 26			21 32	22 07		22 26				23 51	
Deganwy d			20x27								21x35								
Llandudno a			20 34								21 42								
Conwy d				20x28										22x28				23x54	
Penmaenmawr d				20x34										22x34				23x58	
Llanfairfechan d				20x38										22x38				00x04	
Bangor (Gwynedd) a	20 09	20 27		20 47			21 25	21 42				22 22		22 47				00 12	
d	20 11	20 28		20 48			21 27	21 43				22 24		22 48				00 13	
Llanfairpwll d								21x50										00x20	
Bodorgan d								22x00										00x30	
Ty Croes d								22x04										00x34	
Rhosneigr d								22x07										00x37	
Valley d								22x12										00x42	
Holyhead a	20 49	20 59		21 21			21 59	22 24				22 56		23 21				00 53	

	AW	AW	AW	AW	AW	AW
					◇ ⊼	◇
London Euston 15 ⊖65 d						
Birmingham New Street 12 65 d					22 55	
Manchester Airport 84,85 ✈ d	21 32					
Cardiff Central 7 131 d						20 53
Crewe 10 d			23 23		23 57	00e02
Manchester Piccadilly 10 ⇌ d	21 50	22 12		23 14		
Manchester Oxford Road 90 d	21 53	22c29		23 17		
Newton-le-Willows 90 d	22 12	22 47		23 36		
Earlestown 8 90 d	22 15	22 50		23 39		
Warrington Bank Quay 90 d	22 24	22 59		23 48		
Runcorn East d	22 31	23 06		23 55		
Frodsham d	22 35	23 10		23 59		
Helsby d	22 39	23 14		00 03		
Liverpool Lime Street 10 106 d						
Chester a	22 51	23 26	23 44	00 15	00 18	00 27
d					00 40	
Shotton d						
Flint d					00 53	
Prestatyn d					01 06	
Rhyl d					01 12	
Abergele & Pensarn d						
Colwyn Bay d					01 23	
Llandudno Junction a					01 28	
d					01 29	
Deganwy d						
Llandudno a						
Conwy d						
Penmaenmawr d						
Llanfairfechan d						
Bangor (Gwynedd) a					01 45	
d					01 45	
Llanfairpwll d						
Bodorgan d						
Ty Croes d						
Rhosneigr d						
Valley d						
Holyhead a					02 15	

c arr. 2214 e arr. 2353

Crewe and Manchester - Chester and North Wales

	NT	AW	AW	AW	VT	AW	AW	AW	AW	AW	AW	AW	AW	AW	AW
					◇1 ⊏	◇ ⊼	◇ ⊼			◇ ⊼	◇ ⊼			◇ ⊼	◇
London Euston 15 ⊖65 d															
Birmingham New Street 12 65 d					05 30										
Manchester Airport 84,85 ✈ d						05 33									
Cardiff Central 7 131 d											05 20				
Crewe 10 d					06 23		07 03	07 23				08 23			
Manchester Piccadilly 10 ⇌ d						05 50				06 50				07 50	
Manchester Oxford Road 90 d						05 53				06 53				07 53	
Newton-le-Willows 90 d						06 12				07 12				08 12	
Earlestown 8 90 d						06 15				07 15				08 15	
Warrington Bank Quay 90 d	05 52					06 26				07 24				08 24	
Runcorn East d						06 33				07 31				08 31	
Frodsham d						06 37				07 35				08 35	
Helsby d	06a05					06 41				07 39				08 39	
Liverpool Lime Street 10 106 d															
Chester a					06 43	06 53	07 23	07 46		07 51	08 19	08 46		08 51	
d					06 44	06 55	07 26			07 55	08 26			08 55	
Shotton d						07 04				08 04				09 04	
Flint d					06 57	07 10	07 39			08 10	08 39			09 10	
Prestatyn d					07 10	07 23	07 52			08 23	08 52			09 23	
Rhyl d					07 16	07 29	07 58			08 29	08 58			09 29	
Abergele & Pensarn d						07 35				08 35				09 35	
Colwyn Bay d					07 27	07 43	08 09			08 43	09 09			09 43	
Llandudno Junction a					07 33	07 48	08 14			08 48	09 14			09 48	
d		06 13	06 51	07 31	07 33	07 50	08 15		08 25	08 50	09 15		09 26	09 50	10 00
Deganwy d		06x16	06x54	07x34		07x54			08x28	08x54			09x29	09x54	10x03
Llandudno a		06 23	07 01	07 41		08 06			08 35	09 06			09 36	10 06	10 08
Conwy d							08x17								
Penmaenmawr d							08x23								
Llanfairfechan d							08x27								
Bangor (Gwynedd) a					07 49		08 36				09 31				
d					07 50		08 38				09 32				
Llanfairpwll d							08x44								
Bodorgan d							08x54								
Ty Croes d							08x58								
Rhosneigr d							09x01								
Valley d							09x07								
Holyhead a					08 23		09 19				10 05				

	AW	AW	AW	AW	VT	AW	AW	AW	AW	VT	AW	AW	AW	AW	VT	AW	AW	AW
	◇ ⊼			◇ ⊼	◇1 ⊏	◇ ⊼			◇ ⊼	◇1 ⊏	◇ ⊼			◇ ⊼	◇1 ⊏	◇	◇ ⊼	
London Euston 15 ⊖65 d					08 10					08 50					10 10			
Birmingham New Street 12 65 d	07 24										09 24							
Manchester Airport 84,85 ✈ d																		
Cardiff Central 7 131 d						07 20											09 20	
Crewe 10 d		09 23			09 50		10 23			10e45		11 23			11 50			12 23
Manchester Piccadilly 10 ⇌ d				08 50					09 50					10 50				
Manchester Oxford Road 90 d				08 53					09 53					10 53				
Newton-le-Willows 90 d				09 12					10 12					11 12				
Earlestown 8 90 d				09 15					10 15					11 15				
Warrington Bank Quay 90 d				09 26					10 26					11 26				
Runcorn East d				09 33					10 33					11 33				
Frodsham d				09 37					10 37					11 37				
Helsby d				09 41					10 41					11 41				
Liverpool Lime Street 10 106 d																		
Chester a	09 19	09 46		09 53	10 12	10 19	10 46		10 53	11 12	11 19	11 46		11 53	12 12		12 19	12 46
d	09 26			09 55		10 26			10 55	11 15	11 26			11 55			12 26	
Shotton d				10 04					11 04					12 04				
Flint d	09 39			10 10		10 39			11 10		11 39			12 10			12 39	
Prestatyn d	09 52			10 23		10 52			11 23		11 51			12 23			12 52	
Rhyl d	09 58			10 29		10 58			11 29	11 44	11 57			12 29			12 58	
Abergele & Pensarn d				10 35					11 35					12 35				
Colwyn Bay d	10 09			10 43		11 09			11 43	11 57	12 09			12 43			13 09	
Llandudno Junction a	10 14			10 48		11 14			11 48	12 03	12 14			12 48			13 14	
d	10 15		10 26	10 50		11 15		11 26	11 50	12 04	12 14		12 26	12 50		13 00	13 15	
Deganwy d			10x29	10x54				11x29	11x54				12x29	12x54		13x03		
Llandudno a			10 36	11 06				11 36	12 06				12 36	13 06		13 09		
Conwy d	10x17					11x17					12x17							
Penmaenmawr d	10x23					11x23					12x23							
Llanfairfechan d	10x27					11x27					12x27							
Bangor (Gwynedd) a	10 36					11 36				12 22	12 35						13 31	
d	10 38					11 38				12 23	12 38						13 32	
Llanfairpwll d	10x44										12x44						13x39	
Bodorgan d	10x54										12x54						13x49	
Ty Croes d	10x58										12x57						13x53	
Rhosneigr d	11x01										13x00						13x56	
Valley d	11x07										13x07						14x01	
Holyhead a	11 19					12 11				12 58	13 19						14 14	

Crewe and Manchester - Chester and North Wales

		AW		AW	VT	AW		AW	AW	AW	VT	AW			AW	AW	AW	VT	AW	AW		AW		AW	AW
				◇ 🍴	◇[1] ⊡	◇ 🍴				◇ 🍴	◇[1] ⊡	◇ 🍴					◇ 🍴	◇[1] ⊡	◇	◇ 🍴					◇ 🍴
London Euston [15] ⊖65	d				11 10						12 10							13 10							
Birmingham New Street [12] 65	d					11 24														13 23					
Manchester Airport 84,85 ✈	d																								
Cardiff Central [7] 131	d											11 20													
Crewe [10]	d				12 49			13 23			13 49				14 23			14 50				15 23			
Manchester Piccadilly [10] ⇌	d			11 50						12 50							13 50								14 50
Manchester Oxford Road 90	d			11 53						12 53							13 53								14 53
Newton-le-Willows 90	d			12 12						13 12							14 12								15 12
Earlestown [8] 90	d			12 15						13 15							14 15								15 15
Warrington Bank Quay 90	d			12 26						13 26							14 26								15 26
Runcorn East	d			12 33						13 33							14 33								15 33
Frodsham	d			12 37						13 37							14 37								15 37
Helsby	d			12 41						13 41							14 41								15 41
Liverpool Lime Street [10] 106	d																								
Chester	a			12 53	13 12	13 19		13 46		13 53	14 12	14 20			14 46		14 53	15 12		15 21		15 46			15 53
	d			12 55		13 26				13 55		14 25					14 55			15 25					15 55
Shotton	d			13 04						14 04							15 04								16 04
Flint	d			13 10		13 39				14 10		14 38					15 10			15 39					16 10
Prestatyn	d			13 23		13 52				14 23		14 51					15 23			15 52					16 23
Rhyl	d			13 29		13 58				14 29		14 57					15 29			15 58					16 29
Abergele & Pensarn	d			13 35						14 35							15 35								16 35
Colwyn Bay	d			13 43		14 09				14 43		15 08					15 43			16 09					16 43
Llandudno Junction	a			13 48		14 14				14 48		15 13					15 48			16 14					16 48
	d	13 26		13 50		14 15			14 26	14 50		15 15				15 26	15 50		16 00	16 15				16 26	16 50
Deganwy	d	13x29		13x54					14x29	14x54						15x29	15x54		16x03					16x29	16x54
Llandudno	a	13 36		14 06					14 36	15 06						15 36	16 06		16 09					16 36	17 06
Conwy	d					14x17														16x17					
Penmaenmawr	d					14x23														16x23					
Llanfairfechan	d					14x27														16x27					
Bangor (Gwynedd)	a					14 36						15 31								16 36					
	d					14 38						15 32								16 38					
Llanfairpwll	d											15x39													
Bodorgan	d											15x49													
Ty Croes	d											15x53													
Rhosneigr	d											15x56													
Valley	d											16x01													
Holyhead	a					15 11						16 14								17 11					

		VT	AW		AW	AW	AW	VT		AW		AW	AW	AW	AW	VT	AW			AW	AW	AW	VT	AW	AW
		◇[1] ⊡	◇ 🍴				◇ 🍴	◇[1] ⊡		◇ 🍴				◇	◇ 🍴	◇[1] ⊡	◇ 🍴					◇ 🍴	◇[1] ⊡		
London Euston [15] ⊖65	d	14 10						15 10								16 10							17 10		
Birmingham New Street [12] 65	d									15 24															17 24
Manchester Airport 84,85 ✈	d																								
Cardiff Central [7] 131	d		13 20														15 20								
Crewe [10]	d	15 49			16 23			16 49				17 23				17 49				18 23			18 50		
Manchester Piccadilly [10] ⇌	d						15 50								16 50							17 50			
Manchester Oxford Road 90	d						15 53								16 53							17 53			
Newton-le-Willows 90	d						16 12								17 12							18 12			
Earlestown [8] 90	d						16 15								17 15							18 15			
Warrington Bank Quay 90	d						16 26								17 26							18 25			
Runcorn East	d						16 33								17 33							18 32			
Frodsham	d						16 37								17 37							18 36			
Helsby	d						16 41								17 41							18 40			
Liverpool Lime Street [10] 106	d																								
Chester	a	16 10	16 21		16 46		16 53	17 12		17 20		17 46			17 53	18 09	18 20			18 46		18 52	19 10		19 20
	d	16 12	16 26				16 55			17 26					17 55	18 16	18 26					18 55	19 17		19 31
Shotton	d						17 04			17 35					18 04							19 04			19 40
Flint	d	16 25	16 39				17 10			17 41					18 10	18 29	18 39					19 10	19 30		19 46
Prestatyn	d	16 38	16 52				17 23			17 54					18 23	18 42	18 52					19 23	19 43		19 59
Rhyl	d	16 45	16 58				17 29			18 00					18 29	18 49	18 58					19 29	19 50		20 05
Abergele & Pensarn	d						17 35			18 06					18 35							19 35			20 11
Colwyn Bay	d	16 56	17 09				17 43			18 14					18 43	19 00	19 09					19 43	20 01		20 19
Llandudno Junction	a	17 01	17 14				17 48			18 19					18 48	19 05	19 14					19 48	20 06		20 24
	d	17 02	17 15			17 26	17 50			18 21			18 26	18 41	18 50	19 06	19 15				19 26	19 50	20 07	20 24	20 26
Deganwy	d					17x29	17x54						18x29	18x44	18x54						19x29	19x54		20x27	
Llandudno	a					17 36	18 06						18 36	18 49	19 06						19 36	20 06		20 34	
Conwy	d		17x17							18x23															20x28
Penmaenmawr	d		17x23							18x29															20x34
Llanfairfechan	d		17x27							18x33															20x38
Bangor (Gwynedd)	a	17 17	17 36							18 42						19 21	19 31						20 22		20 47
	d	17 19	17 38							18 43						19 23	19 32						20 24		20 48
Llanfairpwll	d		17x44														19x39								
Bodorgan	d		17x54														19x51								
Ty Croes	d		17x58														19x55								
Rhosneigr	d		18x01														19x58								
Valley	d		18x07														20x04								
Holyhead	a	17 51	18 19							19 16						19 55	20 16						20 56		21 21

Table 81

Saturdays
until 04 September

Crewe and Manchester - Chester and North Wales

			AW	AW		VT	AW		AW	AW	AW	AW	AW			AW	AW	AW		AW	AW	AW	AW	AW	
				🍴		◇[1] ⊡	◇ 🍴				◇ 🍴	◇	◇ 🍴					◇				◇ 🍴			
London Euston [15] ⊖65	d					18 10																			
Birmingham New Street [12] 65	d										19 24											21 24			
Manchester Airport 84,85 ✈	d																20 32								
Cardiff Central [7] 131	d						17 20											19 34							
Crewe [10]	d		19 23			19 50			20 23				21 00			21 23				22 23				23 21	
Manchester Piccadilly [10] ⇌	d			18 50						19 50							20 50				21 50		22 26		
Manchester Oxford Road 90	d			18 53						19 53							20 53				21 53		22 29		
Newton-le-Willows 90	d			19 12						20 12							21 12				22 12		22 47		
Earlestown [8] 90	d			19 16						20 15							21 15				22 15		22 50		
Warrington Bank Quay 90	d			19 26						20 30							21 27				22 24		22 59		
Runcorn East	d			19 33						20 37							21 34				22 31		23 06		
Frodsham	d			19 37						20 41							21 38				22 35		23 10		
Helsby	d			19 41						20 45							21 42				22 39		23 14		
Liverpool Lime Street [10] 106	d																								
Chester	a		19 46	19 55		20 12	20 20		20 46	20 57	21 19		21 21			21 46	21 54	22 31		22 45	22 51	23 19	23 26	23 42	
	d						20 35						21 26					22 36							
Shotton	d						20 44						21 35					22 45							
Flint	d						20 50						21 41					22 51							
Prestatyn	d						21 03						21 54					23 05							
Rhyl	d						21 09						22 00					23 11							
Abergele & Pensarn	d												22 06					23 17							
Colwyn Bay	d						21 20						22 14					23 25							
Llandudno Junction	a						21 25						22 19					23 33							
	d						21 26					21 32	22 21												
Deganwy	d											21x35													
Llandudno	a											21 42													
Conwy	d												22x23												
Penmaenmawr	d												22x29												
Llanfairfechan	d												22x33												
Bangor (Gwynedd)	a						21 42						22 42												
	d						21 43						22 43												
Llanfairpwll	d						21x50																		
Bodorgan	d						22x00																		
Ty Croes	d						22x04																		
Rhosneigr	d						22x07																		
Valley	d						22x12																		
Holyhead	a						22 24						23 15												

			AW	AW		AW
				◇ B		🚌
London Euston [15] ⊖65	d					
Birmingham New Street [12] 65	d					
Manchester Airport 84,85 ✈	d					
Cardiff Central [7] 131	d			20 53		
Crewe [10]	d			23 58		
Manchester Piccadilly [10] ⇌	d		23 14			
Manchester Oxford Road 90	d		23 17			
Newton-le-Willows 90	d		23 36			
Earlestown [8] 90	d		23 39			
Warrington Bank Quay 90	d		23 48			
Runcorn East	d		23 55			
Frodsham	d		23 59			
Helsby	d		00 03			
Liverpool Lime Street [10] 106	d					
Chester	a		00 15	00 24		
	d					
Shotton	d					
Flint	d					
Prestatyn	d					
Rhyl	d					
Abergele & Pensarn	d					
Colwyn Bay	d					
Llandudno Junction	a					
	d					23 48
Deganwy	d					
Llandudno	a					
Conwy	d					23 56
Penmaenmawr	d					00 08
Llanfairfechan	d					00 23
Bangor (Gwynedd)	a					00 38
	d					00 38
Llanfairpwll	d					00 47
Bodorgan	d					00 57
Ty Croes	d					01 07
Rhosneigr	d					01 27
Valley	d					01 52
Holyhead	a					02 02

B until 10 July

Table 81

Crewe and Manchester - Chester and North Wales

Saturdays from 11 September

		NT	AW	AW	AW	VT	AW	AW	AW	AW	AW	AW	AW	AW	AW	AW
						◇1 ⊡	◇ ⊤	◇ ⊤			◇ ⊤	◇ ⊤			◇ ⊤	◇
London Euston ⊖65	d															
Birmingham New Street 65	d					05 30										
Manchester Airport 84,85 ✈	d						05 33									
Cardiff Central 131	d											05 20				
Crewe	d					06 23		07 03	07 23				08 23			
Manchester Piccadilly ⇌	d						05 50				06 50				07 50	
Manchester Oxford Road 90	d						05 53				06 53				07 53	
Newton-le-Willows 90	d						06 12				07 12				08 12	
Earlestown 90	d						06 15				07 15				08 15	
Warrington Bank Quay 90	d	05 52					06 26				07 24				08 24	
Runcorn East	d						06 33				07 31				08 31	
Frodsham	d						06 37				07 35				08 35	
Helsby	d	06a05					06 41				07 39				08 39	
Liverpool Lime Street 106	d															
Chester	a					06 43	06 53	07 23	07 46		07 51	08 19	08 46		08 51	
	d					06 44	06 55	07 26			07 55	08 26			08 55	
Shotton	d						07 04				08 04				09 04	
Flint	d					06 57	07 10	07 39			08 10	08 39			09 10	
Prestatyn	d					07 10	07 23	07 52			08 23	08 52			09 23	
Rhyl	d					07 16	07 29	07 58			08 29	08 58			09 29	
Abergele & Pensarn	d						07 35				08 35				09 35	
Colwyn Bay	d					07 27	07 43	08 09			08 43	09 09			09 43	
Llandudno Junction	a					07 33	07 48	08 14			08 48	09 14			09 48	
	d		06 13	06 51	07 31	07 33	07 50	08 15		08 25	08 50	09 15		09 26	09 50	10 00
Deganwy	d		06x16	06x54	07x34		07x54			08x28	08x54			09x29	09x54	10x03
Llandudno	a		06 23	07 01	07 41		08 06			08 35	09 06			09 36	10 06	10 08
Conwy	d							08x17								
Penmaenmawr	d							08x23								
Llanfairfechan	d							08x27								
Bangor (Gwynedd)	a					07 49		08 36				09 31				
	d					07 50		08 38				09 32				
Llanfairpwll	d							08x44								
Bodorgan	d							08x54								
Ty Croes	d							08x58								
Rhosneigr	d							09x01								
Valley	d							09x07								
Holyhead	a					08 23		09 19				10 05				

		AW	AW	AW	AW	VT	AW	AW	AW	AW	VT	AW	AW	AW	AW	VT	AW	AW	AW
		◇ ⊤			◇ ⊤	◇1 ⊡	◇ ⊤			◇ ⊤	◇1 ⊡	◇ ⊤			◇ ⊤	◇1 ⊡	◇	◇ ⊤	
London Euston ⊖65	d					08 10					08 50					10 10			
Birmingham New Street 65	d	07 24										09 24							
Manchester Airport 84,85 ✈	d																		
Cardiff Central 131	d						07 20											09 20	
Crewe	d		09 23			09 50		10 23			10 45		11 23			11 50			12 23
Manchester Piccadilly ⇌	d				08 50					09 50					10 50				
Manchester Oxford Road 90	d				08 53					09 53					10 53				
Newton-le-Willows 90	d				09 12					10 12					11 12				
Earlestown 90	d				09 15					10 15					11 15				
Warrington Bank Quay 90	d				09 26					10 26					11 26				
Runcorn East	d				09 33					10 33					11 33				
Frodsham	d				09 37					10 37					11 37				
Helsby	d				09 41					10 41					11 41				
Liverpool Lime Street 106	d																		
Chester	a	09 19	09 46		09 53	10 12	10 19	10 46		10 53	11 12	11 19	11 46		11 53	12 12		12 19	12 46
	d	09 26			09 55		10 26			10 55	11 15	11 26			11 55			12 26	
Shotton	d				10 04					11 04					12 04				
Flint	d	09 39			10 10		10 39			11 10		11 39			12 10			12 39	
Prestatyn	d	09 52			10 23		10 52			11 23		11 51			12 23			12 52	
Rhyl	d	09 58			10 29		10 58			11 29	11 44	11 57			12 29			12 58	
Abergele & Pensarn	d				10 35					11 35					12 35				
Colwyn Bay	d	10 09			10 43		11 09			11 43	11 57	12 09			12 43			13 09	
Llandudno Junction	a	10 14			10 48		11 14			11 48	12 03	12 14			12 48			13 14	
	d	10 15		10 26	10 50		11 15		11 26	11 50	12 04	12 14		12 26	12 50		13 00	13 15	
Deganwy	d			10x29	10x54				11x29	11x54				12x29	12x54		13x03		
Llandudno	a			10 36	11 06				11 36	12 06				12 36	13 06		13 09		
Conwy	d	10x17					11x17					12x17							
Penmaenmawr	d	10x23					11x23					12x23							
Llanfairfechan	d	10x27					11x27					12x27							
Bangor (Gwynedd)	a	10 36					11 36				12 22	12 35						13 31	
	d	10 38					11 38				12 23	12 38						13 32	
Llanfairpwll	d	10x44										12x44						13x39	
Bodorgan	d	10x54										12x54						13x49	
Ty Croes	d	10x58										12x57						13x53	
Rhosneigr	d	11x01										13x00						13x56	
Valley	d	11x07										13x07						14x01	
Holyhead	a	11 19					12 11				12 58	13 19						14 14	

Table 81

Crewe and Manchester - Chester and North Wales

Saturdays from 11 September

		AW	AW	VT	AW	AW	AW	AW	VT	AW	AW	AW	AW	VT	AW	AW	AW	AW	AW
			◇ ⊤	◇1 ⊡	◇ ⊤			◇ ⊤	◇1 ⊡	◇ ⊤			◇ ⊤	◇1 ⊡	◇	◇ ⊤			◇ ⊤
London Euston ⊖65	d			11 10					12 10					13 10					
Birmingham New Street 65	d				11 24											13 23			
Manchester Airport 84,85 ✈	d																		
Cardiff Central 131	d									11 20									
Crewe	d			12 49		13 23			13 49		14 23			14 50			15 23		
Manchester Piccadilly ⇌	d		11 50					12 50					13 50						14 50
Manchester Oxford Road 90	d		11 53					12 53					13 53						14 53
Newton-le-Willows 90	d		12 12					13 12					14 12						15 12
Earlestown 90	d		12 15					13 15					14 15						15 15
Warrington Bank Quay 90	d		12 26					13 26					14 26						15 26
Runcorn East	d		12 33					13 33					14 33						15 33
Frodsham	d		12 37					13 37					14 37						15 37
Helsby	d		12 41					13 41					14 41						15 41
Liverpool Lime Street 106	d																		
Chester	a		12 53	13 12	13 19	13 46		13 53	14 12	14 20	14 46		14 53	15 12		15 21	15 46		15 53
	d		12 55		13 26			13 55		14 25			14 55			15 25			15 55
Shotton	d		13 04					14 04					15 04						16 04
Flint	d		13 10		13 39			14 10		14 38			15 10			15 39			16 10
Prestatyn	d		13 23		13 52			14 23		14 51			15 23			15 52			16 23
Rhyl	d		13 29		13 58			14 29		14 57			15 29			15 58			16 29
Abergele & Pensarn	d		13 35					14 35					15 35						16 35
Colwyn Bay	d		13 43		14 09			14 43		15 08			15 43			16 09			16 43
Llandudno Junction	a		13 48		14 14			14 48		15 13			15 48		15 56	16 14			16 48
	d	13 26	13 50		14 15		14 26	14 50		15 15		15 26	15 50		16 00	16 15		16 26	16 50
Deganwy	d	13x29	13x54				14x29	14x54				15x29	15x54		16x03			16x29	16x54
Llandudno	a	13 36	14 06				14 36	15 06				15 36	16 06		16 09			16 36	17 06
Conwy	d				14x17											16x17			
Penmaenmawr	d				14x23											16x23			
Llanfairfechan	d				14x27											16x27			
Bangor (Gwynedd)	a				14 36					15 31						16 36			
	d				14 38					15 32						16 38			
Llanfairpwll	d									15x39									
Bodorgan	d									15x49									
Ty Croes	d									15x53									
Rhosneigr	d									15x56									
Valley	d									16x01									
Holyhead	a				15 11					16 14						17 11			

		VT	AW	AW	AW	AW	VT	AW	AW	AW	AW	AW	VT	AW	AW	AW	AW	VT	AW	AW
		◇1 ⊡	◇ ⊤			◇ ⊤	◇1 ⊡	◇ ⊤			◇	◇ ⊤	◇1 ⊡	◇ ⊤			◇ ⊤	◇1 ⊡		
London Euston ⊖65	d	14 10					15 10						16 10					17 10		
Birmingham New Street 65	d							15 24												17 24
Manchester Airport 84,85 ✈	d																			
Cardiff Central 131	d		13 20											15 20						
Crewe	d	15 49		16 23			16 49		17 23				17 49		18 23			18 50		
Manchester Piccadilly ⇌	d					15 50						16 50					17 50			
Manchester Oxford Road 90	d					15 53						16 53					17 53			
Newton-le-Willows 90	d					16 12						17 12					18 12			
Earlestown 90	d					16 15						17 15					18 15			
Warrington Bank Quay 90	d					16 26						17 26					18 25			
Runcorn East	d					16 33						17 33					18 32			
Frodsham	d					16 37						17 37					18 36			
Helsby	d					16 41						17 41					18 40			
Liverpool Lime Street 106	d																			
Chester	a	16 10	16 21	16 46		16 53	17 12	17 20	17 46			17 53	18 09	18 20	18 46		18 52	19 10		19 20
	d	16 12	16 26			16 55		17 26				17 55	18 16	18 26			18 55	19 17		19 31
Shotton	d					17 04		17 35				18 04					19 04			19 40
Flint	d	16 25	16 39			17 10		17 41				18 10	18 29	18 39			19 10	19 30		19 46
Prestatyn	d	16 38	16 52			17 23		17 54				18 23	18 42	18 52			19 23	19 43		19 59
Rhyl	d	16 45	16 58			17 29		18 00				18 29	18 49	18 58			19 29	19 50		20 05
Abergele & Pensarn	d					17 35		18 06				18 35					19 35			20 11
Colwyn Bay	d	16 56	17 09			17 43		18 14				18 43	19 00	19 09			19 43	20 01		20 19
Llandudno Junction	a	17 01	17 14			17 48		18 19				18 48	19 05	19 14			19 48	20 06		20 24
	d	17 02	17 15		17 26	17 50		18 21		18 26	18 41	18 50	19 06	19 15		19 26	19 50	20 07	20 24	20 26
Deganwy	d				17x29	17x54				18x29	18x44	18x54				19x29	19x54		20x27	
Llandudno	a				17 36	18 06				18 36	18 49	19 06				19 36	20 06		20 34	
Conwy	d		17x17					18x23												20x28
Penmaenmawr	d		17x23					18x29												20x34
Llanfairfechan	d		17x27					18x33												20x38
Bangor (Gwynedd)	a	17 17	17 36					18 42					19 21	19 31				20 22		20 47
	d	17 19	17 38					18 43					19 23	19 32				20 24		20 48
Llanfairpwll	d		17x44											19x39						
Bodorgan	d		17x54											19x51						
Ty Croes	d		17x58											19x55						
Rhosneigr	d		18x01											19x58						
Valley	d		18x07											20x04						
Holyhead	a	17 51	18 19					19 16					19 55	20 16				20 56		21 21

Table 81

Crewe and Manchester - Chester and North Wales

Saturdays
from 11 September

	AW	AW ⌶	VT ◇1 □	AW ◇ ⌶	AW	AW	AW ◇ ⌶	AW ◇	AW ◇ ⌶	AW	AW	AW ◇	AW	AW	AW ◇ ⌶	AW B	AW C
London Euston 15 ⊖65 d			18 10														
Birmingham New Street 12 65 d							19 24								21 24		
Manchester Airport 84,85 ✈ d											20 32						
Cardiff Central 7 131 d				17 20								19 34					
Crewe 10 d	19 23		19 50		20 23				21 00	21 23			22 23				
Manchester Piccadilly 10 ⇌ d		18 50				19 50					20 50			21 50		22 21	22 26
Manchester Oxford Road 90 d		18 53				19 53					20 53			21 53		22 24	22 29
Newton-le-Willows 90 d		19 12				20 12					21 12			22 12		22 42	22 47
Earlestown 8 90 d		19 16				20 15					21 15			22 15		22 45	22 50
Warrington Bank Quay 90 d		19 26				20 30					21 27			22 24		22 54	22 59
Runcorn East d		19 33				20 37					21 34			22 31		23 01	23 06
Frodsham d		19 37				20 41					21 38			22 35		23 05	23 10
Helsby d		19 41				20 45					21 42			22 39		23 09	23 14
Liverpool Lime Street 10 106 d																	
Chester a	19 46	19 55	20 12	20 20	20 46	20 57	21 19		21 21	21 46	21 54	22 31	22 45	22 51	23 19	23 21	23 26
d				20 35					21 26			22 36					
Shotton d				20 44					21 35			22 45					
Flint d				20 50					21 41			22 51					
Prestatyn d				21 03					21 54			23 05					
Rhyl d				21 09					22 00			23 11					
Abergele & Pensarn d									22 06			23 17					
Colwyn Bay d				21 20					22 14			23 25					
Llandudno Junction a				21 25					22 19			23 33					
d				21 26				21 32	22 21								
Deganwy d								21x35									
Llandudno a								21 42									
Conwy d									22x23								
Penmaenmawr d									22x29								
Llanfairfechan d									22x33								
Bangor (Gwynedd) a				21 42					22 42								
d				21 43					22 43								
Llanfairpwll d				21x50													
Bodorgan d				22x00													
Ty Croes d				22x04													
Rhosneigr d				22x07													
Valley d				22x12													
Holyhead a				22 24					23 15								

	AW	AW B	AW C	AW ◇	AW B 🚌	AW 🚌
London Euston 15 ⊖65 d						
Birmingham New Street 12 65 d						
Manchester Airport 84,85 ✈ d						
Cardiff Central 7 131 d				20 53		
Crewe 10 d	23 21			23 58		
Manchester Piccadilly 10 ⇌ d		22 55	23 14		23 14	
Manchester Oxford Road 90 d			23 17		23 19	
Newton-le-Willows 90 d			23 36		23 49	
Earlestown 8 90 d			23 39		23 59	
Warrington Bank Quay 90 d			23 48		00 24	
Runcorn East d			23 55		00 44	
Frodsham d			23 59		00 59	
Helsby d			00 03		01 04	
Liverpool Lime Street 10 106 d						
Chester a	23 42	23 58	00 15	00 24	01 24	
d						
Shotton d						
Flint d						
Prestatyn d						
Rhyl d						
Abergele & Pensarn d						
Colwyn Bay d						
Llandudno Junction a						
d						23 48
Deganwy d						
Llandudno a						
Conwy d						23 56
Penmaenmawr d						00 08
Llanfairfechan d						00 23
Bangor (Gwynedd) a						00 38
d						00 38
Llanfairpwll d						00 47
Bodorgan d						00 57
Ty Croes d						01 07
Rhosneigr d						01 27
Valley d						01 52
Holyhead a						02 02

B from 23 October

C from 11 September until 16 October

Table 81

Crewe and Manchester - Chester and North Wales

Sundays
until 05 September

	AW ◇	AW ◇	AW 🚌	AW	AW ◇	AW	NT	AW	AW	VT ◇1 □	AW	AW	AW ◇	AW ◇	AW	AW	NT
London Euston 15 ⊖65 d																	
Birmingham New Street 12 65 d																	
Manchester Airport 84,85 ✈ d																	
Cardiff Central 7 131 d																	
Crewe 10 d		08 27			09 27	09 57				10 42	10 57			11 27		11 57	
Manchester Piccadilly 10 ⇌ d			07 28				09 22								10 55		11 22
Manchester Oxford Road 90 d			07 33												10 59		
Newton-le-Willows 90 d			08 03												11 20		
Earlestown 8 90 d			08 13												11 23		
Warrington Bank Quay 90 d			08 38												11 30		
Runcorn East d			08 58												11 37		
Frodsham d			09 13												11 41		
Helsby d			09 18												11 45		
Liverpool Lime Street 10 106 d																	
Chester a		08 50	09 38		09 45	10 22	10 46			11 02	11 22			11 48	11 57	12 20	12 46
d	06 20	09 02			09 48					11 06				12 03			
Shotton d					09 57									12 12			
Flint d	06 33	09 15			10 03									12 18			
Prestatyn d	06 46	09 28			10 16					11 30				12 31			
Rhyl d	06 52	09 34			10 22					11 36				12 37			
Abergele & Pensarn d					10 28												
Colwyn Bay d	07 03	09 45			10 36					11 47				12 48			
Llandudno Junction a	07 08	09 49			10 41					11 52				12 53			
d	07 09	09 54		10 00	10 43			10 50	11 25	11 54		12 00	12 42	12 54			
Deganwy d				10x03				10x53	11x28			12x03	12x45				
Llandudno a				10 10				11 00	11 35			12 10	12 51				
Conwy d					10x45												
Penmaenmawr d					10x51												
Llanfairfechan d					10x55												
Bangor (Gwynedd) a	07 25	10 11			11 04					12 09				13 10			
d	07 25	10 12			11 05					12 10				13 11			
Llanfairpwll d					11x12												
Bodorgan d					11x22												
Ty Croes d					11x26												
Rhosneigr d					11x29												
Valley d					11x34												
Holyhead a	07 56	10 48			11 48					12 43				13 45			

	AW	AW	AW ◇ ⌶	AW ⌶	AW	AW ◇ ⌶	AW	AW ◇ ⌶	AW ⌶	AW	NT	AW	AW	AW ◇ ⌶	AW ⌶	AW	AW ◇ ⌶	AW	AW	AW ◇ ⌶	AW ⌶	AW
London Euston 15 ⊖65 d																						
Birmingham New Street 12 65 d						11 05											13 24					
Manchester Airport 84,85 ✈ d																						
Cardiff Central 7 131 d																						
Crewe 10 d			12 27		12 57			13 27		13 57				14 27		14 57				15 27		15 57
Manchester Piccadilly 10 ⇌ d				11 56					12 56		13 22				13 56						14 56	
Manchester Oxford Road 90 d				11 59					12 59						13 59						14 59	
Newton-le-Willows 90 d				12 18					13 18						14 18						15 18	
Earlestown 8 90 d				12 21					13 21						14 21						15 21	
Warrington Bank Quay 90 d				12 28					13 29						14 28						15 29	
Runcorn East d				12 35					13 36						14 35						15 36	
Frodsham d				12 39					13 40						14 39						15 40	
Helsby d				12 43					13 44						14 43						15 44	
Liverpool Lime Street 10 106 d																						
Chester a			12 48	12 55	13 18	13 20		13 47	13 56	14 20	14 46			14 47	14 55	15 20	15 30			15 47	15 56	16 20
d			13 02					14 02						15 02						16 02		
Shotton d			13 11					14 11						15 11						16 11		
Flint d			13 17					14 17						15 17						16 17		
Prestatyn d			13 30					14 30						15 30						16 30		
Rhyl d			13 36					14 36						15 36						16 36		
Abergele & Pensarn d			13 42					14 42						15 42						16 42		
Colwyn Bay d			13 50					14 50						15 50						16 50		
Llandudno Junction a			13 55					14 55						15 55						16 55		
d	12 58	13 35	13 57				14 02	14 57				15 00	15 30	15 57				16 04	16 39	16 57		
Deganwy d	13x01	13x38					14x05					15x03	15x33					16x07	16x42			
Llandudno a	13 08	13 45					14 12					15 10	15 40					16 14	16 49			
Conwy d			13x59											15x59								
Penmaenmawr d			14x05											16x05								
Llanfairfechan d			14x09											16x09								
Bangor (Gwynedd) a			14 18					15 12						16 18						17 12		
d			14 19					15 14						16 19						17 14		
Llanfairpwll d								15x20												17x20		
Bodorgan d								15x30												17x30		
Ty Croes d								15x34												17x34		
Rhosneigr d								15x37												17x37		
Valley d								15x43												17x43		
Holyhead a			14 55					15 55						16 55						17 55		

Table 81

Sundays
until 05 September

Crewe and Manchester - Chester and North Wales

	NT		AW	AW	AW	AW	VT	AW	AW	AW	VT		AW	AW	AW	NT	AW	AW	VT	AW	AW		AW	VT
														■	■									
					◇		◇■1	◇			◇■1		◇	A	B		◇		◇■1	◇				◇■1
					🛒	🛒	🍴	🛒		🛒	🍴							🛒	🍴	🛒				🍴
London Euston ■15 ⊖65 d							15 05				16 05								17 05					18 05
Birmingham New Street ■12 65 d								15 24												17 24				
Manchester Airport 84,85 ✈ d																								
Cardiff Central ■7 131 d														15 16	15 22									
Crewe ■10 d					16 27		16 52		17 27		17 52						18 27		18 56		19 27			19 52
Manchester Piccadilly ■10 ⇌ d	15 22					15 56				16 56						17 22		17 56					18 56	
Manchester Oxford Road 90 d						15 59				16 59								17 59					18 59	
Newton-le-Willows 90 d						16 18				17 18								18 18					19 18	
Earlestown ■6 90 d						16 21				17 21								18 21					19 21	
Warrington Bank Quay 90 d						16 28				17 28								18 28					19 29	
Runcorn East d						16 35				17 35								18 35					19 36	
Frodsham d						16 39				17 39								18 39					19 40	
Helsby d						16 43				17 43								18 43					19 44	
Liverpool Lime Street ■10 106 d																								
Chester a	16 46				16 47	16 55	17 14	17 30	17 48	17 55	18 14			18 25	18 25	18 46	18 47	18 55	19 14	19 30	19 48		19 56	20 11
d					17 02			17 32						18 29	18 29		18 52		19 22	19 38				20 18
Shotton d					17 11			17 41						18 38	18 38		19 01			19 47				
Flint d					17 17			17 47						18 44	18 44		19 07		19 35	19 53				20 31
Prestatyn d					17 30			18 00						18 57	18 57		19 21		19 48	20 06				20 44
Rhyl d					17 36			18 06						19 03	19 03		19 27		19 54	20 12				20 51
Abergele & Pensarn d					17 42			18 12						19 09	19 09		19 33			20 18				
Colwyn Bay d					17 50			18 20						19 17	19 17		19 41		20 04	20 26				21 02
Llandudno Junction a					17 55			18 25					18 29	19 22	19 22		19 46		20 09	20 31				21 07
d			17 05	17 40	17 57			18 27					18 30	19 24	19 24		19 47		20 11	20 33				21 08
Deganwy d			17x08	17x43									18x34											
Llandudno a			17 15	17 50									18 40											
Conwy d					17x59									19x26	19x26		19x49			20x35				
Penmaenmawr d					18x05									19x32	19x32		19x55			20x41				
Llanfairfechan d					18x09									19x36	19x36		19x59			20x45				
Bangor (Gwynedd) a					18 18			18 42						19 45	19 45		20 08		20 26	20 54				21 23
d					18 19			18 44						19 45	19 45		20 09		20 27	20 55				21 25
Llanfairpwll d								18x50																
Bodorgan d								19x00																
Ty Croes d								19x04																
Rhosneigr d								19x07																
Valley d								19x13																
Holyhead a					18 55			19 25						20 18	20 18		20 44		20 59	21 30				21 57

A from 18 July until 5 September
B until 11 July

Table 81

Sundays
until 05 September

Crewe and Manchester - Chester and North Wales

	AW	AW	NT	AW	AW	VT	AW		AW	AW	AW	NT	AW	AW	AW	AW	AW		AW	AW	AW			
	■	■																						
	A	B				◇■1	◇		◇				◇		◇					◇ C	◇ D			
						🍴	🛒																	
London Euston ■15 ⊖65 d						19 05																		
Birmingham New Street ■12 65 d							19 24								21 24					22 55	22 55			
Manchester Airport 84,85 ✈ d																								
Cardiff Central ■7 131 d	17 16	17 22																						
Crewe ■10 d				20 27		20 55			21 27		21 57		22 29		23 06		23 38			00e10	00e10			
Manchester Piccadilly ■10 ⇌ d			19 22		19 56					20 56		21 22		21 56		22 56			23 25					
Manchester Oxford Road 90 d					19 59					20 59				21 59		22 59			23 28					
Newton-le-Willows 90 d					20 18					21 18				22 18		23 18			23 46					
Earlestown ■6 90 d					20 21					21 21				22 21		23 21			23 49					
Warrington Bank Quay 90 d					20 30					21 28				22 28		23 28			23 56					
Runcorn East d					20 37					21 35				22 35		23 35			00 03					
Frodsham d					20 41					21 39				22 39		23 39			00 07					
Helsby d					20 45					21 43				22 43		23 43			00 11					
Liverpool Lime Street ■10 106 d																								
Chester a	20 31	20 31	20 46	20 48	20 57	21 14	21 31		21 46	21 55	22 18	22 46	22 50	22 55	23 30	23 55	23 59		00 24	00 30	00 31			
d	20 36	20 36				21 17			22 00				23 00							00 34	00 35			
Shotton d	20 45	20 45							22 09				23 09											
Flint d	20 51	20 51				21 30			22 15				23 15							00 47	00 48			
Prestatyn d	21 04	21 04				21 43			22 28				23 28							01 00	01 01			
Rhyl d	21 10	21 10				21 50			22 34				23 34							01 06	01 07			
Abergele & Pensarn d	21 16	21 16							22 40															
Colwyn Bay d	21 24	21 24				22 01			22 48				23 45							01 17	01 18			
Llandudno Junction a	21 29	21 29				22 06			22 53				23 50							01 23	01 24			
d	21 31	21 31				22 07			22 55				23 51							01 24	01 25			
Deganwy d																								
Llandudno a																								
Conwy d	21x33	21x33											23x53											
Penmaenmawr d	21x39	21x39											00x01											
Llanfairfechan d	21x43	21x43											00x03											
Bangor (Gwynedd) a	21 52	21 52				22 22			23 10				00 12							01 40	01 40			
d	21 54	21 54				22 24			23 12				00 14							01 40	01 41			
Llanfairpwll d	22x00	22x00							23x18															
Bodorgan d	22x10	22x10							23x28															
Ty Croes d	22x14	22x14							23x32															
Rhosneigr d	22x17	22x17							23x35															
Valley d	22x23	22x23							23x41															
Holyhead a	22 38	22 38				22 56			23 52				00 49							02 15	02 15			

A from 18 July until 5 September. ■ from Chester
B until 11 July
C until 18 July
D from 25 July until 5 September
e arr. 2355

Table 81

Crewe and Manchester - Chester and North Wales

Sundays from 12 September

		AW	AW	AW	NT	AW	VT	AW	AW	AW	AW	AW	AW	NT	AW	AW	AW	AW
		🚌	◇			A	◇1 ☕	B		◇		B 🚌			🚌	🚌	◇ ⊼	⊼
London Euston 15 ⊖65	d																	
Birmingham New Street 12 65	d																	
Manchester Airport 84,85 ✈	d																	
Cardiff Central 7 131	d																	
Crewe 10	d		09 24	10 07			10 42		11 05	11 27			11 57				12 27	
Manchester Piccadilly 10	d	07 28			09 22	09 53		09 54			10 55	09 53		11 22				11 56
Manchester Oxford Road 90	d	07 33				09 59					10 59	09 58						11 59
Newton-le-Willows 90	d	08 03				10 18					11 20	10 28						12 18
Earlestown 8 90	d	08 13				10 21					11 23	10 38						12 21
Warrington Bank Quay 90	d	08 38				10 28					11 30	11 03						12 28
Runcorn East	d	08 58				10 35					11 37	11 23						12 35
Frodsham	d	09 13				10 40					11 41	11 38						12 39
Helsby	d	09 18				10 44					11 45	11 43						12 43
Liverpool Lime Street 10 106	d																	
Chester	a	09 38	09 45	10 30	10 46	10 57	11 02	11 04	11 26	11 48	11 57	12 03	12 20	12 46			12 48	12 55
	d		09 48				11 06			12 03							13 02	
Shotton	d		09 57							12 12							13 11	
Flint	d		10 03							12 18							13 17	
Prestatyn	d		10 16				11 30			12 31							13 30	
Rhyl	d		10 22				11 36			12 37							13 36	
Abergele & Pensarn	d		10 28														13 42	
Colwyn Bay	d		10 36				11 47			12 48							13 50	
Llandudno Junction	a		10 41				11 52			12 53							13 55	
	d		10 43				11 54			12 54					13 00	13 04	13 57	
Deganwy	d														13 05	13 09		
Llandudno	a														13 20	13 18		
Conwy	d		10x45														13x59	
Penmaenmawr	d		10x51														14x05	
Llanfairfechan	d		10x55														14x09	
Bangor (Gwynedd)	a		11 04				12 09			13 10							14 18	
	d		11 05				12 10			13 11							14 19	
Llanfairpwll	d		11x11															
Bodorgan	d		11x21															
Ty Croes	d		11x26															
Rhosneigr	d		11x29															
Valley	d		11x34															
Holyhead	a		11 44				12 43			13 45							14 55	

		AW	AW	AW	AW	NT	AW	AW	AW	AW	AW	AW	AW	AW	NT	AW	AW	VT	AW	AW	AW	VT	AW
			◇ ⊼	⊼			◇ ⊼	⊼		🚌	🚌	◇ ⊼	⊼	C		◇ ⊼	⊼	◇1 ☕	🚌	◇	⊼	◇1 ☕	🚌
London Euston 15 ⊖65	d																	15 05				16 05	
Birmingham New Street 12 65	d																						
Manchester Airport 84,85 ✈	d																						
Cardiff Central 7 131	d																						
Crewe 10	d	12 54	13 27		13 57		14 27		14 57			15 27		15 57		16 27		16 52		17 27		17 52	
Manchester Piccadilly 10	d			12 56		13 22		13 56					14 56		15 22		15 56				16 56		
Manchester Oxford Road 90	d			12 59				13 59					14 59				15 59				16 59		
Newton-le-Willows 90	d			13 18				14 18					15 18				16 18				17 18		
Earlestown 8 90	d			13 21				14 21					15 21				16 21				17 21		
Warrington Bank Quay 90	d			13 29				14 28					15 29				16 28				17 28		
Runcorn East	d			13 36				14 35					15 36				16 35				17 35		
Frodsham	d			13 40				14 39					15 40				16 39				17 39		
Helsby	d			13 44				14 43					15 44				16 43				17 43		
Liverpool Lime Street 10 106	d																						
Chester	a	13 15	13 47	13 56	14 18	14 46	14 47	14 55	15 18			15 47	15 56	16 20	16 46	16 47	16 55	17 14		17 47	17 55	18 14	
	d		14 02				15 02					16 02				17 02				18 02			
Shotton	d		14 11				15 11					16 11				17 11				18 11			
Flint	d		14 17				15 17					16 17				17 17				18 17			
Prestatyn	d		14 30				15 30					16 30				17 30				18 30			
Rhyl	d		14 36				15 36					16 36				17 36				18 36			
Abergele & Pensarn	d		14 42				15 42					16 42				17 42				18 42			
Colwyn Bay	d		14 50				15 50					16 50				17 50				18 50			
Llandudno Junction	a		14 55				15 55					16 55				17 55				18 55			
	d		14 57				15 57			16 04	16 10	16 57				17 57			18 17	18 57			19 00
Deganwy	d									16 09	16 15								18 22				19 05
Llandudno	a									16 18	16 30								18 31				19 20
Conwy	d						15x59									17x59							
Penmaenmawr	d						16x05									18x05							
Llanfairfechan	d						16x09									18x09							
Bangor (Gwynedd)	a		15 12				16 18					17 12				18 18				19 12			
	d		15 14				16 19					17 14				18 19				19 14			
Llanfairpwll	d		15x20									17x20								19x20			
Bodorgan	d		15x30									17x30								19x30			
Ty Croes	d		15x34									17x34								19x34			
Rhosneigr	d		15x37									17x37								19x37			
Valley	d		15x43									17x43								19x43			
Holyhead	a		15 55				16 54					17 55				18 55				19 55			

A from 12 September until 17 October B from 24 October C 12 September

Table 81

Crewe and Manchester - Chester and North Wales

Sundays from 12 September

		AW	NT	AW	AW	VT	AW	AW	AW	VT	AW	NT	AW	AW	VT	AW	AW	AW	NT	AW	AW	AW
		■		◇	⊼	◇1 ☕	◇ ⊼			◇1 ☕	■				◇1 ☕	◇				◇		◇
London Euston 15 ⊖65	d					17 05				18 05					19 05							
Birmingham New Street 12 65	d																					
Manchester Airport 84,85 ✈	d																					
Cardiff Central 7 131	d	15 22									17 14											
Crewe 10	d			18 27		18 56		19 27		19 52			20 27		20 55	21 27		22 00		22 29		23 06
Manchester Piccadilly 10	d		17 22		17 56				18 56			19 22		19 56			20 56		21 22		21 56	
Manchester Oxford Road 90	d				17 59				18 59					19 59			20 59				21 59	
Newton-le-Willows 90	d				18 18				19 18					20 18			21 18				22 18	
Earlestown 8 90	d				18 21				19 21					20 21			21 21				22 21	
Warrington Bank Quay 90	d				18 28				19 29					20 30			21 28				22 28	
Runcorn East	d				18 35				19 36					20 37			21 35				22 35	
Frodsham	d				18 39				19 40					20 41			21 39				22 39	
Helsby	d				18 43				19 44					20 45			21 43				22 43	
Liverpool Lime Street 10 106	d																					
Chester	a	18 27	18 46	18 47	18 55	19 14	19 30	19 48	19 56	20 11	20 31	20 46	20 48	20 57	21 14	21 46	21 55	22 21	22 46	22 50	22 55	23 30
	d	18 30		18 52		19 22	19 38			20 18	20 36				21 17	22 00				23 00		
Shotton	d	18 39		19 01			19 47				20 45					22 09				23 09		
Flint	d	18 45		19 07		19 35	19 53			20 31	20 51				21 30	22 15				23 15		
Prestatyn	d	18 59		19 21		19 48	20 06			20 44	21 04				21 43	22 28				23 28		
Rhyl	d	19 05		19 27		19 54	20 12			20 51	21 10				21 50	22 34				23 34		
Abergele & Pensarn	d	19 11		19 33			20 18				21 16					22 40						
Colwyn Bay	d	19 19		19 41		20 04	20 26			21 02	21 24				22 01	22 48				23 45		
Llandudno Junction	a	19 24		19 46		20 09	20 31			21 07	21 29				22 06	22 53				23 50		
	d	19 25		19 47		20 11	20 33			21 08	21 31				22 07	22 55				23 51		
Deganwy	d																					
Llandudno	a																					
Conwy	d	19x27		19x49			20x35				21x33									23x53		
Penmaenmawr	d	19x33		19x55			20x41				21x39									00x01		
Llanfairfechan	d	19x37		19x59			20x45				21x43									00x03		
Bangor (Gwynedd)	a	19 46		20 08		20 26	20 54			21 23	21 52				22 22	23 10				00 12		
	d	19 47		20 09		20 27	20 55			21 25	21 54				22 24	23 12				00 14		
Llanfairpwll	d										22x00					23x18						
Bodorgan	d										22x10					23x28						
Ty Croes	d										22x14					23x32						
Rhosneigr	d										22x17					23x35						
Valley	d										22x23					23x41						
Holyhead	a	20 20		20 44		20 59	21 30			21 57	22 38				22 56	23 52				00 49		

		AW	AW	AW	AW
					◇
London Euston 15 ⊖65	d				
Birmingham New Street 12 65	d				22 55
Manchester Airport 84,85 ✈	d				
Cardiff Central 7 131	d				
Crewe 10	d		23 38		00b10
Manchester Piccadilly 10	d	22 56		23 25	
Manchester Oxford Road 90	d	22 59		23 28	
Newton-le-Willows 90	d	23 18		23 46	
Earlestown 8 90	d	23 21		23 49	
Warrington Bank Quay 90	d	23 28		23 56	
Runcorn East	d	23 35		00 03	
Frodsham	d	23 39		00 07	
Helsby	d	23 43		00 11	
Liverpool Lime Street 10 106	d				
Chester	a	23 55	23 59	00 24	00 31
	d				00 35
Shotton	d				
Flint	d				00 48
Prestatyn	d				01 01
Rhyl	d				01 07
Abergele & Pensarn	d				
Colwyn Bay	d				01 18
Llandudno Junction	a				01 24
	d				01 25
Deganwy	d				
Llandudno	a				
Conwy	d				
Penmaenmawr	d				
Llanfairfechan	d				
Bangor (Gwynedd)	a				01 40
	d				01 41
Llanfairpwll	d				
Bodorgan	d				
Ty Croes	d				
Rhosneigr	d				
Valley	d				
Holyhead	a				02 15

b arr. 2355

North Wales and Chester - Manchester and Crewe

Station	AW	AW	AW	AW	AW	AW	AW	AW	VT	AW	AW	AW	NT	AW	AW	VT	AW	AW	AW
	A													BHX					
				◇				◇ ⌶	◇■1 ⊠	◇ ⌶	◇			◇■1 ⊠		◇■1 ⊠	◇ ⌶		
Holyhead d								04 25	04 50	05 11				05 32		05 51			
Valley d								04x31											
Rhosneigr d																			
Ty Croes d																			
Bodorgan d																			
Llanfairpwll d								04x48											
Bangor (Gwynedd) a								04 55	05 16	05 38				06 00		06 17			
d								04 57	05 16	05 40				06 02		06 18			
Llanfairfechan d										05x47									
Penmaenmawr d										05x51									
Conwy d										05x57									
Llandudno d																	06 34	07 10	
Deganwy d																	06x38	07x14	
Llandudno Junction a								05 13	05 34	06 01				06 19		06 35	06 42	07 20	
d					04 38			05 15	05 34	06 07	05 46			06 21		06 36	06 44		
Colwyn Bay d					04 44			05 21	05 40	06 13	05 52					06 42	06 50		
Abergele & Pensarn d					04 51												06 57		
Rhyl d					04 57			05 31	05 51	06 23	06 02			06 36		06 53	07 03		
Prestatyn d					05 02			05 37		06 29	06 08					06 58	07 08		
Flint d					05 16			05 50		06 42	06 21			06 52		07 12	07 21		
Shotton d					05 22					06 48	06 27						07 27		
Chester a					05 33			06 05	06 19	07 00	06 38			07 07		07 25	07 38		
d	03 36	04 23	04 55	05 15	05 37	05 38	05 51	06 20	06 26	07 22	06 40	06 43		07 08	07 12	07 35	07 40		07 55
Liverpool Lime Street ■10 106 a																			
Helsby d						05 47					06 49		07 06		07 21		07 49		
Frodsham d						05 51					06 53				07 25		07 53		
Runcorn East d						05 56					06 59				07 31		07 59		
Warrington Bank Quay 90 a						06 05					07 06		07 23		07 38		08 06		
Earlestown ■8 90 a						06 12					07 14				07 46		08 15		
Newton-le-Willows 90 a						06 15					07 17				07 49		08 18		
Manchester Oxford Road 90 a						06 35					07 41				08 09		08 41		
Manchester Piccadilly ■10 a	04 43					06 46					07 50				08 18		08 50		
Crewe ■10 a		04 44	05 20		05 58		06 15		06 46			07 04		07 32		07 54			08 18
Cardiff Central ■7 131 a				08 17				09 22						09 58					
Manchester Airport 84,85 ✈ a	05 04																		
Birmingham New Street ■12 65 a		05 58								09 27									
London Euston ■15 ⊖65 a									08 33							09 38			

Station	AW	VT	AW	AW	AW	AW	VT	AW	AW	AW	AW	VT	AW	AW	AW	AW	AW	VT
	◇ ⌶	◇■1 ⊠	◇ ⌶			◇ ⌶	◇■1 ⊠	◇ ⌶			◇ ⌶	◇■1 ⊠	◇ ⌶			◇ ⌶	◇	◇■1 ⊡
Holyhead d	06 29	06 55				07 15					08 05	08 55				09 23		
Valley d	06x35					07x21					08x11					09x29		
Rhosneigr d	06x41					07x26					08x17					09x34		
Ty Croes d	06x44					07x30					08x20					09x38		
Bodorgan d	06x49					07x34					08x25					09x42		
Llanfairpwll d	06x58					07x44					08x34					09x52		
Bangor (Gwynedd) a	07 06	07 21				07 52					08 42	09 21				10 00		
d	07 07	07 22				08 02					09 02	09 22				10 02		
Llanfairfechan d						08x09					09x09					10x09		
Penmaenmawr d						08x13					09x13					10x13		
Conwy d						08x19					09x19					10x19		
Llandudno d			07 45	08 10				08 45	09 10				09 45	10 10			10 20	
Deganwy d			07x49	08x14				08x49	09x14				09x49	10x14			10x24	
Llandudno Junction a	07 23	07 39	07 53	08 20		08 23		08 53	09 20		09 23	09 39	09 53	10 20		10 23	10 30	
d	07 25	07 40	07 54			08 25		08 54			09 25	09 40	09 54			10 25		
Colwyn Bay d	07 31	07 47	08 00			08 31		09 00			09 31	09 47	10 00			10 31		
Abergele & Pensarn d			08 07					09 07					10 07					
Rhyl d	07 41	07 58	08 13			08 41		09 13			09 41	09 58	10 13			10 41		
Prestatyn d	07 47	08 04	08 19			08 47		09 19			09 47	10 04	10 19			10 47		
Flint d	08 00	08 17	08 32			09 00		09 32			10 00	10 17	10 32			11 00		
Shotton d			08 38					09 38					10 38					
Chester a	08 15	08 31	08 50			09 15		09 50			10 15	10 31	10 50			11 15		
d	08 22	08 35	08 52		08 55	09 30	09 35	09 52		09 55	10 22	10 35	10 52		10 55	11 22		11 35
Liverpool Lime Street ■10 106 a																		
Helsby d			09 01					10 01					11 01					
Frodsham d			09 05					10 05					11 05					
Runcorn East d			09 11					10 11					11 11					
Warrington Bank Quay 90 a			09 18					10 18					11 18					
Earlestown ■8 90 a			09 26					10 26					11 26					
Newton-le-Willows 90 a			09 29					10 29					11 29					
Manchester Oxford Road 90 a			09 48					10 48					11 48					
Manchester Piccadilly ■10 a			09 57					10 57					11 57					
Crewe ■10 a		08 54			09 18		09 54			10 18		10 54			11 18			11 54
Cardiff Central ■7 131 a	11 14										13 20							
Manchester Airport 84,85 ✈ a																		
Birmingham New Street ■12 65 a						11 26										13 27		
London Euston ■15 ⊖65 a		10 38					11 38					12 38						13 38

A not 24 May

North Wales and Chester - Manchester and Crewe

Station	AW	AW	AW	AW	VT	AW	AW	AW	AW	VT	AW	AW	AW	AW	AW	VT	AW	AW
	◇ ⌶			◇ ⌶	◇■1 ⊡	◇ ⌶			◇ ⌶	◇■1 ⊡	◇ ⌶			◇ ⌶	◇	◇■1 ⊡	◇ ⌶	
Holyhead d				10 33					11 23					12 38				
Valley d				10x39					11x29									
Rhosneigr d									11x34									
Ty Croes d									11x38									
Bodorgan d									11x42									
Llanfairpwll d				10x56					11x49									
Bangor (Gwynedd) a				11 03					12 00					13 05				
d				11 05					12 02	12 24				13 07				
Llanfairfechan d									12x09									
Penmaenmawr d									12x13									
Conwy d									12x19									
Llandudno d	10 44	11 10				11 44	12 10				12 44	13 10			13 20		13 44	14 10
Deganwy d	10x48	11x14				11x48	12x14				12x48	13x14			13x24		13x48	14x14
Llandudno Junction a	10 52	11 20		11 21		11 52	12 20		12 23	12 40	12 52	13 20		13 23	13 30		13 52	14 20
d	10 53			11 25		11 53			12 25	12 42	12 53			13 25			13 53	
Colwyn Bay d	10 59			11 31		11 59			12 31	12 48	12 59			13 31			13 59	
Abergele & Pensarn d	11 06					12 06					13 06						14 06	
Rhyl d	11 12			11 41		12 12			12 41	12 59	13 12			13 41			14 12	
Prestatyn d	11 18			11 47		12 18			12 47	13 05	13 18			13 47			14 18	
Flint d	11 31			12 00		12 31			13 00	13 18	13 31			14 00			14 31	
Shotton d	11 37					12 37					13 37						14 37	
Chester a	11 49			12 15		12 49			13 15	13 32	13 49			14 15			14 49	
d	11 50		11 55	12 22	12 35	12 50		12 55	13 22	13 35	13 50		13 55	14 22		14 35	14 50	
Liverpool Lime Street ■10 106 a																		
Helsby d	12 00					13 00					14 00						15 00	
Frodsham d	12 04					13 04					14 04						15 04	
Runcorn East d	12 09					13 09					14 09						15 09	
Warrington Bank Quay 90 a	12 18					13 18					14 18						15 18	
Earlestown ■8 90 a	12 26					13 26					14 26						15 26	
Newton-le-Willows 90 a	12 29					13 29					14 29						15 29	
Manchester Oxford Road 90 a	12 48					13 48					14 48						15 48	
Manchester Piccadilly ■10 a	12 57					13 57					14 57						15 57	
Crewe ■10 a			12 18		12 54			13 18		13 54			14 18			14 54		
Cardiff Central ■7 131 a				15 20										17 17				
Manchester Airport 84,85 ✈ a									15 26									
Birmingham New Street ■12 65 a																		
London Euston ■15 ⊖65 a					14 38					15 38						16 38		

Station	AW	AW	VT	AW	AW	NT	AW	AW	VT	AW	AW	AW	AW	VT	AW	AW	AW	AW
		◇ ⌶	◇■1 ⊡	◇ ⌶			◇ ⌶	◇ ⌶	◇■1 ⊡		◇ ⌶	◇ ⌶	◇	◇■1 ⊠		◇ ⌶	◇ ⌶	
Holyhead d		13 23	13 58					14 32				15 23					16 36	
Valley d		13x29										15x29						
Rhosneigr d		13x34										15x34						
Ty Croes d		13x38										15x38						
Bodorgan d		13x42										15x42						
Llanfairpwll d		13x52										15x52						
Bangor (Gwynedd) a		14 00	14 24					14 58				16 00					17 02	
d		14 02	14 25					15 02				16 02					17 04	
Llanfairfechan d		14x09						15x09				16x09						
Penmaenmawr d		14x13						15x13				16x13						
Conwy d		14x19						15x19				16x19						
Llandudno d				14 40			15 08				16 08		16 20			17 07		18 08
Deganwy d				14x44			15x12				16x12		16x24			17x11		18x12
Llandudno Junction a		14 23	14 42	14 48			15 16	15 23			16 16	16 23	16 28			17 15	17 21	18 18
d		14 25	14 43	14 49			15 17	15 25			16 17	16 25				17 16	17 22	
Colwyn Bay d		14 31	14 50	14 55			15 23	15 31			16 23	16 31				17 22	17 28	
Abergele & Pensarn d				15 02				15 38				16 38					17 35	
Rhyl d		14 41	15 00	15 08			15 34	15 44			16 34	16 44				17 33	17 41	
Prestatyn d		14 47		15 14			15 39	15 49			16 39	16 50				17 38	17 47	
Flint d		15 00		15 27			15 53	16 03			16 53	17 03				17 52	18 02	
Shotton d				15 33			15 59				16 59					17 58		
Chester a		15 17	15 28	15 44			16 10	16 17			17 10	17 17				18 11	18 16	
d	14 55	15 22	15 35	15 46	15 55		16 22	16 22	16 35	16 55	17 19	17 22		17 35	17 55	18 16	18 20	
Liverpool Lime Street ■10 106 a																		
Helsby d				15 55		16 11	16 31				17 28					18 25		
Frodsham d				15 59		16 16	16 35				17 33					18 30		
Runcorn East d				16 04		16 22	16 41				17 38					18 35		
Warrington Bank Quay 90 a				16 12		16 34	16 51				17 49					18 45		
Earlestown ■8 90 a				16 26			16 59				17 57					18 57		
Newton-le-Willows 90 a				16 29			17 01				17 59					18 59		
Manchester Oxford Road 90 a				16 48			17 21				18 19					19 21		
Manchester Piccadilly ■10 a				16 57			17 30				18 28					19 29		
Crewe ■10 a	15 18		15 54		16 18				16 54	17 18				17 54	18 18			
Cardiff Central ■7 131 a								19 21									21 19	
Manchester Airport 84,85 ✈ a																		
Birmingham New Street ■12 65 a		17 27										19 26						
London Euston ■15 ⊖65 a			17 38						18 38					19 38				

Table 81

Mondays to Fridays
until 03 September

North Wales and Chester - Manchester and Crewe

	AW	AW	AW ◇	VT ◇1	AW ◇	AW ◇	AW	AW	AW ◇	AW ◇	AW	AW	AW ◇	VT ◇1	AW	AW	AW ◇
Holyhead d			17 21						18 23				19 21				20 37
Valley d			17x27						18x29				19x27				
Rhosneigr d			17x32						18x34				19x32				
Ty Croes d			17x36						18x38				19x36				
Bodorgan d			17x40						18x42				19x40				
Llanfairpwll d			17x50						18x52				19x50				
Bangor (Gwynedd) a			17 58						19 00				19 58				21 04
d			18 00						19 00				20 00	20 20			21 06
Llanfairfechan d			18x07						19x09				20x07				21x13
Penmaenmawr d			18x11						19x13				20x11				21x17
Conwy d			18x17						19x19				20x17				21x23
Llandudno d					18 44	19 03	19 10			19 42	20 08				20 42		
Deganwy d					18x48	19x07	19x14			19x46	20x12				20x46		
Llandudno Junction a			18 21		18 52	19 11	19 20		19 23	19 50	20 18		20 21	20 36	20 50		21 27
d			18 23		18 53				19 25	19 51			20 23	20 38	20 51		21 29
Colwyn Bay d			18 29		18 59				19 31	19 57			20 29	20 44	20 57		21 35
Abergele & Pensarn d					19 06					20 04					21 04		21 42
Rhyl d			18 39		19 12				19 41	20 10			20 39	20 55	21 11		21 48
Prestatyn d			18 45		19 18				19 47	20 16			20 45	21 00	21 16		21 53
Flint d			18 58		19 31				20 00	20 29			20 58	21 14	21 30		22 07
Shotton d					19 37					20 35					21 36		22 13
Chester a			19 15		19 49				20 15	20 47			21 15	21 28	21 47		22 24
d	18 49	18 55		19 35	19 50			19 55	20 17	20 50		20 55	21 21	21 35		21 52	22 26
Liverpool Lime Street 106 a																	
Helsby d	18 59				20 00					20 59						22 01	
Frodsham d	19 03				20 04					21 03						22 05	
Runcorn East d	19 08				20 09					21 09						22 11	
Warrington Bank Quay 90 a	19 18				20 18					21 18						22 18	
Earlestown 90 a	19 26				20 26					21 26						22 26	
Newton-le-Willows 90 a	19 29				20 29					21 29						22 29	
Manchester Oxford Road 90 a	19 48				20 48					21 48						22 50	
Manchester Piccadilly a	19 52				20 52					21 57						22 58	
Crewe a		19 18		19 54				20 18	20 41			21 18		21 54			22 47
Cardiff Central 131 a																	
Manchester Airport 84,85 a	20 13				21 13												
Birmingham New Street 65 a													23 26	22 50			
London Euston ⊖65 a				21 42													

	AW	AW
Holyhead d		
Valley d		
Rhosneigr d		
Ty Croes d		
Bodorgan d		
Llanfairpwll d		
Bangor (Gwynedd) a		
d		
Llanfairfechan d		
Penmaenmawr d		
Conwy d		
Llandudno d	21 45	
Deganwy d	21x49	
Llandudno Junction a	21 53	
d	21 55	
Colwyn Bay d	22 01	
Abergele & Pensarn d	22 09	
Rhyl d	22 16	
Prestatyn d	22 22	
Flint d	22 37	
Shotton d	22 44	
Chester a	22 55	
d	23 01	23 22
Liverpool Lime Street 106 a		
Helsby d		23 31
Frodsham d		23 35
Runcorn East d		23 41
Warrington Bank Quay 90 a		23 49
Earlestown 90 a		23 56
Newton-le-Willows 90 a		23 59
Manchester Oxford Road 90 a		
Manchester Piccadilly a		00 28
Crewe a	23 26	
Cardiff Central 131 a		
Manchester Airport 84,85 a		
Birmingham New Street 65 a		
London Euston ⊖65 a		

Table 81

Mondays to Fridays
from 06 September

North Wales and Chester - Manchester and Crewe

	AW	AW	AW	AW ◇	AW	AW	AW	AW ◇	VT ◇1	AW ◇	AW ◇	AW	NT	AW BHX ◇1	AW	VT ◇1	AW ◇	AW	AW
Holyhead d								04 25	04 50	05 11				05 32		05 51			
Valley d								04x31											
Rhosneigr d																			
Ty Croes d																			
Bodorgan d																			
Llanfairpwll d								04x48											
Bangor (Gwynedd) a								04 55	05 16	05 38				06 00		06 17			
d								04 57	05 16	05 40				06 02		06 18			
Llanfairfechan d										05x47									
Penmaenmawr d										05x51									
Conwy d										05x57									
Llandudno d																	06 34	07 10	
Deganwy d																	06x38	07x14	
Llandudno Junction a								05 13	05 34	06 01				06 19		06 35	06 42	07 20	
d					04 38			05 15	05 34	06 07	05 46			06 21		06 36	06 44		
Colwyn Bay d					04 44			05 21	05 40	06 13	05 52					06 42	06 50		
Abergele & Pensarn d					04 51												06 57		
Rhyl d					04 57			05 31	05 51	06 23	06 02			06 36		06 53	07 03		
Prestatyn d					05 02			05 37		06 29	06 08					06 58	07 08		
Flint d					05 16			05 50		06 42	06 21			06 52		07 12	07 21		
Shotton d					05 22					06 48	06 27						07 27		
Chester a					05 33			06 05	06 19	07 00	06 38			07 07		07 25	07 38		
d	03 36	04 23	04 55	05 15	05 37	05 38	05 51	06 20	06 26	07 22	06 40	06 43		07 08	07 12	07 35	07 40		07 55
Liverpool Lime Street 106 a																			
Helsby d						05 47					06 49		07 06		07 21		07 49		
Frodsham d						05 51					06 53				07 25		07 53		
Runcorn East d						05 56					06 59				07 31		07 59		
Warrington Bank Quay 90 a						06 05					07 06		07 23		07 38		08 06		
Earlestown 90 a						06 12					07 14				07 46		08 15		
Newton-le-Willows 90 a						06 15					07 17				07 49		08 18		
Manchester Oxford Road 90 a						06 35					07 41				08 09		08 41		
Manchester Piccadilly a	04 43					06 46					07 50				08 18		08 50		
Crewe a		04 44	05 20		05 58		06 15		06 46			07 04		07 32		07 54			08 18
Cardiff Central 131 a				08 17				09 22						09 58					
Manchester Airport 84,85 a	05 04																		
Birmingham New Street 65 a		05 58								09 27									
London Euston ⊖65 a									08 33							09 38			

	AW ◇	VT ◇1	AW ◇	AW	AW	AW ◇	VT ◇1	AW ◇	AW	AW	AW ◇	VT ◇1	AW ◇	AW	AW	AW ◇	AW ◇	VT ◇1	AW ◇
Holyhead d	06 29	06 55				07 15					08 05	08 55				09 23			
Valley d	06x35					07x21					08x11					09x29			
Rhosneigr d	06x41					07x26					08x17					09x34			
Ty Croes d	06x44					07x30					08x20					09x38			
Bodorgan d	06x49					07x34					08x25					09x42			
Llanfairpwll d	06x58					07x44					08x34					09x52			
Bangor (Gwynedd) a	07 06	07 21				07 52					08 42	09 21				10 00			
d	07 07	07 22				08 02					09 02	09 22				10 02			
Llanfairfechan d						08x09					09x09					10x09			
Penmaenmawr d						08x13					09x13					10x13			
Conwy d						08x19					09x19					10x19			
Llandudno d			07 45	08 10				08 45	09 10				09 45	10 10			10 20		10 44
Deganwy d			07x49	08x14				08x49	09x14				09x49	10x14			10x24		10x48
Llandudno Junction a	07 23	07 39	07 53	08 20		08 23		08 53	09 20		09 23	09 39	09 53	10 20		10 23	10 30		10 52
d	07 25	07 40	07 54			08 25		08 54			09 25	09 40	09 54			10 25			10 53
Colwyn Bay d	07 31	07 47	08 00			08 31		09 00			09 31	09 47	10 00			10 31			10 59
Abergele & Pensarn d			08 07					09 07					10 07						11 06
Rhyl d	07 41	07 58	08 13			08 41		09 13			09 41	09 58	10 13			10 41			11 12
Prestatyn d	07 47	08 04	08 19			08 47		09 19			09 47	10 04	10 19			10 47			11 18
Flint d	08 00	08 17	08 32			09 00		09 32			10 00	10 17	10 32			11 00			11 31
Shotton d			08 38					09 38					10 38						11 37
Chester a	08 15	08 31	08 50			09 15		09 50			10 15	10 31	10 50			11 15			11 49
d	08 22	08 35	08 52		08 55	09 30	09 35	09 52		09 55	10 22	10 35	10 52		10 55	11 22		11 35	11 50
Liverpool Lime Street 106 a																			
Helsby d			09 01					10 01					11 01						12 00
Frodsham d			09 05					10 05					11 05						12 04
Runcorn East d			09 11					10 11					11 11						12 09
Warrington Bank Quay 90 a			09 18					10 18					11 18						12 18
Earlestown 90 a			09 26					10 26					11 26						12 26
Newton-le-Willows 90 a			09 29					10 29					11 29						12 29
Manchester Oxford Road 90 a			09 48					10 48					11 48						12 48
Manchester Piccadilly a			09 57					10 57					11 57						12 57
Crewe a		08 54			09 18		09 54			10 18		10 54			11 18			11 54	
Cardiff Central 131 a	11 14										13 20								
Manchester Airport 84,85 a																			
Birmingham New Street 65 a						11 26										13 27			
London Euston ⊖65 a		10 38					11 38					12 38						13 38	

Table 81

Mondays to Fridays
from 06 September

North Wales and Chester - Manchester and Crewe

	AW	AW	AW	VT	AW	AW	AW	AW	VT	AW	AW	AW	AW	AW	VT	AW	AW	AW
			◇ 🛒	◇1 🍴	◇ 🛒			◇ 🛒	◇1 🍴	◇ 🛒			◇ 🛒	◇	◇1 🍴	◇ 🛒		
Holyhead d			10 33					11 23					12 38					
Valley d			10x39					11x29										
Rhosneigr d								11x34										
Ty Croes d								11x38										
Bodorgan d								11x42										
Llanfairpwll d			10x56					11x49										
Bangor (Gwynedd) a			11 03					12 00					13 05					
d			11 05					12 02	12 24				13 07					
Llanfairfechan d								12x09										
Penmaenmawr d								12x13										
Conwy d								12x19										
Llandudno d	11 10				11 44	12 10				12 44	13 10			13 20		13 44	14 10	
Deganwy d	11x14				11x48	12x14				12x48	13x14			13x24		13x48	14x14	
Llandudno Junction a	11 20		11 21		11 52	12 20		12 23	12 40	12 52	13 20		13 23	13 30		13 52	14 20	
d			11 25		11 53			12 25	12 42	12 53			13 25			13 53		
Colwyn Bay d			11 31		11 59			12 31	12 48	12 59			13 31			13 59		
Abergele & Pensarn d					12 06					13 06						14 06		
Rhyl d			11 41		12 12			12 41	12 59	13 12			13 41			14 12		
Prestatyn d			11 47		12 18			12 47	13 05	13 18			13 47			14 18		
Flint d			12 00		12 31			13 00	13 18	13 31			14 00			14 31		
Shotton d					12 37					13 37						14 37		
Chester a			12 15		12 49			13 15	13 32	13 49			14 15			14 49		
d		11 55	12 22	12 35	12 50		12 55	13 22	13 35	13 50		13 55	14 22		14 35	14 50		14 55
Liverpool Lime Street 106 a																		
Helsby d					13 00					14 00						15 00		
Frodsham d					13 04					14 04						15 04		
Runcorn East d					13 09					14 09						15 09		
Warrington Bank Quay 90 a					13 18					14 18						15 18		
Earlestown 90 a					13 26					14 26						15 26		
Newton-le-Willows 90 a					13 29					14 29						15 29		
Manchester Oxford Road 90 a					13 48					14 48						15 48		
Manchester Piccadilly ⇌ a					13 57					14 57						15 57		
Crewe a		12 18		12 54			13 18		13 54			14 18			14 54			15 18
Cardiff Central 131 a			15 20										17 17					
Manchester Airport 84,85 ✈ a																		
Birmingham New Street 65 a								15 26										
London Euston ⊖65 a				14 38					15 38						16 38			

	AW	VT	AW	AW	NT	AW	AW	VT	AW	AW	AW	AW	VT	AW	AW	AW	AW	AW
	◇ 🛒	◇1 🍴	◇ 🛒			◇ 🛒	◇ 🛒	◇1 🍴		◇ 🛒	◇ 🛒	◇	◇1 ⊠		◇ 🛒	◇ 🛒		
Holyhead d	13 23	13 58					14 32				15 23					16 36		
Valley d	13x29										15x29							
Rhosneigr d	13x34										15x34							
Ty Croes d	13x38										15x38							
Bodorgan d	13x42										15x42							
Llanfairpwll d	13x52										15x52							
Bangor (Gwynedd) a	14 00	14 24					14 58				16 00					17 02		
d	14 02	14 25					15 02				16 02					17 04		
Llanfairfechan d	14x09						15x09				16x09							
Penmaenmawr d	14x13						15x13				16x13							
Conwy d	14x19						15x19				16x19							
Llandudno d			14 40			15 08				16 08		16 20			17 07		18 08	
Deganwy d			14x44			15x12				16x12		16x24			17x11		18x12	
Llandudno Junction a	14 23	14 42	14 48			15 16	15 23			16 16	16 23	16 28			17 15	17 21	18 18	
d	14 25	14 43	14 49			15 17	15 25			16 17	16 25				17 16	17 22		
Colwyn Bay d	14 31	14 50	14 55			15 23	15 31			16 23	16 31				17 22	17 28		
Abergele & Pensarn d			15 02				15 38				16 38					17 35		
Rhyl d	14 41	15 00	15 08			15 34	15 44			16 34	16 44				17 33	17 41		
Prestatyn d	14 47		15 14			15 39	15 49			16 39	16 50				17 38	17 47		
Flint d	15 00		15 27			15 53	16 03			16 53	17 03				17 52	18 02		
Shotton d			15 33			15 59				16 59					17 58			
Chester a	15 17	15 28	15 44			16 10	16 17			17 10	17 17				18 11	18 16		
d	15 22	15 35	15 46	15 55		16 22	16 22	16 35	16 55	17 19	17 22		17 35	17 55	18 16	18 20		18 49
Liverpool Lime Street 106 a																		
Helsby d			15 55		16 11	16 31				17 28					18 25			18 59
Frodsham d			15 59		16 16	16 35				17 33					18 30			19 03
Runcorn East d			16 04		16 22	16 41				17 38					18 35			19 08
Warrington Bank Quay 90 a			16 12		16 34	16 51				17 49					18 45			19 18
Earlestown 90 a			16 26			16 59				17 57					18 57			19 26
Newton-le-Willows 90 a			16 29			17 01				17 59					18 59			19 29
Manchester Oxford Road 90 a			16 48			17 21				18 19					19 21			19 48
Manchester Piccadilly ⇌ a			16 57			17 30				18 28					19 29			19 52
Crewe a		15 54		16 18				16 54	17 18				17 54	18 18				
Cardiff Central 131 a							19 21									21 19		
Manchester Airport 84,85 ✈ a																		20 13
Birmingham New Street 65 a	17 27										19 26							
London Euston ⊖65 a		17 38						18 38					19 38					

Table 81

Mondays to Fridays
from 06 September

North Wales and Chester - Manchester and Crewe

	AW	AW	VT	AW	AW	AW	AW	AW	AW	AW	AW	AW	VT	AW	AW	AW	AW	AW
		◇ 🛒	◇1 🍴	◇ 🛒	◇			◇ 🛒	◇ 🛒			◇ 🛒	◇1 🍴			◇ 🛒		
Holyhead d		17 21						18 23				19 21				20 37		
Valley d		17x27						18x29				19x27						
Rhosneigr d		17x32						18x34				19x32						
Ty Croes d		17x36						18x38				19x36						
Bodorgan d		17x40						18x42				19x40						
Llanfairpwll d		17x50						18x52				19x50						
Bangor (Gwynedd) a		17 58						19 00				19 58				21 04		
d		18 00						19 00				20 00	20 20			21 06		
Llanfairfechan d		18x07						19x09				20x07				21x13		
Penmaenmawr d		18x11						19x13				20x11				21x17		
Conwy d		18x17						19x19				20x17				21x23		
Llandudno d				18 44	19 03	19 10			19 42	20 08				20 42			21 45	
Deganwy d				18x48	19x07	19x14			19x46	20x12				20x46			21x49	
Llandudno Junction a		18 21		18 52	19 11	19 20		19 23	19 50	20 18		20 21	20 36	20 50		21 27	21 53	
d		18 23		18 53				19 25	19 51			20 23	20 38	20 51		21 29	21 55	
Colwyn Bay d		18 29		18 59				19 31	19 57			20 29	20 44	20 57		21 35	22 01	
Abergele & Pensarn d				19 06					20 04					21 04		21 42	22 09	
Rhyl d		18 39		19 12				19 41	20 10			20 39	20 55	21 11		21 48	22 16	
Prestatyn d		18 45		19 18				19 47	20 16			20 45	21 00	21 16		21 53	22 22	
Flint d		18 58		19 31				20 00	20 29			20 58	21 14	21 30		22 07	22 37	
Shotton d				19 37					20 35					21 36		22 13	22 44	
Chester a		19 15		19 49				20 15	20 47			21 15	21 28	21 47		22 24	22 55	
d	18 55	19 27	19 35	19 50			19 55	20 17	20 50		20 55	21 21	21 35		21 52	22 26	23 01	23 22
Liverpool Lime Street 106 a																		
Helsby d				20 00					20 59						22 01			23 31
Frodsham d				20 04					21 03						22 05			23 35
Runcorn East d				20 09					21 09						22 11			23 41
Warrington Bank Quay 90 a				20 18					21 18						22 18			23 49
Earlestown 90 a				20 26					21 26						22 26			23 56
Newton-le-Willows 90 a				20 29					21 29						22 29			23 59
Manchester Oxford Road 90 a				20 48					21 48						22 50			
Manchester Piccadilly ⇌ a				20 52					21 57						22 58			00 28
Crewe a	19 18		19 54				20 18	20 41			21 18		21 54			22 47	23 26	
Cardiff Central 131 a																		
Manchester Airport 84,85 ✈ a				21 13														
Birmingham New Street 65 a												23 26	22 50					
London Euston ⊖65 a			21 42															

Saturdays
until 04 September

	AW	AW	AW	AW	AW	AW	AW	AW	AW	AW	VT	AW	AW	AW	AW	AW	VT	AW	AW	AW
							◇ 🛒	◇		🛒	◇1 🍴	◇ 🛒	◇ 🛒			◇ 🛒	◇1 🍴	◇ 🛒		
Holyhead d							04 25					05 22				06 35	06 53			
Valley d							04x31					05x28				06x41				
Rhosneigr d												05x33								
Ty Croes d												05x37								
Bodorgan d												05x41								
Llanfairpwll d							04x48					05x51				06x58				
Bangor (Gwynedd) a							04 55					05 59				07 05	07 19			
d							04 57					06 01				07 07	07 20			
Llanfairfechan d												06x08								
Penmaenmawr d												06x12								
Conwy d												06x18								
Llandudno d													06 34	07 10				07 45	08 10	
Deganwy d													06x38	07x14				07x49	08x14	
Llandudno Junction a							05 13					06 22	06 42	07 20		07 23	07 37	07 53	08 20	
d				04 38			05 15		05 37			06 24	06 44			07 25	07 38	07 54		
Colwyn Bay d				04 44			05 21		05 43			06 30	06 50			07 31	07 44	08 00		
Abergele & Pensarn d				04 51					05 50				06 57					08 07		
Rhyl d				04 57			05 31		05 56			06 40	07 03			07 41	07 55	08 13		
Prestatyn d				05 02			05 37		06 01			06 46	07 08			07 47	08 01	08 19		
Flint d				05 16			05 50		06 15			06 59	07 21			08 00	08 15	08 32		
Shotton d				05 22					06 21				07 27					08 38		
Chester a				05 33			06 05		06 33			07 15	07 38			08 15	08 28	08 50		
d	03 36	04 23	04 55	05 37	05 38	05 51	06 12	06 13		07 12	07 17	07 22	07 40		07 55	08 22	08 35	08 52		08 55
Liverpool Lime Street 106 a																				
Helsby d					05 47			06 22		07 21			07 49					09 01		
Frodsham d					05 51			06 26		07 25			07 53					09 05		
Runcorn East d					05 56			06 32		07 31			07 59					09 11		
Warrington Bank Quay 90 a					06 05			06 39		07 38			08 06					09 18		
Earlestown 90 a					06 12			06 47		07 46			08 15					09 26		
Newton-le-Willows 90 a					06 15			06 50		07 49			08 18					09 29		
Manchester Oxford Road 90 a					06 35			07 09		08 09			08 41					09 48		
Manchester Piccadilly ⇌ a	04 45				06 46			07 18		08 18			08 50					09 57		
Crewe a		04 44	05 20	05 58		06 15					07 36				08 18		08 54			09 18
Cardiff Central 131 a							09 22									11 20				
Manchester Airport 84,85 ✈ a	05 12																			
Birmingham New Street 65 a		05 55										09 28								
London Euston ⊖65 a											09 30						10 37			

Table 81

Saturdays
until 04 September

North Wales and Chester - Manchester and Crewe

		AW	VT	AW	AW		AW		AW	VT	AW	AW	AW		AW		AW	VT	AW	AW	AW		AW	VT
		◇	◇1	◇					◇	◇1	◇				◇		◇	◇1	◇				◇	◇1
		⌶	⊡	⌶					⌶	⊡	⌶				⌶			⊡	⌶				⌶	⊡
Holyhead d		07 15	07 55						08 20	08 55					09 23								10 33	
Valley d		07x21							08x26						09x29								10x39	
Rhosneigr d		07x26							08x32						09x34									
Ty Croes d		07x30							08x35						09x38									
Bodorgan d		07x34							08x40						09x42									
Llanfairpwll d		07x44							08x49						09x52								10x56	
Bangor (Gwynedd) a		07 52	08 21						08 57	09 21					10 00								11 03	
d		08 02	08 22						09 02	09 22					10 02								11 05	
Llanfairfechan d		08x09							09x09						10x09									
Penmaenmawr d		08x13							09x13						10x13									
Conwy d		08x19							09x19						10x19									
Llandudno d				08 45	09 10						09 45	10 10					10 20		10 44	11 10				
Deganwy d				08x49	09x14						09x49	10x14					10x24		10x48	11x14				
Llandudno Junction a		08 23	08 39	08 53	09 20				09 23	09 39	09 53	10 20			10 23		10 30		10 52	11 20			11 21	
d		08 25	08 40	08 54					09 25	09 40	09 54				10 25				10 53				11 25	
Colwyn Bay d		08 31	08 47	09 00					09 31	09 47	10 00				10 31				10 59				11 31	
Abergele & Pensarn d				09 07							10 07								11 06					
Rhyl d		08 41	08 58	09 13					09 41	09 58	10 13				10 41				11 12				11 41	
Prestatyn d		08 47	09 04	09 19					09 47	10 03	10 19				10 47				11 18				11 47	
Flint d		09 00	09 18	09 32					10 00		10 32				11 00				11 31				12 00	
Shotton d				09 38							10 38								11 37					
Chester a		09 15	09 31	09 50					10 15	10 28	10 50				11 15				11 49				12 15	
d		09 30	09 35	09 52			09 55		10 22	10 35	10 52		10 55		11 22			11 35	11 50		11 55		12 22	12 35
Liverpool Lime Street 106 a																								
Helsby d				10 01							11 01								12 00					
Frodsham d				10 05							11 05								12 04					
Runcorn East d				10 11							11 11								12 09					
Warrington Bank Quay 90 a				10 18							11 18								12 18					
Earlestown 90 a				10 26							11 26								12 26					
Newton-le-Willows 90 a				10 29							11 29								12 29					
Manchester Oxford Road 90 a				10 48							11 48								12 48					
Manchester Piccadilly a				10 57							11 57								12 57					
Crewe a			09 54				10 18			10 54			11 18					11 54			12 18			12 54
Cardiff Central 131 a									13 20														15 21	
Manchester Airport 84,85 a																								
Birmingham New Street 65 a		11 27													13 26									
London Euston 65 a			11 38							12 38								13 38						14 38

	AW		AW	AW		AW	VT	AW	AW	AW			AW	AW	VT	AW	AW	AW		AW	VT		AW	AW
	◇					◇	◇1	◇					◇	◇	◇1	◇				◇	◇1		◇	◇
	⌶					⌶	⊡	⌶					⌶		⊡	⌶				⌶	⊡		⌶	⌶
Holyhead d						11 23	11 55						12 38							13 23				14 23
Valley d						11x29														13x29				
Rhosneigr d						11x34														13x34				
Ty Croes d						11x38														13x38				
Bodorgan d						11x42														13x42				
Llanfairpwll d						11x52														13x52				
Bangor (Gwynedd) a						12 00	12 20						13 05							14 00				14 53
d						12 02	12 21						13 07							14 02				14 54
Llanfairfechan d						12x09														14x09				15x01
Penmaenmawr d						12x13														14x13				15x05
Conwy d						12x19														14x19				15x11
Llandudno d	11 44		12 10					12 44	13 10					13 20		13 44	14 10						14 42	
Deganwy d	11x48		12x14					12x48	13x14					13x24		13x48	14x14						14x46	
Llandudno Junction a	11 52		12 20			12 23	12 38	12 52	13 20				13 23	13 30		13 52	14 20			14 23			14 50	15 16
d	11 53					12 25	12 39	12 53					13 25			13 53				14 25			14 51	15 17
Colwyn Bay d	11 59					12 31	12 46	12 59					13 31			13 59				14 31			14 57	15 23
Abergele & Pensarn d	12 06							13 06								14 06							15 04	
Rhyl d	12 12					12 41	12 57	13 12					13 41			14 12				14 41			15 10	15 34
Prestatyn d	12 18					12 47		13 18					13 47			14 18				14 47			15 16	15 39
Flint d	12 31					13 00		13 31					14 00			14 31				15 00			15 29	15 53
Shotton d	12 37							13 37								14 37							15 35	
Chester a	12 49					13 15	13 24	13 49					14 15			14 49				15 17			15 46	16 07
d	12 50			12 55		13 22	13 35	13 50		13 55			14 22		14 35	14 50		14 55		15 22	15 35		15 48	16 22
Liverpool Lime Street 106 a																								
Helsby d	13 00							14 00								15 00							15 57	
Frodsham d	13 04							14 04								15 04							16 02	
Runcorn East d	13 09							14 09								15 09							16 07	
Warrington Bank Quay 90 a	13 18							14 18								15 18							16 16	
Earlestown 90 a	13 26							14 26								15 26							16 26	
Newton-le-Willows 90 a	13 29							14 29								15 29							16 29	
Manchester Oxford Road 90 a	13 48							14 48								15 48							16 48	
Manchester Piccadilly a	13 57							14 57								15 57							16 57	
Crewe a				13 18			13 54			14 18					14 54			15 18			15 54			
Cardiff Central 131 a													17 17											19 21
Manchester Airport 84,85 a																								
Birmingham New Street 65 a						15 26														17 26				
London Euston 65 a							15 38								16 38						17 38			

Table 81

Saturdays
until 04 September

North Wales and Chester - Manchester and Crewe

	AW	AW		VT	AW	AW	AW			AW	AW	VT	AW	AW	AW		AW		AW	AW	AW		AW	AW
				◇1	◇					◇	◇	◇1	◇				◇						◇	◇
				⊡	⌶					⌶		⊡	⌶				⌶						⌶	⌶
Holyhead d				14 36						15 23							16 38						17 21	
Valley d										15x29													17x27	
Rhosneigr d										15x34													17x32	
Ty Croes d										15x38													17x36	
Bodorgan d										15x42													17x40	
Llanfairpwll d										15x52													17x50	
Bangor (Gwynedd) a				15 04						16 00							17 05						17 58	
d				15 06						16 02							17 07						18 00	
Llanfairfechan d										16x09													18x07	
Penmaenmawr d										16x13													18x11	
Conwy d										16x19													18x17	
Llandudno d	15 10				15 44	16 10					16 20		16 44	17 10					17 44	18 08				18 44
Deganwy d	15x14				15x48	16x14					16x24		16x48	17x14					17x48	18x12				18x48
Llandudno Junction a	15 20			15 24	15 52	16 20				16 23	16 30		16 52	17 20			17 23		17 52	18 18			18 21	18 52
d				15 25	15 53					16 25			16 53				17 25		17 53				18 23	18 53
Colwyn Bay d				15 33	15 59					16 31			16 59				17 31		17 59				18 29	18 59
Abergele & Pensarn d					16 06								17 06						18 06					19 06
Rhyl d				15 46	16 12					16 41			17 12				17 41		18 12				18 39	19 12
Prestatyn d					16 18					16 47			17 18				17 47		18 18				18 45	19 18
Flint d					16 31					17 00			17 31				18 00		18 31				18 58	19 31
Shotton d					16 37								17 37						18 37					19 37
Chester a				16 17	16 49					17 14			17 49				18 15		18 49				19 13	19 49
d		15 55		16 20	16 50		16 55			17 22		17 35	17 50		17 55		18 22		18 50		18 55			19 50
Liverpool Lime Street 106 a																								
Helsby d					17 00								18 00						19 00					20 00
Frodsham d					17 04								18 04						19 04					20 04
Runcorn East d					17 09								18 09						19 09					20 09
Warrington Bank Quay 90 a					17 18								18 18						19 18					20 18
Earlestown 90 a					17 26								18 26						19 26					20 26
Newton-le-Willows 90 a					17 29								18 29						19 29					20 29
Manchester Oxford Road 90 a					17 48								18 48						19 48					20 48
Manchester Piccadilly a					17 57								18 57						19 52					20 57
Crewe a		16 18		16 43			17 18					17 54			18 18						19 18			
Cardiff Central 131 a																	21 21							
Manchester Airport 84,85 a																			20 13					
Birmingham New Street 65 a										19 26														
London Euston 65 a				18 37																				

	AW	AW	AW			AW	VT	AW	AW	AW	AW	AW			AW	AW		AW	AW					
	◇					◇	◇	◇			◇					◇								
						⌶	⊡	⌶																
Holyhead d						18 23					19 21					20 37								
Valley d						18x29					19x27													
Rhosneigr d						18x34					19x32													
Ty Croes d						18x38					19x36													
Bodorgan d						18x42					19x40													
Llanfairpwll d						18x52					19x50													
Bangor (Gwynedd) a						19 00					19 58					21 04								
d						19 00					20 00					21 06								
Llanfairfechan d						19x09					20x07					21x13								
Penmaenmawr d						19x13					20x11					21x17								
Conwy d						19x19					20x17					21x23								
Llandudno d	19 03	19 10						19 42	20 08			20 42						21 45						
Deganwy d	19x07	19x14						19x46	20x12			20x46						21x49						
Llandudno Junction a	19 11	19 20				19 23		19 50	20 18		20 21	20 50				21 27		21 53						
d						19 25		19 51			20 23	20 51				21 29		21 55						
Colwyn Bay d						19 31		19 57			20 29	20 57				21 35		22 01						
Abergele & Pensarn d								20 04				21 04				21 42		22 09						
Rhyl d						19 41		20 10			20 39	21 10				21 48		22 16						
Prestatyn d						19 47		20 16			20 45	21 16				21 53		22 22						
Flint d						20 00		20 29			20 58	21 29				22 07		22 37						
Shotton d								20 35				21 35				22 13		22 44						
Chester a						20 15		20 47			21 15	21 47				22 24		22 55						
d			19 55			20 17	20 35	20 50		20 55	21 22				21 52	22 26		23 01	23 22					
Liverpool Lime Street 106 a																								
Helsby d								20 59							22 01				23 31					
Frodsham d								21 03							22 05				23 35					
Runcorn East d								21 09							22 11				23 41					
Warrington Bank Quay 90 a								21 16							22 19				23 50					
Earlestown 90 a								21 26							22 26				23 58					
Newton-le-Willows 90 a								21 29							22 30				00 01					
Manchester Oxford Road 90 a								21 48							22 50									
Manchester Piccadilly a								21 57							22 58				00 26					
Crewe a			20 18			20 41	20 54			21 18						22 47		23 26						
Cardiff Central 131 a																								
Manchester Airport 84,85 a																								
Birmingham New Street 65 a											23 29													
London Euston 65 a																								

Table 81

Saturdays from 11 September

North Wales and Chester - Manchester and Crewe

Station		AW	AW	AW	AW	AW	AW	AW	AW	NT	AW	VT	AW	AW	AW	AW	AW	VT	AW	AW	AW
								◇	◇			◇ 1	◇	◇			◇	◇ 1	◇		
													A								
								🛒			🛒	🍴	🛒	🛒			🛒	🍴	🛒		
Holyhead	d							04 25					05 22				06 35	06 53			
Valley	d							04x31					05x28				06x41				
Rhosneigr	d												05x33								
Ty Croes	d												05x37								
Bodorgan	d												05x41								
Llanfairpwll	d							04x48					05x51				06x58				
Bangor (Gwynedd)	a							04 55					05 59				07 05	07 19			
	d							04 57					06 01				07 07	07 20			
Llanfairfechan	d												06x08								
Penmaenmawr	d												06x12								
Conwy	d												06x18								
Llandudno	d													06 34	07 10				07 45	08 10	
Deganwy	d													06x38	07x14				07x49	08x14	
Llandudno Junction	a							05 13					06 22	06 42	07 20		07 23	07 37	07 53	08 20	
	d				04 38			05 15		05 37			06 24	06 44			07 25	07 38	07 54		
Colwyn Bay	d				04 44			05 21		05 43			06 30	06 50			07 31	07 44	08 00		
Abergele & Pensarn	d				04 51					05 50				06 57					08 07		
Rhyl	d				04 57			05 31		05 56			06 40	07 03			07 41	07 55	08 13		
Prestatyn	d				05 02			05 37		06 01			06 46	07 08			07 47	08 01	08 19		
Flint	d				05 16			05 50		06 15			06 59	07 21			08 00	08 15	08 32		
Shotton	d				05 22					06 21				07 27					08 38		
Chester	a				05 33			06 05		06 33			07 15	07 38			08 15	08 28	08 50		
	d	03 36	04 23	04 55	05 37	05 38	05 51	06 12	06 13		07 12	07 17	07 22	07 40		07 55	08 22	08 35	08 52		08 55
Liverpool Lime Street 106	a																				
Helsby	d					05 47			06 22		07 21			07 49					09 01		
Frodsham	d					05 51			06 26		07 25			07 53					09 05		
Runcorn East	d					05 56			06 32		07 31			07 59					09 11		
Warrington Bank Quay 90	a					06 05			06 39		07 38			08 06					09 18		
Earlestown 90	a					06 12			06 47		07 46			08 15					09 26		
Newton-le-Willows 90	a					06 15			06 50		07 49			08 18					09 29		
Manchester Oxford Road 90	a					06 35			07 09		08 09			08 41					09 48		
Manchester Piccadilly	a	04 45				06 46			07 18		08 18			08 50					09 57		
Crewe	a		04 44	05 20	05 58		06 15					07 36				08 18		08 54			09 18
Cardiff Central 131	a							09 22									11 20				
Manchester Airport 84,85 ✈	a	05 12																			
Birmingham New Street 65	a		05 55										09 28								
London Euston ⊖65	a											09 30						10 37			

Station		AW	VT	AW	AW	AW	AW	VT	AW	AW	AW	AW	AW	VT	AW	AW	AW	AW	VT
																		■	
		◇	◇ 1	◇			◇	◇ 1	◇			◇	◇	◇ 1	◇			◇	◇ 1
		🛒	🍴	🛒			🛒	🍴	🛒			🛒		🍴	🛒			🛒	🍴
Holyhead	d	07 15	07 55				08 20	08 55				09 23						10 33	
Valley	d	07x21					08x26					09x29						10x39	
Rhosneigr	d	07x26					08x32					09x34							
Ty Croes	d	07x30					08x35					09x38							
Bodorgan	d	07x34					08x40					09x42							
Llanfairpwll	d	07x44					08x49					09x52						10x56	
Bangor (Gwynedd)	a	07 52	08 21				08 57	09 21				10 00						11 03	
	d	08 02	08 22				09 02	09 22				10 02						11 05	
Llanfairfechan	d	08x09					09x09					10x09							
Penmaenmawr	d	08x13					09x13					10x13							
Conwy	d	08x19					09x19					10x19							
Llandudno	d			08 45	09 10				09 45	10 10			10 20		10 44	11 10			
Deganwy	d			08x49	09x14				09x49	10x14			10x24		10x48	11x14			
Llandudno Junction	a	08 23	08 39	08 53	09 20		09 23	09 39	09 53	10 20		10 23	10 30		10 52	11 20		11 21	
	d	08 25	08 40	08 54			09 25	09 40	09 54			10 25			10 53			11 25	
Colwyn Bay	d	08 31	08 47	09 00			09 31	09 47	10 00			10 31			10 59			11 31	
Abergele & Pensarn	d			09 07					10 07						11 06				
Rhyl	d	08 41	08 58	09 13			09 41	09 58	10 13			10 41			11 12			11 41	
Prestatyn	d	08 47	09 04	09 19			09 47	10 03	10 19			10 47			11 18			11 47	
Flint	d	09 00	09 18	09 32			10 00		10 32			11 00			11 31			12 00	
Shotton	d			09 38					10 38						11 37				
Chester	a	09 15	09 31	09 50			10 15	10 28	10 50			11 15			11 49			12 15	
	d	09 30	09 35	09 52		09 55	10 22	10 35	10 52		10 55	11 22		11 35	11 50		11 55	12 22	12 35
Liverpool Lime Street 106	a																		
Helsby	d			10 01					11 01						12 00				
Frodsham	d			10 05					11 05						12 04				
Runcorn East	d			10 11					11 11						12 09				
Warrington Bank Quay 90	a			10 18					11 18						12 18				
Earlestown 90	a			10 26					11 26						12 26				
Newton-le-Willows 90	a			10 29					11 29						12 29				
Manchester Oxford Road 90	a			10 48					11 48						12 48				
Manchester Piccadilly	a			10 57					11 57						12 57				
Crewe	a		09 54			10 18		10 54			11 18			11 54			12 18		12 54
Cardiff Central 131	a						13 20											15 21	
Manchester Airport 84,85 ✈	a																		
Birmingham New Street 65	a	11 27										13 26							
London Euston ⊖65	a		11 38					12 38						13 38					14 38

Table 81

Saturdays from 11 September

North Wales and Chester - Manchester and Crewe

Station		AW	AW	AW	AW	VT	AW	AW	AW	AW	AW	VT	AW	AW	AW	AW	VT	AW	AW
		◇			◇	◇ 1	◇			◇	◇	◇ 1	◇			◇	◇ 1	◇	◇
		🛒			🛒	🍴	🛒			🛒		🍴	🛒			🛒	🍴	🛒	🛒
Holyhead	d				11 23					12 38						13 23			14 23
Valley	d				11x29											13x29			
Rhosneigr	d				11x34											13x34			
Ty Croes	d				11x38											13x38			
Bodorgan	d				11x42											13x42			
Llanfairpwll	d				11x52											13x52			
Bangor (Gwynedd)	a				12 00					13 05						14 00			14 53
	d				12 02					13 07						14 02			14 54
Llanfairfechan	d				12x09											14x09			15x01
Penmaenmawr	d				12x13											14x13			15x05
Conwy	d				12x19											14x19			15x11
Llandudno	d	11 44	12 10				12 44	13 10			13 20		13 44	14 10				14 42	
Deganwy	d	11x48	12x14				12x48	13x14			13x24		13x48	14x14				14x46	
Llandudno Junction	a	11 52	12 20		12 23		12 52	13 20		13 23	13 30		13 52	14 20		14 23		14 50	15 16
	d	11 53			12 25		12 53			13 25			13 53			14 25		14 51	15 17
Colwyn Bay	d	11 59			12 31		12 59			13 31			13 59			14 31		14 57	15 23
Abergele & Pensarn	d	12 06					13 06						14 06					15 04	
Rhyl	d	12 12			12 41		13 12			13 41			14 12			14 41		15 10	15 34
Prestatyn	d	12 18			12 47		13 18			13 47			14 18			14 47		15 16	15 39
Flint	d	12 31			13 00		13 31			14 00			14 31			15 00		15 29	15 53
Shotton	d	12 37					13 37						14 37					15 35	
Chester	a	12 49			13 15		13 49			14 15			14 49			15 17		15 46	16 07
	d	12 50		12 55	13 22	13 35	13 50		13 55	14 22		14 35	14 50		14 55	15 22	15 35	15 48	16 22
Liverpool Lime Street 106	a																		
Helsby	d	13 00					14 00						15 00					15 57	
Frodsham	d	13 04					14 04						15 04					16 02	
Runcorn East	d	13 09					14 09						15 09					16 07	
Warrington Bank Quay 90	a	13 18					14 18						15 18					16 16	
Earlestown 90	a	13 26					14 26						15 26					16 26	
Newton-le-Willows 90	a	13 29					14 29						15 29					16 29	
Manchester Oxford Road 90	a	13 48					14 48						15 48					16 48	
Manchester Piccadilly	a	13 57					14 57						15 57					16 57	
Crewe	a			13 18		13 54			14 18			14 54			15 18		15 54		
Cardiff Central 131	a									17 17									19 21
Manchester Airport 84,85 ✈	a																		
Birmingham New Street 65	a				15 26											17 26			
London Euston ⊖65	a					15 38						16 38					17 38		

Station		AW	AW	VT	AW	AW	AW	AW	AW	VT	AW	AW	AW	AW	AW	AW	AW	AW
				◇ 1	◇			◇	◇	◇ 1	◇			◇	◇			◇
				🍴	🛒			🛒		🍴	🛒			🛒	🛒			🛒
Holyhead	d			14 36				15 23						16 38				17 21
Valley	d							15x29										17x27
Rhosneigr	d							15x34										17x32
Ty Croes	d							15x38										17x36
Bodorgan	d							15x42										17x40
Llanfairpwll	d							15x52										17x50
Bangor (Gwynedd)	a			15 04				16 00						17 05				17 58
	d			15 06				16 02						17 07				18 00
Llanfairfechan	d							16x09										18x07
Penmaenmawr	d							16x13										18x11
Conwy	d							16x19										18x17
Llandudno	d	15 10			15 44	16 10			16 20		16 44	17 10			17 44	18 08		
Deganwy	d	15x14			15x48	16x14			16x24		16x48	17x14			17x48	18x12		
Llandudno Junction	a	15 20		15 24	15 52	16 20		16 23	16 30		16 52	17 20		17 23	17 52	18 18		18 21
	d			15 25	15 53			16 25			16 53			17 25	17 53			18 23
Colwyn Bay	d			15 33	15 59			16 31			16 59			17 31	17 59			18 29
Abergele & Pensarn	d				16 06						17 06				18 06			
Rhyl	d			15 46	16 12			16 41			17 12			17 41	18 12			18 39
Prestatyn	d				16 18			16 47			17 18			17 47	18 18			18 45
Flint	d				16 31			17 00			17 31			18 00	18 31			18 58
Shotton	d				16 37						17 37				18 37			
Chester	a			16 17	16 49			17 14			17 49			18 15	18 49			19 13
	d		15 55	16 20	16 50		16 55	17 22		17 35	17 50		17 55	18 22	18 50		18 55	
Liverpool Lime Street 106	a																	
Helsby	d				17 00						18 00				19 00			
Frodsham	d				17 04						18 04				19 04			
Runcorn East	d				17 09						18 09				19 09			
Warrington Bank Quay 90	a				17 18						18 18				19 18			
Earlestown 90	a				17 26						18 26				19 26			
Newton-le-Willows 90	a				17 29						18 29				19 29			
Manchester Oxford Road 90	a				17 48						18 48				19 48			
Manchester Piccadilly	a				17 57						18 57				19 52			
Crewe	a		16 18	16 43			17 18			17 54			18 18				19 18	
Cardiff Central 131	a													21 21				
Manchester Airport 84,85 ✈	a														20 13			
Birmingham New Street 65	a							19 26										
London Euston ⊖65	a			18 37														

North Wales and Chester - Manchester and Crewe

Saturdays from 11 September

	AW	AW	AW	AW	AW	VT	AW	AW	AW	AW	AW	AW	AW	AW	AW	AW
	◇	◇			◇	◇	◇			◇			◇		A	B
	🛒				🛒	☕	🛒									🚌
Holyhead d					18 23					19 21			20 37			
Valley d					18x29					19x27						
Rhosneigr d					18x34					19x32						
Ty Croes d					18x38					19x36						
Bodorgan d					18x42					19x40						
Llanfairpwll d					18x52					19x50						
Bangor (Gwynedd) a					19 00					19 58			21 04			
d					19 00					20 00			21 06			
Llanfairfechan d					19x09					20x07			21x13			
Penmaenmawr d					19x13					20x11			21x17			
Conwy d					19x19					20x17			21x23			
Llandudno d	18 44	19 03	19 10				19 42	20 08			20 42			21 45		
Deganwy d	18x48	19x07	19x14				19x46	20x12			20x46			21x49		
Llandudno Junction a	18 52	19 11	19 20		19 23		19 50	20 18		20 21	20 50		21 27	21 53		
d	18 53				19 25		19 51			20 23	20 51		21 29	21 55		
Colwyn Bay d	18 59				19 31		19 57			20 29	20 57		21 35	22 01		
Abergele & Pensarn d	19 06						20 04				21 04		21 42	22 09		
Rhyl d	19 12				19 41		20 10			20 39	21 10		21 48	22 16		
Prestatyn d	19 18				19 47		20 16			20 45	21 16		21 53	22 22		
Flint d	19 31				20 00		20 29			20 58	21 29		22 07	22 37		
Shotton d	19 37						20 35				21 35		22 13	22 44		
Chester a	19 49				20 15		20 47			21 15	21 47		22 24	22 55		
d	19 50			19 55	20 17	20 35	20 50		20 55	21 22		21 52	22 26	23 01	23 22	23 22
Liverpool Lime Street 10 106 a																
Helsby d	20 00						20 59					22 01			23 31	23 42
Frodsham d	20 04						21 03					22 05			23 35	23 47
Runcorn East d	20 09						21 09					22 11			23 41	00 02
Warrington Bank Quay 90 a	20 18						21 16					22 19			23 50	00 22
Earlestown 8 90 a	20 26						21 26					22 26			23 58	00 47
Newton-le-Willows 90 a	20 29						21 29					22 30			00 01	00 57
Manchester Oxford Road 90 a	20 48						21 48					22 50				01 27
Manchester Piccadilly 10 a	20 57						21 57					22 58			00 26	01 32
Crewe 10 a				20 18	20 41	20 54			21 18				22 47	23 26		
Cardiff Central 7 131 a																
Manchester Airport 84,85 ✈ a																
Birmingham New Street 12 65 a										23 29						
London Euston 15 ⊖65 a																

Sundays until 05 September

	AW	AW	AW	AW	AW	AW	AW	AW	AW	AW	AW	AW	AW	AW	VT	AW	AW	AW
				◇	◇		◇			◇	◇			◇	◇■1			◇
									🛒					🛒	☕	🛒		
Holyhead d				07 16			07 50			08 45								10 20
Valley d							07x56											10x26
Rhosneigr d							08x02											10x31
Ty Croes d							08x05											10x35
Bodorgan d							08x10											10x39
Llanfairpwll d							08x19											10x49
Bangor (Gwynedd) a				07 42			08 27			09 12								10 57
d				07 43			08 28			09 13								10 59
Llanfairfechan d							08x35											11x06
Penmaenmawr d							08x39											11x10
Conwy d							08x45											11x16
Llandudno d											10 22		11 07					
Deganwy d											10x26		11x11					
Llandudno Junction a				07 59			08 50			09 29	10 30		11 17					11 20
d				08 00			08 51			09 35	10 32							11 22
Colwyn Bay d				08 07			08 57			09 41								11 28
Abergele & Pensarn d				08 14						09 48								11 35
Rhyl d				08 20			09 08			09 54								11 41
Prestatyn d				08 25						09 59								11 46
Flint d				08 39						10 13								12 00
Shotton d				08 45			09 28			10 19								12 06
Chester a				08 56			09 39			10 30								12 18
d	07 56	08 27	08 41	08 57	09 11	09 27	09 42	09 57	10 36	10 39		10 57		11 22	11 28	11 36	11 57	12 21
Liverpool Lime Street 10 106 a																		
Helsby d			08 50				09 51		10 45							11 45		
Frodsham d			08 54				09 55		10 49							11 49		
Runcorn East d			08 59				10 00		10 54							11 54		
Warrington Bank Quay 90 a			09 10				10 07		11 03							12 03		
Earlestown 8 90 a			09 16				10 19		11 10							12 10		
Newton-le-Willows 90 a			09 19				10 22		11 13							12 13		
Manchester Oxford Road 90 a			09 39				10 41		11 32							12 32		
Manchester Piccadilly 10 a			09 48				10 50		11 41							12 41		
Crewe 10 a	08 22	08 52		09 22		09 52		10 22		11 01		11 22			11 47		12 22	
Cardiff Central 7 131 a																		15 28
Manchester Airport 84,85 ✈ a																		
Birmingham New Street 12 65 a					11 13									13 24				
London Euston 15 ⊖65 a															13 44			

A until 16 October B from 23 October

D until 11 July.

North Wales and Chester - Manchester and Crewe

Sundays until 05 September

	AW	AW	VT	AW	AW	AW	AW	AW	VT	AW	AW	AW	VT	AW	AW	AW	AW	AW	AW	VT
	◇		◇■1					◇	◇■1				◇■1	◇					◇	◇■1
	A																			
			☕			🛒		🛒	☕		🛒		☕				🛒		🛒	☕
Holyhead d	10 20		10 55						11 50				12 50							13 55
Valley d	10x26																			
Rhosneigr d	10x31																			
Ty Croes d	10x35																			
Bodorgan d	10x39																			
Llanfairpwll d	10x49																			
Bangor (Gwynedd) a	10 57		11 21						12 16				13 16							14 21
d	10 59		11 22						12 17				13 18							14 22
Llanfairfechan d	11x06																			
Penmaenmawr d	11x10																			
Conwy d	11x16																			
Llandudno d				11 40	12 18					13 19				13 30	13 50	14 20				
Deganwy d				11x44	12x22					13x23				13x34	13x54	14x24				
Llandudno Junction a	11 20		11 39	11 50	12 28				12 34	13 29			13 34	13 38	14 00	14 30				14 39
d	11 22		11 40						12 35				13 36							14 40
Colwyn Bay d	11 28		11 47						12 42				13 42							14 46
Abergele & Pensarn d	11 35																			
Rhyl d	11 41		11 58						12 53				13 53							14 57
Prestatyn d	11 46		12 03						12 59				13 59							15 03
Flint d	12 00		12 17										14 13							
Shotton d	12 06																			
Chester a	12 18		12 30						13 23				14 26							15 31
d	12 21	12 24	12 33			12 36	12 57	13 22	13 30		13 36	13 57	14 33				14 36	14 57	15 31	15 33
Liverpool Lime Street 10 106 a																				
Helsby d						12 45					13 45						14 45			
Frodsham d						12 49					13 49						14 49			
Runcorn East d						12 54					13 54						14 54			
Warrington Bank Quay 90 a						13 03					14 03						15 03			
Earlestown 8 90 a						13 10					14 10						15 10			
Newton-le-Willows 90 a						13 13					14 13						15 13			
Manchester Oxford Road 90 a						13 32					14 32						15 32			
Manchester Piccadilly 10 a						13 41					14 41						15 41			
Crewe 10 a		12 45	12 52				13 18		13 49			14 18	14 54					15 18		15 54
Cardiff Central 7 131 a	15 37																			
Manchester Airport 84,85 ✈ a																				
Birmingham New Street 12 65 a								15 24											17 35	
London Euston 15 ⊖65 a			14 45						15 45				16 44							17 44

	AW	AW	AW	AW	AW	AW	AW	AW	AW	VT	AW	AW	AW	AW	AW	AW	AW	VT	AW	AW
														■	■					
					◇				◇	◇■1	◇							◇■1		
														B	C					
		🛒			🛒					☕	🛒			🛒	🛒			☕		
Holyhead d					14 30						15 40			16 25	16 25					
Valley d					14x36									16x31	16x31					
Rhosneigr d					14x42									16x36	16x36					
Ty Croes d					14x45									16x40	16x40					
Bodorgan d					14x50									16x44	16x44					
Llanfairpwll d					14x59									16x54	16x54					
Bangor (Gwynedd) a					15 07						16 06			17 02	17 02					
d					15 08						16 08			17 04	17 04					
Llanfairfechan d											16x15									
Penmaenmawr d											16x19									
Conwy d											16x25									
Llandudno d	15 11					15 45	16 16					16 52				17 20	18 05			
Deganwy d	15x15					15x49	16x20					16x56				17x24	18x09			
Llandudno Junction a	15 21				15 25	15 55	16 26				16 29	17 00		17 20	17 20	17 28	18 13			
d					15 26						16 35			17 25	17 25					
Colwyn Bay d					15 32						16 41			17 31	17 31					
Abergele & Pensarn d					15 39						16 48			17 38	17 38					
Rhyl d					15 45						16 54			17 44	17 44					
Prestatyn d					15 51						16 59			17 49	17 49					
Flint d					16 04						17 13			18 03	18 03					
Shotton d					16 10						17 19			18 11	18 11					
Chester a					16 21						17 32			18 21	18 21					
d		15 36	15 57	16 27	16 36			16 57	17 22	17 35	17 36		17 59	18 24	18 24			18 35	18 36	18 57
Liverpool Lime Street 10 106 a																				
Helsby d		15 45			16 45						17 45								18 45	
Frodsham d		15 49			16 49						17 49								18 49	
Runcorn East d		15 54			16 54						17 54								18 54	
Warrington Bank Quay 90 a		16 03			17 03						18 03								19 03	
Earlestown 8 90 a		16 10			17 10						18 10								19 10	
Newton-le-Willows 90 a		16 13			17 13						18 13								19 13	
Manchester Oxford Road 90 a		16 32			17 32						18 32								19 32	
Manchester Piccadilly 10 a		16 41			17 41						18 41								19 41	
Crewe 10 a			16 21	16 48				17 20		17 53			18 18					18 53		19 18
Cardiff Central 7 131 a														21 36	21 38					
Manchester Airport 84,85 ✈ a																				
Birmingham New Street 12 65 a									19 24											
London Euston 15 ⊖65 a										19 44								20 44		

A from 18 July B until 11 July C from 18 July until 5 September

Table 81

Sundays until 05 September

North Wales and Chester - Manchester and Crewe

	AW	AW	AW	VT	AW	AW	AW	AW	VT	AW	AW	AW	AW	AW	AW	AW	AW
	◇ 🛒		◇	◇ ☕			◇		◇ ☕						◇	◇	
Holyhead d	17 30						18 25								20 35	21 40	
Valley d							18x31								20x41		
Rhosneigr d							18x36								20x46		
Ty Croes d							18x40								20x50		
Bodorgan d							18x44								20x54		
Llanfairpwll d							18x54								21x04		
Bangor (Gwynedd) a	17 57						19 02								21 12	22 09	
d	17 59						19 04								21 14	22 11	
Llanfairfechan d	18x06														21x21		
Penmaenmawr d	18x10														21x25		
Conwy d	18x16														21x31		
Llandudno d		18 55															
Deganwy d		18x59															
Llandudno Junction a	18 20	19 05					19 20								21 35	22 27	
d	18 24						19 24								21 37	22 29	
Colwyn Bay d	18 30						19 30								21 43	22 35	
Abergele & Pensarn d	18 37						19 37								21 50		
Rhyl d	18 43						19 43								21 56	22 45	
Prestatyn d	18 48						19 48								22 01	22 51	
Flint d	19 02						20 02								22 15	23 04	
Shotton d	19 08						20 10								22 21		
Chester a	19 19						20 19								22 32	23 18	
d	19 22		19 26	19 35	19 36	19 57	20 27	20 36	20 37	20 57	21 27	21 36	21 57	22 09	22 35		22 57
Liverpool Lime Street 10 106 a																	
Helsby d					19 45			20 45				21 45		22 18			
Frodsham d					19 49			20 49				21 49		22 22			
Runcorn East d					19 54			20 54				21 54		22 27			
Warrington Bank Quay 90 a					20 03			21 03				22 03		22 36			
Earlestown 8 90 a					20 10			21 10				22 10		22 44			
Newton-le-Willows 90 a					20 13			21 13				22 13		22 47			
Manchester Oxford Road 90 a					20 32			21 32				22 32		23 06			
Manchester Piccadilly 10 a					20 41			21 41				22 41		23 15			
Crewe 10 a	19 44			19 54		20 18	20 48		20 56	21 18	21 48		22 18		22 59		23 18
Cardiff Central 7 131 a																	
Manchester Airport 84,85 ✈ a																	
Birmingham New Street 12 65 a			21 29				21 52										
London Euston 15 ⊖65 a																	

Sundays from 12 September

	AW	AW	AW	AW	AW	AW	AW	AW	AW	AW	AW	VT	AW	AW	AW	VT	AW
		A	B 🚌	◇ B		◇ A	B 🚌	🛒	◇	🚌	🚌	◇1 ☕	🛒	◇		◇1 ☕	🛒
Holyhead d									08 45					10 20		10 55	
Valley d														10x26			
Rhosneigr d														10x31			
Ty Croes d														10x35			
Bodorgan d														10x39			
Llanfairpwll d														10x49			
Bangor (Gwynedd) a									09 12					10 57		11 21	
d									09 13					10 59		11 22	
Llanfairfechan d														11x06			
Penmaenmawr d														11x10			
Conwy d														11x16			
Llandudno d										10 05	10 15						
Deganwy d										10 19	10 30						
Llandudno Junction a									09 29	10 24	10 35			11 20		11 39	
d									09 35					11 22		11 40	
Colwyn Bay d									09 41					11 28		11 47	
Abergele & Pensarn d									09 48					11 35			
Rhyl d									09 54					11 41		11 58	
Prestatyn d									09 59					11 46		12 03	
Flint d									10 13					12 00		12 17	
Shotton d									10 19					12 06			
Chester a									10 30					12 18		12 30	
d	08 40	08 41	08 42	08 56	09 40	09 42	09 42	10 36	10 39			11 28	11 36	12 21	12 24	12 33	12 36
Liverpool Lime Street 10 106 a																	
Helsby d		08 50	09 02			09 51	10 02	10 45					11 45				12 45
Frodsham d		08 54	09 07			09 55	10 07	10 49					11 49				12 49
Runcorn East d		08 59	09 22			10 00	10 22	10 54					11 54				12 54
Warrington Bank Quay 90 a		09 10	09 42			10 07	10 42	11 03					12 03				13 03
Earlestown 8 90 a		09 17	10 07			10 19	11 07	11 10					12 10				13 10
Newton-le-Willows 90 a		09 20	10 17			10 22	11 17	11 13					12 13				13 13
Manchester Oxford Road 90 a		09 39	10 47			10 41	11 47	11 32					12 32				13 32
Manchester Piccadilly 10 a		09 49	10 52	09 59		10 50	11 52	11 41					12 41				13 41
Crewe 10 a	09 01				10 01				11 01			11 47			12 45	12 52	
Cardiff Central 7 131 a														15 27			
Manchester Airport 84,85 ✈ a																	
Birmingham New Street 12 65 a																	
London Euston 15 ⊖65 a												13 44				14 45	

A from 12 September until 17 October

B from 24 October

Table 81

Sundays from 12 September

North Wales and Chester - Manchester and Crewe

	AW	VT	AW	AW	AW	AW	VT	AW	VT	AW	AW	AW	AW	AW	AW	VT	AW	AW	VT
		◇1 ☕	🚌	🚌	🛒		◇1 ☕	🛒	◇1 ☕	🛒		◇ 🛒	🚌	🚌	◇ 🛒	◇1 ☕	◇ 🛒	■ 🛒	◇1 ☕
Holyhead d		11 50					12 50		13 55			14 30			15 30			16 25	
Valley d												14x36						16x31	
Rhosneigr d												14x42						16x36	
Ty Croes d												14x45						16x40	
Bodorgan d												14x50						16x44	
Llanfairpwll d												14x59						16x54	
Bangor (Gwynedd) a		12 16					13 16		14 21			15 07			15 57			17 02	
d		12 17					13 18		14 22			15 08			15 59			17 04	
Llanfairfechan d															16x06				
Penmaenmawr d															16x10				
Conwy d															16x16				
Llandudno d			13 10	13 05									15 45	16 00					
Deganwy d			13 15	13 19									15 59	16 15					
Llandudno Junction a		12 34	13 20	13 24			13 34		14 39			15 25	16 04	16 20	16 20			17 20	
d		12 35					13 36		14 40			15 26			16 25			17 25	
Colwyn Bay d		12 42					13 42		14 46			15 32			16 31			17 31	
Abergele & Pensarn d												15 39			16 38			17 38	
Rhyl d		12 53					13 53		14 57			15 45			16 44			17 44	
Prestatyn d		12 59					13 59		15 03			15 51			16 49			17 49	
Flint d							14 13					16 04			17 03			18 03	
Shotton d												16 10			17 09			18 11	
Chester a		13 23					14 26		15 31			16 21			17 20			18 21	
d	13 18	13 30			13 36	14 20	14 33	14 36	15 33	15 36	16 27	16 36			17 22	17 35	17 36	18 24	18 35
Liverpool Lime Street 10 106 a																			
Helsby d					13 45			14 45		15 45		16 45					17 45		
Frodsham d					13 49			14 49		15 49		16 49					17 49		
Runcorn East d					13 54			14 54		15 54		16 54					17 54		
Warrington Bank Quay 90 a					14 03			15 03		16 03		17 03					18 03		
Earlestown 8 90 a					14 10			15 10		16 10		17 10					18 10		
Newton-le-Willows 90 a					14 13			15 13		16 13		17 13					18 13		
Manchester Oxford Road 90 a					14 32			15 32		16 32		17 32					18 32		
Manchester Piccadilly 10 a					14 41			15 41		16 41		17 41					18 41		
Crewe 10 a	13 39	13 49				14 41	14 54		15 54		16 48				17 43	17 53			18 53
Cardiff Central 7 131 a																		21 36	
Manchester Airport 84,85 ✈ a																			
Birmingham New Street 12 65 a																			
London Euston 15 ⊖65 a		15 45					16 44		17 44							19 44			20 44

	AW	AW	AW	VT	AW	AW	AW	AW	VT	AW	AW	AW	AW	AW	AW	AW	AW
			◇ 🛒	◇ ☕			◇		◇ ☕		◇				◇	◇	
Holyhead d			17 30				18 25				19 40				20 35	21 40	
Valley d							18x31								20x41		
Rhosneigr d							18x36								20x46		
Ty Croes d							18x40								20x50		
Bodorgan d							18x44								20x54		
Llanfairpwll d							18x54								21x04		
Bangor (Gwynedd) a			17 57				19 02				20 07				21 12	22 09	
d			17 59				19 04				20 09				21 14	22 11	
Llanfairfechan d			18x06								20x16				21x21		
Penmaenmawr d			18x10								20x20				21x25		
Conwy d			18x16								20x26				21x31		
Llandudno d																	
Deganwy d																	
Llandudno Junction a			18 20				19 20				20 30				21 35	22 27	
d			18 24				19 24				20 37				21 37	22 29	
Colwyn Bay d			18 30				19 30				20 43				21 43	22 35	
Abergele & Pensarn d			18 37				19 37				20 50				21 50		
Rhyl d			18 43				19 43				20 56				21 56	22 45	
Prestatyn d			18 48				19 48				21 01				22 01	22 51	
Flint d			19 02				20 02				21 15				22 15	23 04	
Shotton d			19 08				20 10				21 21				22 21		
Chester a			19 19				20 19				21 31				22 32	23 18	
d	18 36	18 57	19 22	19 35	19 36	19 50	20 27	20 36	20 37	20 50	21 35	21 36	21 50	22 09	22 35		23 00
Liverpool Lime Street 10 106 a																	
Helsby d	18 45				19 45			20 45				21 45		22 18			
Frodsham d	18 49				19 49			20 49				21 49		22 22			
Runcorn East d	18 54				19 54			20 54				21 54		22 27			
Warrington Bank Quay 90 a	19 03				20 03			21 03				22 03		22 36			
Earlestown 8 90 a	19 10				20 10			21 10				22 10		22 44			
Newton-le-Willows 90 a	19 13				20 13			21 13				22 13		22 47			
Manchester Oxford Road 90 a	19 32				20 32			21 32				22 32		23 06			
Manchester Piccadilly 10 a	19 41				20 41			21 41				22 41		23 15			
Crewe 10 a		19 18	19 44	19 54		20 11	20 48		20 56	21 11	21 59		22 11		22 59		23 21
Cardiff Central 7 131 a																	
Manchester Airport 84,85 ✈ a																	
Birmingham New Street 12 65 a							21 52										
London Euston 15 ⊖65 a																	

Table 81A

Holyhead - Dublin

Holyhead	d	
Dun Laoghaire	a	
Dublin Ferryport §	a	

§ Bus connections to/from city centre and railway stations

Details of service not available at time of going to press

Table 81A

Dublin - Holyhead

Dublin Ferryport ‡	d	
Dun Laoghaire	d	
Holyhead	a	

‡ Bus connections to/from city centre and railway stations

Details of service not available at time of going to press

Network Diagram for Tables 82, 83, 94

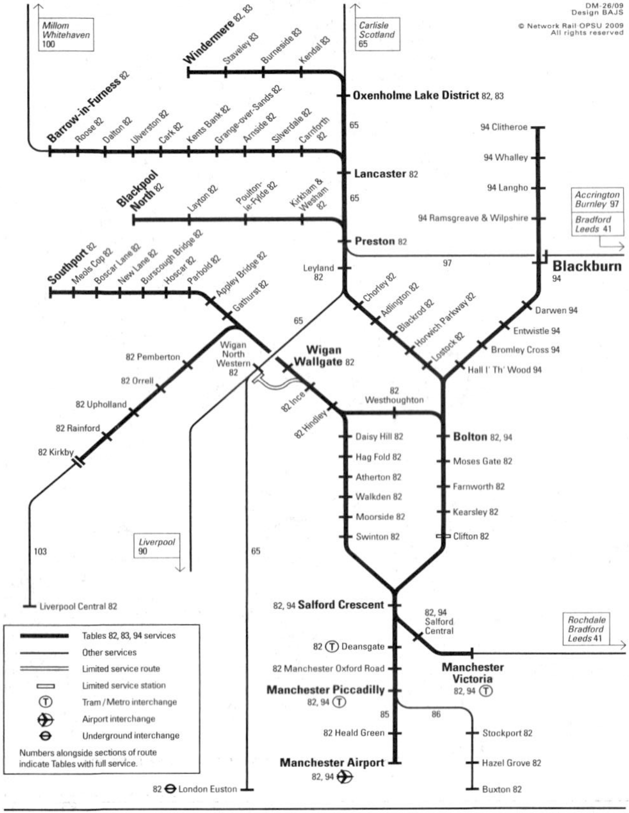

Table 82

Mondays to Fridays
until 03 September

Manchester - Bolton - Wigan, Kirkby, Southport, Preston, Blackpool North and Barrow-in-Furness

		TP	TP	NT	TP	TP	TP	NT	NT	NT	NT	NT	NT	TP
		◇1	◇1		1	◇1	◇1							◇1
Manchester Airport 85 ✈	d	00 01	04 00				05 45							06 18
Heald Green 85	d						05 49							
Buxton 86	d													
Hazel Grove 86	d													
Stockport 84	d													
Manchester Piccadilly 10 ⇌	d	00 16	04 15			05 46	06 03							06 33
Manchester Oxford Road	d						06 06							06 36
Deansgate ⇌	d													
Rochdale 41	d													
Manchester Victoria ⇌	d							05 55	06 00	06 17	06 38	06 45		
Salford Central	d										06 40	06 48		
Salford Crescent	a					05 51		05 59	06 04	06 23	06 44	06 51		
	d					05 52		06 00	06 05	06 24	06 45	06 52		
Swinton	d											06 58		
Moorside	d													
Walkden	d											07 03		
Atherton	d											07 08		
Hag Fold	d													
Daisy Hill	d											07 12		
Kearsley	d										06 52			
Farnworth	d										06 54			
Moses Gate	d										06 57			
Bolton	a	00s31	04s29				06 19	06 11	06 15	06 34	07 00			06 50
	d	00s32	04s29				06 19	06 12	06 15	06 34	07 01			06 50
Westhoughton	d								06 23					
Hindley	d								06 27			07 16		
Ince	d													
Wigan North Western	a		04 44			06 15					07 19			
Wigan Wallgate	a								06 32			07 21		
	d								06 34			07 23		
Pemberton	d								06 38					
Orrell	d								06 42					
Upholland	d								06 45					
Rainford	d								06 49					
Kirkby	a								07 01					
Gathurst	d											07 27		
Appley Bridge	d											07 31		
Parbold	d											07 35		
Hoscar	d													
Burscough Bridge	d											07 39		
New Lane	d													
Bescar Lane	d													
Meols Cop	d											07 47		
Southport	a											07 56		
Lostock	d									06 39				
Horwich Parkway	d									06 43				
Blackrod	d									06 46				
Adlington (Lancashire)	d									06 50				
Chorley	d						06 31			06 55				
Leyland	d					06 28				07 06				
Preston 8 65,97	a	01s03	05s04			06 35	06 42			07 11				07 11
	d	01s05	05s09	05 22		06 37	06 44			07 13				07 14
Kirkham & Wesham 97	a					06 46				07 22				
Poulton-le-Fylde 97	a					06 56				07 30				
Layton 97	a					06 59				07 34				
Blackpool North 97	a	01 30	05 33			07 06				07 41				
Lancaster 8 65	a			05 42			06 59							07 30
	d			05 42	05 46		07 00						07 10	07 30
Oxenholme Lake District 65	a				06 21		07 15							
Windermere 83	a				06 41									
Carnforth	d			05 52									07 20	
Silverdale	d			05 58										
Arnside	d			06 03										
Grange-over-Sands	d			06 09										
Kents Bank	d			06 12										
Cark	d			06 17										
Ulverston	d			06 25										
Dalton	d			06 33										
Roose	d			06 39										
Barrow-in-Furness	a			06 47										

Table 82

Mondays to Fridays
until 03 September

Manchester - Bolton - Wigan, Kirkby, Southport, Preston, Blackpool North and Barrow-in-Furness

			NT	NT	NT	NT	TP	TP	NT	NT	NT	NT	TP	NT	NT	NT	NT	NT	TP	NT	NT	NT
							◇1	◇1 🛒					◇1 🛒						◇1 🛒			
Manchester Airport	85 ✈	d						07 00					07 25						07 58			
Heald Green	85	d											07 30									
Buxton	86	d	05 59									06 23				06 50						
Hazel Grove	86	d	06 33									07 00				07 27						
Stockport	84	d	06 41									07 10				07 37						
Manchester Piccadilly 10	🚊	d	06 54					07 15				07 27	07 45			07 54			08 15			
Manchester Oxford Road		d	06 57					07 18				07 30				07 57			08 19			
Deansgate	🚊	d	06 59									07 32				07 59						
Rochdale	41	d																				
Manchester Victoria	🚊	d		07 01	07 06				07 16	07 23	07 27			07 47			08 00	08 03		08 11		08 22
Salford Central		d		07 04	07 09				07 19	07 26	07 30			07 50			08 03	08 08		08 13		08 25
Salford Crescent		a	07 03	07 07	07 12				07 24	07 29	07 33	07 37		07 53		08 04	08 07	08 12		08 17		08 29
		d	07 03	07 08	07 13				07 25	07 30	07 33	07 37		07 53		08 04	08 08	08 13		08 17		08 30
Swinton		d		07 14										08 00				08 19				
Moorside		d		07 17										08 02				08 22				
Walkden		d		07 20							07 42			08 06				08 25				
Atherton		d		07 26							07 48			08 11				08 31				
Hag Fold		d		07 28										08 14				08 33				
Daisy Hill		d		07 31							07 51			08 17				08 36				
Kearsley		d										07 45										
Farnworth		d										07 47										
Moses Gate		d										07 49										
Bolton		a	07 16		07 23			07 31	07 35	07 41		07 53	07 59			08 14	08 19		08 32	08 27		08 40
		d	07 19		07 23			07 31	07 35	07 42		07 53	07 59			08 15	08 20		08 32	08 28		08 40
Westhoughton		d			07 31	←						08 01								08 35	←	
Hindley		d		07 39	07 35	07 39								08 21				08 43		08 39	08 43	
Ince		d		→		07 42												→		08 42	08 46	
Wigan North Western		a										08 16										
Wigan Wallgate		a			07 40	07 45					08 03			08 26						08 45	08 49	
		d			07 41	07 46								08 28						08 47	08 51	
Pemberton		d				07 50															08 55	
Orrell		d				07 54															08 59	
Upholland		d				07 58															09 02	
Rainford		d				08 01															09 06	
Kirkby		a				08 13															09 18	
Gathurst		d			07 46									08 32						08 51		
Appley Bridge		d			07 49									08 36						08 55		
Parbold		d			07 53															08 59		
Hoscar		d			07 56																	
Burscough Bridge		d			07 59									08 42						09 03		
New Lane		d			08 02																	
Bescar Lane		d			08 05																	
Meols Cop		d			08 10															09 11		
Southport		a			08 20									08 59						09 20		
Lostock		d							07 42							08 20						08 45
Horwich Parkway		d						07 38	07 46							08 24			08 39			08 49
Blackrod		d							07 49													08 52
Adlington (Lancashire)		d							07 53							08 29						08 56
Chorley		d						07 46	07 58				08 11			08 34			08 47			09 01
Leyland		d							08 08							08 43						09 12
Preston 8	65,97	a						07 57	08 14				08 22			08 50			08 58			09 17
		d					07 20	07 59	08 15				08 24		08 38	08 51			08 59			09 19
Kirkham & Wesham	97	a						08 08	08 25													09 28
Poulton-le-Fylde	97	a						08 18	08 33										09 16			09 36
Layton	97	a						08 22	08 37													09 43
Blackpool North	97	a						08 29	08 44							09 17			09 25			09 50
Lancaster 6	65	a					07 36						08 39		08 58							
		d					07 36						08 40		08 58							
Oxenholme Lake District	65	a											08 54									
Windermere	83	a																				
Carnforth		d					07 45								09 08							
Silverdale		d					07 51								09 14							
Arnside		d					07 55								09 19							
Grange-over-Sands		d					08 00								09 25							
Kents Bank		d					08 04								09 28							
Cark		d					08 08								09 33							
Ulverston		d					08 16								09 41							
Dalton		d					08 24								09 49							
Roose		d					08 30								09 55							
Barrow-in-Furness		a					08 39								10 03							

Table 82

Mondays to Fridays
until 03 September

Manchester - Bolton - Wigan, Kirkby, Southport, Preston, Blackpool North and Barrow-in-Furness

			NT	NT	NT	NT	TP	NT	NT	NT	NT	NT	TP	TP	NT	NT	NT	NT	TP	NT	NT	NT
							◇1 🛒						◇1 🛒	◇1					◇1 🛒			
Manchester Airport	85 ✈	d	08 01				08 25						09 00			09 03			09 29			
Heald Green	85	d	08 05				08 29												09 33			
Buxton	86	d																				
Hazel Grove	86	d						08 32												09 32		
Stockport	84	d						08 41												09 41		
Manchester Piccadilly 10	🚊	d	08 22				08 46	08 54					09 16			09 22			09 46	09 54		
Manchester Oxford Road		d	08 26				08 49	08 58					09 19			09 26			09 49	09 58		
Deansgate	🚊	d	08 28				08 51	09 00								09 28			09 51	10 00		
Rochdale	41	d			08 00												09 04					
Manchester Victoria	🚊	d		08 29	08b33	08 46			09 00	09 07	09 10				09 22		09c33	09 46			10 00	10 07
Salford Central		d		08 32	08 36	08 49			09 03	09 10	09 13				09 25		09 36	09 49			10 03	10 10
Salford Crescent		a	08 33	08 37	08 39	08 52	08 56	09 04	09 07	09 13	09 16				09 29	09 33	09 39	09 52	09 56	10 04	10 07	10 13
		d	08 34	08 37	08 40	08 53	08 56	09 04	09 08	09 13	09 17				09 30	09 34	09 40	09 53	09 56	10 04	10 08	10 13
Swinton		d				08 59					09 23							09 59				
Moorside		d									09 26											
Walkden		d				09 04					09 29							10 04				
Atherton		d				09 09					09 35							10 09				
Hag Fold		d									09 37											
Daisy Hill		d				09 13					09 40							10 13				
Kearsley		d			08 47												09 47					
Farnworth		d			08 49												09 49					
Moses Gate		d			08 52												09 52					
Bolton		a	08 44	08 49	08 55		09 06	09 14	09 19	09 23			09 32		09 40	09 45	09 55		10 06	10 14	10 19	10 23
		d	08 45	08 49	08 56		09 07	09 15	09 20	09 24			09 33		09 40	09 45	09 56		10 07	10 15	10 20	10 24
Westhoughton		d	08 53							09 31						09 53						10 31
Hindley		d				09 17				09 35	09 45					09 57		10 17				10 35
Ince		d									09 48											
Wigan North Western		a																				
Wigan Wallgate		a	09 00		09 14	09 22				09 44	09 51					10 02	10 13	10 22				10 44
		d	09 05			09 24					09 52					10 03		10 24				
Pemberton		d									09 56											
Orrell		d									10 00											
Upholland		d									10 04											
Rainford		d									10 07											
Kirkby		a									10 19											
Gathurst		d				09 28												10 28				
Appley Bridge		d	09 11			09 32										10 10		10 32				
Parbold		d	09 15			09 36										10 14		10 36				
Hoscar		d				09 39																
Burscough Bridge		d	09 20			09 42										10 18		10 40				
New Lane		d				09 44																
Bescar Lane		d				09 48																
Meols Cop		d				09 53												10 48				
Southport		a	09 36			10 02										10 35		10 57				
Lostock		d						09 20							09 45					10 20		
Horwich Parkway		d					09 13	09 24							09 49				10 13	10 24		
Blackrod		d													09 52							
Adlington (Lancashire)		d													09 56							
Chorley		d					09 21	09 32					09 44		10 01				10 21	10 32		
Leyland		d						09 42							10 12					10 42		
Preston 8	65,97	a					09 33	09 50					09 55		10 17				10 33	10 51		
		d					09 38						09 58	10 07	10 19				10 38			
Kirkham & Wesham	97	a													10 28							
Poulton-le-Fylde	97	a					09 56								10 36				10 56			
Layton	97	a													10 43							
Blackpool North	97	a					10 05								10 51				11 05			
Lancaster 6	65	a											10 13	10 22								
		d										09 39	10 14	10 23								
Oxenholme Lake District	65	a																				
Windermere	83	a																				
Carnforth		d										09 49		10 32								
Silverdale		d										09 56										
Arnside		d										10 00		10 41								
Grange-over-Sands		d										10 06		10 46								
Kents Bank		d										10 10										
Cark		d										10 14										
Ulverston		d										10 23		10 59								
Dalton		d										10 31										
Roose		d										10 37										
Barrow-in-Furness		a										10 47		11 17								

b arr. 0822

c arr. 0926

Table 82

Manchester - Bolton - Wigan, Kirkby, Southport, Preston, Blackpool North and Barrow-in-Furness

		NT	NT	TP ◇1	TP ◇1 ⌶	NT	NT	NT	NT	TP ◇1 ⌶	NT	NT	NT	NT	NT	TP ◇1 A ⌶	NT	NT	NT	NT	TP ◇1 ⌶	NT	NT
Manchester Airport 85 ✈	d				10 00		10 03			10 29						11 00		11 03			11 29		
Heald Green 85	d									10 33											11 33		
Buxton 86	d																						
Hazel Grove 86	d										10 33											11 33	
Stockport 84	d										10 41											11 41	
Manchester Piccadilly 10 ⇌	d				10 16		10 22			10 46	10 54					11 16		11 22			11 46	11 54	
Manchester Oxford Road	d				10 19		10 26			10 49	10 58					11 19		11 26			11 49	11 58	
Deansgate ⇌	d						10 28			10 51	11 00							11 28			11 51	12 00	
Rochdale 41	d							10 04											11 04				
Manchester Victoria ⇌	d	10 10				10 22		10c33	10 46			11 00	11 07	11 10			11 22		11e33	11 46			12 00
Salford Central	d	10 13				10 25		10 36	10 49			11 03	11 10	11 13			11 25		11 36	11 49			12 03
Salford Crescent	a	10 16				10 29	10 33	10 39	10 52	10 56	11 04	11 07	11 13	11 16			11 29	11 33	11 39	11 52	11 56	12 04	12 07
	d	10 17				10 30	10 34	10 40	10 53	10 56	11 04	11 08	11 13	11 17			11 30	11 34	11 40	11 53	11 56	12 04	12 08
Swinton	d	10 23							10 59					11 23						11 59			
Moorside	d	10 26												11 26									
Walkden	d	10 29							11 04					11 29						12 04			
Atherton	d	10 35							11 09					11 35						12 09			
Hag Fold	d	10 37												11 37									
Daisy Hill	d	10 40							11 13					11 40						12 13			
Kearsley	d							10 47											11 47				
Farnworth	d							10 49											11 49				
Moses Gate	d							10 52											11 52				
Bolton	a				10 32	10 40	10 45	10 55		11 06	11 14	11 19	11 23			11 32	11 40	11 45	11 55		12 06	12 14	12 19
	d				10 33	10 40	10 45	10 56		11 07	11 15	11 20	11 24			11 33	11 40	11 45	11 56		12 07	12 15	12 20
Westhoughton	d						10 53						11 31					11 53					
Hindley	d	10 45					10 57		11 17				11 35	11 45				11 57		12 17			
Ince	d	10 48												11 48									
Wigan North Western	a																						
Wigan Wallgate	a	10 51					11 02	11 13	11 22				11 44	11 51				12 02	12 13	12 22			
	d	10 52					11 03		11 24					11 52				12 03		12 24			
Pemberton	d	10 56												11 56									
Orrell	d	11 00												12 00									
Upholland	d	11 04												12 04									
Rainford	d	11 07												12 07									
Kirkby	a	11 19												12 19									
Gathurst	d								11 28											12 28			
Appley Bridge	d						11 10		11 32									12 10		12 32			
Parbold	d						11 14		11 36									12 14		12 36			
Hoscar	d								11 39														
Burscough Bridge	d						11 18		11 42									12 18		12 41			
New Lane	d								11 44														
Bescar Lane	d								11 48														
Meols Cop	d								11 53											12 49			
Southport	a						11 35		12 02									12 35		12 59			
Lostock	d					10 45					11 20						11 45					12 20	
Horwich Parkway	d					10 49				11 13	11 24						11 49				12 13	12 24	
Blackrod	d					10 52											11 52						
Adlington (Lancashire)	d					10 56											11 56						
Chorley	d				10 44	11 01				11 21	11 32					11 44	12 01				12 21	12 32	
Leyland	d					11 12					11 42						12 12					12 42	
Preston 8 65,97	a				10 55	11 17				11 33	11 50					11 55	12 17				12 33	12 50	
	d			10 45	10 58	11 19				11 38						11 58	12 19				12 38		
Kirkham & Wesham 97	a					11 28											12 28						
Poulton-le-Fylde 97	a					11 36				11 56							12 36				12 56		
Layton 97	a					11 43											12 43						
Blackpool North 97	a					11 50				12 05							12 50				13 05		
Lancaster 6 65	a		10 45	11 00	11 13											12 13							
	d		10 49	11 01	11 14										11 32	12 14							
Oxenholme Lake District 65	a			11 17	11 28																		
Windermere 83	a			11 39																			
Carnforth	d		11b09												11 42	12 23							
Silverdale	d														11 49								
Arnside	d														11 53	12 31							
Grange-over-Sands	d														11 59	12 37							
Kents Bank	d														12 03								
Cark	d														12 07								
Ulverston	d														12 15	12 49							
Dalton	d														12 24								
Roose	d														12 30								
Barrow-in-Furness	a														12 39	13 10							

A ⌶ to Chorley
b arr. 1058
c arr. 1026
e arr. 1126

Table 82

Manchester - Bolton - Wigan, Kirkby, Southport, Preston, Blackpool North and Barrow-in-Furness

		TP ◇1 ⌶	NT	NT	TP ◇1	NT	NT	NT	NT	TP ◇1 ⌶	NT	NT	NT	NT	NT	NT	TP ◇1 ⌶	TP ◇1	NT	NT	NT	NT
Manchester Airport 85 ✈	d	12 00					12 03			12 29							13 00			13 03		
Heald Green 85	d									12 33												
Buxton 86	d																					
Hazel Grove 86	d										12 33											
Stockport 84	d										12 41											
Manchester Piccadilly 10 ⇌	d	12 16					12 22			12 46	12 54						13 16			13 22		
Manchester Oxford Road	d	12 19					12 26			12 49	12 58						13 19			13 26		
Deansgate ⇌	d						12 28			12 51	13 00									13 28		
Rochdale 41	d							12 04													13 04	
Manchester Victoria ⇌	d		12 07	12 10		12 22		12b33	12 46			13 00	13 07	13 10					13 22		13c33	13 46
Salford Central	d		12 10	12 13		12 25		12 36	12 49			13 03	13 10	13 13					13 25		13 36	13 49
Salford Crescent	a		12 13	12 16		12 29	12 33	12 39	12 52	12 56	13 04	13 07	13 13	13 16					13 29	13 33	13 39	13 52
	d		12 13	12 17		12 30	12 34	12 40	12 53	12 56	13 04	13 08	13 13	13 17					13 30	13 34	13 40	13 53
Swinton	d			12 23					12 59					13 23								13 59
Moorside	d			12 26										13 26								
Walkden	d			12 29					13 04					13 29								14 04
Atherton	d			12 35					13 09					13 35								14 09
Hag Fold	d			12 37										13 37								
Daisy Hill	d			12 40					13 13					13 40								14 13
Kearsley	d							12 47													13 47	
Farnworth	d							12 49													13 49	
Moses Gate	d							12 52													13 52	
Bolton	a	12 32	12 23			12 40	12 45	12 55		13 06	13 14	13 19	13 23				13 32		13 40	13 45	13 55	
	d	12 33	12 24			12 40	12 45	12 56		13 07	13 15	13 20	13 24				13 33		13 40	13 45	13 56	
Westhoughton	d		12 31				12 53						13 31							13 53		
Hindley	d		12 35	12 45			12 57		13 17				13 35	13 45						13 57		14 17
Ince	d			12 48										13 48								
Wigan North Western	a																					
Wigan Wallgate	a		12 44	12 51			13 02	13 13	13 22				13 44	13 51						14 02	14 13	14 22
	d			12 52			13 03		13 24					13 52						14 03		14 24
Pemberton	d			12 56										13 56								
Orrell	d			13 00										14 00								
Upholland	d			13 04										14 04								
Rainford	d			13 07										14 07								
Kirkby	a			13 19										14 19								
Gathurst	d								13 28													14 28
Appley Bridge	d						13 10		13 32											14 10		14 32
Parbold	d						13 14		13 36											14 14		14 36
Hoscar	d								13 39													
Burscough Bridge	d						13 18		13 42											14 18		14 41
New Lane	d								13 44													
Bescar Lane	d								13 48													
Meols Cop	d								13 53													14 49
Southport	a						13 35		14 02											14 35		14 59
Lostock	d					12 45					13 20								13 45			
Horwich Parkway	d					12 49				13 13	13 24								13 49			
Blackrod	d					12 52													13 52			
Adlington (Lancashire)	d					12 56													13 56			
Chorley	d	12 44				13 01				13 21	13 32						13 44		14 01			
Leyland	d					13 12					13 42								14 12			
Preston 8 65,97	a	12 55				13 17				13 33	13 50						13 55		14 17			
	d	12 58			13 04	13 19				13 38							13 58	14 04	14 19			
Kirkham & Wesham 97	a					13 28													14 28			
Poulton-le-Fylde 97	a					13 36				13 56									14 36			
Layton 97	a					13 43													14 43			
Blackpool North 97	a					13 50				14 05									14 51			
Lancaster 6 65	a	13 13			13 19											13 42	14 13	14 19				
	d	13 14			13 20										13 32	13 48	14 14	14 20				
Oxenholme Lake District 65	a	13 28			13 36																	
Windermere 83	a				13 56																	
Carnforth	d														13 42	13 58		14 28				
Silverdale	d														13 48							
Arnside	d														13 52			14 37				
Grange-over-Sands	d														13 58			14 42				
Kents Bank	d														14 02							
Cark	d														14 06							
Ulverston	d														14 14			14 55				
Dalton	d														14 22							
Roose	d														14 28							
Barrow-in-Furness	a														14 38			15 15				

b arr. 1225
c arr. 1325

Table 82

Mondays to Fridays
until 03 September

Manchester - Bolton - Wigan, Kirkby, Southport, Preston, Blackpool North and Barrow-in-Furness

		TP ◇1 🛒	NT	NT	TP ◇1 🛒	NT	NT	NT	NT	NT	NT	TP ◇1 A 🛒	TP ◇1 B 🛒	NT	NT	NT	NT	NT	NT	TP ◇1 C 🛒	NT	NT	NT
Manchester Airport 85 ✈	d	13 29			14 00				14 03			14 29	14 29							15 00	15 03		
Heald Green 85	d	13 33										14 33	14 33										
Buxton 86	d																						
Hazel Grove 86	d		13 33											14 33									
Stockport 84	d		13 41											14 41									
Manchester Piccadilly [10] ⇌	d	13 46	13 54		14 16				14 22			14 46	14 46	14 54						15 16	15 22		
Manchester Oxford Road	d	13 49	13 58		14 19				14 26			14 49	14 49	14 58						15 19	15 26		
Deansgate ⇌	d	13 51	14 00						14 28			14 51	14 51	15 00							15 28		
Rochdale 41	d									14 04												15 04	
Manchester Victoria ⇌	d			14 00		14 07	14 10	14 22		14b33	14 46				15 00	15 07	15 10	15 22				15c33	15 40
Salford Central	d			14 03		14 10	14 13	14 25		14 36	14 49				15 03	15 10	15 13	15 25				15 36	15 43
Salford Crescent	a	13 56	14 04	14 07		14 13	14 16	14 29	14 33	14 39	14 52	14 56	14 56	15 04	15 07	15 13	15 16	15 29			15 33	15 39	15 46
	d	13 56	14 04	14 08		14 13	14 17	14 30	14 34	14 40	14 53	14 56	14 56	15 04	15 08	15 13	15 17	15 30			15 34	15 40	15 47
Swinton	d						14 23				14 59						15 23						
Moorside	d						14 26										15 26						
Walkden	d						14 29				15 04						15 29						
Atherton	d						14 35				15 09						15 35						
Hag Fold	d						14 37										15 37						
Daisy Hill	d						14 40				15 13						15 40						
Kearsley	d									14 47												15 47	
Farnworth	d									14 49												15 49	
Moses Gate	d									14 52												15 52	
Bolton	a	14 06	14 14	14 19	14 32	14 23		14 40	14 45	14 55		15 06	15 06	15 14	15 19	15 23		15 40		15 32	15 45	15 55	15 59
	d	14 07	14 15	14 20	14 33	14 24		14 40	14 45	14 56		15 07	15 07	15 15	15 20	15 24		15 40		15 33	15 45	15 56	16 00
Westhoughton	d					14 31			14 53							15 31					15 53		
Hindley	d					14 35	14 45		14 57		15 17					15 35	15 45				15 57		
Ince	d						14 48										15 48						
Wigan North Western	a																						
Wigan Wallgate	a					14 44	14 51		15 02	15 13	15 22					15 44	15 51				16 02	16 13	
	d						14 52		15 03		15 24						15 58				16 03		
Pemberton	d						14 56										16 02						
Orrell	d						15 00										16 06						
Upholland	d						15 04										16 09						
Rainford	d						15 07										16 13						
Kirkby	a						15 19										16 25						
Gathurst	d										15 28										16 08		
Appley Bridge	d								15 10		15 32										16 11		
Parbold	d								15 14		15 36										16 15		
Hoscar	d																				16 18		
Burscough Bridge	d								15 18		15 40										16 21		
New Lane	d																				16 24		
Bescar Lane	d																				16 27		
Meols Cop	d										15 48										16 32		
Southport	a								15 35		15 57										16 42		
Lostock	d		14 20					14 45						15 20				15 45					
Horwich Parkway	d	14 13	14 24					14 49				15 13	15 13	15 24				15 49					
Blackrod	d							14 52										15 52					
Adlington (Lancashire)	d							14 56										15 56					
Chorley	d	14 21	14 32		14 44			15 01				15 21	15 21	15 32				16 01		15 44			
Leyland	d		14 42					15 12						15 42				16 12					
Preston [8] 65,97	a	14 33	14 50		14 55			15 17				15 33	15 33	15 50				16 19		15 55			
	d	14 38			14 58			15 19				15 38	15 42							15 58			
Kirkham & Wesham 97	a							15 28															
Poulton-le-Fylde 97	a	14 56						15 36				15 56	16 02										
Layton 97	a							15 43															
Blackpool North 97	a	15 05						15 50				16 05	16 11										
Lancaster [8] 65	a				15 13															16 13			
	d				15 14														15 34	16 14			
Oxenholme Lake District 65	a				15 28																		
Windermere 83	a																						
Carnforth	d																		15 44	16 22			
Silverdale	d																		15 51	16 28			
Arnside	d																		15 55	16 32			
Grange-over-Sands	d																		16 01	16 38			
Kents Bank	d																		16 05	16 41			
Cark	d																		16 09	16 46			
Ulverston	d																		16 17	16 54			
Dalton	d																		16 26	17 02			
Roose	d																		16 32	17 08			
Barrow-in-Furness	a																		16 39	17 18			

A Does not apply Fridays 2 July to 3 September
B FO from 2 July until 3 September
C 🛒 to Chorley
b arr. 1425
c arr. 1526

Table 82

Mondays to Fridays
until 03 September

Manchester - Bolton - Wigan, Kirkby, Southport, Preston, Blackpool North and Barrow-in-Furness

		NT	TP ◇1 🛒	NT	NT	NT	NT	TP ◇1 🛒	NT	TP ◇1	NT	NT	NT	NT	NT	TP ◇1 🛒	NT	NT	NT	NT	TP ◇1 🛒	NT	TP ◇1
Manchester Airport 85 ✈	d		15 29					16 00					16 03			16 29					17 00		
Heald Green 85	d		15 33													16 33							
Buxton 86	d													15 27									
Hazel Grove 86	d			15 33										16 04				16 30					
Stockport 84	d			15 41										16 12				16 41					
Manchester Piccadilly [10] ⇌	d		15 46	15 54				16 16					16 22	16 27		16 46		16 54			17 15		
Manchester Oxford Road	d		15 49	15 58				16 19					16 26	16 30		16 49		16 58			17 18		
Deansgate ⇌	d		15 51	16 00									16 28	16 33				17 00					
Rochdale 41	d														16 04								
Manchester Victoria ⇌	d	15 46			16 07	16 10					16 20	16 23			16b36		16 46		17 00	17c06		17 10	
Salford Central	d	15 49			16 10	16 13					16 23	16 26			16 39		16 49		17 03	17 09		17 12	
Salford Crescent	a	15 52	15 56	16 04	16 13	16 16					16 26	16 30	16 34	16 38	16 42		16 52	17 04	17 07	17 13		17 16	
	d	15 53	15 56	16 04	16 13	16 17					16 27	16 31	16 34	16 38	16 43		16 53	17 04	17 08	17 14		17 17	
Swinton	d	15 59				16 23											16 59					17 23	
Moorside	d					16 26											17 02					17 26	
Walkden	d	16 04				16 29											17 05					17 31	
Atherton	d	16 09				16 35											17 11			17 26		17 37	
Hag Fold	d					16 37											17 14					17 39	
Daisy Hill	d	16 13				16 40											17 17			17 30		17 43	
Kearsley	d														16 50								
Farnworth	d														16 52								
Moses Gate	d				16 21										16 55								
Bolton	a		16 06	16 19	16 25			16 32			16 37	16 42	16 45	16 48	16 58	17 05		17 14	17 19		17 31		
	d		16 07		16 25			16 33			16 37	16 43	16 45	16 49	16 59	17 06		17 15	17 20		17 32		
Westhoughton	d				16 33								16 53		17 06								
Hindley	d	16 17			16 37	16 45							16 57		17 10		17 21					17 48	
Ince	d					16 48											17 24					17 51	
Wigan North Western	a																						
Wigan Wallgate	a	16 22			16 46	16 51							17 02		17 19		17 31			17 38		17 54	
	d	16 24				16 52							17 03							17 40		17 55	
Pemberton	d					16 56																17 59	
Orrell	d					17 00																18 03	
Upholland	d					17 04																18 07	
Rainford	d					17 07																18 10	
Kirkby	a					17 19																18 22	
Gathurst	d	16 28											17 08							17 44			
Appley Bridge	d	16 32											17 11							17 48			
Parbold	d	16 36											17 15							17 52			
Hoscar	d																						
Burscough Bridge	d	16 40											17 20							17 57			
New Lane	d																						
Bescar Lane	d																						
Meols Cop	d	16 48											17 27							18 05			
Southport	a	16 57											17 37							18 14			
Lostock	d		16 12								16 43			16 54				17 20					
Horwich Parkway	d		16 15								16 47			16 58				17 25					
Blackrod	d										16 51			17 01									
Adlington (Lancashire)	d										16 55			17 05									
Chorley	d		16 23					16 44			17 00			17 10		17 19		17 32			17 44		
Leyland	d										17 11			17 21				17 42					
Preston [8] 65,97	a		16 35					16 55			17 19			17 26		17 30		17 51			17 55		
	d		16 38					17 00		17 04	17 21			17 28		17 32					18 00		18 08
Kirkham & Wesham 97	a		16 47								17 30					17 41							
Poulton-le-Fylde 97	a		16 57								17 38					17 51							
Layton 97	a		17 00								17 43					17 54							
Blackpool North 97	a		17 07								17 50					18 02							
Lancaster [8] 65	a							17 15	17 14	17 23				17 48							18 15		18 23
	d						16 55	17 16	17 19	17 25				17 48							18 16		18 24
Oxenholme Lake District 65	a							17 30		17 43											18 30		
Windermere 83	a									18 08													
Carnforth	d						17 05		17 28					18 00									18 35
Silverdale	d						17 12		17 35					18 06									18 41
Arnside	d						17 16		17 40					18 11									18 45
Grange-over-Sands	d						17 22		17 46					18 19									18 51
Kents Bank	d						17 26		17 49					18 23									18 54
Cark	d						17 30		17 54					18 27									18 59
Ulverston	d						17 39		18 02					18 35									19 07
Dalton	d						17 48		18 10					18 43									19 15
Roose	d						17 54		18 16					18 49									19 21
Barrow-in-Furness	a						18 02		18 25					18 59									19 30

b arr. 1627
c arr. 1658

Table 82

Manchester - Bolton - Wigan, Kirkby, Southport, Preston, Blackpool North and Barrow-in-Furness

Station		NT	TP ◇1	NT	NT	NT	NT	NT	NT	NT	NT	TP ◇1	NT	TP ◇1	NT	NT	NT	NT	NT	TP ◇1	NT	NT	NT
Manchester Airport 85 ✈	d		17 29		17 03							18 00					18 03			18 29			
Heald Green 85	d		17 33																	18 33			
Buxton 86	d					16 30				16 59											17 59		
Hazel Grove 86	d					17 04				17 33											18 33		
Stockport 84	d					17 12				17 41											18 41		
Manchester Piccadilly 10	d		17 46		17 22	17 27				17 54		18 16					18 22			18 46	18 54		
Manchester Oxford Road	d		17 49		17 26	17 30				17 58		18 19					18 26			18 49	18 58		
Deansgate	d		17 51			17 33				18 00							18 28			18 51	19 00		
Rochdale 41	d			17 03												18 02							
Manchester Victoria	d	17 19		17 23			17 36	17 40	17 45		18 00		18 10		18 20	18 23		18 33	18 45			19 00	19 10
Salford Central	d	17 22		17 27			17 39	17 43	17 48		18 03		18 13		18 23	18 26		18 36	18 48			19 03	19 13
Salford Crescent	a	17 25	17 55	17 29	17 34	17 38	17 42	17 46	17 51	18 04	18 07		18 16		18 26	18 30	18 34	18 39	18 51	18 56	19 04	19 07	19 16
	d	17 27	17 55	17 30	17 34	17 38	17 43	17 47	17 52	18 04	18 08		18 17		18 27	18 31	18 34	18 40	18 52	18 56	19 04	19 08	19 17
Swinton	d								17 58				18 23						18 58				19 23
Moorside	d								18 01				18 26						19 01				19 26
Walkden	d								18 05				18 29						19 04				19 29
Atherton	d							17 59	18 11				18 35						19 10				19 35
Hag Fold	d								18 13				18 37						19 12				19 37
Daisy Hill	d							18 03	18 17				18 40						19 15				19 40
Kearsley	d						17 53											18 47					
Farnworth	d						17 55											18 49					
Moses Gate	d						17 57											18 52					
Bolton	a	17 37	18 06	17 42	17 45	17 48	18 01			18 14	18 19	18 32			18 37	18 42	18 45	18 55		19 06	19 19	19 20	
	d	17 37	18 07	17 43	17 45	17 49	18 01			18 15	18 20	18 33			18 37	18 43	18 45	18 56		19 07		19 20	
Westhoughton	d				17 53		18 09										18 53	19 03					
Hindley	d						18 13		18 22				18 45				18 57	19 09	19 20				19 45
Ince	d								18 25				18 48						19 23				19 48
Wigan North Western	a												18 56										
Wigan Wallgate	a				18 01		18 22	18 11	18 28								19 02	19 18	19 30				19 55
	d				18 02			18 15	18 29								19 03						
Pemberton	d								18 33														
Orrell	d								18 37														
Upholland	d								18 41														
Rainford	d								18 44														
Kirkby	a								18 55														
Gathurst	d							18 19									19 08						
Appley Bridge	d				18 09			18 23									19 11						
Parbold	d				18 13			18 28									19 15						
Hoscar	d							18 31															
Burscough Bridge	d				18 17			18 34									19 19						
New Lane	d							18 37															
Bescar Lane	d							18 40															
Meols Cop	d							18 46									19 27						
Southport	a				18 35			18 55									19 37						
Lostock	d	17 43	18 12			17 54				18 20					18 42					19 12			
Horwich Parkway	d	17 47	18 15			17 58				18 24					18 46					19 15			
Blackrod	d	17 51	18 18			18 01									18 49								
Adlington (Lancashire)	d	17 55				18 05									18 53								
Chorley	d	18 00	18 25			18 10				18 32		18 44			18 58					19 23			
Leyland	d	18 11	18 33							18 42					19 10								
Preston 8 65,97	a	18 16	18 38			18 25				18 48		18 55			19 18					19 33			
	d	18 18	18 40			18 26				18 49		19 00		19 04	19 19					19 38			
Kirkham & Wesham 97	a	18 27	18 49												19 28								
Poulton-le-Fylde 97	a	18 35	18 59			18 43									19 36					19 56			
Layton 97	a	18 39	19 02												19 43								
Blackpool North 97	a	18 49	19 09			18 53				19 16					19 52					20 05			
Lancaster 6 65	a											19 15		19 20									
	d											19 16		19 20									
Oxenholme Lake District 65	a											19 30											
Windermere 83	a																						
Carnforth	d													19 29									
Silverdale	d													19 35									
Arnside	d													19 39									
Grange-over-Sands	d													19 44									
Kents Bank	d													19 48									
Cark	d													19 52									
Ulverston	d													20 00									
Dalton	d													20 08									
Roose	d													20 14									
Barrow-in-Furness	a													20 24									

Table 82

Manchester - Bolton - Wigan, Kirkby, Southport, Preston, Blackpool North and Barrow-in-Furness

Station		NT	TP ◇1	NT	NT	TP ◇1	NT	TP ◇1	NT	NT	NT	TP ◇1	NT	NT	NT	NT	NT	TP ◇1	TP ◇1	NT FX
Manchester Airport 85 ✈	d		19 00	19 03		19 29		20 00			20 03	20 29					21 03	21 29	22 00	
Heald Green 85	d					19 33						20 33						21 33		
Buxton 86	d																			
Hazel Grove 86	d																			
Stockport 84	d																			
Manchester Piccadilly 10	d		19 16	19 20		19 46		20 16			20 20	20 46					21 20	21 46	22 16	
Manchester Oxford Road	d		19 19	19 24		19 49		20 19			20 24	20 49					21 24	21 49	22 19	
Deansgate	d			19 26		19 51					20 26	20 51					21 26	21 51		
Rochdale 41	d																			
Manchester Victoria	d				19 28		20 00		20 10	20 22			21 00	21 10		21 22				22 00
Salford Central	d				19 31		20 03		20 13	20 25			21 03	21 13		21 25				
Salford Crescent	a			19 29	19 34	19 56	20 07		20 16	20 29	20 33	20 56	21 07	21 16		21 29	21 33	21 56		22 07
	d			19 30	19 35	19 56	20 08		20 17	20 30	20 34	20 56	21 08	21 17		21 30	21 34	21 56		22 08
Swinton	d								20 23					21 23						
Moorside	d								20 26					21 26						
Walkden	d								20 29					21 29						
Atherton	d								20 35					21 35						
Hag Fold	d								20 37					21 37						
Daisy Hill	d								20 40					21 40						
Kearsley	d																			
Farnworth	d																			
Moses Gate	d																			
Bolton	a		19 32	19 40	19 45	20 06	20 19	20 32		20 40	20 45	21 06	21 19			21 40	21 45	22 06	22 32	22 19
	d		19 33	19 40	19 45	20 07	20 20	20 33		20 40	20 45	21 07	21 20			21 40	21 45	22 07	22 33	22 20
Westhoughton	d			19 48							20 53						21 53			
Hindley	d			19 52					20 45		20 57			21 45			21 57			
Ince	d								20 48					21 48						
Wigan North Western	a																		22 48	
Wigan Wallgate	a			19 57					20 55		21 02			21 55			22 02			
	d			19 59							21 03						22 03			
Pemberton	d																			
Orrell	d																			
Upholland	d																			
Rainford	d																			
Kirkby	a																			
Gathurst	d			20 03							21 08						22 08			
Appley Bridge	d			20 07							21 11						22 11			
Parbold	d			20 11							21 15						22 15			
Hoscar	d										21 18									
Burscough Bridge	d			20 15							21 21						22 20			
New Lane	d										21 24									
Bescar Lane	d										21 27									
Meols Cop	d			20 23							21 32						22 27			
Southport	a			20 32							21 42						22 37			
Lostock	d				19 50					20 45						21 45				
Horwich Parkway	d				19 54	20 13		20 39		20 49		21 13				21 49		22 13		
Blackrod	d				19 57					20 52						21 52				
Adlington (Lancashire)	d				20 01					20 56						21 56				
Chorley	d		19 44		20 06	20 21		20 46		21 01		21 21				22 01		22 21		
Leyland	d				20 18					21 12						22 12				
Preston 8 65,97	a		19 55		20 23	20 33		20 57		21 17		21 33				22 17		22 33	23 09	
	d		19 58		20 25	20 38		20 59		21 19		21 38			21 51	22 19		22 35	23 13	
Kirkham & Wesham 97	a				20 34					21 28						22 28				
Poulton-le-Fylde 97	a				20 42	20 56				21 36		21 56				22 36		22 53		
Layton 97	a				20 46					21 40						22 43				
Blackpool North 97	a				20 57	21 06				21 48		22 06				22 51		23 02		
Lancaster 6 65	a	19 19	20 13					21 14							22 11				23 28	
	d	19 24	20 14					21 15							22 11				23 29	
Oxenholme Lake District 65	a																			
Windermere 83	a																			
Carnforth	d	19 34	20 22					21 23							22 21				23 37	
Silverdale	d		20 28					21 29							22 27				23 43	
Arnside	d		20 32					21 33							22 32				23 47	
Grange-over-Sands	d		20 38					21 39							22 38				23 53	
Kents Bank	d		20 41					21 42							22 41				23 56	
Cark	d		20 46					21 47							22 46				00 02	
Ulverston	d		20 54					21 55							22 54				00 10	
Dalton	d		21 02					22 03							23 02				00 18	
Roose	d		21 08					22 09							23 08				00 24	
Barrow-in-Furness	a		21 18					22 18							23 16				00 32	

Table 82

Mondays to Fridays
until 03 September

Manchester - Bolton - Wigan, Kirkby, Southport, Preston, Blackpool North and Barrow-in-Furness

			NT FO	NT FX	NT FO	NT FX	NT FO	NT	TP	NT	NT FX	NT FO	NT FX	NT FO	NT FX	NT FO
									◇1							
Manchester Airport	85 ✈	d						22 19	22 29							
Heald Green	85	d							22 33							
Buxton	86	d														
Hazel Grove	86	d														
Stockport	84	d								22 34						
Manchester Piccadilly 10	⇌	d						22 36	22 46	22 50						
Manchester Oxford Road		d						22 39	22 49	22 53						
Deansgate	⇌	d						22 41	22 51	22 55						
Rochdale	41	d														
Manchester Victoria	⇌	d	22 00	22 10	22 10	22 22	22 22				23 00	23 00	23 20	23 20	23 23	23 23
Salford Central		d	22 04		22 13		22 25					23 03		23 23		23 26
Salford Crescent		a	22 07	22 17	22 17	22 29	22 29	22 46	22 56	22 59	23 07	23 07	23 25	23 26	23 29	23 29
		d	22 08	22 17	22 17	22 30	22 30	22 46	22 56	22 59	23 08	23 08	23 26	23 26	23 30	23 30
Swinton		d		22 23	22 23								23 33	23 33		
Moorside		d		22 26	22 26								23 35	23 35		
Walkden		d		22 29	22 29								23 39	23 39		
Atherton		d		22 35	22 35								23 44	23 44		
Hag Fold		d		22 37	22 37								23 47	23 47		
Daisy Hill		d		22 40	22 40								23 50	23 50		
Kearsley		d								23 07						
Farnworth		d								23 09						
Moses Gate		d								23 11						
Bolton		a	22 19			22 40	22 40	22 56	23 06	23 15	23 19	23 19			23 40	23 40
		d	22 20			22 40	22 40	22 57	23 07	23 15	23 20	23 20			23 40	23 40
Westhoughton		d						23 04		23 23						
Hindley		d		22 45	22 45			23 08		23 27			23 54	23 54		
Ince		d		22 48	22 48								23 57	23 57		
Wigan North Western		a														
Wigan Wallgate		a		22 57	22 57			23 13		23 38			00 04	00 04		
		d						23 15								
Pemberton		d														
Orrell		d														
Upholland		d														
Rainford		d														
Kirkby		a														
Gathurst		d						23 19								
Appley Bridge		d						23 23								
Parbold		d						23 27								
Hoscar		d														
Burscough Bridge		d						23 31								
New Lane		d														
Bescar Lane		d														
Meols Cop		d						23 39								
Southport		a						23 48								
Lostock		d				22 45	22 45								23 45	23 45
Horwich Parkway		d				22 49	22 49		23 13						23 49	23 49
Blackrod		d				22 52	22 52								23 52	23 52
Adlington (Lancashire)		d				22 56	22 56								23 56	23 56
Chorley		d				23 01	23 01		23 21						00 01	00 01
Leyland		d				23 12	23 12								00 12	00 12
Preston 8	65,97	a				23 17	23 17		23 33						00 17	00 17
		d				23 19	23 19		23 35						00 19	00 19
Kirkham & Wesham	97	a				23 28	23 28								00 28	00 28
Poulton-le-Fylde	97	a				23 36	23 36		23 52						00 36	00 36
Layton	97	a				23 40	23 40								00 43	00 43
Blackpool North	97	a				23 48	23 48		00 02						00 50	00 50
Lancaster 6	65	a														
		d														
Oxenholme Lake District	65	a														
Windermere	83	a														
Carnforth		d														
Silverdale		d														
Arnside		d														
Grange-over-Sands		d														
Kents Bank		d														
Cark		d														
Ulverston		d														
Dalton		d														
Roose		d														
Barrow-in-Furness		a														

Table 82

Mondays to Fridays
from 06 September

Manchester - Bolton - Wigan, Kirkby, Southport, Preston, Blackpool North and Barrow-in-Furness

			TP	TP	NT	TP	TP	TP	NT	NT	NT	NT	NT	NT	TP
			◇1	◇1		1	◇1 ✠	◇1 ✠							◇1 ✠
Manchester Airport	85 ✈	d	00 01	04 00				05 45							06 18
Heald Green	85	d						05 49							
Buxton	86	d													
Hazel Grove	86	d													
Stockport	84	d													
Manchester Piccadilly 10	⇌	d	00 16	04 15			05 46	06 03							06 33
Manchester Oxford Road		d						06 06							06 36
Deansgate	⇌	d													
Rochdale	41	d													
Manchester Victoria	⇌	d							05 55	06 00	06 17	06 38	06 45		
Salford Central		d										06 40	06 48		
Salford Crescent		a					05 51		05 59	06 04	06 23	06 44	06 51		
		d					05 52		06 00	06 05	06 24	06 45	06 52		
Swinton		d											06 58		
Moorside		d													
Walkden		d											07 03		
Atherton		d											07 08		
Hag Fold		d													
Daisy Hill		d											07 12		
Kearsley		d										06 52			
Farnworth		d										06 54			
Moses Gate		d										06 57			
Bolton		a	00s31	04s29				06 19	06 11	06 15	06 34	07 00			06 50
		d	00s32	04s29				06 19	06 12	06 15	06 34	07 01			06 50
Westhoughton		d								06 23					
Hindley		d								06 27			07 16		
Ince		d													
Wigan North Western		a		04 44			06 15					07 19			
Wigan Wallgate		a								06 32			07 21		
		d								06 34			07 23		
Pemberton		d								06 38					
Orrell		d								06 42					
Upholland		d								06 45					
Rainford		d								06 49					
Kirkby		a								07 03					
Gathurst		d											07 27		
Appley Bridge		d											07 31		
Parbold		d											07 35		
Hoscar		d													
Burscough Bridge		d											07 39		
New Lane		d													
Bescar Lane		d													
Meols Cop		d											07 47		
Southport		a											07 58		
Lostock		d									06 39				
Horwich Parkway		d									06 43				
Blackrod		d									06 46				
Adlington (Lancashire)		d									06 50				
Chorley		d						06 31			06 55				
Leyland		d					06 28				07 06				
Preston 8	65,97	a	01s03	05s04			06 35	06 42			07 11				07 11
		d	01s05	05s09	05 22		06 37	06 44			07 13				07 14
Kirkham & Wesham	97	a					06 46				07 22				
Poulton-le-Fylde	97	a					06 56				07 30				
Layton	97	a					06 59				07 34				
Blackpool North	97	a	01 30	05 33			07 06				07 43				
Lancaster 6	65	a			05 42			06 59							07 30
		d			05 42	05 46		07 00						07 10	07 30
Oxenholme Lake District	65	a				06 21		07 15							
Windermere	83	a				06 41									
Carnforth		d			05 52									07 20	
Silverdale		d			05 58										
Arnside		d			06 03										
Grange-over-Sands		d			06 09										
Kents Bank		d			06 12										
Cark		d			06 17										
Ulverston		d			06 25										
Dalton		d			06 33										
Roose		d			06 39										
Barrow-in-Furness		a			06 47										

Manchester - Bolton - Wigan, Kirkby, Southport, Preston, Blackpool North and Barrow-in-Furness

	NT	NT	NT	NT	TP ◇1	TP ◇1 ⌶	NT	NT	NT	NT	TP ◇1 ⌶	NT	NT	NT	NT	NT	TP ◇1 ⌶	NT	NT	NT
Manchester Airport 85 ✈ d						07 00					07 25						07 58			
Heald Green 85 d											07 30									
Buxton 86 d	05 54									06 18				06 45						
Hazel Grove 86 d	06 31									06 58				07 25						
Stockport 84 d	06 41									07 10				07 37						
Manchester Piccadilly 10 ⇌ d	06 54					07 15				07 27	07 45			07 54			08 15			
Manchester Oxford Road d	06 57					07 18				07 30				07 57			08 19			
Deansgate ⇌ d	06 59									07 32				07 59						
Rochdale 41 d																				
Manchester Victoria ⇌ d		07 01	07 06				07 16	07 23	07 27			07 47			08 00	08 03		08 11		08 22
Salford Central d		07 04	07 09				07 19	07 26	07 30			07 50			08 03	08 08		08 13		08 25
Salford Crescent a	07 03	07 07	07 12				07 24	07 29	07 33	07 37		07 53		08 04	08 07	08 12		08 17		08 29
d	07 03	07 08	07 13				07 25	07 30	07 33	07 37		07 53		08 04	08 08	08 13		08 17		08 30
Swinton d		07 14										08 00				08 19				
Moorside d		07 17										08 02				08 22				
Walkden d		07 20							07 42			08 06				08 25				
Atherton d		07 26							07 48			08 11				08 31				
Hag Fold d		07 28										08 14				08 33				
Daisy Hill d		07 31							07 51			08 17				08 36				
Kearsley d										07 45										
Farnworth d										07 47										
Moses Gate d										07 49										
Bolton a	07 16		07 23			07 31	07 35	07 41		07 53	07 59			08 14	08 19		08 32	08 27		08 40
d	07 19		07 23			07 31	07 35	07 42		07 53	07 59			08 15	08 20		08 32	08 28		08 40
Westhoughton d			07 31	←						08 01								08 35	←	
Hindley d		07 39	07 35	07 39								08 21				08 43		08 39	08 43	
Ince d		→		07 42												→		08 42	08 46	
Wigan North Western a										08 18										
Wigan Wallgate a			07 40	07 45					08 05			08 26						08 45	08 49	
d			07 41	07 46								08 28						08 47	08 51	
Pemberton d				07 50															08 55	
Orrell d				07 54															08 59	
Upholland d				07 58															09 02	
Rainford d				08 01															09 06	
Kirkby a				08 15															09 20	
Gathurst d			07 46									08 32						08 51		
Appley Bridge d			07 49									08 36						08 55		
Parbold d			07 53															08 59		
Hoscar d			07 56																	
Burscough Bridge d			07 59									08 42						09 03		
New Lane d			08 02																	
Bescar Lane d			08 05																	
Meols Cop d			08 10															09 11		
Southport a			08 22									09 01						09 22		
Lostock d							07 42							08 20						08 45
Horwich Parkway d						07 38	07 46							08 24			08 39			08 49
Blackrod d							07 49													08 52
Adlington (Lancashire) d							07 53							08 29						08 56
Chorley d						07 46	07 58				08 11			08 34			08 47			09 01
Leyland d							08 08							08 43						09 12
Preston 8 65,97 a						07 57	08 14				08 22			08 50			08 58			09 17
d					07 20	07 59	08 15				08 24		08 38	08 51			08 59			09 19
Kirkham & Wesham 97 a						08 08	08 25													09 28
Poulton-le-Fylde 97 a						08 18	08 33										09 16			09 36
Layton 97 a						08 22	08 37													09 43
Blackpool North 97 a						08 29	08 46							09 19			09 25			09 52
Lancaster 8 65 a					07 36						08 39		08 58							
d					07 36						08 40		08 58							
Oxenholme Lake District 65 a											08 54									
Windermere 83 a																				
Carnforth d					07 45								09 08							
Silverdale d					07 51								09 14							
Arnside d					07 55								09 19							
Grange-over-Sands d					08 00								09 25							
Kents Bank d					08 04								09 28							
Cark d					08 08								09 33							
Ulverston d					08 16								09 41							
Dalton d					08 24								09 49							
Roose d					08 30								09 55							
Barrow-in-Furness a					08 39								10 03							

Manchester - Bolton - Wigan, Kirkby, Southport, Preston, Blackpool North and Barrow-in-Furness

	NT	NT	NT	NT	TP ◇1 ⌶	NT	NT	NT	NT	NT	TP ◇1 ⌶	TP ◇1	NT	NT	NT	NT	TP ◇1 ⌶	NT	NT	NT
Manchester Airport 85 ✈ d	08 01				08 25						09 00			09 03			09 29			
Heald Green 85 d	08 05				08 29												09 33			
Buxton 86 d																				
Hazel Grove 86 d						08 30												09 30		
Stockport 84 d						08 41												09 41		
Manchester Piccadilly 10 ⇌ d	08 22				08 46	08 54					09 16			09 22			09 46	09 54		
Manchester Oxford Road d	08 26				08 49	08 58					09 19			09 26			09 49	09 58		
Deansgate ⇌ d	08 28				08 51	09 00								09 28			09 51	10 00		
Rochdale 41 d			08 00												09 04					
Manchester Victoria ⇌ d		08 29	08b33	08 46			09 00	09 07	09 10				09 22		09c33	09 46			10 00	10 07
Salford Central d		08 32	08 36	08 49			09 03	09 10	09 13				09 25		09 36	09 49			10 03	10 10
Salford Crescent a	08 33	08 37	08 39	08 52	08 56	09 04	09 07	09 13	09 16				09 29	09 33	09 39	09 52	09 56	10 04	10 07	10 13
d	08 34	08 37	08 40	08 53	08 56	09 04	09 08	09 13	09 17				09 30	09 34	09 40	09 53	09 56	10 04	10 08	10 13
Swinton d				08 59					09 23							09 59				
Moorside d									09 26											
Walkden d				09 04					09 29							10 04				
Atherton d				09 09					09 35							10 09				
Hag Fold d									09 37											
Daisy Hill d				09 13					09 40							10 13				
Kearsley d			08 47												09 47					
Farnworth d			08 49												09 49					
Moses Gate d			08 52												09 52					
Bolton a	08 44	08 49	08 55		09 06	09 14	09 19	09 23			09 32		09 40	09 45	09 55		10 06	10 14	10 19	10 23
d	08 45	08 49	08 56		09 07	09 15	09 20	09 24			09 33		09 40	09 45	09 56		10 07	10 15	10 20	10 24
Westhoughton d	08 53							09 31						09 53						10 31
Hindley d				09 17				09 35	09 45					09 57		10 17				10 35
Ince d									09 48											
Wigan North Western a																				
Wigan Wallgate a	09 00		09 16	09 22				09 46	09 51					10 02	10 13	10 22				10 46
d	09 05			09 24					09 52					10 03		10 24				
Pemberton d									09 56											
Orrell d									10 00											
Upholland d									10 04											
Rainford d									10 07											
Kirkby a									10 21											
Gathurst d				09 28												10 28				
Appley Bridge d	09 11			09 32										10 10		10 32				
Parbold d	09 15			09 36										10 14		10 36				
Hoscar d				09 39																
Burscough Bridge d	09 20			09 42										10 18		10 40				
New Lane d				09 44																
Bescar Lane d				09 48																
Meols Cop d				09 53												10 48				
Southport a	09 38			10 04										10 37		10 59				
Lostock d						09 20							09 45					10 20		
Horwich Parkway d					09 13	09 24							09 49				10 13	10 24		
Blackrod d													09 52							
Adlington (Lancashire) d													09 56							
Chorley d					09 21	09 32					09 44		10 01				10 21	10 32		
Leyland d						09 42							10 12					10 42		
Preston 8 65,97 a					09 33	09 50					09 55		10 17				10 33	10 51		
d					09 38						09 58	10 07	10 19				10 38			
Kirkham & Wesham 97 a													10 28							
Poulton-le-Fylde 97 a					09 56								10 36				10 56			
Layton 97 a													10 43							
Blackpool North 97 a					10 05								10 53				11 05			
Lancaster 8 65 a											10 13	10 22								
d										09 39	10 14	10 23								
Oxenholme Lake District 65 a																				
Windermere 83 a																				
Carnforth d										09 49		10 32								
Silverdale d										09 56										
Arnside d										10 00		10 41								
Grange-over-Sands d										10 06		10 46								
Kents Bank d										10 10										
Cark d										10 14										
Ulverston d										10 23		10 59								
Dalton d										10 31										
Roose d										10 37										
Barrow-in-Furness a										10 47		11 17								

b arr. 0822

c arr. 0926

Table 82

Mondays to Fridays
from 06 September

Manchester - Bolton - Wigan, Kirkby, Southport, Preston, Blackpool North and Barrow-in-Furness

	NT	NT	TP	TP	NT	NT	NT	NT	TP	NT	NT	NT	NT	NT	TP	NT	NT	NT	NT	TP	NT	NT
			◇1	◇1 ⊼					◇1 ⊼						◇1 A ⊼					◇1 ⊼		
Manchester Airport 85 ✈ d				10 00		10 03			10 29						11 00		11 03			11 29		
Heald Green 85 d									10 33											11 33		
Buxton 86 d																						
Hazel Grove 86 d										10 31											11 31	
Stockport 84 d										10 41											11 41	
Manchester Piccadilly 10 ⇌ d				10 16		10 22			10 46	10 54					11 16		11 22			11 46	11 54	
Manchester Oxford Road d				10 19		10 26			10 49	10 58					11 19		11 26			11 49	11 58	
Deansgate ⇌ d						10 28			10 51	11 00							11 28			11 51	12 00	
Rochdale 41 d							10 04											11 04				
Manchester Victoria ⇌ d	10 10				10 22		10c33	10 46			11 00	11 07	11 10			11 22		11e33	11 46			12 00
Salford Central d	10 13				10 25		10 36	10 49			11 03	11 10	11 13			11 25		11 36	11 49			12 03
Salford Crescent a	10 16				10 29	10 33	10 39	10 52	10 56	11 04	11 07	11 13	11 16			11 29	11 33	11 39	11 52	11 56	12 04	12 07
d	10 17				10 30	10 34	10 40	10 53	10 56	11 04	11 08	11 13	11 17			11 30	11 34	11 40	11 53	11 56	12 04	12 08
Swinton d	10 23							10 59					11 23						11 59			
Moorside d	10 26												11 26									
Walkden d	10 29							11 04					11 29						12 04			
Atherton d	10 35							11 09					11 35						12 09			
Hag Fold d	10 37												11 37									
Daisy Hill d	10 40							11 13					11 40						12 13			
Kearsley d							10 47											11 47				
Farnworth d							10 49											11 49				
Moses Gate d							10 52											11 52				
Bolton a				10 32	10 40	10 45	10 55		11 06	11 14	11 19	11 23			11 32	11 40	11 45	11 55		12 06	12 14	12 19
d				10 33	10 40	10 45	10 56		11 07	11 15	11 20	11 24			11 33	11 40	11 45	11 56		12 07	12 15	12 20
Westhoughton d						10 53						11 31					11 53					
Hindley d	10 45					10 57		11 17				11 35	11 45				11 57		12 17			
Ince d	10 48												11 48									
Wigan North Western a																						
Wigan Wallgate a	10 51					11 02	11 15	11 22				11 46	11 51				12 02	12 15	12 22			
d	10 52					11 03		11 24					11 52				12 03		12 24			
Pemberton d	10 56												11 56									
Orrell d	11 00												12 00									
Upholland d	11 04												12 04									
Rainford d	11 07												12 07									
Kirkby a	11 21												12 21									
Gathurst d								11 28											12 28			
Appley Bridge d						11 10		11 32									12 10		12 32			
Parbold d						11 14		11 36									12 14		12 36			
Hoscar d								11 39														
Burscough Bridge d						11 18		11 42									12 18		12 41			
New Lane d								11 44														
Bescar Lane d								11 48														
Meols Cop d								11 53											12 49			
Southport a						11 37		12 04									12 37		12 59			
Lostock d					10 45					11 20						11 45					12 20	
Horwich Parkway d					10 49				11 13	11 24						11 49				12 13	12 24	
Blackrod d					10 52											11 52						
Adlington (Lancashire) d					10 56											11 56						
Chorley d				10 44	11 01				11 21	11 32					11 44	12 01				12 21	12 32	
Leyland d					11 12					11 42						12 12					12 42	
Preston 8 65,97 a				10 55	11 17				11 33	11 50					11 55	12 17				12 33	12 50	
d			10 45	10 58	11 19				11 38						11 58	12 19				12 38		
Kirkham & Wesham 97 a					11 28											12 28						
Poulton-le-Fylde 97 a					11 36				11 56							12 36				12 56		
Layton 97 a					11 43											12 43						
Blackpool North 97 a					11 52				12 05							12 52				13 05		
Lancaster 6 65 a		10 45	11 00	11 13											12 13							
d		10 49	11 01	11 14										11 32	12 14							
Oxenholme Lake District 65 a			11 17	11 28																		
Windermere 83 a			11 39																			
Carnforth d		11b09												11 42	12 23							
Silverdale d														11 49								
Arnside d														11 53	12 31							
Grange-over-Sands d														11 59	12 37							
Kents Bank d														12 03								
Cark d														12 07								
Ulverston d														12 15	12 49							
Dalton d														12 24								
Roose d														12 30								
Barrow-in-Furness a														12 39	13 10							

A ⊼ to Chorley
b arr. 1058
c arr. 1026
e arr. 1126

Table 82

Mondays to Fridays
from 06 September

Manchester - Bolton - Wigan, Kirkby, Southport, Preston, Blackpool North and Barrow-in-Furness

	TP	NT	NT	TP	NT	NT	NT	NT	TP	NT	NT	NT	NT	NT	NT	TP	TP	NT	NT	NT	NT
	◇1 ⊼			◇1					◇1 ⊼							◇1 ⊼	◇1				
Manchester Airport 85 ✈ d	12 00					12 03			12 29							13 00			13 03		
Heald Green 85 d									12 33												
Buxton 86 d																					
Hazel Grove 86 d										12 31											
Stockport 84 d										12 41											
Manchester Piccadilly 10 ⇌ d	12 16					12 22			12 46	12 54						13 16			13 22		
Manchester Oxford Road d	12 19					12 26			12 49	12 58						13 19			13 26		
Deansgate ⇌ d						12 28			12 51	13 00									13 28		
Rochdale 41 d							12 04													13 04	
Manchester Victoria ⇌ d		12 07	12 10		12 22		12b33	12 46			13 00	13 07	13 10					13 22		13c33	13 46
Salford Central d		12 10	12 13		12 25		12 36	12 49			13 03	13 10	13 13					13 25		13 36	13 49
Salford Crescent a		12 13	12 16		12 29	12 33	12 39	12 52	12 56	13 04	13 07	13 13	13 16					13 29	13 33	13 39	13 52
d		12 13	12 17		12 30	12 34	12 40	12 53	12 56	13 04	13 08	13 13	13 17					13 30	13 34	13 40	13 53
Swinton d			12 23					12 59					13 23								13 59
Moorside d			12 26										13 26								
Walkden d			12 29					13 04					13 29								14 04
Atherton d			12 35					13 09					13 35								14 09
Hag Fold d			12 37										13 37								
Daisy Hill d			12 40					13 13					13 40								14 13
Kearsley d							12 47													13 47	
Farnworth d							12 49													13 49	
Moses Gate d							12 52													13 52	
Bolton a	12 32	12 23			12 40	12 45	12 55		13 06	13 14	13 19	13 23				13 32		13 40	13 45	13 55	
d	12 33	12 24			12 40	12 45	12 56		13 07	13 15	13 20	13 24				13 33		13 40	13 45	13 56	
Westhoughton d		12 31				12 53						13 31							13 53		
Hindley d		12 35	12 45			12 57		13 17				13 35	13 45						13 57		14 17
Ince d			12 48										13 48								
Wigan North Western a																					
Wigan Wallgate a		12 46	12 51			13 02	13 13	13 22				13 46	13 51						14 02	14 15	14 22
d			12 52			13 03		13 24					13 52						14 03		14 24
Pemberton d			12 56										13 56								
Orrell d			13 00										14 00								
Upholland d			13 04										14 04								
Rainford d			13 07										14 07								
Kirkby a			13 21										14 21								
Gathurst d								13 28													14 28
Appley Bridge d						13 10		13 32											14 10		14 32
Parbold d						13 14		13 36											14 14		14 36
Hoscar d								13 39													
Burscough Bridge d						13 18		13 42											14 18		14 41
New Lane d								13 44													
Bescar Lane d								13 48													
Meols Cop d								13 53													14 49
Southport a						13 37		14 02											14 37		15 01
Lostock d					12 45					13 20								13 45			
Horwich Parkway d					12 49				13 13	13 24								13 49			
Blackrod d					12 52													13 52			
Adlington (Lancashire) d					12 56													13 56			
Chorley d	12 44				13 01				13 21	13 32						13 44		14 01			
Leyland d					13 12					13 42								14 12			
Preston 8 65,97 a	12 55				13 17				13 33	13 50						13 55		14 17			
d	12 58			13 04	13 19				13 38							13 58	14 04	14 19			
Kirkham & Wesham 97 a					13 28													14 28			
Poulton-le-Fylde 97 a					13 36				13 56									14 36			
Layton 97 a					13 43													14 43			
Blackpool North 97 a					13 52				14 05									14 53			
Lancaster 6 65 a	13 13			13 19											13 42	14 13	14 19				
d	13 14			13 20										13 32	13 48	14 14	14 20				
Oxenholme Lake District 65 a	13 28			13 36																	
Windermere 83 a				13 56																	
Carnforth d														13 42	13 58		14 28				
Silverdale d														13 48							
Arnside d														13 52			14 37				
Grange-over-Sands d														13 58			14 42				
Kents Bank d														14 02							
Cark d														14 06							
Ulverston d														14 14			14 55				
Dalton d														14 22							
Roose d														14 28							
Barrow-in-Furness a														14 38			15 15				

b arr. 1225
c arr. 1325

Table 82

Mondays to Fridays
from 06 September

Manchester - Bolton - Wigan, Kirkby, Southport, Preston, Blackpool North and Barrow-in-Furness

	TP ◇1 ⊼	NT	NT	TP ◇1 ⊼	NT	NT	NT	NT	NT		NT	TP ◇1 ⊼	NT	NT	NT	NT	NT	NT	TP ◇1 A ⊼		NT	NT	NT	NT
Manchester Airport 85 ✈ d	13 29			14 00				14 03				14 29							15 00		15 03			
Heald Green 85 d	13 33											14 33												
Buxton 86 d																								
Hazel Grove 86 d		13 31											14 31											
Stockport 84 d		13 41											14 41											
Manchester Piccadilly 10 ⇌ d	13 46	13 54		14 16				14 22				14 46	14 54						15 16		15 22			
Manchester Oxford Road d	13 49	13 58		14 19				14 26				14 49	14 58						15 19		15 26			
Deansgate ⇌ d	13 51	14 00						14 28				14 51	15 00								15 28			
Rochdale 41 d									14 04													15 04		
Manchester Victoria ⇌ d			14 00		14 07	14 10	14 22		14b33		14 46			15 00	15 07	15 10	15 22					15c33	15 40	15 46
Salford Central d			14 03		14 10	14 13	14 25		14 36		14 49			15 03	15 10	15 13	15 25					15 36	15 43	15 49
Salford Crescent a	13 56	14 04	14 07		14 13	14 16	14 29	14 33	14 39		14 52	14 56	15 04	15 07	15 13	15 16	15 29				15 33	15 39	15 46	15 52
d	13 56	14 04	14 08		14 13	14 17	14 30	14 34	14 40		14 53	14 56	15 04	15 08	15 13	15 17	15 30				15 34	15 40	15 47	15 53
Swinton d						14 23					14 59					15 23								15 59
Moorside d						14 26										15 26								
Walkden d						14 29					15 04					15 29								16 04
Atherton d						14 35					15 09					15 35								16 09
Hag Fold d						14 37										15 37								
Daisy Hill d						14 40					15 13					15 40								16 13
Kearsley d									14 47													15 47		
Farnworth d									14 49													15 49		
Moses Gate d									14 52													15 52		
Bolton a	14 06	14 14	14 19	14 32	14 23		14 40	14 45	14 55			15 06	15 14	15 19	15 23		15 40		15 32		15 45	15 55	15 59	
d	14 07	14 15	14 20	14 33	14 24		14 40	14 45	14 56			15 07	15 15	15 20	15 24		15 40		15 33		15 45	15 56	16 00	
Westhoughton d					14 31			14 53							15 31						15 53			
Hindley d					14 35	14 45		14 57			15 17				15 35	15 45					15 57			16 17
Ince d						14 48										15 48								
Wigan North Western a																								
Wigan Wallgate a					14 46	14 51		15 02	15 15		15 22				15 46	15 51					16 02	16 15		16 22
d						14 52		15 03			15 24					15 58					16 03			16 24
Pemberton d						14 56										16 02								
Orrell d						15 00										16 06								
Upholland d						15 04										16 09								
Rainford d						15 07										16 13								
Kirkby a						15 21										16 27								
Gathurst d											15 28										16 08			16 28
Appley Bridge d								15 10			15 32										16 11			16 32
Parbold d								15 14			15 36										16 15			16 36
Hoscar d																					16 18			
Burscough Bridge d								15 18			15 40										16 21			16 40
New Lane d																					16 24			
Bescar Lane d																					16 27			
Meols Cop d											15 48										16 32			16 48
Southport a								15 37			15 59										16 44			16 59
Lostock d		14 20					14 45						15 20				15 45							
Horwich Parkway d	14 13	14 24					14 49					15 13	15 24				15 49							
Blackrod d							14 52										15 52							
Adlington (Lancashire) d							14 56										15 56							
Chorley d	14 21	14 32		14 44			15 01					15 21	15 32				16 01		15 44					
Leyland d		14 42					15 12						15 42				16 12							
Preston 8 65,97 a	14 33	14 50		14 55			15 17					15 33	15 50				16 19		15 55					
d	14 38			14 58			15 19					15 38							15 58					
Kirkham & Wesham 97 a							15 28																	
Poulton-le-Fylde 97 a	14 56						15 36					15 56												
Layton 97 a							15 43																	
Blackpool North 97 a	15 05						15 52					16 05												
Lancaster 6 65 a				15 13															16 13					
d				15 14														15 34	16 14					
Oxenholme Lake District 65 a				15 28																				
Windermere 83 a																								
Carnforth d																		15 44	16 22					
Silverdale d																		15 51	16 28					
Arnside d																		15 55	16 32					
Grange-over-Sands d																		16 01	16 38					
Kents Bank d																		16 05	16 41					
Cark d																		16 09	16 46					
Ulverston d																		16 17	16 54					
Dalton d																		16 26	17 02					
Roose d																		16 32	17 08					
Barrow-in-Furness a																		16 39	17 18					

A ⊼ to Chorley

b arr. 1425

c arr. 1526

Table 82

Mondays to Fridays
from 06 September

Manchester - Bolton - Wigan, Kirkby, Southport, Preston, Blackpool North and Barrow-in-Furness

	TP ◇1 ⊼	NT	NT	NT	NT		TP ◇1 ⊼	NT	TP ◇1	NT	NT	NT	NT	NT	TP ◇1 ⊼		NT	NT	NT	NT	TP ◇1 ⊼	NT	TP ◇1	NT
Manchester Airport 85 ✈ d	15 29						16 00					16 03			16 29						17 00			
Heald Green 85 d	15 33														16 33									
Buxton 86 d													15 22											
Hazel Grove 86 d		15 31											16 02					16 30						
Stockport 84 d		15 41											16 12					16 41						
Manchester Piccadilly 10 ⇌ d	15 46	15 54					16 16					16 22	16 27		16 46			16 54			17 15			
Manchester Oxford Road d	15 49	15 58					16 19					16 26	16 30		16 49			16 58			17 18			
Deansgate ⇌ d	15 51	16 00										16 28	16 33					17 00						
Rochdale 41 d														16 04										
Manchester Victoria ⇌ d			16 07	16 10						16 20	16 23			16b36			16 46		17 00	17c06		17 10		17 19
Salford Central d			16 10	16 13						16 23	16 26			16 39			16 49		17 03	17 09		17 12		17 22
Salford Crescent a	15 56	16 04	16 13	16 16						16 26	16 30	16 34	16 38	16 42			16 52	17 04	17 07	17 13		17 16		17 25
d	15 56	16 04	16 13	16 17						16 27	16 31	16 34	16 38	16 43			16 53	17 04	17 08	17 14		17 17		17 27
Swinton d				16 23													16 59					17 23		
Moorside d				16 26													17 02					17 26		
Walkden d				16 29													17 05					17 31		
Atherton d				16 35													17 11			17 26		17 37		
Hag Fold d				16 37													17 14					17 39		
Daisy Hill d				16 40													17 17			17 30		17 43		
Kearsley d														16 50										
Farnworth d														16 52										
Moses Gate d			16 21											16 55										
Bolton a	16 06	16 19	16 25				16 32			16 37	16 42	16 45	16 48	16 58	17 05			17 14	17 19		17 31			17 37
d	16 07		16 25				16 33			16 37	16 43	16 45	16 49	16 59	17 06			17 15	17 20		17 32			17 37
Westhoughton d			16 33									16 53		17 06										
Hindley d			16 37	16 45								16 57		17 10			17 21					17 48		
Ince d				16 48													17 24					17 51		
Wigan North Western a																								
Wigan Wallgate a			16 48	16 51								17 02		17 21			17 33			17 38		17 54		
d				16 52								17 03								17 40		17 55		
Pemberton d				16 56																		17 59		
Orrell d				17 00																		18 03		
Upholland d				17 04																		18 07		
Rainford d				17 07																		18 10		
Kirkby a				17 21																		18 24		
Gathurst d												17 08								17 44				
Appley Bridge d												17 11								17 48				
Parbold d												17 15								17 52				
Hoscar d																								
Burscough Bridge d												17 20								17 57				
New Lane d																								
Bescar Lane d																								
Meols Cop d												17 27								18 05				
Southport a												17 39								18 16				
Lostock d	16 12									16 43			16 54					17 20						17 43
Horwich Parkway d	16 15									16 47			16 58					17 25						17 47
Blackrod d										16 51			17 01											17 51
Adlington (Lancashire) d										16 55			17 05											17 55
Chorley d	16 23						16 44			17 00			17 10		17 19			17 32			17 44			18 00
Leyland d										17 11			17 21					17 42						18 11
Preston 8 65,97 a	16 35						16 55			17 19			17 26		17 30			17 51			17 55			18 16
d	16 38						17 00		17 04	17 21			17 28		17 32						18 00		18 08	18 18
Kirkham & Wesham 97 a	16 47									17 30					17 41									18 27
Poulton-le-Fylde 97 a	16 57									17 38					17 51									18 35
Layton 97 a	17 00									17 43					17 54									18 39
Blackpool North 97 a	17 07									17 52					18 02									18 51
Lancaster 6 65 a							17 15	17 14	17 23				17 48								18 15		18 23	
d					16 55		17 16	17 19	17 25				17 48								18 16		18 24	
Oxenholme Lake District 65 a							17 30		17 43												18 30			
Windermere 83 a									18 08															
Carnforth d					17 05			17 28					18 00										18 35	
Silverdale d					17 12			17 35					18 06										18 41	
Arnside d					17 16			17 40					18 11										18 45	
Grange-over-Sands d					17 22			17 46					18 19										18 51	
Kents Bank d					17 26			17 49					18 23										18 54	
Cark d					17 30			17 54					18 27										18 59	
Ulverston d					17 39			18 02					18 35										19 07	
Dalton d					17 48			18 10					18 43										19 15	
Roose d					17 54			18 16					18 49										19 21	
Barrow-in-Furness a					18 02			18 25					18 59										19 30	

b arr. 1627

c arr. 1658

Table 82

Mondays to Fridays
from 06 September

Manchester - Bolton - Wigan, Kirkby, Southport, Preston, Blackpool North and Barrow-in-Furness

		NT	TP ◇1	NT	NT	NT	NT	NT	NT	NT	TP ◇1	NT		TP ◇1	NT	NT	NT	NT	NT	TP ◇1	NT	NT		NT	NT
Manchester Airport 85 ✈	d		17 29	17 03							18 00						18 03			18 29					
Heald Green 85	d		17 33																	18 33					
Buxton 86	d				16 25				16 56												17 55				
Hazel Grove 86	d				17 02				17 33												18 33				
Stockport 84	d				17 12				17 41												18 41				
Manchester Piccadilly 10 ⇌	d		17 46	17 22	17 27				17 54		18 16						18 22			18 46	18 54				
Manchester Oxford Road	d		17 49	17 26	17 30				17 58		18 19						18 26			18 49	18 58				
Deansgate ⇌	d		17 51		17 33				18 00								18 28			18 51	19 00				
Rochdale 41	d	17 03														18 02									
Manchester Victoria ⇌	d	17 23				17 36	17 40	17 45		18 00		18 10			18 20	18 23		18 33	18 45			19 00		19 10	
Salford Central	d	17 27				17 39	17 43	17 48		18 03		18 13			18 23	18 26		18 36	18 48			19 03		19 13	
Salford Crescent	a	17 29	17 55	17 34	17 38	17 42	17 46	17 51	18 04	18 07		18 16			18 26	18 30	18 34	18 39	18 51	18 56	19 04	19 07		19 16	
	d	17 30	17 55	17 34	17 38	17 43	17 47	17 52	18 04	18 08		18 17			18 27	18 31	18 34	18 40	18 52	18 56	19 04	19 08		19 17	
Swinton	d							17 58				18 23							18 58					19 23	
Moorside	d							18 01				18 26							19 01					19 26	
Walkden	d							18 05				18 29							19 04					19 29	
Atherton	d						17 59	18 11				18 35							19 10					19 35	
Hag Fold	d							18 13				18 37							19 12					19 37	
Daisy Hill	d						18 03	18 17				18 40							19 15					19 40	
Kearsley	d					17 53												18 47							
Farnworth	d					17 55												18 49							
Moses Gate	d					17 57												18 52							
Bolton	a	17 42	18 06	17 45	17 48	18 01			18 14	18 19	18 32				18 37	18 42	18 45	18 55		19 06	19 19	19 20			
	d	17 43	18 07	17 45	17 49	18 01			18 15	18 20	18 33				18 37	18 43	18 45	18 56		19 07		19 20			
Westhoughton	d			17 53		18 09											18 53	19 03							
Hindley	d					18 13		18 22				18 45					18 57	19 09	19 20					19 45	
Ince	d							18 25				18 48							19 23					19 48	
Wigan North Western	a											18 56													
Wigan Wallgate	a			18 01		18 24	18 11	18 28									19 02	19 20	19 32					19 57	
	d			18 02			18 15	18 29									19 03								
Pemberton	d							18 33																	
Orrell	d							18 37																	
Upholland	d							18 41																	
Rainford	d							18 44																	
Kirkby	a							18 57																	
Gathurst	d						18 19										19 08								
Appley Bridge	d			18 09			18 23										19 11								
Parbold	d			18 13			18 28										19 15								
Hoscar	d																								
Burscough Bridge	d			18 17			18 33										19 19								
New Lane	d																								
Bescar Lane	d																								
Meols Cop	d						18 41										19 27								
Southport	a			18 37			18 52										19 39								
Lostock	d		18 12		17 54				18 20						18 42					19 12					
Horwich Parkway	d		18 15		17 58				18 24						18 46					19 15					
Blackrod	d		18 18		18 01										18 49										
Adlington (Lancashire)	d				18 05										18 53										
Chorley	d		18 25		18 10				18 32		18 44				18 58					19 23					
Leyland	d		18 33						18 42						19 10										
Preston 8 65,97	a		18 38		18 25				18 48		18 55				19 18					19 33					
	d		18 40		18 26				18 49		19 00			19 04	19 19					19 38					
Kirkham & Wesham 97	a		18 49												19 28										
Poulton-le-Fylde 97	a		18 59		18 43										19 36					19 56					
Layton 97	a		19 02												19 43										
Blackpool North 97	a		19 09		18 55				19 18						19 54					20 05					
Lancaster 6 65	a										19 15			19 20											19 19
	d										19 16			19 20											19 24
Oxenholme Lake District 65	a										19 30														
Windermere 83	a																								
Carnforth	d													19 29											19 34
Silverdale	d													19 35											
Arnside	d													19 39											
Grange-over-Sands	d													19 44											
Kents Bank	d													19 48											
Cark	d													19 52											
Ulverston	d													20 00											
Dalton	d													20 08											
Roose	d													20 14											
Barrow-in-Furness	a													20 24											

Table 82

Mondays to Fridays
from 06 September

Manchester - Bolton - Wigan, Kirkby, Southport, Preston, Blackpool North and Barrow-in-Furness

		TP ◇1	NT	NT	TP ◇1	NT	TP ◇1	NT		NT	NT		TP ◇1	NT	NT	NT	NT	NT				TP ◇1	TP ◇1	NT FX	NT FO
Manchester Airport 85 ✈	d	19 00	19 03		19 29		20 00				20 03		20 29					21 03				21 29	22 00		
Heald Green 85	d				19 33								20 33									21 33			
Buxton 86	d																								
Hazel Grove 86	d																								
Stockport 84	d																								
Manchester Piccadilly 10 ⇌	d	19 16	19 20		19 46		20 16				20 20		20 46					21 20				21 46	22 16		
Manchester Oxford Road	d	19 19	19 24		19 49		20 19				20 24		20 49					21 24				21 49	22 19		
Deansgate ⇌	d		19 26		19 51						20 26		20 51					21 26				21 51			
Rochdale 41	d																								
Manchester Victoria ⇌	d			19 28		20 00		20 10		20 22				21 00	21 10		21 22							22 00	22 00
Salford Central	d			19 31		20 03		20 13		20 25				21 03	21 13		21 25								22 04
Salford Crescent	a		19 29	19 34	19 56	20 07		20 16		20 29	20 33		20 56	21 07	21 16		21 29	21 33				21 56		22 07	22 07
	d		19 30	19 35	19 56	20 08		20 17		20 30	20 34		20 56	21 08	21 17		21 30	21 34				21 56		22 08	22 08
Swinton	d							20 23							21 23										
Moorside	d							20 26							21 26										
Walkden	d							20 29							21 29										
Atherton	d							20 35							21 35										
Hag Fold	d							20 37							21 37										
Daisy Hill	d							20 40							21 40										
Kearsley	d																								
Farnworth	d																								
Moses Gate	d																								
Bolton	a	19 32	19 40	19 45	20 06	20 19	20 32			20 40	20 45		21 06	21 19			21 40	21 45				22 06	22 32	22 19	22 19
	d	19 33	19 40	19 45	20 07	20 20	20 33			20 40	20 45		21 07	21 20			21 40	21 45				22 07	22 33	22 20	22 20
Westhoughton	d		19 48								20 53							21 53							
Hindley	d		19 52					20 45			20 57				21 45			21 57							
Ince	d							20 48							21 48										
Wigan North Western	a																						22 48		
Wigan Wallgate	a		19 57					20 57			21 02				21 57			22 02							
	d		19 59								21 03							22 03							
Pemberton	d																								
Orrell	d																								
Upholland	d																								
Rainford	d																								
Kirkby	a																								
Gathurst	d		20 03								21 08							22 08							
Appley Bridge	d		20 07								21 11							22 11							
Parbold	d		20 11								21 15							22 15							
Hoscar	d										21 18														
Burscough Bridge	d		20 15								21 21							22 20							
New Lane	d										21 24														
Bescar Lane	d										21 27														
Meols Cop	d		20 23								21 32							22 27							
Southport	a		20 34								21 42							22 39							
Lostock	d			19 50						20 45							21 45								
Horwich Parkway	d			19 54	20 13		20 39			20 49			21 13				21 49					22 13			
Blackrod	d			19 57						20 52							21 52								
Adlington (Lancashire)	d			20 01						20 56							21 56								
Chorley	d	19 44		20 06	20 21		20 46			21 01			21 21				22 01					22 21			
Leyland	d			20 18						21 12							22 12								
Preston 8 65,97	a	19 55		20 23	20 33		20 57			21 17			21 33				22 17					22 33	23 09		
	d	19 58		20 25	20 38		20 59			21 19			21 38			21 51	22 19					22 35	23 13		
Kirkham & Wesham 97	a			20 34						21 28							22 28								
Poulton-le-Fylde 97	a			20 42	20 56					21 36			21 56				22 36					22 53			
Layton 97	a			20 46						21 40							22 43								
Blackpool North 97	a			20 59	21 06					21 50			22 06				22 53					23 02			
Lancaster 6 65	a	20 13					21 14									22 11							23 28		
	d	20 14					21 15									22 11							23 29		
Oxenholme Lake District 65	a																								
Windermere 83	a																								
Carnforth	d	20 22					21 23									22 21							23 37		
Silverdale	d	20 28					21 29									22 27							23 43		
Arnside	d	20 32					21 33									22 32							23 47		
Grange-over-Sands	d	20 38					21 39									22 38							23 53		
Kents Bank	d	20 41					21 42									22 41							23 56		
Cark	d	20 46					21 47									22 46							00 02		
Ulverston	d	20 54					21 55									22 54							00 10		
Dalton	d	21 02					22 03									23 02							00 18		
Roose	d	21 08					22 09									23 08							00 24		
Barrow-in-Furness	a	21 18					22 18									23 16							00 32		

Table 82

Mondays to Fridays
from 06 September

Manchester - Bolton - Wigan, Kirkby, Southport, Preston, Blackpool North and Barrow-in-Furness

			NT FO	NT FX	NT FX	NT FO	NT	TP ◇1	NT	NT FX	NT FO	NT FX	NT FO	NT FX	NT FO
Manchester Airport	85 ✈	d					22 19	22 29							
Heald Green	85	d						22 33							
Buxton	86	d													
Hazel Grove	86	d													
Stockport	84	d							22 34						
Manchester Piccadilly 10	⇌	d					22 36	22 46	22 50						
Manchester Oxford Road		d					22 39	22 49	22 53						
Deansgate	⇌	d					22 41	22 51	22 55						
Rochdale	41	d													
Manchester Victoria	⇌	d	22 10	22 10	22 22	22 22				23 00	23 00	23 20	23 20	23 23	23 23
Salford Central		d	22 13			22 25					23 03		23 23		23 26
Salford Crescent		a	22 17	22 17	22 29	22 29	22 46	22 56	22 59	23 07	23 07	23 25	23 26	23 29	23 29
		d	22 17	22 17	22 30	22 30	22 46	22 56	22 59	23 08	23 08	23 26	23 26	23 30	23 30
Swinton		d	22 23	22 23								23 33	23 33		
Moorside		d	22 26	22 26								23 35	23 35		
Walkden		d	22 29	22 29								23 39	23 39		
Atherton		d	22 35	22 35								23 44	23 44		
Hag Fold		d	22 37	22 37								23 47	23 47		
Daisy Hill		d	22 40	22 40								23 50	23 50		
Kearsley		d							23 07						
Farnworth		d							23 09						
Moses Gate		d							23 11						
Bolton		a			22 40	22 40	22 56	23 06	23 15	23 19	23 19			23 40	23 40
		d			22 40	22 40	22 57	23 07	23 15	23 20	23 20			23 40	23 40
Westhoughton		d					23 04		23 23						
Hindley		d	22 45	22 45			23 08		23 27			23 54	23 54		
Ince		d	22 48	22 48								23 57	23 57		
Wigan North Western		a													
Wigan Wallgate		a	22 57	22 57			23 13		23 40			00 06	00 06		
		d					23 15								
Pemberton		d													
Orrell		d													
Upholland		d													
Rainford		d													
Kirkby		a													
Gathurst		d					23 19								
Appley Bridge		d					23 23								
Parbold		d					23 27								
Hoscar		d													
Burscough Bridge		d					23 31								
New Lane		d													
Bescar Lane		d													
Meols Cop		d					23 39								
Southport		a					23 50								
Lostock		d			22 45	22 45								23 45	23 45
Horwich Parkway		d			22 49	22 49		23 13						23 49	23 49
Blackrod		d			22 52	22 52								23 52	23 52
Adlington (Lancashire)		d			22 56	22 56								23 56	23 56
Chorley		d			23 01	23 01		23 21						00 01	00 01
Leyland		d			23 12	23 12								00 12	00 12
Preston 8	65,97	a			23 17	23 17		23 33						00 17	00 17
		d			23 19	23 19		23 35						00 19	00 19
Kirkham & Wesham	97	a			23 28	23 28								00 28	00 28
Poulton-le-Fylde	97	a			23 36	23 36		23 52						00 36	00 36
Layton	97	a			23 40	23 40								00 43	00 43
Blackpool North	97	a			23 50	23 50		00 02						00 52	00 52
Lancaster 6	65	a													
		d													
Oxenholme Lake District	65	a													
Windermere	83	a													
Carnforth		d													
Silverdale		d													
Arnside		d													
Grange-over-Sands		d													
Kents Bank		d													
Cark		d													
Ulverston		d													
Dalton		d													
Roose		d													
Barrow-in-Furness		a													

Table 82

Saturdays
until 04 September

Manchester - Bolton - Wigan, Kirkby, Southport, Preston, Blackpool North and Barrow-in-Furness

			TP ◇1	TP ◇1	TP ◇1	NT	NT	NT	TP ◇1 🍴	NT	NT	NT	NT	NT	NT	TP ◇1
Manchester Airport	85 ✈	d	00 01	04 00	05 29				06 18							
Heald Green	85	d			05 33											
Buxton	86	d										05 59				
Hazel Grove	86	d										06 33				
Stockport	84	d										06 41				
Manchester Piccadilly 10	⇌	d	00 16	04 15	05 46				06 33			06 54				
Manchester Oxford Road		d							06 36			06 57				
Deansgate	⇌	d										06 59				
Rochdale	41	d														
Manchester Victoria	⇌	d				05 55	06 00	06 17		06 38	06 45		07 06	07 10		
Salford Central		d								06 40	06 48		07 09	07 13		
Salford Crescent		a			05 51	05 59	06 04	06 23		06 44	06 51	07 03	07 12	07 16		
		d			05 52	06 00	06 05	06 24		06 45	06 52	07 03	07 13	07 16		
Swinton		d									06 58		07 19			
Moorside		d											07 22			
Walkden		d									07 03		07 25			
Atherton		d									07 08		07 31			
Hag Fold		d											07 33			
Daisy Hill		d									07 12		07 36			
Kearsley		d								06 52						
Farnworth		d								06 54						
Moses Gate		d								06 57						
Bolton		a	00s31	04s29	06 02	06 11	06 15	06 34	06 50	07 00		07 16		07 26		
		d	00s32	04s29	06 02	06 12	06 15	06 34	06 50	07 01		07 19		07 27		
Westhoughton		d					06 23							07 34	←	
Hindley		d					06 27				07 16		07 42	07 38	07 42	
Ince		d											→		07 45	
Wigan North Western		a								07 19						
Wigan Wallgate		a					06 32				07 21			07 43	07 48	
		d					06 34				07 23			07 45	07 50	
Pemberton		d					06 38								07 54	
Orrell		d					06 42								07 58	
Upholland		d					06 45								08 01	
Rainford		d					06 49								08 05	
Kirkby		a					07 01								08 17	
Gathurst		d									07 27			07 49		
Appley Bridge		d									07 31			07 53		
Parbold		d									07 35			07 57		
Hoscar		d												08 00		
Burscough Bridge		d									07 39			08 03		
New Lane		d												08 05		
Bescar Lane		d												08 09		
Meols Cop		d									07 47			08 14		
Southport		a									07 56			08 23		
Lostock		d						06 39								
Horwich Parkway		d			06 09			06 43								
Blackrod		d						06 46								
Adlington (Lancashire)		d						06 50								
Chorley		d			06 16			06 55								
Leyland		d			06 28			07 06								
Preston 8	65,97	a	01s03	05s04	06 35			07 11	07 11							
		d	01s05	05s06	06 37			07 13	07 14							07 20
Kirkham & Wesham	97	a			06 46			07 22								
Poulton-le-Fylde	97	a			06 56			07 30								
Layton	97	a			06 59			07 34								
Blackpool North	97	a	01 30	05 33	07 06			07 41								
Lancaster 6	65	a							07 30							07 36
		d							07 30							07 36
Oxenholme Lake District	65	a														
Windermere	83	a														
Carnforth		d														07 45
Silverdale		d														07 51
Arnside		d														07 55
Grange-over-Sands		d														08 00
Kents Bank		d														08 04
Cark		d														08 08
Ulverston		d														08 16
Dalton		d														08 24
Roose		d														08 30
Barrow-in-Furness		a														08 39

Table 82

Saturdays until 04 September

Manchester - Bolton - Wigan, Kirkby, Southport, Preston, Blackpool North and Barrow-in-Furness

		TP ◇1 🍴	NT	NT	NT	NT	TP ◇1 🍴	NT	NT	NT	NT	NT	TP ◇1 🍴	NT	NT	NT	NT	NT	TP ◇1 A 🍴	NT	NT
Manchester Airport 85 ✈	d	07 00					07 25						07 58		08 01				08 25		
Heald Green 85	d						07 30								08 05				08 29		
Buxton 86	d																			07 56	
Hazel Grove 86	d							07 32												08 33	
Stockport 84	d							07 40												08 41	
Manchester Piccadilly [10] 🚊	d	07 15					07 45	07 54					08 15		08 22				08 46	08 54	
Manchester Oxford Road	d	07 18						07 58					08 19		08 25				08 49	08 58	
Deansgate 🚊	d							08 00							08 28				08 51	09 00	
Rochdale 41	d																08 00				
Manchester Victoria 🚊	d		07 16	07 23	07 27				08 00	08 07	08 10			08 22		08 29	08b33	08 46			09 00
Salford Central	d		07 19	07 26	07 30				08 03	08 10	08 13			08 25		08 32	08 36	08 49			09 03
Salford Crescent	a		07 24	07 29	07 33			08 04	08 07	08 13	08 16			08 29	08 33	08 37	08 39	08 52	08 56	09 04	09 07
	d		07 25	07 30	07 33			08 04	08 08	08 13	08 17			08 30	08 34	08 37	08 40	08 53	08 56	09 04	09 08
Swinton	d										08 23							08 59			
Moorside	d										08 26										
Walkden	d				07 42						08 29							09 04			
Atherton	d				07 48						08 35							09 09			
Hag Fold	d										08 37										
Daisy Hill	d				07 51						08 40							09 13			
Kearsley	d																08 47				
Farnworth	d																08 49				
Moses Gate	d																08 52				
Bolton	a	07 31	07 35	07 41			07 59	08 14	08 19	08 23			08 32	08 40	08 44	08 49	08 55		09 06	09 14	09 19
	d	07 31	07 35	07 42			07 59	08 15	08 20	08 24			08 32	08 40	08 45	08 49	08 56		09 07	09 15	09 20
Westhoughton	d									08 31					08 53						
Hindley	d									08 35	08 45							09 17			
Ince	d										08 48										
Wigan North Western	a																				
Wigan Wallgate	a				08 03					08 44	08 51				09 00		09 14	09 22			
	d										08 52				09 05			09 24			
Pemberton	d										08 56										
Orrell	d										09 00										
Upholland	d										09 04										
Rainford	d										09 07										
Kirkby	a										09 19										
Gathurst	d																	09 28			
Appley Bridge	d														09 11			09 32			
Parbold	d														09 15			09 36			
Hoscar	d																	09 39			
Burscough Bridge	d														09 20			09 42			
New Lane	d																	09 44			
Bescar Lane	d																	09 48			
Meols Cop	d																	09 53			
Southport	a														09 36			10 02			
Lostock	d		07 42					08 20						08 45						09 20	
Horwich Parkway	d	07 38	07 46					08 24					08 39	08 49						09 24	
Blackrod	d		07 49											08 52							
Adlington (Lancashire)	d		07 53					08 29						08 56							
Chorley	d	07 46	07 58				08 11	08 34					08 47	09 01					09 19	09 32	
Leyland	d		08 08					08 43						09 12						09 42	
Preston [8] 65,97	a	07 57	08 14				08 22	08 50					08 58	09 17					09 30	09 50	
	d	07 59	08 15				08 24					08 42	08 59	09 19					09 32		
Kirkham & Wesham 97	a	08 08	08 25											09 28							
Poulton-le-Fylde 97	a	08 18	08 33										09 16	09 36							
Layton 97	a	08 22	08 37											09 43							
Blackpool North 97	a	08 29	08 44										09 25	09 50							
Lancaster [6] 65	a						08 39					09 02							09 47		
	d					08 24	08 40					09 02							09 48		
Oxenholme Lake District 65	a						08 54												10 04		
Windermere 83	a																		10 26		
Carnforth	d					08 34						09 12									
Silverdale	d											09 18									
Arnside	d											09 23									
Grange-over-Sands	d											09 29									
Kents Bank	d											09 32									
Cark	d											09 37									
Ulverston	d											09 45									
Dalton	d											09 53									
Roose	d											09 59									
Barrow-in-Furness	a											10 07									

A 🍴 to Chorley

b arr. 0822

Table 82

Saturdays until 04 September

Manchester - Bolton - Wigan, Kirkby, Southport, Preston, Blackpool North and Barrow-in-Furness

		NT	NT	TP ◇1	TP ◇1 🍴	NT	NT	NT	NT	TP ◇1 🍴	NT	NT	NT	NT	NT	TP ◇1	TP ◇1 🍴	NT	NT	NT	NT	TP ◇1 🍴
Manchester Airport 85 ✈	d				09 00		09 03			09 29							10 00		10 03			10 29
Heald Green 85	d									09 33												10 33
Buxton 86	d																					
Hazel Grove 86	d										09 33											
Stockport 84	d										09 41											
Manchester Piccadilly [10] 🚊	d				09 16		09 22			09 46	09 54						10 16		10 22			10 46
Manchester Oxford Road	d				09 19		09 26			09 49	09 58						10 19		10 26			10 49
Deansgate 🚊	d						09 28			09 51	10 00								10 28			10 51
Rochdale 41	d							09 04												10 04		
Manchester Victoria 🚊	d	09 07	09 10			09 22		09b33	09 46			10 00	10 07	10 10				10 22		10e33	10 46	
Salford Central	d	09 10	09 13			09 25		09 36	09 49			10 03	10 10	10 13				10 25		10 36	10 49	
Salford Crescent	a	09 13	09 16			09 29	09 33	09 39	09 52	09 56	10 04	10 07	10 13	10 16				10 29	10 33	10 39	10 52	10 56
	d	09 13	09 17			09 30	09 34	09 40	09 53	09 56	10 04	10 08	10 13	10 17				10 30	10 34	10 40	10 53	10 56
Swinton	d		09 23						09 59					10 23							10 59	
Moorside	d		09 26											10 26								
Walkden	d		09 29						10 04					10 29							11 04	
Atherton	d		09 35						10 09					10 35							11 09	
Hag Fold	d		09 37											10 37								
Daisy Hill	d		09 40						10 13					10 40							11 13	
Kearsley	d							09 47												10 47		
Farnworth	d							09 49												10 49		
Moses Gate	d							09 52												10 52		
Bolton	a	09 23			09 32	09 40	09 45	09 55		10 06	10 14	10 19	10 23				10 32	10 40	10 45	10 55		11 06
	d	09 24			09 33	09 40	09 45	09 56		10 07	10 15	10 20	10 24				10 33	10 40	10 45	10 56		11 07
Westhoughton	d	09 31					09 53						10 31						10 53			
Hindley	d	09 35	09 45				09 57		10 17				10 35	10 45					10 57		11 17	
Ince	d		09 48											10 48								
Wigan North Western	a																					
Wigan Wallgate	a	09 44	09 51				10 02	10 13	10 22				10 44	10 51					11 02	11 13	11 22	
	d		09 52				10 03		10 24					10 52					11 03		11 24	
Pemberton	d		09 56											10 56								
Orrell	d		10 00											11 00								
Upholland	d		10 04											11 04								
Rainford	d		10 07											11 07								
Kirkby	a		10 19											11 19								
Gathurst	d								10 28												11 28	
Appley Bridge	d						10 10		10 32										11 10		11 32	
Parbold	d						10 14		10 36										11 14		11 36	
Hoscar	d																				11 39	
Burscough Bridge	d						10 18		10 40										11 18		11 42	
New Lane	d																				11 44	
Bescar Lane	d																				11 48	
Meols Cop	d								10 48												11 53	
Southport	a						10 35		10 57										11 35		12 02	
Lostock	d					09 45					10 20							10 45				
Horwich Parkway	d					09 49				10 13	10 24							10 49				11 13
Blackrod	d					09 52												10 52				
Adlington (Lancashire)	d					09 56												10 56				
Chorley	d				09 44	10 01				10 21	10 32						10 44	11 01				11 21
Leyland	d					10 12					10 42							11 12				
Preston [8] 65,97	a			09 41	09 55	10 17				10 33	10 50						10 55	11 17				11 33
	d			09 45	09 58	10 19				10 38						10 45	10 58	11 19				11 38
Kirkham & Wesham 97	a					10 28												11 28				
Poulton-le-Fylde 97	a					10 36				10 56								11 36				11 56
Layton 97	a					10 43												11 43				
Blackpool North 97	a					10 50				11 05								11 50				12 05
Lancaster [6] 65	a			10 00	10 13										10 45	11 00	11 13					
	d			10 01	10 14										10 49	11 01	11 14					
Oxenholme Lake District 65	a															11 17	11 28					
Windermere 83	a															11 39						
Carnforth	d			10 09											11c09							
Silverdale	d			10 15																		
Arnside	d			10 19																		
Grange-over-Sands	d			10 25																		
Kents Bank	d			10 28																		
Cark	d			10 33																		
Ulverston	d			10 41																		
Dalton	d			10 49																		
Roose	d			10 55																		
Barrow-in-Furness	a			11 03																		

b arr. 0926

c arr. 1058

e arr. 1026

Manchester - Bolton - Wigan, Kirkby, Southport, Preston, Blackpool North and Barrow-in-Furness

	NT	NT	NT	NT	NT	TP	NT	NT	NT	NT	TP	NT	NT	TP	NT	NT	TP	NT	NT	NT	NT
						◇1 A 🛒					◇1 🛒			◇1 🛒			◇1				
Manchester Airport 85 ✈ d						11 00		11 03			11 29			12 00					12 03		
Heald Green 85 d											11 33										
Buxton 86 d																					
Hazel Grove 86 d	10 33											11 33									
Stockport 84 d	10 41											11 41									
Manchester Piccadilly ■ ⇌ d	10 54					11 16		11 22			11 46	11 54		12 16					12 22		
Manchester Oxford Road d	10 58					11 19		11 26			11 49	11 58		12 19					12 26		
Deansgate ⇌ d	11 00							11 28			11 51	12 00							12 28		
Rochdale 41 d									11 04											12 04	
Manchester Victoria ⇌ d		11 00	11 07	11 10			11 22		11b33	11 46			12 00		12 07	12 10		12 22		12c33	12 46
Salford Central d		11 03	11 10	11 13			11 25		11 36	11 49			12 03		12 10	12 13		12 25		12 36	12 49
Salford Crescent a	11 04	11 07	11 13	11 16			11 29	11 33	11 39	11 52	11 56	12 04	12 07		12 13	12 16		12 29	12 33	12 39	12 52
d	11 04	11 08	11 13	11 17			11 30	11 34	11 40	11 53	11 56	12 04	12 08		12 13	12 17		12 30	12 34	12 40	12 53
Swinton d				11 23						11 59						12 23					12 59
Moorside d				11 26												12 26					
Walkden d				11 29						12 04						12 29					13 04
Atherton d				11 35						12 09						12 35					13 09
Hag Fold d				11 37												12 37					
Daisy Hill d				11 40						12 13						12 40					13 13
Kearsley d									11 47											12 47	
Farnworth d									11 49											12 49	
Moses Gate d									11 52											12 52	
Bolton a	11 14	11 19	11 23			11 32	11 40	11 45	11 55		12 06	12 14	12 19	12 32	12 23			12 40	12 45	12 55	
d	11 15	11 20	11 24			11 33	11 40	11 45	11 56		12 07	12 15	12 20	12 33	12 24			12 40	12 45	12 56	
Westhoughton d			11 31					11 53							12 31				12 53		
Hindley d			11 35	11 45				11 57		12 17					12 35	12 45			12 57		13 17
Ince d				11 48												12 48					
Wigan North Western a																					
Wigan Wallgate a			11 44	11 51				12 02	12 13	12 22					12 44	12 51			13 02	13 13	13 22
d				11 52				12 03		12 24						12 52			13 03		13 24
Pemberton d				11 56												12 56					
Orrell d				12 00												13 00					
Upholland d				12 04												13 04					
Rainford d				12 07												13 07					
Kirkby a				12 19												13 19					
Gathurst d										12 28											13 28
Appley Bridge d								12 10		12 32									13 10		13 32
Parbold d								12 14		12 36									13 14		13 36
Hoscar d																					13 39
Burscough Bridge d								12 18		12 41									13 18		13 42
New Lane d																					13 44
Bescar Lane d																					13 48
Meols Cop d										12 49											13 53
Southport a								12 35		12 59									13 35		14 02
Lostock d	11 20						11 45					12 20						12 45			
Horwich Parkway d	11 24						11 49				12 13	12 24						12 49			
Blackrod d							11 52											12 52			
Adlington (Lancashire) d							11 56											12 56			
Chorley d	11 32					11 44	12 01				12 21	12 32		12 44				13 01			
Leyland d	11 42						12 12					12 42						13 12			
Preston ■ 65,97 a	11 50					11 55	12 17				12 33	12 50		12 55				13 17			
d						11 58	12 19				12 38			12 58			13 04	13 19			
Kirkham & Wesham 97 a							12 28											13 28			
Poulton-le-Fylde 97 a							12 36				12 56							13 36			
Layton 97 a							12 43											13 43			
Blackpool North 97 a							12 50				13 05							13 50			
Lancaster ■ 65 a						12 13								13 13			13 19				
d					11 28	12 14								13 14			13 20				
Oxenholme Lake District 65 a														13 28			13 36				
Windermere 83 a																	13 56				
Carnforth d					11 37	12 23															
Silverdale d					11 43																
Arnside d					11 48	12 31															
Grange-over-Sands d					11 54	12 37															
Kents Bank d					11 57																
Cark d					12 02																
Ulverston d					12 10	12 49															
Dalton d					12 18																
Roose d					12 24																
Barrow-in-Furness a					12 31	13 10															

A 🛒 to Chorley

b arr. 1126
c arr. 1225

Manchester - Bolton - Wigan, Kirkby, Southport, Preston, Blackpool North and Barrow-in-Furness

	TP	NT	NT	NT	NT	NT	NT	TP	NT	NT	NT	NT	TP	NT	NT	NT	NT	NT	TP	TP
	◇1 🛒							◇1 🛒					◇1 🛒						◇1	◇1 🛒
Manchester Airport 85 ✈ d	12 29							13 00		13 03			13 29							14 00
Heald Green 85 d	12 33												13 33							
Buxton 86 d																				
Hazel Grove 86 d		12 33												13 33						
Stockport 84 d		12 41												13 41						
Manchester Piccadilly ■ ⇌ d	12 46	12 54						13 16		13 22			13 46	13 54						14 16
Manchester Oxford Road d	12 49	12 58						13 19		13 26			13 49	13 58						14 19
Deansgate ⇌ d	12 51	13 00								13 28			13 51	14 00						
Rochdale 41 d											13 04									
Manchester Victoria ⇌ d			13 00	13 07	13 10				13 22		13b33	13 46			14 00	14 07	14 10			
Salford Central d			13 03	13 10	13 13				13 25		13 36	13 49			14 03	14 10	14 13			
Salford Crescent a	12 56	13 04	13 07	13 13	13 16				13 29	13 33	13 39	13 52	13 56	14 04	14 07	14 13	14 16			
d	12 56	13 04	13 08	13 13	13 17				13 30	13 34	13 40	13 53	13 56	14 04	14 08	14 13	14 17			
Swinton d					13 23							13 59					14 23			
Moorside d					13 26												14 26			
Walkden d					13 29							14 04					14 29			
Atherton d					13 35							14 09					14 35			
Hag Fold d					13 37												14 37			
Daisy Hill d					13 40							14 13					14 40			
Kearsley d											13 47									
Farnworth d											13 49									
Moses Gate d											13 52									
Bolton a	13 06	13 14	13 19	13 23				13 32	13 40	13 45	13 55		14 06	14 14	14 19	14 23				14 32
d	13 07	13 15	13 20	13 24				13 33	13 40	13 45	13 56		14 07	14 15	14 20	14 24				14 33
Westhoughton d				13 31						13 53						14 31				
Hindley d				13 35	13 45					13 57		14 17				14 35	14 45			
Ince d					13 48												14 48			
Wigan North Western a																				
Wigan Wallgate a				13 44	13 51					14 02	14 13	14 22				14 44	14 51			
d					13 52					14 03		14 24					14 52			
Pemberton d					13 56												14 56			
Orrell d					14 00												15 00			
Upholland d					14 04												15 04			
Rainford d					14 07												15 07			
Kirkby a					14 19												15 19			
Gathurst d												14 28								
Appley Bridge d										14 10		14 32								
Parbold d										14 14		14 36								
Hoscar d																				
Burscough Bridge d										14 18		14 41								
New Lane d																				
Bescar Lane d																				
Meols Cop d												14 49								
Southport a										14 35		14 59								
Lostock d		13 20							13 45					14 20						
Horwich Parkway d	13 13	13 24							13 49				14 13	14 24						
Blackrod d									13 52											
Adlington (Lancashire) d									13 56											
Chorley d	13 21	13 32						13 44	14 01				14 21	14 32						14 44
Leyland d		13 42							14 12					14 42						
Preston ■ 65,97 a	13 33	13 50						13 55	14 17				14 33	14 50						14 55
d	13 38							13 58	14 19				14 38						14 47	14 58
Kirkham & Wesham 97 a									14 28											
Poulton-le-Fylde 97 a	13 56								14 36				14 56							
Layton 97 a									14 43											
Blackpool North 97 a	14 05								14 48				15 05							
Lancaster ■ 65 a							13 42	14 13											15 02	15 13
d						13 32	13 48	14 14										14 22	15 03	15 14
Oxenholme Lake District 65 a								14 28												15 28
Windermere 83 a																				
Carnforth d						13 41	13 58											14 32	15 11	
Silverdale d						13 47												14 38		
Arnside d						13 52												14 42	15 20	
Grange-over-Sands d						13 58												14 48	15 25	
Kents Bank d						14 01												14 52		
Cark d						14 06												14 56		
Ulverston d						14 14												15 04	15 38	
Dalton d						14 22												15 12		
Roose d						14 28												15 18		
Barrow-in-Furness a						14 36												15 26	15 58	

b arr. 1325

Table 82

Saturdays
until 04 September

Manchester - Bolton - Wigan, Kirkby, Southport, Preston, Blackpool North and Barrow-in-Furness

	NT	NT	NT	NT	TP ◇1 🛒	NT	NT	TP ◇1 A 🛒	NT	NT	NT	NT	NT	NT	NT	TP ◇1 🛒	NT	NT	NT	NT	NT	TP ◇1 🛒
Manchester Airport 85 ✈ d		14 03			14 29			15 00				15 03				15 29						16 00
Heald Green 85 d					14 33											15 33						
Buxton 86 d																						
Hazel Grove 86 d						14 33											15 33					
Stockport 84 d						14 41											15 41					
Manchester Piccadilly 10 🚇 d		14 22			14 46	14 54		15 16				15 22				15 46	15 54					16 16
Manchester Oxford Road d		14 26			14 49	14 58		15 19				15 26				15 49	15 58					16 19
Deansgate 🚇 d		14 28			14 51	15 00						15 28				15 51	16 00					
Rochdale 41 d			14 04										15 04									
Manchester Victoria 🚇 d	14 22		14b33	14 46			15 00		15 07	15 10	15 22		15c33	15 40	15 46			16 07	16 10			
Salford Central d	14 25		14 36	14 49			15 03		15 10	15 13	15 25		15 36	15 43	15 49			16 10	16 13			
Salford Crescent a	14 29	14 33	14 39	14 52	14 56	15 04	15 07		15 13	15 16	15 29	15 33	15 39	15 46	15 52	15 56	16 04	16 13	16 16			
d	14 30	14 34	14 40	14 53	14 56	15 04	15 08		15 13	15 17	15 30	15 34	15 40	15 47	15 53	15 56	16 04	16 13	16 17			
Swinton d				14 59						15 23					15 59				16 23			
Moorside d										15 26									16 26			
Walkden d				15 04						15 29					16 04				16 29			
Atherton d				15 09						15 35					16 09				16 35			
Hag Fold d										15 37									16 37			
Daisy Hill d				15 13						15 40					16 13				16 40			
Kearsley d			14 47										15 47									
Farnworth d			14 49										15 49									
Moses Gate d			14 52										15 52									
Bolton a	14 40	14 45	14 55		15 06	15 14	15 19	15 32	15 23		15 40	15 45	15 55	15 59		16 06	16 14	16 23				16 32
d	14 40	14 45	14 56		15 07	15 15	15 20	15 33	15 24		15 40	15 45	15 56	16 00		16 07	16 15	16 24				16 33
Westhoughton d		14 53							15 31			15 53						16 31				
Hindley d		14 57		15 17					15 35	15 45		15 57			16 17			16 35	16 45			
Ince d										15 48									16 48			
Wigan North Western a																						
Wigan Wallgate a		15 02	15 13	15 22					15 44	15 51		16 02	16 13		16 22			16 44	16 51			
d		15 03		15 24						15 52		16 03			16 24				16 52			
Pemberton d										15 56									16 56			
Orrell d										16 00									17 00			
Upholland d										16 04									17 04			
Rainford d										16 07									17 07			
Kirkby a										16 19									17 19			
Gathurst d				15 28								16 08			16 28							
Appley Bridge d		15 10		15 32								16 11			16 32							
Parbold d		15 14		15 36								16 15			16 36							
Hoscar d												16 18										
Burscough Bridge d		15 18		15 40								16 21			16 40							
New Lane d												16 24										
Bescar Lane d												16 27										
Meols Cop d				15 48								16 32			16 48							
Southport a		15 35		15 57								16 42			16 57							
Lostock d	14 45					15 20					15 45						16 20					
Horwich Parkway d	14 49				15 13	15 24					15 49					16 13	16 24					
Blackrod d	14 52										15 52											
Adlington (Lancashire) d	14 56										15 56											
Chorley d	15 01				15 21	15 32		15 44			16 01					16 21	16 32					16 44
Leyland d	15 12					15 42					16 12						16 42					
Preston 8 65,97 a	15 17				15 33	15 50		15 55			16 19					16 33	16 50					16 55
d	15 19				15 38			15 58								16 38						17 00
Kirkham & Wesham 97 a	15 28															16 47						
Poulton-le-Fylde 97 a	15 36				15 56											16 57						
Layton 97 a	15 43															17 00						
Blackpool North 97 a	15 50				16 05											17 07						
Lancaster 6 65 a								16 13												16 30		17 15
d								16 14												16 40	17 00	17 16
Oxenholme Lake District 65 a																						17 30
Windermere 83 a																						
Carnforth d								16 22												16 50	17 10	
Silverdale d								16 28													17 17	
Arnside d								16 32													17 21	
Grange-over-Sands d								16 38													17 27	
Kents Bank d								16 41													17 31	
Cark d								16 46													17 35	
Ulverston d								16 54													17 44	
Dalton d								17 02													17 53	
Roose d								17 08													17 59	
Barrow-in-Furness a								17 18													18 07	

A 🛒 to Chorley b arr. 1425 c arr. 1526

Table 82

Saturdays
until 04 September

Manchester - Bolton - Wigan, Kirkby, Southport, Preston, Blackpool North and Barrow-in-Furness

	TP ◇1	NT	NT	NT	NT	TP ◇1 🛒	NT	NT	NT	NT	NT	NT	TP ◇1 A 🛒	NT	NT	NT	NT	NT	TP ◇1 🛒	NT	NT	NT
Manchester Airport 85 ✈ d				16 03		16 29							17 00			17 03			17 29			
Heald Green 85 d						16 33													17 33			
Buxton 86 d																						
Hazel Grove 86 d								16 30													17 33	
Stockport 84 d								16 41													17 41	
Manchester Piccadilly 10 🚇 d				16 22		16 46		16 54					17 15			17 22			17 46		17 54	
Manchester Oxford Road d				16 26		16 49		16 58					17 18			17 26			17 49		17 58	
Deansgate 🚇 d				16 28				17 00											17 51		18 00	
Rochdale 41 d					16 04										17 03							
Manchester Victoria 🚇 d		16 20	16 23		16b36		16 46		17 00	17 07	17 10			17 19	17 23		17 36	17 40		17 50		18 00
Salford Central d		16 23	16 26		16 39		16 49		17 03	17 10	17 13			17 22	17 26		17 39	17 43		17 53		18 03
Salford Crescent a		16 26	16 30	16 34	16 42		16 52	17 04	17 07	17 13	17 17			17 25	17 30	17 34	17 42	17 46	17 55	17 58	18 04	18 07
d		16 27	16 31	16 34	16 43		16 53	17 04	17 08	17 13	17 17			17 27	17 31	17 34	17 43	17 47	17 55	17 59	18 04	18 08
Swinton d							16 59				17 23									18 05		
Moorside d							17 02				17 26									18 08		
Walkden d							17 05				17 29									18 11		
Atherton d							17 11				17 35							17 59		18 17		
Hag Fold d							17 14				17 37									18 19		
Daisy Hill d							17 17				17 40							18 03		18 22		
Kearsley d					16 50												17 53					
Farnworth d					16 52												17 55					
Moses Gate d					16 55												17 57					
Bolton a		16 37	16 42	16 45	16 58	17 05		17 14	17 19	17 23			17 31	17 37	17 42	17 45	18 01		18 06		18 14	18 19
d		16 37	16 43	16 45	16 59	17 06		17 15	17 20	17 24			17 32	17 37	17 43	17 45	18 01		18 07		18 15	18 20
Westhoughton d				16 53	17 06					17 31						17 53	18 09					
Hindley d				16 57	17 10		17 21			17 35	17 45						18 13			18 27		
Ince d							17 24				17 48											
Wigan North Western a																						
Wigan Wallgate a				17 02	17 19		17 27			17 44	17 51					18 01	18 22	18 11		18 32		
d				17 03			17 29				17 52					18 02		18 15		18 33		
Pemberton d											17 56									18 37		
Orrell d											18 00									18 41		
Upholland d											18 04									18 45		
Rainford d											18 07									18 48		
Kirkby a											18 19									19 00		
Gathurst d				17 08			17 33											18 19				
Appley Bridge d				17 11			17 37									18 09		18 23				
Parbold d				17 15			17 41									18 13		18 28				
Hoscar d																		18 31				
Burscough Bridge d				17 20			17 45									18 17		18 34				
New Lane d																		18 37				
Bescar Lane d																		18 40				
Meols Cop d				17 27			17 53											18 46				
Southport a				17 37			18 02									18 35		18 55				
Lostock d		16 43						17 20						17 43					18 12		18 20	
Horwich Parkway d		16 47						17 24						17 47					18 15		18 24	
Blackrod d		16 51												17 51					18 18			
Adlington (Lancashire) d		16 55												17 55								
Chorley d		17 00				17 19		17 32					17 44	18 00					18 25		18 32	
Leyland d		17 11						17 42						18 11					18 33		18 42	
Preston 8 65,97 a		17 20				17 30		17 50					17 55	18 16					18 38		18 48	
d	17 04	17 21				17 32							17 58	18 18					18 40		18 49	
Kirkham & Wesham 97 a		17 30				17 41								18 27					18 49			
Poulton-le-Fylde 97 a		17 38				17 51								18 35					18 59			
Layton 97 a		17 43				17 54								18 39					19 02			
Blackpool North 97 a		17 48				18 02								18 46					19 09		19 16	
Lancaster 6 65 a	17 20												18 13									
d	17 21											17 33	18 14									
Oxenholme Lake District 65 a	17 38																					
Windermere 83 a	18 00																					
Carnforth d												17 43	18 22									
Silverdale d												17 49	18 28									
Arnside d												17 54	18 32									
Grange-over-Sands d												18 00	18 38									
Kents Bank d												18 03	18 41									
Cark d												18 08	18 46									
Ulverston d												18 16	18 54									
Dalton d												18 24	19 02									
Roose d												18 30	19 08									
Barrow-in-Furness a												18 38	19 18									

A 🛒 to Chorley b arr. 1625

Table 82

Saturdays until 04 September

Manchester - Bolton - Wigan, Kirkby, Southport, Preston, Blackpool North and Barrow-in-Furness

		TP		NT	TP	NT	NT	NT	NT	NT	TP	NT		NT	NT	NT	TP	NT	NT	TP	NT			TP	NT
		◇1			◇1						◇1						◇1			◇1				◇1	
		🛒									🛒														
Manchester Airport	85 ✈ d	18 00						18 03			18 29						19 00	19 03		19 29				20 00	
Heald Green	85 d										18 33									19 33					
Buxton	86 d																								
Hazel Grove	86 d											18 33													
Stockport	84 d											18 41													
Manchester Piccadilly 10	⇌ d	18 16						18 22			18 46	18 54					19 16	19 20		19 46				20 16	
Manchester Oxford Road	d	18 19						18 26			18 49	18 58					19 19	19 24		19 49				20 19	
Deansgate	⇌ d							18 28			18 51	19 00						19 26		19 51					
Rochdale	41 d						18 02																		
Manchester Victoria	⇌ d			18 08		18 20	18 23		18 33	18 45				19 00	19 10				19 28		20 00				20 10
Salford Central	d			18 12		18 23	18 26		18 36	18 48				19 03	19 13				19 31		20 03				20 13
Salford Crescent	a			18 16		18 26	18 30	18 34	18 39	18 51	18 56	19 04		19 07	19 16			19 29	19 34	19 56	20 07				20 16
	d			18 17		18 27	18 31	18 34	18 40	18 52	18 56	19 04		19 08	19 17			19 30	19 35	19 56	20 08				20 17
Swinton	d			18 23						18 58					19 23										20 23
Moorside	d			18 26						19 01					19 26										20 26
Walkden	d			18 29						19 04					19 29										20 29
Atherton	d			18 35						19 10					19 35										20 35
Hag Fold	d			18 37						19 12					19 37										20 37
Daisy Hill	d			18 40						19 15					19 40										20 40
Kearsley	d								18 47																
Farnworth	d								18 49																
Moses Gate	d								18 52																
Bolton	a	18 32				18 37	18 42	18 45	18 55		19 06	19 19		19 20			19 32	19 40	19 45	20 06	20 19			20 32	
	d	18 33				18 37	18 43	18 45	18 56		19 07			19 20			19 33	19 40	19 45	20 07	20 20			20 33	
Westhoughton	d							18 53	19 03									19 48							
Hindley	d			18 45				18 57	19 09	19 20					19 45			19 52							20 45
Ince	d			18 48						19 23					19 48										20 48
Wigan North Western	a			18 56																					
Wigan Wallgate	a							19 02	19 18	19 30					19 55			19 57							20 55
	d							19 03										19 59							
Pemberton	d																								
Orrell	d																								
Upholland	d																								
Rainford	d																								
Kirkby	a																								
Gathurst	d							19 07										20 03							
Appley Bridge	d							19 11										20 07							
Parbold	d							19 15										20 11							
Hoscar	d																								
Burscough Bridge	d							19 19										20 15							
New Lane	d																								
Bescar Lane	d																								
Meols Cop	d							19 27										20 23							
Southport	a							19 37										20 32							
Lostock	d					18 42					19 12								19 50						
Horwich Parkway	d					18 46					19 15								19 54	20 13				20 39	
Blackrod	d					18 49													19 57						
Adlington (Lancashire)	d					18 53													20 01						
Chorley	d	18 44				18 58					19 23						19 44		20 06	20 21				20 46	
Leyland	d					19 10													20 18						
Preston 8	65,97 a	18 55				19 18					19 33						19 58		20 24	20 33				20 57	
	d	19 00			19 04	19 19					19 38						20 02		20 25	20 38				21 02	
Kirkham & Wesham	97 a					19 28													20 34						
Poulton-le-Fylde	97 a					19 36					19 56								20 42	20 56					
Layton	97 a					19 43													20 47						
Blackpool North	97 a					19 50					20 05								20 54	21 06					
Lancaster 6	65 a	19 15			19 20											19 20	20 17							21 17	
	d	19 16			19 20											19 24	20 18							21 18	
Oxenholme Lake District	65 a	19 30																							
Windermere	83 a																								
Carnforth	d				19 29											19 35	20 26							21 26	
Silverdale	d				19 35												20 32							21 32	
Arnside	d				19 39												20 36							21 36	
Grange-over-Sands	d				19 44												20 42							21 42	
Kents Bank	d				19 48												20 45							21 45	
Cark	d				19 52												20 50							21 50	
Ulverston	d				20 00												20 58							21 58	
Dalton	d				20 08												21 06							22 06	
Roose	d				20 14												21 12							22 12	
Barrow-in-Furness	a				20 24												21 20							22 20	

Table 82

Saturdays until 04 September

Manchester - Bolton - Wigan, Kirkby, Southport, Preston, Blackpool North and Barrow-in-Furness

		NT	NT		TP	NT	NT	NT		NT	NT		NT	TP	TP	NT		NT		NT	NT	TP	NT	NT	NT
					◇1									◇1	◇1							◇1			
Manchester Airport	85 ✈ d		20 03		20 29						21 03			21 29	22 00					22 19		22 29			
Heald Green	85 d				20 33									21 33								22 33			
Buxton	86 d																								
Hazel Grove	86 d																								
Stockport	84 d																						22 40		
Manchester Piccadilly 10	⇌ d		20 20		20 46						21 20		21 38	21 46	22 16					22 36		22 46	22 54		
Manchester Oxford Road	d		20 24		20 49						21 24		21 44	21 49	22 19					22 39		22 49	22 58		
Deansgate	⇌ d		20 26		20 51						21 26		21 46	21 51						22 41		22 51	23 00		
Rochdale	41 d																								
Manchester Victoria	⇌ d	20 22				21 00	21 10			21 22						22 00		22 22			22 45			23 05	23 16
Salford Central	d	20 25				21 03	21 13			21 25						22 03		22 25			22 48			23 08	23 19
Salford Crescent	a	20 29	20 33		20 56	21 07	21 16			21 29	21 33			21 56		22 07		22 29		22 46	22 51	22 56	23 02	23 11	23 22
	d	20 30	20 34		20 56	21 08	21 17			21 30	21 34			21 56		22 08		22 30		22 46	22 52	22 56	23 04	23 12	23 22
Swinton	d						21 23														22 58				
Moorside	d						21 26														23 01				
Walkden	d						21 29														23 04				
Atherton	d						21 35														23 10				
Hag Fold	d						21 37														23 12				
Daisy Hill	d						21 40														23 15				
Kearsley	d																						23 11		
Farnworth	d																						23 13		
Moses Gate	d																						23 16		
Bolton	a	20 40	20 45		21 06	21 19				21 40	21 45			22 06	22 32	22 19		22 40		22 56		23 06	23 19	23 23	23 32
	d	20 40	20 45		21 07	21 20				21 40	21 45			22 07	22 33	22 20		22 40		22 57		23 07	23 20	23 24	23 33
Westhoughton	d		20 53								21 53									23 04			23 27		
Hindley	d		20 57				21 45				21 57									23 08	23 20		23 31		
Ince	d						21 48														23 23				
Wigan North Western	a																								
Wigan Wallgate	a		21 02				21 55				22 02									23 13	23 30		23 41		
	d		21 03								22 03									23 15					
Pemberton	d																								
Orrell	d																								
Upholland	d																								
Rainford	d																								
Kirkby	a																								
Gathurst	d		21 08								22 08									23 19					
Appley Bridge	d		21 11								22 11									23 23					
Parbold	d		21 15								22 15									23 27					
Hoscar	d		21 18																						
Burscough Bridge	d		21 21								22 20									23 31					
New Lane	d		21 24																						
Bescar Lane	d		21 27																						
Meols Cop	d		21 32								22 27									23 39					
Southport	a		21 42								22 37									23 48					
Lostock	d	20 45								21 45								22 45							23 38
Horwich Parkway	d	20 49			21 13					21 49				22 13				22 49				23 13			23 42
Blackrod	d	20 52								21 52								22 52							23 45
Adlington (Lancashire)	d	20 56								21 56								22 56							23 49
Chorley	d	21 01			21 21					22 02				22 21				23 01				23 21			23 54
Leyland	d	21 12								22 12								23 12							00 04
Preston 8	65,97 a	21 17			21 33					22 18				22 33	22 54			23 17				23 33			00 10
	d	21 19			21 38			21 59		22 19				22 35	22 55			23 19				23 35			00 11
Kirkham & Wesham	97 a	21 28								22 28								23 28							00 21
Poulton-le-Fylde	97 a	21 36			21 56					22 36				22 53				23 36				23 52			00 29
Layton	97 a	21 40								22 43								23 40							00 33
Blackpool North	97 a	21 48			22 06					22 50				23 02				23 48				00 02			00 40
Lancaster 6	65 a							22 19							23 11										
	d							22 19							23 11										
Oxenholme Lake District	65 a																								
Windermere	83 a																								
Carnforth	d							22 29							23 20										
Silverdale	d							22 35							23 26										
Arnside	d							22 40							23 30										
Grange-over-Sands	d							22 46							23 35										
Kents Bank	d							22 49							23 39										
Cark	d							22 54							23 43										
Ulverston	d							23 02							23 51										
Dalton	d							23 10							23 59										
Roose	d							23 16							00 05										
Barrow-in-Furness	a							23 24							00 15										

Table 82

Saturdays
until 04 September

Manchester - Bolton - Wigan, Kirkby, Southport, Preston, Blackpool North and Barrow-in-Furness

Station	Table		NT
Manchester Airport	85 ✈	d	
Heald Green	85	d	
Buxton	86	d	
Hazel Grove	86	d	
Stockport	84	d	
Manchester Piccadilly 10	⇌	d	
Manchester Oxford Road		d	
Deansgate	⇌	d	
Rochdale	41	d	
Manchester Victoria	⇌	d	23 20
Salford Central		d	23 23
Salford Crescent		a	23 26
		d	23 26
Swinton		d	23 33
Moorside		d	23 35
Walkden		d	23 39
Atherton		d	23 44
Hag Fold		d	23 47
Daisy Hill		d	23 50
Kearsley		d	
Farnworth		d	
Moses Gate		d	
Bolton		a	
		d	
Westhoughton		d	
Hindley		d	23 54
Ince		d	23 57
Wigan North Western		a	
Wigan Wallgate		a	00 04
		d	
Pemberton		d	
Orrell		d	
Upholland		d	
Rainford		d	
Kirkby		a	
Gathurst		d	
Appley Bridge		d	
Parbold		d	
Hoscar		d	
Burscough Bridge		d	
New Lane		d	
Bescar Lane		d	
Meols Cop		d	
Southport		a	
Lostock		d	
Horwich Parkway		d	
Blackrod		d	
Adlington (Lancashire)		d	
Chorley		d	
Leyland		d	
Preston 8	65,97	a	
		d	
Kirkham & Wesham	97	a	
Poulton-le-Fylde	97	a	
Layton	97	a	
Blackpool North	97	a	
Lancaster 6	65	a	
		d	
Oxenholme Lake District	65	a	
Windermere	83	a	
Carnforth		d	
Silverdale		d	
Arnside		d	
Grange-over-Sands		d	
Kents Bank		d	
Cark		d	
Ulverston		d	
Dalton		d	
Roose		d	
Barrow-in-Furness		a	

Table 82

Saturdays
from 11 September

Manchester - Bolton - Wigan, Kirkby, Southport, Preston, Blackpool North and Barrow-in-Furness

Station	Table		TP ◇1	TP ◇1	TP ◇1	TP 1	NT	NT	NT	TP ◇1 ✠	NT	NT	NT	NT	NT	NT	TP ◇1
Manchester Airport	85 ✈	d	00 01	04 00	05 29					06 18							
Heald Green	85	d			05 33												
Buxton	86	d											05 54				
Hazel Grove	86	d											06 31				
Stockport	84	d											06 41				
Manchester Piccadilly 10	⇌	d	00 16	04 15	05 46					06 33			06 54				
Manchester Oxford Road		d								06 36			06 57				
Deansgate	⇌	d											06 59				
Rochdale	41	d															
Manchester Victoria	⇌	d					05 55	06 00	06 17		06 38	06 45		07 01	07 06		
Salford Central		d									06 40	06 48		07 04	07 09		
Salford Crescent		a			05 51		05 59	06 04	06 23		06 44	06 51	07 03	07 07	07 12		
		d			05 52		06 00	06 05	06 24		06 45	06 52	07 03	07 08	07 13		
Swinton		d										06 58		07 14			
Moorside		d												07 17			
Walkden		d										07 03		07 20			
Atherton		d										07 08		07 26			
Hag Fold		d												07 28			
Daisy Hill		d										07 12		07 31			
Kearsley		d									06 52						
Farnworth		d									06 54						
Moses Gate		d									06 57						
Bolton		a	00s31	04s29	06 02		06 11	06 15	06 34	06 50	07 00		07 16		07 23		
		d	00s32	04s29	06 02		06 12	06 15	06 34	06 50	07 01		07 19		07 23		
Westhoughton		d						06 23							07 31	←	
Hindley		d						06 27				07 16		07 39	07 35	07 39	
Ince		d												→		07 42	
Wigan North Western		a									07 19						
Wigan Wallgate		a						06 32				07 21			07 40	07 45	
		d						06 34				07 23			07 41	07 46	
Pemberton		d						06 38								07 50	
Orrell		d						06 42								07 54	
Upholland		d						06 45								07 58	
Rainford		d						06 49								08 01	
Kirkby		a						07 03								08 15	
Gathurst		d										07 27			07 46		
Appley Bridge		d										07 31			07 49		
Parbold		d										07 35			07 53		
Hoscar		d													07 56		
Burscough Bridge		d										07 39			07 59		
New Lane		d													08 02		
Bescar Lane		d													08 05		
Meols Cop		d										07 47			08 10		
Southport		a										07 58			08 22		
Lostock		d							06 39								
Horwich Parkway		d			06 09				06 43								
Blackrod		d							06 46								
Adlington (Lancashire)		d							06 50								
Chorley		d			06 16				06 55								
Leyland		d			06 28				07 06								
Preston 8	65,97	a	01s03	05s04	06 35				07 11	07 11							
		d	01s05	05s06	06 37				07 13	07 14							07 20
Kirkham & Wesham	97	a			06 46				07 22								
Poulton-le-Fylde	97	a			06 56				07 30								
Layton	97	a			06 59				07 34								
Blackpool North	97	a	01 30	05 33	07 06				07 43								
Lancaster 6	65	a								07 30							07 36
		d				05 46				07 30							07 36
Oxenholme Lake District	65	a				06 21											
Windermere	83	a				06 41											
Carnforth		d															07 45
Silverdale		d															07 51
Arnside		d															07 55
Grange-over-Sands		d															08 00
Kents Bank		d															08 04
Cark		d															08 08
Ulverston		d															08 16
Dalton		d															08 24
Roose		d															08 30
Barrow-in-Furness		a															08 39

Table 82

Saturdays from 11 September

Manchester - Bolton - Wigan, Kirkby, Southport, Preston, Blackpool North and Barrow-in-Furness

		TP ◇1 ✠	NT	NT	NT	NT		TP ◇1 ✠	NT	NT		NT	NT	NT	TP ◇1 ✠	NT		NT		NT	NT	NT	TP ◇1 A ✠	NT	NT
Manchester Airport	85 ✈ d	07 00						07 25							07 58			08 01					08 25		
Heald Green	85 d							07 30										08 05					08 29		
Buxton	86 d																							07 51	
Hazel Grove	86 d								07 30															08 31	
Stockport	84 d								07 40															08 41	
Manchester Piccadilly 10	⇌ d	07 15						07 45	07 54						08 15			08 22					08 46	08 54	
Manchester Oxford Road	d	07 18							07 58						08 19			08 25					08 49	08 58	
Deansgate	⇌ d								08 00									08 28					08 51	09 00	
Rochdale	41 d																				08 00				
Manchester Victoria	⇌ d		07 16	07 23	07 27					08 00		08 07	08 10			08 22				08 29	08b33	08 46			09 00
Salford Central	d		07 19	07 26	07 30					08 03		08 10	08 13			08 25				08 32	08 36	08 49			09 03
Salford Crescent	a		07 24	07 29	07 33				08 04	08 07		08 13	08 16			08 29		08 33		08 37	08 39	08 52	08 56	09 04	09 07
	d		07 25	07 30	07 33				08 04	08 08		08 13	08 17			08 30		08 34		08 37	08 40	08 53	08 56	09 04	09 08
Swinton	d												08 23									08 59			
Moorside	d												08 26												
Walkden	d				07 42								08 29									09 04			
Atherton	d				07 48								08 35									09 09			
Hag Fold	d												08 37												
Daisy Hill	d				07 51								08 40									09 13			
Kearsley	d																				08 47				
Farnworth	d																				08 49				
Moses Gate	d																				08 52				
Bolton	a	07 31	07 35	07 41				07 59	08 14	08 19		08 23			08 32	08 40		08 44		08 49	08 55		09 06	09 14	09 19
	d	07 31	07 35	07 42				07 59	08 15	08 20		08 24			08 32	08 40		08 45		08 49	08 56		09 07	09 15	09 20
Westhoughton	d											08 31						08 53							
Hindley	d											08 35	08 45									09 17			
Ince	d												08 48												
Wigan North Western	a																								
Wigan Wallgate	a				08 03							08 46	08 51					09 00			09 14	09 22			
	d												08 52					09 05				09 24			
Pemberton	d												08 56												
Orrell	d												09 00												
Upholland	d												09 04												
Rainford	d												09 07												
Kirkby	a												09 21												
Gathurst	d																					09 28			
Appley Bridge	d																	09 11				09 32			
Parbold	d																	09 15				09 36			
Hoscar	d																					09 39			
Burscough Bridge	d																	09 20				09 42			
New Lane	d																					09 44			
Bescar Lane	d																					09 48			
Meols Cop	d																					09 53			
Southport	a																	09 38				10 04			
Lostock	d		07 42						08 20							08 45								09 20	
Horwich Parkway	d	07 38	07 46						08 24						08 39	08 49								09 24	
Blackrod	d		07 49													08 52									
Adlington (Lancashire)	d		07 53						08 29							08 56									
Chorley	d	07 46	07 58					08 11	08 34						08 47	09 01							09 19	09 32	
Leyland	d		08 08						08 43							09 12								09 42	
Preston 8	65,97 a	07 57	08 14					08 22	08 50						08 58	09 17							09 30	09 50	
	d	07 59	08 15					08 24						08 42	08 59	09 19							09 32		
Kirkham & Wesham	97 a	08 08	08 25													09 28									
Poulton-le-Fylde	97 a	08 18	08 33												09 16	09 36									
Layton	97 a	08 22	08 37													09 43									
Blackpool North	97 a	08 29	08 46												09 25	09 54									
Lancaster 6	65 a							08 39						09 02									09 47		
	d					08 24		08 40						09 02									09 48		
Oxenholme Lake District	65 a							08 54															10 04		
Windermere	83 a																						10 26		
Carnforth	d					08 34								09 12											
Silverdale	d													09 18											
Arnside	d													09 23											
Grange-over-Sands	d													09 29											
Kents Bank	d													09 32											
Cark	d													09 37											
Ulverston	d													09 45											
Dalton	d													09 53											
Roose	d													09 59											
Barrow-in-Furness	a													10 07											

A ✠ to Chorley

b arr. 0822

Table 82

Saturdays from 11 September

Manchester - Bolton - Wigan, Kirkby, Southport, Preston, Blackpool North and Barrow-in-Furness

		NT		NT	TP ◇1	TP ◇1 ✠	NT	NT	NT	NT	TP ◇1 ✠	NT		NT	NT	NT	NT	TP ◇1	TP ◇1 ✠	NT	NT	NT		NT	TP ◇1 ✠
Manchester Airport	85 ✈ d					09 00		09 03			09 29								10 00		10 03				10 29
Heald Green	85 d										09 33														10 33
Buxton	86 d																								
Hazel Grove	86 d											09 33													
Stockport	84 d											09 41													
Manchester Piccadilly 10	⇌ d					09 16		09 22			09 46	09 54							10 16		10 22				10 46
Manchester Oxford Road	d					09 19		09 26			09 49	09 58							10 19		10 26				10 49
Deansgate	⇌ d							09 28			09 51	10 00									10 28				10 51
Rochdale	41 d								09 04													10 04			
Manchester Victoria	⇌ d	09 07		09 10			09 22		09b33	09 46				10 00	10 07	10 10				10 22		10e33		10 46	
Salford Central	d	09 10		09 13			09 25		09 36	09 49				10 03	10 10	10 13				10 25		10 36		10 49	
Salford Crescent	a	09 13		09 16			09 29	09 33	09 39	09 52	09 56	10 04		10 07	10 13	10 16				10 29	10 33	10 39		10 52	10 56
	d	09 13		09 17			09 30	09 34	09 40	09 53	09 56	10 04		10 08	10 13	10 17				10 30	10 34	10 40		10 53	10 56
Swinton	d			09 23						09 59						10 23								10 59	
Moorside	d			09 26												10 26									
Walkden	d			09 29						10 04						10 29								11 04	
Atherton	d			09 35						10 09						10 35								11 09	
Hag Fold	d			09 37												10 37									
Daisy Hill	d			09 40						10 13						10 40								11 13	
Kearsley	d								09 47													10 47			
Farnworth	d								09 49													10 49			
Moses Gate	d								09 52													10 52			
Bolton	a	09 23				09 32	09 40	09 45	09 55		10 06	10 14		10 19	10 23				10 32	10 40	10 45	10 55			11 06
	d	09 24				09 33	09 40	09 45	09 56		10 07	10 15		10 20	10 24				10 33	10 40	10 45	10 56			11 07
Westhoughton	d	09 31						09 53							10 31						10 53				
Hindley	d	09 35		09 45				09 57		10 17					10 35	10 45					10 57			11 17	
Ince	d			09 48												10 48									
Wigan North Western	a																								
Wigan Wallgate	a	09 46		09 51				10 02	10 13	10 22					10 46	10 51					11 02	11 15		11 22	
	d			09 52				10 03		10 24						10 52					11 03			11 24	
Pemberton	d			09 56												10 56									
Orrell	d			10 00												11 00									
Upholland	d			10 04												11 04									
Rainford	d			10 07												11 07									
Kirkby	a			10 21												11 21									
Gathurst	d									10 28														11 28	
Appley Bridge	d							10 10		10 32											11 10			11 32	
Parbold	d							10 14		10 36											11 14			11 36	
Hoscar	d																							11 39	
Burscough Bridge	d							10 18		10 40											11 18			11 42	
New Lane	d																							11 44	
Bescar Lane	d																							11 48	
Meols Cop	d									10 48														11 53	
Southport	a							10 37		10 59											11 37			12 04	
Lostock	d						09 45					10 20								10 45					
Horwich Parkway	d						09 49				10 13	10 24								10 49					11 13
Blackrod	d						09 52													10 52					
Adlington (Lancashire)	d						09 56													10 56					
Chorley	d					09 44	10 01				10 21	10 32							10 44	11 01					11 21
Leyland	d						10 12					10 42								11 12					
Preston 8	65,97 a				09 41	09 55	10 17				10 33	10 50							10 55	11 17					11 33
	d				09 45	09 58	10 19				10 38							10 45	10 58	11 19					11 38
Kirkham & Wesham	97 a						10 28													11 28					
Poulton-le-Fylde	97 a						10 36				10 56									11 36					11 56
Layton	97 a						10 43													11 43					
Blackpool North	97 a						10 50				11 05									11 52					12 05
Lancaster 6	65 a				10 00	10 13											10 45	11 00	11 13						
	d				10 01	10 14											10 49	11 01	11 14						
Oxenholme Lake District	65 a																	11 17	11 28						
Windermere	83 a																	11 39							
Carnforth	d				10 09												11c09								
Silverdale	d				10 15																				
Arnside	d				10 19																				
Grange-over-Sands	d				10 25																				
Kents Bank	d				10 28																				
Cark	d				10 33																				
Ulverston	d				10 41																				
Dalton	d				10 49																				
Roose	d				10 55																				
Barrow-in-Furness	a				11 03																				

b arr. 0926

c arr. 1058

e arr. 1026

Table 82

Saturdays
from 11 September

Manchester - Bolton - Wigan, Kirkby, Southport, Preston, Blackpool North and Barrow-in-Furness

	NT	NT	NT	NT	NT	TP	NT	NT	NT	NT	TP	NT	NT	TP	NT	NT	TP	NT	NT	NT	NT	TP
						◇1 A ✠					◇1 ✠			◇1 ✠			◇1					◇1 ✠
Manchester Airport 85 ✈ d						11 00		11 03			11 29			12 00					12 03			12 29
Heald Green 85 d											11 33											12 33
Buxton 86 d																						
Hazel Grove 86 d	10 31											11 31										
Stockport 84 d	10 41											11 41										
Manchester Piccadilly 10 ⇌ d	10 54					11 16		11 22			11 46	11 54		12 16					12 22			12 46
Manchester Oxford Road d	10 58					11 19		11 26			11 49	11 58		12 19					12 26			12 49
Deansgate ⇌ d	11 00							11 28			11 51	12 00							12 28			12 51
Rochdale 41 d									11 04											12 04		
Manchester Victoria ⇌ d		11 00	11 07	11 10			11 22		11b33	11 46			12 00		12 07	12 10		12 22		12c33	12 46	
Salford Central d		11 03	11 10	11 13			11 25		11 36	11 49			12 03		12 10	12 13		12 25		12 36	12 49	
Salford Crescent a	11 04	11 07	11 13	11 16			11 29	11 33	11 39	11 52	11 56	12 04	12 07		12 13	12 16		12 29	12 33	12 39	12 52	12 56
d	11 04	11 08	11 13	11 17			11 30	11 34	11 40	11 53	11 56	12 04	12 08		12 13	12 17		12 30	12 34	12 40	12 53	12 56
Swinton d				11 23						11 59						12 23					12 59	
Moorside d				11 26												12 26						
Walkden d				11 29						12 04						12 29					13 04	
Atherton d				11 35						12 09						12 35					13 09	
Hag Fold d				11 37												12 37						
Daisy Hill d				11 40						12 13						12 40					13 13	
Kearsley d									11 47											12 47		
Farnworth d									11 49											12 49		
Moses Gate d									11 52											12 52		
Bolton a	11 14	11 19	11 23			11 32	11 40	11 45	11 55		12 06	12 14	12 19	12 32	12 23			12 40	12 45	12 55		13 06
d	11 15	11 20	11 24			11 33	11 40	11 45	11 56		12 07	12 15	12 20	12 33	12 24			12 40	12 45	12 56		13 07
Westhoughton d			11 31					11 53							12 31				12 53			
Hindley d			11 35	11 45				11 57		12 17					12 35	12 45			12 57		13 17	
Ince d				11 48												12 48						
Wigan North Western a																						
Wigan Wallgate a			11 46	11 51				12 02	12 15	12 22					12 46	12 51			13 02	13 13	13 22	
d				11 52				12 03		12 24						12 52			13 03		13 24	
Pemberton d				11 56												12 56						
Orrell d				12 00												13 00						
Upholland d				12 04												13 04						
Rainford d				12 07												13 07						
Kirkby a				12 21												13 21						
Gathurst d										12 28											13 28	
Appley Bridge d								12 10		12 32									13 10		13 32	
Parbold d								12 14		12 36									13 14		13 36	
Hoscar d																					13 39	
Burscough Bridge d								12 18		12 41									13 18		13 42	
New Lane d																					13 44	
Bescar Lane d																					13 48	
Meols Cop d										12 49											13 53	
Southport a								12 37		12 59									13 37		14 02	
Lostock d	11 20						11 45					12 20						12 45				
Horwich Parkway d	11 24						11 49				12 13	12 24						12 49				13 13
Blackrod d							11 52											12 52				
Adlington (Lancashire) d							11 56											12 56				
Chorley d	11 32					11 44	12 01				12 21	12 32		12 44				13 01				13 21
Leyland d	11 42						12 12					12 42						13 12				
Preston 8 65,97 a	11 50					11 55	12 17				12 33	12 50		12 55				13 17				13 33
d						11 58	12 19				12 38			12 58			13 04	13 19				13 38
Kirkham & Wesham 97 a							12 28											13 28				
Poulton-le-Fylde 97 a							12 36				12 56							13 36				13 56
Layton 97 a							12 43											13 43				
Blackpool North 97 a							12 52				13 05							13 52				14 05
Lancaster 6 65 a						12 13								13 13			13 19					
d					11 28	12 14								13 14			13 20					
Oxenholme Lake District 65 a														13 28			13 36					
Windermere 83 a																	13 56					
Carnforth d					11 37	12 23																
Silverdale d					11 43																	
Arnside d					11 48	12 31																
Grange-over-Sands d					11 54	12 37																
Kents Bank d					11 57																	
Cark d					12 02																	
Ulverston d					12 10	12 49																
Dalton d					12 18																	
Roose d					12 24																	
Barrow-in-Furness a					12 31	13 10																

A ✠ to Chorley
b arr. 1126
c arr. 1225

Table 82

Saturdays
from 11 September

Manchester - Bolton - Wigan, Kirkby, Southport, Preston, Blackpool North and Barrow-in-Furness

	NT	NT	NT	NT	NT	NT	TP	NT	NT	NT	NT	TP	NT	NT	NT	NT	NT	TP	TP	NT	NT
							◇1 ✠					◇1 ✠						◇1	◇1 ✠		
Manchester Airport 85 ✈ d							13 00		13 03			13 29							14 00		14 03
Heald Green 85 d												13 33									
Buxton 86 d																					
Hazel Grove 86 d	12 31												13 31								
Stockport 84 d	12 41												13 41								
Manchester Piccadilly 10 ⇌ d	12 54						13 16		13 22			13 46	13 54						14 16		14 22
Manchester Oxford Road d	12 58						13 19		13 26			13 49	13 58						14 19		14 26
Deansgate ⇌ d	13 00								13 28			13 51	14 00								14 28
Rochdale 41 d										13 04											
Manchester Victoria ⇌ d		13 00	13 07	13 10				13 22		13b33	13 46			14 00	14 07	14 10				14 22	
Salford Central d		13 03	13 10	13 13				13 25		13 36	13 49			14 03	14 10	14 13				14 25	
Salford Crescent a	13 04	13 07	13 13	13 16				13 29	13 33	13 39	13 52	13 56	14 04	14 07	14 13	14 16				14 29	14 33
d	13 04	13 08	13 13	13 17				13 30	13 34	13 40	13 53	13 56	14 04	14 08	14 13	14 17				14 30	14 34
Swinton d				13 23							13 59					14 23					
Moorside d				13 26												14 26					
Walkden d				13 29							14 04					14 29					
Atherton d				13 35							14 09					14 35					
Hag Fold d				13 37												14 37					
Daisy Hill d				13 40							14 13					14 40					
Kearsley d										13 47											
Farnworth d										13 49											
Moses Gate d										13 52											
Bolton a	13 14	13 19	13 23				13 32	13 40	13 45	13 55		14 06	14 14	14 19	14 23				14 32	14 40	14 45
d	13 15	13 20	13 24				13 33	13 40	13 45	13 56		14 07	14 15	14 20	14 24				14 33	14 40	14 45
Westhoughton d			13 31						13 53						14 31						14 53
Hindley d			13 35	13 45					13 57		14 17				14 35	14 45					14 57
Ince d				13 48												14 48					
Wigan North Western a																					
Wigan Wallgate a			13 46	13 51					14 02	14 15	14 22				14 46	14 51					15 02
d				13 52					14 03		14 24					14 52					15 03
Pemberton d				13 56												14 56					
Orrell d				14 00												15 00					
Upholland d				14 04												15 04					
Rainford d				14 07												15 07					
Kirkby a				14 21												15 21					
Gathurst d											14 28										
Appley Bridge d									14 10		14 32										15 10
Parbold d									14 14		14 36										15 14
Hoscar d																					
Burscough Bridge d									14 18		14 41										15 18
New Lane d																					
Bescar Lane d																					
Meols Cop d											14 49										
Southport a									14 37		15 01										15 37
Lostock d	13 20							13 45					14 20							14 45	
Horwich Parkway d	13 24							13 49				14 13	14 24							14 49	
Blackrod d								13 52												14 52	
Adlington (Lancashire) d								13 56												14 56	
Chorley d	13 32						13 44	14 01				14 21	14 32						14 44	15 01	
Leyland d	13 42							14 12					14 42							15 12	
Preston 8 65,97 a	13 50						13 55	14 17				14 33	14 50						14 55	15 17	
d							13 58	14 19				14 38						14 47	14 58	15 19	
Kirkham & Wesham 97 a								14 28												15 28	
Poulton-le-Fylde 97 a								14 36				14 56								15 36	
Layton 97 a								14 43												15 43	
Blackpool North 97 a								14 50				15 05								15 52	
Lancaster 6 65 a						13 42	14 13											15 02	15 13		
d					13 32	13 48	14 14										14 22	15 03	15 14		
Oxenholme Lake District 65 a							14 28												15 28		
Windermere 83 a																					
Carnforth d					13 41	13 58											14 32	15 11			
Silverdale d					13 47												14 38				
Arnside d					13 52												14 42	15 20			
Grange-over-Sands d					13 58												14 48	15 25			
Kents Bank d					14 01												14 52				
Cark d					14 06												14 56				
Ulverston d					14 14												15 04	15 38			
Dalton d					14 22												15 12				
Roose d					14 28												15 18				
Barrow-in-Furness a					14 36												15 26	15 58			

b arr. 1325

Table 82

Manchester - Bolton - Wigan, Kirkby, Southport, Preston, Blackpool North and Barrow-in-Furness

	NT	NT	TP	NT	NT	TP	NT	NT	NT	NT	NT	NT	NT	TP	NT	NT	NT	NT	NT	TP	TP	NT
			◇1 🛒			◇1 A 🛒								◇1 🛒						◇1 🛒	◇1	
Manchester Airport 85 ✈ d			14 29			15 00				15 03				15 29						16 00		
Heald Green 85 d			14 33											15 33								
Buxton 86 d																						
Hazel Grove 86 d				14 31											15 31							
Stockport 84 d				14 41											15 41							
Manchester Piccadilly 10 ⇌ d			14 46	14 54		15 16				15 22				15 46	15 54					16 16		
Manchester Oxford Road d			14 49	14 58		15 19				15 26				15 49	15 58					16 19		
Deansgate ⇌ d			14 51	15 00						15 28				15 51	16 00							
Rochdale 41 d	14 04										15 04											
Manchester Victoria ⇌ d	14b33	14 46			15 00		15 07	15 10	15 22		15c33	15 40	15 46			16 07	16 10					16 20
Salford Central d	14 36	14 49			15 03		15 10	15 13	15 25		15 36	15 43	15 49			16 10	16 13					16 23
Salford Crescent a	14 39	14 52	14 56	15 04	15 07		15 13	15 16	15 29	15 33	15 39	15 46	15 52	15 56	16 04	16 13	16 16					16 26
d	14 40	14 53	14 56	15 04	15 08		15 13	15 17	15 30	15 34	15 40	15 47	15 53	15 56	16 04	16 13	16 17					16 27
Swinton d		14 59						15 23					15 59				16 23					
Moorside d								15 26									16 26					
Walkden d		15 04						15 29					16 04				16 29					
Atherton d		15 09						15 35					16 09				16 35					
Hag Fold d								15 37									16 37					
Daisy Hill d		15 13						15 40					16 13				16 40					
Kearsley d	14 47										15 47											
Farnworth d	14 49										15 49											
Moses Gate d	14 52										15 52											
Bolton a	14 55		15 06	15 14	15 19	15 32	15 23		15 40	15 45	15 55	15 59		16 06	16 14	16 23				16 32		16 37
d	14 56		15 07	15 15	15 20	15 33	15 24		15 40	15 45	15 56	16 00		16 07	16 15	16 24				16 33		16 37
Westhoughton d							15 31			15 53						16 31						
Hindley d		15 17					15 35	15 45		15 57			16 17			16 35	16 45					
Ince d								15 48									16 48					
Wigan North Western a																						
Wigan Wallgate a	15 15	15 22					15 46	15 51		16 02	16 15		16 22			16 46	16 51					
d		15 24						15 52		16 03			16 24				16 52					
Pemberton d								15 56									16 56					
Orrell d								16 00									17 00					
Upholland d								16 04									17 04					
Rainford d								16 07									17 07					
Kirkby a								16 21									17 21					
Gathurst d		15 28								16 08			16 28									
Appley Bridge d		15 32								16 11			16 32									
Parbold d		15 36								16 15			16 36									
Hoscar d										16 18												
Burscough Bridge d		15 40								16 21			16 40									
New Lane d										16 24												
Bescar Lane d										16 27												
Meols Cop d		15 48								16 32			16 48									
Southport a		15 59								16 44			16 59									
Lostock d				15 20					15 45						16 20							16 43
Horwich Parkway d			15 13	15 24					15 49					16 13	16 24							16 47
Blackrod d									15 52													16 51
Adlington (Lancashire) d									15 56													16 55
Chorley d			15 21	15 32		15 44			16 01					16 21	16 32					16 44		17 00
Leyland d				15 42					16 12						16 42							17 11
Preston 8 65,97 a			15 33	15 50		15 55			16 19					16 33	16 50					16 55		17 20
d			15 38			15 58								16 38						17 00	17 04	17 21
Kirkham & Wesham 97 a														16 47								17 30
Poulton-le-Fylde 97 a			15 56											16 57								17 38
Layton 97 a														17 00								17 43
Blackpool North 97 a			16 05											17 07								17 50
Lancaster 6 65 a						16 13												16 30		17 15	17 20	
d						16 14												16 40	17 00	17 16	17 21	
Oxenholme Lake District 65 a																				17 30	17 38	
Windermere 83 a																					18 00	
Carnforth d						16 22												16 50	17 10			
Silverdale d						16 28													17 17			
Arnside d						16 32													17 21			
Grange-over-Sands d						16 38													17 27			
Kents Bank d						16 41													17 31			
Cark d						16 46													17 35			
Ulverston d						16 54													17 44			
Dalton d						17 02													17 53			
Roose d						17 08													17 59			
Barrow-in-Furness a						17 18													18 07			

A 🛒 to Chorley

b arr. 1425

c arr. 1526

Table 82

Saturdays
from 11 September

Manchester - Bolton - Wigan, Kirkby, Southport, Preston, Blackpool North and Barrow-in-Furness

	NT	NT	NT	TP	NT	NT	NT	NT	NT	NT	TP	NT	NT	NT	NT	NT	TP	NT	NT
				◇1 🛒							◇1 🛒						◇1 🛒		
Manchester Airport 85 ✈ d		16 03		16 29							17 00			17 03			17 29		
Heald Green 85 d				16 33													17 33		
Buxton 86 d																			
Hazel Grove 86 d						16 30													17 31
Stockport 84 d						16 41													17 41
Manchester Piccadilly 10 ⇌ d		16 22		16 46		16 54					17 15			17 22			17 46		17 54
Manchester Oxford Road d		16 26		16 49		16 58					17 18			17 26			17 49		17 58
Deansgate ⇌ d		16 28				17 00											17 51		18 00
Rochdale 41 d			16 04										17 03						
Manchester Victoria ⇌ d	16 23		16b36		16 46		17 00	17 07	17 10			17 19	17 23		17 36	17 40		17 50	
Salford Central d	16 26		16 39		16 49		17 03	17 10	17 13			17 22	17 26		17 39	17 43		17 53	
Salford Crescent a	16 30	16 34	16 42		16 52	17 04	17 07	17 13	17 17			17 25	17 30	17 34	17 42	17 46	17 55	17 58	18 04
d	16 31	16 34	16 43		16 53	17 04	17 08	17 13	17 17			17 27	17 31	17 34	17 43	17 47	17 55	17 59	18 04
Swinton d					16 59				17 23									18 05	
Moorside d					17 02				17 26									18 08	
Walkden d					17 05				17 29									18 11	
Atherton d					17 11				17 35							17 59		18 17	
Hag Fold d					17 14				17 37									18 19	
Daisy Hill d					17 17				17 40							18 03		18 22	
Kearsley d			16 50												17 53				
Farnworth d			16 52												17 55				
Moses Gate d			16 55												17 57				
Bolton a	16 42	16 45	16 58	17 05		17 14	17 19	17 23			17 31	17 37	17 42	17 45	18 01		18 06		18 14
d	16 43	16 45	16 59	17 06		17 15	17 20	17 24			17 32	17 37	17 43	17 45	18 01		18 07		18 15
Westhoughton d		16 53	17 06					17 31						17 53	18 09				
Hindley d		16 57	17 10		17 21			17 35	17 45						18 13			18 27	
Ince d					17 24				17 48										
Wigan North Western a																			
Wigan Wallgate a		17 02	17 21		17 27			17 44	17 51					18 01	18 24	18 11		18 32	
d		17 03			17 29				17 52					18 02		18 15		18 33	
Pemberton d									17 56									18 37	
Orrell d									18 00									18 41	
Upholland d									18 04									18 45	
Rainford d									18 07									18 48	
Kirkby a									18 21									19 02	
Gathurst d		17 08			17 33											18 19			
Appley Bridge d		17 11			17 37									18 09		18 23			
Parbold d		17 15			17 41									18 13		18 28			
Hoscar d																			
Burscough Bridge d		17 20			17 45									18 17		18 33			
New Lane d																			
Bescar Lane d																			
Meols Cop d		17 27			17 53											18 41			
Southport a		17 39			18 04									18 37		18 52			
Lostock d						17 20						17 43					18 12		18 20
Horwich Parkway d						17 24						17 47					18 15		18 24
Blackrod d												17 51					18 18		
Adlington (Lancashire) d												17 55							
Chorley d				17 19		17 32					17 45	18 00					18 25		18 32
Leyland d						17 42						18 11					18 33		18 42
Preston 8 65,97 a				17 30		17 50					17 55	18 16					18 38		18 48
d				17 32							17 58	18 18					18 40		18 49
Kirkham & Wesham 97 a				17 41								18 27					18 49		
Poulton-le-Fylde 97 a				17 51								18 35					18 59		
Layton 97 a				17 54								18 39					19 02		
Blackpool North 97 a				18 02								18 48					19 09		19 18
Lancaster 6 65 a											18 13								
d										17 33	18 14								
Oxenholme Lake District 65 a																			
Windermere 83 a																			
Carnforth d										17 43	18 22								
Silverdale d										17 49	18 28								
Arnside d										17 54	18 32								
Grange-over-Sands d										18 00	18 38								
Kents Bank d										18 03	18 41								
Cark d										18 08	18 46								
Ulverston d										18 16	18 54								
Dalton d										18 24	19 02								
Roose d										18 30	19 08								
Barrow-in-Furness a										18 38	19 18								

b arr. 1625

Table 82

Saturdays from 11 September

Manchester - Bolton - Wigan, Kirkby, Southport, Preston, Blackpool North and Barrow-in-Furness

		NT	TP ◇1 🚌	NT	TP ◇1	NT	NT	NT	NT	NT	TP ◇1 🚌	NT	NT	NT	NT	TP ◇1	NT	NT	TP ◇1	NT	TP ◇1
Manchester Airport 85 ✈	d		18 00					18 03			18 29					19 00	19 03		19 29		20 00
Heald Green 85	d										18 33								19 33		
Buxton 86	d																				
Hazel Grove 86	d											18 31									
Stockport 84	d											18 41									
Manchester Piccadilly 10	d		18 16					18 22			18 46	18 54				19 16	19 20		19 46		20 16
Manchester Oxford Road	d		18 19					18 26			18 49	18 58				19 19	19 24		19 49		20 19
Deansgate	d							18 28			18 51	19 00					19 26		19 51		
Rochdale 41	d						18 02														
Manchester Victoria	d	18 00		18 08		18 20	18 23		18 33	18 45			19 00	19 10				19 28		20 00	
Salford Central	d	18 03		18 12		18 23	18 26		18 36	18 48			19 03	19 13				19 31		20 03	
Salford Crescent	a	18 07		18 16		18 26	18 30	18 34	18 39	18 51	18 56	19 04	19 07	19 16			19 29	19 34	19 56	20 07	
	d	18 08		18 17		18 27	18 31	18 34	18 40	18 52	18 56	19 04	19 08	19 17			19 30	19 35	19 56	20 08	
Swinton	d			18 23						18 58				19 23							
Moorside	d			18 26						19 01				19 26							
Walkden	d			18 29						19 04				19 29							
Atherton	d			18 35						19 10				19 35							
Hag Fold	d			18 37						19 12				19 37							
Daisy Hill	d			18 40						19 15				19 40							
Kearsley	d								18 47												
Farnworth	d								18 49												
Moses Gate	d								18 52												
Bolton	a	18 19	18 32			18 37	18 42	18 45	18 55		19 06	19 19	19 20			19 32	19 40	19 45	20 06	20 19	20 32
	d	18 20	18 33			18 37	18 43	18 45	18 56		19 07		19 20			19 33	19 40	19 45	20 07	20 20	20 33
Westhoughton	d							18 53	19 03								19 48				
Hindley	d			18 45				18 57	19 09	19 20				19 45			19 52				
Ince	d			18 48						19 23				19 48							
Wigan North Western	a			18 56																	
Wigan Wallgate	a							19 02	19 20	19 32				19 57			19 57				
	d							19 03									19 59				
Pemberton	d																				
Orrell	d																				
Upholland	d																				
Rainford	d																				
Kirkby	a																				
Gathurst	d							19 07									20 03				
Appley Bridge	d							19 11									20 07				
Parbold	d							19 15									20 11				
Hoscar	d																				
Burscough Bridge	d							19 19									20 15				
New Lane	d																				
Bescar Lane	d																				
Meols Cop	d							19 27									20 23				
Southport	a							19 39									20 34				
Lostock	d					18 42					19 12							19 50			
Horwich Parkway	d					18 46					19 15							19 54	20 13		20 39
Blackrod	d					18 49												19 57			
Adlington (Lancashire)	d					18 53												20 01			
Chorley	d		18 44			18 58					19 23					19 44		20 06	20 21		20 46
Leyland	d					19 10												20 18			
Preston 8 65,97	a		18 55			19 18					19 33					19 58		20 24	20 33		20 57
	d		19 00		19 04	19 19					19 38					20 02		20 25	20 38		21 02
Kirkham & Wesham 97	a					19 28												20 34			
Poulton-le-Fylde 97	a					19 36					19 56							20 42	20 56		
Layton 97	a					19 43												20 47			
Blackpool North 97	a					19 52					20 05							20 56	21 06		
Lancaster 6 65	a		19 15		19 20										19 20	20 17					21 17
	d		19 16		19 20										19 24	20 18					21 18
Oxenholme Lake District 65	a		19 30																		
Windermere 83	a																				
Carnforth	d				19 29										19 35	20 26					21 26
Silverdale	d				19 35											20 32					21 32
Arnside	d				19 39											20 36					21 36
Grange-over-Sands	d				19 44											20 42					21 42
Kents Bank	d				19 48											20 45					21 45
Cark	d				19 52											20 50					21 50
Ulverston	d				20 00											20 58					21 58
Dalton	d				20 08											21 06					22 06
Roose	d				20 14											21 12					22 12
Barrow-in-Furness	a				20 24											21 20					22 20

Table 82

Saturdays from 11 September

Manchester - Bolton - Wigan, Kirkby, Southport, Preston, Blackpool North and Barrow-in-Furness

		NT	NT	NT	TP ◇1	NT	NT	NT	NT	NT	NT	TP ◇1	TP ◇1	NT	NT	NT	NT	TP ◇1	NT	NT
Manchester Airport 85 ✈	d			20 03	20 29					21 03		21 29	22 00			22 19		22 29		
Heald Green 85	d				20 33							21 33						22 33		
Buxton 86	d																			
Hazel Grove 86	d																			
Stockport 84	d																		22 40	
Manchester Piccadilly 10	d			20 20	20 46					21 20	21 38	21 46	22 16			22 36		22 46	22 54	
Manchester Oxford Road	d			20 24	20 49					21 24	21 44	21 49	22 19			22 39		22 49	22 58	
Deansgate	d			20 26	20 51					21 26	21 46	21 51				22 41		22 51	23 00	
Rochdale 41	d																			
Manchester Victoria	d	20 10	20 22			21 00	21 10		21 22					22 00	22 22		22 45			23 05
Salford Central	d	20 13	20 25			21 03	21 13		21 25					22 03	22 25		22 48			23 08
Salford Crescent	a	20 16	20 29	20 33	20 56	21 07	21 16		21 29	21 33		21 56		22 07	22 29	22 46	22 51	22 56	23 02	23 11
	d	20 17	20 30	20 34	20 56	21 08	21 17		21 30	21 34		21 56		22 08	22 30	22 46	22 52	22 56	23 04	23 12
Swinton	d	20 23					21 23										22 58			
Moorside	d	20 26					21 26										23 01			
Walkden	d	20 29					21 29										23 04			
Atherton	d	20 35					21 35										23 10			
Hag Fold	d	20 37					21 37										23 12			
Daisy Hill	d	20 40					21 40										23 15			
Kearsley	d																		23 11	
Farnworth	d																		23 13	
Moses Gate	d																		23 16	
Bolton	a		20 40	20 45	21 06	21 19			21 40	21 45		22 06	22 32	22 19	22 40	22 56		23 06	23 19	23 23
	d		20 40	20 45	21 07	21 20			21 40	21 45		22 07	22 33	22 20	22 40	22 57		23 07	23 20	23 24
Westhoughton	d			20 53						21 53						23 04			23 27	
Hindley	d	20 45		20 57			21 45			21 57						23 08	23 20		23 31	
Ince	d	20 48					21 48										23 23			
Wigan North Western	a																			
Wigan Wallgate	a	20 57		21 02			21 57			22 02						23 13	23 32		23 43	
	d			21 03						22 03						23 15				
Pemberton	d																			
Orrell	d																			
Upholland	d																			
Rainford	d																			
Kirkby	a																			
Gathurst	d			21 08						22 08						23 19				
Appley Bridge	d			21 11						22 11						23 23				
Parbold	d			21 15						22 15						23 27				
Hoscar	d			21 18																
Burscough Bridge	d			21 21						22 20						23 31				
New Lane	d			21 24																
Bescar Lane	d			21 27																
Meols Cop	d			21 32						22 27						23 39				
Southport	a			21 42						22 39						23 50				
Lostock	d		20 45						21 45						22 45					
Horwich Parkway	d		20 49		21 13				21 49			22 13			22 49			23 13		
Blackrod	d		20 52						21 52						22 52					
Adlington (Lancashire)	d		20 56						21 56						22 56					
Chorley	d		21 01		21 21				22 02			22 21			23 01			23 21		
Leyland	d		21 12						22 12						23 12					
Preston 8 65,97	a		21 17		21 33				22 18			22 33	22 54		23 17			23 33		
	d		21 19		21 38			21 59	22 19			22 35	22 55		23 19			23 35		
Kirkham & Wesham 97	a		21 28						22 28						23 28					
Poulton-le-Fylde 97	a		21 36		21 56				22 36			22 53			23 36			23 52		
Layton 97	a		21 40						22 43						23 40					
Blackpool North 97	a		21 48		22 06				22 52			23 02			23 50			00 02		
Lancaster 6 65	a							22 19					23 11							
	d							22 19					23 11							
Oxenholme Lake District 65	a																			
Windermere 83	a																			
Carnforth	d							22 29					23 20							
Silverdale	d							22 35					23 26							
Arnside	d							22 40					23 30							
Grange-over-Sands	d							22 46					23 35							
Kents Bank	d							22 49					23 39							
Cark	d							22 54					23 43							
Ulverston	d							23 02					23 51							
Dalton	d							23 10					23 59							
Roose	d							23 16					00 05							
Barrow-in-Furness	a							23 24					00 15							

Table 82

Saturdays from 11 September

Manchester - Bolton - Wigan, Kirkby, Southport, Preston, Blackpool North and Barrow-in-Furness

Station			NT	NT
Manchester Airport	85 ✈	d		
Heald Green	85	d		
Buxton	86	d		
Hazel Grove	86	d		
Stockport	84	d		
Manchester Piccadilly 10	⇌	d		
Manchester Oxford Road		d		
Deansgate	⇌	d		
Rochdale	41	d		
Manchester Victoria	⇌	d	23 16	23 20
Salford Central		d	23 19	23 23
Salford Crescent		a	23 22	23 26
		d	23 22	23 26
Swinton		d		23 33
Moorside		d		23 35
Walkden		d		23 39
Atherton		d		23 44
Hag Fold		d		23 47
Daisy Hill		d		23 50
Kearsley		d		
Farnworth		d		
Moses Gate		d		
Bolton		a	23 32	
		d	23 33	
Westhoughton		d		
Hindley		d		23 54
Ince		d		23 57
Wigan North Western		a		
Wigan Wallgate		a		00 06
		d		
Pemberton		d		
Orrell		d		
Upholland		d		
Rainford		d		
Kirkby		a		
Gathurst		d		
Appley Bridge		d		
Parbold		d		
Hoscar		d		
Burscough Bridge		d		
New Lane		d		
Bescar Lane		d		
Meols Cop		d		
Southport		a		
Lostock		d	23 38	
Horwich Parkway		d	23 42	
Blackrod		d	23 45	
Adlington (Lancashire)		d	23 49	
Chorley		d	23 54	
Leyland		d	00 04	
Preston 8	65,97	a	00 10	
		d	00 11	
Kirkham & Wesham	97	a	00 21	
Poulton-le-Fylde	97	a	00 29	
Layton	97	a	00 33	
Blackpool North	97	a	00 42	
Lancaster 6	65	a		
		d		
Oxenholme Lake District	65	a		
Windermere	83	a		
Carnforth		d		
Silverdale		d		
Arnside		d		
Grange-over-Sands		d		
Kents Bank		d		
Cark		d		
Ulverston		d		
Dalton		d		
Roose		d		
Barrow-in-Furness		a		

Table 82

Sundays until 05 September

Manchester - Bolton - Wigan, Kirkby, Southport, Preston, Blackpool North and Barrow-in-Furness

Station			TP	TP	NT	TP ◇1	NT	NT	TP ◇1	NT	TP ◇1	TP ◇1	NT	NT	TP ◇1	NT	NT	NT	NT
Manchester Airport	85 ✈	d	00 10	05 30		07 55			08 29		09 00				09 30				
Heald Green	85	d																	
Buxton	86	d																	
Hazel Grove	86	d																	
Stockport	84	d						08 22						09 22					10 12
Manchester Piccadilly 10	⇌	d	00 35	05 55		08 11		08 35	08 46		09 16			09 35	09 46				10 26
Manchester Oxford Road		d				08 14		08 38	08 49		09 19			09 38	09 49				10b38
Deansgate	⇌	d				08 16		08 40	08 51					09 40	09 51				10 40
Rochdale	41	d																	
Manchester Victoria	⇌	d			08 01		08 25			09 00			09 25			10 00	10 09	10 25	
Salford Central		d																	
Salford Crescent		a			08 07	08 19	08 29	08 44	08 54	09 06			09 29	09 44	09 54	10 06	10 15	10 29	10 44
		d			08 08	08 20	08 30	08 44	08 55	09 08			09 30	09 44	09 55	10 08	10 17	10 30	10 44
Swinton		d															10 23		
Moorside		d															10 26		
Walkden		d															10 29		
Atherton		d															10 35		
Hag Fold		d															10 37		
Daisy Hill		d															10 40		
Kearsley		d																	
Farnworth		d																	
Moses Gate		d																	
Bolton		a	01s00	06s20	08 19	08 30	08 40	08 54	09 05	09 19	09 32		09 40	09 54	10 05	10 19		10 40	10 54
		d	01s00	06s20	08 20	08 30	08 40	08 55	09 05	09 20	09 33		09 40	09 55	10 05	10 20		10 40	10 55
Westhoughton		d						09 02						10 02					11 02
Hindley		d						09 06						10 06			10 45		11 06
Ince		d																	
Wigan North Western		a																	
Wigan Wallgate		a						09 11						10 11			10 54		11 11
		d						09 13						10 13					11 13
Pemberton		d																	
Orrell		d																	
Upholland		d																	
Rainford		d																	
Kirkby		a																	
Gathurst		d						09 17						10 17					11 17
Appley Bridge		d						09 21						10 21					11 21
Parbold		d						09 25						10 25					11 25
Hoscar		d																	
Burscough Bridge		d						09 29						10 29					11 29
New Lane		d																	
Bescar Lane		d																	
Meols Cop		d						09 37						10 37					11 37
Southport		a						09 46						10 46					11 46
Lostock		d					08 45						09 45					10 45	
Horwich Parkway		d				08 37	08 49		09 12				09 49		10 12			10 49	
Blackrod		d					08 52						09 52					10 52	
Adlington (Lancashire)		d					08 56						09 56					10 56	
Chorley		d				08 45	09 01		09 20		09 44		10 01		10 20			11 01	
Leyland		d					09 12						10 12					11 12	
Preston 8	65,97	a	01s35	06s55		08 56	09 18		09 33		09 57		10 18		10 32			11 18	
		d	01s35	06s55		08 57	09 20		09 34		10 00	10 06	10 20		10 34			11 20	
Kirkham & Wesham	97	a					09 29						10 29					11 29	
Poulton-le-Fylde	97	a				09 14	09 37		09 51				10 37		10 51			11 37	
Layton	97	a					09 42						10 42					11 42	
Blackpool North	97	a	02 15	07 35		09 25	09 49		10 00				10 49		11 00			11 49	
Lancaster 6	65	a									10 16	10 22							
		d									10 16	10 23							
Oxenholme Lake District	65	a									10 30	10 39							
Windermere	83	a										10 58							
Carnforth		d																	
Silverdale		d																	
Arnside		d																	
Grange-over-Sands		d																	
Kents Bank		d																	
Cark		d																	
Ulverston		d																	
Dalton		d																	
Roose		d																	
Barrow-in-Furness		a																	

b arr. 1028

The Sunday service between Manchester Victoria and Wigan Wallgate via Atherton is funded by GMITA and will operate whilst funding exists

Table 82

Sundays
until 05 September

Manchester - Bolton - Wigan, Kirkby, Southport, Preston, Blackpool North and Barrow-in-Furness

			TP	TP	NT		TP			NT	NT	NT	TP	NT	NT	NT	TP		NT	NT	TP	NT	TP	NT	TP	NT
			◇1	◇1			◇1						◇1				◇1 ⌶				◇1		◇1 ⌶		◇1	
Manchester Airport	85 ✈	d		10 29			11 00						11 30				12 00				12 30		13 00			
Heald Green	85	d																								
Buxton	86	d																								
Hazel Grove	86	d																								
Stockport	84	d																		12 21						
Manchester Piccadilly 10	⇌	d		10 46			11 16					11 35	11 46				12 16			12 35	12 46		13 16			
Manchester Oxford Road		d		10 49			11 19					11 38	11 49				12 19			12 38	12 49		13 19			
Deansgate	⇌	d		10 51								11 40	11 51							12 40	12 51					
Rochdale	41	d																								
Manchester Victoria	⇌	d			11 00					11 12	11 25			12 00	12 09				12 25			13 00		13 12		13 25
Salford Central		d																								
Salford Crescent		a		10 54	11 06					11 16	11 29	11 44	11 54	12 06	12 13				12 29	12 44	12 54	13 06		13 16		13 29
		d		10 55	11 08					11 17	11 30	11 44	11 55	12 08	12 17				12 30	12 44	12 55	13 08		13 17		13 30
Swinton		d								11 23					12 23									13 23		
Moorside		d								11 26					12 26									13 26		
Walkden		d								11 29					12 29									13 29		
Atherton		d								11 35					12 35									13 35		
Hag Fold		d								11 37					12 37									13 37		
Daisy Hill		d								11 40					12 40									13 40		
Kearsley		d																								
Farnworth		d																								
Moses Gate		d																								
Bolton		a		11 05	11 19		11 32				11 40	11 54	12 05	12 19			12 32		12 40	12 54	13 05	13 19	13 32			13 40
		d		11 05	11 20		11 33				11 40	11 55	12 05	12 20			12 33		12 40	12 55	13 05	13 20	13 33			13 40
Westhoughton		d										12 02								13 02						
Hindley		d								11 45		12 06			12 45					13 06				13 45		
Ince		d																								
Wigan North Western		a																								
Wigan Wallgate		a								11 54		12 11			12 54					13 11				13 54		
		d										12 13								13 13						
Pemberton		d																								
Orrell		d																								
Upholland		d																								
Rainford		d																								
Kirkby		a																								
Gathurst		d										12 17								13 17						
Appley Bridge		d										12 21								13 21						
Parbold		d										12 25								13 25						
Hoscar		d																								
Burscough Bridge		d										12 29								13 29						
New Lane		d																								
Bescar Lane		d																								
Meols Cop		d										12 37								13 37						
Southport		a										12 46								13 46						
Lostock		d									11 45								12 45							13 45
Horwich Parkway		d		11 12							11 49		12 12						12 49		13 12					13 49
Blackrod		d									11 52								12 52							13 52
Adlington (Lancashire)		d									11 56								12 56							13 56
Chorley		d		11 20			11 44				12 01		12 20				12 44		13 01		13 20		13 44			14 01
Leyland		d									12 12								13 12							14 12
Preston 8	65,97	a		11 32			11 57				12 18		12 32				12 57		13 18		13 32		13 57			14 18
		d		11 34			11 58				12 20		12 34				12 58		13 20		13 34		14 00		14 05	14 20
Kirkham & Wesham	97	a									12 29								13 29							14 29
Poulton-le-Fylde	97	a		11 51							12 37		12 51						13 37		13 51					14 37
Layton	97	a									12 42								13 42							14 42
Blackpool North	97	a		12 00							12 49		13 00						13 49		14 01					14 49
Lancaster 8	65	a					12 13									12 30	13 13						14 15		14 21	
		d	10 28				12 14									12 48	13 14						14 16		14 21	
Oxenholme Lake District	65	a															13 28						14 30			
Windermere	83	a																								
Carnforth		d	10 36				12 22									12 58									14 30	
Silverdale		d	10 42				12 28																		14 36	
Arnside		d	10 46				12 32																		14 40	
Grange-over-Sands		d	10 52				12 38																		14 45	
Kents Bank		d	10 55				12 41																		14 49	
Cark		d	11 00				12 46																		14 53	
Ulverston		d	11 08				12 54																		15 01	
Dalton		d	11 16				13 02																		15 09	
Roose		d	11 22				13 08																		15 15	
Barrow-in-Furness		a	11 30				13 17																		15 25	

b arr. 1056

The Sunday service between Manchester Victoria and Wigan Wallgate via Atherton is funded by GMITA and will operate whilst funding exists

Table 82

Sundays
until 05 September

Manchester - Bolton - Wigan, Kirkby, Southport, Preston, Blackpool North and Barrow-in-Furness

			NT		TP	NT	NT	NT	TP	NT	NT	TP	NT		TP	NT	NT	NT	TP	NT	NT	NT	TP		TP	NT
					◇1				◇1 ⌶			◇1			◇1				◇1				◇1 ⌶		◇1	
Manchester Airport	85 ✈	d			13 30				14 00			14 30			15 00				15 30				16 00			
Heald Green	85	d																								
Buxton	86	d																								
Hazel Grove	86	d																								
Stockport	84	d	13 22								14 21							15 22								
Manchester Piccadilly 10	⇌	d	13 35		13 46				14 16		14 35	14 46			15 16			15 35	15 46				16 16			
Manchester Oxford Road		d	13 38		13 49				14 19		14 38	14 49			15 19			15 38	15 49				16 19			
Deansgate	⇌	d	13 40		13 51						14 40	14 51						15 40	15 51							
Rochdale	41	d																								
Manchester Victoria	⇌	d				14 00	14 12			14 25			15 00			15 12	15 25			16 00	16 12					16 25
Salford Central		d																								
Salford Crescent		a	13 44		13 54	14 06	14 16			14 29	14 44	14 54	15 06			15 16	15 29	15 44	15 54	16 06	16 16					16 29
		d	13 44		13 55	14 08	14 17			14 30	14 44	14 55	15 08			15 17	15 30	15 44	15 55	16 08	16 17					16 30
Swinton		d					14 23									15 23					16 23					
Moorside		d					14 26									15 26					16 26					
Walkden		d					14 29									15 29					16 29					
Atherton		d					14 35									15 35					16 35					
Hag Fold		d					14 37									15 37					16 37					
Daisy Hill		d					14 40									15 40					16 40					
Kearsley		d																								
Farnworth		d																								
Moses Gate		d																								
Bolton		a	13 54		14 05	14 19			14 32	14 40	14 54	15 05	15 19		15 32		15 40	15 54	16 05	16 19			16 32			16 40
		d	13 55		14 05	14 20			14 33	14 40	14 55	15 05	15 20		15 33		15 40	15 55	16 05	16 20			16 33			16 40
Westhoughton		d	14 02								15 02							16 02								
Hindley		d	14 06				14 45				15 06					15 45		16 06			16 45					
Ince		d																								
Wigan North Western		a																								
Wigan Wallgate		a	14 11				14 54				15 11					15 54		16 11			16 54					
		d	14 13								15 13							16 13								
Pemberton		d																								
Orrell		d																								
Upholland		d																								
Rainford		d																								
Kirkby		a																								
Gathurst		d	14 17								15 17							16 17								
Appley Bridge		d	14 21								15 21							16 21								
Parbold		d	14 25								15 25							16 25								
Hoscar		d																								
Burscough Bridge		d	14 29								15 29							16 29								
New Lane		d																								
Bescar Lane		d																								
Meols Cop		d	14 37								15 37							16 37								
Southport		a	14 46								15 46							16 46								
Lostock		d								14 45							15 45									16 45
Horwich Parkway		d			14 12					14 49		15 12					15 49		16 12							16 49
Blackrod		d								14 52							15 52									16 52
Adlington (Lancashire)		d								14 56							15 56									16 56
Chorley		d			14 20				14 44	15 01		15 20			15 44		16 01		16 20				16 44			17 01
Leyland		d								15 12							16 12									17 12
Preston 8	65,97	a			14 32				14 57	15 18		15 32			15 57		16 18		16 32				16 57			17 18
		d			14 34				15 00	15 20		15 34			16 00		16 20		16 34				17 00		17 04	17 20
Kirkham & Wesham	97	a								15 29							16 29									17 29
Poulton-le-Fylde	97	a			14 51					15 37		15 51					16 37		16 51							17 37
Layton	97	a								15 42							16 42									17 42
Blackpool North	97	a			15 00					15 49		16 00					16 49		17 00							17 49
Lancaster 8	65	a							15 15						16 15								17 15		17 22	
		d						14 27	15 16						16 16							17 04	17 16		17 22	
Oxenholme Lake District	65	a							15 30														17 30		17 39	
Windermere	83	a																							17 59	
Carnforth		d						15 00							16 24							17 14				
Silverdale		d													16 30							17 20				
Arnside		d													16 34							17 25				
Grange-over-Sands		d													16 40							17 31				
Kents Bank		d													16 43							17 34				
Cark		d													16 48							17 38				
Ulverston		d													16 56							17 46				
Dalton		d													17 04							17 55				
Roose		d													17 10							18 01				
Barrow-in-Furness		a													17 19							18 08				

The Sunday service between Manchester Victoria and Wigan Wallgate via Atherton is funded by GMITA and will operate whilst funding exists

Manchester - Bolton - Wigan, Kirkby, Southport, Preston, Blackpool North and Barrow-in-Furness

Station		NT	TP	NT	NT	NT	TP	TP		TP	TP	NT	NT	TP	NT	TP	NT	NT		NT	TP	NT	TP	NT	NT
			◇1				◇1	◇1		◇1	◇1			◇1		◇1					◇1		◇1		
							A	A		B	B														
							🍴			🍴						🍴									
Manchester Airport 85 ✈	d		16 30				17 00			17 00				17 30		18 00					18 30		19 00		
Heald Green 85	d																								
Buxton 86	d																								
Hazel Grove 86	d																								
Stockport 84	d	16 21											17 22							18 21					19 22
Manchester Piccadilly 10	d	16 35	16 46				17 16			17 16			17 35	17 46		18 16				18 35	18 46		19 16		19 35
Manchester Oxford Road	d	16 38	16 49				17 19			17 19			17 38	17 49		18 19				18 38	18 49		19 19		19 38
Deansgate	d	16 40	16 51										17 40	17 51						18 40	18 51				19 40
Rochdale 41	d																								
Manchester Victoria	d			17 00	17 12							17 25			18 00		18 12	18 25				19 00		19 25	
Salford Central	d																								
Salford Crescent	a	16 44	16 54	17 06	17 16							17 29	17 44	17 54	18 06		18 16	18 29		18 44	18 54	19 06		19 29	19 44
	d	16 44	16 55	17 08	17 17							17 30	17 44	17 55	18 08		18 17	18 30		18 44	18 55	19 08		19 30	19 44
Swinton	d				17 23												18 23								
Moorside	d				17 26												18 26								
Walkden	d				17 29												18 29								
Atherton	d				17 35												18 35								
Hag Fold	d				17 37												18 37								
Daisy Hill	d				17 40												18 40								
Kearsley	d																								
Farnworth	d																								
Moses Gate	d																								
Bolton	a	16 54	17 05	17 19			17 32			17 32		17 40	17 54	18 05	18 19	18 32		18 40		18 54	19 05	19 19	19 32	19 40	19 54
	d	16 55	17 05	17 20			17 33			17 33		17 40	17 55	18 05	18 20	18 33		18 40		18 55	19 05	19 20	19 33	19 40	19 55
Westhoughton	d	17 02											18 02							19 02					20 02
Hindley	d	17 06			17 45								18 06				18 45			19 06					20 06
Ince	d																								
Wigan North Western	a																								
Wigan Wallgate	a	17 11			17 54								18 11				18 54			19 11					20 11
	d	17 13											18 13							19 13					20 13
Pemberton	d																								
Orrell	d																								
Upholland	d																								
Rainford	d																								
Kirkby	a																								
Gathurst	d	17 17											18 17							19 17					20 17
Appley Bridge	d	17 21											18 21							19 21					20 21
Parbold	d	17 25											18 25							19 25					20 25
Hoscar	d																								
Burscough Bridge	d	17 29											18 29							19 29					20 29
New Lane	d																								
Bescar Lane	d																								
Meols Cop	d	17 37											18 37							19 37					20 37
Southport	a	17 46											18 46							19 46					20 46
Lostock	d											17 45						18 45						19 45	
Horwich Parkway	d		17 12									17 49		18 12				18 49			19 12			19 49	
Blackrod	d											17 52						18 52						19 52	
Adlington (Lancashire)	d											17 56						18 56						19 56	
Chorley	d		17 20				17 44			17 44		18 01		18 20		18 44		19 01			19 20		19 44	20 01	
Leyland	d											18 12						19 12						20 12	
Preston 8 65,97	a		17 32				17 57			17 57		18 18		18 32		18 57		19 18			19 32		19 57	20 18	
	d		17 34				18 00	18 06		18 08	18 12	18 20		18 34		19 00		19 20			19 34		20 00	20 20	
Kirkham & Wesham 97	a											18 29						19 29						20 29	
Poulton-le-Fylde 97	a		17 51									18 37		18 51				19 37			19 51			20 37	
Layton 97	a											18 42						19 42						20 42	
Blackpool North 97	a		18 00									18 49		19 00				19 49			20 00			20 49	
Lancaster 8 65	a					17 55	18 15	18 22		18 23	18 28					19 15							20 15		
	d					18 04	18 16	18 22		18 24	18 28					19 16							20 16		
Oxenholme Lake District 65	a						18 30			18 38						19 30									
Windermere 83	a																								
Carnforth	d					18 14		18 31			18 37												20 24		
Silverdale	d							18 37			18 43												20 30		
Arnside	d							18 41			18 47												20 34		
Grange-over-Sands	d							18 46			18 52												20 40		
Kents Bank	d							18 50			18 56												20 43		
Cark	d							18 54			19 00												20 48		
Ulverston	d							19 02			19 08												20 56		
Dalton	d							19 10			19 16												21 04		
Roose	d							19 16			19 22												21 10		
Barrow-in-Furness	a							19 26			19 32												21 19		

A until 27 June

B from 4 July until 5 September

The Sunday service between Manchester Victoria and Wigan Wallgate via Atherton is funded by GMITA and will operate whilst funding exists

Manchester - Bolton - Wigan, Kirkby, Southport, Preston, Blackpool North and Barrow-in-Furness

Station		TP	NT	NT		NT	NT	TP	NT	TP	NT	NT	TP	NT		NT	NT	TP
		◇1						◇1		◇1			◇1					◇1
Manchester Airport 85 ✈	d	19 30						20 30					21 30					22 30
Heald Green 85	d																	
Buxton 86	d																	
Hazel Grove 86	d																	
Stockport 84	d						20 21					21 22					22 21	
Manchester Piccadilly 10	d	19 46					20 35	20 46				21 35	21 46				22 35	22 46
Manchester Oxford Road	d	19 49					20 38	20 49				21 38	21 49				22 38	22 49
Deansgate	d	19 51					20 40	20 51				21 40	21 51				22 40	22 51
Rochdale 41	d																	
Manchester Victoria	d		20 00			20 25			21 00		21 25			22 00				
Salford Central	d																	
Salford Crescent	a	19 54	20 06			20 29	20 44	20 54	21 06		21 29	21 44	21 54	22 06			22 44	22 54
	d	19 55	20 08			20 30	20 44	20 55	21 08		21 30	21 44	21 55	22 08			22 44	22 55
Swinton	d																	
Moorside	d																	
Walkden	d																	
Atherton	d																	
Hag Fold	d																	
Daisy Hill	d																	
Kearsley	d																	
Farnworth	d																	
Moses Gate	d																	
Bolton	a	20 05	20 19			20 40	20 54	21 05	21 19		21 40	21 54	22 05	22 19			22 54	23 05
	d	20 05	20 20			20 40	20 55	21 05	21 20		21 40	21 55	22 05	22 20			22 55	23 05
Westhoughton	d						21 02					22 02					23 02	
Hindley	d						21 06					22 06					23 06	
Ince	d																	
Wigan North Western	a																	
Wigan Wallgate	a						21 11					22 15					23 15	
	d						21 13											
Pemberton	d																	
Orrell	d																	
Upholland	d																	
Rainford	d																	
Kirkby	a																	
Gathurst	d						21 17											
Appley Bridge	d						21 21											
Parbold	d						21 25											
Hoscar	d																	
Burscough Bridge	d						21 29											
New Lane	d																	
Bescar Lane	d																	
Meols Cop	d						21 37											
Southport	a						21 46											
Lostock	d					20 45					21 45							23 10
Horwich Parkway	d	20 12				20 49		21 12			21 49							23 14
Blackrod	d					20 52					21 52							23 17
Adlington (Lancashire)	d					20 56					21 56							23 20
Chorley	d	20 20				21 01		21 20			22 01		22 17					23 24
Leyland	d					21 12					22 12							23 34
Preston 8 65,97	a	20 32				21 18		21 32			22 18		22 29					23 42
	d	20 34				21 20		21 34			22 20		22 29					23 47
Kirkham & Wesham 97	a					21 29					22 29							23 56
Poulton-le-Fylde 97	a	20 51				21 37		21 51			22 37		22 46					00 05
Layton 97	a					21 42					22 42							
Blackpool North 97	a	21 00				21 49		22 00			22 49		22 55					00 14
Lancaster 8 65	a			20 11						21 18								
	d			20 20						21 23						22 05		
Oxenholme Lake District 65	a																	
Windermere 83	a																	
Carnforth	d			20 30						21 31						22 15		
Silverdale	d									21 37						22 21		
Arnside	d									21 41						22 26		
Grange-over-Sands	d									21 47						22 32		
Kents Bank	d									21 50						22 35		
Cark	d									21 55						22 39		
Ulverston	d									22 03						22 47		
Dalton	d									22 11						22 56		
Roose	d									22 17						23 02		
Barrow-in-Furness	a									22 26						23 09		

The Sunday service between Manchester Victoria and Wigan Wallgate via Atherton is funded by GMITA and will operate whilst funding exists

Table 82

Sundays
from 12 September

Manchester - Bolton - Wigan, Kirkby, Southport, Preston, Blackpool North and Barrow-in-Furness

Station		TP	TP	TP	NT	NT	NT	NT	TP	TP	NT	NT	TP	NT	NT
		🚌	🚌	◇1					◇1	◇1 ✠			◇1		
Manchester Airport 85 ✈	d	00 10	05 30	07 30					08 47	09 00			09 30		
Heald Green 85	d														
Buxton 86	d														
Hazel Grove 86	d														
Stockport 84	d											09 22			
Manchester Piccadilly 10 ⇌	d	00 35	05 55	07 46					09 03	09 16		09 35	09 46		
Manchester Oxford Road	d			07 49					09 06	09 19		09 38	09 49		
Deansgate ⇌	d			07 51					09 08			09 40	09 51		
Rochdale 41	d														
Manchester Victoria ⇌	d				08 01	08 25	08 39	09 00			09 25			10 00	10 09
Salford Central	d														
Salford Crescent	a			07 54	08 07	08 29	08 44	09 06	09 11		09 29	09 44	09 54	10 07	10 15
	d			07 55	08 08	08 30	08 44	09 08	09 12		09 30	09 44	09 55	10 08	10 17
Swinton	d														10 23
Moorside	d														10 26
Walkden	d														10 29
Atherton	d														10 35
Hag Fold	d														10 37
Daisy Hill	d														10 40
Kearsley	d														
Farnworth	d														
Moses Gate	d														
Bolton	a	01s00	06s20	08 05	08 19	08 40	08 54	09 19	09 22	09 32	09 40	09 54	10 05	10 19	
	d	01s00	06s20	08 06	08 20	08 40	08 55	09 20	09 23	09 33	09 40	09 55	10 05	10 20	
Westhoughton	d						09 02					10 02			
Hindley	d						09 06					10 06			10 45
Ince	d														
Wigan North Western	a														
Wigan Wallgate	a						09 11					10 11			10 54
	d						09 13					10 13			
Pemberton	d														
Orrell	d														
Upholland	d														
Rainford	d														
Kirkby	a														
Gathurst	d						09 17					10 17			
Appley Bridge	d						09 21					10 21			
Parbold	d						09 25					10 25			
Hoscar	d														
Burscough Bridge	d						09 29					10 29			
New Lane	d														
Bescar Lane	d														
Meols Cop	d						09 37					10 37			
Southport	a						09 48					10 48			
Lostock	d					08 45					09 45				
Horwich Parkway	d			08 12		08 49			09 30		09 49		10 12		
Blackrod	d					08 52					09 52				
Adlington (Lancashire)	d					08 56					09 56				
Chorley	d			08 20		09 01			09 37	09 44	10 01		10 20		
Leyland	d					09 12					10 12				
Preston 8 65,97	a	01s35	06s55	08 31		09 18			09 50	09 57	10 18		10 32		
	d	01s35	06s55	08 32		09 20			09 51	10 00	10 20		10 34		
Kirkham & Wesham 97	a					09 29					10 29				
Poulton-le-Fylde 97	a			08 49		09 37			10 08		10 37		10 51		
Layton 97	a					09 42					10 42				
Blackpool North 97	a	02 15	07 35	08 58		09 49			10 17		10 49		11 00		
Lancaster 6 65	a									10 15					
	d									10 16					
Oxenholme Lake District 65	a									10 30					
Windermere 83	a														
Carnforth	d														
Silverdale	d														
Arnside	d														
Grange-over-Sands	d														
Kents Bank	d														
Cark	d														
Ulverston	d														
Dalton	d														
Roose	d														
Barrow-in-Furness	a														

The Sunday service between Manchester Victoria and Wigan Wallgate via Atherton is funded by GMITA and will operate whilst funding exists

Table 82

Sundays
from 12 September

Manchester - Bolton - Wigan, Kirkby, Southport, Preston, Blackpool North and Barrow-in-Furness

Station		TP	TP	NT	NT	TP	NT	NT	NT	NT	TP	NT	NT	NT	TP	NT
		◇1 ✠	◇1			◇1					◇1			A	◇1 ✠	
Manchester Airport 85 ✈	d	10 00				10 25					11 30				11 58	
Heald Green 85	d															
Buxton 86	d															
Hazel Grove 86	d															
Stockport 84	d				10 19					11 12						
Manchester Piccadilly 10 ⇌	d	10 16			10 35	10 43				11 27	11 46				12 16	
Manchester Oxford Road	d	10 19			10 38	10 49				11b38	11 49				12 19	
Deansgate ⇌	d				10 40	10 51				11 40	11 51					
Rochdale 41	d															
Manchester Victoria ⇌	d			10 25			11 00	11 12	11 25			12 00	12 09			12 25
Salford Central	d															
Salford Crescent	a			10 29	10 44	10 54	11 06	11 16	11 29	11 44	11 54	12 06	12 13			12 29
	d			10 30	10 44	10 55	11 08	11 17	11 30	11 44	11 55	12 08	12 17			12 30
Swinton	d							11 23					12 23			
Moorside	d							11 26					12 26			
Walkden	d							11 29					12 29			
Atherton	d							11 35					12 35			
Hag Fold	d							11 37					12 37			
Daisy Hill	d							11 40					12 40			
Kearsley	d															
Farnworth	d															
Moses Gate	d															
Bolton	a	10 32		10 40	10 54	11 05	11 19		11 40	11 54	12 05	12 19			12 32	12 40
	d	10 32		10 40	10 55	11 05	11 20		11 40	11 55	12 05	12 20			12 33	12 40
Westhoughton	d				11 02					12 02						
Hindley	d				11 06			11 45		12 06			12 45			
Ince	d															
Wigan North Western	a															
Wigan Wallgate	a				11 11			11 54		12 11			12 54			
	d				11 13					12 13						
Pemberton	d															
Orrell	d															
Upholland	d															
Rainford	d															
Kirkby	a															
Gathurst	d				11 17					12 17						
Appley Bridge	d				11 21					12 21						
Parbold	d				11 25					12 25						
Hoscar	d															
Burscough Bridge	d				11 29					12 29						
New Lane	d															
Bescar Lane	d															
Meols Cop	d				11 37					12 37						
Southport	a				11 48					12 48						
Lostock	d			10 45					11 45							12 45
Horwich Parkway	d			10 49		11 12			11 49		12 12					12 49
Blackrod	d			10 52					11 52							12 52
Adlington (Lancashire)	d			10 56					11 56							12 56
Chorley	d	10 44		11 02		11 20			12 01		12 20				12 44	13 01
Leyland	d			11 12					12 12							13 12
Preston 8 65,97	a	10 55		11 18		11 32			12 18		12 32				12 57	13 18
	d	11 00	11 18	11 20		11 34			12 20		12 34				12 58	13 20
Kirkham & Wesham 97	a			11 29					12 29							13 29
Poulton-le-Fylde 97	a			11 37		11 51			12 37		12 51					13 37
Layton 97	a			11 42					12 42							13 42
Blackpool North 97	a			11 49		12 00			12 49		13 00					13 49
Lancaster 6 65	a	11 15	11 33											12 30	13 13	
	d	11 16	11 34											12 48	13 14	
Oxenholme Lake District 65	a	11 30													13 28	
Windermere 83	a															
Carnforth	d		11 42											12 58		
Silverdale	d		11 48													
Arnside	d		11 52													
Grange-over-Sands	d		11 58													
Kents Bank	d		12 01													
Cark	d		12 06													
Ulverston	d		12 14													
Dalton	d		12 22													
Roose	d		12 28													
Barrow-in-Furness	a		12 37													

A 12 September
b arr. 1129

The Sunday service between Manchester Victoria and Wigan Wallgate via Atherton is funded by GMITA and will operate whilst funding exists

Table 82

Sundays
from 12 September

Manchester - Bolton - Wigan, Kirkby, Southport, Preston, Blackpool North and Barrow-in-Furness

	NT	TP ◇1	NT	NT	TP ◇1	TP ◇1 🛒	NT	NT	TP ◇1	NT	NT	NT A	TP ◇1 🛒	NT	NT	TP ◇1	NT	TP ◇1
Manchester Airport 85 ✈ d		12 30				12 58			13 30				13 58			14 30		15 00
Heald Green 85 d																		
Buxton 86 d																		
Hazel Grove 86 d																		
Stockport 84 d	12 15							13 22							14 21			
Manchester Piccadilly 10 ⇌ d	12 30	12 46				13 16		13 35	13 46				14 16		14 35	14 46		15 16
Manchester Oxford Road d	12b38	12 49				13 19		13 38	13 49				14 19		14 38	14 49		15 19
Deansgate ⇌ d	12 40	12 51						13 40	13 51						14 40	14 51		
Rochdale 41 d																		
Manchester Victoria ⇌ d			13 00	13 12			13 25			14 00	14 12			14 25			15 00	
Salford Central d																		
Salford Crescent a	12 44	12 54	13 06	13 16			13 29	13 44	13 54	14 06	14 16			14 29	14 44	14 54	15 06	
d	12 44	12 55	13 08	13 17			13 30	13 44	13 55	14 08	14 17			14 30	14 44	14 55	15 08	
Swinton d				13 23							14 23							
Moorside d				13 26							14 26							
Walkden d				13 29							14 29							
Atherton d				13 35							14 35							
Hag Fold d				13 37							14 37							
Daisy Hill d				13 40							14 40							
Kearsley d																		
Farnworth d																		
Moses Gate d																		
Bolton a	12 54	13 05	13 19			13 32	13 40	13 54	14 05	14 19			14 32	14 40	14 54	15 05	15 19	15 32
d	12 55	13 05	13 20			13 33	13 40	13 55	14 05	14 20			14 33	14 40	14 55	15 05	15 20	15 33
Westhoughton d	13 02							14 02							15 02			
Hindley d	13 06			13 45				14 06			14 45				15 06			
Ince d																		
Wigan North Western a																		
Wigan Wallgate a	13 11			13 54				14 11			14 54				15 11			
d	13 13							14 13							15 13			
Pemberton d																		
Orrell d																		
Upholland d																		
Rainford d																		
Kirkby a																		
Gathurst d	13 17							14 17							15 17			
Appley Bridge d	13 21							14 21							15 21			
Parbold d	13 25							14 25							15 25			
Hoscar d																		
Burscough Bridge d	13 29							14 29							15 29			
New Lane d																		
Bescar Lane d																		
Meols Cop d	13 37							14 37							15 37			
Southport a	13 48							14 48							15 48			
Lostock d							13 45							14 45				
Horwich Parkway d		13 12					13 49		14 12					14 49		15 12		
Blackrod d							13 52							14 52				
Adlington (Lancashire) d							13 56							14 56				
Chorley d		13 20				13 44	14 01		14 20				14 44	15 01		15 20		15 44
Leyland d							14 12							15 12				
Preston 8 65,97 a		13 32				13 57	14 18		14 32				14 57	15 18		15 32		15 57
d		13 34			13 47	14 00	14 20		14 34				15 00	15 20		15 34		16 00
Kirkham & Wesham 97 a							14 29							15 29				
Poulton-le-Fylde 97 a		13 51					14 37		14 51					15 37		15 51		
Layton 97 a							14 42							15 42				
Blackpool North 97 a		14 01					14 49		15 00					15 49		16 00		
Lancaster 8 65 a					14 03	14 15							15 15					16 15
d					14 03	14 16						14 27	15 16					16 16
Oxenholme Lake District 65 a						14 30							15 30					
Windermere 83 a																		
Carnforth d					14 12							15 00						16 24
Silverdale d					14 18													16 30
Arnside d					14 22													16 34
Grange-over-Sands d					14 27													16 40
Kents Bank d					14 31													16 43
Cark d					14 35													16 48
Ulverston d					14 43													16 56
Dalton d					14 51													17 04
Roose d					14 57													17 10
Barrow-in-Furness a					15 07													17 19

A from 12 September

b arr. 1232

The Sunday service between Manchester Victoria and Wigan Wallgate via Atherton is funded by GMITA and will operate whilst funding exists

Table 82

Sundays
from 12 September

Manchester - Bolton - Wigan, Kirkby, Southport, Preston, Blackpool North and Barrow-in-Furness

	NT	NT	NT	TP ◇1	NT	NT	NT	TP ◇1 🛒	NT	NT	TP ◇1	NT	NT	NT	TP ◇1 🛒	TP ◇1	NT	NT	TP ◇1	NT	TP ◇1 🛒	NT
Manchester Airport 85 ✈ d				15 30				16 00			16 30				17 00				17 30		18 00	
Heald Green 85 d																						
Buxton 86 d																						
Hazel Grove 86 d																						
Stockport 84 d			15 22							16 21								17 22				
Manchester Piccadilly 10 ⇌ d			15 35	15 46				16 16		16 35	16 46				17 16			17 35	17 46		18 16	
Manchester Oxford Road d			15 38	15 49				16 19		16 38	16 49				17 19			17 38	17 49		18 19	
Deansgate ⇌ d			15 40	15 51						16 40	16 51							17 40	17 51			
Rochdale 41 d																						
Manchester Victoria ⇌ d	15 12	15 25			16 00	16 12			16 25			17 00	17 12				17 25			18 00		18 12
Salford Central d																						
Salford Crescent a	15 16	15 29	15 44	15 54	16 06	16 16			16 29	16 44	16 54	17 06	17 16				17 29	17 44	17 54	18 06		18 16
d	15 17	15 30	15 44	15 55	16 08	16 17			16 30	16 44	16 55	17 08	17 17				17 30	17 44	17 55	18 08		18 17
Swinton d	15 23					16 23							17 23									18 23
Moorside d	15 26					16 26							17 26									18 26
Walkden d	15 29					16 29							17 29									18 29
Atherton d	15 35					16 35							17 35									18 35
Hag Fold d	15 37					16 37							17 37									18 37
Daisy Hill d	15 40					16 40							17 40									18 40
Kearsley d																						
Farnworth d																						
Moses Gate d																						
Bolton a		15 40	15 54	16 05	16 19			16 32	16 40	16 54	17 05	17 19			17 32		17 40	17 54	18 05	18 19	18 32	
d		15 40	15 55	16 05	16 20			16 33	16 40	16 55	17 05	17 20			17 33		17 40	17 55	18 05	18 20	18 33	
Westhoughton d			16 02							17 02								18 02				
Hindley d	15 45		16 06			16 45				17 06			17 45					18 06				18 45
Ince d																						
Wigan North Western a																						
Wigan Wallgate a	15 54		16 11			16 54				17 11			17 54					18 11				18 54
d			16 13							17 13								18 13				
Pemberton d																						
Orrell d																						
Upholland d																						
Rainford d																						
Kirkby a																						
Gathurst d			16 17							17 17								18 17				
Appley Bridge d			16 21							17 21								18 21				
Parbold d			16 25							17 25								18 25				
Hoscar d																						
Burscough Bridge d			16 29							17 29								18 29				
New Lane d																						
Bescar Lane d																						
Meols Cop d			16 37							17 37								18 37				
Southport a			16 48							17 48								18 48				
Lostock d		15 45							16 45								17 45					
Horwich Parkway d		15 49		16 12					16 49		17 12						17 49		18 12			
Blackrod d		15 52							16 52								17 52					
Adlington (Lancashire) d		15 56							16 56								17 56					
Chorley d		16 01		16 20				16 44	17 01		17 20				17 44		18 01		18 20		18 44	
Leyland d		16 12							17 12								18 12					
Preston 8 65,97 a		16 18		16 32				16 57	17 18		17 32				17 57		18 18		18 32		18 57	
d		16 20		16 34				17 00	17 20		17 34				18 00	18 06	18 20		18 34		19 00	
Kirkham & Wesham 97 a		16 29							17 29								18 29					
Poulton-le-Fylde 97 a		16 37		16 51					17 37		17 51						18 37		18 51			
Layton 97 a		16 42							17 42								18 42					
Blackpool North 97 a		16 49		17 00					17 49		18 00						18 49		19 00			
Lancaster 8 65 a								17 15						17 55	18 15	18 22					19 15	
d							17 04	17 16						18 04	18 16	18 22					19 16	
Oxenholme Lake District 65 a								17 30							18 30						19 30	
Windermere 83 a																						
Carnforth d							17 14							18 14		18 31						
Silverdale d							17 20									18 37						
Arnside d							17 25									18 41						
Grange-over-Sands d							17 31									18 46						
Kents Bank d							17 34									18 50						
Cark d							17 38									18 54						
Ulverston d							17 46									19 02						
Dalton d							17 55									19 10						
Roose d							18 01									19 16						
Barrow-in-Furness a							18 08									19 26						

The Sunday service between Manchester Victoria and Wigan Wallgate via Atherton is funded by GMITA and will operate whilst funding exists

Table 82

Sundays

from 12 September

Manchester - Bolton - Wigan, Kirkby, Southport, Preston, Blackpool North and Barrow-in-Furness

			NT	NT	TP		NT	TP	NT	NT	TP	NT	NT	NT	NT		TP	NT	TP	NT	NT	TP	NT	NT	NT
					◇1			◇1			◇1						◇1		◇1			◇1			
Manchester Airport	85 ✈	d			18 30			19 00			19 30						20 30					21 30			
Heald Green	85	d																							
Buxton	86	d																							
Hazel Grove	86	d																							
Stockport	84	d		18 21						19 22					20 21						21 22				22 21
Manchester Piccadilly 10	⇌	d		18 35	18 46			19 16		19 35	19 46				20 35		20 46				21 35	21 46			22 35
Manchester Oxford Road		d		18 38	18 49			19 19		19 38	19 49				20 38		20 49				21 38	21 49			22 38
Deansgate	⇌	d		18 40	18 51					19 40	19 51				20 40		20 51				21 40	21 51			22 40
Rochdale	41	d																							
Manchester Victoria	⇌	d	18 25				19 00		19 25			20 00		20 25				21 00		21 25			22 00		
Salford Central		d																							
Salford Crescent		a	18 29	18 44	18 54		19 06		19 29	19 44	19 54	20 06		20 29	20 44		20 54	21 06		21 29	21 44	21 54	22 06		22 44
		d	18 30	18 44	18 55		19 08		19 30	19 44	19 55	20 08		20 30	20 44		20 55	21 08		21 30	21 44	21 55	22 08		22 44
Swinton		d																							
Moorside		d																							
Walkden		d																							
Atherton		d																							
Hag Fold		d																							
Daisy Hill		d																							
Kearsley		d																							
Farnworth		d																							
Moses Gate		d																							
Bolton		a	18 40	18 54	19 05		19 19	19 32	19 40	19 54	20 05	20 19		20 40	20 54		21 05	21 19		21 40	21 54	22 05	22 19		22 54
		d	18 40	18 55	19 05		19 20	19 33	19 40	19 55	20 05	20 20		20 40	20 55		21 05	21 20		21 40	21 55	22 05	22 20		22 55
Westhoughton		d		19 02						20 02					21 02						22 02				23 02
Hindley		d		19 06						20 06					21 06						22 06				23 06
Ince		d																							
Wigan North Western		a																							
Wigan Wallgate		a		19 11						20 11					21 11						22 17				23 17
		d		19 13						20 13					21 13										
Pemberton		d																							
Orrell		d																							
Upholland		d																							
Rainford		d																							
Kirkby		a																							
Gathurst		d		19 17						20 17					21 17										
Appley Bridge		d		19 21						20 21					21 21										
Parbold		d		19 25						20 25					21 25										
Hoscar		d																							
Burscough Bridge		d		19 29						20 29					21 29										
New Lane		d																							
Bescar Lane		d																							
Meols Cop		d		19 37						20 37					21 37										
Southport		a		19 48						20 48					21 48										
Lostock		d	18 45						19 45					20 45						21 45					
Horwich Parkway		d	18 49		19 12				19 49		20 12			20 49			21 12			21 49					
Blackrod		d	18 52						19 52					20 52						21 52					
Adlington (Lancashire)		d	18 56						19 56					20 56						21 56					
Chorley		d	19 01		19 20			19 44	20 01		20 20			21 01			21 20			22 01		22 17			
Leyland		d	19 12						20 12					21 12						22 12					
Preston 8	65,97	a	19 18		19 32			19 57	20 18		20 32			21 18			21 32			22 18		22 29			
		d	19 20		19 34			20 00	20 20		20 34			21 20			21 34			22 20		22 29			
Kirkham & Wesham	97	a	19 29						20 29					21 29						22 29					
Poulton-le-Fylde	97	a	19 37		19 51				20 37		20 51			21 37			21 51			22 37		22 46			
Layton	97	a	19 42						20 42					21 42						22 42					
Blackpool North	97	a	19 49		20 00				20 49		21 00			21 49			22 00			22 49		22 55			
Lancaster 8	65	a						20 15					20 11						21 18						
		d						20 16					20 20						21 23					22 05	
Oxenholme Lake District	65	a																							
Windermere	83	a																							
Carnforth		d						20 24					20 30						21 31					22 15	
Silverdale		d						20 30											21 37					22 21	
Arnside		d						20 34											21 41					22 26	
Grange-over-Sands		d						20 40											21 47					22 32	
Kents Bank		d						20 43											21 50					22 35	
Cark		d						20 48											21 55					22 39	
Ulverston		d						20 56											22 03					22 47	
Dalton		d						21 04											22 11					22 56	
Roose		d						21 10											22 17					23 02	
Barrow-in-Furness		a						21 19											22 26					23 09	

The Sunday service between Manchester Victoria and Wigan Wallgate via Atherton is funded by GMITA and will operate whilst funding exists

Table 82

Sundays

from 12 September

Manchester - Bolton - Wigan, Kirkby, Southport, Preston, Blackpool North and Barrow-in-Furness

			TP
			◇1
Manchester Airport	85 ✈	d	22 30
Heald Green	85	d	
Buxton	86	d	
Hazel Grove	86	d	
Stockport	84	d	
Manchester Piccadilly 10	⇌	d	22 46
Manchester Oxford Road		d	22 49
Deansgate	⇌	d	22 51
Rochdale	41	d	
Manchester Victoria	⇌	d	
Salford Central		d	
Salford Crescent		a	22 54
		d	22 55
Swinton		d	
Moorside		d	
Walkden		d	
Atherton		d	
Hag Fold		d	
Daisy Hill		d	
Kearsley		d	
Farnworth		d	
Moses Gate		d	
Bolton		a	23 05
		d	23 05
Westhoughton		d	
Hindley		d	
Ince		d	
Wigan North Western		a	
Wigan Wallgate		a	
		d	
Pemberton		d	
Orrell		d	
Upholland		d	
Rainford		d	
Kirkby		a	
Gathurst		d	
Appley Bridge		d	
Parbold		d	
Hoscar		d	
Burscough Bridge		d	
New Lane		d	
Bescar Lane		d	
Meols Cop		d	
Southport		a	
Lostock		d	23 10
Horwich Parkway		d	23 14
Blackrod		d	23 17
Adlington (Lancashire)		d	23 20
Chorley		d	23 24
Leyland		d	23 34
Preston 8	65,97	a	23 42
		d	23 47
Kirkham & Wesham	97	a	23 56
Poulton-le-Fylde	97	a	00 05
Layton	97	a	
Blackpool North	97	a	00 14
Lancaster 8	65	a	
		d	
Oxenholme Lake District	65	a	
Windermere	83	a	
Carnforth		d	
Silverdale		d	
Arnside		d	
Grange-over-Sands		d	
Kents Bank		d	
Cark		d	
Ulverston		d	
Dalton		d	
Roose		d	
Barrow-in-Furness		a	

The Sunday service between Manchester Victoria and Wigan Wallgate via Atherton is funded by GMITA and will operate whilst funding exists

Table 82

Mondays to Fridays
until 03 September

Barrow-in-Furness, Blackpool North, Preston, Southport, Kirkby and Wigan - Bolton - Manchester

			TP	TP	TP	NT	NT	TP	NT	NT	NT	TP	NT	NT	NT	NT
			◇1	◇1	◇1			◇1				◇1				
												A				
								🍴				🍴				
Barrow-in-Furness		d		04 35								05 31				
Roose		d														
Dalton		d														
Ulverston		d		04 51								05 47				
Cark		d														
Kents Bank		d														
Grange-over-Sands		d		05 04								06 00				
Arnside		d		05 10								06 06				
Silverdale		d														
Carnforth		d		05 20								06 15			06 44	
Windermere	83	d														
Oxenholme Lake District	65	d														
Lancaster 6	65	a		05 28								06 23			06 53	
		d										06 26				
Blackpool North	97	d	03 36			04 56		05 44						06 19		
Layton	97	d												06 22		
Poulton-le-Fylde	97	d				05 02		05 50						06 27		
Kirkham & Wesham	97	d												06 36		
Preston 8	65,97	a	04u00			05 20		06 08				06 45		06 46		
		d	04u01		05 16	05 22		06 09				06 47		06 48		
Leyland		d												06 53		
Chorley		d			05 26			06 18				06 56		07 01		
Adlington (Lancashire)		d												07 06		
Blackrod		d												07 10		
Horwich Parkway		d			05 35			06 26						07 14		
Lostock		d						06 30						07 20		
Southport		d											06 23			
Meols Cop		d											06 28			
Bescar Lane		d														
New Lane		d														
Burscough Bridge		d											06 36			
Hoscar		d														
Parbold		d											06 41			
Appley Bridge		d											06 45			
Gathurst		d											06 49			
Kirkby		d														
Rainford		d														
Upholland		d														
Orrell		d														
Pemberton		d														
Wigan Wallgate		a											06 54			
		d					06 03		06 31	06 36			06 55			
Wigan North Western		d														
Ince		d					06 06			06 39						
Hindley		d					06 09		06 36	06 42						
Westhoughton		d							06 41				07 03			
Bolton		a	04u30		05 42			06 34	06 52		06 55	07 08	07 11	07 25		07 30
		d	04u30		05 43			06 35	06 53		06 56	07 08	07 12	07 25		07 30
Moses Gate		d									06 59					
Farnworth		d									07 01					
Kearsley		d									07 03					
Daisy Hill		d					06 13			06 46						
Hag Fold		d					06 16			06 49						
Atherton		d					06 19			06 52						
Walkden		d					06 24			06 58						
Moorside		d					06 28			07 01						
Swinton		d					06 30			07 04						
Salford Crescent		a			05 55		06 38	06 47	07 05	07 11	07 15		07 24	07 38		07 43
		d			05 55		06 38	06 47	07 08	07 11	07 15		07 25	07 38		07 43
Salford Central		d					06 41			07 14	07 19			07 41		07 46
Manchester Victoria	⇌	a					06 46			07 20	07 26			07 47		07 53
Rochdale	41	a														
Deansgate	⇌	a						06 51	07 11				07 28			
Manchester Oxford Road		a						06 52	07 13			07 23	07 30			
Manchester Piccadilly 10	⇌	a	04 48		06 01			06 56	07 17			07 27	07 34			
Stockport	84	a							07 34							
Hazel Grove	86	a							07 45							
Buxton	86	a														
Heald Green	85	a						07 10								
Manchester Airport	85 ✈	a	05 07		06 18			07 17				07 47	07 53			

A 🍴 from Preston

Table 82

Mondays to Fridays
until 03 September

Barrow-in-Furness, Blackpool North, Preston, Southport, Kirkby and Wigan - Bolton - Manchester

			TP	NT	NT	NT	NT	NT	NT	NT	TP	NT	NT	NT	NT	TP	NT	NT	NT	NT	NT	NT
			◇1								◇1					◇1						
											A											
			🍴								🍴					🍴						
Barrow-in-Furness		d									06 19						07b00					
Roose		d									06 23						07 04					
Dalton		d									06 30						07 10					
Ulverston		d									06 38						07 19					
Cark		d									06 46						07 27					
Kents Bank		d									06 50						07 32					
Grange-over-Sands		d									06 54						07 36					
Arnside		d									07 00						07 43					
Silverdale		d									07 05						07 48					
Carnforth		d									07 12						07 54					
Windermere	83	d																				
Oxenholme Lake District	65	d																				
Lancaster 6	65	a									07 21					07 47	08 03					
		d									07 22					07 47	08 04					
Blackpool North	97	d	06 34				06 53	07 02						07 18								
Layton	97	d	06 37											07 21								
Poulton-le-Fylde	97	d	06 41					07 08						07 26								
Kirkham & Wesham	97	d	06 50											07 35								
Preston 8	65,97	a	07 01				07 15	07 28			07 41			07 46		08 07	08 29					
		d	07 03				07 17	07 30			07 47			07 47		08 12					08 17	
Leyland		d	07 08				07 22	07 35						07 53							08 23	
Chorley		d	07 15				07 31				07 56			08 01		08 22					08 33	
Adlington (Lancashire)		d					07 36							08 06							08 37	
Blackrod		d	07 21				07 40							08 10							08 41	
Horwich Parkway		d	07 26				07 44							08 14							08 45	
Lostock		d	07 29				07 49							08 20							08 50	
Southport		d			06 53							07 21								07 58		
Meols Cop		d			06 58							07 26								08 03		
Bescar Lane		d			07 03																	
New Lane		d			07 07																	
Burscough Bridge		d			07 09							07 34								08 11		
Hoscar		d			07 13																	
Parbold		d			07 16							07 39								08 16		
Appley Bridge		d			07 20							07 43								08 20		
Gathurst		d			07 23							07 47								08 23		
Kirkby		d							07 11													
Rainford		d							07 19													
Upholland		d							07 23													
Orrell		d							07 27													
Pemberton		d							07 30													
Wigan Wallgate		a			07 29				07 35			07 51								08 28		
		d		07 15	07 29				07 37			07 53	08 00					08 13		08 29		
Wigan North Western		d				07 22		07 50											08 20			
Ince		d		07 18		07 25			07 40									08 16				
Hindley		d		07 21		07 29			07 43			07 58						08 19	08 25	08 34		
Westhoughton		d				07 33						08 03							08 29			
Bolton		a	07 34			07 42	07 54			07 58	08 08	08 11		08 25	08 30	08 34			08 38		08 55	09 02
		d	07 35			07 43	07 55			07 59	08 08	08 12		08 25	08 31	08 35			08 39		08 56	09 02
Moses Gate		d				07 46				08 02									08 42			
Farnworth		d				07 48				08 04									08 44			
Kearsley		d				07 50				08 06									08 46			
Daisy Hill		d		07 26	07 39				07 47				08 07					08 23		08 39		
Hag Fold		d		07 29					07 50									08 26				
Atherton		d		07 32	07 43				07 53				08 12					08 29		08 43		
Walkden		d		07 38					07 59				08 18					08 35		08 49		
Moorside		d		07 41					08 03									08 39				
Swinton		d		07 44					08 06									08 42		08 54		
Salford Crescent		a	07 47	07 51	07 59	08 02	08 07		08 13	08 17		08 24	08 29	08 38	08 43	08 47		08 50	08 56	09 02	09 08	09 15
		d	07 47	07 51	07 59	08 02	08 08		08 13	08 17		08 25	08 30	08 38	08 44	08 47		08 50	08 56	09 02	09 09	09 16
Salford Central		d		07 55	08 02	08 05			08 16	08 20			08 32	08 41	08 46			08 53	08 59	09 04		09 18
Manchester Victoria	⇌	a		08 00	08 08	08 12			08 20	08 25			08 38	08 48	08 52			08 59	09 06	09 11		09 26
Rochdale	41	a							08 51													
Deansgate	⇌	a	07 51				08 11					08 28									09 12	
Manchester Oxford Road		a	07 52				08 14				08 23	08 31				08 52					09 14	
Manchester Piccadilly 10	⇌	a	07 56				08 18				08 27	08 35				08 56					09 18	
Stockport	84	a					08 34														09 34	
Hazel Grove	86	a					08 48														09 45	
Buxton	86	a																				
Heald Green	85	a	08 10									08 47				09 10						
Manchester Airport	85 ✈	a	08 17								08 47	08 53				09 19						

A 🍴 from Preston

b arr. 0642

Table 82

Mondays to Fridays
until 03 September

Barrow-in-Furness, Blackpool North, Preston, Southport, Kirkby and Wigan - Bolton - Manchester

		TP	NT	NT	NT	NT	NT	NT	TP	TP	NT	NT	NT	NT	NT	TP	NT	NT	NT	NT	NT
		◇1 A ⌶							◇1 B ⌶	◇1 C ⌶						◇1 ⌶					
Barrow-in-Furness	d	07 28	08 00																		
Roose	d		08 04																		
Dalton	d	07 37	08 10																		
Ulverston	d	07 45	08 19																		
Cark	d	07 53	08 29																		
Kents Bank	d		08 34																		
Grange-over-Sands	d	08 00	08 38																		
Arnside	d	08 06	08 44																		
Silverdale	d	08 11	08 49																		
Carnforth	d	08 18	08 56																		10 02
Windermere 83	d																				
Oxenholme Lake District 65	d															09 11					
Lancaster 6 65	a	08 26	09 09													09 26					10 12
	d	08 27														09 26					10 19
Blackpool North 97	d					08 20			08 43	08 45									09 20	09 37	
Layton 97	d					08 23													09 23		
Poulton-le-Fylde 97	d					08 28			08 49	08 51									09 28		
Kirkham & Wesham 97	d					08 37													09 37	09 52	
Preston 8 65,97	a	08 45				08 47			09 07	09 09						09 45			09 47	10 02	
	d	08 47				08 49	09 04		09 10	09 10			09 23			09 47			09 49	10 04	
Leyland	d					08 54	09 09						09 29						09 54	10 09	
Chorley	d	08 56				09 02			09 20	09 20			09 36			09 56			10 02		
Adlington (Lancashire)	d					09 07													10 07		
Blackrod	d					09 10													10 10		
Horwich Parkway	d					09 14			09 27	09 27			09 45						10 14		
Lostock	d					09 20							09 50						10 20		
Southport	d			08 25								09 02					09 24				
Meols Cop	d			08 30								09 07									
Bescar Lane	d																				
New Lane	d																				
Burscough Bridge	d			08 38								09 15					09 36				
Hoscar	d																				
Parbold	d			08 43								09 20					09 41				
Appley Bridge	d			08 47								09 24					09 45				
Gathurst	d			08 50								09 27									
Kirkby	d				08 21													09 32			
Rainford	d				08 29													09 40			
Upholland	d				08 33													09 44			
Orrell	d				08 36													09 47			
Pemberton	d				08 39													09 50			
Wigan Wallgate	a			08 55	08 45							09 32					09 51	09 56			
	d			08 56	08 50						09 20	09 32			09 48		09 53	09 58			
Wigan North Western	d						09 24													10 24	
Ince	d				08 53													10 01			
Hindley	d				08 57						09 25	09 37					09 58	10 04			
Westhoughton	d			09 04							09 29						10 02				
Bolton	a	09 08		09 12		09 25		09 30	09 34	09 34	09 38		09 55	10 00	10 02	10 08	10 12		10 25		
	d	09 08		09 13		09 25		09 31	09 35	09 35	09 39		09 56	10 00	10 03	10 08	10 13		10 25		
Moses Gate	d										09 42										
Farnworth	d										09 44										
Kearsley	d										09 46										
Daisy Hill	d				09 01							09 41						10 09			
Hag Fold	d				09 04													10 12			
Atherton	d				09 06							09 45						10 15			
Walkden	d				09 12							09 50						10 20			
Moorside	d				09 15													10 24			
Swinton	d				09 18							09 55						10 26			
Salford Crescent	a			09 25	09 27	09 38		09 43	09 47	09 47	09 56	10 03	10 08	10 13	10 15		10 25	10 34	10 38		
	d			09 26	09 27	09 38		09 44	09 47	09 47	09 56	10 03	10 09	10 13	10 15		10 26	10 34	10 38		
Salford Central	d				09 31	09 41		09 46			09 59	10 05		10 16	10 17			10 36	10 41		
Manchester Victoria ⇌	a				09 38	09 47		09 52			10 06	10 12		10 21	10 25			10 43	10 47		
Rochdale 41	a														10 51						
Deansgate ⇌	a			09 29					09 51	09 51			10 12				10 29				
Manchester Oxford Road	a	09 23		09 31					09 52	09 52			10 14			10 23	10 31				
Manchester Piccadilly 10 ⇌	a	09 27		09 35					09 56	09 56			10 18			10 27	10 35				
Stockport 84	a												10 34								
Hazel Grove 86	a												10 45								
Buxton 86	a																				
Heald Green 85	a								10 10	10 10											
Manchester Airport 85 ✈	a	09 47		09 53					10 17	10 17						10 47	10 53				

A ⌶ from Preston
B FO from 2 July until 3 September
C Does not apply Fridays 2 July to 3 September

Table 82

Mondays to Fridays
until 03 September

Barrow-in-Furness, Blackpool North, Preston, Southport, Kirkby and Wigan - Bolton - Manchester

		NT	TP	NT	NT	NT	NT	TP	NT	NT	NT	NT	NT	NT	TP	NT	NT	NT	NT	TP	NT
			◇1 ⌶					◇1 A ⌶							◇1 ⌶					◇1 A ⌶	
Barrow-in-Furness	d							09 22	10 16												
Roose	d							09 26	10 20												
Dalton	d							09 33	10 26												
Ulverston	d							09 41	10 35												
Cark	d							09 49	10 44												
Kents Bank	d							09 53	10 49												
Grange-over-Sands	d							09 57	10 53												
Arnside	d							10 03	10 59												
Silverdale	d							10 08	11 03												
Carnforth	d							10 15	11 10												
Windermere 83	d																			10 49	
Oxenholme Lake District 65	d																			11 09	
Lancaster 6 65	a							10 25	11 22											11 26	
	d							10 26												11 26	
Blackpool North 97	d											10 20	10 37		10 45						
Layton 97	d											10 23									
Poulton-le-Fylde 97	d											10 28			10 51						
Kirkham & Wesham 97	d											10 37	10 52								
Preston 8 65,97	a		10 04					10 45				10 47	11 02		11 09					11 45	
	d		10 12			10 23		10 47				10 49	11 04		11 10			11 23		11 47	
Leyland	d					10 29						10 54	11 09					11 29			
Chorley	d		10 22			10 36		10 56				11 02			11 20			11 36		11 56	
Adlington (Lancashire)	d											11 07									
Blackrod	d											11 10									
Horwich Parkway	d					10 45						11 14			11 27			11 45			
Lostock	d					10 50						11 20						11 50			
Southport	d				09 55					10 24							10 55				11 24
Meols Cop	d				10 00												11 00				
Bescar Lane	d				10 05												11 05				
New Lane	d				10 09												11 09				
Burscough Bridge	d				10 11					10 36							11 11				11 36
Hoscar	d				10 15												11 15				
Parbold	d				10 18					10 41							11 18				11 41
Appley Bridge	d				10 22					10 45							11 22				11 45
Gathurst	d				10 25												11 25				
Kirkby	d										10 32										
Rainford	d										10 40										
Upholland	d										10 44										
Orrell	d										10 47										
Pemberton	d										10 50										
Wigan Wallgate	a				10 30					10 51	10 56						11 30				11 51
	d			10 20	10 32		10 48			10 53	10 58					11 20	11 32		11 48		11 53
Wigan North Western	d												11 24								
Ince	d										11 01										
Hindley	d			10 25	10 37					10 58	11 04					11 25	11 37				11 58
Westhoughton	d			10 29						11 02						11 29					12 02
Bolton	a	10 30	10 34	10 38		10 55	11 02	11 08		11 12		11 25		11 30	11 34	11 38		11 55	12 02	12 08	12 12
	d	10 31	10 35	10 39		10 56	11 03	11 08		11 13		11 25		11 31	11 35	11 39		11 56	12 03	12 08	12 13
Moses Gate	d			10 42												11 42					
Farnworth	d			10 44												11 44					
Kearsley	d			10 46												11 46					
Daisy Hill	d				10 41						11 09						11 41				
Hag Fold	d										11 12										
Atherton	d				10 45						11 15						11 45				
Walkden	d				10 50						11 20						11 50				
Moorside	d										11 24										
Swinton	d				10 55						11 26						11 55				
Salford Crescent	a	10 43	10 47	10 56	11 02	11 08	11 15			11 25	11 34	11 38		11 43	11 47	11 56	12 02	12 08	12 15		12 25
	d	10 44	10 47	10 56	11 03	11 09	11 15			11 26	11 34	11 38		11 44	11 47	11 56	12 03	12 09	12 15		12 26
Salford Central	d	10 46		10 59	11 05		11 17				11 36	11 41		11 46		11 59	12 05		12 17		
Manchester Victoria ⇌	a	10 52		11 06	11 11		11 25				11 43	11 47		11 52		12 06	12 11		12 25		
Rochdale 41	a						11 51												12 51		
Deansgate ⇌	a		10 51			11 12				11 29					11 51			12 12			12 29
Manchester Oxford Road	a		10 52			11 14		11 23		11 31					11 52			12 14		12 23	12 31
Manchester Piccadilly 10 ⇌	a		10 56			11 18		11 27		11 35					11 56			12 18		12 27	12 35
Stockport 84	a					11 34												12 34			
Hazel Grove 86	a					11 45												12 45			
Buxton 86	a																				
Heald Green 85	a		11 10												12 10						
Manchester Airport 85 ✈	a		11 17					11 50		11 53					12 17					12 47	12 53

A ⌶ from Preston

Table 82

Barrow-in-Furness, Blackpool North, Preston, Southport, Kirkby and Wigan - Bolton - Manchester

		TP ◇1 ⌶	NT	NT	NT	NT	NT	TP ◇1 ⌶	NT	NT	NT	NT	TP ◇1 ⌶	NT	NT	NT	NT	NT	NT	TP ◇1 ⌶
Barrow-in-Furness	d	11 25												12 11						
Roose	d													12 15						
Dalton	d													12 21						
Ulverston	d	11 41												12 29						
Cark	d													12 37						
Kents Bank	d													12 41						
Grange-over-Sands	d	11 53												12 45						
Arnside	d	11 59												12 51						
Silverdale	d													12 56						
Carnforth	d	12 08				12 02								13 02						
Windermere	83 d																			
Oxenholme Lake District	65 d												12 10							
Lancaster ■	65 a	12 18				12 11							12 26	13 15						
	d	12 18				12 28							12 26							
Blackpool North	97 d			11 20	11 37			11 45									12 20	12 37		12 45
Layton	97 d			11 23													12 23			
Poulton-le-Fylde	97 d			11 28				11 51									12 28			12 51
Kirkham & Wesham	97 d			11 37	11 52												12 37	12 52		
Preston ■	65,97 a	12 37		11 47	12 02			12 09					12 45				12 47	13 02		13 09
	d			11 49	12 04			12 10			12 23		12 47				12 49	13 04		13 10
Leyland	d			11 54	12 09						12 29						12 54	13 09		
Chorley	d			12 02				12 20			12 36		12 56				13 02			13 20
Adlington (Lancashire)	d			12 07													13 07			
Blackrod	d			12 10													13 10			
Horwich Parkway	d			12 14				12 27			12 45						13 14			13 27
Lostock	d			12 20							12 50						13 20			
Southport	d									12 00					12 24					
Meols Cop	d									12 05										
Bescar Lane	d																			
New Lane	d																			
Burscough Bridge	d									12 13					12 36					
Hoscar	d																			
Parbold	d									12 18					12 41					
Appley Bridge	d									12 22					12 45					
Gathurst	d									12 25										
Kirkby	d		11 32													12 32				
Rainford	d		11 40													12 40				
Upholland	d		11 44													12 44				
Orrell	d		11 47													12 47				
Pemberton	d		11 50													12 50				
Wigan Wallgate	a		11 56							12 30					12 51	12 56				
	d		11 58						12 20	12 32		12 48			12 53	12 58				
Wigan North Western	d				12 24													13 24		
Ince	d		12 01													13 01				
Hindley	d		12 04						12 25	12 37					12 58	13 04				
Westhoughton	d								12 29						13 02					
Bolton	a			12 25			12 30	12 34	12 38		12 55	13 02	13 08		13 12		13 25		13 30	13 34
	d			12 25			12 31	12 35	12 39		12 56	13 03	13 08		13 13		13 25		13 31	13 35
Moses Gate	d								12 42											
Farnworth	d								12 44											
Kearsley	d								12 46											
Daisy Hill	d		12 09							12 41						13 09				
Hag Fold	d		12 12													13 12				
Atherton	d		12 15							12 45						13 15				
Walkden	d		12 20							12 50						13 20				
Moorside	d		12 24													13 24				
Swinton	d		12 26							12 55						13 26				
Salford Crescent	a		12 34	12 38			12 43	12 47	12 56	13 02	13 08	13 15			13 25	13 34	13 38		13 43	13 47
	d		12 34	12 38			12 44	12 47	12 56	13 03	13 09	13 15			13 26	13 34	13 38		13 44	13 47
Salford Central	d		12 36	12 41			12 46		12 59	13 05		13 17				13 36	13 41		13 46	
Manchester Victoria	⇌ a		12 43	12 47			12 52		13 06	13 11		13 25				13 43	13 47		13 52	
Rochdale	41 a											13 51								
Deansgate	⇌ a							12 51			13 12				13 29					13 51
Manchester Oxford Road	a							12 52			13 14		13 23		13 31					13 52
Manchester Piccadilly ■	⇌ a							12 56			13 18		13 27		13 35					13 56
Stockport	84 a										13 34									
Hazel Grove	86 a										13 45									
Buxton	86 a																			
Heald Green	85 a							13 10												14 10
Manchester Airport	85 ✈ a							13 13					13 47		13 53					14 17

Table 82

Barrow-in-Furness, Blackpool North, Preston, Southport, Kirkby and Wigan - Bolton - Manchester

		NT	NT	NT	NT	TP ◇1 A ⌶	NT	TP ◇1	NT	NT	NT	NT	TP ◇1 ⌶	NT	NT	NT	NT	TP ◇1 ⌶	NT	NT	NT
Barrow-in-Furness	d							13 25													
Roose	d																				
Dalton	d																				
Ulverston	d							13 41													
Cark	d																				
Kents Bank	d																				
Grange-over-Sands	d							13 53													
Arnside	d							13 59													
Silverdale	d																				
Carnforth	d							14 08													
Windermere	83 d					12 51															
Oxenholme Lake District	65 d					13 09												14 10			
Lancaster ■	65 a					13 26		14 18										14 25			
	d					13 26		14 18										14 26			
Blackpool North	97 d									13 20	13 37		13 45								14 20
Layton	97 d									13 23											14 23
Poulton-le-Fylde	97 d									13 28			13 51								14 28
Kirkham & Wesham	97 d									13 37	13 52										14 37
Preston ■	65,97 a					13 45		14 37		13 47	14 02		14 09					14 45			14 47
	d			13 23		13 47				13 49	14 04		14 10			14 23		14 47			14 49
Leyland	d			13 29						13 54	14 09					14 29					14 54
Chorley	d			13 36		13 56				14 02			14 20			14 36		14 56			15 02
Adlington (Lancashire)	d									14 07											15 07
Blackrod	d									14 10											15 10
Horwich Parkway	d			13 45						14 14			14 27			14 45					15 14
Lostock	d			13 50						14 20						14 50					15 20
Southport	d		12 54				13 24								14 00				14 24		
Meols Cop	d		12 59												14 05						
Bescar Lane	d		13 04																		
New Lane	d		13 08																		
Burscough Bridge	d		13 11				13 36								14 13				14 36		
Hoscar	d		13 15																		
Parbold	d		13 18				13 41								14 18				14 41		
Appley Bridge	d		13 22				13 45								14 22				14 45		
Gathurst	d		13 25												14 25						
Kirkby	d								13 32											14 32	
Rainford	d								13 40											14 40	
Upholland	d								13 44											14 44	
Orrell	d								13 47											14 47	
Pemberton	d								13 50											14 50	
Wigan Wallgate	a		13 30				13 51		13 56						14 30				14 51	14 56	
	d	13 20	13 32		13 48		13 53		13 58					14 20	14 32		14 48		14 53	14 58	
Wigan North Western	d										14 24										
Ince	d								14 01											15 01	
Hindley	d	13 25	13 37				13 58		14 04					14 25	14 37				14 58	15 04	
Westhoughton	d	13 29					14 02							14 29					15 02		
Bolton	a	13 38		13 55	14 02	14 08	14 12			14 25		14 30	14 34	14 38		14 55	15 02	15 08	15 12		15 25
	d	13 39		13 56	14 03	14 08	14 13			14 25		14 31	14 35	14 39		14 56	15 03	15 08	15 13		15 25
Moses Gate	d	13 42												14 42							
Farnworth	d	13 44												14 44							
Kearsley	d	13 46												14 46							
Daisy Hill	d		13 41						14 09						14 41					15 09	
Hag Fold	d								14 12											15 12	
Atherton	d		13 45						14 15						14 45					15 15	
Walkden	d		13 50						14 20						14 50					15 20	
Moorside	d								14 24											15 24	
Swinton	d		13 55						14 26						14 55					15 26	
Salford Crescent	a	13 56	14 02	14 08	14 15		14 25		14 34	14 38		14 43	14 47	14 56	15 02	15 08	15 15		15 25	15 33	15 38
	d	13 56	14 03	14 09	14 15		14 26		14 34	14 38		14 44	14 47	14 56	15 03	15 09	15 15		15 26	15 34	15 38
Salford Central	d	13 59	14 05		14 17				14 36	14 41		14 46		14 59	15 05		15 17			15 36	15 41
Manchester Victoria	⇌ a	14 06	14 11		14 25				14 43	14 47		14 52		15 06	15 11		15 25			15 43	15 47
Rochdale	41 a				14 51												15 51				
Deansgate	⇌ a			14 12			14 29						14 51			15 12			15 29		
Manchester Oxford Road	a			14 14		14 23	14 31						14 52			15 14		15 23	15 31		
Manchester Piccadilly ■	⇌ a			14 18		14 27	14 35						14 56			15 18		15 27	15 35		
Stockport	84 a			14 34												15 34					
Hazel Grove	86 a			14 45												15 48					
Buxton	86 a																				
Heald Green	85 a												15 10								
Manchester Airport	85 ✈ a					14 47	14 53						15 17					15 47	15 53		

A ⌶ from Preston

Table 82

Mondays to Fridays
until 03 September

Barrow-in-Furness, Blackpool North, Preston, Southport, Kirkby and Wigan - Bolton - Manchester

		NT	NT	TP ◇1 🛒		NT		NT	NT	NT	TP ◇1 🛒	NT	NT	NT	TP ◇1	NT		NT	NT	NT	TP ◇1 🛒	NT	NT	NT	NT
Barrow-in-Furness	d											14 16			15 25									16 20	
Roose	d											14 20												16 24	
Dalton	d											14 26												16 30	
Ulverston	d											14 35			15 41									16 38	
Cark	d											14 43												16 46	
Kents Bank	d											14 47												16 50	
Grange-over-Sands	d											14 51			15 53									16 54	
Arnside	d											14 57			15 59									17 00	
Silverdale	d											15 02												17 05	
Carnforth	d											15 08		15 38	16 08									17 11	
Windermere 83	d																								
Oxenholme Lake District 65	d										14 58														
Lancaster 6 65	a										15 13	15 20		15 47	16 18									17 25	
	d										15 13			16 03	16 18										
Blackpool North 97	d	14 37		14 45															15 20	15 37	15 45				
Layton 97	d																		15 23						
Poulton-le-Fylde 97	d			14 51															15 28		15 51				
Kirkham & Wesham 97	d	14 52																	15 37	15 52					
Preston 8 65,97	a	15 02		15 09							15 34				16 37				15 47	16 02	16 09				
	d	15 04		15 10					15 23		15 47								15 49	16 04	16 10				16 23
Leyland	d	15 09							15 29										15 54	16 09					16 29
Chorley	d			15 20					15 36		15 56								16 02		16 20				16 36
Adlington (Lancashire)	d																		16 07						
Blackrod	d																		16 10						
Horwich Parkway	d			15 27					15 45										16 14		16 27				16 45
Lostock	d								15 50										16 20						16 50
Southport	d							14 54					15 24										15 58		
Meols Cop	d							14 59															16 03		
Bescar Lane	d							15 04																	
New Lane	d							15 08																	
Burscough Bridge	d							15 11					15 36										16 11		
Hoscar	d							15 15																	
Parbold	d							15 18					15 41										16 16		
Appley Bridge	d							15 22					15 45										16 20		
Gathurst	d							15 25															16 24		
Kirkby	d																	15 32							
Rainford	d																	15 40							
Upholland	d																	15 44							
Orrell	d																	15 47							
Pemberton	d																	15 50							
Wigan Wallgate	a							15 30					15 51					15 56					16 29		
	d					15 20		15 32		15 48			15 53					15 58				16 20	16 30		
Wigan North Western	d	15 24																		16 24					
Ince	d																	16 01					16 33		
Hindley	d					15 25		15 37					15 58					16 04				16 25	16 37		
Westhoughton	d					15 29							16 02									16 29			
Bolton	a		15 30	15 34		15 38			15 55	16 02	16 08		16 12			16 17			16 25		16 34	16 38			16 55
	d		15 31	15 35		15 39			15 56	16 03	16 08		16 13			16 17			16 25		16 35	16 39			16 56
Moses Gate	d					15 42																16 42			
Farnworth	d					15 44																16 44			
Kearsley	d					15 46																16 46			
Daisy Hill	d							15 41										16 09					16 41		
Hag Fold	d																	16 12							
Atherton	d							15 45										16 15					16 45		
Walkden	d							15 50										16 20					16 50		
Moorside	d																	16 24							
Swinton	d							15 55										16 26					16 55		
Salford Crescent	a		15 43	15 47		15 56		16 02	16 08	16 15			16 25			16 30		16 34	16 38		16 47	16 56	17 02		17 08
	d		15 44	15 47		15 56		16 03	16 09	16 15			16 26			16 30		16 34	16 38		16 47	16 56	17 03		17 09
Salford Central	d		15 46			15 59		16 05		16 17						16 33		16 36	16 41			16 59	17 05		
Manchester Victoria ⇌	a		15 54			16 06		16 11		16 23						16 41		16 43	16 47			17 06	17 13		
Rochdale 41	a									16 51															
Deansgate ⇌	a			15 51					16 12												16 51				17 15
Manchester Oxford Road	a			15 52					16 14		16 23		16 31								16 52				17 17
Manchester Piccadilly 10 ⇌	a			15 56					16 18		16 27		16 35								16 56				17 21
Stockport 84	a								16 34																17 32
Hazel Grove 86	a								16 43																17 39
Buxton 86	a								17 22																18 16
Heald Green 85	a			16 10							16 40										17 10				
Manchester Airport 85 ✈	a			16 17							16 47		16 53								17 17				

Table 82

Mondays to Fridays
until 03 September

Barrow-in-Furness, Blackpool North, Preston, Southport, Kirkby and Wigan - Bolton - Manchester

		NT		NT	NT	NT	NT	NT	TP ◇1 🛒	NT	NT	NT		NT	TP ◇1 🛒	NT	NT	NT	NT	TP ◇1 A 🛒	TP ◇1			NT	NT
Barrow-in-Furness	d																				17 21				
Roose	d																								
Dalton	d																				17 30				
Ulverston	d																				17 38				
Cark	d																				17 46				
Kents Bank	d																								
Grange-over-Sands	d																				17 53				
Arnside	d																				17 59				
Silverdale	d																								
Carnforth	d																				18 09				
Windermere 83	d																			17 06					
Oxenholme Lake District 65	d																			17b30					
Lancaster 6 65	a																			17 47	18 20				
	d																			17 48	18 29				
Blackpool North 97	d					16 20	16 35		16 40						17 20				17 37						
Layton 97	d					16 23			16 44						17 23										
Poulton-le-Fylde 97	d					16 28			16 48						17 27										
Kirkham & Wesham 97	d					16 37	16 52		16 57										17 52						
Preston 8 65,97	a					16 47	17 02		17 08						17 45				18 02	18 06					
	d					16 49	17 04		17 09						17 47			17 56	18 04	18 08					
Leyland	d					16 54	17 09											18 01	18 09						
Chorley	d					17 02			17 19						17 56			18 08		18 17					
Adlington (Lancashire)	d					17 07												18 13							
Blackrod	d					17 10												18 17							
Horwich Parkway	d					17 14			17 26									18 20		18 26					
Lostock	d					17 20														18 30					
Southport	d			16 24							16 54					17 24									
Meols Cop	d										16 59					17 29									
Bescar Lane	d										17 04														
New Lane	d										17 08														
Burscough Bridge	d			16 36							17 11					17 37									
Hoscar	d										17 15														
Parbold	d			16 41							17 18					17 42									
Appley Bridge	d			16 45							17 22					17 46									
Gathurst	d										17 25														
Kirkby	d				16 32												17 32								
Rainford	d				16 40												17 40								
Upholland	d				16 44												17 44								
Orrell	d				16 47												17 47								
Pemberton	d				16 50												17 50								
Wigan Wallgate	a			16 51	16 56						17 30					17 52	17 57								
	d	16 48		16 53	16 58					17 20	17 32	17 39				17 54	17 59							18 20	18 32
Wigan North Western	d						17 24												18 24						
Ince	d				17 01												18 02								
Hindley	d			16 58	17 04					17 25	17 37						18 05							18 25	18 37
Westhoughton	d			17 02						17 29		17 47				18 02								18 29	
Bolton	a	17 02		17 12		17 25		17 30	17 34	17 38		17 55		18 01	18 08	18 12		18 30		18 34				18 38	
	d	17 03		17 13		17 25		17 31	17 35	17 39		17 56		18 02	18 08	18 13		18 30		18 35				18 39	
Moses Gate	d									17 42														18 42	
Farnworth	d									17 44														18 44	
Kearsley	d									17 46														18 46	
Daisy Hill	d				17 08						17 41						18 09								18 41
Hag Fold	d				17 11												18 12								
Atherton	d				17 14						17 45						18 15								18 45
Walkden	d				17 19						17 50						18 20								18 50
Moorside	d				17 23												18 24								
Swinton	d				17 25						17 55						18 26								18 55
Salford Crescent	a	17 15		17 25	17 33	17 38		17 43	17 47	17 56	18 02	18 08		18 15		18 25	18 33	18 43		18 47				18 56	19 02
	d	17 15		17 26	17 33	17 38		17 44	17 47	17 56	18 03	18 09		18 15		18 26	18 33	18 43		18 47				18 56	19 03
Salford Central	d	17 17			17 36	17 41		17 46		17 59	18 05			18 17			18 36	18 46						18 59	19 05
Manchester Victoria ⇌	a	17 23			17 43	17 47		17 53		18 06	18 11			18 24			18 43	18 52						19 06	19 11
Rochdale 41	a	17 51												18 47											
Deansgate ⇌	a								17 51			18 12								18 51					
Manchester Oxford Road	a			17 30					17 52			18 14			18 23	18 31				18 52					
Manchester Piccadilly 10 ⇌	a			17 35					17 56			18 18			18 27	18 35				18 56					
Stockport 84	a											18 34													
Hazel Grove 86	a											18 43													
Buxton 86	a											19 22													
Heald Green 85	a								18 10						18 40					19 10					
Manchester Airport 85 ✈	a			17 53					18 17						18 47	18 53				19 17					

A 🛒 from Preston

b arr. 1725

Barrow-in-Furness, Blackpool North, Preston, Southport, Kirkby and Wigan - Bolton - Manchester

Station			NT	TP ◇1	NT	NT	NT	NT	NT	NT	NT	TP ◇1	TP ◇1	NT	NT	NT	TP ◇1	NT	NT	NT	NT	TP ◇1
Barrow-in-Furness		d			17 43									18b03								
Roose		d												18 07								
Dalton		d												18 13								
Ulverston		d			17 59									18 21								
Cark		d												18 29								
Kents Bank		d												18 33								
Grange-over-Sands		d												18 37								
Arnside		d												18 43								
Silverdale		d												18 48								
Carnforth		d			18 25		18 29							18 54								
Windermere	83	d											18 15									
Oxenholme Lake District	65	d											18 36				19 08					
Lancaster ■	65	a		18 26	18 38		18 42						18 52	19 04			19 26					
		d		18 26			18 49						18 52	19 05			19 26					
Blackpool North	97	d							18 20	18 37		18 45							19 20	19 37		19 45
Layton	97	d							18 23										19 23			
Poulton-le-Fylde	97	d							18 28			18 51							19 28			19 51
Kirkham & Wesham	97	d							18 37	18 52									19 37			
Preston ■	65,97	a		18 45					18 47	19 02		19 09	19 11	19 30			19 45		19 47	20 02		20 09
		d		18 47					18 49	19 04		19 10	19 16				19 47		19 49	20 04		20 10
Leyland		d							18 54	19 09									19 54	20 09		
Chorley		d		18 56					19 02			19 20	19 29				19 56		20 02			20 20
Adlington (Lancashire)		d							19 07										20 07			
Blackrod		d							19 10										20 10			
Horwich Parkway		d							19 14			19 27	19 36						20 14			20 27
Lostock		d							19 20										20 20			
Southport		d				18 17									19 00			19 23				
Meols Cop		d				18 22									19 05			19 28				
Bescar Lane		d				18 27																
New Lane		d				18 31																
Burscough Bridge		d				18 33									19 13			19 36				
Hoscar		d				18 37																
Parbold		d				18 40									19 18			19 41				
Appley Bridge		d				18 44									19 22			19 45				
Gathurst		d				18 47									19 25			19 48				
Kirkby		d						18 32														
Rainford		d						18 40														
Upholland		d						18 44														
Orrell		d						18 47														
Pemberton		d						18 50														
Wigan Wallgate		a				18 52		18 56							19 30			19 53				
		d				18 53		18 58							19 32			19 55				
Wigan North Western		d								19 24										20 24		
Ince		d						19 01														
Hindley		d				18 58		19 04							19 37			20 00				
Westhoughton		d				19 02												20 04				
Bolton		a	19 01	19 08		19 12			19 25		19 31	19 34	19 42			20 02	20 08	20 12	20 25		20 30	20 34
		d	19 02	19 08		19 13			19 25		19 31	19 35	19 43			20 02	20 08	20 13	20 25		20 31	20 35
Moses Gate		d																				
Farnworth		d																				
Kearsley		d																				
Daisy Hill		d						19 08							19 41							
Hag Fold		d						19 11														
Atherton		d						19 14							19 45							
Walkden		d						19 19							19 50							
Moorside		d						19 23														
Swinton		d						19 25							19 55							
Salford Crescent		a	19 14			19 25		19 33	19 38		19 44	19 47			20 02	20 15		20 25	20 38		20 43	20 47
		d	19 15			19 26		19 33	19 38		19 44	19 47			20 03	20 15		20 26	20 38		20 44	20 47
Salford Central		d	19 17					19 36	19 41		19 46				20 05	20 17			20 41		20 46	
Manchester Victoria		a	19 23					19 43	19 47		19 53				20 11	20 24			20 47		20 52	
Rochdale	41	a																				
Deansgate		a				19 29						19 51						20 29				20 51
Manchester Oxford Road		a		19 23		19 31						19 52	19 57				20 23	20 31				20 52
Manchester Piccadilly ■		a		19 27		19 35						19 56	20 01				20 27	20 35				20 56
Stockport	84	a																				
Hazel Grove	86	a																				
Buxton	86	a																				
Heald Green	85	a										20 10	20 15									21 10
Manchester Airport	85 ✈	a		19 47		19 53						20 17	20 24				20 47	20 53				21 17

b arr. 1747

Table 82

Mondays to Fridays
until 03 September

Barrow-in-Furness, Blackpool North, Preston, Southport, Kirkby and Wigan - Bolton - Manchester

Station			TP ◇1	NT	NT	NT	NT	TP ◇1	TP ◇1	NT FX	NT FO	NT FX	NT FO	NT FX	NT FO	NT FX	NT FO	TP ◇1	TP FO ◇1	NT	NT FX
Barrow-in-Furness		d							20 07											21 43	
Roose		d							20 11											21 47	
Dalton		d							20 18											21 53	
Ulverston		d							20 26											22 01	
Cark		d							20 34											22 09	
Kents Bank		d							20 38											22 13	
Grange-over-Sands		d							20 42											22 17	
Arnside		d							20 48											22 23	
Silverdale		d							20 53											22 28	
Carnforth		d							21 01											22 34	
Windermere	83	d																			
Oxenholme Lake District	65	d	20 12																22 12		
Lancaster ■	65	a	20 26						21 10										22 26	22 44	
		d	20 26						21 10										22 26	22 45	
Blackpool North	97	d				20 20		20 45						21 20	21 20			21 45			
Layton	97	d				20 23								21 23	21 23						
Poulton-le-Fylde	97	d				20 28		20 51						21 28	21 28			21 51			
Kirkham & Wesham	97	d				20 37								21 37	21 37						
Preston ■	65,97	a	20 45			20 47		21 09	21 29					21 47	21 47			22 09	22 45	23 10	
		d	20 47			20 49		21 10	21 31					21 49	21 49			22 10	22 47		
Leyland		d				20 54								21 54	21 54						
Chorley		d	20 56			21 02		21 20						22 02	22 02			22 20			
Adlington (Lancashire)		d				21 07								22 07	22 07						
Blackrod		d				21 10								22 10	22 10						
Horwich Parkway		d				21 14		21 27						22 14	22 14			22 27			
Lostock		d				21 20								22 20	22 20						
Southport		d			20 23							21 23	21 23								
Meols Cop		d			20 28							21 28	21 28								
Bescar Lane		d																			
New Lane		d																			
Burscough Bridge		d			20 36							21 36	21 36								
Hoscar		d																			
Parbold		d			20 41							21 41	21 41								
Appley Bridge		d			20 45							21 45	21 45								
Gathurst		d			20 48							21 48	21 48								
Kirkby		d																			
Rainford		d																			
Upholland		d																			
Orrell		d																			
Pemberton		d																			
Wigan Wallgate		a			20 53							21 53	21 53								
		d		20 27	20 55					21 27	21 27	21 55	21 55								22 27
Wigan North Western		d							21 48												
Ince		d		20 30						21 30	21 30										22 30
Hindley		d		20 33	21 00					21 33	21 33	22 00	22 00								22 33
Westhoughton		d			21 04							22 04	22 04								
Bolton		a	21 08		21 12	21 25	21 30	21 34				22 12	22 12	22 25	22 25	22 30	22 30	22 34	23 06		
		d	21 08		21 13	21 25	21 31	21 35				22 13	22 13	22 25	22 25	22 31	22 31	22 35	23 06		
Moses Gate		d																			
Farnworth		d																			
Kearsley		d																			
Daisy Hill		d		20 37						21 37	21 37										22 37
Hag Fold		d		20 40						21 40	21 40										22 40
Atherton		d		20 43						21 43	21 43										22 43
Walkden		d		20 49						21 49	21 49										22 49
Moorside		d		20 52						21 52	21 52										22 52
Swinton		d		20 55						21 55	21 55										22 55
Salford Crescent		a		21 02	21 25	21 38	21 43	21 47		22 02	22 02	22 25	22 25	22 38	22 38	22 43	22 43	22 47			23 02
		d		21 03	21 26	21 38	21 44	21 47		22 03	22 03	22 26	22 26	22 38	22 38	22 44	22 44	22 47			23 03
Salford Central		d		21 05		21 41	21 46				22 05		22 28		22 41		22 46				
Manchester Victoria		a		21 11		21 47	21 52			22 11	22 11	22 34	22 34	22 47	22 47	22 52	22 52				23 13
Rochdale	41	a																			
Deansgate		a			21 29			21 51										22 51			
Manchester Oxford Road		a	21 23		21 31			21 52	22 26									22 52	23s21		
Manchester Piccadilly ■		a	21 27		21 35			21 56	22 30									22 56	23 30		
Stockport	84	a																			
Hazel Grove	86	a																			
Buxton	86	a																			
Heald Green	85	a						22 09										23 09			
Manchester Airport	85 ✈	a	21 47		21 53			22 17	22 47									23 17			

Table 82

Mondays to Fridays
until 03 September

Barrow-in-Furness, Blackpool North, Preston, Southport, Kirkby and Wigan - Bolton - Manchester

Station			NT FO	NT	NT	NT	NT	TP ◇1	NT	TP ◇1
Barrow-in-Furness		d								
Roose		d								
Dalton		d								
Ulverston		d								
Cark		d								
Kents Bank		d								
Grange-over-Sands		d								
Arnside		d								
Silverdale		d								
Carnforth		d								
Windermere	83	d								22 45
Oxenholme Lake District	65	d								23 06
Lancaster 6	65	a			23 05					23 23
		d			23 07					23 24
Blackpool North	97	d		22 20				22 45	23 13	
Layton	97	d		22 23					23 16	
Poulton-le-Fylde	97	d		22 28				22 51	23 21	
Kirkham & Wesham	97	d		22 37					23 30	
Preston 8	65,97	a		22 47	23 28			23 09	23 40	23 45
		d		22 49				23 10	23 42	23 51
Leyland		d		22 54					23 48	
Chorley		d		23 02				23 20	23 55	
Adlington (Lancashire)		d		23 07					00 01	
Blackrod		d		23 10					00 04	
Horwich Parkway		d		23 14				23 27	00 08	
Lostock		d		23 20					00 13	
Southport		d				23 10				
Meols Cop		d				23 15				
Bescar Lane		d								
New Lane		d								
Burscough Bridge		d				23 23				
Hoscar		d								
Parbold		d				23 28				
Appley Bridge		d				23 32				
Gathurst		d				23 35				
Kirkby		d								
Rainford		d								
Upholland		d								
Orrell		d								
Pemberton		d								
Wigan Wallgate		a				23 44				
		d	22 27							
Wigan North Western		d								
Ince		d	22 30							
Hindley		d	22 33							
Westhoughton		d								
Bolton		a		23 25			23 30	23 34	00 18	
		d		23 25			23 31	23 35	00 19	
Moses Gate		d								
Farnworth		d								
Kearsley		d								
Daisy Hill		d	22 37							
Hag Fold		d	22 40							
Atherton		d	22 43							
Walkden		d	22 49							
Moorside		d	22 52							
Swinton		d	22 55							
Salford Crescent		a	23 02	23 38			23 43	23 47		
		d	23 03	23 38			23 44	23 47		
Salford Central		d	23 05							
Manchester Victoria	🚊	a	23 13	23 47			23 52		00 36	
Rochdale	41	a								
Deansgate	🚊	a								
Manchester Oxford Road		a								
Manchester Piccadilly 10	🚊	a						23 53		
Stockport	84	a								
Hazel Grove	86	a								
Buxton	86	a								
Heald Green	85	a						00 15		
Manchester Airport	85 ✈	a						00 22		

Table 82

Mondays to Fridays
from 06 September

Barrow-in-Furness, Blackpool North, Preston, Southport, Kirkby and Wigan - Bolton - Manchester

Station			TP ◇1	TP ◇1	TP ◇1	NT	NT	TP ◇1 ✠	NT	NT	NT	TP ◇1 A ✠	NT	NT	NT	NT
Barrow-in-Furness		d		04 35								05 31				
Roose		d														
Dalton		d														
Ulverston		d		04 51								05 47				
Cark		d														
Kents Bank		d														
Grange-over-Sands		d		05 04								06 00				
Arnside		d		05 10								06 06				
Silverdale		d														
Carnforth		d		05 20								06 15			06 44	
Windermere	83	d														
Oxenholme Lake District	65	d														
Lancaster 6	65	a		05 28								06 23			06 53	
		d										06 26				
Blackpool North	97	d	03 36			04 56		05 44						06 19		
Layton	97	d												06 22		
Poulton-le-Fylde	97	d				05 02		05 50						06 27		
Kirkham & Wesham	97	d												06 36		
Preston 8	65,97	a	04u00			05 20		06 08				06 45		06 46		
		d	04u01		05 16	05 22		06 09				06 47		06 48		
Leyland		d												06 53		
Chorley		d			05 26			06 18				06 56		07 01		
Adlington (Lancashire)		d												07 06		
Blackrod		d												07 10		
Horwich Parkway		d			05 35			06 26						07 14		
Lostock		d						06 30						07 20		
Southport		d											06 19			
Meols Cop		d											06 24			
Bescar Lane		d														
New Lane		d														
Burscough Bridge		d											06 32			
Hoscar		d														
Parbold		d											06 37			
Appley Bridge		d											06 41			
Gathurst		d											06 45			
Kirkby		d														
Rainford		d														
Upholland		d														
Orrell		d														
Pemberton		d														
Wigan Wallgate		a											06 52			
		d					06 03		06 31	06 36			06 53			
Wigan North Western		d														
Ince		d					06 06			06 39						
Hindley		d					06 09		06 36	06 42						
Westhoughton		d							06 41				07 01			
Bolton		a	04u30		05 42			06 34	06 52		06 55	07 08	07 11	07 25		07 30
		d	04u30		05 43			06 35	06 53		06 56	07 08	07 12	07 25		07 30
Moses Gate		d									06 59					
Farnworth		d									07 01					
Kearsley		d									07 03					
Daisy Hill		d					06 13			06 46						
Hag Fold		d					06 16			06 49						
Atherton		d					06 19			06 52						
Walkden		d					06 24			06 58						
Moorside		d					06 28			07 01						
Swinton		d					06 30			07 04						
Salford Crescent		a			05 55		06 38	06 47	07 05	07 12	07 16		07 24	07 38		07 43
		d			05 55		06 38	06 47	07 08	07 12	07 16		07 25	07 38		07 43
Salford Central		d					06 41			07 15	07 19			07 41		07 46
Manchester Victoria	🚊	a					06 46			07 21	07 26			07 47		07 52
Rochdale	41	a														
Deansgate	🚊	a						06 51	07 11				07 28			
Manchester Oxford Road		a						06 52	07 13			07 23	07 30			
Manchester Piccadilly 10	🚊	a	04 48		06 01			06 56	07 17			07 27	07 34			
Stockport	84	a							07 34							
Hazel Grove	86	a							07 47							
Buxton	86	a														
Heald Green	85	a						07 10								
Manchester Airport	85 ✈	a	05 07		06 18			07 17				07 47	07 53			

A ✠ from Preston

Barrow-in-Furness, Blackpool North, Preston, Southport, Kirkby and Wigan - Bolton - Manchester

	TP ◇1 ⌶	NT	NT	NT	NT		NT		NT	NT	TP ◇1 A ⌶	NT	NT	NT	NT		TP ◇1 ⌶	NT	NT	NT	NT	NT		NT
Barrow-in-Furness d											06 19							07 00						
Roose d											06 23							07 04						
Dalton d											06 30							07 10						
Ulverston d											06 38							07 19						
Cark d											06 46							07 27						
Kents Bank d											06 50							07 32						
Grange-over-Sands d											06 54							07 36						
Arnside d											07 00							07 43						
Silverdale d											07 05							07 48						
Carnforth d											07 12							07 54						
Windermere 83 d																								
Oxenholme Lake District 65 d																								
Lancaster 65 a											07 21						07 47	08 03						
d											07 22						07 47	08 04						
Blackpool North 97 d	06 34				06 53				07 02					07 18										
Layton 97 d	06 37													07 21										
Poulton-le-Fylde 97 d	06 41								07 08					07 26										
Kirkham & Wesham 97 d	06 50													07 35										
Preston 65,97 a	07 01				07 15				07 28		07 41			07 46			08 07	08 29						
d	07 03				07 17				07 30		07 47			07 47			08 12					08 17		
Leyland d	07 08				07 22				07 35					07 53								08 23		
Chorley d	07 15				07 31						07 56			08 01			08 22					08 33		
Adlington (Lancashire) d					07 36									08 06								08 37		
Blackrod d	07 21				07 40									08 10								08 41		
Horwich Parkway d	07 26				07 44									08 14								08 45		
Lostock d	07 29				07 49									08 20								08 50		
Southport d			06 49									07 18									07 58			
Meols Cop d			06 54									07 23									08 03			
Bescar Lane d			06 59																					
New Lane d			07 03																					
Burscough Bridge d			07 05									07 31									08 11			
Hoscar d			07 09																					
Parbold d			07 12									07 36									08 16			
Appley Bridge d			07 16									07 40									08 20			
Gathurst d			07 19									07 44									08 23			
Kirkby d							07 07																	
Rainford d							07 15																	
Upholland d							07 19																	
Orrell d							07 23																	
Pemberton d							07 26																	
Wigan Wallgate a			07 27				07 33					07 49									08 28			
d		07 15	07 27				07 35					07 51	08 00						08 13		08 29			
Wigan North Western d				07 22					07 50											08 20				
Ince d		07 18		07 25			07 38												08 16					
Hindley d		07 21		07 29			07 41					07 56							08 19	08 25	08 34			
Westhoughton d				07 33								08 01								08 29				
Bolton a	07 34			07 42	07 54					07 58	08 08	08 11		08 25	08 30		08 34			08 38		08 55		09 02
d	07 35			07 43	07 55					07 59	08 08	08 12		08 25	08 31		08 35			08 39		08 56		09 02
Moses Gate d				07 46						08 02										08 42				
Farnworth d				07 48						08 04										08 44				
Kearsley d				07 50						08 06										08 46				
Daisy Hill d		07 26	07 39				07 47						08 07						08 23		08 39			
Hag Fold d		07 29					07 50												08 26					
Atherton d		07 32	07 43				07 53						08 12						08 29		08 43			
Walkden d		07 38					07 59						08 18						08 35		08 49			
Moorside d		07 41					08 03												08 39					
Swinton d		07 44					08 06												08 42		08 54			
Salford Crescent a	07 47	07 51	07 59	08 02	08 07		08 13			08 17		08 24	08 29	08 38	08 43		08 47		08 50	08 56	09 04	09 08		09 15
d	07 47	07 51	07 59	08 02	08 08		08 13			08 17		08 25	08 30	08 38	08 44		08 47		08 50	08 56	09 04	09 09		09 16
Salford Central d		07 55	08 02	08 05			08 16			08 20			08 32	08 41	08 46				08 53	08 59	09 07			09 18
Manchester Victoria ⇌ a		08 00	08 08	08 12			08 20			08 26			08 38	08 48	08 52				08 59	09 06	09 13			09 27
Rochdale 41 a							08 51																	
Deansgate ⇌ a	07 51				08 11							08 28										09 12		
Manchester Oxford Road a	07 52				08 14						08 23	08 31					08 52					09 14		
Manchester Piccadilly [10] ⇌ a	07 56				08 18						08 27	08 35					08 56					09 18		
Stockport 84 a					08 34																	09 34		
Hazel Grove 86 a					08 48																	09 47		
Buxton 86 a																								
Heald Green 85 a	08 10											08 47					09 10							
Manchester Airport 85 ✈ a	08 17										08 47	08 53					09 19							

A ⌶ from Preston

Table 82

Mondays to Fridays
from 06 September

Barrow-in-Furness, Blackpool North, Preston, Southport, Kirkby and Wigan - Bolton - Manchester

	TP ◇1 A ⌶		NT	NT	NT	NT	NT	NT	TP ◇1 ⌶		NT		NT	NT	NT	NT	TP ◇1 ⌶	NT	NT	NT	NT		NT	NT
Barrow-in-Furness d	07 28		08 00																					
Roose d			08 04																					
Dalton d	07 37		08 10																					
Ulverston d	07 45		08 19																					
Cark d	07 53		08 29																					
Kents Bank d			08 34																					
Grange-over-Sands d	08 00		08 38																					
Arnside d	08 06		08 44																					
Silverdale d	08 11		08 49																					
Carnforth d	08 18		08 56																				10 02	
Windermere 83 d																								
Oxenholme Lake District 65 d																	09 11							
Lancaster 65 a	08 26		09 09														09 26						10 12	
d	08 27																09 26						10 19	
Blackpool North 97 d						08 20			08 45											09 20	09 37			
Layton 97 d						08 23														09 23				
Poulton-le-Fylde 97 d						08 28			08 51											09 28				
Kirkham & Wesham 97 d						08 37														09 37	09 52			
Preston 65,97 a	08 45					08 47			09 09								09 45			09 47	10 02			
d	08 47					08 49	09 04		09 10					09 23			09 47			09 49	10 04			
Leyland d						08 54	09 09							09 29						09 54	10 09			
Chorley d	08 56					09 02			09 20					09 36			09 56			10 02				
Adlington (Lancashire) d						09 07														10 07				
Blackrod d						09 10														10 10				
Horwich Parkway d						09 14			09 27					09 45						10 14				
Lostock d						09 20								09 50						10 20				
Southport d				08 22									09 01					09 22						
Meols Cop d				08 27									09 06											
Bescar Lane d																								
New Lane d																								
Burscough Bridge d				08 35									09 14					09 34						
Hoscar d																								
Parbold d				08 40									09 19					09 39						
Appley Bridge d				08 44									09 23					09 43						
Gathurst d				08 47									09 26											
Kirkby d					08 19														09 28					
Rainford d					08 27														09 36					
Upholland d					08 31														09 40					
Orrell d					08 34														09 43					
Pemberton d					08 37														09 46					
Wigan Wallgate a				08 54	08 45								09 32					09 49	09 54					
d				08 55	08 50						09 18		09 32			09 46		09 51	09 56					
Wigan North Western d							09 24														10 24			
Ince d					08 53														09 59					
Hindley d					08 57						09 23		09 37					09 56	10 02					
Westhoughton d				09 03							09 27							10 00						
Bolton a	09 08			09 12		09 25		09 30	09 34		09 38			09 55	10 00	10 02	10 08	10 12		10 25				10 30
d	09 08			09 13		09 25		09 31	09 35		09 39			09 56	10 00	10 03	10 08	10 13		10 25				10 31
Moses Gate d											09 42													
Farnworth d											09 44													
Kearsley d											09 46													
Daisy Hill d					09 01								09 41						10 07					
Hag Fold d					09 04														10 10					
Atherton d					09 06								09 45						10 13					
Walkden d					09 12								09 50						10 18					
Moorside d					09 15														10 22					
Swinton d					09 18								09 55						10 24					
Salford Crescent a				09 25	09 27	09 38		09 43	09 47		09 56		10 03	10 08	10 13	10 15		10 25	10 34	10 38				10 43
d				09 26	09 27	09 38		09 44	09 47		09 56		10 03	10 09	10 13	10 15		10 26	10 34	10 38				10 44
Salford Central d					09 31	09 41		09 46			09 59		10 05		10 16	10 17			10 36	10 41				10 46
Manchester Victoria ⇌ a					09 38	09 47		09 53			10 06		10 12		10 22	10 25			10 43	10 47				10 53
Rochdale 41 a																10 51								
Deansgate ⇌ a				09 29					09 51					10 12				10 29						
Manchester Oxford Road a	09 23			09 31					09 52					10 14			10 23	10 31						
Manchester Piccadilly [10] ⇌ a	09 27			09 35					09 56					10 18			10 27	10 35						
Stockport 84 a														10 34										
Hazel Grove 86 a														10 45										
Buxton 86 a																								
Heald Green 85 a									10 10															
Manchester Airport 85 ✈ a	09 47			09 53					10 17								10 47	10 53						

A ⌶ from Preston

Table 82

Mondays to Fridays
from 06 September

Barrow-in-Furness, Blackpool North, Preston, Southport, Kirkby and Wigan - Bolton - Manchester

			TP		NT	NT	NT	NT	TP		NT	NT	NT	NT	NT	NT	TP		NT		NT	NT	NT	TP	NT	TP
			◇1 [trolley]						◇1 A [trolley]								◇1 [trolley]							◇1 A [trolley]		◇1
Barrow-in-Furness		d							09 22		10b16															11 25
Roose		d							09 26		10 20															
Dalton		d							09 33		10 26															
Ulverston		d							09 41		10 35															11 41
Cark		d							09 49		10 44															
Kents Bank		d							09 53		10 49															
Grange-over-Sands		d							09 57		10 53															11 53
Arnside		d							10 03		10 59															11 59
Silverdale		d							10 08		11 03															
Carnforth		d							10 15		11 10															12 08
Windermere	83	d																						10 49		
Oxenholme Lake District	65	d																						11 09		
Lancaster [8]	65	a							10 25		11 22													11 26		12 18
		d							10 26															11 26		12 18
Blackpool North	97	d												10 20	10 37		10 45									
Layton	97	d												10 23												
Poulton-le-Fylde	97	d												10 28			10 51									
Kirkham & Wesham	97	d												10 37	10 52											
Preston [8]	65,97	a	10 04						10 45					10 47	11 02		11 09							11 45		12 37
		d	10 12				10 23		10 47					10 49	11 04		11 10					11 23		11 47		
Leyland		d					10 29							10 54	11 09							11 29				
Chorley		d	10 22				10 36		10 56					11 02			11 20					11 36		11 56		
Adlington (Lancashire)		d												11 07												
Blackrod		d												11 10												
Horwich Parkway		d					10 45							11 14			11 27					11 45				
Lostock		d					10 50							11 20								11 50				
Southport		d				09 51						10 20									10 51				11 20	
Meols Cop		d				09 56															10 56					
Bescar Lane		d				10 01															11 01					
New Lane		d				10 05															11 05					
Burscough Bridge		d				10 07						10 32									11 07				11 32	
Hoscar		d				10 11															11 11					
Parbold		d				10 14						10 37									11 14				11 37	
Appley Bridge		d				10 18						10 41									11 18				11 41	
Gathurst		d				10 21															11 21					
Kirkby		d											10 28													
Rainford		d											10 36													
Upholland		d											10 40													
Orrell		d											10 43													
Pemberton		d											10 46													
Wigan Wallgate		a				10 28						10 49	10 54								11 28				11 49	
		d			10 18	10 30		10 46				10 51	10 56						11 18		11 30		11 46		11 51	
Wigan North Western		d													11 24											
Ince		d											10 59													
Hindley		d			10 23	10 35						10 56	11 02						11 23		11 35				11 56	
Westhoughton		d			10 27							11 00							11 27						12 00	
Bolton		a	10 34		10 38		10 55	11 02	11 08			11 12		11 25		11 30	11 34		11 38			11 55	12 02	12 08	12 12	
		d	10 35		10 39		10 56	11 03	11 08			11 13		11 25		11 31	11 35		11 39			11 56	12 03	12 08	12 13	
Moses Gate		d			10 42														11 42							
Farnworth		d			10 44														11 44							
Kearsley		d			10 46														11 46							
Daisy Hill		d				10 39							11 07								11 39					
Hag Fold		d											11 10													
Atherton		d				10 43							11 13								11 43					
Walkden		d				10 48							11 18								11 48					
Moorside		d											11 22													
Swinton		d				10 53							11 24								11 53					
Salford Crescent		a	10 47		10 56	11 02	11 08	11 15				11 25	11 34	11 38		11 43	11 47		11 56		12 02	12 08	12 15		12 25	
		d	10 47		10 56	11 03	11 09	11 15				11 26	11 34	11 38		11 44	11 47		11 56		12 03	12 09	12 15		12 26	
Salford Central		d			10 59	11 05		11 17					11 36	11 41		11 46			11 59		12 05		12 17			
Manchester Victoria	[tram]	a			11 06	11 11		11 25					11 43	11 47		11 52			12 06		12 11		12 25			
Rochdale	41	a						11 51															12 51			
Deansgate	[tram]	a	10 51				11 12					11 29					11 51					12 12			12 29	
Manchester Oxford Road		a	10 52				11 14		11 23			11 31					11 52					12 14		12 23	12 31	
Manchester Piccadilly [10]	[tram]	a	10 56				11 18		11 27			11 35					11 56					12 18		12 27	12 35	
Stockport	84	a					11 34															12 34				
Hazel Grove	86	a					11 47															12 47				
Buxton	86	a																								
Heald Green	85	a	11 10														12 10									
Manchester Airport	85 ✈	a	11 17						11 50			11 53					12 17							12 47	12 53	

A [trolley] from Preston

b arr. 1007

Table 82

Mondays to Fridays
from 06 September

Barrow-in-Furness, Blackpool North, Preston, Southport, Kirkby and Wigan - Bolton - Manchester

			NT	NT	NT		NT	NT	TP		NT	NT	NT	NT	TP		NT	NT	NT	NT	NT	NT	TP		NT
									◇1 [trolley]						◇1 [trolley]								◇1 [trolley]		
Barrow-in-Furness		d															12 11								
Roose		d															12 15								
Dalton		d															12 21								
Ulverston		d															12 29								
Cark		d															12 37								
Kents Bank		d															12 41								
Grange-over-Sands		d															12 45								
Arnside		d															12 51								
Silverdale		d															12 56								
Carnforth		d					12 02										13 02								
Windermere	83	d																							
Oxenholme Lake District	65	d													12 10										
Lancaster [8]	65	a					12 11								12 26		13 15								
		d					12 28								12 26										
Blackpool North	97	d		11 20	11 37				11 45											12 20	12 37		12 45		
Layton	97	d		11 23																12 23					
Poulton-le-Fylde	97	d		11 28					11 51											12 28			12 51		
Kirkham & Wesham	97	d		11 37	11 52															12 37	12 52				
Preston [8]	65,97	a		11 47	12 02				12 09						12 45					12 47	13 02		13 09		
		d		11 49	12 04				12 10				12 23		12 47					12 49	13 04		13 10		
Leyland		d		11 54	12 09								12 29							12 54	13 09				
Chorley		d		12 02					12 20				12 36		12 56					13 02			13 20		
Adlington (Lancashire)		d		12 07																13 07					
Blackrod		d		12 10																13 10					
Horwich Parkway		d		12 14					12 27				12 45							13 14			13 27		
Lostock		d		12 20									12 50							13 20					
Southport		d										11 56						12 20							
Meols Cop		d										12 01													
Bescar Lane		d																							
New Lane		d																							
Burscough Bridge		d										12 09						12 32							
Hoscar		d																							
Parbold		d										12 14						12 37							
Appley Bridge		d										12 18						12 41							
Gathurst		d										12 21													
Kirkby		d	11 28																12 28						
Rainford		d	11 36																12 36						
Upholland		d	11 40																12 40						
Orrell		d	11 43																12 43						
Pemberton		d	11 46																12 46						
Wigan Wallgate		a	11 54									12 28						12 49	12 54						
		d	11 56								12 18	12 30		12 46				12 51	12 56						13 18
Wigan North Western		d			12 24																13 24				
Ince		d	11 59																12 59						
Hindley		d	12 02								12 23	12 35						12 56	13 02						13 23
Westhoughton		d									12 27							13 00							13 27
Bolton		a		12 25				12 30	12 34		12 38		12 55	13 02	13 08			13 12		13 25		13 30	13 34		13 38
		d		12 25				12 31	12 35		12 39		12 56	13 03	13 08			13 13		13 25		13 31	13 35		13 39
Moses Gate		d									12 42														13 42
Farnworth		d									12 44														13 44
Kearsley		d									12 46														13 46
Daisy Hill		d	12 07									12 39							13 07						
Hag Fold		d	12 10																13 10						
Atherton		d	12 13									12 43							13 13						
Walkden		d	12 18									12 48							13 18						
Moorside		d	12 22																13 22						
Swinton		d	12 24									12 53							13 24						
Salford Crescent		a	12 34	12 38				12 43	12 47		12 56	13 02	13 08	13 15				13 25	13 34	13 38		13 43	13 47		13 56
		d	12 34	12 38				12 44	12 47		12 56	13 03	13 09	13 15				13 26	13 34	13 38		13 44	13 47		13 56
Salford Central		d	12 36	12 41				12 46			12 59	13 05		13 17					13 36	13 41		13 46			13 59
Manchester Victoria	[tram]	a	12 43	12 47				12 52			13 06	13 11		13 25					13 43	13 47		13 52			14 06
Rochdale	41	a												13 51											
Deansgate	[tram]	a							12 51				13 12					13 29					13 51		
Manchester Oxford Road		a							12 52				13 14		13 23			13 31					13 52		
Manchester Piccadilly [10]	[tram]	a							12 56				13 18		13 27			13 35					13 56		
Stockport	84	a											13 34												
Hazel Grove	86	a											13 47												
Buxton	86	a																							
Heald Green	85	a							13 10														14 10		
Manchester Airport	85 ✈	a							13 17						13 47			13 53					14 17		

Barrow-in-Furness, Blackpool North, Preston, Southport, Kirkby and Wigan - Bolton - Manchester

			NT	NT	NT	TP	NT	TP	NT	NT	NT		NT	TP		NT	NT	NT	NT	TP	NT		NT	NT	NT	NT
						◇1		◇1						◇1						◇1						
						A 🛒								🛒						🛒						
Barrow-in-Furness		d						13 25																		
Roose		d																								
Dalton		d																								
Ulverston		d						13 41																		
Cark		d																								
Kents Bank		d																								
Grange-over-Sands		d						13 53																		
Arnside		d						13 59																		
Silverdale		d																								
Carnforth		d						14 08																		
Windermere	83	d				12 51																				
Oxenholme Lake District	65	d				13 09														14 10						
Lancaster ⑥	65	a				13 26		14 18												14 25						
		d				13 26		14 18												14 26						
Blackpool North	97	d								13 20	13 37			13 45										14 20	14 37	
Layton	97	d								13 23														14 23		
Poulton-le-Fylde	97	d								13 28				13 51										14 28		
Kirkham & Wesham	97	d								13 37	13 52													14 37	14 52	
Preston ⑧	65,97	a				13 45		14 37		13 47	14 02			14 09						14 45				14 47	15 02	
		d		13 23		13 47				13 49	14 04			14 10				14 23		14 47				14 49	15 04	
Leyland		d		13 29						13 54	14 09							14 29						14 54	15 09	
Chorley		d		13 36		13 56				14 02				14 20				14 36		14 56				15 02		
Adlington (Lancashire)		d								14 07														15 07		
Blackrod		d								14 10														15 10		
Horwich Parkway		d		13 45						14 14				14 27				14 45						15 14		
Lostock		d		13 50						14 20								14 50						15 20		
Southport		d	12 50				13 20										13 56				14 20					
Meols Cop		d	12 55														14 01									
Bescar Lane		d	13 00																							
New Lane		d	13 04																							
Burscough Bridge		d	13 07				13 32										14 09				14 32					
Hoscar		d	13 11																							
Parbold		d	13 14				13 37										14 14				14 37					
Appley Bridge		d	13 18				13 41										14 18				14 41					
Gathurst		d	13 21														14 21									
Kirkby		d							13 28														14 28			
Rainford		d							13 36														14 36			
Upholland		d							13 40														14 40			
Orrell		d							13 43														14 43			
Pemberton		d							13 46														14 46			
Wigan Wallgate		a	13 28				13 49		13 54								14 28				14 49		14 54			
		d	13 30		13 46		13 51		13 56							14 18	14 30		14 46		14 51		14 56			
Wigan North Western		d									14 24														15 24	
Ince		d							13 59														14 59			
Hindley		d	13 35				13 56		14 02							14 23	14 35				14 56		15 02			
Westhoughton		d					14 00									14 27					15 00					
Bolton		a		13 55	14 02	14 08	14 12			14 25			14 30	14 34		14 38		14 55	15 02	15 08	15 12			15 25		15 30
		d		13 56	14 03	14 08	14 13			14 25			14 31	14 35		14 39		14 56	15 03	15 08	15 13			15 25		15 31
Moses Gate		d														14 42										
Farnworth		d														14 44										
Kearsley		d														14 46										
Daisy Hill		d	13 39						14 07								14 39						15 07			
Hag Fold		d							14 10														15 10			
Atherton		d	13 43						14 13								14 43						15 13			
Walkden		d	13 48						14 18								14 48						15 18			
Moorside		d							14 22														15 22			
Swinton		d	13 53						14 24								14 53						15 24			
Salford Crescent		a	14 02	14 08	14 15		14 25		14 34	14 38			14 43	14 47		14 56	15 02	15 08	15 15		15 25		15 33	15 38		15 43
		d	14 03	14 09	14 15		14 26		14 34	14 38			14 44	14 47		14 56	15 03	15 09	15 15		15 26		15 34	15 38		15 44
Salford Central		d	14 05		14 17				14 36	14 41			14 46			14 59	15 05		15 17				15 36	15 41		15 46
Manchester Victoria	⇌	a	14 11		14 25				14 43	14 47			14 53			15 06	15 11		15 25				15 43	15 47		15 54
Rochdale	41	a			14 51														15 51							
Deansgate	⇌	a		14 12			14 29							14 51				15 12			15 29					
Manchester Oxford Road		a		14 14		14 23	14 31							14 52				15 14		15 23	15 31					
Manchester Piccadilly ⑩	⇌	a		14 18		14 27	14 35							14 56				15 18		15 27	15 35					
Stockport	84	a		14 34														15 34								
Hazel Grove	86	a		14 47														15 48								
Buxton	86	a																								
Heald Green	85	a												15 10												
Manchester Airport	85 ✈	a				14 47	14 53							15 17						15 47	15 53					

A 🛒 from Preston

Table 82

Mondays to Fridays
from 06 September

Barrow-in-Furness, Blackpool North, Preston, Southport, Kirkby and Wigan - Bolton - Manchester

			TP		NT	NT	NT		NT	TP	NT	NT	NT	TP	NT	NT	NT		NT	TP	NT	NT	NT	NT	NT	NT
			◇1							◇1				◇1						◇1						
			🛒							🛒										🛒						
Barrow-in-Furness		d									14 16			15 25									16 20			
Roose		d									14 20												16 24			
Dalton		d									14 26												16 30			
Ulverston		d									14 35			15 41									16 38			
Cark		d									14 43												16 46			
Kents Bank		d									14 47												16 50			
Grange-over-Sands		d									14 51			15 53									16 54			
Arnside		d									14 57			15 59									17 00			
Silverdale		d									15 02												17 05			
Carnforth		d									15 08		15 38	16 08									17 11			
Windermere	83	d																								
Oxenholme Lake District	65	d								14 58																
Lancaster ⑥	65	a								15 13	15 20		15 47	16 18									17 25			
		d								15 13			16 03	16 18												
Blackpool North	97	d	14 45														15 20		15 37	15 45						
Layton	97	d															15 23									
Poulton-le-Fylde	97	d	14 51														15 28			15 51						
Kirkham & Wesham	97	d															15 37		15 52							
Preston ⑧	65,97	a	15 09							15 34				16 37			15 47		16 02	16 09						
		d	15 10				15 23			15 47							15 49		16 04	16 10				16 23		
Leyland		d					15 29										15 54		16 09					16 29		
Chorley		d	15 20				15 36			15 56							16 02			16 20				16 36		
Adlington (Lancashire)		d															16 07									
Blackrod		d															16 10									
Horwich Parkway		d	15 27				15 45										16 14			16 27				16 45		
Lostock		d					15 50										16 20							16 50		
Southport		d				14 50						15 20										15 56				16 20
Meols Cop		d				14 55																16 01				
Bescar Lane		d				15 00																				
New Lane		d				15 04																				
Burscough Bridge		d				15 07						15 32										16 09				16 32
Hoscar		d				15 11																				
Parbold		d				15 14						15 37										16 14				16 37
Appley Bridge		d				15 18						15 41										16 18				16 41
Gathurst		d				15 21																16 22				
Kirkby		d														15 28										
Rainford		d														15 36										
Upholland		d														15 40										
Orrell		d														15 43										
Pemberton		d														15 46										
Wigan Wallgate		a				15 28						15 49				15 54						16 29				16 49
		d			15 18	15 30			15 46			15 51				15 56					16 18	16 30			16 46	16 51
Wigan North Western		d																	16 24							
Ince		d														15 59						16 33				
Hindley		d			15 23	15 35						15 56				16 02					16 23	16 37				16 56
Westhoughton		d			15 27							16 00									16 27					17 00
Bolton		a	15 34		15 38		15 55		16 02	16 08		16 12			16 17		16 25			16 34	16 38			16 55	17 02	17 12
		d	15 35		15 39		15 56		16 03	16 08		16 13			16 17		16 25			16 35	16 39			16 56	17 03	17 13
Moses Gate		d			15 42																16 42					
Farnworth		d			15 44																16 44					
Kearsley		d			15 46																16 46					
Daisy Hill		d				15 39										16 07						16 41				
Hag Fold		d														16 10										
Atherton		d				15 43										16 13						16 45				
Walkden		d				15 48										16 18						16 50				
Moorside		d														16 22										
Swinton		d				15 53										16 24						16 55				
Salford Crescent		a	15 47		15 56	16 02	16 08		16 15			16 25			16 30	16 34	16 38			16 47	16 56	17 02		17 08	17 15	17 25
		d	15 47		15 56	16 03	16 09		16 15			16 26			16 30	16 34	16 38			16 47	16 56	17 03		17 09	17 15	17 26
Salford Central		d			15 59	16 05			16 17						16 33	16 36	16 41				16 59	17 05			17 17	
Manchester Victoria	⇌	a			16 06	16 11			16 23						16 42	16 43	16 47				17 06	17 13			17 23	
Rochdale	41	a							16 51																17 51	
Deansgate	⇌	a	15 51				16 12													16 51				17 15		
Manchester Oxford Road		a	15 52				16 14			16 23		16 31								16 52				17 17		17 30
Manchester Piccadilly ⑩	⇌	a	15 56				16 18			16 27		16 35								16 56				17 21		17 35
Stockport	84	a					16 34																	17 32		
Hazel Grove	86	a					16 43																	17 39		
Buxton	86	a					17 24																	18 18		
Heald Green	85	a	16 10							16 40										17 10						
Manchester Airport	85 ✈	a	16 17							16 47		16 53								17 17						17 53

Table 82

Mondays to Fridays
from 06 September

Barrow-in-Furness, Blackpool North, Preston, Southport, Kirkby and Wigan - Bolton - Manchester

	NT		NT	NT	NT	TP ◇1 ⊼	NT	NT	NT	NT	TP ◇1 ⊼		NT	NT	NT	NT	TP ◇1 A ⊼	TP ◇1		NT	NT		NT	TP ◇1 ⊼
Barrow-in-Furness d																			17 21						
Roose d																								
Dalton d																			17 30						
Ulverston d																			17 38						
Cark d																			17 46						
Kents Bank d																								
Grange-over-Sands d																			17 53						
Arnside d																			17 59						
Silverdale d																								
Carnforth d																			18 09						
Windermere 83 d																		17 06							
Oxenholme Lake District 65 d																		17b30							
Lancaster 6 65 a																		17 47	18 20						18 26
d																		17 48	18 29						18 26
Blackpool North 97 d			16 20	16 35		16 40						17 20						17 37								
Layton 97 d			16 23			16 44						17 23													
Poulton-le-Fylde 97 d			16 28			16 48						17 27													
Kirkham & Wesham 97 d			16 37	16 52		16 57												17 52								
Preston 8 65,97 a			16 47	17 02		17 08						17 45						18 02	18 06						18 45
d			16 49	17 04		17 09						17 47					17 56	18 04	18 08						18 47
Leyland d			16 54	17 09													18 01	18 09								
Chorley d			17 02			17 19						17 56					18 08		18 17						18 56
Adlington (Lancashire) d			17 07														18 13										
Blackrod d			17 10														18 17										
Horwich Parkway d			17 14			17 26										18 20		18 26								
Lostock d			17 20																18 30								
Southport d								16 50						17 20												
Meols Cop d								16 55						17 25												
Bescar Lane d								17 00																		
New Lane d								17 04																		
Burscough Bridge d								17 07						17 33												
Hoscar d								17 11																		
Parbold d								17 14						17 38												
Appley Bridge d								17 18						17 42												
Gathurst d								17 21																		
Kirkby d	16 30														17 30										
Rainford d	16 38														17 38										
Upholland d	16 42														17 42										
Orrell d	16 45														17 45										
Pemberton d	16 48														17 48										
Wigan Wallgate a	16 56							17 28						17 50	17 57										
d	16 58						17 20	17 30	17 39					17 52	17 59						18 20	18 32			
Wigan North Western d				17 24												18 24								
Ince d	17 01														18 02										
Hindley d	17 04						17 25	17 35						18 05						18 25	18 37			
Westhoughton d							17 29		17 47				18 00							18 29				
Bolton a			17 25		17 30	17 34	17 38		17 55	18 01	18 08		18 12		18 30		18 34			18 38			19 01	19 08
d			17 25		17 31	17 35	17 39		17 56	18 02	18 08		18 13		18 30		18 35			18 39			19 02	19 08
Moses Gate d							17 42												18 42				
Farnworth d							17 44												18 44				
Kearsley d							17 46												18 46				
Daisy Hill d	17 08							17 39						18 09							18 41			
Hag Fold d	17 11														18 12										
Atherton d	17 14							17 43						18 15							18 45			
Walkden d	17 19							17 48						18 20							18 50			
Moorside d	17 23														18 24										
Swinton d	17 25							17 53						18 26							18 55			
Salford Crescent a	17 33		17 38		17 43	17 47	17 56	18 02	18 08	18 15			18 25	18 33	18 43		18 47			18 56	19 02		19 14	
d	17 33		17 38		17 44	17 47	17 56	18 03	18 09	18 15			18 26	18 33	18 43		18 47			18 56	19 03		19 15	
Salford Central d	17 36		17 41		17 46		17 59	18 05		18 17				18 36	18 46					18 59	19 05		19 17	
Manchester Victoria ⇋ a	17 43		17 47		17 53		18 06	18 11		18 24				18 43	18 52					19 06	19 11		19 23	
Rochdale 41 a										18 47														
Deansgate ⇋ a						17 51			18 12								18 51								
Manchester Oxford Road a						17 52			18 14		18 23		18 31				18 52						19 23
Manchester Piccadilly 10 ⇋ a						17 56			18 18		18 27		18 35				18 56						19 27
Stockport 84 a									18 34																
Hazel Grove 86 a									18 43																
Buxton 86 a									19 24																
Heald Green 85 a						18 10					18 40						19 10								
Manchester Airport 85 ✈ a						18 17					18 47		18 53				19 17						19 47

A ⊼ from Preston

b arr. 1725

Table 82

Mondays to Fridays
from 06 September

Barrow-in-Furness, Blackpool North, Preston, Southport, Kirkby and Wigan - Bolton - Manchester

	NT	NT	NT	NT	NT	NT	NT		TP ◇1 ⊼	TP ◇1	NT	NT		NT	TP ◇1 ⊼	NT	NT		NT	NT	TP ◇1		TP ◇1 ⊼	NT
Barrow-in-Furness d	17 43										18 03													
Roose d											18 07													
Dalton d											18 13													
Ulverston d	17 59										18 21													
Cark d											18 29													
Kents Bank d											18 33													
Grange-over-Sands d											18 37													
Arnside d											18 43													
Silverdale d											18 48													
Carnforth d	18 25		18 29								18 54													
Windermere 83 d										18 15														
Oxenholme Lake District 65 d										18 36					19 08								20 12	
Lancaster 6 65 a	18 38		18 42							18 52	19 04				19 26								20 26	
d			18 49							18 52	19 05				19 26								20 26	
Blackpool North 97 d					18 20	18 37			18 45								19 20		19 37		19 45			
Layton 97 d					18 23												19 23						
Poulton-le-Fylde 97 d					18 28				18 51								19 28				19 51			
Kirkham & Wesham 97 d					18 37	18 52											19 37						
Preston 8 65,97 a					18 47	19 02			19 09	19 11	19 30				19 45		19 47		20 02		20 09		20 45	
d					18 49	19 04			19 10	19 16					19 47		19 49		20 04		20 10		20 47	
Leyland d					18 54	19 09											19 54		20 09					
Chorley d					19 02				19 20	19 29					19 56		20 02				20 20		20 56	
Adlington (Lancashire) d					19 07												20 07						
Blackrod d					19 10												20 10						
Horwich Parkway d					19 14				19 27	19 36							20 14				20 27			
Lostock d					19 20												20 20						
Southport d		18 14										18 56				19 19								
Meols Cop d		18 19										19 01				19 24								
Bescar Lane d		18 24																					
New Lane d		18 28																					
Burscough Bridge d		18 30										19 09				19 32								
Hoscar d		18 34																					
Parbold d		18 37										19 14				19 37								
Appley Bridge d		18 41										19 18				19 41								
Gathurst d		18 44										19 21				19 44								
Kirkby d				18 30																				
Rainford d				18 38																				
Upholland d				18 42																				
Orrell d				18 45																				
Pemberton d				18 48																				
Wigan Wallgate a		18 51		18 56								19 28				19 51								
d		18 52		18 58								19 31				19 53								20 27
Wigan North Western d						19 24														20 24					
Ince d				19 01																				20 30
Hindley d		18 57		19 04								19 36				19 58								20 33
Westhoughton d		19 01														20 02								
Bolton a		19 12			19 25		19 31		19 34	19 42				20 02	20 08	20 12	20 25			20 30	20 34		21 08	
d		19 13			19 25		19 31		19 35	19 43				20 02	20 08	20 13	20 25			20 31	20 35		21 08	
Moses Gate d																								
Farnworth d																								
Kearsley d																								
Daisy Hill d				19 08								19 40												20 37
Hag Fold d				19 11																				20 40
Atherton d				19 14								19 44												20 43
Walkden d				19 19								19 49												20 49
Moorside d				19 23																				20 52
Swinton d				19 25								19 54												20 55
Salford Crescent a		19 25		19 33	19 38		19 44		19 47			20 02		20 15		20 25	20 38			20 43	20 47			21 02
d		19 26		19 33	19 38		19 44		19 47			20 03		20 15		20 26	20 38			20 44	20 47			21 03
Salford Central d				19 36	19 41		19 46					20 05		20 17			20 41			20 46				21 05
Manchester Victoria ⇋ a				19 43	19 47		19 53					20 11		20 25			20 47			20 52				21 11
Rochdale 41 a																								
Deansgate ⇋ a		19 29							19 51								20 29					20 51			
Manchester Oxford Road a		19 31							19 52	19 57					20 23	20 31					20 52		21 23	
Manchester Piccadilly 10 ⇋ a		19 35							19 56	20 01					20 27	20 35					20 56		21 27	
Stockport 84 a																								
Hazel Grove 86 a																								
Buxton 86 a																								
Heald Green 85 a									20 10	20 15											21 10			
Manchester Airport 85 ✈ a		19 53							20 17	20 24					20 47	20 53					21 17		21 47	

Barrow-in-Furness, Blackpool North, Preston, Southport, Kirkby and Wigan - Bolton - Manchester

		NT	NT	NT	TP	TP	NT FX	NT FO	NT FX	NT FO	NT FX	NT FO	NT FX	NT FO	TP	TP FO	NT	NT FX	NT FO	NT
					◇1	◇1									◇1	◇1 ✠				
Barrow-in-Furness	d					20 07											21 43			
Roose	d					20 11											21 47			
Dalton	d					20 18											21 53			
Ulverston	d					20 26											22 01			
Cark	d					20 34											22 09			
Kents Bank	d					20 38											22 13			
Grange-over-Sands	d					20 42											22 17			
Arnside	d					20 48											22 23			
Silverdale	d					20 53											22 28			
Carnforth	d					21 01											22 34			
Windermere 83	d																			
Oxenholme Lake District 65	d															22 12				
Lancaster 8 65	a					21 10										22 26	22 44			
	d					21 10										22 26	22 45			
Blackpool North 97	d		20 20		20 45						21 20	21 20			21 45					22 20
Layton 97	d		20 23								21 23	21 23								22 23
Poulton-le-Fylde 97	d		20 28		20 51						21 28	21 28			21 51					22 28
Kirkham & Wesham 97	d		20 37								21 37	21 37								22 37
Preston 8 65,97	a		20 47		21 09	21 29					21 47	21 47			22 09	22 45	23 10			22 47
	d		20 49		21 10	21 31					21 49	21 49			22 10	22 47				22 49
Leyland	d		20 54								21 54	21 54								22 54
Chorley	d		21 02		21 20						22 02	22 02			22 20					23 02
Adlington (Lancashire)	d		21 07								22 07	22 07								23 07
Blackrod	d		21 10								22 10	22 10								23 10
Horwich Parkway	d		21 14		21 27						22 14	22 14			22 27					23 14
Lostock	d		21 20								22 20	22 20								23 20
Southport	d	20 19							21 19	21 19										
Meols Cop	d	20 24							21 24	21 24										
Bescar Lane	d																			
New Lane	d																			
Burscough Bridge	d	20 32							21 32	21 32										
Hoscar	d																			
Parbold	d	20 37							21 37	21 37										
Appley Bridge	d	20 41							21 41	21 41										
Gathurst	d	20 44							21 44	21 44										
Kirkby	d																			
Rainford	d																			
Upholland	d																			
Orrell	d																			
Pemberton	d																			
Wigan Wallgate	a	20 51							21 51	21 51										
	d	20 53					21 27	21 27	21 53	21 53								22 27	22 27	
Wigan North Western	d					21 48														
Ince	d						21 30	21 30										22 30	22 30	
Hindley	d	20 58					21 33	21 33	21 58	21 58								22 33	22 33	
Westhoughton	d	21 02							22 02	22 02										
Bolton	a	21 12	21 25	21 30	21 34				22 12	22 12	22 25	22 25	22 30	22 30	22 34	23 06				23 25
	d	21 13	21 25	21 31	21 35				22 13	22 13	22 25	22 25	22 31	22 31	22 35	23 06				23 25
Moses Gate	d																			
Farnworth	d																			
Kearsley	d																			
Daisy Hill	d						21 37	21 37										22 37	22 37	
Hag Fold	d						21 40	21 40										22 40	22 40	
Atherton	d						21 43	21 43										22 43	22 43	
Walkden	d						21 49	21 49										22 49	22 49	
Moorside	d						21 52	21 52										22 52	22 52	
Swinton	d						21 55	21 55										22 55	22 55	
Salford Crescent	a	21 25	21 38	21 43	21 47		22 02	22 02	22 25	22 25	22 38	22 38	22 43	22 43	22 47			23 02	23 02	23 38
	d	21 26	21 38	21 44	21 47		22 03	22 03	22 26	22 26	22 38	22 38	22 44	22 44	22 47			23 03	23 03	23 38
Salford Central	d		21 41	21 46				22 05		22 28		22 41		22 46					23 05	
Manchester Victoria ⇌	a		21 47	21 52			22 11	22 11	22 34	22 34	22 47	22 47	22 53	22 52				23 13	23 13	23 47
Rochdale 41	a																			
Deansgate ⇌	a	21 29			21 51										22 51					
Manchester Oxford Road	a	21 31			21 52	22 26									22 52	23s21				
Manchester Piccadilly 10 ⇌	a	21 35			21 56	22 30									22 56	23 30				
Stockport 84	a																			
Hazel Grove 86	a																			
Buxton 86	a																			
Heald Green 85	a				22 09										23 09					
Manchester Airport 85 ✈	a	21 53			22 17	22 47									23 17					

Barrow-in-Furness, Blackpool North, Preston, Southport, Kirkby and Wigan - Bolton - Manchester

		NT	NT	NT	TP	NT	TP
					◇1		◇1
Barrow-in-Furness	d						
Roose	d						
Dalton	d						
Ulverston	d						
Cark	d						
Kents Bank	d						
Grange-over-Sands	d						
Arnside	d						
Silverdale	d						
Carnforth	d						
Windermere 83	d						22 45
Oxenholme Lake District 65	d						23 06
Lancaster 8 65	a	23 05					23 23
	d	23 07					23 24
Blackpool North 97	d				22 45	23 13	
Layton 97	d					23 16	
Poulton-le-Fylde 97	d				22 51	23 21	
Kirkham & Wesham 97	d					23 30	
Preston 8 65,97	a	23 28			23 09	23 40	23 45
	d				23 10	23 42	23 51
Leyland	d					23 48	
Chorley	d				23 20	23 55	
Adlington (Lancashire)	d					00 01	
Blackrod	d					00 04	
Horwich Parkway	d				23 27	00 08	
Lostock	d					00 13	
Southport	d		23 10				
Meols Cop	d		23 15				
Bescar Lane	d						
New Lane	d						
Burscough Bridge	d		23 23				
Hoscar	d						
Parbold	d		23 28				
Appley Bridge	d		23 32				
Gathurst	d		23 35				
Kirkby	d						
Rainford	d						
Upholland	d						
Orrell	d						
Pemberton	d						
Wigan Wallgate	a		23 44				
	d						
Wigan North Western	d						
Ince	d						
Hindley	d						
Westhoughton	d						
Bolton	a			23 30	23 34	00 18	
	d			23 31	23 35	00 19	
Moses Gate	d						
Farnworth	d						
Kearsley	d						
Daisy Hill	d						
Hag Fold	d						
Atherton	d						
Walkden	d						
Moorside	d						
Swinton	d						
Salford Crescent	a			23 43	23 47		
	d			23 44	23 47		
Salford Central	d						
Manchester Victoria ⇌	a			23 53		00 36	
Rochdale 41	a						
Deansgate ⇌	a						
Manchester Oxford Road	a						
Manchester Piccadilly 10 ⇌	a				23 53		
Stockport 84	a						
Hazel Grove 86	a						
Buxton 86	a						
Heald Green 85	a				00 15		
Manchester Airport 85 ✈	a				00 22		

Table 82

Saturdays until 04 September

Barrow-in-Furness, Blackpool North, Preston, Southport, Kirkby and Wigan - Bolton - Manchester

		TP ◇1	TP ◇1	TP ◇1	NT	TP ◇1	NT	NT	NT	TP ◇1	NT	NT	NT	TP ◇1 ✠	NT	NT	NT
Barrow-in-Furness	d		04 35							05 31							
Roose	d																
Dalton	d																
Ulverston	d		04 51							05 47							
Cark	d																
Kents Bank	d																
Grange-over-Sands	d		05 04							06 00							
Arnside	d		05 10							06 06							
Silverdale	d																
Carnforth	d		05 20							06 15							
Windermere	83 d																
Oxenholme Lake District	65 d																
Lancaster 6	65 a		05 28							06 23							
	d									06 26							
Blackpool North	97 d	03 36			04 56	05 44						06 19		06 34			06 53
Layton	97 d											06 22		06 37			
Poulton-le-Fylde	97 d				05 02	05 50						06 27		06 41			
Kirkham & Wesham	97 d											06 36		06 50			
Preston 8	65,97 a	03u59			05 20	06 08				06 45		06 46		07 01			07 15
	d	04u01		05 16	05 22	06 09				06 47		06 48		07 03			07 17
Leyland	d											06 53		07 08			07 22
Chorley	d			05 26		06 18				06 56		07 01		07 15			07 31
Adlington (Lancashire)	d											07 06					07 36
Blackrod	d											07 10		07 21			07 40
Horwich Parkway	d			05 35		06 26						07 14		07 26			07 44
Lostock	d					06 30						07 20		07 29			07 49
Southport	d										06 23						
Meols Cop	d										06 28						
Bescar Lane	d																
New Lane	d																
Burscough Bridge	d										06 36						
Hoscar	d																
Parbold	d										06 41						
Appley Bridge	d										06 45						
Gathurst	d										06 49						
Kirkby	d																
Rainford	d																
Upholland	d																
Orrell	d																
Pemberton	d																
Wigan Wallgate	a										06 54						
	d						06 31	06 36			06 55				07 15		
Wigan North Western	d															07 22	
Ince	d							06 39							07 18	07 25	
Hindley	d						06 36	06 42							07 21	07 29	
Westhoughton	d						06 41				07 03					07 33	
Bolton	a	04u30		05 42		06 34	06 52		06 55	07 08	07 11	07 25	07 30	07 34		07 42	07 54
	d	04u30		05 43		06 35	06 53		06 56	07 08	07 12	07 25	07 30	07 35		07 43	07 55
Moses Gate	d								06 59							07 46	
Farnworth	d								07 01							07 48	
Kearsley	d								07 03							07 50	
Daisy Hill	d							06 46							07 26		
Hag Fold	d							06 49							07 29		
Atherton	d							06 52							07 32		
Walkden	d							06 58							07 38		
Moorside	d							07 01							07 41		
Swinton	d							07 04							07 44		
Salford Crescent	a			05 55		06 47	07 05	07 11	07 15		07 24	07 38	07 43	07 47	07 51	08 02	08 07
	d			05 55		06 47	07 08	07 11	07 15		07 25	07 38	07 43	07 47	07 51	08 02	08 08
Salford Central	d							07 14	07 19			07 41	07 46		07 55	08 05	
Manchester Victoria	⇌ a							07 20	07 24			07 47	07 52		08 01	08 12	
Rochdale	41 a																
Deansgate	⇌ a					06 51	07 11				07 28			07 51			08 11
Manchester Oxford Road	a					06 52	07 13			07 23	07 30			07 52			08 14
Manchester Piccadilly 10	⇌ a	04 48		06 01		06 56	07 17			07 27	07 34			07 56			08 18
Stockport	84 a						07 34										08 34
Hazel Grove	86 a						07 45										08 45
Buxton	86 a																
Heald Green	85 a					07 10								08 10			
Manchester Airport	85 ✈ a	05 07		06 18		07 17				07 47	07 53			08 17			

Table 82

Saturdays until 04 September

Barrow-in-Furness, Blackpool North, Preston, Southport, Kirkby and Wigan - Bolton - Manchester

		NT	NT	NT	TP ◇1 A ✠	NT	NT	NT	NT	TP ◇1 ✠	NT	NT	NT	NT	NT	TP ◇1 A ✠	NT	NT	NT	NT	NT
Barrow-in-Furness	d				06 19											07 28					
Roose	d				06 23																
Dalton	d				06 30											07 37					
Ulverston	d				06 38											07 45					
Cark	d				06 46											07 53					
Kents Bank	d				06 50																
Grange-over-Sands	d				06 54											08 00					
Arnside	d				07 00											08 06					
Silverdale	d				07 05											08 11					
Carnforth	d				07 12			07 43								08 18					
Windermere	83 d																				
Oxenholme Lake District	65 d																				
Lancaster 6	65 a				07 21			07 52								08 26					
	d				07 22											08 27					
Blackpool North	97 d	07 02					07 18			07 44									08 20	08 38	
Layton	97 d						07 21			07 47									08 23		
Poulton-le-Fylde	97 d	07 08					07 26			07 51									08 28		
Kirkham & Wesham	97 d						07 35			08 00									08 37		
Preston 8	65,97 a	07 28			07 41		07 46			08 11						08 45			08 47	09 02	
	d	07 30			07 47		07 47			08 12				08 17		08 47			08 49	09 04	
Leyland	d	07 35					07 53							08 23					08 54	09 09	
Chorley	d				07 56		08 01			08 22				08 33		08 56			09 02		
Adlington (Lancashire)	d						08 06							08 37					09 07		
Blackrod	d						08 10							08 41					09 10		
Horwich Parkway	d						08 14							08 45					09 14		
Lostock	d						08 20							08 50					09 20		
Southport	d					07 21							07 53				08 25				
Meols Cop	d					07 26							07 58				08 30				
Bescar Lane	d												08 03								
New Lane	d												08 07								
Burscough Bridge	d					07 34							08 09				08 38				
Hoscar	d												08 13								
Parbold	d					07 39							08 16				08 43				
Appley Bridge	d					07 43							08 20				08 47				
Gathurst	d					07 47							08 23				08 50				
Kirkby	d		07 11															08 21			
Rainford	d		07 19															08 29			
Upholland	d		07 23															08 33			
Orrell	d		07 27															08 36			
Pemberton	d		07 30															08 39			
Wigan Wallgate	a		07 35			07 51							08 28				08 55	08 45			
	d		07 37			07 53					08 13		08 29				08 56	08 50			
Wigan North Western	d	07 50										08 20								09 24	
Ince	d		07 40								08 16							08 53			
Hindley	d		07 43			07 58					08 19	08 25	08 34					08 57			
Westhoughton	d					08 03						08 29					09 04				
Bolton	a			07 58	08 08	08 11	08 25		08 30	08 34		08 38		08 55	09 02	09 08	09 12		09 25		09 30
	d			07 59	08 08	08 12	08 25		08 31	08 35		08 39		08 56	09 02	09 08	09 13		09 25		09 31
Moses Gate	d			08 02								08 42									
Farnworth	d			08 04								08 44									
Kearsley	d			08 06								08 46									
Daisy Hill	d		07 47								08 23		08 39					09 01			
Hag Fold	d		07 50								08 26							09 04			
Atherton	d		07 53								08 29		08 43					09 06			
Walkden	d		07 59								08 35		08 49					09 12			
Moorside	d		08 03								08 39							09 15			
Swinton	d		08 05								08 42		08 54					09 18			
Salford Crescent	a		08 13	08 17		08 24	08 38		08 43	08 47	08 50	08 56	09 03	09 08	09 15		09 25	09 27	09 38		09 43
	d		08 13	08 17		08 25	08 38		08 44	08 47	08 50	08 56	09 03	09 09	09 16		09 26	09 27	09 38		09 44
Salford Central	d		08 16	08 20			08 41		08 46		08 53	08 59	09 06		09 18			09 31	09 41		09 46
Manchester Victoria	⇌ a		08 20	08 25			08 47		08 52		08 59	09 06	09 11		09 26			09 38	09 47		09 52
Rochdale	41 a		08 51												09 54						
Deansgate	⇌ a					08 28								09 12			09 29				
Manchester Oxford Road	a				08 23	08 31				08 52				09 14		09 23	09 31				
Manchester Piccadilly 10	⇌ a				08 27	08 35				08 56				09 18		09 27	09 35				
Stockport	84 a													09 34							
Hazel Grove	86 a													09 45							
Buxton	86 a																				
Heald Green	85 a					08 47				09 12											
Manchester Airport	85 ✈ a				08 47	08 53				09 19						09 47	09 53				

A ✠ from Preston

Table 82

Saturdays until 04 September

Barrow-in-Furness, Blackpool North, Preston, Southport, Kirkby and Wigan - Bolton - Manchester

	TP			NT	NT	NT	NT	NT	TP	NT	NT		NT	NT	NT	TP	NT	NT	TP		NT		NT	NT
	◇1								◇1							◇1			◇1					
	🍴								🍴										🍴					
Barrow-in-Furness d										08 25														
Roose d										08 29														
Dalton d										08 36														
Ulverston d										08 44														
Cark d										08 53														
Kents Bank d										08 58														
Grange-over-Sands d										09 02														
Arnside d										09 08														
Silverdale d										09 13														
Carnforth d										09 20							10 02							
Windermere 83 d																09 38								
Oxenholme Lake District 65 d									09 11							09 58								
Lancaster 6 65 a									09 26	09 33						10 16	10 12							
d									09 26							10 16	10 19							
Blackpool North 97 d	08 45													09 20	09 37				09 45					
Layton 97 d														09 23										
Poulton-le-Fylde 97 d	08 51													09 28					09 51					
Kirkham & Wesham 97 d														09 37										
Preston 8 65,97 a	09 09								09 45					09 47	10 02	10 35			10 09					
d	09 10					09 23			09 47					09 49	10 04				10 10					10 23
Leyland d						09 29								09 54	10 09									10 29
Chorley d	09 20					09 36			09 56					10 02					10 20					10 36
Adlington (Lancashire) d														10 07										
Blackrod d														10 10										
Horwich Parkway d	09 27					09 45								10 14					10 27					10 45
Lostock d						09 50								10 20										10 50
Southport d					09 02						09 24												09 55	
Meols Cop d					09 07																		10 00	
Bescar Lane d																							10 05	
New Lane d																							10 09	
Burscough Bridge d					09 15						09 36												10 11	
Hoscar d																							10 15	
Parbold d					09 20						09 41												10 18	
Appley Bridge d					09 24						09 45												10 22	
Gathurst d					09 27																		10 25	
Kirkby d													09 32											
Rainford d													09 40											
Upholland d													09 44											
Orrell d													09 47											
Pemberton d													09 50											
Wigan Wallgate a					09 32						09 51		09 56										10 30	
d				09 20	09 32			09 48			09 53		09 58								10 20		10 32	
Wigan North Western d															10 24									
Ince d													10 01											
Hindley d				09 25	09 37						09 58		10 04								10 25		10 37	
Westhoughton d				09 29							10 02										10 29			
Bolton a	09 34			09 38		09 55	10 00	10 02	10 08		10 12			10 25				10 30	10 34		10 38			10 55
d	09 35			09 39		09 56	10 00	10 03	10 08		10 13			10 25				10 31	10 35		10 39			10 56
Moses Gate d				09 42																	10 42			
Farnworth d				09 44																	10 44			
Kearsley d				09 46																	10 46			
Daisy Hill d					09 41								10 09										10 41	
Hag Fold d													10 12											
Atherton d					09 45								10 15										10 45	
Walkden d					09 50								10 20										10 50	
Moorside d													10 24											
Swinton d					09 55								10 26										10 55	
Salford Crescent a	09 47			09 56	10 03	10 08	10 13	10 15			10 25		10 34	10 38				10 43	10 47		10 56		11 02	11 08
d	09 47			09 56	10 03	10 09	10 13	10 15			10 26		10 34	10 38				10 44	10 47		10 56		11 03	11 09
Salford Central d				09 59	10 05		10 16	10 17					10 36	10 41				10 46			10 59		11 05	
Manchester Victoria ⇌ a				10 06	10 12		10 21	10 25					10 43	10 47				10 52			11 06		11 11	
Rochdale 41 a								10 51																
Deansgate ⇌ a	09 51					10 12					10 29								10 51					11 12
Manchester Oxford Road a	09 52					10 14			10 23		10 31								10 52					11 14
Manchester Piccadilly 10 ⇌ a	09 56					10 18			10 27		10 35								10 56					11 18
Stockport 84 a						10 34																		11 34
Hazel Grove 86 a						10 45																		11 45
Buxton 86 a																								
Heald Green 85 a	10 10																		11 10					
Manchester Airport 85 ✈ a	10 17								10 47		10 53								11 17					

Table 82

Saturdays until 04 September

Barrow-in-Furness, Blackpool North, Preston, Southport, Kirkby and Wigan - Bolton - Manchester

	NT	TP	NT	NT	NT	NT	NT		NT	TP		NT	NT	NT	NT	TP	NT		NT	NT	NT	NT	TP	TP
		◇1								◇1						◇1							◇1	◇1
		A														A								
		🍴								🍴						🍴							🍴	
Barrow-in-Furness d		09 22	10b16																					11 25
Roose d		09 26	10 20																					
Dalton d		09 33	10 26																					
Ulverston d		09 41	10 34																					11 41
Cark d		09 49	10 43																					
Kents Bank d		09 53	10 47																					
Grange-over-Sands d		09 57	10 51																					11 53
Arnside d		10 03	10 57																					11 59
Silverdale d		10 08	11 02																					
Carnforth d		10 15	11 08																					12 08
Windermere 83 d																10 49								
Oxenholme Lake District 65 d																11 09							11 31	
Lancaster 6 65 a		10 25	11 20													11 26							11 46	12 18
d		10 26														11 26							11 46	12 18
Blackpool North 97 d						10 20	10 37			10 45										11 15	11 37			
Layton 97 d						10 23														11 18				
Poulton-le-Fylde 97 d						10 28				10 51										11 23				
Kirkham & Wesham 97 d						10 37														11 32				
Preston 8 65,97 a		10 45				10 47	11 02			11 09						11 45				11 42	12 02		12 05	12 37
d		10 47				10 49	11 04			11 10				11 23		11 47				11 49	12 04		12 10	
Leyland d						10 54	11 09							11 29						11 54	12 09			
Chorley d		10 56				11 02				11 20				11 36		11 56				12 02			12 20	
Adlington (Lancashire) d						11 07														12 07				
Blackrod d						11 10														12 10				
Horwich Parkway d						11 14				11 27				11 45						12 14			12 27	
Lostock d						11 20								11 50						12 20				
Southport d				10 24									10 55				11 24							
Meols Cop d													11 00											
Bescar Lane d													11 05											
New Lane d													11 09											
Burscough Bridge d				10 36									11 11				11 36							
Hoscar d													11 15											
Parbold d				10 41									11 18				11 41							
Appley Bridge d				10 45									11 22				11 45							
Gathurst d													11 25											
Kirkby d					10 32														11 32					
Rainford d					10 40														11 40					
Upholland d					10 44														11 44					
Orrell d					10 47														11 47					
Pemberton d					10 50														11 50					
Wigan Wallgate a				10 51	10 56								11 30				11 51		11 56					
d	10 48			10 53	10 58							11 20	11 32		11 48		11 53		11 58					
Wigan North Western d							11 24														12 24			
Ince d					11 01														12 01					
Hindley d				10 58	11 04							11 25	11 37				11 58		12 04					
Westhoughton d				11 02								11 29					12 02							
Bolton a	11 02	11 08		11 12		11 25			11 30	11 34		11 38		11 55	12 02	12 08	12 12			12 25		12 30	12 34	
d	11 03	11 08		11 13		11 25			11 31	11 35		11 39		11 56	12 03	12 08	12 13			12 25		12 31	12 35	
Moses Gate d												11 42												
Farnworth d												11 44												
Kearsley d												11 46												
Daisy Hill d					11 09								11 41						12 09					
Hag Fold d					11 12														12 12					
Atherton d					11 15								11 45						12 15					
Walkden d					11 20								11 50						12 20					
Moorside d					11 24														12 24					
Swinton d					11 26								11 55						12 26					
Salford Crescent a	11 15			11 25	11 34	11 38			11 43	11 47		11 56	12 02	12 08	12 15		12 25		12 34	12 38		12 43	12 47	
d	11 15			11 26	11 34	11 38			11 44	11 47		11 56	12 03	12 09	12 15		12 26		12 34	12 38		12 44	12 47	
Salford Central d	11 17				11 36	11 41			11 46			11 59	12 05		12 17				12 36	12 41		12 46		
Manchester Victoria ⇌ a	11 25				11 43	11 47			11 52			12 06	12 11		12 25				12 43	12 47		12 52		
Rochdale 41 a	11 51														12 51									
Deansgate ⇌ a				11 29						11 51				12 12			12 29						12 51	
Manchester Oxford Road a		11 23		11 31						11 52				12 14		12 23	12 31						12 52	
Manchester Piccadilly 10 ⇌ a		11 27		11 35						11 56				12 18		12 27	12 35						12 56	
Stockport 84 a														12 34										
Hazel Grove 86 a														12 45										
Buxton 86 a																								
Heald Green 85 a										12 10													13 10	
Manchester Airport 85 ✈ a		11 47		11 53						12 17						12 47	12 53						13 17	

A 🍴 from Preston

b arr. 1007

Table 82

Saturdays until 04 September

Barrow-in-Furness, Blackpool North, Preston, Southport, Kirkby and Wigan - Bolton - Manchester

		NT	NT	NT	NT	NT	TP ◇1 ✠	NT	NT	NT	NT	NT	NT	TP ◇1 ✠	NT	NT	NT	NT	TP ◇1 A ✠	NT
Barrow-in-Furness	d							12 11												
Roose	d							12 15												
Dalton	d							12 21												
Ulverston	d							12 29												
Cark	d							12 37												
Kents Bank	d							12 41												
Grange-over-Sands	d							12 45												
Arnside	d							12 51												
Silverdale	d							12 56												
Carnforth	d	12 02						13 02												
Windermere 83	d																		12 51	
Oxenholme Lake District 65	d						12 07												13 09	
Lancaster 6 65	a	12 11					12 22	13 15											13 26	
	d	12 25					12 23												13 26	
Blackpool North 97	d										12 20	12 37		12 45						
Layton 97	d										12 23									
Poulton-le-Fylde 97	d										12 28			12 51						
Kirkham & Wesham 97	d										12 37									
Preston 8 65,97	a						12 41				12 47	13 02		13 09					13 45	
	d				12 23		12 47				12 49	13 04		13 10			13 23		13 47	
Leyland	d				12 29						12 54	13 09					13 29			
Chorley	d				12 36		12 56				13 02			13 20			13 36		13 56	
Adlington (Lancashire)	d										13 07									
Blackrod	d										13 10									
Horwich Parkway	d				12 45						13 14			13 27			13 45			
Lostock	d				12 50						13 20						13 50			
Southport	d			12 00					12 24							12 54				13 24
Meols Cop	d			12 05												12 59				
Bescar Lane	d															13 04				
New Lane	d															13 08				
Burscough Bridge	d			12 13					12 36							13 11				13 36
Hoscar	d															13 15				
Parbold	d			12 18					12 41							13 18				13 41
Appley Bridge	d			12 22					12 45							13 22				13 45
Gathurst	d			12 25												13 25				
Kirkby	d									12 32										
Rainford	d									12 40										
Upholland	d									12 44										
Orrell	d									12 47										
Pemberton	d									12 50										
Wigan Wallgate	a			12 30					12 51	12 56						13 30				13 51
	d		12 20	12 32		12 48			12 53	12 58					13 20	13 32		13 48		13 53
Wigan North Western	d											13 24								
Ince	d									13 01										
Hindley	d		12 25	12 37					12 58	13 04					13 25	13 37				13 58
Westhoughton	d		12 29						13 02						13 29					14 02
Bolton	a		12 38		12 55	13 02	13 08		13 12		13 25		13 30	13 34	13 38		13 55	14 02	14 08	14 12
	d		12 39		12 56	13 03	13 08		13 13		13 25		13 31	13 35	13 39		13 56	14 03	14 08	14 13
Moses Gate	d		12 42												13 42					
Farnworth	d		12 44												13 44					
Kearsley	d		12 46												13 46					
Daisy Hill	d			12 41						13 09						13 41				
Hag Fold	d									13 12										
Atherton	d			12 45						13 15						13 45				
Walkden	d			12 50						13 20						13 50				
Moorside	d									13 24										
Swinton	d			12 55						13 26						13 55				
Salford Crescent	a		12 56	13 02	13 08	13 15			13 25	13 34	13 38		13 43	13 47	13 56	14 02	14 08	14 15		14 25
	d		12 56	13 03	13 09	13 15			13 26	13 34	13 38		13 44	13 47	13 56	14 03	14 09	14 15		14 26
Salford Central	d		12 59	13 05		13 17				13 36	13 41		13 46		13 59	14 05		14 17		
Manchester Victoria ⇌	a		13 06	13 11		13 25				13 43	13 47		13 52		14 06	14 11		14 25		
Rochdale 41	a					13 51												14 51		
Deansgate ⇌	a				13 12				13 29					13 51			14 12			14 29
Manchester Oxford Road	a				13 14		13 23		13 31					13 52			14 14		14 23	14 31
Manchester Piccadilly 10 ⇌	a				13 18		13 27		13 35					13 56			14 18		14 27	14 35
Stockport 84	a				13 34												14 34			
Hazel Grove 86	a				13 45												14 45			
Buxton 86	a																			
Heald Green 85	a													14 10						
Manchester Airport 85 ✈	a						13 47		13 53					14 17					14 47	14 53

A ✠ from Preston

Table 82

Saturdays until 04 September

Barrow-in-Furness, Blackpool North, Preston, Southport, Kirkby and Wigan - Bolton - Manchester

		TP ◇1	NT	NT	NT	NT	TP ◇1 ✠	NT	NT	NT	NT	TP ◇1 ✠	NT	NT	NT	NT	NT	NT	TP ◇1 ✠	NT	NT
Barrow-in-Furness	d	13 25											14 16								
Roose	d												14 20								
Dalton	d												14 26								
Ulverston	d	13 41											14 35								
Cark	d												14 44								
Kents Bank	d												14 49								
Grange-over-Sands	d	13 53											14 53								
Arnside	d	13 59											14 59								
Silverdale	d												15 03								
Carnforth	d	14 08											15 10								
Windermere 83	d																				
Oxenholme Lake District 65	d											14 06									
Lancaster 6 65	a	14 18										14 22	15 22								
	d	14 18										14 22									
Blackpool North 97	d			13 20	13 37		13 45									14 20	14 37		14 45		
Layton 97	d			13 23												14 23					
Poulton-le-Fylde 97	d			13 28			13 51									14 28			14 51		
Kirkham & Wesham 97	d			13 37												14 37					
Preston 8 65,97	a	14 37		13 47	14 02		14 09					14 41				14 47	15 02		15 09		
	d			13 49	14 04		14 10			14 23		14 47				14 49	15 04		15 10		
Leyland	d			13 54	14 09					14 29						14 54	15 09				
Chorley	d			14 02			14 20			14 36		14 56				15 02			15 20		
Adlington (Lancashire)	d			14 07												15 07					
Blackrod	d			14 10												15 10					
Horwich Parkway	d			14 14			14 27			14 45						15 14			15 27		
Lostock	d			14 20						14 50						15 20					
Southport	d								14 00					14 24							14 54
Meols Cop	d								14 05												14 59
Bescar Lane	d																				15 04
New Lane	d																				15 08
Burscough Bridge	d								14 13					14 36							15 11
Hoscar	d																				15 15
Parbold	d								14 18					14 41							15 18
Appley Bridge	d								14 22					14 45							15 22
Gathurst	d								14 25												15 25
Kirkby	d		13 32												14 32						
Rainford	d		13 40												14 40						
Upholland	d		13 44												14 44						
Orrell	d		13 47												14 47						
Pemberton	d		13 50												14 50						
Wigan Wallgate	a		13 56						14 30					14 51	14 56						15 30
	d		13 58					14 20	14 32		14 48			14 53	14 58					15 20	15 32
Wigan North Western	d				14 24												15 24				
Ince	d		14 01												15 01						
Hindley	d		14 04					14 25	14 37					14 58	15 04					15 25	15 37
Westhoughton	d							14 29						15 02						15 29	
Bolton	a			14 25		14 30	14 34	14 38		14 55	15 02	15 08		15 12		15 25		15 30	15 34	15 38	
	d			14 25		14 31	14 35	14 39		14 56	15 03	15 08		15 13		15 25		15 31	15 35	15 39	
Moses Gate	d							14 42												15 42	
Farnworth	d							14 44												15 44	
Kearsley	d							14 46												15 46	
Daisy Hill	d		14 09						14 41						15 09						15 41
Hag Fold	d		14 12												15 12						
Atherton	d		14 15						14 45						15 15						15 45
Walkden	d		14 20						14 50						15 20						15 50
Moorside	d		14 24												15 24						
Swinton	d		14 26						14 55						15 26						15 55
Salford Crescent	a		14 34	14 38		14 43	14 47	14 56	15 02	15 08	15 15			15 25	15 34	15 38		15 43	15 47	15 56	16 02
	d		14 34	14 38		14 44	14 47	14 56	15 03	15 09	15 15			15 26	15 34	15 38		15 44	15 47	15 56	16 03
Salford Central	d		14 36	14 41		14 46		14 59	15 05		15 17				15 36	15 41		15 46		15 59	16 05
Manchester Victoria ⇌	a		14 43	14 47		14 52		15 06	15 11		15 25				15 43	15 47		15 54		16 06	16 11
Rochdale 41	a										15 51										
Deansgate ⇌	a						14 51			15 12				15 29					15 51		
Manchester Oxford Road	a						14 52			15 14		15 23		15 31					15 52		
Manchester Piccadilly 10 ⇌	a						14 56			15 18		15 27		15 35					15 56		
Stockport 84	a									15 34											
Hazel Grove 86	a									15 45											
Buxton 86	a																				
Heald Green 85	a						15 10												16 10		
Manchester Airport 85 ✈	a						15 17					15 47		15 53					16 17		

Table 82

Barrow-in-Furness, Blackpool North, Preston, Southport, Kirkby and Wigan - Bolton - Manchester

			NT	NT	TP ◇1 ✠	NT	NT		NT	NT	NT	NT	NT	TP ◇1 ✠		NT	NT	NT	NT	TP ◇1 ✠	TP ◇1	NT	NT	NT	NT	NT
Barrow-in-Furness		d							15 18												16 17					
Roose		d							15 22																	
Dalton		d							15 28												16 26					
Ulverston		d							15 36												16 34					
Cark		d							15 45												16 42					
Kents Bank		d							15 49																	
Grange-over-Sands		d							15 53												16 48					
Arnside		d							15 59												16 54					
Silverdale		d							16 04												16 59					
Carnforth		d					15 36		16 10												17 06					
Windermere	83	d																								
Oxenholme Lake District	65	d			15 09															16 08						
Lancaster 6	65	a			15 26		15 45		16 23											16 25	17 15					
		d			15 26		15 49													16 26	17 15					
Blackpool North	97	d										15 20	15 37	15 45										16 20	16 35	
Layton	97	d										15 23												16 23		
Poulton-le-Fylde	97	d										15 28		15 51										16 28		
Kirkham & Wesham	97	d										15 37												16 37		
Preston 8	65,97	a			15 45							15 47	16 02	16 09						16 45	17 34			16 47	17 02	
		d	15 23		15 47							15 49	16 04	16 10				16 23		16 47				16 49	17 04	
Leyland		d	15 29									15 54	16 09					16 29						16 54	17 09	
Chorley		d	15 36		15 56							16 02		16 20				16 36		16 56				17 02		
Adlington (Lancashire)		d										16 07												17 07		
Blackrod		d										16 10												17 10		
Horwich Parkway		d	15 45									16 14		16 27				16 45						17 14		
Lostock		d	15 50									16 20						16 50						17 20		
Southport		d				15 24											16 00					16 24				
Meols Cop		d															16 05									
Bescar Lane		d																								
New Lane		d																								
Burscough Bridge		d				15 36											16 13					16 36				
Hoscar		d																								
Parbold		d				15 41											16 18					16 41				
Appley Bridge		d				15 45											16 22					16 45				
Gathurst		d															16 25									
Kirkby		d									15 32												16 32			
Rainford		d									15 40												16 40			
Upholland		d									15 44												16 44			
Orrell		d									15 47												16 47			
Pemberton		d									15 50												16 50			
Wigan Wallgate		a				15 51					15 56						16 30					16 51	16 56			
		d		15 48		15 53					15 58					16 20	16 32		16 48			16 53	16 58			
Wigan North Western		d											16 24												17 24	
Ince		d									16 01												17 01			
Hindley		d				15 58					16 04					16 25	16 37					16 58	17 04			
Westhoughton		d				16 02										16 29						17 02				
Bolton		a	15 55	16 02	16 08	16 12				16 17		16 25		16 34		16 38		16 55	17 02	17 08		17 12		17 25		17 30
		d	15 56	16 03	16 08	16 13				16 17		16 25		16 35		16 39		16 56	17 03	17 08		17 13		17 25		17 31
Moses Gate		d														16 42										
Farnworth		d														16 44										
Kearsley		d														16 46										
Daisy Hill		d									16 09						16 41						17 08			
Hag Fold		d									16 12												17 11			
Atherton		d									16 15						16 45						17 14			
Walkden		d									16 20						16 50						17 19			
Moorside		d									16 24												17 23			
Swinton		d									16 26						16 55						17 25			
Salford Crescent		a	16 08	16 15		16 25				16 30	16 33	16 38		16 47		16 56	17 02	17 08	17 15			17 25	17 33	17 38		17 43
		d	16 09	16 15		16 26				16 30	16 34	16 38		16 47		16 56	17 03	17 09	17 15			17 26	17 33	17 38		17 44
Salford Central		d		16 17						16 33	16 37	16 41				16 59	17 05		17 17				17 36	17 41		17 46
Manchester Victoria		a		16 23						16 41	16 43	16 47				17 06	17 11		17 23				17 43	17 47		17 53
Rochdale	41	a		16 51															17 51							
Deansgate		a	16 12											16 51				17 12				17 29				
Manchester Oxford Road		a	16 14		16 23	16 31								16 52				17 14		17 23		17 31				
Manchester Piccadilly 10		a	16 18		16 27	16 35								16 56				17 18		17 27		17 35				
Stockport	84	a	16 34															17 34								
Hazel Grove	86	a	16 45															17 43								
Buxton	86	a																								
Heald Green	85	a			16 40									17 10						17 40						
Manchester Airport	85 ✈	a			16 47	16 53								17 17						17 48		17 53				

Table 82

Barrow-in-Furness, Blackpool North, Preston, Southport, Kirkby and Wigan - Bolton - Manchester

			TP ◇1 ✠			NT	NT	NT	NT	TP ◇1 ✠	NT	NT	NT		NT	TP ◇1 A ✠	TP ◇1		NT	NT	NT	TP ◇1 ✠	NT		NT	NT
Barrow-in-Furness		d															17 21									18 03
Roose		d																								18 07
Dalton		d															17 30									18 13
Ulverston		d															17 38									18 21
Cark		d															17 46									18 29
Kents Bank		d																								18 33
Grange-over-Sands		d															17 53									18 37
Arnside		d															17 59									18 43
Silverdale		d																								18 48
Carnforth		d															18 09								18 26	18 54
Windermere	83	d														17 06										
Oxenholme Lake District	65	d														17b30										
Lancaster 6	65	a														17 47	18 17					18 26			18 38	19 04
		d														17 48	18 17					18 26			18 47	19 05
Blackpool North	97	d	16 40							17 20					17 37											
Layton	97	d	16 44							17 23																
Poulton-le-Fylde	97	d	16 48							17 27																
Kirkham & Wesham	97	d	16 57																							
Preston 8	65,97	a	17 08							17 45					18 02	18 06	18 36					18 45				19 30
		d	17 09					17 23		17 47			17 56		18 04	18 08						18 47				
Leyland		d						17 29					18 01		18 09											
Chorley		d	17 19					17 36		17 56			18 08			18 17						18 56				
Adlington (Lancashire)		d											18 13													
Blackrod		d											18 17													
Horwich Parkway		d	17 26					17 45					18 20			18 26										
Lostock		d						17 50								18 30										
Southport		d					16 54				17 24									17 54			18 17			
Meols Cop		d					16 59				17 29									17 59			18 22			
Bescar Lane		d					17 04													18 04			18 27			
New Lane		d					17 08													18 08			18 31			
Burscough Bridge		d					17 11				17 37									18 11			18 33			
Hoscar		d					17 15													18 15			18 37			
Parbold		d					17 18				17 42									18 18			18 40			
Appley Bridge		d					17 22				17 46									18 22			18 44			
Gathurst		d					17 25													18 25			18 47			
Kirkby		d										17 32														
Rainford		d										17 40														
Upholland		d										17 44														
Orrell		d										17 47														
Pemberton		d										17 50														
Wigan Wallgate		a					17 30				17 52	17 57								18 30			18 52			
		d				17 20	17 32				17 54	17 59							18 20	18 32			18 53			
Wigan North Western		d													18 24											
Ince		d										18 02														
Hindley		d				17 25	17 37					18 05							18 25	18 37			18 58			
Westhoughton		d				17 29					18 02								18 29				19 02			
Bolton		a	17 34			17 38		17 55	18 01	18 08	18 12		18 30			18 34			18 38		19 01	19 08	19 12			
		d	17 35			17 39		17 56	18 02	18 08	18 13		18 30			18 35			18 39		19 02	19 08	19 13			
Moses Gate		d				17 42													18 42							
Farnworth		d				17 44													18 44							
Kearsley		d				17 46													18 46							
Daisy Hill		d					17 41					18 09								18 41						
Hag Fold		d										18 12														
Atherton		d					17 45					18 15								18 45						
Walkden		d					17 50					18 20								18 50						
Moorside		d										18 24														
Swinton		d					17 55					18 26								18 55						
Salford Crescent		a	17 47			17 56	18 02	18 08	18 14		18 25	18 33	18 43			18 47			18 56	19 02	19 14		19 25			
		d	17 47			17 56	18 03	18 09	18 15		18 26	18 33	18 43			18 47			18 56	19 03	19 15		19 26			
Salford Central		d				17 59	18 05		18 17			18 36	18 46						18 59	19 05	19 17					
Manchester Victoria		a				18 06	18 11		18 26			18 43	18 52						19 06	19 11	19 23					
Rochdale	41	a							18 49																	
Deansgate		a	17 51					18 12								18 51							19 29			
Manchester Oxford Road		a	17 52					18 14		18 23	18 31					18 52						19 23	19 31			
Manchester Piccadilly 10		a	17 56					18 18		18 27	18 35					18 56						19 27	19 35			
Stockport	84	a						18 34																		
Hazel Grove	86	a						18 45																		
Buxton	86	a																								
Heald Green	85	a	18 10							18 40						19 10										
Manchester Airport	85 ✈	a	18 17							18 47	18 53					19 17						19 50	19 53			

A ✠ from Preston

b arr. 1725

Table 82

Saturdays until 04 September

Barrow-in-Furness, Blackpool North, Preston, Southport, Kirkby and Wigan - Bolton - Manchester

Station		NT	NT	NT	NT	TP ◇1	NT	NT	TP ◇1	NT	NT	NT	NT	TP ◇1	TP ◇1	TP ◇1	NT	NT	NT	NT	TP ◇1
Barrow-in-Furness	d															19 32					
Roose	d															19 36					
Dalton	d															19 43					
Ulverston	d															19 51					
Cark	d															19 59					
Kents Bank	d															20 03					
Grange-over-Sands	d															20 07					
Arnside	d															20 13					
Silverdale	d															20 18					
Carnforth	d															20 25					
Windermere 83	d																				
Oxenholme Lake District 65	d								19 08						20 12						
Lancaster 6 65	a								19 26						20 26	20 33					
	d								19 26						20 26	20 34					
Blackpool North 97	d		18 20	18 37		18 45					19 20	19 37		19 45					20 20		20 42
Layton 97	d		18 23								19 23								20 23		
Poulton-le-Fylde 97	d		18 28			18 51					19 28			19 51					20 28		20 48
Kirkham & Wesham 97	d		18 37								19 37								20 37		
Preston 8 65,97	a		18 47	19 00		19 09			19 45		19 47	20 02		20 09	20 45	20 54			20 47		21 06
	d		18 49	19 04		19 10			19 47		19 49	20 04		20 10	20 47				20 49		21 10
Leyland	d		18 54	19 09							19 54	20 09							20 54		
Chorley	d		19 02			19 20			19 56		20 02			20 20	20 56				21 02		21 20
Adlington (Lancashire)	d		19 07								20 07								21 07		
Blackrod	d		19 10								20 10								21 10		
Horwich Parkway	d		19 14			19 27					20 14			20 27					21 14		21 27
Lostock	d		19 20								20 20								21 20		
Southport	d						19 00			19 23								20 23			
Meols Cop	d						19 05			19 28								20 28			
Bescar Lane	d																				
New Lane	d																				
Burscough Bridge	d						19 13			19 36								20 36			
Hoscar	d																				
Parbold	d						19 18			19 41								20 41			
Appley Bridge	d						19 22			19 45								20 45			
Gathurst	d						19 25			19 48								20 48			
Kirkby	d	18 32																			
Rainford	d	18 40																			
Upholland	d	18 44																			
Orrell	d	18 47																			
Pemberton	d	18 50																			
Wigan Wallgate	a	18 56					19 30			19 53								20 53			
	d	18 58					19 32			19 55							20 27	20 55			
Wigan North Western	d			19 24								20 24									
Ince	d	19 01															20 30				
Hindley	d	19 04					19 37			20 00							20 33	21 00			
Westhoughton	d									20 04								21 04			
Bolton	a		19 25		19 31	19 34		20 02	20 08	20 12	20 25		20 30	20 34	21 08			21 12	21 25	21 30	21 34
	d		19 25		19 31	19 35		20 02	20 08	20 13	20 25		20 31	20 35	21 08			21 13	21 25	21 31	21 35
Moses Gate	d																				
Farnworth	d																				
Kearsley	d																				
Daisy Hill	d	19 08					19 41										20 37				
Hag Fold	d	19 11															20 40				
Atherton	d	19 14					19 45										20 43				
Walkden	d	19 19					19 50										20 49				
Moorside	d	19 23															20 52				
Swinton	d	19 25					19 55										20 55				
Salford Crescent	a	19 33	19 38		19 44	19 47	20 02	20 15		20 25	20 38		20 43	20 47			21 02	21 25	21 38	21 43	21 47
	d	19 33	19 38		19 44	19 47	20 03	20 15		20 26	20 38		20 44	20 47			21 03	21 26	21 38	21 44	21 47
Salford Central	d	19 36	19 41		19 46		20 05	20 17			20 41		20 46				21 05		21 41	21 46	
Manchester Victoria ⇌	a	19 43	19 47		19 53		20 11	20 24			20 47		20 52				21 11		21 47	21 52	
Rochdale 41	a																				
Deansgate ⇌	a					19 51				20 29				20 51				21 29			21 51
Manchester Oxford Road	a					19 52			20 23	20 31				20 52	21 23			21 31			21 52
Manchester Piccadilly 10 ⇌	a					19 56			20 27	20 35				20 56	21 27			21 35			21 56
Stockport 84	a																				
Hazel Grove 86	a																				
Buxton 86	a																				
Heald Green 85	a					20 10								21 10							22 09
Manchester Airport 85 ✈	a					20 17			20 47	20 53				21 17	21 47			21 53			22 17

Table 82

Saturdays until 04 September

Barrow-in-Furness, Blackpool North, Preston, Southport, Kirkby and Wigan - Bolton - Manchester

Station		NT	NT	NT	TP ◇1	NT	NT	TP ◇1	NT	NT	TP ◇1	NT	NT	NT	NT
Barrow-in-Furness	d					21 43									
Roose	d					21 47									
Dalton	d					21 53									
Ulverston	d					22 01									
Cark	d					22 09									
Kents Bank	d					22 13									
Grange-over-Sands	d					22 17									
Arnside	d					22 23									
Silverdale	d					22 28									
Carnforth	d					22 34									
Windermere 83	d				21 40										
Oxenholme Lake District 65	d				22 01										
Lancaster 6 65	a				22 17	22 44									
	d				22 17	22 45									
Blackpool North 97	d			21 20				21 45		22 20	22 45				23 02
Layton 97	d			21 23						22 23					23 05
Poulton-le-Fylde 97	d			21 28				21 51		22 28	22 51				23 10
Kirkham & Wesham 97	d			21 37						22 37					23 19
Preston 8 65,97	a			21 47	22 38	23 10		22 09		22 47	23 09				23 29
	d			21 49				22 10		22 49	23 10				23 31
Leyland	d			21 54						22 54					23 36
Chorley	d			22 02				22 20		23 02	23 20				23 44
Adlington (Lancashire)	d			22 07						23 07					23 49
Blackrod	d			22 10						23 10					23 52
Horwich Parkway	d			22 14				22 27		23 14	23 27				23 56
Lostock	d			22 20						23 20					00 02
Southport	d		21 23									22 18	23 10		
Meols Cop	d		21 28									22 23	23 15		
Bescar Lane	d											22 28			
New Lane	d											22 32			
Burscough Bridge	d		21 36									22 34	23 23		
Hoscar	d											22 38			
Parbold	d		21 41									22 41	23 28		
Appley Bridge	d		21 45									22 45	23 32		
Gathurst	d		21 48									22 48	23 35		
Kirkby	d														
Rainford	d														
Upholland	d														
Orrell	d														
Pemberton	d														
Wigan Wallgate	a		21 53									22 53	23 44		
	d	21 27	21 55						22 27			22 55			
Wigan North Western	d														
Ince	d	21 30							22 30						
Hindley	d	21 33	22 00						22 33			23 00			
Westhoughton	d		22 04									23 04			
Bolton	a		22 12	22 25			22 30	22 34		23 25	23 34	23 12		23 36	00 07
	d		22 13	22 25			22 31	22 35		23 25	23 35	23 13		23 38	00 07
Moses Gate	d														
Farnworth	d														
Kearsley	d														
Daisy Hill	d	21 37							22 37						
Hag Fold	d	21 40							22 40						
Atherton	d	21 43							22 43						
Walkden	d	21 49							22 49						
Moorside	d	21 52							22 52						
Swinton	d	21 55							22 55						
Salford Crescent	a	22 02	22 25	22 38			22 43	22 47	23 02	23 38	23 47	23 25		23 48	
	d	22 03	22 26	22 38			22 44	22 47	23 03	23 38	23 47	23 26		23 51	
Salford Central	d	22 05	22 28	22 41			22 46		23 05						
Manchester Victoria ⇌	a	22 11	22 34	22 47			22 52		23 13	23 47				23 59	00 26
Rochdale 41	a														
Deansgate ⇌	a							22 51				23 29			
Manchester Oxford Road	a							22 52				23 31			
Manchester Piccadilly 10 ⇌	a							22 56			23 53	23 35			
Stockport 84	a														
Hazel Grove 86	a														
Buxton 86	a														
Heald Green 85	a							23 09			00 15				
Manchester Airport 85 ✈	a							23 17			00 22				

Table 82

Barrow-in-Furness, Blackpool North, Preston, Southport, Kirkby and Wigan - Bolton - Manchester

					TP ◇1	TP ◇1		TP ◇1	NT		TP ◇1		NT	NT	NT	TP ◇1	NT	NT	NT		TP ◇1 ⌶	NT	NT	NT
Barrow-in-Furness d						04 35										05 31								
Roose d																								
Dalton d																								
Ulverston d						04 51										05 47								
Cark d																								
Kents Bank d																								
Grange-over-Sands d						05 04										06 00								
Arnside d						05 10										06 06								
Silverdale d																								
Carnforth d						05 20										06 15								
Windermere 83 d																								
Oxenholme Lake District 65 d																								
Lancaster 6 65 a						05 28										06 23								
d																06 26								
Blackpool North 97 d					03 36				04 56		05 44							06 19			06 34			06 53
Layton 97 d																		06 22			06 37			
Poulton-le-Fylde 97 d									05 02		05 50							06 27			06 41			
Kirkham & Wesham 97 d																		06 36			06 50			
Preston 8 65,97 a					03u59				05 20		06 08					06 45		06 46			07 01			07 15
d					04u01			05 16	05 22		06 09					06 47		06 48			07 03			07 17
Leyland d																		06 53			07 08			07 22
Chorley d								05 26			06 18					06 56		07 01			07 15			07 31
Adlington (Lancashire) d																		07 06						07 36
Blackrod d																		07 10			07 21			07 40
Horwich Parkway d								05 35			06 26							07 14			07 26			07 44
Lostock d											06 30							07 20			07 29			07 49
Southport d																	06 19							
Meols Cop d																	06 24							
Bescar Lane d																								
New Lane d																								
Burscough Bridge d																	06 32							
Hoscar d																								
Parbold d																	06 37							
Appley Bridge d																	06 41							
Gathurst d																	06 45							
Kirkby d																								
Rainford d																								
Upholland d																								
Orrell d																								
Pemberton d																								
Wigan Wallgate a																	06 52							
d													06 31	06 36			06 53					07 15		
Wigan North Western d																							07 22	
Ince d														06 39								07 18	07 25	
Hindley d													06 36	06 42								07 21	07 29	
Westhoughton d													06 41				07 01						07 33	
Bolton a					04u30			05 42			06 34		06 52		06 55	07 08	07 11	07 25	07 30		07 34		07 42	07 54
d					04u30			05 43			06 35		06 53		06 56	07 08	07 12	07 25	07 30		07 35		07 43	07 55
Moses Gate d															06 59								07 46	
Farnworth d															07 01								07 48	
Kearsley d															07 03								07 50	
Daisy Hill d														06 46								07 26		
Hag Fold d														06 49								07 29		
Atherton d														06 52								07 32		
Walkden d														06 58								07 38		
Moorside d														07 01								07 41		
Swinton d														07 04								07 44		
Salford Crescent a								05 55			06 47		07 05	07 12	07 16		07 24	07 38	07 43		07 47	07 51	08 02	08 07
d								05 55			06 47		07 08	07 12	07 16		07 25	07 38	07 43		07 47	07 51	08 02	08 08
Salford Central d														07 15	07 19			07 41	07 46			07 55	08 05	
Manchester Victoria ⇌ a														07 21	07 25			07 47	07 53			08 01	08 12	
Rochdale 41 a																								
Deansgate ⇌ a											06 51		07 11				07 28				07 51			08 11
Manchester Oxford Road a											06 52		07 13			07 23	07 30				07 52			08 14
Manchester Piccadilly 10 ⇌ a					04 48			06 01			06 56		07 17			07 27	07 34				07 56			08 18
Stockport 84 a													07 34											08 34
Hazel Grove 86 a													07 47											08 47
Buxton 86 a																								
Heald Green 85 a											07 10										08 10			
Manchester Airport 85 ✈ a					05 07			06 18			07 17					07 47	07 53				08 17			

Table 82

Barrow-in-Furness, Blackpool North, Preston, Southport, Kirkby and Wigan - Bolton - Manchester

	NT		NT	NT	TP ◇1 A ⌶		NT	NT	NT	NT	TP ◇1 ⌶	NT	NT	NT	NT			NT	TP ◇1 A ⌶	NT	NT	NT	NT	NT
Barrow-in-Furness d					06 19														07 28					
Roose d					06 23																			
Dalton d					06 30														07 37					
Ulverston d					06 38														07 45					
Cark d					06 46														07 53					
Kents Bank d					06 50																			
Grange-over-Sands d					06 54														08 00					
Arnside d					07 00														08 06					
Silverdale d					07 05														08 11					
Carnforth d					07 12				07 43										08 18					
Windermere 83 d																								
Oxenholme Lake District 65 d																								
Lancaster 6 65 a					07 21				07 52										08 26					
d					07 22														08 27					
Blackpool North 97 d			07 02					07 18			07 44											08 20	08 38	
Layton 97 d								07 21			07 47											08 23		
Poulton-le-Fylde 97 d			07 08					07 26			07 51											08 28		
Kirkham & Wesham 97 d								07 35			08 00											08 37		
Preston 8 65,97 a			07 28		07 41			07 46			08 11								08 45			08 47	09 02	
d			07 30		07 47			07 47			08 12				08 17				08 47			08 49	09 04	
Leyland d			07 35					07 53							08 23							08 54	09 09	
Chorley d					07 56			08 01			08 22				08 33				08 56			09 02		
Adlington (Lancashire) d								08 06							08 37							09 07		
Blackrod d								08 10							08 41							09 10		
Horwich Parkway d								08 14							08 45							09 14		
Lostock d								08 20							08 50							09 20		
Southport d							07 18							07 51						08 22				
Meols Cop d							07 23							07 56						08 27				
Bescar Lane d														08 01										
New Lane d														08 05										
Burscough Bridge d							07 31							08 07						08 35				
Hoscar d														08 11										
Parbold d							07 36							08 14						08 40				
Appley Bridge d							07 40							08 18						08 44				
Gathurst d							07 44							08 21						08 47				
Kirkby d	07 07																				08 19			
Rainford d	07 15																				08 27			
Upholland d	07 19																				08 31			
Orrell d	07 23																				08 34			
Pemberton d	07 26																				08 37			
Wigan Wallgate a	07 31						07 49							08 28						08 54	08 45			
d	07 33						07 51					08 13		08 29						08 55	08 50			
Wigan North Western d			07 50										08 20										09 24	
Ince d	07 38											08 16									08 53			
Hindley d	07 41						07 56					08 19	08 25	08 34							08 57			
Westhoughton d							08 01						08 29							09 03				
Bolton a				07 58	08 08		08 11	08 25		08 30	08 34		08 38		08 55			09 02	09 08	09 12		09 25		09 30
d				07 59	08 08		08 12	08 25		08 31	08 35		08 39		08 56			09 02	09 08	09 13		09 25		09 31
Moses Gate d				08 02									08 42											
Farnworth d				08 04									08 44											
Kearsley d				08 06									08 46											
Daisy Hill d	07 45											08 23		08 39							09 01			
Hag Fold d	07 48											08 26									09 04			
Atherton d	07 51											08 29		08 43							09 06			
Walkden d	07 57											08 35		08 49							09 12			
Moorside d	08 01											08 39									09 15			
Swinton d	08 03											08 42		08 54							09 18			
Salford Crescent a	08 13			08 17			08 24	08 38		08 43	08 47	08 50	08 56	09 03	09 08			09 15		09 25	09 27	09 38		09 43
d	08 13			08 17			08 25	08 38		08 44	08 47	08 50	08 56	09 03	09 09			09 16		09 26	09 27	09 38		09 44
Salford Central d	08 16			08 20				08 41		08 46		08 53	08 59	09 06				09 18			09 31	09 41		09 46
Manchester Victoria ⇌ a	08 20			08 26				08 47		08 52		08 59	09 06	09 11				09 26			09 38	09 47		09 53
Rochdale 41 a	08 51																	09 54						
Deansgate ⇌ a							08 28								09 12					09 29				
Manchester Oxford Road a					08 23		08 31				08 52				09 14				09 23	09 31				
Manchester Piccadilly 10 ⇌ a					08 27		08 35				08 56				09 18				09 27	09 35				
Stockport 84 a															09 34									
Hazel Grove 86 a															09 47									
Buxton 86 a																								
Heald Green 85 a							08 47				09 12													
Manchester Airport 85 ✈ a					08 47		08 53				09 19								09 47	09 53				

A ⌶ from Preston

Table 82

Saturdays
from 11 September

Barrow-in-Furness, Blackpool North, Preston, Southport, Kirkby and Wigan - Bolton - Manchester

		TP	NT	NT	NT	NT	NT	TP	NT	NT	NT	NT	NT	TP	NT	NT	TP	NT	NT	NT
		◇1 ⌶						◇1 ⌶						◇1			◇1 ⌶			
Barrow-in-Furness	d								08 25											
Roose	d								08 29											
Dalton	d								08 36											
Ulverston	d								08 44											
Cark	d								08 53											
Kents Bank	d								08 58											
Grange-over-Sands	d								09 02											
Arnside	d								09 08											
Silverdale	d								09 13											
Carnforth	d								09 20						10 02					
Windermere	83 d													09 38						
Oxenholme Lake District	65 d							09 11						09 58						
Lancaster [8]	65 a							09 26	09 33					10 16	10 12					
	d							09 26						10 16	10 19					
Blackpool North	97 d	08 45										09 20	09 37				09 45			
Layton	97 d											09 23								
Poulton-le-Fylde	97 d	08 51										09 28					09 51			
Kirkham & Wesham	97 d											09 37								
Preston [8]	65,97 a	09 09						09 45				09 47	10 02	10 35			10 09			
	d	09 10			09 23			09 47				09 49	10 04				10 10			10 23
Leyland	d				09 29							09 54	10 09							10 29
Chorley	d	09 20			09 36			09 56				10 02					10 20			10 36
Adlington (Lancashire)	d											10 07								
Blackrod	d											10 10								
Horwich Parkway	d	09 27			09 45							10 14					10 27			10 45
Lostock	d				09 50							10 20								10 50
Southport	d			09 01						09 22									09 51	
Meols Cop	d			09 06															09 56	
Bescar Lane	d																		10 01	
New Lane	d																		10 05	
Burscough Bridge	d			09 14						09 34									10 07	
Hoscar	d																		10 11	
Parbold	d			09 19						09 39									10 14	
Appley Bridge	d			09 23						09 43									10 18	
Gathurst	d			09 26															10 21	
Kirkby	d										09 28									
Rainford	d										09 36									
Upholland	d										09 40									
Orrell	d										09 43									
Pemberton	d										09 46									
Wigan Wallgate	a			09 32						09 49	09 54								10 28	
	d		09 18	09 32			09 46			09 51	09 56							10 18	10 30	
Wigan North Western	d												10 24							
Ince	d										09 59									
Hindley	d		09 23	09 37						09 56	10 02							10 23	10 35	
Westhoughton	d		09 27							10 00								10 27		
Bolton	a	09 34	09 38		09 55	10 00	10 02	10 08		10 12		10 25				10 30	10 34	10 38		10 55
	d	09 35	09 39		09 56	10 00	10 03	10 08		10 13		10 25				10 31	10 35	10 39		10 56
Moses Gate	d		09 42															10 42		
Farnworth	d		09 44															10 44		
Kearsley	d		09 46															10 46		
Daisy Hill	d			09 41							10 07								10 39	
Hag Fold	d										10 10									
Atherton	d			09 45							10 13								10 43	
Walkden	d			09 50							10 18								10 48	
Moorside	d										10 22									
Swinton	d			09 55							10 24								10 53	
Salford Crescent	a	09 47	09 56	10 03	10 08	10 13	10 15			10 25	10 34	10 38				10 43	10 47	10 56	11 02	11 08
	d	09 47	09 56	10 03	10 09	10 13	10 15			10 26	10 34	10 38				10 44	10 47	10 56	11 03	11 09
Salford Central	d		09 59	10 05		10 16	10 17				10 36	10 41				10 46		10 59	11 05	
Manchester Victoria	⇌ a		10 06	10 12		10 22	10 25				10 43	10 47				10 53		11 06	11 11	
Rochdale	41 a						10 51													
Deansgate	⇌ a	09 51			10 12					10 29							10 51			11 12
Manchester Oxford Road	a	09 52			10 14			10 23		10 31							10 52			11 14
Manchester Piccadilly [10]	⇌ a	09 56			10 18			10 27		10 35							10 56			11 18
Stockport	84 a				10 34															11 34
Hazel Grove	86 a				10 45															11 47
Buxton	86 a																			
Heald Green	85 a	10 10															11 10			
Manchester Airport	85 ✈ a	10 17						10 47		10 53							11 17			

Table 82

Saturdays
from 11 September

Barrow-in-Furness, Blackpool North, Preston, Southport, Kirkby and Wigan - Bolton - Manchester

		NT	TP	NT	NT	NT	NT	NT	NT	TP	NT	NT	NT	NT	TP	NT	NT	NT	NT	NT	TP	TP
			◇1 A ⌶							◇1 ⌶					◇1 A ⌶						◇1 ⌶	◇1
Barrow-in-Furness	d		09 22	10 16																		11 25
Roose	d		09 26	10 20																		
Dalton	d		09 33	10 26																		
Ulverston	d		09 41	10 34																		11 41
Cark	d		09 49	10 43																		
Kents Bank	d		09 53	10 47																		
Grange-over-Sands	d		09 57	10 51																		
Arnside	d		10 03	10 57																		11 53
Silverdale	d		10 08	11 02																		11 59
Carnforth	d		10 15	11 08																		12 08
Windermere	83 d														10 49							
Oxenholme Lake District	65 d														11 09						11 31	
Lancaster [8]	65 a		10 25	11 20											11 26						11 46	12 18
	d		10 26												11 26						11 46	12 18
Blackpool North	97 d						10 20	10 37		10 45								11 15	11 37			
Layton	97 d						10 23											11 18				
Poulton-le-Fylde	97 d						10 28			10 51								11 23				
Kirkham & Wesham	97 d						10 37											11 32				
Preston [8]	65,97 a		10 45				10 47	11 02		11 09					11 45			11 42	12 02		12 05	12 37
	d		10 47				10 49	11 04		11 10			11 23		11 47			11 49	12 04		12 10	
Leyland	d						10 54	11 09					11 29					11 54	12 09			
Chorley	d		10 56				11 02			11 20			11 36		11 56			12 02			12 20	
Adlington (Lancashire)	d						11 07											12 07				
Blackrod	d						11 10											12 10				
Horwich Parkway	d						11 14			11 27			11 45					12 14			12 27	
Lostock	d						11 20						11 50					12 20				
Southport	d				10 20							10 51				11 20						
Meols Cop	d											10 56										
Bescar Lane	d											11 01										
New Lane	d											11 05										
Burscough Bridge	d				10 32							11 07				11 32						
Hoscar	d											11 11										
Parbold	d				10 37							11 14				11 37						
Appley Bridge	d				10 41							11 18				11 41						
Gathurst	d											11 21										
Kirkby	d					10 28											11 28					
Rainford	d					10 36											11 36					
Upholland	d					10 40											11 40					
Orrell	d					10 43											11 43					
Pemberton	d					10 46											11 46					
Wigan Wallgate	a				10 49	10 54						11 28				11 49	11 54					
	d	10 46			10 51	10 56					11 18	11 30		11 46		11 51	11 56					
Wigan North Western	d							11 24											12 24			
Ince	d					10 59											11 59					
Hindley	d				10 56	11 02					11 23	11 35				11 56	12 02					
Westhoughton	d				11 00						11 27					12 00						
Bolton	a	11 02	11 08		11 12		11 25		11 30	11 34	11 38		11 55	12 02	12 08	12 12		12 25		12 30	12 34	
	d	11 03	11 08		11 13		11 25		11 31	11 35	11 39		11 56	12 03	12 08	12 13		12 25		12 31	12 35	
Moses Gate	d										11 42											
Farnworth	d										11 44											
Kearsley	d										11 46											
Daisy Hill	d					11 07						11 39					12 07					
Hag Fold	d					11 10											12 10					
Atherton	d					11 13						11 43					12 13					
Walkden	d					11 18						11 48					12 18					
Moorside	d					11 22											12 22					
Swinton	d					11 24						11 53					12 24					
Salford Crescent	a	11 15			11 25	11 34	11 38		11 43	11 47	11 56	12 02	12 08	12 15		12 25	12 34	12 38		12 43	12 47	
	d	11 15			11 26	11 34	11 38		11 44	11 47	11 56	12 03	12 09	12 15		12 26	12 34	12 38		12 44	12 47	
Salford Central	d	11 17				11 36	11 41		11 46		11 59	12 05		12 17			12 36	12 41		12 46		
Manchester Victoria	⇌ a	11 25				11 43	11 47		11 52		12 06	12 11		12 25			12 43	12 47		12 52		
Rochdale	41 a	11 51												12 51								
Deansgate	⇌ a				11 29					11 51			12 12			12 29					12 51	
Manchester Oxford Road	a		11 23		11 31					11 52			12 14		12 23	12 31					12 52	
Manchester Piccadilly [10]	⇌ a		11 27		11 35					11 56			12 18		12 27	12 35					12 56	
Stockport	84 a												12 34									
Hazel Grove	86 a												12 47									
Buxton	86 a																					
Heald Green	85 a									12 10											13 10	
Manchester Airport	85 ✈ a		11 47		11 53					12 17					12 47	12 53					13 17	

A ⌶ from Preston

Table 82

Saturdays from 11 September

Barrow-in-Furness, Blackpool North, Preston, Southport, Kirkby and Wigan - Bolton - Manchester

		NT	NT	NT	NT	NT	TP ◇1 ⚭	NT	NT	NT	NT	NT	NT	TP ◇1 ⚭	NT	NT	NT	NT	TP ◇1 A ⚭	NT
Barrow-in-Furness	d							12 11												
Roose	d							12 15												
Dalton	d							12 21												
Ulverston	d							12 29												
Cark	d							12 37												
Kents Bank	d							12 41												
Grange-over-Sands	d							12 45												
Arnside	d							12 51												
Silverdale	d							12 56												
Carnforth	d	12 02						13 02												
Windermere	83 d																		12 51	
Oxenholme Lake District	65 d						12 07												13 09	
Lancaster 6	65 a	12 11					12 22	13 15											13 26	
	d	12 25					12 23												13 26	
Blackpool North	97 d										12 20	12 37		12 45						
Layton	97 d										12 23									
Poulton-le-Fylde	97 d										12 28			12 51						
Kirkham & Wesham	97 d										12 37									
Preston 8	65,97 a						12 41				12 47	13 02		13 09					13 45	
	d				12 23		12 47				12 49	13 04		13 10			13 23		13 47	
Leyland	d				12 29						12 54	13 09					13 29			
Chorley	d				12 36		12 56				13 02			13 20			13 36		13 56	
Adlington (Lancashire)	d										13 07									
Blackrod	d										13 10									
Horwich Parkway	d				12 45						13 14			13 27			13 45			
Lostock	d				12 50						13 20						13 50			
Southport	d			11 56					12 20							12 50				13 20
Meols Cop	d			12 01												12 55				
Bescar Lane	d															13 00				
New Lane	d															13 04				
Burscough Bridge	d			12 09					12 32							13 07				13 32
Hoscar	d															13 11				
Parbold	d			12 14					12 37							13 14				13 37
Appley Bridge	d			12 18					12 41							13 18				13 41
Gathurst	d			12 21												13 21				
Kirkby	d									12 28										
Rainford	d									12 36										
Upholland	d									12 40										
Orrell	d									12 43										
Pemberton	d									12 46										
Wigan Wallgate	a			12 28					12 49	12 54						13 28				13 49
	d		12 18	12 30		12 46			12 51	12 56					13 18	13 30		13 46		13 51
Wigan North Western	d											13 24								
Ince	d									12 59										
Hindley	d		12 23	12 35					12 56	13 02					13 23	13 35				13 56
Westhoughton	d		12 27						13 00						13 27					14 00
Bolton	a		12 38		12 55	13 02	13 08		13 12		13 25		13 30	13 34	13 38		13 55	14 02	14 08	14 12
	d		12 39		12 56	13 03	13 08		13 13		13 25		13 31	13 35	13 39		13 56	14 03	14 08	14 13
Moses Gate	d		12 42												13 42					
Farnworth	d		12 44												13 44					
Kearsley	d		12 46												13 46					
Daisy Hill	d			12 39						13 07						13 39				
Hag Fold	d									13 10										
Atherton	d			12 43						13 13						13 43				
Walkden	d			12 48						13 18						13 48				
Moorside	d									13 22										
Swinton	d			12 53						13 24						13 53				
Salford Crescent	a		12 56	13 02	13 08	13 15			13 25	13 34	13 38		13 43	13 47	13 56	14 02	14 08	14 15		14 25
	d		12 56	13 03	13 09	13 15			13 26	13 34	13 38		13 44	13 47	13 56	14 03	14 09	14 15		14 26
Salford Central	d		12 59	13 05		13 17				13 36	13 41		13 46		13 59	14 05		14 17		
Manchester Victoria	⇌ a		13 06	13 11		13 25				13 43	13 47		13 52		14 06	14 11		14 25		
Rochdale	41 a					13 51												14 51		
Deansgate	⇌ a				13 12				13 29					13 51			14 12			14 29
Manchester Oxford Road	a				13 14		13 23		13 31					13 52			14 14		14 23	14 31
Manchester Piccadilly 10	⇌ a				13 18		13 27		13 35					13 56			14 18		14 27	14 35
Stockport	84 a				13 34												14 34			
Hazel Grove	86 a				13 47												14 47			
Buxton	86 a																			
Heald Green	85 a													14 10						
Manchester Airport	85 ✈ a						13 47		13 53					14 17					14 47	14 53

A ⚭ from Preston

Table 82

Saturdays from 11 September

Barrow-in-Furness, Blackpool North, Preston, Southport, Kirkby and Wigan - Bolton - Manchester

		TP ◇1	NT	NT	NT	NT	TP ◇1 ⚭	NT	NT	NT	NT	TP ◇1 ⚭	NT	NT	NT	NT	NT	NT	TP ◇1 ⚭	NT	NT
Barrow-in-Furness	d	13 25											14 16								
Roose	d												14 20								
Dalton	d												14 26								
Ulverston	d	13 41											14 35								
Cark	d												14 44								
Kents Bank	d												14 49								
Grange-over-Sands	d	13 53											14 53								
Arnside	d	13 59											14 59								
Silverdale	d												15 03								
Carnforth	d	14 08											15 10								
Windermere	83 d																				
Oxenholme Lake District	65 d											14 06									
Lancaster 6	65 a	14 18										14 22	15 22								
	d	14 18										14 22									
Blackpool North	97 d			13 20	13 37		13 45									14 20	14 37		14 45		
Layton	97 d			13 23												14 23					
Poulton-le-Fylde	97 d			13 28			13 51									14 28			14 51		
Kirkham & Wesham	97 d			13 37												14 37					
Preston 8	65,97 a	14 37		13 47	14 02		14 09					14 41				14 47	15 02		15 09		
	d			13 49	14 04		14 10			14 23		14 47				14 49	15 04		15 10		
Leyland	d			13 54	14 09					14 29						14 54	15 09				
Chorley	d			14 02			14 20			14 36		14 56				15 02			15 20		
Adlington (Lancashire)	d			14 07												15 07					
Blackrod	d			14 10												15 10					
Horwich Parkway	d			14 14			14 27			14 45						15 14			15 27		
Lostock	d			14 20						14 50						15 20					
Southport	d								13 56					14 20							14 50
Meols Cop	d								14 01												14 55
Bescar Lane	d																				15 00
New Lane	d																				15 04
Burscough Bridge	d								14 09					14 32							15 07
Hoscar	d																				15 11
Parbold	d								14 14					14 37							15 14
Appley Bridge	d								14 18					14 41							15 18
Gathurst	d								14 21												15 21
Kirkby	d		13 28												14 28						
Rainford	d		13 36												14 36						
Upholland	d		13 40												14 40						
Orrell	d		13 43												14 43						
Pemberton	d		13 46												14 46						
Wigan Wallgate	a		13 54						14 28					14 49	14 54						15 28
	d		13 56					14 18	14 30		14 46			14 51	14 56					15 18	15 30
Wigan North Western	d				14 24												15 24				
Ince	d		13 59												14 59						
Hindley	d		14 02					14 23	14 35					14 56	15 02					15 23	15 35
Westhoughton	d							14 27						15 00						15 27	
Bolton	a			14 25		14 30	14 34	14 38		14 55	15 02	15 08		15 12		15 25		15 30	15 34	15 38	
	d			14 25		14 31	14 35	14 39		14 56	15 03	15 08		15 13		15 25		15 31	15 35	15 39	
Moses Gate	d							14 42												15 42	
Farnworth	d							14 44												15 44	
Kearsley	d							14 46												15 46	
Daisy Hill	d		14 07						14 39						15 07						15 39
Hag Fold	d		14 10												15 10						
Atherton	d		14 13						14 43						15 13						15 43
Walkden	d		14 18						14 48						15 18						15 48
Moorside	d		14 22												15 22						
Swinton	d		14 24						14 53						15 24						15 53
Salford Crescent	a		14 34	14 38		14 43	14 47	14 56	15 02	15 08	15 15			15 25	15 34	15 38		15 43	15 47	15 56	16 02
	d		14 34	14 38		14 44	14 47	14 56	15 03	15 09	15 15			15 26	15 34	15 38		15 44	15 47	15 56	16 03
Salford Central	d		14 36	14 41		14 46		14 59	15 05		15 17				15 36	15 41		15 46		15 59	16 05
Manchester Victoria	⇌ a		14 43	14 47		14 53		15 06	15 11		15 25				15 43	15 47		15 54		16 06	16 11
Rochdale	41 a										15 51										
Deansgate	⇌ a						14 51			15 12				15 29					15 51		
Manchester Oxford Road	a						14 52			15 14		15 23		15 31					15 52		
Manchester Piccadilly 10	⇌ a						14 56			15 18		15 27		15 35					15 56		
Stockport	84 a									15 34											
Hazel Grove	86 a									15 47											
Buxton	86 a																				
Heald Green	85 a						15 10												16 10		
Manchester Airport	85 ✈ a						15 17					15 47		15 53					16 17		

Table 82

Saturdays
from 11 September

Barrow-in-Furness, Blackpool North, Preston, Southport, Kirkby and Wigan - Bolton - Manchester

		NT	NT	TP ◇1 ⊼	NT	NT	NT	NT	NT	NT	NT	TP ◇1 ⊼	NT	NT	NT	NT	TP ◇1 ⊼	TP ◇1	NT	NT	NT	NT	NT
Barrow-in-Furness	d						15 18											16 17					
Roose	d						15 22																
Dalton	d						15 28											16 26					
Ulverston	d						15 36											16 34					
Cark	d						15 45											16 42					
Kents Bank	d						15 49																
Grange-over-Sands	d						15 53											16 48					
Arnside	d						15 59											16 54					
Silverdale	d						16 04											16 59					
Carnforth	d					15 36	16 10											17 06					
Windermere 83	d																						
Oxenholme Lake District 65	d			15 09													16 08						
Lancaster [6] 65	a			15 26		15 45	16 23										16 25	17 15					
	d			15 26		15 49											16 26	17 15					
Blackpool North 97	d									15 20	15 37	15 45									16 20	16 35	
Layton 97	d									15 23											16 23		
Poulton-le-Fylde 97	d									15 28		15 51									16 28		
Kirkham & Wesham 97	d									15 37											16 37		
Preston [8] 65,97	a			15 45						15 47	16 02	16 09					16 45	17 34			16 47	17 02	
	d	15 23		15 47						15 49	16 04	16 10			16 23		16 47				16 49	17 04	
Leyland	d	15 29								15 54	16 09				16 29						16 54	17 09	
Chorley	d	15 36		15 56						16 02		16 20			16 36		16 56				17 02		
Adlington (Lancashire)	d									16 07											17 07		
Blackrod	d									16 10											17 10		
Horwich Parkway	d	15 45								16 14		16 27			16 45						17 14		
Lostock	d	15 50								16 20					16 50						17 20		
Southport	d				15 20									16 00					16 20				
Meols Cop	d													16 05									
Bescar Lane	d																						
New Lane	d																						
Burscough Bridge	d				15 32									16 13					16 32				
Hoscar	d																						
Parbold	d				15 37									16 18					16 37				
Appley Bridge	d				15 41									16 22					16 41				
Gathurst	d													16 25									
Kirkby	d								15 28											16 30			
Rainford	d								15 36											16 38			
Upholland	d								15 40											16 42			
Orrell	d								15 43											16 45			
Pemberton	d								15 46											16 48			
Wigan Wallgate	a				15 49				15 54					16 30					16 49	16 56			
	d		15 46		15 51				15 56				16 18	16 32		16 46			16 51	16 58			
Wigan North Western	d										16 24											17 24	
Ince	d								15 59											17 01			
Hindley	d				15 56				16 02				16 23	16 37					16 56	17 04			
Westhoughton	d				16 00								16 27						17 00				
Bolton	a	15 55	16 02	16 08	16 12			16 17		16 25		16 34	16 38		16 55	17 02	17 08		17 12		17 25		17 30
	d	15 56	16 03	16 08	16 13			16 17		16 25		16 35	16 39		16 56	17 03	17 08		17 13		17 25		17 31
Moses Gate	d												16 42										
Farnworth	d												16 44										
Kearsley	d												16 46										
Daisy Hill	d								16 07					16 41						17 08			
Hag Fold	d								16 10											17 11			
Atherton	d								16 13					16 45						17 14			
Walkden	d								16 18					16 50						17 19			
Moorside	d								16 22											17 23			
Swinton	d								16 24					16 55						17 25			
Salford Crescent	a	16 08	16 15		16 25			16 30	16 33	16 38		16 47	16 56	17 02	17 08	17 15			17 25	17 33	17 38		17 43
	d	16 09	16 15		16 26			16 30	16 34	16 38		16 47	16 56	17 03	17 09	17 15			17 26	17 33	17 38		17 44
Salford Central	d		16 17					16 33	16 37	16 41			16 59	17 05		17 17				17 36	17 41		17 46
Manchester Victoria ⇌	a		16 23					16 42	16 43	16 47			17 06	17 11		17 23				17 43	17 47		17 55
Rochdale 41	a		16 51													17 51							
Deansgate ⇌	a	16 12										16 51			17 12				17 29				
Manchester Oxford Road	a	16 14		16 23	16 31							16 52			17 14		17 23		17 31				
Manchester Piccadilly [10] ⇌	a	16 18		16 27	16 35							16 56			17 18		17 27		17 35				
Stockport 84	a	16 34													17 34								
Hazel Grove 86	a	16 47													17 43								
Buxton 86	a																						
Heald Green 85	a			16 40								17 10					17 40						
Manchester Airport 85 ✈	a			16 47	16 53							17 17					17 48		17 53				

Table 82

Saturdays
from 11 September

Barrow-in-Furness, Blackpool North, Preston, Southport, Kirkby and Wigan - Bolton - Manchester

		TP ◇1 ⊼	NT	NT	NT	NT	TP ◇1 ⊼	NT	NT	NT	NT	TP ◇1 A ⊼	TP ◇1	NT	NT	NT	TP ◇1 ⊼	NT	NT
Barrow-in-Furness	d												17 21						
Roose	d																		
Dalton	d												17 30						
Ulverston	d												17 38						
Cark	d												17 46						
Kents Bank	d																		
Grange-over-Sands	d												17 53						
Arnside	d												17 59						
Silverdale	d																		
Carnforth	d												18 09						18 26
Windermere 83	d											17 06							
Oxenholme Lake District 65	d											17b30							
Lancaster [6] 65	a											17 47	18 17				18 26		18 38
	d											17 48	18 17				18 26		18 47
Blackpool North 97	d	16 40					17 20				17 37								
Layton 97	d	16 44					17 23												
Poulton-le-Fylde 97	d	16 48					17 27												
Kirkham & Wesham 97	d	16 57																	
Preston [8] 65,97	a	17 08					17 45				18 02	18 06	18 36				18 45		
	d	17 09			17 23		17 47			17 56	18 04	18 08					18 47		
Leyland	d				17 29					18 01	18 09								
Chorley	d	17 19			17 36		17 56			18 08		18 17					18 56		
Adlington (Lancashire)	d									18 13									
Blackrod	d									18 17									
Horwich Parkway	d	17 26			17 45					18 20		18 26							
Lostock	d				17 50							18 30							
Southport	d			16 50				17 20							17 54			18 14	
Meols Cop	d			16 55				17 25							17 59			18 19	
Bescar Lane	d			17 00											18 04			18 24	
New Lane	d			17 04											18 08			18 28	
Burscough Bridge	d			17 07				17 33							18 11			18 30	
Hoscar	d			17 11											18 15			18 34	
Parbold	d			17 14				17 38							18 18			18 37	
Appley Bridge	d			17 18				17 42							18 22			18 41	
Gathurst	d			17 21											18 25			18 44	
Kirkby	d								17 30										
Rainford	d								17 38										
Upholland	d								17 42										
Orrell	d								17 45										
Pemberton	d								17 48										
Wigan Wallgate	a			17 28				17 50	17 57						18 30			18 51	
	d		17 20	17 30				17 52	17 59					18 20	18 32			18 52	
Wigan North Western	d										18 24								
Ince	d								18 02										
Hindley	d		17 25	17 35					18 05					18 25	18 37			18 57	
Westhoughton	d		17 29					18 00						18 29				19 01	
Bolton	a	17 34	17 38		17 55	18 01	18 08	18 12		18 30		18 34		18 38		19 01	19 08	19 12	
	d	17 35	17 39		17 56	18 02	18 08	18 13		18 30		18 35		18 39		19 02	19 08	19 13	
Moses Gate	d		17 42											18 42					
Farnworth	d		17 44											18 44					
Kearsley	d		17 46											18 46					
Daisy Hill	d			17 39					18 09						18 41				
Hag Fold	d								18 12										
Atherton	d			17 43					18 15						18 45				
Walkden	d			17 48					18 20						18 50				
Moorside	d								18 24										
Swinton	d			17 53					18 26						18 55				
Salford Crescent	a	17 47	17 56	18 02	18 08	18 14		18 25	18 33	18 43		18 47		18 56	19 02	19 14		19 25	
	d	17 47	17 56	18 03	18 09	18 15		18 26	18 33	18 43		18 47		18 56	19 03	19 15		19 26	
Salford Central	d		17 59	18 05		18 17			18 36	18 46				18 59	19 05	19 17			
Manchester Victoria ⇌	a		18 06	18 11		18 26			18 43	18 52				19 06	19 11	19 23			
Rochdale 41	a					18 49													
Deansgate ⇌	a	17 51			18 12							18 51						19 29	
Manchester Oxford Road	a	17 52			18 14		18 23	18 31				18 52					19 23	19 31	
Manchester Piccadilly [10] ⇌	a	17 56			18 18		18 27	18 35				18 56					19 27	19 35	
Stockport 84	a				18 34														
Hazel Grove 86	a				18 47														
Buxton 86	a																		
Heald Green 85	a	18 10					18 40					19 10							
Manchester Airport 85 ✈	a	18 17					18 47	18 53				19 17					19 50	19 53	

A ⊼ from Preston

b arr. 1725

Barrow-in-Furness, Blackpool North, Preston, Southport, Kirkby and Wigan - Bolton - Manchester

	NT	NT	NT	NT	NT	TP ◇1	NT	NT	TP ◇1 ⊼	NT	NT	NT	NT	TP ◇1	TP ◇1 ⊼	TP ◇1	NT	NT	NT	NT
Barrow-in-Furness d	18 03															19 32				
Roose d	18 07															19 36				
Dalton d	18 13															19 43				
Ulverston d	18 21															19 51				
Cark d	18 29															19 59				
Kents Bank d	18 33															20 03				
Grange-over-Sands d	18 37															20 07				
Arnside d	18 43															20 13				
Silverdale d	18 48															20 18				
Carnforth d	18 54															20 25				
Windermere 83 d																				
Oxenholme Lake District 65 d									19 08						20 12					
Lancaster 6 65 a	19 04								19 26						20 26	20 33				
d	19 05								19 26						20 26	20 34				
Blackpool North 97 d			18 20	18 37		18 45					19 20	19 37		19 45					20 20	
Layton 97 d			18 23								19 23								20 23	
Poulton-le-Fylde 97 d			18 28			18 51					19 28			19 51					20 28	
Kirkham & Wesham 97 d			18 37								19 37								20 37	
Preston 8 65,97 a	19 30		18 47	19 00		19 09			19 45		19 47	20 02		20 09	20 45	20 54			20 47	
d			18 49	19 04		19 10			19 47		19 49	20 04		20 10	20 47				20 49	
Leyland d			18 54	19 09							19 54	20 09							20 54	
Chorley d			19 02			19 20			19 56		20 02			20 20	20 56				21 02	
Adlington (Lancashire) d			19 07								20 07								21 07	
Blackrod d			19 10								20 10								21 10	
Horwich Parkway d			19 14			19 27					20 14			20 27					21 14	
Lostock d			19 20								20 20								21 20	
Southport d							18 56			19 19								20 19		
Meols Cop d							19 01			19 24								20 24		
Bescar Lane d																				
New Lane d																				
Burscough Bridge d							19 09			19 32								20 32		
Hoscar d																				
Parbold d							19 14			19 37								20 37		
Appley Bridge d							19 18			19 41								20 41		
Gathurst d							19 21			19 44								20 44		
Kirkby d		18 30																		
Rainford d		18 38																		
Upholland d		18 42																		
Orrell d		18 45																		
Pemberton d		18 48																		
Wigan Wallgate a		18 56					19 28			19 51								20 51		
d		18 58					19 30			19 53							20 27	20 53		
Wigan North Western d				19 24								20 24								
Ince d		19 01															20 30			
Hindley d		19 04					19 35			19 58							20 33	20 58		
Westhoughton d										20 02								21 02		
Bolton a			19 25		19 31	19 34		20 02	20 08	20 12	20 25		20 30	20 34	21 08			21 12	21 25	21 30
d			19 25		19 31	19 35		20 02	20 08	20 13	20 25		20 31	20 35	21 08			21 13	21 25	21 31
Moses Gate d																				
Farnworth d																				
Kearsley d																				
Daisy Hill d		19 08					19 39										20 37			
Hag Fold d		19 11															20 40			
Atherton d		19 14					19 43										20 43			
Walkden d		19 19					19 48										20 49			
Moorside d		19 23															20 52			
Swinton d		19 25					19 53										20 55			
Salford Crescent a		19 33	19 38		19 44	19 47	20 02	20 15		20 25	20 38		20 43	20 47			21 02	21 25	21 38	21 43
d		19 33	19 38		19 44	19 47	20 03	20 15		20 26	20 38		20 44	20 47			21 03	21 26	21 38	21 44
Salford Central d		19 36	19 41		19 46		20 05	20 17			20 41		20 46				21 05		21 41	21 46
Manchester Victoria ⇌ a		19 43	19 47		19 53		20 11	20 25			20 47		20 52				21 11		21 47	21 52
Rochdale 41 a																				
Deansgate ⇌ a						19 51				20 29				20 51				21 29		
Manchester Oxford Road a						19 52			20 23	20 31				20 52	21 23			21 31		
Manchester Piccadilly 10 ⇌ a						19 56			20 27	20 35				20 56	21 27			21 35		
Stockport 84 a																				
Hazel Grove 86 a																				
Buxton 86 a																				
Heald Green 85 a						20 10								21 10						
Manchester Airport 85 ✈ a						20 17			20 47	20 53				21 17	21 47			21 53		

Barrow-in-Furness, Blackpool North, Preston, Southport, Kirkby and Wigan - Bolton - Manchester

	TP ◇1	NT	NT	NT	TP ◇1	NT	NT	TP ◇1	NT	NT	NT	TP ◇1	NT	NT	NT
Barrow-in-Furness d						21 43									
Roose d						21 47									
Dalton d						21 53									
Ulverston d						22 01									
Cark d						22 09									
Kents Bank d						22 13									
Grange-over-Sands d						22 17									
Arnside d						22 23									
Silverdale d						22 28									
Carnforth d						22 34									
Windermere 83 d					21 40										
Oxenholme Lake District 65 d					22 01										
Lancaster 6 65 a					22 17	22 44									
d					22 17	22 45									
Blackpool North 97 d	20 42			21 20				21 45		22 20		22 45			23 02
Layton 97 d				21 23						22 23					23 05
Poulton-le-Fylde 97 d	20 48			21 28				21 51		22 28		22 51			23 10
Kirkham & Wesham 97 d				21 37						22 37					23 19
Preston 8 65,97 a	21 06			21 47	22 38	23 10		22 09		22 47		23 09			23 29
d	21 10			21 49				22 10		22 49		23 10			23 31
Leyland d				21 54						22 54					23 36
Chorley d	21 20			22 02				22 20		23 02		23 20			23 44
Adlington (Lancashire) d				22 07						23 07					23 49
Blackrod d				22 10						23 10					23 52
Horwich Parkway d	21 27			22 14				22 27		23 14		23 27			23 56
Lostock d				22 20						23 20					00 02
Southport d			21 19								22 18		23 10		
Meols Cop d			21 24								22 23		23 15		
Bescar Lane d											22 28				
New Lane d											22 32				
Burscough Bridge d			21 32								22 34		23 23		
Hoscar d											22 38				
Parbold d			21 37								22 41		23 28		
Appley Bridge d			21 41								22 45		23 32		
Gathurst d			21 44								22 48		23 35		
Kirkby d															
Rainford d															
Upholland d															
Orrell d															
Pemberton d															
Wigan Wallgate a			21 51								22 53		23 44		
d		21 27	21 53						22 27		22 55				
Wigan North Western d															
Ince d		21 30							22 30						
Hindley d		21 33	21 58						22 33		23 00				
Westhoughton d			22 02								23 04				
Bolton a	21 34		22 12	22 25			22 30	22 34		23 25	23 12	23 34		23 36	00 07
d	21 35		22 13	22 25			22 31	22 35		23 25	23 13	23 35		23 38	00 07
Moses Gate d															
Farnworth d															
Kearsley d															
Daisy Hill d		21 37							22 37						
Hag Fold d		21 40							22 40						
Atherton d		21 43							22 43						
Walkden d		21 49							22 49						
Moorside d		21 52							22 52						
Swinton d		21 55							22 55						
Salford Crescent a	21 47	22 02	22 25	22 38			22 43	22 47	23 02	23 38	23 25	23 47		23 48	
d	21 47	22 03	22 26	22 38			22 44	22 47	23 03	23 38	23 26	23 47		23 51	
Salford Central d		22 05	22 28	22 41			22 46		23 05						
Manchester Victoria ⇌ a		22 11	22 34	22 47			22 52		23 13	23 47				23 59	00 26
Rochdale 41 a															
Deansgate ⇌ a	21 51							22 51			23 29				
Manchester Oxford Road a	21 52							22 52			23 31				
Manchester Piccadilly 10 ⇌ a	21 56							22 56			23 35	23 53			
Stockport 84 a															
Hazel Grove 86 a															
Buxton 86 a															
Heald Green 85 a	22 09							23 09				00 15			
Manchester Airport 85 ✈ a	22 17							23 17				00 22			

Table 82

Sundays
until 05 September

Barrow-in-Furness, Blackpool North, Preston, Southport, Kirkby and Wigan - Bolton - Manchester

		TP	TP	TP	NT	NT	NT	NT	TP	NT	NT	NT	NT	NT	TP	NT	NT	TP	NT
				◇1					◇1						◇1			◇1	
		bus	bus				trolley												
Barrow-in-Furness	d																	09 15	
Roose	d																	09 19	
Dalton	d																	09 26	
Ulverston	d																	09 34	
Cark	d																	09 42	
Kents Bank	d																	09 46	
Grange-over-Sands	d																	09 50	
Arnside	d																	09 56	
Silverdale	d																	10 01	
Carnforth	d																	10 08	
Windermere	83 d																		
Oxenholme Lake District	65 d																		
Lancaster ■	65 a																	10 17	
	d																	10 21	
Blackpool North	97 d	03 20	05 20	07 48		08 20	08 36		08 44	08 50			09 20		09 44				10 20
Layton	97 d					08 23							09 23						10 23
Poulton-le-Fylde	97 d			07 54		08 28	08 42		08 50	08 56			09 28		09 50				10 28
Kirkham & Wesham	97 d					08 37	08 51						09 37						10 37
Preston ■	65,97 a	04u00	06u00	08 12		08 47	09 02		09 08	09 14			09 47		10 08			10 40	10 47
	d	04u00	06u00	08 14		08 49	09 05		09 10	09 15			09 49		10 10			10 47	10 49
Leyland	d					08 54				09 21			09 54						10 54
Chorley	d			08 23		09 02			09 20				10 02		10 20			10 56	11 02
Adlington (Lancashire)	d					09 07							10 07						11 07
Blackrod	d					09 10							10 10						11 10
Horwich Parkway	d			08 30		09 14			09 27				10 14		10 27				11 14
Lostock	d					09 20							10 20						11 20
Southport	d											09 09					10 05		
Meols Cop	d											09 14					10 10		
Bescar Lane	d																		
New Lane	d																		
Burscough Bridge	d											09 22					10 18		
Hoscar	d																		
Parbold	d											09 27					10 23		
Appley Bridge	d											09 31					10 27		
Gathurst	d											09 34					10 30		
Kirkby	d																		
Rainford	d																		
Upholland	d																		
Orrell	d																		
Pemberton	d																		
Wigan Wallgate	a											09 39					10 35		
	d				08 40						09 17	09 40				10 17	10 36		
Wigan North Western	d									09 36									
Ince	d																		
Hindley	d				08 45						09 22	09 45				10 22	10 41		
Westhoughton	d				08 49							09 50					10 46		
Bolton	a	04u35	06u35	08 37	08 57	09 25		09 30	09 34			09 58	10 25	10 30	10 34		10 54	11 08	11 25
	d	04u35	06u35	08 37	08 58	09 25		09 31	09 35			09 58	10 25	10 31	10 35		10 54	11 08	11 25
Moses Gate	d																		
Farnworth	d																		
Kearsley	d																		
Daisy Hill	d										09 26					10 26			
Hag Fold	d										09 29					10 29			
Atherton	d										09 31					10 31			
Walkden	d										09 37					10 37			
Moorside	d										09 40					10 40			
Swinton	d										09 43					10 43			
Salford Crescent	a			08 49	09 10	09 38		09 43	09 47		09 50	10 11	10 38	10 43	10 47	10 50	11 07		11 38
	d			08 50	09 11	09 38		09 44	09 47		09 52	10 11	10 38	10 44	10 47	10 51	11 07		11 38
Salford Central	d																		
Manchester Victoria	⇌ a					09 45		09 52			09 58		10 45	10 52		10 57			11 45
Rochdale	41 a																		
Deansgate	⇌ a			08 53	09 14				09 51			10 15			10 51		11 11		
Manchester Oxford Road	a			08 55	09 17				09 53			10 17			10 53		11 13	11 23	
Manchester Piccadilly 10	⇌ a	05u00	07u00	08 59	09 21				09 57			10 23			10 57		11 19	11 27	
Stockport	84 a				09 31												11 30		
Hazel Grove	86 a																		
Buxton	86 a																		
Heald Green	85 a																		
Manchester Airport	85 ✈ a	05 25	07 25	09 19					10 17						11 18			11 47	

The Sunday service between Wigan Wallgate and Manchester Victoria via Atherton is funded by GMITA and will operate whilst funding exists

Table 82

Sundays
until 05 September

Barrow-in-Furness, Blackpool North, Preston, Southport, Kirkby and Wigan - Bolton - Manchester

		NT	NT	TP	NT	NT	NT	NT	NT	TP	NT	NT	NT	TP	NT	NT	NT	TP	NT	NT	NT	TP
				◇1						◇1				◇1				◇1				◇1
																						trolley
Barrow-in-Furness	d													11 23								
Roose	d													11 27								
Dalton	d													11 34								
Ulverston	d													11 42								
Cark	d													11 50								
Kents Bank	d													11 54								
Grange-over-Sands	d													11 58								
Arnside	d													12 04								
Silverdale	d													12 09								
Carnforth	d	10 31												12 17		12 35						
Windermere	83 d																					
Oxenholme Lake District	65 d																					13 10
Lancaster ■	65 a	10 40												12 26		12 44						13 26
	d	10 45												12 26		13 01						13 26
Blackpool North	97 d			10 44	10 50			11 20		11 44	11 50				12 20			12 44	12 50			
Layton	97 d							11 23							12 23							
Poulton-le-Fylde	97 d			10 50	10 56			11 28		11 50	11 56				12 28			12 50	12 56			
Kirkham & Wesham	97 d							11 37							12 37							
Preston ■	65,97 a			11 08	11 14			11 47		12 08	12 14			12 45	12 47			13 08	13 14			13 45
	d			11 10	11 15			11 49		12 10	12 15			12 47	12 49			13 10	13 15			13 47
Leyland	d				11 21			11 54			12 21				12 54				13 21			
Chorley	d			11 20				12 02		12 20				12 56	13 02			13 20				13 56
Adlington (Lancashire)	d							12 07							13 07							
Blackrod	d							12 10							13 10							
Horwich Parkway	d			11 27				12 14		12 27					13 14			13 27				
Lostock	d							12 20							13 20							
Southport	d						11 05						12 05								13 05	
Meols Cop	d						11 10						12 10								13 10	
Bescar Lane	d																					
New Lane	d																					
Burscough Bridge	d						11 18						12 18								13 18	
Hoscar	d																					
Parbold	d						11 23						12 23								13 23	
Appley Bridge	d						11 27						12 27								13 27	
Gathurst	d						11 30						12 30								13 30	
Kirkby	d																					
Rainford	d																					
Upholland	d																					
Orrell	d																					
Pemberton	d																					
Wigan Wallgate	a						11 35						12 35								13 35	
	d					11 17	11 36					12 17	12 36							13 17	13 36	
Wigan North Western	d				11 36						12 36								13 36			
Ince	d																					
Hindley	d					11 22	11 41					12 22	12 41							13 22	13 41	
Westhoughton	d						11 46						12 46								13 46	
Bolton	a		11 30	11 34			11 54	12 25	12 30	12 34			12 54	13 08	13 25		13 30	13 34			13 54	14 08
	d		11 31	11 35			11 54	12 25	12 31	12 35			12 54	13 08	13 25		13 31	13 35			13 54	14 08
Moses Gate	d																					
Farnworth	d																					
Kearsley	d																					
Daisy Hill	d					11 26						12 26								13 26		
Hag Fold	d					11 29						12 29								13 29		
Atherton	d					11 31						12 31								13 31		
Walkden	d					11 37						12 37								13 37		
Moorside	d					11 40						12 40								13 40		
Swinton	d					11 43						12 43								13 43		
Salford Crescent	a		11 43	11 47		11 50	12 07	12 38	12 43	12 47		12 50	13 07		13 38		13 43	13 47		13 50	14 07	
	d		11 44	11 47		11 51	12 07	12 38	12 44	12 47		12 51	13 07		13 38		13 44	13 47		13 51	14 07	
Salford Central	d																					
Manchester Victoria	⇌ a		11 52			11 57		12 45	12 52			12 57			13 45		13 52			13 57		
Rochdale	41 a																					
Deansgate	⇌ a			11 51			12 11			12 51			13 11					13 51			14 11	
Manchester Oxford Road	a			11 53			12 13			12 53			13 13	13 23				13 53			14 13	14 23
Manchester Piccadilly 10	⇌ a			11 57			12 19			12 57			13 19	13 27				13 57			14 19	14 27
Stockport	84 a						12 33						13 30								14 33	
Hazel Grove	86 a																					
Buxton	86 a																					
Heald Green	85 a																					
Manchester Airport	85 ✈ a			12 17						13 17				13 47				14 17				14 47

The Sunday service between Wigan Wallgate and Manchester Victoria via Atherton is funded by GMITA and will operate whilst funding exists

Table 82

Sundays until 05 September

Barrow-in-Furness, Blackpool North, Preston, Southport, Kirkby and Wigan - Bolton - Manchester

			NT			NT	TP ◇1	NT	NT	NT	TP ◇1	NT	NT		TP ◇1	NT	NT	NT	TP ◇1 🛒	NT		NT	TP ◇1		NT	NT
Barrow-in-Furness		d										13 23															
Roose		d										13 27															
Dalton		d										13 34															
Ulverston		d										13 42															
Cark		d										13 50															
Kents Bank		d										13 54															
Grange-over-Sands		d										13 58															
Arnside		d										14 04															
Silverdale		d										14 09															
Carnforth		d										14 17															
Windermere	83	d																								
Oxenholme Lake District	65	d																	15 10							
Lancaster [6]	65	a										14 26								15 25							
		d										14 26								15 25							
Blackpool North	97	d	13 20				13 44	13 50				14 20			14 44	14 50				15 20			15 44		15 50	
Layton	97	d	13 23									14 23								15 23						
Poulton-le-Fylde	97	d	13 28				13 50	13 56				14 28			14 50	14 56				15 28			15 50		15 56	
Kirkham & Wesham	97	d	13 37									14 37								15 37						
Preston [8]	65,97	a	13 47				14 08	14 14			14 45	14 47			15 08	15 14			15 45	15 47			16 08		16 14	
		d	13 49				14 10	14 15			14 47	14 49			15 10	15 15			15 47	15 49			16 10		16 15	
Leyland		d	13 54					14 21				14 54				15 21				15 54					16 21	
Chorley		d	14 02				14 20				14 56	15 02			15 20				15 56	16 02			16 20			
Adlington (Lancashire)		d	14 07									15 07								16 07						
Blackrod		d	14 10									15 10								16 10						
Horwich Parkway		d	14 14				14 27					15 14			15 27					16 14			16 27			
Lostock		d	14 20									15 20								16 20						
Southport		d								14 05								15 05								
Meols Cop		d								14 10								15 10								
Bescar Lane		d																								
New Lane		d																								
Burscough Bridge		d								14 18								15 18								
Hoscar		d																								
Parbold		d								14 23								15 23								
Appley Bridge		d								14 27								15 27								
Gathurst		d								14 30								15 30								
Kirkby		d																								
Rainford		d																								
Upholland		d																								
Orrell		d																								
Pemberton		d																								
Wigan Wallgate		a								14 35								15 35								
		d							14 17	14 36							15 17	15 36								16 17
Wigan North Western		d						14 36								15 36									16 36	
Ince		d																								
Hindley		d							14 22	14 41							15 22	15 41								16 22
Westhoughton		d								14 46								15 46								
Bolton		a	14 25			14 30	14 34			14 54	15 08	15 25	15 30		15 34			15 54	16 08	16 25		16 30	16 34			
		d	14 25			14 31	14 35			14 54	15 08	15 25	15 31		15 35			15 54	16 08	16 25		16 31	16 35			
Moses Gate		d																								
Farnworth		d																								
Kearsley		d																								
Daisy Hill		d							14 26								15 26									16 26
Hag Fold		d							14 29								15 29									16 29
Atherton		d							14 31								15 31									16 31
Walkden		d							14 37								15 37									16 37
Moorside		d							14 40								15 40									16 40
Swinton		d							14 43								15 43									16 43
Salford Crescent		a	14 38			14 43	14 47		14 50	15 07		15 38	15 43		15 47		15 50	16 07		16 38		16 43	16 47			16 50
		d	14 38			14 44	14 47		14 51	15 07		15 38	15 44		15 47		15 51	16 07		16 38		16 44	16 47			16 51
Salford Central		d																								
Manchester Victoria	⇌	a	14 45			14 52			14 57			15 45	15 52				15 57			16 45		16 52				16 57
Rochdale	41	a																								
Deansgate	⇌	a					14 51			15 11					15 51			16 11					16 51			
Manchester Oxford Road		a					14 53			15 13	15 23				15 53			16 13	16 23				16 53			
Manchester Piccadilly [10]	⇌	a					14 57			15 19	15 27				15 57			16 19	16 27				16 57			
Stockport	84	a								15 30								16 33								
Hazel Grove	86	a																								
Buxton	86	a																								
Heald Green	85	a																								
Manchester Airport	85 ✈	a					15 17				15 47				16 17				16 47				17 17			

The Sunday service between Wigan Wallgate and Manchester Victoria via Atherton is funded by GMITA and will operate whilst funding exists

Table 82

Sundays until 05 September

Barrow-in-Furness, Blackpool North, Preston, Southport, Kirkby and Wigan - Bolton - Manchester

			NT	TP ◇1	NT	NT	TP ◇1	NT	TP ◇1		NT	NT	NT	TP ◇1 🛒	TP ◇1	NT		NT	TP ◇1		NT	NT	TP ◇1 🛒	TP ◇1	NT	NT
Barrow-in-Furness		d		15 23			16 25																	18 15		
Roose		d		15 27																				18 19		
Dalton		d		15 34																				18 26		
Ulverston		d		15 42			16 40																	18 34		
Cark		d		15 50																				18 42		
Kents Bank		d		15 54																				18 46		
Grange-over-Sands		d		15 58			16 53																	18 50		
Arnside		d		16 04			16 59																	18 56		
Silverdale		d		16 09																				19 01		
Carnforth		d		16 17		16 37	17 08																	19 08		19 04
Windermere	83	d													16 58										
Oxenholme Lake District	65	d												17 08	17 16								18 10			
Lancaster [6]	65	a		16 26		16 46	17 17							17 23	17 31								18 26	19 17		19 13
		d		16 26		16 51	17 17							17 23	17 32								18 26	19 17		19 23
Blackpool North	97	d			16 20				16 44		16 50					17 20			17 40		17 50				18 20	
Layton	97	d			16 23											17 23									18 23	
Poulton-le-Fylde	97	d			16 28				16 50		16 56					17 28			17 46		17 56				18 28	
Kirkham & Wesham	97	d			16 37											17 37									18 37	
Preston [8]	65,97	a		16 45	16 47		17 37		17 08		17 14			17 42	17 50	17 47			18 04		18 14		18 45	19 37	18 47	
		d		16 47	16 49				17 10		17 15			17 47		17 49			18 10		18 15		18 47		18 49	
Leyland		d			16 54						17 21					17 54					18 21				18 54	
Chorley		d		16 56	17 02				17 20					17 56		18 02			18 20				18 56		19 02	
Adlington (Lancashire)		d			17 07											18 07									19 07	
Blackrod		d			17 10											18 10									19 10	
Horwich Parkway		d			17 14				17 27							18 14			18 27						19 14	
Lostock		d			17 20											18 20									19 20	
Southport		d	16 05										17 05									18 05				
Meols Cop		d	16 10										17 10									18 10				
Bescar Lane		d																								
New Lane		d																								
Burscough Bridge		d	16 18										17 18									18 18				
Hoscar		d																								
Parbold		d	16 23										17 23									18 23				
Appley Bridge		d	16 27										17 27									18 27				
Gathurst		d	16 30										17 30									18 30				
Kirkby		d																								
Rainford		d																								
Upholland		d																								
Orrell		d																								
Pemberton		d																								
Wigan Wallgate		a	16 35										17 35									18 35				
		d	16 36									17 17	17 36									18 36				
Wigan North Western		d									17 36										18 36					
Ince		d																								
Hindley		d	16 41									17 22	17 41									18 41				
Westhoughton		d	16 46										17 46									18 46				
Bolton		a	16 54	17 08	17 25			17 30	17 34				17 54	18 08		18 25		18 30	18 34			18 54	19 08		19 25	
		d	16 54	17 08	17 25			17 31	17 35				17 54	18 08		18 25		18 31	18 35			18 54	19 08		19 25	
Moses Gate		d																								
Farnworth		d																								
Kearsley		d																								
Daisy Hill		d										17 26														
Hag Fold		d										17 29														
Atherton		d										17 31														
Walkden		d										17 37														
Moorside		d										17 40														
Swinton		d										17 43														
Salford Crescent		a	17 07		17 38			17 43	17 47			17 50	18 07			18 38		18 43	18 47			19 07			19 38	
		d	17 07		17 38			17 44	17 47			17 51	18 07			18 38		18 44	18 47			19 07			19 38	
Salford Central		d																								
Manchester Victoria	⇌	a			17 45			17 52				17 57				18 45		18 52							19 45	
Rochdale	41	a																								
Deansgate	⇌	a	17 11						17 51				18 11						18 51			19 11				
Manchester Oxford Road		a	17 13	17 23					17 53				18 13	18 23					18 53			19 13	19 23			
Manchester Piccadilly [10]	⇌	a	17 19	17 27					17 57				18 19	18 27					18 57			19 19	19 27			
Stockport	84	a	17 30										18 33									19 30				
Hazel Grove	86	a																								
Buxton	86	a																								
Heald Green	85	a																								
Manchester Airport	85 ✈	a		17 47					18 17					18 47					19 17				19 47			

The Sunday service between Wigan Wallgate and Manchester Victoria via Atherton is funded by GMITA and will operate whilst funding exists

Sundays
until 05 September

Barrow-in-Furness, Blackpool North, Preston, Southport, Kirkby and Wigan - Bolton - Manchester

			NT	TP ◇1	NT	NT	TP ◇1 🚲	NT	NT	TP ◇1	NT	NT	NT	TP ◇1 🚲	NT	NT	NT	TP ◇1	NT	NT	NT
Barrow-in-Furness		d													20 02						
Roose		d													20 06						
Dalton		d													20 12						
Ulverston		d													20 21						
Cark		d													20 30						
Kents Bank		d													20 35						
Grange-over-Sands		d													20 39						
Arnside		d													20 45						
Silverdale		d													20 49						
Carnforth		d													20 56						
Windermere	83	d																			
Oxenholme Lake District	65	d					19 07							20 10							
Lancaster 6	65	a					19 21							20 26	21 09						
		d					19 22							20 26							
Blackpool North	97	d		18 44	18 50			19 20		19 44	19 50		20 11			20 20		20 44	20 50		21 13
Layton	97	d						19 23								20 23					
Poulton-le-Fylde	97	d		18 50	18 56			19 28		19 50	19 56		20 17			20 28		20 50	20 56		21 19
Kirkham & Wesham	97	d						19 37								20 37					
Preston 8	65,97	a		19 08	19 14		19 41	19 47		20 08	20 14		20 34	20 45		20 47		21 08	21 14		21 36
		d		19 10	19 15		19 47	19 49		20 10	20 15		20 37	20 47		20 49		21 10	21 15		21 39
Leyland		d			19 21			19 54			20 21					20 54			21 21		
Chorley		d		19 20			19 56	20 02		20 20				20 56		21 02		21 20			
Adlington (Lancashire)		d						20 07								21 07					
Blackrod		d						20 10								21 10					
Horwich Parkway		d		19 27				20 14		20 27						21 14		21 27			
Lostock		d						20 20								21 20					
Southport		d				19 05						20 05								21 05	
Meols Cop		d				19 10						20 10								21 10	
Bescar Lane		d																			
New Lane		d																			
Burscough Bridge		d				19 18						20 18								21 18	
Hoscar		d																			
Parbold		d				19 23						20 23								21 23	
Appley Bridge		d				19 27						20 27								21 27	
Gathurst		d				19 30						20 30								21 30	
Kirkby		d																			
Rainford		d																			
Upholland		d																			
Orrell		d																			
Pemberton		d																			
Wigan Wallgate		a				19 35						20 35								21 35	
		d				19 36						20 36								21 36	
Wigan North Western		d			19 36						20 36								21 36		
Ince		d																			
Hindley		d				19 41						20 41								21 41	
Westhoughton		d				19 46						20 46								21 46	
Bolton		a	19 30	19 34		19 54	20 08	20 25	20 30	20 34		20 54		21 08		21 25	21 30	21 34		21 54	
		d	19 31	19 35		19 54	20 08	20 25	20 31	20 35		20 54		21 08		21 25	21 31	21 35		21 54	
Moses Gate		d																			
Farnworth		d																			
Kearsley		d																			
Daisy Hill		d																			
Hag Fold		d																			
Atherton		d																			
Walkden		d																			
Moorside		d																			
Swinton		d																			
Salford Crescent		a	19 43	19 47		20 07		20 38	20 43	20 47		21 07				21 38	21 43	21 47		22 07	
		d	19 44	19 47		20 07		20 38	20 44	20 47		21 07				21 38	21 44	21 47		22 07	
Salford Central		d																			
Manchester Victoria	⇌	a	19 52					20 45	20 52							21 45	21 52				
Rochdale	41	a																			
Deansgate	⇌	a		19 51		20 11				20 51		21 11						21 51		22 11	
Manchester Oxford Road		a		19 53		20 13	20 23			20 53		21 13		21 23				21 53		22 13	
Manchester Piccadilly 10	⇌	a		19 57		20 19	20 27			20 57		21 19		21 27				21 57		22 19	
Stockport	84	a				20 33						21 30								22 33	
Hazel Grove	86	a																			
Buxton	86	a																			
Heald Green	85	a																			
Manchester Airport	85 ✈	a		20 17			20 47			21 17				21 47				22 17			

The Sunday service between Wigan Wallgate and Manchester Victoria via Atherton is funded by GMITA and will operate whilst funding exists

Sundays
until 05 September

Barrow-in-Furness, Blackpool North, Preston, Southport, Kirkby and Wigan - Bolton - Manchester

			NT	NT	NT	TP ◇1 🚲	NT	NT	NT	TP ◇1
Barrow-in-Furness		d								
Roose		d								
Dalton		d								
Ulverston		d								
Cark		d								
Kents Bank		d								
Grange-over-Sands		d								
Arnside		d								
Silverdale		d								
Carnforth		d								
Windermere	83	d								
Oxenholme Lake District	65	d								
Lancaster 6	65	a				22 02				
		d				22 03				
Blackpool North	97	d	21 20	21 50				22 44		23 03
Layton	97	d	21 23							
Poulton-le-Fylde	97	d	21 28	21 56				22 50		23 09
Kirkham & Wesham	97	d	21 37							23 17
Preston 8	65,97	a	21 47	22 14		22 23		23 08		23 28
		d	21 49	22 15		22 29		23 09		23 29
Leyland		d	21 54	22 21				23 15		23 34
Chorley		d	22 02			22 38				23 41
Adlington (Lancashire)		d	22 07							23 45
Blackrod		d	22 10							23 49
Horwich Parkway		d	22 14							23 52
Lostock		d	22 20							23 56
Southport		d					22 05			
Meols Cop		d					22 10			
Bescar Lane		d								
New Lane		d								
Burscough Bridge		d					22 18			
Hoscar		d								
Parbold		d					22 23			
Appley Bridge		d					22 27			
Gathurst		d					22 30			
Kirkby		d								
Rainford		d								
Upholland		d								
Orrell		d								
Pemberton		d								
Wigan Wallgate		a					22 35			
		d					22 36			
Wigan North Western		d		22 36				23 30		
Ince		d								
Hindley		d					22 41			
Westhoughton		d					22 46			
Bolton		a	22 25		22 30	22 50	22 54		23 30	00 02
		d	22 25		22 31	22 51	22 54		23 31	00 02
Moses Gate		d								
Farnworth		d								
Kearsley		d								
Daisy Hill		d								
Hag Fold		d								
Atherton		d								
Walkden		d								
Moorside		d								
Swinton		d								
Salford Crescent		a	22 38		22 43	23 03	23 07		23 43	
		d	22 38		22 44	23 03	23 07		23 44	
Salford Central		d								
Manchester Victoria	⇌	a	22 45		22 52				23 52	
Rochdale	41	a								
Deansgate	⇌	a				23 08	23 11			
Manchester Oxford Road		a				23 10	23 14			
Manchester Piccadilly 10	⇌	a				23 14	23 19			00 18
Stockport	84	a					23 33			
Hazel Grove	86	a								
Buxton	86	a								
Heald Green	85	a								
Manchester Airport	85 ✈	a				23 30				00 32

The Sunday service between Wigan Wallgate and Manchester Victoria via Atherton is funded by GMITA and will operate whilst funding exists

Table 82

Sundays from 12 September

Barrow-in-Furness, Blackpool North, Preston, Southport, Kirkby and Wigan - Bolton - Manchester

Station			TP	TP	NT	TP ◇1	NT	NT A	TP ◇1	NT	TP ◇1	NT A	NT	NT	NT	NT B	NT C	NT	TP ◇1	NT
Barrow-in-Furness		d							09 25											
Roose		d																		
Dalton		d																		
Ulverston		d							09 41											
Cark		d																		
Kents Bank		d																		
Grange-over-Sands		d							09 52											
Arnside		d							09 58											
Silverdale		d																		
Carnforth		d							10 08								10 31			
Windermere	83	d																		
Oxenholme Lake District	65	d																		
Lancaster	65	a							10 17								10 40			
		d							10 21								10 45			
Blackpool North	97	d	03 20	05 20		08 14	08 20	08 36			08 44	08 50			09 20				09 44	
Layton	97	d					08 23								09 23					
Poulton-le-Fylde	97	d				08 20	08 28	08 42			08 50	08 56			09 28				09 50	
Kirkham & Wesham	97	d					08 37	08 51							09 37	09 54				
Preston	65,97	a	04u00	06u00		08 38	08 47	09 02	10 40		09 08	09 14			09 47	10 04			10 08	
		d	04u00	06u00		08 42	08 49	09 05			09 10	09 15			09 49	10 05			10 10	
Leyland		d					08 54					09 21			09 54					
Chorley		d				08 51	09 02				09 20				10 02				10 20	
Adlington (Lancashire)		d					09 07								10 07					
Blackrod		d					09 10								10 10					
Horwich Parkway		d				08 59	09 14				09 27				10 14				10 27	
Lostock		d					09 20								10 20					
Southport		d												09 09						
Meols Cop		d												09 14						
Bescar Lane		d																		
New Lane		d																		
Burscough Bridge		d												09 22						
Hoscar		d																		
Parbold		d												09 27						
Appley Bridge		d												09 31						
Gathurst		d												09 34						
Kirkby		d																		
Rainford		d																		
Upholland		d																		
Orrell		d																		
Pemberton		d																		
Wigan Wallgate		a												09 39						
		d			08 40								09 17	09 40						10 17
Wigan North Western		d										09 36								
Ince		d																		
Hindley		d			08 45								09 22	09 45						10 22
Westhoughton		d			08 49									09 50						
Bolton		a	04u35	06u35	08 57	09 05	09 25			09 30	09 34			09 58	10 25			10 30	10 34	
		d	04u35	06u35	08 58	09 06	09 25			09 31	09 35			09 58	10 25			10 31	10 35	
Moses Gate		d																		
Farnworth		d																		
Kearsley		d																		
Daisy Hill		d											09 26							10 26
Hag Fold		d											09 29							10 29
Atherton		d											09 31							10 31
Walkden		d											09 37							10 37
Moorside		d											09 40							10 40
Swinton		d											09 43							10 43
Salford Crescent		a			09 10	09 18	09 38			09 43	09 47		09 50	10 11	10 38			10 43	10 47	10 50
		d			09 11	09 19	09 38			09 44	09 47		09 52	10 11	10 38			10 44	10 47	10 51
Salford Central		d																		
Manchester Victoria		a					09 45			09 52			09 58		10 45			10 52		10 57
Rochdale	41	a																		
Deansgate		a			09 14	09 22					09 51			10 15					10 51	
Manchester Oxford Road		a			09 17	09 24					09 53			10 17					10 53	
Manchester Piccadilly		a	05u00	07u00	09 21	09 28					09 57			10 22					10 57	
Stockport	84	a			09 31									10 33						
Hazel Grove	86	a																		
Buxton	86	a																		
Heald Green	85	a																		
Manchester Airport	85	a	05 25	07 25		09 53					10 17								11 18	

A from 12 September until 17 October B from 12 September until 7 November C 12 September

The Sunday service between Wigan Wallgate and Manchester Victoria via Atherton is funded by GMITA and will operate whilst funding exists

Table 82

Sundays from 12 September

Barrow-in-Furness, Blackpool North, Preston, Southport, Kirkby and Wigan - Bolton - Manchester

Station			NT	NT	NT	TP ◇1	NT A	NT	NT	NT	NT	TP ◇1	NT A	NT	NT	TP ◇1	NT	NT B	NT
Barrow-in-Furness		d														11 23			
Roose		d														11 27			
Dalton		d														11 34			
Ulverston		d														11 42			
Cark		d														11 50			
Kents Bank		d														11 54			
Grange-over-Sands		d														11 58			
Arnside		d														12 04			
Silverdale		d														12 09			
Carnforth		d														12 17		12 35	
Windermere	83	d																	
Oxenholme Lake District	65	d																	
Lancaster	65	a														12 26		12 44	
		d														12 26		13 01	
Blackpool North	97	d		10 20		10 44	10 50			11 20		11 44	11 50				12 20		
Layton	97	d		10 23						11 23							12 23		
Poulton-le-Fylde	97	d		10 28		10 50	10 56			11 28		11 50	11 56				12 28		
Kirkham & Wesham	97	d		10 37						11 37							12 37		
Preston	65,97	a		10 47		11 08	11 14			11 47		12 08	12 14			12 45	12 47		
		d		10 49		11 10	11 15			11 49		12 10	12 15			12 47	12 49		
Leyland		d		10 54			11 21			11 54			12 21				12 54		
Chorley		d		11 02		11 20				12 02		12 20				12 56	13 02		
Adlington (Lancashire)		d		11 07						12 07							13 07		
Blackrod		d		11 10						12 10							13 10		
Horwich Parkway		d		11 14		11 27				12 14		12 27					13 14		
Lostock		d		11 20						12 20							13 20		
Southport		d	10 01						11 01						12 01				
Meols Cop		d	10 06						11 06						12 06				
Bescar Lane		d																	
New Lane		d																	
Burscough Bridge		d	10 14						11 14						12 14				
Hoscar		d																	
Parbold		d	10 19						11 19						12 19				
Appley Bridge		d	10 23						11 23						12 23				
Gathurst		d	10 26						11 26						12 26				
Kirkby		d																	
Rainford		d																	
Upholland		d																	
Orrell		d																	
Pemberton		d																	
Wigan Wallgate		a	10 33						11 33						12 33				
		d	10 34					11 17	11 34					12 17	12 34				
Wigan North Western		d					11 36						12 36						
Ince		d																	
Hindley		d	10 39					11 22	11 39					12 22	12 39				
Westhoughton		d	10 44						11 44						12 44				
Bolton		a	10 54	11 25	11 30	11 34			11 54	12 25	12 30	12 34			12 54	13 08	13 25		13 30
		d	10 54	11 25	11 31	11 35			11 54	12 25	12 31	12 35			12 54	13 08	13 25		13 31
Moses Gate		d																	
Farnworth		d																	
Kearsley		d																	
Daisy Hill		d						11 26						12 26					
Hag Fold		d						11 29						12 29					
Atherton		d						11 31						12 31					
Walkden		d						11 37						12 37					
Moorside		d						11 40						12 40					
Swinton		d						11 43						12 43					
Salford Crescent		a	11 07	11 38	11 43	11 47		11 50	12 07	12 38	12 43	12 47		12 50	13 07		13 38		13 43
		d	11 07	11 38	11 44	11 47		11 51	12 07	12 38	12 44	12 47		12 51	13 07		13 38		13 44
Salford Central		d																	
Manchester Victoria		a		11 45	11 52			11 57		12 45	12 52			12 57			13 45		13 52
Rochdale	41	a																	
Deansgate		a	11 11			11 51			12 11			12 51			13 11				
Manchester Oxford Road		a	11 13			11 53			12 13			12 52			13 13	13 23			
Manchester Piccadilly		a	11 19			11 57			12 19			12 56			13 19	13 27			
Stockport	84	a	11 30						12 31						13 30				
Hazel Grove	86	a																	
Buxton	86	a																	
Heald Green	85	a																	
Manchester Airport	85	a				12 17						13 17				13 47			

A from 12 September until 17 October B 12 September

The Sunday service between Wigan Wallgate and Manchester Victoria via Atherton is funded by GMITA and will operate whilst funding exists

Table 82

Sundays
from 12 September

Barrow-in-Furness, Blackpool North, Preston, Southport, Kirkby and Wigan - Bolton - Manchester

		TP	NT	NT	NT	TP	NT	NT	NT	TP	NT	NT	NT	TP	NT	NT	TP
		◇1				◇1				◇1				◇1			◇1
			A			🚌		B			A						
Barrow-in-Furness	d							12 45						13 23			
Roose	d							12 49						13 27			
Dalton	d							12 55						13 34			
Ulverston	d							13 04						13 42			
Cark	d							13 13						13 50			
Kents Bank	d							13 18						13 54			
Grange-over-Sands	d							13 22						13 58			
Arnside	d							13 28						14 04			
Silverdale	d							13 32						14 09			
Carnforth	d							13 39						14 17			
Windermere	83 d																
Oxenholme Lake District	65 d					13 10											
Lancaster 6	65 a					13 26		13 52						14 26			
	d					13 26								14 26			
Blackpool North	97 d	12 44	12 50				13 20			13 44	13 50				14 20		14 44
Layton	97 d						13 23								14 23		
Poulton-le-Fylde	97 d	12 50	12 56				13 28			13 50	13 56				14 28		14 50
Kirkham & Wesham	97 d						13 37								14 37		
Preston 8	65,97 a	13 08	13 14			13 45	13 47			14 08	14 14			14 45	14 47		15 08
	d	13 10	13 15			13 47	13 49			14 10	14 15			14 47	14 49		15 10
Leyland	d		13 21				13 54				14 21				14 54		
Chorley	d	13 20				13 56	14 02			14 20				14 56	15 02		15 20
Adlington (Lancashire)	d						14 07								15 07		
Blackrod	d						14 10								15 10		
Horwich Parkway	d	13 27					14 14			14 27					15 14		15 27
Lostock	d						14 20								15 20		
Southport	d				13 01								14 01				
Meols Cop	d				13 06								14 06				
Bescar Lane	d																
New Lane	d																
Burscough Bridge	d				13 14								14 14				
Hoscar	d																
Parbold	d				13 19								14 19				
Appley Bridge	d				13 23								14 23				
Gathurst	d				13 26								14 26				
Kirkby	d																
Rainford	d																
Upholland	d																
Orrell	d																
Pemberton	d																
Wigan Wallgate	a				13 33								14 33				
	d			13 17	13 34							14 17	14 34				
Wigan North Western	d		13 36								14 36						
Ince	d																
Hindley	d			13 22	13 39							14 22	14 39				
Westhoughton	d				13 44								14 44				
Bolton	a	13 34			13 54	14 08	14 25		14 30	14 34			14 54	15 08	15 25	15 30	15 34
	d	13 35			13 54	14 08	14 25		14 31	14 35			14 54	15 08	15 25	15 31	15 35
Moses Gate	d																
Farnworth	d																
Kearsley	d																
Daisy Hill	d			13 26								14 26					
Hag Fold	d			13 29								14 29					
Atherton	d			13 31								14 31					
Walkden	d			13 37								14 37					
Moorside	d			13 40								14 40					
Swinton	d			13 43								14 43					
Salford Crescent	a	13 47		13 50	14 07		14 38		14 43	14 47		14 50	15 07		15 38	15 43	15 47
	d	13 47		13 51	14 07		14 38		14 44	14 47		14 51	15 07		15 38	15 44	15 47
Salford Central	d																
Manchester Victoria	⇌ a			13 57			14 45		14 52			14 57			15 45	15 52	
Rochdale	41 a																
Deansgate	⇌ a	13 51			14 11					14 51			15 11				15 51
Manchester Oxford Road	a	13 53			14 13	14 23				14 53			15 13	15 23			15 53
Manchester Piccadilly 10	⇌ a	13 57			14 19	14 27				14 57			15 19	15 27			15 57
Stockport	84 a				14 33								15 30				
Hazel Grove	86 a																
Buxton	86 a																
Heald Green	85 a																
Manchester Airport	85 ✈ a	14 17				14 47				15 17				15 47			16 17

A from 12 September until 17 October
B not 12 September

The Sunday service between Wigan Wallgate and Manchester Victoria via Atherton is funded by GMITA and will operate whilst funding exists

Table 82

Sundays
from 12 September

Barrow-in-Furness, Blackpool North, Preston, Southport, Kirkby and Wigan - Bolton - Manchester

		NT	NT	NT	TP	NT	NT	TP	NT	NT	NT	TP	NT	NT	NT	TP	NT	NT	NT	TP	NT
					◇1			◇1				◇1				◇1				◇1	
		A			🚌				A								A			🚌	
Barrow-in-Furness	d											15 23									
Roose	d											15 27									
Dalton	d											15 34									
Ulverston	d											15 42									
Cark	d											15 50									
Kents Bank	d											15 54									
Grange-over-Sands	d											15 58									
Arnside	d											16 04									
Silverdale	d											16 09									
Carnforth	d											16 17		16 37							
Windermere	83 d																				
Oxenholme Lake District	65 d				15 10															17 08	
Lancaster 6	65 a				15 25							16 26		16 46						17 23	
	d				15 25							16 26		16 51						17 23	
Blackpool North	97 d	14 50				15 20		15 44	15 50				16 20			16 44	16 50				17 20
Layton	97 d					15 23							16 23								17 23
Poulton-le-Fylde	97 d	14 56				15 28		15 50	15 56				16 28			16 50	16 56				17 28
Kirkham & Wesham	97 d					15 37							16 37								17 37
Preston 8	65,97 a	15 14			15 45	15 47		16 08	16 14			16 45	16 47			17 08	17 14			17 42	17 47
	d	15 15			15 47	15 49		16 10	16 15			16 47	16 49			17 10	17 15			17 47	17 49
Leyland	d	15 21				15 54			16 21				16 54				17 21				17 54
Chorley	d				15 56	16 02		16 20				16 56	17 02			17 20				17 56	18 02
Adlington (Lancashire)	d					16 07							17 07								18 07
Blackrod	d					16 10							17 10								18 10
Horwich Parkway	d					16 14		16 27					17 14			17 27					18 14
Lostock	d					16 20							17 20								18 20
Southport	d			15 01							16 01								17 01		
Meols Cop	d			15 06							16 06								17 06		
Bescar Lane	d																				
New Lane	d																				
Burscough Bridge	d			15 14							16 14								17 14		
Hoscar	d																				
Parbold	d			15 19							16 19								17 19		
Appley Bridge	d			15 23							16 23								17 23		
Gathurst	d			15 26							16 26								17 26		
Kirkby	d																				
Rainford	d																				
Upholland	d																				
Orrell	d																				
Pemberton	d																				
Wigan Wallgate	a			15 33							16 33								17 33		
	d		15 17	15 34						16 17	16 34							17 17	17 34		
Wigan North Western	d	15 36							16 36								17 36				
Ince	d																				
Hindley	d		15 22	15 39						16 22	16 39							17 22	17 39		
Westhoughton	d			15 44							16 44								17 44		
Bolton	a			15 54	16 08	16 25	16 30	16 34			16 54	17 08	17 25		17 30	17 34			17 54	18 08	18 25
	d			15 54	16 08	16 25	16 31	16 35			16 54	17 08	17 25		17 31	17 35			17 54	18 08	18 25
Moses Gate	d																				
Farnworth	d																				
Kearsley	d																				
Daisy Hill	d		15 26							16 26								17 26			
Hag Fold	d		15 29							16 29								17 29			
Atherton	d		15 31							16 31								17 31			
Walkden	d		15 37							16 37								17 37			
Moorside	d		15 40							16 40								17 40			
Swinton	d		15 43							16 43								17 43			
Salford Crescent	a		15 50	16 07		16 38	16 43	16 47		16 50	17 07		17 38		17 43	17 47		17 50	18 07		18 38
	d		15 51	16 07		16 38	16 44	16 47		16 51	17 07		17 38		17 44	17 47		17 51	18 07		18 38
Salford Central	d																				
Manchester Victoria	⇌ a		15 57			16 45	16 52			16 57			17 45		17 52			17 57			18 45
Rochdale	41 a																				
Deansgate	⇌ a			16 11				16 51			17 11					17 51			18 11		
Manchester Oxford Road	a			16 13	16 23			16 53			17 13	17 23				17 53			18 13	18 23	
Manchester Piccadilly 10	⇌ a			16 19	16 27			16 57			17 19	17 27				17 57			18 19	18 27	
Stockport	84 a			16 33							17 30								18 33		
Hazel Grove	86 a																				
Buxton	86 a																				
Heald Green	85 a																				
Manchester Airport	85 ✈ a				16 47			17 17				17 47				18 17				18 47	

A from 12 September until 17 October

The Sunday service between Wigan Wallgate and Manchester Victoria via Atherton is funded by GMITA and will operate whilst funding exists

Table 82

Sundays from 12 September

Barrow-in-Furness, Blackpool North, Preston, Southport, Kirkby and Wigan - Bolton - Manchester

		NT	TP ◇1	NT A	NT	TP ◇1 ✠	TP ◇1	NT	NT	NT	TP ◇1	NT A	NT	TP ◇1 ✠	NT	NT	TP ◇1	NT A	NT	NT	TP ◇1 ✠
Barrow-in-Furness	d						18 15														
Roose	d						18 19														
Dalton	d						18 26														
Ulverston	d						18 34														
Cark	d						18 42														
Kents Bank	d						18 46														
Grange-over-Sands	d						18 50														
Arnside	d						18 56														
Silverdale	d						19 01														
Carnforth	d						19 08		19 04												
Windermere	83 d																				
Oxenholme Lake District	65 d					18 10								19 07							20 10
Lancaster ■	65 a					18 26	19 17		19 13					19 21							20 26
	d					18 26	19 17		19 23					19 22							20 26
Blackpool North	97 d		17 44	17 50				18 20			18 44	18 50			19 20		19 44	19 50		20 11	
Layton	97 d							18 23							19 23						
Poulton-le-Fylde	97 d		17 50	17 56				18 28			18 50	18 56			19 28		19 50	19 56		20 17	
Kirkham & Wesham	97 d							18 37							19 37						
Preston ■	65,97 a		18 08	18 14		18 45	19 37	18 47			19 08	19 14		19 41	19 47		20 08	20 14		20 34	20 45
	d		18 10	18 15		18 47		18 49			19 10	19 15		19 47	19 49		20 10	20 15		20 37	20 47
Leyland	d			18 21				18 54				19 21			19 54			20 21			
Chorley	d		18 20			18 56		19 02			19 20			19 56	20 02		20 20				20 56
Adlington (Lancashire)	d							19 07							20 07						
Blackrod	d							19 10							20 10						
Horwich Parkway	d		18 27					19 14			19 27				20 14		20 27				
Lostock	d							19 20							20 20						
Southport	d				18 01								19 01						20 01		
Meols Cop	d				18 06								19 06						20 06		
Bescar Lane	d																				
New Lane	d																				
Burscough Bridge	d				18 14								19 14						20 14		
Hoscar	d																				
Parbold	d				18 19								19 19						20 19		
Appley Bridge	d				18 23								19 23						20 23		
Gathurst	d				18 26								19 26						20 26		
Kirkby	d																				
Rainford	d																				
Upholland	d																				
Orrell	d																				
Pemberton	d																				
Wigan Wallgate	a				18 33								19 33						20 33		
	d				18 34								19 34						20 34		
Wigan North Western	d			18 36								19 36						20 36			
Ince	d																				
Hindley	d				18 39								19 39						20 39		
Westhoughton	d				18 44								19 44						20 44		
Bolton	a	18 30	18 34		18 54	19 08		19 25		19 30	19 34		19 54	20 08	20 25	20 30	20 34		20 54		21 08
	d	18 31	18 35		18 54	19 08		19 25		19 31	19 35		19 54	20 08	20 25	20 31	20 35		20 54		21 08
Moses Gate	d																				
Farnworth	d																				
Kearsley	d																				
Daisy Hill	d																				
Hag Fold	d																				
Atherton	d																				
Walkden	d																				
Moorside	d																				
Swinton	d																				
Salford Crescent	a	18 43	18 47		19 07			19 38		19 43	19 47		20 07		20 38	20 43	20 47		21 07		
	d	18 44	18 47		19 07			19 38		19 44	19 47		20 07		20 38	20 44	20 47		21 07		
Salford Central	d																				
Manchester Victoria	⇌ a	18 52						19 45		19 52					20 45	20 52					
Rochdale	41 a																				
Deansgate	⇌ a		18 51		19 11						19 51		20 11				20 51		21 11		
Manchester Oxford Road	a		18 53		19 13	19 23					19 53		20 13	20 23			20 53		21 13		21 23
Manchester Piccadilly ■	⇌ a		18 57		19 19	19 27					19 57		20 19	20 27			20 57		21 19		21 27
Stockport	84 a				19 30								20 33						21 30		
Hazel Grove	86 a																				
Buxton	86 a																				
Heald Green	85 a																				
Manchester Airport	85 ✈ a		19 17			19 47					20 17			20 47			21 17				21 47

A from 12 September until 17 October

The Sunday service between Wigan Wallgate and Manchester Victoria via Atherton is funded by GMITA and will operate whilst funding exists

Table 82

Sundays from 12 September

Barrow-in-Furness, Blackpool North, Preston, Southport, Kirkby and Wigan - Bolton - Manchester

		NT	NT	NT	TP ◇1	NT A	NT	NT	NT	NT A	NT	TP ◇1 ✠	NT	NT A	NT	TP ◇1
Barrow-in-Furness	d	20 02														
Roose	d	20 06														
Dalton	d	20 12														
Ulverston	d	20 21														
Cark	d	20 30														
Kents Bank	d	20 35														
Grange-over-Sands	d	20 39														
Arnside	d	20 45														
Silverdale	d	20 49														
Carnforth	d	20 56														
Windermere	83 d															
Oxenholme Lake District	65 d															
Lancaster ■	65 a	21 09										22 02				
	d											22 03				
Blackpool North	97 d		20 20		20 44	20 50		21 13	21 20	21 50				22 44		23 03
Layton	97 d		20 23						21 23							
Poulton-le-Fylde	97 d		20 28		20 50	20 56		21 19	21 28	21 56				22 50		23 09
Kirkham & Wesham	97 d		20 37						21 37							23 17
Preston ■	65,97 a		20 47		21 08	21 14		21 36	21 47	22 14		22 23		23 08		23 28
	d		20 49		21 10	21 15		21 39	21 49	22 15		22 29		23 09		23 29
Leyland	d		20 54			21 21			21 54	22 21				23 15		23 34
Chorley	d		21 02		21 20				22 02			22 38				23 41
Adlington (Lancashire)	d		21 07						22 07							23 45
Blackrod	d		21 10						22 10							23 49
Horwich Parkway	d		21 14		21 27				22 14							23 52
Lostock	d		21 20						22 20							23 56
Southport	d						21 01						22 01			
Meols Cop	d						21 06						22 06			
Bescar Lane	d															
New Lane	d															
Burscough Bridge	d						21 14						22 14			
Hoscar	d															
Parbold	d						21 19						22 19			
Appley Bridge	d						21 23						22 23			
Gathurst	d						21 26						22 26			
Kirkby	d															
Rainford	d															
Upholland	d															
Orrell	d															
Pemberton	d															
Wigan Wallgate	a						21 33						22 33			
	d						21 34						22 34			
Wigan North Western	d					21 36				22 36				23 30		
Ince	d															
Hindley	d						21 39						22 39			
Westhoughton	d						21 44						22 44			
Bolton	a		21 25	21 30	21 34		21 54		22 25		22 30	22 50	22 54		23 30	00 02
	d		21 25	21 31	21 35		21 54		22 25		22 31	22 51	22 54		23 31	00 02
Moses Gate	d															
Farnworth	d															
Kearsley	d															
Daisy Hill	d															
Hag Fold	d															
Atherton	d															
Walkden	d															
Moorside	d															
Swinton	d															
Salford Crescent	a		21 38	21 43	21 47		22 07		22 38		22 43	23 03	23 07		23 43	
	d		21 38	21 44	21 47		22 07		22 38		22 44	23 03	23 07		23 44	
Salford Central	d															
Manchester Victoria	⇌ a		21 45	21 52					22 45		22 52				23 52	
Rochdale	41 a															
Deansgate	⇌ a				21 51		22 11					23 08	23 11			
Manchester Oxford Road	a				21 53		22 13					23 10	23 14			
Manchester Piccadilly ■	⇌ a				21 57		22 19					23 14	23 19			00 18
Stockport	84 a						22 33						23 33			
Hazel Grove	86 a															
Buxton	86 a															
Heald Green	85 a															
Manchester Airport	85 ✈ a				22 17							23 30				00 32

A from 12 September until 17 October

The Sunday service between Wigan Wallgate and Manchester Victoria via Atherton is funded by GMITA and will operate whilst funding exists

Table 83

Mondays to Fridays

Oxenholme- Lake District - Windermere

		TP 1	TP 1	TP 1	TP 1	TP 1	TP ◇1	TP 1	TP ◇1	TP 1	TP 1	TP 1	TP ◇1	TP ◇1	TP 1	TP 1	TP 1	TP 1
Oxenholme Lake District	d	06 21	07 21	08 27	09 14	10 27	11 18	12 28	13 37	14 27	15 38	16 28	17 49	18 46	19 37	20 27	21 15	22 20
Kendal	d	06 26	07 25	08 31	09 18	10 31	11 22	12 32	13 41	14 31	15 43	16 32	17 53	18 50	19 41	20 31	21 19	22 24
Burneside	d		07x29	08x35	09x22		11 26	12x36		14x35	15x46	16x36	17x57	18x54	19x45	20x35	21x23	22x28
Staveley	d		07x34	08x40	09x27		11 31	12x41		14x40	15x51	16x41	18x02	18x59	19x50	20x40	21x28	22x33
Windermere	a	06 41	07 40	08 46	09 33	10 44	11 39	12 47	13 56	14 46	15 59	16 48	18 08	19 08	19 56	20 46	21 34	22 39

Saturdays

		TP 1	TP 1	TP 1	TP 1	TP ◇1	TP ◇1	TP 1	TP ◇1	TP 1	TP 1	TP 1	TP ◇1	TP 1	TP 1	TP 1	TP 1
Oxenholme Lake District	d	06 21	07 21	08 27	09 11	10 05	11 18	12 28	13 37	14 35	15 38	16 28	17 38	18 30	19 37	20 23	21 15
Kendal	d	06 26	07 25	08 31	09 15	10 09	11 22	12 32	13 41	14 39	15 43	16 32	17 42	18 34	19 41	20 27	21 19
Burneside	d		07x29	08x35	09x19	10x13	11x26	12x36		14x43	15x46	16x36	17x46	18x38	19x45	20x31	21x23
Staveley	d		07x34	08x40	09x24	10x18	11x31	12x41		14x48	15x51	16x41	17x51	18x43	19x50	20x36	21x28
Windermere	a	06 41	07 40	08 46	09 30	10 26	11 39	12 47	13 56	14 54	15 59	16 48	18 00	18 49	19 56	20 42	21 34

Sundays

		TP ◇1	TP 1	TP 1	TP 1	TP 1	TP 1	TP 1	TP 1 A	TP ◇1 B	TP 1	TP 1	TP 1
Oxenholme Lake District	d	10 40	11 35	12 29	13 35	14 37	15 35	16 29	17 37	17 39	18 37	19 29	20 16
Kendal	d	10 44	11 39	12 33	13 39	14 41	15 39	16 33	17 41	17 44	18 41	19 33	20 20
Burneside	d		11x43	12x37	13x43	14x45	15x43	16x37	17x45		18x45		20x24
Staveley	d		11x48	12x42	13x48	14x50	15x48	16x42	17x50		18x50		20x29
Windermere	a	10 58	11 54	12 48	13 54	14 56	15 54	16 48	17 56	17 59	18 56	19 45	20 35

A from 12 September

B until 5 September

Table 83

Mondays to Fridays

Windermere - Oxenholme- Lake District

		TP 1	TP 1	TP 1	TP 1	TP ◇1	TP 1	TP ◇1	TP 1	TP 1	TP 1	TP ◇1	TP ◇1	TP 1	TP 1	TP 1	TP 1	TP ◇1
Windermere	d	06 50	07 57	08 50	09 59	10 49	11 59	12 51	14 00	14 59	16 02	17 06	18 15	19 10	20 00	20 50	21 40	22 45
Staveley	d	06x55	08x02		10x04	10x54	12x04		14x05	15x04		17x11	18x20		20x05	20x55	21x45	22x50
Burneside	d	07x00	08x07		10x09	10x59	12x09		14x10	15x09		17x16	18x25		20x10	21x00	21x50	22x55
Kendal	d	07 04	08 11	09 01	10 13	11 03	12 13	13 02	14 14	15 13	16 14	17 20	18 29	19 21	20 14	21 04	21 54	22 59
Oxenholme Lake District	a	07 09	08 16	09 06	10 18	11 08	12 18	13 07	14 19	15 18	16 19	17 25	18 34	19 27	20 19	21 09	21 59	23 04

Saturdays

		TP 1	TP 1	TP 1	TP ◇1	TP ◇1	TP 1	TP ◇1	TP 1	TP 1	TP 1	TP ◇1	TP 1	TP 1	TP 1	TP 1	TP ◇1
Windermere	d	06 57	07 57	08 50	09 38	10 49	11 59	12 51	14 00	14 59	16 02	17 06	18 02	19 00	20 00	20 47	21 40
Staveley	d	07x02	08x02		09x43	10x54	12x04		14x05	15x04		17x11	18x07	19x05	20x05		21x45
Burneside	d	07x07	08x07		09x48	10x59	12x09		14x10	15x09		17x16	18x12	19x10	20x10		21x50
Kendal	d	07 11	08 11	09 01	09 52	11 03	12 13	13 02	14 14	15 13	16 14	17 20	18 16	19 14	20 14	20 58	21 54
Oxenholme Lake District	a	07 16	08 16	09 06	09 57	11 08	12 18	13 07	14 19	15 18	16 19	17 25	18 21	19 19	20 19	21 04	21 59

Sundays

		TP 1	TP 1	TP 1	TP 1	TP 1	TP 1	TP 1 A	TP ◇1 B	TP 1	TP 1	TP 1	TP ◇1
Windermere	d	11 01	11 58	12 58	13 58	15 00	15 58	16 58	16 58	18 04	19 00	19 50	20 40
Staveley	d		12x03	13x03	14x03		16x03	17x03		18x09	19x05		20x45
Burneside	d		12x08	13x08	14x08		16x08	17x08		18x14	19x10		20x50
Kendal	d	11 13	12 12	13 12	14 12	15 12	16 12	17 11	17 09	18 18	19 14	20 01	20 54
Oxenholme Lake District	a	11 18	12 18	13 17	14 17	15 17	16 17	17 17	17 15	18 23	19 19	20 06	20 59

A from 12 September

B until 5 September

Stoke-on-Trent and Crewe - Manchester Airport, Stockport and Manchester

Station		NT MX	TP MO ◇1	NT	NT	VT 1	NT	NT	TP ◇1	AW	NT	NT	NT
London Euston 15 ⊖65	d												
Birmingham New Street 12 68	d												
Wolverhampton 7 68 ⇌	d												
Stafford 65,68	d												
Stoke-on-Trent 50,68	d												
Longport 50	d												
Kidsgrove 50	d												
Crewe 10 65	d	00 44			05 48	06 12				06 27			
Sandbach	d				05 55								
Holmes Chapel	d				06 00								
Goostrey	d				06 03								
Chelford	d				06 07								
Alderley Edge	d				06 11							06 49	
Wilmslow	d			05 46	06 15	06 28				06 45		06 52	
Styal	d												
Manchester Airport ✈	a	01 16		05 53									
Handforth	d				06 18							06 55	
Congleton	d												
Macclesfield	a												
	d							06 22					
Prestbury	d							06 26					
Adlington (Cheshire)	d							06 29					
Poynton	d							06 33					
Bramhall	d							06 35					
Cheadle Hulme	d				06 22			06 38				06 59	
Stockport	a				06 27	06 37		06 43		06 54		07 04	
	d		05 53		06 27	06 38	06 41	06 43	06 53	06 54	06 58	07 04	07 10
Heaton Chapel	d				06 31			06 46				07 08	07 15
Levenshulme	d				06 34			06 49				07 11	07 18
Manchester Piccadilly 10 ⇌	a	01 36	06 05	06 25	06 42	06 49	06 52	06 58	07 02	07 09	07 10	07 21	07 26
	d						06 54						07 27
Manchester Oxford Road	a						06 56						07 29
Deansgate ⇌	a						06 59						07 32

Station		NT	NT	EM ◇	XC ◇1 ⊼	NT	NT	NT	NT	NT	XC ◇1	TP ◇1 ⊼	AW ◇	NT	NT	NT	NT	NT	VT ◇1 ⊠	NT	XC ◇1 ⊼
London Euston 15 ⊖65	d																		06 17		
Birmingham New Street 12 68	d				05 57						06 20										06 57
Wolverhampton 7 68 ⇌	d				06 16						06 40										07 16
Stafford 65,68	d				06 30						06 54										07 30
Stoke-on-Trent 50,68	d	06 30			06 51						07 13					07 17			07 45		
Longport 50	d	06 34														07 21					
Kidsgrove 50	d	06 38														07 25					
Crewe 10 65	d					06 33	06 49						07 27					07 22			07 52
Sandbach	d					06 40	06 56											07 35			
Holmes Chapel	d					06 44	07 00											07 41			
Goostrey	d						07 03											07 45			
Chelford	d						07 08											07 51			
Alderley Edge	d					06 53	07 12			07 30								07 56			
Wilmslow	d					06 57	07 16			07 33			07 44					08 00			08 09
Styal	d																				
Manchester Airport ✈	a					07 04															
Handforth	d						07 19			07 37								08 03			
Congleton	d	06 45			07 03											07 32					
Macclesfield	a	06 52			07 11						07 30					07 39			08 01		
	d	06 53			07 12				07 15		07 31					07 40			08 02		
Prestbury	d	06 57							07 21							07 44					
Adlington (Cheshire)	d	07 00							07 24							07 47					
Poynton	d	07 04							07 27							07 51					
Bramhall	d	07 07							07 31							07 54					
Cheadle Hulme	d	07 11					07 24		07 34	07 42						07 59		08 09			
Stockport	a	07 15			07 27		07 29		07 41	07 47	07 45		07 54			08 03		08 14	08 16		08 20
	d	07 16	07 19	07 22	07 28		07 29	07 31	07 42	07 48	07 49	07 53	07 54	07 57		08 04	08 10	08 14	08 17	08 19	08 21
Heaton Chapel	d						07 33									08 07		08 18			
Levenshulme	d						07 36									08 10		08 21			
Manchester Piccadilly 10 ⇌	a	07 27	07 31	07 34	07 37	07 42	07 44	07 45	07 56	07 59	08 00	08 02	08 08	08 09	08 21	08 21	08 25	08 27	08 28	08 32	08 34
	d			07 34											08 22			08 29			
Manchester Oxford Road	a			07 37											08 24			08 33			
Deansgate ⇌	a														08 28						

Stoke-on-Trent and Crewe - Manchester Airport, Stockport and Manchester

Station		EM ◇	NT	NT	NT	VT ◇1 ⊠	NT	NT	XC ◇1 ⊼	TP ◇1 ⊼	VT ◇1 ⊠	AW ◇ ⊼	NT	VT ◇1 ⊠	NT	NT	EM ◇	XC ◇1 ⊼	NT
London Euston 15 ⊖65	d					06 36					06 55			07 20					
Birmingham New Street 12 68	d								07 31									07 57	
Wolverhampton 7 68 ⇌	d								07 49									08 15	
Stafford 65,68	d																	08 30	
Stoke-on-Trent 50,68	d							07 57	08 19		08 25			08 48				08 55	
Longport 50	d																		
Kidsgrove 50	d							08 04											
Crewe 10 65	d				07 55	08 11						08 28							08 31
Sandbach	d				08 02														08 38
Holmes Chapel	d				08 07														08 42
Goostrey	d																		08 45
Chelford	d																		08 50
Alderley Edge	d		07 53		08 15								08 49						08 54
Wilmslow	d		07 56		08 19	08 27						08 46	08 52						08 57
Styal	d		07 59																
Manchester Airport ✈	a		08 04																09 04
Handforth	d				08 22								08 55						
Congleton	d							08 11											
Macclesfield	a							08 18	08 35		08 41							09 11	
	d			08 06				08 19	08 37		08 41							09 12	
Prestbury	d			08 10				08 23											
Adlington (Cheshire)	d							08 26											
Poynton	d			08 15				08 30											
Bramhall	d			08 17				08 33											
Cheadle Hulme	d			08 20	08 26			08 37					08 59						
Stockport	a			08 27	08 31	08 37		08 41	08 49		08 55	08 58	09 04	09 16				09 27	
	d	08 24		08 28	08 31	08 38	08 41	08 42	08 50	08 53	08 56	08 58	09 04	09 17	09 12	09 21	09 25	09 28	
Heaton Chapel	d				08 35			08 45					09 08		09 16				
Levenshulme	d			08 32				08 48					09 11		09 19				
Manchester Piccadilly 10 ⇌	a	08 36	08 42	08 42	08 45	08 49	08 52	08 56	08 59	09 02	09 07	09 15	09 20	09 28	09 28	09 36	09 36	09 39	09 42
	d	08 37					08 54										09 37		
Manchester Oxford Road	a	08 40					08 56										09 40		
Deansgate ⇌	a						09 00												

Station		NT	VT ◇1 ⊠	NT	NT	XC ◇1 ⊼	TP ◇1 ⊼	VT ◇1 ⊠	AW ◇ ⊼	NT	NT	VT ◇1 ⊠	NT	NT	EM ◇	XC ◇1 ⊼	NT	NT	VT ◇1 ⊠	NT	NT
London Euston 15 ⊖65	d		07 35					08 00				08 20							08 40		
Birmingham New Street 12 68	d					08 31										08 57					
Wolverhampton 7 68 ⇌	d					08 49										09 15					
Stafford 65,68	d					09 01										09 30					
Stoke-on-Trent 50,68	d				08 58	09 20		09 25				09 48				09 55					09 58
Longport 50	d																				
Kidsgrove 50	d				09 05																10 05
Crewe 10 65	d	08 50	09 11						09 28								09 33	09 50	10 11		
Sandbach	d	08 57															09 40	09 57			
Holmes Chapel	d	09 02															09 44	10 02			
Goostrey	d	09 05																10 05			
Chelford	d	09 09																10 09			
Alderley Edge	d	09 13									09 48						09 53	10 13			
Wilmslow	d	09 17	09 27						09 46		09 51						09 57	10 17	10 27		
Styal	d																				
Manchester Airport ✈	a																10 04				
Handforth	d	09 20									09 54							10 20			
Congleton	d				09 12																10 12
Macclesfield	a				09 19			09 41								10 11					10 19
	d				09 20			09 41								10 12					10 20
Prestbury	d				09 24																10 24
Adlington (Cheshire)	d				09 27																10 27
Poynton	d				09 30																10 30
Bramhall	d				09 33																10 33
Cheadle Hulme	d	09 24			09 37						09 59							10 24			10 37
Stockport	a	09 29	09 36		09 41	09 49		09 55	09 58		10 04	10 16				10 27		10 29	10 36		10 41
	d	09 29	09 37	09 41	09 42	09 50	09 53	09 56	09 58		10 04	10 17	10 12	1021	10 26	10 28		10 29	10 37	10 41	10 42
Heaton Chapel	d	09 33			09 45						10 08		10 16					10 33			10 45
Levenshulme	d	09 36			09 48						10 11		10 19					10 36			10 48
Manchester Piccadilly 10 ⇌	a	09 44	09 49	09 52	09 56	09 59	10 02	10 07	10 15	10 18	10 20	10 28	10 28	10 36	10 36	10 39	10 42	10 44	10 49	10 52	10 56
	d			09 54						10 22					10 37					10 54	
Manchester Oxford Road	a			09 56						10 24					10 40					10 56	
Deansgate ⇌	a			10 00						10 28										11 00	

Stoke-on-Trent and Crewe - Manchester Airport, Stockport and Manchester

Station			XC	TP	VT	AW	NT	VT	NT	NT	EM	XC	NT	NT	VT	NT	NT	XC
			◇1 🛒	◇1 🛒	◇1 ⊠	◇ 🛒		◇1 ⊠			◇	◇1 🛒			◇1 ⊠			◇1 🛒
London Euston 15	⊖65	d			09 00			09 20							09 40			
Birmingham New Street 12	68	d	09 31									09 57						10 31
Wolverhampton 7	68	d	09 49									10 15						10 49
Stafford	65,68	d	10 01									10 30						11 01
Stoke-on-Trent	50,68	d	10 20		10 25			10 48				10 55					10 58	11 20
Longport	50	d																
Kidsgrove	50	d															11 05	
Crewe 10	65	d				10 28							10 33	10 50	11 11			
Sandbach		d											10 40	10 57				
Holmes Chapel		d											10 44	11 02				
Goostrey		d												11 05				
Chelford		d												11 09				
Alderley Edge		d					10 49						10 53	11 13				
Wilmslow		d				10 46	10 52						10 57	11 17	11 27			
Styal		d																
Manchester Airport	✈	a											11 04					
Handforth		d					10 55							11 20				
Congleton		d															11 12	
Macclesfield		a			10 41							11 11					11 19	
		d			10 41							11 12					11 20	
Prestbury		d															11 24	
Adlington (Cheshire)		d															11 27	
Poynton		d															11 30	
Bramhall		d															11 33	
Cheadle Hulme		d					10 59							11 24			11 37	
Stockport		a	10 49		10 55	10 58	11 04	11 16				11 27		11 29	11 36		11 41	11 49
		d	10 50	10 53	10 56	10 58	11 04	11 17	11 12	11 21	11 26	11 28		11 29	11 37	11 41	11 42	11 50
Heaton Chapel		d					11 08		11 16					11 33			11 45	
Levenshulme		d					11 11		11 19					11 36			11 48	
Manchester Piccadilly 10		a	10 59	11 02	11 07	11 15	11 20	11 28	11 28	11 36	11 36	11 39	11 42	11 44	11 49	11 52	11 56	11 59
		d									11 37					11 54		
Manchester Oxford Road		a									11 40					11 56		
Deansgate		a														12 00		

Station			TP	VT	AW	NT	VT	NT	NT	EM	XC	NT	NT	VT	NT	NT	XC	TP
			◇1 🛒	◇1 ⊡	◇ 🛒		◇1 ⊡			◇	◇1 🛒			◇1 ⊡			◇1 🛒	◇1 🛒
London Euston 15	⊖65	d		10 00			10 20							10 40				
Birmingham New Street 12	68	d									10 57						11 31	
Wolverhampton 7	68	d									11 15						11 49	
Stafford	65,68	d									11 30						12 01	
Stoke-on-Trent	50,68	d		11 25			11 48				11 55					11 58	12 20	
Longport	50	d																
Kidsgrove	50	d														12 05		
Crewe 10	65	d			11 28							11 33	11 50	12 11				
Sandbach		d										11 40	11 57					
Holmes Chapel		d										11 44	12 02					
Goostrey		d											12 05					
Chelford		d											12 09					
Alderley Edge		d				11 48						11 53	12 13					
Wilmslow		d			11 46	11 51						11 57	12 17	12 27				
Styal		d																
Manchester Airport	✈	a										12 04						
Handforth		d				11 54							12 20					
Congleton		d														12 12		
Macclesfield		a		11 41							12 11					12 19		
		d		11 41							12 12					12 20		
Prestbury		d														12 24		
Adlington (Cheshire)		d														12 27		
Poynton		d														12 30		
Bramhall		d														12 33		
Cheadle Hulme		d				11 59							12 24			12 37		
Stockport		a		11 55	11 58	12 04	12 16				12 27		12 29	12 36		12 41	12 49	
		d	11 53	11 56	11 58	12 04	12 17	12 12	12 21	12 26	12 28		12 29	12 37	12 41	12 42	12 50	12 53
Heaton Chapel		d				12 08		12 16					12 33			12 45		
Levenshulme		d				12 11		12 19					12 36			12 48		
Manchester Piccadilly 10		a	12 02	12 07	12 15	12 20	12 28	12 28	12 36	12 36	12 39	12 42	12 44	12 49	12 52	12 56	12 59	13 02
		d								12 37					12 54			
Manchester Oxford Road		a								12 40					12 56			
Deansgate		a													13 00			

Table 84

Mondays to Fridays

Stoke-on-Trent and Crewe - Manchester Airport, Stockport and Manchester

Station			VT	AW	NT	VT	NT	NT	EM	XC	NT	NT	VT	NT	NT	XC	TP	VT	AW
			◇1 ⊡	◇ 🛒		◇1 ⊡			◇	◇1 🛒			◇1 ⊡			◇1 🛒	◇1 🛒	◇1 ⊡	◇ 🛒
London Euston 15	⊖65	d	11 00			11 20							11 40					12 00	
Birmingham New Street 12	68	d								11 57						12 31			
Wolverhampton 7	68	d								12 15						12 49			
Stafford	65,68	d								12 30						13 01			
Stoke-on-Trent	50,68	d	12 25			12 48				12 55					12 58	13 20		13 25	
Longport	50	d																	
Kidsgrove	50	d													13 05				
Crewe 10	65	d		12 28							12 33	12 50	13 11						13 28
Sandbach		d									12 40	12 57							
Holmes Chapel		d									12 44	13 02							
Goostrey		d										13 05							
Chelford		d										13 09							
Alderley Edge		d			12 49						12 53	13 13							
Wilmslow		d		12 46	12 52						12 57	13 17	13 27						13 46
Styal		d																	
Manchester Airport	✈	a									13 04								
Handforth		d			12 55							13 20							
Congleton		d													13 12				
Macclesfield		a	12 41							13 11					13 19			13 41	
		d	12 41							13 12					13 20			13 42	
Prestbury		d													13 24				
Adlington (Cheshire)		d													13 27				
Poynton		d													13 30				
Bramhall		d													13 33				
Cheadle Hulme		d			12 59							13 24			13 37				
Stockport		a	12 55	12 58	13 04	13 16	13 12	13 21	13 25	13 27		13 29	13 36	13 41	13 41	13 49		13 55	13 58
		d	12 56	12 58	13 04	13 17	13 12	13 21	13 26	13 28		13 29	13 37	13 41	13 42	13 50	13 53	13 56	13 58
Heaton Chapel		d			13 08		13 16					13 33			13 45				
Levenshulme		d			13 11		13 19					13 36			13 48				
Manchester Piccadilly 10		a	13 07	13 15	13 20	13 28	13 28	13 36	13 36	13 39	13 42	13 44	13 49	13 52	13 56	13 59	14 02	14 07	14 15
		d							13 37					13 54					
Manchester Oxford Road		a							13 40					13 56					
Deansgate		a												14 00					

Station			NT	VT	NT	NT	EM	XC	NT	NT	VT	NT	NT	XC	TP	VT	AW	NT	VT
				◇1 ⊡			◇	◇1 🛒			◇1 ⊡			◇1 🛒	◇1 🛒	◇1 ⊡	◇ 🛒		◇1 ⊡
London Euston 15	⊖65	d		12 20							12 40					13 00			13 20
Birmingham New Street 12	68	d						12 57						13 31					
Wolverhampton 7	68	d						13 15						13 49					
Stafford	65,68	d						13 30						14 01					
Stoke-on-Trent	50,68	d		13 48				13 55					13 58	14 20		14 25			14 48
Longport	50	d																	
Kidsgrove	50	d											14 05						
Crewe 10	65	d							13 33	13 50	14 11						14 28		
Sandbach		d							13 40	13 57									
Holmes Chapel		d							13 44	14 02									
Goostrey		d								14 05									
Chelford		d								14 09									
Alderley Edge		d	13 48						13 53	14 13								14 49	
Wilmslow		d	13 51						13 57	14 17	14 27						14 46	14 52	
Styal		d																	
Manchester Airport	✈	a							14 04										
Handforth		d	13 54							14 20								14 55	
Congleton		d											14 12						
Macclesfield		a						14 11					14 19			14 41			
		d						14 12					14 20			14 41			
Prestbury		d											14 24						
Adlington (Cheshire)		d											14 27						
Poynton		d											14 30						
Bramhall		d											14 33						
Cheadle Hulme		d	13 59							14 24			14 37					14 59	
Stockport		a	14 04	14 16				14 27		14 29	14 36		14 41	14 49		14 55	14 58	15 04	15 16
		d	14 04	14 17	14 12	14 21	14 26	14 28		14 29	14 37	14 41	14 42	14 50	14 53	14 56	14 58	15 04	15 17
Heaton Chapel		d	14 08		14 16					14 33			14 45					15 08	
Levenshulme		d	14 11		14 19					14 36			14 48					15 11	
Manchester Piccadilly 10		a	14 20	14 28	14 28	14 36	14 36	14 39	14 42	14 44	14 49	14 52	14 56	14 59	15 02	15 07	15 15	15 20	15 28
		d					14 37					14 54							
Manchester Oxford Road		a					14 40					14 56							
Deansgate		a										15 00							

Stoke-on-Trent and Crewe - Manchester Airport, Stockport and Manchester

	NT	NT	EM	XC	NT	NT	VT	NT	NT	XC	TP	VT	AW	NT	NT	VT	NT	EM	XC
			◇	◇1 ⚒			◇1 ▭			◇1 ⚒	◇1 ⚒	◇1 ▭	◇ ⚒			◇1 ▭		◇	◇1 ⚒
London Euston 15 ⊖65 d							13 40					14 00				14 20			
Birmingham New Street 12 68 d				13 57						14 31									14 57
Wolverhampton 7 68 ⇌ d				14 15						14 49									15 15
Stafford 65,68 d				14 30						15 01									15 30
Stoke-on-Trent 50,68 d				14 55					14 58	15 20		15 25				15 48			15 55
Longport 50 d																			
Kidsgrove 50 d									15 05										
Crewe 10 65 d					14 33	14 50	15 11						15 28						
Sandbach d					14 40	14 57													
Holmes Chapel d					14 44	15 02													
Goostrey d						15 05													
Chelford d						15 09													
Alderley Edge d					14 53	15 13								15 48					
Wilmslow d					14 57	15 17	15 27						15 46	15 51					
Styal d																			
Manchester Airport ✈ a					15 04														
Handforth d						15 20								15 54					
Congleton d									15 12										
Macclesfield a				15 11					15 19			15 41							16 11
d				15 12					15 20			15 41							16 12
Prestbury d									15 24										
Adlington (Cheshire) d									15 27										
Poynton d									15 30										
Bramhall d									15 33										
Cheadle Hulme d						15 24			15 37					15 59					
Stockport a				15 27		15 29	15 36		15 41	15 49		15 55	15 58	16 04		16 16			16 27
d	15 12	15 21	15 26	15 28		15 29	15 37	15 41	15 42	15 50	15 53	15 56	15 58	16 04	16 12	16 17	16 21	16 26	16 28
Heaton Chapel d	15 16					15 33			15 45					16 08	16 16				
Levenshulme d	15 19					15 36			15 48					16 11	16 19				
Manchester Piccadilly 10 ⇌ a	15 28	15 36	15 36	15 39	15 41	15 44	15 49	15 52	15 56	15 59	16 02	16 07	16 15	16 20	16 25	16 28	16 36	16 36	16 39
d			15 37		15 42			15 54							16 27			16 37	
Manchester Oxford Road a			15 40		15 46			15 56							16 29			16 40	
Deansgate ⇌ a								16 00							16 32				

	NT	NT	VT	NT	NT	XC	TP	VT	AW	NT	NT	VT	NT	EM	XC	NT	NT	VT	NT
			◇1 ▭			◇1 ⚒	◇1 ⚒	◇1 ▭	◇ ⚒			◇1 ▭		◇	◇1 ⚒			◇1 ▭	
London Euston 15 ⊖65 d			14 40					15 00				15 20						15 40	
Birmingham New Street 12 68 d						15 31									15 57				
Wolverhampton 7 68 ⇌ d						15 50									16 15				
Stafford 65,68 d															16 30				
Stoke-on-Trent 50,68 d					15 58	16 19		16 25				16 48			16 55				16 58
Longport 50 d																			
Kidsgrove 50 d					16 05														17 05
Crewe 10 65 d	15 33	15 50	16 12						16 28							16 33	16 50	17 11	
Sandbach d	15 40	15 57														16 40	16 57		
Holmes Chapel d	15 44	16 02														16 44	17 02		
Goostrey d		16 05															17 05		
Chelford d		16 09															17 09		
Alderley Edge d	15 53	16 13								16 49						16 53	17 13		
Wilmslow d	15 56	16 17	16 27						16 46	16 52						16 57	17 17	17 27	
Styal d	15 59																		
Manchester Airport ✈ a	16 04															17 04			
Handforth d		16 20								16 55							17 20		
Congleton d					16 12														17 12
Macclesfield a					16 19			16 41							17 11				17 19
d					16 20			16 41							17 12				17 20
Prestbury d					16 24														17 24
Adlington (Cheshire) d					16 27														17 27
Poynton d					16 30														17 30
Bramhall d					16 33														17 33
Cheadle Hulme d		16 24			16 37					16 59							17 24		17 36
Stockport a		16 29	16 36		16 41	16 47		16 54	16 58	17 04		17 16			17 27		17 29	17 36	17 41
d		16 29	16 37	16 41	16 42	16 50	16 53	16 55	16 58	17 04	17 12	17 17	17 21	17 26	17 28		17 29	17 37	17 42
Heaton Chapel d		16 33			16 45					17 08	17 16						17 33		17 45
Levenshulme d		16 36			16 48					17 11	17 19						17 36		17 48
Manchester Piccadilly 10 ⇌ a	16 42	16 44	16 49	16 52	16 56	16 59	17 02	17 07	17 15	17 20	17 25	17 28	17 36	17 37	17 39	17 42	17 44	17 49	17 56
d				16 54							17 27			17 37					
Manchester Oxford Road a				16 56							17 29			17 40					
Deansgate ⇌ a				17 00							17 32								

Stoke-on-Trent and Crewe - Manchester Airport, Stockport and Manchester

	XC	TP	VT	AW	NT	VT	NT	NT	EM	XC	NT	NT	VT	NT	NT	XC	TP
	◇1 ⚒	◇1 ⚒	◇1 ▭	◇ ⚒		◇1 ▭			◇	◇1 ⚒			◇1 ▭			◇1 ⚒	◇1 ⚒
London Euston 15 ⊖65 d			16 00			16 20							16 40				
Birmingham New Street 12 68 d	16 31									16 57						17 31	
Wolverhampton 7 68 ⇌ d	16 49									17 15						17 50	
Stafford 65,68 d	17 01									17 30						18 02	
Stoke-on-Trent 50,68 d	17 20		17 25			17 48				17 55					17 58	18 21	
Longport 50 d																	
Kidsgrove 50 d															18 05		
Crewe 10 65 d				17 29							17 33	17 50	18 11				
Sandbach d											17 40	17 57					
Holmes Chapel d											17 44	18 02					
Goostrey d												18 05					
Chelford d												18 09					
Alderley Edge d					17 48						17 53	18 13					
Wilmslow d				17 47	17 51						17 56	18 17	18 27				
Styal d											17 59						
Manchester Airport ✈ a											18 04						
Handforth d					17 54							18 20					
Congleton d															18 12		
Macclesfield a			17 41							18 11					18 19		
d			17 41							18 12					18 20		
Prestbury d															18 24		
Adlington (Cheshire) d															18 27		
Poynton d															18 30		
Bramhall d															18 33		
Cheadle Hulme d					17 59							18 24			18 37		
Stockport a	17 49		17 55	17 58	18 04	18 16				18 27		18 29	18 37		18 41	18 49	
d	17 50	17 53	17 56	17 58	18 04	18 17	18 12	18 21	18 26	18 28		18 29	18 38	18 41	18 42	18 50	18 53
Heaton Chapel d					18 08		18 16					18 33			18 45		
Levenshulme d					18 11		18 19					18 36			18 48		
Manchester Piccadilly 10 ⇌ a	17 59	18 02	18 07	18 15	18 20	18 28	18 28	18 36	18 36	18 39	18 42	18 44	18 49	18 52	18 56	18 59	19 02
d									18 37					18 54			
Manchester Oxford Road a									18 40					18 56			
Deansgate ⇌ a														19 00			

	VT	AW	NT	VT	NT	NT	EM	XC	NT	VT	NT	XC	TP	VT	AW
	◇1 ⊠	■ ⚒		◇1 ⊠			◇	◇1 ⚒		◇1 ⊠		◇1 ⚒	◇1 ⚒	◇1 ⊠	■ ⚒
London Euston 15 ⊖65 d	17 00			17 20						17 40				18 00	
Birmingham New Street 12 68 d								17 57				18 31			
Wolverhampton 7 68 ⇌ d								18 15				18 49			
Stafford 65,68 d								18 30							
Stoke-on-Trent 50,68 d	18 25			18 49				18 55			18 58	19 19		19 25	
Longport 50 d															
Kidsgrove 50 d											19 05				
Crewe 10 65 d		18 28			18 33				18 50	19 11					19 28
Sandbach d					18 40				18 57						
Holmes Chapel d					18 44				19 02						
Goostrey d									19 05						
Chelford d									19 09						
Alderley Edge d					18 53				19 13						
Wilmslow d		18 46			18 56				19 17	19 27					19 46
Styal d															
Manchester Airport ✈ a					19 04										
Handforth d									19 20						
Congleton d											19 12				
Macclesfield a	18 41							19 11			19 19			19 41	
d	18 41							19 12			19 20			19 41	
Prestbury d											19 24				
Adlington (Cheshire) d											19 27				
Poynton d											19 30				
Bramhall d											19 33				
Cheadle Hulme d									19 24		19 37				
Stockport a	18 55	18 58		19 16				19 27	19 29	19 36	19 41	19 47		19 55	19 58
d	18 56	18 58	19 12	19 17		19 21	19 26	19 28	19 29	19 37	19 42	19 50	19 53	19 56	19 58
Heaton Chapel d			19 16								19 45				
Levenshulme d			19 19								19 48				
Manchester Piccadilly 10 ⇌ a	19 07	19 15	19 28	19 28	19 31	19 35	19 36	19 39	19 43	19 49	19 56	20 00	20 02	20 07	20 15
d					19 32		19 37								
Manchester Oxford Road a					19 36		19 40								
Deansgate ⇌ a															

Stoke-on-Trent and Crewe - Manchester Airport, Stockport and Manchester

		VT	NT	NT	NT	EM	XC	NT	VT	NT	XC	TP	VT	AW	VT	NT	NT	EM
		◇1 ⊠				◇	◇1 ⌶		◇1 ⊠		◇1 ⌶	◇1 ⌶	■ 1 ◫	■ ⌶	■ 1 ◫			◇
London Euston 15 ⊖65	d	18 20							18 40				19 00		19 20			
Birmingham New Street 12 68	d						18 57				19 31							
Wolverhampton 7 68	d						19 15				19 49							
Stafford 65,68	d						19 29				20 01							
Stoke-on-Trent 50,68	d	19 48					19 55			19 58	20 20		20 25		20 48			
Longport 50	d																	
Kidsgrove 50	d									20 05								
Crewe 10 65	d							19 50	20 11					20 28				
Sandbach	d							19 57										
Holmes Chapel	d							20 02										
Goostrey	d							20 05										
Chelford	d							20 09										
Alderley Edge	d							20 13										
Wilmslow	d			19 56				20 17	20 27					20 46			20 56	
Styal	d																	
Manchester Airport ✈	a			20 04													21 04	
Handforth	d							20 20										
Congleton	d									20 12								
Macclesfield	a						20 11			20 19			20 41					
	d						20 12			20 20			20 41					
Prestbury	d									20 24								
Adlington (Cheshire)	d									20 27								
Poynton	d									20 30								
Bramhall	d									20 33								
Cheadle Hulme	d							20 24		20 37								
Stockport	a	20 16					20 27	20 29	20 36	20 41	20 48		20 55	20 58	21 16			
	d	20 17	20 12		20 21	20 26	20 28	20 29	20 37	20 42	20 50	20 53	20 56	20 58	21 17	21 12		21 20
Heaton Chapel	d		20 16							20 45						21 16		
Levenshulme	d		20 19							20 48						21 19		
Manchester Piccadilly 10	a	20 23	20 28	20 32	20 35	20 36	20 39	20 43	20 49	20 56	20 58	21 02	21 07	21 15	21 28	21 28	21 32	21 32
	d			20 32		20 37											21 32	
Manchester Oxford Road	a			20 36		20 40											21 36	
Deansgate	a																	

		NT	XC	NT	VT	NT	XC	VT	AW	NT	NT	XC	NT	NT	VT	NT	TP	VT
			◇1 ⌶		◇1 ◫		◇1	◇1 ◫	◇ ⌶			◇1			◇1 ◫		◇1	◇1 ◫
London Euston 15 ⊖65	d				19 40			20 00							20 40			21 00
Birmingham New Street 12 68	d		19 57				20 31					20 58						
Wolverhampton 7 68	d		20 16				20 49					21 17						
Stafford 65,68	d		20 30		21 04							21 32						
Stoke-on-Trent 50,68	d		20 55			20 58	21 19	21 24				21 55						22 28
Longport 50	d																	
Kidsgrove 50	d					21 05												
Crewe 10 65	d			20 50	21 23				21 28					21 45	22 13			
Sandbach	d			20 57										21 52				
Holmes Chapel	d			21 02										21 58				
Goostrey	d			21 05										22 01				
Chelford	d			21 09										22 07				
Alderley Edge	d			21 13										22 12				
Wilmslow	d			21 17	21 38				21 46		21 55			22 15	22 29			
Styal	d																	
Manchester Airport ✈	a										22 04							
Handforth	d			21 20										22 19				
Congleton	d					21 12												
Macclesfield	a		21 11			21 19		21 40				22 11						22 44
	d		21 12			21 20		21 40				22 12						22 44
Prestbury	d					21 24												
Adlington (Cheshire)	d					21 27												
Poynton	d					21 30												
Bramhall	d					21 33												
Cheadle Hulme	d			21 24		21 37								22 24				
Stockport	a		21 27	21 29		21 41	21 47	21 55	21 58			22 25		22 29	22 38			22 58
	d	21 21	21 28	21 29		21 42	21 50	21 56	21 58	22 12		22 26	22 21	22 29	22 39	22 34	22 53	22 59
Heaton Chapel	d					21 45				22 16						22 38		
Levenshulme	d					21 48				22 19						22 41		
Manchester Piccadilly 10	a	21 35	21 40	21 43	21 57	21 57	22 00	22 07	22 15	22 28	22 31	22 35	22 35	22 43	22 48	22 48	23 02	23 11
	d										22 32					22 50		
Manchester Oxford Road	a										22 36					22 52		
Deansgate	a															22 55		

Stoke-on-Trent and Crewe - Manchester Airport, Stockport and Manchester

		NT	NT	XC	VT	AW	NT	NT	NT	XC MTX	XC MTO	VT
				◇1	◇1 ◫	◇				◇1 A	◇1	◇1 ◫
London Euston 15 ⊖65	d				21 40							22 00
Birmingham New Street 12 68	d			21 57						22 28	22 28	
Wolverhampton 7 68	d			22 16						22 46	22 46	
Stafford 65,68	d			22 30						22 59	22 59	23s39
Stoke-on-Trent 50,68	d	22 18		22 55	23 07					23 21	23 21	
Longport 50	d											
Kidsgrove 50	d	22 25										
Crewe 10 65	d					23 05			23 12			00s05
Sandbach	d								23 19			
Holmes Chapel	d								23 24			
Goostrey	d								23 27			
Chelford	d								23 31			
Alderley Edge	d								23 35			
Wilmslow	d		22 56			23 23			23 39			
Styal	d											
Manchester Airport ✈	a		23 04									
Handforth	d								23 42			
Congleton	d	22 32										
Macclesfield	a	22 40		23 11	23 23							
	d	22 48		23 12	23 23							
Prestbury	d	22 53										
Adlington (Cheshire)	d	22 56										
Poynton	d	22 59										
Bramhall	d	23 02										
Cheadle Hulme	d	23 05							23 46			
Stockport	a	23 10		23 25	23 37	23 32			23 51			00s26
	d	23 10		23 26	23 38	23 33	23 41	23 48	23 51			00s27
Heaton Chapel	d	23 14							23 55			
Levenshulme	d	23 17							23 58			
Manchester Piccadilly 10	a	23 25	23 33	23 37	23 48	23 48	23 54	00 02	00 07	00 12	00 32	00 35
	d											
Manchester Oxford Road	a											
Deansgate	a											

Saturdays
until 10 July

		NT	TP	NT	NT	TP	AW	NT	NT	NT	EM	XC	NT	NT	NT	NT	XC
			◇1			◇1					◇	◇1 ⌶					◇1 ⌶
London Euston 15 ⊖65	d																
Birmingham New Street 12 68	d											05 57					06 31
Wolverhampton 7 68	d											06 16					06 49
Stafford 65,68	d											06 30					07 01
Stoke-on-Trent 50,68	d											06 51				06 57	07 19
Longport 50	d																
Kidsgrove 50	d															07 04	
Crewe 10 65	d	00 44					06 27						06 33	06 49			
Sandbach	d												06 40	06 56			
Holmes Chapel	d												06 44	07 00			
Goostrey	d													07 03			
Chelford	d													07 08			
Alderley Edge	d							06 49					06 53	07 12			
Wilmslow	d			05 46			06 45	06 52					06 57	07 16			
Styal	d																
Manchester Airport ✈	a	01 16		05 53									07 04				
Handforth	d							06 55						07 19			
Congleton	d											07 03				07 11	
Macclesfield	a											07 11				07 18	07 36
	d											07 12				07 19	07 37
Prestbury	d															07 23	
Adlington (Cheshire)	d															07 26	
Poynton	d															07 29	
Bramhall	d															07 32	
Cheadle Hulme	d							06 59						07 24		07 36	
Stockport	a						06 54	07 04				07 27		07 29		07 40	07 49
	d		05 53		06 41	06 53	06 54	07 04	07 12	07 19	07 22	07 28		07 29	07 40	07 41	07 50
Heaton Chapel	d							07 08	07 16					07 33		07 44	
Levenshulme	d							07 11	07 19					07 36		07 47	
Manchester Piccadilly 10	a	01 36	06 05	06 25	06 52	07 02	07 09	07 21	07 28	07 31	07 34	07 38	07 42	07 44	07 52	07 56	08 00
	d				06 54						07 34				07 54		
Manchester Oxford Road	a				06 56						07 37				07 56		
Deansgate	a				06 59										08 00		

Stoke-on-Trent and Crewe - Manchester Airport, Stockport and Manchester

		TP	AW	NT	NT	NT	NT	XC	EM	NT	NT	VT	NT	NT	XC	TP	VT	AW
		◇1						◇1	◇			◇1			◇1	◇1	◇1	◇
London Euston 15 ⊖65	d											06 36					06 55	
Birmingham New Street 12 68	d							06 57							07 31			
Wolverhampton 7 68	d							07 14							07 49			
Stafford 65,68	d							07 29							08 01			
Stoke-on-Trent 50,68	d													07 57	08 20		08 25	
Longport 50	d																	
Kidsgrove 50	d													08 04				
Crewe 10 65	d		07 27					07 53		07 30	07 55	08 11						08 28
Sandbach	d									07 37	08 02							
Holmes Chapel	d									07 41	08 07							
Goostrey	d									07 44								
Chelford	d									07 49								
Alderley Edge	d				07 49					07 53	08 15							
Wilmslow	d		07 44		07 52			08 10		07 56	08 19	08 27						08 46
Styal	d									07 59								
Manchester Airport ✈	a									08 05								
Handforth	d				07 55						08 22							
Congleton	d													08 11				
Macclesfield	a													08 18	08 36		08 41	
	d													08 19	08 37		08 41	
Prestbury	d													08 23				
Adlington (Cheshire)	d													08 26				
Poynton	d													08 30				
Bramhall	d													08 33				
Cheadle Hulme	d				07 59						08 26			08 37				
Stockport	a		07 54		08 04			08 20			08 31	08 37		08 41	08 49		08 55	08 58
	d	07 53	07 54	07 57	08 04	08 12	08 19	08 20	08 24		08 31	08 38	08 41	08 42	08 50	08 53	08 56	08 58
Heaton Chapel	d				08 08	08 16					08 35			08 45				
Levenshulme	d				08 11	08 19								08 48				
Manchester Piccadilly 10	a	08 02	08 08	08 09	08 20	08 28	08 32	08 35	08 36	08 42	08 45	08 49	08 52	08 56	08 59	09 02	09 07	09 14
	d								08 37				08 54					
Manchester Oxford Road	a								08 40				08 56					
Deansgate	a												09 00					

		NT	VT	NT	NT	EM	XC	NT	NT	VT	NT	NT	XC	TP	VT	AW	NT	VT
			◇1			◇	◇1			◇1			◇1	◇1	◇1	◇		◇1
London Euston 15 ⊖65	d		07 20							07 35					08 00			08 20
Birmingham New Street 12 68	d						07 57						08 31					
Wolverhampton 7 68	d						08 15						08 49					
Stafford 65,68	d						08 30						09 01					
Stoke-on-Trent 50,68	d		08 48				08 55					08 58	09 20		09 25			09 48
Longport 50	d																	
Kidsgrove 50	d											09 05						
Crewe 10 65	d							08 31	08 50	09 11						09 28		
Sandbach	d							08 38	08 57									
Holmes Chapel	d							08 42	09 02									
Goostrey	d							08 45	09 05									
Chelford	d							08 50	09 09									
Alderley Edge	d	08 49						08 54	09 13								09 49	
Wilmslow	d	08 52						08 57	09 17	09 27						09 46	09 52	
Styal	d																	
Manchester Airport ✈	a							09 04										
Handforth	d	08 55							09 20								09 55	
Congleton	d											09 12						
Macclesfield	a						09 11					09 19			09 41			
	d						09 12					09 20			09 41			
Prestbury	d											09 24						
Adlington (Cheshire)	d											09 27						
Poynton	d											09 30						
Bramhall	d											09 33						
Cheadle Hulme	d	08 59							09 24			09 37					09 59	
Stockport	a	09 04	09 16				09 27		09 29	09 36		09 41	09 49		09 55	09 58	10 04	10 16
	d	09 04	09 17	09 12	09 21	09 25	09 28		09 29	09 37	09 41	09 42	09 50	09 53	09 56	09 58	10 04	10 17
Heaton Chapel	d	09 08		09 16					09 33			09 45					10 08	
Levenshulme	d	09 11		09 19					09 36			09 48					10 11	
Manchester Piccadilly 10	a	09 20	09 28	09 28	09 36	09 36	09 39	09 42	09 44	09 49	09 52	09 56	09 59	10 02	10 07	10 15	10 20	10 28
	d					09 37					09 54							
Manchester Oxford Road	a					09 40					09 56							
Deansgate	a										10 00							

Table 84

Saturdays until 10 July

Stoke-on-Trent and Crewe - Manchester Airport, Stockport and Manchester

		NT	NT	EM	XC	NT	NT	VT	NT	NT	XC	TP	VT	AW	NT	VT	NT	NT	EM
				◇	◇1			◇1			◇1	◇1	◇1	◇		◇1			◇
London Euston 15 ⊖65	d							08 40					09 00			09 20			
Birmingham New Street 12 68	d				08b57						09 31								
Wolverhampton 7 68	d				09 15						09 49								
Stafford 65,68	d				09 30						10 01								
Stoke-on-Trent 50,68	d				09 55					09 58	10 20		10 25			10 48			
Longport 50	d																		
Kidsgrove 50	d									10 05									
Crewe 10 65	d					09 33	09 50	10 11						10 28					
Sandbach	d					09 40	09 57												
Holmes Chapel	d					09 44	10 02												
Goostrey	d						10 05												
Chelford	d						10 09												
Alderley Edge	d					09 53	10 13								10 49				
Wilmslow	d					09 57	10 17	10 27						10 46	10 52				
Styal	d																		
Manchester Airport ✈	a					10 04													
Handforth	d						10 20								10 55				
Congleton	d									10 12									
Macclesfield	a				10 11					10 19			10 41						
	d				10 12					10 20			10 41						
Prestbury	d									10 24									
Adlington (Cheshire)	d									10 27									
Poynton	d									10 30									
Bramhall	d									10 33									
Cheadle Hulme	d						10 24			10 37					10 59				
Stockport	a				10 27		10 29	10 36		10 41	10 49		10 55	10 58	11 04	11 16			
	d	10 12	10 21	10 26	10 28		10 29	10 37	10 41	10 42	10 50	10 53	10 56	10 58	11 04	11 17	11 12	11 21	11 26
Heaton Chapel	d	10 16					10 33			10 45					11 08		11 16		
Levenshulme	d	10 19					10 36			10 48					11 11		11 19		
Manchester Piccadilly 10	a	10 28	10 36	10 36	10 39	10 42	10 44	10 49	10 52	10 56	10 59	11 02	11 07	11 15	11 20	11 28	11 28	11 36	11 36
	d			10 37					10 54										11 37
Manchester Oxford Road	a			10 40					10 56										11 40
Deansgate	a								11 00										

		XC	NT	NT	VT	NT	NT	XC	TP	VT	AW	NT	VT	NT	NT	EM	XC	NT	NT
		◇1			◇1			◇1	◇1	◇1	◇		◇1			◇	◇1		
London Euston 15 ⊖65	d				09 40					10 00			10 20						
Birmingham New Street 12 68	d	09c57						10 31									10e57		
Wolverhampton 7 68	d	10 15						10 49									11 15		
Stafford 65,68	d	10 30						11 01									11 30		
Stoke-on-Trent 50,68	d	10 55					10 58	11 20		11 25			11 48				11 55		
Longport 50	d																		
Kidsgrove 50	d						11 05												
Crewe 10 65	d		10 33	10 50	11 11						11 28							11 33	11 50
Sandbach	d		10 40	10 57														11 40	11 57
Holmes Chapel	d		10 44	11 02														11 44	12 02
Goostrey	d			11 05															12 05
Chelford	d			11 09															12 09
Alderley Edge	d		10 53	11 13								11 49						11 53	12 13
Wilmslow	d		10 57	11 17	11 27						11 46	11 52						11 57	12 17
Styal	d																		
Manchester Airport ✈	a		11 04															12 04	
Handforth	d			11 20								11 55							12 20
Congleton	d						11 12												
Macclesfield	a	11 11					11 19			11 41							12 11		
	d	11 12					11 20			11 41							12 12		
Prestbury	d						11 24												
Adlington (Cheshire)	d						11 27												
Poynton	d						11 30												
Bramhall	d						11 33												
Cheadle Hulme	d			11 24			11 37					11 59							12 24
Stockport	a	11 27		11 29	11 36		11 41	11 49		11 55	11 58	12 04	12 16				12 27		12 29
	d	11 28		11 29	11 37	11 41	11 42	11 50	11 53	11 56	11 58	12 04	12 17	12 12	12 21	12 26	12 28		12 29
Heaton Chapel	d			11 33			11 45					12 08		12 16					12 33
Levenshulme	d			11 36			11 48					12 11		12 19					12 36
Manchester Piccadilly 10	a	11 39	11 42	11 44	11 49	11 52	11 56	11 59	12 02	12 07	12 15	12 20	12 28	12 28	12 36	12 36	12 39	12 42	12 44
	d					11 54										12 37			
Manchester Oxford Road	a					11 56										12 40			
Deansgate	a					12 00													

b arr. 0848

c arr. 0948

e arr. 1048

Table 84

Saturdays
until 10 July

Stoke-on-Trent and Crewe - Manchester Airport, Stockport and Manchester

	VT ◇1	NT	NT	XC ◇1	VT ◇1	AW ◇	NT	VT ◇1	NT	NT	EM ◇	XC ◇1	NT	NT	VT ◇1	NT	NT	XC ◇1
London Euston 15 ⊖65 d	10 40				11 00			11 20							11 40			
Birmingham New Street 12 68 d				11 31								11b57						12 31
Wolverhampton 7 68 d				11 49								12 15						12 49
Stafford 65,68 d				12 01								12 30						13 01
Stoke-on-Trent 50,68 d			11 58	12 20	12 25			12 48				12 55					12 58	13 20
Longport 50 d																		
Kidsgrove 50 d			12 05														13 05	
Crewe 10 65 d	12 11					12 28							12 33	12 50	13 11			
Sandbach d													12 40	12 57				
Holmes Chapel d													12 44	13 02				
Goostrey d														13 05				
Chelford d														13 09				
Alderley Edge d							12 49						12 53	13 13				
Wilmslow d	12 27					12 46	12 52						12 57	13 17	13 27			
Styal d																		
Manchester Airport ✈ a													13 04					
Handforth d							12 55							13 20				
Congleton d			12 12														13 12	
Macclesfield a			12 19		12 41							13 11					13 19	
d			12 20		12 41							13 12					13 20	
Prestbury d			12 24														13 24	
Adlington (Cheshire) d			12 27														13 27	
Poynton d			12 30														13 30	
Bramhall d			12 33														13 33	
Cheadle Hulme d			12 37				12 59							13 24			13 37	
Stockport a	12 36		12 41	12 49	12 55	12 58	13 04	13 16				13 27		13 29	13 36		13 41	13 49
d	12 37	12 41	12 42	12 50	12 56	12 58	13 04	13 17	13 12	13 21	13 26	13 28		13 29	13 37	13 41	13 42	13 50
Heaton Chapel d			12 45				13 08		13 16					13 33			13 45	
Levenshulme d			12 48				13 11		13 19					13 36			13 48	
Manchester Piccadilly 10 a	12 49	12 52	12 56	12 59	13 07	13 15	13 20	13 28	13 28	13 36	13 36	13 39	13 42	13 44	13 49	13 52	13 56	13 59
d		12 54									13 37					13 54		
Manchester Oxford Road a		12 56									13 40					13 56		
Deansgate a		13 00														14 00		

	TP ◇1	VT ◇1	AW ◇	NT	VT ◇1	NT	NT	EM ◇	XC ◇1	NT	NT	VT ◇1	NT	NT	XC ◇1	TP ◇1	VT ◇1
London Euston 15 ⊖65 d		12 00			12 20							12 40					13 00
Birmingham New Street 12 68 d									12c57						13 31		
Wolverhampton 7 68 d									13 15						13 49		
Stafford 65,68 d									13 30						14 01		
Stoke-on-Trent 50,68 d		13 25			13 48				13 55					13 58	14 20		14 25
Longport 50 d																	
Kidsgrove 50 d														14 05			
Crewe 10 65 d			13 28							13 33	13 50	14 11					
Sandbach d										13 40	13 57						
Holmes Chapel d										13 44	14 02						
Goostrey d											14 05						
Chelford d											14 09						
Alderley Edge d				13 49						13 53	14 13						
Wilmslow d			13 46	13 52						13 57	14 17	14 27					
Styal d																	
Manchester Airport ✈ a										14 04							
Handforth d				13 55							14 20						
Congleton d														14 12			
Macclesfield a		13 41							14 11					14 19			14 41
d		13 42							14 12					14 20			14 41
Prestbury d														14 24			
Adlington (Cheshire) d														14 27			
Poynton d														14 30			
Bramhall d														14 33			
Cheadle Hulme d				13 59							14 24			14 37			
Stockport a		13 55	13 58	14 04	14 16				14 27		14 29	14 36		14 41	14 49		14 55
d	13 53	13 56	13 58	14 04	14 17	14 12	14 21	14 26	14 28		14 29	14 37	14 41	14 42	14 50	14 53	14 56
Heaton Chapel d				14 08		14 16					14 33			14 45			
Levenshulme d				14 11		14 19					14 36			14 48			
Manchester Piccadilly 10 a	14 02	14 07	14 15	14 20	14 28	14 28	14 36	14 36	14 39	14 42	14 44	14 49	14 52	14 56	14 59	15 02	15 07
d								14 37					14 54				
Manchester Oxford Road a								14 40					14 56				
Deansgate a													15 00				

b arr. 1148

c arr. 1248

Table 84

Saturdays
until 10 July

Stoke-on-Trent and Crewe - Manchester Airport, Stockport and Manchester

	AW ◇	NT	VT ◇1	NT	NT	EM ◇	XC ◇1	NT	NT	VT ◇1	NT	NT	XC ◇1	TP ◇1	VT ◇1	AW ◇
London Euston 15 ⊖65 d			13 20							13 40					14 00	
Birmingham New Street 12 68 d							13b57						14 31			
Wolverhampton 7 68 d							14 15						14 49			
Stafford 65,68 d							14 30						15 01			
Stoke-on-Trent 50,68 d			14 48				14 55					14 58	15 20		15 25	
Longport 50 d																
Kidsgrove 50 d												15 05				
Crewe 10 65 d	14 28							14 33	14 50	15 11						15 28
Sandbach d								14 40	14 57							
Holmes Chapel d								14 44	15 02							
Goostrey d									15 05							
Chelford d									15 09							
Alderley Edge d		14 49						14 53	15 13							
Wilmslow d	14 46	14 52						14 57	15 17	15 27						15 46
Styal d																
Manchester Airport ✈ a								15 04								
Handforth d		14 55							15 20							
Congleton d												15 12				
Macclesfield a							15 11					15 19			15 41	
d							15 12					15 20			15 41	
Prestbury d												15 24				
Adlington (Cheshire) d												15 27				
Poynton d												15 30				
Bramhall d												15 33				
Cheadle Hulme d		14 59							15 24			15 37				
Stockport a	14 58	15 04	15 16				15 27		15 29	15 36		15 41	15 49		15 55	15 58
d	14 58	15 04	15 17	15 12	15 21	15 26	15 28		15 29	15 37	15 41	15 42	15 50	15 53	15 56	15 58
Heaton Chapel d		15 08		15 16					15 33			15 45				
Levenshulme d		15 11		15 19					15 36			15 48				
Manchester Piccadilly 10 a	15 15	15 20	15 28	15 28	15 36	15 36	15 39	15 42	15 44	15 49	15 52	15 56	15 59	16 02	16 07	16 15
d						15 37					15 54					
Manchester Oxford Road a						15 40					15 56					
Deansgate a											16 00					

	NT	VT ◇1	NT	NT	EM ◇	XC ◇1	NT	NT	VT ◇1	NT	NT	XC ◇1	TP ◇1	VT ◇1	AW ◇	NT	VT ◇1	NT
London Euston 15 ⊖65 d		14 20							14 40					15 00			15 20	
Birmingham New Street 12 68 d						14c57						15 31						
Wolverhampton 7 68 d						15 15						15 49						
Stafford 65,68 d						15 30						16 01						
Stoke-on-Trent 50,68 d		15 48				15 55					15 58	16 20		16 25			16 48	
Longport 50 d																		
Kidsgrove 50 d											16 05							
Crewe 10 65 d							15 33	15 50	16 12						16 28			
Sandbach d							15 40	15 57										
Holmes Chapel d							15 44	16 02										
Goostrey d								16 05										
Chelford d								16 09										
Alderley Edge d	15 49						15 53	16 13								16 49		
Wilmslow d	15 52						15 56	16 17	16 27						16 46	16 52		
Styal d							15 59											
Manchester Airport ✈ a							16 04											
Handforth d	15 55							16 20								16 55		
Congleton d											16 12							
Macclesfield a						16 11					16 19			16 41				
d						16 12					16 20			16 41				
Prestbury d											16 24							
Adlington (Cheshire) d											16 27							
Poynton d											16 30							
Bramhall d											16 33							
Cheadle Hulme d	15 59							16 24			16 37					16 59		
Stockport a	16 04	16 16				16 27		16 29	16 36		16 41	16 49		16 54	16 58	17 04	17 16	
d	16 04	16 17	16 12	16 21	16 26	16 28		16 29	16 37	16 41	16 42	16 50	16 53	16 55	16 58	17 04	17 17	17 12
Heaton Chapel d	16 08		16 16					16 33			16 45					17 08		17 16
Levenshulme d	16 11		16 19					16 36			16 48					17 11		17 19
Manchester Piccadilly 10 a	16 20	16 28	16 28	16 36	16 36	16 39	16 42	16 44	16 49	16 52	16 56	16 59	17 02	17 07	17 15	17 20	17 28	17 28
d					16 37					16 54								
Manchester Oxford Road a					16 40					16 56								
Deansgate a										17 00								

b arr. 1348

c arr. 1448

Stoke-on-Trent and Crewe - Manchester Airport, Stockport and Manchester

	NT	EM	XC	NT	NT	VT	NT	XC	TP	VT	AW	NT	VT	NT	NT	EM	XC	NT
		◇	◇1 ⌶			◇1 ⊡		◇1 ⊡	◇1 ⌶	◇1 ⊡	◇ ⌶		◇1 ⊡			◇	◇1 ⌶	
London Euston 15 ⊖65 d						15 40				16 00			16 20					
Birmingham New Street 12 68 d			15b57					16 31									16c57	
Wolverhampton 7 68 ⇌ d			16 15					16 49									17 15	
Stafford 65,68 d			16 30					17 01									17 30	
Stoke-on-Trent 50,68 d			16 55				16 58	17 20		17 25			17 48				17 55	
Longport 50 d																		
Kidsgrove 50 d							17 05											
Crewe 10 65 d				16 33	16 50	17 11					17 28							17 33
Sandbach d				16 40	16 57													17 40
Holmes Chapel d				16 44	17 02													17 44
Goostrey d					17 05													
Chelford d					17 09													
Alderley Edge d				16 53	17 13							17 49						17 53
Wilmslow d				16 57	17 17	17 27					17 46	17 52						17 56
Styal d																		17 59
Manchester Airport ✈ a				17 04														18 04
Handforth d					17 20							17 55						
Congleton d							17 12											
Macclesfield a			17 11				17 19			17 41							18 11	
d			17 12				17 20			17 41							18 12	
Prestbury d							17 24											
Adlington (Cheshire) d							17 27											
Poynton d							17 30											
Bramhall d							17 33											
Cheadle Hulme d					17 24		17 37					17 59						
Stockport a			17 27		17 29	17 36	17 41	17 49		17 55	17 58	18 04	18 16				18 27	
d	17 21	17 26	17 28		17 29	17 37	17 42	17 50	17 53	17 56	17 58	18 04	18 17	18 12	18 21	18 26	18 28	
Heaton Chapel d					17 33		17 45					18 08		18 16				
Levenshulme d					17 36		17 48					18 11		18 19				
Manchester Piccadilly 10 ⇌ a	17 36	17 37	17 39	17 42	17 44	17 49	17 56	17 59	18 02	18 07	18 15	18 20	18 28	18 28	18 36	18 36	18 39	18 42
d		17 37														18 37		
Manchester Oxford Road a		17 40														18 40		
Deansgate ⇌ a																		

	NT	VT	NT	NT	XC	TP	VT	AW	VT	NT	NT	NT	EM	XC	NT	VT	NT	XC
		◇1 ⊡			◇1 ⌶	◇1 ⌶	◇1 ⊡	■ ⌶	◇1 ⊡				◇	◇1 ⌶		◇1 ⊡		◇1 ⊡
London Euston 15 ⊖65 d		16 40					17 00		17 20							17 40		
Birmingham New Street 12 68 d					17 31									17e57				18 31
Wolverhampton 7 68 ⇌ d					17 48									18 15				18 49
Stafford 65,68 d					18 00									18 30				19 01
Stoke-on-Trent 50,68 d				17 58	18 20		18 25		18 48					18 55			18 58	19 20
Longport 50 d																		
Kidsgrove 50 d				18 05													19 05	
Crewe 10 65 d	17 50	18 11						18 28			18 33				18 50	19 11		
Sandbach d	17 57										18 40				18 57			
Holmes Chapel d	18 02										18 44				19 02			
Goostrey d	18 05														19 05			
Chelford d	18 09														19 09			
Alderley Edge d	18 13										18 53				19 13			
Wilmslow d	18 17	18 27						18 46			18 56				19 17	19 27		
Styal d																		
Manchester Airport ✈ a											19 04							
Handforth d	18 20														19 20			
Congleton d				18 12													19 12	
Macclesfield a				18 19			18 41							19 11			19 19	
d				18 20			18 41							19 12			19 20	
Prestbury d				18 24													19 24	
Adlington (Cheshire) d				18 27													19 27	
Poynton d				18 30													19 30	
Bramhall d				18 33													19 33	
Cheadle Hulme d	18 24			18 37											19 24		19 37	
Stockport a	18 29	18 36		18 41			18 55	18 58	19 16					19 27	19 29	19 36	19 41	19 49
d	18 29	18 37	18 41	18 42		18 53	18 56	18 58	19 17	19 12		19 21	19 26	19 28	19 29	19 37	19 42	19 50
Heaton Chapel d	18 33			18 45						19 16							19 45	
Levenshulme d	18 36			18 48						19 19							19 48	
Manchester Piccadilly 10 ⇌ a	18 44	18 49	18 52	18 56	18 59	19 02	19 07	19 15	19 28	19 28	19 31	19 35	19 36	19 40	19 43	19 49	19 56	19 59
d			18 54								19 32		19 37					
Manchester Oxford Road a			18 56								19 36		19 40					
Deansgate ⇌ a			19 00															

b arr. 1548 c arr. 1648 e arr. 1748

Stoke-on-Trent and Crewe - Manchester Airport, Stockport and Manchester

	TP	VT	AW	VT	NT	NT	NT	EM	XC	NT	VT	NT	XC	TP	VT	AW
	◇1 ⌶	◇1 ⊡	■ ⌶	◇1 ⊡				◇	◇1 ⌶		◇1 ⊡		◇1 ⊡	◇1 ⌶	◇1 ⊡	■ ⌶
London Euston 15 ⊖65 d		18 00		18 20							18 40				19 00	
Birmingham New Street 12 68 d									18b57				19 31			
Wolverhampton 7 68 ⇌ d									19 15				19 49			
Stafford 65,68 d									19 30				20 01			
Stoke-on-Trent 50,68 d		19 25		19 48					19 55			19 58	20 20		20 25	
Longport 50 d																
Kidsgrove 50 d												20 05				
Crewe 10 65 d			19 28							19 50	20 11					20 28
Sandbach d										19 57						
Holmes Chapel d										20 02						
Goostrey d										20 05						
Chelford d										20 09						
Alderley Edge d										20 13						
Wilmslow d			19 46			19 56				20 17	20 27					20 46
Styal d																
Manchester Airport ✈ a						20 04										
Handforth d										20 20						
Congleton d												20 12				
Macclesfield a		19 41							20 11			20 19	20 36		20 41	
d		19 41							20 12			20 20	20 37		20 41	
Prestbury d												20 24				
Adlington (Cheshire) d												20 27				
Poynton d												20 30				
Bramhall d												20 33				
Cheadle Hulme d										20 24		20 37				
Stockport a		19 55	19 58	20 16					20 27	20 29	20 36	20 41	20 49		20 55	20 58
d	19 53	19 56	19 58	20 17	20 12		20 21	20 26	20 28	20 29	20 37	20 42	20 50	20 53	20 56	20 58
Heaton Chapel d					20 16							20 45				
Levenshulme d					20 19							20 48				
Manchester Piccadilly 10 ⇌ a	20 02	20 07	20 15	20 28	20 28	20 31	20 35	20 37	20 39	20 43	20 49	20 56	20 59	21 02	21 07	21 15
d						20 32										
Manchester Oxford Road a						20 36										
Deansgate ⇌ a																

	VT	NT	NT	EM	NT	XC	NT	VT	NT	XC	AW	NT	NT	NT	XC	NT
	◇1 ⊡			◇		◇1 ⌶		◇1 ⊡		◇1 ⊡	◇ ⌶				◇1 ⌶	
London Euston 15 ⊖65 d	19 20							19 40								
Birmingham New Street 12 68 d						19c57				20 31					21e01	
Wolverhampton 7 68 ⇌ d						20 16				20 49					21 18	
Stafford 65,68 d						20 30				21 01					21 31	
Stoke-on-Trent 50,68 d	20 48					20 55			20 58	21 21						
Longport 50 d																
Kidsgrove 50 d									21 05							
Crewe 10 65 d							20 50	21 19			21 28			21 50	22 03	
Sandbach d							20 57							21 57		
Holmes Chapel d							21 02							22 02		
Goostrey d							21 05							22 05		
Chelford d							21 09							22 09		
Alderley Edge d							21 13							22 13		
Wilmslow d			20 56				21 17	21 34			21 46		21 55	22 17	22 21	
Styal d																
Manchester Airport ✈ a			21 05										22 04			
Handforth d							21 20							22 20		
Congleton d									21 12							
Macclesfield a						21 11			21 19	21 38						
d						21 12			21 20	21 39						
Prestbury d									21 24							
Adlington (Cheshire) d									21 27							
Poynton d									21 30							
Bramhall d									21 33							
Cheadle Hulme d							21 24		21 37					22 24		
Stockport a	21 16					21 27	21 29	21 44	21 41	21 53	21 58			22 29	22 36	
d	21 17	21 12		21 20	21 21	21 28	21 29	21 45	21 42	21 54	21 58	22 12		22 29	22 37	22 40
Heaton Chapel d		21 16							21 45			22 16				22 44
Levenshulme d		21 19							21 48			22 19				22 47
Manchester Piccadilly 10 ⇌ a	21 28	21 28	21 31	21 32	21 35	21 39	21 43	21 53	21 57	22 04	22 15	22 28	22 31	22 43	22 48	22 53
d			21 32										22 32			22 54
Manchester Oxford Road a			21 36										22 36			22 56
Deansgate ⇌ a																23 00

b arr. 1848 c arr. 1948 e arr. 2050

Table 84

Saturdays
until 10 July

Stoke-on-Trent and Crewe - Manchester Airport, Stockport and Manchester

Station		NT	VT	NT	XC	VT	AW	NT	NT	NT	XC
			◇1		◇1	◇1	◇				◇1
London Euston 15 ⊖65	d		20 20			21 00					
Birmingham New Street 12 68	d				21b57						22 31
Wolverhampton 7 68	d				22 16						22 49
Stafford 65,68	d		21 58		22 30	22 34					23 03
Stoke-on-Trent 50,68	d										
Longport 50	d										
Kidsgrove 50	d										
Crewe 10 65	d					23 00	23 06			23 12	
Sandbach	d									23 19	
Holmes Chapel	d									23 24	
Goostrey	d									23 27	
Chelford	d									23 31	
Alderley Edge	d									23 35	
Wilmslow	d		22 38		23 12	23 17	23 24	23 15		23 39	23 43
Styal	d										
Manchester Airport ✈	a							23 23			
Handforth	d									23 42	
Congleton	d										
Macclesfield	a										
	d			22 40							
Prestbury	d			22 44							
Adlington (Cheshire)	d			22 47							
Poynton	d			22 50							
Bramhall	d			22 53							
Cheadle Hulme	d			22 56						23 46	
Stockport	a		22 51	23 01	23 21	23 25	23 32			23 51	23 53
	d	22 48	22 51	23 01	23 22	23 26	23 33		23 41	23 51	23 54
Heaton Chapel	d			23 05						23 55	
Levenshulme	d			23 08						23 58	
Manchester Piccadilly 10	a	23 00	23 04	23 16	23 32	23 38	23 48	23 51	23 54	00 07	00 10
	d										
Manchester Oxford Road	a										
Deansgate	a										

b arr. 2148

Saturdays
17 July to 04 September

Station		NT	TP	NT	NT	TP	AW	NT	NT	NT	EM	XC	NT	NT	NT	NT	XC
			◇1			◇1					◇	◇1					◇1
London Euston 15 ⊖65	d																
Birmingham New Street 12 68	d											05 57					06 31
Wolverhampton 7 68	d											06 16					06 49
Stafford 65,68	d											06 30					07 01
Stoke-on-Trent 50,68	d											06 51				06 57	07 19
Longport 50	d																
Kidsgrove 50	d															07 04	
Crewe 10 65	d	00 44					06 27						06 33	06 49			
Sandbach	d												06 40	06 56			
Holmes Chapel	d												06 44	07 00			
Goostrey	d													07 03			
Chelford	d													07 08			
Alderley Edge	d							06 49					06 53	07 12			
Wilmslow	d			05 46			06 45	06 52					06 57	07 16			
Styal	d																
Manchester Airport ✈	a	01 16		05 53									07 04				
Handforth	d							06 55						07 19			
Congleton	d											07 03				07 11	
Macclesfield	a											07 11				07 18	07 36
	d											07 12				07 19	07 37
Prestbury	d															07 23	
Adlington (Cheshire)	d															07 26	
Poynton	d															07 29	
Bramhall	d															07 32	
Cheadle Hulme	d							06 59						07 24		07 36	
Stockport	a						06 54	07 04				07 27		07 29		07 40	07 49
	d		05 53		06 41	06 53	06 54	07 04	07 12	07 19	07 22	07 28		07 29	07 40	07 41	07 50
Heaton Chapel	d							07 08	07 16					07 33		07 44	
Levenshulme	d							07 11	07 19					07 36		07 47	
Manchester Piccadilly 10	a	01 36	06 05	06 25	06 52	07 02	07 09	07 21	07 28	07 31	07 34	07 38	07 42	07 44	07 52	07 56	08 00
	d				06 54						07 34				07 54		
Manchester Oxford Road	a				06 56						07 37				07 56		
Deansgate	a				06 59										08 00		

Table 84

Saturdays
17 July to 04 September

Stoke-on-Trent and Crewe - Manchester Airport, Stockport and Manchester

Station		TP	AW	NT	NT	NT	NT	XC	EM	NT	NT	VT	NT	NT	XC	TP	VT	AW
		◇1						◇1	◇			◇1			◇1	◇1	◇1	◇
London Euston 15 ⊖65	d											06 36					06 55	
Birmingham New Street 12 68	d							06 57							07 31			
Wolverhampton 7 68	d							07 14							07 49			
Stafford 65,68	d							07 29							08 01			
Stoke-on-Trent 50,68	d													07 57	08 20		08 25	
Longport 50	d																	
Kidsgrove 50	d													08 04				
Crewe 10 65	d		07 27					07 53		07 30	07 55	08 11						08 28
Sandbach	d									07 37	08 02							
Holmes Chapel	d									07 41	08 07							
Goostrey	d									07 44								
Chelford	d									07 49								
Alderley Edge	d				07 49					07 53	08 15							
Wilmslow	d		07 44		07 52			08 10		07 56	08 19	08 27						08 46
Styal	d									07 59								
Manchester Airport ✈	a									08 05								
Handforth	d				07 55						08 22							
Congleton	d													08 11				
Macclesfield	a													08 18	08 36		08 41	
	d													08 19	08 37		08 41	
Prestbury	d													08 23				
Adlington (Cheshire)	d													08 26				
Poynton	d													08 30				
Bramhall	d													08 33				
Cheadle Hulme	d				07 59						08 26			08 37				
Stockport	a		07 54		08 04			08 20			08 31	08 37		08 41	08 49		08 55	08 58
	d	07 53	07 54	07 57	08 04	08 12	08 19	08 20	08 24		08 31	08 38	08 41	08 42	08 50	08 53	08 56	08 58
Heaton Chapel	d				08 08	08 16					08 35			08 45				
Levenshulme	d				08 11	08 19								08 48				
Manchester Piccadilly 10	a	08 02	08 08	08 09	08 20	08 28	08 32	08 35	08 36	08 42	08 45	08 49	08 52	08 56	08 59	09 02	09 07	09 14
	d								08 37				08 54					
Manchester Oxford Road	a								08 40				08 56					
Deansgate	a												09 00					

Station		NT	VT	NT	NT	EM	XC	NT	NT	VT	NT	NT	XC	TP	VT	AW	NT	VT
			◇1			◇	◇1			◇1			◇1	◇1	◇1	◇		◇1
London Euston 15 ⊖65	d		07 20							07 35					08 00			08 20
Birmingham New Street 12 68	d						07b57						08 31					
Wolverhampton 7 68	d						08 15						08 49					
Stafford 65,68	d						08 30						09 01					
Stoke-on-Trent 50,68	d		08 48				08 55					08 58	09 20		09 25			09 48
Longport 50	d																	
Kidsgrove 50	d											09 05						
Crewe 10 65	d							08 31	08 50	09 11						09 28		
Sandbach	d							08 38	08 57									
Holmes Chapel	d							08 42	09 02									
Goostrey	d							08 45	09 05									
Chelford	d							08 50	09 09									
Alderley Edge	d	08 49						08 54	09 13								09 49	
Wilmslow	d	08 52						08 57	09 17	09 27						09 46	09 52	
Styal	d																	
Manchester Airport ✈	a							09 04										
Handforth	d	08 55							09 20								09 55	
Congleton	d											09 12						
Macclesfield	a						09 11					09 19			09 41			
	d						09 12					09 20			09 41			
Prestbury	d											09 24						
Adlington (Cheshire)	d											09 27						
Poynton	d											09 30						
Bramhall	d											09 33						
Cheadle Hulme	d	08 59							09 24			09 37					09 59	
Stockport	a	09 04	09 16				09 27		09 29	09 36		09 41	09 49		09 55	09 58	10 04	10 16
	d	09 04	09 17	09 12	09 21	09 25	09 28		09 29	09 37	09 41	09 42	09 50	09 53	09 56	09 58	10 04	10 17
Heaton Chapel	d	09 08		09 16					09 33			09 45					10 08	
Levenshulme	d	09 11		09 19					09 36			09 48					10 11	
Manchester Piccadilly 10	a	09 20	09 28	09 28	09 36	09 36	09 39	09 42	09 44	09 49	09 52	09 56	09 59	10 02	10 07	10 15	10 20	10 28
	d					09 37					09 54							
Manchester Oxford Road	a					09 40					09 56							
Deansgate	a										10 00							

b arr. 0751

Stoke-on-Trent and Crewe - Manchester Airport, Stockport and Manchester

	NT	NT	EM	XC	NT	NT	VT	NT	NT	XC	TP	VT	AW	NT	VT	NT	NT	EM
			◇	◇1			◇1			◇1	◇1	◇1	◇		◇1			◇
London Euston ⊖65 d							08 40					09 00			09 20			
Birmingham New Street 68 d				08b57						09 31								
Wolverhampton 68 d				09 15						09 49								
Stafford 65,68 d				09 30						10 01								
Stoke-on-Trent 50,68 d				09 55					09 58	10 20		10 25			10 48			
Longport 50 d																		
Kidsgrove 50 d									10 05									
Crewe 65 d					09 33	09 50	10 11						10 28					
Sandbach d					09 40	09 57												
Holmes Chapel d					09 44	10 02												
Goostrey d						10 05												
Chelford d						10 09												
Alderley Edge d					09 53	10 13								10 49				
Wilmslow d					09 57	10 17	10 27						10 46	10 52				
Styal d																		
Manchester Airport ✈ a					10 04													
Handforth d						10 20								10 55				
Congleton d									10 12									
Macclesfield a				10 11					10 19			10 41						
Macclesfield d				10 12					10 20			10 41						
Prestbury d									10 24									
Adlington (Cheshire) d									10 27									
Poynton d									10 30									
Bramhall d									10 33									
Cheadle Hulme d						10 24			10 37					10 59				
Stockport a				10 27		10 29	10 36		10 41	10 49		10 55	10 58	11 04	11 16			
Stockport d	10 12	10 21	10 26	10 28		10 29	10 37	10 41	10 42	10 50	10 53	10 56	10 58	11 04	11 17	11 12	11 21	11 26
Heaton Chapel d	10 16					10 33			10 45					11 08		11 16		
Levenshulme d	10 19					10 36			10 48					11 11		11 19		
Manchester Piccadilly a	10 28	10 36	10 36	10 39	10 42	10 44	10 49	10 52	10 56	10 59	11 02	11 07	11 15	11 20	11 28	11 28	11 36	11 36
Manchester Piccadilly d			10 37					10 54										11 37
Manchester Oxford Road a			10 40					10 56										11 40
Deansgate a								11 00										

	XC	NT	NT	VT	NT	NT	XC	TP	VT	AW	NT	VT	NT	NT	EM	XC	NT	NT
	◇1			◇1			◇1	◇1	◇1	◇		◇1			◇	◇1		
London Euston ⊖65 d				09 40					10 00			10 20						
Birmingham New Street 68 d	09c57						10 31									10e57		
Wolverhampton 68 d	10 15						10 49									11 15		
Stafford 65,68 d	10 30						11 01									11 30		
Stoke-on-Trent 50,68 d	10 55					10 58	11 20		11 25			11 48				11 55		
Longport 50 d																		
Kidsgrove 50 d						11 05												
Crewe 65 d		10 33	10 50	11 11						11 28							11 33	11 50
Sandbach d		10 40	10 57														11 40	11 57
Holmes Chapel d		10 44	11 02														11 44	12 02
Goostrey d			11 05															12 05
Chelford d			11 09															12 09
Alderley Edge d		10 53	11 13								11 49						11 53	12 13
Wilmslow d		10 57	11 17	11 27						11 46	11 52						11 57	12 17
Styal d																		
Manchester Airport ✈ a		11 04															12 04	
Handforth d			11 20								11 55							12 20
Congleton d						11 12												
Macclesfield a	11 11					11 19			11 41							12 11		
Macclesfield d	11 12					11 20			11 41							12 12		
Prestbury d						11 24												
Adlington (Cheshire) d						11 27												
Poynton d						11 30												
Bramhall d						11 33												
Cheadle Hulme d			11 24			11 37					11 59							12 24
Stockport a	11 27		11 29	11 36		11 41	11 49		11 55	11 58	12 04	12 16				12 27		12 29
Stockport d	11 28		11 29	11 37	11 41	11 42	11 50	11 53	11 56	11 58	12 04	12 17	12 12	12 21	12 26	12 28		12 29
Heaton Chapel d			11 33			11 45					12 08		12 16					12 33
Levenshulme d			11 36			11 48					12 11		12 19					12 36
Manchester Piccadilly a	11 39	11 42	11 44	11 49	11 52	11 56	11 59	12 02	12 07	12 15	12 20	12 28	12 28	12 36	12 36	12 39	12 42	12 44
Manchester Piccadilly d					11 54										12 37			
Manchester Oxford Road a					11 56										12 40			
Deansgate a					12 00													

b arr. 0848 c arr. 0948 e arr. 1048

Stoke-on-Trent and Crewe - Manchester Airport, Stockport and Manchester

	VT	NT	NT	XC	TP	VT	AW	NT	VT	NT	NT	EM	XC	NT	NT	VT	NT	NT	XC
	◇1			◇1	◇1	◇1	◇		◇1			◇	◇1			◇1			◇1
London Euston ⊖65 d	10 40					11 00			11 20							11 40			
Birmingham New Street 68 d				11 31									11b57						12 31
Wolverhampton 68 d				11 49									12 15						12 49
Stafford 65,68 d				12 01									12 30						13 01
Stoke-on-Trent 50,68 d			11 58	12 20		12 25			12 48				12 55					12 58	13 20
Longport 50 d																			
Kidsgrove 50 d			12 05															13 05	
Crewe 65 d	12 11						12 28							12 33	12 50	13 11			
Sandbach d														12 40	12 57				
Holmes Chapel d														12 44	13 02				
Goostrey d															13 05				
Chelford d															13 09				
Alderley Edge d								12 49						12 53	13 13				
Wilmslow d	12 27						12 46	12 52						12 57	13 17	13 27			
Styal d																			
Manchester Airport ✈ a														13 04					
Handforth d								12 55							13 20				
Congleton d			12 12															13 12	
Macclesfield a			12 19			12 41							13 11					13 19	
Macclesfield d			12 20			12 41							13 12					13 20	
Prestbury d			12 24															13 24	
Adlington (Cheshire) d			12 27															13 27	
Poynton d			12 30															13 30	
Bramhall d			12 33															13 33	
Cheadle Hulme d			12 37					12 59							13 24			13 37	
Stockport a	12 36	12 41	12 41	12 49		12 55	12 58	13 04	13 16				13 27		13 29	13 36		13 41	13 49
Stockport d	12 37	12 41	12 42	12 50	12 53	12 56	12 58	13 04	13 17	13 12	13 21	13 26	13 28		13 29	13 37	13 41	13 42	13 50
Heaton Chapel d			12 45					13 08		13 16					13 33			13 45	
Levenshulme d			12 48					13 11		13 19					13 36			13 48	
Manchester Piccadilly a	12 49	12 52	12 56	12 59	13 02	13 07	13 15	13 20	13 28	13 28	13 36	13 36	13 39	13 42	13 44	13 49	13 52	13 56	13 59
Manchester Piccadilly d		12 54										13 37					13 54		
Manchester Oxford Road a		12 56										13 40					13 56		
Deansgate a		13 00															14 00		

	TP	VT	AW	NT	VT	NT	NT	EM	XC	NT	NT	VT	NT	NT	XC	TP	VT
	◇1	◇1	◇		◇1			◇	◇1			◇1			◇1	◇1	◇1
London Euston ⊖65 d		12 00			12 20							12 40					13 00
Birmingham New Street 68 d									12c57						13 31		
Wolverhampton 68 d									13 15						13 49		
Stafford 65,68 d									13 30						14 01		
Stoke-on-Trent 50,68 d		13 25			13 48				13 55					13 58	14 20		14 25
Longport 50 d																	
Kidsgrove 50 d														14 05			
Crewe 65 d			13 28							13 33	13 50	14 11					
Sandbach d										13 40	13 57						
Holmes Chapel d										13 44	14 02						
Goostrey d											14 05						
Chelford d											14 09						
Alderley Edge d				13 49						13 53	14 13						
Wilmslow d			13 46	13 52						13 57	14 17	14 27					
Styal d																	
Manchester Airport ✈ a										14 04							
Handforth d				13 55							14 20						
Congleton d														14 12			
Macclesfield a		13 41							14 11					14 19			14 41
Macclesfield d		13 42							14 12					14 20			14 41
Prestbury d														14 24			
Adlington (Cheshire) d														14 27			
Poynton d														14 30			
Bramhall d														14 33			
Cheadle Hulme d				13 59							14 24			14 37			
Stockport a		13 55	13 58	14 04	14 16				14 27		14 29	14 36		14 41	14 49		14 55
Stockport d	13 53	13 56	13 58	14 04	14 17	14 12	14 21	14 26	14 28		14 29	14 37	14 41	14 42	14 50	14 53	14 56
Heaton Chapel d				14 08		14 16					14 33			14 45			
Levenshulme d				14 11		14 19					14 36			14 48			
Manchester Piccadilly a	14 02	14 07	14 15	14 20	14 28	14 28	14 36	14 36	14 39	14 42	14 44	14 49	14 52	14 56	14 59	15 02	15 07
Manchester Piccadilly d								14 37					14 54				
Manchester Oxford Road a								14 40					14 56				
Deansgate a													15 00				

b arr. 1148 c arr. 1248

Table 84

Saturdays
17 July to 04 September

Stoke-on-Trent and Crewe - Manchester Airport, Stockport and Manchester

Station		AW	NT	VT	NT	NT	EM	XC	NT	NT	VT	NT	NT	XC	TP	VT	AW
		◇		◇1			◇	◇1			◇1			◇1	◇1	◇1	◇
London Euston 15 ⊖65	d			13 20							13 40					14 00	
Birmingham New Street 12 68	d							13b57						14 31			
Wolverhampton 7 68	d							14 15						14 49			
Stafford 65,68	d							14 30						15 01			
Stoke-on-Trent 50,68	d			14 48				14 55					14 58	15 20		15 25	
Longport 50	d																
Kidsgrove 50	d												15 05				
Crewe 10 65	d	14 28							14 33	14 50	15 11						15 28
Sandbach	d								14 40	14 57							
Holmes Chapel	d								14 44	15 02							
Goostrey	d									15 05							
Chelford	d									15 09							
Alderley Edge	d		14 49						14 53	15 13							
Wilmslow	d	14 46	14 52						14 57	15 17	15 27						15 46
Styal	d																
Manchester Airport ✈	a								15 04								
Handforth	d		14 55							15 20							
Congleton	d												15 12				
Macclesfield	a							15 11					15 19			15 41	
	d							15 12					15 20			15 41	
Prestbury	d												15 24				
Adlington (Cheshire)	d												15 27				
Poynton	d												15 30				
Bramhall	d												15 33				
Cheadle Hulme	d		14 59							15 24			15 37				
Stockport	a	14 58	15 04	15 16				15 27		15 29	15 36		15 41	15 49		15 55	15 58
	d	14 58	15 04	15 17	15 12	15 21	15 26	15 28		15 29	15 37	15 41	15 42	15 50	15 53	15 56	15 58
Heaton Chapel	d		15 08		15 16					15 33			15 45				
Levenshulme	d		15 11		15 19					15 36			15 48				
Manchester Piccadilly 10	a	15 15	15 20	15 28	15 28	15 36	15 36	15 39	15 42	15 44	15 49	15 52	15 56	15 59	16 02	16 07	16 15
	d						15 37					15 54					
Manchester Oxford Road	a						15 40					15 56					
Deansgate	a											16 00					

Station		NT	VT	NT	NT	EM	XC	NT	NT	VT	NT	NT	XC	TP	VT	AW	NT	VT	NT
			◇1			◇	◇1			◇1			◇1	◇1	◇1	◇		◇1	
London Euston 15 ⊖65	d		14 20							14 40					15 00			15 20	
Birmingham New Street 12 68	d						14c57						15 31						
Wolverhampton 7 68	d						15 15						15 49						
Stafford 65,68	d						15 30						16 01						
Stoke-on-Trent 50,68	d		15 48				15 55					15 58	16 20		16 25			16 48	
Longport 50	d																		
Kidsgrove 50	d											16 05							
Crewe 10 65	d							15 33	15 50	16 12						16 28			
Sandbach	d							15 40	15 57										
Holmes Chapel	d							15 44	16 02										
Goostrey	d								16 05										
Chelford	d								16 09										
Alderley Edge	d	15 49						15 53	16 13								16 49		
Wilmslow	d	15 52						15 56	16 17	16 27						16 46	16 52		
Styal	d							15 59											
Manchester Airport ✈	a							16 04											
Handforth	d	15 55							16 20								16 55		
Congleton	d											16 12							
Macclesfield	a						16 11					16 19			16 41				
	d						16 12					16 20			16 41				
Prestbury	d											16 24							
Adlington (Cheshire)	d											16 27							
Poynton	d											16 30							
Bramhall	d											16 33							
Cheadle Hulme	d	15 59							16 24			16 37					16 59		
Stockport	a	16 04	16 16				16 27		16 29	16 36		16 41	16 49		16 54	16 58	17 04	17 16	
	d	16 04	16 17	16 12	16 21	16 26	16 28		16 29	16 37	16 41	16 42	16 50	16 53	16 55	16 58	17 04	17 17	17 12
Heaton Chapel	d	16 08		16 16					16 33			16 45					17 08		17 16
Levenshulme	d	16 11		16 19					16 36			16 48					17 11		17 19
Manchester Piccadilly 10	a	16 20	16 28	16 28	16 36	16 36	16 39	16 42	16 44	16 49	16 52	16 56	16 59	17 02	17 07	17 15	17 20	17 28	17 28
	d					16 37					16 54								
Manchester Oxford Road	a					16 40					16 56								
Deansgate	a										17 00								

b arr. 1348
c arr. 1448

Table 84

Saturdays
17 July to 04 September

Stoke-on-Trent and Crewe - Manchester Airport, Stockport and Manchester

Station		NT	EM	XC	NT	NT	VT	NT	XC	TP	VT	AW	NT	VT	NT	NT	EM	XC	NT
			◇	◇1			◇1		◇1	◇1	◇1	◇		◇1			◇	◇1	
London Euston 15 ⊖65	d						15 40				16 00			16 20					
Birmingham New Street 12 68	d			15b57					16 31									16c57	
Wolverhampton 7 68	d			16 15					16 49									17 15	
Stafford 65,68	d			16 30					17 01									17 30	
Stoke-on-Trent 50,68	d			16 55				16 58	17 20		17 25			17 48				17 55	
Longport 50	d																		
Kidsgrove 50	d							17 05											
Crewe 10 65	d				16 33	16 50	17 11					17 28							17 33
Sandbach	d				16 40	16 57													17 40
Holmes Chapel	d				16 44	17 02													17 44
Goostrey	d					17 05													
Chelford	d					17 09													
Alderley Edge	d				16 53	17 13							17 49						17 53
Wilmslow	d				16 57	17 17	17 27					17 46	17 52						17 56
Styal	d																		17 59
Manchester Airport ✈	a				17 04														18 04
Handforth	d					17 20							17 55						
Congleton	d							17 12											
Macclesfield	a			17 11				17 19			17 41							18 11	
	d			17 12				17 20			17 41							18 12	
Prestbury	d							17 24											
Adlington (Cheshire)	d							17 27											
Poynton	d							17 30											
Bramhall	d							17 33											
Cheadle Hulme	d					17 24		17 37					17 59						
Stockport	a			17 27		17 29	17 36	17 41	17 49		17 55	17 58	18 04	18 16				18 27	
	d	17 21	17 26	17 28		17 29	17 37	17 42	17 50	17 53	17 56	17 58	18 04	18 17	18 12	18 21	18 26	18 28	
Heaton Chapel	d					17 33		17 45					18 08		18 16				
Levenshulme	d					17 36		17 48					18 11		18 19				
Manchester Piccadilly 10	a	17 36	17 37	17 39	17 42	17 44	17 49	17 56	17 59	18 02	18 07	18 15	18 20	18 28	18 28	18 36	18 36	18 39	18 42
	d		17 37														18 37		
Manchester Oxford Road	a		17 40														18 40		
Deansgate	a																		

Station		NT	VT	NT	NT	XC	TP	VT	AW	VT	NT	NT	NT	EM	XC	NT	VT	NT	XC
			◇1			◇1	◇1	◇1	■	◇1				◇	◇1		◇1		◇1
London Euston 15 ⊖65	d		16 40					17 00		17 20							17 40		
Birmingham New Street 12 68	d					17 31									17e57				18 31
Wolverhampton 7 68	d					17 48									18 15				18 49
Stafford 65,68	d					18 00									18 30				19 01
Stoke-on-Trent 50,68	d				17 58	18 20		18 25		18 48					18 55			18 58	19 20
Longport 50	d																		
Kidsgrove 50	d				18 05													19 05	
Crewe 10 65	d	17 50	18 11						18 28			18 33				18 50	19 11		
Sandbach	d	17 57										18 40				18 57			
Holmes Chapel	d	18 02										18 44				19 02			
Goostrey	d	18 05														19 05			
Chelford	d	18 09														19 09			
Alderley Edge	d	18 13										18 53				19 13			
Wilmslow	d	18 17	18 27						18 46			18 56				19 17	19 27		
Styal	d																		
Manchester Airport ✈	a											19 04							
Handforth	d	18 20														19 20			
Congleton	d				18 12													19 12	
Macclesfield	a				18 19			18 41							19 11			19 19	
	d				18 20			18 41							19 12			19 20	
Prestbury	d				18 24													19 24	
Adlington (Cheshire)	d				18 27													19 27	
Poynton	d				18 30													19 30	
Bramhall	d				18 33													19 33	
Cheadle Hulme	d	18 24			18 37											19 24		19 37	
Stockport	a	18 29	18 36		18 41			18 55	18 58	19 16					19 27	19 29	19 36	19 41	19 49
	d	18 29	18 37	18 41	18 42		18 53	18 56	18 58	19 17	19 12		19 21	19 26	19 23	19 29	19 37	19 42	19 50
Heaton Chapel	d	18 33			18 45						19 16							19 45	
Levenshulme	d	18 36			18 48						19 19							19 48	
Manchester Piccadilly 10	a	18 44	18 49	18 52	18 56	18 59	19 02	19 07	19 15	19 28	19 28	19 31	19 35	19 36	19 43	19 43	19 49	19 56	19 59
	d			18 54								19 32		19 37					
Manchester Oxford Road	a			18 56								19 36		19 40					
Deansgate	a			19 00															

b arr. 1548
c arr. 1648
e arr. 1748

Table 84

Saturdays
17 July to 04 September

Stoke-on-Trent and Crewe - Manchester Airport, Stockport and Manchester

	TP	VT	AW	VT	NT	NT	NT	EM	XC	NT	VT	NT	XC	TP	VT	AW
	◇1	◇1		◇1				◇	◇1		◇1		◇1	◇1	◇1	
London Euston ⊖65 d		18 00		18 20							18 40				19 00	
Birmingham New Street 68 d									18b57				19 31			
Wolverhampton 68 d									19 15				19 49			
Stafford 65,68 d									19 30				20 01			
Stoke-on-Trent 50,68 d		19 25		19 48					19 55			19 58	20 20		20 25	
Longport 50 d																
Kidsgrove 50 d												20 05				
Crewe 65 d			19 28							19 50	20 11					20 28
Sandbach d										19 57						
Holmes Chapel d										20 02						
Goostrey d										20 05						
Chelford d										20 09						
Alderley Edge d										20 13						
Wilmslow d			19 46			19 56				20 17	20 27					20 46
Styal d																
Manchester Airport ✈ a						20 04										
Handforth d										20 20						
Congleton d												20 12				
Macclesfield a		19 41							20 11			20 19	20 36		20 41	
d		19 41							20 12			20 20	20 37		20 41	
Prestbury d												20 24				
Adlington (Cheshire) d												20 27				
Poynton d												20 30				
Bramhall d												20 33				
Cheadle Hulme d										20 24		20 37				
Stockport a		19 55	19 58	20 16					20 27	20 29	20 36	20 41	20 49		20 55	20 58
d	19 53	19 56	19 58	20 17	20 12		20 21	20 26	20 28	20 29	20 37	20 42	20 50	20 53	20 56	20 58
Heaton Chapel d					20 16							20 45				
Levenshulme d					20 19							20 48				
Manchester Piccadilly a	20 02	20 07	20 15	20 28	20 28	20 31	20 35	20 37	20 39	20 43	20 49	20 56	20 59	21 02	21 07	21 15
d						20 32										
Manchester Oxford Road a						20 36										
Deansgate a																

	VT	NT	NT	EM	NT	XC	NT	VT	NT	XC	AW	NT	NT	XC	NT	VT
	◇1			◇		◇1		◇1		◇1	◇			◇1		◇1
London Euston ⊖65 d	19 20							19 40								20 20
Birmingham New Street 68 d						19c57				20 31				21e03		
Wolverhampton 68 d						20 16				20 49				21 19		
Stafford 65,68 d						20 30				21 01				21 32		
Stoke-on-Trent 50,68 d	20 48					20 55			20 58	21 21				21 51		22 05
Longport 50 d																
Kidsgrove 50 d									21 05							
Crewe 65 d							20 50	21 19			21 28				21 50	
Sandbach d							20 57								21 57	
Holmes Chapel d							21 02								22 02	
Goostrey d							21 05								22 05	
Chelford d							21 09								22 09	
Alderley Edge d							21 13								22 13	
Wilmslow d			20 56				21 17	21 34			21 46		21 55		22 17	
Styal d																
Manchester Airport ✈ a			21 05										22 04			
Handforth d							21 20								22 20	
Congleton d									21 12							
Macclesfield a						21 11			21 19	21 38				22 10		22 21
d						21 12			21 20	21 39				22 11		22 21
Prestbury d									21 24							
Adlington (Cheshire) d									21 27							
Poynton d									21 30							
Bramhall d									21 33							
Cheadle Hulme d							21 24		21 37						22 24	
Stockport a	21 16					21 27	21 29	21 44	21 41	21 53	21 58			22 24	22 29	22 35
d	21 17	21 12		21 20	21 21	21 28	21 29	21 45	21 42	21 54	21 58	22 12		22 25	22 29	22 36
Heaton Chapel d		21 16							21 45			22 16				
Levenshulme d		21 19							21 48			22 19				
Manchester Piccadilly a	21 28	21 28	21 31	21 32	21 35	21 39	21 43	21 53	21 57	22 04	22 15	22 28	22 31	22 39	22 43	22 51
d			21 32										22 32			
Manchester Oxford Road a			21 36										22 36			
Deansgate a																

b arr. 1848 c arr. 1948 e arr. 2050

Table 84

Saturdays
17 July to 04 September

Stoke-on-Trent and Crewe - Manchester Airport, Stockport and Manchester

	NT	NT	NT	XC	VT	NT	NT	NT	XC
				◇1	◇1				◇1
London Euston ⊖65 d					21 00				
Birmingham New Street 68 d				21b57					22 31
Wolverhampton 68 d				22 16					22 49
Stafford 65,68 d				22 30	22 34				23 03
Stoke-on-Trent 50,68 d			22 18	22 51					23 21
Longport 50 d									
Kidsgrove 50 d			22 25						
Crewe 65 d					23 00			23 12	
Sandbach d								23 19	
Holmes Chapel d								23 24	
Goostrey d								23 27	
Chelford d								23 31	
Alderley Edge d								23 35	
Wilmslow d					23 17	23 15		23 39	
Styal d									
Manchester Airport ✈ a						23 23			
Handforth d								23 42	
Congleton d			22 32						
Macclesfield a			22 39	23 07					23 38
d			22 40	23 08					23 39
Prestbury d			22 44						
Adlington (Cheshire) d			22 47						
Poynton d			22 50						
Bramhall d			22 53						
Cheadle Hulme d			22 56					23 46	
Stockport a			23 01	23 21	23 25			23 51	23 53
d	22 40	22 48	23 01	23 22	23 26		23 41	23 51	23 54
Heaton Chapel d	22 44		23 05					23 55	
Levenshulme d	22 47		23 08					23 58	
Manchester Piccadilly a	22 53	23 00	23 16	23 32	23 38	23 51	23 54	00 07	00 10
d	22 54								
Manchester Oxford Road a	22 56								
Deansgate a	23 00								

Saturdays
from 11 September

	NT	TP	NT	NT	TP	AW	NT	NT	NT	EM	XC	NT	NT	NT	NT	XC
		◇1			◇1					◇	◇1					◇1
London Euston ⊖65 d																
Birmingham New Street 68 d											05 57					06 31
Wolverhampton 68 d											06 16					06 49
Stafford 65,68 d											06 30					07 01
Stoke-on-Trent 50,68 d											06 51				06 57	07 19
Longport 50 d																
Kidsgrove 50 d															07 04	
Crewe 65 d	00 44					06 27						06 33	06 49			
Sandbach d												06 40	06 56			
Holmes Chapel d												06 44	07 00			
Goostrey d													07 03			
Chelford d													07 08			
Alderley Edge d							06 49					06 53	07 12			
Wilmslow d			05 46			06 45	06 52					06 57	07 16			
Styal d																
Manchester Airport ✈ a	01 16		05 53									07 04				
Handforth d							06 55						07 19			
Congleton d											07 03				07 11	
Macclesfield a											07 11				07 18	07 36
d											07 12				07 19	07 37
Prestbury d															07 23	
Adlington (Cheshire) d															07 26	
Poynton d															07 29	
Bramhall d															07 32	
Cheadle Hulme d							06 59						07 24		07 36	
Stockport a						06 54	07 04				07 27		07 29		07 40	07 49
d		05 53		06 41	06 53	06 54	07 04	07 12	07 19	07 22	07 28		07 29	07 40	07 41	07 50
Heaton Chapel d							07 08	07 16					07 33		07 44	
Levenshulme d							07 11	07 19					07 36		07 47	
Manchester Piccadilly a	01 36	06 05	06 25	06 52	07 02	07 09	07 21	07 28	07 31	07 34	07 38	07 42	07 44	07 52	07 56	07 59
d				06 54						07 34				07 54		
Manchester Oxford Road a				06 56						07 37				07 56		
Deansgate a				06 59										08 00		

b arr. 2148

Stoke-on-Trent and Crewe - Manchester Airport, Stockport and Manchester

Station		TP ◇1 ⊼	AW ◇	NT	NT	NT	NT	XC ◇1 ⊼	EM ◇	NT	NT	VT ◇1 ⊏	NT	NT	XC ◇1 ⊼	TP ◇1 ⊼	VT ◇1 ⊏	AW ◇ ⊼
London Euston 15 ⊖65	d											06 36					06 55	
Birmingham New Street 12 68	d							06 57							07 31			
Wolverhampton 7 68 ⇌	d							07 14							07 49			
Stafford 65,68	d							07 29							08 01			
Stoke-on-Trent 50,68	d													07 57	08 20		08 25	
Longport 50	d																	
Kidsgrove 50	d													08 04				
Crewe 10 65	d		07 27					07 53		07 30	07 55	08 11						08 28
Sandbach	d									07 37	08 02							
Holmes Chapel	d									07 41	08 07							
Goostrey	d									07 44								
Chelford	d									07 49								
Alderley Edge	d				07 49					07 53	08 15							
Wilmslow	d		07 44		07 52			08 10		07 56	08 19	08 27						08 46
Styal	d									07 59								
Manchester Airport ✈	a									08 05								
Handforth	d				07 55						08 22							
Congleton	d													08 11				
Macclesfield	a													08 18	08 36		08 41	
	d													08 19	08 37		08 41	
Prestbury	d													08 23				
Adlington (Cheshire)	d													08 26				
Poynton	d													08 30				
Bramhall	d													08 33				
Cheadle Hulme	d				07 59						08 26			08 37				
Stockport	a		07 54		08 04			08 20			08 31	08 37		08 41	08 49		08 55	08 58
	d	07 53	07 54	07 57	08 04	08 12	08 19	08 20	08 24		08 31	08 38	08 41	08 42	08 50	08 53	08 56	08 58
Heaton Chapel	d				08 08	08 16					08 35			08 45				
Levenshulme	d				08 11	08 19								08 48				
Manchester Piccadilly 10 ⇌	a	08 02	08 08	08 09	08 20	08 28	08 32	08 35	08 36	08 42	08 45	08 49	08 52	08 56	08 59	09 02	09 07	09 14
	d								08 37				08 54					
Manchester Oxford Road	a								08 40				08 56					
Deansgate ⇌	a												09 00					

Station		NT	VT ◇1 ⊏	NT	NT	EM ◇	XC ◇1 ⊼	NT	NT	VT ◇1 ⊏	NT	NT	XC ◇1 ⊏	TP ◇1 ⊼	VT ◇1 ⊏	AW ◇ ⊼	NT	VT ◇1 ⊏
London Euston 15 ⊖65	d		07 20							07 35					08 00			08 20
Birmingham New Street 12 68	d						07b57						08 31					
Wolverhampton 7 68 ⇌	d						08 15						08 49					
Stafford 65,68	d						08 30						09 01					
Stoke-on-Trent 50,68	d		08 48				08 55					08 58	09 20		09 25			09 48
Longport 50	d																	
Kidsgrove 50	d											09 05						
Crewe 10 65	d							08 31	08 50	09 11						09 28		
Sandbach	d							08 38	08 57									
Holmes Chapel	d							08 42	09 02									
Goostrey	d							08 45	09 05									
Chelford	d							08 50	09 09									
Alderley Edge	d	08 49						08 54	09 13								09 49	
Wilmslow	d	08 52						08 57	09 17	09 27						09 46	09 52	
Styal	d																	
Manchester Airport ✈	a							09 04										
Handforth	d	08 55							09 20								09 55	
Congleton	d											09 12						
Macclesfield	a						09 11					09 19			09 41			
	d						09 12					09 20			09 41			
Prestbury	d											09 24						
Adlington (Cheshire)	d											09 27						
Poynton	d											09 30						
Bramhall	d											09 33						
Cheadle Hulme	d	08 59							09 24			09 37					09 59	
Stockport	a	09 04	09 16				09 27		09 29	09 36		09 41	09 49		09 55	09 58	10 04	10 16
	d	09 04	09 17	09 12	09 21	09 25	09 28		09 29	09 37	09 41	09 42	09 50	09 53	09 56	09 58	10 04	10 17
Heaton Chapel	d	09 08		09 16					09 33			09 45					10 08	
Levenshulme	d	09 11		09 19					09 36			09 48					10 11	
Manchester Piccadilly 10 ⇌	a	09 20	09 28	09 28	09 36	09 36	09 39	09 42	09 44	09 49	09 52	09 56	09 59	10 02	10 07	10 15	10 20	10 28
	d					09 37					09 54							
Manchester Oxford Road	a					09 40					09 56							
Deansgate ⇌	a										10 00							

b arr. 0751

Table 84

Saturdays
from 11 September

Stoke-on-Trent and Crewe - Manchester Airport, Stockport and Manchester

Station		NT	NT	EM ◇	XC ◇1 ⊼	NT	NT	VT ◇1 ⊏	NT	NT	XC ◇1 ⊏	TP ◇1 ⊼	VT ◇1 ⊏	AW ◇ ⊼	NT	VT ◇1 ⊏	NT	NT	EM ◇
London Euston 15 ⊖65	d							08 40					09 00			09 20			
Birmingham New Street 12 68	d				08b57						09 31								
Wolverhampton 7 68 ⇌	d				09 15						09 49								
Stafford 65,68	d				09 30						10 01								
Stoke-on-Trent 50,68	d				09 55					09 58	10 20		10 25			10 48			
Longport 50	d																		
Kidsgrove 50	d									10 05									
Crewe 10 65	d					09 33	09 50	10 11						10 28					
Sandbach	d					09 40	09 57												
Holmes Chapel	d					09 44	10 02												
Goostrey	d						10 05												
Chelford	d						10 09												
Alderley Edge	d					09 53	10 13								10 49				
Wilmslow	d					09 57	10 17	10 27						10 46	10 52				
Styal	d																		
Manchester Airport ✈	a					10 04													
Handforth	d						10 20								10 55				
Congleton	d									10 12									
Macclesfield	a				10 11					10 19			10 41						
	d				10 12					10 20			10 41						
Prestbury	d									10 24									
Adlington (Cheshire)	d									10 27									
Poynton	d									10 30									
Bramhall	d									10 33									
Cheadle Hulme	d						10 24			10 37					10 59				
Stockport	a				10 27		10 29	10 36		10 41	10 49		10 55	10 58	11 04	11 16			
	d	10 12	10 21	10 26	10 28		10 29	10 37	10 41	10 42	10 50	10 53	10 56	10 58	11 04	11 17	11 12	11 21	11 26
Heaton Chapel	d	10 16					10 33			10 45					11 08		11 16		
Levenshulme	d	10 19					10 36			10 48					11 11		11 19		
Manchester Piccadilly 10 ⇌	a	10 28	10 36	10 36	10 39	10 42	10 44	10 49	10 52	10 56	10 59	11 02	11 07	11 15	11 20	11 28	11 28	11 36	11 36
	d			10 37					10 54										11 37
Manchester Oxford Road	a			10 40					10 56										11 40
Deansgate ⇌	a								11 00										

Station		XC ◇1 ⊼	NT	NT	VT ◇1 ⊏	NT	NT	XC ◇1 ⊏	TP ◇1 ⊼	VT ◇1 ⊏	AW ◇ ⊼	NT	VT ◇1 ⊏	NT	NT	EM ◇	XC ◇1 ⊼	NT	NT
London Euston 15 ⊖65	d				09 40					10 00			10 20						
Birmingham New Street 12 68	d	09c57						10 31									10e57		
Wolverhampton 7 68 ⇌	d	10 15						10 49									11 15		
Stafford 65,68	d	10 30						11 01									11 30		
Stoke-on-Trent 50,68	d	10 55					10 58	11 20		11 25			11 48				11 55		
Longport 50	d																		
Kidsgrove 50	d						11 05												
Crewe 10 65	d		10 33	10 50	11 11						11 28							11 33	11 50
Sandbach	d		10 40	10 57														11 40	11 57
Holmes Chapel	d		10 44	11 02														11 44	12 02
Goostrey	d			11 05															12 05
Chelford	d			11 09															12 09
Alderley Edge	d		10 53	11 13								11 49						11 53	12 13
Wilmslow	d		10 57	11 17	11 27						11 46	11 52						11 57	12 17
Styal	d																		
Manchester Airport ✈	a		11 04															12 04	
Handforth	d			11 20								11 55							12 20
Congleton	d						11 12												
Macclesfield	a	11 11					11 19			11 41							12 11		
	d	11 12					11 20			11 41							12 12		
Prestbury	d						11 24												
Adlington (Cheshire)	d						11 27												
Poynton	d						11 30												
Bramhall	d						11 33												
Cheadle Hulme	d			11 24			11 37					11 59							12 24
Stockport	a	11 27		11 29	11 36		11 41	11 49		11 55	11 58	12 04	12 16				12 27		12 29
	d	11 28		11 29	11 37	11 41	11 42	11 50	11 53	11 56	11 58	12 04	12 17	12 12	12 21	12 26	12 28		12 29
Heaton Chapel	d			11 33			11 45					12 08		12 16					12 33
Levenshulme	d			11 36			11 48					12 11		12 19					12 36
Manchester Piccadilly 10 ⇌	a	11 39	11 42	11 44	11 49	11 52	11 56	11 59	12 02	12 07	12 15	12 20	12 28	12 28	12 36	12 36	12 39	12 42	12 44
	d					11 54										12 37			
Manchester Oxford Road	a					11 56										12 40			
Deansgate ⇌	a					12 00													

b arr. 0848 c arr. 0948 e arr. 1048

Stoke-on-Trent and Crewe - Manchester Airport, Stockport and Manchester

		VT ◇1	NT	NT	XC ◇1	TP ◇1	VT ◇1	AW ◇	NT	VT ◇1	NT	NT	EM ◇	XC ◇1	NT	NT	VT ◇1	NT	NT	XC ◇1
London Euston 15 ⊖65	d	10 40					11 00			11 20							11 40			
Birmingham New Street 12 68	d				11 31									11b57						12 31
Wolverhampton 7 68	d				11 49									12 15						12 49
Stafford 65,68	d				12 01									12 30						13 01
Stoke-on-Trent 50,68	d			11 58	12 20		12 25			12 48				12 55					12 58	13 20
Longport 50	d																			
Kidsgrove 50	d			12 05															13 05	
Crewe 10 65	d	12 11						12 28							12 33	12 50	13 11			
Sandbach	d														12 40	12 57				
Holmes Chapel	d														12 44	13 02				
Goostrey	d															13 05				
Chelford	d															13 09				
Alderley Edge	d								12 49						12 53	13 13				
Wilmslow	d	12 27						12 46	12 52						12 57	13 17	13 27			
Styal	d																			
Manchester Airport ✈	a														13 04					
Handforth	d								12 55							13 20				
Congleton	d			12 12															13 12	
Macclesfield	a			12 19			12 41							13 11					13 19	
	d			12 20			12 41							13 12					13 20	
Prestbury	d			12 24															13 24	
Adlington (Cheshire)	d			12 27															13 27	
Poynton	d			12 30															13 30	
Bramhall	d			12 33															13 33	
Cheadle Hulme	d			12 37					12 59							13 24			13 37	
Stockport	a	12 36		12 41	12 49		12 55	12 58	13 04	13 16				13 27		13 29	13 36		13 41	13 49
	d	12 37	12 41	12 42	12 50	12 53	12 56	12 58	13 04	13 17	13 12	13 21	13 26	13 28		13 29	13 37	13 41	13 42	13 50
Heaton Chapel	d			12 45					13 08		13 16					13 33			13 45	
Levenshulme	d			12 48					13 11		13 19					13 36			13 48	
Manchester Piccadilly 10	a	12 49	12 52	12 56	12 59	13 02	13 07	13 15	13 20	13 28	13 28	13 36	13 36	13 39	13 42	13 44	13 49	13 52	13 56	13 59
	d		12 54										13 37					13 54		
Manchester Oxford Road	a		12 56										13 40					13 56		
Deansgate	a		13 00															14 00		

		TP ◇1	VT ◇1	AW ◇	NT	VT ◇1	NT	NT	EM ◇	XC ◇1	NT	NT	VT ◇1	NT	NT	XC ◇1	TP ◇1	VT ◇1
London Euston 15 ⊖65	d		12 00			12 20							12 40					13 00
Birmingham New Street 12 68	d									12c57						13 31		
Wolverhampton 7 68	d									13 15						13 49		
Stafford 65,68	d									13 30						14 01		
Stoke-on-Trent 50,68	d		13 25			13 48				13 55					13 58	14 20		14 25
Longport 50	d																	
Kidsgrove 50	d														14 05			
Crewe 10 65	d			13 28							13 33	13 50	14 11					
Sandbach	d										13 40	13 57						
Holmes Chapel	d										13 44	14 02						
Goostrey	d											14 05						
Chelford	d											14 09						
Alderley Edge	d				13 49						13 53	14 13						
Wilmslow	d			13 46	13 52						13 57	14 17	14 27					
Styal	d																	
Manchester Airport ✈	a										14 04							
Handforth	d				13 55							14 20						
Congleton	d														14 12			
Macclesfield	a		13 41							14 11					14 19			14 41
	d		13 42							14 12					14 20			14 41
Prestbury	d														14 24			
Adlington (Cheshire)	d														14 27			
Poynton	d														14 30			
Bramhall	d														14 33			
Cheadle Hulme	d				13 59							14 24			14 37			
Stockport	a		13 55	13 58	14 04	14 16				14 27		14 29	14 36		14 41	14 49		14 55
	d	13 53	13 56	13 58	14 04	14 17	14 12	14 21	14 26	14 28		14 29	14 37	14 41	14 42	14 50	14 53	14 56
Heaton Chapel	d				14 08		14 16					14 33			14 45			
Levenshulme	d				14 11		14 19					14 36			14 48			
Manchester Piccadilly 10	a	14 02	14 07	14 15	14 20	14 28	14 28	14 36	14 36	14 39	14 42	14 44	14 49	14 52	14 56	14 59	15 02	15 07
	d								14 37					14 54				
Manchester Oxford Road	a								14 40					14 56				
Deansgate	a													15 00				

b arr. 1148

c arr. 1248

Stoke-on-Trent and Crewe - Manchester Airport, Stockport and Manchester

		AW ◇	NT	VT ◇1	NT	NT	EM ◇	XC ◇1	NT	NT	VT ◇1	NT	NT	XC ◇1	TP ◇1	VT ◇1	AW ◇
London Euston 15 ⊖65	d			13 20							13 40					14 00	
Birmingham New Street 12 68	d							13b57						14 31			
Wolverhampton 7 68	d							14 15						14 49			
Stafford 65,68	d							14 30						15 01			
Stoke-on-Trent 50,68	d			14 48				14 55					14 58	15 20		15 25	
Longport 50	d																
Kidsgrove 50	d												15 05				
Crewe 10 65	d	14 28							14 33	14 50	15 11						15 28
Sandbach	d								14 40	14 57							
Holmes Chapel	d								14 44	15 02							
Goostrey	d									15 05							
Chelford	d									15 09							
Alderley Edge	d		14 49						14 53	15 13							
Wilmslow	d	14 46	14 52						14 57	15 17	15 27						15 46
Styal	d																
Manchester Airport ✈	a								15 04								
Handforth	d		14 55							15 20							
Congleton	d												15 12				
Macclesfield	a							15 11					15 19			15 41	
	d							15 12					15 20			15 41	
Prestbury	d												15 24				
Adlington (Cheshire)	d												15 27				
Poynton	d												15 30				
Bramhall	d												15 33				
Cheadle Hulme	d		14 59							15 24			15 37				
Stockport	a	14 58	15 04					15 27		15 29	15 36		15 41	15 49		15 55	15 58
	d	14 58	15 04	15 17	15 12	15 21	15 26	15 28		15 29	15 37	15 41	15 42	15 50	15 53	15 56	15 58
Heaton Chapel	d		15 08		15 16					15 33			15 45				
Levenshulme	d		15 11		15 19					15 36			15 48				
Manchester Piccadilly 10	a	15 15	15 20	15 28	15 28	15 36	15 36	15 39	15 42	15 44	15 49	15 52	15 56	15 59	16 02	16 07	16 15
	d						15 37					15 54					
Manchester Oxford Road	a						15 40					15 56					
Deansgate	a											16 00					

		NT	VT ◇1	NT	NT	EM ◇	XC ◇1	NT	NT	VT ◇1	NT	NT	XC ◇1	TP ◇1	VT ◇1	AW ◇	NT	VT ◇1	NT
London Euston 15 ⊖65	d		14 20							14 40					15 00			15 20	
Birmingham New Street 12 68	d						14c57						15 31						
Wolverhampton 7 68	d						15 15						15 49						
Stafford 65,68	d						15 30						16 01						
Stoke-on-Trent 50,68	d		15 48				15 55					15 58	16 20		16 25			16 48	
Longport 50	d																		
Kidsgrove 50	d											16 05							
Crewe 10 65	d							15 33	15 50	16 12						16 28			
Sandbach	d							15 40	15 57										
Holmes Chapel	d							15 44	16 02										
Goostrey	d								16 05										
Chelford	d								16 09										
Alderley Edge	d	15 49						15 53	16 13								16 49		
Wilmslow	d	15 52						15 56	16 17	16 27						16 46	16 52		
Styal	d							15 59											
Manchester Airport ✈	a							16 04											
Handforth	d	15 55							16 20								16 55		
Congleton	d											16 12							
Macclesfield	a						16 11					16 19			16 41				
	d						16 12					16 20			16 41				
Prestbury	d											16 24							
Adlington (Cheshire)	d											16 27							
Poynton	d											16 30							
Bramhall	d											16 33							
Cheadle Hulme	d	15 59							16 24			16 37					16 59		
Stockport	a	16 04	16 16				16 27		16 29	16 36		16 41	16 49		16 54	16 58	17 04	17 16	
	d	16 04	16 17	16 12	16 21	16 26	16 28		16 29	16 37	16 41	16 42	16 50	16 53	16 55	16 58	17 04	17 17	17 12
Heaton Chapel	d	16 08		16 16					16 33			16 45					17 08		17 16
Levenshulme	d	16 11		16 19					16 36			16 48					17 11		17 19
Manchester Piccadilly 10	a	16 20	16 28	16 28	16 36	16 36	16 39	16 42	16 44	16 49	16 52	16 56	16 59	17 02	17 07	17 15	17 20	17 28	17 28
	d					16 37					16 54								
Manchester Oxford Road	a					16 40					16 56								
Deansgate	a										17 00								

b arr. 1348

c arr. 1448

Stoke-on-Trent and Crewe - Manchester Airport, Stockport and Manchester

Station			NT	EM	XC	NT	NT	VT	NT	XC	TP	VT	AW	NT	VT	NT	NT	EM	XC	NT
				◇	◇1			◇1		◇1	◇1	◇1	◇		◇1			◇	◇1	
London Euston 15	⊖65	d						15 40				16 00			16 20					
Birmingham New Street 12	68	d			15b57					16 31									16c57	
Wolverhampton 7	68	d			16 15					16 49									17 15	
Stafford	65,68	d			16 30					17 01									17 30	
Stoke-on-Trent	50,68	d			16 55				16 58	17 20		17 25			17 48				17 55	
Longport	50	d																		
Kidsgrove	50	d							17 05											
Crewe 10	65	d				16 33	16 50	17 11					17 28							17 33
Sandbach		d				16 40	16 57													17 40
Holmes Chapel		d				16 44	17 02													17 44
Goostrey		d					17 05													
Chelford		d					17 09													
Alderley Edge		d				16 53	17 13							17 49						17 53
Wilmslow		d				16 57	17 17	17 27					17 46	17 52						17 56
Styal		d																		17 59
Manchester Airport	✈	a				17 04														18 04
Handforth		d					17 20							17 55						
Congleton		d							17 12											
Macclesfield		a			17 11				17 19			17 41							18 11	
		d			17 12				17 20			17 41							18 12	
Prestbury		d							17 24											
Adlington (Cheshire)		d							17 27											
Poynton		d							17 30											
Bramhall		d							17 33											
Cheadle Hulme		d					17 24		17 37					17 59						
Stockport		a			17 27		17 29	17 36	17 41	17 49		17 55	17 58	18 04	18 16				18 27	
		d	17 21	17 26	17 28		17 29	17 37	17 42	17 50	17 53	17 56	17 58	18 04	18 17	18 12	18 21	18 26	18 28	
Heaton Chapel		d					17 33		17 45					18 08		18 16				
Levenshulme		d					17 36		17 48					18 11		18 19				
Manchester Piccadilly 10	⇌	a	17 36	17 37	17 39	17 42	17 44	17 49	17 56	17 59	18 02	18 07	18 15	18 20	18 28	18 28	18 36	18 36	18 39	18 42
		d		17 37														18 37		
Manchester Oxford Road		a		17 40														18 40		
Deansgate	⇌	a																		

Station			NT	VT	NT	NT	XC	TP	VT	AW	VT	NT	NT	NT	EM	XC	NT	VT	NT	XC
				◇1			◇1	◇1	◇1	■	◇1				◇	◇1		◇1		◇1
London Euston 15	⊖65	d		16 40					17 00		17 20							17 40		
Birmingham New Street 12	68	d					17 31									17e57				18 31
Wolverhampton 7	68	d					17 49									18 15				18 49
Stafford	65,68	d					18 01									18 30				19 01
Stoke-on-Trent	50,68	d				17 58	18 20		18 25		18 48					18 55			18 58	19 20
Longport	50	d																		
Kidsgrove	50	d				18 05													19 05	
Crewe 10	65	d	17 50	18 11						18 28			18 33				18 50	19 11		
Sandbach		d	17 57										18 40				18 57			
Holmes Chapel		d	18 02										18 44				19 02			
Goostrey		d	18 05														19 05			
Chelford		d	18 09														19 09			
Alderley Edge		d	18 13										18 53				19 13			
Wilmslow		d	18 17	18 27						18 46			18 56				19 17	19 27		
Styal		d																		
Manchester Airport	✈	a											19 04							
Handforth		d	18 20														19 20			
Congleton		d				18 12													19 12	
Macclesfield		a				18 19			18 41							19 11			19 19	
		d				18 20			18 41							19 12			19 20	
Prestbury		d				18 24													19 24	
Adlington (Cheshire)		d				18 27													19 27	
Poynton		d				18 30													19 30	
Bramhall		d				18 33													19 33	
Cheadle Hulme		d	18 24			18 37											19 24		19 37	
Stockport		a	18 29	18 36		18 41	18 49		18 55	18 58	19 16					19 27	19 29	19 36	19 41	19 49
		d	18 29	18 37	18 41	18 42	18 50	18 53	18 56	18 58	19 17	19 12		19 21	19 26	19 28	19 29	19 37	19 42	19 50
Heaton Chapel		d	18 33			18 45						19 16							19 45	
Levenshulme		d	18 36			18 48						19 19							19 48	
Manchester Piccadilly 10	⇌	a	18 44	18 49	18 52	18 56	18 59	19 02	19 07	19 15	19 28	19 28	19 31	19 35	19 36	19 40	19 43	19 49	19 56	19 59
		d			18 54								19 32		19 37					
Manchester Oxford Road		a			18 56								19 36		19 40					
Deansgate	⇌	a			19 00															

b arr. 1548 c arr. 1648 e arr. 1748

Table 84

Saturdays from 11 September

Stoke-on-Trent and Crewe - Manchester Airport, Stockport and Manchester

Station			TP	VT	AW	VT	NT	NT	NT	EM	XC	NT	VT	NT	XC	TP	VT	AW
			◇1	◇1	■	◇1				◇	◇1		◇1		◇1	◇1	◇1	■
London Euston 15	⊖65	d		18 00		18 20							18 40				19 00	
Birmingham New Street 12	68	d									18b57				19 31			
Wolverhampton 7	68	d									19 15				19 49			
Stafford	65,68	d									19 30				20 01			
Stoke-on-Trent	50,68	d		19 25		19 48					19 55			19 58	20 20		20 25	
Longport	50	d																
Kidsgrove	50	d												20 05				
Crewe 10	65	d			19 28							19 50	20 11					20 28
Sandbach		d										19 57						
Holmes Chapel		d										20 02						
Goostrey		d										20 05						
Chelford		d										20 09						
Alderley Edge		d										20 13						
Wilmslow		d			19 46			19 56				20 17	20 27					20 46
Styal		d																
Manchester Airport	✈	a						20 04										
Handforth		d										20 20						
Congleton		d												20 12				
Macclesfield		a		19 41							20 11			20 19	20 36		20 41	
		d		19 41							20 12			20 20	20 37		20 41	
Prestbury		d												20 24				
Adlington (Cheshire)		d												20 27				
Poynton		d												20 30				
Bramhall		d												20 33				
Cheadle Hulme		d										20 24		20 37				
Stockport		a		19 55	19 58	20 16					20 27	20 29	20 36	20 41	20 49		20 55	20 58
		d	19 53	19 56	19 58	20 17	20 12		20 21	20 26	20 28	20 29	20 37	20 42	20 50	20 53	20 56	20 58
Heaton Chapel		d					20 16							20 45				
Levenshulme		d					20 19							20 48				
Manchester Piccadilly 10	⇌	a	20 02	20 07	20 15	20 28	20 28	20 31	20 35	20 37	20 39	20 43	20 49	20 56	20 59	21 02	21 07	21 15
		d						20 32										
Manchester Oxford Road		a						20 36										
Deansgate	⇌	a																

Station			VT	NT	NT	EM	NT	XC	NT	VT	NT	XC	AW	NT	NT	XC	NT	VT
			◇1			◇		◇1		◇1		◇1	◇			◇1		◇1
London Euston 15	⊖65	d	19 20							19 40								20 20
Birmingham New Street 12	68	d						19c57				20 31				20e57		
Wolverhampton 7	68	d						20 16				20 49				21 17		
Stafford	65,68	d						20 30				21 01				21 30		
Stoke-on-Trent	50,68	d	20 48					20 55			20 58	21 21				21 55		22 05
Longport	50	d																
Kidsgrove	50	d									21 05							
Crewe 10	65	d							20 50	21 19			21 28				21 50	
Sandbach		d							20 57								21 57	
Holmes Chapel		d							21 02								22 02	
Goostrey		d							21 05								22 05	
Chelford		d							21 09								22 09	
Alderley Edge		d							21 13								22 13	
Wilmslow		d			20 56				21 17	21 34			21 46		21 55		22 17	
Styal		d																
Manchester Airport	✈	a			21 05										22 04			
Handforth		d							21 20								22 20	
Congleton		d									21 12							
Macclesfield		a						21 11			21 19	21 38				22 11		22 21
		d						21 12			21 20	21 39				22 12		22 21
Prestbury		d									21 24							
Adlington (Cheshire)		d									21 27							
Poynton		d									21 30							
Bramhall		d									21 33							
Cheadle Hulme		d							21 24		21 37						22 24	
Stockport		a	21 16					21 27	21 29	21 44	21 41	21 53	21 58			22 27	22 29	22 35
		d	21 17	21 12		21 20	21 21	21 28	21 29	21 45	21 42	21 54	21 58	22 12		22 28	22 29	22 36
Heaton Chapel		d		21 16							21 45			22 16				
Levenshulme		d		21 19							21 48			22 19				
Manchester Piccadilly 10	⇌	a	21 28	21 28	21 31	21 32	21 35	21 39	21 43	21 53	21 57	22 04	22 15	22 28	22 31	22 39	22 43	22 51
		d			21 32										22 32			
Manchester Oxford Road		a			21 36										22 36			
Deansgate	⇌	a																

b arr. 1848 c arr. 1948 e arr. 2048

Stoke-on-Trent and Crewe - Manchester Airport, Stockport and Manchester

		NT	NT	NT	XC	VT	NT	NT	NT	XC
					◇1	◇1				◇1
London Euston 15 ⊖65	d					21 00				
Birmingham New Street 12 68	d				21b57					22 31
Wolverhampton 7 68	d				22 16					22 49
Stafford 65,68	d				22 30	22 34				23 03
Stoke-on-Trent 50,68	d			22 18	22 51					23 21
Longport 50	d									
Kidsgrove 50	d			22 25						
Crewe 10 65	d					23 00			23 2	
Sandbach	d								23 9	
Holmes Chapel	d								23 24	
Goostrey	d								23 27	
Chelford	d								23 31	
Alderley Edge	d								23 35	
Wilmslow	d					23 17	23 15		23 39	
Styal	d									
Manchester Airport	a						23 23			
Handforth	d								23 42	
Congleton	d			22 32						
Macclesfield	a			22 39	23 07					23 38
	d			22 40	23 08					23 39
Prestbury	d			22 44						
Adlington (Cheshire)	d			22 47						
Poynton	d			22 50						
Bramhall	d			22 53						
Cheadle Hulme	d			22 56					2 46	
Stockport	a			23 01	23 21	23 25			2 51	23 53
	d	22 40	22 48	23 01	23 22	23 26		23 41	2 51	23 54
Heaton Chapel	d	22 44		23 05					2 55	
Levenshulme	d	22 47		23 08					2 58	
Manchester Piccadilly 10	a	22 53	23 00	23 16	23 32	23 38	23 51	23 54	[illegible] 07	00 10
	d	22 54								
Manchester Oxford Road	a	22 56								
Deansgate	a	23 00								

Sundays
until 11 July

		NT	TP	AW	NT	NT	NT	TP	AW	NT	NT	XC	VT	NT	TP	VT
			◇1					◇1				◇1	◇1		◇1	◇1
London Euston 15 ⊖65	d												08 10			08 20
Birmingham New Street 12 68	d											09 01				
Wolverhampton 7 68	d											09 19				
Stafford 65,68	d											09 34				10 14
Stoke-on-Trent 50,68	d															
Longport 50	d															
Kidsgrove 50	d															
Crewe 10 65	d			08 28					09 28			09 56	10 17			
Sandbach	d															
Holmes Chapel	d															
Goostrey	d															
Chelford	d															
Alderley Edge	d						09 26							10 19		
Wilmslow	d			08 47			09 30		09 47			10 13	10 32	10 23		10 47
Styal	d															
Manchester Airport	a															
Handforth	d						09 33							10 26		
Congleton	d															
Macclesfield	a															
	d															
Prestbury	d															
Adlington (Cheshire)	d															
Poynton	d															
Bramhall	d															
Cheadle Hulme	d						09 37							10 30		
Stockport	a						09 42					10 22	10 41	10 35		10 56
	d	08 22	08 31		09 [illegible]8	09 22	09 43	09 53		10 04	10 12	10 23	10 42	10 39	10 53	10 57
Heaton Chapel	d				09 [illegible]2		09 47			10 08				10 43		
Levenshulme	d				09 [illegible]5		09 50			10 11				10 46		
Manchester Piccadilly 10	a	08 33	08 42	09 11	09 [illegible]3	09 33	09 58	10 06	10 12	10 20	10 23	10 39	10 55	10 56	11 06	11 10
	d	08 35				09 35					10 26					
Manchester Oxford Road	a	08 37				09 37					10 28					
Deansgate	a	08 40				09 40					10 40					

A not 23 May

b arr. 2148

Stoke-on-Trent and Crewe - Manchester Airport, Stockport and Manchester

		AW	NT	NT	XC	EM	NT	AW	VT	TP	NT	NT	EM	XC	NT	TP	VT	AW	NT	NT	NT
		◇			◇1	◇		◇	◇1	◇1			◇	◇1		◇1	◇1	◇			
London Euston 15 ⊖65	d								09 20								10 20				
Birmingham New Street 12 68	d				10 00									11b01							
Wolverhampton 7 68	d				10 18									11 19							
Stafford 65,68	d				10 33				11 17					11 33			12 18				
Stoke-on-Trent 50,68	d																				
Longport 50	d																				
Kidsgrove 50	d																				
Crewe 10 65	d	10 27					11 02	11 22										12 28			
Sandbach	d	10 38					11 09														
Holmes Chapel	d						11 14														
Goostrey	d						11 17														
Chelford	d						11 21														
Alderley Edge	d			10 40			11 25								12 19					12 51	
Wilmslow	d	10 52		10 43	11 07		11 29	11 41	11 51					12 08	12 23		12 51	12 47		12 54	
Styal	d			10 47																12 58	
Manchester Airport	a			10 56																13 05	
Handforth	d						11 32								12 26						
Congleton	d																				
Macclesfield	a																				
	d																				
Prestbury	d																				
Adlington (Cheshire)	d																				
Poynton	d																				
Bramhall	d																				
Cheadle Hulme	d						11 36								12 30						
Stockport	a	11 01			11 16		11 41		12 00					12 20	12 37		12 59	12 58			
	d	11 01	11 07		11 23	11 26	11 41		12 01	11 53	12 12	12 21	12 26	12 27	12 37	12 53	13 00	12 59	13 12		13 22
Heaton Chapel	d		11 11				11 45				12 16				12 41				13 16		
Levenshulme	d		11 14				11 48				12 19				12 44				13 19		
Manchester Piccadilly 10	a	11 15	11 23	11 25	11 32	11 37	11 54	12 02	12 12	12 06	12 29	12 33	12 37	12 40	12 53	13 06	13 12	13 15	13 27	13 31	13 33
	d			11 26		11 38						12 35	12 38								13 35
Manchester Oxford Road	a			11 30		11 41						12 37	12 41								13 37
Deansgate	a											12 40									13 40

		EM	XC	NT	VT	TP	TP	AW	NT	VT	NT	EM	XC	VT	NT	XC	TP	VT
		◇	◇1		◇1	◇1	◇1	◇		◇1		◇	◇1	◇1		◇1	◇1	◇1
London Euston 15 ⊖65	d				11 20					12 15				12 35				12 55
Birmingham New Street 12 68	d		12c01										13e01			13 31		
Wolverhampton 7 68	d		12 20										13 19			13 49		
Stafford 65,68	d		12 34		13 02								13 34					
Stoke-on-Trent 50,68	d									13 50			13 57			14 21		14 26
Longport 50	d																	
Kidsgrove 50	d																	
Crewe 10 65	d			12 56	13 21			13 29						14 13				
Sandbach	d			13 03														
Holmes Chapel	d			13 08														
Goostrey	d			13 11														
Chelford	d			13 15														
Alderley Edge	d			13 19											14 19			
Wilmslow	d		13 09	13 23	13 37			1349						14 29	14 23			
Styal	d																	
Manchester Airport	a																	
Handforth	d			13 26											14 26			
Congleton	d																	
Macclesfield	a												14 14					14 42
	d												14 15					14 42
Prestbury	d																	
Adlington (Cheshire)	d																	
Poynton	d																	
Bramhall	d																	
Cheadle Hulme	d			13 30											14 30			
Stockport	a		13 19	13 37	13 45			14 00		14 18			14 28	14 38	14 37			14 56
	d	13 26	13 29	13 37	13 46		13 53	14 00	14 12	14 19	14 21	14 26	14 29	14 39	14 37		14 53	14 57
Heaton Chapel	d			13 41					14 16						14 41			
Levenshulme	d			13 44					14 19						14 44			
Manchester Piccadilly 10	a	13 37	13 40	13 53	13 59	14 05	14 06	14 19	14 27	14 30	14 33	14 37	14 40	14 51	14 53	14 57	15 06	15 09
	d	13 38				14 07					14 35	14 38						
Manchester Oxford Road	a	13 41				14 09					14 37	14 41						
Deansgate	a										14 40							

b arr. 1050

c arr. 1150

e arr. 1250

Stoke-on-Trent and Crewe - Manchester Airport, Stockport and Manchester

		NT	NT	EM	XC	VT	NT	TP	NT	VT	NT	EM	XC	VT	NT	XC	TP	VT
				◇	◇1	◇1		◇1		◇1		◇	◇1	◇1		◇1	◇1	◇1
London Euston ⊖65	d					11 20				12 15				12 35				12 55
Birmingham New Street 68	d				12b01								13c01			13 31		
Wolverhampton 68	d				12 20								13 19			13 49		
Stafford 65,68	d				12 34								13 34					
Stoke-on-Trent 50,68	d				12 53	13 09				13 50			13 57			14 21		14 26
Longport 50	d																	
Kidsgrove 50	d																	
Crewe 65	d						12 56							14 13				
Sandbach	d						13 03											
Holmes Chapel	d						13 08											
Goostrey	d						13 11											
Chelford	d						13 15											
Alderley Edge	d	12 51					13 19								14 19			
Wilmslow	d	12 54					13 23							14 29	14 23			
Styal	d	12 58																
Manchester Airport	a	13 05																
Handforth	d						13 26								14 26			
Congleton	d																	
Macclesfield	a				13 09	13 24							14 14					14 42
	d				13 11	13 25							14 15					14 42
Prestbury	d																	
Adlington (Cheshire)	d																	
Poynton	d																	
Bramhall	d																	
Cheadle Hulme	d						13 30								14 30			
Stockport	a				13 28	13 38	13 37			14 18			14 28	14 38	14 37			14 56
	d		13 22	13 26	13 29	13 39	13 37	13 53	14 12	14 19	14 21	14 26	14 29	14 39	14 37		14 53	14 57
Heaton Chapel	d						13 41		14 16						14 41			
Levenshulme	d						13 44		14 19						14 44			
Manchester Piccadilly	a	13 31	13 33	13 37	13 40	13 52	13 53	14 06	14 27	14 30	14 33	14 37	14 40	14 51	14 53	14 57	15 06	15 09
	d		13 35	13 38							14 35	14 38						
Manchester Oxford Road	a		13 37	13 41							14 37	14 41						
Deansgate	a		13 40								14 40							

		AW	NT	VT	NT	NT	EM	XC	VT	NT	XC	TP	VT	AW	NT	VT	NT	EM	XC
		◇		◇1			◇	◇1	◇1		◇1	◇1	◇1	◇		◇1		◇	◇1
London Euston ⊖65	d			13 15					13 35				13 55			14 15			
Birmingham New Street 68	d							14f01			14 31								15g01
Wolverhampton 68	d							14 19			14 49								15 19
Stafford 65,68	d							14 34											15 34
Stoke-on-Trent 50,68	d			14 50				14 57			15 21		15 26			15 50			15 57
Longport 50	d																		
Kidsgrove 50	d																		
Crewe 65	d	14e28							15 13	14 56				15 28					
Sandbach	d									15 03									
Holmes Chapel	d									15 08									
Goostrey	d									15 11									
Chelford	d									15 15									
Alderley Edge	d				14 51					15 19									
Wilmslow	d	14 47			14 54				15 29	15 23				15 47					
Styal	d				14 58														
Manchester Airport	a				15 05														
Handforth	d									15 26									
Congleton	d																		
Macclesfield	a							15 14					15 42						16 14
	d							15 15					15 42						16 15
Prestbury	d																		
Adlington (Cheshire)	d																		
Poynton	d																		
Bramhall	d																		
Cheadle Hulme	d									15 30									
Stockport	a	14 58		15 18				15 28	15 38	15 37			15 56	15 58		16 18			16 28
	d	14 58	15 12	15 19		15 22	15 26	15 29	15 39	15 37		15 53	15 57	15 58	16 12	16 19	16 21	16 26	16 29
Heaton Chapel	d		15 16							15 41					16 16				
Levenshulme	d		15 19							15 44					16 19				
Manchester Piccadilly	a	15 15	15 27	15 30	15 32	15 33	15 37	15 40	15 51	15 53	15 59	16 06	16 09	16 15	16 27	16 30	16 33	16 37	16 40
	d					15 35	15 38										16 35	16 38	
Manchester Oxford Road	a					15 37	15 41										16 37	16 41	
Deansgate	a					15 40											16 40		

b arr. 1150
c arr. 1250
e arr. 1422
f arr. 1348
g arr. 1448

Table 84

Sundays
17 July to 05 September

Stoke-on-Trent and Crewe - Manchester Airport, Stockport and Manchester

		VT	NT	NT	XC	TP	VT	AW	NT	VT	NT	NT	EM	XC	VT	NT	XC	TP	VT
		◇1			◇1	◇1	◇1	■		◇1			◇	◇1	◇1		◇1	◇1	◇1
London Euston ⊖65	d	14 35					14 55			15 15					15 35				15 55
Birmingham New Street 68	d				15 31									16b01			16 31		
Wolverhampton 68	d				15 49									16 19			16 49		
Stafford 65,68	d													16 36					
Stoke-on-Trent 50,68	d			16 01	16 21		16 25			16 50				16 57			17 21		17 26
Longport 50	d																		
Kidsgrove 50	d			16 08															
Crewe 65	d	16 13						16 31							17 13	16 56			
Sandbach	d															17 03			
Holmes Chapel	d															17 08			
Goostrey	d															17 11			
Chelford	d															17 15			
Alderley Edge	d		16 19								16 51					17 19			
Wilmslow	d	16 29	16 23					16 49			16 54				17 29	17 23			
Styal	d										16 58								
Manchester Airport	a										17 05								
Handforth	d		16 26													17 26			
Congleton	d			16 15															
Macclesfield	a			16 22			16 42							17 14					17 42
	d			16 23			16 42							17 15					17 42
Prestbury	d			16 27															
Adlington (Cheshire)	d			16 30															
Poynton	d			16 33															
Bramhall	d			16 36															
Cheadle Hulme	d		16 30	16 39												17 30			
Stockport	a	16 38	16 37	16 44			16 56	16 58		17 18				17 28	17 38	17 37			17 56
	d	16 39	16 37	16 44		16 53	16 57	16 58	17 12	17 19		17 22	17 27	17 29	17 39	17 37		17 53	17 57
Heaton Chapel	d		16 41						17 16							17 41			
Levenshulme	d		16 44						17 19							17 44			
Manchester Piccadilly	a	16 51	16 53	16 58	16 59	17 06	17 09	17 15	17 27	17 30	17 31	17 33	17 37	17 40	17 51	17 53	17 56	18 06	18 09
	d											17 35	17 38						
Manchester Oxford Road	a											17 37	17 41						
Deansgate	a											17 40							

		AW	NT	VT	NT	EM	XC	VT	NT	XC	VT	AW	NT	VT	NT	NT	EM	VT	NT
		■		◇1		◇	◇1	◇1		◇1	◇1	■		◇1			◇	◇1	
London Euston ⊖65	d			16 15				16 35			16 55			17 15				17 35	
Birmingham New Street 68	d						17c01			17 31									
Wolverhampton 68	d						17 19			17 49									
Stafford 65,68	d						17 36												
Stoke-on-Trent 50,68	d			17 50			17 57			18 21	18 26			18 50					
Longport 50	d																		
Kidsgrove 50	d																		
Crewe 65	d	17 28						18 13				18 28						19 13	18 56
Sandbach	d																		19 03
Holmes Chapel	d																		19 08
Goostrey	d																		19 11
Chelford	d																		19 15
Alderley Edge	d								18 19						18 51				19 19
Wilmslow	d	17 45						18 29	18 23			18 47			18 54			19 29	19 23
Styal	d														18 58				
Manchester Airport	a														19 05				
Handforth	d								18 26										19 26
Congleton	d																		
Macclesfield	a						18 14				18 42								
	d						18 15				18 42								
Prestbury	d																		
Adlington (Cheshire)	d																		
Poynton	d																		
Bramhall	d																		
Cheadle Hulme	d								18 30										19 30
Stockport	a	17 58		18 18			18 28	18 38	18 37		18 56	18 58		19 18				19 38	19 37
	d	17 58	18 12	18 19	18 21	18 26	18 29	18 39	18 37		18 57	18 58	19 12	19 19		19 22	19 26	19 39	19 37
Heaton Chapel	d		18 16						18 41				19 16						19 41
Levenshulme	d		18 19						18 44				19 19						19 44
Manchester Piccadilly	a	18 15	18 27	18 30	18 33	18 37	18 40	18 51	18 53	18 56	19 09	19 15	19 27	19 30	19 31	19 33	19 37	19 51	19 53
	d				18 35	18 38										19 35	19 38		
Manchester Oxford Road	a				18 37	18 41										19 37	19 41		
Deansgate	a				18 40											19 40			

b arr. 1548
c arr. 1648

Stoke-on-Trent and Crewe - Manchester Airport, Stockport and Manchester

Sundays
17 July to 05 September

	XC	TP	VT	AW	NT	VT	NT	EM	XC	VT	NT	NT	AW	XC	VT	NT	VT	NT	NT	EM
	◇1	◇1	◇1			◇1		◇	◇1	◇1				◇1	◇1		◇1			◇
London Euston ⊖65 d			17 55			18 15				18 35					18 55		19 15			
Birmingham New Street 68 d	18 31								19b01					19 31						
Wolverhampton 68 d	18 49								19 19					19 49						
Stafford 65,68 d									19 38											
Stoke-on-Trent 50,68 d	19 21		19 26			19 50			19 57			20 01		20 21	20 26		20 50			
Longport 50 d																				
Kidsgrove 50 d												20 08								
Crewe 65 d				19 28						20 13			20 28							
Sandbach d																				
Holmes Chapel d																				
Goostrey d																				
Chelford d																				
Alderley Edge d											20 19							20 51		
Wilmslow d				19 47						20 29	20 23		20 46					20 54		
Styal d																		20 58		
Manchester Airport a																		21 05		
Handforth d											20 26									
Congleton d												20 15								
Macclesfield a			19 42						20 14			20 22			20 42					
d			19 42						20 15			20 23			20 42					
Prestbury d												20 27								
Adlington (Cheshire) d												20 30								
Poynton d												20 33								
Bramhall d												20 36								
Cheadle Hulme d											20 30	20 39								
Stockport a			19 56	19 58		20 18			20 28	20 38	20 37	20 44	20 57		20 56		21 18			
d		19 53	19 57	19 58	20 12	20 19	20 21	20 26	20 29	20 39	20 37	20 44	20 57		20 57	21 12	21 19		21 22	21 24
Heaton Chapel d					20 16						20 41					21 16				
Levenshulme d					20 19						20 44					21 19				
Manchester Piccadilly a	19 58	20 06	20 09	20 15	20 27	20 30	20 33	20 38	20 40	20 51	20 53	20 58	21 14	21 00	21 09	21 27	21 30	21 31	21 33	21 36
d							20 35												21 35	
Manchester Oxford Road a							20 37												21 37	
Deansgate a							20 40												21 40	

	XC	VT	NT	XC	TP	VT	AW	NT	VT	NT	XC	NT	VT	NT	NT	NT	NT	XC
	◇1	◇1		◇1	◇1	◇1			◇1		◇1		◇1					◇1
London Euston ⊖65 d		19 35				19 55			20 15				20 35					
Birmingham New Street 68 d	20c01			20 31							21f01							22g01
Wolverhampton 68 d	20 19			20 49							21 19							22 19
Stafford 65,68 d	20 38										21 38		22 04					22 38
Stoke-on-Trent 50,68 d	20 57			21 21		21 26			21 50		21 57						22 39	22 57
Longport 50 d																		
Kidsgrove 50 d																	22 46	
Crewe 65 d		21 14	20 56				21e28						22 23					
Sandbach d			21 03															
Holmes Chapel d			21 08															
Goostrey d			21 11															
Chelford d			21 15															
Alderley Edge d			21 19									22 19				22 51		
Wilmslow d		21 30	21 23				21 47					22 23	22 38			22 54		
Styal d																22 58		
Manchester Airport a																23 05		
Handforth d			21 26									22 26						
Congleton d																	22 53	
Macclesfield a	21 15					21 42					22 14						23 00	23 12
d	21 15					21 42					22 15						23 01	23 13
Prestbury d																	23 05	
Adlington (Cheshire) d																	23 08	
Poynton d																	23 11	
Bramhall d																	23 14	
Cheadle Hulme d			21 30									22 30					23 17	
Stockport a	21 28	21 39	21 37			21 56	21 58		22 18		22 28	22 37	22 48				23 22	23 27
d	21 29	21 40	21 37		21 53	21 57	21 58	22 12	22 19	22 21	22 29	22 37	22 49	23 12	23 16		23 23	23 28
Heaton Chapel d			21 41					22 16				22 41		23 16				
Levenshulme d			21 44					22 19				22 44		23 19				
Manchester Piccadilly a	21 40	21 52	21 53	21 56	22 06	22 09	22 15	22 27	22 30	22 33	22 40	22 53	23 00	23 27	23 29	23 32	23 37	23 41
d										22 35								
Manchester Oxford Road a										22 37								
Deansgate a										22 40								

b arr. 1848
c arr. 1948
e arr. 2121
f arr. 2048
g arr. 2148

Stoke-on-Trent and Crewe - Manchester Airport, Stockport and Manchester

Sundays
17 July to 05 September

	NT	VT	VT
		◇1	◇1
London Euston ⊖65 d		21 24	21 50
Birmingham New Street 68 d			
Wolverhampton 68 d			
Stafford 65,68 d			23s54
Stoke-on-Trent 50,68 d		23 29	
Longport 50 d			
Kidsgrove 50 d			
Crewe 65 d	22 56		00s13
Sandbach d	23 03		
Holmes Chapel d	23 08		
Goostrey d	23 11		
Chelford d	23 15		
Alderley Edge d	23 19		
Wilmslow d	23 23		
Styal d			
Manchester Airport a			
Handforth d	23 26		
Congleton d			
Macclesfield a		23 45	
d		23 47	
Prestbury d			
Adlington (Cheshire) d			
Poynton d			
Bramhall d			
Cheadle Hulme d	23 30		
Stockport a	23 35	23 59	00s40
d	23 37	00 01	00s41
Heaton Chapel d	23 41		
Levenshulme d	23 44		
Manchester Piccadilly a	23 53	00 13	00 53
d			
Manchester Oxford Road a			
Deansgate a			

Sundays
from 12 September

	NT	TP	AW	NT	NT	NT	TP	AW	NT	NT	XC	VT	NT	VT	AW	NT	NT	NT	XC
		◇1					◇1				◇1	◇1		◇1	◇				◇1
London Euston ⊖65 d												08 10		08 20					
Birmingham New Street 68 d											09 01								10 00
Wolverhampton 68 d											09 19								10 18
Stafford 65,68 d											09 34								10 33
Stoke-on-Trent 50,68 d														10 21					10 52
Longport 50 d																			
Kidsgrove 50 d																			
Crewe 65 d			08 28					09 28			09 56	10 17			10 28				
Sandbach d																			
Holmes Chapel d																			
Goostrey d																			
Chelford d																			
Alderley Edge d						09 19							10 19					10 50	
Wilmslow d			08 47			09 23		09 47			10 13	10 32	10 23		10 47			10 53	
Styal d																		10 57	
Manchester Airport a																		11 04	
Handforth d						09 26							10 26						
Congleton d																			
Macclesfield a														10 36					11 08
d														10 38					11 09
Prestbury d																			
Adlington (Cheshire) d																			
Poynton d																			
Bramhall d																			
Cheadle Hulme d						09 30							10 30						
Stockport a						09 38					10 21	10 41	10 35	10 51	10 58				11 22
d	00 02	08 31		09 08	09 22	09 40	09 53		10 08	10 19	10 22	10 42	10 39	10 52	10 58	11 11	11 12		11 23
Heaton Chapel d				09 12		09 44			10 12				10 43				11 16		
Levenshulme d				09 15		09 47			10 15				10 46				11 19		
Manchester Piccadilly a	00 15	08 42	09 11	09 23	09 33	09 54	10 04	10 13	10 23	10 31	10 34	10 54	10 56	11 04	11 15	11 23	11 25	11 29	11 34
d					09 35					10 35							11 27	11 30	
Manchester Oxford Road a					09 37					10 37							11 29	11 34	
Deansgate a					09 40					10 40							11 40		

Table 84

Sundays from 12 September

Stoke-on-Trent and Crewe - Manchester Airport, Stockport and Manchester

	EM	NT	AW	VT	NT	NT	XC	EM	NT	TP	VT	AW	NT	NT	NT	EM	XC	VT	NT
	◇		◇ [buffet]	◇1 [trolley]			◇1 [buffet]	◇		◇1	◇1 [trolley]	◇ [buffet]				◇	◇1 [buffet]	◇1 [trolley]	
London Euston [15] ⊖65 d				09 20							10 20							11 20	
Birmingham New Street [12] 68 d							11b01										12c01		
Wolverhampton [7] 68 ⇌ d							11 19										12 20		
Stafford 65,68 d							11 33										12 34		
Stoke-on-Trent 50,68 d				11 24			11 52				12 25						12 53	13 09	
Longport 50 d																			
Kidsgrove 50 d																			
Crewe [10] 65 d		10 56	11 22									12 28							12 56
Sandbach d		11 03																	13 03
Holmes Chapel d		11 08																	13 08
Goostrey d		11 11																	13 11
Chelford d		11 15																	13 15
Alderley Edge d		11 19							12 19					12 51					13 19
Wilmslow d		11 23	11 41						12 23			12 47		12 54					13 23
Styal d														12 58					
Manchester Airport ✈ a														13 05					
Handforth d		11 26							12 26										13 26
Congleton d																			
Macclesfield a				11 39			12 09				12 40						13 09	13 24	
d				11 40			12 10				12 41						13 11	13 25	
Prestbury d																			
Adlington (Cheshire) d																			
Poynton d																			
Bramhall d																			
Cheadle Hulme d		11 30							12 30										13 30
Stockport a		11 37		11 53			12 22		12 37		12 54	12 58					13 28	13 38	13 37
d	11 26	11 37		11 54	12 10	12 15	12 22	12 26	12 37	12 53	12 55	12 58	13 12		13 22	13 26	13 29	13 39	13 37
Heaton Chapel d		11 41			12 15				12 41				13 16						13 41
Levenshulme d		11 44			12 18				12 44				13 19						13 44
Manchester Piccadilly [10] ⇌ a	11 37	11 53	12 02	12 06	12 25	12 28	12 34	12 37	12 53	13 02	13 09	13 15	13 27	13 31	13 33	13 37	13 40	13 52	13 53
d	11 38					12 30		12 38							13 35	13 38			
Manchester Oxford Road a	11 41					12 32		12 41							13 37	13 41			
Deansgate ⇌ a						12 40									13 40				

	TP	AW	NT	VT	NT	XC	VT	NT	XC	TP	VT	AW	NT	VT	NT	NT	EM	XC
	◇1	◇ [buffet]		◇1 [trolley]		◇1 [buffet]	◇1 [trolley]		◇1 [buffet]	◇1	◇1 [trolley]	◇ [buffet]		◇1 [trolley]			◇	◇1 [buffet]
London Euston [15] ⊖65 d				12 15			12 35				12 55			13 15				
Birmingham New Street [12] 68 d						13e01			13 31									14g01
Wolverhampton [7] 68 ⇌ d						13 19			13 49									14 19
Stafford 65,68 d						13 34												14 34
Stoke-on-Trent 50,68 d				13 50		13 57			14 21		14 26			14 50				14 57
Longport 50 d																		
Kidsgrove 50 d																		
Crewe [10] 65 d		13 29					14 13					14f28						
Sandbach d																		
Holmes Chapel d																		
Goostrey d																		
Chelford d																		
Alderley Edge d								14 19							14 51			
Wilmslow d		13 49					14 29	14 23				14 47			14 54			
Styal d															14 58			
Manchester Airport ✈ a															15 05			
Handforth d								14 26										
Congleton d																		
Macclesfield a						14 14					14 42							15 14
d						14 15					14 42							15 15
Prestbury d																		
Adlington (Cheshire) d																		
Poynton d																		
Bramhall d																		
Cheadle Hulme d								14 30										
Stockport a		14 00		14 18		14 28	14 38	14 37			14 56	14 58		15 18				15 28
d	13 53	14 00	14 12	14 19	14 21	14 29	14 39	14 37		14 53	14 57	14 58	15 12	15 19		15 22	15 26	15 29
Heaton Chapel d			14 16					14 41					15 16					
Levenshulme d			14 19					14 44					15 19					
Manchester Piccadilly [10] ⇌ a	14 06	14 17	14 27	14 30	14 33	14 40	14 51	14 53	14 57	15 06	15 09	15 15	15 27	15 30	15 32	15 33	15 37	15 40
d					14 35											15 35	15 38	
Manchester Oxford Road a					14 37											15 37	15 41	
Deansgate ⇌ a					14 40											15 40		

b arr. 1050
c arr. 1150
e arr. 1250
f arr. 1422
g arr. 1348

Table 84

Sundays from 12 September

Stoke-on-Trent and Crewe - Manchester Airport, Stockport and Manchester

	VT	NT	XC	TP	VT	AW	NT	VT	NT	EM	XC	VT	NT	NT	XC	TP	VT	AW	NT
	◇1 [trolley]		◇1 [buffet]	◇1	◇1 [trolley]	◇ [buffet]		◇1 [trolley]		◇	◇1 [buffet]	◇1 [trolley]			◇1 [buffet]	◇1	◇1 [trolley]	1 [buffet]	
London Euston [15] ⊖65 d	13 35				13 55			14 15				14 35					14 55		
Birmingham New Street [12] 68 d			14 31								15b01				15 31				
Wolverhampton [7] 68 ⇌ d			14 49								15 19				15 49				
Stafford 65,68 d											15 34								
Stoke-on-Trent 50,68 d			15 21		15 26			15 50			15 57			16 01	16 21		16 25		
Longport 50 d																			
Kidsgrove 50 d														16 08					
Crewe [10] 65 d	15 13	14 56				15 28						16 13						16 31	
Sandbach d		15 03																	
Holmes Chapel d		15 08																	
Goostrey d		15 11																	
Chelford d		15 15																	
Alderley Edge d		15 19											16 19						
Wilmslow d	15 29	15 23				15 47						16 29	16 23					16 49	
Styal d																			
Manchester Airport ✈ a																			
Handforth d		15 26											16 26						
Congleton d														16 15					
Macclesfield a					15 42						16 14			16 22			16 42		
d					15 42						16 15			16 23			16 42		
Prestbury d														16 27					
Adlington (Cheshire) d														16 30					
Poynton d														16 33					
Bramhall d														16 36					
Cheadle Hulme d		15 30											16 30	16 39					
Stockport a	15 38	15 37			15 56	15 58		16 18			16 28	16 38	16 37	16 44			16 56	16 58	
d	15 39	15 37		15 53	15 57	15 58	16 12	16 19	16 21	16 26	16 29	16 39	16 37	16 44		16 53	16 57	16 58	17 12
Heaton Chapel d		15 41					16 16						16 41						17 16
Levenshulme d		15 44					16 19						16 44						17 19
Manchester Piccadilly [10] ⇌ a	15 51	15 53	16 00	16 06	16 09	16 15	16 27	16 30	16 33	16 37	16 40	16 51	16 53	16 58	16 59	17 06	17 09	17 15	17 27
d									16 35	16 38									
Manchester Oxford Road a									16 37	16 41									
Deansgate ⇌ a									16 40										

	VT	NT	NT	EM	XC	VT	NT	XC	TP	VT	AW	NT	VT	NT	EM	XC	VT	NT
	◇1 [trolley]			◇	◇1 [buffet]	◇1 [trolley]		◇1 [buffet]	◇1	◇1 [trolley]	1 [buffet]		◇1 [trolley]		◇	◇1 [buffet]	◇1 [trolley]	
London Euston [15] ⊖65 d	15 15					15 35				15 55			16 15				16 35	
Birmingham New Street [12] 68 d					16c01			16 31								17e01		
Wolverhampton [7] 68 ⇌ d					16 19			16 49								17 19		
Stafford 65,68 d					16 36											17 36		
Stoke-on-Trent 50,68 d	16 50				16 57			17 21		17 26			17 50			17 57		
Longport 50 d																		
Kidsgrove 50 d																		
Crewe [10] 65 d						17 13	16 56				17 28						18 13	
Sandbach d							17 03											
Holmes Chapel d							17 08											
Goostrey d							17 11											
Chelford d							17 15											
Alderley Edge d		16 51					17 19											18 19
Wilmslow d		16 54				17 29	17 23				17 45						18 29	18 23
Styal d		16 58																
Manchester Airport ✈ a		17 05																
Handforth d							17 26											18 26
Congleton d																		
Macclesfield a					17 14					17 42						18 14		
d					17 15					17 42						18 15		
Prestbury d																		
Adlington (Cheshire) d																		
Poynton d																		
Bramhall d																		
Cheadle Hulme d							17 30											18 30
Stockport a	17 18				17 28	17 38	17 37			17 56	17 58		18 18			18 28	18 38	18 37
d	17 19		17 22	17 27	17 29	17 39	17 37		17 53	17 57	17 58	18 12	18 19	18 21	18 26	18 29	18 39	18 37
Heaton Chapel d							17 41					18 16						18 41
Levenshulme d							17 44					18 19						18 44
Manchester Piccadilly [10] ⇌ a	17 30	17 31	17 33	17 37	17 40	17 51	17 53	17 56	18 06	18 09	18 15	18 27	18 30	18 33	18 37	18 40	18 51	18 53
d			17 35	17 38										18 35	18 38			
Manchester Oxford Road a			17 37	17 41										18 37	18 41			
Deansgate ⇌ a			17 40											18 40				

b arr. 1448
c arr. 1548
e arr. 1648

Table 84

Sundays from 12 September

Stoke-on-Trent and Crewe - Manchester Airport, Stockport and Manchester

		XC	VT	AW	NT	VT	NT	NT	EM	VT	NT	XC	TP	VT	AW	NT	VT	NT	EM
		◇1	◇1	■		◇1			◇	◇1		◇1	◇1	◇1	■		◇1		◇
London Euston 15 ⊖65	d		16 55			17 15				17 35				17 55			18 15		
Birmingham New Street 12 68	d	17 31										18 31							
Wolverhampton 7 68	d	17 49										18 49							
Stafford 65,68	d																		
Stoke-on-Trent 50,68	d	18 21	18 26			18 50						19 21		19 26			19 50		
Longport 50	d																		
Kidsgrove 50	d																		
Crewe 10 65	d			18 28						19 13	18 56				19 28				
Sandbach	d										19 03								
Holmes Chapel	d										19 08								
Goostrey	d										19 11								
Chelford	d										19 15								
Alderley Edge	d						18 51				19 19								
Wilmslow	d			18 47			18 54			19 29	19 23				19 47				
Styal	d						18 58												
Manchester Airport ✈	a						19 05												
Handforth	d										19 26								
Congleton	d																		
Macclesfield	a		18 42											19 42					
	d		18 42											19 42					
Prestbury	d																		
Adlington (Cheshire)	d																		
Poynton	d																		
Bramhall	d																		
Cheadle Hulme	d										19 30								
Stockport	a		18 56	18 58		19 18				19 38	19 37			19 56	19 58		20 18		
	d		18 57	18 58	19 12	19 19		19 22	19 26	19 39	19 37		19 53	19 57	19 58	20 12	20 19	20 21	20 26
Heaton Chapel	d				19 16						19 41					20 16			
Levenshulme	d				19 19						19 44					20 19			
Manchester Piccadilly 10	a	18 56	19 09	19 15	19 27	19 30	19 31	19 33	19 37	19 51	19 53	19 58	20 06	20 09	20 15	20 27	20 30	20 33	20 38
	d							19 35	19 38									20 35	
Manchester Oxford Road	a							19 37	19 41									20 37	
Deansgate	a							19 40										20 40	

		XC	VT	NT	NT	AW	XC	VT	VT	NT	NT	EM	XC	VT	NT	XC	TP	VT	AW
		◇1	◇1			■	◇1	◇1	◇1			◇	◇1	◇1		◇1	◇1	◇1	■
London Euston 15 ⊖65	d		18 35					18 55	19 15					19 35				19 55	
Birmingham New Street 12 68	d	19b01					19 31						20c01			20 31			
Wolverhampton 7 68	d	19 19					19 49						20 19			20 49			
Stafford 65,68	d	19 38											20 38						
Stoke-on-Trent 50,68	d	19 57			20 01		20 21	20 26	20 50				20 57			21 21		21 26	
Longport 50	d																		
Kidsgrove 50	d				20 08														
Crewe 10 65	d		20 13			20 28								21 14	20 56				21e28
Sandbach	d														21 03				
Holmes Chapel	d														21 08				
Goostrey	d														21 11				
Chelford	d														21 15				
Alderley Edge	d			20 19						20 51					21 19				
Wilmslow	d		20 29	20 23		20 46				20 54				21 30	21 23				21 47
Styal	d									20 58									
Manchester Airport ✈	a									21 05									
Handforth	d			20 26											21 26				
Congleton	d				20 15														
Macclesfield	a	20 14			20 22			20 42					21 15					21 42	
	d	20 15			20 23			20 42					21 15					21 42	
Prestbury	d				20 27														
Adlington (Cheshire)	d				20 30														
Poynton	d				20 33														
Bramhall	d				20 36														
Cheadle Hulme	d			20 30	20 39										21 30				
Stockport	a	20 28	20 38	20 37	20 44	20 57		20 56	21 18				21 28	21 39	21 37			21 56	21 58
	d	20 29	20 39	20 37	20 44	20 57		20 57	21 19		21 22	21 24	21 29	21 40	21 37		21 53	21 57	21 58
Heaton Chapel	d			20 41											21 41				
Levenshulme	d			20 44											21 44				
Manchester Piccadilly 10	a	20 40	20 51	20 53	20 58	21 14	21 00	21 09	21 30	21 31	21 33	21 36	21 40	21 52	21 53	21 56	22 06	22 09	22 15
	d										21 35								
Manchester Oxford Road	a										21 37								
Deansgate	a										21 40								

b arr. 1848 c arr. 1948 e arr. 2121

Table 84

Sundays from 12 September

Stoke-on-Trent and Crewe - Manchester Airport, Stockport and Manchester

		NT	VT	NT	XC	NT	VT	NT	NT	NT	NT	XC	NT	VT	VT
			◇1		◇1		◇1					◇1		◇1	◇1
London Euston 15 ⊖65	d		20 15				20 35							21 24	21 50
Birmingham New Street 12 68	d				21b01							22c01			
Wolverhampton 7 68	d				21 19							22 19			
Stafford 65,68	d				21 38		22 04					22 38			23s54
Stoke-on-Trent 50,68	d		21 50		21 57						22 39	22 57		23 29	
Longport 50	d														
Kidsgrove 50	d										22 46				
Crewe 10 65	d						22 23						22 56		00s13
Sandbach	d												23 03		
Holmes Chapel	d												23 08		
Goostrey	d												23 11		
Chelford	d												23 15		
Alderley Edge	d					22 19				22 51			23 19		
Wilmslow	d					22 23	22 38			22 54			23 23		
Styal	d									22 58					
Manchester Airport ✈	a									23 05					
Handforth	d					22 26							23 26		
Congleton	d										22 53				
Macclesfield	a				22 14						23 00	23 12		23 45	
	d				22 15						23 01	23 13		23 47	
Prestbury	d										23 05				
Adlington (Cheshire)	d										23 08				
Poynton	d										23 11				
Bramhall	d										23 14				
Cheadle Hulme	d					22 30					23 17		23 30		
Stockport	a		22 18		22 28	22 37	22 48				23 22	23 27	23 35	23 59	00s40
	d	22 12	22 19	22 21	22 29	22 37	22 49	23 12	23 16		23 23	23 28	23 37	00 01	00s41
Heaton Chapel	d	22 16				22 41		23 16					23 41		
Levenshulme	d	22 19				22 44		23 19					23 44		
Manchester Piccadilly 10	a	22 27	22 30	22 33	22 40	22 53	23 00	23 27	23 29	23 32	23 37	23 41	23 53	00 13	00 53
	d			22 35											
Manchester Oxford Road	a			22 37											
Deansgate	a			22 40											

b arr. 2048 c arr. 2148

Table 84

Mondays to Fridays

Manchester, Stockport and Manchester Airport - Crewe and Stoke-on-Trent

				NT	TP	AW	XC	VT	NT	TP		NT	VT	NT	XC	NT	NT	VT	TP MO	NT		NT	NT	VT	AW
					◇1	A	◇1 ⊥	◇1 ⊠		◇1			◇1 ⊠		◇1 ⊥			◇1 ⊠	◇1	1				◇1 ⊠	◇ ⊥
Deansgate	d																								
Manchester Oxford Road	d																								
Manchester Piccadilly 10	a																								
	d			04 15	04 44	04 49	05 00	05 05	05 35	05 44		05 50	05 55	05 58	06 00		06 06	06 10	06 12	06 15		06 17	06 21	06 27	06 30
Levenshulme	d																06 11						06 28		
Heaton Chapel	d																06 14						06 31		
Stockport	a							05 12		05 52		05 59	06 02		06 07		06 18	06 17				06 27	06 34	06 34	06 38
	d							05 13					06 03		06 08		06 19	06 18					06 35	06 35	06 39
Cheadle Hulme	d																06 26								
Bramhall	d																								
Poynton	d																								
Adlington (Cheshire)	d																								
Prestbury	d																								
Macclesfield	a																	06 30						06 47	
	d															06 03		06 31						06 48	
Congleton	d															06 10									
Handforth	d																06 30								
Manchester Airport ✈	d			04a30	05a00	05a04			06b05					06a14					06a29	06a39					
Styal	d																								
Wilmslow	d								06c17				06 11				06 34								06 47
Alderley Edge	d								06 20								06 37								
Chelford	d								06 24																
Goostrey	d								06 29																
Holmes Chapel	d								06 32								06 47								
Sandbach	d								06 36								06 53								
Crewe 10	65 a						05 44	05 34	06 46				06 27		06 32		07 04								07 06
Kidsgrove	50 a															06 16									
Longport	50 a																								
Stoke-on-Trent	50,68 a						06 06									06 26		06 46						07 04	
Stafford	68 a						06 24	05 53							06 57									07 27	
Wolverhampton 7	68 a						06 39								07 12									07 43	
Birmingham New Street 12	68 a						06 58								07 31									08 05	
London Euston 15	⊖65 a							07 28					08 07					08 22						09 34	

		NT	VT	VT	NT	NT		VT	NT	NT	TP	XC	NT	VT	NT	TP	NT	XC	AW	VT	NT	NT	EM	NT	NT
			◇1 ⊠	◇1 ⊠				◇1 ⊠			◇1	◇1 ⊥		◇1 ⊠		◇1 ⊥		◇1 ⊥	◇ ⊥	◇1 ⊠			◇		
Deansgate	d																07 11				07 28				
Manchester Oxford Road	d								06 58								07 15				07 32		07 38		
Manchester Piccadilly 10	a								07 01								07 17				07 34		07 41		
	d	06 32	06 35	06 43	06 46	06 49		07 00	07 03	07 03	07 06	07 06	07 14	07 15	07 17	07 20	07 21	07 26	07 30	07 35	07 36	07 38	07 42	07 46	07 48
Levenshulme	d	06 37				06 55				07 09							07 28					07 43			
Heaton Chapel	d	06 40				06 58				07 12							07 31					07 46			
Stockport	a	06 44	06 43	06 50		07 01		07u07		07 16		07 15		07 22	07 26	07 28	07 34	07 34	07 38	07 43		07 50	07 53		07 57
	d	06 45	06 43	06 51				07u07		07 18		07 16		07 23			07 35	07 35	07 39	07 43		07 51			07 58
Cheadle Hulme	d	06 51								07 24												07 55			08 02
Bramhall	d	06 54																							08 05
Poynton	d	06 57																							08 08
Adlington (Cheshire)	d	07 01																							08 11
Prestbury	d	07 04																							08 14
Macclesfield	a	07 07	06 55															07 47		07 56					08 18
	d	07 08	06 55															07 49		07 56					08 18
Congleton	d	07 15																							08 26
Handforth	d									07 28												07 59			
Manchester Airport ✈	d				07 11				07a22		07a29		07a38								07a53			08 11	
Styal	d																							08 18	
Wilmslow	d			06 59	07 21					07 31									07 47			08 02		08 22	
Alderley Edge	d				07 24					07 34												08a08		08 25	
Chelford	d									07 38															
Goostrey	d									07 43															
Holmes Chapel	d				07 32					07 46														08 33	
Sandbach	d				07 36					07 51														08 37	
Crewe 10	65 a			07 15	07 46					08 01									08 08					08 47	
Kidsgrove	50 a																								08 32
Longport	50 a																								
Stoke-on-Trent	50,68 a	07 30	07 11									07 43		07 48				08 06		08 12					08 42
Stafford	68 a			07 34														08 24							
Wolverhampton 7	68 a											08 13						08 39							
Birmingham New Street 12	68 a											08 31						08 58							
London Euston 15	⊖65 a		08 46	08 52				08 58						09 23						09 52					

A not 24 May

b arr. 0557

c arr. 0611

Table 84

Mondays to Fridays

Manchester, Stockport and Manchester Airport - Crewe and Stoke-on-Trent

		NT		VT	NT	NT	TP	XC	NT	VT	NT	TP		XC	AW	VT	NT	NT	EM	NT	NT	NT	VT	NT	NT
				◇1 ⊠			◇1 ⊥	◇1 ⊥		◇1 ⊠		◇1 ⊥		◇1 ⊥	◇ ⊥	◇1 ⊠			◇				◇1 ⊠		
Deansgate	d																08 29								
Manchester Oxford Road	d				07 58												08 33		08 39					08 58	
Manchester Piccadilly 10	a				08 01												08 35		08 41					09 01	
	d	07 52		07 55	08 03	08 04	08 06	08 07	08 14	08 15	08 17	08 20		08 27	08 30	08 35	08 37	08 38	08 43	08 46	08 48	08 52	08 55	09 03	09 04
Levenshulme	d					08 09												08 43				08 58			09 09
Heaton Chapel	d					08 12												08 46				09 01			09 12
Stockport	a	08 01		08 03		08 16		08 15		08 22	08 27	08 28		08 34	08 38	08 42		08 50	08 53		08 57	09 04	09 03		09 16
	d			08 04		08 17		08 16		08 23				08 35	08 39	08 42		08 51			08 58		09 04		09 17
Cheadle Hulme	d					08 24												08 55			09 02				09 24
Bramhall	d																				09 05				
Poynton	d																				09 08				
Adlington (Cheshire)	d																				09 11				
Prestbury	d																				09 14				
Macclesfield	a													08 47		08 55					09 18				
	d													08 49		08 55					09 18				
Congleton	d																				09 26				
Handforth	d					08 28												08 59							09 28
Manchester Airport ✈	d				08a22		08a26		08a38								08a53			09 11				09a22	
Styal	d																								
Wilmslow	d			08 11		08 31									08 47			09 02		09 21			09 11		09 31
Alderley Edge	d					08 34												09 05		09 24					09 34
Chelford	d					08 38																			09 38
Goostrey	d					08 43																			09 43
Holmes Chapel	d					08 46														09 32					09 46
Sandbach	d					08 52														09 36					09 51
Crewe 10	65 a			08 27		09 04									09 07			09 23		09 46			09 27		10 01
Kidsgrove	50 a																				09 32				
Longport	50 a																								
Stoke-on-Trent	50,68 a							08 43		08 48				09 06		09 11					09 42				
Stafford	68 a							09 02						09 24											
Wolverhampton 7	68 a							09 15						09 39											
Birmingham New Street 12	68 a							09 39						09 58											
London Euston 15	⊖65 a			10 04						10 23						10 42							11 04		

		TP	XC	NT	VT	NT	TP	XC		AW	VT	NT	NT	EM	NT	NT	NT	VT		NT	NT	TP	XC	NT	VT
		◇1 ⊥	◇1 ⊥		◇1 ⊠		◇1 ⊥	◇1 ⊥		◇ ⊥	◇1 ⊠			◇				◇1 ⊠				◇1 ⊥	◇1 ⊥		◇1 ⊐
Deansgate	d											09 29													
Manchester Oxford Road	d											09 33		09 39						09 58					
Manchester Piccadilly 10	a											09 35		09 41						10 01					
	d	09 06	09 07	09 14	09 15	09 17	09 20	09 27		09 30	09 35	09 37	09 38	09 43	09 46	09 48	09 52	09 55		10 03	10 04	10 06	10 07	10 14	10 15
Levenshulme	d												09 43				09 58				10 09				
Heaton Chapel	d												09 46				10 01				10 12				
Stockport	a		09 15		09 22	09 27	09 28	09 34		09 38	09 42		09 50	09 53		09 57	10 04	10 03			10 16		10 15		10 22
	d		09 16		09 23			09 35		09 39	09 42		09 51			09 58		10 04			10 17		10 16		10 23
Cheadle Hulme	d												09 55			10 02					10 24				
Bramhall	d															10 05									
Poynton	d															10 08									
Adlington (Cheshire)	d															10 11									
Prestbury	d															10 14									
Macclesfield	a							09 47			09 55					10 18									
	d							09 49			09 55					10 18									
Congleton	d															10 26									
Handforth	d												09 59								10 28				
Manchester Airport ✈	d	09a33		09a38								09a53			10 11					10a22		10a26		10a38	
Styal	d																								
Wilmslow	d									09 47			10 02		10 21			10 11			10 31				
Alderley Edge	d												10a08		10 24						10 34				
Chelford	d																				10 38				
Goostrey	d																				10 43				
Holmes Chapel	d														10 32						10 46				
Sandbach	d														10 36						10 51				
Crewe 10	65 a									10 06					10 46			10 27			11 01				
Kidsgrove	50 a															10 32									
Longport	50 a																								
Stoke-on-Trent	50,68 a		09 43		09 48			10 06			10 11					10 42							10 43		10 48
Stafford	68 a		10 02					10 24																	
Wolverhampton 7	68 a		10 15					10 39															11 16		
Birmingham New Street 12	68 a		10 39					10 58															11 39		
London Euston 15	⊖65 a				11 23						11 42							12 04							12 23

Manchester, Stockport and Manchester Airport - Crewe and Stoke-on-Trent

		NT	TP	XC	AW	VT	NT	NT	EM	NT	NT	NT	VT	NT	NT	TP	XC	NT	VT	NT	TP	XC
			◇1 ✠	◇1 ✠	◇ ✠	◇1 ⊡			◇				◇1 ⊡			◇1 ✠	◇1 ✠		◇1 ⊡		◇1 ✠	◇1 ✠
Deansgate 🚊	d						10 29															
Manchester Oxford Road	d						10 33		10 39					10 58								
Manchester Piccadilly 10 🚊	a						10 35		10 41													
	d	10 17	10 20	10 27	10 30	10 35	10 37	10 38	10 43	10 46	10 48	10 52	10 55	11 03	11 04	11 06	11 07	11 14	11 15	11 17	11 20	11 27
Levenshulme	d							10 43				10 58			11 09							
Heaton Chapel	d							10 46				11 01			11 12							
Stockport	a	10 27	10 28	10 34	10 38	10 42		10 50	10 53		10 57	11 04	11 03		11 16		11 15		11 22	11 27	11 28	11 34
	d			10 35	10 39	10 42		10 51			10 58		11 04		11 17		11 16		11 23			11 35
Cheadle Hulme	d							10 55			11 02				11 24							
Bramhall	d										11 05											
Poynton	d										11 08											
Adlington (Cheshire)	d										11 11											
Prestbury	d										11 14											
Macclesfield	a			10 47		10 55					11 18											11 47
	d			10 49		10 55					11 18											11 49
Congleton	d										11 26											
Handforth	d							10 59							11 28							
Manchester Airport ✈	d						10a53			11 11				11a22		11a26		11a38				
Styal	d																					
Wilmslow	d				10 47			11 02		11 21			11 11		11 31							
Alderley Edge	d							11a08		11 24					11 34							
Chelford	d														11 38							
Goostrey	d														11 43							
Holmes Chapel	d									11 32					11 46							
Sandbach	d									11 36					11 51							
Crewe 10 65	a				11 06					11 46			11 27		12 01							
Kidsgrove 50	a										11 32											
Longport 50	a																					
Stoke-on-Trent 50,68	a			11 06		11 11					11 42						11 43		11 48			12 06
Stafford 68	a			11 24													12 02					12 24
Wolverhampton 7 68 🚊	a			11 39													12 15					12 39
Birmingham New Street 12 68	a			11 58													12 39					12 58
London Euston 15 ⊖65	a					12 42							13 04						13 23			

		AW	VT	NT	NT	EM	NT	NT	NT	VT	NT	NT	TP	XC	NT	VT	NT	TP	XC	AW	VT	NT	NT
		◇ ✠	◇1 ⊡			◇				◇1 ⊡			◇1 ✠	◇1 ✠		◇1 ⊡		◇1 ✠	◇1 ✠	◇ ✠	◇1 ⊡		
Deansgate 🚊	d			11 29																		12 29	
Manchester Oxford Road	d			11 33		11 39					11 58											12 33	
Manchester Piccadilly 10 🚊	a			11 35		11 41					12 01											12 35	
	d	11 30	11 35	11 37	11 38	11 43	11 46	11 48	11 52	11 55	12 03	12 04	12 06	12 07	12 14	12 15	12 17	12 20	12 27	12 30	12 35	12 37	12 38
Levenshulme	d				11 43				11 58			12 09											12 43
Heaton Chapel	d				11 46				12 01			12 12											12 46
Stockport	a	11 38	11 42		11 50	11 53		11 57	12 04	12 03		12 16		12 15		12 22	12 27	12 28	12 34	12 38	12 42		12 50
	d	11 39	11 42		11 51	11 54		11 58		12 04		12 17		12 16		12 23			12 35	12 39	12 42		12 51
Cheadle Hulme	d				11 55			12 02				12 24											12 55
Bramhall	d							12 05															
Poynton	d							12 08															
Adlington (Cheshire)	d							12 11															
Prestbury	d							12 14															
Macclesfield	a		11 55					12 18											12 47		12 55		
	d		11 55					12 18											12 49		12 55		
Congleton	d							12 26															
Handforth	d				11 59							12 28											12 59
Manchester Airport ✈	d			11a53			12 11				12a22		12a26		12a38							12a53	
Styal	d																						
Wilmslow	d	11 47			12 02		12 21			12 11		12 31								12 47			13 02
Alderley Edge	d				12a08		12 24					12 34											13a08
Chelford	d											12 38											
Goostrey	d											12 43											
Holmes Chapel	d						12 32					12 46											
Sandbach	d						12 36					12 51											
Crewe 10 65	a	12 06					12 46			12 27		13 01								13 06			
Kidsgrove 50	a							12 32															
Longport 50	a																						
Stoke-on-Trent 50,68	a		12 11					12 42						12 43		12 48			13 06		13 11		
Stafford 68	a																		13 24				
Wolverhampton 7 68 🚊	a													13 13					13 39				
Birmingham New Street 12 68	a													13 31					13 58				
London Euston 15 ⊖65	a		13 42							14 04						14 23					14 42		

Table 84 Mondays to Fridays

Manchester, Stockport and Manchester Airport - Crewe and Stoke-on-Trent

		EM	NT	NT	NT	VT	NT	NT	TP	XC	NT	VT	NT	TP	XC	AW	VT	NT	NT	EM	NT	NT	NT
		◇				◇1 ⊡			◇1 ✠	◇1 ✠		◇1 ⊡		◇1 ✠	◇1 ✠	■ ✠	◇1 ⊡			◇			
Deansgate 🚊	d																	13 29					
Manchester Oxford Road	d	12 39					12 58											13 33		13 39			
Manchester Piccadilly 10 🚊	a	12 41					13 01											13 35		13 41			
	d	12 43	12 46	12 48	12 52	12 55	13 03	13 04	13 06	13 07	13 14	13 15	13 17	13 20	13 27	13 30	13 35	13 37	13 38	13 43	13 46	13 48	13 52
Levenshulme	d				12 58			13 09											13 43				13 58
Heaton Chapel	d				13 01			13 12											13 46				14 01
Stockport	a	12 53		12 57	13 04	13 03		13 16		13 15		13 22	13 27	13 28	13 34	13 38	13 42		13 50	13 53		13 57	14 04
	d			12 58		13 04		13 17		13 16		13 23			13 35	13 39	13 42		13 51			13 58	
Cheadle Hulme	d			13 02				13 24											13 55			14 02	
Bramhall	d			13 05																		14 05	
Poynton	d			13 08																		14 08	
Adlington (Cheshire)	d			13 11																		14 11	
Prestbury	d			13 14																		14 14	
Macclesfield	a			13 18											13 47		13 55					14 18	
	d			13 18											13 49		13 55					14 18	
Congleton	d			13 26																		14 26	
Handforth	d							13 28											13 59				
Manchester Airport ✈	d		13 11				13a22		13a26		13a38							13a53			14 11		
Styal	d		13 18																				
Wilmslow	d		13 22			13 11		13 31								13 47			14 02		14 21		
Alderley Edge	d		13 25					13 34											14a08		14 24		
Chelford	d							13 38															
Goostrey	d							13 43															
Holmes Chapel	d		13 33					13 46													14 32		
Sandbach	d		13 37					13 51													14 36		
Crewe 10 65	a		13 47			13 27		14 01								14 06					14 46		
Kidsgrove 50	a			13 32																		14 32	
Longport 50	a																						
Stoke-on-Trent 50,68	a			13 42						13 43		13 48			14 06		14 11					14 42	
Stafford 68	a														14 24								
Wolverhampton 7 68 🚊	a									14 13					14 39								
Birmingham New Street 12 68	a									14 31					14 58								
London Euston 15 ⊖65	a					15 04						15 23					15 42						

		VT	NT	NT	TP	XC	NT	VT	NT	TP	XC	AW	VT	NT	NT	EM	NT	NT	NT	VT	NT	NT
		◇1 ⊡			◇1 ✠	◇1 ✠		◇1 ⊡		◇1 ✠	◇1 ✠	■ ✠	◇1 ⊡			◇				◇1 ⊡		
Deansgate 🚊	d													14 29								
Manchester Oxford Road	d		13 58											14 33		14 39					14 58	
Manchester Piccadilly 10 🚊	a		14 01											14 35		14 41					15 01	
	d	13 55	14 03	14 04	14 06	14 07	14 14	14 15	14 17	14 20	14 27	14 30	14 35	14 37	14 38	14 43	14 46	14 48	14 52	14 55	15 03	15 04
Levenshulme	d			14 09											14 43				14 58			15 09
Heaton Chapel	d			14 12											14 46				15 01			15 12
Stockport	a	14 03		14 16		14 15		14 22	14 27	14 28	14 34	14 38	14 42		14 50	14 53		14 57	15 04	15 03		15 16
	d	14 04		14 17		14 16		14 23			14 35	14 39	14 42		14 51			14 58		15 04		15 17
Cheadle Hulme	d			14 24											14 55			15 02				15 24
Bramhall	d																	15 05				
Poynton	d																	15 08				
Adlington (Cheshire)	d																	15 11				
Prestbury	d																	15 14				
Macclesfield	a										14 47		14 55					15 18				
	d										14 49		14 55					15 18				
Congleton	d																	15 26				
Handforth	d			14 28											14 59							15 28
Manchester Airport ✈	d		14a22		14a26		14a38							14a53			15 11				15a22	
Styal	d																					
Wilmslow	d	14 11		14 31								14 47			15 02		15 21			15 11		15 31
Alderley Edge	d			14 34											15a08		15 24					15 34
Chelford	d			14 38																		15 38
Goostrey	d			14 43																		15 43
Holmes Chapel	d			14 46													15 32					15 46
Sandbach	d			14 51													15 36					15 51
Crewe 10 65	a	14 27		15 01								15 06					15 46			15 27		16 01
Kidsgrove 50	a																	15 32				
Longport 50	a																					
Stoke-on-Trent 50,68	a					14 43		14 48			15 06		15 11					15 42				
Stafford 68	a					15 02					15 24											
Wolverhampton 7 68 🚊	a					15 15					15 39											
Birmingham New Street 12 68	a					15 39					15 58											
London Euston 15 ⊖65	a	16 04						16 23					16 42							17 04		

Manchester, Stockport and Manchester Airport - Crewe and Stoke-on-Trent

		TP	XC	NT	VT	NT	TP	XC	AW	VT	NT	NT	NT	NT	NT	VT	NT	NT	TP	XC	NT	VT	NT
		◇1 ⊼	◇1 ⊼		◇1 ⊡		◇1 ⊼	◇1 ⊼	2 ⊼	◇1 ⊡						◇1 ⊡			◇1 ⊼	◇1 ⊼		◇1 ⊡	
Deansgate ⇌	d										15 29												
Manchester Oxford Road	d										15 33						15 58						
Manchester Piccadilly 10 ⇌	a										15 35						16 01						
	d	15 06	15 07	15 14	15 15	15 17	15 20	15 27	15 30	15 35	15 37	15 38	15 46	15 48	15 52	15 55	16 03	16 04	16 06	16 07	16 14	16 15	16 17
Levenshulme	d											15 43			15 58			16 09					
Heaton Chapel	d											15 46			16 01			16 12					
Stockport	a		15 15		15 22	15 27	15 28	15 34	15 38	15 42		15 50		15 57	16 04	16 03		16 16		16 15		16 22	16 27
	d		15 16		15 23			15 35	15 39	15 42		15 51		15 58		16 04		16 17		16 16		16 23	
Cheadle Hulme	d											15 55		16 02				16 24					
Bramhall	d													16 05									
Poynton	d													16 08									
Adlington (Cheshire)	d													16 11									
Prestbury	d													16 14									
Macclesfield	a							15 47		15 55				16 18									
	d							15 49		15 55				16 18									
Congleton	d													16 26									
Handforth	d											15 59						16 28					
Manchester Airport ✈	d	15a26		15a38							15a53		16 11				16a22		16a26		16a38		
Styal	d																						
Wilmslow	d								15 47			16 02	16 21			16 11		16 31					
Alderley Edge	d											16a08	16 24					16 34					
Chelford	d																	16 38					
Goostrey	d																	16 43					
Holmes Chapel	d												16 32					16 46					
Sandbach	d												16 36					16 51					
Crewe 10 65	a								16 06				16 46			16 27		17 01					
Kidsgrove 50	a													16 32									
Longport 50	a																						
Stoke-on-Trent 50,68	a		15 43		15 48			16 06		16 11				16 42						16 43		16 49	
Stafford 68	a		16 02					16 24												17 02			
Wolverhampton 7 68 ⇌	a		16 15					16 39												17 15			
Birmingham New Street 12 68	a		16 39					16 58												17 39			
London Euston 15 ⊖65	a				17 23					17 42						18 02						18 23	

		TP	XC	AW	VT	NT	NT	EM	NT	NT	NT	VT	NT	NT	NT	TP	XC	NT	NT	VT	NT	TP
		◇1 ⊼	◇1 ⊼	2 ⊼	◇1 ⊡			◇				◇1 ⊡				◇1 ⊼	◇1 ⊼			◇1 ⊠		◇1 ⊼
Deansgate ⇌	d																				17 10	
Manchester Oxford Road	d					16 33		16 39						16 58							17 13	
Manchester Piccadilly 10 ⇌	a					16 35		16 41						17 01							17 15	
	d	16 20	16 27	16 30	16 35	16 37	16 38	16 43	16 46	16 48	16 51	16 55	16 58	17 03	17 03	17 06	17 06	17 09	17 14	17 15	17 17	17 20
Levenshulme	d						16 43						17 03		17 08							
Heaton Chapel	d						16 46						17 06		17 11							
Stockport	a	16 28	16 34	16 38	16 42		16 50	16 53		16 57	17 02	17 03	17 10		17 15			17 17		17 22	17 27	17 28
	d		16 35	16 39	16 42		16 51			16 58		17 04			17 16					17 23	17 28	
Cheadle Hulme	d						16 55			17 02					17 24						17 32	
Bramhall	d									17 05											17 35	
Poynton	d									17 08											17 38	
Adlington (Cheshire)	d									17 11											17 41	
Prestbury	d									17 14											17 44	
Macclesfield	a		16 47		16 56					17 18							17 26				17 48	
	d		16 49		16 56					17 18							17 27				17 48	
Congleton	d									17 26											17 56	
Handforth	d						16 59								17 28							
Manchester Airport ✈	d					16a53			17 11					17a22		17a32			17a39			
Styal	d																					
Wilmslow	d			16 49			17 03		17 21			17 11			17 31							
Alderley Edge	d						17a09		17 24						17 34							
Chelford	d														17 38							
Goostrey	d														17 43							
Holmes Chapel	d								17 32						17 46							
Sandbach	d								17 36						17 51							
Crewe 10 65	a			17 08					17 46			17 27			18 01							
Kidsgrove 50	a									17 32												
Longport 50	a																					
Stoke-on-Trent 50,68	a		17 06		17 12					17 42							17 43			17 49	18 10	
Stafford 68	a		17 24														18 03					
Wolverhampton 7 68 ⇌	a		17 39														18 15					
Birmingham New Street 12 68	a		17 58														18 38					
London Euston 15 ⊖65	a				18 42							19 08								19 23		

Manchester, Stockport and Manchester Airport - Crewe and Stoke-on-Trent

		NT	XC	AW	VT	NT	NT	EM	NT	NT	NT	VT	NT	XC	TP	NT	NT	VT	NT	TP	NT	XC	AW	VT	NT
			◇1 ⊼	2 ⊼	◇1 ⊠			◇				◇1 ⊠		◇1 ⊼	◇1 ⊼			◇1 ⊠		◇1 ⊼		◇1 A ⊼	◇ ⊼	◇1 ⊠	
Deansgate ⇌	d																				18 12				
Manchester Oxford Road	d					17 33		17 39					17 58								18 16				18 33
Manchester Piccadilly 10 ⇌	a					17 35		17 41					18 01								18 18				18 35
	d	17 23	17 27	17 30	17 35	17 37	17 38	17 43	17 46	17 48	17 52	17 55	18 03	18 05	18 06	18 08	18 14	18 15	18 17	18 20	18 21	18 27	18 30	18 35	18 37
Levenshulme	d	17 28					17 43				17 58					18 13					18 28				
Heaton Chapel	d	17 31					17 46				18 01					18 16					18 31				
Stockport	a	17 35	17 35	17 39	17 43		17 50	17 53		17 57	18 04	18 03		18 12		18 20		18 22	18 27	18 28	18 34	18 34	18 38	18 42	
	d		17 35	17 40	17 43		17 51			17 58		18 04		18 13		18 22		18 23				18 35	18 39	18 42	
Cheadle Hulme	d						17 55			18 02						18 30									
Bramhall	d									18 05															
Poynton	d									18 08															
Adlington (Cheshire)	d									18 11															
Prestbury	d									18 14															
Macclesfield	a				17 55					18 17				18 25										18 55	
	d				17 55					18 18				18 26										18 55	
Congleton	d									18 26												18 54			
Handforth	d						17 59									18 34									
Manchester Airport ✈	d					17a53			18 11				18a22		18a26		18a38								18a53
Styal	d								18 18																
Wilmslow	d		17 44	17 48			18 02		18 22			18 11				18 37							18 47		
Alderley Edge	d						18 05		18 25							18 40									
Chelford	d															18 44									
Goostrey	d															18 48									
Holmes Chapel	d								18 33							18 51									
Sandbach	d						18 16		18 37							18 56									
Crewe 10 65	a		18 05	18 11			18 26		18 47			18 27				19 06							19 07		
Kidsgrove 50	a									18 32															
Longport 50	a																								
Stoke-on-Trent 50,68	a				18 11					18 42				18 43				18 48				19 06		19 11	
Stafford 68	a		18 27																			19 24			
Wolverhampton 7 68 ⇌	a		18 39											19 13								19 39			
Birmingham New Street 12 68	a		18 58											19 31								19 58			
London Euston 15 ⊖65	a				19 42							20 06						20 23						20 42	

		NT	EM	NT	NT	NT	VT	NT	NT	TP	XC	NT	VT	NT	TP	NT	XC	AW	NT	EM	NT	NT	NT	AW	VT
			◇				◇1 ⊠			◇1 ⊼	◇1 A ⊼		◇1 ⊡		◇1		◇1 A ⊼	◇		◇					◇1 ⊡
Deansgate ⇌	d																		19 29						
Manchester Oxford Road	d		18 39					18 58											19 33	19 39	19 43			19 49	
Manchester Piccadilly 10 ⇌	a		18 41					19 01											19 35	19 41	19 45			19 52	
	d	18 38	18 43	18 46	18 48	18 52	18 55	19 03	19 04	19 06	19 07	19 14	19 15	19 17	19 18	19 22	19 27	19 30	19 37	19 43	19 46	19 48	19 51	19 54	19 55
Levenshulme	d	18 43				18 58			19 09							19 28							19 58		
Heaton Chapel	d	18 46				19 01			19 12							19 31							20 01		
Stockport	a	18 50	18 53		18 57	19 04	19 03		19 16		19 15		19 22	19 27	19 26	19 34	19 34	19 38		19 53		19 57	20 04		20 03
	d	18 51	18 54		18 58		19 04		19 17		19 16		19 23				19 35	19 39				19 58			20 04
Cheadle Hulme	d	18 55			19 02				19 24													20 02			
Bramhall	d				19 05																	20 05			
Poynton	d				19 08																	20 08			
Adlington (Cheshire)	d				19 11																	20 11			
Prestbury	d				19 14																	20 14			
Macclesfield	a				19 18								19 35				19 47					20 18			
	d				19 18								19 36				19 49					20 18			
Congleton	d				19 26																	20 26			
Handforth	d	18 59							19 28																
Manchester Airport ✈	d			19b14				19a24		19a28		19a38							19a53		20c14			20a13	
Styal	d																								
Wilmslow	d	19 02		19 26			19 11		19 31									19 47			20a24				20 11
Alderley Edge	d	19a08		19a32					19 34																
Chelford	d								19 38																
Goostrey	d								19 43																
Holmes Chapel	d								19 46																
Sandbach	d								19 51																
Crewe 10 65	a						19 27		20 01									20 09							20 27
Kidsgrove 50	a				19 32																	20 32			
Longport 50	a																								
Stoke-on-Trent 50,68	a				19 42						19 43		19 51				20 06					20 42			
Stafford 68	a										20 03						20 25								20 47
Wolverhampton 7 68 ⇌	a										20 16						20 40								
Birmingham New Street 12 68	a										20 33						21 00								
London Euston 15 ⊖65	a						21 06						21 25												22 12

A ⊼ to Wolverhampton

b arr. 1908

c arr. 2007

Manchester, Stockport and Manchester Airport - Crewe and Stoke-on-Trent

		NT		XC ◇1	TP ◇1	TP ◇1	VT ◇1	NT	TP ◇1	XC ◇1	AW ◇	NT	EM ◇		NT	NT	NT	AW ◇	NT	NT	TP ◇1	TP ◇1	VT ◇1	NT	TP ◇1
Deansgate	d											20 29													
Manchester Oxford Road	d				20 07							20 33	20 39		20 43			20 49	20 58			21 07			
Manchester Piccadilly 10	a				20 09							20 35	20 41		20 45			20 52	21 01			21 09			
	d	20 04		20 07	20 11	20 13	20 15	20 17	20 20	20 27	20 30	20 37	20 43		20 46	20 48	20 51	20 54	21 03	21 04	21 06	21 11	21 15	21 17	21 20
Levenshulme	d	20 09															20 58			21 09					
Heaton Chapel	d	20 12															21 01			21 12					
Stockport	a	20 15		20 15			20 22	20 27	20 28	20 34	20 38		20 53			20 58	21 04			21 16			21 22	21 27	21 28
	d	20 17		20 16			20 23			20 35	20 39					20 58				21 17			21 23		
Cheadle Hulme	d	20 24														21 02				21 24					
Bramhall	d															21 05									
Poynton	d															21 08									
Adlington (Cheshire)	d															21 11									
Prestbury	d															21 14									
Macclesfield	a						20 35			20 47						21 18							21 35		
	d						20 36			20 49						21 18							21 36		
Congleton	d															21 26									
Handforth	d	20 28																		21 28					
Manchester Airport ✈	d					20a37						20a53			21b14			21a13	21a24		21a36				
Styal	d																								
Wilmslow	d	20 31									20 47				21a24					21 31					
Alderley Edge	d	20 34																		21 34					
Chelford	d	20 38																		21 38					
Goostrey	d	20 43																		21 43					
Holmes Chapel	d	20 46																		21 46					
Sandbach	d	20 52																		21 51					
Crewe 10 65	a	21 04									21 11									22 01					
Kidsgrove 50	a															21 32									
Longport 50	a																								
Stoke-on-Trent 50,68	a			20 43			20 51			21 06						21 42							21 51		
Stafford 68	a									21 25															
Wolverhampton 7 68	a			21 13						21 39															
Birmingham New Street 12 68	a			21 31						22 00															
London Euston 15 ⊖65	a						22 33																23 48		

		XC ◇1	AW	NT	NT	NT	NT	NT		XC ◇1	NT	TP ◇1	EM ◇	AW ◇	TP FO ◇1	NT	NT	NT		TP ◇1	NT	NT	NT		NT
Deansgate	d			21 29																					
Manchester Oxford Road	d			21 33	21 43								22 24			22 43									
Manchester Piccadilly 10	a			21 35	21 45								22 26			22 45									
	d	21 28	21 35	21 37	21 46	21 48	21 52	22 04		22 07	22 17	22 20	22 28	22 35	22 40	22 46	22 48	23 03		23 06	23 10	23 14	23 17		23 38
Levenshulme	d						21 58	22 09										23 09							23 43
Heaton Chapel	d						22 01	22 12										23 12							23 46
Stockport	a	21 35	21 43			21 57	22 04	22 16		22 15	22 27	22 28	22 37	22 43			22 57	23 16			23 19	23 23	23 26		23 50
	d	21 36	21 44			21 58		22 17		22 16				22 44			22 58	23 16				23 23			23 50
Cheadle Hulme	d					22 02		22 24									23 02	23 23				23 27			23 54
Bramhall	d					22 05											23 05					23 30			
Poynton	d					22 08											23 08					23 33			
Adlington (Cheshire)	d					22 11											23 11					23 37			
Prestbury	d					22 14											23 14					23 40			
Macclesfield	a	21 48				22 18				22 28							23 20					23 46			
	d	21 50				22 18				22 29															
Congleton	d					22 26																			
Handforth	d							22 28										23 27							23 58
Manchester Airport ✈	d			21a53	22 14										22a57	23c14				23a26					
Styal	d																								
Wilmslow	d		21 51		22a22			22 31						22 52		23a22		23 31							00 01
Alderley Edge	d							22 34										23a37							00 04
Chelford	d							22 38																	00 08
Goostrey	d							22 43																	00 12
Holmes Chapel	d							22 46																	00 15
Sandbach	d							22 51																	00 20
Crewe 10 65	a		22 11					23 01						23 10											00 30
Kidsgrove 50	a					22 32																			
Longport 50	a																								
Stoke-on-Trent 50,68	a	22 07				22 42				22 46															
Stafford 68	a	22 25								23 06															
Wolverhampton 7 68	a	22 39								23 19															
Birmingham New Street 12 68	a	22 58								23 38															
London Euston 15 ⊖65	a																								

b arr. 2107
c arr. 2308

Manchester, Stockport and Manchester Airport - Crewe and Stoke-on-Trent

			NT	TP ◇1	AW	XC ◇1	VT ◇1	NT	TP ◇1	NT		VT ◇1	NT	XC ◇1	NT	NT	VT ◇1	TP ◇1	NT	NT		AW ◇	VT ◇1	NT	NT
Deansgate	d																								
Manchester Oxford Road	d																								
Manchester Piccadilly 10	a																								
	d		04 15	04 44	04 58	05 11	05 25	05 35	05 44	05 50		05 55	05 58	06 00		06 06	06 10	06 12	06 15	06 17		06 30	06 35	06 44	06 46
Levenshulme	d															06 11									
Heaton Chapel	d															06 14									
Stockport	a						05 33		05 52	05 59		06 02		06 07		06 18	06 17			06 27		06 38	06 43	06 52	
	d						05 34					06 03		06 08		06 19	06 18					06 39	06 43	06 53	
Cheadle Hulme	d															06 26								06 57	
Bramhall	d																							07 00	
Poynton	d																							07 03	
Adlington (Cheshire)	d																							07 06	
Prestbury	d																							07 09	
Macclesfield	a													06 20			06 30						06 55	07 13	
	d													06 21	06 03		06 31						06 55	07 13	
Congleton	d														06 10									07 21	
Handforth	d															06 30									
Manchester Airport ✈	d		04a30	05a00	05a12			06b05					06a14					06a29	06a39						07 11
Styal	d																								
Wilmslow	d						05 41	06 14				06 11				06 33						06 47			07 21
Alderley Edge	d							06 17								06 36									07 24
Chelford	d							06 21																	
Goostrey	d							06 25																	
Holmes Chapel	d							06 28								06 44									07 32
Sandbach	d							06 33								06 49									07 36
Crewe 10 65	a					05 41	05 57	06 43				06 27				06 59						07 06			07 46
Kidsgrove 50	a														06 16									07 28	
Longport 50	a																								
Stoke-on-Trent 50,68	a					06 07								06 38	06 26		06 46						07 11	07 40	
Stafford 68	a					06 25	06 17							06 57											
Wolverhampton 7 68	a					06 39								07 12											
Birmingham New Street 12 68	a					06 57								07 31											
London Euston 15 ⊖65	a						07 52					08 09					08 28						08 46		

		NT	VT ◇1	XC ◇1	NT	NT		TP ◇1	NT	VT ◇1	NT	TP ◇1	NT	XC ◇1	AW ◇	VT ◇1	NT	NT	EM ◇	NT	NT	NT	VT ◇1	XC ◇1	NT
Deansgate	d												07 11				07 28								
Manchester Oxford Road	d				06 58								07 15				07 32		07 38						07 58
Manchester Piccadilly 10	a				07 01								07 17				07 34		07 41						08 01
	d	06 49	06 55	07 00	07 03	07 03		07 06	07 14	07 15	07 17	07 20	07 21	07 27	07 30	07 35	07 36	07 38	07 42	07 46	07 48	07 52	07 55	07 58	08 03
Levenshulme	d	06 55				07 09							07 28					07 43				07 57			
Heaton Chapel	d	06 58				07 12							07 31					07 46							
Stockport	a	07 01	07 03	07 08		07 16				07 22	07 27	07 28	07 34	07 34	07 38	07 43		07 50	07 53		07 57	08 02	08 03	08 07	
	d		07 04	07 09		07 18				07 23				07 35	07 39	07 43		07 51			07 58		08 04	08 08	
Cheadle Hulme	d					07 24												07 55			08 02				
Bramhall	d																				08 05				
Poynton	d																				08 08				
Adlington (Cheshire)	d																				08 11				
Prestbury	d																				08 14				
Macclesfield	a			07 23										07 47		07 56					08 18			08 23	
	d			07 25										07 49		07 56					08 18			08 25	
Congleton	d																				08 26				
Handforth	d					07 28												07 59							
Manchester Airport ✈	d				07a22			07a29	07a38								07a53			08 11					08a22
Styal	d																			08 18					
Wilmslow	d		07 11			07 31									07 47			08 01		08 22			08 11		
Alderley Edge	d					07 34												08a07		08 25					
Chelford	d					07 38																			
Goostrey	d					07 43																			
Holmes Chapel	d					07 46														08 33					
Sandbach	d					07 51														08 37					
Crewe 10 65	a		07 27			08 01									08 06					08 47			08 27		
Kidsgrove 50	a																				08 32				
Longport 50	a																								
Stoke-on-Trent 50,68	a			07 43						07 48				08 06		08 12					08 42			08 43	
Stafford 68	a			08 03										08 25										09 03	
Wolverhampton 7 68	a			08 17										08 39										09 17	
Birmingham New Street 12 68	a			08 38										08 58										09 39	
London Euston 15 ⊖65	a		09 04							09 23						09 42							10 04		

b arr. 0557

Manchester, Stockport and Manchester Airport - Crewe and Stoke-on-Trent

Saturdays until 10 July

	NT	EM	NT	NT	NT	VT	NT	XC	TP	NT	NT	VT	NT	TP	XC	AW	VT	NT	NT	EM	NT	NT
		◇				◇1		◇1	◇1			◇1		◇1	◇1	◇	◇1			◇		
Deansgate d																						
Manchester Oxford Road d		17 39					17 58											18 33		18 39		
Manchester Piccadilly 10 a		17 41					18 01											18 35		18 41		
Manchester Piccadilly d	17 38	17 43	17 46	17 48	17 52	17 55	18 03	18 05	18 06	18 08	18 14	18 15	18 17	18 20	18 27	18 30	18 35	18 37	18 38	18 43	18 46	18 48
Levenshulme d	17 43				17 58					18 13									18 43			
Heaton Chapel d	17 46				18 01					18 16									18 46			
Stockport a	17 50	17 53		17 57	18 04	18 03		18 12		18 20		18 22	18 27	18 28	18 34	18 38	18 42		18 50	18 53		18 57
Stockport d	17 51	17 54		17 58		18 04		18 13		18 22		18 23			18 35	18 39	18 42		18 51			18 58
Cheadle Hulme d	17 55			18 02						18 30									18 55			19 02
Bramhall d				18 05																		19 05
Poynton d				18 08																		19 08
Adlington (Cheshire) d				18 11																		19 11
Prestbury d				18 14																		19 14
Macclesfield a				18 18				18 25									18 55					19 18
Macclesfield d				18 18				18 26									18 55					19 18
Congleton d				18 26											18 54							19 26
Handforth d	17 59									18 34									18 59			
Manchester Airport d			18 11				18a22		18a26		18a38							18a53			19b14	
Styal d			18 18																			
Wilmslow d	18 02		18 22			18 11				18 37						18 47			19 02		19 26	
Alderley Edge d	18a08		18 25							18 40									19a08		19a32	
Chelford d										18 44												
Goostrey d										18 48												
Holmes Chapel d			18 33							18 51												
Sandbach d			18 37							18 56												
Crewe 10 65 a			18 47			18 27				19 06						19 08						
Kidsgrove 50 a				18 32																		19 32
Longport 50 a																						
Stoke-on-Trent 50,68 a				18 42				18 43				18 48			19 06		19 12					19 42
Stafford 68 a								19 02							19 25							
Wolverhampton 7 68 a								19 16							19 39							
Birmingham New Street 12 68 a								19 33							19 58							
London Euston 15 ⊖65 a						20 04						20 25					20 58					

	NT	VT	NT	NT	TP	XC	NT	NT	TP	NT	XC	AW	VT	NT	EM	NT	NT	NT	AW	NT	TP	XC	TP
		◇1			◇1	◇1			◇1		◇1	◇	◇1		◇						◇1	◇1	◇1
Deansgate d														19 29									
Manchester Oxford Road d			18 58											19 33	19 39	19 43			19 49				20 07
Manchester Piccadilly 10 a			19 01											19 35	19 41	19 45			19 52				20 09
Manchester Piccadilly d	18 52	18 55	19 03	19 04	19 06	19 07	19 14	19 17	19 18	19 22	19 27	19 30	19 35	19 37	19 43	19 46	19 48	19 51	19 54	20 04	20 06	20 07	20 11
Levenshulme d	18 58			19 09						19 28								19 58		20 09			
Heaton Chapel d	19 01			19 12						19 31								20 01		20 12			
Stockport a	19 04	19 03		19 16		19 15		19 27	19 26	19 34	19 34	19 39	19 42		19 53		19 57	20 04		20 16		20 15	
Stockport d		19 04		19 17		19 16					19 35	19 39	19 42				19 58			20 17		20 16	
Cheadle Hulme d				19 24													20 02			20 24			
Bramhall d																	20 05						
Poynton d																	20 08						
Adlington (Cheshire) d																	20 11						
Prestbury d																	20 14						
Macclesfield a											19 47		19 55				20 18						
Macclesfield d											19 49		19 55				20 18						
Congleton d																	20 26						
Handforth d				19 28																20 28			
Manchester Airport d			19a24		19a28		19a38							19a53		20c14			20a13		20a36		
Styal d																							
Wilmslow d		19 11		19 31								19 47				20a24				20 31			
Alderley Edge d				19 34																20 34			
Chelford d				19 38																20 38			
Goostrey d				19 43																20 43			
Holmes Chapel d				19 46																20 46			
Sandbach d				19 51																20 51			
Crewe 10 65 a		19 27		20 01								20 06								21 01			
Kidsgrove 50 a																	20 32						
Longport 50 a																							
Stoke-on-Trent 50,68 a						19 43					20 06		20 12				20 42					20 43	
Stafford 68 a						20 02					20 25											21 02	
Wolverhampton 7 68 a						20 16					20 39											21 15	
Birmingham New Street 12 68 a						20 33					20 58											21 32	
London Euston 15 ⊖65 a		21 18											22 01										

b arr. 1908

c arr. 2007

Table 84

Manchester, Stockport and Manchester Airport - Crewe and Stoke-on-Trent

Saturdays until 10 July

	NT	TP	XC	AW	VT	NT	EM	NT	NT	NT	NT	NT	TP	XC	TP	NT	TP	XC	NT	EM	NT
		◇1	◇1	◇	◇1		◇						◇1	◇1	◇1		◇1	◇1		◇	
Deansgate d						20 29													21 29		
Manchester Oxford Road d						20 33	20 39	20 43			20 58				21 07				21 33	21 39	21 43
Manchester Piccadilly 10 a						20 35	20 41	20 45			21 01				21 09				21 35	21 41	21 45
Manchester Piccadilly d	20 17	20 20	20 27	20 30	20 35	20 37	20 43	20 46	20 48	20 52	21 03	21 04	21 06	21 07	21 11	21 17	21 20	21 28	21 37	21 43	21 46
Levenshulme d										20 58		21 09									
Heaton Chapel d										21 01		21 12									
Stockport a	20 27	20 28	20 34	20 39	20 42		20 53		20 57	21 04		21 16				21 27	21 28	21 35		21 52	
Stockport d			20 35	20 39	20 43				20 58			21 17						21 36			
Cheadle Hulme d									21 02			21 24									
Bramhall d									21 05												
Poynton d									21 08												
Adlington (Cheshire) d									21 11												
Prestbury d									21 14												
Macclesfield a			20 47		20 55				21 18												
Macclesfield d			20 49		20 56				21 18												
Congleton d									21 26												
Handforth d												21 28									
Manchester Airport d						20a53		21b14			21a24		21a36						21a53		22c14
Styal d																					
Wilmslow d				20 47				21a24				21 31						21 45			22a22
Alderley Edge d												21 34									
Chelford d												21 38									
Goostrey d												21 43									
Holmes Chapel d												21 46									
Sandbach d												21 51									
Crewe 10 65 a				21 06								22 01						22 05			
Kidsgrove 50 a									21 32												
Longport 50 a																					
Stoke-on-Trent 50,68 a			21 06		21 11				21 42					21 43							
Stafford 68 a			21 26											22 02				22 32			
Wolverhampton 7 68 a			21 39											22 14				22 50			
Birmingham New Street 12 68 a			21 58											22 32				23 17			
London Euston 15 ⊖65 a					23 04																

	NT	NT	NT	NT	TP	AW	NT	NT	NT	NT	NT	NT	NT
					◇1	◇							
Deansgate d													
Manchester Oxford Road d							22 43						
Manchester Piccadilly 10 a							22 45						
Manchester Piccadilly d	21 48	21 52	22 04	22 17	22 20	22 35	22 46	22 48	23 04	23 10	23 14	23 17	23 37
Levenshulme d		21 58	22 09						23 09				23 42
Heaton Chapel d		22 01	22 12						23 12				23 45
Stockport a	21 58	22 04	22 16	22 27	22 28	22 43		22 57	23 16	23 19	23 23	23 26	23 49
Stockport d	21 58		22 17			22 44		22 58	23 16		23 23		23 50
Cheadle Hulme d	22 02		22 24					23 02	23 21		23 27		23 54
Bramhall d	22 05							23 05			23 30		
Poynton d	22 08							23 08			23 33		
Adlington (Cheshire) d	22 11							23 11			23 37		
Prestbury d	22 14							23 14			23 40		
Macclesfield a	22 20							23 20			23 46		
Macclesfield d													
Congleton d													
Handforth d			22 28						23 25				23 58
Manchester Airport d							23e14						
Styal d													
Wilmslow d			22 31			22 52	23a22		23 28				00 01
Alderley Edge d			22 34						23 31				00a07
Chelford d			22 38						23 35				
Goostrey d			22 43						23 40				
Holmes Chapel d			22 46						23 43				
Sandbach d			22 51						23 48				
Crewe 10 65 a			23 01			23 10			23 53				
Kidsgrove 50 a													
Longport 50 a													
Stoke-on-Trent 50,68 a													
Stafford 68 a													
Wolverhampton 7 68 a													
Birmingham New Street 12 68 a													
London Euston 15 ⊖65 a													

b arr. 2107

c arr. 2208

e arr. 2308

Manchester, Stockport and Manchester Airport - Crewe and Stoke-on-Trent

		NT	TP ◇1	AW	XC ◇1	VT ◇1	NT	TP ◇1	NT	VT ◇1	NT	XC ◇1	NT	NT	VT ◇1	TP ◇1	NT	NT	AW ◇	VT ◇1	NT	NT
Deansgate	d																					
Manchester Oxford Road	d																					
Manchester Piccadilly 10	a																					
	d	04 15	04 44	04 58	05 11	05 25	05 35	05 44	05 50	05 55	05 58	06 00		06 06	06 10	06 12	06 15	06 17	06 30	06 35	06 44	06 46
Levenshulme	d													06 11								
Heaton Chapel	d													06 14								
Stockport	a					05 33		05 52	05 59	06 02		06 07		06 18	06 17			06 27	06 38	06 43	06 52	
	d					05 34				06 03		06 08		06 19	06 18				06 39	06 43	06 53	
Cheadle Hulme	d													06 26							06 57	
Bramhall	d																				07 00	
Poynton	d																				07 03	
Adlington (Cheshire)	d																				07 06	
Prestbury	d																				07 09	
Macclesfield	a											06 20			06 30					06 55	07 13	
	d											06 21	06 03		06 31					06 55	07 13	
Congleton	d												06 10								07 21	
Handforth	d													06 30								
Manchester Airport	d	04a30	05a00	05a12			06b05				06a14					06a29	06a39					07 11
Styal	d																					
Wilmslow	d					05 41	06 14			06 11				06 33					06 47			07 21
Alderley Edge	d						06 17							06 36								07 24
Chelford	d						06 21															
Goostrey	d						06 25															
Holmes Chapel	d						06 28							06 44								07 32
Sandbach	d						06 33							06 49								07 36
Crewe 10	65 a				05 41	05 57	06 43			06 27				06 59					07 06			07 46
Kidsgrove	50 a												06 16								07 28	
Longport	50 a																					
Stoke-on-Trent	50,68 a				06 07							06 38	06 26		06 46					07 11	07 40	
Stafford	68 a				06 25	06 17						06 57										
Wolverhampton 7	68 a				06 39							07 12										
Birmingham New Street 12	68 a				06 57							07 31										
London Euston 15	⊖65 a					07 52				08 09					08 28					08 46		

		NT	VT ◇1	XC ◇1	NT	NT	TP ◇1	NT	VT ◇1	NT	TP ◇1	NT	XC ◇1	AW ◇	VT ◇1	NT	NT	EM ◇	NT	NT	NT	VT ◇1	XC ◇1	NT
Deansgate	d											07 11				07 28								
Manchester Oxford Road	d				06 58							07 15				07 32		07 38						07 58
Manchester Piccadilly 10	a				07 01							07 17				07 34		07 41						08 01
	d	06 49	06 55	07 00	07 03	07 03	07 06	07 14	07 15	07 17	07 20	07 21	07 27	07 30	07 35	07 36	07 38	07 42	07 46	07 48	07 52	07 55	07 58	08 03
Levenshulme	d	06 55				07 09						07 28					07 43				07 57			
Heaton Chapel	d	06 58				07 12						07 31					07 46							
Stockport	a	07 01	07 03	07 08		07 16			07 22	07 27	07 28	07 34	07 34	07 38	07 43		07 50	07 53		07 57	08 02	08 03	08 07	
	d		07 04	07 09		07 18			07 23			07 35	07 35	07 39	07 43		07 51			07 58		08 04	08 08	
Cheadle Hulme	d					07 24											07 55			08 02				
Bramhall	d																			08 05				
Poynton	d																			08 08				
Adlington (Cheshire)	d																			08 11				
Prestbury	d																			08 14				
Macclesfield	a			07 23									07 47		07 56					08 18			08 23	
	d			07 25									07 49		07 56					08 18			08 25	
Congleton	d																			08 26				
Handforth	d					07 28											07 59							
Manchester Airport	d				07a22		07a29	07a38								07a53			08 11					08a22
Styal	d																		08 18					
Wilmslow	d		07 11			07 31								07 47			08 01		08 22			08 11		
Alderley Edge	d					07 34											08a07		08 25					
Chelford	d					07 38																		
Goostrey	d					07 43																		
Holmes Chapel	d					07 46													08 33					
Sandbach	d					07 51													08 37					
Crewe 10	65 a		07 27			08 01								08 06					08 47			08 27		
Kidsgrove	50 a																			08 32				
Longport	50 a																							
Stoke-on-Trent	50,68 a			07 43					07 48				08 06		08 12					08 42			08 43	
Stafford	68 a			08 03									08 25										09 03	
Wolverhampton 7	68 a			08 17									08 39										09 17	
Birmingham New Street 12	68 a			08 38									08 58										09 39	
London Euston 15	⊖65 a		09 04						09 23						09 42							10 04		

b arr. 0557

Table 84

Saturdays
17 July to 04 September

Manchester, Stockport and Manchester Airport - Crewe and Stoke-on-Trent

		NT	TP ◇1	NT	VT ◇1	NT	TP ◇1	XC ◇1	AW	VT ◇1	NT	NT	EM ◇	NT	NT	NT	VT ◇1	NT	NT	TP ◇1	XC ◇1	NT
Deansgate	d										08 29											
Manchester Oxford Road	d										08 33		08 39					08 58				
Manchester Piccadilly 10	a										08 35		08 41					09 01				
	d	08 04	08 06	08 14	08 15	08 17	08 20	08 27	08 30	08 35	08 37	08 38	08 43	08 46	08 48	08 52	08 55	09 03	09 04	09 06	09 07	09 14
Levenshulme	d	08 09										08 43				08 58			09 09			
Heaton Chapel	d	08 12										08 46				09 01			09 12			
Stockport	a	08 16			08 22	08 27	08 28	08 34	08 38	08 42		08 50	08 53		08 57	09 04	09 03		09 16		09 15	
	d	08 17			08 23			08 35	08 39	08 42		08 51			08 58		09 04		09 17		09 16	
Cheadle Hulme	d	08 24										08 55			09 02				09 24			
Bramhall	d														09 05							
Poynton	d														09 08							
Adlington (Cheshire)	d														09 11							
Prestbury	d														09 14							
Macclesfield	a							08 47		08 55					09 18							
	d							08 49		08 55					09 18							
Congleton	d														09 26							
Handforth	d	08 28										08 59							09 28			
Manchester Airport	d		08a26	08a38							08a53			09 11				09a22		09a26		09a38
Styal	d																					
Wilmslow	d	08 31							08 47			09 02		09 21			09 11		09 31			
Alderley Edge	d	08 34										09a08		09 24					09 34			
Chelford	d	08 38																	09 38			
Goostrey	d	08 43																	09 43			
Holmes Chapel	d	08 46												09 32					09 46			
Sandbach	d	08 51												09 36					09 51			
Crewe 10	65 a	09 01							09 06					09 46			09 27		10 01			
Kidsgrove	50 a														09 32							
Longport	50 a																					
Stoke-on-Trent	50,68 a				08 48			09 06		09 12					09 42						09 43	
Stafford	68 a							09 25													10 02	
Wolverhampton 7	68 a							09 39													10 15	
Birmingham New Street 12	68 a							09 58													10 39	
London Euston 15	⊖65 a				10 23					10 42							11 04					

		VT ◇1	NT	TP ◇1	XC ◇1	AW ◇	VT ◇1	NT	NT	EM ◇	NT	NT	NT	VT ◇1	NT	NT	TP ◇1	XC ◇1	NT	VT ◇1	NT	TP ◇1	XC ◇1
Deansgate	d							09 29															
Manchester Oxford Road	d							09 33		09 39					09 58								
Manchester Piccadilly 10	a							09 35		09 41					10 01								
	d	09 15	09 17	09 20	09 27	09 30	09 35	09 37	09 38	09 43	09 46	09 48	09 52	09 55	10 03	10 04	10 06	10 07	10 14	10 15	10 17	10 20	10 27
Levenshulme	d								09 43				09 58			10 09							
Heaton Chapel	d								09 46				10 01			10 12							
Stockport	a	09 22	09 27	09 28	09 34	09 38	09 42		09 50	09 53		09 57	10 04	10 03		10 16		10 15		10 22	10 27	10 28	10 34
	d	09 23			09 35	09 39	09 42		09 51			09 58		10 04		10 17		10 16		10 23			10 35
Cheadle Hulme	d								09 55			10 02				10 24							
Bramhall	d											10 05											
Poynton	d											10 08											
Adlington (Cheshire)	d											10 11											
Prestbury	c											10 14											
Macclesfield	a				09 47		09 55					10 18											10 47
	d				09 49		09 55					10 18											10 49
Congleton	d											10 26											
Handforth	d								09 59							10 28							
Manchester Airport	d							09a53			10 11				10a22		10a26		10a38				
Styal	d																						
Wilmslow	d					09 47			10 02		10 21			10 11		10 31							
Alderley Edge	d								10a08		10 24					10 34							
Chelford	d															10 38							
Goostrey	d															10 43							
Holmes Chapel	d										10 32					10 46							
Sandbach	d										10 36					10 51							
Crewe 10	65 a					10 06					10 46			10 27		11 01							
Kidsgrove	50 a											10 32											
Longport	50 a																						
Stoke-on-Trent	50,68 a	09 48			10 06		10 12					10 42						10 43		10 48			11 06
Stafford	68 a				10 25													11 02					11 25
Wolverhampton 7	68 a				10 39													11 16					11 39
Birmingham New Street 12	68 a				10 58													11 39					11 58
London Euston 15	⊖65 a	11 23					11 42							12 04						12 23			

Table 84

Manchester, Stockport and Manchester Airport - Crewe and Stoke-on-Trent

	AW	VT	NT	NT	EM	NT	NT	NT	VT	NT	NT	TP	XC	NT	VT	NT	TP	XC	AW	VT	NT
	◇	◇1			◇				◇1			◇1	◇1		◇1		◇1	◇1	◇	◇1	
Deansgate d			10 29																		11 29
Manchester Oxford Road d			10 33		10 39					10 58											11 33
Manchester Piccadilly 10 a			10 35		10 41					11 01											11 35
d	10 30	10 35	10 37	10 38	10 43	10 46	10 48	10 52	10 55	11 03	11 04	11 06	11 07	11 14	11 15	11 17	11 20	11 27	11 30	11 35	11 37
Levenshulme d				10 43				10 58			11 09										
Heaton Chapel d				10 46				11 01			11 12										
Stockport a	10 38	10 42		10 50	10 53		10 57	11 04	11 03		11 16		11 15		11 22	11 27	11 28	11 34	11 38	11 42	
d	10 39	10 42		10 51			10 58		11 04		11 17		11 16		11 23			11 35	11 39	11 42	
Cheadle Hulme d				10 55			11 02				11 24										
Bramhall d							11 05														
Poynton d							11 08														
Adlington (Cheshire) d							11 11														
Prestbury d							11 14														
Macclesfield a		10 55					11 18											11 47		11 55	
d		10 55					11 18											11 49		11 55	
Congleton d							11 26														
Handforth d				10 59							11 28										
Manchester Airport d			10a53			11 11				11a22		11a26		11a38							11a53
Styal d																					
Wilmslow d	10 47			11 02		11 21			11 11		11 31								11 47		
Alderley Edge d				11a08		11 24					11 34										
Chelford d											11 38										
Goostrey d											11 43										
Holmes Chapel d						11 32					11 46										
Sandbach d						11 36					11 51										
Crewe 10 65 a	11 06					11 46			11 27		12 01								12 06		
Kidsgrove 50 a							11 32														
Longport 50 a																					
Stoke-on-Trent 50,68 a		11 12					11 42						11 43		11 48			12 06		12 12	
Stafford 68 a													12 02					12 24			
Wolverhampton 7 68 a													12 16					12 39			
Birmingham New Street 12 68 a													12 39					12 58			
London Euston 15 ⊖65 a		12 42							13 04						13 23					13 42	

	NT	EM	NT	NT	NT	VT	NT	NT	TP	XC	NT	VT	NT	TP	XC	AW	VT	NT	NT	EM	NT	NT
		◇				◇1			◇1	◇1		◇1		◇1	◇1	■	◇1			◇		
Deansgate d																		12 29				
Manchester Oxford Road d		11 39					11 58											12 33		12 39		
Manchester Piccadilly 10 a		11 41					12 01											12 35		12 41		
d	11 38	11 43	11 46	11 48	11 52	11 55	12 03	12 04	12 06	12 07	12 14	12 15	12 17	12 20	12 27	12 30	12 35	12 37	12 38	12 43	12 46	12 48
Levenshulme d	11 43				11 58			12 09											12 43			
Heaton Chapel d	11 46				12 01			12 12											12 46			
Stockport a	11 50	11 53		11 57	12 04	12 03		12 16		12 15		12 22	12 27	12 28	12 34	12 38	12 42		12 50	12 53		12 57
d	11 51			11 58		12 04		12 17		12 16		12 23			12 35	12 39	12 42		12 51			12 58
Cheadle Hulme d	11 55			12 02				12 24											12 55			13 02
Bramhall d				12 05																		13 05
Poynton d				12 08																		13 08
Adlington (Cheshire) d				12 11																		13 11
Prestbury d				12 14																		13 14
Macclesfield a				12 18											12 47		12 55					13 18
d				12 18											12 49		12 55					13 18
Congleton d				12 26																		13 26
Handforth d	11 59							12 28											12 59			
Manchester Airport d			12 11				12a22		12a26		12a38							12a53			13 11	
Styal d																					13 18	
Wilmslow d	12 02		12 21			12 11		12 31								12 47			13 02		13 22	
Alderley Edge d	12a08		12 24					12 34											13a08		13 25	
Chelford d								12 38														
Goostrey d								12 43														
Holmes Chapel d			12 32					12 46													13 33	
Sandbach d			12 36					12 51													13 37	
Crewe 10 65 a			12 46			12 27		13 01								13 06					13 47	
Kidsgrove 50 a				12 32																		13 32
Longport 50 a																						
Stoke-on-Trent 50,68 a				12 42						12 43		12 48			13 06		13 12					13 42
Stafford 68 a										13 02					13 25							
Wolverhampton 7 68 a										13 15					13 39							
Birmingham New Street 12 68 a										13 39					13 58							
London Euston 15 ⊖65 a						14 04						14 23					14 42					

Table 84

Saturdays
17 July to 04 September

Manchester, Stockport and Manchester Airport - Crewe and Stoke-on-Trent

	NT	VT	NT	NT	TP	XC	NT	VT	NT	TP	XC	AW	VT	NT	NT	EM	NT	NT	NT	VT	NT	NT
		◇1			◇1	◇1		◇1		◇1	◇1	■	◇1			◇				◇1		
Deansgate d														13 29								
Manchester Oxford Road d			12 58											13 33		13 39					13 58	
Manchester Piccadilly 10 a			13 01											13 35		13 41					14 01	
d	12 52	12 55	13 03	13 04	13 06	13 07	13 14	13 15	13 17	13 20	13 27	13 30	13 35	13 37	13 38	13 43	13 46	13 48	13 52	13 55	14 03	14 04
Levenshulme d	12 58			13 09											13 43				13 58			14 09
Heaton Chapel d	13 01			13 12											13 46				14 01			14 12
Stockport a	13 04	13 03		13 16		13 15		13 22	13 27	13 28	13 34	13 38	13 42		13 50	13 53		13 57	14 04	14 03		14 16
d		13 04		13 17		13 16		13 23			13 35	13 39	13 42		13 51			13 58		14 04		14 17
Cheadle Hulme d				13 24											13 55			14 02				14 24
Bramhall d																		14 05				
Poynton d																		14 08				
Adlington (Cheshire) d																		14 11				
Prestbury d																		14 14				
Macclesfield a											13 47		13 55					14 18				
d											13 49		13 55					14 18				
Congleton d																		14 26				
Handforth d				13 28											13 59							14 28
Manchester Airport d			13a22		13a33		13a38							13a53			14 11				14a22	
Styal d																						
Wilmslow d		13 11		13 31								13 47			14 02		14 21			14 11		14 31
Alderley Edge d				13 34											14a08		14 24					14 34
Chelford d				13 38																		14 38
Goostrey d				13 43																		14 43
Holmes Chapel d				13 46													14 32					14 46
Sandbach d				13 51													14 36					14 51
Crewe 10 65 a		13 27		14 01								14 06					14 46			14 27		15 01
Kidsgrove 50 a																		14 32				
Longport 50 a																						
Stoke-on-Trent 50,68 a						13 43		13 48			14 06		14 12					14 42				
Stafford 68 a						14 02					14 25											
Wolverhampton 7 68 a						14 16					14 39											
Birmingham New Street 12 68 a						14 39					14 58											
London Euston 15 ⊖65 a		15 04						15 23					15 42							16 04		

	TP	XC	NT	VT	NT	TP	XC	AW	VT	NT	NT	EM	NT	NT	NT	VT	NT	NT	TP	XC	NT
	◇1	◇1		◇1		◇1	◇1	■	◇1			◇				◇1			◇1	◇1	
Deansgate d										14 29											
Manchester Oxford Road d										14 33		14 39					14 58				
Manchester Piccadilly 10 a										14 35		14 41					15 01				
d	14 06	14 07	14 14	14 15	14 17	14 20	14 27	14 30	14 35	14 37	14 38	14 43	14 46	14 48	14 52	14 55	15 03	15 04	15 06	15 07	15 14
Levenshulme d											14 43				14 58			15 09			
Heaton Chapel d											14 46				15 01			15 12			
Stockport a		14 15		14 22	14 27	14 28	14 34	14 38	14 42		14 50	14 53		14 57	15 04	15 03		15 16		15 15	
d		14 16		14 23			14 35	14 39	14 42		14 51			14 58		15 04		15 17		15 16	
Cheadle Hulme d											14 55			15 02				15 24			
Bramhall d														15 05							
Poynton d														15 08							
Adlington (Cheshire) d														15 11							
Prestbury d														15 14							
Macclesfield a							14 47		14 55					15 18							
d							14 49		14 55					15 18							
Congleton d														15 26							
Handforth d											14 59							15 28			
Manchester Airport d	14a26		14a38							14a53			15 11				15a22		15a26		15a38
Styal d																					
Wilmslow d								14 47			15 02		15 21			15 11		15 31			
Alderley Edge d											15a08		15 24					15 34			
Chelford d																		15 38			
Goostrey d																		15 43			
Holmes Chapel d													15 32					15 46			
Sandbach d													15 36					15 51			
Crewe 10 65 a								15 06					15 46			15 27		16 01			
Kidsgrove 50 a														15 32							
Longport 50 a																					
Stoke-on-Trent 50,68 a		14 43		14 48			15 06		15 12					15 42						15 43	
Stafford 68 a		15 02					15 25													16 02	
Wolverhampton 7 68 a		15 16					15 39													16 16	
Birmingham New Street 12 68 a		15 39					15 58													16 39	
London Euston 15 ⊖65 a				16 23					16 42							17 04					

Manchester, Stockport and Manchester Airport - Crewe and Stoke-on-Trent

		VT	NT	TP	XC	AW	VT	NT	NT	EM	NT	NT	NT	VT	NT	NT	TP	XC	NT	VT	NT	TP	XC
		◇1		◇1	◇1	■	◇1			◇				◇1			◇1	◇1		◇1		◇1	◇1
Deansgate	d							15 29															
Manchester Oxford Road	d							15 33		15 39					15 58								
Manchester Piccadilly	a							15 35		15 41					16 01								
	d	15 15	15 17	15 20	15 27	15 30	15 35	15 37	15 38	15 43	15 46	15 48	15 52	15 55	16 03	16 04	16 06	16 07	16 14	16 15	16 17	16 20	16 27
Levenshulme	d								15 43				15 58			16 09							
Heaton Chapel	d								15 46				16 01			16 12							
Stockport	a	15 22	15 27	15 28	15 34	15 38	15 42		15 50	15 53		15 57	16 04	16 03		16 16		16 15		16 22	16 27	16 28	16 34
	d	15 23			15 35	15 39	15 42		15 51			15 58		16 04		16 17		16 16		16 23			16 35
Cheadle Hulme	d								15 55			16 02				16 24							
Bramhall	d											16 05											
Poynton	d											16 08											
Adlington (Cheshire)	d											16 11											
Prestbury	d											16 14											
Macclesfield	a				15 47		15 55					16 18											16 47
	d				15 49		15 55					16 18											16 49
Congleton	d											16 26											
Handforth	d								15 59							16 28							
Manchester Airport	d							15a53			16 11				16a22		16a26		16a38				
Styal	d																						
Wilmslow	d					15 47			16 02		16 21			16 11		16 31							
Alderley Edge	d								16a08		16 24					16 34							
Chelford	d															16 38							
Goostrey	d															16 43							
Holmes Chapel	d										16 32					16 46							
Sandbach	d										16 36					16 51							
Crewe 65	a					16 06					16 46			16 27		17 01							
Kidsgrove 50	a											16 32											
Longport 50	a																						
Stoke-on-Trent 50,68	a	15 48			16 06		16 12					16 42						16 43		16 48			17 06
Stafford 68	a				16 24													17 02					17 25
Wolverhampton 68	a				16 39													17 16					17 39
Birmingham New Street 68	a				16 58													17 39					17 58
London Euston ⊖65	a	17 23					17 42							18 04						18 23			

		AW	VT	NT	NT	NT	NT	NT	VT	NT	NT	TP	XC	NT	NT	VT	NT	TP	NT	XC	AW	VT	NT
		■	◇1						◇1			◇1	◇1			◇1		◇1		◇1	■	◇1	
Deansgate	d																		17 12				17 29
Manchester Oxford Road	d			16 33						16 58									17 16				17 33
Manchester Piccadilly	a			16 35						17 01									17 18				17 35
	d	16 30	16 35	16 37	16 38	16 46	16 48	16 51	16 55	17 03	17 03	17 06	17 06	17 09	17 14	17 15	17 17	17 20	17 21	17 27	17 30	17 35	17 37
Levenshulme	d				16 43			16 58			17 08			17 14					17 28				
Heaton Chapel	d				16 46			17 01			17 11			17 17					17 31				
Stockport	a	16 38	16 42		16 50		16 57	17 04	17 03		17 15			17 21		17 22	17 27	17 28	17 34	17 35	17 39	17 43	
	d	16 39	16 42		16 51		16 58	5	17 04		17 16					17 23				17 36	17 40	17 43	
Cheadle Hulme	d				16 55		17 02				17 24												
Bramhall	d						17 05																
Poynton	d						17 08																
Adlington (Cheshire)	d						17 11																
Prestbury	d						17 14																
Macclesfield	a		16 56				17 18						17 25									17 55	
	d		16 56				17 18						17 26									17 55	
Congleton	d						17 26													17 54			
Handforth	d				16 59						17 28												
Manchester Airport	d			16a53		17 11				17a22		17a32			17a38								17a53
Styal	d																						
Wilmslow	d	16 47			17 02	17 21			17 11		17 31										17 48		
Alderley Edge	d				17a08	17 24					17 34												
Chelford	d										17 38												
Goostrey	d										17 43												
Holmes Chapel	d					17 32					17 46												
Sandbach	d					17 36					17 51												
Crewe 65	a	17 06				17 46			17 27		18 01										18 11		
Kidsgrove 50	a						17 32																
Longport 50	a																						
Stoke-on-Trent 50,68	a		17 13				17 42						17 42			17 49				18 07		18 12	
Stafford 68	a												18 03							18 26			
Wolverhampton 68	a												18 16							18 40			
Birmingham New Street 68	a												18 38							18 58			
London Euston ⊖65	a		18 42						19 04							19 23						19 42	

Manchester, Stockport and Manchester Airport - Crewe and Stoke-on-Trent

		NT	EM	NT	NT	NT	VT	NT	XC	TP	NT	NT	VT	NT	TP	XC	AW	VT	NT	NT	EM	NT	NT
			◇				◇1		◇1	◇1			◇1		◇1	◇1	◇	◇1			◇		
Deansgate	d																						
Manchester Oxford Road	d		17 39					17 58											18 33		18 39		
Manchester Piccadilly	a		17 41					18 01											18 35		18 41		
	d	17 38	17 43	17 46	17 48	17 52	17 55	18 03	18 05	18 06	18 08	18 14	18 15	18 17	18 20	18 27	18 30	18 35	18 37	18 38	18 43	18 46	18 48
Levenshulme	d	17 43				17 58					18 13									18 43			
Heaton Chapel	d	17 46				18 01					18 16									18 46			
Stockport	a	17 50	17 53		17 57	18 04	18 03		18 12		18 20		18 22	18 27	18 28	18 34	18 38	18 42		18 50	18 53		18 57
	d	17 51			17 58		18 04		18 13		18 22		18 23			18 35	18 39	18 42		18 51			18 58
Cheadle Hulme	d	17 55			18 02						18 30									18 55			19 02
Bramhall	d				18 05																		19 05
Poynton	d				18 08																		19 08
Adlington (Cheshire)	d				18 11																		19 11
Prestbury	d				18 14																		19 14
Macclesfield	a				18 18				18 25									18 55					19 18
	d				18 18				18 26									18 55					19 18
Congleton	d				18 26											18 54							19 26
Handforth	d	17 59									18 34									18 59			
Manchester Airport	d			18 11				18a22		18a26		18a38							18a53			19b14	
Styal	d			18 18																			
Wilmslow	d	18 02		18 22			18 11				18 37						18 47			19 02		19 26	
Alderley Edge	d	18a08		18 25							18 40									19a08		19a32	
Chelford	d										18 44												
Goostrey	d										18 48												
Holmes Chapel	d			18 33							18 51												
Sandbach	d			18 37							18 56												
Crewe 65	a			18 47			18 27				19 06						19 08						
Kidsgrove 50	a				18 32																		19 32
Longport 50	a																						
Stoke-on-Trent 50,68	a				18 42				18 43				18 48			19 06		19 12					19 42
Stafford 68	a								19 02							19 25							
Wolverhampton 68	a								19 16							19 39							
Birmingham New Street 68	a								19 33							19 58							
London Euston ⊖65	a						20 04						20 25					20 58					

		NT	VT	NT	NT	TP	XC	NT	NT	TP	NT	XC	AW	VT	NT	EM	NT	NT	NT	AW	NT	TP	XC
			◇1			◇1	◇1			◇1		◇1	◇	◇1		◇						◇1	◇1
Deansgate	d														19 29								
Manchester Oxford Road	d			18 58											19 33	19 39	19 43			19 49			
Manchester Piccadilly	a			19 01											19 35	19 41	19 45			19 52			
	d	18 52	18 55	19 03	19 04	19 06	19 07	19 14	19 17	19 18	19 22	19 27	19 30	19 35	19 37	19 43	19 46	19 48	19 51	19 54	20 04	20 06	20 07
Levenshulme	d	18 58			19 09						19 28								19 58		20 09		
Heaton Chapel	d	19 01			19 12						19 31								20 01		20 12		
Stockport	a	19 04	19 03		19 16		19 15		19 27	19 26	19 34	19 34	19 39	19 42		19 53		19 57	20 04		20 16		20 15
	d		19 04		19 17		19 16					19 35	19 39	19 42				19 58			20 17		20 16
Cheadle Hulme	d				19 24													20 02			20 24		
Bramhall	d																	20 05					
Poynton	d																	20 08					
Adlington (Cheshire)	d																	20 11					
Prestbury	d																	20 14					
Macclesfield	a											19 47		19 55				20 18					
	d											19 49		19 55				20 18					
Congleton	d																	20 26					
Handforth	d				19 28																20 28		
Manchester Airport	d			19a24		19a28		19a38							19a53		20c14			20a13		20a36	
Styal	d																						
Wilmslow	d		19 11		19 31								19 47				20a24				20 31		
Alderley Edge	d				19 34																20 34		
Chelford	d				19 38																20 38		
Goostrey	d				19 43																20 43		
Holmes Chapel	d				19 46																20 46		
Sandbach	d				19 51																20 51		
Crewe 65	a		19 27		20 01								20 06								21 01		
Kidsgrove 50	a																	20 32					
Longport 50	a																						
Stoke-on-Trent 50,68	a						19 43					20 06		20 12				20 42					20 43
Stafford 68	a						20 02					20 25											21 02
Wolverhampton 68	a						20 16					20 39											21 15
Birmingham New Street 68	a						20 33					20 58											21 32
London Euston ⊖65	a		21 18											22 01									

b arr. 1908

c arr. 2007

Table 84

Saturdays
17 July to 04 September

Manchester, Stockport and Manchester Airport - Crewe and Stoke-on-Trent

		NT		TP ◇1	XC ◇1	AW ◇	VT ◇1	NT	EM ◇	NT	NT	NT		NT	NT	TP ◇1	XC ◇1	TP ◇1	NT	TP ◇1	XC ◇1	NT		EM ◇	NT
Deansgate ⇌	d							20 29														21 29			
Manchester Oxford Road	d							20 33	20 39	20 43				20 58				21 07				21 33		21 39	21 43
Manchester Piccadilly 10 ⇌	a							20 35	20 41	20 45				21 01				21 09				21 35		21 41	21 45
	d	20 17		20 20	20 27	20 30	20 35	20 37	20 43	20 46	20 48	20 52		21 03	21 04	21 06	21 07	21 11	21 17	21 20	21 28	21 37		21 43	21 46
Levenshulme	d											20 58			21 09										
Heaton Chapel	d											21 01			21 12										
Stockport	a	20 27		20 28	20 34	20 39	20 42		20 53		20 57	21 04			21 16				21 27	21 28	21 35			21 52	
	d				20 35	20 39	20 43				20 58				21 17						21 36				
Cheadle Hulme	d										21 02				21 24										
Bramhall	d										21 05														
Poynton	d										21 08														
Adlington (Cheshire)	d										21 11														
Prestbury	d										21 14														
Macclesfield	a				20 47		20 55				21 18										21 48				
	d				20 49		20 56				21 18										21 50				
Congleton	d										21 26														
Handforth	d														21 28										
Manchester Airport ✈	d							20a53		21b14				21a24		21a36						21a53			22c14
Styal	d																								
Wilmslow	d					20 47				21a24					21 31										22a22
Alderley Edge	d														21 34										
Chelford	d														21 38										
Goostrey	d														21 43										
Holmes Chapel	d														21 46										
Sandbach	d														21 51										
Crewe 10 65	a					21 06									22 01										
Kidsgrove 50	a										21 32														
Longport 50	a																								
Stoke-on-Trent 50,68	a				21 06		21 11				21 42						21 43				22 07				
Stafford 68	a				21 26												22 02				22 33				
Wolverhampton 7 68 ⇌	a				21 39												22 14				22 50				
Birmingham New Street 12 68	a				21 58												22 32				23 17				
London Euston 15 ⊖65	a						23 04																		

		NT	NT	NT	NT	TP ◇1	AW ◇	NT		NT	NT	NT	NT	NT		NT
Deansgate ⇌	d															
Manchester Oxford Road	d							22 43								
Manchester Piccadilly 10 ⇌	a							22 45								
	d	21 48	21 52	22 04	22 17	22 20	22 35	22 46		22 48	23 04	23 10	23 14	23 17		23 37
Levenshulme	d		21 58	22 09							23 09					23 42
Heaton Chapel	d		22 01	22 12							23 12					23 45
Stockport	a	21 58	22 04	22 16	22 27	22 28	22 43			22 57	23 16	23 19	23 23	23 26		23 49
	d	21 58	22 05	22 17			22 44			22 58	23 16		23 23			23 50
Cheadle Hulme	d	22 02		22 24						23 02	23 21		23 27			23 54
Bramhall	d	22 05								23 05			23 30			
Poynton	d	22 08								23 08			23 33			
Adlington (Cheshire)	d	22 11								23 11			23 37			
Prestbury	d	22 14								23 14			23 40			
Macclesfield	a	22 18								23 20			23 46			
	d	22 18														
Congleton	d	22 26														
Handforth	d			22 28							23 25					23 58
Manchester Airport ✈	d							23e14								
Styal	d															
Wilmslow	d			22 31			22 52	23a22			23 28					00 01
Alderley Edge	d			22 34							23 31					00a07
Chelford	d			22 38							23 35					
Goostrey	d			22 43							23 40					
Holmes Chapel	d			22 46							23 43					
Sandbach	d			22 51							23 48					
Crewe 10 65	a			23 01			23 10				23 58					
Kidsgrove 50	a	22 32														
Longport 50	a															
Stoke-on-Trent 50,68	a	22 42														
Stafford 68	a															
Wolverhampton 7 68 ⇌	a															
Birmingham New Street 12 68	a															
London Euston 15 ⊖65	a															

b arr. 2107 c arr. 2208 e arr. 2308

Table 84

Saturdays
from 11 September

Manchester, Stockport and Manchester Airport - Crewe and Stoke-on-Trent

			NT	TP ◇1	AW	XC ◇1	VT ◇1	NT	TP ◇1	NT		VT ◇1	NT	XC ◇1	NT	NT	VT ◇1	TP ◇1	NT	NT		AW ◇	VT ◇1	NT	NT
Deansgate ⇌	d																								
Manchester Oxford Road	d																								
Manchester Piccadilly 10 ⇌	a																								
	d		04 15	04 44	04 58	05 11	05 25	05 35	05 44	05 50		05 55	05 58	06 00		06 06	06 10	06 12	06 15	06 17		06 30	06 35	06 44	06 46
Levenshulme	d															06 11									
Heaton Chapel	d															06 14									
Stockport	a						05 33		05 52	05 59		06 02		06 07		06 18	06 17			06 27		06 38	06 43	06 52	
	d						05 34					06 03		06 08		06 19	06 18					06 39	06 43	06 53	
Cheadle Hulme	d															06 26								06 57	
Bramhall	d																							07 00	
Poynton	d																							07 03	
Adlington (Cheshire)	d																							07 06	
Prestbury	d																							07 09	
Macclesfield	a													06 20			06 30						06 55	07 13	
	d													06 21	06 03		06 31						06 55	07 13	
Congleton	d														06 10									07 21	
Handforth	d															06 30									
Manchester Airport ✈	d		04a30	05a00	05a12			06b05					06a14					06a29	06a39						07 11
Styal	d																								
Wilmslow	d						05 41	06 14				06 11				06 33						06 47			07 21
Alderley Edge	d							06 17								06 36									07 24
Chelford	d							06 21																	
Goostrey	d							06 25																	
Holmes Chapel	d							06 28								06 44									07 32
Sandbach	d							06 33								06 49									07 36
Crewe 10 65	a					05 41	05 57	06 43				06 27				06 59						07 06			07 46
Kidsgrove 50	a														06 16									07 28	
Longport 50	a																								
Stoke-on-Trent 50,68	a					06 07								06 38	06 26		06 46						07 11	07 40	
Stafford 68	a					06 25	06 17							06 57											
Wolverhampton 7 68 ⇌	a					06 39								07 12											
Birmingham New Street 12 68	a					06 57								07 31											
London Euston 15 ⊖65	a						07 52					08 09					08 28						08 46		

		NT	VT ◇1	NT	NT	TP ◇1		XC ◇1	NT	VT ◇1	NT	TP ◇1	NT	XC ◇1	AW	VT ◇1	NT	NT	EM ◇	NT	NT	NT	VT ◇1	NT	NT
Deansgate ⇌	d												07 11				07 28								
Manchester Oxford Road	d			06 58									07 15				07 32		07 38					07 58	
Manchester Piccadilly 10 ⇌	a			07 01									07 17				07 34		07 41					08 01	
	d	06 49	06 55	07 03	07 03	07 06		07 07	07 14	07 15	07 17	07 20	07 21	07 27	07 30	07 35	07 36	07 38	07 42	07 46	07 48	07 52	07 55	08 03	08 04
Levenshulme	d	06 55			07 09								07 28					07 43				07 57			08 09
Heaton Chapel	d	06 58			07 12								07 31					07 46							08 12
Stockport	a	07 01	07 03		07 16			07 15		07 22	07 27	07 28	07 34	07 34	07 38	07 43		07 50	07 53		07 57	08 02	08 03		08 16
	d		07 04		07 18			07 16		07 23				07 35	07 39	07 43		07 51			07 58		08 04		08 17
Cheadle Hulme	d				07 24													07 55			08 02				08 24
Bramhall	d																				08 05				
Poynton	d																				08 08				
Adlington (Cheshire)	d																				08 11				
Prestbury	d																				08 14				
Macclesfield	a													07 47		07 56					08 18				
	d													07 49		07 56					08 18				
Congleton	d																				08 26				
Handforth	d				07 28													07 59							08 28
Manchester Airport ✈	d			07a22		07a29			07a38								07a53			08 11				08a22	
Styal	d																			08 18					
Wilmslow	d		07 11		07 31										07 47			08 01		08 22			08 11		08 31
Alderley Edge	d				07 34													08a07		08 25					08 34
Chelford	d				07 38																				08 38
Goostrey	d				07 43																				08 43
Holmes Chapel	d				07 46															08 33					08 46
Sandbach	d				07 51															08 37					08 51
Crewe 10 65	a		07 27		08 01										08 06					08 47			08 27		09 01
Kidsgrove 50	a																				08 32				
Longport 50	a																								
Stoke-on-Trent 50,68	a							07 43		07 48				08 06		08 12					08 42				
Stafford 68	a							08 02						08 25											
Wolverhampton 7 68 ⇌	a							08 16						08 39											
Birmingham New Street 12 68	a							08 38						08 58											
London Euston 15 ⊖65	a		09 04							09 23						09 42							10 04		

b arr. 0557

Table 84

Saturdays from 11 September

Manchester, Stockport and Manchester Airport - Crewe and Stoke-on-Trent

Station		TP ◇1	XC ◇1	NT	VT ◇1	NT	TP ◇1	XC ◇1	AW ◇	VT ◇1	NT	NT	EM ◇	NT	NT	NT	VT ◇1	NT	NT	TP ◇1	XC ◇1	NT
Deansgate	d										08 29											
Manchester Oxford Road	d										08 33		08 39					08 58				
Manchester Piccadilly	a										08 35		08 41					09 01				
	d	08 06	08 07	08 14	08 15	08 17	08 20	08 27	08 30	08 35	08 37	08 38	08 43	08 46	08 48	08 52	08 55	09 03	09 04	09 06	09 07	09 14
Levenshulme	d											08 43				08 58			09 09			
Heaton Chapel	d											08 46				09 01			09 12			
Stockport	a		08 15		08 22	08 27	08 28	08 34	08 38	08 42		08 50	08 53		08 57	09 04	09 03		09 16		09 15	
	d		08 16		08 23			08 35	08 39	08 42		08 51			08 58		09 04		09 17		09 16	
Cheadle Hulme	d											08 55			09 02				09 24			
Bramhall	d														09 05							
Poynton	d														09 08							
Adlington (Cheshire)	d														09 11							
Prestbury	d														09 14							
Macclesfield	a							08 47		08 55					09 18							
	d							08 49		08 55					09 18							
Congleton	d														09 26							
Handforth	d											08 59							09 28			
Manchester Airport	d	08a26		08a38							08a53			09 11				09a22		09a26		09a38
Styal	d																					
Wilmslow	d								08 47			09 02		09 21			09 11		09 31			
Alderley Edge	d											09a08		09 24					09 34			
Chelford	d																		09 38			
Goostrey	d																		09 43			
Holmes Chapel	d													09 32					09 46			
Sandbach	d													09 36					09 51			
Crewe 65	a								09 06					09 46			09 27		10 01			
Kidsgrove 50	a														09 32							
Longport 50	a																					
Stoke-on-Trent 50,68	a		08 43		08 48			09 06		09 12					09 42						09 43	
Stafford 68	a		09 02					09 25													10 02	
Wolverhampton 68	a		09 15					09 39													10 15	
Birmingham New Street 68	a		09 39					09 58													10 39	
London Euston ⊖65	a				10 23					10 42							11 04					

Station		VT ◇1	NT	TP ◇1	XC ◇1	AW ◇	VT ◇1	NT	NT	EM ◇	NT	NT	NT	VT ◇1	NT	NT	TP ◇1	XC ◇1	NT	VT ◇1	NT	TP ◇1	XC ◇1
Deansgate	d							09 29															
Manchester Oxford Road	d							09 33		09 39					09 58								
Manchester Piccadilly	a							09 35		09 41					10 01								
	d	09 15	09 17	09 20	09 27	09 30	09 35	09 37	09 38	09 43	09 46	09 48	09 52	09 55	10 03	10 04	10 06	10 07	10 14	10 15	10 17	10 20	10 27
Levenshulme	d								09 43				09 58			10 09							
Heaton Chapel	d								09 46				10 01			10 12							
Stockport	a	09 22	09 27	09 28	09 34	09 38	09 42		09 50	09 53		09 57	10 04	10 03		10 16		10 15		10 22	10 27	10 28	10 34
	d	09 23			09 35	09 39	09 42		09 51			09 58		10 04		10 17		10 16		10 23			10 35
Cheadle Hulme	d								09 55			10 02				10 24							
Bramhall	d											10 05											
Poynton	d											10 08											
Adlington (Cheshire)	d											10 11											
Prestbury	d											10 14											
Macclesfield	a				09 47		09 55					10 18											10 47
	d				09 49		09 55					10 18											10 49
Congleton	d											10 26											
Handforth	d								09 59							10 28							
Manchester Airport	d							09a53			10 11				10a22		10a26		10a38				
Styal	d																						
Wilmslow	d					09 47			10 02		10 21			10 11		10 31							
Alderley Edge	d								10a08		10 24					10 34							
Chelford	d															10 38							
Goostrey	d															10 43							
Holmes Chapel	d										10 32					10 46							
Sandbach	d										10 36					10 51							
Crewe 65	a					10 06					10 46			10 27		11 01							
Kidsgrove 50	a											10 32											
Longport 50	a																						
Stoke-on-Trent 50,68	a	09 48			10 06		10 12					10 42						10 43		10 48			11 06
Stafford 68	a				10 25													11 02					11 25
Wolverhampton 68	a				10 39													11 16					11 39
Birmingham New Street 68	a				10 58													11 39					11 58
London Euston ⊖65	a	11 23					11 42							12 04						12 23			

Table 84

Saturdays from 11 September

Manchester, Stockport and Manchester Airport - Crewe and Stoke-on-Trent

Station		AW	VT ◇1	NT	NT	EM ◇	NT	NT	NT	VT ◇1	NT	NT	TP ◇1	XC ◇1	NT	VT ◇1	NT	TP ◇1	XC ◇1	AW ◇	VT ◇1	NT
Deansgate	d			10 29																		11 29
Manchester Oxford Road	d			10 33		10 39					10 58											11 33
Manchester Piccadilly	a			10 35		10 41					11 01											11 35
	d	10 30	10 35	10 37	10 38	10 43	10 46	10 48	10 52	10 55	11 03	11 04	11 06	11 07	11 14	11 15	11 17	11 20	11 27	11 30	11 35	11 37
Levenshulme	d				10 43				10 58			11 09										
Heaton Chapel	d				10 46				11 01			11 12										
Stockport	a	10 38	10 42		10 50	10 53		10 57	11 04	11 03		11 16		11 15		11 22	11 27	11 28	11 34	11 38	11 42	
	d	10 39	10 42		10 51			10 58		11 04		11 17		11 16		11 23			11 35	11 39	11 42	
Cheadle Hulme	d				10 55			11 02				11 24										
Bramhall	d							11 05														
Poynton	d							11 08														
Adlington (Cheshire)	d							11 11														
Prestbury	d							11 14														
Macclesfield	a		10 55					11 18											11 47		11 55	
	d		10 55					11 18											11 49		11 55	
Congleton	d							11 26														
Handforth	d				10 59							11 28										
Manchester Airport	d			10a53			11 11				11a22		11a26		11a38							11a53
Styal	d																					
Wilmslow	d	10 47			11 02		11 21			11 11		11 31								11 47		
Alderley Edge	d				11a08		11 24					11 34										
Chelford	d											11 38										
Goostrey	d											11 43										
Holmes Chapel	d						11 32					11 46										
Sandbach	d						11 36					11 51										
Crewe 65	a	11 06					11 46			11 27		12 01								12 06		
Kidsgrove 50	a							11 32														
Longport 50	a																					
Stoke-on-Trent 50,68	a		11 12					11 42						11 43		11 48			12 06		12 12	
Stafford 68	a													12 02					12 24			
Wolverhampton 68	a													12 16					12 39			
Birmingham New Street 68	a													12 39					12 58			
London Euston ⊖65	a		12 42							13 04						13 23					13 42	

Station		NT	EM ◇	NT	NT	NT	VT ◇1	NT	NT	TP ◇1	XC ◇1	NT	VT ◇1	NT	TP ◇1	XC ◇1	AW	VT ◇1	NT	NT	EM ◇	NT	NT
Deansgate	d																		12 29				
Manchester Oxford Road	d		11 39					11 58											12 33		12 39		
Manchester Piccadilly	a		11 41					12 01											12 35		12 41		
	d	11 38	11 43	11 46	11 48	11 52	11 55	12 03	12 04	12 06	12 07	12 14	12 15	12 17	12 20	12 27	12 30	12 35	12 37	12 38	12 43	12 46	12 48
Levenshulme	d	11 43				11 58			12 09											12 43			
Heaton Chapel	d	11 46				12 01			12 12											12 46			
Stockport	a	11 50	11 53		11 57	12 04	12 03		12 16		12 15		12 22	12 27	12 28	12 34	12 38	12 42		12 50	12 53		12 57
	d	11 51			11 58		12 04		12 17		12 16		12 23			12 35	12 39	12 42		12 51			12 58
Cheadle Hulme	d	11 55			12 02				12 24											12 55			13 02
Bramhall	d				12 05																		13 05
Poynton	d				12 08																		13 08
Adlington (Cheshire)	d				12 11																		13 11
Prestbury	d				12 14																		13 14
Macclesfield	a				12 18											12 47		12 55					13 18
	d				12 18											12 49		12 55					13 18
Congleton	d				12 26																		13 26
Handforth	d	11 59							12 28											12 59			
Manchester Airport	d			12 11				12a22		12a26		12a38							12a53			13 11	
Styal	d																					13 18	
Wilmslow	d	12 02		12 21			12 11		12 31								12 47			13 02		13 22	
Alderley Edge	d	12a08		12 24					12 34											13a08		13 25	
Chelford	d								12 38														
Goostrey	d								12 43														
Holmes Chapel	d			12 32					12 46													13 33	
Sandbach	d			12 36					12 51													13 37	
Crewe 65	a			12 46			12 27		13 01								13 06					13 47	
Kidsgrove 50	a				12 32																		13 32
Longport 50	a																						
Stoke-on-Trent 50,68	a				12 42						12 43		12 48			13 06		13 12					13 42
Stafford 68	a										13 02					13 25							
Wolverhampton 68	a										13 15					13 39							
Birmingham New Street 68	a										13 39					13 58							
London Euston ⊖65	a						14 04						14 23					14 42					

Manchester, Stockport and Manchester Airport - Crewe and Stoke-on-Trent

Saturdays from 11 September

	NT	VT	NT	NT	TP	XC	NT	VT	NT	TP	XC	AW	VT	NT	NT	EM	NT	NT	NT	VT	NT	NT
		◇1			◇1	◇1		◇1		◇1	◇1	■	◇1			◇				◇1		
Deansgate d														13 29								
Manchester Oxford Road d			12 58											13 33		13 39					13 58	
Manchester Piccadilly a			13 01											13 35		13 41					14 01	
d	12 52	12 55	13 03	13 04	13 06	13 07	13 14	13 15	13 17	13 20	13 27	13 30	13 35	13 37	13 38	13 43	13 46	13 48	13 52	13 55	14 03	14 04
Levenshulme d	12 58			13 09											13 43				13 58			14 09
Heaton Chapel d	13 01			13 12											13 46				14 01			14 12
Stockport a	13 04	13 03		13 16		13 15		13 22	13 27	13 28	13 34	13 38	13 42		13 50	13 53		13 57	14 04	14 03		14 16
d		13 04		13 17		13 16		13 23			13 35	13 39	13 42		13 51			13 58		14 04		14 17
Cheadle Hulme d				13 24											13 55			14 02				14 24
Bramhall d																		14 05				
Poynton d																		14 08				
Adlington (Cheshire) d																		14 11				
Prestbury d																		14 14				
Macclesfield a											13 47		13 55					14 18				
d											13 49		13 55					14 18				
Congleton d																		14 26				
Handforth d				13 28											13 59							14 28
Manchester Airport d			13a22		13a33		13a38							13a53			14 11				14a22	
Styal d																						
Wilmslow d		13 11		13 31								13 47			14 02		14 21			14 11		14 31
Alderley Edge d				13 34											14a08		14 24					14 34
Chelford d				13 38																		14 38
Goostrey d				13 43																		14 43
Holmes Chapel d				13 46													14 32					14 46
Sandbach d				13 51													14 36					14 51
Crewe 65 a		13 27		14 01								14 06					14 46			14 27		15 01
Kidsgrove 50 a																		14 32				
Longport 50 a																						
Stoke-on-Trent 50,68 a						13 43		13 48			14 06		14 12					14 42				
Stafford 68 a						14 02					14 25											
Wolverhampton 68 a						14 16					14 39											
Birmingham New Street 68 a						14 39					14 58											
London Euston ⊖65 a		15 04						15 23					15 42							16 04		

	TP	XC	NT	VT	NT	TP	XC	AW	VT	NT	NT	EM	NT	NT	NT	VT	NT	NT	TP	XC
	◇1	◇1		◇1		◇1	◇1		◇1			◇				◇1			◇1	◇1
Deansgate d										14 29										
Manchester Oxford Road d										14 33		14 39					14 58			
Manchester Piccadilly a										14 35		14 41					15 01			
d	14 06	14 07	14 14	14 15	14 17	14 20	14 27	14 30	14 35	14 37	14 38	14 43	14 46	14 48	14 52	14 55	15 03	15 04	15 06	15 07
Levenshulme d											14 43				14 58			15 09		
Heaton Chapel d											14 46				15 01			15 12		
Stockport a		14 15		14 22	14 27	14 28	14 34	14 38	14 42		14 50	14 53		14 57	15 04	15 03		15 16		15 15
d		14 16		14 23			14 35	14 39	14 42		14 51			14 58		15 04		15 17		15 16
Cheadle Hulme d											14 55			15 02				15 24		
Bramhall d														15 05						
Poynton d														15 08						
Adlington (Cheshire) d														15 11						
Prestbury d														15 14						
Macclesfield a							14 47		14 55					15 18						
d							14 49		14 55					15 18						
Congleton d														15 26						
Handforth d											14 59							15 28		
Manchester Airport d	14a26		14a38							14a53			15 11				15a22		15a26	
Styal d																				
Wilmslow d								14 47			15 02		15 21			15 11		15 31		
Alderley Edge d											15a08		15 24					15 34		
Chelford d																		15 38		
Goostrey d																		15 43		
Holmes Chapel d													15 32					15 46		
Sandbach d													15 36					15 51		
Crewe 65 a								15 06					15 46			15 27		16 02		
Kidsgrove 50 a														15 32						
Longport 50 a																				
Stoke-on-Trent 50,68 a		14 43		14 48			15 06		15 12					15 42						15 43
Stafford 68 a		15 02					15 25													16 02
Wolverhampton 68 a		15 16					15 39													16 16
Birmingham New Street 68 a		15 39					15 58													16 39
London Euston ⊖65 a				16 23					16 42							17 04				

Manchester, Stockport and Manchester Airport - Crewe and Stoke-on-Trent

Saturdays from 11 September

	NT	VT	NT	TP	XC	AW	VT	NT	NT	EM	NT	NT	NT	VT	NT	NT	TP	XC	NT	VT	NT	TP
		◇1		◇1	◇1	■	◇1			◇				◇1			◇1	◇1		◇1		◇1
Deansgate d								15 29														
Manchester Oxford Road d								15 33		15 39					15 58							
Manchester Piccadilly a								15 35		15 41					16 01							
d	15 14	15 15	15 17	15 20	15 27	15 30	15 35	15 37	15 38	15 43	15 46	15 48	15 52	15 55	16 03	16 04	16 06	16 07	16 14	16 15	16 17	16 20
Levenshulme d									15 43				15 58			16 09						
Heaton Chapel d									15 46				16 01			16 12						
Stockport a		15 22	15 27	15 28	15 34	15 38	15 42		15 50	15 53		15 57	16 04	16 03		16 16		16 15		16 22	16 27	16 28
d		15 23			15 35	15 39	15 42		15 51			15 58		16 04		16 17		16 16		16 23		
Cheadle Hulme d									15 55			16 02				16 24						
Bramhall d												16 05										
Poynton d												16 08										
Adlington (Cheshire) d												16 11										
Prestbury d												16 14										
Macclesfield a					15 47		15 55					16 18										
d					15 49		15 55					16 18										
Congleton d												16 26										
Handforth d									15 59							16 28						
Manchester Airport d	15a38							15a53			16 11				16a22		16a26		16a38			
Styal d																						
Wilmslow d						15 47			16 02		16 21			16 11		16 31						
Alderley Edge d									16a08		16 24					16 34						
Chelford d																16 38						
Goostrey d																16 43						
Holmes Chapel d											16 32					16 46						
Sandbach d											16 36					16 51						
Crewe 65 a						16 06					16 46			16 27		17 01						
Kidsgrove 50 a												16 32										
Longport 50 a																						
Stoke-on-Trent 50,68 a		15 48			16 06		16 12					16 42						16 43		16 48		
Stafford 68 a					16 24													17 02				
Wolverhampton 68 a					16 39													17 16				
Birmingham New Street 68 a					16 58													17 39				
London Euston ⊖65 a		17 23					17 42							18 04						18 23		

	XC	AW	VT	NT	NT	NT	NT	NT	VT	NT	NT	TP	XC	NT	NT	VT	NT	TP	NT	XC	AW
	◇1	■	◇1						◇1			◇1	◇1			◇1		◇1		◇1	■
Deansgate d																			17 12		
Manchester Oxford Road d				16 33						16 58									17 16		
Manchester Piccadilly a				16 35						17 01									17 18		
d	16 27	16 30	16 35	16 37	16 38	16 46	16 48	16 51	16 55	17 03	17 03	17 06	17 06	17 09	17 14	17 15	17 17	17 20	17 21	17 27	17 30
Levenshulme d					16 43			16 58			17 08			17 14					17 28		
Heaton Chapel d					16 46			17 01			17 11			17 17					17 31		
Stockport a	16 34	16 38	16 42		16 50		16 57	17 04	17 03		17 15			17 21		17 22	17 27	17 28	17 34	17 35	17 39
d	16 35	16 39	16 42		16 51		16 58		17 04		17 16					17 23				17 36	17 40
Cheadle Hulme d					16 55		17 02				17 24										
Bramhall d							17 05														
Poynton d							17 08														
Adlington (Cheshire) d							17 11														
Prestbury d							17 14														
Macclesfield a	16 47		16 56				17 18						17 25								
d	16 49		16 56				17 18						17 26								
Congleton d							17 26													17 54	
Handforth d					16 59						17 28										
Manchester Airport d				16a53		17 11				17a22		17a32			17a38						
Styal d																					
Wilmslow d		16 47			17 02	17 21			17 11		17 31										17 48
Alderley Edge d					17a08	17 24					17 34										
Chelford d											17 38										
Goostrey d											17 43										
Holmes Chapel d						17 32					17 46										
Sandbach d						17 36					17 51										
Crewe 65 a		17 06				17 46			17 27		18 01										18 11
Kidsgrove 50 a							17 32														
Longport 50 a																					
Stoke-on-Trent 50,68 a	17 06		17 13				17 42						17 42			17 49				18 07	
Stafford 68 a	17 25												18 03							18 26	
Wolverhampton 68 a	17 39												18 16							18 40	
Birmingham New Street 68 a	17 58												18 38							18 58	
London Euston ⊖65 a			18 42						19 04							19 23					

Table 84

Manchester, Stockport and Manchester Airport - Crewe and Stoke-on-Trent

		VT	NT	NT	EM	NT	NT	NT	VT	NT		XC	TP	NT	NT	VT	NT	TP	XC	AW		VT	NT	NT	EM
		◇1 ⊐			◇				◇1 ⊐			◇1 ⌶	◇1 ⌶			◇1 ⊐		◇1 ⌶	◇1 ⌶	◇ ⌶		◇1 ⊐			◇
Deansgate	d		17 29																						
Manchester Oxford Road	d		17 33		17 39					17 58													18 33		18 39
Manchester Piccadilly 10	a		17 35		17 41					18 01													18 35		18 41
	d	17 35	17 37	17 38	17 43	17 46	17 48	17 52	17 55	18 03		18 05	18 06	18 08	18 14	18 15	18 17	18 20	18 27	18 30		18 35	18 37	18 38	18 43
Levenshulme	d			17 43				17 58						18 13										18 43	
Heaton Chapel	d			17 46				18 01						18 16										18 46	
Stockport	a	17 43		17 50	17 53		17 57	18 04	18 03			18 12		18 20		18 22	18 27	18 28	18 34	18 38		18 42		18 50	18 53
	d	17 43		17 51			17 58		18 04			18 13		18 22		18 23			18 35	18 39		18 42		18 51	
Cheadle Hulme	d			17 55			18 02							18 30										18 55	
Bramhall	d						18 05																		
Poynton	d						18 08																		
Adlington (Cheshire)	d						18 11																		
Prestbury	d						18 14																		
Macclesfield	a	17 55					18 18					18 25										18 55			
	d	17 55					18 18					18 26										18 55			
Congleton	d						18 26												18 54						
Handforth	d			17 59										18 34										18 59	
Manchester Airport ✈	d		17a53			18 11				18a22			18a26		18a38								18a53		
Styal	d					18 18																			
Wilmslow	d			18 02		18 22			18 11					18 37						18 47				19 02	
Alderley Edge	d			18a08		18 25								18 40										19a08	
Chelford	d													18 44											
Goostrey	d													18 48											
Holmes Chapel	d					18 33								18 51											
Sandbach	d					18 37								18 56											
Crewe 10 65	a					18 47			18 27					19 06						19 08					
Kidsgrove 50	a						18 32																		
Longport 50	a																								
Stoke-on-Trent 50,68	a	18 12					18 42					18 43				18 48			19 06			19 12			
Stafford 68	a											19 02							19 25						
Wolverhampton 7 68	a											19 16							19 39						
Birmingham New Street 12 68	a											19 33							19 58						
London Euston 15 ⊖65	a	19 42							20 04							20 25						20 58			

		NT	NT	NT	VT	NT	NT	TP	XC	NT	NT	TP	NT	XC	AW	VT		NT	EM	NT	NT	NT		AW	NT
					◇1 ⊐			◇1 ⌶	◇1 ⌶			◇1		◇1 ⌶	◇	◇1 ⊐			◇					◇ ⌶	
Deansgate	d																	19 29							
Manchester Oxford Road	d					18 58												19 33	19 39	19 43				19 49	
Manchester Piccadilly 10	a					19 01												19 35	19 41	19 45				19 52	
	d	18 46	18 48	18 52	18 55	19 03	19 04	19 06	19 07	19 14	19 17	19 18	19 22	19 27	19 30	19 35		19 37	19 43	19 46	19 48	19 51		19 54	20 04
Levenshulme	d			18 58			19 09						19 28									19 58			20 09
Heaton Chapel	d			19 01			19 12						19 31									20 01			20 12
Stockport	a		18 57	19 04	19 03		19 16		19 15		19 27	19 26	19 34	19 34	19 39	19 42			19 53		19 57	20 04			20 16
	d		18 58		19 04		19 17		19 16					19 35	19 39	19 42					19 58				20 17
Cheadle Hulme	d		19 02				19 24														20 02				20 24
Bramhall	d		19 05																		20 05				
Poynton	d		19 08																		20 08				
Adlington (Cheshire)	d		19 11																		20 11				
Prestbury	d		19 14																		20 14				
Macclesfield	a		19 18											19 47		19 55					20 18				
	d		19 18											19 49		19 55					20 18				
Congleton	d		19 26																		20 26				
Handforth	d						19 28																		20 28
Manchester Airport ✈	d	19b14				19a24		19a28		19a38								19a53		20c14				20a13	
Styal	d																								
Wilmslow	d	19 26			19 11		19 31								19 47					20a24					20 31
Alderley Edge	d	19a32					19 34																		20 34
Chelford	d						19 38																		20 38
Goostrey	d						19 43																		20 43
Holmes Chapel	d						19 46																		20 46
Sandbach	d						19 51																		20 51
Crewe 10 65	a				19 27		20 01								20 06										21 01
Kidsgrove 50	a		19 32																		20 32				
Longport 50	a																								
Stoke-on-Trent 50,68	a		19 42						19 43					20 06		20 12					20 42				
Stafford 68	a								20 02					20 25											
Wolverhampton 7 68	a								20 16					20 39											
Birmingham New Street 12 68	a								20 33					20 58											
London Euston 15 ⊖65	a				21 18											22 01									

b arr. 1908 c arr. 2007

Table 84

Manchester, Stockport and Manchester Airport - Crewe and Stoke-on-Trent

		TP		XC	TP	NT	TP	XC	AW	VT	NT	EM		NT	NT	NT	NT	NT	TP	XC	TP	NT		TP	XC
		◇1 ⌶		◇1 ⌶	◇1		◇1	◇1 ⌶	◇	◇1 ⊐		◇							◇1 ⌶	◇1 ⌶	◇1			◇1	◇1 ⌶
Deansgate	d										20 29														
Manchester Oxford Road	d				20 07						20 33	20 39		20 43			20 58				21 07				
Manchester Piccadilly 10	a				20 09						20 35	20 41		20 45			21 01				21 09				
	d	20 06		20 07	20 11	20 17	20 20	20 27	20 30	20 35	20 37	20 43		20 46	20 48	20 52	21 03	21 04	21 06	21 07	21 11	21 17		21 20	21 28
Levenshulme	d															20 58		21 09							
Heaton Chapel	d															21 01		21 12							
Stockport	a			20 15		20 27	20 28	20 34	20 39	20 42		20 53			20 57	21 04		21 16				21 27		21 28	21 35
	d			20 16				20 35	20 39	20 43					20 58			21 17							21 36
Cheadle Hulme	d														21 02			21 24							
Bramhall	d														21 05										
Poynton	d														21 08										
Adlington (Cheshire)	d														21 11										
Prestbury	d														21 14										
Macclesfield	a							20 47		20 55					21 18										21 48
	d							20 49		20 56					21 18										21 50
Congleton	d														21 26										
Handforth	d																	21 28							
Manchester Airport ✈	d	20a36									20a53			21b14			21a24		21a36						
Styal	d																								
Wilmslow	d								20 47					21a24				21 31							
Alderley Edge	d																	21 34							
Chelford	d																	21 38							
Goostrey	d																	21 43							
Holmes Chapel	d																	21 46							
Sandbach	d																	21 51							
Crewe 10 65	a								21 06									22 01							
Kidsgrove 50	a														21 32										
Longport 50	a																								
Stoke-on-Trent 50,68	a			20 43				21 06		21 11					21 42					21 43					22 07
Stafford 68	a			21 02				21 26												22 02					22 33
Wolverhampton 7 68	a			21 15				21 39												22 14					22 50
Birmingham New Street 12 68	a			21 32				21 58												22 32					23 17
London Euston 15 ⊖65	a									23 04															

		NT	EM	NT	NT	NT	NT	NT		TP	AW	NT	NT	NT	NT	NT	NT			NT
			◇							◇1	◇									
Deansgate	d	21 29																		
Manchester Oxford Road	d	21 33	21 39	21 43								22 43								
Manchester Piccadilly 10	a	21 35	21 41	21 45								22 45								
	d	21 37	21 43	21 46	21 48	21 52	22 04	22 17		22 20	22 35	22 46	22 48	23 04	23 10	23 14	23 17			23 37
Levenshulme	d					21 58	22 09							23 09						23 42
Heaton Chapel	d					22 01	22 12							23 12						23 45
Stockport	a		21 52		21 58	22 04	22 16	22 27		22 28	22 43		22 57	23 16	23 19	23 23	23 26			23 49
	d		21 52		21 58		22 17				22 44		22 58	23 16		23 23				23 50
Cheadle Hulme	d				22 02		22 24						23 02	23 21		23 27				23 54
Bramhall	d				22 05								23 05			23 30				
Poynton	d				22 08								23 08			23 33				
Adlington (Cheshire)	d				22 11								23 11			23 37				
Prestbury	d				22 14								23 14			23 40				
Macclesfield	a				22 18								23 20			23 46				
	d				22 18															
Congleton	d				22 26															
Handforth	d						22 28							23 25						23 58
Manchester Airport ✈	d	21a53		22c14								23e14								
Styal	d																			
Wilmslow	d			22a22			22 31				22 52	23a22		23 28						00 01
Alderley Edge	d						22 34							23 31						00a07
Chelford	d						22 38							23 35						
Goostrey	d						22 43							23 40						
Holmes Chapel	d						22 46							23 43						
Sandbach	d						22 51							23 48						
Crewe 10 65	a						23 01				23 10			23 58						
Kidsgrove 50	a				22 32															
Longport 50	a																			
Stoke-on-Trent 50,68	a				22 42															
Stafford 68	a																			
Wolverhampton 7 68	a																			
Birmingham New Street 12 68	a																			
London Euston 15 ⊖65	a																			

b arr. 2107 c arr. 2208 e arr. 2308

Table 84

Sundays until 11 July

Manchester, Stockport and Manchester Airport - Crewe and Stoke-on-Trent

		NT	NT	NT	XC	VT	TP	VT	XC	NT	TP	XC	NT	TP	NT	NT		VT	NT		XC	AW	NT	XC
					🚌	◇1 ⊡	◇1	◇1 ⊡	◇1 B ⌶		◇1	🚌		◇1				◇1 ⊡			◇1 B ⌶	◇ C ⌶		🚌
Deansgate d																			09 15					
Manchester Oxford Road d																09 03			09 18					
Manchester Piccadilly 10 a																09 05			09 21					
d		05 41	06 41	07 41		08 05	08 13	08 20	08 27	08 41	08 47		08 55	08 58	09 04	09 07		09 20	09 22		09 27	09 30	09 41	
Levenshulme d													09 00		09 09									
Heaton Chapel d													09 03		09 12									
Stockport a						08 13		08 28	08 34				09 07	09 06	09 16			09 27	09 31		09 35	09 38		
d						08 14		08 29	08 36						09 17			09 28			09 36	09 39		
Cheadle Hulme d															09 21									
Bramhall d																								
Poynton d																								
Adlington (Cheshire) d																								
Prestbury d																								
Macclesfield a																								
d					07 50							08 47												09 43
Congleton d																								
Handforth d															09 25									
Manchester Airport ✈ d		06a03	07a03	08a03			08a33			09 06	09a07					09a22							10a03	
Styal d										09 10														
Wilmslow d						08 22		08 38	08 43	09 15					09 28			09 36			09 44	09 47		
Alderley Edge d										09 20					09a35									
Chelford d										09 24														
Goostrey d										09 28														
Holmes Chapel d										09 31														
Sandbach d										09 36														
Crewe 10 65 a						08 39			09 02	09 46												10 09		
Kidsgrove 50 a																								
Longport 50 a																								
Stoke-on-Trent 50,68 a					08 45							09 42												10 38
Stafford 68 a					09 15	09 00		09 15	09 25			10 12						10 09			10 22			11 08
Wolverhampton 7 68 a									09 40												10 40			
Birmingham New Street 12 68 a									09 58												10 58			
London Euston 15 ⊖65 a						10 56		11 12										12 09						

	NT	NT	NT	TP	VT		XC	AW	VT	NT	XC	NT	VT	TP	NT		AW	XC	VT	NT	XC	NT	VT	NT
				◇1	◇1 ⊡		◇1 B ⌶	■ ⌶	◇1 ⊡		🚌		◇1 ⊡	◇1			■ ⌶	◇1 B ⌶	◇1 ⊡		🚌		◇1 ⊡	
Deansgate d															11 11									
Manchester Oxford Road d			10 00												11 17					11 37				12 00
Manchester Piccadilly 10 a			10 03												11 19					11 41				12 02
d	09 51	10 01	10 08	10 16	10 20		10 24	10 30	10 35	10 41		10 52	11 08	11 18	11 22		11 24	11 27	11 35	11 41		11 52	11 55	12 04
Levenshulme d	09 58	10 07										10 58										11 58		
Heaton Chapel d	10 01	10 10										11 01										12 01		
Stockport a	10 04	10 13			10 28		10 32	10 39	10 44			11 04	11 16	11 27	11 30		11 34	11 34	11 43			12 04	12 03	
d		10 14			10 29		10 33	10 41	10 45				11 18				11 40	11 36	11 44				12 05	
Cheadle Hulme d		10 18																						
Bramhall d																								
Poynton d																								
Adlington (Cheshire) d																								
Prestbury d																								
Macclesfield a																								
d											10 49										11 50			
Congleton d																								
Handforth d		10 22																						
Manchester Airport ✈ d			10a24	10a31						11b08										12a03				12a21
Styal d										11 12														
Wilmslow d		10 25			10 37		10 43	10 47	10 53	11 16			11 26				11 48	11 44	11 53				12 12	
Alderley Edge d		10a36								11 20														
Chelford d										11 24														
Goostrey d										11 37														
Holmes Chapel d										11 40														
Sandbach d										11 44														
Crewe 10 65 a					10 53			11 07		11 54							12 07						12 28	
Kidsgrove 50 a																								
Longport 50 a																								
Stoke-on-Trent 50,68 a											11 44										12 45			
Stafford 68 a							11 18		11 27		12 14		11 59					12 24	12 27		13 15			
Wolverhampton 7 68 a							11 40											12 40						
Birmingham New Street 12 68 a							11 58											12 58						
London Euston 15 ⊖65 a					12 56				13 04				13 32						13 51				14 12	

A not 23 May.
B ⌶ to Wolverhampton
C ◇ to Wilmslow
b arr. 1102

Table 84

Sundays until 11 July

Manchester, Stockport and Manchester Airport - Crewe and Stoke-on-Trent

	NT		TP	VT	TP	NT	XC	VT	NT	EM	NT		VT	NT	NT	XC	TP	VT	TP	NT	XC		AW	VT
			◇1	◇1 ⊡	◇1		◇1 A ⌶	◇1 ⊡		◇			◇1 ⊡			◇1 ⌶	◇1	◇1 ⊡	◇1		◇1 A ⌶		■ ⌶	◇1 ⊡
Deansgate d						12 11														13 11				
Manchester Oxford Road d						12 17								13 00						13 17				
Manchester Piccadilly 10 a						12 19								13 02						13 19				
d	12 04		12 13	12 15	12 18	12 22	12 26	12 35	12 41	12 44	12 52		12 55	13 04	13 04	13 07	13 13	13 15	13 20	13 22	13 27		13 30	13 35
Levenshulme d	12 09										12 58				13 09									
Heaton Chapel d	12 12										13 01				13 12									
Stockport a	12 16			12 22	12 28	12 33		12 44		12 53	13 04		13 03		13 16			13 22	13 28	13 30	13 34		13 39	13 42
d	12 16			12 24				12 45					13 05		13 17			13 22			13 36		13 40	13 42
Cheadle Hulme d	12 20														13 21									
Bramhall d																								
Poynton d																								
Adlington (Cheshire) d																								
Prestbury d																								
Macclesfield a																					13 48			13 55
d																					13 49			13 55
Congleton d																								
Handforth d	12 24														13 25									
Manchester Airport ✈ d			12a29						13 06					13a24			13a29							
Styal d									13 10															
Wilmslow d	12 27			12 32			12 43	12 53	13 15				13 12		13 28								13 47	
Alderley Edge d	12a33								13a21						13 31									
Chelford d															13 35									
Goostrey d															13 40									
Holmes Chapel d															13 43									
Sandbach d															13 48									
Crewe 10 65 a													13 28		13 58								14 07	
Kidsgrove 50 a																								
Longport 50 a																								
Stoke-on-Trent 50,68 a																13 42		13 49			14 06			14 12
Stafford 68 a				13 05			13 25	13 27													14 24			
Wolverhampton 7 68 a							13 40									14 13					14 40			
Birmingham New Street 12 68 a							13 58									14 31					14 58			
London Euston 15 ⊖65 a				14 41				14 52					15 11					15 30						15 48

	NT	EM	NT	VT	NT	NT	XC		TP	VT	TP	NT	XC	AW	VT	NT	NT		EM	NT	VT	NT	NT	XC
		◇		◇1 ⊡			◇1 ⌶		◇1	◇1 ⊡	◇1		◇1 A ⌶	■ ⌶	◇1 ⊡				◇		◇1 ⊡			◇1 ⌶
Deansgate d												14 11												
Manchester Oxford Road d		13 39			14 00							14 17							14 39			15 00		
Manchester Piccadilly 10 a		13 41			14 02							14 19							14 41			15 02		
d	13 41	13 44	13 52	13 55	14 04	14 04	14 07		14 13	14 15	14 20	14 22	14 27	14 30	14 35	14 41	14 41		14 44	14 52	14 55	15 04	15 04	15 07
Levenshulme d			13 58			14 09														14 58			15 09	
Heaton Chapel d			14 01			14 12														15 01			15 12	
Stockport a		13 53	14 04	14 03		14 16				14 22	14 28	14 33	14 34	14 39	14 42		14 49		14 53	15 04	15 03		15 16	
d				14 04		14 17				14 22			14 36	14 39	14 42		14 51				15 04		15 17	
Cheadle Hulme d						14 22											14 56						15 22	
Bramhall d																	14 59							
Poynton d																	15 02							
Adlington (Cheshire) d																	15 04							
Prestbury d																	15 07							
Macclesfield a													14 48		14 55		15 11							
d													14 49		14 55		15 11							
Congleton d																	15 19							
Handforth d						14 26																	15 26	
Manchester Airport ✈ d	14a03				14a21				14a29							15 06						15a21		
Styal d																15 10								
Wilmslow d				14 11		14 29								14 47		15 15					15 11		15 29	
Alderley Edge d						14a35										15a21							15 32	
Chelford d																							15 36	
Goostrey d																							15 40	
Holmes Chapel d																							15 43	
Sandbach d																							15 48	
Crewe 10 65 a				14 27										15 07							15 27		15 58	
Kidsgrove 50 a																	15 25							
Longport 50 a																								
Stoke-on-Trent 50,68 a							14 42			14 49			15 06		15 12		15 37							15 42
Stafford 68 a													15 24											
Wolverhampton 7 68 a							15 13						15 40											16 13
Birmingham New Street 12 68 a							15 31						15 58											16 31
London Euston 15 ⊖65 a				16 11						16 30					16 48						17 11			

A ⌶ to Wolverhampton

Table 84

Sundays until 11 July

Manchester, Stockport and Manchester Airport - Crewe and Stoke-on-Trent

Station		TP	VT	TP	NT	XC	AW	VT	NT	EM	NT	VT	NT	NT	XC	TP	VT	TP	NT	XC	AW	VT
		◇■	◇■	◇■		◇■	■	◇■		◇		◇■			◇■	◇■	◇■	◇■		◇■	■	◇■
			⊐			A ✠	✠	⊐				⊐			✠		⊐			A ✠	✠	⊐
Deansgate	d				15 11														16 11			
Manchester Oxford Road	d				15 17					15 39			16 00						16 17			
Manchester Piccadilly 10	a				15 19					15 41			16 02						16 19			
	d	15 13	15 15	15 20	15 22	15 27	15 30	15 35	15 41	15 44	15 52	15 55	16 04	16 04	16 07	16 13	16 15	16 20	16 22	16 27	16 30	16 35
Levenshulme	d										15 58			16 09								
Heaton Chapel	d										16 01			16 12								
Stockport	a		15 22	15 28	15 30	15 35	15 39	15 42		15 53	16 04	16 03		16 16			16 22	16 28	16 33	16 34	16 39	16 42
	d		15 22			15 36	15 39	15 42				16 04		16 17			16 23			16 36	16 39	16 42
Cheadle Hulme	d													16 22								
Bramhall	d																					
Poynton	d																					
Adlington (Cheshire)	d																					
Prestbury	d																					
Macclesfield	a					15 48		15 55												16 48		16 55
	d					15 49		15 55												16 49		16 55
Congleton	d																					
Handforth	d													16 26								
Manchester Airport ✈	d	15a29							16a03				16a21			16a29						
Styal	d																					
Wilmslow	d						15 47					16 11		16 29							16 47	
Alderley Edge	d													16a35								
Chelford	d																					
Goostrey	d																					
Holmes Chapel	d																					
Sandbach	d																					
Crewe 10 65	a						16 06					16 27									17 06	
Kidsgrove 50	a																					
Longport 50	a																					
Stoke-on-Trent 50,68	a		15 49			16 06		16 12							16 42		16 48			17 06		17 12
Stafford 68	a					16 24														17 25		
Wolverhampton 7 68	a					16 40									17 13					17 40		
Birmingham New Street 12 68	a					16 58									17 31					17 58		
London Euston 15 ⊖65	a		17 30					17 48				18 11					18 30					18 48

Station		NT	EM	NT	VT	NT	NT	XC	TP	VT	TP	NT	XC	AW	VT	NT	EM	NT	VT	NT	NT	XC	TP
			◇		◇■			◇■	◇■	◇■	◇■		◇■	■	◇■		◇		◇■			◇■	◇■
					⊐			✠		⊐			A ✠	✠	⊐				⊐			✠	
Deansgate	d											17 11											
Manchester Oxford Road	d		16 39			17 00						17 17					17 39			18 00			
Manchester Piccadilly 10	a		16 41			17 02						17 19					17 41			18 02			
	d	16 41	16 44	16 52	16 55	17 04	17 04	17 07	17 13	17 15	17 20	17 22	17 27	17 30	17 35	17 41	17 44	17 52	17 55	18 04	18 04	18 07	18 13
Levenshulme	d			16 58			17 09											17 58			18 09		
Heaton Chapel	d			17 01			17 12											18 01			18 12		
Stockport	a		16 53	17 04	17 03		17 16			17 22	17 28	17 30	17 34	17 39	17 42		17 53	18 04	18 03		18 16		
	d				17 04		17 17			17 22			17 36	17 39	17 42				18 04		18 17		
Cheadle Hulme	d						17 22														18 22		
Bramhall	d																						
Poynton	d																						
Adlington (Cheshire)	d																						
Prestbury	d																						
Macclesfield	a												17 48		17 55								
	d												17 49		17 55								
Congleton	d																						
Handforth	d						17 26														18 26		
Manchester Airport ✈	d	17 06				17a21			17a29							18a03				18a21			18a29
Styal	d	17 10																					
Wilmslow	d	17 15			17 11		17 29							17 47					18 11		18 29		
Alderley Edge	d	17a21					17 32														18a35		
Chelford	d						17 36																
Goostrey	d						17 40																
Holmes Chapel	d						17 43																
Sandbach	d						17 48																
Crewe 10 65	a				17 27		17 58							18 07					18 27				
Kidsgrove 50	a																						
Longport 50	a																						
Stoke-on-Trent 50,68	a							17 42		17 49			18 06		18 12							18 42	
Stafford 68	a												18 25										
Wolverhampton 7 68	a							18 13					18 40									19 13	
Birmingham New Street 12 68	a							18 31					18 58									19 31	
London Euston 15 ⊖65	a				19 11					19 30					19 48				20 11				

A ✠ to Wolverhampton

Table 84

Sundays until 11 July

Manchester, Stockport and Manchester Airport - Crewe and Stoke-on-Trent

Station		VT	NT	XC	AW	VT	NT	NT	EM	NT	VT	NT	NT	XC	VT	NT	XC	AW	VT	NT	EM	NT	NT
		◇■		◇■	■	◇■			◇		◇■			◇■	◇■		◇■	◇	◇■		◇		
		⊐		A ✠	✠	⊐					⊐			✠	⊐		A ✠		⊐				
Deansgate	d		18 11													19 11							
Manchester Oxford Road	d		18 17						18 39			19 00				19 17					19 39		20 00
Manchester Piccadilly 10	a		18 19						18 41			19 02				19 19					19 41		20 02
	d	18 15	18 22	18 27	18 30	18 35	18 41	18 42	18 44	18 52	18 55	19 04	19 04	19 07	19 15	19 22	19 27	19 30	19 35	19 41	19 44	19 52	20 04
Levenshulme	d									18 58			19 09									19 58	
Heaton Chapel	d									19 01			19 12									20 01	
Stockport	a	18 22	18 33	18 34	18 39	18 42		18 50	18 53	19 04	19 03		19 16		19 22	19 30	19 34	19 39	19 42		19 53	20 04	
	d			18 36	18 39	18 42		18 52			19 04		19 17		19 22		19 36	19 39	19 42				
Cheadle Hulme	d							18 57					19 22										
Bramhall	d							19 00															
Poynton	d							19 03															
Adlington (Cheshire)	d							19 06															
Prestbury	d							19 09															
Macclesfield	a			18 48		18 55		19 13									19 48		19 55				
	d			18 49		18 55		19 13									19 49		19 55				
Congleton	d							19 21															
Handforth	d												19 26										
Manchester Airport ✈	d						19 06					19a21								20a03			20a21
Styal	d						19 10																
Wilmslow	d				18 47		19 15				19 11		19 29					19 47					
Alderley Edge	d						19a21						19 32										
Chelford	d												19 36										
Goostrey	d												19 40										
Holmes Chapel	d												19 43										
Sandbach	d												19 48										
Crewe 10 65	a				19 06						19 27		19 58					20 07					
Kidsgrove 50	a							19 28															
Longport 50	a																						
Stoke-on-Trent 50,68	a	18 49		19 06		19 12		19 40						19 42	19 49		20 06		20 12				
Stafford 68	a			19 24													20 24						
Wolverhampton 7 68	a			19 40										20 13			20 39						
Birmingham New Street 12 68	a			19 58										20 31			21 00						
London Euston 15 ⊖65	a	20 30				20 48					21 14				21 32				22 04				

Station		NT	XC	TP	TP	VT	NT	AW	NT	EM	NT	VT	NT	NT	XC	TP	NT	AW	NT	NT	NT
			◇■	◇■	◇■	◇■		◇		◇		◇■			◇■	◇■					
			✠			⊐						⊐			✠						
Deansgate	d						20 11										21 11				
Manchester Oxford Road	d						20 17			20 39			21 00				21 17				
Manchester Piccadilly 10	a						20 19			20 41			21 02				21 19				
	d	20 04	20 07	20 13	20 18	20 20	20 22	20 30	20 41	20 44	20 52	20 55	21 04	21 04	21 07	21 20	21 22	21 34	21 41	21 41	21 52
Levenshulme	d	20 09									20 58			21 09							21 58
Heaton Chapel	d	20 12									21 01			21 12							22 01
Stockport	a	20 16	20 15		20 26	20 27	20 33	20 38		20 53	21 04	21 03		21 16	21 15	21 28	21 30			21 49	22 04
	d	20 17	20 16			20 27		20 39				21 03		21 17	21 16					21 52	
Cheadle Hulme	d	20 22												21 22						21 56	
Bramhall	d																			21 59	
Poynton	d																			22 02	
Adlington (Cheshire)	d																			22 05	
Prestbury	d																			22 08	
Macclesfield	a		20 28			20 40						21 15			21 28					22 12	
	d		20 29			20 40						21 15			21 29					22 13	
Congleton	d																			22 20	
Handforth	d	20 26												21 26							
Manchester Airport ✈	d			20a29					21 06				21a21						22a03		
Styal	d								21 10												
Wilmslow	d	20 29						20 47	21 15					21 29				21 50			
Alderley Edge	d	20a37							21a21					21 32							
Chelford	d													21 36							
Goostrey	d													21 40							
Holmes Chapel	d													21 43							
Sandbach	d													21 48							
Crewe 10 65	a							21 07						21 58				22 12			
Kidsgrove 50	a																			22 26	
Longport 50	a																				
Stoke-on-Trent 50,68	a		20 46			20 57						21 32			21 46					22 36	
Stafford 68	a		21 08												22 06						
Wolverhampton 7 68	a		21 21												22 20						
Birmingham New Street 12 68	a		21 39												22 40						
London Euston 15 ⊖65	a					22 56						23 53									

A ✠ to Wolverhampton

Table 84

Sundays until 11 July

Manchester, Stockport and Manchester Airport - Crewe and Stoke-on-Trent

		NT	NT	XC	EM	TP	TP	NT	AW	TP	NT	NT	NT	NT	TP	NT	NT
				◇1	◇	◇1	◇1			◇1					◇1		
Deansgate ⇌	d							22 11								23 11	
Manchester Oxford Road	d	22 00			22 07			22 17		22 37			23 00			23 17	23 59
Manchester Piccadilly 10 ⇌	a	22 02			22 09			22 19		22 39			23 02			23 19	00 02
	d	22 04	22 04	22 07	22 11	22 13	22 15	22 22	22 35	22 42	22 46	22 52	23 04	23 04	23 20	23 22	00 04
Levenshulme	d		22 09									22 58		23 09			
Heaton Chapel	d		22 12									23 01		23 12			
Stockport	a		22 16	22 15	22 20		22 23	22 33				23 04		23 16	23 28	23 33	
	d		22 17	22 16										23 17			
Cheadle Hulme	d		22 22											23 21			
Bramhall	d																
Poynton	d																
Adlington (Cheshire)	d																
Prestbury	d																
Macclesfield	a			22 28													
	d			22 29													
Congleton	d																
Handforth	d		22 26											23 25			
Manchester Airport ✈	d	22a21				22a29					23a09		23a21				00a19
Styal	d																
Wilmslow	d		22 29						22 50					23 28			
Alderley Edge	d		22a35											23a35			
Chelford	d																
Goostrey	d																
Holmes Chapel	d																
Sandbach	d																
Crewe 10	65 a								23 10								
Kidsgrove	50 a																
Longport	50 a																
Stoke-on-Trent	50,68 a			22 46													
Stafford	68 a			23 04													
Wolverhampton 7	68 ⇌ a			23 18													
Birmingham New Street 12	68 a			23 36													
London Euston 15	⊖65 a																

Sundays 18 July to 05 September

		NT	NT	NT	VT	TP	VT	XC	TP	NT	TP	NT	NT	VT	NT	XC	AW	NT	NT	NT	NT
					◇1	◇1	◇1	◇1 A	◇1		◇1			◇1		◇1 A	◇ B				
Deansgate ⇌	d														09 15						
Manchester Oxford Road	d												09 03		09 18						10 00
Manchester Piccadilly 10 ⇌	a												09 05		09 21						10 03
	d	05 41	06 41	07 41	08 05	08 13	08 20	08 27	08 47	08 55	08 58	09 04	09 07	09 20	09 22	09 27	09 30	09 41	09 51	10 01	10 08
Levenshulme	d									09 00		09 09							09 58	10 07	
Heaton Chapel	d									09 03		09 12							10 01	10 10	
Stockport	a				08 13		08 28	08 34		09 07	09 06	09 16		09 27	09 31	09 35	09 38		10 04	10 13	
	d				08 14		08 28	08 36				09 17		09 27		09 36	09 39			10 14	
Cheadle Hulme	d											09 21								10 18	
Bramhall	d																				
Poynton	d																				
Adlington (Cheshire)	d																				
Prestbury	d																				
Macclesfield	a						08 42							09 40		09 48					
	d						08 42							09 40		09 49					
Congleton	d																				
Handforth	d											09 25								10 22	
Manchester Airport ✈	d	06a03	07a03	08a03		08a33			09a07				09a22					10a03			10a24
Styal	d																				
Wilmslow	d				08 22			08 43				09 28					09 47			10 25	
Alderley Edge	d											09 31								10a36	
Chelford	d											09 35									
Goostrey	d											09 40									
Holmes Chapel	d											09 43									
Sandbach	d											09 48									
Crewe 10	65 a				08 39			09 02				09 58					10 09				
Kidsgrove	50 a																				
Longport	50 a																				
Stoke-on-Trent	50,68 a						08 59							09 57		10 05					
Stafford	68 a				09 00			09 25								10 26					
Wolverhampton 7	68 ⇌ a							09 40								10 42					
Birmingham New Street 12	68 a							09 58								10 59					
London Euston 15	⊖65 a				10 56		11 00							12 07							

A ⊼ to Wolverhampton

B ◇ to Wilmslow

Table 84

Sundays 18 July to 05 September

Manchester, Stockport and Manchester Airport - Crewe and Stoke-on-Trent

		TP	VT	XC	AW	VT	NT	NT	NT	NT	VT	TP	NT	AW	XC	VT	NT	NT	VT	NT	NT	TP	VT
		◇1	◇1	◇1 A		◇1					◇1	◇1			◇1 A	◇1			◇1			◇1	◇1
Deansgate ⇌	d												11 11										
Manchester Oxford Road	d									11 00			11 17				11 37			12 00			
Manchester Piccadilly 10 ⇌	a									11 03			11 19				11 41			12 02			
	d	10 16	10 20	10 24	10 30	10 35	10 41	10 52	11 02	11 07	11 15	11 18	11 22	11 24	11 27	11 35	11 41	11 52	11 55	12 04	12 04	12 13	12 15
Levenshulme	d							10 58	11 08									11 58			12 09		
Heaton Chapel	d							11 01	11 11									12 01			12 12		
Stockport	a		10 28	10 32	10 39	10 43		11 04	11 15		11 23	11 27	11 30	11 34	11 34	11 43		12 04	12 03		12 16		12 22
	d		10 29	10 34	10 41	10 43			11 15		11 23			11 40	11 36	11 43			12 05		12 16		12 23
Cheadle Hulme	d								11 22												12 20		
Bramhall	d																						
Poynton	d																						
Adlington (Cheshire)	d																						
Prestbury	d																						
Macclesfield	a			10 46		10 56									11 49	11 56							
	d			10 47		10 56									11 49	11 56							
Congleton	d																						
Handforth	d								11 26												12 24		
Manchester Airport ✈	d	10a31					11b08			11a21							12a03			12a21		12a29	
Styal	d						11 12																
Wilmslow	d		10 37		10 47		11 16		11 29					11 48					12 12		12 27		
Alderley Edge	d						11a21		11 32												12a33		
Chelford	d								11 36														
Goostrey	d								11 41														
Holmes Chapel	d								11 44														
Sandbach	d								11 49														
Crewe 10	65 a		10 53		11 07				11 59					12 07					12 28				
Kidsgrove	50 a																						
Longport	50 a																						
Stoke-on-Trent	50,68 a			11 06		11 13					11 50				12 06	12 13							12 50
Stafford	68 a			11 27											12 24								
Wolverhampton 7	68 ⇌ a			11 42											12 40								
Birmingham New Street 12	68 a			12 00											12 58								
London Euston 15	⊖65 a		12 56			13 00					13 31					13 49			14 12				14 30

		TP	NT	XC	AW	VT	NT	EM	NT	VT	NT	NT	XC	TP	VT	TP	NT	XC	AW	VT	NT	EM
		◇1		◇1 A		◇1		◇		◇1			◇1	◇1	◇1	◇1		◇1 A		◇1		◇
Deansgate ⇌	d		12 11														13 11					
Manchester Oxford Road	d		12 17								13 00						13 17					13 39
Manchester Piccadilly 10 ⇌	a		12 19								13 02						13 19					13 41
	d	12 18	12 22	12 26	12 29	12 35	12 41	12 44	12 52	12 55	13 04	13 04	13 07	13 13	13 15	13 20	13 22	13 27	13 30	13 35	13 41	13 44
Levenshulme	d								12 58			13 09										
Heaton Chapel	d								13 01			13 12										
Stockport	a	12 28	12 33	12 34	12 39	12 44		12 53	13 04	13 03		13 16			13 22	13 28	13 30	13 34	13 39	13 42		13 53
	d			12 36	12 40	12 44				13 05		13 17			13 22			13 36	13 40	13 42		
Cheadle Hulme	d											13 21										
Bramhall	d																					
Poynton	d																					
Adlington (Cheshire)	d																					
Prestbury	d																					
Macclesfield	a			12 48		12 57												13 48		13 55		
	d			12 49		12 57												13 49		13 55		
Congleton	d																					
Handforth	d											13 25										
Manchester Airport ✈	d						13 06				13a24			13a29							14a03	
Styal	d						13 10															
Wilmslow	d				12 48		13 15			13 12		13 28							13 47			
Alderley Edge	d						13a21					13 31										
Chelford	d											13 35										
Goostrey	d											13 40										
Holmes Chapel	d											13 43										
Sandbach	d											13 48										
Crewe 10	65 a				13 08					13 28		13 58							14 07			
Kidsgrove	50 a																					
Longport	50 a																					
Stoke-on-Trent	50,68 a			13 06		13 14							13 42		13 49			14 06		14 12		
Stafford	68 a			13 24														14 24				
Wolverhampton 7	68 ⇌ a			13 40									14 13					14 40				
Birmingham New Street 12	68 a			13 58									14 31					14 58				
London Euston 15	⊖65 a					14 50				15 11					15 30					15 48		

A ⊼ to Wolverhampton

b arr. 1102

Table 84

Manchester, Stockport and Manchester Airport - Crewe and Stoke-on-Trent

		NT	VT	NT	NT	XC	TP	VT	TP	NT	XC	AW	VT	NT	NT	EM	NT	VT	NT	NT	XC	TP	VT
			◇1 ⊏			◇1 ✠	◇1	◇1 ⊏	◇1		◇1 A ✠	■ ✠	◇1 ⊏			◇		◇1 ⊏			◇1 ✠	◇1	◇1 ⊏
Deansgate ⇌	d									14 11													
Manchester Oxford Road	d			14 00						14 17						14 39			15 00				
Manchester Piccadilly 10 ⇌	a			14 02						14 19						14 41			15 02				
	d	13 52	13 55	14 04	14 04	14 07	14 13	14 15	14 20	14 22	14 27	14 30	14 35	14 41	14 41	14 44	14 52	14 55	15 04	15 04	15 07	15 13	15 15
Levenshulme	d	13 58			14 09												14 58			15 09			
Heaton Chapel	d	14 01			14 12												15 01			15 12			
Stockport	a	14 04	14 03		14 16			14 22	14 28	14 33	14 34	14 39	14 42		14 49	14 53	15 04	15 03		15 16			15 22
	d		14 04		14 17			14 22			14 36		14 42		14 51			15 04		15 17			15 22
Cheadle Hulme	d				14 22										14 56					15 22			
Bramhall	d														14 59								
Poynton	d														15 02								
Adlington (Cheshire)	d														15 04								
Prestbury	d														15 07								
Macclesfield	a										14 48		14 55		15 11								
	d										14 49		14 55		15 11								
Congleton	d														15 19								
Handforth	d				14 26															15 26			
Manchester Airport ✈	d			14a21			14a29							15 06					15a21			15a29	
Styal	d													15 10									
Wilmslow	d		14 11		14 29							14 47		15 15				15 11		15 29			
Alderley Edge	d				14a35									15a21						15 32			
Chelford	d																			15 36			
Goostrey	d																			15 40			
Holmes Chapel	d																			15 43			
Sandbach	d																			15 48			
Crewe 10 65	a		14 27									15 07						15 27		15 58			
Kidsgrove 50	a														15 25								
Longport 50	a																						
Stoke-on-Trent 50,68	a					14 42		14 49			15 06		15 12		15 37						15 42		15 49
Stafford 68	a										15 24												
Wolverhampton 7 68 ⇌	a					15 13					15 40										16 13		
Birmingham New Street 12 68	a					15 31					15 58										16 31		
London Euston 15 ⊖65	a		16 11					16 30					16 48					17 11					17 30

		TP	NT	XC	AW	VT	NT	EM	NT	VT	NT	NT	XC	TP	VT	TP	NT	XC	AW	VT	NT	EM
		◇1		◇1 A ✠	■ ✠	◇1 ⊏		◇		◇1 ⊏			◇1 ✠	◇1	◇1 ⊏	◇1		◇1 A ✠	■ ✠	◇1 ⊏		◇
Deansgate ⇌	d		15 11														16 11					
Manchester Oxford Road	d		15 17					15 39			16 00						16 17					16 39
Manchester Piccadilly 10 ⇌	a		15 19					15 41			16 02			16 06		16 09	16 19					16 41
	d	15 20	15 22	15 27	15 30	15 35	15 41	15 44	15 52	15 55	16 04	16 04	16 07	16 13	16 15	16 20	16 22	16 27	16 30	16 35	16 41	16 44
Levenshulme	d								15 58			16 09										
Heaton Chapel	d								16 01			16 12										
Stockport	a	15 28	15 30	15 35	15 39	15 42		15 53	16 04	16 03		16 16			16 22	16 28	16 33	16 34	16 39	16 42		16 53
	d			15 36	15 39	15 42				16 04		16 17			16 23			16 36	16 39	16 42		16 54
Cheadle Hulme	d											16 22										
Bramhall	d																					
Poynton	d																					
Adlington (Cheshire)	d																					
Prestbury	d																					
Macclesfield	a			15 48		15 55												16 48		16 55		
	d			15 49		15 55												16 49		16 55		
Congleton	d																					
Handforth	d											16 26										
Manchester Airport ✈	d						16a03				16a21			16a29							17 06	
Styal	d																				17 10	
Wilmslow	d				15 47					16 11		16 29							16 47		17 15	
Alderley Edge	d											16a35									17a21	
Chelford	d																					
Goostrey	d																					
Holmes Chapel	d																					
Sandbach	d																					
Crewe 10 65	a				16 06					16 27									17 06			
Kidsgrove 50	a																					
Longport 50	a																					
Stoke-on-Trent 50,68	a			16 06		16 12							16 42		16 48			17 06		17 12		
Stafford 68	a			16 24														17 25				
Wolverhampton 7 68 ⇌	a			16 40									17 13					17 40				
Birmingham New Street 12 68	a			16 58									17 31					17 58				
London Euston 15 ⊖65	a					17 48				18 11					18 30					18 48		

A ✠ to Wolverhampton

Table 84

Sundays

18 July to 05 September

Manchester, Stockport and Manchester Airport - Crewe and Stoke-on-Trent

		NT	VT	NT	NT	XC	TP	VT	TP	NT	XC	AW	VT	NT	EM	NT	VT	NT	NT	XC	TP	VT	NT
			◇1 ⊏			◇1 ✠	◇1	◇1 ⊏	◇1		◇1 A ✠	■ ✠	◇1 ⊏		◇		◇1 ⊏			◇1 ✠	◇1	◇1 ⊏	
Deansgate ⇌	d									17 11													18 11
Manchester Oxford Road	d			17 00						17 17					17 39			18 00					18 17
Manchester Piccadilly 10 ⇌	a			17 02						17 19					17 41			18 02					18 19
	d	16 52	16 55	17 04	17 04	17 07	17 13	17 15	17 20	17 22	17 27	17 30	17 35	17 41	17 44	17 52	17 55	18 04	18 04	18 07	18 13	18 15	18 22
Levenshulme	d	16 58			17 09											17 58			18 09				
Heaton Chapel	d	17 01			17 12											18 01			18 12				
Stockport	a	17 04	17 03		17 16			17 22	17 28	17 30	17 34	17 39	17 42		17 53	18 04	18 03		18 16			18 22	18 33
	d		17 04		17 17			17 22			17 36	17 39	17 42				18 04		18 17			18 22	
Cheadle Hulme	d				17 22														18 22				
Bramhall	d																						
Poynton	d																						
Adlington (Cheshire)	d																						
Prestbury	d																						
Macclesfield	a										17 48		17 55										
	d										17 49		17 55										
Congleton	d																						
Handforth	d				17 26														18 26				
Manchester Airport ✈	d			17a21			17a29							18a03				18a21			18a29		
Styal	d																						
Wilmslow	d		17 11		17 29							17 47					18 11		18 29				
Alderley Edge	d				17 32														18a35				
Chelford	d				17 36																		
Goostrey	d				17 40																		
Holmes Chapel	d				17 43																		
Sandbach	d				17 48																		
Crewe 10 65	a		17 27		17 58							18 07					18 27						
Kidsgrove 50	a																						
Longport 50	a																						
Stoke-on-Trent 50,68	a					17 42		17 49			18 06		18 12							18 42		18 49	
Stafford 68	a										18 25												
Wolverhampton 7 68 ⇌	a					18 13					18 40									19 13			
Birmingham New Street 12 68	a					18 31					18 58									19 31			
London Euston 15 ⊖65	a		19 11					19 30					19 48				20 11					20 30	

		XC	AW	VT	NT	NT	EM	NT	VT	NT	NT	XC	VT	NT	XC	AW	VT	NT	EM	NT	NT	NT	XC
		◇1 A ✠	■ ✠	◇1 ⊏			◇		◇1 ⊏			◇1 ✠	◇1 ⊏		◇1 A ✠	◇	◇1 ⊏		◇				◇1 ✠
Deansgate ⇌	d													19 11									
Manchester Oxford Road	d						18 39			19 00				19 17					19 39		20 00		
Manchester Piccadilly 10 ⇌	a						18 41			19 02				19 19					19 41		20 02		
	d	18 27	18 30	18 35	18 41	18 42	18 44	18 52	18 55	19 04	19 04	19 07	19 15	19 22	19 27	19 30	19 35	19 41	19 44	19 52	20 04	20 04	20 07
Levenshulme	d							18 58			19 09									19 58		20 09	
Heaton Chapel	d							19 01			19 12									20 01		20 12	
Stockport	a	18 34	18 39	18 42		18 50	18 53	19 04	19 03		19 16		19 22	19 30	19 34	19 39	19 42		19 53	20 04		20 16	20 15
	d	18 36	18 39	18 42		18 52			19 04		19 17		19 22		19 36	19 39	19 42					20 17	20 16
Cheadle Hulme	d					18 57					19 22											20 22	
Bramhall	d					19 00																	
Poynton	d					19 03																	
Adlington (Cheshire)	d					19 06																	
Prestbury	d					19 09																	
Macclesfield	a	18 48		18 55		19 13									19 48		19 55						20 28
	d	18 49		18 55		19 13									19 49		19 55						20 29
Congleton	d					19 21																	
Handforth	d										19 26											20 26	
Manchester Airport ✈	d				19 06					19a21								20a03			20a21		
Styal	d				19 10																		
Wilmslow	d		18 47		19 15				19 11		19 29					19 47						20 29	
Alderley Edge	d				19a21						19 32											20a37	
Chelford	d										19 36												
Goostrey	d										19 40												
Holmes Chapel	d										19 43												
Sandbach	d										19 48												
Crewe 10 65	a		19 06						19 27		19 58					20 07							
Kidsgrove 50	a					19 28																	
Longport 50	a																						
Stoke-on-Trent 50,68	a	19 06		19 12		19 40						19 42	19 49		20 06		20 12						20 46
Stafford 68	a	19 24													20 24								21 08
Wolverhampton 7 68 ⇌	a	19 40										20 13			20 39								21 21
Birmingham New Street 12 68	a	19 58										20 31			21 00								21 39
London Euston 15 ⊖65	a			20 48					21 14				21 32				22 04						

A ✠ to Wolverhampton

Table 84

Sundays
18 July to 05 September

Manchester, Stockport and Manchester Airport - Crewe and Stoke-on-Trent

	TP	TP	VT	NT	AW	NT	EM	NT	VT	NT	NT	XC	TP	NT	AW	NT	NT	NT	NT	NT
Deansgate d				20 11										21 11						
Manchester Oxford Road d				20 17			20 39			21 00				21 17					22 00	
Manchester Piccadilly a				20 19			20 41			21 02				21 19					22 02	
Manchester Piccadilly d	20 13	20 18	20 20	20 22	20 30	20 41	20 44	20 52	20 55	21 04	21 04	21 07	21 20	21 22	21 34	21 41	21 41	21 52	22 04	22 04
Levenshulme d								20 58			21 09							21 58		22 09
Heaton Chapel d								21 01			21 12							22 01		22 12
Stockport a		20 26	20 27	20 33	20 38		20 53	21 04	21 03		21 16	21 15	21 28	21 30			21 49	22 04		22 16
Stockport d			20 27		20 39				21 03		21 17	21 16					21 52			22 17
Cheadle Hulme d											21 22						21 56			22 22
Bramhall d																	21 59			
Poynton d																	22 02			
Adlington (Cheshire) d																	22 05			
Prestbury d																	22 08			
Macclesfield a			20 40						21 15			21 28					22 12			
Macclesfield d			20 40						21 15			21 29					22 13			
Congleton d																	22 20			
Handforth d											21 26									22 26
Manchester Airport d	20a29					21 06				21a21						22a03			22a21	
Styal d						21 10														
Wilmslow d					20 47	21 15					21 29				21 50					22 29
Alderley Edge d						21a21					21 32									22a35
Chelford d											21 36									
Goostrey d											21 40									
Holmes Chapel d											21 43									
Sandbach d											21 48									
Crewe 65 a					21 07						21 58				22 12					
Kidsgrove 50 a																	22 26			
Longport 50 a																				
Stoke-on-Trent 50,68 a			20 57						21 32			21 46					22 36			
Stafford 68 a												22 06								
Wolverhampton 68 a												22 20								
Birmingham New Street 68 a												22 40								
London Euston ⊖65 a			22 56						23 53											

	XC	EM	TP	TP	NT	AW	NT	NT	NT	NT	TP	NT	NT
Deansgate d					22 11							23 11	
Manchester Oxford Road d		22 07			22 17				23 00			23 17	23 59
Manchester Piccadilly a		22 09			22 19				23 02			23 19	00 02
Manchester Piccadilly d	22 07	22 11	22 13	22 15	22 22	22 35	22 46	22 52	23 04	23 04	23 20	23 22	00 04
Levenshulme d								22 58		23 09			
Heaton Chapel d								23 01		23 12			
Stockport a	22 15	22 20		22 23	22 33			23 04		23 16	23 28	23 33	
Stockport d	22 16									23 17			
Cheadle Hulme d										23 21			
Bramhall d													
Poynton d													
Adlington (Cheshire) d													
Prestbury d													
Macclesfield a	22 28												
Macclesfield d	22 29												
Congleton d													
Handforth d										23 25			
Manchester Airport d			22a29				23a09		23a21				00a19
Styal d													
Wilmslow d						22 50				23 28			
Alderley Edge d										23a35			
Chelford d													
Goostrey d													
Holmes Chapel d													
Sandbach d													
Crewe 65 a						23 10							
Kidsgrove 50 a													
Longport 50 a													
Stoke-on-Trent 50,68 a	22 46												
Stafford 68 a	23 04												
Wolverhampton 68 a	23 18												
Birmingham New Street 68 a	23 36												
London Euston ⊖65 a													

Table 84

Sundays
from 12 September

Manchester, Stockport and Manchester Airport - Crewe and Stoke-on-Trent

	TP	NT	NT	TP	NT	TP	VT	VT	XC	TP	NT	TP	NT	TP	NT	VT	NT	XC	AW	NT
									A									A		
Deansgate d																	09 15			
Manchester Oxford Road d																	09 18			
Manchester Piccadilly a																	09 21			
Manchester Piccadilly d	04u05	05 41	06 41	07 08	07 41	07 50	08 05	08 20	08 26	08 38	08 42	08 47	08 55	08 58	09 04	09 20	09 22	09 27	09 30	09 41
Levenshulme d													09 00		09 09					
Heaton Chapel d													09 03		09 12					
Stockport a							08 13	08 28	08 32				09 07	09 06	09 16	09 27	09 31	09 35	09 38	
Stockport d							08 14	08 28	08 35						09 17	09 27		09 36	09 39	
Cheadle Hulme d															09 21					
Bramhall d																				
Poynton d																				
Adlington (Cheshire) d																				
Prestbury d																				
Macclesfield a								08 42								09 40		09 48		
Macclesfield d								08 42								09 40		09 49		
Congleton d																				
Handforth d															09 25					
Manchester Airport d	04a30	06a03	07a03	07a22	08a03	08a06				08a55	09 09	09a07								10a03
Styal d											09 13									
Wilmslow d							08 22		08 41		09 17				09 28				09 47	
Alderley Edge d											09a22				09 31					
Chelford d															09 35					
Goostrey d															09 40					
Holmes Chapel d															09 43					
Sandbach d															09 48					
Crewe 65 a							08 39		09 01						09 58				10 09	
Kidsgrove 50 a																				
Longport 50 a																				
Stoke-on-Trent 50,68 a								08 59								09 57		10 05		
Stafford 68 a							09 00		09 25									10 26		
Wolverhampton 68 a									09 40									10 42		
Birmingham New Street 68 a									09 58									10 59		
London Euston ⊖65 a							10 56	11 00								12 07				

	NT	NT	NT	TP	VT	NT	XC	AW	VT	TP	NT	NT	NT	NT	VT	TP	NT	XC	AW	VT	NT	NT	VT	NT
							A											A						
Deansgate d						10 15											11 11							
Manchester Oxford Road d			10 00			10 19								11 00			11 17				11 37			12 00
Manchester Piccadilly a			10 02			10 22								11 03			11 19				11 40			12 02
Manchester Piccadilly d	09 51	10 03	10 09	10 14	10 20	10 22	10 27	10 29	10 35	10 38	10 41	10 52	11 02	11 06	11 15	11 18	11 22	11 27	11 30	11 35	11 41	11 52	11 55	12 04
Levenshulme d	09 58	10 08										10 58	11 08									11 58		
Heaton Chapel d	10 01	10 11										11 01	11 11									12 01		
Stockport a	10 04	10 15			10 28	10 33	10 34	10 38	10 42			11 04	11 15		11 23	11 27	11 30	11 34	11 39	11 43		12 04	12 04	
Stockport d		10 17			10 29		10 36	10 39	10 42				11 15		11 23			11 36	11 40	11 43			12 05	
Cheadle Hulme d		10 23											11 22											
Bramhall d																								
Poynton d																								
Adlington (Cheshire) d																								
Prestbury d																								
Macclesfield a							10 48		10 55									11 49		11 56				
Macclesfield d							10 49		10 55									11 49		11 56				
Congleton d																								
Handforth d		10 27											11 26											
Manchester Airport d			10a25	10a29						10a55	11 10			11a21							12a04			12a21
Styal d											11 12													
Wilmslow d		10 30			10 36			10 47			11 16		11 29						11 47				12 12	
Alderley Edge d		10a36									11a23		11 32											
Chelford d													11 36											
Goostrey d													11 41											
Holmes Chapel d													11 44											
Sandbach d													11 49											
Crewe 65 a					10 52			11 07					11 59						12 06				12 28	
Kidsgrove 50 a																								
Longport 50 a																								
Stoke-on-Trent 50,68 a							11 06		11 12						11 50			12 06		12 13				
Stafford 68 a							11 26											12 24						
Wolverhampton 68 a							11 41											12 40						
Birmingham New Street 68 a							12 00											12 58						
London Euston ⊖65 a					12 56				12 59						13 31					13 49			14 12	

A ✠ to Wolverhampton

Table 84

Manchester, Stockport and Manchester Airport - Crewe and Stoke-on-Trent

	NT	VT	TP	NT	XC	AW	VT	NT	EM	NT	VT	NT	NT	XC	TP	VT	TP	NT	XC	AW
		◇1 ☕	◇1		◇1 A 🛒	■ 🛒	◇1 ☕		◇		◇1 ☕			◇1 🛒	◇1	◇1 ☕	◇1		◇1 A 🛒	■ 🛒
Deansgate d				12 11														13 11		
Manchester Oxford Road d				12 17								13 00						13 17		
Manchester Piccadilly a				12 19								13 02						13 19		
d	12 04	12 15	12 18	12 22	12 26	12 30	12 35	12 41	12 44	12 52	12 55	13 04	13 04	13 07	13 13	13 15	13 20	13 22	13 27	13 30
Levenshulme d	12 09									12 58			13 09							
Heaton Chapel d	12 12									13 01			13 12							
Stockport a	12 16	12 23	12 28	12 31	12 35	12 39	12 44		12 53	13 04	13 04		13 16			13 22	13 28	13 30	13 34	13 39
d	12 16	12 23	12 28		12 35	12 40	12 44				13 05		13 17			13 22			13 36	13 40
Cheadle Hulme d	12 22												13 21							
Bramhall d																				
Poynton d																				
Adlington (Cheshire) d																				
Prestbury d																				
Macclesfield a					12 48		12 57												13 48	
d					12 49		12 57												13 49	
Congleton d																				
Handforth d	12 26												13 25							
Manchester Airport ✈ d								13 06				13a21			13a29					
Styal d								13 10												
Wilmslow d	12 29					12 48		13 15			13 12		13 28							13 47
Alderley Edge d	12a35							13a21					13 31							
Chelford d													13 35							
Goostrey d													13 40							
Holmes Chapel d													13 43							
Sandbach d													13 48							
Crewe 10 65 a						13 08					13 28		13 58							14 07
Kidsgrove 50 a																				
Longport 50 a																				
Stoke-on-Trent 50,68 a		12 50			13 06		13 14							13 42		13 49			14 06	
Stafford 68 a					13 24														14 24	
Wolverhampton 7 68 a					13 40									14 13					14 40	
Birmingham New Street 12 68 a					13 58									14 31					14 58	
London Euston 15 ⊖65 a		14 30					14 50				15 11					15 30				

	VT	NT	EM	NT	VT	NT	NT	XC	TP	VT	TP	NT	XC	AW	VT	NT	NT	EM	NT	VT	NT	NT
	◇1 ☕		◇		◇1 ☕			◇1 🛒	◇1	◇1 ☕	◇1		◇1 A 🛒	■ 🛒	◇1 ☕			◇		◇1 ☕		
Deansgate d												14 11										
Manchester Oxford Road d			13 39			14 00						14 17						14 39			15 00	
Manchester Piccadilly a			13 41			14 02						14 19						14 41			15 02	
d	13 35	13 41	13 44	13 52	13 55	14 04	14 04	14 07	14 13	14 15	14 20	14 23	14 27	14 30	14 35	14 41	14 41	14 44	14 52	14 55	15 04	15 04
Levenshulme d				13 58			14 09												14 58			15 09
Heaton Chapel d				14 01			14 12												15 01			15 12
Stockport a	13 42		13 53	14 04	14 03		14 16			14 22	14 28	14 33	14 34	14 39	14 42		14 49	14 53	15 04	15 03		15 16
d	13 42				14 04		14 17			14 22			14 36	14 39	14 42		14 51			15 04		15 17
Cheadle Hulme d							14 22										14 56					15 22
Bramhall d																	14 59					
Poynton d																	15 02					
Adlington (Cheshire) d																	15 04					
Prestbury d																	15 07					
Macclesfield a	13 55												14 48		14 55		15 11					
d	13 55												14 49		14 55		15 11					
Congleton d																	15 19					
Handforth d							14 26															15 26
Manchester Airport ✈ d		14a03				14a21			14a29							15 06					15a21	
Styal d																15 10						
Wilmslow d					14 11		14 29							14 47		15 15				15 11		15 29
Alderley Edge d							14a35									15a21						15 32
Chelford d																						15 36
Goostrey d																						15 40
Holmes Chapel d																						15 43
Sandbach d																						15 48
Crewe 10 65 a					14 27									15 07						15 27		15 58
Kidsgrove 50 a																	15 25					
Longport 50 a																						
Stoke-on-Trent 50,68 a	14 12							14 42		14 49			15 06		15 12		15 37					
Stafford 68 a													15 24									
Wolverhampton 7 68 a								15 13					15 40									
Birmingham New Street 12 68 a								15 31					15 58									
London Euston 15 ⊖65 a	15 48				16 11					16 30					16 48					17 11		

A 🛒 to Wolverhampton

b arr. 1328

Table 84

Manchester, Stockport and Manchester Airport - Crewe and Stoke-on-Trent

	XC	TP	VT	TP	NT	XC	AW	VT	NT	EM	NT	VT	NT	NT	XC	TP	VT	TP	NT	XC	AW
	◇1 🛒	◇1	◇1 ☕	◇1		◇1 A 🛒	■ 🛒	◇1 ☕		◇		◇1 ☕			◇1 🛒	◇1	◇1 ☕	◇1		◇1 A 🛒	■ 🛒
Deansgate d					15 11														16 11		
Manchester Oxford Road d					15 17					15 39			16 00						16 17		
Manchester Piccadilly a					15 19					15 41			16 02						16 19		
d	15 07	15 13	15 15	15 20	15 22	15 27	15 30	15 35	15 41	15 44	15 52	15 55	16 04	16 04	16 07	16 13	16 15	16 20	16 22	16 27	16 30
Levenshulme d											15 58			16 09							
Heaton Chapel d											16 01			16 12							
Stockport a			15 22	15 28	15 30	15 35	15 39	15 42		15 53	16 04	16 03		16 16			16 22	16 28	16 33	16 34	16 39
d			15 22			15 36	15 39	15 42				16 04		16 17			16 23			16 36	16 39
Cheadle Hulme d														16 22							
Bramhall d																					
Poynton d																					
Adlington (Cheshire) d																					
Prestbury d																					
Macclesfield a						15 48		15 55												16 48	
d						15 49		15 55												16 49	
Congleton d																					
Handforth d														16 26							
Manchester Airport ✈ d		15a29							16a03				16a21			16a29					
Styal d																					
Wilmslow d							15 47					16 11		16 29							16 47
Alderley Edge d														16a35							
Chelford d																					
Goostrey d																					
Holmes Chapel d																					
Sandbach d																					
Crewe 10 65 a							16 06					16 27									17 06
Kidsgrove 50 a																					
Longport 50 a																					
Stoke-on-Trent 50,68 a	15 42		15 49			16 06		16 12							16 42		16 48			17 06	
Stafford 68 a						16 24														17 25	
Wolverhampton 7 68 a	16 13					16 40									17 13					17 40	
Birmingham New Street 12 68 a	16 31					16 58									17 31					17 58	
London Euston 15 ⊖65 a			17 30					17 48				18 11					18 30				

	VT	NT	EM	NT	VT	NT	NT	XC	TP	VT	TP	NT	XC	AW	VT	NT	EM	NT	VT	NT	NT	XC
	◇1 ☕		◇		◇1 ☕			◇1 🛒	◇1	◇1 ☕	◇1		◇1 A 🛒	■ 🛒	◇1 ☕		◇		◇1 ☕			◇1 🛒
Deansgate d												17 11										
Manchester Oxford Road d			16 39			17 00						17 17					17 39			18 00		
Manchester Piccadilly a			16 41			17 02						17 19					17 41			18 02		
d	16 35	16 41	16 44	16 52	16 55	17 04	17 04	17 07	17 13	17 15	17 20	17 22	17 27	17 30	17 35	17 41	17 44	17 52	17 55	18 04	18 04	18 07
Levenshulme d				16 58			17 09											17 58			18 09	
Heaton Chapel d				17 01			17 12											18 01			18 12	
Stockport a	16 42		16 53	17 04	17 03		17 16			17 22	17 28	17 30	17 34	17 39	17 42		17 53	18 04	18 03		18 16	
d	16 42				17 04		17 17			17 22			17 36	17 39	17 42				18 04		18 17	
Cheadle Hulme d							17 22														18 22	
Bramhall d																						
Poynton d																						
Adlington (Cheshire) d																						
Prestbury d																						
Macclesfield a	16 55												17 48		17 55							
d	16 55												17 49		17 55							
Congleton d																						
Handforth d							17 26														18 26	
Manchester Airport ✈ d		17 06				17a21			17a29							18a03				18a21		
Styal d		17 10																				
Wilmslow d		17 15			17 11		17 29							17 47					18 11		18 29	
Alderley Edge d		17a21					17 32														18a35	
Chelford d							17 36															
Goostrey d							17 40															
Holmes Chapel d							17 43															
Sandbach d							17 48															
Crewe 10 65 a					17 27		17 58							18 07					18 27			
Kidsgrove 50 a																						
Longport 50 a																						
Stoke-on-Trent 50,68 a	17 12							17 42		17 49			18 06		18 12							18 42
Stafford 68 a													18 25									
Wolverhampton 7 68 a								18 13					18 40									19 13
Birmingham New Street 12 68 a								18 31					18 58									19 31
London Euston 15 ⊖65 a	18 48				19 11					19 30					19 48				20 11			

A 🛒 to Wolverhampton

Table 84

Manchester, Stockport and Manchester Airport - Crewe and Stoke-on-Trent

		TP	VT	NT	XC	AW		VT	NT	NT	EM	NT	VT	NT	NT	XC		VT	NT	XC	AW	VT	NT	EM	NT
		◇1	◇1 ☕		◇1 A 🛒	🛒		◇1 ☕			◇		◇1 ☕			◇1 🛒		◇1 ☕		◇1 A 🛒	◇	◇1 ☕		◇	
Deansgate 🚊	d			18 11															19 11						
Manchester Oxford Road	d			18 17							18 39			19 00					19 17					19 39	
Manchester Piccadilly 10 🚊	a			18 19							18 41			19 02					19 19					19 41	
	d	18 13	18 15	18 22	18 27	18 30		18 35	18 41	18 42	18 44	18 52	18 55	19 04	19 04	19 07		19 15	19 22	19 27	19 30	19 35	19 41	19 44	19 52
Levenshulme	d											18 58			19 09										19 58
Heaton Chapel	d											19 01			19 12										20 01
Stockport	a		18 22	18 33	18 34	18 39		18 42		18 50	18 53	19 04	19 03		19 16			19 22	19 30	19 34	19 39	19 42		19 53	20 04
	d		18 22		18 36	18 39		18 42		18 52			19 04		19 17			19 22		19 36	19 39	19 42			
Cheadle Hulme	d									18 57					19 22										
Bramhall	d									19 00															
Poynton	d									19 03															
Adlington (Cheshire)	d									19 06															
Prestbury	d									19 09															
Macclesfield	a				18 48			18 55		19 13										19 48		19 55			
	d				18 49			18 55		19 13										19 49		19 55			
Congleton	d									19 21															
Handforth	d														19 26										
Manchester Airport ✈	d	18a29							19 06					19a21									20a03		
Styal	d								19 10																
Wilmslow	d					18 47			19 15				19 11		19 29						19 47				
Alderley Edge	d								19a21						19 32										
Chelford	d														19 36										
Goostrey	d														19 40										
Holmes Chapel	d														19 43										
Sandbach	d														19 48										
Crewe 10 65	a					19 06							19 27		19 58						20 07				
Kidsgrove 50	a									19 28															
Longport 50	a																								
Stoke-on-Trent 50,68	a		18 49		19 06			19 12		19 40						19 42		19 49		20 06		20 12			
Stafford 68	a				19 24															20 24					
Wolverhampton 7 68 🚊	a				19 40											20 13				20 39					
Birmingham New Street 12 68	a				19 58											20 31				21 00					
London Euston 15 ⊖65	a		20 30					20 48					21 14					21 32				22 04			

		NT		NT	XC			TP	TP	VT	NT	AW		NT	EM	NT	VT	NT	NT	XC	TP	NT		AW	NT
					◇1 🛒			◇1	◇1	◇1 ☕		◇			◇		◇1 ☕			◇1 🛒	◇1				
Deansgate 🚊	d										20 11											21 11			
Manchester Oxford Road	d	20 00									20 17				20 39			21 00				21 17			
Manchester Piccadilly 10 🚊	a	20 02									20 19				20 41			21 02				21 19			
	d	20 04		20 04	20 07			20 13	20 18	20 20	20 22	20 30		20 41	20 44	20 52	20 55	21 04	21 04	21 07	21 20	21 22		21 34	21 41
Levenshulme	d			20 09												20 58			21 09						
Heaton Chapel	d			20 12												21 01			21 12						
Stockport	a			20 16	20 15				20 26	20 27	20 33	20 38			20 53	21 04	21 03		21 16	21 15	21 28	21 30			
	d			20 17	20 16					20 27		20 39					21 03		21 17	21 16					
Cheadle Hulme	d			20 22															21 22						
Bramhall	d																								
Poynton	d																								
Adlington (Cheshire)	d																								
Prestbury	d																								
Macclesfield	a				20 28					20 40							21 15			21 28					
	d				20 29					20 40							21 15			21 29					
Congleton	d																								
Handforth	d			20 26															21 26						
Manchester Airport ✈	d	20a21						20a29						21 06				21a21							22a03
Styal	d													21 10											
Wilmslow	d			20 29								20 47		21 15					21 29					21 50	
Alderley Edge	d			20a37										21a21					21 32						
Chelford	d																		21 36						
Goostrey	d																		21 40						
Holmes Chapel	d																		21 43						
Sandbach	d																		21 48						
Crewe 10 65	a											21 07							21 58					22 12	
Kidsgrove 50	a																								
Longport 50	a																								
Stoke-on-Trent 50,68	a				20 47					20 57							21 32			21 46					
Stafford 68	a				21 08															22 06					
Wolverhampton 7 68 🚊	a				21 22															22 20					
Birmingham New Street 12 68	a				21 39															22 40					
London Euston 15 ⊖65	a									22 56							23 53								

A 🛒 to Wolverhampton

Table 84

Manchester, Stockport and Manchester Airport - Crewe and Stoke-on-Trent

		NT	NT	NT	NT	XC	EM	TP		TP	NT	AW	TP	NT	NT	NT	NT	TP		NT	NT
						◇1 🛒	◇	◇1		◇1			◇1					◇1			
Deansgate 🚊	d										22 11									23 11	
Manchester Oxford Road	d			22 00			22 07				22 17		22 37			23 00				23 17	23 59
Manchester Piccadilly 10 🚊	a			22 02			22 09				22 19		22 39			23 02				23 19	00 02
	d	21 41	21 52	22 04	22 04	22 07	22 11	22 13		22 15	22 22	22 35	22 42	22 46	22 52	23 04	23 04	23 20		23 22	00 04
Levenshulme	d		21 58		22 09										22 58		23 09				
Heaton Chapel	d		22 01		22 12										23 01		23 12				
Stockport	a	21 49	22 04		22 16	22 15	22 20			22 23	22 33				23 04		23 16	23 28		23 33	
	d	21 52			22 17	22 16											23 17				
Cheadle Hulme	d	21 56			22 22												23 21				
Bramhall	d	21 59																			
Poynton	d	22 02																			
Adlington (Cheshire)	d	22 05																			
Prestbury	d	22 08																			
Macclesfield	a	22 12				22 28															
	d	22 13				22 29															
Congleton	d	22 20																			
Handforth	d				22 26												23 25				
Manchester Airport ✈	d			22a21				22a29						23a09		23a21					00a19
Styal	d																				
Wilmslow	d				22 29							22 50					23 28				
Alderley Edge	d				22a35												23a35				
Chelford	d																				
Goostrey	d																				
Holmes Chapel	d																				
Sandbach	d																				
Crewe 10 65	a											23 10									
Kidsgrove 50	a	22 26																			
Longport 50	a																				
Stoke-on-Trent 50,68	a	22 36				22 46															
Stafford 68	a					23 04															
Wolverhampton 7 68 🚊	a					23 18															
Birmingham New Street 12 68	a					23 36															
London Euston 15 ⊖65	a																				

Manchester - Manchester Airport

		TP	TP	TP	TP	NT	TP	AW	TP	TP	NT	NT	TP	TP	NT	NT	TP	TP	NT	TP	NT
		◇1 A	◇1 B	MX ◇1	◇1		◇1	C	◇1	◇1			◇1	◇1			◇1	◇1 ✠		◇1	
Deansgate	d																	06 51			
Manchester Oxford Road	d																	06 54	06 58		
Manchester Piccadilly	a	00 33	00 43	00 54	03 44	04 14	04 40	04 43	04 48	04 58		05 57	06 01	06 05			06 50	06 56	07 01	07 02	
	d	00 36	00 44	00 54	03 44	04 15	04 44	04 49	04 50	05 00	05 35	05 58	06 03	06 12	06 15	06 46	06 54	06 58	07 03	07 06	07 14
Mauldeth Road	d										05 42				06 22	06 53					07 21
Burnage	d										05 44				06 24	06 55					07 23
East Didsbury	d										05 46				06 26	06 57					07 25
Gatley	d										05 49				06 29	06 59					07 27
Heald Green	d										05 52				06 32	07 02		07 10			07 30
Manchester Airport	a	00 53	01 00	01 10	04 00	04 30	05 00	05 04	05 07	05 19	05 57	06 14	06 18	06 29	06 39	07 07	07 12	07 17	07 22	07 29	07 38
Wilmslow	84 a										06 11					07 20					
Crewe	84 a										06 46					07 46					

		NT	TP	TP	NT	NT	TP	TP	NT	TP	NT	TP	TP	NT	NT	TP	TP	NT	TP	NT	TP	TP	NT	NT
			◇1	◇1 ✠			◇1 ✠	◇1 ✠		◇1 ✠		◇1 ✠	◇1 ✠			◇1 ✠	◇1 ✠		◇1 ✠		◇1 ✠	◇1 ✠		
Deansgate	d	07 11			07 28			07 51						08 29									09 29	
Manchester Oxford Road	d	07 15		07 24	07 32			07 54	07 58				08 24	08 33			08 53	08 58				09 24	09 33	
Manchester Piccadilly	a	07 17	07 19	07 27	07 34		07 51	07 56	08 01	08 02		08 19	08 27	08 35		08 51	08 56	09 01	09 02		09 19	09 27	09 35	
	d	07 21	07 23	07 29	07 36	07 46	07 54	07 58	08 03	08 06	08 14	08 24	08 29	08 37	08 46	08 54	08 58	09 03	09 06	09 14	09 24	09 29	09 37	09 46
Mauldeth Road	d					07 53					08 21				08 53					09 21				09 53
Burnage	d					07 55					08 23				08 55					09 23				09 55
East Didsbury	d					07 57					08 25				08 57				09 16	09 25				09 57
Gatley	d					07 59					08 27				08 59					09 27				09 59
Heald Green	d					08 02		08 10			08 30			08 47	09 02		09 10			09 30				10 02
Manchester Airport	a		07 42	07 47	07 53	08 07	08 12	08 17	08 22	08 26	08 38	08 42	08 47	08 53	09 07	09 12	09 19	09 22	09 33	09 38	09 42	09 47	09 53	10 07
Wilmslow	84 a					08 21									09 20									10 20
Crewe	84 a					08 47									09 46									10 46

		TP	TP	NT	TP	NT	TP	TP	NT	NT	TP	TP	NT	TP	NT	TP	TP	NT	NT	TP	TP	NT
		◇1 ✠	◇1 ✠		◇1 ✠		◇1 ✠	◇1 ✠			◇1 ✠	◇1 ✠		◇1 ✠		◇1 ✠	◇1 ✠			◇1 ✠	◇1 ✠	
Deansgate	d		09 51						10 29			10 51						11 29			11 51	
Manchester Oxford Road	d		09 54	09 58				10 24	10 33			10 54	10 58				11 24	11 33			11 54	11 58
Manchester Piccadilly	a	09 49	09 56	10 01	10 02		10 19	10 27	10 35		10 49	10 56	11 01	11 02		11 19	11 27	11 35		11 49	11 56	12 01
	d	09 54	09 58	10 03	10 06	10 14	10 24	10 29	10 37	10 46	10 54	10 58	11 03	11 06	11 14	11 24	11 29	11 37	11 46	11 54	11 58	12 03
Mauldeth Road	d					10 21				10 53					11 21				11 53			
Burnage	d					10 23				10 55					11 23				11 55			
East Didsbury	d					10 25				10 57					11 25				11 57			
Gatley	d					10 27				10 59					11 27				11 59			
Heald Green	d		10 10			10 30				11 02		11 10			11 30				12 02		12 10	
Manchester Airport	a	10 12	10 17	10 22	10 26	10 38	10 42	10 47	10 53	11 08	11 12	11 17	11 22	11 26	11 38	11 45	11 50	11 53	12 07	12 12	12 17	12 22
Wilmslow	84 a									11 20									12 20			
Crewe	84 a									11 46									12 46			

		TP	NT	TP	TP	NT	NT	TP	TP	NT	TP	NT	TP	TP	NT	NT	TP	TP	NT
		◇1 ✠		◇1 ✠	◇1 ✠			◇1 ✠	◇1 ✠		◇1 ✠		◇1 ✠	◇1 ✠			◇1 ✠	◇1 ✠	
Deansgate	d					12 29			12 51						13 29			13 51	
Manchester Oxford Road	d				12 24	12 33			12 54	12 58				13 24	13 33			13 54	13 58
Manchester Piccadilly	a	12 02		12 19	12 27	12 35		12 49	12 56	13 01	13 02		13 19	13 27	13 35		13 49	13 56	14 01
	d	12 06	12 14	12 24	12 29	12 37	12 46	12 54	12 58	13 03	13 06	13 14	13 24	13 29	13 37	13 46	13 54	13 58	14 03
Mauldeth Road	d		12 21				12 53					13 21				13 53			
Burnage	d		12 23				12 55					13 23				13 55			
East Didsbury	d		12 25				12 57					13 25				13 57			
Gatley	d		12 27				12 59					13 27				13 59			
Heald Green	d		12 30				13 02		13 10			13 30				14 02		14 10	
Manchester Airport	a	12 26	12 38	12 42	12 47	12 53	13 07	13 12	13 17	13 22	13 26	13 39	13 42	13 47	13 53	14 07	14 12	14 17	14 22
Wilmslow	84 a						13 21									14 20			
Crewe	84 a						13 47									14 46			

		TP	NT	TP	TP	NT	NT	TP	TP	NT	TP	NT	TP	TP	NT	NT	TP	TP	NT	TP	NT	TP
		◇1 ✠		◇1 ✠	◇1 ✠			◇1 ✠	◇1 ✠		◇1 ✠		◇1 ✠	◇1 ✠			◇1 ✠	◇1 ✠		◇1 ✠		◇1 ✠
Deansgate	d					14 29			14 51						15 29			15 51				
Manchester Oxford Road	d				14 24	14 33			14 54	14 58				15 24	15 33			15 54	15 58			
Manchester Piccadilly	a	14 02		14 19	14 27	14 35		14 49	14 56	15 01	15 02		15 19	15 27	15 35		15 49	15 56	16 01	16 02		16 19
	d	14 06	14 14	14 24	14 29	14 37	14 46	14 54	14 58	15 03	15 06	15 14	15 24	15 29	15 37	15 46	15 54	15 58	16 03	16 06	16 14	16 24
Mauldeth Road	d		14 21				14 53					15 21				15 53					16 21	
Burnage	d		14 23				14 55					15 23				15 55					16 23	
East Didsbury	d		14 25				14 57					15 25				15 57					16 25	
Gatley	d		14 27				14 59					15 27				15 59					16 27	
Heald Green	d		14 30				15 02		15 10			15 30				16 02		16 10			16 30	
Manchester Airport	a	14 26	14 38	14 42	14 47	14 53	15 07	15 12	15 17	15 22	15 26	15 38	15 42	15 47	15 53	16 07	16 12	16 17	16 22	16 26	16 38	16 42
Wilmslow	84 a						15 20									16 20						
Crewe	84 a						15 46									16 46						

A MO from 19 July until 6 September
B MO until 12 July, MO from 13 September
C not 24 May

Manchester - Manchester Airport

		TP	NT	NT	TP	TP	NT	TP	NT	TP	NT	NT	TP	TP	NT	TP	NT	NT	TP	TP	NT	NT	TP	NT
		◇1 ✠			◇1 ✠	◇1 ✠		◇1 ✠		◇1 ✠			◇1 ✠	◇1 ✠		◇1 ✠			◇1 ✠	◇1 ✠			◇1 ✠	
Deansgate	d					16 51								17 51				18 12						
Manchester Oxford Road	d	16 24	16 33			16 54	16 58			17 24	17 33			17 54	17 58			18 16		18 24	18 33			18 58
Manchester Piccadilly	a	16 27	16 35		16 49	16 56	17 01	17 02		17 27	17 35		17 49	17 56	18 01	18 02		18 18	18 19	18 27	18 35		18 49	19 01
	d	16 29	16 37	16 46	16 54	16 58	17 03	17 06	17 14	17 29	17 37	17 46	17 54	17 58	18 03	18 06	18 14	18 21	18 24	18 29	18 37	18 46	18 54	19 03
Mauldeth Road	d			16 53					17 21			17 53					18 21					18 53		
Burnage	d			16 55					17 23			17 55					18 23					18 55		
East Didsbury	d			16 57				17 19	17 25			17 57					18 25					18 57		
Gatley	d			16 59				17 22	17 27			17 59					18 27					18 59		
Heald Green	d	16 40		17 02		17 10		17 25	17 30	17 40		18 02		18 10			18 30			18 40		19 02		
Manchester Airport	a	16 47	16 53	17 07	17 12	17 17	17 22	17 32	17 39	17 48	17 53	18 07	18 12	18 17	18 22	18 26	18 38		18 42	18 47	18 53	19 08	19 13	19 24
Wilmslow	84 a			17 20								18 21										19 23		
Crewe	84 a			17 46								18 47												

		TP	TP	NT	TP	NT	TP	NT	TP	TP	TP	TP	NT	TP	NT	TP	NT	TP	TP	NT	TP
		◇1 A ✠	◇1 B ✠		◇1 ✠		◇1 ✠		◇1 ✠	◇1	◇1 ✠	◇1 ✠		◇1		◇1		◇1 ✠	◇1 ✠		◇1
Deansgate	d					19 29			19 51				20 29			20 51				21 29	
Manchester Oxford Road	d				19 24	19 33		19 43	19 54	19 59		20 24	20 33		20 43	20 54	20 58		21 24	21 33	
Manchester Piccadilly	a	19 02	19 02		19 27	19 35	19 32	19 45	19 56	20 01	20 02	20 27	20 35	20 33	20 45	20 56	21 01	21 02	21 27	21 35	21 33
	d	19 06	19 06	19 14	19 29	19 37	19 40	19 46	19 58	20 03	20 13	20 29	20 37	20 40	20 46	20 58	21 03	21 06	21 29	21 37	21 40
Mauldeth Road	d			19 21				19 53			20 21				20 53			21 15			
Burnage	d			19 23				19 55			20 23				20 55			21 17			
East Didsbury	d			19 25				19 57			20 26				20 57			21 20			
Gatley	d			19 27				19 59			20 29				20 59			21 23			
Heald Green	d			19 30				20 02	20 10	20 15	20 32				21 02	21 10		21 26			
Manchester Airport	a	19 28	19 33	19 38	19 47	19 53	19 59	20 07	20 17	20 24	20 37	20 47	20 53	20 57	21 07	21 17	21 24	21 36	21 47	21 53	21 57
Wilmslow	84 a							20 24							21 24						
Crewe	84 a																				

		NT	TP	TP	TP	NT	TP	TP	TP
			◇1	◇1	◇1		◇1	◇1	◇1
Deansgate	d		21 51				22 51		
Manchester Oxford Road	d	21 43	21 54	22 27		22 43	22 54		
Manchester Piccadilly	a	21 45	21 56	22 30	22 33	22 45	22 56	23 02	23 53
	d	21 46	21 58	22 32	22 40	22 46	22 58	23 06	23 55
Mauldeth Road	d	21 53				22 53			00 04
Burnage	d	21 55				22 55			00 06
East Didsbury	d	21 57				22 57			00 09
Gatley	d	21 59				22 59			00 12
Heald Green	d	22 02	22 09			23 02	23 09		00 15
Manchester Airport	a	22 10	22 17	22 47	22 57	23 08	23 17	23 26	00 22
Wilmslow	84 a	22 22				23 22			
Crewe	84 a								

Saturdays

		TP	TP	NT	TP	TP	TP	AW	NT	NT	TP	TP	TP	NT	NT	TP	TP	NT	TP	NT	NT	TP	TP
		◇1	◇1		◇1	◇1	◇1				◇1	◇1	◇1			◇1	◇1		◇1			◇1	◇1
Deansgate	d																06 51				07 11		
Manchester Oxford Road	d																06 54	06 58			07 15		07 24
Manchester Piccadilly	a	00 54	03 44	04 14	04 40	04 48	04 52	04 45		05 57	06 01	06 02	06 05			06 50	06 56	07 01	07 02		07 17	07 19	07 27
	d	00 54	03 44	04 15	04 44	04 50	04 54	04 58	05 35	05 58	06 03	06 08	06 12	06 15	06 46	06 54	06 58	07 03	07 06	07 14	07 21	07 23	07 29
Mauldeth Road	d								05 42					06 22	06 53					07 21			
Burnage	d								05 44					06 24	06 55					07 23			
East Didsbury	d								05 46					06 26	06 57					07 25			
Gatley	d								05 49					06 29	06 59					07 27			
Heald Green	d								05 52					06 32	07 02		07 10			07 30			
Manchester Airport	a	01 10	04 00	04 30	05 00	05 07	05 10	05 12	05 57	06 14	06 18	06 24	06 29	06 39	07 07	07 12	07 17	07 22	07 29	07 38		07 42	07 47
Wilmslow	84 a								06 11						07 20								
Crewe	84 a								06 43						07 46								

		NT	NT	TP	NT	TP	NT	TP	TP	NT	NT	TP	TP	NT	TP	NT	TP	TP	NT	NT	TP	TP	NT
				◇1		◇1 ✠		◇1	◇1 ✠			◇1	◇1 ✠		◇1 ✠		◇1 ✠	◇1 ✠			◇1 ✠	◇1 ✠	
Deansgate	d	07 28								08 29									09 29			09 51	
Manchester Oxford Road	d	07 32			07 58				08 24	08 33			08 53	08 58				09 24	09 33			09 54	09 58
Manchester Piccadilly	a	07 34		07 51	08 01	08 02		08 19	08 27	08 35		08 51	08 56	09 01	09 02		09 19	09 27	09 35		09 49	09 56	10 01
	d	07 36	07 46	07 54	08 03	08 06	08 14	08 24	08 29	08 37	08 46	08 54	08 58	09 03	09 06	09 14	09 24	09 29	09 37	09 46	09 54	09 58	10 03
Mauldeth Road	d		07 53				08 21				08 53					09 21				09 53			
Burnage	d		07 55				08 23				08 55					09 23				09 55			
East Didsbury	d		07 57				08 25				08 57				09 16	09 25				09 57			
Gatley	d		07 59				08 27				08 59					09 27				09 59			
Heald Green	d		08 02				08 30			08 47	09 02		09 12			09 30				10 02		10 10	
Manchester Airport	a	07 53	08 07	08 12	08 22	08 26	08 38	08 42	08 47	08 53	09 08	09 12	09 19	09 22	09 26	09 38	09 42	09 47	09 53	10 07	10 12	10 17	10 22
Wilmslow	84 a		08 21								09 21									10 20			
Crewe	84 a		08 47								09 46									10 46			

A Does not apply Fridays 2 July to 3 september
B FO from 2 July until 3 September

Table 85

Manchester - Manchester Airport

Saturdays

	TP ◇1 ⊼		NT	TP ◇1 ⊼	TP ◇1 ⊼	NT	NT	TP ◇1 ⊼	TP ◇1 ⊼	NT	TP ◇1 ⊼		NT	TP ◇1 ⊼	TP ◇1 ⊼	NT	NT	TP ◇1 ⊼	TP ◇1 ⊼	NT	TP ◇1 ⊼		NT	TP ◇1 ⊼
Deansgate d						10 29			10 51							11 29			11 51					
Manchester Oxford Road d					10 24	10 33			10 54	10 58					11 24	11 33			11 54	11 58				
Manchester Piccadilly 10 a	10 02			10 19	10 27	10 35		10 49	10 56	11 01	11 02			11 19	11 27	11 35		11 49	11 56	12 01	12 02			12 19
d	10 06		10 14	10 24	10 29	10 37	10 46	10 54	10 58	11 03	11 06		11 14	11 24	11 29	11 37	11 46	11 54	11 58	12 03	12 06		12 14	12 24
Mauldeth Road d			10 21				10 53						11 21				11 53						12 21	
Burnage d			10 23				10 55						11 23				11 55						12 23	
East Didsbury d			10 25				10 57						11 25				11 57						12 25	
Gatley d			10 27				10 59						11 27				11 59						12 27	
Heald Green d			10 30				11 02		11 10				11 30				12 02		12 10				12 30	
Manchester Airport a	10 26		10 38	10 42	10 47	10 53	11 07	11 12	11 17	11 22	11 26		11 38	11 42	11 47	11 53	12 07	12 12	12 17	12 22	12 26		12 38	12 42
Wilmslow 84 a							11 20										12 20							
Crewe 10 84 a							11 46										12 46							

	TP ◇1 ⊼	NT	NT	TP ◇1 ⊼	TP ◇1 ⊼	NT	TP ◇1 ⊼		NT	TP ◇1 ⊼	TP ◇1 ⊼	NT	NT	TP ◇1 ⊼	TP ◇1 ⊼	NT	TP ◇1 ⊼		NT	TP ◇1 ⊼	TP ◇1 ⊼	NT	NT	TP ◇1 ⊼
Deansgate d		12 29			12 51							13 29			13 51							14 29		
Manchester Oxford Road d	12 24	12 33			12 54	12 58					13 24	13 33			13 54	13 58					14 24	14 33		
Manchester Piccadilly 10 a	12 27	12 35		12 49	12 56	13 01	13 02			13 19	13 27	13 35		13 49	13 56	14 01	14 02			14 19	14 27	14 35		14 49
d	12 29	12 37	12 46	12 54	12 58	13 03	13 06		13 14	13 24	13 29	13 37	13 46	13 54	13 58	14 03	14 06		14 14	14 24	14 29	14 37	14 46	14 54
Mauldeth Road d			12 53						13 21				13 53						14 21				14 53	
Burnage d			12 55						13 23				13 55						14 23				14 55	
East Didsbury d			12 57						13 25				13 57						14 25				14 57	
Gatley d			12 59						13 27				13 59						14 27				14 59	
Heald Green d			13 02		13 10				13 30				14 02		14 10				14 30				15 02	
Manchester Airport a	12 47	12 53	13 07	13 12	13 17	13 22	13 33		13 38	13 42	13 47	13 53	14 07	14 12	14 17	14 22	14 26		14 38	14 42	14 47	14 53	15 07	15 12
Wilmslow 84 a			13 21										14 20										15 20	
Crewe 10 84 a			13 47										14 46										15 46	

	TP ◇1 ⊼	NT	TP ◇1 ⊼		NT	TP ◇1 ⊼	TP ◇1 ⊼	NT	NT	TP ◇1 ⊼	TP ◇1 ⊼	NT	TP ◇1 ⊼		NT	TP ◇1 ⊼	TP ◇1 ⊼	NT	NT	TP ◇1 ⊼	TP ◇1 ⊼	NT	TP ◇1 ⊼	
Deansgate d	14 51							15 29			15 51										16 51			
Manchester Oxford Road d	14 54	14 58					15 24	15 33			15 54	15 58					16 24	16 33			16 54	16 58		
Manchester Piccadilly 10 a	14 56	15 01	15 02			15 19	15 27	15 35		15 49	15 56	16 01	16 02			16 19	16 27	16 35		16 49	16 56	17 01	17 02	
d	14 58	15 03	15 06		15 14	15 24	15 29	15 37	15 46	15 54	15 58	16 03	16 06		16 14	16 24	16 29	16 37	16 46	16 54	16 58	17 03	17 06	
Mauldeth Road d					15 21				15 53						16 21				16 53					
Burnage d					15 23				15 55						16 23				16 55					
East Didsbury d					15 25				15 57						16 25				16 57				17 19	
Gatley d					15 27				15 59						16 27				16 59				17 22	
Heald Green d	15 10				15 30				16 02		16 10				16 30		16 40		17 02		17 10		17 25	
Manchester Airport a	15 17	15 22	15 26		15 38	15 42	15 47	15 53	16 07	16 12	16 17	16 22	16 26		16 38	16 42	16 47	16 53	17 07	17 12	17 17	17 22	17 32	
Wilmslow 84 a									16 20										17 20					
Crewe 10 84 a									16 46										17 46					

	NT	TP ◇1 ⊼	NT	NT	TP ◇1 ⊼	TP ◇1 ⊼	NT	TP ◇1 ⊼	NT		TP ◇1 ⊼	TP ◇1 ⊼	NT	NT	TP ◇1 ⊼		NT	TP ◇1 ⊼	NT	TP ◇1 ⊼	NT	TP ◇1	NT	
Deansgate d			17 29			17 51															19 29			
Manchester Oxford Road d		17 24	17 33			17 54	17 58					18 24	18 33				18 58			19 24	19 33		19 43	
Manchester Piccadilly 10 a		17 27	17 35		17 49	17 56	18 01	18 02			18 19	18 27	18 35		18 49		19 01	19 02		19 27	19 35	19 33	19 45	
d	17 14	17 29	17 37	17 46	17 54	17 58	18 03	18 06	18 14		18 24	18 29	18 37	18 46	18 54		19 03	19 06	19 14	19 32	19 37	19 40	19 46	
Mauldeth Road d	17 21			17 53					18 21					18 53					19 21				19 53	
Burnage d	17 23			17 55					18 23					18 55					19 23				19 55	
East Didsbury d	17 25			17 57					18 25					18 57					19 25				19 57	
Gatley d	17 27			17 59					18 27					18 59					19 27				19 59	
Heald Green d	17 30	17 40		18 02		18 10			18 30			18 40		19 02					19 30				20 02	
Manchester Airport a	17 38	17 48	17 53	18 07	18 12	18 17	18 22	18 26	18 38		18 42	18 47	18 53	19 08	19 13		19 24	19 28	19 38	19 50	19 53	19 59	20 07	
Wilmslow 84 a				18 21										19 23									20 24	
Crewe 10 84 a				18 47																				

	AW	TP ◇1	TP ◇1 ⊼	TP ◇1 ⊼	NT		TP ◇1	NT	TP ◇1	NT	TP ◇1 ⊼	TP ◇1 ⊼	NT	TP ◇1	NT		TP ◇1	TP ◇1	NT	TP ◇1	TP ◇1			
Deansgate d		19 51			20 29				20 51				21 29				21 51			22 51				
Manchester Oxford Road d	19 49	19 54		20 24	20 33			20 43	20 54	20 58		21 24	21 33		21 43		21 54		22 43	22 54				
Manchester Piccadilly 10 a	19 52	19 56	20 02	20 27	20 35		20 33	20 45	20 56	21 01	21 02	21 27	21 35	21 33	21 45		21 56	22 33	22 45	22 56	23 53			
d	19 54	19 58	20 06	20 32	20 37		20 40	20 46	20 58	21 03	21 06	21 29	21 37	21 40	21 46		21 58	22 40	22 46	22 58	23 55			
Mauldeth Road d			20 15					20 53			21 15				21 53				22 53		00 04			
Burnage d			20 17					20 55			21 17				21 55				22 55		00 06			
East Didsbury d			20 20					20 57			21 20				21 57				22 57		00 09			
Gatley d			20 23					20 59			21 23				21 59				22 59		00 12			
Heald Green d		20 10	20 26					21 02	21 10		21 26				22 02		22 09		23 02	23 09	00 15			
Manchester Airport a	20 13	20 17	20 36	20 47	20 53		20 57	21 07	21 17	21 24	21 36	21 47	21 53	21 57	22 08		22 17	22 57	23 08	23 17	00 22			
Wilmslow 84 a								21 24							22 22				23 22					
Crewe 10 84 a																								

Table 85

Manchester - Manchester Airport

Sundays until 11 July

	TP ◇1 A	TP ◇1	TP 🚌	TP ◇1	NT	TP ◇1	NT	TP 🚌		TP ◇1	NT	TP ◇1	TP ◇1	TP ◇1	TP ◇1	NT	TP ◇1	NT	TP ◇1		NT	TP ◇1	NT	TP ◇1
Deansgate d															08 53			09 15				09 51		
Manchester Oxford Road d															08 56	09 03		09 18				09 54	10 00	
Manchester Piccadilly 10 a	00 41	04 02	05u00	05 17		06 34		07u00		07 34			08 34	08 42	08 59	09 05	09 11	09 21	09 34			09 57	10 03	
d	00 45	04 06	05u00	05 21	05 41	06 38	06 41	07u00		07 38	07 41	08 13	08 38	08 47	09 00	09 07	09 17	09 22	09 38		09 41	09 58	10 08	10 16
Mauldeth Road d	⌇				05 48		06 48				07 48										09 48			
Burnage d	⌇				05 50		06 50				07 50										09 50			
East Didsbury d	⌇				05 52		06 52				07 52										09 52			
Gatley d	⌇				05 54		06 54				07 54										09 54			
Heald Green d	⌇				05 57		06 57				07 57										09 57			
Manchester Airport a	01 00	04 23	05 25	05 38	06 03	06 55	07 03	07 25		07 55	08 03	08 33	08 55	09 07	09 19	09 22	09 34		09 55		10 03	10 17	10 24	10 31
Wilmslow 84 a																								
Crewe 10 84 a																								

	TP ◇1	TP ◇1	NT	TP ◇1	NT	TP ◇1		TP ◇1	NT	TP ◇1	NT	TP ◇1	NT	TP ◇1	NT	TP ◇1	NT	TP ◇1	NT	TP ◇1	TP ◇1	NT	TP ◇1	NT
Deansgate d				10 51	11 11					11 51			12 11			12 51			13 11				13 51	
Manchester Oxford Road d				10 54	11 17	11 24			11 37	11 54	12 00		12 17			12 54	13 00		13 17	13 24			13 54	14 00
Manchester Piccadilly 10 a		10 34		10 57	11 19	11 27		11 34	11 41	11 57	12 02	12 06	12 19	12 34		12 57	13 02	13 06	13 19	13 27	13 34		13 57	14 02
d	10 23	10 38	10 41	10 58	11 22	11 29		11 38	11 41	11 58	12 04	12 13	12 22	12 38	12 41	12 58	13 04	13 13	13 22	13 29	13 38	13 41	13 58	14 04
Mauldeth Road d			10 48						11 48						12 48							13 48		
Burnage d			10 50						11 50						12 50							13 50		
East Didsbury d			10 52						11 52						12 52							13 52		
Gatley d			10 54						11 54						12 54							13 54		
Heald Green d			10 57						11 57						12 57							13 57		
Manchester Airport a	10 37	10 55	11 02	11 18		11 47		11 55	12 03	12 17	12 21	12 29		12 55	13 02	13 17	13 24	13 29		13 47	13 55	14 03	14 17	14 21
Wilmslow 84 a			11 16												13 13									
Crewe 10 84 a			11 54																					

	TP ◇1		NT	TP ◇1 ⊼	TP ◇1	NT	TP ◇1	NT	TP ◇1	NT	TP ◇1		TP ◇1	NT	TP ◇1	NT	TP ◇1	NT	TP ◇1 ⊼	TP ◇1	NT		TP ◇1	NT
Deansgate d			14 11				14 51			15 11					15 51			16 11					16 51	
Manchester Oxford Road d			14 17	14 24			14 54	15 00		15 17	15 24				15 54	16 00		16 17	16 24				16 54	17 00
Manchester Piccadilly 10 a	14 06		14 19	14 27	14 34		14 57	15 02	15 06	15 19	15 27		15 34		15 57	16 02	16 06	16 19	16 27	16 34			16 57	17 02
d	14 13		14 22	14 29	14 38	14 41	14 58	15 04	15 13	15 22	15 29		15 38	15 41	15 58	16 04	16 13	16 22	16 29	16 38	16 41		16 58	17 04
Mauldeth Road d						14 48								15 48							16 48			
Burnage d						14 50								15 50							16 50			
East Didsbury d						14 52								15 52							16 52			
Gatley d						14 54								15 54							16 54			
Heald Green d						14 57								15 57							16 57			
Manchester Airport a	14 29			14 47	14 55	15 02	15 17	15 21	15 29		15 47		15 55	16 03	16 17	16 21	16 29		16 47	16 55	17 02		17 17	17 21
Wilmslow 84 a						15 14															17 13			
Crewe 10 84 a																								

	TP ◇1	NT	TP ◇1	TP ◇1	NT	TP ◇1	NT		TP ◇1	NT	TP ◇1 ⊼	TP ◇1	NT	TP ◇1	NT	TP ◇1	NT	TP ◇1 ⊼	TP ◇1	NT	TP ◇1	NT	TP ◇1	NT
Deansgate d		17 11				17 51				18 11				18 51			19 11				19 51			20 11
Manchester Oxford Road d		17 17	17 24			17 54	18 00			18 17	18 24			18 54	19 00		19 17	19 24			19 54	20 00		20 17
Manchester Piccadilly 10 a	17 06	17 19	17 27	17 34		17 57	18 02		18 06	18 19	18 27	18 34		18 57	19 02	19 06	19 19	19 27	19 34		19 57	20 02	20 06	20 19
d	17 13	17 22	17 29	17 38	17 41	17 58	18 04		18 13	18 22	18 29	18 38	18 41	18 58	19 04	19 13	19 22	19 29	19 38	19 41	19 58	20 04	20 13	20 22
Mauldeth Road d					17 48								18 48							19 48				
Burnage d					17 50								18 50							19 50				
East Didsbury d					17 52								18 52							19 52				
Gatley d					17 54								18 54							19 54				
Heald Green d					17 57								18 57							19 57				
Manchester Airport a	17 29		17 47	17 55	18 03	18 17	18 21		18 29		18 47	18 55	19 02	19 17	19 21	19 29		19 47	19 55	20 03	20 17	20 21	20 29	
Wilmslow 84 a													19 13											
Crewe 10 84 a																								

	TP ◇1 ⊼	TP ◇1	NT		TP ◇1	NT	TP ◇1 ⊼	NT	TP ◇1 ⊼	AW	NT	TP ◇1	NT	TP ◇1	NT	AW	TP ◇1	NT	NT	TP ◇1 ⊼	NT	NT		
Deansgate d					20 51			21 11				21 51			22 11					23 09	23 11			
Manchester Oxford Road d	20 24				20 54	21 00		21 17	21 24			21 54	22 00		22 17				23 00	23 12	23 17	23 59		
Manchester Piccadilly 10 a	20 27	20 34			20 57	21 02	21 06	21 19	21 27			21 57	22 02	22 06	22 19		22 36		23 02	23 14	23 19	00 02		
d	20 30	20 38	20 41		20 58	21 04	21 13	21 22	21 29	21 34	21 41	21 58	22 04	22 13	22 22	22 35	22 38	22 46	23 04	23 15	23 22	00 04		
Mauldeth Road d			20 48								21 48							22 53						
Burnage d			20 50								21 50							22 55						
East Didsbury d			20 52								21 52							22 57						
Gatley d			20 54								21 54							22 59						
Heald Green d			20 57								21 57							23 02						
Manchester Airport a	20 47	20 55	21 02		21 17	21 21	21 29		21 47		22 03	22 17	22 21	22 29			22 55	23 09	23 21	23 30		00 19		
Wilmslow 84 a			21 13							21 49						22 49								
Crewe 10 84 a										22 12						23 10								

A not 23 May

Table 85

Manchester - Manchester Airport

Sundays

18 July to 05 September

	TP	TP	TP	TP	NT	TP	NT	TP	TP	NT	TP	TP	TP	TP	NT	TP	NT	TP	NT	TP	NT	TP
	◇1	◇1	(bus)	◇1		◇1		(bus)	◇1		◇1	◇1	◇1	◇1		◇1		◇1		◇1		◇1
Deansgate d														08 53			09 15			09 51		
Manchester Oxford Road d														08 56	09 03		09 18			09 54	10 00	
Manchester Piccadilly [10] a	00 41	04 02	05u00	05 17		06 34		07u00	07 34			08 34	08 42	08 59	09 05	09 11	09 21	09 34		09 57	10 03	
d	00 45	04 06	05u00	05 21	05 41	06 38	06 41	07u00	07 38	07 41	08 13	08 38	08 47	09 00	09 07	09 17	09 22	09 38	09 41	09 58	10 08	10 16
Mauldeth Road d					05 48		06 48			07 48									09 48			
Burnage d					05 50		06 50			07 50									09 50			
East Didsbury d					05 52		06 52			07 52									09 52			
Gatley d					05 54		06 54			07 54									09 54			
Heald Green d					05 57		06 57			07 57									09 57			
Manchester Airport ✈ a	01 00	04 23	05 25	05 38	06 03	06 55	07 03	07 25	07 55	08 03	08 33	08 55	09 07	09 19	09 22	09 34		09 55	10 03	10 17	10 24	10 31
Wilmslow 84 a																						
Crewe [10] 84 a																						

	TP	TP	NT	TP	NT	NT	TP	TP	NT	TP	NT	TP	NT	TP	NT	TP	NT	TP	NT	TP	TP	NT	TP
	◇1	◇1		◇1			◇1	◇1		◇1		◇1		◇1		◇1		◇1		◇1	◇1		◇1
Deansgate d				10 51		11 11				11 51			12 11			12 51			13 11				13 51
Manchester Oxford Road d				10 54	11 00	11 17	11 24		11 37	11 54	12 00		12 17			12 54	13 00		13 17	13 24			13 54
Manchester Piccadilly [10] a		10 34		10 57	11 03	11 19	11 27	11 34	11 41	11 57	12 02	12 06	12 19	12 34		12 57	13 02	13 06	13 19	13 27	13 34		13 57
d	10 23	10 38	10 41	10 58	11 07	11 22	11 29	11 38	11 41	11 58	12 04	12 13	12 22	12 38	12 41	12 58	13 04	13 13	13 22	13 29	13 38	13 41	13 58
Mauldeth Road d			10 48						11 48						12 48							13 48	
Burnage d			10 50						11 50						12 50							13 50	
East Didsbury d			10 52						11 52						12 52							13 52	
Gatley d			10 54						11 54						12 54							13 54	
Heald Green d			10 57						11 57						12 57							13 57	
Manchester Airport ✈ a	10 37	10 55	11 02	11 18	11 21		11 47	11 55	12 03	12 17	12 21	12 29		12 55	13 02	13 17	13 24	13 29		13 47	13 55	14 03	14 17
Wilmslow 84 a			11 16												13 13								
Crewe [10] 84 a																							

	NT	TP	NT	TP	TP	NT	TP	NT	TP	NT	TP	TP	NT	TP	NT	TP	NT	TP	TP	NT	TP
		◇1		◇1 (trolley)	◇1		◇1		◇1		◇1	◇1		◇1		◇1		◇1 (trolley)	◇1		◇1
Deansgate d			14 11				14 51			15 11				15 51			16 11				16 51
Manchester Oxford Road d	14 00		14 17	14 24			14 54	15 00		15 17	15 24			15 54	16 00		16 17	16 24			16 54
Manchester Piccadilly [10] a	14 02	14 06	14 19	14 27	14 34		14 57	15 02	15 06	15 19	15 27	15 34		15 57	16 02	16 06	16 19	16 27	16 34		16 57
d	14 04	14 13	14 22	14 29	14 38	14 41	14 58	15 04	15 13	15 22	15 29	15 38	15 41	15 58	16 04	16 13	16 22	16 29	16 38	16 41	16 58
Mauldeth Road d						14 48							15 48							16 48	
Burnage d						14 50							15 50							16 50	
East Didsbury d						14 52							15 52							16 52	
Gatley d						14 54							15 54							16 54	
Heald Green d						14 57							15 57							16 57	
Manchester Airport ✈ a	14 21	14 29		14 47	14 55	15 02	15 17	15 21	15 29		15 47	15 55	16 03	16 17	16 21	16 29		16 47	16 55	17 02	17 17
Wilmslow 84 a						15 14														17 13	
Crewe [10] 84 a																					

	NT	TP	NT	TP	TP	NT	TP	NT	TP	NT	TP	TP	NT	TP	NT	TP	NT	TP	TP	NT	TP	NT	TP
		◇1		◇1	◇1		◇1		◇1		◇1 (trolley)	◇1		◇1		◇1		◇1 (trolley)	◇1		◇1		◇1
Deansgate d			17 11				17 51			18 11				18 51			19 11				19 51		
Manchester Oxford Road d	17 00		17 17	17 24			17 54	18 00		18 17	18 24			18 54	19 00		19 17	19 24			19 54	20 00	
Manchester Piccadilly [10] a	17 02	17 06	17 19	17 27	17 34		17 57	18 02	18 06	18 19	18 27	18 34		18 57	19 02	19 06	19 19	19 27	19 34		19 57	20 02	20 06
d	17 04	17 13	17 22	17 29	17 38	17 41	17 58	18 04	18 13	18 22	18 29	18 38	18 41	18 58	19 04	19 13	19 22	19 29	19 38	19 41	19 58	20 04	20 13
Mauldeth Road d						17 48							18 48							19 48			
Burnage d						17 50							18 50							19 50			
East Didsbury d						17 52							18 52							19 52			
Gatley d						17 54							18 54							19 54			
Heald Green d						17 57							18 57							19 57			
Manchester Airport ✈ a	17 21	17 29		17 47	17 55	18 03	18 17	18 21	18 29		18 47	18 55	19 02	19 17	19 21	19 29		19 47	19 55	20 03	20 17	20 21	20 29
Wilmslow 84 a													19 13										
Crewe [10] 84 a																							

	NT	TP	TP	NT	TP	NT	TP	NT	TP	AW	NT	TP	NT	TP	NT	AW	TP	NT	NT	TP	NT	NT
		◇1 (trolley)	◇1		◇1		◇1 (trolley)		◇1 (trolley)			◇1		◇1			◇1			◇1 (trolley)		
Deansgate d	20 11				20 51			21 11				21 51			22 11					23 09	23 11	
Manchester Oxford Road d	20 17	20 24			20 54	21 00		21 17	21 24			21 54	22 00		22 17				23 00	23 12	23 17	23 59
Manchester Piccadilly [10] a	20 19	20 27	20 34		20 57	21 02	21 06	21 19	21 27			21 57	22 02	22 06	22 19		22 36		23 02	23 14	23 19	00 02
d	20 22	20 30	20 38	20 41	20 58	21 04	21 13	21 22	21 29	21 34	21 41	21 58	22 04	22 13	22 22	22 35	22 38	22 46	23 04	23 15	23 22	00 04
Mauldeth Road d				20 48							21 48							22 53				
Burnage d				20 50							21 50							22 55				
East Didsbury d				20 52							21 52							22 57				
Gatley d				20 54							21 54							22 59				
Heald Green d				20 57							21 57							23 02				
Manchester Airport ✈ a		20 47	20 55	21 02	21 17	21 21	21 29		21 47		22 03	22 17	22 21	22 29			22 55	23 09	23 21	23 30		00 19
Wilmslow 84 a				21 13						21 49						22 49						
Crewe [10] 84 a										22 12						23 10						

Table 85

Manchester - Manchester Airport

Sundays

from 12 September

	TP	TP	TP	NT	TP	NT	TP	TP	TP	NT	TP	TP	TP	NT	TP	NT	TP	NT	TP	NT	TP
	(bus)	(bus)	(bus)		(bus)		(bus)	◇1	(bus)		◇1	◇1	(bus)		◇1		◇1		◇1		◇1
Deansgate d																09 15	09 23		09 51		
Manchester Oxford Road d																09 18	09 26		09 54	10 00	
Manchester Piccadilly [10] a	04 05	04u05	05u00		06 00		07u00		07 25				08s40		08 42	09 21	09 28		09 57	10 02	
d	04 05	04u05	05u00	05 41	06 00	06 41	07u00	07 08	07 25	07 41	07 50	08 38	08s40	08 42	08 47	09 22	09 33	09 41	09 58	10 09	10 14
Mauldeth Road d				05 48		06 48				07 48				08 49				09 48			
Burnage d				05 50		06 50				07 50				08 51				09 50			
East Didsbury d				05 52		06 52				07 52				08 53				09 52			
Gatley d				05 54		06 54				07 54				08 56				09 54			
Heald Green d				05 57		06 57				07 57				08 59				09 57			
Manchester Airport ✈ a	04 30	04 30	05 25	06 03	06 25	07 03	07 25	07 22	07 50	08 03	08 06	08 55	09 05	09 04	09 07		09 53	10 03	10 17	10 25	10 29
Wilmslow 84 a														09 17							
Crewe [10] 84 a																					

	NT	TP	TP	NT	TP	NT	NT	TP	NT	TP	NT	NT	TP	NT	TP	TP	NT	TP	NT	TP	NT	TP
		◇1	◇1		◇1			◇1		◇1			◇1		◇1	◇1		◇1		◇1		◇1
Deansgate d	10 15		10 51			11 11		11 51			12 11		12 51				13 11			13 51		
Manchester Oxford Road d	10 19		10 54	11 00		11 17	11 37	11 54	12 00		12 17		12 54	13 00			13 17	13 24		13 54	14 00	
Manchester Piccadilly [10] a	10 22	10 33	10 57	11 03	11 08	11 19	11 40	11 57	12 02	12 06	12 19		12 56	13 02	13 08	13 02	13 19	13 27		13 57	14 02	14 08
d	10 22	10 38	10 58	11 06	11 10	11 22	11 41	11 58	12 04	12 12	12 22	12 41	12 58	13 04	13 10	13 13	13 22	13 29	13 41	13 58	14 04	14 10
Mauldeth Road d							11 48					12 48							13 48			
Burnage d							11 50					12 50							13 50			
East Didsbury d							11 52					12 52							13 52			
Gatley d							11 54					12 54							13 54			
Heald Green d							11 57					12 57							13 57			
Manchester Airport ✈ a		10 55	11 18	11 21	11 25		12 04	12 17	12 21	12 29		13 02	13 17	13 21	13 25	13 29		13 47	14 03	14 17	14 21	14 25
Wilmslow 84 a												13 13										
Crewe [10] 84 a																						

	TP	NT	TP	NT	TP	NT	TP	TP	NT	TP	TP	NT	TP	NT	TP	NT	TP	TP	NT	TP	NT
	◇1		◇1 (trolley)		◇1		◇1	◇1		◇1	◇1		◇1		◇1		◇1 (trolley)	◇1		◇1	
Deansgate d		14 11			14 51				15 11				15 51			16 11				16 51	
Manchester Oxford Road d		14 17	14 24		14 54	15 00		15 10	15 17	15 24			15 54	16 00		16 17	16 24			16 54	17 00
Manchester Piccadilly [10] a	14 06	14 19	14 27		14 57	15 02	15 06	15 14	15 19	15 27	15 34		15 57	16 02	16 06	16 19	16 27	16 34		16 57	17 02
d	14 13	14 23	14 29	14 41	14 58	15 04	15 13	15 18	15 22	15 29	15 38	15 41	15 58	16 04	16 13	16 22	16 29	16 38	16 41	16 58	17 04
Mauldeth Road d				14 48								15 48							16 48		
Burnage d				14 50								15 50							16 50		
East Didsbury d				14 52								15 52							16 52		
Gatley d				14 54								15 54							16 54		
Heald Green d				14 57								15 57							16 57		
Manchester Airport ✈ a	14 29		14 47	15 02	15 17	15 21	15 29	15 35		15 47	15 55	16 03	16 17	16 21	16 29		16 47	16 55	17 02	17 17	17 21
Wilmslow 84 a				15 14															17 13		
Crewe [10] 84 a																					

	TP	NT	TP	TP	NT	TP	NT	TP	NT	TP	TP	NT	TP	NT	TP	NT	TP	TP	NT	TP	NT	TP	NT
	◇1		◇1	◇1		◇1		◇1		◇1 (trolley)	◇1		◇1		◇1		◇1 (trolley)	◇1		◇1		◇1	
Deansgate d		17 11				17 51			18 11				18 51			19 11				19 51			20 11
Manchester Oxford Road d		17 17	17 24			17 54	18 00		18 17	18 24			18 54	19 00		19 17	19 24			19 54	20 00		20 17
Manchester Piccadilly [10] a	17 06	17 19	17 27	17 34		17 57	18 02	18 06	18 19	18 27	18 34		18 57	19 02	19 06	19 19	19 27	19 34		19 57	20 02	20 06	20 19
d	17 13	17 22	17 29	17 38	17 41	17 58	18 04	18 13	18 22	18 29	18 38	18 41	18 58	19 04	19 13	19 22	19 29	19 38	19 41	19 58	20 04	20 13	20 22
Mauldeth Road d					17 48							18 48							19 48				
Burnage d					17 50							18 50							19 50				
East Didsbury d					17 52							18 52							19 52				
Gatley d					17 54							18 54							19 54				
Heald Green d					17 57							18 57							19 57				
Manchester Airport ✈ a	17 29		17 47	17 55	18 03	18 17	18 21	18 29		18 47	18 55	19 02	19 17	19 21	19 29		19 47	19 55	20 03	20 17	20 21	20 29	
Wilmslow 84 a												19 13											
Crewe [10] 84 a																							

	TP	TP	NT	TP	NT	TP	NT	TP	AW	NT	TP	NT	TP	NT	AW	TP	NT	NT	TP	NT	NT
	◇1 (trolley)	◇1		◇1		◇1 (trolley)		◇1 (trolley)			◇1		◇1			◇1			◇1 (trolley)		
Deansgate d				20 51			21 11				21 51			22 11					23 09	23 11	
Manchester Oxford Road d	20 24			20 54	21 00		21 17	21 24			21 54	22 00		22 17				23 00	23 12	23 17	23 59
Manchester Piccadilly [10] a	20 27	20 34		20 57	21 02	21 06	21 19	21 27			21 57	22 02	22 06	22 19		22 36		23 02	23 14	23 19	00 02
d	20 30	20 38	20 41	20 58	21 04	21 13	21 22	21 29	21 34	21 41	21 58	22 04	22 13	22 22	22 35	22 38	22 46	23 04	23 15	23 22	00 04
Mauldeth Road d			20 48							21 48							22 53				
Burnage d			20 50							21 50							22 55				
East Didsbury d			20 52							21 52							22 57				
Gatley d			20 54							21 54							22 59				
Heald Green d			20 57							21 57							23 02				
Manchester Airport ✈ a	20 47	20 55	21 02	21 17	21 21	21 29		21 47		22 03	22 17	22 21	22 29			22 55	23 09	23 21	23 30		00 19
Wilmslow 84 a			21 13						21 49						22 49						
Crewe [10] 84 a									22 12						23 10						

Manchester Airport - Manchester

		TP MO	TP MX	TP MX	TP MO	NT MX	TP	TP	NT			TP	AW	TP	TP	NT	TP	TP	NT	NT		TP	TP	TP	NT
		◇1	◇1	◇1	◇1		◇1	◇1				◇1	◇ ⊼	◇1	◇1 ⊼		◇1 ⊼	◇1 ⊼				◇1 ⊼	◇1 ⊼	◇1 ⊼	
Crewe 10	84 d					00 44																			06 33
Wilmslow	84 d															05 46									06 57
Manchester Airport	✈ d	00 01	00 01	00 38	00 48	01 20	04 00	04 12	04 34			05 15	05 33	05 37	05 45	06b01	06 18	06 23	06 41	06 46		06 55	07 00	07 05	07c17
Heald Green	d														05 49	06 04				06 49					07 20
Gatley	d															06 07				06 52					07 23
East Didsbury	d															06 10				06 55					07 26
Burnage	d															06 12				06 57					07 28
Mauldeth Road	d															06 14				06 59					07 30
Manchester Piccadilly 10	a	00 15	00 15	00 51	01 01	01 36	04 13	04 27	04 47			05 33	05 48	05 51	06 00	06 25	06 31	06 39	06 56	07 11		07 13	07 14	07 22	07 42
	d	00 16	00 16	00 53	01 03		04 15	04 30	04 49			05 44	05 50	05 57	06 03		06 33	06 54	06 58			07 20	07 15	07 26	
Manchester Oxford Road	a												05 52		06 05		06 35		07 00				07 17		
Deansgate	a																								

		TP	TP	NT	NT	TP	TP	NT	TP	NT	NT	TP	NT	NT	TP	TP	NT	TP	NT	TP	TP	NT	NT	TP
		◇1 ⊼	◇1 ⊼			◇1 ⊼	◇1 ⊼		◇1 ⊼			◇1 ⊼			◇1 ⊼	◇1 ⊼		◇1 ⊼		◇1 ⊼	◇1 ⊼			◇1 ⊼
Crewe 10	84 d									07 22									08 31					
Wilmslow	84 d									08 00	07 56								08 57					
Manchester Airport	✈ d	07 25	07 35	07 41	07 46	07 54	07 58	08 01	08 05		08e17	08 25	08 41	08 46	08 55	09 00	09 03	09 05	09f17	09 29	09 35	09 41	09 46	09 55
Heald Green	d	07 30			07 49			08 05			08 20	08 29		08 49					09 20	09 33			09 49	
Gatley	d				07 52		08 03				08 23	08 32		08 52					09 23				09 52	
East Didsbury	d				07 55	08 00					08 26	08 35		08 55					09 26				09 55	
Burnage	d				07 57						08 28			08 57					09 28				09 57	
Mauldeth Road	d				07 59						08 30			08 59					09 30				09 59	
Manchester Piccadilly 10	a	07 43	07 49	07 56	08 11	08 13	08 14	08 21	08 22	08 27	08 42	08 44	08 58	09 11	09 13	09 14	09 18	09 22	09 42	09 44	09 52	09 59	10 11	10 13
	d	07 45	07 56	07 58		08 20	08 15	08 22	08 26	08 29		08 46	09 01		09 20	09 16	09 22	09 26		09 46	09 57	10 01		10 20
Manchester Oxford Road	a			08 00			08 17	08 24		08 33		08 48	09 03			09 18	09 24			09 48		10 03		
Deansgate	a							08 28				08 51					09 28			09 51				

		TP		NT	TP	NT	TP	TP	NT	NT	TP	TP			NT	TP	NT	TP	TP	NT	NT	TP	TP	NT	TP
		◇1 ⊼			◇1 ⊼		◇1 ⊼	◇1 ⊼			◇1 ⊼	◇1 ⊼				◇1 ⊼		◇1 ⊼	◇1 ⊼			◇1 ⊼	◇1 ⊼		◇1 ⊼
Crewe 10	84 d					09 33											10 33								
Wilmslow	84 d					09 57											10 57								
Manchester Airport	✈ d	10 00		10 03	10 05	10g17	10 29	10 35	10 41	10 46	10 55	11 00			11 03	11 05	11h17	11 29	11 35	11 41	11 46	11 55	12 00	12 03	12 05
Heald Green	d					10 20	10 33			10 49							11 20	11 33			11 49				
Gatley	d					10 23				10 52							11 23				11 52				
East Didsbury	d					10 26				10 55							11 26				11 55				
Burnage	d					10 28				10 57							11 28				11 57				
Mauldeth Road	d					10 30				10 59							11 30				11 59				
Manchester Piccadilly 10	a	10 14		10 18	10 22	10 42	10 44	10 52	10 59	11 11	11 13	11 14			11 18	11 22	11 42	11 44	11 52	11 59	12 11	12 13	12 14	12 18	12 22
	d	10 16		10 22	10 27		10 46	10 57	11 01		11 20	11 16			11 22	11 27		11 46	11 57	12 01		12 20	12 16	12 22	12 27
Manchester Oxford Road	a	10 18		10 24			10 48		11 03			11 18			11 24			11 48		12 03			12 18	12 24	
Deansgate	a			10 28			10 51								11 28			11 51						12 28	

		NT	TP	TP	NT	NT	TP	TP		NT	TP	NT	TP	TP	NT	NT	TP	TP		NT	TP	NT	TP	TP	NT
			◇1 ⊼	◇1 ⊼			◇1 ⊼	◇1 ⊼			◇1 ⊼		◇1 ⊼	◇1 ⊼			◇1 ⊼	◇1 ⊼			◇1 ⊼		◇1 ⊼	◇1 ⊼	
Crewe 10	84 d	11 33										12 33										13 33			
Wilmslow	84 d	11 57										12 57										13 57			
Manchester Airport	✈ d	12i17	12 29	12 35	12 41	12 46	12 55	13 00		13 03	13 05	13j17	13 29	13 35	13 41	13 46	13 55	14 00		14 03	14 05	14k17	14 29	14 35	14 41
Heald Green	d	12 20	12 33			12 49						13 20	13 33			13 49						14 20	14 33		
Gatley	d	12 23				12 52						13 23				13 52						14 23			
East Didsbury	d	12 26				12 55						13 26				13 55						14 26			
Burnage	d	12 28				12 57						13 28				13 57						14 28			
Mauldeth Road	d	12 30				12 59						13 30				13 59						14 30			
Manchester Piccadilly 10	a	12 42	12 44	12 52	12 59	13 11	13 13	13 14		13 18	13 22	13 42	13 44	13 52	13 59	14 11	14 13	14 14		14 18	14 22	14 42	14 44	14 52	14 59
	d		12 46	12 57	13 01		13 20	13 16		13 22	13 27		13 46	13 57	14 01		14 20	14 16		14 22	14 27		14 46	14 57	15 01
Manchester Oxford Road	a		12 48		13 03			13 18		13 24			13 48		14 03			14 18		14 24			14 48		15 03
Deansgate	a		12 51							13 28			13 51							14 28			14 51		

		NT	TP	TP	NT	TP	NT	TP	TP	NT	NT	TP	TP	NT	TP	NT	TP	TP	NT	NT	TP	TP	NT	TP	NT
			◇1 ⊼	◇1 ⊼		◇1 ⊼		◇1 ⊼	◇1 ⊼			◇1 ⊼	◇1 ⊼		◇1 ⊼		◇1 ⊼	◇1 ⊼			◇1 ⊼	◇1 ⊼		◇1 ⊼	
Crewe 10	84 d						14 33									15 33									16 33
Wilmslow	84 d						14 57									15 56									16 57
Manchester Airport	✈ d	14 46	14 55	15 00	15 03	15 05	15 17	15 29	15 35	15 41	15 46	15 55	16 00	16 03	16 05	16m17	16 29	16 35	16 41	16 46	16 55	17 00	17 03	17 05	17b17
Heald Green	d	14 49					15 20	15 33			15 49					16 20	16 33			16 49					17 20
Gatley	d	14 52					15 23				15 52					16 23				16 52					17 23
East Didsbury	d	14 55					15 26				15 55					16 26				16 55					17 26
Burnage	d	14 57					15 28				15 57					16 28				16 57					17 28
Mauldeth Road	d	14 59					15 30				15 59					16 30				16 59					17 30
Manchester Piccadilly 10	a	15 11	15 13	15 14	15 18	15 22	15 41	15 44	15 52	15 59	16 11	16 13	16 14	16 18	16 22	16 42	16 44	16 52	16 59	17 11	17 13	17 14	17 21	17 22	17 42
	d		15 20	15 16	15 22	15 27	15 42	15 46	15 57	16 01		16 20	16 16	16 22	16 27		16 46	16 56	17 01		17 20	17 15	17 22	17 26	
Manchester Oxford Road	a			15 18	15 24		15 46	15 48		16 03			16 18	16 24			16 48		17 03			17 17	17 25		
Deansgate	a				15 28			15 51						16 28											

b arr. 0553
c arr. 0704
e arr. 0804
f arr. 0904
g arr. 1004
h arr. 1104
i arr. 1204
j arr. 1304
k arr. 1404
l arr. 1504
m arr. 1604

Table 85 Mondays to Fridays

Manchester Airport - Manchester

		TP	NT	NT	TP	TP	NT	NT	TP	TP	NT	NT	TP	TP	NT	NT	TP	TP	NT	NT	TP	TP	NT	NT	TP
		◇1			◇1 ⊼	◇1 ⊼			◇1 ⊼	◇1			◇1	◇1			◇1	◇1			◇1	◇1			◇1
Crewe 10	84 d							17 33								18 33									
Wilmslow	84 d							17 56								18 56								19 56	
Manchester Airport	✈ d	17 29	17 41	17 46	17 55	18 00	18 03	18c17	18 29	18 35	18 41	18 46	18 15	18 55	19 03	19 09	19 20	19 29	19 41	19 46	19 55	20 00	20 03	20 09	20 20
Heald Green	d	17 33		17 49				18 20	18 33			18 49				19 12		19 33		19 49				20 12	
Gatley	d			17 52				18 23				18 52				19 15				19 52				20 15	
East Didsbury	d			17 55				18 26				18 55				19 18				19 55				20 18	
Burnage	d			17 57				18 28				18 57				19 20				19 57				20 20	
Mauldeth Road	d			17 59				18 30				18 59				19 22				19 59				20 22	
Manchester Piccadilly 10	a	17 44	17 59	18 11	18 13	18 14	18 18	18 42	18 44	18 52	18 59	19 11	19 14	19 13	19 18	19 31	19 36	19 44	19 59	20 11	20 13	20 14	20 18	20 32	20 36
	d	17 46	18 01		18 20	18 16	18 22		18 46	18 57	19 01		19 16	19 18	19 20	19 32	19 42	19 46	20 01		20 20	20 16	20 20	20 32	20 42
Manchester Oxford Road	a	17 48	18 03			18 18	18 24		18 48		19 03		19 18		19 22	19 36		19 48	20 03			20 18	20 22	20 36	
Deansgate	a	17 51					18 28		18 51						19 26			19 51					20 26		

		TP	AW	TP	NT	NT		TP	TP	AW	NT	TP	TP	NT	NT	TP		TP	NT	TP FX	TP
		◇1		◇1				◇1	◇1			◇1	◇1			◇1		◇1		◇1	◇1
Crewe 10	84 d																				
Wilmslow	84 d					20 56								21 55					22 56		
Manchester Airport	✈ d	20 29	20 32	20 47	21 03	21 09		21 20	21 29	21 32	21 41	21 47	22 00	22 08	22 19	22 22		22 29	23 09	23 18	23 52
Heald Green	d	20 33		20 51		21 12			21 33			21 51		22 12				22 33	23 12		
Gatley	d			20 54		21 15						21 54		22 15					23 15		
East Didsbury	d			20 57		21 18						21 57		22 17					23 18		
Burnage	d			20 59		21 20						21 59		22 19					23 20		
Mauldeth Road	d			21 02		21 22						22 02		22 21					23 22		
Manchester Piccadilly 10	a	20 44	20 48	21 13	21 18	21 32		21 36	21 44	21 48	21 59	22 13	22 14	22 31	22 34	22 36		22 44	23 33	23 34	00 09
	d	20 46	20 50	21 20	21 20	21 32		21 42	21 46	21 50	22 01	22 20	22 16	22 32	22 36	22 42		22 46		23 38	00 15
Manchester Oxford Road	a	20 48	20 52		21 22	21 36			21 48	21 52	22 03		22 18	22 36	22 38			22 48			
Deansgate	a	20 51			21 26				21 51						22 41			22 51			

Saturdays

		TP	TP	NT	TP	TP	NT	TP	TP		AW	TP	NT	TP	TP	NT	NT	TP	TP	TP		NT	TP	TP	NT
		◇1	◇1		◇1	◇1		◇1	◇1		◇ ⊼	◇1		◇1 ⊼	◇1 ⊼			◇1 ⊼	◇1 ⊼	◇1 ⊼			◇1 ⊼	◇1 ⊼	
Crewe 10	84 d			00 44																		06 33			
Wilmslow	84 d												05 46									06 57			
Manchester Airport	✈ d	00 01	00 38	01 20	04 00	04 15	04 34	05 15	05 29		05 33	05 37	06e01	06 18	06 23	06 41	06 46	06 55	07 00	07 05		07f17	07 25	07 33	07 41
Heald Green	d								05 33				06 04				06 49					07 20	07 30		
Gatley	d												06 07				06 52					07 23			
East Didsbury	d												06 10				06 55					07 26			
Burnage	d												06 12				06 57					07 28			
Mauldeth Road	d												06 14				06 59					07 30			
Manchester Piccadilly 10	a	00 15	00 51	01 36	04 13	04 29	04 47	05 33	05 44		05 48	05 51	06 25	06 31	06 39	06 56	07 11	07 13	07 14	07 22		07 42	07 43	07 48	07 56
	d	00 16	00 53		04 15	04 30	04 49	05 44	05 46		05 50	05 57		06 33	06 54	06 58		07 20	07 15	07 26			07 45	07 55	07 58
Manchester Oxford Road	a										05 52			06 35		07 00			07 17						08 00
Deansgate	a																								

		NT	TP	TP	NT	TP	NT	TP	NT	TP	NT	NT	TP	TP	NT	TP		NT	TP	TP	NT	NT	TP	TP	NT
			◇1 ⊼	◇1 ⊼		◇1 ⊼		◇1 ⊼		◇1 ⊼			◇1 ⊼	◇1 ⊼		◇1 ⊼			◇1 ⊼	◇1 ⊼			◇1 ⊼	◇1 ⊼	
Crewe 10	84 d						07 30		07 30									08 31							
Wilmslow	84 d						07 56		07 56									08 57							
Manchester Airport	✈ d	07 46	07 54	07 58	08 01	08 05	08g17	08 25	08g17	08 35	08 41	08 46	08 55	09 00	09 03	09 05		09h17	09 29	09 35	09 41	09 46	09 55	10 00	10 03
Heald Green	d	07 49			08 05		08 20	08 29	08 20			08 49						09 20	09 33			09 49			
Gatley	d	07 52		08 03			08 23	08 32	08 23			08 52						09 23				09 52			
East Didsbury	d	07 55	08 00				08 26	08 35	08 26			08 55						09 26				09 55			
Burnage	d	07 57					08 28		08 28			08 57						09 28				09 57			
Mauldeth Road	d	07 59					08 30		08 30			08 59						09 30				09 59			
Manchester Piccadilly 10	a	08 11	08 13	08 14	08 21	08 22	08 42	08 44	08 42	08 49	08 59	09 11	09 13	09 14	09 18	09 22		09 42	09 44	09 52	09 59	10 11	10 13	10 14	10 18
	d		08 20	08 15	08 22	08 26		08 46		08 57	09 01		09 20	09 16	09 22	09 26			09 46	09 57	10 01		10 20	10 16	10 22
Manchester Oxford Road	a			08 17	08 24			08 48			09 03			09 18	09 24				09 48		10 03			10 18	10 24
Deansgate	a				08 28			08 51							09 28				09 51						10 28

		TP		NT	TP	TP	NT	NT	TP	TP	NT	TP		NT	TP	TP	NT	NT	TP	TP	NT	TP		NT	TP
		◇1			◇1 ⊼	◇1 ⊼			◇1 ⊼	◇1 ⊼		◇1 ⊼			◇1 ⊼	◇1 ⊼			◇1 ⊼	◇1 ⊼		◇1 ⊼			◇1 ⊼
Crewe 10	84 d			09 33										10 33										11 33	
Wilmslow	84 d			09 57										10 57										11 57	
Manchester Airport	✈ d	10 05		10i17	10 29	10 35	10 41	10 46	10 55	11 00	11 03	11 05		11j17	11 29	11 35	11 41	11 46	11 55	12 00	12 03	12 05		12k17	12 29
Heald Green	d			10 20	10 33			10 49						11 20	11 33			11 49						12 20	12 33
Gatley	d			10 23				10 52						11 23				11 52						12 23	
East Didsbury	d			10 26				10 55						11 26				11 55						12 26	
Burnage	d			10 28				10 57						11 28				11 57						12 28	
Mauldeth Road	d			10 30				10 59						11 30				11 59						12 30	
Manchester Piccadilly 10	a	10 22		10 42	10 44	10 52	10 59	11 11	11 13	11 14	11 18	11 22		11 42	11 44	11 52	11 59	12 11	12 13	12 14	12 18	12 22		12 42	12 44
	d	10 27			10 46	10 57	11 01		11 20	11 16	11 22	11 27			11 46	11 57	12 01		12 20	12 16	12 22	12 27			12 46
Manchester Oxford Road	a				10 48		11 03			11 18	11 24				11 48		12 03			12 18	12 24				12 48
Deansgate	a				10 51						11 28				11 51						12 28				12 51

b arr. 1704
c arr. 1804
e arr. 0553
f arr. 0704
g arr. 0805
h arr. 0904
i arr. 1004
j arr. 1104
k arr. 1204

Table 85

Saturdays

Manchester Airport - Manchester

	TP ◇1 ⌶	NT	NT	TP ◇1 ⌶	TP ◇1 ⌶	NT	TP ◇1 ⌶	NT	TP ◇1 ⌶	TP ◇1 ⌶	NT	NT	TP ◇1 ⌶	TP ◇1 ⌶	NT	TP ◇1 ⌶	NT	TP ◇1 ⌶	TP ◇1	NT	NT	TP ◇1 ⌶
Crewe [10] 84 d								12 33									13 33					
Wilmslow 84 d								12 57									13 57					
Manchester Airport ✈ d	12 35	12 41	12 46	12 55	13 00	13 03	13 05	13b17	13 29	13 35	13 41	13 46	13 55	14 00	14 03	14 05	14c17	14 29	14 35	14 41	14 46	14 55
Heald Green d			12 49					13 20	13 33			13 49					14 20	14 33			14 49	
Gatley d			12 52					13 23				13 52					14 23				14 52	
East Didsbury d			12 55					13 26				13 55					14 26				14 55	
Burnage d			12 57					13 28				13 57					14 28				14 57	
Mauldeth Road d			12 59					13 30				13 59					14 30				14 59	
Manchester Piccadilly [10] ⇌ a	12 52	12 59	13 11	13 13	13 14	13 18	13 22	13 42	13 44	13 52	13 59	14 11	14 13	14 14	14 18	14 22	14 42	14 44	14 52	14 59	15 11	15 13
d	12 57	13 01		13 20	13 16	13 22	13 27		13 46	13 57	14 01		14 20	14 16	14 22	14 27		14 46	14 57	15 01		15 20
Manchester Oxford Road a		13 03			13 18	13 24			13 48		14 03			14 18	14 24			14 48		15 03		
Deansgate ⇌ a						13 28			13 51						14 28			14 51				

	TP ◇1 ⌶	NT	TP ◇1 ⌶	NT	TP ◇1 ⌶	TP ◇1 ⌶	NT	NT	TP ◇1 ⌶	TP ◇1 ⌶	NT	TP ◇1	NT	TP ◇1 ⌶	TP ◇1	NT	NT	TP ◇1 ⌶	TP ◇1 ⌶	NT	TP ◇1	NT
Crewe [10] 84 d				14 33									15 33									16 33
Wilmslow 84 d				14 57									15 56									16 57
Manchester Airport ✈ d	15 00	15 03	15 05	15e17	15 29	15 35	15 41	15 46	15 55	16 00	16 03	16 05	16f17	16 29	16 35	16 41	16 46	16 55	17 00	17 03	17 05	17g17
Heald Green d				15 20	15 33			15 49					16 20	16 33			16 49					17 20
Gatley d				15 23				15 52					16 23				16 52					17 23
East Didsbury d				15 26				15 55					16 26				16 55					17 26
Burnage d				15 28				15 57					16 28				16 57					17 28
Mauldeth Road d				15 30				15 59					16 30				16 59					17 30
Manchester Piccadilly [10] ⇌ a	15 14	15 18	15 22	15 42	15 44	15 52	15 59	16 11	16 13	16 14	16 18	16 22	16 42	16 44	16 52	16 59	17 11	17 13	17 14	17 21	17 22	17 42
d	15 16	15 22	15 27		15 46	15 57	16 01		16 20	16 16	16 22	16 27		16 46	16 56	17 01		17 20	17 15	17 22	17 26	
Manchester Oxford Road a	15 18	15 24			15 48		16 03			16 18	16 24			16 48		17 03			17 17	17 25		
Deansgate ⇌ a		15 28			15 51						16 28											

	TP ◇1	TP ◇1	NT	NT	TP ◇1 ⌶	TP ◇1 ⌶	NT	NT	TP ◇1	TP ◇1	NT	NT	TP ◇1	TP ◇1	NT	NT	TP ◇1	TP ◇1	NT	NT	TP ◇1	TP ◇1	NT	NT
Crewe [10] 84 d								17 33								18 33								
Wilmslow 84 d								17 56								18 56								19 56
Manchester Airport ✈ d	17 29	17 35	17 41	17 46	17 55	18 00	18 03	18h17	18 35	18 29	18 41	18 46	18 55	19 00	19 03	19 09	19 19	19 29	19 41	19 46	19 55	20 00	20 03	20 09
Heald Green d	17 33			17 49				18 20		18 33		18 49				19 12		19 33		19 49				20 12
Gatley d				17 52				18 23				18 52				19 15				19 52				20 15
East Didsbury d				17 55				18 26				18 55				19 18				19 55				20 18
Burnage d				17 57				18 28				18 57				19 20				19 57				20 20
Mauldeth Road d				17 59				18 30				18 59				19 22				19 59				20 22
Manchester Piccadilly [10] ⇌ a	17 44	17 52	17 59	18 11	18 13	18 14	18 18	18 42	18 52	18 44	18 59	19 11	19 13	19 14	19 18	19 31	19 36	19 44	19 59	20 11	20 13	20 14	20 18	20 31
d	17 46	17 56	18 01		18 20	18 16	18 22		18 57	18 46	19 01		19 18	19 16	19 20	19 32	19 42	19 46	20 01		20 20	20 16	20 20	20 32
Manchester Oxford Road a	17 48		18 03			18 18	18 24			18 48	19 03			19 18	19 22	19 36		19 48	20 03			20 18	20 22	20 36
Deansgate ⇌ a	17 51						18 28			18 51					19 26			19 51					20 26	

	TP ◇1	TP ◇1	AW	TP ◇1	NT	NT	TP ◇1	TP ◇1	NT	TP ◇1	TP ◇1	NT	NT	TP ◇1	TP ◇1	TP ◇1 A	TP B 🚌	TP ◇1 B	NT
Crewe [10] 84 d																			
Wilmslow 84 d						20 56						21 55							23 15
Manchester Airport ✈ d	20 20	20 29	20 32	20 47	21 03	21 09	21 20	21 29	21 41	21 47	22 00	22 08	22 19	22 22	22 29	23 24	23 24	23 24	23 27
Heald Green d		20 33		20 51		21 12		21 33		21 51		22 12			22 33				23 30
Gatley d				20 54		21 15				21 54		22 15							23 33
East Didsbury d				20 57		21 18				21 57		22 17							23 36
Burnage d				20 59		21 20				21 59		22 19							23 38
Mauldeth Road d				21 02		21 22				22 02		22 21							23 40
Manchester Piccadilly [10] ⇌ a	20 36	20 44	20 48	21 13	21 18	21 31	21 36	21 44	22 00	22 13	22 14	22 31	22 34	22 36	22 44	23 39	23u49	23 39	23 51
d	20 42	20 46	20 50	21 20	21 20	21 32	21 42	21 46	22 01	22 20	22 16	22 32	22 36	22 42	22 46	23 41	23u49		
Manchester Oxford Road a		20 48	20 52		21 22	21 36		21 48	22 03		22 18	22 36	22 38		22 48				
Deansgate ⇌ a		20 51			21 26			21 51					22 41		22 51				

Sundays
until 11 July

	TP 🚌	TP ◇1	TP ◇1	TP 🚌	NT	TP ◇1	TP ◇1	NT	TP ◇1	TP ◇1	NT	TP ◇1	NT	TP ◇1	TP ◇1 ⌶	NT	TP ◇1	TP ◇1	NT	NT	TP ◇1	TP ◇1	NT
Crewe [10] 84 d																							
Wilmslow 84 d																							
Manchester Airport ✈ d	00 10	01 22	04 43	05 30	06 09	06 24	07 24	07 30	07 55	08 06	08 09	08 29	08 34	08 39	09 00	09 06	09 20	09 30	09 35	10 08	10 19	10 29	10 32
Heald Green d					06 12			07 33			08 12					09 09				10 11			
Gatley d					06 15			07 36			08 15					09 12				10 14			
East Didsbury d					06 18			07 39			08 18					09 15				10 17			
Burnage d					06 20			07 41			08 20					09 17				10 19			
Mauldeth Road d					06 22			07 43			08 22					09 19				10 21			
Manchester Piccadilly [10] ⇌ a	00 35	01 35	04 56	05 55	06 31	06 37	07 37	07 54	08 08	08 24	08 31	08 44	08 49	08 54	09 14	09 29	09 37	09 44	09 48	10 30	10 34	10 43	10 48
d	00 35	01 42	05 02	05 55		06 42	07 42		08 11	08 28		08 46	08 50	08 58	09 16		09 42	09 46	09 50		10 42	10 46	10 50
Manchester Oxford Road a									08 13			08 48	08 52		09 18			09 48	09 52			10 48	10 52
Deansgate ⇌ a									08 16			08 51						09 51				10 51	

A until 4 September
B from 11 September
b arr. 1304
c arr. 1404
e arr. 1504
f arr. 1604
g arr. 1704
h arr. 1804

Table 85

Sundays
until 11 July

Manchester Airport - Manchester

	TP ◇1	TP ◇1	NT	TP ◇1	TP ◇1	TP ◇1 ⌶	NT	TP ◇1	TP ◇1	NT	TP ◇1	TP ◇1 ⌶	NT	TP ◇1	TP ◇1	NT	TP ◇1	TP ◇1 ⌶	NT	TP ◇1	TP ◇1	NT
Crewe [10] 84 d																						
Wilmslow 84 d			10 43										12 54									
Manchester Airport ✈ d	10 44	11 00	11b03	11 17	11 30	12 00	12 09	12 20	12 30	12 35	12 55	13 00	13 09	13 20	13 30	13 35	13 55	14 00	14 09	14 20	14 30	14 35
Heald Green d			11 07				12 12						13 12						14 12			
Gatley d			11 10				12 15						13 15						14 15			
East Didsbury d			11 12				12 18						13 18						14 18			
Burnage d			11 14				12 20						13 20						14 20			
Mauldeth Road d			11 16				12 22						13 22						14 22			
Manchester Piccadilly [10] ⇌ a	10 58	11 14	11 25	11 34	11 44	12 14	12 31	12 37	12 44	12 48	13 09	13 14	13 31	13 37	13 44	13 48	14 09	14 14	14 31	14 37	14 44	14 48
d	11 18	11 16	11 26	11 42	11 46	12 16		12 42	12 46	12 50	13 20	13 16		13 42	13 46	13 50	14 20	14 16		14 42	14 46	14 50
Manchester Oxford Road a		11 18	11 30		11 48	12 18			12 48	12 52		13 18			13 48	13 52		14 18			14 48	14 52
Deansgate ⇌ a					11 51				12 51						13 51						14 51	

	TP ◇1	TP ◇1	NT	TP ◇1	TP ◇1	NT	TP ◇1	TP ◇1 ⌶	NT	TP ◇1	TP ◇1	NT	TP ◇1	TP ◇1 ⌶	NT	TP ◇1	TP ◇1	NT	TP ◇1	TP ◇1 ⌶	NT	TP ◇1
Crewe [10] 84 d																						
Wilmslow 84 d			14 54												16 54							
Manchester Airport ✈ d	14 55	15 00	15 09	15 20	15 30	15 35	15 55	16 00	16 09	16 20	16 30	16 35	16 55	17 00	17 09	17 20	17 30	17 35	17 55	18 00	18 09	18 20
Heald Green d			15 12						16 12						17 12						18 12	
Gatley d			15 15						16 15						17 15						18 15	
East Didsbury d			15 18						16 18						17 18						18 18	
Burnage d			15 20						16 20						17 20						18 20	
Mauldeth Road d			15 22						16 22						17 22						18 22	
Manchester Piccadilly [10] ⇌ a	15 09	15 14	15 32	15 37	15 44	15 48	16 09	16 14	16 31	16 37	16 44	16 48	17 09	17 14	17 31	17 37	17 44	17 48	18 20	18 14	18 31	18 37
d	15 20	15 16		15 42	15 46	15 50	16 20	16 16		16 42	16 46	16 50	17 20	17 16		17 42	17 46	17 50	18 20	18 16		18 42
Manchester Oxford Road a		15 18			15 48	15 52		16 18			16 48	16 52		17 18			17 48	17 52		18 18		
Deansgate ⇌ a					15 51						16 51						17 51					

	TP ◇1	NT	TP ◇1	TP ◇1	NT	TP ◇1	TP ◇1	NT	TP ◇1	NT	TP ◇1	TP ◇1	NT	TP ◇1	NT	TP ◇1	TP ◇1	NT	TP ◇1	NT	NT	TP ◇1	NT	TP ◇1
Crewe [10] 84 d																								
Wilmslow 84 d					18 54										20 54								22 54	
Manchester Airport ✈ d	18 30	18 35	18 55	19 00	19 09	19 20	19 30	19 35	19 55	20 09	20 20	20 30	20 35	20 55	21 09	21 20	21 30	21 35	21 55	22 09	22 35	22 55	23 09	23 20
Heald Green d					19 12					20 12					21 12					22 12			23 12	
Gatley d					19 15					20 15					21 15					22 15			23 15	
East Didsbury d					19 18					20 18					21 18					22 18			23 18	
Burnage d					19 20					20 20					21 20					22 20			23 20	
Mauldeth Road d					19 22					20 22					21 22					22 22			23 22	
Manchester Piccadilly [10] ⇌ a	18 44	18 48	19 09	19 14	19 31	19 37	19 44	19 48	20 09	20 31	20 37	20 44	20 48	21 09	21 31	21 37	21 44	21 48	22 09	22 31	22 48	23 09	23 32	23 37
d	18 46	18 50	19 20	19 16		19 42	19 46	19 50	20 18		20 42	20 46	20 50	21 20		21 42	21 46	21 50	22 15		22 50	23 20		23 42
Manchester Oxford Road a	18 48	18 52		19 18			19 48	19 52				20 48	20 52				21 48	21 52			22 52			
Deansgate ⇌ a	18 51						19 51					20 51					21 51							

Sundays
18 July to 05 September

	TP 🚌	TP ◇1	TP ◇1	TP 🚌	NT	TP ◇1	TP ◇1	NT	TP ◇1	TP ◇1	NT	TP ◇1	NT	TP ◇1	TP ◇1 ⌶	NT	TP ◇1	TP ◇1	NT	NT	TP ◇1	TP ◇1	NT
Crewe [10] 84 d																							
Wilmslow 84 d																							
Manchester Airport ✈ d	00 10	01 22	04 43	05 30	06 09	06 24	07 24	07 30	07 55	08 06	08 09	08 29	08 34	08 39	09 00	09 06	09 20	09 30	09 35	10 08	10 19	10 29	10 32
Heald Green d					06 12			07 33			08 12					09 09				10 11			
Gatley d					06 15			07 36			08 15					09 12				10 14			
East Didsbury d					06 18			07 39			08 18					09 15				10 17			
Burnage d					06 20			07 41			08 20					09 17				10 19			
Mauldeth Road d					06 22			07 43			08 22					09 19				10 21			
Manchester Piccadilly [10] ⇌ a	00 35	01 35	04 56	05 55	06 31	06 37	07 37	07 54	08 08	08 24	08 31	08 44	08 49	08 54	09 14	09 29	09 37	09 44	09 48	10 30	10 34	10 43	10 48
d	00 35	01 42	05 02	05 55		06 42	07 42		08 11	08 28		08 46	08 50	08 58	09 16		09 42	09 46	09 50		10 42	10 46	10 50
Manchester Oxford Road a									08 13			08 48	08 52		09 18			09 48	09 52			10 48	10 52
Deansgate ⇌ a									08 16			08 51						09 51				10 51	

b arr. 1056

Table 85

Manchester Airport - Manchester

Sundays
18 July to 05 September

	TP ◇1	TP ◇1	NT	TP ◇1	TP ◇1	NT	TP ◇1 ⟂	NT	TP ◇1	TP ◇1	NT	TP ◇1	TP ◇1 ⟂	NT	TP ◇1	TP ◇1	NT	TP ◇1	TP ◇1 ⟂	NT	TP ◇1	TP ◇1
Crewe 10 84 d																						
Wilmslow 84 d			10 43											12 54								
Manchester Airport ✈ d	10 44	11 00	11b03	11 17	11 30	11 35	12 00	12 09	12 20	12 30	12 35	12 55	13 00	13 09	13 20	13 30	13 35	13 55	14 00	14 09	14 20	14 30
Heald Green d			11 07					12 12						13 12						14 12		
Gatley d			11 10					12 15						13 15						14 15		
East Didsbury d			11 12					12 18						13 18						14 18		
Burnage d			11 14					12 20						13 20						14 20		
Mauldeth Road d			11 16					12 22						13 22						14 22		
Manchester Piccadilly 10 ⇌ a	10 58	11 14	11 25	11 34	11 44	11 48	12 14	12 31	12 37	12 44	12 48	13 09	13 14	13 31	13 37	13 44	13 48	14 09	14 14	14 31	14 37	14 44
d	11 18	11 16	11 26	11 42	11 46	11 50	12 16		12 42	12 46	12 50	13 20	13 16		13 42	13 46	13 50	14 20	14 16		14 42	14 46
Manchester Oxford Road a		11 18	11 30		11 48	11 52	12 18			12 48	12 52		13 18			13 48	13 52		14 18			14 48
Deansgate ⇌ a					11 51					12 51						13 51						14 51

	NT	TP ◇1	TP ◇1	NT	TP ◇1	TP ◇1	NT	TP ◇1	TP ◇1 ⟂	NT	TP ◇1	TP ◇1	NT	TP ◇1	TP ◇1 ⟂	NT	TP ◇1	TP ◇1	NT	TP ◇1	TP ◇1 ⟂	NT
Crewe 10 84 d																						
Wilmslow 84 d				14 54												16 54						
Manchester Airport ✈ d	14 35	14 55	15 00	15 09	15 20	15 30	15 35	15 55	16 00	16 09	16 20	16 30	16 35	16 55	17 00	17 09	17 20	17 30	17 35	17 55	18 00	18 09
Heald Green d				15 12						16 12						17 12						18 12
Gatley d				15 15						16 15						17 15						18 15
East Didsbury d				15 18						16 18						17 18						18 18
Burnage d				15 20						16 20						17 20						18 20
Mauldeth Road d				15 22						16 22						17 22						18 22
Manchester Piccadilly 10 ⇌ a	14 48	15 09	15 14	15 32	15 37	15 44	15 48	16 09	16 14	16 31	16 37	16 44	16 48	17 09	17 14	17 31	17 37	17 44	17 48	18 20	18 14	18 31
d	14 50	15 20	15 16		15 42	15 46	15 50	16 20	16 16		16 42	16 46	16 50	17 20	17 16		17 42	17 46	17 50	18 20	18 16	
Manchester Oxford Road a	14 52		15 18			15 48	15 52		16 18			16 48	16 52		17 18			17 48	17 52		18 18	
Deansgate ⇌ a						15 51						16 51						17 51				

	TP ◇1	TP ◇1	NT	TP ◇1	TP ◇1	NT	TP ◇1	TP ◇1	NT	TP ◇1	NT	TP ◇1	TP ◇1	NT	TP ◇1	NT	TP ◇1	TP ◇1	NT	TP ◇1	NT	NT	TP ◇1
Crewe 10 84 d																							
Wilmslow 84 d						18 54										20 54							
Manchester Airport ✈ d	18 20	18 30	18 35	18 55	19 00	19 09	19 20	19 30	19 35	19 55	20 09	20 20	20 30	20 35	20 55	21 09	21 20	21 30	21 35	21 55	22 09	22 35	22 55
Heald Green d						19 12					20 12					21 12					22 12		
Gatley d						19 15					20 15					21 15					22 15		
East Didsbury d						19 18					20 18					21 18					22 18		
Burnage d						19 20					20 20					21 20					22 20		
Mauldeth Road d						19 22					20 22					21 22					22 22		
Manchester Piccadilly 10 ⇌ a	18 37	18 44	18 48	19 09	19 14	19 31	19 37	19 44	19 48	20 09	20 31	20 37	20 44	20 48	21 09	21 31	21 37	21 44	21 48	22 09	22 31	22 48	23 09
d	18 42	18 46	18 50	19 20	19 16		19 42	19 46	19 50	20 18		20 42	20 46	20 50	21 20		21 42	21 46	21 50	22 15		22 50	23 20
Manchester Oxford Road a		18 48	18 52		19 18			19 48	19 52				20 48	20 52				21 48	21 52			22 52	
Deansgate ⇌ a		18 51						19 51					20 51					21 51					

	NT	TP ◇1
Crewe 10 84 d		
Wilmslow 84 d	22 54	
Manchester Airport ✈ d	23 09	23 20
Heald Green d	23 12	
Gatley d	23 15	
East Didsbury d	23 18	
Burnage d	23 20	
Mauldeth Road d	23 22	
Manchester Piccadilly 10 ⇌ a	23 32	23 37
d		23 42
Manchester Oxford Road a		
Deansgate ⇌ a		

Sundays
from 12 September

	TP 🚌	TP 🚌	TP 🚌	TP 🚌	NT	TP 🚌	NT	TP 🚌	TP ◇1	TP ◇1	NT	TP ◇1	TP ◇1	TP ◇1 ⟂	TP ◇1	NT	TP ◇1	TP ◇1 ⟂	TP ◇1	NT	TP ◇1	NT
Crewe 10 84 d																						
Wilmslow 84 d																						
Manchester Airport ✈ d	00 10	01 40	05 15	05 30	06 09	06 15	07 09	07 10	07 30	07 40	08 24	08 39	08 47	09 00	09 03	09 06	09 30	10 00	10 03	10 07	10 25	10 31
Heald Green d					06 12		07 12				08 27					09 09				10 10		
Gatley d					06 15		07 15				08 30					09 12				10 13		
East Didsbury d					06 18		07 18				08 33					09 15				10 16		
Burnage d					06 20		07 20				08 35					09 17				10 18		
Mauldeth Road d					06 22		07 22				08 37					09 19				10 20		
Manchester Piccadilly 10 ⇌ a	00 35	02 05	05 40	05 55	06 31	06 40	07 31	07 35	07 44	07 53	08 47	08 54	09 01	09 14	09 18	09 29	09 44	10 14	10 18	10 30	10 39	10 45
d	00 35	02 05	05 40	05 55		06 40			07 46	07 55		08 58	09 03	09 16	09 20		09 46	10 16	10 20		10 43	10 50
Manchester Oxford Road a									07 48				09 05	09 18			09 48	10 18			10 45	10 52
Deansgate ⇌ a									07 51				09 08				09 51				10 51	

b arr. 1056

Table 85

Manchester Airport - Manchester

Sundays
from 12 September

	TP ◇1	TP ◇1	NT	TP ◇1	NT	TP ◇1 ⟂	TP ◇1	NT	TP ◇1	NT	TP ◇1	TP ◇1 ⟂	TP ◇1	NT	TP ◇1	NT	TP ◇1	TP ◇1 ⟂	NT	TP ◇1	TP ◇1	NT
Crewe 10 84 d																						
Wilmslow 84 d			10 53											12 54								
Manchester Airport ✈ d	10 44	11 03	11 08	11 30	11 33	11 58	12 03	12 09	12 30	12 35	12 55	12 58	13 03	13 09	13 30	13 35	13 55	13 58	14 09	14 20	14 30	14 35
Heald Green d			11 11					12 12						13 12					14 12			
Gatley d			11 14					12 15						13 15					14 15			
East Didsbury d			11 17					12 18						13 18					14 18			
Burnage d			11 19					12 20						13 20					14 20			
Mauldeth Road d			11 21					12 22						13 22					14 22			
Manchester Piccadilly 10 ⇌ a	10 58	11 18	11 29	11 44	11 48	12 14	12 18	12 31	12 44	12 48	13 09	13 14	13 18	13 31	13 44	13 48	14 09	14 14	14 31	14 37	14 44	14 48
d	11 18	11 20	11 30	11 46	11 50	12 16	12 20		12 46	12 50	13 20	13 16	13 20		13 46	13 50	14 20	14 16		14 42	14 46	14 50
Manchester Oxford Road a			11 34	11 48	11 52	12 18			12 48	12 52		13 18			13 48	13 52		14 18			14 48	14 52
Deansgate ⇌ a				11 51					12 51						13 51						14 51	

	TP ◇1	TP ◇1	NT	TP ◇1	TP ◇1	NT	TP ◇1	TP ◇1 ⟂	NT	TP ◇1	TP ◇1	NT	TP ◇1	TP ◇1 ⟂	NT	TP ◇1	TP ◇1	NT	TP ◇1	TP ◇1 ⟂	NT	TP ◇1
Crewe 10 84 d																						
Wilmslow 84 d			14 54												16 54							
Manchester Airport ✈ d	14 55	15 00	15 09	15 20	15 30	15 35	15 55	16 00	16 09	16 20	16 30	16 35	16 55	17 00	17 09	17 20	17 30	17 35	17 55	18 00	18 09	18 20
Heald Green d			15 12						16 12						17 12						18 12	
Gatley d			15 15						16 15						17 15						18 15	
East Didsbury d			15 18						16 18						17 18						18 18	
Burnage d			15 20						16 20						17 20						18 20	
Mauldeth Road d			15 22						16 22						17 22						18 22	
Manchester Piccadilly 10 ⇌ a	15 09	15 14	15 32	15 37	15 44	15 48	16 09	16 14	16 31	16 37	16 44	16 48	17 09	17 14	17 31	17 37	17 44	17 48	18 20	18 14	18 31	18 37
d	15 20	15 16		15 42	15 46	15 50	16 20	16 16		16 42	16 46	16 50	17 20	17 16		17 42	17 46	17 50	18 20	18 16		18 42
Manchester Oxford Road a		15 18			15 48	15 52		16 18			16 48	16 52		17 18			17 48	17 52		18 18		
Deansgate ⇌ a					15 51						16 51						17 51					

	TP ◇1	NT	TP ◇1	TP ◇1	NT	TP ◇1	TP ◇1	NT	TP ◇1	NT	TP ◇1	TP ◇1	NT	TP ◇1	NT	TP ◇1	TP ◇1	NT	TP ◇1	NT	NT	TP ◇1	NT	TP ◇1
Crewe 10 84 d																								
Wilmslow 84 d					18 54										20 54								22 54	
Manchester Airport ✈ d	18 30	18 35	18 55	19 00	19 09	19 20	19 30	19 35	19 55	20 09	20 20	20 30	20 35	20 55	21 09	21 20	21 30	21 35	21 55	22 09	22 35	22 55	23 09	23 20
Heald Green d					19 12					20 12					21 12					22 12			23 12	
Gatley d					19 15					20 15					21 15					22 15			23 15	
East Didsbury d					19 18					20 18					21 18					22 18			23 18	
Burnage d					19 20					20 20					21 20					22 20			23 20	
Mauldeth Road d					19 22					20 22					21 22					22 22			23 22	
Manchester Piccadilly 10 ⇌ a	18 44	18 48	19 09	19 14	19 31	19 37	19 44	19 48	20 09	20 31	20 37	20 44	20 48	21 09	21 31	21 37	21 44	21 48	22 09	22 31	22 48	23 09	23 32	23 37
d	18 46	18 50	19 20	19 16		19 42	19 46	19 50	20 18		20 42	20 46	20 50	21 20		21 42	21 46	21 50	22 15		22 50	23 20		23 42
Manchester Oxford Road a	18 48	18 52		19 18			19 48	19 52				20 48	20 52				21 48	21 52			22 52			
Deansgate ⇌ a	18 51						19 51					20 51					21 51							

Table 86

Manchester - Hazel Grove and Buxton

Mondays to Fridays
until 03 September

	NT	NT	NT	NT	NT	NT	NT	NT	NT	NT	NT	NT	NT	NT	NT	NT	NT	NT	NT	NT	NT
Deansgate d				07 11		08 12		09 12		10 12		11 12		12 12		13 12		14 12		15 12	
Manchester Oxford Road d				07 15		08 15		09 16		10 16		11 16		12 16		13 16		14 16		15 16	
Manchester Piccadilly 84 d	05 50	06 21	06 49	07 21	07 52	08 20	08 52	09 21	09 52	10 21	10 52	11 21	11 52	12 21	12 52	13 21	13 52	14 21	14 52	15 21	15 52
Levenshulme 84 d		06 28	06 55	07 28		08 28	08 58	09 28	09 58	10 28	10 58	11 28	11 58	12 28	12 58	13 28	13 58	14 28	14 58	15 28	15 58
Heaton Chapel 84 d		06 31	06 58	07 31		08 31	09 01	09 31	10 01	10 31	11 01	11 31	12 01	12 31	13 01	13 31	14 01	14 31	15 01	15 31	16 01
Stockport 84 d	06 00	06 35	07 02	07 35	08 01	08 35	09 05	09 35	10 05	10 35	11 05	11 35	12 05	12 35	13 05	13 35	14 05	14 35	15 05	15 35	16 05
Davenport d		06 39	07 06	07 39	08 05	08 39	09 09	09 39	10 09	10 39	11 09	11 39	12 09	12 39	13 09	13 39	14 09	14 39	15 09	15 39	16 09
Woodsmoor d		06 41	07 08	07 41	08 07	08 41	09 11	09 41	10 11	10 41	11 11	11 41	12 11	12 41	13 11	13 41	14 11	14 41	15 11	15 41	16 11
Hazel Grove a	06 06	06 45	07 10	07 45	08 09	08 48	09 13	09 45	10 13	10 45	11 13	11 45	12 13	12 45	13 13	13 45	14 13	14 45	15 13	15 48	16 13
d	06 07		07 10		08 10		09 13		10 13		11 13		12 13		13 13		14 13		15 13		16 13
Middlewood d			07 15				09 18		10 18				12 18				14 18				16 18
Disley d			07 19		08 17		09 22		10 22		11 20		12 22		13 20		14 22		15 20		16 22
New Mills Newtown d			07 22		08 20		09 25		10 25		11 24		12 25		13 24		14 25		15 24		16 25
Furness Vale d			07 25		08 23		09 28		10 28		11 26		12 28		13 26		14 28		15 26		16 28
Whaley Bridge d			07 28		08 26		09 31		10 31		11 29		12 31		13 29		14 31		15 29		16 31
Chapel-en-le-Frith d			07 35		08 33		09 38		10 38		11 36		12 38		13 36		14 38		15 36		16 38
Dove Holes d			07 40				09 43		10 43				12 43				14 43				16 43
Buxton a			07 50		08 44		09 53		10 53		11 50		12 53		13 50		14 53		15 50		16 53

	NT	NT	NT	NT	NT	NT	NT	NT	NT	NT	NT	NT	NT
Deansgate d	16 12			17 15			18 12						
Manchester Oxford Road d	16 16			17 19			18 16						
Manchester Piccadilly 84 d	16 21	16 51	16 58	17 23	17 23	17 52	18 21	18 52	19 22	19 51	20 51	21 52	23 10
Levenshulme 84 d	16 28		17 03		17 28	17 58	18 28	18 58	19 28	19 58	20 58	21 58	
Heaton Chapel 84 d	16 31		17 06		17 31	18 01	18 31	19 01	19 31	20 01	21 01	22 01	
Stockport 84 d	16 35	17 03	17 10	17 32	17 35	18 05	18 35	19 05	19 35	20 05	21 05	22 05	23 20
Davenport d	16 39	17 06	17 14		17 39	18 09	18 39	19 09	19 39	20 09	21 09	22 09	23 23
Woodsmoor d	16 41	17 08	17 16		17 41	18 11	18 41	19 11	19 41	20 11	21 11	22 11	23 25
Hazel Grove a	16 43	17 10	17 20	17 39	17 45	18 13	18 43	19 13	19 45	20 13	21 13	22 13	23 27
d	16 46	17 11		17 39		18 13	18 46	19 13		20 13	21 13	22 13	23 28
Middlewood d		17 15				18 18		19 18		20 18	21 18	22 18	23 32
Disley d	16 53	17 19		17 46		18 22	18 53	19 22		20 22	21 22	22 22	23 36
New Mills Newtown d	16 56	17 23		17 50		18 25	18 56	19 25		20 25	21 25	22 25	23 40
Furness Vale d	16 59	17 26		17 52		18 28	18 59	19 28		20 28	21 28	22 28	23 42
Whaley Bridge d	17 02	17 29		17 55		18 31	19 02	19 31		20 31	21 31	22 31	23 45
Chapel-en-le-Frith d	17 09	17 36		18 03		18 38	19 09	19 38		20 38	21 38	22 38	23 52
Dove Holes d		17 41				18 43		19 43		20 43	21 43	22 43	23 57
Buxton a	17 22	17 51		18 16		18 54	19 22	19 53		20 53	21 53	22 53	00 07

Mondays to Fridays
from 06 September

	NT	NT	NT	NT	NT	NT	NT	NT	NT	NT	NT	NT	NT	NT	NT	NT	NT	NT	NT	NT	NT
Deansgate d				07 11		08 12		09 12		10 12		11 12		12 12		13 12		14 12		15 12	
Manchester Oxford Road d				07 15		08 15		09 16		10 16		11 16		12 16		13 16		14 16		15 16	
Manchester Piccadilly 84 d	05 50	06 21	06 49	07 21	07 52	08 20	08 52	09 21	09 52	10 21	10 52	11 21	11 52	12 21	12 52	13 21	13 52	14 21	14 52	15 21	15 52
Levenshulme 84 d		06 28	06 55	07 28		08 28	08 58	09 28	09 58	10 28	10 58	11 28	11 58	12 28	12 58	13 28	13 58	14 28	14 58	15 28	15 58
Heaton Chapel 84 d		06 31	06 58	07 31		08 31	09 01	09 31	10 01	10 31	11 01	11 31	12 01	12 31	13 01	13 31	14 01	14 31	15 01	15 31	16 01
Stockport 84 d	06 00	06 35	07 02	07 35	08 01	08 35	09 05	09 35	10 05	10 35	11 05	11 35	12 05	12 35	13 05	13 35	14 05	14 35	15 05	15 35	16 05
Davenport d		06 39	07 06	07 39	08 05	08 39	09 09	09 39	10 09	10 39	11 09	11 39	12 09	12 39	13 09	13 39	14 09	14 39	15 09	15 39	16 09
Woodsmoor d		06 41	07 08	07 41	08 07	08 41	09 11	09 41	10 11	10 41	11 11	11 41	12 11	12 41	13 11	13 41	14 11	14 41	15 11	15 41	16 11
Hazel Grove a	06 06	06 47	07 10	07 47	08 09	08 48	09 13	09 47	10 13	10 45	11 13	11 47	12 13	12 47	13 13	13 47	14 13	14 47	15 13	15 48	16 13
d	06 07		07 10		08 10		09 13		10 13		11 13		12 13		13 13		14 13		15 13		16 13
Middlewood d			07 15				09 18		10 18				12 18				14 18				16 18
Disley d			07 19		08 17		09 22		10 22		11 20		12 22		13 20		14 22		15 20		16 22
New Mills Newtown d			07 22		08 20		09 25		10 25		11 24		12 25		13 24		14 25		15 24		16 25
Furness Vale d			07 25		08 23		09 28		10 28		11 26		12 28		13 26		14 28		15 26		16 28
Whaley Bridge d			07 28		08 26		09 31		10 31		11 29		12 31		13 29		14 31		15 29		16 31
Chapel-en-le-Frith d			07 35		08 33		09 38		10 38		11 36		12 38		13 36		14 38		15 36		16 38
Dove Holes d			07 40				09 43		10 43				12 43				14 43				16 43
Buxton a			07 52		08 44		09 55		10 55		11 52		12 55		13 52		14 55		15 52		16 55

	NT	NT	NT	NT	NT	NT	NT	NT	NT	NT	NT	NT	NT
Deansgate d	16 12			17 15			18 12						
Manchester Oxford Road d	16 16			17 19			18 16						
Manchester Piccadilly 84 d	16 21	16 51	16 58	17 23	17 23	17 52	18 21	18 52	19 22	19 51	20 51	21 52	23 10
Levenshulme 84 d	16 28		17 03		17 28	17 58	18 28	18 58	19 28	19 58	20 58	21 58	
Heaton Chapel 84 d	16 31		17 06		17 31	18 01	18 31	19 01	19 31	20 01	21 01	22 01	
Stockport 84 d	16 35	17 03	17 10	17 32	17 35	18 05	18 35	19 05	19 35	20 05	21 05	22 05	23 20
Davenport d	16 39	17 06	17 14		17 39	18 09	18 39	19 09	19 39	20 09	21 09	22 09	23 23
Woodsmoor d	16 41	17 08	17 16		17 41	18 11	18 41	19 11	19 41	20 11	21 11	22 11	23 25
Hazel Grove a	16 43	17 10	17 22	17 39	17 47	18 13	18 43	19 13	19 47	20 13	21 13	22 13	23 27
d	16 46	17 11		17 39		18 13	18 46	19 13		20 13	21 13	22 13	23 28
Middlewood d		17 15				18 18		19 18		20 18	21 18	22 18	23 32
Disley d	16 53	17 19		17 46		18 22	18 53	19 22		20 22	21 22	22 22	23 36
New Mills Newtown d	16 56	17 23		17 50		18 25	18 56	19 25		20 25	21 25	22 25	23 40
Furness Vale d	16 59	17 26		17 52		18 28	18 59	19 28		20 28	21 28	22 28	23 42
Whaley Bridge d	17 02	17 29		17 55		18 31	19 02	19 31		20 31	21 31	22 31	23 45
Chapel-en-le-Frith d	17 09	17 36		18 03		18 38	19 09	19 38		20 38	21 38	22 38	23 52
Dove Holes d		17 41				18 43		19 43		20 43	21 43	22 43	23 57
Buxton a	17 24	17 53		18 18		18 56	19 24	19 55		20 55	21 55	22 55	00 09

Table 86

Manchester - Hazel Grove and Buxton

Saturdays
until 04 September

	NT	NT	NT	NT	NT	NT	NT	NT	NT	NT	NT	NT	NT	NT	NT	NT	NT	NT	NT	NT	NT
Deansgate d			07 11		08 12		09 12		10 12		11 12		12 12		13 12		14 12		15 12		16 12
Manchester Oxford Road d			07 15		08 15		09 16		10 16		11 16		12 16		13 16		14 16		15 16		16 16
Manchester Piccadilly 84 d	05 50	06 49	07 21	07 52	08 20	08 52	09 21	09 52	10 21	10 52	11 21	11 52	12 21	12 52	13 21	13 52	14 21	14 52	15 21	15 52	16 21
Levenshulme 84 d		06 55	07 28	07 57	08 28	08 58	09 28	09 58	10 28	10 58	11 28	11 58	12 28	12 58	13 28	13 58	14 28	14 58	15 28	15 58	16 28
Heaton Chapel 84 d		06 58	07 31		08 31	09 01	09 31	10 01	10 31	11 01	11 31	12 01	12 31	13 01	13 31	14 01	14 31	15 01	15 31	16 01	16 31
Stockport 84 d	06 00	07 02	07 35	08 02	08 35	09 05	09 35	10 05	10 35	11 05	11 35	12 05	12 35	13 05	13 35	14 05	14 35	15 05	15 35	16 05	16 35
Davenport d		07 06	07 39	08 06	08 39	09 09	09 39	10 09	10 39	11 09	11 39	12 09	12 39	13 09	13 39	14 09	14 39	15 09	15 39	16 09	16 39
Woodsmoor d		07 08	07 41	08 08	08 41	09 11	09 41	10 11	10 41	11 11	11 41	12 11	12 41	13 11	13 41	14 11	14 41	15 11	15 41	16 11	16 41
Hazel Grove a	06 06	07 10	07 45	08 11	08 45	09 13	09 45	10 13	10 45	11 13	11 45	12 13	12 45	13 13	13 45	14 13	14 45	15 13	15 45	16 13	16 45
d	06 07	07 10		08 11		09 13		10 13		11 13		12 13		13 13		14 13		15 13		16 13	
Middlewood d		07 15				09 18		10 18				12 18				14 18				16 18	
Disley d		07 19		08 18		09 22		10 22		11 20		12 22		13 20		14 22		15 20		16 22	
New Mills Newtown d		07 22		08 21		09 25		10 25		11 24		12 25		13 24		14 25		15 24		16 25	
Furness Vale d		07 25		08 24		09 28		10 28		11 26		12 28		13 26		14 28		15 26		16 28	
Whaley Bridge d		07 28		08 27		09 31		10 31		11 29		12 31		13 29		14 31		15 29		16 31	
Chapel-en-le-Frith d		07 35		08 34		09 38		10 38		11 36		12 38		13 36		14 38		15 36		16 38	
Dove Holes d		07 40				09 43		10 43				12 43				14 43				16 43	
Buxton a		07 50		08 48		09 53		10 53		11 50		12 53		13 50		14 53		15 50		16 53	

	NT	NT	NT	NT	NT	NT	NT	NT	NT	NT	NT
Deansgate d			17 12		18 12						
Manchester Oxford Road d			17 16		18 16						
Manchester Piccadilly 84 d	16 51	17 09	17 21	17 52	18 21	18 52	19 22	19 51	20 52	21 52	23 10
Levenshulme 84 d	16 58	17 14	17 28	17 58	18 28	18 58	19 28	19 58	20 58	21 58	
Heaton Chapel 84 d	17 01	17 17	17 31	18 01	18 31	19 01	19 31	20 01	21 01	22 01	
Stockport 84 d	17 05	17b32	17 35	18 05	18 35	19 05	19 35	20 05	21 05	22 05	23 20
Davenport d	17 09		17 39	18 09	18 39	19 09	19 39	20 09	21 09	22 09	23 23
Woodsmoor d	17 11		17 41	18 11	18 41	19 11	19 41	20 11	21 11	22 11	23 25
Hazel Grove a	17 13	17 39	17 43	18 13	18 45	19 13	19 45	20 13	21 13	22 13	23 27
d	17 13		17 46	18 13		19 13		20 13	21 13	22 13	23 28
Middlewood d			17 50			19 18		20 18	21 18	22 18	23 32
Disley d	17 20		17 54	18 20		19 22		20 22	21 22	22 22	23 36
New Mills Newtown d	17 24		17 58	18 24		19 25		20 25	21 25	22 25	23 40
Furness Vale d	17 26		18 00	18 26		19 28		20 28	21 28	22 28	23 42
Whaley Bridge d	17 29		18 03	18 29		19 31		20 31	21 31	22 31	23 45
Chapel-en-le-Frith d	17 36		18 10	18 36		19 38		20 38	21 38	22 38	23 52
Dove Holes d			18 15			19 43		20 43	21 43	22 43	23 57
Buxton a	17 50		18 25	18 50		19 53		20 53	21 53	22 53	00 07

Saturdays
from 11 September

	NT	NT	NT	NT	NT	NT	NT	NT	NT	NT	NT	NT	NT	NT	NT	NT	NT	NT	NT	NT	NT
Deansgate d			07 11		08 12		09 12		10 12		11 12		12 12		13 12		14 12		15 12		16 12
Manchester Oxford Road d			07 15		08 15		09 16		10 16		11 16		12 16		13 16		14 16		15 16		16 16
Manchester Piccadilly 84 d	05 50	06 49	07 21	07 52	08 20	08 52	09 21	09 52	10 21	10 52	11 21	11 52	12 21	12 52	13 21	13 52	14 21	14 52	15 21	15 52	16 21
Levenshulme 84 d		06 55	07 28	07 57	08 28	08 58	09 28	09 58	10 28	10 58	11 28	11 58	12 28	12 58	13 28	13 58	14 28	14 58	15 28	15 58	16 28
Heaton Chapel 84 d		06 58	07 31		08 31	09 01	09 31	10 01	10 31	11 01	11 31	12 01	12 31	13 01	13 31	14 01	14 31	15 01	15 31	16 01	16 31
Stockport 84 d	06 00	07 02	07 35	08 02	08 35	09 05	09 35	10 05	10 35	11 05	11 35	12 05	12 35	13 05	13 35	14 05	14 35	15 05	15 35	16 05	16 35
Davenport d		07 06	07 39	08 06	08 39	09 09	09 39	10 09	10 39	11 09	11 39	12 09	12 39	13 09	13 39	14 09	14 39	15 09	15 39	16 09	16 39
Woodsmoor d		07 08	07 41	08 08	08 41	09 11	09 41	10 11	10 41	11 11	11 41	12 11	12 41	13 11	13 41	14 11	14 41	15 11	15 41	16 11	16 41
Hazel Grove a	06 06	07 10	07 47	08 11	08 47	09 13	09 47	10 13	10 45	11 13	11 47	12 13	12 47	13 13	13 47	14 13	14 47	15 13	15 47	16 13	16 47
d	06 07	07 10		08 11		09 13		10 13		11 13		12 13		13 13		14 13		15 13		16 13	
Middlewood d		07 15				09 18		10 18				12 18				14 18				16 18	
Disley d		07 19		08 18		09 22		10 22		11 20		12 22		13 20		14 22		15 20		16 22	
New Mills Newtown d		07 22		08 21		09 25		10 25		11 24		12 25		13 24		14 25		15 24		16 25	
Furness Vale d		07 25		08 24		09 28		10 28		11 26		12 28		13 26		14 28		15 26		16 28	
Whaley Bridge d		07 28		08 27		09 31		10 31		11 29		12 31		13 29		14 31		15 29		16 31	
Chapel-en-le-Frith d		07 35		08 34		09 38		10 38		11 36		12 38		13 36		14 38		15 36		16 38	
Dove Holes d		07 40				09 43		10 43				12 43				14 43				16 43	
Buxton a		07 52		08 48		09 55		10 55		11 52		12 55		13 52		14 55		15 52		16 55	

	NT	NT	NT	NT	NT	NT	NT	NT	NT	NT	NT
Deansgate d			17 12		18 12						
Manchester Oxford Road d			17 16		18 16						
Manchester Piccadilly 84 d	16 51	17 09	17 21	17 52	18 21	18 52	19 22	19 51	20 52	21 52	23 10
Levenshulme 84 d	16 58	17 14	17 28	17 58	18 28	18 58	19 28	19 58	20 58	21 58	
Heaton Chapel 84 d	17 01	17 17	17 31	18 01	18 31	19 01	19 31	20 01	21 01	22 01	
Stockport 84 d	17 05	17b32	17 35	18 05	18 35	19 05	19 35	20 05	21 05	22 05	23 20
Davenport d	17 09		17 39	18 09	18 39	19 09	19 39	20 09	21 09	22 09	23 23
Woodsmoor d	17 11		17 41	18 11	18 41	19 11	19 41	20 11	21 11	22 11	23 25
Hazel Grove a	17 13	17 41	17 43	18 13	18 47	19 13	19 47	20 13	21 13	22 13	23 27
d	17 13		17 46	18 13		19 13		20 13	21 13	22 13	23 28
Middlewood d			17 50			19 18		20 18	21 18	22 18	23 32
Disley d	17 20		17 54	18 20		19 22		20 22	21 22	22 22	23 36
New Mills Newtown d	17 24		17 58	18 24		19 25		20 25	21 25	22 25	23 40
Furness Vale d	17 26		18 00	18 26		19 28		20 28	21 28	22 28	23 42
Whaley Bridge d	17 29		18 03	18 29		19 31		20 31	21 31	22 31	23 45
Chapel-en-le-Frith d	17 36		18 10	18 36		19 38		20 38	21 38	22 38	23 52
Dove Holes d			18 15			19 43		20 43	21 43	22 43	23 57
Buxton a	17 52		18 27	18 52		19 55		20 55	21 55	22 55	00 09

b arr. 1721

Table 86

Manchester - Hazel Grove and Buxton

Sundays until 05 September

		NT	NT	NT	NT	NT	NT	NT	NT	NT	NT	NT	NT	NT	NT	NT
Deansgate	d															
Manchester Oxford Road	d															
Manchester Piccadilly 10 84	d	08 55	09 51	10 52	11 52	12 52	13 52	14 52	15 52	16 52	17 52	18 52	19 52	20 52	21 52	22 52
Levenshulme 84	d	09 00	09 58	10 58	11 58	12 58	13 58	14 58	15 58	16 58	17 58	18 58	19 58	20 58	21 58	22 58
Heaton Chapel 84	d	09 03	10 01	11 01	12 01	13 01	14 01	15 01	16 01	17 01	18 01	19 01	20 01	21 01	22 01	23 01
Stockport 84	d	09 10	10 05	11 05	12 05	13 05	14 05	15 05	16 05	17 05	18 05	19 05	20 05	21 05	22 05	23 05
Davenport	d	09 13	10 09	11 09	12 09	13 09	14 09	15 09	16 09	17 09	18 09	19 09	20 09	21 09	22 09	23 09
Woodsmoor	d	09 15	10 11	11 11	12 11	13 11	14 11	15 11	16 11	17 11	18 11	19 11	20 11	21 11	22 11	23 11
Hazel Grove	a	09 17	10 13	11 13	12 13	13 13	14 13	15 13	16 13	17 13	18 13	19 13	20 13	21 13	22 13	23 13
	d	09 18	10 13	11 13	12 13	13 13	14 13	15 13	16 13	17 13	18 13	19 13	20 13	21 13	22 13	23 13
Middlewood	d	09 22	10 18	11 18	12 18	13 18	14 18	15 18	16 18	17 18	18 18	19 18	20 18	21 18	22 18	23 18
Disley	d	09 26	10 22	11 22	12 22	13 22	14 22	15 22	16 22	17 22	18 22	19 22	20 22	21 22	22 22	23 22
New Mills Newtown	d	09 30	10 25	11 25	12 25	13 25	14 25	15 25	16 25	17 25	18 25	19 25	20 25	21 25	22 25	23 25
Furness Vale	d	09 32	10 28	11 28	12 28	13 28	14 28	15 28	16 28	17 28	18 28	19 28	20 28	21 28	22 28	23 28
Whaley Bridge	d	09 35	10 31	11 31	12 31	13 31	14 31	15 31	16 31	17 31	18 31	19 31	20 31	21 31	22 31	23 31
Chapel-en-le-Frith	d	09 42	10 38	11 38	12 38	13 38	14 38	15 38	16 38	17 38	18 38	19 38	20 38	21 38	22 38	23 38
Dove Holes	d	09 47	10 43	11 43	12 43	13 43	14 43	15 43	16 43	17 43	18 43	19 43	20 43	21 43	22 43	23 43
Buxton	a	09 57	10 53	11 53	12 53	13 53	14 53	15 53	16 53	17 53	18 53	19 53	20 53	21 53	22 53	23 53

Sundays from 12 September

		NT	NT	NT	NT	NT	NT	NT	NT	NT	NT	NT	NT	NT	NT	NT
Deansgate	d															
Manchester Oxford Road	d															
Manchester Piccadilly 10 84	d	08 55	09 51	10 52	11 52	12 52	13 52	14 52	15 52	16 52	17 52	18 52	19 52	20 52	21 52	22 52
Levenshulme 84	d	09 00	09 58	10 58	11 58	12 58	13 58	14 58	15 58	16 58	17 58	18 58	19 58	20 58	21 58	22 58
Heaton Chapel 84	d	09 03	10 01	11 01	12 01	13 01	14 01	15 01	16 01	17 01	18 01	19 01	20 01	21 01	22 01	23 01
Stockport 84	d	09 10	10 05	11 05	12 05	13 05	14 05	15 05	16 05	17 05	18 05	19 05	20 05	21 05	22 05	23 05
Davenport	d	09 13	10 09	11 09	12 09	13 09	14 09	15 09	16 09	17 09	18 09	19 09	20 09	21 09	22 09	23 09
Woodsmoor	d	09 15	10 11	11 11	12 11	13 11	14 11	15 11	16 11	17 11	18 11	19 11	20 11	21 11	22 11	23 11
Hazel Grove	a	09 17	10 13	11 13	12 13	13 13	14 13	15 13	16 13	17 13	18 13	19 13	20 13	21 13	22 13	23 13
	d	09 18	10 13	11 13	12 13	13 13	14 13	15 13	16 13	17 13	18 13	19 13	20 13	21 13	22 13	23 13
Middlewood	d	09 22	10 18	11 18	12 18	13 18	14 18	15 18	16 18	17 18	18 18	19 18	20 18	21 18	22 18	23 18
Disley	d	09 26	10 22	11 22	12 22	13 22	14 22	15 22	16 22	17 22	18 22	19 22	20 22	21 22	22 22	23 22
New Mills Newtown	d	09 30	10 25	11 25	12 25	13 25	14 25	15 25	16 25	17 25	18 25	19 25	20 25	21 25	22 25	23 25
Furness Vale	d	09 32	10 28	11 28	12 28	13 28	14 28	15 28	16 28	17 28	18 28	19 28	20 28	21 28	22 28	23 28
Whaley Bridge	d	09 35	10 31	11 31	12 31	13 31	14 31	15 31	16 31	17 31	18 31	19 31	20 31	21 31	22 31	23 31
Chapel-en-le-Frith	d	09 42	10 38	11 38	12 38	13 38	14 38	15 38	16 38	17 38	18 38	19 38	20 38	21 38	22 38	23 38
Dove Holes	d	09 47	10 43	11 43	12 43	13 43	14 43	15 43	16 43	17 43	18 43	19 43	20 43	21 43	22 43	23 43
Buxton	a	09 59	10 55	11 55	12 55	13 55	14 55	15 55	16 55	17 55	18 55	19 55	20 55	21 55	22 55	23 55

Table 86

Buxton and Hazel Grove - Manchester

Mondays to Fridays until 03 September

		NT	NT	NT	NT	NT	NT	NT	EM ◇	NT	NT	NT	NT	NT	NT	NT	NT	NT	NT	NT	NT	NT	NT
Buxton	d	05 59		06 23		06 50		07 24		07 48		08 27		09 27		10 30		11 27		12 30		13 25	
Dove Holes	d			06 29		06 56		07 30				08 33		09 33				11 33				13 31	
Chapel-en-le-Frith	d	06 08		06 34		07 01		07 35		07 57		08 38		09 38		10 39		11 38		12 39		13 36	
Whaley Bridge	d	06 14		06 40		07 07		07 41		08 03		08 44		09 44		10 45		11 44		12 45		13 42	
Furness Vale	d	06 17		06 43		07 10		07 44		08 06		08 47		09 47		10 48		11 47		12 48		13 45	
New Mills Newtown	d	06 20		06 46		07 13		07 47		08 10		08 50		09 50		10 51		11 50		12 51		13 48	
Disley	d	06 24		06 49		07 17		07 51		08 14		08 53		09 53		10 55		11 53		12 55		13 51	
Middlewood	d			06 53		07 21		07 55				08 57		09 57				11 57				13 55	
Hazel Grove	a	06 32		06 59		07 27		08 00	08 16	08 22		09 03		10 03		11 03		12 03		13 03		14 01	
	d	06 33	06 50	07 00	07 22	07 27	07 48	08 01	08 17	08 22	08 32	09 04	09 32	10 04	10 33	11 04	11 33	12 04	12 33	13 04	13 33	14 01	14 33
Woodsmoor	d	06 35	06 52	07 02	07 24	07 30	07 50	08 03			08 34	09 06	09 34	10 06	10 35	11 06	11 35	12 06	12 35	13 06	13 35	14 03	14 35
Davenport	d	06 37	06 54	07 04	07 27	07 32	07 53	08 06			08 37	09 08	09 37	10 08	10 37	11 08	11 37	12 08	12 37	13 08	13 37	14 05	14 37
Stockport 84	a	06 41	06 58	07 08	07 31	07 37	07 57	08 10	08 24		08 41	09 12	09 41	10 12	10 41	11 12	11 41	12 12	12 41	13 12	13 41	14 09	14 41
Heaton Chapel 84	a			07 15		07 41						09 16		10 16		11 16		12 16		13 16		14 16	
Levenshulme 84	a			07 18		07 44						09 19		10 19		11 19		12 19		13 19		14 19	
Manchester Piccadilly 10 84	a	06 52	07 10	07 26	07 45	07 52	08 09	08 25	08 36	08 39	08 52	09 28	09 52	10 28	10 52	11 28	11 52	12 28	12 52	13 28	13 52	14 28	14 52
Manchester Oxford Road	a	06 56		07 29		07 56			08 40		08 56		09 56		10 56		11 56		12 56		13 56		14 56
Deansgate	a	06 59		07 32		07 59					09 00		10 00		11 00		12 00		13 00		14 00		15 00

		NT	NT	NT	NT	NT	NT	NT	NT	NT	NT	NT	NT	NT
Buxton	d	14 30		15 27		16 30	16 59	17 27	17 59	18 27	19 27	20 27	21 27	22 56
Dove Holes	d			15 33				17 33		18 33	19 33	20 33	21 33	23 02
Chapel-en-le-Frith	d	14 39		15 38		16 39	17 08	17 38	18 08	18 38	19 38	20 38	21 38	23 07
Whaley Bridge	d	14 45		15 44		16 45	17 14	17 44	18 14	18 44	19 44	20 44	21 44	23 13
Furness Vale	d	14 48		15 47		16 48	17 17	17 47	18 17	18 47	19 47	20 47	21 47	23 16
New Mills Newtown	d	14 51		15 50		16 51	17 20	17 50	18 20	18 50	19 50	20 50	21 50	23 19
Disley	d	14 55		15 53		16 55	17 24	17 53	18 24	18 53	19 53	20 53	21 53	23 22
Middlewood	d			15 57				17 57		18 57	19 57	20 57	21 57	23 26
Hazel Grove	a	15 03		16 03		17 03	17 32	18 03	18 32	19 03	20 03	21 03	22 03	23 31
	d	15 04	15 33	16 04	16 30	17 04	17 33	18 04	18 33	19 04	20 04	21 04	22 04	23 32
Woodsmoor	d	15 06	15 35	16 06	16 32	17 06	17 35	18 06	18 35	19 06	20 06	21 06	22 06	23 34
Davenport	d	15 08	15 37	16 08	16 35	17 08	17 37	18 08	18 37	19 08	20 08	21 08	22 08	23 36
Stockport 84	a	15 12	15 41	16 12	16 40	17 12	17 41	18 12	18 41	19 12	20 12	21 12	22 12	23 40
Heaton Chapel 84	a	15 16		16 16		17 16		18 16		19 16	20 16	21 16	22 16	
Levenshulme 84	a	15 19		16 19		17 19		18 19		19 19	20 19	21 19	22 19	
Manchester Piccadilly 10 84	a	15 28	15 52	16 25	16 52	17 25	17 52	18 28	18 52	19 28	20 28	21 28	22 28	23 54
Manchester Oxford Road	a		15 56	16 29	16 56	17 29	17 56		18 56					
Deansgate	a		16 00	16 32	17 00	17 32	18 00		19 00					

Mondays to Fridays from 06 September

		NT	NT	NT	NT	NT	NT	NT	EM ◇	NT	NT	NT	NT	NT	NT	NT	NT	NT	NT	NT	NT	NT	NT
Buxton	d	05 54		06 18		06 45		07 19		07 43		08 22		09 22		10 25		11 22		12 25		13 20	
Dove Holes	d			06 24		06 51		07 25				08 28		09 28				11 28				13 26	
Chapel-en-le-Frith	d	06 03		06 29		06 56		07 30		07 52		08 33		09 33		10 34		11 33		12 34		13 31	
Whaley Bridge	d	06 09		06 35		07 02		07 36		07 58		08 39		09 39		10 40		11 39		12 40		13 37	
Furness Vale	d	06 12		06 38		07 05		07 39		08 01		08 42		09 42		10 43		11 42		12 43		13 40	
New Mills Newtown	d	06 15		06 41		07 08		07 42		08 05		08 45		09 45		10 46		11 45		12 46		13 43	
Disley	d	06 19		06 44		07 12		07 46		08 09		08 48		09 48		10 50		11 48		12 50		13 46	
Middlewood	d			06 48		07 16		07 50				08 52		09 52				11 52				13 50	
Hazel Grove	a	06 30		06 57		07 25		07 58	08 16	08 21		09 01		10 01		11 01		12 01		13 01		14 01	
	d	06 31	06 49	06 58	07 20	07 25	07 48	07 59	08 17	08 21	08 30	09 02	09 30	10 02	10 31	11 02	11 31	12 02	12 31	13 02	13 31	14 01	14 31
Woodsmoor	d	06 33	06 51	07 00	07 22	07 28	07 50	08 01			08 32	09 04	09 32	10 04	10 33	11 04	11 33	12 04	12 33	13 04	13 33	14 03	14 33
Davenport	d	06 35	06 53	07 02	07 25	07 30	07 53	08 04			08 35	09 06	09 35	10 06	10 35	11 06	11 35	12 06	12 35	13 06	13 35	14 05	14 35
Stockport 84	a	06 41	06 58	07 08	07 31	07 37	07 57	08 10	08 24		08 41	09 12	09 41	10 12	10 41	11 12	11 41	12 12	12 41	13 12	13 41	14 09	14 41
Heaton Chapel 84	a			07 15		07 41						09 16		10 16		11 16		12 16		13 16		14 16	
Levenshulme 84	a			07 18		07 44						09 19		10 19		11 19		12 19		13 19		14 19	
Manchester Piccadilly 10 84	a	06 52	07 10	07 26	07 45	07 52	08 09	08 25	08 36	08 39	08 52	09 28	09 52	10 28	10 52	11 28	11 52	12 28	12 52	13 28	13 52	14 28	14 52
Manchester Oxford Road	a	06 56		07 29		07 56			08 40		08 56		09 56		10 56		11 56		12 56		13 56		14 56
Deansgate	a	06 59		07 32		07 59					09 00		10 00		11 00		12 00		13 00		14 00		15 00

		NT	NT	NT	NT	NT	NT	NT	NT	NT	NT	NT	NT	NT
Buxton	d	14 25		15 22		16 25	16 56	17 25	17 55	18 22	19 22	20 22	21 22	22 51
Dove Holes	d			15 28				17 31		18 28	19 28	20 28	21 28	22 57
Chapel-en-le-Frith	d	14 34		15 33		16 34	17 05	17 36	18 04	18 33	19 33	20 33	21 33	23 02
Whaley Bridge	d	14 40		15 39		16 40	17 11	17 42	18 10	18 39	19 39	20 39	21 39	23 08
Furness Vale	d	14 43		15 42		16 43	17 14	17 45	18 13	18 42	19 42	20 42	21 42	23 11
New Mills Newtown	d	14 46		15 45		16 46	17 17	17 48	18 16	18 45	19 45	20 45	21 45	23 14
Disley	d	14 50		15 48		16 50	17 21	17 51	18 20	18 48	19 48	20 48	21 48	23 17
Middlewood	d			15 52				17 55		18 52	19 52	20 52	21 52	23 21
Hazel Grove	a	15 01		16 01		17 01	17 32	18 03	18 32	19 01	20 01	21 01	22 01	23 29
	d	15 02	15 31	16 02	16 30	17 02	17 33	18 04	18 33	19 02	20 02	21 02	22 02	23 30
Woodsmoor	d	15 04	15 33	16 04	16 32	17 04	17 35	18 06	18 35	19 04	20 04	21 04	22 04	23 32
Davenport	d	15 06	15 35	16 06	16 35	17 06	17 37	18 08	18 37	19 06	20 06	21 06	22 06	23 34
Stockport 84	a	15 12	15 41	16 12	16 40	17 12	17 41	18 12	18 41	19 12	20 12	21 12	22 12	23 40
Heaton Chapel 84	a	15 16		16 16		17 16		18 16		19 16	20 16	21 16	22 16	
Levenshulme 84	a	15 19		16 19		17 19		18 19		19 19	20 19	21 19	22 19	
Manchester Piccadilly 10 84	a	15 28	15 52	16 25	16 52	17 25	17 52	18 28	18 52	19 28	20 28	21 28	22 28	23 54
Manchester Oxford Road	a		15 56	16 29	16 56	17 29	17 56		18 56					
Deansgate	a		16 00	16 32	17 00	17 32	18 00		19 00					

Table 86

Buxton and Hazel Grove - Manchester

Saturdays
until 04 September

		NT	NT	NT	NT	NT	EM ◇	NT	NT	NT	NT	NT	NT	NT	NT	NT	NT	NT	NT	NT	NT	NT	NT
Buxton	d	05 59	06 27			07 27		07 56	08 27		09 27		10 30		11 27		12 30		13 27		14 30		15 27
Dove Holes	d		06 33			07 33		08 02	08 33		09 33				11 33				13 33				15 33
Chapel-en-le-Frith	d	06 08	06 38			07 38		08 07	08 38		09 38		10 39		11 38		12 39		13 38		14 39		15 38
Whaley Bridge	d	06 14	06 44			07 44		08 13	08 44		09 44		10 45		11 44		12 45		13 44		14 45		15 44
Furness Vale	d	06 17	06 47			07 47		08 16	08 47		09 47		10 48		11 47		12 48		13 47		14 48		15 47
New Mills Newtown	d	06 20	06 50			07 50		08 19	08 50		09 50		10 51		11 50		12 51		13 50		14 51		15 50
Disley	d	06 24	06 53			07 53		08 22	08 53		09 53		10 55		11 53		12 55		13 53		14 55		15 53
Middlewood	d		06 57			07 57		08 26	08 57		09 57				11 57				13 57				15 57
Hazel Grove	a	06 32	07 03			08 03	08 16	08 32	09 03		10 03		11 03		12 03		13 03		14 03		15 03		16 03
	d	06 33	07 03	07 32	07 48	08 03	08 17	08 33	09 04	09 33	10 04	10 33	11 04	11 33	12 04	12 33	13 04	13 33	14 04	14 33	15 04	15 33	16 04
Woodsmoor	d	06 35	07 05	07 34	07 50	08 05		08 35	09 06	09 35	10 06	10 35	11 06	11 35	12 06	12 35	13 06	13 35	14 06	14 35	15 06	15 35	16 06
Davenport	d	06 37	07 07	07 36	07 53	08 07		08 37	09 08	09 37	10 08	10 37	11 08	11 37	12 08	12 37	13 08	13 37	14 08	14 37	15 08	15 37	16 08
Stockport 84	a	06 41	07 12	07 40	07 57	08 12	08 24	08 41	09 12	09 41	10 12	10 41	11 12	11 41	12 12	12 41	13 12	13 41	14 12	14 41	15 12	15 41	16 12
Heaton Chapel 84	a		07 16			08 16			09 16		10 16		11 16		12 16		13 16		14 16		15 16		16 16
Levenshulme 84	a		07 19			08 19			09 19		10 19		11 19		12 19		13 19		14 19		15 19		16 19
Manchester Piccadilly 10 84 ⇌	a	06 52	07 28	07 52	08 09	08 28	08 36	08 52	09 28	09 52	10 28	10 52	11 28	11 52	12 28	12 52	13 28	13 52	14 28	14 52	15 28	15 52	16 28
Manchester Oxford Road	a	06 56		07 56			08 40	08 56		09 56		10 56		11 56		12 56		13 56		14 56		15 56	
Deansgate ⇌	a	06 59		08 00				09 00		10 00		11 00		12 00		13 00		14 00		15 00		16 00	

		NT	NT	NT	NT	NT	NT	NT	NT	NT	NT
Buxton	d		16 30		17 27		18 27	19 27	20 27	21 27	22 56
Dove Holes	d				17 33		18 33	19 33	20 33	21 33	23 02
Chapel-en-le-Frith	d		16 39		17 38		18 38	19 38	20 38	21 38	23 07
Whaley Bridge	d		16 45		17 44		18 44	19 44	20 44	21 44	23 13
Furness Vale	d		16 48		17 47		18 47	19 47	20 47	21 47	23 16
New Mills Newtown	d		16 51		17 50		18 50	19 50	20 50	21 50	23 19
Disley	d		16 55		17 53		18 53	19 53	20 53	21 53	23 22
Middlewood	d				17 57		18 57	19 57	20 57	21 57	23 26
Hazel Grove	a		17 03		18 03		19 03	20 03	21 03	22 03	23 31
	d	16 30	17 04	17 33	18 04	18 33	19 04	20 04	21 04	22 04	23 32
Woodsmoor	d	16 32	17 06	17 35	18 06	18 35	19 06	20 06	21 06	22 06	23 34
Davenport	d	16 34	17 08	17 37	18 08	18 37	19 08	20 08	21 08	22 08	23 36
Stockport 84	a	16 40	17 12	17 41	18 12	18 41	19 12	20 12	21 12	22 12	23 40
Heaton Chapel 84	a		17 16		18 16		19 16	20 16	21 16	22 16	
Levenshulme 84	a		17 19		18 19		19 19	20 19	21 19	22 19	
Manchester Piccadilly 10 84 ⇌	a	16 52	17 28	17 52	18 28	18 52	19 28	20 28	21 28	22 28	23 54
Manchester Oxford Road	a	16 56		17 56		18 56					
Deansgate ⇌	a	17 00		18 00		19 00					

Saturdays
from 11 September

		NT	NT	NT	NT	NT	EM ◇	NT	NT	NT	NT	NT	NT	NT	NT	NT	NT	NT	NT	NT	NT	NT	NT
Buxton	d	05 54	06 22			07 22		07 51	08 22		09 22		10 25		11 22		12 25		13 22		14 25		15 22
Dove Holes	d		06 28			07 28		07 57	08 28		09 28				11 28				13 28				15 28
Chapel-en-le-Frith	d	06 03	06 33			07 33		08 02	08 33		09 33		10 34		11 33		12 34		13 33		14 34		15 33
Whaley Bridge	d	06 09	06 39			07 39		08 08	08 39		09 39		10 40		11 39		12 40		13 39		14 40		15 39
Furness Vale	d	06 12	06 42			07 42		08 11	08 42		09 42		10 43		11 42		12 43		13 42		14 43		15 42
New Mills Newtown	d	06 15	06 45			07 45		08 14	08 45		09 45		10 46		11 45		12 46		13 45		14 46		15 45
Disley	d	06 19	06 48			07 48		08 17	08 48		09 48		10 50		11 48		12 50		13 48		14 50		15 48
Middlewood	d		06 52			07 52		08 21	08 52		09 52				11 52				13 52				15 52
Hazel Grove	a	06 30	07 01			08 01	08 16	08 30	09 01		10 01		11 01		12 01		13 01		14 01		15 01		16 01
	d	06 31	07 01	07 30	07 48	08 01	08 17	08 31	09 02	09 33	10 02	10 31	11 02	11 31	12 02	12 31	13 02	13 31	14 02	14 31	15 02	15 31	16 02
Woodsmoor	d	06 33	07 03	07 32	07 50	08 03		08 33	09 04	09 35	10 04	10 33	11 04	11 33	12 04	12 33	13 04	13 33	14 04	14 33	15 04	15 33	16 04
Davenport	d	06 35	07 05	07 34	07 53	08 05		08 35	09 06	09 37	10 06	10 35	11 06	11 35	12 06	12 35	13 06	13 35	14 06	14 35	15 06	15 35	16 06
Stockport 84	a	06 41	07 12	07 40	07 57	08 12	08 24	08 41	09 12	09 41	10 12	10 41	11 12	11 41	12 12	12 41	13 12	13 41	14 12	14 41	15 12	15 41	16 12
Heaton Chapel 84	a		07 16			08 16			09 16		10 16		11 16		12 16		13 16		14 16		15 16		16 16
Levenshulme 84	a		07 19			08 19			09 19		10 19		11 19		12 19		13 19		14 19		15 19		16 19
Manchester Piccadilly 10 84 ⇌	a	06 52	07 28	07 52	08 09	08 28	08 36	08 52	09 28	09 52	10 28	10 52	11 28	11 52	12 28	12 52	13 28	13 52	14 28	14 52	15 28	15 52	16 28
Manchester Oxford Road	a	06 56		07 56			08 40	08 56		09 56		10 56		11 56		12 56		13 56		14 56		15 56	
Deansgate ⇌	a	06 59		08 00				09 00		10 00		11 00		12 00		13 00		14 00		15 00		16 00	

		NT	NT	NT	NT	NT	NT	NT	NT	NT	NT
Buxton	d		16 25		17 22		18 22	19 22	20 22	21 22	22 51
Dove Holes	d				17 28		18 28	19 28	20 28	21 28	22 57
Chapel-en-le-Frith	d		16 34		17 33		18 33	19 33	20 33	21 33	23 02
Whaley Bridge	d		16 40		17 39		18 39	19 39	20 39	21 39	23 08
Furness Vale	d		16 43		17 42		18 42	19 42	20 42	21 42	23 11
New Mills Newtown	d		16 46		17 45		18 45	19 45	20 45	21 45	23 14
Disley	d		16 50		17 48		18 48	19 48	20 48	21 48	23 17
Middlewood	d				17 52		18 52	19 52	20 52	21 52	23 21
Hazel Grove	a		17 01		18 01		19 01	20 01	21 01	22 01	23 29
	d	16 30	17 02	17 31	18 02	18 31	19 02	20 02	21 02	22 02	23 30
Woodsmoor	d	16 32	17 04	17 33	18 04	18 33	19 04	20 04	21 04	22 04	23 32
Davenport	d	16 34	17 06	17 35	18 06	18 35	19 06	20 06	21 06	22 06	23 34
Stockport 84	a	16 40	17 12	17 41	18 12	18 41	19 12	20 12	21 12	22 12	23 40
Heaton Chapel 84	a		17 16		18 16		19 16	20 16	21 16	22 16	
Levenshulme 84	a		17 19		18 19		19 19	20 19	21 19	22 19	
Manchester Piccadilly 10 84 ⇌	a	16 52	17 28	17 52	18 28	18 52	19 28	20 28	21 28	22 28	23 54
Manchester Oxford Road	a	16 56		17 56		18 56					
Deansgate ⇌	a	17 00		18 00		19 00					

Table 86

Buxton and Hazel Grove - Manchester

Sundays
until 05 September

		NT	NT	NT	NT	NT	NT	NT	NT	NT	NT	NT	NT	NT	NT	NT
Buxton	d	08 23	09 19	10 23	11 27	12 27	13 27	14 27	15 27	16 27	17 27	18 27	19 27	20 27	21 27	22 27
Dove Holes	d	08 29	09 25	10 29	11 33	12 33	13 33	14 33	15 33	16 33	17 33	18 33	19 33	20 33	21 33	22 33
Chapel-en-le-Frith	d	08 34	09 30	10 34	11 38	12 38	13 38	14 38	15 38	16 38	17 38	18 38	19 38	20 38	21 38	22 38
Whaley Bridge	d	08 40	09 36	10 40	11 44	12 44	13 44	14 44	15 44	16 44	17 44	18 44	19 44	20 44	21 44	22 44
Furness Vale	d	08 43	09 39	10 43	11 47	12 47	13 47	14 47	15 47	16 47	17 47	18 47	19 47	20 47	21 47	22 47
New Mills Newtown	d	08 46	09 42	10 46	11 50	12 50	13 50	14 50	15 50	16 50	17 50	18 50	19 50	20 50	21 50	22 50
Disley	d	08 49	09 45	10 49	11 53	12 53	13 53	14 53	15 53	16 53	17 53	18 53	19 53	20 53	21 53	22 53
Middlewood	d	08 53	09 49	10 53	11 57	12 57	13 57	14 57	15 57	16 57	17 57	18 57	19 57	20 57	21 57	22 57
Hazel Grove	a	08 59	09 55	10 58	12 03	13 03	14 03	15 03	16 03	17 03	18 03	19 03	20 03	21 03	22 03	23 03
	d	09 00	09 55	10 59	12 04	13 04	14 04	15 04	16 04	17 04	18 04	19 04	20 04	21 04	22 04	23 04
Woodsmoor	d	09 02	09 57	11 01	12 06	13 06	14 06	15 06	16 06	17 06	18 06	19 06	20 06	21 06	22 06	23 06
Davenport	d	09 04	09 59	11 03	12 08	13 08	14 08	15 08	16 08	17 08	18 08	19 08	20 08	21 08	22 08	23 08
Stockport 84	a	09 08	10 04	11 07	12 12	13 12	14 12	15 12	16 12	17 12	18 12	19 12	20 12	21 12	22 12	23 12
Heaton Chapel 84	a	09 12	10 08	11 11	12 16	13 16	14 16	15 16	16 16	17 16	18 16	19 16	20 16	21 16	22 16	23 16
Levenshulme 84	a	09 15	10 11	11 14	12 19	13 19	14 19	15 19	16 19	17 19	18 19	19 19	20 19	21 19	22 19	23 19
Manchester Piccadilly 10 84 ⇌	a	09 23	10 20	11 23	12 29	13 27	14 27	15 27	16 27	17 27	18 27	19 27	20 27	21 27	22 27	23 27
Manchester Oxford Road	a															
Deansgate ⇌	a															

Sundays
from 12 September

		NT	NT	NT	NT	NT	NT	NT	NT	NT	NT	NT	NT	NT	NT	NT
Buxton	d	08 21	09 18	10 22	11 22	12 22	13 22	14 22	15 22	16 22	17 22	18 22	19 22	20 22	21 22	22 22
Dove Holes	d	08 27	09 24	10 28	11 28	12 28	13 28	14 28	15 28	16 28	17 28	18 28	19 28	20 28	21 28	22 28
Chapel-en-le-Frith	d	08 32	09 29	10 33	11 33	12 33	13 33	14 33	15 33	16 33	17 33	18 33	19 33	20 33	21 33	22 33
Whaley Bridge	d	08 38	09 35	10 39	11 39	12 39	13 39	14 39	15 39	16 39	17 39	18 39	19 39	20 39	21 39	22 39
Furness Vale	d	08 41	09 38	10 42	11 42	12 42	13 42	14 42	15 42	16 42	17 42	18 42	19 42	20 42	21 42	22 42
New Mills Newtown	d	08 44	09 41	10 45	11 45	12 45	13 45	14 45	15 45	16 45	17 45	18 45	19 45	20 45	21 45	22 45
Disley	d	08 47	09 44	10 48	11 48	12 48	13 48	14 48	15 48	16 48	17 48	18 48	19 48	20 48	21 48	22 48
Middlewood	d	08 51	09 48	10 52	11 52	12 52	13 52	14 52	15 52	16 52	17 52	18 52	19 52	20 52	21 52	22 52
Hazel Grove	a	08 57	09 57	11 00	12 01	13 01	14 01	15 01	16 01	17 01	18 01	19 01	20 01	21 01	22 01	23 01
	d	08 58	09 57	11 01	12 02	13 02	14 02	15 02	16 02	17 02	18 02	19 02	20 02	21 02	22 02	23 02
Woodsmoor	d	09 00	09 59	11 03	12 04	13 04	14 04	15 04	16 04	17 04	18 04	19 04	20 04	21 04	22 04	23 04
Davenport	d	09 02	10 01	11 05	12 06	13 06	14 06	15 06	16 06	17 06	18 06	19 06	20 06	21 06	22 06	23 06
Stockport 84	a	09 08	10 08	11 11	12 10	13 12	14 12	15 12	16 12	17 12	18 12	19 12	20 12	21 12	22 12	23 12
Heaton Chapel 84	a	09 12	10 12		12 15	13 16	14 16	15 16	16 16	17 16	18 16	19 16	20 16	21 16	22 16	23 16
Levenshulme 84	a	09 15	10 15		12 18	13 19	14 19	15 19	16 19	17 19	18 19	19 19	20 19	21 19	22 19	23 19
Manchester Piccadilly 10 84 ⇌	a	09 23	10 23	11 23	12 25	13 27	14 27	15 27	16 27	17 27	18 27	19 27	20 27	21 27	22 27	23 27
Manchester Oxford Road	a															
Deansgate ⇌	a															

Network Diagram for Tables 88, 89, 90, 91

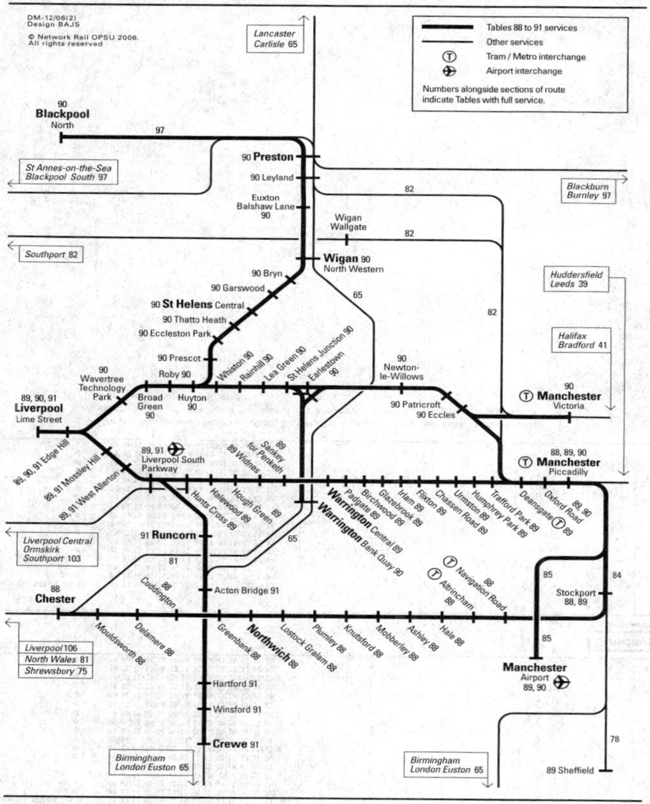

Table 88

Manchester - Northwich and Chester

Mondays to Fridays
until 03 September

		NT	NT	NT	NT	NT	NT	NT	NT	NT	NT	NT	NT	NT	NT	NT	NT	NT	NT	NT	NT
Manchester Piccadilly	84 d	06 17	07 17	08 17	09 17	10 17	11 17	12 17	13 17	14 17	15 17	16 17		17 09		18 17	19 17	20 17	21 17	22 17	23 17
Stockport	84 d	06 30	07 30	08 30	09 30	10 30	11 30	12 30	13 30	14 30	15 30	16 30	16 58	17 19	17 58	18 30	19 30	20 30	21 30	22 30	23 27
Navigation Road	d	06 44	07 44	08 44	09 44	10 44	11 44	12 44	13 44	14 44	15 44	16 44	17 12	17 33	18 12	18 44	19 44	20 44	21 44	22 44	23 41
Altrincham	a	06 46	07 46	08 46	09 46	10 46	11 46	12 46	13 46	14 46	15 46	16 46	17 14	17 35	18 14	18 46	19 46	20 46	21 46	22 46	23 43
	d	06 46	07 46	08 46	09 46	10 46	11 46	12 46	13 46	14 46	15 46	16 46	17 14	17 35	18 14	18 46	19 46	20 46	21 46	22 46	23 43
Hale	d	06 49	07 49	08 49	09 49	10 49	11 49	12 49	13 49	14 49	15 49	16 49	17 17	17 38	18 17	18 49	19 49	20 49	21 49	22 49	23 46
Ashley	d	06x52	07x52	08x52	09x52	10x52	11x52	12x52	13x52	14x52	15x52	16x52	17x20	17x41	18x20	18x52	19x52	20x52	21x52	22x52	23x49
Mobberley	d	06x55	07x55	08x55	09x55	10x55	11x55	12x55	13x55	14x55	15x55	16x55	17x23	17x44	18x23	18x55	19x55	20x55	21x55	22x55	23x52
Knutsford	d	06 59	07 59	08 59	09 59	10 59	11 59	12 59	13 59	14 59	15 59	16 59	17 27	17 49	18 27	18 59	19 59	20 59	21 59	22 59	23 57
Plumley	d	07 03	08 03	09 03	10 03	11 03	12 03	13 03	14 03	15 03	16 03	17 03	17 31	17 53	18 31	19 03	20 03	21 03	22 03	23 03	00 01
Lostock Gralam	d	07 07	08 07	09 07	10 07	11 07	12 07	13 07	14 07	15 07	16 07	17 07	17 35	17 56	18 35	19 07	20 07	21 07	22 07	23 07	00 04
Northwich	d	07 12	08 12	09 12	10 12	11 12	12 12	13 12	14 12	15 12	16 12	17 12	17 40	18 02	18 40	19 12	20 12	21 12	22 12	23 12	00 10
Greenbank	d	07 17	08 17	09 17	10 17	11 17	12 17	13 17	14 17	15 17	16 17	17 17	17 45	18 06	18 45	19 17	20 17	21 17	22 17	23 17	00 14
Cuddington	d	07 22	08 22	09 22	10 22	11 22	12 22	13 22	14 22	15 22	16 22	17 22	17 50	18 11	18 50	19 22	20 22	21 22	22 22	23 22	00 19
Delamere	d	07x26	08x26	09x26	10x26	11x26	12x26	13x26	14x26	15x26	16x26	17x26	17x54	18x16	18x54	19x26	20x26	21x26	22x26	23x26	00x24
Mouldsworth	d	07 31	08 31	09 31	10 31	11 31	12 31	13 31	14 31	15 31	16 31	17 31	17 59	18 21	18 59	19 31	20 31	21 31	22 31	23 31	00 28
Chester	81 a	07 45	08 45	09 45	10 45	11 45	12 45	13 45	14 45	15 45	16 45	17 45	18 13	18 35	19 13	19 45	20 45	21 45	22 45	23 45	00 43

Mondays to Fridays
from 06 September

		NT	NT	NT	NT	NT	NT	NT	NT	NT	NT	NT	NT	NT	NT	NT	NT	NT	NT	NT	NT
Manchester Piccadilly	84 d	06 17	07 17	08 17	09 17	10 17	11 17	12 17	13 17	14 17	15 17	16 17		17 09		18 17	19 17	20 17	21 17	22 17	23 17
Stockport	84 d	06 30	07 30	08 30	09 30	10 30	11 30	12 30	13 30	14 30	15 30	16 30	16 58	17 19	17 58	18 30	19 30	20 30	21 30	22 30	23 27
Navigation Road	d	06 44	07 44	08 44	09 44	10 44	11 44	12 44	13 44	14 44	15 44	16 44	17 12	17 33	18 12	18 44	19 44	20 44	21 44	22 44	23 41
Altrincham	a	06 46	07 46	08 46	09 46	10 46	11 46	12 46	13 46	14 46	15 46	16 46	17 14	17 35	18 14	18 46	19 46	20 46	21 46	22 46	23 43
	d	06 46	07 46	08 46	09 46	10 46	11 46	12 46	13 46	14 46	15 46	16 46	17 14	17 35	18 14	18 46	19 46	20 46	21 46	22 46	23 43
Hale	d	06 49	07 49	08 49	09 49	10 49	11 49	12 49	13 49	14 49	15 49	16 49	17 17	17 38	18 17	18 49	19 49	20 49	21 49	22 49	23 46
Ashley	d	06x52	07x52	08x52	09x52	10x52	11x52	12x52	13x52	14x52	15x52	16x52	17x20	17x41	18x20	18x52	19x52	20x52	21x52	22x52	23x49
Mobberley	d	06x55	07x55	08x55	09x55	10x55	11x55	12x55	13x55	14x55	15x55	16x55	17x23	17x44	18x23	18x55	19x55	20x55	21x55	22x55	23x52
Knutsford	d	06 59	07 59	08 59	09 59	10 59	11 59	12 59	13 59	14 59	15 59	16 59	17 27	17 49	18 27	18 59	19 59	20 59	21 59	22 59	23 57
Plumley	d	07 03	08 03	09 03	10 03	11 03	12 03	13 03	14 03	15 03	16 03	17 03	17 31	17 53	18 31	19 03	20 03	21 03	22 03	23 03	00 01
Lostock Gralam	d	07 07	08 07	09 07	10 07	11 07	12 07	13 07	14 07	15 07	16 07	17 07	17 35	17 56	18 35	19 07	20 07	21 07	22 07	23 07	00 04
Northwich	d	07 12	08 12	09 12	10 12	11 12	12 12	13 12	14 12	15 12	16 12	17 12	17 40	18 02	18 40	19 12	20 12	21 12	22 12	23 12	00 10
Greenbank	d	07 17	08 17	09 17	10 17	11 17	12 17	13 17	14 17	15 17	16 17	17 17	17 45	18 06	18 45	19 17	20 17	21 17	22 17	23 17	00 14
Cuddington	d	07 22	08 22	09 22	10 22	11 22	12 22	13 22	14 22	15 22	16 22	17 22	17 50	18 11	18 50	19 22	20 22	21 22	22 22	23 22	00 19
Delamere	d	07x26	08x26	09x26	10x26	11x26	12x26	13x26	14x26	15x26	16x26	17x26	17x54	18x16	18x54	19x26	20x26	21x26	22x26	23x26	00x24
Mouldsworth	d	07 31	08 31	09 31	10 31	11 31	12 31	13 31	14 31	15 31	16 31	17 31	17 59	18 21	18 59	19 31	20 31	21 31	22 31	23 31	00 28
Chester	81 a	07 47	08 47	09 47	10 47	11 47	12 47	13 47	14 47	15 47	16 47	17 47	18 15	18 37	19 15	19 47	20 47	21 47	22 47	23 47	00 45

Saturdays
until 04 September

		NT	NT	NT	NT	NT	NT	NT	NT	NT	NT	NT	NT	NT	NT	NT	NT	NT	NT
Manchester Piccadilly	84 d	06 17	07 17	08 17	09 17	10 17	11 17	12 17	13 17	14 17	15 17	16 17	17 17	18 17	19 17	20 17	21 17	22 17	23 17
Stockport	84 d	06 30	07 30	08 30	09 30	10 30	11 30	12 30	13 30	14 30	15 30	16 30	17 30	18 30	19 30	20 30	21 30	22 30	23 27
Navigation Road	d	06 44	07 44	08 44	09 44	10 44	11 44	12 44	13 44	14 44	15 44	16 44	17 44	18 44	19 44	20 44	21 44	22 44	23 41
Altrincham	a	06 46	07 46	08 46	09 46	10 46	11 46	12 46	13 46	14 46	15 46	16 46	17 46	18 46	19 46	20 46	21 46	22 46	23 43
	d	06 46	07 46	08 46	09 46	10 46	11 46	12 46	13 46	14 46	15 46	16 46	17 46	18 46	19 46	20 46	21 46	22 46	23 43
Hale	d	06 49	07 49	08 49	09 49	10 49	11 49	12 49	13 49	14 49	15 49	16 49	17 49	18 49	19 49	20 49	21 49	22 49	23 46
Ashley	d	06x52	07x52	08x52	09x52	10x52	11x52	12x52	13x52	14x52	15x52	16x52	17x52	18x52	19x52	20x52	21x52	22x52	23x49
Mobberley	d	06x55	07x55	08x55	09x55	10x55	11x55	12x55	13x55	14x55	15x55	16x55	17x55	18x55	19x55	20x55	21x55	22x55	23x52
Knutsford	d	06 59	07 59	08 59	09 59	10 59	11 59	12 59	13 59	14 59	15 59	16 59	17 59	18 59	19 59	20 59	21 59	22 59	23 57
Plumley	d	07 03	08 03	09 03	10 03	11 03	12 03	13 03	14 03	15 03	16 03	17 03	18 03	19 03	20 03	21 03	22 03	23 03	00 01
Lostock Gralam	d	07 07	08 07	09 07	10 07	11 07	12 07	13 07	14 07	15 07	16 07	17 07	18 07	19 07	20 07	21 07	22 07	23 07	00 04
Northwich	d	07 12	08 12	09 12	10 12	11 12	12 12	13 12	14 12	15 12	16 12	17 12	18 12	19 12	20 12	21 12	22 12	23 12	00 10
Greenbank	d	07 17	08 17	09 17	10 17	11 17	12 17	13 17	14 17	15 17	16 17	17 17	18 17	19 17	20 17	21 17	22 17	23 17	00 14
Cuddington	d	07 22	08 22	09 22	10 22	11 22	12 22	13 22	14 22	15 22	16 22	17 22	18 22	19 22	20 22	21 22	22 22	23 22	00 19
Delamere	d	07x26	08x26	09x26	10x26	11x26	12x26	13x26	14x26	15x26	16x26	17x26	18x26	19x26	20x26	21x26	22x26	23x26	00x24
Mouldsworth	d	07 31	08 31	09 31	10 31	11 31	12 31	13 31	14 31	15 31	16 31	17 31	18 31	19 31	20 31	21 31	22 31	23 31	00 28
Chester	81 a	07 45	08 45	09 45	10 45	11 45	12 45	13 45	14 45	15 45	16 45	17 45	18 45	19 45	20 45	21 45	22 45	23 45	00 43

Saturdays
from 11 September

		NT	NT	NT	NT	NT	NT	NT	NT	NT	NT	NT	NT	NT	NT	NT	NT	NT	NT
Manchester Piccadilly	84 d	06 17	07 17	08 17	09 17	10 17	11 17	12 17	13 17	14 17	15 17	16 17	17 17	18 17	19 17	20 17	21 17	22 17	23 17
Stockport	84 d	06 30	07 30	08 30	09 30	10 30	11 30	12 30	13 30	14 30	15 30	16 30	17 30	18 30	19 30	20 30	21 30	22 30	23 27
Navigation Road	d	06 44	07 44	08 44	09 44	10 44	11 44	12 44	13 44	14 44	15 44	16 44	17 44	18 44	19 44	20 44	21 44	22 44	23 41
Altrincham	a	06 46	07 46	08 46	09 46	10 46	11 46	12 46	13 46	14 46	15 46	16 46	17 46	18 46	19 46	20 46	21 46	22 46	23 43
	d	06 46	07 46	08 46	09 46	10 46	11 46	12 46	13 46	14 46	15 46	16 46	17 46	18 46	19 46	20 46	21 46	22 46	23 43
Hale	d	06 49	07 49	08 49	09 49	10 49	11 49	12 49	13 49	14 49	15 49	16 49	17 49	18 49	19 49	20 49	21 49	22 49	23 46
Ashley	d	06x52	07x52	08x52	09x52	10x52	11x52	12x52	13x52	14x52	15x52	16x52	17x52	18x52	19x52	20x52	21x52	22x52	23x49
Mobberley	d	06x55	07x55	08x55	09x55	10x55	11x55	12x55	13x55	14x55	15x55	16x55	17x55	18x55	19x55	20x55	21x55	22x55	23x52
Knutsford	d	06 59	07 59	08 59	09 59	10 59	11 59	12 59	13 59	14 59	15 59	16 59	17 59	18 59	19 59	20 59	21 59	22 59	23 57
Plumley	d	07 03	08 03	09 03	10 03	11 03	12 03	13 03	14 03	15 03	16 03	17 03	18 03	19 03	20 03	21 03	22 03	23 03	00 01
Lostock Gralam	d	07 07	08 07	09 07	10 07	11 07	12 07	13 07	14 07	15 07	16 07	17 07	18 07	19 07	20 07	21 07	22 07	23 07	00 04
Northwich	d	07 12	08 12	09 12	10 12	11 12	12 12	13 12	14 12	15 12	16 12	17 12	18 12	19 12	20 12	21 12	22 12	23 12	00 10
Greenbank	d	07 17	08 17	09 17	10 17	11 17	12 17	13 17	14 17	15 17	16 17	17 17	18 17	19 17	20 17	21 17	22 17	23 17	00 14
Cuddington	d	07 22	08 22	09 22	10 22	11 22	12 22	13 22	14 22	15 22	16 22	17 22	18 22	19 22	20 22	21 22	22 22	23 22	00 19
Delamere	d	07x26	08x26	09x26	10x26	11x26	12x26	13x26	14x26	15x26	16x26	17x26	18x26	19x26	20x26	21x26	22x26	23x26	00x24
Mouldsworth	d	07 31	08 31	09 31	10 31	11 31	12 31	13 31	14 31	15 31	16 31	17 31	18 31	19 31	20 31	21 31	22 31	23 31	00 28
Chester	81 a	07 47	08 47	09 47	10 47	11 47	12 47	13 47	14 47	15 47	16 47	17 47	18 47	19 47	20 47	21 47	22 47	23 47	00 45

Table 88

Manchester - Northwich and Chester

Sundays
until 05 September

		NT	NT	NT	NT	NT	NT	NT
Manchester Piccadilly [10] 84 ⇌	d	09 22	11 22	13 22	15 22	17 22	19 22	21 22
Stockport 84	d	09 31	11 31	13 31	15 31	17 31	19 31	21 31
Navigation Road ⇌	d	09 45	11 45	13 45	15 45	17 45	19 45	21 45
Altrincham ⇌	a	09 47	11 47	13 47	15 47	17 47	19 47	21 47
	d	09 47	11 47	13 47	15 47	17 47	19 47	21 47
Hale	d	09 50	11 50	13 50	15 50	17 50	19 50	21 50
Ashley	d	09x53	11x53	13x53	15x53	17x53	19x53	21x53
Mobberley	d	09x56	11x56	13x56	15x56	17x56	19x56	21x56
Knutsford	d	10 00	12 00	14 00	16 00	18 00	20 00	22 00
Plumley	d	10 05	12 04	14 04	16 04	18 04	20 04	22 04
Lostock Gralam	d	10 08	12 08	14 08	16 08	18 08	20 08	22 08
Northwich	d	10 13	12 13	14 13	16 13	18 13	20 13	22 13
Greenbank	d	10 18	12 18	14 18	16 18	18 18	20 18	22 18
Cuddington	d	10 23	12 23	14 23	16 23	18 23	20 23	22 23
Delamere	d	10x27	12x27	14x27	16x27	18x27	20x27	22x27
Mouldsworth	d	10 32	12 32	14 32	16 32	18 32	20 32	22 32
Chester 81	a	10 46	12 46	14 46	16 46	18 46	20 46	22 46

Sundays
from 12 September

		NT	NT	NT	NT	NT	NT	NT
Manchester Piccadilly [10] 84 ⇌	d	09 22	11 22	13 22	15 22	17 22	19 22	21 22
Stockport 84	d	09 31	11 31	13 31	15 31	17 31	19 31	21 31
Navigation Road ⇌	d	09 45	11 45	13 45	15 45	17 45	19 45	21 45
Altrincham ⇌	a	09 47	11 47	13 47	15 47	17 47	19 47	21 47
	d	09 47	11 47	13 47	15 47	17 47	19 47	21 47
Hale	d	09 50	11 50	13 50	15 50	17 50	19 50	21 50
Ashley	d	09x53	11x53	13x53	15x53	17x53	19x53	21x53
Mobberley	d	09x56	11x56	13x56	15x56	17x56	19x56	21x56
Knutsford	d	10 00	12 00	14 00	16 00	18 00	20 00	22 00
Plumley	d	10 05	12 04	14 04	16 04	18 04	20 04	22 04
Lostock Gralam	d	10 08	12 08	14 08	16 08	18 08	20 08	22 08
Northwich	d	10 13	12 13	14 13	16 13	18 13	20 13	22 13
Greenbank	d	10 18	12 18	14 18	16 18	18 18	20 18	22 18
Cuddington	d	10 23	12 23	14 23	16 23	18 23	20 23	22 23
Delamere	d	10x27	12x27	14x27	16x27	18x27	20x27	22x27
Mouldsworth	d	10 32	12 32	14 32	16 32	18 32	20 32	22 32
Chester 81	a	10 46	12 46	14 46	16 46	18 46	20 46	22 46

On Sundays only, National Rail Tickets to stations between Hale and Mouldsworth inclusive are valid for travel on Metrolink services between Manchester City Centre and Altrincham

Table 88

Chester and Northwich - Manchester

Mondays to Fridays
until 03 September

		NT	NT	NT	NT	NT	NT	NT	NT
Chester 81	d	06 05	06 35	07 03	07 35	08 07	09 07	10 07	11 07
Mouldsworth	d	06 16	06 46	07 14	07 46	08 18	09 18	10 18	11 18
Delamere	d	06x21	06x51	07x19	07x51	08x23	09x23	10x23	11x23
Cuddington	d	06 25	06 55	07 23	07 55	08 27	09 27	10 27	11 27
Greenbank	d	06 30	07 00	07 28	08 00	08 32	09 32	10 32	11 32
Northwich	d	06 35	07 05	07 33	08 05	08 37	09 37	10 37	11 37
Lostock Gralam	d	06 38	07 08	07 36	08 08	08 40	09 40	10 40	11 40
Plumley	d	06 41	07 11	07 40	08 11	08 43	09 43	10 43	11 43
Knutsford	d	06 46	07 17	07 45	08 17	08 49	09 49	10 49	11 49
Mobberley	d	06x50	07x21	07x49	08x21	08x53	09x53	10x53	11x53
Ashley	d	06x54	07x24	07x53	08x24	08x56	09x56	10x56	11x56
Hale	d	06 57	07 28	07 57	08 28	08 59	09 59	10 59	11 59
Altrincham ⇌	a	07 01	07 32	08 01	08 32	09 04	10 04	11 04	12 04
	d	07 02	07 33	08 02	08 33	09 04	10 04	11 04	12 04
Navigation Road ⇌	d	07 04	07 35	08 04	08 35	09 06	10 06	11 06	12 06
Stockport 84	a	07 18	07 56	08 19	08 56	09 21	10 21	11 21	12 21
Manchester Piccadilly [10] 84 ⇌	a	07 31		08 32		09 36	10 36	11 36	12 36

		NT	NT	NT	NT	NT	NT	NT	NT	NT	NT	NT
Chester 81	d	12 07	13 07	14 07	15 07	16 07	17 07	18 07	19 07	20 07	21 07	22 48
Mouldsworth	d	12 18	13 18	14 18	15 18	16 18	17 18	18 18	19 18	20 18	21 18	22 59
Delamere	d	12x23	13x23	14x23	15x23	16x23	17x23	18x23	19x23	20x23	21x23	23x04
Cuddington	d	12 27	13 27	14 27	15 27	16 27	17 27	18 27	19 27	20 27	21 27	23 08
Greenbank	d	12 32	13 32	14 32	15 32	16 32	17 32	18 32	19 32	20 32	21 32	23 13
Northwich	d	12 37	13 37	14 37	15 37	16 37	17 37	18 37	19 37	20 37	21 37	23 17
Lostock Gralam	d	12 40	13 40	14 40	15 40	16 40	17 40	18 40	19 40	20 40	21 40	23 20
Plumley	d	12 43	13 43	14 43	15 43	16 43	17 43	18 43	19 43	20 43	21 43	23 24
Knutsford	d	12 49	13 49	14 49	15 49	16 49	17 49	18 49	19 49	20 49	21 49	23 29
Mobberley	d	12x53	13x53	14x53	15x53	16x53	17x53	18x53	19x53	20x53	21x53	23x33
Ashley	d	12x56	13x56	14x56	15x56	16x56	17x56	18x56	19x56	20x56	21x56	23x36
Hale	d	12 59	13 59	14 59	15 59	16 59	17 59	18 59	19 59	20 59	21 59	23 39
Altrincham ⇌	a	13 04	14 04	15 04	16 04	17 04	18 04	19 04	20 04	21 04	22 04	23 44
	d	13 04	14 04	15 04	16 04	17 04	18 04	19 04	20 04	21 04	22 04	23 44
Navigation Road ⇌	d	13 06	14 06	15 06	16 06	17 06	18 06	19 06	20 06	21 06	22 06	23 46
Stockport 84	a	13 21	14 21	15 21	16 21	17 21	18 21	19 21	20 21	21 21	22 21	00 02
Manchester Piccadilly [10] 84 ⇌	a	13 36	14 36	15 36	16 36	17 36	18 36	19 35	20 35	21 35	22 35	00 18

Mondays to Fridays
from 06 September

		NT	NT	NT	NT	NT	NT	NT	NT	NT
Chester 81	d	06 01	06 35	06 59	07 35	08 03	09 03	10 03	11 03	12 03
Mouldsworth	d	06 12	06 46	07 10	07 46	08 14	09 14	10 14	11 14	12 14
Delamere	d	06x17	06x51	07x15	07x51	08x19	09x19	10x19	11x19	12x19
Cuddington	d	06 21	06 55	07 19	07 55	08 23	09 23	10 23	11 23	12 23
Greenbank	d	06 26	07 00	07 24	08 00	08 28	09 28	10 28	11 28	12 28
Northwich	d	06 31	07 05	07 29	08 05	08 33	09 33	10 33	11 33	12 33
Lostock Gralam	d	06 34	07 08	07 32	08 08	08 36	09 36	10 36	11 36	12 36
Plumley	d	06 37	07 11	07 36	08 11	08 39	09 39	10 39	11 39	12 39
Knutsford	d	06 42	07 17	07 41	08 17	08 45	09 45	10 45	11 45	12 45
Mobberley	d	06x46	07x21	07x45	08x21	08x49	09x49	10x49	11x49	12x49
Ashley	d	06x50	07x24	07x49	08x24	08x52	09x52	10x52	11x52	12x52
Hale	d	06 53	07 28	07 53	08 28	08 55	09 55	10 55	11 55	12 55
Altrincham ⇌	a	06 57	07 32	07 57	08 32	09 00	10 00	11 00	12 00	13 00
	d	06 58	07 33	07 58	08 33	09 00	10 00	11 00	12 00	13 00
Navigation Road ⇌	d	07 00	07 35	08 00	08 35	09 02	10 02	11 02	12 02	13 02
Stockport 84	a	07 18	07 56	08 19	08 56	09 21	10 21	11 21	12 21	13 21
Manchester Piccadilly [10] 84 ⇌	a	07 31		08 32		09 36	10 36	11 36	12 36	13 36

		NT	NT	NT	NT	NT	NT	NT	NT	NT	NT
Chester 81	d	13 03	14 03	15 03	16 03	17 03	18 03	19 03	20 03	21 03	22 44
Mouldsworth	d	13 14	14 14	15 14	16 14	17 14	18 14	19 14	20 14	21 14	22 55
Delamere	d	13x19	14x19	15x19	16x19	17x19	18x19	19x19	20x19	21x19	23x00
Cuddington	d	13 23	14 23	15 23	16 23	17 23	18 23	19 23	20 23	21 23	23 04
Greenbank	d	13 28	14 28	15 28	16 28	17 28	18 28	19 28	20 28	21 28	23 09
Northwich	d	13 33	14 33	15 33	16 33	17 33	18 33	19 33	20 33	21 33	23 13
Lostock Gralam	d	13 36	14 36	15 36	16 36	17 36	18 36	19 36	20 36	21 36	23 16
Plumley	d	13 39	14 39	15 39	16 39	17 39	18 39	19 39	20 39	21 39	23 20
Knutsford	d	13 45	14 45	15 45	16 45	17 45	18 45	19 45	20 45	21 45	23 25
Mobberley	d	13x49	14x49	15x49	16x49	17x49	18x49	19x49	20x49	21x49	23x29
Ashley	d	13x52	14x52	15x52	16x52	17x52	18x52	19x52	20x52	21x52	23x32
Hale	d	13 55	14 55	15 55	16 55	17 55	18 55	19 55	20 55	21 55	23 35
Altrincham ⇌	a	14 00	15 00	16 00	17 00	18 00	19 00	20 00	21 00	22 00	23 40
	d	14 00	15 00	16 00	17 00	18 00	19 00	20 00	21 00	22 00	23 40
Navigation Road ⇌	d	14 02	15 02	16 02	17 02	18 02	19 02	20 02	21 02	22 02	23 42
Stockport 84	a	14 21	15 21	16 21	17 21	18 21	19 21	20 21	21 21	22 21	00 02
Manchester Piccadilly [10] 84 ⇌	a	14 36	15 36	16 36	17 36	18 36	19 35	20 35	21 35	22 35	00 18

Saturdays
until 04 September

		NT	NT	NT	NT	NT	NT	NT	NT	NT
Chester 81	d	06 05	07 03	08 07	09 07	10 07	11 07	12 07	13 07	14 07
Mouldsworth	d	06 16	07 14	08 18	09 18	10 18	11 18	12 18	13 18	14 18
Delamere	d	06x21	07x19	08x23	09x23	10x23	11x23	12x23	13x23	14x23
Cuddington	d	06 25	07 23	08 27	09 27	10 27	11 27	12 27	13 27	14 27
Greenbank	d	06 30	07 28	08 32	09 32	10 32	11 32	12 32	13 32	14 32
Northwich	d	06 35	07 33	08 37	09 37	10 37	11 37	12 37	13 37	14 37
Lostock Gralam	d	06 38	07 36	08 40	09 40	10 40	11 40	12 40	13 40	14 40
Plumley	d	06 41	07 40	08 43	09 43	10 43	11 43	12 43	13 43	14 43
Knutsford	d	06 46	07 45	08 49	09 49	10 49	11 49	12 49	13 49	14 49
Mobberley	d	06x50	07x49	08x53	09x53	10x53	11x53	12x53	13x53	14x53
Ashley	d	06x54	07x53	08x56	09x56	10x56	11x56	12x56	13x56	14x56
Hale	d	06 57	07 57	08 59	09 59	10 59	11 59	12 59	13 59	14 59
Altrincham ⇌	a	07 01	08 01	09 04	10 04	11 04	12 04	13 04	14 04	15 04
	d	07 02	08 02	09 04	10 04	11 04	12 04	13 04	14 04	15 04
Navigation Road ⇌	d	07 04	08 04	09 06	10 06	11 06	12 06	13 06	14 06	15 06
Stockport 84	a	07 18	08 19	09 21	10 21	11 21	12 21	13 21	14 21	15 21
Manchester Piccadilly [10] 84 ⇌	a	07 31	08 32	09 36	10 36	11 36	12 36	13 36	14 36	15 36

		NT	NT	NT	NT	NT	NT	NT	NT
Chester 81	d	15 07	16 07	17 07	18 07	19 07	20 07	21 33	22 49
Mouldsworth	d	15 18	16 18	17 18	18 18	19 18	20 18	21 45	23 00
Delamere	d	15x23	16x23	17x23	18x23	19x23	20x23	21x49	23x05
Cuddington	d	15 27	16 27	17 27	18 27	19 27	20 27	21 54	23 09
Greenbank	d	15 32	16 32	17 32	18 32	19 32	20 32	21 58	23 14
Northwich	d	15 37	16 37	17 37	18 37	19 37	20 37	22 03	23 18
Lostock Gralam	d	15 40	16 40	17 40	18 40	19 40	20 40	22 06	23 21
Plumley	d	15 43	16 43	17 43	18 43	19 43	20 43	22 10	23 25
Knutsford	d	15 49	16 49	17 49	18 49	19 49	20 49	22 15	23 30
Mobberley	d	15x53	16x53	17x53	18x53	19x53	20x53	22x19	23x34
Ashley	d	15x56	16x56	17x56	18x56	19x56	20x56	22x23	23x37
Hale	d	15 59	16 59	17 59	18 59	19 59	20 59	22 26	23 40
Altrincham ⇌	a	16 04	17 04	18 04	19 04	20 04	21 04	22 30	23 45
	d	16 04	17 04	18 04	19 04	20 04	21 04	22 31	23 45
Navigation Road ⇌	d	16 06	17 06	18 06	19 06	20 06	21 06	22 33	23 47
Stockport 84	a	16 21	17 21	18 21	19 21	20 21	21 21	22 47	00 02
Manchester Piccadilly [10] 84 ⇌	a	16 36	17 36	18 36	19 35	20 35	21 35	23 00	00 15

Saturdays
from 11 September

		NT	NT	NT	NT	NT	NT	NT	NT	NT
Chester 81	d	06 01	06 59	08 03	09 03	10 03	11 03	12 03	13 03	14 03
Mouldsworth	d	06 12	07 10	08 14	09 14	10 14	11 14	12 14	13 14	14 14
Delamere	d	06x17	07x15	08x19	09x19	10x19	11x19	12x19	13x19	14x19
Cuddington	d	06 21	07 19	08 23	09 23	10 23	11 23	12 23	13 23	14 23
Greenbank	d	06 26	07 24	08 28	09 28	10 28	11 28	12 28	13 28	14 28
Northwich	d	06 31	07 29	08 33	09 33	10 33	11 33	12 33	13 33	14 33
Lostock Gralam	d	06 34	07 32	08 36	09 36	10 36	11 36	12 36	13 36	14 36
Plumley	d	06 37	07 36	08 39	09 39	10 39	11 39	12 39	13 39	14 39
Knutsford	d	06 42	07 41	08 45	09 45	10 45	11 45	12 45	13 45	14 45
Mobberley	d	06x46	07x45	08x49	09x49	10x49	11x49	12x49	13x49	14x49
Ashley	d	06x50	07x49	08x52	09x52	10x52	11x52	12x52	13x52	14x52
Hale	d	06 53	07 53	08 55	09 55	10 55	11 55	12 55	13 55	14 55
Altrincham ⇌	a	06 57	07 57	09 00	10 00	11 00	12 00	13 00	14 00	15 00
	d	06 58	07 58	09 00	10 00	11 00	12 00	13 00	14 00	15 00
Navigation Road ⇌	d	07 00	08 00	09 02	10 02	11 02	12 02	13 02	14 02	15 02
Stockport 84	a	07 18	08 19	09 21	10 21	11 21	12 21	13 21	14 21	15 21
Manchester Piccadilly [10] 84 ⇌	a	07 31	08 32	09 36	10 36	11 36	12 36	13 36	14 36	15 36

		NT	NT	NT	NT	NT	NT	NT	NT
Chester 81	d	15 03	16 03	17 03	18 03	19 03	20 03	21 33	22 45
Mouldsworth	d	15 14	16 14	17 14	18 14	19 14	20 14	21 45	22 56
Delamere	d	15x19	16x19	17x19	18x19	19x19	20x19	21x49	23x01
Cuddington	d	15 23	16 23	17 23	18 23	19 23	20 23	21 54	23 05
Greenbank	d	15 28	16 28	17 28	18 28	19 28	20 28	21 58	23 10
Northwich	d	15 33	16 33	17 33	18 33	19 33	20 33	22 03	23 14
Lostock Gralam	d	15 36	16 36	17 36	18 36	19 36	20 36	22 06	23 17
Plumley	d	15 39	16 39	17 39	18 39	19 39	20 39	22 10	23 21
Knutsford	d	15 45	16 45	17 45	18 45	19 45	20 45	22 15	23 26
Mobberley	d	15x49	16x49	17x49	18x49	19x49	20x49	22x19	23x30
Ashley	d	15x52	16x52	17x52	18x52	19x52	20x52	22x23	23x33
Hale	d	15 55	16 55	17 55	18 55	19 55	20 55	22 26	23 36
Altrincham ⇌	a	16 00	17 00	18 00	19 00	20 00	21 00	22 30	23 41
	d	16 00	17 00	18 00	19 00	20 00	21 00	22 31	23 41
Navigation Road ⇌	d	16 02	17 02	18 02	19 02	20 02	21 02	22 33	23 43
Stockport 84	a	16 21	17 21	18 21	19 21	20 21	21 21	22 47	00 02
Manchester Piccadilly [10] 84 ⇌	a	16 36	17 36	18 36	19 35	20 35	21 35	23 00	00 15

Table 88

Chester and Northwich - Manchester

Sundays
until 05 September

		NT	NT	NT	NT	NT	NT	NT
Chester	81 d	08 58	11 07	13 07	15 07	17 07	19 07	21 07
Mouldsworth	d	09 09	11 18	13 18	15 18	17 18	19 18	21 18
Delamere	d	09x14	11x23	13x23	15x23	17x23	19x23	21x23
Cuddington	d	09 18	11 27	13 27	15 27	17 27	19 27	21 27
Greenbank	d	09 23	11 32	13 32	15 32	17 32	19 32	21 32
Northwich	d	09 28	11 37	13 37	15 37	17 37	19 37	21 37
Lostock Gralam	d	09 31	11 40	13 40	15 40	17 40	19 40	21 40
Plumley	d	09 34	11 43	13 43	15 43	17 43	19 43	21 43
Knutsford	d	09 40	11 49	13 49	15 49	17 49	19 49	21 49
Mobberley	d	09x44	11x53	13x53	15x53	17x53	19x53	21x53
Ashley	d	09x47	11x56	13x56	15x56	17x56	19x56	21x56
Hale	d	09 50	11 59	13 59	15 59	17 59	19 59	21 59
Altrincham	⇌ a	09 55	12 04	14 04	16 04	18 04	20 04	22 04
	d	09 55	12 04	14 04	16 04	18 04	20 04	22 04
Navigation Road	⇌ d	09 57	12 06	14 06	16 06	18 06	20 06	22 06
Stockport	84 a	10 12	12 21	14 21	16 21	18 21	20 21	22 21
Manchester Piccadilly 10	84 ⇌ a	10 23	12 33	14 33	16 33	18 33	20 33	22 33

Sundays
from 12 September

		NT	NT	NT	NT	NT	NT	NT
Chester	81 d	09 01	10 58	13 03	15 03	17 03	19 03	21 03
Mouldsworth	d	09 12	11 09	13 14	15 14	17 14	19 14	21 14
Delamere	d	09x17	11x14	13x19	15x19	17x19	19x19	21x19
Cuddington	d	09 21	11 18	13 23	15 23	17 23	19 23	21 23
Greenbank	d	09 26	11 23	13 28	15 28	17 28	19 28	21 28
Northwich	d	09 31	11 28	13 33	15 33	17 33	19 33	21 33
Lostock Gralam	d	09 34	11 31	13 36	15 36	17 36	19 36	21 36
Plumley	d	09 37	11 34	13 39	15 39	17 39	19 39	21 39
Knutsford	d	09 43	11 40	13 45	15 45	17 45	19 45	21 45
Mobberley	d	09x47	11x44	13x49	15x49	17x49	19x49	21x49
Ashley	d	09x50	11x47	13x52	15x52	17x52	19x52	21x52
Hale	d	09 53	11 50	13 55	15 55	17 55	19 55	21 55
Altrincham	⇌ a	09 58	11 55	14 00	16 00	18 00	20 00	22 00
	d	09 58	11 55	14 00	16 00	18 00	20 00	22 00
Navigation Road	⇌ d	10 00	11 57	14 02	16 02	18 02	20 02	22 02
Stockport	84 a	10 19	12 15	14 21	16 21	18 21	20 21	22 21
Manchester Piccadilly 10,84	⇌ a	10 31	12 28	14 33	16 33	18 33	20 33	22 33

On Sundays only, National Rail Tickets to stations between Hale and Mouldsworth inclusive are valid for travel on Metrolink services between Manchester City Centre and Altrincham

Table 89

Mondays to Fridays

Liverpool - Warrington Central - Manchester and Manchester Airport

		NT	NT	NT	NT	NT	TP	NT	EM	NT	NT	NT	TP
							◇1 ⌶		◇				◇1 ⌶
Liverpool Lime Street 10	90,91 d	03 38	05 13		05 49	06 13	06 16	06 21	06 47	06 50	07 13		07 16
Edge Hill	90,91 d				05 53					06 54			
Mossley Hill	91 d				05 58			06 29		06 59			
West Allerton	91 d				06 00			06 31		07 01			
Liverpool Central 10	103 d												
L'pool Sth Parkway 7	91,103 ✈ d				06 03			06 34	06 57	07 04			
Hunts Cross	103 d				06 07					07 08			
Halewood	d				06 09					07 10			
Hough Green	d				06 13			06 41		07 14			
Widnes	d				06 17			06 44	07 07	07 18			07 33
Sankey for Penketh	d				06 22					07 23			
Warrington Central	a				06 28		06 37	06 52	07 15	07 29			07 39
	d			06 02			06 38	06 53	07 15			07 22	07 40
Padgate	d			06 05				06 56				07 25	
Birchwood	d			06 08			06 43	06 59	07 20			07 28	07 45
Glazebrook	d			06 13				07 04				07 33	
Irlam	d			06 16				07 07				07 36	07 50
Flixton	d			06 20				07 11				07 40	
Chassen Road	d			06 22				07 13				07 42	
Urmston	d			06 24				07 15				07 44	
Humphrey Park	d			06 26				07 17				07 46	
Trafford Park	d			06 29				07 20				07 49	
Deansgate	84,85 ⇌ a			06 36				07 29				07 58	
Manchester Oxford Road	84,85 a			06 41		06 57	07 00	07 36	07 38		07 57	08 03	08 04
Manchester Picc 10	78,84,85 ⇌ a	04 14	05 57			07 01	07 09		07 41		08 01		08 08
Stockport	84 a								07 53				
Sheffield 7	78 ⇌ a								08 34				
Manchester Airport	85 ✈ a	04 30	06 14			07 22					08 22		

		NT	EM	NT	NT	TP	NT	EM	NT	NT	TP	NT	EM
			◇			◇1 ⌶		◇			◇1 ⌶		◇
Liverpool Lime Street 10	90,91 d	07 26	07 43	07 51	08 13	08 22	08 26	08 52	08 55	09 13	09 22	09 27	09 52
Edge Hill	90,91 d	07 30					08 30		08 59				
Mossley Hill	91 d	07 35		07 59			08 35		09 04			09 35	
West Allerton	91 d	07 37		08 01			08 37		09 06			09 37	
Liverpool Central 10	103 d												
L'pool Sth Parkway 7	91,103 ✈ d	07 40	07 53	08 04			08 40	09 03	09 09			09 40	10 03
Hunts Cross	103 d		07 59	08 08					09 13				
Halewood	d			08 10					09 16				
Hough Green	d	07 47		08 14			08 47		09 20			09 47	
Widnes	d		08 05	08 18			08 50	09 11	09 23			09 50	10 11
Sankey for Penketh	d			08 23					09 28				
Warrington Central	a	07 56	08 13	08 28		08 43	08 58	09 18	09 33		09 43	09 58	10 18
	d	07 57	08 13	08 28		08 44	08 59	09 19	09 34		09 44	09 59	10 19
Padgate	d	08 00					09 02					10 02	
Birchwood	d	08 03	08 18	08 33		08 49	09 05		09 38		09 49	10 05	
Glazebrook	d	08 08										10 10	
Irlam	d	08 11		08 39			09 11		09 44			10 13	
Flixton	d	08 15		08 43			09 15					10 17	
Chassen Road	d	08 17		08 45								10 19	
Urmston	d	08 19		08 47			09 18		09 49			10 21	
Humphrey Park	d	08 21		08 49			09 20						
Trafford Park	d	08 24		08 52			09 23						
Deansgate	84,85 ⇌ a	08 32		09 00			09 31		09 59			10 31	
Manchester Oxford Road	84,85 a	08 36	08 38	09 04	08 57	09 05	09 36	09 39	10 04	09 57	10 05	10 36	10 39
Manchester Picc 10	78,84,85 ⇌ a		08 41		09 01	09 09		09 41		10 01	10 09		10 41
Stockport	84 a		08 53					09 53					10 53
Sheffield 7	78 ⇌ a		09 35					10 33					11 34
Manchester Airport	85 ✈ a				09 22					10 22			

		NT	NT	TP	NT	EM	NT	NT	TP	NT	EM	NT	NT
				◇1 ⌶		◇			◇1 ⌶		◇		
Liverpool Lime Street 10	90,91 d	09 55	10 13	10 22	10 27	10 52	10 55	11 13	11 22	11 27	11 52	11 55	12 13
Edge Hill	90,91 d	09 59					10 59					11 59	
Mossley Hill	91 d	10 04			10 35		11 04			11 35		12 04	
West Allerton	91 d	10 06			10 37		11 06			11 37		12 06	
Liverpool Central 10	103 d												
L'pool Sth Parkway 7	91,103 ✈ d	10 09			10 40	11 03	11 09			11 40	12 03	12 09	
Hunts Cross	103 d	10 13					11 13					12 13	
Halewood	d	10 16					11 16					12 16	
Hough Green	d	10 20			10 47		11 20			11 47		12 20	
Widnes	d	10 23			10 50	11 11	11 23			11 50	12 11	12 23	
Sankey for Penketh	d	10 28					11 28					12 28	
Warrington Central	a	10 33		10 43	10 58	11 18	11 33		11 43	11 58	12 18	12 33	
	d	10 34		10 44	10 59	11 19	11 34		11 44	11 59	12 19	12 34	
Padgate	d				11 02					12 02			
Birchwood	d	10 38		10 49	11 05		11 38		11 49	12 05		12 38	
Glazebrook	d									12 10			
Irlam	d	10 44			11 11		11 44			12 13		12 44	
Flixton	d				11 15					12 17			
Chassen Road	d									12 19			
Urmston	d	10 49			11 18		11 49			12 21		12 49	
Humphrey Park	d				11 20								
Trafford Park	d				11 23								
Deansgate	84,85 ⇌ a	10 59			11 31		11 59			12 31		12 59	
Manchester Oxford Road	84,85 a	11 04	10 57	11 05	11 36	11 39	12 04	11 57	12 05	12 36	12 39	13 04	12 57
Manchester Picc 10	78,84,85 ⇌ a		11 01	11 09		11 41		12 01	12 09		12 41		13 01
Stockport	84 a					11 53					12 53		
Sheffield 7	78 ⇌ a					12 34					13 34		
Manchester Airport	85 ✈ a		11 22					12 22					13 22

		TP	NT	EM	NT	NT	TP	NT	EM	NT	NT	TP	NT
		◇1 ⌶		◇			◇1 ⌶		◇			◇1 ⌶	
Liverpool Lime Street 10	90,91 d	12 22	12 27	12 52	12 55	13 13	13 22	13 27	13 52	13 55	14 13	14 22	14 27
Edge Hill	90,91 d				12 59					13 59			
Mossley Hill	91 d		12 35		13 04			13 35		14 04			14 35
West Allerton	91 d		12 37		13 06			13 37		14 06			14 37
Liverpool Central 10	103 d												
L'pool Sth Parkway 7	91,103 ✈ d		12 40	13 03	13 09			13 40	14 03	14 09			14 40
Hunts Cross	103 d				13 13					14 13			
Halewood	d				13 16					14 16			
Hough Green	d		12 47		13 20			13 47		14 20			14 47
Widnes	d		12 50	13 11	13 23			13 50	14 11	14 23			14 50
Sankey for Penketh	d				13 28					14 28			
Warrington Central	a	12 43	12 58	13 18	13 33		13 43	13 58	14 18	14 33		14 43	14 58
	d	12 44	12 59	13 19	13 34		13 44	13 59	14 19	14 34		14 44	14 59
Padgate	d		13 02					14 02					15 02
Birchwood	d	12 49	13 05		13 38		13 49	14 05		14 38		14 49	15 05
Glazebrook	d							14 10					
Irlam	d		13 11		13 44			14 13		14 44			15 11
Flixton	d		13 15					14 17					15 15
Chassen Road	d							14 19					
Urmston	d		13 18		13 49			14 21		14 49			15 18
Humphrey Park	d		13 20										15 20
Trafford Park	d		13 23										15 23
Deansgate	84,85 ⇌ a		13 31		13 59			14 31		14 59			15 31
Manchester Oxford Road	84,85 a	13 05	13 36	13 39	14 04	13 57	14 05	14 36	14 39	15 04	14 57	15 05	15 36
Manchester Picc 10	78,84,85 ⇌ a	13 09		13 41		14 01	14 09		14 41		15 01	15 09	
Stockport	84 a			13 53					14 53				
Sheffield 7	78 ⇌ a			14 35					15 34				
Manchester Airport	85 ✈ a					14 22					15 22		

Table 89

Liverpool - Warrington Central - Manchester and Manchester Airport

	NT	NT	TP	NT	EM	NT	NT	TP	NT	EM	NT	NT	TP	NT	EM	NT	NT	TP	NT	EM	NT	TP	EM	NT
			◇1		◇			◇1		◇			◇1		◇			◇1		◇		◇1	◇	
Liverpool Lime Street 10 90,91 d	14 55	15 13	15 22	15 27	15 52	15 55	16 13	16 22	16 27	16 52	16 55	17 06	17 22	17 25	17 52	17 55	18 13	18 22	18 25	18 52	18 55	19 22	19 52	19 55
Edge Hill 90,91 d	14 59					15 59					16 59			17 29		17 59			18 29		18 59			19 59
Mossley Hill 91 d	15 04			15 35		16 04			16 35		17 04			17 34		18 04			18 34		19 04			20 04
West Allerton 91 d	15 06			15 37		16 06			16 37		17 06			17 36		18 06			18 36		19 06			20 06
Liverpool Central 10 103 d																								
L'pool Sth Parkway 7 91,103 ✈ d	15 09			15 40	16 03	16 09			16 40	17 03	17 09			17 39	18 03	18 09			18 39	19 03	19 09		20 03	20 09
Hunts Cross 103 d	15 13					16 13					17 13			17 43		18 13			18 43		19 13			20 13
Halewood d	15 16					16 16					17 16			17 46		18 16			18 46		19 16			20 16
Hough Green d	15 20			15 47		16 20			16 47		17 20			17 50		18 20			18 50		19 20			20 20
Widnes d	15 23			15 50	16 11	16 23			16 50	17 11	17 23			17 53	18 11	18 23			18 53	19 11	19 23		20 11	20 23
Sankey for Penketh d	15 28					16 28					17 28			17 58		18 28			18 58		19 28			20 28
Warrington Central a	15 33		15 43	15 58	16 18	16 33		16 43	16 58	17 18	17 33		17 43	18 03	18 18	18 33		18 43	19 03	19 18	19 34	19 43	20 18	20 34
d	15 34		15 44	15 59	16 19	16 34		16 44	16 59	17 19	17 34		17 44	18 04	18 19	18 34		18 44	19 04	19 19		19 44	20 19	
Padgate d				16 02					17 02					18 07					19 07					
Birchwood d	15 38		15 49	16 05		16 38		16 49	17 05		17 38		17 49	18 10		18 38		18 49	19 10			19 49		
Glazebrook d				16 10															19 15					
Irlam d	15 44			16 13		16 44			17 11		17 44			18 16		18 44			19 18					
Flixton d				16 17					17 15					18 20										
Chassen Road d				16 19																				
Urmston d	15 49			16 18		16 49			17 18		17 49			18 23		18 49			19 23					
Humphrey Park d				16 21					17 20															
Trafford Park d									17 23															
Deansgate 84,85 a	15 59			16 31		16 59			17 31		17 59			18 31		18 59			19 31					
Manchester Oxford Road 84,85 a	16 04	15 57	16 05	16 36	16 38	17 04	16 57	17 05	17 36	17 38	18 04	17 57	18 05	18 36	18 39	19 04	18 57	19 05	19 36	19 39		20 05	20 39	
Manchester Picc 10 78,84,85 a		16 01	16 09		16 41		17 01	17 09		17 41		18 01	18 09		18 41		19 01	19 09		19 41		20 09	20 41	
Stockport 84 a					16 53					17 53					18 53					19 53			20 53	
Sheffield 7 78 a					17 37					18 41					19 33					20 36			21 35	
Manchester Airport 85 ✈ a		16 22					17 22					18 22					19 24							

	NT	TP	NT	EM	NT	TP	NT
		◇1		◇		◇1	
Liverpool Lime Street 10 90,91 d	20 09	20 22	20 55	21 37	21 55	22 30	23 38
Edge Hill 90,91 d			20 59		21 59		23 42
Mossley Hill 91 d			21 04		22 04		23 47
West Allerton 91 d			21 06		22 06		23 50
Liverpool Central 10 103 d							
L'pool Sth Parkway 7 91,103 ✈ d			21 09	21 47	22 09		23 53
Hunts Cross 103 d			21 13		22 13		23 56
Halewood d			21 16		22 16		23 59
Hough Green d			21 20		22 20		00 03
Widnes d			21 23	21 55	22 23		00 06
Sankey for Penketh d			21 28		22 28		00 11
Warrington Central a		20 43	21 33	22 03	22 33	22 52	00 16
d		20 44	21 34	22 03	22 34	22 52	00 17
Padgate d			21 37		22 37		
Birchwood d		20 49	21 40		22 40	22 57	
Glazebrook d			21 45		22 45		
Irlam d			21 48		22 48		
Flixton d			21 52		22 52		
Chassen Road d			21 54		22 54		
Urmston d			21 56		22 56		
Humphrey Park d			21 58		22 58		
Trafford Park d			22 01		23 01		
Deansgate 84,85 a			22 08		23 08		
Manchester Oxford Road 84,85 a	20 57	21 05	22 13	22 23	23 13	23 14	
Manchester Picc 10 78,84,85 a	21 01	21 09		22 26		23 19	00 40
Stockport 84 a				22 37			
Sheffield 7 78 a				23 35			
Manchester Airport 85 ✈ a	21 24						

Table 89

Liverpool - Warrington Central - Manchester and Manchester Airport

	NT	NT	NT	NT	TP	NT	EM	NT	NT	TP	NT	EM	NT	NT	TP	NT	EM	NT	NT	TP	NT	EM	NT	NT
					◇1		◇			◇1		◇			◇1		◇			◇1		◇		
Liverpool Lime Street 10 90,91 d	03 38	05 13	05 49	06 13	06 16	06 25	06 49	06 55	07 13	07 16	07 26	07 42	07 51	08 13	08 22	08 26	08 52	08 55	09 13	09 22	09 27	09 52	09 55	10 13
Edge Hill 90,91 d			05 53					06 59			07 30					08 30		08 59					09 59	
Mossley Hill 91 d			05 58			06 33		07 04			07 35		07 59			08 35		09 04			09 35		10 04	
West Allerton 91 d			06 00			06 35		07 06			07 37		08 01			08 37		09 06			09 37		10 06	
Liverpool Central 10 103 d																								
L'pool Sth Parkway 7 91,103 ✈ d			06 03			06 38	06 59	07 09			07 40	07 52	08 04			08 40	09 03	09 09			09 40	10 03	10 09	
Hunts Cross 103 d			06 07					07 13				07 59	08 08					09 13					10 13	
Halewood d			06 09					07 16					08 10					09 16					10 16	
Hough Green d			06 13			06 46		07 20			07 47		08 14			08 47		09 20			09 47		10 20	
Widnes d			06 17			06 49	07 07	07 23		07 33		08 05	08 18			08 50	09 11	09 23			09 50	10 11	10 23	
Sankey for Penketh d			06 22					07 28					08 23					09 28					10 28	
Warrington Central a			06 28		06 37	06 57	07 15	07 34		07 39	07 56	08 13	08 28		08 43	08 58	09 18	09 33		09 43	09 58	10 18	10 33	
d					06 38	06 58	07 15			07 40	07 57	08 13	08 28		08 44	08 59	09 19	09 34		09 44	09 59	10 19	10 34	
Padgate d						07 01					08 00					09 02					10 02			
Birchwood d					06 43	07 04	07 20			07 45	08 03	08 18	08 33		08 49	09 05		09 38		09 49	10 05		10 38	
Glazebrook d						07 09					08 08										10 10			
Irlam d						07 12				07 50	08 11		08 39			09 11		09 44			10 13		10 44	
Flixton d						07 16					08 15		08 43			09 15					10 17			
Chassen Road d						07 18					08 17		08 45								10 19			
Urmston d						07 20					08 19		08 47			09 18		09 49			10 21		10 49	
Humphrey Park d						07 22					08 21		08 49			09 20								
Trafford Park d						07 25					08 24		08 52			09 23								
Deansgate 84,85 a						07 32					08 32		09 00			09 31		09 59			10 31		10 59	
Manchester Oxford Road 84,85 a				06 57	07 00	07 37	07 38		07 57	08 04	08 36	08 38	09 04	08 57	09 05	09 36	09 39	10 04	09 57	10 05	10 36	10 39	11 04	10 57
Manchester Picc 10 78,84,85 a	04 14	05 57		07 01	07 09		07 41		08 01	08 08		08 41		09 01	09 09		09 41		10 01	10 09		10 41		11 01
Stockport 84 a							07 53					08 53					09 53					10 53		
Sheffield 7 78 a							08 34					09 34					10 34					11 34		
Manchester Airport 85 ✈ a	04 30	06 14		07 22					08 22					09 22					10 22					11 22

	TP	NT	EM	NT	NT	TP	NT	EM	NT	NT	TP	NT	EM	NT	NT	TP	NT	EM	NT	NT	TP	NT	EM	NT
	◇1		◇			◇1		◇			◇1		◇			◇1		◇			◇1		◇	
Liverpool Lime Street 10 90,91 d	10 22	10 27	10 52	10 55	11 13	11 22	11 27	11 52	11 55	12 13	12 22	12 27	12 52	12 55	13 13	13 22	13 27	13 52	13 55	14 13	14 22	14 27	14 52	14 55
Edge Hill 90,91 d				10 59					11 59					12 59					13 59					14 59
Mossley Hill 91 d		10 35		11 04			11 35		12 04			12 35		13 04			13 35		14 04			14 35		15 04
West Allerton 91 d		10 37		11 06			11 37		12 06			12 37		13 06			13 37		14 06			14 37		15 06
Liverpool Central 10 103 d																								
L'pool Sth Parkway 7 91,103 ✈ d		10 40	11 03	11 09			11 40	12 03	12 09			12 40	13 03	13 09			13 40	14 03	14 09			14 40	15 03	15 09
Hunts Cross 103 d				11 13					12 13					13 13					14 13					15 13
Halewood d				11 16					12 16					13 16					14 16					15 16
Hough Green d		10 47		11 20			11 47		12 20			12 47		13 20			13 47		14 20			14 47		15 20
Widnes d		10 50	11 11	11 23			11 50	12 11	12 23			12 50	13 11	13 23			13 50	14 11	14 23			14 50	15 11	15 23
Sankey for Penketh d				11 28					12 28					13 28					14 28					15 28
Warrington Central a	10 43	10 58	11 18	11 33		11 43	11 58	12 18	12 33		12 43	12 58	13 18	13 33		13 43	13 58	14 18	14 33		14 43	14 58	15 18	15 33
d	10 44	10 59	11 19	11 34		11 44	11 59	12 19	12 34		12 44	12 59	13 19	13 34		13 44	13 59	14 19	14 34		14 44	14 59	15 19	15 34
Padgate d		11 02					12 02					13 02					14 02					15 02		
Birchwood d	10 49	11 05		11 38		11 49	12 05		12 38		12 49	13 05		13 38		13 49	14 05		14 38		14 49	15 05		15 38
Glazebrook d							12 10										14 10							
Irlam d		11 11		11 44			12 13		12 44			13 11		13 44			14 13		14 44			15 11		15 44
Flixton d		11 15					12 17					13 15					14 17					15 15		
Chassen Road d							12 19										14 19							
Urmston d		11 18		11 49			12 21		12 49			13 18		13 49			14 21		14 49			15 18		15 49
Humphrey Park d		11 20										13 20										15 20		
Trafford Park d		11 23										13 23										15 23		
Deansgate 84,85 a		11 31		11 59			12 31		12 59			13 31		13 59			14 31		14 59			15 31		15 59
Manchester Oxford Road 84,85 a	11 05	11 36	11 39	12 04	11 57	12 05	12 36	12 39	13 04	12 57	13 05	13 36	13 39	14 04	13 57	14 05	14 36	14 39	15 04	14 57	15 05	15 36	15 39	16 04
Manchester Picc 10 78,84,85 a	11 09		11 41		12 01	12 09		12 41		13 01	13 09		13 41		14 01	14 09		14 41		15 01	15 09		15 41	
Stockport 84 a			11 53					12 53					13 53					14 53					15 53	
Sheffield 7 78 a			12 34					13 34					14 34					15 34					16 35	
Manchester Airport 85 ✈ a					12 22					13 22					14 22					15 22				

Table 89

Saturdays

Liverpool - Warrington Central - Manchester and Manchester Airport

	NT	TP	NT	NT	NT	TP	NT	EM	NT	NT	TP	NT	EM	NT	NT	TP	NT	EM	NT	TP	EM	NT	NT	TP
		◇■1				◇■1		◇			◇■1		◇			◇■1		◇		◇■1	◇			◇■1
Liverpool Lime Street ■10 90,91 d	15 13	15 22	15 27	15 55	16 13	16 22	16 27	16 52	16 55	17 06	17 22	17 25	17 52	17 55	18 13	18 22	18 25	18 52	18 55	19 22	19 52	19 55	20 09	20 22
Edge Hill 90,91 d				15 59					16 59			17 29		17 59			18 29		18 59			19 59		
Mossley Hill 91 d			15 35	16 04			16 35		17 04			17 34		18 04			18 34		19 04			20 04		
West Allerton 91 d			15 37	16 06			16 37		17 06			17 36		18 06			18 36		19 06			20 06		
Liverpool Central ■10 103 d																								
L'pool Sth Parkway ■7 91,103 ✈ d			15 40	16 09			16 40	17 03	17 09			17 39	18 03	18 09			18 39	19 03	19 09		20 03	20 09		
Hunts Cross 103 d				16 13					17 13			17 43		18 13			18 43		19 13			20 13		
Halewood d				16 16					17 16			17 46		18 16			18 46		19 16			20 16		
Hough Green d			15 47	16 20			16 47		17 20			17 50		18 20			18 50		19 20			20 20		
Widnes d			15 50	16 23			16 50	17 11	17 23			17 54	18 11	18 23			18 53	19 11	19 23		20 11	20 23		
Sankey for Penketh d				16 28					17 28			17 58		18 28			18 58		19 28			20 28		
Warrington Central a		15 43	15 58	16 33		16 43	16 58	17 18	17 33		17 43	18 03	18 18	18 33		18 43	19 03	19 18	19 34	19 43	20 18	20 34		20 43
d		15 44	15 59	16 34		16 44	16 59	17 19	17 34		17 44	18 04	18 19	18 34		18 44	19 04	19 19		19 44	20 19			20 44
Padgate d			16 02				17 02					18 07					19 07							
Birchwood d		15 49	16 05	16 38		16 49	17 05		17 38		17 49	18 10		18 38		18 49	19 10			19 49				20 49
Glazebrook d			16 10														19 15							
Irlam d			16 13	16 44			17 11		17 44			18 16		18 44			19 18							
Flixton d			16 17				17 15					18 20												
Chassen Road d			16 19																					
Urmston d			16 18	16 49			17 18		17 49			18 23		18 49			19 23							
Humphrey Park d			16 21				17 20																	
Trafford Park d							17 23																	
Deansgate 84,85 ⇌ a			16 31	16 59			17 31		17 59			18 31		18 59			19 31							
Manchester Oxford Road 84,85 a	15 57	16 05	16 36	17 04	16 57	17 05	17 36	17 38	18 04	17 57	18 05	18 36	18 39	19 04	18 57	19 05	19 36	19 39		20 05	20 39		20 57	21 05
Manchester Picc ■10 78,84,85 ⇌ a	16 01	16 09			17 01	17 09		17 41		18 01	18 09		18 41		19 01	19 09		19 41		20 09	20 41		21 01	21 09
Stockport 84 a								17 53					18 53					19 53			20 53			
Sheffield ■7 78 ⇌ a								18 35					19 35					20 35			21 34			
Manchester Airport 85 ✈ a	16 22				17 22					18 22					19 24								21 24	

	EM	NT	NT	TP	NT
	◇			◇■1	
Liverpool Lime Street ■10 90,91 d	20 52	20 55	21 55	22 30	23 38
Edge Hill 90,91 d		20 59	21 59		23 42
Mossley Hill 91 d		21 04	22 04		23 47
West Allerton 91 d		21 06	22 06		23 49
Liverpool Central ■10 103 d					
L'pool Sth Parkway ■7 91,103 ✈ d	21 03	21 09	22 09		23 52
Hunts Cross 103 d		21 13	22 13		23 56
Halewood d		21 16	22 16		23 59
Hough Green d		21 20	22 20		00 03
Widnes d	21 11	21 23	22 23		00 06
Sankey for Penketh d		21 28	22 28		00 11
Warrington Central a	21 18	21 33	22 33	22 52	00 16
d	21 19	21 34	22 34	22 52	00 17
Padgate d		21 37	22 37		
Birchwood d		21 40	22 40	22 57	
Glazebrook d		21 45	22 45		
Irlam d		21 48	22 48		
Flixton d		21 52	22 52		
Chassen Road d		21 54	22 54		
Urmston d		21 56	22 56		
Humphrey Park d		21 58	22 58		
Trafford Park d		22 01	23 01		
Deansgate 84,85 ⇌ a		22 08	23 08		
Manchester Oxford Road 84,85 a	21 38	22 13	23 13	23 14	
Manchester Picc ■10 78,84,85 ⇌ a	21 41			23 19	00 39
Stockport 84 a	21 52				
Sheffield ■7 78 ⇌ a	22 31				
Manchester Airport 85 ✈ a					

Table 89

Sundays

until 05 September

Liverpool - Warrington Central - Manchester and Manchester Airport

	NT	TP	NT	NT	TP	NT	NT	NT	TP	NT	NT	TP	NT	NT	TP	NT	EM	EM	NT	TP	NT	EM
		◇■1			◇■1		B	C	◇■1			◇■1			◇■1		◇ C	◇ B		◇■1		◇
Liverpool Lime Street ■10 90,91 d	08 05	08 22	08 26	09 01	09 22	09 26	10 01	10 01	10 22	10 26	11 01	11 22	11 26	12 01	12 22	12 26	12 52	12 52	13 01	13 22	13 26	13 52
Edge Hill 90,91 d																						
Mossley Hill 91 d			08 34			09 34				10 34			11 34			12 34					13 34	
West Allerton 91 d			08 36			09 36				10 36			11 36			12 36					13 36	
Liverpool Central ■10 103 d																						
L'pool Sth Parkway ■7 91,103 ✈ d			08 39			09 39				10 39			11 39			12 39	13 03	13 03			13 39	14 03
Hunts Cross 103 d			08 43			09 43				10 43			11 43			12 43					13 43	
Halewood d			08 46			09 46				10 46			11 46			12 46					13 46	
Hough Green d			08 50			09 50				10 50			11 50			12 50					13 50	
Widnes d			08 53			09 53				10 53			11 53			12 53	13 11	13 11			13 53	14 11
Sankey for Penketh d																						
Warrington Central a		08 43	09 01		09 43	10 01			10 43	11 01		11 43	12 01		12 43	13 01	13 18	13 18		13 43	14 01	14 18
d		08 44	09 02		09 44	10 02			10 44	11 02		11 44	12 02		12 44	13 02	13 19	13 19		13 44	14 02	14 19
Padgate d																						
Birchwood d		08 49	09 06		09 49	10 06			10 49	11 06		11 49	12 06		12 49	13 06				13 49	14 06	
Glazebrook d																						
Irlam d			09 12			10 12				11 12			12 12			13 12					14 12	
Flixton d																						
Chassen Road d																						
Urmston d			09 17			10 17				11 17			12 17			13 17					14 17	
Humphrey Park d																						
Trafford Park d																						
Deansgate 84,85 ⇌ a			09 27			10 27				11 27			12 27			13 27					14 27	
Manchester Oxford Road 84,85 a	09 01	09 05	09 31	09 59	10 05	10 31	10 59	10 59	11 05	11 31	11 59	12 05	12 31	12 59	13 05	13 31	13 39	13 39	13 59	14 05	14 31	14 39
Manchester Picc ■10 78,84,85 ⇌ a	09 05	09 09		10 03	10 09			11 03	11 09		12 02	12 09		13 02	13 09		13 41	13 41	14 02	14 09		14 41
Stockport 84 a																	13 53	13 53				14 53
Sheffield ■7 78 ⇌ a																	14 42	14 39				15 33
Manchester Airport 85 ✈ a	09 22			10 24				11 21			12 21			13 24					14 21			

	NT	TP	NT	EM	NT	TP	NT	EM	NT	TP	NT	EM	NT	TP	NT	EM	NT	TP	NT	EM	NT	TP
		◇■1		◇		◇■1		◇		◇■1		◇		◇■1		◇		◇■1		◇		◇■1
Liverpool Lime Street ■10 90,91 d	14 01	14 22	14 26	14 52	15 01	15 22	15 26	15 52	16 01	16 22	16 26	16 52	17 01	17 22	17 26	17 52	18 01	18 22	18 26	18 52	19 01	19 22
Edge Hill 90,91 d																						
Mossley Hill 91 d			14 34				15 34				16 34				17 34				18 34			
West Allerton 91 d			14 36				15 36				16 36				17 36				18 36			
Liverpool Central ■10 103 d																						
L'pool Sth Parkway ■7 91,103 ✈ d			14 39	15 03			15 39	16 03			16 39	17 03			17 39	18 03			18 39	19 03		
Hunts Cross 103 d			14 43				15 43				16 43				17 43				18 43			
Halewood d			14 46				15 46				16 46				17 46				18 46			
Hough Green d			14 50				15 50				16 50				17 50				18 50			
Widnes d			14 53	15 11			15 53	16 11			16 53	17 11			17 53	18 11			18 53	19 11		
Sankey for Penketh d																						
Warrington Central a		14 43	15 01	15 18		15 43	16 01	16 18		16 43	17 01	17 18		17 43	18 01	18 18		18 43	19 01	19 18		19 43
d		14 44	15 02	15 19		15 44	16 02	16 19		16 44	17 02	17 19		17 44	18 02	18 19		18 44	19 02	19 19		19 44
Padgate d																						
Birchwood d		14 49	15 06			15 49	16 06			16 49	17 06			17 49	18 06			18 49	19 06			19 49
Glazebrook d																						
Irlam d			15 12				16 12				17 12				18 12				19 12			
Flixton d																						
Chassen Road d																						
Urmston d			15 17				16 17				17 17				18 17				19 17			
Humphrey Park d																						
Trafford Park d																						
Deansgate 84,85 ⇌ a			15 27				16 27				17 27				18 27				19 27			
Manchester Oxford Road 84,85 a	14 59	15 05	15 31	15 39	15 59	16 05	16 31	16 38	16 59	17 05	17 31	17 38	17 59	18 05	18 31	18 39	18 59	19 05	19 31	19 39	19 59	20 05
Manchester Picc ■10 78,84,85 ⇌ a	15 02	15 09		15 41	16 02	16 09		16 41	17 02	17 09		17 41	18 02	18 09		18 41	19 02	19 09		19 41	20 02	20 09
Stockport 84 a				15 53				16 53				17 53				18 53				19 53		
Sheffield ■7 78 ⇌ a				16 36				17 36				18 37				19 34				20 34		
Manchester Airport 85 ✈ a	15 21				16 21				17 21				18 21				19 21				20 21	

B until 11 July

C from 18 July until 5 September

Sundays
until 05 September

Liverpool - Warrington Central - Manchester and Manchester Airport

		NT	EM ◇	NT	TP ◇■	NT	NT	EM ◇	NT	TP ◇■	NT	NT	NT
Liverpool Lime Street ■ 90,91	d	19 26	19 52	20 01	20 22	20 26	21 01	21 22	21 26	21 52	22 01	22 26	23 01
Edge Hill 90,91	d												
Mossley Hill 91	d	19 34				20 34			21 34			22 34	
West Allerton 91	d	19 36				20 36			21 36			22 36	
Liverpool Central ■ 103	d												
L'pool Sth Parkway ■ 91,103 ✈	d	19 39	20 03			20 39			21 39			22 39	
Hunts Cross 103	d	19 43				20 43			21 43			22 43	
Halewood	d	19 46				20 46			21 46			22 46	
Hough Green	d	19 50				20 50			21 50			22 50	
Widnes	d	19 53	20 11			20 53		21 39	21 53			22 53	
Sankey for Penketh	d												
Warrington Central	a	20 01	20 18		20 43	21 01		21 47	22 01	22 13		23 01	
	d	20 02	20 19		20 44	21 02		21 47	22 02	22 14		23 02	
Padgate	d												
Birchwood	d	20 06			20 49	21 06			22 06	22 19		23 06	
Glazebrook	d												
Irlam	d	20 12				21 12			22 12			23 12	
Flixton	d												
Chassen Road	d												
Urmston	d	20 17				21 17			22 17			23 17	
Humphrey Park	d												
Trafford Park	d												
Deansgate 84,85	a	20 27				21 27			22 27			23 27	
Manchester Oxford Road 84,85	a	20 31	20 39	20 59	21 05	21 31	21 59	22 07	22 31	22 35	22 59	23 31	23 59
Manchester Picc ■ 78,84,85	a		20 41	21 02	21 09		22 02	22 09		22 39	23 02		00 02
Stockport 84	a		20 53					22 20					
Sheffield ■ 78	a		21 36					23 25					
Manchester Airport 85 ✈	a			21 21			22 21				23 21		00 19

Sundays
from 12 September

		NT	NT	NT	NT	NT	NT	NT	NT	NT	NT	EM ◇	NT	NT	EM ◇	NT	TP ◇■	NT	EM ◇	NT	TP ◇■	NT
Liverpool Lime Street ■ 90,91	d	08 22	08 26	09 01	09 26	10 01	10 26	11 01	11 26	12 01	12 26	12 52	13 01	13 26	13 52	14 01	14 22	14 26	14 52	15 01	15 22	15 26
Edge Hill 90,91	d																					
Mossley Hill 91	d		08 34		09 34		10 34		11 34		12 34			13 34				14 34				15 34
West Allerton 91	d		08 36		09 36		10 36		11 36		12 36			13 36				14 36				15 36
Liverpool Central ■ 103	d																					
L'pool Sth Parkway ■ 91,103 ✈	d		08 39		09 39		10 39		11 39		12 39	13 03		13 39	14 03			14 39	15 03			15 39
Hunts Cross 103	d		08 43		09 43		10 43		11 43		12 43			13 43				14 43				15 43
Halewood	d		08 46		09 46		10 46		11 46		12 46			13 46				14 46				15 46
Hough Green	d		08 50		09 50		10 50		11 50		12 50			13 50				14 50				15 50
Widnes	d		08 53		09 53		10 53		11 53		12 53	13 11		13 53	14 11			14 53	15 11			15 53
Sankey for Penketh	d																					
Warrington Central	a		09 01		10 01		11 01		12 01		13 01	13 18		14 01	14 18		14 43	15 01	15 18		15 43	16 01
	d		09 02		10 02		11 02		12 02		13 02	13 19		14 02	14 19		14 44	15 02	15 19		15 44	16 02
Padgate	d																					
Birchwood	d		09 06		10 06		11 06		12 06		13 06			14 06			14 49	15 06			15 49	16 06
Glazebrook	d																					
Irlam	d		09 12		10 12		11 12		12 12		13 12			14 12				15 12				16 12
Flixton	d																					
Chassen Road	d																					
Urmston	d		09 17		10 17		11 17		12 17		13 17			14 17				15 17				16 17
Humphrey Park	d																					
Trafford Park	d																					
Deansgate 84,85	a		09 27		10 27		11 27		12 27		13 27			14 27				15 27				16 27
Manchester Oxford Road 84,85	a	09 20	09 31	09 59	10 31	10 59	11 31	11 59	12 31	12 59	13 31	13 39	13 59	14 31	14 39	14 59	15 05	15 31	15 39	15 59	16 05	16 31
Manchester Picc ■ 78,84,85	a			10 02		11 03		12 02		13 02		13 41	14 02		14 41	15 02	15 09		15 41	16 02	16 09	
Stockport 84	a											13 53			14 53				15 53			
Sheffield ■ 78	a											14 39			15 37				16 36			
Manchester Airport 85 ✈	a			10 25		11 21		12 21		13 21			14 21			15 21				16 21		

Table 89

Sundays
from 12 September

Liverpool - Warrington Central - Manchester and Manchester Airport

		EM ◇	NT	TP ◇■	NT	EM ◇	NT	TP ◇■	NT	EM ◇	NT	TP ◇■	NT	EM ◇	NT	TP ◇■	NT	EM ◇	NT	TP ◇■	NT	NT	EM ◇
Liverpool Lime Street ■ 90,91	d	15 52	16 01	16 22	16 26	16 52	17 01	17 22	17 26	17 52	18 01	18 22	18 26	18 52	19 01	19 22	19 26	19 52	20 01	20 22	20 26	21 01	21 22
Edge Hill 90,91	d																						
Mossley Hill 91	d				16 34				17 34				18 34				19 34				20 34		
West Allerton 91	d				16 36				17 36				18 36				19 36				20 36		
Liverpool Central ■ 103	d																						
L'pool Sth Parkway ■ 91,103 ✈	d	16 03			16 39	17 03			17 39	18 03			18 39	19 03			19 39	20 03			20 39		
Hunts Cross 103	d				16 43				17 43				18 43				19 43				20 43		
Halewood	d				16 46				17 46				18 46				19 46				20 46		
Hough Green	d				16 50				17 50				18 50				19 50				20 50		
Widnes	d	16 11			16 53	17 11			17 53	18 11			18 53	19 11			19 53	20 11			20 53		21 39
Sankey for Penketh	d																						
Warrington Central	a	16 18		16 43	17 01	17 18		17 43	18 01	18 18		18 43	19 01	19 18		19 43	20 01	20 18		20 43	21 01		21 47
	d	16 19		16 44	17 02	17 19		17 44	18 02	18 19		18 44	19 02	19 19		19 44	20 02	20 19		20 44	21 02		21 47
Padgate	d																						
Birchwood	d			16 49	17 06			17 49	18 06			18 49	19 06			19 49	20 06			20 49	21 06		
Glazebrook	d																						
Irlam	d				17 12				18 12				19 12				20 12				21 12		
Flixton	d																						
Chassen Road	d																						
Urmston	d				17 17				18 17				19 17				20 17				21 17		
Humphrey Park	d																						
Trafford Park	d																						
Deansgate 84,85	a				17 27				18 27				19 27				20 27				21 27		
Manchester Oxford Road 84,85	a	16 38	16 59	17 05	17 31	17 38	17 59	18 05	18 31	18 39	18 59	19 05	19 31	19 39	19 59	20 05	20 31	20 39	20 59	21 05	21 31	21 59	22 06
Manchester Picc ■ 78,84,85	a	16 41	17 02	17 09		17 41	18 02	18 09		18 41	19 02	19 09		19 41	20 02	20 09		20 41	21 02	21 09		22 02	22 09
Stockport 84	a	16 53				17 53				18 53				19 53				20 53					22 20
Sheffield ■ 78	a	17 36				18 37				19 34				20 34				21 36					23 25
Manchester Airport 85 ✈	a		17 21				18 21				19 21				20 21				21 21			22 21	

		NT	TP ◇■	NT	NT	NT
Liverpool Lime Street ■ 90,91	d	21 26	21 52	22 01	22 26	23 01
Edge Hill 90,91	d					
Mossley Hill 91	d	21 34			22 34	
West Allerton 91	d	21 36			22 36	
Liverpool Central ■ 103	d					
L'pool Sth Parkway ■ 91,103 ✈	d	21 39			22 39	
Hunts Cross 103	d	21 43			22 43	
Halewood	d	21 46			22 46	
Hough Green	d	21 50			22 50	
Widnes	d	21 53			22 53	
Sankey for Penketh	d					
Warrington Central	a	22 01	22 13		23 01	
	d	22 02	22 14		23 02	
Padgate	d					
Birchwood	d	22 06	22 19		23 06	
Glazebrook	d					
Irlam	d	22 12			23 12	
Flixton	d					
Chassen Road	d					
Urmston	d	22 17			23 17	
Humphrey Park	d					
Trafford Park	d					
Deansgate 84,85	a	22 27			23 27	
Manchester Oxford Road 84,85	a	22 31	22 35	22 59	23 31	23 59
Manchester Picc ■ 78,84,85	a		22 39	23 02		00 02
Stockport 84	a					
Sheffield ■ 78	a					
Manchester Airport 85 ✈	a			23 21		00 19

Manchester Airport and Manchester - Warrington Central - Liverpool

	NT	NT	NT	NT	NT	NT	TP	NT	EM	NT	NT	TP	NT	EM	NT	NT	TP	NT	EM	NT	NT
							◇1		◇			◇1 ☕		◇			◇1 ☕		◇		
Manchester Airport 85 ✈ d	04 34					06 41					07 41					08 41					09 41
Sheffield 7 78 ⇌ d									06 20					07 35					08 42		
Stockport 84 d									07 22					08 24					09 25		
Manchester Picc 10 78,84,85 ⇌ d	04 49					06 58	07 07		07 34		07 58	08 07		08 37		09 01	09 07		09 37		10 01
Manchester Oxford Road 84,85 d				06 27	06 46	07 01	07 11		07 37	07 39	08 03	08 11	08 15	08 41	08 44	09 04	09 11	09 15	09 41	09 44	10 04
Deansgate 84,85 ⇌ d				06 29						07 41			08 17		08 46			09 17		09 46	
Trafford Park d				06 34						07 46								09 22			
Humphrey Park d				06 36														09 24			
Urmston d				06 38	06 53					07 49			08 24		08 52			09 27		09 52	
Chassen Road d				06 40									08 26								
Flixton d				06 43						07 52			08 29					09 30			
Irlam d				06 47	06 58					07 56			08 33		08 57			09 34		09 57	
Glazebrook d				06 50						07 59			08 36								
Birchwood d				06 54	07 04		07 24			08 04		08 24	08 40		09 03		09 24	09 40		10 03	
Padgate d				06 57						08 07					09 06					10 06	
Warrington Central a				07 01	07 12		07 29		07 53	08 10		08 29	08 45	08 57	09 09		09 29	09 45	09 57	10 09	
d		06 03	06 37	07 01			07 29	07 35	07 53	08 11		08 29	08 46	08 57	09 10		09 29	09 45	09 57	10 10	
Sankey for Penketh d		06 07	06 41	07 05				07 39		08 15					09 14					10 14	
Widnes d		06 12	06 46	07 11				07 44	08 01	08 20			08 54	09 05	09 19			09 53	10 05	10 19	
Hough Green d		06 15	06 49	07 14				07 47	08 05	08 24			08 57		09 23			09 56		10 23	
Halewood d		06 20	06 54	07 18				07 52		08 28					09 27					10 27	
Hunts Cross 89 d		06 23	06 57	07 22				07 55	08s10	08 32					09 30					10 30	
L'pool South Parkway 7 91,103 ✈ a																					
Liverpool Central 10 103 a																					
West Allerton 91 a		06 31	07 05	07 30				08 03		08 40			09 10		09 39			10 10		10 39	
Mossley Hill 91 a		06 33	07 07	07 33				08 06		08 43			09 13		09 41			10 12		10 41	
Edge Hill 90,91 a		06 39	07 13	07 40				08 11		08 48					09 47					10 47	
Liverpool Lime Street 10 90,91 a	05 32	06 45	07 19	07 48		07 49	07 57	08 18	08 31	08 55	08 59	08 57	09 24	09 31	09 53	09 48	09 57	10 24	10 31	10 53	10 48

	TP	NT	EM	NT	NT	TP	NT	EM	NT	NT	TP	NT	EM	NT	NT	TP	NT	EM	NT	NT	TP	NT
	◇1 ☕		◇			◇1 ☕		◇			◇1 ☕		◇			◇1 ☕		◇			◇1 ☕	
Manchester Airport 85 ✈ d					10 41					11 41					12 41					13 41		
Sheffield 7 78 ⇌ d			09 42					10 42					11 42					12 42				
Stockport 84 d			10 26					11 26					12 26					13 26				
Manchester Picc 10 78,84,85 ⇌ d	10 07		10 37		11 01	11 07		11 37		12 01	12 07		12 37		13 01	13 07		13 37		14 01	14 07	
Manchester Oxford Road 84,85 d	10 11	10 16	10 41	10 44	11 04	11 11	11 16	11 41	11 44	12 04	12 11	12 16	12 41	12 44	13 04	13 11	13 16	13 41	13 44	14 04	14 11	14 16
Deansgate 84,85 ⇌ d		10 18		10 46			11 18		11 46			12 18		12 46			13 18		13 46			14 18
Trafford Park d							11 23										13 23					
Humphrey Park d							11 25										13 25					
Urmston d		10 24		10 52			11 27		11 52			12 24		12 52			13 27		13 52			14 24
Chassen Road d		10 26										12 26										14 26
Flixton d		10 29					11 30					12 29					13 30					14 29
Irlam d		10 33		10 57			11 34		11 57			12 33		12 57			13 34		13 57			14 33
Glazebrook d		10 36										12 36										14 36
Birchwood d	10 24	10 40		11 03		11 24	11 40		12 03		12 24	12 40		13 03		13 24	13 40		14 03		14 24	14 40
Padgate d				11 06					12 06					13 06					14 06			
Warrington Central a	10 29	10 45	10 57	11 09		11 29	11 45	11 57	12 09		12 29	12 45	12 57	13 09		13 29	13 45	13 57	14 09		14 29	14 45
d	10 29	10 46	10 57	11 10		11 29	11 46	11 57	12 10		12 29	12 46	12 57	13 10		13 29	13 46	13 57	14 10		14 29	14 46
Sankey for Penketh d				11 14					12 14					13 14					14 14			
Widnes d		10 54	11 05	11 19			11 54	12 05	12 19			12 54	13 05	13 19			13 54	14 05	14 19			14 54
Hough Green d		10 57		11 23			11 57		12 23			12 57		13 23			13 57		14 23			14 57
Halewood d				11 27					12 27					13 27					14 27			
Hunts Cross 89 d				11 30					12 30					13 30					14 30			
L'pool South Parkway 7 91,103 ✈ a																						
Liverpool Central 10 103 a																						
West Allerton 91 a		11 10		11 39			12 10		12 39			13 10		13 39			14 10		14 39			15 10
Mossley Hill 91 a		11 13		11 41			12 13		12 41			13 13		13 41			14 13		14 41			15 13
Edge Hill 90,91 a				11 47					12 47					13 47					14 47			
Liverpool Lime Street 10 90,91 a	10 57	11 24	11 31	11 53	11 48	11 57	12 24	12 31	12 53	12 48	12 57	13 24	13 31	13 53	13 48	13 57	14 24	14 31	14 53	14 48	14 57	15 24

Table 89 Mondays to Fridays

Manchester Airport and Manchester - Warrington Central - Liverpool

	EM	NT	NT	TP	NT	EM	NT	NT	TP	NT	EM	NT	NT	TP	NT	EM	NT	NT	TP	EM	NT
	◇			◇1 ☕		◇			◇1 ☕		◇			◇1 ☕		◇			◇1 ☕	◇	
Manchester Airport 85 ✈ d			14 41					15 41					16 41					17 41			
Sheffield 7 78 ⇌ d	13 42					14 42					15 42					16 42				17 40	
Stockport 84 d	14 26					15 26					16 26					17 26				18 26	
Manchester Picc 10 78,84,85 ⇌ d	14 37		15 01	15 07		15 37		16 01	16 07		16 37		17 01	17 07		17 37		18 01	18 07	18 37	
Manchester Oxford Road 84,85 d	14 41	14 44	15 04	15 11	15 16	15 41	15 44	16 04	16 11	16 16	16 41	16 43	17 04	17 11	17 13	17 42	17 44	18 04	18 11	18 41	18 44
Deansgate 84,85 ⇌ d		14 46			15 18		15 46			16 18		16 45			17 15		17 46				18 46
Trafford Park d					15 23							16 51			17 20		17 51				18 51
Humphrey Park d					15 25										17 22		17 53				18 53
Urmston d		14 52			15 27		15 52			16 24		16 54			17 25		17 55				18 55
Chassen Road d										16 26					17 27		17 57				18 57
Flixton d					15 30					16 29		16 57			17 29		18 00				19 00
Irlam d		14 57			15 34		15 57			16 33		17 01			17 33	17 52	18 04				19 04
Glazebrook d										16 36					17 36		18 07				19 07
Birchwood d		15 03		15 24	15 40		16 03		16 24	16 40		17 07		17 24	17 41	17 58	18 12		18 24		19 11
Padgate d		15 06					16 06			16 43		17 10			17 44		18 15				19 14
Warrington Central a	14 57	15 09		15 29	15 45	15 57	16 09		16 29	16 47	16 57	17 13		17 29	17 48	18 03	18 18		18 29	18 57	19 20
d	14 57	15 10		15 29	15 45	15 57	16 10		16 29	16 47	16 57	17 14		17 29	17 48	18 03	18 19		18 29	18 57	
Sankey for Penketh d		15 14					16 14					17 18			17 52						
Widnes d	15 05	15 19			15 53	16 05	16 19			16 55	17 05	17 23			17 58	18 11				19 05	
Hough Green d		15 23			15 56		16 23			16 58		17 27			18 01		18 28				
Halewood d		15 27			16 01		16 27					17 31			18 06						
Hunts Cross 89 d		15 30					16 30					17 34		17 40	18 09		18 33			19 12	
L'pool South Parkway 7 91,103 ✈ a																					
Liverpool Central 10 103 a																					
West Allerton 91 a		15 39			16 11		16 39			17 11		17 42			18 18		18 42				
Mossley Hill 91 a		15 41			16 13		16 42			17 13		17 45			18 20		18 44				
Edge Hill 90,91 a		15 47					16 47					17 50			18 30		18 50				
Liverpool Lime Street 10 90,91 a	15 31	15 53	15 48	15 57	16 25	16 31	16 54	16 48	16 57	17 25	17 31	17 58	17 48	18 00	18 38	18 35	18 57	19 00	18 59	19 35	

	NT	TP	NT	EM	NT	NT	TP	NT	EM	NT	TP	NT	NT	NT	TP	NT	NT
		◇1 ☕		◇			◇1		◇		◇1				◇1		
Manchester Airport 85 ✈ d	18 41					19 41								21 41			
Sheffield 7 78 ⇌ d				18 42					19 42								
Stockport 84 d				19 26					20 26								
Manchester Picc 10 78,84,85 ⇌ d	19 01	19 07		19 37		20 01	20 07		20 37		21 07	21 38		22 01	22 07		
Manchester Oxford Road 84,85 d	19 04	19 11		19 41	19 44	20 04	20 11		20 41	20 44	21 11	21 44		22 04	22 11		23 27
Deansgate 84,85 ⇌ d					19 46					20 46		21 46					23 29
Trafford Park d					19 51					20 51		21 51					23 34
Humphrey Park d					19 53					20 53		21 53					23 36
Urmston d					19 55					20 55		21 55					23 38
Chassen Road d					19 57					20 57		21 57					23 40
Flixton d					20 00					21 00		22 00					23 43
Irlam d					20 04					21 04		22 04					23 47
Glazebrook d					20 07					21 07		22 07					23 50
Birchwood d		19 24			20 11		20 24			21 11	21 24	22 11			22 24		23 54
Padgate d					20 14					21 14		22 14					23 57
Warrington Central a		19 29		19 57	20 18		20 29		20 57	21 20	21 29	22 20			22 29		00 01
d		19 29	19 34	19 57	20 18		20 29	20 49	20 57		21 29		21 49		22 29	22 49	00 02
Sankey for Penketh d			19 38					20 53					21 53			22 53	00 05
Widnes d			19 43	20 05				20 58	21 05				21 58			22 58	00 11
Hough Green d			19 46		20 28			21 01					22 01			23 01	00 13
Halewood d			19 51					21 06					22 06			23 06	00 18
Hunts Cross 89 d			19 54		20 33			21 09					22 09			23 09	00 21
L'pool South Parkway 7 91,103 ✈ a																	
Liverpool Central 10 103 a																	
West Allerton 91 a			20 03		20 41			21 15					22 15			23 16	
Mossley Hill 91 a			20 05		20 44			21 18					22 18			23 18	
Edge Hill 90,91 a			20 11					21 23					22 23			23 23	
Liverpool Lime Street 10 90,91 a	19 48	19 57	20 18	20 35	20 56	20 48	20 59	21 30	21 35		21 57		22 30	22 48	22 59	23 30	00 41

Manchester Airport and Manchester - Warrington Central - Liverpool

	NT	NT	NT	NT	NT	TP	NT	EM	NT	NT	TP	NT	EM	NT	NT	TP	NT	EM	NT	NT	TP
						◇1		◇			◇1 🛒		◇			◇1 🛒		◇			◇1 🛒
Manchester Airport 85 ✈ d	04 34				06 41					07 41					08 41					09 41	
Sheffield 7 78 ⇌ d								06 20					07 35					08 42			
Stockport 84 d								07 22					08 24					09 25			
Manchester Picc 10 78,84,85 ⇌ d	04 49				06 58	07 07		07 34		07 58	08 07		08 37		09 01	09 07		09 37		10 01	10 07
Manchester Oxford Road 84,85 d				06 22	07 01	07 11		07 37	07 39	08 03	08 11	08 15	08 41	08 44	09 04	09 11	09 16	09 41	09 44	10 04	10 11
Deansgate 84,85 ⇌ d				06 24					07 41			08 17		08 46			09 18		09 46		
Trafford Park d				06 29					07 46								09 23				
Humphrey Park d				06 31													09 25				
Urmston d				06 33					07 49			08 24		08 52			09 27		09 52		
Chassen Road d				06 35								08 26									
Flixton d				06 38					07 52			08 29					09 30				
Irlam d				06 42					07 56			08 33		08 57			09 34		09 57		
Glazebrook d				06 45					07 59			08 36									
Birchwood d				06 49		07 24			08 04		08 24	08 40		09 03		09 24	09 40		10 03		10 24
Padgate d				06 52					08 07					09 06					10 06		
Warrington Central a				06 56		07 29		07 53	08 10		08 29	08 45	08 57	09 09		09 29	09 45	09 57	10 09		10 29
d		06 03	06 37	06 56		07 29	07 40	07 53	08 11		08 29	08 46	08 57	09 10		09 29	09 46	09 57	10 10		10 29
Sankey for Penketh d		06 07	06 41	07 00			07 44		08 15					09 14					10 14		
Widnes d		06 12	06 46	07 06			07 49	08 01	08 20			08 54	09 05	09 19			09 54	10 05	10 19		
Hough Green d		06 15	06 49	07 09			07 52	08 05	08 24			08 57		09 23			09 57		10 23		
Halewood d		06 20	06 54	07 13			07 57		08 28					09 27					10 27		
Hunts Cross 89 d		06 23	06 57	07 17			08 00	08s10	08 32					09 30					10 30		
L'pool South Parkway 7 91,103 ✈ a																					
Liverpool Central 10 103 a																					
West Allerton 91 a		06 31	07 05	07 25			08 06		08 40			09 10		09 39			10 10		10 39		
Mossley Hill 91 a		06 33	07 07	07 28			08 09		08 43			09 12		09 41			10 13		10 41		
Edge Hill 90,91 a		06 39	07 13	07 34			08 14		08 48					09 47					10 47		
Liverpool Lime Street 10 90,91 a	05 32	06 45	07 20	07 40	07 49	07 57	08 21	08 31	08 55	08 59	08 57	09 24	09 31	09 53	09 48	09 57	10 24	10 31	10 53	10 48	10 57

	NT	EM	NT	NT	TP	NT	EM	NT	NT	TP	NT	EM	NT	NT	TP	NT	EM	NT	NT	TP	NT	EM
		◇			◇1		◇			◇1 🛒		◇			◇1 🛒		◇			◇1		◇
Manchester Airport 85 ✈ d				10 41					11 41					12 41					13 41			
Sheffield 7 78 ⇌ d		09 42					10 42					11 42					12 42					13 42
Stockport 84 d		10 26					11 26					12 26					13 26					14 26
Manchester Picc 10 78,84,85 ⇌ d		10 37		11 01	11 07		11 37		12 01	12 07		12 37		13 01	13 07		13 37		14 01	14 07		14 37
Manchester Oxford Road 84,85 d	10 16	10 41	10 44	11 04	11 11	11 16	11 41	11 44	12 04	12 11	12 16	12 41	12 44	13 04	13 11	13 16	13 41	13 44	14 04	14 11	14 16	14 41
Deansgate 84,85 ⇌ d	10 18		10 46			11 18		11 46			12 18		12 46			13 18		13 46			14 18	
Trafford Park d						11 23										13 23						
Humphrey Park d						11 25										13 25						
Urmston d	10 24		10 52			11 27		11 52			12 24		12 52			13 27		13 52			14 24	
Chassen Road d	10 26										12 26										14 26	
Flixton d	10 29					11 30					12 29					13 30					14 29	
Irlam d	10 33		10 57			11 34		11 57			12 33		12 57			13 34		13 57			14 33	
Glazebrook d	10 36										12 36										14 36	
Birchwood d	10 40		11 03		11 24	11 40		12 03		12 24	12 40		13 03		13 24	13 40		14 03		14 24	14 40	
Padgate d			11 06					12 06					13 06					14 06				
Warrington Central a	10 45	10 57	11 09		11 29	11 45	11 57	12 09		12 29	12 45	12 57	13 09		13 29	13 45	13 57	14 09		14 29	14 45	14 57
d	10 46	10 57	11 10		11 29	11 46	11 57	12 10		12 29	12 46	12 57	13 10		13 29	13 46	13 57	14 10		14 29	14 46	14 57
Sankey for Penketh d			11 14					12 14					13 14					14 14				
Widnes d	10 54	11 05	11 19			11 54	12 05	12 19			12 54	13 05	13 19			13 54	14 05	14 19			14 54	15 05
Hough Green d	10 57		11 23			11 57		12 23			12 57		13 23			13 57		14 23			14 57	
Halewood d			11 27					12 27					13 27					14 27				
Hunts Cross 89 d			11 30					12 30					13 30					14 30				
L'pool South Parkway 7 91,103 ✈ a																						
Liverpool Central 10 103 a																						
West Allerton 91 a	11 10		11 39			12 10		12 39			13 10		13 39			14 10		14 39			15 10	
Mossley Hill 91 a	11 13		11 41			12 13		12 41			13 13		13 41			14 13		14 41			15 13	
Edge Hill 90,91 a			11 47					12 47					13 47					14 47				
Liverpool Lime Street 10 90,91 a	11 24	11 31	11 53	11 48	11 57	12 24	12 31	12 53	12 48	12 57	13 24	13 31	13 53	13 48	13 57	14 24	14 31	14 53	14 48	14 57	15 24	15 31

Table 89

Saturdays

Manchester Airport and Manchester - Warrington Central - Liverpool

	NT	NT	TP	NT	EM	NT	NT	TP	NT	EM	NT	NT	TP	NT	EM	NT	NT	TP	EM	NT	NT
			◇1 🛒		◇			◇1 🛒		◇			◇1 🛒		◇			◇1 🛒	◇		
Manchester Airport 85 ✈ d		14 41					15 41					16 41					17 41				18 41
Sheffield 7 78 ⇌ d					14 42					15 42					16 42				17 40		
Stockport 84 d					15 26					16 26					17 26				18 26		
Manchester Picc 10 78,84,85 ⇌ d		15 01	15 07		15 37		16 01	16 07		16 37		17 01	17 07		17 37		18 01	18 07	18 37		19 01
Manchester Oxford Road 84,85 d	14 44	15 04	15 11	15 16	15 41	15 44	16 04	16 11	16 16	16 41	16 43	17 04	17 11	17 13	17 42	17 44	18 04	18 11	18 41	18 44	19 04
Deansgate 84,85 ⇌ d	14 46			15 18		15 46			16 18		16 45			17 15		17 46				18 46	
Trafford Park d				15 23							16 51			17 20		17 51				18 51	
Humphrey Park d				15 25										17 22		17 53				18 53	
Urmston d	14 52			15 27		15 52			16 24		16 54			17 25		17 55				18 55	
Chassen Road d									16 26					17 27		17 57				18 57	
Flixton d				15 30					16 29		16 57			17 29		18 00				19 00	
Irlam d	14 57			15 34		15 57			16 33		17 01			17 33	17 52	18 04				19 04	
Glazebrook d									16 36					17 36		18 07				19 07	
Birchwood d	15 03		15 24	15 40		16 03		16 24	16 40		17 07		17 24	17 41	17 58	18 12		18 24		19 11	
Padgate d	15 06					16 06			16 43		17 10			17 44		18 15				19 14	
Warrington Central a	15 09		15 29	15 45	15 57	16 09		16 29	16 47	16 57	17 13		17 29	17 48	18 03	18 18		18 29	18 57	19 20	
d	15 10		15 29	15 45	15 57	16 10		16 29	16 47	16 57	17 14		17 29	17 48	18 03	18 19		18 29	18 57		
Sankey for Penketh d	15 14					16 14					17 18			17 52							
Widnes d	15 19			15 53	16 05	16 19			16 55	17 05	17 23			17 58	18 11				19 05		
Hough Green d	15 23			15 56		16 23			16 58		17 27			18 01		18 28					
Halewood d	15 27			16 01		16 27					17 31			18 06							
Hunts Cross 89 d	15 30					16 30					17 34		17 40	18 09		18 33			19 12		
L'pool South Parkway 7 91,103 ✈ a																					
Liverpool Central 10 103 a																					
West Allerton 91 a	15 39			16 11		16 39			17 11		17 42			18 18		18 42					
Mossley Hill 91 a	15 41			16 13		16 41			17 13		17 45			18 20		18 44					
Edge Hill 90,91 a	15 47					16 47					17 50			18 30		18 50					
Liverpool Lime Street 10 90,91 a	15 53	15 48	15 57	16 25	16 31	16 54	16 48	16 57	17 25	17 31	17 58	17 48	18 00	18 38	18 35	18 57	19 00	18 59	19 35		19 48

	TP	NT	EM	NT	NT	TP	NT	NT	TP	NT	NT	NT	TP	NT	NT
	◇1		◇			◇1			◇1				◇1		
Manchester Airport 85 ✈ d					19 41							21 41			
Sheffield 7 78 ⇌ d			18 42												
Stockport 84 d			19 26												
Manchester Picc 10 78,84,85 ⇌ d	19 07		19 37		20 01	20 07			21 07	21 38		22 01	22 07		
Manchester Oxford Road 84,85 d	19 11		19 41	19 44	20 04	20 11	20 44		21 11	21 44		22 04	22 11		23 20
Deansgate 84,85 ⇌ d				19 46			20 46			21 46					23 22
Trafford Park d				19 51			20 51			21 51					23 27
Humphrey Park d				19 53			20 53			21 53					23 29
Urmston d				19 55			20 55			21 55					23 31
Chassen Road d				19 57			20 57			21 57					23 33
Flixton d				20 00			21 00			22 00					23 36
Irlam d				20 04			21 04			22 04					23 40
Glazebrook d				20 07			21 07			22 07					23 43
Birchwood d	19 24			20 11		20 24	21 11		21 24	22 11			22 24		23 47
Padgate d				20 14			21 14			22 14					23 50
Warrington Central a	19 29		19 57	20 18		20 29	21 20		21 29	22 20			22 29		23 54
d	19 29	19 34	19 57	20 18		20 29		20 49	21 29		21 49		22 29	22 49	23 54
Sankey for Penketh d		19 38						20 53			21 53			22 53	23 58
Widnes d		19 43	20 05					20 58			21 58			22 58	00 04
Hough Green d		19 46		20 28				21 01			22 01			23 01	00 06
Halewood d		19 51						21 06			22 06			23 06	00 11
Hunts Cross 89 d		19 54		20 33				21 09			22 09			23 09	00 14
L'pool South Parkway 7 91,103 ✈ a															
Liverpool Central 10 103 a															
West Allerton 91 a		20 03		20 41				21 19			22 15			23 15	
Mossley Hill 91 a		20 05		20 44				21 21			22 18			23 18	
Edge Hill 90,91 a		20 11						21 27			22 23			23 23	
Liverpool Lime Street 10 90,91 a	19 57	20 18	20 34	20 55	20 48	20 59		21 34	21 57		22 30	22 48	22 58	23 30	00 34

Table 89

Sundays
until 05 September

Manchester Airport and Manchester - Warrington Central - Liverpool

		NT	NT	NT	TP ◇1	NT	TP ◇1	NT	NT	TP ◇1	EM ◇	NT	NT B	NT C	TP ◇1	EM ◇	NT	NT	TP ◇1	EM ◇	NT	NT
Manchester Airport 85 ✈	d			08 34					10 32				11 35					12 35				13 35
Sheffield 7 78	d										10 41					11 38				12 41		
Stockport 84	d										11 26					12 26				13 26		
Manchester Picc 10 78,84,85	d			08 50	09 07		10 07		10 50	11 07	11 38		11 50	11 50	12 07	12 38		12 50	13 07	13 38		13 50
Manchester Oxford Road 84,85	d	08 06	08 45	08 53	09 11	09 45	10 11	10 45	10 53	11 11	11 42	11 45	11 53	11 53	12 11	12 42	12 45	12 53	13 11	13 42	13 45	13 53
Deansgate 84,85	d	08 08	08 47			09 47		10 47				11 47					12 47				13 47	
Trafford Park	d																					
Humphrey Park	d																					
Urmston	d	08 14	08 53			09 53		10 53				11 53					12 53				13 53	
Chassen Road	d																					
Flixton	d																					
Irlam	d	08 19	08 58			09 58		10 58				11 58					12 58				13 58	
Glazebrook	d																					
Birchwood	d	08 25	09 04		09 24	10 04	10 24	11 04		11 24		12 04			12 24		13 04		13 24		14 04	
Padgate	d																					
Warrington Central	a	08 30	09 09		09 29	10 09	10 29	11 09		11 29	11 58	12 09			12 29	12 58	13 09		13 29	13 58	14 09	
	d	08 30	09 09		09 29	10 09	10 29	11 09		11 29	11 59	12 09			12 29	12 58	13 09		13 29	13 58	14 09	
Sankey for Penketh	d																					
Widnes	d	08 38	09 17			10 17		11 17			12 06	12 17				13 06	13 17			14 06	14 17	
Hough Green	d	08 42	09 21			10 21		11 21				12 21					13 21				14 21	
Halewood	d	08 46	09 25			10 25		11 25				12 25					13 25				14 25	
Hunts Cross 89	d	08 49	09 28			10 28		11 28				12 28					13 28				14 28	
L'pool South Parkway 7 91,103 ✈	a																					
Liverpool Central 10 103	a																					
West Allerton 91	a	08 57	09 36			10 36		11 36				12 36					13 36				14 36	
Mossley Hill 91	a	09 00	09 39			10 39		11 39				12 39					13 39				14 39	
Edge Hill 90,91	a																					
Liverpool Lime Street 10 90,91	a	09 11	09 49	09 54	09 57	10 50	10 57	11 50	11 54	11 57	12 30	12 50	12 54	12 54	12 57	13 30	13 50	13 54	13 57	14 30	14 50	14 54

		TP ◇1	EM ◇	NT	NT	TP ◇1	EM ◇	NT	NT	TP ◇1	EM ◇	NT	NT	TP ◇1	EM ◇	NT	NT	TP ◇1	EM ◇	NT	NT	TP ◇1	EM ◇
Manchester Airport 85 ✈	d				14 35				15 35				16 35				17 35				18 35		
Sheffield 7 78	d		13 38				14 39				15 38				16 44				17 44				18 37
Stockport 84	d		14 26				15 26				16 26				17 27				18 26				19 26
Manchester Picc 10 78,84,85	d	14 07	14 38		14 50	15 07	15 38		15 50	16 07	16 38		16 50	17 07	17 38		17 50	18 07	18 38		18 50	19 07	19 38
Manchester Oxford Road 84,85	d	14 11	14 42	14 45	14 53	15 11	15 42	15 45	15 53	16 11	16 42	16 45	16 53	17 11	17 42	17 45	17 53	18 11	18 42	18 45	18 53	19 11	19 42
Deansgate 84,85	d			14 47				15 47				16 47				17 47				18 47			
Trafford Park	d																						
Humphrey Park	d																						
Urmston	d			14 53				15 53				16 53				17 53				18 53			
Chassen Road	d																						
Flixton	d																						
Irlam	d			14 58				15 58				16 58				17 58				18 58			
Glazebrook	d																						
Birchwood	d	14 24		15 04		15 24		16 04		16 24		17 04		17 24		18 04		18 24		19 04		19 24	
Padgate	d																						
Warrington Central	a	14 29	14 58	15 09		15 29	15 58	16 09		16 29	16 58	17 09		17 29	17 58	18 09		18 29	18 58	19 09		19 29	19 58
	d	14 29	14 58	15 09		15 29	15 58	16 09		16 29	16 58	17 09		17 29	17 58	18 09		18 29	18 58	19 09		19 29	19 58
Sankey for Penketh	d																						
Widnes	d		15 06	15 17			16 06	16 17			17 06	17 17			18 06	18 17			19 06	19 17			20 06
Hough Green	d			15 21				16 21				17 21				18 21				19 21			
Halewood	d			15 25				16 25				17 25				18 25				19 25			
Hunts Cross 89	d			15 28				16 28				17 28				18 28				19 28			
L'pool South Parkway 7 91,103 ✈	a																						
Liverpool Central 10 103	a																						
West Allerton 91	a			15 36				16 36				17 36				18 36				19 36			
Mossley Hill 91	a			15 39				16 39				17 39				18 39				19 39			
Edge Hill 90,91	a																						
Liverpool Lime Street 10 90,91	a	14 57	15 30	15 50	15 54	15 57	16 30	16 50	16 54	16 57	17 30	17 50	17 54	17 57	18 30	18 50	18 54	18 57	19 30	19 50	19 54	19 57	20 30

B from 18 July until 5 September

C until 11 July

Table 89

Sundays
until 05 September

Manchester Airport and Manchester - Warrington Central - Liverpool

		NT	NT	TP ◇1	NT	NT	TP ◇1	NT	NT	TP ◇1	NT	NT
Manchester Airport 85 ✈	d		19 35			20 35			21 35			22 35
Sheffield 7 78	d											
Stockport 84	d											
Manchester Picc 10 78,84,85	d		19 50	20 07		20 50	21 07		21 50	22 07		22 50
Manchester Oxford Road 84,85	d	19 45	19 53	20 11	20 45	20 53	21 11	21 45	21 53	22 11	22 45	22 53
Deansgate 84,85	d	19 47			20 47			21 47			22 47	
Trafford Park	d											
Humphrey Park	d											
Urmston	d	19 53			20 53			21 53			22 53	
Chassen Road	d											
Flixton	d											
Irlam	d	19 58			20 58			21 58			22 58	
Glazebrook	d											
Birchwood	d	20 04		20 24	21 04		21 24	22 04		22 24	23 04	
Padgate	d											
Warrington Central	a	20 09		20 29	21 09		21 29	22 09		22 29	23 09	
	d	20 09		20 29	21 09		21 29	22 09		22 29	23 09	
Sankey for Penketh	d											
Widnes	d	20 17			21 17			22 17			23 17	
Hough Green	d	20 21			21 21			22 21			23 21	
Halewood	d	20 25			21 25			22 25			23 25	
Hunts Cross 89	d	20 28			21 28			22 28			23 28	
L'pool South Parkway 7 91,103 ✈	a											
Liverpool Central 10 103	a											
West Allerton 91	a	20 36			21 36			22 36			23 36	
Mossley Hill 91	a	20 39			21 39			22 39			23 39	
Edge Hill 90,91	a											
Liverpool Lime Street 10 90,91	a	20 50	20 54	20 57	21 50	21 54	21 57	22 50	22 54	22 57	23 50	23 54

Sundays
from 12 September

		NT	NT	NT	NT	NT	NT	EM ◇	NT	NT	EM ◇	NT	NT	EM ◇	NT	NT	NT	NT	EM ◇	NT	NT	TP ◇1
Manchester Airport 85 ✈	d						10 31			11 33			12 35			13 35		14 35			15 35	
Sheffield 7 78	d							10 41			11 38			12 41					14 39			
Stockport 84	d							11 26			12 26			13 26					15 26			
Manchester Picc 10 78,84,85	d				09 50		10 50	11 38		11 50	12 38		12 50	13 38		13 50		14 50	15 38		15 50	16 07
Manchester Oxford Road 84,85	d	07 45	09 13	09 45	09 53	10 45	10 53	11 42	11 45	11 53	12 42	12 45	12 53	13 42	13 45	13 53	14 45	14 53	15 42	15 45	15 53	16 11
Deansgate 84,85	d	07 47	09 15	09 47		10 47			11 47			12 47			13 47		14 47			15 47		
Trafford Park	d																					
Humphrey Park	d																					
Urmston	d	07 53	09 21	09 53		10 53			11 53			12 53			13 53		14 53			15 53		
Chassen Road	d																					
Flixton	d																					
Irlam	d	07 58	09 26	09 58		10 58			11 58			12 58			13 58		14 58			15 58		
Glazebrook	d																					
Birchwood	d	08 04	09 32	10 04		11 04			12 04			13 04			14 04		15 04			16 04		16 24
Padgate	d																					
Warrington Central	a	08 09	09 37	10 09		11 09		11 58	12 09		12 58	13 09		13 58	14 09		15 09		15 58	16 09		16 29
	d	08 31	09 37	10 09		11 09		11 59	12 09		12 58	13 09		13 58	14 09		15 09		15 58	16 09		16 29
Sankey for Penketh	d																					
Widnes	d	08 39	09 45	10 17		11 17		12 06	12 17		13 06	13 17		14 06	14 17		15 17		16 06	16 17		
Hough Green	d	08 42	09 49	10 21		11 21			12 21			13 21			14 21		15 21			16 21		
Halewood	d	08 46	09 53	10 25		11 25			12 25			13 25			14 25		15 25			16 25		
Hunts Cross 89	d	08 49	09 56	10 28		11 28			12 28			13 28			14 28		15 28			16 28		
L'pool South Parkway 7 91,103 ✈	a																					
Liverpool Central 10 103	a																					
West Allerton 91	a	08 58	10 04	10 36		11 36			12 36			13 36			14 36		15 36			16 36		
Mossley Hill 91	a	09 00	10 07	10 39		11 39			12 39			13 39			14 39		15 39			16 39		
Edge Hill 90,91	a																					
Liverpool Lime Street 10 90,91	a	09 12	10 18	10 50	10 54	11 50	11 54	12 30	12 50	12 54	13 30	13 50	13 54	14 30	14 50	14 54	15 50	15 54	16 30	16 50	16 54	16 57

Table 89

Sundays from 12 September

Manchester Airport and Manchester - Warrington Central - Liverpool

	EM ◇	NT	NT	TP ◇1	EM ◇	NT	NT	TP ◇1	EM ◇	NT	NT	TP ◇1	EM ◇	NT	NT	TP ◇1	NT	NT	TP ◇1	NT	NT	TP ◇1
Manchester Airport 85 d			16 35				17 35				18 35				19 35			20 35			21 35	
Sheffield 78 d	15 38				16 44				17 44				18 37									
Stockport 84 d	16 26				17 27				18 26				19 26									
Manchester Picc 78,84,85 d	16 38		16 50	17 07	17 38		17 50	18 07	18 38		18 50	19 07	19 38		19 50	20 07		20 50	21 07		21 50	22 07
Manchester Oxford Road 84,85 d	16 42	16 45	16 53	17 11	17 42	17 45	17 53	18 11	18 42	18 45	18 53	19 11	19 42	19 45	19 53	20 11	20 45	20 53	21 11	21 45	21 53	22 11
Deansgate 84,85 d		16 47				17 47				18 47				19 47			20 47			21 47		
Trafford Park d																						
Humphrey Park d																						
Urmston d		16 53				17 53				18 53				19 53			20 53			21 53		
Chassen Road d																						
Flixton d																						
Irlam d		16 58				17 58				18 58				19 58			20 58			21 58		
Glazebrook d																						
Birchwood d		17 04		17 24		18 04		18 24		19 04		19 24		20 04		20 24	21 04		21 24	22 04		22 24
Padgate d																						
Warrington Central a	16 58	17 09		17 29	17 58	18 09		18 29	18 58	19 09		19 29	19 58	20 09		20 29	21 09		21 29	22 09		22 29
d	16 58	17 09		17 29	17 58	18 09		18 29	18 58	19 09		19 29	19 58	20 09		20 29	21 09		21 29	22 09		22 29
Sankey for Penketh d																						
Widnes d	17 06	17 17			18 06	18 17			19 06	19 17			20 06	20 17			21 17			22 17		
Hough Green d		17 21				18 21				19 21				20 21			21 21			22 21		
Halewood d		17 25				18 25				19 25				20 25			21 25			22 25		
Hunts Cross 89 d		17 28				18 28				19 28				20 28			21 28			22 28		
L'pool South Parkway 91,103 a																						
Liverpool Central 103 a																						
West Allerton 91 a		17 36				18 36				19 36				20 36			21 36			22 36		
Mossley Hill 91 a		17 39				18 39				19 39				20 39			21 39			22 39		
Edge Hill 90,91 a																						
Liverpool Lime Street 90,91 a	17 30	17 50	17 54	17 57	18 30	18 50	18 54	18 57	19 30	19 50	19 54	19 57	20 30	20 50	20 54	20 57	21 50	21 54	21 57	22 50	22 54	22 57

	NT		NT
Manchester Airport 85 d			22 35
Sheffield 78 d			
Stockport 84 d			
Manchester Picc 78,84,85 d			22 50
Manchester Oxford Road 84,85 d	22 45		22 53
Deansgate 84,85 d	22 47		
Trafford Park d			
Humphrey Park d			
Urmston d	22 53		
Chassen Road d			
Flixton d			
Irlam d	22 58		
Glazebrook d			
Birchwood d	23 04		
Padgate d			
Warrington Central a	23 09		
d	23 09		
Sankey for Penketh d			
Widnes d	23 17		
Hough Green d	23 21		
Halewood d	23 25		
Hunts Cross 89 d	23 28		
L'pool South Parkway 91,103 a			
Liverpool Central 103 a			
West Allerton 91 a	23 36		
Mossley Hill 91 a	23 39		
Edge Hill 90,91 a			
Liverpool Lime Street 90,91 a	23 50		23 54

Table 90

Mondays to Fridays

Liverpool and St Helens - Newton-le-Willows, Wigan, Preston and Manchester

	NT	NT	AW	NT	NT	NT	NT	NT	AW ◇	NT	NT	NT	NT	AW	NT
Liverpool Lime Street 89,91 d	05 13	05 31		05 46	06 01	06 13	06 16	06 31		06 46	06 57	07 01	07 13		07 16
Edge Hill 89,91 d		05 35		05 50	06 05		06 20	06 35		06 50		07 05			07 20
Wavertree Technology Park d	05 19	05 37		05 52	06 07	06 19	06 22	06 37		06 52		07 07	07 19		07 22
Broad Green d		05 40		05 55	06 10		06 25	06 40		06 55		07 10			07 25
Roby d		05 44		05 59	06 14		06 29	06 44		06 59		07 14			07 29
Huyton d		05 46		06 01	06 16		06 31	06 46		07 01	07 06	07 16			07 31
Prescot d		05 51			06 21			06 51				07 21			
Eccleston Park d		05 53			06 23			06 53				07 23			
Thatto Heath d		05 56			06 26			06 56				07 26			
St Helens Central a		05 59			06 29			06 59			07 15	07 29			
d		06 00			06 30			07 00			07 15	07 30			
Garswood d		06 07			06 37			07 07				07 37			
Bryn d		06 10			06 40			07 10				07 40			
Whiston d				06 05			06 35			07 05					07 35
Rainhill d				06 08			06 38			07 08					07 38
Lea Green d				06 11			06 41			07 11			07 28		07 41
St Helens Junction d	05 29			06 14		06 29	06 44			07 14			07 31		07 44
Warrington Bank Quay d			06 06						07 07					07 39	
Earlestown d			06 12	06 19			06 50		07 14	07 19				07 46	07 49
Warrington Bank Quay a							07 01								
Newton-le-Willows d	05 35		06 15	06 22		06 35			07 17	07 22			07 37	07 49	07 52
Wigan North Western 65 a		06 21			06 51			07 21			07 30	07 51			
d											07 31				
Euxton Balshaw Lane d											07 41				
Leyland 82 a											07 46				
Preston 65,82 a											07 56				
Blackpool North 97 a															
Patricroft d				06 34						07 34					08 04
Eccles d				06 36						07 36					08 06
Manchester Victoria a				06 49						07 49					08 19
Manchester Oxford Road a			06 35			06 57			07 41				07 57	08 09	
Manchester Piccadilly a	05 57		06 46			07 01			07 50				08 01	08 18	
Manchester Airport 85 a	06 14					07 22							08 22		

	NT	AW ◇	NT	NT	NT	NT	NT	NT	NT	NT	NT	AW ◇	NT	NT	NT	NT	NT	NT	AW ◇	NT	NT	NT	NT
Liverpool Lime Street 89,91 d	07 31		07 46	07 57	08 01	08 13	08 16	08 31	08 44	08 57	09 01		09 13	09 18	09 31	09 46	09 57	10 01		10 13	10 16	10 31	10 46
Edge Hill 89,91 d	07 35		07 50		08 05		08 20	08 35	08 50		09 05			09 20	09 35	09 50		10 05			10 20	10 35	10 50
Wavertree Technology Park d	07 37		07 52		08 07	08 19	08 22	08 37	08 52		09 07		09 19	09 22	09 37	09 52		10 07		10 19	10 22	10 37	10 52
Broad Green d	07 40		07 55		08 10		08 25	08 40	08 55		09 10			09 25	09 40	09 55		10 10			10 25	10 40	10 55
Roby d	07 44		07 59		08 14		08 29	08 44	08 59		09 14			09 29	09 44	09 59		10 14			10 29	10 44	10 59
Huyton d	07 46		08 01	08 06	08 16		08 31	08 46	09 01	09 06	09 16			09 31	09 46	10 01	10 06	10 16			10 31	10 46	11 01
Prescot d	07 51				08 21			08 51			09 21				09 51			10 21				10 51	
Eccleston Park d	07 53				08 23			08 53			09 23				09 53			10 23				10 53	
Thatto Heath d	07 56				08 26			08 56			09 26				09 56			10 26				10 56	
St Helens Central a	07 59			08 15	08 29			08 59		09 15	09 29				09 59		10 15	10 29				10 59	
d	08 00			08 15	08 30			09 00		09 15	09 30				10 00		10 15	10 30				11 00	
Garswood d	08 07				08 37			09 07			09 37				10 07			10 37				11 07	
Bryn d	08 10				08 40			09 10			09 40				10 10			10 40				11 10	
Whiston d			08 05				08 35		09 05					09 35		10 05					10 35		11 05
Rainhill d			08 08				08 38		09 08					09 38		10 08					10 38		11 08
Lea Green d			08 11				08 41		09 11					09 41		10 11					10 41		11 11
St Helens Junction d			08 14			08 29	08 44		09 14				09 29	09 44		10 14				10 29	10 44		11 14
Warrington Bank Quay d		08 08										09 19							10 19				
Earlestown d		08 16	08 19				08 50		09 19			09 26		09 50		10 19			10 26		10 50		11 19
Warrington Bank Quay a							09 01							10 01							11 01		
Newton-le-Willows d		08 19	08 22			08 35			09 22			09 29	09 35			10 22			10 29	10 35			11 22
Wigan North Western 65 a	08 21			08 30	08 51			09 21		09 30	09 51				10 21		10 30	10 51				11 21	
d				08 31						09 31							10 31						
Euxton Balshaw Lane d				08 41						09 41							10 41						
Leyland 82 a				08 46						09 46							10 46						
Preston 65,82 a				08 56						09 54							10 54						
Blackpool North 97 a										10 21							11 21						
Patricroft d			08 34						09 34							10 34							11 34
Eccles d			08 36						09 36							10 36							11 36
Manchester Victoria a			08 50						09 47							10 49							11 49
Manchester Oxford Road a		08 41				08 57						09 48	09 57						10 48	10 57			
Manchester Piccadilly a		08 50				09 01						09 57	10 01						10 57	11 01			
Manchester Airport 85 a						09 22							10 22							11 22			

Liverpool and St Helens - Newton-le-Willows, Wigan, Preston and Manchester

	NT	NT	AW	NT	NT	NT	NT	NT	NT	AW	NT	NT	NT	NT	NT	NT	AW	NT	NT	NT	NT
			◇							◇							◇				
Liverpool Lime Street [10] 89,91 d	10 57	11 01		11 13	11 16	11 31	11 46	11 57	12 01		12 13	12 16	12 31	12 46	12 57	13 01		13 13	13 16	13 31	13 46
Edge Hill 89,91 d		11 05			11 20	11 35	11 50		12 05			12 20	12 35	12 50		13 05			13 20	13 35	13 50
Wavertree Technology Park d		11 07		11 19	11 22	11 37	11 52		12 07		12 19	12 22	12 37	12 52		13 07		13 19	13 22	13 37	13 52
Broad Green d		11 10			11 25	11 40	11 55		12 10			12 25	12 40	12 55		13 10			13 25	13 40	13 55
Roby d		11 14			11 29	11 44	11 59		12 14			12 29	12 44	12 59		13 14			13 29	13 44	13 59
Huyton d	11 06	11 16			11 31	11 46	12 01	12 06	12 16			12 31	12 46	13 01	13 06	13 16			13 31	13 46	14 01
Prescot d		11 21				11 51			12 21				12 51			13 21				13 51	
Eccleston Park d		11 23				11 53			12 23				12 53			13 23				13 53	
Thatto Heath d		11 26				11 56			12 26				12 56			13 26				13 56	
St Helens Central a	11 15	11 29				11 59		12 15	12 29				12 59		13 15	13 29				13 59	
d	11 15	11 30				12 00		12 15	12 30				13 00		13 15	13 30				14 00	
Garswood d		11 37				12 07			12 37				13 07			13 37				14 07	
Bryn d		11 40				12 10			12 40				13 10			13 40				14 10	
Whiston d					11 35		12 05					12 35		13 05					13 35		14 05
Rainhill d					11 38		12 08					12 38		13 08					13 38		14 08
Lea Green d					11 41		12 11					12 41		13 11					13 41		14 11
St Helens Junction d				11 29	11 44		12 14				12 29	12 44		13 14				13 29	13 44		14 14
Warrington Bank Quay d			11 19							12 19							13 19				
Earlestown [8] d			11 26		11 50		12 19			12 26		12 50		13 19			13 26		13 50		14 19
Warrington Bank Quay a					12 01							13 01							14 01		
Newton-le-Willows d			11 29	11 35			12 22			12 29	12 35			13 22			13 29	13 35			14 22
Wigan North Western 65 a	11 30	11 51				12 21		12 30	12 51				13 21		13 30	13 51				14 21	
d	11 31							12 31							13 31						
Euxton Balshaw Lane d	11 41							12 41							13 41						
Leyland 82 a	11 46							12 46							13 46						
Preston [8] 65,82 a	11 54							12 54							13 54						
Blackpool North 97 a	12 21							13 21							14 21						
Patricroft d							12 34							13 34							14 34
Eccles d							12 36							13 36							14 36
Manchester Victoria a							12 50							13 47							14 50
Manchester Oxford Road a			11 48	11 57						12 48	12 57						13 48	13 57			
Manchester Piccadilly [10] a			11 57	12 01						12 57	13 01						13 57	14 01			
Manchester Airport 85 a				12 22							13 22							14 22			

	NT	NT	AW	NT	NT	NT	NT	NT	NT	AW	NT	NT	NT	NT	NT	NT	AW	NT	NT	NT	NT	AW
			◇							◇							◇					◇
Liverpool Lime Street [10] 89,91 d	13 57	14 01		14 13	14 16	14 31	14 46	14 57	15 01		15 13	15 16	15 31	15 46	15 57	16 01		16 13	16 16	16 27	16 31	
Edge Hill 89,91 d		14 05			14 20	14 35	14 50		15 05			15 20	15 35	15 50		16 05			16 20		16 35	
Wavertree Technology Park d		14 07		14 19	14 22	14 37	14 52		15 07		15 19	15 22	15 37	15 52		16 07		16 19	16 22		16 37	
Broad Green d		14 10			14 25	14 40	14 55		15 10			15 25	15 40	15 55		16 10			16 25		16 40	
Roby d		14 14			14 29	14 44	14 59		15 14			15 29	15 44	15 59		16 14			16 29		16 44	
Huyton d	14 06	14 16			14 31	14 46	15 01	15 06	15 16			15 31	15 46	16 01	16 06	16 16			16 31		16 46	
Prescot d		14 21				14 51			15 21				15 51			16 21					16 51	
Eccleston Park d		14 23				14 53			15 23				15 53			16 23					16 53	
Thatto Heath d		14 26				14 56			15 26				15 56			16 26					16 56	
St Helens Central a	14 15	14 29				14 59		15 15	15 29				15 59		16 15	16 29					16 59	
d	14 15	14 30				15 00		15 15	15 30				16 00		16 15	16 30					17 00	
Garswood d		14 37				15 07			15 37				16 07			16 37					17 07	
Bryn d		14 40				15 10			15 40				16 10			16 40					17 10	
Whiston d					14 35		15 05					15 35		16 05					16 35			
Rainhill d					14 38		15 08					15 38		16 08					16 38			
Lea Green d					14 41		15 11					15 41		16 11					16 41			
St Helens Junction d				14 29	14 44		15 14				15 29	15 44		16 14				16 29	16 44			
Warrington Bank Quay d			14 19							15 19							16 19					16 51
Earlestown [8] d			14 26		14 50		15 19			15 26		15 50		16 19			16 26		16 49			16 59
Warrington Bank Quay a					15 01							16 01										
Newton-le-Willows d			14 29	14 35			15 22			15 29	15 35			16 22			16 29	16 35	16 52			17 02
Wigan North Western 65 a	14 30	14 51				15 21		15 30	15 51				16 21		16 29	16 51					17 21	
d	14 31							15 31							16 31							
Euxton Balshaw Lane d	14 41							15 41							16 42							
Leyland 82 a	14 46							15 46							16 47							
Preston [8] 65,82 a	14 54							15 54							16 56							
Blackpool North 97 a	15 21							16 21							17 24							
Patricroft d							15 34							16 34					17 04			
Eccles d							15 36							16 36					17 06			
Manchester Victoria a							15 49							16 49					17 20			
Manchester Oxford Road a			14 48	14 57						15 48	15 57						16 48	16 57		17 36		17 21
Manchester Piccadilly [10] a			14 57	15 01						15 57	16 01						16 57	17 01				17 30
Manchester Airport 85 a				15 22							16 22							17 22				

Table 90 — Mondays to Fridays

Liverpool and St Helens - Newton-le-Willows, Wigan, Preston and Manchester

	NT	NT	NT	NT	NT	NT	NT	AW	NT	NT	NT	NT	NT	NT	NT	AW	NT	NT	AW	NT	NT
								◇								◇					
Liverpool Lime Street [10] 89,91 d	16 46	16 57	17 01	17 06	17 10	17 19	17 27		17 35	17 44	17 48	18 01	18 13	18 16	18 31		18 46	19 01		19 12	19 23
Edge Hill 89,91 d	16 50		17 05		17 14		17 31		17 39		17 52	18 05		18 20	18 35		18 50	19 05		19 16	
Wavertree Technology Park d	16 52		17 07	17 12	17 16		17 33		17 41	17 49	17 54	18 07	18 19	18 22	18 37		18 52	19 07		19 18	
Broad Green d	16 55		17 10		17 19		17 36		17 44	17 52	17 57	18 10		18 25	18 40		18 55	19 10		19 21	
Roby d	16 59		17 14		17 23		17 40		17 48		18 01	18 14		18 29	18 44		18 59	19 14		19 25	
Huyton d	17 01	17 06	17 16	17 19	17 25	17 29	17 42		17 50	17 57	18 03	18 16		18 31	18 46		19 01	19 16		19 27	19 32
Prescot d			17 21			17 33				18 02		18 21			18 51			19 21			
Eccleston Park d			17 23			17 36				18 05		18 23			18 53			19 23			
Thatto Heath d			17 26			17 38				18 07		18 26			18 56			19 26			
St Helens Central a		17 15	17 29			17 42	17 51			18 11		18 29			18 59			19 29			19 40
d		17 15	17 30			17 42	17 51			18 11		18 30			19 00			19 30			19 41
Garswood d			17 37			17 49				18 19		18 37			19 07			19 37			
Bryn d			17 40			17 52				18 22		18 40			19 10			19 40			
Whiston d	17 05				17 28				17 54		18 07			18 35			19 05			19 31	
Rainhill d	17 08				17 32				17 57		18 10			18 38			19 08			19 34	
Lea Green d	17 11			17 26	17 35				18 00		18 13			18 41			19 11			19 37	
St Helens Junction d	17 14			17 29	17 39				18 03		18 16		18 29	18 44			19 14			19 40	
Warrington Bank Quay d								17 49								18 46			19 19		
Earlestown [8] d	17 19				17 44			17 57	18 08		18 21			18 50		18 57	19 19		19 26	19 45	
Warrington Bank Quay a														19 01							
Newton-le-Willows d	17 22			17 35	17 47			18 00	18 11		18 24		18 35			19 00	19 22		19 29	19 48	
Wigan North Western 65 a		17 30	17 52			18 04	18 04			18 30		18 49			19 21			19 51			19 54
d		17 31					18 05			18 31		18 49									19 55
Euxton Balshaw Lane d		17 41					18 16			18 41		19 01									20 05
Leyland 82 a		17 46					18 21			18 46		19 06									20 10
Preston [8] 65,82 a		17 54					18 31			18 54		19 15									20 18
Blackpool North 97 a		18 24								19 23											20 44
Patricroft d	17 34				17 59				18 23								19 34			20 00	
Eccles d	17 36				18 01				18 25		18 36						19 36			20 02	
Manchester Victoria a	17 47				18 14				18 41		18 49						19 49			20 16	
Manchester Oxford Road a				17 57				18 19					18 57			19 21			19 48		
Manchester Piccadilly [10] a				18 01				18 28					19 01			19 29			19 52		
Manchester Airport 85 a				18 22									19 24						20 13		

	NT	AW	NT	NT	NT	NT	AW	NT	TP	NT	AW	NT	NT	NT	AW
		◇					◇		◇ [1]						
Liverpool Lime Street [10] 89,91 d	19 42		20 09	20 12	20 25	20 42		21 12		21 42		22 12	23 02	23 16	
Edge Hill 89,91 d	19 46			20 16		20 46		21 16		21 46		22 16	23 06	23 20	
Wavertree Technology Park d	19 48		20 15	20 18		20 48		21 18		21 48		22 18	23 08	23 22	
Broad Green d	19 51			20 21		20 51		21 21		21 51		22 21	23 11	23 26	
Roby d	19 55			20 25		20 55		21 25		21 55		22 25	23 15	23 30	
Huyton d	19 57			20 27	20 34	20 57		21 27		21 57		22 27	23 17	23 32	
Prescot d	20 02					21 02				22 02			23 22		
Eccleston Park d	20 04					21 04				22 04			23 24		
Thatto Heath d	20 07					21 07				22 07			23 27		
St Helens Central a	20 10				20 42	21 10				22 10			23 30		
d	20 11				20 43	21 11				22 11			23 31		
Garswood d	20 18					21 18				22 18			23 38		
Bryn d	20 21					21 21				22 21			23 41		
Whiston d				20 31				21 31				22 31		23 36	
Rainhill d				20 34				21 34				22 34		23 39	
Lea Green d				20 37				21 37				22 37		23 42	
St Helens Junction d			20 25	20 40				21 40				22 40		23 45	
Warrington Bank Quay d		20 19					21 19				22 19				23 49
Earlestown [8] d		20 26		20 45			21 26	21 45			22 26	22 45		23 50	23 56
Warrington Bank Quay a															
Newton-le-Willows d		20 29	20 35	20 48			21 29	21 48			22 29	22 48		23 53	23 59
Wigan North Western 65 a	20 32				20 57	21 32			21 47	22 28			23 48		
d					20 57				21 48	22 28			23 48		
Euxton Balshaw Lane d					21 08					22 39			23 59		
Leyland 82 a					21 16					22 44			00 04		
Preston [8] 65,82 a					21 22					22 55			00 13		
Blackpool North 97 a					21 53					23 22					
Patricroft d				21 00				22 00				23 00		00 05	
Eccles d				21 02				22 02				23 02		00 08	
Manchester Victoria a				21 15				22 15				23 15		00 21	
Manchester Oxford Road a		20 48	20 57				21 48		22 26		22 50				
Manchester Piccadilly [10] a		20 52	21 01				21 57		22 30		22 58				00 28
Manchester Airport 85 a		21 13	21 24						22 47						

Table 90

Liverpool and St Helens - Newton-le-Willows, Wigan, Preston and Manchester

Saturdays until 16 October

	NT	NT	AW	NT	NT	NT	NT	NT	NT	AW ◇	NT	NT	NT	NT	AW 🛒	NT	NT	NT
Liverpool Lime Street 89,91 d	05 13	05 31		05 46	06 01	06 13	06 16	06 25	06 31		06 46	06 57	07 01	07 13		07 16	07 26	07 31
Edge Hill 89,91 d		05 35		05 50	06 05		06 20		06 35		06 50		07 05			07 20	07 30	07 35
Wavertree Technology Park d	05 19	05 37		05 52	06 07	06 19	06 22		06 37		06 52		07 07	07 19		07 22		07 37
Broad Green d		05 40		05 55	06 10		06 25		06 40		06 55		07 10			07 25		07 40
Roby d		05 44		05 59	06 14		06 29		06 44		06 59		07 14			07 29		07 44
Huyton d		05 46		06 01	06 16		06 31		06 46		07 01	07 06	07 16			07 31		07 46
Prescot d		05 51			06 21				06 51				07 21					07 51
Eccleston Park d		05 53			06 23				06 53				07 23					07 53
Thatto Heath d		05 56			06 26				06 56				07 26					07 56
St Helens Central a		05 59			06 29				06 59			07 15	07 29					07 59
d		06 00			06 30				07 00			07 15	07 30					08 00
Garswood d		06 07			06 37				07 07				07 37					08 07
Bryn d		06 10			06 40				07 10				07 40					08 10
Whiston d				06 05			06 35				07 05					07 35		
Rainhill d				06 08			06 38				07 08					07 38		
Lea Green d				06 11			06 41				07 11			07 28		07 41		
St Helens Junction d	05 29			06 14		06 29	06 44				07 14			07 31		07 44		
Warrington Bank Quay d			06 06							06 40					07 39			
Earlestown ■ d			06 12	06 19			06 50			06 47	07 19				07 46	07 49		
Warrington Bank Quay a							07 01											
Newton-le-Willows d	05 35		06 15	06 22		06 35				06 50	07 22			07 37	07 49	07 52		
Wigan North Western 65 a		06 21			06 51				07 21			07 30	07 51					08 21
d												07 31						
Euxton Balshaw Lane d												07 41						
Leyland 82 a												07 46						
Preston ■ 65,82 a												07 54						
Blackpool North 97 a												08 21						
Patricroft d				06 34							07 34					08 04		
Eccles d				06 36							07 36					08 06		
Manchester Victoria a				06 49							07 49					08 19		
Manchester Oxford Road a			06 35			06 57		07 37		07 09				07 57	08 09		08 36	
Manchester Piccadilly ■ a	05 57		06 46			07 01				07 18				08 01	08 18			
Manchester Airport 85 a	06 14					07 22								08 22				

	AW ◇ 🛒	NT	NT	NT	NT	NT	NT	NT	NT	NT	AW ◇ 🛒	NT	NT	NT	NT	NT	AW ◇ 🛒	NT	NT	NT	NT	NT	NT	AW ◇ 🛒
Liverpool Lime Street 89,91 d		07 46	07 57	08 01	08 13	08 16	08 31	08 44	08 57	09 01		09 13	09 31	09 46	09 57	10 01		10 13	10 16	10 31	10 46	10 57	11 01	
Edge Hill 89,91 d		07 50		08 05		08 20	08 35	08 50		09 05			09 35	09 50		10 05			10 20	10 35	10 50		11 05	
Wavertree Technology Park d		07 52		08 07	08 19	08 22	08 37	08 52		09 07		09 19	09 37	09 52		10 07		10 19	10 22	10 37	10 52		11 07	
Broad Green d		07 55		08 10		08 25	08 40	08 55		09 10			09 40	09 55		10 10			10 25	10 40	10 55		11 10	
Roby d		07 59		08 14		08 29	08 44	08 59		09 14			09 44	09 59		10 14			10 29	10 44	10 59		11 14	
Huyton d		08 01	08 06	08 16		08 31	08 46	09 01	09 06	09 16			09 46	10 01	10 06	10 16			10 31	10 46	11 01	11 06	11 16	
Prescot d				08 21			08 51			09 21			09 51			10 21				10 51			11 21	
Eccleston Park d				08 23			08 53			09 23			09 53			10 23				10 53			11 23	
Thatto Heath d				08 26			08 56			09 26			09 56			10 26				10 56			11 26	
St Helens Central a			08 15	08 29			08 59		09 15	09 29			09 59		10 15	10 29				10 59		11 15	11 29	
d			08 15	08 30			09 00		09 15	09 30			10 00		10 15	10 30				11 00		11 15	11 30	
Garswood d				08 37			09 07			09 37			10 07			10 37				11 07			11 37	
Bryn d				08 40			09 10			09 40			10 10			10 40				11 10			11 40	
Whiston d		08 05				08 35		09 05						10 05					10 35		11 05			
Rainhill d		08 08				08 38		09 08						10 08					10 38		11 08			
Lea Green d		08 11				08 41		09 11						10 11					10 41		11 11			
St Helens Junction d		08 14			08 29	08 44		09 14				09 29		10 14				10 29	10 44		11 14			
Warrington Bank Quay d	08 08										09 19						10 19							11 19
Earlestown ■ d	08 16	08 19				08 50		09 19			09 26			10 19			10 26		10 50		11 19			11 26
Warrington Bank Quay a						09 01													11 01					
Newton-le-Willows d	08 19	08 22			08 35			09 22			09 29	09 35		10 22			10 29	10 35			11 22			11 29
Wigan North Western 65 a			08 30	08 51			09 21		09 30	09 51			10 21		10 30	10 51				11 21		11 30	11 51	
d			08 31						09 31						10 31							11 31		
Euxton Balshaw Lane d			08 41						09 41						10 41							11 41		
Leyland 82 a			08 46						09 46						10 46							11 46		
Preston ■ 65,82 a			08 54						09 54						10 54							11 54		
Blackpool North 97 a			09 21						10 21						11 21							12 21		
Patricroft d		08 34						09 34						10 34							11 34			
Eccles d		08 36						09 36						10 36							11 36			
Manchester Victoria a		08 50						09 47						10 49							11 49			
Manchester Oxford Road a	08 41				08 57						09 48	09 57					10 48	10 57						11 48
Manchester Piccadilly ■ a	08 50				09 01						09 57	10 01					10 57	11 01						11 57
Manchester Airport 85 a					09 22							10 22						11 22						

Table 90

Liverpool and St Helens - Newton-le-Willows, Wigan, Preston and Manchester

Saturdays until 16 October

	NT	NT	NT	NT	NT	NT	AW ◇ 🛒	NT	NT	NT	NT	NT	NT	AW ◇ 🛒	NT	NT	NT	NT	NT	NT	AW ◇ 🛒
Liverpool Lime Street 89,91 d	11 13	11 16	11 31	11 46	11 57	12 01		12 13	12 16	12 31	12 46	12 57	13 01		13 13	13 16	13 31	13 46	13 57	14 01	
Edge Hill 89,91 d		11 20	11 35	11 50		12 05			12 20	12 35	12 50		13 05			13 20	13 35	13 50		14 05	
Wavertree Technology Park d	11 19	11 22	11 37	11 52		12 07		12 19	12 22	12 37	12 52		13 07		13 19	13 22	13 37	13 52		14 07	
Broad Green d		11 25	11 40	11 55		12 10			12 25	12 40	12 55		13 10			13 25	13 40	13 55		14 10	
Roby d		11 29	11 44	11 59		12 14			12 29	12 44	12 59		13 14			13 29	13 44	13 59		14 14	
Huyton d		11 31	11 46	12 01	12 06	12 16			12 31	12 46	13 01	13 06	13 16			13 31	13 46	14 01	14 06	14 16	
Prescot d			11 51			12 21				12 51			13 21				13 51			14 21	
Eccleston Park d			11 53			12 23				12 53			13 23				13 53			14 23	
Thatto Heath d			11 56			12 26				12 56			13 26				13 56			14 26	
St Helens Central a			11 59		12 15	12 29				12 59		13 15	13 29				13 59		14 15	14 29	
d			12 00		12 15	12 30				13 00		13 15	13 30				14 00		14 15	14 30	
Garswood d			12 07			12 37				13 07			13 37				14 07			14 37	
Bryn d			12 10			12 40				13 10			13 40				14 10			14 40	
Whiston d		11 35		12 05					12 35		13 05					13 35		14 05			
Rainhill d		11 38		12 08					12 38		13 08					13 38		14 08			
Lea Green d		11 41		12 11					12 41		13 11					13 41		14 11			
St Helens Junction d	11 29	11 44		12 14				12 29	12 44		13 14				13 29	13 44		14 14			
Warrington Bank Quay d							12 19							13 19							14 19
Earlestown ■ d		11 50		12 19			12 26		12 50		13 19			13 26		13 50		14 19			14 26
Warrington Bank Quay a		12 01							13 01							14 01					
Newton-le-Willows d	11 35			12 22			12 29	12 35			13 22			13 29	13 35			14 22			14 29
Wigan North Western 65 a			12 21		12 30	12 51				13 21		13 30	13 51				14 21		14 30	14 51	
d					12 31							13 31							14 31		
Euxton Balshaw Lane d					12 41							13 41							14 41		
Leyland 82 a					12 46							13 46							14 46		
Preston ■ 65,82 a					12 54							13 54							14 54		
Blackpool North 97 a					13 21							14 21							15 21		
Patricroft d				12 34							13 34							14 34			
Eccles d				12 36							13 36							14 36			
Manchester Victoria a				12 49							13 49							14 50			
Manchester Oxford Road a	11 57						12 48	12 57						13 48	13 57						14 48
Manchester Piccadilly ■ a	12 01						12 57	13 01						13 57	14 01						14 57
Manchester Airport 85 a	12 22							13 22							14 22						

	NT	NT	NT	NT	NT	NT	AW ◇ 🛒	NT	NT	NT	NT	NT	NT	AW ◇ 🛒	NT	NT	NT	NT	NT	NT	AW ◇ 🛒	NT
Liverpool Lime Street 89,91 d	14 13	14 16	14 31	14 46	14 57	15 01		15 13	15 16	15 31	15 46	15 57	16 01		16 13	16 16	16 31	16 46	16 57	17 01		17 06
Edge Hill 89,91 d		14 20	14 35	14 50		15 05			15 20	15 35	15 50		16 05			16 20	16 35	16 50		17 05		
Wavertree Technology Park d	14 19	14 22	14 37	14 52		15 07		15 19	15 22	15 37	15 52		16 07		16 19	16 22	16 37	16 52		17 07		17 12
Broad Green d		14 25	14 40	14 55		15 10			15 25	15 40	15 55		16 10			16 25	16 40	16 55		17 10		
Roby d		14 29	14 44	14 59		15 14			15 29	15 44	15 59		16 14			16 29	16 44	16 59		17 14		
Huyton d		14 31	14 46	15 01	15 06	15 16			15 31	15 46	16 01	16 06	16 16			16 31	16 46	17 01	17 06	17 16		17 19
Prescot d			14 51			15 21				15 51			16 21				16 51			17 21		
Eccleston Park d			14 53			15 23				15 53			16 23				16 53			17 23		
Thatto Heath d			14 56			15 26				15 56			16 26				16 56			17 26		
St Helens Central a			14 59		15 15	15 29				15 59		16 15	16 29				16 59		17 15	17 29		
d			15 00		15 15	15 30				16 00		16 15	16 30				17 00		17 15	17 30		
Garswood d			15 07			15 37				16 07			16 37				17 07			17 37		
Bryn d			15 10			15 40				16 10			16 40				17 10			17 40		
Whiston d		14 35		15 05					15 35		16 05					16 35		17 05				
Rainhill d		14 38		15 08					15 38		16 08					16 38		17 08				
Lea Green d		14 41		15 11					15 41		16 11					16 41		17 11				17 26
St Helens Junction d	14 29	14 44		15 14				15 29	15 44		16 14				16 29	16 44		17 14				17 29
Warrington Bank Quay d							15 19							16 19							17 19	
Earlestown ■ d		14 50		15 19			15 26		15 50		16 19			16 26		16 49		17 19			17 26	
Warrington Bank Quay a		15 01							16 01													
Newton-le-Willows d	14 35			15 22			15 29	15 35			16 22			16 29	16 35	16 52		17 22			17 29	17 35
Wigan North Western 65 a			15 21		15 30	15 51				16 21		16 30	16 51				17 21		17 30	17 52		
d					15 31							16 31							17 31			
Euxton Balshaw Lane d					15 41							16 41							17 41			
Leyland 82 a					15 46							16 46							17 46			
Preston ■ 65,82 a					15 54							16 54							17 54			
Blackpool North 97 a					16 21							17 21							18 24			
Patricroft d				15 34							16 34					17 04		17 34				
Eccles d				15 36							16 36					17 06		17 36				
Manchester Victoria a				15 49							16 49					17 20		17 47				
Manchester Oxford Road a	14 57						15 48	15 57						16 48	16 57						17 48	17 57
Manchester Piccadilly ■ a	15 01						15 57	16 01						16 57	17 01						17 57	18 01
Manchester Airport 85 a	15 22							16 22							17 22							18 22

Table 90

Saturdays
until 16 October

Liverpool and St Helens - Newton-le-Willows, Wigan, Preston and Manchester

		NT	NT	NT	NT	NT	NT	NT	AW ◇ ✠	NT	NT	NT	NT	NT	AW	NT	NT	NT	AW ◇ ✠	NT	NT	NT
Liverpool Lime Street 10 89,91	d	17 10	17 19	17 27	17 35	17 44	17 48	18 01		18 13	18 16	18 31	18 46	19 01		19 12	19 23	19 42		20 09	20 12	20 25
Edge Hill 89,91	d	17 14		17 31	17 39		17 52	18 05			18 20	18 35	18 50	19 05		19 16		19 46			20 16	
Wavertree Technology Park	d	17 16		17 33	17 41	17 49	17 54	18 07		18 19	18 22	18 37	18 52	19 07		19 18		19 48		20 15	20 18	
Broad Green	d	17 19		17 36	17 44	17 52	17 57	18 10			18 25	18 40	18 55	19 10		19 21		19 51			20 21	
Roby	d	17 23		17 40	17 48		18 01	18 14			18 29	18 44	18 59	19 14		19 25		19 55			20 25	
Huyton	d	17 25	17 29	17 42	17 50	17 57	18 03	18 16			18 31	18 46	19 01	19 16		19 27	19 32	19 57			20 27	20 34
Prescot	d		17 33			18 02		18 21				18 51		19 21				20 02				
Eccleston Park	d		17 36			18 05		18 23				18 53		19 23				20 04				
Thatto Heath	d		17 38			18 07		18 26				18 56		19 26				20 07				
St Helens Central	a		17 42	17 51		18 11		18 29				18 59		19 29			19 40	20 10				20 42
	d		17 42	17 51		18 11		18 30				19 00		19 30			19 41	20 11				20 43
Garswood	d		17 49			18 19		18 37				19 07		19 37				20 18				
Bryn	d		17 52			18 22		18 40				19 10		19 40				20 21				
Whiston	d	17 28			17 54		18 07				18 35		19 05			19 31					20 31	
Rainhill	d	17 32			17 57		18 10				18 38		19 08			19 34					20 34	
Lea Green	d	17 35			18 00		18 13				18 41		19 11			19 37					20 37	
St Helens Junction	d	17 39			18 03		18 16			18 29	18 44		19 14			19 40				20 25	20 40	
Warrington Bank Quay	d								18 19						19 19				20 19			
Earlestown 8	d	17 44			18 08		18 21		18 26		18 50		19 19		19 26	19 45			20 26		20 45	
Warrington Bank Quay	a										19 01											
Newton-le-Willows	d	17 47			18 11		18 24		18 29	18 35			19 22		19 29	19 48			20 29	20 35	20 48	
Wigan North Western 65	a		18 04	18 05		18 30		18 49				19 21		19 51			19 54	20 32				20 57
	d			18 05		18 31		18 49									19 55					20 57
Euxton Balshaw Lane	d			18 16		18 41		19 01									20 05					21 08
Leyland 82	a			18 21		18 46		19 06									20 10					21 16
Preston 8 65,82	a			18 31		18 54		19 15									20 18					21 22
Blackpool North 97	a					19 21											20 44					21 53
Patricroft	d	17 59			18 23								19 34			20 00					21 00	
Eccles	d	18 01			18 25		18 36						19 36			20 02					21 02	
Manchester Victoria ⇌	a	18 15			18 41		18 49						19 49			20 15					21 15	
Manchester Oxford Road	a								18 48	18 57					19 48				20 48	20 57		
Manchester Piccadilly 10 ⇌	a								18 57	19 01					19 52				20 57	21 01		
Manchester Airport 85 ✈	a									19 24					20 13					21 24		

		NT	AW ◇ ✠	NT	NT	AW	NT	NT	NT	AW
Liverpool Lime Street 10 89,91	d	20 42		21 12	21 42		22 12	23 02	23 16	
Edge Hill 89,91	d	20 46		21 16	21 46		22 16	23 06	23 20	
Wavertree Technology Park	d	20 48		21 18	21 48		22 18	23 08	23 22	
Broad Green	d	20 51		21 21	21 51		22 21	23 11	23 26	
Roby	d	20 55		21 25	21 55		22 25	23 15	23 30	
Huyton	d	20 57		21 27	21 57		22 27	23 17	23 32	
Prescot	d	21 02			22 02			23 22		
Eccleston Park	d	21 04			22 04			23 24		
Thatto Heath	d	21 07			22 07			23 27		
St Helens Central	a	21 10			22 10			23 30		
	d	21 11			22 11			23 31		
Garswood	d	21 18			22 18			23 38		
Bryn	d	21 21			22 21			23 41		
Whiston	d			21 31			22 31		23 36	
Rainhill	d			21 34			22 34		23 39	
Lea Green	d			21 37			22 37		23 42	
St Helens Junction	d			21 40			22 40		23 45	
Warrington Bank Quay	d		21 19			22 19				23 50
Earlestown 8	d		21 26	21 45		22 27	22 45		23 50	23 58
Warrington Bank Quay	a									
Newton-le-Willows	d		21 29	21 48		22 30	22 48		23 53	00 01
Wigan North Western 65	a	21 32			22 28			23 48		
	d				22 28			23 48		
Euxton Balshaw Lane	d				22 39			23 59		
Leyland 82	a				22 44			00 04		
Preston 8 65,82	a				22 55			00 13		
Blackpool North 97	a				23 22					
Patricroft	d			22 00			23 00		00 05	
Eccles	d			22 02			23 02		00 08	
Manchester Victoria ⇌	a			22 15			23 15		00 21	
Manchester Oxford Road	a		21 48			22 50				
Manchester Piccadilly 10 ⇌	a		21 57			22 58				00 26
Manchester Airport 85 ✈	a									

Table 90

Saturdays
from 23 October

Liverpool and St Helens - Newton-le-Willows, Wigan, Preston and Manchester

		NT	NT	AW	NT	NT	NT	NT	NT	NT	AW ◇	NT	NT	NT	NT	AW ✠	NT	NT	NT
Liverpool Lime Street 10 89,91	d	05 13	05 31		05 46	06 01	06 13	06 16	06 25	06 31		06 46	06 57	07 01	07 13		07 16	07 26	07 31
Edge Hill 89,91	d		05 35		05 50	06 05		06 20		06 35		06 50		07 05			07 20	07 30	07 35
Wavertree Technology Park	d	05 19	05 37		05 52	06 07	06 19	06 22		06 37		06 52		07 07	07 19		07 22		07 37
Broad Green	d		05 40		05 55	06 10		06 25		06 40		06 55		07 10			07 25		07 40
Roby	d		05 44		05 59	06 14		06 29		06 44		06 59		07 14			07 29		07 44
Huyton	d		05 46		06 01	06 16		06 31		06 46		07 01	07 06	07 16			07 31		07 46
Prescot	d		05 51			06 21				06 51				07 21					07 51
Eccleston Park	d		05 53			06 23				06 53				07 23					07 53
Thatto Heath	d		05 56			06 26				06 56				07 26					07 56
St Helens Central	a		05 59			06 29				06 59			07 15	07 29					07 59
	d		06 00			06 30				07 00			07 15	07 30					08 00
Garswood	d		06 07			06 37				07 07				07 37					08 07
Bryn	d		06 10			06 40				07 10				07 40					08 10
Whiston	d				06 05			06 35				07 05					07 35		
Rainhill	d				06 08			06 38				07 08					07 38		
Lea Green	d				06 11			06 41				07 11			07 28		07 41		
St Helens Junction	d	05 29			06 14		06 29	06 44				07 14			07 31		07 44		
Warrington Bank Quay	d			06 06							06 40					07 39			
Earlestown 8	d			06 12	06 19			06 50			06 47	07 19				07 46	07 49		
Warrington Bank Quay	a							07 01											
Newton-le-Willows	d	05 35		06 15	06 22		06 35				06 50	07 22			07 37	07 49	07 52		
Wigan North Western 65	a		06 21			06 51				07 21			07 30	07 51					08 21
	d												07 31						
Euxton Balshaw Lane	d												07 41						
Leyland 82	a												07 46						
Preston 8 65,82	a												07 54						
Blackpool North 97	a												08 21						
Patricroft	d				06 34							07 34					08 04		
Eccles	d				06 36							07 36					08 06		
Manchester Victoria ⇌	a				06 49							07 49					08 19		
Manchester Oxford Road	a			06 35			06 57		07 37		07 09				07 57	08 09		08 36	
Manchester Piccadilly 10 ⇌	a	05 57		06 46			07 01				07 18				08 01	08 18			
Manchester Airport 85 ✈	a	06 14					07 22								08 22				

		AW ◇ ✠	NT	NT	NT	NT	NT	NT	NT	NT	NT	AW ◇ ✠	NT	NT	NT	NT	NT	AW ◇ ✠	NT	NT	NT	NT	NT	NT	AW ◇ ✠
Liverpool Lime Street 10 89,91	d		07 46	07 57	08 01	08 13	08 31	08 16	08 44	08 57	09 01		09 13	09 31	09 46	09 57	10 01		10 13	10 16	10 31	10 46	10 57	11 01	
Edge Hill 89,91	d		07 50		08 05		08 35	08 20	08 50		09 05			09 35	09 50		10 05			10 20	10 35	10 50		11 05	
Wavertree Technology Park	d		07 52		08 07	08 19	08 37	08 22	08 52		09 07		09 19	09 37	09 52		10 07		10 19	10 22	10 37	10 52		11 07	
Broad Green	d		07 55		08 10		08 40	08 25	08 55		09 10			09 40	09 55		10 10			10 25	10 40	10 55		11 10	
Roby	d		07 59		08 14		08 44	08 29	08 59		09 14			09 44	09 59		10 14			10 29	10 44	10 59		11 14	
Huyton	d		08 01	08 06	08 16		08 46	08 31	09 01	09 06	09 16			09 46	10 01	10 06	10 16			10 31	10 46	11 01	11 06	11 16	
Prescot	d				08 21		08 51				09 21			09 51			10 21				10 51			11 21	
Eccleston Park	d				08 23		08 53				09 23			09 53			10 23				10 53			11 23	
Thatto Heath	d				08 26		08 56				09 26			09 56			10 26				10 56			11 26	
St Helens Central	a			08 15	08 29		08 59			09 15	09 29			09 59		10 15	10 29				10 59		11 15	11 29	
	d			08 15	08 30		09 00			09 15	09 30			10 00		10 15	10 30				11 00		11 15	11 30	
Garswood	d				08 37		09 07				09 37			10 07			10 37				11 07			11 37	
Bryn	d				08 40		09 10				09 40			10 10			10 40				11 10			11 40	
Whiston	d		08 05					08 35	09 05						10 05					10 35		11 05			
Rainhill	d		08 08					08 38	09 08						10 08					10 38		11 08			
Lea Green	d		08 11					08 41	09 11						10 11					10 41		11 11			
St Helens Junction	d		08 14			08 29		08 44	09 14				09 29		10 14				10 29	10 44		11 14			
Warrington Bank Quay	d	08 08										09 19						10 19							11 19
Earlestown 8	d	08 16	08 19					08 50	09 19			09 26			10 19			10 26		10 50		11 19			11 26
Warrington Bank Quay	a							09 01												11 01					
Newton-le-Willows	d	08 19	08 22			08 35			09 22			09 29	09 35		10 22			10 29	10 35			11 22			11 29
Wigan North Western 65	a			08 30	08 51		09 21			09 30	09 51			10 21		10 30	10 51				11 21		11 30	11 51	
	d			08 31						09 31						10 31							11 31		
Euxton Balshaw Lane	d			08 41						09 41						10 41							11 41		
Leyland 82	a			08 46						09 46						10 46							11 46		
Preston 8 65,82	a			08 54						09 54						10 54							11 54		
Blackpool North 97	a			09 21						10 21						11 21							12 21		
Patricroft	d		08 34						09 34						10 34							11 34			
Eccles	d		08 36						09 36						10 36							11 36			
Manchester Victoria ⇌	a		08 50						09 47						10 49							11 49			
Manchester Oxford Road	a	08 41				08 57						09 48	09 57					10 48	10 57						11 48
Manchester Piccadilly 10 ⇌	a	08 50				09 01						09 57	10 01					10 57	11 01						11 57
Manchester Airport 85 ✈	a					09 22							10 22						11 22						

Table 90

Saturdays from 23 October

Liverpool and St Helens - Newton-le-Willows, Wigan, Preston and Manchester

Station		NT	NT	NT	NT	NT	NT	AW ◇	NT	NT	NT	NT
Liverpool Lime Street 10 89,91	d	11 13	11 16	11 31	11 46	11 57	12 01		12 13	12 16	12 31	12 46
Edge Hill 89,91	d		11 20	11 35	11 50		12 05			12 20	12 35	12 50
Wavertree Technology Park	d	11 19	11 22	11 37	11 52		12 07		12 19	12 22	12 37	12 52
Broad Green	d		11 25	11 40	11 55		12 10			12 25	12 40	12 55
Roby	d		11 29	11 44	11 59		12 14			12 29	12 44	12 59
Huyton	d		11 31	11 46	12 01	12 06	12 16			12 31	12 46	13 01
Prescot	d			11 51			12 21				12 51	
Eccleston Park	d			11 53			12 23				12 53	
Thatto Heath	d			11 56			12 26				12 56	
St Helens Central	a			11 59		12 15	12 29				12 59	
	d			12 00		12 15	12 30				13 00	
Garswood	d			12 07			12 37				13 07	
Bryn	d			12 10			12 40				13 10	
Whiston	d		11 35		12 05					12 35		13 05
Rainhill	d		11 38		12 08					12 38		13 08
Lea Green	d		11 41		12 11					12 41		13 11
St Helens Junction	d	11 29	11 44		12 14				12 29	12 44		13 14
Warrington Bank Quay	d							12 19				
Earlestown 8	d		11 50		12 19			12 26		12 50		13 19
Warrington Bank Quay	a		12 01							13 01		
Newton-le-Willows	d	11 35			12 22			12 29	12 35			13 22
Wigan North Western 65	a			12 21		12 30	12 51				13 21	
	d					12 31						
Euxton Balshaw Lane	d					12 41						
Leyland 82	a					12 46						
Preston 8 65,82	a					12 54						
Blackpool North 97	a					13 21						
Patricroft	d				12 34							13 34
Eccles	d				12 36							13 36
Manchester Victoria	a				12 49							13 49
Manchester Oxford Road	a	11 57						12 48	12 57			
Manchester Piccadilly 10	a	12 01						12 57	13 01			
Manchester Airport 85	a	12 22							13 22			

Station		NT	NT	AW ◇	NT	NT	NT	NT	NT	NT	AW ◇
Liverpool Lime Street 10 89,91	d	12 57	13 01		13 13	13 16	13 31	13 46	13 57	14 01	
Edge Hill 89,91	d		13 05			13 20	13 35	13 50		14 05	
Wavertree Technology Park	d		13 07		13 19	13 22	13 37	13 52		14 07	
Broad Green	d		13 10			13 25	13 40	13 55		14 10	
Roby	d		13 14			13 29	13 44	13 59		14 14	
Huyton	d	13 06	13 16			13 31	13 46	14 01	14 06	14 16	
Prescot	d		13 21				13 51			14 21	
Eccleston Park	d		13 23				13 53			14 23	
Thatto Heath	d		13 26				13 56			14 26	
St Helens Central	a	13 15	13 29				13 59		14 15	14 29	
	d	13 15	13 30				14 00		14 15	14 30	
Garswood	d		13 37				14 07			14 37	
Bryn	d		13 40				14 10			14 40	
Whiston	d					13 35		14 05			
Rainhill	d					13 38		14 08			
Lea Green	d					13 41		14 11			
St Helens Junction	d				13 29	13 44		14 14			
Warrington Bank Quay	d			13 19							14 19
Earlestown 8	d			13 26		13 50		14 19			14 26
Warrington Bank Quay	a					14 01					
Newton-le-Willows	d			13 29	13 35			14 22			14 29
Wigan North Western 65	a	13 30	13 51				14 21		14 30	14 51	
	d	13 31							14 31		
Euxton Balshaw Lane	d	13 41							14 41		
Leyland 82	a	13 46							14 46		
Preston 8 65,82	a	13 54							14 54		
Blackpool North 97	a	14 21							15 21		
Patricroft	d							14 34			
Eccles	d							14 36			
Manchester Victoria	a							14 50			
Manchester Oxford Road	a			13 48	13 57						14 48
Manchester Piccadilly 10	a			13 57	14 01						14 57
Manchester Airport 85	a				14 22						

Station		NT	NT	NT	NT	NT	NT	AW ◇	NT	NT	NT	NT
Liverpool Lime Street 10 89,91	d	14 13	14 16	14 31	14 46	14 57	15 01		15 13	15 16	15 31	15 46
Edge Hill 89,91	d		14 20	14 35	14 50		15 05			15 20	15 35	15 50
Wavertree Technology Park	d	14 19	14 22	14 37	14 52		15 07		15 19	15 22	15 37	15 52
Broad Green	d		14 25	14 40	14 55		15 10			15 25	15 40	15 55
Roby	d		14 29	14 44	14 59		15 14			15 29	15 44	15 59
Huyton	d		14 31	14 46	15 01	15 06	15 16			15 31	15 46	16 01
Prescot	d			14 51			15 21				15 51	
Eccleston Park	d			14 53			15 23				15 53	
Thatto Heath	d			14 56			15 26				15 56	
St Helens Central	a			14 59		15 15	15 29				15 59	
	d			15 00		15 15	15 30				16 00	
Garswood	d			15 07			15 37				16 07	
Bryn	d			15 10			15 40				16 10	
Whiston	d		14 35		15 05					15 35		16 05
Rainhill	d		14 38		15 08					15 38		16 08
Lea Green	d		14 41		15 11					15 41		16 11
St Helens Junction	d	14 29	14 44		15 14				15 29	15 44		16 14
Warrington Bank Quay	d							15 19				
Earlestown 8	d		14 50		15 19			15 26		15 50		16 19
Warrington Bank Quay	a		15 01							16 01		
Newton-le-Willows	d	14 35			15 22			15 29	15 35			16 22
Wigan North Western 65	a			15 21		15 30	15 51				16 21	
	d					15 31						
Euxton Balshaw Lane	d					15 41						
Leyland 82	a					15 46						
Preston 8 65,82	a					15 54						
Blackpool North 97	a					16 21						
Patricroft	d				15 34							16 34
Eccles	d				15 36							16 36
Manchester Victoria	a				15 49							16 49
Manchester Oxford Road	a	14 57						15 48	15 57			
Manchester Piccadilly 10	a	15 01						15 57	16 01			
Manchester Airport 85	a	15 22							16 22			

Station		NT	NT	AW ◇	NT	NT	NT	NT	NT	NT	AW ◇	NT
Liverpool Lime Street 10 89,91	d	15 57	16 01		16 13	16 16	16 31	16 46	16 57	17 01		17 06
Edge Hill 89,91	d		16 05			16 20	16 35	16 50		17 05		
Wavertree Technology Park	d		16 07		16 19	16 22	16 37	16 52		17 07		17 12
Broad Green	d		16 10			16 25	16 40	16 55		17 10		
Roby	d		16 14			16 29	16 44	16 59		17 14		
Huyton	d	16 06	16 16			16 31	16 46	17 01	17 06	17 16		17 19
Prescot	d		16 21				16 51			17 21		
Eccleston Park	d		16 23				16 53			17 23		
Thatto Heath	d		16 26				16 56			17 26		
St Helens Central	a	16 15	16 29				16 59		17 15	17 29		
	d	16 15	16 30				17 00		17 15	17 30		
Garswood	d		16 37				17 07			17 37		
Bryn	d		16 40				17 10			17 40		
Whiston	d					16 35		17 05				
Rainhill	d					16 38		17 08				
Lea Green	d					16 41		17 11				17 26
St Helens Junction	d				16 29	16 44		17 14				17 29
Warrington Bank Quay	d			16 19							17 19	
Earlestown 8	d			16 26		16 49		17 19			17 26	
Warrington Bank Quay	a											
Newton-le-Willows	d			16 29	16 35	16 52		17 22			17 29	17 35
Wigan North Western 65	a	16 30	16 51				17 21		17 30	17 52		
	d	16 31							17 31			
Euxton Balshaw Lane	d	16 41							17 41			
Leyland 82	a	16 46							17 46			
Preston 8 65,82	a	16 54							17 54			
Blackpool North 97	a	17 21							18 24			
Patricroft	d					17 04		17 34				
Eccles	d					17 06		17 36				
Manchester Victoria	a					17 20		17 47				
Manchester Oxford Road	a			16 48	16 57						17 48	17 57
Manchester Piccadilly 10	a			16 57	17 01						17 57	18 01
Manchester Airport 85	a				17 22							18 22

Table 90

Saturdays from 23 October

Liverpool and St Helens - Newton-le-Willows, Wigan, Preston and Manchester

Station		NT	NT	NT	NT	NT	NT	NT	AW ◇	NT	NT	NT
Liverpool Lime Street 10 89,91	d	17 10	17 19	17 27	17 35	17 44	17 48	18 01		18 13	18 16	18 31
Edge Hill 89,91	d	17 14		17 31	17 39		17 52	18 05			18 20	18 35
Wavertree Technology Park	d	17 16		17 33	17 41	17 49	17 54	18 07		18 19	18 22	18 37
Broad Green	d	17 19		17 36	17 44	17 52	17 57	18 10			18 25	18 40
Roby	d	17 23		17 40	17 48		18 01	18 14			18 29	18 44
Huyton	d	17 25	17 29	17 42	17 50	17 57	18 03	18 16			18 31	18 46
Prescot	d		17 33			18 02		18 21				18 51
Eccleston Park	d		17 36			18 05		18 23				18 53
Thatto Heath	d		17 38			18 07		18 26				18 56
St Helens Central	a		17 42	17 51		18 11		18 29				18 59
	d		17 42	17 51		18 11		18 30				19 00
Garswood	d		17 49			18 19		18 37				19 07
Bryn	d		17 52			18 22		18 40				19 10
Whiston	d	17 28			17 54		18 07				18 35	
Rainhill	d	17 32			17 57		18 10				18 38	
Lea Green	d	17 35			18 00		18 13				18 41	
St Helens Junction	d	17 39			18 03		18 16			18 29	18 44	
Warrington Bank Quay	d								18 19			
Earlestown 8	d	17 44			18 08		18 21		18 26		18 50	
Warrington Bank Quay	a										19 01	
Newton-le-Willows	d	17 47			18 11		18 24		18 29	18 35		
Wigan North Western 65	a		18 04	18 05		18 30		18 49				19 21
	d			18 05		18 31		18 49				
Euxton Balshaw Lane	d			18 16		18 41		19 01				
Leyland 82	a			18 21		18 46		19 06				
Preston 8 65,82	a			18 31		18 54		19 15				
Blackpool North 97	a					19 21						
Patricroft	d	17 59			18 23							
Eccles	d	18 01			18 25		18 36					
Manchester Victoria	a	18 15			18 41		18 49					
Manchester Oxford Road	a								18 48	18 57		
Manchester Piccadilly 10	a								18 57	19 01		
Manchester Airport 85	a									19 24		

Station		NT	NT	AW ◇	NT	NT	NT	AW ◇	NT	NT
Liverpool Lime Street 10 89,91	d	18 46	19 01		19 12	19 23	19 42		20 09	20 12
Edge Hill 89,91	d	18 50	19 05		19 16		19 46			20 16
Wavertree Technology Park	d	18 52	19 07		19 18		19 48		20 15	20 18
Broad Green	d	18 55	19 10		19 21		19 51			20 21
Roby	d	18 59	19 14		19 25		19 55			20 25
Huyton	d	19 01	19 16		19 27	19 32	19 57			20 27
Prescot	d		19 21				20 02			
Eccleston Park	d		19 23				20 04			
Thatto Heath	d		19 26				20 07			
St Helens Central	a		19 29			19 40	20 10			
	d		19 30			19 41	20 11			
Garswood	d		19 37				20 18			
Bryn	d		19 40				20 21			
Whiston	d	19 05			19 31					20 31
Rainhill	d	19 08			19 34					20 34
Lea Green	d	19 11			19 37					20 37
St Helens Junction	d	19 14			19 40				20 25	20 40
Warrington Bank Quay	d			19 19				20 19		
Earlestown 8	d	19 19		19 26	19 45			20 26		20 45
Warrington Bank Quay	a									
Newton-le-Willows	d	19 22		19 29	19 48			20 29	20 35	20 48
Wigan North Western 65	a		19 51			19 54	20 32			
	d					19 55				
Euxton Balshaw Lane	d					20 05				
Leyland 82	a					20 10				
Preston 8 65,82	a					20 18				
Blackpool North 97	a					20 44				
Patricroft	d	19 34			20 00					21 00
Eccles	d	19 36			20 02					21 02
Manchester Victoria	a	19 49			20 15					21 15
Manchester Oxford Road	a			19 48				20 48	20 57	
Manchester Piccadilly 10	a			19 52				20 57	21 01	
Manchester Airport 85	a			20 13					21 24	

Station		NT	NT	AW ◇	NT	NT	AW	NT	TP ◇1	NT	NT
Liverpool Lime Street 10 89,91	d	20 25	20 42		21 12	21 42		22 12	22 30	23 02	23 16
Edge Hill 89,91	d		20 46		21 16	21 46		22 16		23 06	23 20
Wavertree Technology Park	d		20 48		21 18	21 48		22 18		23 08	23 22
Broad Green	d		20 51		21 21	21 51		22 21		23 11	23 26
Roby	d		20 55		21 25	21 55		22 25		23 15	23 30
Huyton	d	20 34	20 57		21 27	21 57		22 27		23 17	23 32
Prescot	d		21 02			22 02				23 22	
Eccleston Park	d		21 04			22 04				23 24	
Thatto Heath	d		21 07			22 07				23 27	
St Helens Central	a	20 42	21 10			22 10				23 34	
	d	20 43	21 11			22 11					
Garswood	d		21 18			22 18					
Bryn	d		21 21			22 21					
Whiston	d				21 31			22 31			23 36
Rainhill	d				21 34			22 34			23 39
Lea Green	d				21 37			22 37			23 42
St Helens Junction	d				21 40			22 40			23 45
Warrington Bank Quay	d			21 19			22 19				
Earlestown 8	d			21 26	21 45		22 27	22 45			23 50
Warrington Bank Quay	a										
Newton-le-Willows	d			21 29	21 48		22 30	22 48			23 53
Wigan North Western 65	a	20 57	21 32			22 28					
	d	20 57				22 28					
Euxton Balshaw Lane	d	21 08				22 39					
Leyland 82	a	21 16				22 44					
Preston 8 65,82	a	21 22				22 55					
Blackpool North 97	a	21 53				23 22					
Patricroft	d				22 00			23 00			00 05
Eccles	d				22 02			23 02			00 08
Manchester Victoria	a				22 15			23 15			00 21
Manchester Oxford Road	a			21 48			22 50		23 14		
Manchester Piccadilly 10	a			21 57			22 58		23 19		
Manchester Airport 85	a										

Table 90

Sundays until 05 September

Liverpool and St Helens - Newton-le-Willows, Wigan, Preston and Manchester

		NT	NT	AW	NT	NT	AW ◇	NT B	NT C	VT ◇1 ⊡	NT	AW 🚌	NT	NT	AW 🚌	NT	NT	AW 🚌	NT	NT
Liverpool Lime Street 10 89,91	d	08 05	08 31		09 01	09 31		10 01	10 01		10 31		11 01	11 31		12 01	12 31		13 01	13 31
Edge Hill 89,91	d																			
Wavertree Technology Park	d	08 11	08 37		09 07	09 37		10 07	10 07		10 37		11 07	11 37		12 07	12 37		13 07	13 37
Broad Green	d	08 14	08 40		09 10	09 40		10 10	10 10		10 40		11 10	11 40		12 10	12 40		13 10	13 40
Roby	d	08 17	08 43		09 13	09 43		10 13	10 13		10 43		11 13	11 43		12 13	12 43		13 13	13 43
Huyton	d	08 19	08 46		09 16	09 46		10 16	10 16		10 46		11 16	11 46		12 16	12 46		13 16	13 46
Prescot	d		08 50			09 50					10 50			11 50			12 50			13 50
Eccleston Park	d																			
Thatto Heath	d		08 54			09 54					10 54			11 54			12 54			13 54
St Helens Central	a		08 57			09 57					10 57			11 57			12 57			13 57
	d		08 58			09 58					10 58			11 58			12 58			13 58
Garswood	d		09 05			10 05					11 05			12 05			13 05			14 05
Bryn	d																			
Whiston	d	08 23			09 19			10 19	10 19				11 19			12 19			13 19	
Rainhill	d	08 26			09 22			10 22	10 22				11 22			12 22			13 22	
Lea Green	d	08 29			09 26			10 26	10 26				11 26			12 26			13 26	
St Helens Junction	d	08 32			09 29			10 29	10 29				11 29			12 29			13 29	
Warrington Bank Quay	d			09 10			10 12					11 03			12 03			13 03		
Earlestown 8	d	08 37		09 16	09 33		10 19	10 33	10 33			11 10	11 33		12 10	12 33		13 10	13 33	
Warrington Bank Quay	a									10 37										
Newton-le-Willows	d	08 40		09 19	09 36		10 22	10 36	10 36			11 13	11 36		12 13	12 36		13 13	13 36	
Wigan North Western 65	a		09 13			10 13				10 48	11 13			12 13			13 13			14 13
	d		09 14			10 14				10 48	11 14			12 14			13 14			14 14
Euxton Balshaw Lane	d		09 24			10 26					11 24			12 24			13 24			14 24
Leyland 82	a		09 29			10 31					11 29			12 29			13 29			14 29
Preston 8 65,82	a		09 37			10 39				11 04	11 37			12 37			13 37			14 37
Blackpool North 97	a		10 07			11 09					12 07			13 07			14 09			15 07
Patricroft	d																			
Eccles	d	08 52			09 49			10 49	10 49				11 49			12 49			13 49	
Manchester Victoria ⇌	a																			
Manchester Oxford Road	a	09 01		09 39	09 59		10 41	10 59	10 59			11 32	11 59		12 32	12 59		13 32	13 59	
Manchester Piccadilly 10 ⇌	a	09 05		09 48	10 03		10 50		11 03			11 41	12 02		12 41	13 02		13 41	14 02	
Manchester Airport 85 ✈	a	09 22			10 24				11 21				12 21			13 24			14 21	

		AW 🚌	NT	NT	AW 🚌	NT	NT	AW 🚌	NT	NT	AW ◇ 🚌	NT	NT	AW ◇ 🚌	NT	NT	AW	NT	NT	AW	NT	NT	AW
Liverpool Lime Street 10 89,91	d		14 01	14 31		15 01	15 31		16 01	16 31		17 01	17 31		18 01	18 31		19 01	19 31		20 01	20 31	
Edge Hill 89,91	d																						
Wavertree Technology Park	d		14 07	14 37		15 07	15 37		16 07	16 37		17 07	17 37		18 07	18 37		19 07	19 37		20 07	20 37	
Broad Green	d		14 10	14 40		15 10	15 40		16 10	16 40		17 10	17 40		18 10	18 40		19 10	19 40		20 10	20 40	
Roby	d		14 13	14 43		15 13	15 43		16 13	16 43		17 13	17 43		18 13	18 43		19 13	19 43		20 13	20 43	
Huyton	d		14 16	14 46		15 16	15 46		16 16	16 46		17 16	17 46		18 16	18 46		19 16	19 46		20 16	20 46	
Prescot	d			14 50			15 50			16 50			17 50			18 50			19 50			20 50	
Eccleston Park	d																						
Thatto Heath	d			14 54			15 54			16 54			17 54			18 54			19 54			20 54	
St Helens Central	a			14 57			15 57			16 57			17 57			18 57			19 57			20 57	
	d			14 58			15 58			16 58			17 58			18 58			19 58			20 58	
Garswood	d			15 05			16 05			17 05			18 05			19 05			20 05			21 05	
Bryn	d																						
Whiston	d		14 19			15 19			16 19			17 19			18 19			19 19			20 19		
Rainhill	d		14 22			15 22			16 22			17 22			18 22			19 22			20 22		
Lea Green	d		14 26			15 26			16 26			17 26			18 26			19 26			20 26		
St Helens Junction	d		14 29			15 29			16 29			17 29			18 29			19 29			20 29		
Warrington Bank Quay	d	14 03			15 03			16 03			17 03			18 03			19 03			20 03			21 03
Earlestown 8	d	14 10	14 33		15 10	15 33		16 10	16 33		17 10	17 33		18 10	18 33		19 10	19 33		20 10	20 33		21 10
Warrington Bank Quay	a																						
Newton-le-Willows	d	14 13	14 36		15 13	15 36		16 13	16 36		17 13	17 36		18 13	18 36		19 13	19 36		20 13	20 36		21 13
Wigan North Western 65	a			15 13			16 13			17 13			18 13			19 13			20 13			21 13	
	d			15 14			16 14			17 14			18 14			19 14			20 14			21 14	
Euxton Balshaw Lane	d			15 24			16 24			17 24			18 24			19 24			20 24			21 24	
Leyland 82	a			15 29			16 29			17 29			18 29			19 29			20 29			21 29	
Preston 8 65,82	a			15 37			16 37			17 37			18 37			19 37			20 37			21 37	
Blackpool North 97	a			16 07			17 07			18 07			19 07			20 07			21 07			22 07	
Patricroft	d																						
Eccles	d		14 49			15 49			16 49			17 49			18 49			19 49			20 49		
Manchester Victoria ⇌	a																						
Manchester Oxford Road	a	14 32	14 59		15 32	15 59		16 32	16 59		17 32	17 59		18 32	18 59		19 32	19 59		20 32	20 59		21 32
Manchester Piccadilly 10 ⇌	a	14 41	15 02		15 41	16 02		16 41	17 02		17 41	18 02		18 41	19 02		19 41	20 02		20 41	21 02		21 41
Manchester Airport 85 ✈	a		15 21			16 21			17 21			18 21			19 21			20 21			21 21		

B until 11 July

C from 18 July until 5 September

Table 90

Sundays until 05 September

Liverpool and St Helens - Newton-le-Willows, Wigan, Preston and Manchester

		NT	NT	AW	NT	NT	AW	NT
Liverpool Lime Street 10 89,91	d	21 01	21 31		22 01	22 31		23 01
Edge Hill 89,91	d							
Wavertree Technology Park	d	21 07	21 37		22 07	22 37		23 07
Broad Green	d	21 10	21 40		22 10	22 40		23 10
Roby	d	21 13	21 43		22 13	22 43		23 13
Huyton	d	21 16	21 46		22 16	22 46		23 16
Prescot	d		21 50			22 50		
Eccleston Park	d							
Thatto Heath	d		21 54			22 54		
St Helens Central	a		21 57			22 57		
	d		21 58			22 58		
Garswood	d		22 05			23 05		
Bryn	d							
Whiston	d	21 19			22 19			23 19
Rainhill	d	21 22			22 22			23 22
Lea Green	d	21 26			22 26			23 26
St Helens Junction	d	21 29			22 29			23 29
Warrington Bank Quay	d			22 03			22 36	
Earlestown 8	d	21 33		22 10	22 33		22 44	23 33
Warrington Bank Quay	a							
Newton-le-Willows	d	21 36		22 13	22 36		22 47	23 36
Wigan North Western 65	a		22 13			23 13		
	d		22 14			23 14		
Euxton Balshaw Lane	d		22 24					
Leyland 82	a		22 29			23 27		
Preston 8 65,82	a		22 37			23 35		
Blackpool North 97	a		23 07			00 05		
Patricroft	d							
Eccles	d	21 49			22 49			23 49
Manchester Victoria ⇌	a							
Manchester Oxford Road	a	21 59		22 32	22 59		23 06	23 59
Manchester Piccadilly 10 ⇌	a	22 02		22 41	23 02		23 15	00 02
Manchester Airport 85 ✈	a	22 21			23 21			00 19

Sundays 12 September to 17 October

		NT	NT	AW	NT	NT	AW ◇	NT	VT ◇1 ⊡	NT	AW 🚌	NT	NT	AW 🚌	NT	NT	AW 🚌	NT	NT	AW 🚌
Liverpool Lime Street 10 89,91	d	08 22	08 31		09 01	09 31		10 01		10 31		11 01	11 31		12 01	12 31		13 01	13 31	
Edge Hill 89,91	d																			
Wavertree Technology Park	d	08 28	08 37		09 07	09 37		10 07		10 37		11 07	11 37		12 07	12 37		13 07	13 37	
Broad Green	d	08 31	08 40		09 10	09 40		10 10		10 40		11 10	11 40		12 10	12 40		13 10	13 40	
Roby	d	08 34	08 43		09 13	09 43		10 13		10 43		11 13	11 43		12 13	12 43		13 13	13 43	
Huyton	d	08 36	08 46		09 16	09 46		10 16		10 46		11 16	11 46		12 16	12 46		13 16	13 46	
Prescot	d		08 50			09 50				10 50			11 50			12 50			13 50	
Eccleston Park	d																			
Thatto Heath	d		08 54			09 54				10 54			11 54			12 54			13 54	
St Helens Central	a		08 57			09 57				10 57			11 57			12 57			13 57	
	d		08 58			09 58				10 58			11 58			12 58			13 58	
Garswood	d		09 05			10 05				11 05			12 05			13 05			14 05	
Bryn	d																			
Whiston	d	08 40			09 19			10 19				11 19			12 19			13 19		
Rainhill	d	08 43			09 22			10 22				11 22			12 22			13 22		
Lea Green	d	08 46			09 26			10 26				11 26			12 26			13 26		
St Helens Junction	d	08 49			09 29			10 29				11 29			12 29			13 29		
Warrington Bank Quay	d			09 10			10 12				11 03			12 03			13 03			14 03
Earlestown 8	d	08 54		09 17	09 33		10 19	10 33			11 10	11 33		12 10	12 33		13 10	13 33		14 10
Warrington Bank Quay	a								10 37											
Newton-le-Willows	d	08 57		09 20	09 36		10 22	10 36			11 13	11 36		12 13	12 36		13 13	13 36		14 13
Wigan North Western 65	a		09 13			10 13			10 48	11 13			12 13			13 13			14 13	
	d		09 14			10 14			10 48	11 14			12 14			13 14			14 14	
Euxton Balshaw Lane	d		09 24			10 26				11 24			12 24			13 24			14 24	
Leyland 82	a		09 29			10 31				11 29			12 29			13 29			14 29	
Preston 8 65,82	a		09 37			10 39			11 04	11 37			12 37			13 37			14 37	
Blackpool North 97	a		10 07			11 09				12 07			13 07			14 09			15 07	
Patricroft	d																			
Eccles	d	09 09			09 49			10 49				11 49			12 49			13 49		
Manchester Victoria ⇌	a																			
Manchester Oxford Road	a	09 20		09 39	09 59		10 41	10 59			11 32	11 59		12 32	12 59		13 32	13 59		14 32
Manchester Piccadilly 10 ⇌	a			09 49	10 02		10 50	11 03			11 41	12 02		12 41	13 02		13 41	14 02		14 41
Manchester Airport 85 ✈	a				10 25			11 21				12 21			13 21			14 21		

Table 90

Sundays
12 September to 17 October

Liverpool and St Helens - Newton-le-Willows, Wigan, Preston and Manchester

	NT	NT	AW	NT	NT	AW	NT	NT	AW	NT	NT
			H			H			◇ H		
Liverpool Lime Street ■10 89,91 d	14 01	14 31		15 01	15 31		16 01	16 31		17 01	17 31
Edge Hill 89,91 d											
Wavertree Technology Park d	14 07	14 37		15 07	15 37		16 07	16 37		17 07	17 37
Broad Green d	14 10	14 40		15 10	15 40		16 10	16 40		17 10	17 40
Roby d	14 13	14 43		15 13	15 43		16 13	16 43		17 13	17 43
Huyton d	14 16	14 46		15 16	15 46		16 16	16 46		17 16	17 46
Prescot d		14 50			15 50			16 50			17 50
Eccleston Park d											
Thatto Heath d		14 54			15 54			16 54			17 54
St Helens Central a		14 57			15 57			16 57			17 57
d		14 58			15 58			16 58			17 58
Garswood d		15 05			16 05			17 05			18 05
Bryn d											
Whiston d	14 19			15 19			16 19			17 19	
Rainhill d	14 22			15 22			16 22			17 22	
Lea Green d	14 26			15 26			16 26			17 26	
St Helens Junction d	14 29			15 29			16 29			17 29	
Warrington Bank Quay d			15 03			16 03			17 03		
Earlestown ■ d	14 33		15 10	15 33		16 10	16 33		17 10	17 33	
Warrington Bank Quay a											
Newton-le-Willows d	14 36		15 13	15 36		16 13	16 36		17 13	17 36	
Wigan North Western 65 a		15 13			16 13			17 13			18 13
d		15 14			16 14			17 14			18 14
Euxton Balshaw Lane d		15 24			16 24			17 24			18 24
Leyland 82 a		15 29			16 29			17 29			18 29
Preston ■ 65,82 a		15 37			16 37			17 37			18 37
Blackpool North 97 a		16 07			17 07			18 07			19 07
Patricroft d											
Eccles d	14 49			15 49			16 49			17 49	
Manchester Victoria a											
Manchester Oxford Road a	14 59		15 32	15 59		16 32	16 59		17 32	17 59	
Manchester Piccadilly ■10 a	15 02		15 41	16 02		16 41	17 02		17 41	18 02	
Manchester Airport 85 a	15 21			16 21			17 21			18 21	

	AW	NT	NT	AW	NT	NT	AW	NT	NT	AW	NT
	◇ H										
Liverpool Lime Street ■10 89,91 d		18 01	18 31		19 01	19 31		20 01	20 31		21 01
Edge Hill 89,91 d											
Wavertree Technology Park d		18 07	18 37		19 07	19 37		20 07	20 37		21 07
Broad Green d		18 10	18 40		19 10	19 40		20 10	20 40		21 10
Roby d		18 13	18 43		19 13	19 43		20 13	20 43		21 13
Huyton d		18 16	18 46		19 16	19 46		20 16	20 46		21 16
Prescot d			18 50			19 50			20 50		
Eccleston Park d											
Thatto Heath d			18 54			19 54			20 54		
St Helens Central a			18 57			19 57			20 57		
d			18 58			19 58			20 58		
Garswood d			19 05			20 05			21 05		
Bryn d											
Whiston d		18 19			19 19			20 19			21 19
Rainhill d		18 22			19 22			20 22			21 22
Lea Green d		18 26			19 26			20 26			21 26
St Helens Junction d		18 29			19 29			20 29			21 29
Warrington Bank Quay d	18 03			19 03			20 03			21 03	
Earlestown ■ d	18 10	18 33		19 10	19 33		20 10	20 33		21 10	21 33
Warrington Bank Quay a											
Newton-le-Willows d	18 13	18 36		19 13	19 36		20 13	20 36		21 13	21 36
Wigan North Western 65 a			19 13			20 13			21 13		
d			19 14			20 14			21 14		
Euxton Balshaw Lane d			19 24			20 24			21 24		
Leyland 82 a			19 29			20 29			21 29		
Preston ■ 65,82 a			19 37			20 37			21 37		
Blackpool North 97 a			20 07			21 07			22 07		
Patricroft d											
Eccles d		18 49			19 49			20 49			21 49
Manchester Victoria a											
Manchester Oxford Road a	18 32	18 59		19 32	19 59		20 32	20 59		21 32	21 59
Manchester Piccadilly ■10 a	18 41	19 02		19 41	20 02		20 41	21 02		21 41	22 02
Manchester Airport 85 a		19 21			20 21			21 21			22 21

	NT	AW	NT	NT	AW	NT
Liverpool Lime Street ■10 89,91 d	21 31		22 01	22 31		23 01
Edge Hill 89,91 d						
Wavertree Technology Park d	21 37		22 07	22 37		23 07
Broad Green d	21 40		22 10	22 40		23 10
Roby d	21 43		22 13	22 43		23 13
Huyton d	21 46		22 16	22 46		23 16
Prescot d	21 50			22 50		
Eccleston Park d						
Thatto Heath d	21 54			22 54		
St Helens Central a	21 57			22 57		
d	21 58			22 58		
Garswood d	22 05			23 05		
Bryn d						
Whiston d			22 19			23 19
Rainhill d			22 22			23 22
Lea Green d			22 26			23 26
St Helens Junction d			22 29			23 29
Warrington Bank Quay d		22 03			22 36	
Earlestown ■ d		22 10	22 33		22 44	23 33
Warrington Bank Quay a						
Newton-le-Willows d		22 13	22 36		22 47	23 36
Wigan North Western 65 a	22 13			23 13		
d	22 14			23 14		
Euxton Balshaw Lane d	22 24					
Leyland 82 a	22 29			23 27		
Preston ■ 65,82 a	22 37			23 35		
Blackpool North 97 a	23 07			00 05		
Patricroft d						
Eccles d			22 49			23 49
Manchester Victoria a						
Manchester Oxford Road a		22 32	22 59		23 06	23 59
Manchester Piccadilly ■10 a		22 41	23 02		23 15	00 02
Manchester Airport 85 a			23 21			00 19

Table 90

Sundays
from 24 October

Liverpool and St Helens - Newton-le-Willows, Wigan, Preston and Manchester

	AW	NT	NT	NT	NT	AW	NT	NT	AW	AW	NT
	🚌					🚌			🚌	H	
Liverpool Lime Street ■10 89,91 d		08 22	08 31	09 01	09 31		10 01	10 31			11 01
Edge Hill 89,91 d											
Wavertree Technology Park d		08 28	08 37	09 07	09 37		10 07	10 37			11 07
Broad Green d		08 31	08 40	09 10	09 40		10 10	10 40			11 10
Roby d		08 34	08 43	09 13	09 43		10 13	10 43			11 13
Huyton d		08 36	08 46	09 16	09 46		10 16	10 46			11 16
Prescot d			08 50		09 50			10 50			
Eccleston Park d											
Thatto Heath d			08 54		09 54			10 54			
St Helens Central a			09 01		09 59			11 01			
d											
Garswood d											
Bryn d											
Whiston d		08 40		09 19			10 19				11 19
Rainhill d		08 43		09 22			10 22				11 22
Lea Green d		08 46		09 26			10 26				11 26
St Helens Junction d		08 49		09 29			10 29				11 29
Warrington Bank Quay d	00 22					09 42			10 42	11 03	
Earlestown ■ d	00 47	08 54		09 33		10 07	10 33		11 07	11 10	11 33
Warrington Bank Quay a											
Newton-le-Willows d	00 57	08 57		09 36		10 17	10 36		11 17	11 13	11 36
Wigan North Western 65 a											
d											
Euxton Balshaw Lane d											
Leyland 82 a											
Preston ■ 65,82 a											
Blackpool North 97 a											
Patricroft d											
Eccles d		09 09		09 49			10 49				11 49
Manchester Victoria a											
Manchester Oxford Road a	01 27	09 20		09 59		10 47	10 59		11 47	11 32	11 59
Manchester Piccadilly ■10 a	01 32			10 02		10 52	11 03		11 52	11 41	12 02
Manchester Airport 85 a				10 25			11 21				12 21

	NT	AW	NT	NT	AW	NT	NT	AW	NT	NT
		H			H			H		
Liverpool Lime Street ■10 89,91 d	11 31		12 01	12 31		13 01	13 31		14 01	14 31
Edge Hill 89,91 d										
Wavertree Technology Park d	11 37		12 07	12 37		13 07	13 37		14 07	14 37
Broad Green d	11 40		12 10	12 40		13 10	13 40		14 10	14 40
Roby d	11 43		12 13	12 43		13 13	13 43		14 13	14 43
Huyton d	11 46		12 16	12 46		13 16	13 46		14 16	14 46
Prescot d	11 50			12 50			13 50			14 50
Eccleston Park d										
Thatto Heath d	11 54			12 54			13 54			14 54
St Helens Central a	12 01			13 01			14 01			15 01
d										
Garswood d										
Bryn d										
Whiston d			12 19			13 19			14 19	
Rainhill d			12 22			13 22			14 22	
Lea Green d			12 26			13 26			14 26	
St Helens Junction d			12 29			13 29			14 29	
Warrington Bank Quay d		12 03			13 03			14 03		
Earlestown ■ d		12 10	12 33		13 10	13 33		14 10	14 33	
Warrington Bank Quay a										
Newton-le-Willows d		12 13	12 36		13 13	13 36		14 13	14 36	
Wigan North Western 65 a										
d										
Euxton Balshaw Lane d										
Leyland 82 a										
Preston ■ 65,82 a										
Blackpool North 97 a										
Patricroft d										
Eccles d			12 49			13 49			14 49	
Manchester Victoria a										
Manchester Oxford Road a		12 32	12 59		13 32	13 59		14 32	14 59	
Manchester Piccadilly ■10 a		12 41	13 02		13 41	14 02		14 41	15 02	
Manchester Airport 85 a			13 21			14 21			15 21	

	AW	NT	NT	AW	NT	NT	AW	NT	NT	AW	NT
	H			H			◇ H			◇ H	
Liverpool Lime Street ■10 89,91 d		15 01	15 31		16 01	16 31		17 01	17 31		18 01
Edge Hill 89,91 d											
Wavertree Technology Park d		15 07	15 37		16 07	16 37		17 07	17 37		18 07
Broad Green d		15 10	15 40		16 10	16 40		17 10	17 40		18 10
Roby d		15 13	15 43		16 13	16 43		17 13	17 43		18 13
Huyton d		15 16	15 46		16 16	16 46		17 16	17 46		18 16
Prescot d			15 50			16 50			17 50		
Eccleston Park d											
Thatto Heath d			15 54			16 54			17 54		
St Helens Central a			16 01			17 01			18 01		
d											
Garswood d											
Bryn d											
Whiston d		15 19			16 19			17 19			18 19
Rainhill d		15 22			16 22			17 22			18 22
Lea Green d		15 26			16 26			17 26			18 26
St Helens Junction d		15 29			16 29			17 29			18 29
Warrington Bank Quay d	15 03			16 03			17 03			18 03	
Earlestown ■ d	15 10	15 33		16 10	16 33		17 10	17 33		18 10	18 33
Warrington Bank Quay a											
Newton-le-Willows d	15 13	15 36		16 13	16 36		17 13	17 36		18 13	18 36
Wigan North Western 65 a											
d											
Euxton Balshaw Lane d											
Leyland 82 a											
Preston ■ 65,82 a											
Blackpool North 97 a											
Patricroft d											
Eccles d		15 49			16 49			17 49			18 49
Manchester Victoria a											
Manchester Oxford Road a	15 32	15 59		16 32	16 59		17 32	17 59		18 32	18 59
Manchester Piccadilly ■10 a	15 41	16 02		16 41	17 02		17 41	18 02		18 41	19 02
Manchester Airport 85 a		16 21			17 21			18 21			19 21

	NT	AW	NT	NT	AW	NT	NT	AW	NT	NT	AW
Liverpool Lime Street ■10 89,91 d	18 31		19 01	19 31		20 01	20 31		21 01	21 31	
Edge Hill 89,91 d											
Wavertree Technology Park d	18 37		19 07	19 37		20 07	20 37		21 07	21 37	
Broad Green d	18 40		19 10	19 40		20 10	20 40		21 10	21 40	
Roby d	18 43		19 13	19 43		20 13	20 43		21 13	21 43	
Huyton d	18 46		19 16	19 46		20 16	20 46		21 16	21 46	
Prescot d	18 50			19 50			20 50			21 50	
Eccleston Park d											
Thatto Heath d	18 54			19 54			20 54			21 54	
St Helens Central a	19 01			20 01			21 01			22 01	
d											
Garswood d											
Bryn d											
Whiston d			19 19			20 19			21 19		
Rainhill d			19 22			20 22			21 22		
Lea Green d			19 26			20 26			21 26		
St Helens Junction d			19 29			20 29			21 29		
Warrington Bank Quay d		19 03			20 03			21 03			22 03
Earlestown ■ d		19 10	19 33		20 10	20 33		21 10	21 33		22 10
Warrington Bank Quay a											
Newton-le-Willows d		19 13	19 36		20 13	20 36		21 13	21 36		22 13
Wigan North Western 65 a											
d											
Euxton Balshaw Lane d											
Leyland 82 a											
Preston ■ 65,82 a											
Blackpool North 97 a											
Patricroft d											
Eccles d			19 49			20 49			21 49		
Manchester Victoria a											
Manchester Oxford Road a		19 32	19 59		20 32	20 59		21 32	21 59		22 32
Manchester Piccadilly ■10 a		19 41	20 02		20 41	21 02		21 41	22 02		22 41
Manchester Airport 85 a			20 21			21 21			22 21		

Liverpool and St Helens - Newton-le-Willows, Wigan, Preston and Manchester

		NT	NT	AW	NT
Liverpool Lime Street 10 89,91	d	22 01	22 31		23 01
Edge Hill 89,91	d				
Wavertree Technology Park	d	22 07	22 37		23 07
Broad Green	d	22 10	22 40		23 10
Roby	d	22 13	22 43		23 13
Huyton	d	22 16	22 46		23 16
Prescot	d		22 50		
Eccleston Park	d				
Thatto Heath	d		22 54		
St Helens Central	a		23 01		
	d				
Garswood	d				
Bryn	d				
Whiston	d	22 19			23 19
Rainhill	d	22 22			23 22
Lea Green	d	22 26			23 26
St Helens Junction	d	22 29			23 29
Warrington Bank Quay	d			22 36	
Earlestown 8	d	22 33		22 44	23 33
Warrington Bank Quay	a				
Newton-le-Willows	d	22 36		22 47	23 36
Wigan North Western 65	a				
	d				
Euxton Balshaw Lane	d				
Leyland 82	a				
Preston 8 65,82	a				
Blackpool North 97	a				
Patricroft	d				
Eccles	d	22 49			23 49
Manchester Victoria ⇌	a				
Manchester Oxford Road	a	22 59		23 06	23 59
Manchester Piccadilly 10 ⇌	a	23 02		23 15	00 02
Manchester Airport 85 ✈	a	23 21			00 19

Manchester, Preston, Wigan and Newton-le-Willows - St Helens and Liverpool

		NT	NT	NT	AW ◇	NT	NT	NT	AW ◇	NT	NT	NT	NT	NT	NT	NT	AW ◇	NT	NT	NT	NT	NT	AW ◇	NT	NT
Manchester Airport 85 ✈	d				05 33					06 41								07 41						08 41	
Manchester Piccadilly 10 ⇌	d				05 50				06 50	06 58							07 50	07 58					08 50	09 01	
Manchester Oxford Road	d				05 53				06 53	07 01							07 53	08 03					08 53	09 04	
Manchester Victoria ⇌	d		05 39			06 09						07 09			07 39				08 09			08 39			
Eccles	d		05 46			06 16						07 16			07 46				08 16			08 46			
Patricroft	d		05 49			06 19						07 19			07 49				08 19			08 49			
Blackpool North 97	d													07 02											
Preston 8 65,82	d													07 30											
Leyland 82	d													07 35											
Euxton Balshaw Lane	d													07 40											
Wigan North Western 65	a													07 50											
	d			06 08			06 38	06 47			07 08		07 38	07 50		07 58				08 28					09 08
Newton-le-Willows	d		06 01		06 12	06 31		07 00	07 12	07 19		07 31			08 01		08 12	08 21	08 31			09 01	09 12	09 22	
Warrington Bank Quay	d																								
Earlestown 8	d		06 04		06 15	06 34		07 03	07 15			07 34			08 04		08 15		08 34			09 04	09 15		
Warrington Bank Quay	a				06 25				07 22								08 23						09 25		
St Helens Junction	d		06 09			06 39		07 09		07 24		07 39			08 09			08 26	08 39			09 09		09 27	
Lea Green	d		06 12			06 42		07 12				07 42			08 12			08 29	08 42			09 12			
Rainhill	d		06 16			06 46		07 16		07 29		07 46			08 16			08 34	08 46			09 16			
Whiston	d		06 19			06 49		07 19				07 49			08 19			08 37	08 49			09 19			
Bryn	d			06 15			06 45				07 15		07 45			08 05				08 35					09 15
Garswood	d			06 19			06 49				07 19		07 49	07 59		08 09				08 39					09 19
St Helens Central	a			06 25			06 55				07 25		07 55	08 06		08 15				08 45					09 25
	d	05 56		06 26			06 56				07 26		07 56	08 06		08 16				08 46	08 56				09 26
Thatto Heath	d	05 59		06 29			06 59				07 29		07 59			08 19				08 49	08 59				09 29
Eccleston Park	d	06 02		06 32			07 02				07 32		08 02			08 22				08 52	09 02				09 32
Prescot	d	06 04		06 34			07 04				07 34		08 04	08 12		08 24				08 54	09 04				09 34
Huyton	d	06 08	06 23	06 38		06 53	07 08	07 23		07 34	07 38	07 53	08 08	08 16	08 23	08 28		08 41	08 53	08 58	09 08	09 23			09 38
Roby	d	06 10	06 25	06 40		06 55	07 10	07 25			07 40	07 55	08 10		08 25	08 30			08 55	09 00	09 10	09 25			09 40
Broad Green	d	06 13	06 28	06 43		06 58	07 13	07 28			07 43	07 58	08 13	08 20	08 28	08 33		08 45	08 58	09 03	09 13	09 28			09 43
Wavertree Technology Park	d	06 16	06 31	06 46		07 01	07 16	07 31		07 39	07 46	08 01	08 16	08 24	08 31	08 36		08 48	09 01	09 06	09 16	09 31		09 38	09 46
Edge Hill 89,91	d	06 19	06 34	06 49		07 04	07 19	07 34			07 49	08 04	08 19		08 34	08 39			09 04	09 09	09 19	09 34			09 49
Liverpool Lime Street 10 89,91	a	06 28	06 43	06 58		07 13	07 28	07 43		07 49	07 58	08 13	08 28	08 35	08 43	08 50		08 59	09 13	09 18	09 28	09 43		09 48	09 58

		NT	NT	NT	AW ◇	NT	NT	NT	NT	NT	NT	AW ◇	NT	NT	NT	NT	NT	NT	AW ◇	NT	NT	NT	NT	NT	NT
Manchester Airport 85 ✈	d					09 41							10 41							11 41					
Manchester Piccadilly 10 ⇌	d				09 50	10 01						10 50	11 01						11 50	12 01					
Manchester Oxford Road	d				09 53	10 04						10 53	11 04						11 53	12 04					
Manchester Victoria ⇌	d			09 39							10 39							11 39							12 39
Eccles	d			09 46							10 46							11 46							12 46
Patricroft	d			09 49							10 49							11 49							12 49
Blackpool North 97	d							09 37							10 37							11 37			
Preston 8 65,82	d	09 04						10 04							11 04							12 04			
Leyland 82	d	09 09						10 09							11 09							12 09			
Euxton Balshaw Lane	d	09 14						10 14							11 14							12 14			
Wigan North Western 65	a	09 24						10 24							11 24							12 24			
	d	09 24					10 08	10 24		10 38				11 08	11 24		11 38				12 08	12 24		12 38	
Newton-le-Willows	d			10 01	10 12	10 22					11 01	11 12	11 22					12 01	12 12	12 22					13 01
Warrington Bank Quay	d		09 22						10 22							11 22							12 22		
Earlestown 8	d		09 34	10 04	10 15				10 34		11 04	11 15				11 34		12 04	12 15				12 34		13 04
Warrington Bank Quay	a				10 25							11 25							12 25						
St Helens Junction	d		09 39	10 09		10 27			10 39		11 09		11 27			11 39		12 09		12 27			12 39		13 09
Lea Green	d		09 42	10 12					10 42		11 12					11 42		12 12					12 42		13 12
Rainhill	d		09 46	10 16					10 46		11 16					11 46		12 16					12 46		13 16
Whiston	d		09 49	10 19					10 49		11 19					11 49		12 19					12 49		13 19
Bryn	d						10 15			10 45				11 15			11 45				12 15			12 45	
Garswood	d						10 19			10 49				11 19			11 49				12 19			12 49	
St Helens Central	a	09 39					10 25	10 39		10 55				11 25	11 39		11 55				12 25	12 39		12 55	
	d	09 39					10 26	10 39		10 56				11 26	11 39		11 56				12 26	12 39		12 56	
Thatto Heath	d						10 29			10 59				11 29			11 59				12 29			12 59	
Eccleston Park	d						10 32			11 02				11 32			12 02				12 32			13 02	
Prescot	d						10 34			11 04				11 34			12 04				12 34			13 04	
Huyton	d	09 48	09 53	10 23			10 38	10 48	10 53	11 08	11 23			11 38	11 48	11 53	12 08	12 23			12 38	12 48	12 53	13 08	13 23
Roby	d		09 55	10 25			10 40		10 55	11 10	11 25			11 40		11 55	12 10	12 25			12 40		12 55	13 10	13 25
Broad Green	d		09 58	10 28			10 43		10 58	11 13	11 28			11 43		11 58	12 13	12 28			12 43		12 58	13 13	13 28
Wavertree Technology Park	d		10 01	10 31		10 38	10 46		11 01	11 16	11 31		11 38	11 46		12 01	12 16	12 31		12 38	12 46		13 01	13 16	13 31
Edge Hill 89,91	d		10 04	10 34			10 49		11 04	11 19	11 34			11 49		12 04	12 19	12 34			12 49		13 04	13 19	13 34
Liverpool Lime Street 10 89,91	a	10 02	10 13	10 43		10 48	10 58	11 02	11 13	11 28	11 43		11 48	11 58	12 02	12 13	12 28	12 43		12 48	12 58	13 02	13 13	13 28	13 43

Manchester, Preston, Wigan and Newton-le-Willows - St Helens and Liverpool

	AW ◇	NT	NT	NT	NT	NT	NT	AW ◇	NT	NT	NT	NT	NT	NT	AW ◇	NT	NT	NT	NT	NT	NT	AW ◇	NT	NT
Manchester Airport 85 ✈ d		12 41							13 41							14 41							15 41	
Manchester Piccadilly 10 d	12 50	13 01						13 50	14 01						14 50	15 01						15 50	16 01	
Manchester Oxford Road d	12 53	13 04						13 53	14 04						14 53	15 04						15 53	16 04	
Manchester Victoria d							13 39							14 39							15 39			
Eccles d							13 46							14 46							15 46			
Patricroft d							13 49							14 49							15 49			
Blackpool North 97 d				12 37							13 37							14 37						
Preston 8 65,82 d				13 04							14 04							15 04						
Leyland 82 d				13 09							14 09							15 09						
Euxton Balshaw Lane d				13 14							14 14							15 14						
Wigan North Western 65 a				13 24							14 24							15 24						
d			13 08	13 24		13 38				14 08	14 24		14 38				15 08	15 24		15 38				16 08
Newton-le-Willows d	13 12	13 22					14 01	14 12	14 22					15 01	15 12	15 22					16 01	16 12	16 22	
Warrington Bank Quay d					13 22							14 22							15 22					
Earlestown 8 d	13 15				13 34		14 04	14 15				14 34		15 04	15 15				15 34		16 04	16 15		
Warrington Bank Quay a	13 25							14 25							15 25							16 26		
St Helens Junction d		13 27			13 39		14 09		14 27			14 39		15 09		15 27			15 39		16 09		16 27	
Lea Green d					13 42		14 12					14 42		15 12					15 42		16 12			
Rainhill d					13 46		14 16					14 46		15 16					15 46		16 16			
Whiston d					13 49		14 19					14 49		15 19					15 49		16 19			
Bryn d			13 15			13 45				14 15			14 45				15 15			15 45				16 15
Garswood d			13 19			13 49				14 19			14 49				15 19			15 49				16 19
St Helens Central a			13 25	13 39		13 55				14 25	14 39		14 55				15 25	15 39		15 55				16 25
d			13 26	13 39		13 56				14 26	14 39		14 56				15 26	15 39		15 56				16 26
Thatto Heath d			13 29			13 59				14 29			14 59				15 29			15 59				16 29
Eccleston Park d			13 32			14 02				14 32			15 02				15 32			16 02				16 32
Prescot d			13 34			14 04				14 34			15 04				15 34			16 04				16 34
Huyton d			13 38	13 48	13 53	14 08	14 23			14 38	14 48	14 53	15 08	15 23			15 38	15 48	15 53	16 08	16 23			16 38
Roby d			13 40		13 55	14 10	14 25			14 40		14 55	15 10	15 25			15 40		15 55	16 10	16 25			16 40
Broad Green d			13 43		13 58	14 13	14 28			14 43		14 58	15 13	15 28			15 43		15 58	16 13	16 28			16 43
Wavertree Technology Park d		13 38	13 46		14 01	14 16	14 31		14 38	14 46		15 01	15 16	15 31		15 38	15 46		16 01	16 16	16 31		16 38	16 46
Edge Hill 89,91 d			13 49		14 04	14 19	14 34			14 49		15 04	15 19	15 34			15 49		16 04	16 19	16 34			16 49
Liverpool Lime Street 10 89,91 a		13 48	13 58	14 02	14 13	14 28	14 43		14 48	14 58	15 02	15 13	15 28	15 43		15 48	15 58	16 02	16 13	16 28	16 43		16 48	16 58

	NT	NT	NT	NT	AW ◇	NT	NT	NT	NT	AW	NT	NT	AW ◇	NT	NT	NT	NT	NT	NT	AW	NT	NT	NT	NT
Manchester Airport 85 ✈ d						16 41									17 41						18 41			
Manchester Piccadilly 10 d					16 50	17 01				17 19			17 50		18 01					18 50	19 01			
Manchester Oxford Road d					16 53	17 04				17 22			17 53		18 04					18 53	19 04			
Manchester Victoria d				16 39					17 09			17 37						18 39						
Eccles d				16 46					17 16			17 46			18 11			18 46						
Patricroft d				16 49					17 19			17 49						18 49						
Blackpool North 97 d	15 37							16 35											17 37				18 37	
Preston 8 65,82 d	16 04							17 04											18 04				19 04	
Leyland 82 d	16 09							17 09											18 09				19 09	
Euxton Balshaw Lane d	16 14							17 14											18 14				19 14	
Wigan North Western 65 a	16 24							17 24											18 24				19 24	
d	16 24		16 38				17 08	17 24			17 38			18 08		18 21	18 35		18 24			19 08	19 24	
Newton-le-Willows d				17 01	17 12	17 22			17 31	17 40		18 01	18 12		18 24	18 33		19 01		19 12	19 22			
Warrington Bank Quay d		16 22																						19 22
Earlestown 8 d		16 34		17 04	17 15				17 34	17 44		18 04	18 15			18 36		19 04		19 16				19 34
Warrington Bank Quay a					17 25					17 52			18 23							19 24				
St Helens Junction d		16 39		17 09		17 27			17 39			18 09			18 29	18 41		19 09			19 27			19 39
Lea Green d		16 42		17 12					17 42			18 12			18 32	18 44		19 12						19 42
Rainhill d		16 46		17 16					17 46			18 16			18 36	18 48		19 16						19 46
Whiston d		16 49		17 19					17 49			18 19				18 51		19 19						19 49
Bryn d			16 45				17 15				17 45			18 15			18 45					19 15		
Garswood d			16 49				17 19				17 49			18 19			18 49					19 19		
St Helens Central a	16 39		16 55				17 25	17 39			17 55			18 25			18 55		18 39			19 25	19 39	
d	16 39		16 56				17 26	17 39			17 56			18 26			18 56		18 39			19 26	19 39	
Thatto Heath d			16 59				17 29				17 59			18 29			18 59					19 29		
Eccleston Park d			17 02				17 32				18 02			18 32			19 02					19 32		
Prescot d			17 04				17 34				18 04			18 34			19 04					19 34		
Huyton d	16 48	16 53	17 08	17 23			17 38	17 48	17 53		18 08	18 23		18 38	18 41	18 55	19 08	19 23	18 48			19 38	19 48	19 53
Roby d		16 55	17 10	17 25			17 40		17 55		18 10	18 25			18 43	18 57	19 10	19 25				19 40		19 55
Broad Green d		16 58	17 13	17 28			17 43		17 58		18 13	18 28			18 47	19 00	19 13	19 28				19 43		19 58
Wavertree Technology Park d		17 01	17 16	17 31		17 38	17 46		18 01		18 16	18 31		18 43	18 50	19 03	19 16	19 31			19 38	19 46		20 01
Edge Hill 89,91 d		17 04	17 19	17 34			17 49		18 04		18 19	18 34		18 46		19 06	19 19	19 34				19 49		20 04
Liverpool Lime Street 10 89,91 a	17 05	17 13	17 28	17 43		17 48	17 58	18 02	18 13		18 28	18 43		18 54	19 00	19 16	19 28	19 43	19 03		19 48	19 58	20 02	20 13

	NT	NT	NT	NT	NT	NT	NT	NT	NT	AW	NT	AW	NT	NT	AW	NT	NT	NT	AW
Manchester Airport 85 ✈ d			19 41							20 32		21 32	21 41						
Manchester Piccadilly 10 d		19 50	20 01							20 50		21 50	22 01		22 12				23 14
Manchester Oxford Road d		19 53	20 04							20 53		21 53	22 04		22b29				23 17
Manchester Victoria d	19 39							20 39			21 39					22 39		23 09	
Eccles d	19 46							20 46			21 46					22 46		23 16	
Patricroft d	19 49							20 49			21 49					22 49		23 19	
Blackpool North 97 d						19 37			20 37								22 14		
Preston 8 65,82 d						20 04			21 04								22 43		
Leyland 82 d						20 09			21 09								22 48		
Euxton Balshaw Lane d						20 14			21 14								22 53		
Wigan North Western 65 a						20 23			21 23								23 02		
d				20 08	20 08	20 24	20 38		21 23					22 25			23 03		
Newton-le-Willows d	20 01	20 12	20 22					21 01		21 12	22 01	22 12	22 22		22 47	23 01		23 31	23 36
Warrington Bank Quay d																			
Earlestown 8 d	20 04	20 15						21 04		21 15	22 04	22 15			22 50	23 04		23 34	23 39
Warrington Bank Quay a		20 25								21 24		22 23			22 58				23 47
St Helens Junction d	20 09		20 27					21 09			22 09		22 27			23 09		23 39	
Lea Green d	20 12							21 12			22 12					23 12		23 42	
Rainhill d	20 16							21 16			22 16					23 16		23 46	
Whiston d	20 19							21 19			22 19					23 19		23 49	
Bryn d				20 15	20 15		20 45		21 30					22 32			23 10		
Garswood d				20 19	20 19		20 49		21 34					22 36			23 14		
St Helens Central a				20 25	20 25	20 39	20 55		21 40					22 42			23 20		
d				20 26	20 26	20 39	20 56		21 41					22 43			23 21		
Thatto Heath d				20 29	20 29		20 59		21 44					22 46			23 24		
Eccleston Park d				20 32	20 32		21 02		21 47					22 49			23 27		
Prescot d				20 34	20 34		21 04		21 49					22 51			23 29		
Huyton d	20 23			20 38	20 38	20 48	21 08	21 23	21 53		22 23			22 55		23 23	23 33	23 53	
Roby d	20 25			20 40	20 40		21 10	21 25	21 55		22 25			22 57		23 25	23 35	23 55	
Broad Green d	20 28			20 43	20 43		21 13	21 28	21 58		22 28			23 00		23 28	23 38	23 58	
Wavertree Technology Park d	20 31		20 38	20 46	20 46		21 16	21 31	22 03		22 31		22 38	23 03		23 31	23 41	00 01	
Edge Hill 89,91 d	20 34			20 49	20 49		21 19	21 34	22 06		22 34			23 06		23 34	23 46	00 04	
Liverpool Lime Street 10 89,91 a	20 43		20 48	20 58	20 58	21 02	21 28	21 43	22 16		22 43		22 48	23 15		23 43	23 54	00 13	

Saturdays
until 16 October

	NT	NT	AW ◇	NT	NT	NT	NT	AW ◇	NT	NT	NT	NT	NT	NT	NT	AW ◇	NT	NT	NT	NT	NT	AW ◇	NT	NT
Manchester Airport 85 ✈ d			05 33						06 41								07 41						08 41	
Manchester Piccadilly 10 d			05 50					06 50	06 58							07 50	07 58					08 50	09 01	
Manchester Oxford Road d			05 53					06 53	07 01							07 53	08 03					08 53	09 04	
Manchester Victoria d		05 39			06 09						07 09			07 39				08 09			08 39			
Eccles d		05 46			06 16						07 16			07 46				08 16			08 46			
Patricroft d		05 49			06 19						07 19			07 49				08 19			08 49			
Blackpool North 97 d													07 02											
Preston 8 65,82 d													07 30											
Leyland 82 d													07 35											
Euxton Balshaw Lane d													07 40											
Wigan North Western 65 a													07 50											
d				06 08		06 38	06 47			07 08		07 38	07 50		07 58				08 28					09 08
Newton-le-Willows d		06 01	06 12		06 31		07 00	07 12	07 19		07 31			08 01		08 12	08 21	08 31			09 01	09 12	09 22	
Warrington Bank Quay d																								
Earlestown 8 d		06 04	06 15		06 34		07 03	07 15			07 34			08 04		08 15		08 34			09 04	09 15		
Warrington Bank Quay a			06 25					07 23								08 23						09 25		
St Helens Junction d		06 09			06 39		07 09		07 24		07 39			08 09			08 26	08 39			09 09		09 27	
Lea Green d		06 12			06 42		07 12				07 42			08 12			08 29	08 42			09 12			
Rainhill d		06 16			06 46		07 16		07 29		07 46			08 16			08 33	08 46			09 16			
Whiston d		06 19			06 49		07 19				07 49			08 19			08 37	08 49			09 19			
Bryn d				06 15		06 45				07 15		07 45			08 05				08 35					09 15
Garswood d				06 19		06 49				07 19		07 49	07 59		08 09				08 39					09 19
St Helens Central a				06 25		06 55				07 25		07 55	08 06		08 15				08 45					09 25
d	05 56			06 26		06 56				07 26		07 56	08 06		08 16				08 46	08 56				09 26
Thatto Heath d	05 59			06 29		06 59				07 29		07 59			08 19				08 49	08 59				09 29
Eccleston Park d	06 02			06 32		07 02				07 32		08 02			08 22				08 52	09 02				09 32
Prescot d	06 04			06 34		07 04				07 34		08 04	08 12		08 24				08 54	09 04				09 34
Huyton d	06 08	06 23		06 38	06 53	07 08	07 23		07 34	07 38	07 53	08 08	08 16	08 23	08 28		08 41	08 53	08 58	09 08	09 23			09 38
Roby d	06 10	06 25		06 40	06 55	07 10	07 25			07 40	07 55	08 10		08 25	08 30			08 55	09 00	09 10	09 25			09 40
Broad Green d	06 13	06 28		06 43	06 58	07 13	07 28			07 43	07 58	08 13	08 20	08 28	08 33		08 45	08 58	09 03	09 13	09 28			09 43
Wavertree Technology Park d	06 16	06 31		06 46	07 01	07 16	07 31		07 39	07 46	08 01	08 16	08 24	08 31	08 36		08 48	09 01	09 06	09 16	09 31		09 38	09 46
Edge Hill 89,91 d	06 19	06 34		06 49	07 04	07 19	07 34			07 49	08 04	08 19		08 34	08 39			09 04	09 09	09 19	09 34			09 49
Liverpool Lime Street 10 89,91 a	06 28	06 43		06 58	07 13	07 28	07 43		07 49	07 58	08 13	08 28	08 34	08 43	08 48		08 59	09 13	09 18	09 28	09 43		09 48	09 58

b arr. 2214

Table 90

Saturdays
until 16 October

Manchester, Preston, Wigan and Newton-le-Willows - St Helens and Liverpool

	NT	NT	NT	NT	AW ◇ 🛒	NT	NT	NT	NT	NT	NT	AW ◇ 🛒	NT	NT	NT	NT	NT	NT	AW ◇ 🛒	NT	NT	NT	NT	NT
Manchester Airport 85 ✈ d						09 41							10 41							11 41				
Manchester Piccadilly 10 ⛴ d					09 50	10 01						10 50	11 01						11 50	12 01				
Manchester Oxford Road d					09 53	10 04						10 53	11 04						11 53	12 04				
Manchester Victoria ⛴ d				09 39							10 39							11 39						
Eccles d				09 46							10 46							11 46						
Patricroft d				09 49							10 49							11 49						
Blackpool North 97 d	08 38							09 37							10 37							11 37		
Preston 8 65,82 d	09 04							10 04							11 04							12 04		
Leyland 82 d	09 09							10 09							11 09							12 09		
Euxton Balshaw Lane d	09 14							10 14							11 14							12 14		
Wigan North Western 65 a	09 24							10 24							11 24							12 24		
d	09 24		09 38				10 08	10 24	10 38					11 08	11 24		11 38				12 08	12 24		12 38
Newton-le-Willows d				10 01	10 12	10 22					11 01	11 12	11 22					12 01	12 12	12 22				
Warrington Bank Quay d		09 22								10 22						11 22							12 22	
Earlestown 8 d		09 34		10 04	10 15					10 34	11 04	11 15				11 34		12 04	12 15				12 34	
Warrington Bank Quay a					10 25							11 25							12 25					
St Helens Junction d		09 39		10 09		10 27				10 39	11 09		11 27			11 39		12 09		12 27			12 39	
Lea Green d		09 42		10 12						10 42	11 12					11 42		12 12					12 42	
Rainhill d		09 46		10 16						10 46	11 16					11 46		12 16					12 46	
Whiston d		09 49		10 19						10 49	11 19					11 49		12 19					12 49	
Bryn d			09 45				10 15		10 45					11 15			11 45				12 15			12 45
Garswood d			09 49				10 19		10 49					11 19			11 49				12 19			12 49
St Helens Central a	09 39		09 55				10 25	10 39	10 55					11 25	11 39		11 55				12 25	12 39		12 55
d	09 39		09 56				10 26	10 39	10 56					11 26	11 39		11 56				12 26	12 39		12 56
Thatto Heath d			09 59				10 29		10 59					11 29			11 59				12 29			12 59
Eccleston Park d			10 02				10 32		11 02					11 32			12 02				12 32			13 02
Prescot d			10 04				10 34		11 04					11 34			12 04				12 34			13 04
Huyton d	09 48	09 53	10 08	10 23			10 38	10 48	11 08	10 53	11 23			11 38	11 48	11 53	12 08	12 23			12 38	12 48	12 53	13 08
Roby d		09 55	10 10	10 25			10 40		11 10	10 55	11 25			11 40		11 55	12 10	12 25			12 40		12 55	13 10
Broad Green d		09 58	10 13	10 28			10 43		11 13	10 58	11 28			11 43		11 58	12 13	12 28			12 43		12 58	13 13
Wavertree Technology Park d		10 01	10 16	10 31		10 38	10 46		11 16	11 01	11 31		11 38	11 46		12 01	12 16	12 31		12 38	12 46		13 01	13 16
Edge Hill 89,91 d		10 04	10 21	10 34			10 49		11 19	11 04	11 34			11 49		12 04	12 19	12 34			12 49		13 04	13 19
Liverpool Lime Street 10 89,91 a	10 02	10 13	10 29	10 43		10 48	10 58	11 02	11 28	11 13	11 43		11 48	11 58	12 02	12 13	12 28	12 43		12 48	12 58	13 02	13 13	13 28

	NT	AW ◇ 🛒	NT	NT	NT	NT	NT	NT	NT	AW ◇ 🛒	NT	NT	NT	NT	NT	NT	AW ◇ 🛒	NT	NT	NT	NT	NT	NT	AW ◇ 🛒
Manchester Airport 85 ✈ d			12 41								13 41							14 41						
Manchester Piccadilly 10 ⛴ d		12 50	13 01							13 50	14 01						14 50	15 01						15 50
Manchester Oxford Road d		12 53	13 04							13 53	14 04						14 53	15 04						15 53
Manchester Victoria ⛴ d	12 39								13 39							14 39							15 39	
Eccles d	12 46								13 46							14 46							15 46	
Patricroft d	12 49								13 49							14 49							15 49	
Blackpool North 97 d						12 37							13 37							14 37				
Preston 8 65,82 d						13 04							14 04							15 04				
Leyland 82 d						13 09							14 09							15 09				
Euxton Balshaw Lane d						13 14							14 14							15 14				
Wigan North Western 65 a						13 24							14 24							15 24				
d				13 38	13 08	13 24		13 38				14 08	14 24		14 38				15 08	15 24		15 38		
Newton-le-Willows d	13 01	13 12	13 22						14 01	14 12	14 22					15 01	15 12	15 22					16 01	16 12
Warrington Bank Quay d							13 22							14 22							15 22			
Earlestown 8 d	13 04	13 15					13 34		14 04	14 15				14 34		15 04	15 15				15 34		16 04	16 15
Warrington Bank Quay a		13 25								14 25							15 25							16 25
St Helens Junction d	13 09		13 27				13 39		14 09		14 27			14 39		15 09		15 27			15 39		16 09	
Lea Green d	13 12						13 42		14 12					14 42		15 12					15 42		16 12	
Rainhill d	13 16						13 46		14 16					14 46		15 16					15 46		16 16	
Whiston d	13 19						13 49		14 19					14 49		15 19					15 49		16 19	
Bryn d				13 45	13 15			13 45				14 15			14 45				15 15			15 45		
Garswood d				13 49	13 19			13 49				14 19			14 49				15 19			15 49		
St Helens Central a				13 55	13 25	13 39		13 55				14 25	14 39		14 55				15 25	15 39		15 55		
d				13 56	13 26	13 39		13 56				14 26	14 39		14 56				15 26	15 39		15 56		
Thatto Heath d				13 59	13 29			13 59				14 29			14 59				15 29			15 59		
Eccleston Park d				14 02	13 32			14 02				14 32			15 02				15 32			16 02		
Prescot d				14 04	13 34			14 04				14 34			15 04				15 34			16 04		
Huyton d	13 23			14 08	13 38	13 48	13 53	14 08	14 23			14 38	14 48	14 53	15 08	15 23			15 38	15 48	15 53	16 08	16 23	
Roby d	13 25			14 10	13 40		13 55	14 10	14 25			14 40		14 55	15 10	15 25			15 40		15 55	16 10	16 25	
Broad Green d	13 28			14 13	13 43		13 58	14 13	14 28			14 43		14 58	15 13	15 28			15 43		15 58	16 13	16 28	
Wavertree Technology Park d	13 31		13 38	14 16	13 46		14 01	14 16	14 31		14 38	14 46		15 01	15 16	15 31		15 38	15 46		16 01	16 16	16 31	
Edge Hill 89,91 d	13 34			14 19	13 49		14 04	14 19	14 34			14 49		15 04	15 19	15 34			15 49		16 04	16 19	16 34	
Liverpool Lime Street 10 89,91 a	13 43		13 48	14 28	13 58	14 02	14 13	14 28	14 43		14 48	14 58	15 02	15 13	15 28	15 43		15 48	15 58	16 02	16 13	16 28	16 43	

Table 90

Saturdays
until 16 October

Manchester, Preston, Wigan and Newton-le-Willows - St Helens and Liverpool

	NT	NT	NT	NT	NT	NT	AW ◇ 🛒	NT	NT	NT	NT	NT	NT	AW ◇ 🛒	NT	NT	NT	NT	NT	NT	AW 🛒	NT	NT	NT
Manchester Airport 85 ✈ d	15 41							16 41								17 41						18 41		
Manchester Piccadilly 10 ⛴ d	16 01						16 50	17 01						17 50		18 01					18 50	19 01		
Manchester Oxford Road d	16 04						16 53	17 04						17 53		18 04					18 53	19 04		
Manchester Victoria ⛴ d						16 39					17 09		17 39							18 39				
Eccles d						16 46					17 16		17 46			18 11				18 46				
Patricroft d						16 49					17 19		17 49							18 49				
Blackpool North 97 d			15 37							16 35							17 37							18 37
Preston 8 65,82 d			16 04							17 04							18 04							19 04
Leyland 82 d			16 09							17 09							18 09							19 09
Euxton Balshaw Lane d			16 14							17 14							18 14							19 14
Wigan North Western 65 a			16 24							17 24							18 24							19 24
d		16 08	16 24		16 38				17 08	17 24		17 38			18 08		18 24	18 21	18 35				19 08	19 24
Newton-le-Willows d	16 22					17 01	17 12	17 22			17 31		18 01	18 12		18 24		18 33		19 01	19 12	19 22		
Warrington Bank Quay d				16 22																				
Earlestown 8 d				16 34		17 04	17 15				17 34		18 04	18 15				18 36		19 04	19 16			
Warrington Bank Quay a							17 25							18 24							19 25			
St Helens Junction d	16 27			16 39		17 09		17 27			17 39		18 09			18 29		18 41		19 09		19 27		
Lea Green d				16 42		17 12					17 42		18 12			18 32		18 44		19 12				
Rainhill d				16 46		17 16					17 46		18 16			18 36		18 48		19 16				
Whiston d				16 49		17 19					17 49		18 19					18 51		19 19				
Bryn d		16 15			16 45				17 15			17 45			18 15				18 45				19 15	
Garswood d		16 19			16 49				17 19			17 49			18 19				18 49				19 19	
St Helens Central a		16 25	16 39		16 55				17 25	17 39		17 55			18 25		18 39		18 55				19 25	19 39
d		16 26	16 39		16 56				17 26	17 39		17 56			18 26		18 39		18 56				19 26	19 39
Thatto Heath d		16 29			16 59				17 29			17 59			18 29				18 59				19 29	
Eccleston Park d		16 32			17 02				17 32			18 02			18 32				19 02				19 32	
Prescot d		16 34			17 04				17 34			18 04			18 34				19 04				19 34	
Huyton d		16 38	16 48	16 53	17 08	17 23			17 38	17 48	17 53	18 08	18 23		18 38	18 41	18 48	18 55	19 08	19 23			19 38	19 48
Roby d		16 40		16 55	17 10	17 25			17 40		17 55	18 10	18 25			18 43		18 57	19 10	19 25			19 40	
Broad Green d		16 43		16 58	17 13	17 28			17 43		17 58	18 13	18 28			18 47		19 00	19 13	19 28			19 43	
Wavertree Technology Park d	16 38	16 46		17 01	17 16	17 31		17 38	17 46		18 01	18 16	18 31		18 43	18 50		19 03	19 16	19 31		19 38	19 46	
Edge Hill 89,91 d		16 49		17 04	17 19	17 34			17 49		18 04	18 19	18 34		18 46			19 06	19 19	19 34			19 49	
Liverpool Lime Street 10 89,91 a	16 48	16 58	17 05	17 13	17 28	17 43		17 48	17 58	18 02	18 13	18 28	18 43		18 54	19 00	19 02	19 15	19 28	19 43		19 48	19 58	20 02

	NT	NT	AW	NT	NT	NT	NT	NT	AW	NT	NT	AW	NT	NT	AW	NT	NT	NT	AW
Manchester Airport 85 ✈ d				19 41					20 32				21 41						
Manchester Piccadilly 10 ⛴ d			19 50	20 01					20 50			21 50	22 01		22 26				23 14
Manchester Oxford Road d			19 53	20 04					20 53			21 53	22 04		22 29				23 17
Manchester Victoria ⛴ d		19 39						20 39			21 39					22 39		23 09	
Eccles d		19 46						20 46			21 46					22 46		23 16	
Patricroft d		19 49						20 49			21 49					22 49		23 19	
Blackpool North 97 d						19 37				20 37							22 14		
Preston 8 65,82 d						20 04				21 04							22 43		
Leyland 82 d						20 09				21 09							22 48		
Euxton Balshaw Lane d						20 14				21 14							22 53		
Wigan North Western 65 a						20 24				21 23							23 02		
d					20 08	20 24	20 38			21 23				22 25			23 03		
Newton-le-Willows d		20 01	20 12	20 22				21 01	21 12		22 01	22 12	22 22		22 47	23 01		23 31	23 36
Warrington Bank Quay d	19 22																		
Earlestown 8 d	19 34	20 04	20 15					21 04	21 15		22 04	22 15			22 50	23 04		23 34	23 39
Warrington Bank Quay a			20 29						21 26			22 23			22 58				23 47
St Helens Junction d	19 39	20 09		20 27				21 09			22 09		22 27			23 09		23 39	
Lea Green d	19 42	20 12						21 12			22 12					23 12		23 42	
Rainhill d	19 46	20 16						21 16			22 16					23 16		23 46	
Whiston d	19 49	20 19						21 19			22 19					23 19		23 49	
Bryn d					20 15		20 45			21 30				22 32			23 10		
Garswood d					20 19		20 49			21 34				22 36			23 14		
St Helens Central a					20 25	20 39	20 55			21 40				22 42			23 20		
d					20 26	20 39	20 56			21 41				22 43			23 21		
Thatto Heath d					20 29		20 59			21 44				22 46			23 24		
Eccleston Park d					20 32		21 02			21 47				22 49			23 27		
Prescot d					20 34		21 04			21 49				22 51			23 29		
Huyton d	19 53	20 23			20 38	20 48	21 08	21 23		21 53	22 23			22 55		23 23	23 33	23 53	
Roby d	19 55	20 25			20 40		21 10	21 25		21 55	22 25			22 57		23 25	23 35	23 55	
Broad Green d	19 58	20 28			20 43		21 13	21 28		21 58	22 28			23 00		23 28	23 38	23 57	
Wavertree Technology Park d	20 01	20 31		20 38	20 46		21 16	21 31		22 03	22 31		22 38	23 03		23 31	23 41	00 01	
Edge Hill 89,91 d	20 04	20 34			20 49		21 19	21 34		22 06	22 34			23 06		23 34	23 46	00 04	
Liverpool Lime Street 10 89,91 a	20 13	20 43		20 48	20 58	21 02	21 28	21 43		22 14	22 43		22 48	23 15		23 43	23 54	00 13	

Manchester, Preston, Wigan and Newton-le-Willows - St Helens and Liverpool

	NT	NT	AW	NT	NT	NT	NT	AW	NT	NT	NT	NT	NT	NT	NT	AW	NT	NT	NT	NT	NT	AW	NT	NT
			◇ 🛒					◇ 🛒								◇ 🛒						◇ 🛒		
Manchester Airport 85 ✈ d			05 33						06 41								07 41						08 41	
Manchester Piccadilly 10 ⇌ d			05 50					06 50	06 58							07 50	07 58					08 50	09 01	
Manchester Oxford Road d			05 53					06 53	07 01							07 53	08 03					08 53	09 04	
Manchester Victoria ⇌ d		05 39			06 09						07 09			07 39				08 09			08 39			
Eccles d		05 46			06 16						07 16			07 46				08 16			08 46			
Patricroft d		05 49			06 19						07 19			07 49				08 19			08 49			
Blackpool North 97 d													07 02											
Preston 8 65,82 d													07 30											
Leyland 82 d													07 35											
Euxton Balshaw Lane d													07 40											
Wigan North Western 65 a													07 50											
d				06 08		06 38	06 47			07 08		07 38	07 50		07 58				08 28					09 08
Newton-le-Willows d		06 01	06 12		06 31		07 00	07 12	07 19		07 31			08 01		08 12	08 21	08 31			09 01	09 12	09 22	
Warrington Bank Quay d																								
Earlestown 8 d		06 04	06 15		06 34		07 03	07 15			07 34			08 04		08 15		08 34			09 04	09 15		
Warrington Bank Quay a			06 25					07 23								08 23						09 25		
St Helens Junction d		06 09			06 39		07 09		07 24		07 39			08 09			08 26	08 39			09 09		09 27	
Lea Green d		06 12			06 42		07 12				07 42			08 12			08 29	08 42			09 12			
Rainhill d		06 16			06 46		07 16		07 29		07 46			08 16			08 33	08 46			09 16			
Whiston d		06 19			06 49		07 19				07 49			08 19			08 37	08 49			09 19			
Bryn d				06 15		06 45				07 15		07 45			08 05				08 35					09 15
Garswood d				06 19		06 49				07 19		07 49	07 59		08 09				08 39					09 19
St Helens Central a				06 25		06 55				07 25		07 55	08 06		08 15				08 45					09 25
d	05 56			06 26		06 56				07 26		07 56	08 06		08 16				08 46	08 56				09 26
Thatto Heath d	05 59			06 29		06 59				07 29		07 59			08 19				08 49	08 59				09 29
Eccleston Park d	06 02			06 32		07 02				07 32		08 02			08 22				08 52	09 02				09 32
Prescot d	06 04			06 34		07 04				07 34		08 04	08 12		08 24				08 54	09 04				09 34
Huyton d	06 08	06 23		06 38	06 53	07 08	07 23		07 34	07 38	07 53	08 08	08 16	08 23	08 28		08 41	08 53	08 58	09 08	09 23			09 38
Roby d	06 10	06 25		06 40	06 55	07 10	07 25			07 40	07 55	08 10		08 25	08 30			08 55	09 00	09 10	09 25			09 40
Broad Green d	06 13	06 28		06 43	06 58	07 13	07 28			07 43	07 58	08 13	08 20	08 28	08 33		08 45	08 58	09 03	09 13	09 28			09 43
Wavertree Technology Park d	06 16	06 31		06 46	07 01	07 16	07 31		07 39	07 46	08 01	08 16	08 24	08 31	08 36		08 48	09 01	09 06	09 16	09 31		09 38	09 46
Edge Hill 89,91 d	06 19	06 34		06 49	07 04	07 19	07 34			07 49	08 04	08 19		08 34	08 39			09 04	09 09	09 19	09 34			09 49
Liverpool Lime Street 10 89,91 a	06 28	06 43		06 58	07 13	07 28	07 43		07 49	07 58	08 13	08 28	08 34	08 43	08 48		08 59	09 13	09 18	09 28	09 43		09 48	09 58

	NT	NT	NT	NT	AW	NT	NT	NT	NT	NT	NT	AW	NT	NT	NT	NT	NT	NT	AW	NT	NT	NT	NT	NT
					◇ 🛒							◇ 🛒							◇ 🛒					
Manchester Airport 85 ✈ d						09 41							10 41							11 41				
Manchester Piccadilly 10 ⇌ d					09 50	10 01						10 50	11 01						11 50	12 01				
Manchester Oxford Road d					09 53	10 04						10 53	11 04						11 53	12 04				
Manchester Victoria ⇌ d				09 39							10 39							11 39						
Eccles d				09 46							10 46							11 46						
Patricroft d				09 49							10 49							11 49						
Blackpool North 97 d	08 38							09 37							10 37							11 37		
Preston 8 65,82 d	09 04							10 04							11 04							12 04		
Leyland 82 d	09 09							10 09							11 09							12 09		
Euxton Balshaw Lane d	09 14							10 14							11 14							12 14		
Wigan North Western 65 a	09 24							10 24							11 24							12 24		
d	09 24		09 38				10 08	10 24		10 38				11 08	11 24		11 38				12 08	12 24		12 38
Newton-le-Willows d				10 01	10 12	10 22					11 01	11 12	11 22					12 01	12 12	12 22				
Warrington Bank Quay d		09 22							10 22							11 22							12 22	
Earlestown 8 d		09 34		10 04	10 15				10 34		11 04	11 15				11 34		12 04	12 15				12 34	
Warrington Bank Quay a					10 25							11 25							12 25					
St Helens Junction d		09 39		10 09		10 27			10 39		11 09		11 27			11 39		12 09		12 27			12 39	
Lea Green d		09 42		10 12					10 42		11 12					11 42		12 12					12 42	
Rainhill d		09 46		10 16					10 46		11 16					11 46		12 16					12 46	
Whiston d		09 49		10 19					10 49		11 19					11 49		12 19					12 49	
Bryn d			09 45				10 15			10 45				11 15			11 45				12 15			12 45
Garswood d			09 49				10 19			10 49				11 19			11 49				12 19			12 49
St Helens Central a	09 39		09 55				10 25	10 39		10 55				11 25	11 39		11 55				12 25	12 39		12 55
d	09 39		09 56				10 26	10 39		10 56				11 26	11 39		11 56				12 26	12 39		12 56
Thatto Heath d			09 59				10 29			10 59				11 29			11 59				12 29			12 59
Eccleston Park d			10 02				10 32			11 02				11 32			12 02				12 32			13 02
Prescot d			10 04				10 34			11 04				11 34			12 04				12 34			13 04
Huyton d	09 48	09 53	10 08	10 23			10 38	10 48	10 53	11 08	11 23			11 38	11 48	11 53	12 08	12 23			12 38	12 48	12 53	13 08
Roby d		09 55	10 10	10 25			10 40		10 55	11 10	11 25			11 40		11 55	12 10	12 25			12 40		12 55	13 10
Broad Green d		09 58	10 13	10 28			10 43		10 58	11 13	11 28			11 43		11 58	12 13	12 28			12 43		12 58	13 13
Wavertree Technology Park d		10 01	10 16	10 31		10 38	10 46		11 01	11 16	11 31		11 38	11 46		12 01	12 16	12 31		12 38	12 46		13 01	13 16
Edge Hill 89,91 d		10 04	10 21	10 34			10 49		11 04	11 19	11 34			11 49		12 04	12 19	12 34			12 49		13 04	13 19
Liverpool Lime Street 10 89,91 a	10 02	10 13	10 29	10 43		10 48	10 58	11 02	11 13	11 28	11 43		11 48	11 58	12 02	12 13	12 28	12 43		12 48	12 58	13 02	13 13	13 28

Manchester, Preston, Wigan and Newton-le-Willows - St Helens and Liverpool

	NT	AW	NT	NT	NT	NT	NT	NT	AW	NT	NT	NT	NT	NT	NT	AW	NT	NT	NT	NT	NT	NT	AW	NT
		◇ 🛒							◇ 🛒							◇ 🛒							◇ 🛒	
Manchester Airport 85 ✈ d			12 41							13 41							14 41							15 41
Manchester Piccadilly 10 ⇌ d		12 50	13 01						13 50	14 01						14 50	15 01						15 50	16 01
Manchester Oxford Road d		12 53	13 04						13 53	14 04						14 53	15 04						15 53	16 04
Manchester Victoria ⇌ d	12 39							13 39							14 39							15 39		
Eccles d	12 46							13 46							14 46							15 46		
Patricroft d	12 49							13 49							14 49							15 49		
Blackpool North 97 d					12 37							13 37							14 37					
Preston 8 65,82 d					13 04							14 04							15 04					
Leyland 82 d					13 09							14 09							15 09					
Euxton Balshaw Lane d					13 14							14 14							15 14					
Wigan North Western 65 a					13 24							14 24							15 24					
d				13 08	13 24		13 38				14 08	14 24		14 38				15 08	15 24		15 38			
Newton-le-Willows d	13 01	13 12	13 22					14 01	14 12	14 22					15 01	15 12	15 22					16 01	16 12	16 22
Warrington Bank Quay d						13 22							14 22							15 22				
Earlestown 8 d	13 04	13 15				13 34		14 04	14 15				14 34		15 04	15 15				15 34		16 04	16 15	
Warrington Bank Quay a		13 25							14 25							15 25							16 25	
St Helens Junction d	13 09		13 27			13 39		14 09		14 27			14 39		15 09		15 27			15 39		16 09		16 27
Lea Green d	13 12					13 42		14 12					14 42		15 12					15 42		16 12		
Rainhill d	13 16					13 46		14 16					14 46		15 16					15 46		16 16		
Whiston d	13 19					13 49		14 19					14 49		15 19					15 49		16 19		
Bryn d				13 15			13 45				14 15			14 45				15 15			15 45			
Garswood d				13 19			13 49				14 19			14 49				15 19			15 49			
St Helens Central a				13 25	13 39		13 55				14 25	14 39		14 55				15 25	15 39		15 55			
d				13 26	13 39		13 56				14 26	14 39		14 56				15 26	15 39		15 56			
Thatto Heath d				13 29			13 59				14 29			14 59				15 29			15 59			
Eccleston Park d				13 32			14 02				14 32			15 02				15 32			16 02			
Prescot d				13 34			14 04				14 34			15 04				15 34			16 04			
Huyton d	13 23			13 38	13 48	13 53	14 08	14 23			14 38	14 48	14 53	15 08	15 23			15 38	15 48	15 53	16 08	16 23		
Roby d	13 25			13 40		13 55	14 10	14 25			14 40		14 55	15 10	15 25			15 40		15 55	16 10	16 25		
Broad Green d	13 28			13 43		13 58	14 13	14 28			14 43		14 58	15 13	15 28			15 43		15 58	16 13	16 28		
Wavertree Technology Park d	13 31		13 38	13 46		14 01	14 16	14 31		14 38	14 46		15 01	15 16	15 31		15 38	15 46		16 01	16 16	16 31		16 38
Edge Hill 89,91 d	13 34			13 49		14 04	14 19	14 34			14 49		15 04	15 19	15 34			15 49		16 04	16 19	16 34		
Liverpool Lime Street 10 89,91 a	13 43		13 48	13 58	14 02	14 13	14 28	14 43		14 48	14 58	15 02	15 13	15 28	15 43		15 48	15 58	16 02	16 13	16 28	16 43		16 48

	NT	NT	NT	NT	NT	AW	NT	NT	NT	NT	NT	NT	AW	NT	NT	NT	NT	NT	AW	NT	NT	NT	NT	NT
						◇ 🛒							◇ 🛒						🛒					
Manchester Airport 85 ✈ d							16 41								17 41					18 41				
Manchester Piccadilly 10 ⇌ d						16 50	17 01						17 50		18 01				18 50	19 01				
Manchester Oxford Road d						16 53	17 04						17 53		18 04				18 53	19 04				
Manchester Victoria ⇌ d					16 39					17 09		17 39						18 39						19 39
Eccles d					16 46					17 16		17 46			18 11			18 46						19 46
Patricroft d					16 49					17 19		17 49						18 49						19 49
Blackpool North 97 d		15 37							16 35							17 37						18 37		
Preston 8 65,82 d		16 04							17 04							18 04						19 04		
Leyland 82 d		16 09							17 09							18 09						19 09		
Euxton Balshaw Lane d		16 14							17 14							18 14						19 14		
Wigan North Western 65 a		16 24							17 24							18 24						19 24		
d	16 08	16 24		16 38				17 08	17 24		17 38			18 08		18 24	18 35				19 08	19 24		
Newton-le-Willows d					17 01	17 12	17 22			17 31		18 01	18 12		18 24			19 01	19 12	19 22				20 01
Warrington Bank Quay d			16 22																				19 22	
Earlestown 8 d			16 34		17 04	17 15				17 34		18 04	18 15					19 04	19 16				19 34	20 04
Warrington Bank Quay a						17 25							18 24						19 25					
St Helens Junction d			16 39		17 09		17 27			17 39		18 09			18 29			19 09		19 27			19 39	20 09
Lea Green d			16 42		17 12					17 42		18 12			18 32			19 12					19 42	20 12
Rainhill d			16 46		17 16					17 46		18 16			18 36			19 16					19 46	20 16
Whiston d			16 49		17 19					17 49		18 19						19 19					19 49	20 19
Bryn d	16 15			16 45				17 15			17 45			18 15			18 45				19 15			
Garswood d	16 19			16 49				17 19			17 49			18 19			18 49				19 19			
St Helens Central a	16 25	16 39		16 55				17 25	17 39		17 55			18 25		18 39	18 55				19 25	19 39		
d	16 26	16 39		16 56				17 26	17 39		17 56			18 26		18 39	18 56				19 26	19 39		
Thatto Heath d	16 29			16 59				17 29			17 59			18 29			18 59				19 29			
Eccleston Park d	16 32			17 02				17 32			18 02			18 32			19 02				19 32			
Prescot d	16 34			17 04				17 34			18 04			18 34			19 04				19 34			
Huyton d	16 38	16 48	16 53	17 08	17 23			17 38	17 48	17 53	18 08	18 23		18 38	18 41	18 48	19 08	19 23			19 38	19 48	19 53	20 23
Roby d	16 40		16 55	17 10	17 25			17 40		17 55	18 10	18 25			18 43		19 10	19 25			19 40		19 55	20 25
Broad Green d	16 43		16 58	17 13	17 28			17 43		17 58	18 13	18 28			18 47		19 13	19 28			19 43		19 58	20 28
Wavertree Technology Park d	16 46		17 01	17 16	17 31		17 38	17 46		18 01	18 16	18 31		18 43	18 50		19 16	19 31		19 38	19 46		20 01	20 31
Edge Hill 89,91 d	16 49		17 04	17 19	17 34			17 49		18 04	18 19	18 34		18 46			19 19	19 34			19 49		20 04	20 34
Liverpool Lime Street 10 89,91 a	16 58	17 05	17 13	17 28	17 43		17 48	17 58	18 02	18 13	18 28	18 43		18 54	19 00	19 02	19 28	19 43		19 48	19 58	20 02	20 13	20 43

Saturdays from 23 October

Manchester, Preston, Wigan and Newton-le-Willows - St Helens and Liverpool

	AW	NT	NT	NT	NT	NT	NT	AW	NT	AW	NT	AW	NT	NT	NT	AW
Manchester Airport 85 ✈ d		19 41						20 32			21 41					
Manchester Piccadilly 10 d	19 50	20 01						20 50		21 50	22 01	22 21				23 14
Manchester Oxford Road d	19 53	20 04						20 53		21 53	22 04	22 24				23 19
Manchester Victoria d						20 39			21 39					22 39		
Eccles d						20 46			21 46					22 46		
Patricroft d						20 49			21 49					22 49		
Blackpool North 97 d				19 37			20 37								22 14	
Preston 8 65,82 d				20 04			21 04								22 43	
Leyland 82 d				20 09			21 09								22 48	
Euxton Balshaw Lane d				20 14			21 14								22 53	
Wigan North Western 65 a				20 24			21 23								23 02	
d			20 08	20 24	20 38		21 23						22 25		23 03	
Newton-le-Willows d	20 12	20 22				21 01		21 12	22 01	22 12	22 22	22 42		23 01		23 49
Warrington Bank Quay d																
Earlestown 8 d	20 15					21 04		21 15	22 04	22 15		22 45		23 04		23 59
Warrington Bank Quay a	20 29							21 26		22 23		22 53				00 24
St Helens Junction d		20 27				21 09			22 09		22 27			23 09		
Lea Green d						21 12			22 12					23 12		
Rainhill d						21 16			22 16					23 16		
Whiston d						21 19			22 19					23 19		
Bryn d			20 15		20 45		21 30						22 32		23 10	
Garswood d			20 19		20 49		21 34						22 36		23 14	
St Helens Central a			20 25	20 39	20 55		21 40						22 42		23 20	
d			20 26	20 39	20 56		21 41						22 43		23 21	
Thatto Heath d			20 29		20 59		21 44						22 46		23 24	
Eccleston Park d			20 32		21 02		21 47						22 49		23 27	
Prescot d			20 34		21 04		21 49						22 51		23 29	
Huyton d			20 38	20 48	21 08	21 23	21 53		22 23				22 55	23 23	23 33	
Roby d			20 40		21 10	21 25	21 55		22 25				22 57	23 25	23 35	
Broad Green d			20 43		21 13	21 28	21 58		22 28				23 00	23 28	23 38	
Wavertree Technology Park d		20 38	20 46		21 16	21 31	22 03		22 31		22 38		23 03	23 31	23 41	
Edge Hill 89,91 d			20 49		21 19	21 34	22 06		22 34				23 06	23 34	23 46	
Liverpool Lime Street 10 89,91 a		20 48	20 58	21 02	21 28	21 43	22 14		22 43		22 48		23 15	23 43	23 54	

Sundays until 05 September

	AW	NT	NT	NT	NT	NT	NT	NT	AW	NT B	NT C	NT	AW	NT	NT	AW	NT	NT	AW	NT	NT	AW	NT
Manchester Airport 85 ✈ d			08 34				10 32			11 35				12 35			13 35			14 35			15 35
Manchester Piccadilly 10 d	07 28		08 50		09 50		10 50		10 55	11 50	11 50		11 56	12 50		12 56	13 50		13 56	14 50		14 56	15 50
Manchester Oxford Road d	07 33		08 53		09 53		10 53		10 59	11 53	11 53		11 59	12 53		12 59	13 53		13 59	14 53		14 59	15 53
Manchester Victoria d																							
Eccles d			09 00		10 00		11 00			12 00	12 00			13 00			14 00			15 00			16 00
Patricroft d																							
Blackpool North 97 d				08 50		09 50		10 50				11 50			12 50			13 50			14 50		
Preston 8 65,82 d				09 15		10 15		11 15				12 15			13 15			14 15			15 15		
Leyland 82 d				09 21		10 21		11 21				12 21			13 21			14 21			15 21		
Euxton Balshaw Lane d				09 26		10 26		11 25				12 25			13 25			14 25			15 25		
Wigan North Western 65 a				09 35		10 35		11 35				12 35			13 35			14 35			15 35		
d		08 36		09 36		10 36		11 36				12 36			13 36			14 36			15 36		
Newton-le-Willows d	08 03		09 13		10 13		11 13		11 20	12 13	12 13		12 18	13 13		13 18	14 13		14 18	15 13		15 18	16 13
Warrington Bank Quay d																							
Earlestown 8 d	08 13		09 16		10 16		11 16		11 23	12 16	12 16		12 21	13 16		13 21	14 16		14 21	15 16		15 21	16 16
Warrington Bank Quay a	08 38								11 29				12 27			13 28			14 27			15 28	
St Helens Junction d			09 21		10 21		11 21			12 21	12 21			13 21			14 21			15 21			16 21
Lea Green d			09 24		10 24		11 24			12 24	12 24			13 24			14 24			15 24			16 24
Rainhill d			09 28		10 28		11 28			12 28	12 28			13 28			14 28			15 28			16 28
Whiston d			09 31		10 31		11 31			12 31	12 31			13 31			14 31			15 31			16 31
Bryn d																							
Garswood d		08 46		09 46		10 46		11 46				12 46			13 46			14 46			15 46		
St Helens Central a		08 52		09 52		10 52		11 52				12 52			13 52			14 52			15 52		
d		08 53		09 53		10 53		11 53				12 53			13 53			14 53			15 53		
Thatto Heath d		08 56		09 56		10 56		11 56				12 56			13 56			14 56			15 56		
Eccleston Park d																							
Prescot d		09 00		10 00		11 00		12 00				13 00			14 00			15 00			16 00		
Huyton d		09 05	09 35	10 05	10 35	11 05	11 35	12 05		12 35	12 35	13 05		13 35	14 05		14 35	15 05		15 35	16 05		16 35
Roby d		09 07	09 37	10 07	10 37	11 07	11 37	12 07		12 37	12 37	13 07		13 37	14 07		14 37	15 07		15 37	16 07		16 37
Broad Green d		09 10	09 40	10 10	10 40	11 10	11 40	12 10		12 40	12 40	13 10		13 40	14 10		14 40	15 10		15 40	16 10		16 40
Wavertree Technology Park d		09 13	09 43	10 13	10 43	11 13	11 43	12 13		12 43	12 43	13 13		13 43	14 13		14 43	15 13		15 43	16 13		16 43
Edge Hill 89,91 d																							
Liverpool Lime Street 10 89,91 a		09 24	09 54	10 24	10 54	11 24	11 54	12 24		12 54	12 54	13 24		13 54	14 24		14 54	15 24		15 54	16 24		16 54

B from 18 July until 5 September **C** until 11 July

Sundays until 05 September

Manchester, Preston, Wigan and Newton-le-Willows - St Helens and Liverpool

	NT	AW	NT	NT	AW	NT	NT	AW	NT	NT	AW	NT	NT	AW	NT	NT	AW	NT	NT	AW	NT	NT
Manchester Airport 85 ✈ d			16 35			17 35			18 35			19 35			20 35			21 35			22 35	
Manchester Piccadilly 10 d		15 56	16 50		16 56	17 50		17 56	18 50		18 56	19 50		19 56	20 50		20 56	21 50		21 56	22 50	
Manchester Oxford Road d		15 59	16 53		16 59	17 53		17 59	18 53		18 59	19 53		19 59	20 53		20 59	21 53		21 59	22 53	
Manchester Victoria d																						
Eccles d			17 00			18 00			19 00			20 00			21 00			22 00			23 00	
Patricroft d																						
Blackpool North 97 d	15 50			16 50			17 50			18 50			19 50			20 50			21 50			22 44
Preston 8 65,82 d	16 15			17 15			18 15			19 15			20 15			21 15			22 15			23 09
Leyland 82 d	16 21			17 21			18 21			19 21			20 21			21 21			22 21			23 15
Euxton Balshaw Lane d	16 25			17 25			18 25			19 25			20 25			21 25			22 25			23 19
Wigan North Western 65 a	16 35			17 35			18 35			19 35			20 35			21 35			22 35			23 29
d	16 36			17 36			18 36			19 36			20 36			21 36			22 36			23 30
Newton-le-Willows d		16 18	17 13		17 18	18 13		18 18	19 13		19 18	20 13		20 18	21 13		21 18	22 13		22 18	23 13	
Warrington Bank Quay d																						
Earlestown 8 d		16 21	17 16		17 21	18 16		18 21	19 16		19 21	20 16		20 21	21 16		21 21	22 16		22 21	23 16	
Warrington Bank Quay a		16 27			17 27			18 27			19 28			20 29			21 27			22 27		
St Helens Junction d			17 21			18 21			19 21			20 21			21 21			22 21			23 21	
Lea Green d			17 24			18 24			19 24			20 24			21 24			22 24			23 24	
Rainhill d			17 28			18 28			19 28			20 28			21 28			22 28			23 28	
Whiston d			17 31			18 31			19 31			20 31			21 31			22 31			23 31	
Bryn d																						
Garswood d	16 46			17 46			18 46			19 46			20 46			21 46			22 46			23 40
St Helens Central a	16 52			17 52			18 52			19 52			20 52			21 52			22 53			23 46
d	16 53			17 53			18 53			19 53			20 53			21 53			22 53			23 47
Thatto Heath d	16 56			17 56			18 56			19 56			20 56			21 56			22 56			23 50
Eccleston Park d																						
Prescot d	17 00			18 00			19 00			20 00			21 00			22 00			23 00			23 54
Huyton d	17 05		17 35	18 05		18 35	19 05		19 35	20 05		20 35	21 05		21 35	22 05		22 35	23 04		23 35	23 59
Roby d	17 07		17 37	18 07		18 37	19 07		19 37	20 07		20 37	21 07		21 37	22 07		22 37	23 07		23 37	00 01
Broad Green d	17 10		17 40	18 10		18 40	19 10		19 40	20 10		20 40	21 10		21 40	22 10		22 40	23 10		23 40	00 04
Wavertree Technology Park d	17 13		17 43	18 13		18 43	19 13		19 43	20 13		20 43	21 13		21 43	22 13		22 43	23 13		23 43	00 07
Edge Hill 89,91 d																						
Liverpool Lime Street 10 89,91 a	17 24		17 54	18 24		18 54	19 24		19 54	20 24		20 54	21 24		21 54	22 24		22 54	23 24		23 54	00 18

	AW	AW
Manchester Airport 85 ✈ d		
Manchester Piccadilly 10 d	22 56	23 25
Manchester Oxford Road d	22 59	23 28
Manchester Victoria d		
Eccles d		
Patricroft d		
Blackpool North 97 d		
Preston 8 65,82 d		
Leyland 82 d		
Euxton Balshaw Lane d		
Wigan North Western 65 a		
d		
Newton-le-Willows d	23 18	23 46
Warrington Bank Quay d		
Earlestown 8 d	23 21	23 49
Warrington Bank Quay a	23 27	23 55
St Helens Junction d		
Lea Green d		
Rainhill d		
Whiston d		
Bryn d		
Garswood d		
St Helens Central a		
d		
Thatto Heath d		
Eccleston Park d		
Prescot d		
Huyton d		
Roby d		
Broad Green d		
Wavertree Technology Park d		
Edge Hill 89,91 d		
Liverpool Lime Street 10 89,91 a		

Manchester, Preston, Wigan and Newton-le-Willows - St Helens and Liverpool

Sundays
12 September to 17 October

	AW	NT	NT	TP	NT	NT	NT	AW	NT	NT	AW	NT	NT	AW	NT	NT	AW	NT	NT
	🚌			◇1										🛒			🛒		
Manchester Airport 85 ✈ d									10 31			11 33			12 35			13 35	
Manchester Piccadilly 10 ⇌ d	07 28					09 50		09 53	10 50		10 55	11 50		11 56	12 50		12 56	13 50	
Manchester Oxford Road d	07 33					09 53		09 59	10 53		10 59	11 53		11 59	12 53		12 59	13 53	
Manchester Victoria ⇌ d			08 53	09 15															
Eccles d			09 00			10 00			11 00			12 00			13 00			14 00	
Patricroft d																			
Blackpool North 97 d					08 50		09 50			10 50			11 50			12 50			13 50
Preston 8 65,82 d					09 15		10 15			11 15			12 15			13 15			14 15
Leyland 82 d					09 21		10 21			11 21			12 21			13 21			14 21
Euxton Balshaw Lane d					09 26		10 26			11 25			12 25			13 25			14 25
Wigan North Western 65 a					09 35		10 35			11 35			12 35			13 35			14 35
d		08 36			09 36		10 36			11 36			12 36			13 36			14 36
Newton-le-Willows d	08 03		09 13	09 33		10 13		10 18	11 13		11 20	12 13		12 18	13 13		13 18	14 13	
Warrington Bank Quay d																			
Earlestown 8 d	08 13		09 16			10 16		10 21	11 16		11 23	12 16		12 21	13 16		13 21	14 16	
Warrington Bank Quay a	08 38							10 27			11 29			12 27			13 28		
St Helens Junction d			09 20			10 21			11 21			12 21			13 21			14 21	
Lea Green d			09 23			10 24			11 24			12 24			13 24			14 24	
Rainhill d			09 27			10 28			11 28			12 28			13 28			14 28	
Whiston d			09 30			10 31			11 31			12 31			13 31			14 31	
Bryn d																			
Garswood d		08 46			09 46		10 46			11 46			12 46			13 46			14 46
St Helens Central a		08 52			09 52		10 52			11 52			12 52			13 52			14 52
d		08 53			09 53		10 53			11 53			12 53			13 53			14 53
Thatto Heath d		08 56			09 56		10 56			11 56			12 56			13 56			14 56
Eccleston Park d																			
Prescot d		09 00			10 00		11 00			12 00			13 00			14 00			15 00
Huyton d		09 05	09 34		10 05	10 35	11 05		11 35	12 05		12 35	13 05		13 35	14 05		14 35	15 05
Roby d		09 07	09 36		10 07	10 37	11 07		11 37	12 07		12 37	13 07		13 37	14 07		14 37	15 07
Broad Green d		09 10	09 40		10 10	10 40	11 10		11 40	12 10		12 40	13 10		13 40	14 10		14 40	15 10
Wavertree Technology Park d		09 13	09 43		10 13	10 43	11 13		11 43	12 13		12 43	13 13		13 43	14 13		14 43	15 13
Edge Hill 89,91 d																			
Liverpool Lime Street 10 89,91 a		09 24	09 53	09 57	10 24	10 54	11 24		11 54	12 24		12 54	13 24		13 54	14 24		14 54	15 24

	AW	NT	NT	AW	NT	NT	AW	NT	NT	AW	NT	NT	AW	NT	NT	AW	NT	NT	AW	NT	NT	AW
	🛒			🛒			🛒			🛒			🛒									
Manchester Airport 85 ✈ d		14 35			15 35			16 35			17 35			18 35			19 35			20 35		
Manchester Piccadilly 10 ⇌ d	13 56	14 50		14 56	15 50		15 56	16 50		16 56	17 50		17 56	18 50		18 56	19 50		19 56	20 50		20 56
Manchester Oxford Road d	13 59	14 53		14 59	15 53		15 59	16 53		16 59	17 53		17 59	18 53		18 59	19 53		19 59	20 53		20 59
Manchester Victoria ⇌ d																						
Eccles d		15 00			16 00			17 00			18 00			19 00			20 00			21 00		
Patricroft d																						
Blackpool North 97 d			14 50			15 50			16 50			17 50			18 50			19 50			20 50	
Preston 8 65,82 d			15 15			16 15			17 15			18 15			19 15			20 15			21 15	
Leyland 82 d			15 21			16 21			17 21			18 21			19 21			20 21			21 21	
Euxton Balshaw Lane d			15 25			16 25			17 25			18 25			19 25			20 25			21 25	
Wigan North Western 65 a			15 35			16 35			17 35			18 35			19 35			20 35			21 35	
d			15 36			16 36			17 36			18 36			19 36			20 36			21 36	
Newton-le-Willows d	14 18	15 13		15 18	16 13		16 18	17 13		17 18	18 13		18 18	19 13		19 18	20 13		20 18	21 13		21 18
Warrington Bank Quay d																						
Earlestown 8 d	14 21	15 16		15 21	16 16		16 21	17 16		17 21	18 16		18 21	19 16		19 21	20 16		20 21	21 16		21 21
Warrington Bank Quay a	14 27			15 28			16 27			17 27			18 27			19 28			20 29			21 27
St Helens Junction d		15 21			16 21			17 21			18 21			19 21			20 21			21 21		
Lea Green d		15 24			16 24			17 24			18 24			19 24			20 24			21 24		
Rainhill d		15 28			16 28			17 28			18 28			19 28			20 28			21 28		
Whiston d		15 31			16 31			17 31			18 31			19 31			20 31			21 31		
Bryn d																						
Garswood d			15 46			16 46			17 46			18 46			19 46			20 46			21 46	
St Helens Central a			15 52			16 52			17 52			18 52			19 52			20 52			21 52	
d			15 53			16 53			17 53			18 53			19 53			20 53			21 53	
Thatto Heath d			15 56			16 56			17 56			18 56			19 56			20 56			21 56	
Eccleston Park d																						
Prescot d			16 00			17 00			18 00			19 00			20 00			21 00			22 00	
Huyton d		15 35	16 05		16 35	17 05		17 35	18 05		18 35	19 05		19 35	20 05		20 35	21 05		21 35	22 05	
Roby d		15 37	16 07		16 37	17 07		17 37	18 07		18 37	19 07		19 37	20 07		20 37	21 07		21 37	22 07	
Broad Green d		15 40	16 10		16 40	17 10		17 40	18 10		18 40	19 10		19 40	20 10		20 40	21 10		21 40	22 10	
Wavertree Technology Park d		15 43	16 13		16 43	17 13		17 43	18 13		18 43	19 13		19 43	20 13		20 43	21 13		21 43	22 13	
Edge Hill 89,91 d																						
Liverpool Lime Street 10 89,91 a		15 54	16 24		16 54	17 24		17 54	18 24		18 54	19 24		19 54	20 24		20 54	21 24		21 54	22 24	

Table 90

Manchester, Preston, Wigan and Newton-le-Willows - St Helens and Liverpool

Sundays
12 September to 17 October

	NT	NT	AW	NT	NT	AW	AW
Manchester Airport 85 ✈ d	21 35			22 35			
Manchester Piccadilly 10 ⇌ d	21 50		21 56	22 50		22 56	23 25
Manchester Oxford Road d	21 53		21 59	22 53		22 59	23 28
Manchester Victoria ⇌ d							
Eccles d	22 00			23 00			
Patricroft d							
Blackpool North 97 d		21 50			22 44		
Preston 8 65,82 d		22 15			23 09		
Leyland 82 d		22 21			23 15		
Euxton Balshaw Lane d		22 25			23 19		
Wigan North Western 65 a		22 35			23 29		
d		22 36			23 30		
Newton-le-Willows d	22 13		22 18	23 13		23 18	23 46
Warrington Bank Quay d							
Earlestown 8 d	22 16		22 21	23 16		23 21	23 49
Warrington Bank Quay a			22 27			23 27	23 55
St Helens Junction d	22 21			23 21			
Lea Green d	22 24			23 24			
Rainhill d	22 28			23 28			
Whiston d	22 31			23 31			
Bryn d							
Garswood d		22 46			23 40		
St Helens Central a		22 53			23 46		
d		22 53			23 47		
Thatto Heath d		22 56			23 50		
Eccleston Park d							
Prescot d		23 00			23 54		
Huyton d	22 35	23 04		23 35	23 59		
Roby d	22 37	23 07		23 37	00 01		
Broad Green d	22 40	23 10		23 40	00 04		
Wavertree Technology Park d	22 43	23 13		23 43	00 07		
Edge Hill 89,91 d							
Liverpool Lime Street 10 89,91 a	22 54	23 24		23 54	00 18		

Sundays
from 24 October

	TP	TP	TP	AW	NT	NT	TP	NT	NT	AW	NT	AW	NT	NT	AW	NT	NT	AW	NT	NT	AW
	🚌	🚌	🚌	🚌			◇1			🚌					🛒			🛒			🛒
Manchester Airport 85 ✈ d	01 40	06 15	07 10								10 31			11 33			12 35			13 35	
Manchester Piccadilly 10 ⇌ d	02 05	06 40	07a35	07 28					09 50	09 53	10 50	10 55		11 50	11 56		12 50	12 56		13 50	13 56
Manchester Oxford Road d				07 33					09 53	09 58	10 53	10 59		11 53	11 59		12 53	12 59		13 53	13 59
Manchester Victoria ⇌ d						08 53	09 15														
Eccles d						09 00			10 00		11 00			12 00			13 00			14 00	
Patricroft d																					
Blackpool North 97 d																					
Preston 8 65,82 d																					
Leyland 82 d																					
Euxton Balshaw Lane d																					
Wigan North Western 65 a																					
d																					
Newton-le-Willows d				08 03		09 13	09 33		10 13	10 28	11 13	11 20		12 13	12 18		13 13	13 18		14 13	14 18
Warrington Bank Quay d																					
Earlestown 8 d				08 13		09 16			10 16	10 38	11 16	11 23		12 16	12 21		13 16	13 21		14 16	14 21
Warrington Bank Quay a				08 38						11 03		11 29			12 27			13 28			14 27
St Helens Junction d						09 20			10 21		11 21			12 21			13 21			14 21	
Lea Green d						09 23			10 24		11 24			12 24			13 24			14 24	
Rainhill d						09 27			10 28		11 28			12 28			13 28			14 28	
Whiston d						09 30			10 31		11 31			12 31			13 31			14 31	
Bryn d																					
Garswood d																					
St Helens Central a																					
d					08 53			09 53					11 53			12 53			13 53		
Thatto Heath d					08 56			09 56					11 56			12 56			13 56		
Eccleston Park d																					
Prescot d					09 00			10 00					12 00			13 00			14 00		
Huyton d					09 05	09 34		10 05	10 35		11 35		12 05	12 35		13 05	13 35		14 05	14 35	
Roby d					09 07	09 36		10 07	10 37		11 37		12 07	12 37		13 07	13 37		14 07	14 37	
Broad Green d					09 10	09 40		10 10	10 40		11 40		12 10	12 40		13 10	13 40		14 10	14 40	
Wavertree Technology Park d					09 13	09 43		10 13	10 43		11 43		12 13	12 43		13 13	13 43		14 13	14 43	
Edge Hill 89,91 d																					
Liverpool Lime Street 10 89,91 a					09 24	09 53	09 57	10 24	10 54		11 54		12 24	12 54		13 24	13 54		14 24	14 54	

Table 90

Sundays
from 24 October

Manchester, Preston, Wigan and Newton-le-Willows - St Helens and Liverpool

	NT	NT	AW	NT	NT		AW	NT	NT	AW	NT	NT	AW	NT	NT		AW	NT	NT	AW	NT	NT	AW	NT
Manchester Airport 85 ✈ d		14 35			15 35				16 35			17 35			18 35				19 35			20 35		
Manchester Piccadilly 10 d		14 50	14 56		15 50		15 56		16 50	16 56		17 50	17 56		18 50		18 56		19 50	19 56		20 50	20 56	
Manchester Oxford Road d		14 53	14 59		15 53		15 59		16 53	16 59		17 53	17 59		18 53		18 59		19 53	19 59		20 53	20 59	
Manchester Victoria d																								
Eccles d		15 00			16 00				17 00			18 00			19 00				20 00			21 00		
Patricroft d																								
Blackpool North 97 d																								
Preston 8 65,82 d																								
Leyland 82 d																								
Euxton Balshaw Lane d																								
Wigan North Western 65 a																								
d																								
Newton-le-Willows d		15 13	15 18		16 13		16 18		17 13	17 18		18 13	18 18		19 13		19 18		20 13	20 18		21 13	21 18	
Warrington Bank Quay d																								
Earlestown 8 d		15 16	15 21		16 16		16 21		17 16	17 21		18 16	18 21		19 16		19 21		20 16	20 21		21 16	21 21	
Warrington Bank Quay a			15 28				16 27			17 27			18 27				19 28			20 29			21 27	
St Helens Junction d		15 21			16 21				17 21			18 21			19 21				20 21			21 21		
Lea Green d		15 24			16 24				17 24			18 24			19 24				20 24			21 24		
Rainhill d		15 28			16 28				17 28			18 28			19 28				20 28			21 28		
Whiston d		15 31			16 31				17 31			18 31			19 31				20 31			21 31		
Bryn d																								
Garswood d																								
St Helens Central a																								
d	14 53			15 53				16 53			17 53			18 53				19 53			20 53			21 53
Thatto Heath d	14 56			15 56				16 56			17 56			18 56				19 56			20 56			21 56
Eccleston Park d																								
Prescot d	15 00			16 00				17 00			18 00			19 00				20 00			21 00			22 00
Huyton d	15 05	15 35		16 05	16 35			17 05	17 35		18 05	18 35		19 05	19 35			20 05	20 35		21 05	21 35		22 05
Roby d	15 07	15 37		16 07	16 37			17 07	17 37		18 07	18 37		19 07	19 37			20 07	20 37		21 07	21 37		22 07
Broad Green d	15 10	15 40		16 10	16 40			17 10	17 40		18 10	18 40		19 10	19 40			20 10	20 40		21 10	21 40		22 10
Wavertree Technology Park d	15 13	15 43		16 13	16 43			17 13	17 43		18 13	18 43		19 13	19 43			20 13	20 43		21 13	21 43		22 13
Edge Hill 89,91 d																								
Liverpool Lime Street 10 89,91 a	15 24	15 54		16 24	16 54			17 24	17 54		18 24	18 54		19 24	19 54			20 24	20 54		21 24	21 54		22 24

	NT		AW	NT	NT	AW	AW	NT
Manchester Airport 85 ✈ d	21 35				22 35			
Manchester Piccadilly 10 d	21 50		21 56		22 50	22 56	23 25	
Manchester Oxford Road d	21 53		21 59		22 53	22 59	23 28	
Manchester Victoria d								
Eccles d	22 00				23 00			
Patricroft d								
Blackpool North 97 d								
Preston 8 65,82 d								
Leyland 82 d								
Euxton Balshaw Lane d								
Wigan North Western 65 a								
d								
Newton-le-Willows d	22 13		22 18		23 13	23 18	23 46	
Warrington Bank Quay d								
Earlestown 8 d	22 16		22 21		23 16	23 21	23 49	
Warrington Bank Quay a			22 27			23 27	23 55	
St Helens Junction d	22 21				23 21			
Lea Green d	22 24				23 24			
Rainhill d	22 28				23 28			
Whiston d	22 31				23 31			
Bryn d								
Garswood d								
St Helens Central a								
d				22 53				23 47
Thatto Heath d				22 56				23 50
Eccleston Park d								
Prescot d				23 00				23 54
Huyton d	22 35			23 04	23 35			23 59
Roby d	22 37			23 07	23 37			00 01
Broad Green d	22 40			23 10	23 40			00 04
Wavertree Technology Park d	22 43			23 13	23 43			00 07
Edge Hill 89,91 d								
Liverpool Lime Street 10 89,91 a	22 54			23 24	23 54			00 18

Table 91

Mondays to Fridays

Liverpool - Runcorn and Crewe

	VT	NT	VT	NT	LM	EM	NT	VT	LM	NT	LM	EM	VT	NT	LM	NT	LM	VT	EM	NT	LM	NT	LM	VT
	◇1 ⊠		◇1 ⊠		1	◇		◇1 ⊠	1		1	◇	◇1 ⊠		1		1	◇1 ⊠	◇		1		1	◇1 ⊠
Liverpool Lime Street 10 90 d	05 27	05 49	06 05	06 21	06 30	06 47	06 50	07 00	07 04	07 26	07 34	07 43	07 48	07 51	08 04	08 26	08 34	08 48	08 52	08 55	09 04	09 27	09 34	09 48
Edge Hill 90 d		05 53					06 54			07 30						08 30				08 59				
Mossley Hill d		05 58		06 29			06 59			07 35				07 59		08 35				09 04		09 35		
West Allerton d		06 00		06 31			07 01			07 37				08 01		08 37				09 06		09 37		
Liverpool South Parkway 7 ✈ a		06 03		06 34	06 39	06 57	07 04		07 13	07 40	07 43	07 53		08 04	08 15	08 40	08 43		09 02	09 09	09 15	09 40	09 43	
d					06 40				07 14		07 44				08 15		08 44				09 15		09 44	
Runcorn a	05 42		06 20		06 47			07u15	07 21		07 51		08 03		08 24		08 51	09 03			09 24		09 51	10 03
d	05 43		06 21		06 48			07u15	07 22		07 52		08 04		08 24		08 52	09 04			09 25		09 52	10 04
Acton Bridge d					06 57				07 32						08 34		09 02							
Hartford d					07 02				07 36		08 04						09 06						10 04	
Winsford d					07 06						08 08												10 08	
Crewe 10 65 a	06 00				07 14				07 48		08 19				08 47		09 20				09 44		10 19	
Birmingham New Street 12 65 a					08 17				08 47		09 18				09 47		10 17				10 47		11 18	
London Euston ⊖65 a	07 50		08 22					09 01					09 56					10 55						11 56

	EM	NT	LM	NT	LM	VT	EM	NT	LM	NT	LM	VT	EM	NT	LM	NT	LM	VT	EM	NT	LM	NT	LM	VT
	◇		1		1	◇1 trolley	◇		1		1	◇1 trolley	◇		1		1	◇1 trolley	◇		1		1	◇1 trolley
Liverpool Lime Street 10 90 d	09 52	09 55	10 04	10 27	10 34	10 48	10 52	10 55	11 04	11 27	11 34	11 48	11 52	11 55	12 04	12 27	12 34	12 48	12 52	12 55	13 04	13 27	13 34	13 48
Edge Hill 90 d		09 59						10 59						11 59						12 59				
Mossley Hill d		10 04		10 35				11 04		11 35				12 04		12 35				13 04		13 35		
West Allerton d		10 06		10 37				11 06		11 37				12 06		12 37				13 06		13 37		
Liverpool South Parkway 7 ✈ a	10 02	10 09	10 15	10 40	10 43		11 02	11 09	11 15	11 40	11 43		12 02	12 09	12 15	12 40	12 43		13 02	13 09	13 15	13 40	13 43	
d			10 15		10 44				11 15		11 44				12 15		12 44				13 15		13 44	
Runcorn a			10 24		10 51	11 03			11 24		11 51	12 03			12 24		12 51	13 03			13 24		13 51	14 03
d			10 25		10 52	11 04			11 25		11 52	12 04			12 25		12 52	13 04			13 25		13 52	14 04
Acton Bridge d																	13 02							
Hartford d					11 04						12 04						13 06						14 04	
Winsford d					11 08						12 08												14 08	
Crewe 10 65 a			10 45		11 19				11 45		12 19				12 45		13 20				13 45		14 19	
Birmingham New Street 12 65 a			11 47		12 17				12 47		13 17				13 47		14 17				14 47		15 20	
London Euston ⊖65 a						12 58						13 56						14 56						15 56

	EM	NT	LM	NT	LM	VT	EM	NT	LM	NT	LM	VT	EM	NT	LM	NT	LM	VT	EM	NT	LM	NT	LM	VT
	◇		1		1	◇1 trolley	◇		1		1	◇1 trolley	◇		1		1	◇1 trolley	◇		1		1	◇1 ⊠
Liverpool Lime Street 10 90 d	13 52	13 55	14 04	14 27	14 34	14 48	14 52	14 55	15 04	15 27	15 34	15 48	15 52	15 55	16 04	16 27	16 34	16 48	16 52	16 55	17 04	17 25	17 34	17 48
Edge Hill 90 d		13 59						14 59						15 59						16 59		17 29		
Mossley Hill d		14 04		14 35				15 04		15 35				16 04		16 35				17 04		17 34		
West Allerton d		14 06		14 37				15 06		15 37				16 06		16 37				17 06		17 36		
Liverpool South Parkway 7 ✈ a	14 02	14 09	14 15	14 40	14 43		15 02	15 09	15 15	15 40	15 43		16 02	16 09	16 15	16 40	16 43		17 02	17 09	17 15	17 39	17 43	
d			14 15		14 44			15 09	15 15		15 44			16 09	16 15		16 44				17 15		17 44	
Runcorn a			14 24		14 51	15 03			15 24		15 51	16 03			16 24		16 52	17 03			17 24		17 51	18 03
d					14 52	15 04			15 25		15 52	16 04			16 25		16 52	17 04			17 25		17 52	18 04
Acton Bridge d																	17 01						18 01	
Hartford d					15 04						16 04						17 06						18 06	
Winsford d					15 08						16 08										17 39			
Crewe 10 65 a					15 19				15 45		16 19				16 45		17 19				17 47		18 20	
Birmingham New Street 12 65 a					16 17				16 47		17 20				17 47		18 17				18 48		19 17	
London Euston ⊖65 a						16 56						17 56						18 59						20 02

	EM	NT	LM	NT	LM	VT	EM	NT	LM	LM	VT	EM	NT	LM	LM	VT	NT	LM	EM	NT	LM	LM	NT
	◇		1		1	◇1 ⊠	◇		1	1	◇1 trolley	◇		1	1	◇1 trolley		1	◇		1	1	
Liverpool Lime Street 10 90 d	17 52	17 55	18 04	18 25	18 34	18 48	18 52	18 55	19 11	19 34	19 48	19 52	19 55	20 04	20 34	20 48	20 55	21 34	21 37	21 55	22 34	23 34	23 38
Edge Hill 90 d		17 59		18 29				18 59					19 59				20 59			21 59			23 42
Mossley Hill d		18 04		18 34				19 04					20 04				21 04			22 04			23 47
West Allerton d		18 06		18 36				19 06					20 06				21 06			22 06			23 50
Liverpool South Parkway 7 ✈ a	18 02	18 09	18 14	18 39	18 43		19 02	19 09	19 20	19 43		20 02	20 09	20 15	20 43		21 09	21 43	21 47	22 09	22 44	23 44	23 53
d			18 15		18 44				19 21	19 44				20 15	20 44			21 44			22 44	23 45	
Runcorn a			18 24		18 51	19 03			19 28	19 51	20 03			20 24	20 51	21 03		21 51			22 52	23 53	
d			18 24		18 52	19 04			19 29	19 52	20 04			20 24	20 52	21 04		21 52			22 52	23 53	
Acton Bridge d									19 40												23 02	00 03	
Hartford d					19 04					20 04					21 04			22 04			23 08	00 08	
Winsford d			18 38		19 08					20 08					21 08			22 08			23 11	00 12	
Crewe 10 65 a			18 47		19 16	19 21			19 53	20 16	20 21			20 45	21 16	21 22		22 18			23 22		
Birmingham New Street 12 65 a			19 47		20 18				20 47	21 18				21 47	22 17			23 18					
London Euston ⊖65 a						21 05					22 09					23 58							

Table 91

Liverpool - Runcorn and Crewe

Saturdays

	VT	NT	NT	LM	VT	EM	NT	LM	VT	NT	LM	EM	VT	NT	LM	NT	LM	VT	EM	NT	LM	LM	VT
	◇1			1	◇1	◇		1	◇1		1	◇	◇1		1		1	◇1	◇		1	1	◇1
Liverpool Lime Street 10 90 d	05 47	05 49	06 25	06 32	06 45	06 49	06 55	07 04	07 19	07 26	07 34	07 42	07 48	07 51	08 04	08 26	08 34	08 48	08 52	08 55	09 04	09 34	09 48
Edge Hill 90 d		05 53					06 59			07 30						08 30				08 59			
Mossley Hill d		05 58	06 33				07 04			07 35				07 59		08 35				09 04			
West Allerton d		06 00	06 35				07 06			07 37				08 01		08 37				09 06			
Liverpool South Parkway 7 ✈ a		06 03	06 38	06 41		06 59	07 09	07 14		07 40	07 43	07 52		08 04	08 14	08 40	08 43		09 02	09 09	09 15	09 43	
d				06 42				07 14			07 44				08 15		08 44				09 15	09 44	
Runcorn a	06 02			06 49	07 00			07 22	07 35		07 51		08 03		08 24		08 51	09 03			09 24	09 51	10 03
d	06 03			06 50	07 01			07 22	07 36		07 52		08 04		08 24		08 52	09 04			09 24	09 52	10 04
Acton Bridge d								07 32							08 34		09 02						
Hartford d				07 02				07 36			08 04						09 06					10 04	
Winsford d				07 06							08 08											10 08	
Crewe 10 65 a				07 14	07 18			07 47	07 52		08 19				08 47		09 20				09 44	10 19	
Birmingham New Street 12 65 a				08 17				08 47			09 18				09 47		10 17				10 47	11 17	
London Euston ⊖65 a	08 05				08 59				09 46				10 00					11 01					11 56

	EM	NT	LM	NT	LM	VT	EM	NT	LM	NT	LM	VT	EM	NT	LM	NT	LM	VT	EM	NT	LM	NT	LM	VT
	◇		1		1	◇1	◇		1		1	◇1	◇		1		1	◇1	◇		1		1	◇1
Liverpool Lime Street 10 90 d	09 52	09 55	10 04	10 27	10 34	10 48	10 52	10 55	11 04	11 27	11 34	11 48	11 52	11 55	12 04	12 27	12 34	12 48	12 52	12 55	13 04	13 27	13 34	13 48
Edge Hill 90 d		09 59						10 59						11 59						12 59				
Mossley Hill d		10 04		10 35				11 04		11 35				12 04		12 35				13 04		13 35		
West Allerton d		10 06		10 37				11 06		11 37				12 06		12 37				13 06		13 37		
Liverpool South Parkway 7 ✈ a	10 02	10 09	10 15	10 40	10 43		11 02	11 09	11 15	11 40	11 43		12 02	12 09	12 15	12 40	12 43		13 02	13 09	13 15	13 40	13 43	
d			10 15		10 44				11 15		11 44				12 15		12 44				13 15		13 44	
Runcorn a			10 24		10 51	11 03			11 24		11 51	12 03			12 24		12 51	13 03			13 24		13 51	14 03
d			10 25		10 52	11 04			11 25		11 52	12 04			12 25		12 52	13 04			13 25		13 52	14 04
Acton Bridge d																	13 02							
Hartford d					11 04						12 04						13 06						14 04	
Winsford d					11 08						12 08												14 08	
Crewe 10 65 a			10 45		11 19				11 45		12 19				12 45		13 20				13 45		14 19	
Birmingham New Street 12 65 a			11 47		12 17				12 47		13 17				13 47		14 17				14 47		15 18	
London Euston ⊖65 a						12 56						13 56						14 56						15 56

	EM	NT	LM	NT	LM	VT	EM	NT	LM	NT	LM	VT	EM	NT	LM	NT	LM	VT	EM	NT	LM	NT	LM	VT
	◇		1		1	◇1	◇		1		1	◇1	◇		1		1	◇1	◇		1		1	◇1
Liverpool Lime Street 10 90 d	13 52	13 55	14 04	14 27	14 34	14 48	14 52	14 55	15 04	15 27	15 34	15 48	15 52	15 55	16 04	16 27	16 34	16 48	16 52	16 55	17 04	17 25	17 34	17 48
Edge Hill 90 d		13 59						14 59						15 59						16 59		17 29		
Mossley Hill d		14 04		14 35				15 04		15 35				16 04		16 35				17 04		17 34		
West Allerton d		14 06		14 37				15 06		15 37				16 06		16 37				17 06		17 36		
Liverpool South Parkway 7 ✈ a	14 02	14 09	14 15	14 40	14 43		15 02	15 09	15 15	15 40	15 43		16 02	16 09	16 15	16 40	16 43		17 02	17 09	17 15	17 39	17 43	
d			14 15		14 44				15 15		15 44				16 15		16 44				17 15		17 44	
Runcorn a			14 24		14 51	15 03			15 24		15 51	16 03			16 24		16 51	17 03			17 24		17 51	18 03
d			14 25		14 52	15 04			15 25		15 52	16 04			16 25		16 52	17 04			17 25		17 52	18 04
Acton Bridge d																	17 02						18 02	
Hartford d					15 04						16 04						17 06						18 06	
Winsford d					15 08						16 08										17 39			
Crewe 10 65 a			14 45		15 19				15 45		16 19				16 45		17 20				17 47		18 20	
Birmingham New Street 12 65 a			15 47		16 17				16 47		17 18				17 47		18 17				18 47		19 17	
London Euston ⊖65 a						16 56						17 55						18 56						19 56

	EM	NT	LM	NT	LM	VT	EM	NT	LM	LM	VT	EM	NT	LM	EM	NT	LM	NT	LM	NT
	◇		1		1	◇1	◇		1	1	◇1	◇		1	◇		1		1	
Liverpool Lime Street 10 90 d	17 52	17 55	18 04	18 25	18 34	18 48	18 52	18 55	19 04	19 34	19 48	19 52	19 55	20 34	20 52	20 55	21 34	21 55	22 04	23 38
Edge Hill 90 d		17 59		18 29				18 59					19 59			20 59		21 59		23 42
Mossley Hill d		18 04		18 34				19 04					20 04			21 04		22 04		23 47
West Allerton d		18 06		18 36				19 06					20 06			21 06		22 06		23 49
Liverpool South Parkway 7 ✈ a	18 02	18 09	18 14	18 39	18 43		19 02	19 09	19 14	19 43		20 02	20 09	20 43	21 02	21 09	21 43	22 09	22 13	23 52
d			18 15		18 44				19 14	19 44				20 44			21 44	22 09	22 13	
Runcorn a			18 24		18 51	19 03			19 23	19 51	20 03			20 51			21 51		22 20	
d			18 24		18 52	19 04			19 23	19 52	20 04			20 52			21 52		22 21	
Acton Bridge d									19 36											
Hartford d					19 04					20 04				21 03			22 04		22 33	
Winsford d			18 38		19 08					20 08				21 08			22 08		22 37	
Crewe 10 65 a			18 46		19 19				19 49	20 16				21 16			22 21		22 48	
Birmingham New Street 12 65 a			19 47		20 17				20 47	21 17				22 20			23 21			
London Euston ⊖65 a						21 15					22 14									

Table 91

Liverpool - Runcorn and Crewe

Sundays

	VT	NT	VT	NT	VT	NT	VT	NT	LM		VT	NT	LM	VT	EM	NT	LM	VT	EM		NT	LM	VT	EM
	◇1		◇1		◇1		◇1		1		◇1		1	◇1	◇		1	◇1	◇			1	◇1	◇
Liverpool Lime Street 10 90 d	08 15	08 26	08 38	09 26	09 38	10 26	10 38	11 26	11 34		11 48	12 26	12 34	12 48	12 52	13 26	13 34	13 48	13 52		14 26	14 34	14 48	14 52
Edge Hill 90 d																								
Mossley Hill d		08 34		09 34		10 34		11 34				12 34				13 34					14 34			
West Allerton d		08 36		09 36		10 36		11 36				12 36				13 36					14 36			
Liverpool South Parkway 7 ✈ a		08 39		09 39		10 39		11 39	11 43			12 39	12 43		13 02	13 39	13 43		14 02		14 39	14 43		15 02
d									11 44				12 44				13 44					14 44		
Runcorn a	08 34		08 53		09 53		10 53		11 51		12 03		12 51	13 03			13 51	14 03				14 51	15 03	
d	08 35		08 54		09 54		10 54		11 52		12 04		12 52	13 04			13 52	14 04				14 52	15 04	
Acton Bridge d																								
Hartford d									12 04				13 03				14 03					15 03		
Winsford d									12 08				13 08				14 08					15 08		
Crewe 10 65 a	08 52		09 11		10 12		11 12		12 19				13 19				14 18					15 20		
Birmingham New Street 12 65 a									13 16				14 15				15 15					16 15		
London Euston ⊖65 a	11 06		11 39		12 37		13 15				14 06			15 03				16 03					17 03	

	NT	LM	VT	EM	VT		NT	LM	VT	EM	NT	LM	VT	EM	NT		LM	VT	EM	NT	LM	VT	EM	NT
		1	◇1	◇	◇1			1	◇1	◇		1	◇1	◇			1	◇1	◇		1	◇1	◇	
Liverpool Lime Street 10 90 d	15 26	15 34	15 48	15 52	16 18		16 26	16 34	16 48	16 52	17 26	17 34	17 48	17 52	18 26		18 34	18 48	18 52	19 26	19 34	19 48	19 52	20 26
Edge Hill 90 d																								
Mossley Hill d	15 34						16 34				17 34				18 34					19 34				20 34
West Allerton d	15 36						16 36				17 36				18 36					19 36				20 36
Liverpool South Parkway 7 ✈ a	15 39	15 43		16 02			16 39	16 43		17 02	17 39	17 43		18 02	18 39		18 43		19 02	19 39	19 43		20 02	20 39
d		15 44						16 44				17 44					18 44				19 44			
Runcorn a		15 51	16 03		16 33			16 51	17 03			17 51	18 03				18 51	19 03			19 51	20 03		
d		15 52	16 04		16 34			16 52	17 04			17 52	18 04				18 52	19 04			19 52	20 04		
Acton Bridge d																								
Hartford d		16 03						17 03				18 03					19 03				20 03			
Winsford d		16 08						17 08				18 08					19 08				20 08			
Crewe 10 65 a		16 18			16 50			17 18				18 20					19 20				20 16	20 22		
Birmingham New Street 12 65 a		17 15						18 15				19 15					20 15				21 15			
London Euston ⊖65 a			18 04		18 42				19 03				20 03					21 04				22 29		

	LM		VT	NT	LM	NT
	1		◇1		1	
Liverpool Lime Street 10 90 d	20 34		20 48	21 26	21 34	22 26
Edge Hill 90 d						
Mossley Hill d				21 34		22 34
West Allerton d				21 36		22 36
Liverpool South Parkway 7 ✈ a	20 43			21 39	21 43	22 39
d	20 44			21 39	21 44	
Runcorn a	20 51		21 03		21 51	
d	20 52		21 04		21 52	
Acton Bridge d						
Hartford d	21 03				22 03	
Winsford d	21 08				22 08	
Crewe 10 65 a	21 16		21 21		22 18	
Birmingham New Street 12 65 a	22 15				23 17	
London Euston ⊖65 a			23 57			

Crewe and Runcorn - Liverpool

Mondays to Fridays

	NT MX	NT	LM	NT	LM	NT	LM	VT	NT	LM	EM	LM	NT	LM	VT	NT	EM	LM	NT	LM
			■		◇■		◇■	◇■ ⊠		◇■	◇	◇■		◇■	◇■ ⊠		◇	◇■		◇■
London Euston ⊖65 d								05 27							07 07					
Birmingham New Street ■ 65 d							06 01			06 36		07 01		07 36				08 01		08 36
Crewe ■ 65 d			06 02		06 32		06 57	07 24		07 33		07 58		08 31				08 58		09 31
Winsford d			06 10		06 41		07 04			07 42		08 05						09 07		
Hartford d			06 15		06 46		07 09			07 47		08 10						09 12		
Acton Bridge d			06 19		06 51		07 14			07 51		08 14								
Runcorn a			06 27		06 59		07 23	07 42		07 59		08 22		08 50	08 55			09 22		09 50
d			06 28		06 59		07 23	07 42		08 00		08 23		08 50	08 55			09 22		09 50
Liverpool South Parkway ■ ✈ a			06 36		07 08		07 32			08 08		08 31		08 59				09 31		09 59
d	00 27	06 27	06 37	07 01	07 08	07 27	07 32		07 59	08 09	08 18	08 32	08 37	08 59		09 06	09 15	09 31	09 36	09 59
West Allerton d		06 31		07 05		07 30			08 03				08 40			09 10			09 39	
Mossley Hill d		06 33		07 07		07 33			08 06				08 43			09 13			09 41	
Edge Hill 90 d		06 39		07 13		07 40			08 11				08 48						09 47	
Liverpool Lime Street ■ 90 a	00 41	06 45	06 49	07 19	07 22	07 48	07 42	08 01	08 18	08 21	08 31	08 44	08 55	09 10	09 15	09 24	09 31	09 43	09 53	10 10

	VT	NT	EM	LM	NT	LM	VT	NT	EM	LM	NT	LM	VT	NT	EM	LM	NT	LM	VT	NT	EM	LM
	◇■ ⊠		◇	◇■		◇■	◇■ ⊠		◇	◇■		◇■	◇■ ⊐		◇	◇■		◇■	◇■ ⊐		◇	◇■
London Euston ⊖65 d	08 07						09 07						10 07						11 07			
Birmingham New Street ■ 65 d				09 01		09 36				10 01		10 36				11 01		11 36				12 01
Crewe ■ 65 d				09 57		10 31				10 57		11 31				11 57		12 31				12 57
Winsford d										11 06												13 06
Hartford d				10 10						11 11						12 10						13 11
Acton Bridge d				10 14												12 14						
Runcorn a	09 55			10 22		10 50	10 55			11 21		11 50	11 55			12 23		12 50	12 55			13 21
d	09 55			10 23		10 50	10 55			11 22		11 50	11 55			12 23		12 50	12 55			13 22
Liverpool South Parkway ■ ✈ a				10 31		10 59				11 30		11 59				12 32		12 59				13 30
d		10 06	10 15	10 32	10 36	10 59		11 06	11 15	11 31	11 36	11 59		12 06	12 15	12 32	12 36	12 59		13 06	13 15	13 31
West Allerton d		10 10			10 39			11 10			11 39			12 10			12 39			13 10		
Mossley Hill d		10 12			10 41			11 13			11 41			12 13			12 41			13 13		
Edge Hill 90 d					10 47						11 47						12 47					
Liverpool Lime Street ■ 90 a	10 15	10 24	10 31	10 44	10 53	11 10	11 15	11 24	11 31	11 43	11 53	12 10	12 15	12 24	12 31	12 44	12 53	13 10	13 15	13 24	13 31	13 43

	NT	LM	VT	NT	EM	LM	NT	LM	VT	NT	EM	LM	NT	LM	VT	NT	EM	LM	NT	LM	VT
		◇■	◇■ ⊐		◇	◇■		◇■	◇■ ⊐		◇	◇■		◇■	◇■ ⊐		◇	◇■		◇■	◇■ ⊐
London Euston ⊖65 d			12 07						13 07						14 07						15 07
Birmingham New Street ■ 65 d		12 36				13 01		13 36				14 01		14 36				15 01		15 36	
Crewe ■ 65 d		13 31				13 57		14 31				14 57		15 31				15 57		16 31	
Winsford d						14 06						15 06									
Hartford d						14 11						15 11						16 10			
Acton Bridge d																		16 14			
Runcorn a		13 50	13 55			14 21		14 50	14 55			15 21		15 50	15 55			16 22		16 50	16 55
d		13 50	13 55			14 22		14 50	14 55			15 22		15 50	15 55			16 22		16 50	16 55
Liverpool South Parkway ■ ✈ a		13 59				14 30		14 59				15 30		15 59				16 31		16 59	
d	13 36	13 59		14 06	14 15	14 31	14 36	14 59		15 06	15 15	15 31	15 36	15 59		16 07	16 15	16 31	16 36	16 59	
West Allerton d	13 39			14 10			14 39			15 10			15 39			16 11			16 39		
Mossley Hill d	13 41			14 13			14 41			15 13			15 41			16 13			16 42		
Edge Hill 90 d	13 47						14 47						15 47						16 47		
Liverpool Lime Street ■ 90 a	13 53	14 10	14 15	14 24	14 31	14 43	14 53	15 10	15 15	15 24	15 31	15 43	15 53	16 10	16 15	16 25	16 31	16 45	16 54	17 10	17 15

	NT	EM	LM	NT	LM	VT	NT	EM	LM	NT	LM	VT	NT	EM	LM	VT	NT	LM	VT	EM	VT	NT	LM
		◇	◇■		◇■	◇■ ⊐		◇	◇■		◇■	◇■ ⊠		◇	◇■	◇■ ⊠		◇■	◇■ ⊠	◇	◇■ ⊠		◇■
London Euston ⊖65 d						16 07						17 07				17 33			18 07		18 33		
Birmingham New Street ■ 65 d			16 01		16 36				17 01		17 36				18 01			18 36					19 36
Crewe ■ 65 d			16 57		17 31				18 01		18 33	18 45			19 02	19 17		19 31	19 44		20 17		20 31
Winsford d			17 07						18 09						19 10			19 42					20 40
Hartford d			17 12						18 14		18 45							19 47					20 45
Acton Bridge d											18 50												
Runcorn a			17 21		17 50	17 55			18 23		18 58	19 02			19 22	19 34		19 57	20 01		20 34		20 56
d			17 22		17 50	17 55			18 24		18 58	19 02			19 23	19 34		19 57	20 01		20 34		20 56
Liverpool South Parkway ■ ✈ a			17 30		17 59				18 32		19 07				19 31			20 06					21 05
d	17 07	17 15	17 31	17 39	17 59		18 14	18 22	18 33	18 38	19 07		19 13	19 18	19 32		19 59	20 06		20 15		20 38	21 05
West Allerton d	17 11			17 42			18 18			18 42			19 16				20 03					20 41	
Mossley Hill d	17 13			17 45			18 20			18 44			19 18				20 05					20 44	
Edge Hill 90 d				17 50			18 30			18 50			19 26				20 11						
Liverpool Lime Street ■ 90 a	17 25	17 31	17 43	17 58	18 10	18 15	18 38	18 35	18 44	18 57	19 18	19 23	19 35	19 35	19 44	19 52	20 18	20 18	20 21	20 35	20 53	20 56	21 16

Crewe and Runcorn - Liverpool

	VT	NT	EM	LM	VT	NT	LM	NT	VT
	■ ■ ⊐		◇	◇■	◇■ ⊐		◇■		◇■ ⊐
London Euston ⊖65 d	19 07				20 07				21 07
Birmingham New Street ■ 65 d				20 36			21 36		
Crewe ■ 65 d				21 31			22 31		22 48
Winsford d				21 39			22 39		
Hartford d				21 44			22 44		
Acton Bridge d							22 48		
Runcorn a	21 01			21 54	21 59		22 56		23 07
d	21 01			21 54	21 59		22 57		23 07
Liverpool South Parkway ■ ✈ a				22 05		22 12	23 07		
d		21 12	21 20	22 05		22 12	23 08	23 13	
West Allerton d		21 15				22 15		23 16	
Mossley Hill d		21 18				22 18		23 18	
Edge Hill 90 d		21 23				22 23		23 23	
Liverpool Lime Street ■ 90 a	21 21	21 30	21 35	22 15	22 20	22 30	23 23	23 30	23 31

Saturdays

	NT	NT	NT	LM	NT	LM	NT	LM	EM	LM	NT	LM	VT	NT	EM	LM	NT	LM	VT	NT	EM	LM
				◇■		◇■		◇■	◇	◇■		◇■	◇■ ⊐		◇	◇■		◇■	◇■ ⊐		◇	◇■
London Euston ⊖65 d													07 07						08 07			
Birmingham New Street ■ 65 d						06 01		06 36		07 01		07 36				08 01		08 36				09 01
Crewe ■ 65 d				06 32		06 57		07 35		08 00		08 31	08 43			08 58		09 31				09 57
Winsford d				06 41		07 05		07 44		08 07						09 07						
Hartford d				06 46		07 10		07 49		08 12						09 12						10 10
Acton Bridge d				06 51				07 53		08 16												10 14
Runcorn a				06 59		07 20		08 02		08 24		08 50	09 00			09 21		09 50	09 55			10 22
d				06 59		07 21		08 03		08 25		08 50	09 00			09 22		09 50	09 55			10 23
Liverpool South Parkway ■ ✈ a				07 08		07 30		08 11		08 33		08 59				09 30		09 59				10 31
d	00 27	06 27	07 01	07 08	07 22	07 30	08 03	08 12	08 18	08 34	08 37	08 59		09 06	09 15	09 31	09 36	09 59		10 06	10 15	10 32
West Allerton d		06 31	07 05		07 25		08 06				08 40			09 10			09 39			10 10		
Mossley Hill d		06 33	07 07		07 28		08 09				08 43			09 12			09 41			10 13		
Edge Hill 90 d		06 39	07 13		07 34		08 14				08 48						09 47					
Liverpool Lime Street ■ 90 a	00 41	06 45	07 20	07 22	07 40	07 42	08 21	08 24	08 31	08 46	08 55	09 12	09 21	09 24	09 31	09 43	09 53	10 10	10 15	10 24	10 31	10 44

	NT	LM	VT	NT	EM	LM	NT	LM	VT	NT	EM	LM	NT	LM	VT	NT	EM	LM	NT	LM	VT	NT
		◇■	◇■ ⊐		◇	◇■		◇■	◇■ ⊐		◇	◇■		◇■	◇■ ⊐		◇	◇■		◇■	◇■ ⊐	
London Euston ⊖65 d			09 07						10 07						11 07						12 07	
Birmingham New Street ■ 65 d		09 36				10 01		10 36				11 01		11 36				12 01		12 36		
Crewe ■ 65 d		10 31				10 57		11 31				11 57		12 31				12 57		13 31		
Winsford d						11 06												13 06				
Hartford d						11 11						12 10						13 11				
Acton Bridge d												12 14										
Runcorn a		10 50	10 55			11 21		11 50	11 55			12 22		12 50	12 55			13 21		13 50	13 55	
d		10 50	10 55			11 22		11 50	11 55			12 23		12 50	12 55			13 22		13 50	13 55	
Liverpool South Parkway ■ ✈ a		10 59				11 30		11 59				12 31		12 59				13 30		13 59		
d	10 36	10 59		11 06	11 15	11 31	11 36	11 59		12 06	12 15	12 32	12 36	12 59		13 06	13 15	13 31	13 36	13 59		14 06
West Allerton d	10 39			11 10			11 39			12 10			12 39			13 10			13 39			14 10
Mossley Hill d	10 41			11 13			11 41			12 13			12 41			13 13			13 41			14 13
Edge Hill 90 d	10 47						11 47						12 47						13 47			
Liverpool Lime Street ■ 90 a	10 53	11 10	11 15	11 24	11 31	11 43	11 53	12 10	12 15	12 24	12 31	12 44	12 53	13 10	13 15	13 24	13 31	13 43	13 53	14 10	14 15	14 24

	EM	LM	NT	LM	VT	NT	EM	LM	NT	LM	VT	NT	EM	LM	NT	LM	VT	NT	EM	LM	NT
	◇	◇■		◇■	◇■ ⊐		◇	◇■		◇■	◇■ ⊐		◇	◇■		◇■	◇■ ⊐		◇	◇■	
London Euston ⊖65 d					13 07						14 07						15 07				
Birmingham New Street ■ 65 d		13 01		13 36				14 01		14 36				15 01		15 36				16 01	
Crewe ■ 65 d		13 57		14 31				14 57		15 31				15 57		16 31				16 57	
Winsford d		14 06						15 06												17 06	
Hartford d		14 11						15 11						16 11						17 11	
Acton Bridge d														16 15							
Runcorn a		14 21		14 50	14 55			15 21		15 50	15 55			16 23		16 50	16 55			17 21	
d		14 22		14 50	14 55			15 22		15 50	15 55			16 24		16 50	16 55			17 22	
Liverpool South Parkway ■ ✈ a		14 30		14 59				15 30		15 59				16 32		16 59				17 30	
d	14 15	14 31	14 36	14 59		15 06	15 15	15 31	15 36	15 59		16 07	16 15	16 33	16 36	16 59		17 07	17 15	17 31	17 39
West Allerton d			14 39			15 10			15 39			16 11			16 39			17 11			17 42
Mossley Hill d			14 41			15 13			15 41			16 13			16 41			17 13			17 45
Edge Hill 90 d			14 47						15 47						16 47						17 50
Liverpool Lime Street ■ 90 a	14 31	14 43	14 53	15 10	15 15	15 24	15 31	15 43	15 53	16 10	16 15	16 25	16 31	16 44	16 54	17 10	17 15	17 25	17 31	17 43	17 58

Crewe and Runcorn - Liverpool

Saturdays

	LM	VT	NT	EM	LM	VT	NT	LM	VT	NT	EM	LM	VT	NT	EM	LM	VT	NT	VT	NT	LM	NT	VT
	◇1	◇1 ☕		◇	◇1	◇1 ☕		◇1	◇1 ☕		◇	◇1	◇1 ☕		◇	◇1	◇1 ☕		◇1 ☕		◇1		◇1 ☕
London Euston ⊖65 d		16 07				16 33			17 07				18 07				18 33		19 07				20 11
Birmingham New Street [12] 65 d	16 36				17 01			17 36				18 01				19 01					20 01		
Crewe [10] 65 d	17 31				18 00			18 33				18 59				19 58			20 47		21 05		22 14
Winsford d					18 08							19 08				20 07					21 14		
Hartford d					18 13			18 44				19 13				20 12					21 19		
Acton Bridge d																20 16							
Runcorn a	17 50	17 55			18 23	18 31		18 52	18 59			19 22	19 55			20 24	20 32		21 05		21 29		22 32
d	17 50	17 55			18 23	18 31		18 53	18 59			19 23	19 55			20 25	20 32		21 05		21 29		22 32
Liverpool South Parkway [7] ✈ a	17 59				18 32			19 02				19 31				20 33					21 38		
d	17 59		18 14	18 22	18 32		18 38	19 02		19 11	19 18	19 32		19 59	20 20	20 34		20 38		21 15	21 38	22 12	
West Allerton d			18 18				18 42			19 15				20 03				20 41		21 19		22 15	
Mossley Hill d			18 20				18 44			19 18				20 05				20 44		21 21		22 18	
Edge Hill 90 d			18 30				18 50			19 26				20 11						21 27		22 23	
Liverpool Lime Street [10] 90 a	18 10	18 15	18 38	18 35	18 44	18 53	18 57	19 14	19 17	19 35	19 35	19 44	20 15	20 18	20 34	20 46	20 52	20 55	21 25	21 34	21 50	22 30	22 54

	NT
London Euston ⊖65 d	
Birmingham New Street [12] 65 d	
Crewe [10] 65 d	
Winsford d	
Hartford d	
Acton Bridge d	
Runcorn a	
d	
Liverpool South Parkway [7] ✈ a	
d	23 12
West Allerton d	23 15
Mossley Hill d	23 18
Edge Hill 90 d	23 23
Liverpool Lime Street [10] 90 a	23 30

Sundays

	NT	NT	NT	NT	NT	NT	VT	LM	LM	NT	VT	LM	LM	EM	NT	VT	LM	LM	EM	NT	VT	LM
	A	B	C	B	C		◇1 ☕	◇1 D	◇1 E		◇1 ☕	◇1 D	◇1 E	◇		◇1 ☕	◇1 D	◇1 E	◇		◇1 ☕	◇1
London Euston ⊖65 d							08 15				09 15					10 15					11 15	
Birmingham New Street [12] 65 d								09 42	09 42			10 42	10 42				11 42	11 42				12 35
Crewe [10] 65 d							10 30	10 38	10 39		11 32	11 38	11 39			12 33	12 38	12 39			13 17	13 31
Winsford d								10 45	10 46			11 45	11 46				12 45	12 46				13 38
Hartford d								10 50	10 51			11 50	11 51				12 50	12 51				13 43
Acton Bridge d																						
Runcorn a							10 47	11 00	11 00		11 49	12 01	12 02			12 50	13 01	13 02			13 34	13 54
d							10 47	11 00	11 01		11 49	12 01	12 02			12 50	13 01	13 02			13 34	13 54
Liverpool South Parkway [7] ✈ a								11 10	11 10			12 11	12 12				13 11	13 12				14 04
d	00 20	08 54	08 55	09 33	10 02	10 33		11 10	11 11	11 33		12 11	12 12	12 17	12 33		13 11	13 12	13 17	13 33		14 04
West Allerton d		08 57	08 58	09 36	10 04	10 36				11 36					12 36					13 36		
Mossley Hill d		09 00	09 00	09 39	10 07	10 39				11 39					12 39					13 39		
Edge Hill 90 d																						
Liverpool Lime Street [10] 90 a	00 34	09 11	09 12	09 49	10 18	10 50	11 09	11 20	11 21	11 50	12 10	12 21	12 22	12 30	12 50	13 11	13 21	13 22	13 30	13 50	13 57	14 14

	VT	EM	NT	LM	VT	EM	NT	LM	VT	EM	NT	LM	VT	EM	NT	LM	VT	EM	NT	LM	VT	EM
	◇1 ☕	◇		◇1	◇1 ☕	◇ B		◇1	◇1 ☕	◇		◇1	◇1 ☕	◇		◇1	◇1 ☕	◇		◇1	◇1 ☕	◇
London Euston ⊖65 d	12 02				13 02				14 02				15 02				16 02				17 02	
Birmingham New Street [12] 65 d				13 35				14 35				15 35				16 35				17 35		
Crewe [10] 65 d	13 44			14 31	14 42			15 31	15 45			16 34				17 31				18 31		
Winsford d				14 38				15 38				16 41				17 38				18 38		
Hartford d				14 43				15 43				16 46				17 43				18 43		
Acton Bridge d																						
Runcorn a	14 01			14 54	14 59			15 54	16 02			16 56	16 59			17 54	17 57			18 54	18 57	
d	14 01			14 54	14 59			15 54	16 02			16 57	16 59			17 54	17 57			18 54	18 57	
Liverpool South Parkway [7] ✈ a				15 04				16 04				17 06				18 04				19 04		
d		14 16	14 33	15 04		15 16	15 33	16 04		16 16	16 33	17 07		17 16	17 33	18 04		18 16	18 33	19 04		19 17
West Allerton d			14 36				15 36				16 36				17 36				18 36			
Mossley Hill d			14 39				15 39				16 39				17 39				18 39			
Edge Hill 90 d																						
Liverpool Lime Street [10] 90 a	14 23	14 30	14 50	15 14	15 21	15 30	15 50	16 14	16 23	16 30	16 50	17 17	17 23	17 30	17 50	18 14	18 20	18 30	18 50	19 14	19 20	19 30

A not 23 May
B until 5 September
C from 12 September
D from 18 July
E until 11 July

Crewe and Runcorn - Liverpool

Sundays

	NT	LM	VT	EM	NT	LM	VT	NT	VT	VT	NT	NT	VT	VT
		◇1	◇1 ☕	◇		◇1	◇1 ☕		◇1 ☕	◇1 ☕			◇1 A ☕	◇1 B ☕
London Euston ⊖65 d			18 02				19 02		20 02	20 05			21 21	21 21
Birmingham New Street [12] 65 d		18 35				19 35								
Crewe [10] 65 d		19 31				20 31	20 50		21 46	21 55			23 41	23 41
Winsford d		19 38				20 38								
Hartford d		19 43				20 43								
Acton Bridge d														
Runcorn a		19 54	19 58			20 54	21 07		22 03	22 12			00 02	00 04
d		19 54	19 58			20 54	21 07		22 03	22 12			00 02	00 04
Liverpool South Parkway [7] ✈ a		20 04				21 04								
d	19 33	20 04		20 16	20 33	21 04		21 33			22 33	23 33		
West Allerton d	19 36				20 36			21 36			22 36	23 36		
Mossley Hill d	19 39				20 39			21 39			22 39	23 39		
Edge Hill 90 d														
Liverpool Lime Street [10] 90 a	19 50	20 14	20 20	20 30	20 50	21 14	21 28	21 50	22 24	22 33	22 50	23 50	00 29	00 31

A until 5 September
B from 12 September

Table 94

Manchester and Bolton - Blackburn - Clitheroe

Mondays to Fridays
until 03 September

	NT	NT	NT	NT	NT	NT	NT	NT	NT	NT	NT	NT	NT	NT	NT	NT	NT	NT	NT	NT	NT	NT
Manchester Victoria 82 d		05 55		07 23	08 00	08 29	09 00	10 00	11 00	12 00	13 00	14 00	15 00	15 40	16 23	17 00	17 23	18 00	18 23	19 00	20 00	21 00
Salford Central 82 d				07 26	08 03	08 32	09 03	10 03	11 03	12 03	13 03	14 03	15 03	15 43	16 26	17 03	17 27	18 03	18 26	19 03	20 03	21 03
Manchester Piccadilly 10 82 d			06 54																			
Salford Crescent 82 d		06 00	07 03	07 30	08 08	08 37	09 08	10 08	11 08	12 08	13 08	14 08	15 08	15 47	16 31	17 08	17 30	18 08	18 31	19 08	20 08	21 08
Bolton 82 d		06 12	07 19	07 42	08 20	08 49	09 20	10 20	11 20	12 20	13 20	14 20	15 20	16 00	16 43	17 20	17 43	18 20	18 43	19 20	20 20	21 20
Hall I' Th' Wood d		06 17	07 24	07 47	08 25	08 54	09 25	10 25	11 25	12 25	13 25	14 25	15 25	16 05	16 48	17 25	17 48	18 25	18 48	19 25	20 25	21 25
Bromley Cross d		06 20	07 27	07 53	08 28	08 57	09 28	10 28	11 28	12 28	13 28	14 28	15 28	16 10	16 51	17 28	17 55	18 28	18 54	19 28	20 28	21 28
Entwistle d				07x59	08x34		09x34	10x34	11x34	12x34	13x34	14x34	15x34	16x16	16x57	17x34		18x34		19x34	20x34	21x34
Darwen a		06 31	07 39	08 06	08 41	09 09	09 41	10 41	11 41	12 41	13 41	14 41	15 41	16 23	17 04	17 41	18 07	18 41	19 06	19 41	20 41	21 41
d		06 42	07 39	08 11	08 41	09 11	09 41	10 41	11 41	12 41	13 41	14 41	15 41	16 23	17 11	17 41	18 07	18 41	19 11	19 41	20 41	21 41
Blackpool North 97 d																						
Preston 8 97 d																						
Blackburn a		06 49	07 46	08 20	08 51	09 20	09 50	10 50	11 50	12 50	13 50	14 50	15 49	16 30	17 19	17 51	18 16	18 48	19 21	19 51	20 50	21 50
d	06 25	06 52	07 47		08 52		09 52	10 52	11 52	12 52	13 52	14 52	15 52	16 31	17 19	17 53		18 49		19 52	20 52	21 52
Ramsgreave & Wilpshire d	06 31	06 58	07 53		08 58		09 58	10 58	11 58	12 58	13 58	14 58	15 58	16 37	17 25	17 59		18 55		19 58	20 58	21 58
Langho d	06 35	07 02	07 57		09 02		10 02	11 02	12 02	13 02	14 02	15 02	16 02	16 41	17 30	18 03		18 59		20 02	21 02	22 02
Whalley d	06 39	07 06	08 01		09 06		10 06	11 06	12 06	13 06	14 06	15 06	16 06	16 45	17 34	18 07		19 03		20 06	21 06	22 06
Clitheroe a	06 50	07 17	08 12		09 17		10 17	11 17	12 17	13 17	14 17	15 17	16 17	16 56	17 44	18 18		19 14		20 17	21 17	22 17

	NT FO	NT FX	NT FO	NT FX
Manchester Victoria 82 d	22 00	22 00	23 00	23 00
Salford Central 82 d	22 04		23 03	
Manchester Piccadilly 10 82 d				
Salford Crescent 82 d	22 08	22 08	23 08	23 08
Bolton 82 d	22 20	22 20	23 20	23 20
Hall I' Th' Wood d	22 25	22 25	23 25	23 25
Bromley Cross d	22 28	22 28	23 28	23 28
Entwistle d	22x34	22x34	23x34	23x34
Darwen a	22 41	22 41	23 41	23 41
d	22 41	22 41	23 41	23 41
Blackpool North 97 d				
Preston 8 97 d				
Blackburn a	22 50	22 50	23 51	23 51
d	22 51	22 51		
Ramsgreave & Wilpshire d	22 57	22 57		
Langho d	23 01	23 01		
Whalley d	23 05	23 05		
Clitheroe a	23 16	23 16		

Mondays to Fridays
from 06 September

	NT	NT	NT	NT	NT	NT	NT	NT	NT	NT	NT	NT	NT	NT	NT	NT	NT	NT	NT	NT	NT	NT
Manchester Victoria 82 d		05 55		07 23	08 00	08 29	09 00	10 00	11 00	12 00	13 00	14 00	15 00	15 40	16 23	17 00	17 23	18 00	18 23	19 00	20 00	21 00
Salford Central 82 d				07 26	08 03	08 32	09 03	10 03	11 03	12 03	13 03	14 03	15 03	15 43	16 26	17 03	17 27	18 03	18 26	19 03	20 03	21 03
Manchester Piccadilly 10 82 d			06 54																			
Salford Crescent 82 d		06 00	07 03	07 30	08 08	08 37	09 08	10 08	11 08	12 08	13 08	14 08	15 08	15 47	16 31	17 08	17 30	18 08	18 31	19 08	20 08	21 08
Bolton 82 d		06 12	07 19	07 42	08 20	08 49	09 20	10 20	11 20	12 20	13 20	14 20	15 20	16 00	16 43	17 20	17 43	18 20	18 43	19 20	20 20	21 20
Hall I' Th' Wood d		06 17	07 24	07 47	08 25	08 54	09 25	10 25	11 25	12 25	13 25	14 25	15 25	16 05	16 48	17 25	17 48	18 25	18 48	19 25	20 25	21 25
Bromley Cross d		06 20	07 27	07 53	08 28	08 57	09 28	10 28	11 28	12 28	13 28	14 28	15 28	16 10	16 51	17 28	17 55	18 28	18 54	19 28	20 28	21 28
Entwistle d				07x59	08x34		09x34	10x34	11x34	12x34	13x34	14x34	15x34	16x16	16x57	17x34		18x34		19x34	20x34	21x34
Darwen a		06 31	07 39	08 06	08 41	09 09	09 41	10 41	11 41	12 41	13 41	14 41	15 41	16 23	17 04	17 41	18 07	18 41	19 06	19 41	20 41	21 41
d		06 42	07 39	08 11	08 41	09 11	09 41	10 41	11 41	12 41	13 41	14 41	15 41	16 23	17 11	17 41	18 07	18 41	19 11	19 41	20 41	21 41
Blackpool North 97 d																						
Preston 8 97 d																						
Blackburn a		06 49	07 46	08 20	08 51	09 20	09 50	10 50	11 50	12 50	13 50	14 50	15 49	16 30	17 19	17 51	18 16	18 48	19 21	19 51	20 50	21 50
d	06 25	06 52	07 47		08 52		09 52	10 52	11 52	12 52	13 52	14 52	15 52	16 31	17 19	17 53		18 49		19 52	20 52	21 52
Ramsgreave & Wilpshire d	06 31	06 58	07 53		08 58		09 58	10 58	11 58	12 58	13 58	14 58	15 58	16 37	17 25	17 59		18 55		19 58	20 58	21 58
Langho d	06 35	07 02	07 57		09 02		10 02	11 02	12 02	13 02	14 02	15 02	16 02	16 41	17 30	18 03		18 59		20 02	21 02	22 02
Whalley d	06 39	07 06	08 01		09 06		10 06	11 06	12 06	13 06	14 06	15 06	16 06	16 45	17 34	18 07		19 03		20 06	21 06	22 06
Clitheroe a	06 52	07 19	08 14		09 19		10 19	11 19	12 19	13 19	14 19	15 19	16 19	16 58	17 46	18 20		19 16		20 17	21 19	22 19

	NT FX	NT FO	NT FO	NT FX
Manchester Victoria 82 d	22 00	22 00	23 00	23 00
Salford Central 82 d		22 04	23 03	
Manchester Piccadilly 10 82 d				
Salford Crescent 82 d	22 08	22 08	23 08	23 08
Bolton 82 d	22 20	22 20	23 20	23 20
Hall I' Th' Wood d	22 25	22 25	23 25	23 25
Bromley Cross d	22 28	22 28	23 28	23 28
Entwistle d	22x34	22x34	23x34	23x34
Darwen a	22 41	22 41	23 41	23 41
d	22 41	22 41	23 41	23 41
Blackpool North 97 d				
Preston 8 97 d				
Blackburn a	22 50	22 50	23 51	23 51
d	22 51	22 51		
Ramsgreave & Wilpshire d	22 57	22 57		
Langho d	23 01	23 01		
Whalley d	23 05	23 05		
Clitheroe a	23 18	23 18		

Table 94

Manchester and Bolton - Blackburn - Clitheroe

Saturdays
until 04 September

	NT	NT	NT	NT	NT	NT	NT	NT	NT	NT	NT	NT	NT	NT	NT	NT	NT	NT	NT	NT	NT	NT	NT	NT
Manchester Victoria 82 d		05 55		07 23	08 00	08 29	09 00	10 00	11 00	12 00	13 00	14 00	15 00	15 40	16 23	17 00	17 23	18 00	18 23	19 00	20 00	21 00	22 00	23 05
Salford Central 82 d				07 26	08 03	08 32	09 03	10 03	11 03	12 03	13 03	14 03	15 03	15 43	16 26	17 03	17 26	18 03	18 26	19 03	20 03	21 03	22 03	23 08
Manchester Piccadilly 10 82 d			06 54																					
Salford Crescent 82 d		06 00	07 03	07 30	08 08	08 37	09 08	10 08	11 08	12 08	13 08	14 08	15 08	15 47	16 31	17 08	17 31	18 08	18 31	19 08	20 08	21 08	22 08	23 12
Bolton 82 d		06 12	07 19	07 42	08 20	08 49	09 20	10 20	11 20	12 20	13 20	14 20	15 20	16 00	16 43	17 20	17 43	18 20	18 43	19 20	20 20	21 20	22 20	23 24
Hall I' Th' Wood d		06 17	07 24	07 47	08 25	08 54	09 25	10 25	11 25	12 25	13 25	14 25	15 25	16 05	16 48	17 25	17 48	18 25	18 48	19 25	20 25	21 25	22 25	23 29
Bromley Cross d		06 20	07 27	07 53	08 28	08 57	09 28	10 28	11 28	12 28	13 28	14 28	15 28	16 10	16 51	17 28	17 55	18 28	18 54	19 28	20 28	21 28	22 28	23 32
Entwistle d				07x59	08x34		09x34	10x34	11x34	12x34	13x34	14x34	15x34	16x16	16x57	17x34		18x34		19x34	20x34	21x34	22x34	23x38
Darwen a		06 31	07 39	08 06	08 41	09 09	09 41	10 41	11 41	12 41	13 41	14 41	15 41	16 23	17 04	17 41	18 07	18 41	19 06	19 41	20 41	21 41	22 41	23 45
d		06 42	07 39	08 11	08 41	09 11	09 41	10 41	11 41	12 41	13 41	14 41	15 41	16 23	17 11	17 41	18 07	18 41	19 11	19 41	20 41	21 41	22 41	23 45
Blackpool North 97 d																								
Preston 8 97 d																								
Blackburn a		06 49	07 46	08 20	08 51	09 20	09 50	10 50	11 50	12 50	13 50	14 50	15 49	16 30	17 19	17 51	18 21	18 48	19 21	19 51	20 50	21 50	22 50	23 54
d	06 25	06 52	07 47		08 52		09 52	10 52	11 52	12 52	13 52	14 52	15 52	16 31	17 19	17 53		18 49		19 52	20 52	21 52	22 51	
Ramsgreave & Wilpshire d	06 31	06 58	07 53		08 58		09 58	10 58	11 58	12 58	13 58	14 58	15 58	16 37	17 25	17 59		18 55		19 58	20 58	21 58	22 57	
Langho d	06 35	07 02	07 57		09 02		10 02	11 02	12 02	13 02	14 02	15 02	16 02	16 41	17 30	18 03		18 59		20 02	21 02	22 02	23 01	
Whalley d	06 39	07 06	08 01		09 06		10 06	11 06	12 06	13 06	14 06	15 06	16 06	16 45	17 34	18 07		19 03		20 06	21 06	22 06	23 05	
Clitheroe a	06 50	07 17	08 12		09 17		10 17	11 17	12 17	13 17	14 17	15 17	16 17	16 56	17 44	18 18		19 14		20 17	21 17	22 17	23 16	

Saturdays
from 11 September

	NT	NT	NT	NT	NT	NT	NT	NT	NT	NT	NT	NT	NT	NT	NT	NT	NT	NT	NT	NT	NT	NT	NT	NT
Manchester Victoria 82 d		05 55		07 23	08 00	08 29	09 00	10 00	11 00	12 00	13 00	14 00	15 00	15 40	16 23	17 00	17 23	18 00	18 23	19 00	20 00	21 00	22 00	23 05
Salford Central 82 d				07 26	08 03	08 32	09 03	10 03	11 03	12 03	13 03	14 03	15 03	15 43	16 26	17 03	17 26	18 03	18 26	19 03	20 03	21 03	22 03	23 08
Manchester Piccadilly 10 82 d			06 54																					
Salford Crescent 82 d		06 00	07 03	07 30	08 08	08 37	09 08	10 08	11 08	12 08	13 08	14 08	15 08	15 47	16 31	17 08	17 31	18 08	18 31	19 08	20 08	21 08	22 08	23 12
Bolton 82 d		06 12	07 19	07 42	08 20	08 49	09 20	10 20	11 20	12 20	13 20	14 20	15 20	16 00	16 43	17 20	17 43	18 20	18 43	19 20	20 20	21 20	22 20	23 24
Hall I' Th' Wood d		06 17	07 24	07 47	08 25	08 54	09 25	10 25	11 25	12 25	13 25	14 25	15 25	16 05	16 48	17 25	17 48	18 25	18 48	19 25	20 25	21 25	22 25	23 29
Bromley Cross d		06 20	07 27	07 53	08 28	08 57	09 28	10 28	11 28	12 28	13 28	14 28	15 28	16 10	16 51	17 28	17 55	18 28	18 54	19 28	20 28	21 28	22 28	23 32
Entwistle d				07x59	08x34		09x34	10x34	11x34	12x34	13x34	14x34	15x34	16x16	16x57	17x34		18x34		19x34	20x34	21x34	22x34	23x38
Darwen a		06 31	07 39	08 06	08 41	09 09	09 41	10 41	11 41	12 41	13 41	14 41	15 41	16 23	17 04	17 41	18 07	18 41	19 06	19 41	20 41	21 41	22 41	23 45
d		06 42	07 39	08 11	08 41	09 11	09 41	10 41	11 41	12 41	13 41	14 41	15 41	16 23	17 11	17 41	18 07	18 41	19 11	19 41	20 41	21 41	22 41	23 45
Blackpool North 97 d																								
Preston 8 97 d																								
Blackburn a		06 49	07 46	08 20	08 51	09 20	09 50	10 50	11 50	12 50	13 50	14 50	15 49	16 30	17 19	17 51	18 21	18 48	19 21	19 51	20 50	21 50	22 50	23 54
d	06 25	06 52	07 47		08 52		09 52	10 52	11 52	12 52	13 52	14 52	15 52	16 31	17 19	17 53		18 49		19 52	20 52	21 52	22 51	
Ramsgreave & Wilpshire d	06 31	06 58	07 53		08 58		09 58	10 58	11 58	12 58	13 58	14 58	15 58	16 37	17 25	17 59		18 55		19 58	20 58	21 58	22 57	
Langho d	06 35	07 02	07 57		09 02		10 02	11 02	12 02	13 02	14 02	15 02	16 02	16 41	17 30	18 03		18 59		20 02	21 02	22 02	23 01	
Whalley d	06 39	07 06	08 01		09 06		10 06	11 06	12 06	13 06	14 06	15 06	16 06	16 45	17 34	18 07		19 03		20 06	21 06	22 06	23 05	
Clitheroe a	06 52	07 19	08 14		09 19		10 19	11 19	12 19	13 19	14 19	15 19	16 19	16 58	17 46	18 20		19 16		20 19	21 19	22 19	23 18	

Sundays

	NT	NT A	NT	NT B	NT	NT	NT	NT	NT	NT	NT	NT	NT	NT	NT	NT	NT
Manchester Victoria 82 d	08 01		09 00		10 00	11 00	12 00	13 00	14 00	15 00	16 00	17 00	18 00	19 00	20 00	21 00	22 00
Salford Central 82 d																	
Manchester Piccadilly 10 82 d																	
Salford Crescent 82 d	08 08		09 08		10 08	11 08	12 08	13 08	14 08	15 08	16 08	17 08	18 08	19 08	20 08	21 08	22 08
Bolton 82 d	08 20		09 20		10 20	11 20	12 20	13 20	14 20	15 20	16 20	17 20	18 20	19 20	20 20	21 20	22 20
Hall I' Th' Wood d	08 25		09 25		10 25	11 25	12 25	13 25	14 25	15 25	16 25	17 25	18 25	19 25	20 25	21 25	22 25
Bromley Cross d	08 28		09 28		10 28	11 28	12 28	13 28	14 28	15 28	16 28	17 28	18 28	19 28	20 28	21 28	22 28
Entwistle d	08x34		09x34		10x34	11x34	12x34	13x34	14x34	15x34	16x34	17x34	18x34	19x34	20x34	21x34	22x34
Darwen a	08 41		09 41		10 41	11 41	12 41	13 41	14 41	15 41	16 41	17 41	18 41	19 41	20 41	21 41	22 41
d	08 41		09 41		10 41	11 41	12 41	13 41	14 41	15 41	16 41	17 41	18 41	19 41	20 41	21 41	22 41
Blackpool North 97 d		08 36															
Preston 8 97 d		09 05		10 00													
Blackburn a	08 48	09 25	09 48	10 19	10 48	11 48	12 48	13 48	14 48	15 48	16 48	17 48	18 48	19 48	20 48	21 48	22 50
d	08 57	09 27	09 50	10 22	10 50	11 50	12 50	13 50	14 50	15 50	16 50	17 50	18 50	19 50	20 50	21 50	
Ramsgreave & Wilpshire d	09 03	09 34	09 56	10 28	10 56	11 56	12 56	13 56	14 56	15 56	16 56	17 56	18 56	19 56	20 56	21 56	
Langho d	09 07	09 39	10 00	10 33	11 00	12 00	13 00	14 00	15 00	16 00	17 00	18 00	19 00	20 00	21 00	22 00	
Whalley d	09 11	09 43	10 04	10 38	11 04	12 04	13 04	14 04	15 04	16 04	17 04	18 04	19 04	20 04	21 04	22 04	
Clitheroe a	09 22	09 50	10 15	10 44	11 15	12 15	13 15	14 15	15 15	16 15	17 15	18 15	19 15	20 15	21 15	22 15	

A until 17 October

B until 5 September

Table 94

Clitheroe - Blackburn - Bolton and Manchester

Mondays to Fridays
until 03 September

		NT	NT	NT	NT	NT	NT	NT	NT	NT	NT	NT	NT	NT	NT	NT	NT	NT	NT	NT	NT	NT	NT FX	NT FO	NT
Clitheroe	d		06 40	07 07	07 40		08 26		09 40	10 40	11 40	12 40	13 40	14 40	15 26	16 40	17 09	18 09	18 40		19 40	20 40	21 40	21 40	22 40
Whalley	d		06 46	07 13	07 46		08 32		09 46	10 46	11 46	12 46	13 46	14 46	15 32	16 46	17 15	18 15	18 46		19 46	20 46	21 46	21 46	22 46
Langho	d		06 50	07 17	07 50		08 36		09 50	10 50	11 50	12 50	13 50	14 50	15 36	16 50	17 19	18 19	18 50		19 50	20 50	21 50	21 50	22 50
Ramsgreave & Wilpshire	d		06 55	07 22	07 55		08 41		09 55	10 55	11 55	12 55	13 55	14 55	15 41	16 55	17 24	18 24	18 55		19 55	20 55	21 55	21 55	22 55
Blackburn	a		07 01	07 29	08 02		08 47		10 01	11 01	12 01	13 01	14 01	15 01	15 47	17 01	17 30	18 30	19 01		20 01	21 01	22 01	22 01	23 01
	d	06 28	07 01	07 29	08 03	08 32	09 03	09 31	10 03	11 03	12 03	13 03	14 03	15 03	15 51	17 03	17 31	18 31	19 03	19 31	20 03	21 03	22 03	22 03	23 03
Preston 8 97	a																								
Blackpool North 97	a																								
Darwen	a	06 35	07 09	07 37	08 10	08 39	09 11	09 38	10 10	11 10	12 10	13 10	14 10	15 10	15 58	17 10	17 38	18 38	19 10	19 38	20 10	21 10	22 10	22 10	23 10
	d	06 35	07 09	07 40	08 10	08 42	09 11	09 41	10 10	11 10	12 10	13 10	14 10	15 10	15 58	17 10	17 41	18 41	19 10	19 42	20 10	21 10	22 10	22 10	23 10
Entwistle	d	06x42	07x16		08x17				10x17	11x17	12x17	13x17	14x17	15x17		17x17	17x48	18x48	19x17	19x49	20x17	21x17	22x17	22x17	23x17
Bromley Cross	d	06 48	07 21	07 51	08 23	08 52	09 22	09 52	10 23	11 23	12 23	13 23	14 23	15 23	16 09	17 23	17 54	18 54	19 23	19 54	20 23	21 23	22 23	22 23	23 23
Hall I' Th' Wood	d	06 50	07 24	07 53	08 25	08 55	09 25	09 55	10 25	11 25	12 25	13 25	14 25	15 25	16 12	17 25	17 56	18 56	19 25	19 57	20 25	21 25	22 25	22 25	23 25
Bolton 82	a	06 55	07 30	07 58	08 30	09 02	09 30	10 00	10 30	11 30	12 30	13 30	14 30	15 30	16 17	17 30	18 01	19 01	19 31	20 02	20 30	21 30	22 30	22 30	23 30
Salford Crescent 82	a	07 15	07 43	08 17	08 43	09 15	09 43	10 13	10 43	11 43	12 43	13 43	14 43	15 43	16 30	17 43	18 15	19 14	19 44	20 15	20 43	21 43	22 43	22 43	23 43
Manchester Piccadilly 10 82 ⇌	a																								
Salford Central 82	a	07 18	07 46	08 20	08 46	09 18	09 46	10 16	10 46	11 46	12 46	13 46	14 46	15 46	16 33	17 46	18 17	19 17	19 46	20 17	20 46	21 46		22 46	
Manchester Victoria 82 ⇌	a	07 26	07 53	08 25	08 52	09 26	09 52	10 21	10 52	11 52	12 52	13 52	14 52	15 54	16 41	17 53	18 24	19 23	19 53	20 24	20 52	21 52	22 52	22 52	23 52

Mondays to Fridays
from 06 September

		NT	NT	NT	NT	NT	NT	NT	NT	NT	NT	NT	NT	NT	NT	NT	NT	NT	NT	NT	NT	NT	NT FO	NT FX	NT
Clitheroe	d		06 40	07 07	07 40		08 26		09 40	10 40	11 40	12 40	13 40	14 40	15 26	16 40	17 09	18 09	18 40		19 40	20 40	21 40	21 40	22 40
Whalley	d		06 46	07 13	07 46		08 32		09 46	10 46	11 46	12 46	13 46	14 46	15 32	16 46	17 15	18 15	18 46		19 46	20 46	21 46	21 46	22 46
Langho	d		06 50	07 17	07 50		08 36		09 50	10 50	11 50	12 50	13 50	14 50	15 36	16 50	17 19	18 19	18 50		19 50	20 50	21 50	21 50	22 50
Ramsgreave & Wilpshire	d		06 55	07 22	07 55		08 41		09 55	10 55	11 55	12 55	13 55	14 55	15 41	16 55	17 24	18 24	18 55		19 55	20 55	21 55	21 55	22 55
Blackburn	a		07 01	07 29	08 02		08 47		10 01	11 01	12 01	13 01	14 01	15 01	15 47	17 01	17 30	18 30	19 01		20 01	21 01	22 01	22 01	23 01
	d	06 28	07 01	07 29	08 03	08 32	09 03	09 31	10 03	11 03	12 03	13 03	14 03	15 03	15 51	17 03	17 31	18 31	19 03	19 31	20 03	21 03	22 03	22 03	23 03
Preston 8 97	a																								
Blackpool North 97	a																								
Darwen	a	06 35	07 09	07 37	08 10	08 39	09 11	09 38	10 10	11 10	12 10	13 10	14 10	15 10	15 58	17 10	17 38	18 38	19 10	19 38	20 10	21 10	22 10	22 10	23 10
	d	06 35	07 09	07 40	08 10	08 42	09 11	09 41	10 10	11 10	12 10	13 10	14 10	15 10	15 58	17 10	17 41	18 41	19 10	19 42	20 10	21 10	22 10	22 10	23 10
Entwistle	d	06x42	07x16		08x17				10x17	11x17	12x17	13x17	14x17	15x17		17x17	17x48	18x48	19x17	19x49	20x17	21x17	22x17	22x17	23x17
Bromley Cross	d	06 48	07 21	07 51	08 23	08 52	09 22	09 52	10 23	11 23	12 23	13 23	14 23	15 23	16 09	17 23	17 54	18 54	19 23	19 54	20 23	21 23	22 23	22 23	23 23
Hall I' Th' Wood	d	06 50	07 24	07 53	08 25	08 55	09 25	09 55	10 25	11 25	12 25	13 25	14 25	15 25	16 12	17 25	17 56	18 56	19 25	19 57	20 25	21 25	22 25	22 25	23 25
Bolton 82	a	06 55	07 30	07 58	08 30	09 02	09 30	10 00	10 30	11 30	12 30	13 30	14 30	15 30	16 17	17 30	18 01	19 01	19 31	20 02	20 30	21 30	22 30	22 30	23 30
Salford Crescent 82	a	07 16	07 43	08 17	08 43	09 15	09 43	10 13	10 43	11 43	12 43	13 43	14 43	15 43	16 30	17 43	18 15	19 14	19 44	20 15	20 43	21 43	22 43	22 43	23 43
Manchester Piccadilly 10 82 ⇌	a																								
Salford Central 82	a	07 19	07 46	08 20	08 46	09 18	09 46	10 16	10 46	11 46	12 46	13 46	14 46	15 46	16 33	17 46	18 17	19 17	19 46	20 17	20 46	21 46	22 46		
Manchester Victoria 82 ⇌	a	07 26	07 52	08 26	08 52	09 27	09 53	10 22	10 53	11 52	12 52	13 52	14 53	15 54	16 42	17 53	18 24	19 23	19 53	20 25	20 52	21 52	22 52	22 53	23 53

Table 94

Clitheroe - Blackburn - Bolton and Manchester

Saturdays
until 04 September

		NT	NT	NT	NT	NT	NT	NT	NT	NT	NT	NT	NT	NT	NT	NT	NT	NT	NT	NT	NT	NT	NT	NT
Clitheroe	d			07 07	07 40		08 26		09 40	10 40	11 40	12 40	13 40	14 40	15 26	16 40	17 09	18 09	18 40		19 40	20 40	21 40	22 46
Whalley	d			07 13	07 46		08 32		09 46	10 46	11 46	12 46	13 46	14 46	15 32	16 46	17 15	18 15	18 46		19 46	20 46	21 46	22 52
Langho	d			07 17	07 50		08 36		09 50	10 50	11 50	12 50	13 50	14 50	15 36	16 50	17 19	18 19	18 50		19 50	20 50	21 50	22 56
Ramsgreave & Wilpshire	d			07 22	07 55		08 41		09 55	10 55	11 55	12 55	13 55	14 55	15 41	16 55	17 24	18 24	18 55		19 55	20 55	21 55	23 01
Blackburn	a			07 28	08 02		08 47		10 01	11 01	12 01	13 01	14 01	15 01	15 47	17 01	17 30	18 30	19 01		20 01	21 01	22 01	23 07
	d	06 28	07 00	07 29	08 03	08 32	09 03	09 31	10 03	11 03	12 03	13 03	14 03	15 03	15 51	17 03	17 31	18 31	19 03	19 31	20 03	21 03	22 03	23 09
Preston 8 97	a																							
Blackpool North 97	a																							
Darwen	a	06 35	07 07	07 37	08 10	08 39	09 11	09 38	10 10	11 10	12 10	13 10	14 10	15 10	15 58	17 10	17 38	18 38	19 10	19 38	20 10	21 10	22 10	23 16
	d	06 35	07 08	07 40	08 10	08 42	09 11	09 41	10 10	11 10	12 10	13 10	14 10	15 10	15 58	17 10	17 41	18 41	19 10	19 42	20 10	21 10	22 10	23 16
Entwistle	d	06x42	07x15		08x17				10x17	11x17	12x17	13x17	14x17	15x17		17x17	17x48	18x48	19x17	19x49	20x17	21x17	22x17	23x23
Bromley Cross	d	06 48	07 20	07 51	08 23	08 52	09 22	09 52	10 23	11 23	12 23	13 23	14 23	15 23	16 09	17 23	17 54	18 54	19 23	19 54	20 23	21 23	22 23	23 29
Hall I' Th' Wood	d	06 50	07 23	07 53	08 25	08 55	09 25	09 55	10 25	11 25	12 25	13 25	14 25	15 25	16 12	17 25	17 56	18 56	19 25	19 57	20 25	21 25	22 25	23 31
Bolton 82	a	06 55	07 30	07 58	08 30	09 02	09 30	10 00	10 30	11 30	12 30	13 30	14 30	15 30	16 17	17 30	18 01	19 01	19 31	20 02	20 30	21 30	22 30	23 36
Salford Crescent 82	a	07 15	07 43	08 17	08 43	09 15	09 43	10 13	10 43	11 43	12 43	13 43	14 43	15 43	16 30	17 43	18 14	19 14	19 44	20 15	20 43	21 43	22 43	23 48
Manchester Piccadilly 10 82 ⇌	a																							
Salford Central 82	a	07 19	07 46	08 20	08 46	09 18	09 46	10 16	10 46	11 46	12 46	13 46	14 46	15 46	16 33	17 46	18 17	19 17	19 46	20 17	20 46	21 46	22 46	
Manchester Victoria 82 ⇌	a	07 24	07 52	08 25	08 52	09 26	09 52	10 21	10 52	11 52	12 52	13 52	14 52	15 54	16 41	17 53	18 26	19 23	19 53	20 24	20 52	21 52	22 52	23 59

Saturdays
from 11 September

		NT	NT	NT	NT	NT	NT	NT	NT	NT	NT	NT	NT	NT	NT	NT	NT	NT	NT	NT	NT	NT	NT	NT
Clitheroe	d			07 07	07 40		08 26		09 40	10 40	11 40	12 40	13 40	14 40	15 26	16 40	17 09	18 09	18 40		19 40	20 40	21 40	22 46
Whalley	d			07 13	07 46		08 32		09 46	10 46	11 46	12 46	13 46	14 46	15 32	16 46	17 15	18 15	18 46		19 46	20 46	21 46	22 52
Langho	d			07 17	07 50		08 36		09 50	10 50	11 50	12 50	13 50	14 50	15 36	16 50	17 19	18 19	18 50		19 50	20 50	21 50	22 56
Ramsgreave & Wilpshire	d			07 22	07 55		08 41		09 55	10 55	11 55	12 55	13 55	14 55	15 41	16 55	17 24	18 24	18 55		19 55	20 55	21 55	23 01
Blackburn	a			07 28	08 02		08 47		10 01	11 01	12 01	13 01	14 01	15 01	15 47	17 01	17 30	18 30	19 01		20 01	21 01	22 01	23 07
	d	06 28	07 00	07 29	08 03	08 32	09 03	09 31	10 03	11 03	12 03	13 03	14 03	15 03	15 51	17 03	17 31	18 31	19 03	19 31	20 03	21 03	22 03	23 09
Preston 8 97	a																							
Blackpool North 97	a																							
Darwen	a	06 35	07 07	07 37	08 10	08 39	09 11	09 38	10 10	11 10	12 10	13 10	14 10	15 10	15 58	17 10	17 38	18 38	19 10	19 38	20 10	21 10	22 10	23 16
	d	06 35	07 08	07 40	08 10	08 42	09 11	09 41	10 10	11 10	12 10	13 10	14 10	15 10	15 58	17 10	17 41	18 41	19 10	19 42	20 10	21 10	22 10	23 16
Entwistle	d	06x42	07x15		08x17				10x17	11x17	12x17	13x17	14x17	15x17		17x17	17x48	18x48	19x17	19x49	20x17	21x17	22x17	23x23
Bromley Cross	d	06 48	07 20	07 51	08 23	08 52	09 22	09 52	10 23	11 23	12 23	13 23	14 23	15 23	16 09	17 23	17 54	18 54	19 23	19 54	20 23	21 23	22 23	23 29
Hall I' Th' Wood	d	06 50	07 23	07 53	08 25	08 55	09 25	09 55	10 25	11 25	12 25	13 25	14 25	15 25	16 12	17 25	17 56	18 56	19 25	19 57	20 25	21 25	22 25	23 31
Bolton 82	a	06 55	07 30	07 58	08 30	09 02	09 30	10 00	10 30	11 30	12 30	13 30	14 30	15 30	16 17	17 30	18 01	19 01	19 31	20 02	20 30	21 30	22 30	23 36
Salford Crescent 82	a	07 15	07 43	08 17	08 43	09 15	09 43	10 13	10 43	11 43	12 43	13 43	14 43	15 43	16 30	17 43	18 14	19 14	19 44	20 15	20 43	21 43	22 43	23 48
Manchester Piccadilly 10 82 ⇌	a																							
Salford Central 82	a	07 19	07 46	08 20	08 46	09 18	09 46	10 16	10 46	11 46	12 46	13 46	14 46	15 46	16 33	17 46	18 17	19 17	19 46	20 17	20 46	21 46	22 46	
Manchester Victoria 82 ⇌	a	07 24	07 52	08 25	08 52	09 26	09 52	10 21	10 52	11 52	12 52	13 52	14 52	15 54	16 41	17 53	18 26	19 23	19 53	20 24	20 52	21 52	22 52	23 59

Clitheroe - Blackburn - Bolton and Manchester

Sundays

		NT	NT	NT	NT	NT	NT	NT	NT	NT	NT	NT A	NT	NT	NT B	NT	NT	NT
Clitheroe	d		09 40	10 40	11 40	12 40	13 40	14 40	15 40	16 40	17 40	17 58	18 40	19 40	19 57	20 40	21 40	22 40
Whalley	d		09 46	10 46	11 46	12 46	13 46	14 46	15 46	16 46	17 46	18 04	18 46	19 46	20 04	20 46	21 46	22 46
Langho	d		09 50	10 50	11 50	12 50	13 50	14 50	15 50	16 50	17 50	18 09	18 50	19 50	20 09	20 50	21 50	22 50
Ramsgreave & Wilpshire	d		09 55	10 55	11 55	12 55	13 55	14 55	15 55	16 55	17 55	18 14	18 55	19 55	20 14	20 55	21 55	22 55
Blackburn	a		10 01	11 02	12 01	13 01	14 01	15 01	16 01	17 01	18 01	18 23	19 01	20 01	20 22	21 01	22 01	23 01
	d	09 03	10 03	11 03	12 03	13 03	14 03	15 03	16 03	17 03	18 03	18 28	19 03	20 03	20 25	21 03	22 03	23 03
Preston 8 97	a											18 50			20 47			
Blackpool North 97	a														21 16			
Darwen	a	09 10	10 10	11 10	12 10	13 10	14 10	15 10	16 10	17 10	18 10		19 10	20 10		21 10	22 10	23 10
	d	09 10	10 10	11 10	12 10	13 10	14 10	15 10	16 10	17 10	18 10		19 10	20 10		21 10	22 10	23 10
Entwistle	d	09x17	10x17	11x17	12x17	13x17	14x17	15x17	16x17	17x17	18x17		19x17	20x17		21x17	22x17	23x17
Bromley Cross	d	09 23	10 23	11 23	12 23	13 23	14 23	15 23	16 23	17 23	18 23		19 23	20 23		21 23	22 23	23 23
Hall I' Th' Wood	d	09 25	10 25	11 25	12 25	13 25	14 25	15 25	16 25	17 25	18 25		19 25	20 25		21 25	22 25	23 25
Bolton 82	a	09 30	10 30	11 30	12 30	13 30	14 30	15 30	16 30	17 30	18 30		19 30	20 30		21 30	22 30	23 30
Salford Crescent 82	a	09 43	10 43	11 43	12 43	13 43	14 43	15 43	16 43	17 43	18 43		19 43	20 43		21 43	22 43	23 43
Manchester Piccadilly 10 82 ⇌	a																	
Salford Central 82	a																	
Manchester Victoria 82 ⇌	a	09 52	10 52	11 52	12 52	13 52	14 52	15 52	16 52	17 52	18 52		19 52	20 52		21 52	22 52	23 52

A until 5 September

B until 17 October

Network Diagram for Tables 97, 98, 99, 100

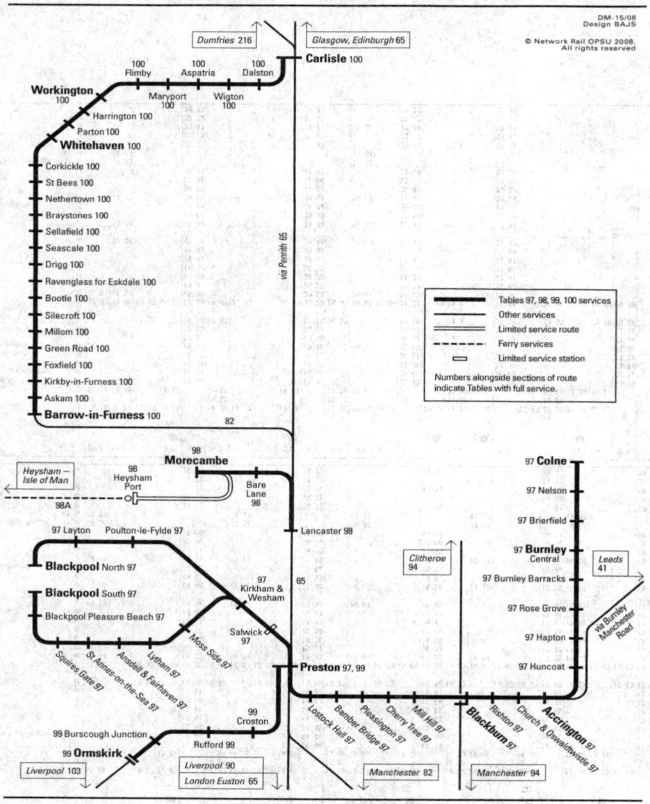

Blackpool - Preston - Blackburn, Accrington, Burnley and Colne

		TP	NT	NT	NT	TP	NT	NT	NT	TP	NT	NT	NT	TP	NT	NT	TP	NT	NT	NT	TP	NT
		◇1				◇1 🛒				◇1 🛒				◇1 🛒			◇1 🛒				◇1 A 🛒	
Blackpool North	d	03 36		04 56	05 29	05 44		06 19	06 28	06 34		06 53	07 02	07 10	07 18	07 29	07 36		08 20	08 29	08 43	
Layton	d							06 22		06 37				07 13	07 21		07 39		08 23			
Poulton-le-Fylde	d			05 02	05 35	05 50		06 27	06 34	06 41			07 08	07 17	07 26	07 35	07 43		08 28	08 35	08 49	
Blackpool South	d						05 42				06 42							07 42				08 44
Blackpool Pleasure Beach	d						05 44				06 44							07 44				08 46
Squires Gate	d						05 46				06 46							07 46				08 48
St Annes-on-the-Sea	d						05 50				06 50							07 50				08 52
Ansdell & Fairhaven	d						05 53				06 53							07 53				08 55
Lytham	d						05 56				06 56							07 56				08 58
Moss Side	d						06 01				07 01							08 01				09 03
Kirkham & Wesham	d						06 08	06 36		06 50	07 09			07 26	07 35		07 52	08 09	08 37			09 10
Salwick	d										07 13							08 13				
Preston 8	a	04u00		05 20	05 52	06 08	06 19	06 46	06 52	07 01	07 20	07 15	07 28	07 37	07 46	07 52	08 03	08 20	08 47	08 52	09 07	09 20
	d		04 47	05 22	05 54		06 21		06 54		07 22					07 54		08 22		08 54		09 22
Lostock Hall	d						06 26				07 27							08 27				09 27
Bamber Bridge	d						06 29				07 30							08 30				09 30
Pleasington	d						06 37				07 38							08 38				09 38
Cherry Tree	d						06 40				07 41							08 41				09 41
Mill Hill (Lancashire)	d						06 42				07 43							08 43				09 43
Blackburn	a		05 03	05 38	06 09		06 45		07 09		07 50					08 09		08 46		09 09		09 46
Clitheroe 94	a																					
Blackburn	d		05 04	05 39	06 10		06 48		07 10		07 51					08 10		08 48		09 10		09 48
Rishton	d			05 44			06 53				07 56							08 53				09 53
Church & Oswaldtwistle	d			05 47			06 56				07 59							08 56				09 56
Accrington	d		05 11	05 50	06 17		06 59		07 17		08 02					08 17		08 59		09 17		09 59
Huncoat	d			05 54			07 03				08 06							09 03				10 03
Hapton	d			05 57			07 06				08 09							09 06				10 06
Rose Grove	d			06 00			07 09				08 12							09 09				10 09
Burnley Manchester Road 41	a				06 26				07 26							08 26				09 26		
Leeds 10 41	a				07 39				08 39							09 39				10 39		
Burnley Barracks	d						07 12				08 15							09 12				10 12
Burnley Central	d		05 21	06 05			07 15				08 18							09 15				10 15
Brierfield	d			06 09			07 19				08 22							09 19				10 19
Nelson	d			06 12			07 22				08 25							09 22				10 22
Colne	a		05 35	06 22			07 32				08 35							09 32				10 32

		TP	NT	NT	NT	TP	NT	NT	NT	NT	NT	TP	NT	NT	NT	NT	TP	NT	NT	NT	NT	TP	NT
		◇1 B 🛒				◇1 🛒						◇1 🛒					◇1 🛒					◇1 🛒	
Blackpool North	d	08 45	09 20	09 29	09 37	09 43		10 20	10 29	10 37		10 45	11 20	11 29	11 37		11 45	12 20	12 29	12 37		12 45	13 20
Layton	d		09 23					10 23					11 23					12 23					13 23
Poulton-le-Fylde	d	08 51	09 28	09 35		09 49		10 28	10 35			10 51	11 28	11 35			11 51	12 28	12 35			12 51	13 28
Blackpool South	d						09 44				10 44					11 44					12 44		
Blackpool Pleasure Beach	d						09 46				10 46					11 46					12 46		
Squires Gate	d						09 48				10 48					11 48					12 48		
St Annes-on-the-Sea	d						09 52				10 52					11 52					12 52		
Ansdell & Fairhaven	d						09 55				10 55					11 55					12 55		
Lytham	d						09 58				10 58					11 58					12 58		
Moss Side	d						10 03				11 03					12 03					13 03		
Kirkham & Wesham	d		09 37		09 52		10 10	10 37		10 52	11 10		11 37		11 52	12 10		12 37		12 52	13 10		13 37
Salwick	d																						
Preston 8	a	09 09	09 47	09 52	10 02	10 07	10 20	10 47	10 52	11 02	11 20	11 09	11 47	11 52	12 02	12 20	12 09	12 47	12 52	13 02	13 20	13 09	13 47
	d			09 54			10 22		10 54		11 22			11 54		12 22			12 54		13 22		
Lostock Hall	d						10 27				11 27					12 27					13 27		
Bamber Bridge	d						10 30				11 30					12 30					13 30		
Pleasington	d						10 38				11 38					12 38					13 38		
Cherry Tree	d						10 41				11 41					12 41					13 41		
Mill Hill (Lancashire)	d						10 43				11 43					12 43					13 43		
Blackburn	a			10 09			10 46		11 09		11 46			12 09		12 46			13 09		13 46		
Clitheroe 94	a																						
Blackburn	d			10 10			10 48		11 10		11 48			12 10		12 48			13 10		13 48		
Rishton	d						10 53				11 53					12 53					13 53		
Church & Oswaldtwistle	d						10 56				11 56					12 56					13 56		
Accrington	d			10 17			10 59		11 17		11 59			12 17		12 59			13 17		13 59		
Huncoat	d						11 03				12 03					13 03					14 03		
Hapton	d						11 06				12 06					13 06					14 06		
Rose Grove	d						11 09				12 09					13 09					14 09		
Burnley Manchester Road 41	a			10 26					11 27					12 26					13 26				
Leeds 10 41	a			11 39					12 39					13 39					14 39				
Burnley Barracks	d						11 12				12 12					13 12					14 12		
Burnley Central	d						11 15				12 15					13 15					14 15		
Brierfield	d						11 19				12 19					13 19					14 19		
Nelson	d						11 22				12 22					13 22					14 22		
Colne	a						11 32				12 32					13 32					14 32		

A FO 2 July until 3 September

B Does not apply Fridays 2 July to 3 September

Table 97

Blackpool - Preston - Blackburn, Accrington, Burnley and Colne

		NT		NT	TP ◇1 ⊼	NT	NT	NT	NT	TP ◇1 ⊼	NT	NT	NT	NT	TP ◇1 ⊼	NT	NT	NT	NT	TP ◇1 ⊼	NT	NT	TP ◇1 ⊼	NT	NT
Blackpool North	d	13 29		13 37	13 45		14 20	14 29	14 37	14 45		15 20	15 29	15 37	15 45		16 20	16 29	16 35	16 40		17 14	17 20	17 37	
Layton	d						14 23					15 23					16 23			16 44			17 23		
Poulton-le-Fylde	d	13 35			13 51		14 28	14 35		14 51		15 28	15 35		15 51		16 28	16 35		16 48		17 20	17 27		
Blackpool South	d					13 44					14 44					15 44					16 44				17 44
Blackpool Pleasure Beach	d					13 46					14 46					15 46					16 46				17 46
Squires Gate	d					13 48					14 48					15 48					16 48				17 48
St Annes-on-the-Sea	d					13 52					14 52					15 52					16 52				17 52
Ansdell & Fairhaven	d					13 55					14 55					15 55					16 55				17 55
Lytham	d					13 58					14 58					15 58					16 58				17 58
Moss Side	d					14 03					15 03					16 02					17 03				18 03
Kirkham & Wesham	d			13 52		14 10	14 37		14 52		15 10	15 37		15 52		16 10	16 37		16 52	16 57	17 10	17 29		17 52	18 10
Salwick	d																								
Preston 8	a	13 52		14 02	14 09	14 20	14 47	14 52	15 02	15 09	15 20	15 47	15 52	16 02	16 09	16 22	16 47	16 52	17 02	17 08	17 20	17 44	17 45	18 02	18 20
	d	13 54				14 22		14 54			15 22		15 54			16 22		16 54			17 22	17 44			18 24
Lostock Hall	d					14 27					15 27					16 27					17 27	17 51			18 30
Bamber Bridge	d					14 30					15 30					16 30					17 30	17 54			18 33
Pleasington	d					14 38					15 38					16 38					17 38	18 01			18 41
Cherry Tree	d					14 41					15 41					16 41					17 41	18 05			18 44
Mill Hill (Lancashire)	d					14 43					15 43					16 43					17 43	18 08			18 46
Blackburn	a	14 10				14 46		15 09			15 46		16 09			16 48		17 09			17 48	18 11			18 52
Clitheroe	94 a																								
Blackburn	d	14 10				14 48		15 10			15 48		16 10			16 50		17 10			17 58	18 11			18 53
Rishton	d					14 53					15 53					16 55					18 03				18 58
Church & Oswaldtwistle	d					14 56					15 56					16 58					18 06				19 01
Accrington	d	14 17				14 59		15 17			15 59		16 17			17 01		17 17			18 09	18 19			19 04
Huncoat	d					15 03					16 03					17 05					18 13				19 08
Hapton	d					15 06					16 06					17 08					18 16				19 11
Rose Grove	d					15 09					16 09					17 11					18 19				19 14
Burnley Manchester Road	41 a	14 26						15 26					16 26					17 26				18 27			
Leeds 10	41 a	15 39						16 39					17 39					18 39				19 39			
Burnley Barracks	d					15 12					16 12					17 14					18 22				19 17
Burnley Central	d					15 15					16 15					17 18					18 25				19 20
Brierfield	d					15 19					16 19					17 21					18 29				19 24
Nelson	d					15 22					16 22					17 24					18 32				19 27
Colne	a					15 32					16 32					17 34					18 42				19 37

		NT	NT	NT	TP ◇1 ⊼	NT	NT	NT		TP ◇1	NT	NT	NT	NT	NT	TP ◇1	NT	TP ◇1	NT	NT	NT	TP ◇1	NT	NT	
Blackpool North	d	18 20	18 29	18 37	18 45		19 20	19 37		19 45		20 20	20 29	20 37		20 45	21 20	21 45		22 14	22 20	22 45	23 13		
Layton	d	18 23					19 23					20 23					21 23				22 23		23 16		
Poulton-le-Fylde	d	18 28	18 35		18 51		19 28			19 51		20 28	20 35			20 51	21 28	21 51			22 28	22 51	23 21		
Blackpool South	d					18 44					19 44				20 44				22 00					23 30	
Blackpool Pleasure Beach	d					18 46					19 46				20 46				22 02					23 32	
Squires Gate	d					18 48					19 48				20 48				22 04					23 34	
St Annes-on-the-Sea	d					18 52					19 52				20 52				22 08					23 38	
Ansdell & Fairhaven	d					18 55					19 55				20 55				22 11					23 41	
Lytham	d					18 58					19 58				20 58				22 14					23 44	
Moss Side	d					19 03					20 03				21 03				22 19					23 49	
Kirkham & Wesham	d	18 37		18 52		19 10	19 37				20 10	20 37			21 10		21 37		22 26		22 37		23 30	23 56	
Salwick	d																								
Preston 8	a	18 47	18 52	19 02	19 09	19 20	19 47	20 02		20 09	20 20	20 47	20 53	21 04	21 20	21 09	21 47	22 09	22 36	22 41	22 47	23 09	23 40	00 08	
	d		18 54			19 22					20 22		20 54		21 22				22 38						
Lostock Hall	d					19 27					20 27				21 27				22 43						
Bamber Bridge	d					19 30					20 30				21 30				22 46						
Pleasington	d					19 38					20 38				21 38				22 54						
Cherry Tree	d					19 41					20 41				21 41				22 57						
Mill Hill (Lancashire)	d					19 43					20 43				21 43				22 59						
Blackburn	a		19 09			19 46					20 46		21 09		21 46				23 04						
Clitheroe	94 a																								
Blackburn	d		19 10			19 48					20 48		21 10		21 48				23 05						
Rishton	d					19 53					20 53				21 53				23 10						
Church & Oswaldtwistle	d					19 56					20 56				21 56				23 13						
Accrington	d		19 17			19 59					20 59		21 17		21 59				23 16						
Huncoat	d					20 03					21 03				22 03				23 20						
Hapton	d					20 06					21 06				22 06				23 23						
Rose Grove	d					20 09					21 09				22 09				23 26						
Burnley Manchester Road	41 a		19 26										21 28												
Leeds 10	41 a		20 41										22 41												
Burnley Barracks	d					20 12					21 12				22 12				23 29						
Burnley Central	d					20 15					21 15				22 15				23 32						
Brierfield	d					20 19					21 19				22 19				23 36						
Nelson	d					20 22					21 22				22 22				23 39						
Colne	a					20 32					21 32				22 32				23 49						

Table 97

Blackpool - Preston - Blackburn, Accrington, Burnley and Colne

			TP ◇1	NT	NT	NT	NT	TP ◇1	NT	NT		TP ◇1 ⊼	NT	NT	NT	NT	NT	TP ◇1 ⊼	NT	NT		NT	NT	NT	TP ◇1 ⊼
Blackpool North	d		03 36		04 56	05 29		05 44	06 19	06 28		06 34	06 53		07 02	07 18	07 29	07 44		08 20		08 29	08 38		08 45
Layton	d								06 22			06 37				07 21		07 47		08 23					
Poulton-le-Fylde	d				05 02	05 35		05 50	06 27	06 34		06 41			07 08	07 26	07 35	07 51		08 28		08 35			08 51
Blackpool South	d						05 42							06 42					07 42					08 44	
Blackpool Pleasure Beach	d						05 44							06 44					07 44					08 46	
Squires Gate	d						05 46							06 46					07 46					08 48	
St Annes-on-the-Sea	d						05 50							06 50					07 50					08 52	
Ansdell & Fairhaven	d						05 53							06 53					07 53					08 55	
Lytham	d						05 56							06 56					07 56					08 58	
Moss Side	d						06 01							07 01					08 01					09 03	
Kirkham & Wesham	d						06 08		06 36			06 50		07 09		07 35		08 00	08 09	08 37				09 10	
Salwick	d													07 13					08 13						
Preston 8	a		03u59		05 20	05 52	06 19	06 08	06 46	06 52		07 01	07 15	07 20	07 28	07 46	07 52	08 11	08 20	08 47		08 52	09 02	09 20	09 09
	d			04 47	05 22	05 54	06 21			06 54				07 22			07 54		08 22			08 54		09 22	
Lostock Hall	d						06 26							07 27					08 27					09 27	
Bamber Bridge	d						06 29							07 30					08 30					09 30	
Pleasington	d						06 37							07 38					08 38					09 38	
Cherry Tree	d						06 40							07 41					08 41					09 41	
Mill Hill (Lancashire)	d						06 42							07 43					08 43					09 43	
Blackburn	a			05 03	05 38	06 09	06 45			07 09				07 50			08 09		08 46			09 09		09 46	
Clitheroe	94 a																								
Blackburn	d			05 04	05 39	06 10	06 48			07 10				07 51			08 10		08 48			09 10		09 48	
Rishton	d				05 44		06 53							07 56					08 53					09 53	
Church & Oswaldtwistle	d				05 47		06 56							07 59					08 56					09 56	
Accrington	d			05 11	05 50	06 17	06 59			07 17				08 02			08 17		08 59			09 17		09 59	
Huncoat	d				05 54		07 03							08 06					09 03					10 03	
Hapton	d				05 57		07 06							08 09					09 06					10 06	
Rose Grove	d				06 00		07 09							08 12					09 09					10 09	
Burnley Manchester Road	41 a					06 26				07 26							08 26					09 26			
Leeds 10	41 a					07 39				08 39							09 39					10 39			
Burnley Barracks	d						07 12							08 15					09 12					10 12	
Burnley Central	d			05 21	06 05		07 15							08 18					09 15					10 15	
Brierfield	d				06 09		07 19							08 22					09 19					10 19	
Nelson	d				06 12		07 22							08 25					09 22					10 22	
Colne	a			05 35	06 22		07 32							08 35					09 32					10 32	

		TP ◇1	NT	NT	NT	TP ◇1 ⊼	NT		NT	NT	NT	TP ◇1 ⊼	NT	NT	NT	TP ◇1		NT	NT	NT	NT	NT	TP ◇1 ⊼	NT	TP ◇1 A
Blackpool North	d	09 14	09 20	09 29	09 37	09 45			10 20	10 29	10 37	10 45		11 15	11 24	11 32		11 37		12 20	12 29	12 37	12 45		13 15
Layton	d		09 23						10 23					11 18						12 23					
Poulton-le-Fylde	d	09 20	09 28	09 35		09 51			10 28	10 35		10 51		11 23	11 31	11 38				12 28	12 35		12 51		
Blackpool South	d						09 44						10 44						11 44					12 44	
Blackpool Pleasure Beach	d						09 46						10 46						11 46					12 46	
Squires Gate	d						09 48						10 48						11 48					12 48	
St Annes-on-the-Sea	d						09 52						10 52						11 52					12 52	
Ansdell & Fairhaven	d						09 55						10 55						11 55					12 55	
Lytham	d						09 58						10 58						11 58					12 58	
Moss Side	d						10 03						11 03						12 03					13 03	
Kirkham & Wesham	d		09 37				10 10		10 37				11 10	11 32					12 10	12 37				13 10	
Salwick	d																								
Preston 8	a	09 41	09 47	09 52	10 02	10 09	10 20		10 47	10 52	11 02	11 09	11 20	11 42	11 52	11 58		12 02	12 20	12 47	12 52	13 02	13 09	13 20	13 38
	d			09 54			10 22			10 54			11 22		11 54				12 22		12 54			13 22	
Lostock Hall	d						10 27						11 27						12 27					13 27	
Bamber Bridge	d						10 30						11 30						12 30					13 30	
Pleasington	d						10 38						11 38						12 38					13 38	
Cherry Tree	d						10 41						11 41						12 41					13 41	
Mill Hill (Lancashire)	d						10 43						11 43						12 43					13 43	
Blackburn	a			10 09			10 46			11 09			11 46		12 09				12 46		13 09			13 46	
Clitheroe	94 a																								
Blackburn	d			10 10			10 48			11 10			11 48		12 10				12 48		13 10			13 48	
Rishton	d						10 53						11 53						12 53					13 53	
Church & Oswaldtwistle	d						10 56						11 56						12 56					13 56	
Accrington	d			10 17			10 59			11 17			11 59		12 17				12 59		13 17			13 59	
Huncoat	d						11 03						12 03						13 03					14 03	
Hapton	d						11 06						12 06						13 06					14 06	
Rose Grove	d						11 09						12 09						13 09					14 09	
Burnley Manchester Road	41 a			10 26						11 27					12 26						13 26				
Leeds 10	41 a			11 39						12 39					13 39						14 39				
Burnley Barracks	d						11 12						12 12						13 12					14 12	
Burnley Central	d						11 15						12 15						13 15					14 15	
Brierfield	d						11 19						12 19						13 19					14 19	
Nelson	d						11 22						12 22						13 22					14 22	
Colne	a						11 32						12 32						13 32					14 32	

A from 3 July until 4 September

Blackpool - Preston - Blackburn, Accrington, Burnley and Colne

		NT	NT	NT	TP ◇1	NT	NT	NT	NT	TP ◇1	NT	NT	NT	NT	TP ◇1	NT	NT	NT	NT	TP ◇1	NT	NT
Blackpool North	d	13 20	13 29	13 37	13 45		14 20	14 29	14 37	14 45		15 20	15 29	15 37	15 45		16 20	16 29	16 35	16 40		17 14
Layton	d	13 23					14 23					15 23					16 23			16 44		
Poulton-le-Fylde	d	13 28	13 35		13 51		14 28	14 35		14 51		15 28	15 35		15 51		16 28	16 35		16 48		17 20
Blackpool South	d					13 44					14 44					15 44					16 44	
Blackpool Pleasure Beach	d					13 46					14 46					15 46					16 46	
Squires Gate	d					13 48					14 48					15 48					16 48	
St Annes-on-the-Sea	d					13 52					14 52					15 52					16 52	
Ansdell & Fairhaven	d					13 55					14 55					15 55					16 55	
Lytham	d					13 58					14 58					15 58					16 58	
Moss Side	d					14 03					15 03					16 03					17 03	
Kirkham & Wesham	d	13 37				14 10	14 37				15 10	15 37				16 10	16 37			16 57	17 10	17 29
Salwick	d															16 15						
Preston	a	13 47	13 53	14 02	14 09	14 20	14 47	14 52	15 02	15 09	15 20	15 47	15 52	16 02	16 09	16 22	16 47	16 52	17 02	17 08	17 20	17 42
	d		13 54			14 22		14 54			15 22		15 54			16 22		16 54			17 22	17 44
Lostock Hall	d					14 27					15 27					16 27					17 27	17 51
Bamber Bridge	d					14 30					15 30					16 30					17 30	17 54
Pleasington	d					14 38					15 38					16 38					17 38	18 01
Cherry Tree	d					14 41					15 41					16 41					17 41	18 05
Mill Hill (Lancashire)	d					14 43					15 43					16 43					17 43	18 08
Blackburn	a		14 10			14 46		15 09			15 46		16 09			16 48		17 09			17 47	18 11
Clitheroe 94	a																					
Blackburn	d		14 10			14 48		15 10			15 48		16 10			16 50		17 10			17 48	18 11
Rishton	d					14 53					15 53					16 55					17 53	
Church & Oswaldtwistle	d					14 56					15 56					16 58					17 56	
Accrington	d		14 17			14 59		15 17			15 59		16 17			17 01		17 17			17 59	18 19
Huncoat	d					15 03					16 03					17 05					18 03	
Hapton	d					15 06					16 06					17 08					18 06	
Rose Grove	d					15 09					16 09					17 11					18 09	
Burnley Manchester Road 41	a		14 26					15 26					16 26					17 26				18 27
Leeds 41	a		15 39					16 39					17 39					18 39				19 39
Burnley Barracks	d					15 12					16 12					17 14					18 12	
Burnley Central	d					15 15					16 15					17 16					18 15	
Brierfield	d					15 19					16 19					17 21					18 19	
Nelson	d					15 22					16 22					17 24					18 22	
Colne	a					15 32					16 32					17 34					18 32	

		TP ◇1	NT	NT	NT	NT	NT	TP ◇1	NT	NT	NT	TP ◇1	NT	NT	NT	NT	TP ◇1	NT	NT	TP ◇1	NT	NT A	NT	TP ◇1	NT
Blackpool North	d	17 20	17 37		18 20	18 29	18 37	18 45		19 20	19 37	19 45		20 20	20 29	20 37	20 42		21 20	21 45		22 14	22 20	22 45	23 02
Layton	d	17 23			18 23					19 23				20 23					21 23				22 23		23 05
Poulton-le-Fylde	d	17 27			18 28	18 35		18 51		19 28		19 51		20 28	20 35		20 48		21 28	21 51			22 28	22 51	23 10
Blackpool South	d			17 44					18 44				19 44					20 44			22 00				
Blackpool Pleasure Beach	d			17 46					18 46				19 46					20 46			22 02				
Squires Gate	d			17 48					18 48				19 48					20 48			22 04				
St Annes-on-the-Sea	d			17 52					18 52				19 52					20 52			22 08				
Ansdell & Fairhaven	d			17 55					18 55				19 55					20 55			22 11				
Lytham	d			17 58					18 58				19 58					20 58			22 14				
Moss Side	d			18 03					19 03				20 03					21 03			22 19				
Kirkham & Wesham	d			18 10	18 37				19 10	19 37			20 10	20 37				21 10	21 37		22 26		22 37		23 19
Salwick	d																								
Preston	a	17 45	18 02	18 22	18 47	18 52	19 00	19 09	19 20	19 47	20 02	20 09	20 20	20 47	20 53	21 01	21 06	21 20	21 47	22 09	22 36	22 41	22 47	23 09	23 29
	d			18 24		18 54			19 22				20 22		20 54			21 22			22 38				
Lostock Hall	d			18 30					19 27				20 27					21 27			22 43				
Bamber Bridge	d			18 33					19 30				20 30					21 30			22 46				
Pleasington	d			18 41					19 38				20 38					21 38			22 54				
Cherry Tree	d			18 44					19 41				20 41					21 41			22 57				
Mill Hill (Lancashire)	d			18 46					19 43				20 43					21 43			22 59				
Blackburn	a			18 52		19 09			19 46				20 46		21 09			21 46			23 06				
Clitheroe 94	a																								
Blackburn	d			18 53		19 10			19 48				20 48		21 10			21 48							
Rishton	d			18 58					19 53				20 53					21 53							
Church & Oswaldtwistle	d			19 01					19 56				20 56					21 56							
Accrington	d			19 04		19 17			19 59				20 59		21 17			21 59							
Huncoat	d			19 08					20 03				21 03					22 03							
Hapton	d			19 11					20 06				21 06					22 06							
Rose Grove	d			19 14					20 09				21 09					22 09							
Burnley Manchester Road 41	a					19 26									21 28										
Leeds 41	a					20 41									22 41										
Burnley Barracks	d			19 17					20 12				21 12					22 12							
Burnley Central	d			19 20					20 15				21 15					22 15							
Brierfield	d			19 24					20 19				21 19					22 19							
Nelson	d			19 27					20 22				21 22					22 22							
Colne	a			19 37					20 32				21 32					22 32							

A Until 16 October

Blackpool - Preston - Blackburn, Accrington, Burnley and Colne

		NT	NT
Blackpool North	d		
Layton	d		
Poulton-le-Fylde	d		
Blackpool South	d	23 30	
Blackpool Pleasure Beach	d	23 32	
Squires Gate	d	23 34	
St Annes-on-the-Sea	d	23 38	
Ansdell & Fairhaven	d	23 41	
Lytham	d	23 44	
Moss Side	d	23 49	
Kirkham & Wesham	d	23 56	
Salwick	d		
Preston	a	00 08	
	d		
Lostock Hall	d		
Bamber Bridge	d		
Pleasington	d		
Cherry Tree	d		
Mill Hill (Lancashire)	d		
Blackburn	a		
Clitheroe 94	a		
Blackburn	d		23 14
Rishton	d		23 24
Church & Oswaldtwistle	d		23 36
Accrington	d		23 40
Huncoat	d		23 46
Hapton	d		23 52
Rose Grove	d		23 58
Burnley Manchester Road 41	a		
Leeds 41	a		
Burnley Barracks	d		00 02
Burnley Central	d		00 07
Brierfield	d		00 15
Nelson	d		00 20
Colne	a		00 28

Sundays
until 17 October

		TP	TP	TP ◇1 B	TP ◇1 C	NT	NT	NT	TP ◇1	NT	NT C	NT B	NT	NT	TP ◇1	NT	NT B	NT	NT	TP ◇1	NT	NT	NT
Blackpool North	d	03 20	05 20	07 48	08 14		08 20	08 36	08 44	08 50	09 01	09 11	09 20		09 44	09 50		10 11	10 20	10 44	10 50	11 13	11 20
Layton	d						08 23						09 23						10 23				11 23
Poulton-le-Fylde	d			07 54	08 20		08 28	08 42	08 50	08 56	09 07	09 17	09 28		09 50	09 56		10 17	10 28	10 50	10 56	11 19	11 28
Blackpool South	d													09 28									
Blackpool Pleasure Beach	d													09 30									
Squires Gate	d													09 32									
St Annes-on-the-Sea	d													09 36									
Ansdell & Fairhaven	d													09 39									
Lytham	d													09 42									
Moss Side	d													09 47									
Kirkham & Wesham	d						08 37	08 51					09 37	09 54					10 37				11 37
Salwick	d																						
Preston	a	04u00	06u00	08 12	08 38		08 47	09 02	09 08	09 14	09 24	09 34	09 47	10 04	10 08	10 14		10 34	10 47	11 08	11 14	11 36	11 47
	d					08 16		09 05			09 27	09 37		10 05			10 00	10 37				11 37	
Lostock Hall	d					08 21		09 11						10 11			10 05						
Bamber Bridge	d					08 24		09 14						10 14			10 08						
Pleasington	d													10 21									
Cherry Tree	d													10 24									
Mill Hill (Lancashire)	d													10 27									
Blackburn	a					08 35		09 25			09 42	09 52		10 30			10 19	10 52				11 53	
Clitheroe 94	a							09 50									10 44						
Blackburn	d					08 37					09 44	09 54		10 31				10 54				11 54	
Rishton	d													10 36									
Church & Oswaldtwistle	d													10 39									
Accrington	d					08 44					09 51	10 01		10 42				11 01				12 01	
Huncoat	d													10 47									
Hapton	d													10 50									
Rose Grove	d					08 51								10 53									
Burnley Manchester Road 41	a										10 00	10 10						11 10				12 10	
Leeds 41	a										11 21	11 21						12 22				13 22	
Burnley Barracks	d													10 56									
Burnley Central	d					08 56								10 58									
Brierfield	d					09 00								11 03									
Nelson	d					09 03								11 06									
Colne	a					09 13								11 15									

B until 5 September

C from 12 September until 17 October

Table 97

Sundays
until 17 October

Blackpool - Preston - Blackburn, Accrington, Burnley and Colne

		NT	TP ◇1	NT	NT	NT	NT	TP ◇1	NT	NT	NT	NT
Blackpool North	d		11 44	11 50	12 11	12 20		12 44	12 50	13 13	13 20	
Layton	d					12 23					13 23	
Poulton-le-Fylde	d		11 50	11 56	12 17	12 28		12 50	12 56	13 19	13 28	
Blackpool South	d	11 27					12 27					13 27
Blackpool Pleasure Beach	d	11 29					12 29					13 29
Squires Gate	d	11 31					12 31					13 31
St Annes-on-the-Sea	d	11 35					12 35					13 35
Ansdell & Fairhaven	d	11 38					12 38					13 38
Lytham	d	11 41					12 41					13 41
Moss Side	d	11 46					12 46					13 46
Kirkham & Wesham	d	11 53				12 37	12 53				13 37	13 53
Salwick	d											
Preston	a	12 03	12 08	12 14	12 34	12 47	13 05	13 08	13 14	13 36	13 47	14 03
	d	12 05			12 37					13 37		14 05
Lostock Hall	d	12 11										14 11
Bamber Bridge	d	12 14										14 14
Pleasington	d	12 21										14 21
Cherry Tree	d	12 24										14 24
Mill Hill (Lancashire)	d	12 27										14 27
Blackburn	a	12 30			12 52					13 53		14 30
Clitheroe 94	a											
Blackburn	d	12 31			12 54					13 54		14 31
Rishton	d	12 36										14 36
Church & Oswaldtwistle	d	12 39										14 39
Accrington	d	12 42			13 01					14 01		14 42
Huncoat	d	12 47										14 47
Hapton	d	12 50										14 50
Rose Grove	d	12 53										14 53
Burnley Manchester Road 41	a				13 10					14 10		
Leeds 41	a				14 22					15 22		
Burnley Barracks	d	12 56										14 56
Burnley Central	d	12 58										14 58
Brierfield	d	13 03										15 03
Nelson	d	13 06										15 06
Colne	a	13 15										15 15

		TP ◇1	NT	NT	NT	NT	TP ◇1	NT	NT	NT	NT	TP ◇1
Blackpool North	d	13 44	13 50	14 11	14 20		14 44	14 50	15 13	15 20		15 44
Layton	d				14 23					15 23		
Poulton-le-Fylde	d	13 50	13 56	14 17	14 28		14 50	14 56	15 19	15 28		15 50
Blackpool South	d					14 27					15 27	
Blackpool Pleasure Beach	d					14 29					15 29	
Squires Gate	d					14 31					15 31	
St Annes-on-the-Sea	d					14 35					15 35	
Ansdell & Fairhaven	d					14 38					15 38	
Lytham	d					14 41					15 41	
Moss Side	d					14 46					15 46	
Kirkham & Wesham	d				14 37	14 53				15 37	15 53	
Salwick	d											
Preston	a	14 08	14 14	14 34	14 47	15 05	15 08	15 14	15 36	15 47	16 03	16 08
	d			14 37					15 37		16 05	
Lostock Hall	d										16 11	
Bamber Bridge	d										16 14	
Pleasington	d										16 21	
Cherry Tree	d										16 24	
Mill Hill (Lancashire)	d										16 27	
Blackburn	a			14 52					15 53		16 30	
Clitheroe 94	a											
Blackburn	d			14 54					15 54		16 31	
Rishton	d										16 36	
Church & Oswaldtwistle	d										16 39	
Accrington	d			15 01					16 01		16 42	
Huncoat	d										16 47	
Hapton	d										16 50	
Rose Grove	d										16 53	
Burnley Manchester Road 41	a			15 10					16 10			
Leeds 41	a			16 22					17 21			
Burnley Barracks	d										16 56	
Burnley Central	d										16 58	
Brierfield	d										17 03	
Nelson	d										17 06	
Colne	a										17 15	

		NT	NT	NT	NT	TP ◇1	NT	NT	NT	NT	TP ◇1 A
Blackpool North	d	15 50	16 11	16 20		16 44	16 50	17 11	17 20		17 30
Layton	d			16 23					17 23		
Poulton-le-Fylde	d	15 56	16 17	16 28		16 50	16 56	17 17	17 28		
Blackpool South	d				16 27					17 24	
Blackpool Pleasure Beach	d				16 29					17 26	
Squires Gate	d				16 31					17 28	
St Annes-on-the-Sea	d				16 35					17 32	
Ansdell & Fairhaven	d				16 38					17 35	
Lytham	d				16 41					17 38	
Moss Side	d				16 46					17 43	
Kirkham & Wesham	d			16 37	16 53				17 37	17 50	
Salwick	d										
Preston	a	16 14	16 34	16 47	17 05	17 08	17 14	17 34	17 47	18 00	17 53
	d		16 37					17 37		18 05	
Lostock Hall	d									18 11	
Bamber Bridge	d									18 14	
Pleasington	d									18 21	
Cherry Tree	d									18 24	
Mill Hill (Lancashire)	d									18 27	
Blackburn	a		16 52					17 52		18 30	
Clitheroe 94	a										
Blackburn	d		16 54					17 54		18 31	
Rishton	d									18 36	
Church & Oswaldtwistle	d									18 39	
Accrington	d		17 01					18 01		18 42	
Huncoat	d									18 47	
Hapton	d									18 50	
Rose Grove	d									18 53	
Burnley Manchester Road 41	a		17 10					18 10			
Leeds 41	a		18 21					19 21			
Burnley Barracks	d									18 56	
Burnley Central	d									18 58	
Brierfield	d									19 03	
Nelson	d									19 06	
Colne	a									19 15	

		TP ◇1 B	TP ◇1 C	NT	NT	NT	NT	TP ◇1	NT	NT	NT	NT
Blackpool North	d	17 40	17 44	17 50	18 11	18 20		18 44	18 50	19 13	19 20	
Layton	d					18 23					19 23	
Poulton-le-Fylde	d	17 46	17 50	17 56	18 17	18 28		18 50	18 56	19 19	19 28	
Blackpool South	d						18 27					19 27
Blackpool Pleasure Beach	d						18 29					19 29
Squires Gate	d						18 31					19 31
St Annes-on-the-Sea	d						18 35					19 35
Ansdell & Fairhaven	d						18 38					19 38
Lytham	d						18 41					19 41
Moss Side	d						18 46					19 46
Kirkham & Wesham	d					18 37	18 53				19 37	19 53
Salwick	d											
Preston	a	18 04	18 08	18 14	18 34	18 47	19 05	19 08	19 14	19 36	19 47	20 03
	d				18 37					19 37		20 05
Lostock Hall	d											20 11
Bamber Bridge	d											20 14
Pleasington	d											20 21
Cherry Tree	d											20 24
Mill Hill (Lancashire)	d											20 27
Blackburn	a				18 52					19 53		20 30
Clitheroe 94	a											
Blackburn	d				18 54					19 54		20 31
Rishton	d											20 36
Church & Oswaldtwistle	d											20 39
Accrington	d				19 01					20 01		20 42
Huncoat	d											20 47
Hapton	d											20 50
Rose Grove	d											20 53
Burnley Manchester Road 41	a				19 10					20 10		
Leeds 41	a				20 23					21 22		
Burnley Barracks	d											20 56
Burnley Central	d											20 58
Brierfield	d											21 03
Nelson	d											21 06
Colne	a											21 15

A from 4 July until 5 September **B** until 5 September **C** from 12 September until 17 October

Table 97

Sundays
until 17 October

Blackpool - Preston - Blackburn, Accrington, Burnley and Colne

		TP ◇1	NT	NT	NT	NT	TP ◇1	NT	NT	NT	NT	NT	TP ◇1	NT	TP ◇1
Blackpool North	d	19 44	19 50	20 11	20 20		20 44	20 50	21 13	21 20		21 50	21 56	22 44	23 03
Layton	d				20 23					21 23					
Poulton-le-Fylde	d	19 50	19 56	20 17	20 28		20 50	20 56	21 19	21 28		21 56	22 02	22 50	23 09
Blackpool South	d					20 27					21 27				
Blackpool Pleasure Beach	d					20 29					21 29				
Squires Gate	d					20 31					21 31				
St Annes-on-the-Sea	d					20 35					21 35				
Ansdell & Fairhaven	d					20 38					21 38				
Lytham	d					20 41					21 41				
Moss Side	d					20 46					21 46				
Kirkham & Wesham	d				20 37	20 53				21 37	21 53				23 17
Salwick	d														
Preston	a	20 08	20 14	20 34	20 47	21 03	21 08	21 14	21 36	21 47	22 03	22 14	22 20	23 08	23 28
	d			20 37		21 05			21 39		22 05				
Lostock Hall	d					21 11					22 11				
Bamber Bridge	d					21 14					22 14				
Pleasington	d					21 21					22 21				
Cherry Tree	d					21 24					22 24				
Mill Hill (Lancashire)	d					21 27					22 27				
Blackburn	a			20 52		21 30			21 54		22 30				
Clitheroe 94	a														
Blackburn	d			20 54		21 31			21 55		22 31				
Rishton	d					21 36					22 36				
Church & Oswaldtwistle	d					21 39					22 39				
Accrington	d			21 01		21 42			22 02		22 42				
Huncoat	d					21 47					22 47				
Hapton	d					21 50					22 50				
Rose Grove	d					21 53					22 53				
Burnley Manchester Road 41	a			21 10					22 12						
Leeds 41	a			22 22					23 23						
Burnley Barracks	d					21 56					22 56				
Burnley Central	d					22a02					22 58				
Brierfield	d										23 03				
Nelson	d										23 06				
Colne	a										23 15				

Sundays
24 October to 07 November

		TP bus	TP bus	TP ◇1	NT	NT	TP ◇1	NT	NT	NT	TP ◇1	NT
Blackpool North	d	03 20	05 20	08 14		08 20	08 44	09 01	09 20		09 44	09 50
Layton	d					08 23			09 23			
Poulton-le-Fylde	d			08 20		08 28	08 50	09 07	09 28		09 50	09 58
Blackpool South	d									09 28		
Blackpool Pleasure Beach	d									09 30		
Squires Gate	d									09 32		
St Annes-on-the-Sea	d									09 36		
Ansdell & Fairhaven	d									09 39		
Lytham	d									09 42		
Moss Side	d									09 47		
Kirkham & Wesham	d					08 37			09 37	09 54		
Salwick	d											
Preston	a	04u00	06u00	08 38		08 47	09 08	09 24	09 47	10 04	10 08	10 14
	d				08 16			09 27		10 05		
Lostock Hall	d				08 21					10 11		
Bamber Bridge	d				08 24					10 14		
Pleasington	d									10 21		
Cherry Tree	d									10 24		
Mill Hill (Lancashire)	d									10 27		
Blackburn	a				08 35			09 42		10 30		
Clitheroe 94	a											
Blackburn	d				08 37			09 44		10 31		
Rishton	d									10 36		
Church & Oswaldtwistle	d									10 39		
Accrington	d				08 44			09 51		10 42		
Huncoat	d									10 47		
Hapton	d									10 50		
Rose Grove	d				08 51					10 53		
Burnley Manchester Road 41	a							10 00				
Leeds 41	a							11 21				
Burnley Barracks	d									10 56		
Burnley Central	d				08 56					10 58		
Brierfield	d				09 00					11 03		
Nelson	d				09 03					11 06		
Colne	a				09 13					11 15		

		NT	NT	TP ◇1	NT	NT	NT	TP ◇1	NT	NT	NT	TP ◇1
Blackpool North	d	10 11	10 20	10 44	11 13	11 20		11 44	12 11	12 20		12 44
Layton	d		10 23			11 23				12 23		
Poulton-le-Fylde	d	10 17	10 28	10 50	11 19	11 28		11 50	12 17	12 28		12 50
Blackpool South	d						11 27				12 27	
Blackpool Pleasure Beach	d						11 29				12 29	
Squires Gate	d						11 31				12 31	
St Annes-on-the-Sea	d						11 35				12 35	
Ansdell & Fairhaven	d						11 38				12 38	
Lytham	d						11 41				12 41	
Moss Side	d						11 46				12 46	
Kirkham & Wesham	d		10 37			11 37	11 53			12 37	12 53	
Salwick	d											
Preston	a	10 34	10 47	11 08	11 36	11 47	12 03	12 08	12 34	12 47	13 05	13 08
	d	10 37			11 37		12 05		12 37			
Lostock Hall	d						12 11					
Bamber Bridge	d						12 14					
Pleasington	d						12 21					
Cherry Tree	d						12 24					
Mill Hill (Lancashire)	d						12 27					
Blackburn	a	10 52			11 53		12 30		12 52			
Clitheroe 94	a											
Blackburn	d	10 54			11 54		12 31		12 54			
Rishton	d						12 36					
Church & Oswaldtwistle	d						12 39					
Accrington	d	11 01			12 01		12 42		13 01			
Huncoat	d						12 47					
Hapton	d						12 50					
Rose Grove	d						12 53					
Burnley Manchester Road 41	a	11 10			12 10				13 10			
Leeds 41	a	12 22			13 22				14 22			
Burnley Barracks	d						12 56					
Burnley Central	d						12 58					
Brierfield	d						13 03					
Nelson	d						13 06					
Colne	a						13 15					

Table 97

Sundays

24 October to 07 November

Blackpool - Preston - Blackburn, Accrington, Burnley and Colne

		NT	NT	NT	TP	NT		NT	NT	TP	NT	NT	NT	TP	NT	NT		NT	TP	NT	NT	NT	TP	NT	NT
					◇1					◇1				◇1					◇1				◇1		
Blackpool North	d	13 13	13 20		13 44	14 11		14 20		14 44	15 13	15 20		15 44	16 11	16 20			16 44	17 11	17 20		17 44	18 11	18 20
Layton	d		13 23					14 23				15 23				16 23					17 23				18 23
Poulton-le-Fylde	d	13 19	13 28		13 50	14 17		14 28		14 50	15 19	15 28		15 50	16 17	16 28			16 50	17 17	17 28		17 50	18 17	18 28
Blackpool South	d			13 27					14 27				15 27					16 27				17 24			
Blackpool Pleasure Beach	d			13 29					14 29				15 29					16 29				17 26			
Squires Gate	d			13 31					14 31				15 31					16 31				17 28			
St Annes-on-the-Sea	d			13 35					14 35				15 35					16 35				17 32			
Ansdell & Fairhaven	d			13 38					14 38				15 38					16 38				17 35			
Lytham	d			13 41					14 41				15 41					16 41				17 38			
Moss Side	d			13 46					14 46				15 46					16 46				17 43			
Kirkham & Wesham	d		13 37	13 53				14 37	14 53			15 37	15 53			16 37		16 53			17 37	17 50			18 37
Salwick	d																								
Preston 8	a	13 36	13 47	14 03	14 08	14 34		14 47	15 05	15 08	15 36	15 47	16 03	16 08	16 34	16 47		17 05	17 08	17 34	17 47	18 00	18 08	18 34	18 47
	d	13 37		14 05		14 37					15 37		16 05		16 37					17 37		18 05		18 37	
Lostock Hall	d			14 11									16 11									18 11			
Bamber Bridge	d			14 14									16 14									18 14			
Pleasington	d			14 21									16 21									18 21			
Cherry Tree	d			14 24									16 24									18 24			
Mill Hill (Lancashire)	d			14 27									16 27									18 27			
Blackburn	a	13 53		14 30		14 52					15 53		16 30		16 52					17 52		18 30		18 52	
Clitheroe 94	a																								
Blackburn	d	13 54		14 31		14 54					15 54		16 31		16 54					17 54		18 31		18 54	
Rishton	d			14 36									16 36									18 36			
Church & Oswaldtwistle	d			14 39									16 39									18 39			
Accrington	d	14 01		14 42		15 01					16 01		16 42		17 01					18 01		18 42		19 01	
Huncoat	d			14 47									16 47									18 47			
Hapton	d			14 50									16 50									18 50			
Rose Grove	d			14 53									16 53									18 53			
Burnley Manchester Road 41	a	14 10				15 10					16 10				17 10					18 10				19 10	
Leeds 10 41	a	15 22				16 22					17 21				18 21					19 21				20 23	
Burnley Barracks	d			14 56									16 56									18 56			
Burnley Central	d			14 58									16 58									18 58			
Brierfield	d			15 03									17 03									19 03			
Nelson	d			15 06									17 06									19 06			
Colne	a			15 15									17 15									19 15			

		NT		TP	NT	NT	NT	TP	NT	NT	NT	TP		NT	NT	NT	TP	TP
				◇1				◇1				◇1					◇1	◇1
Blackpool North	d			18 44	19 13	19 20		19 44	20 11	20 20		20 44		21 13	21 20		21 56	23 03
Layton	d					19 23				20 23					21 23			
Poulton-le-Fylde	d			18 50	19 19	19 28		19 50	20 17	20 28		20 50		21 19	21 28		22 02	23 09
Blackpool South	d	18 27					19 27				20 27					21 27		
Blackpool Pleasure Beach	d	18 29					19 29				20 29					21 29		
Squires Gate	d	18 31					19 31				20 31					21 31		
St Annes-on-the-Sea	d	18 35					19 35				20 35					21 35		
Ansdell & Fairhaven	d	18 38					19 38				20 38					21 38		
Lytham	d	18 41					19 41				20 41					21 41		
Moss Side	d	18 46					19 46				20 46					21 46		
Kirkham & Wesham	d	18 53				19 37	19 53			20 37	20 53				21 37	21 53		23 17
Salwick	d																	
Preston 8	a	19 05		19 08	19 36	19 47	20 03	20 08	20 34	20 47	21 03	21 08		21 36	21 47	22 03	22 20	23 28
	d				19 37		20 05		20 37		21 05			21 39		22 05		
Lostock Hall	d						20 11				21 11					22 11		
Bamber Bridge	d						20 14				21 14					22 14		
Pleasington	d						20 21				21 21					22 21		
Cherry Tree	d						20 24				21 24					22 24		
Mill Hill (Lancashire)	d						20 27				21 27					22 27		
Blackburn	a				19 53		20 30		20 52		21 30			21 54		22 30		
Clitheroe 94	a																	
Blackburn	d				19 54		20 31		20 54		21 31			21 55		22 31		
Rishton	d						20 36				21 36					22 36		
Church & Oswaldtwistle	d						20 39				21 39					22 39		
Accrington	d				20 01		20 42		21 01		21 42			22 02		22 42		
Huncoat	d						20 47				21 47					22 47		
Hapton	d						20 50				21 50					22 50		
Rose Grove	d						20 53				21 53					22 53		
Burnley Manchester Road 41	a				20 10				21 10					22 12				
Leeds 10 41	a				21 22				22 22					23 23				
Burnley Barracks	d						20 56				21 56					22 56		
Burnley Central	d						20 58				22a02					22 58		
Brierfield	d						21 03									23 03		
Nelson	d						21 06									23 06		
Colne	a						21 15									23 15		

Table 97

Sundays

from 14 November

Blackpool - Preston - Blackburn, Accrington, Burnley and Colne

		TP	TP	TP	NT	NT	TP	NT	NT	TP	NT	NT	NT	NT	TP	NT	NT	TP	NT		NT	NT	TP	NT
		(bus)	(bus)	◇1			◇1			◇1					◇1			◇1					◇1	
Blackpool North	d	03 20	05 20	08 14		08 20	08 44	09 01	09 20	09 44	09 50		10 11	10 20	10 44	11 13	11 20	11 44			12 11	12 20	12 44	13 13
Layton	d					08 23			09 23					10 23			11 23					12 23		
Poulton-le-Fylde	d			08 20		08 28	08 50	09 07	09 28	09 50	09 56		10 17	10 28	10 50	11 19	11 28	11 50			12 17	12 28	12 50	13 19
Blackpool South	d																							
Blackpool Pleasure Beach	d																							
Squires Gate	d																							
St Annes-on-the-Sea	d																							
Ansdell & Fairhaven	d																							
Lytham	d																							
Moss Side	d																							
Kirkham & Wesham	d					08 37			09 37					10 37			11 37					12 37		
Salwick	d																							
Preston 8	a	04u00	06u00	08 38		08 47	09 08	09 24	09 47	10 08	10 14		10 34	10 47	11 08	11 36	11 47	12 08			12 34	12 47	13 08	13 36
	d				08 16			09 27				10 05	10 37			11 37			12 05		12 37			13 37
Lostock Hall	d				08 21							10 11							12 11					
Bamber Bridge	d				08 24							10 14							12 14					
Pleasington	d											10 21							12 21					
Cherry Tree	d											10 24							12 24					
Mill Hill (Lancashire)	d											10 27							12 27					
Blackburn	a				08 35			09 42				10 30	10 52			11 53			12 30		12 52			13 53
Clitheroe 94	a																							
Blackburn	d				08 37			09 44				10 31	10 54			11 54			12 31		12 54			13 54
Rishton	d											10 36							12 36					
Church & Oswaldtwistle	d											10 39							12 39					
Accrington	d				08 44			09 51				10 42	11 01			12 01			12 42		13 01			14 01
Huncoat	d											10 47							12 47					
Hapton	d											10 50							12 50					
Rose Grove	d				08 51							10 53							12 53					
Burnley Manchester Road 41	a							10 00					11 10			12 10					13 10			14 10
Leeds 10 41	a							11 21					12 22			13 22					14 22			15 22
Burnley Barracks	d											10 56							12 56					
Burnley Central	d				08 56							10 58							12 58					
Brierfield	d				09 00							11 03							13 03					
Nelson	d				09 03							11 06							13 06					
Colne	a				09 13							11 15							13 15					

		NT	TP	NT	NT	NT		TP	NT	NT	TP	NT	NT	NT	TP	NT		NT	TP	NT	NT	NT	TP	NT	NT
			◇1					◇1			◇1				◇1				◇1				◇1		
Blackpool North	d	13 20	13 44		14 11	14 20		14 44	15 13	15 20	15 44		16 11	16 20	16 44	17 11		17 20	17 44		18 11	18 20	18 44	19 13	19 20
Layton	d	13 23				14 23				15 23				16 23				17 23				18 23			19 23
Poulton-le-Fylde	d	13 28	13 50		14 17	14 28		14 50	15 19	15 28	15 50		16 17	16 28	16 50	17 17		17 28	17 50		18 17	18 28	18 50	19 19	19 28
Blackpool South	d																								
Blackpool Pleasure Beach	d																								
Squires Gate	d																								
St Annes-on-the-Sea	d																								
Ansdell & Fairhaven	d																								
Lytham	d																								
Moss Side	d																								
Kirkham & Wesham	d	13 37				14 37				15 37				16 37				17 37				18 37			19 37
Salwick	d																								
Preston 8	a	13 47	14 08		14 34	14 47		15 08	15 36	15 47	16 08		16 34	16 47	17 08	17 34		17 47	18 08		18 34	18 47	19 08	19 36	19 47
	d			14 05	14 37				15 37			16 05	16 37			17 37				18 05	18 37			19 37	
Lostock Hall	d			14 11								16 11								18 11					
Bamber Bridge	d			14 14								16 14								18 14					
Pleasington	d			14 21								16 21								18 21					
Cherry Tree	d			14 24								16 24								18 24					
Mill Hill (Lancashire)	d			14 27								16 27								18 27					
Blackburn	a			14 30	14 52				15 53			16 30	16 52			17 52				18 30	18 52			19 53	
Clitheroe 94	a																								
Blackburn	d			14 31	14 54				15 54			16 31	16 54			17 54				18 31	18 54			19 54	
Rishton	d			14 36								16 36								18 36					
Church & Oswaldtwistle	d			14 39								16 39								18 39					
Accrington	d			14 42	15 01				16 01			16 42	17 01			18 01				18 42	19 01			20 01	
Huncoat	d			14 47								16 47								18 47					
Hapton	d			14 50								16 50								18 50					
Rose Grove	d			14 53								16 53								18 53					
Burnley Manchester Road 41	a				15 10				16 10				17 10			18 10					19 10			20 10	
Leeds 10 41	a				16 22				17 21				18 21			19 21					20 23			21 22	
Burnley Barracks	d			14 56								16 56								18 56					
Burnley Central	d			14 58								16 58								18 58					
Brierfield	d			15 03								17 03								19 03					
Nelson	d			15 06								17 06								19 06					
Colne	a			15 15								17 15								19 15					

Table 97

Sundays from 14 November

Blackpool - Preston - Blackburn, Accrington, Burnley and Colne

			TP ◇1	NT	NT	NT	TP ◇1	NT	NT	TP ◇1	NT	TP ◇1
Blackpool North		d	19 44		20 11	20 20	20 44	21 13	21 20	21 56		23 03
Layton		d				20 23			21 23			
Poulton-le-Fylde		d	19 50		20 17	20 28	20 50	21 19	21 28	22 02		23 09
Blackpool South		d										
Blackpool Pleasure Beach		d										
Squires Gate		d										
St Annes-on-the-Sea		d										
Ansdell & Fairhaven		d										
Lytham		d										
Moss Side		d										
Kirkham & Wesham		d				20 37			21 37			23 17
Salwick		d										
Preston 8		a	20 08		20 34	20 47	21 08	21 36	21 47	22 20		23 28
		d		20 05	20 37			21 39			22 05	
Lostock Hall		d		20 11							22 11	
Bamber Bridge		d		20 14							22 14	
Pleasington		d		20 21							22 21	
Cherry Tree		d		20 24							22 24	
Mill Hill (Lancashire)		d		20 27							22 27	
Blackburn		a		20 30	20 52			21 54			22 30	
Clitheroe	94	a										
Blackburn		d		20 31	20 54			21 55			22 31	
Rishton		d		20 36							22 36	
Church & Oswaldtwistle		d		20 39							22 39	
Accrington		d		20 42	21 01			22 02			22 42	
Huncoat		d		20 47							22 47	
Hapton		d		20 50							22 50	
Rose Grove		d		20 53							22 53	
Burnley Manchester Road	41	a			21 10			22 12				
Leeds 10	41	a			22 22			23 23				
Burnley Barracks		d		20 56							22 56	
Burnley Central		d		20 58							22 58	
Brierfield		d		21 03							23 03	
Nelson		d		21 06							23 06	
Colne		a		21 15							23 15	

Table 97

Mondays to Fridays

Colne, Burnley, Accrington and Blackburn - Preston - Blackpool

			NT MX	TP ◇1	TP ◇1	TP ◇1 ✠	NT	NT	NT	TP ◇1 ✠	NT	NT	NT	NT	TP ◇1 ✠	NT	NT	NT	TP ◇1 ✠
Colne		d					05 40				06 46					07 47			
Nelson		d					05 45				06 51					07 52			
Brierfield		d					05 48				06 54					07 55			
Burnley Central		d					05 53				06 59					08 00			
Burnley Barracks		d					05 55				07 01					08 02			
Leeds 10	41	d							05 51				06 51					07 51	
Burnley Manchester Road	41	d							06 57				07 57					08 57	
Rose Grove		d					05 58				07 05					08 05			
Hapton		d					06 01									08 08			
Huncoat		d					06 04				07 09					08 11			
Accrington		d					06 09		07 06		07 14		08 06			08 16		09 06	
Church & Oswaldtwistle		d					06 11				07 16					08 18			
Rishton		d					06 14				07 19					08 21			
Blackburn		a					06 23		07 16		07 24		08 14			08 27		09 14	
Clitheroe	94	d																	
Blackburn		d					06 25		07 16		07 35		08 15			08 35		09 15	
Mill Hill (Lancashire)		d					06 28				07 38		08 18			08 38			
Cherry Tree		d					06 30				07 40					08 40			
Pleasington		d					06 32				07 42					08 42			
Bamber Bridge		d					06 39		07 26		07 49		08 27			08 49			
Lostock Hall		d					06 42		07 28		07 52		08 30			08 52			
Preston 8		a		01s03			06 50		07 36		08 00		08 38			09 00		09 32	
		d	00 19	01s05	05s09	06 37	07 00	07 13	07 38	07 59	08 02	08 15	08 40	08 51	08 59	09 02	09 19	09 34	09 38
Salwick		d					07 07				08 09								
Kirkham & Wesham		d	00 28			06 46	07 11	07 22		08 09	08 13	08 25				09 11	09 28		
Moss Side		d					07 17				08 19					09 17			
Lytham		d					07 21				08 23					09 21			
Ansdell & Fairhaven		d					07 24				08 26					09 24			
St Annes-on-the-Sea		d					07 28				08 30					09 28			
Squires Gate		d					07 32				08 34					09 32			
Blackpool Pleasure Beach		d					07 34				08 36					09 34			
Blackpool South		a					07 38				08 41					09 39			
Poulton-le-Fylde		d	00 36			06 56		07 30	07 54	08 18		08 33	08 56		09 16		09 36	09 50	09 56
Layton		d	00 43			06 59		07 34		08 22		08 37					09 43		
Blackpool North		a	00 50	01 30	05 33	07 06		07 41	08 05	08 29		08 44	09 05	09 17	09 25		09 50	10 00	10 05

			NT	NT	NT	NT	TP ◇1 ✠	NT	NT	NT	NT	TP ◇1 ✠	NT	NT	NT	NT	TP ◇1 ✠	NT	NT	NT	NT	TP ◇1 ✠	NT	NT
Colne		d		08 50					09 50					10 50					11 50					12 50
Nelson		d		08 55					09 55					10 55					11 55					12 55
Brierfield		d		08 58					09 58					10 58					11 58					12 58
Burnley Central		d		09 03					10 03					11 03					12 03					13 03
Burnley Barracks		d		09 05					10 05					11 05					12 05					13 05
Leeds 10	41	d				08 51					09 51					10 51					11 51			
Burnley Manchester Road	41	d				09 57					10 57					11 57					12 57			
Rose Grove		d		09 08					10 08					11 08					12 08					13 08
Hapton		d		09 11					10 11					11 11					12 11					13 11
Huncoat		d		09 14					10 14					11 14					12 14					13 14
Accrington		d		09 19		10 06			10 19		11 06			11 19		12 06			12 19		13 06			13 19
Church & Oswaldtwistle		d		09 21					10 21					11 21					12 21					13 21
Rishton		d		09 24					10 24					11 24					12 24					13 24
Blackburn		a		09 33		10 14			10 33		11 14			11 33		12 14			12 33		13 14			13 33
Clitheroe	94	d																						
Blackburn		d		09 35		10 15			10 35		11 15			11 35		12 15			12 35		13 15			13 35
Mill Hill (Lancashire)		d		09 38					10 38					11 38					12 38					13 38
Cherry Tree		d		09 40					10 40					11 40					12 40					13 40
Pleasington		d		09 42					10 42					11 42					12 42					13 42
Bamber Bridge		d		09 49					10 49					11 49					12 49					13 49
Lostock Hall		d		09 52					10 52					11 52					12 52					13 52
Preston 8		a		10 00		10 32			11 00		11 32			12 00		12 32			13 00		13 32			14 00
		d	09 55	10 02	10 19	10 34	10 38	10 55	11 02	11 19	11 34	11 38	11 55	12 02	12 19	12 34	12 38	12 55	13 02	13 19	13 34	13 38	13 55	14 02
Salwick		d												12 09										
Kirkham & Wesham		d	10 05	10 11	10 28			11 05	11 11	11 28			12 05	12 13	12 28			13 05	13 11	13 28			14 05	14 11
Moss Side		d		10 17					11 17					12 19					13 17					14 17
Lytham		d		10 21					11 21					12 23					13 21					14 21
Ansdell & Fairhaven		d		10 24					11 24					12 26					13 24					14 24
St Annes-on-the-Sea		d		10 28					11 28					12 30					13 28					14 28
Squires Gate		d		10 32					11 32					12 34					13 32					14 32
Blackpool Pleasure Beach		d		10 34					11 34					12 36					13 34					14 34
Blackpool South		a		10 39					11 39					12 41					13 39					14 39
Poulton-le-Fylde		d			10 36	10 50	10 56			11 36	11 50	11 56			12 36	12 50	12 56			13 36	13 50	13 56		
Layton		d			10 43					11 43					12 43					13 43				
Blackpool North		a	10 21		10 51	11 00	11 05	11 21		11 50	12 00	12 05	12 21		12 50	13 00	13 05	13 21		13 50	14 00	14 05	14 21	

Table 97

Mondays to Fridays

Colne, Burnley, Accrington and Blackburn - Preston - Blackpool

Station		NT		NT	TP	NT	NT	NT	NT	TP	TP			NT	NT	NT	TP	NT	NT	NT	TP	NT		NT	NT
					◇1 ⌶					◇1 A ⌶	◇1 B ⌶						◇1 ⌶				◇1 ⌶				
Colne	d						13 50								14 50				15 50						16 50
Nelson	d						13 55								14 55				15 55						16 55
Brierfield	d						13 58								14 58				15 58						16 58
Burnley Central	d						14 03								15 03				16 03						17 03
Burnley Barracks	d						14 05								15 05				16 05						17 05
Leeds 10	41 d			12 51					13 51							14 51						15 51			
Burnley Manchester Road	41 d			13 57					14 57							15 57						16 58			
Rose Grove	d						14 08								15 08				16 08						17 08
Hapton	d						14 11								15 11				16 11						17 11
Huncoat	d						14 14								15 14				16 14						17 14
Accrington	d			14 06			14 19		15 06						15 19	16 06			16 19			17 06			17 19
Church & Oswaldtwistle	d						14 21								15 21				16 21						17 21
Rishton	d						14 24								15 24				16 24						17 24
Blackburn	a			14 14			14 33		15 14						15 33	16 14			16 33			17 14			17 34
Clitheroe	94 d																								
Blackburn	d			14 15			14 35		15 15						15 35	16 15			16 35			17 15			17 35
Mill Hill (Lancashire)	d						14 38								15 38				16 38						17 38
Cherry Tree	d						14 40								15 40				16 40						17 40
Pleasington	d						14 42								15 42				16 42						17 42
Bamber Bridge	d						14 49								15 49				16 49						17 49
Lostock Hall	d						14 52								15 52				16 52						17 52
Preston 8	a			14 32			15 00		15 32						16 00	16 32			17 00			17 32			18 00
	d	14 19		14 34	14 38	14 55	15 02	15 19	15 34	15 38	15 42			15 55	16 02	16 34	16 38	16 58	17 02	17 21	17 32	17 36		17 55	18 02
Salwick	d														16 09										
Kirkham & Wesham	d	14 28				15 05	15 11	15 28						16 05	16 13		16 47	17 07	17 11	17 30	17 41			18 05	18 11
Moss Side	d						15 17								16 19				17 17						18 17
Lytham	d						15 21								16 23				17 21						18 21
Ansdell & Fairhaven	d						15 24								16 26				17 24						18 24
St Annes-on-the-Sea	d						15 28								16 30				17 28						18 28
Squires Gate	d						15 32								16 34				17 32						18 32
Blackpool Pleasure Beach	d						15 34								16 36				17 34						18 34
Blackpool South	a						15 39								16 41				17 39						18 39
Poulton-le-Fylde	d	14 36		14 50	14 56			15 36	15 50	15 56	16 02					16 50	16 57			17 38	17 51	17 56		18 13	
Layton	d	14 43						15 43									17 00			17 43	17 54				
Blackpool North	a	14 51		15 00	15 05	15 21		15 50	16 00	16 05	16 11			16 21		17 00	17 07	17 24		17 50	18 02	18 06		18 24	

Station		NT	NT	NT	NT	TP	NT	NT	NT	NT	NT	TP	NT	NT	NT	NT	TP	NT		NT	NT	TP	NT	NT	NT
						◇1 ⌶						◇1 ⌶					◇1					◇1			
Colne	d							17 50					18 55					19 50					20 50		
Nelson	d							17 55					19 00					19 55					20 55		
Brierfield	d							17 58					19 03					19 58					20 58		
Burnley Central	d							18 03					19 08					20 03					21 03		
Burnley Barracks	d							18 05					19 10					20 05					21 05		
Leeds 10	41 d			16 51							17 51					18 51									20 51
Burnley Manchester Road	41 d			17 57							18 57					19 57									21 56
Rose Grove	d							18 08					19 13					20 08					21 08		
Hapton	d							18 11					19 16					20 11					21 11		
Huncoat	d							18 14					19 19					20 14					21 14		
Accrington	d			18 06				18 19			19 06		19 24			20 06		20 19					21 19		22 05
Church & Oswaldtwistle	d							18 21					19 26					20 21					21 21		
Rishton	d							18 24					19 29					20 24					21 24		
Blackburn	a			18 14				18 34			19 14		19 34			20 14		20 33					21 33		22 13
Clitheroe	94 d																								
Blackburn	d			18 15				18 35	18 44		19 15		19 35			20 15		20 35					21 35		22 14
Mill Hill (Lancashire)	d							18 38					19 38					20 38					21 38		
Cherry Tree	d							18 40					19 40					20 40					21 40		
Pleasington	d							18 42					19 42					20 42					21 42		
Bamber Bridge	d							18 49					19 49					20 49					21 49		
Lostock Hall	d							18 52					19 52					20 52					21 52		
Preston 8	a			18 33				19 00	19 05		19 32		20 00			20 32		21 00					22 02		22 31
	d	18 18	18 26	18 34	18 49	18 40	18 55	19 02	19 08	19 19	19 34	19 38	20 02	20 19	20 25	20 34	20 38	21 02		21 19	21 24	21 38		22 19	22 32
Salwick	d																								
Kirkham & Wesham	d	18 27					19 05	19 11		19 28			20 11		20 34			21 11		21 28				22 28	
Moss Side	d							19 17					20 17					21 17							
Lytham	d							19 21					20 21					21 21							
Ansdell & Fairhaven	d							19 24					20 24					21 24							
St Annes-on-the-Sea	d							19 28					20 28					21 28							
Squires Gate	d							19 32					20 32					21 32							
Blackpool Pleasure Beach	d							19 34					20 34					21 34							
Blackpool South	a							19 39					20 39					21 39							
Poulton-le-Fylde	d	18 35	18 43	18 50		18 59				19 36	19 50	19 56			20 42	20 50	20 56			21 36		21 56		22 36	22 49
Layton	d	18 39				19 02				19 43					20 47					21 40				22 43	
Blackpool North	a	18 49	18 53	19 00	19 16	19 09	19 23		19 33	19 52	20 00	20 05		20 44	20 57	21 00	21 06			21 48	21 53	22 06		22 51	22 59

A Does not apply Fridays 2 July to 3 september **B** FO from 2 July until 3 September

Table 97

Mondays to Fridays

Colne, Burnley, Accrington and Blackburn - Preston - Blackpool

Station		TP	NT	NT		NT	TP	TP	NT	NT
		◇1					◇1	◇1		
Colne	d		21 45						22 55	
Nelson	d		21 50						23 00	
Brierfield	d		21 53						23 03	
Burnley Central	d		21 58						23 08	
Burnley Barracks	d		22 00						23 10	
Leeds 10	41 d									
Burnley Manchester Road	41 d									
Rose Grove	d		22 03						23 13	
Hapton	d		22 06							
Huncoat	d		22 09							
Accrington	d		22 14						23 20	
Church & Oswaldtwistle	d		22 16							
Rishton	d		22 19							
Blackburn	a		22 24						23 28	
Clitheroe	94 d									
Blackburn	d		22 25						23 30	
Mill Hill (Lancashire)	d		22 28						23 33	
Cherry Tree	d		22 30							
Pleasington	d		22 32							
Bamber Bridge	d		22 39						23 41	
Lostock Hall	d		22 42						23 43	
Preston 8	a		22 50						23 54	
	d	22 35	22 51	22 57		23 19	23 35	23 51		23 55
Salwick	d									
Kirkham & Wesham	d		23 01			23 28				
Moss Side	d		23 07							
Lytham	d		23 11							
Ansdell & Fairhaven	d		23 14							
St Annes-on-the-Sea	d		23 18							
Squires Gate	d		23 21							
Blackpool Pleasure Beach	d		23 24							
Blackpool South	a		23 28							
Poulton-le-Fylde	d	22 53				23 36	23 52	00 08		00 11
Layton	d					23 40				
Blackpool North	a	23 02		23 22		23 48	00 02	00 16		00 21

Colne, Burnley, Accrington and Blackburn - Preston - Blackpool

		NT		TP ◇1	TP ◇1	TP ◇1	NT	NT	NT		NT	TP ◇1 ⌶	NT	NT	NT	NT	TP ◇1 ⌶	NT	NT		NT	NT	NT	TP ◇1 ⌶
Colne d							05 40						06 50					07 50					08 50	
Nelson d							05 45						06 55					07 55					08 55	
Brierfield d							05 48						06 58					07 58					08 58	
Burnley Central d							05 53						07 03					08 03					09 03	
Burnley Barracks d							05 55						07 05					08 05					09 05	
Leeds 10 41 d									05 51						06 51						07 51			
Burnley Manchester Road 41 d									06 57						07 57						08 57			
Rose Grove d							05 58						07 08					08 08					09 08	
Hapton d							06 01						07 11					08 11					09 11	
Huncoat d							06 04						07 14					08 14					09 14	
Accrington d							06 09		07 06				07 19		08 06			08 19			09 06		09 19	
Church & Oswaldtwistle d							06 11						07 21					08 21					09 21	
Rishton d							06 14						07 24					08 24					09 24	
Blackburn a							06 23		07 16				07 33		08 14			08 33			09 14		09 33	
Clitheroe 94 d																								
Blackburn d							06 25		07 16				07 35		08 15			08 35			09 15		09 35	
Mill Hill (Lancashire) d							06 28						07 38		08 18			08 38					09 38	
Cherry Tree d							06 30						07 40					08 40					09 40	
Pleasington d							06 32						07 42					08 42					09 42	
Bamber Bridge d							06 39		07 26				07 49		08 27			08 49					09 49	
Lostock Hall d							06 42		07 28				07 52		08 30			08 52					09 52	
Preston 8 a							06 50		07 36				08 00		08 38			09 00			09 32		10 00	
d		00 19		01s05	05s06	06 37	07 00	07 13	07 38		07 55	07 59	08 02	08 15	08 40	08 55	08 59	09 02	09 19		09 34	09 55	10 02	10 08
Salwick d							07 07						08 09											
Kirkham & Wesham d						06 46	07 11	07 22				08 09	08 13	08 25				09 11	09 28				10 11	
Moss Side d							07 17						08 19					09 17					10 17	
Lytham d							07 21						08 23					09 21					10 21	
Ansdell & Fairhaven d							07 24						08 26					09 24					10 24	
St Annes-on-the-Sea d							07 28						08 30					09 28					10 28	
Squires Gate d							07 32						08 34					09 32					10 32	
Blackpool Pleasure Beach d							07 34						08 36					09 34					10 34	
Blackpool South a							07 38						08 41					09 39					10 39	
Poulton-le-Fylde d						06 56		07 30	07 54			08 18		08 33	08 56		09 16		09 36		09 50			10 27
Layton d						06 59		07 34				08 22		08 37					09 43					
Blackpool North a		00 52		01 30	05 33	07 06		07 41	08 05		08 21	08 29		08 44	09 05	09 21	09 25		09 50		10 00	10 21		10 35

	NT	NT	TP ◇1 ⌶	NT	NT		NT	NT	TP ◇1 ⌶	NT	NT	NT	NT	TP ◇1 ⌶	TP ◇1 A		NT	NT	NT	NT	TP ◇1 ⌶	NT	NT	NT
Colne d					09 50						10 50							11 50					12 50	
Nelson d					09 55						10 55							11 55					12 55	
Brierfield d					09 58						10 58							11 58					12 58	
Burnley Central d					10 03						11 03							12 03					13 03	
Burnley Barracks d					10 05						11 05							12 05					13 05	
Leeds 10 41 d		08 51						09 51					10 51							11 51				
Burnley Manchester Road 41 d		09 57						10 57					11 57							12 57				
Rose Grove d					10 08						11 08							12 08					13 08	
Hapton d					10 11						11 11							12 11					13 11	
Huncoat d					10 14						11 14							12 14					13 14	
Accrington d		10 06			10 19			11 06			11 19		12 06					12 19		13 06			13 19	
Church & Oswaldtwistle d					10 21						11 21							12 21					13 21	
Rishton d					10 24						11 24							12 24					13 24	
Blackburn a		10 14			10 33			11 14			11 33		12 14					12 33		13 14			13 33	
Clitheroe 94 d																								
Blackburn d		10 15			10 35			11 15			11 35		12 15					12 35		13 15			13 35	
Mill Hill (Lancashire) d					10 38						11 38							12 38					13 38	
Cherry Tree d					10 40						11 40							12 40					13 40	
Pleasington d					10 42						11 42							12 42					13 42	
Bamber Bridge d					10 49						11 49							12 49					13 49	
Lostock Hall d					10 52						11 52							12 52					13 52	
Preston 8 a		10 32			11 00			11 32			12 00		12 32					13 00		13 32			14 00	
d	10 19	10 34	10 38	10 55	11 02		11 19	11 34	11 38	11 55	12 02	12 19	12 34	12 38	12 48		12 55	13 02	13 19	13 34	13 38	13 55	14 02	14 19
Salwick d											12 09													
Kirkham & Wesham d	10 28				11 11		11 28				12 13	12 28						13 11	13 28				14 11	14 28
Moss Side d					11 17						12 19							13 17					14 17	
Lytham d					11 21						12 23							13 21					14 21	
Ansdell & Fairhaven d					11 24						12 26							13 24					14 24	
St Annes-on-the-Sea d					11 28						12 30							13 28					14 28	
Squires Gate d					11 32						12 34							13 32					14 32	
Blackpool Pleasure Beach d					11 34						12 36							13 34					14 34	
Blackpool South a					11 39						12 41							13 39					14 39	
Poulton-le-Fylde d	10 36	10 50	10 56				11 36	11 50	11 56			12 36	12 50	12 56					13 36	13 50	13 56			14 36
Layton d	10 43						11 43					12 43							13 43					14 43
Blackpool North a	10 50	11 00	11 05	11 21			11 50	12 00	12 05	12 21		12 50	13 00	13 05	13 12		13 21		13 50	14 00	14 05	14 21		14 48

A from 3 July until 4 September

Table 97 Saturdays

Colne, Burnley, Accrington and Blackburn - Preston - Blackpool

	NT		TP ◇1 ⌶	NT	NT	NT	NT	TP ◇1 ⌶	NT	NT	NT		TP ◇1 ⌶	NT	NT	NT	TP ◇1 ⌶	NT	NT	NT	NT		NT	TP ◇1 ⌶
Colne d					13 50					14 50					15 50					16 50				
Nelson d					13 55					14 55					15 55					16 55				
Brierfield d					13 58					14 58					15 58					16 58				
Burnley Central d					14 03					15 03					16 03					17 03				
Burnley Barracks d					14 05					15 05					16 05					17 05				
Leeds 10 41 d	12 51						13 51				14 51							15 51					16 51	
Burnley Manchester Road 41 d	13 57						14 57				15 57							16 58					17 57	
Rose Grove d					14 08					15 08					16 08					17 08				
Hapton d					14 11					15 11					16 11					17 11				
Huncoat d					14 14					15 14					16 14					17 14				
Accrington d	14 06				14 19		15 06			15 19	16 06				16 19			17 06		17 19			18 06	
Church & Oswaldtwistle d					14 21					15 21					16 21					17 21				
Rishton d					14 24					15 24					16 24					17 24				
Blackburn a	14 14				14 33		15 14			15 33	16 14				16 33			17 14		17 34			18 14	
Clitheroe 94 d																								
Blackburn d	14 15				14 35		15 15			15 35	16 15				16 35			17 15		17 35			18 15	
Mill Hill (Lancashire) d					14 38					15 38					16 38					17 38				
Cherry Tree d					14 40					15 40					16 40					17 40				
Pleasington d					14 42					15 42					16 42					17 42				
Bamber Bridge d					14 49					15 49					16 49					17 49				
Lostock Hall d					14 52					15 52					16 52					17 52				
Preston 8 a	14 32				15 00		15 32			16 00	16 32				17 00			17 32		18 00			18 33	
d	14 34		14 38	14 55	15 02	15 19	15 34	15 38	15 55	16 02	16 34		16 38	16 55	17 02	17 21	17 32	17 36	17 55	18 02	18 18		18 34	18 40
Salwick d										16 09														
Kirkham & Wesham d					15 11	15 28				16 13			16 47		17 11	17 30	17 41			18 11	18 27			18 49
Moss Side d					15 17					16 19					17 17					18 17				
Lytham d					15 21					16 23					17 21					18 21				
Ansdell & Fairhaven d					15 24					16 26					17 24					18 24				
St Annes-on-the-Sea d					15 28					16 30					17 28					18 28				
Squires Gate d					15 32					16 34					17 32					18 32				
Blackpool Pleasure Beach d					15 34					16 36					17 34					18 34				
Blackpool South a					15 39					16 41					17 39					18 39				
Poulton-le-Fylde d	14 50		14 56			15 36	15 50	15 56			16 50		16 57			17 38	17 51	17 56			18 35		18 50	18 59
Layton d						15 43							17 00			17 43	17 54				18 39			19 02
Blackpool North a	15 00		15 05	15 21		15 50	16 00	16 05	16 21		17 00		17 07	17 21		17 48	18 02	18 06	18 24		18 46		19 00	19 09

	NT	NT	NT	NT	NT	TP ◇1 ⌶	NT		NT	NT	NT	TP ◇1	NT	NT	NT	TP ◇1	NT		NT	NT	TP ◇1	NT	NT	NT
Colne d			17 50				18 50						19 50				20 50					21 45		
Nelson d			17 55				18 55						19 55				20 55					21 50		
Brierfield d			17 58				18 58						19 58				20 58					21 53		
Burnley Central d			18 03				19 03						20 03				21 03					21 58		
Burnley Barracks d			18 05				19 05						20 05				21 05					22 00		
Leeds 10 41 d					17 51						18 51									20 51				
Burnley Manchester Road 41 d					18 57						19 57									21 56				
Rose Grove d			18 08				19 08						20 08				21 08					22 03		
Hapton d			18 11				19 11						20 11				21 11					22 06		
Huncoat d			18 14				19 14						20 14				21 14					22 09		
Accrington d			18 19		19 06		19 19				20 06		20 19				21 19			22 05		22 14		
Church & Oswaldtwistle d			18 21				19 21						20 21				21 21					22 16		
Rishton d			18 24				19 24						20 24				21 24					22 19		
Blackburn a			18 34		19 14		19 33				20 14		20 33				21 33			22 13		22 24		
Clitheroe 94 d																								
Blackburn d			18 35		19 15		19 35				20 15		20 35				21 35			22 14		22 25		
Mill Hill (Lancashire) d			18 38				19 38						20 38				21 38					22 28		
Cherry Tree d			18 40				19 40						20 40				21 40					22 30		
Pleasington d			18 42				19 42						20 42				21 42					22 32		
Bamber Bridge d			18 49				19 49						20 49				21 49					22 39		
Lostock Hall d			18 52				19 52						20 52				21 52					22 42		
Preston 8 a			19 00		19 32		20 00				20 32		21 00				22 02			22 31		22 50		
d	18 49	18 55	19 02	19 19	19 34	19 38	20 02		20 19	20 25	20 34	20 38	21 02	21 19	21 24	21 38			22 19	22 32	22 35	22 51	22 57	23 19
Salwick d																								
Kirkham & Wesham d			19 11	19 28			20 11			20 34			21 11	21 28					22 28			23 01		23 28
Moss Side d			19 17				20 17						21 17									23 07		
Lytham d			19 21				20 21						21 21									23 11		
Ansdell & Fairhaven d			19 24				20 24						21 24									23 14		
St Annes-on-the-Sea d			19 28				20 28						21 28									23 18		
Squires Gate d			19 32				20 32						21 32									23 21		
Blackpool Pleasure Beach d			19 34				20 34						21 34									23 24		
Blackpool South a			19 39				20 39						21 39									23 28		
Poulton-le-Fylde d				19 36	19 50	19 56				20 42	20 50	20 56		21 36		21 56			22 36	22 49	22 53			23 36
Layton d				19 43						20 47				21 40					22 43					23 40
Blackpool North a	19 16	19 21		19 50	20 00	20 05			20 44	20 54	21 00	21 06		21 48	21 53	22 06			22 50	22 59	23 02		23 22	23 48

Table 97

Saturdays

Colne, Burnley, Accrington and Blackburn - Preston - Blackpool

		TP ◇1	NT
Colne	d		22 55
Nelson	d		23 00
Brierfield	d		23 03
Burnley Central	d		23 08
Burnley Barracks	d		23 10
Leeds 10 41	d		
Burnley Manchester Road 41	d		
Rose Grove	d		23 13
Hapton	d		
Huncoat	d		
Accrington	d		23 20
Church & Oswaldtwistle	d		
Rishton	d		
Blackburn	a		23 28
Clitheroe 94	d		
Blackburn	d		23 30
Mill Hill (Lancashire)	d		23 33
Cherry Tree	d		
Pleasington	d		
Bamber Bridge	d		23 41
Lostock Hall	d		23 43
Preston 8	a		23 54
	d	23 35	
Salwick	d		
Kirkham & Wesham	d		
Moss Side	d		
Lytham	d		
Ansdell & Fairhaven	d		
St Annes-on-the-Sea	d		
Squires Gate	d		
Blackpool Pleasure Beach	d		
Blackpool South	a		
Poulton-le-Fylde	d	23 52	
Layton	d		
Blackpool North	a	00 02	

Table 97

Sundays
until 17 October

Colne, Burnley, Accrington and Blackburn - Preston - Blackpool

		NT	NT	TP	TP	TP	NT	TP	NT	TP	NT	TP	NT	NT	NT	TP	NT	NT	NT	TP	NT	NT
						◇1		◇1		◇1		◇1				◇1				◇1		
		B	C	bus	bus	B		D		D		B										
Colne	d													09 16								
Nelson	d													09 21								
Brierfield	d													09 24								
Burnley Central	d													09 29								
Burnley Barracks	d													09 31								
Leeds 10 41	d														08 45			09 35				10 35
Burnley Manchester Road 41	d														09 50			10 39				11 39
Rose Grove	d													09 34								
Hapton	d													09 37								
Huncoat	d													09 40								
Accrington	d													09 45	09 59			10 48				11 47
Church & Oswaldtwistle	d													09 47								
Rishton	d													09 50								
Blackburn	a													09 55	10 07			10 56				11 55
Clitheroe 94	d																					
Blackburn	d													09 57	10 07			10 56				11 56
Mill Hill (Lancashire)	d													10 00								
Cherry Tree	d													10 02								
Pleasington	d													10 04								
Bamber Bridge	d													10 11								
Lostock Hall	d													10 14								
Preston 8	a	00 10	00 10											10 22	10 27			11 13				12 13
	d	00 11	00 11	01s35	06s55	08 32	08 49	08 57	09 20	09 34	09 39	09 51	10 20	10 24	10 29	10 34	10 40	11 15	11 20	11 34	11 39	12 14
Salwick	d																					
Kirkham & Wesham	d	00 21	00 21				08 58		09 29				10 29	10 33					11 29			
Moss Side	d						09 04							10 39								
Lytham	d						09 08							10 43								
Ansdell & Fairhaven	d						09 11							10 46								
St Annes-on-the-Sea	d						09 15							10 50								
Squires Gate	d						09 19							10 54								
Blackpool Pleasure Beach	d						09 21							10 56								
Blackpool South	a						09 26							11 01								
Poulton-le-Fylde	d	00 29	00 29			08 49		09 14	09 37	09 51	09 57	10 08	10 37		10 46	10 51	10 57	11 32	11 37	11 51	11 57	12 31
Layton	d	00 33	00 33						09 42				10 42						11 42			
Blackpool North	a	00 42	00 40	02 15	07 35	08 58		09 25	09 49	10 00	10 07	10 17	10 49		10 53	11 00	11 09	11 39	11 49	12 00	12 07	12 38

		NT	NT	TP	NT	NT	NT	NT	TP	NT	NT	NT	NT	TP	NT	NT	NT	NT	TP	NT	NT	NT	NT
				◇1					◇1					◇1					◇1				
Colne	d					11 35										13 35							
Nelson	d					11 40										13 40							
Brierfield	d					11 43										13 43							
Burnley Central	d					11 48										13 48							
Burnley Barracks	d					11 50										13 50							
Leeds 10 41	d						11 35				12 35						13 35				14 35		
Burnley Manchester Road 41	d						12 39				13 39						14 39				15 39		
Rose Grove	d					11 53										13 53							
Hapton	d					11 56										13 56							
Huncoat	d					11 59										13 59							
Accrington	d					12 04	12 47				13 47					14 04	14 47				15 47		
Church & Oswaldtwistle	d					12 06										14 06							
Rishton	d					12 09										14 09							
Blackburn	a					12 14	12 55				13 55					14 14	14 55				15 55		
Clitheroe 94	d																						
Blackburn	d					12 16	12 56				13 56					14 16	14 56				15 56		
Mill Hill (Lancashire)	d					12 19										14 19							
Cherry Tree	d					12 21										14 21							
Pleasington	d					12 23										14 23							
Bamber Bridge	d					12 30										14 30							
Lostock Hall	d					12 33										14 33							
Preston 8	a					12 42	13 13				14 13					14 42	15 13				16 13		
	d	11 44	12 20	12 34	12 39	12 44	13 14	13 20	13 34	13 41	14 14	13 44	14 20	14 34	14 39	14 43	15 14	15 20	15 34	15 39	16 14	15 44	16 20
Salwick	d																						
Kirkham & Wesham	d	11 53	12 29			12 53		13 29				13 53	14 29			14 51		15 29				15 53	16 29
Moss Side	d	11 59				12 59						13 59				14 57						15 59	
Lytham	d	12 03				13 03						14 03				15 01						16 03	
Ansdell & Fairhaven	d	12 06				13 06						14 06				15 04						16 06	
St Annes-on-the-Sea	d	12 10				13 10						14 10				15 08						16 10	
Squires Gate	d	12 14				13 14						14 14				15 12						16 14	
Blackpool Pleasure Beach	d	12 16				13 16						14 16				15 14						16 16	
Blackpool South	a	12 21				13 21						14 21				15 20						16 21	
Poulton-le-Fylde	d		12 37	12 51	12 57		13 31	13 37	13 51	13 57	14 30		14 37	14 51	14 57		15 32	15 37	15 51	15 57	16 31		16 37
Layton	d		12 42					13 42					14 42					15 42					16 42
Blackpool North	a		12 49	13 00	13 07		13 38	13 49	14 01	14 09	14 38		14 49	15 00	15 07		15 39	15 49	16 00	16 07	16 38		16 49

B from 12 September until 17 October

C from 30 May until 5 September

D until 5 September

Table 97

Sundays until 17 October

Colne, Burnley, Accrington and Blackburn - Preston - Blackpool

		TP ◇1		NT	NT	NT	NT	TP ◇1	NT	NT	NT	NT		TP ◇1	NT	NT	NT	NT	TP ◇1	NT	NT	NT		NT	TP ◇1
Colne	d				15 35											17 35									
Nelson	d				15 40											17 40									
Brierfield	d				15 43											17 43									
Burnley Central	d				15 48											17 48									
Burnley Barracks	d				15 50											17 50									
Leeds 10 41	d					15 35				16 35							17 35				18 35				
Burnley Manchester Road 41	d					16 39				17 39							18 39				19 39				
Rose Grove	d				15 53											17 53									
Hapton	d				15 56											17 56									
Huncoat	d				15 59											17 59									
Accrington	d				16 04	16 47				17 47						18 04	18 47				19 47				
Church & Oswaldtwistle	d				16 06											18 06									
Rishton	d				16 09											18 09									
Blackburn	a				16 14	16 55				17 55						18 14	18 55				19 56				
Clitheroe 94	d																								
Blackburn	d				16 16	16 56				17 56						18 16	18 56				19 57				
Mill Hill (Lancashire)	d				16 19											18 19									
Cherry Tree	d				16 21											18 21									
Pleasington	d				16 23											18 23									
Bamber Bridge	d				16 30											18 30									
Lostock Hall	d				16 33											18 33									
Preston 8	a				16 42	17 13				18 13						18 42	19 13				20 14				
	d	16 34		16 39	16 43	17 14	17 20	17 34	17 39	18 14	17 44	18 20		18 34	18 39	18 43	19 14	19 20	19 34	19 39	20 15	19 44		20 20	20 34
Salwick	d																								
Kirkham & Wesham	d				16 51		17 29				17 53	18 29				18 51		19 29				19 53		20 29	
Moss Side	d				16 57						17 59					18 57						19 59			
Lytham	d				17 01						18 03					19 01						20 03			
Ansdell & Fairhaven	d				17 04						18 06					19 04						20 06			
St Annes-on-the-Sea	d				17 08						18 10					19 08						20 10			
Squires Gate	d				17 12						18 14					19 12						20 14			
Blackpool Pleasure Beach	d				17 14						18 16					19 14						20 16			
Blackpool South	a				17 20						18 21					19 20						20 21			
Poulton-le-Fylde	d	16 51		16 57		17 31	17 37	17 51	17 57	18 31		18 37		18 51	18 57		19 31	19 37	19 51	19 57	20 32			20 37	20 51
Layton	d						17 42					18 42						19 42						20 42	
Blackpool North	a	17 00		17 07		17 38	17 49	18 00	18 07	18 38		18 49		19 00	19 07		19 38	19 49	20 00	20 07	20 39			20 49	21 00

		NT	NT	NT 🚌	NT	NT	TP ◇1	NT		NT	NT	TP ◇1	NT	NT	NT	TP ◇1
Colne	d		19 35											21 35		
Nelson	d		19 40											21 40		
Brierfield	d		19 43											21 43		
Burnley Central	d		19 48											21 48		
Burnley Barracks	d		19 50											21 50		
Leeds 10 41	d				19 35					20 35						
Burnley Manchester Road 41	d				20 39					21 39						
Rose Grove	d		19 53											21 53		
Hapton	d		19 56											21 56		
Huncoat	d		19 59											21 59		
Accrington	d		20 04		20 47					21 47				22 04		
Church & Oswaldtwistle	d		20 06											22 06		
Rishton	d		20 09											22 09		
Blackburn	a		20 14		20 55					21 55				22 14		
Clitheroe 94	d			19 57												
Blackburn	d		20 16	20 25	20 56					21 56				22 16		
Mill Hill (Lancashire)	d		20 19											22 19		
Cherry Tree	d		20 21											22 21		
Pleasington	d		20 23											22 23		
Bamber Bridge	d		20 30	20 34										22 30		
Lostock Hall	d		20 33	20 38										22 33		
Preston 8	a		20 42	20 47	21 13					22 13				22 44		
	d	20 39	20 43	20 49	21 14	21 20	21 34	21 39		22 14	22 20	22 29	22 39		23 39	23 47
Salwick	d															
Kirkham & Wesham	d		20 51	20 59		21 29					22 29					23 56
Moss Side	d		20 57													
Lytham	d		21 01													
Ansdell & Fairhaven	d		21 04													
St Annes-on-the-Sea	d		21 08													
Squires Gate	d		21 12													
Blackpool Pleasure Beach	d		21 14													
Blackpool South	a		21 20													
Poulton-le-Fylde	d	20 57		21 07	21 31	21 37	21 51	21 57		22 31	22 37	22 46	22 57		23 56	00 05
Layton	d					21 42					22 42					
Blackpool North	a	21 07		21 16	21 38	21 49	22 00	22 07		22 38	22 49	22 55	23 07		00 05	00 14

Table 97

Sundays 24 October to 07 November

Colne, Burnley, Accrington and Blackburn - Preston - Blackpool

			NT	TP 🚌	TP 🚌	TP ◇1	NT	NT	TP ◇1	NT		NT	NT	TP ◇1	NT	NT	TP ◇1	NT	NT	NT		TP ◇1	NT	NT	NT
Colne	d											09 16											11 35		
Nelson	d											09 21											11 40		
Brierfield	d											09 24											11 43		
Burnley Central	d											09 29											11 48		
Burnley Barracks	d											09 31											11 50		
Leeds 10 41	d												08 45		09 35			10 35						11 35	
Burnley Manchester Road 41	d												09 50		10 39			11 39						12 39	
Rose Grove	d											09 34											11 53		
Hapton	d											09 37											11 56		
Huncoat	d											09 40											11 59		
Accrington	d											09 45	09 59		10 48			11 47					12 04	12 47	
Church & Oswaldtwistle	d											09 47											12 06		
Rishton	d											09 50											12 09		
Blackburn	a											09 55	10 07		10 56			11 55					12 14	12 55	
Clitheroe 94	d																								
Blackburn	d											09 57	10 07		10 56			11 56					12 16	12 56	
Mill Hill (Lancashire)	d											10 00											12 19		
Cherry Tree	d											10 02											12 21		
Pleasington	d											10 04											12 23		
Bamber Bridge	d											10 11											12 30		
Lostock Hall	d											10 14											12 33		
Preston 8	a		00 10									10 22	10 27		11 13			12 13					12 42	13 13	
	d		00 11	01s35	06s55	08 32	08 49	09 20	09 51	10 20		10 24	10 29	10 34	11 15	11 20	11 34	12 14	11 44	12 20		12 34	12 44	13 14	13 20
Salwick	d																								
Kirkham & Wesham	d		00 21				08 58	09 29		10 29		10 33				11 29			11 53	12 29			12 53		13 29
Moss Side	d						09 04					10 39							11 59				12 59		
Lytham	d						09 08					10 43							12 03				13 03		
Ansdell & Fairhaven	d						09 11					10 46							12 06				13 06		
St Annes-on-the-Sea	d						09 15					10 50							12 10				13 10		
Squires Gate	d						09 19					10 54							12 14				13 14		
Blackpool Pleasure Beach	d						09 21					10 56							12 16				13 16		
Blackpool South	a						09 26					11 01							12 21				13 21		
Poulton-le-Fylde	d		00 29			08 49		09 37	10 08	10 37			10 46	10 51	11 32	11 37	11 51	12 31		12 37		12 51		13 31	13 37
Layton	d		00 33					09 42		10 42						11 42				12 42					13 42
Blackpool North	a		00 42	02 15	07 35	08 58		09 49	10 17	10 49			10 53	11 00	11 39	11 49	12 00	12 38		12 49		13 00		13 38	13 49

		TP ◇1	NT	NT	NT	TP ◇1		NT	NT	NT	TP ◇1	NT	NT	NT	TP ◇1	NT		NT	NT	TP ◇1	NT	NT	NT	TP ◇1	NT
Colne	d							13 35								15 35									17 35
Nelson	d							13 40								15 40									17 40
Brierfield	d							13 43								15 43									17 43
Burnley Central	d							13 48								15 48									17 48
Burnley Barracks	d							13 50								15 50									17 50
Leeds 10 41	d		12 35						13 35			14 35						15 35			16 35				
Burnley Manchester Road 41	d		13 39						14 39			15 39						16 39			17 39				
Rose Grove	d							13 53								15 53									17 53
Hapton	d							13 56								15 56									17 56
Huncoat	d							13 59								15 59									17 59
Accrington	d		13 47					14 04	14 47			15 47				16 04		16 47			17 47				18 04
Church & Oswaldtwistle	d							14 06								16 06									18 06
Rishton	d							14 09								16 09									18 09
Blackburn	a		13 55					14 14	14 55			15 55				16 14		16 55			17 55				18 14
Clitheroe 94	d																								
Blackburn	d		13 56					14 16	14 56			15 56				16 16		16 56			17 56				18 16
Mill Hill (Lancashire)	d							14 19								16 19									18 19
Cherry Tree	d							14 21								16 21									18 21
Pleasington	d							14 23								16 23									18 23
Bamber Bridge	d							14 30								16 30									18 30
Lostock Hall	d							14 33								16 33									18 33
Preston 8	a		14 13					14 42	15 13			16 13				16 42		17 13			18 13				18 42
	d	13 34	14 14	13 44	14 20	14 34		14 43	15 14	15 20	15 34	16 14	15 44	16 20	16 34	16 43		17 14	17 20	17 34	18 14	17 44	18 20	18 34	18 43
Salwick	d																								
Kirkham & Wesham	d			13 53	14 29			14 51		15 29			15 53	16 29		16 51			17 29			17 53	18 29		18 51
Moss Side	d			13 59				14 57					15 59			16 57						17 59			18 57
Lytham	d			14 03				15 01					16 03			17 01						18 03			19 01
Ansdell & Fairhaven	d			14 06				15 04					16 06			17 04						18 06			19 04
St Annes-on-the-Sea	d			14 10				15 08					16 10			17 08						18 10			19 08
Squires Gate	d			14 14				15 12					16 14			17 12						18 14			19 12
Blackpool Pleasure Beach	d			14 16				15 14					16 16			17 14						18 16			19 14
Blackpool South	a			14 21				15 20					16 21			17 20						18 21			19 20
Poulton-le-Fylde	d	13 51	14 30		14 37	14 51			15 32	15 37	15 51	16 31		16 37	16 51			17 31	17 37	17 51	18 31		18 37	18 51	
Layton	d				14 42					15 42				16 42					17 42				18 42		
Blackpool North	a	14 01	14 38		14 49	15 00			15 39	15 49	16 00	16 38		16 49	17 00			17 38	17 49	18 00	18 38		18 49	19 00	

Table 97

Sundays
24 October to 07 November

Colne, Burnley, Accrington and Blackburn - Preston - Blackpool

Station		NT		NT	TP ◇[1]	NT	NT	NT	TP ◇[1]	NT	NT	NT		TP ◇[1]	NT	NT	TP ◇[1]	NT	TP ◇[1]
Colne	d									19 35								21 35	
Nelson	d									19 40								21 40	
Brierfield	d									19 43								21 43	
Burnley Central	d									19 48								21 48	
Burnley Barracks	d									19 50								21 50	
Leeds [10] 41	d	17 35				18 35					19 35				20 35				
Burnley Manchester Road 41	d	18 39				19 39					20 39				21 39				
Rose Grove	d									19 53								21 53	
Hapton	d									19 56								21 56	
Huncoat	d									19 59								21 59	
Accrington	d	18 47				19 47				20 04	20 47				21 47			22 04	
Church & Oswaldtwistle	d									20 06								22 06	
Rishton	d									20 09								22 09	
Blackburn	a	18 55				19 56				20 14	20 55				21 55			22 14	
Clitheroe 94	d																		
Blackburn	d	18 56				19 57				20 16	20 56				21 56			22 16	
Mill Hill (Lancashire)	d									20 19								22 19	
Cherry Tree	d									20 21								22 21	
Pleasington	d									20 23								22 23	
Bamber Bridge	d									20 30								22 30	
Lostock Hall	d									20 33								22 33	
Preston [8]	a	19 13				20 14				20 42	21 13				22 13			22 44	
	d	19 14		19 20	19 34	20 15	19 44	20 20	20 34	20 43	21 14	21 20		21 34	22 14	22 20	22 29		23 47
Salwick	d																		
Kirkham & Wesham	d			19 29			19 53	20 29		20 51		21 29				22 29			23 56
Moss Side	d						19 59			20 57									
Lytham	d						20 03			21 01									
Ansdell & Fairhaven	d						20 06			21 04									
St Annes-on-the-Sea	d						20 10			21 08									
Squires Gate	d						20 14			21 12									
Blackpool Pleasure Beach	d						20 16			21 14									
Blackpool South	a						20 21			21 20									
Poulton-le-Fylde	d	19 31		19 37	19 51	20 32		20 37	20 51		21 31	21 37		21 51	22 31	22 37	22 46		00 05
Layton	d			19 42				20 42				21 42				22 42			
Blackpool North	a	19 38		19 49	20 00	20 39		20 49	21 00		21 38	21 49		22 00	22 38	22 49	22 55		00 14

Sundays
from 14 November

Station			NT	TP	TP	TP ◇[1]	NT	TP ◇[1]	NT	NT		NT	TP ◇[1]	NT	NT	TP ◇[1]	NT	NT	TP ◇[1]	NT		NT	NT	TP ◇[1]	NT
Colne	d									09 16										11 35					
Nelson	d									09 21										11 40					
Brierfield	d									09 24										11 43					
Burnley Central	d									09 29										11 48					
Burnley Barracks	d									09 31										11 50					
Leeds [10] 41	d											08 45		09 35			10 35					11 35			12 35
Burnley Manchester Road 41	d											09 50		10 39			11 39					12 39			13 39
Rose Grove	d									09 34										11 53					
Hapton	d									09 37										11 56					
Huncoat	d									09 40										11 59					
Accrington	d									09 45		09 59		10 48			11 47			12 04		12 47			13 47
Church & Oswaldtwistle	d									09 47										12 06					
Rishton	d									09 50										12 09					
Blackburn	a									09 55		10 07		10 56			11 55			12 14		12 55			13 55
Clitheroe 94	d																								
Blackburn	d									09 57		10 07		10 56			11 56			12 16		12 56			13 56
Mill Hill (Lancashire)	d									10 00										12 19					
Cherry Tree	d									10 02										12 21					
Pleasington	d									10 04										12 23					
Bamber Bridge	d									10 11										12 30					
Lostock Hall	d									10 14										12 33					
Preston [8]	a		00 10							10 24		10 27		11 13			12 13			12 44		13 13			14 13
	d		00 11	01s35	06s55	08 32	09 20	09 51	10 20			10 29	10 34	11 15	11 20	11 34	12 14	12 20	12 34			13 14	13 20	13 34	14 14
Salwick	d																								
Kirkham & Wesham	d		00 21				09 29		10 29						11 29			12 29					13 29		
Moss Side	d																								
Lytham	d																								
Ansdell & Fairhaven	d																								
St Annes-on-the-Sea	d																								
Squires Gate	d																								
Blackpool Pleasure Beach	d																								
Blackpool South	a																								
Poulton-le-Fylde	d		00 29			08 49	09 37	10 08	10 37			10 46	10 51	11 32	11 37	11 51	12 31	12 37	12 51			13 31	13 37	13 51	14 30
Layton	d		00 33				09 42		10 42						11 42			12 42					13 42		
Blackpool North	a		00 42	02 15	07 35	08 58	09 49	10 17	10 49			10 53	11 00	11 39	11 49	12 00	12 38	12 49	13 00			13 38	13 49	14 01	14 38

Table 97

Sundays
from 14 November

Colne, Burnley, Accrington and Blackburn - Preston - Blackpool

Station		NT	TP ◇[1]	NT	NT	NT		TP ◇[1]	NT	NT	TP ◇[1]	NT	NT	NT	TP ◇[1]	NT		NT	TP ◇[1]	NT	NT	NT	TP ◇[1]	NT	NT
Colne	d			13 35								15 35								17 35					
Nelson	d			13 40								15 40								17 40					
Brierfield	d			13 43								15 43								17 43					
Burnley Central	d			13 48								15 48								17 48					
Burnley Barracks	d			13 50								15 50								17 50					
Leeds [10] 41	d				13 35				14 35				15 35			16 35					17 35			18 35	
Burnley Manchester Road 41	d				14 39				15 39				16 39			17 39					18 39			19 39	
Rose Grove	d			13 53								15 53								17 53					
Hapton	d			13 56								15 56								17 56					
Huncoat	d			13 59								15 59								17 59					
Accrington	d			14 04	14 47				15 47			16 04	16 47			17 47				18 04	18 47			19 47	
Church & Oswaldtwistle	d			14 06								16 06								18 06					
Rishton	d			14 09								16 09								18 09					
Blackburn	a			14 14	14 55				15 55			16 14	16 55			17 55				18 14	18 55			19 56	
Clitheroe 94	d																								
Blackburn	d			14 16	14 56				15 56			16 16	16 56			17 56				18 16	18 56			19 57	
Mill Hill (Lancashire)	d			14 19								16 19								18 19					
Cherry Tree	d			14 21								16 21								18 21					
Pleasington	d			14 23								16 23								18 23					
Bamber Bridge	d			14 30								16 30								18 30					
Lostock Hall	d			14 33								16 33								18 33					
Preston [8]	a			14 44	15 13				16 13			16 44	17 13			18 13				18 44	19 13			20 14	
	d	14 20	14 34		15 14	15 20		15 34	16 14	16 20	16 34		17 14	17 20	17 34	18 14		18 20	18 34		19 14	19 20	19 34	20 15	20 20
Salwick	d																								
Kirkham & Wesham	d	14 29				15 29				16 29				17 29				18 29				19 29			20 29
Moss Side	d																								
Lytham	d																								
Ansdell & Fairhaven	d																								
St Annes-on-the-Sea	d																								
Squires Gate	d																								
Blackpool Pleasure Beach	d																								
Blackpool South	a																								
Poulton-le-Fylde	d	14 37	14 51		15 32	15 37		15 51	16 31	16 37	16 51		17 31	17 37	17 51	18 31		18 37	18 51		19 31	19 37	19 51	20 32	20 37
Layton	d	14 42				15 42				16 42				17 42				18 42				19 42			20 42
Blackpool North	a	14 49	15 00		15 39	15 49		16 00	16 38	16 49	17 00		17 38	17 49	18 00	18 38		18 49	19 00		19 38	19 49	20 00	20 39	20 49

Station		TP ◇[1]		NT	NT	NT	TP ◇[1]	NT	NT	TP ◇[1]	NT	TP ◇[1]
Colne	d			19 35							21 35	
Nelson	d			19 40							21 40	
Brierfield	d			19 43							21 43	
Burnley Central	d			19 48							21 48	
Burnley Barracks	d			19 50							21 50	
Leeds [10] 41	d				19f35			20 35				
Burnley Manchester Road 41	d				20 39			21 39				
Rose Grove	d			19 53							21 53	
Hapton	d			19 56							21 56	
Huncoat	d			19 59							21 59	
Accrington	d			20 04	20 47			21 47			22 04	
Church & Oswaldtwistle	d			20 06							22 06	
Rishton	d			20 09							22 09	
Blackburn	a			20 14	20 55			21 55			22 14	
Clitheroe 94	d											
Blackburn	d			20 16	20 56			21 56			22 16	
Mill Hill (Lancashire)	d			20 19							22 19	
Cherry Tree	d			20 21							22 21	
Pleasington	d			20 23							22 23	
Bamber Bridge	d			20 30							22 30	
Lostock Hall	d			20 33							22 33	
Preston [8]	a			20 44	21 13			22 13			22 44	
	d	20 34			21 14	21 20	21 34	22 14	22 20	22 29		23 47
Salwick	d											
Kirkham & Wesham	d					21 29			22 29			23 56
Moss Side	d											
Lytham	d											
Ansdell & Fairhaven	d											
St Annes-on-the-Sea	d											
Squires Gate	d											
Blackpool Pleasure Beach	d											
Blackpool South	a											
Poulton-le-Fylde	d	20 51			21 31	21 37	21 51	22 31	22 37	22 46		00 05
Layton	d					21 42			22 42			
Blackpool North	a	21 00			21 38	21 49	22 00	22 38	22 49	22 55		00 14

Table 98

Lancaster - Morecambe and Heysham

			TP 1	NT	NT	NT	NT	NT	NT	NT	NT	NT	NT	NT	NT	NT	NT	NT	NT	NT	NT	NT	NT	NT
Lancaster 6	82	d	05 46	06 38	07 25	07 58	08 35	09 15	10 04	10 19	11 22	12 02	12 28	13 44	14 27	15 25	16 03	16 19	16 49	17 38	18 33	18 49	19 40	20 22
Bare Lane		d	05 52	06 44	07 31	08 04	08 41	09 21	10 10	10 26	11 28	12 08	12 34	13 50	14 33	15 31	16 09	16 26	16 55	17 44	18 39	18 55	19 46	20 28
Morecambe		a	05 56	06 49	07 36	08 09	08 46	09 26	10 15	10 32	11 33	12 13	12 39	13 55	14 38	15 36	16 13	16 30	17 00	17 49	18 44	19 01	19 50	20 32
		d	05 59										12 42											
Heysham Port		a											12 57											

			NT	NT	NT
Lancaster 6	82	d	21 03	22 06	22 35
Bare Lane		d	21 09	22 12	22 41
Morecambe		a	21 13	22 16	22 45
		d			
Heysham Port		a			

Saturdays

			TP 1	NT	NT	NT	NT	NT	NT	NT	NT	NT	NT	NT	NT	NT	NT	NT	NT	NT	NT	NT	NT	NT
Lancaster 6	82	d	05 46	06 38	07 25	07 57	08 35	09 15	10 05	10 19	11 23	12 02	12 25	13 24	14 27	15 25	15 49	16 03	17 04	17 37	18 21	18 47	19 40	20 22
Bare Lane		d	05 52	06 44	07 31	08 03	08 41	09 21	10 11	10 26	11 29	12 08	12 31	13 30	14 33	15 31	15 56	16 09	17 10	17 43	18 27	18 53	19 46	20 28
Morecambe		a	05 56	06 49	07 36	08 08	08 46	09 26	10 16	10 32	11 34	12 13	12 36	13 35	14 38	15 36	16 02	16 14	17 15	17 48	18 32	18 59	19 50	20 32
		d	05 59										12 39											
Heysham Port		a											12 54											

			NT	NT	NT
Lancaster 6	82	d	21 03	22 06	22 35
Bare Lane		d	21 09	22 12	22 41
Morecambe		a	21 13	22 16	22 45
		d			
Heysham Port		a			

Sundays
until 12 September

			NT	NT	NT	NT	NT	NT	NT	NT	NT	NT	NT	NT	NT
Lancaster 6	82	d	10 45	11 05	12 00	12 05	13 01	13 20	14 27	15 04	15 45	16 26	16 51	19 23	21 18
Bare Lane		d	10 51	11 11	12 06	12 11	13 07	13 26	14 34	15 10	15 51	16 32	16 56	19 29	21 24
Morecambe		a	10 57	11 16	12 11	12 16	13 11	13 31	14 38	15 15	15 56	16 37	17 03	19 35	21 29
		d			12 14			13 34	14 46						
Heysham Port		a			12 29			13 49							

Sundays
from 19 September

			NT	NT	NT	NT
Lancaster 6	82	d	15 04	16 51	19 23	21 18
Bare Lane		d	15 10	16 56	19 29	21 24
Morecambe		a	15 15	17 03	19 35	21 29
		d				
Heysham Port		a				

Table 98

Heysham and Morecambe - Lancaster

			TP 1	NT	NT	NT	NT	NT	NT	NT	NT	NT	NT	NT	NT	NT	NT	NT	NT	NT	NT	NT	NT	NT
Heysham Port		d												13 15										
Morecambe		a												13 25										
		d	05 59	06 19	07 03	07 42	08 11	08 51	09 32	10 34	10 55	11 39	12 32	13 29	13 58	14 42	15 45	16 19	16 34	17 03	17 56	19 00	19 08	19 55
Bare Lane		d	06 03	06 23	07 07	07 46	08 15	08 55	09 36	10 38	10 59	11 43	12 36	13 36	14 02	14 46	15 49	16 23	16 38	17 07	18 00	19 04	19 12	19 59
Lancaster 6	82	a		06 30	07 14	07 53	08 21	09 03	09 43	10 45	11 06	11 50	12 43	13 42	14 09	14 53	15 56		16 45	17 14	18 07	19 11	19 19	20 06

			NT	NT	NT	NT
Heysham Port		d				
Morecambe		a				
		d	20 40	21 36	22 20	22 55
Bare Lane		d	20 44	21 40	22 24	22 59
Lancaster 6	82	a	20 51	21 47	22 31	23 05

Saturdays

			TP 1	NT	NT	NT	NT	NT	NT	NT	NT	NT	NT	NT	NT	NT	NT	NT	NT	NT	NT	NT	NT	NT
Heysham Port		d												13 15										
Morecambe		a												13 25										
		d	05 59	06 19	07 03	07 38	08 11	08 51	09 41	10 34	10 54	11 40	12 32	13 29	13 58	14 42	15 44	16 19	16 40	17 20	17 56	18 58	19 09	19 55
Bare Lane		d	06 03	06 23	07 07	07 42	08 15	08 55	09 45	10 38	10 58	11 44	12 36	13 36	14 02	14 46	15 48	16 24	16 44	17 24	18 00	19 02	19 13	19 59
Lancaster 6	82	a		06 30	07 14	07 49	08 22	09 03	09 52	10 45	11 05	11 51	12 43	13 42	14 09	14 53	15 55	16 30	16 50	17 31	18 07	19 09	19 20	20 06

			NT	NT	NT
Heysham Port		d			
Morecambe		a			
		d	20 40	21 36	22 20
Bare Lane		d	20 44	21 40	22 24
Lancaster 6	82	a	20 51	21 47	22 31

Sundays
until 12 September

			NT	NT	NT	NT	NT	NT	NT	NT	NT	NT	NT	NT	NT
Heysham Port		d				12 42		14 00							
Morecambe		a				12 52		14 10							
		d	11 20	11 35	12 20	12 56	13 23	14 17	14 46	15 21	16 03	16 42	17 45	20 00	21 41
Bare Lane		d	11 24	11 39	12 24	13 03	13 27	14 24	14 50	15 25	16 07	16 46	17 49	20 04	21 45
Lancaster 6	82	a	11 31	11 46	12 30	13 12	13 34	14 31		15 32	16 15	16 53	17 55	20 11	21 51

Sundays
from 19 September

			NT	NT	NT	NT
Heysham Port		d				
Morecambe		a				
		d	15 21	17 45	20 00	21 41
Bare Lane		d	15 25	17 49	20 04	21 45
Lancaster 6	82	a	15 32	17 55	20 11	21 51

Table 98A

Mondays to Fridays

To and from The Isle of Man via Heysham and Liverpool

One Class only on ship

Liverpool Landing Stage	⛴	d
Heysham Port	⛴	d
Douglas (Isle of Man)	⛴	a

Saturdays

Liverpool Landing Stage	⛴	d
Heysham Port	⛴	d
Douglas (Isle of Man)	⛴	a

Sundays

Liverpool Landing Stage	⛴	d
Heysham Port	⛴	d
Douglas (Isle of Man)	⛴	a

Mondays to Fridays

Douglas (Isle of Man)	⛴	d
Heysham Port	⛴	a
Liverpool Landing Stage	⛴	a

Saturdays

Douglas (Isle of Man)	⛴	d
Heysham Port	⛴	a
Liverpool Landing Stage	⛴	a

Sundays

Douglas (Isle of Man)	⛴	d
Heysham Port	⛴	a
Liverpool Landing Stage	⛴	a

Details of service not available at time of going to press

Table 99

Mondays to Saturdays

Ormskirk - Preston

		NT	NT	NT	NT	NT	NT	NT	NT	NT	NT	NT	NT
Ormskirk	d	06 58	08 06	09 17	10 54	12 17	13 40	14 53	16 38	17 52	19 08	20 19	22 17
Burscough Junction	d	07 02	08 10	09 21	10 58	12 21	13 44	14 57	16 42	17 56	19 12	20 23	22 21
Rufford	d	07 07	08 15	09 25	11 03	12 25	13 49	15 01	16 46	18 01	19 17	20 27	22 25
Croston	d	07 11	08 19	09 30	11 07	12 30	13 54	15 06	16 51	18 06	19 21	20 32	22 30
Preston 8	a	07 29	08 36	09 47	11 24	12 47	14 12	15 23	17 07	18 23	19 39	20 49	22 46

Mondays to Saturdays

		NT	NT	NT	NT	NT	NT	NT	NT	NT	NT	NT	NT
Preston 8	d	06 25	07 33	08 41	10 07	11 32	12 59	14 17	15 39	17 10	18 34	19 42	21 37
Croston	d	06 36	07 45	08 52	10 19	11 43	13 11	14 28	15 51	17 22	18 47	19 53	21 49
Rufford	d	06 41	07 50	08 57	10 24	11 48	13 16	14 33	15 56	17 27	18 51	19 58	21 53
Burscough Junction	d	06 46	07 55	09 02	10 29	11 53	13 21	14 38	16 01	17 32	18 56	20 03	21 58
Ormskirk	a	06 55	08 04	09 11	10 38	12 00	13 30	14 45	16 10	17 41	19 05	20 12	22 07

For connections to and from Liverpool Central please refer to Table 103

No Sunday Service

Table 100

Barrow-in-Furness - Whitehaven and Carlisle

Mondays to Fridays

		NT	NT	NT	NT	NT	NT	NT	NT	NT	NT	NT	NT	NT	NT	NT	NT	NT	NT	NT	NT
Lancaster 82	d			05 42				08 58						15 34		16 55					
Barrow-in-Furness	d		06 00	06 49	08 01		09 10	10b11	11 22		12 31	13 31	14 54	16 41	17 28	18 05		19 35			21 25
Askam	d		06 10	06 59	08 11		09 20	10 21	11 32		12 41	13 41	15 04	16 51	17 40	18 15		19 45			21 35
Kirkby-in-Furness	d		06 14	07x04	08x15		09x24	10x25	11x36		12x45	13x45	15x08	16x55	17x44	18x19		19x49			21x39
Foxfield	d		06x18	07x08	08x18		09x27	10x28	11x39		12x48	13x48	15x11	16x58	17x48	18x22		19x52			21x42
Green Road	d		06x22	07x12	08x22		09x31	10x32	11x43		12x52	13x52	15x15	17x02	17x51	18x26		19x56			21x46
Millom	a		06 29	07 18	08 28		09 37	10 38	11 49		12 58	13 58	15 21	17 08	17 58	18 35		20 05			21 55
	d		06 29	07 19	08 29		09 38	10 39	11 49		12 59	13 58	15 22	17 09	17 58						
Silecroft	d		06x34	07x24			09x42	10x43	11x54		13x03	14x03	15x26	17x13	18x03						
Bootle	d		06x41	07x31			09x49	10x50	12x00		13x10	14x09	15x33	17x20	18x09						
Ravenglass for Eskdale	d		06 47	07 37	08 44		09 55	10 56	12 06		13 15	14 15	15 39	17 26	18 15						
Drigg	d		06x51	07x40			09x58	10x59	12x09		13x18	14x18	15x42	17x29	18x18						
Seascale	d		06x54	07x44	08x49		10x01	11x02	12x12		13x21	14x21	15x45	17x32	18x21						
Sellafield	d		07 02	07 50	08a58		10 10	11 07	12 18		13 28	14 27	15 51	17 39	18 27						
Braystones	d		07x05	07x54								14x31			18x31						
Nethertown	d		07x08	07x56								14x33			18x33						
St Bees	d		07 12	08 01			10 20	11 20	12 27		13 38	14 38	16 00	17 49	18c45						
Corkickle	d		07x17	08x06			10x25	11x25	12x32		13x43	14x43	16x05	17x54	18x50						
Whitehaven	a		07 20	08 09			10 27	11 27	12 36		13 45	14 46	16 09	17 57	18 53						
	d	06 30	07 25	08 11		09 02	10 28	11 29	12 37	13 05	13 47	14 48	16 11	17 58	18 55		19 31		20 30	21 50	
Parton	d	06x33	07x29	08x14		09x05	10x31	11x32	12x41		13x50	14x51	16x15	18x02	18x58		19x34		20x33	21x53	
Harrington	d	06x41	07x37	08x22		09x13	10x40	11x40	12x49		13x58	14x59	16x23	18x10	19x06		19x42		20x41	22x01	
Workington	d	06 48	07 43	08 29		09 20	10 46	11 47	12 55	13 22	14 05	15 06	16 29	18 16	19 12		19 49		20 48	22a10	
Flimby	d	06x52	07x48	08x33		09x24	10x50	11x51	13x00		14x09	15x10	16x34	18x21	19x17		19x53		20x52		
Maryport	d	06 56	07 51	08 37		09 28	10 54	11 55	13 03	13 30	14 13	15 14	16 37	18 26	19 20		19 57		20 56		
Aspatria	d	07x05	08x01	08x46		09x37	11x03	12x04	13x13		14x22	15x23	16x47	18x36	19x30		20x06		21x05		
Wigton	d	07 15	08 11	08 56		09 47	11 13	12 14	13 23	13 50	14 32	15 33	16 57	18 46	19 40		20 16		21 15		
Dalston	d	07x24	08x19	09x05		09x56	11x22	12x23	13x31		14x41	15x42	17x05	18x54	19x48		20x25		21x24		
Carlisle	a	07 38	08 35	09 21		10 13	11 37	12 39	13 47	14 11	14 57	15 58	17 21	19 08	20 04		20 41		21 39		

Saturdays

		NT	NT	NT	NT	NT	NT	NT	NT	NT	NT	NT	NT	NT	NT	NT	NT	NT	NT	NT
Lancaster 82	d							09 02			11 28		13 32	14 22		17 00				
Barrow-in-Furness	d		06 00	07 05	08 01		09 07	10 10	11 22		12 33	13 50	14 50	15 32	17 25	18 10	19 30			21 25
Askam	d		06 10	07 15	08 11		09 17	10 20	11 32		12 43	14 00	15 00	15 42	17 35	18 20	19 40			21 35
Kirkby-in-Furness	d		06x14	07x19	08x15		09x21	10x24	11x36		12x47	14x04	15x04	15x46	17x39	18x24	19x44			21x39
Foxfield	d		06x17	07x23	08x18		09x24	10x28	11x39		12x51	14x07	15x07	15x50	17x42	18x27	19x47			21x42
Green Road	d		06x21	07x27	08x22		09x28	10x31	11x43		12x54	14x11	15x11	15x53	17x46	18x31	19x51			21x46
Millom	a		06 25	07 34	08 28		09 34	10 38	11 49		13 01	14 17	15 17	16 00	17 52	18 40	20 00			21 55
	d		06 26	07 34	08 29		09 35	10 38	11 50		13 01	14 18	15 18	16 00	17 53					
Silecroft	d		06x30	07x39			09x39	10x43	11x54		13x06	14x22	15x22	16x05	17x57					
Bootle	d		06x37	07x46			09x46	10x49	12x01		13x12	14x29	15x29	16x11	18x04					
Ravenglass for Eskdale	d		06 42	07 52	08 44		09 52	10 55	12 07		13 18	14 35	15 35	16 17	18 10					
Drigg	d		06x45	07x56			09x55	10x58	12x10		13x21	14x38	15x38	16x20	18x13					
Seascale	d		06x50	07x59	08x49		09x58	11x03	12x13		13x24	14x41	15x41	16x23	18x16					
Sellafield	d		06 55	08 06	08a58		10 04	11 09	12 19		13 30	14 47	15f51	16 30	18 22					
Braystones	d		06x59	08x09										16x33	18x26					
Nethertown	d		07x01	08x12										16x36	18x28					
St Bees	d		07 06	08 16			10 14	11 19	12 29		13 40	14 56	16 01	16h45	18 33					
Corkickle	d		07x11	08x21			10x19	11x24	12x34		13x45	15x01	16x06	16x50	18x38					
Whitehaven	a		07 15	08 25			10 22	11 27	12 41		13 48	15 05	16 09	16 54	18 41					
	d	06 30	07 19	08 26		09 15	10 24	11 28		12 54	13 50	15 06	16 11	16 56	18 43			19 31	20 30	
Parton	d	06x33	07x23	08x30		09x18	10x27	11x32		12x57	13x54	15x10	16x15	16x59	18x46			19x34	20x33	
Harrington	d	06x41	07x31	08x38		09x26	10x35	11x40		13x05	14x02	15x18	16x23	17x07	18x54			19x42	20x41	
Workington	d	06 48	07 37	08 44		09 33	10 42	11 46		13 12	14 08	15 24	16 29	17 14	19 01			19 49	20 48	
Flimby	d	06x52	07x42	08x49		09x37	10x46	11x51		13x16	14x13	15x29	16x34	17x18	19x05			19x53	20x52	
Maryport	d	06 56	07 45	08 52		09 41	10 50	11 54		13 20	14 16	15 32	16 37	17 22	19 09			19 57	20 56	
Aspatria	d	07x05	07x55	09x02		09x50	10x59	12x04		13x29	14x26	15x42	16x47	17x31	19x18			20x06	21x05	
Wigton	d	07 15	08 05	09 12		10 00	11 09	12 14		13 39	14 36	15 52	16 57	17 41	19 28			20 16	21 15	
Dalston	d	07x24	08x13	09x20		10x08	11x18	12x22		13x48	14x44	16x00	17x05	17x50	19x37			20x25	21x24	
Carlisle	a	07 38	08 27	09 36		10 24	11 34	12 39		14 04	15 01	16 16	17 21	18 06	19 53			20 41	21 39	

b arr. 1003
c arr. 1838
f arr. 1546
h arr. 1640

Table 100

Barrow-in-Furness - Whitehaven and Carlisle

Sundays
until 11 July

		NT	NT	NT
Lancaster 82	d			
Barrow-in-Furness	d			
Askam	d			
Kirkby-in-Furness	d			
Foxfield	d			
Green Road	d			
Millom	a			
	d			
Silecroft	d			
Bootle	d			
Ravenglass for Eskdale	d			
Drigg	d			
Seascale	d			
Sellafield	d			
Braystones	d			
Nethertown	d			
St Bees	d			
Corkickle	d			
Whitehaven	a			
	d	12 57	16 28	20 28
Parton	d	13x00	16x31	20x31
Harrington	d	13x08	16x39	20x39
Workington	d	13 15	16 46	20 46
Flimby	d	13x19	16x50	20x50
Maryport	d	13 23	16 54	20 54
Aspatria	d	13x32	17x03	21x03
Wigton	d	13 42	17 13	21 13
Dalston	d	13x50	17x21	21x21
Carlisle	a	14 07	17 37	21 38

Sundays
18 July to 05 September

		NT	NT	NT
Lancaster 82	d			
Barrow-in-Furness	d			
Askam	d			
Kirkby-in-Furness	d			
Foxfield	d			
Green Road	d			
Millom	a			
	d			
Silecroft	d			
Bootle	d			
Ravenglass for Eskdale	d			
Drigg	d			
Seascale	d			
Sellafield	d			
Braystones	d			
Nethertown	d			
St Bees	d			
Corkickle	d			
Whitehaven	a			
	d	12 57	16 28	20 28
Parton	d	13x02	16x33	20x33
Harrington	d	13x12	16x43	20x43
Workington	d	13 22	16 53	20 53
Flimby	d	13b32	17x03	21x03
Maryport	d	13 37	17 08	21 08
Aspatria	d	13x57	17x28	21x28
Wigton	d	14 17	17 48	21 48
Dalston	d	14x36	18x07	22x07
Carlisle	a	14 54	18 25	22 25

b stops on request, arr. 1325

No Sunday Service Whitehaven to Barrow-in-Furness

Table 100

Sundays from 12 September

Barrow-in-Furness - Whitehaven and Carlisle

			NT	NT	NT
Lancaster 🅱	82	d			
Barrow-in-Furness		d			
Askam		d			
Kirkby-in-Furness		d			
Foxfield		d			
Green Road		d			
Millom		a			
		d			
Silecroft		d			
Bootle		d			
Ravenglass for Eskdale		d			
Drigg		d			
Seascale		d			
Sellafield		d			
Braystones		d			
Nethertown		d			
St Bees		d			
Corkickle		d			
Whitehaven		a			
		d	12 57	16 28	20 28
Parton		d	13x00	16x31	20x31
Harrington		d	13x08	16x39	20x39
Workington		d	13 15	16 46	20 46
Flimby		d	13x19	16x50	20x50
Maryport		d	13 23	16 54	20 54
Aspatria		d	13x32	17x03	21x03
Wigton		d	13 42	17 13	21 13
Dalston		d	13x50	17x21	21x21
Carlisle 🅱		a	14 07	17 37	21 38

No Sunday Service Whitehaven to Barrow-in-Furness

Table 100

Mondays to Fridays

Carlisle and Whitehaven - Barrow-in-Furness

			NT	NT	NT	NT	NT	NT	NT	NT	NT	NT	NT	NT	NT	NT	NT	NT	NT	NT	NT	NT
Carlisle 🅱		d				07 44		08 44	09 40	10 43	11 50	12 47	14 20	15 12	16 31	17 27	18c13	19 15		20 33	21 50	
Dalston		d				07x52		08x52	09x48	10x51	11x58	12x55	14x28	15x20	16x39	17x35	18x21	19x23		20x41	21x58	
Wigton		d				08 01		09 01	09 57	11 00	12 07	13 04	14 37	15 29	16 48	17 44	18 30	19 32		20 50	22 07	
Aspatria		d				08x11		09x11	10x07	11x10	12x17	13x14	14x47	15x39	16x58	17x54	18x40	19x42		21x00	22x17	
Maryport		d		06 00		08 21		09 21	10 17	11 20	12 27	13 24	14 57	15 49	17 08	18 04	18 50	19 52		21 10	22 27	
Flimby		d		06x03		08x24		09x24	10x20	11x23	12x30	13x27	15x00	15x52	17x11	18x07	18x53	19x55		21x13	22x30	
Workington		d		06 09		08 33		09 33	10 29	11 32	12 39	13 36	15 09	16 01	17 20	18 16	19 02	20 04		21 22	22 39	
Harrington		d		06x13		08x36		09x36	10x32	11x35	12x42	13x39	15x12	16x04	17x23	18x19	19x05	20x07		21x25	22x42	
Parton		d		06x21		08x45		09x45	10x42	11x44	12x52	13x48	15x21	16x13	17x32	18x28	19x14	20x16		21x34	22x51	
Whitehaven		a		06 26		08 54		09 49	10 47	11 50	13 00	13 54	15 27	16 19	17 38	18 34	19 23	20 25		21 43	23 00	
		d		06 28	07 28			09 51	10 48	11 51		13 56	15 28	16 20	17 39	18 35						
Corkickle		d		06x30	07x30			09x53	10x50	11x53		13x58	15x30	16x22	17x41	18x37						
St Bees		d		06 35	07 35			09 58	10 56	11 59		14 03	15 36	16 28	17 50	18 43						
Nethertown		d		06x39						12x03			15x40		17x54							
Braystones		d		06x42						12x05			15x42		17x57							
Sellafield		d		06 48	07 48		09 07	10 09	11 08	12 11		14 14	15b54	16 42	18 03	18 54						
Seascale		d		06x51	07x51		09x10	10x14	11x11	12x14		14x17	15x57	16x45	18x07	18x57						
Drigg		d		06x54	07x54		09x13	10x17	11x14	12x17		14x20	16x01	16x49	18x11	19x00						
Ravenglass for Eskdale		d		06 57	07 57		09 16	10 20	11 18	12 21		14 23	16 04	16 52	18 14	19 03						
Bootle		d		07x03	08x03		09x22	10x26	11x23	12x26		14x29	16x10	16x58	18x20	19x09						
Silecroft		d		07x09	08x09		09x28	10x32	11x30	12x33		14x35	16x17	17x05	18x27	19x15						
Millom		a		07 16	08 14		09 35	10 39	11 37	12 40		14 42	16 24	17 12	18 34	19 22						
		d	06 10	07 17	08 15		09 36	10 40	11 37	12 40		14 43	16 25	17 13	18 34	19 23			20 12			22 02
Green Road		d	06x14	07x21	08x19		09x40	10x44	11x41	12x44		14x47	16x29	17x17	18x39	19x27			20x16			22x06
Foxfield		d	06x17	07x24	08x22		09x43	10x47	11x44	12x47		14x50	16x33	17x21	18x43	19x30			20x19			22x09
Kirkby-in-Furness		d	06x21	07x28	08x26		09x47	10x51	11x48	12x51		14x54	16x38	17x26	18x47	19x34			20x23			22x13
Askam		d	06 26	07 33	08 31		09 52	10 56	11 53	12 56		14 59	16 43	17 31	18 52	19 39			20 28			22 18
Barrow-in-Furness		a	06 42	07 49	08 49		10 07	11 14	12 09	13 14		15 17	17 01	17 47	19 10	19 57			20 45			22 35
Lancaster 🅱	82	a	08 03	09 09			11 22		13 15					19 04								

Saturdays

			NT	NT	NT	NT	NT	NT	NT	NT	NT	NT	NT	NT	NT	NT	NT	NT	NT	NT	NT	NT
Carlisle 🅱		d			07 44		08 37	09 40	10 43	11 39		12 48	14 21	15 25	16 30	17 40	18 11	19 00	20 05		21 45	
Dalston		d			07x52		08x45	09x48	10x51	11x47		12x56	14x29	15x33	16x38	17x48	18 19	19x08	20x13		21x53	
Wigton		d			08 01		08 54	09 57	11 00	11 56		13 05	14 38	15 42	16 47	17 57	18 28	19 17	20 22		22 02	
Aspatria		d			08x11		09x04	10x07	11x10	12x06		13x15	14x48	15x52	16x57	18x07	18 39	19x27	20x32		22x12	
Maryport		d		06 26	08 21		09 14	10 17	11 20	12 16		13 25	14 58	16 02	17 07	18 17	18 49	19 37	20 42		22 22	
Flimby		d		06x29	08x24		09x17	10x20	11x23	12x19		13x28	15x01	16x05	17x10	18x20	18 53	19x40	20x45		22x25	
Workington		d		06 37	08 33		09 26	10 29	11 32	12 28		13 37	15 10	16 14	17 19	18 29	19 01	19 49	20 54		22 34	
Harrington		d		06x41	08x36		09x29	10x32	11x35	12x31		13x40	15x14	16x18	17x23	18x32	19 05	19x52	20x57		22x37	
Parton		d		06x49	08x45		09x38	10x40	11x44	12x40		13x49	15x22	16x26	17x31	18x41	19x14	20x01	21x06		22x46	
Whitehaven		a		06 55	08 54		09 44	10 47	11 50	12 49		13 55	15 28	16 32	17 37	18 47	19 23	20 10	21 15		22 55	
		d		06 57			09 45	10 48	11 51		12 54	13 57	15 30	16 34	17 39	18 48						
Corkickle		d		06x59			09x47	10x50	11x53		12x56	13x59	15x32	16x36	17x41	18x50						
St Bees		d		07e10			09 53	10 56	11 59		13 01	14 04	15 37	16 43	17 46	18 56						
Nethertown		d		07x14				11x00					15x41		17x50							
Braystones		d		07x16				11x02					15x44		17x53							
Sellafield		d		07 22		09 07	10 03	11 08	12 10		13 12	14 15	15 50	16 53	17 59	19 06						
Seascale		d		07x25		09x10	10x06	11x11	12x13		13x15	14x18	15x53	16x56	18x02	19x09						
Drigg		d		07x28		09x13	10x09	11x14	12x16		13x18	14x21	15x56	16x59	18x05	19x12						
Ravenglass for Eskdale		d		07 32		09 16	10 13	11 18	12 20		13 21	14 24	15 59	17 03	18 08	19 16						
Bootle		d		07x37		09x22	10x18	11x23	12x25		13x27	14x30	16x05	17x08	18x14	19x21						
Silecroft		d		07x44		09x28	10x25	11x30	12x32		13x33	14x36	16x11	17x15	18x20	19x28						
Millom		a		07 51		09 35	10 32	11 37	12 39		13 40	14 43	16 18	17 22	18 27	19 35						
		d	06 10	07 51		09 36	10 32	11 37	12 39		13 41	14 44	16 19	17 22	18 28	19 36				20 10		22 02
Green Road		d	06x14	07x55		09x40	10x36	11x41	12x43		13x45	14x48	16x23	17x26	18x32	19x40				20x14		22x06
Foxfield		d	06x17	07x59		09x43	10x40	11x44	12x47		13x48	14x51	16x26	17x30	18x35	19x43				20x17		22x09
Kirkby-in-Furness		d	06x21	08x03		09x47	10x44	11x48	12x51		13x52	14x55	16x30	17x34	18x39	19x47				20x21		22x13
Askam		d	06 26	08 08		09 52	10 49	11 53	12 56		13 57	15 00	16 35	17 39	18 44	19 52				20 26		22 18
Barrow-in-Furness		a	06 42	08 24		10 07	11 07	12 09	13 14		14 13	15 16	16 53	17 55	19 02	20 10				20 44		22 35
Lancaster 🅱	82	a		09 33		11 20		13 15			15 22	16 23		19 04								

b arr. 1548

c arr. 1800

e arr. 0704

Table 100

Carlisle and Whitehaven - Barrow-in-Furness

Sundays
until 11 July

		NT	NT	NT
Carlisle	d	15 00	19 00	21 50
Dalston	d	15x08	19x08	21x58
Wigton	d	15 17	19 17	22 07
Aspatria	d	15x27	19x27	22x17
Maryport	d	15 37	19 37	22 27
Flimby	d	15x40	19x40	22x30
Workington	d	15 49	19 49	22 39
Harrington	d	15x52	19x52	22x42
Parton	d	16x01	20x01	22x51
Whitehaven	a	16 10	20 10	23 00
	d			
Corkickle	d			
St Bees	d			
Nethertown	d			
Braystones	d			
Sellafield	d			
Seascale	d			
Drigg	d			
Ravenglass for Eskdale	d			
Bootle	d			
Silecroft	d			
Millom	a			
	d			
Green Road	d			
Foxfield	d			
Kirkby-in-Furness	d			
Askam	d			
Barrow-in-Furness	a			
Lancaster 82	a			

Sundays
18 July to 05 September

		NT 🚌	NT 🚌	NT 🚌
Carlisle	d	15 00	19 00	21 50
Dalston	d	15x15	19x15	22x05
Wigton	d	15 35	19 35	22 25
Aspatria	d	15x55	19x55	22x45
Maryport	d	16 15	20 15	23 05
Flimby	d	16x20	20x20	23x10
Workington	d	16 30	20 30	23 20
Harrington	d	16x40	20x40	23x30
Parton	d	16x50	20x50	23x40
Whitehaven	a	16 56	20 56	23 46
	d			
Corkickle	d			
St Bees	d			
Nethertown	d			
Braystones	d			
Sellafield	d			
Seascale	d			
Drigg	d			
Ravenglass for Eskdale	d			
Bootle	d			
Silecroft	d			
Millom	a			
	d			
Green Road	d			
Foxfield	d			
Kirkby-in-Furness	d			
Askam	d			
Barrow-in-Furness	a			
Lancaster 82	a			

No Sunday Service Whitehaven to Barrow-in-Furness

Table 100

Carlisle and Whitehaven - Barrow-in-Furness

Sundays
from 12 September

		NT	NT	NT
Carlisle	d	15 00	19 00	21 50
Dalston	d	15x08	19x08	21x58
Wigton	d	15 17	19 17	22 07
Aspatria	d	15x27	19x27	22x17
Maryport	d	15 37	19 37	22 27
Flimby	d	15x40	19x40	22x30
Workington	d	15 49	19 49	22 39
Harrington	d	15x52	19x52	22x42
Parton	d	16x01	20x01	22x51
Whitehaven	a	16 10	20 10	23 00
	d			
Corkickle	d			
St Bees	d			
Nethertown	d			
Braystones	d			
Sellafield	d			
Seascale	d			
Drigg	d			
Ravenglass for Eskdale	d			
Bootle	d			
Silecroft	d			
Millom	a			
	d			
Green Road	d			
Foxfield	d			
Kirkby-in-Furness	d			
Askam	d			
Barrow-in-Furness	a			
Lancaster 82	a			

No Sunday Service Whitehaven to Barrow-in-Furness

Network Diagram for Tables 101, 103, 106, 109

DM-14/06(2)
Design BAJS

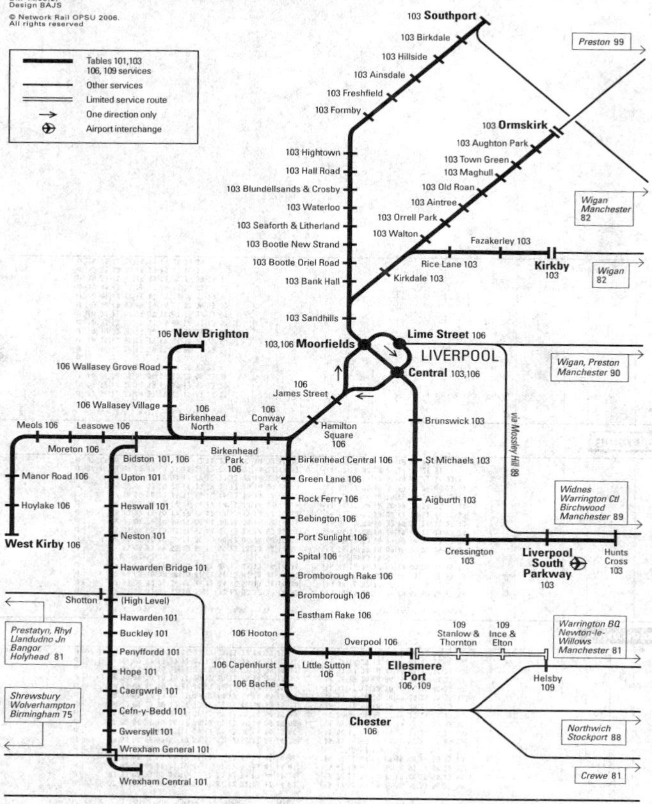

Table 101

Wrexham - Bidston

Mondays to Fridays

		AW	AW BHX	AW	AW BHX	AW	AW BHX	AW	AW BHX	AW	AW BHX	AW	AW BHX	AW	AW
Wrexham Central	d		07 28	08 30	09 30	10 30	11 30	12 30	13 30	14 30	15 30	16 30	17 43	19 44	21 55
Wrexham General	a		07 30	08 32	09 32	10 32	11 32	12 32	13 32	14 32	15 32	16 32	17 45	19 46	21 57
	d	06 31	07 30	08 32	09 32	10 32	11 32	12 32	13 32	14 32	15 32	16 32	17 45	19 46	21 57
Gwersyllt	d	06 35	07 34	08 36	09 36	10 36	11 36	12 36	13 36	14 36	15 36	16 36	17 49	19 50	22 01
Cefn-y-Bedd	d	06 40	07 39	08 41	09 41	10 41	11 41	12 41	13 41	14 41	15 41	16 41	17 54	19 55	22 06
Caergwrle	d	06 42	07 41	08 43	09 43	10 43	11 43	12 43	13 43	14 43	15 43	16 43	17 56	19 57	22 08
Hope (Flintshire)	d	06 44	07 43	08 45	09 45	10 45	11 45	12 45	13 45	14 45	15 45	16 45	17 58	19 59	22 10
Penyffordd	d	06 48	07 47	08 49	09 49	10 49	11 49	12 49	13 49	14 49	15 49	16 49	18 02	20 03	22 14
Buckley	d	06 51	07 50	08 52	09 52	10 52	11 52	12 52	13 52	14 52	15 52	16 52	18 05	20 06	22 17
Hawarden	d	06 55	07 54	08 56	09 56	10 56	11 56	12 56	13 56	14 56	15 56	16 56	18 09	20 10	22 21
Shotton High Level	d	06 59	07 59	09 00	10 00	11 00	12 00	13 00	14 00	15 00	16 00	17 00	18 13	20 14	22 25
Hawarden Bridge	d	07x01	08x01									17x02			
Neston	d	07 10	08 10	09 10	10 10	11 10	12 10	13 10	14 10	15 10	16 10	17 11	18 23	20 24	22 35
Heswall	d	07 15	08 15	09 15	10 15	11 15	12 15	13 15	14 15	15 15	16 15	17 16	18 28	20 29	22 40
Upton	d	07 21	08 21	09 21	10 21	11 21	12 21	13 21	14 21	15 21	16 21	17 22	18 34	20 35	22 46
Bidston	a	07 29	08 29	09 29	10 29	11 29	12 29	13 29	14 29	15 29	16 29	17 29	18 44	20 43	22 54

Saturdays

		AW	AW	AW	AW	AW	AW	AW	AW	AW	AW	AW	AW	AW	AW
Wrexham Central	d		07 28	08 30	09 30	10 30	11 30	12 30	13 30	14 30	15 30	16 30	17 43	19 44	21 55
Wrexham General	a		07 30	08 32	09 32	10 32	11 32	12 32	13 32	14 32	15 32	16 32	17 45	19 46	21 57
	d	06 31	07 30	08 32	09 32	10 32	11 32	12 32	13 32	14 32	15 32	16 32	17 45	19 46	21 57
Gwersyllt	d	06 35	07 34	08 36	09 36	10 36	11 36	12 36	13 36	14 36	15 36	16 36	17 49	19 50	22 01
Cefn-y-Bedd	d	06 40	07 39	08 41	09 41	10 41	11 41	12 41	13 41	14 41	15 41	16 41	17 54	19 55	22 06
Caergwrle	d	06 42	07 41	08 43	09 43	10 43	11 43	12 43	13 43	14 43	15 43	16 43	17 56	19 57	22 08
Hope (Flintshire)	d	06 44	07 43	08 45	09 45	10 45	11 45	12 45	13 45	14 45	15 45	16 45	17 58	19 59	22 10
Penyffordd	d	06 48	07 47	08 49	09 49	10 49	11 49	12 49	13 49	14 49	15 49	16 49	18 02	20 03	22 14
Buckley	d	06 51	07 50	08 52	09 52	10 52	11 52	12 52	13 52	14 52	15 52	16 52	18 05	20 06	22 17
Hawarden	d	06 55	07 54	08 56	09 56	10 56	11 56	12 56	13 56	14 56	15 56	16 56	18 09	20 10	22 21
Shotton High Level	d	06 59	07 59	09 00	10 00	11 00	12 00	13 00	14 00	15 00	16 00	17 00	18 13	20 14	22 25
Hawarden Bridge	d	07x01	08x01									17x02			
Neston	d	07 10	08 10	09 10	10 10	11 10	12 10	13 10	14 10	15 10	16 10	17 11	18 23	20 24	22 35
Heswall	d	07 15	08 15	09 15	10 15	11 15	12 15	13 15	14 15	15 15	16 15	17 16	18 28	20 29	22 40
Upton	d	07 21	08 21	09 21	10 21	11 21	12 21	13 21	14 21	15 21	16 21	17 22	18 34	20 35	22 46
Bidston	a	07 29	08 29	09 29	10 29	11 29	12 29	13 29	14 29	15 29	16 29	17 29	18 44	20 43	22 54

Sundays

		AW	AW	AW	AW	AW	AW
Wrexham Central	d		11 11	13 41	16 11	18 41	21 11
Wrexham General	a		11 13	13 43	16 13	18 43	21 13
	d	08 44	11 14	13 44	16 14	18 44	21 14
Gwersyllt	d	08 48	11 18	13 48	16 18	18 48	21 18
Cefn-y-Bedd	d	08 53	11 23	13 53	16 23	18 53	21 23
Caergwrle	d	08 55	11 25	13 55	16 25	18 55	21 25
Hope (Flintshire)	d	08 57	11 27	13 57	16 27	18 57	21 27
Penyffordd	d	09 01	11 31	14 01	16 31	19 01	21 31
Buckley	d	09 04	11 34	14 04	16 34	19 04	21 34
Hawarden	d	09 08	11 38	14 08	16 38	19 08	21 38
Shotton High Level	d	09 12	11 42	14 12	16 42	19 12	21 42
Hawarden Bridge	d						
Neston	d	09 22	11 52	14 22	16 52	19 22	21 52
Heswall	d	09 27	11 57	14 27	16 57	19 27	21 57
Upton	d	09 33	12 03	14 33	17 03	19 33	22 03
Bidston	a	09 41	12 11	14 41	17 11	19 41	22 11

For connections to Liverpool Lime Street please refer to Table 106

Table 101

Bidston - Wrexham

		AW BHX	AW	AW BHX	AW	AW BHX	AW	AW BHX	AW	AW BHX	AW	AW BHX	AW	AW BHX	AW	AW
Bidston	d		07 31	08 31	09 32	10 32	11 32	12 32	13 32	14 32	15 32	16 31	17 45	18 46	20 56	22 56
Upton	d		07 33	08 33	09 34	10 34	11 34	12 34	13 34	14 34	15 34	16 33	17 47	18 48	20 58	22 58
Heswall	d		07 40	08 40	09 41	10 41	11 41	12 41	13 41	14 41	15 41	16 40	17 54	18 55	21 05	23 05
Neston	d		07 45	08 45	09 46	10 46	11 46	12 46	13 46	14 46	15 46	16 45	17 59	19 00	21 10	23 10
Hawarden Bridge	d		07x53	08x53								16x53	18x07			
Shotton High Level	d		07 55	08 55	09 55	10 55	11 55	12 55	13 55	14 55	15 55	16 55	18 09	19 09	21 19	23 20
Hawarden	d		08 00	09 00	10 00	11 00	12 00	13 00	14 00	15 00	16 00	17 00	18 14	19 14	21 24	23 25
Buckley	d		08 05	09 05	10 05	11 05	12 05	13 05	14 05	15 05	16 05	17 05	18 19	19 19	21 29	23 30
Penyffordd	d		08 08	09 08	10 08	11 08	12 08	13 08	14 08	15 08	16 08	17 08	18 22	19 22	21 32	23 33
Hope (Flintshire)	d		08 12	09 12	10 12	11 12	12 12	13 12	14 12	15 12	16 12	17 12	18 26	19 26	21 36	23 37
Caergwrle	d		08 14	09 14	10 14	11 14	12 14	13 14	14 14	15 14	16 14	17 14	18 28	19 28	21 38	23 39
Cefn-y-Bedd	d		08 16	09 16	10 16	11 16	12 16	13 16	14 16	15 16	16 16	17 16	18 30	19 30	21 40	23 41
Gwersyllt	d		08 20	09 20	10 20	11 20	12 20	13 20	14 20	15 20	16 20	17 20	18 34	19 34	21 44	23 47
Wrexham General	a		08 27	09 27	10 27	11 27	12 27	13 27	14 27	15 27	16 27	17 27	18 41	19 41	21 51	23 54
	d	07 10	08 27	09 27	10 27	11 27	12 27	13 27	14 27	15 27	16 27	17 27	18 41	19 41	21 51	
Wrexham Central	a	07 13	08 32	09 32	10 32	11 32	12 32	13 32	14 32	15 32	16 32	17 32	18 46	19 46	21 56	

Saturdays

		AW	AW	AW	AW	AW	AW	AW	AW	AW	AW	AW	AW	AW	AW	AW
Bidston	d		07 31	08 31	09 32	10 32	11 32	12 32	13 32	14 32	15 32	16 31	17 45	18 46	20 56	22 56
Upton	d		07 33	08 33	09 34	10 34	11 34	12 34	13 34	14 34	15 34	16 33	17 47	18 48	20 58	22 58
Heswall	d		07 40	08 40	09 41	10 41	11 41	12 41	13 41	14 41	15 41	16 40	17 54	18 55	21 05	23 05
Neston	d		07 45	08 45	09 46	10 46	11 46	12 46	13 46	14 46	15 46	16 45	17 59	19 00	21 10	23 10
Hawarden Bridge	d		07x53	08x53								16x53	18x07			
Shotton High Level	d		07 55	08 55	09 55	10 55	11 55	12 55	13 55	14 55	15 55	16 55	18 09	19 09	21 19	23 20
Hawarden	d		08 00	09 00	10 00	11 00	12 00	13 00	14 00	15 00	16 00	17 00	18 14	19 14	21 24	23 25
Buckley	d		08 05	09 05	10 05	11 05	12 05	13 05	14 05	15 05	16 05	17 05	18 19	19 19	21 29	23 30
Penyffordd	d		08 08	09 08	10 08	11 08	12 08	13 08	14 08	15 08	16 08	17 08	18 22	19 22	21 32	23 33
Hope (Flintshire)	d		08 12	09 12	10 12	11 12	12 12	13 12	14 12	15 12	16 12	17 12	18 26	19 26	21 36	23 37
Caergwrle	d		08 14	09 14	10 14	11 14	12 14	13 14	14 14	15 14	16 14	17 14	18 28	19 28	21 38	23 39
Cefn-y-Bedd	d		08 16	09 16	10 16	11 16	12 16	13 16	14 16	15 16	16 16	17 16	18 30	19 30	21 40	23 41
Gwersyllt	d		08 20	09 20	10 20	11 20	12 20	13 20	14 20	15 20	16 20	17 20	18 34	19 34	21 44	23 47
Wrexham General	a		08 27	09 27	10 27	11 27	12 27	13 27	14 27	15 27	16 27	17 27	18 41	19 41	21 51	23 54
	d	07 10	08 27	09 27	10 27	11 27	12 27	13 27	14 27	15 27	16 27	17 27	18 41	19 41	21 51	
Wrexham Central	a	07 13	08 32	09 32	10 32	11 32	12 32	13 32	14 32	15 32	16 32	17 32	18 46	19 46	21 56	

Sundays

		AW	AW	AW	AW	AW	AW
Bidston	d	09 57	12 27	14 57	17 27	19 57	22 27
Upton	d	09 59	12 29	14 59	17 29	19 59	22 29
Heswall	d	10 06	12 36	15 06	17 36	20 06	22 36
Neston	d	10 11	12 41	15 11	17 41	20 11	22 41
Hawarden Bridge	d						
Shotton High Level	d	10 20	12 50	15 20	17 50	20 20	22 50
Hawarden	d	10 25	12 55	15 25	17 55	20 25	22 55
Buckley	d	10 30	13 00	15 30	18 00	20 30	23 00
Penyffordd	d	10 33	13 03	15 33	18 03	20 33	23 03
Hope (Flintshire)	d	10 37	13 07	15 37	18 07	20 37	23 07
Caergwrle	d	10 39	13 09	15 39	18 09	20 39	23 09
Cefn-y-Bedd	d	10 41	13 11	15 41	18 11	20 41	23 11
Gwersyllt	d	10 45	13 15	15 45	18 15	20 45	23 15
Wrexham General	a	10 52	13 22	15 52	18 22	20 52	23 25
	d	10 53	13 23	15 53	18 23	20 53	
Wrexham Central	a	10 58	13 28	15 58	18 28	20 58	

Table 102

Llandudno - Blaenau Ffestiniog

			AW ◇	AW ◇	AW ◇	AW ◇	AW ◇	AW ◇
Llandudno	81	d			10 20	13 20	16 20	19 03
Deganwy	81	d			10x24	13x24	16x24	19x07
Llandudno Junction	81	d	05 35	07 39	10 33	13 33	16 33	19b20
Glan Conwy		d		07x42	10x36	13x36	16x36	19x23
Tal-y-Cafn		d	05 43	07 48	10 42	13 42	16 42	19 29
Dolgarrog		d		07x53	10x47	13x47	16x47	19x34
North Llanrwst		d	05 52	08x00	10x53	13x53	16x53	19x40
Llanrwst		d	05 53	08 02	10 55	13 55	16 55	19 42
Betws-y-Coed		d	05 59	08 08	11 01	14 01	17 01	19 48
Pont-y-Pant		d		08x16	11x09	14x09	17x09	19x56
Dolwyddelan		d		08x19	11x12	14x12	17x12	19x59
Roman Bridge		d		08x23	11x16	14x16	17x16	20x03
Blaenau Ffestiniog		a	06 26	08 40	11 33	14 33	17 33	20 19

Saturdays

			AW ◇	AW ◇	AW ◇	AW ◇	AW ◇	AW ◇
Llandudno	81	d			10 20	13 20	16 20	19 03
Deganwy	81	d			10x24	13x24	16x24	19x07
Llandudno Junction	81	d	05 35	07 39	10 33	13 33	16 33	19b20
Glan Conwy		d		07x42	10x36	13x36	16x36	19x23
Tal-y-Cafn		d	05 43	07 48	10 42	13 42	16 42	19 29
Dolgarrog		d		07x53	10x47	13x47	16x47	19x34
North Llanrwst		d	05 52	08x00	10x53	13x53	16x53	19x40
Llanrwst		d	05 53	08 02	10 55	13 55	16 55	19 42
Betws-y-Coed		d	05 59	08 08	11 01	14 01	17 01	19 48
Pont-y-Pant		d		08x16	11x09	14x09	17x09	19x56
Dolwyddelan		d		08x19	11x12	14x12	17x12	19x59
Roman Bridge		d		08x23	11x16	14x16	17x16	20x03
Blaenau Ffestiniog		a	06 26	08 40	11 33	14 33	17 33	20 19

Sundays
until 05 September

			AW ◇	AW ◇	AW ◇
Llandudno	81	d	10 22	13 30	
Deganwy	81	d	10x26	13x34	
Llandudno Junction	81	d	10 32	13 40	16 15
Glan Conwy		d	10x35	13x43	16x18
Tal-y-Cafn		d	10 41	13 49	16 24
Dolgarrog		d	10x46	13x54	16x29
North Llanrwst		d	10x52	14x00	16x35
Llanrwst		d	10 54	14 02	16 37
Betws-y-Coed		d	11 00	14 08	16 43
Pont-y-Pant		d	11x08	14x16	16x51
Dolwyddelan		d	11x11	14x19	16x54
Roman Bridge		d	11x15	14x23	16x58
Blaenau Ffestiniog		a	11 30	14 38	17 13

Sundays
from 12 September

			AW 🚌	AW 🚌	AW 🚌	AW 🚌	AW 🚌	AW 🚌
Llandudno	81	d	10 05	10 15	13 05	13 10	15 45	16 00
Deganwy	81	d	10 19	10 30	13 19	13 15	15 59	16 15
Llandudno Junction	81	d	10 24	10 35	13 24	13c35	16 04	16 20
Glan Conwy		d		10 40		13 40		16 25
Tal-y-Cafn		d		10 48		13 48		16 33
Dolgarrog		d		10 53		13 53		16 38
North Llanrwst		d		10 58		13 58		16 43
Llanrwst		d	10 50	11 00	14 03	14 00	16 30	16 45
Betws-y-Coed		d	11a00	11 10	14a14	14 10	16a40	16 55
Pont-y-Pant		d		11 20		14 20		17 05
Dolwyddelan		d		11 25		14 25		17 10
Roman Bridge		d		11 32		14 32		17 17
Blaenau Ffestiniog		a		11 45		14 45		17 30

b arr. 1911

c arr. 1320

For connections from Crewe, Chester, Rhyl and Bangor (Gwynedd) please refer to Table 81

Table 102

Mondays to Fridays

Blaenau Ffestiniog - Llandudno

		AW ◇	AW ◇	AW ◇	AW ◇	AW ◇	AW ◇
Blaenau Ffestiniog	d	06 30	08 46	11 46	14 57	17 37	20 23
Roman Bridge	d	06x40	08x56	11x56	15x07	17x47	20x33
Dolwyddelan	d	06x43	09x00	12x00	15x11	17x51	20x37
Pont-y-Pant	d	06x46	09x03	12x03	15x14	17x54	20x40
Betws-y-Coed	d	06 56	09 13	12 13	15 24	18 04	20 50
Llanrwst	d	07 02	09 19	12 19	15 30	18 10	20 56
North Llanrwst	d	07x03	09x20	12x20	15x31	18x11	20x57
Dolgarrog	d	07x09	09x27	12x27	15x38	18x18	21x04
Tal-y-Cafn	d	07x15	09x33	12x33	15x44	18x24	21x10
Glan Conwy	d	07x21	09x39	12x39	15x50	18x30	21x16
Llandudno Junction	81 a	07 26	09 45	12 45	15 56	18 35	21 21
Deganwy	81 a		10x03	13x03	16x07	18x44	21x35
Llandudno	81 a		10 08	13 09	16 13	18 49	21 42

Saturdays

		AW ◇	AW ◇	AW ◇	AW ◇	AW ◇	AW ◇
Blaenau Ffestiniog	d	06 30	08 46	11 46	14 57	17 37	20 23
Roman Bridge	d	06x40	08x56	11x56	15x07	17x47	20x33
Dolwyddelan	d	06x43	09x00	12x00	15x11	17x51	20x37
Pont-y-Pant	d	06x46	09x03	12x03	15x14	17x54	20x40
Betws-y-Coed	d	06 56	09 13	12 13	15 24	18 04	20 50
Llanrwst	d	07 02	09 19	12 19	15 30	18 10	20 56
North Llanrwst	d	07x03	09x20	12x20	15x31	18x11	20x57
Dolgarrog	d	07x09	09x27	12x27	15x38	18x18	21x04
Tal-y-Cafn	d	07x15	09x33	12x33	15x44	18x24	21x10
Glan Conwy	d	07x21	09x39	12x39	15x50	18x30	21x16
Llandudno Junction	81 a	07 26	09 45	12 45	15 56	18 35	21 21
Deganwy	81 a		10x03	13x03	16x03	18x44	21x35
Llandudno	81 a		10 08	13 09	16 09	18 49	21 42

Sundays
until 05 September

		AW ◇	AW ◇	AW ◇
Blaenau Ffestiniog	d	11 45	15 03	17 30
Roman Bridge	d	11x55	15x13	17x40
Dolwyddelan	d	11x58	15x16	17x44
Pont-y-Pant	d	12x01	15x19	17x48
Betws-y-Coed	d	12 11	15 29	17 57
Llanrwst	d	12 17	15 35	18 03
North Llanrwst	d	12x18	15x36	18x05
Dolgarrog	d	12x24	15x42	18x11
Tal-y-Cafn	d	12x29	15x47	18x17
Glan Conwy	d	12x35	15x53	18x23
Llandudno Junction	81 a	12 40	15 59	18 29
Deganwy	81 a	12x45		18x34
Llandudno	81 a	12 51		18 40

Sundays
from 12 September

		AW 🚌	AW 🚌	AW 🚌	AW 🚌	AW 🚌	AW 🚌
Blaenau Ffestiniog	d	11 50	12 00	15 00	15 00	17 15	17 50
Roman Bridge	d	12 00	12 10	15 10	15 10	17 25	18 00
Dolwyddelan	d	12 05	12 13	15 13	15 15	17 28	18 05
Pont-y-Pant	d	12 09	12 16	15 16	15 19	17 31	18 09
Betws-y-Coed	d	12 20	12a25	15a25	15 30	17a40	18 20
Llanrwst	d	12 30			15 40		18 30
North Llanrwst	d	12 33			15 43		18 33
Dolgarrog	d	12 38			15 48		18 38
Tal-y-Cafn	d	12 43			15 53		18 43
Glan Conwy	d	12 51			16 01		18 51
Llandudno Junction	81 a	13 00			16 10		19 00
Deganwy	81 a	13 05			16 15		19 05
Llandudno	81 a	13 20			16 30		19 20

Table 103

Mondays to Saturdays

Hunts Cross and Liverpool - Kirkby, Ormskirk and Southport

		ME	ME	ME	ME	ME	ME	ME	ME	ME	ME	ME	ME	ME	ME	ME	ME	ME
Hunts Cross	89 d					06 06		06 21			06 36		06 51			07 06		
Liverpool Sth Parkway 7 89 ✈	d					06 09		06 24			06 39		06 54			07 09		
Cressington	d					06 12		06 27			06 42		06 57			07 12		
Aigburth	d					06 14		06 29			06 44		06 59			07 14		
St Michaels	d					06 16		06 31			06 46		07 01			07 16		
Brunswick	d					06 19		06 34			06 49		07 04			07 19		
Liverpool Central 10	a					06 23		06 38			06 53		07 08			07 23		
	d	05 55		06 08	06 10	06 23	06 25	06 38	06 40	06 50	06 53	06 55	07 08	07 10	07 20	07 23	07 25	07 35
Moorfields 10	d	05 57		06 10	06 12	06 25	06 27	06 40	06 42	06 52	06 55	06 57	07 10	07 12	07 22	07 25	07 27	07 37
Sandhills	d	06 01	05 59	06 14	06 16	06 29	06 31	06 44	06 46	06 56	06 59	07 01	07 14	07 16	07 26	07 29	07 31	07 41
Kirkdale	d	06 04			06 19		06 34		06 49	06 59		07 04		07 19	07 29		07 34	07 44
Rice Lane	d	06 07					06 37			07 02					07 32			07 47
Fazakerley	d	06 10					06 40			07 03					07 34			07 49
Kirkby	a	06 13					06 43			07 08					07 38			07 53
Walton (Merseyside)	d				06 22				06 52			07 07		07 22			07 37	
Orrell Park	d				06 23				06 53			07 08		07 23			07 38	
Aintree	d				06 26				06 56			07 11		07 26			07 41	
Old Roan	d				06 28				06 58			07 13		07 28			07 43	
Maghull	d				06 31				07 01			07 16		07 31			07 46	
Town Green	d				06 35				07 05			07 20		07 35			07 50	
Aughton Park	d				06 37				07 07			07 22		07 37			07 52	
Ormskirk	a				06 42				07 12			07 27		07 42			07 57	
Bank Hall	d		06 01	06 16		06 31		06 46			07 01		07 16			07 31		
Bootle Oriel Road	d		06 03	06 18		06 33		06 48			07 03		07 18			07 33		
Bootle New Strand	d		06 05	06 20		06 35		06 50			07 05		07 20			07 35		
Seaforth & Litherland	d		06 07	06 22		06 37		06 52			07 07		07 22			07 37		
Waterloo (Merseyside)	d		06 09	06 24		06 39		06 54			07 09		07 24			07 39		
Blundellsands & Crosby	d		06 12	06 27		06 42		06 57			07 12		07 27			07 42		
Hall Road	d		06 14	06 29		06 44		06 59			07 14		07 29			07 44		
Hightown	d		06 17	06 32		06 47		07 02			07 17		07 32			07 47		
Formby	d		06 21	06 36		06 51		07 06			07 21		07 36			07 51		
Freshfield	d		06 23	06 38		06 53		07 08			07 23		07 38			07 53		
Ainsdale	d		06 27	06 42		06 57		07 12			07 27		07 42			07 57		
Hillside	d		06 30	06 45		07 00		07 15			07 30		07 45			08 00		
Birkdale	d		06 32	06 47		07 02		07 17			07 32		07 47			08 02		
Southport	a		06 37	06 52		07 07		07 22			07 37		07 52			08 07		

		ME	ME	ME	ME	ME	ME	ME	ME	ME	ME	ME	ME	ME	ME SO	ME SX	ME	ME	ME SO	ME SX	ME	ME	ME
Hunts Cross	89 d	07 21			07 36			07 51			08 06			08 21				08 36				08 51	
Liverpool Sth Parkway 7 89 ✈	d	07 24			07 39			07 54			08 09			08 24				08 39				08 54	
Cressington	d	07 27			07 42			07 57			08 12			08 27				08 42				08 57	
Aigburth	d	07 29			07 44			07 59			08 14			08 29				08 44				08 59	
St Michaels	d	07 31			07 46			08 01			08 16			08 31				08 46				09 01	
Brunswick	d	07 34			07 49			08 04			08 19			08 34				08 49				09 04	
Liverpool Central 10	a	07 38			07 53			08 08			08 23			08 38				08 53				09 08	
	d	07 38	07 40	07 50	07 53	07 55	08 05	08 08	08 10	08 20	08 23	08 25	08 35	08 38	08 40	08 40	08 50	08 53	08 55	08 55	09 05	09 08	09 10
Moorfields 10	d	07 40	07 42	07 52	07 55	07 57	08 07	08 10	08 12	08 22	08 25	08 27	08 37	08 40	08 42	08 42	08 52	08 55	08 57	08 57	09 07	09 10	09 12
Sandhills	d	07 44	07 46	07 56	07 59	08 01	08 11	08 14	08 16	08 26	08 29	08 31	08 41	08 44	08 46	08 46	08 56	08 59	09 01	09 01	09 11	09 14	09 16
Kirkdale	d		07 49	07 59		08 04	08 14		08 19	08 29		08 34	08 44		08 49	08 49	08 59		09 04	09 04	09 14		09 19
Rice Lane	d			08 02			08 17			08 32			08 47				09 02				09 17		
Fazakerley	d			08 04			08 19			08 34			08 49				09 05				09 19		
Kirkby	a			08 08			08 23			08 38			08 53				09 08				09 23		
Walton (Merseyside)	d		07 52			08 07			08 22			08 37			08 52	08 52			09 07	09 07			09 22
Orrell Park	d		07 53			08 08			08 23			08 38			08 53	08 53			09 08	09 08			09 23
Aintree	d		07 56			08 11			08 26			08 41			08 56	08 56			09 11	09 11			09 26
Old Roan	d		07 58			08 13			08 28			08 43			08 58	08 58			09 13	09 13			09 28
Maghull	d		08 01			08 16			08 31			08 46			09 01	09 01			09 16	09 16			09 31
Town Green	d		08 05			08 20			08 35			08 50			09 05	09 05			09 20	09 20			09 35
Aughton Park	d		08 07			08 22			08 37			08 52			09 07	09 07			09 22	09 22			09 37
Ormskirk	a		08 12			08 27			08 42			08 57			09 12	09 13			09 27	09 28			09 42
Bank Hall	d	07 46			08 01			08 16			08 31			08 46				09 01				09 16	
Bootle Oriel Road	d	07 48			08 03			08 18			08 33			08 48				09 03				09 18	
Bootle New Strand	d	07 50			08 05			08 20			08 35			08 50				09 05				09 20	
Seaforth & Litherland	d	07 52			08 07			08 22			08 37			08 52				09 07				09 22	
Waterloo (Merseyside)	d	07 54			08 09			08 24			08 39			08 54				09 09				09 24	
Blundellsands & Crosby	d	07 57			08 12			08 27			08 42			08 57				09 12				09 27	
Hall Road	d	07 59			08 14			08 29			08 44			08 59				09 14				09 29	
Hightown	d	08 02			08 17			08 32			08 47			09 02				09 17				09 32	
Formby	d	08 06			08 21			08 36			08 51			09 06				09 21				09 36	
Freshfield	d	08 08			08 23			08 38			08 53			09 08				09 23				09 38	
Ainsdale	d	08 12			08 27			08 42			08 57			09 12				09 27				09 42	
Hillside	d	08 15			08 30			08 45			09 00			09 15				09 30				09 45	
Birkdale	d	08 17			08 32			08 47			09 02			09 17				09 32				09 47	
Southport	a	08 22			08 37			08 52			09 07			09 22				09 37				09 52	

Hunts Cross and Liverpool - Kirkby, Ormskirk and Southport

		ME	ME	ME	ME	ME	ME SO	ME SX	ME	ME	ME	ME	ME	ME	ME	ME	ME	ME	ME	ME	ME	ME
Hunts Cross 89	d		09 06			09 21				09 36			09 51			10 06			10 21			10 36
Liverpool Sth Parkway 7 89 ✈	d		09 09			09 24				09 39			09 54			10 09			10 24			10 39
Cressington	d		09 12			09 27				09 42			09 57			10 12			10 27			10 42
Aigburth	d		09 14			09 29				09 44			09 59			10 14			10 29			10 44
St Michaels	d		09 16			09 31				09 46			10 01			10 16			10 31			10 46
Brunswick	d		09 19			09 34				09 49			10 04			10 19			10 34			10 49
Liverpool Central 10	a		09 23			09 38				09 53			10 08			10 23			10 38			10 53
	d	09 20	09 23	09 25	09 35	09 38	09 40	09 40	09 50	09 53	09 55	10 05	10 08	10 10	10 20	10 23	10 25	10 35	10 38	10 40	10 50	10 53
Moorfields 10	d	09 22	09 25	09 27	09 37	09 40	09 42	09 42	09 52	09 55	09 57	10 07	10 10	10 12	10 22	10 25	10 27	10 37	10 40	10 42	10 52	10 55
Sandhills	d	09 26	09 29	09 31	09 41	09 44	09 46	09 46	09 56	09 59	10 01	10 11	10 14	10 16	10 26	10 29	10 31	10 41	10 44	10 46	10 56	10 59
Kirkdale	d	09 29		09 34	09 44		09 49	09 49	09 59		10 04	10 14		10 19	10 29		10 34	10 44		10 49	10 59	
Rice Lane	d	09 32			09 47				10 02			10 17			10 32			10 47			11 02	
Fazakerley	d	09 34			09 49				10 04			10 19			10 34			10 49			11 04	
Kirkby	a	09 38			09 53				10 08			10 23			10 38			10 53			11 08	
Walton (Merseyside)	d			09 37			09 52	09 52			10 07			10 22			10 37			10 52		
Orrell Park	d			09 38			09 53	09 53			10 08			10 23			10 38			10 53		
Aintree	d			09 41			09 56	09 56			10 11			10 26			10 41			10 56		
Old Roan	d			09 43			09 58	09 58			10 13			10 28			10 43			10 58		
Maghull	d			09 46			10 01	10 01			10 16			10 31			10 46			11 01		
Town Green	d			09 50			10 05	10 05			10 20			10 35			10 50			11 05		
Aughton Park	d			09 52			10 07	10 07			10 22			10 37			10 52			11 07		
Ormskirk	a			09 57			10 12	10 13			10 27			10 42			10 57			11 12		
Bank Hall	d		09 31			09 46				10 01			10 16			10 31			10 46			11 01
Bootle Oriel Road	d		09 33			09 48				10 03			10 18			10 33			10 48			11 03
Bootle New Strand	d		09 35			09 50				10 05			10 20			10 35			10 50			11 05
Seaforth & Litherland	d		09 37			09 52				10 07			10 22			10 37			10 52			11 07
Waterloo (Merseyside)	d		09 39			09 54				10 09			10 24			10 39			10 54			11 09
Blundellsands & Crosby	d		09 42			09 57				10 12			10 27			10 42			10 57			11 12
Hall Road	d		09 44			09 59				10 14			10 29			10 44			10 59			11 14
Hightown	d		09 47			10 02				10 17			10 32			10 47			11 02			11 17
Formby	d		09 51			10 06				10 21			10 36			10 51			11 06			11 21
Freshfield	d		09 53			10 08				10 23			10 38			10 53			11 08			11 23
Ainsdale	d		09 57			10 12				10 27			10 42			10 57			11 12			11 27
Hillside	d		10 00			10 15				10 30			10 45			11 00			11 15			11 30
Birkdale	d		10 02			10 17				10 32			10 47			11 02			11 17			11 32
Southport	a		10 07			10 22				10 37			10 52			11 07			11 22			11 37

		ME	ME	ME	ME	ME	ME	ME	ME	ME	ME	ME	ME	ME	ME	ME	ME	ME	ME	ME	ME	ME	ME
Hunts Cross 89	d			10 51			11 06			11 21			11 36			11 51			12 06			12 21	
Liverpool Sth Parkway 7 89 ✈	d			10 54			11 09			11 24			11 39			11 54			12 09			12 24	
Cressington	d			10 57			11 12			11 27			11 42			11 57			12 12			12 27	
Aigburth	d			10 59			11 14			11 29			11 44			11 59			12 14			12 29	
St Michaels	d			11 01			11 16			11 31			11 46			12 01			12 16			12 31	
Brunswick	d			11 04			11 19			11 34			11 49			12 04			12 19			12 34	
Liverpool Central 10	a			11 08			11 23			11 38			11 53			12 08			12 23			12 38	
	d	10 55	11 05	11 08	11 10	11 20	11 23	11 25	11 35	11 38	11 40	11 50	11 53	11 55	12 05	12 08	12 10	12 20	12 23	12 25	12 35	12 38	12 40
Moorfields 10	d	10 57	11 07	11 10	11 12	11 22	11 25	11 27	11 37	11 40	11 42	11 52	11 55	11 57	12 07	12 10	12 12	12 22	12 25	12 27	12 37	12 40	12 42
Sandhills	d	11 01	11 11	11 14	11 16	11 26	11 29	11 31	11 41	11 44	11 46	11 56	11 59	12 01	12 11	12 14	12 16	12 26	12 29	12 31	12 41	12 44	12 46
Kirkdale	d	11 04	11 14		11 19	11 29		11 34	11 44		11 49	11 59		12 04	12 14		12 19	12 29		12 34	12 44		12 49
Rice Lane	d		11 17			11 32			11 47			12 02			12 17			12 32			12 47		
Fazakerley	d		11 19			11 34			11 49			12 04			12 19			12 34			12 49		
Kirkby	a		11 23			11 38			11 53			12 08			12 23			12 38			12 53		
Walton (Merseyside)	d	11 07			11 22			11 37			11 52			12 07			12 22			12 37			12 52
Orrell Park	d	11 08			11 23			11 38			11 53			12 08			12 23			12 38			12 53
Aintree	d	11 11			11 26			11 41			11 56			12 11			12 26			12 41			12 56
Old Roan	d	11 13			11 28			11 43			11 58			12 13			12 28			12 43			12 58
Maghull	d	11 16			11 31			11 46			12 01			12 16			12 31			12 46			13 01
Town Green	d	11 20			11 35			11 50			12 05			12 20			12 35			12 50			13 05
Aughton Park	d	11 22			11 37			11 52			12 07			12 22			12 37			12 52			13 07
Ormskirk	a	11 27			11 42			11 57			12 12			12 27			12 42			12 57			13 12
Bank Hall	d			11 16			11 31			11 46			12 01			12 16			12 31			12 46	
Bootle Oriel Road	d			11 18			11 33			11 48			12 03			12 18			12 33			12 48	
Bootle New Strand	d			11 20			11 35			11 50			12 05			12 20			12 35			12 50	
Seaforth & Litherland	d			11 22			11 37			11 52			12 07			12 22			12 37			12 52	
Waterloo (Merseyside)	d			11 24			11 39			11 54			12 09			12 24			12 39			12 54	
Blundellsands & Crosby	d			11 27			11 42			11 57			12 12			12 27			12 42			12 57	
Hall Road	d			11 29			11 44			11 59			12 14			12 29			12 44			12 59	
Hightown	d			11 32			11 47			12 02			12 17			12 32			12 47			13 02	
Formby	d			11 36			11 51			12 06			12 21			12 36			12 51			13 06	
Freshfield	d			11 38			11 53			12 08			12 23			12 38			12 53			13 08	
Ainsdale	d			11 42			11 57			12 12			12 27			12 42			12 57			13 12	
Hillside	d			11 45			12 00			12 15			12 30			12 45			13 00			13 15	
Birkdale	d			11 47			12 02			12 17			12 32			12 47			13 02			13 17	
Southport	a			11 52			12 07			12 22			12 37			12 52			13 07			13 22	

Table 103 Mondays to Saturdays

Hunts Cross and Liverpool - Kirkby, Ormskirk and Southport

		ME	ME	ME	ME	ME	ME	ME	ME	ME	ME	ME	ME	ME	ME	ME	ME	ME	ME	ME	ME	ME
Hunts Cross 89	d		12 36			12 51			13 06			13 21			13 36			13 51			14 06	
Liverpool Sth Parkway 7 89 ✈	d		12 39			12 54			13 09			13 24			13 39			13 54			14 09	
Cressington	d		12 42			12 57			13 12			13 27			13 42			13 57			14 12	
Aigburth	d		12 44			12 59			13 14			13 29			13 44			13 59			14 14	
St Michaels	d		12 46			13 01			13 16			13 31			13 46			14 01			14 16	
Brunswick	d		12 49			13 04			13 19			13 34			13 49			14 04			14 19	
Liverpool Central 10	a		12 53			13 08			13 23			13 38			13 53			14 08			14 23	
	d	12 50	12 53	12 55	13 05	13 08	13 10	13 20	13 23	13 25	13 35	13 38	13 40	13 50	13 53	13 55	14 05	14 08	14 10	14 20	14 23	14 25
Moorfields 10	d	12 52	12 55	12 57	13 07	13 10	13 12	13 22	13 25	13 27	13 37	13 40	13 42	13 52	13 55	13 57	14 07	14 10	14 12	14 22	14 25	14 27
Sandhills	d	12 56	12 59	13 01	13 11	13 14	13 16	13 26	13 29	13 31	13 41	13 44	13 46	13 56	13 59	14 01	14 11	14 14	14 16	14 26	14 29	14 31
Kirkdale	d	12 59		13 04	13 14		13 19	13 29		13 34	13 44		13 49	13 59		14 04	14 14		14 19	14 29		14 34
Rice Lane	d	13 02			13 17			13 32			13 47			14 02			14 17			14 32		
Fazakerley	d	13 04			13 19			13 34			13 49			14 04			14 19			14 34		
Kirkby	a	13 08			13 23			13 38			13 53			14 08			14 23			14 38		
Walton (Merseyside)	d			13 07			13 22			13 37			13 52			14 07			14 22			14 37
Orrell Park	d			13 08			13 23			13 38			13 53			14 08			14 23			14 38
Aintree	d			13 11			13 26			13 41			13 56			14 11			14 26			14 41
Old Roan	d			13 13			13 28			13 43			13 58			14 13			14 28			14 43
Maghull	d			13 16			13 31			13 46			14 01			14 16			14 31			14 46
Town Green	d			13 20			13 35			13 50			14 05			14 20			14 35			14 50
Aughton Park	d			13 22			13 37			13 52			14 07			14 22			14 37			14 52
Ormskirk	a			13 27			13 42			13 57			14 12			14 27			14 42			14 57
Bank Hall	d		13 01			13 16			13 31			13 46			14 01			14 16			14 31	
Bootle Oriel Road	d		13 03			13 18			13 33			13 48			14 03			14 18			14 33	
Bootle New Strand	d		13 05			13 20			13 35			13 50			14 05			14 20			14 35	
Seaforth & Litherland	d		13 07			13 22			13 37			13 52			14 07			14 22			14 37	
Waterloo (Merseyside)	d		13 09			13 24			13 39			13 54			14 09			14 24			14 39	
Blundellsands & Crosby	d		13 12			13 27			13 42			13 57			14 12			14 27			14 42	
Hall Road	d		13 14			13 29			13 44			13 59			14 14			14 29			14 44	
Hightown	d		13 17			13 32			13 47			14 02			14 17			14 32			14 47	
Formby	d		13 21			13 36			13 51			14 06			14 21			14 36			14 51	
Freshfield	d		13 23			13 38			13 53			14 08			14 23			14 38			14 53	
Ainsdale	d		13 27			13 42			13 57			14 12			14 27			14 42			14 57	
Hillside	d		13 30			13 45			14 00			14 15			14 30			14 45			15 00	
Birkdale	d		13 32			13 47			14 02			14 17			14 32			14 47			15 02	
Southport	a		13 37			13 52			14 07			14 22			14 37			14 52			15 07	

		ME	ME	ME	ME	ME	ME	ME	ME	ME	ME	ME	ME	ME	ME	ME	ME	ME	ME	ME	ME	ME
Hunts Cross 89	d		14 21			14 36			14 51			15 06			15 21			15 36			15 51	
Liverpool Sth Parkway 7 89 ✈	d		14 24			14 39			14 54			15 09			15 24			15 39			15 54	
Cressington	d		14 27			14 42			14 57			15 12			15 27			15 42			15 57	
Aigburth	d		14 29			14 44			14 59			15 14			15 29			15 44			15 59	
St Michaels	d		14 31			14 46			15 01			15 16			15 31			15 46			16 01	
Brunswick	d		14 34			14 49			15 04			15 19			15 34			15 49			16 04	
Liverpool Central 10	a		14 38			14 53			15 08			15 23			15 38			15 53			16 08	
	d	14 35	14 38	14 40	14 50	14 53	14 55	15 05	15 08	15 10	15 20	15 23	15 25	15 35	15 38	15 40	15 50	15 53	15 55	16 05	16 08	16 10
Moorfields 10	d	14 37	14 40	14 42	14 52	14 55	14 57	15 07	15 10	15 12	15 22	15 25	15 27	15 37	15 40	15 42	15 52	15 55	15 57	16 07	16 10	16 12
Sandhills	d	14 41	14 44	14 46	14 56	14 59	15 01	15 11	15 14	15 16	15 26	15 29	15 31	15 41	15 44	15 46	15 56	15 59	16 01	16 11	16 14	16 16
Kirkdale	d	14 44		14 49	14 59		15 04	15 14		15 19	15 29		15 34	15 44		15 49	15 59		16 04	16 14		16 19
Rice Lane	d	14 47			15 02			15 17			15 32			15 47			16 02			16 17		
Fazakerley	d	14 49			15 04			15 19			15 34			15 49			16 04			16 19		
Kirkby	a	14 53			15 08			15 23			15 38			15 53			16 08			16 23		
Walton (Merseyside)	d			14 52			15 07			15 22			15 37			15 52			16 07			16 22
Orrell Park	d			14 53			15 08			15 23			15 38			15 53			16 08			16 23
Aintree	d			14 56			15 11			15 26			15 41			15 56			16 11			16 26
Old Roan	d			14 58			15 13			15 28			15 43			15 58			16 13			16 28
Maghull	d			15 01			15 16			15 31			15 46			16 01			16 16			16 31
Town Green	d			15 05			15 20			15 35			15 50			16 05			16 20			16 35
Aughton Park	d			15 07			15 22			15 37			15 52			16 07			16 22			16 37
Ormskirk	a			15 12			15 27			15 42			15 57			16 12			16 27			16 42
Bank Hall	d		14 46			15 01			15 16			15 31			15 46			16 01			16 16	
Bootle Oriel Road	d		14 48			15 03			15 18			15 33			15 48			16 03			16 18	
Bootle New Strand	d		14 50			15 05			15 20			15 35			15 50			16 05			16 20	
Seaforth & Litherland	d		14 52			15 07			15 22			15 37			15 52			16 07			16 22	
Waterloo (Merseyside)	d		14 54			15 09			15 24			15 39			15 54			16 09			16 24	
Blundellsands & Crosby	d		14 57			15 12			15 27			15 42			15 57			16 12			16 27	
Hall Road	d		14 59			15 14			15 29			15 44			15 59			16 14			16 29	
Hightown	d		15 02			15 17			15 32			15 47			16 02			16 17			16 32	
Formby	d		15 06			15 21			15 36			15 51			16 06			16 21			16 36	
Freshfield	d		15 08			15 23			15 38			15 53			16 08			16 23			16 38	
Ainsdale	d		15 12			15 27			15 42			15 57			16 12			16 27			16 42	
Hillside	d		15 15			15 30			15 45			16 00			16 15			16 30			16 45	
Birkdale	d		15 17			15 32			15 47			16 02			16 17			16 32			16 47	
Southport	a		15 22			15 37			15 52			16 07			16 22			16 37			16 52	

Hunts Cross and Liverpool - Kirkby, Ormskirk and Southport

	ME	ME	ME	ME	ME	ME	ME	ME	ME	ME	ME	ME	ME SX	ME	ME	ME	ME	ME	ME	ME	ME	ME
Hunts Cross 89 d		16 06			16 21			16 36			16 51				17 06			17 21			17 36	
Liverpool Sth Parkway 7 89 ✈ d		16 09			16 24			16 39			16 54				17 09			17 24			17 39	
Cressington d		16 12			16 27			16 42			16 57				17 12			17 27			17 42	
Aigburth d		16 14			16 29			16 44			16 59				17 14			17 29			17 44	
St Michaels d		16 16			16 31			16 46			17 01				17 16			17 31			17 46	
Brunswick d		16 19			16 34			16 49			17 04				17 19			17 34			17 49	
Liverpool Central 10 a		16 23			16 38			16 53			17 08				17 23			17 38			17 53	
d	16 20	16 23	16 25	16 35	16 38	16 40	16 50	16 53	16 55	17 05	17 08	17 10	17 13	17 20	17 23	17 25	17 35	17 38	17 40	17 50	17 53	17 55
Moorfields 10 d	16 22	16 25	16 27	16 37	16 40	16 42	16 52	16 55	16 57	17 07	17 10	17 12	17 15	17 22	17 25	17 27	17 37	17 40	17 42	17 52	17 55	17 57
Sandhills d	16 26	16 29	16 31	16 41	16 44	16 46	16 56	16 59	17 01	17 11	17 14	17 16	17 19	17 26	17 29	17 31	17 41	17 44	17 46	17 56	17 59	18 01
Kirkdale d	16 29		16 34	16 44		16 49	16 59		17 04	17 14		17 19		17 29		17 34	17 44		17 49	17 59		18 04
Rice Lane d	16 32			16 47			17 02			17 17				17 32			17 47			18 02		
Fazakerley d	16 34			16 49			17 04			17 19				17 34			17 49			18 04		
Kirkby a	16 38			16 53			17 08			17 23				17 38			17 53			18 08		
Walton (Merseyside) d			16 37			16 52			17 07			17 22				17 37			17 52			18 07
Orrell Park d			16 38			16 53			17 08			17 23				17 38			17 53			18 08
Aintree d			16 41			16 56			17 11			17 26				17 41			17 56			18 11
Old Roan d			16 43			16 58			17 13			17 28				17 43			17 58			18 13
Maghull d			16 46			17 01			17 16			17 31				17 46			18 01			18 16
Town Green d			16 50			17 05			17 20			17 35				17 50			18 05			18 20
Aughton Park d			16 52			17 07			17 22			17 37				17 52			18 07			18 22
Ormskirk a			16 57			17 12			17 27			17 42				17 57			18 12			18 27
Bank Hall d		16 31			16 46			17 01			17 16		17 21		17 31			17 46			18 01	
Bootle Oriel Road d		16 33			16 48			17 03			17 18		17 23		17 33			17 48			18 03	
Bootle New Strand d		16 35			16 50			17 05			17 20		17 25		17 35			17 50			18 05	
Seaforth & Litherland d		16 37			16 52			17 07			17 22		17 27		17 37			17 52			18 07	
Waterloo (Merseyside) d		16 39			16 54			17 09			17 24		17 29		17 39			17 54			18 09	
Blundellsands & Crosby d		16 42			16 57			17 12			17 27		17 32		17 42			17 57			18 12	
Hall Road d		16 44			16 59			17 14			17 29		17 34		17 44			17 59			18 14	
Hightown d		16 47			17 02			17 17			17 32		17 37		17 47			18 02			18 17	
Formby d		16 51			17 06			17 21			17 36		17 41		17 51			18 06			18 21	
Freshfield d		16 53			17 08			17 23			17 38		17 43		17 53			18 08			18 23	
Ainsdale d		16 57			17 12			17 27			17 42		17 47		17 57			18 12			18 27	
Hillside d		17 00			17 15			17 30			17 45		17 50		18 00			18 15			18 30	
Birkdale d		17 02			17 17			17 32			17 47		17 52		18 02			18 17			18 32	
Southport a		17 07			17 22			17 37			17 52		17 57		18 07			18 22			18 37	

	ME	ME	ME	ME	ME	ME	ME	ME	ME	ME	ME	ME	ME	ME	ME	ME	ME	ME	ME	ME
Hunts Cross 89 d		17 51			18 06			18 21			18 36			18 51		19 06		19 21		19 36
Liverpool Sth Parkway 7 89 ✈ d		17 54			18 09			18 24			18 39			18 54		19 09		19 24		19 39
Cressington d		17 57			18 12			18 27			18 42			18 57		19 12		19 27		19 42
Aigburth d		17 59			18 14			18 29			18 44			18 59		19 14		19 29		19 44
St Michaels d		18 01			18 16			18 31			18 46			19 01		19 16		19 31		19 46
Brunswick d		18 04			18 19			18 34			18 49			19 04		19 19		19 34		19 49
Liverpool Central 10 a		18 08			18 23			18 38			18 53			19 08		19 23		19 38		19 53
d	18 05	18 08	18 10	18 20	18 23	18 25	18 35	18 38	18 40	18 50	18 53	18 55	19 05	19 08	19 10	19 23	19 25	19 38	19 40	19 53
Moorfields 10 d	18 07	18 10	18 12	18 22	18 25	18 27	18 37	18 40	18 42	18 52	18 55	18 57	19 07	19 10	19 12	19 25	19 27	19 40	19 42	19 55
Sandhills d	18 11	18 14	18 16	18 26	18 29	18 31	18 41	18 44	18 46	18 56	18 59	19 01	19 11	19 14	19 16	19 29	19 31	19 44	19 46	19 59
Kirkdale d	18 14		18 19	18 29		18 34	18 44		18 49	18 59		19 04	19 14		19 19		19 34		19 49	
Rice Lane d	18 17			18 32			18 47			19 02			19 17				19 37			
Fazakerley d	18 19			18 34			18 49			19 04			19 19				19 40			
Kirkby a	18 23			18 38			18 53			19 08			19 23				19 45			
Walton (Merseyside) d			18 22			18 37			18 52			19 07			19 22				19 52	
Orrell Park d			18 23			18 38			18 53			19 08			19 23				19 53	
Aintree d			18 26			18 41			18 56			19 11			19 26				19 56	
Old Roan d			18 28			18 43			18 58			19 13			19 28				19 58	
Maghull d			18 31			18 46			19 01			19 16			19 31				20 01	
Town Green d			18 35			18 50			19 05			19 20			19 35				20 05	
Aughton Park d			18 37			18 52			19 07			19 22			19 37				20 07	
Ormskirk a			18 42			18 57			19 12			19 27			19 42				20 13	
Bank Hall d		18 16			18 31			18 46			19 01			19 16		19 31		19 46		20 01
Bootle Oriel Road d		18 18			18 33			18 48			19 03			19 18		19 33		19 48		20 03
Bootle New Strand d		18 20			18 35			18 50			19 05			19 20		19 35		19 50		20 05
Seaforth & Litherland d		18 22			18 37			18 52			19 07			19 22		19 37		19 52		20 07
Waterloo (Merseyside) d		18 24			18 39			18 54			19 09			19 24		19 39		19 54		20 09
Blundellsands & Crosby d		18 27			18 42			18 57			19 12			19 27		19 42		19 57		20 12
Hall Road d		18 29			18 44			18 59			19 14			19 29		19 44		19 59		20 14
Hightown d		18 32			18 47			19 02			19 17			19 32		19 47		20 02		20 17
Formby d		18 36			18 51			19 06			19 21			19 36		19 51		20 06		20 21
Freshfield d		18 38			18 53			19 08			19 23			19 38		19 53		20 08		20 23
Ainsdale d		18 42			18 57			19 12			19 27			19 42		19 57		20 12		20 27
Hillside d		18 45			19 00			19 15			19 30			19 45		20 00		20 15		20 30
Birkdale d		18 47			19 02			19 17			19 32			19 47		20 02		20 17		20 32
Southport a		18 52			19 07			19 22			19 37			19 52		20 07		20 22		20 37

Hunts Cross and Liverpool - Kirkby, Ormskirk and Southport

	ME SO	ME SX	ME	ME	ME	ME	ME	ME	ME	ME	ME	ME	ME	ME	ME	ME	ME	ME	ME	ME	ME	ME
Hunts Cross 89 d			19 51		20 06		20 21		20 36		20 51		21 06		21 21		21 36		21 51		22 06	
Liverpool Sth Parkway 7 89 ✈ d			19 54		20 09		20 24		20 39		20 54		21 09		21 24		21 39		21 54		22 09	
Cressington d			19 57		20 12		20 27		20 42		20 57		21 12		21 27		21 42		21 57		22 12	
Aigburth d			19 59		20 14		20 29		20 44		20 59		21 14		21 29		21 44		21 59		22 14	
St Michaels d			20 01		20 16		20 31		20 46		21 01		21 16		21 31		21 46		22 01		22 16	
Brunswick d			20 04		20 19		20 34		20 49		21 04		21 19		21 34		21 49		22 04		22 19	
Liverpool Central 10 a			20 08		20 23		20 38		20 53		21 08		21 23		21 38		21 53		22 08		22 23	
d	19 55	19 55	20 08	20 10	20 23	20 25	20 38	20 40	20 53	20 55	21 08	21 10	21 23	21 25	21 38	21 40	21 53	21 55	22 08	22 10	22 23	22 25
Moorfields 10 d	19 57	19 57	20 10	20 12	20 25	20 27	20 40	20 42	20 55	20 57	21 10	21 12	21 25	21 27	21 40	21 42	21 55	21 57	22 10	22 12	22 25	22 27
Sandhills d	20 01	20 01	20 14	20 16	20 29	20 31	20 44	20 46	20 59	21 01	21 14	21 16	21 29	21 31	21 44	21 46	21 59	22 01	22 14	22 16	22 29	22 31
Kirkdale d	20 04	20 04		20 19		20 34		20 49		21 04		21 19		21 34		21 49		22 04		22 19		22 34
Rice Lane d	20 07	20 07				20 37				21 07				21 37				22 07				22 37
Fazakerley d	20 10	20 10				20 40				21 10				21 40				22 10				22 40
Kirkby a	20 13	20 15				20 43				21 13				21 43				22 13				22 43
Walton (Merseyside) d				20 22				20 52				21 22				21 52				22 22		
Orrell Park d				20 23				20 53				21 23				21 53				22 23		
Aintree d				20 26				20 56				21 26				21 56				22 26		
Old Roan d				20 28				20 58				21 28				21 58				22 28		
Maghull d				20 31				21 01				21 31				22 01				22 31		
Town Green d				20 35				21 05				21 35				22 05				22 35		
Aughton Park d				20 37				21 07				21 37				22 07				22 37		
Ormskirk a				20 42				21 12				21 42				22 12				22 42		
Bank Hall d			20 16		20 31		20 46		21 01		21 16		21 31		21 46		22 01		22 16		22 31	
Bootle Oriel Road d			20 18		20 33		20 48		21 03		21 18		21 33		21 48		22 03		22 18		22 33	
Bootle New Strand d			20 20		20 35		20 50		21 05		21 20		21 35		21 50		22 05		22 20		22 35	
Seaforth & Litherland d			20 22		20 37		20 52		21 07		21 22		21 37		21 52		22 07		22 22		22 37	
Waterloo (Merseyside) d			20 24		20 39		20 54		21 09		21 24		21 39		21 54		22 09		22 24		22 39	
Blundellsands & Crosby d			20 27		20 42		20 57		21 12		21 27		21 42		21 57		22 12		22 27		22 42	
Hall Road d			20 29		20 44		20 59		21 14		21 29		21 44		21 59		22 14		22 29		22 44	
Hightown d			20 32		20 47		21 02		21 17		21 32		21 47		22 02		22 17		22 32		22 47	
Formby d			20 36		20 51		21 06		21 21		21 36		21 51		22 06		22 21		22 36		22 51	
Freshfield d			20 38		20 53		21 08		21 23		21 38		21 53		22 08		22 23		22 38		22 53	
Ainsdale d			20 42		20 57		21 12		21 27		21 42		21 57		22 12		22 27		22 42		22 57	
Hillside d			20 45		21 00		21 15		21 30		21 45		22 00		22 15		22 30		22 45		23 00	
Birkdale d			20 47		21 02		21 17		21 32		21 47		22 02		22 17		22 32		22 47		23 02	
Southport a			20 52		21 07		21 22		21 37		21 52		22 07		22 22		22 37		22 52		23 07	

	ME	ME	ME	ME	ME	ME	ME	ME	ME	ME	ME
Hunts Cross 89 d	22 21		22 36		22 51		23 06		23 21		
Liverpool Sth Parkway 7 89 ✈ d	22 24		22 39		22 54		23 09		23 24		
Cressington d	22 27		22 42		22 57		23 12		23 27		
Aigburth d	22 29		22 44		22 59		23 14		23 29		
St Michaels d	22 31		22 46		23 01		23 16		23 31		
Brunswick d	22 34		22 49		23 04		23 19		23 34		
Liverpool Central 10 a	22 38		22 53		23 08		23 23		23 38		
d	22 38	22 40	22 53	22 55	23 08	23 10	23 23	23 25	23 38	23 40	23 55
Moorfields 10 d	22 40	22 42	22 55	22 57	23 10	23 12	23 25	23 27	23 40	23 42	23 57
Sandhills d	22 44	22 46	22 59	23 01	23 14	23 16	23 29	23 31	23 44	23 46	00 01
Kirkdale d		22 49		23 04		23 19		23 34		23 49	00 04
Rice Lane d				23 07				23 37			00 07
Fazakerley d				23 10				23 40			00 10
Kirkby a				23 13				23 43			00 13
Walton (Merseyside) d		22 52				23 22				23 52	
Orrell Park d		22 53				23 23				23 53	
Aintree d		22 56				23 26				23 56	
Old Roan d		22 58				23 28				23 58	
Maghull d		23 01				23 31				00 01	
Town Green d		23 05				23 35				00 05	
Aughton Park d		23 07				23 37				00 07	
Ormskirk a		23 12				23 42				00 12	
Bank Hall d	22 46		23 01		23 16		23 31		23 46		
Bootle Oriel Road d	22 48		23 03		23 18		23 33		23 48		
Bootle New Strand d	22 50		23 05		23 20		23 35		23 50		
Seaforth & Litherland d	22 52		23 07		23 22		23 37		23 52		
Waterloo (Merseyside) d	22 54		23 09		23 24		23 39		23 54		
Blundellsands & Crosby d	22 57		23 12		23 27		23 42		23 57		
Hall Road d	22 59		23 14		23 29		23 44		23 59		
Hightown d	23 02		23 17		23 32		23 47		00 02		
Formby d	23 06		23 21		23 36		23 51		00 06		
Freshfield d	23 08		23 23		23 38		23 53		00 08		
Ainsdale d	23 12		23 27		23 42		23 57		00 12		
Hillside d	23 15		23 30		23 45		23 59		00 15		
Birkdale d	23 17		23 32		23 47		00 02		00 17		
Southport a	23 22		23 37		23 52		00 07		00 22		

Table 103

Sundays until 26 September

Hunts Cross and Liverpool - Kirkby, Ormskirk and Southport

	ME	ME	ME	ME	ME	ME	ME	ME	ME	ME	ME	ME	ME	ME	ME	ME	ME	ME
Hunts Cross 89 d			08 06			08 36			09 06			09 36				10 06		
Liverpool Sth Parkway ■ 89 ✈ d			08 09			08 39			09 09			09 39				10 09		
Cressington d			08 12			08 42			09 12			09 42				10 12		
Aigburth d			08 14			08 44			09 14			09 44				10 14		
St Michaels d			08 16			08 46			09 16			09 46				10 16		
Brunswick d			08 19			08 49			09 19			09 49				10 19		
Liverpool Central ■ a			08 23			08 53			09 23			09 53				10 23		
d	08 08	08 10	08 23	08 25	08 40	08 53	08 55	09 10	09 23	09 25	09 40	09 53	09 55	10 08	10 10	10 23	10 25	10 38
Moorfields ■ d	08 10	08 12	08 25	08 27	08 42	08 55	08 57	09 12	09 25	09 27	09 42	09 55	09 57	10 10	10 12	10 25	10 27	10 40
Sandhills d	08 14	08 16	08 29	08 31	08 46	08 59	09 01	09 16	09 29	09 31	09 46	09 59	10 01	10 14	10 16	10 29	10 31	10 44
Kirkdale d		08 19		08 34	08 49		09 04	09 19		09 34	09 49		10 04		10 19		10 34	
Rice Lane d				08 37			09 07			09 37			10 07				10 37	
Fazakerley d				08 40			09 10			09 40			10 10				10 40	
Kirkby a				08 43			09 13			09 43			10 13				10 43	
Walton (Merseyside) d		08 22			08 52			09 22			09 52				10 22			
Orrell Park d		08 23			08 53			09 23			09 53				10 23			
Aintree d		08 26			08 56			09 26			09 56				10 26			
Old Roan d		08 28			08 58			09 28			09 58				10 28			
Maghull d		08 31			09 01			09 31			10 01				10 31			
Town Green d		08 35			09 05			09 35			10 05				10 35			
Aughton Park d		08 37			09 07			09 37			10 07				10 37			
Ormskirk a		08 42			09 12			09 42			10 12				10 42			
Bank Hall d	08 16		08 31			09 01			09 31			10 01		10 16		10 31		10 46
Bootle Oriel Road d	08 18		08 33			09 03			09 33			10 03		10 18		10 33		10 48
Bootle New Strand d	08 20		08 35			09 05			09 35			10 05		10 20		10 35		10 50
Seaforth & Litherland d	08 22		08 37			09 07			09 37			10 07		10 22		10 37		10 52
Waterloo (Merseyside) d	08 24		08 39			09 09			09 39			10 09		10 24		10 39		10 54
Blundellsands & Crosby d	08 27		08 42			09 12			09 42			10 12		10 27		10 42		10 57
Hall Road d	08 29		08 44			09 14			09 44			10 14		10 29		10 44		10 59
Hightown d	08 32		08 47			09 17			09 47			10 17		10 32		10 47		11 02
Formby d	08 36		08 51			09 21			09 51			10 21		10 36		10 51		11 06
Freshfield d	08 38		08 53			09 23			09 53			10 23		10 38		10 53		11 08
Ainsdale d	08 42		08 57			09 27			09 57			10 27		10 42		10 57		11 12
Hillside d	08 45		09 00			09 30			10 00			10 30		10 45		11 00		11 15
Birkdale d	08 47		09 02			09 32			10 02			10 32		10 47		11 02		11 17
Southport a	08 52		09 07			09 37			10 07			10 37		10 52		11 07		11 22

	ME	ME	ME	ME	ME	ME	ME	ME	ME	ME	ME	ME	ME	ME	ME	ME	ME	ME	ME	ME	ME	ME
Hunts Cross 89 d		10 36				11 06				11 36				12 06				12 36				13 06
Liverpool Sth Parkway ■ 89 ✈ d		10 39				11 09				11 39				12 09				12 39				13 09
Cressington d		10 42				11 12				11 42				12 12				12 42				13 12
Aigburth d		10 44				11 14				11 44				12 14				12 44				13 14
St Michaels d		10 46				11 16				11 46				12 16				12 46				13 16
Brunswick d		10 49				11 19				11 49				12 19				12 49				13 19
Liverpool Central ■ a		10 53				11 23				11 53				12 23				12 53				13 23
d	10 40	10 53	10 55	11 08	11 10	11 23	11 25	11 38	11 40	11 53	11 55	12 08	12 10	12 23	12 25	12 38	12 40	12 53	12 55	13 08	13 10	13 23
Moorfields ■ d	10 42	10 55	10 57	11 10	11 12	11 25	11 27	11 40	11 42	11 55	11 57	12 10	12 12	12 25	12 27	12 40	12 42	12 55	12 57	13 10	13 12	13 25
Sandhills d	10 46	10 59	11 01	11 14	11 16	11 29	11 31	11 44	11 46	11 59	12 01	12 14	12 16	12 29	12 31	12 44	12 46	12 59	13 01	13 14	13 16	13 29
Kirkdale d	10 49		11 04		11 19		11 34		11 49		12 04		12 19		12 34		12 49		13 04		13 19	
Rice Lane d			11 07				11 37				12 07				12 37				13 07			
Fazakerley d			11 10				11 40				12 10				12 40				13 10			
Kirkby a			11 13				11 43				12 13				12 43				13 13			
Walton (Merseyside) d	10 52				11 22				11 52				12 22				12 52				13 22	
Orrell Park d	10 53				11 23				11 53				12 23				12 53				13 23	
Aintree d	10 56				11 26				11 56				12 26				12 56				13 26	
Old Roan d	10 58				11 28				11 58				12 28				12 58				13 28	
Maghull d	11 01				11 31				12 01				12 31				13 01				13 31	
Town Green d	11 05				11 35				12 05				12 35				13 05				13 35	
Aughton Park d	11 07				11 37				12 07				12 37				13 07				13 37	
Ormskirk a	11 12				11 42				12 12				12 42				13 12				13 42	
Bank Hall d		11 01		11 16		11 31		11 46		12 01		12 16		12 31		12 46		13 01		13 16		13 31
Bootle Oriel Road d		11 03		11 18		11 33		11 48		12 03		12 18		12 33		12 48		13 03		13 18		13 33
Bootle New Strand d		11 05		11 20		11 35		11 50		12 05		12 20		12 35		12 50		13 05		13 20		13 35
Seaforth & Litherland d		11 07		11 22		11 37		11 52		12 07		12 22		12 37		12 52		13 07		13 22		13 37
Waterloo (Merseyside) d		11 09		11 24		11 39		11 54		12 09		12 24		12 39		12 54		13 09		13 24		13 39
Blundellsands & Crosby d		11 12		11 27		11 42		11 57		12 12		12 27		12 42		12 57		13 12		13 27		13 42
Hall Road d		11 14		11 29		11 44		11 59		12 14		12 29		12 44		12 59		13 14		13 29		13 44
Hightown d		11 17		11 32		11 47		12 02		12 17		12 32		12 47		13 02		13 17		13 32		13 47
Formby d		11 21		11 36		11 51		12 06		12 21		12 36		12 51		13 06		13 21		13 36		13 51
Freshfield d		11 23		11 38		11 53		12 08		12 23		12 38		12 53		13 08		13 23		13 38		13 53
Ainsdale d		11 27		11 42		11 57		12 12		12 27		12 42		12 57		13 12		13 27		13 42		13 57
Hillside d		11 30		11 45		12 00		12 15		12 30		12 45		13 00		13 15		13 30		13 45		14 00
Birkdale d		11 32		11 47		12 02		12 17		12 32		12 47		13 02		13 17		13 32		13 47		14 02
Southport a		11 37		11 52		12 07		12 22		12 37		12 52		13 07		13 22		13 37		13 52		14 07

Table 103

Sundays until 26 September

Hunts Cross and Liverpool - Kirkby, Ormskirk and Southport

	ME	ME	ME	ME	ME	ME	ME	ME	ME	ME	ME	ME	ME	ME	ME	ME	ME	ME	ME	ME	ME
Hunts Cross 89 d				13 36				14 06				14 36				15 06				15 36	
Liverpool Sth Parkway ■ 89 ✈ d				13 39				14 09				14 39				15 09				15 39	
Cressington d				13 42				14 12				14 42				15 12				15 42	
Aigburth d				13 44				14 14				14 44				15 14				15 44	
St Michaels d				13 46				14 16				14 46				15 16				15 46	
Brunswick d				13 49				14 19				14 49				15 19				15 49	
Liverpool Central ■ a				13 53				14 23				14 53				15 23				15 53	
d	13 25	13 38	13 40	13 53	13 55	14 08	14 10	14 23	14 25	14 38	14 40	14 53	14 55	15 08	15 10	15 23	15 25	15 38	15 40	15 53	15 55
Moorfields ■ d	13 27	13 40	13 42	13 55	13 57	14 10	14 12	14 25	14 27	14 40	14 42	14 55	14 57	15 10	15 12	15 25	15 27	15 40	15 42	15 55	15 57
Sandhills d	13 31	13 44	13 46	13 59	14 01	14 14	14 16	14 29	14 31	14 44	14 46	14 59	15 01	15 14	15 16	15 29	15 31	15 44	15 46	15 59	16 01
Kirkdale d	13 34		13 49		14 04		14 19		14 34		14 49		15 04		15 19		15 34		15 49		16 04
Rice Lane d	13 37				14 07				14 37				15 07				15 37				16 07
Fazakerley d	13 40				14 10				14 40				15 10				15 40				16 10
Kirkby a	13 43				14 13				14 43				15 13				15 43				16 13
Walton (Merseyside) d			13 52				14 22				14 52				15 22				15 52		
Orrell Park d			13 53				14 23				14 53				15 23				15 53		
Aintree d			13 56				14 26				14 56				15 26				15 56		
Old Roan d			13 58				14 28				14 58				15 28				15 58		
Maghull d			14 01				14 31				15 01				15 31				16 01		
Town Green d			14 05				14 35				15 05				15 35				16 05		
Aughton Park d			14 07				14 37				15 07				15 37				16 07		
Ormskirk a			14 12				14 42				15 12				15 42				16 12		
Bank Hall d		13 46		14 01		14 16		14 31		14 46		15 01		15 16		15 31		15 46		16 01	
Bootle Oriel Road d		13 48		14 03		14 18		14 33		14 48		15 03		15 18		15 33		15 48		16 03	
Bootle New Strand d		13 50		14 05		14 20		14 35		14 50		15 05		15 20		15 35		15 50		16 05	
Seaforth & Litherland d		13 52		14 07		14 22		14 37		14 52		15 07		15 22		15 37		15 52		16 07	
Waterloo (Merseyside) d		13 54		14 09		14 24		14 39		14 54		15 09		15 24		15 39		15 54		16 09	
Blundellsands & Crosby d		13 57		14 12		14 27		14 42		14 57		15 12		15 27		15 42		15 57		16 12	
Hall Road d		13 59		14 14		14 29		14 44		14 59		15 14		15 29		15 44		15 59		16 14	
Hightown d		14 02		14 17		14 32		14 47		15 02		15 17		15 32		15 47		16 02		16 17	
Formby d		14 06		14 21		14 36		14 51		15 06		15 21		15 36		15 51		16 06		16 21	
Freshfield d		14 08		14 23		14 38		14 53		15 08		15 23		15 38		15 53		16 08		16 23	
Ainsdale d		14 12		14 27		14 42		14 57		15 12		15 27		15 42		15 57		16 12		16 27	
Hillside d		14 15		14 30		14 45		15 00		15 15		15 30		15 45		16 00		16 15		16 30	
Birkdale d		14 17		14 32		14 47		15 02		15 17		15 32		15 47		16 02		16 17		16 32	
Southport a		14 22		14 37		14 52		15 07		15 22		15 37		15 52		16 07		16 22		16 37	

	ME	ME	ME	ME	ME	ME	ME	ME	ME	ME	ME	ME	ME	ME	ME	ME	ME	ME	ME	ME	ME	ME
Hunts Cross 89 d			16 06				16 36				17 06				17 36				18 06			
Liverpool Sth Parkway ■ 89 ✈ d			16 09				16 39				17 09				17 39				18 09			
Cressington d			16 12				16 42				17 12				17 42				18 12			
Aigburth d			16 14				16 44				17 14				17 44				18 14			
St Michaels d			16 16				16 46				17 16				17 46				18 16			
Brunswick d			16 19				16 49				17 19				17 49				18 19			
Liverpool Central ■ a			16 23				16 53				17 23				17 53				18 23			
d	16 08	16 10	16 23	16 25	16 38	16 40	16 53	16 55	17 08	17 10	17 23	17 25	17 38	17 40	17 53	17 55	18 08	18 10	18 23	18 25	18 38	18 40
Moorfields ■ d	16 10	16 12	16 25	16 27	16 40	16 42	16 55	16 57	17 10	17 12	17 25	17 27	17 40	17 42	17 55	17 57	18 10	18 12	18 25	18 27	18 40	18 42
Sandhills d	16 14	16 16	16 29	16 31	16 44	16 46	16 59	17 01	17 14	17 16	17 29	17 31	17 44	17 46	17 59	18 01	18 14	18 16	18 29	18 31	18 44	18 46
Kirkdale d		16 19		16 34		16 49		17 04		17 19		17 34		17 49		18 04		18 19		18 34		18 49
Rice Lane d				16 37				17 07				17 37				18 07				18 37		
Fazakerley d				16 40				17 10				17 40				18 10				18 40		
Kirkby a				16 43				17 13				17 43				18 13				18 43		
Walton (Merseyside) d		16 22				16 52				17 22				17 52				18 22				18 52
Orrell Park d		16 23				16 53				17 23				17 53				18 23				18 53
Aintree d		16 26				16 56				17 26				17 56				18 26				18 56
Old Roan d		16 28				16 58				17 28				17 58				18 28				18 58
Maghull d		16 31				17 01				17 31				18 01				18 31				19 01
Town Green d		16 35				17 05				17 35				18 05				18 35				19 05
Aughton Park d		16 37				17 07				17 37				18 07				18 37				19 07
Ormskirk a		16 42				17 12				17 42				18 12				18 42				19 12
Bank Hall d	16 16		16 31		16 46		17 01		17 16		17 31		17 46		18 01		18 16		18 31		18 46	
Bootle Oriel Road d	16 18		16 33		16 48		17 03		17 18		17 33		17 48		18 03		18 18		18 33		18 48	
Bootle New Strand d	16 20		16 35		16 50		17 05		17 20		17 35		17 50		18 05		18 20		18 35		18 50	
Seaforth & Litherland d	16 22		16 37		16 52		17 07		17 22		17 37		17 52		18 07		18 22		18 37		18 52	
Waterloo (Merseyside) d	16 24		16 39		16 54		17 09		17 24		17 39		17 54		18 09		18 24		18 39		18 54	
Blundellsands & Crosby d	16 27		16 42		16 57		17 12		17 27		17 42		17 57		18 12		18 27		18 42		18 57	
Hall Road d	16 29		16 44		16 59		17 14		17 29		17 44		17 59		18 14		18 29		18 44		18 59	
Hightown d	16 32		16 47		17 02		17 17		17 32		17 47		18 02		18 17		18 32		18 47		19 02	
Formby d	16 36		16 51		17 06		17 21		17 36		17 51		18 06		18 21		18 36		18 51		19 06	
Freshfield d	16 38		16 53		17 08		17 23		17 38		17 53		18 08		18 23		18 38		18 53		19 08	
Ainsdale d	16 42		16 57		17 12		17 27		17 42		17 57		18 12		18 27		18 42		18 57		19 12	
Hillside d	16 45		17 00		17 15		17 30		17 45		18 00		18 15		18 30		18 45		19 00		19 15	
Birkdale d	16 47		17 02		17 17		17 32		17 47		18 02		18 17		18 32		18 47		19 02		19 17	
Southport a	16 52		17 07		17 22		17 37		17 52		18 07		18 22		18 37		18 52		19 07		19 22	

Table 103

Hunts Cross and Liverpool - Kirkby, Ormskirk and Southport

Sundays
until 26 September

		ME	ME	ME	ME	ME	ME	ME	ME	ME	ME	ME	ME	ME	ME	ME	ME	ME	ME	ME	ME	ME
Hunts Cross 89	d	18 36				19 06				19 36				20 06				20 36				21 06
Liverpool Sth Parkway 89 ✈	d	18 39				19 09				19 39				20 09				20 39				21 09
Cressington	d	18 42				19 12				19 42				20 12				20 42				21 12
Aigburth	d	18 44				19 14				19 44				20 14				20 44				21 14
St Michaels	d	18 46				19 16				19 46				20 16				20 46				21 16
Brunswick	d	18 49				19 19				19 49				20 19				20 49				21 19
Liverpool Central	a	18 53				19 23				19 53				20 23				20 53				21 23
	d	18 53	18 55	19 08	19 10	19 23	19 25	19 38	19 40	19 53	19 55	20 08	20 10	20 23	20 25	20 38	20 40	20 53	20 55	21 08	21 10	21 23
Moorfields	d	18 55	18 57	19 10	19 12	19 25	19 27	19 40	19 42	19 55	19 57	20 10	20 12	20 25	20 27	20 40	20 42	20 55	20 57	21 10	21 12	21 25
Sandhills	d	18 59	19 01	19 14	19 16	19 29	19 31	19 44	19 46	19 59	20 01	20 14	20 16	20 29	20 31	20 44	20 46	20 59	21 01	21 14	21 16	21 29
Kirkdale	d		19 04		19 19		19 34		19 49		20 04		20 19		20 34		20 49		21 04		21 19	
Rice Lane	d		19 07				19 37				20 07				20 37				21 07			
Fazakerley	d		19 10				19 40				20 10				20 40				21 10			
Kirkby	a		19 13				19 43				20 13				20 43				21 13			
Walton (Merseyside)	d				19 22				19 52				20 22				20 52				21 22	
Orrell Park	d				19 23				19 53				20 23				20 53				21 23	
Aintree	d				19 26				19 56				20 26				20 56				21 26	
Old Roan	d				19 28				19 58				20 28				20 58				21 28	
Maghull	d				19 31				20 01				20 31				21 01				21 31	
Town Green	d				19 35				20 05				20 35				21 05				21 35	
Aughton Park	d				19 37				20 07				20 37				21 07				21 37	
Ormskirk	a				19 42				20 12				20 42				21 12				21 42	
Bank Hall	d	19 01		19 16		19 31		19 46		20 01		20 16		20 31		20 46		21 01		21 16		21 31
Bootle Oriel Road	d	19 03		19 18		19 33		19 48		20 03		20 18		20 33		20 48		21 03		21 18		21 33
Bootle New Strand	d	19 05		19 20		19 35		19 50		20 05		20 20		20 35		20 50		21 05		21 20		21 35
Seaforth & Litherland	d	19 07		19 22		19 37		19 52		20 07		20 22		20 37		20 52		21 07		21 22		21 37
Waterloo (Merseyside)	d	19 09		19 24		19 39		19 54		20 09		20 24		20 39		20 54		21 09		21 24		21 39
Blundellsands & Crosby	d	19 12		19 27		19 42		19 57		20 12		20 27		20 42		20 57		21 12		21 27		21 42
Hall Road	d	19 14		19 29		19 44		19 59		20 14		20 29		20 44		20 59		21 14		21 29		21 44
Hightown	d	19 17		19 32		19 47		20 02		20 17		20 32		20 47		21 02		21 17		21 32		21 47
Formby	d	19 21		19 36		19 51		20 06		20 21		20 36		20 51		21 06		21 21		21 36		21 51
Freshfield	d	19 23		19 38		19 53		20 08		20 23		20 38		20 53		21 08		21 23		21 38		21 53
Ainsdale	d	19 27		19 42		19 57		20 12		20 27		20 42		20 57		21 12		21 27		21 42		21 57
Hillside	d	19 30		19 45		20 00		20 15		20 30		20 45		21 00		21 15		21 30		21 45		22 00
Birkdale	d	19 32		19 47		20 02		20 17		20 32		20 47		21 02		21 17		21 32		21 47		22 02
Southport	a	19 37		19 52		20 07		20 22		20 37		20 52		21 07		21 22		21 37		21 52		22 07

		ME	ME	ME	ME	ME	ME	ME	ME	ME	ME	ME	ME	ME	ME	ME	ME	ME	ME	ME	ME
Hunts Cross 89	d				21 36				22 06				22 36				23 06				
Liverpool Sth Parkway 89 ✈	d				21 39				22 09				22 39				23 09				
Cressington	d				21 42				22 12				22 42				23 12				
Aigburth	d				21 44				22 14				22 44				23 14				
St Michaels	d				21 46				22 16				22 46				23 16				
Brunswick	d				21 49				22 19				22 49				23 19				
Liverpool Central	a				21 53				22 23				22 53				23 23				
	d	21 25	21 38	21 40	21 53	21 55	22 08	22 10	22 23	22 25	22 38	22 40	22 53	22 55	23 08	23 10	23 23	23 25	23 38	23 40	23 55
Moorfields	d	21 27	21 40	21 42	21 55	21 57	22 10	22 12	22 25	22 27	22 40	22 42	22 55	22 57	23 10	23 12	23 25	23 27	23 40	23 42	23 57
Sandhills	d	21 31	21 44	21 46	21 59	22 01	22 14	22 16	22 29	22 31	22 44	22 46	22 59	23 01	23 14	23 16	23a29	23 31	23 44	23 46	00 01
Kirkdale	d	21 34		21 49		22 04		22 19		22 34		22 49		23 04		23 19		23 34		23 49	00 04
Rice Lane	d	21 37				22 07				22 37				23 07				23 37			00 07
Fazakerley	d	21 40				22 10				22 40				23 10				23 40			00 10
Kirkby	a	21 43				22 13				22 43				23 13				23 43			00 13
Walton (Merseyside)	d			21 52				22 22				22 52				23 22				23 52	
Orrell Park	d			21 53				22 23				22 53				23 23				23 53	
Aintree	d			21 56				22 26				22 56				23 26				23 56	
Old Roan	d			21 58				22 28				22 58				23 28				23 58	
Maghull	d			22 01				22 31				23 01				23 31				00 01	
Town Green	d			22 05				22 35				23 05				23 35				00 05	
Aughton Park	d			22 07				22 37				23 07				23 37				00 07	
Ormskirk	a			22 12				22 42				23 12				23 42				00 12	
Bank Hall	d		21 46		22 01		22 16		22 31		22 46		23 01		23 16				23 46		
Bootle Oriel Road	d		21 48		22 03		22 18		22 33		22 48		23 03		23 18				23 48		
Bootle New Strand	d		21 50		22 05		22 20		22 35		22 50		23 05		23 20				23 50		
Seaforth & Litherland	d		21 52		22 07		22 22		22 37		22 52		23 07		23 22				23 52		
Waterloo (Merseyside)	d		21 54		22 09		22 24		22 39		22 54		23 09		23 24				23 54		
Blundellsands & Crosby	d		21 57		22 12		22 27		22 42		22 57		23 12		23 27				23 57		
Hall Road	d		21 59		22 14		22 29		22 44		22 59		23 14		23 29				23 59		
Hightown	d		22 02		22 17		22 32		22 47		23 02		23 17		23 32				00 02		
Formby	d		22 06		22 21		22 36		22 51		23 06		23 21		23 36				00 06		
Freshfield	d		22 08		22 23		22 38		22 53		23 08		23 23		23 38				00 08		
Ainsdale	d		22 12		22 27		22 42		22 57		23 12		23 27		23 42				00 12		
Hillside	d		22 15		22 30		22 45		23 00		23 15		23 30		23 45				00 15		
Birkdale	d		22 17		22 32		22 47		23 02		23 17		23 32		23 47				00 17		
Southport	a		22 22		22 37		22 52		23 07		23 22		23 37		23 52				00 22		

Table 103

Hunts Cross and Liverpool - Kirkby, Ormskirk and Southport

Sundays
from 03 October

		ME	ME	ME	ME	ME	ME	ME	ME	ME	ME	ME	ME	ME	ME	ME	ME	ME	ME
Hunts Cross 89	d			08 06			08 36			09 06			09 36			10 06			10 36
Liverpool Sth Parkway 89 ✈	d			08 09			08 39			09 09			09 39			10 09			10 39
Cressington	d			08 12			08 42			09 12			09 42			10 12			10 42
Aigburth	d			08 14			08 44			09 14			09 44			10 14			10 44
St Michaels	d			08 16			08 46			09 16			09 46			10 16			10 46
Brunswick	d			08 19			08 49			09 19			09 49			10 19			10 49
Liverpool Central	a			08 23			08 53			09 23			09 53			10 23			10 53
	d	08 08	08 10	08 23	08 25	08 40	08 53	08 55	09 10	09 23	09 25	09 40	09 53	09 55	10 10	10 23	10 25	10 40	10 53
Moorfields	d	08 10	08 12	08 25	08 27	08 42	08 55	08 57	09 12	09 25	09 27	09 42	09 55	09 57	10 12	10 25	10 27	10 42	10 55
Sandhills	d	08 14	08 16	08 29	08 31	08 46	08 59	09 01	09 16	09 29	09 31	09 46	09 59	10 01	10 16	10 29	10 31	10 46	10 59
Kirkdale	d		08 19		08 34	08 49		09 04	09 19		09 34	09 49		10 04	10 19		10 34	10 49	
Rice Lane	d				08 37			09 07			09 37			10 07			10 37		
Fazakerley	d				08 40			09 10			09 40			10 10			10 40		
Kirkby	a				08 43			09 13			09 43			10 13			10 43		
Walton (Merseyside)	d		08 22			08 52			09 22			09 52			10 22			10 52	
Orrell Park	d		08 23			08 53			09 23			09 53			10 23			10 53	
Aintree	d		08 26			08 56			09 26			09 56			10 26			10 56	
Old Roan	d		08 28			08 58			09 28			09 58			10 28			10 58	
Maghull	d		08 31			09 01			09 31			10 01			10 31			11 01	
Town Green	d		08 35			09 05			09 35			10 05			10 35			11 05	
Aughton Park	d		08 37			09 07			09 37			10 07			10 37			11 07	
Ormskirk	a		08 42			09 12			09 42			10 12			10 42			11 12	
Bank Hall	d	08 16		08 31			09 01			09 31			10 01			10 31			11 01
Bootle Oriel Road	d	08 18		08 33			09 03			09 33			10 03			10 33			11 03
Bootle New Strand	d	08 20		08 35			09 05			09 35			10 05			10 35			11 05
Seaforth & Litherland	d	08 22		08 37			09 07			09 37			10 07			10 37			11 07
Waterloo (Merseyside)	d	08 24		08 39			09 09			09 39			10 09			10 39			11 09
Blundellsands & Crosby	d	08 27		08 42			09 12			09 42			10 12			10 42			11 12
Hall Road	d	08 29		08 44			09 14			09 44			10 14			10 44			11 14
Hightown	d	08 32		08 47			09 17			09 47			10 17			10 47			11 17
Formby	d	08 36		08 51			09 21			09 51			10 21			10 51			11 21
Freshfield	d	08 38		08 53			09 23			09 53			10 23			10 53			11 23
Ainsdale	d	08 42		08 57			09 27			09 57			10 27			10 57			11 27
Hillside	d	08 45		09 00			09 30			10 00			10 30			11 00			11 30
Birkdale	d	08 47		09 02			09 32			10 02			10 32			11 02			11 32
Southport	a	08 52		09 07			09 37			10 07			10 37			11 07			11 37

		ME	ME	ME	ME	ME	ME	ME	ME	ME	ME	ME	ME	ME	ME	ME	ME	ME	ME	ME	ME	ME	ME
Hunts Cross 89	d			11 06			11 36			12 06			12 36			13 06			13 36			14 06	
Liverpool Sth Parkway 89 ✈	d			11 09			11 39			12 09			12 39			13 09			13 39			14 09	
Cressington	d			11 12			11 42			12 12			12 42			13 12			13 42			14 12	
Aigburth	d			11 14			11 44			12 14			12 44			13 14			13 44			14 14	
St Michaels	d			11 16			11 46			12 16			12 46			13 16			13 46			14 16	
Brunswick	d			11 19			11 49			12 19			12 49			13 19			13 49			14 19	
Liverpool Central	a			11 23			11 53			12 23			12 53			13 23			13 53			14 23	
	d	10 55	11 10	11 23	11 25	11 40	11 53	11 55	12 10	12 23	12 25	12 40	12 53	12 55	13 10	13 23	13 25	13 40	13 53	13 55	14 10	14 23	14 25
Moorfields	d	10 57	11 12	11 25	11 27	11 42	11 55	11 57	12 12	12 25	12 27	12 42	12 55	12 57	13 12	13 25	13 27	13 42	13 55	13 57	14 12	14 25	14 27
Sandhills	d	11 01	11 16	11 29	11 31	11 46	11 59	12 01	12 16	12 29	12 31	12 46	12 59	13 01	13 16	13 29	13 31	13 46	13 59	14 01	14 16	14 29	14 31
Kirkdale	d	11 04	11 19		11 34	11 49		12 04	12 19		12 34	12 49		13 04	13 19		13 34	13 49		14 04	14 19		14 34
Rice Lane	d	11 07			11 37			12 07			12 37			13 07			13 37			14 07			14 37
Fazakerley	d	11 10			11 40			12 10			12 40			13 10			13 40			14 10			14 40
Kirkby	a	11 13			11 43			12 13			12 43			13 13			13 43			14 13			14 43
Walton (Merseyside)	d		11 22			11 52			12 22			12 52			13 22			13 52			14 22		
Orrell Park	d		11 23			11 53			12 23			12 53			13 23			13 53			14 23		
Aintree	d		11 26			11 56			12 26			12 56			13 26			13 56			14 26		
Old Roan	d		11 28			11 58			12 28			12 58			13 28			13 58			14 28		
Maghull	d		11 31			12 01			12 31			13 01			13 31			14 01			14 31		
Town Green	d		11 35			12 05			12 35			13 05			13 35			14 05			14 35		
Aughton Park	d		11 37			12 07			12 37			13 07			13 37			14 07			14 37		
Ormskirk	a		11 42			12 12			12 42			13 12			13 42			14 12			14 42		
Bank Hall	d			11 31			12 01			12 31			13 01			13 31			14 01			14 31	
Bootle Oriel Road	d			11 33			12 03			12 33			13 03			13 33			14 03			14 33	
Bootle New Strand	d			11 35			12 05			12 35			13 05			13 35			14 05			14 35	
Seaforth & Litherland	d			11 37			12 07			12 37			13 07			13 37			14 07			14 37	
Waterloo (Merseyside)	d			11 39			12 09			12 39			13 09			13 39			14 09			14 39	
Blundellsands & Crosby	d			11 42			12 12			12 42			13 12			13 42			14 12			14 42	
Hall Road	d			11 44			12 14			12 44			13 14			13 44			14 14			14 44	
Hightown	d			11 47			12 17			12 47			13 17			13 47			14 17			14 47	
Formby	d			11 51			12 21			12 51			13 21			13 51			14 21			14 51	
Freshfield	d			11 53			12 23			12 53			13 23			13 53			14 23			14 53	
Ainsdale	d			11 57			12 27			12 57			13 27			13 57			14 27			14 57	
Hillside	d			12 00			12 30			13 00			13 30			14 00			14 30			15 00	
Birkdale	d			12 02			12 32			13 02			13 32			14 02			14 32			15 02	
Southport	a			12 07			12 37			13 07			13 37			14 07			14 37			15 07	

Hunts Cross and Liverpool - Kirkby, Ormskirk and Southport

	ME		ME	ME	ME	ME	ME	ME	ME	ME	ME		ME	ME	ME	ME	ME	ME	ME	ME	ME		ME	ME
Hunts Cross 89 d			14 36			15 06			15 36				16 06			16 36			17 06				17 36	
Liverpool Sth Parkway [7] 89 d			14 39			15 09			15 39				16 09			16 39			17 09				17 39	
Cressington d			14 42			15 12			15 42				16 12			16 42			17 12				17 42	
Aigburth d			14 44			15 14			15 44				16 14			16 44			17 14				17 44	
St Michaels d			14 46			15 16			15 46				16 16			16 46			17 16				17 46	
Brunswick d			14 49			15 19			15 49				16 19			16 49			17 19				17 49	
Liverpool Central [10] a			14 53			15 23			15 53				16 23			16 53			17 23				17 53	
d	14 40		14 53	14 55	15 10	15 23	15 25	15 40	15 53	15 55	16 10		16 23	16 25	16 40	16 53	16 55	17 10	17 23	17 25	17 40		17 53	17 55
Moorfields [10] d	14 42		14 55	14 57	15 12	15 25	15 27	15 42	15 55	15 57	16 12		16 25	16 27	16 42	16 55	16 57	17 12	17 25	17 27	17 42		17 55	17 57
Sandhills d	14 46		14 59	15 01	15 16	15 29	15 31	15 46	15 59	16 01	16 16		16 29	16 31	16 46	16 59	17 01	17 16	17 29	17 31	17 46		17 59	18 01
Kirkdale d	14 49			15 04	15 19		15 34	15 49		16 04	16 19			16 34	16 49		17 04	17 19		17 34	17 49			18 04
Rice Lane d				15 07			15 37			16 07				16 37			17 07			17 37				18 07
Fazakerley d				15 10			15 40			16 10				16 40			17 10			17 40				18 10
Kirkby a				15 13			15 43			16 13				16 43			17 13			17 43				18 13
Walton (Merseyside) d	14 52				15 22			15 52			16 22				16 52			17 22			17 52			
Orrell Park d	14 53				15 23			15 53			16 23				16 53			17 23			17 53			
Aintree d	14 56				15 26			15 56			16 26				16 56			17 26			17 56			
Old Roan d	14 58				15 28			15 58			16 28				16 58			17 28			17 58			
Maghull d	15 01				15 31			16 01			16 31				17 01			17 31			18 01			
Town Green d	15 05				15 35			16 05			16 35				17 05			17 35			18 05			
Aughton Park d	15 07				15 37			16 07			16 37				17 07			17 37			18 07			
Ormskirk a	15 12				15 42			16 12			16 42				17 12			17 42			18 12			
Bank Hall d			15 01			15 31			16 01				16 31			17 01			17 31				18 01	
Bootle Oriel Road d			15 03			15 33			16 03				16 33			17 03			17 33				18 03	
Bootle New Strand d			15 05			15 35			16 05				16 35			17 05			17 35				18 05	
Seaforth & Litherland d			15 07			15 37			16 07				16 37			17 07			17 37				18 07	
Waterloo (Merseyside) d			15 09			15 39			16 09				16 39			17 09			17 39				18 09	
Blundellsands & Crosby d			15 12			15 42			16 12				16 42			17 12			17 42				18 12	
Hall Road d			15 14			15 44			16 14				16 44			17 14			17 44				18 14	
Hightown d			15 17			15 47			16 17				16 47			17 17			17 47				18 17	
Formby d			15 21			15 51			16 21				16 51			17 21			17 51				18 21	
Freshfield d			15 23			15 53			16 23				16 53			17 23			17 53				18 23	
Ainsdale d			15 27			15 57			16 27				16 57			17 27			17 57				18 27	
Hillside d			15 30			16 00			16 30				17 00			17 30			18 00				18 30	
Birkdale d			15 32			16 02			16 32				17 02			17 32			18 02				18 32	
Southport a			15 37			16 07			16 37				17 07			17 37			18 07				18 37	

	ME	ME	ME	ME	ME	ME	ME		ME	ME	ME	ME	ME	ME	ME	ME	ME		ME	ME	ME	ME	ME	ME
Hunts Cross 89 d		18 06			18 36				19 06			19 36			20 06				20 36			21 06		
Liverpool Sth Parkway [7] 89 d		18 09			18 39				19 09			19 39			20 09				20 39			21 09		
Cressington d		18 12			18 42				19 12			19 42			20 12				20 42			21 12		
Aigburth d		18 14			18 44				19 14			19 44			20 14				20 44			21 14		
St Michaels d		18 16			18 46				19 16			19 46			20 16				20 46			21 16		
Brunswick d		18 19			18 49				19 19			19 49			20 19				20 49			21 19		
Liverpool Central [10] a		18 23			18 53				19 23			19 53			20 23				20 53			21 23		
d	18 10	18 23	18 25	18 40	18 53	18 55	19 10		19 23	19 25	19 40	19 53	19 55	20 10	20 23	20 25	20 40		20 53	20 55	21 10	21 23	21 25	21 40
Moorfields [10] d	18 12	18 25	18 27	18 42	18 55	18 57	19 12		19 25	19 27	19 42	19 55	19 57	20 12	20 25	20 27	20 42		20 55	20 57	21 12	21 25	21 27	21 42
Sandhills d	18 16	18 29	18 31	18 46	18 59	19 01	19 16		19 29	19 31	19 46	19 59	20 01	20 16	20 29	20 31	20 46		20 59	21 01	21 16	21 29	21 31	21 46
Kirkdale d	18 19		18 34	18 49		19 04	19 19			19 34	19 49		20 04	20 19		20 34	20 49			21 04	21 19		21 34	21 49
Rice Lane d			18 37			19 07				19 37			20 07			20 37				21 07			21 37	
Fazakerley d			18 40			19 10				19 40			20 10			20 40				21 10			21 40	
Kirkby a			18 43			19 13				19 43			20 13			20 43				21 13			21 43	
Walton (Merseyside) d	18 22			18 52			19 22				19 52			20 22			20 52				21 22			21 52
Orrell Park d	18 23			18 53			19 23				19 53			20 23			20 53				21 23			21 53
Aintree d	18 26			18 56			19 26				19 56			20 26			20 56				21 26			21 56
Old Roan d	18 28			18 58			19 28				19 58			20 28			20 58				21 28			21 58
Maghull d	18 31			19 01			19 31				20 01			20 31			21 01				21 31			22 01
Town Green d	18 35			19 05			19 35				20 05			20 35			21 05				21 35			22 05
Aughton Park d	18 37			19 07			19 37				20 07			20 37			21 07				21 37			22 07
Ormskirk a	18 42			19 12			19 42				20 12			20 42			21 12				21 42			22 12
Bank Hall d		18 31			19 01				19 31			20 01			20 31				21 01			21 31		
Bootle Oriel Road d		18 33			19 03				19 33			20 03			20 33				21 03			21 33		
Bootle New Strand d		18 35			19 05				19 35			20 05			20 35				21 05			21 35		
Seaforth & Litherland d		18 37			19 07				19 37			20 07			20 37				21 07			21 37		
Waterloo (Merseyside) d		18 39			19 09				19 39			20 09			20 39				21 09			21 39		
Blundellsands & Crosby d		18 42			19 12				19 42			20 12			20 42				21 12			21 42		
Hall Road d		18 44			19 14				19 44			20 14			20 44				21 14			21 44		
Hightown d		18 47			19 17				19 47			20 17			20 47				21 17			21 47		
Formby d		18 51			19 21				19 51			20 21			20 51				21 21			21 51		
Freshfield d		18 53			19 23				19 53			20 23			20 53				21 23			21 53		
Ainsdale d		18 57			19 27				19 57			20 27			20 57				21 27			21 57		
Hillside d		19 00			19 30				20 00			20 30			21 00				21 30			22 00		
Birkdale d		19 02			19 32				20 02			20 32			21 02				21 32			22 02		
Southport a		19 07			19 37				20 07			20 37			21 07				21 37			22 07		

Hunts Cross and Liverpool - Kirkby, Ormskirk and Southport

	ME	ME	ME		ME	ME	ME	ME	ME	ME	ME	ME	ME		ME	ME
Hunts Cross 89 d	21 36				22 06			22 36			23 06					
Liverpool Sth Parkway [7] 89 d	21 39				22 09			22 39			23 09					
Cressington d	21 42				22 12			22 42			23 12					
Aigburth d	21 44				22 14			22 44			23 14					
St Michaels d	21 46				22 16			22 46			23 16					
Brunswick d	21 49				22 19			22 49			23 19					
Liverpool Central [10] a	21 53				22 23			22 53			23 23					
d	21 53	21 55	22 10		22 23	22 25	22 40	22 53	22 55	23 10	23 23	23 25	23 38		23 40	23 55
Moorfields [10] d	21 55	21 57	22 12		22 25	22 27	22 42	22 55	22 57	23 12	23 25	23 27	23 40		23 42	23 57
Sandhills d	21 59	22 01	22 16		22 29	22 31	22 46	22 59	23 01	23 16	23 29	23 31	23 44		23 46	00 01
Kirkdale d		22 04	22 19			22 34	22 49		23 04	23 19		23 34			23 49	00 04
Rice Lane d		22 07				22 37			23 07			23 37				00 07
Fazakerley d		22 10				22 40			23 10			23 40				00 10
Kirkby a		22 13				22 43			23 13			23 43				00 13
Walton (Merseyside) d			22 22				22 52			23 22					23 52	
Orrell Park d			22 23				22 53			23 23					23 53	
Aintree d			22 26				22 56			23 26					23 56	
Old Roan d			22 28				22 58			23 28					23 58	
Maghull d			22 31				23 01			23 31					00 01	
Town Green d			22 35				23 05			23 35					00 05	
Aughton Park d			22 37				23 07			23 37					00 07	
Ormskirk a			22 42				23 12			23 42					00 12	
Bank Hall d	22 01				22 31			23 01			23 31		23 46			
Bootle Oriel Road d	22 03				22 33			23 03			23 33		23 48			
Bootle New Strand d	22 05				22 35			23 05			23 35		23 50			
Seaforth & Litherland d	22 07				22 37			23 07			23 37		23 52			
Waterloo (Merseyside) d	22 09				22 39			23 09			23 39		23 54			
Blundellsands & Crosby d	22 12				22 42			23 12			23 42		23 57			
Hall Road d	22 14				22 44			23 14			23 44		23 59			
Hightown d	22 17				22 47			23 17			23 47		00 02			
Formby d	22 21				22 51			23 21			23 51		00 06			
Freshfield d	22 23				22 53			23 23			23 53		00 08			
Ainsdale d	22 27				22 57			23 27			23 57		00 12			
Hillside d	22 30				23 00			23 30			23 59		00 15			
Birkdale d	22 32				23 02			23 32			00 02		00 17			
Southport a	22 37				23 07			23 37			00 07		00 22			

Southport, Ormskirk and Kirkby - Liverpool and Hunts Cross

				ME	ME	ME	ME	ME SO	ME SX	ME		ME	ME	ME	ME	ME	ME	ME	ME	ME SX		ME SO	ME	ME	ME
Southport	d						05 43			05 58			06 13		06 28		06 43			06 58		06 58			07 13
Birkdale	d						05 47			06 02			06 17		06 32		06 47			07 02		07 02			07 17
Hillside	d						05 49			06 04			06 19		06 34		06 49			07 04		07 04			07 19
Ainsdale	d						05 52			06 07			06 22		06 37		06 52			07 07		07 07			07 22
Freshfield	d						05 56			06 11			06 26		06 41		06 56			07 11		07 11			07 26
Formby	d						05 58			06 13			06 28		06 43		06 58			07 13		07 13			07 28
Hightown	d						06 02			06 17			06 32		06 47		07 02			07 17		07 17			07 32
Hall Road	d						06 05			06 20			06 35		06 50		07 05			07 20		07 20			07 35
Blundellsands & Crosby	d						06 07			06 22			06 37		06 52		07 07			07 22		07 22			07 37
Waterloo (Merseyside)	d						06 10			06 25			06 40		06 55		07 10			07 25		07 25			07 40
Seaforth & Litherland	d						06 12			06 27			06 42		06 57		07 12			07 27		07 27			07 42
Bootle New Strand	d						06 15			06 30			06 45		07 00		07 15			07 30		07 30			07 45
Bootle Oriel Road	d						06 16			06 31			06 46		07 01		07 16			07 31		07 31			07 46
Bank Hall	d						06 18			06 33			06 48		07 03		07 18			07 33		07 33			07 48
Ormskirk	d					05 50						06 20				06 50			07 05					07 20	
Aughton Park	d					05 53						06 23				06 53			07 08					07 23	
Town Green	d					05 55						06 25				06 55			07 10					07 25	
Maghull	d					06 00						06 30				07 00			07 15					07 30	
Old Roan	d					06 03						06 33				07 03			07 18					07 33	
Aintree	d					06 05						06 35				07 05			07 20					07 35	
Orrell Park	d					06 07						06 37				07 07			07 22					07 37	
Walton (Merseyside)	d					06 09						06 39				07 09			07 24					07 39	
Kirkby	d			05 48				06 18	06 18					06 48				07 13					07 28		
Fazakerley	d			05 51				06 21	06 21					06 51				07 16					07 31		
Rice Lane	d			05 54				06 24	06 24					06 54				07 19					07 34		
Kirkdale	d			05 57		06 12		06 27	06 27			06 42		06 57		07 12		07 22	07 27				07 37	07 42	
Sandhills	d			06 00	06 06	06 14	06 21	06 30	06 30	06 36		06 44	06 51	07 00	07 06	07 14	07 21	07 25	07 29	07 36		07 36	07 40	07 44	07 51
Moorfields 10	d			06 03	06 10	06 18	06 25	06 33	06 33	06 40		06 48	06 55	07 03	07 10	07 18	07 25	07 28	07 33	07 40		07 40	07 43	07 48	07 55
Liverpool Central 10	a			06 06	06 13	06 20	06 28	06 36	06 36	06 43		06 50	06 58	07 06	07 13	07 20	07 28	07 31	07 35	07 43		07 43	07 46	07 50	07 58
	d				06 14		06 29			06 43			06 59		07 14		07 29			07 44		07 44			07 59
Brunswick	d				06 17		06 32			06 47			07 02		07 17		07 32			07 47		07 47			08 02
St Michaels	d				06 20		06 35			06 49			07 05		07 20		07 35			07 50		07 50			08 05
Aigburth	d				06 22		06 37			06 52			07 07		07 22		07 37			07 52		07 52			08 07
Cressington	d				06 24		06 39			06 54			07 09		07 24		07 39			07 54		07 54			08 09
Liverpool Sth Parkway 7 89 ✈	d				06 27		06 42			06 56			07 12		07 27		07 42			07 57		07 57			08 12
Hunts Cross 89	a				06 31		06 46			07 01			07 16		07 31		07 46			08 01		08 01			08 16

		ME	ME	ME	ME	ME		ME	ME	ME SX	ME		ME	ME	ME SX	ME			ME	ME	ME	ME	ME	ME	ME
Southport	d			07 28				07 43		07 48			07 58		08 03				08 13			08 28			08 43
Birkdale	d			07 32				07 47		07 52			08 02		08 07				08 17			08 32			08 47
Hillside	d			07 34				07 49		07 54			08 04		08 09				08 19			08 34			08 49
Ainsdale	d			07 37				07 52		07 57			08 07		08 12				08 22			08 37			08 52
Freshfield	d			07 41				07 56		08 01			08 11		08 16				08 26			08 41			08 56
Formby	d			07 43				07 58		08 03			08 13		08 18				08 28			08 43			08 58
Hightown	d			07 47				08 02		08 07			08 17		08 22				08 32			08 47			09 02
Hall Road	d			07 50				08 05		08 10			08 20		08 25				08 35			08 50			09 05
Blundellsands & Crosby	d			07 52				08 07		08 12			08 22		08 27				08 37			08 52			09 07
Waterloo (Merseyside)	d			07 55				08 10		08 15			08 25		08 30				08 40			08 55			09 10
Seaforth & Litherland	d			07 57				08 12		08 17			08 27		08 32				08 42			08 57			09 12
Bootle New Strand	d			08 00				08 15		08 20			08 30		08 35				08 45			09 00			09 15
Bootle Oriel Road	d			08 01				08 16		08 21			08 31		08 36				08 46			09 01			09 16
Bank Hall	d			08 03				08 18		08 23			08 33		08 38				08 48			09 03			09 18
Ormskirk	d		07 35			07 50					08 05					08 20					08 35			08 50	
Aughton Park	d		07 38			07 53					08 08					08 23					08 38			08 53	
Town Green	d		07 40			07 55					08 10					08 25					08 40			08 55	
Maghull	d		07 45			08 00					08 15					08 30					08 45			09 00	
Old Roan	d		07 48			08 03					08 18					08 33					08 48			09 03	
Aintree	d		07 50			08 05					08 20					08 35					08 50			09 05	
Orrell Park	d		07 52			08 07					08 22					08 37					08 52			09 07	
Walton (Merseyside)	d		07 54			08 09					08 24					08 39					08 54			09 09	
Kirkby	d	07 43			07 58				08 13					08 28						08 43			08 58		
Fazakerley	d	07 46			08 01				08 16					08 31						08 46			09 01		
Rice Lane	d	07 49			08 04				08 19					08 34						08 49			09 04		
Kirkdale	d	07 52	07 57		08 07	08 12			08 22		08 27			08 37		08 42				08 52	08 57		09 07	09 12	
Sandhills	d	07 55	07 59	08 06	08 10	08 14		08 21	08 25	08 27	08 29		08 36	08 40	08 42	08 44			08 51	08 55	08 59	09 06	09 10	09 14	09 21
Moorfields 10	d	07 58	08 03	08 10	08 13	08 18		08 25	08 28	08 31	08 33		08 40	08 43	08 46	08 48			08 55	08 58	09 03	09 10	09 13	09 18	09 25
Liverpool Central 10	a	08 01	08 05	08 13	08 16	08 20		08 28	08 31	08 33	08 35		08 43	08 46	08 48	08 50			08 58	09 01	09 05	09 13	09 16	09 20	09 28
	d			08 14				08 29					08 44						08 59			09 14			09 29
Brunswick	d			08 17				08 32					08 47						09 02			09 17			09 32
St Michaels	d			08 20				08 35					08 50						09 05			09 20			09 35
Aigburth	d			08 22				08 37					08 52						09 07			09 22			09 37
Cressington	d			08 24				08 39					08 54						09 09			09 24			09 39
Liverpool Sth Parkway 7 89 ✈	d			08 27				08 42					08 57						09 12			09 27			09 42
Hunts Cross 89	a			08 31				08 46					09 01						09 16			09 31			09 46

Southport, Ormskirk and Kirkby - Liverpool and Hunts Cross

		ME		ME	ME	ME	ME	ME	ME	ME	ME	ME		ME	ME	ME	ME	ME	ME	ME	ME	ME		ME	ME
Southport	d				08 58			09 13			09 28				09 43			09 58			10 13				10 28
Birkdale	d				09 02			09 17			09 32				09 47			10 02			10 17				10 32
Hillside	d				09 04			09 19			09 34				09 49			10 04			10 19				10 34
Ainsdale	d				09 07			09 22			09 37				09 52			10 07			10 22				10 37
Freshfield	d				09 11			09 26			09 41				09 56			10 11			10 26				10 41
Formby	d				09 13			09 28			09 43				09 58			10 13			10 28				10 43
Hightown	d				09 17			09 32			09 47				10 02			10 17			10 32				10 47
Hall Road	d				09 20			09 35			09 50				10 05			10 20			10 35				10 50
Blundellsands & Crosby	d				09 22			09 37			09 52				10 07			10 22			10 37				10 52
Waterloo (Merseyside)	d				09 25			09 40			09 55				10 10			10 25			10 40				10 55
Seaforth & Litherland	d				09 27			09 42			09 57				10 12			10 27			10 42				10 57
Bootle New Strand	d				09 30			09 45			10 00				10 15			10 30			10 45				11 00
Bootle Oriel Road	d				09 31			09 46			10 01				10 16			10 31			10 46				11 01
Bank Hall	d				09 33			09 48			10 03				10 18			10 33			10 48				11 03
Ormskirk	d			09 05			09 20			09 35				09 50			10 05			10 20				10 35	
Aughton Park	d			09 08			09 23			09 38				09 53			10 08			10 23				10 38	
Town Green	d			09 10			09 25			09 40				09 55			10 10			10 25				10 40	
Maghull	d			09 15			09 30			09 45				10 00			10 15			10 30				10 45	
Old Roan	d			09 18			09 33			09 48				10 03			10 18			10 33				10 48	
Aintree	d			09 20			09 35			09 50				10 05			10 20			10 35				10 50	
Orrell Park	d			09 22			09 37			09 52				10 07			10 22			10 37				10 52	
Walton (Merseyside)	d			09 24			09 39			09 54				10 09			10 24			10 39				10 54	
Kirkby	d	09 13				09 28			09 43			09 58				10 13			10 28			10 43			
Fazakerley	d	09 16				09 31			09 46			10 01				10 16			10 31			10 46			
Rice Lane	d	09 19				09 34			09 49			10 04				10 19			10 34			10 49			
Kirkdale	d	09 22		09 27		09 37	09 42		09 52	09 57		10 07		10 12		10 22	10 27		10 37	10 42		10 52		10 57	
Sandhills	d	09 25		09 29	09 36	09 40	09 44	09 51	09 55	09 59	10 06	10 10		10 14	10 21	10 25	10 29	10 36	10 40	10 44	10 51	10 55		10 59	11 06
Moorfields 10	d	09 28		09 33	09 40	09 43	09 48	09 55	09 58	10 03	10 10	10 13		10 18	10 25	10 28	10 33	10 40	10 43	10 48	10 55	10 58		11 03	11 10
Liverpool Central 10	a	09 31		09 35	09 43	09 46	09 50	09 58	10 01	10 05	10 13	10 16		10 20	10 28	10 31	10 35	10 43	10 46	10 50	10 58	11 01		11 05	11 13
	d				09 44			09 59			10 14				10 29			10 44			10 59				11 14
Brunswick	d				09 47			10 02			10 17				10 32			10 47			11 02				11 17
St Michaels	d				09 50			10 05			10 20				10 35			10 50			11 05				11 20
Aigburth	d				09 52			10 07			10 22				10 37			10 52			11 07				11 22
Cressington	d				09 54			10 09			10 24				10 39			10 54			11 09				11 24
Liverpool Sth Parkway 7 89 ✈	d				09 57			10 12			10 27				10 42			10 57			11 12				11 27
Hunts Cross 89	a				10 01			10 16			10 31				10 46			11 01			11 16				11 31

		ME	ME	ME	ME	ME	ME	ME		ME	ME	ME	ME	ME	ME	ME	ME	ME		ME	ME	ME	ME	ME	ME
Southport	d			10 43			10 58				11 13			11 28			11 43				11 58			12 13	
Birkdale	d			10 47			11 02				11 17			11 32			11 47				12 02			12 17	
Hillside	d			10 49			11 04				11 19			11 34			11 49				12 04			12 19	
Ainsdale	d			10 52			11 07				11 22			11 37			11 52				12 07			12 22	
Freshfield	d			10 56			11 11				11 26			11 41			11 56				12 11			12 26	
Formby	d			10 58			11 13				11 28			11 43			11 58				12 13			12 28	
Hightown	d			11 02			11 17				11 32			11 47			12 02				12 17			12 32	
Hall Road	d			11 05			11 20				11 35			11 50			12 05				12 20			12 35	
Blundellsands & Crosby	d			11 07			11 22				11 37			11 52			12 07				12 22			12 37	
Waterloo (Merseyside)	d			11 10			11 25				11 40			11 55			12 10				12 25			12 40	
Seaforth & Litherland	d			11 12			11 27				11 42			11 57			12 12				12 27			12 42	
Bootle New Strand	d			11 15			11 30				11 45			12 00			12 15				12 30			12 45	
Bootle Oriel Road	d			11 16			11 31				11 46			12 01			12 16				12 31			12 46	
Bank Hall	d			11 18			11 33				11 48			12 03			12 18				12 33			12 48	
Ormskirk	d		10 50			11 05				11 20			11 35			11 50				12 05			12 20		
Aughton Park	d		10 53			11 08				11 23			11 38			11 53				12 08			12 23		
Town Green	d		10 55			11 10				11 25			11 40			11 55				12 10			12 25		
Maghull	d		11 00			11 15				11 30			11 45			12 00				12 15			12 30		
Old Roan	d		11 03			11 18				11 33			11 48			12 03				12 18			12 33		
Aintree	d		11 05			11 20				11 35			11 50			12 05				12 20			12 35		
Orrell Park	d		11 07			11 22				11 37			11 52			12 07				12 22			12 37		
Walton (Merseyside)	d		11 09			11 24				11 39			11 54			12 09				12 24			12 39		
Kirkby	d	10 58			11 13			11 28				11 43			11 58			12 13				12 28			12 43
Fazakerley	d	11 01			11 16			11 31				11 46			12 01			12 16				12 31			12 46
Rice Lane	d	11 04			11 19			11 34				11 49			12 04			12 19				12 34			12 49
Kirkdale	d	11 07	11 12		11 22	11 27		11 37		11 42		11 52	11 57		12 07	12 12		12 22		12 27		12 37	12 42		12 52
Sandhills	d	11 10	11 14	11 21	11 25	11 29	11 36	11 40		11 44	11 51	11 55	11 59	12 06	12 10	12 14	12 21	12 25		12 29	12 36	12 40	12 44	12 51	12 55
Moorfields 10	d	11 13	11 18	11 25	11 28	11 33	11 40	11 43		11 48	11 55	11 58	12 03	12 10	12 13	12 18	12 25	12 28		12 33	12 40	12 43	12 48	12 55	12 58
Liverpool Central 10	a	11 16	11 20	11 28	11 31	11 35	11 43	11 46		11 50	11 58	12 01	12 05	12 13	12 16	12 20	12 28	12 31		12 35	12 43	12 46	12 50	12 58	13 01
	d			11 29			11 44				11 59			12 14			12 29				12 44			12 59	
Brunswick	d			11 32			11 47				12 02			12 17			12 32				12 47			13 02	
St Michaels	d			11 35			11 50				12 05			12 20			12 35				12 50			13 05	
Aigburth	d			11 37			11 52				12 07			12 22			12 37				12 52			13 07	
Cressington	d			11 39			11 54				12 09			12 24			12 39				12 54			13 09	
Liverpool Sth Parkway 7 89 ✈	d			11 42			11 57				12 12			12 27			12 42				12 57			13 12	
Hunts Cross 89	a			11 46			12 01				12 16			12 31			12 46				13 01			13 16	

Southport, Ormskirk and Kirkby - Liverpool and Hunts Cross

		ME	ME	ME	ME	ME	ME	ME	ME	ME	ME	ME	ME	ME	ME	ME	ME	ME	ME	ME	ME	ME
Southport	d		12 28			12 43			12 58			13 13			13 28			13 43			13 58	
Birkdale	d		12 32			12 47			13 02			13 17			13 32			13 47			14 02	
Hillside	d		12 34			12 49			13 04			13 19			13 34			13 49			14 04	
Ainsdale	d		12 37			12 52			13 07			13 22			13 37			13 52			14 07	
Freshfield	d		12 41			12 56			13 11			13 26			13 41			13 56			14 11	
Formby	d		12 43			12 58			13 13			13 28			13 43			13 58			14 13	
Hightown	d		12 47			13 02			13 17			13 32			13 47			14 02			14 17	
Hall Road	d		12 50			13 05			13 20			13 35			13 50			14 05			14 20	
Blundellsands & Crosby	d		12 52			13 07			13 22			13 37			13 52			14 07			14 22	
Waterloo (Merseyside)	d		12 55			13 10			13 25			13 40			13 55			14 10			14 25	
Seaforth & Litherland	d		12 57			13 12			13 27			13 42			13 57			14 12			14 27	
Bootle New Strand	d		13 00			13 15			13 30			13 45			14 00			14 15			14 30	
Bootle Oriel Road	d		13 01			13 16			13 31			13 46			14 01			14 16			14 31	
Bank Hall	d		13 03			13 18			13 33			13 48			14 03			14 18			14 33	
Ormskirk	d	12 35			12 50			13 05			13 20			13 35			13 50			14 05		
Aughton Park	d	12 38			12 53			13 08			13 23			13 38			13 53			14 08		
Town Green	d	12 40			12 55			13 10			13 25			13 40			13 55			14 10		
Maghull	d	12 45			13 00			13 15			13 30			13 45			14 00			14 15		
Old Roan	d	12 48			13 03			13 18			13 33			13 48			14 03			14 18		
Aintree	d	12 50			13 05			13 20			13 35			13 50			14 05			14 20		
Orrell Park	d	12 52			13 07			13 22			13 37			13 52			14 07			14 22		
Walton (Merseyside)	d	12 54			13 09			13 24			13 39			13 54			14 09			14 24		
Kirkby	d			12 58			13 13			13 28			13 43			13 58			14 13			14 28
Fazakerley	d			13 01			13 16			13 31			13 46			14 01			14 16			14 31
Rice Lane	d			13 04			13 19			13 34			13 49			14 04			14 19			14 34
Kirkdale	d	12 57		13 07	13 12		13 22	13 27		13 37	13 42		13 52	13 57		14 07	14 12		14 22	14 27		14 37
Sandhills	d	12 59	13 06	13 10	13 14	13 21	13 25	13 29	13 36	13 40	13 44	13 51	13 55	13 59	14 06	14 10	14 14	14 21	14 25	14 29	14 36	14 40
Moorfields ■10	d	13 03	13 10	13 13	13 18	13 25	13 28	13 33	13 40	13 43	13 48	13 55	13 58	14 03	14 10	14 13	14 18	14 25	14 28	14 33	14 40	14 43
Liverpool Central ■10	a	13 05	13 13	13 16	13 20	13 28	13 31	13 35	13 43	13 46	13 50	13 58	14 01	14 05	14 13	14 16	14 20	14 28	14 31	14 35	14 43	14 46
	d		13 14			13 29			13 44			13 59			14 14			14 29			14 44	
Brunswick	d		13 17			13 32			13 47			14 02			14 17			14 32			14 47	
St Michaels	d		13 20			13 35			13 50			14 05			14 20			14 35			14 50	
Aigburth	d		13 22			13 37			13 52			14 07			14 22			14 37			14 52	
Cressington	d		13 24			13 39			13 54			14 09			14 24			14 39			14 54	
Liverpool Sth Parkway ■7 89 ✈	d		13 27			13 42			13 57			14 12			14 27			14 42			14 57	
Hunts Cross 89	a		13 31			13 46			14 01			14 16			14 31			14 46			15 01	

		ME	ME	ME	ME	ME	ME	ME	ME	ME	ME	ME	ME	ME	ME	ME	ME	ME	ME	ME	ME	ME	ME
Southport	d		14 13			14 28			14 43			14 58			15 13			15 28			15 43		
Birkdale	d		14 17			14 32			14 47			15 02			15 17			15 32			15 47		
Hillside	d		14 19			14 34			14 49			15 04			15 19			15 34			15 49		
Ainsdale	d		14 22			14 37			14 52			15 07			15 22			15 37			15 52		
Freshfield	d		14 26			14 41			14 56			15 11			15 26			15 41			15 56		
Formby	d		14 28			14 43			14 58			15 13			15 28			15 43			15 58		
Hightown	d		14 32			14 47			15 02			15 17			15 32			15 47			16 02		
Hall Road	d		14 35			14 50			15 05			15 20			15 35			15 50			16 05		
Blundellsands & Crosby	d		14 37			14 52			15 07			15 22			15 37			15 52			16 07		
Waterloo (Merseyside)	d		14 40			14 55			15 10			15 25			15 40			15 55			16 10		
Seaforth & Litherland	d		14 42			14 57			15 12			15 27			15 42			15 57			16 12		
Bootle New Strand	d		14 45			15 00			15 15			15 30			15 45			16 00			16 15		
Bootle Oriel Road	d		14 46			15 01			15 16			15 31			15 46			16 01			16 16		
Bank Hall	d		14 48			15 03			15 18			15 33			15 48			16 03			16 18		
Ormskirk	d	14 20			14 35			14 50			15 05			15 20			15 35			15 50			16 05
Aughton Park	d	14 23			14 38			14 53			15 08			15 23			15 38			15 53			16 08
Town Green	d	14 25			14 40			14 55			15 10			15 25			15 40			15 55			16 10
Maghull	d	14 30			14 45			15 00			15 15			15 30			15 45			16 00			16 15
Old Roan	d	14 33			14 48			15 03			15 18			15 33			15 48			16 03			16 18
Aintree	d	14 35			14 50			15 05			15 20			15 35			15 50			16 05			16 20
Orrell Park	d	14 37			14 52			15 07			15 22			15 37			15 52			16 07			16 22
Walton (Merseyside)	d	14 39			14 54			15 09			15 24			15 39			15 54			16 09			16 24
Kirkby	d			14 43			14 58			15 13			15 28			15 43			15 58			16 13	
Fazakerley	d			14 46			15 01			15 16			15 31			15 46			16 01			16 16	
Rice Lane	d			14 49			15 04			15 19			15 34			15 49			16 04			16 19	
Kirkdale	d	14 42		14 52	14 57		15 07	15 12		15 22	15 27		15 37	15 42		15 52	15 57		16 07	16 12		16 22	16 27
Sandhills	d	14 44	14 51	14 55	14 59	15 06	15 10	15 14	15 21	15 25	15 29	15 36	15 40	15 44	15 51	15 55	15 59	16 06	16 10	16 14	16 21	16 25	16 29
Moorfields ■10	d	14 48	14 55	14 58	15 03	15 10	15 13	15 18	15 25	15 28	15 33	15 40	15 43	15 48	15 55	15 58	16 03	16 10	16 13	16 18	16 25	16 28	16 33
Liverpool Central ■10	a	14 50	14 58	15 01	15 05	15 13	15 16	15 20	15 28	15 31	15 35	15 43	15 46	15 50	15 58	16 01	16 05	16 13	16 16	16 20	16 28	16 31	16 35
	d		14 59			15 14			15 29			15 44			15 59			16 14			16 29		
Brunswick	d		15 02			15 17			15 32			15 47			16 02			16 17			16 32		
St Michaels	d		15 05			15 20			15 35			15 50			16 05			16 20			16 35		
Aigburth	d		15 07			15 22			15 37			15 52			16 07			16 22			16 37		
Cressington	d		15 09			15 24			15 39			15 54			16 09			16 24			16 39		
Liverpool Sth Parkway ■7 89 ✈	d		15 12			15 27			15 42			15 57			16 12			16 27			16 42		
Hunts Cross 89	a		15 16			15 31			15 46			16 01			16 16			16 31			16 46		

Table 103 Mondays to Saturdays

Southport, Ormskirk and Kirkby - Liverpool and Hunts Cross

		ME	ME	ME	ME	ME	ME SX	ME SO	ME	ME SO	ME SX	ME	ME	ME	ME	ME	ME	ME	ME	ME	ME	ME	ME
Southport	d	15 58			16 13				16 28				16 43			16 58			17 13			17 28	
Birkdale	d	16 02			16 17				16 32				16 47			17 02			17 17			17 32	
Hillside	d	16 04			16 19				16 34				16 49			17 04			17 19			17 34	
Ainsdale	d	16 07			16 22				16 37				16 52			17 07			17 22			17 37	
Freshfield	d	16 11			16 26				16 41				16 56			17 11			17 26			17 41	
Formby	d	16 13			16 28				16 43				16 58			17 13			17 28			17 43	
Hightown	d	16 17			16 32				16 47				17 02			17 17			17 32			17 47	
Hall Road	d	16 20			16 35				16 50				17 05			17 20			17 35			17 50	
Blundellsands & Crosby	d	16 22			16 37				16 52				17 07			17 22			17 37			17 52	
Waterloo (Merseyside)	d	16 25			16 40				16 55				17 10			17 25			17 40			17 55	
Seaforth & Litherland	d	16 27			16 42				16 57				17 12			17 27			17 42			17 57	
Bootle New Strand	d	16 30			16 45				17 00				17 15			17 30			17 45			18 00	
Bootle Oriel Road	d	16 31			16 46				17 01				17 16			17 31			17 46			18 01	
Bank Hall	d	16 33			16 48				17 03				17 18			17 33			17 48			18 03	
Ormskirk	d			16 20			16 35	16 35				16 50			17 05			17 20			17 35		
Aughton Park	d			16 23			16 38	16 38				16 53			17 08			17 23			17 38		
Town Green	d			16 25			16 40	16 40				16 55			17 10			17 25			17 40		
Maghull	d			16 30			16 45	16 45				17 00			17 15			17 30			17 45		
Old Roan	d			16 33			16 48	16 48				17 03			17 18			17 33			17 48		
Aintree	d			16 35			16 50	16 50				17 05			17 20			17 35			17 50		
Orrell Park	d			16 37			16 52	16 52				17 07			17 22			17 37			17 52		
Walton (Merseyside)	d			16 39			16 54	16 54				17 09			17 24			17 39			17 54		
Kirkby	d		16 28			16 43				16 58	16 58			17 13			17 28			17 43			17 58
Fazakerley	d		16 31			16 46				17 01	17 01			17 16			17 31			17 46			18 01
Rice Lane	d		16 34			16 49				17 04	17 04			17 19			17 34			17 49			18 04
Kirkdale	d		16 37	16 42		16 52	16 57	16 57		17 07	17 07	17 12		17 22	17 27		17 37	17 42		17 52	17 57		18 07
Sandhills	d	16 36	16 40	16 44	16 51	16 55	16 59	16 59	17 06	17 10	17 10	17 14	17 21	17 25	17 29	17 36	17 40	17 44	17 51	17 55	17 59	18 06	18 10
Moorfields ■10	d	16 40	16 43	16 48	16 55	16 58	17 03	17 03	17 10	17 13	17 13	17 18	17 25	17 28	17 33	17 40	17 43	17 48	17 55	17 58	18 03	18 10	18 13
Liverpool Central ■10	a	16 43	16 46	16 50	16 58	17 01	17 05	17 05	17 13	17 16	17 16	17 20	17 28	17 31	17 35	17 43	17 46	17 50	17 58	18 01	18 05	18 13	18 16
	d	16 44			16 59				17 14				17 29			17 44			17 59			18 14	
Brunswick	d	16 47			17 02				17 17				17 32			17 47			18 02			18 17	
St Michaels	d	16 50			17 05				17 20				17 35			17 50			18 05			18 20	
Aigburth	d	16 52			17 07				17 22				17 37			17 52			18 07			18 22	
Cressington	d	16 54			17 09				17 24				17 39			17 54			18 09			18 24	
Liverpool Sth Parkway ■7 89 ✈	d	16 57			17 12				17 27				17 42			17 57			18 12			18 27	
Hunts Cross 89	a	17 01			17 16				17 31				17 46			18 01			18 16			18 31	

		ME	ME	ME	ME	ME	ME	ME	ME	ME	ME	ME	ME	ME	ME	ME	ME	ME	ME	ME	ME	ME
Southport	d		17 43			17 58			18 13			18 28			18 43			18 58			19 13	
Birkdale	d		17 47			18 02			18 17			18 32			18 47			19 02			19 17	
Hillside	d		17 49			18 04			18 19			18 34			18 49			19 04			19 19	
Ainsdale	d		17 52			18 07			18 22			18 37			18 52			19 07			19 22	
Freshfield	d		17 56			18 11			18 26			18 41			18 56			19 11			19 26	
Formby	d		17 58			18 13			18 28			18 43			18 58			19 13			19 28	
Hightown	d		18 02			18 17			18 32			18 47			19 02			19 17			19 32	
Hall Road	d		18 05			18 20			18 35			18 50			19 05			19 20			19 35	
Blundellsands & Crosby	d		18 07			18 22			18 37			18 52			19 07			19 22			19 37	
Waterloo (Merseyside)	d		18 10			18 25			18 40			18 55			19 10			19 25			19 40	
Seaforth & Litherland	d		18 12			18 27			18 42			18 57			19 12			19 27			19 42	
Bootle New Strand	d		18 15			18 30			18 45			19 00			19 15			19 30			19 45	
Bootle Oriel Road	d		18 16			18 31			18 46			19 01			19 16			19 31			19 46	
Bank Hall	d		18 18			18 33			18 48			19 03			19 18			19 33			19 48	
Ormskirk	d	17 50			18 05			18 20			18 35			18 50			19 05			19 20		
Aughton Park	d	17 53			18 08			18 23			18 38			18 53			19 08			19 23		
Town Green	d	17 55			18 10			18 25			18 40			18 55			19 10			19 25		
Maghull	d	18 00			18 15			18 30			18 45			19 00			19 15			19 30		
Old Roan	d	18 03			18 18			18 33			18 48			19 03			19 18			19 33		
Aintree	d	18 05			18 20			18 35			18 50			19 05			19 20			19 35		
Orrell Park	d	18 07			18 22			18 37			18 52			19 07			19 22			19 37		
Walton (Merseyside)	d	18 09			18 24			18 39			18 54			19 09			19 24			19 39		
Kirkby	d			18 13			18 28			18 43			18 58			19 13			19 28			19 48
Fazakerley	d			18 16			18 31			18 46			19 01			19 16			19 31			19 51
Rice Lane	d			18 19			18 34			18 49			19 04			19 19			19 34			19 54
Kirkdale	d	18 12		18 22	18 27		18 37	18 42		18 52	18 57		19 07	19 12		19 22	19 27		19 37	19 42		19 57
Sandhills	d	18 14	18 21	18 25	18 29	18 36	18 40	18 44	18 51	18 55	18 59	19 06	19 10	19 14	19 21	19 25	19 29	19 36	19 40	19 44	19 51	20 00
Moorfields ■10	d	18 18	18 25	18 28	18 33	18 40	18 43	18 48	18 55	18 58	19 03	19 10	19 13	19 18	19 25	19 28	19 33	19 40	19 43	19 48	19 55	20 03
Liverpool Central ■10	a	18 20	18 28	18 31	18 35	18 43	18 46	18 50	18 58	19 01	19 05	19 13	19 16	19 20	19 28	19 31	19 35	19 43	19 46	19 50	19 58	20 06
	d		18 29			18 44			18 59			19 14			19 29			19 44			19 59	
Brunswick	d		18 32			18 47			19 02			19 17			19 32			19 47			20 02	
St Michaels	d		18 35			18 50			19 05			19 20			19 35			19 50			20 05	
Aigburth	d		18 37			18 52			19 07			19 22			19 37			19 52			20 07	
Cressington	d		18 39			18 54			19 09			19 24			19 39			19 54			20 09	
Liverpool Sth Parkway ■7 89 ✈	d		18 42			18 57			19 12			19 27			19 42			19 57			20 12	
Hunts Cross 89	a		18 46			19 01			19 16			19 31			19 46			20 01			20 16	

Table 103

Mondays to Saturdays

Southport, Ormskirk and Kirkby - Liverpool and Hunts Cross

		ME	ME	ME	ME SO	ME SX	ME	ME		ME	ME	ME	ME	ME	ME	ME	ME	ME		ME	ME	ME	ME	ME	ME
Southport	d	19 28		19 43			19 58			20 13		20 28		20 43		20 58		21 13			21 28		21 43		21 58
Birkdale	d	19 32		19 47			20 02			20 17		20 32		20 47		21 02		21 17			21 32		21 47		22 02
Hillside	d	19 34		19 49			20 04			20 19		20 34		20 49		21 04		21 19			21 34		21 49		22 04
Ainsdale	d	19 37		19 52			20 07			20 22		20 37		20 52		21 07		21 22			21 37		21 52		22 07
Freshfield	d	19 41		19 56			20 11			20 26		20 41		20 56		21 11		21 26			21 41		21 56		22 11
Formby	d	19 43		19 58			20 13			20 28		20 43		20 58		21 13		21 28			21 43		21 58		22 13
Hightown	d	19 47		20 02			20 17			20 32		20 47		21 02		21 17		21 32			21 47		22 02		22 17
Hall Road	d	19 50		20 05			20 20			20 35		20 50		21 05		21 20		21 35			21 50		22 05		22 20
Blundellsands & Crosby	d	19 52		20 07			20 22			20 37		20 52		21 07		21 22		21 37			21 52		22 07		22 22
Waterloo (Merseyside)	d	19 55		20 10			20 25			20 40		20 55		21 10		21 25		21 40			21 55		22 10		22 25
Seaforth & Litherland	d	19 57		20 12			20 27			20 42		20 57		21 12		21 27		21 42			21 57		22 12		22 27
Bootle New Strand	d	20 00		20 15			20 30			20 45		21 00		21 15		21 30		21 45			22 00		22 15		22 30
Bootle Oriel Road	d	20 01		20 16			20 31			20 46		21 01		21 16		21 31		21 46			22 01		22 16		22 31
Bank Hall	d	20 03		20 18			20 33			20 48		21 03		21 18		21 33		21 48			22 03		22 18		22 33
Ormskirk	d		19 50					20 20					20 50				21 20					21 50			
Aughton Park	d		19 53					20 23					20 53				21 23					21 53			
Town Green	d		19 55					20 25					20 55				21 25					21 55			
Maghull	d		20 00					20 30					21 00				21 30					22 00			
Old Roan	d		20 03					20 33					21 03				21 33					22 03			
Aintree	d		20 05					20 35					21 05				21 35					22 05			
Orrell Park	d		20 07					20 37					21 07				21 37					22 07			
Walton (Merseyside)	d		20 09					20 39					21 09				21 39					22 09			
Kirkby	d				20 18	20 18					20 48				21 18					21 48				22 18	
Fazakerley	d				20 21	20 21					20 51				21 21					21 51				22 21	
Rice Lane	d				20 24	20 24					20 54				21 24					21 54				22 24	
Kirkdale	d		20 12		20 27	20 27		20 42			20 57		21 12		21 27		21 42			21 57		22 12		22 27	
Sandhills	d	20 06	20 14	20 21	20 30	20 30	20 36	20 44		20 51	21 00	21 06	21 14	21 21	21 30	21 36	21 44	21 51		22 00	22 06	22 14	22 21	22 30	22 36
Moorfields 10	d	20 10	20 18	20 25	20 33	20 33	20 40	20 48		20 55	21 03	21 10	21 18	21 25	21 33	21 40	21 48	21 55		22 03	22 10	22 18	22 25	22 33	22 40
Liverpool Central 10	a	20 13	20 20	20 28	20 36	20 36	20 43	20 50		20 58	21 06	21 13	21 20	21 28	21 36	21 43	21 50	21 58		22 06	22 13	22 20	22 28	22 36	22 43
	d	20 14		20 29			20 44			20 59		21 14		21 29		21 44		21 59			22 14		22 29		22 44
Brunswick	d	20 17		20 32			20 47			21 02		21 17		21 32		21 47		22 02			22 17		22 32		22 47
St Michaels	d	20 20		20 35			20 50			21 05		21 20		21 35		21 50		22 05			22 20		22 35		22 50
Aigburth	d	20 22		20 37			20 52			21 07		21 22		21 37		21 52		22 07			22 22		22 37		22 52
Cressington	d	20 24		20 39			20 54			21 09		21 24		21 39		21 54		22 09			22 24		22 39		22 54
Liverpool Sth Parkway 7 89 ✈	d	20 27		20 42			20 57			21 12		21 27		21 42		21 57		22 12			22 27		22 42		22 57
Hunts Cross 89	a	20 31		20 46			21 01			21 16		21 31		21 46		22 01		22 16			22 31		22 46		23 01

		ME	ME	ME		ME	ME	ME	ME	ME	ME	ME
Southport	d		22 13			22 28		22 43		22 58		23 16
Birkdale	d		22 17			22 32		22 47		23 02		23 20
Hillside	d		22 19			22 34		22 49		23 04		23 22
Ainsdale	d		22 22			22 37		22 52		23 07		23 25
Freshfield	d		22 26			22 41		22 56		23 11		23 29
Formby	d		22 28			22 43		22 58		23 13		23 31
Hightown	d		22 32			22 47		23 02		23 17		23 35
Hall Road	d		22 35			22 50		23 05		23 20		23 38
Blundellsands & Crosby	d		22 37			22 52		23 07		23 22		23 40
Waterloo (Merseyside)	d		22 40			22 55		23 10		23 25		23 43
Seaforth & Litherland	d		22 42			22 57		23 12		23 27		23 45
Bootle New Strand	d		22 45			23 00		23 15		23 30		23 48
Bootle Oriel Road	d		22 46			23 01		23 16		23 31		23 49
Bank Hall	d		22 48			23 03		23 18		23 33		23 51
Ormskirk	d	22 20					22 50				23 20	
Aughton Park	d	22 23					22 53				23 23	
Town Green	d	22 25					22 55				23 25	
Maghull	d	22 30					23 00				23 30	
Old Roan	d	22 33					23 03				23 33	
Aintree	d	22 35					23 05				23 35	
Orrell Park	d	22 37					23 07				23 37	
Walton (Merseyside)	d	22 39					23 09				23 39	
Kirkby	d			22 48					23 18			
Fazakerley	d			22 51					23 21			
Rice Lane	d			22 54					23 24			
Kirkdale	d	22 42		22 57			23 12		23 27		23 42	
Sandhills	d	22 44	22 51	23 00		23 06	23 14	23 21	23 30	23 36	23 44	23 55
Moorfields 10	d	22 48	22 55	23 03		23 10	23 18	23 25	23 33	23 40	23 48	23 58
Liverpool Central 10	a	22 50	22 58	23 06		23 13	23 20	23 28	23 36	23 43	23 50	00 01
	d		22 59			23 14		23 29		23 44		
Brunswick	d		23 02			23 17		23 32		23 47		
St Michaels	d		23 05			23 20		23 35		23 50		
Aigburth	d		23 07			23 22		23 37		23 52		
Cressington	d		23 09			23 24		23 39		23 54		
Liverpool Sth Parkway 7 89 ✈	d		23 12			23 27		23 42		23 57		
Hunts Cross 89	a		23 18			23 32		23 46		00 01		

Table 103

Sundays

until 26 September

Southport, Ormskirk and Kirkby - Liverpool and Hunts Cross

				ME	ME	ME	ME	ME	ME	ME		ME	ME	ME	ME	ME	ME	ME	ME	ME		ME	ME	ME	ME
Southport	d					07 58			08 28				08 58			09 28			09 58			10 13		10 28	
Birkdale	d					08 02			08 32				09 02			09 32			10 02			10 17		10 32	
Hillside	d					08 04			08 34				09 04			09 34			10 04			10 19		10 34	
Ainsdale	d					08 07			08 37				09 07			09 37			10 07			10 22		10 37	
Freshfield	d					08 11			08 41				09 11			09 41			10 11			10 26		10 41	
Formby	d					08 13			08 43				09 13			09 43			10 13			10 28		10 43	
Hightown	d					08 17			08 47				09 17			09 47			10 17			10 32		10 47	
Hall Road	d					08 20			08 50				09 20			09 50			10 20			10 35		10 50	
Blundellsands & Crosby	d					08 22			08 52				09 22			09 52			10 22			10 37		10 52	
Waterloo (Merseyside)	d					08 25			08 55				09 25			09 55			10 25			10 40		10 55	
Seaforth & Litherland	d					08 27			08 57				09 27			09 57			10 27			10 42		10 57	
Bootle New Strand	d					08 30			09 00				09 30			10 00			10 30			10 45		11 00	
Bootle Oriel Road	d					08 31			09 01				09 31			10 01			10 31			10 46		11 01	
Bank Hall	d					08 33			09 03				09 33			10 03			10 33			10 48		11 03	
Ormskirk	d						08 20			08 50				09 20			09 50			10 20					10 50
Aughton Park	d						08 23			08 53				09 23			09 53			10 23					10 53
Town Green	d						08 25			08 55				09 25			09 55			10 25					10 55
Maghull	d						08 30			09 00				09 30			10 00			10 30					11 00
Old Roan	d						08 33			09 03				09 33			10 03			10 33					11 03
Aintree	d						08 35			09 05				09 35			10 05			10 35					11 05
Orrell Park	d						08 37			09 07				09 37			10 07			10 37					11 07
Walton (Merseyside)	d						08 39			09 09				09 39			10 09			10 39					11 09
Kirkby	d				08 18			08 48				09 18			09 48			10 18					10 48		
Fazakerley	d				08 21			08 51				09 21			09 51			10 21					10 51		
Rice Lane	d				08 24			08 54				09 24			09 54			10 24					10 54		
Kirkdale	d				08 27		08 42	08 57		09 12		09 27		09 42	09 57		10 12	10 27		10 42			10 57		11 12
Sandhills	d				08 30	08 36	08 44	09 00	09 06	09 14		09 30	09 36	09 44	10 00	10 06	10 14	10 30	10 36	10 44		10 51	11 00	11 06	11 14
Moorfields 10	d				08 33	08 40	08 48	09 03	09 10	09 18		09 33	09 40	09 48	10 03	10 10	10 18	10 33	10 40	10 48		10 55	11 03	11 10	11 18
Liverpool Central 10	a				08 36	08 43	08 50	09 06	09 13	09 20		09 36	09 43	09 50	10 06	10 13	10 20	10 36	10 43	10 50		10 58	11 06	11 13	11 20
	d			08 14		08 44			09 14				09 44			10 14			10 44					11 14	
Brunswick	d			08 17		08 47			09 17				09 47			10 17			10 47					11 17	
St Michaels	d			08 20		08 50			09 20				09 50			10 20			10 50					11 20	
Aigburth	d			08 22		08 52			09 22				09 52			10 22			10 52					11 22	
Cressington	d			08 24		08 54			09 24				09 54			10 24			10 54					11 24	
Liverpool Sth Parkway 7 89 ✈	d			08 27		08 57			09 27				09 57			10 27			10 57					11 27	
Hunts Cross 89	a			08 31		09 01			09 31				10 01			10 31			11 01					11 31	

		ME	ME	ME	ME	ME		ME	ME	ME	ME	ME	ME	ME	ME	ME		ME	ME	ME	ME	ME	ME	ME	ME
Southport	d	10 43		10 58		11 13			11 28		11 43		11 58		12 13			12 28		12 43		12 58		13 13	
Birkdale	d	10 47		11 02		11 17			11 32		11 47		12 02		12 17			12 32		12 47		13 02		13 17	
Hillside	d	10 49		11 04		11 19			11 34		11 49		12 04		12 19			12 34		12 49		13 04		13 19	
Ainsdale	d	10 52		11 07		11 22			11 37		11 52		12 07		12 22			12 37		12 52		13 07		13 22	
Freshfield	d	10 56		11 11		11 26			11 41		11 56		12 11		12 26			12 41		12 56		13 11		13 26	
Formby	d	10 58		11 13		11 28			11 43		11 58		12 13		12 28			12 43		12 58		13 13		13 28	
Hightown	d	11 02		11 17		11 32			11 47		12 02		12 17		12 32			12 47		13 02		13 17		13 32	
Hall Road	d	11 05		11 20		11 35			11 50		12 05		12 20		12 35			12 50		13 05		13 20		13 35	
Blundellsands & Crosby	d	11 07		11 22		11 37			11 52		12 07		12 22		12 37			12 52		13 07		13 22		13 37	
Waterloo (Merseyside)	d	11 10		11 25		11 40			11 55		12 10		12 25		12 40			12 55		13 10		13 25		13 40	
Seaforth & Litherland	d	11 12		11 27		11 42			11 57		12 12		12 27		12 42			12 57		13 12		13 27		13 42	
Bootle New Strand	d	11 15		11 30		11 45			12 00		12 15		12 30		12 45			13 00		13 15		13 30		13 45	
Bootle Oriel Road	d	11 16		11 31		11 46			12 01		12 16		12 31		12 46			13 01		13 16		13 31		13 46	
Bank Hall	d	11 18		11 33		11 48			12 03		12 18		12 33		12 48			13 03		13 18		13 33		13 48	
Ormskirk	d				11 20					11 50				12 20					12 50				13 20		
Aughton Park	d				11 23					11 53				12 23					12 53				13 23		
Town Green	d				11 25					11 55				12 25					12 55				13 25		
Maghull	d				11 30					12 00				12 30					13 00				13 30		
Old Roan	d				11 33					12 03				12 33					13 03				13 33		
Aintree	d				11 35					12 05				12 35					13 05				13 35		
Orrell Park	d				11 37					12 07				12 37					13 07				13 37		
Walton (Merseyside)	d				11 39					12 09				12 39					13 09				13 39		
Kirkby	d		11 18					11 48				12 18				12 48					13 18				13 48
Fazakerley	d		11 21					11 51				12 21				12 51					13 21				13 51
Rice Lane	d		11 24					11 54				12 24				12 54					13 24				13 54
Kirkdale	d		11 27		11 42			11 57		12 12		12 27		12 42		12 57			13 12		13 27		13 42		13 57
Sandhills	d	11 21	11 30	11 36	11 44	11 51		12 00	12 06	12 14	12 21	12 30	12 36	12 44	12 51	13 00		13 06	13 14	13 21	13 30	13 36	13 44	13 51	14 00
Moorfields 10	d	11 25	11 33	11 40	11 48	11 55		12 03	12 10	12 18	12 25	12 33	12 40	12 48	12 55	13 03		13 10	13 18	13 25	13 33	13 40	13 48	13 55	14 03
Liverpool Central 10	a	11 28	11 36	11 43	11 50	11 58		12 06	12 13	12 20	12 28	12 36	12 43	12 50	12 58	13 06		13 13	13 20	13 28	13 36	13 43	13 50	13 58	14 06
	d			11 44					12 14				12 44					13 14				13 44			
Brunswick	d			11 47					12 17				12 47					13 17				13 47			
St Michaels	d			11 50					12 20				12 50					13 20				13 50			
Aigburth	d			11 52					12 22				12 52					13 22				13 52			
Cressington	d			11 54					12 24				12 54					13 24				13 54			
Liverpool Sth Parkway 7 89 ✈	d			11 57					12 27				12 57					13 27				13 57			
Hunts Cross 89	a			12 01					12 31				13 01					13 31				14 01			

Table 103

Sundays
until 26 September

Southport, Ormskirk and Kirkby - Liverpool and Hunts Cross

		ME		ME	ME	ME	ME	ME	ME	ME	ME	ME		ME	ME	ME	ME	ME	ME	ME	ME	ME		ME	ME
Southport	d	13 28			13 43		13 58		14 13		14 28			14 43		14 58		15 13		15 28		15 43			15 58
Birkdale	d	13 32			13 47		14 02		14 17		14 32			14 47		15 02		15 17		15 32		15 47			16 02
Hillside	d	13 34			13 49		14 04		14 19		14 34			14 49		15 04		15 19		15 34		15 49			16 04
Ainsdale	d	13 37			13 52		14 07		14 22		14 37			14 52		15 07		15 22		15 37		15 52			16 07
Freshfield	d	13 41			13 56		14 11		14 26		14 41			14 56		15 11		15 26		15 41		15 56			16 11
Formby	d	13 43			13 58		14 13		14 28		14 43			14 58		15 13		15 28		15 43		15 58			16 13
Hightown	d	13 47			14 02		14 17		14 32		14 47			15 02		15 17		15 32		15 47		16 02			16 17
Hall Road	d	13 50			14 05		14 20		14 35		14 50			15 05		15 20		15 35		15 50		16 05			16 20
Blundellsands & Crosby	d	13 52			14 07		14 22		14 37		14 52			15 07		15 22		15 37		15 52		16 07			16 22
Waterloo (Merseyside)	d	13 55			14 10		14 25		14 40		14 55			15 10		15 25		15 40		15 55		16 10			16 25
Seaforth & Litherland	d	13 57			14 12		14 27		14 42		14 57			15 12		15 27		15 42		15 57		16 12			16 27
Bootle New Strand	d	14 00			14 15		14 30		14 45		15 00			15 15		15 30		15 45		16 00		16 15			16 30
Bootle Oriel Road	d	14 01			14 16		14 31		14 46		15 01			15 16		15 31		15 46		16 01		16 16			16 31
Bank Hall	d	14 03			14 18		14 33		14 48		15 03			15 18		15 33		15 48		16 03		16 18			16 33
Ormskirk	d			13 50				14 20				14 50					15 20				15 50				
Aughton Park	d			13 53				14 23				14 53					15 23				15 53				
Town Green	d			13 55				14 25				14 55					15 25				15 55				
Maghull	d			14 00				14 30				15 00					15 30				16 00				
Old Roan	d			14 03				14 33				15 03					15 33				16 03				
Aintree	d			14 05				14 35				15 05					15 35				16 05				
Orrell Park	d			14 07				14 37				15 07					15 37				16 07				
Walton (Merseyside)	d			14 09				14 39				15 09					15 39				16 09				
Kirkby	d					14 18				14 48					15 18				15 48					16 18	
Fazakerley	d					14 21				14 51					15 21				15 51					16 21	
Rice Lane	d					14 24				14 54					15 24				15 54					16 24	
Kirkdale	d			14 12		14 27		14 42		14 57		15 12			15 27		15 42		15 57		16 12			16 27	
Sandhills	d	14 06		14 14	14 21	14 30	14 36	14 44	14 51	15 00	15 06	15 14		15 21	15 30	15 36	15 44	15 51	16 00	16 06	16 14	16 21		16 30	16 36
Moorfields	d	14 10		14 18	14 25	14 33	14 40	14 48	14 55	15 03	15 10	15 18		15 25	15 33	15 40	15 48	15 55	16 03	16 10	16 18	16 25		16 33	16 40
Liverpool Central	a	14 13		14 20	14 28	14 36	14 43	14 50	14 58	15 06	15 13	15 20		15 28	15 36	15 43	15 50	15 58	16 06	16 13	16 20	16 28		16 36	16 43
	d	14 14					14 44				15 14					15 44				16 14					16 44
Brunswick	d	14 17					14 47				15 17					15 47				16 17					16 47
St Michaels	d	14 20					14 50				15 20					15 50				16 20					16 50
Aigburth	d	14 22					14 52				15 22					15 52				16 22					16 52
Cressington	d	14 24					14 54				15 24					15 54				16 24					16 54
Liverpool Sth Parkway 89 ✈	d	14 27					14 57				15 27					15 57				16 27					16 57
Hunts Cross 89	a	14 31					15 01				15 31					16 01				16 31					17 01

		ME	ME	ME	ME	ME	ME	ME		ME	ME	ME	ME	ME	ME	ME	ME	ME		ME	ME	ME	ME	ME	ME
Southport	d		16 13		16 28		16 43			16 58		17 13		17 28		17 43		17 58			18 13		18 28		18 43
Birkdale	d		16 17		16 32		16 47			17 02		17 17		17 32		17 47		18 02			18 17		18 32		18 47
Hillside	d		16 19		16 34		16 49			17 04		17 19		17 34		17 49		18 04			18 19		18 34		18 49
Ainsdale	d		16 22		16 37		16 52			17 07		17 22		17 37		17 52		18 07			18 22		18 37		18 52
Freshfield	d		16 26		16 41		16 56			17 11		17 26		17 41		17 56		18 11			18 26		18 41		18 56
Formby	d		16 28		16 43		16 58			17 13		17 28		17 43		17 58		18 13			18 28		18 43		18 58
Hightown	d		16 32		16 47		17 02			17 17		17 32		17 47		18 02		18 17			18 32		18 47		19 02
Hall Road	d		16 35		16 50		17 05			17 20		17 35		17 50		18 05		18 20			18 35		18 50		19 05
Blundellsands & Crosby	d		16 37		16 52		17 07			17 22		17 37		17 52		18 07		18 22			18 37		18 52		19 07
Waterloo (Merseyside)	d		16 40		16 55		17 10			17 25		17 40		17 55		18 10		18 25			18 40		18 55		19 10
Seaforth & Litherland	d		16 42		16 57		17 12			17 27		17 42		17 57		18 12		18 27			18 42		18 57		19 12
Bootle New Strand	d		16 45		17 00		17 15			17 30		17 45		18 00		18 15		18 30			18 45		19 00		19 15
Bootle Oriel Road	d		16 46		17 01		17 16			17 31		17 46		18 01		18 16		18 31			18 46		19 01		19 16
Bank Hall	d		16 48		17 03		17 18			17 33		17 48		18 03		18 18		18 33			18 48		19 03		19 18
Ormskirk	d	16 20				16 50					17 20				17 50					18 20				18 50	
Aughton Park	d	16 23				16 53					17 23				17 53					18 23				18 53	
Town Green	d	16 25				16 55					17 25				17 55					18 25				18 55	
Maghull	d	16 30				17 00					17 30				18 00					18 30				19 00	
Old Roan	d	16 33				17 03					17 33				18 03					18 33				19 03	
Aintree	d	16 35				17 05					17 35				18 05					18 35				19 05	
Orrell Park	d	16 37				17 07					17 37				18 07					18 37				19 07	
Walton (Merseyside)	d	16 39				17 09					17 39				18 09					18 39				19 09	
Kirkby	d			16 48				17 18					17 48				18 18					18 48			
Fazakerley	d			16 51				17 21					17 51				18 21					18 51			
Rice Lane	d			16 54				17 24					17 54				18 24					18 54			
Kirkdale	d	16 42		16 57		17 12		17 27			17 42		17 57		18 12		18 27			18 42		18 57		19 12	
Sandhills	d	16 44	16 51	17 00	17 06	17 14	17 21	17 30		17 36	17 44	17 51	18 00	18 06	18 14	18 21	18 30	18 36		18 44	18 51	19 00	19 06	19 14	19 21
Moorfields	d	16 48	16 55	17 03	17 10	17 18	17 25	17 33		17 40	17 48	17 55	18 03	18 10	18 18	18 25	18 33	18 40		18 48	18 55	19 03	19 10	19 18	19 25
Liverpool Central	a	16 50	16 58	17 06	17 13	17 20	17 28	17 36		17 43	17 50	17 58	18 06	18 13	18 20	18 28	18 36	18 43		18 50	18 58	19 06	19 13	19 20	19 28
	d				17 14					17 44				18 14				18 44					19 14		
Brunswick	d				17 17					17 47				18 17				18 47					19 17		
St Michaels	d				17 20					17 50				18 20				18 50					19 20		
Aigburth	d				17 22					17 52				18 22				18 52					19 22		
Cressington	d				17 24					17 54				18 24				18 54					19 24		
Liverpool Sth Parkway 89 ✈	d				17 27					17 57				18 27				18 57					19 27		
Hunts Cross 89	a				17 31					18 01				18 31				19 01					19 31		

Table 103

Sundays
until 26 September

Southport, Ormskirk and Kirkby - Liverpool and Hunts Cross

		ME	ME	ME		ME	ME	ME	ME	ME	ME	ME	ME	ME		ME	ME	ME	ME	ME	ME	ME	ME	ME	
Southport	d		18 58			19 13		19 28		19 43		19 58		20 13			20 28		20 43		20 58		21 13		
Birkdale	d		19 02			19 17		19 32		19 47		20 02		20 17			20 32		20 47		21 02		21 17		
Hillside	d		19 04			19 19		19 34		19 49		20 04		20 19			20 34		20 49		21 04		21 19		
Ainsdale	d		19 07			19 22		19 37		19 52		20 07		20 22			20 37		20 52		21 07		21 22		
Freshfield	d		19 11			19 26		19 41		19 56		20 11		20 26			20 41		20 56		21 11		21 26		
Formby	d		19 13			19 28		19 43		19 58		20 13		20 28			20 43		20 58		21 13		21 28		
Hightown	d		19 17			19 32		19 47		20 02		20 17		20 32			20 47		21 02		21 17		21 32		
Hall Road	d		19 20			19 35		19 50		20 05		20 20		20 35			20 50		21 05		21 20		21 35		
Blundellsands & Crosby	d		19 22			19 37		19 52		20 07		20 22		20 37			20 52		21 07		21 22		21 37		
Waterloo (Merseyside)	d		19 25			19 40		19 55		20 10		20 25		20 40			20 55		21 10		21 25		21 40		
Seaforth & Litherland	d		19 27			19 42		19 57		20 12		20 27		20 42			20 57		21 12		21 27		21 42		
Bootle New Strand	d		19 30			19 45		20 00		20 15		20 30		20 45			21 00		21 15		21 30		21 45		
Bootle Oriel Road	d		19 31			19 46		20 01		20 16		20 31		20 46			21 01		21 16		21 31		21 46		
Bank Hall	d		19 33			19 48		20 03		20 18		20 33		20 48			21 03		21 18		21 33		21 48		
Ormskirk	d			19 20					19 50				20 20					20 50				21 20			
Aughton Park	d			19 23					19 53				20 23					20 53				21 23			
Town Green	d			19 25					19 55				20 25					20 55				21 25			
Maghull	d			19 30					20 00				20 30					21 00				21 30			
Old Roan	d			19 33					20 03				20 33					21 03				21 33			
Aintree	d			19 35					20 05				20 35					21 05				21 35			
Orrell Park	d			19 37					20 07				20 37					21 07				21 37			
Walton (Merseyside)	d			19 39					20 09				20 39					21 09				21 39			
Kirkby	d	19 18					19 48				20 18					20 48				21 18				21 48	
Fazakerley	d	19 21					19 51				20 21					20 51				21 21				21 51	
Rice Lane	d	19 24					19 54				20 24					20 54				21 24				21 54	
Kirkdale	d	19 27		19 42			19 57		20 12		20 27		20 42			20 57		21 12		21 27		21 42		21 57	
Sandhills	d	19 30	19 36	19 44		19 51	20 00	20 06	20 14	20 21	20 30	20 36	20 44	20 51		21 00	21 06	21 14	21 21	21 30	21 36	21 44	21 51	22 00	
Moorfields	d	19 33	19 40	19 48		19 55	20 03	20 10	20 18	20 25	20 33	20 40	20 48	20 55		21 03	21 10	21 18	21 25	21 33	21 40	21 48	21 55	22 03	
Liverpool Central	a	19 36	19 43	19 50		19 58	20 06	20 13	20 20	20 28	20 36	20 43	20 50	20 58		21 06	21 13	21 20	21 28	21 36	21 43	21 50	21 58	22 06	
	d		19 44					20 14				20 44					21 14				21 44				
Brunswick	d		19 47					20 17				20 47					21 17				21 47				
St Michaels	d		19 50					20 20				20 50					21 20				21 50				
Aigburth	d		19 52					20 22				20 52					21 22				21 52				
Cressington	d		19 54					20 24				20 54					21 24				21 54				
Liverpool Sth Parkway 89 ✈	d		19 57					20 27				20 57					21 27				21 57				
Hunts Cross 89	a		20 01					20 31				21 01					21 31				22 01				

		ME	ME	ME	ME	ME	ME	ME	ME	ME		ME	ME	ME	ME	ME	ME
Southport	d	21 28		21 43		21 58		22 13		22 28			22 43		22 58		23 16
Birkdale	d	21 32		21 47		22 02		22 17		22 32			22 47		23 02		23 20
Hillside	d	21 34		21 49		22 04		22 19		22 34			22 49		23 04		23 22
Ainsdale	d	21 37		21 52		22 07		22 22		22 37			22 52		23 07		23 25
Freshfield	d	21 41		21 56		22 11		22 26		22 41			22 56		23 11		23 29
Formby	d	21 43		21 58		22 13		22 28		22 43			22 58		23 13		23 31
Hightown	d	21 47		22 02		22 17		22 32		22 47			23 02		23 17		23 35
Hall Road	d	21 50		22 05		22 20		22 35		22 50			23 05		23 20		23 38
Blundellsands & Crosby	d	21 52		22 07		22 22		22 37		22 52			23 07		23 22		23 40
Waterloo (Merseyside)	d	21 55		22 10		22 25		22 40		22 55			23 10		23 25		23 43
Seaforth & Litherland	d	21 57		22 12		22 27		22 42		22 57			23 12		23 27		23 45
Bootle New Strand	d	22 00		22 15		22 30		22 45		23 00			23 15		23 30		23 48
Bootle Oriel Road	d	22 01		22 16		22 31		22 46		23 01			23 16		23 31		23 49
Bank Hall	d	22 03		22 18		22 33		22 48		23 03			23 18		23 33		23 51
Ormskirk	d		21 50				22 20					22 50				23 20	
Aughton Park	d		21 53				22 23					22 53				23 23	
Town Green	d		21 55				22 25					22 55				23 25	
Maghull	d		22 00				22 30					23 00				23 30	
Old Roan	d		22 03				22 33					23 03				23 33	
Aintree	d		22 05				22 35					23 05				23 35	
Orrell Park	d		22 07				22 37					23 07				23 37	
Walton (Merseyside)	d		22 09				22 39					23 09				23 39	
Kirkby	d				22 18				22 48					23 18			
Fazakerley	d				22 21				22 51					23 21			
Rice Lane	d				22 24				22 54					23 24			
Kirkdale	d		22 12		22 27		22 42		22 57			23 12		23 27		23 42	
Sandhills	d	22 06	22 14	22 21	22 30	22 36	22 44	22 51	23 00	23 06		23 14	23 21	23 30	23 36	23 44	23 55
Moorfields	d	22 10	22 18	22 25	22 33	22 40	22 48	22 55	23 03	23 10		23 18	23 25	23 33	23 40	23 48	23 58
Liverpool Central	a	22 13	22 20	22 28	22 36	22 43	22 50	22 58	23 06	23 13		23 20	23 28	23 36	23 43	23 50	00 01
	d	22 14				22 44				23 14					23 44		
Brunswick	d	22 17				22 47				23 17					23 47		
St Michaels	d	22 20				22 50				23 20					23 50		
Aigburth	d	22 22				22 52				23 22					23 52		
Cressington	d	22 24				22 54				23 24					23 54		
Liverpool Sth Parkway 89 ✈	d	22 27				22 57				23 27					23 57		
Hunts Cross 89	a	22 31				23 01				23 31					00 01		

Table 103

Sundays
from 03 October

Southport, Ormskirk and Kirkby - Liverpool and Hunts Cross

				ME	ME	ME	ME	ME	ME	ME		ME	ME	ME	ME	ME	ME	ME	ME	ME		ME	ME	ME	ME
Southport	d					07 58			08 28				08 58			09 28			09 58				10 28		
Birkdale	d					08 02			08 32				09 02			09 32			10 02				10 32		
Hillside	d					08 04			08 34				09 04			09 34			10 04				10 34		
Ainsdale	d					08 07			08 37				09 07			09 37			10 07				10 37		
Freshfield	d					08 11			08 41				09 11			09 41			10 11				10 41		
Formby	d					08 13			08 43				09 13			09 43			10 13				10 43		
Hightown	d					08 17			08 47				09 17			09 47			10 17				10 47		
Hall Road	d					08 20			08 50				09 20			09 50			10 20				10 50		
Blundellsands & Crosby	d					08 22			08 52				09 22			09 52			10 22				10 52		
Waterloo (Merseyside)	d					08 25			08 55				09 25			09 55			10 25				10 55		
Seaforth & Litherland	d					08 27			08 57				09 27			09 57			10 27				10 57		
Bootle New Strand	d					08 30			09 00				09 30			10 00			10 30				11 00		
Bootle Oriel Road	d					08 31			09 01				09 31			10 01			10 31				11 01		
Bank Hall	d					08 33			09 03				09 33			10 03			10 33				11 03		
Ormskirk	d						08 20			08 50				09 20			09 50			10 20				10 50	
Aughton Park	d						08 23			08 53				09 23			09 53			10 23				10 53	
Town Green	d						08 25			08 55				09 25			09 55			10 25				10 55	
Maghull	d						08 30			09 00				09 30			10 00			10 30				11 00	
Old Roan	d						08 33			09 03				09 33			10 03			10 33				11 03	
Aintree	d						08 35			09 05				09 35			10 05			10 35				11 05	
Orrell Park	d						08 37			09 07				09 37			10 07			10 37				11 07	
Walton (Merseyside)	d						08 39			09 09				09 39			10 09			10 39				11 09	
Kirkby	d				08 18			08 48				09 18			09 48			10 18				10 48			11 18
Fazakerley	d				08 21			08 51				09 21			09 51			10 21				10 51			11 21
Rice Lane	d				08 24			08 54				09 24			09 54			10 24				10 54			11 24
Kirkdale	d				08 27		08 42	08 57		09 12		09 27		09 42	09 57		10 12	10 27		10 42		10 57		11 12	11 27
Sandhills	d				08 30	08 36	08 44	09 00	09 06	09 14		09 30	09 36	09 44	10 00	10 06	10 14	10 30	10 36	10 44		11 00	11 06	11 14	11 30
Moorfields 10	d				08 33	08 40	08 48	09 03	09 10	09 18		09 33	09 40	09 48	10 03	10 10	10 18	10 33	10 40	10 48		11 03	11 10	11 18	11 33
Liverpool Central 10	a				08 36	08 43	08 50	09 06	09 13	09 20		09 36	09 43	09 50	10 06	10 13	10 20	10 36	10 43	10 50		11 06	11 13	11 20	11 36
	d			08 14		08 44			09 14				09 44			10 14			10 44				11 14		
Brunswick	d			08 17		08 47			09 17				09 47			10 17			10 47				11 17		
St Michaels	d			08 20		08 50			09 20				09 50			10 20			10 50				11 20		
Aigburth	d			08 22		08 52			09 22				09 52			10 22			10 52				11 22		
Cressington	d			08 24		08 54			09 24				09 54			10 24			10 54				11 24		
Liverpool Sth Parkway 7 89 ✈	d			08 27		08 57			09 27				09 57			10 27			10 57				11 27		
Hunts Cross 89	a			08 31		09 01			09 31				10 01			10 31			11 01				11 31		

		ME	ME	ME	ME	ME		ME	ME	ME	ME	ME	ME	ME	ME	ME		ME	ME	ME	ME	ME	ME	ME	ME
Southport	d	10 58			11 28				11 58			12 28			12 58				13 28			13 58			14 28
Birkdale	d	11 02			11 32				12 02			12 32			13 02				13 32			14 02			14 32
Hillside	d	11 04			11 34				12 04			12 34			13 04				13 34			14 04			14 34
Ainsdale	d	11 07			11 37				12 07			12 37			13 07				13 37			14 07			14 37
Freshfield	d	11 11			11 41				12 11			12 41			13 11				13 41			14 11			14 41
Formby	d	11 13			11 43				12 13			12 43			13 13				13 43			14 13			14 43
Hightown	d	11 17			11 47				12 17			12 47			13 17				13 47			14 17			14 47
Hall Road	d	11 20			11 50				12 20			12 50			13 20				13 50			14 20			14 50
Blundellsands & Crosby	d	11 22			11 52				12 22			12 52			13 22				13 52			14 22			14 52
Waterloo (Merseyside)	d	11 25			11 55				12 25			12 55			13 25				13 55			14 25			14 55
Seaforth & Litherland	d	11 27			11 57				12 27			12 57			13 27				13 57			14 27			14 57
Bootle New Strand	d	11 30			12 00				12 30			13 00			13 30				14 00			14 30			15 00
Bootle Oriel Road	d	11 31			12 01				12 31			13 01			13 31				14 01			14 31			15 01
Bank Hall	d	11 33			12 03				12 33			13 03			13 33				14 03			14 33			15 03
Ormskirk	d		11 20			11 50				12 20			12 50			13 20				13 50			14 20		
Aughton Park	d		11 23			11 53				12 23			12 53			13 23				13 53			14 23		
Town Green	d		11 25			11 55				12 25			12 55			13 25				13 55			14 25		
Maghull	d		11 30			12 00				12 30			13 00			13 30				14 00			14 30		
Old Roan	d		11 33			12 03				12 33			13 03			13 33				14 03			14 33		
Aintree	d		11 35			12 05				12 35			13 05			13 35				14 05			14 35		
Orrell Park	d		11 37			12 07				12 37			13 07			13 37				14 07			14 37		
Walton (Merseyside)	d		11 39			12 09				12 39			13 09			13 39				14 09			14 39		
Kirkby	d			11 48				12 18			12 48			13 18				13 48			14 18			14 48	
Fazakerley	d			11 51				12 21			12 51			13 21				13 51			14 21			14 51	
Rice Lane	d			11 54				12 24			12 54			13 24				13 54			14 24			14 54	
Kirkdale	d		11 42	11 57		12 12		12 27		12 42	12 57		13 12	13 27		13 42		13 57		14 12	14 27		14 42	14 57	
Sandhills	d	11 36	11 44	12 00	12 06	12 14		12 30	12 36	12 44	13 00	13 06	13 14	13 30	13 36	13 44		14 00	14 06	14 14	14 30	14 36	14 44	15 00	15 06
Moorfields 10	d	11 40	11 48	12 03	12 10	12 18		12 33	12 40	12 48	13 03	13 10	13 18	13 33	13 40	13 48		14 03	14 10	14 18	14 33	14 40	14 48	15 03	15 10
Liverpool Central 10	a	11 43	11 50	12 06	12 13	12 20		12 36	12 43	12 50	13 06	13 13	13 20	13 36	13 43	13 50		14 06	14 13	14 20	14 36	14 43	14 50	15 06	15 13
	d	11 44			12 14				12 44			13 14			13 44				14 14			14 44			15 14
Brunswick	d	11 47			12 17				12 47			13 17			13 47				14 17			14 47			15 17
St Michaels	d	11 50			12 20				12 50			13 20			13 50				14 20			14 50			15 20
Aigburth	d	11 52			12 22				12 52			13 22			13 52				14 22			14 52			15 22
Cressington	d	11 54			12 24				12 54			13 24			13 54				14 24			14 54			15 24
Liverpool Sth Parkway 7 89 ✈	d	11 57			12 27				12 57			13 27			13 57				14 27			14 57			15 27
Hunts Cross 89	a	12 01			12 31				13 01			13 31			14 01				14 31			15 01			15 31

Table 103

Sundays
from 03 October

Southport, Ormskirk and Kirkby - Liverpool and Hunts Cross

		ME		ME	ME	ME	ME	ME	ME	ME	ME	ME		ME	ME	ME	ME	ME	ME	ME	ME	ME		ME	ME
Southport	d				14 58			15 28			15 58				16 28			16 58			17 28				17 58
Birkdale	d				15 02			15 32			16 02				16 32			17 02			17 32				18 02
Hillside	d				15 04			15 34			16 04				16 34			17 04			17 34				18 04
Ainsdale	d				15 07			15 37			16 07				16 37			17 07			17 37				18 07
Freshfield	d				15 11			15 41			16 11				16 41			17 11			17 41				18 11
Formby	d				15 13			15 43			16 13				16 43			17 13			17 43				18 13
Hightown	d				15 17			15 47			16 17				16 47			17 17			17 47				18 17
Hall Road	d				15 20			15 50			16 20				16 50			17 20			17 50				18 20
Blundellsands & Crosby	d				15 22			15 52			16 22				16 52			17 22			17 52				18 22
Waterloo (Merseyside)	d				15 25			15 55			16 25				16 55			17 25			17 55				18 25
Seaforth & Litherland	d				15 27			15 57			16 27				16 57			17 27			17 57				18 27
Bootle New Strand	d				15 30			16 00			16 30				17 00			17 30			18 00				18 30
Bootle Oriel Road	d				15 31			16 01			16 31				17 01			17 31			18 01				18 31
Bank Hall	d				15 33			16 03			16 33				17 03			17 33			18 03				18 33
Ormskirk	d	14 50				15 20			15 50			16 20				16 50			17 20			17 50			
Aughton Park	d	14 53				15 23			15 53			16 23				16 53			17 23			17 53			
Town Green	d	14 55				15 25			15 55			16 25				16 55			17 25			17 55			
Maghull	d	15 00				15 30			16 00			16 30				17 00			17 30			18 00			
Old Roan	d	15 03				15 33			16 03			16 33				17 03			17 33			18 03			
Aintree	d	15 05				15 35			16 05			16 35				17 05			17 35			18 05			
Orrell Park	d	15 07				15 37			16 07			16 37				17 07			17 37			18 07			
Walton (Merseyside)	d	15 09				15 39			16 09			16 39				17 09			17 39			18 09			
Kirkby	d			15 18			15 48			16 18				16 48			17 18			17 48				18 18	
Fazakerley	d			15 21			15 51			16 21				16 51			17 21			17 51				18 21	
Rice Lane	d			15 24			15 54			16 24				16 54			17 24			17 54				18 24	
Kirkdale	d	15 12		15 27		15 42	15 57		16 12	16 27		16 42		16 57		17 12	17 27		17 42	17 57		18 12		18 27	
Sandhills	d	15 14		15 30	15 36	15 44	16 00	16 06	16 14	16 30	16 36	16 44		17 00	17 06	17 14	17 30	17 36	17 44	18 00	18 06	18 14		18 30	18 36
Moorfields 10	d	15 18		15 33	15 40	15 48	16 03	16 10	16 18	16 33	16 40	16 48		17 03	17 10	17 18	17 33	17 40	17 48	18 03	18 10	18 18		18 33	18 40
Liverpool Central 10	a	15 20		15 36	15 43	15 50	16 06	16 13	16 20	16 36	16 43	16 50		17 06	17 13	17 20	17 36	17 43	17 50	18 06	18 13	18 20		18 36	18 43
	d				15 44			16 14			16 44				17 14			17 44			18 14				18 44
Brunswick	d				15 47			16 17			16 47				17 17			17 47			18 17				18 47
St Michaels	d				15 50			16 20			16 50				17 20			17 50			18 20				18 50
Aigburth	d				15 52			16 22			16 52				17 22			17 52			18 22				18 52
Cressington	d				15 54			16 24			16 54				17 24			17 54			18 24				18 54
Liverpool Sth Parkway 7 89 ✈	d				15 57			16 27			16 57				17 27			17 57			18 27				18 57
Hunts Cross 89	a				16 01			16 31			17 01				17 31			18 01			18 31				19 01

		ME	ME	ME	ME	ME	ME	ME		ME	ME	ME	ME	ME	ME	ME	ME	ME		ME	ME	ME	ME	ME	ME
Southport	d			18 28			18 58				19 28			19 58			20 28				20 58			21 28	
Birkdale	d			18 32			19 02				19 32			20 02			20 32				21 02			21 32	
Hillside	d			18 34			19 04				19 34			20 04			20 34				21 04			21 34	
Ainsdale	d			18 37			19 07				19 37			20 07			20 37				21 07			21 37	
Freshfield	d			18 41			19 11				19 41			20 11			20 41				21 11			21 41	
Formby	d			18 43			19 13				19 43			20 13			20 43				21 13			21 43	
Hightown	d			18 47			19 17				19 47			20 17			20 47				21 17			21 47	
Hall Road	d			18 50			19 20				19 50			20 20			20 50				21 20			21 50	
Blundellsands & Crosby	d			18 52			19 22				19 52			20 22			20 52				21 22			21 52	
Waterloo (Merseyside)	d			18 55			19 25				19 55			20 25			20 55				21 25			21 55	
Seaforth & Litherland	d			18 57			19 27				19 57			20 27			20 57				21 27			21 57	
Bootle New Strand	d			19 00			19 30				20 00			20 30			21 00				21 30			22 00	
Bootle Oriel Road	d			19 01			19 31				20 01			20 31			21 01				21 31			22 01	
Bank Hall	d			19 03			19 33				20 03			20 33			21 03				21 33			22 03	
Ormskirk	d	18 20			18 50			19 20				19 50			20 20			20 50				21 20			21 50
Aughton Park	d	18 23			18 53			19 23				19 53			20 23			20 53				21 23			21 53
Town Green	d	18 25			18 55			19 25				19 55			20 25			20 55				21 25			21 55
Maghull	d	18 30			19 00			19 30				20 00			20 30			21 00				21 30			22 00
Old Roan	d	18 33			19 03			19 33				20 03			20 33			21 03				21 33			22 03
Aintree	d	18 35			19 05			19 35				20 05			20 35			21 05				21 35			22 05
Orrell Park	d	18 37			19 07			19 37				20 07			20 37			21 07				21 37			22 07
Walton (Merseyside)	d	18 39			19 09			19 39				20 09			20 39			21 09				21 39			22 09
Kirkby	d		18 48			19 18				19 48			20 18			20 48				21 18			21 48		
Fazakerley	d		18 51			19 21				19 51			20 21			20 51				21 21			21 51		
Rice Lane	d		18 54			19 24				19 54			20 24			20 54				21 24			21 54		
Kirkdale	d	18 42	18 57		19 12	19 27		19 42		19 57		20 12	20 27		20 42	20 57		21 12		21 27		21 42	21 57		22 12
Sandhills	d	18 44	19 00	19 06	19 14	19 30	19 36	19 44		20 00	20 06	20 14	20 30	20 36	20 44	21 00	21 06	21 14		21 30	21 36	21 44	22 00	22 06	22 14
Moorfields 10	d	18 48	19 03	19 10	19 18	19 33	19 40	19 48		20 03	20 10	20 18	20 33	20 40	20 48	21 03	21 10	21 18		21 33	21 40	21 48	22 03	22 10	22 18
Liverpool Central 10	a	18 50	19 06	19 13	19 20	19 36	19 43	19 50		20 06	20 13	20 20	20 36	20 43	20 50	21 06	21 13	21 20		21 36	21 43	21 50	22 06	22 13	22 20
	d			19 14			19 44				20 14			20 44			21 14				21 44			22 14	
Brunswick	d			19 17			19 47				20 17			20 47			21 17				21 47			22 17	
St Michaels	d			19 20			19 50				20 20			20 50			21 20				21 50			22 20	
Aigburth	d			19 22			19 52				20 22			20 52			21 22				21 52			22 22	
Cressington	d			19 24			19 54				20 24			20 54			21 24				21 54			22 24	
Liverpool Sth Parkway 7 89 ✈	d			19 27			19 57				20 27			20 57			21 27				21 57			22 27	
Hunts Cross 89	a			19 31			20 01				20 31			21 01			21 31				22 01			22 31	

Table 103

Sundays
from 03 October

Southport, Ormskirk and Kirkby - Liverpool and Hunts Cross

		ME	ME	ME	ME	ME	ME	ME	ME	ME	ME
Southport	d		21 58			22 28			22 58		23 16
Birkdale	d		22 02			22 32			23 02		23 20
Hillside	d		22 04			22 34			23 04		23 22
Ainsdale	d		22 07			22 37			23 07		23 25
Freshfield	d		22 11			22 41			23 11		23 29
Formby	d		22 13			22 43			23 13		23 31
Hightown	d		22 17			22 47			23 17		23 35
Hall Road	d		22 20			22 50			23 20		23 38
Blundellsands & Crosby	d		22 22			22 52			23 22		23 40
Waterloo (Merseyside)	d		22 25			22 55			23 25		23 43
Seaforth & Litherland	d		22 27			22 57			23 27		23 45
Bootle New Strand	d		22 30			23 00			23 30		23 48
Bootle Oriel Road	d		22 31			23 01			23 31		23 49
Bank Hall	d		22 33			23 03			23 33		23 51
Ormskirk	d			22 20			22 50			23 20	
Aughton Park	d			22 23			22 53			23 23	
Town Green	d			22 25			22 55			23 25	
Maghull	d			22 30			23 00			23 30	
Old Roan	d			22 33			23 03			23 33	
Aintree	d			22 35			23 05			23 35	
Orrell Park	d			22 37			23 07			23 37	
Walton (Merseyside)	d			22 39			23 09			23 39	
Kirkby	d	22 18			22 48			23 18			
Fazakerley	d	22 21			22 51			23 21			
Rice Lane	d	22 24			22 54			23 24			
Kirkdale	d	22 27		22 42	22 57		23 12	23 27		23 42	
Sandhills	d	22 30	22 36	22 44	23 00	23 06	23 14	23 30	23 36	23 44	23 55
Moorfields 10	d	22 33	22 40	22 48	23 03	23 10	23 18	23 33	23 40	23 48	23 58
Liverpool Central 10	a	22 36	22 43	22 50	23 06	23 13	23 20	23 36	23 43	23 50	00 01
	d		22 44			23 14			23 44		
Brunswick	d		22 47			23 17			23 47		
St Michaels	d		22 50			23 20			23 50		
Aigburth	d		22 52			23 22			23 52		
Cressington	d		22 54			23 24			23 54		
Liverpool Sth Parkway 7 89 ✈	d		22 57			23 27			23 57		
Hunts Cross 89	a		23 01			23 31			00 01		

Table 106

Mondays to Saturdays

Liverpool and Birkenhead - New Brighton, West Kirby, Ellesmere Port and Chester

		ME	ME	ME	ME	ME	ME	ME	ME	ME	ME	ME	ME	ME	ME	ME	ME	ME	ME
Moorfields 10	d	05 36	05 56	06 06	06 16	06 21	06 26	06 41	06 46	06 51	06 56	07 11	07 16	07 21	07 26	07 31	07 36	07 41	07 46
Liverpool Lime Street 10	d	05 38	05 58	06 08	06 18	06 23	06 28	06 43	06 48	06 53	06 58	07 13	07 18	07 23	07 28	07 33	07 38	07 43	07 48
Liverpool Central 10	d	05 40	06 00	06 10	06 20	06 25	06 30	06 45	06 50	06 55	07 00	07 15	07 20	07 25	07 30	07 35	07 40	07 45	07 50
James Street	d	05 42	06 02	06 12	06 22	06 27	06 32	06 47	06 52	06 57	07 02	07 17	07 22	07 27	07 32	07 37	07 42	07 47	07 52
Hamilton Square	d	05 45	06 05	06 15	06 25	06 30	06 35	06 50	06 55	07 00	07 05	07 20	07 25	07 30	07 35	07 40	07 45	07 50	07 55
Conway Park	d				06 27	06 32			06 57	07 02			07 27	07 32		07 42	07 47		07 57
Birkenhead Park	d				06 29	06 34			06 59	07 04			07 29	07 34		07 44	07 49		07 59
Birkenhead North	d				06 32	06 37			07 02	07 07			07 32	07 37		07 47	07 52		08 02
Wallasey Village	d				06 37				07 07				07 37			07 52			08 07
Wallasey Grove Road	d				06 38				07 08				07 38			07 53			08 08
New Brighton	a				06 43				07 13				07 43			07 58			08 13
Bidston	d					06 40				07 10				07 40			07 55		
Leasowe	d					06 42				07 12				07 42			07 57		
Moreton (Merseyside)	d					06 44				07 14				07 44			07 59		
Meols	d					06 48				07 18				07 48			08 03		
Manor Road	d					06 50				07 20				07 50			08 05		
Hoylake	d					06 52				07 22				07 52			08 07		
West Kirby	a					06 57				07 27				07 57			08 12		
Birkenhead Central	d	05 47	06 07	06 17			06 37	06 52			07 07	07 22			07 37			07 52	
Green Lane	d	05 49	06 09	06 19			06 39	06 54			07 09	07 24			07 39			07 54	
Rock Ferry	d	05 52	06 12	06 22			06 42	06 57			07 12	07 27			07 42			07 57	
Bebington	d	05 54	06 14	06 24			06 44	06 59			07 14	07 29			07 44			07 59	
Port Sunlight	d	05 56	06 16	06 26			06 46	07 01			07 16	07 31			07 46			08 01	
Spital	d	05 58	06 18	06 28			06 48	07 03			07 18	07 33			07 48			08 03	
Bromborough Rake	d	06 00	06 20	06 30			06 50	07 05			07 20	07 35			07 50			08 05	
Bromborough	d	06 02	06 22	06 32			06 52	07 07			07 22	07 37			07 52			08 07	
Eastham Rake	d	06 05	06 25	06 35			06 55	07 10			07 25	07 40			07 55			08 10	
Hooton	d	06 07	06 27	06 37			06 57	07 12			07 27	07 42			07 57			08 12	
Little Sutton	d		06 31				07 01				07 31				08 01				
Overpool	d		06 33				07 03				07 33				08 03				
Ellesmere Port	a		06 37				07 07				07 37				08 07				
Capenhurst	d	06 12		06 42				07 17				07 47						08 17	
Bache	d	06 17		06 47				07 22				07 52						08 22	
Chester	a	06 26		06 56				07 26				07 56						08 26	

		ME	ME	ME	ME	ME	ME	ME	ME	ME	ME	ME	ME	ME	ME	ME	ME SO	ME SX	ME	ME	ME	ME	ME
Moorfields 10	d	07 51	07 56	08 01	08 06	08 11	08 16	08 21	08 26	08 31	08 36	08 41	08 46	08 51	08 56	09 01	09 06	09 06	09 11	09 16	09 21	09 26	09 31
Liverpool Lime Street 10	d	07 53	07 58	08 03	08 08	08 13	08 18	08 23	08 28	08 33	08 38	08 43	08 48	08 53	08 58	09 03	09 08	09 08	09 13	09 18	09 23	09 28	09 33
Liverpool Central 10	d	07 55	08 00	08 05	08 10	08 15	08 20	08 25	08 30	08 35	08 40	08 45	08 50	08 55	09 00	09 05	09 10	09 10	09 15	09 20	09 25	09 30	09 35
James Street	d	07 57	08 02	08 07	08 12	08 17	08 22	08 27	08 32	08 37	08 42	08 47	08 52	08 57	09 02	09 07	09 12	09 12	09 17	09 22	09 27	09 32	09 37
Hamilton Square	d	08 00	08 05	08 10	08 15	08 20	08 25	08 30	08 35	08 40	08 45	08 50	08 55	09 00	09 05	09 10	09 15	09 15	09 20	09 25	09 30	09 35	09 40
Conway Park	d	08 02		08 12	08 17		08 27	08 32		08 42	08 47		08 57	09 02		09 12	09 17	09 17		09 27	09 32		09 42
Birkenhead Park	d	08 04		08 14	08 19		08 29	08 34		08 44	08 49		08 59	09 04		09 14	09 19	09 19		09 29	09 34		09 44
Birkenhead North	d	08 07		08 17	08 22		08 32	08 37		08 47	08 52		09 02	09 07		09 17	09 22	09 22		09 32	09 37		09 47
Wallasey Village	d			08 22			08 37			08 52			09 07			09 22				09 37			09 52
Wallasey Grove Road	d			08 23			08 38			08 53			09 08			09 23				09 38			09 53
New Brighton	a			08 28			08 43			08 58			09 13			09 28				09 43			09 58
Bidston	d	08 10			08 25			08 40			08 55			09 10			09 25	09 25			09 40		
Leasowe	d	08 12			08 27			08 42			08 57			09 12			09 27	09 27			09 42		
Moreton (Merseyside)	d	08 14			08 29			08 44			08 59			09 14			09 29	09 29			09 44		
Meols	d	08 18			08 33			08 48			09 03			09 18			09 33	09 33			09 48		
Manor Road	d	08 20			08 35			08 50			09 05			09 20			09 35	09 35			09 50		
Hoylake	d	08 22			08 37			08 52			09 07			09 22			09 37	09 37			09 52		
West Kirby	a	08 27			08 42			08 57			09 12			09 27			09 42	09 42			09 57		
Birkenhead Central	d		08 07			08 22			08 37			08 52			09 07				09 22			09 37	
Green Lane	d		08 09			08 24			08 39			08 54			09 09				09 24			09 39	
Rock Ferry	d		08 12			08 27			08 42			08 57			09 12				09 27			09 42	
Bebington	d		08 14			08 29			08 44			08 59			09 14				09 29			09 44	
Port Sunlight	d		08 16			08 31			08 46			09 01			09 16				09 31			09 46	
Spital	d		08 18			08 33			08 48			09 03			09 18				09 33			09 48	
Bromborough Rake	d		08 20			08 35			08 50			09 05			09 20				09 35			09 50	
Bromborough	d		08 22			08 37			08 52			09 07			09 22				09 37			09 52	
Eastham Rake	d		08 25			08 40			08 55			09 10			09 25				09 40			09 55	
Hooton	d		08 27			08 42			08 57			09 12			09 27				09 42			09 57	
Little Sutton	d		08 31						09 01						09 31							10 01	
Overpool	d		08 33						09 03						09 33							10 03	
Ellesmere Port	a		08 37						09 07						09 37							10 07	
Capenhurst	d					08 47						09 17							09 47				
Bache	d					08 52						09 22							09 52				
Chester	a					08 56						09 26							09 56				

Table 106

Mondays to Saturdays

Liverpool and Birkenhead - New Brighton, West Kirby, Ellesmere Port and Chester

		ME		ME	ME	ME	ME	ME	ME	ME	ME	ME		ME	ME	ME	ME	ME	ME	ME	ME	ME		ME	ME
Moorfields	d	09 36		09 41	09 46	09 51	09 56	10 01	10 06	10 11	10 16	10 21		10 26	10 31	10 36	10 41	10 46	10 51	10 56	11 01	11 06		11 11	11 16
Liverpool Lime Street	d	09 38		09 43	09 48	09 53	09 58	10 03	10 08	10 13	10 18	10 23		10 28	10 33	10 38	10 43	10 48	10 53	10 58	11 03	11 08		11 13	11 18
Liverpool Central	d	09 40		09 45	09 50	09 55	10 00	10 05	10 10	10 15	10 20	10 25		10 30	10 35	10 40	10 45	10 50	10 55	11 00	11 05	11 10		11 15	11 20
James Street	d	09 42		09 47	09 52	09 57	10 02	10 07	10 12	10 17	10 22	10 27		10 32	10 37	10 42	10 47	10 52	10 57	11 02	11 07	11 12		11 17	11 22
Hamilton Square	d	09 45		09 50	09 55	10 00	10 05	10 10	10 15	10 20	10 25	10 30		10 35	10 40	10 45	10 50	10 55	11 00	11 05	11 10	11 15		11 20	11 25
Conway Park	d	09 47			09 57	10 02		10 12	10 17		10 27	10 32			10 42	10 47		10 57	11 02		11 12	11 17			11 27
Birkenhead Park	d	09 49			09 59	10 04		10 14	10 19		10 29	10 34			10 44	10 49		10 59	11 04		11 14	11 19			11 29
Birkenhead North	d	09 52			10 02	10 07		10 17	10 22		10 32	10 37			10 47	10 52		11 02	11 07		11 17	11 22			11 32
Wallasey Village	d				10 07			10 22			10 37				10 52			11 07			11 22				11 37
Wallasey Grove Road	d				10 08			10 23			10 38				10 53			11 08			11 23				11 38
New Brighton	a				10 13			10 28			10 43				10 58			11 13			11 28				11 43
Bidston	d	09 55				10 10			10 25			10 40				10 55			11 10			11 25			
Leasowe	d	09 57				10 12			10 27			10 42				10 57			11 12			11 27			
Moreton (Merseyside)	d	09 59				10 14			10 29			10 44				10 59			11 14			11 29			
Meols	d	10 03				10 18			10 33			10 48				11 03			11 18			11 33			
Manor Road	d	10 05				10 20			10 35			10 50				11 05			11 20			11 35			
Hoylake	d	10 07				10 22			10 37			10 52				11 07			11 22			11 37			
West Kirby	a	10 12				10 27			10 42			10 57				11 12			11 27			11 42			
Birkenhead Central	d			09 52			10 07			10 22				10 37			10 52			11 07				11 22	
Green Lane	d			09 54			10 09			10 24				10 39			10 54			11 09				11 24	
Rock Ferry	d			09 57			10 12			10 27				10 42			10 57			11 12				11 27	
Bebington	d			09 59			10 14			10 29				10 44			10 59			11 14				11 29	
Port Sunlight	d			10 01			10 16			10 31				10 46			11 01			11 16				11 31	
Spital	d			10 03			10 18			10 33				10 48			11 03			11 18				11 33	
Bromborough Rake	d			10 05			10 20			10 35				10 50			11 05			11 20				11 35	
Bromborough	d			10 07			10 22			10 37				10 52			11 07			11 22				11 37	
Eastham Rake	d			10 10			10 25			10 40				10 55			11 10			11 25				11 40	
Hooton	d			10 12			10 27			10 42				10 57			11 12			11 27				11 42	
Little Sutton	d						10 31							11 01						11 31					
Overpool	d						10 33							11 03						11 33					
Ellesmere Port	a						10 37							11 07						11 37					
Capenhurst	d			10 17						10 47							11 17							11 47	
Bache	d			10 22						10 52							11 22							11 52	
Chester	a			10 26						10 56							11 26							11 56	

		ME	ME	ME	ME	ME	ME	ME		ME	ME	ME	ME	ME	ME	ME	ME	ME		ME	ME	ME	ME	ME	ME
Moorfields	d	11 21	11 26	11 31	11 36	11 41	11 46	11 51		11 56	12 01	12 06	12 11	12 16	12 21	12 26	12 31	12 36		12 41	12 46	12 51	12 56	13 01	13 06
Liverpool Lime Street	d	11 23	11 28	11 33	11 38	11 43	11 48	11 53		11 58	12 03	12 08	12 13	12 18	12 23	12 28	12 33	12 38		12 43	12 48	12 53	12 58	13 03	13 08
Liverpool Central	d	11 25	11 30	11 35	11 40	11 45	11 50	11 55		12 00	12 05	12 10	12 15	12 20	12 25	12 30	12 35	12 40		12 45	12 50	12 55	13 00	13 05	13 10
James Street	d	11 27	11 32	11 37	11 42	11 47	11 52	11 57		12 02	12 07	12 12	12 17	12 22	12 27	12 32	12 37	12 42		12 47	12 52	12 57	13 02	13 07	13 12
Hamilton Square	d	11 30	11 35	11 40	11 45	11 50	11 55	12 00		12 05	12 10	12 15	12 20	12 25	12 30	12 35	12 40	12 45		12 50	12 55	13 00	13 05	13 10	13 15
Conway Park	d	11 32		11 42	11 47		11 57	12 02			12 12	12 17		12 27	12 32		12 42	12 47			12 57	13 02		13 12	13 17
Birkenhead Park	d	11 34		11 44	11 49		11 59	12 04			12 14	12 19		12 29	12 34		12 44	12 49			12 59	13 04		13 14	13 19
Birkenhead North	d	11 37		11 47	11 52		12 02	12 07			12 17	12 22		12 32	12 37		12 47	12 52			13 02	13 07		13 17	13 22
Wallasey Village	d			11 52			12 07				12 22			12 37			12 52				13 07			13 22	
Wallasey Grove Road	d			11 53			12 08				12 23			12 38			12 53				13 08			13 23	
New Brighton	a			11 58			12 13				12 28			12 43			12 58				13 13			13 28	
Bidston	d	11 40			11 55			12 10				12 25			12 40			12 55				13 10			13 25
Leasowe	d	11 42			11 57			12 12				12 27			12 42			12 57				13 12			13 27
Moreton (Merseyside)	d	11 44			11 59			12 14				12 29			12 44			12 59				13 14			13 29
Meols	d	11 48			12 03			12 18				12 33			12 48			13 03				13 18			13 33
Manor Road	d	11 50			12 05			12 20				12 35			12 50			13 05				13 20			13 35
Hoylake	d	11 52			12 07			12 22				12 37			12 52			13 07				13 22			13 37
West Kirby	a	11 57			12 12			12 27				12 42			12 57			13 12				13 27			13 42
Birkenhead Central	d		11 37			11 52				12 07			12 22			12 37				12 52			13 07		
Green Lane	d		11 39			11 54				12 09			12 24			12 39				12 54			13 09		
Rock Ferry	d		11 42			11 57				12 12			12 27			12 42				12 57			13 12		
Bebington	d		11 44			11 59				12 14			12 29			12 44				12 59			13 14		
Port Sunlight	d		11 46			12 01				12 16			12 31			12 46				13 01			13 16		
Spital	d		11 48			12 03				12 18			12 33			12 48				13 03			13 18		
Bromborough Rake	d		11 50			12 05				12 20			12 35			12 50				13 05			13 20		
Bromborough	d		11 52			12 07				12 22			12 37			12 52				13 07			13 22		
Eastham Rake	d		11 55			12 10				12 25			12 40			12 55				13 10			13 25		
Hooton	d		11 57			12 12				12 27			12 42			12 57				13 12			13 27		
Little Sutton	d		12 01							12 31						13 01							13 31		
Overpool	d		12 03							12 33						13 03							13 33		
Ellesmere Port	a		12 07							12 37						13 07							13 37		
Capenhurst	d					12 17							12 47							13 17					
Bache	d					12 22							12 52							13 22					
Chester	a					12 26							12 56							13 26					

Table 106

Mondays to Saturdays

Liverpool and Birkenhead - New Brighton, West Kirby, Ellesmere Port and Chester

		ME	ME	ME		ME	ME	ME	ME	ME	ME	ME	ME	ME		ME	ME	ME	ME	ME	ME	ME	ME	ME	
Moorfields	d	13 11	13 16	13 21		13 26	13 31	13 36	13 41	13 46	13 51	13 56	14 01	14 06		14 11	14 16	14 21	14 26	14 31	14 36	14 41	14 46	14 51	
Liverpool Lime Street	d	13 13	13 18	13 23		13 28	13 33	13 38	13 43	13 48	13 53	13 58	14 03	14 08		14 13	14 18	14 23	14 28	14 33	14 38	14 43	14 48	14 53	
Liverpool Central	d	13 15	13 20	13 25		13 30	13 35	13 40	13 45	13 50	13 55	14 00	14 05	14 10		14 15	14 20	14 25	14 30	14 35	14 40	14 45	14 50	14 55	
James Street	d	13 17	13 22	13 27		13 32	13 37	13 42	13 47	13 52	13 57	14 02	14 07	14 12		14 17	14 22	14 27	14 32	14 37	14 42	14 47	14 52	14 57	
Hamilton Square	d	13 20	13 25	13 30		13 35	13 40	13 45	13 50	13 55	14 00	14 05	14 10	14 15		14 20	14 25	14 30	14 35	14 40	14 45	14 50	14 55	15 00	
Conway Park	d		13 27	13 32			13 42	13 47		13 57	14 02		14 12	14 17			14 27	14 32		14 42	14 47		14 57	15 02	
Birkenhead Park	d		13 29	13 34			13 44	13 49		13 59	14 04		14 14	14 19			14 29	14 34		14 44	14 49		14 59	15 04	
Birkenhead North	d		13 32	13 37			13 47	13 52		14 02	14 07		14 17	14 22			14 32	14 37		14 47	14 52		15 02	15 07	
Wallasey Village	d		13 37				13 52			14 07			14 22				14 37			14 52			15 07		
Wallasey Grove Road	d		13 38				13 53			14 08			14 23				14 38			14 53			15 08		
New Brighton	a		13 43				13 58			14 13			14 28				14 43			14 58			15 13		
Bidston	d			13 40				13 55			14 10			14 25				14 40			14 55			15 10	
Leasowe	d			13 42				13 57			14 12			14 27				14 42			14 57			15 12	
Moreton (Merseyside)	d			13 44				13 59			14 14			14 29				14 44			14 59			15 14	
Meols	d			13 48				14 03			14 18			14 33				14 48			15 03			15 18	
Manor Road	d			13 50				14 05			14 20			14 35				14 50			15 05			15 20	
Hoylake	d			13 52				14 07			14 22			14 37				14 52			15 07			15 22	
West Kirby	a			13 57				14 12			14 27			14 42				14 57			15 12			15 27	
Birkenhead Central	d	13 22				13 37			13 52			14 07				14 22			14 37			14 52			
Green Lane	d	13 24				13 39			13 54			14 09				14 24			14 39			14 54			
Rock Ferry	d	13 27				13 42			13 57			14 12				14 27			14 42			14 57			
Bebington	d	13 29				13 44			13 59			14 14				14 29			14 44			14 59			
Port Sunlight	d	13 31				13 46			14 01			14 16				14 31			14 46			15 01			
Spital	d	13 33				13 48			14 03			14 18				14 33			14 48			15 03			
Bromborough Rake	d	13 35				13 50			14 05			14 20				14 35			14 50			15 05			
Bromborough	d	13 37				13 52			14 07			14 22				14 37			14 52			15 07			
Eastham Rake	d	13 40				13 55			14 10			14 25				14 40			14 55			15 10			
Hooton	d	13 42				13 57			14 12			14 27				14 42			14 57			15 12			
Little Sutton	d					14 01						14 31							15 01						
Overpool	d					14 03						14 33							15 03						
Ellesmere Port	a					14 07						14 37							15 07						
Capenhurst	d	13 47							14 17							14 47						15 17			
Bache	d	13 52							14 22							14 52						15 22			
Chester	a	13 56							14 26							14 56						15 26			

		ME	ME	ME	ME	ME	ME	ME	ME	ME		ME	ME	ME	ME	ME	ME SX	ME	ME	ME		ME SX	ME	ME	ME
Moorfields	d	14 56	15 01	15 06	15 11	15 16	15 21	15 26	15 31	15 36		15 41	15 46	15 51	15 56	16 01	16 03	16 06	16 11	16 16		16 18	16 21	16 26	16 31
Liverpool Lime Street	d	14 58	15 03	15 08	15 13	15 18	15 23	15 28	15 33	15 38		15 43	15 48	15 53	15 58	16 03	16 05	16 08	16 13	16 18		16 20	16 23	16 28	16 33
Liverpool Central	d	15 00	15 05	15 10	15 15	15 20	15 25	15 30	15 35	15 40		15 45	15 50	15 55	16 00	16 05	16 07	16 10	16 15	16 20		16 22	16 25	16 30	16 35
James Street	d	15 02	15 07	15 12	15 17	15 22	15 27	15 32	15 37	15 42		15 47	15 52	15 57	16 02	16 07	16 09	16 12	16 17	16 22		16 24	16 27	16 32	16 37
Hamilton Square	d	15 05	15 10	15 15	15 20	15 25	15 30	15 35	15 40	15 45		15 50	15 55	16 00	16 05	16 10	16a12	16 15	16 20	16 25		16a27	16 30	16 35	16 40
Conway Park	d		15 12	15 17		15 27	15 32		15 42	15 47			15 57	16 02		16 12		16 17		16 27			16 32		16 42
Birkenhead Park	d		15 14	15 19		15 29	15 34		15 44	15 49			15 59	16 04		16 14		16 19		16 29			16 34		16 44
Birkenhead North	d		15 17	15 22		15 32	15 37		15 47	15 52			16 02	16 07		16 17		16 22		16 32			16 37		16 47
Wallasey Village	d		15 22			15 37			15 52				16 07			16 22				16 37					16 52
Wallasey Grove Road	d		15 23			15 38			15 53				16 08			16 23				16 38					16 53
New Brighton	a		15 28			15 43			15 58				16 13			16 28				16 43					16 58
Bidston	d			15 25			15 40			15 55				16 10				16 25					16 40		
Leasowe	d			15 27			15 42			15 57				16 12				16 27					16 42		
Moreton (Merseyside)	d			15 29			15 44			15 59				16 14				16 29					16 44		
Meols	d			15 33			15 48			16 03				16 18				16 33					16 48		
Manor Road	d			15 35			15 50			16 05				16 20				16 35					16 50		
Hoylake	d			15 37			15 52			16 07				16 22				16 37					16 52		
West Kirby	a			15 42			15 57			16 12				16 27				16 42					16 57		
Birkenhead Central	d	15 07			15 22			15 37				15 52			16 07				16 22					16 37	
Green Lane	d	15 09			15 24			15 39				15 54			16 09				16 24					16 39	
Rock Ferry	d	15 12			15 27			15 42				15 57			16 12				16 27					16 42	
Bebington	d	15 14			15 29			15 44				15 59			16 14				16 29					16 44	
Port Sunlight	d	15 16			15 31			15 46				16 01			16 16				16 31					16 46	
Spital	d	15 18			15 33			15 48				16 03			16 18				16 33					16 48	
Bromborough Rake	d	15 20			15 35			15 50				16 05			16 20				16 35					16 50	
Bromborough	d	15 22			15 37			15 52				16 07			16 22				16 37					16 52	
Eastham Rake	d	15 25			15 40			15 55				16 10			16 25				16 40					16 55	
Hooton	d	15 27			15 42			15 57				16 12			16 27				16 42					16 57	
Little Sutton	d	15 31						16 01							16 31									17 01	
Overpool	d	15 33						16 03							16 33									17 03	
Ellesmere Port	a	15 37						16 07							16 37									17 07	
Capenhurst	d				15 47							16 17							16 47						
Bache	d				15 52							16 22							16 52						
Chester	a				15 56							16 26							16 56						

Liverpool and Birkenhead - New Brighton, West Kirby, Ellesmere Port and Chester

		ME SX	ME	ME SO	ME	ME SX	ME	ME	ME	ME SX	ME	ME SO	ME	ME SX	ME	ME	ME	ME SX	ME	ME SO	ME	ME SX	ME
Moorfields	d	16 33	16 36	16 41	16 46	16 48	16 51	16 56	17 01	17 03	17 06	17 11	17 16	17 18	17 21	17 26	17 31	17 33	17 36	17 41	17 46	17 48	17 51
Liverpool Lime Street	d	16 35	16 38	16 43	16 48	16 50	16 53	16 58	17 03	17 05	17 08	17 13	17 18	17 20	17 23	17 28	17 33	17 35	17 38	17 43	17 48	17 50	17 53
Liverpool Central	d	16 37	16 40	16 45	16 50	16 52	16 55	17 00	17 05	17 07	17 10	17 15	17 20	17 22	17 25	17 30	17 35	17 37	17 40	17 45	17 50	17 52	17 55
James Street	d	16 39	16 42	16 47	16 52	16 54	16 57	17 02	17 07	17 09	17 12	17 17	17 22	17 24	17 27	17 32	17 37	17 39	17 42	17 47	17 52	17 54	17 57
Hamilton Square	d	16 42	16 45	16 50	16 55	16 57	17 00	17 05	17 10	17 12	17 15	17 20	17 25	17 27	17 30	17 35	17 40	17 42	17 45	17 50	17 55	17 57	18 00
Conway Park	d		16 47		16 57		17 02		17 12		17 17		17 27		17 32		17 42		17 47		17 57		18 02
Birkenhead Park	d		16 49		16 59		17 04		17 14		17 19		17 29		17 34		17 44		17 49		17 59		18 04
Birkenhead North	d		16 52		17 02		17 07		17 17		17 22		17 32		17 37		17 47		17 52		18 02		18 07
Wallasey Village	d				17 07				17 22				17 37				17 52				18 07		
Wallasey Grove Road	d				17 08				17 23				17 38				17 53				18 08		
New Brighton	a				17 13				17 28				17 43				17 58				18 13		
Bidston	d		16 55				17 10				17 25				17 40				17 55				18 10
Leasowe	d		16 57				17 12				17 27				17 42				17 57				18 12
Moreton (Merseyside)	d		16 59				17 14				17 29				17 44				17 59				18 14
Meols	d		17 03				17 18				17 33				17 48				18 03				18 18
Manor Road	d		17 05				17 20				17 35				17 50				18 05				18 20
Hoylake	d		17 07				17 22				17 37				17 52				18 07				18 22
West Kirby	a		17 12				17 27				17 42				17 57				18 12				18 27
Birkenhead Central	d	16 45		16 52		17 00		17 07		17 15		17 22		17 30		17 37		17 45		17 52		18 00	
Green Lane	d	16 47		16 54		17 02		17 09		17 17		17 24		17 32		17 39		17 47		17 54		18 02	
Rock Ferry	d	16 49		16 57		17 04		17 12		17 19		17 27		17 34		17 42		17 49		17 57		18 04	
Bebington	d	16 52		16 59		17 07		17 14		17 22		17 29		17 37		17 44		17 52		17 59		18 07	
Port Sunlight	d	16 54		17 01		17 09		17 16		17 24		17 31		17 39		17 46		17 54		18 01		18 09	
Spital	d	16 56		17 03		17 11		17 18		17 26		17 33		17 41		17 48		17 56		18 03		18 11	
Bromborough Rake	d	16 58		17 05		17 13		17 20		17 28		17 35		17 43		17 50		17 58		18 05		18 13	
Bromborough	d	17 00		17 07		17 15		17 22		17 30		17 37		17 45		17 52		18 00		18 07		18 15	
Eastham Rake	d	17 02		17 10		17 17		17 25		17 32		17 40		17 47		17 55		18 02		18 10		18 17	
Hooton	d	17 04		17 12		17 19		17 27		17 34		17 42		17 49		17 57		18 04		18 12		18 19	
Little Sutton	d							17 31								18 01							
Overpool	d							17 33								18 03							
Ellesmere Port	a							17 37								18 07							
Capenhurst	d	17 09		17 17		17 24				17 39		17 47		17 54				18 09		18 17		18 24	
Bache	d	17 15		17 22		17 30				17 45		17 52		18 00				18 15		18 22		18 30	
Chester	a	17 18		17 26		17 33				17 48		17 56		18 03				18 18		18 26		18 33	

		ME	ME	ME	ME	ME	ME	ME	ME	ME	ME	ME	ME	ME	ME	ME	ME	ME	ME	ME	ME	ME
Moorfields	d	17 56	18 01	18 06	18 11	18 16	18 21	18 26	18 31	18 36	18 41	18 46	18 51	18 56	19 01	19 06	19 11	19 16	19 26	19 31	19 41	19 46
Liverpool Lime Street	d	17 58	18 03	18 08	18 13	18 18	18 23	18 28	18 33	18 38	18 43	18 48	18 53	18 58	19 03	19 08	19 13	19 18	19 28	19 33	19 43	19 48
Liverpool Central	d	18 00	18 05	18 10	18 15	18 20	18 25	18 30	18 35	18 40	18 45	18 50	18 55	19 00	19 05	19 10	19 15	19 20	19 30	19 35	19 45	19 50
James Street	d	18 02	18 07	18 12	18 17	18 22	18 27	18 32	18 37	18 42	18 47	18 52	18 57	19 02	19 07	19 12	19 17	19 22	19 32	19 37	19 47	19 52
Hamilton Square	d	18 05	18 10	18 15	18 20	18 25	18 30	18 35	18 40	18 45	18 50	18 55	19 00	19 05	19 10	19 15	19 20	19 25	19 35	19 40	19 50	19 55
Conway Park	d		18 12	18 17		18 27	18 32		18 42	18 47		18 57	19 02		19 12	19 17		19 27		19 42		19 57
Birkenhead Park	d		18 14	18 19		18 29	18 34		18 44	18 49		18 59	19 04		19 14	19 19		19 29		19 44		19 59
Birkenhead North	d		18 17	18 22		18 32	18 37		18 47	18 52		19 02	19 07		19 17	19 22		19 32		19 47		20 02
Wallasey Village	d		18 22			18 37			18 52			19 07			19 22			19 37				20 07
Wallasey Grove Road	d		18 23			18 38			18 53			19 08			19 23			19 38				20 08
New Brighton	a		18 28			18 43			18 58			19 13			19 28			19 43				20 13
Bidston	d			18 25			18 40			18 55			19 10			19 25				19 50		
Leasowe	d			18 27			18 42			18 57			19 12			19 27				19 52		
Moreton (Merseyside)	d			18 29			18 44			18 59			19 14			19 29				19 54		
Meols	d			18 33			18 48			19 03			19 18			19 33				19 58		
Manor Road	d			18 35			18 50			19 05			19 20			19 35				20 00		
Hoylake	d			18 37			18 52			19 07			19 22			19 37				20 02		
West Kirby	a			18 42			18 57			19 12			19 27			19 42				20 07		
Birkenhead Central	d	18 07			18 22			18 37			18 52			19 07			19 22		19 37		19 52	
Green Lane	d	18 09			18 24			18 39			18 54			19 09			19 24		19 39		19 54	
Rock Ferry	d	18 12			18 27			18 42			18 57			19 12			19 27		19 42		19 57	
Bebington	d	18 14			18 29			18 44			18 59			19 14			19 29		19 44		19 59	
Port Sunlight	d	18 16			18 31			18 46			19 01			19 16			19 31		19 46		20 01	
Spital	d	18 18			18 33			18 48			19 03			19 18			19 33		19 48		20 03	
Bromborough Rake	d	18 20			18 35			18 50			19 05			19 20			19 35		19 50		20 05	
Bromborough	d	18 22			18 37			18 52			19 07			19 22			19 37		19 52		20 07	
Eastham Rake	d	18 25			18 40			18 55			19 10			19 25			19 40		19 55		20 10	
Hooton	d	18 27			18 42			18 57			19 12			19 27			19 42		19 57		20 12	
Little Sutton	d	18 31						19 01						19 31					20 01			
Overpool	d	18 33						19 03						19 33					20 03			
Ellesmere Port	a	18 37						19 07						19 37					20 07			
Capenhurst	d				18 47						19 17						19 47				20 17	
Bache	d				18 52						19 22						19 52				20 22	
Chester	a				18 56						19 26						19 56				20 26	

Table 106 Mondays to Saturdays

Liverpool and Birkenhead - New Brighton, West Kirby, Ellesmere Port and Chester

		ME	ME	ME	ME	ME	ME	ME	ME	ME	ME	ME	ME	ME	ME	ME	ME	ME	ME	ME	ME	ME	ME
Moorfields	d	19 56	20 01	20 11	20 16	20 26	20 31	20 41	20 46	20 56	21 01	21 11	21 16	21 26	21 31	21 41	21 46	21 56	22 01	22 11	22 16	22 26	22 31
Liverpool Lime Street	d	19 58	20 03	20 13	20 18	20 28	20 33	20 43	20 48	20 58	21 03	21 13	21 18	21 28	21 33	21 43	21 48	21 58	22 03	22 13	22 18	22 28	22 33
Liverpool Central	d	20 00	20 05	20 15	20 20	20 30	20 35	20 45	20 50	21 00	21 05	21 15	21 20	21 30	21 35	21 45	21 50	22 00	22 05	22 15	22 20	22 30	22 35
James Street	d	20 02	20 07	20 17	20 22	20 32	20 37	20 47	20 52	21 02	21 07	21 17	21 22	21 32	21 37	21 47	21 52	22 02	22 07	22 17	22 22	22 32	22 37
Hamilton Square	d	20 05	20 10	20 20	20 25	20 35	20 40	20 50	20 55	21 05	21 10	21 20	21 25	21 35	21 40	21 50	21 55	22 05	22 10	22 20	22 25	22 35	22 40
Conway Park	d		20 12		20 27		20 42		20 57		21 12		21 27		21 42		21 57		22 12		22 27		22 42
Birkenhead Park	d		20 14		20 29		20 44		20 59		21 14		21 29		21 44		21 59		22 14		22 29		22 44
Birkenhead North	d		20 17		20 32		20 47		21 02		21 17		21 32		21 47		22 02		22 17		22 32		22 47
Wallasey Village	d				20 37				21 07				21 37				22 07				22 37		
Wallasey Grove Road	d				20 38				21 08				21 38				22 08				22 38		
New Brighton	a				20 43				21 13				21 43				22 13				22 43		
Bidston	d		20 20				20 50				21 20				21 50				22 20				22 50
Leasowe	d		20 22				20 52				21 22				21 52				22 22				22 52
Moreton (Merseyside)	d		20 24				20 54				21 24				21 54				22 24				22 54
Meols	d		20 28				20 58				21 28				21 58				22 28				22 58
Manor Road	d		20 30				21 00				21 30				22 00				22 30				23 00
Hoylake	d		20 32				21 02				21 32				22 02				22 32				23 02
West Kirby	a		20 37				21 07				21 37				22 07				22 37				23 07
Birkenhead Central	d	20 07		20 22		20 37		20 52		21 07		21 22		21 37		21 52		22 07		22 22		22 37	
Green Lane	d	20 09		20 24		20 39		20 54		21 09		21 24		21 39		21 54		22 09		22 24		22 39	
Rock Ferry	d	20 12		20 27		20 42		20 57		21 12		21 27		21 42		21 57		22 12		22 27		22 42	
Bebington	d	20 14		20 29		20 44		20 59		21 14		21 29		21 44		21 59		22 14		22 29		22 44	
Port Sunlight	d	20 16		20 31		20 46		21 01		21 16		21 31		21 46		22 01		22 16		22 31		22 46	
Spital	d	20 18		20 33		20 48		21 03		21 18		21 33		21 48		22 03		22 18		22 33		22 48	
Bromborough Rake	d	20 20		20 35		20 50		21 05		21 20		21 35		21 50		22 05		22 20		22 35		22 50	
Bromborough	d	20 22		20 37		20 52		21 07		21 22		21 37		21 52		22 07		22 22		22 37		22 52	
Eastham Rake	d	20 25		20 40		20 55		21 10		21 25		21 40		21 55		22 10		22 25		22 40		22 55	
Hooton	d	20 27		20 42		20 57		21 12		21 27		21 42		21 57		22 12		22 27		22 42		22 57	
Little Sutton	d	20 31				21 01				21 31				22 01				22 31				23 01	
Overpool	d	20 33				21 03				21 33				22 03				22 33				23 03	
Ellesmere Port	a	20 37				21 07				21 37				22 07				22 37				23 07	
Capenhurst	d			20 47				21 17				21 47				22 17				22 47			
Bache	d			20 52				21 22				21 52				22 22				22 52			
Chester	a			20 56				21 26				21 56				22 26				22 56			

		ME	ME	ME	ME	ME	ME	ME	ME	ME	ME	ME
Moorfields	d	22 41	22 46	22 56	23 01	23 11	23 16	23 26	23 31	23 41	23 46	23 56
Liverpool Lime Street	d	22 43	22 48	22 58	23 03	23 13	23 18	23 28	23 33	23 43	23 48	23 58
Liverpool Central	d	22 45	22 50	23 00	23 05	23 15	23 20	23 30	23 35	23 45	23 50	23 59
James Street	d	22 47	22 52	23 02	23 07	23 17	23 22	23 32	23 37	23 47	23 52	00 02
Hamilton Square	d	22 50	22 55	23 05	23 10	23 20	23 25	23 35	23 40	23 50	23 55	00a05
Conway Park	d		22 57		23 12		23 27		23 42		23 57	
Birkenhead Park	d		22 59		23 14		23 29		23 44		23 59	
Birkenhead North	d		23 02		23 17		23 32		23 47		00 02	
Wallasey Village	d		23 07				23 37				00 07	
Wallasey Grove Road	d		23 08				23 38				00 08	
New Brighton	a		23 13				23 43				00 13	
Bidston	d				23 20				23 50			
Leasowe	d				23 22				23 52			
Moreton (Merseyside)	d				23 24				23 54			
Meols	d				23 28				23 58			
Manor Road	d				23 30				23 59			
Hoylake	d				23 32				00 02			
West Kirby	a				23 37				00 07			
Birkenhead Central	d	22 52		23 07		23 22		23 37		23 52		
Green Lane	d	22 54		23 09		23 24		23 39		23 54		
Rock Ferry	d	22 57		23 12		23 27		23 42		23 57		
Bebington	d	22 59		23 14		23 29		23 44		23 59		
Port Sunlight	d	23 01		23 16		23 31		23 46		00 01		
Spital	d	23 03		23 18		23 33		23 48		00 03		
Bromborough Rake	d	23 05		23 20		23 35		23 50		00 05		
Bromborough	d	23 07		23 22		23 37		23 52		00 07		
Eastham Rake	d	23 10		23 25		23 40		23 55		00 10		
Hooton	d	23 12		23 27		23 42		23 57		00 12		
Little Sutton	d			23 31				00 01				
Overpool	d			23 33				00 03				
Ellesmere Port	a			23 37				00 07				
Capenhurst	d	23 17				23 47				00 17		
Bache	d	23 22				23 52				00 22		
Chester	a	23 26				23 56				00 26		

Table 106

Sundays

Liverpool and Birkenhead - New Brighton, West Kirby, Ellesmere Port and Chester

				ME			ME	ME	ME	ME		ME	ME	ME	ME	ME	ME	ME	ME	ME		ME	ME	ME	ME
Moorfields 10	d			07 56			08 11	08 16	08 26	08 31		08 41	08 46	08 56	09 01	09 11	09 16	09 26	09 31	09 41		09 46	09 56	10 01	10 11
Liverpool Lime Street 10	d			07 58			08 13	08 18	08 28	08 33		08 43	08 48	08 58	09 03	09 13	09 18	09 28	09 33	09 43		09 48	09 58	10 03	10 13
Liverpool Central 10	d			08 00			08 15	08 20	08 30	08 35		08 45	08 50	09 00	09 05	09 15	09 20	09 30	09 35	09 45		09 50	10 00	10 05	10 15
James Street	d			08 02			08 17	08 22	08 32	08 37		08 47	08 52	09 02	09 07	09 17	09 22	09 32	09 37	09 47		09 52	10 02	10 07	10 17
Hamilton Square	d			08 05			08 20	08 25	08 35	08 40		08 50	08 55	09 05	09 10	09 20	09 25	09 35	09 40	09 50		09 55	10 05	10 10	10 20
Conway Park	d							08 27		08 42			08 57		09 12		09 27		09 42			09 57		10 12	
Birkenhead Park	d							08 29		08 44			08 59		09 14		09 29		09 44			09 59		10 14	
Birkenhead North	d							08 32		08 47			09 02		09 17		09 32		09 47			10 02		10 17	
Wallasey Village	d							08 37					09 07				09 37					10 07			
Wallasey Grove Road	d							08 38					09 08				09 38					10 08			
New Brighton	a							08 43					09 13				09 43					10 13			
Bidston	d									08 50					09 20				09 50					10 20	
Leasowe	d									08 52					09 22				09 52					10 22	
Moreton (Merseyside)	d									08 54					09 24				09 54					10 24	
Meols	d									08 58					09 28				09 58					10 28	
Manor Road	d									09 00					09 30				10 00					10 30	
Hoylake	d									09 02					09 32				10 02					10 32	
West Kirby	a									09 07					09 37				10 07					10 37	
Birkenhead Central	d			08 07			08 22		08 37			08 52		09 07		09 22		09 37		09 52			10 07		10 22
Green Lane	d			08 09			08 24		08 39			08 54		09 09		09 24		09 39		09 54			10 09		10 24
Rock Ferry	d			08 12			08 27		08 42			08 57		09 12		09 27		09 42		09 57			10 12		10 27
Bebington	d			08 14			08 29		08 44			08 59		09 14		09 29		09 44		09 59			10 14		10 29
Port Sunlight	d			08 16			08 31		08 46			09 01		09 16		09 31		09 46		10 01			10 16		10 31
Spital	d			08 18			08 33		08 48			09 03		09 18		09 33		09 48		10 03			10 18		10 33
Bromborough Rake	d			08 20			08 35		08 50			09 05		09 20		09 35		09 50		10 05			10 20		10 35
Bromborough	d			08 22			08 37		08 52			09 07		09 22		09 37		09 52		10 07			10 22		10 37
Eastham Rake	d			08 25			08 40		08 55			09 10		09 25		09 40		09 55		10 10			10 25		10 40
Hooton	d			08 27			08 42		08 57			09 12		09 27		09 42		09 57		10 12			10 27		10 42
Little Sutton	d			08 31					09 01					09 31				10 01					10 31		
Overpool	d			08 33					09 03					09 33				10 03					10 33		
Ellesmere Port	a			08 37					09 07					09 37				10 07					10 37		
Capenhurst	d						08 47					09 17				09 47				10 17					10 47
Bache	d						08 52					09 22				09 52				10 22					10 52
Chester	a						08 56					09 26				09 56				10 26					10 56

		ME	ME	ME	ME	ME		ME	ME	ME	ME	ME	ME	ME	ME	ME		ME	ME	ME	ME	ME	ME	ME	ME
Moorfields 10	d	10 16	10 26	10 31	10 41	10 46		10 56	11 01	11 11	11 16	11 26	11 31	11 41	11 46	11 56		12 01	12 11	12 16	12 26	12 31	12 41	12 46	12 56
Liverpool Lime Street 10	d	10 18	10 28	10 33	10 43	10 48		10 58	11 03	11 13	11 18	11 28	11 33	11 43	11 48	11 58		12 03	12 13	12 18	12 28	12 33	12 43	12 48	12 58
Liverpool Central 10	d	10 20	10 30	10 35	10 45	10 50		11 00	11 05	11 15	11 20	11 30	11 35	11 45	11 50	12 00		12 05	12 15	12 20	12 30	12 35	12 45	12 50	13 00
James Street	d	10 22	10 32	10 37	10 47	10 52		11 02	11 07	11 17	11 22	11 32	11 37	11 47	11 52	12 02		12 07	12 17	12 22	12 32	12 37	12 47	12 52	13 02
Hamilton Square	d	10 25	10 35	10 40	10 50	10 55		11 05	11 10	11 20	11 25	11 35	11 40	11 50	11 55	12 05		12 10	12 20	12 25	12 35	12 40	12 50	12 55	13 05
Conway Park	d	10 27		10 42		10 57			11 12		11 27		11 42		11 57			12 12		12 27		12 42		12 57	
Birkenhead Park	d	10 29		10 44		10 59			11 14		11 29		11 44		11 59			12 14		12 29		12 44		12 59	
Birkenhead North	d	10 32		10 47		11 02			11 17		11 32		11 47		12 02			12 17		12 32		12 47		13 02	
Wallasey Village	d	10 37				11 07					11 37				12 07					12 37				13 07	
Wallasey Grove Road	d	10 38				11 08					11 38				12 08					12 38				13 08	
New Brighton	a	10 43				11 13					11 43				12 13					12 43				13 13	
Bidston	d			10 50					11 20				11 50					12 20				12 50			
Leasowe	d			10 52					11 22				11 52					12 22				12 52			
Moreton (Merseyside)	d			10 54					11 24				11 54					12 24				12 54			
Meols	d			10 58					11 28				11 58					12 28				12 58			
Manor Road	d			11 00					11 30				12 00					12 30				13 00			
Hoylake	d			11 02					11 32				12 02					12 32				13 02			
West Kirby	a			11 07					11 37				12 07					12 37				13 07			
Birkenhead Central	d		10 37		10 52			11 07		11 22		11 37		11 52		12 07			12 22		12 37		12 52		13 07
Green Lane	d		10 39		10 54			11 09		11 24		11 39		11 54		12 09			12 24		12 39		12 54		13 09
Rock Ferry	d		10 42		10 57			11 12		11 27		11 42		11 57		12 12			12 27		12 42		12 57		13 12
Bebington	d		10 44		10 59			11 14		11 29		11 44		11 59		12 14			12 29		12 44		12 59		13 14
Port Sunlight	d		10 46		11 01			11 16		11 31		11 46		12 01		12 16			12 31		12 46		13 01		13 16
Spital	d		10 48		11 03			11 18		11 33		11 48		12 03		12 18			12 33		12 48		13 03		13 18
Bromborough Rake	d		10 50		11 05			11 20		11 35		11 50		12 05		12 20			12 35		12 50		13 05		13 20
Bromborough	d		10 52		11 07			11 22		11 37		11 52		12 07		12 22			12 37		12 52		13 07		13 22
Eastham Rake	d		10 55		11 10			11 25		11 40		11 55		12 10		12 25			12 40		12 55		13 10		13 25
Hooton	d		10 57		11 12			11 27		11 42		11 57		12 12		12 27			12 42		12 57		13 12		13 27
Little Sutton	d		11 01					11 31				12 01				12 31					13 01				13 31
Overpool	d		11 03					11 33				12 03				12 33					13 03				13 33
Ellesmere Port	a		11 07					11 37				12 07				12 37					13 07				13 37
Capenhurst	d				11 17					11 47				12 17					12 47				13 17		
Bache	d				11 22					11 52				12 22					12 52				13 22		
Chester	a				11 26					11 56				12 26					12 56				13 26		

Table 106

Sundays

Liverpool and Birkenhead - New Brighton, West Kirby, Ellesmere Port and Chester

		ME		ME	ME	ME	ME	ME	ME	ME	ME	ME		ME	ME	ME	ME	ME	ME	ME	ME	ME		ME	ME
Moorfields 10	d	13 01		13 11	13 16	13 26	13 31	13 41	13 46	13 56	14 01	14 11		14 16	14 26	14 31	14 41	14 46	14 56	15 01	15 11	15 16		15 26	15 31
Liverpool Lime Street 10	d	13 03		13 13	13 18	13 28	13 33	13 43	13 48	13 58	14 03	14 13		14 18	14 28	14 33	14 43	14 48	14 58	15 03	15 13	15 18		15 28	15 33
Liverpool Central 10	d	13 05		13 15	13 20	13 30	13 35	13 45	13 50	14 00	14 05	14 15		14 20	14 30	14 35	14 45	14 50	15 00	15 05	15 15	15 20		15 30	15 35
James Street	d	13 07		13 17	13 22	13 32	13 37	13 47	13 52	14 02	14 07	14 17		14 22	14 32	14 37	14 47	14 52	15 02	15 07	15 17	15 22		15 32	15 37
Hamilton Square	d	13 10		13 20	13 25	13 35	13 40	13 50	13 55	14 05	14 10	14 20		14 25	14 35	14 40	14 50	14 55	15 05	15 10	15 20	15 25		15 35	15 40
Conway Park	d	13 12			13 27		13 42		13 57		14 12			14 27		14 42		14 57		15 12		15 27			15 42
Birkenhead Park	d	13 14			13 29		13 44		13 59		14 14			14 29		14 44		14 59		15 14		15 29			15 44
Birkenhead North	d	13 17			13 32		13 47		14 02		14 17			14 32		14 47		15 02		15 17		15 32			15 47
Wallasey Village	d				13 37				14 07					14 37				15 07				15 37			
Wallasey Grove Road	d				13 38				14 08					14 38				15 08				15 38			
New Brighton	a				13 43				14 13					14 43				15 13				15 43			
Bidston	d	13 20					13 50				14 20					14 50				15 20					15 50
Leasowe	d	13 22					13 52				14 22					14 52				15 22					15 52
Moreton (Merseyside)	d	13 24					13 54				14 24					14 54				15 24					15 54
Meols	d	13 28					13 58				14 28					14 58				15 28					15 58
Manor Road	d	13 30					14 00				14 30					15 00				15 30					16 00
Hoylake	d	13 32					14 02				14 32					15 02				15 32					16 02
West Kirby	a	13 37					14 07				14 37					15 07				15 37					16 07
Birkenhead Central	d			13 22		13 37		13 52		14 07		14 22			14 37		14 52		15 07		15 22			15 37	
Green Lane	d			13 24		13 39		13 54		14 09		14 24			14 39		14 54		15 09		15 24			15 39	
Rock Ferry	d			13 27		13 42		13 57		14 12		14 27			14 42		14 57		15 12		15 27			15 42	
Bebington	d			13 29		13 44		13 59		14 14		14 29			14 44		14 59		15 14		15 29			15 44	
Port Sunlight	d			13 31		13 46		14 01		14 16		14 31			14 46		15 01		15 16		15 31			15 46	
Spital	d			13 33		13 48		14 03		14 18		14 33			14 48		15 03		15 18		15 33			15 48	
Bromborough Rake	d			13 35		13 50		14 05		14 20		14 35			14 50		15 05		15 20		15 35			15 50	
Bromborough	d			13 37		13 52		14 07		14 22		14 37			14 52		15 07		15 22		15 37			15 52	
Eastham Rake	d			13 40		13 55		14 10		14 25		14 40			14 55		15 10		15 25		15 40			15 55	
Hooton	d			13 42		13 57		14 12		14 27		14 42			14 57		15 12		15 27		15 42			15 57	
Little Sutton	d					14 01				14 31					15 01				15 31					16 01	
Overpool	d					14 03				14 33					15 03				15 33					16 03	
Ellesmere Port	a					14 07				14 37					15 07				15 37					16 07	
Capenhurst	d			13 47				14 17				14 47					15 17				15 47				
Bache	d			13 52				14 22				14 52					15 22				15 52				
Chester	a			13 56				14 26				14 56					15 26				15 56				

		ME	ME	ME	ME	ME	ME	ME		ME	ME	ME	ME	ME	ME	ME	ME	ME		ME	ME	ME	ME	ME	ME
Moorfields 10	d	15 41	15 46	15 56	16 01	16 11	16 16	16 26		16 31	16 41	16 46	16 56	17 01	17 11	17 16	17 26	17 31		17 41	17 46	17 56	18 01	18 11	18 16
Liverpool Lime Street 10	d	15 43	15 48	15 58	16 03	16 13	16 18	16 28		16 33	16 43	16 48	16 58	17 03	17 13	17 18	17 28	17 33		17 43	17 48	17 58	18 03	18 13	18 18
Liverpool Central 10	d	15 45	15 50	16 00	16 05	16 15	16 20	16 30		16 35	16 45	16 50	17 00	17 05	17 15	17 20	17 30	17 35		17 45	17 50	18 00	18 05	18 15	18 20
James Street	d	15 47	15 52	16 02	16 07	16 17	16 22	16 32		16 37	16 47	16 52	17 02	17 07	17 17	17 22	17 32	17 37		17 47	17 52	18 02	18 07	18 17	18 22
Hamilton Square	d	15 50	15 55	16 05	16 10	16 20	16 25	16 35		16 40	16 50	16 55	17 05	17 10	17 20	17 25	17 35	17 40		17 50	17 55	18 05	18 10	18 20	18 25
Conway Park	d		15 57		16 12		16 27			16 42		16 57		17 12		17 27		17 42			17 57		18 12		18 27
Birkenhead Park	d		15 59		16 14		16 29			16 44		16 59		17 14		17 29		17 44			17 59		18 14		18 29
Birkenhead North	d		16 02		16 17		16 32			16 47		17 02		17 17		17 32		17 47			18 02		18 17		18 32
Wallasey Village	d		16 07				16 37					17 07				17 37					18 07				18 37
Wallasey Grove Road	d		16 08				16 38					17 08				17 38					18 08				18 38
New Brighton	a		16 13				16 43					17 13				17 43					18 13				18 43
Bidston	d				16 20					16 50				17 20				17 50					18 20		
Leasowe	d				16 22					16 52				17 22				17 52					18 22		
Moreton (Merseyside)	d				16 24					16 54				17 24				17 54					18 24		
Meols	d				16 28					16 58				17 28				17 58					18 28		
Manor Road	d				16 30					17 00				17 30				18 00					18 30		
Hoylake	d				16 32					17 02				17 32				18 02					18 32		
West Kirby	a				16 37					17 07				17 37				18 07					18 37		
Birkenhead Central	d	15 52		16 07		16 22		16 37			16 52		17 07		17 22		17 37			17 52		18 07		18 22	
Green Lane	d	15 54		16 09		16 24		16 39			16 54		17 09		17 24		17 39			17 54		18 09		18 24	
Rock Ferry	d	15 57		16 12		16 27		16 42			16 57		17 12		17 27		17 42			17 57		18 12		18 27	
Bebington	d	15 59		16 14		16 29		16 44			16 59		17 14		17 29		17 44			17 59		18 14		18 29	
Port Sunlight	d	16 01		16 16		16 31		16 46			17 01		17 16		17 31		17 46			18 01		18 16		18 31	
Spital	d	16 03		16 18		16 33		16 48			17 03		17 18		17 33		17 48			18 03		18 18		18 33	
Bromborough Rake	d	16 05		16 20		16 35		16 50			17 05		17 20		17 35		17 50			18 05		18 20		18 35	
Bromborough	d	16 07		16 22		16 37		16 52			17 07		17 22		17 37		17 52			18 07		18 22		18 37	
Eastham Rake	d	16 10		16 25		16 40		16 55			17 10		17 25		17 40		17 55			18 10		18 25		18 40	
Hooton	d	16 12		16 27		16 42		16 57			17 12		17 27		17 42		17 57			18 12		18 27		18 42	
Little Sutton	d			16 31				17 01					17 31				18 01					18 31			
Overpool	d			16 33				17 03					17 33				18 03					18 33			
Ellesmere Port	a			16 37				17 07					17 37				18 07					18 37			
Capenhurst	d	16 17				16 47					17 17				17 47					18 17				18 47	
Bache	d	16 22				16 52					17 22				17 52					18 22				18 52	
Chester	a	16 26				16 56					17 26				17 56					18 26				18 56	

Table 106

Sundays

Liverpool and Birkenhead - New Brighton, West Kirby, Ellesmere Port and Chester

		ME	ME	ME	ME	ME	ME	ME	ME	ME	ME	ME	ME	ME	ME	ME	ME	ME	ME	ME	ME	ME
Moorfields 10	d	18 26	18 31	18 41	18 46	18 56	19 01	19 11	19 16	19 26	19 31	19 41	19 46	19 56	20 01	20 11	20 16	20 26	20 31	20 41	20 46	20 56
Liverpool Lime Street 10	d	18 28	18 33	18 43	18 48	18 58	19 03	19 13	19 18	19 28	19 33	19 43	19 48	19 58	20 03	20 13	20 18	20 28	20 33	20 43	20 48	20 58
Liverpool Central 10	d	18 30	18 35	18 45	18 50	19 00	19 05	19 15	19 20	19 30	19 35	19 45	19 50	20 00	20 05	20 15	20 20	20 30	20 35	20 45	20 50	21 00
James Street	d	18 32	18 37	18 47	18 52	19 02	19 07	19 17	19 22	19 32	19 37	19 47	19 52	20 02	20 07	20 17	20 22	20 32	20 37	20 47	20 52	21 02
Hamilton Square	d	18 35	18 40	18 50	18 55	19 05	19 10	19 20	19 25	19 35	19 40	19 50	19 55	20 05	20 10	20 20	20 25	20 35	20 40	20 50	20 55	21 05
Conway Park	d		18 42		18 57		19 12		19 27		19 42		19 57		20 12		20 27		20 42		20 57	
Birkenhead Park	d		18 44		18 59		19 14		19 29		19 44		19 59		20 14		20 29		20 44		20 59	
Birkenhead North	d		18 47		19 02		19 17		19 32		19 47		20 02		20 17		20 32		20 47		21 02	
Wallasey Village	d				19 07				19 37				20 07				20 37				21 07	
Wallasey Grove Road	d				19 08				19 38				20 08				20 38				21 08	
New Brighton	a				19 13				19 43				20 13				20 43				21 13	
Bidston	d		18 50				19 20				19 50				20 20				20 50			
Leasowe	d		18 52				19 22				19 52				20 22				20 52			
Moreton (Merseyside)	d		18 54				19 24				19 54				20 24				20 54			
Meols	d		18 58				19 28				19 58				20 28				20 58			
Manor Road	d		19 00				19 30				20 00				20 30				21 00			
Hoylake	d		19 02				19 32				20 02				20 32				21 02			
West Kirby	a		19 07				19 37				20 07				20 37				21 07			
Birkenhead Central	d	18 37		18 52		19 07		19 22		19 37		19 52		20 07		20 22		20 37		20 52		21 07
Green Lane	d	18 39		18 54		19 09		19 24		19 39		19 54		20 09		20 24		20 39		20 54		21 09
Rock Ferry	d	18 42		18 57		19 12		19 27		19 42		19 57		20 12		20 27		20 42		20 57		21 12
Bebington	d	18 44		18 59		19 14		19 29		19 44		19 59		20 14		20 29		20 44		20 59		21 14
Port Sunlight	d	18 46		19 01		19 16		19 31		19 46		20 01		20 16		20 31		20 46		21 01		21 16
Spital	d	18 48		19 03		19 18		19 33		19 48		20 03		20 18		20 33		20 48		21 03		21 18
Bromborough Rake	d	18 50		19 05		19 20		19 35		19 50		20 05		20 20		20 35		20 50		21 05		21 20
Bromborough	d	18 52		19 07		19 22		19 37		19 52		20 07		20 22		20 37		20 52		21 07		21 22
Eastham Rake	d	18 55		19 10		19 25		19 40		19 55		20 10		20 25		20 40		20 55		21 10		21 25
Hooton	d	18 57		19 12		19 27		19 42		19 57		20 12		20 27		20 42		20 57		21 12		21 27
Little Sutton	d	19 01				19 31				20 01				20 31				21 01				21 31
Overpool	d	19 03				19 33				20 03				20 33				21 03				21 33
Ellesmere Port	a	19 07				19 37				20 07				20 37				21 07				21 37
Capenhurst	d			19 17				19 47				20 17				20 47				21 17		
Bache	d			19 22				19 52				20 22				20 52				21 22		
Chester	a			19 26				19 56				20 26				20 56				21 26		

		ME	ME	ME	ME	ME	ME	ME	ME	ME	ME	ME	ME	ME	ME	ME	ME	ME	ME	ME	ME	ME	ME
Moorfields 10	d	21 01	21 11	21 16	21 26	21 31	21 41	21 46	21 56	22 01	22 11	22 16	22 26	22 31	22 41	22 46	22 56	23 01	23 11	23 16	23 26	23 31	23 41
Liverpool Lime Street 10	d	21 03	21 13	21 18	21 28	21 33	21 43	21 48	21 58	22 03	22 13	22 18	22 28	22 33	22 43	22 48	22 58	23 03	23 13	23 18	23 28	23 33	23 43
Liverpool Central 10	d	21 05	21 15	21 20	21 30	21 35	21 45	21 50	22 00	22 05	22 15	22 20	22 30	22 35	22 45	22 50	23 00	23 05	23 15	23 20	23 30	23 35	23 45
James Street	d	21 07	21 17	21 22	21 32	21 37	21 47	21 52	22 02	22 07	22 17	22 22	22 32	22 37	22 47	22 52	23 02	23 07	23 17	23 22	23 32	23 37	23 47
Hamilton Square	d	21 10	21 20	21 25	21 35	21 40	21 50	21 55	22 05	22 10	22 20	22 25	22 35	22 40	22 50	22 55	23 05	23 10	23 20	23 25	23 35	23 40	23 50
Conway Park	d	21 12		21 27		21 42		21 57		22 12		22 27		22 42		22 57		23 12		23 27		23 42	
Birkenhead Park	d	21 14		21 29		21 44		21 59		22 14		22 29		22 44		22 59		23 14		23 29		23 44	
Birkenhead North	d	21 17		21 32		21 47		22 02		22 17		22 32		22 47		23 02		23 17		23 32		23 47	
Wallasey Village	d			21 37				22 07				22 37				23 07				23 37			
Wallasey Grove Road	d			21 38				22 08				22 38				23 08				23 38			
New Brighton	a			21 43				22 13				22 43				23 13				23 43			
Bidston	d	21 20				21 50				22 20				22 50				23 20				23 50	
Leasowe	d	21 22				21 52				22 22				22 52				23 22				23 52	
Moreton (Merseyside)	d	21 24				21 54				22 24				22 54				23 24				23 54	
Meols	d	21 28				21 58				22 28				22 58				23 28				23 58	
Manor Road	d	21 30				22 00				22 30				23 00				23 30				23 59	
Hoylake	d	21 32				22 02				22 32				23 02				23 32				00 02	
West Kirby	a	21 37				22 07				22 37				23 07				23 37				00 07	
Birkenhead Central	d		21 22		21 37		21 52		22 07		22 22		22 37		22 52		23 07		23 22		23 37		23 52
Green Lane	d		21 24		21 39		21 54		22 09		22 24		22 39		22 54		23 09		23 24		23 39		23 54
Rock Ferry	d		21 27		21 42		21 57		22 12		22 27		22 42		22 57		23 12		23 27		23 42		23 57
Bebington	d		21 29		21 44		21 59		22 14		22 29		22 44		22 59		23 14		23 29		23 44		23 59
Port Sunlight	d		21 31		21 46		22 01		22 16		22 31		22 46		23 01		23 16		23 31		23 46		00 01
Spital	d		21 33		21 48		22 03		22 18		22 33		22 48		23 03		23 18		23 33		23 48		00 03
Bromborough Rake	d		21 35		21 50		22 05		22 20		22 35		22 50		23 05		23 20		23 35		23 50		00 05
Bromborough	d		21 37		21 52		22 07		22 22		22 37		22 52		23 07		23 22		23 37		23 52		00 07
Eastham Rake	d		21 40		21 55		22 10		22 25		22 40		22 55		23 10		23 25		23 40		23 55		00 10
Hooton	d		21 42		21 57		22 12		22 27		22 42		22 57		23 12		23 27		23 42		23 57		00 12
Little Sutton	d				22 01				22 31				23 01				23 31				00 01		
Overpool	d				22 03				22 33				23 03				23 33				00 03		
Ellesmere Port	a				22 07				22 37				23 07				23 37				00 07		
Capenhurst	d		21 47				22 17				22 47				23 17				23 47				00 17
Bache	d		21 52				22 22				22 52				23 22				23 52				00 22
Chester	a		21 56				22 26				22 56				23 26				23 56				00 26

Table 106

Sundays

Liverpool and Birkenhead - New Brighton, West Kirby, Ellesmere Port and Chester

		ME	ME
Moorfields 10	d	23 46	23 56
Liverpool Lime Street 10	d	23 48	23 58
Liverpool Central 10	d	23 50	23 59
James Street	d	23 52	00 02
Hamilton Square	d	23 55	00a05
Conway Park	d	23 57	
Birkenhead Park	d	23 59	
Birkenhead North	d	00 02	
Wallasey Village	d	00 07	
Wallasey Grove Road	d	00 08	
New Brighton	a	00 13	
Bidston	d		
Leasowe	d		
Moreton (Merseyside)	d		
Meols	d		
Manor Road	d		
Hoylake	d		
West Kirby	a		
Birkenhead Central	d		
Green Lane	d		
Rock Ferry	d		
Bebington	d		
Port Sunlight	d		
Spital	d		
Bromborough Rake	d		
Bromborough	d		
Eastham Rake	d		
Hooton	d		
Little Sutton	d		
Overpool	d		
Ellesmere Port	a		
Capenhurst	d		
Bache	d		
Chester	a		

Table 106

Mondays to Saturdays

Chester, Ellesmere Port, West Kirby and New Brighton - Birkenhead and Liverpool

		ME	ME	ME	ME	ME	ME	ME	ME	ME	ME	ME	ME	ME	ME	ME	ME	ME	ME	ME	ME	ME SX	ME	ME SX	ME SO
Chester	d						06 00				06 30						07 00					07 22			07 30
Bache	d						06 03				06 33						07 03					07 26			07 33
Capenhurst	d						06 09				06 39						07 09					07 32			07 39
Ellesmere Port	d									06 19				06 49						07 19				07 31	
Overpool	d									06 22				06 52						07 22				07 34	
Little Sutton	d									06 24				06 54						07 24				07 36	
Hooton	d		05 39			05 59	06 14			06 29	06 44			06 59			07 14			07 29		07 36		07 44	07 44
Eastham Rake	d		05 41			06 01	06 16			06 31	06 46			07 01			07 16			07 31		07 38		07 46	07 46
Bromborough	d		05 43			06 03	06 18			06 33	06 48			07 03			07 18			07 33		07 41		07 48	07 48
Bromborough Rake	d		05 45			06 05	06 20			06 35	06 50			07 05			07 20			07 35		07 43		07 50	07 50
Spital	d		05 47			06 07	06 22			06 37	06 52			07 07			07 22			07 37		07 45		07 52	07 52
Port Sunlight	d		05 49			06 09	06 24			06 39	06 54			07 09			07 24			07 39		07 47		07 54	07 54
Bebington	d		05 51			06 11	06 26			06 41	06 56			07 11			07 26			07 41		07 49		07 56	07 56
Rock Ferry	d	05 44	05 54			06 14	06 29			06 44	06 59			07 14			07 29			07 44		07 52		07 59	07 59
Green Lane	d	05 47	05 57			06 17	06 32			06 47	07 02			07 17			07 32			07 47		07 54		08 02	08 02
Birkenhead Central	d	05 49	05 59			06 19	06 34			06 49	07 04			07 19			07 34			07 49		07 57		08 04	08 04
West Kirby	d				05 51				06 21				06 51			07 06			07 21				07 36		
Hoylake	d				05 54				06 24				06 54			07 09			07 24				07 39		
Manor Road	d				05 56				06 26				06 56			07 11			07 26				07 41		
Meols	d				05 58				06 28				06 58			07 13			07 28				07 43		
Moreton (Merseyside)	d				06 01				06 31				07 01			07 16			07 31				07 46		
Leasowe	d				06 03				06 33				07 03			07 18			07 33				07 48		
Bidston	d				06 06				06 36				07 06			07 21			07 36				07 51		
New Brighton	d			05 53				06 23				06 53			07 08			07 23			07 38				
Wallasey Grove Road	d			05 57				06 27				06 57			07 12			07 27			07 42				
Wallasey Village	d			05 59				06 29				06 59			07 14			07 29			07 44				
Birkenhead North	d			06 04	06 09			06 34	06 39			07 04	07 09		07 19	07 24		07 34	07 39		07 49		07 54		
Birkenhead Park	d			06 06	06 11			06 36	06 41			07 06	07 11		07 21	07 26		07 36	07 41		07 51		07 56		
Conway Park	d			06 09	06 14			06 39	06 44			07 09	07 14		07 24	07 29		07 39	07 44		07 54		07 59		
Hamilton Square	d	05 51	06 01	06 11	06 16	06 21	06 36	06 41	06 46	06 51	07 06	07 11	07 16	07 21	07 26	07 31	07 36	07 41	07 46	07 51	07 56	07 59	08 01	08 06	08 06
James Street	d	05 54	06 04	06 14	06 19	06 24	06 39	06 44	06 49	06 54	07 09	07 14	07 19	07 24	07 29	07 34	07 39	07 44	07 49	07 54	07 59	08 02	08 04	08 09	08 09
Moorfields 10	a	05 56	06 06	06 16	06 21	06 26	06 41	06 46	06 51	06 56	07 11	07 16	07 21	07 26	07 31	07 36	07 41	07 46	07 51	07 56	08 01	08 03	08 06	08 11	08 11
Liverpool Lime Street 10	a	05 58	06 08	06 18	06 23	06 28	06 43	06 48	06 53	06 58	07 13	07 18	07 23	07 28	07 33	07 38	07 43	07 48	07 53	07 58	08 03	08 05	08 08	08 13	08 13
Liverpool Central 10	a	06 00	06 10	06 20	06 25	06 30	06 45	06 50	06 55	07 00	07 15	07 20	07 25	07 30	07 35	07 40	07 45	07 50	07 55	08 00	08 05	08 07	08 10	08 15	08 15

		ME	ME SX	ME	ME	ME	ME SX	ME	ME SX	ME SO	ME	ME SX	ME	ME	ME	ME SX	ME	ME	ME	ME SX	ME	ME	ME	ME	ME
Chester	d		07 37				07 52			08 00		08 07						08 30							09 00
Bache	d		07 41				07 56			08 03		08 11						08 33							09 03
Capenhurst	d		07 47				08 02			08 09		08 17						08 39							09 09
Ellesmere Port	d				07 49				08 01					08 19								08 49			
Overpool	d				07 52				08 04					08 22								08 52			
Little Sutton	d				07 54				08 06					08 24								08 54			
Hooton	d		07 51		07 59		08 06		08 14	08 14		08 21		08 29		08 36		08 44		08 51		08 59			09 14
Eastham Rake	d		07 53		08 01		08 08		08 16	08 16		08 23		08 31		08 38		08 46		08 53		09 01			09 16
Bromborough	d		07 56		08 03		08 11		08 18	08 18		08 26		08 33		08 41		08 48		08 56		09 03			09 18
Bromborough Rake	d		07 58		08 05		08 13		08 20	08 20		08 28		08 35		08 43		08 50		08 58		09 05			09 20
Spital	d		08 00		08 07		08 15		08 22	08 22		08 30		08 37		08 45		08 52		09 00		09 07			09 22
Port Sunlight	d		08 02		08 09		08 17		08 24	08 24		08 32		08 39		08 47		08 54		09 02		09 09			09 24
Bebington	d		08 04		08 11		08 19		08 26	08 26		08 34		08 41		08 49		08 56		09 04		09 11			09 26
Rock Ferry	d		08 07		08 14		08 22		08 29	08 29		08 37		08 44		08 52		08 59		09 07		09 14			09 29
Green Lane	d		08 09		08 17		08 24		08 32	08 32		08 39		08 47		08 54		09 02		09 09		09 17			09 32
Birkenhead Central	d		08 12		08 19		08 27		08 34	08 34		08 42		08 49		08 57		09 04		09 12		09 19			09 34
West Kirby	d			07 51				08 06					08 21				08 36				08 51			09 06	
Hoylake	d			07 54				08 09					08 24				08 39				08 54			09 09	
Manor Road	d			07 56				08 11					08 26				08 41				08 56			09 11	
Meols	d			07 58				08 13					08 28				08 43				08 58			09 13	
Moreton (Merseyside)	d			08 01				08 16					08 31				08 46				09 01			09 16	
Leasowe	d			08 03				08 18					08 33				08 48				09 03			09 18	
Bidston	d			08 06				08 21					08 36				08 51				09 06			09 21	
New Brighton	d	07 53				08 08					08 23				08 38				08 53				09 08		
Wallasey Grove Road	d	07 57				08 12					08 27				08 42				08 57				09 12		
Wallasey Village	d	07 59				08 14					08 29				08 44				08 59				09 14		
Birkenhead North	d	08 04		08 09		08 19		08 24			08 34		08 39		08 49		08 54		09 04		09 09		09 19	09 24	
Birkenhead Park	d	08 06		08 11		08 21		08 26			08 36		08 41		08 51		08 56		09 06		09 11		09 21	09 26	
Conway Park	d	08 09		08 14		08 24		08 29			08 39		08 44		08 54		08 59		09 09		09 14		09 24	09 29	
Hamilton Square	d	08 11	08 14	08 16	08 21	08 26	08 29	08 31	08 36	08 36	08 41	08 44	08 46	08 51	08 56	08 59	09 01	09 06	09 11	09 14	09 16	09 21	09 26	09 31	09 36
James Street	d	08 14	08 17	08 19	08 24	08 29	08 32	08 34	08 39	08 39	08 44	08 47	08 49	08 54	08 59	09 02	09 04	09 09	09 14	09 17	09 19	09 24	09 29	09 34	09 39
Moorfields 10	a	08 16	08 18	08 21	08 26	08 31	08 33	08 36	08 41	08 41	08 46	08 48	08 51	08 56	09 01	09 03	09 06	09 11	09 16	09 18	09 21	09 26	09 31	09 36	09 41
Liverpool Lime Street 10	a	08 18	08 20	08 23	08 28	08 33	08 35	08 38	08 43	08 43	08 48	08 50	08 53	08 58	09 03	09 05	09 08	09 13	09 18	09 20	09 23	09 28	09 33	09 38	09 43
Liverpool Central 10	a	08 20	08 22	08 25	08 30	08 35	08 37	08 40	08 45	08 45	08 50	08 52	08 55	09 00	09 05	09 07	09 10	09 15	09 20	09 22	09 25	09 30	09 35	09 40	09 45

Table 106

Mondays to Saturdays

Chester, Ellesmere Port, West Kirby and New Brighton - Birkenhead and Liverpool

		ME	ME	ME	ME	ME	ME	ME	ME	ME	ME	ME		ME	ME	ME	ME	ME	ME	ME	ME	ME		ME	ME
Chester	d						09 30							10 00						10 30					
Bache	d						09 33							10 03						10 33					
Capenhurst	d						09 39							10 09						10 39					
Ellesmere Port	d			09 19						09 49							10 19							10 49	
Overpool	d			09 22						09 52							10 22							10 52	
Little Sutton	d			09 24						09 54							10 24							10 54	
Hooton	d			09 29			09 44			09 59				10 14			10 29			10 44				10 59	
Eastham Rake	d			09 31			09 46			10 01				10 16			10 31			10 46				11 01	
Bromborough	d			09 33			09 48			10 03				10 18			10 33			10 48				11 03	
Bromborough Rake	d			09 35			09 50			10 05				10 20			10 35			10 50				11 05	
Spital	d			09 37			09 52			10 07				10 22			10 37			10 52				11 07	
Port Sunlight	d			09 39			09 54			10 09				10 24			10 39			10 54				11 09	
Bebington	d			09 41			09 56			10 11				10 26			10 41			10 56				11 11	
Rock Ferry	d			09 44			09 59			10 14				10 29			10 44			10 59				11 14	
Green Lane	d			09 47			10 02			10 17				10 32			10 47			11 02				11 17	
Birkenhead Central	d			09 49			10 04			10 19				10 34			10 49			11 04				11 19	
West Kirby	d		09 21			09 36			09 51			10 06				10 21			10 36			10 51			
Hoylake	d		09 24			09 39			09 54			10 09				10 24			10 39			10 54			
Manor Road	d		09 26			09 41			09 56			10 11				10 26			10 41			10 56			
Meols	d		09 28			09 43			09 58			10 13				10 28			10 43			10 58			
Moreton (Merseyside)	d		09 31			09 46			10 01			10 16				10 31			10 46			11 01			
Leasowe	d		09 33			09 48			10 03			10 18				10 33			10 48			11 03			
Bidston	d		09 36			09 51			10 06			10 21				10 36			10 51			11 06			
New Brighton	d	09 23			09 38			09 53			10 08				10 23			10 38			10 53				11 08
Wallasey Grove Road	d	09 27			09 42			09 57			10 12				10 27			10 42			10 57				11 12
Wallasey Village	d	09 29			09 44			09 59			10 14				10 29			10 44			10 59				11 14
Birkenhead North	d	09 34	09 39		09 49	09 54		10 04	10 09		10 19	10 24			10 34	10 39		10 49	10 54		11 04	11 09			11 19
Birkenhead Park	d	09 36	09 41		09 51	09 56		10 06	10 11		10 21	10 26			10 36	10 41		10 51	10 56		11 06	11 11			11 21
Conway Park	d	09 39	09 44		09 54	09 59		10 09	10 14		10 24	10 29			10 39	10 44		10 54	10 59		11 09	11 14			11 24
Hamilton Square	d	09 41	09 46	09 51	09 56	10 01	10 06	10 11	10 16	10 21	10 26	10 31		10 36	10 41	10 46	10 51	10 56	11 01	11 06	11 11	11 16		11 21	11 26
James Street	d	09 44	09 49	09 54	09 59	10 04	10 09	10 14	10 19	10 24	10 29	10 34		10 39	10 44	10 49	10 54	10 59	11 04	11 09	11 14	11 19		11 24	11 29
Moorfields 10	a	09 46	09 51	09 56	10 01	10 06	10 11	10 16	10 21	10 26	10 31	10 36		10 41	10 46	10 51	10 56	11 01	11 06	11 11	11 16	11 21		11 26	11 31
Liverpool Lime Street 10	a	09 48	09 53	09 58	10 03	10 08	10 13	10 18	10 23	10 28	10 33	10 38		10 43	10 48	10 53	10 58	11 03	11 08	11 13	11 18	11 23		11 28	11 33
Liverpool Central 10	a	09 50	09 55	10 00	10 05	10 10	10 15	10 20	10 25	10 30	10 35	10 40		10 45	10 50	10 55	11 00	11 05	11 10	11 15	11 20	11 25		11 30	11 35

		ME	ME	ME	ME	ME	ME	ME		ME	ME	ME	ME	ME	ME	ME	ME	ME		ME	ME	ME	ME	ME	ME
Chester	d		11 00							11 30						12 00							12 30		
Bache	d		11 03							11 33						12 03							12 33		
Capenhurst	d		11 09							11 39						12 09							12 39		
Ellesmere Port	d					11 19							11 49							12 19					
Overpool	d					11 22							11 52							12 22					
Little Sutton	d					11 24							11 54							12 24					
Hooton	d		11 14			11 29				11 44			11 59			12 14				12 29			12 44		
Eastham Rake	d		11 16			11 31				11 46			12 01			12 16				12 31			12 46		
Bromborough	d		11 18			11 33				11 48			12 03			12 18				12 33			12 48		
Bromborough Rake	d		11 20			11 35				11 50			12 05			12 20				12 35			12 50		
Spital	d		11 22			11 37				11 52			12 07			12 22				12 37			12 52		
Port Sunlight	d		11 24			11 39				11 54			12 09			12 24				12 39			12 54		
Bebington	d		11 26			11 41				11 56			12 11			12 26				12 41			12 56		
Rock Ferry	d		11 29			11 44				11 59			12 14			12 29				12 44			12 59		
Green Lane	d		11 32			11 47				12 02			12 17			12 32				12 47			13 02		
Birkenhead Central	d		11 34			11 49				12 04			12 19			12 34				12 49			13 04		
West Kirby	d	11 06			11 21			11 36				11 51			12 06			12 21				12 36			12 51
Hoylake	d	11 09			11 24			11 39				11 54			12 09			12 24				12 39			12 54
Manor Road	d	11 11			11 26			11 41				11 56			12 11			12 26				12 41			12 56
Meols	d	11 13			11 28			11 43				11 58			12 13			12 28				12 43			12 58
Moreton (Merseyside)	d	11 16			11 31			11 46				12 01			12 16			12 31				12 46			13 01
Leasowe	d	11 18			11 33			11 48				12 03			12 18			12 33				12 48			13 03
Bidston	d	11 21			11 36			11 51				12 06			12 21			12 36				12 51			13 06
New Brighton	d			11 23			11 38				11 53			12 08			12 23				12 38			12 53	
Wallasey Grove Road	d			11 27			11 42				11 57			12 12			12 27				12 42			12 57	
Wallasey Village	d			11 29			11 44				11 59			12 14			12 29				12 44			12 59	
Birkenhead North	d	11 24		11 34	11 39		11 49	11 54			12 04	12 09		12 19	12 24		12 34	12 39			12 49	12 54		13 04	13 09
Birkenhead Park	d	11 26		11 36	11 41		11 51	11 56			12 06	12 11		12 21	12 26		12 36	12 41			12 51	12 56		13 06	13 11
Conway Park	d	11 29		11 39	11 44		11 54	11 59			12 09	12 14		12 24	12 29		12 39	12 44			12 54	12 59		13 09	13 14
Hamilton Square	d	11 31	11 36	11 41	11 46	11 51	11 56	12 01		12 06	12 11	12 16	12 21	12 26	12 31	12 36	12 41	12 46		12 51	12 56	13 01	13 06	13 11	13 16
James Street	d	11 34	11 39	11 44	11 49	11 54	11 59	12 04		12 09	12 14	12 19	12 24	12 29	12 34	12 39	12 44	12 49		12 54	12 59	13 04	13 09	13 14	13 19
Moorfields 10	a	11 36	11 41	11 46	11 51	11 56	12 01	12 06		12 11	12 16	12 21	12 26	12 31	12 36	12 41	12 46	12 51		12 56	13 01	13 06	13 11	13 16	13 21
Liverpool Lime Street 10	a	11 38	11 43	11 48	11 53	11 58	12 03	12 08		12 13	12 18	12 23	12 28	12 33	12 38	12 43	12 48	12 53		12 58	13 03	13 08	13 13	13 18	13 23
Liverpool Central 10	a	11 40	11 45	11 50	11 55	12 00	12 05	12 10		12 15	12 20	12 25	12 30	12 35	12 40	12 45	12 50	12 55		13 00	13 05	13 10	13 15	13 20	13 25

Chester, Ellesmere Port, West Kirby and New Brighton - Birkenhead and Liverpool

		ME	ME	ME		ME	ME	ME	ME	ME	ME	ME	ME	ME		ME	ME	ME	ME	ME	ME	ME	ME	ME
Chester	d					13 00						13 30							14 00					
Bache	d					13 03						13 33							14 03					
Capenhurst	d					13 09						13 39							14 09					
Ellesmere Port	d	12 49							13 19						13 49					14 19		
Overpool	d	12 52							13 22						13 52					14 22		
Little Sutton	d	12 54							13 24						13 54					14 24		
Hooton	d	12 59				13 14			13 29			13 44				13 59			14 14			14 29		
Eastham Rake	d	13 01				13 16			13 31			13 46				14 01			14 16			14 31		
Bromborough	d	13 03				13 18			13 33			13 48				14 03			14 18			14 33		
Bromborough Rake	d	13 05				13 20			13 35			13 50				14 05			14 20			14 35		
Spital	d	13 07				13 22			13 37			13 52				14 07			14 22			14 37		
Port Sunlight	d	13 09				13 24			13 39			13 54				14 09			14 24			14 39		
Bebington	d	13 11				13 26			13 41			13 56				14 11			14 26			14 41		
Rock Ferry	d	13 14				13 29			13 44			13 59				14 14			14 29			14 44		
Green Lane	d	13 17				13 32			13 47			14 02				14 17			14 32			14 47		
Birkenhead Central	d	13 19				13 34			13 49			14 04				14 19			14 34			14 49		
West Kirby	d			13 06				13 21			13 36			13 51				14 06			14 21			14 36
Hoylake	d			13 09				13 24			13 39			13 54				14 09			14 24			14 39
Manor Road	d			13 11				13 26			13 41			13 56				14 11			14 26			14 41
Meols	d			13 13				13 28			13 43			13 58				14 13			14 28			14 43
Moreton (Merseyside)	d			13 16				13 31			13 46			14 01				14 16			14 31			14 46
Leasowe	d			13 18				13 33			13 48			14 03				14 18			14 33			14 48
Bidston	d			13 21				13 36			13 51			14 06				14 21			14 36			14 51
New Brighton	d		13 08				13 23			13 38			13 53				14 08			14 23			14 38	
Wallasey Grove Road	d		13 12				13 27			13 42			13 57				14 12			14 27			14 42	
Wallasey Village	d		13 14				13 29			13 44			13 59				14 14			14 29			14 44	
Birkenhead North	d		13 19	13 24			13 34	13 39		13 49	13 54		14 04	14 09			14 19	14 24		14 34	14 39		14 49	14 54
Birkenhead Park	d		13 21	13 26			13 36	13 41		13 51	13 56		14 06	14 11			14 21	14 26		14 36	14 41		14 51	14 56
Conway Park	d		13 24	13 29			13 39	13 44		13 54	13 59		14 09	14 14			14 24	14 29		14 39	14 44		14 54	14 59
Hamilton Square	d	13 21	13 26	13 31		13 36	13 41	13 46	13 51	13 56	14 01	14 06	14 11	14 16		14 21	14 26	14 31	14 36	14 41	14 46	14 51	14 56	15 01
James Street	d	13 24	13 29	13 34		13 39	13 44	13 49	13 54	13 59	14 04	14 09	14 14	14 19		14 24	14 29	14 34	14 39	14 44	14 49	14 54	14 59	15 04
Moorfields	a	13 26	13 31	13 36		13 41	13 46	13 51	13 56	14 01	14 06	14 11	14 16	14 21		14 26	14 31	14 36	14 41	14 46	14 51	14 56	15 01	15 06
Liverpool Lime Street	a	13 28	13 33	13 38		13 43	13 48	13 53	13 58	14 03	14 08	14 13	14 18	14 23		14 28	14 33	14 38	14 43	14 48	14 53	14 58	15 03	15 08
Liverpool Central	a	13 30	13 35	13 40		13 45	13 50	13 55	14 00	14 05	14 10	14 15	14 20	14 25		14 30	14 35	14 40	14 45	14 50	14 55	15 00	15 05	15 10

		ME	ME	ME	ME	ME	ME	ME	ME	ME		ME	ME	ME	ME	ME	ME	ME	ME	ME		ME	ME	ME	ME
Chester	d	14 30						15 00							15 30							16 00			
Bache	d	14 33						15 03							15 33							16 03			
Capenhurst	d	14 39						15 09							15 39							16 09			
Ellesmere Port	d				14 49							15 19						15 49							16 19
Overpool	d				14 52							15 22						15 52							16 22
Little Sutton	d				14 54							15 24						15 54							16 24
Hooton	d	14 44			14 59			15 14				15 29			15 44			15 59				16 14			16 29
Eastham Rake	d	14 46			15 01			15 16				15 31			15 46			16 01				16 16			16 31
Bromborough	d	14 48			15 03			15 18				15 33			15 48			16 03				16 18			16 33
Bromborough Rake	d	14 50			15 05			15 20				15 35			15 50			16 05				16 20			16 35
Spital	d	14 52			15 07			15 22				15 37			15 52			16 07				16 22			16 37
Port Sunlight	d	14 54			15 09			15 24				15 39			15 54			16 09				16 24			16 39
Bebington	d	14 56			15 11			15 26				15 41			15 56			16 11				16 26			16 41
Rock Ferry	d	14 59			15 14			15 29				15 44			15 59			16 14				16 29			16 44
Green Lane	d	15 02			15 17			15 32				15 47			16 02			16 17				16 32			16 47
Birkenhead Central	d	15 04			15 19			15 34				15 49			16 04			16 19				16 34			16 49
West Kirby	d			14 51			15 06			15 21				15 36			15 51			16 06				16 21	
Hoylake	d			14 54			15 09			15 24				15 39			15 54			16 09				16 24	
Manor Road	d			14 56			15 11			15 26				15 41			15 56			16 11				16 26	
Meols	d			14 58			15 13			15 28				15 43			15 58			16 13				16 28	
Moreton (Merseyside)	d			15 01			15 16			15 31				15 46			16 01			16 16				16 31	
Leasowe	d			15 03			15 18			15 33				15 48			16 03			16 18				16 33	
Bidston	d			15 06			15 21			15 36				15 51			16 06			16 21				16 36	
New Brighton	d		14 53			15 08			15 23				15 38			15 53			16 08				16 23		
Wallasey Grove Road	d		14 57			15 12			15 27				15 42			15 57			16 12				16 27		
Wallasey Village	d		14 59			15 14			15 29				15 44			15 59			16 14				16 29		
Birkenhead North	d		15 04	15 09		15 19	15 24		15 34	15 39			15 49	15 54		16 04	16 09		16 19	16 24			16 34	16 39	
Birkenhead Park	d		15 06	15 11		15 21	15 26		15 36	15 41			15 51	15 56		16 06	16 11		16 21	16 26			16 36	16 41	
Conway Park	d		15 09	15 14		15 24	15 29		15 39	15 44			15 54	15 59		16 09	16 14		16 24	16 29			16 39	16 44	
Hamilton Square	d	15 06	15 11	15 16	15 21	15 26	15 31	15 36	15 41	15 46		15 51	15 56	16 01	16 06	16 11	16 16	16 21	16 26	16 31		16 36	16 41	16 46	16 51
James Street	d	15 09	15 14	15 19	15 24	15 29	15 34	15 39	15 44	15 49		15 54	15 59	16 04	16 09	16 14	16 19	16 24	16 29	16 34		16 39	16 44	16 49	16 54
Moorfields	a	15 11	15 16	15 21	15 26	15 31	15 36	15 41	15 46	15 51		15 56	16 01	16 06	16 11	16 16	16 21	16 26	16 31	16 36		16 41	16 46	16 51	16 56
Liverpool Lime Street	a	15 13	15 18	15 23	15 28	15 33	15 38	15 43	15 48	15 53		15 58	16 03	16 08	16 13	16 18	16 23	16 28	16 33	16 38		16 43	16 48	16 53	16 58
Liverpool Central	a	15 15	15 20	15 25	15 30	15 35	15 40	15 45	15 50	15 55		16 00	16 05	16 10	16 15	16 20	16 25	16 30	16 35	16 40		16 45	16 50	16 55	17 00

Chester, Ellesmere Port, West Kirby and New Brighton - Birkenhead and Liverpool

		ME	ME	ME	ME	ME		ME	ME	ME	ME	ME	ME	ME	ME	ME		ME	ME	ME	ME	ME	ME	ME	ME
Chester	d			16 30							17 00						17 30						18 00	
Bache	d			16 33							17 03						17 33						18 03	
Capenhurst	d			16 39							17 09						17 39						18 09	
Ellesmere Port	d							16 49						17 19							17 49				
Overpool	d							16 52						17 22							17 52				
Little Sutton	d							16 54						17 24							17 54				
Hooton	d			16 44				16 59			17 14			17 29				17 44			17 59			18 14	
Eastham Rake	d			16 46				17 01			17 16			17 31				17 46			18 01			18 16	
Bromborough	d			16 48				17 03			17 18			17 33				17 48			18 03			18 18	
Bromborough Rake	d			16 50				17 05			17 20			17 35				17 50			18 05			18 20	
Spital	d			16 52				17 07			17 22			17 37				17 52			18 07			18 22	
Port Sunlight	d			16 54				17 09			17 24			17 39				17 54			18 09			18 24	
Bebington	d			16 56				17 11			17 26			17 41				17 56			18 11			18 26	
Rock Ferry	d			16 59				17 14			17 29			17 44				17 59			18 14			18 29	
Green Lane	d			17 02				17 17			17 32			17 47				18 02			18 17			18 32	
Birkenhead Central	d			17 04				17 19			17 34			17 49				18 04			18 19			18 34	
West Kirby	d		16 36			16 51				17 06			17 21			17 36				17 51			18 06		
Hoylake	d		16 39			16 54				17 09			17 24			17 39				17 54			18 09		
Manor Road	d		16 41			16 56				17 11			17 26			17 41				17 56			18 11		
Meols	d		16 43			16 58				17 13			17 28			17 43				17 58			18 13		
Moreton (Merseyside)	d		16 46			17 01				17 16			17 31			17 46				18 01			18 16		
Leasowe	d		16 48			17 03				17 18			17 33			17 48				18 03			18 18		
Bidston	d		16 51			17 06				17 21			17 36			17 51				18 06			18 21		
New Brighton	d	16 38			16 53				17 08			17 23			17 38				17 53			18 08			18 23
Wallasey Grove Road	d	16 42			16 57				17 12			17 27			17 42				17 57			18 12			18 27
Wallasey Village	d	16 44			16 59				17 14			17 29			17 44				17 59			18 14			18 29
Birkenhead North	d	16 49	16 54		17 04	17 09			17 19	17 24		17 34	17 39		17 49	17 54			18 04	18 09		18 19	18 24		18 34
Birkenhead Park	d	16 51	16 56		17 06	17 11			17 21	17 26		17 36	17 41		17 51	17 56			18 06	18 11		18 21	18 26		18 36
Conway Park	d	16 54	16 59		17 09	17 14			17 24	17 29		17 39	17 44		17 54	17 59			18 09	18 14		18 24	18 29		18 39
Hamilton Square	d	16 56	17 01	17 06	17 11	17 16		17 21	17 26	17 31	17 36	17 41	17 46	17 51	17 56	18 01		18 06	18 11	18 16	18 21	18 26	18 31	18 36	18 41
James Street	d	16 59	17 04	17 09	17 14	17 19		17 24	17 29	17 34	17 39	17 44	17 49	17 54	17 59	18 04		18 09	18 14	18 19	18 24	18 29	18 34	18 39	18 44
Moorfields	a	17 01	17 06	17 11	17 16	17 21		17 26	17 31	17 36	17 41	17 46	17 51	17 56	18 01	18 06		18 11	18 16	18 21	18 26	18 31	18 36	18 41	18 46
Liverpool Lime Street	a	17 03	17 08	17 13	17 18	17 23		17 28	17 33	17 38	17 43	17 48	17 53	17 58	18 03	18 08		18 13	18 18	18 23	18 28	18 33	18 38	18 43	18 48
Liverpool Central	a	17 05	17 10	17 15	17 20	17 25		17 30	17 35	17 40	17 45	17 50	17 55	18 00	18 05	18 10		18 15	18 20	18 25	18 30	18 35	18 40	18 45	18 50

		ME		ME	ME	ME	ME	ME	ME	ME	ME	ME		ME	ME	ME	ME	ME	ME	ME	ME	ME		ME	ME
Chester	d						18 30				19 00					19 30				20 00					20 30
Bache	d						18 33				19 03					19 33				20 03					20 33
Capenhurst	d						18 39				19 09					19 39				20 09					20 39
Ellesmere Port	d			18 19					18 49					19 19				19 49				20 19			
Overpool	d			18 22					18 52					19 22				19 52				20 22			
Little Sutton	d			18 24					18 54					19 24				19 54				20 24			
Hooton	d			18 29			18 44		18 59		19 14			19 29		19 44		19 59		20 14		20 29			20 44
Eastham Rake	d			18 31			18 46		19 01		19 16			19 31		19 46		20 01		20 16		20 31			20 46
Bromborough	d			18 33			18 48		19 03		19 18			19 33		19 48		20 03		20 18		20 33			20 48
Bromborough Rake	d			18 35			18 50		19 05		19 20			19 35		19 50		20 05		20 20		20 35			20 50
Spital	d			18 37			18 52		19 07		19 22			19 37		19 52		20 07		20 22		20 37			20 52
Port Sunlight	d			18 39			18 54		19 09		19 24			19 39		19 54		20 09		20 24		20 39			20 54
Bebington	d			18 41			18 56		19 11		19 26			19 41		19 56		20 11		20 26		20 41			20 56
Rock Ferry	d			18 44			18 59		19 14		19 29			19 44		19 59		20 14		20 29		20 44			20 59
Green Lane	d			18 47			19 02		19 17		19 32			19 47		20 02		20 17		20 32		20 47			21 02
Birkenhead Central	d			18 49			19 04		19 19		19 34			19 49		20 04		20 19		20 34		20 49			21 04
West Kirby	d	18 21				18 36				19 01					19 31				20 01					20 31	
Hoylake	d	18 24				18 39				19 04					19 34				20 04					20 34	
Manor Road	d	18 26				18 41				19 06					19 36				20 06					20 36	
Meols	d	18 28				18 43				19 08					19 38				20 08					20 38	
Moreton (Merseyside)	d	18 31				18 46				19 11					19 41				20 11					20 41	
Leasowe	d	18 33				18 48				19 13					19 43				20 13					20 43	
Bidston	d	18 36				18 51				19 16					19 46				20 16					20 46	
New Brighton	d				18 38			18 53				19 23					19 53				20 23				
Wallasey Grove Road	d				18 42			18 57				19 27					19 57				20 27				
Wallasey Village	d				18 44			18 59				19 29					19 59				20 29				
Birkenhead North	d	18 39			18 49	18 54		19 04		19 19		19 34			19 49		20 04		20 19		20 34			20 49	
Birkenhead Park	d	18 41			18 51	18 56		19 06		19 21		19 36			19 51		20 06		20 21		20 36			20 51	
Conway Park	d	18 44			18 54	18 59		19 09		19 24		19 39			19 54		20 09		20 24		20 39			20 54	
Hamilton Square	d	18 46		18 51	18 56	19 01	19 06	19 11	19 21	19 26	19 36	19 41		19 51	19 56	20 06	20 11	20 21	20 26	20 36	20 41	20 51		20 56	21 06
James Street	d	18 49		18 54	18 59	19 04	19 09	19 14	19 24	19 29	19 39	19 44		19 54	19 59	20 09	20 14	20 24	20 29	20 39	20 44	20 54		20 59	21 09
Moorfields	a	18 51		18 56	19 01	19 06	19 11	19 16	19 26	19 31	19 41	19 46		19 56	20 01	20 11	20 16	20 26	20 31	20 41	20 46	20 56		21 01	21 11
Liverpool Lime Street	a	18 53		18 58	19 03	19 08	19 13	19 18	19 28	19 33	19 43	19 48		19 58	20 03	20 13	20 18	20 28	20 33	20 43	20 48	20 58		21 03	21 13
Liverpool Central	a	18 55		19 00	19 05	19 10	19 15	19 20	19 30	19 35	19 45	19 50		20 00	20 05	20 15	20 20	20 30	20 35	20 45	20 50	21 00		21 05	21 15

Table 106

Mondays to Saturdays

Chester, Ellesmere Port, West Kirby and New Brighton - Birkenhead and Liverpool

		ME	ME	ME	ME	ME	ME	ME	ME	ME	ME	ME	ME	ME	ME	ME	ME	ME	ME	ME	ME	ME	ME
Chester	d				21 00				21 30				22 00				22 30				23 00		
Bache	d				21 03				21 33				22 03				22 33				23 03		
Capenhurst	d				21 09				21 39				22 09				22 39				23 09		
Ellesmere Port	d		20 49				21 19				21 49				22 19				22 49				23 19
Overpool	d		20 52				21 22				21 52				22 22				22 52				23 22
Little Sutton	d		20 54				21 24				21 54				22 24				22 54				23 24
Hooton	d		20 59		21 14		21 29		21 44		21 59		22 14		22 29		22 44		22 59		23 14		23 29
Eastham Rake	d		21 01		21 16		21 31		21 46		22 01		22 16		22 31		22 46		23 01		23 16		23 31
Bromborough	d		21 03		21 18		21 33		21 48		22 03		22 18		22 33		22 48		23 03		23 18		23 33
Bromborough Rake	d		21 05		21 20		21 35		21 50		22 05		22 20		22 35		22 50		23 05		23 20		23 35
Spital	d		21 07		21 22		21 37		21 52		22 07		22 22		22 37		22 52		23 07		23 22		23 37
Port Sunlight	d		21 09		21 24		21 39		21 54		22 09		22 24		22 39		22 54		23 09		23 24		23 39
Bebington	d		21 11		21 26		21 41		21 56		22 11		22 26		22 41		22 56		23 11		23 26		23 41
Rock Ferry	d		21 14		21 29		21 44		21 59		22 14		22 29		22 44		22 59		23 14		23 29		23 44
Green Lane	d		21 17		21 32		21 47		22 02		22 17		22 32		22 47		23 02		23 17		23 32		23 47
Birkenhead Central	d		21 19		21 34		21 49		22 04		22 19		22 34		22 49		23 04		23 19		23 34		23 49
West Kirby	d			21 01				21 31				22 01				22 31				23 01			
Hoylake	d			21 04				21 34				22 04				22 34				23 04			
Manor Road	d			21 06				21 36				22 06				22 36				23 06			
Meols	d			21 08				21 38				22 08				22 38				23 08			
Moreton (Merseyside)	d			21 11				21 41				22 11				22 41				23 11			
Leasowe	d			21 13				21 43				22 13				22 43				23 13			
Bidston	d			21 16				21 46				22 16				22 46				23 16			
New Brighton	d	20 53				21 23				21 53				22 23				22 53				23 23	
Wallasey Grove Road	d	20 57				21 27				21 57				22 27				22 57				23 27	
Wallasey Village	d	20 59				21 29				21 59				22 29				22 59				23 29	
Birkenhead North	d	21 04		21 19		21 34		21 49		22 04		22 19		22 34		22 49		23 04		23 19		23 34	
Birkenhead Park	d	21 06		21 21		21 36		21 51		22 06		22 21		22 36		22 51		23 06		23 21		23 36	
Conway Park	d	21 09		21 24		21 39		21 54		22 09		22 24		22 39		22 54		23 09		23 24		23 39	
Hamilton Square	d	21 11	21 21	21 26	21 36	21 41	21 51	21 56	22 06	22 11	22 21	22 26	22 36	22 41	22 51	22 56	23 06	23 11	23 21	23 26	23 36	23 41	23 51
James Street	d	21 14	21 24	21 29	21 39	21 44	21 54	21 59	22 09	22 14	22 24	22 29	22 39	22 44	22 54	22 59	23 09	23 14	23 24	23 29	23 39	23 44	23 54
Moorfields	a	21 16	21 26	21 31	21 41	21 46	21 56	22 01	22 11	22 16	22 26	22 31	22 41	22 46	22 56	23 01	23 11	23 16	23 26	23 31	23 41	23 46	23 56
Liverpool Lime Street	a	21 18	21 28	21 33	21 43	21 48	21 58	22 03	22 13	22 18	22 28	22 33	22 43	22 48	22 58	23 03	23 13	23 18	23 28	23 33	23 43	23 48	23 58
Liverpool Central	a	21 20	21 30	21 35	21 45	21 50	22 00	22 05	22 15	22 20	22 30	22 35	22 45	22 50	23 00	23 05	23 15	23 20	23 30	23 35	23 45	23 50	23 59

Sundays

		ME	ME	ME	ME	ME	ME	ME	ME	ME	ME	ME	ME	ME	ME	ME	ME	ME	ME	ME	ME	ME	ME
Chester	d					08 00				08 30				09 00				09 30				10 00	
Bache	d					08 03				08 33				09 03				09 33				10 03	
Capenhurst	d					08 09				08 39				09 09				09 39				10 09	
Ellesmere Port	d			07 49				08 19				08 49				09 19				09 49			
Overpool	d			07 52				08 22				08 52				09 22				09 52			
Little Sutton	d			07 54				08 24				08 54				09 24				09 54			
Hooton	d			07 59		08 14		08 29		08 44		08 59		09 14		09 29		09 44		09 59		10 14	
Eastham Rake	d			08 01		08 16		08 31		08 46		09 01		09 16		09 31		09 46		10 01		10 16	
Bromborough	d			08 03		08 18		08 33		08 48		09 03		09 18		09 33		09 48		10 03		10 18	
Bromborough Rake	d			08 05		08 20		08 35		08 50		09 05		09 20		09 35		09 50		10 05		10 20	
Spital	d			08 07		08 22		08 37		08 52		09 07		09 22		09 37		09 52		10 07		10 22	
Port Sunlight	d			08 09		08 24		08 39		08 54		09 09		09 24		09 39		09 54		10 09		10 24	
Bebington	d			08 11		08 26		08 41		08 56		09 11		09 26		09 41		09 56		10 11		10 26	
Rock Ferry	d	07 49		08 14		08 29		08 44		08 59		09 14		09 29		09 44		09 59		10 14		10 29	
Green Lane	d	07 52		08 17		08 32		08 47		09 02		09 17		09 32		09 47		10 02		10 17		10 32	
Birkenhead Central	d	07 54		08 19		08 34		08 49		09 04		09 19		09 34		09 49		10 04		10 19		10 34	
West Kirby	d				08 01				08 31				09 01				09 31				10 01		
Hoylake	d				08 04				08 34				09 04				09 34				10 04		
Manor Road	d				08 06				08 36				09 06				09 36				10 06		
Meols	d				08 08				08 38				09 08				09 38				10 08		
Moreton (Merseyside)	d				08 11				08 41				09 11				09 41				10 11		
Leasowe	d				08 13				08 43				09 13				09 43				10 13		
Bidston	d				08 16				08 46				09 16				09 46				10 16		
New Brighton	d		07 53				08 23				08 53				09 23				09 53				10 23
Wallasey Grove Road	d		07 57				08 27				08 57				09 27				09 57				10 27
Wallasey Village	d		07 59				08 29				08 59				09 29				09 59				10 29
Birkenhead North	d		08 04		08 19		08 34		08 49		09 04		09 19		09 34		09 49		10 04		10 19		10 34
Birkenhead Park	d		08 06		08 21		08 36		08 51		09 06		09 21		09 36		09 51		10 06		10 21		10 36
Conway Park	d		08 09		08 24		08 39		08 54		09 09		09 24		09 39		09 54		10 09		10 24		10 39
Hamilton Square	d	07 56	08 11	08 21	08 26	08 36	08 41	08 51	08 56	09 06	09 11	09 21	09 26	09 36	09 41	09 51	09 56	10 06	10 11	10 21	10 26	10 36	10 41
James Street	d	07 59	08 14	08 24	08 29	08 39	08 44	08 54	08 59	09 09	09 14	09 24	09 29	09 39	09 44	09 54	09 59	10 09	10 14	10 24	10 29	10 39	10 44
Moorfields	a	08 01	08 16	08 26	08 31	08 41	08 46	08 56	09 01	09 11	09 16	09 26	09 31	09 41	09 46	09 56	10 01	10 11	10 16	10 26	10 31	10 41	10 46
Liverpool Lime Street	a	08 03	08 18	08 28	08 33	08 43	08 48	08 58	09 03	09 13	09 18	09 28	09 33	09 43	09 48	09 58	10 03	10 13	10 18	10 28	10 33	10 43	10 48
Liverpool Central	a	08 05	08 20	08 30	08 35	08 45	08 50	09 00	09 05	09 15	09 20	09 30	09 35	09 45	09 50	10 00	10 05	10 15	10 20	10 30	10 35	10 45	10 50

Table 106

Sundays

Chester, Ellesmere Port, West Kirby and New Brighton - Birkenhead and Liverpool

		ME	ME	ME	ME	ME	ME	ME	ME	ME	ME	ME	ME	ME	ME	ME	ME	ME	ME	ME	ME	ME	ME
Chester	d			10 30				11 00				11 30				12 00				12 30			
Bache	d			10 33				11 03				11 33				12 03				12 33			
Capenhurst	d			10 39				11 09				11 39				12 09				12 39			
Ellesmere Port	d	10 19				10 49				11 19				11 49				12 19				12 49	
Overpool	d	10 22				10 52				11 22				11 52				12 22				12 52	
Little Sutton	d	10 24				10 54				11 24				11 54				12 24				12 54	
Hooton	d	10 29		10 44		10 59		11 14		11 29		11 44		11 59		12 14		12 29		12 44		12 59	
Eastham Rake	d	10 31		10 46		11 01		11 16		11 31		11 46		12 01		12 16		12 31		12 46		13 01	
Bromborough	d	10 33		10 48		11 03		11 18		11 33		11 48		12 03		12 18		12 33		12 48		13 03	
Bromborough Rake	d	10 35		10 50		11 05		11 20		11 35		11 50		12 05		12 20		12 35		12 50		13 05	
Spital	d	10 37		10 52		11 07		11 22		11 37		11 52		12 07		12 22		12 37		12 52		13 07	
Port Sunlight	d	10 39		10 54		11 09		11 24		11 39		11 54		12 09		12 24		12 39		12 54		13 09	
Bebington	d	10 41		10 56		11 11		11 26		11 41		11 56		12 11		12 26		12 41		12 56		13 11	
Rock Ferry	d	10 44		10 59		11 14		11 29		11 44		11 59		12 14		12 29		12 44		12 59		13 14	
Green Lane	d	10 47		11 02		11 17		11 32		11 47		12 02		12 17		12 32		12 47		13 02		13 17	
Birkenhead Central	d	10 49		11 04		11 19		11 34		11 49		12 04		12 19		12 34		12 49		13 04		13 19	
West Kirby	d		10 31				11 01				11 31				12 01				12 31				13 01
Hoylake	d		10 34				11 04				11 34				12 04				12 34				13 04
Manor Road	d		10 36				11 06				11 36				12 06				12 36				13 06
Meols	d		10 38				11 08				11 38				12 08				12 38				13 08
Moreton (Merseyside)	d		10 41				11 11				11 41				12 11				12 41				13 11
Leasowe	d		10 43				11 13				11 43				12 13				12 43				13 13
Bidston	d		10 46				11 16				11 46				12 16				12 46				13 16
New Brighton	d				10 53				11 23				11 53				12 23				12 53		
Wallasey Grove Road	d				10 57				11 27				11 57				12 27				12 57		
Wallasey Village	d				10 59				11 29				11 59				12 29				12 59		
Birkenhead North	d		10 49		11 04		11 19		11 34		11 49		12 04		12 19		12 34		12 49		13 04		13 19
Birkenhead Park	d		10 51		11 06		11 21		11 36		11 51		12 06		12 21		12 36		12 51		13 06		13 21
Conway Park	d		10 54		11 09		11 24		11 39		11 54		12 09		12 24		12 39		12 54		13 09		13 24
Hamilton Square	d	10 51	10 56	11 06	11 11	11 21	11 26	11 36	11 41	11 51	11 56	12 06	12 11	12 21	12 26	12 36	12 41	12 51	12 56	13 06	13 11	13 21	13 26
James Street	d	10 54	10 59	11 09	11 14	11 24	11 29	11 39	11 44	11 54	11 59	12 09	12 14	12 24	12 29	12 39	12 44	12 54	12 59	13 09	13 14	13 24	13 29
Moorfields	a	10 56	11 01	11 11	11 16	11 26	11 31	11 41	11 46	11 56	12 01	12 11	12 16	12 26	12 31	12 41	12 46	12 56	13 01	13 11	13 16	13 26	13 31
Liverpool Lime Street	a	10 58	11 03	11 13	11 18	11 28	11 33	11 43	11 48	11 58	12 03	12 13	12 18	12 28	12 33	12 43	12 48	12 58	13 03	13 13	13 18	13 28	13 33
Liverpool Central	a	11 00	11 05	11 15	11 20	11 30	11 35	11 45	11 50	12 00	12 05	12 15	12 20	12 30	12 35	12 45	12 50	13 00	13 05	13 15	13 20	13 30	13 35

		ME	ME	ME	ME	ME	ME	ME	ME	ME	ME	ME	ME	ME	ME	ME	ME	ME	ME	ME	ME	ME
Chester	d	13 00				13 30				14 00				14 30				15 00				15 30
Bache	d	13 03				13 33				14 03				14 33				15 03				15 33
Capenhurst	d	13 09				13 39				14 09				14 39				15 09				15 39
Ellesmere Port	d			13 19				13 49				14 19				14 49				15 19		
Overpool	d			13 22				13 52				14 22				14 52				15 22		
Little Sutton	d			13 24				13 54				14 24				14 54				15 24		
Hooton	d	13 14		13 29		13 44		13 59		14 14		14 29		14 44		14 59		15 14		15 29		15 44
Eastham Rake	d	13 16		13 31		13 46		14 01		14 16		14 31		14 46		15 01		15 16		15 31		15 46
Bromborough	d	13 18		13 33		13 48		14 03		14 18		14 33		14 48		15 03		15 18		15 33		15 48
Bromborough Rake	d	13 20		13 35		13 50		14 05		14 20		14 35		14 50		15 05		15 20		15 35		15 50
Spital	d	13 22		13 37		13 52		14 07		14 22		14 37		14 52		15 07		15 22		15 37		15 52
Port Sunlight	d	13 24		13 39		13 54		14 09		14 24		14 39		14 54		15 09		15 24		15 39		15 54
Bebington	d	13 26		13 41		13 56		14 11		14 26		14 41		14 56		15 11		15 26		15 41		15 56
Rock Ferry	d	13 29		13 44		13 59		14 14		14 29		14 44		14 59		15 14		15 29		15 44		15 59
Green Lane	d	13 32		13 47		14 02		14 17		14 32		14 47		15 02		15 17		15 32		15 47		16 02
Birkenhead Central	d	13 34		13 49		14 04		14 19		14 34		14 49		15 04		15 19		15 34		15 49		16 04
West Kirby	d				13 31				14 01				14 31				15 01				15 31	
Hoylake	d				13 34				14 04				14 34				15 04				15 34	
Manor Road	d				13 36				14 06				14 36				15 06				15 36	
Meols	d				13 38				14 08				14 38				15 08				15 38	
Moreton (Merseyside)	d				13 41				14 11				14 41				15 11				15 41	
Leasowe	d				13 43				14 13				14 43				15 13				15 43	
Bidston	d				13 46				14 16				14 46				15 16				15 46	
New Brighton	d		13 23				13 53				14 23				14 53				15 23			
Wallasey Grove Road	d		13 27				13 57				14 27				14 57				15 27			
Wallasey Village	d		13 29				13 59				14 29				14 59				15 29			
Birkenhead North	d		13 34		13 49		14 04		14 19		14 34		14 49		15 04		15 19		15 34		15 49	
Birkenhead Park	d		13 36		13 51		14 06		14 21		14 36		14 51		15 06		15 21		15 36		15 51	
Conway Park	d		13 39		13 54		14 09		14 24		14 39		14 54		15 09		15 24		15 39		15 54	
Hamilton Square	d	13 36	13 41	13 51	13 56	14 06	14 11	14 21	14 26	14 36	14 41	14 51	14 56	15 06	15 11	15 21	15 26	15 36	15 41	15 51	15 56	16 06
James Street	d	13 39	13 44	13 54	13 59	14 09	14 14	14 24	14 29	14 39	14 44	14 54	14 59	15 09	15 14	15 24	15 29	15 39	15 44	15 54	15 59	16 09
Moorfields	a	13 41	13 46	13 56	14 01	14 11	14 16	14 26	14 31	14 41	14 46	14 56	15 01	15 11	15 16	15 26	15 31	15 41	15 46	15 56	16 01	16 11
Liverpool Lime Street	a	13 43	13 48	13 58	14 03	14 13	14 18	14 28	14 33	14 43	14 48	14 58	15 03	15 13	15 18	15 28	15 33	15 43	15 48	15 58	16 03	16 13
Liverpool Central	a	13 45	13 50	14 00	14 05	14 15	14 20	14 30	14 35	14 45	14 50	15 00	15 05	15 15	15 20	15 30	15 35	15 45	15 50	16 00	16 05	16 15

Chester, Ellesmere Port, West Kirby and New Brighton - Birkenhead and Liverpool

		ME	ME	ME	ME	ME	ME	ME	ME	ME	ME	ME	ME	ME	ME	ME	ME	ME	ME	ME	ME	ME	ME
Chester	d				16 00				16 30				17 00				17 30				18 00		
Bache	d				16 03				16 33				17 03				17 33				18 03		
Capenhurst	d				16 09				16 39				17 09				17 39				18 09		
Ellesmere Port	d		15 49				16 19				16 49				17 19				17 49				18 19
Overpool	d		15 52				16 22				16 52				17 22				17 52				18 22
Little Sutton	d		15 54				16 24				16 54				17 24				17 54				18 24
Hooton	d		15 59		16 14		16 29		16 44		16 59		17 14		17 29		17 44		17 59		18 14		18 29
Eastham Rake	d		16 01		16 16		16 31		16 46		17 01		17 16		17 31		17 46		18 01		18 16		18 31
Bromborough	d		16 03		16 18		16 33		16 48		17 03		17 18		17 33		17 48		18 03		18 18		18 33
Bromborough Rake	d		16 05		16 20		16 35		16 50		17 05		17 20		17 35		17 50		18 05		18 20		18 35
Spital	d		16 07		16 22		16 37		16 52		17 07		17 22		17 37		17 52		18 07		18 22		18 37
Port Sunlight	d		16 09		16 24		16 39		16 54		17 09		17 24		17 39		17 54		18 09		18 24		18 39
Bebington	d		16 11		16 26		16 41		16 56		17 11		17 26		17 41		17 56		18 11		18 26		18 41
Rock Ferry	d		16 14		16 29		16 44		16 59		17 14		17 29		17 44		17 59		18 14		18 29		18 44
Green Lane	d		16 17		16 32		16 47		17 02		17 17		17 32		17 47		18 02		18 17		18 32		18 47
Birkenhead Central	d		16 19		16 34		16 49		17 04		17 19		17 34		17 49		18 04		18 19		18 34		18 49
West Kirby	d			16 01				16 31				17 01				17 31				18 01			
Hoylake	d			16 04				16 34				17 04				17 34				18 04			
Manor Road	d			16 06				16 36				17 06				17 36				18 06			
Meols	d			16 08				16 38				17 08				17 38				18 08			
Moreton (Merseyside)	d			16 11				16 41				17 11				17 41				18 11			
Leasowe	d			16 13				16 43				17 13				17 43				18 13			
Bidston	d			16 16				16 46				17 16				17 46				18 16			
New Brighton	d	15 53				16 23				16 53				17 23				17 53				18 23	
Wallasey Grove Road	d	15 57				16 27				16 57				17 27				17 57				18 27	
Wallasey Village	d	15 59				16 29				16 59				17 29				17 59				18 29	
Birkenhead North	d	16 04		16 19		16 34		16 49		17 04		17 19		17 34		17 49		18 04		18 19		18 34	
Birkenhead Park	d	16 06		16 21		16 36		16 51		17 06		17 21		17 36		17 51		18 06		18 21		18 36	
Conway Park	d	16 09		16 24		16 39		16 54		17 09		17 24		17 39		17 54		18 09		18 24		18 39	
Hamilton Square	d	16 11	16 21	16 26	16 36	16 41	16 51	16 56	17 06	17 11	17 21	17 26	17 36	17 41	17 51	17 56	18 06	18 11	18 21	18 26	18 36	18 41	18 51
James Street	d	16 14	16 24	16 29	16 39	16 44	16 54	16 59	17 09	17 14	17 24	17 29	17 39	17 44	17 54	17 59	18 09	18 14	18 24	18 29	18 39	18 44	18 54
Moorfields ■	a	16 16	16 26	16 31	16 41	16 46	16 56	17 01	17 11	17 16	17 26	17 31	17 41	17 46	17 56	18 01	18 11	18 16	18 26	18 31	18 41	18 46	18 56
Liverpool Lime Street ■	a	16 18	16 28	16 33	16 43	16 48	16 58	17 03	17 13	17 18	17 28	17 33	17 43	17 48	17 58	18 03	18 13	18 18	18 28	18 33	18 43	18 48	18 58
Liverpool Central ■	a	16 20	16 30	16 35	16 45	16 50	17 00	17 05	17 15	17 20	17 30	17 35	17 45	17 50	18 00	18 05	18 15	18 20	18 30	18 35	18 45	18 50	19 00

		ME	ME	ME	ME	ME	ME	ME	ME	ME	ME	ME	ME	ME	ME	ME	ME	ME	ME	ME	ME	ME
Chester	d		18 30				19 00				19 30				20 00				20 30			
Bache	d		18 33				19 03				19 33				20 03				20 33			
Capenhurst	d		18 39				19 09				19 39				20 09				20 39			
Ellesmere Port	d				18 49				19 19				19 49				20 19				20 49	
Overpool	d				18 52				19 22				19 52				20 22				20 52	
Little Sutton	d				18 54				19 24				19 54				20 24				20 54	
Hooton	d		18 44		18 59		19 14		19 29		19 44		19 59		20 14		20 29		20 44		20 59	
Eastham Rake	d		18 46		19 01		19 16		19 31		19 46		20 01		20 16		20 31		20 46		21 01	
Bromborough	d		18 48		19 03		19 18		19 33		19 48		20 03		20 18		20 33		20 48		21 03	
Bromborough Rake	d		18 50		19 05		19 20		19 35		19 50		20 05		20 20		20 35		20 50		21 05	
Spital	d		18 52		19 07		19 22		19 37		19 52		20 07		20 22		20 37		20 52		21 07	
Port Sunlight	d		18 54		19 09		19 24		19 39		19 54		20 09		20 24		20 39		20 54		21 09	
Bebington	d		18 56		19 11		19 26		19 41		19 56		20 11		20 26		20 41		20 56		21 11	
Rock Ferry	d		18 59		19 14		19 29		19 44		19 59		20 14		20 29		20 44		20 59		21 14	
Green Lane	d		19 02		19 17		19 32		19 47		20 02		20 17		20 32		20 47		21 02		21 17	
Birkenhead Central	d		19 04		19 19		19 34		19 49		20 04		20 19		20 34		20 49		21 04		21 19	
West Kirby	d	18 31				19 01				19 31				20 01				20 31				21 01
Hoylake	d	18 34				19 04				19 34				20 04				20 34				21 04
Manor Road	d	18 36				19 06				19 36				20 06				20 36				21 06
Meols	d	18 38				19 08				19 38				20 08				20 38				21 08
Moreton (Merseyside)	d	18 41				19 11				19 41				20 11				20 41				21 11
Leasowe	d	18 43				19 13				19 43				20 13				20 43				21 13
Bidston	d	18 46				19 16				19 46				20 16				20 46				21 16
New Brighton	d			18 53				19 23				19 53				20 23				20 53		
Wallasey Grove Road	d			18 57				19 27				19 57				20 27				20 57		
Wallasey Village	d			18 59				19 29				19 59				20 29				20 59		
Birkenhead North	d	18 49		19 04		19 19		19 34		19 49		20 04		20 19		20 34		20 49		21 04		21 19
Birkenhead Park	d	18 51		19 06		19 21		19 36		19 51		20 06		20 21		20 36		20 51		21 06		21 21
Conway Park	d	18 54		19 09		19 24		19 39		19 54		20 09		20 24		20 39		20 54		21 09		21 24
Hamilton Square	d	18 56	19 06	19 11	19 21	19 26	19 36	19 41	19 51	19 56	20 06	20 11	20 21	20 26	20 36	20 41	20 51	20 56	21 06	21 11	21 21	21 26
James Street	d	18 59	19 09	19 14	19 24	19 29	19 39	19 44	19 54	19 59	20 09	20 14	20 24	20 29	20 39	20 44	20 54	20 59	21 09	21 14	21 24	21 29
Moorfields ■	a	19 01	19 11	19 16	19 26	19 31	19 41	19 46	19 56	20 01	20 11	20 16	20 26	20 31	20 41	20 46	20 56	21 01	21 11	21 16	21 26	21 31
Liverpool Lime Street ■	a	19 03	19 13	19 18	19 28	19 33	19 43	19 48	19 58	20 03	20 13	20 18	20 28	20 33	20 43	20 48	20 58	21 03	21 13	21 18	21 28	21 33
Liverpool Central ■	a	19 05	19 15	19 20	19 30	19 35	19 45	19 50	20 00	20 05	20 15	20 20	20 30	20 35	20 45	20 50	21 00	21 05	21 15	21 20	21 30	21 35

Table 106

Sundays

Chester, Ellesmere Port, West Kirby and New Brighton - Birkenhead and Liverpool

		ME	ME	ME	ME	ME	ME	ME	ME	ME	ME	ME	ME	ME	ME	ME	ME	ME	ME	ME
Chester	d	21 00				21 30				22 00				22 30				23 00		
Bache	d	21 03				21 33				22 03				22 33				23 03		
Capenhurst	d	21 09				21 39				22 09				22 39				23 09		
Ellesmere Port	d			21 19				21 49				22 19				22 49				23 19
Overpool	d			21 22				21 52				22 22				22 52				23 22
Little Sutton	d			21 24				21 54				22 24				22 54				23 24
Hooton	d	21 14		21 29		21 44		21 59		22 14		22 29		22 44		22 59		23 14		23 29
Eastham Rake	d	21 16		21 31		21 46		22 01		22 16		22 31		22 46		23 01		23 16		23 31
Bromborough	d	21 18		21 33		21 48		22 03		22 18		22 33		22 48		23 03		23 18		23 33
Bromborough Rake	d	21 20		21 35		21 50		22 05		22 20		22 35		22 50		23 05		23 20		23 35
Spital	d	21 22		21 37		21 52		22 07		22 22		22 37		22 52		23 07		23 22		23 37
Port Sunlight	d	21 24		21 39		21 54		22 09		22 24		22 39		22 54		23 09		23 24		23 39
Bebington	d	21 26		21 41		21 56		22 11		22 26		22 41		22 56		23 11		23 26		23 41
Rock Ferry	d	21 29		21 44		21 59		22 14		22 29		22 44		22 59		23 14		23 29		23 44
Green Lane	d	21 32		21 47		22 02		22 17		22 32		22 47		23 02		23 17		23 32		23 47
Birkenhead Central	d	21 34		21 49		22 04		22 19		22 34		22 49		23 04		23 19		23 34		23 49
West Kirby	d				21 31				22 01				22 31				23 01			
Hoylake	d				21 34				22 04				22 34				23 04			
Manor Road	d				21 36				22 06				22 36				23 06			
Meols	d				21 38				22 08				22 38				23 08			
Moreton (Merseyside)	d				21 41				22 11				22 41				23 11			
Leasowe	d				21 43				22 13				22 43				23 13			
Bidston	d				21 46				22 16				22 46				23 16			
New Brighton	d		21 23				21 53				22 23				22 53				23 23	
Wallasey Grove Road	d		21 27				21 57				22 27				22 57				23 27	
Wallasey Village	d		21 29				21 59				22 29				22 59				23 29	
Birkenhead North	d		21 34		21 49		22 04		22 19		22 34		22 49		23 04		23 19		23 34	
Birkenhead Park	d		21 36		21 51		22 06		22 21		22 36		22 51		23 06		23 21		23 36	
Conway Park	d		21 39		21 54		22 09		22 24		22 39		22 54		23 09		23 24		23 39	
Hamilton Square	d	21 36	21 41	21 51	21 56	22 06	22 11	22 21	22 26	22 36	22 41	22 51	22 56	23 06	23 11	23 21	23 26	23 36	23 41	23 51
James Street	d	21 39	21 44	21 54	21 59	22 09	22 14	22 24	22 29	22 39	22 44	22 54	22 59	23 09	23 14	23 24	23 29	23 39	23 44	23 54
Moorfields ■	a	21 41	21 46	21 56	22 01	22 11	22 16	22 26	22 31	22 41	22 46	22 56	23 01	23 11	23 16	23 26	23 31	23 41	23 46	23 56
Liverpool Lime Street ■	a	21 43	21 48	21 58	22 03	22 13	22 18	22 28	22 33	22 43	22 48	22 58	23 03	23 13	23 18	23 28	23 33	23 43	23 48	23 58
Liverpool Central ■	a	21 45	21 50	22 00	22 05	22 15	22 20	22 30	22 35	22 45	22 50	23 00	23 05	23 15	23 20	23 30	23 35	23 45	23 50	23 59

Table 109

Mondays to Saturdays

Helsby - Ellesmere Port

		NT	NT	NT	NT
Warrington Bank Quay 81	d	05 49			
Helsby	d	06 03	06 33	15 17	15 48
Ince & Elton	d	06 06	06 36	15 20	15 51
Stanlow & Thornton	d	06 08	06 38	15 22	15 53
Ellesmere Port	a	06 15	06 45	15 28	15 59

No Sunday Service

Table 109

Mondays to Saturdays

Ellesmere Port - Helsby

		NT	NT SO	NT SX	NT	NT
Ellesmere Port	d	06 19	06 56	06 56	15 34	16 04
Stanlow & Thornton	d	06 23	07 00	07 00	15 38	16 08
Ince & Elton	d	06 26	07 03	07 03	15 41	16 11
Helsby	a	06 30	07 07	07 06	15 45	16 14
Warrington Bank Quay 81	a			07 23		16 34

No Sunday Service

Network Diagram for Tables 114, 115

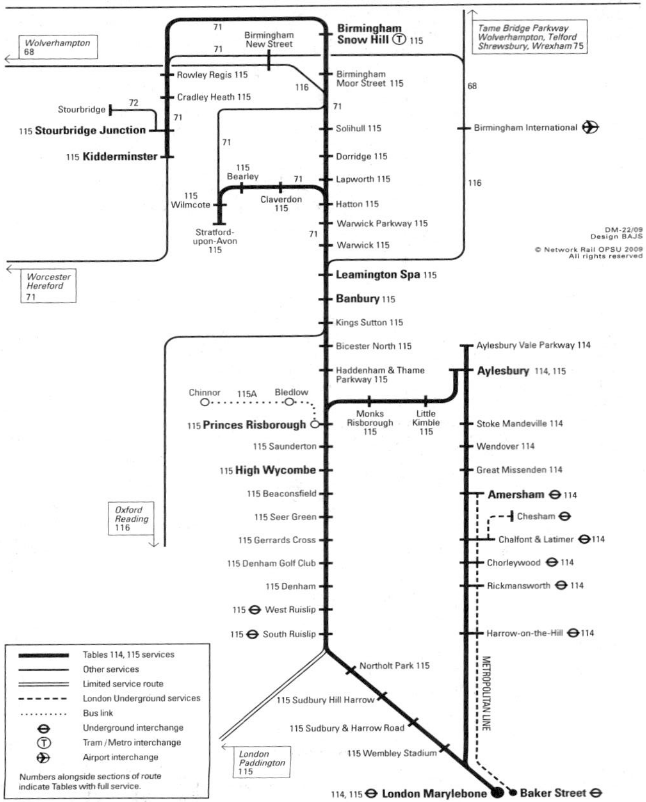

Table 114

London - Amersham and Aylesbury

Mondays to Fridays

until 01 October

Station			CH MX	CH ◇	CH MX	CH	CH ◇	CH	CH	CH	CH ◇		CH ◇	CH ◇	CH	CH ◇	CH	CH	CH	CH	CH ◇		CH	CH	CH ◇	CH
London Marylebone 10	⊖	d	22p57	23p27	23p57	06 32	07 04	07 26	07 56	08 27	08 57		09 27	09 57	10 27	10 57	11 27	11 57	12 27	12 57	13 27		13 57	14 27	14 57	15 27
Harrow-on-the-Hill 3 §	⊖	d	23p09	23p39	00 09	06 45	07 16	07 38	08 08	08 39	09 09		09 39	10 09	10 39	11 09	11 39	12 09	12 39	13 09	13 39		14 09	14 39	15 09	15 39
Rickmansworth §	⊖	d	23p19	23p49	00 19	06 55	07 27	07 48	08 18	08 49	09 19		09 49	10 19	10 49	11 19	11 49	12 19	12 49	13 19	13 49		14 19	14 49	15 19	15 49
Chorleywood §	⊖	d	23p24	23p54	00 24	07 00	07 31	07 53	08 23	08 54	09 24		09 54	10 24	10 54	11 24	11 54	12 24	12 54	13 24	13 54		14 24	14 54	15 24	15 54
Chalfont & Latimer §	⊖	d	23p28	23p58	00 28	07 04	07 35	07 57	08 27	08 58	09 28		09 58	10 28	10 58	11 28	11 58	12 28	12 58	13 28	13 58		14 28	14 58	15 28	15 58
Amersham §	⊖	d	23p32	00 02	00 32	07 08	07 39	08 01	08 31	09 02	09 32		10 02	10 32	11 02	11 32	12 02	12 32	13 02	13 32	14 02		14 32	15 02	15 32	16 02
Great Missenden		d	23p38	00 08	00 38	07 14	07 46	08 07	08 37	09 08	09 38		10 08	10 38	11 08	11 38	12 08	12 38	13 08	13 38	14 08		14 38	15 08	15 38	16 08
Wendover		d	23p44	00 14	00 44	07 20	07 52	08 13	08 43	09 14	09 44		10 14	10 44	11 14	11 44	12 14	12 44	13 14	13 44	14 14		14 44	15 14	15 44	16 14
Stoke Mandeville		d	23p48	00 18	00 48	07 24	07 56	08 17	08 47	09 18	09 48		10 18	10 48	11 18	11 48	12 18	12 48	13 18	13 48	14 18		14 48	15 18	15 48	16 18
Aylesbury		d	23p53	00a26	00a56	07 30	08 01	08a25	08 52	09a26	09 53		10a26	10 53	11a26	11 53	12a26	12 53	13a26	13 53	14a26		14 53	15a26	15 53	16a26
Aylesbury Vale Parkway		a	00 01			07 39	08 08		09 00		10 01			11 01		12 01		13 01		14 01			15 01		16 01	

Station			CH	CH	CH	CH	CH		CH	CH	CH	CH	CH	CH	CH	CH	CH		CH	CH ◇	CH	CH	CH	CH	CH ◇	CH
London Marylebone 10	⊖	d	15 57	16 27	16 42	16 57	17 16		17 27	17 47	18 03	18 18	18 36	18 51	19 09	19 25	19 57		20 27	20 57	21 27	21 57	22 27	22 57	23 27	23 57
Harrow-on-the-Hill 3 §	⊖	d	16 09	16 39		17 09			17 40		18 15		18 48	19 03		19 37	20 09		20 39	21 09	21 39	22 09	22 39	23 09	23 39	00 09
Rickmansworth §	⊖	d	16 19	16 49		17 19			17 50							19 47	20 19		20 49	21 19	21 49	22 19	22 49	23 19	23 49	00 19
Chorleywood §	⊖	d	16 24	16 54		17 24			17 55		18 29		19 02	19 17		19 52	20 24		20 54	21 24	21 54	22 24	22 54	23 24	23 54	00 24
Chalfont & Latimer §	⊖	d	16 28	16 58		17 28			17 59		18 33		19 06	19 21		19 56	20 28		20 58	21 28	21 58	22 28	22 58	23 28	23 58	00 28
Amersham §	⊖	d	16 32	17 02	17 15	17 32			18 03	18 18	18 38		19 10	19 25		20 00	20 32		21 02	21 32	22 02	22 32	23 02	23 32	00 02	00 32
Great Missenden		d	16 38	17 08	17 22	17 38	17 51		18 09	18 25	18 44	18 56	19 16	19 31	19 46	20 06	20 38		21 08	21 38	22 08	22 38	23 08	23 38	00 08	00 38
Wendover		d	16 44	17 14	17 28	17 44	17 57		18 15	18 31	18 50	19 02	19 22	19 37	19 52	20 12	20 44		21 14	21 44	22 14	22 44	23 14	23 44	00 14	00 44
Stoke Mandeville		d	16 48	17 18	17 32	17 48	18 01		18 19	18 35	18 54	19 06	19 26	19 41	19 57	20 16	20 48		21 18	21 48	22 18	22 48	23 18	23 48	00 18	00 48
Aylesbury		d	16 53	17a26	17 37	17a56	18 06		18a26	18 40	19a02	19 11	19a34	19a49	20 09	20a24	20 53		21a26	21 53	22a26	22 53	23a26	23 53	00a26	00a56
Aylesbury Vale Parkway		a	17 02		17 42		18 15			18 46		19 17			20 15		21 01			22 01		23 01		00 01		

Mondays to Fridays

from 04 October

Station			CH MX	CH ◇	CH MX	CH	CH ◇	CH	CH	CH	CH ◇		CH ◇	CH ◇	CH	CH ◇	CH	CH	CH	CH	CH ◇		CH	CH	CH ◇	CH
London Marylebone 10	⊖	d	22p57	23p27	23p57	06 32	07 04	07 26	07 56	08 27	08 57		09 27	09 57	10 27	10 57	11 27	11 57	12 27	12 57	13 27		13 57	14 27	14 57	15 27
Harrow-on-the-Hill 3 §	⊖	d	23p09	23p39	00 09	06 45	07 16	07 38	08 08	08 39	09 09		09 39	10 09	10 39	11 09	11 39	12 09	12 39	13 09	13 39		14 09	14 39	15 09	15 39
Rickmansworth §	⊖	d	23p19	23p49	00 19	06 55	07 27	07 48	08 18	08 49	09 19		09 49	10 19	10 49	11 19	11 49	12 19	12 49	13 19	13 49		14 19	14 49	15 19	15 49
Chorleywood §	⊖	d	23p24	23p54	00 24	07 00	07 31	07 53	08 23	08 54	09 24		09 54	10 24	10 54	11 24	11 54	12 24	12 54	13 24	13 54		14 24	14 54	15 24	15 54
Chalfont & Latimer §	⊖	d	23p28	23p58	00 28	07 04	07 35	07 57	08 27	08 58	09 28		09 58	10 28	10 58	11 28	11 58	12 28	12 58	13 28	13 58		14 28	14 58	15 28	15 58
Amersham §	⊖	d	23p32	00 02	00 32	07 08	07 39	08 01	08 31	09 02	09 32		10 02	10 32	11 02	11 32	12 02	12 32	13 02	13 32	14 02		14 32	15 02	15 32	16 02
Great Missenden		d	23p38	00 08	00 38	07 14	07 46	08 07	08 37	09 08	09 38		10 08	10 38	11 08	11 38	12 08	12 38	13 08	13 38	14 08		14 38	15 08	15 38	16 08
Wendover		d	23p44	00 14	00 44	07 20	07 52	08 13	08 43	09 14	09 44		10 14	10 44	11 14	11 44	12 14	12 44	13 14	13 44	14 14		14 44	15 14	15 44	16 14
Stoke Mandeville		d	23p48	00 18	00 48	07 24	07 56	08 17	08 47	09 18	09 48		10 18	10 48	11 18	11 48	12 18	12 48	13 18	13 48	14 18		14 48	15 18	15 48	16 18
Aylesbury		d	23p53	00a26	00a59	07 30	08 01	08a28	08 52	09a29	09 53		10a29	10 53	11a29	11 53	12a29	12 53	13a29	13 53	14a29		14 53	15a29	15 53	16a29
Aylesbury Vale Parkway		a	00 04			07 42	08 11		09 03		10 04			11 04		12 04		13 04		14 04			15 04		16 04	

Station			CH	CH	CH	CH	CH		CH	CH	CH	CH	CH	CH	CH	CH	CH		CH	CH ◇	CH	CH	CH	CH	CH ◇	CH
London Marylebone 10	⊖	d	15 57	16 27	16 42	16 57	17 16		17 27	17 47	18 03	18 18	18 36	18 51	19 09	19 25	19 57		20 27	20 57	21 27	21 57	22 27	22 57	23 27	23 57
Harrow-on-the-Hill 3 §	⊖	d	16 09	16 39		17 09			17 40		18 15		18 48	19 03		19 37	20 09		20 39	21 09	21 39	22 09	22 39	23 09	23 39	00 09
Rickmansworth §	⊖	d	16 19	16 49		17 19			17 50							19 47	20 19		20 49	21 19	21 49	22 19	22 49	23 19	23 49	00 19
Chorleywood §	⊖	d	16 24	16 54		17 24			17 55		18 29		19 02	19 17		19 52	20 24		20 54	21 24	21 54	22 24	22 54	23 24	23 54	00 24
Chalfont & Latimer §	⊖	d	16 28	16 58		17 28			17 59		18 33		19 06	19 21		19 56	20 28		20 58	21 28	21 58	22 28	22 58	23 28	23 58	00 28
Amersham §	⊖	d	16 32	17 02	17 15	17 32			18 03	18 18	18 38		19 10	19 25		20 00	20 32		21 02	21 32	22 02	22 32	23 02	23 32	00 02	00 32
Great Missenden		d	16 38	17 08	17 22	17 38	17 51		18 09	18 25	18 44	18 56	19 16	19 31	19 46	20 06	20 38		21 08	21 38	22 08	22 38	23 08	23 38	00 08	00 38
Wendover		d	16 44	17 14	17 28	17 44	17 57		18 15	18 31	18 50	19 02	19 22	19 37	19 52	20 12	20 44		21 14	21 44	22 14	22 44	23 14	23 44	00 14	00 44
Stoke Mandeville		d	16 48	17 18	17 32	17 48	18 01		18 19	18 35	18 54	19 06	19 26	19 41	19 57	20 16	20 48		21 18	21 48	22 18	22 48	23 18	23 48	00 18	00 48
Aylesbury		d	16 53	17a29	17 37	17a59	18 06		18a29	18 40	19a05	19 11	19a37	19a52	20 09	20a27	20 53		21a29	21 53	22a26	22 53	23a26	23 53	00a26	00a59
Aylesbury Vale Parkway		a	17 05		17 45		18 18			18 49		19 20			20 18		21 04			22 04		23 04		00 04		

Saturdays

until 02 October

Station			CH	CH ◇	CH	CH	CH ◇	CH	CH	CH ◇	CH		CH	CH	CH	CH ◇	CH	CH	CH	CH ◇	CH		CH	CH ◇	CH	CH
London Marylebone 10	⊖	d	22p57	23p27	23p57		07 27	07 57	08 27	08 57	09 27		09 57	10 27	10 57	11 27	11 57	12 27	12 57	13 27	13 57		14 27	14 57	15 27	15 57
Harrow-on-the-Hill 3 §	⊖	d	23p09	23p39	00 09		07 39	08 09	08 39	09 09	09 39		10 09	10 39	11 09	11 39	12 09	12 39	13 09	13 39	14 09		14 39	15 09	15 39	16 09
Rickmansworth §	⊖	d	23p19	23p49	00 19		07 49	08 19	08 49	09 19	09 49		10 19	10 49	11 19	11 49	12 19	12 49	13 19	13 49	14 19		14 49	15 19	15 49	16 19
Chorleywood §	⊖	d	23p24	23p54	00 24		07 54	08 24	08 54	09 24	09 54		10 24	10 54	11 24	11 54	12 24	12 54	13 24	13 54	14 24		14 54	15 24	15 54	16 24
Chalfont & Latimer §	⊖	d	23p28	23p58	00 28		07 58	08 28	08 58	09 28	09 58		10 28	10 58	11 28	11 58	12 28	12 58	13 28	13 58	14 28		14 58	15 28	15 58	16 28
Amersham §	⊖	d	23p32	00 02	00 32	07 05	08 02	08 32	09 02	09 32	10 02		10 32	11 02	11 32	12 02	12 32	13 02	13 32	14 02	14 32		15 02	15 32	16 02	16 32
Great Missenden		d	23p38	00 08	00 38	07 11	08 08	08 38	09 08	09 38	10 08		10 38	11 08	11 38	12 08	12 38	13 08	13 38	14 08	14 38		15 08	15 38	16 08	16 38
Wendover		d	23p44	00 14	00 44	07 17	08 14	08 44	09 14	09 44	10 14		10 44	11 14	11 44	12 14	12 44	13 14	13 44	14 14	14 44		15 14	15 44	16 14	16 44
Stoke Mandeville		d	23p48	00 18	00 48	07 21	08 18	08 48	09 18	09 48	10 18		10 48	11 18	11 48	12 18	12 48	13 18	13 48	14 18	14 48		15 18	15 48	16 18	16 48
Aylesbury		d	23p53	00a26	00a56	07a29	08a26	08 53	09a26	09 53	10a26		10 53	11a26	11 53	12a26	12 53	13a26	13 53	14a26	14 53		15a26	15 53	16a26	16 53
Aylesbury Vale Parkway		a	00 01					09 01		10 01			11 01		12 01		13 01		14 01		15 01			16 01		17 01

§ London Underground Limited (Metropolitan Line) services operate between Harrow-on-the-Hill, Rickmansworth, Chorleywood, Chalfont & Latimer and Amersham

London - Amersham and Aylesbury

Saturdays until 02 October

		CH	CH	CH	CH	CH	CH	CH	CH	CH	CH	CH	CH
										◇			
London Marylebone [10]	⊖ d	16 27	16 57	17 27	17 57	18 27	18 57	19 27	19 57	20 57	21 57	22 57	23 57
Harrow-on-the-Hill [3] ‡	⊖ d	16 39	17 09	17 39	18 09	18 39	19 09	19 39	20 09	21 09	22 09	23 09	00 09
Rickmansworth ‡	⊖ d	16 49	17 19	17 49	18 19	18 49	19 19	19 49	20 19	21 19	22 19	23 19	00 19
Chorleywood ‡	⊖ d	16 54	17 24	17 54	18 24	18 54	19 24	19 54	20 24	21 24	22 24	23 24	00 24
Chalfont & Latimer ‡	⊖ d	16 58	17 28	17 58	18 28	18 58	19 28	19 58	20 28	21 28	22 28	23 28	00 28
Amersham ‡	⊖ d	17 02	17 32	18 02	18 32	19 02	19 32	20 02	20 32	21 32	22 32	23 32	00 32
Great Missenden	d	17 08	17 38	18 08	18 38	19 08	19 38	20 08	20 38	21 38	22 38	23 38	00 38
Wendover	d	17 14	17 44	18 14	18 44	19 14	19 44	20 14	20 44	21 44	22 44	23 44	00 44
Stoke Mandeville	d	17 18	17 48	18 18	18 48	19 18	19 48	20 18	20 48	21 48	22 48	23 48	00 48
Aylesbury	d	17a26	17 53	18a26	18 53	19a26	19 53	20a26	20 53	21 53	22 53	23 53	00a56
Aylesbury Vale Parkway	a		18 01		19 01		20 01		21 01	22 01	23 01	00 01	

Saturdays from 09 October

		CH	CH	CH	CH	CH	CH	CH	CH	CH	CH	CH	CH	CH	CH	CH	CH	CH	CH	CH	CH	CH	CH
			◇			◇			◇					◇				◇			◇		
London Marylebone [10]	⊖ d	22p57	23p27	23p57		07 27	07 57	08 27	08 57	09 27	09 57	10 27	10 57	11 27	11 57	12 27	12 57	13 27	13 57	14 27	14 57	15 27	15 57
Harrow-on-the-Hill [3] ‡	⊖ d	23p09	23p39	00 09		07 39	08 09	08 39	09 09	09 39	10 09	10 39	11 09	11 39	12 09	12 39	13 09	13 39	14 09	14 39	15 09	15 39	16 09
Rickmansworth ‡	⊖ d	23p19	23p49	00 19		07 49	08 19	08 49	09 19	09 49	10 19	10 49	11 19	11 49	12 19	12 49	13 19	13 49	14 19	14 49	15 19	15 49	16 19
Chorleywood ‡	⊖ d	23p24	23p54	00 24		07 54	08 24	08 54	09 24	09 54	10 24	10 54	11 24	11 54	12 24	12 54	13 24	13 54	14 24	14 54	15 24	15 54	16 24
Chalfont & Latimer ‡	⊖ d	23p28	23p58	00 28		07 58	08 28	08 58	09 28	09 58	10 28	10 58	11 28	11 58	12 28	12 58	13 28	13 58	14 28	14 58	15 28	15 58	16 28
Amersham ‡	⊖ d	23p32	00 02	00 32	07 05	08 02	08 32	09 02	09 32	10 02	10 32	11 02	11 32	12 02	12 32	13 02	13 32	14 02	14 32	15 02	15 32	16 02	16 32
Great Missenden	d	23p38	00 08	00 38	07 11	08 08	08 38	09 08	09 38	10 08	10 38	11 08	11 38	12 08	12 38	13 08	13 38	14 08	14 38	15 08	15 38	16 08	16 38
Wendover	d	23p44	00 14	00 44	07 17	08 14	08 44	09 14	09 44	10 14	10 44	11 14	11 44	12 14	12 44	13 14	13 44	14 14	14 44	15 14	15 44	16 14	16 44
Stoke Mandeville	d	23p48	00 18	00 48	07 21	08 18	08 48	09 18	09 48	10 18	10 48	11 18	11 48	12 18	12 48	13 18	13 48	14 18	14 48	15 18	15 48	16 18	16 48
Aylesbury	d	23p53	00a29	00a59	07a32	08a29	08 53	09a29	09 53	10a29	10 53	11a29	11 53	12a29	12 53	13a29	13 53	14a29	14 53	15a29	15 53	16a29	16 53
Aylesbury Vale Parkway	a	00 04					09 04		10 04		11 04		12 04		13 04		14 04		15 04		16 04		17 04

		CH	CH	CH	CH	CH	CH	CH	CH	CH	CH	CH	CH
										◇			
London Marylebone [10]	⊖ d	16 27	16 57	17 27	17 57	18 27	18 57	19 27	19 57	20 57	21 57	22 57	23 57
Harrow-on-the-Hill [3] ‡	⊖ d	16 39	17 09	17 39	18 09	18 39	19 09	19 39	20 09	21 09	22 09	23 09	00 09
Rickmansworth ‡	⊖ d	16 49	17 19	17 49	18 19	18 49	19 19	19 49	20 19	21 19	22 19	23 19	00 19
Chorleywood ‡	⊖ d	16 54	17 24	17 54	18 24	18 54	19 24	19 54	20 24	21 24	22 24	23 24	00 24
Chalfont & Latimer ‡	⊖ d	16 58	17 28	17 58	18 28	18 58	19 28	19 58	20 28	21 28	22 28	23 28	00 28
Amersham ‡	⊖ d	17 02	17 32	18 02	18 32	19 02	19 32	20 02	20 32	21 32	22 32	23 32	00 32
Great Missenden	d	17 08	17 38	18 08	18 38	19 08	19 38	20 08	20 38	21 38	22 38	23 38	00 38
Wendover	d	17 14	17 44	18 14	18 44	19 14	19 44	20 14	20 44	21 44	22 44	23 44	00 44
Stoke Mandeville	d	17 18	17 48	18 18	18 48	19 18	19 48	20 18	20 48	21 48	22 48	23 48	00 48
Aylesbury	d	17a29	17 53	18a29	18 53	19a29	19 53	20a29	20 53	21 53	22 53	23 53	00a59
Aylesbury Vale Parkway	a		18 04		19 04		20 04		21 04	22 04	23 04	00 04	

Sundays until 26 September

		CH	CH	CH	CH	CH	CH	CH	CH	CH	CH	CH	CH	CH	CH	CH	CH	CH	CH	CH	CH	CH	CH
						◇				◇				◇									
		A		A																			
London Marylebone [10]	⊖ d	22p57		23p57		08 27	09 27	10 27	11 27	12 27	13 27	14 27		15 27		16 27		17 27		18 27		19 27	
Harrow-on-the-Hill [3] ‡	⊖ d	23p09		00 09		08 39	09 39	10 39	11 39	12 39	13 39	14 39		15 39		16 39		17 39		18 39		19 39	
Rickmansworth ‡	⊖ d	23p19		00 19		08 49	09 49	10 49	11 49	12 49	13 49	14 49		15 49		16 49		17 49		18 49		19 49	
Chorleywood ‡	⊖ d	23p24		00 24		08 54	09 54	10 54	11 54	12 54	13 54	14 54		15 54		16 54		17 54		18 54		19 54	
Chalfont & Latimer ‡	⊖ d	23p28		00 28		08 58	09 58	10 58	11 58	12 58	13 58	14 58		15 58		16 58		17 58		18 58		19 58	
Amersham ‡	⊖ d	23p32	00 02	00 32	08 32	09 02	10 02	11 02	12 02	13 02	14 02	15 02	15 32	16 02	16 32	17 02	17 32	18 02	18 32	19 02	19 32	20 02	20 32
Great Missenden	d	23p38	00 08	00 38	08 38	09 08	10 08	11 08	12 08	13 08	14 08	15 08	15 38	16 08	16 38	17 08	17 38	18 08	18 38	19 08	19 38	20 08	20 38
Wendover	d	23p44	00 14	00 44	08 44	09 14	10 14	11 14	12 14	13 14	14 14	15 14	15 44	16 14	16 44	17 14	17 44	18 14	18 44	19 14	19 44	20 14	20 44
Stoke Mandeville	d	23p48	00 18	00 48	08 48	09 18	10 18	11 18	12 18	13 18	14 18	15 18	15 48	16 18	16 48	17 18	17 48	18 18	18 48	19 18	19 48	20 18	20 48
Aylesbury	d	23p53	00a26	00a56	08a56	09 23	10 23	11 23	12 23	13 23	14 23	15 23	15a56	16 23	16a56	17 23	17a56	18 23	18a56	19 23	19a56	20 23	20a56
Aylesbury Vale Parkway	a	00 01				09 31	10 31	11 31	12 31	13 31	14 31	15 31		16 31		17 31		18 31		19 31		20 31	

		CH	CH	CH	CH	CH
						◇
London Marylebone [10]	⊖ d	20 27		21 27	22 27	23 27
Harrow-on-the-Hill [3] ‡	⊖ d	20 39		21 39	22 39	23 39
Rickmansworth ‡	⊖ d	20 49		21 49	22 49	23 49
Chorleywood ‡	⊖ d	20 54		21 54	22 54	23 54
Chalfont & Latimer ‡	⊖ d	20 58		21 58	22 58	23 58
Amersham ‡	⊖ d	21 02	21 32	22 02	23 02	00 02
Great Missenden	d	21 08	21 38	22 08	23 08	00 08
Wendover	d	21 14	21 44	22 14	23 14	00 14
Stoke Mandeville	d	21 18	21 48	22 18	23 18	00 18
Aylesbury	d	21 23	21a56	22 23	23 23	00a26
Aylesbury Vale Parkway	a	21 31		22 31	23 31	

‡ London Underground Limited (Metropolitan Line) services operate between Harrow-on-the-Hill, Rickmansworth, Chorleywood, Chalfont & Latimer and Amersham

A not 23 May

London - Amersham and Aylesbury

Sundays from 03 October

		CH	CH	CH	CH	CH	CH	CH	CH	CH	CH	CH	CH	CH	CH	CH	CH	CH	CH	CH	CH	CH	CH
							◇				◇				◇								
		A	B																				
London Marylebone [10]	⊖ d	22p57	22p57		23p57		08 27	09 27	10 27	11 27	12 27	13 27	14 27		15 27		16 27		17 27		18 27		19 27
Harrow-on-the-Hill [3] †	⊖ d	23p09	23p09		00 09		08 39	09 39	10 39	11 39	12 39	13 39	14 39		15 39		16 39		17 39		18 39		19 39
Rickmansworth †	⊖ d	23p19	23p19		00 19		08 49	09 49	10 49	11 49	12 49	13 49	14 49		15 49		16 49		17 49		18 49		19 49
Chorleywood †	⊖ d	23p24	23p24		00 24		08 54	09 54	10 54	11 54	12 54	13 54	14 54		15 54		16 54		17 54		18 54		19 54
Chalfont & Latimer †	⊖ d	23p28	23p28		00 28		08 58	09 58	10 58	11 58	12 58	13 58	14 58		15 58		16 58		17 58		18 58		19 58
Amersham †	⊖ d	23p32	23p32	00 02	00 32	08 32	09 02	10 02	11 02	12 02	13 02	14 02	15 02	15 32	16 02	16 32	17 02	17 32	18 02	18 32	19 02	19 32	20 02
Great Missenden	d	23p38	23p38	00 08	00 38	08 38	09 08	10 08	11 08	12 08	13 08	14 08	15 08	15 38	16 08	16 38	17 08	17 38	18 08	18 38	19 08	19 38	20 08
Wendover	d	23p44	23p44	00 14	00 44	08 44	09 14	10 14	11 14	12 14	13 14	14 14	15 14	15 44	16 14	16 44	17 14	17 44	18 14	18 44	19 14	19 44	20 14
Stoke Mandeville	d	23p48	23p48	00 18	00 48	08 48	09 18	10 18	11 18	12 18	13 18	14 18	15 18	15 48	16 18	16 48	17 18	17 48	18 18	18 48	19 18	19 48	20 18
Aylesbury	d	23p53	23p53	00a29	00a56	08a59	09 23	10 23	11 23	12 23	13 23	14 23	15 23	15a59	16 23	16a59	17 23	17a59	18 23	18a59	19 23	19a59	20 23
Aylesbury Vale Parkway	a	00 04	00 01				09 34	10 34	11 34	12 34	13 34	14 34	15 34		16 34		17 34		18 34		19 34		20 34

		CH	CH	CH	CH	CH	CH
							◇
London Marylebone [10]	⊖ d		20 27		21 27	22 27	23 27
Harrow-on-the-Hill [3] †	⊖ d		20 39		21 39	22 39	23 39
Rickmansworth †	⊖ d		20 49		21 49	22 49	23 49
Chorleywood †	⊖ d		20 54		21 54	22 54	23 54
Chalfont & Latimer †	⊖ d		20 58		21 58	22 58	23 58
Amersham †	⊖ d	20 32	21 02	21 32	22 02	23 02	00 02
Great Missenden	d	20 38	21 08	21 38	22 08	23 08	00 08
Wendover	d	20 44	21 14	21 44	22 14	23 14	00 14
Stoke Mandeville	d	20 48	21 18	21 48	22 18	23 18	00 18
Aylesbury	d	20a59	21 23	21a59	22 23	23 23	00a29
Aylesbury Vale Parkway	a		21 34		22 34	23 34	

† London Underground Limited (Metropolitan Line) services operate between Harrow-on-the-Hill, Rickmansworth, Chorleywood, Chalfont & Latimer and Amersham

A not 3 October
B 3 October

Table 114

Aylesbury and Amersham - London

Mondays to Fridays until 01 October

Station		CH	CH	CH	CH	CH	CH	CH	CH	CH
Aylesbury Vale Parkway	d	05 26	06 05		06 42		07 13		07 45	
Aylesbury	d	05 31	06 10	06 26	06 47	07 00	07 18	07 32	07 50	08 06
Stoke Mandeville	d	05 35	06 14	06 30	06 51	07 04	07 22	07 36	07 54	08 10
Wendover	d	05 39	06 18	06 34	06 55	07 08	07 26	07 40	07 58	08 14
Great Missenden	d	05 45	06 24	06 40	07 01	07 14	07 32	07 46	08 04	08 20
Amersham ?	⊖ d	05 52	06 31	06 47		07 21	07 39	07 53	08 11	08 27
Chalfont & Latimer ?	⊖ d		06 35	06 51		07 25		07 57		08 31
Chorleywood ?	⊖ d		06 38	06 54		07 28		08 00		08 34
Rickmansworth ?	⊖ d			06 59				08 05		
Harrow-on-the-Hill 3 ?	⊖ d	06 11	06 53	07 10		07 43		08 16		08 49
London Marylebone 10	⊖ a	06 25	07 10	07 25	07 42	07 58	08 15	08 31	08 44	09 05

Station		CH	CH	CH ◇	CH	CH	CH	CH	CH	CH ◇
Aylesbury Vale Parkway	d	08 17		09 05	09 30		10 30		11 30	
Aylesbury	d	08 22	08 35	09 10	09 35	10 05	10 35	11 05	11 35	12 05
Stoke Mandeville	d	08 26	08 39	09 14	09 39	10 09	10 39	11 09	11 39	12 09
Wendover	d	08 30	08 43	09 18	09 43	10 13	10 43	11 13	11 43	12 13
Great Missenden	d	08 36	08 49	09 24	09 49	10 19	10 49	11 19	11 49	12 19
Amersham ?	⊖ d		08 56	09 31	09 56	10 26	10 56	11 26	11 56	12 26
Chalfont & Latimer ?	⊖ d		09 00	09 35	10 00	10 30	11 00	11 30	12 00	12 30
Chorleywood ?	⊖ d		09 03	09 38	10 03	10 33	11 03	11 33	12 03	12 33
Rickmansworth ?	⊖ d		09 08	09 43	10 08	10 38	11 08	11 38	12 08	12 38
Harrow-on-the-Hill 3 ?	⊖ d		09 19	09 54	10 19	10 49	11 19	11 49	12 19	12 49
London Marylebone 10	⊖ a	09 16	09 35	10 10	10 35	11 05	11 35	12 05	12 35	13 05

Station		CH ◇	CH	CH ◇	CH
Aylesbury Vale Parkway	d	12 30		13 30	
Aylesbury	d	12 35	13 05	13 35	14 05
Stoke Mandeville	d	12 39	13 09	13 39	14 09
Wendover	d	12 43	13 13	13 43	14 13
Great Missenden	d	12 49	13 19	13 49	14 19
Amersham ?	⊖ d	12 56	13 26	13 56	14 26
Chalfont & Latimer ?	⊖ d	13 00	13 30	14 00	14 30
Chorleywood ?	⊖ d	13 03	13 33	14 03	14 33
Rickmansworth ?	⊖ d	13 08	13 38	14 08	14 38
Harrow-on-the-Hill 3 ?	⊖ d	13 19	13 49	14 19	14 49
London Marylebone 10	⊖ a	13 35	14 05	14 35	15 05

Station		CH	CH ◇	CH	CH	CH ◇	CH	CH	CH	CH	CH	CH ◇	CH ◇	CH	CH ◇	CH	CH	CH
Aylesbury Vale Parkway	d	14 30		15 30		16 30		17 30		18 20			19 30		20 30		21 30	22 30
Aylesbury	d	14 35	15 05	15 35	16 05	16 35	17 05	17 35	17 55	18 25	18 45	19 15	19 35	20 05	20 35	21 05	21 35	22 35
Stoke Mandeville	d	14 39	15 09	15 39	16 09	16 39	17 09	17 39	17 59	18 29	18 49	19 19	19 39	20 09	20 39	21 09	21 39	22 39
Wendover	d	14 43	15 13	15 43	16 13	16 43	17 13	17 43	18 03	18 33	18 53	19 23	19 43	20 13	20 43	21 13	21 43	22 43
Great Missenden	d	14 49	15 19	15 49	16 19	16 49	17 19	17 49	18 09	18 39	18 59	19 29	19 49	20 19	20 49	21 19	21 49	22 49
Amersham ?	⊖ d	14 56	15 26	15 56	16 26	16 56	17 26	17 56	18 16	18 46	19 06	19 36	19 56	20 26	20 56	21 26	21 56	22 56
Chalfont & Latimer ?	⊖ d	15 00	15 30	16 00	16 30	17 00	17 30	18 00	18 20	18 50	19 10	19 40	20 00	20 30	21 00	21 30	22 00	23 00
Chorleywood ?	⊖ d	15 03	15 33	16 03	16 33	17 03	17 33	18 03	18 23	18 53	19 13	19 43	20 03	20 33	21 03	21 33	22 03	23 03
Rickmansworth ?	⊖ d	15 08	15 38	16 08	16 38	17 08	17 38	18 08	18 28	18 58	19 18	19 48	20 08	20 38	21 08	21 38	22 08	23 08
Harrow-on-the-Hill 3 ?	⊖ d	15 19	15 49	16 19	16 49	17 19	17 49	18 19	18 39	19 09	19 29	19 59	20 19	20 49	21 19	21 49	22 19	23 19
London Marylebone 10	⊖ a	15 35	16 05	16 35	17 05	17 35	18 05	18 35	18 55	19 25	19 45	20 15	20 35	21 05	21 35	22 05	22 35	23 35

Mondays to Fridays from 04 October

Station		CH	CH	CH	CH	CH	CH	CH	CH	CH
Aylesbury Vale Parkway	d	05 23	06 02		06 39		07 10		07 42	
Aylesbury	d	05 28	06 07	06 23	06 44	06 57	07 15	07 29	07 47	08 03
Stoke Mandeville	d	05 32	06 11	06 27	06 48	07 01	07 19	07 33	07 51	08 07
Wendover	d	05 36	06 15	06 31	06 52	07 05	07 23	07 37	07 55	08 11
Great Missenden	d	05 42	06 21	06 37	06 58	07 11	07 29	07 43	08 01	08 17
Amersham ?	⊖ d	05 49	06 28	06 44		07 18	07 36	07 50	08 08	08 24
Chalfont & Latimer ?	⊖ d		06 32	06 48		07 22		07 54		08 28
Chorleywood ?	⊖ d		06 37	06 53		07 27		07 59		08 33
Rickmansworth ?	⊖ d			06 59				08 05		
Harrow-on-the-Hill 3 ?	⊖ d	06 11	06 53	07 10		07 43		08 16		08 49
London Marylebone 10	⊖ a	06 25	07 10	07 25	07 42	07 58	08 15	08 31	08 44	09 05

Station		CH	CH	CH ◇	CH	CH	CH	CH	CH	CH ◇
Aylesbury Vale Parkway	d	08 14		09 02	09 27		10 27		11 27	
Aylesbury	d	08 19	08 32	09 07	09 32	10 02	10 32	11 02	11 32	12 02
Stoke Mandeville	d	08 23	08 36	09 11	09 36	10 06	10 36	11 06	11 36	12 06
Wendover	d	08 27	08 40	09 15	09 40	10 10	10 40	11 10	11 40	12 10
Great Missenden	d	08 33	08 46	09 21	09 46	10 16	10 46	11 16	11 46	12 16
Amersham ?	⊖ d		08 53	09 28	09 53	10 23	10 53	11 23	11 53	12 23
Chalfont & Latimer ?	⊖ d		08 57	09 32	09 57	10 27	10 57	11 27	11 57	12 27
Chorleywood ?	⊖ d		09 02	09 37	10 02	10 32	11 02	11 32	12 02	12 32
Rickmansworth ?	⊖ d		09 08	09 43	10 08	10 38	11 08	11 38	12 08	12 38
Harrow-on-the-Hill 3 ?	⊖ d		09 19	09 54	10 19	10 49	11 19	11 49	12 19	12 49
London Marylebone 10	⊖ a	09 16	09 35	10 10	10 35	11 05	11 35	12 05	12 35	13 05

Station		CH ◇	CH	CH ◇	CH
Aylesbury Vale Parkway	d	12 27		13 27	
Aylesbury	d	12 32	13 02	13 32	14 02
Stoke Mandeville	d	12 36	13 06	13 36	14 06
Wendover	d	12 40	13 10	13 40	14 10
Great Missenden	d	12 46	13 16	13 46	14 16
Amersham ?	⊖ d	12 53	13 23	13 53	14 23
Chalfont & Latimer ?	⊖ d	12 57	13 27	13 57	14 27
Chorleywood ?	⊖ d	13 02	13 32	14 02	14 32
Rickmansworth ?	⊖ d	13 08	13 38	14 08	14 38
Harrow-on-the-Hill 3 ?	⊖ d	13 19	13 49	14 19	14 49
London Marylebone 10	⊖ a	13 35	14 05	14 35	15 05

Station		CH	CH ◇	CH	CH	CH ◇	CH	CH	CH	CH	CH	CH ◇	CH ◇	CH	CH ◇	CH	CH	CH
Aylesbury Vale Parkway	d	14 27		15 27		16 27		17 27		18 17			19 27		20 27		21 27	22 27
Aylesbury	d	14 32	15 02	15 32	16 02	16 32	17 02	17 32	17 52	18 22	18 42	19 12	19 32	20 02	20 32	21 02	21 32	22 32
Stoke Mandeville	d	14 36	15 06	15 36	16 06	16 36	17 06	17 36	17 56	18 26	18 46	19 16	19 36	20 06	20 36	21 06	21 36	22 36
Wendover	d	14 40	15 10	15 40	16 10	16 40	17 10	17 40	18 00	18 30	18 50	19 20	19 40	20 10	20 40	21 10	21 40	22 40
Great Missenden	d	14 46	15 16	15 46	16 16	16 46	17 16	17 46	18 06	18 36	18 56	19 26	19 46	20 16	20 46	21 16	21 46	22 46
Amersham ?	⊖ d	14 53	15 23	15 53	16 23	16 53	17 23	17 53	18 13	18 43	19 03	19 33	19 53	20 23	20 53	21 23	21 53	22 53
Chalfont & Latimer ?	⊖ d	14 57	15 27	15 57	16 27	16 57	17 27	17 57	18 17	18 47	19 07	19 37	19 57	20 27	20 57	21 27	21 57	22 57
Chorleywood ?	⊖ d	15 02	15 32	16 02	16 32	17 02	17 32	18 02	18 22	18 52	19 12	19 42	20 02	20 32	21 02	21 32	22 02	23 02
Rickmansworth ?	⊖ d	15 08	15 38	16 08	16 38	17 08	17 38	18 08	18 28	18 58	19 18	19 48	20 08	20 38	21 08	21 38	22 08	23 08
Harrow-on-the-Hill 3 ?	⊖ d	15 19	15 49	16 19	16 49	17 19	17 49	18 19	18 39	19 09	19 29	19 59	20 19	20 49	21 19	21 49	22 19	23 19
London Marylebone 10	⊖ a	15 35	16 05	16 35	17 05	17 35	18 05	18 35	18 55	19 25	19 45	20 15	20 35	21 05	21 35	22 08	22 35	23 35

Saturdays until 02 October

Station		CH ◇	CH	CH	CH	CH	CH	CH	CH	CH
Aylesbury Vale Parkway	d			07 00	07 30		08 30		09 30	
Aylesbury	d	06 05	06 35	07 05	07 35	08 05	08 35	09 05	09 35	10 05
Stoke Mandeville	d	06 09	06 39	07 09	07 39	08 09	08 39	09 09	09 39	10 09
Wendover	d	06 13	06 43	07 13	07 43	08 13	08 43	09 13	09 43	10 13
Great Missenden	d	06 19	06 49	07 19	07 49	08 19	08 49	09 19	09 49	10 19
Amersham ?	⊖ d	06 26	06a58	07 26	07 56	08 26	08 56	09 26	09 56	10 26
Chalfont & Latimer ?	⊖ d	06 30		07 30	08 00	08 30	09 00	09 30	10 00	10 30
Chorleywood ?	⊖ d	06 33		07 33	08 03	08 33	09 03	09 33	10 03	10 33
Rickmansworth ?	⊖ d	06 38		07 38	08 08	08 38	09 08	09 38	10 08	10 38
Harrow-on-the-Hill 3 ?	⊖ d	06 49		07 49	08 19	08 49	09 19	09 49	10 19	10 49
London Marylebone 10	⊖ a	07 05		08 04	08 34	09 04	09 34	10 05	10 35	11 05

Station		CH	CH	CH	CH	CH	CH	CH ◇	CH	CH ◇
Aylesbury Vale Parkway	d	10 30		11 30		12 30		13 30		14 30
Aylesbury	d	10 35	11 05	11 35	12 05	12 35	13 05	13 35	14 05	14 35
Stoke Mandeville	d	10 39	11 09	11 39	12 09	12 39	13 09	13 39	14 09	14 39
Wendover	d	10 43	11 13	11 43	12 13	12 43	13 13	13 43	14 13	14 43
Great Missenden	d	10 49	11 19	11 49	12 19	12 49	13 19	13 49	14 19	14 49
Amersham ?	⊖ d	10 56	11 26	11 56	12 26	12 56	13 26	13 56	14 26	14 56
Chalfont & Latimer ?	⊖ d	11 00	11 30	12 00	12 30	13 00	13 30	14 00	14 30	15 00
Chorleywood ?	⊖ d	11 03	11 33	12 03	12 33	13 03	13 33	14 03	14 33	15 03
Rickmansworth ?	⊖ d	11 08	11 38	12 08	12 38	13 08	13 38	14 08	14 38	15 08
Harrow-on-the-Hill 3 ?	⊖ d	11 19	11 49	12 19	12 49	13 19	13 49	14 19	14 49	15 19
London Marylebone 10	⊖ a	11 35	12 05	12 35	13 05	13 35	14 05	14 35	15 05	15 35

Station		CH	CH	CH ◇	CH
Aylesbury Vale Parkway	d		15 30		16 30
Aylesbury	d	15 05	15 35	16 05	16 35
Stoke Mandeville	d	15 09	15 39	16 09	16 39
Wendover	d	15 13	15 43	16 13	16 43
Great Missenden	d	15 19	15 49	16 19	16 49
Amersham ?	⊖ d	15 26	15 56	16 26	16 56
Chalfont & Latimer ?	⊖ d	15 30	16 00	16 30	17 00
Chorleywood ?	⊖ d	15 33	16 03	16 33	17 03
Rickmansworth ?	⊖ d	15 38	16 08	16 38	17 08
Harrow-on-the-Hill 3 ?	⊖ d	15 49	16 19	16 49	17 19
London Marylebone 10	⊖ a	16 05	16 34	17 05	17 35

? London Underground Limited (Metropolitan Line) services operate between Harrow-on-the-Hill, Rickmansworth, Chorleywood, Chalfont & Latimer and Amersham

Table 114

Aylesbury and Amersham - London

Saturdays until 02 October

Station		CH	CH	CH ◇	CH	CH	CH	CH ◇	CH	CH
Aylesbury Vale Parkway	d		17 30		18 30		19 46	20 46	21 46	
Aylesbury	d	17 05	17 35	18 05	18 35	19 05	20b05	21c05	22e05	23 20
Stoke Mandeville	d	17 09	17 39	18 09	18 39	19 09	20 09	21 09	22 09	23 24
Wendover	d	17 13	17 43	18 13	18 43	19 13	20 13	21 13	22 13	23 28
Great Missenden	d	17 19	17 49	18 19	18 49	19 19	20 19	21 19	22 19	23 34
Amersham ??	⊖ d	17 26	17 56	18 26	18 56	19 26	20 26	21 26	22 26	23a43
Chalfont & Latimer ??	⊖ d	17 30	18 00	18 30	19 00	19 30	20 30	21 30	22 30	
Chorleywood ??	⊖ d	17 33	18 03	18 33	19 03	19 33	20 33	21 33	22 33	
Rickmansworth ??	⊖ d	17 38	18 08	18 38	19 08	19 38	20 38	21 38	22 38	
Harrow-on-the-Hill 3 ??	⊖ d	17 49	18 19	18 49	19 19	19 49	20 49	21 49	22 49	
London Marylebone 10	⊖ a	18 05	18 35	19 05	19 35	20 05	21 05	22 05	23 05	

Saturdays from 09 October

Station		CH ◇	CH	CH	CH	CH	CH	CH	CH	CH
Aylesbury Vale Parkway	d			06 57	07 27		08 27		09 27	
Aylesbury	d	06 02	06 32	07 02	07 32	08 02	08 32	09 02	09 32	10 02
Stoke Mandeville	d	06 06	06 36	07 06	07 36	08 06	08 36	09 06	09 36	10 06
Wendover	d	06 10	06 40	07 10	07 40	08 10	08 40	09 10	09 40	10 10
Great Missenden	d	06 16	06 46	07 16	07 46	08 16	08 46	09 16	09 46	10 16
Amersham ??	⊖ d	06 23	06a55	07 23	07 53	08 23	08 53	09 23	09 53	10 23
Chalfont & Latimer ??	⊖ d	06 27		07 27	07 57	08 27	08 57	09 27	09 57	10 27
Chorleywood ??	⊖ d	06 32		07 32	08 02	08 32	09 02	09 32	10 02	10 32
Rickmansworth ??	⊖ d	06 38		07 38	08 08	08 38	09 08	09 38	10 08	10 38
Harrow-on-the-Hill 3 ??	⊖ d	06 49		07 49	08 19	08 49	09 19	09 49	10 19	10 49
London Marylebone 10	⊖ a	07 05		08 04	08 34	09 04	09 34	10 05	10 35	11 05

Station		CH	CH	CH	CH	CH	CH	CH ◇	CH	CH ◇
Aylesbury Vale Parkway	d	10 27		11 27		12 27		13 27		14 27
Aylesbury	d	10 32	11 02	11 32	12 02	12 32	13 02	13 32	14 02	14 32
Stoke Mandeville	d	10 36	11 06	11 36	12 06	12 36	13 06	13 36	14 06	14 36
Wendover	d	10 40	11 10	11 40	12 10	12 40	13 10	13 40	14 10	14 40
Great Missenden	d	10 46	11 16	11 46	12 16	12 46	13 16	13 46	14 16	14 46
Amersham ??	⊖ d	10 53	11 23	11 53	12 23	12 53	13 23	13 53	14 23	14 53
Chalfont & Latimer ??	⊖ d	10 57	11 27	11 57	12 27	12 57	13 27	13 57	14 27	14 57
Chorleywood ??	⊖ d	11 02	11 32	12 02	12 32	13 02	13 32	14 02	14 32	15 02
Rickmansworth ??	⊖ d	11 08	11 38	12 08	12 38	13 08	13 38	14 08	14 38	15 08
Harrow-on-the-Hill 3 ??	⊖ d	11 19	11 49	12 19	12 49	13 19	13 49	14 19	14 49	15 19
London Marylebone 10	⊖ a	11 35	12 05	12 35	13 05	13 35	14 05	14 35	15 05	15 35

Station		CH	CH	CH ◇	CH
Aylesbury Vale Parkway	d		15 27		16 27
Aylesbury	d	15 02	15 32	16 02	16 32
Stoke Mandeville	d	15 06	15 36	16 06	16 36
Wendover	d	15 10	15 40	16 10	16 40
Great Missenden	d	15 16	15 46	16 16	16 46
Amersham ??	⊖ d	15 23	15 53	16 23	16 53
Chalfont & Latimer ??	⊖ d	15 27	15 57	16 27	16 57
Chorleywood ??	⊖ d	15 32	16 02	16 32	17 02
Rickmansworth ??	⊖ d	15 38	16 08	16 38	17 08
Harrow-on-the-Hill 3 ??	⊖ d	15 49	16 19	16 49	17 19
London Marylebone 10	⊖ a	16 05	16 34	17 05	17 35

Station		CH	CH	CH ◇	CH	CH	CH	CH ◇	CH	CH
Aylesbury Vale Parkway	d		17 27		18 27		19 46	20 46	21 46	
Aylesbury	d	17 02	17 32	18 02	18 32	19 02	20b02	21c02	22e02	23 17
Stoke Mandeville	d	17 06	17 36	18 06	18 36	19 06	20 06	21 06	22 06	23 21
Wendover	d	17 10	17 40	18 10	18 40	19 10	20 10	21 10	22 10	23 25
Great Missenden	d	17 16	17 46	18 16	18 46	19 16	20 16	21 16	22 16	23 31
Amersham ??	⊖ d	17 23	17 53	18 23	18 53	19 23	20 23	21 23	22 23	23a40
Chalfont & Latimer ??	⊖ d	17 27	17 57	18 27	18 57	19 27	20 27	21 27	22 27	
Chorleywood ??	⊖ d	17 32	18 02	18 32	19 02	19 32	20 32	21 32	22 32	
Rickmansworth ??	⊖ d	17 38	18 08	18 38	19 08	19 38	20 38	21 38	22 38	
Harrow-on-the-Hill 3 ??	⊖ d	17 49	18 19	18 49	19 19	19 49	20 49	21 49	22 49	
London Marylebone 10	⊖ a	18 05	18 35	19 05	19 35	20 05	21 05	22 05	23 05	

Sundays until 26 September

Station		CH ◇	CH	CH	CH	CH	CH	CH	CH ◇	CH
Aylesbury Vale Parkway	d	07 30	08 30	09 00	10 00	11 00	12 00	13 00	14 00	15 00
Aylesbury	d	07 35	08 35	09 05	10 05	11 05	12 05	13 05	14 05	15 05
Stoke Mandeville	d	07 39	08 39	09 09	10 09	11 09	12 09	13 09	14 09	15 09
Wendover	d	07 43	08 43	09 13	10 13	11 13	12 13	13 13	14 13	15 13
Great Missenden	d	07 49	08 49	09 19	10 19	11 19	12 19	13 19	14 19	15 19
Amersham ??	⊖ d	07 56	08 56	09 26	10 26	11 26	12 26	13 26	14 26	15 26
Chalfont & Latimer ??	⊖ d	08 00	09 00	09 30	10 30	11 30	12 30	13 30	14 30	15 30
Chorleywood ??	⊖ d	08 03	09 03	09 33	10 33	11 33	12 33	13 33	14 33	15 33
Rickmansworth ??	⊖ d	08 08	09 08	09 38	10 38	11 38	12 38	13 38	14 38	15 38
Harrow-on-the-Hill 3 ??	⊖ d	08 19	09 19	09 49	10 49	11 49	12 49	13 49	14 49	15 49
London Marylebone 10	⊖ a	08 35	09 35	10 05	11 05	12 05	13 05	14 05	15 05	16 05

Station		CH	CH	CH	CH	CH	CH	CH	CH ◇	CH
Aylesbury Vale Parkway	d		16 00		17 00		18 00		19 00	
Aylesbury	d	15 35	16 05	16 35	17 05	17 35	18 05	18 35	19 05	19 35
Stoke Mandeville	d	15 39	16 09	16 39	17 09	17 39	18 09	18 39	19 09	19 39
Wendover	d	15 43	16 13	16 43	17 13	17 43	18 13	18 43	19 13	19 43
Great Missenden	d	15 49	16 19	16 49	17 19	17 49	18 19	18 49	19 19	19 49
Amersham ??	⊖ d	15a58	16 26	16a58	17 26	17a58	18 26	18a58	19 26	19a58
Chalfont & Latimer ??	⊖ d		16 30		17 30		18 30		19 30	
Chorleywood ??	⊖ d		16 33		17 33		18 33		19 33	
Rickmansworth ??	⊖ d		16 38		17 38		18 38		19 38	
Harrow-on-the-Hill 3 ??	⊖ d		16 49		17 49		18 49		19 49	
London Marylebone 10	⊖ a		17 05		18 05		19 05		20 05	

Station		CH	CH	CH	CH
Aylesbury Vale Parkway	d	20 00		21 00	
Aylesbury	d	20 05	20 35	21 05	21 35
Stoke Mandeville	d	20 09	20 39	21 09	21 39
Wendover	d	20 13	20 43	21 13	21 43
Great Missenden	d	20 19	20 49	21 19	21 49
Amersham ??	⊖ d	20 26	20a58	21 26	21a58
Chalfont & Latimer ??	⊖ d	20 30		21 30	
Chorleywood ??	⊖ d	20 33		21 33	
Rickmansworth ??	⊖ d	20 38		21 38	
Harrow-on-the-Hill 3 ??	⊖ d	20 49		21 49	
London Marylebone 10	⊖ a	21 05		22 05	

Station		CH	CH ◇
Aylesbury Vale Parkway	d	22 00	
Aylesbury	d	22 05	22 35
Stoke Mandeville	d	22 09	22 39
Wendover	d	22 13	22 43
Great Missenden	d	22 19	22 49
Amersham ??	⊖ d	22a28	22 56
Chalfont & Latimer ??	⊖ d		23 00
Chorleywood ??	⊖ d		23 03
Rickmansworth ??	⊖ d		23 08
Harrow-on-the-Hill 3 ??	⊖ d		23 19
London Marylebone 10	⊖ a		23 35

?? London Underground Limited (Metropolitan Line) services operate between Harrow-on-the-Hill, Rickmansworth, Chorleywood, Chalfont & Latimer and Amersham

b arr. 1950

c arr. 2050

e arr. 2150

Table 114

Sundays
from 03 October

Aylesbury and Amersham - London

		CH	CH	CH	CH	CH	CH	CH	CH	CH	CH	CH	CH	CH	CH	CH	CH	CH	CH	CH	CH	CH	CH
		◇							◇									◇					
Aylesbury Vale Parkway	d	07 27	08 27	08 57	09 57	10 57	11 57	12 57	13 57	14 57		15 57		16 57		17 57		18 57		19 57		20 57	
Aylesbury	d	07 32	08 32	09 02	10 02	11 02	12 02	13 02	14 02	15 02	15 32	16 02	16 32	17 02	17 32	18 02	18 32	19 02	19 32	20 02	20 32	21 02	21 32
Stoke Mandeville	d	07 36	08 36	09 06	10 06	11 06	12 06	13 06	14 06	15 06	15 36	16 06	16 36	17 06	17 36	18 06	18 36	19 06	19 36	20 06	20 36	21 06	21 36
Wendover	d	07 40	08 40	09 10	10 10	11 10	12 10	13 10	14 10	15 10	15 40	16 10	16 40	17 10	17 40	18 10	18 40	19 10	19 40	20 10	20 40	21 10	21 40
Great Missenden	d	07 46	08 46	09 16	10 16	11 16	12 16	13 16	14 16	15 16	15 46	16 16	16 46	17 16	17 46	18 16	18 46	19 16	19 46	20 16	20 46	21 16	21 46
Amersham ??? ⊖	d	07 53	08 53	09 23	10 23	11 23	12 23	13 23	14 23	15 23	15a55	16 23	16a55	17 23	17a55	18 23	18a55	19 23	19a55	20 23	20a55	21 23	21a55
Chalfont & Latimer ??? ⊖	d	07 57	08 57	09 27	10 27	11 27	12 27	13 27	14 27	15 27		16 27		17 27		18 27		19 27		20 27		21 27	
Chorleywood ??? ⊖	d	08 02	09 02	09 32	10 32	11 32	12 32	13 32	14 32	15 32		16 32		17 32		18 32		19 32		20 32		21 32	
Rickmansworth ??? ⊖	d	08 08	09 08	09 38	10 38	11 38	12 38	13 38	14 38	15 38		16 38		17 38		18 38		19 38		20 38		21 38	
Harrow-on-the-Hill ■3 ??? ⊖	d	08 19	09 19	09 49	10 49	11 49	12 49	13 49	14 49	15 49		16 49		17 49		18 49		19 49		20 49		21 49	
London Marylebone ■10 ⊖	a	08 35	09 35	10 05	11 05	12 05	13 05	14 05	15 05	16 05		17 05		18 05		19 05		20 05		21 05		22 05	

		CH	CH
			◇
Aylesbury Vale Parkway	d	21 57	
Aylesbury	d	22 02	22 32
Stoke Mandeville	d	22 06	22 36
Wendover	d	22 10	22 40
Great Missenden	d	22 16	22 46
Amersham ??? ⊖	d	22a25	22 53
Chalfont & Latimer ??? ⊖	d		22 57
Chorleywood ??? ⊖	d		23 02
Rickmansworth ??? ⊖	d		23 08
Harrow-on-the-Hill ■3 ??? ⊖	d		23 19
London Marylebone ■10 ⊖	a		23 35

??? London Underground Limited (Metropolitan Line) services operate between Harrow-on-the-Hill, Rickmansworth, Chorleywood, Chalfont & Latimer and Amersham

Table 115

Mondays to Fridays
until 01 October

London - High Wycombe, Aylesbury, Banbury, Stratford-upon-Avon, Birmingham Snow Hill and Kidderminster

		CH MX	CH MX	CH MO	CH MX	CH MX	CH MX	CH MO	CH MO	CH MX	CH	CH	CH		CH	CH	CH	CH	CH	CH	CH	CH	CH	WS	CH
		◇					◇											◇			◇	◇		◇■1	
London Marylebone ■10 ⊖	d	22p20	22p40	22p45	23p10	23p30	23p54	23p45		00 10			06 00		06 10	06 27		06 50	06 53			07 15	07 18	07 33	07 36
London Paddington ■15 ⊖	d																								
Wembley Stadium	d		22p49	22p54	23p19	23p39		23p54		00 19			06 09			06 36			07 02				07 27		
Sudbury & Harrow Road	d																								
Sudbury Hill Harrow	d																								
Northolt Park	d			22p59		23p44		23p59		00 24			06 14			06 41									
South Ruislip § ⊖	d		22p56	23p03		23p48		00 03		00 28			06 18			06 45									
West Ruislip ■3 § ⊖	d			23p06		23p51		00 06		00 31					06 27	06 48			07 11				07 36		
Denham	d		23p02	23p11		23p56		00 11		00 36			06 24		06 32	06 53			07 16				07 41		
Denham Golf Club	d			23p13		23p58		00 13		00 38						06 55									
Gerrards Cross ■1	d		23p07	23p16	23p33	00 01	00 15	00 16		00 41			06 28		06 37	06 58			07 21			07 36	07 45		
Seer Green	d		23p11	23p21		00 06		00 21		00 46			06 33						07 26				07 50		
Beaconsfield	d		23p15	23p24	23p39	00 09	00 21	00 24		00 49			06 36		06 43	07 04			07 29			07 42	07 53		
High Wycombe ■1	d		23p21	23p30	23p45	00 15	00 27	00 30		00 55		06 10	06a45		06 50	07a14		07 20	07a38			07 50	08a02		08 06
Saunderton	d			23p37		00 22	00 34	00 37		01 02		06 16			06 56										08 12
Princes Risborough ■2	d		23p31	23p43	23p56	00 27	00 40	00 43	00 48	01 07		06 21			07 03		07 10	07 31		08 23		08 00			08 18
Monks Risborough	d					00 31			00 51	01 11							07 13			08 26					
Little Kimble	d					00 34			00 55	01 14							07 17			08 30					
Aylesbury	a					00 49			01 06	01 29							07 28			08 41					
Haddenham & Thame Parkway	d	23p02	23p38	23p50	00 03		00 47	00 50				06 28			07 10			07 38				08 06			08 24
Bicester North ■3	d	23p13	23p52	00 04	00 16		01 00	01 04				06 43			07 22			07 50				08 17			08a39
Kings Sutton	d		00 04	00 16			01 12					06 56			07 32							08 29			
Banbury	d	23p31	00a14	00a25	00a40		01a21	01a24				07 02			07a47			08 05				08 34		08 37	
Leamington Spa ■8	d	23p48									06 55	07 22						08 24			08 30	08 52		08a54	
Warwick	d	23p53									06 59	07 26						08 28			08 34	08 57			
Warwick Parkway	d	23p56									07 02	07 30						08 32			08 37	09 00			
Hatton	d										07 07	07 34									08 42	09 07			
Claverdon	d										07 12										08 47				
Bearley	d										07 17										08 52				
Wilmcote	d										07 21										08 56				
Stratford-upon-Avon	a										07 30										09 05				
Lapworth	a																					09 12			
Dorridge	a	00 07										07 42						08 42				09 16			
Solihull	a	00 12										07 50						08 48				09 20			
Birmingham Moor Street	a	00 22										08 03						08 59				09 32			
Birmingham Snow Hill	a	00 32										08 11						09 07				09 41			
Rowley Regis	a																								
Cradley Heath	a																								
Stourbridge Junction ■2	a																								
Kidderminster	a																								

		CH	CH	CH	CH	CH	CH	CH	CH	CH	CH	CH	CH	CH	CH	CH	CH	CH	CH	CH	WS	CH	CH	CH	CH
			◇			◇	◇		◇		◇		◇	◇				◇	◇		◇■1	◇	◇		
London Marylebone ■10 ⊖	d	07 39	07 50	07 53	08 00	08 20	08 24	08 30	08 50		08 53	09 00	09 17	09 20		09 24	09 30	09 50	09 54	10 00	10 17	10 20	10 24	10 30	
London Paddington ■15 ⊖	d																								
Wembley Stadium	d				08 09			08 39				09 09					09 39			10 09				10 39	
Sudbury & Harrow Road	d																								
Sudbury Hill Harrow	d	07 50			08 13			08 43									09 43							10 43	
Northolt Park	d	07 53					08 36										09 46			10 14				10 46	
South Ruislip § ⊖	d	07 56			08 18							09 16								10 18					
West Ruislip ■3 § ⊖	d				08 21			08 50									09 51							10 51	
Denham	d				08 26			08 54				09 22					09 55			10 24				10 55	
Denham Golf Club	d	08 03						08 57									09 58							10 58	
Gerrards Cross ■1	d	08a10		08 14	08 30		08 46	09 00			09 14	09 27				09 45	10 01		10 15	10 28			10 45	11 01	
Seer Green	d			08 19	08 35		08 50					09 31					10 06			10 33				11 06	
Beaconsfield	d			08 22	08 38		08 54	09 06			09 20	09 35				09 51	10 09		10 21	10 36			10 51	11 09	
High Wycombe ■1	d			08 29	08a49	08 51	09 00	09a15	09 20		09 27	09a44		09 50		09 58	10a19	10 20	10 28	10a45		10 50	10 58	11a18	
Saunderton	d			08 35			09 07									10 04							11 04		
Princes Risborough ■2	d			08 41		09 03	09 12			09 17	09 36			10 01	10 11	10a13			10 38			11 01	11 10		11 11
Monks Risborough	d									09 20					10 14										11 14
Little Kimble	d									09 24					10 18										11 18
Aylesbury	a									09 35					10 29										11 29
Haddenham & Thame Parkway	d			08 48		09 09	09 19				09 43			10 07					10 45			11 07	11 16		
Bicester North ■3	d		08 43	09a07		09 20	09a38				09 57		10 10	10 19					11a01			11 19	11a33		
Kings Sutton	d										10 08														
Banbury	d		08 58			09 35			09 57		10a18		10 29	10 35				10 57			11a29	11 35			
Leamington Spa ■8	d		09 15			09 54			10 15				10 49	10 54				11 15				11 54			
Warwick	d		09 19			09 58			10 19				10 53	10 59				11 19				11 59			
Warwick Parkway	d		09 22			10 02			10 22					11 02				11 22				12 02			
Hatton	d					10 07																12 07			
Claverdon	d																								
Bearley	d																								
Wilmcote	d																								
Stratford-upon-Avon	a												11 16												
Lapworth	a					10 12																12 13			
Dorridge	a		09 33			10 16			10 33					11 13				11 33				12 17			
Solihull	a		09 38			10 22			10 38					11 18				11 38				12 22			
Birmingham Moor Street	a		09 49			10 33			10 49					11 30				11 49				12 34			
Birmingham Snow Hill	a		10 01			10 41			11 01					11 41				12 01				12 42			
Rowley Regis	a																								
Cradley Heath	a																								
Stourbridge Junction ■2	a																								
Kidderminster	a																								

§ London Underground Limited (Central Line) also operate services between South Ruislip and West Ruislip at frequent intervals

Table 115

Mondays to Fridays
until 01 October

London - High Wycombe, Aylesbury, Banbury, Stratford-upon-Avon, Birmingham Snow Hill and Kidderminster

		CH ◇ ⌶	CH ◇ ⌶	CH	WS ◇1 ⊡	CH ⌶	CH ◇ ⌶	CH	CH	CH	CH ◇	CH	CH	CH	CH	CH ◇	CH	CH	CH	CH	CH	CH	CH	CH ◇ ⌶	CH ◇
London Marylebone 10 ⊖	d	10 50	10 54	11 00	11 20	11 24	11 50		11 30		11 54	12 00	12 20	12 24	12 30	12 50		12 54	13 00	13 20		13 24	13 30	13 50	13 54
London Paddington 15 ⊖	d									11 36															
Wembley Stadium	d			11 09					11 39			12 09			12 39				13 09				13 39		
Sudbury & Harrow Road	d																								
Sudbury Hill Harrow	d								11 43						12 43								13 43		
Northolt Park	d			11 14					11 46			12 14			12 46				13 14				13 46		
South Ruislip § ⊖	d			11 18								12 18							13 18						
West Ruislip 3 § ⊖	d								11 51						12 51								13 51		
Denham	d			11 24					11 55			12 24			12 55				13 24				13 55		
Denham Golf Club	d														12 58								13 58		
Gerrards Cross 1	d		11 15	11 28					12 00	12 03	12 15	12 28		12 45	13 01			13 15	13 28			13 45	14 01		14 15
Seer Green	d			11 33						12 08		12 33			13 06				13 33				14 06		
Beaconsfield	d		11 21	11 36					12 06	12 11	12 21	12 36		12 51	13 09			13 21	13 36			13 51	14 09		14 21
High Wycombe 1	d		11 28	11a45		11 54			12 12	12a19	12 28	12a45	12 50	12 58	13a19			13 28	13a45	13 50		13 58	14a18		14 28
Saunderton	d								12 19					13 04								14 04			
Princes Risborough 2	d		11 38			12 04		12 11	12a27		12 38		13 01	13 10			13 11	13 38		14 02	14 11	14a13			14 38
Monks Risborough	d							12 14									13 14				14 14				
Little Kimble	d							12 18									13 18				14 18				
Aylesbury	a							12 29									13 29				14 29				
Haddenham & Thame Parkway	d		11 45			12 10					12 45		13 07	13 16				13 45		14 08					14 45
Bicester North 3	d	11 41	11 59			12 22	12 40				13a01		13 19	13a34		13 39		13 59		14 20				14 41	14 56
Kings Sutton	d		12 12																						15 07
Banbury	d	11 59	12 17		12 30	12 38	12 57						13 35			13 57		14a18		14 35				14 59	15 13
Leamington Spa 8	d	12 16	12 38		12a47	12 56	13 15						13 54			14 15				14 54				15 17	15 33
Warwick	d	12 20	12 42			13 00	13 19						13 59			14 19				14 59				15 21	15 38
Warwick Parkway	d	12 23				13 04	13 22						14 02			14 22				15 02				15 24	
Hatton	d		12 49										14 07												15 45
Claverdon	d		12 54																						15 50
Bearley	d		12 59																						15 55
Wilmcote	d																								16 00
Stratford-upon-Avon	a		13 11																						16 12
Lapworth	a												14 13												
Dorridge	a	12 33				13 14	13 33						14 17			14 32				15 13				15 34	
Solihull	a	12 38				13 20	13 38						14 22			14 39				15 18				15 39	
Birmingham Moor Street	a	12 49				13 31	13 49						14 34			14 49				15 33				15 49	
Birmingham Snow Hill ⇌	a	13 02				13 41	14 01						14 42			15 02				15 41				16 01	
Rowley Regis	a																								
Cradley Heath	a																								
Stourbridge Junction 2	a																								
Kidderminster	a																								

		CH	CH	CH	CH	CH ◇	CH	CH ◇	CH		CH	CH	CH	CH	CH	CH ◇ ⌶	CH	CH	CH	WS ◇1 ⊡	CH ⌶	CH	CH	CH	CH
London Marylebone 10 ⊖	d	14 00	14 20	14 24	14 30	14 50		14 54	15 00		15 20		15 23	15 30	15 43	16 00	16 03	16 06	16 09	16 30	16 33		16 36	16 39	16 46
London Paddington 15 ⊖	d																								
Wembley Stadium	d	14 09			14 39				15 09				15 33	15 39					16 19					16 49	
Sudbury & Harrow Road	d																		16 22						
Sudbury Hill Harrow	d				14 43									15 43					16 24						
Northolt Park	d	14 14			14 46				15 14					15 46					16 27						16 58
South Ruislip § ⊖	d	14 18							15 18									16 21							17 02
West Ruislip 3 § ⊖	d				14 51									15 51					16 32					16 58	
Denham	d	14 24			14 55				15 24					15 55					16 36					17 03	
Denham Golf Club	d				14 58									15 58					16 39						
Gerrards Cross 1	d	14 28		14 45	15 01			15 15	15 28				15 48	16 01	16 05			16 29	16 42					17 07	17 10
Seer Green	d	14 33			15 06				15 33				15 53					16 33							17 15
Beaconsfield	d	14 36		14 51	15 09			15 21	15 36				15 56	16 07	16 11			16 37	16 48					17 13	17 18
High Wycombe 1	d	14a45	14 50	14 58	15a18			15 28	15a45		15 50		16 02	16a16	16 18		16 32	16 43	16a57				17 05	17 20	17a27
Saunderton	d			15 04									16 09					16 50							
Princes Risborough 2	d		15 01	15 10			15 11	15 38			16 01	16 07	16a21		16 27		16 43	16a58				17 00	17 16	17a33	
Monks Risborough	d						15 14					16 10										17 03			
Little Kimble	d						15 18					16 14										17 07			
Aylesbury	a						15 29					16 25										17 18			
Haddenham & Thame Parkway	d		15 07	15 16				15 45			16 07				16 34		16 49						17 22		
Bicester North 3	d		15 19	15a34		15 39		16a01			16 19				16a50		17 01				17 25		17 34		
Kings Sutton	d																17 12								
Banbury	d		15 35			15 57					16 36					17 03	17 25			17 32	17 40		18 09		
Leamington Spa 8	d		15 54			16 15					16 54					17 22				17a50	17 58		18 28		
Warwick	d		15 59			16 19					16 59					17 27					18 02		18 32		
Warwick Parkway	d		16 02			16 22					17 03					17 30					18 05		18 36		
Hatton	d		16 07																		18 10		18 42		
Claverdon	d																						18 48		
Bearley	d																						18 53		
Wilmcote	d																						18 58		
Stratford-upon-Avon	a																						19 06		
Lapworth	a		16 13								17 10										18 15				
Dorridge	a		16 17			16 33					17 14					17 42					18 19				
Solihull	a		16 22			16 38					17 20					17 48					18 24				
Birmingham Moor Street	a		16 34			16 49					17 32					17 58					18 33				
Birmingham Snow Hill ⇌	a		16 42			17 01					17 41					18 12					18 42				
Rowley Regis	a																								
Cradley Heath	a																								
Stourbridge Junction 2	a																								
Kidderminster	a																								

§ London Underground Limited (Central Line) also operate services between South Ruislip and West Ruislip at frequent intervals

Table 115

Mondays to Fridays
until 01 October

London - High Wycombe, Aylesbury, Banbury, Stratford-upon-Avon, Birmingham Snow Hill and Kidderminster

			CH	CH	CH	CH	CH	CH	CH	CH	CH	CH	CH	CH	CH	CH	CH	CH	CH	CH	CH	CH	CH	CH	CH ◇
London Marylebone 10 ⊖	d			17 07	17 10	17 20	17 30	17 33	17 38	17 44	17 51	18 03	18 09	18 12	18 15	18 21	18 33	18 40	18 43	18 46	19 03	19 06	19 12	19 30	19 33
London Paddington 15 ⊖	d																								
Wembley Stadium	d			17 17	17 21				17 47						18 25					18 56			19 22		
Sudbury & Harrow Road	d				17 24											18 32							19 25		
Sudbury Hill Harrow	d							17 45								18 34							19 27		
Northolt Park	d				17 28			17 47			18 04					18 37			18 56				19 30		
South Ruislip § ⊖	d				17 31					17 59					18 32					19 03		19 21			
West Ruislip 3 § ⊖	d			17 26					17 56					18 29					19 01				19 35		
Denham	d			17 30				17 55		18 05				18 33						19 09			19 39		
Denham Golf Club	d			17 33											18 38								19 42		
Gerrards Cross 1	d			17 36		17 42			18 03	18 09			18 31	18 38	18 42	18a49			19 07	19 13		19 29	19 45		
Seer Green	d					17 47		18 01			18 16			18 42					19 12			19 33			
Beaconsfield	d				17 44	17 50		18 05		18 15	18 20			18 46	18 49			19 05	19 15	19 19		19 37			19 58
High Wycombe 1	d			17 47	17a54	17 57		18a14	18 15	18 21	18a29		18 41	18 53	18a58			19 12	19a24	19 26	19 34	19 43	19a59		20 04
Saunderton	d			17 54						18 28			18 48							19 32		19 50			
Princes Risborough 2	d		17 50	17 59		18a09			18 24	18 33		18 44	18 53	19 02				19 22		19 38	19 43	19a59			20 15
Monks Risborough	d		17 53							18 37										19 41					
Little Kimble	d		17 57							18 40										19 45					
Aylesbury	a		18 08							18 56				19 21						19 59					
Haddenham & Thame Parkway	d			18 06			18 15		18 31			18 51	19 01					19 29			19 50			20 12	20 21
Bicester North 3	d			18a23			18 26		18 44			19 03	19a17				19 25	19a46			20 03			20 23	20 33
Kings Sutton	d											19 12									20 15				
Banbury	d						18 41		19 09			19a28					19 40				20a29			20 38	20 49
Leamington Spa 8	d						19 00		19 28								19 59							20 56	21 07
Warwick	d						19 04		19 32								20 03							21 00	21 12
Warwick Parkway	d						19 08		19a41								20 07							21 04	
Hatton	d						19 13										20 12							21 09	21 19
Claverdon	d																								21 25
Bearley	d																								21 30
Wilmcote	d																								21 34
Stratford-upon-Avon	a																								21 45
Lapworth	a						19 18										20 17							21 14	
Dorridge	a						19 22										20 23							21 18	
Solihull	a						19 28										20 28							21 24	
Birmingham Moor Street	a						19 38										20 37							21 36	
Birmingham Snow Hill ⇌	a						19 48										20 48							21 47	
Rowley Regis	a																								
Cradley Heath	a																								
Stourbridge Junction 2	a																								
Kidderminster	a																								

		CH	CH	CH	CH ◇	CH	CH ◇	CH		CH	CH	CH	CH	CH	CH ◇	CH	CH ◇	CH	CH		CH FX	CH FO	CH	CH FX ◇	CH FO ◇
London Marylebone 10 ⊖	d	19 37	19 50	20 00	20 06	20 10	20 30	20 33		21 00	21 03	21 18	21 40		21 33	22 03	22 20	22 23	22 40		23 10	23 10	23 30	23 54	23 54
London Paddington 15 ⊖	d																								
Wembley Stadium	d	19 46				20 19		20 42			21 12		21 49					22 32	22 49		23 19	23 19	23 39		
Sudbury & Harrow Road	d							20 45																	
Sudbury Hill Harrow	d							20 48																	
Northolt Park	d	19 51				20 24					21 17		21 54					22 37					23 44		
South Ruislip § ⊖	d		20 05					20 53					21 58						22 56				23 48		
West Ruislip 3 § ⊖	d	19 56				20 29					21 22							22 42					23 51		
Denham	d	20 01				20 34		20 58			21 27		22 04					22 47	23 02				23 56		
Denham Golf Club	d					20 36					21 29							22 49					23 58		
Gerrards Cross 1	d	20 06	20 13		20 27	20 40		21 03			21 33	21 39	22 08			22 24		22 53	23 07		23 33	23 33	00 01	00 15	00 15
Seer Green	d	20 10				20 44		21 07			21 37		22 13					22 57	23 11				00 06		
Beaconsfield	d	20 14	20 19		20 33	20 47		21 11			21 41	21 47	22 16			22 30		23 01	23 15		23 39	23 39	00 09	00 21	00 21
High Wycombe 1	d	20 21	20a29		20 40	20 54	21 00	21 17			21 47	21 53	22 23			22 36		23 07	23 21		23 45	23 45	00 15	00 27	00 27
Saunderton	d	20 27				21 00					21 54		22 29					23 14					00 22	00 34	00 34
Princes Risborough 2	d	20 34			20 49	21 06	21 11	21a30			21 59	22 03	22 36			22 46		23 19	23 31		23 56	23 56	00 27	00 40	00 40
Monks Risborough	d	20 37				21 09					22 03							23 23					00 31		
Little Kimble	d	20 41				21 13					22 06							23 26					00 34		
Aylesbury	a	20 55				21 27					22 20		22 54					23 40					00 49		
Haddenham & Thame Parkway	d				20 56		21 17			21 41		22 09			22 16	22 53	23 02		23 38		00 03	00 03		00 47	00 47
Bicester North 3	d			20 51	21a13		21 28			21 54		22a25			22 28	23a09	23 13		23 52		00 16	00 16		01 00	01 00
Kings Sutton	d						21 41												00 04					01 12	01 12
Banbury	d			21 07			21 47			22 10					22 43		23 31		00a14		00a40	00 33		01a21	01 19
Leamington Spa 8	d			21 26			22 05			22 30				22 25	23 00		23 48					00 52			01a39
Warwick	d						22 10							22 29	23 05		23 53					00 56			
Warwick Parkway	d			21 31			22 14			22 35					23 07		23 56					01a06			
Hatton	d						22 19																		
Claverdon	d																								
Bearley	d																								
Wilmcote	d																								
Stratford-upon-Avon	a													22 55											
Lapworth	a						22 24																		
Dorridge	a			21 41			22 28			22 46					23 18		00 07								
Solihull	a			21 47			22 35			22 51					23 23		00 12								
Birmingham Moor Street	a			21 58			22 49			23 00					23 33		00 22								
Birmingham Snow Hill ⇌	a			22 04			22 58			23 05					23 45		00 32								
Rowley Regis	a			22 24						23 38															
Cradley Heath	a			22 29						23 44															
Stourbridge Junction 2	a			22 35						23 52															
Kidderminster	a			22 50																					

§ London Underground Limited (Central Line) also operate services between South Ruislip and West Ruislip at frequent intervals

Table 115

Mondays to Fridays
from 04 October

London - High Wycombe, Aylesbury, Banbury, Stratford-upon-Avon, Birmingham Snow Hill and Kidderminster

		CH MX	CH MX	CH MO	CH MX	CH MX	CH MX	CH MO	CH MO	CH MX	CH	CH	CH		CH	CH	CH	CH	CH	CH	CH	CH			CH
		◇					◇										◇			◇	◇				
London Marylebone 10 ⊖	d	22p20	22p40	22p45	23p10	23p30	23p54	23p45		00 10			06 00		06 27		06 50	06 53			07 15	07 18			07 36
London Paddington 15 ⊖	d																								
Wembley Stadium	d		22p49	22p54	23p19	23p39		23p54		00 19			06 09		06 36			07 02				07 27			
Sudbury & Harrow Road	d																								
Sudbury Hill Harrow	d																								
Northolt Park	d			22p59		23p44		23p59		00 24			06 14		06 41										
South Ruislip § ⊖	d		22p56	23p03		23p48		00 03		00 28			06 18		06 45										
West Ruislip 3 § ⊖	d			23p06		23p51		00 06		00 31					06 48			07 11				07 36			
Denham	d		23p02	23p11		23p56		00 11		00 36			06 24		06 53			07 16				07 41			
Denham Golf Club	d			23p13		23p58		00 13		00 38					06 55										
Gerrards Cross 1	d		23p07	23p16	23p33	00 01	00 15	00 16		00 41			06 28		06 58			07 21			07 36	07 45			
Seer Green	d		23p11	23p21		00 06		00 21		00 46			06 33					07 26				07 50			
Beaconsfield	d		23p15	23p24	23p39	00 09	00 21	00 24		00 49			06 36		07 04			07 29			07 42	07 53			
High Wycombe 1	d		23p21	23p30	23p45	00 15	00 27	00 30		00 55		06 07	06a48		07a17		07 20	07a41			07 50	08a05			08 06
Saunderton	d			23p37		00 22	00 34	00 37		01 02		06 13													08 12
Princes Risborough 2	d		23p31	23p43	23p56	00 27	00 40	00 43	00 48	01 07		06 19				07 10	07 31		08 23		08 00				08 18
Monks Risborough	d					00 31			00 51	01 11						07 13			08 26						
Little Kimble	d					00 34			00 55	01 14						07 17			08 30						
Aylesbury	a					00 52			01 09	01 32						07 31			08 44						
Haddenham & Thame Parkway	d	23p02	23p38	23p50	00 03		00 47	00 50				06 26					07 38				08 06				08 24
Bicester North 3	d	23p13	23p52	00 04	00 16		01 00	01 04				06 41					07 50				08 17				08a40
Kings Sutton	d		00 04	00 16			01 12					06 54									08 29				
Banbury	d	23p31	00a17	00a28	00a43		01a24	01a27				07 02					08 05				08 34				
Leamington Spa 8	d	23p48									06 55	07 22					08 24			08 30	08 52				
Warwick	d	23p53									06 59	07 26					08 28			08 34	08 57				
Warwick Parkway	d	23p56									07 02	07 30					08 32			08 37	09 00				
Hatton	d										07 07	07 34								08 42	09 07				
Claverdon	d										07 12									08 47					
Bearley	d										07 17									08 52					
Wilmcote	d										07 21									08 56					
Stratford-upon-Avon	a										07 33									09 08					
Lapworth	a																				09 12				
Dorridge	a	00 07										07 42					08 42				09 16				
Solihull	a	00 12										07 50					08 48				09 20				
Birmingham Moor Street	a	00 22										08 03					08 59				09 32				
Birmingham Snow Hill	a	00 35										08 14					09 10				09 44				
Rowley Regis	a																								
Cradley Heath	a																								
Stourbridge Junction 2	a																								
Kidderminster	a																								

		CH	CH	CH	CH	CH	CH	CH	CH	CH	CH	CH	CH	CH	CH	CH	CH		CH	CH		CH	CH	CH	CH
			◇			◇	◇		◇ H		◇ H		◇ H	◇ H					◇			◇ H	◇		
London Marylebone 10 ⊖	d	07 39	07 50	07 53	08 00	08 20	08 24	08 30	08 50		08 53	09 00	09 17	09 20		09 24	09 30		09 54	10 00		10 20	10 24	10 30	
London Paddington 15 ⊖	d																								
Wembley Stadium	d				08 09			08 39				09 09					09 39			10 09				10 39	
Sudbury & Harrow Road	d																								
Sudbury Hill Harrow	d	07 50			08 13			08 43									09 43							10 43	
Northolt Park	d	07 53					08 36										09 46			10 14				10 46	
South Ruislip § ⊖	d	07 56			08 18							09 16								10 18					
West Ruislip 3 § ⊖	d				08 21			08 50									09 51							10 51	
Denham	d				08 26			08 54				09 22					09 55			10 24				10 55	
Denham Golf Club	d	08 03						08 57									09 58							10 58	
Gerrards Cross 1	d	08a13		08 14	08 30		08 46	09 00			09 14	09 27				09 45	10 01		10 15	10 28			10 45	11 01	
Seer Green	d			08 19	08 35		08 50					09 31					10 06			10 33				11 06	
Beaconsfield	d			08 22	08 38		08 54	09 06			09 20	09 35				09 51	10 09		10 21	10 36			10 51	11 09	
High Wycombe 1	d			08 29	08a50	08 51	09 00	09a18	09 20		09 27	09a47		09 50		09 58	10a19		10 28	10a48		10 50	10 58	11a21	
Saunderton	d			08 35			09 07									10 04							11 04		
Princes Risborough 2	d			08 41		09 03	09 12			09 17	09 36			10 01	10 11	10a16			10 38			11 01	11 10		11 11
Monks Risborough	d									09 20					10 14										11 14
Little Kimble	d									09 24					10 18										11 18
Aylesbury	a									09 38					10 32										11 32
Haddenham & Thame Parkway	d			08 48		09 09	09 19				09 43			10 07					10 45			11 07	11 16		
Bicester North 3	d		08 43	09a10		09 20	09a41				09 57		10 10	10 19					11a04			11 19	11a36		
Kings Sutton	d										10 08														
Banbury	d		08 58			09 35			09 57		10a21		10 29	10 35								11 35			
Leamington Spa 8	d		09 15			09 54			10 15				10 49	10 54								11 54			
Warwick	d		09 19			09 58			10 19				10 53	10 59								11 59			
Warwick Parkway	d		09 22			10 02			10 22					11 02								12 02			
Hatton	d					10 07																12 07			
Claverdon	d																								
Bearley	d																								
Wilmcote	d																								
Stratford-upon-Avon	a												11 18												
Lapworth	a					10 12																12 13			
Dorridge	a		09 33			10 16			10 33					11 13								12 17			
Solihull	a		09 38			10 22			10 38					11 18								12 22			
Birmingham Moor Street	a		09 49			10 33			10 49					11 30								12 34			
Birmingham Snow Hill	a		10 04			10 44			11 04					11 44								12 45			
Rowley Regis	a																								
Cradley Heath	a																								
Stourbridge Junction 2	a																								
Kidderminster	a																								

§ London Underground Limited (Central Line) also operate services between South Ruislip and West Ruislip at frequent intervals

Table 115

Mondays to Fridays
from 04 October

London - High Wycombe, Aylesbury, Banbury, Stratford-upon-Avon, Birmingham Snow Hill and Kidderminster

			CH	CH		CH	CH	CH	CH	CH	CH	CH	CH	CH	CH	CH	CH	CH	CH	CH	CH	CH	CH		CH
			◇ H			H	◇ H				◇					◇									◇
London Marylebone 10 ⊖	d		10 54	11 00		11 24	11 50		11 30		11 54	12 00	12 20	12 24	12 30	12 50		12 54	13 00	13 20		13 24	13 30		13 54
London Paddington 15 ⊖	d									11 36															
Wembley Stadium	d			11 09					11 39			12 09			12 39				13 09				13 39		
Sudbury & Harrow Road	d																								
Sudbury Hill Harrow	d								11 43						12 43								13 43		
Northolt Park	d			11 14					11 46			12 14			12 46				13 14				13 46		
South Ruislip § ⊖	d			11 18								12 18							13 18						
West Ruislip 3 § ⊖	d								11 51						12 51								13 51		
Denham	d			11 24					11 55			12 24			12 55				13 24				13 55		
Denham Golf Club	d														12 58								13 58		
Gerrards Cross 1	d		11 15	11 28					12 00	12 03	12 15	12 28		12 45	13 01			13 15	13 28			13 45	14 01		14 15
Seer Green	d			11 33						12 08		12 33			13 06				13 33				14 06		
Beaconsfield	d		11 21	11 36					12 06	12 11	12 21	12 36		12 51	13 09			13 21	13 36			13 51	14 09		14 21
High Wycombe 1	d		11 28	11a48		11 54			12 12	12a22	12 28	12a48	12 50	12 58	13a22			13 28	13a48	13 50		13 58	14a21		14 28
Saunderton	d								12 19					13 04								14 04			
Princes Risborough 2	d		11 38			12 04		12 11	12a30		12 38		13 01	13 10			13 11	13 38		14 02	14 11	14a16			14 38
Monks Risborough	d							12 14									13 14				14 14				
Little Kimble	d							12 18									13 18				14 18				
Aylesbury	a							12 32									13 32				14 32				
Haddenham & Thame Parkway	d		11 45			12 10					12 45		13 07	13 16				13 45		14 08					14 45
Bicester North 3	d		11 59			12 22	12 40				13a04		13 19	13a36		13 39		13 59		14 20					14 56
Kings Sutton	d		12 12																						15 07
Banbury	d		12 17			12 38	12 57						13 35			13 57		14a21		14 35					15 13
Leamington Spa 8	d		12 38			12 56	13 15						13 54			14 15				14 54					15 33
Warwick	d		12 42			13 00	13 19						13 59			14 19				14 59					15 38
Warwick Parkway	d					13 04	13 22						14 02			14 22				15 02					
Hatton	d		12 49										14 07												15 45
Claverdon	d		12 54																						15 50
Bearley	d		12 59																						15 55
Wilmcote	d																								16 00
Stratford-upon-Avon	a		13 14																						16 15
Lapworth	a												14 13												
Dorridge	a					13 14	13 33						14 17			14 32				15 13					
Solihull	a					13 20	13 38						14 22			14 39				15 18					
Birmingham Moor Street	a					13 31	13 49						14 34			14 49				15 33					
Birmingham Snow Hill	a					13 44	14 04						14 45			15 05				15 44					
Rowley Regis	a																								
Cradley Heath	a																								
Stourbridge Junction 2	a																								
Kidderminster	a																								

		CH	CH	CH	CH	CH	CH	CH	CH		CH	CH	CH	CH	CH			CH	CH		CH	CH	CH	CH	CH
						◇		◇													H				
London Marylebone 10 ⊖	d	14 00	14 20	14 24	14 30	14 50		14 54	15 00		15 20		15 23	15 30	15 43			16 06	16 09		16 33		16 36	16 39	16 46
London Paddington 15 ⊖	d																								
Wembley Stadium	d	14 09			14 39				15 09				15 33	15 39					16 19					16 49	
Sudbury & Harrow Road	d																		16 22						
Sudbury Hill Harrow	d				14 43									15 43					16 24						
Northolt Park	d	14 14			14 46				15 14					15 46					16 27						16 58
South Ruislip § ⊖	d	14 18							15 18									16 21							17 02
West Ruislip 3 § ⊖	d				14 51									15 51					16 32					16 58	
Denham	d	14 24			14 55				15 24					15 55					16 36					17 03	
Denham Golf Club	d				14 58									15 58					16 39						
Gerrards Cross 1	d	14 28		14 45	15 01			15 15	15 28				15 48	16 01	16 05			16 29	16 42					17 07	17 10
Seer Green	d	14 33			15 06				15 33				15 53					16 33							17 15
Beaconsfield	d	14 36		14 51	15 09			15 21	15 36				15 56	16 07	16 11			16 37	16 48					17 13	17 18
High Wycombe 1	d	14a48	14 50	14 58	15a21			15 28	15a48		15 50		16 02	16a19	16 18			16 43	17a00				17 05	17 20	17a30
Saunderton	d			15 04									16 09					16 50							
Princes Risborough 2	d		15 01	15 10			15 11	15 38			16 01	16 07	16a24		16 27			16a58				17 00	17 16	17a36	
Monks Risborough	d						15 14					16 10										17 03			
Little Kimble	d						15 18					16 14										17 07			
Aylesbury	a						15 32					16 28										17 21			
Haddenham & Thame Parkway	d		15 07	15 16				15 45			16 07				16 34								17 22		
Bicester North 3	d		15 19	15a36		15 39		16a04			16 19				16a53						17 25		17 34		
Kings Sutton	d																								
Banbury	d		15 35			15 57					16 36										17 40		18 09		
Leamington Spa 8	d		15 54			16 15					16 54										17 58		18 28		
Warwick	d		15 59			16 19					16 59										18 02		18 32		
Warwick Parkway	d		16 02			16 22					17 03										18 05		18 36		
Hatton	d		16 07																		18 10		18 42		
Claverdon	d																						18 48		
Bearley	d																						18 53		
Wilmcote	d																						18 58		
Stratford-upon-Avon	a																						19 09		
Lapworth	a		16 13								17 10										18 15				
Dorridge	a		16 17			16 33					17 14										18 19				
Solihull	a		16 22			16 38					17 20										18 24				
Birmingham Moor Street	a		16 34			16 49					17 32										18 33				
Birmingham Snow Hill	a		16 45			17 04					17 44										18 45				
Rowley Regis	a																								
Cradley Heath	a																								
Stourbridge Junction 2	a																								
Kidderminster	a																								

§ London Underground Limited (Central Line) also operate services between South Ruislip and West Ruislip at frequent intervals

Table 115

Mondays to Fridays

from 04 October

London - High Wycombe, Aylesbury, Banbury, Stratford-upon-Avon, Birmingham Snow Hill and Kidderminster

		CH	CH	CH	CH	CH	CH	CH	CH	CH	CH	CH	CH	CH	CH	CH	CH	CH	CH	CH	CH	CH
																						◇
London Marylebone 10 ⊖	d	17 30		17 07	17 20	17 10	17 38	17 33	17 44	17 51	18 09	18 12	18 15	18 21	18 33	18 40	18 43	18 46	19 06	19 12	19 30	19 33
London Paddington 15 ⊖	d																					
Wembley Stadium	d			17 17		17 21	17 47						18 25					18 56		19 22		
Sudbury & Harrow Road	d					17 24								18 32						19 25		
Sudbury Hill Harrow	d							17 45						18 34						19 27		
Northolt Park	d					17 28		17 47		18 04				18 37			18 56			19 30		
South Ruislip § ⊖	d					17 31			17 59				18 32					19 03	19 21			
West Ruislip 3 § ⊖	d			17 26			17 56					18 29					19 01			19 35		
Denham	d			17 30				17 55	18 05			18 33						19 09		19 39		
Denham Golf Club	d			17 33									18 38							19 42		
Gerrards Cross 1	d			17 36	17 42		18 03		18 09		18 31	18 38	18 42	18a52			19 07	19 13	19 29	19 45		
Seer Green	d				17 47			18 01		18 16		18 42					19 12		19 33			
Beaconsfield	d				17 50	17 44		18 05	18 15	18 20		18 46	18 49			19 05	19 15	19 19	19 37			19 58
High Wycombe 1	d			17 47	17 57	17a57	18 15	18a17	18 21	18a32	18 41	18 53	19a01			19 12	19a27	19 26	19 43	20a02		20 04
Saunderton	d			17 54					18 28		18 48							19 32	19 50			
Princes Risborough 2	d		17 50	17 59	18a11		18 24		18 33		18 53	19 02				19 22		19 38	20a02			20 15
Monks Risborough	d		17 53						18 37									19 41				
Little Kimble	d		17 57						18 40									19 45				
Aylesbury	a		18 11						18 59			19 24						20 02				
Haddenham & Thame Parkway	d	18 15		18 06			18 31				19 01					19 29					20 12	20 21
Bicester North 3	d	18 26		18a26			18 44				19a20				19 25	19a49					20 23	20 33
Kings Sutton	d																					
Banbury	d	18 41					19 09								19 40						20 38	20 49
Leamington Spa 8	d	19 00					19 28								19 59						20 56	21 07
Warwick	d	19 04					19 32								20 03						21 00	21 12
Warwick Parkway	d	19 08					19a44								20 07						21 04	
Hatton	d	19 13													20 12						21 09	21 19
Claverdon	d																					21 25
Bearley	d																					21 30
Wilmcote	d																					21 34
Stratford-upon-Avon	a																					21 48
Lapworth	a	19 18													20 17						21 14	
Dorridge	a	19 22													20 23						21 18	
Solihull	a	19 28													20 28						21 24	
Birmingham Moor Street	a	19 38													20 37						21 36	
Birmingham Snow Hill	a	19 51													20 51						21 50	
Rowley Regis	a																					
Cradley Heath	a																					
Stourbridge Junction 2	a																					
Kidderminster	a																					

		CH	CH	CH	CH	CH	CH	CH	CH	CH	CH	CH	CH	CH	CH	CH	CH	CH FX	CH FO	CH	CH FX	CH FO
					◇		◇				◇				◇						◇	◇
London Marylebone 10 ⊖	d	19 37	19 50	20 00	20 06	20 10	20 30	20 33	21 03		21 33	21 18	21 40	22 03	22 20	22 23	22 40	23 10	23 10	23 30	23 54	23 54
London Paddington 15 ⊖	d																					
Wembley Stadium	d	19 46				20 19		20 42	21 12				21 49			22 32	22 49	23 19	23 19	23 39		
Sudbury & Harrow Road	d							20 45														
Sudbury Hill Harrow	d							20 48														
Northolt Park	d	19 51				20 24			21 17				21 54			22 37				23 44		
South Ruislip § ⊖	d		20 05					20 53					21 58				22 56			23 48		
West Ruislip 3 § ⊖	d	19 56				20 29			21 22							22 42				23 51		
Denham	d	20 01				20 34		20 58	21 27				22 04			22 47	23 02			23 56		
Denham Golf Club	d					20 36			21 29							22 49				23 58		
Gerrards Cross 1	d	20 06	20 13		20 27	20 40		21 03	21 33			21 39	22 08	22 24		22 53	23 07	23 33	23 33	00 01	00 15	00 15
Seer Green	d	20 10				20 44		21 07	21 37				22 13			22 57	23 11			00 06		
Beaconsfield	d	20 14	20 19		20 33	20 47		21 11	21 41			21 47	22 16	22 30		23 01	23 15	23 39	23 39	00 09	00 21	00 21
High Wycombe 1	d	20 21	20a32		20 40	20 54	21 00	21 17	21 47			21 53	22 23	22 36		23 07	23 21	23 45	23 45	00 15	00 27	00 27
Saunderton	d	20 27				21 00			21 54				22 29			23 14				00 22	00 34	00 34
Princes Risborough 2	d	20 34			20 49	21 06	21 11	21a33	21 59			22 03	22 36	22 46		23 19	23 31	23 56	23 56	00 27	00 40	00 40
Monks Risborough	d	20 37				21 09			22 03							23 23				00 31		
Little Kimble	d	20 41				21 13			22 06							23 26				00 34		
Aylesbury	a	20 58				21 30			22 23				22 57			23 43				00 52		
Haddenham & Thame Parkway	d				20 56		21 17				22 16	22 09		22 53	23 02		23 38	00 03	00 03		00 47	00 47
Bicester North 3	d			20 51	21a16		21 28				22 28	22a28		23a12	23 13		23 52	00 16	00 16		01 00	01 00
Kings Sutton	d						21 41										00 04				01 12	01 12
Banbury	d			21 07			21 47				22 43				23 31		00a17	00a43	00 33		01a24	01 19
Leamington Spa 8	d			21 26			22 05			22 25	23 00				23 48				00 52			01a42
Warwick	d						22 10			22 29	23 05				23 53				00 56			
Warwick Parkway	d			21 31			22 14				23 07				23 56				01a09			
Hatton	d						22 19															
Claverdon	d																					
Bearley	d																					
Wilmcote	d																					
Stratford-upon-Avon	a									22 58												
Lapworth	a						22 24															
Dorridge	a			21 41			22 28				23 18				00 07							
Solihull	a			21 47			22 35				23 23				00 12							
Birmingham Moor Street	a			21 58			22 49				23 33				00 22							
Birmingham Snow Hill	a			22 04			23 01				23 48				00 35							
Rowley Regis	a			22 24																		
Cradley Heath	a			22 29																		
Stourbridge Junction 2	a			22 35																		
Kidderminster	a			22 53																		

§ London Underground Limited (Central Line) also operate services between South Ruislip and West Ruislip at frequent intervals

Table 115

Saturdays

until 02 October

London - High Wycombe, Aylesbury, Banbury, Stratford-upon-Avon, Birmingham Snow Hill and Kidderminster

		CH	CH	CH	CH	CH	CH	CH	CH	CH	CH	CH	CH	WS	CH	CH	CH	CH	CH	CH	CH	CH	CH	CH	CH
		◇				◇		◇	◇				◇	◇ 1	◇		◇		◇	◇	◇			◇	
London Marylebone 10 ⊖	d	22p20	22p40	23p10	23p30	23p54	00 10		06 24				07 24	08 14	08 18	08 24	08 45		08 53	09 12	09 15	09 24		09 45	10 00
London Paddington 15 ⊖	d																								
Wembley Stadium	d		22p49	23p19	23p39		00 19		06 33				07 33			08 33						09 33			10 09
Sudbury & Harrow Road	d																								
Sudbury Hill Harrow	d																								
Northolt Park	d				23p44		00 24		06 38				07 38			08 38						09 38			10 14
South Ruislip § ⊖	d		22p56		23p48		00 28		06 42				07 42			08 42						09 42			10 18
West Ruislip 3 § ⊖	d				23p51		00 31		06 45				07 45			08 45						09 45			
Denham	d		23p02		23p56		00 36		06 50				07 50			08 50						09 50			10 24
Denham Golf Club	d				23p58		00 38		06 52				07 52			08 52						09 52			
Gerrards Cross 1	d		23p07	23p33	00 01	00 15	00 41		06 55				07 55		08 39	08 55			09 14		09 36	09 55			10 28
Seer Green	d		23p11		00 06		00 46		07 00				08 00			09 00						10 00			10 33
Beaconsfield	d		23p15	23p39	00 09	00 21	00 49		07 03				08 03		08 45	09 03			09 20		09 42	10 03			10 36
High Wycombe 1	d		23p21	23p45	00 15	00 27	00 55	06 10	07 10				08 10		08 51	09a13	09 15		09 27		09 48	10a13		10 15	10a45
Saunderton	d				00 22	00 34	01 02	06 16	07 16				08 16		08 58						09 55				
Princes Risborough 2	d		23p31	23p56	00 27	00 40	01 07	06 21	07 22	07 30	08 30		08 22		09 04		09 26	09 28	09 37		10 01		10 11	10 25	
Monks Risborough	d				00 31		01 11			07 33	08 33							09 31					10 14		
Little Kimble	d				00 34		01 14			07 37	08 37							09 35					10 18		
Aylesbury	a				00 49		01 29			07 47	08 47							09 45					10 28		
Haddenham & Thame Parkway	d	23p02	23p38	00 03		00 47		06 28	07 29				08 29		09 11		09 32		09 43		10 08			10 31	
Bicester North 3	d	23p13	23p52	00 16		01 00		06 43	07 44				08 42		09 22		09 43		09 58	10 05	10 22			10 43	
Kings Sutton	d		00 04			01 12		06 53					08 53						10 09						
Banbury	d	23p31	00a14	00 33		01 19		07 02	08 01				08 58	09 30	09 39		09 58		10a18	10 20	10 38			10 58	
Leamington Spa 8	d	23p48		00 52		01a39		07 22	08 21			08 30	09 17	09a48	09 58		10 17			10 38	10 58			11 17	
Warwick	d	23p53		00 56				07 26	08 24			08 34	09 21		10 02		10 21			10 42	11 02			11 21	
Warwick Parkway	d	23p56		01a06				07 30	08 28			08 37	09 25		10 06		10 25				11 05			11 25	
Hatton	d							07 34	08 33			08 42					10 30								
Claverdon	d											08 48													
Bearley	d											08 53													
Wilmcote	d											08 57													
Stratford-upon-Avon	a											09 09								11 11					
Lapworth	a								08 38								10 35								
Dorridge	a	00 07						07 42	08 42				09 35		10 16		10 39				11 16			11 35	
Solihull	a	00 12						07 50	08 50				09 41		10 22		10 45				11 23			11 42	
Birmingham Moor Street	a	00 22						08 03	08 59				09 51		10 33		10 54				11 33			11 51	
Birmingham Snow Hill	a	00 32						08 11	09 08				10 02		10 41		11 04				11 41			12 01	
Rowley Regis	a																								
Cradley Heath	a																								
Stourbridge Junction 2	a																								
Kidderminster	a																								

		CH	CH	CH	CH	CH	CH	CH	CH	CH	CH	CH	CH	WS	CH	CH	CH	CH	CH	CH	CH	CH	CH	CH
		◇		◇		◇				◇				◇ 1		◇		◇			◇			◇
London Marylebone 10 ⊖	d	10 18	10 24	10 50		10 53	11 00	11 20	11 24	11 50		11 53	12 20	12 24	12 30	12 50		12 53	13 20	13 24	13 50		13 53	14 20
London Paddington 15 ⊖	d																							
Wembley Stadium	d		10 33				11 09		11 33			12 02			12 39			13 02		13 33			14 02	
Sudbury & Harrow Road	d																							
Sudbury Hill Harrow	d																							
Northolt Park	d		10 38				11 14		11 38						12 44					13 38				
South Ruislip § ⊖	d						11 18		11 42						12 48					13 42				
West Ruislip 3 § ⊖	d		10 43						11 45						12 51					13 45				
Denham	d		10 48				11 24		11 50						12 56					13 50				
Denham Golf Club	d		10 50						11 52						12 58					13 52				
Gerrards Cross 1	d		10 54			11 14	11 28		11 55			12 16			13 01			13 16		13 55			14 16	
Seer Green	d		10 58				11 33		12 00						13 06					14 00				
Beaconsfield	d		11 01			11 20	11 36		12 03			12 22			13 09			13 22		14 03			14 22	
High Wycombe 1	d	10 48	11a11			11 27	11a45	11 50	12a13			12 28	12 49		13a19			13 28	13 50	14a13			14 28	14 50
Saunderton	d	10 54				11 33						12 35						13 35					14 35	
Princes Risborough 2	d	11 01			11 08	11 39		12 01			12 11	12 40	12 59				13 09	13 40	14 01			14 11	14 40	15 01
Monks Risborough	d				11 11						12 14						13 12					14 14		
Little Kimble	d				11 15						12 18						13 16					14 18		
Aylesbury	a				11 25						12 28						13 26					14 28		
Haddenham & Thame Parkway	d	11 07				11 45		12 07				12 47	13 05					13 47	14 07				14 47	15 07
Bicester North 3	d	11 19		11 42		12 00		12 19		12 42		13a03	13 17			13 42		14 02	14 19		14 42		14 59	15 19
Kings Sutton	d					12 11																	15 10	
Banbury	d	11 35		11 58		12 19		12 35		12 58			13 32	13 37		13 58		14a21	14 35		14 58		15 16	15 35
Leamington Spa 8	d	11 54		12 17		12 38		12 54		13 17			13 51	13a55		14 17			14 54		15 17		15 34	15 54
Warwick	d	11 59		12 21		12 42		12 59		13 21			13 58			14 21			14 59		15 21		15 38	15 59
Warwick Parkway	d	12 02		12 25				13 02		13 25			14 02			14 25			15 02		15 25			16 02
Hatton	d	12 07				12 50							14 07										15 45	16 07
Claverdon	d																						15 51	
Bearley	d					12 59																	15 56	
Wilmcote	d					13 03																	16 00	
Stratford-upon-Avon	a					13 13																	16 12	
Lapworth	a	12 13											14 13											16 13
Dorridge	a	12 17		12 35				13 13		13 36			14 17			14 36			15 13		15 36			16 17
Solihull	a	12 22		12 41				13 19		13 42			14 22			14 41			15 19		15 41			16 22
Birmingham Moor Street	a	12 34		12 52				13 32		13 52			14 34			14 52			15 32		15 52			16 33
Birmingham Snow Hill	a	12 42		13 01				13 41		14 01			14 42			15 01			15 41		16 01			16 41
Rowley Regis	a																							
Cradley Heath	a																							
Stourbridge Junction 2	a																							
Kidderminster	a																							

§ London Underground Limited (Central Line) also operate services between South Ruislip and West Ruislip at frequent intervals

Table 115

Saturdays until 02 October

London - High Wycombe, Aylesbury, Banbury, Stratford-upon-Avon, Birmingham Snow Hill and Kidderminster

	CH	CH ◇	CH	CH ◇	CH	CH	CH	CH	CH	CH	CH	CH	CH	CH	CH	CH	CH	CH	WS ◇1	CH	CH ◇	CH
London Marylebone ⊖ d	14 24	14 50		14 53	15 00	15 20	15 24	15 50		15 53	16 00	16 20	16 24	16 50		16 53	17 00	17 20	17 24	17 30	17 50	
London Paddington ⊖ d																						
Wembley Stadium d	14 33				15 09		15 33				16 09		16 33				17 09			17 39		
Sudbury & Harrow Road d																						
Sudbury Hill Harrow d																						
Northolt Park d	14 38				15 14		15 38				16 14		16 38				17 14			17 44		
South Ruislip § ⊖ d	14 42				15 18						16 18		16 42				17 18					
West Ruislip § ⊖ d	14 45						15 43						16 45							17 49		
Denham d	14 50				15 24		15 48				16 24		16 50				17 24			17 54		
Denham Golf Club d	14 52						15 50						16 52							17 56		
Gerrards Cross d	14 55			15 14	15 28		15 54			16 14	16 28		16 55			17 14	17 28			18 00		
Seer Green d	15 00				15 33		15 58				16 33		17 00				17 33			18 04		
Beaconsfield d	15 03			15 20	15 36		16 01			16 20	16 36		17 03			17 20	17 36			18 07		
High Wycombe d	15a13			15 27	15a45	15 50	16a11			16 27	16a45	16 50	17a13			17 27	17a45	17 49		18a17		
Saunderton d				15 33						16 33						17 33						
Princes Risborough d			15 05	15 39		16 01			16 05	16 39		17 01			17 11	17 39		17 59				18 08
Monks Risborough d			15 08						16 08						17 14							18 11
Little Kimble d			15 12						16 12						17 18							18 15
Aylesbury a			15 22						16 22						17 28							18 25
Haddenham & Thame Parkway d				15 45		16 07				16 45		17 07				17 45		18 05				
Bicester North d		15 42		16a03		16 19		16 42		17a02		17 19		17 42		18 00		18 17			18 45	
Kings Sutton d																18 11						
Banbury d		15 58				16 35		16 58				17 35		17 58		18 19		18 32	18 37		19 03	
Leamington Spa d		16 17				16 54		17 17				17 54		18 17		18 38		18 51	18a55		19 23	
Warwick d		16 21				16 59		17 21				17 59		18 21		18 42		18 58			19 27	
Warwick Parkway d		16 25				17 02		17 25				18 02		18 25				19 02			19 30	
Hatton d						17 07						18 07				18 49		19 07				
Claverdon d																18 55						
Bearley d																19 00						
Wilmcote d																19 04						
Stratford-upon-Avon a																19 15						
Lapworth a						17 13						18 13						19 13				
Dorridge a		16 35				17 17		17 35				18 17		18 36				19 17			19 41	
Solihull a		16 42				17 22		17 42				18 22		18 41				19 22			19 48	
Birmingham Moor Street a		16 53				17 33		17 53				18 33		18 54				19 33			19 58	
Birmingham Snow Hill a		17 02				17 41		18 02				18 41		19 04				19 41			20 06	
Rowley Regis a																						
Cradley Heath a																						
Stourbridge Junction a																						
Kidderminster a																						

	CH	CH	CH	CH	CH ◇	CH	CH	CH	CH	CH	CH	CH ◇	CH	CH	CH ◇	CH	CH	CH ◇	CH	CH	CH	CH
London Marylebone ⊖ d	17 53	18 00	18 20	18 30	18 50		18 53	19 00	19 20		19 30	20 00	20 05	20 40	20 50	21 15	21 40	22 00	22 10	23 10	23 14	23 45
London Paddington ⊖ d																						
Wembley Stadium d		18 09		18 39				19 09			19 39		20 14			21 24			22 19	23 19	23 23	23 54
Sudbury & Harrow Road d																						
Sudbury Hill Harrow d																						
Northolt Park d		18 14		18 44				19 14			19 44		20 19			21 29			22 24		23 28	
South Ruislip § ⊖ d		18 18						19 18					20 23			21 33			22 28		23 32	
West Ruislip § ⊖ d				18 49							19 49		20 26			21 36			22 31		23 35	
Denham d		18 24		18 54				19 24			19 54		20 31			21 41			22 36		23 40	
Denham Golf Club d				18 56							19 56		20 33			21 43			22 38		23 42	
Gerrards Cross d	18 14	18 28		19 00			19 14	19 28			20 00		20 36	21 01		21 46	22 01		22 41	23 33	23 45	00 08
Seer Green d		18 33		19 04				19 33			20 04		20 41			21 51			22 46		23 50	
Beaconsfield d	18 20	18 36		19 07			19 20	19 36			20 07		20 44	21 07		21 54	22 07		22 49	23 39	23 53	00 14
High Wycombe d	18 27	18a45	18 50	19a17			19 27	19 43	19 49		20 13	20 30	20 50	21 13	21 21	22 00	22 13		22 55	23 45	23 59	00 20
Saunderton d	18 33						19 33				20 20			21 20		22 07			23 02		00 06	
Princes Risborough d	18 39		19 01			19 08	19 39	19 54	19 59	20 05	20 27	20 41	21 00	21 27	21 31	22 14	22 24		23 07	23 56	00 12	00 32
Monks Risborough d						19 11				20 08	20 30			21 30		22 17			23 11		00 16	
Little Kimble d						19 15				20 12	20 34			21 34		22 21			23 14		00 19	
Aylesbury a						19 25		20 12		20 22	20 47		21 19	21 47		22 35			23 29		00 34	
Haddenham & Thame Parkway d	18 45		19 07				19 45		20 05			20 48			21 38		22 31			00 03		00 38
Bicester North d	19a02		19 19		19 45		20 00		20 17			21 00			21 51		22a47	22 51		00 16		00 52
Kings Sutton d							20 11															01 03
Banbury d			19 35		20 03		20 19		20 32			21 19			22 07			23 06		00a36		01a14
Leamington Spa d			19 54		20 23		20 38		20 51			21 38			22 27			23 24				
Warwick d			19 59		20 27		20 42		20 58			21 42			22 31			23 28				
Warwick Parkway d			20 02		20 30				21 02			21 46			22 35			23 32				
Hatton d			20 07				20 49		21 07													
Claverdon d							20 54															
Bearley d																						
Wilmcote d																						
Stratford-upon-Avon a							21 10															
Lapworth a			20 13						21 13													
Dorridge a			20 17		20 41				21 17			21 57			22 46			23 42				
Solihull a			20 22		20 47				21 22			22 03			22 51			23 49				
Birmingham Moor Street a			20 34		20 58				21 33			22 15			23 02			23 59				
Birmingham Snow Hill a			20 42		21 06				21 41			22 26			23 10			00 10				
Rowley Regis a																						
Cradley Heath a																						
Stourbridge Junction a																						
Kidderminster a																						

§ London Underground Limited (Central Line) also operate services between South Ruislip and West Ruislip at frequent intervals

Table 115

Saturdays from 09 October

London - High Wycombe, Aylesbury, Banbury, Stratford-upon-Avon, Birmingham Snow Hill and Kidderminster

	CH ◇	CH	CH	CH	CH ◇	CH	CH ◇	CH	CH	CH	CH ◇	CH ◇	CH	CH ◇	CH	CH ◇	CH ◇	CH ◇	CH	CH	CH ◇	CH
London Marylebone ⊖ d	22p20	22p40	23p10	23p30	23p54	00 10	06 24				07 24	08 18	08 24	08 45		08 53	09 12	09 15	09 24		09 45	10 00
London Paddington ⊖ d																						
Wembley Stadium d		22p49	23p19	23p39		00 19	06 33				07 33		08 33						09 33			10 09
Sudbury & Harrow Road d																						
Sudbury Hill Harrow d																						
Northolt Park d				23p44		00 24	06 38				07 38		08 38						09 38			10 14
South Ruislip § ⊖ d		22p56		23p48		00 28	06 42				07 42		08 42						09 42			10 18
West Ruislip § ⊖ d				23p51		00 31	06 45				07 45		08 45						09 45			
Denham d		23p02		23p56		00 36	06 50				07 50		08 50						09 50			10 24
Denham Golf Club d				23p58		00 38	06 52				07 52		08 52						09 52			
Gerrards Cross d		23p07	23p33	00 01	00 15	00 41	06 55				07 55	08 39	08 55			09 14		09 36	09 55			10 28
Seer Green d		23p11		00 06		00 46	07 00				08 00		09 00						10 00			10 33
Beaconsfield d		23p15	23p39	00 09	00 21	00 49	07 03				08 03	08 45	09 03			09 20		09 42	10 03			10 36
High Wycombe d		23p21	23p45	00 15	00 27	00 55	07 10				08 10	08 51	09a14	09 15		09 27		09 48	10a14		10 15	10a47
Saunderton d				00 22	00 34	01 02	07 16				08 16	08 58						09 55				
Princes Risborough d		23p31	23p56	00 27	00 40	01 07	07 22	07 30	08 30		08 22	09 04		09 26	09 28	09 37		10 01		10 11	10 25	
Monks Risborough d				00 31		01 11		07 33	08 33						09 31					10 14		
Little Kimble d				00 34		01 14		07 37	08 37						09 35					10 18		
Aylesbury a				00 52		01 32		07 50	08 50						09 48					10 31		
Haddenham & Thame Parkway d	23p02	23p38	00 03		00 47		07 29				08 29	09 11		09 32		09 43		10 08			10 31	
Bicester North d	23p13	23p52	00 16		01 00		07 44				08 42	09 22		09 43		09 58	10 05	10 22			10 43	
Kings Sutton d		00 04			01 12						08 53					10 09						
Banbury d	23p31	00a17	00 33		01 19		08 01				08 58	09 39		09 58		10a21	10 20	10 38			10 58	
Leamington Spa d	23p48		00 52		01a42		08 21			08 30	09 17	09 58		10 17			10 38	10 58			11 17	
Warwick d	23p53		00 56				08 24			08 34	09 21	10 02		10 21			10 42	11 02			11 21	
Warwick Parkway d	23p56		01a09				08 28			08 37	09 25	10 06		10 25				11 05			11 25	
Hatton d							08 33			08 42				10 30								
Claverdon d										08 48												
Bearley d										08 53												
Wilmcote d										08 57												
Stratford-upon-Avon a										09 12							11 14					
Lapworth a							08 38							10 35								
Dorridge a	00 07						08 42				09 35	10 16		10 39				11 16			11 35	
Solihull a	00 12						08 50				09 41	10 22		10 45				11 23			11 42	
Birmingham Moor Street a	00 22						08 59				09 51	10 33		10 54				11 33			11 51	
Birmingham Snow Hill a	00 35						09 11				10 05	10 44		11 07				11 44			12 04	
Rowley Regis a																						
Cradley Heath a																						
Stourbridge Junction a																						
Kidderminster a																						

	CH ◇	CH	CH ◇	CH	CH ◇	CH	CH	CH	CH ◇	CH	CH	CH	CH	CH ◇	CH	CH ◇	CH	CH	CH ◇	CH	CH	CH ◇
London Marylebone ⊖ d	10 18	10 24	10 50		10 53	11 00	11 20	11 24	11 50		11 53	12 20	12 30	12 50		12 53	13 20	13 24	13 50		13 53	14 20
London Paddington ⊖ d																						
Wembley Stadium d		10 33				11 09		11 33			12 02		12 39			13 02		13 33			14 02	
Sudbury & Harrow Road d																						
Sudbury Hill Harrow d																						
Northolt Park d		10 38				11 14		11 38					12 44					13 38				
South Ruislip § ⊖ d						11 18		11 42					12 48					13 42				
West Ruislip § ⊖ d		10 43						11 45					12 51					13 45				
Denham d		10 48				11 24		11 50					12 56					13 50				
Denham Golf Club d		10 50						11 52					12 58					13 52				
Gerrards Cross d		10 54			11 14	11 28		11 55			12 16		13 01			13 16		13 55			14 16	
Seer Green d		10 58				11 33		12 00					13 06					14 00				
Beaconsfield d		11 01			11 20	11 36		12 03			12 22		13 09			13 22		14 03			14 22	
High Wycombe d	10 48	11a14			11 27	11a48	11 50	12a16			12 28	12 49	13a22			13 28	13 50	14a16			14 28	14 50
Saunderton d	10 54				11 33						12 35					13 35					14 35	
Princes Risborough d	11 01			11 08	11 39		12 01			12 11	12 40	12 59			13 09	13 40	14 01			14 11	14 40	15 01
Monks Risborough d				11 11						12 14					13 12					14 14		
Little Kimble d				11 15						12 18					13 16					14 18		
Aylesbury a				11 28						12 31					13 29					14 31		
Haddenham & Thame Parkway d	11 07				11 45		12 07				12 47	13 05				13 47	14 07				14 47	15 07
Bicester North d	11 19		11 42		12 00		12 19		12 42		13a06	13 17		13 42		14 02	14 19		14 42		14 59	15 19
Kings Sutton d					12 11																15 10	
Banbury d	11 35		11 58		12 19		12 35		12 58			13 32		13 58		14a24	14 35		14 58		15 16	15 35
Leamington Spa d	11 54		12 17		12 38		12 54		13 17			13 51		14 17			14 54		15 17		15 34	15 54
Warwick d	11 59		12 21		12 42		12 59		13 21			13 58		14 21			14 59		15 21		15 38	15 59
Warwick Parkway d	12 02		12 25				13 02		13 25			14 02		14 25			15 02		15 25			16 02
Hatton d	12 07				12 50							14 07									15 45	16 07
Claverdon d																					15 51	
Bearley d					12 59																15 56	
Wilmcote d					13 03																16 00	
Stratford-upon-Avon a					13 16																16 15	
Lapworth a	12 13											14 13										16 13
Dorridge a	12 17		12 35				13 13		13 36			14 17		14 36			15 13		15 36			16 17
Solihull a	12 22		12 41				13 19		13 42			14 22		14 41			15 19		15 41			16 22
Birmingham Moor Street a	12 34		12 52				13 32		13 52			14 34		14 52			15 32		15 52			16 33
Birmingham Snow Hill a	12 45		13 04				13 44		14 04			14 45		15 04			15 44		16 04			16 44
Rowley Regis a																						
Cradley Heath a																						
Stourbridge Junction a																						
Kidderminster a																						

§ London Underground Limited (Central Line) also operate services between South Ruislip and West Ruislip at frequent intervals

Table 115

Saturdays from 09 October

London - High Wycombe, Aylesbury, Banbury, Stratford-upon-Avon, Birmingham Snow Hill and Kidderminster

		CH	CH ◇	CH	CH ◇	CH	CH	CH	CH	CH	CH	CH	CH	CH	CH	CH	CH	CH	CH	CH	CH ◇	CH
London Marylebone 10 ⊖	d	14 24	14 50		14 53	15 00	15 20	15 24	15 50		15 53	16 00	16 20	16 24	16 50		16 53	17 00	17 20	17 30	17 50	
London Paddington 15 ⊖	d																					
Wembley Stadium	d	14 33				15 09		15 33				16 09		16 33				17 09		17 39		
Sudbury & Harrow Road	d																					
Sudbury Hill Harrow	d																					
Northolt Park	d	14 38				15 14		15 38				16 14		16 38				17 14		17 44		
South Ruislip § ⊖	d	14 42				15 18						16 18		16 42				17 18				
West Ruislip 3 § ⊖	d	14 45						15 43						16 45						17 49		
Denham	d	14 50				15 24		15 48				16 24		16 50				17 24		17 54		
Denham Golf Club	d	14 52						15 50						16 52						17 56		
Gerrards Cross 1	d	14 55			15 14	15 28		15 54			16 14	16 28		16 55			17 14	17 28		18 00		
Seer Green	d	15 00				15 33		15 58				16 33		17 00				17 33		18 04		
Beaconsfield	d	15 03			15 20	15 36		16 01			16 20	16 36		17 03			17 20	17 36		18 07		
High Wycombe 1	d	15a16			15 27	15a48	15 50	16a14			16 27	16a48	16 50	17a16			17 27	17a48	17 49	18a20		
Saunderton	d				15 33						16 33						17 33					
Princes Risborough 2	d			15 05	15 39		16 01			16 05	16 39		17 01			17 11	17 39		17 59			18 08
Monks Risborough	d			15 08						16 08						17 14						18 11
Little Kimble	d			15 12						16 12						17 18						18 15
Aylesbury	a			15 25						16 25						17 31						18 28
Haddenham & Thame Parkway	d				15 45		16 07				16 45		17 07				17 45		18 05			
Bicester North 3	d		15 42		16a06		16 19		16 42		17a05		17 19		17 42		18 00		18 17		18 45	
Kings Sutton	d																18 11					
Banbury	d		15 58				16 35		16 58				17 35		17 58		18 19		18 32		19 03	
Leamington Spa 8	d		16 17				16 54		17 17				17 54		18 17		18 38		18 51		19 23	
Warwick	d		16 21				16 59		17 21				17 59		18 21		18 42		18 58		19 27	
Warwick Parkway	d		16 25				17 02		17 25				18 02		18 25				19 02		19 30	
Hatton	d						17 07						18 07				18 49		19 07			
Claverdon	d																18 55					
Bearley	d																19 00					
Wilmcote	d																19 04					
Stratford-upon-Avon	a																19 18					
Lapworth	a						17 13						18 13						19 13			
Dorridge	a		16 35				17 17		17 35				18 17		18 36				19 17		19 41	
Solihull	a		16 42				17 22		17 42				18 22		18 41				19 22		19 48	
Birmingham Moor Street	a		16 53				17 33		17 53				18 33		18 54				19 33		19 58	
Birmingham Snow Hill	a		17 05				17 44		18 05				18 44		19 07				19 44		20 09	
Rowley Regis	a																					
Cradley Heath	a																					
Stourbridge Junction 2	a																					
Kidderminster	a																					

		CH	CH	CH	CH	CH ◇	CH	CH	CH	CH	CH	CH	CH ◇	CH	CH	CH ◇	CH	CH	CH ◇	CH	CH	CH	CH
London Marylebone 10 ⊖	d	17 53	18 00	18 20	18 30	18 50		18 53	19 00	19 20		19 30	20 00	20 05	20 40	20 50	21 15	21 40	22 00	22 10	23 10	23 14	23 45
London Paddington 15 ⊖	d																						
Wembley Stadium	d		18 09		18 39				19 09			19 39		20 14			21 24			22 19	23 19	23 23	23 54
Sudbury & Harrow Road	d																						
Sudbury Hill Harrow	d																						
Northolt Park	d		18 14		18 44				19 14			19 44		20 19			21 29			22 24		23 28	
South Ruislip § ⊖	d		18 18						19 18					20 23			21 33			22 28		23 32	
West Ruislip 3 § ⊖	d				18 49							19 49		20 26			21 36			22 31		23 35	
Denham	d		18 24		18 54				19 24			19 54		20 31			21 41			22 36		23 40	
Denham Golf Club	d				18 56							19 56		20 33			21 43			22 38		23 42	
Gerrards Cross 1	d	18 14	18 28		19 00			19 14	19 28			20 00		20 36	21 01		21 46	22 01		22 41	23 33	23 45	00 08
Seer Green	d		18 33		19 04				19 33			20 04		20 41			21 51			22 46		23 50	
Beaconsfield	d	18 20	18 36		19 07			19 20	19 36			20 07		20 44	21 07		21 54	22 07		22 49	23 39	23 53	00 14
High Wycombe 1	d	18 27	18a48	18 50	19a20			19 27	19 43	19 49		20 13	20 30	20 50	21 13	21 21	22 00	22 13		22 55	23 45	23 59	00 20
Saunderton	d	18 33						19 33				20 20			21 20		22 07			23 02		00 06	
Princes Risborough 2	d	18 39		19 01			19 08	19 39	19 54	19 59	20 05	20 27	20 41	21 00	21 27	21 31	22 14	22 24		23 07	23 56	00 12	00 32
Monks Risborough	d						19 11				20 08	20 30			21 30		22 17			23 11		00 16	
Little Kimble	d						19 15				20 12	20 34			21 34		22 21			23 14		00 19	
Aylesbury	a						19 28		20 15		20 25	20 50		21 22	21 50		22 38			23 32		00 37	
Haddenham & Thame Parkway	d	18 45		19 07				19 45		20 05			20 48			21 38		22 31			00 03		00 38
Bicester North 3	d	19a05		19 19		19 45		20 00		20 17			21 00			21 51		22a48	22 51		00 16		00 52
Kings Sutton	d							20 11															01 03
Banbury	d			19 35		20 03		20 19		20 32			21 19			22 07			23 06		00a39		01a17
Leamington Spa 8	d			19 54		20 23		20 38		20 51			21 38			22 27			23 24				
Warwick	d			19 59		20 27		20 42		20 58			21 42			22 31			23 28				
Warwick Parkway	d			20 02		20 30				21 02			21 46			22 35			23 32				
Hatton	d			20 07				20 49		21 07													
Claverdon	d							20 54															
Bearley	d																						
Wilmcote	d																						
Stratford-upon-Avon	a							21 13															
Lapworth	a			20 13						21 13													
Dorridge	a			20 17		20 41				21 17			21 57			22 46			23 42				
Solihull	a			20 22		20 47				21 22			22 03			22 51			23 49				
Birmingham Moor Street	a			20 34		20 58				21 33			22 15			23 02			23 59				
Birmingham Snow Hill	a			20 45		21 09				21 44			22 29			23 13			00 13				
Rowley Regis	a																						
Cradley Heath	a																						
Stourbridge Junction 2	a																						
Kidderminster	a																						

§ London Underground Limited (Central Line) also operate services between South Ruislip and West Ruislip at frequent intervals

Table 115

Sundays until 26 September

London - High Wycombe, Aylesbury, Banbury, Stratford-upon-Avon, Birmingham Snow Hill and Kidderminster

		CH	CH	CH	CH	CH	CH	CH ◇	CH	CH ◇	WS ◇1	CH ◇	CH	CH ◇	CH ◇	CH	CH	CH ◇	CH ◇	CH	CH	CH	CH ◇
London Marylebone 10 ⊖	d	23p10	23p14	23p45	00 10	07 35	07 50	08 10	08 54	09 15	09 33	09 45	09 54	10 15	10 50	10 54	11 20	11 45	11 50	11 54	12 20	12 33	12 50
London Paddington 15 ⊖	d																						
Wembley Stadium	d	23p19	23p23	23p54	00 19	07 44	07 59		09 03				10 03			11 03				12 03		12 42	
Sudbury & Harrow Road	d																						
Sudbury Hill Harrow	d																						
Northolt Park	d		23p28		00 24		08 04		09 08				10 08			11 08				12 08			
South Ruislip § ⊖	d		23p32		00 28	07 51	08 08		09 12				10 12			11 12				12 12			
West Ruislip 3 § ⊖	d		23p35		00 31		08 11		09 15				10 15			11 15				12 15			
Denham	d		23p40		00 36	07 57	08 16		09 20				10 20			11 20				12 20			
Denham Golf Club	d		23p42		00 38		08 18		09 22							11 22							
Gerrards Cross 1	d	23p33	23p45	00 08	00 41	08 02	08 21		09 25	09 36			10 24	10 36		11 25	11 41			12 24	12 41	12 56	
Seer Green	d		23p50		00 46		08 26		09 30				10 28			11 30				12 28			
Beaconsfield	d	23p39	23p53	00 14	00 49	08 08	08 29		09 33	09 42			10 32	10 42		11 33	11 47			12 32	12 47	13 02	
High Wycombe 1	d	23p45	23p59	00 20	00 55	08 14	08 35	08 40	09 39	09 49			10 38	10 49		11 39	11 54			12 38	12 54	13 08	
Saunderton	d		00 06		01 02		08 42		09 46				10 45			11 46				12 45			
Princes Risborough 2	d	23p56	00 12	00 32	01 07	08 25	08 47	08 51	09 51	09 59			10 50	10 59		11 51	12 04			12 50	13 04	13 18	
Monks Risborough	d		00 16		01 11		08 51		09 55				10 54			11 55				12 54			
Little Kimble	d		00 19		01 14		08 54		09 58				10 57			11 58				12 57			
Aylesbury	a		00 34		01 29		09 09		10 13				11 11			12 13				13 11			
Haddenham & Thame Parkway	d	00 03		00 38		08 32		08 58		10 05				11 06			12 11				13 11	13 25	
Bicester North 3	d	00 16		00 52		08a48		09 09		10 18		10 40		11 20	11 45		12 25	12 40	12 45		13 25	13a41	13 45
Kings Sutton	d			01 03				09 21						11 33							13 36		
Banbury	d	00a36		01a14				09 27		10 41	10 37	11 00		11 38	12 02		12 41	13 00	13 05		13 41		14 02
Leamington Spa 8	d							09 46		11 01	10a55	11 20		11 58	12 22		13 01	13 20	13 25		14 00		14 22
Warwick	d							09 51		11 05		11 24		12 02			13 05	13 24			14 04		
Warwick Parkway	d							09 54		11 09				12 06	12 27		13 09		13 31		14 08		14 27
Hatton	d							09 59				11 31		12 11				13 31					
Claverdon	d																						
Bearley	d																						
Wilmcote	d											11 43						13 43					
Stratford-upon-Avon	a											11 59						13 54					
Lapworth	a							10 05						12 16							14 16		
Dorridge	a							10 09		11 19				12 19	12 38		13 19		13 42		14 20		14 38
Solihull	a							10 14		11 26				12 25	12 44		13 25		13 47		14 26		14 44
Birmingham Moor Street	a							10 26		11 35				12 35	12 55		13 37		13 58		14 37		14 54
Birmingham Snow Hill	a							10 39		11 45				12 44	13 03		13 46		14 08		14 47		15 03
Rowley Regis	a																						
Cradley Heath	a																						
Stourbridge Junction 2	a																						
Kidderminster	a																						

		CH	CH	CH ◇	CH ◇	CH	CH ◇	CH	CH ◇	CH	CH	CH ◇	CH	CH	CH	CH	CH	CH	CH	CH ◇	CH	CH	CH
London Marylebone 10 ⊖	d	12 54	13 20	13 33	13 50	13 54	14 20	14 33	14 50	14 54	15 20	15 33	15 57	16 00	16 22	16 36	16 57	17 00	17 20	17 36	17 57	18 00	18 20
London Paddington 15 ⊖	d																						
Wembley Stadium	d	13 03		13 42		14 03		14 42		15 03		15 42		16 09		16 45		17 09		17 45		18 09	
Sudbury & Harrow Road	d																						
Sudbury Hill Harrow	d																						
Northolt Park	d	13 08				14 08				15 08				16 14				17 14				18 14	
South Ruislip § ⊖	d	13 12				14 12				15 12				16 18				17 18				18 18	
West Ruislip 3 § ⊖	d	13 15				14 15				15 15				16 21				17 21				18 21	
Denham	d	13 20				14 20				15 20				16 26				17 26				18 26	
Denham Golf Club	d	13 22								15 22								17 28					
Gerrards Cross 1	d	13 25	13 41	13 56		14 24	14 41	14 56		15 25	15 41	15 56		16 30	16 43	16 59		17 31	17 41	17 59		18 30	18 41
Seer Green	d	13 30				14 28				15 30				16 34				17 36				18 34	
Beaconsfield	d	13 33	13 47	14 02		14 32	14 47	15 02		15 33	15 47	16 02		16 38	16 49	17 05		17 39	17 47	18 05		18 38	18 47
High Wycombe 1	d	13 39	13 54	14 08		14 38	14 54	15 08		15 39	15 54	16 08		16 44	16 56	17 11		17 45	17 54	18 11		18 44	18 54
Saunderton	d	13 46				14 45				15 46				16 51				17 52				18 51	
Princes Risborough 2	d	13 51	14 04	14 18		14 50	15 04	15 18		15 51	16 04	16 18		16 56	17 06	17 21		17 57	18 04	18 21		18 56	19 04
Monks Risborough	d	13 55				14 54				15 55				17 00				18 01				19 00	
Little Kimble	d	13 58				14 57				15 58				17 03				18 04				19 03	
Aylesbury	a	14 13				15 11				16 13				17 18				18 19				19 17	
Haddenham & Thame Parkway	d		14 11	14 25			15 11	15 25			16 11	16 25			17 13	17 28			18 11	18 28			19 10
Bicester North 3	d		14 25	14 40	14 45		15 25	15a41	15 45		16 25	16 40	16 52		17 27	17a44	17 52		18 25	18 42	18 52		19 23
Kings Sutton	d			14 53								16 53								18 53			
Banbury	d		14 41	15 00	15 05		15 40		16 02		16 41	17 00	17 07		17 43		18 09		18 41	19 00	19 09		19 46
Leamington Spa 8	d		15 01	15 20	15 25		15 59		16 22		17 01	17 20	17 25		18 03		18 29		19 01	19 20	19 29		20 05
Warwick	d		15 05	15 24			16 03				17 05	17 24			18 07				19 05	19 24			20 09
Warwick Parkway	d		15 09		15 31		16 06		16 27		17 09		17 31		18 10		18 34		19 09		19 34		20 13
Hatton	d			15 31			16 11					17 31			18 15					19 31			
Claverdon	d																						
Bearley	d																						
Wilmcote	d			15 43								17 43								19 43			
Stratford-upon-Avon	a			15 54								17 54								19 54			
Lapworth	a						16 16								18 20								20 21
Dorridge	a		15 19		15 42		16 20		16 38		17 19		17 41		18 24		18 45		19 19		19 45		20 25
Solihull	a		15 25		15 47		16 26		16 44		17 25		17 48		18 31		18 51		19 27		19 51		20 32
Birmingham Moor Street	a		15 35		15 57		16 35		16 54		17 37		17 57		18 41		19 01		19 38		20 01		20 42
Birmingham Snow Hill	a		15 49		16 06		16 49		17 03		17 46		18 07		18 49		19 10		19 46		20 10		20 53
Rowley Regis	a																						
Cradley Heath	a																						
Stourbridge Junction 2	a																						
Kidderminster	a																						

§ London Underground Limited (Central Line) also operate services between South Ruislip and West Ruislip at frequent intervals

Table 115

Sundays
until 26 September

London - High Wycombe, Aylesbury, Banbury, Stratford-upon-Avon, Birmingham Snow Hill and Kidderminster

		CH	CH	CH	CH ◇	CH	CH	CH	CH ◇	CH ◇	CH	CH	CH ◇	CH	CH	CH	CH
London Marylebone [10] ⊖	d	18 36	18 57	19 00	19 22	19 36	19 57	20 00	20 20	20 50	21 10	21 40	22 00	22 10	22 45		23 45
London Paddington [15] ⊖	d																
Wembley Stadium	d	18 45		19 09		19 45		20 09			21 19			22 19	22 54		23 54
Sudbury & Harrow Road	d																
Sudbury Hill Harrow	d																
Northolt Park	d			19 14				20 14			21 24			22 24	22 59		23 59
South Ruislip § ⊖	d			19 18				20 18			21 28			22 28	23 03		00 03
West Ruislip [3] § ⊖	d			19 21				20 21			21 31			22 31	23 06		00 06
Denham	d			19 26				20 26			21 36			22 36	23 11		00 11
Denham Golf Club	d			19 28							21 38				23 13		00 13
Gerrards Cross [1]	d	18 59		19 31	19 43	19 59		20 30	20 41	21 11	21 41	22 01		22 40	23 16		00 16
Seer Green	d			19 36				20 34			21 46			22 44	23 21		00 21
Beaconsfield	d	19 05		19 39	19 49	20 05		20 38	20 47	21 17	21 49	22 07		22 48	23 24		00 24
High Wycombe [1]	d	19 11		19 45	19 56	20 11		20 44	20 54	21 24	21 55	22 13		22 54	23 30		00 30
Saunderton	d			19 52				20 51			22 02			23 01	23 37		00 37
Princes Risborough [2]	d	19 21		19 57	20 07	20 21		20 56	21 04	21 34	22 07	22 24		23 06	23 43	23 48	00 43
Monks Risborough	d			20 01				21 00			22 11			23 10		23 51	
Little Kimble	d			20 04				21 03			22 14			23 13		23 55	
Aylesbury	a			20 19				21 18			22 29			23 27		00 06	
Haddenham & Thame Parkway	d	19 28			20 14	20 28			21 11	21 41		22 31			23 50		00 50
Bicester North [3]	d	19 42	19 52		20 27	20 42	20 52		21 25	21 55		22a47	22 51		00 04		01 04
Kings Sutton	d					20 53									00 16		
Banbury	d	20a02	20 09		20 44	21a04	21 09		21 41	22 11			23 06		00a25		01a24
Leamington Spa [8]	d		20 29		21 03		21 29		22 01	22 31			23 24				
Warwick	d				21 08				22 05	22 35			23 28				
Warwick Parkway	d		20 34		21 11		21 34		22 09	22 39			23 32				
Hatton	d									22 43							
Claverdon	d																
Bearley	d																
Wilmcote	d																
Stratford-upon-Avon	a																
Lapworth	a									22 48							
Dorridge	a		20 45		21 22		21 45		22 20	22 52			23 43				
Solihull	a		20 51		21 29		21 51		22 25	22 59			23 47				
Birmingham Moor Street	a		21 01		21 40		22 01		22 37	23 10			23 58				
Birmingham Snow Hill	a		21 10		21 48		22 10		22 45	23 18			00 08				
Rowley Regis	a																
Cradley Heath	a																
Stourbridge Junction [2]	a																
Kidderminster	a																

Sundays
from 03 October

		CH	CH A	CH B	CH	CH	CH	CH	CH ◇	CH	CH ◇	CH ◇	CH	CH ◇	CH ◇	CH	CH	CH ◇	CH ◇	CH	CH
London Marylebone [10] ⊖	d	23p10	23p14	23p14	23p45	00 10	07 35	07 50	08 10	08 54	09 15	09 45	09 54	10 15	10 50	10 54	11 20	11 45	11 50	11 54	12 20
London Paddington [15] ⊖	d																				
Wembley Stadium	d	23p19	23p23	23p23	23p54	00 19	07 44	07 59		09 03			10 03			11 03				12 03	
Sudbury & Harrow Road	d																				
Sudbury Hill Harrow	d																				
Northolt Park	d		23p28	23p28		00 24		08 04		09 08			10 08			11 08				12 08	
South Ruislip § ⊖	d		23p32	23p32		00 28	07 51	08 08		09 12			10 12			11 12				12 12	
West Ruislip [3] § ⊖	d		23p35	23p35		00 31		08 11		09 15			10 15			11 15				12 15	
Denham	d		23p40	23p40		00 36	07 57	08 16		09 20			10 20			11 20				12 20	
Denham Golf Club	d		23p42	23p42		00 38		08 18		09 22						11 22					
Gerrards Cross [1]	d	23p33	23p45	23p45	00 08	00 41	08 02	08 21		09 25	09 36		10 24	10 36		11 25	11 41			12 24	12 41
Seer Green	d		23p50	23p50		00 46		08 26		09 30			10 28			11 30				12 28	
Beaconsfield	d	23p39	23p53	23p53	00 14	00 49	08 08	08 29		09 33	09 42		10 32	10 42		11 33	11 47			12 32	12 47
High Wycombe [1]	d	23p45	23p59	23p59	00 20	00 55	08 14	08 35	08 40	09 39	09 49		10 38	10 49		11 39	11 54			12 38	12 54
Saunderton	d		00 06	00 06		01 02		08 42		09 46			10 45			11 46				12 45	
Princes Risborough [2]	d	23p56	00 12	00 12	00 32	01 07	08 25	08 47	08 51	09 51	09 59		10 50	10 59		11 51	12 04			12 50	13 04
Monks Risborough	d		00 16	00 16		01 11		08 51		09 55			10 54			11 55				12 54	
Little Kimble	d		00 19	00 19		01 14		08 54		09 58			10 57			11 58				12 57	
Aylesbury	a		00 34	00 37		01 32		09 12		10 16			11 14			12 16				13 14	
Haddenham & Thame Parkway	d	00 03			00 38		08 32		08 58		10 05			11 06			12 11				13 11
Bicester North [3]	d	00 16			00 52		08a51		09 09		10 18	10 40		11 20	11 45		12 25	12 40	12 45		13 25
Kings Sutton	d				01 03				09 21					11 33							13 36
Banbury	d	00a36			01a14				09 27		10 41	11 00		11 38	12 02		12 41	13 00	13 05		13 41
Leamington Spa [8]	d								09 46		11 01	11 20		11 58	12 22		13 01	13 20	13 25		14 00
Warwick	d								09 51		11 05	11 24		12 02			13 05	13 24			14 04
Warwick Parkway	d								09 54		11 09			12 06	12 27		13 09		13 31		14 08
Hatton	d								09 59			11 31		12 11				13 31			
Claverdon	d																				
Bearley	d																				
Wilmcote	d											11 43						13 43			
Stratford-upon-Avon	a											12 02						13 57			
Lapworth	a								10 05					12 16							14 16
Dorridge	a								10 09		11 19			12 19	12 38		13 19		13 42		14 20
Solihull	a								10 14		11 26			12 25	12 44		13 25		13 47		14 26
Birmingham Moor Street	a								10 26		11 35			12 35	12 55		13 37		13 58		14 37
Birmingham Snow Hill	a								10 42		11 48			12 47	13 06		13 49		14 11		14 50
Rowley Regis	a																				
Cradley Heath	a																				
Stourbridge Junction [2]	a																				
Kidderminster	a																				

§ London Underground Limited (Central Line) also operate services between South Ruislip and West Ruislip at frequent intervals

A 3 October
B not 3 October

Table 115

Sundays
from 03 October

London - High Wycombe, Aylesbury, Banbury, Stratford-upon-Avon, Birmingham Snow Hill and Kidderminster

		CH	CH ◇	CH	CH	CH ◇	CH ◇	CH	CH ◇	CH	CH ◇	CH	CH	CH ◇	CH	CH	CH	CH	CH	CH	CH	CH ◇	CH
London Marylebone [10] ⊖	d	12 33	12 50	12 54	13 20	13 33	13 50	13 54	14 20	14 33	14 50	14 54	15 20	15 33	15 57	16 00	16 22	16 36	16 57	17 00	17 20	17 36	17 57
London Paddington [15] ⊖	d																						
Wembley Stadium	d	12 42		13 03		13 42		14 03		14 42		15 03		15 42		16 09		16 45		17 09		17 45	
Sudbury & Harrow Road	d																						
Sudbury Hill Harrow	d																						
Northolt Park	d			13 08				14 08				15 08				16 14				17 14			
South Ruislip § ⊖	d			13 12				14 12				15 12				16 18				17 18			
West Ruislip [3] § ⊖	d			13 15				14 15				15 15				16 21				17 21			
Denham	d			13 20				14 20				15 20				16 26				17 26			
Denham Golf Club	d			13 22								15 22								17 28			
Gerrards Cross [1]	d	12 56		13 25	13 41	13 56		14 24	14 41	14 56		15 25	15 41	15 56		16 30	16 43	16 59		17 31	17 41	17 59	
Seer Green	d			13 30				14 28				15 30				16 34				17 36			
Beaconsfield	d	13 02		13 33	13 47	14 02		14 32	14 47	15 02		15 33	15 47	16 02		16 38	16 49	17 05		17 39	17 47	18 05	
High Wycombe [1]	d	13 08		13 39	13 54	14 08		14 38	14 54	15 08		15 39	15 54	16 08		16 44	16 56	17 11		17 45	17 54	18 11	
Saunderton	d			13 46				14 45				15 46				16 51				17 52			
Princes Risborough [2]	d	13 18		13 51	14 04	14 18		14 50	15 04	15 18		15 51	16 04	16 18		16 56	17 06	17 21		17 57	18 04	18 21	
Monks Risborough	d			13 55				14 54				15 55				17 00				18 01			
Little Kimble	d			13 58				14 57				15 58				17 03				18 04			
Aylesbury	a			14 16				15 14				16 16				17 21				18 22			
Haddenham & Thame Parkway	d	13 25			14 11	14 25			15 11	15 25			16 11	16 25			17 13	17 28			18 11	18 28	
Bicester North [3]	d	13a42	13 45		14 25	14 40	14 45		15 25	15a42	15 45		16 25	16 40	16 52		17 27	17a47	17 52		18 25	18 42	18 52
Kings Sutton	d					14 53								16 53								18 53	
Banbury	d		14 02		14 41	15 00	15 05		15 40		16 02		16 41	17 00	17 07		17 43		18 09		18 41	19 00	19 09
Leamington Spa [8]	d		14 22		15 01	15 20	15 25		15 59		16 22		17 01	17 20	17 25		18 03		18 29		19 01	19 20	19 29
Warwick	d				15 05	15 24			16 03				17 05	17 24			18 07				19 05	19 24	
Warwick Parkway	d		14 27		15 09		15 31		16 06		16 27		17 09		17 31		18 10		18 34		19 09		19 34
Hatton	d					15 31			16 11					17 31			18 15					19 31	
Claverdon	d																						
Bearley	d																						
Wilmcote	d					15 43								17 43								19 43	
Stratford-upon-Avon	a					15 57								17 57								19 57	
Lapworth	a								16 16								18 20						
Dorridge	a		14 38		15 19		15 42		16 20		16 38		17 19		17 41		18 24		18 45		19 19		19 45
Solihull	a		14 44		15 25		15 47		16 26		16 44		17 25		17 48		18 31		18 51		19 27		19 51
Birmingham Moor Street	a		14 54		15 35		15 57		16 35		16 54		17 37		17 57		18 41		19 01		19 38		20 01
Birmingham Snow Hill	a		15 06		15 52		16 09		16 52		17 06		17 49		18 10		18 52		19 13		19 49		20 13
Rowley Regis	a																						
Cradley Heath	a																						
Stourbridge Junction [2]	a																						
Kidderminster	a																						

		CH	CH	CH	CH	CH	CH ◇	CH	CH	CH	CH ◇	CH ◇	CH	CH	CH ◇	CH	CH	CH	CH
London Marylebone [10] ⊖	d	18 00	18 20	18 36	18 57	19 00	19 22	19 36	19 57	20 00	20 20	20 50	21 10	21 40	22 00	22 10	22 45		23 45
London Paddington [15] ⊖	d																		
Wembley Stadium	d	18 09		18 45		19 09		19 45		20 09			21 19			22 19	22 54		23 54
Sudbury & Harrow Road	d																		
Sudbury Hill Harrow	d																		
Northolt Park	d	18 14				19 14				20 14			21 24			22 24	22 59		23 59
South Ruislip § ⊖	d	18 18				19 18				20 18			21 28			22 28	23 03		00 03
West Ruislip [3] § ⊖	d	18 21				19 21				20 21			21 31			22 31	23 06		00 06
Denham	d	18 26				19 26				20 26			21 36			22 36	23 11		00 11
Denham Golf Club	d					19 28							21 38				23 13		00 13
Gerrards Cross [1]	d	18 30	18 41	18 59		19 31	19 43	19 59		20 30	20 41	21 11	21 41	22 01		22 40	23 16		00 16
Seer Green	d	18 34				19 36				20 34			21 46			22 44	23 21		00 21
Beaconsfield	d	18 38	18 47	19 05		19 39	19 49	20 05		20 38	20 47	21 17	21 49	22 07		22 48	23 24		00 24
High Wycombe [1]	d	18 44	18 54	19 11		19 45	19 56	20 11		20 44	20 54	21 24	21 55	22 13		22 54	23 30		00 30
Saunderton	d	18 51				19 52				20 51			22 02			23 01	23 37		00 37
Princes Risborough [2]	d	18 56	19 04	19 21		19 57	20 07	20 21		20 56	21 04	21 34	22 07	22 24		23 06	23 43	23 48	00 43
Monks Risborough	d	19 00				20 01				21 00			22 11			23 10		23 51	
Little Kimble	d	19 03				20 04				21 03			22 14			23 13		23 55	
Aylesbury	a	19 20				20 22				21 21			22 32			23 30		00 09	
Haddenham & Thame Parkway	d		19 10	19 28			20 14	20 28			21 11	21 41		22 31			23 50		00 50
Bicester North [3]	d		19 23	19 42	19 52		20 27	20 42	20 52		21 25	21 55		22a48	22 51		00 04		01 04
Kings Sutton	d							20 53									00 16		
Banbury	d		19 46	20a05	20 09		20 44	21a07	21 09		21 41	22 11			23 06		00a28		01a27
Leamington Spa [8]	d		20 05		20 29		21 03		21 29		22 01	22 31			23 24				
Warwick	d		20 09				21 08				22 05	22 35			23 28				
Warwick Parkway	d		20 13		20 34		21 11		21 34		22 09	22 39			23 32				
Hatton	d											22 43							
Claverdon	d																		
Bearley	d																		
Wilmcote	d																		
Stratford-upon-Avon	a																		
Lapworth	a		20 21									22 48							
Dorridge	a		20 25		20 45		21 22		21 45		22 20	22 52			23 43				
Solihull	a		20 32		20 51		21 29		21 51		22 25	22 59			23 47				
Birmingham Moor Street	a		20 42		21 01		21 40		22 01		22 37	23 10			23 58				
Birmingham Snow Hill	a		20 56		21 13		21 51		22 13		22 48	23 21			00 11				
Rowley Regis	a																		
Cradley Heath	a																		
Stourbridge Junction [2]	a																		
Kidderminster	a																		

§ London Underground Limited (Central Line) also operate services between South Ruislip and West Ruislip at frequent intervals

Table 115

Mondays to Fridays
until 01 October

Kidderminster, Birmingham Snow Hill, Stratford-upon-Avon, Banbury, Aylesbury and High Wycombe - London

	CH	CH	CH	CH	CH	CH	CH	CH	CH	CH	CH	CH	CH	CH	CH	CH	CH	CH	CH	CH	CH	WS
								⌶					◇ ⌶									◇1 ⊐
Kidderminster d																						
Stourbridge Junction 2 d																						
Cradley Heath d																						
Rowley Regis d																						
Birmingham Snow Hill d													05 43									
Birmingham Moor Street d													05 46									
Solihull d													05 56									
Dorridge d													06 01									
Lapworth d																						
Stratford-upon-Avon d														06 10								
Wilmcote d														06 14								
Bearley d														06 20								
Claverdon d														06 25								
Hatton d														06 31								
Warwick Parkway d								05 40					06 12									
Warwick d													06 15	06 38								
Leamington Spa 8 d								05 45					06 20	06a45							06 55	07 29
Banbury d			05 24					06 03				06 25	06 38				06 53				07 18	07 48
Kings Sutton d			05 28									06 29										
Bicester North 3 d			05 40		05 54			06 17				06 42	06 53			06 59	07 10				07 33	
Haddenham & Thame Parkway d			05 53		06 07			06 30				06 55				07 12	07 23				07 46	
Aylesbury d	05 05	05 35		05 49			06 19			06 29										07 28		
Little Kimble d	05 13			05 57						06 37										07 36		
Monks Risborough d	05 17			06 01						06 41										07 40		
Princes Risborough 2 d	05 20	05 48	06 01	06 05	06 14		06 32	06 36		06 45		07 03				07 19	07 30			07 44	07 53	
Saunderton d	05 25			06 10						06 50						07 24						
High Wycombe 1 d	05 32	05 58	06 12	06 17	06 24	06 28	06 50		06 55	07 02	07 08	07 13			07 21	07 31		07 45	07 50	07 55		
Beaconsfield d	05 38	06 04	06 18	06 23		06 34	06 56		07 01	07 08		07 20			07 27	07 37			07 56	08 01		
Seer Green d	05 41	06 07				06 37					07 17				07 30					08 04		
Gerrards Cross 1 d	05 45	06 11	06 24	06 28		06 41	07 01		07 06	07 14	07 21				07 34	07 43		07 54	08 02			
Denham Golf Club d	05 48					06 44			07 09										08 05			
Denham d	05 50	06 15				06 46			07 12						07 38				08 08		08 16	
West Ruislip 3 § ⊖ d	05 55			06 37		06 51	07 08													08 14		
South Ruislip § ⊖ d	05 58		06 32	06 41					07 18						07 44				08 14			
Northolt Park d	06 02			06 44		06 56	07 13											08 04				
Sudbury Hill Harrow d						06 58																
Sudbury & Harrow Road d				06 48																		
Wembley Stadium d	06 07		06 39	06 51		07 02				07 28					07 51			08 09	08 21		08 26	
London Paddington 15 ⊖ a																						
London Marylebone 10 ⊖ a	06 21	06 39	06 51	07 07	06 58	07 15	07 29	07 18	07 36	07 41	07 47	07 50	07 53		08 05	08 08	08 11	08 25	08 34	08 37	08 40	08 57

	CH	CH	CH	CH	CH	CH	CH	CH	CH	CH	CH	CH	CH	CH	CH	CH	CH	CH	CH	CH	CH	CH
							◇ ⌶					⌶	◇ ⌶			◇ ⌶	◇				◇ ⌶	
Kidderminster d							06 30						06 56			07 30					08 09	
Stourbridge Junction 2 d							06 39						07 07			07 40					08 23	
Cradley Heath d							06 44						07 14			07 45					08 28	
Rowley Regis d							06 50						07 22			07 53					08 34	
Birmingham Snow Hill d							07 14						07 45			08 12					08 52	
Birmingham Moor Street d							07 17						07 48			08 15					08 55	
Solihull d							07 28						07 58			08 25					09 05	
Dorridge d							07 34						08 03			08 30					09 10	
Lapworth d													08 07									
Stratford-upon-Avon d			06 46					07 36														
Wilmcote d								07 40														
Bearley d								07 46														
Claverdon d								07 51														
Hatton d			07 03					07 56					08 13									
Warwick Parkway d			07 09				07 47						08 19			08 41					09 21	
Warwick d			07 13				07 50	08 05					08 23			08 44					09 24	
Leamington Spa 8 d			07 18				07 54	08a11					08 27			08 49					09 29	
Banbury d			07 36			08 00	08 12						08 45			09 10	09 15				09 47	
Kings Sutton d													08 50				09 19					
Bicester North 3 d		07 40	07 51			08 14	08 26					08 47	09 00		09 12		09 31			09 47	10 04	
Haddenham & Thame Parkway d		07 53	08 03			08 25	08 37					09 00	09 12		09 25		09 44			10 00		
Aylesbury d				08 02							08 44							09 40				
Little Kimble d				08 10							08 52							09 48				
Monks Risborough d				08 14							08 56							09 52				
Princes Risborough 2 d		07 59		08a21		08 31				08 56	09a01	09 08			09 32		09 51	09a59		10 06		
Saunderton d		08 04				08 36				09 01					09 37							
High Wycombe 1 d		08 11			08 31	08 43			08 55	09 08		09 18		09 32	09 44	09 51	10 01		10 04	10 17		10 30
Beaconsfield d		08 17			08 37	08 49			09 01	09 14		09 24		09 38	09 50				10 10	10 23		10 36
Seer Green d					08 40					09 17				09 41					10 13			10 39
Gerrards Cross 1 d	08 17	08 22			08 45	08 55			09 06	09 21		09 30		09 46	09 55				10 17	10 29		10 43
Denham Golf Club d									09 09					09 49								10 46
Denham d	08 21				08 49				09 12						09 59				10 21			10 48
West Ruislip 3 § ⊖ d	08 41								09 16					09 54								10 56
South Ruislip § ⊖ d						09 04				09 29					10 05				10 27			
Northolt Park d	08 46								09 21					09 59					10 30			11 01
Sudbury Hill Harrow d	08 48								09 24										10 33			
Sudbury & Harrow Road d	08 51								09 26													
Wembley Stadium d						09 11			09 29					10 04					10 37			11 06
London Paddington 15 ⊖ a																						
London Marylebone 10 ⊖ a	09 09	08 48	08 51		09 13	09 25	09 27		09 44	09 48		09 55	09 59	10 18	10 25	10 28	10 38		10 52	10 55	10 59	11 25

§ London Underground Limited (Central Line) also operate services between South Ruislip and West Ruislip at frequent intervals

Table 115

Mondays to Fridays
until 01 October

Kidderminster, Birmingham Snow Hill, Stratford-upon-Avon, Banbury, Aylesbury and High Wycombe - London

	CH	CH	CH	CH	CH	CH	CH	CH	CH	CH	CH	CH	CH	CH	CH	CH	CH	CH	CH	CH	CH	CH
		◇			◇	◇		◇	◇				◇			◇						
Kidderminster d																						
Stourbridge Junction 2 d																						
Cradley Heath d																						
Rowley Regis d																						
Birmingham Snow Hill d		09 12				09 52			10 12				10 52			11 12				11 52		
Birmingham Moor Street d		09 15				09 55			10 15				10 55			11 15				11 55		
Solihull d		09 25				10 05			10 25				11 05			11 25				12 05		
Dorridge d		09 30				10 10			10 30				11 10			11 30				12 10		
Lapworth d		09 34							10 34													
Stratford-upon-Avon d					09 36														11 40			
Wilmcote d					09 40																	
Bearley d					09 46																	
Claverdon d					09 51														11 51			
Hatton d		09 40			09 57				10 40										11 57			
Warwick Parkway d		09 45			10 01	10 21			10 45				11 21			11 41				12 21		
Warwick d		09 49			10 04	10 24			10 49				11 24			11 45			12 04	12 24		
Leamington Spa 8 d		09 54			10 09	10 29			10 54				11 29			11 52			12 09	12 29		
Banbury d		10 12			10 28	10 47			11 12				11 47			12 09			12 28	12 47		
Kings Sutton d					10 33														12 33			
Bicester North 3 d		10 28			10 45	11 04		11 16	11 28			11 47	12 04			12 24			12 45	13 04		13 16
Haddenham & Thame Parkway d		10 40			10 58			11 29	11 40			12 00				12 36			12 58			13 29
Aylesbury d			10 38							11 39							12 38					
Little Kimble d			10 46							11 47							12 46					
Monks Risborough d			10 50							11 51							12 50					
Princes Risborough 2 d	10 38	10 47	10a56		11 06			11 36	11 47	11a58		12 06			12 36	12 43	12a56		13 06			13 36
Saunderton d	10 43							11 41							12 41							13 41
High Wycombe 1 d	10 49	10 57		11 02	11 17		11 32	11 47	11 57		12 02	12 17		12 32	12 47	12 53		13 02	13 17		13 32	13 47
Beaconsfield d	10 55			11 08	11 23		11 38	11 54			12 08	12 23		12 38	12 54			13 08	13 23		13 38	13 54
Seer Green d				11 11			11 41				12 11			12 41				13 11			13 41	
Gerrards Cross 1 d	11 01			11 15	11 29		11 45	11 59			12 15	12 29		12 45	12 59			13 15	13 29		13 45	13 59
Denham Golf Club d							11 48							12 48							13 48	
Denham d				11 19			11 50				12 19			12 50				13 19			13 50	
West Ruislip 3 § ⊖ d							11 55							12 55							13 55	
South Ruislip § ⊖ d				11 25							12 25							13 25				
Northolt Park d				11 28			12 00				12 28			13 00				13 28			14 00	
Sudbury Hill Harrow d				11 31							12 31							13 31				
Sudbury & Harrow Road d																						
Wembley Stadium d				11 35			12 05				12 35			13 05				13 35			14 05	
London Paddington 15 ⊖ a																						
London Marylebone 10 ⊖ a	11 29	11 32		11 49	11 58	12 02	12 19	12 25	12 31		12 48	12 55	12 59	13 18	13 25	13 29		13 49	13 55	13 59	14 18	14 25

	CH	CH	CH	CH	CH	WS	CH	CH	CH	CH	CH	CH	CH	CH	CH	CH	CH	CH	CH	CH	CH	CH	CH	CH
	◇				◇	◇1 ⊐			◇			◇	◇		◇	◇			◇	◇			◇	
Kidderminster d																								
Stourbridge Junction 2 d																								
Cradley Heath d																								
Rowley Regis d																								
Birmingham Snow Hill d	12 12				12 52				13 12				13 52			14 12				14 52			15 12	
Birmingham Moor Street d	12 15				12 55				13 15				13 55			14 15				14 55			15 15	
Solihull d	12 25				13 05				13 25				14 05			14 25				15 05			15 25	
Dorridge d	12 30				13 10				13 30				14 10			14 30				15 10			15 30	
Lapworth d	12 34															14 34								
Stratford-upon-Avon d																			14 36					
Wilmcote d																			14 40					
Bearley d																			14 46					
Claverdon d																			14 51					
Hatton d	12 40															14 40			14 57					
Warwick Parkway d	12 45				13 21				13 41				14 21			14 45				15 21			15 41	
Warwick d	12 49				13 24				13 45				14 24			14 49			15 04	15 24			15 44	
Leamington Spa 8 d	12 54				13 29	13 46			13 52				14 29			14 54			15 09	15 29			15 49	
Banbury d	13 12				13 47	14 04			14 09				14 47		15 00	15 12			15 28	15 47			16 07	
Kings Sutton d																			15 33					
Bicester North 3 d	13 28			13 47	14 04				14 24			14 47	15 04		15 16	15 28			15 44	16 04			16 24	
Haddenham & Thame Parkway d	13 40			14 00					14 36			15 00			15 29	15 40			15 57				16 36	
Aylesbury d		13 41								14 38							15 38							16 39
Little Kimble d		13 49								14 46							15 46							16 47
Monks Risborough d		13 53								14 50							15 50							16 51
Princes Risborough 2 d	13 47	13a59		14 06				14 38	14 43	14a56		15 06			15 36	15 47	15a56		16 04			16 36	16 43	16a57
Saunderton d								14 43							15 41							16 41		
High Wycombe 1 d	13 57		14 02	14 17			14 32	14 49	14 53		15 02	15 17		15 32	15 47	15 57		16 02	16 15		16 32	16 47	16 53	
Beaconsfield d			14 08	14 23			14 38	14 55			15 08	15 23		15 38	15 54			16 08	16 21		16 38	16 54		
Seer Green d			14 11				14 41				15 11			15 41				16 11			16 41			
Gerrards Cross 1 d			14 15	14 29			14 45	15 01			15 15	15 29		15 45	15 59			16 15	16 27		16 45	16 59		
Denham Golf Club d							14 48							15 48							16 48			
Denham d			14 19				14 50				15 19			15 50				16 19			16 50			
West Ruislip 3 § ⊖ d							14 55							15 55							16 55			
South Ruislip § ⊖ d			14 25								15 25							16 25						
Northolt Park d			14 28				15 00				15 28			16 00				16 28			17 00			
Sudbury Hill Harrow d			14 31								15 31							16 31						
Sudbury & Harrow Road d																								
Wembley Stadium d			14 35				15 05				15 35			16 05				16 35			17 05			
London Paddington 15 ⊖ a																								
London Marylebone 10 ⊖ a	14 31		14 48	14 55	14 59	15 15	15 23	15 26	15 29		15 48	15 55	16 02	16 18	16 26	16 32		16 51	16 54	17 02	17 21	17 25	17 31	

§ London Underground Limited (Central Line) also operate services between South Ruislip and West Ruislip at frequent intervals

Table 115

Mondays to Fridays
until 01 October

Kidderminster, Birmingham Snow Hill, Stratford-upon-Avon, Banbury, Aylesbury and High Wycombe - London

	CH	CH	CH		CH	CH	CH	CH	CH	CH	CH	CH	CH	CH	CH	CH	CH	CH	CH	CH	CH	CH	CH
		◇	◇			◇									◇								◇
Kidderminster d																							
Stourbridge Junction 2 d																							
Cradley Heath d																							
Rowley Regis d																							
Birmingham Snow Hill ⇌ d			15 52					16 12				16 52			17 10				17 52				18 12
Birmingham Moor Street d			15 55					16 15				16 55			17 13				17 55				18 15
Solihull d			16 05					16 25				17 05			17 23				18 05				18 25
Dorridge d			16 10					16 30				17 10			17 30				18 12				18 30
Lapworth d								16 34							17 34								18 34
Stratford-upon-Avon d																17 40							
Wilmcote d																							
Bearley d																							
Claverdon d																							
Hatton d								16 40							17 40								18 40
Warwick Parkway d			16 21					16 45				17 20			17 45				18 23				18 45
Warwick d			16 24					16 49				17 23			17 49	18 04			18 26				18 49
Leamington Spa 8 d			16 29					16 54				17 28			17 54	18 08			18 30				18 54
Banbury d			16 47					17 12				17 46			18 12	18 26			18 48				19 12
Kings Sutton d												17 51											19 17
Bicester North 3 d		16 44	17 04			17 17		17 27				18 02			18 28	18 41		18 48	19 04			19 25	19 30
Haddenham & Thame Parkway d		16 57				17 30		17 39				18 14			18 40			19 02					19 42
Aylesbury d							17 23						18 08							19 20			
Little Kimble d							17 31						18 16										
Monks Risborough d							17 35						18 20							19 31			
Princes Risborough 2 d		17 06				17 37	17a42	17 46	17 51		18 15		18 24		18 47			19 10		19a38		19 43	19 49
Saunderton d		17 12				17 42							18 29									19 48	
High Wycombe 1 d	17 05	17 19	17 26		17 38	17 48		17 56	18 01	18 06	18 25	18 30	18 35	18 47	18 57		19 06	19 20	19 28		19 36	19 55	20 00
Beaconsfield d	17 11	17 25			17 44	17 55			18 07	18 12	18 31		18 41	18 53			19 12	19 26			19 42	20 01	
Seer Green d	17 14				17 47					18 15				18 56			19 15				19 45		
Gerrards Cross 1 d	17 18	17 30			17 51	18 00			18 13	18 19	18 36		18 47	19 00			19 19	19 31			19 49	20 06	
Denham Golf Club d	17 21									18 22							19 22						
Denham d	17 23				17 55					18 24			18 51	19 04			19 24				19 53		
West Ruislip 3 § ⊖ d					17 59				18 19				18 57								19 57		
South Ruislip § ⊖ d	17 29									18 30				19 10			19 30						
Northolt Park d	17 33				18 04					18 34			19 02				19 34				20 02		
Sudbury Hill Harrow d	17 35									18 36							19 36						
Sudbury & Harrow Road d																							
Wembley Stadium d	17 39				18 09				18 28				19 07	19 17			19 40				20 07		
London Paddington 15 ⊖ a																							
London Marylebone 10 ⊖ a	17 53	17 55	18 04		18 23	18 27		18 33	18 41	18 52	19 02	19 08	19 24	19 30	19 35	19 39	19 55	19 58	20 06		20 21	20 31	20 37

	CH	CH	CH	CH	CH	CH	CH	CH	CH		CH	CH	CH
		◇				◇	◇		◇		◇		
Kidderminster d													
Stourbridge Junction 2 d													
Cradley Heath d													
Rowley Regis d													
Birmingham Snow Hill ⇌ d				19 12			20 12		21 15				
Birmingham Moor Street d				19 15			20 15		21 18				
Solihull d				19 25			20 25		21 27				
Dorridge d				19 32			20 32		21 33				
Lapworth d				19 36			20 36		21 37				
Stratford-upon-Avon d						19 48							23 00
Wilmcote d						19 53							
Bearley d						19 59							
Claverdon d						20 04							
Hatton d				19 42		20 10	20 42		21 42				
Warwick Parkway d				19 47		20 16	20 47		21 47				
Warwick d				19 50		20 19	20 50		21 51				23 21
Leamington Spa 8 d				19 54		20 24	20 54		21 55				23 25
Banbury d		19 44		20 12		20 44	21 12		22 15				23 44
Kings Sutton d						20 49			22 20				
Bicester North 3 d		19 59		20 27		21 02	21 27		22 32		22 39		
Haddenham & Thame Parkway d		20 10		20 39		21 16	21 39		22 43				
Aylesbury d			20 16					21 37				23 00	
Little Kimble d			20 24					21 45				23 08	
Monks Risborough d			20 28					21 49				23 12	
Princes Risborough 2 d		20 17	20 31	20 46		21 23	21 46	21 52	22 49		22 56	23 15	
Saunderton d			20 36					21 57			23 01		
High Wycombe 1 d	20 06	20 27	20 43	20 56	21 06	21 33	21 56	22 06	22 59		23 09	23 25	
Beaconsfield d	20 12	20 33	20 49		21 12	21 39		22 12			23 15	23 31	
Seer Green d	20 15				21 15			22 15			23 18		
Gerrards Cross 1 d	20 19	20 38	20 54		21 19	21 44		22 19			23 22	23 37	
Denham Golf Club d	20 22				21 22			22 22			23 25		
Denham d	20 24				21 24			22 24			23 27		
West Ruislip 3 § ⊖ d	20 29				21 29			22 29			23 32		
South Ruislip § ⊖ d	20 32				21 32			22 32			23 35		
Northolt Park d	20 36				21 36			22 36			23 39		
Sudbury Hill Harrow d													
Sudbury & Harrow Road d													
Wembley Stadium d	20 41	20 53		21 18	21 41		22 18	22 41	23 20		23 44	23 50	
London Paddington 15 ⊖ a													
London Marylebone 10 ⊖ a	20 55	21 08	21 19	21 32	21 54	22 11	22 32	22 55	23 34		23 58	00 04	

§ London Underground Limited (Central Line) also operate services between South Ruislip and West Ruislip at frequent intervals

Table 115

Mondays to Fridays
from 04 October

Kidderminster, Birmingham Snow Hill, Stratford-upon-Avon, Banbury, Aylesbury and High Wycombe - London

	CH	CH	CH	CH	CH	CH	CH		CH	CH	CH	CH	CH	CH	CH	CH	CH		CH	CH	CH	CH	CH
									H					◇ H									
Kidderminster d																							
Stourbridge Junction 2 d																							
Cradley Heath d																							
Rowley Regis d																							
Birmingham Snow Hill ⇌ d														05 43									
Birmingham Moor Street d														05 46									
Solihull d														05 56									
Dorridge d														06 01									
Lapworth d																							
Stratford-upon-Avon d															06 10								
Wilmcote d															06 14								
Bearley d															06 20								
Claverdon d															06 25								
Hatton d															06 31								
Warwick Parkway d									05 40					06 12									
Warwick d														06 15	06 38								
Leamington Spa 8 d									05 45					06 20	06a48								06 55
Banbury d			05 24						06 03				06 25	06 38					06 53				07 18
Kings Sutton d			05 28										06 29										
Bicester North 3 d			05 40		05 54				06 17				06 42	06 53			06 59		07 10				07 33
Haddenham & Thame Parkway d			05 53		06 07				06 30				06 55				07 12		07 23				07 46
Aylesbury d	05 02	05 35		05 49			06 19				06 29											07 28	
Little Kimble d	05 10			05 57							06 37											07 36	
Monks Risborough d	05 14			06 01							06 41											07 40	
Princes Risborough 2 d	05 18	05 48	06 01	06 05	06 14		06 32		06 36		06 45		07 03				07 19		07 30			07 44	07 53
Saunderton d	05 23			06 10							06 50						07 24						
High Wycombe 1 d	05 30	05 58	06 12	06 17	06 24	06 28	06 50			06 55	07 02	07 08	07 13			07 21	07 31			07 45	07 50	07 55	
Beaconsfield d	05 37	06 04	06 18	06 23		06 34	06 56			07 01	07 08		07 20			07 27	07 37				07 56	08 01	
Seer Green d	05 40	06 07				06 37						07 17				07 30						08 04	
Gerrards Cross 1 d	05 45	06 11	06 24	06 28		06 41	07 01			07 06	07 14	07 21				07 34	07 43			07 54	08 02		
Denham Golf Club d	05 48					06 44				07 09											08 05		
Denham d	05 50	06 15				06 46				07 12						07 38					08 08		08 16
West Ruislip 3 § ⊖ d	05 55			06 37		06 51	07 08															08 14	
South Ruislip § ⊖ d	05 58		06 32	06 41						07 18						07 44					08 14		
Northolt Park d	06 02			06 44		06 56	07 13													08 04			
Sudbury Hill Harrow d						06 58																	
Sudbury & Harrow Road d				06 48																			
Wembley Stadium d	06 07		06 39	06 51		07 02					07 28					07 51				08 09	08 21		08 26
London Paddington 15 ⊖ a																							
London Marylebone 10 ⊖ a	06 24	06 42	06 54	07 10	07 01	07 18	07 32		07 21	07 39	07 44	07 50	07 53	07 56		08 08	08 11		08 14	08 28	08 37	08 40	08 43

	CH	CH	CH	CH		CH	CH	CH	CH	CH	CH	CH		CH	CH	CH	CH	CH	CH	CH	CH	CH	CH
								◇ H						H	◇ H			◇ H	◇				◇ H
Kidderminster d								06 30							06 56			07 30					08 09
Stourbridge Junction 2 d								06 39							07 07			07 40					08 23
Cradley Heath d								06 44							07 14			07 45					08 28
Rowley Regis d								06 50							07 22			07 53					08 34
Birmingham Snow Hill ⇌ d								07 14							07 45			08 12					08 52
Birmingham Moor Street d								07 17							07 48			08 15					08 55
Solihull d								07 28							07 58			08 25					09 05
Dorridge d								07 34							08 03			08 30					09 10
Lapworth d															08 07								
Stratford-upon-Avon d			06 46						07 36														
Wilmcote d									07 40														
Bearley d									07 46														
Claverdon d									07 51														
Hatton d			07 03						07 56						08 13								
Warwick Parkway d			07 09					07 47							08 19			08 41					09 21
Warwick d			07 13					07 50	08 05						08 23			08 44					09 24
Leamington Spa 8 d			07 18					07 54	08a14						08 27			08 49					09 29
Banbury d			07 36				08 00	08 12							08 45			09 10	09 15				09 47
Kings Sutton d															08 50				09 19				
Bicester North 3 d		07 40	07 51				08 14	08 26						08 47	09 00		09 12		09 31			09 47	10 04
Haddenham & Thame Parkway d		07 53	08 03				08 25	08 37						09 00	09 12		09 25		09 44			10 00	
Aylesbury d				08 02								08 44								09 40			
Little Kimble d				08 10								08 52								09 48			
Monks Risborough d				08 14								08 56								09 52			
Princes Risborough 2 d		07 59		08a24			08 31				08 56	09a01		09 08			09 32		09 51	09a59		10 06	
Saunderton d		08 04					08 36				09 01						09 37						
High Wycombe 1 d		08 11				08 31	08 43			08 55	09 08			09 18		09 32	09 44	09 51	10 01		10 04	10 17	
Beaconsfield d		08 17				08 37	08 49			09 01	09 14			09 24		09 38	09 50				10 10	10 23	
Seer Green d						08 40					09 17					09 41					10 13		
Gerrards Cross 1 d	08 17	08 22				08 45	08 55			09 06	09 21			09 30		09 46	09 55				10 17	10 29	
Denham Golf Club d										09 09						09 49							
Denham d	08 21					08 49				09 12							09 59				10 21		
West Ruislip 3 § ⊖ d	08 41									09 16						09 54							
South Ruislip § ⊖ d							09 04				09 29						10 05				10 27		
Northolt Park d	08 46									09 21						09 59					10 30		
Sudbury Hill Harrow d	08 48									09 24											10 33		
Sudbury & Harrow Road d	08 51									09 26													
Wembley Stadium d							09 11			09 29						10 04					10 37		
London Paddington 15 ⊖ a																							
London Marylebone 10 ⊖ a	09 12	08 51	08 54			09 16	09 28	09 30		09 47	09 51			09 58	09 59	10 21	10 28	10 31	10 41		10 55	10 58	11 02

§ London Underground Limited (Central Line) also operate services between South Ruislip and West Ruislip at frequent intervals

Table 115

Mondays to Fridays
from 04 October

Kidderminster, Birmingham Snow Hill, Stratford-upon-Avon, Banbury, Aylesbury and High Wycombe - London

		CH	CH ◇	CH	CH	CH ◇	CH ◇	CH	CH ◇	CH ◇	CH	CH	CH	CH ◇	CH	CH	CH ◇	CH	CH	CH	CH	CH
Kidderminster	d																					
Stourbridge Junction 2	d																					
Cradley Heath	d																					
Rowley Regis	d																					
Birmingham Snow Hill	d		09 12				09 52			10 12				10 52			11 12				11 52	
Birmingham Moor Street	d		09 15				09 55			10 15				10 55			11 15				11 55	
Solihull	d		09 25				10 05			10 25				11 05			11 25				12 05	
Dorridge	d		09 30				10 10			10 30				11 10			11 30				12 10	
Lapworth	d		09 34							10 34												
Stratford-upon-Avon	d					09 36														11 40		
Wilmcote	d					09 40																
Bearley	d					09 46																
Claverdon	d					09 51														11 51		
Hatton	d		09 40			09 57				10 40										11 57		
Warwick Parkway	d		09 45			10 01	10 21			10 45				11 21			11 41				12 21	
Warwick	d		09 49			10 04	10 24			10 49				11 24			11 45			12 04	12 24	
Leamington Spa 8	d		09 54			10 09	10 29			10 54				11 29			11 52			12 09	12 29	
Banbury	d		10 12			10 28	10 47			11 12				11 47			12 09			12 28	12 47	
Kings Sutton	d					10 33														12 33		
Bicester North 3	d		10 28			10 45	11 04		11 16	11 28			11 47	12 04			12 24			12 45	13 04	
Haddenham & Thame Parkway	d		10 40			10 58			11 29	11 40			12 00				12 36			12 58		
Aylesbury	d			10 38							11 39							12 38				
Little Kimble	d			10 46							11 47							12 46				
Monks Risborough	d			10 50							11 51							12 50				
Princes Risborough 2	d	10 38	10 47	10a59		11 06			11 36	11 47	12a01		12 06			12 36	12 43	12a59		13 06		
Saunderton	d	10 43							11 41							12 41						
High Wycombe 1	d	10 49	10 57		11 02	11 17		11 32	11 47	11 57		12 02	12 17		12 32	12 47	12 53		13 02	13 17		13 32
Beaconsfield	d	10 55			11 08	11 23		11 38	11 54			12 08	12 23		12 38	12 54			13 08	13 23		13 38
Seer Green	d				11 11			11 41				12 11			12 41				13 11			13 41
Gerrards Cross 1	d	11 01			11 15	11 29		11 45	11 59			12 15	12 29		12 45	12 59			13 15	13 29		13 45
Denham Golf Club	d							11 48							12 48							13 48
Denham	d				11 19			11 50				12 19			12 50				13 19			13 50
West Ruislip 3 § ⊖	d							11 55							12 55							13 55
South Ruislip § ⊖	d				11 25							12 25							13 25			
Northolt Park	d				11 28			12 00				12 28			13 00				13 28			14 00
Sudbury Hill Harrow	d				11 31							12 31							13 31			
Sudbury & Harrow Road	d																					
Wembley Stadium	d				11 35			12 05				12 35			13 05				13 35			14 05
London Paddington 15 ⊖	a																					
London Marylebone 10 ⊖	a	11 32	11 35		11 52	12 01	12 05	12 22	12 28	12 34		12 51	12 58	13 02	13 21	13 28	13 32		13 52	13 58	14 02	14 21

		CH	CH ◇	CH	CH	CH	CH ◇	CH	CH ◇	CH	CH	CH ◇	CH ◇	CH	CH ◇	CH ◇	CH	CH	CH ◇	CH ◇	CH	CH	CH ◇
Kidderminster	d																						
Stourbridge Junction 2	d																						
Cradley Heath	d																						
Rowley Regis	d																						
Birmingham Snow Hill	d		12 12				12 52		13 12				13 52			14 12				14 52			15 12
Birmingham Moor Street	d		12 15				12 55		13 15				13 55			14 15				14 55			15 15
Solihull	d		12 25				13 05		13 25				14 05			14 25				15 05			15 25
Dorridge	d		12 30				13 10		13 30				14 10			14 30				15 10			15 30
Lapworth	d		12 34													14 34							
Stratford-upon-Avon	d																		14 36				
Wilmcote	d																		14 40				
Bearley	d																		14 46				
Claverdon	d																		14 51				
Hatton	d		12 40													14 40			14 57				
Warwick Parkway	d		12 45				13 21		13 41				14 21			14 45				15 21			15 41
Warwick	d		12 49				13 24		13 45				14 24			14 49			15 04	15 24			15 44
Leamington Spa 8	d		12 54				13 29		13 52				14 29			14 54			15 09	15 29			15 49
Banbury	d		13 12				13 47		14 09				14 47		15 00	15 12			15 28	15 47			16 07
Kings Sutton	d																		15 33				
Bicester North 3	d	13 16	13 28			13 47	14 04		14 24			14 47	15 04		15 16	15 28			15 44	16 04			16 24
Haddenham & Thame Parkway	d	13 29	13 40			14 00			14 36			15 00			15 29	15 40			15 57				16 36
Aylesbury	d			13 41						14 38							15 38						
Little Kimble	d			13 49						14 46							15 46						
Monks Risborough	d			13 53						14 50							15 50						
Princes Risborough 2	d	13 36	13 47	14a00		14 06		14 38	14 43	14a59		15 06			15 36	15 47	15a59		16 04			16 36	16 43
Saunderton	d	13 41						14 43							15 41							16 41	
High Wycombe 1	d	13 47	13 57		14 02	14 17		14 49	14 53		15 02	15 17		15 32	15 47	15 57		16 02	16 15		16 32	16 47	16 53
Beaconsfield	d	13 54			14 08	14 23		14 55			15 08	15 23		15 38	15 54			16 08	16 21		16 38	16 54	
Seer Green	d				14 11						15 11			15 41				16 11			16 41		
Gerrards Cross 1	d	13 59			14 15	14 29		15 01			15 15	15 29		15 45	15 59			16 15	16 27		16 45	16 59	
Denham Golf Club	d													15 48							16 48		
Denham	d				14 19						15 19			15 50				16 19			16 50		
West Ruislip 3 § ⊖	d													15 55							16 55		
South Ruislip § ⊖	d				14 25						15 25							16 25					
Northolt Park	d				14 28						15 28			16 00				16 28			17 00		
Sudbury Hill Harrow	d				14 31						15 31							16 31					
Sudbury & Harrow Road	d																						
Wembley Stadium	d				14 35						15 35			16 05				16 35			17 05		
London Paddington 15 ⊖	a																						
London Marylebone 10 ⊖	a	14 28	14 34		14 51	14 58	15 02	15 29	15 32		15 51	15 58	16 05	16 21	16 29	16 35		16 54	16 57	17 05	17 24	17 28	17 34

§ London Underground Limited (Central Line) also operate services between South Ruislip and West Ruislip at frequent intervals

Table 115

Mondays to Fridays
from 04 October

Kidderminster, Birmingham Snow Hill, Stratford-upon-Avon, Banbury, Aylesbury and High Wycombe - London

		CH	CH	CH ◇	CH ◇	CH	CH ◇	CH	CH	CH	CH	CH	CH	CH	CH ◇	CH	CH	CH	CH	CH	CH	CH
Kidderminster	d																					
Stourbridge Junction 2	d																					
Cradley Heath	d																					
Rowley Regis	d																					
Birmingham Snow Hill	d				15 52				16 12				16 52		17 10				17 52			
Birmingham Moor Street	d				15 55				16 15				16 55		17 13				17 55			
Solihull	d				16 05				16 25				17 05		17 23				18 05			
Dorridge	d				16 10				16 30				17 10		17 30				18 12			
Lapworth	d								16 34						17 34							
Stratford-upon-Avon	d															17 40						
Wilmcote	d																					
Bearley	d																					
Claverdon	d																					
Hatton	d								16 40						17 40							
Warwick Parkway	d				16 21				16 45				17 20		17 45				18 23			
Warwick	d				16 24				16 49				17 23		17 49	18 04			18 26			
Leamington Spa 8	d				16 29				16 54				17 28		17 54	18 08			18 30			
Banbury	d				16 47				17 12				17 46		18 12	18 26			18 48			
Kings Sutton	d												17 51									
Bicester North 3	d			16 44	17 04		17 17		17 27				18 02		18 28	18 41		18 48	19 04			19 25
Haddenham & Thame Parkway	d			16 57			17 30		17 39				18 14		18 40			19 02				
Aylesbury	d	16 39						17 23												19 20		
Little Kimble	d	16 47						17 31														
Monks Risborough	d	16 51						17 35												19 31		
Princes Risborough 2	d	17a00		17 06			17 37	17a42	17 46	17 51		18 15			18 47			19 10		19a41		19 43
Saunderton	d			17 12			17 42															19 48
High Wycombe 1	d		17 05	17 19	17 26	17 38	17 48		17 56	18 01	18 06	18 25	18 30	18 47	18 57		19 06	19 20	19 28		19 36	19 55
Beaconsfield	d		17 11	17 25		17 44	17 55			18 07	18 12	18 31		18 53			19 12	19 26			19 42	20 01
Seer Green	d		17 14			17 47					18 15			18 56			19 15				19 45	
Gerrards Cross 1	d		17 18	17 30		17 51	18 00			18 13	18 19	18 36		19 00			19 19	19 31			19 49	20 06
Denham Golf Club	d		17 21								18 22						19 22					
Denham	d		17 23			17 55					18 24			19 04			19 24				19 53	
West Ruislip 3 § ⊖	d					17 59				18 19											19 57	
South Ruislip § ⊖	d		17 29								18 30			19 10			19 30					
Northolt Park	d		17 33			18 04					18 34						19 34				20 02	
Sudbury Hill Harrow	d		17 35								18 36						19 36					
Sudbury & Harrow Road	d																					
Wembley Stadium	d		17 39			18 09				18 28				19 17			19 40				20 07	
London Paddington 15 ⊖	a																					
London Marylebone 10 ⊖	a		17 56	17 58	18 07	18 26	18 30		18 36	18 44	18 55	19 05	19 11	19 33	19 38	19 42	19 58	20 01	20 09		20 24	20 34

		CH ◇	CH	CH ◇	CH	CH	CH	CH ◇	CH ◇	CH	CH ◇	CH ◇	CH	CH
Kidderminster	d													
Stourbridge Junction 2	d													
Cradley Heath	d													
Rowley Regis	d													
Birmingham Snow Hill	d	18 12				19 12			20 12		21 15			
Birmingham Moor Street	d	18 15				19 15			20 15		21 18			
Solihull	d	18 25				19 25			20 25		21 27			
Dorridge	d	18 30				19 32			20 32		21 33			
Lapworth	d	18 34				19 36			20 36		21 37			
Stratford-upon-Avon	d							19 48						23 00
Wilmcote	d							19 53						
Bearley	d							19 59						
Claverdon	d							20 04						
Hatton	d	18 40				19 42		20 10	20 42		21 42			
Warwick Parkway	d	18 45				19 47		20 16	20 47		21 47			
Warwick	d	18 49				19 50		20 19	20 50		21 51			23 21
Leamington Spa 8	d	18 54				19 54		20 24	20 54		21 55			23 25
Banbury	d	19 12		19 44		20 12		20 44	21 12		22 15			23 44
Kings Sutton	d	19 17						20 49			22 20			
Bicester North 3	d	19 30		19 59		20 27		21 02	21 27		22 32	22 39		
Haddenham & Thame Parkway	d	19 42		20 10		20 39		21 16	21 39		22 43			
Aylesbury	d				20 16					21 37			23 00	
Little Kimble	d				20 24					21 45			23 08	
Monks Risborough	d				20 28					21 49			23 12	
Princes Risborough 2	d	19 49		20 17	20 31	20 46		21 23	21 46	21 52	22 49	22 56	23 15	
Saunderton	d				20 36					21 57		23 01		
High Wycombe 1	d	20 00	20 06	20 27	20 43	20 56	21 06	21 33	21 56	22 06	22 59	23 09	23 25	
Beaconsfield	d		20 12	20 33	20 49		21 12	21 39		22 12		23 15	23 31	
Seer Green	d		20 15				21 15			22 15		23 18		
Gerrards Cross 1	d		20 19	20 38	20 54		21 19	21 44		22 19		23 22	23 37	
Denham Golf Club	d		20 22				21 22			22 22		23 25		
Denham	d		20 24				21 24			22 24		23 27		
West Ruislip 3 § ⊖	d		20 29				21 29			22 29		23 32		
South Ruislip § ⊖	d		20 32				21 32			22 32		23 35		
Northolt Park	d		20 36				21 36			22 36		23 39		
Sudbury Hill Harrow	d													
Sudbury & Harrow Road	d													
Wembley Stadium	d		20 41	20 53		21 18	21 41		22 18	22 41	23 20	23 44	23 50	
London Paddington 15 ⊖	a													
London Marylebone 10 ⊖	a	20 40	20 58	21 11	21 22	21 35	21 57	22 14	22 35	22 58	23 37	00 01	00 07	

§ London Underground Limited (Central Line) also operate services between South Ruislip and West Ruislip at frequent intervals

Table 115

Saturdays
until 02 October

Kidderminster, Birmingham Snow Hill, Stratford-upon-Avon, Banbury, Aylesbury and High Wycombe - London

		CH	CH	CH	CH	CH	CH	CH	CH	CH	CH	CH	CH	CH	CH	CH	CH	CH	CH	CH	CH	CH	CH
							◇	◇		◇		◇		◇					◇				◇
Kidderminster	d									06 37													09 03
Stourbridge Junction	d									06 45													09 15
Cradley Heath	d									06 50													09 21
Rowley Regis	d									06 56													09 27
Birmingham Snow Hill	d						06 12	06 36		07 12				08 12					09 12				09 52
Birmingham Moor Street	d						06 15	06 39		07 15				08 15					09 15				09 55
Solihull	d						06 25	06 49		07 25				08 25					09 25				10 05
Dorridge	d						06 31	06 54		07 31				08 32					09 31				10 11
Lapworth	d									07 35				08 36					09 35				
Stratford-upon-Avon	d											07 35										09 36	
Wilmcote	d																					09 41	
Bearley	d																					09 47	
Claverdon	d											07 47										09 52	
Hatton	d									07 41		07 57		08 42								09 57	
Warwick Parkway	d						06 41	07 05		07 45				08 46					09 44				10 22
Warwick	d						06 45	07 08		07 48		08 04		08 49					09 47			10 04	10 25
Leamington Spa	d						06 49	07 13		07 53		08 09		08 53					09 53			10 09	10 30
Banbury	d			06 05	06 33		07 07	07 33		08 13		08 29		09 13			09 29		10 13			10 29	10 49
Kings Sutton	d			06 09								08 33					09 33						
Bicester North	d			06 22	06 48		07 24	07 48		08 28		08 46		09 28			09 46		10 28			10 46	11 04
Haddenham & Thame Parkway	d			06 35	07 01		07 35	08 01		08 40		08 59		09 40			09 59		10 40			10 59	
Aylesbury	d	05 15	05 57			06 57			07 57				09 07		09 48					10 38			
Little Kimble	d	05 23	06 05			07 05			08 05				09 15		09 56					10 46			
Monks Risborough	d	05 27	06 09			07 09			08 09				09 19		10 00					10 50			
Princes Risborough	d	05 30	06 12	06 43		07 12	07 43		08 12	08 47		09 06	09 22	09 47	10a06		10 09		10 47	10a59		11 06	
Saunderton	d	05 35	06 17			07 17			08 17				09 27				10 13					11 11	
High Wycombe	d	05 42	06 24	06 53		07 24	07 53		08 24	08 57	09 04	09 18	09 34	09 57		10 04	10 20	10 34	10 57		11 04	11 18	
Beaconsfield	d	05 48	06 30	06 59		07 30	07 59		08 30		09 10	09 24	09 40			10 10	10 26	10 40			11 10	11 24	
Seer Green	d	05 51	06 33			07 33			08 33		09 13		09 43			10 13		10 43			11 13		
Gerrards Cross	d	05 55	06 37	07 04		07 37	08 04		08 37		09 17	09 30	09 47			10 17	10 32	10 47			11 17	11 30	
Denham Golf Club	d	05 58	06 40			07 40			08 40				09 50					10 50					
Denham	d	06 00	06 42			07 42			08 42		09 21		09 52			10 21		10 52			11 21		
West Ruislip §	⊖ d	06 05	06 47			07 47			08 47				09 57					10 57					
South Ruislip §	⊖ d	06 08	06 50			07 50			08 50		09 27					10 27					11 27		
Northolt Park	d	06 12	06 54			07 54			08 54		09 30		10 02			10 30		11 02			11 30		
Sudbury Hill Harrow	d																						
Sudbury & Harrow Road	d																						
Wembley Stadium	d	06 17	06 59	07 17		07 59			08 59		09 35		10 07			10 35		11 07			11 35		
London Paddington	⊖ a																						
London Marylebone	⊖ a	06 29	07 12	07 31	07 48	08 12	08 29	08 49	09 13	09 30	09 50	09 55	10 23	10 34		10 50	10 58	11 26	11 32		11 50	11 56	11 59

		CH	CH	CH	CH	CH	CH	CH	CH	CH	CH	CH	CH	CH	CH	CH	CH	CH	CH	CH	CH	CH	CH	CH
			◇				◇		◇										◇		◇	◇		
Kidderminster	d																							
Stourbridge Junction	d																							
Cradley Heath	d																							
Rowley Regis	d																							
Birmingham Snow Hill	d		10 12				10 52		11 12			11 52		12 12			12 52		13 12			13 52		14 12
Birmingham Moor Street	d		10 15				10 55		11 15			11 55		12 15			12 55		13 15			13 55		14 15
Solihull	d		10 25				11 05		11 25			12 05		12 25			13 05		13 25			14 05		14 25
Dorridge	d		10 31				11 11		11 31			12 11		12 31			13 11		13 31			14 11		14 31
Lapworth	d		10 35											12 35										14 35
Stratford-upon-Avon	d										11 36													
Wilmcote	d										11 41													
Bearley	d										11 47													
Claverdon	d										11 52													
Hatton	d		10 41								11 57			12 41										14 41
Warwick Parkway	d		10 45				11 22		11 41			12 22		12 45			13 22		13 41			14 22		14 45
Warwick	d		10 48				11 25		11 45		12 04	12 25		12 48			13 25		13 45			14 25		14 48
Leamington Spa	d		10 53				11 30		11 49		12 09	12 30		12 53			13 30		13 53			14 30		14 53
Banbury	d		11 13			11 29	11 49		12 07		12 29	12 49		13 13			13 49		14 13			14 49		15 13
Kings Sutton	d					11 33					12 33													
Bicester North	d		11 28			11 46	12 04		12 24		12 46	13 04		13 28		13 46	14 04		14 28		14 46	15 04		15 28
Haddenham & Thame Parkway	d		11 40			11 59			12 35		12 59			13 40		13 59			14 40		14 59			15 40
Aylesbury	d			11 38						12 38					13 38					14 38				
Little Kimble	d			11 46						12 46					13 46					14 46				
Monks Risborough	d			11 50						12 50					13 50					14 50				
Princes Risborough	d		11 47	11a56		12 06			12 43	12a56	13 06			13 47	13a56	14 06			14 47	14a56	15 06			15 47
Saunderton	d					12 11					13 11					14 11					15 11			
High Wycombe	d	11 34	11 57		12 04	12 18		12 34	12 53		13 18		13 34	13 57		14 18		14 34	14 57		15 18		15 34	15 57
Beaconsfield	d	11 40			12 10	12 24		12 40			13 24		13 40			14 24		14 40			15 24		15 40	
Seer Green	d	11 43			12 13			12 43					13 43					14 43					15 43	
Gerrards Cross	d	11 47			12 17	12 30		12 47			13 30		13 47			14 30		14 47			15 30		15 47	
Denham Golf Club	d	11 50						12 50					13 50					14 50					15 50	
Denham	d	11 52			12 21			12 52					13 52					14 52					15 52	
West Ruislip §	⊖ d	11 57						12 57					13 57					14 57					15 57	
South Ruislip §	⊖ d				12 27			13 00					14 00					15 00					16 00	
Northolt Park	d	12 02			12 30			13 04					14 04					15 04					16 04	
Sudbury Hill Harrow	d																							
Sudbury & Harrow Road	d																							
Wembley Stadium	d	12 07			12 35			13 09			13 43		14 09			14 43		15 09			15 43		16 09	
London Paddington	⊖ a																							
London Marylebone	⊖ a	12 26	12 30		12 48	12 58	13 01	13 23	13 26		13 58	14 02	14 22	14 32		14 58	15 01	15 27	15 31		15 58	16 01	16 21	16 37

§ London Underground Limited (Central Line) also operate services between South Ruislip and West Ruislip at frequent intervals

Table 115

Saturdays
until 02 October

Kidderminster, Birmingham Snow Hill, Stratford-upon-Avon, Banbury, Aylesbury and High Wycombe - London

		CH	CH	CH	CH	CH	CH	CH	CH	CH	CH	CH	CH	CH	CH	CH	CH	CH	CH	CH	CH	CH
					◇						◇						◇					
Kidderminster	d																					
Stourbridge Junction	d																					
Cradley Heath	d																					
Rowley Regis	d																					
Birmingham Snow Hill	d				14 52		15 12				15 52		16 12				16 52		17 12			
Birmingham Moor Street	d				14 55		15 15				15 55		16 15				16 55		17 15			
Solihull	d				15 05		15 25				16 05		16 25				17 05		17 25			
Dorridge	d				15 11		15 31				16 11		16 31				17 11		17 31			
Lapworth	d												16 35						17 35			
Stratford-upon-Avon	d			14 36																17 40		
Wilmcote	d			14 41																		
Bearley	d			14 47																		
Claverdon	d			14 52																		
Hatton	d			14 57									16 41						17 41			
Warwick Parkway	d				15 22		15 41				16 22		16 45				17 22		17 45			
Warwick	d			15 04	15 25		15 45				16 25		16 48				17 25		17 48	18 02		
Leamington Spa	d			15 09	15 30		15 49				16 30		16 53				17 30		17 53	18 06		
Banbury	d			15 29	15 49		16 07				16 49		17 13				17 49		18 13	18 24		
Kings Sutton	d			15 33																		
Bicester North	d			15 46	16 04		16 24			16 46	17 04		17 28			17 46	18 04		18 28	18 38		
Haddenham & Thame Parkway	d			15 59			16 35			16 59			17 40			17 59			18 40			
Aylesbury	d	15 38						16 38						17 38							18 38	
Little Kimble	d	15 46						16 46						17 46							18 46	
Monks Risborough	d	15 50						16 50						17 50							18 50	
Princes Risborough	d	15a56		16 06			16 43	16a56		17 06			17 47	17a56		18 06			18 47		18a58	
Saunderton	d			16 11						17 11						18 11						
High Wycombe	d		16 04	16 18		16 34	16 53		17 04	17 18		17 34	17 57		18 04	18 18	18 28	18 34	18 57			19 04
Beaconsfield	d		16 10	16 24		16 40			17 10	17 24		17 40			18 10	18 24		18 40				19 10
Seer Green	d		16 13			16 43			17 13			17 43			18 13			18 43				19 13
Gerrards Cross	d		16 17	16 30		16 47			17 17	17 30		17 47			18 17	18 30		18 47				19 17
Denham Golf Club	d					16 50						17 50						18 50				
Denham	d		16 21			16 52			17 21			17 52			18 21			18 52				19 21
West Ruislip §	⊖ d					16 57						17 57						18 57				
South Ruislip §	⊖ d		16 27						17 27						18 27							19 27
Northolt Park	d		16 30			17 02			17 30			18 02			18 30			19 02				19 30
Sudbury Hill Harrow	d																					
Sudbury & Harrow Road	d																					
Wembley Stadium	d		16 35			17 07			17 35			18 07			18 35			19 07				19 35
London Paddington	⊖ a																					
London Marylebone	⊖ a		16 49	16 56	16 59	17 20	17 29		17 49	17 58	18 01	18 25	18 32		18 48	18 58	19 02	19 21	19 30	19 37		19 50

		CH	CH	CH	CH	CH	CH	CH	CH	CH	CH	CH	CH	CH
		◇				◇		◇	◇	◇			◇	
Kidderminster	d													
Stourbridge Junction	d													
Cradley Heath	d													
Rowley Regis	d													
Birmingham Snow Hill	d		17 52			18 12		19 10		20 10			21 15	
Birmingham Moor Street	d		17 55			18 15		19 13		20 13			21 18	
Solihull	d		18 05			18 25		19 23		20 23			21 27	
Dorridge	d		18 11			18 32		19 30		20 30			21 34	
Lapworth	d					18 36		19 34		20 34			21 38	
Stratford-upon-Avon	d								19 48		21 15			
Wilmcote	d								19 53					
Bearley	d								19 59					
Claverdon	d								20 04					
Hatton	d					18 42		19 40	20 10	20 40	21a33		21 43	
Warwick Parkway	d		18 22			18 46		19 44	20 16	20 44			21 48	
Warwick	d		18 25			18 49		19 47	20 19	20 47			21 51	
Leamington Spa	d		18 30			18 53		19 52	20 23	20 52			21 55	
Banbury	d	18 32	18 49			19 13		20 13	20 42	21 15			22 15	
Kings Sutton	d	18 36							20 47				22 20	
Bicester North	d	18 48	19 04			19 29	20 00	20 29	21 00	21 30			22 32	
Haddenham & Thame Parkway	d	19 01				19 42	20 13	20 42	21 13	21 43			22 45	
Aylesbury	d			19 30								21 55		22 45
Little Kimble	d			19 38								22 03		22 53
Monks Risborough	d			19 42								22 07		22 57
Princes Risborough	d	19 08		19a48		19 50	20 21	20 50	21 21	21 52		22 10	22 54	23 00
Saunderton	d	19 13					20 26		21 26			22 15		23 05
High Wycombe	d	19 20	19 28		19 34	20 00	20 34	21 00	21 34	22 02		22 22	23 04	23 12
Beaconsfield	d	19 26			19 40	20 06	20 40	21 06	21 40	22 08		22 28		23 18
Seer Green	d				19 43		20 43		21 43			22 31		23 21
Gerrards Cross	d	19 31			19 47	20 11	20 47	21 11	21 47	22 13		22 36		23 26
Denham Golf Club	d				19 50		20 50		21 50			22 39		23 29
Denham	d				19 52		20 52		21 52			22 41		23 31
West Ruislip §	⊖ d				19 57		20 57		21 57			22 46		23 36
South Ruislip §	⊖ d				20 00		21 00		22 00			22 49		23 39
Northolt Park	d				20 04		21 04		22 04			22 53		23 43
Sudbury Hill Harrow	d													
Sudbury & Harrow Road	d													
Wembley Stadium	d				20 09		21 09		22 09	22 27		22 59	23 27	23 49
London Paddington	⊖ a													
London Marylebone	⊖ a	19 58	20 02		20 23	20 37	21 27	21 37	22 22	22 40		23 15	23 40	00 03

§ London Underground Limited (Central Line) also operate services between South Ruislip and West Ruislip at frequent intervals

Kidderminster, Birmingham Snow Hill, Stratford-upon-Avon, Banbury, Aylesbury and High Wycombe - London

		CH	CH	CH	CH	CH	CH	CH		CH	CH	CH	CH	CH	CH	CH	CH	CH			CH	CH	CH	CH	CH
							◇	◇			◇		◇		◇						◇				◇
Kidderminster	d										06 37														09 03
Stourbridge Junction	d										06 45														09 15
Cradley Heath	d										06 50														09 21
Rowley Regis	d										06 56														09 27
Birmingham Snow Hill	d						06 12	06 36			07 12				08 12						09 12				09 52
Birmingham Moor Street	d						06 15	06 39			07 15				08 15						09 15				09 55
Solihull	d						06 25	06 49			07 25				08 25						09 25				10 05
Dorridge	d						06 31	06 54			07 31				08 32						09 31				10 11
Lapworth	d										07 35				08 36						09 35				
Stratford-upon-Avon	d												07 35											09 36	
Wilmcote	d																							09 41	
Bearley	d																							09 47	
Claverdon	d												07 47											09 52	
Hatton	d										07 41		07 57		08 42									09 57	
Warwick Parkway	d						06 41	07 05			07 45				08 46						09 44				10 22
Warwick	d						06 45	07 08			07 48		08 04		08 49						09 47			10 04	10 25
Leamington Spa	d						06 49	07 13			07 53		08 09		08 53						09 53			10 09	10 30
Banbury	d			06 05	06 33		07 07	07 33			08 13		08 29		09 13			09 29			10 13			10 29	10 49
Kings Sutton	d			06 09									08 33					09 33							
Bicester North	d			06 22	06 48		07 24	07 48			08 28		08 46		09 28			09 46			10 28			10 46	11 04
Haddenham & Thame Parkway	d			06 35	07 01		07 35	08 01			08 40		08 59		09 40			09 59			10 40			10 59	
Aylesbury	d	05 15	05 57			06 57				07 57				09 07		09 48						10 38			
Little Kimble	d	05 23	06 05			07 05				08 05				09 15		09 56						10 46			
Monks Risborough	d	05 27	06 09			07 09				08 09				09 19		10 00						10 50			
Princes Risborough	d	05 30	06 12	06 43		07 12	07 43			08 12	08 47		09 06	09 22	09 47	10a07		10 09			10 47	10a59		11 06	
Saunderton	d	05 35	06 17			07 17				08 17				09 27				10 13						11 11	
High Wycombe	d	05 42	06 24	06 53		07 24	07 53			08 24	08 57	09 04	09 18	09 34	09 57		10 04	10 20			10 57		11 04	11 18	
Beaconsfield	d	05 48	06 30	06 59		07 30	07 59			08 30		09 10	09 24	09 40			10 10	10 26					11 10	11 24	
Seer Green	d	05 51	06 33			07 33				08 33		09 13		09 43			10 13						11 13		
Gerrards Cross	d	05 55	06 37	07 04		07 37	08 04			08 37		09 17	09 30	09 47			10 17	10 32					11 17	11 30	
Denham Golf Club	d	05 58	06 40			07 40				08 40				09 50											
Denham	d	06 00	06 42			07 42				08 42		09 21		09 52			10 21						11 21		
West Ruislip §	d	06 05	06 47			07 47				08 47				09 57											
South Ruislip §	d	06 08	06 50			07 50				08 50		09 27					10 27						11 27		
Northolt Park	d	06 12	06 54			07 54				08 54		09 30		10 02			10 30						11 30		
Sudbury Hill Harrow	d																								
Sudbury & Harrow Road	d																								
Wembley Stadium	d	06 17	06 59	07 17		07 59				08 59		09 35		10 07			10 35						11 35		
London Paddington	a																								
London Marylebone	a	06 32	07 15	07 34	07 51	08 15	08 32	08 52		09 16	09 33	09 53	09 58	10 26	10 37		10 53	11 01			11 35		11 53	11 59	12 02

			CH	CH	CH	CH		CH	CH	CH	CH	CH	CH	CH	CH	CH		CH	CH	CH	CH	CH	CH	CH	CH
			◇					◇		◇											◇		◇	◇	
Kidderminster	d																								
Stourbridge Junction	d																								
Cradley Heath	d																								
Rowley Regis	d																								
Birmingham Snow Hill	d		10 12					10 52		11 12			11 52		12 12				12 52		13 12			13 52	
Birmingham Moor Street	d		10 15					10 55		11 15			11 55		12 15				12 55		13 15			13 55	
Solihull	d		10 25					11 05		11 25			12 05		12 25				13 05		13 25			14 05	
Dorridge	d		10 31					11 11		11 31			12 11		12 31				13 11		13 31			14 11	
Lapworth	d		10 35												12 35										
Stratford-upon-Avon	d											11 36													
Wilmcote	d											11 41													
Bearley	d											11 47													
Claverdon	d											11 52													
Hatton	d		10 41									11 57			12 41										
Warwick Parkway	d		10 45					11 22		11 41			12 22		12 45				13 22		13 41			14 22	
Warwick	d		10 48					11 25		11 45		12 04	12 25		12 48				13 25		13 45			14 25	
Leamington Spa	d		10 53					11 30		11 49		12 09	12 30		12 53				13 30		13 53			14 30	
Banbury	d		11 13			11 29		11 49		12 07		12 29	12 49		13 13				13 49		14 13			14 49	
Kings Sutton	d					11 33						12 33													
Bicester North	d		11 28			11 46		12 04		12 24		12 46	13 04		13 28			13 46	14 04		14 28		14 46	15 04	
Haddenham & Thame Parkway	d		11 40			11 59				12 35		12 59			13 40			13 59			14 40		14 59		
Aylesbury	d			11 38							12 38					13 38						14 38			
Little Kimble	d			11 46							12 46					13 46						14 46			
Monks Risborough	d			11 50							12 50					13 50						14 50			
Princes Risborough	d		11 47	11a59		12 06				12 43	12a59	13 06			13 47	13a59		14 06			14 47	14a59	15 06		
Saunderton	d					12 11						13 11						14 11					15 11		
High Wycombe	d		11 57		12 04	12 18			12 34	12 53		13 18		13 34	13 57			14 18		14 34	14 57		15 18		15 34
Beaconsfield	d				12 10	12 24			12 40			13 24		13 40				14 24		14 40			15 24		15 40
Seer Green	d				12 13				12 43					13 43						14 43					15 43
Gerrards Cross	d				12 17	12 30			12 47			13 30		13 47				14 30		14 47			15 30		15 47
Denham Golf Club	d								12 50					13 50						14 50					15 50
Denham	d				12 21				12 52					13 52						14 52					15 52
West Ruislip §	d								12 57					13 57						14 57					15 57
South Ruislip §	d				12 27				13 00					14 00						15 00					16 00
Northolt Park	d				12 30				13 04					14 04						15 04					16 04
Sudbury Hill Harrow	d																								
Sudbury & Harrow Road	d																								
Wembley Stadium	d				12 35				13 09			13 43		14 09				14 43		15 09			15 43		16 09
London Paddington	a																								
London Marylebone	a		12 33		12 51	13 01		13 04	13 26	13 29		14 01	14 05	14 25	14 35			15 01	15 04	15 30	15 34		16 01	16 04	16 24

§ London Underground Limited (Central Line) also operate services between South Ruislip and West Ruislip at frequent intervals

Table 115

Saturdays
from 09 October

Kidderminster, Birmingham Snow Hill, Stratford-upon-Avon, Banbury, Aylesbury and High Wycombe - London

		CH		CH	CH	CH	CH	CH	CH	CH	CH	CH		CH		CH	CH	CH	CH	CH	CH	CH	CH		CH
							◇							◇						◇					
Kidderminster	d																								
Stourbridge Junction	d																								
Cradley Heath	d																								
Rowley Regis	d																								
Birmingham Snow Hill	d	14 12					14 52		15 12					15 52		16 12				16 52		17 12			
Birmingham Moor Street	d	14 15					14 55		15 15					15 55		16 15				16 55		17 15			
Solihull	d	14 25					15 05		15 25					16 05		16 25				17 05		17 25			
Dorridge	d	14 31					15 11		15 31					16 11		16 31				17 11		17 31			
Lapworth	d	14 35														16 35						17 35			
Stratford-upon-Avon	d					14 36																	17 40		
Wilmcote	d					14 41																			
Bearley	d					14 47																			
Claverdon	d					14 52																			
Hatton	d	14 41				14 57										16 41						17 41			
Warwick Parkway	d	14 45					15 22		15 41					16 22		16 45				17 22		17 45			
Warwick	d	14 48				15 04	15 25		15 45					16 25		16 48				17 25		17 48	18 02		
Leamington Spa	d	14 53				15 09	15 30		15 49					16 30		16 53				17 30		17 53	18 06		
Banbury	d	15 13				15 29	15 49		16 07					16 49		17 13				17 49		18 13	18 24		
Kings Sutton	d					15 33																			
Bicester North	d	15 28				15 46	16 04		16 24			16 46		17 04		17 28			17 46	18 04		18 28	18 38		
Haddenham & Thame Parkway	d	15 40				15 59			16 35			16 59				17 40			17 59			18 40			
Aylesbury	d			15 38						16 38							17 38								18 38
Little Kimble	d			15 46						16 46							17 46								18 46
Monks Risborough	d			15 50						16 50							17 50								18 50
Princes Risborough	d	15 47		15a59		16 06			16 43	16a59		17 06				17 47	17a59		18 06			18 47			18a59
Saunderton	d					16 11						17 11							18 11						
High Wycombe	d	15 57			16 04	16 18		16 34	16 53		17 04	17 18				17 57		18 04	18 18	18 28	18 34	18 57			
Beaconsfield	d				16 10	16 24		16 40			17 10	17 24						18 10	18 24		18 40				
Seer Green	d				16 13			16 43			17 13							18 13			18 43				
Gerrards Cross	d				16 17	16 30		16 47			17 17	17 30						18 17	18 30		18 47				
Denham Golf Club	d							16 50													18 50				
Denham	d				16 21			16 52			17 21							18 21			18 52				
West Ruislip §	d							16 57													18 57				
South Ruislip §	d				16 27						17 27							18 27							
Northolt Park	d				16 30			17 02			17 30							18 30			19 02				
Sudbury Hill Harrow	d																								
Sudbury & Harrow Road	d																								
Wembley Stadium	d				16 35			17 07			17 35							18 35			19 07				
London Paddington	a																								
London Marylebone	a	16 40			16 52	16 59	17 02	17 23	17 32		17 52	18 01		18 04		18 35		18 51	19 01	19 05	19 24	19 33	19 40		

		CH	CH	CH	CH	CH	CH	CH	CH		CH	CH	CH	CH	CH	CH
			◇				◇		◇		◇	◇			◇	
Kidderminster	d															
Stourbridge Junction	d															
Cradley Heath	d															
Rowley Regis	d															
Birmingham Snow Hill	d			17 52			18 12		19 10			20 10			21 15	
Birmingham Moor Street	d			17 55			18 15		19 13			20 13			21 18	
Solihull	d			18 05			18 25		19 23			20 23			21 27	
Dorridge	d			18 11			18 32		19 30			20 30			21 34	
Lapworth	d						18 36		19 34			20 34			21 38	
Stratford-upon-Avon	d										19 48		21 15			
Wilmcote	d										19 53					
Bearley	d										19 59					
Claverdon	d										20 04					
Hatton	d						18 42		19 40		20 10	20 40	21a36		21 43	
Warwick Parkway	d			18 22			18 46		19 44		20 16	20 44			21 48	
Warwick	d			18 25			18 49		19 47		20 19	20 47			21 51	
Leamington Spa	d			18 30			18 53		19 52		20 23	20 52			21 55	
Banbury	d		18 32	18 49			19 13		20 13		20 42	21 15			22 15	
Kings Sutton	d		18 36								20 47				22 20	
Bicester North	d		18 48	19 04			19 29	20 00	20 29		21 00	21 30			22 32	
Haddenham & Thame Parkway	d		19 01				19 42	20 13	20 42		21 13	21 43			22 45	
Aylesbury	d				19 30									21 55		22 45
Little Kimble	d				19 38									22 03		22 53
Monks Risborough	d				19 42									22 07		22 57
Princes Risborough	d		19 08		19a48		19 50	20 21	20 50		21 21	21 52		22 10	22 54	23 00
Saunderton	d		19 13					20 26			21 26			22 15		23 05
High Wycombe	d	19 04	19 20	19 28		19 34	20 00	20 34	21 00		21 34	22 02		22 22	23 04	23 12
Beaconsfield	d	19 10	19 26			19 40	20 06	20 40	21 06		21 40	22 08		22 28		23 18
Seer Green	d	19 13				19 43		20 43			21 43			22 31		23 21
Gerrards Cross	d	19 17	19 31			19 47	20 11	20 47	21 11		21 47	22 13		22 36		23 26
Denham Golf Club	d					19 50		20 50			21 50			22 39		23 29
Denham	d	19 21				19 52		20 52			21 52			22 41		23 31
West Ruislip §	d					19 57		20 57			21 57			22 46		23 36
South Ruislip §	d	19 27				20 00		21 00			22 00			22 49		23 39
Northolt Park	d	19 30				20 04		21 04			22 04			22 53		23 43
Sudbury Hill Harrow	d															
Sudbury & Harrow Road	d															
Wembley Stadium	d	19 35				20 09		21 09			22 09	22 27		22 59	23 27	23 49
London Paddington	a															
London Marylebone	a	19 53	20 01	20 05		20 26	20 40	21 30	21 40		22 25	22 43		23 18	23 43	00 06

§ London Underground Limited (Central Line) also operate services between South Ruislip and West Ruislip at frequent intervals

Table 115

Sundays
until 26 September

Kidderminster, Birmingham Snow Hill, Stratford-upon-Avon, Banbury, Aylesbury and High Wycombe - London

		CH	CH	CH	CH	CH	CH	CH	CH	CH	CH	CH	CH	CH	CH	CH	CH	CH	CH	CH	CH	CH
								◇		◇			◇	◇		◇		◇			◇	
Kidderminster	d																					
Stourbridge Junction [2]	d																					
Cradley Heath	d																					
Rowley Regis	d																					
Birmingham Snow Hill	d							08 40		09 10		09 40		10 10		10 40		11 10		11 40		12 10
Birmingham Moor Street	d							08 43		09 13		09 43		10 13		10 43		11 13		11 43		12 13
Solihull	d							08 52		09 22		09 52		10 22		10 52		11 22		11 52		12 22
Dorridge	d							08 58		09 28		09 58		10 28		10 58		11 28		11 58		12 28
Lapworth	d															11 02						
Stratford-upon-Avon	d												10 00								12 00	
Wilmcote	d												10 04								12 04	
Bearley	d																					
Claverdon	d																					
Hatton	d												10 17			11 07					12 17	
Warwick Parkway	d							09 09		09 38		10 09		10 38		11 12		11 38		12 09		12 38
Warwick	d							09 12		09 41			10 25	10 41				11 41			12 25	12 41
Leamington Spa [8]	d							09 17		09 47		10 16	10 29	10 47		11 18		11 47		12 16	12 29	12 47
Banbury	d					09 03		09 36	09 47	10 06		10 35	10 48	11 06		11 37		12 06		12 35	12 48	13 06
Kings Sutton	d					09 08							10 53								12 53	
Bicester North [3]	d			08 24	09 02	09 20		09 52	10 02	10 22		10 51	11 06	11 22		11 53	12 06	12 22		12 51	13 06	13 22
Haddenham & Thame Parkway	d			08 35	09 15	09 33			10 15			11 04	11 19			12 06	12 19			13 04	13 19	
Aylesbury	d	07 26	08 20				09 30				10 28				11 30				12 28			
Little Kimble	d	07 34	08 28				09 38				10 36				11 38				12 36			
Monks Risborough	d	07 38	08 32				09 42				10 40				11 42				12 40			
Princes Risborough [2]	d	07 41	08 35	08 43	09 22	09 41	09 45		10 22		10 43	11 12	11 26		11 45	12 15	12 26		12 43	13 12	13 26	
Saunderton	d	07 46		08 48			09 50				10 48				11 50				12 48			
High Wycombe [1]	d	07 53	08 45	08 55	09 32	09 52	09 57		10 32		10 55	11 22	11 36		11 57	12 25	12 36		12 55	13 22	13 36	
Beaconsfield	d	07 59	08 51	09 01	09 38		10 03		10 38		11 01	11 28	11 42		12 03	12 31	12 42		13 01	13 28	13 42	
Seer Green	d	08 02		09 04			10 06				11 04				12 06				13 04			
Gerrards Cross [1]	d	08 06	08 57	09 08	09 43		10 10		10 43		11 08	11 34	11 48		12 10	12 36	12 48		13 08	13 34	13 48	
Denham Golf Club	d	08 09					10 13								12 13							
Denham	d	08 12		09 12			10 16				11 12				12 16				13 12			
West Ruislip [3] § ⊖	d	08 16		09 17			10 20				11 16				12 20				13 16			
South Ruislip § ⊖	d	08 20		09 20			10 24				11 20				12 24				13 20			
Northolt Park	d	08 23		09 24			10 27				11 23				12 27				13 23			
Sudbury Hill Harrow	d																					
Sudbury & Harrow Road	d																					
Wembley Stadium	d	08 28		09 29			10 32				11 28		12 01		12 32		13 01		13 28		14 01	
London Paddington [15] ⊖	a																					
London Marylebone [10] ⊖	a	08 41	09 22	09 43	10 09	10 25	10 47	10 51	11 10	11 23	11 42	11 58	12 17	12 22	12 47	13 01	13 14	13 22	13 42	13 58	14 16	14 22

		CH	CH	CH	CH	CH	CH	CH	CH	CH	CH	CH	CH	CH	CH	CH	CH	CH	CH	CH	CH	CH	CH
					◇			◇	◇						◇								◇
Kidderminster	d																						
Stourbridge Junction [2]	d																						
Cradley Heath	d																						
Rowley Regis	d																						
Birmingham Snow Hill	d		12 40		13 10		13 40		14 10		14 40			15 40		16 10		16 40		17 10		17 40	
Birmingham Moor Street	d		12 43		13 13		13 43		14 13		14 43			15 43		16 13		16 43		17 13		17 43	
Solihull	d		12 52		13 22		13 52		14 22		14 52			15 52		16 22		16 52		17 22		17 52	
Dorridge	d		12 58		13 28		13 58		14 28		14 58			15 58		16 28		16 58		17 28		17 58	
Lapworth	d						14 02							16 02								18 02	
Stratford-upon-Avon	d							14 00							16 00								18 00
Wilmcote	d							14 04							16 04								18 04
Bearley	d																						
Claverdon	d																						
Hatton	d						14 07	14 17						16 07	16 17							18 07	18 17
Warwick Parkway	d		13 09		13 38		14 12		14 38		15 09			16 12		16 38		17 09		17 38		18 12	
Warwick	d				13 41			14 25	14 41						16 25	16 41				17 41			18 25
Leamington Spa [8]	d		13 16		13 47		14 18	14 29	14 47		15 16			16 18	16 29	16 47		17 16		17 47		18 18	18 29
Banbury	d		13 35		14 06		14 37	14 48	15 06		15 35			16 37	16 48	17 06		17 35		18 06		18 37	18 48
Kings Sutton	d							14 53							16 53								18 53
Bicester North [3]	d		13 51	14 06	14 22		14 53	15 06	15 22		15 51	16 06		16 53	17 06	17 22		17 51	18 06	18 22		18 53	19 06
Haddenham & Thame Parkway	d		14 04	14 19			15 06	15 19			16 04	16 19		17 06	17 19			18 04	18 19			19 06	19 19
Aylesbury	d	13 28				14 28				15 30			16 30				17 30				18 28		
Little Kimble	d	13 36				14 36				15 38			16 38				17 38				18 36		
Monks Risborough	d	13 40				14 40				15 42			16 42				17 42				18 40		
Princes Risborough [2]	d	13 43	14 12	14 26		14 43	15 15	15 26		15 45	16 12	16 26	16 45	17 15	17 26		17 45	18 12	18 26		18 43	19 15	19 26
Saunderton	d	13 48				14 48				15 50			16 50				17 50				18 48		
High Wycombe [1]	d	13 55	14 22	14 36		14 55	15 25	15 36		15 57	16 22	16 41	16 57	17 25	17 36		17 57	18 22	18 36		18 55	19 25	19 36
Beaconsfield	d	14 01	14 28	14 42		15 01	15 31	15 42		16 03	16 28	16 47	17 03	17 31	17 42		18 03	18 28	18 42		19 01	19 31	19 42
Seer Green	d	14 04				15 04				16 06			17 06				18 06				19 04		
Gerrards Cross [1]	d	14 08	14 34	14 48		15 08	15 36	15 48		16 10	16 34	16 52	17 10	17 36	17 48		18 10	18 34	18 48		19 08	19 36	19 48
Denham Golf Club	d	14 11								16 13							18 13						
Denham	d	14 13				15 12				16 16			17 14				18 16				19 12		
West Ruislip [3] § ⊖	d	14 20				15 16				16 20			17 20				18 20				19 16		
South Ruislip § ⊖	d	14 24				15 20				16 24			17 24				18 24				19 20		
Northolt Park	d	14 27				15 23				16 27			17 27				18 27				19 23		
Sudbury Hill Harrow	d																						
Sudbury & Harrow Road	d																						
Wembley Stadium	d	14 32		15 01		15 28		16 01		16 32		17 05	17 32		18 01		18 32		19 01		19 28		20 01
London Paddington [15] ⊖	a																						
London Marylebone [10] ⊖	a	14 48	15 00	15 14	15 23	15 42	16 02	16 16	16 22	16 47	16 58	17 20	17 49	18 02	18 16	18 21	18 48	18 59	19 14	19 22	19 42	20 02	20 16

§ London Underground Limited (Central Line) also operate services between South Ruislip and West Ruislip at frequent intervals

Table 115

Sundays
until 26 September

Kidderminster, Birmingham Snow Hill, Stratford-upon-Avon, Banbury, Aylesbury and High Wycombe - London

		CH	CH	CH	CH	CH	CH	CH	CH
		◇			◇	◇	◇		◇
Kidderminster	d								
Stourbridge Junction [2]	d								
Cradley Heath	d								
Rowley Regis	d								
Birmingham Snow Hill	d	18 10		18 40	19 10		20 15		21 15
Birmingham Moor Street	d	18 13		18 43	19 13		20 18		21 18
Solihull	d	18 22		18 52	19 21		20 28		21 28
Dorridge	d	18 28		18 58	19 28		20 35		21 35
Lapworth	d				19 32				
Stratford-upon-Avon	d					19 57			
Wilmcote	d					20 01			
Bearley	d								
Claverdon	d								
Hatton	d				19 39	20 14			
Warwick Parkway	d	18 38		19 09	19 43		20 46		21 46
Warwick	d	18 41			19 46	20 22	20 49		21 49
Leamington Spa [8]	d	18 47		19 16	19 50	20 26	20 54		21 54
Banbury	d	19 06		19 35	20 10	20 46	21 13		22 15
Kings Sutton	d				20 15				22 20
Bicester North [3]	d	19 22		19 51	20 28	21 02	21 30		22 34
Haddenham & Thame Parkway	d			20 04	20 41		21 43		22 47
Aylesbury	d		19 30					22 32	
Little Kimble	d		19 38					22 40	
Monks Risborough	d		19 42					22 44	
Princes Risborough [2]	d		19 45	20 12	20 48		21 51	22a50	22 55
Saunderton	d		19 50		20 53		21 56		23 00
High Wycombe [1]	d		19 57	20 22	21 04		22 03		23 07
Beaconsfield	d		20 03	20 28	21 10		22 09		23 13
Seer Green	d		20 06		21 13		22 12		23 16
Gerrards Cross [1]	d		20 10	20 34	21 17		22 16		23 20
Denham Golf Club	d		20 13				22 19		
Denham	d		20 16		21 21		22 21		23 24
West Ruislip [3] § ⊖	d		20 20		21 26		22 26		23 28
South Ruislip § ⊖	d		20 24		21 29		22 29		23 32
Northolt Park	d		20 27		21 33		22 33		23 35
Sudbury Hill Harrow	d								
Sudbury & Harrow Road	d								
Wembley Stadium	d		20 32		21 38		22 38		23 40
London Paddington [15] ⊖	a								
London Marylebone [10] ⊖	a	20 21	20 48	20 58	21 53	22 01	22 52		23 54

Sundays
from 03 October

		CH	CH	CH	CH	CH	CH	CH	CH	CH	CH	CH	CH	CH	CH	CH	CH	CH	CH	CH	CH
								◇		◇			◇	◇		◇		◇			◇
Kidderminster	d																				
Stourbridge Junction [2]	d																				
Cradley Heath	d																				
Rowley Regis	d																				
Birmingham Snow Hill	d							08 40		09 10		09 40		10 10		10 40		11 10		11 40	
Birmingham Moor Street	d							08 43		09 13		09 43		10 13		10 43		11 13		11 43	
Solihull	d							08 52		09 22		09 52		10 22		10 52		11 22		11 52	
Dorridge	d							08 58		09 28		09 58		10 28		10 58		11 28		11 58	
Lapworth	d															11 02					
Stratford-upon-Avon	d												10 00								12 00
Wilmcote	d												10 04								12 04
Bearley	d																				
Claverdon	d																				
Hatton	d												10 17			11 07					12 17
Warwick Parkway	d							09 09		09 38		10 09		10 38		11 12		11 38		12 09	
Warwick	d							09 12		09 41			10 25	10 41				11 41			12 25
Leamington Spa [8]	d							09 17		09 47		10 16	10 29	10 47		11 18		11 47		12 16	12 29
Banbury	d					09 03		09 36	09 47	10 06		10 35	10 48	11 06		11 37		12 06		12 35	12 48
Kings Sutton	d					09 08							10 53								12 53
Bicester North [3]	d			08 24	09 02	09 20		09 52	10 02	10 22		10 51	11 06	11 22		11 53	12 06	12 22		12 51	13 06
Haddenham & Thame Parkway	d			08 35	09 15	09 33			10 15			11 04	11 19			12 06	12 19			13 04	13 19
Aylesbury	d	07 26	08 20				09 30				10 28				11 30				12 28		
Little Kimble	d	07 34	08 28				09 38				10 36				11 38				12 36		
Monks Risborough	d	07 38	08 32				09 42				10 40				11 42				12 40		
Princes Risborough [2]	d	07 41	08 35	08 43	09 22	09 41	09 45		10 22		10 43	11 12	11 26		11 45	12 15	12 26		12 43	13 12	13 26
Saunderton	d	07 46		08 48			09 50				10 48				11 50				12 48		
High Wycombe [1]	d	07 53	08 45	08 55	09 32	09 52	09 57		10 32		10 55	11 22	11 36		11 57	12 25	12 36		12 55	13 22	13 36
Beaconsfield	d	07 59	08 51	09 01	09 38		10 03		10 38		11 01	11 28	11 42		12 03	12 31	12 42		13 01	13 28	13 42
Seer Green	d	08 02		09 04			10 06				11 04				12 06				13 04		
Gerrards Cross [1]	d	08 06	08 57	09 08	09 43		10 10		10 43		11 08	11 34	11 48		12 10	12 36	12 48		13 08	13 34	13 48
Denham Golf Club	d	08 09					10 13								12 13						
Denham	d	08 12		09 12			10 16				11 12				12 16				13 12		
West Ruislip [3] § ⊖	d	08 16		09 17			10 20				11 16				12 20				13 16		
South Ruislip § ⊖	d	08 20		09 20			10 24				11 20				12 24				13 20		
Northolt Park	d	08 23		09 24			10 27				11 23				12 27				13 23		
Sudbury Hill Harrow	d																				
Sudbury & Harrow Road	d																				
Wembley Stadium	d	08 28		09 29			10 32				11 28		12 01		12 32		13 01		13 28		14 01
London Paddington [15] ⊖	a																				
London Marylebone [10] ⊖	a	08 44	09 25	09 46	10 12	10 28	10 50	10 54	11 13	11 26	11 45	12 01	12 20	12 25	12 50	13 04	13 17	13 25	13 45	14 01	14 19

§ London Underground Limited (Central Line) also operate services between South Ruislip and West Ruislip at frequent intervals

Table 115

Kidderminster, Birmingham Snow Hill, Stratford-upon-Avon, Banbury, Aylesbury and High Wycombe - London

Sundays from 03 October

		CH	CH	CH	CH	CH	CH	CH	CH	CH	CH	CH	CH	CH	CH	CH	CH	CH	CH	CH	CH	CH	CH
						◇			◇	◇						◇							
Kidderminster	d																						
Stourbridge Junction 2	d																						
Cradley Heath	d																						
Rowley Regis	d																						
Birmingham Snow Hill	d	12 10		12 40		13 10		13 40		14 10		14 40			15 40		16 10		16 40		17 10		17 40
Birmingham Moor Street	d	12 13		12 43		13 13		13 43		14 13		14 43			15 43		16 13		16 43		17 13		17 43
Solihull	d	12 22		12 52		13 22		13 52		14 22		14 52			15 52		16 22		16 52		17 22		17 52
Dorridge	d	12 28		12 58		13 28		13 58		14 28		14 58			15 58		16 28		16 58		17 28		17 58
Lapworth	d							14 02							16 02								18 02
Stratford-upon-Avon	d								14 00							16 00							
Wilmcote	d								14 04							16 04							
Bearley	d																						
Claverdon	d																						
Hatton	d							14 07	14 17						16 07	16 17							18 07
Warwick Parkway	d	12 38		13 09		13 38		14 12		14 38		15 09			16 12		16 38		17 09		17 38		18 12
Warwick	d	12 41				13 41			14 25	14 41						16 25	16 41				17 41		
Leamington Spa 8	d	12 47		13 16		13 47		14 18	14 29	14 47		15 16			16 18	16 29	16 47		17 16		17 47		18 18
Banbury	d	13 06		13 35		14 06		14 37	14 48	15 06		15 35			16 37	16 48	17 06		17 35		18 06		18 37
Kings Sutton	d								14 53							16 53							
Bicester North 3	d	13 22		13 51	14 06	14 22		14 53	15 06	15 22		15 51	16 06		16 53	17 06	17 22		17 51	18 06	18 22		18 53
Haddenham & Thame Parkway	d			14 04	14 19			15 06	15 19			16 04	16 19		17 06	17 19			18 04	18 19			19 06
Aylesbury	d		13 28				14 28				15 30			16 30				17 30				18 28	
Little Kimble	d		13 36				14 36				15 38			16 38				17 38				18 36	
Monks Risborough	d		13 40				14 40				15 42			16 42				17 42				18 40	
Princes Risborough 2	d		13 43	14 12	14 26		14 43	15 15	15 26		15 45	16 12	16 26	16 45	17 15	17 26		17 45	18 12	18 26		18 43	19 15
Saunderton	d		13 48				14 48				15 50			16 50				17 50				18 48	
High Wycombe 1	d		13 55	14 22	14 36		14 55	15 25	15 36		15 57	16 22	16 41	16 57	17 25	17 36		17 57	18 22	18 36		18 55	19 25
Beaconsfield	d		14 01	14 28	14 42		15 01	15 31	15 42		16 03	16 28	16 47	17 03	17 31	17 42		18 03	18 28	18 42		19 01	19 31
Seer Green	d		14 04				15 04				16 06			17 06				18 06				19 04	
Gerrards Cross 1	d		14 08	14 34	14 48		15 08	15 36	15 48		16 10	16 34	16 52	17 10	17 36	17 48		18 10	18 34	18 48		19 08	19 36
Denham Golf Club	d		14 11								16 13							18 13					
Denham	d		14 13				15 12				16 16			17 14				18 16				19 12	
West Ruislip 3 § ⊖	d		14 20				15 16				16 20			17 20				18 20				19 16	
South Ruislip § ⊖	d		14 24				15 20				16 24			17 24				18 24				19 20	
Northolt Park	d		14 27				15 23				16 27			17 27				18 27				19 23	
Sudbury Hill Harrow	d																						
Sudbury & Harrow Road	d																						
Wembley Stadium	d		14 32		15 01		15 28		16 01		16 32		17 05	17 32		18 01		18 32		19 01		19 28	
London Paddington 15 ⊖	a																						
London Marylebone 10 ⊖	a	14 25	14 51	15 03	15 17	15 26	15 45	16 05	16 19	16 25	16 50	17 01	17 23	17 52	18 05	18 19	18 24	18 51	19 02	19 17	19 25	19 45	20 05

		CH	CH	CH	CH	CH	CH	CH	CH
		◇	◇			◇	◇		◇
Kidderminster	d								
Stourbridge Junction 2	d								
Cradley Heath	d								
Rowley Regis	d								
Birmingham Snow Hill	d		18 10		18 40		20 15		21 15
Birmingham Moor Street	d		18 13		18 43		20 18		21 18
Solihull	d		18 22		18 52		20 28		21 28
Dorridge	d		18 28		18 58		20 35		21 35
Lapworth	d								
Stratford-upon-Avon	d	18 00				19 57			
Wilmcote	d	18 04				20 01			
Bearley	d								
Claverdon	d								
Hatton	d	18 17				20 14			
Warwick Parkway	d		18 38		19 09		20 46		21 46
Warwick	d	18 25	18 41			20 22	20 49		21 49
Leamington Spa 8	d	18 29	18 47		19 16	20 26	20 54		21 54
Banbury	d	18 48	19 06		19 35	20 46	21 13		22 15
Kings Sutton	d	18 53							22 20
Bicester North 3	d	19 06	19 22		19 51	21 02	21 30		22 34
Haddenham & Thame Parkway	d	19 19			20 04		21 43		22 47
Aylesbury	d			19 30				22 32	
Little Kimble	d			19 38				22 40	
Monks Risborough	d			19 42				22 44	
Princes Risborough 2	d	19 26		19 45	20 12		21 51	22a53	22 55
Saunderton	d			19 50			21 56		23 00
High Wycombe 1	d	19 36		19 57	20 22		22 03		23 07
Beaconsfield	d	19 42		20 03	20 28		22 09		23 13
Seer Green	d			20 06			22 12		23 16
Gerrards Cross 1	d	19 48		20 10	20 34		22 16		23 20
Denham Golf Club	d			20 13			22 19		
Denham	d			20 16			22 21		23 24
West Ruislip 3 § ⊖	d			20 20			22 26		23 28
South Ruislip § ⊖	d			20 24			22 29		23 32
Northolt Park	d			20 27			22 33		23 35
Sudbury Hill Harrow	d								
Sudbury & Harrow Road	d								
Wembley Stadium	d	20 01		20 32			22 38		23 40
London Paddington 15 ⊖	a								
London Marylebone 10 ⊖	a	20 19	20 24	20 51	21 01	22 04	22 55		23 57

§ London Underground Limited (Central Line) also operate services between South Ruislip and West Ruislip at frequent intervals

Table 115A

Mondays to Fridays

Chinnor - Princes Risborough

Bus Service

		CH	CH	CH	CH	CH	CH
Chinnor, Lower Road	d	06 08	06 41	07 30	08 03	09 09	09 40
Chinnor, Estover Way	d	06 10	06 43	07 32	08 05	09 11	09 42
Chinnor, The Wheatsheaf	d	06 11	06 44	07 33	08 06	09 12	09 43
Chinnor, The Red Lion	d	06 14	06 47	07 36	08 09	09 15	09 46
Bledlow, Village Hall	d	06 17	06 50	07 39	08 12	09 18	09 49
Princes Risborough	a	06 24	06 57	07 46	08 19	09 25	09 56

No Saturday or Sunday service

Table 115A

Mondays to Fridays

Princes Risborough - Chinnor

Bus Service

		CH 🚌	CH 🚌	CH 🚌	CH 🚌	CH 🚌	CH 🚌	CH 🚌
Princes Risborough	d	16 48	17 21	18 13	18 50	19 25	20 04	20 54
Bledlow, Village Hall	d	16 55	17 28	18 20	18 57	19 32	20 11	21 01
Chinnor, Lower Road	d	16 58	17 31	18 23	19 00	19 35	20 14	21 04
Chinnor, Estover Way	d	17 00	17 35	18 25	19 02	19 37	20 16	21 06
Chinnor, The Wheatsheaf	d	17 01	17 36	18 26	19 03	19 38	20 17	21 07
Chinnor, The Red Lion	a	17 04	17 39	18 29	19 06	19 41	20 20	21 10

Network Diagram for Tables 116, 117, 118, 119, 120, 121, 122, 126

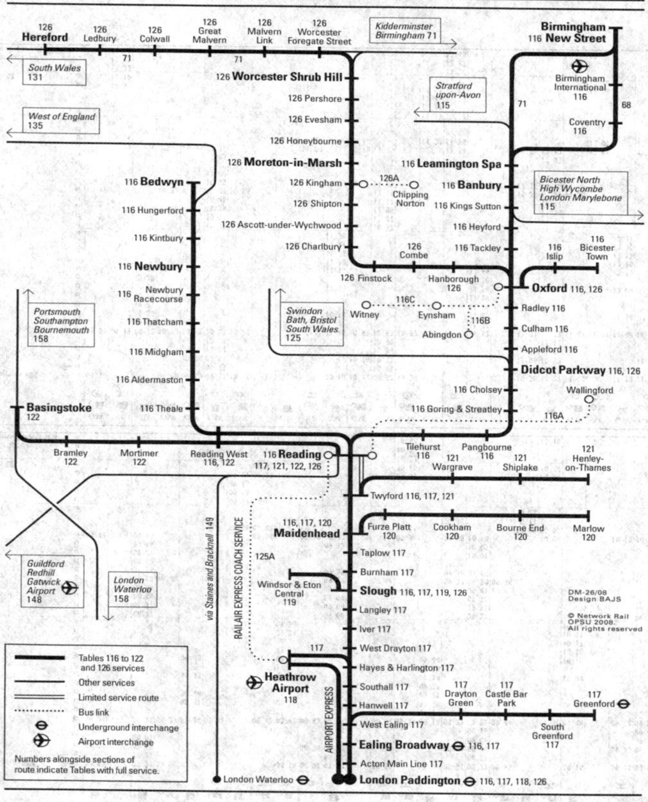

Table 116

London and Reading - Bedwyn, Oxford, Bicester, Banbury and Birmingham

		CH A	CH B	GW MX 1	GW MX ◇1	GW MX ◇1 ☕	GW MX ◇1 ☕	GW MO 🚌	GW MO ◇1 ☕	GW MO 🚌	GW MX 1	GW MX 1	GW MX ◇1	GW 1	GW 1	GW 1	GW 1	GW 1	GW ◇1 ☕	XC ◇1 🛒
London Paddington 15 ⊖	d			22p45	23p20	23p30	23p30		23p37		23p29		00 20				05 17		05 36	
Ealing Broadway ⊖	d			22p54							23p37									
Slough 3	d			23p12	23p39				23p55		23p54		00 39				05 33		05 52	
Maidenhead 3	d			23p23							00 01									
Twyford 3	d			23p31							00 09									
Reading 7	d			23p40	00 04	00 08	00 08		00 15		00 19	00 20	01 00	05 21			05 52	05 57	06 07	06 11
Reading West	d											00s23		05 23						
Theale	d											00s29		05 29						
Aldermaston	d											00s34		05 34						
Midgham	d											00s37		05 38						
Thatcham	d											00s42		05 43						
Newbury Racecourse	d											00s47		05 47						
Newbury	a											00 52		05 50						
	d													05 50						
Kintbury	d													05 57						
Hungerford	d													06 01						
Bedwyn	a													06 11						
Tilehurst	d			23p44							00 23							06 01		
Pangbourne	d			23p49							00 28							06 05		
Goring & Streatley	d			23p54							00 33							06 10		
Cholsey	d			23p59							00 38							06 15		
Didcot Parkway	a			00 06		00 25	00 25		00s32		00 45		01 19				06 07	06 22	06 20	
	d			00 06				00 25		00 40	00 45		01 19				06 08	06 25		
Appleford	d										00 50									
Culham	d										00 52							06 31		
Radley	d			00 14				00 40			00 56									
Oxford	a			00 23	00 33			00 55		01 05	01 07		01 34				06 22	06 41		06 34
	d	00 20	00 20												05 45	05 51		06 41		06 36
Islip	d															06 04				
Bicester Town	a															06 16				
Tackley	d														05 54			06 49		
Heyford	d														05 58			06 55		
Kings Sutton	d														06 07			07 02		
Banbury	a	00 50	00 47												06 14			07 10		06 52
Leamington Spa 8	a																			07 10
Coventry	a																			07 22
Birmingham International	a																			07 37
Birmingham New Street 12	a																			07 48

		GW 1	GW 1	XC ◇1 🛒	GW 1	GW 1	GW 1	GW ◇1 ☕	GW 1	XC ◇1 🛒	GW 1	GW 1 🛒	GW ◇1 ☕	GW ◇1 ☕	XC ◇1 🛒	GW 1	GW 1	GW 1	GW 1	XC ◇1 🛒	GW 1	GW ◇1 ☕	GW 1
London Paddington 15 ⊖	d		05 22		06 20	05 57		06 30				06 48	07 00	07 15			07 18	07 22	06 57			07 48	
Ealing Broadway ⊖	d		05 30			06 05													07 05				
Slough 3	d		05 54		06 35	06 29						07 04						07 36	07 29				
Maidenhead 3	d		06 02			06 37													07 37				
Twyford 3	d		06 10			06 45													07 45				
Reading 7	d	06 15	06 21	06 41	06 51	06 53		06 56	07 01	07 11	07 19	07 22	07 26	07 41	07 41	07 43	07 48	07 52	07 53	08 11	08 12	08 16	
Reading West	d	06 17							07 03		07 21										08 14		
Theale	d	06 23							07 09		07 28						07 56				08 20		
Aldermaston	d	06 28							07 14		07 33						08 01				08 25		
Midgham	d	06 32							07 18		07 36										08 29		
Thatcham	d	06 37							07 23		07 41						08 08				08 34		
Newbury Racecourse	d	06 41							07 27		07 46										08 38		
Newbury	a	06 47							07 30		07 51						08 13				08 42		
	d								07 30								08 13				08 42		
Kintbury	d								07 37								08 20				08 49		
Hungerford	d								07 41								08 24				08 53		
Bedwyn	a								07 51								08 34				09 03		
Tilehurst	d		06 25			06 57						07 27							07 57				
Pangbourne	d		06 29			07 01						07 31							08 01				
Goring & Streatley	d		06 34			07 06						07 36							08 06				
Cholsey	d		06 39			07 11						07 41							08 11				
Didcot Parkway	a		06 47			07 19		07 10				07 49	07 40	07 55		08 02			08 20			08 32	
	d		06 48			07 33	07 09					07 50				08 08			08 25				
Appleford	d					07 37										08 13							
Culham	d					07 39	07 13									08 15							
Radley	d					07 43	07 17									08 19			08 33				
Oxford	a		07 00	07 05	07 18	07 53	07 26			07 35		08 02			08 05	08 30		08 19	08 42	08 34			
	d			07 07			07 27			07 36					08 07					08 36			08 35
Islip	d						07 41																08 48
Bicester Town	a						07 53																09 01
Tackley	d																						
Heyford	d																						
Kings Sutton	d																						
Banbury	a			07 24						07 54					08 26					08 52			
Leamington Spa 8	a			07 42						08 11					08 43					09 10			
Coventry	a									08 23										09 22			
Birmingham International	a									08 37										09 37			
Birmingham New Street 12	a			08 16						08 48					09 18					09 48			

A MX from 5 October
B MX until 1 October

Table 116

Mondays to Fridays

London and Reading - Bedwyn, Oxford, Bicester, Banbury and Birmingham

		GW 1	GW 1	GW ◇1 ☕	GW 1	GW ◇1 ☕	GW 1	XC ◇1 🛒	GW ◇1 ☕	GW ◇1 ☕	GW 1	GW ◇1 ☕	XC ◇1 🛒	GW 1	GW 1	GW 1	GW ◇1 ☕	GW 1	XC ◇1 🛒	GW 1	GW ◇1 🛒	GW 1
London Paddington 15 ⊖	d	07 50	07 27	08 00		08 15			08 18	08 22	07 57	08 30			08 51	08 27	09 15			09 18	09 21	08 57
Ealing Broadway ⊖	d		07 35								08 05					08 35						09 05
Slough 3	d	08 05	07 59							08 36	08 29				09 06	08 59					09 36	09 27
Maidenhead 3	d		08 07								08 37					09 06						09 34
Twyford 3	d		08 15								08 45					09 16						09 42
Reading 7	d	08 21	08 23	08 27	08 34	08 41		08 41	08 48	08 52	08 55	08 57	09 11	09 12	09 22	09 23	09 41		09 41	09 48	09 52	09 53
Reading West	d													09 14								
Theale	d				08 41				08 56					09 20						09 56		
Aldermaston	d				08 46									09 25								
Midgham	d													09 29								
Thatcham	d				08 53				09 04					09 34						10 04		
Newbury Racecourse	d													09 38								
Newbury	a				09 03				09 12					09 44						10 10		
	d								09 12											10 10		
Kintbury	d																			10 17		
Hungerford	d								09 21											10 21		
Bedwyn	a								09 30											10 31		
Tilehurst	d		08 27								09 00					09 27						09 57
Pangbourne	d		08 31								09 04					09 31						10 01
Goring & Streatley	d		08 36								09 09					09 36						10 06
Cholsey	d		08 41								09 14					09 41						10 11
Didcot Parkway	a		08 50	08 40		08 55					09 22	09 11			09 37	09 50	09 55					10 18
	d		08 55								09 25				09 38	09 55						10 25
Appleford	d		09 00																			
Culham	d		09 01													10 01						
Radley	d		09 06								09 33					10 03						
Oxford	a	08 48	09 15					09 05		09 20	09 42		09 34		09 52	10 14			10 04		10 18	10 40
	d						08 53	09 07					09 36					10 00	10 07			
Islip	d																	10 13				
Bicester Town	a																	10 25				
Tackley	d						09 02															
Heyford	d						09 06															
Kings Sutton	d						09 15															
Banbury	a						09 21	09 25					09 52						10 24			
Leamington Spa 8	a							09 42					10 10						10 44			
Coventry	a												10 22									
Birmingham International	a												10 37									
Birmingham New Street 12	a							10 18					10 48						11 18			

		GW ◇1 Ø	XC ◇1 🛒	GW 1	GW ◇1 ☕	GW ◇1	GW 1	GW ◇1 ☕	GW 1	XC ◇1 🛒	GW 1	GW ◇1 ☕	GW 1	GW ◇1 Ø	GW 1	XC ◇1 🛒	GW 1	GW ◇1	GW 1	GW ◇1 ☕	XC ◇1 🛒	GW 1	GW ◇1 ☕
London Paddington 15 ⊖	d	09 30			09 48	09 50	09 27	10 15			10 18	10 22	09 57	10 30				10 50	10 27	11 15		11 18	11 22
Ealing Broadway ⊖	d						09 35						10 05						10 35				
Slough 3	d					10 06	09 57					10 36	10 27					11 06	10 57				11 36
Maidenhead 3	d						10 04						10 34						11 04				
Twyford 3	d						10 12						10 42						11 12				
Reading 7	d	09 57	10 11	10 12	10 16	10 22	10 23	10 41		10 41	10 48	10 52	10 53	10 57		11 11	11 12	11 21	11 23	11 41	11 41	11 48	11 52
Reading West	d			10 14													11 14						
Theale	d			10 20							10 56						11 20					11 56	
Aldermaston	d			10 25													11 25						
Midgham	d			10 29													11 29						
Thatcham	d			10 34							11 04						11 34					12 04	
Newbury Racecourse	d			10 38													11 38						
Newbury	a			10 44							11 10						11 44					12 10	
	d										11 10											12 10	
Kintbury	d										11 17											12 17	
Hungerford	d										11 21											12 21	
Bedwyn	a										11 31											12 31	
Tilehurst	d						10 27						10 57						11 27				
Pangbourne	d						10 31						11 01						11 31				
Goring & Streatley	d						10 36						11 06						11 36				
Cholsey	d						10 41						11 11						11 41				
Didcot Parkway	a	10 11			10 32		10 49	10 55					11 19	11 11				11 37	11 50	11 55			
	d						10 55						11 25					11 38	11 55				
Appleford	d						11 00																
Culham	d																						
Radley	d						11 03												12 03				
Oxford	a		10 34			10 48	11 14			11 04		11 18	11 40			11 34		11 50	12 12		12 05		12 18
	d		10 36						11 00	11 07		11 19			11 24	11 36					12 07		12 19
Islip	d								11 13														
Bicester Town	a								11 25														
Tackley	d														11 33								
Heyford	d														11 37								
Kings Sutton	d														11 46								
Banbury	a		10 52							11 24					11 52	11 55					12 26		
Leamington Spa 8	a		11 10							11 41						12 12					12 44		
Coventry	a		11 22													12 24							
Birmingham International	a		11 37													12 37							
Birmingham New Street 12	a		11 48							12 18						12 48					13 18		

London and Reading - Bedwyn, Oxford, Bicester, Banbury and Birmingham

		GW 1	GW ◇1 ⊏	XC ◇1 ⚒	GW 1	GW ◇1 ⊏	GW ◇1 ⚒	GW 1	GW ◇1 ⊏	XC ◇1 ⚒	GW ◇1 ⊏	GW ◇1	GW 1	GW ◇1 ⊏	GW 1	XC ◇1 ⚒	GW 1	GW ◇1	GW 1	XC ◇1 ⚒	GW ◇1 ⊏	GW 1	GW ◇1 ⚒
London Paddington 15 ⊖	d	10 57	11 30			11 48	11 50	11 27	12 15		12 18	12 21	11 57	12 30				12 50	12 27		13 15	13 18	13 21
Ealing Broadway ⊖	d	11 05						11 35					12 05						12 35				
Slough 3	d	11 27					12 06	11 57				12 36	12 27					13 06	12 57				13 36
Maidenhead 3	d	11 34						12 04					12 34						13 04				
Twyford 3	d	11 42						12 12					12 42						13 12				
Reading 7	d	11 53	11 57	12 11	12 12	12 16	12 22	12 23	12 41	12 41	12 48	12 52	12 53	12 57		13 11	13 12	13 22	13 23	13 41	13 41	13 48	13 52
Reading West	d				12 14												13 14						
Theale	d				12 20						12 56						13 20					13 56	
Aldermaston	d				12 25												13 25						
Midgham	d				12 29												13 29						
Thatcham	d				12 34						13 04						13 34					14 04	
Newbury Racecourse	d				12 38												13 38						
Newbury	a				12 44						13 12						13 44					14 10	
	d										13 12											14 10	
Kintbury	d																					14 17	
Hungerford	d										13 21											14 21	
Bedwyn	a										13 30											14 31	
Tilehurst	d	11 57						12 27					12 57						13 27				
Pangbourne	d	12 01						12 31					13 01						13 31				
Goring & Streatley	d	12 06						12 36					13 06						13 36				
Cholsey	d	12 11						12 41					13 11						13 41				
Didcot Parkway	a	12 20	12 11			12 32		12 49	12 55				13 19	13 11				13 37	13 49		13 55		
	d	12 25						12 55					13 25					13 38	13 55				
Appleford	d							13 00											14 01				
Culham	d																						
Radley	d							13 03											14 03				
Oxford	a	12 40		12 34			12 48	13 14		13 04		13 19	13 40			13 34		13 50	14 14	14 04			14 18
	d			12 36						13 07					13 30	13 36				14 07			
Islip	d														13 43								
Bicester Town	a														13 55								
Tackley	d																						
Heyford	d																						
Kings Sutton	d																						
Banbury	a			12 52						13 24						13 52				14 27			
Leamington Spa 8	a			13 10						13 42						14 10				14 44			
Coventry	a			13 22												14 22							
Birmingham International	a			13 37												14 37							
Birmingham New Street 12	a			13 48						14 18						14 48				15 18			

		GW 1	GW ◇1 ⊏	GW 1	XC ◇1 ⚒	GW 1	GW ◇1 ⊏	GW ◇1	GW 1	GW ◇1 ⊏	GW 1	XC ◇1 ⚒	GW 1	GW ◇1	GW 1	GW ◇1 ⊏	XC ◇1 ⚒	GW 1	GW ◇1 ⚒	GW 1	GW ◇1 ⊏	XC ◇1 ⚒	GW 1
London Paddington 15 ⊖	d	12 57	13 30				13 48	13 50	13 27	14 15			14 18	14 21	13 57	14 30			14 50	14 27	15 15		15 18
Ealing Broadway ⊖	d	13 05							13 35						14 05					14 35			
Slough 3	d	13 27						14 06	13 57					14 36	14 27				15 06	14 57			
Maidenhead 3	d	13 34							14 04						14 34					15 04			
Twyford 3	d	13 42							14 12						14 42					15 12			
Reading 7	d	13 53	13 57		14 11	14 12	14 16	14 22	14 23	14 41		14 41	14 48	14 52	14 53	14 57	15 11	15 12	15 22	15 23	15 41	15 41	15 48
Reading West	d					14 14												15 14					
Theale	d					14 20							14 56					15 20					15 56
Aldermaston	d					14 25												15 25					
Midgham	d					14 29												15 29					
Thatcham	d					14 34							15 04					15 34					16 04
Newbury Racecourse	d					14 38												15 38					
Newbury	a					14 44							15 10					15 44					16 10
	d												15 10										16 10
Kintbury	d												15 17										16 17
Hungerford	d												15 21										16 21
Bedwyn	a												15 31										16 31
Tilehurst	d	13 57							14 27						14 57					15 27			
Pangbourne	d	14 01							14 31						15 01					15 31			
Goring & Streatley	d	14 06							14 36						15 06					15 36			
Cholsey	d	14 11							14 41						15 11					15 41			
Didcot Parkway	a	14 20	14 11				14 32		14 49	14 55					15 22	15 11			15 37	15 49	15 55		
	d	14 25							14 55						15 25				15 38	15 55			
Appleford	d								15 00											16 01			
Culham	d																						
Radley	d								15 03											16 03			
Oxford	a	14 40			14 34			14 48	15 14			15 05		15 18	15 40		15 34		15 50	16 14		16 04	
	d			14 24	14 36						15 00	15 07					15 36					16 07	
Islip	d										15 13												
Bicester Town	a										15 25												
Tackley	d			14 33																			
Heyford	d			14 37																			
Kings Sutton	d			14 46																			
Banbury	a			14 52	14 55							15 24					15 52					16 29	
Leamington Spa 8	a				15 13							15 42					16 10					16 48	
Coventry	a				15 24												16 22						
Birmingham International	a				15 37												16 37						
Birmingham New Street 12	a				15 48							16 18					16 48					17 18	

London and Reading - Bedwyn, Oxford, Bicester, Banbury and Birmingham

		GW ◇1	GW 1	GW ◇1 ⊏	GW 1	GW 1	XC ◇1 ⚒	GW 1	GW ◇1 ⊏	GW ◇1 ⊏	GW 1	GW ◇1 ⊏	XC ◇1 ⚒	GW 1	GW 1	GW 1	GW 1	GW ◇1 ⊏	GW ◇1 ⊏	XC ◇1 ⚒	GW 1	GW 1	GW 1
London Paddington 15 ⊖	d	15 22	14 57	15 30					15 48	15 51	15 27	16 15			16 18	16 22	15 57	16 30	16 36			16 48	16 27
Ealing Broadway ⊖	d		15 05								15 35						16 05						16 35
Slough 3	d	15 36	15 27							16 06	15 55					16 36	16 26					17 04	16 53
Maidenhead 3	d		15 34								16 03						16 33						17 04
Twyford 3	d		15 42								16 11						16 41						17 12
Reading 7	d	15 52	15 53	15 57			16 11	16 12	16 16	16 22	16 24	16 41	16 41		16 48	16 52	16 53	16 57	17 03	17 11	17 12	17 20	17 23
Reading West	d							16 14													17 14		
Theale	d							16 20							16 56						17 20		
Aldermaston	d							16 25							17 01						17 25		
Midgham	d							16 29													17 29		
Thatcham	d							16 34							17 08						17 34		
Newbury Racecourse	d							16 38													17 38		
Newbury	a							16 44							17 14				17 18		17 44		
	d													17 08	17 24				17 19				
Kintbury	d													17 14	17 31								
Hungerford	d													17 19	17 35				17 29				
Bedwyn	a													17 28	17 45								
Tilehurst	d		15 57								16 27						16 57						17 27
Pangbourne	d		16 01								16 31						17 01						17 31
Goring & Streatley	d		16 06								16 36						17 06						17 36
Cholsey	d		16 11								16 41						17 11						17 41
Didcot Parkway	a		16 19	16 11					16 32		16 49	16 54				17 08	17 20	17 11				17 35	17 49
	d		16 25								16 55					17 09	17 25					17 37	17 55
Appleford	d										17 00						17 30						
Culham	d										17 01						17 32						
Radley	d		16 33								17 06						17 36						18 03
Oxford	a	16 18	16 42				16 34			16 47	17 15		17 04			17 23	17 44			17 34		17 50	18 11
	d				16 23	16 30	16 36						17 07				17 45			17 36			
Islip	d					16 43																	
Bicester Town	a					16 55																	
Tackley	d				16 32												17 54						
Heyford	d				16 36												17 58						
Kings Sutton	d				16 45												18 07						
Banbury	a				16 51		16 54						17 27				18 15			17 54			
Leamington Spa 8	a						17 12						17 44							18 11			
Coventry	a						17 23													18 22			
Birmingham International	a						17 37													18 37			
Birmingham New Street 12	a						17 48						18 18							18 48			

		GW ◇1 ⊏	GW ◇1 ⊏	GW ◇1 ⊏	GW ◇1 ⊏	GW 1	XC ◇1 ⚒	GW ◇1 ⊏	GW ◇1 ⊏	GW 1	GW ◇1 ⊏	XC ◇1 ⚒	GW 1	GW 1	GW ◇1 ⊏	GW 1	GW ◇1 ⊏	GW ◇1 ⊏	GW 1	GW ◇1 ⊏	GW ◇1 ⊏	XC ◇1 ⚒
London Paddington 15 ⊖	d	17 00	17 03	17 06	17 15			17 22	17 30	17 18	17 36				17 48	17 33	17 50	18 00	17 25	18 06	18 15	
Ealing Broadway ⊖	d																		17 33			
Slough 3	d																		17 58			
Maidenhead 3	d									17 40						17 53	18 09		18 10			
Twyford 3	d			17 28						17 48						18 07			18 17	18 28		
Reading 7	d	17 26	17 31	17 36	17 41		17 41	17 50	17 56	17 57	18 03	18 11		18 12	18 16	18 18	18 22	18 27	18 27	18 37	18 41	18 41
Reading West	d													18 14								
Theale	d			17 45										18 20						18 45		
Aldermaston	d													18 25								
Midgham	d													18 29								
Thatcham	d			17 55										18 34						18 55		
Newbury Racecourse	d													18 38								
Newbury	a		17 47	18 02							18 18			18 44						19 02		
	d			18 02									18 26							19 02		
Kintbury	d			18 10									18 32							19 10		
Hungerford	d			18 16									18 37							19 16		
Bedwyn	a			18 24									18 46							19 24		
Tilehurst	d									18 01						18 24			18 31			
Pangbourne	d									18 06						18 30			18 35			
Goring & Streatley	d									18 11						18 36			18 40			
Cholsey	d									18 16						18 42			18 45			
Didcot Parkway	a	17 40			17 55				18 10	18 22					18 32	18 50		18 40	18 54		18 55	
	d									18 25						18 50			18 55			
Appleford	d																		19 02			
Culham	d									18 31												
Radley	d									18 35									19 07			
Oxford	a						18 05	18 15		18 45		18 34				19 06	18 47		19 16			19 11
	d					17 54	18 07	18 16				18 36					18 54		19 16			19 12
Islip	d					18 07																
Bicester Town	a					18 19																
Tackley	d																		19 27			
Heyford	d																		19 31			
Kings Sutton	d																		19 40			
Banbury	a						18 26					18 54							19 46			19 30
Leamington Spa 8	a						18 44					19 10										19 47
Coventry	a											19 22										
Birmingham International	a											19 37										
Birmingham New Street 12	a						19 18					19 48										20 18

Table 116

London and Reading - Bedwyn, Oxford, Bicester, Banbury and Birmingham

	GW	GW	GW	GW	GW	XC	GW	GW	GW	GW	GW
	◇■ ☕	◇■ ☕	■	◇■ ☕	■	◇■ ⊼	■	■	◇■ ☕	■	◇■ ☕
London Paddington ⊖ d	18 22	18 30	18 18	18 33				18 15	18 47	18 51	19 00
Ealing Broadway ⊖ d								18 23			
Slough d								18 47		19 06	
Maidenhead d			18 40					18 57			
Twyford d			18 48					19 05	19 09		
Reading d	18 50	18 56	18 57	19 01		19 11	19 12	19 18	19 18	19 22	19 27
Reading West d							19 14				
Theale d							19 20				
Aldermaston d							19 25				
Midgham d							19 29				
Thatcham d							19 34				
Newbury Racecourse d							19 38				
Newbury a				19 16			19 44				
d				19 17							
Kintbury d											
Hungerford d				19 27							
Bedwyn a				19 35							
Tilehurst d			19 01					19 24			
Pangbourne d			19 06					19 28			
Goring & Streatley d			19 11					19 33			
Cholsey d			19 16					19 38			
Didcot Parkway a		19 10	19 22					19 47	19 32		19 41
d			19 25					19 55			19 42
Appleford d											
Culham d			19 33								
Radley d			19 37					20 03			
Oxford a	19 20		19 47			19 34		20 14		19 50	
d					19 30	19 36					
Islip d					19 43						
Bicester Town a					19 55						
Tackley d											
Heyford d											
Kings Sutton d											
Banbury a						19 52					
Leamington Spa a						20 10					
Coventry a						20 22					
Birmingham International a						20 37					
Birmingham New Street a						20 48					

	GW	GW	GW	XC	GW	GW	GW	GW	GW	GW	XC
	■	■ ✕	◇■ ☕	◇■ ⊼	■	■	◇■ ☕	◇■ ☕	■	◇■ ☕	◇■
London Paddington ⊖ d	18 25	19 03	19 15				19 22	19 30	19 18	19 45	
Ealing Broadway ⊖ d	18 33										
Slough d	18 59						19 36				
Maidenhead d	19 10								19 40		
Twyford d	19 18								19 48		
Reading d	19 27	19u32	19 41	19 41		19 42	19 52	19 57	19 57	20 11	20 11
Reading West d						19 44					
Theale d						19 50					
Aldermaston d						19 55					
Midgham d						19 59					
Thatcham d						20 04					
Newbury Racecourse d						20 08					
Newbury a		19 48				20 11				20 27	
d					19 57	20 32					
Kintbury d					20 03	20 38					
Hungerford d					20 08	20 42					
Bedwyn a					20 17	20 52					
Tilehurst d	19 31								20 01		
Pangbourne d	19 35								20 06		
Goring & Streatley d	19 40								20 11		
Cholsey d	19 46								20 16		
Didcot Parkway a	19 53		19 55					20 11	20 22		
d	20 08								20 25		
Appleford d	20 13										
Culham d									20 31		
Radley d	20 18								20 35		
Oxford a	20 27			20 05			20 18		20 45		20 34
d				20 07							20 36
Islip d											
Bicester Town a											
Tackley d											
Heyford d											
Kings Sutton d											
Banbury a				20 27							20 52
Leamington Spa a				20 45							21 10
Coventry a											21 22
Birmingham International a											21 37
Birmingham New Street a				21 22							21 48

	GW	GW	GW	GW	GW	GW	GW	GW	XC	GW	GW
	◇■ ☕	◇■	■	■	■	◇■ ☕	◇■ ☕	■	◇■	◇■ ⊼	■
London Paddington ⊖ d	19 48	19 50			19 27	20 00	20 15			20 20	19 57
Ealing Broadway ⊖ d					19 35						20 05
Slough d		20 06			19 59					20 36	20 27
Maidenhead d					20 09						20 34
Twyford d					20 17						20 42
Reading d	20 16	20 22			20 23	20 27	20 41	20 41	20 41	20 52	20 53
Reading West d								20 44			
Theale d								20 50			
Aldermaston d								20 55			
Midgham d								20 58			
Thatcham d								21 03			
Newbury Racecourse d								21 08			
Newbury a								21 11			
d								21 22			
Kintbury d								21 29			
Hungerford d								21 33			
Bedwyn a								21 43			
Tilehurst d					20 27						20 57
Pangbourne d					20 31						21 01
Goring & Streatley d					20 36						21 06
Cholsey d					20 41						21 11
Didcot Parkway a	20 32				20 51	20 41	20 55		21 04		21 19
d					20 55				21 08		21 25
Appleford d					20 59						
Culham d											
Radley d					21 04						21 33
Oxford a		20 48			21 12				21 21	21 16	21 42
d			20 55	21 00					21 23		
Islip d				21 13							
Bicester Town a				21 25							
Tackley d			21 04								
Heyford d			21 08								
Kings Sutton d			21 17								
Banbury a			21 23						21 40		
Leamington Spa a									21 59		
Coventry a											
Birmingham International a											
Birmingham New Street a									22 30		

	GW	GW	XC	GW	GW	GW	GW	GW FX	XC	GW
	◇■ ☕	◇■ ☕	◇■	■	◇■ ⊼	■	◇■ ☕	◇■ ☕	◇■	◇■
London Paddington ⊖ d	20 35	20 45			20 51	20 27	21 15	21 15		21 21
Ealing Broadway ⊖ d						20 35				
Slough d					21 06	20 57				21 36
Maidenhead d						21 04				
Twyford d						21 12				
Reading d	21 01	21 11	21 11		21 22	21 27	21 41	21 41	21 46	21 52
Reading West d										
Theale d										
Aldermaston d										
Midgham d										
Thatcham d										
Newbury Racecourse d										
Newbury a	21 17									
d										
Kintbury d										
Hungerford d										
Bedwyn a										
Tilehurst d						21 32				
Pangbourne d						21 36				
Goring & Streatley d						21 41				
Cholsey d						21 46				
Didcot Parkway a		21 25				21 54	22 00	22 00		
d						21 55	22 00	22 00		
Appleford d						21 59				
Culham d						22 01				
Radley d						22 05				
Oxford a			21 34		21 53	22 15			22 28	22 24
d			21 36	21 41					22 30	
Islip d										
Bicester Town a										
Tackley d				21 50						
Heyford d				21 54						
Kings Sutton d				22 03						
Banbury a			21 52	22 09					22 52	
Leamington Spa a			22 10						23 12	
Coventry a			22 22						23 25	
Birmingham International a			22 33						23 36	
Birmingham New Street a			22 45						23 49	

Table 116

London and Reading - Bedwyn, Oxford, Bicester, Banbury and Birmingham

	GW	GW	GW	GW	GW FO	GW	GW FO	GW FX	GW FX
	■	■	◇■ ☕	■	■	■	◇■ ☕	◇■ ☕	◇■ ☕
London Paddington ⊖ d	20 57		21 45			21 27	22 15	22 15	22 15
Ealing Broadway ⊖ d	21 05					21 35			
Slough d	21 27					21 54			
Maidenhead d	21 34					22 01			
Twyford d	21 42					22 09			
Reading d	21 57	22 01	22 11			22 27	22 41	22 50	22 50
Reading West d		22 03							
Theale d		22 10							
Aldermaston d		22 15							
Midgham d		22 18							
Thatcham d		22 23							
Newbury Racecourse d		22 28							
Newbury a		22 31							
d		22 31							
Kintbury d		22 37							
Hungerford d		22 42							
Bedwyn a		22 52							
Tilehurst d	22 02					22 32			
Pangbourne d	22 07					22 37			
Goring & Streatley d	22 12					22 42			
Cholsey d	22 17					22 47			
Didcot Parkway a	22 25		22 30			22 55	23 01	23 07	23 07
d	22 25					22 55			
Appleford d						23 00			
Culham d						23 01			
Radley d						23 04			
Oxford a	22 39					23 16			
d				22 57	23 09				
Islip d					23 22				
Bicester Town a					23 34				
Tackley d				23 06					
Heyford d				23 10					
Kings Sutton d				23 19					
Banbury a				23 26					
Leamington Spa a									
Coventry a									
Birmingham International a									
Birmingham New Street a									

	GW FO	GW	GW	GW FX	GW FO	GW FX	GW FX	GW FO	GW FX	GW	GW FO	GW FX	GW FO
	◇■	■	■	◇■	◇■ ☕	◇■ ☕	◇■ ☕	◇■	◇■	■	◇■	◇■	◇■ ☕
London Paddington ⊖ d	22 21	21 57		22 21	22 45	22 45	22 45	22 48	22 48	22 45	23 20	23 20	23 30
Ealing Broadway ⊖ d		22 05								22 54			
Slough d	22 36	22 33		22 42				23 06	23 06	23 12	23 39	23 39	
Maidenhead d		22 41								23 23			
Twyford d		22 49								23 31			
Reading d	22 52	22 58	23 00	23 06	23 11	23 15	23 21	23 22	23 34	23 40	23 54	00 04	00 05
Reading West d			23 02										
Theale d			23 08										
Aldermaston d			23 13										
Midgham d			23 17										
Thatcham d			23 22										
Newbury Racecourse d			23 26										
Newbury a			23 29										
d			23 29										
Kintbury d			23 36										
Hungerford d			23 40										
Bedwyn a			23 50										
Tilehurst d		23 02								23 44			
Pangbourne d		23 06								23 49			
Goring & Streatley d		23 11								23 54			
Cholsey d		23 16								23 59			
Didcot Parkway a		23 25			23 29	23 32	23 38			00 06			00 23
d		23 28								00 06			
Appleford d													
Culham d													
Radley d										00 14			
Oxford a	23 26	23 44		23 38				23 48	00 13	00 23	00 28	00 33	
d													
Islip d													
Bicester Town a													
Tackley d													
Heyford d													
Kings Sutton d													
Banbury a													
Leamington Spa a													
Coventry a													
Birmingham International a													
Birmingham New Street a													

	GW FX	GW FX	GW
	◇■ ☕	◇■ ☕	■
London Paddington ⊖ d	23 30	23 30	23 29
Ealing Broadway ⊖ d			23 37
Slough d			23 54
Maidenhead d			00 01
Twyford d			00 09
Reading d	00 08	00 08	00 19
Reading West d			
Theale d			
Aldermaston d			
Midgham d			
Thatcham d			
Newbury Racecourse d			
Newbury a			
d			
Kintbury d			
Hungerford d			
Bedwyn a			
Tilehurst d			00 23
Pangbourne d			00 28
Goring & Streatley d			00 33
Cholsey d			00 38
Didcot Parkway a	00 25	00 25	00 45
d			00 45
Appleford d			00 50
Culham d			00 52
Radley d			00 56
Oxford a			01 07
d			
Islip d			
Bicester Town a			
Tackley d			
Heyford d			
Kings Sutton d			
Banbury a			
Leamington Spa a			
Coventry a			
Birmingham International a			
Birmingham New Street a			

Table 116

Saturdays

London and Reading - Bedwyn, Oxford, Bicester, Banbury and Birmingham

		CH	CH	GW	GW	GW	GW	GW	GW	GW	GW	GW	XC	GW	GW	GW	GW	XC	GW	GW	GW	GW	XC
				1	◇1	1	1	◇1	1	1	1	1	◇1	1	1	1	◇1	◇1	1	◇1	1	◇1	◇1
		A	B																				
					☕								🛒					🛒				☕	🛒
London Paddington 15 ⊖	d			22p45	23p30	23p29		00 20								05 25	05 50			06 21	05 57	06 30	
Ealing Broadway ⊖	d			22p54		23p37										05 33					06 05		
Slough 3	d			23p12		23p54		00 39								05 51	06 06			06 38	06 31		
Maidenhead 3	d			23p23		00 01										06 02					06 42		
Twyford 3	d			23p31		00 09										06 10					06 50		
Reading 7	d			23p40	00 05	00 19	00 20	00 56	05 10	05 41		05 45	06 10	06 12		06 21	06 22	06 46	06 48	06 54	06 56	06 59	07 11
Reading West	d						00s23		05 13	05 44				06 14									
Theale	d						00s29		05 19	05 50				06 20					06 55				
Aldermaston	d						00s34		05 24	05 55				06 25									
Midgham	d						00s37		05 27	05 58				06 29									
Thatcham	d						00s42		05 32	06 03				06 34					07 04				
Newbury Racecourse	d						00s47		05 37	06 08				06 38									
Newbury	a						00 52		05 39	06 10				06 44					07 09				
	d								05 39	06 10									07 09				
Kintbury	d								05 46	06 17									07 16				
Hungerford	d								05 50	06 21									07 20				
Bedwyn	a								05 59	06 30									07 29				
Tilehurst	d			23p44		00 23						05 49				06 25					07 00		
Pangbourne	d			23p49		00 28						05 53				06 29					07 04		
Goring & Streatley	d			23p54		00 33						05 58				06 34					07 09		
Cholsey	d			23p59		00 38						06 03				06 39					07 14		
Didcot Parkway	a			00 06	00 23	00 45		01 13				06 12				06 46	06 37				07 30	07 12	
	d			00 06		00 45		01 14				06 13				06 47	06 38				07 30		
Appleford	d					00 50						06 17											
Culham	d					00 52						06 20											
Radley	d			00 14		00 56						06 24				06 54							
Oxford	a			00 23		01 07		01 28				06 32	06 36			07 03	06 52	07 10		07 19	07 43		07 34
	d	00 20	00 20								06 16		06 38		07 00			07 12					07 36
Islip	d														07 13								
Bicester Town	a														07 25								
Tackley	d										06 25												
Heyford	d										06 29												
Kings Sutton	d										06 38												
Banbury	a	00 50	00 47								06 46		06 54					07 32					07 52
Leamington Spa 6	a												07 12					07 50					08 10
Coventry	a												07 24										08 22
Birmingham International	a												07 39										08 37
Birmingham New Street 12	a												07 51					08 17					08 48

		GW	GW	GW	GW	GW	GW	XC	GW	GW	GW	GW	GW	XC	GW	GW	GW	XC	GW	GW	GW	GW	GW
		1	◇1	1	1	1	1	◇1	1	1	◇1	▣ 1	◇1	◇1	1	◇1	1	◇1	◇1	1	1	◇1	1
							C		D			C	D								C	D	
								🛒			🛒	☕	☕	🛒				🛒	☕			☕	
London Paddington 15 ⊖	d		06 50			06 27				06 57	07 21	07 30	07 30			07 50	07 27		08 15		08 18	08 18	07 57
Ealing Broadway ⊖	d					06 35				07 05							07 35						08 05
Slough 3	d		07 06			06 57				07 27	07 38					08 06	07 57						08 27
Maidenhead 3	d					07 04				07 34							08 04						08 34
Twyford 3	d					07 12				07 42							08 12						08 42
Reading 7	d	07 11	07 22			07 23	07 35	07 47	07 48	07 53	07 53	07 57	07 57	08 11	08 18	08 22	08 23	08 40	08 41		08 48	08 49	08 53
Reading West	d	07 14													08 20								
Theale	d	07 21					07 44		07 57						08 27						08 57	08 58	
Aldermaston	d	07 26													08 32								
Midgham	d	07 29													08 36								
Thatcham	d	07 34					07 52		08 05						08 41						09 04	09 07	
Newbury Racecourse	d	07 39													08 45								
Newbury	a	07 43					07 58		08 11						08 51						09 11	09 13	
	d						07 58		08 11											08 58	09 27	09 14	
Kintbury	d						08 04		08 17											09 04	09 33		
Hungerford	d						08 09		08 22											09 09	09 38	09 23	
Bedwyn	a						08 18		08 31											09 17	09 47	09 30	
Tilehurst	d					07 27				07 57							08 27						08 57
Pangbourne	d					07 31				08 01							08 31						09 01
Goring & Streatley	d					07 36				08 06							08 36						09 06
Cholsey	d					07 41				08 11							08 41						09 11
Didcot Parkway	a					07 49				08 19		08 11	08 12				08 48		08 54				09 19
	d					07 51				08 25							08 55						09 25
Appleford	d																09 00						
Culham	d					07 56																	
Radley	d					08 00											09 03						
Oxford	a		07 48			08 09		08 13		08 40	08 19			08 34		08 48	09 14	09 04					09 40
	d			07 53	08 07			08 15						08 36				09 07					
Islip	d				08 20																		
Bicester Town	a				08 32																		
Tackley	d			08 02																			
Heyford	d			08 06																			
Kings Sutton	d			08 15																			
Banbury	a			08 23				08 34						08 52				09 23					
Leamington Spa 6	a							08 54						09 10				09 41					
Coventry	a													09 22									
Birmingham International	a													09 37									
Birmingham New Street 12	a							09 19						09 48				10 17					

A from 9 October
B until 2 October
C until 4 September
D from 11 September

Table 116

Saturdays

London and Reading - Bedwyn, Oxford, Bicester, Banbury and Birmingham

		GW	GW	GW	GW	XC	GW	GW	GW	XC	GW	GW	GW	GW	GW	XC	GW	GW	GW	GW	XC	GW
		◇1	◇1	▣ 1	1	◇1	1	◇1	1	◇1	1	1	1	◇1	◇1	◇1	1	◇1	1	1	◇1	◇1
				A																		
		☕	☕	☕		🛒				🛒					☕	🛒					🛒	☕
London Paddington 15 ⊖	d	08 21	08 30	08 35				08 50	08 27		09 18	08 57		09 21	09 30			09 50	09 27			10 15
Ealing Broadway ⊖	d								08 35			09 05							09 35			
Slough 3	d	08 39						09 06	08 57			09 27		09 39				10 06	09 57			
Maidenhead 3	d								09 04			09 34							10 04			
Twyford 3	d								09 12			09 42							10 12			
Reading 7	d	08 54	08 57	09u04		09 11	09 12	09 22	09 23	09 40	09 48	09 53		09 54	09 57	10 11	10 12	10 22	10 23		10 40	10 41
Reading West	d						09 14										10 14					
Theale	d						09 20				09 56						10 20					
Aldermaston	d						09 25										10 25					
Midgham	d						09 29										10 29					
Thatcham	d						09 34				10 04						10 34					
Newbury Racecourse	d						09 38										10 38					
Newbury	a			09 20			09 44				10 10						10 44					
	d										10 10											
Kintbury	d										10 17											
Hungerford	d										10 21											
Bedwyn	a										10 30											
Tilehurst	d								09 27			09 57							10 27			
Pangbourne	d								09 31			10 01							10 31			
Goring & Streatley	d								09 36			10 06							10 36			
Cholsey	d								09 41			10 11							10 41			
Didcot Parkway	a		09 12						09 48			10 18			10 12				10 48			10 54
	d								09 55			10 25							10 55			
Appleford	d																		11 00			
Culham	d								10 01													
Radley	d								10 03										11 03			
Oxford	a	09 18				09 34		09 48	10 14	10 04		10 40		10 19		10 34		10 48	11 14		11 04	
	d				09 27	09 36				10 07			10 16			10 36				11 00	11 07	
Islip	d				09 41															11 13		
Bicester Town	a				09 53															11 25		
Tackley	d												10 25									
Heyford	d												10 29									
Kings Sutton	d												10 40									
Banbury	a					09 52				10 23			10 48			10 52					11 23	
Leamington Spa 6	a					10 10				10 41						11 10					11 41	
Coventry	a					10 22										11 22						
Birmingham International	a					10 37										11 37						
Birmingham New Street 12	a					10 48				11 17						11 48					12 17	

		GW	GW	GW	GW	GW	XC	GW	GW	GW	XC	GW	GW	GW	GW	GW	GW	GW	XC	GW	GW	GW	GW
		1	1	1	◇1	◇1	◇1	1	◇1	1	◇1	1	1	1	1	◇1	◇1	1	◇1	1	1	◇1	1
		B	C									B	C							B	C		
					☕	☕	🛒				🛒					🛒	⌀		🛒				
London Paddington 15 ⊖	d	10 18	10 18	09 57	10 21	10 30			10 50	10 27		11 18	11 18	10 57		11 21	11 30					11 50	11 27
Ealing Broadway ⊖	d			10 05						10 35				11 05									11 35
Slough 3	d			10 27	10 39				11 06	10 57				11 27		11 39						12 06	11 57
Maidenhead 3	d			10 34						11 04				11 34									12 04
Twyford 3	d			10 42						11 12				11 42									12 12
Reading 7	d	10 48	10 48	10 53	10 54	10 57	11 11	11 12	11 22	11 23	11 40	11 48	11 48	11 53		11 55	11 58		12 11	12 12	12 14	12 22	12 23
Reading West	d							11 14												12 14	12 16		
Theale	d	10 56	10 56					11 20				11 56	11 56							12 20	12 22		
Aldermaston	d							11 25												12 25	12 27		
Midgham	d							11 29												12 29	12 31		
Thatcham	d	11 04	11 04					11 34				12 04	12 04							12 34	12 36		
Newbury Racecourse	d							11 38												12 38	12 40		
Newbury	a	11 10	11 10					11 44				12 10	12 10							12 44	12 46		
	d	11 10	11 21									12 10	12 24										
Kintbury	d	11 17	11 28									12 17	12 30										
Hungerford	d	11 21	11 32									12 21	12 35										
Bedwyn	a	11 31	11 42									12 31	12 44										
Tilehurst	d			10 57						11 27				11 57									12 27
Pangbourne	d			11 01						11 31				12 01									12 31
Goring & Streatley	d			11 06						11 36				12 06									12 36
Cholsey	d			11 11						11 41				12 11									12 41
Didcot Parkway	a			11 19		11 12				11 49				12 19			12 12						12 48
	d			11 25						11 55				12 25									12 55
Appleford	d																						13 00
Culham	d																						
Radley	d									12 03													13 03
Oxford	a			11 40	11 19		11 34		11 48	12 14	12 04			12 40		12 20			12 34			12 48	13 14
	d						11 36				12 07				12 16			12 30	12 36				
Islip	d																	12 43					
Bicester Town	a																	12 55					
Tackley	d														12 25								
Heyford	d														12 29								
Kings Sutton	d														12 39								
Banbury	a						11 52				12 23				12 46				12 52				
Leamington Spa 6	a						12 10				12 43								13 10				
Coventry	a						12 22												13 22				
Birmingham International	a						12 37												13 37				
Birmingham New Street 12	a						12 48				13 17								13 48				

A until 4 September. The Torbay Express
B from 11 September
C until 4 September

London and Reading - Bedwyn, Oxford, Bicester, Banbury and Birmingham

		XC	GW	GW	GW	GW	GW	GW	GW	XC	GW	GW	GW	GW	GW	XC	GW	GW	GW	GW	GW	XC
		◇1	◇1	1	◇1	1	◇1	◇1	1	◇1	1	1	1	◇1	1	◇1	1	1	1	◇1	◇1	◇1
				A	B				C		A											
		⌶	⊡		⊡			⊡	⊡	⌶						⌶				⌶	⊡	⌶
London Paddington 15 ⊖	d		12 15	12 18	12 18	11 57	12 21	12 30	12 35					12 50	12 27		13 18	12 57		13 21	13 30	
Ealing Broadway ⊖	d					12 05									12 35			13 05				
Slough 3	d					12 27	12 39							13 06	12 57			13 27		13 39		
Maidenhead 3	d					12 34									13 04			13 34				
Twyford 3	d					12 42									13 12			13 42				
Reading 7	d	12 40	12 41	12 49	12 49	12 53	12 54	12 57	13u03	13 11		13 12		13 22	13 23	13 40	13 48	13 53		13 55	13 59	14 11
Reading West	d											13 14										
Theale	d			12 57	12 58							13 20					13 56					
Aldermaston	d											13 25										
Midgham	d											13 29										
Thatcham	d			13 04	13 07							13 34					14 04					
Newbury Racecourse	d											13 38										
Newbury	a			13 11	13 13				13 20			13 44					14 10					
	d				13 14						13 25						14 10					
Kintbury	d										13 31						14 17					
Hungerford	d				13 23						13 36						14 21					
Bedwyn	a				13 30						13 42						14 31					
Tilehurst	d					12 57									13 27			13 57				
Pangbourne	d					13 01									13 31			14 01				
Goring & Streatley	d					13 06									13 36			14 06				
Cholsey	d					13 11									13 41			14 11				
Didcot Parkway	a		12 54			13 19		13 12							13 48			14 19			14 12	
	d					13 25									13 55			14 25				
Appleford	d														14 01							
Culham	d														14 03							
Radley	d																					
Oxford	a	13 04				13 40	13 19			13 34				13 48	14 14	14 04		14 40		14 19		14 34
	d	13 07								13 36			13 41			14 07			14 16			14 36
Islip	d												13 54									
Bicester Town	a												14 06									
Tackley	d																		14 25			
Heyford	d																		14 29			
Kings Sutton	d																		14 38			
Banbury	a	13 23								13 52						14 23			14 46			14 52
Leamington Spa 8	a	13 41								14 10						14 44						15 10
Coventry	a									14 22												15 22
Birmingham International	a									14 37												15 37
Birmingham New Street 12	a	14 17								14 48						15 17						15 48

		GW	GW	GW	GW	XC	GW	GW	GW	GW	GW	XC	GW	GW	GW	GW	XC	GW	GW	GW	GW	GW	XC
		1	◇1	1	1	◇1	◇1	1	1	◇1	◇1	◇1	1	◇1	1	1	◇1	1	1	1	◇1	◇1	◇1
						⌶	⊡			⌶	⊡	⌶					⌶				⌶	⊡	⌶
London Paddington 15 ⊖	d		13 50	13 27			14 15	14 18	13 57	14 21	14 30			14 50	14 27			15 18	14 57		15 21	15 30	
Ealing Broadway ⊖	d			13 35					14 05						14 35				15 05				
Slough 3	d		14 06	13 57					14 27	14 39				15 06	14 57				15 27		15 39		
Maidenhead 3	d			14 04					14 34						15 04				15 34				
Twyford 3	d			14 12					14 42						15 12				15 42				
Reading 7	d	14 12	14 22	14 23		14 40	14 41	14 48	14 53	14 54	14 57	15 11	15 12	15 22	15 23		15 40	15 48	15 53		15 55	15 59	16 11
Reading West	d	14 14											15 14										
Theale	d	14 20						14 56					15 20					15 56					
Aldermaston	d	14 25											15 25										
Midgham	d	14 29											15 29										
Thatcham	d	14 34						15 04					15 34					16 04					
Newbury Racecourse	d	14 38											15 38										
Newbury	a	14 44						15 10					15 44					16 10					
	d							15 10										16 10					
Kintbury	d							15 17										16 17					
Hungerford	d							15 21										16 21					
Bedwyn	a							15 31										16 31					
Tilehurst	d			14 27					14 57						15 27				15 57				
Pangbourne	d			14 31					15 01						15 31				16 01				
Goring & Streatley	d			14 36					15 06						15 36				16 06				
Cholsey	d			14 41					15 11						15 41				16 11				
Didcot Parkway	a			14 48			14 54		15 19		15 12				15 48				16 19			16 12	
	d			14 55					15 25						15 55				16 25				
Appleford	d			15 00																			
Culham	d														16 01								
Radley	d			15 03											16 03								
Oxford	a		14 48	15 13		15 04			15 40	15 18		15 34		15 48	16 14		16 04		16 40		16 19		16 34
	d				14 57	15 07						15 36				16 01	16 07			16 16			16 36
Islip	d				15 10											16 14							
Bicester Town	a				15 22											16 26							
Tackley	d																			16 25			
Heyford	d																			16 29			
Kings Sutton	d																			16 39			
Banbury	a					15 23						15 52					16 23			16 46			16 52
Leamington Spa 8	a					15 41						16 10					16 47						17 10
Coventry	a											16 22											17 22
Birmingham International	a											16 37											17 37
Birmingham New Street 12	a					16 17						16 48					17 17						17 48

A until 4 September
B from 11 September
C until 4 September. The Torbay Express

Table 116

Saturdays

London and Reading - Bedwyn, Oxford, Bicester, Banbury and Birmingham

		GW	GW	GW	XC	GW	GW	GW	GW	GW	GW	XC	GW	GW	GW	XC	GW	GW	GW	GW	GW	XC
		1	◇1	1	◇1	◇1	1	1	1	◇1	◇1	◇1	1	◇1	1	◇1	1	1	1	◇1	◇1	◇1
					⌶	⊡				⊡	⊡	⌶				⌶				⊡	⊡	⌶
London Paddington 15 ⊖	d		15 50	15 27		16 15	16 18	15 57		16 21	16 30			16 50	16 27		17 18	16 57		17 21	17 30	
Ealing Broadway ⊖	d			15 35				16 05							16 35			17 05				
Slough 3	d		16 06	15 57				16 27		16 39				17 06	16 57			17 27		17 39		
Maidenhead 3	d			16 04				16 34							17 04			17 34				
Twyford 3	d			16 12				16 42							17 12			17 42				
Reading 7	d	16 12	16 22	16 23	16 40	16 41	16 48	16 53		16 54	16 57	17 11	17 15	17 22	17 23	17 40	17 48	17 54		17 55	17 57	18 11
Reading West	d	16 14											17 17									
Theale	d	16 20					16 56						17 23				17 56					
Aldermaston	d	16 25											17 28									
Midgham	d	16 29											17 32									
Thatcham	d	16 34					17 04						17 37				18 04					
Newbury Racecourse	d	16 38											17 41									
Newbury	a	16 44					17 10						17 47				18 10					
	d						17 10										18 10					
Kintbury	d						17 17										18 17					
Hungerford	d						17 21										18 21					
Bedwyn	a						17 31										18 30					
Tilehurst	d			16 27				16 57							17 27			17 57				
Pangbourne	d			16 31				17 01							17 31			18 01				
Goring & Streatley	d			16 36				17 06							17 36			18 06				
Cholsey	d			16 41				17 11							17 41			18 11				
Didcot Parkway	a			16 48		16 54		17 19			17 12				17 48			18 19			18 12	
	d			16 55				17 25							17 55			18 25				
Appleford	d			17 00																		
Culham	d														18 01							
Radley	d			17 03											18 03							
Oxford	a		16 48	17 14	17 04			17 40		17 18		17 34		17 47	18 14	18 04		18 40		18 18		18 34
	d				17 07				17 10			17 36				18 07			18 16			18 36
Islip	d								17 23													
Bicester Town	a								17 35													
Tackley	d																		18 25			
Heyford	d																		18 29			
Kings Sutton	d																		18 39			
Banbury	a				17 23							17 52				18 23			18 46			18 52
Leamington Spa 8	a				17 41							18 10				18 44						19 10
Coventry	a											18 22										19 22
Birmingham International	a											18 37										19 37
Birmingham New Street 12	a				18 17							18 48				19 17						19 48

		GW	GW	GW	GW	XC	GW	GW	GW	GW	GW	XC	GW	GW	GW	GW	GW	XC	GW	GW	GW	GW
		1	1	◇1	1	◇1	◇1	1	1	◇1	◇1	◇1	◇1	1	◇1	1	1	◇1	◇1	1	◇1	1
																			C			
						⌶	⊡			⊡	⊡	⌶			⊡			⌶	⊡			
London Paddington 15 ⊖	d			17 50	17 27		18 15	18 18	17 57	18 21	18 30		18 50	18 27	19 06				19 15		19 21	18 57
Ealing Broadway ⊖	d				17 35				18 05					18 35								19 05
Slough 3	d			18 06	17 57				18 27	18 39			19 06	18 57							19 38	19 27
Maidenhead 3	d				18 04				18 34					19 04								19 34
Twyford 3	d				18 12				18 42					19 12								19 42
Reading 7	d	18 12		18 22	18 23	18 40	18 41	18 48	18 53	18 54	18 57	19 11	19 22	19 23	19 32			19 40	19 41	19 49	19 52	19 53
Reading West	d	18 14																		19 52		
Theale	d	18 20						18 56												19 58		
Aldermaston	d	18 25																		20 03		
Midgham	d	18 29																		20 06		
Thatcham	d	18 34						19 04												20 11		
Newbury Racecourse	d	18 38																		20 16		
Newbury	a	18 44						19 10							19 48					20 18		
	d							19 10												20 18		
Kintbury	d							19 17												20 25		
Hungerford	d							19 21												20 29		
Bedwyn	a							19 30												20 38		
Tilehurst	d				18 27				18 57					19 27								19 57
Pangbourne	d				18 31				19 01					19 31								20 01
Goring & Streatley	d				18 36				19 06					19 36								20 06
Cholsey	d				18 41				19 11					19 41								20 11
Didcot Parkway	a				18 48		18 54		19 19		19 12			19 48					19 54			20 19
	d				18 55				19 25					19 55								20 25
Appleford	d				19 00																	
Culham	d													20 01								
Radley	d				19 03									20 03								
Oxford	a			18 48	19 14	19 04			19 40	19 18		19 34	19 48	20 14				20 04			20 20	20 40
	d		18 41			19 07						19 36				19 48	19 56	20 07				
Islip	d		18 54													20 01						
Bicester Town	a		19 06													20 13						
Tackley	d																20 05					
Heyford	d																20 09					
Kings Sutton	d																20 18					
Banbury	a					19 23						19 52					20 25	20 28				
Leamington Spa 8	a					19 41						20 10						20 46				
Coventry	a											20 22										
Birmingham International	a											20 37										
Birmingham New Street 12	a					20 18						20 48						21 16				

C from 11 September

Table 116

Saturdays

London and Reading - Bedwyn, Oxford, Bicester, Banbury and Birmingham

		GW	XC	GW	GW	GW	GW	GW	XC	GW	GW	GW	GW	GW	GW	XC	GW	GW	XC	GW	GW	GW	GW
		◇■	◇■	◇■	■	◇■	◇■	■	◇■	◇■	■	◇■	■	◇■	■	◇■	◇■	■	◇■	◇■	■	■	◇■
London Paddington 15 ⊖	d	19 30		19 50	19 27	20 00	20 06			20 15		20 21	19 57	20 30			20 50	20 27		21 17		20 57	21 30
Ealing Broadway ⊖	d				19 35								20 05					20 35				21 05	
Slough 3	d			20 06	19 57							20 36	20 27				21 06	20 57		21 35		21 27	
Maidenhead 3	d				20 04								20 34					21 04				21 34	
Twyford 3	d				20 12								20 42					21 12				21 42	
Reading 7	d	19 57	20 11	20 22	20 23	20 27	20 32		20 40	20 41	20 49	20 52	20 53	20 59		21 11	21 22	21 23	21 40	21 52		21 53	21 57
Reading West	d										20 52												
Theale	d										20 58												
Aldermaston	d										21 03												
Midgham	d										21 06												
Thatcham	d										21 11												
Newbury Racecourse	d										21 16												
Newbury	a						20 46				21 18												
	d										21 32												
Kintbury	d										21 39												
Hungerford	d										21 43												
Bedwyn	a										21 52												
Tilehurst	d				20 27								20 57					21 27				21 57	
Pangbourne	d				20 31								21 01					21 31				22 01	
Goring & Streatley	d				20 36								21 06					21 36				22 06	
Cholsey	d				20 41								21 11					21 41				22 11	
Didcot Parkway	a	20 11			20 48	20 41				20 54			21 19	21 13			21 39	21 48		22 07		22 19	22 12
	d				20 55								21 25				21 40	21 55		22 08		22 25	
Appleford	d				21 00																		
Culham	d																	22 01					
Radley	d				21 03													22 03				22 34	
Oxford	a		20 34	20 47	21 14				21 04			21 20	21 40			21 34	21 53	22 14	22 04	22 20		22 43	
	d		20 36					21 00	21 07						21 20	21 36			22 07		22 25		
Islip	d							21 13													22 38		
Bicester Town	a							21 25													22 50		
Tackley	d														21 29								
Heyford	d														21 33								
Kings Sutton	d														21 42								
Banbury	a		20 52						21 23						21 49	21 52			22 23				
Leamington Spa 8	a		21 10						21 44							22 10			22 41				
Coventry	a		21 22						21 55							22 22							
Birmingham International	a		21 37						22 12							22 37							
Birmingham New Street 12	a		21 48						22 25							22 48			23 09				

		GW	GW	GW	GW	GW	GW	GW	GW	GW	GW	GW	GW	GW	GW	GW
		■	◇■	◇■	■	◇■	■		◇■	◇■	■	■	◇■	◇■	■	■
									A	B	B	A		A	B	A
London Paddington 15 ⊖	d		22 00	22 06	21 57	22 35			23 00	23 00	22 45	22 45	23 30	23 33	23 20	23 20
Ealing Broadway ⊖	d				22 05						22 55	22 55			23 28	23 28
Slough 3	d			22 24	22 27				23 17	23 17	23 21	23 21		23 50	23 54	23 54
Maidenhead 3	d				22 34						23 32	23 32			00 05	00 05
Twyford 3	d				22 42						23 39	23 39			00 13	00 13
Reading 7	d	22 03	22 27	22 41	22 53	23 02	23 12		23 34	23 34	23 49	23 49	23 59	00 10	00 20	00 20
Reading West	d	22 06					23 14									
Theale	d	22 12					23 20									
Aldermaston	d	22 17					23 25									
Midgham	d	22 20					23 29									
Thatcham	d	22 25					23 34									
Newbury Racecourse	d	22 30					23 38									
Newbury	a	22 32					23 41									
	d	22 32					23 41									
Kintbury	d	22 39					23 48									
Hungerford	d	22 43					23 52									
Bedwyn	a	22 51					00 01									
Tilehurst	d				22 57						23 53	23 53			00 24	00 24
Pangbourne	d				23 01						23 58	23 58				
Goring & Streatley	d				23 06						00 03	00 03			00 31	00 31
Cholsey	d				23 11						00 08	00 08			00 36	00 36
Didcot Parkway	a		22 41	22 56	23 19	23 21			23 51	23 51	00 16	00 16	00 18	00 26	00 46	00 46
	d			22 57	23 20				23 51			00 17		00 27		00 47
Appleford	d															00s51
Culham	d															00s54
Radley	d				23 27							00s24				00s58
Oxford	a			23 09	23 37				00 03			00 32		00 39		01 06
	d							23 47								
Islip	d															
Bicester Town	a															
Tackley	d							00s06								
Heyford	d							00s20								
Kings Sutton	d															
Banbury	a							00 45								
Leamington Spa 8	a															
Coventry	a															
Birmingham International	a															
Birmingham New Street 12	a															

A until 4 September
B from 11 September

Table 116

Sundays
until 05 September

London and Reading - Bedwyn, Oxford, Bicester, Banbury and Birmingham

		GW	GW	GW	GW	GW	GW	GW	GW	GW	GW	XC	GW	GW	GW	GW	GW	GW	GW	GW	GW	GW
		■	◇■	■	■		◇■	◇■		◇■	■	◇■	◇■	◇■	■	◇■	◇■	◇■	■	■	■	◇■
		A											B	C								
London Paddington 15 ⊖	d	22p45	23p33		23p20		07 57	08 00		08 03	07 44		08 33	08 37		08 42	08 57	09 00		08 44	09 04	09 30
Ealing Broadway ⊖	d	22p55			23p28						07 52									08 52		
Slough 3	d	23p21	23p50		23p54					08 27	08 20					09 00				09 16	09 23	
Maidenhead 3	d	23p32			00 05					08 36	08 29									09 27	09 33	
Twyford 3	d	23p39			00 13						08 37									09 35		
Reading 7	d	23p49	00 10	00 15	00 20	08 14	08 37	08 42	08 44	08 50	08 53	09 11	09 14	09 14		09 26	09 32	09 37		09 43	09 47	10 05
Reading West	d			00s18		08 17															09 50	
Theale	d			00s24		08 23			08 51												09 56	
Aldermaston	d			00s29		08 28															10 01	
Midgham	d			00s32		08 31															10 04	
Thatcham	d			00s37		08 36			09 00												10 09	
Newbury Racecourse	d			00s42																		
Newbury	a			00 45		08 43			09 05								09 47				10 15	
	d								09 06												10 15	
Kintbury	d								09 12												10 21	
Hungerford	d								09 17												10 26	
Bedwyn	a								09 24												10 35	
Tilehurst	d	23p53			00 24						08 57									09 47		
Pangbourne	d	23p58									09 02									09 52		
Goring & Streatley	d	00 03			00 31						09 07									09 57		
Cholsey	d	00 08			00 36						09 12									10 02		
Didcot Parkway	a	00 16	00 26		00 46		08 53	08 58		09 05	09 17		09 28	09 28		09 41		09 53		10 09		10 18
	d	00 17	00 27		00 47					09 05	09 27					09 42				10 10		
Appleford	d				00s51															10 14		
Culham	d				00s54																	
Radley	d	00s24			00s58						09 34									10 19		
Oxford	a	00 32	00 39		01 06					09 17	09 43	09 34				09 55				10 27		
	d											09 37			09 36				10 00			
Islip	d														09 49							
Bicester Town	a														10 01							
Tackley	d																		10 09			
Heyford	d																		10 13			
Kings Sutton	d																		10 22			
Banbury	a											09 53							10 30			
Leamington Spa 8	a											10 11										
Coventry	a											10 22										
Birmingham International	a											10 38										
Birmingham New Street 12	a											10 50										

		XC	GW	GW	GW	GW	GW	GW	XC	GW	GW	GW	GW	GW	GW	XC	GW	GW	GW	GW	GW	XC
		◇■	◇■	◇■	■	■	■	◇■	◇■	◇■	◇■	■	■	◇■	■	◇■	◇■	◇■	◇■	■	■	◇■
London Paddington 15 ⊖	d		09 35	10 00		09 44	10 04	10 30		10 42	11 00	10 43	11 04	11 30			11 42	11 57	12 00	11 43	12 04	
Ealing Broadway ⊖	d					09 52						10 50								11 50		
Slough 3	d		09 51			10 16	10 23			10 59		11 16	11 23				12 00			12 16	12 23	
Maidenhead 3	d					10 27	10 32					11 27	11 31							12 27	12 31	
Twyford 3	d					10 35						11 35								12 35		
Reading 7	d	10 11	10 12	10 37		10 43	10 47	11 05	11 11	11 21	11 37	11 43	11 47	12 05		12 11	12 21	12 32	12 37	12 43	12 47	12 54
Reading West	d						10 50														12 50	
Theale	d						10 56						11 54								12 56	
Aldermaston	d						11 01														13 01	
Midgham	d						11 04														13 04	
Thatcham	d						11 09						12 03								13 09	
Newbury Racecourse	d						11 14														13 14	
Newbury	a						11 18						12 08					12 47			13 18	
	d												12 09									
Kintbury	d												12 15									
Hungerford	d												12 20									
Bedwyn	a												12 29									
Tilehurst	d					10 47						11 47								12 47		
Pangbourne	d					10 52						11 52								12 52		
Goring & Streatley	d					10 57						11 57								12 57		
Cholsey	d					11 02						12 02								13 02		
Didcot Parkway	a		10 28	10 50		11 09		11 18		11 36	11 50	12 09		12 18			12 37		12 50	13 09		
	d		10 28			11 10				11 37	11 51	12 10					12 38			13 10		
Appleford	d																			13 15		
Culham	d																					
Radley	d					11 17						12 17								13 19		
Oxford	a	10 35	10 42			11 27			11 35	11 50		12 27				12 35	12 50			13 28		13 15
	d	10 37			10 56				11 37						12 33	12 37						13 17
Islip	d				11 09										12 46							
Bicester Town	a				11 21										12 58							
Tackley	d																					
Heyford	d																					
Kings Sutton	d																					
Banbury	a	10 53							11 53							12 53						13 33
Leamington Spa 8	a	11 11							12 11							13 11						13 51
Coventry	a	11 22							12 22							13 22						
Birmingham International	a	11 38							12 38							13 37						
Birmingham New Street 12	a	11 50							12 50							13 48						14 19

A not 23 May
B until 11 July
C from 18 July until 5 September

Table 116

Sundays until 05 September

London and Reading - Bedwyn, Oxford, Bicester, Banbury and Birmingham

Station		GW	XC	GW	GW	GW	XC	GW	GW	GW	GW	XC	GW	GW	GW	XC	GW	GW	GW	GW	XC	GW	GW
		◇1	◇1	◇1	◇1	1	◇1	1	1	1	◇1	◇1	◇1	◇1	◇1	◇1	1	1	1	◇1	◇1	1	◇1
		🍴	🛒	🍴	🍴		🛒				🍴	🛒	🍴	🍴	🍴	🛒				🍴	🛒		🍴
London Paddington 15 ⊖	d	12 30		12 42	13 00				12 43	13 04	13 30		13 42	13 57	14 00		13 43	14 06		14 30		14 43	15 00
Ealing Broadway ⊖	d								12 50								13 50					14 50	
Slough 3	d			12 58					13 16	13 23			13 58				14 16	14 23				15 16	
Maidenhead 3	d								13 27	13 31							14 27	14 31				15 27	
Twyford 3	d								13 35								14 35					15 35	
Reading 7	d	13 05	13 11	13 21	13 37		13 40		13 43	13 47	14 05	14 11	14 21	14 32	14 37	14 40	14 43	14 47		15 05	15 11	15 43	15 37
Reading West	d																	14 50					
Theale	d									13 54								14 56					
Aldermaston	d																	15 01					
Midgham	d																	15 04					
Thatcham	d									14 03								15 09					
Newbury Racecourse	d																	15 14					
Newbury	a									14 08				14 47				15 18					
	d									14 09													
Kintbury	d									14 15													
Hungerford	d									14 20													
Bedwyn	a									14 29													
Tilehurst	d								13 47								14 47					15 47	
Pangbourne	d								13 52								14 52					15 52	
Goring & Streatley	d								13 57								14 57					15 57	
Cholsey	d								14 02								15 02					16 02	
Didcot Parkway	a	13 18		13 36	13 50				14 09		14 18		14 36		14 50		15 09			15 18		16 09	15 50
	d			13 36					14 10				14 36				15 10					16 10	
Appleford	d																15 14					16 14	
Culham	d																						
Radley	d								14 17								15 19					16 17	
Oxford	a		13 35	13 51			14 03		14 27			14 35	14 50			15 03	15 27				15 35	16 25	
	d		13 37			13 56	14 06	14 20				14 37				15 06			15 33		15 37		
Islip	d					14 09													15 46				
Bicester Town	a					14 21													15 58				
Tackley	d							14 29															
Heyford	d							14 33															
Kings Sutton	d							14 42															
Banbury	a		13 53				14 23	14 50				14 53				15 23					15 53		
Leamington Spa 8	a		14 11				14 41					15 11				15 41					16 11		
Coventry	a		14 22									15 22									16 22		
Birmingham International	a		14 35									15 35									16 35		
Birmingham New Street 12	a		14 48				15 10					15 48				16 09					16 48		

Station		XC	GW	GW	XC	GW	GW	GW	XC	GW	GW	GW	GW	XC	GW	XC	GW	GW	GW	GW	XC	GW	GW
		◇1	1	◇1	◇1	◇1	◇1	1	◇1	1	1	1	◇1	◇1	◇1	◇1	1	1	1	◇1	◇1	◇1	◇1
				A									A										
		🛒		🍴	🛒	🍴	🍴		🛒				🍴	🛒	🍴	🛒				🍴	🛒	🍴	🍴
London Paddington 15 ⊖	d		15 06	15 30		15 57	16 00				15 43	16 06	16 30		17 00			16 43	17 06	17 30		17 57	18 00
Ealing Broadway ⊖	d										15 50							16 50					
Slough 3	d		15 23								16 16	16 23						17 16	17 23				
Maidenhead 3	d		15 31								16 27	16 31						17 27	17 31				
Twyford 3	d										16 35							17 35					
Reading 7	d	15 40	15 47	16 05	16 11	16 32	16 37		16 40		16 43	16 47	17 05	17 11	17 37	17 40		17 43	17 47	18 05	18 11	18 32	18 37
Reading West	d											16 50											
Theale	d		15 54									16 56							17 54				
Aldermaston	d											17 01											
Midgham	d											17 04											
Thatcham	d		16 03									17 09							18 03				
Newbury Racecourse	d											17 14											
Newbury	a		16 08			16 47						17 18							18 08			18 47	
	d		16 09																18 09				
Kintbury	d		16 15																18 15				
Hungerford	d		16 20																18 20				
Bedwyn	a		16 29																18 29				
Tilehurst	d										16 47							17 47					
Pangbourne	d										16 52							17 52					
Goring & Streatley	d										16 57							17 57					
Cholsey	d										17 02							18 02					
Didcot Parkway	a			16 18			16 50				17 09		17 18		17 50			18 09		18 18			18 50
	d										17 10							18 10					
Appleford	d																	18 14					
Culham	d																						
Radley	d										17 17							18 19					
Oxford	a	16 03			16 35				17 03		17 25			17 35		18 03		18 27			18 35		
	d	16 06			16 37			16 56	17 06	17 19				17 37		18 06	18 26				18 37		
Islip	d							17 09									18 39						
Bicester Town	a							17 21									18 51						
Tackley	d									17 28													
Heyford	d									17 32													
Kings Sutton	d									17 41													
Banbury	a	16 23			16 53				17 23	17 50				17 53		18 23					18 53		
Leamington Spa 8	a	16 41			17 11				17 41					18 11		18 41					19 11		
Coventry	a				17 22									18 22							19 22		
Birmingham International	a				17 35									18 35							19 35		
Birmingham New Street 12	a	17 09			17 48				18 09					18 48		19 09					19 48		

A until 1 July

Table 116

Sundays until 05 September

London and Reading - Bedwyn, Oxford, Bicester, Banbury and Birmingham

Station		XC	GW	GW	GW	GW	XC	GW	GW	XC	GW	GW	XC	GW	GW	GW	XC	GW	GW	GW	XC	GW	GW
		◇1	1	1	◇1	1	◇1	◇1	1	◇1	1	◇1	◇1	1	◇1	◇1	◇1	1	◇1	1	◇1	◇1	◇1
					A							A											
		🛒			🍴		🛒	🍴		🛒		🍴	🛒		🍴	🍴	🛒		🍴		🛒		🍴
London Paddington 15 ⊖	d		17 43	18 12	18 30	18 43		19 00			19 06	19 30		19 43	19 57	20 00			20 30			20 42	21 00
Ealing Broadway ⊖	d		17 50			18 50								19 50									
Slough 3	d		18 16	18 29		19 16					19 23			20 16								20 59	
Maidenhead 3	d		18 27	18 40		19 27					19 31			20 27									
Twyford 3	d		18 35			19 35								20 35									
Reading 7	d	18 40	18 43	18 56	19 05	19 43	19 11	19 37		19 40	19 54	20 05	20 11	20 43	20 32	20 37	20 40	20 44	21 05		21 11	21 21	21 37
Reading West	d			18 59														20 47					
Theale	d			19 05							20 03							20 53					
Aldermaston	d			19 10														20 58					
Midgham	d			19 13														21 02					
Thatcham	d			19 18							20 12							21 07					
Newbury Racecourse	d			19 23														21 11					
Newbury	a			19 27							20 17				20 48			21 16					
	d										20 18				20 49								
Kintbury	d										20 24												
Hungerford	d										20 29												
Bedwyn	a										20 38												
Tilehurst	d		18 47			19 47								20 47									
Pangbourne	d		18 52			19 52								20 52									
Goring & Streatley	d		18 57			19 57								20 57									
Cholsey	d		19 02			20 02								21 02									
Didcot Parkway	a		19 09		19 18	20 09		19 50				20 18		21 09		20 50			21 18			21 38	21 52
	d		19 10		19 19	20 10		19 51				20 19		21 10		20 51			21 19			21 38	21 52
Appleford	d																						
Culham	d																						
Radley	d		19 17			20 17								21 17									
Oxford	a	19 03	19 25			20 25	19 35			20 03			20 35	21 27			21 03				21 35	21 51	
	d	19 06					19 37		19 56	20 06			20 37				21 06			21 33	21 37		
Islip	d								20 09											21 46			
Bicester Town	a								20 21											21 58			
Tackley	d																						
Heyford	d																						
Kings Sutton	d																						
Banbury	a	19 23					19 53			20 24			20 53				21 23				21 53		
Leamington Spa 8	a	19 41					20 11			20 41			21 11				21 41				22 11		
Coventry	a	19 53					20 22			20 53			21 22				21 53				22 22		
Birmingham International	a	20 03					20 35			21 03			21 35				22 03				22 32		
Birmingham New Street 12	a	20 15					20 48			21 15			21 48				22 15				22 42		

Station		XC	GW	GW	GW	GW	GW	GW	GW	GW	GW	GW	GW	GW	GW	GW
		◇1	1	1	◇1	◇1	1	◇1	1	1		◇1		1	◇1	◇1
		🛒				🍴		🍴			🚌		🚌		🍴	🍴
London Paddington 15 ⊖	d			20 43	21 27	21 37		22 03	21 43	22 15		22 42		22 43	23 03	23 37
Ealing Broadway ⊖	d			20 50					21 50	22 24				22 50		
Slough 3	d			21 16	21 49				22 16	22 46		22 59		23 16		23 55
Maidenhead 3	d			21 27					22 31	22 56				23 24		
Twyford 3	d			21 35					22 39	23 04				23 32		
Reading 7	d	21 40	21 44	21 45	22 08	22 14	22 44	22 50	22 54	23 12		23 21		23 52	23 47	00 15
Reading West	d						22 47			23 15						
Theale	d		21 51				22 53			23 21						
Aldermaston	d						22 58									
Midgham	d						23 01									
Thatcham	d		22 00				23 06			23 30						
Newbury Racecourse	d						23 11									
Newbury	a		22 05				23 15			23 37						
	d		22 06													
Kintbury	d		22 12													
Hungerford	d		22 17													
Bedwyn	a		22 24													
Tilehurst	d			21 47					22 58					23 57		
Pangbourne	d			21 52					23 03					00 01		
Goring & Streatley	d			21 57					23 07					00 07		
Cholsey	d			22 03					23 12					00 12		
Didcot Parkway	a			22 09	22 24	22 29		23 05	23 21			23 37		00 20	00s02	00s32
	d			22 10	22 24						23 26		23 45			
Appleford	d															
Culham	d															
Radley	d			22 17							23 41					
Oxford	a	22 03		22 27	22 37						23 56		00 10			
	d	22 06														
Islip	d															
Bicester Town	a															
Tackley	d															
Heyford	d															
Kings Sutton	d															
Banbury	a	22 23														
Leamington Spa 8	a	22 41														
Coventry	a	22 53														
Birmingham International	a	23 03														
Birmingham New Street 12	a	23 14														

A until 11 July

Table 116

Sundays from 12 September

London and Reading - Bedwyn, Oxford, Bicester, Banbury and Birmingham

		GW	GW	GW	GW	GW	GW	GW	GW	GW	GW	GW	GW	XC	GW	GW	GW	GW	GW	GW	GW	XC	GW	GW	GW
		bus	1	1	bus	1	bus		◇1 ⊏	◇1 ⌶		1	◇1 ⊏	◇1 ⌶	1	◇1	◇1 ⊏	◇1 ⊏	1	1	◇1 ⊏	◇1 ⌶	◇1 ⊏	◇1 ⊏	1
London Paddington 15 ⊖	d		22p45			23p20			07 57	08 00		07 29	08 30			08 42	08 57	09 03	08 44		09 30		09 35	10 03	
Ealing Broadway ⊖	d		22p55			23p28						07 36							08 52						
Slough 3	d		23p21			23p54				08 24		07 58				09 05			09 16				09 57		
Maidenhead 3	d		23p32			00 05				08 31		08 08							09 24						
Twyford 3	d		23p39			00 13						08 16							09 32						
Reading 7	d		23p49	00 15		00 20		08 14	08 33	08 44	08 44	08 48	09 05	09 11		09 21	09 32	09 37	09 43	09 44	10 05	10 11	10 11	10 37	
Reading West	d			00s18				08 17												09 47					
Theale	d			00s24				08 23			08 51									09 53					
Aldermaston	d			00s29				08 28												09 58					
Midgham	d			00s32				08 31												10 01					
Thatcham	d			00s37				08 36			09 00									10 06					
Newbury Racecourse	d			00s42																					
Newbury	a			00 45				08 43			09 05						09 47			10 12					
	d										09 06									10 12					
Kintbury	d										09 12									10 18					
Hungerford	d										09 17									10 23					
Bedwyn	a										09 24									10 31					
Tilehurst	d		23p53			00 24						08 52							09 47						
Pangbourne	d		23p58									08 56							09 52						
Goring & Streatley	d		00 03			00 31						09 01							09 57						
Cholsey	d		00 08			00 36						09 06							10 02						
Didcot Parkway	a		00 16			00 46			08 48	08 59		09 11	09 21			09 37		09 53	10 09		10 18		10 27	10 50	
	d	00 01			00 28		00 56			09 05		09 14				09 38			10 10				10 27		
Appleford	d						01s06												10 14						
Culham	d						01s16																		
Radley	d				00s43		01s26					09 21							10 19						
Oxford	a	00 26			00 58		01 41			09 16		09 30		09 34		09 51			10 27			10 35	10 41		
	d													09 37	09 36							10 37			10 56
Islip	d														09 49										11 09
Bicester Town	a														10 01										11 21
Tackley	d																								
Heyford	d																								
Kings Sutton	d																								
Banbury	a													09 53								10 53			
Leamington Spa 8	a													10 11								11 11			
Coventry	a													10 22								11 22			
Birmingham International	a													10 38								11 38			
Birmingham New Street 12	a													10 50								11 50			

		GW	GW	GW	XC	GW	GW	GW	GW	GW	GW	XC	GW	GW	GW	GW	GW	XC	GW	XC	GW	GW	GW	XC	GW
		1	1	◇1 ⊏	◇1 ⌶	◇1 ⊏	1	◇1 ⊏	1	1	◇1 ⊏	◇1 ⌶	◇1	1	◇1 ⊏	◇1 ⊏	1	◇1 ⌶	◇1 ⊏	◇1 ⌶	◇1 ⊏	◇1 ⊏	1	◇1 ⌶	1
London Paddington 15 ⊖	d	09 44		10 37		10 42	10 43	11 03			11 37		11 42	11 43	11 57	12 03			12 37		12 42	13 03			12 43
Ealing Broadway ⊖	d	09 52					10 50							11 50											12 50
Slough 3	d	10 16				11 05	11 16						12 03	12 16							13 05				13 16
Maidenhead 3	d	10 27					11 27							12 27											13 27
Twyford 3	d	10 35					11 35							12 35											13 35
Reading 7	d	10 43	10 44	11 11	11 11	11 20	11 43	11 37	11 44		12 11	12 11	12 21	12 43	12 32	12 37	12 44	12 54	13 11	13 11	13 21	13 37		13 40	13 43
Reading West	d		10 47														12 47								
Theale	d		10 53						11 51								12 53								
Aldermaston	d		10 58														12 58								
Midgham	d		11 01														13 01								
Thatcham	d		11 06						12 00								13 06								
Newbury Racecourse	d		11 11														13 11								
Newbury	a		11 15						12 05						12 47		13 15								
	d								12 06																
Kintbury	d								12 12																
Hungerford	d								12 17																
Bedwyn	a								12 25																
Tilehurst	d	10 47					11 47							12 47											13 47
Pangbourne	d	10 52					11 52							12 52											13 52
Goring & Streatley	d	10 57					11 57							12 57											13 57
Cholsey	d	11 02					12 02							13 02											14 02
Didcot Parkway	a	11 09		11 24		11 35	12 09	11 50			12 24		12 37	13 09		12 50			13 24		13 35	13 50			14 09
	d	11 10				11 36	12 10						12 38	13 10							13 36				14 10
Appleford	d																								
Culham	d																								
Radley	d	11 17					12 17							13 17											14 17
Oxford	a	11 27			11 35	11 49	12 27					12 35	12 50	13 27				13 15		13 35	13 51			14 03	14 27
	d				11 37					12 33		12 37						13 17		13 37			13 56	14 06	
Islip	d									12 46													14 09		
Bicester Town	a									12 58													14 21		
Tackley	d																								
Heyford	d																								
Kings Sutton	d																								
Banbury	a				11 53							12 53						13 33		13 53				14 23	
Leamington Spa 8	a				12 11							13 11						13 51		14 11				14 41	
Coventry	a				12 22							13 22								14 22					
Birmingham International	a				12 38							13 37								14 35					
Birmingham New Street 12	a				12 50							13 48						14 19		14 48				15 10	

Table 116

Sundays from 12 September

London and Reading - Bedwyn, Oxford, Bicester, Banbury and Birmingham

		GW	GW	XC	GW	GW	GW	GW	XC	GW	GW	GW	XC	GW	GW	XC	GW	GW	XC	GW	GW	GW	GW	XC	GW
		1	◇1 ⊏	◇1 ⌶	◇1 ⊏	1	◇1 ⊏	◇1 ⊏	◇1 ⌶	1	1	◇1 ⊏	◇1 ⌶	1	◇1 ⊏	◇1 ⌶	1	◇1 ⊏	◇1 ⌶	1	◇1 ⊏	◇1 ⊏	1	◇1 ⌶	1
London Paddington 15 ⊖	d		13 37		13 42	13 43	13 57	14 03				14 37		14 43	15 03			15 37		15 43	15 57	16 03			
Ealing Broadway ⊖	d					13 50								14 50						15 50					
Slough 3	d				14 05	14 16								15 16						16 16					
Maidenhead 3	d					14 27								15 27						16 27					
Twyford 3	d					14 35								15 35						16 35					
Reading 7	d	13 44	14 11	14 11	14 21	14 43	14 32	14 37	14 40		14 44	15 11	15 11	15 43	15 37	15 40	15 44	16 11	16 11	16 43	16 32	16 37		16 40	16 44
Reading West	d										14 47														16 47
Theale	d	13 51									14 53						15 51								16 53
Aldermaston	d										14 58														16 58
Midgham	d										15 01														17 01
Thatcham	d	14 00									15 06						16 00								17 06
Newbury Racecourse	d										15 11														17 11
Newbury	a	14 05					14 47				15 15						16 05				16 47				17 15
	d	14 06															16 06				16 48				
Kintbury	d	14 12															16 12								
Hungerford	d	14 17															16 17								
Bedwyn	a	14 25															16 25								
Tilehurst	d					14 47								15 47						16 47					
Pangbourne	d					14 52								15 52						16 52					
Goring & Streatley	d					14 57								15 57						16 57					
Cholsey	d					15 02								16 02						17 02					
Didcot Parkway	a		14 24		14 36	15 09		14 50				15 24		16 09	15 50			16 24		17 09		16 50			
	d				14 36	15 10								16 10						17 10					
Appleford	d																								
Culham	d																								
Radley	d					15 17								16 17						17 17					
Oxford	a			14 35	14 50	15 27			15 03				15 35	16 27		16 03			16 35	17 25				17 03	
	d			14 37					15 06	15 33			15 37			16 06			16 37				16 56	17 06	
Islip	d									15 46													17 09		
Bicester Town	a									15 58													17 21		
Tackley	d																								
Heyford	d																								
Kings Sutton	d																								
Banbury	a			14 53					15 23				15 53			16 23			16 53					17 23	
Leamington Spa 8	a			15 11					15 41				16 11			16 41			17 11					17 41	
Coventry	a			15 22									16 22						17 22						
Birmingham International	a			15 35									16 35						17 35						
Birmingham New Street 12	a			15 48					16 09				16 48			17 09			17 48					18 09	

		GW	XC	GW	GW	XC	GW	GW	GW	XC	GW	GW	GW	XC	GW	GW	XC	GW	GW	GW	XC	GW	GW	XC	GW
		◇1 ⊏	◇1 ⌶	1	◇1 ⊏	◇1 ⌶	1	◇1 ⊏	1	◇1 ⌶	1	◇1 ⊏	◇1 ⊏	◇1 ⌶	1	◇1 ⊏	◇1 ⌶	1	◇1 ⊏	1	◇1 ⌶	1	◇1 ⊏	◇1 ⌶	1
London Paddington 15 ⊖	d	16 37		16 43	17 03			17 37			17 43	17 57	18 03			18 37		18 43	19 03				19 37		19 43
Ealing Broadway ⊖	d			16 50							17 50							18 50							19 50
Slough 3	d			17 16							18 16							19 16							20 16
Maidenhead 3	d			17 27							18 27							19 27							20 27
Twyford 3	d			17 35							18 35							19 35							20 35
Reading 7	d	17 11	17 11	17 43	17 37	17 40	17 44	18 11		18 11	18 43	18 32	18 37	18 40	18 44	19 11	19 11	19 43	19 37		19 40	19 44	20 11	20 11	20 43
Reading West	d														18 47										
Theale	d						17 51								18 53							19 51			
Aldermaston	d														18 58										
Midgham	d														19 01										
Thatcham	d						18 00								19 06							20 00			
Newbury Racecourse	d														19 11										
Newbury	a						18 05					18 47			19 15							20 05			
	d						18 06															20 06			
Kintbury	d						18 12															20 12			
Hungerford	d						18 17															20 17			
Bedwyn	a						18 25															20 25			
Tilehurst	d			17 47							18 47							19 47							20 47
Pangbourne	d			17 52							18 52							19 52							20 52
Goring & Streatley	d			17 57							18 57							19 57							20 57
Cholsey	d			18 02							19 02							20 02							21 02
Didcot Parkway	a	17 24		18 09	17 50			18 24			19 09		18 50			19 24		20 09	19 50				20 24		21 09
	d			18 10							19 10							20 10							21 10
Appleford	d																								
Culham	d																								
Radley	d			18 19							19 17							20 17							21 17
Oxford	a		17 35	18 27		18 03				18 35	19 25			19 03			19 35	20 25			20 03			20 35	21 27
	d		17 37			18 06			18 35	18 37				19 06			19 37			19 56	20 06			20 37	
Islip	d								18 48											20 09					
Bicester Town	a								19 00											20 21					
Tackley	d																								
Heyford	d																								
Kings Sutton	d																								
Banbury	a		17 53			18 23				18 53				19 23			19 53				20 24			20 53	
Leamington Spa 8	a		18 11			18 41				19 11				19 41			20 11				20 41			21 11	
Coventry	a		18 22							19 22				19 53			20 22				20 53			21 22	
Birmingham International	a		18 35							19 35				20 03			20 35				21 03			21 35	
Birmingham New Street 12	a		18 48			19 09				19 48				20 15			20 48				21 15			21 48	

Table 116

Sundays
from 12 September

London and Reading - Bedwyn, Oxford, Bicester, Banbury and Birmingham

		GW	GW	XC	GW	GW	GW	XC	GW	GW	GW	XC	GW	GW	GW	GW	GW	GW
		◇1	◇1	◇1	1	◇1	1	◇1	◇1	1	◇1	◇1	1	◇1	◇1	1	1	◇1
		☕	☕	🛒		☕		🛒			☕	🛒			☕			☕
London Paddington 15 ⊖	d	19 57	20 03			20 37			20 42	20 43	21 03			21 27	21 37	21 43		22 03
Ealing Broadway ⊖	d									20 50						21 50		
Slough 3	d								21 04	21 16				21 53		22 16		
Maidenhead 3	d									21 27						22 31		
Twyford 3	d									21 35						22 39		
Reading 7	d	20 32	20 37	20 40	20 44	21 11		21 11	21 21	21 47	21 37	21 40	21 44	22 08	22 14	22 54	22 44	22 50
Reading West	d				20 47												22 47	
Theale	d				20 53								21 51				22 53	
Aldermaston	d				20 58												22 58	
Midgham	d				21 02												23 01	
Thatcham	d				21 07								22 00				23 06	
Newbury Racecourse	d				21 11												23 11	
Newbury	a	20 48			21 16								22 05				23 15	
	d												22 06					
Kintbury	d												22 12					
Hungerford	d												22 17					
Bedwyn	a												22 24					
Tilehurst	d									21 52						22 58		
Pangbourne	d									21 56						23 03		
Goring & Streatley	d									22 01						23 07		
Cholsey	d									22 06						23 12		
Didcot Parkway	a		20 50			21 24			21 38	22 13	21 52			22 24	22 29	23 21		23 05
	d								21 38	22 14				22 24				23 05
Appleford	d																	
Culham	d																	
Radley	d									22 21								
Oxford	a			21 03				21 35	21 51	22 29		22 03		22 37				
	d			21 06			21 33	21 37				22 06						
Islip	d						21 46											
Bicester Town	a						21 58											
Tackley	d																	
Heyford	d																	
Kings Sutton	d																	
Banbury	a			21 23				21 53				22 23						
Leamington Spa 8	a			21 41				22 11				22 41						
Coventry	a			21 53				22 22				22 53						
Birmingham International	a			22 03				22 32				23 03						
Birmingham New Street 12	a			22 15				22 42				23 14						

		GW	GW	GW	GW	GW	GW	GW	GW
		◇1	1		◇1	◇1		1	◇1
		☕		🚌	☕		🚌		☕
London Paddington 15 ⊖	d	23 37	22 15		22 37	22 42		22 43	23 03
Ealing Broadway ⊖	d		22 24					22 50	
Slough 3	d	23 55	22 46			22 59		23 16	
Maidenhead 3	d		22 56					23 24	
Twyford 3	d		23 04					23 32	
Reading 7	d	00 15	23 12		23 16	23 21		23 53	23 47
Reading West	d		23 15						
Theale	d		23 21						
Aldermaston	d								
Midgham	d								
Thatcham	d		23 30						
Newbury Racecourse	d								
Newbury	a		23 37						
	d								
Kintbury	d								
Hungerford	d								
Bedwyn	a								
Tilehurst	d							23 57	
Pangbourne	d							00 01	
Goring & Streatley	d							00 07	
Cholsey	d							00 12	
Didcot Parkway	a	00s32			23s30	23 37		00 20	00s02
	d			23 26			23 45		
Appleford	d								
Culham	d								
Radley	d			23 41					
Oxford	a			23 56			00 10		
	d								
Islip	d								
Bicester Town	a								
Tackley	d								
Heyford	d								
Kings Sutton	d								
Banbury	a								
Leamington Spa 8	a								
Coventry	a								
Birmingham International	a								
Birmingham New Street 12	a								

Table 116

Mondays to Fridays

Birmingham, Banbury, Bicester, Oxford and Bedwyn - Reading and London

		GW	GW	CH	CH	GW	GW	GW	GW	GW	GW	GW	GW	GW	GW	GW	GW	GW	GW	GW	GW	GW	GW
		MO	MX			MX			MO	MO	MO	MX			MX								
		◇1	◇1			◇1	1	1	1	1	◇1	1		1	1	1	1	◇1	1	1	1	1	1
				A	B		C	D					E	F		E							
		☕				☕							🚌					☕					
Birmingham New Street 12	d																						
Birmingham International	d																						
Coventry	d																						
Leamington Spa 8	d			23p25	23p25																		
Banbury	d			23p44	23p44							23p50											
Kings Sutton	d											23p54											
Heyford	d											00 03											
Tackley	d											00 07											
Bicester Town	d																						
Islip	d																						
Oxford	a			00 14	00 17							00 19											
	d		23p05									00 19	03 38	04 00	04 00		05 03		05 34		05 45		05 59
Radley	d											00 26					05 09				05 51		
Culham	d											00 30											
Appleford	d											00 32											
Didcot Parkway	a		23p18									00 39	04 03	04 11	04 12		05 17		05 46		06 00		06 12
	d	23p11	23p18			23p35	23p40	23p40	23p50		00 35	00 43		04 12	04 12	04 12	05 18	05 41	05 46		06 00		06 13
Cholsey	d								23p56			00 49		04 18	04 18	04 18	05 23		05 52				
Goring & Streatley	d								00 01			00 54		04 23	04 23	04 23	05 28		05 57				
Pangbourne	d								00 05			00 59		04 28	04 28	04 28	05 33		06 02				
Tilehurst	d								00 10			01 03		04 32	04 32	04 32	05 37		06 06				
Bedwyn	d																						
Hungerford	d																						
Kintbury	d																						
Newbury	a																						
	d									23p45										05 40		05 58	
Newbury Racecourse	d									23p47										05 42			
Thatcham	d									23p52										05 47		06 02	
Midgham	d									23p57										05 51			
Aldermaston	d									00 01										05 55			
Theale	d									00 06										06 00		06 10	
Reading West	d									00s13										06 07		06 17	
Reading 7	a	23p27	23p35			23p54	23p55	23p55	00 15	00 17	00 51	01 09		04 38	04 38	04 38	05 43	05 56	06 12	06 12	06 16	06 21	06 30
	d	23p29	23p40			23p55	23p56	23p56	00 15		00 53	01 10		04 39	04 39	04 39	05 44	05 57	06 15		06 16	06 22	06 31
Twyford 3	a								00 21		00 59	01 17		04 45	04 45	04 45	05 50		06 21		06 23		
Maidenhead 3	a		23p53						00 29		01 06	01 25		04 53	04 53	04 53	05 58		06 28		06 31		06 42
Slough 3	a		00 01				00 14	00 14	00 36		01 14	01 32		05 00	05 00	05 00	06 10		06 40			06 40	06 50
Ealing Broadway ⊖	a								00 59		01 30	01 48		05 25	05 25	05 25	06 35		07 05				
London Paddington 15 ⊖	a	00 13	00 26			00 33	00 38	00 42	01 11		01 39	02 00		05 41	05 41	05 41	06 49	06 24	07 17		06 54	07 00	07 09

A MX until 1 October
B MX from 5 October
C MO from 13 September
D MO until 6 September
E MO until 6 September, MO from 25 October
F MO from 13 September until 18 October

Birmingham, Banbury, Bicester, Oxford and Bedwyn - Reading and London

		GW	GW	GW	GW	GW	GW	GW	GW	GW	GW	GW	GW	GW	GW	GW	GW	GW	GW	XC	GW	GW
		1	1	◇1	1	1	◇1	◇1	1	1	◇1	1	◇1	◇1	1	1	◇1	1	◇1	◇1	◇1	1
				🛒			🛒	🛒			🛒		🛒	🛒		🍴	🛒		🛒	🍴	🛒	
Birmingham New Street 12	d																			06 03		
Birmingham International	d																			06 14		
Coventry	d																			06 25		
Leamington Spa 8	d																			06 38		
Banbury	d								06 08									06 30		06 57		
Kings Sutton	d								06 12									06 34				
Heyford	d								06 21									06 43				
Tackley	d								06 25									06 47				
Bicester Town	d											06 23										
Islip	d											06 34										
Oxford	a								06 36			06 49						06 59		07 14		
	d		06 07				06 27		06 37			06 50		06 56		07 09		07 00		07 16		
Radley	d		06 13						06 43									07 06				
Culham	d		06 17						06 47									07 10				
Appleford	d		06 19						06 49									07 12				
Didcot Parkway	a		06 26				06 39		06 56			07 05		07 07				07 22				
	d	06 20	06 31	06 29		06 35	06 39	06 47	07 01		06 59			07 09			07 20	07 28			07 29	
Cholsey	d	06 25	06 37			06 42			07 07							07 24		07 34				
Goring & Streatley	d	06 30	06 42			06 48			07 12							07 30		07 39				
Pangbourne	d	06 35	06 47			06 54			07 17							07 37		07 44				
Tilehurst	d	06 40	06 51			06 59			07 21							07 43		07 48				
Bedwyn	d				06 08					06 23									06 46			07 07
Hungerford	d				06 14					06 28			06 39						06 53			07 12
Kintbury	d				06 18					06 33									06 59			07 17
Newbury	a				06 25					06 40			06 49						07 08			07 24
	d				06 25					06 40			06 50		06 56				07 09			07 24
Newbury Racecourse	d									06 42					06 58							07 26
Thatcham	d				06 30					06 47			06 57		07 03				07 16			07 32
Midgham	d									06 52					07 07							07 36
Aldermaston	d									06 55					07 11							07 40
Theale	d				06 38					07 00			07 07		07 16				07 25			07 45
Reading West	d				06 45					07 07					07 23				07 34			07 52
Reading 7	a	06 46	06 58	06 43	06 49	07 05	06 54	07 00	07 28	07 12	07 13		07 19	07 25	07 28		07 34	07 53	07 37	07 39	07 43	07 56
	d	06 46	07 10	06 44	06 50	07 07	06 56	07 01	07 30		07 15		07 21	07 27			07 36	07 55	07 39		07 45	
Twyford 3	a	06 53	07 16						07 37									08 02				
Maidenhead 3	a	07 02	07 24			07 17	07 07		07 45							07 59		08 10				
Slough 3	a		07 36	06 58					07 56									08 19				
Ealing Broadway ⊖	a		08 03						08 19													
London Paddington 15 ⊖	a	07 27	08 14	07 16	07 23	07 39	07 29	07 32	08 32		07 44		07 53	07 59		08 25	08 07	08 50	08 09		08 14	

		GW	GW	GW	GW	XC	GW	GW	GW	GW	GW	GW	GW	XC	GW	GW	GW	GW	GW	GW	GW	XC
		1	1	◇1	◇1	◇1	◇1	◇1	◇1	1	1	1	1	◇1	◇1	1	1	◇1	◇1	1	◇1	◇1
			🍴	🛒	🛒⊘	🍴	🛒	🛒	🛒				🍴	🍴	🛒			🛒	🛒		🛒	🍴
Birmingham New Street 12	d					06 33								07 03								07 33
Birmingham International	d													07 14								
Coventry	d													07 25								
Leamington Spa 8	d					07 00								07 38								08 04
Banbury	d					07 22				07 27				07 55								08 21
Kings Sutton	d									07 31												
Heyford	d									07 40												
Tackley	d									07 44												
Bicester Town	d																07 57					
Islip	d																08 08					
Oxford	a					07 41				07 55				08 14			08 23					08 40
	d	07 21	07 33			07 43			07 51	07 56			08 05	08 15		08 21				08 37		08 43
Radley	d	07 27								08 02						08 27						
Culham	d	07 31								08 06												
Appleford	d	07 33								08 09										08 45		
Didcot Parkway	a	07 40		07 45			07 53	08 00		08 15			08 18		08 28	08 36			08 46	08 51	08 52	
	d	07 49		07 47			07 55	08 01		08 15			08 20		08 29	08 37			08 47	09 01	08 53	
Cholsey	d	07 55								08 22						08 43				09 07		
Goring & Streatley	d	08 00								08 27						08 48				09 12		
Pangbourne	d	08 04								08 32						08 53				09 17		
Tilehurst	d	08 09								08 37						08 57				09 21		
Bedwyn	d											07 56										
Hungerford	d				07 36							08 01										
Kintbury	d											08 06										
Newbury	a				07 46							08 14										
	d				07 47						07 55							08 29				
Newbury Racecourse	d										07 57											
Thatcham	d										08 02											
Midgham	d										08 07											
Aldermaston	d										08 10											
Theale	d										08 16											
Reading West	d										08 23											
Reading 7	a	08 15	07 58	08 00	08 06	08 08	08 12	08 16	08 21	08 43	08 27		08 36	08 40	08 44	09 03		08 50	09 01	09 28	09 07	09 08
	d	08 19	07 59	08 02	08 08		08 13	08 17	08 23	08 48			08 38		08 45	09 03		08 52	09 02	09 33	09 08	
Twyford 3	a	08 25								08 54						09 09				09 39		
Maidenhead 3	a	08 33								09 02						09 17				09 47		
Slough 3	a															09 29				09 54		
Ealing Broadway ⊖	a															09 54				10 19		
London Paddington 15 ⊖	a	08 59	08 30	08 33	08 38		08 40	08 44	08 51	09 26			09 06		09 14	10 03		09 21	09 29	10 31	09 39	

Birmingham, Banbury, Bicester, Oxford and Bedwyn - Reading and London

		GW	GW	GW	GW	GW	GW	XC	GW	GW	GW	GW	GW	GW	XC	GW	GW	GW	GW	GW	XC	GW	GW
		1	◇1	◇1	1	◇1	1	1	◇1	1	◇1	1	1	◇1	◇1	1	◇1	◇1	1	1	◇1	◇1	1
			🛒	🛒				🍴	🛒					🛒	🍴			🛒			🍴	🛒	
Birmingham New Street 12	d							08 03							08 33						09 03		
Birmingham International	d							08 14													09 14		
Coventry	d							08 25													09 25		
Leamington Spa 8	d							08 38							09 00						09 38		
Banbury	d							08 55							09 19					09 39	09 55		
Kings Sutton	d																			09 43			
Heyford	d																			09 52			
Tackley	d																			09 56			
Bicester Town	d											09 07											
Islip	d											09 18											
Oxford	a							09 14				09 32			09 41					10 10	10 14		
	d			08 51		09 01	09 07	09 16			09 31		09 37		09 42		10 01		10 07		10 16		
Radley	d						09 13												10 13				
Culham	d						09 17																
Appleford	d																		10 17				
Didcot Parkway	a					09 14	09 24						09 50						10 24				
	d		08 59			09 15	09 31		09 29				10 01	09 53				10 16	10 31			10 29	
Cholsey	d						09 37						10 07						10 37				
Goring & Streatley	d						09 42						10 12						10 42				
Pangbourne	d						09 47						10 17						10 47				
Tilehurst	d						09 51						10 21						10 51				
Bedwyn	d				08 40											09 36							
Hungerford	d				08 45											09 41							
Kintbury	d				08 50											09 46							
Newbury	a				08 57											09 53							
	d	08 36			08 57					09 22						09 53							10 13
Newbury Racecourse	d	08 38								09 24													10 15
Thatcham	d	08 43			09 02					09 29						09 58							10 20
Midgham	d	08 47								09 33													10 24
Aldermaston	d	08 51								09 37													10 28
Theale	d	08 56			09 10					09 42						10 06							10 33
Reading West	d	09 03								09 49													10 40
Reading 7	a	09 08	09 13	09 14	09 20	09 32	09 57	09 39	09 44	09 54	09 54		10 28	10 06	10 08	10 16	10 25	10 31	10 58		10 39	10 44	10 45
	d		09 15	09 18	09 21	09 37	10 03		09 45		09 55		10 33	10 08		10 18	10 25	10 32	11 03			10 45	
Twyford 3	a						10 09						10 39						11 09				
Maidenhead 3	a						10 17						10 47						11 17				
Slough 3	a					09 51	10 24				10 10		10 54				10 39		11 24				
Ealing Broadway ⊖	a						10 49						11 19						11 49				
London Paddington 15 ⊖	a		09 44	09 47	09 55	10 09	11 01		10 14		10 29		11 31	10 37		10 54	11 00	11 07	12 01			11 14	

		GW	GW	GW	XC	GW	GW	GW	GW	GW	XC	GW	GW	GW	GW	GW	XC	GW	GW	GW	GW	GW
		◇1	◇1	1	◇1	1	1	◇1	◇1	1	◇1	◇1	1	◇1	1	◇1	◇1	1	1	◇1	◇1	1
		🍴	🛒		🍴				🛒		🍴	🛒		🍴		🛒	🍴				🛒	
Birmingham New Street 12	d				09 33						10 03						10 33					
Birmingham International	d										10 14											
Coventry	d										10 25											
Leamington Spa 8	d				10 00						10 38						11 00					
Banbury	d				10 19						10 55						11 19					
Kings Sutton	d																					
Heyford	d																					
Tackley	d																					
Bicester Town	d					10 30												11 30				
Islip	d					10 41												11 41				
Oxford	a				10 41	10 56					11 14						11 40	11 56				
	d	10 31		10 37	10 43			11 01		11 07	11 16			11 31	11 37		11 43			12 01		12 07
Radley	d									11 13												12 13
Culham	d																					
Appleford	d																					12 17
Didcot Parkway	a			10 51						11 22					11 51							12 24
	d		10 47	11 01					11 16	11 31		11 29			12 01	11 53					12 16	12 31
Cholsey	d			11 07						11 37					12 07							12 37
Goring & Streatley	d			11 12						11 42					12 12							12 42
Pangbourne	d			11 17						11 47					12 17							12 47
Tilehurst	d			11 21						11 51					12 21							12 51
Bedwyn	d						10 36												11 36			
Hungerford	d						10 41												11 41			
Kintbury	d						10 46												11 46			
Newbury	a						10 53												11 53			
	d						10 53						11 13						11 53			
Newbury Racecourse	d												11 15									
Thatcham	d						10 58						11 20						11 58			
Midgham	d												11 24									
Aldermaston	d												11 28									
Theale	d						11 06						11 33						12 06			
Reading West	d												11 40									
Reading 7	a	10 54	11 00	11 27	11 08		11 16	11 24	11 30	11 58	11 39	11 43	11 45	11 54	12 27	12 06	12 08		12 16	12 25	12 30	12 57
	d	10 55	11 02	11 33			11 18	11 25	11 32	12 03		11 44		11 55	12 33	12 08			12 18	12 25	12 32	13 03
Twyford 3	a			11 39						12 09					12 39							13 09
Maidenhead 3	a			11 47						12 17					12 47							13 17
Slough 3	a	11 09		11 54				11 39		12 24				12 09	12 54					12 39		13 24
Ealing Broadway ⊖	a			12 19						12 49					13 19							13 49
London Paddington 15 ⊖	a	11 29	11 32	12 31			11 55	11 57	12 00	13 01		12 14		12 29	13 31	12 37			12 54	13 00	13 06	14 01

Birmingham, Banbury, Bicester, Oxford and Bedwyn - Reading and London

		XC	GW	GW	GW	GW	GW	XC	GW	GW	GW	GW	XC	GW	GW	GW	GW	GW	GW	XC	GW	GW	GW
		◇1	◇1	1	◇1	◇1	1	◇1	◇1	◇1	1	1	◇1	◇1	1	1	◇1	1	◇1	◇1	◇1	◇1	◇1
Birmingham New Street 12	d	11 03						11 33					12 03							12 33			
Birmingham International	d	11 14											12 14										
Coventry	d	11 25											12 25										
Leamington Spa 8	d	11 38						12 00					12 38							13 00			
Banbury	d	11 55						12 19				12 39	12 55							13 19			
Kings Sutton	d											12 43											
Heyford	d											12 52											
Tackley	d											12 56											
Bicester Town	d																						
Islip	d																						
Oxford	a	12 14						12 40				13 10	13 14							13 40			
	d	12 16			12 31		12 37	12 43	13 01		13 07		13 16				13 31	13 37		13 43		14 01	
Radley	d										13 13												
Culham	d										13 17												
Appleford	d																						
Didcot Parkway	a						12 49				13 24							13 49					
	d		12 29			12 47	13 01			13 16	13 31			13 29				14 01	13 53				14 16
Cholsey	d						13 07				13 37							14 07					
Goring & Streatley	d						13 12				13 42							14 12					
Pangbourne	d						13 17				13 47							14 17					
Tilehurst	d						13 21				13 51							14 21					
Bedwyn	d															13 12					13 32		
Hungerford	d															13 17					13 39		
Kintbury	d															13 22							
Newbury	a															13 29					13 49		
	d			12 13											13 13	13 29					13 49		
Newbury Racecourse	d			12 15											13 15								
Thatcham	d			12 20											13 20	13 34					13 56		
Midgham	d			12 24											13 24								
Aldermaston	d			12 28											13 28								
Theale	d			12 33											13 33	13 42					14 05		
Reading West	d			12 40											13 40								
Reading 7	a	12 39	12 43	12 45	12 54	13 00	13 27	13 08	13 24	13 30	13 58		13 39	13 43	13 45	13 51	13 54	14 27	14 06	14 08	14 15	14 24	14 31
	d		12 44		12 55	13 02	13 33		13 25	13 32	14 03			13 44		13 52	13 55	14 33	14 08		14 17	14 25	14 32
Twyford 3	a						13 39				14 09							14 39					
Maidenhead 3	a						13 47				14 17							14 47					
Slough 3	a				13 09		13 54		13 39		14 24						14 09	14 54				14 39	
Ealing Broadway ⊖	a						14 19				14 49							15 19					
London Paddington 15 ⊖	a		13 14		13 29	13 32	14 31		14 01	14 06	15 01			14 14		14 25	14 29	15 32	14 37		14 44	15 01	15 08

		GW	XC	GW	GW	GW	GW	GW	GW	XC	GW	GW	GW	GW	XC	GW	GW	GW	GW	GW	GW	XC	GW	GW
		1	◇1	1	◇1	1	◇1	1	◇1	◇1	1	◇1	◇1	1	◇1	◇1	1	◇1	1	1	◇1	◇1	1	1
Birmingham New Street 12	d		13 03							13 33					14 03							14 33		
Birmingham International	d		13 14												14 14									
Coventry	d		13 25												14 25									
Leamington Spa 8	d		13 38							14 00					14 38							15 00		
Banbury	d		13 55							14 19					14 55				15 07			15 19		
Kings Sutton	d																		15 11					
Heyford	d																		15 20					
Tackley	d																		15 24					
Bicester Town	d			14 00																			15 30	
Islip	d			14 11																			15 41	
Oxford	a		14 14	14 28						14 40					15 14				15 37			15 41	15 56	
	d	14 07	14 16				14 31	14 37		14 43		15 01		15 07	15 16			15 31		15 37		15 43		
Radley	d	14 13						14 43						15 13						15 43				
Culham	d													15 17										
Appleford	d	14 17																						
Didcot Parkway	a	14 24						14 51						15 24						15 51				
	d	14 31			14 29			15 01	14 47				15 16	15 31		15 29				16 01	15 53			
Cholsey	d	14 37						15 07						15 37						16 07				
Goring & Streatley	d	14 42						15 12						15 42						16 12				
Pangbourne	d	14 47						15 17						15 47						16 17				
Tilehurst	d	14 51						15 21						15 51						16 21				
Bedwyn	d										14 36													15 36
Hungerford	d										14 41													15 41
Kintbury	d										14 46													15 46
Newbury	a										14 53													15 53
	d					14 13					14 53						15 13							15 53
Newbury Racecourse	d					14 15											15 15							
Thatcham	d					14 20					14 58						15 20							15 58
Midgham	d					14 24											15 24							
Aldermaston	d					14 28											15 28							
Theale	d					14 33					15 06						15 33							16 06
Reading West	d					14 40											15 40							
Reading 7	a	14 58	14 39		14 43	14 45	14 54	15 27	15 00	15 08	15 16	15 24	15 31	15 58	15 39	15 43	15 45	15 54		16 27	16 06	16 08		16 16
	d	15 03			14 44		14 55	15 33	15 02		15 18	15 25	15 32	16 03		15 44		15 55		16 33	16 08			16 18
Twyford 3	a	15 09						15 39						16 09						16 39				
Maidenhead 3	a	15 17						15 47						16 17						16 47				
Slough 3	a	15 24					15 09	15 54				15 39		16 24				16 09		16 54				
Ealing Broadway ⊖	a	15 49						16 19						16 49						17 19				
London Paddington 15 ⊖	a	16 01			15 14		15 29	16 31	15 32		15 54	16 01	16 09	17 01		16 14		16 27		17 31	16 39			16 57

Birmingham, Banbury, Bicester, Oxford and Bedwyn - Reading and London

		GW	GW	GW	XC	GW	GW	GW	GW	GW	XC	GW	GW	GW	GW	GW	GW	XC	GW	GW	GW	GW	GW
		1	◇1	1	◇1	◇1	1	◇1	◇1	1	◇1	◇1	1	1	1	◇1	1	◇1	1	◇1	1	1	◇1
Birmingham New Street 12	d				15 03						15 33							16 03					
Birmingham International	d				15 14													16 14					
Coventry	d				15 25													16 25					
Leamington Spa 8	d				15 38						16 00							16 38					
Banbury	d				15 55						16 19							16 55					
Kings Sutton	d																						
Heyford	d																						
Tackley	d																						
Bicester Town	d																		17 00				
Islip	d																		17 11				
Oxford	a				16 14						16 40							17 14	17 26				
	d	16 01		16 07	16 16			16 31		16 37	16 43			16 47	17 01		17 07	17 16				17 31	17 36
Radley	d			16 13						16 43							17 13					17 37	
Culham	d																						
Appleford	d			16 17													17 17					17 41	
Didcot Parkway	a			16 24						16 51				17 04			17 24					17 48	
	d		16 16	16 31		16 29			16 47	17 01						17 16	17 31			17 29		18 01	
Cholsey	d			16 37						17 07							17 37					18 07	
Goring & Streatley	d			16 42						17 12							17 42					18 12	
Pangbourne	d			16 47						17 17							17 47					18 17	
Tilehurst	d			16 51						17 21							17 51					18 21	
Bedwyn	d												16 44										
Hungerford	d											16 39	16 49										
Kintbury	d												16 54										
Newbury	a											16 49	17 03										
	d						16 13					16 49									17 13		
Newbury Racecourse	d						16 15														17 15		
Thatcham	d						16 20					16 56									17 20		
Midgham	d						16 24														17 24		
Aldermaston	d						16 28														17 28		
Theale	d						16 33					17 05									17 33		
Reading West	d						16 40														17 40		
Reading 7	a	16 24	16 31	16 59	16 39	16 43	16 45	16 54	17 00	17 29	17 08	17 15			17 24	17 31	17 57	17 39		17 43	17 45	18 27	18 01
	d	16 25	16 34	17 03		16 44		16 55	17 02	17 33		17 17			17 25	17 32	18 00			17 44		18 33	18 02
Twyford 3	a			17 09						17 39							18 06					18 39	
Maidenhead 3	a			17 17						17 47		17 28					18 17					18 47	
Slough 3	a	16 40		17 24				17 09		17 54					17 39		18 24					18 54	
Ealing Broadway ⊖	a			17 49						18 19							18 48					19 19	
London Paddington 15 ⊖	a	17 00	17 06	18 01		17 14		17 27	17 30	18 31		17 54			17 59	18 02	19 00			18 14		19 31	18 30

		GW	XC	GW	GW	GW	GW	GW	XC	GW	GW	GW	GW	GW	XC	GW	GW	GW	GW	XC	GW	GW	GW
		◇1	◇1	1	1	1	◇1	1	◇1	◇1	1	1	◇1	1	◇1	1	1	◇1	1	◇1	1	◇1	◇1
Birmingham New Street 12	d		16 33						17 03						17 33					18 03			
Birmingham International	d								17 14											18 14			
Coventry	d								17 25											18 25			
Leamington Spa 8	d		17 00						17 38						18 00					18 38			
Banbury	d		17 19	17 22					17 55						18 19					18 55			
Kings Sutton	d			17 26																			
Heyford	d			17 35																			
Tackley	d			17 39																			
Bicester Town	d															18 30							
Islip	d															18 41							
Oxford	a		17 41	17 53					18 14						18 40	18 56				19 14			
	d		17 43			18 01		18 07	18 16			18 31		18 37	18 43			19 01	19 01	19 16			19 31
Radley	d							18 13						18 43					19 07				
Culham	d							18 17															
Appleford	d													18 47									
Didcot Parkway	a							18 24						18 56					19 16				
	d	17 53					18 16	18 31		18 29			18 47	19 01					19 32			19 29	
Cholsey	d							18 37						19 07					19 37				
Goring & Streatley	d							18 42						19 12					19 42				
Pangbourne	d							18 47						19 17					19 47				
Tilehurst	d							18 51						19 21					19 51				
Bedwyn	d				17 36						17 55										19 03		
Hungerford	d				17 41						18 00										19 08		
Kintbury	d				17 46						18 05										19 13		
Newbury	a				17 53						18 12										19 22		
	d				17 53						18 13						18 53						
Newbury Racecourse	d										18 15												
Thatcham	d				17 58						18 20						18 58						
Midgham	d										18 24												
Aldermaston	d				18 04						18 28												
Theale	d				18 09						18 33						19 06						
Reading West	d										18 40												
Reading 7	a	18 06	18 08		18 21	18 24	18 31	19 00	18 39	18 44	18 45	18 54	19 01	19 27	19 08		19 16	19 25	19 57	19 39		19 44	19 54
	d	18 08			18 22	18 25	18 32	19 03		18 45		18 55	19 02	19 33			19 18	19 25	19 58			19 45	19 54
Twyford 3	a							19 09						19 42					20 04				
Maidenhead 3	a							19 21						19 50					20 12				
Slough 3	a					18 39		19 29				19 09		19 57				19 39	20 19				20 09
Ealing Broadway ⊖	a							19 53						20 22					20 49				
London Paddington 15 ⊖	a	18 39			18 54	18 59	19 02	20 01		19 14		19 31	19 32	20 31			19 54	20 00	20 59			20 14	20 29

Table 116

Saturdays

Birmingham, Banbury, Bicester, Oxford and Bedwyn - Reading and London

		GW	GW	GW	GW	GW	XC	GW	GW	GW	GW	GW	XC	GW	GW	GW	GW	GW	GW	GW	XC	GW	GW
		1	◇1	1	◇1	1	◇1	◇1	1	◇1	◇1	1	◇1	◇1	1	◇1	◇1	◇1	◇1	1	◇1	1	1
		A						B	A							A	B	C	B				
					⊡		✕	⊡			⊡		✕	⊡		⊡	⊡	⊡	⊡		✕		
Birmingham New Street 12	d						12 33						13 03								13 33		
Birmingham International	d												13 15										
Coventry	d												13 25										
Leamington Spa 8	d						13 02						13 38								14 00		
Banbury	d			13 02			13 21						13 55								14 19		
Kings Sutton	d			13 07																			
Heyford	d			13 15																			
Tackley	d			13 20																			
Bicester Town	d																					14 17	
Islip	d																					14 28	
Oxford	a			13 32			13 40						14 14								14 40	14 44	
	d		13 31			13 37	13 43			14 01		14 07	14 16			14 31	14 31			14 37	14 43		
Radley	d											14 13											
Culham	d																						
Appleford	d											14 17											
Didcot Parkway	a					13 49						14 24								14 49			
	d				13 47	14 01					14 22	14 31		14 29				14 47	14 47	15 01			
Cholsey	d					14 07						14 37								15 07			
Goring & Streatley	d					14 12						14 42								15 12			
Pangbourne	d					14 17						14 47								15 17			
Tilehurst	d					14 21						14 51								15 21			
Bedwyn	d							13 33	13 40														14 37
Hungerford	d							13 40	13 46														14 41
Kintbury	d								13 50														14 46
Newbury	a							13 49	13 57														14 53
	d	13 28						13 50	13 57						14 13								14 53
Newbury Racecourse	d														14 15								
Thatcham	d	13 33						13 57	14 02						14 20								14 58
Midgham	d														14 24								
Aldermaston	d														14 28								
Theale	d	13 41						14 06	14 10						14 33								15 06
Reading West	d														14 40								
Reading 7	a	13 51	13 54		14 00	14 27	14 08	14 19	14 18	14 25	14 36	14 58	14 39	14 43	14 45	14 54	14 54	15 00	15 00	15 27	15 08		15 17
	d	13 51	13 55		14 02	14 33		14 19	14 18	14 25	14 38	15 03		14 45		14 55	14 56	15 02	15 02	15 33			15 19
Twyford 3	a					14 39						15 09								15 39			
Maidenhead 3	a					14 47						15 17								15 47			
Slough 3	a		14 09			14 54				14 40		15 24				15 09	15 10			15 54			
Ealing Broadway ⊖	a					15 19						15 49								16 19			
London Paddington 15 ⊖	a	14 24	14 29		14 32	15 31		14 45	14 55	14 59	15 09	16 01		15 14		15 29	15 29	15 32	15 32	16 31			15 54

		GW	GW	GW	XC	GW	GW	GW	GW	GW	GW	GW	XC	GW	GW	GW	GW	GW	GW	GW	GW	GW	XC
		◇1	1	1	◇1	◇1	1	◇1	1	◇1	◇1	1	◇1	1	1	1	◇1	◇1	◇1	◇1	◇1	1	◇1
			A				B			B	A				B	A	A	B	A	B	A		
					✕	⊡				⊡	⊡		✕						⊡	⊡	⊡		✕
Birmingham New Street 12	d				14 03								14 33										15 03
Birmingham International	d				14 14																		15 14
Coventry	d				14 25																		15 25
Leamington Spa 8	d				14 38								15 00										15 38
Banbury	d				14 55				15 02				15 20										15 55
Kings Sutton	d								15 07														
Heyford	d								15 15														
Tackley	d								15 20														
Bicester Town	d													15 28									
Islip	d													15 39									
Oxford	a				15 14				15 32				15 41	15 55									16 14
	d	15 01		15 07	15 16			15 31				15 37	15 43				16 01	16 01				16 07	16 16
Radley	d			15 13																		16 13	
Culham	d			15 17																			
Appleford	d																					16 17	
Didcot Parkway	a			15 24								15 49										16 24	
	d			15 31		15 29				15 47	15 47	16 01								16 22	16 22	16 31	
Cholsey	d			15 37								16 07										16 37	
Goring & Streatley	d			15 42								16 12										16 42	
Pangbourne	d			15 47								16 17										16 47	
Tilehurst	d			15 51								16 21										16 51	
Bedwyn	d														15 37	15 42							
Hungerford	d														15 41	15 46							
Kintbury	d														15 46	15 52							
Newbury	a														15 53	15 58							
	d		15 05				15 13								15 53	15 58			16 06				
Newbury Racecourse	d		15 07				15 15																
Thatcham	d		15 12				15 20								15 58	16 03							
Midgham	d		15 16				15 24																
Aldermaston	d		15 20				15 28																
Theale	d		15 25				15 33								16 06	16 11							
Reading West	d		15 32				15 40																
Reading 7	a	15 25	15 37	15 59	15 39	15 44	15 45	15 54		16 01	16 01	16 29	16 08		16 16	16 20	16 24	16 24	16 27	16 36	16 36	16 58	16 39
	d	15 25		16 03		15 45		15 55		16 02	16 02	16 33			16 18	16 21	16 25	16 25	16 28	16 38	16 38	17 03	
Twyford 3	a			16 09								16 39										17 09	
Maidenhead 3	a			16 17								16 47										17 17	
Slough 3	a	15 40		16 24				16 10				16 54					16 40	16 40				17 24	
Ealing Broadway ⊖	a			16 49								17 19										17 49	
London Paddington 15 ⊖	a	15 59		17 01		16 14		16 29		16 32	16 37	17 31			16 52	16 53	16 59	17 00	17 06	17 06	17 09	18 01	

A until 4 September
B from 11 September
C until 4 September. The Pembroke Coast Express

Table 116

Saturdays

Birmingham, Banbury, Bicester, Oxford and Bedwyn - Reading and London

		GW	GW	GW	GW	GW	GW	XC	GW	GW	GW	GW	GW	XC	GW	GW	GW	GW	GW	XC	GW	GW
		◇1	1	◇1	◇1	◇1	1	◇1	1	◇1	1	1	1	◇1	◇1	1	◇1	◇1	1	◇1	1	1
					A				B			A				B		C				
		⊡		✕	⊡	⊡		✕						✕	⊡		⊡	⊡		✕		
Birmingham New Street 12	d							15 33						16 03						16 33		
Birmingham International	d													16 14								
Coventry	d													16 25								
Leamington Spa 8	d							16 02						16 38						17 00		
Banbury	d							16 20						16 55						17 19	17 23	
Kings Sutton	d																				17 28	
Heyford	d																				17 36	
Tackley	d																				17 41	
Bicester Town	d										16 35											
Islip	d										16 46											
Oxford	a							16 40			17 02			17 14						17 41	17 53	
	d			16 31			16 37	16 43		17 01			17 07	17 16			17 30		17 37	17 43		
Radley	d												17 13									
Culham	d												17 17									
Appleford	d																					
Didcot Parkway	a						16 49						17 24						17 49			
	d	16 29				16 47	17 01						17 31		17 29			17 47	18 01			
Cholsey	d						17 07						17 37						18 07			
Goring & Streatley	d						17 12						17 42						18 12			
Pangbourne	d						17 17						17 47						18 17			
Tilehurst	d						17 21						17 51						18 21			
Bedwyn	d				16 36				16 40			16 56										17 37
Hungerford	d				16 43				16 46			17 00										17 41
Kintbury	d								16 50			17 05										17 46
Newbury	a				16 53				16 57			17 12										17 53
	d		16 13		16 54				16 57			17 12				17 15						17 53
Newbury Racecourse	d		16 15									17 15				17 17						
Thatcham	d		16 20		17 00				17 02			17 20				17 22						17 58
Midgham	d		16 24									17 25				17 27						
Aldermaston	d		16 28									17 28				17 30						
Theale	d		16 33		17 09				17 10			17 33				17 35						18 06
Reading West	d		16 40									17 40				17 42						
Reading 7	a	16 44	16 45	16 54	17 19	17 00	17 27	17 08	17 17	17 25		17 44	17 57	17 39	17 44	17 47	17 54	18 00	18 27	18 08		18 17
	d	16 45		16 55	17 20	17 02	17 33		17 19	17 25			18 03		17 45		17 54	18 02	18 33			18 19
Twyford 3	a						17 39						18 09						18 39			
Maidenhead 3	a						17 47						18 17						18 47			
Slough 3	a			17 09			17 54			17 40			18 24				18 09		18 54			
Ealing Broadway ⊖	a						18 19						18 49						19 19			
London Paddington 15 ⊖	a	17 14		17 29	17 51	17 32	18 31		17 54	17 59			19 01		18 14		18 29	18 32	19 31			18 52

		GW	GW	GW	XC	GW	GW	GW	GW	GW	GW	GW	GW	XC	GW	GW	GW	XC	GW	GW	GW	GW	GW
		◇1	◇1	1	◇1	◇1	1	◇1	◇1	◇1	1	◇1	1	◇1	1	◇1	1	◇1	◇1	1	◇1	1	◇1
								D	E	D		C							A				D
			⊡		✕	⊡		⊡	✕	✕		⊡		✕				✕	⊡		✕		⊡
Birmingham New Street 12	d				17 03									17 33				18 03					
Birmingham International	d				17 14													18 14					
Coventry	d				17 25													18 25					
Leamington Spa 8	d				17 38									18 00				18 38					
Banbury	d				17 55									18 19				18 55				19 02	
Kings Sutton	d																					19 07	
Heyford	d																					19 15	
Tackley	d																					19 20	
Bicester Town	d										18 04												
Islip	d										18 15												
Oxford	a				18 14						18 31			18 40				19 14				19 32	
	d	18 01		18 07	18 16				18 31	18 31			18 37	18 43		19 01	19 07	19 16			19 31		
Radley	d			18 13													19 13						
Culham	d																19 17						
Appleford	d			18 17																			
Didcot Parkway	a			18 24									18 49				19 24						
	d		18 22	18 31		18 29		18 38				18 47	19 01				19 31		19 29				19 44
Cholsey	d			18 37									19 07				19 37						
Goring & Streatley	d			18 42									19 12				19 42						
Pangbourne	d			18 47									19 17				19 47						
Tilehurst	d			18 51									19 21				19 51						
Bedwyn	d														18 37								
Hungerford	d														18 41								
Kintbury	d														18 46								
Newbury	a														18 53								
	d						18 13								18 53					19 13			
Newbury Racecourse	d						18 15													19 15			
Thatcham	d						18 20								18 58					19 20			
Midgham	d						18 24													19 24			
Aldermaston	d						18 28													19 28			
Theale	d						18 33								19 06					19 33			
Reading West	d						18 40													19 40			
Reading 7	a	18 25	18 36	18 58	18 39	18 44	18 45	18 52	18 54	18 56		19 00	19 27	19 08	19 17	19 25	19 57	19 39	19 44	19 45	19 54		19 59
	d	18 25	18 38	19 03		18 45		18 54	18 55	18 57		19 02	19 33		19 19	19 25	20 03		19 45		19 55		20 01
Twyford 3	a			19 09									19 39				20 09						
Maidenhead 3	a			19 17									19 47				20 17						
Slough 3	a	18 40		19 24					19 09	19 12			19 54			19 40	20 24				20 09		
Ealing Broadway ⊖	a			19 49									20 19				20 49						
London Paddington 15 ⊖	a	18 59	19 08	20 01		19 14		19 29	19 29	19 32		19 32	20 31		19 52	19 59	21 01		20 14		20 29		20 32

A from 11 September
B until 4 September
C until 10 July, from 11 September
D from 17 July until 4 September
E until 10 July

Saturdays

Birmingham, Banbury, Bicester, Oxford and Bedwyn - Reading and London

		GW	XC	GW	GW	GW	GW	GW	GW	GW	XC	GW	GW	GW	GW	GW	XC	GW	GW	GW	GW	XC
		1	◇1	1	◇1	◇1	◇1	1	◇1	1	◇1	◇1	◇1	◇1	◇1	1	◇1	1	◇1	1	1	◇1
					A	B								C	D							
Birmingham New Street 12	d		18 33								19 03						19 33					20 03
Birmingham International	d										19 14											20 14
Coventry	d										19 25											20 25
Leamington Spa 8	d		19 00								19 38						20 03					20 38
Banbury	d		19 19								19 55						20 21			20 38		20 55
Kings Sutton	d																			20 43		
Heyford	d																			20 51		
Tackley	d																			20 56		
Bicester Town	d			19 18														20 30				
Islip	d			19 29														20 41				
Oxford	a		19 40	19 45							20 14						20 40	20 56		21 08		21 14
	d	19 37	19 43				20 01			20 07	20 16		20 31			20 37	20 43		21 01			21 16
Radley	d									20 13												
Culham	d																					
Appleford	d									20 17												
Didcot Parkway	a	19 49								20 24						20 49						
	d	20 01							20 22	20 31		20 29		20 47	20 47	21 01						
Cholsey	d	20 07								20 37						21 07						
Goring & Streatley	d	20 12								20 47						21 12						
Pangbourne	d	20 17								20 47						21 17						
Tilehurst	d	20 21								20 51						21 21						
Bedwyn	d							19 39													20 48	
Hungerford	d							19 45													20 54	
Kintbury	d							19 49													20 58	
Newbury	a							19 56													21 05	
	d				19 50	19 49		19 56													21 05	
Newbury Racecourse	d							19 58													21 07	
Thatcham	d							20 03													21 12	
Midgham	d							20 08													21 17	
Aldermaston	d							20 11													21 20	
Theale	d							20 16													21 25	
Reading West	d							20 23													21 32	
Reading 7	a	20 27	20 08		20 07	20 08	20 25	20 29	20 36	20 57	20 39	20 44	20 54	21 06	21 06	21 27	21 08		21 25		21 37	21 39
	d	20 33			20 09	20 12	20 25		20 38	21 03	20 46	20 45	20 54	21 08	21 08	21 33			21 25			
Twyford 3	a	20 39								21 09						21 39						
Maidenhead 3	a	20 47								21 17						21 47						
Slough 3	a	20 54					20 40			21 24			21 09			21 54			21 40			
Ealing Broadway ⊖	a	21 19								21 49						22 19						
London Paddington 15 ⊖	a	21 31			20 37	20 39	20 59		21 07	22 01		21 14	21 29	21 37	21 36	22 31			21 59			

		GW	GW	GW	GW	XC	GW	GW	GW	XC	GW	GW	GW	GW	GW	GW	GW	GW	GW
		◇1	◇1	◇1	◇1	◇1	1	1	◇1	◇1	1	◇1	◇1	1	◇1	1	◇1	1	1
		C	D	C								A	B						
Birmingham New Street 12	d					20 33				21 03									
Birmingham International	d									21 14									
Coventry	d									21 25									
Leamington Spa 8	d					21 00				21 38									
Banbury	d					21 20				21 55				22 02					
Kings Sutton	d													22 07					
Heyford	d													22 15					
Tackley	d													22 20					
Bicester Town	d							21 37											22 53
Islip	d							21 48											23 04
Oxford	a					21 41		22 03		22 16				22 32					23 19
	d				21 36	21 43	21 50		22 08	22 18		22 31	22 31					23 07	
Radley	d						21 56											23 13	
Culham	d																	23 17	
Appleford	d																	23 20	
Didcot Parkway	a				21 49		22 04		22 19									23 25	
	d	21 29	21 34	21 34	21 50		22 04		22 20						22 49		23 32	23 36	
Cholsey	d						22 10											23 42	
Goring & Streatley	d						22 15											23 47	
Pangbourne	d						22 21											23 51	
Tilehurst	d						22 24											23 56	
Bedwyn	d										22 00					23 00			
Hungerford	d										22 06					23 06			
Kintbury	d										22 10					23 10			
Newbury	a										22 17					23 17			
	d										22 17					23 17			
Newbury Racecourse	d										22 19					23 19			
Thatcham	d										22 24					23 24			
Midgham	d										22 29					23 29			
Aldermaston	d										22 32					23 32			
Theale	d										22 37					23 37			
Reading West	d										22 44					23 44			
Reading 7	a	21 42	21 48	21 49	22 04	22 10	22 31		22 35	22 41	22 50	22 54	22 54		23 04	23 50	23 52	00 01	
	d	21 44	21 50	21 51	22 05		22 33		22 36			22 55	22 55		23 05		23 53	00 03	
Twyford 3	a						22 39											00 09	
Maidenhead 3	a						22 47											00 17	
Slough 3	a				22 22		22 54		22 50			23 12	23 17					00 28	
Ealing Broadway ⊖	a						23 19											00 52	
London Paddington 15 ⊖	a	22 14	22 16	22 21	22 39		23 28		23 09			23 31	23 36		23 38		00 33	01 02	

A from 11 September
B until 4 September
C from 17 July until 4 September
D until 10 July, from 11 September

Sundays
until 05 September

Birmingham, Banbury, Bicester, Oxford and Bedwyn - Reading and London

		GW	GW	GW	GW	GW	GW	GW	GW	GW	GW	GW	GW	GW	GW	XC	GW	GW	GW	GW	GW	GW	XC
		◇1	1	1		1	◇1	◇1	◇1	1	1	◇1	◇1	1	1	◇1	1	◇1	◇1	◇1	1	1	◇1
																			B	C			
Birmingham New Street 12	d															09 03							10 03
Birmingham International	d															09 14							10 14
Coventry	d															09 25							10 25
Leamington Spa 8	d															09 38							10 38
Banbury	d															09 55							10 55
Kings Sutton	d																						
Heyford	d																						
Tackley	d																						
Bicester Town	d																10 04						
Islip	d																10 15						
Oxford	a															10 14	10 31						11 14
	d		23p07		07 45	08 05		08 38			09 05		09 38		10 05	10 16						11 05	11 16
Radley	d		23p13			08 12					09 11				10 11							11 11	
Culham	d		23p17																				
Appleford	d		23p20												10 16								
Didcot Parkway	a		23p25		08 10	08 20		08 50			09 21		09 50		10 21							11 21	
	d	23p32	23p36	07 45		08 20	08 43	08 50	09 14		09 26	09 46	09 50		10 21				10 46	10 54		11 21	
Cholsey	d		23p42			08 26					09 32				10 27							11 27	
Goring & Streatley	d		23p47	07 53		08 32					09 37				10 33							11 33	
Pangbourne	d		23p51			08 36					09 41				10 37							11 37	
Tilehurst	d		23p56			08 41					09 46				10 42							11 42	
Bedwyn	d													09 35							10 54		
Hungerford	d													09 41							11 00		
Kintbury	d													09 46							11 04		
Newbury	a													09 52							11 11		
	d									09 05				09 53				10 27			11 11		
Newbury Racecourse	d									09 07				09 55									
Thatcham	d									09 12				10 00							11 16		
Midgham	d									09 17				10 05									
Aldermaston	d									09 20				10 08									
Theale	d									09 25				10 13							11 24		
Reading West	d									09 32				10 21									
Reading 7	a	23p52	00 01	08 03		08 47	08 59	09 06	09 28	09 35	09 51	09 59	10 06	10 25	10 49	10 42		10 47	11 00	11 09	11 37	11 46	11 42
	d	23p53	00 03	08 03		08 50	09 01	09 06	09 29	09 36	09 52	10 01	10 10	10 26	10 52			10 49	11 02	11 09	11 38	11 52	
Twyford 3	a		00 09			08 56					09 58				10 58							11 58	
Maidenhead 3	a		00 17			09 04				09 48	10 06			10 39	11 06						11 50	12 06	
Slough 3	a		00 28	08 22		09 11		09 25		09 57	10 13		10 32	10 50	11 14						12 03	12 14	
Ealing Broadway ⊖	a		00 52			09 34					10 36				11 37							12 37	
London Paddington 15 ⊖	a	00 33	01 02	08 44		09 44	09 39	09 45	10 06	10 16	10 47	10 39	10 53	11 10	11 47			11 24	11 38	11 51	12 22	12 47	

		GW	GW	GW	GW	GW	GW	GW	GW	XC	GW	GW	XC	GW	GW	XC	GW	GW	GW	GW	GW	XC	GW	GW
		1	◇1	◇1	◇1	◇1	1	1	1	◇1	◇1	◇1	◇1	1	1	◇1	1	◇1	◇1	◇1	◇1	◇1	1	1
					B																			
Birmingham New Street 12	d									11 03			11 33			12 03						12 33		
Birmingham International	d									11 14						12 14								
Coventry	d									11 25						12 25								
Leamington Spa 8	d									11 38			12 00			12 38						13 00		
Banbury	d	11 00								11 55			12 19			12 55						13 19		
Kings Sutton	d	11 05																						
Heyford	d	11 14																						
Tackley	d	11 19																						
Bicester Town	d						11 33										13 03							
Islip	d						11 44										13 14							
Oxford	a	11 29					12 00			12 14			12 48			13 14	13 30					13 41		
	d					11 38			12 05	12 16			12 49		13 05	13 16					13 38	13 43		14 05
Radley	d								12 11						13 11									14 11
Culham	d																							
Appleford	d								12 16															14 16
Didcot Parkway	a					11 50			12 21						13 21						13 50			14 21
	d		11 29		11 47	11 50			12 21		12 29	12 47			13 21			13 29		13 47	13 50			14 21
Cholsey	d								12 27						13 27									14 27
Goring & Streatley	d								12 33						13 33									14 33
Pangbourne	d								12 37						13 37									14 37
Tilehurst	d								12 42						13 42									14 42
Bedwyn	d													13 37										
Hungerford	d													13 00										
Kintbury	d													13 04										
Newbury	a													13 11										
	d			11 26				12 03						13 11					13 31				14 03	
Newbury Racecourse	d							12 05															14 05	
Thatcham	d							12 10						13 16									14 10	
Midgham	d							12 15															14 15	
Aldermaston	d							12 18															14 18	
Theale	d							12 23						13 37									14 23	
Reading West	d							12 31															14 31	
Reading 7	a		11 42	11 47	12 00	12 07		12 34	12 47	12 42	12 42	13 00	13 15	13 37	13 46	13 42		13 42	13 48	14 00	14 07	14 10	14 34	14 46
	d		11 44	11 49	12 02	12 10		12 36	12 52		12 44	13 02		13 37	13 52			13 44	13 49	14 02	14 10		14 36	14 52
Twyford 3	a								12 58						13 58									14 58
Maidenhead 3	a							12 48	13 06					13 48	14 06								14 48	15 06
Slough 3	a					12 32		12 59	13 13					14 00	14 14						14 30		14 59	15 14
Ealing Broadway ⊖	a								13 36						14 37									15 37
London Paddington 15 ⊖	a		12 24	12 29	12 38	12 51		13 23	13 47		13 24	13 38		14 23	14 47			14 24	14 30	14 38	14 52		15 23	15 47

B from 18 July until 5 September
C until 11 July

Table 116

Sundays
until 05 September

Birmingham, Banbury, Bicester, Oxford and Bedwyn - Reading and London

		XC	GW	GW	XC	GW	GW	GW	XC	GW	GW	XC	GW	GW	XC	GW	GW	GW	GW	GW	XC
		◇1	◇1	◇1	◇1	1	1	1	◇1	◇1	◇1	◇1	1	1	◇1	1	1	◇1	◇1	◇1	◇1
Birmingham New Street 12	d	13 03			13 33				14 03			14 33			15 03						15 33
Birmingham International	d	13 14							14 14						15 14						
Coventry	d	13 25							14 25						15 25						
Leamington Spa 8	d	13 38			14 00				14 38			15 00			15 38						16 00
Banbury	d	13 55			14 19				14 55			15 19			15 55		16 00				16 19
Kings Sutton	d																16 05				
Heyford	d																16 14				
Tackley	d																16 18				
Bicester Town	d					14 33										16 03					
Islip	d					14 44										16 14					
Oxford	a	14 14			14 45	15 00			15 14			15 41			16 14	16 30	16 33				16 41
	d	14 16			14 45			15 05	15 16			15 43		16 05	16 16						16 43
Radley	d							15 11						16 11							
Culham	d																				
Appleford	d													16 16							
Didcot Parkway	a							15 21						16 21							
	d		14 29	14 47				15 21		15 29	15 47			16 21				16 29		16 47	
Cholsey	d							15 27						16 27							
Goring & Streatley	d							15 33						16 33							
Pangbourne	d							15 37						16 37							
Tilehurst	d							15 42						16 42							
Bedwyn	d						14 54														
Hungerford	d						15 00														
Kintbury	d						15 04														
Newbury	a						15 11														
	d						15 11						16 03						16 29		
Newbury Racecourse	d												16 05								
Thatcham	d						15 16						16 10								
Midgham	d												16 15								
Aldermaston	d												16 18								
Theale	d						15 24						16 23								
Reading West	d												16 31								
Reading 7	a	14 42	14 42	15 00	15 15		15 37	15 46	15 42	15 42	16 00	16 09	16 34	16 46	16 42			16 42	16 47	17 00	17 09
	d		14 44	15 02			15 37	15 52		15 44	16 02		16 36	16 52				16 44	16 49	17 02	
Twyford 3	a							15 58						16 58							
Maidenhead 3	a						15 48	16 06					16 48	17 06							
Slough 3	a						16 00	16 14					16 59	17 14							
Ealing Broadway ⊖	a							16 37						17 37							
London Paddington 15 ⊖	a		15 24	15 38			16 23	16 48		16 24	16 38		17 23	17 48				17 24	17 29	17 38	

		GW	GW	XC	GW	GW	XC	GW	GW	GW	GW	XC	GW	GW	GW	GW	GW	XC	GW	GW	GW	XC
		1	1	◇1	◇1	◇1	◇1	1	◇1	1	1	◇1	1	◇1	◇1	◇1	◇1	◇1	1	◇1	1	◇1
															A	B						
Birmingham New Street 12	d			16 04			16 33					17 03						17 33				18 03
Birmingham International	d			16 14								17 14										18 14
Coventry	d			16 25								17 25										18 25
Leamington Spa 8	d			16 38			17 00					17 38						18 00				18 38
Banbury	d			16 55			17 19					17 55	18 00					18 19				18 55
Kings Sutton	d												18 07									
Heyford	d												18 16									
Tackley	d												18 20									
Bicester Town	d							17 33														
Islip	d							17 44														
Oxford	a			17 14			17 38	18 00				18 14	18 31					18 44				19 14
	d		17 05	17 16			17 43				18 05	18 16						18 45			19 05	19 16
Radley	d		17 11								18 11										19 11	
Culham	d																					
Appleford	d										18 16											
Didcot Parkway	a		17 21								18 21										19 21	
	d		17 21		17 29	17 47			17 58		18 21				18 47	18 47	18 59			19 19	19 21	
Cholsey	d		17 27								18 27										19 27	
Goring & Streatley	d		17 33								18 33										19 33	
Pangbourne	d		17 37								18 37										19 37	
Tilehurst	d		17 42								18 42										19 42	
Bedwyn	d	16 54																	18 47			
Hungerford	d	17 00																	18 53			
Kintbury	d	17 04																	18 57			
Newbury	a	17 11																	19 04			
	d	17 11								18 03				18 31					19 04			
Newbury Racecourse	d									18 05												
Thatcham	d	17 16								18 10									19 09			
Midgham	d									18 15												
Aldermaston	d									19 18												
Theale	d	17 24								18 23									19 17			
Reading West	d									18 31												
Reading 7	a	17 35	17 46	17 39	17 42	18 00	18 09		18 12	18 34	18 46	18 42		18 48	19 00	19 00	19 12	19 15	19 28	19 32	19 46	19 42
	d	17 36	17 52		17 44	18 02			18 14	18 37	18 52			18 50	19 02	19 02	19 14		19 29	19 34	19 52	
Twyford 3	a		17 58								18 58										19 58	
Maidenhead 3	a	17 48	18 06							18 51	19 06								19 41		20 06	
Slough 3	a	17 58	18 14							19 02	19 14								19 51		20 14	
Ealing Broadway ⊖	a		18 37								19 37										20 37	
London Paddington 15 ⊖	a	18 18	18 48		18 24	18 38			18 51	19 23	19 47			19 29	19 39	19 39	19 54		20 23	20 10	20 47	

A until 11 July
B from 18 July until 5 September

Table 116

Sundays
until 05 September

Birmingham, Banbury, Bicester, Oxford and Bedwyn - Reading and London

		GW	XC	GW	GW	GW	GW	GW	XC	XC	GW	GW	GW	GW	GW	GW	XC	GW	XC	GW	GW	GW
		1	◇1	◇1	1	◇1	1	◇1	◇1	◇1	◇1	◇1	◇1	1	◇1	1	◇1	1	◇1	◇1	◇1	1
											A	B			A							
Birmingham New Street 12	d		18 33						19 03	19 33							20 03		20 33			
Birmingham International	d								19 14								20 14					
Coventry	d								19 25								20 25					
Leamington Spa 8	d		19 00						19 38	20 00							20 38		21 00			
Banbury	d		19 19						19 55	20 19							20 55		21 19			
Kings Sutton	d																					
Heyford	d																					
Tackley	d																					
Bicester Town	d	19 03												20 33								
Islip	d	19 14												20 44								
Oxford	a	19 30	19 38						20 14	20 40				21 00			21 14		21 38			
	d		19 43				20 05		20 16	20 43			20 50				21 16	21 21	21 40		21 50	
Radley	d						20 11											21 27				
Culham	d																					
Appleford	d																					
Didcot Parkway	a						20 21						21 04					21 35			22 03	
	d			19 59		20 17	20 21				20 59	20 59	21 04		21 17			21 35		22 01	22 05	
Cholsey	d						20 27											21 41				
Goring & Streatley	d						20 33											21 46				
Pangbourne	d						20 37											21 51				
Tilehurst	d						20 42											21 55				
Bedwyn	d															20 54						
Hungerford	d															21 00						
Kintbury	d															21 04						
Newbury	a															21 11						
	d				19 53			20 17								21 12						21 53
Newbury Racecourse	d				19 55																	21 55
Thatcham	d				20 00											21 17						22 00
Midgham	d				20 05																	22 05
Aldermaston	d				20 08																	22 08
Theale	d				20 13											21 25						22 13
Reading West	d				20 21																	22 21
Reading 7	a		20 09	20 12	20 24	20 32	20 46	20 34	20 42	21 09	21 16	21 15	21 19		21 32	21 33	21 42	22 02	22 05	22 17	22 22	22 24
	d			20 14		20 32	20 52	20 37			21 17	21 17	21 19		21 32			22 10		22 19	22 24	
Twyford 3	a						20 57											22 16				
Maidenhead 3	a						21 05						21 33					22 24				
Slough 3	a						21 14						21 42					22 34			22 47	
Ealing Broadway ⊖	a						21 38											22 56				
London Paddington 15 ⊖	a			20 51		21 09	21 48	21 12			21 56	21 56	22 04		22 12			23 05		23 08	23 13	

		GW	XC	GW	GW	GW	GW	GW	GW	GW	GW	GW	GW	GW
		◇1	◇1	1	1	◇1	◇1	1	◇1			1	1	1
						B	A							
Birmingham New Street 12	d		21 03											
Birmingham International	d		21 14											
Coventry	d		21 24											
Leamington Spa 8	d		21 35											
Banbury	d													
Kings Sutton	d													
Heyford	d													
Tackley	d													
Bicester Town	d				22 03									
Islip	d				22 14									
Oxford	a		22 08		22 30									
	d		22 10	22 14						23 00				
Radley	d			22 20						23 15				
Culham	d													
Appleford	d													
Didcot Parkway	a			22 28						23 35				
	d			22 28		22 37	22 37		23 11			23 40	23 50	
Cholsey	d			22 34									23 56	
Goring & Streatley	d			22 39									00 01	
Pangbourne	d			22 44									00 05	
Tilehurst	d			22 48									00 10	
Bedwyn	d							22 35						
Hungerford	d							22 41						
Kintbury	d							22 45						
Newbury	a							22 52						
	d	22 12						22 53			23 23			23 45
Newbury Racecourse	d													23 47
Thatcham	d							22 58			23 28			23 52
Midgham	d													23 57
Aldermaston	d													00 01
Theale	d							23 06			23 36			00 06
Reading West	d													00s13
Reading 7	a	22 29	22 35	22 53		22 55	22 56	23 18	23 27		23 45	23 55	00 15	00 17
	d	22 30		23 00		22 56	22 57		23 29			23 56	00 15	
Twyford 3	a			23 06									00 21	
Maidenhead 3	a			23 14									00 29	
Slough 3	a			23 22								00 14	00 36	
Ealing Broadway ⊖	a			23 44									00 59	
London Paddington 15 ⊖	a	23 16		23 54		23 46	23 46		00 13			00 42	01 11	

A until 11 July
B from 18 July until 5 September

Table 116

Sundays from 12 September

Birmingham, Banbury, Bicester, Oxford and Bedwyn - Reading and London

		GW ◇1 ☕	GW 1	GW 1	GW 🚌	GW 1	GW ◇1 ☕	GW 1	GW 1	GW ◇1 ☕	GW ◇1 ☕	GW 1	GW 1	XC ◇1 🍴	GW 1	GW ◇1 ☕	GW ◇1 ☕	GW 1	GW 1	XC ◇1 ☕	GW ◇1 ☕	GW ◇1 ☕	GW ◇1 ☕
Birmingham New Street 12	d													09 03						10 03			
Birmingham International	d													09 14						10 14			
Coventry	d													09 25						10 25			
Leamington Spa 8	d													09 38						10 38			
Banbury	d													09 55						10 55			
Kings Sutton	d																						
Heyford	d																						
Tackley	d																						
Bicester Town	d														10 04								
Islip	d														10 15								
Oxford	a													10 14	10 31					11 14			
	d		23p07		07 45				09 01		09 50		10 05	10 16					11 05	11 16			
Radley	d		23p13						09 07				10 11						11 11				
Culham	d		23p17																				
Appleford	d		23p20										10 16										
Didcot Parkway	a		23p25		08 10				09 16		10 02		10 20						11 20				
	d	23p32	23p36	07 45		08 20	08 43		09 16	09 46	10 03		10 21				10 46		11 21		11 29		11 47
Cholsey	d		23p42			08 26			09 22				10 27						11 27				
Goring & Streatley	d		23p47	07 53		08 32			09 27				10 33						11 33				
Pangbourne	d		23p51			08 36			09 32				10 37						11 37				
Tilehurst	d		23p56			08 41			09 36				10 42						11 42				
Bedwyn	d											09 35						10 42					
Hungerford	d											09 41						10 48					
Kintbury	d											09 46						10 52					
Newbury	a											09 52						10 59					
	d							08 53				09 53				10 32		11 00				11 26	
Newbury Racecourse	d							08 55				09 55											
Thatcham	d							09 00				10 00						11 05					
Midgham	d							09 05				10 05											
Aldermaston	d							09 08				10 08											
Theale	d							09 13				10 13						11 13					
Reading West	d							09 21				10 21											
Reading 7	a	23p52	00 01	08 03		08 47	09 01	09 24	09 42	09 59	10 18	10 24	10 49	10 42		10 48	11 00	11 21	11 46	11 42	11 42	11 47	12 01
	d	23p53	00 03	08 03		08 50	09 03		09 52	10 01	10 20		10 52			10 49	11 02		11 52		11 44	11 49	12 02
Twyford 3	a		00 09			08 56			09 58				10 58						11 58				
Maidenhead 3	a		00 17			09 04			10 06				11 06						12 06				
Slough 3	a		00 28	08 22		09 11			10 14		10 35		11 14						12 14				
Ealing Broadway ⊖	a		00 52			09 40			10 40				11 40						12 40				
London Paddington 15 ⊖	a	00 33	01 02	08 44		09 50	09 39		10 50	10 39	10 58		11 50			11 29	11 39		12 50		12 21	12 29	12 39

		GW ◇1	GW 1	GW 1	GW 1	XC ◇1 ☕	GW ◇1 ☕	GW ◇1 ☕	XC ◇1 🍴	GW 1	GW 1	XC ◇1 ☕	GW 1	GW ◇1 ☕	GW ◇1 ☕	GW ◇1 ☕	XC ◇1 🍴	GW ◇1	GW 1	GW 1	XC ◇1 ☕	GW ◇1 ☕	GW ◇1 ☕
Birmingham New Street 12	d					11 03			11 33			12 03					12 33				13 03		
Birmingham International	d					11 14						12 14									13 14		
Coventry	d					11 25						12 25									13 25		
Leamington Spa 8	d					11 38			12 00			12 38					13 00				13 38		
Banbury	d					11 55			12 19			12 55					13 19				13 55		
Kings Sutton	d																						
Heyford	d																						
Tackley	d																						
Bicester Town	d		11 33										13 03										
Islip	d		11 44										13 14										
Oxford	a		12 00			12 14			12 38			13 14	13 30				13 41				14 14		
	d	11 50			12 05	12 16			12 43		13 05	13 16					13 43	13 50		14 05	14 16		
Radley	d				12 11						13 11									14 11			
Culham	d																						
Appleford	d				12 16															14 16			
Didcot Parkway	a	12 02			12 20			12 46			13 20							14 02		14 20			
	d	12 03			12 21		12 29	12 47			13 21			13 29		13 47		14 03		14 21		14 29	14 47
Cholsey	d				12 27						13 27									14 27			
Goring & Streatley	d				12 33						13 33									14 33			
Pangbourne	d				12 37						13 37									14 37			
Tilehurst	d				12 42						13 42									14 42			
Bedwyn	d									12 42													
Hungerford	d									12 48													
Kintbury	d									12 52													
Newbury	a									12 59													
	d			11 53						13 00					13 31				13 53				
Newbury Racecourse	d			11 55															13 55				
Thatcham	d			12 00						13 05									14 00				
Midgham	d			12 05															14 05				
Aldermaston	d			12 08															14 08				
Theale	d			12 13						13 13									14 13				
Reading West	d			12 21															14 21				
Reading 7	a	12 18		12 24	12 47	12 42	12 42	13 00	13 09	13 21	13 46	13 42		13 42	13 48	14 00	14 10	14 18	14 24	14 46	14 42	14 42	15 00
	d	12 19			12 52		12 44	13 02			13 52			13 44	13 51	14 02		14 19		14 52		14 44	15 02
Twyford 3	a				12 58						13 58									14 58			
Maidenhead 3	a				13 06						14 06									15 06			
Slough 3	a	12 33			13 14						14 14							14 35		15 14			
Ealing Broadway ⊖	a				13 40						14 40									15 40			
London Paddington 15 ⊖	a	12 59			13 50		13 21	13 39			14 50			14 21	14 29	14 39		14 58		15 50		15 21	15 39

Table 116

Sundays from 12 September

Birmingham, Banbury, Bicester, Oxford and Bedwyn - Reading and London

		XC ◇1 🍴	GW 1	GW 1	GW 1	XC ◇1 ☕	GW ◇1 ☕	GW ◇1 ☕	XC ◇1 🍴	GW 1	GW 1	XC ◇1 ☕	GW 1	GW ◇1 ☕	GW ◇1 ☕	GW ◇1 ☕	XC ◇1 🍴	GW 1	GW 1	XC ◇1 ☕	GW ◇1 ☕	GW ◇1 ☕
Birmingham New Street 12	d	13 33				14 03			14 33			15 03					15 33			16 04		
Birmingham International	d					14 14						15 14								16 14		
Coventry	d					14 25						15 25								16 25		
Leamington Spa 8	d	14 00				14 38			15 00			15 38					16 00			16 38		
Banbury	d	14 19				14 55			15 19			15 55					16 19			16 55		
Kings Sutton	d																					
Heyford	d																					
Tackley	d																					
Bicester Town	d		14 33										16 03									
Islip	d		14 44										16 14									
Oxford	a	14 37	15 00			15 14			15 41			16 14	16 30				16 41			17 14		
	d	14 41			15 05	15 16			15 43		16 05	16 16					16 43		17 05	17 16		
Radley	d				15 11						16 11								17 11			
Culham	d																					
Appleford	d										16 16											
Didcot Parkway	a				15 20						16 20								17 20			
	d				15 21		15 29	15 47			16 21			16 29		16 47			17 21		17 29	17 47
Cholsey	d				15 27						16 27								17 27			
Goring & Streatley	d				15 33						16 33								17 33			
Pangbourne	d				15 37						16 37								17 37			
Tilehurst	d				15 42						16 42								17 42			
Bedwyn	d			14 42														16 42				
Hungerford	d			14 48														16 48				
Kintbury	d			14 52														16 52				
Newbury	a			14 59														16 59				
	d			15 00						15 53					16 29			17 00				
Newbury Racecourse	d									15 55												
Thatcham	d			15 05						16 00								17 05				
Midgham	d									16 05												
Aldermaston	d									16 08												
Theale	d			15 13						16 13								17 13				
Reading West	d									16 21												
Reading 7	a	15 09		15 21	15 46	15 42	15 42	16 00	16 09	16 24	16 46	16 42		16 42	16 47	17 00	17 09	17 21	17 46	17 39	17 42	18 00
	d				15 52		15 44	16 02			16 52			16 44	16 49	17 02			17 52		17 44	18 02
Twyford 3	a				15 58						16 58								17 58			
Maidenhead 3	a				16 06						17 06								18 06			
Slough 3	a				16 14						17 14								18 14			
Ealing Broadway ⊖	a				16 41						17 41								18 41			
London Paddington 15 ⊖	a				16 50		16 21	16 39			17 50			17 22	17 29	17 39			18 50		18 21	18 39

		XC ◇1 🍴	GW 1	GW ◇1 ☕	GW 1	GW 1	XC ◇1 ☕	GW ◇1 ☕	GW ◇1 ☕	XC ◇1 🍴	GW ◇1 ☕	GW 1	GW ◇1 ☕	GW 1	XC ◇1 ☕	GW 1	XC ◇1 🍴	GW ◇1 ☕	GW 1	GW ◇1 ☕	GW 1	XC ◇1 ☕	XC ◇1 🍴
Birmingham New Street 12	d	16 33					17 03			17 33					18 03		18 33					19 03	19 33
Birmingham International	d						17 14								18 14							19 14	
Coventry	d						17 25								18 25							19 25	
Leamington Spa 8	d	17 00					17 38			18 00					18 38		19 00					19 38	20 00
Banbury	d	17 19					17 55			18 19					18 55		19 19					19 55	20 19
Kings Sutton	d																						
Heyford	d																						
Tackley	d																						
Bicester Town	d		17 33													19 03							
Islip	d		17 44													19 14							
Oxford	a	17 38	18 00				18 14			18 39					19 14	19 30	19 38					20 14	20 40
	d	17 43				18 05	18 16			18 43				19 05	19 16		19 43				20 05	20 16	20 43
Radley	d					18 11								19 11							20 11		
Culham	d																						
Appleford	d					18 16																	
Didcot Parkway	a					18 20								19 20							20 20		
	d			17 59		18 21			18 47		18 59		19 19	19 21				19 59		20 17	20 21		
Cholsey	d					18 27								19 27							20 27		
Goring & Streatley	d					18 33								19 33							20 33		
Pangbourne	d					18 37								19 37							20 37		
Tilehurst	d					18 42								19 42							20 42		
Bedwyn	d											18 42											
Hungerford	d											18 48											
Kintbury	d											18 52											
Newbury	a											18 59											
	d				17 53			18 34				19 00							19 53				
Newbury Racecourse	d				17 55														19 55				
Thatcham	d				18 00							19 05							20 00				
Midgham	d				18 05														20 05				
Aldermaston	d				18 08														20 08				
Theale	d				18 13							19 13							20 13				
Reading West	d				18 21														20 21				
Reading 7	a	18 09		18 12	18 24	18 46	18 42	18 52	19 00	19 09	19 12	19 21	19 32	19 46	19 42		20 09	20 12	20 24	20 32	20 46	20 42	21 09
	d			18 14		18 52		18 53	19 03		19 14		19 34	19 52				20 14		20 32	20 52		
Twyford 3	a					18 58								19 58							20 58		
Maidenhead 3	a					19 06								20 06							21 06		
Slough 3	a					19 15								20 14							21 14		
Ealing Broadway ⊖	a					19 41								20 41							21 41		
London Paddington 15 ⊖	a			18 59		19 51		19 29	19 39		19 59		20 09	20 51				20 59		21 09	21 51		

Table 116

Sundays from 12 September

Birmingham, Banbury, Bicester, Oxford and Bedwyn - Reading and London

		GW ◇1	GW ◇1	GW 1		GW ◇1	GW 1	XC ◇1	GW ◇1	GW 1	XC ◇1	GW ◇1	GW ◇1	GW 1		GW ◇1	XC ◇1	GW 1	GW 1	GW 1	GW ◇1	GW	GW	GW 1
Birmingham New Street 12	d							20 03			20 33						21 03							
Birmingham International	d							20 14									21 14							
Coventry	d							20 25									21 24							
Leamington Spa 8	d							20 38			21 00						21 35							
Banbury	d							20 55			21 19													
Kings Sutton	d																							
Heyford	d																							
Tackley	d																							
Bicester Town	d			20 33															22 03					
Islip	d			20 44															22 14					
Oxford	a			21 00				21 14			21 38						22 08		22 30					
	d		20 50					21 16		21 21	21 40		21 50				22 10	22 21				23 00		
Radley	d									21 27								22 27				23 15		
Culham	d																							
Appleford	d																							
Didcot Parkway	a		21 04							21 35			22 03					22 35				23 35		
	d	20 59	21 05			21 17			21 31	21 35		22 01	22 05					22 35			23 11			23 40
Cholsey	d									21 41								22 41						
Goring & Streatley	d									21 46								22 46						
Pangbourne	d									21 51								22 51						
Tilehurst	d									21 55								22 55						
Bedwyn	d						20 54													22 35				
Hungerford	d						21 00													22 41				
Kintbury	d						21 04													22 45				
Newbury	a						21 11													22 52				
	d						21 12							21 53		22 12				22 53			23 23	
Newbury Racecourse	d													21 55										
Thatcham	d						21 17							22 00						22 58			23 28	
Midgham	d													22 05										
Aldermaston	d													22 08										
Theale	d						21 25							22 13						23 06			23 36	
Reading West	d													22 21										
Reading 7	a	21 15	21 19			21 32	21 33	21 42	21 45	22 02	22 05	22 17	22 21	22 24		22 29	22 35	23 00		23 15	23 27		23 44	23 55
	d	21 17	21 19			21 32			21 47	22 10		22 19	22 24			22 30		23 00			23 29			23 56
Twyford 3	a									22 16								23 06						
Maidenhead 3	a		21 33							22 24								23 14						
Slough 3	a		21 39							22 34			22 47					23 22						00 14
Ealing Broadway ⊖	a									22 56								23 44						
London Paddington 15 ⊖	a	22 02	22 05			22 09			22 29	23 05		23 08	23 13			23 16		23 54			00 13			00 38

		GW 1	GW 1
Birmingham New Street 12	d		
Birmingham International	d		
Coventry	d		
Leamington Spa 8	d		
Banbury	d		
Kings Sutton	d		
Heyford	d		
Tackley	d		
Bicester Town	d		
Islip	d		
Oxford	a		
	d		
Radley	d		
Culham	d		
Appleford	d		
Didcot Parkway	a		
	d	23 50	
Cholsey	d	23 56	
Goring & Streatley	d	00 01	
Pangbourne	d	00 05	
Tilehurst	d	00 10	
Bedwyn	d		
Hungerford	d		
Kintbury	d		
Newbury	a		
	d		23 45
Newbury Racecourse	d		23 47
Thatcham	d		23 52
Midgham	d		23 57
Aldermaston	d		00 01
Theale	d		00 06
Reading West	d		00s13
Reading 7	a	00 15	00 17
	d	00 15	
Twyford 3	a	00 21	
Maidenhead 3	a	00 29	
Slough 3	a	00 36	
Ealing Broadway ⊖	a	00 59	
London Paddington 15 ⊖	a	01 11	

b arr. 2027

Table 116A

Mondays to Fridays

Reading - Wallingford

Bus Service

		GW BHX	GW BHX	GW BHX	GW BHX	GW BHX	GW BHX	GW BHX	GW BHX	GW BHX	GW BHX	GW BHX	GW BHX	GW BHX	GW BHX	GW BHX	GW BHX	GW BHX	GW BHX	GW BHX	GW BHX	GW BHX	GW BHX
Reading	d	06 55	07 20	07 50	08 25	09 05	09 30	10 05	10 30	11 05	11 30	12 05	12 30	13 05	13 30	14 05	14 30	15 05	15 30	16 05	16 35	17 05	17 35
Wallingford Town Hall	a	07 23	07 55	08 20	09 00	09 35	10 05	10 35	11 05	11 35	12 05	12 35	13 05	13 35	14 05	14 35	15 05	15 35	16 05	16 35	17 14	17 39	18 14

		GW BHX	GW BHX	GW BHX	GW BHX	GW BHX	GW BHX	GW BHX	GW BHX
Reading	d	18 05	18 35	19 05	19 35	20 05	21 05	22 05	23 05
Wallingford Town Hall	a	18 37	19 10	19 35	20 08	20 38	21 38	22 38	23 38

Saturdays

		GW BHX	GW BHX	GW BHX	GW	GW	GW	GW	GW	GW	GW	GW	GW	GW	GW	GW	GW	GW	GW	GW	GW	GW	GW
Reading	d	00 05	01 05	02 05	07 00	08 30	09 30	10 05	10 30	11 05	11 30	12 05	12 30	13 05	13 30	14 05	14 30	15 05	15 30	16 05	16 30	17 05	17 30
Wallingford Town Hall	a	00 38	01 38	02 38	07 27	09 05	10 05	10 35	11 05	11 35	12 05	12 35	13 05	13 35	14 05	14 35	15 05	15 35	16 05	16 35	17 05	17 39	18 09

		GW	GW	GW	GW	GW	GW	GW	GW
Reading	d	18 05	18 35	19 05	19 35	20 05	21 05	22 05	23 05
Wallingford Town Hall	a	18 37	19 10	19 32	20 08	20 38	21 38	22 38	23 38

Sundays

		GW	GW	GW	GW	GW	GW	GW	GW	GW	GW	GW	GW	GW	GW	GW	GW
Reading	d	00 05	01 05	02 05	09 35	10 35	11 35	12 35	13 35	14 35	15 35	16 35	17 35	19 35	20 35	22 05	23 05
Wallingford Town Hall	a	00 38	01 38	02 38	10 08	11 08	12 08	13 08	14 08	15 08	16 08	17 08	18 08	20 08	21 08	22 38	23 38

Table 116A

Wallingford - Reading

Bus Service

		GW BHX	GW BHX	GW BHX	GW BHX	GW BHX	GW BHX	GW BHX	GW BHX	GW BHX	GW BHX	GW BHX	GW BHX	GW BHX	GW BHX	GW BHX	GW BHX	GW BHX	GW BHX	GW BHX	GW BHX	GW BHX	GW BHX
Wallingford Market Place	d	06 10	06 35	07 15	07 40	08 10	08 50	09 25	09 50	10 20	10 50	11 20	11 50	12 20	12 50	13 20	13 50	14 20	14 50	15 20	15 50	16 20	16 50
Reading	a	06 48	07 13	07 45	08 20	08 40	09 28	09 55	10 28	10 50	11 28	11 50	12 28	12 50	13 28	13 50	14 28	14 50	15 28	15 50	16 28	16 50	17 28

		GW BHX	GW BHX	GW BHX	GW BHX	GW BHX	GW BHX	GW BHX	GW BHX	GW FO BHX
Wallingford Market Place	d	17 25	17 55	18 25	18 50	19 50	20 50	21 55	22 55	23 55
Reading	a	17 55	18 33	18 55	19 28	20 28	21 28	22 33	23 33	00 33

Saturdays

		GW BHX	GW BHX	GW BHX	GW	GW	GW	GW	GW	GW	GW	GW	GW	GW	GW	GW	GW	GW	GW	GW	GW	GW	GW
Wallingford Market Place	d	23p55	00 55	01 55	07 50	08 50	09 20	09 50	10 20	10 50	11 20	11 50	12 20	12 50	13 20	13 50	14 20	14 50	15 20	15 50	16 20	16 50	17 20
Reading	a	00 33	01 33	02 33	08 25	09 28	09 50	10 28	10 50	11 28	11 50	12 28	12 50	13 28	13 50	14 28	14 50	15 28	15 50	16 28	16 50	17 28	17 50

		GW	GW	GW	GW	GW	GW	GW	GW	GW
Wallingford Market Place	d	17 50	18 20	18 50	19 20	19 50	20 50	21 55	22 55	23 55
Reading	a	18 28	18 50	19 28	19 50	20 28	21 28	22 33	23 33	00 33

Sundays

		GW A	GW	GW	GW	GW	GW	GW	GW	GW	GW	GW	GW	GW	GW	GW	GW
Wallingford Market Place	d	23p55	00 55	01 55	09 20	10 20	11 20	12 20	13 20	14 20	15 20	16 20	17 20	18 20	19 25	21 25	22 25
Reading	a	00 33	01 33	02 33	09 53	10 53	11 53	12 53	13 53	14 53	15 53	16 53	17 53	18 53	19 58	21 58	22 58

A not 23 May

Table 116B

Mondays to Fridays

Oxford - Abingdon

Bus Service

		GW MX BHX	GW BHX	GW BHX	GW BHX	GW BHX	GW BHX	GW BHX	GW BHX	GW BHX	GW BHX	GW BHX	GW BHX	GW BHX	GW BHX	GW BHX	GW BHX	GW BHX	GW BHX	GW BHX	GW BHX	GW BHX	GW BHX
Oxford	d	23p40	06 11	06 30	06 50	07 14	07 32	07 52	08 12	08 34	08 56	09 20	09 40	10 00	10 20	10 40	11 00	11 20	11 40	12 00	12 20	12 40	13 00
Abingdon Stratton Way	a	00 10	06 41	07 00	07 20	07 44	08 02	08 22	08 42	09 04	09 26	09 50	10 10	10 30	10 50	11 10	11 30	11 50	12 10	12 30	12 50	13 10	13 30

		GW BHX	GW BHX	GW BHX	GW BHX	GW BHX	GW BHX	GW BHX	GW BHX	GW BHX	GW BHX	GW BHX	GW BHX	GW BHX	GW BHX	GW BHX	GW BHX	GW BHX	GW BHX	GW BHX	GW BHX	GW BHX	GW BHX
Oxford	d	13 20	13 40	14 00	14 20	14 40	15 00	15 15	15 25	15 45	16 05	16 25	16 45	17 05	17 25	17 45	18 05	18 23	18 40	19 10	19 40	20 10	20 40
Abingdon Stratton Way	a	13 50	14 10	14 30	14 50	15 10	15 30	15 45	15 55	16 15	16 35	16 55	17 15	17 35	17 55	18 15	18 35	18 53	19 10	19 40	20 10	20 40	21 10

		GW BHX	GW BHX	GW BHX	GW BHX	GW BHX	GW BHX
Oxford	d	21 10	21 40	22 10	22 40	23 10	23 40
Abingdon Stratton Way	a	21 40	22 10	22 40	23 10	23 40	00 10

Saturdays

		GW BHX	GW	GW	GW	GW	GW	GW	GW	GW	GW	GW	GW	GW	GW	GW	GW	GW	GW	GW	GW	GW	GW
Oxford	d	23p40	06 40	07 10	07 40	08 10	08 40	09 00	09 20	09 40	10 00	10 20	10 40	11 00	11 20	11 40	12 00	12 20	12 40	13 00	13 20	13 40	14 00
Abingdon Stratton Way	a	00 10	07 10	07 40	08 10	08 40	09 10	09 30	09 50	10 10	10 30	10 50	11 10	11 30	11 50	12 10	12 30	12 50	13 10	13 30	13 50	14 10	14 30

		GW	GW	GW	GW	GW	GW	GW	GW	GW	GW	GW	GW	GW	GW	GW	GW	GW	GW	GW	GW	GW	GW
Oxford	d	14 20	14 40	15 00	15 20	15 40	16 00	16 20	16 40	17 00	17 20	17 40	18 00	18 20	18 40	19 10	19 40	20 10	20 40	21 10	21 40	22 10	22 40
Abingdon Stratton Way	a	14 50	15 10	15 30	15 50	16 10	16 30	16 50	17 10	17 30	17 50	18 10	18 30	18 50	19 10	19 40	20 10	20 40	21 10	21 40	22 10	22 40	23 10

		GW	GW
Oxford	d	23 10	23 40
Abingdon Stratton Way	a	23 40	00 10

Sundays

		GW A	GW	GW	GW	GW	GW	GW	GW	GW	GW	GW	GW	GW	GW	GW	GW	GW	GW	GW	GW	GW	GW
Oxford	d	23p40	08 10	08 40	09 10	09 40	10 10	10 40	11 10	11 40	12 10	12 40	13 10	13 40	14 10	14 40	15 10	15 40	16 10	16 40	17 10	17 40	18 10
Abingdon Stratton Way	a	00 10	08 40	09 10	09 40	10 10	10 40	11 10	11 40	12 10	12 40	13 10	13 40	14 10	14 40	15 10	15 40	16 10	16 40	17 10	17 40	18 10	18 40

		GW	GW	GW	GW	GW	GW	GW	GW	GW	GW
Oxford	d	18 40	19 10	19 40	20 10	20 40	21 10	21 40	22 10	22 40	23 10
Abingdon Stratton Way	a	19 10	19 40	20 10	20 40	21 10	21 40	22 10	22 40	23 10	23 40

A not 23 May

Table 116B

Mondays to Fridays

Abingdon - Oxford

Bus Service

		GW BHX	GW BHX	GW BHX	GW BHX	GW BHX	GW BHX	GW BHX	GW BHX	GW BHX		GW BHX	GW BHX	GW BHX	GW BHX	GW BHX	GW BHX	GW BHX	GW BHX	GW BHX		GW BHX	GW BHX	GW BHX	GW BHX
Abingdon Stratton Way	d	05 40	05 57	06 15	06 35	06 52	07 12	07 32	07 52	08 12	....	08 32	08 52	09 14	09 37	10 00	10 20	10 40	11 00	11 20	....	11 40	12 00	12 20	12 40
Oxford	a	06 05	06 22	06 40	07 00	07 17	07 37	07 57	08 17	08 37		08 57	09 17	09 39	10 02	10 25	10 45	11 05	11 25	11 45		12 05	12 25	12 45	13 05

		GW BHX	GW BHX	GW BHX	GW BHX	GW BHX		GW BHX	GW BHX	GW BHX	GW BHX	GW BHX	GW BHX	GW BHX	GW BHX	GW BHX		GW BHX	GW BHX	GW BHX	GW BHX	GW BHX	GW BHX	GW BHX	GW BHX
Abingdon Stratton Way	d	13 00	13 20	13 40	14 00	14 20	....	14 40	15 00	15 20	15 40	15 57	16 17	16 37	16 57	17 17	....	17 37	17 57	18 17	18 37	19 00	19 30	20 00	20 30
Oxford	a	13 25	13 45	14 05	14 25	14 45		15 05	15 25	15 45	16 05	16 22	16 42	17 02	17 22	17 42		18 02	18 22	18 42	19 02	19 25	19 55	20 25	20 55

		GW BHX		GW BHX	GW BHX	GW BHX	GW BHX
Abingdon Stratton Way	d	21 00	....	21 30	22 00	22 30	23 00
Oxford	a	21 25		21 55	22 25	22 55	23 25

Saturdays

		GW	GW	GW	GW	GW	GW	GW	GW	GW		GW	GW	GW	GW	GW	GW	GW	GW	GW		GW	GW	GW	GW
Abingdon Stratton Way	d	06 00	06 30	07 00	07 30	08 00	08 20	08 40	09 00	09 20	....	09 40	10 00	10 20	10 40	11 00	11 20	11 40	12 00	12 20	....	12 40	13 00	13 20	13 40
Oxford	a	06 25	06 55	07 25	07 55	08 25	08 45	09 05	09 25	09 45		10 05	10 25	10 45	11 05	11 25	11 45	12 05	12 25	12 45		13 05	13 25	13 45	14 05

		GW	GW	GW	GW	GW		GW	GW	GW	GW	GW	GW	GW	GW	GW		GW	GW	GW	GW	GW	GW	GW	GW
Abingdon Stratton Way	d	14 00	14 20	14 40	15 00	15 20	....	15 40	16 00	16 20	16 40	17 00	17 20	17 40	18 00	18 20	....	18 40	19 00	19 30	20 00	20 30	21 00	21 30	22 00
Oxford	a	14 25	14 45	15 05	15 25	15 45		16 05	16 25	16 45	17 05	17 25	17 45	18 05	18 25	18 45		19 05	19 25	19 55	20 25	20 55	21 25	21 55	22 25

		GW		GW
Abingdon Stratton Way	d	22 30	....	23 00
Oxford	a	22 55		23 25

Sundays

		GW	GW	GW	GW	GW	GW	GW	GW	GW		GW	GW	GW	GW	GW	GW	GW	GW	GW		GW	GW	GW	GW
Abingdon Stratton Way	d	07 30	08 00	08 30	09 00	09 30	10 00	10 30	11 00	11 30	....	12 00	12 30	13 00	13 30	14 00	14 30	15 00	15 30	16 00	....	16 30	17 00	17 30	18 00
Oxford	a	07 55	08 25	08 55	09 25	09 55	10 25	10 55	11 25	11 55		12 25	12 55	13 25	13 55	14 25	14 55	15 25	15 55	16 25		16 55	17 25	17 55	18 25

		GW	GW	GW	GW	GW		GW	GW	GW	GW	GW
Abingdon Stratton Way	d	18 30	19 00	19 30	20 00	20 30	....	21 00	21 30	22 00	22 30	23 00
Oxford	a	18 55	19 25	19 55	20 25	20 55		21 25	21 55	22 25	22 55	23 25

Table 116C

Mondays to Fridays

Oxford - Eynsham - Witney

Bus Service

Oxford Frideswide Square	d
Eynsham Church	a
Witney Market Place	a

Saturdays

Oxford Frideswide Square	d
Eynsham Church	a
Witney Market Place	a

Sundays

Oxford Frideswide Square	d
Eynsham Church	a
Witney Market Place	a

Details of service not available at time of going to press

Table 116C

Witney - Eynsham - Oxford

Bus Service

Witney Market Place	d
Eynsham Witney Road	d
Oxford Frideswide Square	a

Saturdays

Witney Market Place	d
Eynsham Witney Road	d
Oxford Frideswide Square	a

Sundays

Witney Market Place	d
Eynsham Witney Road	d
Oxford Frideswide Square	a

Details of service not available at time of going to press

Table 117

London - Greenford and Reading

	GW MX 1	GW MX ◇1	GW MO 1	GW MX ◇1	GW MX 1	GW MX 1	GW MX ◇1 ☕	GW MX ◇1 ☕	GW MO ◇1 ☕	GW MO ◇1	GW MX 1	GW MO 1	GW MX 1	GW MX ◇1	GW MO 1	GW MX 1	GW 1	GW 1	HC
London Paddington 15 ⊖ d	22p45	22p48	23p15	23p20		23p29	23p30	23p30	23p37	23p47	23p48	23p53		00 20	00 34	00 34	01 34	03 34	04 42
Acton Main Line d	22p51										23p54								
Ealing Broadway ⊖ d	22p54		23p24			23p37				23p55	23p58	00 02			00 42	00 42	01 42	03 42	04 50
West Ealing d											00 01								
Drayton Green d																			
Castle Bar Park d																			
South Greenford d																			
Greenford ⊖ a																			
Hanwell d											00 03								
Southall d			23p29								00 07	00 07			00 47	00 47	01 47	03 48	04 54
Hayes & Harlington d	23p02		23p33			23p44					00 12	00 11			00 51	00 51	01 51	03 52	04 58
Heathrow Terminals 1-2-3 2 ✈ a																			05 04
Heathrow Terminal 4 ✈ a													←						05 10
West Drayton d			23p37								00 16 →	00 15	00 16		00 55	00 55	01 55	03 56	
Iver d													00 19						
Langley d			23p42									00 20	00 22		01 00	01 00			
Slough 3 a	23p12	23p06	23p46	23p38		23p53			23p54	00 08		00 24	00 28	00 39	01 05	01 05	02 04	04 04	
d	23p12	23p06	23p46	23p39		23p54			23p55	00 08		00 24	00 28	00 39	01 05	01 05	02 04	04 05	
Burnham d	23p16		23p51									00 28	00 32		01 09	01 09			
Taplow d	23p19												00 35			01 13			
Maidenhead 3 d	23p23		23p56			00 01				00 16		00 34	00 39		01 15	01 16	02 11	04 12	
Twyford 3 d	23p31		00 04		00 07	00 09						00 42	00 47		01 23	01 24	02 19	04 20	
Reading 7 a	23p40	23p34	00 13	00 04	00 16	00 19	00 06	00 06	00 15	00 28		00 49	00 57	01 00	01 32	01 33	02 29	04 30	
Oxford a	00 23	00 13		00 33		01 07								01 34					

	HX 1	HC	GW 1	GW 1	HX 1	GW ◇1 ☕	HC	GW ◇1 ☕	HX 1	GW 1	GW 1	HX 1	GW 1	HC	HX 1	GW 1	GW 1	GW 1	HX 1	GW 1	GW ◇1 ☕	HC
London Paddington 15 ⊖ d	05 10	05 13	05 17	05 22	05 25	05 30	05 33	05 36	05 40	05 42	05 45	05 55	05 57	06 03	06 10	06 12	06 15	06 20	06 25	06 27	06 30	06 33
Acton Main Line d											05 51						06 21					
Ealing Broadway ⊖ d		05 21		05 30			05 41			05 50	05 54		06 05	06 11		06 20	06 24			06 35		06 41
West Ealing d							05 43				05 57			06 13			06 27					06 43
Drayton Green d											05 59						06 29					
Castle Bar Park d											06 01						06 31					
South Greenford d											06 04						06 34					
Greenford ⊖ a											06 09						06 39					
Hanwell d							05 45							06 15								06 45
Southall d		05 25		05 35			05 49			05 58			06 10	06 19		06 28						06 49
Hayes & Harlington d		05 29		05 39			05 53			06 02			06 14	06 23		06 32				06 45		06 53
Heathrow Terminals 1-2-3 2 ✈ a	05 26	05 35			05 40		06 05		05 55			06 10		06 35	06 25				06 40			07 05
Heathrow Terminal 4 ✈ a		05 41																				
West Drayton d				05 43						06 06			06 18			06 40				06 49		
Iver d				05 46									06 21							06 52		
Langley d				05 50									06 25							06 56		
Slough 3 a			05 33	05 54				05 51		06 13			06 29			06 47		06 35		07 00		
d			05 33	05 54				05 52		06 13			06 29			06 47		06 35		07 00		
Burnham d										06 17						06 51						
Taplow d										06 21						06 54						
Maidenhead 3 d				06 02						06 28			06 37			06 58				07 08		
Twyford 3 d				06 10						06 35			06 45			07 06				07 16		
Reading 7 a			05 51	06 20		05 55		06 05		06 44			06 53			07 15		06 49		07 25	06 54	
Oxford a			06 22	07 00									07 53					07 18				

	HX 1	GW 1	GW 1	GW ◇1 ☕	GW 1 🍴	HX 1	GW 1	GW ◇1 ☕	HC	HX 1	GW 1	GW 1	GW ◇1 ☕	GW 1	GW 1	HX 1	GW 1	GW ◇1 Ø	HC	HX 1	GW 1
London Paddington 15 ⊖ d	06 40	06 42	06 45	06 45	06 48	06 55	06 57	07 00	07 03	07 10	07 12	07 15	07 15	07 18	07 22	07 25	07 27	07 30	07 33	07 40	07 42
Acton Main Line d			06 51									07 21									
Ealing Broadway ⊖ d		06 50	06 54				07 05		07 11		07 20	07 24					07 35		07 41		07 50
West Ealing d			06 57						07 13			07 27							07 43		
Drayton Green d			06 59									07 29									
Castle Bar Park d			07 01									07 31									
South Greenford d			07 04									07 34									
Greenford ⊖ a			07 09									07 39									
Hanwell d									07 15										07 45		
Southall d		06 58					07 10		07 19		07 28						07 40		07 49		07 58
Hayes & Harlington d		07 02					07 14		07 23		07 32						07 44		07 53		08 02
Heathrow Terminals 1-2-3 2 ✈ a	06 55					07 10			07 35	07 25						07 40			08 05	07 55	
Heathrow Terminal 4 ✈ a																					
West Drayton d		07 06					07 18				07 36						07 48				08 06
Iver d							07 21										07 51				
Langley d							07 25										07 55				
Slough 3 a		07 13			07 04		07 29				07 43				07 36		07 59				08 13
d		07 13			07 04		07 29				07 43				07 36		07 59				08 13
Burnham d		07 17									07 47										08 17
Taplow d		07 21									07 51										08 21
Maidenhead 3 d		07 25					07 37				07 55						08 07				08 25
Twyford 3 d		07 33					07 45				08 03						08 15				08 33
Reading 7 a		07 44		07 09	07 19		07 52	07 24			08 12		07 39	07 47	07 51		08 23	07 56			08 42
Oxford a					08 02		08 42								08 19		09 15				

Table 117

London - Greenford and Reading

	GW 1	GW ◇1 Ø	GW ◇1 🍴	GW 1	HX 1	GW 1	GW ◇1 🍴	HC	GW 1	GW 1	HX 1	GW 1	GW 1	GW ◇1 🍴	GW ◇1 🍴	GW ◇1 🍴	HX 1	GW 1	GW ◇1 🍴	HC	GW 1	HX 1
London Paddington 15 ⊖ d	07 45	07 45	07 48	07 50	07 55	07 57	08 00	08 03	08 06		08 10	08 12	08 15	08 15	08 18	08 22	08 25	08 27	08 30	08 33	08 38	08 40
Acton Main Line d	07 51												08 21									
Ealing Broadway ⊖ d	07 54					08 05		08 11				08 20	08 24					08 35		08 41	08 47	
West Ealing d	07 57							08 13					08 27							08 43		
Drayton Green d	07 59												08 29									
Castle Bar Park d	08 01												08 31									
South Greenford d	08 04												08 34									
Greenford ⊖ a	08 09												08 39									
Hanwell d								08 15												08 45		
Southall d						08 10		08 19				08 28						08 40		08 49	08 53	
Hayes & Harlington d						08 14		08 23				08 32						08 44		08 53	08 57	
Heathrow Terminals 1-2-3 2 ✈ a					08 10			08 35			08 25						08 40			09 05		08 55
Heathrow Terminal 4 ✈ a																						
West Drayton d						08 18						08 36						08 48				
Iver d						08 21												08 51				
Langley d						08 25												08 55				
Slough 3 a				08 05		08 29			08 25			08 43				08 36		08 59			09 05	
d				08 05		08 29			08 26			08 43				08 36		08 59			09 05	
Burnham d												08 47									09 09	
Taplow d												08 51									09 13	
Maidenhead 3 d						08 37			08 34	←		08 55						09 06			09 17	
Twyford 3 d						08 45			08 42	08 45		09 03						09 16			09 25	
Reading 7 a		08 09	08 14	08 21		→	08 25		08 52	08 55		09 12		08 39	08 44	08 51		09 23	08 56		09 35	
Oxford a				08 48						09 42						09 20		10 14				

	GW 1	GW ◇1 🍴	GW 1	GW 1	HX 1	GW 1	GW ◇1 Ø	HC	GW ◇1	HX 1	GW 1	GW 1	GW ◇1 🍴	GW 1	GW ◇1 ⊥	HX 1	GW 1	GW ◇1 Ø	HC	HX 1
London Paddington 15 ⊖ d	08 42	08 45	08 45	08 51	08 55	08 57	09 00	09 03	09 06	09 10	09 12	09 15	09 15	09 18	09 21	09 25	09 27	09 30	09 33	09 40
Acton Main Line d			08 50									09 21								
Ealing Broadway ⊖ d	08 50		08 54			09 05		09 11			09 20	09 24					09 35		09 41	
West Ealing d	08 53		08 57					09 13				09 27							09 43	
Drayton Green d			08 59									09 29								
Castle Bar Park d			09 01									09 31								
South Greenford d			09 04									09 34								
Greenford ⊖ a			09 10									09 39								
Hanwell d	08 56							09 15											09 45	
Southall d	09 00							09 19			09 28								09 49	
Hayes & Harlington d	09 04					09 12		09 23			09 32						09 42		09 53	
Heathrow Terminals 1-2-3 2 ✈ a					09 10			09 35		09 25						09 40			10 05	09 55
Heathrow Terminal 4 ✈ a																				
West Drayton d	09 08					09 16					09 36						09 46			
Iver d	09 11					09 19											09 49			
Langley d	09 14					09 22											09 52			
Slough 3 a	09 19			09 06		09 27					09 43				09 36		09 57			
d	09 19			09 06		09 27					09 43				09 36		09 57			
Burnham d											09 47									
Taplow d											09 51									
Maidenhead 3 d	09 26					09 34					09 55						10 04			
Twyford 3 d	09a35					09 42					10 03						10 12			
Reading 7 a		09 09		09 20		09 52	09 25		09 30		10 17		09 39	09 48	09 52		10 22	09 56		
Oxford a				09 52		10 40									10 18		11 14			

	GW 1	GW 1	GW ◇1 Ø	GW ◇1 🍴	GW ◇1	HX 1	GW 1	GW ◇1 🍴	HC	GW ◇1 Ø	HX 1	GW 1	GW 1	GW ◇1 🍴	GW 1	GW ◇1 🍴	HX 1	GW 1	GW ◇1 Ø	HC	HX 1	GW 1
London Paddington 15 ⊖ d	09 42	09 45	09 45	09 48	09 50	09 55	09 57	10 00	10 03	10 06	10 10	10 12	10 15	10 15	10 18	10 22	10 25	10 27	10 30	10 33	10 40	10 42
Acton Main Line d		09 51											10 21									
Ealing Broadway ⊖ d	09 50	09 54					10 05		10 11			10 20	10 24					10 35		10 41		10 50
West Ealing d		09 57							10 13				10 27							10 43		
Drayton Green d		09 59											10 29									
Castle Bar Park d		10 01											10 31									
South Greenford d		10 04											10 34									
Greenford ⊖ a		10 09											10 39									
Hanwell d									10 15											10 45		
Southall d	09 58								10 19			10 28								10 49		10 58
Hayes & Harlington d	10 02						10 12		10 23			10 32						10 42		10 53		11 02
Heathrow Terminals 1-2-3 2 ✈ a						10 10			10 35		10 25						10 40			11 05	10 55	
Heathrow Terminal 4 ✈ a																						
West Drayton d	10 06						10 16					10 36						10 46				11 06
Iver d							10 19											10 49				
Langley d							10 22											10 52				
Slough 3 a	10 13				10 06		10 27					10 43				10 36		10 57				11 13
d	10 13				10 06		10 27					10 43				10 36		10 57				11 13
Burnham d	10 17											10 47										11 17
Taplow d	10 21											10 51										11 21
Maidenhead 3 d	10 25						10 34					10 55						11 04				11 25
Twyford 3 d	10 33						10 42					11 03						11 12				11 33
Reading 7 a	10 43		10 09	10 14	10 22		10 52	10 25		10 30		11 12		10 39	10 48	10 51		11 22	10 56			11 43
Oxford a					10 48		11 40									11 18		12 12				

Table 117

London - Greenford and Reading

	GW 1	GW ◇1 Ø	GW ◇1	HX 1	GW 1	GW ◇1 🍴	HC	GW ◇1 Ø	HX 1	GW 1	GW 1	GW ◇1 🍴	GW 1	GW ◇1 🍴	HX 1	GW 1	GW ◇1 🍴	HC	HX 1	GW 1	GW 1	GW ◇1 Ø
London Paddington 15 ⊖ d	10 45	10 45	10 50	10 55	10 57	11 00	11 03	11 06	11 10	11 12	11 15	11 15	11 18	11 22	11 25	11 27	11 30	11 33	11 40	11 42	11 45	11 45
Acton Main Line d	10 51										11 21										11 51	
Ealing Broadway ⊖ d	10 54				11 05		11 11			11 20	11 24					11 35		11 41		11 50	11 54	
West Ealing d	10 57						11 13				11 27							11 43			11 57	
Drayton Green d	10 59										11 29										11 59	
Castle Bar Park d	11 01										11 31										12 01	
South Greenford d	11 04										11 34										12 04	
Greenford ⊖ a	11 09										11 39										12 09	
Hanwell d							11 15											11 45				
Southall d							11 19			11 28								11 49		11 58		
Hayes & Harlington d					11 12		11 23			11 32						11 42		11 53		12 02		
Heathrow Terminals 1-2-3 2 ✈ a				11 10			11 35		11 25						11 40			12 05	11 55			
Heathrow Terminal 4 ✈ a																						
West Drayton d					11 16					11 36						11 46				12 06		
Iver d					11 19											11 49						
Langley d					11 22											11 52						
Slough 3 a			11 06		11 27					11 43				11 36		11 57				12 13		
d			11 06		11 27					11 43				11 36		11 57				12 13		
Burnham d										11 47										12 17		
Taplow d										11 51										12 21		
Maidenhead 3 d					11 34					11 55						12 04				12 25		
Twyford 3 d					11 42					12 03						12 12				12 33		
Reading 7 a		11 09	11 21		11 52	11 25		11 30		12 17		11 39	11 48	11 51		12 22	11 56			12 43		12 09
Oxford a			11 50		12 40									12 18		13 14						

	GW ◇1 🍴	GW ◇1 ⊥	HX 1	GW 1	GW ◇1 🍴	HC	GW ◇1 Ø	HX 1	GW 1	GW 1	GW ◇1 🍴	GW ◇1 🍴	GW ◇1	HX 1	GW 1	GW ◇1 🍴	HC	HX 1	GW 1	GW 1	GW ◇1 Ø
London Paddington 15 ⊖ d	11 48	11 50	11 55	11 57	12 00	12 03	12 06	12 10	12 12	12 15	12 15	12 18	12 21	12 25	12 27	12 30	12 33	12 40	12 42	12 45	12 45
Acton Main Line d										12 21										12 51	
Ealing Broadway ⊖ d				12 05		12 11			12 20	12 24					12 35		12 41		12 50	12 54	
West Ealing d						12 13				12 27							12 43			12 57	
Drayton Green d										12 29										12 59	
Castle Bar Park d										12 31										13 01	
South Greenford d										12 34										13 04	
Greenford ⊖ a										12 39										13 10	
Hanwell d						12 15											12 45				
Southall d						12 19			12 28								12 49		12 58		
Hayes & Harlington d				12 12		12 23			12 32						12 42		12 53		13 02		
Heathrow Terminals 1-2-3 2 ✈ a			12 10			12 35		12 25						12 40			13 05	12 55			
Heathrow Terminal 4 ✈ a																					
West Drayton d				12 16					12 36						12 46				13 06		
Iver d				12 19											12 49						
Langley d				12 22											12 52						
Slough 3 a		12 06		12 27					12 43				12 36		12 57				13 13		
d		12 06		12 27					12 43				12 36		12 57				13 13		
Burnham d									12 47										13 17		
Taplow d									12 51										13 21		
Maidenhead 3 d				12 34					12 55						13 04				13 25		
Twyford 3 d				12 42					13 03						13 12				13 33		
Reading 7 a	12 14	12 22		12 50	12 25		12 30		13 12		12 39	12 44	12 51		13 22	12 56			13 43		13 09
Oxford a		12 48		13 40									13 19		14 14						

	GW ◇1	HX 1	GW 1	GW ◇1 🍴	HC	GW ◇1 Ø	HX 1	GW ◇1 🍴	GW 1	GW 1	GW 1	GW ◇1 ⊥	HX 1	GW 1	GW ◇1 🍴	HC	HX 1	GW 1	GW 1	GW ◇1 🍴	GW ◇1 🍴	GW ◇1	HX 1
London Paddington 15 ⊖ d	12 50	12 55	12 57	13 00	13 03	13 06	13 10	13 15	13 12	13 15	13 18	13 21	13 25	13 27	13 30	13 33	13 40	13 42	13 45	13 45	13 48	13 50	13 55
Acton Main Line d										13 21									13 51				
Ealing Broadway ⊖ d			13 05		13 11				13 20	13 24				13 35		13 41		13 50	13 54				
West Ealing d					13 13					13 27						13 43			13 57				
Drayton Green d										13 29									13 59				
Castle Bar Park d										13 31									14 01				
South Greenford d										13 34									14 04				
Greenford ⊖ a										13 39									14 09				
Hanwell d					13 15											13 45							
Southall d					13 19				13 28							13 49		13 58					
Hayes & Harlington d			13 12		13 23				13 32					13 42		13 53		14 02					
Heathrow Terminals 1-2-3 2 ✈ a		13 10			13 35		13 25						13 40			14 05	13 55						14 10
Heathrow Terminal 4 ✈ a																							
West Drayton d			13 16						13 36					13 46				14 06					
Iver d			13 19											13 49									
Langley d			13 22											13 52									
Slough 3 a	13 06		13 27						13 43			13 36		13 57				14 13				14 06	
d	13 06		13 27						13 43			13 36		13 57				14 13				14 06	
Burnham d									13 47									14 17					
Taplow d									13 51									14 21					
Maidenhead 3 d			13 34						13 55					14 04				14 25					
Twyford 3 d			13 42						14 03					14 12				14 33					
Reading 7 a	13 22		13 52	13 25		13 30		13 39	14 17		13 47	13 52		14 21	13 56			14 43		14 09	14 14	14 21	
Oxford a	13 50		14 40									14 18		15 14								14 48	

London - Greenford and Reading

		GW 1	GW ◇1 🍴	HC	GW ◇1 Ø	HX 1	GW 1	GW 1	GW ◇1 🍴	GW 1	GW ◇1	HX 1	GW 1	GW ◇1 🍴	HC	HX 1	GW 1	GW 1	GW ◇1 🍴	GW ◇1 🍽	HX 1	GW 1
London Paddington 15 ⊖	d	13 57	14 00	14 03	14 06	14 10	14 12	14 15	14 15	14 18	14 21	14 25	14 27	14 30	14 33	14 40	14 42	14 45	14 45	14 50	14 55	14 57
Acton Main Line	d							14 21										14 51				
Ealing Broadway ⊖	d	14 05		14 11			14 20	14 24					14 35		14 41		14 50	14 54				15 05
West Ealing	d			14 13				14 27							14 43			14 57				
Drayton Green	d							14 29										14 59				
Castle Bar Park	d							14 31										15 01				
South Greenford	d							14 34										15 04				
Greenford ⊖	a							14 39										15 09				
Hanwell	d			14 15											14 45							
Southall	d			14 19			14 28								14 49		14 58					
Hayes & Harlington	d	14 12		14 23			14 32						14 42		14 53		15 02					15 12
Heathrow Terminals 1-2-3 2 ✈	a			14 35		14 25						14 40			15 05	14 55					15 10	
Heathrow Terminal 4 ✈	a																					
West Drayton	d	14 16					14 36						14 46				15 06					15 16
Iver	d	14 19											14 49									15 19
Langley	d	14 22											14 52									15 22
Slough 3	a	14 27					14 43				14 36		14 57				15 13			15 06		15 27
	d	14 27					14 43				14 36		14 57				15 13			15 06		15 27
Burnham	d						14 47										15 17					
Taplow	d						14 51										15 21					
Maidenhead 3	d	14 34					14 55						15 04				15 25					15 34
Twyford 3	d	14 42					15 03						15 12				15 33					15 42
Reading 7	a	14 52	14 25		14 30		15 12		14 39	14 47	14 52		15 22	14 56			15 42		15 09	15 22		15 52
Oxford	a	15 40									15 18		16 14							15 50		16 42

		GW ◇1 🍴	HC	GW ◇1 Ø	HX 1	GW 1	GW 1	GW ◇1 🍴	GW 1	GW ◇1	HX 1	GW 1	GW ◇1 🍴	HC	HX 1	GW 1	GW 1	GW ◇1 🍴	GW ◇1 🍴	GW ◇1 🍴	HX 1	GW 1	GW ◇1 🍴
London Paddington 15 ⊖	d	15 00	15 03	15 06	15 10	15 12	15 15	15 15	15 18	15 22	15 25	15 27	15 30	15 33	15 40	15 42	15 45	15 45	15 48	15 51	15 55	15 57	16 00
Acton Main Line	d						15 21										15 51						
Ealing Broadway ⊖	d		15 11			15 20	15 24					15 35		15 41		15 50	15 54					16 05	
West Ealing	d		15 13				15 27							15 43			15 57						
Drayton Green	d						15 29										15 59						
Castle Bar Park	d						15 31										16 01						
South Greenford	d						15 34										16 04						
Greenford ⊖	a						15 39										16 09						
Hanwell	d		15 15											15 45									
Southall	d		15 19			15 28						15 40		15 49		15 58						16 10	
Hayes & Harlington	d		15 23			15 32						15 44		15 53		16 02						16 14	
Heathrow Terminals 1-2-3 2 ✈	a		15 35		15 25						15 40			16 05	15 55						16 10		
Heathrow Terminal 4 ✈	a																						
West Drayton	d					15 36						15 48				16 06						16 19	
Iver	d					15 39										16 09							
Langley	d					15 43										16 13							
Slough 3	a					15 47				15 36		15 55				16 17				16 06		16 26	
	d					15 47				15 36		15 55				16 17				16 06		16 26	
Burnham	d					15 51										16 21							
Taplow	d					15 55										16 25							
Maidenhead 3	d					15 59						16 03				16 29						16 33	
Twyford 3	d					16 07						16 11				16 37						16 41	
Reading 7	a	15 25		15 30		16 17		15 39	15 47	15 51		16 22	15 56			16 45		16 09	16 14	16 20		16 52	16 25
Oxford	a									16 18		17 15								16 47		17 44	

		HC	GW ◇1 🍴	HX 1	GW 1	GW 1	GW ◇1 🍴	GW 1	GW 1	HX 1	GW 1	GW ◇1 🍴	HC	GW ◇1 🍴	HX 1	GW 1	GW 1	GW ◇1 🍴	GW 1	HX 1	GW 1	GW ◇1 🍴	HC
London Paddington 15 ⊖	d	16 03	16 06	16 10	16 12	16 15	16 15	16 18	16 22	16 25	16 27	16 30	16 33	16 36	16 40	16 42	16 45	16 45	16 48	16 55	16 57	17 00	17 03
Acton Main Line	d					16 21											16 51						
Ealing Broadway ⊖	d	16 11			16 20	16 24					16 35		16 41			16 50	16 54				17 05		17 11
West Ealing	d	16 13				16 27							16 43				16 57						17 13
Drayton Green	d					16 29											16 59						
Castle Bar Park	d					16 31											17 01						
South Greenford	d					16 34											17 04						
Greenford ⊖	a					16 39											17 09						
Hanwell	d	16 15											16 45										17 15
Southall	d	16 19			16 28						16 40		16 49			16 58					17 10		17 19
Hayes & Harlington	d	16 23			16 32						16 44		16 53			17 02					17 14		17 23
Heathrow Terminals 1-2-3 2 ✈	a	16 35		16 25						16 40			17 05		16 55					17 10			17 35
Heathrow Terminal 4 ✈	a																						
West Drayton	d				16 36											17 07					17 19		
Iver	d				16 40											17 10					17 22		
Langley	d				16 44											17 14					17 26		
Slough 3	a				16 48				16 36		16 53					17 18			17 04		17 30		
	d				16 48				16 36		16 53					17 18			17 04		17 30		
Burnham	d				16 52											17 22					17 34		
Taplow	d				16 56											17 26					17 38		
Maidenhead 3	d				17 00						17 04					17 30					17 43		
Twyford 3	d				17 08						17 12					17 38					17 51		
Reading 7	a		16 30		17 16		16 39	16 48	16 52		17 22	16 56		17 01		→		17 09	17 19		→	17 24	
Oxford	a								17 23		18 11								17 50				

		GW ◇1 🍴	GW ◇1 🍴	HX 1	GW 1	GW 1	GW ◇1 🍴	GW 1	GW 1	GW 1	GW ◇1 🍴	HX 1	GW 1	GW ◇1 🍴	GW 1	HC	GW 1	GW ◇1 🍴	HX 1	GW 1	GW 1	GW ◇1 🍴
London Paddington 15 ⊖	d	17 03	17 06	17 10	17 12	17 15	17 15		17 18	17 18	17 22	17 25	17 25	17 30		17 33	17 33	17 36	17 40	17 42	17 45	17 45
Acton Main Line	d								17 24													
Ealing Broadway ⊖	d					17 23			17 27				17 33			17 41					17 53	
West Ealing	d								17 30							17 43						
Drayton Green	d								17 32													
Castle Bar Park	d								17 34													
South Greenford	d								17 37													
Greenford ⊖	a								17 12													
Hanwell	d															17 45						
Southall	d					17 29							17 38			17 49					17 59	
Hayes & Harlington	d					17 33							17 42			17 53					18 03	
Heathrow Terminals 1-2-3 2 ✈	a			17 25								17 40				18 05			17 55			
Heathrow Terminal 4 ✈	a																					
West Drayton	d					17 38							17 47								18 08	
Iver	d					17 41							17 50									
Langley	d					17 44							17 54								18 12	
Slough 3	a				17 35	17 49							17 58							18 04	18 16	
	d				17 36	17 49							17 58							18 05	18 16	
Burnham	d					17 53							18 02								18 21	
Taplow	d					17 57							18 06									
Maidenhead 3	d				17 48	18a05		←		17 40			18 10		←		17 53			18 14	18 26	
Twyford 3	d		17 28		17a58			17 38		17 48			18 17		17 51		18 07				18 34	
Reading 7	a	17 29	17 35				17 40	17 46		17 56	17 49		→	17 54	18 00		18 15	18 01			→	18 09
Oxford	a									18 45	18 15						19 06					

		GW 1	GW ◇1 🍴	GW ◇1 🍴	GW 1	HX 1	GW 1	GW ◇1 🍴	HC	GW ◇1 🍴	HX 1	GW 1	GW 1	GW ◇1 🍴	GW 1	GW 1	GW 1	GW ◇1 🍴	HX 1	GW 1	GW ◇1 🍴	HC
London Paddington 15 ⊖	d	17 48	17 48	17 50		17 55	17 57	18 00	18 03	18 06	18 10	18 12	18 15	18 15		18 18	18 18	18 22	18 25	18 25	18 30	18 33
Acton Main Line	d	17 54														18 24						
Ealing Broadway ⊖	d	17 57					18 05		18 11				18 23			18 27				18 33		18 41
West Ealing	d	18 00							18 13							18 30						18 43
Drayton Green	d	18 02														18 32						
Castle Bar Park	d	18 04														18 34						
South Greenford	d	18 07														18 37						
Greenford ⊖	a	18 12														18 42						
Hanwell	d								18 15													18 45
Southall	d						18 10		18 19				18 29							18 38		18 49
Hayes & Harlington	d						18 14		18 23				18 33							18 42		18 53
Heathrow Terminals 1-2-3 2 ✈	a					18 10			18 35		18 25								18 40			19 05
Heathrow Terminal 4 ✈	a																					
West Drayton	d						18 19						18 38							18 46		
Iver	d						18 22													18 49		
Langley	d						18 26						18 42							18 52		
Slough 3	a						18 30					18 35	18 47							18 59		
	d						18 30					18 36	18 47							18 59		
Burnham	d						18 35						18 51							19 03		
Taplow	d						18 39													19 06		
Maidenhead 3	d			18 09	←		18 44					18 48	18 57		←		18 40			19 10		
Twyford 3	d				18 17		18 51			18 28		18a58	19 05		18 34		18 48			19 18		
Reading 7	a		18 14	18 20	18 26		→	18 25		18 35			→	18 40	18 43		18 56	18 49		→	18 54	
Oxford	a			18 47	19 16												19 47	19 20				

		GW ◇1 🍴	GW 1	GW 1	HX 1	GW 1	GW ◇1 🍴	GW 1	GW ◇1 🍴	GW 1	GW 1	GW 1	GW 1	HX 1	GW 1	GW ◇1 🍴	HC	GW 1	HX 1	GW 1	GW 1
London Paddington 15 ⊖	d	18 33		18 36	18 40	18 45	18 45		18 47	18 48	18 51			18 55	18 57	19 00	19 03	19 06	19 10	19 12	19 15
Acton Main Line	d									18 54											19 21
Ealing Broadway ⊖	d					18 53				18 57					19 05		19 11			19 20	19 24
West Ealing	d									19 00							19 13				19 27
Drayton Green	d									19 02											19 29
Castle Bar Park	d									19 04											19 31
South Greenford	d									19 07											19 34
Greenford ⊖	a									19 12											19 39
Hanwell	d																19 15				
Southall	d					18 59									19 10		19 19			19 28	
Hayes & Harlington	d					19 03									19 14		19 23			19 32	
Heathrow Terminals 1-2-3 2 ✈	a				18 55									19 10			19 35		19 25		
Heathrow Terminal 4 ✈	a																				
West Drayton	d														19 19						
Iver	d														19 22						
Langley	d														19 26						
Slough 3	a			18 54		19 11					19 06				19 30					19 41	
	d			18 55		19 11					19 06				19 30					19 41	
Burnham	d					19 15									19 34					19 45	
Taplow	d														19 38					19 48	
Maidenhead 3	d		←	19a06		19 21		←				←	←		19 43			19 27		19 52	
Twyford 3	d		18 51			19 37		19 05	19 09			19 18	19 37		19 51			19a38		20 00	
Reading 7	a	18 59	19 01			→	19 09	19 13	19 17		19 22	19 26	19 45		→	19 27				→	
Oxford	a							20 14			19 50	20 27									

Table 117

Mondays to Fridays

London - Greenford and Reading

Station	GW ◇1 ☕	GW 1	GW 1	GW 1	GW ◇1 ☕	HX 1	GW 1	GW ◇1 ☕	HC		HX 1	GW 1	GW 1	GW ◇1 ☕	GW ◇1 ☕	GW ◇1	HX 1	GW 1	GW ◇1 ☕		HC	HX 1	GW 1	GW 1
London Paddington 15 ⊖ d	19 15	19 18			19 22	19 25	19 27	19 30	19 33		19 40	19 42	19 45	19 45	19 48	19 50	19 55	19 57	20 00		20 03	20 10	20 12	20 15
Acton Main Line d													19 51											20 21
Ealing Broadway ⊖ d							19 35		19 41			19 50	19 54					20 05			20 11		20 20	20 24
West Ealing d									19 43				19 57								20 13			20 27
Drayton Green d													19 59											20 29
Castle Bar Park d													20 01											20 31
South Greenford d													20 04											20 34
Greenford ⊖ a													20 09											20 39
Hanwell d									19 45												20 15			
Southall d							19 40		19 49			19 58									20 19		20 28	
Hayes & Harlington d							19 44		19 53			20 02						20 12			20 23		20 32	
Heathrow Terminals 1-2-3 2 ✈ a						19 40			20 05		19 55						20 10				20 35	20 25		
Heathrow Terminal 4 ✈ a																								
West Drayton d							19 48					20 06						20 16					20 36	
Iver d							19 51					20 09						20 19						
Langley d							19 55					20 13						20 22						
Slough 3 a					19 36		19 59					20 17				20 06		20 27					20 43	
d					19 36		19 59					20 17				20 06		20 27					20 43	
Burnham d							20 03					20 21											20 47	
Taplow d												20 25											20 51	
Maidenhead 3 d		19 40	←	←			20 09					20 29						20 34					20 55	
Twyford 3 d		19 48	19 51	20 00			20 17					20 37						20 42					21 03	
Reading 7 a	19 39	19 56	20 00	20 10	19 51		20 23	19 56				20 45		20 09	20 14	20 22		20 52	20 25				21 12	
Oxford a		20 45			20 18		21 12									20 48		21 42						

Station	GW ◇1 ☕	GW ◇1 🍴	HX 1	GW 1	HC		GW ◇1 ☕	HX 1	GW 1	GW 1	GW ◇1 ☕	GW ◇1 🍴	HX 1	GW 1	HC		HX 1	GW 1	GW ◇1 ☕	GW FX ◇1 ☕	GW 1	GW ◇1	HX 1	GW 1
London Paddington 15 ⊖ d	20 15	20 20	20 25	20 27	20 33		20 35	20 40	20 42	20 45	20 45	20 51	20 55	20 57	21 03		21 10	21 12	21 15	21 15	21 15	21 21	21 25	21 27
Acton Main Line d										20 51											21 21			
Ealing Broadway ⊖ d				20 35	20 41				20 50	20 54				21 05	21 11			21 20			21 24			21 35
West Ealing d					20 43					20 57					21 13						21 27			
Drayton Green d										20 59											21 29			
Castle Bar Park d										21 01											21 31			
South Greenford d										21 04											21 34			
Greenford ⊖ a										21 09											21 39			
Hanwell d					20 45										21 15									
Southall d					20 49				20 58						21 19			21 28						
Hayes & Harlington d				20 42	20 53				21 02					21 12	21 23			21 32						21 42
Heathrow Terminals 1-2-3 2 ✈ a			20 40		21 05			20 55					21 10		21 35		21 25						21 40	
Heathrow Terminal 4 ✈ a																								
West Drayton d				20 46					21 06					21 16				21 36						21 46
Iver d				20 49										21 19										
Langley d				20 52										21 22										
Slough 3 a		20 35		20 57					21 13			21 06		21 27				21 43				21 36		21 54
d		20 36		20 57					21 13			21 06		21 27				21 43				21 36		21 54
Burnham d									21 17									21 47						
Taplow d									21 21									21 51						
Maidenhead 3 d				21 04					21 25					21 34				21 55						22 01
Twyford 3 d				21 12					21 33					21 42				22 03						22 09
Reading 7 a	20 39	20 50		21 21			20 59		21 43		21 09	21 22		21 51				22 12	21 39	21 39		21 52		22 20
Oxford a		21 16		22 15								21 53		22 39								22 24		23 16

Station	HC		HX 1	GW 1	GW ◇1 ☕	HX 1	GW 1	HC	HX 1	GW FX 1	GW FO 1		GW FO ◇1 ☕	GW FX ◇1 ☕	GW FX ◇1 ☕	GW FO ◇1	GW FX ◇1	HX 1	HC	HX 1	GW 1		GW FO ◇1 ☕	GW FX ◇1 ☕
London Paddington 15 ⊖ d	21 33		21 40	21 42	21 45	21 55	21 57	22 03	22 10	22 10	22 10		22 15	22 15	22 15	22 21	22 21	22 25	22 33	22 40	22 45		22 45	22 45
Acton Main Line d																					22 51			
Ealing Broadway ⊖ d	21 41			21 50			22 05	22 11		22 18	22 18								22 41		22 54			
West Ealing d	21 43							22 13											22 43					
Drayton Green d																								
Castle Bar Park d																								
South Greenford d																								
Greenford ⊖ a																								
Hanwell d	21 45							22 15											22 45					
Southall d	21 49			21 58				22 19		22 23	22 23								22 49					
Hayes & Harlington d	21 53			22 02			22 12	22 23		22 27	22 27								22 53		23 02			
Heathrow Terminals 1-2-3 2 ✈ a	22 05		21 55			22 10		22 35	22 25									22 40	23 05	22 55				
Heathrow Terminal 4 ✈ a																								
West Drayton d				22 06			22 16			22 31	22 31													
Iver d				22 09			22 19				22 34													
Langley d				22 13			22 22				22 38													
Slough 3 a				22 18			22 28			22 39	22 43					22 36	22 42				23 12			
d				22 19			22 33			22 45	22 45					22 36	22 42				23 12			
Burnham d				22 22						22 49	22 49										23 16			
Taplow d				22 26						22 52	22 52										23 19			
Maidenhead 3 d				22 30			22 41			22 56	22 56										23 23			
Twyford 3 d				22 38			22 49			23 04	23 04										23 31			
Reading 7 a				22 46	22 09		22 58			23 14	23 14		22 39	22 48	22 48	22 52	23 06				23 40		23 09	23 13
Oxford a							23 44									23 26	23 38				00 23			

Table 117

Mondays to Fridays

London - Greenford and Reading

Station	GW FX ◇1 ☕	GW FO ◇1	GW FX ◇1	HX 1	GW 1	HC	HX 1		GW FO ◇1	GW FX ◇1	HX 1	GW 1	GW FO ◇1 ☕	GW FX ◇1 ☕	GW FX ◇1 ☕				GW 1
London Paddington 15 ⊖ d	22 45	22 48	22 48	22 55	22 59	23 03	23 10		23 20	23 20	23 25	23 29	23 30	23 30	23 30				23 48
Acton Main Line d																			23 54
Ealing Broadway ⊖ d					23 07	23 11						23 37							23 58
West Ealing d						23 13													00 01
Drayton Green d																			
Castle Bar Park d																			
South Greenford d																			
Greenford ⊖ a																			
Hanwell d						23 15													00 03
Southall d					23 12	23 19													00 07
Hayes & Harlington d					23 18	23 23						23 44							00 12
Heathrow Terminals 1-2-3 2 ✈ a				23 10		23 35	23 25				23 40								
Heathrow Terminal 4 ✈ a						23 41													
West Drayton d					23 22														00 16
Iver d					23 25														00 19
Langley d					23 28														00 22
Slough 3 a		23 06	23 06		23 34				23 36	23 38		23 53							00 28
d		23 06	23 06		23 34				23 39	23 39		23 54							00 28
Burnham d																			00 32
Taplow d																			00 35
Maidenhead 3 d					23 41							00 01							00 39
Twyford 3 d					23 49							00 09							00 47
Reading 7 a	23 19	23 21	23 34		23 59				23 54	00 04		00 19	00 03	00 06	00 06				00 57
Oxford a		23 48	00 13						00 28	00 33		01 07							

Saturdays

Station	GW 1	GW ◇1	GW 1	GW 1	GW ◇1 ☕		GW 1	GW ◇1	GW 1		GW 1	GW 1	HC	HX 1	HC	HX 1	GW 1	HC	HX 1	GW 1	GW ◇1	HX 1	GW 1	HC
London Paddington 15 ⊖ d	22p45	23p20		23p29	23p30		23p48	00 20	00 34		01 44	03 34	04 42	05 10	05 13	05 25	05 25	05 33	05 40	05 45	05 50	05 55	05 57	06 03
Acton Main Line d	22p51						23p54													05 51				
Ealing Broadway ⊖ d	22p54			23p37			23p58		00 42		01 52	03 42	04 50		05 21		05 33	05 41		05 54			06 05	06 11
West Ealing d							00 01											05 43		05 57				06 13
Drayton Green d																				05 59				
Castle Bar Park d																				06 01				
South Greenford d																				06 04				
Greenford ⊖ a																				06 09				
Hanwell d							00 03											05 45						06 15
Southall d							00 07		00 47		01 57	03 47	04 54		05 25		05 38	05 49					06 10	06 19
Hayes & Harlington d	23p02			23p44			00 12		00 51		02 01	03 51	04 58		05 29		05 42	05 53					06 14	06 23
Heathrow Terminals 1-2-3 2 ✈ a													05 04	05 26	05 35	05 40		06 05	05 55			06 10		06 35
Heathrow Terminal 4 ✈ a													05 10		05 41									
West Drayton d							00 16		00 55		02 05	03 55											06 18	
Iver d							00 19																06 21	
Langley d							00 22		01 00														06 25	
Slough 3 a	23p12	23p36		23p53			00 28	00 38	01 05		02 13	04 03					05 50				06 06		06 30	
d	23p12	23p39		23p54			00 28	00 39	01 05		02 13	04 03					05 51				06 06		06 31	
Burnham d	23p16						00 32		01 09								05 55						06 35	
Taplow d	23p19						00 35		01 13								05 58						06 38	
Maidenhead 3 d	23p23			00 01			00 39		01 16		02 21	04 11					06 02						06 42	
Twyford 3 d	23p31		00 07	00 09			00 47		01 24		02 29	04 19					06 10						06 50	
Reading 7 a	23p40	23p54	00 16	00 19	00 03		00 57	00 55	01 33		02 38	04 30					06 17				06 37		06 56	
Oxford a	00 23	00 28		01 07				01 28									07 03				06 52		07 43	

Station	HX 1	GW 1	GW 1	GW ◇1	HX 1		GW 1	GW ◇1 ☕	HC	HX 1	GW 1	GW 1	GW ◇1	HX 1	GW 1		GW ◇1 ☕	HC	HX 1	GW 1	GW 1	GW ◇1 🍴	HX 1	GW 1
London Paddington 15 ⊖ d	06 10	06 12	06 15	06 21	06 25		06 27	06 30	06 33	06 40	06 42	06 45	06 50	06 55	06 57		07 00	07 03	07 10	07 12	07 15	07 21	07 25	07 27
Acton Main Line d			06 21									06 51									07 21			
Ealing Broadway ⊖ d		06 20	06 24				06 35		06 41		06 50	06 54			07 05			07 11		07 20	07 24			07 35
West Ealing d			06 27						06 43			06 57						07 13			07 27			
Drayton Green d			06 29									06 59									07 29			
Castle Bar Park d			06 31									07 01									07 31			
South Greenford d			06 34									07 04									07 34			
Greenford ⊖ a			06 39									07 09									07 39			
Hanwell d									06 45									07 15						
Southall d		06 28							06 49		06 58							07 19		07 28				
Hayes & Harlington d		06 32					06 42		06 53		07 02				07 12			07 23		07 32				07 42
Heathrow Terminals 1-2-3 2 ✈ a	06 25				06 40				07 05	06 55				07 10				07 35	07 25				07 40	
Heathrow Terminal 4 ✈ a																								
West Drayton d		06 36					06 46				07 06				07 16					07 36				07 46
Iver d							06 49								07 19									07 49
Langley d							06 52								07 22									07 52
Slough 3 a		06 43		06 37			06 57				07 13		07 06		07 27					07 43		07 37		07 57
d		06 43		06 38			06 57				07 13		07 06		07 27					07 43		07 38		07 57
Burnham d		06 47									07 17									07 47				
Taplow d		06 51									07 21									07 51				
Maidenhead 3 d		06 55					07 04				07 25				07 34					07 55				08 04
Twyford 3 d		07 03					07 12				07 33				07 42					08 03				08 12
Reading 7 a		07 13		06 53			07 20	06 57			07 43		07 22		07 52		07 26			08 13		07 53		08 22
Oxford a				07 19			08 09						07 48		08 40							08 19		09 14

London - Greenford and Reading

		GW	GW	HC	HX	GW	GW	GW	GW	HX	GW	GW	HC	HX	GW	GW	GW	GW	GW	GW	HX
		1 A ⊏P	◇1 B ⊏P		1	1	1	◇1 ⊏P	◇1	1	1	◇1 ⊏P		1	1	1	◇1 ⊏P	◇1 B ⊏P	1 A	◇1 ⊏P	1
London Paddington 15 ⊖	d	07 30	07 30	07 33	07 40	07 42	07 45	07 45	07 50	07 55	07 57	08 00	08 03	08 10	08 12	08 15	08 15	08 18	08 18	08 21	08 25
Acton Main Line	d						07 51									08 21					
Ealing Broadway ⊖	d			07 41		07 50	07 54				08 05		08 11		08 20	08 24					
West Ealing	d			07 43			07 57						08 13			08 27					
Drayton Green	d						07 59									08 29					
Castle Bar Park	d						08 01									08 31					
South Greenford	d						08 04									08 34					
Greenford ⊖	a						08 09									08 39					
Hanwell	d			07 45									08 15								
Southall	d			07 49		07 58							08 19		08 28						
Hayes & Harlington	d			07 53		08 02					08 12		08 23		08 32						
Heathrow Terminals 1-2-3 2 ✈	a			08 05	07 55					08 10			08 35	08 25							08 40
Heathrow Terminal 4 ✈	a																				
West Drayton	d					08 06					08 16				08 36						
Iver	d										08 19										
Langley	d										08 22										
Slough 3	a					08 13			08 06		08 27				08 43					08 38	
	d					08 13			08 06		08 27				08 43					08 39	
Burnham	d					08 17									08 47						
Taplow	d					08 21									08 51						
Maidenhead 3	d					08 25					08 34				08 55						
Twyford 3	d					08 33					08 42				09 03						
Reading 7	a	07 55	07 57			08 43		08 09	08 22		08 52	08 26			09 13		08 40	08 45	08 48	08 53	
Oxford	a								08 48		09 40									09 18	

		GW	GW	HC	HX	GW	GW	GW	GW	GW	HX	GW	GW	HC	GW	HX	GW	GW	GW	GW	HX
		1	◇1 ⊏P		1	1	1	◇1 B ⊏P	◇1 A ⊏P	◇1	1	1	◇1 ⊏P		◇1 B ⊘	1	1	1	1	◇1	1
London Paddington 15 ⊖	d	08 27	08 30	08 33	08 40	08 42	08 45	08 45	08 45	08 50	08 55	08 57	09 00	09 03	09 06	09 10	09 12	09 15	09 18	09 21	09 25
Acton Main Line	d						08 51											09 21			
Ealing Broadway ⊖	d	08 35		08 41		08 50	08 54					09 05		09 11			09 20	09 24			
West Ealing	d			08 43			08 57							09 13				09 27			
Drayton Green	d						08 59											09 29			
Castle Bar Park	d						09 01											09 31			
South Greenford	d						09 04											09 34			
Greenford ⊖	a						09 09											09 39			
Hanwell	d			08 45										09 15							
Southall	d			08 49		08 58								09 19			09 28				
Hayes & Harlington	d	08 42		08 53		09 02						09 12		09 23			09 32				
Heathrow Terminals 1-2-3 2 ✈	a			09 05	08 55						09 10			09 35		09 25					09 40
Heathrow Terminal 4 ✈	a																				
West Drayton	d	08 46				09 06						09 16					09 36				
Iver	d	08 49										09 19									
Langley	d	08 52										09 22									
Slough 3	a	08 57				09 13				09 06		09 27					09 43			09 38	
	d	08 57				09 13				09 06		09 27					09 43			09 39	
Burnham	d					09 17											09 47				
Taplow	d					09 21											09 51				
Maidenhead 3	d	09 04				09 25						09 34					09 55				
Twyford 3	d	09 12				09 33						09 42					10 03				
Reading 7	a	09 23	08 56			09 43		09 09	09 10	09 22		09 52	09 26		09 30		10 13		09 48	09 54	
Oxford	a	10 14								09 48		10 40								10 19	

A until 4 September

B from 11 September

Table 117

Saturdays

London - Greenford and Reading

		GW	GW	HC	HX	GW	GW	GW	GW	HX	GW	GW	HC	GW	HX	GW	GW	GW	GW	GW	HX
		1	◇1 ⊏P		1	1	1	◇1 ⊏P	◇1	1	1	◇1 ⊏P		◇1 A ⊘	1	1	1	◇1 ⊏P	1	◇1 ⊏P	1
London Paddington 15 ⊖	d	09 27	09 30	09 33	09 40	09 42	09 45	09 45	09 50	09 55	09 57	10 00	10 03	10 06	10 10	10 12	10 15	10 15	10 18	10 21	10 25
Acton Main Line	d						09 51										10 21				
Ealing Broadway ⊖	d	09 35		09 41		09 50	09 54				10 05		10 11			10 20	10 24				
West Ealing	d			09 43			09 57						10 13				10 27				
Drayton Green	d						09 59										10 29				
Castle Bar Park	d						10 01										10 31				
South Greenford	d						10 04										10 34				
Greenford ⊖	a						10 09										10 39				
Hanwell	d			09 45									10 15								
Southall	d			09 49		09 58							10 19			10 28					
Hayes & Harlington	d	09 42		09 53		10 02					10 12		10 23			10 32					
Heathrow Terminals 1-2-3 2 ✈	a			10 05	09 55					10 10			10 35		10 25						10 40
Heathrow Terminal 4 ✈	a																				
West Drayton	d	09 46				10 06					10 16					10 36					
Iver	d	09 49									10 19										
Langley	d	09 52									10 22										
Slough 3	a	09 57				10 13			10 06		10 27					10 43				10 38	
	d	09 57				10 13			10 06		10 27					10 43				10 39	
Burnham	d					10 17										10 47					
Taplow	d					10 21										10 51					
Maidenhead 3	d	10 04				10 25					10 34					10 55					
Twyford 3	d	10 12				10 33					10 42					11 03					
Reading 7	a	10 22	09 57			10 43		10 09	10 22		10 52	10 26		10 30		11 13		10 40	10 48	10 53	
Oxford	a	11 14							10 48		11 40									11 19	

		GW	GW	HC	HX	GW	GW	GW	GW	HX	GW	GW	HC	GW	HX	GW	GW	GW	GW	HX	GW
		1	◇1 ⊏P		1	1	1	◇1 ⊘	◇1	1	1	◇1 ⊏P		◇1 D ⊘	1	1	1	1	◇1 🍴	1	1
London Paddington 15 ⊖	d	10 27	10 30	10 33	10 40	10 42	10 45	10 45	10 50	10 55	10 57	11 00	11 03	11 06	11 10	11 12	11 15	11 18	11 21	11 25	11 27
Acton Main Line	d						10 51										11 21				
Ealing Broadway ⊖	d	10 35		10 41		10 50	10 54				11 05		11 11			11 20	11 24				11 35
West Ealing	d			10 43			10 57						11 13				11 27				
Drayton Green	d						10 59										11 29				
Castle Bar Park	d						11 01										11 31				
South Greenford	d						11 04										11 34				
Greenford ⊖	a						11 09										11 39				
Hanwell	d			10 45									11 15								
Southall	d			10 49		10 58							11 19			11 28					
Hayes & Harlington	d	10 42		10 53		11 02					11 12		11 23			11 32					11 42
Heathrow Terminals 1-2-3 2 ✈	a			11 05	10 55					11 10			11 35		11 25					11 40	
Heathrow Terminal 4 ✈	a																				
West Drayton	d	10 46				11 06					11 16					11 36					11 46
Iver	d	10 49									11 19										11 49
Langley	d	10 52									11 22										11 52
Slough 3	a	10 57				11 13			11 06		11 27					11 43			11 38		11 57
	d	10 57				11 13			11 06		11 27					11 43			11 39		11 57
Burnham	d					11 17										11 47					
Taplow	d					11 21										11 51					
Maidenhead 3	d	11 04				11 25					11 34					11 55					12 04
Twyford 3	d	11 12				11 33					11 42					12 03					12 12
Reading 7	a	11 22	10 57			11 43		11 09	11 22		11 52	11 26		11 30		12 13		11 48	11 54		12 22
Oxford	a	12 14							11 48		12 40								12 20		13 14

A from 11 September. The Cornish Riviera

D from 11 September

Table 117

London - Greenford and Reading

		GW	HC	HX	GW	GW	GW	GW	HX	GW	GW	HC	GW	HX	GW	GW	GW	GW	GW	GW	HX
		◇1 Ø		1	1	1	◇1 Ø	◇1	1	1	◇1 ⊐		◇1 B Ø	1	1	1	◇1 ⊐	◇1 D ⊐	1 A	◇1	1
London Paddington 15 ⊖	d	11 30	11 33	11 40	11 42	11 45	11 45	11 50	11 55	11 57	12 00	12 03	12 06	12 10	12 12	12 15	12 15	12 18	12 18	12 21	12 25
Acton Main Line	d					11 51										12 21					
Ealing Broadway ⊖	d		11 41		11 50	11 54				12 05		12 11			12 20	12 24					
West Ealing	d		11 43			11 57						12 13				12 27					
Drayton Green	d					11 59										12 29					
Castle Bar Park	d					12 01										12 31					
South Greenford	d					12 04										12 34					
Greenford ⊖	a					12 09										12 39					
Hanwell	d		11 45									12 15									
Southall	d		11 49		11 58							12 19			12 28						
Hayes & Harlington	d		11 53		12 02					12 12		12 23			12 32						
Heathrow Terminals 1-2-3 2 ✈	a		12 05	11 55					12 10			12 35		12 25							12 40
Heathrow Terminal 4 ✈	a																				
West Drayton	d				12 06					12 16					12 36						
Iver	d									12 19											
Langley	d									12 22											
Slough 3	a				12 13			12 06		12 27					12 43					12 38	
	d				12 13			12 06		12 27					12 43					12 39	
Burnham	d				12 17										12 47						
Taplow	d				12 21										12 51						
Maidenhead 3	d				12 25					12 34					12 55						
Twyford 3	d				12 33					12 42					13 03						
Reading 7	a	11 58			12 43		12 09	12 22		12 52	12 26		12 30		13 13		12 40	12 45	12 49	12 54	
Oxford	a							12 48		13 40										13 19	

		GW	GW	HC	HX	GW	GW	GW	GW	HX	GW	GW	HC	GW	HX	GW	GW	GW	GW	HX
		1	◇1 ⊐		1	1	1	◇1 ⊐	◇1	1	1	◇1 ⊐		◇1 D ⊐	1	1	1	1	◇1 ✕	1
London Paddington 15 ⊖	d	12 27	12 30	12 33	12 40	12 42	12 45	12 45	12 50	12 55	12 57	13 00	13 03	13 06	13 10	13 12	13 15	13 18	13 21	13 25
Acton Main Line	d						12 51										13 21			
Ealing Broadway ⊖	d	12 35		12 41		12 50	12 54				13 05		13 11			13 20	13 24			
West Ealing	d			12 43			12 57						13 13				13 27			
Drayton Green	d						12 59										13 29			
Castle Bar Park	d						13 01										13 31			
South Greenford	d						13 04										13 34			
Greenford ⊖	a						13 09										13 39			
Hanwell	d			12 45									13 15							
Southall	d			12 49		12 58							13 19			13 28				
Hayes & Harlington	d	12 42		12 53		13 02					13 12		13 23			13 32				
Heathrow Terminals 1-2-3 2 ✈	a			13 05	12 55					13 10			13 35		13 25					13 40
Heathrow Terminal 4 ✈	a																			
West Drayton	d	12 46				13 06					13 16					13 36				
Iver	d	12 49									13 19									
Langley	d	12 52									13 22									
Slough 3	a	12 57				13 13			13 06		13 27					13 43			13 38	
	d	12 57				13 13			13 06		13 27					13 43			13 39	
Burnham	d					13 17										13 47				
Taplow	d					13 21										13 51				
Maidenhead 3	d	13 04				13 25					13 34					13 55				
Twyford 3	d	13 12				13 33					13 42					14 03				
Reading 7	a	13 22	12 57			13 43		13 09	13 22		13 52	13 26		13 30		14 13		13 48	13 54	
Oxford	a	14 14							13 48		14 40								14 19	

		GW	GW	HC	HX	GW	GW	GW	GW	HX	GW	GW	HC	GW	HX	GW	GW	GW	GW	GW	HX	GW	GW
		1	◇1 ⊐		1	1	1	◇1 ⊐	◇1	1	1	◇1 ⊐		◇1 ⊐	1	1	1	◇1 ⊐	1	◇1 ✕	1	1	◇1 ⊐
London Paddington 15 ⊖	d	13 27	13 30	13 33	13 40	13 42	13 45	13 45	13 50	13 55	13 57	14 00	14 03	14 06	14 10	14 12	14 15	14 15	14 18	14 21	14 25	14 27	14 30
Acton Main Line	d						13 51										14 21						
Ealing Broadway ⊖	d	13 35		13 41		13 50	13 54				14 05		14 11			14 20	14 24					14 35	
West Ealing	d			13 43			13 57						14 13				14 27						
Drayton Green	d						13 59										14 29						
Castle Bar Park	d						14 01										14 31						
South Greenford	d						14 04										14 34						
Greenford ⊖	a						14 09										14 39						
Hanwell	d			13 45									14 15										
Southall	d			13 49		13 58							14 19			14 28							
Hayes & Harlington	d	13 42		13 53		14 02					14 12		14 23			14 32						14 42	
Heathrow Terminals 1-2-3 2 ✈	a			14 05	13 55					14 10			14 35		14 25						14 40		
Heathrow Terminal 4 ✈	a																						
West Drayton	d	13 46				14 06					14 16					14 36						14 46	
Iver	d	13 49									14 19											14 49	
Langley	d	13 52									14 22											14 52	
Slough 3	a	13 57				14 13			14 06		14 27					14 43				14 38		14 57	
	d	13 57				14 13			14 06		14 27					14 43				14 39		14 57	
Burnham	d					14 17										14 47							
Taplow	d					14 21										14 51							
Maidenhead 3	d	14 04				14 25					14 34					14 55						15 04	
Twyford 3	d	14 12				14 33					14 42					15 03						15 12	
Reading 7	a	14 22	13 58			14 43		14 09	14 22		14 52	14 26		14 30		15 13		14 40	14 48	14 53		15 22	14 57
Oxford	a	15 13							14 48		15 40									15 18		16 14	

A until 4 September
B from 11 September. The Royal Duchy
D from 11 September

Table 117

London - Greenford and Reading

		HC	HX	GW	GW	GW	GW	HX	GW	GW	HC	HX	GW	GW	GW	GW	HX	GW	GW	HC	HX
			1	1	1	◇1 ⊐	◇1	1	1	◇1 ⊐		1	1	1	1	◇1 ✕	1	1	◇1 ⊐		1
London Paddington 15 ⊖	d	14 33	14 40	14 42	14 45	14 45	14 50	14 55	14 57	15 00	15 03	15 10	15 12	15 15	15 18	15 21	15 25	15 27	15 30	15 33	15 40
Acton Main Line	d				14 51									15 21							
Ealing Broadway ⊖	d	14 41		14 50	14 54				15 05		15 11		15 20	15 24				15 35		15 41	
West Ealing	d	14 43			14 57						15 13			15 27						15 43	
Drayton Green	d				14 59									15 29							
Castle Bar Park	d				15 01									15 31							
South Greenford	d				15 04									15 34							
Greenford ⊖	a				15 09									15 39							
Hanwell	d	14 45									15 15									15 45	
Southall	d	14 49		14 58							15 19		15 28							15 49	
Hayes & Harlington	d	14 53		15 02					15 12		15 23		15 32					15 42		15 53	
Heathrow Terminals 1-2-3 2 ✈	a	15 05	14 55					15 10			15 35	15 25					15 40			16 05	15 55
Heathrow Terminal 4 ✈	a																				
West Drayton	d			15 06					15 16				15 36					15 46			
Iver	d								15 19									15 49			
Langley	d								15 22									15 52			
Slough 3	a			15 13			15 06		15 27				15 43			15 38		15 57			
	d			15 13			15 06		15 27				15 43			15 39		15 57			
Burnham	d			15 17									15 47								
Taplow	d			15 21									15 51								
Maidenhead 3	d			15 25					15 34				15 55					16 04			
Twyford 3	d			15 33					15 42				16 03					16 12			
Reading 7	a			15 43		15 09	15 22		15 52	15 26			16 13		15 48	15 54		16 22	15 58		
Oxford	a						15 48		16 40							16 19		17 14			

		GW	GW	GW	GW	HX	GW	GW	HC	GW	HX	GW	GW	GW	GW	GW	HX	GW	GW	GW	HC	HX	GW
		1	1	◇1 ⊐	◇1	1	1	◇1 ⊐		◇1 ⊐	1	1	1	◇1 ⊐	1	◇1 ⊐	1	1	◇1 A ⊐	◇1 B ⊐		1	1
London Paddington 15 ⊖	d	15 42	15 45	15 45	15 50	15 55	15 57	16 00	16 03	16 06	16 10	16 12	16 15	16 15	16 18	16 21	16 25	16 27	16 30	16 30	16 33	16 40	16 42
Acton Main Line	d		15 51										16 21										
Ealing Broadway ⊖	d	15 50	15 54				16 05		16 11			16 20	16 24					16 35			16 41		16 50
West Ealing	d		15 57						16 13				16 27								16 43		
Drayton Green	d		15 59										16 29										
Castle Bar Park	d		16 01										16 31										
South Greenford	d		16 04										16 34										
Greenford ⊖	a		16 09										16 39										
Hanwell	d								16 15												16 45		
Southall	d	15 58							16 19			16 28									16 49		16 58
Hayes & Harlington	d	16 02					16 12		16 23			16 32						16 42			16 53		17 02
Heathrow Terminals 1-2-3 2 ✈	a					16 10			16 35		16 25						16 40				17 05	16 55	
Heathrow Terminal 4 ✈	a																						
West Drayton	d	16 06					16 16					16 36						16 46					17 06
Iver	d						16 19											16 49					
Langley	d						16 22											16 52					
Slough 3	a	16 13			16 06		16 27					16 43				16 38		16 57					17 13
	d	16 13			16 06		16 27					16 43				16 39		16 57					17 13
Burnham	d	16 17										16 47											17 17
Taplow	d	16 21										16 51											17 21
Maidenhead 3	d	16 25					16 34					16 55						17 04					17 25
Twyford 3	d	16 33					16 42					17 03						17 12					17 33
Reading 7	a	16 43		16 09	16 22		16 52	16 26		16 31		17 13		16 40	16 48	16 53		17 22	16 57	16 57			17 43
Oxford	a				16 48		17 40									17 18		18 14					

		GW	GW	GW	HX	GW	GW	HC	HX	GW	GW	GW	GW	HX	GW	GW	HC	HX	GW	GW	GW	GW
		1	◇1 ⊐	◇1	1	1	◇1 ⊐		1	1	1	1	◇1 ⊐	1	1	◇1 ⊐		1	1	1	◇1 ⊐	◇1
London Paddington 15 ⊖	d	16 45	16 45	16 50	16 55	16 57	17 00	17 03	17 10	17 12	17 15	17 18	17 21	17 25	17 27	17 30	17 33	17 40	17 42	17 45	17 45	17 50
Acton Main Line	d	16 51									17 21									17 51		
Ealing Broadway ⊖	d	16 54				17 05		17 11		17 20	17 24				17 35		17 41		17 50	17 54		
West Ealing	d	16 57						17 13			17 27						17 43			17 57		
Drayton Green	d	16 59									17 29									17 59		
Castle Bar Park	d	17 01									17 31									18 01		
South Greenford	d	17 04									17 34									18 04		
Greenford ⊖	a	17 09									17 39									18 09		
Hanwell	d							17 15									17 45					
Southall	d							17 19		17 28							17 49		17 58			
Hayes & Harlington	d					17 12		17 23		17 32					17 42		17 53		18 02			
Heathrow Terminals 1-2-3 2 ✈	a				17 10			17 35	17 25					17 40			18 05	17 55				
Heathrow Terminal 4 ✈	a																					
West Drayton	d					17 16				17 36					17 46				18 06			
Iver	d					17 19									17 49							
Langley	d					17 22									17 52							
Slough 3	a			17 06		17 27				17 43			17 38		17 57				18 13			18 06
	d			17 06		17 27				17 43			17 39		17 57				18 13			18 06
Burnham	d									17 47									18 17			
Taplow	d									17 51									18 21			
Maidenhead 3	d					17 34				17 55					18 04				18 25			
Twyford 3	d					17 42				18 03					18 12				18 33			
Reading 7	a		17 09	17 22		17 52	17 26			18 13		17 48	17 53		18 22	17 57			18 43		18 09	18 22
Oxford	a			17 47		18 40							18 18		19 14							18 48

A from 11 September. The Torbay Express
B until 4 September

London - Greenford and Reading

		HX 1	GW 1	GW ◇1 ☕	HC	GW ◇1 ☕	HX 1	GW 1	GW 1	GW ◇1 ☕	GW 1	GW ◇1 ☕	HX 1	GW 1	GW ◇1 ☕	HC	HX 1	GW 1	GW 1	GW ◇1 ☕	GW ◇1	HX 1
London Paddington 15 ⊖	d	17 55	17 57	18 00	18 03	18 06	18 10	18 12	18 15	18 15	18 18	18 21	18 25	18 27	18 30	18 33	18 40	18 42	18 45	18 45	18 50	18 55
Acton Main Line	d								18 21										18 51			
Ealing Broadway ⊖	d		18 05		18 11			18 20	18 24					18 35		18 41		18 50	18 54			
West Ealing	d				18 13				18 27							18 43			18 57			
Drayton Green	d								18 29										18 59			
Castle Bar Park	d								18 31										19 01			
South Greenford	d								18 34										19 04			
Greenford ⊖	a								18 39										19 09			
Hanwell	d				18 15											18 45						
Southall	d				18 19			18 28								18 49		18 58				
Hayes & Harlington	d		18 12		18 23			18 32						18 42		18 53		19 02				
Heathrow Terminals 1-2-3 2 ✈	a	18 10			18 35		18 25						18 40			19 05	18 55					19 10
Heathrow Terminal 4 ✈	a																					
West Drayton	d		18 16					18 36						18 46				19 06				
Iver	d		18 19											18 49								
Langley	d		18 22											18 52								
Slough 3	a		18 27					18 43				18 38		18 57				19 13			19 06	
	d		18 27					18 43				18 39		18 57				19 13			19 06	
Burnham	d							18 47										19 17				
Taplow	d							18 51										19 21				
Maidenhead 3	d		18 34					18 55						19 04				19 25				
Twyford 3	d		18 42					19 03						19 12				19 33				
Reading 7	a		18 52	18 27		18 30		19 13		18 40	18 48	18 53		19 22	18 57			19 43		19 09	19 22	
Oxford	a		19 40									19 18		20 14							19 48	

		GW 1	GW ◇1 ☕	HC	GW ◇1 ☕	HX 1	GW 1	GW 1	GW ◇1 A ☕	GW ◇1	HX 1	GW 1	GW ◇1 ☕	HC	HX 1	GW 1	GW 1	GW ◇1 ☕	GW ◇1 🍴	HX 1	GW 1	GW ◇1 ☕	HC
London Paddington 15 ⊖	d	18 57	19 00	19 03	19 06	19 10	19 12	19 15	19 15	19 21	19 25	19 27	19 30	19 33	19 40	19 42	19 45	19 45	19 50	19 55	19 57	20 00	20 03
Acton Main Line	d							19 21									19 51						
Ealing Broadway ⊖	d	19 05		19 11			19 20	19 24				19 35		19 41		19 50	19 54				20 05		20 11
West Ealing	d			19 13				19 27						19 43			19 57						20 13
Drayton Green	d							19 29									19 59						
Castle Bar Park	d							19 31									20 01						
South Greenford	d							19 34									20 04						
Greenford ⊖	a							19 39									20 09						
Hanwell	d			19 15										19 45									20 15
Southall	d			19 19			19 28							19 49		19 58							20 19
Hayes & Harlington	d	19 12		19 23			19 32					19 42		19 53		20 02					20 12		20 23
Heathrow Terminals 1-2-3 2 ✈	a			19 35		19 25					19 40			20 05	19 55					20 10			20 35
Heathrow Terminal 4 ✈	a																						
West Drayton	d	19 16					19 36					19 46				20 06					20 16		
Iver	d	19 19										19 49									20 19		
Langley	d	19 22										19 52									20 22		
Slough 3	a	19 27					19 43			19 37		19 57				20 13			20 06		20 27		
	d	19 27					19 43			19 38		19 57				20 13			20 06		20 27		
Burnham	d						19 47									20 17							
Taplow	d						19 51									20 21							
Maidenhead 3	d	19 34					19 55					20 04				20 25					20 34		
Twyford 3	d	19 42					20 03					20 12				20 33					20 42		
Reading 7	a	19 52	19 26		19 30		20 13		19 39	19 52		20 22	19 57			20 43		20 09	20 21		20 52	20 27	
Oxford	a	20 40								20 20		21 14							20 47		21 40		

		GW ◇1 ☕	HX 1	GW 1	GW 1	GW ◇1 ☕	GW ◇1	HX 1	GW 1	GW ◇1 ☕	HC	HX 1	GW 1	GW ◇1 ☕	GW 1	GW ◇1	HX 1	GW 1	HC	HX 1	GW 1	GW 1
London Paddington 15 ⊖	d	20 06	20 10	20 12	20 15	20 15	20 21	20 25	20 27	20 30	20 33	20 40	20 42	20 45	20 45	20 50	20 55	20 57	21 03	21 10	21 12	21 15
Acton Main Line	d				20 21										20 51							21 21
Ealing Broadway ⊖	d			20 20	20 24				20 35		20 41		20 50		20 54			21 05	21 11		21 20	21 24
West Ealing	d				20 27						20 43				20 57				21 13			21 27
Drayton Green	d				20 29										20 59							21 29
Castle Bar Park	d				20 31										21 01							21 31
South Greenford	d				20 34										21 04							21 34
Greenford ⊖	a				20 39										21 09							21 39
Hanwell	d										20 45								21 15			
Southall	d			20 28							20 49		20 58						21 19		21 28	
Hayes & Harlington	d			20 32					20 42		20 53		21 02					21 12	21 23		21 32	
Heathrow Terminals 1-2-3 2 ✈	a		20 25					20 40			21 05	20 55					21 10		21 35	21 25		
Heathrow Terminal 4 ✈	a																					
West Drayton	d			20 36					20 46				21 06					21 16			21 36	
Iver	d								20 49									21 19				
Langley	d								20 52									21 22				
Slough 3	a			20 43			20 36		20 57				21 13			21 06		21 27			21 43	
	d			20 43			20 36		20 57				21 13			21 06		21 27			21 43	
Burnham	d			20 47									21 17								21 47	
Taplow	d			20 51									21 21								21 51	
Maidenhead 3	d			20 55					21 04				21 25					21 34			21 55	
Twyford 3	d			21 03					21 12				21 33					21 42			22 03	
Reading 7	a	20 30		21 13		20 40	20 52		21 22	20 59			21 43	21 09		21 22		21 52			22 13	
Oxford	a						21 20		22 14							21 53		22 43				

A from 11 September

Table 117

Saturdays

London - Greenford and Reading

		GW ◇1	HX 1	GW ◇1 ☕	HC	HX 1	GW 1	HX 1	GW 1	GW ◇1 ☕	HC	GW ◇1	HX 1	GW 1	HX 1	HC	GW ◇1 ☕	HX 1	GW 1 A	GW 1 B	HX 1	GW ◇1 B	GW ◇1 A
London Paddington 15 ⊖	d	21 17	21 25	21 30	21 33	21 40	21 42	21 55	21 57	22 00	22 03	22 06	22 10	22 12	22 25	22 33	22 35	22 40	22 45	22 45	22 55	23 00	23 00
Acton Main Line	d																		22 51	22 51			
Ealing Broadway ⊖	d				21 41		21 50		22 05		22 11			22 20		22 41			22 55	22 55			
West Ealing	d				21 43						22 13					22 43							
Drayton Green	d																						
Castle Bar Park	d																						
South Greenford	d																						
Greenford ⊖	a																						
Hanwell	d				21 45						22 15					22 45							
Southall	d				21 49		21 58				22 19			22 28		22 49			23 00	23 00			
Hayes & Harlington	d				21 53		22 02		22 12		22 23			22 32		22 53			23 04	23 04			
Heathrow Terminals 1-2-3 2 ✈	a		21 40		22 05	21 55		22 10			22 35		22 25		22 40	23 05		22 55			23 10		
Heathrow Terminal 4 ✈	a																						
West Drayton	d						22 06		22 16					22 36					23 08	23 08			
Iver	d								22 19										23 11	23 11			
Langley	d								22 22										23 14	23 14			
Slough 3	a	21 34					22 13		22 27			22 23		22 43					23 19	23 19		23 16	23 16
	d	21 35					22 13		22 27			22 24		22 43					23 21	23 21		23 17	23 17
Burnham	d						22 17							22 47					23 25	23 25			
Taplow	d						22 21							22 51									
Maidenhead 3	d						22 25		22 34					22 55					23 32	23 32			
Twyford 3	d						22 33		22 42					23 03					23 39	23 39			
Reading 7	a	21 51		21 55			22 43		22 52	22 27		22 40		23 13			23 00		23 46	23 46		23 33	23 33
Oxford	a	22 20							23 37			23 09								00 32		00 03	

		HC	HX 1	GW 1 A	GW 1 B	HX 1	GW ◇1 ☕	GW ◇1 A	GW ◇1 B	GW 1
London Paddington 15 ⊖	d	23 03	23 10	23 20	23 20	23 25	23 30	23 33	23 33	23 42
Acton Main Line	d									
Ealing Broadway ⊖	d	23 11		23 28	23 28					23 50
West Ealing	d	23 13								
Drayton Green	d									
Castle Bar Park	d									
South Greenford	d									
Greenford ⊖	a									
Hanwell	d	23 15								
Southall	d	23 19		23 33	23 33					23 56
Hayes & Harlington	d	23 23		23 37	23 37					00 01
Heathrow Terminals 1-2-3 2 ✈	a	23 35	23 25			23 40				
Heathrow Terminal 4 ✈	a	23 41								
West Drayton	d			23 41	23 41					00 06
Iver	d			23 44	23 44					
Langley	d			23 48	23 48					
Slough 3	a			23 53	23 53			23 49	23 49	00 13
	d			23 54	23 54			23 50	23 50	00 14
Burnham	d			23 57	23 57					00 18
Taplow	d			00 01	00 01					00 21
Maidenhead 3	d			00 05	00 05					00 25
Twyford 3	d			00 13	00 13					00 33
Reading 7	a			00 20	00 20		23 59	00 07	00 08	00 43
Oxford	a				01 06				00 39	

A from 11 September

B until 4 September

Table 117

London - Greenford and Reading

Sundays
until 05 September

		GW	GW	GW	GW	GW	GW	GW	GW	HX		HX	HX	HX	HX	HC	HX	HX	GW	HX		HX	HC	HX	HX
London Paddington	d	22p45	23p00	23p20	23p33	23p42	00 05	00 30	01 00	05 10		05 25	05 40	05 55	06 10	06 12	06 25	06 40	06 44	06 55		07 10	07 12	07 25	07 40
Acton Main Line	d	22p51																							
Ealing Broadway	d	22p55		23p28		23p50	00 13	00 38	01 08							06 20			06 52				07 20		
West Ealing	d																								
Drayton Green	d																								
Castle Bar Park	d																								
South Greenford	d																								
Greenford	a																								
Hanwell	d																								
Southall	d	23p00		23p33		23p56	00 19	00 44	01 13							06 24			06 58				07 24		
Hayes & Harlington	d	23p04		23p37		00 01	00 23	00 48	01 17							06 28			07 02				07 28		
Heathrow Terminals 1-2-3	a									05 26		05 41	05 56	06 11	06 26	06 34	06 41	06 56		07 11		07 26	07 34	07 41	07 56
Heathrow Terminal 4	a															06 41							07 41		
West Drayton	d	23p08		23p41		00 06	00 27	00 52											07 06						
Iver	d	23p11		23p44			00 30																		
Langley	d	23p14		23p48			00 33	00 56											07 11						
Slough	a	23p19	23p16	23p53	23p49	00 13	00 37	01 00	01 25										07 16						
	d	23p21	23p17	23p54	23p50	00 14	00 38	01 01	01 26										07 16						
Burnham	d	23p25		23p57		00 18	00 42												07 20						
Taplow	d			00 01		00 21	00 45																		
Maidenhead	d	23p32		00 05		00 25	00 49	01 08	01 33										07 26						
Twyford	d	23p39		00 13		00 33	00 57	01 16	01 41										07 34						
Reading	a	23p46	23p33	00 20	00 08	00 43	01 05	01 24	01 50										07 43						
Oxford	a	00 32	00 03	01 06	00 39																				

		GW	HX	GW	GW	GW		HX	HC	GW	HX	GW	GW	HX	GW	GW		HX	GW	GW	GW	HC	HX	GW	HX
												B	C												
London Paddington	d	07 44	07 55	07 57	08 00	08 03		08 10	08 12	08 14	08 25	08 33	08 37	08 40	08 42	08 44		08 55	08 57	09 00	09 04	09 07	09 10	09 15	09 25
Acton Main Line	d																								
Ealing Broadway	d	07 52							08 20	08 24						08 52						09 15		09 24	
West Ealing	d																								
Drayton Green	d																								
Castle Bar Park	d																								
South Greenford	d																								
Greenford	a																								
Hanwell	d																								
Southall	d	07 58							08 24	08 29						08 58						09 19		09 29	
Hayes & Harlington	d	08 02							08 28	08 33						09 02						09 24		09 33	
Heathrow Terminals 1-2-3	a		08 11					08 26	08 34		08 41			08 56				09 11				09 29	09 25		09 40
Heathrow Terminal 4	a								08 41													09 39			
West Drayton	d	08 06								08 37						09 06								09 37	
Iver	d																								
Langley	d	08 11								08 42						09 10								09 42	
Slough	a	08 14				08 26				08 46					08 59	09 14					09 23			09 46	
	d	08 20				08 27				08 46					09 00	09 16					09 23			09 46	
Burnham	d	08 25														09 20									
Taplow	d																								
Maidenhead	d	08 29				08 36				08 54						09 27					09 33			09 54	
Twyford	d	08 37								09 02						09 35								10 02	
Reading	a	08 47		08 35	08 40	08 50				09 10		09 12	09 12		09 24	09 43			09 30	09 35	09 46			10 10	
Oxford	a	09 43				09 17									09 55	10 27									

		GW		GW	HC	HX	GW	HX	GW	GW	GW	HC		HX	GW	HX	GW	HC	GW	HX	GW	GW		HX	GW
London Paddington	d	09 30		09 35	09 37	09 40	09 44	09 55	09 57	10 00	10 04	10 07		10 10	10 15	10 25	10 30	10 37	10 37	10 40	10 42	10 43		10 55	10 57
Acton Main Line	d																								
Ealing Broadway	d				09 45		09 52					10 15			10 24			10 45				10 50			
West Ealing	d																								
Drayton Green	d																								
Castle Bar Park	d																								
South Greenford	d																								
Greenford	a																								
Hanwell	d																								
Southall	d				09 49		09 58					10 19			10 29			10 49				10 56			
Hayes & Harlington	d				09 54		10 02					10 24			10 33			10 54				11 02			
Heathrow Terminals 1-2-3	a				09 59	09 55		10 10				10 29		10 25		10 40		10 59		10 55				11 10	
Heathrow Terminal 4	a				10 09							10 39						11 09							
West Drayton	d						10 06								10 37							11 06			
Iver	d																								
Langley	d						10 10								10 42							11 10			
Slough	a			09 50			10 14				10 23				10 46						10 58	11 14			
	d			09 51			10 16				10 23				10 46						10 59	11 16			
Burnham	d						10 20															11 20			
Taplow	d																								
Maidenhead	d						10 27				10 32				10 54							11 27			
Twyford	d						10 35								11 02							11 35			
Reading	a	10 03		10 12			10 43		10 30	10 35	10 46				11 10		11 03		11 12		11 19	11 43			11 30
Oxford	a			10 42			11 27														11 50	12 27			

B until 11 July

C from 18 July until 5 September

Table 117

London - Greenford and Reading

Sundays
until 05 September

		GW	GW	HC	HX	GW	HX	GW		HC	GW	HX	GW	GW	HX	GW	GW	GW		HC	HX	GW	HX	GW	HC
London Paddington	d	11 00	11 04	11 07	11 10	11 15	11 25	11 30		11 37	11 37	11 40	11 42	11 43	11 55	11 57	12 00	12 04		12 07	12 10	12 15	12 25	12 30	12 37
Acton Main Line	d																								
Ealing Broadway	d			11 15		11 24				11 45				11 50						12 15		12 24			12 45
West Ealing	d																								
Drayton Green	d																								
Castle Bar Park	d																								
South Greenford	d																								
Greenford	a																								
Hanwell	d																								
Southall	d			11 19		11 29				11 49				11 56						12 19		12 29			12 49
Hayes & Harlington	d			11 24		11 33				11 54				12 02						12 24		12 33			12 54
Heathrow Terminals 1-2-3	a			11 29	11 25		11 40			11 59		11 55			12 10					12 29	12 25		12 40		12 59
Heathrow Terminal 4	a			11 39						12 09										12 39					13 09
West Drayton	d					11 37								12 06								12 37			
Iver	d																								
Langley	d					11 42								12 10								12 42			
Slough	a		11 22			11 46							11 59	12 14				12 22				12 46			
	d		11 23			11 46							12 00	12 16				12 23				12 46			
Burnham	d													12 20											
Taplow	d																								
Maidenhead	d		11 31			11 54								12 27				12 31				12 54			
Twyford	d					12 02								12 35								13 02			
Reading	a	11 35	11 46			12 10		12 03			12 12		12 19	12 43		12 30	12 35	12 46				13 10		13 03	
Oxford	a												12 50	13 28											

		GW	HX	GW		GW	HX	GW	GW	GW	HC	HX	GW	HX	GW		GW	HC	HX	GW	GW	HX	GW	GW	GW	
London Paddington	d	12 37	12 40	12 42		12 43	12 55	12 57	13 00	13 04	13 07	13 10	13 15	13 25			13 30	13 37	13 40	13 42	13 43	13 55	13 57	14 00	14 06	
Acton Main Line	d																									
Ealing Broadway	d					12 50					13 15		13 24					13 45			13 50					
West Ealing	d																									
Drayton Green	d																									
Castle Bar Park	d																									
South Greenford	d																									
Greenford	a																									
Hanwell	d																									
Southall	d					12 56					13 19		13 29					13 49			13 56					
Hayes & Harlington	d					13 02					13 24		13 33					13 54			14 02					
Heathrow Terminals 1-2-3	a		12 55				13 10				13 29	13 25		13 40				13 59	13 55			14 10				
Heathrow Terminal 4	a										13 39							14 09								
West Drayton	d					13 06							13 37								14 06					
Iver	d																									
Langley	d					13 10							13 42								14 10					
Slough	a			12 57		13 14				13 22			13 46							13 57	14 14				14 22	
	d			12 58		13 16				13 23			13 46							13 58	14 16				14 23	
Burnham	d					13 20															14 20					
Taplow	d																									
Maidenhead	d					13 27				13 31			13 54								14 27				14 31	
Twyford	d					13 35							14 02								14 35					
Reading	a	13 12		13 20		13 43		13 30	13 35	13 46			14 10				14 03			14 19	14 43		14 30	14 35	14 46	
Oxford	a			13 51		14 27														14 50	15 27					

		HC	HX	GW	HX	GW	HC	GW	HX	GW	HX	GW	GW	GW	HC	HX	GW	HX	GW	HC	HX	GW	HX	GW	GW
																			A						
London Paddington	d	14 07	14 10	14 15	14 25	14 30	14 37	14 37	14 40	14 43	14 55	14 57	15 00	15 06	15 07	15 10	15 15	15 25	15 30	15 37	15 40	15 43	15 55	15 57	16 00
Acton Main Line	d																								
Ealing Broadway	d	14 15		14 24			14 45			14 50					15 15		15 24			15 45		15 50			
West Ealing	d																								
Drayton Green	d																								
Castle Bar Park	d																								
South Greenford	d																								
Greenford	a																								
Hanwell	d																								
Southall	d	14 19		14 29			14 49			14 56					15 19		15 29			15 49		15 56			
Hayes & Harlington	d	14 24		14 33			14 54			15 02					15 24		15 33			15 54		16 02			
Heathrow Terminals 1-2-3	a	14 29	14 25		14 40		14 59		14 55		15 10				15 29	15 25		15 40		15 59	15 55		16 10		
Heathrow Terminal 4	a	14 39					15 09								15 39					16 09					
West Drayton	d			14 37						15 06							15 37					16 06			
Iver	d																								
Langley	d			14 42						15 10							15 42					16 10			
Slough	a			14 46						15 14				15 22			15 46					16 14			
	d			14 46						15 16				15 23			15 46					16 16			
Burnham	d									15 20							15 51					16 20			
Taplow	d																								
Maidenhead	d			14 54						15 27				15 31			15 56					16 27			
Twyford	d			15 02						15 35							16 04					16 35			
Reading	a			15 10		15 03		15 12		15 43		15 30	15 35	15 46			16 12		16 03			16 43		16 30	16 35
Oxford	a									16 25												17 25			

A until 11 July

Table 117

London - Greenford and Reading

Sundays until 05 September

	GW 1	HC	HX 1	GW 1	HX 1		GW ◇1 A	HC	GW ◇1	HX 1	GW 1	HX 1	GW ◇1	GW ◇1	GW 1		HC	HX 1	GW 1	HX 1	GW ◇1	HC	GW ◇1	HX 1
London Paddington 15 ⊖ d	16 06	16 07	16 10	16 15	16 25		16 30	16 37	16 37	16 40	16 43	16 55	16 57	17 00	17 06		17 07	17 10	17 15	17 25	17 30	17 37	17 37	17 40
Acton Main Line d																								
Ealing Broadway ⊖ d		16 15		16 24				16 45			16 50						17 15		17 24			17 45		
West Ealing d																								
Drayton Green d																								
Castle Bar Park d																								
South Greenford d																								
Greenford ⊖ a																								
Hanwell d																								
Southall d		16 19		16 29				16 49			16 56						17 19		17 29			17 49		
Hayes & Harlington d		16 24		16 33				16 54			17 02						17 24		17 33			17 54		
Heathrow Terminals 1-2-3 2 ✈ a		16 29	16 25		16 40			16 59		16 55		17 10					17 29	17 25		17 40		17 59		17 55
Heathrow Terminal 4 ✈ a		16 39						17 09									17 39					18 09		
West Drayton d				16 37							17 06								17 37					
Iver d																								
Langley d				16 42							17 10								17 42					
Slough 3 a	16 22			16 46							17 14				17 22				17 46					
d	16 23			16 46							17 16				17 23				17 46					
Burnham d				16 51							17 20								17 51					
Taplow d																								
Maidenhead 3 d	16 31			16 56							17 27				17 31				17 56					
Twyford 3 d				17 04							17 35								18 04					
Reading 7 a	16 46			17 12			17 03		17 14		17 43		17 30	17 35	17 46				18 12		18 03		18 14	
Oxford a											18 27													

	GW 1		HX 1	GW ◇1	GW ◇1	HC	HX 1	GW 1	GW 1	HX 1	GW ◇1 A	HC	GW ◇1	HX 1	GW 1	HX 1	GW ◇1	GW ◇1	GW 1	HC	HX 1		GW 1	HX 1
London Paddington 15 ⊖ d	17 43		17 55	17 57	18 00	18 07	18 10	18 12	18 15	18 25	18 30	18 37	18 37	18 40	18 43	18 55	18 57	19 00	19 06	19 07	19 10		19 15	19 25
Acton Main Line d																								
Ealing Broadway ⊖ d	17 50					18 15			18 24			18 45			18 50					19 15			19 24	
West Ealing d																								
Drayton Green d																								
Castle Bar Park d																								
South Greenford d																								
Greenford ⊖ a																								
Hanwell d																								
Southall d	17 56					18 19			18 29			18 49			18 56					19 19			19 29	
Hayes & Harlington d	18 02					18 24			18 33			18 54			19 02					19 24			19 33	
Heathrow Terminals 1-2-3 2 ✈ a			18 10			18 29	18 25			18 40		18 59		18 55		19 10				19 29	19 25			19 40
Heathrow Terminal 4 ✈ a						18 39						19 09								19 39				
West Drayton d	18 06								18 37						19 06								19 37	
Iver d																								
Langley d	18 10								18 42						19 10								19 42	
Slough 3 a	18 14							18 28	18 46						19 14				19 22				19 46	
d	18 16							18 29	18 46						19 16				19 23				19 46	
Burnham d	18 20								18 51						19 20								19 51	
Taplow d																								
Maidenhead 3 d	18 27							18 40	18 56						19 27				19 31				19 56	
Twyford 3 d	18 35								19 04						19 35								20 04	
Reading 7 a	18 43			18 30	18 35			18 55	19 12		19 03		19 14		19 43		19 30	19 35	19 51				20 12	
Oxford a	19 25														20 25									

	GW ◇1 A	HC	GW ◇1	HX 1	GW 1	HX 1	GW ◇1	GW ◇1	HC	HX 1	GW 1	HX 1		GW ◇1	HC	GW ◇1	HX 1		GW ◇1	GW 1	HX 1	GW ◇1	GW ◇1	HC
London Paddington 15 ⊖ d	19 30	19 37	19 37	19 40	19 43	19 55	19 57	20 00	20 07	20 10	20 15	20 25		20 30	20 37	20 37	20 40		20 42	20 43	20 55	20 57	21 00	21 07
Acton Main Line d																								
Ealing Broadway ⊖ d		19 45			19 50				20 15		20 24				20 45					20 50				21 15
West Ealing d																								
Drayton Green d																								
Castle Bar Park d																								
South Greenford d																								
Greenford ⊖ a																								
Hanwell d																								
Southall d		19 49			19 56				20 19		20 29				20 49					20 56				21 19
Hayes & Harlington d		19 54			20 02				20 24		20 33				20 54					21 02				21 24
Heathrow Terminals 1-2-3 2 ✈ a		19 59		19 55		20 10			20 29	20 25		20 40			20 59		20 55				21 10			21 29
Heathrow Terminal 4 ✈ a		20 09							20 39						21 09									21 39
West Drayton d					20 06						20 37									21 06				
Iver d																								
Langley d					20 10						20 42									21 10				
Slough 3 a					20 14						20 46								20 59	21 14				
d					20 16						20 46								20 59	21 16				
Burnham d					20 20						20 51									21 20				
Taplow d																								
Maidenhead 3 d					20 27						20 56									21 27				
Twyford 3 d					20 35						21 04									21 35				
Reading 7 a	20 03		20 14		20 43		20 30	20 35			21 12			21 03		21 15			21 19	21 43		21 30	21 35	
Oxford a					21 27														21 51	22 27				

A until 11 July

Table 117

London - Greenford and Reading

Sundays until 05 September

	HX 1	GW 1	HX 1		GW ◇1	GW ◇1	HX 1	GW 1	HX 1	GW ◇1	HX 1	HC	GW 1		HX 1	HX 1	GW ◇1	GW 1	HX 1	GW ◇1	HX 1	HC	GW 1	HX 1
London Paddington 15 ⊖ d	21 10	21 15	21 25		21 27	21 37	21 40	21 43	21 55	22 03	22 10	22 12	22 15		22 25	22 40	22 42	22 43	22 55	23 03	23 10	23 12	23 15	23 25
Acton Main Line d																								
Ealing Broadway ⊖ d		21 24						21 50				22 20	22 24					22 50				23 20	23 24	
West Ealing d																								
Drayton Green d																								
Castle Bar Park d																								
South Greenford d																								
Greenford ⊖ a																								
Hanwell d																								
Southall d		21 29						21 56				22 24	22 29					22 56				23 24	23 29	
Hayes & Harlington d		21 33						22 02				22 28	22 33					23 02				23 28	23 33	
Heathrow Terminals 1-2-3 2 ✈ a	21 25		21 40				21 56		22 11		22 26	22 34			22 41	22 56			23 11		23 26	23 34		23 41
Heathrow Terminal 4 ✈ a												22 41										23 41		
West Drayton d		21 37						22 06					22 37					23 06					23 37	
Iver d																								
Langley d		21 42						22 10					22 42					23 10					23 42	
Slough 3 a		21 46			21 48			22 14					22 46				22 59	23 14					23 46	
d		21 59			21 49			22 16					22 46				22 59	23 16					23 46	
Burnham d		22 03						22 20					22 50					23 20					23 51	
Taplow d																								
Maidenhead 3 d		22 08						22 31					22 56					23 24					23 56	
Twyford 3 d		22 16						22 39					23 04					23 32					00 04	
Reading 7 a		22 23			22 08	22 12		22 46		22 49			23 11				23 19	23 46		23 45			00 13	
Oxford a					22 37																			

	GW ◇1	GW ◇1		GW 1
London Paddington 15 ⊖ d	23 37	23 47		23 53
Acton Main Line d				
Ealing Broadway ⊖ d		23 55		00 02
West Ealing d				
Drayton Green d				
Castle Bar Park d				
South Greenford d				
Greenford ⊖ a				
Hanwell d				
Southall d				00 07
Hayes & Harlington d				00 11
Heathrow Terminals 1-2-3 2 ✈ a				
Heathrow Terminal 4 ✈ a				
West Drayton d				00 15
Iver d				
Langley d				00 20
Slough 3 a	23 54	00 08		00 24
d	23 55	00 08		00 24
Burnham d				00 28
Taplow d				
Maidenhead 3 d		00 16		00 34
Twyford 3 d				00 42
Reading 7 a	00 15	00 28		00 49
Oxford a				

Sundays from 12 September

	GW 1	GW ◇1	GW 1	GW 1	GW 1	GW 1	HX 1	HX 1	HX 1		HX 1	HX 1	HC	HX 1	HX 1	GW 1	HX 1	HX 1	HC		HX 1	GW 1	HX 1	HX 1
London Paddington 15 ⊖ d	23p20	23p33	23p42	00 05	00 30	01 00	05 10	05 25	05 40		05 55	06 10	06 12	06 25	06 40	06 44	06 55	07 10	07 12		07 25	07 29	07 40	07 55
Acton Main Line d																								
Ealing Broadway ⊖ d	23p28		23p50	00 13	00 38	01 08							06 20			06 52			07 20			07 36		
West Ealing d																								
Drayton Green d																								
Castle Bar Park d																								
South Greenford d																								
Greenford ⊖ a																								
Hanwell d																								
Southall d	23p33		23p56	00 19	00 44	01 13							06 24			06 58			07 24			07 42		
Hayes & Harlington d	23p37		00 01	00 23	00 48	01 17							06 28			07 02			07 28			07 46		
Heathrow Terminals 1-2-3 2 ✈ a							05 26	05 41	05 56		06 11	06 26	06 34	06 41	06 56		07 11	07 26	07 34		07 41		07 56	08 11
Heathrow Terminal 4 ✈ a													06 41						07 41					
West Drayton d	23p41		00 06	00 27	00 52											07 06						07 50		
Iver d	23p44			00 30																				
Langley d	23p48			00 33	00 56											07 11						07 55		
Slough 3 a	23p53	23p49	00 13	00 37	01 00	01 25										07 16						07 58		
d	23p54	23p50	00 14	00 38	01 01	01 26										07 16						07 58		
Burnham d	23p57		00 18	00 42												07 20						08 03		
Taplow d	00 01		00 21	00 45																				
Maidenhead 3 d	00 05		00 25	00 49	01 08	01 33										07 26						08 08		
Twyford 3 d	00 13		00 33	00 57	01 16	01 41										07 34						08 16		
Reading 7 a	00 20	00 07	00 43	01 05	01 24	01 50										07 43						08 25		
Oxford a																						09 30		

Table 117

Sundays from 12 September

London - Greenford and Reading

		GW	GW	HX	HC	GW	HX	GW	HX	GW	GW	HX	GW	GW	HX	HC	GW	HX	GW	GW	HX	GW	HX	GW	GW
		◇1 🍴	◇1 🍽	1		1	1	◇1 🍴	1	◇1	1	1	◇1 🍴	◇1 🍴	1		1	1	◇1 🍴	◇1 🍴	1	1	1	◇1 🍴	◇1 🍴
London Paddington 15 ⊖	d	07 57	08 00	08 10	08 12	08 14	08 25	08 30	08 40	08 42	08 44	08 55	08 57	09 03	09 10	09 12	09 15	09 25	09 30	09 35	09 40	09 44	09 55	09 57	10 03
Acton Main Line	d																								
Ealing Broadway ⊖	d				08 20	08 24					08 52					09 20	09 24					09 52			
West Ealing	d																								
Drayton Green	d																								
Castle Bar Park	d																								
South Greenford	d																								
Greenford ⊖	a																								
Hanwell	d																								
Southall	d				08 24	08 29					08 58					09 24	09 29					09 58			
Hayes & Harlington	d				08 28	08 33					09 02					09 28	09 33					10 02			
Heathrow Terminals 1-2-3 2 ✈	a			08 26	08 34		08 41		08 56			09 11			09 26	09 34		09 41			09 56		10 11		
Heathrow Terminal 4 ✈	a				08 41											09 41									
West Drayton	d					08 37					09 06						09 37					10 06			
Iver	d																								
Langley	d					08 42					09 10						09 42					10 10			
Slough 3	a		08 23			08 46				09 04	09 14						09 46			09 56		10 14			
	d		08 24			08 46				09 05	09 16						09 46			09 57		10 16			
Burnham	d										09 20											10 20			
Taplow	d																								
Maidenhead 3	d		08 31			08 54					09 24						09 54					10 27			
Twyford 3	d					09 02					09 32						10 02					10 35			
Reading 7	a	08 31	08 44			09 10		09 03		09 19	09 43		09 30	09 35			10 10		10 01	10 11		10 43		10 30	10 35
Oxford	a		09 16							09 51	10 27									10 41		11 27			

		HX	HC	GW	HX	GW	HX	GW	GW	HX	GW	GW	HX	HC	GW	HX	GW	GW	HX	GW	GW	HX	GW	GW	HX
		1		1	1	◇1 🍴	1	◇1 🍴	1	1	◇1 🍴	◇1 🍴	1		1	1	◇1 🍴	◇1 🍴	1	◇1	1	1	◇1 🍴	◇1 🍴	1
London Paddington 15 ⊖	d	10 10	10 12	10 15	10 25	10 37	10 40	10 42	10 43	10 55	10 57	11 03	11 10	11 12	11 15	11 25	11 27	11 37	11 40	11 42	11 43	11 55	11 57	12 03	12 10
Acton Main Line	d																								
Ealing Broadway ⊖	d		10 20	10 24					10 50					11 20	11 24						11 50				
West Ealing	d																								
Drayton Green	d																								
Castle Bar Park	d																								
South Greenford	d																								
Greenford ⊖	a																								
Hanwell	d																								
Southall	d		10 24	10 29					10 56					11 24	11 29						11 56				
Hayes & Harlington	d		10 28	10 33					11 02					11 28	11 33						12 02				
Heathrow Terminals 1-2-3 2 ✈	a	10 26	10 34		10 41		10 56			11 11			11 26	11 34		11 41			11 56			12 11			12 26
Heathrow Terminal 4 ✈	a		10 41											11 41											
West Drayton	d			10 37					11 06						11 37						12 06				
Iver	d																								
Langley	d			10 42					11 10						11 42						12 10				
Slough 3	a			10 46				11 04	11 14						11 46					12 03	12 14				
	d			10 46				11 05	11 16						11 46					12 03	12 16				
Burnham	d								11 20												12 20				
Taplow	d																								
Maidenhead 3	d			10 54					11 27						11 54						12 27				
Twyford 3	d			11 02					11 35						12 02						12 35				
Reading 7	a			11 10		11 09		11 19	11 43		11 30	11 35			12 10		12 00	12 10		12 19	12 43		12 30	12 35	
Oxford	a							11 49	12 27											12 50	13 28				

		HC	GW	HX	GW	HX	GW	GW	HX	GW	GW	HX	HC	GW	HX	GW	HX	GW	GW	HX	GW	GW	HX	HC	GW
			1	1	◇1 🍴	1	◇1 🍴	1	1	◇1 🍴	◇1 🍴	1		1	1	◇1 🍴	1	◇1 🍴	1	1	◇1 🍴	◇1 🍴	1		1
London Paddington 15 ⊖	d	12 12	12 15	12 25	12 37	12 40	12 42	12 43	12 55	12 57	13 03	13 10	13 12	13 15	13 25	13 37	13 40	13 42	13 43	13 55	13 57	14 03	14 10	14 12	14 15
Acton Main Line	d																								
Ealing Broadway ⊖	d	12 20	12 24					12 50					13 20	13 24					13 50					14 20	14 24
West Ealing	d																								
Drayton Green	d																								
Castle Bar Park	d																								
South Greenford	d																								
Greenford ⊖	a																								
Hanwell	d																								
Southall	d	12 24	12 29					12 56					13 24	13 29					13 56					14 24	14 29
Hayes & Harlington	d	12 28	12 33					13 02					13 28	13 33					14 02					14 28	14 33
Heathrow Terminals 1-2-3 2 ✈	a	12 34		12 41		12 56			13 11			13 26	13 34		13 41		13 56			14 11			14 26	14 34	
Heathrow Terminal 4 ✈	a	12 41											13 41											14 41	
West Drayton	d		12 37					13 06						13 37					14 06						14 37
Iver	d																								
Langley	d		12 42					13 10						13 42					14 10						14 42
Slough 3	a		12 46				13 04	13 14						13 46				14 04	14 14						14 46
	d		12 46				13 05	13 16						13 46				14 05	14 16						14 46
Burnham	d							13 20											14 20						
Taplow	d																								
Maidenhead 3	d		12 54					13 27						13 54					14 27						14 54
Twyford 3	d		13 02					13 35						14 02					14 35						15 02
Reading 7	a		13 10		13 09		13 20	13 43		13 30	13 35			14 10		14 09		14 19	14 43		14 30	14 35			15 10
Oxford	a						13 51	14 27										14 50	15 27						

Table 117

Sundays from 12 September

London - Greenford and Reading

		HX	GW	HX	GW	HX	GW	GW	HX	HC	GW	HX	GW	HX	GW	HX	GW	GW	HX	HC	GW	HX	GW	GW	HX
		1	◇1 🍴	1	1	1	◇1 🍴	◇1 🍴	1		1	1	◇1 🍴	1	1	1	◇1 🍴	◇1 🍴	1		1	1	◇1 🍴	◇1 🍴	1
London Paddington 15 ⊖	d	14 25	14 30	14 40	14 43	14 55	14 57	15 03	15 10	15 12	15 15	15 25	15 37	15 40	15 43	15 55	15 57	16 03	16 10	16 12	16 15	16 25	16 27	16 37	16 40
Acton Main Line	d																								
Ealing Broadway ⊖	d				14 50					15 20	15 24				15 50					16 20	16 24				
West Ealing	d																								
Drayton Green	d																								
Castle Bar Park	d																								
South Greenford	d																								
Greenford ⊖	a																								
Hanwell	d																								
Southall	d				14 56					15 24	15 29				15 56					16 24	16 29				
Hayes & Harlington	d				15 02					15 28	15 33				16 02					16 28	16 33				
Heathrow Terminals 1-2-3 2 ✈	a	14 41		14 56		15 11			15 26	15 34		15 41		15 56		16 11			16 26	16 34		16 41			16 56
Heathrow Terminal 4 ✈	a									15 41										16 41					
West Drayton	d				15 06						15 37				16 06						16 37				
Iver	d																								
Langley	d				15 10						15 42				16 10						16 42				
Slough 3	a				15 14						15 46				16 14						16 46				
	d				15 16						15 46				16 16						16 46				
Burnham	d				15 20						15 50				16 20						16 50				
Taplow	d																								
Maidenhead 3	d				15 27						15 56				16 27						16 56				
Twyford 3	d				15 35						16 04				16 35						17 04				
Reading 7	a		15 03		15 43		15 30	15 36			16 12		16 09		16 43		16 30	16 35			17 12		17 03	17 09	
Oxford	a				16 27										17 27										

		GW	HX	GW	GW	HX	HC	GW	HX	GW	GW	HX	GW	HX	GW	GW	HX	HC	GW	HX	GW	GW	HX	GW	HX
		1	1	◇1 🍴	◇1 🍴	1		1	1	◇1 🍴	◇1 🍴	1	1	1	◇1 🍴	◇1 🍴	1		1	1	◇1 🍴	◇1 🍴	1	1	1
London Paddington 15 ⊖	d	16 43	16 55	16 57	17 03	17 10	17 12	17 15	17 25	17 30	17 37	17 40	17 43	17 55	17 57	18 03	18 10	18 12	18 15	18 25	18 27	18 37	18 40	18 43	18 55
Acton Main Line	d																								
Ealing Broadway ⊖	d	16 50					17 20	17 24					17 50					18 20	18 24					18 50	
West Ealing	d																								
Drayton Green	d																								
Castle Bar Park	d																								
South Greenford	d																								
Greenford ⊖	a																								
Hanwell	d																								
Southall	d	16 56					17 24	17 29					17 56					18 24	18 29					18 56	
Hayes & Harlington	d	17 02					17 28	17 33					18 02					18 28	18 33					19 02	
Heathrow Terminals 1-2-3 2 ✈	a		17 11			17 26	17 34		17 41			17 56		18 11			18 26	18 34		18 41			18 56		19 11
Heathrow Terminal 4 ✈	a						17 41											18 41							
West Drayton	d	17 06						17 37					18 06						18 37					19 06	
Iver	d																								
Langley	d	17 10						17 42					18 10						18 42					19 10	
Slough 3	a	17 14						17 46					18 14						18 46					19 14	
	d	17 16						17 46					18 16						18 46					19 16	
Burnham	d	17 20						17 50					18 20						18 50					19 20	
Taplow	d																								
Maidenhead 3	d	17 27						17 56					18 27						18 56					19 27	
Twyford 3	d	17 35						18 04					18 35						19 04					19 35	
Reading 7	a	17 43		17 30	17 35			18 12		18 04	18 09		18 43		18 30	18 35			19 12		19 03	19 09		19 43	
Oxford	a	18 27											19 27											20 27	

		GW	GW	HX	HC	GW	HX	GW	GW	HX	GW	HX	GW	GW	HX	HC	GW	HX	GW	GW	HX	GW	GW	HX	GW
		◇1 🍴	◇1 🍴	1		1	1	◇1 🍴	◇1 🍴	1	1	1	◇1 🍴	◇1 🍴	1		1	1	◇1 🍴	◇1 🍴	1	◇1	1	1	◇1 🍴
London Paddington 15 ⊖	d	18 57	19 03	19 10	19 12	19 15	19 25	19 30	19 37	19 40	19 43	19 55	19 57	20 03	20 10	20 12	20 15	20 25	20 30	20 37	20 40	20 42	20 43	20 55	20 57
Acton Main Line	d																								
Ealing Broadway ⊖	d				19 20	19 24					19 50					20 20	20 24						20 50		
West Ealing	d																								
Drayton Green	d																								
Castle Bar Park	d																								
South Greenford	d																								
Greenford ⊖	a																								
Hanwell	d																								
Southall	d				19 24	19 29					19 56					20 24	20 29						20 56		
Hayes & Harlington	d				19 28	19 33					20 02					20 28	20 33						21 02		
Heathrow Terminals 1-2-3 2 ✈	a			19 26	19 34		19 41			19 56		20 11			20 26	20 34		20 41			20 56			21 11	
Heathrow Terminal 4 ✈	a				19 41											20 41									
West Drayton	d					19 37					20 06						20 37						21 06		
Iver	d																								
Langley	d					19 42					20 10						20 42						21 10		
Slough 3	a					19 46					20 14						20 46					21 03	21 14		
	d					19 46					20 16						20 46					21 04	21 16		
Burnham	d					19 50					20 20						20 50						21 20		
Taplow	d																								
Maidenhead 3	d					19 56					20 27						20 56						21 27		
Twyford 3	d					20 04					20 35						21 04						21 35		
Reading 7	a	19 30	19 35			20 12		20 02	20 09		20 43		20 30	20 36			21 12		21 03	21 09		21 19	21 43		21 30
Oxford	a										21 27											21 51	22 29		

London - Greenford and Reading

		GW ◇1 ☕	HX 1	HC	GW 1	HX 1	GW ◇1	GW ◇1 ☕	HX 1	GW 1	HX 1	GW ◇1 ☕	HX 1	HC	GW 1	HX 1	GW ◇1 ☕	HX 1	GW ◇1	GW 1	HX 1	GW ◇1 ☕	HX 1	HC	GW 1
London Paddington 15 ⊖	d	21 03	21 10	21 12	21 15	21 25	21 27	21 37	21 40	21 43	21 55	22 03	22 10	22 12	22 15	22 25	22 37	22 40	22 42	22 43	22 55	23 03	23 10	23 12	23 15
Acton Main Line	d																								
Ealing Broadway ⊖	d			21 20	21 24					21 50				22 20	22 24					22 50				23 20	23 24
West Ealing	d																								
Drayton Green	d																								
Castle Bar Park	d																								
South Greenford	d																								
Greenford ⊖	a																								
Hanwell	d																								
Southall	d			21 24	21 29					21 56				22 24	22 29					22 56				23 24	23 29
Hayes & Harlington	d			21 28	21 33					22 02				22 28	22 33					23 02				23 28	23 33
Heathrow Terminals 1-2-3 2 ✈	a		21 26	21 34		21 41			21 56		22 11		22 26	22 34		22 41		22 56			23 11		23 26	23 34	
Heathrow Terminal 4 ✈	a			21 41										22 41										23 41	
West Drayton	d				21 37					22 06					22 37					23 06					23 37
Iver	d																								
Langley	d				21 41					22 10					22 42					23 10					23 42
Slough 3	a				21 46		21 52			22 14					22 46				22 59	23 14					23 46
	d				21 46		21 53			22 16					22 46				22 59	23 16					23 46
Burnham	d				21 50					22 20					22 50					23 20					23 50
Taplow	d																								
Maidenhead 3	d				21 55					22 31					22 56					23 24					23 56
Twyford 3	d				22 03					22 39					23 04					23 32					00 04
Reading 7	a	21 35			22 10		22 07	22 12		22 46		22 49			23 11		23 14		23 19	23 43		23 45			00 13
Oxford	a						22 37																		

		HX 1	GW ◇1 ☕	GW ◇1	GW 1
London Paddington 15 ⊖	d	23 25	23 37	23 47	23 53
Acton Main Line	d				
Ealing Broadway ⊖	d			23 55	00 02
West Ealing	d				
Drayton Green	d				
Castle Bar Park	d				
South Greenford	d				
Greenford ⊖	a				
Hanwell	d				
Southall	d				00 07
Hayes & Harlington	d				00 11
Heathrow Terminals 1-2-3 2 ✈	a	23 41			
Heathrow Terminal 4 ✈	a				
West Drayton	d				00 15
Iver	d				
Langley	d				00 20
Slough 3	a		23 54	00 08	00 24
	d		23 55	00 08	00 24
Burnham	d				00 28
Taplow	d				
Maidenhead 3	d			00 16	00 34
Twyford 3	d				00 42
Reading 7	a		00 15	00 28	00 49
Oxford	a				

Reading and Greenford - London

		GW MX 1	GW MX 1	HX MX	HX MO 1	GW MO ◇1 ☕	HX MX	HC MO	HC MX	GW 1 A	GW 1 B	HX MO	GW MX ◇1	GW MX ◇1 ☕	GW 1 A	GW 1 B	GW MO 1	GW MX 1	GW MO ◇1	GW MX 1	GW 1	GW 1
Oxford	d												23p05							00 19		
Reading 7	d	22p46	23p15			23p29				23p35	23p35		23p40	23p55	23p56	23p56	00 15	00 15	00 53	01 10	02 24	03 54
Twyford 3	d	22p54	23p22							23p41	23p41						00 21	00 21	00 59	01 17	02 30	04 00
Maidenhead 3	d	23p02	23p29							23p49	23p49		23p53				00 29	00 29	01 07	01 25	02 38	04 08
Taplow	d	23p06	23p33															00 32				
Burnham	d	23p09	23p36							23p54	23p54							00 35				
Slough 3	a	23p15	23p41							23p58	23p58		00 01		00 14	00 14	00 36	00 40	01 14	01 32	02 45	04 15
	d	23p27	23p41							23p59	23p59		00 01		00 14	00 14	00 36	00 40	01 14	01 32	02 45	04 15
Langley	d	23p31	23p45							00 03	00 03						00 40	00 44				
Iver	d	23p34	23p48																			
West Drayton	d	23p38	23p51							00 08	00 08						00 45	00 49			02 52	04 22
Heathrow Terminal 4 ✈	d							00 01	00 01													
Heathrow Terminals 1-2-3 2 ✈	d			23p48	23p53		23p57	00 07	00 07			00 02										
Hayes & Harlington	d	23p43	23p56					00 13	00 13	00 16	00 16						00 50	00 54	01 23	01 41	02 57	04 27
Southall	d	23p47	23p59					00 16	00 17	00 20	00 20						00 53	00 57			03 00	04 30
Hanwell	d																					
Greenford ⊖	d																					
South Greenford	d																					
Castle Bar Park	d																					
Drayton Green	d																					
West Ealing	d																					
Ealing Broadway ⊖	d	23p52	00 06					00 21	00 22	00 25	00 25						00 59	01 03	01 30	01 48	03 06	04 36
Acton Main Line	d																					
London Paddington 15 ⊖	a	00 03	00 17	00 04	00 09	00 13	00 18	00 30	00 30	00 34	00 38	00 18	00 26	00 33	00 38	00 42	01 11	01 14	01 39	02 00	03 18	04 47

		HX 1	GW 1 C	GW 1 D	HX 1	HC	HX 1	GW 1	HX 1	HC	GW 1	GW 1	GW 1	GW ◇1 ☕	HX 1	GW 1	HX 1	HC	GW 1	GW 1	GW 1	GW 1
Oxford	d		04 00										05 03								05 34	05 45
Reading 7	d		04 39	04 39				05 14			05 39		05 44	05 57		06 02			06 07		06 15	06 16
Twyford 3	d		04 45	04 45				05 20			05 45		05 50						06 13		06 21	06 23
Maidenhead 3	d		04 53	04 53				05 28			05 53		05 58						06 21		06 28	06 31
Taplow	d							05 32					06 02						06 24		06 32	
Burnham	d							05 35					06 05						06 27		06 35	
Slough 3	a		05 00	05 00				05 40			06 01		06 10			06 17			06 32		06 40	
	d		05 00	05 00				05 40			06 01		06 10			06 17			06 32		06 40	
Langley	d		05 04	05 04				05 44					06 14						06 36		06 44	
Iver	d		05 07	05 07				05 47					06 17								06 47	
West Drayton	d		05 11	05 11				05 51					06 21						06 41		06 51	
Heathrow Terminal 4 ✈	d					05 23				05 51												
Heathrow Terminals 1-2-3 2 ✈	d	05 12			05 33	05 29	05 48		06 03	05 57					06 18		06 33	06 27				
Hayes & Harlington	d		05 16	05 16		05 35		05 56		06 03	06 10		06 26					06 33	06 46		06 56	
Southall	d		05 19	05 19		05 38		05 59		06 06	06 13		06 29					06 36	06 50		07 00	
Hanwell	d					05 41				06 09								06 39				
Greenford ⊖	d											06 16								06 46		
South Greenford	d											06 19								06 49		
Castle Bar Park	d											06 22								06 52		
Drayton Green	d											06 24								06 54		
West Ealing	d					05 43				06 11		06 26						06 41		06 56		
Ealing Broadway ⊖	d		05 28	05 28		05 46		06 05		06 14	06 19	06 29	06 35					06 44	06 55	06 59	07 05	
Acton Main Line	d		05 31	05 31				06 08				06 33	06 38							07 03		
London Paddington 15 ⊖	a	05 28	05 41	05 41	05 49	05 56	06 04	06 16	06 19	06 24	06 31	06 42	06 49	06 24	06 34	06 36	06 49	06 54	07 07	07 12	07 17	06 54

A MO from 13 September
B MO until 6 September
C MX until 3 September, from 7 September until 22 October, MX from 26 October
D MO until 6 September, MO from 25 October

Table 117

Mondays to Fridays

Reading and Greenford - London

	GW		HX	GW	HC	GW	GW	GW	GW	GW	HX		GW	GW	GW	GW		HX	HC	GW	GW		GW	GW
	■1		■1	■1		■1	■1	■1	◇■1 🛒	■1	■1		■1	◇■1 🛒	■1	◇■1 🛒		■1		■1	■1		■1	■1
Oxford d				05 59										06 27										06 07
Reading 7 d	06 22			06 31		06 32		06 37	06 44	06 46			06 50	06 56	06 57	07 01				07 02	07 07			07 10
Twyford 5 d						06 38		06 43		06 53					07 03					07 08				07 16
Maidenhead 5 d				06 43		06 46		06 53		07 03				07 08	07 11					07 16	07 19			07 24
Taplow d								06 57																07 28
Burnham d						06 50		07 01												07 22				07 31
Slough 5 a	06 40			06 50		06 56		07 06	06 58						07 19					07 26				07 36
d	06 40			06 50		06 56		07 06	06 59						07 20					07 27				07 36
Langley d						06 59		07 11												07 31				07 41
Iver d						07 03		07 14																07 44
West Drayton d						07 07		07 18												07 35				07 48
Heathrow Terminal 4 ✈ d																								
Heathrow Terminals 1-2-3 2 ✈ d			06 48		06 57						07 03							07 18	07 27					
Hayes & Harlington d					07 03	07 12		07 23											07 33	07 40				07 53
Southall d					07 06	07 16		07 27											07 36	07 43				07 57
Hanwell d					07 09														07 39					
Greenford ⊖ d							07 16																07 46	
South Greenford d							07 19																07 49	
Castle Bar Park d							07 22																07 52	
Drayton Green d							07 24																07 54	
West Ealing d					07 11		07 26												07 41				07 56	
Ealing Broadway ⊖ d					07 14	07 21	07 29	07 33											07 44	07 50			07 59	08 03
Acton Main Line d							07 33																08 03	
London Paddington 15 ⊖ a	07 00		07 05	07 09	07 24	07 33	07 42	07 44	07 16	07 27	07 19		07 23	07 29	07 47	07 32		07 35	07 54	08 02	07 39		08 12	08 14

	GW	HX	GW	GW	GW	GW	GW		HX	HC	GW	GW	GW	GW	GW	GW	HX		GW	GW	GW	GW	GW	GW
	◇■1 🛒	■1	◇■1 🛒	■1	◇■1 🛒	◇■1 🛒	■1		■1		■1	◇■1 🛒	◇■1 🛒	■1	■1	◇■1 🛒	■1		■1 🍴	■1	■1	■1 🍴	◇■1 🛒	■1
Oxford d					06 56						06 37								07 09		07 00	07 33		
Reading 7 d	07 15		07 21		07 27	07 30					07 30	07 36	07 39		07 40	07 45					07 55	07 59	08 02	08 06
Twyford 5 d				07 22							07 37				07 46					07 56	08 02			08 14
Maidenhead 5 d				07 31			07 41				07 45				07 54				08 00	08 04	08 11			
Taplow d															07 58									
Burnham d											07 51				08 01						08 16			
Slough 5 a							07 49				07 56				08 06						08 19			
d							07 50				07 56				08 08						08 20			
Langley d											08 01				08 12									
Iver d															08 15									
West Drayton d											08 05				08 19									
Heathrow Terminal 4 ✈ d																								
Heathrow Terminals 1-2-3 2 ✈ d		07 33							07 48	07 57							08 03							
Hayes & Harlington d										08 03	08 10				08 24									
Southall d										08 06	08 13				08 28									
Hanwell d										08 09														
Greenford ⊖ d														08 16										
South Greenford d														08 19										
Castle Bar Park d														08 22										
Drayton Green d														08 24										
West Ealing d										08 11				08 26										
Ealing Broadway ⊖ d										08 14	08 19			08 29	08 33									
Acton Main Line d														08 33										
London Paddington 15 ⊖ a	07 44	07 49	07 53	07 56	07 59	08 02	08 17		08 04	08 24	08 32	08 07	08 09	08 42	08 47	08 14	08 19		08 25	08 29	08 50	08 30	08 33	

	HX	GW	HC		GW	GW	GW	GW	GW	GW	HX	GW	GW		HC	GW	GW	HX	GW	GW	GW	HX	GW	
	■1	◇■1 🛒			■1	■1	■1	◇■1 🛒	◇■1 🛒	■1	■1	◇■1 🛒	■1			■1	◇■1 🛒	■1	■1 🍴	◇■1 🛒	■1	■1	◇■1 🛒	
Oxford d										07 21		07 51							08 05		07 56			
Reading 7 d		08 08					08 12	08 13	08 17	08 19		08 23				08 31	08 34		08 38	08 45	08 48		08 52	
Twyford 5 d							08 18			08 25						08 37					08 54			
Maidenhead 5 d							08 26			08 34			08 41			08 45					09 03			
Taplow d							08 29									08 49								
Burnham d							08 32									08 50								
Slough 5 a							08 38						08 49			08 57								
d					08 25		08 38						08 50			08 57								
Langley d					08 30		08 42									09 01								
Iver d							08 45									09 04								
West Drayton d					08 35		08 49									09 08								
Heathrow Terminal 4 ✈ d																								
Heathrow Terminals 1-2-3 2 ✈ d	08 18		08 27								08 33				08 57			08 48				09 03		
Hayes & Harlington d			08 33		08 39		08 53								09 03	09 13								
Southall d			08 36		08 43		08 57								09 06	09 17								
Hanwell d			08 39												09 09									
Greenford ⊖ d						08 46																		
South Greenford d						08 49																		
Castle Bar Park d						08 52																		
Drayton Green d						08 54																		
West Ealing d			08 41			08 56									09 11									
Ealing Broadway ⊖ d			08 44		08 49	08 59	09 03								09 14	09 23								
Acton Main Line d						09 03																		
London Paddington 15 ⊖ a	08 35	08 38	08 54		09 01	09 12	09 17	08 40	08 44	08 59	08 49	08 51	09 20		09 24	09 35	09 00	09 04	09 06	09 14	09 26	09 19	09 21	

Table 117

Mondays to Fridays

Reading and Greenford - London

	GW	HX	GW	GW	HC	GW	GW	GW	GW		GW	GW	HX	GW	GW	HC	GW	GW	HX		GW	GW	HX	GW
	◇■1 🛒	■1	■1	■1		■1	◇■1 🛒	◇■1 🛒	■1		■1	◇■1 🛒	■1	■1	◇■1 🛒		■1	◇■1 🛒	■1		◇■1	◇■1 🛒	■1	■1
Oxford d						08 21						08 51					08 37				09 01			
Reading 7 d	09 02					09 03	09 08	09 15			09 17	09 18		09 21	09 27		09 33	09 34			09 37	09 45		
Twyford 5 d						09 09					09 24						09 39							
Maidenhead 5 d						09 17					09 33						09 47							
Taplow d						09 21					09 36													
Burnham d						09 24					09 39													
Slough 5 a						09 29					09 44						09 54				09 51			
d				09 14		09 29					09 44						09 54				09 51			
Langley d						09 33											09 58							
Iver d						09 36											10 01							
West Drayton d				09 21		09 40					09 51						10 05							
Heathrow Terminal 4 ✈ d																								
Heathrow Terminals 1-2-3 2 ✈ d		09 18			09 27								09 33			09 57			09 48				10 03	
Hayes & Harlington d				09 26	09 33	09 45					09 56					10 03	10 10							
Southall d				09 30	09 36	09 48										10 06	10 13							
Hanwell d					09 39											10 09								
Greenford ⊖ d			09 16						09 46															10 16
South Greenford d			09 19						09 49															10 19
Castle Bar Park d			09 22						09 52															10 22
Drayton Green d			09 24						09 54															10 24
West Ealing d			09 26		09 41				09 56							10 11								10 26
Ealing Broadway ⊖ d			09 29	09 36	09 44	09 54			09 59		10 03					10 14	10 19							10 29
Acton Main Line d			09 33						10 03															10 33
London Paddington 15 ⊖ a	09 29	09 35	09 42	09 47	09 54	10 03	09 39	09 44	10 12		10 16	09 47	09 49	09 55	09 59	10 24	10 31	10 02	10 05		10 09	10 14	10 19	10 42

	GW	GW	GW	HX	HC		GW	GW	GW	HX	GW	GW	GW	GW	HX		GW	HC	GW	GW	HX	GW	GW	GW
	■1	◇■1	◇■1 🛒	■1			■1	◇■1 🛒	◇■1 🛒	■1	■1	■1	■1	◇■1	■1		◇■1 🛒		■1	◇■1 🛒	■1	■1	■1	◇■1 🛒
Oxford d		09 31					09 07							10 01					09 37					
Reading 7 d	09 48	09 55	10 02				10 03	10 08	10 12		10 18		10 18	10 25			10 32		10 33	10 45			10 48	10 52
Twyford 5 d	09 54						10 09						10 24						10 39				10 54	
Maidenhead 5 d	10 02						10 17						10 32						10 47				11 02	
Taplow d	10 06												10 36										11 06	
Burnham d	10 09												10 39										11 09	
Slough 5 a	10 14	10 10					10 24						10 44	10 39					10 54				11 14	
d	10 14	10 11					10 24						10 44	10 40					10 54				11 14	
Langley d							10 28												10 58					
Iver d							10 31												11 01					
West Drayton d	10 21						10 35						10 51						11 05				11 21	
Heathrow Terminal 4 ✈ d																								
Heathrow Terminals 1-2-3 2 ✈ d				10 18	10 27					10 33					10 48			10 57			11 03			
Hayes & Harlington d	10 26				10 33		10 40						10 56					11 03	11 10				11 26	
Southall d					10 36		10 43											11 06	11 13					
Hanwell d					10 39													11 09						
Greenford ⊖ d												10 46										11 16		
South Greenford d												10 49										11 19		
Castle Bar Park d												10 52										11 22		
Drayton Green d												10 54										11 24		
West Ealing d					10 41							10 56						11 11				11 26		
Ealing Broadway ⊖ d	10 33				10 44		10 49					10 59	11 03					11 14	11 19			11 29	11 33	
Acton Main Line d												11 03										11 33		
London Paddington 15 ⊖ a	10 46	10 29	10 32	10 34	10 54		11 01	10 37	10 39	10 49	10 54	11 12	11 16	11 00	11 05		11 07	11 24	11 31	11 14	11 19	11 42	11 46	11 24

	GW		GW	HX	HC	GW	GW	HX	GW	GW	GW		GW	GW	HX	HC	GW	GW	HX	GW	GW		GW	GW
	◇■1 🍴		◇■1 🛒	■1		■1	◇■1 🛒	■1	■1	■1	■1		◇■1	◇■1 🛒	■1		■1	◇■1 🛒	■1	■1	■1		◇■1 🛒	◇■1 🍴
Oxford d	10 31					10 07							11 01				10 37							11 31
Reading 7 d	10 55		11 02			11 03	11 09		11 18		11 18		11 25	11 32			11 33	11 44			11 48		11 52	11 55
Twyford 5 d						11 09					11 24						11 39				11 54			
Maidenhead 5 d						11 17					11 32						11 47				12 02			
Taplow d											11 36										12 06			
Burnham d											11 39										12 09			
Slough 5 a	11 09					11 24					11 44		11 39				11 54				12 14			12 09
d	11 10					11 24					11 44		11 40				11 54				12 14			12 10
Langley d						11 28											11 58							
Iver d						11 31											12 01							
West Drayton d						11 35					11 51						12 05				12 21			
Heathrow Terminal 4 ✈ d																								
Heathrow Terminals 1-2-3 2 ✈ d				11 18	11 27			11 33							11 48	11 57			12 03					
Hayes & Harlington d					11 33	11 40					11 56					12 03	12 10				12 26			
Southall d					11 36	11 43										12 06	12 13							
Hanwell d					11 39											12 09								
Greenford ⊖ d										11 46										12 16				
South Greenford d										11 49										12 19				
Castle Bar Park d										11 52										12 22				
Drayton Green d										11 54										12 24				
West Ealing d					11 41					11 56						12 11				12 26				
Ealing Broadway ⊖ d					11 44	11 49				11 59	12 03					12 14	12 19			12 29	12 33			
Acton Main Line d										12 03										12 33				
London Paddington 15 ⊖ a	11 29		11 32	11 34	11 54	12 01	11 38	11 49	11 55	12 12	12 16		11 57	12 00	12 04	12 24	12 31	12 14	12 19	12 42	12 46		12 23	12 29

Reading and Greenford - London

	GW ◇1 ☕	HX 1	HC	GW 1	GW ◇1 ☕	GW ◇1 ☕	HX 1	GW 1	GW 1	GW 1	GW ◇1	HX 1	GW ◇1 ☕	HC	GW 1	GW ◇1 ☕	HX 1	GW 1	GW 1	GW ◇1	GW ◇1 ☕	HX 1
Oxford d				11 07							12 01				11 37					12 31		
Reading [7] d	12 02			12 03	12 08	12 12		12 18		12 18	12 25		12 32		12 33	12 44			12 48	12 55	13 02	
Twyford [3] d				12 09						12 24					12 39				12 54			
Maidenhead [3] d				12 17						12 32					12 47				13 02			
Taplow d										12 36									13 06			
Burnham d										12 39									13 09			
Slough [3] a				12 24						12 44	12 39				12 54				13 14	13 09		
d				12 24						12 44	12 40				12 54				13 14	13 10		
Langley d				12 28											12 58							
Iver d				12 31											13 01							
West Drayton d				12 35						12 51					13 05				13 21			
Heathrow Terminal 4 ✈ d																						
Heathrow Terminals 1-2-3 [2] ✈ d		12 18	12 27				12 33					12 48		12 57			13 03					13 18
Hayes & Harlington d			12 33	12 40						12 56				13 03	13 10				13 26			
Southall d			12 36	12 43										13 06	13 13							
Hanwell d			12 39											13 09								
Greenford ⊖ d									12 46									13 16				
South Greenford d									12 49									13 19				
Castle Bar Park d									12 52									13 22				
Drayton Green d									12 54									13 24				
West Ealing d			12 41						12 56					13 11				13 26				
Ealing Broadway ⊖ d			12 44	12 49					12 59	13 03				13 14	13 19			13 29	13 33			
Acton Main Line d									13 03									13 33				
London Paddington [15] ⊖ a	12 32	12 34	12 54	13 01	12 37	12 40	12 49	12 54	13 12	13 16	13 00	13 04	13 06	13 24	13 31	13 14	13 19	13 42	13 46	13 29	13 32	13 35

	HC	GW 1	GW ◇1 ☕	GW R 1 ☕	HX 1	GW 1	GW 1	GW ◇1	HX 1	GW ◇1 ☕	HC	GW 1	GW ◇1 ☕	HX 1	GW 1	GW 1	GW 1	GW ◇1 ⊼	GW ◇1 ☕	HX 1	HC
Oxford d		12 07						13 01				12 37						13 31			
Reading [7] d		13 03	13 09	13 16			13 18	13 25		13 32		13 33	13 44			13 48	13 52	13 55	14 02		
Twyford [3] d		13 09					13 24					13 39				13 54					
Maidenhead [3] d		13 17					13 32					13 47				14 02					
Taplow d							13 36									14 06					
Burnham d							13 39									14 09					
Slough [3] a		13 24					13 44	13 39				13 54				14 14		14 09			
d		13 24					13 44	13 40				13 54				14 14		14 10			
Langley d		13 28										13 58									
Iver d		13 31										14 01									
West Drayton d		13 35					13 51					14 05				14 21					
Heathrow Terminal 4 ✈ d																					
Heathrow Terminals 1-2-3 [2] ✈ d	13 27				13 33				13 48		13 57			14 03						14 18	14 27
Hayes & Harlington d	13 33	13 40					13 56				14 03	14 10				14 26					14 33
Southall d	13 36	13 43									14 06	14 13									14 36
Hanwell d	13 39										14 09										14 39
Greenford ⊖ d						13 46									14 16						
South Greenford d						13 49									14 19						
Castle Bar Park d						13 52									14 22						
Drayton Green d						13 54									14 24						
West Ealing d	13 41					13 56					14 11				14 26						14 41
Ealing Broadway ⊖ d	13 44	13 49				13 59	14 03				14 14	14 19			14 29	14 33					14 44
Acton Main Line d						14 03									14 33						
London Paddington [15] ⊖ a	13 54	14 01	13 38	13 43	13 49	14 12	14 16	14 01	14 04	14 06	14 24	14 31	14 14	14 19	14 42	14 46	14 25	14 29	14 32	14 34	14 54

	GW 1	GW ◇1 ☕	GW ◇1 ☕	GW ◇1 ☕	HX 1	GW 1	GW 1	GW ◇1	HX 1	GW ◇1 ☕	HC	GW 1	GW ◇1 ☕	HX 1	GW 1	GW 1	GW R 1 ☕	GW ◇1	GW ◇1 ☕	HX 1	HC	GW 1
Oxford d	13 07							14 01				13 37						14 31				14 07
Reading [7] d	14 03	14 08	14 12	14 17			14 18	14 25		14 32		14 33	14 44			14 48	14 52	14 55	15 02			15 03
Twyford [3] d	14 09						14 24					14 39				14 54						15 09
Maidenhead [3] d	14 17						14 32					14 47				15 02						15 17
Taplow d							14 36									15 06						
Burnham d							14 39									15 09						
Slough [3] a	14 24						14 44	14 39				14 54				15 14		15 09				15 24
d	14 24						14 44	14 40				14 54				15 14		15 10				15 24
Langley d	14 28											14 58										15 28
Iver d	14 31											15 01										15 31
West Drayton d	14 35						14 51					15 05				15 21						15 35
Heathrow Terminal 4 ✈ d																						
Heathrow Terminals 1-2-3 [2] ✈ d					14 33				14 48		14 57			15 03						15 18	15 27	
Hayes & Harlington d	14 40						14 56				15 03	15 10				15 26					15 33	15 40
Southall d	14 43										15 06	15 13									15 36	15 43
Hanwell d											15 09										15 39	
Greenford ⊖ d						14 46									15 16							
South Greenford d						14 49									15 19							
Castle Bar Park d						14 52									15 22							
Drayton Green d						14 54									15 24							
West Ealing d						14 56					15 11				15 26						15 41	
Ealing Broadway ⊖ d	14 49					14 59	15 03				15 14	15 19			15 29	15 33					15 44	15 49
Acton Main Line d						15 03									15 33							
London Paddington [15] ⊖ a	15 01	14 37	14 40	14 44	14 49	15 12	15 16	15 01	15 04	15 08	15 24	15 32	15 14	15 19	15 42	15 46	15 24	15 29	15 32	15 35	15 54	16 01

Reading and Greenford - London

	GW ◇1 ☕	HX 1	GW 1	GW 1	GW 1	GW ◇1	HX 1	GW ◇1 ☕	GW 1	GW ◇1 ☕	HC	HX 1	GW 1	GW 1	GW ◇1 ☕	GW ◇1 ☕	GW ◇1 ☕	HX 1	HC	GW 1	GW ◇1 ☕	GW ◇1 ☕	HX 1
Oxford d						15 01			14 37							15 31				15 07			
Reading [7] d	15 09		15 18		15 18	15 25		15 32	15 33	15 44				15 48	15 52	15 55	16 02			16 03	16 08	16 12	
Twyford [3] d					15 24				15 39					15 54						16 09			
Maidenhead [3] d					15 32				15 47					16 02						16 17			
Taplow d					15 36									16 06									
Burnham d					15 39									16 09									
Slough [3] a					15 44	15 39			15 54					16 14		16 09				16 24			
d					15 44	15 40			16 54					16 14		16 10				16 24			
Langley d									15 58											16 28			
Iver d									16 01											16 31			
West Drayton d					15 51				16 05					16 21						16 35			
Heathrow Terminal 4 ✈ d																							
Heathrow Terminals 1-2-3 [2] ✈ d		15 33					15 48				15 57	16 03						16 18	16 27				16 33
Hayes & Harlington d					15 56				16 10		16 03			16 26					16 33	16 40			
Southall d									16 13		16 06								16 36	16 43			
Hanwell d											16 09								16 39				
Greenford ⊖ d				15 46									16 16										
South Greenford d				15 49									16 19										
Castle Bar Park d				15 52									16 22										
Drayton Green d				15 54									16 24										
West Ealing d				15 56							16 11		16 26						16 41				
Ealing Broadway ⊖ d				15 59	16 03				16 19		16 14		16 29	16 33					16 44	16 49			
Acton Main Line d				16 03									16 33										
London Paddington [15] ⊖ a	15 38	15 49	15 54	16 12	16 16	16 01	16 05	16 09	16 31	16 14	16 24	16 19	16 42	16 46	16 22	16 27	16 30	16 35	16 54	17 01	16 39	16 44	16 49

	GW 1	GW 1	GW 1	GW 1	HX 1	HC	GW 1	GW ◇1 ☕	GW ◇1 ☕	HX 1	GW 1	GW 1	GW ◇1 ☕	GW ◇1 ☕	GW ◇1 ☕	HX 1	HC	GW 1	GW ◇1 ☕	HX 1	GW ◇1 ☕
Oxford d				16 01			15 37							16 31				16 07			
Reading [7] d	16 18		16 18	16 25			16 33	16 34	16 44			16 48	16 52	16 55	17 02			17 03	17 09		17 17
Twyford [3] d			16 24				16 39					16 54						17 09			
Maidenhead [3] d			16 32				16 47					17 02						17 17			17 29
Taplow d			16 36									17 06									
Burnham d			16 39									17 09									
Slough [3] a			16 44	16 40			16 54					17 14		17 09				17 24			
d			16 44	16 40			16 54					17 14		17 10				17 24			
Langley d							16 58											17 28			
Iver d							17 01											17 31			
West Drayton d			16 51				17 05					17 21						17 35			
Heathrow Terminal 4 ✈ d																					
Heathrow Terminals 1-2-3 [2] ✈ d					16 48	16 57				17 03						17 18	17 27			17 33	
Hayes & Harlington d			16 56			17 03	17 10					17 26					17 33	17 40			
Southall d						17 06	17 13										17 36	17 43			
Hanwell d						17 09											17 39				
Greenford ⊖ d		16 46									17 16										
South Greenford d		16 49									17 19										
Castle Bar Park d		16 52									17 22										
Drayton Green d		16 54									17 24										
West Ealing d		16 56				17 11					17 26						17 41				
Ealing Broadway ⊖ d		16 59	17 03			17 14	17 19				17 29	17 33					17 44	17 49			
Acton Main Line d		17 03									17 33										
London Paddington [15] ⊖ a	16 57	17 12	17 16	17 00	17 04	17 24	17 31	17 06	17 14	17 19	17 42	17 46	17 24	17 27	17 30	17 35	17 54	18 01	17 39	17 49	17 54

	GW 1	GW 1	GW 1	GW ◇1 ☕	HX 1	HC	GW 1	GW 1	GW ◇1 ☕	HX 1	GW ◇1 ☕	GW 1	GW 1	GW ◇1 ☕	GW 1	GW ◇1 ☕	HX 1	GW ◇1 ☕	GW ◇1 ☕	HX 1	HC	GW 1	GW 1
Oxford d			17 01				16 37								17 07	17 36							
Reading [7] d		17 18	17 25	17 32			17 33	17 42	17 44		17 52		17 54	17 56	18 00	18 02		18 08	18 12				
Twyford [3] d		17 24					17 39	17 48							18 10								
Maidenhead [3] d		17 32					17 47	17 56					18 08		18 17							18 25	
Taplow d		17 36						17 59															
Burnham d		17 39						18 02															
Slough [3] a		17 44	17 39				17 54	18 07					18 14		18 24							18 33	
d		17 44	17 40				17 54	18 07					18 14		18 24							18 33	
Langley d							17 58								18 28								
Iver d							18 01								18 32								
West Drayton d		17 51					18 05	18 14							18 35								
Heathrow Terminal 4 ✈ d																							
Heathrow Terminals 1-2-3 [2] ✈ d					17 48	17 57				18 03							18 18			18 33	18 27		
Hayes & Harlington d		17 56				18 03	18 10	18 19					18 26		18 39						18 33	18 45	
Southall d						18 06	18 13								18 43						18 36		
Hanwell d						18 09															18 39		
Greenford ⊖ d	17 46											18 16											18 46
South Greenford d	17 49											18 19											18 49
Castle Bar Park d	17 52											18 22											18 52
Drayton Green d	17 54											18 24											18 54
West Ealing d	17 56					18 11						18 26									18 41		18 56
Ealing Broadway ⊖ d	17 59	18 03				18 14	18 19	18 26				18 29	18 33		18 48						18 44	18 54	18 59
Acton Main Line d	18 03											18 33											19 03
London Paddington [15] ⊖ a	18 12	18 16	17 59	18 02	18 05	18 24	18 31	18 37	18 14	18 19	18 21	18 42	18 46	18 24	19 00	18 30	18 35	18 39	18 44	18 49	18 54	19 05	19 12

Table 117

Reading and Greenford - London

Mondays to Fridays

		GW 1	GW 1	GW 1	GW ◇1 ☕	HX 1	HC	GW 1	GW ◇1 ☕	HX 1	GW 1	GW 1	GW ◇1 ☕	GW 1	GW ◇1 ☕	HX 1	HC	GW 1	GW ◇1 ☕	HX 1	GW 1	GW 1
Oxford	d			18 01				17 31						18 31				18 07				
Reading 7	d	18 18	18 22	18 25	18 32			18 33	18 45			18 48	18 51	18 55	19 02			19 03	19 09		19 18	
Twyford 3	d	18 24						18 39				18 54						19 09				
Maidenhead 3	d	18 32						18 48				19 02						19 21				
Taplow	d	18 36										19 06										
Burnham	d	18 39										19 09										
Slough 3	a	18 44		18 39				18 54				19 14		19 09				19 29				
	d	18 44		18 40				18 54				19 14		19 10				19 29				
Langley	d							18 58										19 33				
Iver	d							19 01										19 36				
West Drayton	d	18 51						19 05				19 21						19 39				
Heathrow Terminal 4 ✈	d																					
Heathrow Terminals 1-2-3 2 ✈	d					18 48	18 57			19 03						19 18	19 27			19 33		
Hayes & Harlington	d	18 56					19 03	19 10				19 26					19 33	19 44				
Southall	d						19 06	19 13									19 36	19 47				
Hanwell	d						19 09										19 39					
Greenford ⊖	d										19 16											19 46
South Greenford	d										19 19											19 49
Castle Bar Park	d										19 22											19 52
Drayton Green	d										19 24											19 54
West Ealing	d						19 11				19 26						19 41					19 56
Ealing Broadway ⊖	d	19 05					19 14	19 19			19 29	19 33					19 44	19 53				19 59
Acton Main Line	d										19 33											20 03
London Paddington 15 ⊖	a	19 18	18 54	18 59	19 02	19 05	19 24	19 31	19 14	19 19	19 42	19 46	19 24	19 31	19 32	19 35	19 54	20 02	19 38	19 49	19 54	20 12

		GW 1	GW ◇1 ☕	GW ◇1 🛒	HX 1	HC	GW 1	GW ◇1 ☕	HX 1	GW 1	GW 1	GW ◇1	HC	GW 1	GW ◇1 ☕	HX 1	GW ◇1 ☕	GW ◇1 ☕	HX 1	GW 1	GW 1	GW ◇1	HX 1
Oxford	d			19 01			18 37					19 31		19 01								20 01	
Reading 7	d	19 18	19 25	19 25			19 33	19 45			19 48	19 54		19 58	20 02		20 08	20 15			20 18	20 25	
Twyford 3	d	19 24					19 42				19 54			20 04							20 24		
Maidenhead 3	d	19 32					19 50				20 02			20 12							20 32		
Taplow	d	19 36									20 06										20 36		
Burnham	d	19 39									20 09										20 39		
Slough 3	a	19 44		19 39			19 57				20 14	20 09		20 19							20 44	20 39	
	d	19 44		19 40			19 57				20 14	20 10		20 24							20 44	20 40	
Langley	d						20 01							20 28									
Iver	d						20 04							20 31									
West Drayton	d	19 51					20 08				20 21			20 35							20 51		
Heathrow Terminal 4 ✈	d																						
Heathrow Terminals 1-2-3 2 ✈	d				19 48	19 57			20 03				20 27			20 18			20 33				20 48
Hayes & Harlington	d	19 56				20 03	20 13				20 26		20 33	20 40							20 56		
Southall	d					20 06	20 16						20 36	20 43									
Hanwell	d					20 09							20 39										
Greenford ⊖	d									20 16										20 46			
South Greenford	d									20 19										20 49			
Castle Bar Park	d									20 22										20 52			
Drayton Green	d									20 24										20 54			
West Ealing	d					20 11				20 26			20 41							20 56			
Ealing Broadway ⊖	d	20 03				20 14	20 22			20 29	20 33		20 44	20 49						20 59	21 03		
Acton Main Line	d									20 33										21 03			
London Paddington 15 ⊖	a	20 16	19 54	20 00	20 04	20 24	20 31	20 14	20 19	20 42	20 46	20 29	20 54	20 59	20 32	20 34	20 39	20 46	20 49	21 12	21 18	21 01	21 04

		HC	GW 1	GW ◇1	GW ◇1 ☕	HX 1	GW 1	GW 1	GW ◇1 ☕	GW ◇1 ☕	GW ◇1 ☕	HX 1	HX 1	HC	GW 1	GW 1	GW ◇1	HX 1	HC	GW 1	GW ◇1 ☕	HX 1	GW ◇1 ☕
Oxford	d		19 37							20 31						20 07	21 01			20 37			
Reading 7	d		20 33	20 34	20 45			20 48	20 52	20 55	21 02					21 14	21 25			21 33	21 45		22 01
Twyford 3	d		20 39					20 54								21 20				21 39			
Maidenhead 3	d		20 47					21 02								21 28				21 47			
Taplow	d							21 06								21 32				21 50			
Burnham	d							21 09								21 35				21 53			
Slough 3	a		20 54					21 13		21 09						21 40	21 39			21 58			
	d		20 54					21 14		21 10						21 40	21 40			21 59			
Langley	d		20 58					21 17								21 44				22 02			
Iver	d		21 01					21 20								21 47				22 05			
West Drayton	d		21 05					21 24								21 51				22 09			
Heathrow Terminal 4 ✈	d																						
Heathrow Terminals 1-2-3 2 ✈	d	20 57				21 03						21 18	21 33	21 27				21 48	21 57			22 03	
Hayes & Harlington	d	21 03	21 10					21 28						21 33		21 56			22 03	22 14			
Southall	d	21 06	21 13											21 36		21 59			22 06				
Hanwell	d	21 09												21 39					22 09				
Greenford ⊖	d						21 16								21 46								
South Greenford	d						21 19								21 49								
Castle Bar Park	d						21 22								21 52								
Drayton Green	d						21 24								21 54								
West Ealing	d	21 11					21 26							21 41	21 56				22 11				
Ealing Broadway ⊖	d	21 14	21 19				21 29	21 35						21 44	21 59	22 05			22 14	22 21			
Acton Main Line	d						21 33								22 03								
London Paddington 15 ⊖	a	21 24	21 31	21 07	21 14	21 19	21 42	21 48	21 21	21 29	21 32	21 34	21 49	21 54	22 14	22 16	22 00	22 04	22 24	22 32	22 14	22 19	22 30

		HX 1	GW FX ◇1	GW FO ◇1	GW ◇1 ☕	HX 1	HC	HX 1	GW 1	HX 1	GW ◇1	HC	HX 1	HC	GW 1	GW FO ◇1 ☕	GW FX ◇1 ☕	GW FO ◇1 ☕	HX 1	GW FX ◇1 ☕	HX	GW FX 1
Oxford	d		21 31	21 31							22 11											
Reading 7	d		22 06	22 06	22 11				22 15		22 46				22 46	23 05	23 05	23 08		23 08		23 15
Twyford 3	d								22 22						22 54							23 22
Maidenhead 3	d								22 30						23 02							23 29
Taplow	d								22 33						23 06							23 33
Burnham	d								22 36						23 09							23 36
Slough 3	a		22 22	22 22					22 41		23 03				23 15							23 41
	d		22 22	22 22					22 41		23 04				23 27							23 41
Langley	d								22 45						23 31							23 45
Iver	d								22 48						23 34							23 48
West Drayton	d								22 51						23 38							23 51
Heathrow Terminal 4 ✈	d																					
Heathrow Terminals 1-2-3 2 ✈	d	22 18				22 33	22 27	22 48		23 03		22 57	23 18	23 27					23 33		23 48	
Hayes & Harlington	d						22 33		22 56			23 03		23 33	23 43							23 56
Southall	d						22 36		23 00			23 06		23 36	23 47							23 59
Hanwell	d						22 39					23 09		23 39								
Greenford ⊖	d																					
South Greenford	d																					
Castle Bar Park	d																					
Drayton Green	d																					
West Ealing	d						22 41					23 11		23 41								
Ealing Broadway ⊖	d						22 44		23 05			23 14		23 44	23 52							00 06
Acton Main Line	d																					
London Paddington 15 ⊖	a	22 34	22 43	22 43	22 45	22 49	22 54	23 04	23 17	23 19	23 24	23 24	23 34	23 54	00 03	23 36	23 40	23 42	23 49	23 50	00 04	00 17

		GW FO 1	HX	GW FO ◇1	GW FX ◇1	GW FO ◇1 ☕	GW FX ◇1 ☕
Oxford	d			23 05	23 05		
Reading 7	d	23 15		23 35	23 40	23 55	23 55
Twyford 3	d	23 22					
Maidenhead 3	d	23 29		23 47	23 53		
Taplow	d	23 33					
Burnham	d	23 36					
Slough 3	a	23 41		23 54	00 01		
	d	23 41		23 55	00 01		
Langley	d	23 45					
Iver	d	23 48					
West Drayton	d	23 52					
Heathrow Terminal 4 ✈	d						
Heathrow Terminals 1-2-3 2 ✈	d		23 57				
Hayes & Harlington	d	23 56					
Southall	d	23 59					
Hanwell	d						
Greenford ⊖	d						
South Greenford	d						
Castle Bar Park	d						
Drayton Green	d						
West Ealing	d						
Ealing Broadway ⊖	d	00 06					
Acton Main Line	d						
London Paddington 15 ⊖	a	00 17	00 18	00 22	00 26	00 27	00 33

Saturdays

		GW 1	HX	GW 1	HX	GW ◇1	GW ◇1 ☕	HC	GW 1	GW 1	GW 1	HX 1	GW 1	HX 1	HC	HX 1	GW 1	HX 1	HC	GW 1	HX 1	GW 1
Oxford	d					23p05				00 19			03 59									
Reading 7	d	22p46		23p15		23p35	23p55		00 15	01 10	04 10		04 40				05 10			05 33		
Twyford 3	d	22p54		23p22					00 21	01 17	04 16		04 46				05 16			05 39		
Maidenhead 3	d	23p02		23p29		23p47			00 29	01 25	04 24		04 54				05 24			05 47		
Taplow	d	23p06		23p33					00 32								05 28					
Burnham	d	23p09		23p36					00 35								05 31					
Slough 3	a	23p15		23p41		23p54			00 40	01 32	04 31		05 01				05 35			05 54		
	d	23p27		23p41		23p55			00 40	01 32	04 32		05 02				05 36			05 54		
Langley	d	23p31		23p45					00 44								05 40			05 58		
Iver	d	23p34		23p48													05 43			06 01		
West Drayton	d	23p38		23p52					00 49		04 38						05 45			06 05		
Heathrow Terminal 4 ✈	d							00 01							05 23				05 51			
Heathrow Terminals 1-2-3 2 ✈	d		23p48		23p57			00 07				05 12		05 33	05 29	05 48		06 03	05 57		06 18	
Hayes & Harlington	d	23p43		23p56				00 13	00 54	01 41	04 43		05 11		05 35		05 51		06 03	06 10		
Southall	d	23p47		23p59				00 16	00 57		04 46		05 14		05 38		05 54		06 06	06 13		
Hanwell	d														05 41				06 09			
Greenford ⊖	d																					06 16
South Greenford	d																					06 19
Castle Bar Park	d																					06 22
Drayton Green	d																					06 24
West Ealing	d														05 43				06 11			06 26
Ealing Broadway ⊖	d	23p52		00 06				00 21	01 03	01 48	04 52		05 20		05 46		06 00		06 14	06 19		06 29
Acton Main Line	d												05 23				06 03					06 33
London Paddington 15 ⊖	a	00 03	00 04	00 17	00 18	00 22	00 27	00 30	01 14	02 00	05 01	05 28	05 31	05 49	05 56	06 04	06 11	06 19	06 24	06 31	06 34	06 42

Table 117

Saturdays

Reading and Greenford - London

		GW 1	HX 1	HC	GW 1	HX 1		GW 1	GW 1	HC	GW 1	GW ◇1 ☕	HX 1	GW 1	GW 1	GW 1		HX 1	GW ◇1	HC	GW 1	GW ◇1 ☕	HX 1	GW 1	GW 1
Oxford	d				05 14						05 50								06 31		06 07				
Reading 7	d	05 48			06 03				06 18		06 33	06 45			06 48	06 52			07 00		07 03	07 15			07 18
Twyford 3	d	05 54			06 09				06 24		06 39				06 54						07 09				07 24
Maidenhead 3	d	06 02			06 17				06 32		06 47				07 02						07 17				07 32
Taplow	d	06 06							06 36						07 06										07 36
Burnham	d	06 09							06 39						07 09										07 39
Slough 3	a	06 14			06 24				06 44		06 54				07 14				07 16		07 24				07 44
	d	06 14			06 24				06 44		06 54				07 14				07 17		07 24				07 44
Langley	d				06 28						06 58										07 28				
Iver	d				06 31						07 01										07 31				
West Drayton	d	06 21			06 35				06 51		07 05				07 21						07 35				07 51
Heathrow Terminal 4 ✈	d																								
Heathrow Terminals 1-2-3 2 ✈	d		06 33	06 27		06 48				06 57			07 03					07 18		07 27			07 33		
Hayes & Harlington	d	06 26		06 33	06 40				06 56	07 03	07 10				07 26					07 33	07 40				07 56
Southall	d			06 36	06 43					07 06	07 13									07 36	07 43				
Hanwell	d			06 39						07 09										07 39					
Greenford ⊖	d							06 46						07 16										07 46	
South Greenford	d							06 49						07 19										07 49	
Castle Bar Park	d							06 52						07 22										07 52	
Drayton Green	d							06 54						07 24										07 54	
West Ealing	d			06 41				06 56		07 11				07 26						07 41				07 56	
Ealing Broadway ⊖	d	06 33		06 44	06 49			06 59	07 03	07 14	07 19			07 29	07 33					07 44	07 49			07 59	08 03
Acton Main Line	d							07 03						07 33										08 02	
London Paddington 15 ⊖	a	06 46	06 49	06 54	07 01	07 04		07 12	07 16	07 24	07 31	07 14	07 19	07 42	07 46	07 22		07 34	07 37	07 54	08 01	07 44	07 49	08 12	08 16

		GW 1		GW ◇1	GW ◇1 ☕	HX 1	HC	GW 1	GW ◇1 ☕	HX 1	GW 1	GW 1		GW ◇1 ☕	HC	GW 1 A	GW ◇1 ☕	GW 1 B	HX 1	GW ◇1 ☕	HX 1	GW 1		GW 1	GW 1
Oxford	d			07 01				06 42						07 31		07 07		07 07							
Reading 7	d	07 21		07 27	07 32			07 33	07 46			07 48		07 54		07 58	08 02	08 03		08 16				08 18	08 20
Twyford 3	d							07 39				07 54				08 09		08 09						08 24	
Maidenhead 3	d							07 47				08 02				08 17		08 17						08 32	
Taplow	d											08 06												08 36	
Burnham	d											08 09												08 39	
Slough 3	a							07 54				08 14		08 09		08 24		08 24						08 44	
	d							07 54				08 14		08 09		08 24		08 24						08 44	
Langley	d							07 58								08 28		08 28							
Iver	d							08 01								08 31		08 31							
West Drayton	d							08 05				08 21				08 35		08 35						08 51	
Heathrow Terminal 4 ✈	d																								
Heathrow Terminals 1-2-3 2 ✈	d					07 48	07 57			08 03					08 27				08 18		08 33				
Hayes & Harlington	d						08 03	08 10				08 26			08 33	08 40		08 40						08 56	
Southall	d						08 06	08 13							08 36	08 43		08 43							
Hanwell	d						08 09								08 39										
Greenford ⊖	d										08 16											08 46			
South Greenford	d										08 19											08 49			
Castle Bar Park	d										08 22											08 52			
Drayton Green	d										08 24											08 54			
West Ealing	d						08 11				08 26				08 41							08 56			
Ealing Broadway ⊖	d						08 14	08 19			08 29	08 33			08 44	08 49		08 49				08 59		09 03	
Acton Main Line	d										08 33											09 03			
London Paddington 15 ⊖	a	07 54		07 59	08 02	08 04	08 24	08 31	08 14	08 19	08 42	08 46		08 29	08 54	09 01	08 32	09 01	08 34	08 44	08 49	09 12		09 16	08 52

		GW ◇1	GW ◇1 ☕	HX 1	HC	GW 1	GW ◇1 ☕	HX 1		GW 1	GW 1	GW ◇1 ☕	GW ◇1 ☕	GW ◇1 ☕	HX 1	HC	GW 1	GW ◇1 ☕		GW ◇1 ☕	HX 1	GW 1	GW 1	GW 1	GW ◇1
Oxford	d	08 01				07 37							08 31				08 07								09 01
Reading 7	d	08 26	08 33			08 33	08 46				08 48	08 52	08 55	09 02			09 03	09 09		09 16			09 18	09 20	09 24
Twyford 3	d					08 39					08 54						09 09						09 24		
Maidenhead 3	d					08 47					09 02						09 17						09 32		
Taplow	d										09 06												09 36		
Burnham	d										09 09												09 39		
Slough 3	a	08 40				08 54					09 14		09 09				09 24						09 44		09 40
	d	08 41				08 54					09 14		09 11				09 24						09 44		09 40
Langley	d					08 58											09 28								
Iver	d					09 01											09 31								
West Drayton	d					09 05					09 21						09 35						09 51		
Heathrow Terminal 4 ✈	d																								
Heathrow Terminals 1-2-3 2 ✈	d			08 48	08 57			09 03							09 18	09 27					09 33				
Hayes & Harlington	d				09 03	09 10					09 26					09 33	09 40						09 56		
Southall	d				09 06	09 13										09 36	09 43								
Hanwell	d				09 09											09 39									
Greenford ⊖	d									09 16												09 46			
South Greenford	d									09 19												09 49			
Castle Bar Park	d									09 22												09 52			
Drayton Green	d									09 24												09 54			
West Ealing	d				09 11					09 26						09 41						09 56			
Ealing Broadway ⊖	d				09 14	09 19				09 29	09 33					09 44	09 49					09 59	10 03		
Acton Main Line	d									09 33												10 03			
London Paddington 15 ⊖	a	08 59	09 02	09 04	09 24	09 31	09 14	09 19		09 42	09 46	09 21	09 29	09 32	09 34	09 54	10 01	09 37		09 44	09 49	10 12	10 16	09 52	09 59

A until 4 September
B from 11 September

Table 117

Saturdays

Reading and Greenford - London

		GW ◇1 ☕	HX 1	HC		GW 1	GW ◇1 ☕	GW ◇1 ☕	HX 1	GW 1	GW 1	GW ◇1 ☕	GW ◇1 ☕	HX 1		HC	GW 1	GW ◇1 ☕	HX 1	GW 1	GW 1	GW 1	GW ◇1	GW ◇1 B ☕	
Oxford	d					08 37						09 31					09 07						10 01		
Reading 7	d	09 33				09 33	09 37	09 45			09 48	09 55	10 02				10 03	10 10		10 18		10 18	10 25	10 33	
Twyford 3	d					09 39					09 54						10 09					10 24			
Maidenhead 3	d					09 47					10 02						10 17					10 32			
Taplow	d										10 06											10 36			
Burnham	d										10 09											10 39			
Slough 3	a					09 54					10 14	10 09					10 24					10 44	10 40		
	d					09 54					10 14	10 10					10 24					10 44	10 40		
Langley	d					09 58											10 28								
Iver	d					10 01											10 31								
West Drayton	d					10 05					10 21						10 35					10 51			
Heathrow Terminal 4 ✈	d																								
Heathrow Terminals 1-2-3 2 ✈	d		09 48	09 57					10 03					10 18		10 27			10 33						
Hayes & Harlington	d			10 03		10 10					10 26					10 33	10 40					10 56			
Southall	d			10 06		10 13										10 36	10 43								
Hanwell	d			10 09												10 39									
Greenford ⊖	d									10 16											10 46				
South Greenford	d									10 19											10 49				
Castle Bar Park	d									10 22											10 52				
Drayton Green	d									10 24											10 54				
West Ealing	d			10 11						10 26						10 41					10 56				
Ealing Broadway ⊖	d			10 14		10 19				10 29	10 33					10 44	10 49				10 59	11 03			
Acton Main Line	d									10 33											11 03				
London Paddington 15 ⊖	a	10 02	10 04	10 24		10 31	10 08	10 14	10 19	10 42	10 46	10 29	10 32	10 34		10 54	11 01	10 38	10 49	10 52	11 12	11 16	10 59	11 02	

		HX 1	HC	GW 1	GW ◇1 ☕		GW ◇1 ☕	HX 1	GW 1	GW 1		GW ◇1 ☕	GW ◇1 ☕	GW ◇1 ☕	HX 1	HC	GW 1	GW ◇1 ☕	HX 1	GW 1		GW 1	GW 1	GW ◇1	HX 1
Oxford	d			09 37									10 31				10 07							11 01	
Reading 7	d			10 33	10 38		10 45			10 48		10 53	10 55	11 02			11 03	11 13				11 18	11 21	11 25	
Twyford 3	d			10 39						10 54							11 09					11 24			
Maidenhead 3	d			10 47						11 02							11 17					11 32			
Taplow	d									11 06												11 36			
Burnham	d									11 09												11 39			
Slough 3	a			10 54						11 14			11 09				11 24					11 44		11 39	
	d			10 54						11 14			11 10				11 24					11 44		11 40	
Langley	d			10 58													11 28								
Iver	d			11 01													11 31								
West Drayton	d			11 05						11 21							11 35					11 51			
Heathrow Terminal 4 ✈	d																								
Heathrow Terminals 1-2-3 2 ✈	d	10 48	10 57					11 03							11 18	11 27			11 33						11 48
Hayes & Harlington	d		11 03	11 10						11 26						11 33	11 40					11 56			
Southall	d		11 06	11 13												11 36	11 43								
Hanwell	d		11 09													11 39									
Greenford ⊖	d								11 16											11 46					
South Greenford	d								11 19											11 49					
Castle Bar Park	d								11 22											11 52					
Drayton Green	d								11 24											11 54					
West Ealing	d		11 11						11 26							11 41				11 56					
Ealing Broadway ⊖	d		11 14	11 19					11 29	11 33						11 44	11 49			11 59		12 03			
Acton Main Line	d								11 33											12 03					
London Paddington 15 ⊖	a	11 04	11 24	11 31	11 08		11 14	11 19	11 42	11 46		11 24	11 29	11 33	11 34	11 54	12 01	11 40	11 49	12 12		12 16	11 52	11 59	12 04

B from 11 September

Reading and Greenford - London

		HC	GW	GW	HX	GW	GW	GW	GW	GW	GW	HX	HC	GW	GW	HX	GW	GW	GW	GW	GW	GW	HX
			■	◇■ ⊡	■	■	■	■ ⊡	◇■ A ✕	◇■ B ✕	◇■ ⊡	■		■	◇■ ⊡	■	■ B	■	■	◇■ A	◇■ B	■ A	■
Oxford	d		10 37						11 31	11 31				11 07						12 01	12 01		
Reading 7	d		11 33	11 45			11 48	11 53	11 55	11 55	12 02			12 03	12 11		12 17		12 18	12 24	12 25	12 27	
Twyford 3	d		11 39				11 54							12 09					12 24				
Maidenhead 3	d		11 47				12 02							12 17					12 32				
Taplow	d						12 06												12 36				
Burnham	d						12 09												12 39				
Slough 3	a		11 54				12 14			12 09				12 24					12 44	12 39	12 40		
	d		11 54				12 14			12 11				12 24					12 44	12 39	12 40		
Langley	d		11 58											12 28									
Iver	d		12 01											12 31									
West Drayton	d		12 05				12 21							12 35					12 51				
Heathrow Terminal 4 ✈	d																						
Heathrow Terminals 1-2-3 2 ✈	d	11 57			12 03							12 18	12 27			12 33							12 48
Hayes & Harlington	d	12 03	12 10				12 26						12 33	12 40					12 56				
Southall	d	12 06	12 13										12 36	12 43									
Hanwell	d	12 09											12 39										
Greenford ⊖	d					12 16												12 46					
South Greenford	d					12 19												12 49					
Castle Bar Park	d					12 22												12 52					
Drayton Green	d					12 24												12 54					
West Ealing	d	12 11				12 26							12 41					12 56					
Ealing Broadway ⊖	d	12 14	12 19			12 29	12 33						12 44	12 49				12 59	13 03				
Acton Main Line	d					12 33												13 03					
London Paddington 15 ⊖	a	12 24	12 31	12 14	12 19	12 42	12 46	12 23	12 29	12 29	12 32	12 34	12 54	13 01	12 39	12 49	12 52	13 12	13 16	13 00	12 59	13 03	13 04

		HC	GW	GW	GW	GW	GW	HX	GW	GW	GW	GW	GW	HX	HC	GW	GW	GW	GW	GW	HX	GW
			■	◇■ A ⊡	◇■ B ⊡	■ A ⊡	◇■ B ⊡	■	■	■	◇■ A ⊡	◇■ B ⊡	◇■ ⊡	■		■	◇■ ⊡	■	■	◇■ C ⊡	■	■ D ⊡
Oxford	d		11 37													12 07						
Reading 7	d		12 33	12 37	12 38	12 43	12 44			12 48	12 50	12 54	13 02			13 03	13 12		13 18	13 20		13 20
Twyford 3	d		12 39							12 54						13 09			13 24			
Maidenhead 3	d		12 47							13 02						13 17			13 32			
Taplow	d									13 06									13 36			
Burnham	d									13 09									13 39			
Slough 3	a		12 54							13 14						13 24			13 44			
	d		12 54							13 14						13 24			13 44			
Langley	d		12 58													13 28						
Iver	d		13 01													13 31						
West Drayton	d		13 05							13 21						13 35			13 51			
Heathrow Terminal 4 ✈	d																					
Heathrow Terminals 1-2-3 2 ✈	d	12 57						13 03						13 18	13 27						13 33	
Hayes & Harlington	d	13 03	13 10							13 26					13 33	13 40			13 56			
Southall	d	13 06	13 13												13 36	13 43						
Hanwell	d	13 09													13 39							
Greenford ⊖	d								13 16									13 46				
South Greenford	d								13 19									13 49				
Castle Bar Park	d								13 22									13 52				
Drayton Green	d								13 24									13 54				
West Ealing	d	13 11							13 26						13 41			13 56				
Ealing Broadway ⊖	d	13 14	13 19						13 29	13 33					13 44	13 49		13 59	14 03			
Acton Main Line	d								13 33									14 03				
London Paddington 15 ⊖	a	13 24	13 31	13 10	13 06	13 14	13 14	13 19	13 42	13 46	13 22	13 21	13 32	13 34	13 54	14 01	13 41	14 12	14 16	13 46	13 49	13 54

A until 4 September
B from 11 September
C from 11 September. The Cornish Riveira
D until 4 September. The Cornish Riveira

Reading and Greenford - London

		GW	HX	HC	GW	GW	HX	GW	GW	GW	GW	GW	GW	HX	HC	GW	GW	GW	GW	GW	GW	HX	GW
		◇■	■		■	◇■ ⊡	■	■	■	■ A	■ B	◇■	◇■ ⊡	■		■	◇■ ⊡	■ B	■	■	◇■ A ⊡	■	◇■
Oxford	d	13 01			12 37							13 31				13 07							14 01
Reading 7	d	13 25			13 33	13 45			13 48	13 51	13 51	13 55	14 02			14 03	14 11	14 18		14 18	14 19		14 25
Twyford 3	d				13 39				13 54							14 09				14 24			
Maidenhead 3	d				13 47				14 02							14 17				14 32			
Taplow	d								14 06											14 36			
Burnham	d								14 09											14 39			
Slough 3	a	13 40			13 54				14 14			14 09				14 24				14 44			14 40
	d	13 40			13 54				14 14			14 10				14 24				14 44			14 40
Langley	d				13 58											14 28							
Iver	d				14 01											14 31							
West Drayton	d				14 05				14 21							14 35				14 51			
Heathrow Terminal 4 ✈	d																						
Heathrow Terminals 1-2-3 2 ✈	d		13 48	13 57			14 03							14 18	14 27							14 33	
Hayes & Harlington	d			14 03	14 10				14 26						14 33	14 40				14 56			
Southall	d			14 06	14 13										14 36	14 43							
Hanwell	d			14 09											14 39								
Greenford ⊖	d							14 16											14 46				
South Greenford	d							14 19											14 49				
Castle Bar Park	d							14 22											14 52				
Drayton Green	d							14 24											14 54				
West Ealing	d			14 11				14 26							14 41				14 56				
Ealing Broadway ⊖	d			14 14	14 19			14 29	14 33						14 44	14 49			14 59	15 03			
Acton Main Line	d							14 33											15 03				
London Paddington 15 ⊖	a	13 59	14 04	14 24	14 31	14 14	14 19	14 42	14 46	14 23	14 24	14 29	14 32	14 34	14 54	15 01	14 39	14 55	15 12	15 16	14 45	14 49	14 59

		HX	HC	GW	GW	GW	HX	GW	GW	GW	GW	GW	GW	GW	GW	HX	HC	GW	GW	HX	GW	GW
		■		■	◇■ ⊡	◇■ ⊡	■	■	■	◇■ A ⊡	■ B ⊡	◇■ B ⊡	◇■ A ⊡	◇■ C ⊡	◇■ A ⊡	■		■	◇■ ⊡	■	■	■
Oxford	d			13 37								14 31	14 31					14 07				
Reading 7	d			14 33	14 38	14 45			14 48	14 53	14 53	14 55	14 56	15 02	15 02			15 03	15 11			15 18
Twyford 3	d			14 39					14 54									15 09				15 24
Maidenhead 3	d			14 47					15 02									15 17				15 32
Taplow	d								15 06													15 36
Burnham	d								15 09													15 39
Slough 3	a			14 54					15 14			15 09	15 10					15 24				15 44
	d			14 54					15 14			15 10	15 11					15 24				15 44
Langley	d			14 58														15 28				
Iver	d			15 01														15 31				
West Drayton	d			15 05					15 21									15 35				15 51
Heathrow Terminal 4 ✈	d																					
Heathrow Terminals 1-2-3 2 ✈	d	14 48	14 57				15 03									15 18	15 27			15 33		
Hayes & Harlington	d		15 03	15 10					15 26								15 33	15 40				15 56
Southall	d		15 06	15 13													15 36	15 43				
Hanwell	d		15 09														15 39					
Greenford ⊖	d							15 16													15 46	
South Greenford	d							15 19													15 49	
Castle Bar Park	d							15 22													15 52	
Drayton Green	d							15 24													15 54	
West Ealing	d		15 11					15 26									15 41				15 56	
Ealing Broadway ⊖	d		15 14	15 19				15 29	15 33								15 44	15 49			15 59	16 03
Acton Main Line	d							15 33													16 03	
London Paddington 15 ⊖	a	15 04	15 24	15 31	15 09	15 14	15 19	15 42	15 46	15 22	15 23	15 29	15 29	15 32	15 32	15 34	15 54	16 01	15 39	15 49	16 12	16 16

A from 11 September
B until 4 September
C until 4 September. The Pembroke Coast Express

Table 117

Reading and Greenford - London

		GW	GW	HX	HC	GW	GW	HX	GW	GW	GW	GW	GW	GW	GW	HX	GW	HC	GW	GW	HX	GW	GW
		[1]	◇[1]	[1]		[1]	◇[1] ☕	[1]	[1]	[1]	[R] [1] A ☕	◇[1] B ☕	◇[1]	◇[1] A ☕	◇[1] B ☕	[1]	◇[1] A ☕		[1]	◇[1] ☕	[1]	[1] B	[1]
Oxford	d		15 01			14 37							15 31						15 07				
Reading [7]	d	15 19	15 25			15 33	15 45			15 48	15 53	15 53	15 55	16u01	16 02		16 02		16 03	16 11		16 18	
Twyford [3]	d					15 39				15 54									16 09				
Maidenhead [3]	d					15 47				16 02									16 17				
Taplow	d									16 06													
Burnham	d									16 09													
Slough [3]	a		15 40			15 54				16 14			16 10						16 24				
	d		15 40			15 54				16 14			16 11						16 24				
Langley	d					15 58													16 28				
Iver	d					16 01													16 31				
West Drayton	d					16 05				16 21									16 35				
Heathrow Terminal 4 ✈	d																						
Heathrow Terminals 1-2-3 [2] ✈	d			15 48	15 57			16 03								16 18		16 27			16 33		
Hayes & Harlington	d				16 03	16 10				16 26								16 33	16 40				
Southall	d				16 06	16 13												16 36	16 43				
Hanwell	d				16 09													16 39					
Greenford ⊖	d								16 16														16 46
South Greenford	d								16 19														16 49
Castle Bar Park	d								16 22														16 52
Drayton Green	d								16 24														16 54
West Ealing	d				16 11				16 26									16 41					16 56
Ealing Broadway ⊖	d				16 14	16 19			16 29	16 33								16 44	16 49				16 59
Acton Main Line	d								16 33														17 03
London Paddington [15] ⊖	a	15 54	15 59	16 04	16 24	16 31	16 14	16 19	16 42	16 46	16 21	16 23	16 29	16 32	16 32	16 34	16 37	16 54	17 01	16 41	16 49	16 52	17 12

		GW	GW	GW	GW	HX	GW	HC	GW	GW	GW	GW	HX	GW	GW	GW	GW	GW	GW	HX	HC	GW	GW
		[1]	[1] A	◇[1] A	◇[1] B	[1]	◇[1] A ☕		[1]	◇[1] B ☕	◇[1] A ☕	◇[1] ☕	[1]	[1]	[1]	◇[1] B ☕	[R] [1] A ☕	◇[1] 🍴	◇[1] ☕	[1]		[1]	◇[1] ☕
Oxford	d			16 01	16 01				15 37									16 31				16 07	
Reading [7]	d	16 18	16 21	16 25	16 25		16 28		16 33	16 38	16 38	16 45			16 48	16 50	16 51	16 55	17 02			17 03	17 11
Twyford [3]	d	16 24							16 39						16 54							17 09	
Maidenhead [3]	d	16 32							16 47						17 02							17 17	
Taplow	d	16 36													17 06								
Burnham	d	16 39													17 09								
Slough [3]	a	16 44		16 40	16 40				16 54						17 14			17 09				17 24	
	d	16 44		16 40	16 40				16 54						17 14			17 11				17 24	
Langley	d								16 58													17 28	
Iver	d								17 01													17 31	
West Drayton	d	16 51							17 05						17 21							17 35	
Heathrow Terminal 4 ✈	d																						
Heathrow Terminals 1-2-3 [2] ✈	d					16 48		16 57					17 03							17 18	17 27		
Hayes & Harlington	d	16 56						17 03	17 10						17 26						17 33	17 40	
Southall	d							17 06	17 13												17 36	17 43	
Hanwell	d							17 09													17 39		
Greenford ⊖	d													17 16									
South Greenford	d													17 19									
Castle Bar Park	d													17 22									
Drayton Green	d													17 24									
West Ealing	d							17 11						17 26							17 41		
Ealing Broadway ⊖	d	17 03						17 14	17 19					17 29	17 33						17 44	17 49	
Acton Main Line	d													17 33									
London Paddington [15] ⊖	a	17 16	16 53	16 59	17 00	17 04	17 06	17 24	17 31	17 06	17 09	17 14	17 19	17 42	17 46	17 21	17 21	17 29	17 32	17 34	17 54	18 01	17 38

A until 4 September
B from 11 September

Table 117

Reading and Greenford - London

		HX	GW	GW	GW	GW	GW	HX	HC	GW	GW	GW	HX	GW	GW	GW	GW	GW	GW	HX	HC	GW
		[1]	[1]	[1]	[1] A	◇[1] B ☕	◇[1]	[1]		[1]	◇[1] C ☕	◇[1] ☕	[1]	[1]	[1]	[R] [1] A ☕	◇[1] B ☕	◇[1] ☕	◇[1] D ☕	[1]		[1]
Oxford	d						17 01			16 37								17 30				17 07
Reading [7]	d			17 18	17 19	17 20	17 25			17 33	17 36	17 45			17 48	17 52	17 54	17 54	18 02			18 03
Twyford [3]	d			17 24						17 39					17 54							18 09
Maidenhead [3]	d			17 32						17 47					18 02							18 17
Taplow	d			17 36											18 06							
Burnham	d			17 39											18 09							
Slough [3]	a			17 44			17 40			17 54					18 14			18 09				18 24
	d			17 44			17 40			17 54					18 14			18 11				18 24
Langley	d									17 58												18 28
Iver	d									18 01												18 31
West Drayton	d			17 51						18 05					18 21							18 35
Heathrow Terminal 4 ✈	d																					
Heathrow Terminals 1-2-3 [2] ✈	d	17 33						17 48	17 57				18 03							18 18	18 27	
Hayes & Harlington	d			17 56					18 03	18 10					18 26						18 33	18 40
Southall	d								18 06	18 13											18 36	18 43
Hanwell	d								18 09												18 39	
Greenford ⊖	d		17 46											18 16								
South Greenford	d		17 49											18 19								
Castle Bar Park	d		17 52											18 22								
Drayton Green	d		17 54											18 24								
West Ealing	d		17 56						18 11					18 26							18 41	
Ealing Broadway ⊖	d		17 59	18 03					18 14	18 19				18 29	18 33						18 44	18 49
Acton Main Line	d		18 03											18 33								
London Paddington [15] ⊖	a	17 49	18 12	18 16	17 54	17 51	17 59	18 04	18 24	18 31	18 08	18 14	18 19	18 42	18 46	18 23	18 21	18 29	18 32	18 34	18 54	19 01

		GW	HX	GW	GW	GW	GW	HX	HC	GW	GW	GW	HX	GW	GW	GW	GW	GW	GW	GW	HX	HC	GW
		◇[1] ☕	[1]	[1]	[1]	[1]	◇[1]	[1]		[1]	◇[1] ☕	◇[1] ☕	[1]	[1]	[1]	◇[1] E ☕	◇[1] F ☕	◇[1] G 🍴	◇[1] F 🍴	◇[1] D ☕	[1]		[1]
Oxford	d						18 01			17 37								18 31	18 31				18 07
Reading [7]	d	18 11			18 18	18 19	18 25			18 33	18 38	18 45			18 48	18 50	18 54	18 55	18 57	19 02			19 03
Twyford [3]	d				18 24					18 39					18 54								19 09
Maidenhead [3]	d				18 32					18 47					19 02								19 17
Taplow	d				18 36										19 06								
Burnham	d				18 39										19 09								
Slough [3]	a				18 44		18 40			18 54					19 14			19 09	19 12				19 24
	d				18 44		18 40			18 54					19 14			19 10	19 13				19 24
Langley	d									18 58													19 28
Iver	d									19 01													19 31
West Drayton	d				18 51					19 05					19 21								19 35
Heathrow Terminal 4 ✈	d																						
Heathrow Terminals 1-2-3 [2] ✈	d		18 33					18 48	18 57				19 03								19 18	19 27	
Hayes & Harlington	d				18 56				19 03	19 10					19 26							19 33	19 40
Southall	d								19 06	19 13												19 36	19 43
Hanwell	d								19 09													19 39	
Greenford ⊖	d			18 46										19 16									
South Greenford	d			18 49										19 19									
Castle Bar Park	d			18 52										19 22									
Drayton Green	d			18 54										19 24									
West Ealing	d			18 56					19 11					19 26								19 41	
Ealing Broadway ⊖	d			18 59	19 03				19 14	19 19				19 29	19 33							19 44	19 49
Acton Main Line	d			19 03										19 33									
London Paddington [15] ⊖	a	18 38	18 49	19 12	19 16	18 52	18 59	19 04	19 24	19 31	19 08	19 14	19 19	19 42	19 46	19 22	19 29	19 29	19 32	19 32	19 34	19 54	20 01

A until 4 September
B from 11 September
C until 4 September. The Torbay Express
D until 10 July, from 11 September
E The Royal Duchy
F from 17 July until 4 September
G until 10 July

Table 117

Reading and Greenford - London

Saturdays

	GW ◇1	HX 1	GW 1	GW 1	GW 1	GW ◇1	HX 1	HC	GW 1	GW ◇1 A	HX 1	GW 1	GW 1	GW ◇1	GW ◇1 B	GW ◇1 C	HX 1	HC	GW 1	GW ◇1 A	GW ◇1 D
Oxford d						19 01			18 37					19 31					19 07		
Reading 7 d	19 11			19 18	19 19	19 25			19 33	19 45			19 48	19 55	20 01	20 02			20 03	20 09	20 12
Twyford 3 d				19 24					19 39				19 54						20 09		
Maidenhead 3 d				19 32					19 47				20 02						20 17		
Taplow d				19 36									20 06								
Burnham d				19 39									20 09								
Slough 3 a				19 44		19 40			19 54				20 14	20 09					20 24		
d				19 44		19 40			19 54				20 14	20 10					20 24		
Langley d									19 58										20 28		
Iver d									20 01										20 31		
West Drayton d				19 51					20 05				20 21						20 35		
Heathrow Terminal 4 d																					
Heathrow Terminals 1-2-3 2 d		19 33					19 48	19 57			20 03						20 18	20 27			
Hayes & Harlington d				19 56				20 03	20 10				20 26					20 33	20 40		
Southall d								20 06	20 13									20 36	20 43		
Hanwell d								20 09										20 39			
Greenford d			19 46									20 16									
South Greenford d			19 49									20 19									
Castle Bar Park d			19 52									20 22									
Drayton Green d			19 54									20 24									
West Ealing d			19 56					20 11				20 26						20 41			
Ealing Broadway d			19 59	20 03				20 14	20 19			20 29	20 33					20 44	20 49		
Acton Main Line d			20 03									20 33									
London Paddington 15 a	19 39	19 49	20 12	20 16	19 52	19 59	20 04	20 24	20 31	20 14	20 19	20 42	20 46	20 29	20 32	20 32	20 34	20 54	21 01	20 37	20 39

	HX 1	GW 1	GW 1	GW ◇1	HX 1	HC	GW 1	GW ◇1	GW ◇1	HX 1	GW 1	GW 1	GW ◇1	GW ◇1	HX 1	HC	GW 1	GW ◇1	HX 1	GW 1	GW 1	GW ◇1
Oxford d				20 01			19 37						20 31				20 07					21 01
Reading 7 d			20 18	20 25			20 33	20 38	20 45			20 48	20 54	21 01			21 03	21 08			21 18	21 25
Twyford 3 d			20 24				20 39					20 54					21 09				21 24	
Maidenhead 3 d			20 32				20 47					21 02					21 17				21 32	
Taplow d			20 36									21 06									21 36	
Burnham d			20 39									21 09									21 39	
Slough 3 a			20 44	20 40			20 54					21 14	21 09				21 24				21 44	21 40
d			20 44	20 40			20 54					21 14	21 09				21 24				21 44	21 40
Langley d							20 58										21 28					
Iver d							21 01										21 31					
West Drayton d			20 51				21 05					21 21					21 35				21 51	
Heathrow Terminal 4 d																						
Heathrow Terminals 1-2-3 2 d	20 33				20 48	20 57				21 03					21 18	21 27			21 33			
Hayes & Harlington d			20 56			21 03	21 10					21 26				21 33	21 40				21 56	
Southall d						21 06	21 13									21 36	21 43					
Hanwell d						21 09										21 39						
Greenford d		20 46									21 16									21 46		
South Greenford d		20 49									21 19									21 49		
Castle Bar Park d		20 52									21 22									21 52		
Drayton Green d		20 54									21 24									21 54		
West Ealing d		20 56				21 11					21 26					21 41				21 56		
Ealing Broadway d		20 59	21 03			21 14	21 19				21 29	21 33				21 44	21 49			21 59	22 03	
Acton Main Line d		21 03									21 33									22 03		
London Paddington 15 a	20 49	21 12	21 16	20 59	21 04	21 24	21 31	21 07	21 14	21 19	21 42	21 46	21 29	21 32	21 34	21 54	22 01	21 37	21 49	22 12	22 16	21 59

	HX 1	HC	GW 1	GW ◇1 B	GW 1	GW ◇1 C	HX 1	GW ◇1 B	GW ◇1 D	GW ◇1 C	HX 1	GW ◇1	HX 1	HC	GW 1	GW ◇1 B	HX 1	HC	GW 1	GW ◇1	GW 1	HX 1	GW ◇1 A	HX 1
Oxford d			20 37									21 36							21 50	22 08			22 31	
Reading 7 d			21 33	21 44	21 48	21 50		21 51	21 59	22 02		22 05			22 18	22 25			22 33	22 36	22 48		22 55	
Twyford 3 d			21 39		21 54										22 24				22 39		22 54			
Maidenhead 3 d			21 47		22 02										22 32				22 47		23 02			
Taplow d					22 06										22 36						23 06			
Burnham d					22 09										22 39						23 09			
Slough 3 a			21 54		22 14							22 22			22 44				22 54	22 50	23 14		23 12	
d			21 54		22 14							22 22			22 44				22 54	22 51	23 14		23 12	
Langley d			21 58																22 58					
Iver d			22 01																23 01					
West Drayton d			22 05		22 21										22 51				23 05		23 21			
Heathrow Terminal 4 d																								
Heathrow Terminals 1-2-3 2 d	21 48	21 57					22 03				22 18		22 33	22 27			22 48	22 57				23 03		23 18
Hayes & Harlington d		22 03	22 10		22 26									22 33	22 56			23 03	23 10		23 26			
Southall d		22 06	22 13											22 36				23 06	23 13					
Hanwell d		22 09												22 39				23 09						
Greenford d																								
South Greenford d																								
Castle Bar Park d																								
Drayton Green d																								
West Ealing d		22 11												22 41				23 11						
Ealing Broadway d		22 14	22 19		22 33									22 44	23 03			23 14	23 19		23 33			
Acton Main Line d																								
London Paddington 15 a	22 04	22 24	22 31	22 14	22 46	22 16	22 19	22 21	22 26	22 30	22 34	22 39	22 49	22 54	23 16	22 59	23 04	23 24	23 28	23 09	23 46	23 19	23 31	23 34

A from 11 September
B from 17 July until 4 September
C until 10 July, from 11 September
D until 4 September

Table 117

Reading and Greenford - London

Saturdays

	GW ◇1 A	GW ◇1	HX 1	HC	HX 1	GW 1	HX	GW ◇1	GW 1
Oxford d	22 31								23 07
Reading 7 d	22 55	23 05				23 18		23 53	00 03
Twyford 3 d						23 24			00 09
Maidenhead 3 d						23 32			00 17
Taplow d						23 36			00 21
Burnham d						23 39			00 24
Slough 3 a	23 17					23 44			00 28
d	23 18					23 44			00 29
Langley d									00 33
Iver d									00 36
West Drayton d						23 51			00 39
Heathrow Terminal 4 d									
Heathrow Terminals 1-2-3 2 d			23 33	23 27	23 48		23 57		
Hayes & Harlington d				23 33		23 56			00 44
Southall d				23 36					00 47
Hanwell d				23 39					
Greenford d									
South Greenford d									
Castle Bar Park d									
Drayton Green d									
West Ealing d				23 41					
Ealing Broadway d				23 44		00 03			00 53
Acton Main Line d									
London Paddington 15 a	23 36	23 38	23 49	23 54	00 04	00 16	00 19	00 33	01 02

Sundays
until 05 September

	HX 1	GW 1	HX	HC	GW ◇1	GW 1	HX 1	HX 1	HX 1	HX 1	HX 1	HC	HX 1	HX 1	HX 1	GW 1	HX 1	HC	HX 1	HX 1	HX 1	GW 1
Oxford d						23p07																
Reading 7 d		23p18			23p53	00 03										06 22						07 22
Twyford 3 d		23p24				00 09										06 28						07 28
Maidenhead 3 d		23p32				00 17										06 36						07 36
Taplow d		23p36				00 21																
Burnham d		23p39				00 24										06 40						07 40
Slough 3 a		23p44				00 28										06 45						07 45
d		23p44				00 29										06 46						07 46
Langley d						00 33										06 50						07 50
Iver d						00 36																
West Drayton d		23p51				00 39										06 55						07 55
Heathrow Terminal 4 d				00 01								06 07						07 07				
Heathrow Terminals 1-2-3 2 d	23p48		23p57	00 07			05 08	05 23	05 38	05 53	06 08	06 13	06 23	06 38	06 53		07 08	07 13	07 23	07 38	07 53	
Hayes & Harlington d		23p56		00 13		00 44						06 19				07 02		07 19				08 02
Southall d				00 16		00 47						06 22				07 05		07 22				08 05
Hanwell d																						
Greenford d																						
South Greenford d																						
Castle Bar Park d																						
Drayton Green d																						
West Ealing d																						
Ealing Broadway d		00 03		00 21		00 53						06 27				07 11		07 27				08 11
Acton Main Line d																						
London Paddington 15 a	00 04	00 16	00 19	00 30	00 33	01 02	05 24	05 39	05 54	06 09	06 24	06 36	06 39	06 54	07 09	07 22	07 24	07 36	07 39	07 54	08 09	08 22

	HX 1	HC	HX 1	GW 1	HX 1	HX 1	GW 1	GW 1	HX 1	HX 1	GW ◇1	GW ◇1	HX 1	HC	GW 1	HX 1	GW ◇1	GW 1	HX 1	HC	GW ◇1	GW 1
Oxford d								08 05				08 38										09 05
Reading 7 d				08 03			08 22	08 50			09 01	09 06			09 18		09 29	09 36			09 43	09 52
Twyford 3 d							08 28	08 56							09 24							09 58
Maidenhead 3 d							08 36	09 04							09 36			09 48				10 06
Taplow d																						
Burnham d							08 40								09 40							
Slough 3 a				08 22			08 45	09 11				09 25			09 45			09 57				10 13
d				08 23			08 46	09 12				09 25			09 45			09 58				10 14
Langley d							08 50	09 16							09 49							10 18
Iver d																						
West Drayton d							08 55	09 21							09 54							10 23
Heathrow Terminal 4 d		08 07												09 21						09 51		
Heathrow Terminals 1-2-3 2 d	08 08	08 13	08 23		08 38	08 53			09 06	09 19			09 33	09 27		09 48			10 03	09 57		
Hayes & Harlington d		08 19					09 02	09 25						09 33	09 59					10 03		10 27
Southall d		08 22					09 05	09 29						09 36	10 02					10 06		10 31
Hanwell d																						
Greenford d																						
South Greenford d																						
Castle Bar Park d																						
Drayton Green d																						
West Ealing d																						
Ealing Broadway d		08 27					09 11	09 34						09 41	10 08					10 11		10 36
Acton Main Line d																						
London Paddington 15 a	08 24	08 36	08 39	08 44	08 54	09 09	09 20	09 44	09 22	09 35	09 39	09 45	09 49	09 50	10 18	10 04	10 06	10 16	10 19	10 20	10 23	10 47

A until 4 September

Table 117

Reading and Greenford - London

Sundays until 05 September

	HX ■	GW ◇■ ☕	HX ■	HC	GW ◇■	GW ■	HX ■	GW ■	HX ■	HC	GW ◇■ ☕	GW ◇■ ☕	GW ■	HX ■	GW ◇■ A ☕	HX ■	HC	GW ◇■ B ☕	HX ■	GW ■	HX ■
Oxford d					09 38								10 05								
Reading d		10 01			10 10	10 18		10 26			10 44	10 49	19 52		11 02			11 09		11 18	
Twyford d						10 24							10 58							11 24	
Maidenhead d						10 36		10 40					11 06							11 36	
Taplow d																					
Burnham d						10 40														11 40	
Slough a					10 32	10 45		10 50					11 14							11 45	
d					10 32	10 45		10 51					11 15							11 45	
Langley d						10 47							11 19							11 47	
Iver d																					
West Drayton d						10 53							11 24							11 53	
Heathrow Terminal 4 ✈ d				10 21						10 51							11 21				
Heathrow Terminals 1-2-3 ✈ d	10 18		10 33	10 27			10 48		11 03	10 57				11 18		11 33	11 27		11 48		12 03
Hayes & Harlington d				10 33		10 59				11 03			11 28				11 33			11 59	
Southall d				10 36		11 02				11 06			11 32				11 36			12 02	
Hanwell d																					
Greenford ⊖ d																					
South Greenford d																					
Castle Bar Park d																					
Drayton Green d																					
West Ealing d																					
Ealing Broadway ⊖ d				10 41		11 08				11 11			11 37				11 41			12 08	
Acton Main Line d																					
London Paddington ⊖ a	10 34	10 39	10 49	10 50	10 53	11 18	11 04	11 10	11 19	11 20	11 21	11 24	11 47	11 34	11 38	11 49	11 50	11 51	12 04	12 18	12 19

	HC	GW ■	GW ◇■ ☕	GW ◇■ ☕	GW ■	HX ■	GW ◇■ A ☕	HX ■	HC	GW ◇■	HX ■	GW ■	HX ■	HC	GW ■	GW ◇■ ☕	GW ■	HX ■	GW ◇■ ☕	HX ■	HC	GW ■
Oxford d					11 05					11 38							12 05					
Reading d		11 38	11 44	11 49	11 52		12 02			12 10		12 18			12 36	12 44	12 52		13 02			13 18
Twyford d					11 58							12 24					12 58					13 24
Maidenhead d		11 50			12 06							12 36			12 49		13 06					13 36
Taplow d																						
Burnham d												12 40										13 40
Slough a		12 03			12 14					12 32		12 45			12 59		13 13					13 45
d		12 03			12 15					12 32		12 45			13 00		13 14					13 45
Langley d					12 19							12 49					13 18					13 49
Iver d																						
West Drayton d					12 24							12 54					13 23					13 54
Heathrow Terminal 4 ✈ d	11 51								12 21					12 51							13 21	
Heathrow Terminals 1-2-3 ✈ d	11 57					12 18		12 33	12 27		12 48		13 03	12 57				13 18		13 33	13 27	
Hayes & Harlington d	12 03				12 28				12 33			12 59		13 03			13 27				13 33	13 59
Southall d	12 06				12 32				12 36			13 02		13 06			13 31				13 36	14 02
Hanwell d																						
Greenford ⊖ d																						
South Greenford d																						
Castle Bar Park d																						
Drayton Green d																						
West Ealing d																						
Ealing Broadway ⊖ d	12 11				12 37				12 41			13 08		13 11			13 36				13 41	14 08
Acton Main Line d																						
London Paddington ⊖ a	12 20	12 22	12 24	12 29	12 47	12 34	12 38	12 49	12 50	12 51	13 04	13 18	13 19	13 20	13 23	13 24	13 47	13 34	13 38	13 49	13 50	14 18

	HX ■	GW ◇■ ☕	HX ■	HC	GW ■	GW ◇■ ☕	GW ◇■ ☕	GW ■	HX ■	GW ◇■ ☕	HX ■	HC	GW ◇■	HX ■	GW ■	HX ■	HC	GW ■	GW ◇■ ☕	GW ◇■ ☕	GW ■	HX ■
Oxford d								13 05					13 38								14 05	
Reading d		13 23			13 37	13 44	13 49	13 52		14 02			14 10		14 18			14 36	14 44	14 50	14 52	
Twyford d								13 58							14 24						14 58	
Maidenhead d					13 49			14 06							14 36			14 49			15 06	
Taplow d																						
Burnham d															14 40							
Slough a					14 00			14 14					14 30		14 45			14 59			15 14	
d					14 00			14 15					14 30		14 45			15 00			15 15	
Langley d								14 19							14 49						15 19	
Iver d																						
West Drayton d								14 24							14 54						15 24	
Heathrow Terminal 4 ✈ d				13 51								14 21					14 51					
Heathrow Terminals 1-2-3 ✈ d	13 48		14 03	13 57					14 18		14 33	14 27		14 48		15 03	14 57					15 18
Hayes & Harlington d				14 03				14 28				14 33			14 59		15 03				15 28	
Southall d				14 06				14 32				14 36			15 02		15 06				15 32	
Hanwell d																						
Greenford ⊖ d																						
South Greenford d																						
Castle Bar Park d																						
Drayton Green d																						
West Ealing d																						
Ealing Broadway ⊖ d				14 11				14 37				14 41			15 08		15 11				15 37	
Acton Main Line d																						
London Paddington ⊖ a	14 04	14 06	14 19	14 20	14 23	14 24	14 30	14 47	14 34	14 38	14 49	14 50	14 52	15 04	15 18	15 19	15 20	15 23	15 24	15 29	15 47	15 34

A from 18 July until 5 September
B until 11 July

Table 117

Reading and Greenford - London

Sundays until 05 September

	GW ◇■ ☕	HX ■	HC	GW ■	HX ■	GW ◇■ ☕	HX ■	HC	GW ■	GW ◇■ ☕	GW ◇■ ☕	GW ■	HX ■	GW ◇■ ☕	HX ■	HC	HX ■	GW ■	HX ■	HC	GW ■	GW ◇■ ☕
Oxford d												15 05										
Reading d	15 02			15 18		15 23			15 37	15 44	15 50	15 52		16 02				16 18			16 36	16 44
Twyford d				15 24								15 58						16 24				
Maidenhead d				15 36					15 49			16 06						16 36			16 49	
Taplow d																						
Burnham d				15 40								16 11						16 40				
Slough a				15 45					16 00			16 14						16 45			16 59	
d				15 45					16 00			16 15						16 45			17 00	
Langley d				15 49								16 20						16 49				
Iver d																						
West Drayton d				15 54								16 24						16 54				
Heathrow Terminal 4 ✈ d			15 21					15 51								16 21				16 51		
Heathrow Terminals 1-2-3 ✈ d		15 33	15 27		15 48		16 03	15 57					16 18		16 33	16 27	16 48		17 03	16 57		
Hayes & Harlington d			15 33	15 59				16 03				16 30				16 33		16 59		17 03		
Southall d			15 36	16 02				16 06				16 32				16 36		17 02		17 06		
Hanwell d																						
Greenford ⊖ d																						
South Greenford d																						
Castle Bar Park d																						
Drayton Green d																						
West Ealing d																						
Ealing Broadway ⊖ d			15 41	16 08				16 11				16 37				16 41		17 08		17 11		
Acton Main Line d																						
London Paddington ⊖ a	15 38	15 49	15 50	16 18	16 04	16 06	16 19	16 20	16 23	16 24	16 30	16 48	16 34	16 38	16 49	16 51	17 04	17 18	17 19	17 20	17 23	17 24

	GW ◇■ ☕	GW ■	HX ■	GW ◇■ ☕	HX ■	HC	GW ■	HX ■	GW ◇■ ☕	GW ■	HC	HX ■	GW ◇■ ☕	GW ◇■ ☕	GW ■	HX ■	GW ◇■ ☕	HX ■	GW ◇■ ☕	HC	HX ■	GW ■
Oxford d		16 05													17 05							
Reading d	16 49	16 52		17 02			17 18		17 21	17 36			17 44	17 49	17 52		18 02		18 14			18 18
Twyford d		16 58					17 24								17 58							18 24
Maidenhead d		17 06					17 36			17 49					18 06							18 36
Taplow d																						
Burnham d		17 11					17 40								18 11							18 40
Slough a		17 14					17 45			17 58					18 14							18 45
d		17 15					17 45			17 59					18 15							18 45
Langley d		17 21					17 49								18 21							18 49
Iver d																						
West Drayton d		17 24					17 54								18 24							18 54
Heathrow Terminal 4 ✈ d						17 21					17 51									18 21		
Heathrow Terminals 1-2-3 ✈ d			17 18		17 33	17 27		17 48			17 57	18 03				18 18		18 33		18 27	18 48	
Hayes & Harlington d		17 30				17 33	17 59				18 03				18 30					18 33		18 59
Southall d		17 32				17 36	18 02				18 06				18 32					18 36		19 02
Hanwell d																						
Greenford ⊖ d																						
South Greenford d																						
Castle Bar Park d																						
Drayton Green d																						
West Ealing d																						
Ealing Broadway ⊖ d		17 37				17 41	18 08				18 11				18 37					18 41		19 08
Acton Main Line d																						
London Paddington ⊖ a	17 29	17 48	17 34	17 38	17 49	17 50	18 18	18 04	18 06	18 18	18 20	18 20	18 24	18 29	18 48	18 34	18 38	18 49	18 51	18 51	19 04	19 18

	HX ■	HC	GW ■	GW ◇■ ☕	GW ◇■ ☕	GW ■	HX ■	GW ◇■ ☕	HX ■	HC	GW ◇■ ☕	GW ■	HX ■	GW ◇■ ☕	GW ■	GW ◇■ ☕	HX ■	HC	GW ◇■ ☕	GW ◇■ ☕
Oxford d						18 05														
Reading d			18 37	18 46	18 50	18 52		19 02			19 14	19 18		19 25	19 29	19 34			19 44	19 47
Twyford d						18 58						19 24								
Maidenhead d			18 51			19 06						19 36			19 42					
Taplow d																				
Burnham d						19 11						19 40								
Slough a			19 02			19 14						19 45			19 51					
d			19 02			19 15						19 45			19 59					
Langley d						19 20						19 49								
Iver d																				
West Drayton d						19 24						19 54								
Heathrow Terminal 4 ✈ d		18 51								19 21								19 51		
Heathrow Terminals 1-2-3 ✈ d	19 03	18 57					19 18		19 33	19 27			19 48				20 03	19 57		
Hayes & Harlington d		19 03				19 29				19 33		19 59						20 03		
Southall d		19 06				19 32				19 36		20 02						20 06		
Hanwell d																				
Greenford ⊖ d																				
South Greenford d																				
Castle Bar Park d																				
Drayton Green d																				
West Ealing d																				
Ealing Broadway ⊖ d		19 11				19 37				19 41		20 08						20 11		
Acton Main Line d																				
London Paddington ⊖ a	19 19	19 20	19 23	19 26	19 29	19 47	19 34	19 39	19 49	19 51	19 54	20 17	20 04	20 06	20 23	20 10	20 19	20 20	20 22	20 24

Table 117

Reading and Greenford - London

Sundays
until 05 September

		HX	GW	HX	HC	GW	GW	HX		GW	GW	HX	HC	GW	HX	GW	HX	HC		GW	GW	GW	GW	HX	GW
		1	1	1		◇1 ☕	1	1		◇1 ☕	◇1 ☕	1		◇1 ☕	1	1	1			◇1 ☕	◇1 ☕	◇1 🛒	◇1 ☕	1	◇1 A ☕
Oxford	d		19 05													20 05						20 50			
Reading 7	d		19 52			20 14	20 18			20 32	20 37			20 44		20 52				21 14	21 17	21 19	21 26		21 32
Twyford 3	d		19 58				20 24									20 57									
Maidenhead 3	d		20 06				20 36									21 05						21 34			
Taplow	d																								
Burnham	d		20 11				20 40									21 11									
Slough 3	a		20 14				20 45									21 14						21 42			
	d		20 15				20 45									21 15						21 42			
Langley	d		20 20				20 49									21 20									
Iver	d																								
West Drayton	d		20 24				20 54									21 24									
Heathrow Terminal 4 ✈	d				20 21								20 51					21 21							
Heathrow Terminals 1-2-3 2 ✈	d	20 18		20 33	20 27			20 48				21 03	20 57		21 18		21 33	21 27						21 53	
Hayes & Harlington	d		20 29		20 33		20 59						21 03			21 29		21 33							
Southall	d		20 32		20 36		21 02						21 06			21 32		21 36							
Hanwell	d																								
Greenford ⊖	d																								
South Greenford	d																								
Castle Bar Park	d																								
Drayton Green	d																								
West Ealing	d																								
Ealing Broadway ⊖	d		20 37		20 41		21 08						21 11			21 38		21 41							
Acton Main Line	d																								
London Paddington 15 ⊖	a	20 34	20 47	20 49	20 50	20 51	21 18	21 04		21 09	21 12	21 19	21 20	21 21	21 34	21 48	21 49	21 50		21 53	21 56	22 04	22 07	22 09	22 12

		HX	HC	GW		HX	HX	GW	GW	HX	GW	GW	HX	HC		GW	HX	GW	GW	GW	HX	HX	GW	GW	
		1		1		1	1	1	◇1 ☕	1	◇1	◇1 ☕	1			1	1	◇1 B ☕	◇1 A ☕	1	1	1	◇1 ☕	1	
Oxford	d							21 21			21 50									22 14					
Reading 7	d			21 40				22 10	22 19		22 24	22 30				22 40		22 56	22 57	23 00			23 29	23 35	
Twyford 3	d			21 46				22 16								22 46				23 07				23 41	
Maidenhead 3	d			21 54				22 24								22 54				23 15				23 49	
Taplow	d																								
Burnham	d			21 59				22 29								22 58								23 54	
Slough 3	a			22 03				22 34			22 47					23 03				23 22				23 58	
	d			22 08				22 34			22 48					23 03				23 22				23 59	
Langley	d			22 12				22 38								23 07				23 26				00 03	
Iver	d																								
West Drayton	d			22 17				22 43								23 12				23 31				00 08	
Heathrow Terminal 4 ✈	d		22 07											23 07											
Heathrow Terminals 1-2-3 2 ✈	d	22 08	22 13			22 23	22 38			22 53			23 08	23 13			23 23				23 38	23 53			
Hayes & Harlington	d		22 19	22 22				22 47						23 19		23 23				23 36				00 16	
Southall	d		22 22	22 26				22 51						23 22						23 39				00 20	
Hanwell	d																								
Greenford ⊖	d																								
South Greenford	d																								
Castle Bar Park	d																								
Drayton Green	d																								
West Ealing	d																								
Ealing Broadway ⊖	d		22 27	22 31				22 56						23 27		23 31				23 45				00 25	
Acton Main Line	d																								
London Paddington 15 ⊖	a	22 24	22 36	22 40		22 43	22 54	23 05	23 08	23 10	23 13	23 16	23 24	23 36		23 40	23 43	23 46	23 46	23 54	23 56	00 09	00 13	00 38	

		GW
		1
Oxford	d	
Reading 7	d	23 56
Twyford 3	d	
Maidenhead 3	d	
Taplow	d	
Burnham	d	
Slough 3	a	00 14
	d	00 14
Langley	d	
Iver	d	
West Drayton	d	
Heathrow Terminal 4 ✈	d	
Heathrow Terminals 1-2-3 2 ✈	d	
Hayes & Harlington	d	
Southall	d	
Hanwell	d	
Greenford ⊖	d	
South Greenford	d	
Castle Bar Park	d	
Drayton Green	d	
West Ealing	d	
Ealing Broadway ⊖	d	
Acton Main Line	d	
London Paddington 15 ⊖	a	00 42

A until 11 July
B from 18 July until 5 September

Table 117

Reading and Greenford - London

Sundays
from 12 September

		HX	GW	HX	HC	GW	GW	HX	HX	HX		HX	HX	HC	HX	HX	HX	GW	HX	HC		HX	HX	HX	GW
		1	1			◇1 ☕	1	1	1	1		1	1		1	1	1	1	1			1	1	1	1
Oxford	d						23p07																		
Reading 7	d		23p18			23p53	00 03											06 22							07 22
Twyford 3	d		23p24				00 09											06 28							07 28
Maidenhead 3	d		23p32				00 17											06 36							07 36
Taplow	d		23p36				00 21																		
Burnham	d		23p39				00 24											06 40							07 40
Slough 3	a		23p44				00 28											06 45							07 45
	d		23p44				00 29											06 46							07 46
Langley	d						00 33											06 50							07 50
Iver	d						00 36																		
West Drayton	d		23p51				00 39											06 55							07 55
Heathrow Terminal 4 ✈	d				00 01									06 07						07 07					
Heathrow Terminals 1-2-3 2 ✈	d	23p48		23p57	00 07			05 08	05 23	05 38		05 53	06 08	06 13	06 23	06 38	06 53		07 08	07 13		07 23	07 38	07 53	
Hayes & Harlington	d		23p56		00 13		00 44							06 19				07 02		07 19					08 02
Southall	d				00 16		00 47							06 22				07 05		07 22					08 05
Hanwell	d																								
Greenford ⊖	d																								
South Greenford	d																								
Castle Bar Park	d																								
Drayton Green	d																								
West Ealing	d																								
Ealing Broadway ⊖	d		00 03		00 21		00 53							06 27				07 11		07 27					08 11
Acton Main Line	d																								
London Paddington 15 ⊖	a	00 04	00 16	00 19	00 30	00 33	01 02	05 24	05 39	05 54		06 09	06 24	06 36	06 39	06 54	07 09	07 20	07 24	07 36		07 39	07 54	08 09	08 20

		HX	HC	HX	GW	HX		HX	GW	HX	HC	GW	GW	GW	HX	HX		GW	HX	GW	HX	HC	GW	GW	GW
		1		1	1	1		1	1	1		1	◇1 ☕	1	1	1		◇1	1	◇1 ☕	1		1	◇1 ☕	1
Oxford	d																						09 01		
Reading 7	d				08 03				08 22			08 50	09 03	09 18				09 19		09 44			09 52	10 01	10 18
Twyford 3	d								08 28			08 56		09 24									09 58		10 24
Maidenhead 3	d								08 36			09 04		09 36									10 06		10 36
Taplow	d																								
Burnham	d								08 40					09 40											10 40
Slough 3	a				08 22				08 45			09 11		09 46				09 35					10 14		10 45
	d				08 23				08 46			09 18		09 46				09 37					10 18		10 48
Langley	d								08 50			09 22		09 50									10 22		10 50
Iver	d																								
West Drayton	d								08 55			09 27		09 55									10 27		10 56
Heathrow Terminal 4 ✈	d		08 07								09 07											10 07			
Heathrow Terminals 1-2-3 2 ✈	d	08 08	08 13	08 23		08 38		08 53		09 08	09 13				09 23	09 38			09 53		10 08	10 13			
Hayes & Harlington	d		08 19						09 02		09 19	09 32		10 02								10 19	10 32		11 01
Southall	d		08 22						09 05		09 22	09 35										10 22	10 35		
Hanwell	d																								
Greenford ⊖	d																								
South Greenford	d																								
Castle Bar Park	d																								
Drayton Green	d																								
West Ealing	d																								
Ealing Broadway ⊖	d		08 27						09 11		09 27	09 41		10 09								10 27	10 41		11 08
Acton Main Line	d																								
London Paddington 15 ⊖	a	08 24	08 36	08 39	08 44	08 54		09 09	09 20	09 24	09 36	09 50	09 39	10 18	09 41	09 54		09 58	10 09	10 19	10 24	10 36	10 50	10 39	11 18

		HX		HX	GW	HX	GW	HX	GW	HC	GW	GW		HX	HX	HX	GW	GW	HX	GW	HC	GW		GW	GW
		1		1	◇1	1	◇1 ☕	1	◇1 ☕		1	◇1 ☕		1	1	1	1	◇1 ☕	1	◇1 ☕		1		◇1 ☕	1
Oxford	d				09 50						10 05											11 05			
Reading 7	d				10 20		10 44		10 49		10 52	11 02					11 18	11 44		11 49		11 52		12 02	12 18
Twyford 3	d										10 58						11 24					11 58			12 24
Maidenhead 3	d										11 06						11 36					12 06			12 36
Taplow	d																								
Burnham	d																11 40								12 40
Slough 3	a				10 35						11 14						11 45					12 14			12 45
	d				10 35						11 18						11 48					12 18			12 48
Langley	d										11 22						11 52					12 22			12 52
Iver	d																								
West Drayton	d										11 27						11 56					12 27			12 56
Heathrow Terminal 4 ✈	d									11 07											12 07				
Heathrow Terminals 1-2-3 2 ✈	d	10 23		10 38		10 53		11 08		11 13				11 23	11 38	11 53			12 08		12 13				
Hayes & Harlington	d									11 19	11 32						12 01				12 19	12 32			13 01
Southall	d									11 22	11 35										12 22	12 35			
Hanwell	d																								
Greenford ⊖	d																								
South Greenford	d																								
Castle Bar Park	d																								
Drayton Green	d																								
West Ealing	d																								
Ealing Broadway ⊖	d									11 27	11 41						12 08				12 27	12 41			13 08
Acton Main Line	d																								
London Paddington 15 ⊖	a	10 41		10 54	10 58	11 09	11 21	11 24	11 29	11 36	11 50	11 39		11 41	11 54	12 09	12 18	12 21	12 24	12 29	12 36	12 50		12 39	13 18

Table 117

Reading and Greenford - London

Sundays from 12 September

	HX 1	HX 1	GW ◇1	HX 1	GW ◇1 ☕	HX 1	HC		GW 1	GW ◇1 ☕	HX 1	HX 1	HX 1	GW 1	GW ◇1 ☕	HX 1	GW ◇1 ☕		HC	GW 1	GW ◇1 ☕	GW 1	HX 1	HX 1
Oxford d			11 50						12 05											13 05				
Reading 7 d			12 19		12 44				12 52	13 02				13 18	13 44		13 51			13 52	14 02	14 18		
Twyford 3 d									12 58					13 24						13 58		14 24		
Maidenhead 3 d									13 06					13 36						14 06		14 36		
Taplow d																								
Burnham d														13 40								14 40		
Slough 3 a			12 33						13 14					13 45						14 14		14 45		
d			12 34						13 18					13 48						14 18		14 48		
Langley d									13 22					13 52						14 22		14 52		
Iver d																								
West Drayton d									13 27					13 56						14 27		14 56		
Heathrow Terminal 4 ✈ d							13 07												14 07					
Heathrow Terminals 1-2-3 2 ✈ d	12 23	12 38		12 53		13 08	13 13				13 23	13 38	13 53			14 08			14 13				14 23	14 38
Hayes & Harlington d							13 19		13 32					14 01					14 19	14 32		15 01		
Southall d							13 22		13 35										14 22	14 35				
Hanwell d																								
Greenford ⊖ d																								
South Greenford d																								
Castle Bar Park d																								
Drayton Green d																								
West Ealing d																								
Ealing Broadway ⊖ d							13 27		13 41					14 08					14 27	14 41		15 08		
Acton Main Line d																								
London Paddington 15 ⊖ a	12 41	12 54	12 59	13 09	13 21	13 24	13 36		13 50	13 39	13 41	13 54	14 09	14 19	14 21	14 24	14 29		14 36	14 50	14 39	15 18	14 41	14 54

	GW ◇1	HX 1	GW ◇1 ☕		HX 1	GW ◇1 ☕	HC	GW 1	GW ◇1 ☕	HX 1	HX 1	HX 1	GW 1		GW ◇1 ☕	HX 1	GW ◇1 ☕	HC	GW 1	GW ◇1 ☕	HX 1	HX 1	HX 1	
Oxford d	13 50							14 05											15 05					
Reading 7 d	14 19		14 44			14 50		14 52	15 02				15 18		15 44		15 50		15 52	16 02				
Twyford 3 d								14 58					15 24						15 58					
Maidenhead 3 d								15 06					15 36						16 06					
Taplow d																								
Burnham d													15 40						16 11					
Slough 3 a	14 35							15 14					15 45						16 14					
d	14 36							15 18					15 48						16 18					
Langley d								15 22					15 52						16 22					
Iver d																								
West Drayton d								15 27					15 56						16 27					
Heathrow Terminal 4 ✈ d							15 07											16 07						
Heathrow Terminals 1-2-3 2 ✈ d		14 53			15 08		15 13			15 23	15 38	15 53				16 08		16 13			16 23	16 38	16 53	
Hayes & Harlington d							15 19	15 32					16 02					16 19	16 32					
Southall d							15 22	15 35										16 22	16 35					
Hanwell d																								
Greenford ⊖ d																								
South Greenford d																								
Castle Bar Park d																								
Drayton Green d																								
West Ealing d																								
Ealing Broadway ⊖ d							15 27	15 41					16 08					16 27	16 41					
Acton Main Line d																								
London Paddington 15 ⊖ a	14 58	15 09	15 21		15 24	15 29	15 36	15 50	15 39	15 41	15 54	16 09	16 18		16 21	16 24	16 29	16 36	16 50	16 39	16 41	16 54	17 09	

	GW 1	GW ◇1 ☕	HX 1	GW ◇1 ☕	HC	GW 1	GW ◇1 ☕	GW 1	HX 1		HX 1	GW ◇1 ☕	HX 1	GW ◇1 ☕	HX 1	GW ◇1 ☕	HC	GW 1	GW ◇1 ☕		HX 1	HX 1	GW ◇1 ☕	HX 1
Oxford d						16 05												17 05						
Reading 7 d	16 18	16 44		16 49		16 52	17 02	17 18				17 21		17 44		17 49		17 52	18 02				18 14	
Twyford 3 d	16 24					16 58		17 24										17 58						
Maidenhead 3 d	16 36					17 06		17 36										18 06						
Taplow d																								
Burnham d	16 40					17 11		17 40										18 11						
Slough 3 a	16 45					17 14		17 45										18 14						
d	16 48					17 18		17 48										18 18						
Langley d	16 52					17 22		17 52										18 22						
Iver d																								
West Drayton d	16 56					17 28		17 56										18 27						
Heathrow Terminal 4 ✈ d					17 07												18 07							
Heathrow Terminals 1-2-3 2 ✈ d			17 08		17 13				17 23		17 38		17 53		18 08		18 13				18 23	18 38		18 53
Hayes & Harlington d	17 01				17 19	17 32		18 01									18 19	18 32						
Southall d					17 22	17 36											18 22	18 35						
Hanwell d																								
Greenford ⊖ d																								
South Greenford d																								
Castle Bar Park d																								
Drayton Green d																								
West Ealing d																								
Ealing Broadway ⊖ d	17 08				17 27	17 41		18 08									18 27	18 41						
Acton Main Line d																								
London Paddington 15 ⊖ a	17 19	17 22	17 24	17 29	17 36	17 50	17 39	18 18	17 41		17 54	17 59	18 09	18 21	18 24	18 29	18 36	18 50	18 39		18 41	18 54	18 59	19 09

Table 117

Reading and Greenford - London

Sundays from 12 September

	GW 1	GW ◇1 ☕	HX 1	HC	GW 1		GW ◇1 ☕	GW ◇1 ☕	HX 1	HX 1	GW ◇1 ☕	GW 1	GW ◇1 ☕	GW ◇1 ☕	HX 1		GW ◇1 ☕	HX 1	GW ◇1 ☕	HC	HX 1	GW 1	HX 1	GW ◇1 ☕
Oxford d					18 05																	19 05		
Reading 7 d	18 18	18 46			18 52		18 53	19 03			19 14	19 18	19 23	19 34			19 44		19 49			19 52		20 14
Twyford 3 d	18 24				18 58							19 24										19 58		
Maidenhead 3 d	18 36				19 06							19 36										20 06		
Taplow d																								
Burnham d	18 40				19 11							19 40										20 11		
Slough 3 a	18 45				19 15							19 45										20 14		
d	18 48				19 18							19 48										20 18		
Langley d	18 52				19 22							19 52										20 22		
Iver d																								
West Drayton d	18 56				19 27							19 56										20 27		
Heathrow Terminal 4 ✈ d				19 07																20 07				
Heathrow Terminals 1-2-3 2 ✈ d			19 08	19 13					19 23	19 38					19 53			20 08		20 13	20 23		20 38	
Hayes & Harlington d	19 01			19 19	19 32							20 01								20 19		20 32		
Southall d				19 22	19 35															20 22		20 35		
Hanwell d																								
Greenford ⊖ d																								
South Greenford d																								
Castle Bar Park d																								
Drayton Green d																								
West Ealing d																								
Ealing Broadway ⊖ d	19 08			19 27	19 41							20 08								20 27		20 41		
Acton Main Line d																								
London Paddington 15 ⊖ a	19 18	19 21	19 24	19 36	19 51		19 29	19 39	19 41	19 54	19 59	20 18	20 06	20 09	20 11		20 21	20 24	20 29	20 36	20 39	20 51	20 54	20 59

	GW 1		GW ◇1 ☕	HX 1	GW ◇1 ☕	HX 1	GW ◇1 ☕	HC	HX 1	GW 1	HX 1	GW ◇1 ☕		GW ◇1 ☕	GW ◇1 🛒	GW 1	GW ◇1 ☕	HX 1	HX 1	GW ◇1 ☕	HC	HX 1	HX 1	GW 1
Oxford d										20 05					20 50									21 21
Reading 7 d	20 18		20 32		20 44		20 47			20 52		21 14		21 17	21 19	21 24	21 32			21 47				22 10
Twyford 3 d	20 24									20 58						21 30								22 16
Maidenhead 3 d	20 36									21 06					21 33	21 38								22 24
Taplow d																								
Burnham d	20 40									21 11						21 43								22 29
Slough 3 a	20 45									21 14					21 39	21 48								22 34
d	20 48									21 19					21 39	21 48								22 34
Langley d	20 52									21 23						21 52								22 38
Iver d																								
West Drayton d	20 56									21 28						21 56								22 43
Heathrow Terminal 4 ✈ d								21 07													22 07			
Heathrow Terminals 1-2-3 2 ✈ d				20 53		21 08		21 13	21 23		21 38							21 53	22 08		22 13	22 23	22 38	
Hayes & Harlington d	21 01							21 19		21 32						22 01					22 19			22 47
Southall d								21 22		21 36						22 05					22 22			22 51
Hanwell d																								
Greenford ⊖ d																								
South Greenford d																								
Castle Bar Park d																								
Drayton Green d																								
West Ealing d																								
Ealing Broadway ⊖ d	21 08							21 27		21 41						22 11					22 27			22 56
Acton Main Line d																								
London Paddington 15 ⊖ a	21 18		21 09	21 12	21 21	21 24	21 27	21 36	21 39	21 51	21 54	21 59		22 02	22 05	22 20	22 09	22 11	22 24	22 29	22 36	22 39	22 54	23 05

	GW ◇1 ☕	HX 1	GW ◇1	GW ◇1 ☕	GW ◇1 ☕	HX 1	HC		GW 1	HX 1	GW 1	HX 1	HX 1	GW ◇1 ☕	GW 1	GW 1
Oxford d			21 50								22 21					
Reading 7 d	22 19		22 24	22 30	22 39				22 43		23 00			23 29	23 35	23 56
Twyford 3 d									22 49		23 07				23 41	
Maidenhead 3 d									22 57		23 15				23 49	
Taplow d																
Burnham d									23 01						23 54	
Slough 3 a			22 47						23 06		23 22				23 58	00 14
d			22 48						23 06		23 22				23 59	00 14
Langley d									23 10		23 26				00 03	
Iver d																
West Drayton d									23 15		23 31				00 08	
Heathrow Terminal 4 ✈ d							23 07									
Heathrow Terminals 1-2-3 2 ✈ d		22 53				23 08	23 13			23 23		23 38	23 53			
Hayes & Harlington d							23 19		23 23		23 36				00 16	
Southall d							23 22				23 39				00 20	
Hanwell d																
Greenford ⊖ d																
South Greenford d																
Castle Bar Park d																
Drayton Green d																
West Ealing d																
Ealing Broadway ⊖ d							23 27		23 31		23 45				00 25	
Acton Main Line d																
London Paddington 15 ⊖ a	23 08	23 10	23 13	23 16	23 20	23 24	23 36		23 40	23 43	23 54	23 56	00 09	00 13	00 34	00 38

Table 118

Mondays to Fridays

London - Heathrow Airport

	HC	HC	HX 1	HC	HX 1	HC	HX 1	HC	HX 1		HC	HX 1	HC	HX 1	HC	HX 1	HC	HX 1	HC		HX 1	HC	HX 1	HC
London Paddington ⊖ d	04 42		05 10	05 13	05 25		05 40		05 55			06 10		06 25		06 40		06 55			07 10		07 25	
Heathrow Terminals 1-2-3 ✈ a	05 04		05 26	05 35	05 40		05 55		06 10			06 25		06 40		06 55		07 10			07 25		07 40	
d	05 05	05 16	05 29	05 36	05 41	05 44	05 56	06 03	06 11		06 18	06 26	06 33	06 41	06 48	06 56	07 03	07 11	07 18		07 26	07 33	07 41	07 48
Heathrow Terminal 4 ✈ a	05 10	05 20		05 41		05 48		06 07			06 22		06 37		06 52		07 07		07 22			07 37		07 52
Heathrow Terminal 5 ✈ a			05 33		05 46		06 01		06 16			06 31		06 46		07 01		07 16			07 31		07 46	

	HX 1	HC	HX 1	HC	HX 1		HC	HX 1	HC	HX 1	HC	HX 1	HC	HX 1	HC		HX 1	HC	HX 1	HC	HX 1	HC	HX 1	HC
London Paddington ⊖ d	07 40		07 55		08 10			08 25		08 40		08 55		09 10			09 25		09 40		09 55		10 10	
Heathrow Terminals 1-2-3 ✈ a	07 55		08 10		08 25			08 40		08 55		09 10		09 25			09 40		09 55		10 10		10 25	
d	07 56	08 03	08 11	08 18	08 26		08 33	08 41	08 48	08 56	09 03	09 11	09 18	09 26	09 33		09 41	09 48	09 56	10 03	10 11	10 18	10 26	10 33
Heathrow Terminal 4 ✈ a		08 07		08 22			08 37		08 52		09 07		09 22		09 37			09 52		10 07		10 22		10 37
Heathrow Terminal 5 ✈ a	08 01		08 16		08 31			08 46		09 01		09 16		09 31			09 46		10 01		10 16		10 31	

	HX 1		HC	HX 1	HC	HX 1	HC	HX 1	HC	HX 1	HC		HX 1	HC	HX 1	HC	HX 1	HC	HX 1	HC	HX 1		HC	HX 1
London Paddington ⊖ d	10 25			10 40		10 55		11 10		11 25			11 40		11 55		12 10		12 25		12 40			12 55
Heathrow Terminals 1-2-3 ✈ a	10 40			10 55		11 10		11 25		11 40			11 55		12 10		12 25		12 40		12 55			13 10
d	10 41		10 48	10 56	11 03	11 11	11 18	11 26	11 33	11 41	11 48		11 56	12 03	12 11	12 18	12 26	12 33	12 41	12 48	12 56		13 03	13 11
Heathrow Terminal 4 ✈ a			10 52		11 07		11 22		11 37		11 52			12 07		12 22		12 37		12 52			13 07	
Heathrow Terminal 5 ✈ a	10 46			11 01		11 16		11 31		11 46			12 01		12 16		12 31		12 46		13 01			13 16

	HC	HX 1	HC	HX 1	HC	HX 1	HC		HX 1	HC	HX 1	HC	HX 1	HC	HX 1	HC	HX 1		HC	HX 1	HC	HX 1	HC	HX 1
London Paddington ⊖ d		13 10		13 25		13 40			13 55		14 10		14 25		14 40		14 55			15 10		15 25		15 40
Heathrow Terminals 1-2-3 ✈ a		13 25		13 40		13 55			14 10		14 25		14 40		14 55		15 10			15 25		15 40		15 55
d	13 18	13 26	13 33	13 41	13 48	13 56	14 03		14 11	14 18	14 26	14 33	14 41	14 48	14 56	15 03	15 11		15 18	15 26	15 33	15 41	15 48	15 56
Heathrow Terminal 4 ✈ a	13 22		13 37		13 52		14 07			14 22		14 37		14 52		15 07			15 22		15 37		15 52	
Heathrow Terminal 5 ✈ a		13 31		13 46		14 01			14 16		14 31		14 46		15 01		15 16			15 31		15 46		16 01

	HC	HX 1	HC		HX 1	HC	HX 1	HC	HX 1	HC	HX 1	HC	HX 1		HC	HX 1	HC	HX 1	HC	HX 1	HC	HX 1	HC	
London Paddington ⊖ d		15 55			16 10		16 25		16 40		16 55		17 10			17 25		17 40		17 55		18 10		
Heathrow Terminals 1-2-3 ✈ a		16 10			16 25		16 40		16 55		17 10		17 25			17 40		17 55		18 10		18 25		
d	16 03	16 11	16 18		16 26	16 33	16 41	16 48	16 56	17 03	17 11	17 18	17 26		17 33	17 41	17 48	17 56	18 03	18 11	18 18	18 26	18 33	
Heathrow Terminal 4 ✈ a	16 07		16 22			16 37		16 52		17 07		17 22			17 37		17 52		18 07		18 22		18 37	
Heathrow Terminal 5 ✈ a		16 16			16 31		16 46		17 01		17 16		17 31			17 46		18 01		18 16		18 31		

	HX 1	HC	HX 1	HC	HX 1	HC	HX 1	HC	HX 1		HC	HX 1	HC	HX 1	HC	HX 1	HC	HX 1	HC		HX 1	HC	HX 1	HC
London Paddington ⊖ d	18 25		18 40		18 55		19 10		19 25			19 40		19 55		20 10		20 25			20 40		20 55	
Heathrow Terminals 1-2-3 ✈ a	18 40		18 55		19 10		19 25		19 40			19 55		20 10		20 25		20 40			20 55		21 10	
d	18 41	18 48	18 56	19 03	19 11	19 18	19 26	19 33	19 41		19 48	19 56	20 03	20 11	20 18	20 26	20 33	20 41	20 48		20 56	21 03	21 11	21 18
Heathrow Terminal 4 ✈ a		18 52		19 07		19 22		19 37			19 52		20 07		20 22		20 37		20 52			21 07		21 22
Heathrow Terminal 5 ✈ a	18 46		19 01		19 16		19 31		19 46			20 01		20 16		20 31		20 46			21 01		21 16	

	HX 1	HC	HX 1	HC	HX 1		HC	HX 1	HC	HX 1	HC	HX 1	HC	HX 1	HC		HX 1	HC	HX 1	HC	HC	HX 1	HC	
London Paddington ⊖ d	21 10		21 25		21 40			21 55		22 10		22 25		22 40			22 55		23 10		23 03	23 25		
Heathrow Terminals 1-2-3 ✈ a	21 25		21 40		21 55			22 10		22 25		22 40		22 55			23 10		23 25		23 35	23 40		
d	21 26	21 33	21 41	21 48	21 56		22 03	22 11	22 18	22 26	22 33	22 41	22 48	22 56	23 03		23 11	23 18	23 26	23 33	23 37	23 41	23 48	
Heathrow Terminal 4 ✈ a		21 37		21 52			22 07		22 22		22 37		22 52		23 07			23 22		23 37	23 41		23 52	
Heathrow Terminal 5 ✈ a	21 31		21 46		22 01			22 16		22 31		22 46		23 01			23 16		23 31			23 46		

Saturdays

	HC	HC	HX 1	HC	HX 1	HC	HX 1	HC	HX 1		HC	HX 1	HC	HX 1	HC	HX 1	HC	HX 1	HC		HX 1	HC	HX 1	HC
London Paddington ⊖ d	04 42		05 10	05 13	05 25		05 40		05 55			06 10		06 25		06 40		06 55			07 10		07 25	
Heathrow Terminals 1-2-3 ✈ a	05 04		05 26	05 35	05 40		05 55		06 10			06 25		06 40		06 55		07 10			07 25		07 40	
d	05 05	05 16	05 29	05 36	05 41	05 44	05 56	06 03	06 11		06 18	06 26	06 33	06 41	06 48	06 56	07 03	07 11	07 18		07 26	07 33	07 41	07 48
Heathrow Terminal 4 ✈ a	05 10	05 20		05 41		05 48		06 07			06 22		06 37		06 52		07 07		07 22			07 37		07 52
Heathrow Terminal 5 ✈ a			05 33		05 46		06 01		06 16			06 31		06 46		07 01		07 16			07 31		07 46	

	HX 1	HC	HX 1	HC	HX 1		HC	HX 1	HC	HX 1	HC	HX 1	HC	HX 1	HC		HX 1	HC	HX 1	HC	HX 1	HC	HX 1	HC
London Paddington ⊖ d	07 40		07 55		08 10			08 25		08 40		08 55		09 10			09 25		09 40		09 55		10 10	
Heathrow Terminals 1-2-3 ✈ a	07 55		08 10		08 25			08 40		08 55		09 10		09 25			09 40		09 55		10 10		10 25	
d	07 56	08 03	08 11	08 18	08 26		08 33	08 41	08 48	08 56	09 03	09 11	09 18	09 26	09 33		09 41	09 48	09 56	10 03	10 11	10 18	10 26	10 33
Heathrow Terminal 4 ✈ a		08 07		08 22			08 37		08 52		09 07		09 22		09 37			09 52		10 07		10 22		10 37
Heathrow Terminal 5 ✈ a	08 01		08 16		08 31			08 46		09 01		09 16		09 31			09 46		10 01		10 16		10 31	

	HX 1		HC	HX 1	HC	HX 1	HC	HX 1	HC	HX 1	HC		HX 1	HC	HX 1	HC	HX 1	HC	HX 1	HC	HX 1		HC	HX 1
London Paddington ⊖ d	10 25			10 40		10 55		11 10		11 25			11 40		11 55		12 10		12 25		12 40			12 55
Heathrow Terminals 1-2-3 ✈ a	10 40			10 55		11 10		11 25		11 40			11 55		12 10		12 25		12 40		12 55			13 10
d	10 41		10 48	10 56	11 03	11 11	11 18	11 26	11 33	11 41	11 48		11 56	12 03	12 11	12 18	12 26	12 33	12 41	12 48	12 56		13 03	13 11
Heathrow Terminal 4 ✈ a			10 52		11 07		11 22		11 37		11 52			12 07		12 22		12 37		12 52			13 07	
Heathrow Terminal 5 ✈ a	10 46			11 01		11 16		11 31		11 46			12 01		12 16		12 31		12 46		13 01			13 16

Table 118

Saturdays

London - Heathrow Airport

	HC	HX 1	HC	HX 1	HC	HX 1	HC		HX 1	HC	HX 1	HC	HX 1	HC	HX 1	HC	HX 1		HC	HX 1	HC	HX 1	HC	HX 1
London Paddington ⊖ d		13 10		13 25		13 40			13 55		14 10		14 25		14 40		14 55			15 10		15 25		15 40
Heathrow Terminals 1-2-3 ✈ a		13 25		13 40		13 55			14 10		14 25		14 40		14 55		15 10			15 25		15 40		15 55
d	13 18	13 26	13 33	13 41	13 48	13 56	14 03		14 11	14 18	14 26	14 33	14 41	14 48	14 56	15 03	15 11		15 18	15 26	15 33	15 41	15 48	15 56
Heathrow Terminal 4 ✈ a	13 22		13 37		13 52		14 07			14 22		14 37		14 52		15 07			15 22		15 37		15 52	
Heathrow Terminal 5 ✈ a		13 31		13 46		14 01			14 16		14 31		14 46		15 01		15 16			15 31		15 46		16 01

	HC	HX 1	HC		HX 1	HC	HX 1	HC	HX 1	HC	HX 1	HC	HX 1		HC	HX 1	HC	HX 1	HC	HX 1	HC	HX 1	HC	
London Paddington ⊖ d		15 55			16 10		16 25		16 40		16 55		17 10			17 25		17 40		17 55		18 10		
Heathrow Terminals 1-2-3 ✈ a		16 10			16 25		16 40		16 55		17 10		17 25			17 40		17 55		18 10		18 25		
d	16 03	16 11	16 18		16 26	16 33	16 41	16 48	16 56	17 03	17 11	17 18	17 26		17 33	17 41	17 48	17 56	18 03	18 11	18 18	18 26	18 33	
Heathrow Terminal 4 ✈ a	16 07		16 22			16 37		16 52		17 07		17 22			17 37		17 52		18 07		18 22		18 37	
Heathrow Terminal 5 ✈ a		16 16			16 31		16 46		17 01		17 16		17 31			17 46		18 01		18 16		18 31		

	HX 1	HC	HX 1	HC	HX 1	HC	HX 1	HC	HX 1		HC	HX 1	HC	HX 1	HC	HX 1	HC	HX 1	HC		HX 1	HC	HX 1	HC
London Paddington ⊖ d	18 25		18 40		18 55		19 10		19 25			19 40		19 55		20 10		20 25			20 40		20 55	
Heathrow Terminals 1-2-3 ✈ a	18 40		18 55		19 10		19 25		19 40			19 55		20 10		20 25		20 40			20 55		21 10	
d	18 41	18 48	18 56	19 03	19 11	19 18	19 26	19 33	19 41		19 48	19 56	20 03	20 11	20 18	20 26	20 33	20 41	20 48		20 56	21 03	21 11	21 18
Heathrow Terminal 4 ✈ a		18 52		19 07		19 22		19 37			19 52		20 07		20 22		20 37		20 52			21 07		21 22
Heathrow Terminal 5 ✈ a	18 46		19 01		19 16		19 31		19 46			20 01		20 16		20 31		20 46			21 01		21 16	

	HX 1	HC	HX 1	HC	HX 1		HC	HX 1	HC	HX 1	HC	HX 1	HC	HX 1	HC		HX 1	HC	HX 1	HC	HC	HX 1	HC	
London Paddington ⊖ d	21 10		21 25		21 40			21 55		22 10		22 25		22 40			22 55		23 10		23 03	23 25		
Heathrow Terminals 1-2-3 ✈ a	21 25		21 40		21 55			22 10		22 25		22 40		22 55			23 10		23 25		23 35	23 40		
d	21 26	21 33	21 41	21 48	21 56		22 03	22 11	22 18	22 26	22 33	22 41	22 48	22 56	23 03		23 11	23 18	23 26	23 33	23 37	23 41	23 48	
Heathrow Terminal 4 ✈ a		21 37		21 52			22 07		22 22		22 37		22 52		23 07			23 22		23 37	23 41		23 52	
Heathrow Terminal 5 ✈ a	21 31		21 46		22 01			22 16		22 31		22 46		23 01			23 16		23 31			23 46		

Sundays

until 05 September

	HX 1	HX 1	HC	HX 1	HC	HX 1	HC	HX 1	HC	HC	HX 1	HC	HX 1	HC	HX 1	HC	HX 1	HC	HC		HX 1	HC	HX 1	HC
London Paddington ⊖ d	05 10	05 25		05 40		05 55		06 10		06 12	06 25		06 40		06 55		07 10		07 12		07 25		07 40	
Heathrow Terminals 1-2-3 ✈ a	05 26	05 41		05 56		06 11		06 26		06 34	06 41		06 56		07 11		07 26		07 34		07 41		07 56	
d	05 27	05 42	05 47	05 59	06 01	06 13	06 19	06 31	06 33	06 37	06 47	06 49	06 59	07 01	07 13	07 19	07 31	07 33	07 37		07 47	07 49	07 59	08 01
Heathrow Terminal 4 ✈ a			05 51		06 05		06 23		06 37	06 41		06 53		07 05		07 23		07 37	07 41			07 53		08 05
Heathrow Terminal 5 ✈ a	05 32	05 47		06 03		06 17		06 35			06 51		07 03		07 17		07 35				07 51		08 03	

	HX 1	HC	HX 1	HC	HC		HX 1	HC	HX 1	HC	HX 1	HC	HX 1	HC	HX 1		HC	HX 1	HC	HX 1	HC	HX 1	HC	HX 1
London Paddington ⊖ d	07 55		08 10		08 12		08 25		08 40		08 55		09 10	09 07	09 25			09 40	09 37	09 55		10 10	10 07	10 25
Heathrow Terminals 1-2-3 ✈ a	08 11		08 26		08 34		08 41		08 56		09 11		09 25	09 29	09 40			09 55	09 59	10 10		10 25	10 29	10 40
d	08 13	08 19	08 31	08 33	08 37		08 47	08 49	08 59	09 01	09 13	09 15	09 26	09 35	09 41		09 44	09 56	10 05	10 11	10 14	10 26	10 35	10 41
Heathrow Terminal 4 ✈ a		08 23		08 37	08 41			08 53		09 05		09 19		09 39			09 48		10 09		10 18		10 39	
Heathrow Terminal 5 ✈ a	08 17		08 35				08 51		09 03		09 17		09 31		09 46			10 01		10 16		10 31		10 46

	HC		HX 1	HC	HX 1	HC	HX 1	HC	HX 1	HC	HX 1		HC	HX 1	HC	HX 1	HC	HX 1	HC	HX 1	HC		HX 1	HC
London Paddington ⊖ d			10 40	10 37	10 55		11 10	11 07	11 25		11 40		11 37	11 55		12 10	12 07	12 25		12 40	12 37		12 55	
Heathrow Terminals 1-2-3 ✈ a			10 55	10 59	11 10		11 25	11 29	11 40		11 55		11 59	12 10		12 25	12 29	12 40		12 55	12 59		13 10	
d	10 44		10 56	11 05	11 11	11 14	11 26	11 35	11 41	11 44	11 56		12 05	12 11	12 14	12 26	12 35	12 41	12 44	12 56	13 05		13 11	13 14
Heathrow Terminal 4 ✈ a	10 48			11 09		11 18		11 39		11 48			12 09		12 18		12 39		12 48		13 09			13 18
Heathrow Terminal 5 ✈ a			11 01		11 16		11 31		11 46		12 01			12 16		12 31		12 46		13 01			13 16	

	HX 1	HC	HX 1	HC	HX 1	HC	HX 1		HC	HX 1	HC	HX 1	HC	HX 1	HC	HX 1	HC		HX 1	HC	HX 1	HC	HX 1	HC
London Paddington ⊖ d	13 10	13 07	13 25		13 40	13 37	13 55			14 10	14 07	14 25		14 40	14 37	14 55			15 10	15 07	15 25		15 40	15 37
Heathrow Terminals 1-2-3 ✈ a	13 25	13 29	13 40		13 55	13 59	14 10			14 25	14 29	14 40		14 55	14 59	15 10			15 25	15 29	15 40		15 55	15 59
d	13 26	13 35	13 41	13 44	13 56	14 05	14 11		14 14	14 26	14 35	14 41	14 44	14 56	15 05	15 11	15 14		15 26	15 35	15 41	15 44	15 56	16 05
Heathrow Terminal 4 ✈ a		13 39		13 48		14 09			14 18		14 39		14 48		15 09		15 18			15 39		15 48		16 09
Heathrow Terminal 5 ✈ a	13 31		13 46		14 01		14 16			14 31		14 46		15 01		15 16			15 31		15 46		16 01	

	HX 1	HC	HX 1		HC	HX 1	HC	HX 1	HC	HX 1	HC	HX 1	HC		HX 1	HC	HX 1	HC	HX 1	HC	HX 1	HC	HX 1	
London Paddington ⊖ d	15 55		16 10		16 07	16 25		16 40	16 37	16 55		17 10	17 07		17 25		17 40	17 37	17 55		18 10	18 07	18 25	
Heathrow Terminals 1-2-3 ✈ a	16 10		16 25		16 29	16 40		16 55	16 59	17 10		17 25	17 29		17 40		17 55	17 59	18 10		18 25	18 29	18 40	
d	16 11	16 14	16 26		16 35	16 41	16 44	16 56	17 05	17 11	17 14	17 26	17 35		17 41	17 44	17 56	18 05	18 11	18 14	18 26	18 35	18 41	
Heathrow Terminal 4 ✈ a		16 18			16 39		16 48		17 09		17 18		17 39			17 48		18 09		18 18		18 39		
Heathrow Terminal 5 ✈ a	16 16		16 31			16 46		17 01		17 16		17 31			17 46		18 01		18 16		18 31		18 46	

	HC	HX 1	HC	HX 1	HC	HX 1	HC	HX 1	HC		HX 1	HC	HX 1	HC	HX 1	HC	HX 1	HC	HX 1		HC	HX 1	HC	HX 1
London Paddington ⊖ d		18 40	18 37	18 55		19 10	19 07	19 25			19 40	19 37	19 55		20 10	20 07	20 25		20 40		20 37	20 55		21 10
Heathrow Terminals 1-2-3 ✈ a		18 55	18 59	19 10		19 25	19 29	19 40			19 55	19 59	20 10		20 25	20 29	20 40		20 55		20 59	21 10		21 25
d	18 44	18 56	19 05	19 11	19 14	19 26	19 35	19 41	19 44		19 56	20 05	20 11	20 14	20 26	20 35	20 41	20 44	20 56		21 05	21 11	21 14	21 26
Heathrow Terminal 4 ✈ a	18 48		19 09		19 18		19 39		19 48			20 09		20 18		20 39		20 48			21 09		21 18	
Heathrow Terminal 5 ✈ a		19 01		19 16		19 31		19 46			20 01		20 16		20 31		20 46		21 01			21 16		21 31

Table 118

London - Heathrow Airport

Sundays until 05 September

	HC	HX 1	HC	HX 1	HC		HX 1	HC	HX 1	HC	HC	HX 1	HC	HX 1	HC		HX 1	HC	HX 1	HC	HC	HX 1	HC	
London Paddington ⊖ d	21 07	21 25		21 40			21 55		22 10		22 12	22 25		22 40			22 55		23 10		23 12	23 25		
Heathrow Terminals 1-2-3 ✈ a	21 29	21 40		21 56			22 11		22 26		22 34	22 41		22 56			23 11		23 26		23 34	23 41		
d	21 35	21 41	21 49	21 59	22 01		22 13	22 19	22 31	22 33	22 37	22 47	22 49	22 59	23 01		23 13	23 19	23 31	23 33	23 37	23 47	23 49	
Heathrow Terminal 4 ✈ a	21 39		21 53		22 05			22 23		22 37	22 41		22 53		23 05			23 23		23 37	23 41		23 53	
Heathrow Terminal 5 ✈ a		21 46		22 03			22 17		22 35			22 51		23 03			23 17		23 35			23 51		

Sundays from 12 September

	HX 1	HX 1	HC	HX 1	HC	HX 1	HC	HX 1	HC	HC	HX 1	HC	HX 1	HC	HX 1	HC	HX 1	HC	HC		HX 1	HC	HX 1	HC
London Paddington ⊖ d	05 10	05 25		05 40		05 55		06 10		06 12	06 25		06 40		06 55		07 10		07 12		07 25		07 40	
Heathrow Terminals 1-2-3 ✈ a	05 26	05 41		05 56		06 11		06 26		06 34	06 41		06 56		07 11		07 26		07 34		07 41		07 56	
d	05 27	05 42	05 47	05 59	06 01	06 13	06 19	06 31	06 33	06 37	06 47	06 49	06 59	07 01	07 13	07 19	07 31	07 33	07 37		07 47	07 49	07 59	08 01
Heathrow Terminal 4 ✈ a			05 51		06 05		06 23		06 37	06 41		06 53		07 05		07 23		07 37	07 41			07 53		08 05
Heathrow Terminal 5 ✈ a	05 32	05 47		06 03		06 17		06 35			06 51		07 03		07 17		07 35				07 51		08 03	

	HX 1	HC	HX 1	HC	HC		HX 1	HC	HX 1	HC	HX 1	HC	HX 1	HC	HC		HX 1	HC	HX 1	HC	HX 1	HC	HX 1	HC
London Paddington ⊖ d	07 55		08 10		08 12		08 25		08 40		08 55		09 10		09 12		09 25		09 40		09 55		10 10	
Heathrow Terminals 1-2-3 ✈ a	08 11		08 26		08 34		08 41		08 56		09 11		09 26		09 34		09 41		09 56		10 11		10 26	
d	08 13	08 19	08 31	08 33	08 37		08 47	08 49	08 59	09 01	09 13	09 19	09 31	09 33	09 37		09 47	09 49	09 59	10 01	10 13	10 19	10 31	10 33
Heathrow Terminal 4 ✈ a		08 23		08 37	08 41			08 53		09 05		09 23		09 37	09 41			09 53		10 05		10 23		10 37
Heathrow Terminal 5 ✈ a	08 17		08 35				08 51		09 03		09 17		09 35				09 51		10 03		10 17		10 35	

	HC		HX 1	HC	HX 1	HC	HX 1	HC	HX 1	HC	HC		HX 1	HC	HX 1	HC	HX 1	HC	HX 1	HC	HC		HX 1	HC
London Paddington ⊖ d	10 12		10 25		10 40		10 55		11 10		11 12		11 25		11 40		11 55		12 10		12 12		12 25	
Heathrow Terminals 1-2-3 ✈ a	10 34		10 41		10 56		11 11		11 26		11 34		11 41		11 56		12 11		12 26		12 34		12 41	
d	10 37		10 47	10 49	10 59	11 01	11 13	11 19	11 31	11 33	11 37		11 47	11 49	11 59	12 01	12 13	12 19	12 31	12 33	12 37		12 47	12 49
Heathrow Terminal 4 ✈ a	10 41			10 53		11 05		11 23		11 37	11 41			11 53		12 05		12 23		12 37	12 41			12 53
Heathrow Terminal 5 ✈ a			10 51		11 03		11 17		11 35				11 51		12 03		12 17		12 35				12 51	

	HX 1	HC	HX 1	HC	HX 1	HC	HC		HX 1	HC	HX 1	HC	HX 1	HC	HX 1	HC	HC		HX 1	HC	HX 1	HC	HX 1	HC
London Paddington ⊖ d	12 40		12 55		13 10		13 12		13 25		13 40		13 55		14 10		14 12		14 25		14 40		14 55	
Heathrow Terminals 1-2-3 ✈ a	12 56		13 11		13 26		13 34		13 41		13 56		14 11		14 26		14 34		14 41		14 56		15 11	
d	12 59	13 01	13 13	13 19	13 31	13 33	13 37		13 47	13 49	13 59	14 01	14 13	14 19	14 31	14 33	14 37		14 47	14 49	14 59	15 01	15 13	15 19
Heathrow Terminal 4 ✈ a		13 05		13 23		13 37	13 41			13 53		14 05		14 23		14 37	14 41			14 53		15 05		15 23
Heathrow Terminal 5 ✈ a	13 03		13 17		13 35				13 51		14 03		14 17		14 35				14 51		15 03		15 17	

	HX 1	HC	HC		HX 1	HC	HX 1	HC	HX 1	HC	HX 1	HC	HC		HX 1	HC	HX 1	HC	HX 1	HC	HX 1	HC	HC	
London Paddington ⊖ d	15 10		15 12		15 25		15 40		15 55		16 10		16 12		16 25		16 40		16 55		17 10		17 12	
Heathrow Terminals 1-2-3 ✈ a	15 26		15 34		15 41		15 56		16 11		16 26		16 34		16 41		16 56		17 11		17 26		17 34	
d	15 31	15 33	15 37		15 47	15 49	15 59	16 01	16 13	16 19	16 31	16 33	16 37		16 47	16 49	16 59	17 01	17 13	17 19	17 31	17 33	17 37	
Heathrow Terminal 4 ✈ a		15 37	15 41			15 53		16 05		16 23		16 37	16 41			16 53		17 05		17 23		17 37	17 41	
Heathrow Terminal 5 ✈ a	15 35				15 51		16 03		16 17		16 35				16 51		17 03		17 17		17 35			

	HX 1	HC	HX 1	HC	HX 1	HC	HX 1	HC	HC		HX 1	HC	HX 1	HC	HX 1	HC	HX 1	HC	HC		HX 1	HC	HX 1	HC
London Paddington ⊖ d	17 25		17 40		17 55		18 10		18 12		18 25		18 40		18 55		19 10		19 12		19 25		19 40	
Heathrow Terminals 1-2-3 ✈ a	17 41		17 56		18 11		18 26		18 34		18 41		18 56		19 11		19 26		19 34		19 41		19 56	
d	17 47	17 49	17 59	18 01	18 13	18 19	18 31	18 33	18 37		18 47	18 49	18 59	19 01	19 13	19 19	19 31	19 33	19 37		19 47	19 49	19 59	20 01
Heathrow Terminal 4 ✈ a		17 53		18 05		18 23		18 37	18 41			18 53		19 05		19 23		19 37	19 41			19 53		20 05
Heathrow Terminal 5 ✈ a	17 51		18 03		18 17		18 35				18 51		19 03		19 17		19 35				19 51		20 03	

	HX 1	HC	HX 1	HC	HC		HX 1	HC	HX 1	HC	HX 1	HC	HX 1	HC	HC		HX 1	HC	HX 1	HC	HX 1	HC	HX 1	HC
London Paddington ⊖ d	19 55		20 10		20 12		20 25		20 40		20 55		21 10		21 12		21 25		21 40		21 55		22 10	
Heathrow Terminals 1-2-3 ✈ a	20 11		20 26		20 34		20 41		20 56		21 11		21 26		21 34		21 41		21 56		22 11		22 26	
d	20 13	20 19	20 31	20 33	20 37		20 47	20 49	20 59	21 01	21 13	21 19	21 31	21 33	21 37		21 47	21 49	21 59	22 01	22 13	22 19	22 31	22 33
Heathrow Terminal 4 ✈ a		20 23		20 37	20 41			20 53		21 05		21 23		21 37	21 41			21 53		22 05		22 23		22 37
Heathrow Terminal 5 ✈ a	20 17		20 35				20 51		21 03		21 17		21 35				21 51		22 03		22 17		22 35	

	HC		HX 1	HC	HX 1	HC	HX 1	HC	HX 1	HC	HC		HX 1	HC										
London Paddington ⊖ d	22 12		22 25		22 40		22 55		23 10		23 12		23 25											
Heathrow Terminals 1-2-3 ✈ a	22 34		22 41		22 56		23 11		23 26		23 34		23 41											
d	22 37		22 47	22 49	22 59	23 01	23 13	23 19	23 31	23 33	23 37		23 47	23 49										
Heathrow Terminal 4 ✈ a	22 41			22 53		23 05		23 23		23 37	23 41			23 53										
Heathrow Terminal 5 ✈ a			22 51		23 03		23 17		23 35				23 51											

Table 118

Mondays to Fridays

Heathrow Airport - London

				HX MO	HC	HX 1	HC	HX 1	HC		HX 1	HC	HC	HX 1	HC	HX 1	HC	HX 1	HC		HX 1	HC	HX 1	HC
Heathrow Terminal 5 ✈ d				23p58		05 07		05 27			05 42			05 57		06 12		06 27			06 42		06 57	
Heathrow Terminal 4 ✈ d					00 01		05 23		05 32			05 51	05 57		06 12		06 27		06 42			06 57		07 12
Heathrow Terminals 1-2-3 ✈ a				00 02	00 05	05 11	05 27	05 31	05 36		05 46	05 55	06 01	06 01	06 16	06 16	06 31	06 31	06 46		06 46	07 01	07 01	07 16
d				00 02	00 07	05 12	05 29	05 33			05 48	05 57		06 03		06 18		06 33			06 48		07 03	
London Paddington ⊖ a				00 18	00 30	05 28	05 56	05 49			06 04	06 24		06 19		06 34		06 49			07 05		07 19	

	HX 1	HC	HX 1	HC	HX 1		HC	HX 1	HC	HX 1	HC	HX 1	HC	HX 1	HC		HX 1	HC	HX 1	HC	HX 1	HC	HX 1	HC
Heathrow Terminal 5 ✈ d	07 12		07 27		07 42			07 57		08 12		08 27		08 42			08 57		09 12		09 27		09 42	
Heathrow Terminal 4 ✈ d		07 27		07 42			07 57		08 12		08 27		08 42		08 57			09 12		09 27		09 42		09 57
Heathrow Terminals 1-2-3 ✈ a	07 16	07 31	07 31	07 46	07 46		08 01	08 01	08 16	08 16	08 31	08 31	08 46	08 46	09 01		09 01	09 16	09 16	09 31	09 31	09 46	09 46	10 01
d	07 18		07 33		07 48			08 03		08 18		08 33		08 48			09 03		09 18		09 33		09 48	
London Paddington ⊖ a	07 35		07 49		08 04			08 19		08 35		08 49		09 04			09 19		09 35		09 49		10 05	

	HX 1		HC	HX 1	HC	HX 1	HC	HX 1	HC	HX 1	HC		HX 1	HC	HX 1	HC	HX 1	HC	HX 1	HC	HX 1		HC	HX 1
Heathrow Terminal 5 ✈ d	09 57			10 12		10 27		10 42		10 57			11 12		11 27		11 42		11 57		12 12			12 27
Heathrow Terminal 4 ✈ d			10 12		10 27		10 42		10 57		11 12			11 27		11 42		11 57		12 12			12 27	
Heathrow Terminals 1-2-3 ✈ a	10 01		10 16	10 16	10 31	10 31	10 46	10 46	11 01	11 01	11 16		11 16	11 31	11 31	11 46	11 46	12 01	12 01	12 16	12 16		12 31	12 31
d	10 03			10 18		10 33		10 48		11 03			11 18		11 33		11 48		12 03		12 18			12 33
London Paddington ⊖ a	10 19			10 34		10 49		11 05		11 19			11 34		11 49		12 04		12 19		12 34			12 49

	HC	HX 1	HC	HX 1	HC	HX 1	HC		HX 1	HC	HX 1	HC	HX 1	HC	HX 1	HC	HX 1		HC	HX 1	HC	HX 1	HC	HX 1
Heathrow Terminal 5 ✈ d		12 42		12 57		13 12			13 27		13 42		13 57		14 12		14 27			14 42		14 57		15 12
Heathrow Terminal 4 ✈ d	12 42		12 57		13 12		13 27			13 42		13 57		14 12		14 27			14 42		14 57		15 12	
Heathrow Terminals 1-2-3 ✈ a	12 46	12 46	13 01	13 01	13 16	13 16	13 31		13 31	13 46	13 46	14 01	14 01	14 16	14 16	14 31	14 31		14 46	14 46	15 01	15 01	15 16	15 16
d		12 48		13 03		13 18			13 33		13 48		14 03		14 18		14 33			14 48		15 03		15 18
London Paddington ⊖ a		13 04		13 19		13 35			13 49		14 04		14 19		14 34		14 49			15 04		15 19		15 35

	HC	HX 1	HC		HX 1	HC	HX 1	HC	HX 1	HC	HX 1	HC	HX 1		HC	HX 1	HC	HX 1	HC	HX 1	HC	HX 1	HC	
Heathrow Terminal 5 ✈ d		15 27			15 42		15 57		16 12		16 27		16 42			16 57		17 12		17 27		17 42		
Heathrow Terminal 4 ✈ d	15 27		15 42			15 57		16 12		16 27		16 42			16 57		17 12		17 27		17 42		17 57	
Heathrow Terminals 1-2-3 ✈ a	15 31	15 31	15 46		15 46	16 01	16 01	16 16	16 16	16 31	16 31	16 46	16 46		17 01	17 01	17 16	17 16	17 31	17 31	17 46	17 46	18 01	
d		15 33			15 48		16 03		16 18		16 33		16 48			17 03		17 18		17 33		17 48		
London Paddington ⊖ a		15 49			16 05		16 19		16 35		16 49		17 04			17 19		17 35		17 49		18 05		

	HX 1	HC	HX 1	HC	HX 1	HC	HX 1	HC	HX 1		HC	HX 1	HC	HX 1	HC	HX 1	HC	HX 1	HC		HX 1	HC	HX 1	HC
Heathrow Terminal 5 ✈ d	17 57		18 12		18 27		18 42		18 57			19 12		19 27		19 42		19 57			20 12		20 27	
Heathrow Terminal 4 ✈ d		18 12		18 27		18 42		18 57			19 12		19 27		19 42		19 57		20 12			20 27		20 42
Heathrow Terminals 1-2-3 ✈ a	18 01	18 16	18 16	18 31	18 31	18 46	18 46	19 01	19 01		19 16	19 16	19 31	19 31	19 46	19 46	20 01	20 01	20 16		20 16	20 31	20 31	20 46
d	18 03		18 18		18 33		18 48		19 03			19 18		19 33		19 48		20 03			20 18		20 33	
London Paddington ⊖ a	18 19		18 35		18 49		19 05		19 19			19 35		19 49		20 04		20 19			20 34		20 49	

	HX 1	HC	HX 1	HC	HX 1		HC	HX 1	HC	HX 1	HC	HX 1	HC	HX 1	HC		HX 1	HC	HX 1	HC	HX 1	HC	HX 1	HC
Heathrow Terminal 5 ✈ d	20 42		20 57		21 12			21 27		21 42		21 57		22 12			22 27		22 42		22 57		23 12	
Heathrow Terminal 4 ✈ d		20 57		21 12			21 27		21 42		21 57		22 12		22 27			22 42		22 57		23 12		23 27
Heathrow Terminals 1-2-3 ✈ a	20 46	21 01	21 01	21 16	21 16		21 31	21 31	21 46	21 46	22 01	22 01	22 16	22 16	22 31		22 31	22 46	22 46	23 01	23 01	23 16	23 16	23 31
d	20 48		21 03		21 18			21 33		21 48		22 03		22 18			22 33		22 48		23 03		23 18	
London Paddington ⊖ a	21 04		21 19		21 34			21 49		22 04		22 19		22 34			22 49		23 04		23 19		23 34	

	HX 1	HC	HX		HX																			
Heathrow Terminal 5 ✈ d	23 27		23 42		23 53																			
Heathrow Terminal 4 ✈ d		23 42																						
Heathrow Terminals 1-2-3 ✈ a	23 31	23 46	23 46		23 57																			
d	23 33		23 48																					
London Paddington ⊖ a	23 49		00 04																					

Saturdays

			HC	HX 1	HC	HX 1	HC	HX 1	HC		HC	HX 1	HC	HX 1	HC	HX 1	HC	HX 1	HC		HX 1	HC	HX 1	HC
Heathrow Terminal 5 ✈ d				05 07		05 27		05 42				05 57		06 12		06 27		06 42			06 57		07 12	
Heathrow Terminal 4 ✈ d			00 01		05 23		05 32		05 51		05 57		06 12		06 27		06 42		06 57			07 12		07 27
Heathrow Terminals 1-2-3 ✈ a			00 05	05 11	05 27	05 31	05 36	05 46	05 55		06 01	06 01	06 16	06 16	06 31	06 31	06 46	06 46	07 01		07 01	07 16	07 16	07 31
d			00 07	05 12	05 29	05 33		05 48	05 57			06 03		06 18		06 33		06 48			07 03		07 18	
London Paddington ⊖ a			00 30	05 28	05 56	05 49		06 04	06 24			06 19		06 34		06 49		07 04			07 19		07 34	

	HX 1	HC	HX 1	HC	HX 1		HC	HX 1	HC	HX 1	HC	HX 1	HC	HX 1	HC		HX 1	HC	HX 1	HC	HX 1	HC	HX 1	HC
Heathrow Terminal 5 ✈ d	07 27		07 42		07 57			08 12		08 27		08 42		08 57			09 12		09 27		09 42		09 57	
Heathrow Terminal 4 ✈ d		07 42		07 57			08 12		08 27		08 42		08 57		09 12			09 27		09 42		09 57		10 12
Heathrow Terminals 1-2-3 ✈ a	07 31	07 46	07 46	08 01	08 01		08 16	08 16	08 31	08 31	08 46	08 46	09 01	09 01	09 16		09 16	09 31	09 31	09 46	09 46	10 01	10 01	10 16
d	07 33		07 48		08 03			08 18		08 33		08 48		09 03			09 18		09 33		09 48		10 03	
London Paddington ⊖ a	07 49		08 04		08 19			08 34		08 49		09 04		09 19			09 34		09 49		10 04		10 19	

Table 118

Heathrow Airport - London

Saturdays

	HX 1		HC	HX 1	HC	HX 1	HC	HX 1	HC	HX 1	HC		HX 1	HC	HX 1	HC	HX 1	HC	HX 1	HC	HX 1		HC	HX 1
Heathrow Terminal 5 ✈ d	10 12			10 27		10 42		10 57		11 12			11 27		11 42		11 57		12 12		12 27			12 42
Heathrow Terminal 4 ✈ d			10 27		10 42		10 57		11 12		11 27			11 42		11 57		12 12		12 27			12 42	
Heathrow Terminals 1-2-3 2 ✈ a	10 16		10 31	10 31	10 46	10 46	11 01	11 01	11 16	11 16	11 31		11 31	11 46	11 46	12 01	12 01	12 16	12 16	12 31	12 31		12 46	12 46
d	10 18			10 33		10 48		11 03		11 18			11 33		11 48		12 03		12 18		12 33			12 48
London Paddington 15 ⊖ a	10 34			10 49		11 04		11 19		11 34			11 49		12 04		12 19		12 34		12 49			13 04

	HC	HX 1	HC	HX 1	HC	HX 1	HC		HX 1	HC	HX 1	HC	HX 1	HC	HX 1	HC	HX 1		HC	HX 1	HC	HX 1	HC	HX 1
Heathrow Terminal 5 ✈ d		12 57		13 12		13 27			13 42		13 57		14 12		14 27		14 42			14 57		15 12		15 27
Heathrow Terminal 4 ✈ d	12 57		13 12		13 27		13 42			13 57		14 12		14 27		14 42			14 57		15 12		15 27	
Heathrow Terminals 1-2-3 2 ✈ a	13 01	13 01	13 16	13 16	13 31	13 31	13 46		13 46	14 01	14 01	14 16	14 16	14 31	14 31	14 46	14 46		15 01	15 01	15 16	15 16	15 31	15 31
d		13 03		13 18		13 33			13 48		14 03		14 18		14 33		14 48			15 03		15 18		15 33
London Paddington 15 ⊖ a		13 19		13 34		13 49			14 04		14 19		14 34		14 49		15 04			15 19		15 34		15 49

	HC	HX 1	HC		HX 1	HC	HX 1	HC	HX 1	HC	HX 1	HC	HX 1		HC	HX 1	HC	HX 1	HC	HX 1	HC	HX 1	HC	
Heathrow Terminal 5 ✈ d		15 42			15 57		16 12		16 27		16 42		16 57			17 12		17 27		17 42		17 57		
Heathrow Terminal 4 ✈ d	15 42		15 57			16 12		16 27		16 42		16 57			17 12		17 27		17 42		17 57		18 12	
Heathrow Terminals 1-2-3 2 ✈ a	15 46	15 46	16 01		16 01	16 16	16 16	16 31	16 31	16 46	16 46	17 01	17 01		17 16	17 16	17 31	17 31	17 46	17 46	18 01	18 01	18 16	
d		15 48			16 03		16 18		16 33		16 48		17 03			17 18		17 33		17 48		18 03		
London Paddington 15 ⊖ a		16 04			16 19		16 34		16 49		17 04		17 19			17 34		17 49		18 04		18 19		

	HX 1	HC	HX 1	HC	HX 1	HC	HX 1	HC	HX 1		HC	HX 1	HC	HX 1	HC	HX 1	HC	HX 1	HC		HX 1	HC	HX 1	HC
Heathrow Terminal 5 ✈ d	18 12		18 27		18 42		18 57		19 12			19 27		19 42		19 57		20 12			20 27		20 42	
Heathrow Terminal 4 ✈ d		18 27		18 42		18 57		19 12			19 27		19 42		19 57		20 12		20 27			20 42		20 57
Heathrow Terminals 1-2-3 2 ✈ a	18 16	18 31	18 31	18 46	18 46	19 01	19 01	19 16	19 16		19 31	19 31	19 46	19 46	20 01	20 01	20 16	20 16	20 31		20 31	20 46	20 46	21 01
d	18 18		18 33		18 48		19 03		19 18			19 33		19 48		20 03		20 18			20 33		20 48	
London Paddington 15 ⊖ a	18 34		18 49		19 04		19 19		19 34			19 49		20 04		20 19		20 34			20 49		21 04	

	HX 1	HC	HX 1	HC	HX 1		HC	HX 1	HC	HX 1	HC	HX 1	HC	HX 1	HC		HX 1	HC	HX 1	HC	HX 1	HC	HX 1	
Heathrow Terminal 5 ✈ d	20 57		21 12		21 27			21 42		21 57		22 12		22 27			22 42		22 57		23 12		23 27	
Heathrow Terminal 4 ✈ d		21 12		21 27			21 42		21 57		22 12		22 27		22 42			22 57		23 12		23 27		
Heathrow Terminals 1-2-3 2 ✈ a	21 01	21 16	21 16	21 31	21 31		21 46	21 46	22 01	22 01	22 16	22 16	22 31	22 31	22 46		22 46	23 01	23 01	23 16	23 16	23 31	23 31	
d	21 03		21 18		21 33			21 48		22 03		22 18		22 33			22 48		23 03		23 18		23 33	
London Paddington 15 ⊖ a	21 19		21 34		21 49			22 04		22 19		22 34		22 49			23 04		23 19		23 34		23 49	

	HC	HX 1	HX
Heathrow Terminal 5 ✈ d		23 42	23 53
Heathrow Terminal 4 ✈ d	23 42		
Heathrow Terminals 1-2-3 2 ✈ a	23 46	23 46	23 57
d		23 48	
London Paddington 15 ⊖ a		00 04	

Sundays

until 05 September

	HX 1		HC	HX 1	HX 1	HX 1	HX 1	HC	HX 1		HC	HC	HX 1	HC	HX 1	HC	HX 1	HC	HX 1		HC	HC	HX 1	HC
Heathrow Terminal 5 ✈ d	23p42			05 03	05 18	05 33	05 48		06 03				06 18		06 33		06 48		07 03				07 18	
Heathrow Terminal 4 ✈ d			00 01					05 53			06 07	06 13		06 25		06 41		06 53			07 07	07 13		07 25
Heathrow Terminals 1-2-3 2 ✈ a	23p46		00 05	05 07	05 22	05 37	05 52	05 57	06 07		06 11	06 17	06 22	06 29	06 37	06 45	06 52	06 57	07 07		07 11	07 17	07 22	07 29
d	23p48		00 07	05 08	05 23	05 38	05 53		06 08		06 13		06 23		06 38		06 53		07 08		07 13		07 23	
London Paddington 15 ⊖ a	00 04		00 30	05 24	05 39	05 54	06 09		06 24		06 36		06 39		06 54		07 09		07 24		07 36		07 39	

	HX 1	HC	HX 1	HC	HX 1		HC	HC	HX 1	HC	HX 1	HC	HX 1	HC	HX 1		HC	HX 1	HC	HX 1	HC	HX 1	HC	HX 1
Heathrow Terminal 5 ✈ d	07 33		07 48		08 03				08 18		08 33		08 48		09 00			09 13		09 27		09 42		09 57
Heathrow Terminal 4 ✈ d		07 41		07 53			08 07	08 13		08 25		08 41		08 53			09 06		09 21		09 31		09 51	
Heathrow Terminals 1-2-3 2 ✈ a	07 37	07 45	07 52	07 57	08 07		08 11	08 17	08 22	08 29	08 37	08 45	08 52	08 57	09 04		09 10	09 17	09 25	09 31	09 35	09 46	09 55	10 01
d	07 38		07 53		08 08		08 13		08 23		08 38		08 53		09 06			09 19	09 27	09 33		09 48	09 57	10 03
London Paddington 15 ⊖ a	07 54		08 09		08 24		08 36		08 39		08 54		09 09		09 22			09 35	09 50	09 49		10 04	10 20	10 19

	HC		HX 1	HC	HX 1	HC	HX 1	HC	HX 1	HC	HX 1		HC	HX 1	HC	HX 1	HC	HX 1	HC	HX 1	HC		HX 1	HC
Heathrow Terminal 5 ✈ d			10 12		10 27		10 42		10 57		11 12			11 27		11 42		11 57		12 12			12 27	
Heathrow Terminal 4 ✈ d	10 01			10 21		10 31		10 51		11 01			11 21		11 31		11 51		12 01		12 21			12 31
Heathrow Terminals 1-2-3 2 ✈ a	10 05		10 16	10 25	10 31	10 35	10 46	10 55	11 01	11 05	11 16		11 25	11 31	11 35	11 46	11 55	12 01	12 05	12 16	12 25		12 31	12 35
d			10 18	10 27	10 33		10 48	10 57	11 03		11 18		11 27	11 33		11 48	11 57	12 03		12 18	12 27		12 33	
London Paddington 15 ⊖ a			10 34	10 50	10 49		11 04	11 20	11 19		11 34		11 50	11 49		12 04	12 20	12 19		12 34	12 50		12 49	

	HX 1	HC	HX 1	HC	HX 1	HC	HX 1		HC	HX 1	HC	HX 1	HC	HX 1	HC	HX 1	HC		HX 1	HC	HX 1	HC	HX 1	HC
Heathrow Terminal 5 ✈ d	12 42		12 57		13 12		13 27			13 42		13 57		14 12		14 27			14 42		14 57		15 12	
Heathrow Terminal 4 ✈ d		12 51		13 01		13 21			13 31		13 51		14 01		14 21		14 31			14 51		15 01		15 21
Heathrow Terminals 1-2-3 2 ✈ a	12 46	12 55	13 01	13 05	13 16	13 25	13 31		13 35	13 46	13 55	14 01	14 05	14 16	14 25	14 31	14 35		14 46	14 55	15 01	15 05	15 16	15 25
d	12 48	12 57	13 03		13 18	13 27	13 33			13 48	13 57	14 03		14 18	14 27	14 33			14 48	14 57	15 03		15 18	15 27
London Paddington 15 ⊖ a	13 04	13 20	13 19		13 34	13 50	13 49			14 04	14 20	14 19		14 34	14 50	14 49			15 04	15 20	15 19		15 34	15 50

Table 118

Heathrow Airport - London

Sundays

until 05 September

	HX 1	HC	HX 1		HC	HX 1	HC	HX 1	HC	HX 1	HC	HX 1	HC		HX 1	HC	HX 1	HC	HX 1	HC	HX 1	HC	HX 1	
Heathrow Terminal 5 ✈ d	15 27		15 42			15 57		16 12		16 27		16 42			16 57		17 12		17 27		17 42		17 57	
Heathrow Terminal 4 ✈ d		15 31			15 51		16 01		16 21		16 31		16 51			17 01		17 21		17 31		17 51		
Heathrow Terminals 1-2-3 2 ✈ a	15 31	15 35	15 46		15 55	16 01	16 05	16 16	16 25	16 31	16 35	16 46	16 55		17 01	17 05	17 16	17 25	17 31	17 35	17 46	17 55	18 01	
d	15 33		15 48		15 57	16 03		16 18	16 27	16 33		16 48	16 57		17 03		17 18	17 27	17 33		17 48	17 57	18 03	
London Paddington 15 ⊖ a	15 49		16 04		16 20	16 19		16 34	16 51	16 49		17 04	17 20		17 19		17 34	17 50	17 49		18 04	18 20	18 20	

	HC	HX 1	HC	HX 1	HC	HX 1	HC	HX 1	HC		HX 1	HC	HX 1	HC	HX 1	HC	HX 1	HC	HX 1		HC	HX 1	HC	HX 1
Heathrow Terminal 5 ✈ d		18 12		18 27		18 42		18 57			19 12		19 27		19 42		19 57		20 12			20 27		20 42
Heathrow Terminal 4 ✈ d	18 01		18 21		18 31		18 51		19 01			19 21		19 31		19 51		20 01			20 21		20 31	
Heathrow Terminals 1-2-3 2 ✈ a	18 05	18 16	18 25	18 31	18 35	18 46	18 55	19 01	19 05		19 16	19 25	19 31	19 35	19 46	19 55	20 01	20 05	20 16		20 25	20 31	20 35	20 46
d		18 18	18 27	18 33		18 48	18 57	19 03			19 18	19 27	19 33		19 48	19 57	20 03		20 18		20 27	20 33		20 48
London Paddington 15 ⊖ a		18 34	18 51	18 49		19 04	19 20	19 19			19 34	19 51	19 49		20 04	20 20	20 19		20 34		20 50	20 49		21 04

	HC	HX 1	HC	HX 1			HC	HX 1	HC	HX 1	HC	HX 1	HC	HC	HX 1		HC	HX 1	HC	HX 1	HC	HX 1	HC	HC
Heathrow Terminal 5 ✈ d		20 57		21 12				21 27		21 48		22 03			22 18			22 33		22 48		23 03		
Heathrow Terminal 4 ✈ d	20 51		21 01				21 21		21 41		21 53		22 07	22 13			22 25		22 41		22 53		23 07	23 13
Heathrow Terminals 1-2-3 2 ✈ a	20 55	21 01	21 05	21 16			21 25	21 31	21 45	21 52	21 57	22 07	22 11	22 17	22 22		22 29	22 37	22 45	22 52	22 57	23 07	23 11	23 17
d	20 57	21 03		21 18			21 27	21 33		21 53		22 08	22 13		22 23			22 38		22 53		23 08	23 13	
London Paddington 15 ⊖ a	21 20	21 19		21 34			21 50	21 49		22 09		22 24	22 36		22 43			22 54		23 10		23 24	23 36	

	HX 1		HC	HX 1	HC	HX 1	HX
Heathrow Terminal 5 ✈ d	23 18			23 33		23 48	23 58
Heathrow Terminal 4 ✈ d			23 25		23 41		
Heathrow Terminals 1-2-3 2 ✈ a	23 22		23 29	23 37	23 45	23 52	00 02
d	23 23			23 38		23 53	
London Paddington 15 ⊖ a	23 43			23 56		00 09	

Sundays

from 12 September

			HC	HX 1	HX 1	HX 1	HX 1	HC	HX 1		HC	HC	HX 1	HC	HX 1	HC	HX 1	HC	HX 1		HC	HC	HX 1	HC
Heathrow Terminal 5 ✈ d				05 03	05 18	05 33	05 48		06 03				06 18		06 33		06 48		07 03				07 18	
Heathrow Terminal 4 ✈ d			00 01					05 53			06 07	06 13		06 25		06 41		06 53			07 07	07 13		07 25
Heathrow Terminals 1-2-3 2 ✈ a			00 05	05 07	05 22	05 37	05 52	05 57	06 07		06 11	06 17	06 22	06 29	06 37	06 45	06 52	06 57	07 07		07 11	07 17	07 22	07 29
d			00 07	05 08	05 23	05 38	05 53		06 08		06 13		06 23		06 38		06 53		07 08		07 13		07 23	
London Paddington 15 ⊖ a			00 30	05 24	05 39	05 54	06 09		06 24		06 36		06 39		06 54		07 09		07 24		07 36		07 39	

	HX 1	HC	HX 1	HC	HX 1		HC	HC	HX 1	HC	HX 1	HC	HX 1	HC	HX 1		HC	HC	HX 1	HC	HX 1	HC	HX 1	HC
Heathrow Terminal 5 ✈ d	07 33		07 48		08 03				08 18		08 33		08 48		09 03				09 18		09 33		09 48	
Heathrow Terminal 4 ✈ d		07 41		07 53			08 07	08 13		08 25		08 41		08 53			09 07	09 13		09 25		09 41		09 53
Heathrow Terminals 1-2-3 2 ✈ a	07 37	07 45	07 52	07 57	08 07		08 11	08 17	08 22	08 29	08 37	08 45	08 52	08 57	09 07		09 11	09 17	09 22	09 29	09 37	09 45	09 52	09 57
d	07 38		07 53		08 08		08 13		08 23		08 38		08 53		09 08		09 13		09 23		09 38		09 53	
London Paddington 15 ⊖ a	07 54		08 09		08 24		08 36		08 39		08 54		09 09		09 24		09 36		09 41		09 54		10 09	

	HX 1		HC	HC	HX 1	HC	HX 1	HC	HX 1	HC	HX 1		HC	HC	HX 1	HC	HX 1	HC	HX 1	HC	HX 1		HC	HC
Heathrow Terminal 5 ✈ d	10 03				10 18		10 33		10 48		11 03				11 18		11 33		11 48		12 03			
Heathrow Terminal 4 ✈ d			10 07	10 13		10 25		10 41		10 53			11 07	11 13		11 25		11 41		11 53			12 07	12 13
Heathrow Terminals 1-2-3 2 ✈ a	10 07		10 11	10 17	10 22	10 29	10 37	10 45	10 52	10 57	11 07		11 11	11 17	11 22	11 29	11 37	11 45	11 52	11 57	12 07		12 11	12 17
d	10 08		10 13		10 23		10 38		10 53		11 08		11 13		11 23		11 38		11 53		12 08		12 13	
London Paddington 15 ⊖ a	10 24		10 36		10 41		10 54		11 09		11 24		11 36		11 41		11 54		12 09		12 24		12 36	

	HX 1	HC	HX 1	HC	HX 1	HC	HX 1		HC	HC	HX 1	HC	HX 1	HC	HX 1	HC	HX 1		HC	HC	HX 1	HC	HX 1	HC
Heathrow Terminal 5 ✈ d	12 18		12 33		12 48		13 03				13 18		13 33		13 48		14 03				14 18		14 33	
Heathrow Terminal 4 ✈ d		12 25		12 41		12 53			13 07	13 13		13 25		13 41		13 53			14 07	14 13		14 25		14 41
Heathrow Terminals 1-2-3 2 ✈ a	12 22	12 29	12 37	12 45	12 52	12 57	13 07		13 11	13 17	13 22	13 29	13 37	13 45	13 52	13 57	14 07		14 11	14 17	14 22	14 29	14 37	14 45
d	12 23		12 38		12 53		13 08		13 13		13 23		13 38		13 53		14 08		14 13		14 23		14 38	
London Paddington 15 ⊖ a	12 41		12 54		13 09		13 24		13 36		13 41		13 54		14 09		14 24		14 36		14 41		14 54	

	HX 1	HC	HX 1		HC	HC	HX 1	HC	HX 1	HC	HX 1	HC	HX 1		HC	HC	HX 1	HC	HX 1	HC	HX 1	HC	HX 1	
Heathrow Terminal 5 ✈ d	14 48		15 03				15 18		15 33		15 48		16 03				16 18		16 33		16 48		17 03	
Heathrow Terminal 4 ✈ d		14 53			15 07	15 13		15 25		15 41		15 53			16 07	16 13		16 25		16 41		16 53		
Heathrow Terminals 1-2-3 2 ✈ a	14 52	14 57	15 07		15 11	15 17	15 22	15 29	15 37	15 45	15 52	15 57	16 07		16 11	16 17	16 22	16 29	16 37	16 45	16 52	16 57	17 07	
d	14 53		15 08		15 13		15 23		15 38		15 53		16 08		16 13		16 23		16 38		16 53		17 08	
London Paddington 15 ⊖ a	15 09		15 24		15 36		15 41		15 54		16 09		16 24		16 36		16 41		16 54		17 09		17 24	

	HC	HC	HX 1	HC	HX 1	HC	HX 1	HC	HX 1		HC	HC	HX 1	HC	HX 1	HC	HX 1	HC	HX 1		HC	HC	HX 1	HC
Heathrow Terminal 5 ✈ d			17 18		17 33		17 48		18 03				18 18		18 33		18 48		19 03				19 18	
Heathrow Terminal 4 ✈ d	17 07	17 13		17 25		17 41		17 53			18 07	18 13		18 25		18 41		18 53			19 07	19 13		19 25
Heathrow Terminals 1-2-3 2 ✈ a	17 11	17 17	17 22	17 29	17 37	17 45	17 52	17 57	18 07		18 11	18 17	18 22	18 29	18 37	18 45	18 52	18 57	19 07		19 11	19 17	19 22	19 29
d	17 13		17 23		17 38		17 53		18 08		18 13		18 23		18 38		18 53		19 08		19 13		19 23	
London Paddington 15 ⊖ a	17 36		17 41		17 54		18 09		18 24		18 36		18 41		18 54		19 09		19 24		19 36		19 41	

Table 118

Sundays from 12 September

Heathrow Airport - London

		HX 1	HC	HX 1	HC	HX 1		HC	HC	HX 1	HC	HX 1	HC	HX 1	HC	HX 1		HC	HC	HX 1	HC	HX 1	HC	HX 1	HC
Heathrow Terminal 5	d	19 33		19 48		20 03				20 18		20 33		20 48		21 03				21 18		21 33		21 48	
Heathrow Terminal 4	d		19 41		19 53			20 07	20 13		20 25		20 41		20 53			21 07	21 13		21 25		21 41		21 53
Heathrow Terminals 1-2-3	a	19 37	19 45	19 52	19 57	20 07		20 11	20 17	20 22	20 29	20 37	20 45	20 52	20 57	21 07		21 11	21 17	21 22	21 29	21 37	21 45	21 52	21 57
	d	19 38		19 53		20 08		20 13		20 23		20 38		20 53		21 08		21 13		21 23		21 38		21 53	
London Paddington ⊖	a	19 54		20 11		20 24		20 36		20 39		20 54		21 12		21 24		21 36		21 39		21 54		22 11	

		HX 1		HC	HC	HX 1	HC	HX 1	HC	HX 1	HC	HX 1		HC	HC	HX 1	HC	HX 1	HC	HX 1	HX				
Heathrow Terminal 5	d	22 03				22 18		22 33		22 48		23 03				23 18		23 33		23 48	23 58				
Heathrow Terminal 4	d			22 07	22 13		22 25		22 41		22 53			23 07	23 13		23 25		23 41						
Heathrow Terminals 1-2-3	a	22 07		22 11	22 17	22 22	22 29	22 37	22 45	22 52	22 57	23 07		23 11	23 17	23 22	23 29	23 37	23 45	23 52	00 02				
	d	22 08		22 13		22 23		22 38		22 53		23 08		23 13		23 23		23 38		23 53					
London Paddington ⊖	a	22 24		22 36		22 39		22 54		23 10		23 24		23 36		23 43		23 56		00 09					

Table 119

Mondays to Fridays

Slough - Windsor & Eton

		GW 1	GW 1	GW 1	GW 1	GW 1	GW 1	GW 1	GW 1	GW 1		GW 1	GW 1	GW 1	GW 1	GW 1	GW 1	GW 1	GW 1	GW 1		GW 1	GW 1	GW 1	GW 1
Slough	d	05 38	05 58	06 18	06 37	06 55	07 13	07 31	07 54	08 13		08 31	08 54	09 14	09 33	09 53	10 11	10 30	10 50	11 10		11 30	11 50	12 10	12 30
Windsor & Eton Central	a	05 44	06 04	06 24	06 43	07 01	07 19	07 37	08 00	08 19		08 37	09 00	09 20	09 39	09 59	10 17	10 36	10 56	11 16		11 36	11 56	12 16	12 36

		GW 1	GW 1	GW 1	GW 1	GW 1		GW 1	GW 1	GW 1	GW 1	GW 1	GW 1	GW 1	GW 1	GW 1		GW 1	GW 1	GW 1	GW 1	GW 1	GW 1	GW 1	GW 1
Slough	d	12 50	13 10	13 30	13 50	14 10		14 30	14 50	15 10	15 30	15 50	16 21	16 43	17 01	17 21		17 40	17 58	18 16	18 40	18 58	19 16	19 40	20 00
Windsor & Eton Central	a	12 56	13 16	13 36	13 56	14 16		14 36	14 56	15 16	15 36	15 56	16 27	16 49	17 07	17 27		17 46	18 04	18 22	18 46	19 04	19 22	19 46	20 06

		GW 1		GW 1	GW 1	GW 1	GW 1	GW 1	GW 1	GW 1	GW 1	GW 1
Slough	d	20 20		20 40	21 00	21 20	21 40	22 00	22 20	22 40	23 00	23 20
Windsor & Eton Central	a	20 26		20 46	21 06	21 26	21 46	22 06	22 26	22 46	23 06	23 26

Saturdays

		GW 1	GW 1	GW 1	GW 1	GW 1	GW 1	GW 1	GW 1	GW 1		GW 1	GW 1	GW 1	GW 1	GW 1	GW 1	GW 1	GW 1	GW 1		GW 1	GW 1	GW 1	GW 1
Slough	d	06 17	06 47	07 17	07 47	08 17	08 47	09 17	09 47	10 17		10 47	11 17	11 47	12 17	12 47	13 17	13 47	14 17	14 47		15 17	15 47	16 17	16 47
Windsor & Eton Central	a	06 23	06 53	07 23	07 53	08 23	08 53	09 23	09 53	10 23		10 53	11 23	11 53	12 23	12 53	13 23	13 53	14 23	14 53		15 23	15 53	16 23	16 53

		GW 1	GW 1	GW 1	GW 1	GW 1		GW 1	GW 1	GW 1	GW 1	GW 1	GW 1	GW 1	GW 1	GW 1
Slough	d	17 17	17 47	18 17	18 47	19 17		19 47	20 17	20 47	21 17	21 47	22 17	22 53	23 22	23 56
Windsor & Eton Central	a	17 23	17 53	18 23	18 53	19 23		19 53	20 23	20 53	21 23	21 53	22 23	22 59	23 28	00 02

Sundays

		GW 1 A	GW 1	GW 1	GW 1	GW 1	GW 1	GW 1	GW 1	GW 1		GW 1	GW 1	GW 1	GW 1	GW 1	GW 1	GW 1	GW 1	GW 1		GW 1	GW 1	GW 1	GW 1
Slough	d	23p56	08 22	08 52	09 22	09 52	10 22	10 52	11 22	11 52		12 22	12 52	13 22	13 52	14 22	14 52	15 22	15 52	16 22		16 52	17 22	17 52	18 22
Windsor & Eton Central	a	00 02	08 28	08 58	09 28	09 58	10 28	10 58	11 28	11 58		12 28	12 58	13 28	13 58	14 28	14 58	15 28	15 58	16 28		16 58	17 28	17 58	18 28

		GW 1	GW 1	GW 1	GW 1	GW 1		GW 1	GW 1	GW 1	GW 1	GW 1
Slough	d	18 52	19 22	19 52	20 22	20 52		21 22	21 52	22 22	22 52	23 22
Windsor & Eton Central	a	18 58	19 28	19 58	20 28	20 58		21 28	21 58	22 28	22 58	23 28

A not 23 May

Table 119

Mondays to Fridays

Windsor & Eton - Slough

		GW 1	GW 1	GW 1	GW 1	GW 1	GW 1	GW 1	GW 1	GW 1		GW 1	GW 1	GW 1	GW 1	GW 1	GW 1	GW 1	GW 1	GW 1		GW 1	GW 1	GW 1	GW 1
Windsor & Eton Central	d	05 48	06 08	06 28	06 46	07 04	07 22	07 40	08 04	08 22		08 40	09 04	09 24	09 42	10 02	10 20	10 40	11 00	11 20		11 40	12 00	12 20	12 40
Slough 3	a	05 54	06 14	06 34	06 52	07 10	07 28	07 46	08 10	08 28		08 46	09 10	09 30	09 48	10 08	10 26	10 46	11 06	11 26		11 46	12 06	12 26	12 46

		GW 1	GW 1	GW 1	GW 1	GW 1		GW 1	GW 1	GW 1	GW 1	GW 1	GW 1	GW 1	GW 1	GW 1		GW 1	GW 1	GW 1	GW 1	GW 1	GW 1	GW 1	GW 1
Windsor & Eton Central	d	13 00	13 20	13 40	14 00	14 20		14 40	15 00	15 20	15 40	16 00	16 30	16 52	17 10	17 30		17 49	18 07	18 28	18 49	19 07	19 27	19 50	20 10
Slough 3	a	13 06	13 26	13 46	14 06	14 26		14 46	15 06	15 26	15 46	16 06	16 36	16 58	17 16	17 36		17 55	18 13	18 34	18 55	19 13	19 33	19 56	20 16

		GW 1		GW 1	GW 1	GW 1	GW 1	GW 1	GW 1	GW 1	GW 1	GW 1
Windsor & Eton Central	d	20 30		20 50	21 10	21 30	21 50	22 10	22 30	22 50	23 10	23 30
Slough 3	a	20 36		20 56	21 16	21 36	21 56	22 16	22 36	22 56	23 16	23 36

Saturdays

		GW 1	GW 1	GW 1	GW 1	GW 1	GW 1	GW 1	GW 1	GW 1		GW 1	GW 1	GW 1	GW 1	GW 1	GW 1	GW 1	GW 1	GW 1		GW 1	GW 1	GW 1	GW 1
Windsor & Eton Central	d	06 27	06 57	07 27	07 57	08 27	08 57	09 27	09 57	10 27		10 57	11 27	11 57	12 27	12 57	13 27	13 57	14 27	14 57		15 27	15 57	16 27	16 57
Slough 3	a	06 33	07 03	07 33	08 03	08 33	09 03	09 33	10 03	10 33		11 03	11 33	12 03	12 33	13 03	13 33	14 03	14 33	15 03		15 33	16 03	16 33	17 03

		GW 1	GW 1	GW 1	GW 1	GW 1		GW 1	GW 1	GW 1	GW 1	GW 1	GW 1	GW 1	GW 1
Windsor & Eton Central	d	17 27	17 57	18 27	18 57	19 27		19 57	20 27	20 57	21 26	21 57	22 27	23 02	23 32
Slough 3	a	17 33	18 03	18 33	19 03	19 33		20 03	20 33	21 03	21 32	22 03	22 33	23 08	23 38

Sundays

		GW 1	GW 1	GW 1	GW 1	GW 1	GW 1	GW 1	GW 1	GW 1		GW 1	GW 1	GW 1	GW 1	GW 1	GW 1	GW 1	GW 1	GW 1		GW 1	GW 1	GW 1	GW 1
Windsor & Eton Central	d	00 05	08 32	09 02	09 32	10 02	10 32	11 02	11 32	12 02		12 32	13 02	13 32	14 02	14 32	15 02	15 32	16 02	16 32		17 02	17 32	18 02	18 32
Slough 3	a	00 11	08 38	09 08	09 38	10 08	10 38	11 08	11 38	12 08		12 38	13 08	13 38	14 08	14 38	15 08	15 38	16 08	16 38		17 08	17 38	18 08	18 38

		GW 1	GW 1	GW 1	GW 1	GW 1		GW 1	GW 1	GW 1	GW 1	GW 1
Windsor & Eton Central	d	19 02	19 32	20 02	20 32	21 02		21 32	22 02	22 32	23 02	23 32
Slough 3	a	19 08	19 38	20 08	20 38	21 08		21 38	22 08	22 38	23 08	23 38

Table 120

Mondays to Fridays

Maidenhead - Marlow

		GW MX 1	GW 1	GW 1	GW 1	GW 1	GW 1	GW 1	GW 1	GW 1		GW 1	GW 1	GW 1	GW 1	GW 1	GW 1	GW 1	GW 1	GW 1		GW 1	GW 1	GW 1	GW 1
London Paddington 15 ⊖	d																								
Maidenhead 3	d	23p45	05 25	05 49		06 31		07 09		07 42			08 13		09 04	09 38	10 38	11 38	12 38	13 38		14 38	15 38	16 38	17 46
Furze Platt	d	23p49	05 29	05 53		06 35		07 13		07 46			08 17		09 08	09 42	10 42	11 42	12 42	13 42		14 42	15 42	16 42	17 50
Cookham	d	23p52	05 32	05 57		06 39		07 17		07 49			08 20		09 11	09 45	10 45	11 45	12 45	13 45		14 45	15 45	16 45	17 53
Bourne End 3	a	23p56	05 36	06 01		06 43		07 21		07 53			08 24		09 15	09 49	10 49	11 49	12 49	13 49		14 49	15 49	16 49	17 57
	d	00 01	05 40		06 18		06 49		07 28			07 58		08 27		09 53	10 53	11 53	12 53	13 53		14 53	15 53	16 53	18 01
Marlow	a	00 08	05 48		06 25		06 56		07 35			08 05		08 34		10 01	11 01	12 01	13 01	14 01		15 01	16 01	17 01	18 09

		GW 1	GW 1	GW 1	GW 1	GW 1		GW 1	GW 1	GW 1	GW 1	GW 1	GW 1	GW 1
London Paddington 15 ⊖	d	17 42				18 36								
Maidenhead 3	d	18 14		18 45		19b13			19 51		20 42	21 38	22 46	23 45
Furze Platt	d	18 19		18 49		19 18			19 55		20 46	21 42	22 50	23 49
Cookham	d	18 22		18 52		19 21			19 58		20 49	21 45	22 53	23 52
Bourne End 3	a	18 28		18 56		19 25			20 02		20 53	21 49	22 57	23 56
	d		18 31		19 01			19 30		20 05	20 57	21 53	23 01	00 01
Marlow	a		18 38		19 08			19 37		20 12	21 05	22 01	23 09	00 08

Saturdays

		GW 1	GW 1	GW 1	GW 1	GW 1	GW 1	GW 1	GW 1	GW 1		GW 1	GW 1	GW 1	GW 1	GW 1	GW 1	GW 1	GW 1	GW 1		GW 1
London Paddington 15 ⊖	d																					
Maidenhead 3	d	23p45	06 38	07 38	08 38	09 38	10 38	11 38	12 38	13 38		14 38	15 38	16 38	17 38	18 38	19 38	20 38	21 38	22 38		23 38
Furze Platt	d	23p49	06 42	07 42	08 42	09 42	10 42	11 42	12 42	13 42		14 42	15 42	16 42	17 42	18 42	19 42	20 42	21 42	22 42		23 42
Cookham	d	23p52	06 45	07 45	08 45	09 45	10 45	11 45	12 45	13 45		14 45	15 45	16 45	17 45	18 45	19 45	20 45	21 45	22 45		23 45
Bourne End 3	a	23p56	06 49	07 49	08 49	09 49	10 49	11 49	12 49	13 49		14 49	15 49	16 49	17 49	18 49	19 49	20 49	21 49	22 49		23 49
	d	00 01	06 53	07 53	08 53	09 53	10 53	11 53	12 53	13 53		14 53	15 53	16 53	17 53	18 53	19 53	20 53	21 53	22 53		23 53
Marlow	a	00 08	07 01	08 01	09 01	10 01	11 01	12 01	13 01	14 01		15 01	16 01	17 01	18 01	19 01	20 01	21 01	22 01	23 01		00 01

Sundays

		GW 1 A	GW 1	GW 1	GW 1	GW 1	GW 1	GW 1	GW 1	GW 1		GW 1	GW 1	GW 1	GW 1	GW 1	GW 1
London Paddington 15 ⊖	d																
Maidenhead 3	d	23p38	08 35	09 35	10 35	11 35	12 35	13 35	14 35	15 35		16 35	17 35	18 35	19 35	20 35	21 40
Furze Platt	d	23p42	08 39	09 39	10 39	11 39	12 38	13 39	14 39	15 39		16 39	17 39	18 39	19 39	20 39	21 44
Cookham	d	23p45	08 42	09 42	10 42	11 42	12 41	13 42	14 42	15 42		16 42	17 42	18 42	19 42	20 42	21 47
Bourne End 3	a	23p49	08 47	09 47	10 47	11 47	12 47	13 47	14 47	15 47		16 47	17 47	18 47	19 47	20 47	21 52
	d	23p53	08 51	09 51	10 51	11 51	12 50	13 51	14 51	15 51		16 51	17 51	18 51	19 51	20 51	21 56
Marlow	a	00 01	08 58	09 58	10 58	11 58	12 58	13 58	14 58	15 58		16 58	17 58	18 58	19 58	20 58	22 03

A not 23 May

b arr. 1906

Table 120

Marlow - Maidenhead

Mondays to Fridays

		GW MX 1	GW 1	GW 1	GW 1	GW 1	GW 1	GW 1	GW 1	GW 1	GW 1	GW 1	GW 1	GW 1	GW 1	GW 1	GW 1	GW 1	GW 1	GW 1	GW 1	GW 1	GW 1
Marlow	d	00 11	06 04		06 39		07 18		07 47		08 17		08 37		10 06	11 06	12 06	13 06	14 06	15 06	16 06	17 06	18 20
Bourne End 3	a	00 18	06 11		06 46		07 25		07 54		08 24		08 44		10 13	11 13	12 13	13 13	14 13	15 13	16 13	17 13	18 27
	d	00 22		06 14		06 49		07 28		07 57		08 28	08 48	09 19	10 17	11 17	12 17	13 17	14 17	15 17	16 17	17 17	
Cookham	d	00 26		06 17		06 52		07 31		08 00		08 31	08 52	09 22	10 21	11 21	12 21	13 21	14 21	15 21	16 21	17 21	
Furze Platt	d	00 29		06 21		06 56		07 35		08 04		08 35	08 55	09 26	10 24	11 24	12 24	13 24	14 24	15 24	16 24	17 24	
Maidenhead 3	a	00 34		06 25		07 00		07 39		08 08		08 39	09 00	09 30	10 29	11 29	12 29	13 29	14 29	15 29	16 29	17 29	
London Paddington 15 ⊖	a							08 17				09 20											

		GW 1	GW 1	GW 1	GW 1	GW 1	GW 1	GW 1	GW 1	GW 1	GW 1	GW 1
Marlow	d		18 50		19 20		19 55		20 15	21 08	22 04	23 13
Bourne End 3	a		18 57		19 27		20 02		20 22	21 15	22 11	23 20
	d	18 30		19 00		19 35		20 10	20 26	21 19	22 15	23 24
Cookham	d	18 33		19 03		19 38		20 13	20 30	21 23	22 19	23 28
Furze Platt	d	18 37		19 07		19 42		20 17	20 33	21 26	22 22	23 31
Maidenhead 3	a	18 41		19 11		19 46		20 21	20 38	21 31	22 27	23 36
London Paddington 15 ⊖	a											

Saturdays

		GW 1	GW 1	GW 1	GW 1	GW 1	GW 1	GW 1	GW 1	GW 1	GW 1	GW 1	GW 1	GW 1	GW 1	GW 1	GW 1	GW 1	GW 1
Marlow	d	00 11	07 06	08 06	09 06	10 06	11 06	12 06	13 06	14 06	15 06	16 06	17 06	18 06	19 06	20 06	21 06	22 06	23 06
Bourne End 3	a	00 18	07 13	08 13	09 13	10 13	11 13	12 13	13 13	14 13	15 13	16 13	17 13	18 13	19 13	20 13	21 13	22 13	23 13
	d	00 22	07 17	08 17	09 17	10 17	11 17	12 17	13 17	14 17	15 17	16 17	17 17	18 17	19 17	20 17	21 17	22 17	23 17
Cookham	d	00 26	07 21	08 21	09 21	10 21	11 21	12 21	13 21	14 21	15 21	16 21	17 21	18 21	19 21	20 21	21 21	22 21	23 21
Furze Platt	d	00 29	07 24	08 24	09 24	10 24	11 24	12 24	13 24	14 24	15 24	16 24	17 24	18 24	19 24	20 24	21 24	22 24	23 24
Maidenhead 3	a	00 34	07 29	08 29	09 29	10 29	11 29	12 29	13 29	14 29	15 29	16 29	17 29	18 29	19 29	20 29	21 29	22 29	23 29
London Paddington 15 ⊖	a																		

Sundays

		GW 1	GW 1	GW 1	GW 1	GW 1	GW 1	GW 1	GW 1	GW 1	GW 1	GW 1	GW 1	GW 1	GW 1	GW 1
Marlow	d	00 06	09 01	10 01	11 01	12 01	13 01	14 01	15 01	16 01	17 01	18 01	19 01	20 01	21 01	22 06
Bourne End 3	a	00 13	09 08	10 08	11 08	12 08	13 08	14 08	15 08	16 08	17 08	18 08	19 08	20 08	21 08	22 13
	d	00 17	09 12	10 12	11 12	12 12	13 12	14 12	15 12	16 12	17 12	18 12	19 12	20 12	21 12	22 17
Cookham	d	00 21	09 16	10 16	11 16	12 16	13 16	14 16	15 16	16 16	17 16	18 16	19 16	20 16	21 16	22 20
Furze Platt	d	00 24	09 20	10 20	11 20	12 20	13 20	14 20	15 20	16 20	17 20	18 20	19 20	20 20	21 20	22 24
Maidenhead 3	a	00 29	09 24	10 24	11 24	12 24	13 24	14 24	15 24	16 24	17 24	18 24	19 24	20 24	21 24	22 28
London Paddington 15 ⊖	a															

Table 121

Twyford - Henley-on-Thames

Mondays to Fridays

		GW 1	GW 1	GW 1	GW 1	GW 1	GW 1	GW 1	GW 1	GW 1	GW 1	GW 1	GW 1	GW 1	GW 1	GW 1	GW 1	GW 1	GW 1	GW 1	GW 1	GW 1	GW 1
London Paddington 15 ⊖	d																			17 12		18 12	19 06
Reading 7	d					08 06																	
Twyford 3	d	05 42	06 21	06 50	07 27	08 14	08 45	09 21	09 53	10 36	11 21	12 06	12 51	13 36	14 21	15 06	15 48	16 47	17 31	17 58	18 31	18 58	19 38
Wargrave	d	05 46	06 25	06 54	07 31	08 19	08 49	09 25	09 57	10 40	11 25	12 10	12 55	13 40	14 25	15 10	15 52	16 51	17 35	18 03	18 35	19 03	19 42
Shiplake	d	05 49	06 28	06 57	07 34	08 22	08 52	09 28	10 00	10 43	11 28	12 13	12 58	13 43	14 28	15 13	15 55	16 54	17 38	18 06	18 38	19 06	19 45
Henley-on-Thames	a	05 54	06 33	07 02	07 39	08 26	08 57	09 33	10 05	10 48	11 33	12 18	13 03	13 48	14 33	15 18	16 00	16 59	17 43	18 13	18 43	19 13	19 52

		GW 1	GW 1	GW 1	GW 1	GW 1
London Paddington 15 ⊖	d					
Reading 7	d					
Twyford 3	d	20 09	20 48	21 48	22 52	23 37
Wargrave	d	20 13	20 52	21 52	22 56	23 41
Shiplake	d	20 16	20 55	21 55	22 59	23 44
Henley-on-Thames	a	20 21	21 00	22 00	23 04	23 49

Saturdays

		GW 1	GW 1	GW 1	GW 1	GW 1	GW 1	GW 1	GW 1	GW 1	GW 1	GW 1	GW 1	GW 1	GW 1	GW 1	GW 1	GW 1	GW 1
London Paddington 15 ⊖	d																		
Reading 7	d																		
Twyford 3	d	06 57	07 50	08 50	09 50	10 50	11 50	12 50	13 50	14 50	15 50	16 50	17 50	18 50	19 50	20 50	21 50	22 50	23 50
Wargrave	d	07 01	07 54	08 54	09 54	10 54	11 54	12 54	13 54	14 54	15 54	16 54	17 54	18 54	19 54	20 54	21 54	22 54	23 54
Shiplake	d	07 04	07 57	08 57	09 57	10 57	11 57	12 57	13 57	14 57	15 57	16 57	17 57	18 57	19 57	20 57	21 57	22 57	23 57
Henley-on-Thames	a	07 09	08 02	09 02	10 02	11 02	12 02	13 02	14 02	15 02	16 02	17 02	18 02	19 02	20 02	21 02	22 02	23 02	00 02

Sundays

		GW 1 A	GW 1	GW 1	GW 1	GW 1	GW 1	GW 1	GW 1	GW 1	GW 1	GW 1	GW 1	GW 1	GW 1
London Paddington 15 ⊖	d														
Reading 7	d														
Twyford 3	d	23p50	09 38	10 38	11 38	12 38	13 38	14 38	15 38	16 38	17 38	18 38	19 38	20 38	21 38
Wargrave	d	23p54	09 42	10 42	11 42	12 42	13 42	14 42	15 42	16 42	17 42	18 42	19 42	20 42	21 42
Shiplake	d	23p57	09 45	10 45	11 45	12 45	13 45	14 45	15 45	16 45	17 45	18 45	19 45	20 45	21 45
Henley-on-Thames	a	00 02	09 50	10 50	11 50	12 50	13 50	14 50	15 50	16 50	17 50	18 50	19 50	20 50	21 50

A not 23 May

Table 121

Mondays to Fridays

Henley-on-Thames - Twyford

		GW MX	GW	GW	GW	GW	GW	GW	GW	GW	GW	GW	GW	GW	GW	GW	GW	GW	GW	GW	GW	GW	GW
Henley-on-Thames	d	23p52	06 06	06 36	07 09	07 44	08 29	09 01	09 36	10 09	10 54	11 39	12 24	13 09	13 54	14 39	15 24	16 20	17 09	17 46	18 17	18 46	19 16
Shiplake	d	23p56	06 10	06 40	07 13	07 48	08 33	09 05	09 40	10 13	10 58	11 43	12 28	13 13	13 58	14 43	15 28	16 24	17 13	17 50	18 21	18 50	19 20
Wargrave	d	23p59	06 13	06 43	07 16	07 51	08 36	09 08	09 43	10 16	11 01	11 46	12 31	13 16	14 01	14 46	15 31	16 27	17 16	17 53	18 24	18 53	19 23
Twyford	a	00 04	06 18	06 48	07 21	07 56	08 41	09 13	09 48	10 21	11 06	11 51	12 36	13 21	14 06	14 51	15 36	16 32	17 21	17 58	18 29	18 58	19 28
Reading	a	00 16																					
London Paddington ⊖	a				07 56	08 29																	

		GW	GW	GW	GW	GW	GW
Henley-on-Thames	d	19 55	20 24	21 05	22 07	23 07	23 52
Shiplake	d	19 59	20 28	21 09	22 11	23 11	23 56
Wargrave	d	20 02	20 31	21 12	22 14	23 14	23 59
Twyford	a	20 07	20 36	21 17	22 19	23 19	00 04
Reading	a						00 16
London Paddington ⊖	a						

Saturdays

		GW	GW	GW	GW	GW	GW	GW	GW	GW	GW	GW	GW	GW	GW	GW	GW	GW	GW
Henley-on-Thames	d	23p52	07 24	08 24	09 24	10 24	11 24	12 24	13 24	14 24	15 24	16 24	17 24	18 24	19 24	20 24	21 24	22 24	23 24
Shiplake	d	23p56	07 28	08 28	09 28	10 28	11 28	12 28	13 28	14 28	15 28	16 28	17 28	18 28	19 28	20 28	21 28	22 28	23 28
Wargrave	d	23p59	07 31	08 31	09 31	10 31	11 31	12 31	13 31	14 31	15 31	16 31	17 31	18 31	19 31	20 31	21 31	22 31	23 31
Twyford	a	00 04	07 36	08 36	09 36	10 36	11 36	12 36	13 36	14 36	15 36	16 36	17 36	18 36	19 36	20 36	21 36	22 36	23 36
Reading	a	00 16																	
London Paddington ⊖	a																		

Sundays

		GW	GW	GW	GW	GW	GW	GW	GW	GW	GW	GW	GW	GW	GW
Henley-on-Thames	d	00 08	10 03	11 03	12 03	13 03	14 03	15 03	16 03	17 03	18 03	19 03	20 03	21 03	22 01
Shiplake	d	00 12	10 07	11 07	12 07	13 07	14 07	15 07	16 07	17 07	18 07	19 07	20 07	21 07	22 05
Wargrave	d	00 15	10 10	11 10	12 10	13 10	14 10	15 10	16 10	17 10	18 10	19 10	20 10	21 10	22 08
Twyford	a	00 20	10 15	11 15	12 15	13 15	14 15	15 15	16 15	17 15	18 15	19 15	20 15	21 15	22 13
Reading	a														
London Paddington ⊖	a														

Table 122

Mondays to Fridays

Reading - Basingstoke

		GW MO	GW	GW	GW	GW	GW	XC	GW	GW	XC	GW	GW	XC	GW	GW	XC	GW	GW	XC	GW	GW	XC
Reading	d	23p37	05 39	06 07	06 39	07 07	07 39	07b46	08 07	08 39	08 45	09 07	09 39	09c46	10 07	10 39	10e46	11 07	11 39	11f46	12 07	12 39	12g46
Reading West	d	23p40	05 42	06 10	06 42	07 10	07 42		08 10	08 42		09 10	09 42		10 10	10 42		11 10	11 42		12 10	12 42	
Mortimer	d	23p48	05 50	06 18	06 50	07 18	07 50		08 18	08 50		09 18	09 50		10 18	10 50		11 18	11 50		12 18	12 50	
Bramley (Hants)	d	23p53	05 55	06 23	06 55	07 23	07 55		08 23	08 55		09 23	09 55		10 23	10 55		11 23	11 55		12 23	12 55	
Basingstoke	a	00 01	06 03	06 31	07 03	07 31	08 03	08 08	08 31	09 03	09 08	09 34	10 03	10 08	10 31	11 03	11 08	11 31	12 03	12 08	12 34	13 03	13 08

		GW	GW	XC	GW	GW	XC	GW	GW	XC	GW	GW	XC	GW	GW	XC	GW	GW	XC	GW	GW	XC	GW
Reading	d	13 07	13 39	13h46	14 07	14 39	14i46	15 07	15 39	15j46	16 07	16 39	16k46	17 07	17 39	17l46	18 07	18 39	18m46	19 07	19 37	19n46	20 07
Reading West	d	13 10	13 42		14 10	14 42		15 10	15 42		16 10	16 42		17 10	17 42		18 10	18 42		19 10	19 40		20 10
Mortimer	d	13 18	13 50		14 18	14 50		15 18	15 50		16 18	16 50		17 18	17 50		18 18	18 50		19 18	19 48		20 18
Bramley (Hants)	d	13 23	13 55		14 23	14 55		15 23	15 55		16 23	16 55		17 23	17 55		18 23	18 55		19 23	19 53		20 23
Basingstoke	a	13 31	14 03	14 08	14 31	15 03	15 08	15 31	16 03	16 08	16 31	17 03	17 08	17 31	18 05	18 08	18 31	19 05	19 08	19 31	20 01	20 09	20 32

		GW	XC	GW	GW	XC	GW	XC	GW	GW
Reading	d	20 37	20o46	21 07	21 39	21q46	22 10	22r48	22 55	23 34
Reading West	d	20 40		21 10	21 42		22 13		22 58	23 37
Mortimer	d	20 48		21 18	21 50		22 21		23 06	23 45
Bramley (Hants)	d	20 53		21 23	21 55		22 26		23 11	23 50
Basingstoke	a	21 01	21 09	21 31	22 03	22 09	22 34	23 12	23 19	23 58

Saturdays

		GW	GW	GW	GW	XC	GW A	GW B	GW	XC	GW	GW	XC	GW	GW	XC	GW A	GW B	GW	XC	GW A	GW B	GW
Reading	d	06 07	06 39	07 07	07 39	07b46	08 07	08 10	08 39	08t46	09 07	09 39	09c46	10 07	10 39	10e46	11 07	11 07	11 39	11f46	12 07	12 10	12 39
Reading West	d	06 10	06 42	07 10	07 42		08 10	08 13	08 42		09 10	09 42		10 10	10 42		11 10	11 10	11 42		12 10	12 13	12 42
Mortimer	d	06 18	06 50	07 18	07 50		08 18	08 21	08 50		09 18	09 50		10 18	10 50		11 17	11 18	11 50		12 18	12 21	12 50
Bramley (Hants)	d	06 23	06 55	07 23	07 55		08 23	08 26	08 55		09 23	09 55		10 23	10 55		11 22	11 23	11 55		12 23	12 26	12 55
Basingstoke	a	06 32	07 03	07 32	08 03	08 08	08 31	08 34	09 03	09 08	09 31	10 03	10 08	10 31	11 03	11 08	11 31	11 32	12 03	12 08	12 31	12 34	13 03

		XC	GW A	GW B	GW	XC	GW	GW	XC	GW	GW	XC	GW	GW	XC	GW	GW	XC	GW	GW	XC	GW	GW
Reading	d	12g46	13 07	13 08	13 39	13h46	14 07	14 39	14i46	15 07	15 39	15j46	16 07	16 39	16k46	17 07	17 39	17l46	18 07	18 39	18m46	19 07	19 39
Reading West	d		13 10	13 10	13 42		14 10	14 42		15 10	15 42		16 10	16 42		17 10	17 42		18 10	18 42		19 10	19 42
Mortimer	d		13 16	13 18	13 50		14 18	14 50		15 18	15 50		16 18	16 50		17 18	17 50		18 18	18 50		19 18	19 50
Bramley (Hants)	d		13 21	13 23	13 55		14 23	14 55		15 23	15 55		16 23	16 55		17 23	17 55		18 23	18 55		19 23	19 55
Basingstoke	a	13 08	13 31	13 33	14 03	14 08	14 31	15 03	15 08	15 31	16 03	16 08	16 31	17 03	17 08	17 31	18 03	18 08	18 31	19 03	19 08	19 31	20 03

		XC	GW	GW	XC	GW	GW	XC	GW	GW	XC	GW
Reading	d	19n46	20 07	20 39	20o46	21 07	21 39	21v46	22 07	22 39	22r48	23 07
Reading West	d		20 10	20 42		21 10	21 42		22 10	22 42		23 10
Mortimer	d		20 18	20 50		21 18	21 50		22 18	22 50		23 18
Bramley (Hants)	d		20 23	20 55		21 23	21 55		22 23	22 55		23 23
Basingstoke	a	20 08	20 31	21 03	21 08	21 31	22 03	22 08	22 31	23 03	23 11	23 31

Sundays

		GW	GW	GW	XC	GW	XC	GW	XC	GW	XC	GW	XC	GW	XC	GW	XC	GW	XC	GW	XC	GW	XC
Reading	d	07 37	08 37	09 37	09 51	10 37	10w51	11 37	11y51	12 37	12z51	13 37	13aa51	14 37	14bb51	15 37	15cc51	16 37	16dd51	17 37	17l51	18 37	18ee51
Reading West	d	07 40	08 40	09 40		10 40		11 40		12 40		13 40		14 40		15 40		16 40		17 40		18 40	
Mortimer	d	07 48	08 48	09 48		10 48		11 48		12 48		13 48		14 48		15 48		16 48		17 48		18 48	
Bramley (Hants)	d	07 53	08 53	09 53		10 53		11 53		12 53		13 53		14 53		15 53		16 53		17 53		18 53	
Basingstoke	a	08 01	09 01	10 01	10 09	11 01	11 09	12 01	12 09	13 01	13 09	14 01	14 09	15 01	15 09	16 01	16 09	17 01	17 09	18 01	18 09	19 01	19 09

A from 11 September
B until 4 September
b arr. 0739
c arr. 0939
e arr. 1039
f arr. 1139
g arr. 1239
h arr. 1339
i arr. 1439
j arr. 1539
k arr. 1639
l arr. 1739
m arr. 1839
n arr. 1939
o arr. 2039
q arr. 2140
r arr. 2241
t arr. 0839
v arr. 2139
w arr. 1042
y arr. 1142
z arr. 1242
aa arr. 1342
bb arr. 1442
cc arr. 1542
dd arr. 1642
ee arr. 1842

Reading - Basingstoke

Sundays

		GW 1	XC ◇1	GW 1	XC ◇1	GW 1	XC ◇1	GW 1	GW 1
Reading 7	d	19 37	19b51	20 37	20c51	21 37	21e51	22 37	23 37
Reading West	d	19 40		20 40		21 40		22 41	23 40
Mortimer	d	19 48		20 48		21 48		22 49	23 48
Bramley (Hants)	d	19 53		20 53		21 53		22 54	23 53
Basingstoke	a	20 01	20 09	21 01	21 09	22 01	22 11	23 02	00 01

b arr. 1942 c arr. 2042 e arr. 2142

Basingstoke - Reading

Mondays to Fridays

		GW MX 1	GW MO 1	XC ◇1	GW 1	GW 1	XC ◇1	GW 1	GW 1	XC ◇1	GW 1	GW 1	XC ◇1	GW 1	GW 1	XC ◇1	GW 1	GW 1	XC ◇1	GW 1	GW 1	XC ◇1	GW 1
Basingstoke	d	00 02	00 07	05 47	06 07	06 37	06 47	07 07	07 37	07 47	08 07	08 37	08 47	09 07	09 37	09 47	10 07	10 37	10 47	11 07	11 37	11 47	12 07
Bramley (Hants)	d	00 09	00 14		06 14	06 44		07 14	07 44		08 14	08 44		09 14	09 44		10 14	10 44		11 14	11 44		12 14
Mortimer	d	00 14	00 19		06 19	06 49		07 19	07 49		08 19	08 49		09 19	09 49		10 19	10 49		11 19	11 49		12 19
Reading West	d	00 22	00 26		06 27	06 57		07 27	07 57		08 27	08 57		09 27	09 57		10 27	10 57		11 27	11 57		12 27
Reading 7	a	00 26	00 30	06 04	06 32	07 00	07 04	07 31	08 00	08 04	08 30	09 00	09 04	09 30	10 00	10 04	10 30	11 00	11 04	11 30	12 00	12 04	12 30

		GW 1	XC ◇1	GW 1	GW 1	XC ◇1	GW 1	GW 1	XC ◇1	GW 1	GW 1	XC ◇1	GW 1	GW 1	XC ◇1	GW 1	GW 1	XC ◇1	GW 1	GW 1	XC ◇1	GW 1	GW 1
Basingstoke	d	12 37	12 47	13 07	13 37	13 47	14 07	14 37	14 47	15 07	15 37	15 47	16 07	16 37	16 47	17 07	17 37	17 47	18 07	18 37	18 47	19 07	19 37
Bramley (Hants)	d	12 44		13 14	13 44		14 14	14 44		15 14	15 44		16 14	16 44		17 14	17 44		18 14	18 44		19 14	19 44
Mortimer	d	12 49		13 19	13 49		14 19	14 49		15 19	15 49		16 19	16 49		17 19	17 49		18 19	18 49		19 19	19 49
Reading West	d	12 57		13 27	13 57		14 27	14 57		15 27	15 57		16 27	16 57		17 27	17 57		18 27	18 57		19 27	19 57
Reading 7	a	13 00	13 04	13 30	14 00	14 04	14 30	15 00	15 04	15 30	16 00	16 04	16 30	17 00	17 04	17 30	18 00	18 04	18 31	19 00	19 04	19 31	20 00

		XC ◇1	GW 1	GW 1	XC ◇1	GW 1	GW 1	GW 1	GW 1	GW 1
Basingstoke	d	19 47	20 07	20 37	20 47	21 07	21 42	22 24	22 55	23 30
Bramley (Hants)	d		20 14	20 44		21 14	21 49	22 31	23 02	23 37
Mortimer	d		20 19	20 49		21 19	21 54	22 36	23 07	23 42
Reading West	d		20 27	20 57		21 27	22 02	22 44	23 15	23 50
Reading 7	a	20 04	20 30	21 01	21 04	21 30	22 05	22 47	23 18	23 53

Saturdays

		GW 1	XC ◇1	GW 1	XC ◇1	GW 1	XC ◇1	GW 1	XC ◇1	GW 1	GW 1	XC ◇1	GW 1	GW 1	XC ◇1	GW 1	GW 1	XC ◇1	GW 1	GW 1	XC ◇1	GW 1	GW 1
Basingstoke	d	00 02	05 41	06 37	06 47	07 07	07 25	07 37	07 47	08 07	08 37	08 47	09 07	09 37	09 47	10 07	10 37	10 47	11 07	11 37	11 47	12 07	12 37
Bramley (Hants)	d	00 09		06 44		07 14		07 44		08 14	08 44		09 14	09 44		10 14	10 44		11 14	11 44		12 14	12 44
Mortimer	d	00 14		06 49		07 19		07 49		08 19	08 49		09 19	09 49		10 19	10 49		11 19	11 49		12 19	12 49
Reading West	d	00 22		06 57		07 27		07 57		08 27	08 57		09 27	09 57		10 27	10 57		11 27	11 57		12 27	12 57
Reading 7	a	00 26	05 59	07 00	07 04	07 31	07 42	08 00	08 04	08 31	09 00	09 04	09 31	10 00	10 04	10 31	11 00	11 04	11 31	12 00	12 04	12 31	13 00

		XC ◇1	GW 1	GW 1	XC ◇1	GW 1	GW 1	XC ◇1	GW 1	GW 1 A	GW 1 B	XC ◇1	GW 1	GW 1	XC ◇1	GW 1	GW 1	XC ◇1	GW 1	GW 1	XC ◇1	GW 1	GW 1
Basingstoke	d	12 47	13 07	13 37	13 47	14 07	14 37	14 47	15 07	15 37	15 37	15 47	16 07	16 37	16 47	17 07	17 37	17 47	18 07	18 37	18 47	19 07	19 37
Bramley (Hants)	d		13 14	13 44		14 14	14 44		15 14	15 44	15 44		16 14	16 44		17 14	17 44		18 14	18 44		19 14	19 44
Mortimer	d		13 19	13 49		14 19	14 49		15 19	15 49	15 49		16 19	16 49		17 19	17 49		18 19	18 49		19 19	19 49
Reading West	d		13 27	13 57		14 27	14 57		15 27	15 57	15 57		16 27	16 57		17 27	17 57		18 27	18 57		19 27	19 57
Reading 7	a	13 04	13 31	14 00	14 04	14 31	15 00	15 04	15 31	16 00	16 02	16 05	16 31	17 00	17 04	17 31	18 00	18 04	18 31	19 00	19 04	19 31	20 01

		XC ◇1	GW 1	GW 1	XC ◇1	GW 1	GW 1	GW 1	GW 1	GW 1	GW 1
Basingstoke	d	19 47	20 08	20 37	20 47	21 07	21 39	22 07	22 37	23 07	23 37
Bramley (Hants)	d		20 14	20 44		21 14	21 46	22 14	22 44	23 14	23 44
Mortimer	d		20 19	20 49		21 19	21 51	22 19	22 49	23 19	23 49
Reading West	d		20 27	20 57		21 27	21 57	22 27	22 57	23 27	23 57
Reading 7	a	20 04	20 33	21 01	21 04	21 31	22 02	22 31	23 00	23 31	00 01

Sundays

		GW 1 C	GW 1	GW 1	XC ◇1	GW 1	XC ◇1	GW 1	XC ◇1	GW 1	XC ◇1	GW 1	XC ◇1	GW 1	XC ◇1	GW 1	GW 1	XC ◇1	GW 1	XC ◇1	GW 1	XC ◇1	GW 1
Basingstoke	d	23p37	08 07	09 07	09 47	10 07	10 47	11 07	11 47	12 07	12 47	13 07	13 47	14 07	14 47	15 07	16 07	16 47	17 07	17 47	18 07	18 47	19 07
Bramley (Hants)	d	23p44	08 14	09 14		10 14		11 14		12 14		13 14		14 14		15 14	16 14		17 14		18 14		19 14
Mortimer	d	23p49	08 19	09 19		10 19		11 19		12 19		13 19		14 19		15 19	16 19		17 19		18 19		19 19
Reading West	d	23p57	08 27	09 27		10 27		11 27		12 27		13 27		14 27		15 27	16 27		17 27		18 27		19 28
Reading 7	a	00 01	08 30	09 30	10 04	10 30	11 04	11 30	12 04	12 30	13 04	13 30	14 04	14 30	15 04	15 30	16 30	17 04	17 30	18 04	18 30	19 04	19 31

		XC ◇1	GW 1	XC ◇1	GW 1	GW 1	GW 1
Basingstoke	d	19 47	20 07	20 47	21 07	22 07	23 07
Bramley (Hants)	d		20 14		21 14	22 15	23 14
Mortimer	d		20 19		21 19	22 20	23 19
Reading West	d		20 27		21 27	22 30	23 27
Reading 7	a	20 04	20 30	21 04	21 30	22 33	23 30

A from 11 September B until 4 September C not 23 May

Network Diagram for Table 123

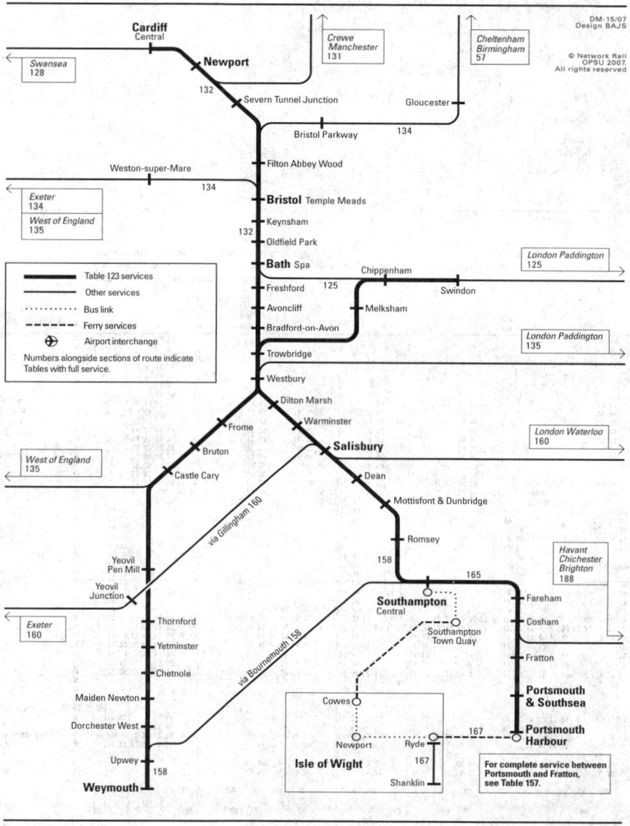

Table 123

Mondays to Fridays

South Wales and Bristol - Weymouth and Portsmouth

		GW MX		GW	GW	GW	GW	GW	GW	GW		GW	GW	GW	GW	SW	GW	GW	GW	GW	GW	GW	GW	GW	GW
							◇					◇ H		■ H		◇[1]		◇[1]	◇ H			◇ H			◇ H
Cardiff Central [7]	d											06 28		07 30					08 30			09 30			10 30
Newport (South Wales)	d											06 42		07 44					08 44			09 44			10 44
Severn Tunnel Jn	d											06 53		07 55					08 55						
Filton Abbey Wood	d											07 09	07 25	08 09	08 23				09 09		09 23	10 09		10 25	11 09
Bristol Temple Meads [10]	d	23p20					05 44			06f47		07 23	07 49	08 23	08 40	08 51	09 05		09 23		09g49	10 23		10h49	11 23
Keynsham	d	23p27					05 51			06 54			07 56		08 47	08 58					09 56			10 56	
Oldfield Park	d	23p34					05 58			07 01			08 03		08 54		09 17				10 03			11 03	
London Paddington [15] ⊖	d																	08 18							
Swindon	d								06e16																
Chippenham	d								06 32																
Melksham	d								06 41																
Bath Spa [7]	d	23p38					06 02			07 05		07 36	08 07	08 36	08 58	09 07	09 21		09 36		10 07	10 36		11 07	11 36
Freshford	d	23p47					06 12			07 15			08 16		09 07						10 16			11 16	
Avoncliff	d	23b50					06x14			07x17			08x18		09x09						10x18			11x18	
Bradford-on-Avon	d	23p53					06 18			07 21		07 47	08 22	08 47	09 13	09 20	09 33				10 22	10 47		11 22	11 47
Trowbridge	d	23p59					06 25		06 50	07 27		07 53	08 28	08 53	09 19	09 27	09 39		09 51		10 28	10 53		11 28	11 53
Westbury	a	00 06					06 32		06 57	07 34		08 01	08 36	09 01	09 27	09 33	09 49	09 58	09 58		10 36	11 00		11 36	12 01
	d	00 07		05 24	05 49	06 25	06 37	06 47	07 01			08 01		09 01	09 31	09 39		10 00	09 58	10 08	10 37	11 01	11 07		12 01
Frome	d	00a18				06a35		06 56							09 40						10 46				
Bruton	d							07 08							09 52						10 58				
Castle Cary	a							07 13							09 57			10 17			11 03				
	d							07 14							09 58			10 17			11 03				
Yeovil Pen Mill	d							07c35							10 12						11 17				
Thornford	d							07x39							10x16						11x22				
Yetminster	d							07x42							10x19						11x25				
Chetnole	d							07x46							10x23						11x29				
Maiden Newton	d							07 58							10 35						11 41				
Dorchester West	d							08 09							10 46						11 54				
Upwey	a							08 16							10 54						12 02				
Weymouth	a							08 23							11 02						12 08				
Dilton Marsh	d								07x03											10x10			11x09		
Warminster	d			05 32	05 56		06 43		07 12			08 08		09 08		09 46			10 06	10a19		11 08	11 16		12 08
Salisbury	a			05 53	06 19		07 10		07 36			08 32		09 32		10 09			10 28			11 32	11 38		12 32
	d				06 20		07 11		07 36			08 32		09 32					10 30			11 32	11 39		12 32
Romsey	d				06 38		07 30		07 56			08 50		09 50					10 50			11 50	12 00		12 50
Southampton Central	a				06 49		07 41		08 09			09 04		10 04					11 04			12 02	12 19		13 04
Fareham	a				07 14		08 05					09 27		10 27					11 27			12 27			13 27
	d				07 15		08 06					09 27		10 27					11 27			12 27			13 27
Cosham	a				07 23		08 14					09 35		10 35					11 35			12 35			13 35
Fratton	a				07 34		08 21					09 42		10 42					11 42			12 42			13 42
Portsmouth & Southsea	a				07 38		08 24					09 46		10 46					11 46			12 46			13 46
Portsmouth Harbour	a				07 45		08 30					09 54		10 54					11 54			12 54			13 54
Havant	a																								
Chichester [4]	a																								
Barnham	a																								
Worthing [4]	a																								
Shoreham-by-Sea	a																								
Hove [2]	a																								
Brighton [10]	a																								

b previous night, stops on request
c arr. 0729
e arr. 0606
f arr. 0641
g arr. 0935
h arr. 1038

For connections from Swansea please refer to Table 128. For connections from Plymouth and Exeter St Davids please refer to Table 135. For connections to Bournemouth please refer to Table 158

Table 123

South Wales and Bristol - Weymouth and Portsmouth

		GW	GW	GW	GW	SW		GW	GW	GW	GW	GW	GW	GW	GW	GW	SW	GW	GW	GW	GW	GW	GW	GW	GW
		◇1 ⊘		◇ 🛒	◇ A	◇1 ☕		◇1 ☕	◇ 🛒		◇ 🛒			◇ 🛒	◇1 ⊘		◇1	◇ 🛒					◇1 ☕	■ 🛒	
Cardiff Central 7	d			11 30					12 30		13 30			14 30				15 30						16 30	
Newport (South Wales)	d			11 44					12 44		13 44			14 44				15 44						16 44	
Severn Tunnel Jn	d																							16 55	
Filton Abbey Wood	d		11 23	12 09	12 25				13 09	13 23	14 09		14 25	15 09		15 23		16 09		16 25	16 48	16 55		17 09	17 23
Bristol Temple Meads 10	d		11b49	12 23	12 39	13 10			13c23	13e49	14 23		14f48	15 23		15g44	15 54	16 23		16h49	17 05	17i11		17 23	17j49
Keynsham	d		11 56		12 46					13 56			14 55			15 51				16 56		17 19			17 56
Oldfield Park	d		12 03		12 53					14 03			15 02			15 58				17 03	17 17	17 26		17 33	18 03
London Paddington 15 ⊖	d	11 06						12 18							15 06								16 36		
Swindon	d																								
Chippenham	d																								
Melksham	d																								
Bath Spa 7	d		12 07	12 36	12 57	13 23			13 36	14 07	14 36		15 06	15 36		16 02	16 07	16 36		17 07	17 22	17 30		17 37	18 07
Freshford	d		12 16		13 06					14 16			15 15			16 10				17 16		17 39			18 16
Avoncliff	d		12x18		13x07					14x18			15x17			16x13				17x18		17 41			18x18
Bradford-on-Avon	d		12 22	12 47	13 12	13 35			13 47	14 22	14 47		15 22	15 47		16 16	16 22	16 47		17 22	17 33			17 49	18 22
Trowbridge	d		12 28	12 53	13 18	13 42			13 53	14 28	14 53		15 28	15 53		16 22	16 28	16 53		17 28	17 39	17 49		17 55	18 28
Westbury	a	12 21	12 36	13 01	13 25	13 48		13 57	14 01	14 36	15 01	15 08	15 36	16 01	16 22	16 29	16 36	17 01		17 36	17 47	17 59	18 02	18 04	18 36
	d	12 22	12 37	13 01	13 27	13 53		13 59	14 02	14 37	15 01	15 11	15 38	16 01	16 23		16 39	17 01	17 11	17 38	17 54		18 03	18 04	18 39
Frome	d		12 47							14a48			15 47							17 47					18 49
Bruton	d		12 57										15 58							17 59					19 00
Castle Cary	a	12 39	13 03					14 16					16 04		16 41					18 04			18 20		19 05
	d	12 39	13 04					14 16					16 09		16 41					18 05			18 21		19 06
Yeovil Pen Mill	d		13 17										16 24							18 21					19 19
Thornford	d		13x22										16x28							18x26					19x24
Yetminster	d		13x25										16x31							18x29					19x27
Chetnole	d		13x29										16x35							18x33					19x31
Maiden Newton	d		13 41										16 47							18 45					19 43
Dorchester West	d		13 54										16 58							18 58					19 54
Upwey	a		14 02										17 05							19 06					20 01
Weymouth	a		14 09										17 10							19 13					20 08
Dilton Marsh	d				13x29							15x13							17x13		17x56				
Warminster	d			13 08	13 36	14 00			14 08		15 08	15a22		16 08			16 47	17 08	17a21		18a05			18 11	
Salisbury	a			13 32	13 58	14 28			14 32		15 32			16 32			17 09	17 32						18 34	
	d			13 32	13 59	14 45			14 32		15 32			16 32				17 32						18 34	
Romsey	d			13 50	14 20				14 50		15 50			16 50				17 50						18 53	
Southampton Central	a			14 04	14 32				15 04		16 04			17 04				18 04						19 04	
Fareham	a			14 27	14 55				15 27		16 27			17 27				18 27						19 27	
	d			14 27	14 56				15 27		16 27			17 27				18 27						19 27	
Cosham	a			14 35	15 04				15 35		16 35			17 35				18 35						19 35	
Fratton	a			14 42					15 42		16 42			17 42				18 48						19 42	
Portsmouth & Southsea	a			14 46					15 46		16 46			17 46				18 52						19 46	
Portsmouth Harbour	a			14 54					15 54		16 54			17 54				18 58						19 54	
Havant	a				15 10																				
Chichester 4	a				15 21																				
Barnham	a				15 29																				
Worthing 4	a				15 45																				
Shoreham-by-Sea	a				15 56																				
Hove 2	a				16 07																				
Brighton 10	a				16 14																				

A ◇ from Bristol Temple Meads
b arr. 1135
c arr. 1317
e arr. 1336
f arr. 1438
g arr. 1537
h arr. 1638
i arr. 1703
j arr. 1737

For connections from Swansea please refer to Table 128. For connections from Plymouth and Exeter St Davids please refer to Table 135. For connections to Bournemouth please refer to Table 158

Table 123

South Wales and Bristol - Weymouth and Portsmouth

		GW	GW	GW	GW	GW	GW	GW	GW	GW	GW	GW		GW	GW	GW	GW	GW	SW	GW
		◇1 ☕		■ 🛒	◇1 ☕			◇1 ☕	◇ 🛒	◇1 ☕		◇		◇1 ☕		◇1 ☕	◇		1	
Cardiff Central 7	d			17 30					18 30			19 30					20 30			
Newport (South Wales)	d			17 44					18 44			19 44					20 44			
Severn Tunnel Jn	d			17 55					18 55											
Filton Abbey Wood	d		17 49	18 09		18 23			19 09		19 23	20 09			20 25		21 09			
Bristol Temple Meads 10	d		18 07	18 23		18b49			19 23		19c49	20 23			20e49		21 23	22 00	22 25	23 20
Keynsham	d		18 14			18 56					19 56				20 56			22 07		23 27
Oldfield Park	d		18 21			19 03					20 03				21 03			22 14		23 34
London Paddington 15 ⊖	d	17 06			17 36			18 06		18 33				19 45		20 35				
Swindon	d						18 44													
Chippenham	d						19 01													
Melksham	d						19 11													
Bath Spa 7	d		18 25	18 36		19 07			19 36		20 07	20 36			21 07		21 36	22 18	22 38	23 38
Freshford	d		18 34			19 16					20 16				21 16			22 28		23 47
Avoncliff	d		18x36			19x18					20x18				21x18			22x29		23x50
Bradford-on-Avon	d		18 40	18 47		19 22			19 47		20 22	20 47			21 22		21 47	22 34	22 51	23 53
Trowbridge	d		18 46	18 53		19 28	19 20		19 53		20 28	20 53			21 28		21 53	22 40	22 57	23 59
Westbury	a	18 52	18 56	19 00	18 59	19 36	19 27	19 52	20 01	20 04	20 36	21 01		21 05	21 36	21 56	22 01	22 47	23 04	00 06
	d			19 01	19 01		19 40	19 53	20 01	20 05	20 36	21 01		21 05	21 38	21 57	22 01		23 08	00 07
Frome	d							20a02			20a47				21 49					00a18
Bruton	d														22 01					
Castle Cary	a				19 17					20 22				21 27	22 06	22 14				
	d				19 19					20 22				21 27	22 06	22 15				
Yeovil Pen Mill	d														22 20					
Thornford	d														22x25					
Yetminster	d														22x28					
Chetnole	d														22x32					
Maiden Newton	d														22 44					
Dorchester West	d														22 54					
Upwey	a														23 02					
Weymouth	a														23 09					
Dilton Marsh	d						19x42										22x04			
Warminster	d			19 08			19 49		20 08			21 08					22 08		23 15	
Salisbury	a			19 32			20 12		20 32			21 32					22 32		23 35	
	d			19 32			20 13		20 32			21 32					22 32			
Romsey	d			19 50			20 35		20 50			21 50					22 50			
Southampton Central	a			20 04			20 48		21 04			22 02					23 03			
Fareham	a			20 27					21 27			22 42					23 27			
	d			20 27					21 27			22 42					23 27			
Cosham	a																			
Fratton	a			20 42					21 41			22 56					23 44			
Portsmouth & Southsea	a			20 46					21 45			22 59					23 48			
Portsmouth Harbour	a			20 54					21 52			23 04					23 54			
Havant	a																			
Chichester 4	a																			
Barnham	a																			
Worthing 4	a																			
Shoreham-by-Sea	a																			
Hove 2	a																			
Brighton 10	a																			

b arr. 1837
c arr. 1936
e arr. 2038

For connections from Swansea please refer to Table 128. For connections from Plymouth and Exeter St Davids please refer to Table 135. For connections to Bournemouth please refer to Table 158

Table 123

Saturdays

South Wales and Bristol - Weymouth and Portsmouth

		GW	GW	GW	GW	GW	GW	GW	GW	GW		GW	GW	GW	SW	GW	GW	GW	GW	GW	GW	GW	GW	GW	GW
			■ 🛏 □P			◇				◇			◇		◇1	■ 1 A □P	◇1 B □P	C	◇			◇ Ħ			■ 1 A □P
Cardiff Central 7	d									06 30			07 30						08 30			09 30			
Newport (South Wales)	d									06 44			07 44						08 44			09 44			
Severn Tunnel Jn	d									06 55			07 55						08 55						
Filton Abbey Wood	d									07 09			08 09	08 23					09 09		09 23	10 09		10 28	
Bristol Temple Meads 10	d	23p20				05 49			06 49	07 23		07 49	08 23	08 40	08 51			09 09	09 23		09c49	10 23		10 49	
Keynsham	d	23p27				05 56			06 56			07 56		08 47	08 58			09 17			09 56			10 56	
Oldfield Park	d	23p34				06 03			07 03			08 03		08 54				09 24			10 03			11 03	
London Paddington 15 ⊖	d		23p45													08 35	08 18								10 35
Swindon	d																								
Chippenham	d																								
Melksham	d																								
Bath Spa 7	d	23p38				06 07			07 07	07 36		08 07	08 36	08 58	09 07			09 28	09 36		10 07	10 36		11 07	
Freshford	d	23p47				06 16			07 16			08 16		09 07							10 16			11 16	
Avoncliff	d	23b50				06x18			07x18			08x18		09x09							10x18			11x18	
Bradford-on-Avon	d	23p53				06 22			07 22	07 47		08 22	08 47	09 13	09 20			09 41	09 47		10 22	10 47		11 22	
Trowbridge	d	23p59				06 28			07 28	07 53		08 28	08 53	09 19	09 27			09 49	09 53		10 28	10 53		11 28	
Westbury	a	00 06	01 35			06 35			07 35	08 01		08 35	09 01	09 27	09 34	09 56	09 59	09 56	10 03		10 36	11 00		11 35	11 53
	d	00 07	01 37	05 26	06 01	06 43	06 47	07 03		08 01			09 01	09 27	09 39	09 58	10 00	10 02	10 03	10 10	10 37	11 01	11 07		11 54
Frome	d	00a18					06 56							09 36				10 10			10 46				
Bruton	d						07 08							09 48				10 21			10 58				
Castle Cary	a						07 14							09 53		10 14	10 17	10 25			11 03				12 11
	d						07 15							09 53		10 15	10 18	10 26			11 03				12 12
Yeovil Pen Mill	d						07 31							10 07				10 49			11 17				
Thornford	d						07x35							10x12							11x22				
Yetminster	d						07x38							10x15							11x25				
Chetnole	d						07x42							10x19							11x29				
Maiden Newton	d						07 54							10 31				11 14			11 41				
Dorchester West	d						08 05							10 38				11 30			11 54				
Upwey	a						08 12							10 49							12 02				
Weymouth	a						08 18							10 56				11 42			12 08				
Dilton Marsh	d							07x06												10x13			11x09		
Warminster	d			05 34	06 08	06 50		07 12		08 08			09 08		09 46				10 08	10a19		11 08	11 16		
Salisbury	a			05 58	06 32	07 15		07 35		08 32			09 32		10 09				10 31			11 32	11 38		
	d				06 32	07 24		07 37		08 32			09 32						10 32			11 32	11 39		
Romsey	d				06 50	07 44		07 56		08 50			09 50						10 50			11 50	12 00		
Southampton Central	a				07 02	08 02		08 07		09 02			10 02						11 02			12 02	12 20		
Fareham	a				07 27	08 27				09 27			10 27						11 27			12 27			
	d				07 27	08 27				09 27			10 27						11 27			12 27			
Cosham	a				07 35	08 35				09 35			10 35						11 35			12 35			
Fratton	a				07 42	08 42				09 42			10 42						11 42			12 42			
Portsmouth & Southsea	a				07 46	08 46				09 46			10 46						11 46			12 46			
Portsmouth Harbour	a				07 52	08 52				09 52			10 52						11 52			12 51			
Havant	a																								
Chichester 4	a																								
Barnham	a																								
Worthing 4	a																								
Shoreham-by-Sea	a																								
Hove 2	a																								
Brighton 10	a																								

A until 4 September. The Torbay Express
B from 11 September
C until 4 September
b previous night, stops on request
c arr. 0935

For connections from Swansea please refer to Table 128. For connections from Plymouth and Exeter St Davids please refer to Table 135. For connections to Bournemouth please refer to Table 158

Table 123

Saturdays

South Wales and Bristol - Weymouth and Portsmouth

		GW	GW	GW	GW	GW	SW		GW	GW	GW	GW	GW	GW	GW	GW	GW	GW	GW	GW	GW	GW	SW	GW	GW
		◇ Ħ	◇1 A ⌀		◇ Ħ		◇1 □P		◇1 A □P	■ 1 B □P	◇ Ħ		◇		A Ħ	C Ħ	◇	A	C	◇1 C □P	◇1 A □P		◇1	◇	A
Cardiff Central 7	d	10 30			11 30						12 30		13 30				14 30							15 30	
Newport (South Wales)	d	10 44			11 44						12 44		13 44				14 44							15 44	
Severn Tunnel Jn	d																								
Filton Abbey Wood	d	11 09		11 23	12 09	12 28					13 09	13 23	14 09		14 25	14 25	15 09					15 22		16 09	
Bristol Temple Meads 10	d	11 23		11b49	12 23	12 43	13 15				13 23	13c49	14 23		14e49	14e49	15 23					15 38	15 54	16 23	
Keynsham	d			11 56		12 50						13 56			14 56	14 56						15 45			
Oldfield Park	d			12 03		12 57						14 03			15 03	15 03						15 52			
London Paddington 15 ⊖	d		11 06						12 18	12 35										15 06	15 06				
Swindon	d																	15 20	15 20						
Chippenham	d																	15 36	15 36						
Melksham	d																	15 46	15 46						
Bath Spa 7	d	11 36		12 07	12 36	13 00	13 28				13 36	14 07	14 36		15 07	15 07	15 36					15 56	16 07	16 36	
Freshford	d			12 16								14 16			15 16	15 16						16 06			
Avoncliff	d			12x18								14x18			15x18	15x18						16x09			
Bradford-on-Avon	d	11 47		12 22	12 47	13 13	13 40				13 47	14 22	14 47		15 22	15 22	15 47					16 12	16 24	16 47	
Trowbridge	d	11 53		12 28	12 53	13 19	13 47				13 53	14 28	14 53		15 28	15 28	15 53	15 58	15 58			16 18	16 30	16 53	
Westbury	a	12 01	12 22	12 36	13 01	13 26	13 53		13 59	13 58	14 01	14 35	15 01	15 08	15 36	15 36	16 01	16 05	16 05	16 22	16 23	16 28	16 37	17 01	
	d	12 01	12 22	12 37	13 01	13 27	13 54		13 59	13 59	14 01	14 36	15 01	15 11	15 36	15 36	16 01		16 10	16 22	16 23		16 39	17 01	17 08
Frome	d			12 47								14a48			15 46	15 46									
Bruton	d			12 57											15 57	15 57									
Castle Cary	a		12 40	13 03					14 16	14 16					16 03	16 02				16 40	16 41				
	d		12 40	13 04					14 16	14 17					16 09	16 02				16 40	16 41				
Yeovil Pen Mill	d			13 17											16 24	16 17									
Thornford	d			13x22											16x28	16x21									
Yetminster	d			13x25											16x31	16x24									
Chetnole	d			13x29											16x35	16x28									
Maiden Newton	d			13 41											16 47	16f47									
Dorchester West	d			13 54											16 58	16 58									
Upwey	a			14 02																					
Weymouth	a			14 08											17 09	17 09									
Dilton Marsh	d					13x30								15x13					16x13						17x10
Warminster	d	12 08			13 08	13 36	14 02				14 08		15 08	15a22			16 08		16a19				16 47	17 08	17a19
Salisbury	a	12 32			13 32	13 58	14 25				14 32		15 32				16 32						17 09	17 32	
	d	12 32			13 32	13 59	14 45				14 32		15 32				16 32							17 32	
Romsey	d	12 50			13 50	14 19					14 50		15 50				16 50							17 50	
Southampton Central	a	13 02			14 02	14 32					15 02		16 02				17 02							18 02	
Fareham	a	13 27			14 27	14 54					15 27		16 27				17 27							18 27	
	d	13 27			14 27	14 55					15 27		16 27				17 27							18 27	
Cosham	a	13 35			14 35	15 03					15 35		16 35				17 35							18 35	
Fratton	a	13 42			14 42						15 42		16 42				17 42							18 42	
Portsmouth & Southsea	a	13 46			14 46						15 46		16 46				17 46							18 46	
Portsmouth Harbour	a	13 51			14 51						15 51		16 51				17 51							18 52	
Havant	a					15 03																			
Chichester 4	a					15 21																			
Barnham	a					15 29																			
Worthing 4	a					15 45																			
Shoreham-by-Sea	a					15 55																			
Hove 2	a					16 07																			
Brighton 10	a					16 14																			

A from 11 September
B until 4 September. The Torbay Express
C until 4 September
b arr. 1135
c arr. 1335
e arr. 1440
f arr. 1639

For connections from Swansea please refer to Table 128. For connections from Plymouth and Exeter St Davids please refer to Table 135. For connections to Bournemouth please refer to Table 158

Table 123

Saturdays

South Wales and Bristol - Weymouth and Portsmouth

		GW	GW	GW	GW	GW	GW	GW	GW	GW	GW	GW	GW	GW	GW	GW	GW	GW	SW	GW
			■	◇1 A ☕	◇1 B ☕		◇			◇	◇1 ☕		◇	◇1 ☕			◇		1	
Cardiff Central 7	d		16 30				17 30			18 30			19 30				20 30			
Newport (South Wales)	d		16 44				17 44			18 44			19 44				20 44			
Severn Tunnel Jn	d		16 55				17 55													
Filton Abbey Wood	d	16 25	17 09			17 23	18 09		18 28	19 09		19 24	20 09		20 25		21 09			
Bristol Temple Meads 10	d	16 49	17 23			17b49	18 23		18c49	19 23		19e49	20 23		20 49		21 23	21 54	22 23	23 11
Keynsham	d	16 56				17 56			18 56			19 56			20 56			21 59		23 18
Oldfield Park	d	17 03				18 03			19 03			20 03			21 03			22 06		23 25
London Paddington 15 ⊖	d			17 06	17 06						19 06			20 06						
Swindon	d															21 08				
Chippenham	d															21 24				
Melksham	d															21 34				
Bath Spa 7	d	17 07	17 36			18 07	18 36		19 07	19 36		20 07	20 36		21 07		21 36	22 10	22 36	23 29
Freshford	d	17 16				18 16			19 16			20 16			21 16			22 19		23 38
Avoncliff	d	17x18				18x18			19x18			20x18			21x18			22x21		23x41
Bradford-on-Avon	d	17 22	17 47			18 22	18 47		19 22	19 47		20 22	20 47		21 22		21 47	22 25	22 47	23 44
Trowbridge	d	17 28	17 53			18 28	18 53		19 28	19 53		20 28	20 53		21 28	21 43	21 53	22 31	22 53	23 50
Westbury	a	17 36	18 01	18 21	18 22	18 36	19 01		19 35	20 01	20 27	20 35	21 01	21 24	21 36	21 51	22 01	22 40	23 00	23 57
	d	17 38	18 01	18 21	18 22	18 39	19 01	19 09		20 01	20 28	20 37	21 01	21 25	21 38		22 01		23 04	23 57
Frome	d	17 47				18 49						20a46			21 49					00a07
Bruton	d	17 59				19 00									22 01					
Castle Cary	a	18 04		18 39	18 40	19 05					20 45			21 43	22 06					
	d	18 05		18 40	18 41	19 06					20 45			21 43	22 06					
Yeovil Pen Mill	d	18 21				19 19									22 20					
Thornford	d	18x26				19x24									22x25					
Yetminster	d	18x29				19x27									22x28					
Chetnole	d	18x33				19x31									22x32					
Maiden Newton	d	18 44				19 43									22 44					
Dorchester West	d	18 54				19 54									22 54					
Upwey	a	19 02				20 01									23 02					
Weymouth	a	19 09				20 08									23 09					
Dilton Marsh	d							19x12									22x04			
Warminster	d		18 08				19 08	19 18		20 08			21 08				22 08		23 11	
Salisbury	a		18 32				19 32	19 41		20 32			21 32				22 31		23 34	
	d		18 32				19 32	19 41		20 32			21 32				22 32			
Romsey	d		18 50				19 50	20 04		20 50			21 50				22 50			
Southampton Central	a		19 02				20 02	20 18		21 02			22 02				23 02			
Fareham	a		19 27				20 27			21 27			22 26				23 27			
	d		19 27				20 27			21 27			22 27				23 27			
Cosham	a		19 35																	
Fratton	a		19 42				20 42			21 42			22 42				23 41			
Portsmouth & Southsea	a		19 46				20 46			21 46			22 46				23 45			
Portsmouth Harbour	a		19 52				20 52			21 52			22 52				23 52			
Havant	a																			
Chichester 4	a																			
Barnham	a																			
Worthing 4	a																			
Shoreham-by-Sea	a																			
Hove 2	a																			
Brighton 10	a																			

A until 4 September
B from 11 September
b arr. 1737
c arr. 1839
e arr. 1938

For connections from Swansea please refer to Table 128. For connections from Plymouth and Exeter St Davids please refer to Table 135. For connections to Bournemouth please refer to Table 158

Table 123

Sundays until 11 July

South Wales and Bristol - Weymouth and Portsmouth

		GW	GW	GW	GW	GW	GW	GW	GW	GW	GW	GW	GW	GW	GW	GW	SW	GW	GW	GW	GW	GW	GW
			◇		◇1 ☕	◇	◇1 ☕	◇	■ ◇ A 🚌	◇1 ☕	◇		◇1 ☕	◇	◇1 ☕	◇	◇1	◇	◇1 ☕	◇	◇		◇
Cardiff Central 7	d		08 05			09 15		10 08	11 08		12 08			13 08		14 08		15 05		16 08	16 35		17 08
Newport (South Wales)	d		08 23			09 29		10 22	11 22		12 22			13 22		14 22		15 19		16 22	16 49		17 23
Severn Tunnel Jn	d		08 39			09 46		10 39	11 39		12 39			13 39		14 39		15 36		16 39			17 40
Filton Abbey Wood	d		08 54			10 03		10 54	11 54		12 57			13 54		14 55		15 53		16 55	17 20		17 55
Bristol Temple Meads 10	d		09b10	09 14		10 15		11c10	12e15		13 10			14g15		15 10	16 04	16h10		17i15	17j40	17 44	18 10
Keynsham	d		09 17	09 21				11 17			13 17					15 17	16 11			17 22		17 51	18 17
Oldfield Park	d		09 24	09 29				11 24			13 24					15 24				17 29		17 58	18 24
London Paddington 15 ⊖	d				08 57		09 57			11 37			12 57		13 57				15 57				
Swindon	d																						
Chippenham	d																						
Melksham	d																						
Bath Spa 7	d		09 27	09 33		10 29		11 27	12 27		13 27			14 28		15 27	16 20	16 24		17 32	17 52	18 01	18 27
Freshford	d					10 39			12 37					14 37				16 35				18 11	
Avoncliff	d					10x41			12x39					14x39				16x37				18x14	
Bradford-on-Avon	d		09 39	09 48		10 45		11 39	12 43		13 39			14 43		15 39	16 31	16 41		17 44	18 04	18 17	18 39
Trowbridge	d		09 45	09 55		10 51		11 46	12 49		13 46			14 49		15 45	16 37	16 47		17 50	18 11	18 23	18 45
Westbury	a		09 53	10 02	10 22	10 58		11 53	12 59	13 04	13 53		14 17	14 56		15 52	16 44	16 54	17 22	17 57	18 18	18 30	18 54
	d	09 00	09 58	10 05	10 23	11 00		12 03	13 00	13 05	14 03	14 13	14 19	15 00		15 58	16 46	16 55	17 24	18 00	18 19	18 30	18 58
Frome	d	09 10		10 15								14f29										18 39	
Bruton	d	09 22		10 27								14 41										18 51	
Castle Cary	a	09 26		10 31			11 33			13 22		14 45			15 34				17 40			18 56	
	d	09 28		10 33			11 34			13 22		14 48			15 35				17 41			18 58	
Yeovil Pen Mill	d	09 42		10 47								15 02										19 12	
Thornford	d	09x47		10x52																		19x16	
Yetminster	d	09x50		10x55																		19x19	
Chetnole	d	09x54		10x59																		19x23	
Maiden Newton	d	10 05		11 11								15 22										19 35	
Dorchester West	d	10 13		11 25								15 36										19 47	
Upwey	a																					19 54	
Weymouth	a	10 27		11 41								15 49										20 01	
Dilton Marsh	d		10x01					12x06			14x06					16x01		16x58			18x22		
Warminster	d		10 07			11 07		12 12	13 07		14 12			15 07		16 07	16 53	17 04		18 07	18 28		19 05
Salisbury	a		10 32			11 29		12 34	13 30		14 39			15 30		16 32	17 16	17 29		18 32	18 53		19 32
	d		10 32			11 31		12 36	13 32		14 48			15 32		16 32		17 29		18 32	18 57		19 32
Romsey	d		10 50			11 50		12 54	13 50		15 10			15 50		16 50		17 47		18 50	19 15		19 50
Southampton Central	a		11 02			12 02		13 06	14 02		15 20			16 02		17 02		17 59		19 02	19 26		20 02
Fareham	a		11 27			12 26		13 33	14 25		15 50			16 26		17 27		18 24		19 27	19 48		20 27
	d		11 27			12 27		13 34	14 26		15 51			16 27		17 27		18 24		19 27	19 49		20 27
Cosham	a		11 35			12 35		13 41	14 34		16 00			16 35		17 35		18 32		19 35	19 58		
Fratton	a		11 42			12 42			14 41					16 42		17 42		18 39		19 42			20 42
Portsmouth & Southsea	a		11 45			12 45			14 44					16 45		17 45		18 42		19 46			20 45
Portsmouth Harbour	a		11 52			12 52			14 50					16 53		17 52		18 49		19 52			20 52
Havant	a							14 03			16 11										20 10		
Chichester 4	a							14 19			16 22										20 21		
Barnham	a							14 27			16 30										20 29		
Worthing 4	a							14 44			16 45										20 51		
Shoreham-by-Sea	a							14 51			16 51										20 57		
Hove 2	a							14 59			16 58										21 04		
Brighton 10	a							15 06			17 05										21 10		

A 🚌 from Bristol Temple Meads ◇ from Bristol Temple Meads ■ to Filton Abbey Wood
b arr. 0904
c arr. 1103
e arr. 1204
f arr. 1422
g arr. 1404
h arr. 1603
i arr. 1706
j arr. 1729

For connections from Swansea please refer to Table 128. For connections from Plymouth and Exeter St Davids please refer to Table 135. For connections to Bournemouth please refer to Table 158

Table 123

Sundays until 11 July

South Wales and Bristol - Weymouth and Portsmouth

		GW	GW	GW	GW	GW	GW	GW	GW	GW	SW	GW	GW
			◇1 🍴	1	◇	◇1 🍴	◇	◇1 🍴		◇	1		◇
Cardiff Central 7	d			17 40	18 08		19 08			20 18			22 00
Newport (South Wales)	d			17 54	18 22		19 22			20 31			22 18
Severn Tunnel Jn	d				18 39		19 40			20 48			22 35
Filton Abbey Wood	d			18 25	18 56		19 55			21 05			22 52
Bristol Temple Meads 10	d			18b50	19 10		20c15		20 50	21e22	21 35	22 15	23 10
Keynsham	d				19 17				20 57			22 22	
Oldfield Park	d				19 24				21 04			22 29	
London Paddington 15 ⊖	d		17 57			18 57		19 57					
Swindon	d	18 19											
Chippenham	d	18 35											
Melksham	d	18 45											
Bath Spa 7	d			19 02	19 27		20 27		21 07	21 35	21 49	22 32	23 22
Freshford	d						20 37		21 18			22 43	
Avoncliff	d						20x39		21x21			22x45	
Bradford-on-Avon	d			19 14	19 39		20 43		21 24	21 46	22 00	22 49	23 34
Trowbridge	d	18 54		19 20	19 45		20 49		21 30	21 52	22 06	22 55	23 40
Westbury	a	19 06	19 26	19 27	19 52		20 56	21 27	21 37	21 59	22 13	23 02	23 47
	d		19 28	19 31	19 53		20 57	21 28	21 38	22 00	22 15		23 50
Frome	d								21 48				
Bruton	d								21 59				
Castle Cary	a					20 29		21 45	22 04				
	d					20 29		21 46	22 05				
Yeovil Pen Mill	d								22 19				
Thornford	d								22x23				
Yetminster	d								22x26				
Chetnole	d								22x30				
Maiden Newton	d								22 42				
Dorchester West	d								22 53				
Upwey	a								23 00				
Weymouth	a								23 06				
Dilton Marsh	d				19x56								23x53
Warminster	d			19 38	20 02		21 05			22 08	22 22		23a59
Salisbury	a			19 59	20 25		21 27			22 30	22 46		
	d			20 00	20 30		21 32			22 31			
Romsey	d			20 19	20 48		21 51			22 50			
Southampton Central	a			20 29	20 59		22 01			23 00			
Fareham	a			20 54	21 23		22 26			23 23			
	d			20 55	21 24		22 27			23 24			
Cosham	a												
Fratton	a			21 09	21 37		22 40			23 37			
Portsmouth & Southsea	a			21 15	21 41		22 43			23 41			
Portsmouth Harbour	a			21 26	21 48		22 51			23 49			
Havant	a												
Chichester 4	a												
Barnham	a												
Worthing 4	a												
Shoreham-by-Sea	a												
Hove 2	a												
Brighton 10	a												

b arr. 1833 c arr. 2005 e arr. 2113

For connections from Swansea please refer to Table 128. For connections from Plymouth and Exeter St Davids please refer to Table 135. For connections to Bournemouth please refer to Table 158

Table 123

Sundays 18 July to 05 September

South Wales and Bristol - Weymouth and Portsmouth

		GW	GW	GW	GW	GW	GW	GW	GW	GW	GW	GW
			◇		◇1 🍴	◇	◇1 🍴	◇	1 ◇ A ✕	◇1 🍴	◇	
Cardiff Central 7	d		08 05			09 15		10 08	11 08		12 08	
Newport (South Wales)	d		08 23			09 33		10 26	11 26		12 26	
Severn Tunnel Jn	d		08 39			09 46		10 39	11 39		12 39	
Filton Abbey Wood	d		08 54			10 03		10 54	11 54		12 57	
Bristol Temple Meads 10	d		09b10	09 14		10 15		11c10	12e15		13 10	
Keynsham	d		09 17	09 21				11 17			13 17	
Oldfield Park	d		09 24	09 29				11 24			13 24	
London Paddington 15 ⊖	d				08 57		09 57			11 37		
Swindon	d											
Chippenham	d											
Melksham	d											
Bath Spa 7	d		09 27	09 33		10 29		11 27	12 27		13 27	
Freshford	d					10 39			12 37			
Avoncliff	d					10x41			12x39			
Bradford-on-Avon	d		09 39	09 48		10 45		11 39	12 43		13 39	
Trowbridge	d		09 45	09 55		10 51		11 46	12 49		13 46	
Westbury	a		09 53	10 02	10 22	10 58		11 53	12 59	13 04	13 53	
	d	09 00	09 58	10 05	10 23	11 00		12 03	13 00	13 05	14 03	14 13
Frome	d	09 10		10 15								14f29
Bruton	d	09 22		10 27								14 41
Castle Cary	a	09 26		10 31			11 33			13 22		14 45
	d	09 28		10 33			11 34			13 22		14 48
Yeovil Pen Mill	d	09 42		10 47								15 02
Thornford	d	09x47		10x52								
Yetminster	d	09x50		10x55								
Chetnole	d	09x54		10x59								
Maiden Newton	d	10 05		11 11								15 22
Dorchester West	d	10 13		11 25								15 36
Upwey	a											
Weymouth	a	10 27		11 41								15 49
Dilton Marsh	d		10x01					12x06			14x06	
Warminster	d		10 07			11 07		12 12	13 07		14 12	
Salisbury	a		10 32			11 32		12 34	13 30		14 39	
	d		10 32			11 32		12 36	13 32		14 48	
Romsey	d		10 50			11 50		12 54	13 50		15 10	
Southampton Central	a		11 02			12 02		13 06	14 02		15 20	
Fareham	a		11 27			12 27		13 33	14 25		15 50	
	d		11 27			12 27		13 34	14 26		15 51	
Cosham	a		11 35			12 35		13 41	14 34		16 00	
Fratton	a		11 42			12 42			14 41			
Portsmouth & Southsea	a		11 45			12 45			14 44			
Portsmouth Harbour	a		11 52			12 52			14 50			
Havant	a							14 03			16 11	
Chichester 4	a							14 19			16 22	
Barnham	a							14 27			16 30	
Worthing 4	a							14 44			16 45	
Shoreham-by-Sea	a							14 51			16 51	
Hove 2	a							14 59			16 58	
Brighton 10	a							15 06			17 05	

		GW	GW	GW	GW	GW	SW	GW	GW	GW	GW	GW	GW
		◇1 🍴	◇	◇1 🍴	◇		◇1	◇	◇1 🍴	◇	◇		◇
Cardiff Central 7	d		13 08		14 08			15 08		16 08	16 35		17 08
Newport (South Wales)	d		13 28		14 26			15 29		16 26	16 53		17 26
Severn Tunnel Jn	d		13 39		14 39			15 39		16 39			17 39
Filton Abbey Wood	d		13 54		14 55			15 57		16 55	17 20		17 54
Bristol Temple Meads 10	d		14g15		15 10		16 04	16h15		17i15	17j40	17 44	18k10
Keynsham	d				15 17		16 11			17 22		17 51	18 17
Oldfield Park	d				15 24					17 29		17 58	18 24
London Paddington 15 ⊖	d	12 57		13 57					15 57				
Swindon	d												
Chippenham	d												
Melksham	d												
Bath Spa 7	d		14 28		15 27		16 20	16 27		17 32	17 52	18 01	18 27
Freshford	d		14 37					16 38				18 11	
Avoncliff	d		14x39					16x40				18x14	
Bradford-on-Avon	d		14 43		15 39		16 31	16 44		17 44	18 04	18 17	18 39
Trowbridge	d		14 49		15 45		16 37	16 50		17 50	18 11	18 23	18 45
Westbury	a	14 17	14 56		15 52		16 44	16 57	17 22	17 57	18 18	18 30	18 54
	d	14 19	15 00		15 58		16 46	16 58	17 24	18 00	18 19	18 30	18 58
Frome	d											18 39	
Bruton	d											18 51	
Castle Cary	a			15 34					17 40			18 56	
	d			15 35					17 41			18 58	
Yeovil Pen Mill	d											19 12	
Thornford	d											19x16	
Yetminster	d											19x19	
Chetnole	d											19x23	
Maiden Newton	d											19 35	
Dorchester West	d											19 47	
Upwey	a											19 54	
Weymouth	a											20 01	
Dilton Marsh	d				16x01			17x01			18x22		
Warminster	d		15 07		16 07		16 53	17 07		18 07	18 28		19 05
Salisbury	a		15 32		16 32		17 16	17 32		18 32	18 53		19 32
	d		15 32		16 32			17 32		18 32	18 57		19 32
Romsey	d		15 50		16 50			17 50		18 50	19 15		19 50
Southampton Central	a		16 02		17 02			18 02		19 02	19 26		20 02
Fareham	a		16 27		17 27			18 27		19 27	19 48		20 27
	d		16 27		17 27			18 27		19 27	19 49		20 27
Cosham	a		16 35		17 35			18 35		19 35	19 58		
Fratton	a		16 42		17 42			18 42		19 42			20 42
Portsmouth & Southsea	a		16 45		17 45			18 45		19 45			20 45
Portsmouth Harbour	a		16 52		17 52			18 52		19 52			20 52
Havant	a										20 10		
Chichester 4	a										20 21		
Barnham	a										20 29		
Worthing 4	a										20 51		
Shoreham-by-Sea	a										20 57		
Hove 2	a										21 04		
Brighton 10	a										21 10		

A ✕ from Bristol Temple Meads ◇ from Bristol Temple Meads 1 to Filton Abbey Wood
b arr. 0904
c arr. 1103
e arr. 1204
f arr. 1422
g arr. 1404
h arr. 1606
i arr. 1706
j arr. 1729
k arr. 1804

For connections from Swansea please refer to Table 128. For connections from Plymouth and Exeter St Davids please refer to Table 135. For connections to Bournemouth please refer to Table 158

Table 123

Sundays
18 July to 05 September

South Wales and Bristol - Weymouth and Portsmouth

		GW	GW	GW	GW	GW	GW	GW	GW	GW	SW	GW	GW
			◇1 ☕	■	◇	◇1 ☕	◇	◇1 ☕		◇	1		◇
Cardiff Central 7	d			17 40	18 08		19 08			20 18			22 00
Newport (South Wales)	d			17 58	18 26		19 26			20 35			22 18
Severn Tunnel Jn	d				18 39		19 40			20 48			22 35
Filton Abbey Wood	d			18 25	18 56		19 55			21 05			22 52
Bristol Temple Meads 10	d			18b50	19 10		20c15		20 50	21e22	21 35	22 15	23 10
Keynsham	d				19 17				20 57			22 22	
Oldfield Park	d				19 24				21 04			22 29	
London Paddington 15 ⊖	d		17 57			18 57		19 57					
Swindon	d	18 19											
Chippenham	d	18 35											
Melksham	d	18 45											
Bath Spa 7	d			19 02	19 27		20 27		21 07	21 35	21 49	22 32	23 22
Freshford	d						20 37		21 18			22 43	
Avoncliff	d						20x39		21x21			22x45	
Bradford-on-Avon	d			19 14	19 39		20 43		21 24	21 46	22 00	22 49	23 34
Trowbridge	d	18 54		19 20	19 45		20 49		21 30	21 52	22 06	22 55	23 40
Westbury	a	19 06	19 26	19 27	19 52		20 56	21 27	21 37	21 59	22 13	23 02	23 47
	d		19 28	19 31	19 53		20 57	21 28	21 38	22 00	22 15		23 50
Frome	d								21 48				
Bruton	d								21 59				
Castle Cary	a					20 29		21 45	22 04				
	d					20 29		21 46	22 05				
Yeovil Pen Mill	d								22 19				
Thornford	d								22x23				
Yetminster	d								22x26				
Chetnole	d								22x30				
Maiden Newton	d								22 42				
Dorchester West	d								22 53				
Upwey	a								23 00				
Weymouth	a								23 06				
Dilton Marsh	d				19x56								23x53
Warminster	d			19 38	20 02		21 05			22 08	22 22		23a59
Salisbury	a			19 59	20 25		21 27			22 30	22 46		
	d			20 00	20 30		21 32			22 31			
Romsey	d			20 19	20 48		21 51			22 50			
Southampton Central	a			20 29	20 59		22 01			23 00			
Fareham	a			20 54	21 23		22 26			23 23			
	d			20 55	21 24		22 27			23 24			
Cosham	a												
Fratton	a			21 09	21 37		22 40			23 37			
Portsmouth & Southsea	a			21 15	21 41		22 43			23 41			
Portsmouth Harbour	a			21 26	21 48		22 51			23 49			
Havant	a												
Chichester 4	a												
Barnham	a												
Worthing 4	a												
Shoreham-by-Sea	a												
Hove 2	a												
Brighton 10	a												

b arr. 1833
c arr. 2005
e arr. 2113

For connections from Swansea please refer to Table 128. For connections from Plymouth and Exeter St Davids please refer to Table 135. For connections to Bournemouth please refer to Table 158

Table 123

Sundays
from 12 September

South Wales and Bristol - Weymouth and Portsmouth

		GW	GW	GW	GW	GW	GW	GW	GW	GW
		◇	◇1 ☕	◇	◇1 ☕	◇	■ ◇ A 🍴	◇1 ☕	◇	◇1 ☕
Cardiff Central 7	d	08 05		09 15		10 08	11 08		12 08	
Newport (South Wales)	d	08 23		09 29		10 22	11 22		12 22	
Severn Tunnel Jn	d	08 39		09 46		10 39	11 39		12 39	
Filton Abbey Wood	d	08 54		10 03		10 54	11 54		12 57	
Bristol Temple Meads 10	d	09b10		10 15		11c10	12e15		13 10	
Keynsham	d	09 17				11 17			13 17	
Oldfield Park	d	09 24				11 24			13 24	
London Paddington 15 ⊖	d		08 57		09 57			11 27		12 57
Swindon	d									
Chippenham	d									
Melksham	d									
Bath Spa 7	d	09 27		10 29		11 27	12 27		13 27	
Freshford	d			10 39			12 37			
Avoncliff	d			10x41			12x39			
Bradford-on-Avon	d	09 39		10 45		11 39	12 43		13 39	
Trowbridge	d	09 45		10 51		11 46	12 49		13 46	
Westbury	a	09 53	10 22	10 58		11 53	12 59	13 01	13 53	14 17
	d	09 58	10 23	11 00		12 03	13 00	13 05	14 03	14 19
Frome	d									
Bruton	d									
Castle Cary	a				11 33			13 22		
	d				11 34			13 22		
Yeovil Pen Mill	d									
Thornford	d									
Yetminster	d									
Chetnole	d									
Maiden Newton	d									
Dorchester West	d									
Upwey	a									
Weymouth	a									
Dilton Marsh	d	10x01				12x06			14x06	
Warminster	d	10 07		11 07		12 12	13 07		14 12	
Salisbury	a	10 32		11 32		12 34	13 32		14 39	
	d	10 32		11 32		12 36	13 32		14 48	
Romsey	d	10 50		11 50		12 54	13 50		15 10	
Southampton Central	a	11 02		12 02		13 06	14 02		15 20	
Fareham	a	11 27		12 27		13 33	14 25		15 50	
	d	11 27		12 27		13 34	14 26		15 51	
Cosham	a	11 35		12 35		13 41	14 34		16 00	
Fratton	a	11 42		12 42			14 41			
Portsmouth & Southsea	a	11 45		12 45			14 45			
Portsmouth Harbour	a	11 52		12 52			14 52			
Havant	a					14 03			16 11	
Chichester 4	a					14 19			16 22	
Barnham	a					14 27			16 30	
Worthing 4	a					14 44			16 45	
Shoreham-by-Sea	a					14 51			16 51	
Hove 2	a					14 59			16 58	
Brighton 10	a					15 06			17 05	

		GW	GW	GW	GW	SW	GW	GW	GW	GW	GW	GW	GW	GW
			◇	◇1 ☕	◇	◇1	◇	◇1 ☕	◇	◇		◇		◇1 ☕
Cardiff Central 7	d		13 08		14 08		15 08		16 08	16 35		17 08		
Newport (South Wales)	d		13 22		14 22		15 22		16 22	16 49		17 22		
Severn Tunnel Jn	d		13 39		14 39		15 39		16 39			17 39		
Filton Abbey Wood	d		13 54		14 55		15 56		16 55	17 20		17 54		
Bristol Temple Meads 10	d	13 55	14f15		15 10	16 04	16g15		17h15	17i40	17 44	18j10		
Keynsham	d	14 02			15 17	16 11			17 22		17 51	18 17		
Oldfield Park	d	14 09			15 24				17 29		17 58	18 24		
London Paddington 15 ⊖	d			13 57				15 57						17 57
Swindon	d												18 19	
Chippenham	d												18 35	
Melksham	d												18 45	
Bath Spa 7	d	14 13	14 28		15 27	16 20	16 26		17 32	17 52	18 01	18 27		
Freshford	d	14 23	14 37				16 37				18 11			
Avoncliff	d	14 26	14x39				16x39				18x14			
Bradford-on-Avon	d	14 29	14 43		15 39	16 31	16 43		17 44	18 04	18 17	18 39		
Trowbridge	d	14 35	14 49		15 45	16 37	16 49		17 50	18 11	18 23	18 45	18 54	
Westbury	a	14 42	14 56		15 52	16 44	16 56	17 22	17 59	18 18	18 30	18 54	19 06	19 26
	d	14 45	15 00		15 58	16 46	16 58	17 24	18 00	18 19	18 30	18 58		19 28
Frome	d	14 54									18 39			
Bruton	d	15 06									18 51			
Castle Cary	a	15 10		15 34				17 40			18 56			
	d	15 11		15 35				17 41			18 58			
Yeovil Pen Mill	d	15 25									19 12			
Thornford	d	15 31									19x16			
Yetminster	d	15 34									19x19			
Chetnole	d	15 38									19x23			
Maiden Newton	d	15 49									19 35			
Dorchester West	d	16 00									19 47			
Upwey	a	16 09									19 54			
Weymouth	a	16 14									20 01			
Dilton Marsh	d				16x01		17x01			18x22				
Warminster	d		15 07		16 07	16 53	17 07		18 07	18 28		19 05		
Salisbury	a		15 32		16 32	17 16	17 32		18 32	18 53		19 32		
	d		15 32		16 32		17 32		18 32	18 57		19 32		
Romsey	d		15 50		16 50		17 50		18 50	19 15		19 50		
Southampton Central	a		16 02		17 02		18 02		19 02	19 26		20 02		
Fareham	a		16 27		17 27		18 27		19 27	19 48		20 27		
	d		16 27		17 27		18 27		19 27	19 49		20 27		
Cosham	a		16 35		17 35		18 35		19 35	19 58				
Fratton	a		16 42		17 42		18 42		19 42			20 42		
Portsmouth & Southsea	a		16 46		17 45		18 45		19 46			20 45		
Portsmouth Harbour	a		16 52		17 52		18 52		19 52			20 52		
Havant	a									20 10				
Chichester 4	a									20 21				
Barnham	a									20 29				
Worthing 4	a									20 51				
Shoreham-by-Sea	a									20 57				
Hove 2	a									21 04				
Brighton 10	a									21 10				

A 🍴 from Bristol Temple Meads ◇ from Bristol Temple Meads ■ to Filton Abbey Wood
b arr. 0904
c arr. 1103
e arr. 1204
f arr. 1404
g arr. 1606
h arr. 1706
i arr. 1729
j arr. 1804

For connections from Swansea please refer to Table 128. For connections from Plymouth and Exeter St Davids please refer to Table 135. For connections to Bournemouth please refer to Table 158

Table 123

Sundays
from 12 September

South Wales and Bristol - Weymouth and Portsmouth

		GW	GW	GW	GW	GW	GW	GW	SW	GW	GW
		■	◇	◇1 ☕	◇	◇1 ☕		◇	1		◇
Cardiff Central 7	d	17 40	18 08		19 08			20 18			22 00
Newport (South Wales)	d	17 54	18 22		19 22			20 31			22 18
Severn Tunnel Jn	d		18 39		19 40			20 48			22 35
Filton Abbey Wood	d	18 25	18 56		19 55			21 05			22 52
Bristol Temple Meads 10	d	18b50	19 10		20c15		20 50	21e22	21 35	22 15	23 10
Keynsham	d		19 17				20 57			22 22	
Oldfield Park	d		19 24				21 04			22 29	
London Paddington 15 ⊖	d			18 57		19 57					
Swindon	d										
Chippenham	d										
Melksham	d										
Bath Spa 7	d	19 02	19 27		20 27		21 07	21 35	21 49	22 32	23 22
Freshford	d				20 37		21 18			22 43	
Avoncliff	d				20x39		21x21			22x45	
Bradford-on-Avon	d	19 14	19 39		20 43		21 24	21 46	22 00	22 49	23 34
Trowbridge	d	19 20	19 45		20 49		21 30	21 52	22 06	22 55	23 40
Westbury	a	19 27	19 52		20 56	21 27	21 37	21 59	22 13	23 02	23 47
	d	19 31	19 53		20 57	21 28	21 38	22 00	22 15		23 50
Frome	d						21 48				
Bruton	d						21 59				
Castle Cary	a			20 29		21 45	22 04				
	d			20 29		21 46	22 05				
Yeovil Pen Mill	d						22 19				
Thornford	d						22x23				
Yetminster	d						22x26				
Chetnole	d						22x30				
Maiden Newton	d						22 42				
Dorchester West	d						22 53				
Upwey	a						23 00				
Weymouth	a						23 06				
Dilton Marsh	d		19x56								23x53
Warminster	d	19 38	20 02		21 05			22 08	22 22		23a59
Salisbury	a	19 59	20 25		21 27			22 30	22 46		
	d	20 00	20 30		21 32			22 31			
Romsey	d	20 19	20 48		21 51			22 50			
Southampton Central	a	20 29	20 59		22 01			23 00			
Fareham	a	20 54	21 23		22 26			23 23			
	d	20 55	21 24		22 27			23 24			
Cosham	a										
Fratton	a	21 09	21 37		22 40			23 37			
Portsmouth & Southsea	a	21 15	21 41		22 43			23 41			
Portsmouth Harbour	a	21 26	21 48		22 51			23 49			
Havant	a										
Chichester 4	a										
Barnham	a										
Worthing 4	a										
Shoreham-by-Sea	a										
Hove 2	a										
Brighton 10	a										

b arr. 1833　　c arr. 2005　　e arr. 2113

For connections from Swansea please refer to Table 128. For connections from Plymouth and Exeter St Davids please refer to Table 135. For connections to Bournemouth please refer to Table 158

Table 123

Mondays to Fridays

Portsmouth and Weymouth - Bristol and South Wales

		GW MO	GW	GW	GW	GW	GW	GW	GW	SW	GW	GW	GW	GW	GW	GW	GW	GW	GW	GW	GW	GW	GW
				◇1 ☕	◇1 ☕			◇1 A Ø		1			◇1 ☕	■ ◇ B 🛒			◇ 🛒	◇	◇1 A Ø	◇ 🛒			◇1
Brighton 10	d																						
Hove 2	d																						
Shoreham-by-Sea	d																						
Worthing 4	d																						
Barnham	d																						
Chichester 4	d																						
Havant	d																						
Portsmouth Harbour	d	22p03												06 00			06 51			08 23			
Portsmouth & Southsea	d	22p12												06 04			06 55			08 27			
Fratton	d	22p16												06 08			06 59			08 31			
Cosham	d													06 15			07 07			08 39			
Fareham	a	22p31												06 23			07 17			08 46			
	d	22p32												06 24			07 18			08 47			
Southampton Central	d	22p57												06 46			07 47	08 23		09 10			
Romsey	d	23p09												07 00			08 00	08 35		09 21			
Salisbury	a	23p27												07 18			08 20	09 00		09 40			
	d	23p28				06 04				06 40				07 19			08 21	09 03		09 41			
Warminster	d	23p53				06 25				07 00		07 23		07 39			08 41	09 23		10 01		10 25	
Dilton Marsh	d	23b58				06x29						07x27		07x43				09x28				10x29	
Weymouth	d										05 33				06 40						08 50		
Upwey	d										05 37				06 45						08 55		
Dorchester West	d										05 45				06 53						09 03		
Maiden Newton	d										05 57				07 05						09 15		
Chetnole	d										06x06				07x13						09x23		
Yetminster	d										06x08				07x16						09x26		
Thornford	d										06x10				07x18						09x28		
Yeovil Pen Mill	d										06 20				07 30						09 38		
Castle Cary	a							06 37			06 33		07 25		07 43				09 40		09 51		
	d							06 38			06 45		07 27		07 44				09 41		09 52		
Bruton	d										06 51				07 49						09 58		
Frome	d				06 07		06 45				07 04				08 02						10 15		
Westbury	a	00 02			06 17	06 34	06 54	07 00		07 08	07 12	07 32	07 45	07 47	08 13		08 49	09 35	09 59	10 09	10 24	10 33	11 02
	d		05 58	06 08	06 18	06 38	06 55	07 05	07 02	07 09	07 18	07 38	07 51	07 54	08 17	08 45	08 56	09 38	10 00	10 10	10 38		11 03
Trowbridge	d		06 04			06 44	07 01		07 08	07 15	07 24	07 44		08 00	08 23	08 51	09 02	09 44		10 16	10 44		
Bradford-on-Avon	d		06 10			06 49	07 07			07 21	07 30	07 50		08 06	08 29	08 57	09 08	09 50		10 22	10 50		
Avoncliff	d		06x12			06x52	07x09				07x32	07x52			08x31	08x59		09x52			10x52		
Freshford	d		06 15			06 55	07 13				07 36	07 55		08 10	08 34	09 02		09 55			10 55		
Bath Spa 7	a		06 26			07 06	07 24			07 33	07 47	08 06		08 20	08 45	09 13	09 20	10 06		10 34	11 06		
Melksham	d								07 17														
Chippenham	a								07 30														
Swindon	a								07 48														
London Paddington 15 ⊖	a			07 53	08 09			08 38					09 21						11 24				12 23
Oldfield Park	a		06 30			07 10	07 28			07 37	07 51	08 10		08 23	08 49	09 17		10 10			11 10		
Keynsham	a		06 37			07 17	07 35			07 44	07 57	08 17		08 31	08 56	09 24	09 30	10 17			11 17		
Bristol Temple Meads 10	a		06 45			07 27	07 45			07 52	08 06	08 29		08 39	09 05	09 35	09 39	10 29		10 48	11 29		
Filton Abbey Wood	a		07 01			07 42	08 00				08 21	08 48		09 01	09 21	09 48	10 00	10 48		11 00	11 48		
Severn Tunnel Jn	a		07 14																				
Newport (South Wales)	a		07 26				08 27							09 25			10 25			11 25			
Cardiff Central 7	a		07 44				08 46							09 43			10 43			11 43			

A Ø to Westbury　　B ◇ from Westbury ■ to Dilton Marsh　　b previous night, stops on request

For connections to Swansea please refer to Table 128. For connections to Exeter St Davids and Plymouth please refer to Table 135. For connections from Bournemouth please refer to Table 158

Portsmouth and Weymouth - Bristol and South Wales

		GW	SW	GW	GW	GW		GW	GW	GW	GW	GW	SW
		◇ 🍴	◇ 1	◇	◇ 🍴			◇ 1 🛒	◇ 🍴		◇	◇ 🍴	◇ 1
Brighton 10	d			09 00									
Hove 2	d			09 04									
Shoreham-by-Sea	d			09 13									
Worthing 4	d			09 22									
Barnham	d			09 38									
Chichester 4	d			09 47									
Havant	d			09 59									
Portsmouth Harbour	d	09 23			10 23				11 23			12 23	
Portsmouth & Southsea	d	09 27			10 27				11 27			12 27	
Fratton	d	09 31			10 31				11 31			12 31	
Cosham	d	09 39		10 05	10 39				11 39			12 39	
Fareham	a	09 46		10 14	10 46				11 46			12 46	
	d	09 47		10 14	10 47				11 47			12 47	
Southampton Central	d	10 10		10 42	11 10				12 10		12 26	13 10	
Romsey	d	10 21		10 54	11 21				12 21		12 39	13 21	
Salisbury	a	10 40		11 13	11 40				12 40		13 02	13 40	
	d	10 41	10 52	11 14	11 41				12 41		13 06	13 41	13 52
Warminster	d	11 01	11 12	11 33	12 01				13 01		13 33	14 01	14 12
Dilton Marsh	d										13x38		
Weymouth	d					11 10							
Upwey	d					11 15							
Dorchester West	d					11 23							
Maiden Newton	d					11b43							
Chetnole	d					11x50							
Yetminster	d					11x53							
Thornford	d					11x55							
Yeovil Pen Mill	d					12 05							
Castle Cary	a					12 19		12 45					
	d					12 22		12 45					
Bruton	d					12 27							
Frome	d					12 39							
Westbury	a	11 09	11 20	11 38	12 09	12 48		13 04	13 09		13 42	14 09	14 20
	d	11 10	11 21	11 38	12 10	12 49		13 05	13 10	13 38	13 44	14 10	14 21
Trowbridge	d	11 16	11 27	11 44	12 16	12 55			13 16	13 44	13 50	14 16	14 27
Bradford-on-Avon	d	11 22	11 33	11 50	12 22	13 01			13 23	13 50	13 57	14 22	14 33
Avoncliff	d			11x52		13x03				13x52	13x59		
Freshford	d			11 55		13 05				13 55	14 02		
Bath Spa 7	a	11 34	11 46	12 06	12 34	13 17			13 34	14 06	14 13	14 34	14 46
Melksham	d												
Chippenham	a												
Swindon	a												
London Paddington 15 ⊖	a							14 44					
Oldfield Park	a			12 10		13 20					14 17		
Keynsham	a			12 17		13 27					14 25		
Bristol Temple Meads 10	a	11 48	12 05	12 29	12 48	13 36			13 48		14 35	14 48	15 05
Filton Abbey Wood	a	12 00		12 48	13 00	13 48			14 00	14 29	14 47	15 00	
Severn Tunnel Jn	a												
Newport (South Wales)	a	12 25			13 25				14 25			15 24	
Cardiff Central 7	a	12 43			13 43				14 43			15 43	

		GW	GW	GW		GW	GW	GW	GW	GW	GW	GW	GW
			◇ 1 A 🛒	◇ 🍴			◇ 1 🛒	◇ 1 🛒	■ 🍴		■ 🍴		■ 🍴
Brighton 10	d												
Hove 2	d												
Shoreham-by-Sea	d												
Worthing 4	d												
Barnham	d												
Chichester 4	d												
Havant	d												
Portsmouth Harbour	d			13 23					14 23		15 23		16 23
Portsmouth & Southsea	d			13 27					14 27		15 27		16 27
Fratton	d			13 31					14 31		15 31		16 31
Cosham	d			13 39					14 39		15 39		16 39
Fareham	a			13 46					14 46		15 46		16 46
	d			13 47					14 47		15 47		16 47
Southampton Central	d			14 10					15 10		16 10		17 10
Romsey	d			14 21					15 21		16 21		17 21
Salisbury	a			14 40					15 40		16 40		17 40
	d			14 41					15 41		16 41		17 41
Warminster	d			15 01		15 28			16 01		17 01	17 28	18 01
Dilton Marsh	d					15x32						17x32	
Weymouth	d	13 10								15 08			
Upwey	d	13 15								15 13			
Dorchester West	d	13 23								15 21			
Maiden Newton	d	13c43								15 33			
Chetnole	d	13x51								15x42			
Yetminster	d	13x54								15x45			
Thornford	d	13x56								15x47			
Yeovil Pen Mill	d	14 06								15 56			
Castle Cary	a	14 19	14 43				15 51			16 09			
	d	14 20	14 44				15 51			16 10			
Bruton	d	14 26								16 16			
Frome	d	14 39						15 55		16 29			
Westbury	a	14 48	15 02	15 09		15 36		16 06	16 09	16 38	17 09	17 36	18 09
	d	14 48	15 03	15 10		15 38		16 06	16 10	16 38	17 10	17 38	18 10
Trowbridge	d	14 54		15 16		15 44			16 16	16 44	17 16	17 44	18 16
Bradford-on-Avon	d	15 00		15 22		15 50			16 22	16 50	17 22	17 50	18 22
Avoncliff	d	15x02				15x52				16x52		17x52	
Freshford	d	15 06				15 55				16 55		17 55	
Bath Spa 7	a	15 17		15 34		16 06			16 34	17 06	17 34	18 06	18 34
Melksham	d												
Chippenham	a												
Swindon	a												
London Paddington 15 ⊖	a		16 22				17 24	17 54					
Oldfield Park	a	15 21				16 09				17 10		18 10	
Keynsham	a	15 28				16 17				17 17		18 16	
Bristol Temple Meads 10	a	15 36		15 48		16 29			16 48	17 29	17 48	18 28	18 49
Filton Abbey Wood	a	15 48		16 00		16 48			17 00	17 48	18 00	18 48	19 00
Severn Tunnel Jn	a								17 14		18 13		19 13
Newport (South Wales)	a			16 25					17 25		18 25		19 25
Cardiff Central 7	a			16 43					17 43		18 43		19 43

A Restaurant service available for customers joining at Plymouth, Totnes, Newton Abbot, Exeter St.Davids, Taunton and Castle Cary. 🛒 from Westbury

b arr. 1134

c arr. 1333

For connections to Swansea please refer to Table 128. For connections to Exeter St Davids and Plymouth please refer to Table 135. For connections from Bournemouth please refer to Table 158

Portsmouth and Weymouth - Bristol and South Wales

		GW		GW	GW	GW FX	GW FO	GW	GW	GW	GW	GW	
						◇ 🍴	◇ 🍴	◇ 1 🛒		◇ 1		◇	
Brighton 10	d											17 00	
Hove 2	d											17 04	
Shoreham-by-Sea	d											17 13	
Worthing 4	d											17 22	
Barnham	d											17 39	
Chichester 4	d											17 47	
Havant	d											17 58	
Portsmouth Harbour	d					17 23	17 23						
Portsmouth & Southsea	d					17 27	17 27						
Fratton	d					17 31	17 31						
Cosham	d					17 39	17 39					18 05	
Fareham	a					17 46	17 46					18 12	
	d					17 47	17 47					18 13	
Southampton Central	d					18 10	18 10					18 42	
Romsey	d					18 21	18 21					18 54	
Salisbury	a					18 40	18 40					19 12	
	d					18 41	18 41					19 13	
Warminster	d			18 18		19 01	19 01					19 32	
Dilton Marsh	d			18x22								19x37	
Weymouth	d	17 30											
Upwey	d	17 35											
Dorchester West	d	17 43											
Maiden Newton	d	17 54											
Chetnole	d	18x03											
Yetminster	d	18x06											
Thornford	d	18x08											
Yeovil Pen Mill	d	18b23											
Castle Cary	a	18 36						18 52					
	d	18 37						18 53					
Bruton	d	18 43											
Frome	d	19 05							←				
Westbury	a	19 17		18 28		19 09	19 09	19 11	19 17			19 40	
	d	19 17			18 38	19 10	19 10	19 11	19 17	19 17	19 32	19 41	
Trowbridge	d	→			18 44	19 16	19 16		19 23		19 38	19 47	
Bradford-on-Avon	d				18 50	19 22	19 22		19 29			19 53	
Avoncliff	d				18x52				19x31			19x55	
Freshford	d				18 55				19 35			19 57	
Bath Spa 7	a				19 06	19 34	19 34		19 46			20 11	
Melksham	d										19 47		
Chippenham	a										20 01		
Swindon	a										20 21		
London Paddington 15 ⊖	a							20 39		21 07			
Oldfield Park	a				19 10				19 50			20 13	
Keynsham	a				19 17				19 57			20 20	
Bristol Temple Meads 10	a				19 29	19 49	19 49		20 05			20 29	
Filton Abbey Wood	a				19 48		20 00					20 48	
Severn Tunnel Jn	a						20 19						
Newport (South Wales)	a						20 30						
Cardiff Central 7	a						20 48						

		GW	GW	GW	GW FO	GW FX	GW	GW	SW	GW		GW FO	GW FX
		◇ 🍴	1		◇ 1 🛒	◇ 1 🛒	◇		◇ 1			◇	◇
Brighton 10	d												
Hove 2	d												
Shoreham-by-Sea	d												
Worthing 4	d												
Barnham	d												
Chichester 4	d												
Havant	d												
Portsmouth Harbour	d	18 23					19 23					20 23	20 23
Portsmouth & Southsea	d	18 27					19 27					20 27	20 27
Fratton	d	18 31					19 31					20 31	20 31
Cosham	d	18 39					19 39						
Fareham	a	18 46					19 46					20 46	20 46
	d	18 47					19 47					20 47	20 47
Southampton Central	d	19 10					20 10					21 10	21 10
Romsey	d	19 21					20 21					21 21	21 21
Salisbury	a	19 40					20 40					21 40	21 40
	d	19 41					20 41		20 57			21 41	21 41
Warminster	d	20 01					21 01		21 17			22 01	22 01
Dilton Marsh	d												
Weymouth	d									20 21			
Upwey	d									20 26			
Dorchester West	d									20 34			
Maiden Newton	d									20 45			
Chetnole	d									20x54			
Yetminster	d									20x57			
Thornford	d									20x59			
Yeovil Pen Mill	d									21 09			
Castle Cary	a				20 44	20 44				21 22			
	d				20 45	20 45				21 23			
Bruton	d									21 29			
Frome	d		20 15					21 01		21 42			
Westbury	a	20 09	20 26		21 03	21 03	21 08	21 11	21 25	21 51		22 09	22 09
	d	20 10		20 38	21 04	21 04	21 10		21 25	21 55		22 10	22 10
Trowbridge	d	20 16		20 44			21 16		21 31	22 01		22 16	22 16
Bradford-on-Avon	d	20 22		20 50			21 22		21 37	22 07		22 22	22 22
Avoncliff	d			20x52						22x09			
Freshford	d			20 55						22 13			
Bath Spa 7	a	20 34		21 06			21 34		21 50	22 24		22 34	22 34
Melksham	d												
Chippenham	a												
Swindon	a												
London Paddington 15 ⊖	a				22 30	22 30							
Oldfield Park	a			21 10						22 28			
Keynsham	a			21 17					21 58	22 35			
Bristol Temple Meads 10	a	20 50		21 29			21 49		22 06	22 44		22 48	22 48
Filton Abbey Wood	a	21 00					22 00					23 00	23 00
Severn Tunnel Jn	a	21 15					22 17					23 16	23 16
Newport (South Wales)	a	21 27					22 37					23 35	23 34
Cardiff Central 7	a	21 45					23 00					23 57	23 57

b arr. 1816

For connections to Swansea please refer to Table 128. For connections to Exeter St Davids and Plymouth please refer to Table 135. For connections from Bournemouth please refer to Table 158

Table 123

Portsmouth and Weymouth - Bristol and South Wales

Mondays to Fridays

		GW	GW	GW
Brighton 10	d			
Hove 2	d			
Shoreham-by-Sea	d			
Worthing 4	d			
Barnham	d			
Chichester 4	d			
Havant	d			
Portsmouth Harbour	d			21 23
Portsmouth & Southsea	d			21 27
Fratton	d			21 31
Cosham	d			
Fareham	a			21 47
	d			21 47
Southampton Central	d	21 20		22 22
Romsey	d	21 31		22 33
Salisbury	a	21 51		22 58
	d	21 53		23 00
Warminster	d	22 15		23 20
Dilton Marsh	d	22x20		23x24
Weymouth	d			
Upwey	d			
Dorchester West	d			
Maiden Newton	d			
Chetnole	d			
Yetminster	d			
Thornford	d			
Yeovil Pen Mill	d			
Castle Cary	a			
	d			
Bruton	d			
Frome	d			
Westbury	a	22 25		23 30
	d		22 32	
Trowbridge	d		22 38	
Bradford-on-Avon	d		22 44	
Avoncliff	d		22x46	
Freshford	d		22 49	
Bath Spa 7	a		23 00	
Melksham	d			
Chippenham	a			
Swindon	a			
London Paddington 15 ⊖	a			
Oldfield Park	a		23 04	
Keynsham	a		23 12	
Bristol Temple Meads 10	a		23 22	
Filton Abbey Wood	a			
Severn Tunnel Jn	a			
Newport (South Wales)	a			
Cardiff Central 7	a			

For connections to Swansea please refer to Table 128. For connections to Exeter St Davids and Plymouth please refer to Table 135. For connections from Bournemouth please refer to Table 158

Table 123

Portsmouth and Weymouth - Bristol and South Wales

Saturdays

		GW	GW	SW	GW	GW	GW	GW	GW	GW	GW	GW	GW	GW	GW	GW	GW	SW	GW	GW	GW	GW	GW
				1		◇1	◇		◇		◇	◇1	◇			1	◇	◇1	◇	1	◇		◇1
												A								B			C
						⊏			≍			⊘	≍			⊏	≍			⊏	≍		⊏
Brighton 10	d																		09 00				
Hove 2	d																		09 04				
Shoreham-by-Sea	d																		09 13				
Worthing 4	d																		09 22				
Barnham	d																		09 41				
Chichester 4	d																		09 49				
Havant	d																		10 00				
Portsmouth Harbour	d						06 00		07 05				08 23				09 23				10 23		
Portsmouth & Southsea	d						06 04		07 09				08 27				09 27				10 27		
Fratton	d						06 08		07 14				08 31				09 31				10 31		
Cosham	d						06 19		07 21				08 39				09 39		10 06		10 39		
Fareham	a						06 27		07 29				08 46				09 46		10 15		10 46		
	d						06 28		07 30				08 47				09 47		10 16		10 47		
Southampton Central	d						06 53		07 54		08 27		09 10				10 10		10 42		11 10		
Romsey	d						07 11		08 12		08 38		09 21				10 21		10 53		11 21		
Salisbury	a						07 29		08 30		09 03		09 40				10 40		11 13		11 40		
	d	06 03		06 40			07 30		08 34		09 03		09 41				10 41	10 52	11 13		11 41		
Warminster	d	06 23		07 00	07 23		07 50		08 54		09 23		10 01		10 25		11 01	11 12	11 34		12 01		
Dilton Marsh	d	06x27			07x27		07x54				09x28				10x29								
Weymouth	d							06 40						08 50								11 10	
Upwey	d							06 45						08 55								11 15	
Dorchester West	d							06 53						09 03								11 26	
Maiden Newton	d							07 05						09 15								11b43	
Chetnole	d							07x13						09x23								11x50	
Yetminster	d							07x16						09x26								11x53	
Thornford	d							07x18						09x28								11x56	
Yeovil Pen Mill	d							07 30						09 38								12 05	
Castle Cary	a					07 31		07 43				09 39		09 51						11 23		12 19	12 44
	d					07 33		07 44				09 40		09 54						11 24		12 22	12 45
Bruton	d							07 49						10 00								12 27	
Frome	d		06 37					08 02						10 19								12 39	
Westbury	a	06 34	06 46	07 08	07 31	07 51	07 59	08 13	09 00		09 34	09 58	10 09	10 28	10 33	10 59	11 09	11 20	11 42	11 42	12 09	12 48	13 03
	d	06 38	06 51	07 09	07 38	07 56	08 10	08 17	09 10	09 03	09 38	09 59	10 10	10 38		11 02	11 10	11 21	11 42	11 45	12 10	12 49	13 05
Trowbridge	d	06 44	06 57	07 15	07 44		08 16	08 23	09 16	09 09	09 44		10 16	10 44			11 16	11 27	11 48		12 16	12 55	
Bradford-on-Avon	d	06 50	07 03	07 21	07 50		08 22	08 29	09 22		09 50		10 22	10 50			11 22	11 33	11 54		12 22	13 01	
Avoncliff	d	06x52	07x05		07x52			08x31			09x52			10x52					11x57			13x03	
Freshford	d	06 55	07 09		07 55			08 34			09 55			10 55					12 00			13 05	
Bath Spa 7	a	07 06	07 20	07 33	08 06		08 34	08 45	09 34		10 06		10 34	11 06			11 34	11 46	12 10		12 34	13 17	
Melksham	d									09 18													
Chippenham	a									09 30													
Swindon	a									09 49													
London Paddington 15 ⊖	a					09 21						11 24				12 23				13 14			14 45
Oldfield Park	a	07 10	07 24	07 37	08 10			08 49			10 10			11 10					12 14			13 20	
Keynsham	a	07 17	07 31	07 44	08 17			08 56			10 17			11 17					12 21			13 27	
Bristol Temple Meads 10	a	07 29	07 39	07 53	08 29		08 47	09 05	09 48		10 29		10 48	11 29			11 48	12 05	12 29		12 48	13 36	
Filton Abbey Wood	a	07 48	08 01		08 48		09 00		10 00		10 48		11 00	11 48			12 00		12 48		13 00	13 48	
Severn Tunnel Jn	a																						
Newport (South Wales)	a		08 25				09 25		10 25				11 25				12 25				13 25		
Cardiff Central 7	a		08 43				09 43		10 43				11 43				12 43				13 43		

A ⊘ to Westbury
B until 4 September
C from 11 September
b arr. 1136

For connections to Swansea please refer to Table 128. For connections to Exeter St Davids and Plymouth please refer to Table 135. For connections from Bournemouth please refer to Table 158

Table 123

Saturdays

Portsmouth and Weymouth - Bristol and South Wales

		GW	GW	GW	SW	GW	GW	GW	GW	GW	GW	GW	GW	GW	GW	GW	GW	GW	GW	GW	GW	GW	GW
		◇	◇	◇	◇1		◇1 A		◇	◇1 B		◇1 C	◇1 C	◇	C	◇1 D	E	F	◇	C	B	■	B
Brighton 10	d																						
Hove 2	d																						
Shoreham-by-Sea	d																						
Worthing 4	d																						
Barnham	d																						
Chichester 4	d																						
Havant	d																						
Portsmouth Harbour	d	11 23		12 23					13 23					14 23					15 23			16 23	
Portsmouth & Southsea	d	11 27		12 27					13 27					14 27					15 27			16 27	
Fratton	d	11 31		12 31					13 31					14 31					15 31			16 31	
Cosham	d	11 39		12 39					13 39					14 39					15 39			16 39	
Fareham	a	11 46		12 46					13 46					14 46					15 46			16 46	
	d	11 47		12 47					13 47					14 47					15 47			16 47	
Southampton Central	d	12 10	12 27	13 10					14 10					15 10					16 10			17 10	
Romsey	d	12 21	12 38	13 21					14 21					15 21					16 21			17 21	
Salisbury	a	12 40	13 03	13 40					14 40					15 40					16 40			17 40	
	d	12 41	13 04	13 41	13 52				14 41					15 41					16 41			17 41	
Warminster	d	13 01	13 25	14 01	14 12				15 01		15 28			16 01			16 28	16 28	17 01	17 28		18 01	
Dilton Marsh	d		13x29								15x33						16 33	16 33		17 32			
Weymouth	d					13 10									15 08						16 08		16 55
Upwey	d					13 15									15 13						16 13		
Dorchester West	d					13 23									15 21						16 23		17 07
Maiden Newton	d					13b43									15 33						16c42		17 21
Chetnole	d					13x51									15x42						16 51		
Yetminster	d					13x54									15x45						16 54		
Thornford	d					13x56									15x47						16 56		
Yeovil Pen Mill	d					14 06									15 56						17 05		17 41
Castle Cary	a					14 19	14 43			15 07		15 48			16 09	16 18					17 18		18 02
	d					14 20	14 44			15 08		15 49			16 10	16 19					17 19		18 05
Bruton	d					14 26									16 16						17 25		18 11
Frome	d					14 39							15 55		16 29						17 38		18 23
Westbury	a	13 09	13 34	14 09	14 20	14 48	15 02		15 09	15 26	15 36		16 05	16 09	16 38	16 36	16 36	16 36	17 09	17 36	17 47	18 09	18 33
	d	13 10	13 38	14 10	14 21	14 48	15 03	15 06	15 10	15 28	15 38		16 08	16 10	16 38	16 38	16 38	16 38	17 10	17 38	17 48	18 10	18 38
Trowbridge	d	13 16	13 44	14 16	14 27	14 54		15 12	15 16		15 44			16 16	16 44		16 44	16 44	17 16	17 44	17 54	18 16	18 44
Bradford-on-Avon	d	13 22	13 50	14 22	14 33	15 00			15 22		15 50			16 22	16 50		16 50	16 50	17 22	17 50	18 00	18 22	18 50
Avoncliff	d		13x52			15x02					15x52				16x52		16x52	16x52		17x52	18x02		
Freshford	d		13 55			15 06					15 55				16 55		16 55	16 55		17 55	18 05		
Bath Spa 7	a	13 34	14 06	14 34	14 46	15 17			15 35		16 06			16 34	17 06		17 10	17 06	17 34	18 06	18 16	18 34	19 06
Melksham	d							15 21															
Chippenham	a							15 29															
Swindon	a							15 49															
London Paddington 15 ⊖	a						16 23			17 06		17 21	17 51			18 08							
Oldfield Park	a		14 10			15 21					16 10				17 10		17 14	17 10		18 10	18 20		19 09
Keynsham	a		14 17			15 28					16 17				17 17		17 21	17 17		18 16	18 26		19 17
Bristol Temple Meads 10	a	13 48	14 29	14 48	15 05	15 36			15 49		16 29			16 48	17 29		17 30	17 29	17 48	18 29	18 35	18 48	19 29
Filton Abbey Wood	a	14 00	14 48	15 00		15 48			16 00		16 48			17 00	17 48		17 48	17 48	18 00	18 48	18 48	19 00	
Severn Tunnel Jn	a													17 14					18 13				
Newport (South Wales)	a	14 25		15 25					16 25					17 25					18 25			19 25	
Cardiff Central 7	a	14 43		15 43					16 43					17 43					18 43			19 42	

A from 11 September. ⊘ to Westbury
B until 4 September
C from 11 September
D until 4 September. The Torbay Express
E from 17 July until 4 September
F until 10 July
b arr. 1333
c arr. 1633

For connections to Swansea please refer to Table 128. For connections to Exeter St Davids and Plymouth please refer to Table 135. For connections from Bournemouth please refer to Table 158

Table 123

Saturdays

Portsmouth and Weymouth - Bristol and South Wales

		GW	GW	GW	GW	GW	GW	GW	GW	GW	GW	GW	GW	GW	SW	GW	GW	GW
			A	◇	◇1 A	◇1 B		■ ◇ C	◇1	◇	D	E	1	◇	◇1		◇	
Brighton 10	d							17 00										
Hove 2	d							17 04										
Shoreham-by-Sea	d							17 13										
Worthing 4	d							17 22										
Barnham	d							17 38										
Chichester 4	d							17 46										
Havant	d							18 00										
Portsmouth Harbour	d			17 23						18 23				19 23			20 23	
Portsmouth & Southsea	d			17 27						18 27				19 27			20 27	
Fratton	d			17 31						18 31				19 31			20 31	
Cosham	d			17 39				18 06		18 39				19 39				
Fareham	a			17 46				18 14		18 46				19 46			20 45	
	d			17 47				18 15		18 47				19 47			20 47	
Southampton Central	d			18 10				18 45		19 10				20 10			21 10	21 27
Romsey	d			18 21				18 56		19 21				20 21			21 21	21 38
Salisbury	a			18 40				19 15		19 40				20 40			21 41	22 03
	d			18 41				19 16		19 41				20 41	20 57		21 41	22 04
Warminster	d			19 01				19 37		20 01				21 01	21 17		22 01	22 25
Dilton Marsh	d							19x42										22x29
Weymouth	d	17 30														20 21		
Upwey	d	17 35														20 26		
Dorchester West	d	17 43														20 34		
Maiden Newton	d	17 54														20 45		
Chetnole	d	18x03														20x54		
Yetminster	d	18x06														20x57		
Thornford	d	18x08														20x59		
Yeovil Pen Mill	d	18b23														21 09		
Castle Cary	a	18 31			18 52	18 52			19 46							21 22		
	d	18 32			18 53	18 53			19 47							21 23		
Bruton	d	18 38														21 29		
Frome	d	19c05					←						20 53			21 42		
Westbury	a	19 14		19 09	19 11	19 11	19 14	19 46	20 05	20 09			21 02	21 09	21 25	21 51	22 10	22 34
	d	19 17	18 38	19 10	19 12	19 12	19 17	19 49	20 06	20 10	20 38	20 38		21 10	21 25	21 55	22 10	22 38
Trowbridge	d	→	18 44	19 16			19 23	19 55		20 16	20 44	20 44		21 16	21 31	22 01	22 16	22 44
Bradford-on-Avon	d		18 50	19 22			19 29	20 01		20 22	20 50	20 50		21 22	21 37	22 07	22 22	22 50
Avoncliff	d		18x52				19x31	20x03			20x52	20x52				22x09		22x52
Freshford	d		18 55				19 35	20 06			20 55	20 55				22 13		22 55
Bath Spa 7	a		19 06	19 34			19 46	20 16		20 34	21 06	21 09		21 37	21 50	22 24	22 36	23 06
Melksham	d																	
Chippenham	a																	
Swindon	a																	
London Paddington 15 ⊖	a				20 37	20 39			21 32									
Oldfield Park	a		19 10				19 50	20 20			21 10	21 13				22 28		23 10
Keynsham	a		19 17				19 57	20 27			21 17	21 19			21 58	22 35		23 17
Bristol Temple Meads 10	a		19 29	19 48			20 05	20 35		20 48	21 29	21 32		21 51	22 06	22 44	22 50	23 29
Filton Abbey Wood	a		19 48	20 00				20 48		21 00				22 00			23 00	
Severn Tunnel Jn	a													22 17			23 17	
Newport (South Wales)	a			20 25						21 25				22 36			23 35	
Cardiff Central 7	a			20 43						21 43				22 56			23 55	

A from 11 September
B until 4 September
C ◇ to Dilton Marsh ■ from Westbury
D until 10 July, from 11 September
E from 17 July until 4 September
b arr. 1816
c arr. 1856

For connections to Swansea please refer to Table 128. For connections to Exeter St Davids and Plymouth please refer to Table 135. For connections from Bournemouth please refer to Table 158

Table 123

Sundays until 11 July

Portsmouth and Weymouth - Bristol and South Wales

		GW	GW	GW	GW	GW	GW	GW	GW	GW	SW	GW	GW	GW	GW	GW	GW	GW	GW	GW	GW	GW	GW
		◇1 🍴		◇1 🍴	■		◇1 🍴	◇	◇	◇1 🍴	◇1	◇		◇1 🍴	◇	■			◇1 🍴	◇	◇	◇1 🍴	◇
Brighton 10	d								11 08												15 45		
Hove 2	d								11 12												15 49		
Shoreham-by-Sea	d								11 18												15 55		
Worthing 4	d								11 27												16 06		
Barnham	d								11 46												16 23		
Chichester 4	d								11 54												16 34		
Havant	d								12b10												16 48		
Portsmouth Harbour	d				09 08			11 08				13 08			14 08	15 08				16 08			17 08
Portsmouth & Southsea	d				09 12			11 12				13 12			14 12	15 12				16 12			17 12
Fratton	d				09 16			11 16				13 16			14 16	15 16				16 16			17 16
Cosham	d				09 23			11 23	12c23			13 23			14 23	15 23				16 23	16 55		17 23
Fareham	a				09 31			11 31	12 31			13 31			14 31	15 31				16 31	17 02		17 31
	d				09 32			11 32	12 32			13 32			14 32	15 32				16 32	17 03		17 32
Southampton Central	d				09 54			11 54	12 54			13 54			14 54	15 54				16 54	17 26		17 54
Romsey	d				10 05			12 06	13 06			14 06			15 06	16 06				17 06	17 39		18 06
Salisbury	a				10 24			12 24	13 24			14 24			15 24	16 24				17 24	18 01		18 24
	d				10 30			12 28	13 28		13 55	14 28			15 28	16 28				17 28	18 02		18 28
Warminster	d				10 50			12 48	13 47		14 15	14 48			15 48	16 48				17 48	18 22		18 48
Dilton Marsh	d				10x55							14x53			15x53	16x53					18x27		
Weymouth	d					11 10							14 10					16 10					
Upwey	d					11 15							14 15					16 15					
Dorchester West	d					11 26							14 23					16 23					
Maiden Newton	d					11 39							14 35					16 35					
Chetnole	d					11x46							14x43					16x43					
Yetminster	d					11x49							14x46					16x46					
Thornford	d					11x52							14x48					16x48					
Yeovil Pen Mill	d					12 01							15 01					16 58					
Castle Cary	a	09 28				12 14	12 33						15 13	15 32				17 10	17 33				
	d	09 29				12 16	12 34						15 16	15 33				17 13	17 34				
Bruton	d					12 22							15 21					17 18					
Frome	d		09 33			12 35							15 34					17 31					
Westbury	a	09 46	09 42	10 50	10 58	12 44	12 52	12 55	13 56	13 51	14 23	14 56	15 43	15 50	15 56	16 56		17 40	17 51	17 58	18 31	18 53	18 55
	d	09 49	09 58	10 53	10 59		12 53	12 56	13 56	13 59	14 23	15 02	15 44	15 50	15 59	17 00	17 09	17 41	17 53	18 02	18 32	18 58	19 01
Trowbridge	d		10 04		11 05			13 02	14 02		14 29	15 08	15 50		16 05	17 06	17 15	17 47		18 08	18 38		19 07
Bradford-on-Avon	d		10 09		11 11			13 08	14 08		14 35	15 14	15 56		16 11	17 12		17 53			18 44		19 13
Avoncliff	d		10x12					13x11	14x11				15 59		16x14			17x56			18x47		
Freshford	d		10 15					13 14	14 14				16 02		16 17			17 59			18 49		
Bath Spa 7	a		10 26		11 25			13 25	14 24		14 48	15 27	16 12		16 28	17 25		18 10		18 25	18 59		19 26
Melksham	d																17 25						
Chippenham	a																17 38						
Swindon	a																17 56						
London Paddington 15 ⊖	a	11 24		12 29			14 30			15 29				17 29					19 29			20 22	
Oldfield Park	a		10 30		11 28			13 28	14 27				16 16			17 28		18 13			19 03		
Keynsham	a		10 37		11 35			13 35	14 35				16 23			17 35		18 21			19 10		
Bristol Temple Meads 10	a		10 45		11 43			13 43	14 43		15 02	15 40	16 31		16 41	17 43		18 33		18 38	19 18		19 39
Filton Abbey Wood	a				11 55			13 55	14 55			15 55			16 55	17 55				18 55			19 55
Severn Tunnel Jn	a				12 10			14 07	15 07			16 07			17 10	18 07				19 07			20 10
Newport (South Wales)	a				12 30			14 22	15 27			16 27			17 30	18 27				19 27			20 29
Cardiff Central 7	a				12 45			14 42	15 42			16 45			17 47	18 44				19 43			20 47

b arr. 1204 **c** arr. 1216

For connections to Swansea please refer to Table 128. For connections to Exeter St Davids and Plymouth please refer to Table 135. For connections from Bournemouth please refer to Table 158

Table 123

Sundays until 11 July

Portsmouth and Weymouth - Bristol and South Wales

		GW	GW	GW	SW	GW	GW	GW	GW	GW	GW	GW
				◇	◇1	◇1 🍴	◇	◇	◇1 🍴		◇	
Brighton 10	d						17 45					
Hove 2	d						17 49					
Shoreham-by-Sea	d						17 55					
Worthing 4	d						18 06					
Barnham	d						18 23					
Chichester 4	d						18 34					
Havant	d						18 48					
Portsmouth Harbour	d			18 08				19 08			20 08	22 03
Portsmouth & Southsea	d			18 12				19 12			20 12	22 12
Fratton	d			18 16				19 16			20 16	22 16
Cosham	d			18 23			18 55	19 23				
Fareham	a			18 31			19 02	19 31			20 31	22 31
	d			18 32			19 03	19 32			20 32	22 32
Southampton Central	d			18 54			19 30	19 54			20 54	22 57
Romsey	d			19 06			19 42	20 06			21 06	23 09
Salisbury	a			19 24			20 00	20 24			21 24	23 27
	d			19 25	19 55		20 03	20 28			21 28	23 28
Warminster	d			19 48	20 15		20 23	20 48			21 48	23 53
Dilton Marsh	d						20x28				21x53	23x58
Weymouth	d	17 56								20 09		
Upwey	d	18 01								20 14		
Dorchester West	d	18 09								20 22		
Maiden Newton	d	18 21								20 34		
Chetnole	d	18x29								20x42		
Yetminster	d	18x32								20x45		
Thornford	d	18x34								20x47		
Yeovil Pen Mill	d	18 44								20 57		
Castle Cary	a	18 56				20 06			21 13	21 09		
	d	18 59				20 07			21 15	21 19		
Bruton	d	19 05								21 25		
Frome	d	19 18								21 38		
Westbury	a	19 27		19 55	20 23	20 26	20 32	20 56	21 33	21 47	21 56	00 02
	d	19 30	19 35	20 01	20 23	20 27	20 37	21 02	21 33	21 49	22 02	
Trowbridge	d	19 36	19 42	20 07	20 29		20 43	21 08		21 55	22 08	
Bradford-on-Avon	d	19 42		20 13	20 35		20 49	21 14		22 01	22 14	
Avoncliff	d	19x45					20x52			22x04		
Freshford	d	19 48					20 54			22 07		
Bath Spa 7	a	19 59		20 26	20 48		21 05	21 27		22 18	22 28	
Melksham	d		19 52									
Chippenham	a		20 02									
Swindon	a		20 20									
London Paddington 15 ⊖	a					21 53			23 16			
Oldfield Park	a	20 02					21 08			22 21		
Keynsham	a	20 10			20 56		21 16			22 29		
Bristol Temple Meads 10	a	20 18		20 39	21 04		21 24	21 40		22 37	22 41	
Filton Abbey Wood	a			20 55				21 57			22 55	
Severn Tunnel Jn	a			21 07				22 12			23 07	
Newport (South Wales)	a			21 27				22 32			23 28	
Cardiff Central 7	a			21 43				22 54			23 49	

For connections to Swansea please refer to Table 128. For connections to Exeter St Davids and Plymouth please refer to Table 135. For connections from Bournemouth please refer to Table 158

Table 123

Sundays
18 July to 05 September

Portsmouth and Weymouth - Bristol and South Wales

		GW	GW	GW	GW	GW	GW	GW	GW	GW	SW	GW	GW	GW	GW	GW	GW	GW	GW	GW	GW	GW	GW
		◇1 ☕		◇1 ☕	■		◇1 ☕	◇	◇	◇1 ☕	◇1	◇		◇1 ☕	◇	■			◇1 ☕	◇	◇	◇1 ☕	◇
Brighton 10	d								11 08												15 45		
Hove 2	d								11 12												15 49		
Shoreham-by-Sea	d								11 18												15 55		
Worthing 4	d								11 27												16 06		
Barnham	d								11 46												16 23		
Chichester 4	d								11 54												16 34		
Havant	d								12b10												16 48		
Portsmouth Harbour	d				09 08			11 08				13 08			14 08	15 08				16 08			17 08
Portsmouth & Southsea	d				09 12			11 12				13 12			14 12	15 12				16 12			17 12
Fratton	d				09 16			11 16				13 16			14 16	15 16				16 16			17 16
Cosham	d				09 23			11 23	12c23			13 23			14 23	15 23				16 23	16 55		17 23
Fareham	a				09 31			11 31	12 31			13 31			14 31	15 31				16 31	17 02		17 31
	d				09 32			11 32	12 32			13 32			14 32	15 32				16 32	17 03		17 32
Southampton Central	d				09 54			11 54	12 54			13 54			14 54	15 54				16 54	17 26		17 54
Romsey	d				10 05			12 06	13 06			14 06			15 06	16 06				17 06	17 39		18 06
Salisbury	a				10 24			12 24	13 24			14 24			15 24	16 24				17 24	18 01		18 24
	d				10 30			12 28	13 28		13 55	14 28			15 28	16 28				17 28	18 02		18 28
Warminster	d				10 50			12 48	13 47		14 15	14 48			15 48	16 48				17 48	18 22		18 48
Dilton Marsh	d				10x55							14x53			15x53	16x53					18x27		
Weymouth	d					11 10							14 10					16 10					
Upwey	d					11 15							14 15					16 15					
Dorchester West	d					11 26							14 23					16 23					
Maiden Newton	d					11 39							14 35					16 35					
Chetnole	d					11x46							14x43					16x43					
Yetminster	d					11x49							14x46					16x46					
Thornford	d					11x52							14x48					16x48					
Yeovil Pen Mill	d					12 01							15 01					16 58					
Castle Cary	a	09 28				12 14	12 33						15 13	15 32				17 10	17 33				
	d	09 29				12 16	12 34						15 16	15 33				17 13	17 34				
Bruton	d					12 22							15 21					17 18					
Frome	d		09 33			12 35							15 34					17 31					
Westbury	a	09 46	09 42	10 50	10 58	12 44	12 52	12 55	13 56	13 51	14 23	14 56	15 43	15 50	15 56	16 56		17 40	17 51	17 58	18 31	18 53	18 55
	d	09 49	09 58	10 53	10 59		12 53	12 56	13 56	13 59	14 23	15 02	15 44	15 50	15 59	17 00	17 09	17 41	17 53	18 02	18 32	18 58	19 01
Trowbridge	d		10 04		11 05			13 02	14 02		14 29	15 08	15 50		16 05	17 06	17 15	17 47		18 08	18 38		19 07
Bradford-on-Avon	d		10 09		11 11			13 08	14 08		14 35	15 14	15 56		16 11	17 12		17 53			18 44		19 13
Avoncliff	d		10x12					13x11	14x11				15 59		16x14			17x56			18x47		
Freshford	d		10 15					13 14	14 14				16 02		16 17			17 59			18 49		
Bath Spa 7	a		10 26		11 25			13 25	14 24		14 48	15 27	16 12		16 28	17 25		18 10		18 25	19 04		19 26
Melksham	d																17 25						
Chippenham	a																17 38						
Swindon	a																17 56						
London Paddington 15 ⊖	a	11 24		12 29			14 30			15 29				17 29					19 29			20 22	
Oldfield Park	a		10 30		11 28			13 28	14 27				16 16			17 28		18 13			19 08		
Keynsham	a		10 37		11 35			13 35	14 35				16 23			17 35		18 21			19 15		
Bristol Temple Meads 10	a		10 45		11 43			13 43	14 43		15 02	15 40	16 31		16 41	17 43		18 33		18 38	19 23		19 39
Filton Abbey Wood	a				11 55			13 55	14 55			15 55			16 55	17 55				18 55			19 55
Severn Tunnel Jn	a				12 10			14 07	15 07			16 07			17 10	18 07				19 07			20 10
Newport (South Wales)	a				12 26			14 22	15 23			16 23			17 26	18 23				19 23			20 27
Cardiff Central 7	a				12 45			14 46	15 42			16 45			17 46	18 45				19 43			20 49

b arr. 1204

c arr. 1216

For connections to Swansea please refer to Table 128. For connections to Exeter St Davids and Plymouth please refer to Table 135. For connections from Bournemouth please refer to Table 158

Table 123

Sundays
18 July to 05 September

Portsmouth and Weymouth - Bristol and South Wales

		GW	GW	GW	SW	GW	GW	GW	GW	GW	GW	GW
				◇	◇1	◇1 ☕	◇	◇	◇1 ☕		◇	
Brighton 10	d						17 45					
Hove 2	d						17 49					
Shoreham-by-Sea	d						17 55					
Worthing 4	d						18 06					
Barnham	d						18 23					
Chichester 4	d						18 34					
Havant	d						18 48					
Portsmouth Harbour	d			18 08				19 08			20 08	22 03
Portsmouth & Southsea	d			18 12				19 12			20 12	22 12
Fratton	d			18 16				19 16			20 16	22 16
Cosham	d			18 23			18 55	19 23				
Fareham	a			18 31			19 02	19 31			20 31	22 31
	d			18 32			19 03	19 32			20 32	22 32
Southampton Central	d			18 54			19 30	19 54			20 54	22 57
Romsey	d			19 06			19 42	20 06			21 06	23 09
Salisbury	a			19 24			20 00	20 24			21 24	23 27
	d			19 25	19 55		20 03	20 28			21 28	23 28
Warminster	d			19 48	20 15		20 23	20 48			21 48	23 53
Dilton Marsh	d						20x28				21x53	23x58
Weymouth	d	17 56								20 09		
Upwey	d	18 01								20 14		
Dorchester West	d	18 09								20 22		
Maiden Newton	d	18 21								20 34		
Chetnole	d	18x29								20x42		
Yetminster	d	18x32								20x45		
Thornford	d	18x34								20x47		
Yeovil Pen Mill	d	18 44								20 57		
Castle Cary	a	18 56				20 06			21 13	21 09		
	d	18 59				20 07			21 15	21 19		
Bruton	d	19 05								21 25		
Frome	d	19 18								21 38		
Westbury	a	19 27		19 55	20 23	20 26	20 32	20 56	21 33	21 47	21 56	00 02
	d	19 32	19 35	20 01	20 23	20 27	20 37	21 02	21 33	21 49	22 02	
Trowbridge	d	19 38	19 42	20 07	20 29		20 43	21 08		21 55	22 08	
Bradford-on-Avon	d	19 44		20 13	20 35		20 49	21 14		22 01	22 14	
Avoncliff	d	19x47					20x52			22x04		
Freshford	d	19 50					20 54			22 07		
Bath Spa 7	a	20 04		20 26	20 48		21 05	21 27		22 18	22 28	
Melksham	d		19 52									
Chippenham	a		20 02									
Swindon	a		20 20									
London Paddington 15 ⊖	a					21 53			23 16			
Oldfield Park	a	20 07					21 08			22 21		
Keynsham	a	20 16			20 56		21 16			22 29		
Bristol Temple Meads 10	a	20 24		20 39	21 04		21 24	21 40		22 37	22 41	
Filton Abbey Wood	a			20 55				21 57			22 55	
Severn Tunnel Jn	a			21 07				22 12			23 07	
Newport (South Wales)	a			21 23				22 32			23 28	
Cardiff Central 7	a			21 44				22 54			23 49	

For connections to Swansea please refer to Table 128. For connections to Exeter St Davids and Plymouth please refer to Table 135. For connections from Bournemouth please refer to Table 158

Table 123

Portsmouth and Weymouth - Bristol and South Wales

		GW	GW	GW	GW	GW	GW	GW	GW	SW	GW	GW
		◇1 ☕		◇1 ☕	■	◇1 ☕	◇	◇	◇1 ☕	◇1	◇	
Brighton 10	d							11 10				
Hove 2	d							11 14				
Shoreham-by-Sea	d							11 20				
Worthing 4	d							11 29				
Barnham	d							11 46				
Chichester 4	d							11 54				
Havant	d							12b10				
Portsmouth Harbour	d				09 08		11 08				13 08	
Portsmouth & Southsea	d				09 12		11 12				13 12	
Fratton	d				09 16		11 16				13 16	
Cosham	d				09 23		11 23	12c23			13 23	
Fareham	a				09 31		11 31	12 31			13 31	
	d				09 32		11 32	12 32			13 32	
Southampton Central	d				09 54		11 54	12 54			13 54	
Romsey	d				10 05		12 06	13 06			14 06	
Salisbury	a				10 24		12 24	13 24			14 24	
	d				10 30		12 28	13 28		13 55	14 28	
Warminster	d				10 50		12 48	13 47		14 15	14 48	
Dilton Marsh	d				10x55						14x53	
Weymouth	d											14 00
Upwey	d											14 05
Dorchester West	d											14 13
Maiden Newton	d											14 25
Chetnole	d											14x33
Yetminster	d											14x36
Thornford	d											14x38
Yeovil Pen Mill	d											14 48
Castle Cary	a	09 33				12 33						15 00
	d	09 34				12 34						15 03
Bruton	d											15 08
Frome	d		09 39									15 21
Westbury	a	09 51	09 48	10 50	10 58	12 52	12 55	13 56	13 51	14 23	14 56	15 30
	d	09 54	09 58	10 53	10 59	12 53	12 56	13 56	13 59	14 23	15 02	15 31
Trowbridge	d		10 04		11 05		13 02	14 02		14 29	15 08	15 37
Bradford-on-Avon	d		10 09		11 11		13 08	14 08		14 35	15 14	15 43
Avoncliff	d		10x12				13x11	14x11				15x46
Freshford	d		10 15				13 14	14 14				15 49
Bath Spa 7	a		10 26		11 25		13 25	14 24		14 48	15 27	16 00
Melksham	d											
Chippenham	a											
Swindon	a											
London Paddington 15 ⊖	a	11 29		12 29		14 29			15 29			
Oldfield Park	a		10 30		11 28		13 28	14 27				16 03
Keynsham	a		10 37		11 35		13 35	14 35				16 11
Bristol Temple Meads 10	a		10 45		11 43		13 43	14 43		15 02	15 40	16 23
Filton Abbey Wood	a				11 55		13 55	14 55			15 55	
Severn Tunnel Jn	a				12 10		14 07	15 07			16 07	
Newport (South Wales)	a				12 30		14 27	15 27			16 27	
Cardiff Central 7	a				12 45		14 51	15 42			16 45	

		GW	GW	GW	GW	GW	GW	GW	GW	GW	GW	GW
		◇1 ☕	◇	■		◇1 ☕	◇	◇	◇1 ☕	◇		
Brighton 10	d							15 46				
Hove 2	d							15 50				
Shoreham-by-Sea	d							15 56				
Worthing 4	d							16 08				
Barnham	d							16 25				
Chichester 4	d							16 34				
Havant	d							16 48				
Portsmouth Harbour	d		14 08	15 08			16 08			17 08		
Portsmouth & Southsea	d		14 12	15 12			16 12			17 12		
Fratton	d		14 16	15 16			16 16			17 16		
Cosham	d		14 23	15 23			16 23	16 55		17 23		
Fareham	a		14 31	15 31			16 31	17 02		17 31		
	d		14 32	15 32			16 32	17 03		17 32		
Southampton Central	d		14 54	15 54			16 54	17 26		17 54		
Romsey	d		15 06	16 06			17 06	17 39		18 06		
Salisbury	a		15 24	16 24			17 24	18 01		18 24		
	d		15 28	16 28			17 28	18 02		18 28		
Warminster	d		15 48	16 48			17 48	18 22		18 48		
Dilton Marsh	d		15x53	16x53				18x27				
Weymouth	d										17 56	
Upwey	d										18 01	
Dorchester West	d										18 09	
Maiden Newton	d										18 21	
Chetnole	d										18x29	
Yetminster	d										18x32	
Thornford	d										18x34	
Yeovil Pen Mill	d										18 44	
Castle Cary	a	15 32				17 36					18 56	
	d	15 33				17 37					18 59	
Bruton	d										19 05	
Frome	d										19 18	
Westbury	a	15 50	15 56	16 56		17 54	17 58	18 31	18 53	18 55	19 27	
	d	15 50	15 59	17 00	17 05	17 56	18 02	18 32	18 58	19 01	19 30	19 35
Trowbridge	d		16 05	17 06	17 11		18 08	18 38		19 07	19 36	19 42
Bradford-on-Avon	d		16 11	17 12				18 44		19 13	19 42	
Avoncliff	d		16x14					18x47			19x45	
Freshford	d		16 17					18 49			19 48	
Bath Spa 7	a		16 28	17 25			18 25	18 59		19 26	19 59	
Melksham	d				17 21							19 52
Chippenham	a				17 31							20 02
Swindon	a				17 48							20 20
London Paddington 15 ⊖	a	17 29				19 29			20 29			
Oldfield Park	a			17 28				19 03			20 02	
Keynsham	a			17 35				19 10			20 10	
Bristol Temple Meads 10	a		16 41	17 43			18 38	19 18		19 39	20 18	
Filton Abbey Wood	a		16 55	17 55			18 55			19 55		
Severn Tunnel Jn	a		17 10	18 07			19 07			20 10		
Newport (South Wales)	a		17 30	18 27			19 27			20 29		
Cardiff Central 7	a		17 47	18 45			19 43			20 47		

b arr. 1204 c arr. 1216

For connections to Swansea please refer to Table 128. For connections to Exeter St Davids and Plymouth please refer to Table 135. For connections from Bournemouth please refer to Table 158

Table 123

Portsmouth and Weymouth - Bristol and South Wales

		GW	SW	GW	GW	GW	GW	GW	GW	GW
		◇	◇1	◇1 ☕	◇	◇	◇1 ☕		◇	
Brighton 10	d				17 46					
Hove 2	d				17 50					
Shoreham-by-Sea	d				17 56					
Worthing 4	d				18 08					
Barnham	d				18 25					
Chichester 4	d				18 34					
Havant	d				18 48					
Portsmouth Harbour	d	18 08				19 08			20 08	22 03
Portsmouth & Southsea	d	18 12				19 12			20 12	22 12
Fratton	d	18 16				19 16			20 16	22 16
Cosham	d	18 23			18 55	19 23				
Fareham	a	18 31			19 02	19 31			20 31	22 31
	d	18 32			19 03	19 32			20 32	22 32
Southampton Central	d	18 54			19b30	19 54			20 54	22 57
Romsey	d	19 06			19 42	20 06			21 06	23 09
Salisbury	a	19 24			20 00	20 24			21 24	23 27
	d	19 25	19 55		20 03	20 28			21 28	23 28
Warminster	d	19 48	20 15		20 23	20 48			21 48	23 53
Dilton Marsh	d				20x28				21x53	23x58
Weymouth	d							20 09		
Upwey	d							20 14		
Dorchester West	d							20 22		
Maiden Newton	d							20 34		
Chetnole	d							20x42		
Yetminster	d							20x45		
Thornford	d							20x47		
Yeovil Pen Mill	d							20 57		
Castle Cary	a			20 06			21 13	21 09		
	d			20 07			21 15	21 19		
Bruton	d							21 25		
Frome	d							21 38		
Westbury	a	19 55	20 23	20 26	20 32	20 56	21 33	21 47	21 56	00 02
	d	20 01	20 23	20 27	20 37	21 02	21 33	21 49	22 02	
Trowbridge	d	20 07	20 29		20 43	21 08		21 55	22 08	
Bradford-on-Avon	d	20 13	20 35		20 49	21 14		22 01	22 14	
Avoncliff	d				20x52			22x04		
Freshford	d				20 54			22 07		
Bath Spa 7	a	20 26	20 48		21 08	21 27		22 18	22 28	
Melksham	d									
Chippenham	a									
Swindon	a									
London Paddington 15 ⊖	a			21 59			23 16			
Oldfield Park	a				21 11			22 21		
Keynsham	a		20 56		21 19			22 29		
Bristol Temple Meads 10	a	20 39	21 04		21 27	21 40		22 37	22 41	
Filton Abbey Wood	a	20 55				21 57			22 55	
Severn Tunnel Jn	a	21 07				22 15			23 07	
Newport (South Wales)	a	21 27				22 36			23 28	
Cardiff Central 7	a	21 43				22 59			23 49	

b arr. 1924

Route Diagram for Table 125

DM 12/06
Design BAJS

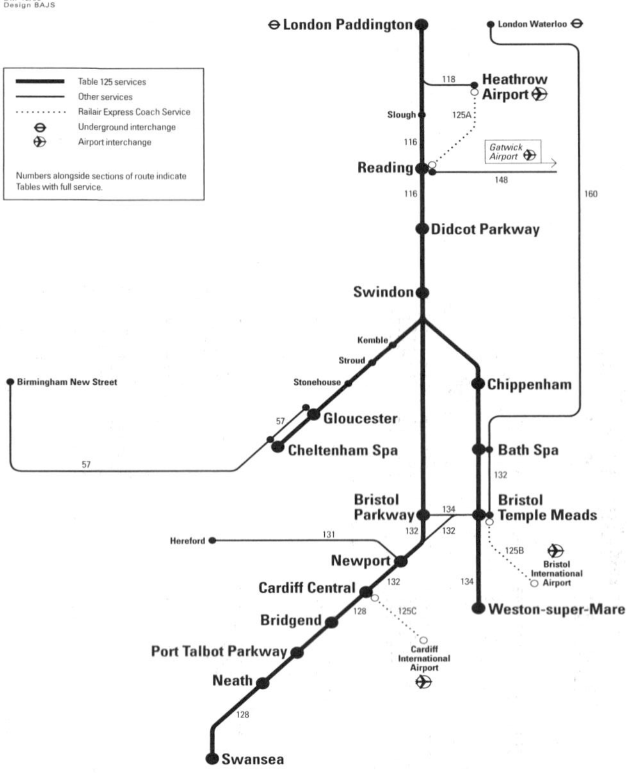

London - Swindon, Cheltenham Spa, Bristol, Weston-super-Mare and South Wales

		GW MX	GW	GW MX	GW MO	GW MX	GW MO	GW
			◇1 C ⊐	◇1 ⊐	◇1 ⊐	◇1 ⊐	◇1 ⊐	
London Paddington 15 ⊖	d		22p37	22p45	23p03	23p30	23p37	
Slough 3	d						23p55	
Reading 7	d		23p16	23p15	23p47	00 08	00 15	
Didcot Parkway	d		23b33	23p33	00s03	00 25	00s33	
Swindon	a		23b48	23p51	00s21	00 44	00s52	06 06
	d	23p33	23b52	23p52	00s23	00 45	00s53	06 16
Kemble	d	23p47						
Stroud	d	00 02						
Stonehouse	d	00 07						
Gloucester 7	a	00 24						
Cheltenham Spa	a							
Chippenham	d				00s38	01 00	01s09	06 32
Bath Spa 7	a				00s51	01 13	01s22	
Bristol Parkway 7	a		00s16	00 17				
	d		00s18	00 18				
Bristol Temple Meads 10	a		00 30		01 05	01 29	01 36	
Weston-super-Mare	a							
Newport (South Wales)	a			00 46		02s10		
Cardiff Central 7	a			01 06		02 31		
Bridgend	a			01 32				
Port Talbot Parkway	a			01 45				
Neath	a			01 52				
Swansea	a			02 07				

		GW	GW	GW	GW	GW	GW	GW	GW	GW	GW	GW	GW	GW	GW	GW	GW	GW	GW	GW	GW	GW	GW
		◇1 ⊐	◇1 ⊐	◇1 ⊐	◇1 ⊐	◇1 ⊐	◇1 ⊐	◇1 ⊘	◇1 D ⊐⊘	◇1 ⊐	◇1 ⊐	◇1 ⊐	◇1 ⊐	◇1 ⊐	◇1 E ⊐⊘		◇1 ⊐	◇1 E ⊐⊘	◇1 D ⊐⊘	◇1 ⊐	◇1 ⊐	◇1 ⊐	◇1 E ⊐⊘
London Paddington 15 ⊖	d	05 30	05 36	06 30	06 45	07 00	07 15	07 30	07 45	07 48	08 00	08 15	08 30	08 45	09 00		09 15	09 30	09 45	09 48	10 00	10 15	10 30
Slough 3	d		05 52																				
Reading 7	d	05 56	06 07	06 56	07 11	07 26	07 41	07 57	08 11	08 16	08 27	08 41	08 57	09 11	09 27		09 41	09 57	10 11	10 16	10 27	10 41	10 57
Didcot Parkway	d		06 21	07 12		07 42	07 56			08 33	08 42	08 56	09 12				09 56	10 12		10 33		10 56	11 12
Swindon	a	06 23	06 41	07 28	07 38	07 58	08 13	08 27	08 38	08 53	08 59	09 13	09 30	09 38	09 54		10 13	10 30	10 38	10 53	10 55	11 13	11 30
	d	06 25	06 50	07 30	07 38	08 00	08 13	08 27	08 38	08 54	09 00	09 13	09 30	09 38	09 55	09 54	10 13	10 30	10 38	10 54	10 55	11 13	11 30
Kemble	d		07 07							09 07						10 07				11 07			
Stroud	d		07 22							09 22						10 22				11 22			
Stonehouse	d		07 28							09 28						10 28				11 28			
Gloucester 7	a		07 45							09 44						10 50				11 44			
Cheltenham Spa	a		08 01							10 01						11 03				12 01			
Chippenham	d	06 40		07 45		08 15		08 41			09 15		09 45		10 10			10 45			11 10		11 45
Bath Spa 7	a	06 52		07 57		08 27		08 55			09 29		09 59		10 23			10 59			11 24		11 59
Bristol Parkway 7	a				08 04		08 39		09 04			09 39		10 04			10 39		11 04			11 39	
	d				08 07		08 40		09 07			09 40		10 07			10 40		11 07			11 40	
Bristol Temple Meads 10	a	07 07		08 17		08 44		09 10			09 44		10 15		10 38			11 15			11 40		12 15
Weston-super-Mare	a																				12 06		
Newport (South Wales)	a	07 44			08 31		09 07		09 31			10 04		10 31			11 04		11 31			12 04	
Cardiff Central 7	a	08 00			08 48		09 24		09 47			10 21		10 46			11 23		11 46			12 21	
Bridgend	a	08 23			09 09				10 09					11 09					12 09				
Port Talbot Parkway	a	08 36			09 22				10 22					11 22					12 22				
Neath	a	08 44			09 30				10 30					11 30					12 30				
Swansea	a	08 57			09 45				10 44					11 43					12 43				

		GW	GW	GW	GW	GW	GW	GW	GW	GW	GW	GW	GW	GW	GW	GW	GW	GW	GW	GW	GW	GW	GW
		◇1 D ⊐⊘		◇1 ⊐	◇1 ⊐	◇1 ⊐	◇1 D ⊐⊘	◇1 ⊐	◇1 ⊐	◇1 ⊐	◇1 ⊐	◇1 D ⊐⊘	◇1 ⊐		◇1 ⊐	◇1 ⊐	◇1 ⊐	◇1 ⊐	◇1 ⊐	◇1 ⊐	◇1 ⊐	◇1 ⊐	
London Paddington 15 ⊖	d	10 45		11 00	11 15	11 30	11 45	11 48	12 00	12 15	12 30	12 45	13 00		13 15	13 30	13 45	13 48	14 00	14 15	14 30	14 45	
Slough 3	d																						
Reading 7	d	11 11		11 27	11 41	11 57	12 11	12 16	12 27	12 41	12 57	13 11	13 27		13 41	13 57	14 11	14 16	14 27	14 41	14 57	15 11	
Didcot Parkway	d				11 56	12 12		12 33		12 56	13 12				13 56	14 12		14 33		14 56	15 12		
Swindon	a	11 38		11 55	12 13	12 30	12 38	12 53	12 55	13 13	13 30	13 38	13 54		14 13	14 30	14 38	14 54	14 55	15 13	15 30	15 38	
	d	11 38	11 54	11 55	12 13	12 30	12 38	12 54	12 55	13 13	13 30	13 38	13 55	13 54	14 13	14 30	14 38	14 54	14 55	15 13	15 30	15 38	15 54
Kemble	d		12 07					13 07						14 07				15 07					16 07
Stroud	d		12 22					13 22						14 22				15 22					16 22
Stonehouse	d		12 28					13 28						14 28				15 28					16 28
Gloucester 7	a		12 50					13 44						14 50				15 44					16 50
Cheltenham Spa	a		13 03					14 01						15 03				16 01					17 03
Chippenham	d			12 10		12 45			13 10		13 45		14 10			14 45			15 10		15 45		
Bath Spa 7	a			12 23		12 59			13 24		13 59		14 23			14 59			15 24		15 59		
Bristol Parkway 7	a	12 04			12 39		13 04			13 39		14 04			14 39		15 04			15 39		16 05	
	d	12 07			12 40		13 07			13 40		14 07			14 40		15 07			15 40		16 07	
Bristol Temple Meads 10	a			12 39		13 15			13 41		14 15		14 39			15 15			15 40		16 15		
Weston-super-Mare	a																				16 50		
Newport (South Wales)	a	12 31			13 04		13 31			14 04		14 31			14 04		15 31			16 04		16 31	
Cardiff Central 7	a	12 46			13 22		13 46			14 22		14 46			15 23		15 46			16 22		16 46	
Bridgend	a	13 09					14 09					15 09					16 09					17 09	
Port Talbot Parkway	a	13 22					14 22					15 22					16 22					17 22	
Neath	a	13 30					14 30					15 30					16 30					17 30	
Swansea	a	13 43					14 43					15 43					16 43					17 43	

A MO from 19 July until 6 September
B MO until 12 July
C MO from 13 September
D ⊐ from Bridgend ⊘ to Cardiff Central
E ⊐ from Chippenham ⊘ to Swindon
b previous night, stops to set down only

For connections from Heathrow Airport, Gatwick Airport and Oxford please refer to Tables 125A, 148 and 116. For connections to Birmingham New Street and Hereford please refer to Tables 57 and 131

Table 125

London - Swindon, Cheltenham Spa, Bristol, Weston-super-Mare and South Wales

	GW	GW	GW	GW	GW	GW	GW	GW	GW	GW	GW
	◇1 🛒	◇1 🛒	◇1 🛒	◇1 🛒	◇1 🛒	◇1 🛒	◇1 🛒	◇1 🛒	◇1 🛒		◇1 🛒
London Paddington 15 ⊖ d	15 00	15 15	15 30	15 45	15 48	16 00	16 15	16 30	16 45		17 00
Slough 3 d											
Reading 7 d	15 27	15 41	15 57	16 11	16 16	16 27	16 41	16 57	17 11		17 26
Didcot Parkway d		15 56	16 12		16 33		16 56	17 12			17 42
Swindon a	15 55	16 13	16 30	16 38	16 53	16 55	17 13	17 30	17 38		17 58
d	15 55	16 13	16 30	16 38	16 54	16 55	17 13	17 30	17 38	17 54	18 00
Kemble d					17 07					18 07	
Stroud d					17 22					18 22	
Stonehouse d					17 28					18 28	
Gloucester 7 a					17 46					18 49	
Cheltenham Spa a					18 01					19 03	
Chippenham d	16 10		16 45			17 10		17 45			18 15
Bath Spa 7 a	16 24		16 59			17 24		18 00			18 27
Bristol Parkway 7 a		16 39		17 04			17 40		18 04		
d		16 40		17 07			17 40		18 07		
Bristol Temple Meads 10 a	16 39		17 15			17 41		18 15			18 44
Weston-super-Mare a			17 49					18 55			
Newport (South Wales) a		17 04		17 31			18 04		18 31		
Cardiff Central 7 a		17 22		17 46			18 20		18 48		
Bridgend a				18 09			18 45		19 09		
Port Talbot Parkway a				18 22			18 58		19 22		
Neath a				18 30			19 05		19 30		
Swansea a				18 48			19 19		19 45		

	GW	GW	GW	GW	GW	GW	GW	GW	GW FX	GW FO	GW
	◇1 🛒	◇1 🛒	◇1 🛒		◇1 🛒	◇1 🛒	◇1 🛒	◇1 🛒	◇1 🛒	◇1 🛒	◇1 🛒
London Paddington 15 ⊖ d	17 15	17 30	17 45		17 48	18 00	18 15	18 30	18 45	18 45	18 47
Slough 3 d											
Reading 7 d	17 41	17 56	18 11		18 16	18 27	18 41	18 56	19 11	19 11	19 18
Didcot Parkway d	17 56	18 12			18 33	18 42	18 56	19 12			19 33
Swindon a	18 13	18 28	18 38	18 41	18 53	18 59	19 13	19 28	19 38	19 38	19 53
d	18 13	18 30	18 38	18 44	18 54	19 00	19 13	19 30	19 38	19 38	19 54
Kemble d					19 07						20 07
Stroud d					19 22						20 22
Stonehouse d					19 28						20 28
Gloucester 7 a					19 45						20 45
Cheltenham Spa a					20 01						21 01
Chippenham d		18 45		19 01		19 15		19 45			
Bath Spa 7 a		18 57				19 28		19 57			
Bristol Parkway 7 a	18 40		19 06				19 40		20 04	20 04	
d	18 40		19 10				19 40		20 07	20 07	
Bristol Temple Meads 10 a		19 12				19 43		20 13			
Weston-super-Mare a		19 48						20 53			
Newport (South Wales) a	19 11		19 38				20 07		20 31	20 35	
Cardiff Central 7 a	19 26		19 53				20 22		20 45	20 51	
Bridgend a	19 49		20 16				20 45		21 09	21 15	
Port Talbot Parkway a	20 02		20 29				20 58		21 22	21 28	
Neath a	20 10		20 37				21 05		21 30	21 36	
Swansea a	20 23		20 50				21 19		21 43	21 49	

	GW	GW	GW	GW	GW	GW	GW	GW	GW	GW FX	GW
	◇1 🛒	◇1 🛒	◇1 🛒	◇1 🛒	◇1 🛒	◇1 🛒	◇1 🛒		◇1 🛒	◇1 🛒	◇1 🛒
London Paddington 15 ⊖ d	19 00	19 15	19 30	19 48	20 00	20 15	20 45		21 15	21 15	21 45
Slough 3 d											
Reading 7 d	19 27	19 41	19 57	20 16	20 27	20 41	21 11		21 41	21 41	22 11
Didcot Parkway d	19 42	19 56	20 12	20 33	20 42	20 56	21 26		22 00	22 00	22 30
Swindon a	20 00	20 13	20 30	20 52	20 59	21 13	21 43		22 18	22 18	22 48
d	20 00	20 13	20 30	20 54	21 00	21 13	21 43	21 54	22 19	22 19	22 49
Kemble d				21 11				22 07			
Stroud d				21 26				22 22			
Stonehouse d				21 31				22 28			
Gloucester 7 a				21 46				22 44			
Cheltenham Spa a				22 02				23 03			
Chippenham d	20 15		20 45		21 15		21 59				23 04
Bath Spa 7 a	20 29		20 59		21 28		22 10				23 17
Bristol Parkway 7 a		20 39				21 39			22 45	22 45	
d		20 40				21 40			22 45	22 45	
Bristol Temple Meads 10 a	20 44		21 15		21 44		22 30				23 33
Weston-super-Mare a			21 48								00s06
Newport (South Wales) a		21 04				22 03			23 18	23 18	
Cardiff Central 7 a		21 19				22 23			23 39	23 39	
Bridgend a		21 45				22 46			00 01	00 27	
Port Talbot Parkway a		21 58				22 59			00 14	00 40	
Neath a		22 06				23 07			00 22	00 48	
Swansea a		22 19				23 20			00 37	01 01	

	GW FO	GW FX	GW FX	GW	GW	GW FO	GW FX	GW FX	GW FO	GW FX
	◇1 🛒	◇1 🛒	◇1 🛒	◇1 🛒		◇1 🛒	◇1 🛒	◇1 🛒	◇1 🛒	◇1 🛒
London Paddington 15 ⊖ d	22 15	22 15	22 15			22 45	22 45	22 45	23 30	23 30
Slough 3 d										
Reading 7 d	22 41	22 50	22 50			23 11	23 15	23 21	00 05	00 08
Didcot Parkway d	23 01	23 08	23 08			23 30	23 33	23 39	00 25	00 25
Swindon a	23 19	23 25	23 25	23 26		23 48	23 51	23 57	00 40	00 44
d	23 20	23 25	23 25	23 33	23 33	23 49	23 52	23 58	00 42	00 45
Kemble d					23 47					
Stroud d					00 02					
Stonehouse d					00 07					
Gloucester 7 a					00 24					
Cheltenham Spa a										
Chippenham d	23 34	23 40							00 57	01 00
Bath Spa 7 a	23 47	23 54							01 11	01 13
Bristol Parkway 7 a						00 14	00 17	00 23		
d						00 16	00 18	00 24		
Bristol Temple Meads 10 a	00 03	00 10	00 10	00 15					01 27	01 29
Weston-super-Mare a										
Newport (South Wales) a						00 38	00 46	00 52	02s02	02s10
Cardiff Central 7 a						00 53	01 06	01 12	02 18	02 31
Bridgend a						01 19	01 32	01 59		
Port Talbot Parkway a						01 32	01 45	02 12		
Neath a						01 39	01 52	02 20		
Swansea a						01 53	02 07	02 34		

	GW FX
	◇1 🛒
London Paddington 15 ⊖ d	23 30
Slough 3 d	
Reading 7 d	00 08
Didcot Parkway d	00 25
Swindon a	00 44
d	00 45
Kemble d	
Stroud d	
Stonehouse d	
Gloucester 7 a	
Cheltenham Spa a	
Chippenham d	
Bath Spa 7 a	
Bristol Parkway 7 a	
d	
Bristol Temple Meads 10 a	01 23
Weston-super-Mare a	
Newport (South Wales) a	02s10
Cardiff Central 7 a	02 31
Bridgend a	
Port Talbot Parkway a	
Neath a	
Swansea a	

For connections from Heathrow Airport, Gatwick Airport and Oxford please refer to Tables 125A, 148 and 116. For connections to Birmingham New Street and Hereford please refer to Tables 57 and 131

Table 125

London - Swindon, Cheltenham Spa, Bristol, Weston-super-Mare and South Wales

	GW	GW	GW	GW	GW	GW	GW	GW	GW	GW	GW
	◇1 🛒	◇1 🛒	◇1 🛒	◇1 🛒		◇1 🛒	◇1 🛒		◇1 🛒	◇1 🛒	1 🛒
London Paddington 15 ⊖ d	21p15	21p45	22p15			22p45	23p30		06 30	07 00	07 30
Slough 3 d											
Reading 7 d	21p41	22p11	22p41			23p11	00 05		06 59	07 27	07 57
Didcot Parkway d	22p00	22p30	23p01			23p30	00 25		07 12		08 12
Swindon a	22p18	22p48	23p19	23p26		23p48	00 40		07 30	07 54	08 29
d	22p19	22p49	23p20	23p33	23p33	23p49	00 42	07 16	07 30	07 55	08 30
Kemble d					23p47			07 30			
Stroud d					00 02			07 45			
Stonehouse d					00 07			07 50			
Gloucester 7 a					00 24			08 06			
Cheltenham Spa a								08 24			
Chippenham d		23p04	23p34				00 57		07 45	08 10	08 45
Bath Spa 7 a		23p17	23p47				01 11		08 00	08 24	08 59
Bristol Parkway 7 a	22p45					00 14					
d	22p45					00 16					
Bristol Temple Meads 10 a		23p33	00 03	00 15			01 27		08 15	08 39	09 14
Weston-super-Mare a		00 06									
Newport (South Wales) a	23p18					00 38	02s02				
Cardiff Central 7 a	23p39					00 53	02 18				
Bridgend a	00 01					01 19					
Port Talbot Parkway a	00 14					01 32					
Neath a	00 22					01 39					
Swansea a	00 37					01 53					

	GW	GW	GW	GW	GW	GW	GW	GW	GW	GW	GW
	◇1 🛒	◇1 🛒	◇1 🛒	◇1 🛒	◇1 🛒	◇1 🛒		◇1 🛒	◇1 🛒	◇1 🛒	◇1 🛒
London Paddington 15 ⊖ d	07 45	08 00	08 15	08 30	08 45	09 00		09 30	09 45	10 00	10 15
Slough 3 d											
Reading 7 d	08 11	08 27	08 41	08 57	09 11	09 27		09 57	10 11	10 27	10 41
Didcot Parkway d			08 55	09 12				10 12			10 55
Swindon a	08 38	08 55	09 15	09 30	09 38	09 54		10 30	10 38	10 54	11 15
d	08 38	08 55	09 15	09 30	09 38	09 55	10 14	10 30	10 38	10 55	11 15
Kemble d			09 30				10 28				11 30
Stroud d			09 45				10 43				11 45
Stonehouse d			09 50				10 48				11 50
Gloucester 7 a			10 06				11 07				12 07
Cheltenham Spa a			10 22				11 22				12 22
Chippenham d		09 10		09 45		10 10		10 45		11 10	
Bath Spa 7 a		09 24		10 00		10 24		11 00		11 24	
Bristol Parkway 7 a	09 04				10 05				11 04		
d	09 07				10 07				11 07		
Bristol Temple Meads 10 a		09 39		10 15		10 39		11 15		11 39	
Weston-super-Mare a						11 07					
Newport (South Wales) a	09 31				10 31				11 31		
Cardiff Central 7 a	09 47				10 47				11 46		
Bridgend a	10 09				11 09				12 09		
Port Talbot Parkway a	10 22				11 22				12 22		
Neath a	10 30				11 30				12 30		
Swansea a	10 43				11 43				12 43		

	GW	GW	GW	GW	GW	GW	GW	GW	GW	GW	GW
	◇1 🛒	◇1 A 🛒⊘	◇1 🛒		◇1 B 🛒⊘	◇1 A 🛒⊘	◇1 🛒	◇1 🛒	◇1 🛒	◇1 🛒	◇1 🛒
London Paddington 15 ⊖ d	10 30	10 45	11 00		11 30	11 45	12 00	12 15	12 30	12 45	13 00
Slough 3 d											
Reading 7 d	10 57	11 11	11 27		11 58	12 11	12 27	12 41	12 57	13 11	13 27
Didcot Parkway d	11 12				12 12			12 55	13 12		
Swindon a	11 30	11 38	11 54		12 30	12 38	12 54	13 15	13 30	13 38	13 55
d	11 30	11 38	11 55	12 14	12 30	12 38	12 55	13 15	13 30	13 38	13 55
Kemble d				12 28				13 30			
Stroud d				12 43				13 45			
Stonehouse d				12 48				13 50			
Gloucester 7 a				13 03				14 06			
Cheltenham Spa a				13 22				14 22			
Chippenham d	11 45		12 10		12 45		13 10		13 45		14 10
Bath Spa 7 a	12 00		12 24		13 00		13 24		14 00		14 24
Bristol Parkway 7 a		12 04				13 04				14 04	
d		12 07				13 07				14 07	
Bristol Temple Meads 10 a	12 15		12 39		13 15		13 42		14 15		14 39
Weston-super-Mare a	12 36								14 36		
Newport (South Wales) a		12 31				13 31				14 31	
Cardiff Central 7 a		12 46				13 47				14 46	
Bridgend a		13 09				14 09				15 09	
Port Talbot Parkway a		13 22				14 22				15 22	
Neath a		13 30				14 30				15 30	
Swansea a		13 43				14 43				15 43	

	GW	GW	GW	GW	GW	GW	GW	GW	GW	GW	GW
		◇1 🛒	◇1 🛒	◇1 🛒	◇1 🛒		◇1 🛒	◇1 🛒	◇1 🛒		◇1 🛒
London Paddington 15 ⊖ d		13 30	13 45	14 00	14 15		14 30	14 45	15 00		15 30
Slough 3 d											
Reading 7 d		13 59	14 11	14 27	14 41		14 57	15 11	15 27		15 59
Didcot Parkway d		14 12			14 55		15 12				16 12
Swindon a		14 30	14 38	14 54	15 15		15 30	15 38	15 54		16 30
d	14 14	14 30	14 38	14 55	15 15	15 20	15 30	15 38	15 55	16 14	16 30
Kemble d	14 28				15 30					16 28	
Stroud d	14 43				15 45					16 43	
Stonehouse d	14 48				15 50					16 48	
Gloucester 7 a	15 03				16 06					17 03	
Cheltenham Spa a	15 25				16 22					17 25	
Chippenham d		14 45		15 10		15 36	15 45		16 10		16 45
Bath Spa 7 a		15 00		15 24			16 00		16 24		17 00
Bristol Parkway 7 a			15 04					16 04			
d			15 07					16 07			
Bristol Temple Meads 10 a		15 15		15 41			16 15		16 39		17 15
Weston-super-Mare a							16 36				17 36
Newport (South Wales) a			15 31					16 31			
Cardiff Central 7 a			15 46					16 47			
Bridgend a			16 09					17 09			
Port Talbot Parkway a			16 22					17 22			
Neath a			16 30					17 30			
Swansea a			16 43					17 43			

	GW	GW	GW	GW	GW	GW	GW	GW	GW	GW
	◇1 🛒	◇1 🛒	◇1 🛒	◇1 🛒	◇1 🛒	◇1 🛒		◇1 🛒	◇1 🛒	◇1 🛒
London Paddington 15 ⊖ d	15 45	16 00	16 15	16 30	16 45	17 00		17 30	17 45	18 00
Slough 3 d										
Reading 7 d	16 11	16 27	16 41	16 57	17 11	17 27		17 57	18 11	18 27
Didcot Parkway d			16 55	17 12				18 12		
Swindon a	16 38	16 54	17 15	17 30	17 38	17 54		18 30	18 38	18 54
d	16 38	16 55	17 15	17 30	17 38	17 55	18 14	18 30	18 38	18 55
Kemble d			17 30				18 28			
Stroud d			17 45				18 43			
Stonehouse d			17 50				18 48			
Gloucester 7 a			18 06				19 03			
Cheltenham Spa a			18 22				19 25			
Chippenham d		17 10		17 45		18 10		18 45		19 10
Bath Spa 7 a		17 24		18 00		18 24		19 00		19 24
Bristol Parkway 7 a	17 04				18 04				19 12	
d	17 07				18 07				19 12	
Bristol Temple Meads 10 a		17 39		18 15		18 39		19 15		19 39
Weston-super-Mare a				18 36				19 50		
Newport (South Wales) a	17 30				18 31				19 37	
Cardiff Central 7 a	17 46				18 47				19 52	
Bridgend a	18 09				19 09				20 15	
Port Talbot Parkway a	18 22				19 22				20 28	
Neath a	18 30				19 30				20 36	
Swansea a	18 46				19 44				20 49	

	GW	GW	GW	GW	GW	GW	GW	GW	GW	GW	GW
	◇1 🛒	◇1 🛒	◇1 🛒	◇1 🛒		◇1 🛒	◇1 🛒	◇1 🛒		◇1 🛒	◇1 🛒
London Paddington 15 ⊖ d	18 15	18 30	18 45	19 00		19 30	19 45	20 00		20 15	20 30
Slough 3 d											
Reading 7 d	18 41	18 57	19 11	19 27		19 57	20 11	20 27		20 41	20 59
Didcot Parkway d	18 55	19 12				20 12		20 42		20 55	21 13
Swindon a	19 15	19 29	19 38	19 54		20 30	20 38	21 00	21 03	21 15	21 31
d	19 15	19 30	19 38	19 55	20 00	20 30	20 38	21 00	21 08	21 15	21 31
Kemble d	19 30				20 15					21 30	
Stroud d	19 45				20 30					21 45	
Stonehouse d	19 50				20 35					21 50	
Gloucester 7 a	20 06				20 51					22 05	
Cheltenham Spa a	20 22				21 05					22 20	
Chippenham d		19 45		20 10		20 45		21 15	21 24		21 47
Bath Spa 7 a		19 59		20 24		21 00		21 29			21 58
Bristol Parkway 7 a			20 05				21 04				
d			20 07				21 07				
Bristol Temple Meads 10 a		20 15		20 40		21 15		21 45			22 15
Weston-super-Mare a		20 36		21 26							22s48
Newport (South Wales) a			20 31				21 30				
Cardiff Central 7 a			20 45				21 47				
Bridgend a			21 09				22 09				
Port Talbot Parkway a			21 22				22 22				
Neath a			21 30				22 30				
Swansea a			21 43				22 43				

A 🛒 from Bridgend ⊘ to Cardiff Central

B 🛒 from Chippenham ⊘ to Swindon

For connections from Heathrow Airport, Gatwick Airport and Oxford please refer to Tables 125A, 148 and 116. For connections to Birmingham New Street and Hereford please refer to Tables 57 and 131

Table 125

Saturdays until 10 July

London - Swindon, Cheltenham Spa, Bristol, Weston-super-Mare and South Wales

		GW	GW	GW	GW	GW	GW
		◇1	◇1		◇1	◇1	◇1
		🛒	🛒		🛒	🛒	🛒
London Paddington 15 ⊖	d	20 45	21 30		22 00	22 35	23 30
Slough 3	d						
Reading 7	d	21 11	21 57		22 27	23 02	23 59
Didcot Parkway	d		22 12		22 41	23 22	00 18
Swindon	a	21 40	22 30		22 59	23 40	00 36
	d	21 41	22 30	22 35	22 59	23 41	00 36
Kemble	d			22 49			
Stroud	d			23 04			
Stonehouse	d			23 09			
Gloucester 7	a			23 25			
Cheltenham Spa	a						
Chippenham	d		22 45			23 56	00 52
Bath Spa 7	a		23 00			00 10	01 07
Bristol Parkway 7	a	22 06			23 27		
	d	22 11			23 28		
Bristol Temple Meads 10	a		23 15			00 25	01 21
Weston-super-Mare	a						
Newport (South Wales)	a	22 46			23 58		
Cardiff Central 7	a	23 06			00 20		
Bridgend	a	23 28					
Port Talbot Parkway	a	23 41					
Neath	a	23 49					
Swansea	a	00 02					

Saturdays 17 July to 04 September

		GW	GW	GW	GW	GW	GW	GW	GW	GW	GW	GW	GW	GW	GW	GW	GW	GW	GW	GW	GW	GW	GW
		◇1	◇1	◇1	◇1		◇1	◇1		◇1	◇1	1	◇1	◇1	◇1	◇1	◇1	◇1		◇1	◇1	◇1	◇1
		🛒	🛒	🛒	🛒		🛒	🛒		🛒	🛒	🛒	🛒	🛒	🛒	🛒	🛒	🛒		🛒	🛒	🛒	🛒
London Paddington 15 ⊖	d	21p15	21p45	22p15			22p45	23p30		06 30	07 00	07 30	07 45	08 00	08 15	08 30	08 45	09 00		09 30	09 45	10 00	10 15
Slough 3	d																						
Reading 7	d	21p41	22p11	22p41			23p11	00 05		06 59	07 27	07 57	08 11	08 27	08 41	08 57	09 11	09 27		09 57	10 11	10 27	10 41
Didcot Parkway	d	22p00	22p30	23p01			23p30	00 25		07 12		08 12			08 55	09 12				10 12			10 55
Swindon	a	22p18	22p48	23p19	23p26		23p48	00 40		07 30	07 54	08 29	08 38	08 55	09 15	09 30	09 38	09 54		10 30	10 38	10 54	11 15
	d	22p19	22p49	23p20	23p33	23p33	23p49	00 42	07 16	07 30	07 55	08 30	08 38	08 55	09 15	09 30	09 38	09 55	10 14	10 30	10 38	10 55	11 15
Kemble	d					23p47			07 30						09 30				10 28				11 30
Stroud	d					00 02			07 45						09 45				10 43				11 45
Stonehouse	d					00 07			07 50						09 50				10 48				11 50
Gloucester 7	a					00 24			08 06						10 06				11 07				12 07
Cheltenham Spa	a								08 24						10 22				11 22				12 22
Chippenham	d		23p04	23p34				00 57		07 45	08 10	08 45		09 10		09 45		10 10		10 45		11 10	
Bath Spa 7	a		23p17	23p47				01 11		08 00	08 24	08 59		09 24		10 00		10 24		11 00		11 24	
Bristol Parkway 7	a	22p45					00 14						09 04				10 05				11 04		
	d	22p45					00 16						09 07				10 07				11 07		
Bristol Temple Meads 10	a		23p33	00 03	00 15			01 27		08 15	08 39	09 14		09 39		10 15		10 39		11 15		11 39	
Weston-super-Mare	a		00s06															11 07					
Newport (South Wales)	a	23p18					00 38	02s02					09 31				10 31				11 31		
Cardiff Central 7	a	23p39					00 53	02 18					09 47				10 47				11 46		
Bridgend	a	00 01					01 19						10 09				11 09				12 09		
Port Talbot Parkway	a	00 14					01 32						10 22				11 22				12 22		
Neath	a	00 22					01 39						10 30				11 30				12 30		
Swansea	a	00 37					01 53						10 43				11 43				12 43		

		GW	GW	GW	GW	GW	GW	GW	GW	GW	GW	GW	GW	GW	GW	GW	GW	GW	GW	GW	GW	GW	GW
		◇1	◇1	◇1		◇1	◇1	◇1	◇1	◇1	◇1	◇1		◇1	◇1	◇1	◇1		◇1	◇1	◇1		◇1
			A			B	A																
		🛒	🛒⊘	🛒		🛒⊘	🛒⊘	🛒	🛒	🛒	🛒	🛒		🛒	🛒	🛒	🛒		🛒	🛒	🛒		🛒
London Paddington 15 ⊖	d	10 30	10 45	11 00		11 30	11 45	12 00	12 15	12 30	12 45	13 00		13 30	13 45	14 00	14 15		14 30	14 45	15 00		15 30
Slough 3	d																						
Reading 7	d	10 57	11 11	11 27		11 58	12 11	12 27	12 41	12 57	13 11	13 27		13 59	14 11	14 27	14 41		14 57	15 11	15 27		15 59
Didcot Parkway	d	11 12				12 12			12 55	13 12				14 12			14 55		15 12				16 12
Swindon	a	11 30	11 38	11 54		12 30	12 38	12 54	13 15	13 30	13 38	13 55		14 30	14 38	14 54	15 15		15 30	15 38	15 54		16 30
	d	11 30	11 38	11 55	12 14	12 30	12 38	12 55	13 15	13 30	13 38	13 55	14 14	14 30	14 38	14 55	15 15	15 20	15 30	15 38	15 55	16 14	16 30
Kemble	d				12 28				13 30				14 28				15 30					16 28	
Stroud	d				12 43				13 45				14 43				15 45					16 43	
Stonehouse	d				12 48				13 50				14 48				15 50					16 48	
Gloucester 7	a				13 03				14 06				15 03				16 06					17 03	
Cheltenham Spa	a				13 22				14 22				15 25				16 22					17 25	
Chippenham	d	11 45		12 10		12 45		13 10		13 45		14 10		14 45		15 10		15 36	15 45		16 10		16 45
Bath Spa 7	a	12 00		12 24		13 00		13 24		14 00		14 24		15 00		15 24			16 00		16 24		17 00
Bristol Parkway 7	a		12 04				13 04				14 04				15 04					16 04			
	d		12 07				13 07				14 07				15 07					16 07			
Bristol Temple Meads 10	a	12 15		12 39		13 15		13 42		14 15		14 39		15 15		15 41			16 15		16 39		17 15
Weston-super-Mare	a	12 36								14 36									16 36				17 36
Newport (South Wales)	a		12 31				13 31				14 31				15 31					16 31			
Cardiff Central 7	a		12 46				13 47				14 46				15 46					16 47			
Bridgend	a		13 09				14 09				15 09				16 09					17 09			
Port Talbot Parkway	a		13 22				14 22				15 22				16 22					17 22			
Neath	a		13 30				14 30				15 30				16 30					17 30			
Swansea	a		13 43				14 43				15 43				16 43					17 43			

A 🛒 from Bridgend ⊘ to Cardiff Central

B 🛒 from Chippenham ⊘ to Swindon

For connections from Heathrow Airport, Gatwick Airport and Oxford please refer to Tables 125A, 148 and 116. For connections to Birmingham New Street and Hereford please refer to Tables 57 and 131

Table 125

Saturdays 17 July to 04 September

London - Swindon, Cheltenham Spa, Bristol, Weston-super-Mare and South Wales

		GW	GW	GW	GW	GW	GW	GW	GW	GW	GW	GW	GW	GW	GW	GW	GW	GW	GW	GW	GW	GW
		◇1	◇1	◇1	◇1	◇1	◇1		◇1	◇1	◇1	◇1	◇1	◇1	◇1		◇1	◇1	◇1		◇1	◇1
		🛒	🛒	🛒	🛒	🛒	🛒		🛒	🛒	🛒	🛒	🛒	🛒	🛒		🛒	🛒	🛒		🛒	🛒
London Paddington 15 ⊖	d	15 45	16 00	16 15	16 30	16 45	17 00		17 30	17 45	18 00	18 15	18 30	18 45	19 00		19 30	19 45	20 00		20 15	20 30
Slough 3	d																					
Reading 7	d	16 11	16 27	16 41	16 57	17 11	17 27		17 57	18 11	18 27	18 41	18 57	19 11	19 27		19 57	20 11	20 27		20 41	20 59
Didcot Parkway	d			16 55	17 12				18 12			18 55	19 12				20 12		20 42		20 55	21 13
Swindon	a	16 38	16 54	17 15	17 30	17 38	17 54		18 30	18 38	18 54	19 15	19 29	19 38	19 54		20 30	20 38	21 00	21 03	21 15	21 31
	d	16 38	16 55	17 15	17 30	17 38	17 55	18 14	18 30	18 38	18 55	19 15	19 30	19 38	19 55	20 00	20 30	20 38	21 00	21 08	21 15	21 31
Kemble	d			17 30				18 28				19 30				20 15					21 30	
Stroud	d			17 45				18 43				19 45				20 30					21 45	
Stonehouse	d			17 50				18 48				19 50				20 35					21 50	
Gloucester 7	a			18 06				19 03				20 06				20 51					22 05	
Cheltenham Spa	a			18 22				19 25				20 22				21 05					22 20	
Chippenham	d		17 10		17 45		18 10		18 45		19 10		19 45		20 10		20 45		21 15	21 24		21 47
Bath Spa 7	a		17 24		18 00		18 24		19 00		19 24		19 59		20 24		21 00		21 29			21 58
Bristol Parkway 7	a	17 34				18 32				19 26				20 27				21 30				
	d	17 41				18 40				19 37				20 31				21 40				
Bristol Temple Meads 10	a		17 39		18 15		18 39		19 15		19 39		20 15		20 40		21 15		21 45			22 15
Weston-super-Mare	a				18 36				19 50				20 36		21 26							22s48
Newport (South Wales)	a	18 09				19 05				20 11				21 05				22 14				
Cardiff Central 7	a	18 25				19 22				20 27				21 20				22 35				
Bridgend	a	18 50				19 48				20 49				21 44				22 57				
Port Talbot Parkway	a	19 03				20 01				21 02				21 57				23 10				
Neath	a	19 10				20 08				21 10				22 05				23 18				
Swansea	a	19 25				20 23				21 23				22 18				23 31				

		GW	GW	GW	GW	GW	GW
		◇1	◇1		◇1	◇1	◇1
		🛒	🛒		🛒	🛒	🛒
London Paddington 15 ⊖	d	20 45	21 30		22 00	22 35	23 30
Slough 3	d						
Reading 7	d	21 11	21 57		22 27	23 02	23 59
Didcot Parkway	d		22 12		22 41	23 22	00 18
Swindon	a	21 40	22 30		22 59	23 40	00 36
	d	21 41	22 30	22 35	22 59	23 41	00 36
Kemble	d			22 49			
Stroud	d			23 04			
Stonehouse	d			23 09			
Gloucester 7	a			23 25			
Cheltenham Spa	a						
Chippenham	d		22 45			23 56	00 52
Bath Spa 7	a		23 00			00 10	01 07
Bristol Parkway 7	a	22 32			23 40		
	d	22 37			23 47		
Bristol Temple Meads 10	a		23 15			00 25	01 21
Weston-super-Mare	a						
Newport (South Wales)	a	23 07			00 17		
Cardiff Central 7	a	23 28			00 39		
Bridgend	a	23 49					
Port Talbot Parkway	a	00 02					
Neath	a	00 11					
Swansea	a	00 23					

Saturdays from 11 September

		GW	GW	GW	GW	GW	GW	GW	GW	GW	GW	GW	GW	GW	GW	GW	GW	GW	GW	GW	GW	GW	GW
		◇1	◇1	◇1	◇1		◇1	◇1		◇1	◇1	◇1	◇1	◇1	◇1	◇1	◇1	◇1		◇1	◇1	◇1	◇1
		🛒	🛒	🛒	🛒		🛒	🛒		🛒	🛒	🛒	🛒	🛒	🛒	🛒	🛒	🛒		🛒	🛒	🛒	🛒
London Paddington 15 ⊖	d	21p15	21p45	22p15			22p45	23p30		06 30	07 00	07 30	07 45	08 00	08 15	08 30	08 45	09 00		09 30	09 45	10 00	10 15
Slough 3	d																						
Reading 7	d	21p41	22p11	22p41			23p11	00 05		06 59	07 27	07 57	08 11	08 27	08 41	08 57	09 11	09 27		09 57	10 11	10 27	10 41
Didcot Parkway	d	22p00	22p30	23p01			23p30	00 25		07 12		08 12			08 55	09 12				10 12			10 55
Swindon	a	22p18	22p48	23p19	23p26		23p48	00 40		07 30	07 54	08 30	08 38	08 55	09 15	09 30	09 38	09 54		10 30	10 38	10 54	11 15
	d	22p19	22p49	23p20	23p33	23p33	23p49	00 42	07 16	07 30	07 55	08 30	08 38	08 55	09 15	09 30	09 38	09 55	10 14	10 30	10 38	10 55	11 15
Kemble	d					23p47			07 30						09 30				10 28				11 30
Stroud	d					00 02			07 45						09 45				10 43				11 45
Stonehouse	d					00 07			07 50						09 50				10 48				11 50
Gloucester 7	a					00 24			08 06						10 06				11 07				12 07
Cheltenham Spa	a								08 24						10 22				11 22				12 22
Chippenham	d		23p04	23p34				00 57		07 45	08 10	08 45		09 10		09 45		10 10		10 45		11 10	
Bath Spa 7	a		23p17	23p47				01 11		08 00	08 24	09 00		09 24		10 00		10 24		11 00		11 24	
Bristol Parkway 7	a	22p45					00 14						09 04				10 04				11 04		
	d	22p45					00 16						09 07				10 07				11 07		
Bristol Temple Meads 10	a		23p33	00 03	00 15			01 27		08 15	08 39	09 15		09 39		10 15		10 39		11 15		11 39	
Weston-super-Mare	a		00s06																				
Newport (South Wales)	a	23p18					00 38	02s02					09 31				10 31				11 31		
Cardiff Central 7	a	23p39					00 53	02 18					09 47				10 46				11 46		
Bridgend	a	00 01					01 19						10 09				11 09				12 09		
Port Talbot Parkway	a	00 14					01 32						10 22				11 22				12 22		
Neath	a	00 22					01 39						10 30				11 30				12 30		
Swansea	a	00 37					01 53						10 43				11 43				12 43		

For connections from Heathrow Airport, Gatwick Airport and Oxford please refer to Tables 125A, 148 and 116. For connections to Birmingham New Street and Hereford please refer to Tables 57 and 131

Table 125

Saturdays from 11 September

London - Swindon, Cheltenham Spa, Bristol, Weston-super-Mare and South Wales

Station		GW	GW	GW	GW	GW	GW	GW	GW	GW	GW	GW	GW	GW	GW	GW	GW	GW	GW	GW	GW	GW	GW
		◇1	◇1	◇1		◇1	◇1	◇1	◇1	◇1	◇1	◇1		◇1	◇1	◇1	◇1		◇1	◇1	◇1		◇1
			A			B	A																
		🛒	🛒⊘	🛒		🛒⊘	🛒⊘	🛒	🛒	🛒	🛒	🛒		🛒	🛒	🛒	🛒		🛒	🛒	🛒		🛒
London Paddington 15 ⊖	d	10 30	10 45	11 00		11 30	11 45	12 00	12 15	12 30	12 45	13 00		13 30	13 45	14 00	14 15		14 30	14 45	15 00		15 30
Slough 3	d																						
Reading 7	d	10 57	11 11	11 27		11 58	12 11	12 27	12 41	12 57	13 11	13 27		13 59	14 11	14 27	14 41		14 57	15 11	15 27		15 59
Didcot Parkway	d	11 12				12 12			12 55	13 12				14 12			14 55		15 12				16 12
Swindon	a	11 30	11 38	11 54		12 30	12 38	12 54	13 15	13 30	13 38	13 55		14 30	14 38	14 54	15 15		15 30	15 38	15 54		16 30
	d	11 30	11 38	11 55	12 14	12 30	12 38	12 55	13 15	13 30	13 38	13 55	14 14	14 30	14 38	14 55	15 15	15 20	15 30	15 38	15 55	16 14	16 30
Kemble	d				12 28				13 30				14 28				15 30					16 28	
Stroud	d				12 43				13 45				14 43				15 45					16 43	
Stonehouse	d				12 48				13 50				14 48				15 50					16 48	
Gloucester 7	a				13 03				14 06				15 03				16 06					17 03	
Cheltenham Spa	a				13 22				14 22				15 25				16 22					17 25	
Chippenham	d	11 45		12 10		12 45		13 10		13 45		14 10		14 45		15 10		15 36	15 45		16 10		16 45
Bath Spa 7	a	12 00		12 24		13 00		13 24		14 00		14 24		15 00		15 24			16 00		16 24		17 00
Bristol Parkway 7	a		12 04				13 04				14 04				15 04					16 04			
	d		12 07				13 07				14 07				15 07					16 07			
Bristol Temple Meads 10	a	12 15		12 39		13 15		13 42		14 15		14 39		15 15		15 41			16 15		16 39		17 15
Weston-super-Mare	a																						
Newport (South Wales)	a		12 31				13 31				14 31				15 31					16 31			
Cardiff Central 7	a		12 46				13 47				14 46				15 46					16 47			
Bridgend	a		13 09				14 09				15 09				16 09					17 09			
Port Talbot Parkway	a		13 22				14 22				15 22				16 22					17 22			
Neath	a		13 30				14 30				15 30				16 30					17 30			
Swansea	a		13 43				14 43				15 43				16 43					17 43			

Station		GW	GW	GW	GW	GW	GW	GW	GW	GW	GW	GW	GW	GW	GW	GW	GW	GW	GW	GW	GW	GW
		◇1	◇1	◇1	◇1	◇1	◇1		◇1	◇1	◇1	◇1	◇1	◇1	◇1		◇1	◇1	◇1	◇1		◇1
					C																	
		🛒	🛒	🛒	🛒	🛒	🛒		🛒	🛒	🛒	🛒	🛒	🛒	🛒		🛒	🛒	🛒	🛒		🛒
London Paddington 15 ⊖	d	15 45	16 00	16 15	16 30	16 45	17 00		17 30	17 45	18 00	18 15	18 30	18 45	19 00		19 15	19 30	19 45	20 00		20 15
Slough 3	d																					
Reading 7	d	16 11	16 27	16 41	16 57	17 11	17 27		17 57	18 11	18 27	18 41	18 57	19 11	19 27		19 41	19 57	20 11	20 27		20 41
Didcot Parkway	d			16 55	17 12				18 12			18 55	19 12				19 55	20 12		20 42		20 55
Swindon	a	16 38	16 54	17 15	17 30	17 38	17 54		18 30	18 38	18 54	19 15	19 29	19 38	19 54		20 13	20 30	20 38	21 00	21 03	21 15
	d	16 38	16 55	17 15	17 30	17 38	17 55	18 14	18 30	18 38	18 55	19 15	19 30	19 38	19 55	20 00	20 13	20 30	20 38	21 00	21 08	21 15
Kemble	d			17 30				18 28				19 30				20 15						21 30
Stroud	d			17 45				18 43				19 45				20 30						21 45
Stonehouse	d			17 50				18 48				19 50				20 35						21 50
Gloucester 7	a			18 06				19 03				20 06				20 51						22 05
Cheltenham Spa	a			18 22				19 25				20 22				21 05						22 20
Chippenham	d		17 10		17 45		18 10		18 45		19 10		19 45		20 10			20 45		21 15	21 24	
Bath Spa 7	a		17 24		18 00		18 24		19 00		19 24		19 59		20 24			21 00		21 29		
Bristol Parkway 7	a	17 04				18 04				19 12				20 05			20 40		21 04			
	d	17 07				18 07				19 12				20 07			20 40		21 07			
Bristol Temple Meads 10	a		17 39		18 15		18 39		19 15		19 39		20 15		20 40			21 15		21 45		
Weston-super-Mare	a				18 36				19 50				20 36		21 26							
Newport (South Wales)	a	17 30				18 31				19 37				20 31			21 04		21 30			
Cardiff Central 7	a	17 46				18 47				19 52				20 45			21 22		21 47			
Bridgend	a	18 09				19 09				20 15				21 09			21 45		22 09			
Port Talbot Parkway	a	18 22				19 22				20 28				21 22			21 58		22 22			
Neath	a	18 30				19 30				20 36				21 30			22 06		22 30			
Swansea	a	18 46				19 44				20 49				21 43			22 18		22 43			

Station		GW	GW	GW	GW	GW	GW	GW
		◇1	◇1	◇1		◇1	◇1	◇1
		🛒	🛒	🛒		🛒	🛒	🛒
London Paddington 15 ⊖	d	20 30	20 45	21 30		22 00	22 35	23 30
Slough 3	d							
Reading 7	d	20 59	21 11	21 57		22 27	23 02	23 59
Didcot Parkway	d	21 13		22 12		22 41	23 22	00 18
Swindon	a	21 31	21 40	22 30		22 59	23 40	00 36
	d	21 31	21 41	22 30	22 35	22 59	23 41	00 36
Kemble	d				22 49			
Stroud	d				23 04			
Stonehouse	d				23 09			
Gloucester 7	a				23 25			
Cheltenham Spa	a							
Chippenham	d	21 47		22 45			23 56	00 52
Bath Spa 7	a	21 58		23 00			00 10	01 07
Bristol Parkway 7	a		22 06			23 27		
	d		22 11			23 28		
Bristol Temple Meads 10	a	22 15		23 15			00 25	01 21
Weston-super-Mare	a	22s48						
Newport (South Wales)	a		22 46			23 58		
Cardiff Central 7	a		23 06			00 20		
Bridgend	a		23 28					
Port Talbot Parkway	a		23 41					
Neath	a		23 49					
Swansea	a		00 02					

A 🛒 from Bridgend ⊘ to Cardiff Central   B 🛒 from Chippenham ⊘ to Swindon   C The Torbay Express

For connections from Heathrow Airport, Gatwick Airport and Oxford please refer to Tables 125A, 148 and 116. For connections to Birmingham New Street and Hereford please refer to Tables 57 and 131

Table 125

Sundays until 11 July

London - Swindon, Cheltenham Spa, Bristol, Weston-super-Mare and South Wales

Station		GW	GW	GW	GW	GW	GW	GW	GW	GW	GW	GW	GW	GW	GW	GW	GW	GW	GW	GW	GW	GW	GW
		◇1	◇1	◇1	◇1	◇1	◇1	◇1	◇1	◇1		◇1	◇1	◇1	◇1	◇1	◇1	◇1	◇1	◇1		◇1	◇1
		A	A	A	A																		
		🛒	🛒	🛒	🛒	🛒	🛒	🛒	🛒	🛒		🛒	🛒	🛒	🛒	🛒	🛒	🛒	🛒	🛒		🛒	🛒
London Paddington 15 ⊖	d	20p45	22p00	22p35	23p30	07 57	08 00	08 33	09 00	09 30		10 00	10 30	10 37	11 00	11 30	12 00	12 30	12 37	13 00		13 30	14 00
Slough 3	d																						
Reading 7	d	21p11	22p27	23p02	23p59	08 37	08 42	09 14	09 37	10 05		10 37	11 05	11 14	11 37	12 05	12 37	13 05	13 14	13 37		14 05	14 37
Didcot Parkway	d		22p41	23p22	00 18	08 54	08 58	09 29	09 53	10 19		10 51	11 19		11 51	12 19	12 51	13 19		13 51		14 19	14 51
Swindon	a	21p40	22p59	23p40	00 36	09 12	09 18	09 47	10 09	10 37		11 09	11 37	11 41	12 09	12 37	13 09	13 37	13 42	14 09		14 36	15 09
	d	21p41	22p59	23p41	00 36	09 13	09 18	09 50	10 10	10 38	10 47	11 09	11 38	11 53	12 09	12 38	13 09	13 38	13 43	14 09	14 21	14 38	15 09
Kemble	d							10 03			11 01			12 07					13 57		14 36		
Stroud	d							10 18			11 16			12 22					14 12		14 51		
Stonehouse	d							10 23			11 21			12 27					14 17		14 56		
Gloucester 7	a							10 40			11 37			12 43					14 33		15 19		
Cheltenham Spa	a							10 56			11 50			13 03					14 49		15 33		
Chippenham	d			23p56	00 52		09 35		10 27			11 25			12 25		13 25			14 25			15 25
Bath Spa 7	a			00 10	01 07		09 48		10 41			11 38			12 38		13 38			14 38			15 38
Bristol Parkway 7	a	22p06	23p27			09 38				11 03			12 03			13 03		14 03				15 03	
	d	22p11	23p28			09 40				11 04			12 04			13 04		14 04				15 04	
Bristol Temple Meads 10	a			00 25	01 21		10 02		10 56			11 54			12 53		13 54			14 54			15 53
Weston-super-Mare	a											12 31					14 25						
Newport (South Wales)	a	22p46	23p58			10 05				11 34			12 34			13 30		14 32				15 32	
Cardiff Central 7	a	23p06	00 20			10 23				11 52			12 50			13 48		14 50				15 50	
Bridgend	a	23p28				11 11				12 40			13 49			14 36		15 51				16 38	
Port Talbot Parkway	a	23p41				11 24				12 53			14 02			14 49		16 04				16 51	
Neath	a	23p49				11 31				13 00			14 10			14 57		16 12				16 59	
Swansea	a	00 02				11 45				13 14			14 23			15 11		16 25				17 12	

Station		GW	GW	GW	GW	GW	GW	GW	GW	GW	GW	GW	GW	GW	GW	GW	GW	GW	GW	GW	GW	GW	GW	GW
		◇1	◇1	◇1	◇1	◇1	◇1	◇1	◇1			◇1	◇1	◇1	◇1	◇1	◇1	◇1	◇1	◇1	◇1	◇1	◇1	◇1
		🛒	🛒	🛒	🛒	🛒	🛒	🛒	🛒			🛒	🛒	🛒	🛒	🛒	🛒	🛒	🛒	🛒	🛒	🛒	🛒	🛒
London Paddington 15 ⊖	d	14 30	14 37	15 00	15 30	16 00	16 30	16 37	17 00			17 30	17 37	18 00	18 30	18 37	19 00	19 30	19 37	20 00	20 30	20 37	21 00	21 37
Slough 3	d																							
Reading 7	d	15 05	15 14	15 37	16 05	16 37	17 05	17 15	17 37			18 05	18 16	18 37	19 05	19 15	19 37	20 05	20 16	20 37	21 05	21 16	21 37	22 14
Didcot Parkway	d	15 19		15 51	16 19	16 51	17 19		17 51			18 19		18 51	19 19		19 51	20 19		20 51	21 19		21 52	22 30
Swindon	a	15 36	15 42	16 09	16 36	17 09	17 37	17 46	18 09			18 37	18 43	19 09	19 37	19 45	20 09	20 38	20 43	21 09	21 38	21 45	22 13	22 48
	d	15 38	15 43	16 09	16 38	17 09	17 38	17 46	18 09	18 19	18 22	18 38	18 43	19 09	19 38	19 46	20 09	20 38	20 43	21 09	21 38	21 46	22 14	22 51
Kemble	d		15 56					18 00			18 36					20 00						22 00		
Stroud	d		16 11					18 15			18 50					20 15						22 15		
Stonehouse	d		16 16					18 20			18 55					20 19						22 20		
Gloucester 7	a		16 33					18 35			19 21					20 35						22 35		
Cheltenham Spa	a		16 49					18 51								20 50						22 58		
Chippenham	d			16 25		17 25			18 25	18 35			18 59	19 25			20 25		20 59	21 25			22 27	
Bath Spa 7	a			16 38		17 41			18 38				19 12	19 38			20 38		21 12	21 38			22 41	
Bristol Parkway 7	a	16 03			17 03		18 06					19 03			20 07			21 03			22 03			23 15
	d	16 04			17 04		18 08					19 04			20 10			21 04			22 04			23 17
Bristol Temple Meads 10	a			16 54		17 57			18 53				19 27	19 53			20 54		21 29	21 53			22 56	
Weston-super-Mare	a			17 26									20 00				21 25			22 26				
Newport (South Wales)	a	16 32			17 34		18 36					19 32			20 37			21 33			22 40			23 45
Cardiff Central 7	a	16 53			17 51		18 52					19 51			20 53			21 56			23 02			00 06
Bridgend	a	17 56			18 39		19 50					20 38			21 49			22 45			23 50			00 55
Port Talbot Parkway	a	18 09			18 52		20 03					20 51			22 02			22 58			00 03			01 08
Neath	a	18 16			19 00		20 11					20 58			22 09			23 05			00 10			01 15
Swansea	a	18 30			19 13		20 24					21 12			22 23			23 19			00 24			01 29

Station		GW	GW	GW	GW
			◇1	◇1	◇1
			🛒	🛒	🛒
London Paddington 15 ⊖	d		22 03	23 03	23 37
Slough 3	d				23 55
Reading 7	d		22 50	23 47	00 15
Didcot Parkway	d		23 05	00s03	00s33
Swindon	a		23 25	00s21	00s52
	d	22 57	23 25	00s23	00s53
Kemble	d	23 11			
Stroud	d	23 26			
Stonehouse	d	23 31			
Gloucester 7	a	23 47			
Cheltenham Spa	a	00 05			
Chippenham	d		23 41	00s38	01s09
Bath Spa 7	a		23 54	00s51	01s22
Bristol Parkway 7	a				
	d				
Bristol Temple Meads 10	a		00 09	01 05	01 36
Weston-super-Mare	a				
Newport (South Wales)	a				
Cardiff Central 7	a				
Bridgend	a				
Port Talbot Parkway	a				
Neath	a				
Swansea	a				

A not 23 May

For connections from Heathrow Airport, Gatwick Airport and Oxford please refer to Tables 125A, 148 and 116. For connections to Birmingham New Street and Hereford please refer to Tables 57 and 131

Table 125

London - Swindon, Cheltenham Spa, Bristol, Weston-super-Mare and South Wales

Sundays
18 July to 05 September

		GW ◇1 ⊡	GW ◇1 ⊡	GW ◇1 ⊡	GW ◇1 ⊡	GW ◇1 ⊡	GW ◇1 ⊡	GW	GW ◇1 ⊡	GW ◇1 ⊡	GW ◇1 ⊡	GW ◇1 ⊡	GW ◇1 ⊡	GW ◇1 ⊡	GW ◇1 ⊡	GW ◇1 ⊡	GW ◇1 ⊡	GW	GW ◇1 ⊡	GW ◇1 ⊡	GW ◇1 ⊡	GW ◇1 ⊡	GW ◇1 ⊡	GW ◇1 ⊡	GW ◇1 ⊡
London Paddington 15 ⊖	d	23p30	07 57	08 00	08 37	09 00	09 30		10 00	10 30	10 37	11 00	11 30	12 00	12 37	12 30	13 00		13 30	14 00	14 30	14 37	15 00	15 30	16 00
Slough 3	d																								
Reading 7	d	23p59	08 37	08 42	09 14	09 37	10 05		10 37	11 05	11 14	11 37	12 05	12 37	13 14	12 05	13 37		13 05	14 37	15 05	15 14	15 37	16 05	16 37
Didcot Parkway	d	00 18	08 54	08 58	09 29	09 53	10 19		10 51	11 19		11 51	12 19	12 51		12 19	13 51		13 19	14 51	15 19		15 51	16 19	16 51
Swindon	a	00 36	09 12	09 18	09 47	10 09	10 37		11 09	11 37	11 41	12 09	12 37	13 09	13 42	12 37	14 09		14 36	15 09	15 37	15 42	16 09	16 36	17 09
	d	00 36	09 13	09 18	09 50	10 10	10 38	10 47	11 09	11 38	11 53	12 09	12 38	13 09	13 43	12 38	14 09	14 21	14 38	15 09	15 38	15 43	16 09	16 38	17 09
Kemble	d				10 03			11 01			12 07				13 57			14 36				15 56			
Stroud	d				10 18			11 16			12 22				14 12			14 51				16 11			
Stonehouse	d				10 23			11 21			12 27				14 17			14 56				16 16			
Gloucester 7	a				10 40			11 37			12 43				14 33			15 19				16 33			
Cheltenham Spa	a				10 55			11 50			13 03				14 49			15 33				16 49			
Chippenham	d	00 52		09 35		10 27			11 25			12 25		13 25			14 25			15 25			16 25		17 25
Bath Spa 7	a	01 07		09 48		10 41			11 38			12 38		13 38			14 38			15 38			16 38		17 41
Bristol Parkway 7	a		10 00				11 18			12 19			13 19			14 19			15 19		16 19			17 19	
	d		10 07				11 25			12 26			13 28			14 26			15 26		16 26			17 26	
Bristol Temple Meads 10	a	01 21		10 02		10 56			11 54			12 53		13 54			14 54			15 53			16 54		17 57
Weston-super-Mare	a								12 31					14 25									17 26		
Newport (South Wales)	a		10 32				11 48			12 48			13 48			14 48			15 50		16 48			17 48	
Cardiff Central 7	a		10 50				12 08			13 08			14 11			15 10			16 12		17 10			18 10	
Bridgend	a		11 13				12 31			13 31			14 33			15 33			16 35		17 33			18 33	
Port Talbot Parkway	a		11 26				12 44			13 44			14 46			15 46			16 48		17 46			18 49	
Neath	a		11 34				12 52			13 52			14 54			15 54			16 56		17 54			18 58	
Swansea	a		11 48				13 07			14 05			15 07			16 07			17 09		18 10			19 11	

		GW ◇1 ⊡	GW ◇1 ⊡	GW ◇1 ⊡	GW	GW	GW ◇1 ⊡		GW ◇1 ⊡	GW ◇1 ⊡	GW ◇1 ⊡	GW ◇1 ⊡	GW ◇1 ⊡	GW ◇1 ⊡	GW ◇1 ⊡	GW ◇1 ⊡	GW ◇1 ⊡	GW ◇1 ⊡	GW ◇1 ⊡		GW ◇1 ⊡	GW	GW ◇1 ⊡	GW ◇1 ⊡	GW ◇1 ⊡
London Paddington 15 ⊖	d	16 30	16 37	17 00			17 30		17 37	18 00	18 37	18 45	19 00	19 30	19 37	20 00	20 30	20 37	21 00		21 37		22 03	23 03	23 37
Slough 3	d																								23 55
Reading 7	d	17 05	17 15	17 37			18 05		18 16	18 37	19 15	19 11	19 37	20 05	20 16	20 37	21 05	21 16	21 37		22 14		22 50	23 47	00 15
Didcot Parkway	d	17 19		17 51			18 19			18 51			19 51	20 19		20 51	21 19		21 52		22 30		23 05	00s03	00s33
Swindon	a	17 37	17 46	18 09			18 37		18 43	19 09	19 45	19 38	20 09	20 38	20 43	21 09	21 38	21 45	22 13		22 49		23 25	00s21	00s52
	d	17 38	17 46	18 09	18 19	18 22	18 38		18 43	19 09	19 46	19 38	20 09	20 38	20 43	21 09	21 38	21 46	22 14		22 51	22 57	23 25	00s23	00s53
Kemble	d		18 00			18 36					20 00							22 00				23 11			
Stroud	d		18 15			18 50					20 15							22 15				23 26			
Stonehouse	d		18 20			18 55					20 19							22 20				23 31			
Gloucester 7	a		18 35			19 21					20 35							22 35				23 47			
Cheltenham Spa	a		18 51								20 50							22 58				00 05			
Chippenham	d			18 25	18 35				18 59	19 25			20 25		20 59	21 25			22 27				23 41	00s38	01s09
Bath Spa 7	a			18 38					19 12	19 38			20 38		21 12	21 38			22 41				23 54	00s51	01s22
Bristol Parkway 7	a	18 22					19 19					20 27		21 20			22 24				23 31				
	d	18 26					19 26					20 31		21 26			22 30				23 38				
Bristol Temple Meads 10	a			18 53					19 27	19 53			20 54		21 29	21 53			22 56				00 09	01 05	01 36
Weston-super-Mare	a								20 00				21 25			22 26									
Newport (South Wales)	a	18 49					19 50					21 05		21 48			23 00				00 03				
Cardiff Central 7	a	19 12					20 14					21 20		22 11			23 21				00 25				
Bridgend	a	19 34					20 36					21 44		22 34			23 44				00 48				
Port Talbot Parkway	a	19 47					20 49					21 57		22 47			23 58				01 01				
Neath	a	19 55					20 57					22 05		22 54			00 04				01 09				
Swansea	a	20 08					21 10					22 18		23 08			00 19				01 22				

Sundays
from 12 September

		GW ◇1 ⊡	GW ◇1 ⊡	GW ◇1 ⊡	GW ◇1 ⊡	GW ◇1 ⊡	GW ◇1 ⊡	GW	GW ◇1 ⊡		GW ◇1 ⊡	GW ◇1 ⊡	GW ◇1 ⊡	GW ◇1 ⊡	GW ◇1 ⊡	GW ◇1 ⊡	GW ◇1 ⊡	GW ◇1 ⊡	GW	GW ◇1 ⊡	GW ◇1 ⊡	GW ◇1 ⊡	GW ◇1 ⊡	GW ◇1 ⊡	GW ◇1 ⊡
London Paddington 15 ⊖	d	23p30	07 57	08 30		09 03	09 30		10 03		10 37		11 03	11 37	12 03		12 37	13 03		13 37	14 03		14 37	15 03	15 37
Slough 3	d																								
Reading 7	d	23p59	08 33	09 05		09 37	10 05		10 37		11 11		11 37	12 11	12 37		13 11	13 37		14 11	14 37		15 11	15 37	16 11
Didcot Parkway	d	00 18	08 48	09 22		09 53	10 19		10 51		11 25		11 51	12 25	12 51		13 25	13 51		14 25	14 51		15 25	15 51	16 25
Swindon	a	00 36	09 07	09 40		10 09	10 37		11 09		11 42		12 09	12 43	13 09		13 42	14 09		14 42	15 09		15 42	16 09	16 42
	d	00 36	09 08	09 41	09 50	10 10	10 38	10 47	11 09		11 45	11 53	12 09	12 44	13 09	13 40	13 45	14 09	14 21	14 44	15 09	15 35	15 44	16 09	16 44
Kemble	d				10 03			11 01				12 07				13 54			14 36			15 48			
Stroud	d				10 18			11 16				12 22				14 09			14 51			16 03			
Stonehouse	d				10 23			11 21				12 27				14 14			14 56			16 08			
Gloucester 7	a				10 39			11 36				12 43				14 33			15 19			16 25			
Cheltenham Spa	a				10 55			11 49				13 03				14 48			15 33			16 46			
Chippenham	d	00 52	09 24			10 27			11 25				12 25		13 25			14 25			15 25			16 25	
Bath Spa 7	a	01 07	09 36			10 41			11 38				12 38		13 38			14 38			15 38			16 39	
Bristol Parkway 7	a			10 06			11 03				12 09			13 10			14 09			15 09			16 09		17 09
	d			10 07			11 04				12 10			13 11			14 10			15 10			16 10		17 10
Bristol Temple Meads 10	a	01 21	09 51			10 56			11 54				12 53		13 54			14 54			15 53			16 54	
Weston-super-Mare	a								12 31						14 25									17 25	
Newport (South Wales)	a			10 32			11 32				12 36			13 35			14 36			15 36			16 36		17 40
Cardiff Central 7	a			10 50			11 50				12 54			13 55			14 54			15 54			16 54		17 57
Bridgend	a			11 13			12 13				13 18			14 17			15 18			16 18			17 18		18 20
Port Talbot Parkway	a			11 26			12 26				13 30			14 30			15 30			16 30			17 30		18 33
Neath	a			11 34			12 33				13 37			14 38			15 37			16 37			17 37		18 41
Swansea	a			11 48			12 47				13 51			14 51			15 51			16 51			17 52		18 54

For connections from Heathrow Airport, Gatwick Airport and Oxford please refer to Tables 125A, 148 and 116. For connections to Birmingham New Street and Hereford please refer to Tables 57 and 131

Table 125

London - Swindon, Cheltenham Spa, Bristol, Weston-super-Mare and South Wales

Sundays
from 12 September

		GW ◇1 ⊡	GW ◇1 ⊡	GW ◇1 ⊡	GW ◇1 ⊡	GW		GW	GW ◇1 ⊡	GW ◇1 ⊡	GW ◇1 ⊡	GW ◇1 ⊡	GW ◇1 ⊡	GW ◇1 ⊡	GW ◇1 ⊡	GW ◇1 ⊡		GW ◇1 ⊡	GW ◇1 ⊡	GW ◇1 ⊡	GW ◇1 ⊡	GW ◇1 ⊡	GW	GW ◇1 ⊡	GW ◇1 ⊡
London Paddington 15 ⊖	d	16 03	16 27	16 37	17 03				17 30	17 37	18 03	18 27	18 37	19 03	19 30	19 37		20 03	20 30	20 37	21 03	21 37		22 03	22 37
Slough 3	d																								
Reading 7	d	16 37	17 05	17 11	17 37				18 06	18 11	18 37	19 05	19 11	19 37	20 05	20 11		20 37	21 05	21 11	21 37	22 14		22 50	23 16
Didcot Parkway	d	16 51		17 25	17 51					18 25	18 51		19 25	19 51		20 25		20 51		21 25	21 52	22 30		23 05	23s33
Swindon	a	17 09	17 35	17 43	18 09				18 33	18 44	19 09	19 34	19 43	20 09	20 33	20 44		21 09	21 34	21 44	22 13	22 49		23 25	23s48
	d	17 09	17 35	17 44	18 09	18 19		18 22	18 33	18 45	19 09	19 35	19 44	20 09	20 33	20 44		21 09	21 35	21 44	22 14	22 51	22 57	23 25	23s52
Kemble	d		17 49					18 36				19 49							21 49				23 11		
Stroud	d		18 04					18 50				20 04							22 04				23 26		
Stonehouse	d		18 08					18 55				20 08							22 09				23 31		
Gloucester 7	a		18 24					19 21				20 31							22 24				23 47		
Cheltenham Spa	a		18 47									20 48							22 45				00 05		
Chippenham	d	17 25			18 25	18 35			18 49		19 25			20 25	20 48			21 25			22 27			23 41	
Bath Spa 7	a	17 41			18 38				19 07		19 38			20 38	21 01			21 38			22 41			23 54	
Bristol Parkway 7	a			18 09						19 13			20 09			21 09				22 09		23 15			00s16
	d			18 10						19 14			20 10			21 10				22 10		23 17			00s18
Bristol Temple Meads 10	a	17 56			18 53				19 24		19 53			20 54	21 16			21 53			22 56			00 09	00 30
Weston-super-Mare	a								19 56					21 25				22 26							
Newport (South Wales)	a			18 36						19 41			20 36			21 36				22 40		23 45			
Cardiff Central 7	a			18 54						19 59			20 53			21 58				23 02		00 06			
Bridgend	a			19 18						20 22			21 18			22 21				23 24		00 29			
Port Talbot Parkway	a			19 30						20 35			21 30			22 34				23 37		00 42			
Neath	a			19 37						20 43			21 37			22 42				23 45		00 50			
Swansea	a			19 51						20 56			21 52			22 55				23 58		01 03			

		GW ◇1 ⊡	GW ◇1 ⊡
London Paddington 15 ⊖	d	23 03	23 37
Slough 3	d		23 55
Reading 7	d	23 47	00 15
Didcot Parkway	d	00s03	00s33
Swindon	a	00s21	00s52
	d	00s23	00s53
Kemble	d		
Stroud	d		
Stonehouse	d		
Gloucester 7	a		
Cheltenham Spa	a		
Chippenham	d	00s38	01s09
Bath Spa 7	a	00s51	01s22
Bristol Parkway 7	a		
	d		
Bristol Temple Meads 10	a	01 05	01 36
Weston-super-Mare	a		
Newport (South Wales)	a		
Cardiff Central 7	a		
Bridgend	a		
Port Talbot Parkway	a		
Neath	a		
Swansea	a		

For connections from Heathrow Airport, Gatwick Airport and Oxford please refer to Tables 125A, 148 and 116. For connections to Birmingham New Street and Hereford please refer to Tables 57 and 131

South Wales, Weston-super-Mare, Bristol, Cheltenham Spa and Swindon - London

		GW MO	GW MX	GW MX	GW	GW	GW	GW	GW	GW	GW	GW	GW	GW	GW	GW	GW	GW	GW	GW	GW	GW	GW
		◇1	◇1	1	◇1	◇1	◇1	◇1	◇1	◇1	◇1	◇1	◇1	◇1	◇1	◇1		◇1	◇1	◇1	◇1	◇1	◇1
							A	E					B							C			D
		🍴	🍴	🍴	🍴	🍴	🍴	🍴	🍴	🍴	🍴	🍴	🍴	🍴	🍴	🍴		⊘	🍴	🍴⊘	🍴	🍴	🍴⊘
Swansea	d						03 53	03 58		04 58				05 27				05 58		06 28			06 58
Neath	d						04 05	04 10		05 10				05 39				06 10		06 40			07 10
Port Talbot Parkway	d						04 13	04 18		05 18				05 47				06 18		06 48			07 18
Bridgend	d						04 26	04 30		05 30				05 59				06 30		07 00			07 30
Cardiff Central 7	d						05 15	05 15		05 55				06 24				06 55		07 25			07 55
Newport (South Wales)	d						05 33	05 33		06 09				06 38				07 09		07 39			08 09
Weston-super-Mare	d		22p01													06 20			06 49			07 24	
Bristol Temple Meads 10	d	22p05	22p35		04 47	05 30			06 00			06 30	06 40			07 00			07e30			08 00	
Bristol Parkway 7	a				04u56		05 59	05 59		06 29				06 58				07 29		07 59			08 30
	d				04u57		06 01	06 01		06 31				07 01				07 31		08 01			08 31
Bath Spa 7	d	22p19	22p47			05 43			06 13			06 43	06 52			07 13			07 43			08 13	
Chippenham	d	22p31	23p00			05 55			06 25			06 55	07 05			07 25	07 30		07 55			08 25	
Cheltenham Spa	d										05 53				06 30						07 29		
Gloucester 7	d										06b10				06c47						07f45		
Stonehouse	d										06 23				06 59						07 59		
Stroud	d										06 29				07 05						08 05		
Kemble	d										06 43				07 19						08 19		
Swindon	a	22p46	23p14	03 15	05 22	06 10	06 27	06 27	06 40	06 57	06 58	07 10	07 19	07 27	07 35	07 40	07 48	07 57	08 10	08 27	08 33	08 40	08 57
	d	22p52	23p16	03 17	05 23	06 11	06 28	06 28	06 41	06 58	07 01	07 11	07 20	07 28	07 35	07 41	07 54	07 58	08 11	08 28	08 35	08 41	08 59
Didcot Parkway	a	23p10	23p33		05 41	06 28	06 46	06 46	06 58		07 19	07 28		07 45	07 53	08 00			08 28	08 46	08 52	08 58	
Reading 7	a	23p27	23p54	04s02	05 56	06 43	07 00	07 00	07 13	07 28	07 34	07 43		08 00	08 12	08 16			08 44	09 01	09 07	09 13	09 25
Slough 3	a					06 58																	
London Paddington 15 ⊖	a	00 13	00 33	05 43	06 24	07 16	07 32	07 32	07 44	08 02	08 07	08 14	08 16	08 33	08 40	08 44		08 54	09 14	09 29	09 39	09 44	09 59

		GW	GW	GW	GW	GW	GW	GW	GW	GW	GW	GW	GW	GW	GW	GW	GW	GW	GW	GW	GW	GW	GW
			◇1	◇1	◇1	◇1	◇1	◇1	◇1	◇1		◇1	◇1	◇1	◇1	◇1	◇1	◇1	◇1	◇1		◇1	◇1
							C																
			🍴	🍴	🍴	🍴	🍴⊘	🍴	🍴	🍴		🍴	🍴	🍴	🍴	🍴	🍴	🍴	🍴	🍴		🍴	🍴
Swansea	d			07 28			07 58		08j28					09 28					10 28				
Neath	d			07 40			08 10		08 40					09 40					10 40				
Port Talbot Parkway	d			07 48			08 18		08 48					09 48					10 48				
Bridgend	d			08 00			08 30		09 00					10 00					11 00				
Cardiff Central 7	d			08 25			08 55		09 25			09 55		10 25			10 55		11 25			11 55	
Newport (South Wales)	d			08 39			09 09		09 39			10 09		10 39			11 09		11 39			12 09	
Weston-super-Mare	d		07h49							09 29													
Bristol Temple Meads 10	d	08g13	08 30			09 00		09 30		10 00			10 30			11 00		11 30		12 00			12 30
Bristol Parkway 7	a			08 59			09 30		09 59			10 30		10 59			11 30		11 59			12 30	
	d			09 01			09 31		10 01			10 31		11 01			11 31		12 01			12 31	
Bath Spa 7	d	08 31	08 43			09 13		09 43		10 13			10 43			11 13		11 43		12 13			12 43
Chippenham	d	08 45	08 55			09 25		09 55		10 25			10 55			11 25		11 55		12 25			12 55
Cheltenham Spa	d				08 31						09 40				10 31						11 40		
Gloucester 7	d				08i46						09 54				10k46						11 54		
Stonehouse	d				08 59						10 06				10 59						12 06		
Stroud	d				09 05						10 11				11 05						12 11		
Kemble	d				09 19						10 27				11 19						12 27		
Swindon	a	09 04	09 10	09 27	09 33	09 40	09 57	10 10	10 27	10 40	10 43	10 57	11 10	11 27	11 33	11 40	11 57	12 10	12 27	12 41	12 43	12 57	13 10
	d		09 11	09 29	09 35	09 41	09 59	10 11	10 29	10 41		10 59	11 11	11 29	11 35	11 41	11 59	12 11	12 29	12 41		12 59	13 11
Didcot Parkway	a		09 28		09 52		10 16	10 28	10 46			11 16	11 28		11 52		12 16	12 28	12 46			13 16	13 28
Reading 7	a		09 44	09 59	10 06	10 10	10 31	10 44	11 00	11 08		11 30	11 43	11 59	12 06	12 10	12 30	12 43	13 00	13 09		13 30	13 43
Slough 3	a																						
London Paddington 15 ⊖	a		10 14	10 32	10 37	10 39	11 07	11 14	11 32	11 38		12 00	12 14	12 32	12 37	12 40	13 06	13 14	13 32	13 38		14 06	14 14

A MO until 12 July
B until 2 July, from 6 September
C 🍴 from Reading ⊘ to Didcot Parkway
D 🍴 from Reading ⊘ to Swindon
E not MO until 12 July

b arr. 0603
c arr. 0640
e arr. 0724
f arr. 0739
g arr. 0801

h arr. 0741
i arr. 0840
j arr. 0821
k arr. 1040

For connections from Hereford and Birmingham New Street please refer to Tables 131 and 57. For connections to Oxford, Gatwick Airport and Heathrow Airport please refer to Tables 116, 148 and 125A

South Wales, Weston-super-Mare, Bristol, Cheltenham Spa and Swindon - London

		GW	GW	GW	GW	GW	GW	GW	GW	GW	GW	GW	GW	GW	GW	GW	GW	GW	GW	GW	GW	GW
		◇1	◇1	◇1	◇1	◇1	◇1	◇1		◇1	◇1	◇1	◇1	◇1	◇1	◇1	◇1	◇1		◇1	◇1	◇1
		A																				
		🍴⊘	🍴	🍴	🍴	🍴	🍴	🍴		🍴	🍴	🍴	🍴	🍴	🍴	🍴	🍴	🍴		🍴	🍴	🍴
Swansea	d	11 28					12 28					13 28					14 28					15 28
Neath	d	11 40					12 40					13 40					14 40					15 40
Port Talbot Parkway	d	11 48					12 48					13 48					14 48					15 48
Bridgend	d	12 00					13 00					14 00					15 00					16 00
Cardiff Central 7	d	12 25			12 55		13 25			13 55		14 25			14 55		15 25			15 55		16 25
Newport (South Wales)	d	12 39			13 09		13 39			14 09		14 39			15 09		15 39			16 09		16 39
Weston-super-Mare	d																					
Bristol Temple Meads 10	d			13 00		13 30		14 00			14 30			15 00		15 30		16 00			16 30	
Bristol Parkway 7	a	12 59			13 30		13 59			14 30		15 00			15 30		15 59			16 30		16 59
	d	13 01			13 31		14 01			14 31		15 01			15 31		16 01			16 31		17 01
Bath Spa 7	d			13 13		13 43		14 13			14 43			15 13		15 43		16 13			16 43	
Chippenham	d			13 25		13 55		14 25			14 55			15 25		15 55		16 25			16 55	
Cheltenham Spa	d		12 31						13 40				14 31						15 40			
Gloucester 7	d		12b46						13 54				14c46						15 54			
Stonehouse	d		12 59						14 06				14 59						16 06			
Stroud	d		13 05						14 11				15 05						16 11			
Kemble	d		13 19						14 27				15 19						16 27			
Swindon	a	13 27	13 33	13 40	13 57	14 10	14 27	14 40	14 43	14 57	15 10	15 27	15 33	15 40	15 57	16 10	16 27	16 40	16 43	16 57	17 10	17 27
	d	13 29	13 35	13 41	13 59	14 11	14 29	14 41		14 59	15 11	15 29	15 35	15 41	15 59	16 11	16 29	16 41		16 59	17 11	17 29
Didcot Parkway	a		13 52		14 15	14 28	14 46			15 15	15 28		15 52		16 16	16 28	16 46			17 16	17 28	
Reading 7	a	13 59	14 06	14 10	14 31	14 43	15 00	15 08		15 31	15 43	16 00	16 06	16 10	16 31	16 43	17 00	17 08		17 31	17 43	17 55
Slough 3	a																					
London Paddington 15 ⊖	a	14 32	14 37	14 40	15 08	15 14	15 32	15 38		16 09	16 14	16 30	16 39	16 44	17 06	17 14	17 30	17 39		18 02	18 14	18 24

		GW	GW	GW	GW	GW	GW	GW	GW	GW	GW	GW	GW	GW	GW	GW	GW	GW	GW FO	GW FX	GW FO	GW FX	GW
		◇1	◇1	◇1	◇1	◇1	◇1	◇1	◇1	◇1	◇1	◇1		◇1		◇1	◇1	1	◇1	◇1	◇1	◇1	
		🍴	🍴	🍴	🍴	🍴	🍴	🍴	🍴	🍴	🍴	🍴		🍴		🍴	🍴		🍴	🍴	🍴	🍴	
Swansea	d					16 28				17 28				18 28			19 29		20 28	20 28			
Neath	d					16 40				17 40				18 40			19 40		20 40	20 40			
Port Talbot Parkway	d					16 48				17 48				18 48			19 48		20 48	20 48			
Bridgend	d					17 00				18 00				19 00			20 00		21 00	21 00			
Cardiff Central 7	d			16 55		17 25		17 55		18 25				19 25			20 25		21 25	21 25			
Newport (South Wales)	d			17 09		17 39		18 09		18 39				19 39			20 39		21 39	21 39			
Weston-super-Mare	d				17 10				18 09														
Bristol Temple Meads 10	d		17 00		17 30		18 00		18 30			19 30				20 30					21 50	21 50	
Bristol Parkway 7	a			17 30		17 59		18 30		18 59				19 59			21 00		21 59	21 59			
	d			17 31		18 01		18 31		19 01				20 01			21 01		22 01	22 01			
Bath Spa 7	d		17 13		17 43		18 13		18 43			19 43				20 43					22 02	22 02	
Chippenham	d		17 25		17 55		18 25		18 55			19 55	20 02			20 55					22 15	22 15	
Cheltenham Spa	d	16 31									18 34				20 00			20 48					22 00
Gloucester 7	d	16e46									18f52				20 13			21g05					22 13
Stonehouse	d	16 59									19 05				20 25			21 17					22 26
Stroud	d	17 05									19 10				20 30			21 23					22 31
Kemble	d	17 19									19 24				20 44			21 37					22 46
Swindon	a	17 33	17 40	17 57	18 10	18 27	18 40	18 57	19 10	19 27	19 39	20 10	20 21	20 27	21 02	21 10	21 28	21 51	22 27	22 27	22 33	22 33	23 02
	d	17 35	17 41	17 59	18 11	18 29	18 41	18 59	19 11	19 29	19 41	20 11	20 24	20 29		21 11	21 29		22 28	22 28	22 34	22 34	
Didcot Parkway	a	17 52		18 16	18 28	18 46			19 28	19 46	19 58	20 28		20 46		21 28	21 49				22 50	22 50	
Reading 7	a	18 06	18 12	18 31	18 44	19 01	19 08	19 25	19 44	20 00	20 13	20 44		21 00		21 43	22 09		23 03	23 03	23 06	23 06	
Slough 3	a																						
London Paddington 15 ⊖	a	18 39	18 44	19 02	19 14	19 32	19 38	19 54	20 14	20 32	20 46	21 14		21 32		22 14	22 45		23 36	23 40	23 42	23 50	

		GW FO	GW FX
		◇1	◇1
		🍴	🍴
Swansea	d		
Neath	d		
Port Talbot Parkway	d		
Bridgend	d		
Cardiff Central 7	d		
Newport (South Wales)	d		
Weston-super-Mare	d	22 01	22 01
Bristol Temple Meads 10	d	22 35	22 35
Bristol Parkway 7	a		
	d		
Bath Spa 7	d	22 47	22 47
Chippenham	d	23 00	23 00
Cheltenham Spa	d		
Gloucester 7	d		
Stonehouse	d		
Stroud	d		
Kemble	d		
Swindon	a	23 14	23 14
	d	23 16	23 16
Didcot Parkway	a	23 33	23 33
Reading 7	a	23 54	23 54
Slough 3	a		
London Paddington 15 ⊖	a	00 27	00 33

A 🍴 from Reading ⊘ to Swindon
b arr. 1240

c arr. 1440
e arr. 1640

f arr. 1845
g arr. 2058

For connections from Hereford and Birmingham New Street please refer to Tables 131 and 57. For connections to Oxford, Gatwick Airport and Heathrow Airport please refer to Tables 116, 148 and 125A

Table 125

Saturdays until 10 July

South Wales, Weston-super-Mare, Bristol, Cheltenham Spa and Swindon - London

		GW	GW	GW	GW	GW	GW	GW	GW	GW	GW	GW	GW	GW	GW	GW	GW	GW	GW	GW	GW	GW	GW
		◇1 ☕	🛏 ☕	◇1 ☕		◇1 ☕	◇1 ☕	◇1 ☕	◇1 ☕	◇1 ☕	◇1 ☕	◇1 ☕	◇1 ☕	◇1 ☕	◇1 ☕	◇1 A ☕⊘	◇1 ☕	◇1 A ☕⊘	◇1 ☕		◇1 ☕	◇1 ☕	◇1 ☕
Swansea	d					03 58	04 58		05 28		05 58		06 28			06 58		07 28					08 28
Neath	d					04 10	05 10		05 40		06 10		06 40			07 10		07 40					08 40
Port Talbot Parkway	d					04 18	05 18		05 48		06 18		06 48			07 18		07 48					08 48
Bridgend	d					04 30	05 30		06 00		06 30		07 00			07 30		08 00					09 00
Cardiff Central 7	d					04 55	05 55		06 25		06 55		07 25			07 55		08 25					09 25
Newport (South Wales)	d					05 09	06 09		06 39		07 09		07 39			08 09		08 39					09 39
Weston-super-Mare	d	22p01								06 24					07 24				08 29				
Bristol Temple Meads 10	d	22p35		05 30		06b00		06 30		07 00		07 30			08 00		08 30		09 00			09 30	
Bristol Parkway 7	a						06 29		06 59		07 29		07 59			08 30		08 59					09 59
	d						06 31		07 01		07 31		08 01			08 31		09 01					10 01
Bath Spa 7	d	22p47		05 43		06 13		06 43		07 13		07 43			08 13		08 43		09 13			09 43	
Chippenham	d	23p00		05 55		06 25		06 55		07 25		07 55			08 25		08 55		09 25	09 30		09 55	
Cheltenham Spa	d				05 30									07 30							08 59		
Gloucester 7	d				05 44									07c46							09e16		
Stonehouse	d				05 56									07 58							09 29		
Stroud	d				06 01									08 03							09 34		
Kemble	d				06 16									08 17							09 48		
Swindon	a	23p14	03 15	06 09	06 32	06 39	06 57	07 09	07 27	07 40	07 57	08 09	08 27	08 33	08 39	08 58	09 09	09 27	09 39	09 49	10 02	10 10	10 28
	d	23p16	03 17	06 11		06 41	06 59	07 11	07 29	07 41	07 58	08 11	08 29	08 35	08 41	08 59	09 11	09 29	09 41		10 04	10 11	10 29
Didcot Parkway	a	23p33		06 28		06 58	07 16	07 28	07 46	07 59	08 16	08 28	08 46	08 51	08 58	09 16	09 28	09 46			10 21	10 28	10 47
Reading 7	a	23p54	04s00	06 43		07 14	07 31	07 44	08 00	08 14	08 32	08 44	09 00	09 07	09 14	09 32	09 44	10 00	10 08		10 36	10 45	11 01
Slough 3	a																						
London Paddington 15 ⊖	a	00 27	05 43	07 14		07 44	08 02	08 14	08 32	08 44	09 02	09 14	09 32	09 37	09 44	10 02	10 14	10 32	10 38		11 08	11 14	11 33

		GW	GW	GW	GW	GW	GW	GW	GW	GW	GW	GW	GW	GW	GW	GW	GW	GW	GW	GW	GW	GW	GW
		◇1 ☕		◇1 ☕	◇1 ☕	◇1 ☕	◇1 ☕	◇1 ☕	◇1 ☕	◇1 ☕		◇1 ☕	◇1 ☕	◇1 ☕	◇1 ☕	◇1 ☕	◇1 B ☕	◇1 ☕		◇1 ☕	◇1 ☕	◇1 ☕	
Swansea	d				09 28				10h28				11 28				12l28				13 28		
Neath	d				09 40				10 40				11 40				12 40				13 40		
Port Talbot Parkway	d				09 48				10 48				11 48				12 48				13 48		
Bridgend	d				10 00				11 00				12 00				13 00				14 00		
Cardiff Central 7	d				10 25				11 25				12 25				13 25				14 25		
Newport (South Wales)	d				10 39				11 39				12 39				13 39				14 39		
Weston-super-Mare	d									11 33						13 01							
Bristol Temple Meads 10	d	10 00		10 30		11 00		11 30		12 00		12 30		13 00		13 30		14 00		14 30		15 00	
Bristol Parkway 7	a				10 59				11 59				12 59				13 59				14 59		
	d				11 01				12 01				13 01				14 01				15 01		
Bath Spa 7	d	10 13		10 43		11 13		11 43		12 13		12 43		13 13		13 43		14 13		14 43		15 13	
Chippenham	d	10 25		10 55		11 25		11 55		12 25		12 55		13 25		13 55		14 25		14 55		15 25	15 29
Cheltenham Spa	d		10 01				11 00				12 01				13 00				14 01				
Gloucester 7	d		10 15				11f16				12 15				13j16				14 15				
Stonehouse	d		10 27				11 29				12 27				13 29				14 27				
Stroud	d		10 32				11 34				12 32				13 34				14 32				
Kemble	d		10 47				11 48				12 47				13 48				14 47				
Swindon	a	10 39	11 02	11 09	11 27	11 39	12 02	12 09	12 27	12 40	13 02	13 09	13 27	13 39	14 02	14 09	14 27	14 39	15 02	15 09	15 27	15 39	15 49
	d	10 41		11 11	11 29	11 41	12 04	12 11	12 29	12 41		13 11	13 29	13 41	14 04	14 11	14 29	14 41		15 11	15 29	15 41	
Didcot Parkway	a			11 28	11 46		12 21	12 28	12 46			13 28	13 46		14 21	14 28	14 46			15 28	15 46		
Reading 7	a	11 11		11 44	12 00	12 09	12 35	12 48	13 00	13 10		13 44	14 00	14 09	14 36	14 43	15 00	15 09		15 44	16 01	16 09	
Slough 3	a																						
London Paddington 15 ⊖	a	11 40		12 14	12 31	12 39	13 10	13 22	13 32	13 41		14 14	14 32	14 39	15 09	15 14	15 32	15 39		16 14	16 37	16 41	

		GW	GW	GW	GW	GW	GW	GW	GW	GW	GW	GW	GW	GW	GW	GW	GW	GW	GW	GW	GW	GW	GW
		◇1 ☕	◇1 ☕	◇1 ☕	◇1 ☕		◇1 ☕	◇1 ☕	◇1 ☕	◇1 ☕	◇1 ☕	◇1 ☕	◇1 ☕		◇1 ☕	◇1 ☕	◇1 ☕	◇1 ☕	◇1 ☕		◇1 ☕	◇1 ☕	◇1 ☕
Swansea	d			14 28				15 28				16 28			17q28			18 28			19 28		
Neath	d			14 40				15 40				16 40			17 40			18 40			19 40		
Port Talbot Parkway	d			14 48				15 48				16 48			17 48			18 48			19 48		
Bridgend	d			15 00				16 00				17 00			18 00			19 00			20 00		
Cardiff Central 7	d			15 25				16 25				17 25			18 25			19 25			20 25		
Newport (South Wales)	d			15 39				16 39				17 39			18 39			19 39			20 39		
Weston-super-Mare	d		15 01								17 01								20 10				21 59
Bristol Temple Meads 10	d		15 30		16 00		16 30		17 00		17 30		18 00				19 30		20 33			21 47	22 33
Bristol Parkway 7	a			15 59				16 59				17 59			18 59			19 59			21 01		
	d			16 01				17 01				18 01			19 01			20 01			21 01		
Bath Spa 7	d		15 43		16 13		16 43		17 13		17 43		18 13				19 43		20 46			22 02	22 46
Chippenham	d		15 55		16 25		16 55		17 25		17 55		18 25				19 55		20 58			22 15	22 58
Cheltenham Spa	d	15 00				16 01				17 00				18 01		19 00				21 19			
Gloucester 7	d	15 16				16 15				17 16				18 15		19 16				21 35			
Stonehouse	d	15 29				16 27				17 29				18 27		19 29				21 47			
Stroud	d	15 34				16 32				17 34				18 32		19 34				21 52			
Kemble	d	15 48				16 47				17 48				18 47		19 48				22 07			
Swindon	a	16 02	16 09	16 27	16 39	17 02	17 09	17 27	17 39	18 02	18 09	18 27	18 39	19 02	19 27	20 02	20 09	20 27	21 13	22 22	21 29	22 29	23 13
	d	16 04	16 11	16 29	16 41		17 11	17 29	17 41	18 04	18 11	18 29	18 41		19 29	20 04	20 11	20 29	21 14		21 29	22 31	23 14
Didcot Parkway	a	16 21	16 28	16 46			17 28	17 46		18 21	18 28	18 46				20 21	20 28	20 46	21 31		21 47	22 48	23 31
Reading 7	a	16 36	16 44	17 00	17 09		17 44	18 00	18 09	18 36	18 44	19 00	19 09		19 59	20 36	20 44	21 06	21 48		21 59	23 04	23 52
Slough 3	a																						
London Paddington 15 ⊖	a	17 09	17 14	17 32	17 38		18 14	18 32	18 38	19 08	19 14	19 32	19 39		20 32	21 07	21 14	21 36	22 16		22 30	23 38	00 33

A ☕ from Reading ⊘ to Didcot Parkway

B The Pembroke Coast Express

For connections from Hereford and Birmingham New Street please refer to Tables 131 and 57. For connections to Oxford, Gatwick Airport and Heathrow Airport please refer to Tables 116, 148 and 125A

Table 125

Saturdays 17 July to 04 September

South Wales, Weston-super-Mare, Bristol, Cheltenham Spa and Swindon - London

		GW	GW	GW	GW	GW	GW	GW	GW	GW	GW	GW	GW	GW	GW	GW	GW	GW	GW	GW	GW	GW	GW
		◇1 ☕	🛏 ☕	◇1 ☕		◇1 ☕	◇1 ☕	◇1 ☕	◇1 ☕	◇1 ☕	◇1 ☕	◇1 ☕	◇1 ☕	◇1 ☕	◇1 ☕	◇1 A ☕⊘	◇1 ☕	◇1 A ☕⊘	◇1 ☕		◇1 ☕	◇1 ☕	◇1 ☕
Swansea	d					03 58	04 58		05 28		05 58		06 28			06 58		07 28					08 28
Neath	d					04 10	05 10		05 40		06 10		06 40			07 10		07 40					08 40
Port Talbot Parkway	d					04 18	05 18		05 48		06 18		06 48			07 18		07 48					08 48
Bridgend	d					04 30	05 30		06 00		06 30		07 00			07 30		08 00					09 00
Cardiff Central 7	d					04 55	05 55		06 25		06 55		07 25			07 55		08 25					09 25
Newport (South Wales)	d					05 09	06 09		06 39		07 09		07 39			08 09		08 39					09 39
Weston-super-Mare	d	22p01								06 24					07 24				08 29				
Bristol Temple Meads 10	d	22p35		05 30		06 00		06 30		07 00		07 30			08 00		08 30		09 00			09 30	
Bristol Parkway 7	a						06 29		06 59		07 29		07 59			08 30		08 59					09 59
	d						06 31		07 01		07 31		08 01			08 31		09 01					10 01
Bath Spa 7	d	22p47		05 43		06 13		06 43		07 13		07 43			08 13		08 43		09 13			09 43	
Chippenham	d	23p00		05 55		06 25		06 55		07 25		07 55			08 25		08 55		09 25	09 30		09 55	
Cheltenham Spa	d				05 30									07 30							08 59		
Gloucester 7	d				05 44									07 46							09 16		
Stonehouse	d				05 56									07 58							09 29		
Stroud	d				06 01									08 03							09 34		
Kemble	d				06 16									08 17							09 48		
Swindon	a	23p14	03 15	06 09	06 32	06 39	06 57	07 09	07 27	07 40	07 57	08 09	08 27	08 33	08 39	08 58	09 09	09 27	09 39	09 49	10 02	10 10	10 28
	d	23p16	03 17	06 11		06 41	06 59	07 11	07 29	07 41	07 58	08 11	08 29	08 35	08 41	08 59	09 11	09 29	09 41		10 04	10 11	10 29
Didcot Parkway	a	23p33		06 28		06 58	07 16	07 28	07 46	07 59	08 16	08 28	08 46	08 51	08 58	09 16	09 28	09 46			10 21	10 28	10 47
Reading 7	a	23p54	04s00	06 43		07 14	07 31	07 44	08 00	08 14	08 32	08 44	09 00	09 07	09 14	09 32	09 44	10 00	10 08		10 36	10 45	11 01
Slough 3	a																						
London Paddington 15 ⊖	a	00 27	05 43	07 14		07 44	08 02	08 14	08 32	08 44	09 02	09 14	09 32	09 37	09 44	10 02	10 14	10 32	10 38		11 08	11 14	11 33

		GW	GW	GW	GW	GW	GW	GW	GW	GW	GW	GW	GW	GW	GW	GW	GW	GW	GW	GW	GW	GW	GW
		◇1 ☕		◇1 ☕	◇1 ☕	◇1 ☕	◇1 ☕	◇1 ☕	◇1 ☕	◇1 ☕		◇1 ☕	◇1 ☕	◇1 ☕	◇1 ☕	◇1 ☕	◇1 B ☕	◇1 ☕		◇1 ☕	◇1 ☕	◇1 ☕	
Swansea	d				09 28				10h28				11 28				12l28				13 28		
Neath	d				09 40				10 40				11 40				12 40				13 40		
Port Talbot Parkway	d				09 48				10 48				11 48				12 48				13 48		
Bridgend	d				10 00				11 00				12 00				13 00				14 00		
Cardiff Central 7	d				10 25				11 25				12 25				13 25				14 25		
Newport (South Wales)	d				10 39				11 39				12 39				13 39				14 39		
Weston-super-Mare	d									11 33						13 01							
Bristol Temple Meads 10	d	10 00		10 30		11 00		11 30		12 00		12 30		13 00		13 30		14 00		14 30		15 00	
Bristol Parkway 7	a				10 59				11 59				12 59				13 59				14 59		
	d				11 01				12 01				13 01				14 01				15 01		
Bath Spa 7	d	10 13		10 43		11 13		11 43		12 13		12 43		13 13		13 43		14 13		14 43		15 13	
Chippenham	d	10 25		10 55		11 25		11 55		12 25		12 55		13 25		13 55		14 25		14 55		15 25	15 29
Cheltenham Spa	d		10 01				11 00				12 01				13 00				14 01				
Gloucester 7	d		10 15				11 16				12 15				13 16				14 15				
Stonehouse	d		10 27				11 29				12 27				13 29				14 27				
Stroud	d		10 32				11 34				12 32				13 34				14 32				
Kemble	d		10 47				11 48				12 47				13 48				14 47				
Swindon	a	10 39	11 02	11 09	11 27	11 39	12 02	12 09	12 27	12 40	13 02	13 09	13 27	13 39	14 02	14 09	14 27	14 39	15 02	15 09	15 27	15 39	15 49
	d	10 41		11 11	11 29	11 41	12 04	12 11	12 29	12 41		13 11	13 29	13 41	14 04	14 11	14 29	14 41		15 11	15 29	15 41	
Didcot Parkway	a			11 28	11 46		12 21	12 28	12 46			13 28	13 46		14 21	14 28	14 46			15 28	15 46		
Reading 7	a	11 11		11 44	12 00	12 09	12 35	12 48	13 00	13 10		13 44	14 00	14 09	14 36	14 43	15 00	15 09		15 44	16 01	16 09	
Slough 3	a																						
London Paddington 15 ⊖	a	11 40		12 14	12 31	12 39	13 10	13 22	13 32	13 41		14 14	14 32	14 39	15 09	15 14	15 32	15 39		16 14	16 37	16 41	

		GW	GW	GW	GW	GW	GW	GW	GW	GW	GW	GW	GW	GW	GW	GW	GW	GW	GW	GW	GW	GW
		◇1 ☕	◇1 ☕	◇1 ☕	◇1 ☕		◇1 ☕	◇1 ☕	◇1 ☕	◇1 ☕	◇1 ☕	◇1 ☕		◇1 ☕	◇1 ☕	◇1 ☕	◇1 ☕	◇1 ☕	◇1 ☕		◇1 ☕	◇1 ☕
Swansea	d			14 28							15 37			16 37			17 37	18 28				
Neath	d			14 40							15 49			16 49			17 49	18 40				
Port Talbot Parkway	d			14 48							15 57			16 57			17 57	18 48				
Bridgend	d			15 00							16 09			17 09			18 09	19 00				
Cardiff Central 7	d			15 25							16r40			17 40			18 40	19 25				
Newport (South Wales)	d			15 39							16 55			17 55			18 55	19 39				
Weston-super-Mare	d		15 01							17 01									20 10			21 59
Bristol Temple Meads 10	d		15 30		16 00		16 30	17 00		17 30		18 00				19 30			20 33		21 47	22 33
Bristol Parkway 7	a			15 59							17 15			18 16			19 15	20 13				
	d			16 01							17 29			18 33			19 32	20 20				
Bath Spa 7	d		15 43		16 13		16 43	17 13		17 43		18 13				19 43			20 46		22 02	22 46
Chippenham	d		15 55		16 25		16 55	17 25		17 55		18 25				19 55			20 58		22 15	22 58
Cheltenham Spa	d	15 00				16 01			17 00				18 01		19 00					21 19		
Gloucester 7	d	15 16				16 15			17 16				18 15		19 16					21 35		
Stonehouse	d	15 29				16 27			17 29				18 27		19 29					21 47		
Stroud	d	15 34				16 32			17 34				18 32		19 34					21 52		
Kemble	d	15 48				16 47			17 48				18 47		19 48					22 07		
Swindon	a	16 02	16 09	16 27	16 39	17 02	17 09	17 39	18 02	18 09	18 16	18 39	19 02	19 21	20 02	20 09	20 18	21 07	21 13	22 22	22 29	23 13
	d	16 04	16 11	16 29	16 41		17 11	17 41	18 04	18 11	18 17	18 41		19 23	20 04	20 11	20 20	21 08	21 14		22 31	23 14
Didcot Parkway	a	16 21	16 28	16 46			17 28		18 21	18 28	18 34			19 40	20 21	20 28	20 37	21 27	21 31		22 48	23 31
Reading 7	a	16 36	16 44	17 00	17 09		17 44	18 09	18 36	18 44	18 52	19 09		19 59	20 36	20 44	21 06	21 42	21 49		23 04	23 52
Slough 3	a																					
London Paddington 15 ⊖	a	17 09	17 14	17 32	17 38		18 14	18 38	19 08	19 14	19 29	19 39		20 32	21 07	21 14	21 37	22 14	22 21		23 38	00 33

A ☕ from Reading ⊘ to Didcot Parkway

B The Pembroke Coast Express

For connections from Hereford and Birmingham New Street please refer to Tables 131 and 57. For connections to Oxford, Gatwick Airport and Heathrow Airport please refer to Tables 116, 148 and 125A

Table 125

Saturdays
from 11 September

South Wales, Weston-super-Mare, Bristol, Cheltenham Spa and Swindon - London

		GW	GW	GW	GW	GW	GW	GW	GW	GW		GW	GW	GW	GW	GW	GW	GW	GW	GW		GW	GW	GW	GW
		◇1	■	◇1		◇1	◇1	◇1	◇1	◇1		◇1	◇1	◇1	◇1	◇1	◇1	◇1	◇1	◇1			◇1	◇1	◇1
																	A		A						B
		🛒	🛏 🛒	🛒		🛒	🛒	🛒	🛒	🛒		🛒	🛒	🛒	🛒	🛒	🛒⊘	🛒	🛒⊘	🛒			🛒	🛒	🛒
Swansea	d					03 58	04 58		05 28			05 58		06 28			06 58		07 28				07 58		
Neath	d					04 10	05 10		05 40			06 10		06 40			07 10		07 40				08 10		
Port Talbot Parkway	d					04 18	05 18		05 48			06 18		06 48			07 18		07 48				08 18		
Bridgend	d					04 30	05 30		06 00			06 30		07 00			07 30		08 00				08 30		
Cardiff Central 7	d					04 55	05 55		06 25			06 55		07 25			07 55		08 25				08 55		
Newport (South Wales)	d					05 09	06 09		06 39			07 09		07 39			08 09		08 39				09 09		
Weston-super-Mare	d	22p01								06 24						07 24				08 29					09 02
Bristol Temple Meads 10	d	22p35		05 30		06 00		06 30		07 00			07 30			08 00		08 30		09 00					09 30
Bristol Parkway 7	a						06 29		06 59			07 29		07 59			08 30		08 59				09 30		
	d						06 31		07 01			07 31		08 01			08 31		09 01				09 31		
Bath Spa 7	d	22p47		05 43		06 13		06 43		07 13			07 43			08 13		08 43		09 13					09 43
Chippenham	d	23p00		05 55		06 25		06 55		07 25			07 55			08 25		08 55		09 25		09 30			09 55
Cheltenham Spa	d				05 30										07 30									08 59	
Gloucester 7	d				05 44										07 46									09 16	
Stonehouse	d				05 56										07 58									09 29	
Stroud	d				06 01										08 03									09 34	
Kemble	d				06 16										08 17									09 48	
Swindon	a	23p14	03 15	06 09	06 32	06 39	06 57	07 09	07 27	07 40		07 57	08 09	08 27	08 33	08 39	08 58	09 09	09 27	09 39		09 49	09 57	10 02	10 10
	d	23p16	03 17	06 11		06 41	06 59	07 11	07 29	07 41		07 58	08 11	08 29	08 35	08 41	08 59	09 11	09 29	09 41			09 59	10 04	10 11
Didcot Parkway	a	23p33		06 28		06 58	07 16	07 28	07 46	07 59		08 16	08 28	08 46	08 51	08 58	09 16	09 28	09 46				10 15	10 21	10 28
Reading 7	a	23p54	04s00	06 43		07 14	07 31	07 44	08 00	08 14		08 32	08 44	09 00	09 07	09 14	09 32	09 44	10 00	10 08			10 32	10 36	10 45
Slough 3	a																								
London Paddington 15 ⊖	a	00 27	05 43	07 14		07 44	08 02	08 14	08 32	08 44		09 02	09 14	09 32	09 37	09 44	10 02	10 14	10 32	10 38			11 02	11 08	11 14

		GW	GW	GW	GW	GW		GW	GW	GW	GW	GW	GW	GW	GW	GW		GW	GW	GW	GW	GW	GW	GW	GW
		◇1	◇1		◇1	◇1		◇1	◇1	◇1	◇1	◇1		◇1	◇1	◇1		◇1	◇1	◇1	◇1		◇1	◇1	◇1
		🛒	🛒		🛒	🛒		🛒	🛒	🛒	🛒	🛒		🛒	🛒	🛒		🛒	🛒	🛒	🛒		🛒	🛒	🛒
Swansea	d	08 28				09 28					10h28				11 28					12 28				13 28	
Neath	d	08 40				09 40					10 40				11 40					12 40				13 40	
Port Talbot Parkway	d	08 48				09 48					10 48				11 48					12 48				13 48	
Bridgend	d	09 00				10 00					11 00				12 00					13 00				14 00	
Cardiff Central 7	d	09 25				10 25					11 25				12 25					13 25				14 25	
Newport (South Wales)	d	09 39				10 39					11 39				12 39					13 39				14 39	
Weston-super-Mare	d																								
Bristol Temple Meads 10	d		10 00		10 30			11 00		11 30		12 00		12 30		13 00			13 30		14 00		14 30		15 00
Bristol Parkway 7	a	09 59				10 59					11 59				12 59					13 59				14 59	
	d	10 01				11 01					12 01				13 01					14 01				15 01	
Bath Spa 7	d		10 13		10 43			11 13		11 43		12 13		12 43		13 13			13 43		14 13		14 43		15 13
Chippenham	d		10 25		10 55			11 25		11 55		12 25		12 55		13 25			13 55		14 25		14 55		15 25
Cheltenham Spa	d			10 01					11 00				12 01					13 00				14 01			
Gloucester 7	d			10 15					11 16				12 15					13i16				14 15			
Stonehouse	d			10 27					11 29				12 27					13 29				14 27			
Stroud	d			10 32					11 34				12 32					13 34				14 32			
Kemble	d			10 47					11 48				12 47					13 48				14 47			
Swindon	a	10 28	10 39	11 02	11 09	11 27		11 39	12 02	12 09	12 27	12 40	13 02	13 09	13 27	13 39		14 02	14 09	14 27	14 39	15 02	15 09	15 27	15 39
	d	10 29	10 41		11 11	11 29		11 41	12 04	12 11	12 29	12 41		13 11	13 29	13 41		14 04	14 11	14 29	14 41		15 11	15 29	15 41
Didcot Parkway	a	10 47			11 28	11 46			12 21	12 27	12 46			13 28	13 46			14 21	14 28	14 46			15 28	15 46	
Reading 7	a	11 01	11 11		11 44	12 00		12 09	12 36	12 43	13 00	13 10		13 44	14 00	14 09		14 36	14 43	15 00	15 09		15 44	16 01	16 09
Slough 3	a																								
London Paddington 15 ⊖	a	11 33	11 40		12 14	12 32		12 39	13 06	13 14	13 32	13 41		14 14	14 32	14 39		15 09	15 14	15 32	15 39		16 14	16 32	16 41

		GW		GW	GW	GW	GW	GW	GW	GW	GW	GW		GW	GW	GW	GW	GW	GW	GW	GW	GW		GW	GW
				◇1	◇1	◇1	◇1		◇1	◇1	◇1	◇1		◇1	◇1	◇1		◇1	◇1	◇1	◇1	◇1		◇1	
				🛒	🛒	🛒	🛒		🛒	🛒	🛒	🛒		🛒	🛒	🛒		🛒	🛒	🛒	🛒	🛒		🛒	
Swansea	d					14 28				15 28					16 28				17 28			18 28			
Neath	d					14 40				15 40					16 40				17 40			18 40			
Port Talbot Parkway	d					14 48				15 48					16 48				17 48			18 48			
Bridgend	d					15 00				16 00					17 00				18 00			19 00			
Cardiff Central 7	d					15 25				16 25					17 25				18 25			19 25			
Newport (South Wales)	d					15 39				16 39					17 39				18 39			19 39			
Weston-super-Mare	d																							20 10	
Bristol Temple Meads 10	d				15 30		16 00		16 30		17 00			17 30		18 00		18 30			19 30			20 33	
Bristol Parkway 7	a					15 59				16 59					17 59				18 59			19 59			
	d					16 01				17 01					18 01				19 01			20 01			
Bath Spa 7	d				15 43		16 13		16 43		17 13			17 43		18 13		18 43			19 43			20 46	
Chippenham	d	15 29			15 55		16 25		16 55		17 25			17 55		18 25		18 55			19 55			20 58	
Cheltenham Spa	d			15 00				16 01				17 00					18 01			19 00					21 19
Gloucester 7	d			15 16				16 15				17 16					18 15			19 16					21 35
Stonehouse	d			15 29				16 27				17 29					18 27			19 29					21 47
Stroud	d			15 34				16 32				17 34					18 32			19 34					21 52
Kemble	d			15 48				16 47				17 48					18 47			19 48					22 07
Swindon	a	15 49		16 02	16 09	16 27	16 39	17 02	17 09	17 27	17 39	18 02		18 09	18 27	18 39	19 02	19 09	19 27	20 02	20 09	20 27		21 13	22 22
	d			16 04	16 11	16 29	16 41		17 11	17 29	17 41	18 04		18 11	18 29	18 41		19 11	19 29	20 04	20 11	20 29		21 14	
Didcot Parkway	a			16 21	16 28	16 46			17 28	17 46		18 21		18 28	18 46			19 28		20 21	20 28	20 46		21 31	
Reading 7	a			16 36	16 44	17 00	17 09		17 44	18 00	18 09	18 36		18 44	19 00	19 09		19 44	19 59	20 36	20 44	21 06		21 48	
Slough 3	a																								
London Paddington 15 ⊖	a			17 06	17 14	17 32	17 38		18 14	18 32	18 38	19 08		19 14	19 32	19 39		20 14	20 32	21 07	21 14	21 36		22 16	

A 🛒 from Reading ⊘ to Didcot Parkway

B The Torbay Express

For connections from Hereford and Birmingham New Street please refer to Tables 131 and 57. For connections to Oxford, Gatwick Airport and Heathrow Airport please refer to Tables 116, 148 and 125A

Table 125

Saturdays
from 11 September

South Wales, Weston-super-Mare, Bristol, Cheltenham Spa and Swindon - London

		GW	GW
		◇1	◇1
		🛒	🛒
Swansea	d		
Neath	d		
Port Talbot Parkway	d		
Bridgend	d		
Cardiff Central 7	d		
Newport (South Wales)	d		
Weston-super-Mare	d		21 59
Bristol Temple Meads 10	d	21 47	22 33
Bristol Parkway 7	a		
	d		
Bath Spa 7	d	22 02	22 46
Chippenham	d	22 15	22 58
Cheltenham Spa	d		
Gloucester 7	d		
Stonehouse	d		
Stroud	d		
Kemble	d		
Swindon	a	22 29	23 13
	d	22 31	23 14
Didcot Parkway	a	22 48	23 31
Reading 7	a	23 04	23 52
Slough 3	a		
London Paddington 15 ⊖	a	23 38	00 33

Sundays
until 11 July

		GW	GW	GW	GW	GW	GW	GW	GW	GW		GW	GW	GW	GW	GW	GW	GW	GW	GW		GW	GW	GW	GW
		◇1	◇1	◇1	◇1	◇1	◇1		◇1	◇1		◇1	◇1	◇1	◇1		◇1	◇1	◇1	◇1		◇1	◇1	◇1	◇1
		A																							
		🛒	🛒	🛒	🛒	🛒	🛒		🛒	🛒		🛒	🛒	🛒	🛒		🛒	🛒	🛒	🛒		🛒	🛒	🛒	🛒
Swansea	d						07 40						09 55				10 55		11 55				12 55		13 55
Neath	d						07 52						10 07				11 07		12 07				13 07		14 07
Port Talbot Parkway	d						08 00						10 15				11 15		12 15				13 15		14 15
Bridgend	d						08 14						10 27				11 27		12 27				13 27		14 27
Cardiff Central 7	d				08 00		09 05						11 15				12 15		13 15				14 15		15 15
Newport (South Wales)	d				08 18		09 19						11 32				12 32		13 32				14 32		15 32
Weston-super-Mare	d	21p59				08 11				09 56								12 51						14 52	
Bristol Temple Meads 10	d	22p33	07 45	08 15		08 45			09 55	10 30		11 30			12 30			13 30				14 30		15 30	
Bristol Parkway 7	a				08 46		09 46						11 59				12 59		13 59				14 59		15 59
	d				08 48		09 48						12 01				13 01		14 01				15 01		16 01
Bath Spa 7	d	22p46	07 58	08 28		08 58			10 07	10 43		11 43			12 43			13 43				14 43		15 43	
Chippenham	d	22p58	08 10	08 40		09 10			10 19	10 55		11 55			12 55			13 55				14 55		15 55	
Cheltenham Spa	d							09 30						11 46		12 24				13 46					
Gloucester 7	d							09 44						12 02		12 38				14 02					
Stonehouse	d							09 56						12 15		12 50				14 15					
Stroud	d							10 01						12 20		12 55				14 20					
Kemble	d							10 15						12 35		13 09				14 35					
Swindon	a	23p13	08 25	08 55	09 13	09 25	10 13	10 30	10 34	11 10		12 10	12 28	12 48	13 10	13 24	13 28	14 10	14 28	14 50		15 10	15 28	16 10	16 27
	d	23p14	08 26	08 55	09 14	09 28	10 13		10 35	11 11		12 11	12 29	12 53	13 11		13 29	14 11	14 29	14 51		15 11	15 29	16 11	16 29
Didcot Parkway	a	23p31	08 43	09 13		09 46			10 53	11 28		12 28	12 46		13 28		13 46	14 28	14 46			15 28	15 46	16 28	16 46
Reading 7	a	23p52	08 59	09 28	09 43	09 59	10 42		11 09	11 42		12 42	13 00	13 21	13 42		14 00	14 42	15 00	15 17		15 42	16 00	16 42	17 00
Slough 3	a																								
London Paddington 15 ⊖	a	00 33	09 39	10 06	10 23	10 39	11 21		11 51	12 24		13 24	13 38	14 06	14 24		14 38	15 24	15 38	16 06		16 24	16 38	17 24	17 38

		GW	GW	GW	GW	GW		GW	GW	GW	GW	GW	GW	GW	GW	GW		GW	GW	GW	GW	GW	GW	GW	GW
		◇1	◇1	◇1		◇1			◇1	◇1	◇1	◇1	◇1	◇1	◇1	◇1		◇1			◇1	◇1	◇1	◇1	◇1
		🛒	🛒	🛒		🛒			🛒	🛒	🛒	🛒	🛒	🛒	🛒	🛒		🛒			🛒	🛒	🛒	🛒	🛒
Swansea	d			14 55						15 55			16 25			17 25							18 25		19 45
Neath	d			15 07						16 07			16 37			17 37							18 37		19 57
Port Talbot Parkway	d			15 15						16 15			16 44			17 44							18 44		20 04
Bridgend	d			15 27						16 27			16 57			18 00							18 57		20 17
Cardiff Central 7	d			16 15						17 15			17 50			18 50							19o50		21 05
Newport (South Wales)	d			16 32						17 32			18 04			19 04							20 04		21 22
Weston-super-Mare	d								17 01		17 26							18 53						20 38	
Bristol Temple Meads 10	d		16 30			17 00			17 30		18 00			18 30	19 00			19 30			20 00			21 00	
Bristol Parkway 7	a			16 59						17 59			18 31			19 31							20 31		21 49
	d			17 01						18 01			18 33			19 33							20 33		21 51
Bath Spa 7	d		16 43			17 13			17 43		18 13			18 43	19 13			19 43			20 13			21 13	
Chippenham	d		16 55			17 25		17 39	17 55		18 25			18 55	19 25			19 55		20 04	20 25			21 25	
Cheltenham Spa	d	15 46			16 33							17 46										19 46			
Gloucester 7	d	16 02			16 47							18 04							19 34			20 04			
Stonehouse	d	16 15			16 59							18 17							19 48			20 17			
Stroud	d	16 20			17 04							18 22							19 53			20 22			
Kemble	d	16 35			17 19							18 38							20 07			20 38			
Swindon	a	16 50	17 10	17 28	17 34	17 39		17 56	18 10	18 28	18 40	18 51	18 59	19 11	19 40	19 59		20 10	20 23	20 20	20 40	20 51	20 59	21 41	22 19
	d	16 51	17 11	17 29		17 40			18 11	18 29	18 41	18 51	18 59	19 11	19 41	20 01		20 11		20 24	20 41	20 51	20 59	21 41	22 19
Didcot Parkway	a		17 28	17 46		17 57				18 46	18 59		19 18		19 58	20 16					20 59		21 16	22 00	22 37
Reading 7	a	17 18	17 42	18 00		18 12			18 42	19 00	19 12	19 21	19 32	19 42	20 12	20 32		20 42			21 16	21 25	21 32	22 17	22 56
Slough 3	a																								
London Paddington 15 ⊖	a	18 06	18 24	18 38		18 51			19 26	19 39	19 54	20 06	20 10	20 24	20 51	21 09		21 21			21 56	22 07	22 12	23 08	23 46

A not 23 May

For connections from Hereford and Birmingham New Street please refer to Tables 131 and 57. For connections to Oxford, Gatwick Airport and Heathrow Airport please refer to Tables 116, 148 and 125A

Table 125

Sundays until 11 July

South Wales, Weston-super-Mare, Bristol, Cheltenham Spa and Swindon - London

		GW	GW ◇1 🍴
Swansea	d		
Neath	d		
Port Talbot Parkway	d		
Bridgend	d		
Cardiff Central 7	d		
Newport (South Wales)	d		
Weston-super-Mare	d		
Bristol Temple Meads 10	d		22 05
Bristol Parkway 7	a		
	d		
Bath Spa 7	d		22 19
Chippenham	d		22 31
Cheltenham Spa	d	21 46	
Gloucester 7	d	21 59	
Stonehouse	d	22 12	
Stroud	d	22 17	
Kemble	d	22 32	
Swindon	a	22 47	22 46
	d		22 52
Didcot Parkway	a		23 10
Reading 7	a		23 27
Slough 3	a		
London Paddington 15 ⊖	a		00 13

Sundays 18 July to 05 September

		GW ◇1 🍴	GW ◇1 🍴	GW ◇1 🍴	GW ◇1 🍴	GW ◇1 🍴	GW ◇1 🍴	GW	GW ◇1 🍴	GW ◇1 🍴		GW ◇1 🍴	GW ◇1 🍴
Swansea	d						07 40			08 45			
Neath	d						07 52			08 57			
Port Talbot Parkway	d						08 00			09 04			
Bridgend	d						08 11			09 16			
Cardiff Central 7	d				07 35		08 40			09 45			
Newport (South Wales)	d				07 53		08 58			10 03			
Weston-super-Mare	d	21p59				08 11						10 14	
Bristol Temple Meads 10	d	22p33	07 45	08 15		08 45			09 48			10 48	11 30
Bristol Parkway 7	a				08 22		09 24			10 23			
	d				08 27		09 30			10 30			
Bath Spa 7	d	22p46	07 58	08 28		08 58			10 00			11 01	11 43
Chippenham	d	22p58	08 10	08 40		09 10			10 12			11 13	11 55
Cheltenham Spa	d							09 24					
Gloucester 7	d							09 38					
Stonehouse	d							09 50					
Stroud	d							09 55					
Kemble	d							10 09					
Swindon	a	23p13	08 25	08 55	09 06	09 25	10 13	10 24	10 27	11 10		11 28	12 10
	d	23p14	08 26	08 55	09 14	09 28	10 13		10 29	11 11		11 29	12 11
Didcot Parkway	a	23p31	08 43	09 13		09 46			10 45	11 28		11 46	12 28
Reading 7	a	23p52	08 59	09 28	09 43	09 59	10 43		11 00	11 42		12 00	12 42
Slough 3	a												
London Paddington 15 ⊖	a	00 33	09 39	10 06	10 23	10 39	11 21		11 38	12 24		12 38	13 24

		GW ◇1 🍴	GW ◇1 🍴	GW ◇1 🍴	GW	GW ◇1 🍴	GW ◇1 🍴	GW ◇1 🍴		GW ◇1 🍴	GW ◇1 🍴	GW ◇1 🍴	GW ◇1 🍴
Swansea	d	09 55				10 55		11 55				12 55	
Neath	d	10 07				11 07		12 07				13 07	
Port Talbot Parkway	d	10 15				11 15		12 15				13 15	
Bridgend	d	10 27				11 27		12 27				13 27	
Cardiff Central 7	d	10 50				11 50		12 50				13 50	
Newport (South Wales)	d	11 13				12 13		13 13				14 13	
Weston-super-Mare	d						12 51						14 52
Bristol Temple Meads 10	d			12 30			13 30				14 30		15 30
Bristol Parkway 7	a	11 34				12 34		13 34				14 34	
	d	11 40				12 45		13 45				14 45	
Bath Spa 7	d			12 43			13 43				14 43		15 43
Chippenham	d			12 55			13 55				14 55		15 55
Cheltenham Spa	d		11 46		12 24					13 46			
Gloucester 7	d		12 02		12 38					14 02			
Stonehouse	d		12 15		12 50					14 15			
Stroud	d		12 20		12 55					14 20			
Kemble	d		12 35		13 09					14 35			
Swindon	a	12 25	12 48	13 10	13 24	13 27	14 10	14 25		14 50	15 10	15 26	16 10
	d	12 29	12 53	13 11		13 29	14 11	14 29		14 51	15 11	15 29	16 11
Didcot Parkway	a	12 46		13 28		13 46	14 28	14 46			15 28	15 46	16 28
Reading 7	a	13 00	13 21	13 42		14 00	14 42	15 00		15 17	15 42	16 00	16 42
Slough 3	a												
London Paddington 15 ⊖	a	13 38	14 06	14 24		14 38	15 24	15 38		16 06	16 24	16 38	17 24

		GW ◇1 🍴	GW ◇1 🍴	GW ◇1 🍴	GW ◇1 🍴	GW		GW ◇1 🍴	GW	GW ◇1 🍴	GW ◇1 🍴	GW ◇1 🍴	GW ◇1 🍴
Swansea	d	13 55			14 55						15 55		
Neath	d	14 07			15 07						16 07		
Port Talbot Parkway	d	14 15			15 15						16 15		
Bridgend	d	14 27			15 27						16 27		
Cardiff Central 7	d	14 50			15 50						16 50		
Newport (South Wales)	d	15 13			16 13						17 14		
Weston-super-Mare	d									17 01		17 26	
Bristol Temple Meads 10	d			16 30				17 00		17 30		18 00	
Bristol Parkway 7	a	15 34			16 34						17 34		
	d	15 45			16 45						17 45		
Bath Spa 7	d			16 43				17 13		17 43		18 13	
Chippenham	d			16 55				17 25	17 39	17 55		18 25	
Cheltenham Spa	d		15 46			16 33							17 46
Gloucester 7	d		16 02			16 47							18 4
Stonehouse	d		16 15			16 59							18 17
Stroud	d		16 20			17 04							18 22
Kemble	d		16 35			17 19							18 38
Swindon	a	16 25	16 50	17 10	17 25	17 34		17 39	17 56	18 10	18 28	18 40	18 51
	d	16 29	16 51	17 11	17 29			17 40		18 11	18 29	18 41	18 51
Didcot Parkway	a	16 46		17 28	17 46			17 57			18 46	18 59	
Reading 7	a	17 00	17 18	17 42	18 00			18 12		18 42	19 00	19 12	19 21
Slough 3	a												
London Paddington 15 ⊖	a	17 38	18 06	18 24	18 38			18 51		19 26	19 39	19 54	20 06

		GW ◇1 🍴	GW ◇1 🍴	GW ◇1 🍴		GW ◇1 🍴	GW ◇1 🍴	GW	GW	GW ◇1 🍴	GW ◇1 🍴	GW ◇1 🍴	GW ◇1 🍴
Swansea	d	16 25				17 25							19 55
Neath	d	16 37				17 37							20 07
Port Talbot Parkway	d	16 44				17 44							20 14
Bridgend	d	16 57				17 57							20 26
Cardiff Central 7	d	17 25				18 25							20 50
Newport (South Wales)	d	17 43				18 43							21 11
Weston-super-Mare	d						18 53					20 38	
Bristol Temple Meads 10	d		18 30	19 00			19 30			20 00		21 00	
Bristol Parkway 7	a	18 04				19 04							21 31
	d	18 15				19 15							21 38
Bath Spa 7	d		18 43	19 13			19 43			20 13		21 13	
Chippenham	d		18 55	19 25			19 55		20 04	20 25		21 25	
Cheltenham Spa	d										19 46		
Gloucester 7	d							19 34			20 04		
Stonehouse	d							19 48			20 17		
Stroud	d							19 53			20 22		
Kemble	d							20 07			20 38		
Swindon	a	18 55	19 11	19 40		19 53	20 10	20 23	20 20	20 40	20 51	21 41	22 19
	d	18 59	19 11	19 41		19 59	20 11		20 24	20 41	20 51	21 41	22 19
Didcot Parkway	a	19 16		19 58		20 16				20 59		22 00	22 37
Reading 7	a	19 32	19 42	20 12		20 32	20 42			21 15	21 25	22 17	22 55
Slough 3	a												
London Paddington 15 ⊖	a	20 10	20 24	20 51		21 09	21 21			21 56	22 07	23 08	23 46

For connections from Hereford and Birmingham New Street please refer to Tables 131 and 57. For connections to Oxford, Gatwick Airport and Heathrow Airport please refer to Tables 116, 148 and 125A

Table 125

Sundays 18 July to 05 September

South Wales, Weston-super-Mare, Bristol, Cheltenham Spa and Swindon - London

		GW	GW ◇1 🍴
Swansea	d		
Neath	d		
Port Talbot Parkway	d		
Bridgend	d		
Cardiff Central 7	d		
Newport (South Wales)	d		
Weston-super-Mare	d		
Bristol Temple Meads 10	d		22 05
Bristol Parkway 7	a		
	d		
Bath Spa 7	d		22 19
Chippenham	d		22 31
Cheltenham Spa	d	21 46	
Gloucester 7	d	21 59	
Stonehouse	d	22 12	
Stroud	d	22 17	
Kemble	d	22 32	
Swindon	a	22 47	22 46
	d		22 52
Didcot Parkway	a		23 10
Reading 7	a		23 27
Slough 3	a		
London Paddington 15 ⊖	a		00 13

Sundays from 12 September

		GW ◇1 🍴	GW ◇1 🍴	GW 1 🍴	GW ◇1 🍴	GW ◇1 🍴	GW ◇1 🍴	GW	GW ◇1 🍴	GW ◇1 🍴		GW ◇1 🍴	GW ◇1 🍴
Swansea	d						08 07					09 21	
Neath	d						08 19					09 33	
Port Talbot Parkway	d						08 26					09 40	
Bridgend	d						08 38					09 52	
Cardiff Central 7	d				07 55		09 05					10 15	
Newport (South Wales)	d				08 13		09 19					10 32	
Weston-super-Mare	d	21p59				08 11				09 56			
Bristol Temple Meads 10	d	22p33	07 45	08 20		08 45			09 48	10 30			11 30
Bristol Parkway 7	a				08 41		09 46					10 59	
	d				08 42		09 48					11 01	
Bath Spa 7	d	22p46	07 58	08 33		08 58			10 00	10 43			11 43
Chippenham	d	22p58	08 10	08 45		09 10			10 12	10 55			11 55
Cheltenham Spa	d							09 24					
Gloucester 7	d							09 38					
Stonehouse	d							09 50					
Stroud	d							09 55					
Kemble	d							10 09					
Swindon	a	23p13	08 25	09 00	09 07	09 24	10 13	10 24	10 27	11 10		11 26	12 10
	d	23p14	08 26		09 08	09 28	10 13		10 29	11 11		11 29	12 11
Didcot Parkway	a	23p31	08 43			09 46			10 45	11 28		11 46	12 28
Reading 7	a	23p52	09 01		09 42	09 59	10 42		11 00	11 42		12 01	12 42
Slough 3	a												
London Paddington 15 ⊖	a	00 33	09 39		10 19	10 39	11 21		11 39	12 21		12 39	13 21

		GW ◇1 🍴	GW ◇1 🍴	GW ◇1 🍴	GW	GW ◇1 🍴	GW ◇1 🍴	GW ◇1 🍴		GW ◇1 🍴	GW ◇1 🍴	GW ◇1 🍴	GW ◇1 🍴
Swansea	d		10 21			11 21		12 21				13 21	
Neath	d		10 33			11 33		12 33				13 33	
Port Talbot Parkway	d		10 40			11 40		12 40				13 40	
Bridgend	d		10 52			11 52		12 52				13 52	
Cardiff Central 7	d		11 15			12 15		13 15				14 15	
Newport (South Wales)	d		11 32			12 32		13 32				14 32	
Weston-super-Mare	d						12 51						14 52
Bristol Temple Meads 10	d			12c30			13e30				14 30		15f30
Bristol Parkway 7	a		11 59			12 59		13 59				14 59	
	d		12 01			13 02		14 01				15 01	
Bath Spa 7	d			12 43			13 43				14 43		15 43
Chippenham	d			12 55			13 55				14 55		15 55
Cheltenham Spa	d	11 20			12 24					13 46			
Gloucester 7	d	11b37			12 38					14 02			
Stonehouse	d	11 50			12 50					14 15			
Stroud	d	11 55			12 55					14 20			
Kemble	d	12 10			13 09					14 38			
Swindon	a	12 23	12 27	13 10	13 24	13 27	14 10	14 27		14 52	15 10	15 27	16 10
	d		12 29	13 11		13 29	14 11	14 29			15 11	15 29	16 11
Didcot Parkway	a		12 46	13 28		13 46	14 28	14 46			15 28	15 46	16 28
Reading 7	a		13 00	13 42		14 00	14 42	15 00			15 42	16 00	16 42
Slough 3	a												
London Paddington 15 ⊖	a		13 39	14 21		14 39	15 21	15 39			16 21	16 39	17 22

		GW ◇1 🍴	GW ◇1 🍴	GW ◇1 🍴	GW ◇1 🍴	GW		GW ◇1 🍴	GW	GW ◇1 🍴	GW ◇1 🍴	GW ◇1 🍴	GW ◇1 🍴
Swansea	d	14 21			15 21						16h21		
Neath	d	14 33			15 33						16 33		
Port Talbot Parkway	d	14 40			15 40						16 40		
Bridgend	d	14 52			15 52						16 52		
Cardiff Central 7	d	15 15			16 15						17 15		
Newport (South Wales)	d	15 32			16 32						17 32		
Weston-super-Mare	d									17 00		17 26	
Bristol Temple Meads 10	d			16 30				17 00		17g30		18 00	
Bristol Parkway 7	a	15 59			16 59						17 59		
	d	16 01			17 01						18 01		
Bath Spa 7	d			16 43				17 13		17 43		18 13	
Chippenham	d			16 55				17 25	17 31	17 55		18 25	
Cheltenham Spa	d		15 46			16 33							17 46
Gloucester 7	d		16 02			16 47							18i04
Stonehouse	d		16 15			16 59							18 17
Stroud	d		16 20			17 04							18 22
Kemble	d		16 35			17 19							18 38
Swindon	a	16 27	16 50	17 10	17 27	17 34		17 40	17 48	18 10	18 28	18 40	18 51
	d	16 29	16 51	17 11	17 29			17 41		18 11	18 29	18 41	18 51
Didcot Parkway	a	16 46		17 28	17 46			17 58			18 46	18 59	
Reading 7	a	17 00	17 18	17 42	18 00			18 12		18 42	19 00	19 12	19 21
Slough 3	a												
London Paddington 15 ⊖	a	17 39	17 59	18 21	18 39			18 59		19 21	19 39	19 59	20 06

		GW ◇1 🍴	GW ◇1 🍴	GW ◇1 🍴		GW ◇1 🍴	GW ◇1 🍴	GW	GW	GW ◇1 🍴	GW ◇1 🍴	GW ◇1 🍴	GW ◇1 🍴
Swansea	d	16 51				17j51					18 51		
Neath	d	17 03				18 03					19 03		
Port Talbot Parkway	d	17 10				18 10					19 10		
Bridgend	d	17 22				18 22					19 22		
Cardiff Central 7	d	17 50				18 50					19 50		
Newport (South Wales)	d	18 04				19 04					20 04		
Weston-super-Mare	d						18 53						20 38
Bristol Temple Meads 10	d		18 30	19 00			19k30			20 00			21 00
Bristol Parkway 7	a	18 31				19 31					20 31		
	d	18 33				19 33					20 33		
Bath Spa 7	d		18 43	19 13			19 43			20 13			21 13
Chippenham	d		18 55	19 25			19 55		20 04	20 25			21 25
Cheltenham Spa	d											20 05	
Gloucester 7	d							19 34				20l23	
Stonehouse	d							19 48				20 36	
Stroud	d							19 53				20 42	
Kemble	d							20 07				20 57	
Swindon	a	18 59	19 11	19 40		19 58	20 10	20 23	20 20	20 40	20 59	21 11	21 41
	d	19 01	19 11	19 41		19 59	20 11		20 28	20 41	20 59	21 11	21 41
Didcot Parkway	a	19 18		19 58		20 16				20 59	21 16	21 30	22 00
Reading 7	a	19 32	19 42	20 12		20 32	20 42			21 15	21 32	21 45	22 17
Slough 3	a												
London Paddington 15 ⊖	a	20 09	20 21	20 59		21 09	21 21			22 02	22 09	22 29	23 08

b arr. 1130
c arr. 1223
e arr. 1319
f arr. 1523
g arr. 1721
h arr. 1614
i arr. 1757
j arr. 1739
k arr. 1924
l arr. 2015

For connections from Hereford and Birmingham New Street please refer to Tables 131 and 57. For connections to Oxford, Gatwick Airport and Heathrow Airport please refer to Tables 116, 148 and 125A

Table 125

Sundays
from 12 September

South Wales, Weston-super-Mare, Bristol, Cheltenham Spa and Swindon - London

		GW		GW	GW
		◇1			◇1
		⊡			⊡
Swansea	d	19b59			
Neath	d	20 11			
Port Talbot Parkway	d	20 18			
Bridgend	d	20 30			
Cardiff Central 7	d	20 55			
Newport (South Wales)	d	21 09			
Weston-super-Mare	d				
Bristol Temple Meads 10	d				22 05
Bristol Parkway 7	a	21 36			
	d	21 38			
Bath Spa 7	d				22 19
Chippenham	d				22 31
Cheltenham Spa	d			21 46	
Gloucester 7	d			21 59	
Stonehouse	d			22 12	
Stroud	d			22 17	
Kemble	d			22 32	
Swindon	a	22 04		22 47	22 46
	d	22 05			22 52
Didcot Parkway	a				23 10
Reading 7	a	22 37			23 27
Slough 3	a				
London Paddington 15 ⊖	a	23 20			00 13

b arr. 1953

Table 125A

Mondays to Fridays

Reading - Heathrow Railair Link

Express Coach Service

Reading 7	d
Heathrow Terminal 5 Bus ✈	a
Heathrow Terminal 1 Bus ✈	a
Heathrow Terminal 2 Bus ✈	a
Heathrow Terminal 3 Bus ✈	a

Saturdays

Reading 7	d
Heathrow Terminal 5 Bus ✈	a
Heathrow Terminal 1 Bus ✈	a
Heathrow Terminal 2 Bus ✈	a
Heathrow Terminal 3 Bus ✈	a

Sundays

Reading 7	d
Heathrow Terminal 5 Bus ✈	a
Heathrow Terminal 1 Bus ✈	a
Heathrow Terminal 2 Bus ✈	a
Heathrow Terminal 3 Bus ✈	a

Reading 7	d
Heathrow Terminal 5 Bus ✈	a
Heathrow Terminal 1 Bus ✈	a
Heathrow Terminal 2 Bus ✈	a
Heathrow Terminal 3 Bus ✈	a

Details of service not available at time of going to press

Table 125A

Mondays to Fridays

Heathrow - Reading Railair Link
Express Coach Service

Heathrow Central Bus Stn ✈	d																							
Heathrow Terminal 5 Bus ✈	d																							
Reading 7	a																							

Saturdays

Heathrow Central Bus Stn ✈	d																							
Heathrow Terminal 5 Bus ✈	d																							
Reading 7	a																							

Sundays

Heathrow Central Bus Stn ✈	d																							
Heathrow Terminal 5 Bus ✈	d																							
Reading 7	a																							

Details of service not available at time of going to press

Table 125B

Mondays to Saturdays

Bristol - Bristol International Airport
Bus Service

		GW	GW	GW	GW	GW	GW	GW	GW	GW		GW SX	GW	GW	GW	GW	GW	GW	GW	GW		GW	GW	GW	GW
Bristol Temple Meads 10	d	02 40	03 55	05 25	06 10	06 25	06 40	06 55	07 10	07 25		07 40	07 55	08 10	08 25	08 40	08 55	09 10	09 25	09 40		09 55	10 10	10 25	10 40
Bristol Internatl Airport ✈	a	03 05	04 20	05 50	06 35	06 50	07 05	07 20	07 35	07 50		08 05	08 20	08 35	08 50	09 05	09 20	09 35	09 50	10 05		10 20	10 35	10 50	11 05

		GW	GW	GW	GW	GW		GW	GW	GW	GW	GW	GW	GW	GW	GW		GW	GW	GW	GW	GW	GW	GW	GW SX
Bristol Temple Meads 10	d	10 55	11 10	11 25	11 40	11 55		12 10	12 25	12 40	12 55	13 10	13 25	13 40	13 55	14 10		14 25	14 40	14 55	15 10	15 25	15 40	15 55	16 10
Bristol Internatl Airport ✈	a	11 20	11 35	11 50	12 05	12 20		12 35	12 50	13 05	13 20	13 35	13 50	14 05	14 20	14 35		14 50	15 05	15 20	15 35	15 50	16 05	16 20	16 35

		GW		GW SX	GW SX	GW SX	GW	GW SX	GW	GW SX	GW	GW SX		GW	GW SX	GW	GW	GW	GW	GW	GW	GW		GW	
Bristol Temple Meads 10	d	16 25		16 40	16 55	17 10	17 25	17 40	17 55	18 10	18 25	18 40		18 55	19 10	19 25	19 55	20 25	20 55	21 25	21 55	22 25		22 55	
Bristol Internatl Airport ✈	a	16 50		17 05	17 20	17 35	17 50	18 05	18 20	18 35	18 50	19 05		19 20	19 35	19 50	20 20	20 50	21 20	21 50	22 20	22 50		23 20	

Sundays

		GW	GW	GW	GW	GW	GW	GW	GW	GW		GW	GW	GW	GW	GW	GW	GW	GW	GW		GW	GW	GW	GW
Bristol Temple Meads 10	d	02 40	03 55	05 25	05 55	06 25	06 55	07 25	07 55	08 25		08 55	09 25	09 55	10 25	10 55	11 25	11 55	12 25	12 55		13 25	13 55	14 25	14 40
Bristol Internatl Airport ✈	a	03 05	04 20	05 45	06 20	06 50	07 20	07 50	08 20	08 50		09 20	09 50	10 20	10 50	11 20	11 50	12 20	12 50	13 20		13 50	14 20	14 50	15 05

		GW	GW	GW	GW	GW		GW	GW	GW	GW	GW	GW	GW	GW	GW		GW	GW	GW	GW	GW	GW	GW	GW
Bristol Temple Meads 10	d	14 55	15 10	15 25	15 40	15 55		16 10	16 25	16 40	16 55	17 10	17 25	17 40	17 55	18 10		18 25	18 40	18 55	19 10	19 25	19 55	20 10	20 25
Bristol Internatl Airport ✈	a	15 20	15 35	15 50	16 05	16 20		16 35	16 50	17 05	17 20	17 35	17 50	18 05	18 20	18 35		18 50	19 05	19 20	19 35	19 50	20 20	20 35	20 50

		GW		GW	GW	GW	GW	GW	GW	GW															
Bristol Temple Meads 10	d	20 40		20 55	21 10	21 40	21 55	22 10	22 25	22 55															
Bristol Internatl Airport ✈	a	21 05		21 20	21 35	22 05	22 20	22 35	22 50	23 20															

Table 125B

Mondays to Saturdays

Bristol International Airport - Bristol

Bus Service

		GW MX	GW	GW	GW	GW	GW	GW	GW	GW	GW	GW	GW	GW	GW	GW	GW	GW	GW	GW	GW	GW	GW
Bristol Internatl Airport	✈ d	23p45	03 05	04 20	06 15	06 45	07 00	07 15	07 30	07 45	08 00	08 15	08 30	08 45	09 00	09 15	09 30	09 45	10 00	10 15	10 30	10 45	11 00
Bristol Temple Meads 10	a	00 10	03 30	04 45	06 40	07 10	07 25	07 40	07 55	08 10	08 25	08 40	08 55	09 10	09 25	09 40	09 55	10 10	10 25	10 40	10 55	11 10	11 25

		GW	GW	GW	GW	GW	GW	GW	GW	GW	GW	GW	GW	GW	GW	GW	GW	GW	GW	GW	GW	GW SX	GW
Bristol Internatl Airport	✈ d	11 15	11 30	11 45	12 00	12 15	12 30	12 45	13 00	13 15	13 30	13 45	14 00	14 15	14 30	14 45	15 00	15 15	15 30	15 45	16 00	16 15	16 30
Bristol Temple Meads 10	a	11 40	11 55	12 10	12 25	12 40	12 55	13 10	13 25	13 40	13 55	14 10	14 25	14 40	14 55	15 10	15 25	15 40	15 55	16 10	16 25	16 40	16 55

		GW SX	GW	GW SX	GW	GW SX	GW	GW SX	GW	GW SX	GW	GW SX	GW	GW	GW	GW	GW	GW	GW	GW	GW	GW
Bristol Internatl Airport	✈ d	16 45	17 00	17 15	17 30	17 45	18 00	18 15	18 30	18 45	19 00	19 15	19 30	20 00	20 30	21 00	21 30	22 00	22 15	22 45	23 15	23 45
Bristol Temple Meads 10	a	17 10	17 25	17 40	17 55	18 10	18 25	18 40	18 55	19 10	19 25	19 40	19 55	20 25	20 55	21 25	21 55	22 25	22 40	23 10	23 40	00 10

Sundays

		GW A	GW	GW	GW	GW	GW	GW	GW	GW	GW	GW	GW	GW	GW	GW	GW	GW	GW	GW	GW	GW	GW
Bristol Internatl Airport	✈ d	23p45	03 05	04 20	06 00	07 00	07 30	08 00	08 30	09 00	09 30	10 00	10 30	11 00	12 00	12 30	13 00	13 30	14 00	14 30	14 45	15 00	15 15
Bristol Temple Meads 10	a	00 10	03 30	04 45	06 25	07 25	07 55	08 25	08 55	09 25	09 55	10 25	10 55	11 25	12 25	12 55	13 25	13 55	14 25	14 55	15 10	15 25	15 40

		GW	GW	GW	GW	GW	GW	GW	GW	GW	GW	GW	GW	GW	GW	GW	GW	GW	GW	GW	GW	GW	GW
Bristol Internatl Airport	✈ d	15 30	15 45	16 00	16 15	16 30	16 45	17 00	17 15	17 30	17 45	18 00	18 30	18 45	19 00	19 15	19 30	19 45	20 00	20 15	20 30	20 45	21 15
Bristol Temple Meads 10	a	15 55	16 10	16 25	16 40	16 55	17 10	17 25	17 40	17 55	18 10	18 25	18 55	19 10	19 25	19 40	19 55	20 10	20 25	20 40	20 55	21 10	21 40

		GW	GW	GW	GW	GW	GW	GW	GW	GW
Bristol Internatl Airport	✈ d	21 30	21 45	22 00	22 15	22 30	22 45	23 00	23 15	23 30
Bristol Temple Meads 10	a	21 55	22 10	22 25	22 40	22 55	23 10	23 25	23 40	23 55

A not 23 May

Table 125C

Mondays to Fridays

Cardiff - Cardiff International Airport

Bus Service

		GW	GW	GW	GW	GW	GW	GW	GW	GW	GW	GW	GW	GW
Cardiff Central Bus Stn	d	05 10	08 00	08 57	10 02	11 02	12 02	13 02	14 02	15 02	16 02	17 12	17 40	18 20
Cardiff International Apt	✈ a	05 39	08 35	09 26	10 31	11 31	12 31	13 31	14 31	15 31	16 33	17 50	18 12	18 50

Saturdays

		GW	GW	GW	GW	GW	GW	GW	GW	GW	GW	GW	GW	GW
Cardiff Central Bus Stn	d	05 10	08 02	09 02	10 02	11 02	12 02	13 02	14 02	15 02	16 02	17 12	17 40	18 20
Cardiff International Apt	✈ a	05 39	08 31	09 31	10 31	11 31	12 31	13 31	14 31	15 31	16 31	17 41	18 12	18 49

Sundays

		GW	GW	GW	GW	GW	GW	GW
Cardiff Central Bus Stn	d	08 30	10 02	12 02	14 02	16 02	18 02	19 15
Cardiff International Apt	✈ a	08 59	10 31	12 31	14 31	16 31	18 31	19 44

Table 125C

Cardiff International Airport - Cardiff

Bus Service

		GW	GW	GW	GW	GW	GW	GW	GW	GW	GW	GW	GW	GW	GW	GW
		🚌	🚌	🚌	🚌	🚌	🚌	🚌	🚌	🚌	🚌	🚌	🚌	🚌	🚌	🚌
Cardiff International Apt ✈	d	07 16	07 51	09 35	10 35	11 05	11 35	12 35	13 35	14 35	15 05	15 35	16 40	17 41	18 51	20 25
Cardiff Central Bus Stn	a	07 50	08 32	10 06	11 06	11 36	12 06	13 06	14 06	15 06	15 36	16 06	17 16	18 12	19 21	20 55

Saturdays

		GW	GW	GW	GW	GW	GW	GW	GW	GW	GW	GW	GW	GW
		🚌	🚌	🚌	🚌	🚌	🚌	🚌	🚌	🚌	🚌	🚌	🚌	🚌
Cardiff International Apt ✈	d	07 25	08 00	09 35	10 35	11 35	12 35	13 35	14 35	15 35	16 40	17 40	18 51	20 25
Cardiff Central Bus Stn	a	07 56	08 31	10 06	11 06	12 06	13 06	14 06	15 06	16 06	17 11	18 11	19 23	20 55

Sundays

		GW	GW	GW	GW	GW	GW	GW
		🚌	🚌	🚌	🚌	🚌	🚌	🚌
Cardiff International Apt ✈	d	09 05	10 40	12 40	14 40	16 40	18 40	20 25
Cardiff Central Bus Stn	a	09 35	11 10	13 10	15 10	17 10	19 10	21 01

Table 126

London and Oxford - Worcester and Hereford

		GW	GW	GW	GW	GW	GW	GW	GW	GW	GW	GW	GW	GW	GW	GW
		■1	■1	◇■1	◇■1	◇■1	◇■1	◇■1	◇■1	◇■1	■1	◇■1	◇■1	◇■1	◇■1	◇■1
			🍴	🛒	🍴	🛒	🛒	🍴		🛒		🛒	🛒	🛒	🛒	🍴
London Paddington ■15 ⊖	d		06 48	08 22	09 21	10 22	11 22	13 21	14 21	15 51		17 22	17 50	18 22	19 22	20 20
Slough ■3	d		07 04	08 36	09 36	10 36	11 36	13 36	14 36	16 06					19 36	20 36
Reading ■7	d		07 22	08 52	09 52	10 52	11 52	13 52	14 52	16 22		17 50	18 22	18 50	19 52	20 52
Didcot Parkway	d		07 50													
Oxford	d		08 04	09 21	10 25	11 19	12 19	14 19	15 19	16 47	17 31	18 16	18 54	19 21	20 20	21 18
Hanborough	d			09 31	10 35	11 29	12 29	14 29	15 30	16 58	17 40	18 26		19 31	20 30	21 27
Combe	d										17 43					
Finstock	d										17 48					
Charlbury	d			09 39	10 42	11 37	12 37	14 37	15 37	17 06	17 52	18 35	19 09	19 40	20 38	21 35
Ascott-under-Wychwood	d										17 57					
Shipton	d										18 00		19 16			
Kingham	d		08 25	09 49	10 51	11 47	12 47	14 46	15 46	17 15	18 05	18 45	19 23	19 50	20 48	21 45
Moreton-in-Marsh	a		08 33	09 58	11 00	11 56	12 56	14 54	15 56	17 24	18 13	18 54	19 32	19 59	20 57	21 54
	d	05 37	08 34	09 59	11 01	11 57	12 57	14 58		17 25	18 14	18 55	19 35	20 00	20 58	21 54
Honeybourne	d		08 46	10 11		12 09	13 09	15 09		17 37	18 26	19 07		20 11	21 10	22 06
Evesham	a	05 51	08 53	10 19	11 16	12 17	13 17	15 16		17 45	18 33	19 15	19 52	20 19	21 18	22 14
	d	06 06	08 54	10 29	11 18	12 29	13 19	15 19		17 47	18 41	19 21	19 57	20 20	21 25	22 15
Pershore	d	06 14	09 02	10 37		12 37	13 27	15 27		17 55	18 49	19 29	20 05	20 28	21 33	22 23
Worcester Shrub Hill ■7	a	06 32	09 16	10 51	11 35	12 50	13 39	15 39		18 07	19 11	19 44	20 23	20 41	21 46	22 39
Worcester Foregate Street ■7	a	06 38	09 19	10 55	11 39	12 54	13 43	15 47			19 17	19 48		20 45	21 52	22 44
Malvern Link	a		09 28	11 05		13 03	13 53	15 57				19 58		20 54	22 04	22 53
Great Malvern	a		09 31	11 09		13 07	13 57	16 00				20 02		20 58	22 08	22 57
Colwall	a			11 15		13 15						20 08		21 04	22 25	
Ledbury	a			11 23		13 23						20 16		21 12	22 33	
Hereford ■7	a			11 44		13 45						20 34		21 31	22 52	

Saturdays

		GW	GW	GW	GW	GW	GW	GW	GW	GW	GW	GW	GW
		◇■1	◇■1	◇■1	◇■1	◇■1	◇■1	◇■1	◇■1	◇■1	◇■1	◇■1	◇■1
			🍴	🛒	🛒	🍴	🍴	🍴	🍴	🛒	🛒	🛒	🍴
London Paddington ■15 ⊖	d	06 21	07 21	08 21	10 21	11 21	13 21	14 21	15 21	16 21	17 21	18 21	19 50
Slough ■3	d	06 38	07 38	08 39	10 39	11 39	13 39	14 39	15 39	16 39	17 39	18 39	20 06
Reading ■7	d	06 54	07 53	08 54	10 54	11 55	13 55	14 54	15 55	16 54	17 55	18 54	20 22
Didcot Parkway	d												
Oxford	d	07 21	08 21	09 21	11 21	12 23	14 21	15 21	16 21	17 21	18 21	19 21	20 49
Hanborough	d	07 31	08 31	09 31	11 31	12 33	14 31	15 31	16 31	17 31	18 31	19 31	20 58
Combe	d												
Finstock	d												
Charlbury	d	07 39	08 39	09 39	11 39	12 41	14 39	15 39	16 39	17 39	18 39	19 39	21 06
Ascott-under-Wychwood	d												
Shipton	d						14 46			17 46			21 12
Kingham	d	07 49	08 49	09 49	11 49	12 51	14 49	15 49	16 49	17 50	18 49	19 49	21 17
Moreton-in-Marsh	a	07 58	08 58	09 59	11 58	13 00	14 59	15 57	16 57	18 00	18 57	19 58	21 25
	d	08 00	09 00	10 00	12 00	13 02	15 00	16 00	17 00	18 00	19 00	20 00	21 28
Honeybourne	d	08 11	09 11	10 11	12 11	13 13	15 11	16 11	17 11	18 11	19 11	20 11	21 39
Evesham	a	08 22	09 22	10 21	12 19	13 21	15 21	16 18	17 22	18 22	19 19	20 19	21 46
	d	08 24	09 24	10 24	12 24	13 24	15 24	16 24	17 24	18 24	19 22	20 27	21 49
Pershore	d	08 32	09 32	10 32	12 32	13 32	15 32	16 32	17 32	18 32	19 30	20 35	21 56
Worcester Shrub Hill ■7	a	08 43	09 43	10 44	12 43	13 44	15 43	16 44	17 43	18 44	19 41	20 46	22 08
Worcester Foregate Street ■7	a	08 47	09 46	10 48	12 48	13 47	15 47	16 48	17 47	18 54	19 45	20 50	22 11
Malvern Link	a	08 57	09 57	10 57	12 57	13 57	15 57	16 57	17 57	19 03		21 00	22 20
Great Malvern	a	09 04	10 04	11 04	13 04	14 04	16 04	17 04	18 04	19 07		21 04	22 27
Colwall	a			11 13	13 13					19 13		21 10	
Ledbury	a			11 21	13 21					19 21		21 18	
Hereford ■7	a			11 42	13 42					19 45		21 36	

Sundays

until 05 September

		GW	GW	GW	GW	GW	GW
		◇■1	◇■1	◇■1	◇■1	◇■1	◇■1
		🍴	🛒	🛒	🛒	🛒	
London Paddington ■15 ⊖	d	08 03	09 35	10 42	12 42	13 42	21 27
Slough ■3	d	08 27	09 51	10 59	12 58	13 58	21 49
Reading ■7	d	08 50	10 12	11 21	13 21	14 21	22 08
Didcot Parkway	d	09 05	10 28	11 37	13 36	14 36	22 24
Oxford	d	09 17	10 44	11 51	13 51	14 51	22 40
Hanborough	d	09 27	10 55	12 02	14 01		22 55
Combe	d						
Finstock	d						
Charlbury	d	09 34	11 03	12 09	14 09	15 05	23 03
Ascott-under-Wychwood	d						
Shipton	d						
Kingham	d	09 43	11 13	12 20	14 19	15 14	23 13
Moreton-in-Marsh	a	09 51	11 21	12 28	14 28	15 24	23 21
	d	09 57	11 22	12 30	14 29	15 24	23 23
Honeybourne	d	10 08	11 34	12 42		15 38	23 35
Evesham	a	10 15	11 41	12 49	14 47	15 46	23 41
	d	10 17	11 44	12 49	14 48	15 49	23 44
Pershore	d	10 25	11 52	12 59	14 57	15 57	23 52
Worcester Shrub Hill ■7	a	10 36	12 03	13 10	15 09	16 08	00 03
Worcester Foregate Street ■7	a	10 39	12 07	13 14	15 13		
Malvern Link	a	10 49	12 17	13 24	15 22		
Great Malvern	a	10 54	12 20	13 28	15 26		
Colwall	a		12 27	13 34	15 33		
Ledbury	a		12 35	13 42	15 41		
Hereford ■7	a		12 58	14 04	16 07		

Table 126

Sundays from 12 September

London and Oxford - Worcester and Hereford

		GW	GW	GW	GW	GW	GW
		◇1	◇1	◇1	◇1	◇1	◇1
		🛒	☕	☕	☕	☕	
London Paddington 15 ⊖	d	08 00	09 35	10 42	12 42	13 42	21 27
Slough 3	d	08 24	09 57	11 05	13 05	14 05	21 53
Reading 7	d	08 44	10 11	11 20	13 21	14 21	22 08
Didcot Parkway	d	09 05	10 27	11 36	13 36	14 36	22 24
Oxford	d	09 17	10 43	11 50	13 51	14 51	22 40
Hanborough	d	09 27	10 54	12 01	14 01		22 55
Combe	d						
Finstock	d						
Charlbury	d	09 34	11 02	12 09	14 09	15 05	23 03
Ascott-under-Wychwood	d						
Shipton	d						
Kingham	d	09 43	11 12	12 19	14 19	15 14	23 13
Moreton-in-Marsh	a	09 51	11 20	12 27	14 28	15 24	23 21
	d	09 57	11 22	12 29	14 29	15 24	23 23
Honeybourne	d	10 08	11 34	12 42		15 37	23 35
Evesham	a	10 15	11 41	12 49	14 47	15 46	23 41
	d	10 17	11 44	12 49	14 48	15 49	23 44
Pershore	d	10 25	11 52	12 59	14 57	15 57	23 52
Worcester Shrub Hill 7	a	10 36	12 03	13 10	15 09	16 08	00 03
Worcester Foregate Street 7	a	10 39	12 07	13 14	15 13		
Malvern Link	a	10 49	12 17	13 24	15 22		
Great Malvern	a	10 54	12 20	13 28	15 26		
Colwall	a		12 27	13 34	15 33		
Ledbury	a		12 35	13 42	15 41		
Hereford 7	a		12 54	14 05	16 07		

Table 126

Mondays to Fridays

Hereford and Worcester - Oxford and London

		GW	GW	GW	GW	GW	GW	GW	GW	GW	GW	GW	GW	GW	GW	GW	GW
		◇1	◇1	◇1	1	◇1	1	◇1	◇1	◇1	◇1	◇1	1	◇1	◇1	◇1	1
		☕	☕	☕Ø		☕Ø		🛒	🛒	🛒	☕	☕		☕	🛒	☕	
Hereford 7	d			05 34		06 43					13 11			15 11			
Ledbury	d			05 50		07 00					13 30			15 27			
Colwall	d			05 58		07 09					13 37			15 35			
Great Malvern	d		05 17	06 03		07 14		08 58	09 54		13 47	14 34		15 40	17 00		
Malvern Link	d		05 20	06 07		07 18		09 00	09 56		13 51	14 37		15 44	17 02		
Worcester Foregate Street 7	d		05 31	06 18	06 51	07 30		09 09	10 05	12 06	14 02	14 52		16 02	17 20	18 49	19 27
Worcester Shrub Hill 7	d	05 02	05 35	06 26	06 53	07 35		09 12	10 08	12 08	14 06	14 56		16 06	17 24	18 53	19 29
Pershore	d		05 44	06 35	07 02	07 44		09 21	10 17	12 17	14 15	15 05		16 16	17 34	19 08	19 45
Evesham	a	05 16	05 53	06 44	07 10	07 53		09 29	10 26	12 26	14 24	15 14		16 25	17 42	19 17	19 54
	d	05 18	05 55	06 45	07 11	07 54		09 30	10 27	12 27	14 26	15 22		16 30	17 51	19 19	20 22
Honeybourne	d		06 02	06 52		08 01		09 37	10 34	12 34	14 33	15 29		16 37	17 57		20 29
Moreton-in-Marsh	a	05 34	06 14	07 05	07 27	08 14		09 49	10 47	12 47	14 45	15 41		16 49	18 09	19 35	20 42
	d	05 48	06 16	07 06	07 27	08 15	09 29	09 50	10 47	12 47	14 47	15 43	16 14	16 51	18 12	19 36	20 43
Kingham	d	05 56	06 24	07 15	07 36	08 24	09 37	09 58	10 56	12 56	14 55	15 51	16 21	16 59	18 20	19 45	20 52
Shipton	d				07 40									17 05			
Ascott-under-Wychwood	d				07 44												
Charlbury	d	06 06	06 34	07 26	07 49	08 35	09 52	10 08	11 05	13 05	15 05	16 01	16 31	17 18	18 47	19 55	21 01
Finstock	d				07 53												
Combe	d				07 58												
Hanborough	d	06 14	06 42	07 34	08 01			10 15	11 13	13 13	15 13	16 09		17 26		20 03	21 09
Oxford	a	06 25	06 54	07 46	08 12	08 49	10 05	10 26	11 28	13 25	15 25	16 27	16 46	17 36	19 01	20 18	21 20
Didcot Parkway	a	06 39	07 07				10 24						17 04				
Reading 7	a	06 54	07 25	08 21		09 14	10 58	10 54	11 54	13 54	15 54	16 54		18 01	19 25	20 54	
Slough 3	a						11 24	11 09	12 09	14 09	16 09	17 09			19 39	21 09	
London Paddington 15 ⊖	a	07 29	07 59	08 51		09 47	12 01	11 29	12 29	14 29	16 27	17 27		18 30	20 00	21 29	

Saturdays

		GW	GW	GW	GW	GW	GW	GW	GW	GW	GW	GW	GW	GW	GW	GW	GW
		◇1	◇1	◇1	◇1	◇1	◇1	◇1	◇1	◇1	◇1	◇1	◇1	◇1	◇1	◇1	1
				A		B	C	B	C			D	E				
		☕	☕	☕Ø	☕	🛒	🛒	☕	☕	🛒	☕	🛒	🛒	🛒	🛒		
Hereford 7	d			07 10				12 13	12 13		15 10						
Ledbury	d			07 30				12 31	12 31		15 29						
Colwall	d			07 38				12 39	12 39		15 36						
Great Malvern	d	05 39	06 35	07 43	08 43	09 43	09 43	12 43	12 43	14 32	15 42	16 32	16 32	17 43	18 29		22 40
Malvern Link	d	05 42	06 39	07 46	08 46	09 46	09 46	12 46	12 46	14 35	15 45	16 35	16 35	17 46	18 31		22 43
Worcester Foregate Street 7	d	05 52	06 50	07 57	08 57	09 57	09 57	12 57	12 57	14 57	15 56	16 57	16 57	17 57	18 42	20 02	22 51
Worcester Shrub Hill 7	d	05 56	06 54	08 02	09 02	10 02	10 02	13 02	13 02	15 02	16 02	17 02	17 02	18 02	19 00	20 06	22 54
Pershore	d	06 06	07 03	08 11	09 11	10 11	10 11	13 11	13 11	15 11	16 11	17 11	17 11	18 11	19 09	20 15	23 03
Evesham	a	06 14	07 11	08 20	09 20	10 19	10 19	13 21	13 21	15 19	16 20	17 19	17 19	18 20	19 17	20 23	23 12
	d	06 23	07 25	08 27	09 27	10 27	10 27	13 27	13 27	15 27	16 26	17 27	17 27	18 27	19 27	20 37	
Honeybourne	d	06 30	07 32	08 33	09 33	10 33	10 33	13 33	13 33	15 33	16 32	17 33	17 33	18 33	19 33	20 44	
Moreton-in-Marsh	a	06 42	07 43	08 45	09 46	10 46	10 46	13 45	13 45	15 45	16 46	17 46	17 46	18 46	19 45	20 57	
	d	06 45	07 45	08 48	09 48	10 48	10 48	13 48	13 48	15 48	16 47	17 48	17 48	18 48	19 48	20 58	
Kingham	d	06 54	07 54	08 56	09 56	10 56	10 56	13 56	13 56	15 56	16 56	17 56	17 56	18 56	19 56	21 07	
Shipton	d		08 00	09 02							17 01						
Ascott-under-Wychwood	d																
Charlbury	d	07 04	08 08	09 08	10 08	11 08	11 08	14 08	14 08	16 08	17 08	18 08	18 08	19 08	20 08	21 18	
Finstock	d																
Combe	d																
Hanborough	d	07 12	08 16	09 16	10 16	11 16	11 16	14 16	14 16	16 16	17 16	18 16	18 16	19 16	20 16	21 26	
Oxford	a	07 22	08 28	09 28	10 28	11 28	11 28	14 28	14 28	16 28	17 28	18 28	18 28	19 28	20 28	21 36	
Didcot Parkway	a															21 49	
Reading 7	a	07 54	08 54	09 54	10 54	11 54	11 54	14 54	14 54	16 54	17 54	18 54	18 56	19 54	20 54	22 04	
Slough 3	a	08 09	09 09	10 09	11 09	12 09		15 10	15 09	17 09	18 09	19 09	19 12	20 09	21 09	22 22	
London Paddington 15 ⊖	a	08 29	09 29	10 29	11 29	12 29	12 29	15 29	15 29	17 29	18 29	19 29	19 32	20 29	21 29	22 39	

B from 11 September
C until 4 September
D until 10 July
E from 17 July until 4 September

Table 126

Sundays until 05 September

Hereford and Worcester - Oxford and London

		GW	GW	GW	GW	GW	GW	GW	GW	GW	GW	GW	GW
		◇1	◇1	◇1	◇1	◇1	◇1	◇1	◇1	◇1	◇1	◇1	◇1
		A	B										
		🛒	🛒	🛒		☕	☕	☕	☕	☕	🛒		
Hereford 7	d					13 28	14 30		16 33		18 30		
Ledbury	d					13 46	14 55		16 50		18 48		
Colwall	d					13 53	15 02		16 58		18 55		
Great Malvern	d	09 00	09 00	11 07	13 10	13 59	15 08		17 03		19b08	20 08	20 55
Malvern Link	d	09 03	09 03	11 10	13 13	14 03	15 12		17 07		19 12	20 11	20 59
Worcester Foregate Street 7	d	09 12	09 12	11 19	13 23	14 14	15 23		17 21	18 25	19 25	20 25	21 10
Worcester Shrub Hill 7	d	09 17	09 17	11 22	13 27	14 19	15 27	16 27	17 27	18 27	19 27	20 27	21c18
Pershore	d	09 26	09 26	11 31	13 36	14 28	15 36	16 36	17 36	18 36	19 36	20 36	21 28
Evesham	a	09 34	09 34	11 40	13 44	14 36	15 45	16 45	17 45	18 45	19 45	20 46	21 36
	d	09 36	09 36	11 46	13 47	14 51	15 52	16 52	17 50	18 52	19 52	20 52	21 51
Honeybourne	d	09 42	09 42	11 52	13 52		15 58	16 58		19 00	20 00	21 00	21 59
Moreton-in-Marsh	a	09 55	09 55	12 04	14 05	15 06	16 11	17 11	18 05	19 13	20 12	21 12	22 12
	d	09 56	09 56	12 07	14 07	15 09	16 12	17 12	18 07	19 13	20 13	21 13	22 12
Kingham	d	10 04	10 04	12 15	14 15	15 16	16 20	17 20	18 15	19 22	20 22	21 22	22 22
Shipton	d												
Ascott-under-Wychwood	d												
Charlbury	d	10 15	10 15	12 24	14 25	15 27	16 29	17 30	18 25	19 31	20 31	21 32	22 31
Finstock	d												
Combe	d												
Hanborough	d	10 22	10 22	12 32	14 33	15 35	16 38	17 38		19 40	20 40	21 40	22 40
Oxford	a	10 33	10 33	12 40	14 40	15 48	16 50	17 50	18 39	19 49	20 49	21 49	22 48
Didcot Parkway	a	10 52	10 52	12 55	14 55	16 02	17 03	18 03	18 53	20 04	21 04	22 03	
Reading 7	a	11 08	11 09	13 12	15 12	16 19	17 20	18 20	19 09	20 22	21 19	22 22	
Slough 3	a	11 30	11 35	13 30	15 31	16 48	17 50	18 50	19 34	20 48	21 42	22 47	
London Paddington 15 ⊖	a	11 52	11 54	13 53	15 53	17 06	18 09	19 07	19 52	21 07	22 04	23 13	

Sundays from 12 September

		GW	GW	GW	GW	GW	GW	GW	GW	GW	GW	GW
		◇1	◇1	◇1	◇1	◇1	◇1	◇1	◇1	◇1	◇1	◇1
		🛒	🛒		☕	☕	☕	☕	☕	🛒		
Hereford 7	d				13 28	14 30		16 33		18 30		
Ledbury	d				13 46	14 55		16 50		18 48		
Colwall	d				13 53	15 02		16 58		18 55		
Great Malvern	d	09 00	11 07	13 10	13 59	15 08		17 03		19b11	20 10	20 55
Malvern Link	d	09 03	11 10	13 13	14 03	15 12		17 07		19 14	20 11	20 59
Worcester Foregate Street 7	d	09 12	11 19	13 23	14 14	15 23		17 22	18 25	19 25	20 24	21 10
Worcester Shrub Hill 7	d	09 17	11 22	13 27	14 19	15 27	16 27	17 27	18 27	19 27	20 27	21c18
Pershore	d	09 26	11 31	13 36	14 28	15 36	16 36	17 36	18 36	19 36	20 36	21 28
Evesham	a	09 34	11 40	13 44	14 36	15 45	16 45	17 45	18 45	19 45	20 46	21 36
	d	09 36	11 46	13 47	14 50	15 51	16 52	17 50	18 51	19 52	20 52	21 51
Honeybourne	d	09 42	11 52	13 52		15 57	16 58	17 59	18 58	19 59	20 59	21 59
Moreton-in-Marsh	a	09 55	12 04	14 05	15 05	16 11	17 11	18 11	19 10	20 12	21 12	22 12
	d	09 56	12 07	14 07	15 07	16 12	17 12	18 12	19 12	20 12	21 12	22 12
Kingham	d	10 04	12 15	14 15	15 15	16 20	17 20	18 22	19 21	20 22	21 22	22 22
Shipton	d											
Ascott-under-Wychwood	d											
Charlbury	d	10 15	12 25	14 25	15 25	16 29	17 30	18 32	19 30	20 32	21 32	22 31
Finstock	d											
Combe	d											
Hanborough	d	10 22	12 33	14 33	15 33	16 38	17 38		19 39	20 40	21 40	22 40
Oxford	a	10 34	12 48	14 50	15 48	16 50	17 50	18 49	19 49	20 49	21 49	22 48
Didcot Parkway	a	11 02	13 02	15 02	16 01	17 03	18 03	19 03	20 04	21 04	22 03	
Reading 7	a	11 20	13 20	15 20	16 19	17 20	18 20	19 19	20 22	21 19	22 21	
Slough 3	a	11 38	11 36	15 35	16 34	17 39	18 35	19 35	20 38	21 39	22 47	
London Paddington 15 ⊖	a	11 59	13 59	15 58	16 59	18 05	19 02	20 02	21 02	22 05	23 13	

A from 18 July
B until 11 July
b arr. 1900
c arr. 2112

Table 126A

Mondays to Fridays

Kingham - Chipping Norton

Bus Service

		GW	GW	GW	GW	GW	GW	GW	GW	GW	GW	GW	GW	GW	GW	GW	GW	GW
		BHX	BHX	BHX	BHX	BHX	BHX	BHX	BHX	BHX	BHX	BHX	BHX	BHX	BHX	BHX	BHX	BHX
		🚌	🚌	🚌	🚌	🚌	🚌	🚌	🚌	🚌	🚌	🚌	🚌	🚌	🚌	🚌	🚌	🚌
Kingham	d	06 30	07 00	07 30	08 30	09 55	10 55	11 55	12 55	13 55	14 55	15 50	16 35	17 20	18 10	18 50	19 25	19 50
Chipping Norton West St	a	06 43	07 13	07 43	08 43	10 08	11 08	12 08	13 08	14 08	15 08	16 03	16 48	17 33	18 23	19 03	19 38	20 03

Saturdays

		GW	GW	GW	GW	GW	GW	GW	GW	GW	GW	GW	GW	GW
		🚌	🚌	🚌	🚌	🚌	🚌	🚌	🚌	🚌	🚌	🚌	🚌	🚌
Kingham	d	08 15	08 55	09 55	10 55	11 55	12 55	13 55	14 55	15 50	16 50	17 55	18 50	19 50
Chipping Norton West St	a	08 28	09 08	10 08	11 08	12 08	13 08	14 08	15 08	16 03	17 03	18 08	19 03	20 03

Sundays

		GW	GW	GW
		🚌	🚌	🚌
Kingham	d	13 17	17 17	18 22
Chipping Norton West St	a	13 29	17 29	18 34

Table 126A

Mondays to Fridays

Chipping Norton - Kingham

Bus Service

		GW BHX	GW BHX	GW BHX	GW BHX	GW BHX	GW BHX	GW BHX	GW BHX	GW BHX	GW BHX	GW BHX	GW BHX	GW BHX	GW BHX	GW BHX	GW BHX
Chipping Norton West St	d	06 07	06 45	07 15	08 00	09 30	10 35	11 35	12 35	13 35	14 35	15 30	16 20	16 55	17 45	18 25	19 10
Kingham	a	06 19	06 58	07 28	08 14	09 44	10 50	11 50	12 50	13 50	14 50	15 45	16 35	17 10	18 00	18 40	19 25

Saturdays

		GW	GW	GW	GW	GW	GW	GW	GW	GW	GW	GW	GW	GW
Chipping Norton West St	d	08 00	08 30	09 30	10 35	11 35	12 35	13 35	14 35	15 30	16 35	17 30	18 25	19 10
Kingham	a	08 14	08 44	09 44	10 50	11 50	12 50	13 50	14 50	15 45	16 50	17 45	18 40	19 25

Sundays

		GW	GW	GW
Chipping Norton West St	d	09 25	13 33	17 59
Kingham	a	09 39	13 47	18 13

Route Diagram for Tables 127, 128

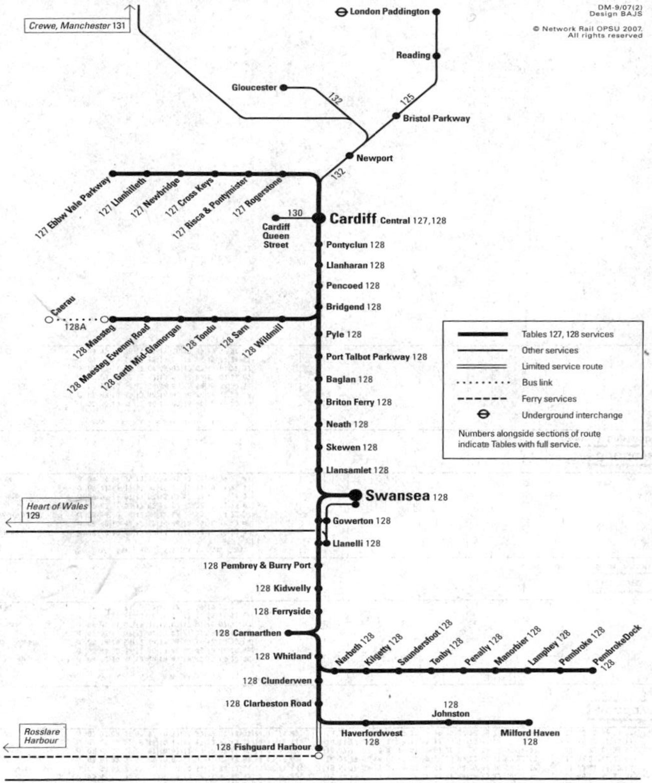

Table 127

Mondays to Saturdays

Cardiff Central - Ebbw Vale Parkway

		AW	AW	AW	AW	AW	AW	AW	AW	AW	AW	AW	AW	AW	AW	AW	AW	AW
Cardiff Central 7	d	06 35	07 39	08 35	09 35	10 35	11 35	12 35	13 35	14 35	15 35	16 35	17 35	18 35	19 35	20 35	21 35	22 35
Rogerstone	d	06 57	08 00	08 57	09 57	10 57	11 57	12 57	13 57	14 57	15 57	16 57	17 57	18 57	19 57	20 57	21 57	22 57
Risca & Pontymister	d	07 00	08 04	09 00	10 00	11 00	12 00	13 00	14 00	15 00	16 00	17 00	18 00	19 00	20 00	21 00	22 00	23 00
Cross Keys	d	07 06	08 09	09 06	10 06	11 06	12 06	13 06	14 06	15 06	16 06	17 06	18 06	19 06	20 06	21 06	22 06	23 06
Newbridge (Ebbw Vale)	d	07 14	08 17	09 14	10 14	11 14	12 14	13 14	14 14	15 14	16 14	17 14	18 14	19 14	20 14	21 14	22 14	23 14
Llanhilleth	d	07 20	08 23	09 20	10 20	11 20	12 20	13 20	14 20	15 20	16 20	17 20	18 20	19 20	20 20	21 20	22 20	23 20
Ebbw Vale Parkway	a	07 31	08 32	09 31	10 31	11 31	12 31	13 31	14 31	15 31	16 31	17 31	18 31	19 31	20 31	21 31	22 31	23 31

Sundays
until 11 July

		AW	AW	AW	AW	AW	AW	AW
Cardiff Central 7	d	07 40	09 35	11 30	13 30	15 30	17 30	19 30
Rogerstone	d	08 03	09 56	11 51	13 51	15 51	17 51	19 51
Risca & Pontymister	d	08 07	10 00	11 55	13 55	15 55	17 55	19 55
Cross Keys	d	08 13	10 06	12 01	14 01	16 01	18 01	20 01
Newbridge (Ebbw Vale)	d	08 21	10 14	12 09	14 09	16 09	18 09	20 09
Llanhilleth	d	08 28	10 21	12 16	14 16	16 16	18 16	20 16
Ebbw Vale Parkway	a	08 39	10 32	12 27	14 27	16 27	18 27	20 27

Sundays
18 July to 05 September

		AW	AW	AW	AW	AW	AW	AW
Cardiff Central 7	d	07 40	09 35	11 30	13 30	15 30	17 30	19 30
Rogerstone	d	08 03	09 58	11 53	13 53	15 53	17 53	19 53
Risca & Pontymister	d	08 07	10 02	11 57	13 57	15 57	17 57	19 57
Cross Keys	d	08 13	10 08	12 03	14 03	16 03	18 03	20 03
Newbridge (Ebbw Vale)	d	08 21	10 16	12 11	14 11	16 11	18 11	20 11
Llanhilleth	d	08 28	10 23	12 18	14 18	16 18	18 18	20 18
Ebbw Vale Parkway	a	08 39	10 34	12 29	14 29	16 29	18 29	20 29

Sundays
from 12 September

		AW	AW	AW	AW	AW	AW	AW
Cardiff Central 7	d	07 40	09 35	11 30	13 30	15 30	17 30	19 30
Rogerstone	d	08 03	09 56	11 51	13 51	15 51	17 51	19 51
Risca & Pontymister	d	08 07	10 00	11 55	13 55	15 55	17 55	19 55
Cross Keys	d	08 13	10 06	12 01	14 01	16 01	18 01	20 01
Newbridge (Ebbw Vale)	d	08 21	10 14	12 09	14 09	16 09	18 09	20 09
Llanhilleth	d	08 28	10 21	12 16	14 16	16 16	18 16	20 16
Ebbw Vale Parkway	a	08 39	10 32	12 27	14 27	16 27	18 27	20 27

Table 127

Mondays to Saturdays

Ebbw Vale Parkway - Cardiff Central

		AW	AW	AW	AW	AW	AW	AW	AW	AW	AW	AW	AW	AW SO	AW SX	AW SO	AW SX	AW	AW FO	AW FSX	AW SO	AW
Ebbw Vale Parkway	d	06 40	07 40	08 40	09 40	10 40	11 40	12 40	13 40	14 40	15 40	16 40	17 40	18 40	18 40	19 40	19 40	20 40	21 40	21 40	21 40	22 40
Llanhilleth	d	06 48	07 48	08 48	09 48	10 48	11 48	12 48	13 48	14 48	15 48	16 48	17 48	18 48	18 48	19 48	19 48	20 48	21 48	21 48	21 48	22 48
Newbridge (Ebbw Vale)	d	06 54	07 54	08 54	09 54	10 54	11 54	12 54	13 54	14 54	15 54	16 54	17 54	18 54	18 54	19 54	19 54	20 54	21 54	21 54	21 54	22 54
Cross Keys	d	07 02	08 02	09 02	10 02	11 02	12 02	13 02	14 02	15 02	16 02	17 02	18 02	19 02	19 02	20 02	20 02	21 02	22 02	22 02	22 02	23 02
Risca & Pontymister	d	07 07	08 07	09 07	10 07	11 07	12 07	13 07	14 07	15 07	16 07	17 07	18 07	19 07	19 07	20 07	20 07	21 07	22 07	22 07	22 07	23 07
Rogerstone	d	07 11	08 11	09 11	10 11	11 11	12 11	13 11	14 11	15 11	16 11	17 11	18 11	19 11	19 11	20 11	20 11	21 11	22 11	22 11	22 11	23 11
Cardiff Central 7	a	07 37	08 37	09 37	10 37	11 37	12 37	13 37	14 37	15 37	16 37	17 36	18 37	19 37	19 39	20 37	20 39	21 37	22 41	22 40	22 39	23 37

Sundays
until 11 July

		AW	AW	AW	AW	AW	AW	AW
Ebbw Vale Parkway	d	08 40	10 40	12 40	14 40	16 40	18 40	20 40
Llanhilleth	d	08 48	10 48	12 48	14 48	16 48	18 48	20 48
Newbridge (Ebbw Vale)	d	08 54	10 54	12 54	14 54	16 54	18 54	20 54
Cross Keys	d	09 02	11 02	13 02	15 02	17 02	19 02	21 02
Risca & Pontymister	d	09 07	11 07	13 07	15 07	17 07	19 07	21 07
Rogerstone	d	09 11	11 11	13 11	15 11	17 11	19 11	21 11
Cardiff Central 7	a	09 37	11 38	13 37	15 38	17 39	19 37	21 40

Sundays
18 July to 05 September

		AW	AW	AW	AW	AW	AW	AW
Ebbw Vale Parkway	d	08 40	10 40	12 40	14 40	16 40	18 40	20 40
Llanhilleth	d	08 48	10 48	12 48	14 48	16 48	18 48	20 48
Newbridge (Ebbw Vale)	d	08 54	10 54	12 54	14 54	16 54	18 54	20 54
Cross Keys	d	09 02	11 02	13 02	15 02	17 02	19 02	21 02
Risca & Pontymister	d	09 07	11 07	13 07	15 07	17 07	19 07	21 07
Rogerstone	d	09 11	11 11	13 11	15 11	17 11	19 11	21 11
Cardiff Central 7	a	09 39	11 39	13 37	15 41	17 41	19 39	21 41

Sundays
from 12 September

		AW	AW	AW	AW	AW	AW	AW
Ebbw Vale Parkway	d	08 40	10 40	12 40	14 40	16 40	18 40	20 40
Llanhilleth	d	08 48	10 48	12 48	14 48	16 48	18 48	20 48
Newbridge (Ebbw Vale)	d	08 54	10 54	12 54	14 54	16 54	18 54	20 54
Cross Keys	d	09 02	11 02	13 02	15 02	17 02	19 02	21 02
Risca & Pontymister	d	09 07	11 07	13 07	15 07	17 07	19 07	21 07
Rogerstone	d	09 11	11 11	13 11	15 11	17 11	19 11	21 11
Cardiff Central 7	a	09 37	11 38	13 37	15 38	17 39	19 37	21 40

Cardiff - Maesteg, Swansea and West Wales

	AW MX	AW	AW	AW MX	AW	AW	AW	GW	AW MX		GW	AW MX	GW MX	GW MX	GW	GW	GW	GW MX	GW MX	AW	AW	AW	AW	AW
	■	◇ A	◇ B	◇	◇ A	◇ B	◇ C	◇1 B			◇1 C		◇1	◇1	◇1 A	◇1 B	◇1 C	◇1	◇1	◇				
	H							⊐P			⊐P		⊐P	⊐P	⊐P	⊐P	⊐P	⊐P	⊐P					
London Paddington 15 ⊖ d								20p30			20p30		21p15	21p15	21p37	21p37	21p37	22p45	22p45					
Reading 7 d								21p05			21p05		21p41	21p41	22p14	22p14	22p14	23p15	23p21					
Manchester Piccadilly 10 d	17p30																							
Gloucester 7 d																								
Bristol Parkway 7 d								22p30			22p04		22p45	22p45	23p17	23p38	23p17	00 18	00 24					
Newport (South Wales) d	20p42							23p00			22p40		23p18	23p18	23p45	00 04	23p45	00 48	00 54					
Cardiff Central 7 d	21p06	22p30	22p30				22p20	23p24	23p15		23p04	23p15	23p42	23p42	00 09	00 28	00 09	01 09	01 15					
Pontyclun d									23p29															
Llanharan d									23p34															
Pencoed d									23p39															
Bridgend d	21p28	22p51	22p51				23p03	23p44	23p45		23p50	23p59	00 01	00 27	00 30	00 49	00 56	01 32	01 59					
Wildmill d																								
Sarn d																								
Tondu d																								
Garth (Mid Glamorgan) d																								
Maesteg (Ewenny Road) d																								
Maesteg a																								
Pyle d	21p36								23p53			00 08												
Port Talbot Parkway d	21p45	23p05	23p05				23p16	23p59	00 01		00 04	00 17	00 14	00 40	00 43	01 02	01 09	01 45	02 12					
Baglan d									00 05			00 20												
Briton Ferry d									00 08			00 24												
Neath d	21p52	23p13	23p13				23p24	00 06	00 12		00 11	00 28	00 22	00 48	00 51	01 10	01 16	01 52	02 20					
Skewen d									00 16			00 31												
Llansamlet d									00 20			00 35												
Swansea a	22p07	23p25	23p25				23p37	00 19	00 28		00 24	00 41	00 37	01 01	01 03	01 22	01 29	02 07	02 34					
d	22p26	23p38	23p39	23p45			23p45		00 45			01 11								04 36				05 50
Gowerton d	22c36	23c49	23c50				23c56		00x56			01x22												06x00
Llanelli a	22p42	23p56	23p57	00 01			00 03		01s03			01s28								04 52				06 07
d	22p44	23p58	23p59	00 02			00 05		01s03			01s30												06 09
Pembrey & Burry Port d	22p49	00 04	00 05	00 07			00 11		01s09			01s36												06 15
Kidwelly d	22c55	00x11	00x12				00x18		01s15			01s42												06x22
Ferryside d	23c01	00x17	00x18		←	←	00x24		01s21			01s48												06x28
Carmarthen a	23p14	00 30	00 31	00 27	00 30	00 31	00 37		01 40			02 06												06 42
d	23p17	00 34	00 34	00 30	00 34	00 34	00 40														04 53	05 43	06 00	06 43
Whitland a	23p30	→	→	00 45	00 50	00 50	00 56														05 06	05 59	06 14	07 00
d	23p30			00 45	00 50	00 50	00 56														05 06	05 59	06 15	07 00
Narberth d																						06x08		07x09
Kilgetty d																						06x18		07x19
Saundersfoot d																						06x20		07x21
Tenby a																						06 27		07 28
d																						06 30		07 42
Penally d																						06x33		07x45
Manorbier d																						06 40		07 52
Lamphey d																						06x47		07x59
Pembroke d																						06 50		08 02
Pembroke Dock a																						07 04		08 17
Clunderwen d	23c37																				05x13		06x19	
Clarbeston Road d	23c44			00x59	01x03	01x03	01x09														05x21		06x27	
Haverfordwest d	23p53																				05 32		06 35	
Johnston d	00x01																				05x40		06x43	
Milford Haven a	00 18																				05 54		06 58	
Fishguard Harbour ⛴ a				01 26	01 32	01 32	01 38																	
d																								
Rosslare Harbour ⛴ a																								

A MO from 13 September
B MO from 19 July until 6 September
C MO until 12 July
c previous night, stops on request

Cardiff - Maesteg, Swansea and West Wales

	AW	AW	AW	AW	AW	GW	AW	AW	GW	AW	AW	AW	AW	GW	AW	AW	GW	AW	AW	AW	AW	AW	GW	AW	AW
	◇		◇		◇	◇1	◇	◇	◇1	◇				◇1	◇		◇1	◇	◇				◇1	◇	
	H				H	⊐P			⊐P	H				⊐P⊘	H		⊐P	H	H				⊐P⊘	H	
London Paddington 15 ⊖ d						05 30			06 45					07 45			08 45						09 45		
Reading 7 d						05 56			07 11					08 11			09 11						10 11		
Manchester Piccadilly 10 d															06 30				07 30					08 30	
Gloucester 7 d				05 50									07 58			08 58									10 58
Bristol Parkway 7 d									08 07					09 07			10 07						11 07		
Newport (South Wales) d			06 17	06 44	07 35	07 44		08 01	08 31	08 34			08 52	09 31	09 37	09 52	10 31		10 37				11 31	11 37	11 52
Cardiff Central 7 d	05 39	05 51	06 42	07 04	07 58	08 02	08 09	08 20	08 50	09 04		09 14	09 18	09 48	10 04	10 18	10 48	10 54	11 04		11 14	11 18	11 48	12 04	12 18
Pontyclun d	05 51	06 03		07 16				08 32					09 30			10 30						11 30			12 30
Llanharan d	05 56	06 08		07 21				08 37					09 35			10 35						11 35			12 35
Pencoed d	06 00	06 12		07 25				08 41					09 39			10 39						11 39			12 39
Bridgend d	06 06	06 20	07 02	07 32	08 17	08 23	08 29	08 49	09 09	09 23		09 34	09 46	10 09	10 23	10 46	11 09		11 24		11 34	11 46	12 09	12 23	12 46
Wildmill d		06 22		07 35				08 51					09 49			10 49						11 49			12 49
Sarn d		06 25		07 38				08 54					09 52			10 52						11 52			12 52
Tondu d		06 29		07 41				08 58					09 55			10 55						11 55			12 55
Garth (Mid Glamorgan) d		06 38		07 51				09 07					10 05			11 05						12 05			13 05
Maesteg (Ewenny Road) d		06 41		07 53				09 10					10 07			11 07						12 07			13 07
Maesteg a		06 46		07 59				09 14					10 12			11 12						12 12			13 12
Pyle d	06 14		07 10									09 42									11 42				
Port Talbot Parkway d	06 23		07 18		08 30	08 36	08 45	45	09 22	09 36		09 50		10 22	10 36		11 22		11 37		11 50		12 22	12 36	
Baglan d	06 26		07 22				08 49					09 54									11 54				
Briton Ferry d	06 30		07 25				08 52					09 57									11 57				
Neath d	06 34		07 29		08 37	08 44	08 56		09 30	09 43		10 01		10 30	10 43		11 30		11 44		12 01		12 30	12 43	
Skewen d	06 37		07 33				09 00					10 05									12 05				
Llansamlet d	06 41		07 37				09 04					10 09									12 09				
Swansea a	06 50		07 45		08 49	08 57	09 13		09 45	09 56		10 20		10 44	10 55		11 43		11 55		12 20		12 43	12 55	
d	06 53		07 50		09 02		09 15			10 00	10 05				11 00				12 00	12 05				13 02	
Gowerton d			08x00		09x17						10x16									12x16					
Llanelli a	07 09		08 07		09 23		09 32			10 15	10 23				11 17			11 58	12 15	12 23				13 18	
d	07 09		08 08		09 24					10 16	10 25				11 17			11 58	12 16	12 25				13 18	
Pembrey & Burry Port d	07 15		08 14		09 30					10 21	10 31				11 23				12 21	12 31				13 24	
Kidwelly d	07x21		08x20		09x36						10x38									12x38					
Ferryside d	07x27		08x26		09x41						10x44									12x44					
Carmarthen a	07 41		08 40		09 54					10 47	10 58				11 43				12 47	12 58				13 44	
d	07 44		08 45		09 57						11 00				11 47					12 58				13 47	
Whitland a	07 58		08 59		10 12						11 14				12 00			12 34		13 14				14 00	
d	07 58		08 59		10 12						11 15				12 00			12 34		13 15				14 00	
Narberth d			09x08								11x23									13x23					
Kilgetty d			09x18								11x32									13x32					
Saundersfoot d			09x20								11x34									13x34					
Tenby a			09 27								11 41									13 41					
d			09 43								11 45									13 45					
Penally d			09x46								11x48									13x48					
Manorbier d			09 53								11 54									13 54					
Lamphey d			10x00								12x02									14x02					
Pembroke d			10 03								12 05									14 05					
Pembroke Dock a			10 17								12 19									14 19					
Clunderwen d	08x05				10x18										12x06									14x06	
Clarbeston Road d	08x12				10x26										12x14			12 48						14x14	
Haverfordwest d	08 21				10 34										12 22									14 22	
Johnston d	08x29				10x42										12x30									14x30	
Milford Haven a	08 46				11 00										12 47									14 45	
Fishguard Harbour ⛴ a																		13 15							
d																									
Rosslare Harbour ⛴ a																									

Cardiff - Maesteg, Swansea and West Wales

		AW		GW	AW	AW	AW	AW	GW	AW	AW	GW		AW	AW	AW	AW	GW	AW	AW	GW	AW	AW	AW	AW
																			■				■		
		◇		◇1	◇				◇1	◇		◇1		◇				◇1	◇		◇1			◇	◇
				⊡⊘	⌶				⊡⊘	⌶		⊡⊘		⌶				⊡	⌶		⊡		⌶	⌶	
London Paddington [15] ⊖	d			10 45					11 45			12 45						13 45			14 45				
Reading [7]	d			11 11					12 11			13 11						14 11			15 11				
Manchester Piccadilly [10]	d				09 30					10 30				11 30					12 30				13 30		
Gloucester [7]	d							11 58									13 58			14 58					
Bristol Parkway [7]	d			12 07					13 07			14 07						15 07			16 07				
Newport (South Wales)	d			12 31	12 37			12 52	13 31	13 37		14 31		14 38			14 52	15 31	15 37	15 52	16 31		16 37	17 00	
Cardiff Central [7]	d			12 48	13 04		13 14	13 18	13 48	14 04	14 21	14 48		15 04		15 14	15 18	15 48	16 04	16 18	16 48		17 04	17 21	
Pontyclun	d							13 30			14 33						15 30			16 30				17 33	
Llanharan	d							13 35			14 38						15 35			16 35				17 38	
Pencoed	d							13 39			14 42						15 39			16 39				17 42	
Bridgend	d			13 09	13 23		13 34	13 46	14 09	14 23	14 49	15 09		15 23		15 34	15 46	16 09	16 23	16 46	17 09		17 25	17 49	
Wildmill	d							13 49			14 52						15 49			16 49				17 52	
Sarn	d							13 52			14 55						15 52			16 52				17 55	
Tondu	d							13 55			14 58						15 55			16 55				17 58	
Garth (Mid Glamorgan)	d							14 05			15 08						16 05			17 05				18 08	
Maesteg (Ewenny Road)	d							14 07			15 10						16 07			17 07				18 10	
Maesteg	a							14 12			15 15						16 12			17 12				18 15	
Pyle	d						13 42									15 42			16 31				17 31		
Port Talbot Parkway	d			13 22	13 36		13 50		14 22	14 36		15 22		15 36		15 50		16 22	16 39		17 22		17 39		
Baglan	d						13 54									15 54							17 40		
Briton Ferry	d						13 57									15 57							17 45		
Neath	d			13 30	13 43		14 01		14 30	14 43		15 30		15 43		16 01		16 30	16 46		17 30		17 49		
Skewen	d						14 05									16 05							17 52		
Llansamlet	d						14 09									16 09							17 56		
Swansea	a			13 43	13 55		14 20		14 43	14 55		15 43		15 55		16 20		16 43	16 58		17 43		18 05		
	d	13 16			14 00	14 05				15 00				16 00	16 05				17 05			17 51	18 09		18 21
Gowerton	d					14x16									16x16				17x17			18x01	18x19		
Llanelli	a	13 32			14 15	14 23				15 18				16 15	16 23				17 24			18 08	18 25		18 37
	d				14 16	14 25				15 18				16 16	16 25				17 25			18 10	18 27		
Pembrey & Burry Port	d				14 21	14 31				15 24				16 21	16 31				17 31			18 16	18 32		
Kidwelly	d					14x38									16x38				17x37			18x23	18x38		
Ferryside	d					14x44									16x44				17x42			18x29	18x44		
Carmarthen	a				14 47	14 58				15 44				16 47	16 58				17 55			18 43	19 00		
	d					14 58				15 47					16 58				17 58			19 05			
Whitland	a					15 14				16 00					17 14				18 15			19 19			
	d					15 15				16 00					17 15				18 15			19 19			
Narberth	d					15x23									17x23							19x28			
Kilgetty	d					15x32									17x32							19x38			
Saundersfoot	d					15x34									17x34							19x40			
Tenby	a					15 41									17 41							19 47			
	d					15 45									17 45							19 52			
Penally	d					15x48									17x48							19x55			
Manorbier	d					15 54									17 54							20 02			
Lamphey	d					16x02									18x02							20x09			
Pembroke	d					16 05									18 05							20 12			
Pembroke Dock	a					16 19									18 19							20 22			
Clunderwen	d									16x06									18x21						
Clarbeston Road	d									16x14									18x28						
Haverfordwest	d									16 22									18 37						
Johnston	d									16x30									18x45						
Milford Haven	a									16 45									19 00						
Fishguard Harbour ⛴	a																								
	d																								
Rosslare Harbour ⛴	a																								

Cardiff - Maesteg, Swansea and West Wales

		AW	GW	AW	GW	AW	GW	AW		AW	GW	GW	AW	GW	AW	GW	GW	GW	AW	AW	GW	AW	GW	AW	AW
																	FX	FO							
				■				■					■						■			■			
			◇1		◇1		◇1				◇1	◇1		◇1		◇1	◇1	◇1			◇1		◇1		◇
			⊡	⌶	⊡		⊡	⌶			⊡	⊡	⌶	⊡		⊡	⊡	⊡	⌶		⊡	⌶	⊡		
London Paddington [15] ⊖	d		15 45		16 15		16 45				17 15	17 45				18 15	18 45	18 45			19 15		20 15		
Reading [7]	d		16 11		16 41		17 11				17 41	18 11				18 41	19 11	19 11			19 41		20 41		
Manchester Piccadilly [10]	d			14 30				15 30					16 30						17 30			18 30			
Gloucester [7]	d					16 58				17 59					18 58					19 58					
Bristol Parkway [7]	d		17 07		17 40		18 07				18 40	19 10				19 40	20 07	20 07			20 40		21 40		
Newport (South Wales)	d		17 31	17 34	18 04	17 52	18 31	18 40		18 53	19 11	19 38	19 33		19 52	20 08	20 31	20 37	20 42	20 52	21 04	21 50	22 05		
Cardiff Central [7]	d	17 38	17 48	18 04	18 22	18 12	18 50	19 04		19 12	19 28	19 56	19 59		20 13	20 24	20 49	20 55	21 06	21 10	21 22	22 12	22 26	22 35	
Pontyclun	d					18 24				19 28					20 25					21 22					
Llanharan	d					18 29				19 33					20 30					21 27					
Pencoed	d					18 33				19 37					20 34					21 32					
Bridgend	d	17 59	18 09	18 23	18 45	18 49	19 09	19 23		19 45	19 49	20 16	20 20		20 41	20 45	21 09	21 16	21 28	21 41	21 45	22 41	22 46	22 59	
Wildmill	d					18 52				19 48					20 44					21 43				23 01	
Sarn	d					18 55				19 51					20 47					21 46				23 04	
Tondu	d					18 58				19 54					20 50					21 50				23 08	
Garth (Mid Glamorgan)	d					19 08				20 04					21 00					21 59				23 17	
Maesteg (Ewenny Road)	d					19 10				20 06					21 02					22 02				23 20	
Maesteg	a					19 15				20 11					21 05					22 06				23 25	
Pyle	d	18 07		18 31				19 30											21 36						
Port Talbot Parkway	d	18 16	18 22	18 39	18 58		19 22	19 38			20 02	20 29	20 34			20 58	21 22	21 29	21 45		21 58	22 55	22 59		
Baglan	d	18 20						19 41																	
Briton Ferry	d	18 23						19 44																	
Neath	d	18 27	18 30	18 46	19 05		19 30	19 48			20 10	20 37				21 05	21 30	21 37	21 52		22 06	23 03	23 07		
Skewen	d	18 31						19 53																	
Llansamlet	d	18 35						19 57																	
Swansea	a	18 46	18 48	18 58	19 19		19 45	20 04			20 23	20 50				21 19	21 43	21 49	22 07		22 19	23 15	23 20		
	d			19 05				20 08				21 00							22 26			23 20	23 20		23 45
Gowerton	d			19x17				20x19						←					22x36			23x30			
Llanelli	a			19 24				20 25				21 16	21 04	21 16					22 42			23 37			00 01
	d			19 25				20 26				21 16	21 04	21 16					22 44			23 39			00 02
Pembrey & Burry Port	d			19 31				20 31				→	21 10	21 23					22 49			23 44			00 07
Kidwelly	d							20x37											22x55			23x51			
Ferryside	d							20x43											23x01			23x57			
Carmarthen	a			19 51				20 56					21 31	21 45					23 14			00 16			00 27
	d			19 55				20 58					22 04						23 17						00 30
Whitland	a			20 08				21 13					22 19						23 30						00 45
	d			20 08				21 13					22 19						23 30						00 45
Narberth	d							21x22																	
Kilgetty	d							21x31																	
Saundersfoot	d							21x33																	
Tenby	a							21 40																	
	d							21 43																	
Penally	d							21x46																	
Manorbier	d							21 52																	
Lamphey	d							22x00																	
Pembroke	d							22 03																	
Pembroke Dock	a							22 18																	
Clunderwen	d			20x14									22x25						23x37						
Clarbeston Road	d			20x22									22x33						23x44						00x59
Haverfordwest	d			20 30									22 41						23 53						
Johnston	d			20x38									22x49						00x01						
Milford Haven	a			20 55									23 06						00 18						
Fishguard Harbour ⛴	a																								01 26
	d																								
Rosslare Harbour ⛴	a																								

Cardiff - Maesteg, Swansea and West Wales

		AW	AW	GW	GW FX	GW FO	GW FX	GW FX
				◇1 ☕	◇1 ☕	◇1 ☕	◇1 ☕	◇1 ☕
London Paddington 15 ⊖	d			21 15	21 15	22 45	22 45	22 45
Reading 7	d			21 41	21 41	23 11	23 15	23 21
Manchester Piccadilly 10	d							
Gloucester 7	d							
Bristol Parkway 7	d			22 45	22 45	00 16	00 18	00 24
Newport (South Wales)	d			23 18	23 18	00 38	00 48	00 54
Cardiff Central 7	d	23 15	23 15	23 42	23 42	00 55	01 09	01 15
Pontyclun	d	23 29						
Llanharan	d	23 34						
Pencoed	d	23 39						
Bridgend	d	23 45	23 59	00 01	00 27	01 19	01 32	01 59
Wildmill	d							
Sarn	d							
Tondu	d							
Garth (Mid Glamorgan)	d							
Maesteg (Ewenny Road)	d							
Maesteg	a							
Pyle	d	23 53	00 08					
Port Talbot Parkway	d	00 01	00 17	00 14	00 40	01 32	01 45	02 12
Baglan	d	00 05	00 20					
Briton Ferry	d	00 08	00 24					
Neath	d	00 12	00 28	00 22	00 48	01 39	01 52	02 20
Skewen	d	00 16	00 31					
Llansamlet	d	00 20	00 35					
Swansea	a	00 28	00 41	00 37	01 01	01 53	02 07	02 34
	d	00 45	01 11					
Gowerton	d	00x56	01x22					
Llanelli	a	01s03	01s28					
	d	01s03	01s30					
Pembrey & Burry Port	d	01s09	01s36					
Kidwelly	d	01s15	01s42					
Ferryside	d	01s21	01s48					
Carmarthen	a	01 40	02 06					
	d							
Whitland	a							
	d							
Narberth	d							
Kilgetty	d							
Saundersfoot	d							
Tenby	a							
	d							
Penally	d							
Manorbier	d							
Lamphey	d							
Pembroke	d							
Pembroke Dock	a							
Clunderwen	d							
Clarbeston Road	d							
Haverfordwest	d							
Johnston	d							
Milford Haven	a							
Fishguard Harbour ⛴	a							
	d							
Rosslare Harbour ⛴	a							

Cardiff - Maesteg, Swansea and West Wales

		AW	AW	AW	AW	AW	GW	GW	AW	AW	AW	AW	AW
		2 🚌	◇				◇1 ☕	◇1 ☕			🚌		◇ 🚌
London Paddington 15 ⊖	d						21p15	22p45					
Reading 7	d						21p41	23p11					
Manchester Piccadilly 10	d	17p30											
Gloucester 7	d												
Bristol Parkway 7	d						22p45	00 16					
Newport (South Wales)	d	20p42					23p18	00 38					
Cardiff Central 7	d	21p06			23p15	23p15	23p42	00 55					05 39
Pontyclun	d				23p29								05 51
Llanharan	d				23p34								05 56
Pencoed	d				23p39								06 01
Bridgend	d	21p28			23p45	23p59	00 01	01 19					06 07
Wildmill	d												
Sarn	d												
Tondu	d												
Garth (Mid Glamorgan)	d												
Maesteg (Ewenny Road)	d												
Maesteg	a												
Pyle	d	21p36			23p53	00 08							06 15
Port Talbot Parkway	d	21p45			00 01	00 17	00 14	01 32					06 23
Baglan	d				00 05	00 20							06 27
Briton Ferry	d				00 08	00 24							06 30
Neath	d	21p52			00 12	00 28	00 22	01 39					06 34
Skewen	d				00 16	00 31							06 38
Llansamlet	d				00 20	00 35							06 42
Swansea	a	22p07			00 28	00 41	00 37	01 53					06 50
	d	22p26	23p45	00 05	00 45	01 11						05 50	06 53
Gowerton	d	22c36		00 15	00x56	01x22						06x00	
Llanelli	a	22p42	00 01	00 22	01s03	01s28						06 07	07 09
	d	22p44	00 02	00 24	01s03	01s30						06 09	07 09
Pembrey & Burry Port	d	22p49	00 07	00 30	01s09	01s36						06 15	07 15
Kidwelly	d	22c55		00 37	01s15	01s42						06x22	07x21
Ferryside	d	23c01		00 43	01s21	01s48						06x28	07x28
Carmarthen	a	23p14	00 27	00 59	01 40	02 06						06 42	07 41
	d	23p17	00 30						04 53	05 43	06 00	06 43	07 44
Whitland	a	23p30	00 45						05 06	05 59	06 13	07 00	07 58
	d	23p30	00 45						05 06	05 59	06 13	07 00	07 58
Narberth	d									06x08		07x09	
Kilgetty	d									06x18		07x19	
Saundersfoot	d									06x20		07x21	
Tenby	a									06 27		07 28	
	d									06 30		07 42	
Penally	d									06x33		07x45	
Manorbier	d									06 40		07 52	
Lamphey	d									06x47		07x59	
Pembroke	d									06 50		08 02	
Pembroke Dock	a									07 04		08 17	
Clunderwen	d	23c37							05x13		06x19		08x05
Clarbeston Road	d	23c44	00x59						05x21		06x27		08x12
Haverfordwest	d	23p53							05 32		06 35		08 21
Johnston	d	00x01							05x40		06x43		08x29
Milford Haven	a	00 18							05 54		06 58		08 46
Fishguard Harbour ⛴	a		01 26										
	d												
Rosslare Harbour ⛴	a												

		AW	GW	AW	AW	GW	GW	AW	AW	AW	AW	AW	AW
			◇1	◇		1	◇1		◇ 🚌	◇		🚌	◇ 🚌
London Paddington 15 ⊖	d												
Reading 7	d												
Manchester Piccadilly 10	d												
Gloucester 7	d				05 50								
Bristol Parkway 7	d						07 11						
Newport (South Wales)	d				06 44		07 31		07 38		08 01		08 35
Cardiff Central 7	d	05 51		06 42	07 04		07 48		08 04	08 09	08 22		09 04
Pontyclun	d	06 03			07 16						08 34		
Llanharan	d	06 08			07 21						08 38		
Pencoed	d	06 12			07 25						08 42		
Bridgend	d	06 20		07 02	07 32		08 09		08 23	08 29	08 49		09 23
Wildmill	d	06 22			07 35						08 52		
Sarn	d	06 25			07 38						08 55		
Tondu	d	06 29			07 41						08 58		
Garth (Mid Glamorgan)	d	06 38			07 51						09 08		
Maesteg (Ewenny Road)	d	06 41			07 53						09 10		
Maesteg	a	06 46			07 59						09 15		
Pyle	d			07 10									
Port Talbot Parkway	d			07 18			08 22		08 36	08 45			09 36
Baglan	d			07 22						08 49			
Briton Ferry	d			07 25						08 52			
Neath	d			07 29			08 30		08 43	08 56			09 43
Skewen	d			07 33						09 00			
Llansamlet	d			07 37						09 04			
Swansea	a			07 45			08 45		08 55	09 13			09 56
	d		07 24	07 50		08 15			09 00	09 16		09 48	10 05
Gowerton	d			08x00					09x16			09x58	
Llanelli	a		07 42	08 07		08 31			09 23	09 32		10 05	10 20
	d		07 43	08 08		08 36			09 24			10 07	10 22
Pembrey & Burry Port	d		07 50	08 14		08 43			09 30			10 13	10 27
Kidwelly	d			08x20					09x36			10x20	
Ferryside	d			08x26					09x41			10x26	
Carmarthen	a		08 11	08 42		09 08			09 54			10 40	10 51
	d		08 18					09 40	09 57			10 56	
Whitland	a		08 35					09 56	10 12			11 10	
	d		08 37					09 56	10 12			11 10	
Narberth	d		08x46					10x05				11x19	
Kilgetty	d		08x55					10x15				11x29	
Saundersfoot	d		08x58					10x17				11x31	
Tenby	a		09 06					10 29				11 38	
	d		09 10									11 39	
Penally	d		09x14									11x42	
Manorbier	d		09 22									11 49	
Lamphey	d		09x31									11x56	
Pembroke	d		09 36									11 59	
Pembroke Dock	a		09 43									12 14	
Clunderwen	d								10x18				
Clarbeston Road	d								10x26				
Haverfordwest	d								10 34				
Johnston	d								10x42				
Milford Haven	a								10 59				
Fishguard Harbour ⛴	a												
	d												
Rosslare Harbour ⛴	a												

c previous night, stops on request

Table 128

Saturdays until 04 September

Cardiff - Maesteg, Swansea and West Wales

Station		AW	AW	GW ◇1 ⊏⊐	AW ◇ ⊥	AW	AW ◇ ⊥	GW ◇1 ⊏⊐	AW ◇ ⊥	AW	AW	AW ⊥
London Paddington ⊖	d			07 45				08 45				
Reading	d			08 11				09 11				
Manchester Piccadilly	d				06 30				07 30			
Gloucester	d		07 58			08 58						
Bristol Parkway	d			09 07				10 07				
Newport (South Wales)	d		08 52	09 31	09 37	09 52		10 31	10 37			
Cardiff Central	d	09 14	09 18	09 48	10 04	10 18	10 55	10 48	11 04	11 14	11 21	
Pontyclun	d		09 30			10 30					11 33	
Llanharan	d		09 35			10 35					11 38	
Pencoed	d		09 39			10 39					11 42	
Bridgend	d	09 34	09 46	10 09	10 23	10 46		11 09	11 23	11 34	11 49	
Wildmill	d		09 49			10 49					11 52	
Sarn	d		09 52			10 52					11 55	
Tondu	d		09 55			10 55					11 58	
Garth (Mid Glamorgan)	d		10 05			11 05					12 08	
Maesteg (Ewenny Road)	d		10 07			11 07					12 10	
Maesteg	a		10 12			11 12					12 15	
Pyle	d	09 42								11 42		
Port Talbot Parkway	d	09 50		10 22	10 36			11 22	11 36	11 50		
Baglan	d	09 54								11 54		
Briton Ferry	d	09 57								11 57		
Neath	d	10 01		10 30	10 43			11 30	11 43	12 01		
Skewen	d	10 05								12 05		
Llansamlet	d	10 09								12 09		
Swansea	a	10 20		10 43	10 55			11 43	11 55	12 20		
	d				11 00			11 50	12 00			12 35
Gowerton	d											12x50
Llanelli	a				11 17		12 00	12 06	12 21			12 57
	d				11 17		12 00	12 08	12 21			12 59
Pembrey & Burry Port	d				11 23			12 14	12 27			13 05
Kidwelly	d											13x12
Ferryside	d											13x18
Carmarthen	a				11 42			12 39	12 57			13 32
	d				11 47			12 46				
Whitland	a				12 00		12 35	13 03				
	d				12 00		12 36	13 05				
Narberth	d											
Kilgetty	d											
Saundersfoot	d							13 25				
Tenby	a							13 35				
	d							13 41				
Penally	d											
Manorbier	d							13 51				
Lamphey	d											
Pembroke	d							14 03				
Pembroke Dock	a							14 14				
Clunderwen	d				12x06							
Clarbeston Road	d				12x14		12 50					
Haverfordwest	d				12 22							
Johnston	d				12x30							
Milford Haven	a				12 47							
Fishguard Harbour ⛴	a						13 17					
	d											
Rosslare Harbour ⛴	a											

Station		GW ◇1 ⊏⊐	AW ◇ ⊥	AW	AW ◇	AW ⊥	GW ◇1 ⊏⊐⊘	AW ◇ ⊥	AW	AW	GW ◇1 ⊏⊐⊘	AW ◇ ⊥
London Paddington ⊖	d	09 45					10 45				11 45	
Reading	d	10 11					11 11				12 11	
Manchester Piccadilly	d		08 30					09 30				10 30
Gloucester	d			10 58						11 58		
Bristol Parkway	d	11 07					12 07				13 07	
Newport (South Wales)	d	11 31	11 37	11 52			12 31	12 37		12 52	13 31	13 37
Cardiff Central	d	11 48	12 04	12 18			12 48	13 04	13 14	13 18	13 48	14 04
Pontyclun	d			12 30						13 30		
Llanharan	d			12 35						13 35		
Pencoed	d			12 39						13 39		
Bridgend	d	12 09	12 23	12 46			13 09	13 23	13 34	13 46	14 09	14 23
Wildmill	d			12 49						13 49		
Sarn	d			12 52						13 52		
Tondu	d			12 55						13 55		
Garth (Mid Glamorgan)	d			13 05						14 05		
Maesteg (Ewenny Road)	d			13 07						14 07		
Maesteg	a			13 12						14 12		
Pyle	d								13 42			
Port Talbot Parkway	d	12 22	12 36				13 22	13 36	13 50		14 22	14 36
Baglan	d								13 54			
Briton Ferry	d								13 57			
Neath	d	12 30	12 43				13 30	13 43	14 01		14 30	14 43
Skewen	d								14 05			
Llansamlet	d								14 09			
Swansea	a	12 43	12 55				13 43	13 55	14 20		14 43	14 55
	d		13 00		13 16	13 35		14 00				15 00
Gowerton	d					13x45						
Llanelli	a		13 18		13 32	13 52		14 15				15 20
	d		13 18			13 54		14 16				15 21
Pembrey & Burry Port	d		13 24			14 00		14 21				15 26
Kidwelly	d					14x07						
Ferryside	d					14x13						
Carmarthen	a		13 44			14 30		14 47				15 47
	d		13 49			14 45						15 49
Whitland	a		14 02			15 01						16 02
	d		14 02			15 02						16 02
Narberth	d					15x11						
Kilgetty	d					15x20						
Saundersfoot	d					15x22						
Tenby	a					15 29						
	d					15 33						
Penally	d					15x36						
Manorbier	d					15 42						
Lamphey	d					15x50						
Pembroke	d					15 53						
Pembroke Dock	a					16 07						
Clunderwen	d		14x08									16x09
Clarbeston Road	d		14x16									16x16
Haverfordwest	d		14 24									16 25
Johnston	d		14x32									16x33
Milford Haven	a		14 47									16 50
Fishguard Harbour ⛴	a											
	d											
Rosslare Harbour ⛴	a											

Table 128

Saturdays until 04 September

Cardiff - Maesteg, Swansea and West Wales

Station		AW	GW ◇1 ⊏⊐	AW ◇ ⊥	AW ⊥	AW	AW	GW ◇1 ⊏⊐	AW ■ ⊥	AW	GW ◇1 ⊏⊐	AW ⊥
London Paddington ⊖	d		12 45					13 45			14 45	
Reading	d		13 11					14 11			15 11	
Manchester Piccadilly	d			11 30					12 30			
Gloucester	d						13 58			14 58		
Bristol Parkway	d		14 07					15 07			16 07	
Newport (South Wales)	d		14 31	14 38			14 52	15 31	15 37	15 52	16 31	
Cardiff Central	d	14 21	14 48	15 04		15 14	15 18	15 48	16 04	16 18	16 48	
Pontyclun	d	14 33					15 30			16 30		
Llanharan	d	14 38					15 35			16 35		
Pencoed	d	14 42					15 39			16 39		
Bridgend	d	14 49	15 09	15 23		15 34	15 46	16 09	16 23	16 46	17 09	
Wildmill	d	14 52					15 49			16 49		
Sarn	d	14 55					15 52			16 52		
Tondu	d	14 58					15 55			16 55		
Garth (Mid Glamorgan)	d	15 08					16 05			17 05		
Maesteg (Ewenny Road)	d	15 10					16 07			17 07		
Maesteg	a	15 15					16 12			17 12		
Pyle	d					15 42			16 31			
Port Talbot Parkway	d		15 22	15 36		15 50		16 22	16 39		17 22	
Baglan	d					15 54						
Briton Ferry	d					15 57						
Neath	d		15 30	15 43		16 01		16 30	16 46		17 30	
Skewen	d					16 05						
Llansamlet	d					16 09						
Swansea	a		15 43	15 55		16 20		16 43	16 58		17 43	
	d			16 00	16 05				17 05			17 51
Gowerton	d				16x16				17x16			18x01
Llanelli	a			16 15	16 23				17 23			18 08
	d			16 16	16 24				17 24			18 10
Pembrey & Burry Port	d			16 21	16 30				17 30			18 16
Kidwelly	d				16x37				17x36			18x23
Ferryside	d				16x43				17x41			18x29
Carmarthen	a			16 47	16 57				17 54			18 43
	d				17 08				17 58			19 02
Whitland	a				17 24				18 15			19 16
	d				17 29				18 15			19 17
Narberth	d				17x38							19x26
Kilgetty	d				17x48							19x36
Saundersfoot	d				17x50							19x38
Tenby	a				17 57							19 45
	d				18 00							19 50
Penally	d				18x03							19x53
Manorbier	d				18 10							20 00
Lamphey	d				18x17							20x07
Pembroke	d				18 20							20 10
Pembroke Dock	a				18 34							20 20
Clunderwen	d								18x21			
Clarbeston Road	d								18x28			
Haverfordwest	d								18 37			
Johnston	d								18x45			
Milford Haven	a								19 00			
Fishguard Harbour ⛴	a											
	d											
Rosslare Harbour ⛴	a											

Station		AW ■ ⊥	AW ◇	AW ■ ⊥	AW	GW ◇1 A ⊏⊐	AW ■ ⊥	AW	GW ◇1 B ⊏⊐	GW ◇1 A ⊏⊐	AW ■ ⊥	AW
London Paddington ⊖	d					15 45			15 45	16 45		
Reading	d					16 11			16 11	17 11		
Manchester Piccadilly	d	13 30					14 30				15 30	
Gloucester	d							16 58				17 58
Bristol Parkway	d					17 07			17 41	18 07		
Newport (South Wales)	d	16 37		17 00		17 30	17 34	17 52	18 10	18 31	18 38	18 52
Cardiff Central	d	17 04		17 21	17 38	17 49	18 04	18 18	18 28	18 50	19 04	19 16
Pontyclun	d			17 33				18 30				19 28
Llanharan	d			17 38				18 35				19 33
Pencoed	d			17 42				18 39				19 37
Bridgend	d	17 25		17 49	17 58	18 09	18 23	18 46	18 50	19 09	19 23	19 45
Wildmill	d			17 52				18 49				19 48
Sarn	d			17 55				18 52				19 51
Tondu	d			17 58				18 55				19 54
Garth (Mid Glamorgan)	d			18 08				19 05				20 04
Maesteg (Ewenny Road)	d			18 10				19 07				20 06
Maesteg	a			18 15				19 12				20 11
Pyle	d	17 31			18 06		18 31				19 30	
Port Talbot Parkway	d	17 39			18 14	18 22	18 39		19 03	19 22	19 38	
Baglan	d	17 40			18 18						19 41	
Briton Ferry	d	17 45			18 21						19 44	
Neath	d	17 49			18 25	18 30	18 46		19 10	19 30	19 48	
Skewen	d	17 52			18 29						19 53	
Llansamlet	d	17 56			18 33						19 57	
Swansea	a	18 04			18 44	18 46	18 58		19 25	19 44	20 04	
	d	18 09	18 21				19 05				20 08	
Gowerton	d	18x19					19x16				20x19	
Llanelli	a	18 25	18 37				19 23				20 25	
	d	18 27					19 24				20 26	
Pembrey & Burry Port	d	18 32					19 30				20 31	
Kidwelly	d	18x38									20x37	
Ferryside	d	18x44									20x43	
Carmarthen	a	19 00					19 50				20 56	
	d						19 55				20 58	
Whitland	a						20 08				21 13	
	d						20 08				21 13	
Narberth	d										21x22	
Kilgetty	d										21x31	
Saundersfoot	d										21x33	
Tenby	a										21 40	
	d										21 43	
Penally	d										21x46	
Manorbier	d										21 52	
Lamphey	d										22x00	
Pembroke	d										22 03	
Pembroke Dock	a										22 18	
Clunderwen	d						20x14					
Clarbeston Road	d						20x22					
Haverfordwest	d						20 30					
Johnston	d						20x38					
Milford Haven	a						20 55					
Fishguard Harbour ⛴	a											
	d											
Rosslare Harbour ⛴	a											

A until 10 July

B from 17 July until 4 September

Table 128

Saturdays until 04 September

Cardiff - Maesteg, Swansea and West Wales

		GW	GW	AW	GW	AW	GW	GW	AW	AW	GW	GW	AW	GW	AW	GW	GW
		◇1 A 🍴	◇1 B 🍴	■ ⊼	◇1 B 🍴		◇1 A 🍴	◇1 B 🍴	■ ⊼		◇1 A 🍴	◇1 B 🍴	◇ ⊼	◇1 A 🍴		◇1 B 🍴	◇1 A 🍴
London Paddington ⊖	d	16 45	17 45				17 45	18 45			18 45	19 45		19 45		20 45	20 45
Reading	d	17 11	18 11				18 11	19 11			19 11	20 11		20 11		21 11	21 11
Manchester Piccadilly	d			16 30					17 30				18 30				
Gloucester	d					18 58				19 58							
Bristol Parkway	d	18 40	19 12				19 37	20 07			20 31	21 07		21 40		22 11	22 37
Newport (South Wales)	d	19 05	19 37	19 31		19 52	20 11	20 31	20 40	20 52	21 06	21 31	21 44	22 15		22 46	23 08
Cardiff Central	d	19 25	19 55	20 00		20 13	20 29	20 48	21 06	21 10	21 24	21 48	22 12	22 36	22 43	23 07	23 30
Pontyclun	d					20 25				21 22					22 55		
Llanharan	d					20 30				21 27					23 00		
Pencoed	d					20 34				21 30					23 04		
Bridgend	d	19 48	20 15	20 22		20 41	20 49	21 09	21 25	21 41	21 44	22 09	22 33	22 57	23 10	23 28	23 49
Wildmill	d					20 44				21 43							
Sarn	d					20 47				21 46							
Tondu	d					20 50				21 50							
Garth (Mid Glamorgan)	d					21 00				21 59							
Maesteg (Ewenny Road)	d					21 02				22 02							
Maesteg	a					21 07				22 06							
Pyle	d								21 32						23 18		
Port Talbot Parkway	d	20 01	20 28	20 35			21 02	21 22	21 40		21 57	22 22	22 47	23 10	23 27	23 41	00 02
Baglan	d														23 30		
Briton Ferry	d														23 34		
Neath	d	20 08	20 36				21 10	21 30	21 47		22 05	22 30	22 55	23 18	23 38	23 49	00 11
Skewen	d														23 41		
Llansamlet	d														23 45		
Swansea	a	20 23	20 49				21 23	21 43	22 00		22 18	22 43	23 07	23 31	23 53	00 22	00 23
	d		21 00				21 30		22 26				23 12		00 08		
Gowerton	d				←				22x36				23x23		00x19		
Llanelli	a		21 16	21 05	21 16		21 46		22 42				23 29		00s26		
	d		21 16	21 05	21 16		21 46		22 44				23 31		00s27		
Pembrey & Burry Port	d		→	21 11	21 23		21 53		22 49				23 36		00s33		
Kidwelly	d								22x55				23x43		00s39		
Ferryside	d								23x01				23x49		00s45		
Carmarthen	a			21 31	21 45		22 16		23 18				00 09		01 03		
	d			22 03													
Whitland	a			22 18													
	d			22 18													
Narberth	d																
Kilgetty	d																
Saundersfoot	d																
Tenby	a																
	d																
Penally	d																
Manorbier	d																
Lamphey	d																
Pembroke	d																
Pembroke Dock	a																
Clunderwen	d			22x24													
Clarbeston Road	d			22x32													
Haverfordwest	d			22 40													
Johnston	d			22x48													
Milford Haven	a			23 05													
Fishguard Harbour ⛴	a																
	d																
Rosslare Harbour ⛴	a																

A from 17 July until 4 September

B until 10 July

Table 128

Saturdays from 11 September

Cardiff - Maesteg, Swansea and West Wales

		AW	AW	AW	AW	AW	GW	GW	AW	AW	AW	AW	AW
		■ ⊼	◇				◇1 🍴	◇1 🍴					◇ ⊼
London Paddington ⊖	d						21p15	22p45					
Reading	d						21p41	23p11					
Manchester Piccadilly	d	17p30											
Gloucester	d												
Bristol Parkway	d						22p45	00 16					
Newport (South Wales)	d	20p42					23p18	00 38					
Cardiff Central	d	21p06			23p15	23p15	23p42	00 55					05 39
Pontyclun	d				23p29								05 51
Llanharan	d				23p34								05 56
Pencoed	d				23p39								06 01
Bridgend	d	21p28			23p45	23p59	00 01	01 19					06 07
Wildmill	d												
Sarn	d												
Tondu	d												
Garth (Mid Glamorgan)	d												
Maesteg (Ewenny Road)	d												
Maesteg	a												
Pyle	d	21p36			23p53	00 08							06 15
Port Talbot Parkway	d	21p45			00 01	00 17	00 14	01 32					06 23
Baglan	d				00 05	00 20							06 27
Briton Ferry	d				00 08	00 24							06 30
Neath	d	21p52			00 12	00 28	00 22	01 39					06 34
Skewen	d				00 16	00 31							06 38
Llansamlet	d				00 20	00 35							06 42
Swansea	a	22p07			00 28	00 41	00 37	01 53					06 50
	d	22p26	23p45	00 05	00 45	01 11						05 50	06 53
Gowerton	d	22c36		00 15	00x56	01x22						06x00	
Llanelli	a	22p42	00 01	00 22	01s03	01s28						06 07	07 09
	d	22p44	00 02	00 24	01s03	01s30						06 09	07 09
Pembrey & Burry Port	d	22p49	00 07	00 30	01s09	01s36						06 15	07 15
Kidwelly	d	22c55		00 37	01s15	01s42						06x22	07x21
Ferryside	d	23c01		00 43	01s21	01s48						06x28	07x28
Carmarthen	a	23p14	00 27	00 59	01 40	02 06						06 42	07 41
	d	23p17	00 30						04 53	05 43	06 00	06 43	07 44
Whitland	a	23p30	00 45						05 06	05 59	06 13	07 00	07 58
	d	23p30	00 45						05 06	05 59	06 13	07 00	07 58
Narberth	d									06x08		07x09	
Kilgetty	d									06x18		07x19	
Saundersfoot	d									06x20		07x21	
Tenby	a									06 27		07 28	
	d									06 30		07 42	
Penally	d									06x33		07x45	
Manorbier	d									06 40		07 52	
Lamphey	d									06x47		07x59	
Pembroke	d									06 50		08 02	
Pembroke Dock	a									07 04		08 17	
Clunderwen	d	23c37							05x13		06x19		08x05
Clarbeston Road	d	23c44	00x59						05x21		06x27		08x12
Haverfordwest	d	23p53							05 32		06 35		08 21
Johnston	d	00x01							05x40		06x43		08x29
Milford Haven	a	00 18							05 54		06 58		08 46
Fishguard Harbour ⛴	a		01 26										
	d												
Rosslare Harbour ⛴	a												

		AW	AW	AW	GW	GW	AW	AW	AW	AW	AW	AW	AW
			◇		1	◇1	◇ ⊼		◇		◇ ⊼		
London Paddington ⊖	d												
Reading	d												
Manchester Piccadilly	d												
Gloucester	d			05 50									07 58
Bristol Parkway	d					07 11							
Newport (South Wales)	d			06 44		07 31	07 38	08 01			08 35		08 52
Cardiff Central	d	05 51	06 42	07 04		07 48	08 04	08 22	08 09		09 04	09 14	09 18
Pontyclun	d	06 03		07 16				08 34					09 30
Llanharan	d	06 08		07 21				08 38					09 35
Pencoed	d	06 12		07 25				08 42					09 39
Bridgend	d	06 20	07 02	07 32		08 09	08 23	08 49	08 29		09 23	09 34	09 46
Wildmill	d	06 22		07 35				08 52					09 49
Sarn	d	06 25		07 38				08 55					09 52
Tondu	d	06 29		07 41				08 58					09 55
Garth (Mid Glamorgan)	d	06 38		07 51				09 08					10 05
Maesteg (Ewenny Road)	d	06 41		07 53				09 10					10 07
Maesteg	a	06 46		07 59				09 15					10 12
Pyle	d		07 10									09 42	
Port Talbot Parkway	d		07 18			08 22	08 36		08 45		09 36	09 50	
Baglan	d		07 22						08 49			09 54	
Briton Ferry	d		07 25						08 52			09 57	
Neath	d		07 29			08 30	08 43		08 56		09 43	10 01	
Skewen	d		07 33						09 00			10 05	
Llansamlet	d		07 37						09 04			10 09	
Swansea	a		07 45			08 45	08 55		09 13		09 56	10 20	
	d		07 50		08 15		09 00		09 16	09 48	10 05		
Gowerton	d		08x00				09x16			09x58			
Llanelli	a		08 07		08 31		09 23		09 32	10 05	10 20		
	d		08 08		08 36		09 24			10 07	10 22		
Pembrey & Burry Port	d		08 14		08 43		09 30			10 13	10 27		
Kidwelly	d		08x20				09x36			10x20			
Ferryside	d		08x26				09x41			10x26			
Carmarthen	a		08 40		09 08		09 54			10 40	10 51		
	d		08 53				09 57			10 56			
Whitland	a		09 09				10 12			11 10			
	d		09 09				10 12			11 10			
Narberth	d		09x18							11x19			
Kilgetty	d		09x28							11x29			
Saundersfoot	d		09x30							11x31			
Tenby	a		09 37							11 38			
	d		09 43							11 41			
Penally	d		09x46							11x44			
Manorbier	d		09 53							11 51			
Lamphey	d		10x00							11x58			
Pembroke	d		10 03							12 01			
Pembroke Dock	a		10 17							12 16			
Clunderwen	d						10x18						
Clarbeston Road	d						10x26						
Haverfordwest	d						10 34						
Johnston	d						10x42						
Milford Haven	a						10 59						
Fishguard Harbour ⛴	a												
	d												
Rosslare Harbour ⛴	a												

c previous night, stops on request

Table 128

Saturdays from 11 September

Cardiff - Maesteg, Swansea and West Wales

		GW	AW	AW	GW	AW		AW	AW	AW	AW	GW	AW	AW	AW	GW		AW	AW	AW	AW	GW	AW	AW	GW
		◇[1]	◇		◇[1]	◇		◇				◇[1]	◇		◇	◇[1]		◇				◇[1]	◇		◇[1]
		☕	🛒		☕	🛒		🛒				☕	🛒			☕⊘		🛒				☕⊘	🛒		☕
London Paddington [15] ⊖	d	07 45			08 45							09 45				10 45						11 45			12 45
Reading [7]	d	08 11			09 11							10 11				11 11						12 11			13 11
Manchester Piccadilly [10]	d		06 30					07 30					08 30					09 30					10 30		
Gloucester [7]	d			08 58										10 58							11 58				
Bristol Parkway [7]	d	09 07			10 07							11 07				12 07						13 07			14 07
Newport (South Wales)	d	09 31	09 37	09 52	10 31			10 37				11 31	11 37	11 52		12 31		12 37			12 52	13 31	13 37		14 31
Cardiff Central [7]	d	09 48	10 04	10 18	10 48	10 55		11 04		11 14	11 21	11 48	12 04	12 18		12 48		13 04		13 14	13 18	13 48	14 04	14 21	14 48
Pontyclun	d			10 30							11 33			12 30							13 30			14 33	
Llanharan	d			10 35							11 38			12 35							13 35			14 38	
Pencoed	d			10 39							11 42			12 39							13 39			14 42	
Bridgend	d	10 09	10 23	10 46	11 09			11 23		11 34	11 49	12 09	12 23	12 46		13 09		13 23		13 34	13 46	14 09	14 23	14 49	15 09
Wildmill	d			10 49							11 52			12 49							13 49			14 52	
Sarn	d			10 52							11 55			12 52							13 52			14 55	
Tondu	d			10 55							11 58			12 55							13 55			14 58	
Garth (Mid Glamorgan)	d			11 05							12 08			13 05							14 05			15 08	
Maesteg (Ewenny Road)	d			11 07							12 10			13 07							14 07			15 10	
Maesteg	a			11 12							12 15			13 12							14 12			15 15	
Pyle	d									11 42										13 42					
Port Talbot Parkway	d	10 22	10 36		11 22			11 36		11 50		12 22	12 36			13 22		13 36		13 50		14 22	14 36		15 22
Baglan	d									11 54										13 54					
Briton Ferry	d									11 57										13 57					
Neath	d	10 30	10 43		11 30			11 43		12 01		12 30	12 43			13 30		13 43		14 01		14 30	14 43		15 30
Skewen	d									12 05										14 05					
Llansamlet	d									12 09										14 09					
Swansea	a	10 43	10 55		11 43			11 55		12 20		12 43	12 55			13 43		13 55		14 20		14 43	14 55		15 43
	d		11 00					12 00	12 05				13 00		13 16			14 00	14 05				15 00		
Gowerton	d								12x16										14x16						
Llanelli	a		11 17			12 00		12 15	12 23				13 18		13 32			14 15	14 23				15 23		
	d		11 17			12 00		12 16	12 24				13 18					14 16	14 24				15 23		
Pembrey & Burry Port	d		11 23					12 21	12 30				13 24					14 21	14 30				15 29		
Kidwelly	d								12x37										14x37						
Ferryside	d								12x43										14x43						
Carmarthen	a		11 42					12 47	12 57				13 44					14 47	14 57				15 49		
	d		11 47						12 58				13 49						14 58				15 52		
Whitland	a		12 00			12 35			13 14				14 02						15 14				16 04		
	d		12 00			12 36			13 14				14 02						15 14				16 05		
Narberth	d								13x23										15x23						
Kilgetty	d								13x33										15x33						
Saundersfoot	d								13x35										15x35						
Tenby	a								13 42										15 42						
	d								13 46										15 46						
Penally	d								13x49										15x49						
Manorbier	d								13 55										15 55						
Lamphey	d								14x03										16x03						
Pembroke	d								14 06										16 06						
Pembroke Dock	a								14 20										16 20						
Clunderwen	d		12x06										14x08										16x11		
Clarbeston Road	d		12x14			12 50							14x16										16x19		
Haverfordwest	d		12 22										14 24										16 27		
Johnston	d		12x30										14x32										16x35		
Milford Haven	a		12 47										14 47										16 52		
Fishguard Harbour ⛴	a					13 17																			
	d																								
Rosslare Harbour ⛴	a																								

Table 128

Saturdays from 11 September

Cardiff - Maesteg, Swansea and West Wales

		AW		AW	AW	AW	GW	AW	AW	GW	AW	AW	AW	AW	AW	GW	AW	AW	GW	AW	AW	GW		AW	GW
		◇					◇[1]	■		◇[1]		■	◇	■		◇[1]	■		◇[1]	■		◇[1]		■	◇[1]
		🛒					☕	🛒		☕		🛒		🛒		☕	🛒		☕	🛒		☕		🛒	☕
London Paddington [15] ⊖	d						13 45			14 45						15 45			16 45			17 45			
Reading [7]	d						14 11			15 11						16 11			17 11			18 11			
Manchester Piccadilly [10]	d	11 30						12 30				13 30					14 30			15 30				16 30	
Gloucester [7]	d					13 58			14 58									16 58			17 58				
Bristol Parkway [7]	d						15 07			16 07						17 07			18 07			19 12			
Newport (South Wales)	d	14 38				14 52	15 31	15 37	15 52	16 31		16 37		17 00		17 30	17 34	17 52	18 31	18 38	18 52	19 37		19 31	
Cardiff Central [7]	d	15 04			15 14	15 18	15 48	16 04	16 18	16 48		17 04		17 21	17 38	17 49	18 04	18 18	18 50	19 04	19 16	19 55		20 00	
Pontyclun	d					15 30			16 30					17 33				18 30			19 28				
Llanharan	d					15 35			16 35					17 38				18 35			19 33				
Pencoed	d					15 39			16 39					17 42				18 39			19 37				
Bridgend	d	15 23			15 34	15 46	16 09	16 23	16 46	17 09		17 25		17 49	17 58	18 09	18 23	18 46	19 09	19 23	19 45	20 15		20 22	
Wildmill	d					15 49			16 49					17 52				18 49			19 48				
Sarn	d					15 52			16 52					17 55				18 52			19 51				
Tondu	d					15 55			16 55					17 58				18 55			19 54				
Garth (Mid Glamorgan)	d					16 05			17 05					18 08				19 05			20 04				
Maesteg (Ewenny Road)	d					16 07			17 07					18 10				19 07			20 06				
Maesteg	a					16 12			17 12					18 15				19 12			20 11				
Pyle	d				15 42			16 31				17 31			18 06		18 31			19 30					
Port Talbot Parkway	d	15 36			15 50		16 22	16 39		17 22		17 39			18 14	18 22	18 39		19 22	19 38		20 28		20 35	
Baglan	d				15 54							17 40			18 18					19 41					
Briton Ferry	d				15 57							17 45			18 21					19 44					
Neath	d	15 43			16 01		16 30	16 46		17 30		17 49			18 25	18 30	18 46		19 30	19 48		20 36			
Skewen	d				16 05							17 52			18 29					19 53					
Llansamlet	d				16 09							17 56			18 33					19 57					
Swansea	a	15 55			16 20		16 43	16 58		17 43		18 04			18 44	18 46	18 58		19 44	20 04		20 49			
	d	16 00		16 05				17 05			17 51	18 09	18 21				19 05			20 08		21 00			
Gowerton	d			16x16				17x17			18x01	18x19					19x20			20x19					←
Llanelli	a	16 15		16 23				17 24			18 08	18 25	18 37				19 27			20 25		21 16		21 05	21 16
	d	16 16		16 24				17 25			18 10	18 27					19 28			20 26		21 16		21 05	21 16
Pembrey & Burry Port	d	16 21		16 30				17 31			18 16	18 32					19 34			20 31		→		21 11	21 23
Kidwelly	d			16x37				17x37			18x23	18x38								20x37					
Ferryside	d			16x43				17x42			18x29	18x44								20x43					
Carmarthen	a	16 47		16 57				17 55			18 43	19 00					19 54			20 56				21 31	21 45
	d			16 58				17 58			19 02						19 58			20 58				22 03	
Whitland	a			17 14				18 16			19 16						20 11			21 13				22 18	
	d			17 14				18 17			19 17						20 11			21 13				22 18	
Narberth	d			17x23							19x26									21x22					
Kilgetty	d			17x33							19x36									21x31					
Saundersfoot	d			17x35							19x38									21x33					
Tenby	a			17 42							19 45									21 40					
	d			17 46							19 50									21 43					
Penally	d			17x49							19x53									21x46					
Manorbier	d			17 55							20 00									21 52					
Lamphey	d			18x03							20x07									22x00					
Pembroke	d			18 06							20 10									22 03					
Pembroke Dock	a			18 20							20 20									22 18					
Clunderwen	d							18x22									20x17							22x24	
Clarbeston Road	d							18x30									20x25							22x32	
Haverfordwest	d							18 38									20 33							22 40	
Johnston	d							18x46									20x41							22x48	
Milford Haven	a							19 01									20 58							23 05	
Fishguard Harbour ⛴	a																								
	d																								
Rosslare Harbour ⛴	a																								

Table 128

Cardiff - Maesteg, Swansea and West Wales

Saturdays
from 11 September

		AW	GW	AW	AW	GW	GW	AW	AW	GW
			◇1	■		◇1	◇1	◇		◇1
			🍴	🛒		🍴	🍴	🛒		🍴
London Paddington 15 ⊖	d		18 45			19 15	19 45			20 45
Reading 7	d		19 11			19 41	20 11			21 11
Manchester Piccadilly 10	d			17 30				18 30		
Gloucester 7	d	18 58			19 58					
Bristol Parkway 7	d		20 07			20 40	21 07			22 11
Newport (South Wales)	d	19 52	20 31	20 40	20 52	21 04	21 31	21 44		22 46
Cardiff Central 7	d	20 13	20 48	21 06	21 10	21 22	21 48	22 12	22 43	23 07
Pontyclun	d	20 25			21 22				22 55	
Llanharan	d	20 30			21 27				23 00	
Pencoed	d	20 34			21 30				23 04	
Bridgend	d	20 41	21 09	21 25	21 41	21 45	22 09	22 33	23 10	23 28
Wildmill	d	20 44			21 43					
Sarn	d	20 47			21 46					
Tondu	d	20 50			21 50					
Garth (Mid Glamorgan)	d	21 00			21 59					
Maesteg (Ewenny Road)	d	21 02			22 02					
Maesteg	a	21 07			22 06					
Pyle	d			21 32					23 18	
Port Talbot Parkway	d		21 22	21 40		21 58	22 22	22 47	23 27	23 41
Baglan	d								23 30	
Briton Ferry	d								23 34	
Neath	d		21 30	21 47		22 06	22 30	22 55	23 38	23 49
Skewen	d								23 41	
Llansamlet	d								23 45	
Swansea	a		21 43	22 00		22 18	22 43	23 07	23 53	00 02
	d			22 26				23 12	00 08	
Gowerton	d			22x36				23x23	00x19	
Llanelli	a			22 42				23 29	00s26	
	d			22 44				23 31	00s27	
Pembrey & Burry Port	d			22 49				23 36	00s33	
Kidwelly	d			22x55				23x43	00s39	
Ferryside	d			23x01				23x49	00s45	
Carmarthen	a			23 18				00 09	01 03	
	d									
Whitland	a									
	d									
Narberth	d									
Kilgetty	d									
Saundersfoot	d									
Tenby	a									
	d									
Penally	d									
Manorbier	d									
Lamphey	d									
Pembroke	d									
Pembroke Dock	a									
Clunderwen	d									
Clarbeston Road	d									
Haverfordwest	d									
Johnston	d									
Milford Haven	a									
Fishguard Harbour ⛴	a									
	d									
Rosslare Harbour ⛴	a									

Table 128

Cardiff - Maesteg, Swansea and West Wales

Sundays
until 11 July

		AW	AW	GW	AW	AW	AW	AW	AW	AW	AW	GW	AW
		◇		◇1						◇	◇	◇1	◇
		🛒		🍴		🚌				🛒		🍴	🛒
London Paddington 15 ⊖	d			20p45								07 57	
Reading 7	d			21p11								08 37	
Manchester Piccadilly 10	d	18p30											
Gloucester 7	d												
Bristol Parkway 7	d			22p11								09 40	
Newport (South Wales)	d	21p44		22p46		08 45				09 13		10 05	
Cardiff Central 7	d	22p12	22p43	23p07		09 15				09 37		10 25	10 38
Pontyclun	d		22p55			09 40							
Llanharan	d		23p00			09 48							
Pencoed	d		23p04			09 55							
Bridgend	d	22p33	23p10	23p28		10a10				10 20		11 12	11 23
Wildmill	d												
Sarn	d												
Tondu	d												
Garth (Mid Glamorgan)	d												
Maesteg (Ewenny Road)	d												
Maesteg	a												
Pyle	d		23p18							10 28			
Port Talbot Parkway	d	22p47	23p27	23p41						10 37		11 25	11 37
Baglan	d		23p30										
Briton Ferry	d		23p34										
Neath	d	22p55	23p38	23p49						10 45		11 32	11 45
Skewen	d		23p41										
Llansamlet	d		23p45										
Swansea	a	23p07	23p53	00 02						10 58		11 45	11 58
	d	23p12	00 08							11 01	11 07		12 14
Gowerton	d	23c23	00x19								11 16		12x24
Llanelli	a	23p29	00s26							11 17	11 23		12 32
	d	23p31	00s27							11 19			12 32
Pembrey & Burry Port	d	23p36	00s33							11 25			12 38
Kidwelly	d	23c43	00s39							11x32			12x44
Ferryside	d	23c49	00s45							11x38			12x50
Carmarthen	a	00 09	01 03							11 51			13 04
	d				08 20		09 06	09 55	10 19	11 57			13 06
Whitland	a				08 36		09 22	10 11	10 33	12 13			13 21
	d				08 37		09 22	10 11	10 34	12 13			13 22
Narberth	d						09x31		10x43				
Kilgetty	d						09x41		10x52				
Saundersfoot	d						09x43		10x54				
Tenby	a						09 50		11 01				
	d						09 51		11 07				
Penally	d						09x54		11x10				
Manorbier	d						10 01		11 16				
Lamphey	d						10x08		11x24				
Pembroke	d						10 11		11 27				
Pembroke Dock	a						10 21		11 40				
Clunderwen	d				08x45			10x19		12x21			
Clarbeston Road	d				08x53			10x27		12x29			13 35
Haverfordwest	d				09 01			10 35		12 37			
Johnston	d				09x10			10x44		12x46			
Milford Haven	a				09 21			10 55		12 57			
Fishguard Harbour ⛴	a												13 58
	d												
Rosslare Harbour ⛴	a												

		AW	GW	GW	AW	AW	AW	GW	AW	AW	GW	AW
		◇	◇1	◇1			◇	◇1		■	◇1	
			🍴	🍴		🛒		🍴	🚌	🛒	🍴	
London Paddington 15 ⊖	d		09 30	10 30				11 30			12 30	
Reading 7	d		10 05	11 05				12 05			13 05	
Manchester Piccadilly 10	d									10 30		
Gloucester 7	d											
Bristol Parkway 7	d		11 04	12 04				13 04			14 04	
Newport (South Wales)	d		11 34	12 36				13 34		13 29	14 32	
Cardiff Central 7	d	11 40	11 53	12 53				13 50	13 51	14 09	14 51	
Pontyclun	d								14 16			
Llanharan	d								14 24			
Pencoed	d								14 32			
Bridgend	d	12 23	12 41	13 49				14 36	14a47	14 52	15 51	
Wildmill	d											
Sarn	d											
Tondu	d											
Garth (Mid Glamorgan)	d											
Maesteg (Ewenny Road)	d											
Maesteg	a											
Pyle	d	12 31								15 00		
Port Talbot Parkway	d	12 39	12 54	14 03				14 50		15 08	16 05	
Baglan	d											
Briton Ferry	d											
Neath	d		13 01	14 10				14 57		15 16	16 12	
Skewen	d											
Llansamlet	d											
Swansea	a		13 14	14 23				15 11		15 29	16 25	
	d		13 24			14 28	15 04	15 18		15 32		16 30
Gowerton	d					14x39	15x15					16x41
Llanelli	a	13 08	13 40			14 46	15 22	15 34		15 48		16 48
	d	13 08	13 41			14 48	15 26	15 35		15 49		16 50
Pembrey & Burry Port	d	13 15	13 48			14 54		15 42		15 55		16 56
Kidwelly	d					15x00						17x03
Ferryside	d					15x06						17x09
Carmarthen	a	13 38	14 09			15 21		16 03		16 17		17 22
	d				14 21	15 23				16 23		17 26
Whitland	a				14 37	15 39				16 39		17 40
	d				14 37	15 39				16 40		17 48
Narberth	d					15x47						17x57
Kilgetty	d					15x57						18x07
Saundersfoot	d					15x59						18x09
Tenby	a					16 06						18 16
	d					16 10						18 19
Penally	d					16x13						18x22
Manorbier	d					16 19						18 29
Lamphey	d					16x27						18x36
Pembroke	d					16 30						18 40
Pembroke Dock	a					16 43						18 54
Clunderwen	d				14x45					16x48		
Clarbeston Road	d				14x53					16x56		
Haverfordwest	d				15 01					17 05		
Johnston	d				15x10					17x13		
Milford Haven	a				15 24					17 28		
Fishguard Harbour ⛴	a											
	d											
Rosslare Harbour ⛴	a											

c previous night, stops on request

Table 128

Sundays
until 11 July

Cardiff - Maesteg, Swansea and West Wales

		GW	GW	AW	GW	AW	AW	AW	GW	AW	GW	AW	AW	GW	GW	AW	GW	GW
		◇■	◇■		◇■			■	◇■		◇■	■	◇	◇■	◇■	◇	◇■	◇■
London Paddington ■ ⊖	d	13 30	14 45		15 30				16 30		17 30			18 30	19 30		20 30	21 37
Reading ■	d	14 05	15 11		16 05				17 05		18 05			19 05	20 05		21 05	22 14
Manchester Piccadilly ■	d							14 30										
Gloucester ■	d																	
Bristol Parkway ■	d	15 04	16 07		17 04				18 08		19 04			20 10	21 04		22 04	23 17
Newport (South Wales)	d	15 32	16 31		17 34			17 34	18 37		19 32			20 38	21 33		22 40	23 45
Cardiff Central ■	d	15 51	16 48		17 53	17 46		18 04	18 58		19 53		20 13	20 55	21 57	22 20	23 04	00 09
Pontyclun	d					18 11												
Llanharan	d					18 19												
Pencoed	d					18 27												
Bridgend	d	16 38	17 09		18 40	18a42		18 52	19 50		20 38		20 56	21 50	22 46	23 03	23 50	00 56
Wildmill	d																	
Sarn	d																	
Tondu	d																	
Garth (Mid Glamorgan)	d																	
Maesteg (Ewenny Road)	d																	
Maesteg	a																	
Pyle	d							19 00					21 04					
Port Talbot Parkway	d	16 52	17 22		18 53			19 09	20 03		20 51		21 12	22 02	22 58	23 16	00 04	01 09
Baglan	d																	
Briton Ferry	d																	
Neath	d	16 59	16 59		19 01			19 17	20 12		20 58		21 20	22 10	23 06	23 24	00 11	01 16
Skewen	d																	
Llansamlet	d																	
Swansea	a	17 12	17 43		19 13			19 29	20 24		21 12		21 33	22 23	23 19	23 37	00 24	01 29
	d	17 19		18 35				19 40		20 35			21 39			23 45		
Gowerton	d			18x46						20x46						23x56		
Llanelli	a	17 35		18 53				19 56		20 54			21 54			00 03		
	d	17 36		18 55				19 58		20 55			21 55			00 05		
Pembrey & Burry Port	d	17 43		19 01				20 04		21 01			22 02			00 11		
Kidwelly	d			19x08						21x08						00x18		
Ferryside	d			19x14						21x14						00x24		
Carmarthen	a	18 04		19 27				20 26		21 32			22 25			00 37		
	d						19 45	20 29					22 26			00 40		
Whitland	a						20 01	20 45					22 42			00 56		
	d						20 01	20 51				20 47	22 43			00 56		
Narberth	d											20x56						
Kilgetty	d											21x05						
Saundersfoot	d											21x07						
Tenby	a											21 16						
	d											21 18						
Penally	d											21x21						
Manorbier	d											21 27						
Lamphey	d											21x35						
Pembroke	d											21 38						
Pembroke Dock	a											21 53						
Clunderwen	d						20x09	20x59					22x50					
Clarbeston Road	d						20x17	21x07					22x58			01x09		
Haverfordwest	d						20a25	21 15					23 07					
Johnston	d							21x24					23x15					
Milford Haven	a							21 39					23 29					
Fishguard Harbour ⛴	a															01 38		
	d																	
Rosslare Harbour ⛴	a																	

Table 128

Sundays
18 July to 05 September

Cardiff - Maesteg, Swansea and West Wales

		AW	GW	AW	AW	AW	AW	AW	GW	AW	AW	GW	GW	GW
			◇■				◇	◇	◇■	◇	◇	◇■	◇■	◇■
London Paddington ■ ⊖	d		20p45						07 57			09 30	10 30	11 30
Reading ■	d		21p11						08 37			10 05	11 05	12 05
Manchester Piccadilly ■	d													
Gloucester ■	d													
Bristol Parkway ■	d		22p37						10 07			11 25	12 26	13 28
Newport (South Wales)	d		23p08				09 27		10 32			11 48	12 48	13 48
Cardiff Central ■	d	22p43	23p30				09 50		10 53	11 26	12 05	12 11	13 11	14 14
Pontyclun	d	22p55					10 03							
Llanharan	d	23p00					10 08							
Pencoed	d	23p04					10 13							
Bridgend	d	23p10	23p49				10 20		11 14	11 46	12 26	12 31	13 31	14 33
Wildmill	d													
Sarn	d													
Tondu	d													
Garth (Mid Glamorgan)	d													
Maesteg (Ewenny Road)	d													
Maesteg	a													
Pyle	d	23p18					10 28				12 34			
Port Talbot Parkway	d	23p27	00 02				10 37		11 27	12 00	12 43	12 45	13 45	14 47
Baglan	d	23p30												
Briton Ferry	d	23p34												
Neath	d	23p38	00 11				10 45		11 35	12 08		12 52	13 52	14 54
Skewen	d	23p41												
Llansamlet	d	23p45												
Swansea	a	23p53	00 23				10 58		11 48	12 20		13 07	14 05	15 07
	d	00 08					11 01	11 07		12 24		13 17		15 15
Gowerton	d	00x19						11 16		12x34				
Llanelli	a	00s26					11 17	11 23		12 42	13 11	13 33		15 31
	d	00s27					11 19			12 42	13 12	13 34		15 32
Pembrey & Burry Port	d	00s33					11 25			12 48	13 18	13 41		15 39
Kidwelly	d	00s39					11x32			12x54				
Ferryside	d	00s45					11x38			13x00				
Carmarthen	a	01 03					11 51			13 14	13 41	14 02		16 00
	d			08 20	09 55	10 19	11 57			13 17	14 07			
Whitland	a			08 36	10 11	10 33	12 13			13 32	14 23			
	d			08 37	10 11	10 34	12 13			13 32	14 23			
Narberth	d					10x43								
Kilgetty	d					10x52								
Saundersfoot	d					10x54								
Tenby	a					11 01								
	d					11 07								
Penally	d					11x10								
Manorbier	d					11 16								
Lamphey	d					11x24								
Pembroke	d					11 27								
Pembroke Dock	a					11 40								
Clunderwen	d			08x45	10x19		12x21	20x35			14x31			
Clarbeston Road	d			08x53	10x27		12x29	20x43		13 46	14x39			
Haverfordwest	d			09 01	10 35		12 37	20 52			14 47			
Johnston	d			09x10	10x44		12x46	21x00			14x56			
Milford Haven	a			09 21	10 55		12 57	21 15			15 10			
Fishguard Harbour ⛴	a									14 08				
	d													
Rosslare Harbour ⛴	a													

		AW	AW	AW	GW	AW	AW	GW	AW	GW	AW	GW	GW
			■	◇	◇■		■	◇■		◇■	■	◇■	◇■
London Paddington ■ ⊖	d				12 30			13 30		14 30		15 30	16 30
Reading ■	d				13 05			14 05		15 05		16 05	17 05
Manchester Piccadilly ■	d		10 30				12 29				14 30		
Gloucester ■	d												
Bristol Parkway ■	d				14 26			15 26		16 26		17 26	18 26
Newport (South Wales)	d		13 29		14 48		15 43	15 50		16 48	17 38	17 48	18 50
Cardiff Central ■	d		13 50		15 13		16 04	16 15		17 13	17 58	18 10	19 13
Pontyclun	d		14 03								18 12		
Llanharan	d		14 08								18 17		
Pencoed	d		14 13								18 22		
Bridgend	d		14 20		15 33		16 26	16 35		17 33	18 29	18 34	19 34
Wildmill	d												
Sarn	d												
Tondu	d												
Garth (Mid Glamorgan)	d												
Maesteg (Ewenny Road)	d												
Maesteg	a												
Pyle	d		14 28				16 34				18 37		
Port Talbot Parkway	d		14 36		15 47		16 42	16 49		17 47	18 46	18 50	19 47
Baglan	d												
Briton Ferry	d												
Neath	d				15 54			16 56		17 54	18 54	18 59	19 56
Skewen	d												
Llansamlet	d												
Swansea	a				16 07			17 09		18 10	19 06	19 11	20 08
	d	14 11		15 20		16 30		17 16	18 11		19 18		
Gowerton	d	14x22		15x31		16x41			18x22				
Llanelli	a	14 29	15 08	15 44		16 48	17 12	17 32	18 29		19 34		
	d	14 31	15 09	15 51		16 50	17 12	17 33	18 31		19 35		
Pembrey & Burry Port	d	14 37	15 15			16 56	17 19	17 40	18 37		19 42		
Kidwelly	d	14x43				17x03			18x44				
Ferryside	d	14x49				17x09			18x50				
Carmarthen	a	15 04	15 37		16 00	17 22	17 42	18 01	19 03		20 04		
	d	15 07	16 09			17 26	18 06		19 06		20 08		
Whitland	a	15 23	16 25			17 40	18 22		19 22		20 24		
	d	15 23	16 26			17 48	18 23		19 22		20 28		
Narberth	d	15x31				17x57							
Kilgetty	d	15x41				18x07							
Saundersfoot	d	15x43				18x09							
Tenby	a	15 50				18 16							
	d	15 54				18 19							
Penally	d	15x57				18x22							
Manorbier	d	16 03				18 29							
Lamphey	d	16x11				18x36							
Pembroke	d	16 14				18 40							
Pembroke Dock	a	16 27				18 54							
Clunderwen	d		16x34				18x31		19x30		20x35		
Clarbeston Road	d		16x42				18x39		19x38		20x43		
Haverfordwest	d		16 50				18 47		19a46		20 52		
Johnston	d		16x59				18x56				21x00		
Milford Haven	a		17 14				19 11				21 15		
Fishguard Harbour ⛴	a												
	d												
Rosslare Harbour ⛴	a												

Table 128

Cardiff - Maesteg, Swansea and West Wales

Sundays
18 July to 05 September

		AW	AW	GW	AW	GW	GW	AW	GW	GW
		■ ✕		◇1 ⊐	◇	◇1 ⊐	◇1 ⊐	◇	◇1 ⊐	◇1 ⊐
London Paddington 15 ⊖	d			17 30		18 30	19 30		20 30	21 37
Reading 7	d			18 05		19 05	20 05		21 05	22 14
Manchester Piccadilly 10	d									
Gloucester 7	d									
Bristol Parkway 7	d			19 26		20 30	21 26		22 30	23 38
Newport (South Wales)	d			19 51		20 50	21 48		23 00	00 04
Cardiff Central 7	d			20 17	20 21	22 13	21 14	22 30	23 24	00 28
Pontyclun	d									
Llanharan	d									
Pencoed	d									
Bridgend	d			20 36	20 43	22 35	21 36	22 51	23 44	00 49
Wildmill	d									
Sarn	d									
Tondu	d									
Garth (Mid Glamorgan)	d									
Maesteg (Ewenny Road)	d									
Maesteg	a									
Pyle	d				20 51					
Port Talbot Parkway	d			20 49	20 59	22 47	21 48	23 05	23 59	01 02
Baglan	d									
Briton Ferry	d									
Neath	d			20 57	21 07	22 55	21 57	23 13	00 06	01 10
Skewen	d									
Llansamlet	d									
Swansea	a			21 10	21 20	23 08	22 09	23 25	00 19	01 22
	d		20 35		21 23			23 39		
Gowerton	d		20x46					23x50		
Llanelli	a		20 54		21 38			23 57		
	d		20 55		21 40			23 59		
Pembrey & Burry Port	d		21 01		21 46			00 05		
Kidwelly	d		21x08					00x12		
Ferryside	d		21x14					00x18		
Carmarthen	a		21 32		22 09			00 31		
	d				22 11			00 34		
Whitland	a				22 27			00 50		
	d	20 29			22 28			00 50		
Narberth	d	20x38								
Kilgetty	d	20x47								
Saundersfoot	d	20x49								
Tenby	a	20 58								
	d	21 00								
Penally	d	21x03								
Manorbier	d	21 09								
Lamphey	d	21x17								
Pembroke	d	21 20								
Pembroke Dock	a	21 35								
Clunderwen	d				22x35					
Clarbeston Road	d				22x43			01x03		
Haverfordwest	d				22 52					
Johnston	d				23x00					
Milford Haven	a				23 14					
Fishguard Harbour ⛴	a							01 32		
	d									
Rosslare Harbour ⛴	a									

Table 128

Cardiff - Maesteg, Swansea and West Wales

Sundays
from 12 September

		AW	AW	GW	AW	AW	AW	AW	GW	AW	GW	AW	GW	AW	AW
		◇ ✕		◇1 ⊐			◇ ✕	◇	◇1 ⊐	◇ ✕	◇1 ⊐	◇ ✕	◇1 ⊐		■ ✕
London Paddington 15 ⊖	d			20p45					08 30		09 30		10 37		
Reading 7	d			21p11					09 05		10 05		11 11		
Manchester Piccadilly 10	d	18p30													10 29
Gloucester 7	d														
Bristol Parkway 7	d			22p11					10 07		11 04		12 10		
Newport (South Wales)	d	21p44		22p46			09 27		10 32	11 00	11 32		12 36		13 29
Cardiff Central 7	d	22p12	22p43	23p07			09 50		10 53	11 18	11 53	12 05	12 56		14 01
Pontyclun	d		22p55				10 03								14 15
Llanharan	d		23p00				10 08								14 20
Pencoed	d		23p04				10 13								14 24
Bridgend	d	22p33	23p10	23p28			10 20		11 18	11 14	12 14	12 26	13 18		14 31
Wildmill	d														
Sarn	d														
Tondu	d														
Garth (Mid Glamorgan)	d														
Maesteg (Ewenny Road)	d														
Maesteg	a														
Pyle	d		23p18				10 28					12 34			14 39
Port Talbot Parkway	d	22p47	23p27	23p41			10 37		15 31	11 27	12 27	12 43	13 31		14 48
Baglan	d		23p30												
Briton Ferry	d		23p34												
Neath	d	22p55	23p38	23p49			10 45		15 37	11 35	12 34		13 37		14 56
Skewen	d		23p41												
Llansamlet	d		23p45												
Swansea	a	23p07	23p53	00 02			10 58		15 51	11 48	12 47		13 51		15 08
	d	23p12	00 08				11 01	11 07			12 54			14 11	15 11
Gowerton	d	23c23	00x19					11 16						14x22	
Llanelli	a	23p29	00s26				11 17	11 23			13 10	13 17		14 29	15 27
	d	23p31	00s27				11 19				13 11	13 18		14 31	15 27
Pembrey & Burry Port	d	23p36	00s33				11 25				13 18	13 24		14 37	15 34
Kidwelly	d	23c43	00s39				11x32							14x43	
Ferryside	d	23c49	00s45				11x38							14x49	
Carmarthen	a	00 09	01 03				11 51				13 39	13 49		15 04	15 56
	d				09 55	10 19	11 55					14 04		15 07	16 09
Whitland	a				10 11	10 33	12 11					14 20		15 23	16 25
	d				10 11	10 34	12 11					14 20		15 23	16 26
Narberth	d					10x43								15x31	
Kilgetty	d					10x52								15x41	
Saundersfoot	d					10x54								15x43	
Tenby	a					11 01								15 50	
	d					11 07								15 54	
Penally	d					11x10								15x57	
Manorbier	d					11 16								16 03	
Lamphey	d					11x24								16x11	
Pembroke	d					11 27								16 14	
Pembroke Dock	a					11 40								16 27	
Clunderwen	d				10x19		12x19					14x28			16x34
Clarbeston Road	d				10x27		12x27			13 36		14x36			16x42
Haverfordwest	d				10 35		12 35					14 44			16 50
Johnston	d				10x44		12x44					14x53			16x59
Milford Haven	a				10 55		12 55					15 07			17 14
Fishguard Harbour ⛴	a									13 59					
	d														
Rosslare Harbour ⛴	a														

		AW	GW	AW	GW	AW	GW	AW	GW	AW	GW	AW	AW	GW
		◇	◇1 ⊐		◇1 ⊐	■ ✕	◇1 ⊐		◇1 ⊐	■ ✕	◇1 ⊐	■ ✕		◇1 ⊐
London Paddington 15 ⊖	d		12 37		13 37		14 37		15 37		16 37			17 37
Reading 7	d		13 11		14 11		15 11		16 11		17 11			18 11
Manchester Piccadilly 10	d					12 30				14 30				
Gloucester 7	d													
Bristol Parkway 7	d		14 10		15 10		16 10		17 10		18 10			19 14
Newport (South Wales)	d		14 36		15 36	15 45	16 36		17 40	17 34	18 36			19 41
Cardiff Central 7	d		14 56		15 56	16 16	16 56		18 00	18 04	18 56			20 00
Pontyclun	d									18 19				
Llanharan	d									18 24				
Pencoed	d									18 28				
Bridgend	d		15 18		16 18	16 37	17 19		18 21	18 36	19 18			20 22
Wildmill	d													
Sarn	d													
Tondu	d													
Garth (Mid Glamorgan)	d													
Maesteg (Ewenny Road)	d													
Maesteg	a													
Pyle	d					16 45				18 44				
Port Talbot Parkway	d		15 31		16 31	16 54	17 31		18 34	18 52	19 31			20 35
Baglan	d													
Briton Ferry	d													
Neath	d		15 37		16 37	17 02	17 37		18 42	19 00	19 37			20 43
Skewen	d													
Llansamlet	d													
Swansea	a		15 51		16 51	17 14	17 52		18 54	19 13	19 51			20 56
	d	15 26		16 16	17 04	17 25		18 11		19 19			20 35	
Gowerton	d	15 36		16x27				18x22					20x46	
Llanelli	a	15 44		16 34	17 20	17 41		18 29		19 35			20 54	
	d			16 36	17 21	17 41		18 31		19 36			20 55	
Pembrey & Burry Port	d			16 42	17 28	17 48		18 37		19 43			21 01	
Kidwelly	d			16x49				18x44					21x08	
Ferryside	d			16x55				18x50					21x14	
Carmarthen	a			17 08	17 49	18 17		19 03		20 05			21 32	
	d			17 25		18 20		19 06		20 09				
Whitland	a			17 39		18 36		19 22		20 25				
	d			17 48		18 37		19 22		20 32		20 27		
Narberth	d			17x57								20x36		
Kilgetty	d			18x07								20x45		
Saundersfoot	d			18x09								20x47		
Tenby	a			18 16								20 56		
	d			18 19								20 58		
Penally	d			18x22								21x01		
Manorbier	d			18 29								21 07		
Lamphey	d			18x36								21x15		
Pembroke	d			18 40								21 18		
Pembroke Dock	a			18 54								21 33		
Clunderwen	d					18x45		19x30		20x39				
Clarbeston Road	d					18x53		19x38		20x47				
Haverfordwest	d					19 01		19a46		20 56				
Johnston	d					19x10				21x04				
Milford Haven	a					19 25				21 19				
Fishguard Harbour ⛴	a													
	d													
Rosslare Harbour ⛴	a													

Table 128

Sundays
from 12 September

Cardiff - Maesteg, Swansea and West Wales

		AW	GW	GW	AW	GW	GW
		◇	◇■ ▭	◇■ ▭	◇	◇■ ▭	◇■ ▭
London Paddington ⊖	d		18 37	19 37		20 37	21 37
Reading	d		19 11	20 11		21 11	22 14
Manchester Piccadilly	d						
Gloucester	d						
Bristol Parkway	d		20 10	21 10		22 10	23 17
Newport (South Wales)	d		20 36	21 36		22 40	23 45
Cardiff Central	d	20 15	20 55	22 00	22 30	23 04	00 09
Pontyclun	d						
Llanharan	d						
Pencoed	d						
Bridgend	d	20 37	21 18	22 22	22 51	23 24	00 30
Wildmill	d						
Sarn	d						
Tondu	d						
Garth (Mid Glamorgan)	d						
Maesteg (Ewenny Road)	d						
Maesteg	a						
Pyle	d	20 45					
Port Talbot Parkway	d	20 54	21 31	22 34	23 05	23 38	00 43
Baglan	d						
Briton Ferry	d						
Neath	d	21 02	21 37	22 43	23 13	23 46	00 51
Skewen	d						
Llansamlet	d						
Swansea	a	21 14	21 52	22 55	23 25	23 58	01 03
	d	21 18			23 38		
Gowerton	d				23x49		
Llanelli	a	21 33			23 56		
	d	21 34			23 58		
Pembrey & Burry Port	d	21 41			00 04		
Kidwelly	d				00x11		
Ferryside	d				00x17		
Carmarthen	a	22 04			00 30		
	d	22 05			00 34		
Whitland	a	22 21			00 50		
	d	22 22			00 50		
Narberth	d						
Kilgetty	d						
Saundersfoot	d						
Tenby	a						
	d						
Penally	d						
Manorbier	d						
Lamphey	d						
Pembroke	d						
Pembroke Dock	a						
Clunderwen	d	22x29					
Clarbeston Road	d	22x37			01x03		
Haverfordwest	d	22 46					
Johnston	d	22x54					
Milford Haven	a	23 08					
Fishguard Harbour ⛴	a				01 32		
	d						
Rosslare Harbour ⛴	a						

Table 128

Mondays to Fridays

West Wales, Swansea and Maesteg - Cardiff

		AW MX	AW	AW	AW	AW	AW MX	AW	AW	AW MX	AW	GW	GW	GW	GW	AW	GW	GW	AW	AW	GW	AW	GW
			◇ A	◇ B	◇ C	B		A	C		◇	◇■ C ▭	◇■ D ▭	◇■ ▭	◇■ ▭	◇ ⫨	◇■ ⌀	◇■ ▭⌀		◇ ⫨	◇■ ▭⌀		◇■ ▭
Rosslare Harbour ⛴	d																						
Fishguard Harbour ⛴	a																						
	d										01 50												
Milford Haven	d		21p29	21p33	21p44	23p15	23p19	23p21	23p45	00 19													
Johnston	d		21b37	21b41	21b52	23b23	23b27	23b29	23b53	00x27													
Haverfordwest	d		21p47	21p49	21p59	23p30	23p34	23p36	00 03	00 34													
Clarbeston Road	d		21b55	21b57	22b08	23b39	23b42	23b45	00x12	00x42	02x10												
Clunderwen	d		22b03	22b05	22b15	23b46	23b49	23b52	00x19	00x49													
Pembroke Dock	d																						
Pembroke	d																						
Lamphey	d																						
Manorbier	d																						
Penally	d																						
Tenby	a																						
	d																						
Saundersfoot	d																						
Kilgetty	d																						
Narberth	d																						
Whitland	a		22p09	22p11	22p22	23p53	23p55	23p59	00 26	00 55	02 22												
	d		22p12	22p14	22p24	23p53	23p57	23p59	00 27	00 57	02 22												
Carmarthen	a		22p29	22p31	22p42	00 11	00 18	00 17	00 49	01 13	02 39												
	d		22p32	22p34	22p44						02 44					05 04				05 50		06 16	
Ferryside	d		22b42	22b44	22b55															06x00		06x26	
Kidwelly	d		22b48	22b50	23b01															06x05		06x31	
Pembrey & Burry Port	d		22p56	22p58	23p08											05 22				06 12		06 38	
Llanelli	a		23p02	23p04	23p14						03 06					05 27				06 17		06 43	
	d		23p02	23p04	23p15						03 06					05 28				06 18		06 44	
Gowerton	d		23b10	23b12	23b22															06x24		06x51	
Swansea	a		23p27	23p29	23p39						03 25									06 38		07 05	
	d		23p28	23p30	23p41							03 53	03 58	04 58	05 27		05 58	06 28		06 45	06 58	07 09	07 28
Llansamlet	d																					07 16	
Skewen	d																					07 20	
Neath	d		23p40	23p42	23p52							04 05	04 10	05 10	05 39		06 10	06 40		06 56	07 10	07 24	07 40
Briton Ferry	d																					07 27	
Baglan	d																					07 31	
Port Talbot Parkway	d		23p47	23p49	23p59							04 13	04 18	05 18	05 47	06 01	06 18	06 48		07 03	07 18	07 35	07 48
Pyle	d		23p54	23p56	00 06															07 09		07 42	
Maesteg	d	22p15																	06 46				
Maesteg (Ewenny Road)	d	22p17																	06 48				
Garth (Mid Glamorgan)	d	22p20																	06 51				
Tondu	d	22p29																	07 00				
Sarn	d	22p32																	07 03				
Wildmill	d	22p34																	07 05				
Bridgend	d	22p38	00 02	00 04	00 15							04 26	04 30	05 30	05 59	06 15	06 30	07 00	07 09	07 17	07 30	07 50	08 00
Pencoed	d	22p44														06 21			07 15			08 07	
Llanharan	d	22p48														06 24				07 24		08 11	
Pontyclun	d	22p52														06 29			07 22			08 15	
Cardiff Central	a	23p07	00 27	00 29	00 57							05 12	05 15	05 52	06 21	06 43	06 52	07 22	07 36	07 40	07 52	08 34	08 22
Newport (South Wales)	a	23p39										05 32	05 32	06 09	06 37	07 02	07 09	07 39		08 03	08 09		08 39
Bristol Parkway	a											05 59	05 59	06 29	06 58		07 29	07 59			08 30		08 59
Gloucester	a	00 39																					
Manchester Piccadilly	a															10 15				11 15			
Reading	a											07 00	07 00	07 28	08 00			09 01			09 25		09 59
London Paddington ⊖	a											07 32	07 32	08 02	08 33		08 54	09 29			09 59		10 32

A MO from 19 July until 6 September
B MO from 13 September
C MO until 12 July
D MO from 19 July MSX all dates
b previous night, stops on request

Table 128

West Wales, Swansea and Maesteg - Cardiff

Mondays to Fridays

		AW	AW	GW	GW	AW	AW	AW	GW	AW	AW	AW	GW	AW	AW	AW	AW	GW	AW	AW	GW	AW	AW	AW	AW
		◇		◇ 1	◇ 1	◇		◇	◇ 1	◇			◇ 1	◇				◇ 1	◇		◇ 1	◇	◇		
Rosslare Harbour ⛴	d																								
Fishguard Harbour ⛴	a																								
	d																								
Milford Haven	d	06 00				07 03								09 08								11 08			
Johnston	d	06x08				07x11								09x16								11x16			
Haverfordwest	d	06 15				07 18								09 23								11 23			
Clarbeston Road	d	06x23				07x26								09x31								11x31			
Clunderwen	d	06x30				07x33								09x38								11x38			
Pembroke Dock	d									07 09							09 05							11 05	
Pembroke	d									07 17							09 13							11 13	
Lamphey	d									07x20							09x16							11x16	
Manorbier	d									07 29							09 25							11 25	
Penally	d									07x34							09x30							11x30	
Tenby	a									07 37							09 33							11 33	
	d									07 37							09 38							11 42	
Saundersfoot	d									07x45							09x46							11x50	
Kilgetty	d									07x47							09x48							11x51	
Narberth	d									07x57							09x58							12x01	
Whitland	a	06 36				07 39				08 05				09 44			10 06					11 44		12 09	
	d	06 38				07 41				08 07				09 46			10 09					11 46		12 11	
Carmarthen	a	06 54				07 57				08 25				10 03			10 26					12 02		12 29	
	d	06 57			07 30	08 01				08 30	09 00			10 06			10 29		11 04			12 05		12 31	
Ferryside	d				07 42	08x11				08x40	09x10								11x14						
Kidwelly	d				07 49	08x16				08x46	09x16								11x19						
Pembrey & Burry Port	d	07 15			07 56	08 23				08 53	09 23			10 22			10 48		11 25			12 23		12 50	
Llanelli	a	07 20			08 02	08 28				08 59	09 29			10 29			10 54		11 31			12 28		12 56	
	d	07 21			08 04	08 29		08 45		09 00	09 30			10 29			10 55		11 31			12 29		12 57	
Gowerton	d	07x27				08x35		08 53		09x08							11x02		11x38				12 37	13x04	
Swansea	a	07 41			08 21	08 48		09 08		09 23	09 51			10 47			11 23		11 51			12 46	13 06	13 23	
	d	07 45		07 58	08 28	08 55		09 11	09 28	09 55			10 28	10 55		11 10		11 28	11 55		12 28	12 55	13 10		
Llansamlet	d							09 18								11 17							13 17		
Skewen	d							09 22								11 21							13 21		
Neath	d	07 56		08 10	08 40	09 06		09 26	09 40	10 06			10 40	11 06		11 25		11 40	12 06		12 40	13 06	13 25		
Briton Ferry	d							09 31								11 28							13 28		
Baglan	d							09 33								11 32							13 32		
Port Talbot Parkway	d	08 03		08 18	08 48	09 13		09 37	09 48	10 13			10 48	11 13		11 36		11 48	12 13		12 48	13 13	13 36		
Pyle	d	08 09						09 45								11 43							13 43		
Maesteg	d		08 00				09 15					10 15			11 15					12 15					13 15
Maesteg (Ewenny Road)	d		08 02				09 17					10 17			11 17					12 17					13 17
Garth (Mid Glamorgan)	d		08 05				09 20					10 20			11 20					12 20					13 20
Tondu	d		08 14				09 29					10 29			11 29					12 29					13 29
Sarn	d		08 17				09 32					10 32			11 32					12 32					13 32
Wildmill	d		08 19				09 34					10 34			11 34					12 34					13 34
Bridgend	d	08 17	08 23	08 30	09 00	09 25	09 38	09 54	10 00	10 25		10 38	11 00	11 25	11 38	11 55		12 00	12 25	12 38	13 00	13 25	13 52		13 38
Pencoed	d	08 23					09 44					10 44			11 44					12 44					13 44
Llanharan	d		08 31				09 48					10 48			11 48					12 48					13 48
Pontyclun	d	08 30					09 52					10 52			11 52					12 52					13 52
Cardiff Central [7]	a	08 44	08 48	08 52	09 22	09 47	10 07	10 19	10 22	10 48		11 09	11 22	11 47	12 08	12 17		12 22	12 47	13 07	13 22	13 47	14 15		14 07
Newport (South Wales)	a	09 03	09 25	09 09	09 39	10 03	10 25		10 39	11 03			11 39	12 03	12 25			12 39	13 03	13 25	13 39	14 03			
Bristol Parkway [7]	a			09 30	09 59				10 59				11 59					12 59			13 59				
Gloucester [7]	a		10 20				11 20								13 20					14 20					
Manchester Piccadilly [10]	a	12 15				13 15				14 15				15 15					16 15			17 15			
Reading [7]	a			10 31	11 00				11 59				13 00					13 59			15 00				
London Paddington [15] ⊖	a			11 07	11 32				12 32				13 32					14 32			15 32				

Table 128

West Wales, Swansea and Maesteg - Cardiff

Mondays to Fridays

		GW		AW	AW	GW	AW	AW	AW	AW	AW	GW	AW	AW	GW	AW	AW	AW	AW	AW	GW	AW		AW	GW
		◇ 1		◇		◇ 1	■	■				◇ 1	■		◇ 1	■	◇				◇ 1	◇			◇ 1
Rosslare Harbour ⛴	d																								
Fishguard Harbour ⛴	a																								
	d							13 30																	
Milford Haven	d						13 08									15 08									
Johnston	d						13x16									15x16									
Haverfordwest	d						13 23									15 23									
Clarbeston Road	d						13x31	13 50								15x31									
Clunderwen	d						13x38									15x38									
Pembroke Dock	d										13 05									15 05					
Pembroke	d										13 13									15 13					
Lamphey	d										13x16									15x16					
Manorbier	d										13 25									15 25					
Penally	d										13x30									15x30					
Tenby	a										13 33									15 33					
	d										13 42									15 42					
Saundersfoot	d										13x50									15x49					
Kilgetty	d										13x51									15x51					
Narberth	d										14x01									16x00					
Whitland	a						13 44	14 02			14 09					15 44				16 08					
	d						13 46	14 02			14 11					15 46				16 11					
Carmarthen	a						14 02	14 19			14 29					16 02				16 28					
	d			13 04			14 05	14 22			14 31		15 05			16 05				16 31		17 04			
Ferryside	d			13x14							14x42									16x41		17x14			
Kidwelly	d			13x19							14x48									16x47		17x19			
Pembrey & Burry Port	d			13 25			14 23				14 55		15 23			16 23				16 54		17 25			
Llanelli	a			13 31			14 28	14 44			15 01		15 28			16 28				17 00		17 31			
	d			13 31			14 29	14 45			15 01		15 29			16 29	17 38			17 01		17 31			
Gowerton	d						14x35									16x35	17 45			17x08					
Swansea	a			13 49			14 49				15 23		15 47			16 48	18 06			17 24		17 49			
	d	13 28		13 55		14 28	14 55			15 10		15 28	15 55		16 28	16 55			17 10		17 28	17 55			18 28
Llansamlet	d									15 17									17 17						
Skewen	d									15 21									17 21						
Neath	d	13 40		14 06		14 40	15 06			15 25		15 40	16 06		16 40	17 06			17 25		17 40	18 06			18 40
Briton Ferry	d									15 28									17 28						
Baglan	d									15 32									17 32						
Port Talbot Parkway	d	13 48		14 13		14 48	15 13			15 36		15 48	16 13		16 48	17 13			17 36		17 48	18 13			18 48
Pyle	d									15 43									17 43						
Maesteg	d				14 15				15 17					16 15				17 15						18 20	
Maesteg (Ewenny Road)	d				14 17				15 19					16 17				17 17						18 22	
Garth (Mid Glamorgan)	d				14 20				15 22					16 20				17 20						18 25	
Tondu	d				14 29				15 31					16 29				17 29						18 34	
Sarn	d				14 32				15 34					16 32				17 32						18 37	
Wildmill	d				14 34				15 36					16 34				17 34						18 39	
Bridgend	d	14 00		14 25	14 38	15 00	15 25		15 40	15 52		16 00	16 25	16 38	17 00	17 25		17 38	17 54		18 00	18 26		18 43	19 00
Pencoed	d				14 44				15 46					16 44				17 44						18 49	
Llanharan	d				14 48				15 50					16 48				17 48						18 53	
Pontyclun	d				14 52				15 54					16 52				17 52	18 04					18 57	
Cardiff Central [7]	a	14 22		14 47	15 07	15 22	15 47	16 04	16 09	16 15		16 22	16 47	17 07	17 22	17 47		18 07	18 18		18 22	18 47		19 13	19 22
Newport (South Wales)	a	14 39		15 03	15 26	15 39	16 03	16 18				16 39	17 03	17 25	17 39	18 03		18 25			18 39	19 03			19 39
Bristol Parkway [7]	a	15 00				15 59						16 59			17 59						18 59				19 59
Gloucester [7]	a				16 21			17 15						18 21				19 20							
Manchester Piccadilly [10]	a			18 15			19 15						20 15			21 15						22 15			
Reading [7]	a	16 00				17 00						17 55			19 01						20 00				21 00
London Paddington [15] ⊖	a	16 30				17 30						18 24			19 32						20 32				21 32

Table 128

Mondays to Fridays

West Wales, Swansea and Maesteg - Cardiff

		AW	AW	AW	AW	GW ◇1	AW ◇	AW	GW FO ◇1	GW FX ◇1	AW ◇	AW	AW	AW ◇	AW	AW FX	AW FO	AW	AW	AW	AW
Rosslare Harbour ⛴	d																				
Fishguard Harbour ⛴	a																				
	d																				
Milford Haven	d			17 08							19 08				21 18						23 19
Johnston	d			17x16							19x16				21x26						23x27
Haverfordwest	d			17 23							19 23				21 33						23 34
Clarbeston Road	d			17x31							19x31				21x41						23x42
Clunderwen	d			17x38							19x38				21x48						23x49
Pembroke Dock	d				17 05								19 16						21 11	22 23	
Pembroke	d				17 13								19 24						21 19	22 31	
Lamphey	d				17x16								19x27						21x22	22x34	
Manorbier	d				17 25								19 36						21 31	22 42	
Penally	d				17x30								19x41						21x36	22x48	
Tenby	a				17 33								19 44						21 39	22 50	
	d				17 42								19 48						21 44	22 50	
Saundersfoot	d				17x49								19x56						21x52	22x58	
Kilgetty	d				17x51								19x58						21x54	23x00	
Narberth	d				18x00								20x08						22x04	23x09	
Whitland	a			17 44	18 08						19 44		20 16		21 54				22 12	23 17	23 55
	d			17 47	18 11						19 46		20 19		21 56				22 14	23 20	23 57
Carmarthen	a			18 05	18 28						20 02		20 36		22 16				22 32	23 39	00 18
	d			18 07	18 31		19 08				20 05		20 39						22 35		
Ferryside	d			18x17	18x41								20x49						22x45		
Kidwelly	d			18x23	18x47								20x55						22x51		
Pembrey & Burry Port	d			18 30	18 54		19 26				20 23		21 02						22 58		
Llanelli	a			18 35	19 00		19 31				20 28		21 08						23 04		
	d			18 36	19 01		19 32				20 29		21 09	21 43					23 05		
Gowerton	d				19x08									21 50					23x12		
Swansea	a			18 54	19 23		19 49				20 47		21 33	22 10					23 28		
	d	19 00		19 10		19 29	20 00		20 28	20 28	20 55		21 35					22 32			
Llansamlet	d			19 17									21 42					22 39			
Skewen	d			19 21									21 46					22 43			
Neath	d	19 11		19 25		19 40	20 11		20 40	20 40	21 06		21 50					22 47			
Briton Ferry	d			19 28									21 53					22 50			
Baglan	d			19 32									21 57					22 54			
Port Talbot Parkway	d	19 18		19 36		19 48	20 18		20 48	20 48	21 13		22 01					22 58			
Pyle	d			19 43									22 08					23 05			
Maesteg	d		19 17					20 15				21 15				22 15	22 15				
Maesteg (Ewenny Road)	d		19 19					20 17				21 17				22 17	22 17				
Garth (Mid Glamorgan)	d		19 22					20 20				21 20				22 20	22 20				
Tondu	d		19 31					20 29				21 29				22 29	22 29				
Sarn	d		19 34					20 32				21 32				22 32	22 32				
Wildmill	d		19 36					20 34				21 34				22 34	22 34				
Bridgend	d	19 32	19 40	19 51		20 00	20 30	20 38	21 00	21 00	21 25	21 38	22 16			22 38	22 38	23 13			
Pencoed	d		19 46					20 44				21 44				22 44	22 44				
Llanharan	d		19 49					20 48				21 48				22 48	22 48				
Pontyclun	d		19 54					20 52				21 52				22 52	22 52				
Cardiff Central 7	a	19 59	20 10	20 16		20 22	20 51	21 07	21 22	21 22	21 47	22 10	22 39			23 07	23 07	23 38			
Newport (South Wales)	a					20 38	21 08	21 25	21 38	21 38						23 39	23 38				
Bristol Parkway 7	a					21 00			21 59	21 59											
Gloucester 7	a							22 22								00 39	00 39				
Manchester Piccadilly 10	a																				
Reading 7	a					22 09			23 03	23 03											
London Paddington 15 ⊖	a					22 45			23 36	23 40											

Table 128

Saturdays

until 04 September

West Wales, Swansea and Maesteg - Cardiff

		AW	AW	AW	AW ◇	GW ◇1	GW ◇1	GW ◇1	AW ◇	GW ◇1	GW ◇1	AW	AW ◇	GW ◇1	AW	GW ◇1	AW ◇	AW	GW ◇1	AW ◇	AW	AW	AW ◇	GW ◇1
Rosslare Harbour ⛴	d																							
Fishguard Harbour ⛴	a																							
	d				01 50																			
Milford Haven	d		23p19	00 19													06 00			07 03				
Johnston	d		23b27	00x27													06x08			07x11				
Haverfordwest	d		23p34	00 34													06 15			07 18				
Clarbeston Road	d		23b42	00x42	02x10												06x23			07x26				
Clunderwen	d		23b49	00x49													06x30			07x33				
Pembroke Dock	d																							
Pembroke	d																							
Lamphey	d																							
Manorbier	d																							
Penally	d																							
Tenby	a																							
	d																							
Saundersfoot	d																							
Kilgetty	d																							
Narberth	d																							
Whitland	a		23p55	00 55	02 22												06 36			07 39				
	d		23p57	00 57	02 22												06 38			07 41				
Carmarthen	a		00 18	01 13	02 39												06 54			07 57				
	d				02 44				05 04				05 50		06 16		06 57			08 01	08 30			
Ferryside	d												06x00		06x26					08x11	08x40			
Kidwelly	d												06x05		06x31					08x16	08x46			
Pembrey & Burry Port	d								05 22				06 12		06 38		07 15			08 23	08 53			
Llanelli	a				03 06				05 27				06 17		06 43		07 20			08 28	08 59			
	d				03 06				05 28				06 18		06 44		07 21			08 29	09 00		08 45	
Gowerton	d												06x24		06x51		07x27			08x35	09x07		08 53	
Swansea	a				03 26								06 38		07 05		07 41			08 49	09 23		09 08	
	d					03 58	04 58	05 28		05 58	06 28		06 45	06 58	07 09	07 28	07 45		08 28	08 55			09 11	09 28
Llansamlet	d														07 16								09 19	
Skewen	d														07 20								09 23	
Neath	d					04 10	05 10	05 40		06 10	06 40		06 56	07 10	07 24	07 40	07 56		08 40	09 06			09 27	09 40
Briton Ferry	d														07 27								09 31	
Baglan	d														07 31								09 34	
Port Talbot Parkway	d					04 18	05 18	05 48	06 01	06 18	06 48		07 03	07 18	07 35	07 48	08 03		08 48	09 13			09 38	09 48
Pyle	d												07 09		07 42		08 09						09 46	
Maesteg	d	22p15										06 46						08 00				09 17		
Maesteg (Ewenny Road)	d	22p17										06 48						08 02				09 19		
Garth (Mid Glamorgan)	d	22p20										06 51						08 05				09 22		
Tondu	d	22p29										07 00						08 14				09 31		
Sarn	d	22p32										07 03						08 17				09 34		
Wildmill	d	22p34										07 05						08 19				09 36		
Bridgend	d	22p38				04 30	05 30	06 00	06 13	06 30	07 00	07 09	07 17	07 30	07 50	08 00	08 17	08 23	09 00	09 25		09 40	09 54	10 00
Pencoed	d	22p44							06 19			07 15			08 07		08 23					09 46		
Llanharan	d	22p48							06 23				07 24		08 11			08 30				09 50		
Pontyclun	d	22p52							06 28			07 22			08 15		08 30					09 54		
Cardiff Central 7	a	23p07				04 52	05 52	06 22	06 43	06 52	07 22	07 36	07 40	07 52	08 34	08 22	08 43	08 47	09 22	09 47		10 09	10 20	10 22
Newport (South Wales)	a	23p38				05 09	06 09	06 38	07 02	07 08	07 39		08 03	08 08		08 38	09 03	09 24	09 39	10 03		10 25		10 39
Bristol Parkway 7	a					05 36	06 29	06 59		07 29	07 59			08 30		08 59			09 59					10 59
Gloucester 7	a	00 39																10 21				11 21		
Manchester Piccadilly 10	a								10 15				11 15				12 15			13 15				
Reading 7	a					07 14	07 31	08 00		08 32	09 00			09 32		10 00			11 01					12 00
London Paddington 15 ⊖	a					07 44	08 02	08 32		09 02	09 32			10 02		10 32			11 33					12 31

b previous night, stops on request

Table 128

Saturdays until 04 September

West Wales, Swansea and Maesteg - Cardiff

	AW	AW	AW	GW	AW		AW	AW	AW	GW	AW	AW
	◇ ⌶	⌶		◇ 1 ⊡	◇ ⌶					◇ 1 ⊡	◇ ⌶	
Rosslare Harbour ⛴ d												
Fishguard Harbour ⛴ a												
d												
Milford Haven d					09 08							
Johnston d					09x16							
Haverfordwest d					09 23							
Clarbeston Road d					09x31							
Clunderwen d					09x38							
Pembroke Dock d	07 09	08 35										
Pembroke d	07 17	08 43										
Lamphey d	07x20	08x46										
Manorbier d	07 29	08 55										
Penally d	07x34	09x00										
Tenby a	07 37	09 03										
d	07 37	09 10										
Saundersfoot d	07x45	09x18										
Kilgetty d	07x47	09x20										
Narberth d	07x57	09x30										
Whitland a	08 05	09 38			09 44							
d	08 07				09 46				10 08			
Carmarthen a	08 24				10 03				10 26			
d	09 00			09 35	10 06				10 29		11 01	
Ferryside d	09x10										11x11	
Kidwelly d	09x15										11x16	
Pembrey & Burry Port d	09 21			09 56	10 23				10 48		11 23	
Llanelli a	09 27			10 01	10 29				10 54		11 28	
d	09 27			10 03	10 29				10 56		11 29	
Gowerton d									11x03		11x35	
Swansea a	09 47			10 21	10 47				11 17		11 49	
d	09 55			10 28	10 55			11 10		11 28	11 55	
Llansamlet d								11 17				
Skewen d								11 21				
Neath d	10 06			10 40	11 06			11 25		11 40	12 06	
Briton Ferry d								11 28				
Baglan d								11 32				
Port Talbot Parkway d	10 13			10 48	11 13			11 36		11 48	12 13	
Pyle d								11 43				
Maesteg d			10 15				11 15					12 17
Maesteg (Ewenny Road) d			10 17				11 17					12 19
Garth (Mid Glamorgan) d			10 20				11 20					12 22
Tondu d			10 29				11 29					12 31
Sarn d			10 32				11 32					12 34
Wildmill d			10 34				11 34					12 36
Bridgend d	10 25		10 38	11 00	11 25		11 38	11 55		12 00	12 25	12 40
Pencoed d			10 44				11 44					12 46
Llanharan d			10 48				11 48					12 50
Pontyclun d			10 52				11 52					12 54
Cardiff Central 7 a	10 47		11 13	11 22	11 47		12 07	12 17		12 22	12 47	13 09
Newport (South Wales) 7 a	11 03			11 39	12 03		12 25			12 39	13 03	13 25
Bristol Parkway 7 a				11 59						12 59		
Gloucester 7 a							13 21					14 21
Manchester Piccadilly 10 a	14 15				15 15						16 15	
Reading 7 a				13 00						14 00		
London Paddington 15 ⊖ a				13 32						14 32		

	GW	AW	AW	AW	AW	GW	AW	AW	GW	AW	AW	AW
	◇ 1 A ⊡	◇ ⌶	⌶		◇	◇ 1 ⊡	◇ ⌶		◇ 1 ⊡	■ ⌶	■ ◇ ⌶	
Rosslare Harbour ⛴ d												
Fishguard Harbour ⛴ a												
d											13 30	
Milford Haven d		11 08								13 08		
Johnston d		11x16								13x16		
Haverfordwest d		11 23								13 23		
Clarbeston Road d		11x31								13x31	13 50	
Clunderwen d		11x38								13x38		
Pembroke Dock d	10 00											
Pembroke d	10 10											
Lamphey d												
Manorbier d	10 23											
Penally d												
Tenby a	10 32											
d	10 36		11 41									
Saundersfoot d	10 46		11x49									
Kilgetty d			11x51									
Narberth d			12x01									
Whitland a	11 06	11 44	12 09							13 44	14 02	
d	11 07	11 46	12 11							13 46	14 02	
Carmarthen a	11 25	12 02	12 29							14 02	14 19	
d	11 35	12 05	12 31				13 04			14 05	14 22	
Ferryside d							13x14					
Kidwelly d							13x19					
Pembrey & Burry Port d	11 56	12 23	12 50				13 25			14 23		
Llanelli a	12 01	12 28	12 56				13 31			14 28	14 44	
d	12 03	12 29	12 57		12 37		13 31			14 29	14 45	
Gowerton d			13x04							14x35		
Swansea a	12 21	12 47	13 23		13 01		13 49			14 49		
d	12 28	12 55			13 10	13 28	13 55		14 28	14 55		
Llansamlet d					13 17							
Skewen d					13 21							
Neath d	12 40	13 06			13 25	13 40	14 06		14 40	15 06		
Briton Ferry d					13 28							
Baglan d					13 32							
Port Talbot Parkway d	12 48	13 13			13 36	13 48	14 13		14 48	15 13		
Pyle d					13 43							
Maesteg d				13 15				14 15				15 17
Maesteg (Ewenny Road) d				13 17				14 17				15 19
Garth (Mid Glamorgan) d				13 20				14 20				15 22
Tondu d				13 29				14 29				15 31
Sarn d				13 32				14 32				15 34
Wildmill d				13 34				14 34				15 36
Bridgend d	13 00	13 25		13 38	13 52	14 00	14 25	14 38	15 00	15 25		15 40
Pencoed d				13 44				14 44				15 46
Llanharan d				13 48				14 48				15 50
Pontyclun d				13 52				14 52				15 54
Cardiff Central 7 a	13 22	13 47		14 09	14 15	14 22	14 47	15 07	15 22	15 47	16 02	16 09
Newport (South Wales) 7 a	13 38	14 03				14 39	15 03	15 25	15 39	16 03		16 23
Bristol Parkway 7 a	13 59					14 59			15 59			
Gloucester 7 a								16 21				17 21
Manchester Piccadilly 10 a		17 15					18 15			19 15		
Reading 7 a	15 00					16 01			17 00			
London Paddington 15 ⊖ a	15 32					16 37			17 32			

A The Pembroke Coast Express

Table 128

Saturdays until 04 September

West Wales, Swansea and Maesteg - Cardiff

	AW		AW	GW	GW	AW	AW	GW	GW	AW	AW	
			⌶	◇ 1 A ⊡	◇ 1 B ⊡	■ ⌶		◇ 1 A ⊡	◇ 1 B ⊡	■ ⌶		
Rosslare Harbour ⛴ d												
Fishguard Harbour ⛴ a												
d												
Milford Haven d										15 08		
Johnston d										15x16		
Haverfordwest d										15 23		
Clarbeston Road d										15x31		
Clunderwen d										15x38		
Pembroke Dock d			13 05									
Pembroke d			13 13									
Lamphey d			13x16									
Manorbier d			13 25									
Penally d			13x30									
Tenby a			13 33									
d			13 41									
Saundersfoot d			13x49									
Kilgetty d			13x51									
Narberth d			14x01									
Whitland a			14 09							15 44		
d			14 11							15 46		
Carmarthen a			14 29							16 02		
d			14 31			15 05				16 05		
Ferryside d			14x42									
Kidwelly d			14x48									
Pembrey & Burry Port d			14 55			15 23				16 23		
Llanelli a			15 01			15 28				16 28		
d			15 01			15 29				16 29		
Gowerton d										16x35		
Swansea a			15 23			15 47				16 49		
d	15 10			15 28	15 37	15 55		16 28	16 37	16 55		
Llansamlet d	15 17											
Skewen d	15 21											
Neath d	15 25			15 40	15 49	16 06		16 40	16 49	17 06		
Briton Ferry d	15 28											
Baglan d	15 32											
Port Talbot Parkway d	15 36			15 48	15 57	16 13		16 48	16 57	17 13		
Pyle d	15 43											
Maesteg d							16 15				17 15	
Maesteg (Ewenny Road) d							16 17				17 17	
Garth (Mid Glamorgan) d							16 20				17 20	
Tondu d							16 29				17 29	
Sarn d							16 32				17 32	
Wildmill d							16 34				17 34	
Bridgend d	15 52			16 00	16 09	16 25	16 38	17 00	17 09	17 25	17 38	
Pencoed d							16 44				17 44	
Llanharan d							16 48				17 48	
Pontyclun d							16 52				17 52	
Cardiff Central 7 a	16 16			16 22	16 33	16 47	17 07	17 22	17 33	17 47	18 07	
Newport (South Wales) 7 a	16 32			16 39	16 54	17 03	17 27	17 39	17 54	18 03	18 25	
Bristol Parkway 7 a				16 59	17 15			17 59	18 16			
Gloucester 7 a							18 20				19 20	
Manchester Piccadilly 10 a						20 15				21 15		
Reading 7 a				18 00	18 52			19 00	19 59			
London Paddington 15 ⊖ a				18 32	19 29			19 32	20 32			

	AW	GW	GW	AW	AW	AW	GW	GW	AW		AW	AW
		◇ 1 A ⊡	◇ 1 B ⊡	◇ ⌶	⌶		◇ 1 A ⊡	◇ 1 B ⊡				
Rosslare Harbour ⛴ d												
Fishguard Harbour ⛴ a												
d												
Milford Haven d												17 08
Johnston d												17x16
Haverfordwest d												17 23
Clarbeston Road d												17x31
Clunderwen d												17x38
Pembroke Dock d		14 55	14 55		16 30							
Pembroke d		15 05	15 05		16 38							
Lamphey d		15x08	15x08		16x41							
Manorbier d		15 20	15 20		16 50							
Penally d		15x26	15x26		16x55							
Tenby a		15 29	15 29		16 58							
d		15 36	15 36		17 00							
Saundersfoot d		15 46	15 46		17x08							
Kilgetty d		15x49	15x49		17x10							
Narberth d		15x58	15x58		17x20							
Whitland a		16 08	16 08		17 28							17 44
d		16 09	16 09		17 31							17 47
Carmarthen a		16 27	16 27		17 48							18 05
d		16 33	16 33	17 04	18 30							18 07
Ferryside d		16x45	16x45	17x14	18x40							18x17
Kidwelly d		16x50	16x50	17x19	18x46							18x23
Pembrey & Burry Port d		16 58	16 58	17 25	18 53							18 30
Llanelli a		17 03	17 03	17 31	18 59							18 35
d		17 05	17 05	17 31	19 00							18 36
Gowerton d					→							
Swansea a		17 21	17 22	17 49								18 54
d	17 10	17 28	17 37	17 55			18 28	18 28	19 00			19 10
Llansamlet d	17 17											19 17
Skewen d	17 21											19 21
Neath d	17 25	17 40	17 49	18 06			18 40	18 40	19 11			19 25
Briton Ferry d	17 28											19 28
Baglan d	17 32											19 32
Port Talbot Parkway d	17 36	17 48	17 57	18 13			18 48	18 48	19 19			19 36
Pyle d	17 43											19 43
Maesteg d						18 20					19 15	
Maesteg (Ewenny Road) d						18 22					19 17	
Garth (Mid Glamorgan) d						18 25					19 20	
Tondu d						18 34					19 29	
Sarn d						18 37					19 32	
Wildmill d						18 39					19 34	
Bridgend d	17 55	18 00	18 09	18 25		18 43	19 00	19 00	19 32		19 38	19 51
Pencoed d						18 49					19 44	
Llanharan d						18 53					19 48	
Pontyclun d	18 05					18 57					19 52	
Cardiff Central 7 a	18 18	18 22	18 36	18 47		19 13	19 22	19 22	19 59		20 09	20 16
Newport (South Wales) 7 a		18 39	18 54	19 03			19 39	19 39				
Bristol Parkway 7 a		18 59	19 15				19 59	20 13				
Gloucester 7 a												
Manchester Piccadilly 10 a				22 15								
Reading 7 a		19 59	21 06				21 06	21 42				
London Paddington 15 ⊖ a		20 32	21 37				21 36	22 14				

A until 10 July

B from 17 July until 4 September

Table 128

Saturdays until 04 September

West Wales, Swansea and Maesteg - Cardiff

		AW	AW	AW	AW	AW	AW	AW	AW	AW	AW	AW	AW	AW	AW	AW
				◇		◇	◇									
						A	B									
		🛒														
Rosslare Harbour ⛴	d															
Fishguard Harbour ⛴	a															
	d															
Milford Haven	d					19 08	19 08				21 18					23 18
Johnston	d					19x16	19x16				21x26					23x26
Haverfordwest	d					19 23	19 23				21 33					23 33
Clarbeston Road	d					19x31	19x31				21x41					23x41
Clunderwen	d					19x38	19x38				21x48					23x48
Pembroke Dock	d								19 16					21 11	22 23	
Pembroke	d								19 24					21 19	22 31	
Lamphey	d								19x27					21x22	22x34	
Manorbier	d								19 36					21 31	22 42	
Penally	d								19x41					21x36	22x48	
Tenby	a								19 44					21 39	22 50	
	d								19 47					21 44	22 50	
Saundersfoot	d								19x55					21x52	22x58	
Kilgetty	d								19x57					21x54	23x00	
Narberth	d								20x07					22x04	23x09	
Whitland	a					19 44	19 44		20 15		21 54			22 12	23 17	23 54
	d					19 46	19 46		20 17		21 56			22 14	23 20	23 56
Carmarthen	a					20 02	20 02		20 36		22 15			22 32	23 39	00 17
	d			19 08		20 05	20 05		20 40					22 36		
Ferryside	d								20x51					22x47		
Kidwelly	d								20x57					22x53		
Pembrey & Burry Port	d	←		19 26		20 23	20 23		21 05					23 00		
Llanelli	a	18 59		19 31		20 28	20 28		21 11					23 06		
	d	19 00		19 32		20 29	20 29		21 11	21 40				23 06		
Gowerton	d	19x07								21 49				23x14		
Swansea	a	19 22		19 50		20 50	20 50		21 31	22 10				23 32		
	d		19 28	20 00		20 55	20 55		21 35				22 20			
Llansamlet	d								21 42				22 27			
Skewen	d								21 46				22 31			
Neath	d		19 40	20 11		21 06	21 06		21 50				22 35			
Briton Ferry	d								21 53				22 38			
Baglan	d								21 57				22 42			
Port Talbot Parkway	d		19 48	20 18		21 13	21 13		22 01				22 46			
Pyle	d								22 08				22 53			
Maesteg	d				20 15			21 15				22 15				
Maesteg (Ewenny Road)	d				20 17			21 17				22 17				
Garth (Mid Glamorgan)	d				20 20			21 20				22 20				
Tondu	d				20 29			21 29				22 29				
Sarn	d				20 32			21 32				22 32				
Wildmill	d				20 34			21 34				22 34				
Bridgend	d		20 00	20 30	20 38	21 25	21 25	21 38	22 16			22 39	23 01			
Pencoed	d				20 44			21 44				22 45				
Llanharan	d				20 48			21 48				22 49				
Pontyclun	d				20 52			21 52				22 53				
Cardiff Central 7	a			20 51	21 07	21 49	21 46	22 09	22 39			23 08	23 26			
Newport (South Wales)	a			21 08	21 25		22 05					23 37				
Bristol Parkway 7	a															
Gloucester 7	a				22 19							00 42				
Manchester Piccadilly 10	a															
Reading 7	a															
London Paddington 15 ⊖	a															

A from 17 July until 4 September

B until 10 July

Table 128

Saturdays from 11 September

West Wales, Swansea and Maesteg - Cardiff

		AW	AW	AW	AW	GW	GW	GW	AW	GW	GW	AW	AW	GW	AW	GW	AW	AW	GW	GW	AW	AW	AW
					◇	◇1	◇1	◇1	◇	◇1	◇1		◇	◇1		◇1	◇		◇1	◇1	◇		
						🍴	🍴	🍴	🛒	🍴	🍴		🛒	🍴⊘		🍴⊘	🛒		🍴	🍴	🛒		
Rosslare Harbour ⛴	d																						
Fishguard Harbour ⛴	a																						
	d				01 50																		
Milford Haven	d		23p19	00 19													06 00				07 03		
Johnston	d		23b27	00x27													06x08				07x11		
Haverfordwest	d		23p34	00 34													06 15				07 18		
Clarbeston Road	d		23b42	00x42	02x10												06x23				07x26		
Clunderwen	d		23b49	00x49													06x30				07x33		
Pembroke Dock	d																						
Pembroke	d																						
Lamphey	d																						
Manorbier	d																						
Penally	d																						
Tenby	a																						
	d																						
Saundersfoot	d																						
Kilgetty	d																						
Narberth	d																						
Whitland	a		23p55	00 55	02 22												06 36				07 39		
	d		23p57	00 57	02 22												06 38				07 41		
Carmarthen	a		00 18	01 13	02 39												06 54				07 57		
	d				02 44				05 04				05 50		06 16		06 57				08 01	08 30	
Ferryside	d												06x00		06x26						08x11	08x40	
Kidwelly	d												06x05		06x31						08x16	08x46	
Pembrey & Burry Port	d								05 22				06 12		06 38		07 15				08 23	08 53	
Llanelli	a				03 06				05 27				06 17		06 43		07 20				08 28	08 59	
	d				03 06				05 28				06 18		06 44		07 21				08 29	09 00	
Gowerton	d												06x24		06x51		07x27				08x35	09x07	
Swansea	a				03 26								06 38		07 05		07 41				08 49	09 23	
	d					03 58	04 58	05 28		05 58	06 28		06 45	06 58	07 09	07 28	07 45		07 58	08 28	08 55		
Llansamlet	d														07 16								
Skewen	d														07 20								
Neath	d					04 10	05 10	05 40		06 10	06 40		06 56	07 10	07 24	07 40	07 56		08 10	08 40	09 06		
Briton Ferry	d														07 27								
Baglan	d														07 31								
Port Talbot Parkway	d					04 18	05 18	05 48	06 01	06 18	06 48		07 03	07 18	07 35	07 48	08 03		08 18	08 48	09 13		
Pyle	d												07 09		07 42		08 09						
Maesteg	d	22p15										06 46						08 00					09 17
Maesteg (Ewenny Road)	d	22p17										06 48						08 02					09 19
Garth (Mid Glamorgan)	d	22p20										06 51						08 05					09 22
Tondu	d	22p29										07 00						08 14					09 31
Sarn	d	22p32										07 03						08 17					09 34
Wildmill	d	22p34										07 05						08 19					09 36
Bridgend	d	22p38				04 30	05 30	06 00	06 13	06 30	07 00	07 09	07 17	07 30	07 50	08 00	08 17	08 23	08 30	09 00	09 25		09 40
Pencoed	d	22p44							06 19			07 15			08 07		08 23						09 46
Llanharan	d	22p48							06 23				07 24		08 11			08 30					09 50
Pontyclun	d	22p52							06 28			07 22			08 15		08 30						09 54
Cardiff Central 7	a	23p07				04 52	05 52	06 22	06 43	06 52	07 22	07 36	07 40	07 52	08 34	08 22	08 43	08 47	08 52	09 22	09 47		10 09
Newport (South Wales)	a	23p38				05 09	06 09	06 38	07 02	07 08	07 39		08 03	08 08		08 38	09 03	09 24	09 08	09 39	10 03		10 25
Bristol Parkway 7	a					05 36	06 29	06 59		07 29	07 59			08 30		08 59			09 30	09 59			
Gloucester 7	a	00 39																10 21					11 21
Manchester Piccadilly 10	a								10 15				11 15				12 15				13 15		
Reading 7	a					07 14	07 31	08 00		08 32	09 00			09 32		10 00			10 32	11 01			
London Paddington 15 ⊖	a					07 44	08 02	08 32		09 02	09 32			10 02		10 32			11 02	11 33			

b previous night, stops on request

Table 128

West Wales, Swansea and Maesteg - Cardiff

Saturdays
from 11 September

	AW	GW	AW	AW	GW	AW	AW	AW	AW	GW	AW	AW
	◇	◇1 ⊐	◇ ⌶		◇1 ⊐	◇ ⌶				◇1 ⊐	◇ ⌶	
Rosslare Harbour ⛴ d												
Fishguard Harbour ⛴ a												
d												
Milford Haven d						09 08						
Johnston d						09x16						
Haverfordwest d						09 23						
Clarbeston Road d						09x31						
Clunderwen d						09x38						
Pembroke Dock d			07 09						09 05			
Pembroke d			07 17						09 13			
Lamphey d			07x20						09x16			
Manorbier d			07 29						09 25			
Penally d			07x34						09x30			
Tenby a			07 37						09 33			
d			07 37						09 38			
Saundersfoot d			07x45						09x46			
Kilgetty d			07x47						09x48			
Narberth d			07x57						09x58			
Whitland a			08 05			09 44			10 06			
d			08 07			09 46			10 09			
Carmarthen a			08 24			10 03			10 26			
d			09 00		09 35	10 06			10 29		11 01	
Ferryside d			09x10								11x11	
Kidwelly d			09x15								11x16	
Pembrey & Burry Port d			09 21		09 56	10 23			10 48		11 23	
Llanelli a			09 27		10 01	10 29			10 54		11 28	
d	08 45		09 27		10 03	10 29			10 55		11 29	
Gowerton d	08 53								11x02		11x35	
Swansea a	09 08		09 47		10 21	10 47			11 23		11 49	
d	09 11	09 28	09 55		10 28	10 55		11 10		11 28	11 55	
Llansamlet d	09 19							11 17				
Skewen d	09 23							11 21				
Neath d	09 27	09 40	10 06		10 40	11 06		11 25		11 40	12 06	
Briton Ferry d	09 31							11 28				
Baglan d	09 34							11 32				
Port Talbot Parkway d	09 38	09 48	10 13		10 48	11 13		11 36		11 48	12 13	
Pyle d	09 46							11 43				
Maesteg d				10 15			11 15					12 17
Maesteg (Ewenny Road) d				10 17			11 17					12 19
Garth (Mid Glamorgan) d				10 20			11 20					12 22
Tondu d				10 29			11 29					12 31
Sarn d				10 32			11 32					12 34
Wildmill d				10 34			11 34					12 36
Bridgend d	09 54	10 00	10 25	10 38	11 00	11 25	11 38	11 55		12 00	12 25	12 40
Pencoed d				10 44			11 44					12 46
Llanharan d				10 48			11 48					12 50
Pontyclun d				10 52			11 52					12 54
Cardiff Central 7 a	10 20	10 22	10 47	11 13	11 22	11 47	12 07	12 17		12 22	12 47	13 09
Newport (South Wales) a		10 39	11 03		11 39	12 03	12 25			12 39	13 03	13 25
Bristol Parkway 7 a		10 59			11 59					12 59		
Gloucester 7 a							13 21					14 21
Manchester Piccadilly 10 a			14 15			15 15					16 15	
Reading 7 a		12 00			13 00					14 00		
London Paddington 15 ⊖ a		12 32			13 32					14 32		

	GW	AW	AW	AW	GW	AW	AW	AW	GW	AW	AW	AW
	◇1 ⊐	◇ ⌶			◇1 ⊐	◇	◇ ⌶		◇1 ⊐	■ ⌶	■ ◇ ⌶	
Rosslare Harbour ⛴ d												
Fishguard Harbour ⛴ a												
d											13 30	
Milford Haven d		11 08								13 08		
Johnston d		11x16								13x16		
Haverfordwest d		11 23								13 23		
Clarbeston Road d		11x31								13x31	13 50	
Clunderwen d		11x38								13x38		
Pembroke Dock d			11 05									
Pembroke d			11 13									
Lamphey d			11x16									
Manorbier d			11 25									
Penally d			11x30									
Tenby a			11 33									
d			11 39									
Saundersfoot d			11x47									
Kilgetty d			11x49									
Narberth d			11x59									
Whitland a		11 44	12 07							13 44	14 02	
d		11 46	12 10							13 46	14 02	
Carmarthen a		12 02	12 27							14 02	14 19	
d		12 05	12 31				13 04			14 05	14 22	
Ferryside d							13x14					
Kidwelly d							13x19					
Pembrey & Burry Port d		12 23	12 50				13 25			14 23		
Llanelli a		12 28	12 56				13 31			14 28	14 44	
d		12 29	12 57			12 37	13 31			14 29	14 45	
Gowerton d			13x04							14x35		
Swansea a		12 47	13 23			13 01	13 49			14 49		
d	12 28	12 55			13 28	13 10	13 55		14 28	14 55		
Llansamlet d						13 17						
Skewen d						13 21						
Neath d	12 40	13 06			13 40	13 25	14 06		14 40	15 06		
Briton Ferry d						13 28						
Baglan d						13 32						
Port Talbot Parkway d	12 48	13 13			13 48	13 36	14 13		14 48	15 13		
Pyle d						13 43						
Maesteg d				13 15				14 15				15 17
Maesteg (Ewenny Road) d				13 17				14 17				15 19
Garth (Mid Glamorgan) d				13 20				14 20				15 22
Tondu d				13 29				14 29				15 31
Sarn d				13 32				14 32				15 34
Wildmill d				13 34				14 34				15 36
Bridgend d	13 00	13 25		13 38	14 00	13 52	14 25	14 38	15 00	15 25		15 40
Pencoed d				13 44				14 44				15 46
Llanharan d				13 48				14 48				15 50
Pontyclun d				13 52				14 52				15 54
Cardiff Central 7 a	13 22	13 47		14 09	14 22	14 15	14 47	15 07	15 22	15 47	16 02	16 09
Newport (South Wales) a	13 38	14 03			14 39		15 03	15 25	15 39	16 03		16 23
Bristol Parkway 7 a	13 59				14 59				15 59			
Gloucester 7 a								16 21				17 21
Manchester Piccadilly 10 a		17 15					18 15			19 15		
Reading 7 a	15 00				16 01				17 00			
London Paddington 15 ⊖ a	15 32				16 32				17 32			

Table 128

West Wales, Swansea and Maesteg - Cardiff

Saturdays
from 11 September

	AW	AW	GW	AW	AW	GW	AW	AW	AW	AW	GW	AW
			◇1 ⊐	■ ⌶		◇1 ⊐	■ ⌶				◇1 ⊐	◇ ⌶
Rosslare Harbour ⛴ d												
Fishguard Harbour ⛴ a												
d												
Milford Haven d							15 08					
Johnston d							15x16					
Haverfordwest d							15 23					
Clarbeston Road d							15x31					
Clunderwen d							15x38					
Pembroke Dock d		13 05								15 05		
Pembroke d		13 13								15 13		
Lamphey d		13x16								15x16		
Manorbier d		13 25								15 25		
Penally d		13x30								15x30		
Tenby a		13 33								15 33		
d		13 43								15 43		
Saundersfoot d		13x51								15x51		
Kilgetty d		13x53								15x53		
Narberth d		14x03								16x03		
Whitland a		14 11					15 44			16 11		
d		14 14					15 46			16 14		
Carmarthen a		14 31					16 02			16 31		
d		14 34		15 05			16 05			16 34		17 04
Ferryside d		14x44								16x44		17x14
Kidwelly d		14x50								16x50		17x19
Pembrey & Burry Port d		14 57		15 23			16 23			16 57		17 25
Llanelli a		15 03		15 28			16 28			17 03		17 31
d		15 04		15 29			16 29			17 04		17 31
Gowerton d							16x35					
Swansea a		15 25		15 47			16 49			17 23		17 49
d	15 10		15 28	15 55		16 28	16 55		17 10		17 28	17 55
Llansamlet d	15 17								17 17			
Skewen d	15 21								17 21			
Neath d	15 25		15 40	16 06		16 40	17 06		17 25		17 40	18 06
Briton Ferry d	15 28								17 28			
Baglan d	15 32								17 32			
Port Talbot Parkway d	15 36		15 48	16 13		16 48	17 13		17 36		17 48	18 13
Pyle d	15 43								17 43			
Maesteg d					16 15			17 15				
Maesteg (Ewenny Road) d					16 17			17 17				
Garth (Mid Glamorgan) d					16 20			17 20				
Tondu d					16 29			17 29				
Sarn d					16 32			17 32				
Wildmill d					16 34			17 34				
Bridgend d	15 52		16 00	16 25	16 38	17 00	17 25	17 38	17 55		18 00	18 25
Pencoed d					16 44			17 44				
Llanharan d					16 48			17 48				
Pontyclun d					16 52			17 52	18 05			
Cardiff Central 7 a	16 16		16 22	16 47	17 07	17 22	17 47	18 07	18 18		18 22	18 47
Newport (South Wales) a	16 32		16 39	17 03	17 27	17 39	18 03	18 25			18 39	19 03
Bristol Parkway 7 a			16 59			17 59					18 59	
Gloucester 7 a					18 20			19 20				
Manchester Piccadilly 10 a				20 15			21 15					22 15
Reading 7 a			18 00			19 00					19 59	
London Paddington 15 ⊖ a			18 32			19 32					20 32	

	AW	GW	AW	AW	AW	GW	AW	AW	AW		AW	AW
		◇1 ⊐				◇1 ⊐		◇			◇	
Rosslare Harbour ⛴ d												
Fishguard Harbour ⛴ a												
d												
Milford Haven d					17 08						19 08	
Johnston d					17x16						19x16	
Haverfordwest d					17 23						19 23	
Clarbeston Road d					17x31						19x31	
Clunderwen d					17x38						19x38	
Pembroke Dock d							17 05					
Pembroke d							17 13					
Lamphey d							17x16					
Manorbier d							17 25					
Penally d							17x30					
Tenby a							17 33					
d							17 43					
Saundersfoot d							17x51					
Kilgetty d							17x53					
Narberth d							18x03					
Whitland a					17 44		18 11				19 44	
d					17 47		18 14				19 46	
Carmarthen a					18 05		18 31				20 04	
d					18 07		18 34	19 08			20 07	
Ferryside d					18x17		18x44					
Kidwelly d					18x23		18x50					
Pembrey & Burry Port d					18 30		18 57	19 26			20 25	
Llanelli a					18 35		19 03	19 31			20 30	
d					18 36		19 04	19 32			20 31	
Gowerton d							19x12					
Swansea a					18 54		19 26	19 50			20 50	
d		18 28		19 00	19 10	19 28		20 00			20 55	
Llansamlet d					19 17							
Skewen d					19 21							
Neath d		18 40		19 11	19 25	19 40		20 11			21 06	
Briton Ferry d					19 28							
Baglan d					19 32							
Port Talbot Parkway d		18 48		19 19	19 36	19 48		20 18			21 13	
Pyle d					19 43							
Maesteg d	18 20		19 15						20 15			21 15
Maesteg (Ewenny Road) d	18 22		19 17						20 17			21 17
Garth (Mid Glamorgan) d	18 25		19 20						20 20			21 20
Tondu d	18 34		19 29						20 29			21 29
Sarn d	18 37		19 32						20 32			21 32
Wildmill d	18 39		19 34						20 34			21 34
Bridgend d	18 43	19 00	19 38	19 32	19 51	20 00		20 30	20 38		21 25	21 38
Pencoed d	18 49		19 44						20 44			21 44
Llanharan d	18 53		19 47						20 48			21 48
Pontyclun d	18 57		19 52						20 52			21 52
Cardiff Central 7 a	19 13	19 22	20 05	19 59	20 16	20 25		20 51	21 07		21 46	22 09
Newport (South Wales) a		19 39	20 24			20 39		21 08	21 25		22 05	
Bristol Parkway 7 a		19 59				21 01						
Gloucester 7 a									22 19			
Manchester Piccadilly 10 a			23 48									
Reading 7 a		21 06				22 02						
London Paddington 15 ⊖ a		21 36				22 30						

Table 128

West Wales, Swansea and Maesteg - Cardiff

Saturdays
from 11 September

		AW	AW	AW	AW	AW	AW	AW	AW
Rosslare Harbour ⛴	d								
Fishguard Harbour ⛴	a								
	d								
Milford Haven	d			21 18					23 18
Johnston	d			21x26					23x26
Haverfordwest	d			21 33					23 33
Clarbeston Road	d			21x41					23x41
Clunderwen	d			21x48					23x48
Pembroke Dock	d	19 16					21 11	22 23	
Pembroke	d	19 24					21 19	22 31	
Lamphey	d	19x27					21x22	22x34	
Manorbier	d	19 36					21 31	22 42	
Penally	d	19x41					21x36	22x48	
Tenby	a	19 44					21 39	22 50	
	d	19 47					21 44	22 50	
Saundersfoot	d	19x55					21x52	22x58	
Kilgetty	d	19x57					21x54	23x00	
Narberth	d	20x07					22x04	23x09	
Whitland	a	20 15		21 54			22 12	23 17	23 54
	d	20 17		21 56			22 14	23 20	23 56
Carmarthen	a	20 36		22 15			22 32	23 39	00 17
	d	20 40					22 36		
Ferryside	d	20x51					22x47		
Kidwelly	d	20x57					22x53		
Pembrey & Burry Port	d	21 05					23 00		
Llanelli	a	21 11					23 06		
	d	21 11	21 40				23 06		
Gowerton	d		21 47				23x14		
Swansea	a	21 31	22 10				23 32		
	d	21 35				22 20			
Llansamlet	d	21 42				22 27			
Skewen	d	21 46				22 31			
Neath	d	21 50				22 35			
Briton Ferry	d	21 53				22 38			
Baglan	d	21 57				22 42			
Port Talbot Parkway	d	22 01				22 46			
Pyle	d	22 08				22 53			
Maesteg	d				22 15				
Maesteg (Ewenny Road)	d				22 17				
Garth (Mid Glamorgan)	d				22 20				
Tondu	d				22 29				
Sarn	d				22 32				
Wildmill	d				22 34				
Bridgend	d	22 16			22 39	23 01			
Pencoed	d				22 45				
Llanharan	d				22 49				
Pontyclun	d				22 53				
Cardiff Central 7	a	22 39			23 08	23 26			
Newport (South Wales)	a				23 37				
Bristol Parkway 7	a								
Gloucester 7	a				00 42				
Manchester Piccadilly 10	a								
Reading 7	a								
London Paddington 15 ⊖	a								

Table 128

West Wales, Swansea and Maesteg - Cardiff

Sundays
until 11 July

		AW	AW	GW	GW	AW	GW	AW	AW	GW		AW	AW
				◇1	◇1		◇1		◇	◇1			
				⊐	⊐		⊐	🚌	H	⊐			
Rosslare Harbour ⛴	d												
Fishguard Harbour ⛴	a												
	d												
Milford Haven	d		23p18						09 30				
Johnston	d		23b26						09x38				
Haverfordwest	d		23p33						09 45				
Clarbeston Road	d		23b41						09x54				
Clunderwen	d		23b48						10x01				
Pembroke Dock	d												10 36
Pembroke	d												10 44
Lamphey	d												10x47
Manorbier	d												10 56
Penally	d												11x01
Tenby	a												11 02
	d												11 06
Saundersfoot	d												11x14
Kilgetty	d												11x16
Narberth	d												11x26
Whitland	a		23p54						10 08				11 34
	d		23p56						10 08				11 38
Carmarthen	a		00 17						10 26				11 55
	d					09 40			10 28			11 18	
Ferryside	d					09x50						11x28	
Kidwelly	d					09x56						11x34	
Pembrey & Burry Port	d					10 03			10 48			11 42	
Llanelli	a					10 09			10 54			11 48	
	d					10 10			10 54			11 48	
Gowerton	d					10x17						11x56	
Swansea	a					10 33			11 14			12 12	
	d			07 40	09 55		10 55		11 17	11 55			
Llansamlet	d												
Skewen	d												
Neath	d			07 52	10 07		11 07		11 28	12 07			
Briton Ferry	d												
Baglan	d												
Port Talbot Parkway	d			08 00	10 15		11 15		11 35	12 15			
Pyle	d								11 42				
Maesteg	d	22p15											
Maesteg (Ewenny Road)	d	22p17											
Garth (Mid Glamorgan)	d	22p20											
Tondu	d	22p29											
Sarn	d	22p32											
Wildmill	d	22p34											
Bridgend	d	22p39		08 14	10 27		11 27	11 34	11 51	12 27			
Pencoed	d	22p45						11 49					
Llanharan	d	22p49						11 57					
Pontyclun	d	22p53						12 05					
Cardiff Central 7	a	23p08		08 58	11 13		12 13	12 30	12 33	13 14			
Newport (South Wales)	a	23p37		09 18	11 31		12 31		12 57	13 31			
Bristol Parkway 7	a			09 46	11 59		12 59			13 59			
Gloucester 7	a	00 42											
Manchester Piccadilly 10	a								16 15				
Reading 7	a			10 42	13 00		14 00			15 00			
London Paddington 15 ⊖	a			11 21	13 38		14 38			15 38			

		GW	AW	GW	AW	GW	AW	AW	AW	GW	AW	GW	AW
			■					■	■				
		◇1		◇1		◇1				◇1		◇1	
		⊐	H	⊐		⊐	🚌	H		⊐	H	⊐	🚌
Rosslare Harbour ⛴	d												
Fishguard Harbour ⛴	a												
	d										14 18		
Milford Haven	d		11 30					13 16					
Johnston	d		11x38					13x24					
Haverfordwest	d		11 45					13 31					
Clarbeston Road	d		11x54					13x40			14 38		
Clunderwen	d		12x01					13x48					
Pembroke Dock	d				11 55								
Pembroke	d				12 03								
Lamphey	d				12x06								
Manorbier	d				12 15								
Penally	d				12x20								
Tenby	a				12 23								
	d				12 23								
Saundersfoot	d				12x31								
Kilgetty	d				12x33								
Narberth	d				12x43								
Whitland	a		12 06		12 51			13 54			14 50		
	d		12 08		12 53			13 56			14 50		
Carmarthen	a		12 26		13 13			14 14			15 10		
	d		12 30		13 16			14 16			15 13	15 34	
Ferryside	d				13x27						15x25		
Kidwelly	d				13x33						15x32		
Pembrey & Burry Port	d		12 49		13 40			14 36			15 40	15 55	
Llanelli	a		12 55		13 46			14 42			15 47	16 00	
	d		12 56		13 47			14 42	15 44		15 51	16 02	
Gowerton	d				13x54						15x58		
Swansea	a		13 14		14 12			15 01	16 04		16 14	16 18	
	d	12 55	13 19	13 55		14 55		15 09		15 55		16 25	
Llansamlet	d												
Skewen	d												
Neath	d	13 07	13 30	14 07		15 07		15 20		16 07		16 37	
Briton Ferry	d												
Baglan	d												
Port Talbot Parkway	d	13 15	13 37	14 15		15 15		15 27		16 15		16 44	
Pyle	d		13 44					15 35					
Maesteg	d												
Maesteg (Ewenny Road)	d												
Garth (Mid Glamorgan)	d												
Tondu	d												
Sarn	d												
Wildmill	d												
Bridgend	d	13 27	13 57	14 27		15 27	15 34	15 43		16 27		16 57	17 49
Pencoed	d						15 49						18 04
Llanharan	d						15 57						18 12
Pontyclun	d						16 05						18 20
Cardiff Central 7	a	14 14	14 40	15 14		16 14	16 30	16 31		17 14		17 42	18 45
Newport (South Wales)	a	14 31	15 12	15 31		16 31		16 52		17 31		18 03	
Bristol Parkway 7	a	14 59		15 59		16 59				17 59		18 31	
Gloucester 7	a												
Manchester Piccadilly 10	a		18 15					20 15					
Reading 7	a	16 00		17 00		18 00				19 00		19 32	
London Paddington 15 ⊖	a	16 38		17 38		18 38				19 39		20 10	

b previous night, stops on request

Table 128

West Wales, Swansea and Maesteg - Cardiff

Sundays
until 11 July

Station		GW	AW	GW	AW	AW	GW	AW	AW	AW	AW	AW	AW	AW
		◇1 🍴	■ 🛒	◇1 🍴	🛒		◇1 🍴	■			◇	◇		
Rosslare Harbour ⛴	d													
Fishguard Harbour ⛴	a													
	d													
Milford Haven	d		15 31			17 51				19 48		21 44		23 45
Johnston	d		15x39			17x59				19x56		21x52		23x53
Haverfordwest	d		15 46			18 06				20 03		21 59		00 03
Clarbeston Road	d		15x55			18x14				20x11		22x08		00x12
Clunderwen	d		16x02			18x21				20x18		22x15		00x19
Pembroke Dock	d				16 50				19 00				22 00	
Pembroke	d				16 58				19 08				22 08	
Lamphey	d				17x01				19x11				22x11	
Manorbier	d				17 10				19 20				22 20	
Penally	d				17x15				19x25				22x25	
Tenby	a				17 18				19 28				22 28	
	d				17 18				19 30				22 28	
Saundersfoot	d				17x26				19x38				22x36	
Kilgetty	d				17x28				19x40				22x38	
Narberth	d				17x38				19x50				22x48	
Whitland	a		16 09		17 46	18 27			19 58	20 24		22 22	22 56	00 26
	d		16 10		17 49	18 29			19 59	20 27		22 24	22 59	00 27
Carmarthen	a		16 29		18 10	18 46			20 17	20 45		22 42	23 20	00 49
	d		16 35	17 30	18 18		18 55		20 19		20 54	22 44		
Ferryside	d		16x45		18x29				20x30			22x55		
Kidwelly	d		16x51		18x35				20x36			23x01		
Pembrey & Burry Port	d		16 59	17 50	18 42		19 15		20 43		21 13	23 08		
Llanelli	a		17 05	17 56	18 48		19 21		20 49		21 19	23 14		
	d		17 05	17 57	18 50		19 22	19 52	20 51		21 19	23 15		
Gowerton	d				18x58			20 01	20x58			23x22		
Swansea	a		17 24	18 14	19 12		19 39	20 15	21 10		21 39	23 39		
	d	17 25	17 35	18 25			19 45				21 42	23 41		
Llansamlet	d													
Skewen	d													
Neath	d	17 37	17 46	18 37			19 57	20 51			21 53	23 52		
Briton Ferry	d													
Baglan	d													
Port Talbot Parkway	d	17 44	17 53	18 44			20 04	20 59			22 00	23 59		
Pyle	d		18 00								22 07	00 06		
Maesteg	d													
Maesteg (Ewenny Road)	d													
Garth (Mid Glamorgan)	d													
Tondu	d													
Sarn	d													
Wildmill	d													
Bridgend	d	18 00	18 12	18 57			20 17	21 14			22 16	00 15		
Pencoed	d													
Llanharan	d													
Pontyclun	d													
Cardiff Central 7	a	18 46	18 55	19 44			21 04	22 03			22 58	00 57		
Newport (South Wales)	a	19 03	19 12	20 03			21 21				23 18			
Bristol Parkway 7	a	19 31		20 31			21 49							
Gloucester 7	a													
Manchester Piccadilly 10	a		22 24											
Reading 7	a	20 32		21 32			22 56							
London Paddington 15 ⊖	a	21 09		22 12			23 46							

Table 128

West Wales, Swansea and Maesteg - Cardiff

Sundays
18 July to 05 September

Station		AW	AW	AW	GW	GW	GW	AW	GW	AW	GW	AW	AW
				◇	◇1 🍴	◇1 🍴	◇1 🍴		◇1 🍴	◇ 🛒	◇1 🍴		
Rosslare Harbour ⛴	d												
Fishguard Harbour ⛴	a												
	d			01 50									
Milford Haven	d		23p18							09 30			
Johnston	d		23b26							09x38			
Haverfordwest	d		23p33							09 45			
Clarbeston Road	d		23b41	02 10						09x54			
Clunderwen	d		23b48							10x01			
Pembroke Dock	d												10 36
Pembroke	d												10 44
Lamphey	d												10x47
Manorbier	d												10 56
Penally	d												11x01
Tenby	a												11 02
	d												11 06
Saundersfoot	d												11x14
Kilgetty	d												11x16
Narberth	d												11x26
Whitland	a		23p54	02 22						10 08			11 34
	d		23p56	02 22						10 08			11 38
Carmarthen	a		00 17	02 40						10 26			11 55
	d			02 43				09 40		10 30		11 18	
Ferryside	d							09x50				11x28	
Kidwelly	d							09x56				11x34	
Pembrey & Burry Port	d							10 03		10 49		11 42	
Llanelli	a			03 06				10 09		10 55		11 48	
	d			03 07				10 10		10 56		11 48	
Gowerton	d							10x17				11x56	
Swansea	a			03 26				10 33		11 15		12 12	
	d			03 35	07 40	08 45	09 55		10 55	11 32	11 55		
Llansamlet	d												
Skewen	d												
Neath	d			03 46	07 52	08 57	10 07		11 07	11 43	12 07		
Briton Ferry	d												
Baglan	d												
Port Talbot Parkway	d			03 53	08 00	09 04	10 15		11 15	11 50	12 15		
Pyle	d									11 57			
Maesteg	d	22p15											
Maesteg (Ewenny Road)	d	22p17											
Garth (Mid Glamorgan)	d	22p20											
Tondu	d	22p29											
Sarn	d	22p32											
Wildmill	d	22p34											
Bridgend	d	22p39		04 06	08 11	09 16	10 27		11 27	12 05	12 27		
Pencoed	d	22p45								12 11			
Llanharan	d	22p49								12 15			
Pontyclun	d	22p53								12 20			
Cardiff Central 7	a	23p08		04 38	08 34	09 39	10 48		11 48	12 34	12 48		
Newport (South Wales)	a	23p37			08 56	10 02	11 12		12 12	12 57	13 12		
Bristol Parkway 7	a				09 24	10 23	11 34		12 34		13 34		
Gloucester 7	a	00 42											
Manchester Piccadilly 10	a									16 15			
Reading 7	a				10 43	11 42	13 00		14 00		15 00		
London Paddington 15 ⊖	a				11 21	12 24	13 38		14 38		15 38		

Station		GW	AW	GW	AW	GW	AW	AW	GW	AW	GW	GW
		◇1 🍴	■ 🛒	◇1 🍴		◇1 🍴	■ 🛒	■	◇1 🍴	🛒	◇1 🍴	◇1 🍴
Rosslare Harbour ⛴	d											
Fishguard Harbour ⛴	a											
	d									14 23		
Milford Haven	d		11 30				13 30					
Johnston	d		11x38				13x38					
Haverfordwest	d		11 45				13 45					
Clarbeston Road	d		11x54				13x54			14 45		
Clunderwen	d		12x01				14x01					
Pembroke Dock	d				12 05							
Pembroke	d				12 13							
Lamphey	d				12x16							
Manorbier	d				12 25							
Penally	d				12x30							
Tenby	a				12 33							
	d				12 33							
Saundersfoot	d				12x41							
Kilgetty	d				12x43							
Narberth	d				12x53							
Whitland	a		12 06		13 01		14 08			14 57		
	d		12 08		13 03		14 08			14 57		
Carmarthen	a		12 26		13 23		14 26			15 17		
	d		12 30		13 26		14 28			15 18	15 30	
Ferryside	d				13x36					15x28		
Kidwelly	d				13x42					15x34		
Pembrey & Burry Port	d		12 49		13 49		14 47			15 41	15 51	
Llanelli	a		12 55		13 55		14 53			15 47	15 56	
	d		12 56		13 56		14 54	15 41		15 48	15 58	
Gowerton	d				14x03			15 48		15x55		
Swansea	a		13 14		14 21		15 12	16 02		16 13	16 18	
	d	12 55	13 40	13 55		14 55	15 25		15 55		16 25	17 25
Llansamlet	d											
Skewen	d											
Neath	d	13 07	13 51	14 07		15 07	15 36		16 07		16 37	17 37
Briton Ferry	d											
Baglan	d											
Port Talbot Parkway	d	13 15	13 58	14 15		15 15	15 43		16 15		16 44	17 44
Pyle	d		14 06				15 50					
Maesteg	d											
Maesteg (Ewenny Road)	d											
Garth (Mid Glamorgan)	d											
Tondu	d											
Sarn	d											
Wildmill	d											
Bridgend	d	13 27	14 14	14 27		15 27	15 58		16 27		16 57	17 57
Pencoed	d						16 04					
Llanharan	d						16 08					
Pontyclun	d						16 13					
Cardiff Central 7	a	13 48	14 37	14 48		15 48	16 28		16 48		17 18	18 19
Newport (South Wales)	a	14 12	15 06	15 12		16 12	16 57		17 12		17 42	18 42
Bristol Parkway 7	a	14 34		15 34		16 34			17 34		18 04	19 04
Gloucester 7	a											
Manchester Piccadilly 10	a		18 15				20 15					
Reading 7	a	16 00		17 00		18 00			19 00		19 32	20 32
London Paddington 15 ⊖	a	16 38		17 38		18 38			19 39		20 10	21 09

b previous night, stops on request

Table 128

Sundays

18 July to 05 September

West Wales, Swansea and Maesteg - Cardiff

		AW	AW	AW	GW	AW	AW	AW	AW	AW	AW	AW
		■ ╤	╤		◇1 ⊡		■		◇	◇		
Rosslare Harbour ⛴	d											
Fishguard Harbour ⛴	a											
	d											
Milford Haven	d	15 30		17 30				19 33		21 29		23 21
Johnston	d	15x38		17x38				19x41		21x37		23x29
Haverfordwest	d	15 45		17 45				19 48		21 47		23 36
Clarbeston Road	d	15x54		17x53				19x56		21x55		23x45
Clunderwen	d	16x01		18x00				20x03		22x03		23x52
Pembroke Dock	d		16 50			19 00					22 00	
Pembroke	d		16 58			19 08					22 08	
Lamphey	d		17x01			19x11					22x11	
Manorbier	d		17 10			19 20					22 20	
Penally	d		17x15			19x25					22x25	
Tenby	a		17 18			19 28					22 28	
	d		17 18			19 30					22 28	
Saundersfoot	d		17x26			19x38					22x36	
Kilgetty	d		17x28			19x40					22x38	
Narberth	d		17x38			19x50					22x48	
Whitland	a	16 08	17 46	18 06		19 58		20 09		22 09	22 56	23 59
	d	16 09	17 49	18 08		19 59		20 12		22 12	22 59	23 59
Carmarthen	a	16 27	18 16	18 25		20 17		20 30		22 29	23 20	00 17
	d	16 30	18 16		19 05	20 19			20 54	22 32		
Ferryside	d	16x41	18x27			20x30				22x42		
Kidwelly	d	16x47	18x33			20x36				22x48		
Pembrey & Burry Port	d	16 54	18 40		19 25	20 43			21 13	22 56		
Llanelli	a	17 00	18 46		19 30	20 49			21 19	23 02		
	d	17 01	18 48		19 32	20 51	19 52		21 19	23 02		
Gowerton	d		18x55			20x58	19 59			23x10		
Swansea	a	17 22	19 09		19 48	21 10	20 13		21 39	23 27		
	d	17 31			19 55				21 52	23 28		
Llansamlet	d											
Skewen	d											
Neath	d	17 42			20 07		20 51		22 03	23 40		
Briton Ferry	d											
Baglan	d											
Port Talbot Parkway	d	17 49			20 14		20 58		22 10	23 47		
Pyle	d	17 56							22 17	23 54		
Maesteg	d											
Maesteg (Ewenny Road)	d											
Garth (Mid Glamorgan)	d											
Tondu	d											
Sarn	d											
Wildmill	d											
Bridgend	d	18 04			20 26		21 11		22 25	00 02		
Pencoed	d	18 10										
Llanharan	d	18 14										
Pontyclun	d	18 19										
Cardiff Central 7	a	18 34			20 49		21 36		22 49	00 27		
Newport (South Wales)	a	18 56			21 09				23 18			
Bristol Parkway 7	a				21 31							
Gloucester 7	a											
Manchester Piccadilly 10	a	22 15										
Reading 7	a				22 55							
London Paddington 15 ⊖	a				23 46							

Table 128

Sundays

from 12 September

West Wales, Swansea and Maesteg - Cardiff

		AW	AW	AW	GW	GW	GW	AW	GW	AW		AW	GW	GW	AW	AW	GW	GW	AW	AW	AW	GW	GW	AW	GW
				◇	◇1 ⊡	◇1 ⊡	◇1 ⊡		◇1 ⊡	◇ ╤			◇1 ⊡	◇1 ⊡	■ ╤		◇1 ⊡	◇1 ⊡	■ ╤		■	◇1 ⊡	◇1 ⊡	■ ╤	◇1 ⊡
Rosslare Harbour ⛴	d																								
Fishguard Harbour ⛴	a																								
	d			01 50																14 23					
Milford Haven	d		23p18												11 28				13 23					15 30	
Johnston	d		23b26												11x36				13x31					15x38	
Haverfordwest	d		23p33												11 43				13 38					15 45	
Clarbeston Road	d		23b41	02 10											11x52				13x47	14 43				15x54	
Clunderwen	d		23b48												11x59				13x54					16x01	
Pembroke Dock	d															11 55									
Pembroke	d															12 03									
Lamphey	d															12x06									
Manorbier	d															12 15									
Penally	d															12x20									
Tenby	a															12 23									
	d															12 23									
Saundersfoot	d															12x31									
Kilgetty	d															12x33									
Narberth	d															12x43									
Whitland	a		23p54	02 22											12 06	12 51			14 01	14 55				16 08	
	d		23p56	02 22											12 08	12 54			14 02	14 55				16 09	
Carmarthen	a		00 17	02 40											12 26	13 14			14 20	15 15				16 26	
	d			02 43				09 40		10 30		11 18			12 30	13 17			14 23	15 16		15 30		16 30	16 55
Ferryside	d							09x50				11x28				13x27				15x26				16x40	
Kidwelly	d							09x56				11x34				13x33				15x32				16x46	
Pembrey & Burry Port	d							10 03		10 49		11 42			12 49	13 40			14 42	15 39		15 50		16 54	17 15
Llanelli	a			03 06				10 09		10 55		11 48			12 55	13 46			14 48	15 45		15 57		17 00	17 21
	d			03 07				10 10		10 56		11 48			12 56	13 47			14 49	15 46	15 41	15 59		17 00	17 22
Gowerton	d							10x17				11x56				13x54				15x53					
Swansea	a			03 26				10 33		11 14		12 12			13 14	14 12			15 07	16 09	15 59	16 14		17 19	17 39
	d			03 35	08 07	09 21	10 21		11 21	11 32			12 21	13 21	13 40		14 21	15 21	15 33			16 21	16 51	17 30	17 51
Llansamlet	d																								
Skewen	d																								
Neath	d			03 46	08 19	09 33	10 33		11 33	11 43			12 33	13 33	13 51		14 33	15 33	15 44			16 33	17 03	17 41	18 03
Briton Ferry	d																								
Baglan	d																								
Port Talbot Parkway	d			03 53	08 26	09 40	10 40		11 40	11 50			12 40	13 40	13 58		14 40	15 40	15 51			16 40	17 10	17 48	18 10
Pyle	d									11 57					14 06				15 58					17 55	
Maesteg	d	22p15																							
Maesteg (Ewenny Road)	d	22p17																							
Garth (Mid Glamorgan)	d	22p20																							
Tondu	d	22p29																							
Sarn	d	22p32																							
Wildmill	d	22p34																							
Bridgend	d	22p39		04 06	08 38	09 52	10 52		11 52	12 05			12 52	13 52	14 14		14 52	15 52	16 06			16 52	17 22	18 03	18 22
Pencoed	d	22p45								12 11									16 12					18 09	
Llanharan	d	22p49								12 15									16 16					18 13	
Pontyclun	d	22p53								12 20									16 21					18 18	
Cardiff Central 7	a	23p08		04 35	09 01	10 14	11 14		12 14	12 35			13 14	14 14	14 37		15 14	16 14	16 36			17 14	17 45	18 34	18 45
Newport (South Wales)	a	23p37			09 18	10 31	11 31		12 31	12 52			13 31	14 31	15 12		15 31	16 31	16 52			17 31	18 03	18 52	19 03
Bristol Parkway 7	a				09 46	10 59	11 59		12 59				13 59	14 59			15 59	16 59				17 59	18 31		19 31
Gloucester 7	a	00 42																							
Manchester Piccadilly 10	a									16 15					18 15				20 15					22 15	
Reading 7	a				10 42	12 01	13 00		14 00				15 00	16 00			17 00	18 00				19 00	19 32		20 32
London Paddington 15 ⊖	a				11 21	12 39	13 39		14 39				15 39	16 39			17 39	18 39				19 39	20 09		21 09

b previous night, stops on request

Table 128

Sundays from 12 September

West Wales, Swansea and Maesteg - Cardiff

		GW ◇1	AW	AW	GW ◇1	AW	AW ■	AW	AW ◇	AW ◇	AW	AW
Rosslare Harbour	d											
Fishguard Harbour	a											
	d											
Milford Haven	d			17 30				19 38		21 33		23 15
Johnston	d			17x38				19x46		21x41		23x23
Haverfordwest	d			17 45				19 53		21 49		23 30
Clarbeston Road	d			17x53				20x01		21x57		23x39
Clunderwen	d			18x00				20x08		22x05		23x46
Pembroke Dock	d		16 50			19 00					22 00	
Pembroke	d		16 58			19 08					22 08	
Lamphey	d		17x01			19x11					22x11	
Manorbier	d		17 10			19 20					22 20	
Penally	d		17x15			19x25					22x25	
Tenby	a		17 18			19 28					22 28	
	d		17 18			19 30					22 28	
Saundersfoot	d		17x26			19x38					22x36	
Kilgetty	d		17x28			19x40					22x38	
Narberth	d		17x38			19x50					22x48	
Whitland	a		17 46	18 06		19 58		20 14		22 11	22 56	23 53
	d		17 49	18 08		19 59		20 17		22 14	22 59	23 53
Carmarthen	a		18 10	18 27		20 17		20 35		22 31	23 20	00 11
	d		18 10		19 09	20 19			21 05	22 34		
Ferryside	d		18x20			20x30				22x44		
Kidwelly	d		18x26			20x36				22x50		
Pembrey & Burry Port	d		18 34		19 29	20 43			21 24	22 58		
Llanelli	a		18 40		19 35	20 49			21 30	23 04		
	d		18 41		19 36	20 51	19 59		21 30	23 04		
Gowerton	d		18x49			20x58	20 02			23x12		
Swansea	a		19 03		19 53	21 12	20 16		21 50	23 29		
	d	18 51			19 59		20 40		21 52	23 30		
Llansamlet	d											
Skewen	d											
Neath	d	19 03			20 11		20 51		22 03	23 42		
Briton Ferry	d											
Baglan	d											
Port Talbot Parkway	d	19 10			20 18		20 58		22 10	23 49		
Pyle	d								22 17	23 56		
Maesteg	d											
Maesteg (Ewenny Road)	d											
Garth (Mid Glamorgan)	d											
Tondu	d											
Sarn	d											
Wildmill	d											
Bridgend	d	19 22			20 30		21 11		22 25	00 04		
Pencoed	d											
Llanharan	d											
Pontyclun	d											
Cardiff Central 7	a	19 45			20 53		21 36		22 49	00 29		
Newport (South Wales)	a	20 03			21 08				23 18			
Bristol Parkway 7	a	20 31			21 36							
Gloucester 7	a											
Manchester Piccadilly 10	a											
Reading 7	a	21 32			22 37							
London Paddington 15 ⊖	a	22 09			23 20							

Table 128A

Mondays to Fridays

Maesteg - Caerau

Bus Service

		AW	AW	AW	AW	AW	AW	AW	AW	AW	AW	AW	AW	AW	AW	AW	AW	AW
Maesteg	d	06 51	08 05	09 20	10 20	11 20	12 20	13 20	14 20	15 20	16 20	17 20	18 20	19 20	20 20	21 20	22 11	23 34
Caerau (Square)	a	07 01	08 15	09 30	10 30	11 30	12 30	13 30	14 30	15 30	16 30	17 30	18 30	19 30	20 30	21 30	22 21	23 43
Caerau Park	a	07 10	08 24	09 39	10 39	11 39	12 39	13 39	14 39	15 39	16 39	17 39	18 39	19 39	20 39	21 39	22 30	23 53

Saturdays

		AW	AW	AW	AW	AW	AW	AW	AW	AW	AW	AW	AW	AW	AW	AW	AW
Maesteg	d	06 51	08 05	09 20	10 20	11 20	12 20	13 20	14 20	15 20	16 20	17 20	18 20	19 20	20 20	21 20	22 11
Caerau (Square)	a	07 01	08 15	09 30	10 30	11 30	12 30	13 30	14 30	15 30	16 30	17 30	18 30	19 30	20 30	21 30	22 21
Caerau Park	a	07 10	08 24	09 39	10 39	11 39	12 39	13 39	14 39	15 39	16 39	17 39	18 39	19 39	20 39	21 39	22 30

No Sunday Service

For connections from Cardiff and Bridgend please refer to Table 128

Table 128A

Mondays to Fridays

Caerau - Maesteg
Bus Service

		AW 🚌	AW 🚌	AW 🚌	AW 🚌	AW 🚌	AW 🚌	AW 🚌	AW 🚌	AW 🚌		AW 🚌	AW 🚌	AW 🚌	AW 🚌	AW 🚌	AW 🚌	AW 🚌
Caerau Park	d	06 21	07 35	08 50	09 50	10 50	11 50	12 50	13 50	14 50		15 50	16 50	17 50	18 40	19 40	20 40	21 40
Caerau (Square)	d	06 31	07 45	09 00	10 00	11 00	12 00	13 00	14 00	15 00		16 00	17 00	18 00	18 50	19 50	20 50	21 50
Maesteg	a	06 41	07 55	09 10	10 10	11 10	12 10	13 10	14 10	15 10		16 10	17 10	18 10	19 00	20 00	21 00	22 00

Saturdays

		AW 🚌	AW 🚌	AW 🚌	AW 🚌	AW 🚌	AW 🚌	AW 🚌	AW 🚌	AW 🚌		AW 🚌	AW 🚌	AW 🚌	AW 🚌	AW 🚌	AW 🚌	AW 🚌
Caerau Park	d	06 21	07 35	08 50	09 50	10 50	11 50	12 50	13 50	14 50		15 50	16 50	17 50	18 40	19 40	20 40	21 40
Caerau (Square)	d	06 31	07 45	09 00	10 00	11 00	12 00	13 00	14 00	15 00		16 00	17 00	18 00	18 50	19 50	20 50	21 50
Maesteg	a	06 41	07 55	09 10	10 10	11 10	12 10	13 10	14 10	15 10		16 10	17 10	18 10	19 00	20 00	21 00	22 00

Network Diagram for Tables 129, 131

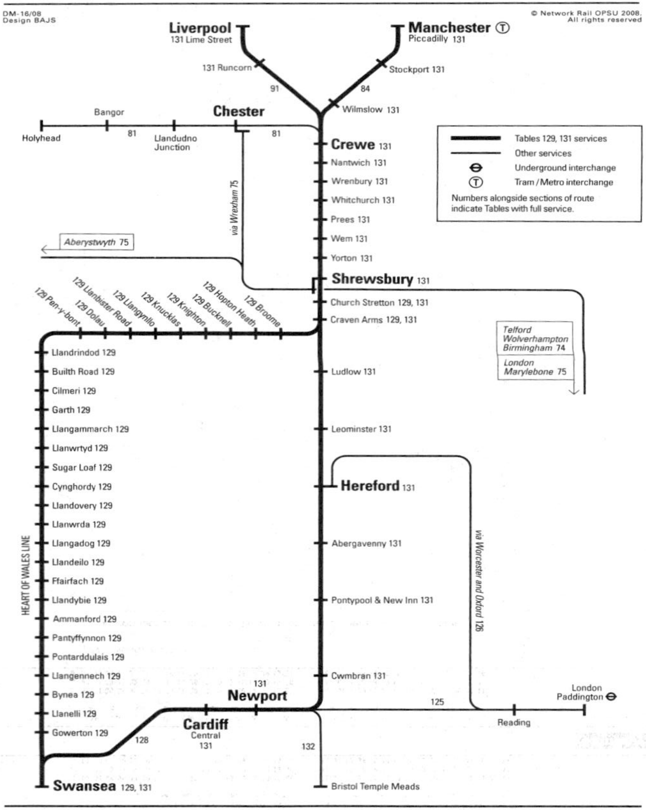

Table 129

Mondays to Fridays

Swansea - Shrewsbury
HEART OF WALES LINE

		AW ◇	AW ◇	AW ◇	AW ◇
Swansea	d	04 36	09 15	13 16	18 21
Gowerton	d				
Llanelli	d	04 53	09 34	13 35	18 39
Bynea	d	04x58	09x39	13x39	18x44
Llangennech	d	05x01	09x43	13x43	18x47
Pontarddulais	d	05x05	09x47	13x48	18x51
Pantyffynnon	d	05 13	09 55	13 55	18 59
Ammanford	d	05 16	09 58	13 58	19 02
Llandybie	d	05 20	10 02	14 03	19 06
Ffairfach	d	05x27	10x10	14x10	19x13
Llandeilo	a	05 30	10 12	14 12	19 16
	d	05 32	10 15	14 15	19 18
Llangadog	d	05 42	10 24	14 24	19 28
Llanwrda	d	05 45	10 28	14 28	19 31
Llandovery	a	05 52	10 34	14 34	19 38
	d	05 54	10 37	14 37	19 40
Cynghordy	d	06x02	10x45	14x45	19x48
Sugar Loaf	d	06x10	10x54	14x53	19x56
Llanwrtyd	a	06 16	11 00	14 59	20 02
	d	06 19	11 05	15 01	20 07
Llangammarch	d	06x24	11x11	15x07	20x12
Garth (Powys)	d	06x28	11x15	15x11	20x16
Cilmeri	d	06x33	11x20	15x16	20x21
Builth Road	d	06x36	11x23	15x19	20x24
Llandrindod	a	06 47	11 35	15 31	20 36
	d	06 55	11 39	15 39	20 40
Pen-y-bont	d	07x02	11x46	15x46	20x47
Dolau	d	07 07	11 51	15 51	20 52
Llanbister Road	d	07x12	11x57	15x56	20x58
Llangynllo	d	07x17	12x02	16x01	21x03
Knucklas	d	07x23	12x08	16x07	21x09
Knighton	a	07 29	12 13	16 13	21 14
	d	07 32	12 16	16 15	21 15
Bucknell	d	07 38	12 22	16 21	21 21
Hopton Heath	d	07x42	12x26	16x25	21x25
Broome	d	07x46	12x30	16x29	21x29
Craven Arms	a	07 53	12 37	16 36	21 36
Church Stretton	a	08 06	12 50	16 49	21 49
Shrewsbury	a	08 22	13 08	17 10	22 06

Saturdays

		AW ◇	AW ◇	AW ◇	AW ◇
Swansea	d	04 36	09 16	13 16	18 21
Gowerton	d				
Llanelli	d	04 53	09 34	13 35	18 39
Bynea	d	04x58	09x39	13x39	18x44
Llangennech	d	05x01	09x43	13x43	18x47
Pontarddulais	d	05x05	09x47	13x48	18x51
Pantyffynnon	d	05 13	09 55	13 55	18 59
Ammanford	d	05 16	09 58	13 58	19 02
Llandybie	d	05 20	10 02	14 03	19 06
Ffairfach	d	05x27	10x10	14x10	19x13
Llandeilo	a	05 30	10 12	14 12	19 16
	d	05 32	10 15	14 15	19 18
Llangadog	d	05 42	10 24	14 24	19 28
Llanwrda	d	05 45	10 28	14 28	19 31
Llandovery	a	05 52	10 34	14 34	19 38
	d	05 54	10 37	14 37	19 40
Cynghordy	d	06x02	10x45	14x45	19x48
Sugar Loaf	d	06x10	10x54	14x53	19x56
Llanwrtyd	a	06 16	11 00	14 59	20 02
	d	06 19	11 05	15 01	20 07
Llangammarch	d	06x24	11x11	15x07	20x12
Garth (Powys)	d	06x28	11x15	15x11	20x16
Cilmeri	d	06x33	11x20	15x16	20x21
Builth Road	d	06x36	11x23	15x19	20x24
Llandrindod	a	06 47	11 35	15 31	20 36
	d	06 55	11 39	15 39	20 40
Pen-y-bont	d	07x02	11x46	15x46	20x47
Dolau	d	07 07	11 51	15 51	20 52
Llanbister Road	d	07x12	11x57	15x56	20x58
Llangynllo	d	07x17	12x02	16x01	21x03
Knucklas	d	07x23	12x08	16x07	21x09
Knighton	a	07 29	12 13	16 13	21 14
	d	07 32	12 16	16 15	21 17
Bucknell	d	07 38	12 22	16 21	21 23
Hopton Heath	d	07x42	12x26	16x25	21x27
Broome	d	07x46	12x30	16x29	21x31
Craven Arms	a	07 53	12 37	16 36	21 38
Church Stretton	a	08 06	12 50	16 49	21 51
Shrewsbury	a	08 22	13 08	17 10	22 08

Table 129

Sundays

Swansea - Shrewsbury
HEART OF WALES LINE

		AW ◇	AW ◇ A	AW ◇ B	AW ◇ C
Swansea	d	11 06	15 04	15 26	15 20
Gowerton	d	11x16	15x15	15x36	15x31
Llanelli	d	11 29	15 26	15b51	15b51
Bynea	d	11x34	15x31	15x56	15x56
Llangennech	d	11x38	15x35	16x00	16x00
Pontarddulais	d	11x42	15x40	16x04	16x05
Pantyffynnon	d	11 50	15 47	16 12	16 12
Ammanford	d	11 53	15 50	16 15	16 15
Llandybie	d	11 57	15 55	16 19	16 20
Ffairfach	d	12 05	16x02	16x27	16x27
Llandeilo	a	12 07	16 05	16 29	16 30
	d	12 10	16 07	16 32	16 32
Llangadog	d	12 19	16 17	16 41	16 42
Llanwrda	d	12 23	16 20	16 45	16 45
Llandovery	a	12 29	16 27	16 51	16 52
	d	12 32	16 29	16 54	16 54
Cynghordy	d	12x40	16x38	17x02	17x03
Sugar Loaf	d	12x49	16x46	17x11	17x11
Llanwrtyd	a	12 55	16 52	17 17	17 17
	d	12 57	16 55	17 19	17 20
Llangammarch	d	13x03	17x01	17x25	17x26
Garth (Powys)	d	13x07	17x05	17x29	17x30
Cilmeri	d	13x13	17x10	17x35	17x35
Builth Road	d	13x16	17x14	17x38	17x39
Llandrindod	a	13 28	17 25	17 50	17 50
	d	13 41	17 57	17 57	17 57
Pen-y-bont	d	13x49	18x04	18x04	18x04
Dolau	d	13 54	18 09	18 09	18 09
Llanbister Road	d	14x00	18x15	18x15	18x15
Llangynllo	d	14x05	18x21	18x21	18x21
Knucklas	d	14x12	18x27	18x27	18x27
Knighton	a	14 17	18 33	18 33	18 33
	d	14 20	18 35	18 35	18 35
Bucknell	d	14 26	18 41	18 41	18 41
Hopton Heath	d	14x30	18x46	18x46	18x46
Broome	d	14x35	18x50	18x50	18x50
Craven Arms	a	14 42	18 57	18 57	18 57
Church Stretton	a	14 55	19 12	19 12	19 11
Shrewsbury	a	15 13	19 29	19 31	19 29

A until 11 July
B from 18 July until 5 September
C from 12 September
b arr. 1544

Table 129

Shrewsbury - Swansea

HEART OF WALES LINE

		AW ◇	AW ◇	AW ◇	AW ◇
Shrewsbury	d	05 19	09 05	14 05	18 05
Church Stretton	d	05 36	09 22	14 23	18 23
Craven Arms	d	05 47	09 34	14 36	18 35
Broome	d	05x52	09x39	14x14	18x40
Hopton Heath	d	05x56	09x43	14x45	18x44
Bucknell	d	06 00	09 47	14 49	18 48
Knighton	d	06 11	09 56	14 58	18 57
Knucklas	d	06x15	10x01	15x03	19x02
Llangynllo	d	06x22	10x09	15x11	19x10
Llanbister Road	d	06x27	10x14	15x15	19x15
Dolau	d	06 33	10 19	15 21	19 20
Pen-y-bont	d	06x37	10x24	15x25	19x24
Llandrindod	a	06 48	10 33	15 34	19 33
	d	06 52	10 33	15 36	19 34
Builth Road	d	07x01	10x43	15x46	19x43
Cilmeri	d	07x04	10x46	15x49	19x46
Garth (Powys)	d	07x09	10x51	15x55	19x52
Llangammarch	d	07x12	10x55	15x59	19x55
Llanwrtyd	a	07 18	11 01	16 05	20 01
	d	07 21	11 06	16 07	20 10
Sugar Loaf	d	07x27	11x13	16x14	20x16
Cynghordy	d	07x33	11x20	16x21	20x23
Llandovery	a	07 43	11 29	16 30	20 33
	d	07 45	11 32	16 33	20 35
Llanwrda	d	07 51	11 37	16 39	20 41
Llangadog	d	07 54	11 41	16 43	20 45
Llandeilo	a	08 03	11 50	16 52	20 54
	d	08 06	11 53	16 54	20 57
Ffairfach	d	08x08	11x55	16x57	20x59
Llandybie	d	08 15	12 02	17 04	21 07
Ammanford	d	08 20	12 07	17 09	21 11
Pantyffynnon	d	08 23	12 10	17 12	21 14
Pontarddulais	d	08x30	12x17	17x19	21x21
Llangennech	d	08x34	12x21	17x23	21x26
Bynea	d	08x37	12x24	17x29	21x29
Llanelli	a	08 42	12 29	17 32	21 34
Gowerton	a	08x53		17x45	21x50
Swansea	a	09 08	13 06	18 06	22 10

Saturdays

		AW ◇	AW ◇	AW ◇	AW ◇
Shrewsbury	d	05 19	09 05	14 05	18 05
Church Stretton	d	05 36	09 22	14 23	18 23
Craven Arms	d	05 47	09 34	14 36	18 35
Broome	d	05x52	09x39	14x14	18x40
Hopton Heath	d	05x56	09x43	14x45	18x44
Bucknell	d	06 00	09 47	14 49	18 48
Knighton	d	06 11	09 56	14 58	18 57
Knucklas	d	06x15	10x01	15x03	19x02
Llangynllo	d	06x22	10x09	15x11	19x10
Llanbister Road	d	06x27	10x14	15x15	19x15
Dolau	d	06 33	10 19	15 21	19 20
Pen-y-bont	d	06x37	10x24	15x25	19x24
Llandrindod	a	06 48	10 33	15 34	19 33
	d	06 52	10 33	15 36	19 34
Builth Road	d	07x01	10x43	15x46	19x43
Cilmeri	d	07x04	10x46	15x49	19x46
Garth (Powys)	d	07x09	10x51	15x55	19x52
Llangammarch	d	07x12	10x55	15x59	19x55
Llanwrtyd	a	07 18	11 01	16 05	20 01
	d	07 21	11 06	16 07	20 10
Sugar Loaf	d	07x27	11x13	16x14	20x16
Cynghordy	d	07x33	11x20	16x21	20x23
Llandovery	a	07 43	11 29	16 30	20 33
	d	07 45	11 32	16 33	20 35
Llanwrda	d	07 51	11 37	16 39	20 41
Llangadog	d	07 54	11 41	16 43	20 45
Llandeilo	a	08 03	11 50	16 52	20 54
	d	08 06	11 53	16 54	20 57
Ffairfach	d	08x08	11x55	16x57	20x59
Llandybie	d	08 15	12 02	17 04	21 07
Ammanford	d	08 20	12 07	17 09	21 11
Pantyffynnon	d	08 23	12 10	17 12	21 14
Pontarddulais	d	08x30	12x17	17x19	21x21
Llangennech	d	08x34	12x21	17x23	21x26
Bynea	d	08x37	12x24	17x29	21x29
Llanelli	a	08 42	12 29	17 32	21 34
Gowerton	a	08x53		17x45	21x47
Swansea	a	09 08	13 01	18 06	22 10

Table 129

Shrewsbury - Swansea

HEART OF WALES LINE

		AW ◇ A	AW ◇ C	AW ◇ B	AW ◇ B	AW ◇ A	AW ◇ C
Shrewsbury	d	12 07	12 07	12 07	16 18	16 18	16 18
Church Stretton	d	12 25	12 25	12 25	16 36	16 36	16 36
Craven Arms	d	12 36	12 36	12 36	16 47	16 47	16 47
Broome	d	12x42	12x42	12x42	16x53	16x53	16x53
Hopton Heath	d	12x46	12x46	12x46	16x57	16x57	16x57
Bucknell	d	12 51	12 51	12 51	17 02	17 02	17 02
Knighton	d	13 00	13 00	13 00	17 11	17 11	17 11
Knucklas	d	13x06	13x06	13x06	17x16	17x16	17x16
Llangynllo	d	13x14	13x14	13x14	17x24	17x24	17x24
Llanbister Road	d	13x19	13x19	13x19	17x29	17x29	17x29
Dolau	d	13 25	13 25	13 25	17 35	17 35	17 35
Pen-y-bont	d	13x29	13x29	13x29	17x40	17x40	17x40
Llandrindod	a	13 38	13 38	13 38	17 49	17 49	17 49
	d	13 41	13 41	13 41	17 51	17 51	17 54
Builth Road	d	13x50	13x50	13x50	18x01	18x01	18x04
Cilmeri	d	13x54	13x54	13x54	18x04	18x04	18x07
Garth (Powys)	d	13x59	13x59	13x59	18x10	18x10	18x13
Llangammarch	d	14x03	14x03	14x03	18x14	18x14	18x17
Llanwrtyd	a	14 09	14 09	14 09	18 20	18 20	18 23
	d	14 12	14 12	14 12	18 22	18 22	18 25
Sugar Loaf	d	14x18	14x18	14x18	18x29	18x29	18x32
Cynghordy	d	14x25	14x25	14x25	18x36	18x36	18x39
Llandovery	a	14 35	14 35	14 35	18 45	18 45	18 48
	d	14 37	14 37	14 37	18 48	18 48	18 51
Llanwrda	d	14 43	14 43	14 43	18 54	18 54	18 57
Llangadog	d	14 47	14 47	14 47	18 58	18 58	19 01
Llandeilo	a	14 56	14 56	14 56	19 07	19 07	19 10
	d	15 01	14 59	14 59	19 09	19 09	19 12
Ffairfach	d	15x03	15x01	15x01	19x12	19x12	19x15
Llandybie	d	15 11	15 09	15 09	19 19	19 19	19 22
Ammanford	d	15 15	15 13	15 13	19 24	19 24	19 27
Pantyffynnon	d	15 18	15 16	15 16	19 27	19 27	19 30
Pontarddulais	d	15x25	15x23	15x23	19x34	19x34	19x37
Llangennech	d	15x30	15x28	15x28	19x38	19x38	19x41
Bynea	d	15x33	15x31	15x31	19x42	19x42	19x45
Llanelli	a	15 38	15 36	15 36	19 47	19 47	19 50
Gowerton	a			15x48	19x59	20x01	20x02
Swansea	a	16 04	15 59	16 02	20 13	20 15	20 16

A until 11 July
B from 18 July until 5 September
C from 12 September

Network Diagram for Table 130

DM-27/08
Design BAJS

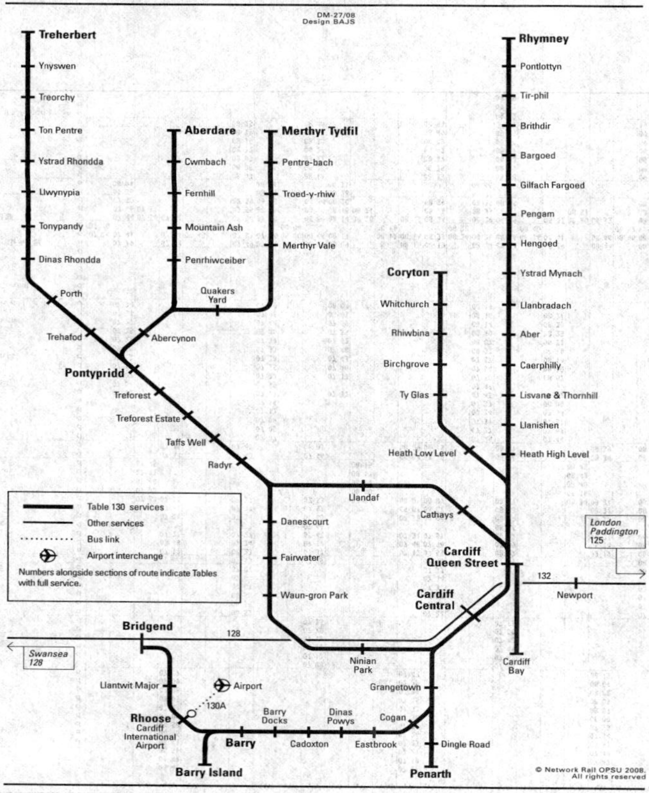

Treherbert, Aberdare, Merthyr, Pontypridd, Rhymney and Coryton - Cardiff, Penarth, Barry, Barry Island and Bridgend

		AW	AW	AW	AW	AW	AW	AW	AW	AW		AW	AW	AW	AW	AW	AW	AW	AW	AW	AW	AW	AW	AW	AW
Treherbert	d											05 47								06 17					
Ynyswen	d											05 49								06 19					
Treorchy	d											05 51								06 21					
Ton Pentre	d											05 53								06 23					
Ystrad Rhondda	a											05 56								06 26					
	d											05 58								06 28					
Llwynypia	d											06 00								06 30					
Tonypandy	d											06 03								06 33					
Dinas Rhondda	d											06 05								06 35					
Porth	a											06 08								06 38					
	d											06 09								06 39					
Trehafod	d											06 12								06 42					
Merthyr Tydfil	d																								06 38
Pentre-bach	d																								06 42
Troed Y Rhiw	d																								06 45
Merthyr Vale	a																								06 48
	d																								06 50
Quakers Yard	d																								06 55
Aberdare ■	d																					06 22			
Cwmbach	d																					06 25			
Fernhill	d																					06 28			
Mountain Ash	a																					06 31			
	d																					06 34			
Penrhiwceiber	d																					06 37			
Abercynon	d																					06 43			06 59
Pontypridd ■	a											06 17								06 47		06 53			07 07
	d				05 24							06 18								06 48		06 54			07 09
Trefforest	d				05 27							06 21								06 51		06 57			07 12
Trefforest Estate	d				05 31							06 25										07 01			07 16
Taffs Well ■	d				05 34							06 28								06 58	06 53	07 04			07 20
Radyr ■	a				05 37							06 31								07 01	06 56	07 07			07 23
	d				05 37							06 31								07 01	07 04	07 07			07 23
Danescourt	d																				07 08				
Fairwater	d																				07 10				
Waun-gron Park	d																				07 12				
Ninian Park	d																				07 15				
Llandaf	d				05 40							06 34								07 04		07 10			07 26
Cathays	d				05 45							06 39								07 09		07 15			07 31
Rhymney ■	d																	06 10						06 34	
Pontlottyn	d																	06 13						06 37	
Tir-phil	d																	06 17						06 41	
Brithdir	d																	06 20						06 44	
Bargoed	a																	06 23						06 47	
	d																	06 29						06 48	
Gilfach Fargoed	d																	06 31							
Pengam	d																	06 34						06 52	
Hengoed	d																	06 37						06 56	
Ystrad Mynach ■	d																	06 40						06 58	
Llanbradach	d																	06 45						07 03	
Aber	d																	06 49						07 07	
Caerphilly ■	d							06 10										06 52						07 10	
Lisvane & Thornhill	d							06 14										06 56						07 14	
Llanishen	d							06 16										06 58						07 16	
Heath High Level	d							06 19										07 01						07 19	
Coryton	d																								
Whitchurch (Cardiff)	d																								
Rhiwbina	d																								
Birchgrove	d																								
Ty Glas	d																								
Heath Low Level	d																								
Cardiff Queen Street ■	a				05 48			06 25				06 44						07 06		07 14		07 20		07 24	07 35
	d				05 51			06 26	06 36			06 44	06 48		07 00			07 08	07 12	07 16		07 21	07 24	07 26	07 36
Cardiff Bay	a								06 40				06 52		07 04				07 16				07 28		
Cardiff Central ■	a				05 54			06 29				06 48						07 11		07 18	07 20	07 24		07 29	07 40
	d	05 20	05 41	05 46	05 55	06 16	06 25	06 41		06 36				06 55		07 01	07 10	07 16			07 21	07 25		07 31	07 41
Grangetown	d	05 24	05 45	05 50	05 59	06 20	06 29	06 45		06 40				06 59		07 05	07 14	07 20				07 29		07 35	07 45
Dingle Road	d			05 54		06 24				06 44						07 11		07 26						07 42	
Penarth	a			05 59		06 28				06 49						07 16		07 31						07 46	
Cogan	d	05 28	05 48		06 03		06 33	06 48						07 03			07 18					07 33			07 48
Eastbrook	d	05 30	05 51		06 05		06 35	06 51						07 05			07 20					07 35			07 51
Dinas Powys	d	05 32	05 53		06 07		06 37	06 53						07 07			07 22					07 37			07 53
Cadoxton	d	05 37	05 57		06 12		06 42	06 57						07 12			07 27					07 42			07 57
Barry Docks	d	05 40	06 00		06 15		06 45	07 00						07 15			07 30					07 45			08 00
Barry ■	d	05 44	06 05		06 19		06 49	07 05						07 19			07 34					07 49			08 05
Barry Island	a	05 50			06 25		06 55							07 25			07 40					07 55			
Rhoose Cardiff Int Airport ✈	d		06 12					07 12																	08 12
Llantwit Major	d		06 22					07 22																	08 22
Bridgend	a		06 39					07 39																	08 39

Table 130

Mondays to Fridays
until 03 September

Treherbert, Aberdare, Merthyr, Pontypridd, Rhymney and Coryton - Cardiff, Penarth, Barry, Barry Island and Bridgend

		AW	AW	AW	AW	AW		AW	AW	AW	AW	AW	AW	AW	AW	AW	AW	AW	AW	AW	AW	AW	AW	AW	AW
Treherbert	d				06 47										07 17								07 45		
Ynyswen	d				06 49										07 19								07 47		
Treorchy	d				06 51										07 21								07 49		
Ton Pentre	d				06 53										07 23								07 51		
Ystrad Rhondda	a				06 56										07 26								07 54		
	d				06 58										07 28								07 58		
Llwynypia	d				07 00										07 30								08 00		
Tonypandy	d				07 03										07 33								08 03		
Dinas Rhondda	d				07 05										07 35								08 05		
Porth	a				07 08										07 38								08 08		
	d				07 09										07 39								08 09		
Trehafod	d				07 12										07 42								08 12		
Merthyr Tydfil	d										07 08								07 38						
Pentre-bach	d										07 12								07 42						
Troed Y Rhiw	d										07 15								07 45						
Merthyr Vale	a										07 18								07 48						
	d										07 20								07 50						
Quakers Yard	d										07 25								07 55						
Aberdare ■	d							06 52								07 22									07 52
Cwmbach	d							06 55								07 25									07 55
Fernhill	d							06 58								07 28									07 58
Mountain Ash	a							07 01								07 31									08 01
	d							07 04								07 34									08 04
Penrhiwceiber	d							07 07								07 37									08 07
Abercynon	d							07 13			07 29					07 43			07 59						08 13
Pontypridd ■	a				07 17			07 23			07 37				07 47	07 53			08 07				08 17		08 23
	d				07 18			07 24			07 39				07 48	07 54			08 09				08 18		08 24
Trefforest	d				07 21			07 27			07 42				07 51	07 57			08 12				08 21		08 27
Trefforest Estate	d										07 46								08 16						
Taffs Well ■	d				07 28			07 34			07 50				07 58	08 04			08 20				08 28		08 34
Radyr ■	a				07 31			07 37			07 53				08 01	08 07			08 23				08 31		08 37
	d			07 34	07 31			07 37			07 53		08 04		08 01	08 07			08 23			08 34	08 31		08 37
Danescourt	d			07 38									08 08									08 38			
Fairwater	d			07 40									08 10									08 40			
Waun-gron Park	d			07 42									08 12									08 42			
Ninian Park	d			07 45									08 15									08 45			
Llandaf	d				07 34			07 40			07 56				08 04	08 10			08 26				08 34		08 40
Cathays	d				07 39			07 45			08 01				08 09	08 15			08 31				08 39		08 45
Rhymney ■	d								07 02									07 24			07 44				
Pontlottyn	d								07 05									07 27			07 47				
Tir-phil	d								07 09									07 31			07 51				
Brithdir	d								07 12									07 34			07 54				
Bargoed	a								07 15									07 37			08 00				
	d		07 02						07 17			07 32						07 45			08 02				
Gilfach Fargoed	d		07 04						07 19									07 47							
Pengam	d		07 07						07 22			07 37						07 50			08 07				
Hengoed	d		07 10						07 25			07 40						07 54			08 10				
Ystrad Mynach ■	d		07 13						07 28			07 43						07 57			08 13				
Llanbradach	d		07 18						07 33			07 48						08 02			08 18				
Aber	d		07 22						07 37			07 52						08 07			08 22				
Caerphilly ■	d		07 25						07 40			07 55						08 10			08 25				
Lisvane & Thornhill	d		07 29						07 44			07 59						08 14			08 29				
Llanishen	d		07 31						07 46			08 01						08 16			08 31				
Heath High Level	d		07 34						07 49			08 04						08 19			08 34				
Coryton	d																								
Whitchurch (Cardiff)	d																								
Rhiwbina	d																								
Birchgrove	d																								
Ty Glas	d																								
Heath Low Level	d																								
Cardiff Queen Street ■	a		07 39		07 44			07 49	07 54		08 04	08 09			08 14	08 19		08 24	08 34		08 39		08 44		08 49
	d	07 36	07 41		07 46	07 48		07 51	07 56	08 00	08 06	08 11		08 12	08 16	08 21	08 24	08 26	08 36	08 36	08 41		08 46	08 48	08 51
Cardiff Bay	a	07 40				07 52				08 04				08 16			08 28			08 40				08 52	
Cardiff Central ■	a		07 44	07 50	07 51			07 54	07 59		08 09	08 14	08 20		08 22	08 24		08 29	08 39		08 47	08 50	08 52		08 54
	d		07 46	07 51				07 55	08 01		08 10	08 16	08 21			08 25		08 31	08 41			08 51			08 55
Grangetown	d		07 50					07 59	08 05		08 14	08 20				08 29		08 35	08 45						08 59
Dingle Road	d		07 56						08 11			08 26						08 41							
Penarth	a		08 01						08 16			08 31						08 46							
Cogan	d							08 03			08 18					08 33			08 48						09 03
Eastbrook	d							08 05			08 20					08 35			08 51						09 05
Dinas Powys	d							08 07			08 22					08 37			08 53						09 07
Cadoxton	d							08 12			08 27					08 42			08 57						09 12
Barry Docks	d							08 15			08 30					08 45			09 00						09 15
Barry ■	d							08 19			08 34					08 49			09 05						09 19
Barry Island	a							08 25			08 40					08 55									09 25
Rhoose Cardiff Int Airport ✈	d																		09 12						
Llantwit Major	d																		09 22						
Bridgend	a																		09 39						

Table 130

Mondays to Fridays
until 03 September

Treherbert, Aberdare, Merthyr, Pontypridd, Rhymney and Coryton - Cardiff, Penarth, Barry, Barry Island and Bridgend

		AW	AW	AW	AW	AW	AW	AW	AW	AW	AW	AW	AW	AW	AW	AW	AW	AW	AW	AW	AW	AW		AW	AW
Treherbert	d							08 17								08 47									
Ynyswen	d							08 19								08 49									
Treorchy	d							08 21								08 51									
Ton Pentre	d							08 23								08 53									
Ystrad Rhondda	a							08 26								08 56									
	d							08 28								08 58									
Llwynypia	d							08 30								09 00									
Tonypandy	d							08 33								09 03									
Dinas Rhondda	d							08 35								09 05									
Porth	a							08 38								09 08									
	d							08 39								09 09									
Trehafod	d							08 42								09 12									
Merthyr Tydfil	d			08 08								08 38									09 08				
Pentre-bach	d			08 12								08 42									09 12				
Troed Y Rhiw	d			08 15								08 45									09 15				
Merthyr Vale	a			08 18								08 48									09 18				
	d			08 20								08 50									09 20				
Quakers Yard	d			08 25								08 55									09 25				
Aberdare ■	d								08 22									08 52							
Cwmbach	d								08 25									08 55							
Fernhill	d								08 28									08 58							
Mountain Ash	a								08 31									09 01							
	d								08 34									09 04							
Penrhiwceiber	d								08 37									09 07							
Abercynon	d			08 29					08 43			08 59						09 13			09 29				
Pontypridd ■	a			08 37				08 47	08 53			09 07				09 17		09 23			09 37				
	d			08 39				08 48	08 54			09 09				09 18		09 24			09 39				
Trefforest	d			08 42				08 51	08 57			09 12				09 21		09 27			09 42				
Trefforest Estate	d			08 46								09 16									09 46				
Taffs Well ■	d			08 50				08 58	09 04			09 20				09 28		09 34			09 50				
Radyr ■	a			08 53				09 01	09 07			09 23				09 31		09 37			09 53				
	d			08 53		09 04		09 01	09 07			09 23			09 34	09 31		09 37			09 53			10 04	
Danescourt	d					09 08									09 38									10 08	
Fairwater	d					09 10									09 40									10 10	
Waun-gron Park	d					09 12									09 42									10 12	
Ninian Park	d					09 15									09 45									10 15	
Llandaf	d			08 56				09 04	09 10			09 26				09 34		09 40			09 56				
Cathays	d			09 01				09 09	09 15			09 31				09 39		09 45			10 01				
Rhymney ■	d										08 30														
Pontlottyn	d										08 33														
Tir-phil	d										08 37														
Brithdir	d										08 40														
Bargoed	a										08 44														
	d	08 17			08 32						08 47			09 02					09 17			09 32			
Gilfach Fargoed	d	08 19																	09 19						
Pengam	d	08 22			08 37						08 52			09 07					09 22			09 37			
Hengoed	d	08 25			08 40						08 55			09 10					09 25			09 40			
Ystrad Mynach ■	d	08 28			08 43						08 58			09 13					09 28			09 43			
Llanbradach	d	08 33			08 48						09 03			09 18					09 33			09 48			
Aber	d	08 37			08 52						09 07			09 22					09 37			09 52			
Caerphilly ■	d	08 40			08 55						09 10			09 25					09 40			09 55			
Lisvane & Thornhill	d	08 44			08 59						09 14			09 29					09 44			09 59			
Llanishen	d	08 46			09 01						09 16			09 31					09 46			10 01			
Heath High Level	d	08 49			09 04						09 19			09 34					09 49			10 04			
Coryton	d																								
Whitchurch (Cardiff)	d																								
Rhiwbina	d																								
Birchgrove	d																								
Ty Glas	d																								
Heath Low Level	d																								
Cardiff Queen Street ■	a	08 54		09 04	09 09			09 14	09 19		09 24	09 34		09 39		09 44		09 49	09 54		10 04	10 09			
	d	08 56	09 00	09 06	09 11		09 12	09 16	09 21	09 24	09 26	09 36	09 36	09 41		09 46	09 48	09 51	09 56	10 00	10 06	10 11			10 12
Cardiff Bay	a		09 04				09 16			09 28			09 40				09 52			10 04					10 16
Cardiff Central ■	a	08 59		09 09	09 14	09 20		09 22	09 24		09 29	09 39		09 44	09 50	09 52		09 54	09 59		10 09	10 14		10 20	
	d	09 01		09 10	09 16	09 21			09 25		09 31	09 41		09 46	09 51			09 55	10 01		10 10	10 16		10 21	
Grangetown	d	09 05		09 14	09 20				09 29		09 35	09 45		09 50				09 59	10 05		10 14	10 20			
Dingle Road	d	09 11			09 26						09 41			09 56					10 11			10 26			
Penarth	a	09 16			09 31						09 46			10 01					10 16			10 31			
Cogan	d			09 18					09 33			09 48						10 03			10 18				
Eastbrook	d			09 20					09 35			09 51						10 05			10 20				
Dinas Powys	d			09 22					09 37			09 53						10 07			10 22				
Cadoxton	d			09 27					09 42			09 57						10 12			10 27				
Barry Docks	d			09 30					09 45			10 00						10 15			10 30				
Barry ■	d			09 34					09 49			10 05						10 19			10 34				
Barry Island	a			09 40					09 55									10 25			10 40				
Rhoose Cardiff Int Airport ✈	d											10 12													
Llantwit Major	d											10 22													
Bridgend	a											10 39													

Table 130

Mondays to Fridays
until 03 September

Treherbert, Aberdare, Merthyr, Pontypridd, Rhymney and Coryton - Cardiff, Penarth, Barry, Barry Island and Bridgend

		AW	AW	AW	AW	AW	AW	AW	AW	AW	AW	AW	AW	AW	AW	AW	AW	AW	AW	AW	AW	AW	AW	AW
Treherbert	d	09 17								09 47													10 17	
Ynyswen	d	09 19								09 49													10 19	
Treorchy	d	09 21								09 51													10 21	
Ton Pentre	d	09 23								09 53													10 23	
Ystrad Rhondda	a	09 26								09 56													10 26	
	d	09 28								09 58													10 28	
Llwynypia	d	09 30								10 00													10 30	
Tonypandy	d	09 33								10 03													10 33	
Dinas Rhondda	d	09 35								10 05													10 35	
Porth	a	09 38								10 08													10 38	
	d	09 39								10 09													10 52	
Trehafod	d	09 42								10 12													10 55	
Merthyr Tydfil	d					09 38							10 04											10 38
Pentre-bach	d					09 42							10 08											10 42
Troed Y Rhiw	d					09 45							10 11											10 45
Merthyr Vale	a					09 48							10 14											10 48
	d					09 50							10 16											10 50
Quakers Yard	d					09 55							10 22											10 55
Aberdare 3	d		09 22									09 52								10 22				
Cwmbach	d		09 25									09 55								10 25				
Fernhill	d		09 28									09 58								10 28				
Mountain Ash	a		09 31									10 01								10 31				
	d		09 34									10 04								10 34				
Penrhiwceiber	d		09 37									10 07								10 37				
Abercynon	d		09 43			09 59						10 13	10 26							10 43				10 59
Pontypridd 3	a	09 47	09 53			10 07				10 17		10 23	10 32							10 53			11 00	11 08
	d	09 48	09 54			10 09				10 18		10 24				10 39				10 54			11 04	11 09
Trefforest	d	09 51	09 57			10 12				10 21		10 27				10 42				10 57			11 07	11 12
Trefforest Estate	d					10 16										10 46								11 16
Taffs Well 3	d	09 58	10 04			10 20				10 28		10 34				10 50				11 04			11 13	11 20
Radyr 3	a	10 01	10 07			10 23				10 31		10 37				10 53				11 07			11 17	11 23
	d	10 01	10 07			10 23			10 34	10 31		10 37				10 53		11 04		11 07			11 17	11 23
Danescourt	d								10 38									11 08						
Fairwater	d								10 40									11 10						
Waun-gron Park	d								10 42									11 12						
Ninian Park	d								10 45									11 15						
Llandaf	d	10 04	10 10			10 26				10 34		10 40				10 56				11 10				11 26
Cathays	d	10 09	10 15			10 31				10 39		10 45				11 01				11 15				11 31
Rhymney 3	d				09 29																	10 29		
Pontlottyn	d				09 32																	10 32		
Tir-phil	d				09 36																	10 36		
Brithdir	d				09 39																	10 39		
Bargoed	a				09 42																	10 42		
	d				09 47			10 02						10 17			10 32					10 47		
Gilfach Fargoed	d													10 19										
Pengam	d				09 52			10 07						10 22			10 37					10 52		
Hengoed	d				09 55			10 10						10 25			10 40					10 55		
Ystrad Mynach 3	d				09 58			10 13						10 28			10 43					10 58		
Llanbradach	d				10 03			10 18						10 33			10 48					11 03		
Aber	d				10 07			10 22						10 37			10 52					11 07		
Caerphilly 3	d				10 10			10 25						10 40			10 55					11 10		
Lisvane & Thornhill	d				10 14			10 29						10 44			10 59					11 14		
Llanishen	d				10 16			10 31						10 46			11 01					11 16		
Heath High Level	d				10 19			10 34						10 49			11 04					11 19		
Coryton	d																							
Whitchurch (Cardiff)	d																							
Rhiwbina	d																							
Birchgrove	d																							
Ty Glas	d																							
Heath Low Level	d																							
Cardiff Queen Street 3	a	10 14	10 19		10 24	10 34		10 39		10 44		10 49		10 54		11 04	11 09			11 19		11 24		11 34
	d	10 16	10 21	10 24	10 26	10 36	10 36	10 41		10 46	10 48	10 51		10 56	11 00	11 06	11 11		11 12	11 21	11 24	11 26		11 36
Cardiff Bay	a			10 28			10 40				10 52				11 04				11 16		11 28			
Cardiff Central 7	a	10 22	10 24		10 29	10 39		10 44	10 50	10 52		10 54		10 59		11 09	11 14	11 20		11 24		11 29	11 34	11 39
	d		10 25		10 31	10 41		10 46	10 51			10 55		11 01		11 10	11 16	11 21		11 25		11 31		11 41
Grangetown	d		10 29		10 35	10 45		10 50				10 59		11 05		11 14	11 20			11 29		11 35		11 45
Dingle Road	d				10 41			10 56						11 11			11 26					11 41		
Penarth	a				10 46			11 01						11 16			11 31					11 46		
Cogan	d		10 33			10 48						11 03				11 18				11 33				11 48
Eastbrook	d		10 35			10 51						11 05				11 20				11 35				11 51
Dinas Powys	d		10 37			10 53						11 07				11 22				11 37				11 53
Cadoxton	d		10 42			10 57						11 12				11 27				11 42				11 57
Barry Docks	d		10 45			11 00						11 15				11 30				11 45				12 00
Barry 3	d		10 49			11 05						11 19				11 34				11 49				12 05
Barry Island	a		10 55									11 25				11 41				11 55				
Rhoose Cardiff Int Airport ✈	d					11 12																		12 12
Llantwit Major	d					11 22																		12 22
Bridgend	a					11 39																		12 39

Table 130

Mondays to Fridays
until 03 September

Treherbert, Aberdare, Merthyr, Pontypridd, Rhymney and Coryton - Cardiff, Penarth, Barry, Barry Island and Bridgend

		AW	AW	AW	AW	AW	AW	AW	AW	AW	AW	AW	AW	AW	AW	AW	AW	AW	AW	AW	AW	AW
Treherbert	d				10 47									11 17								11 47
Ynyswen	d				10 49									11 19								11 49
Treorchy	d				10 51									11 21								11 51
Ton Pentre	d				10 53									11 23								11 53
Ystrad Rhondda	a				10 56									11 26								11 56
	d				10 58									11 28								11 58
Llwynypia	d				11 00									11 30								12 00
Tonypandy	d				11 03									11 33								12 03
Dinas Rhondda	d				11 05									11 35								12 05
Porth	a				11 08									11 38								12 08
	d				11 09									11 39								12 09
Trehafod	d				11 12									11 42								12 12
Merthyr Tydfil	d									11 08								11 38				
Pentre-bach	d									11 12								11 42				
Troed Y Rhiw	d									11 15								11 45				
Merthyr Vale	a									11 18								11 48				
	d									11 20								11 50				
Quakers Yard	d									11 25								11 55				
Aberdare 3	d						10 52								11 22							
Cwmbach	d						10 55								11 25							
Fernhill	d						10 58								11 28							
Mountain Ash	a						11 01								11 31							
	d						11 04								11 34							
Penrhiwceiber	d						11 07								11 37							
Abercynon	d						11 13			11 29					11 43			11 59				
Pontypridd 3	a				11 17		11 23			11 37				11 47	11 53			12 07				12 17
	d				11 18		11 24			11 39				11 48	11 54			12 09				12 18
Trefforest	d				11 21		11 27			11 42				11 51	11 57			12 12				12 21
Trefforest Estate	d									11 46								12 16				
Taffs Well 3	d				11 28		11 34			11 50				11 58	12 04			12 20				12 28
Radyr 3	a				11 31		11 37			11 53				12 01	12 07			12 23				12 31
	d			11 34	11 31		11 37			11 53		12 04		12 01	12 07			12 23			12 34	12 31
Danescourt	d			11 38								12 08									12 38	
Fairwater	d			11 40								12 10									12 40	
Waun-gron Park	d			11 42								12 12									12 42	
Ninian Park	d			11 45								12 15									12 45	
Llandaf	d				11 34		11 40			11 56				12 04	12 10			12 26				12 34
Cathays	d				11 39		11 45			12 01				12 09	12 15			12 31				12 39
Rhymney 3	d																11 29					
Pontlottyn	d																11 32					
Tir-phil	d																11 36					
Brithdir	d																11 39					
Bargoed	a																11 42					
	d		11 02					11 17			11 32						11 47			12 02		
Gilfach Fargoed	d							11 19														
Pengam	d		11 07					11 22			11 37						11 52			12 07		
Hengoed	d		11 10					11 25			11 40						11 55			12 10		
Ystrad Mynach 3	d		11 13					11 28			11 43						11 58			12 13		
Llanbradach	d		11 18					11 33			11 48						12 03			12 18		
Aber	d		11 22					11 37			11 52						12 07			12 22		
Caerphilly 3	d		11 25					11 40			11 55						12 10			12 25		
Lisvane & Thornhill	d		11 29					11 44			11 59						12 14			12 29		
Llanishen	d		11 31					11 46			12 01						12 16			12 31		
Heath High Level	d		11 34					11 49			12 04						12 19			12 34		
Coryton	d																					
Whitchurch (Cardiff)	d																					
Rhiwbina	d																					
Birchgrove	d																					
Ty Glas	d																					
Heath Low Level	d																					
Cardiff Queen Street 3	a		11 39		11 44		11 49	11 54		12 04	12 09			12 14	12 19		12 24	12 34		12 39		12 44
	d	11 36	11 41		11 46	11 48	11 51	11 56	12 00	12 06	12 11		12 12	12 16	12 21	12 24	12 26	12 36	12 36	12 41		12 46
Cardiff Bay	a	11 40				11 52			12 04				12 16			12 28			12 40			
Cardiff Central 7	a		11 44	11 50	11 52		11 54	11 59		12 09	12 14	12 20		12 22	12 24		12 29	12 39		12 44	12 50	12 52
	d		11 46	11 51			11 55	12 01		12 10	12 16	12 21			12 25		12 31	12 41		12 46	12 51	
Grangetown	d		11 50				11 59	12 05		12 14	12 20				12 29		12 35	12 45		12 50		
Dingle Road	d		11 56					12 11			12 26						12 41			12 56		
Penarth	a		12 01					12 16			12 31						12 46			13 01		
Cogan	d						12 03			12 18					12 33			12 48				
Eastbrook	d						12 05			12 20					12 35			12 51				
Dinas Powys	d						12 07			12 22					12 37			12 53				
Cadoxton	d						12 12			12 27					12 42			12 57				
Barry Docks	d						12 15			12 30					12 45			13 00				
Barry 3	d						12 19			12 34					12 49			13 05				
Barry Island	a						12 25			12 40					12 55							
Rhoose Cardiff Int Airport ✈	d																	13 12				
Llantwit Major	d																	13 22				
Bridgend	a																	13 39				

Table 130

Mondays to Fridays
until 03 September

Treherbert, Aberdare, Merthyr, Pontypridd, Rhymney and Coryton - Cardiff, Penarth, Barry, Barry Island and Bridgend

		AW	AW	AW	AW	AW	AW	AW	AW	AW	AW	AW	AW	AW	AW	AW	AW	AW	AW	AW	AW	AW	AW
Treherbert	d									12 17								12 47					
Ynyswen	d									12 19								12 49					
Treorchy	d									12 21								12 51					
Ton Pentre	d									12 23								12 53					
Ystrad Rhondda	a									12 26								12 56					
	d									12 28								12 58					
Llwynypia	d									12 30								13 00					
Tonypandy	d									12 33								13 03					
Dinas Rhondda	d									12 35								13 05					
Porth	a									12 38								13 08					
	d									12 39								13 09					
Trehafod	d									12 42								13 12					
Merthyr Tydfil	d					12 08								12 38									13 08
Pentre-bach	d					12 12								12 42									13 12
Troed Y Rhiw	d					12 15								12 45									13 15
Merthyr Vale	a					12 18								12 48									13 18
	d					12 20								12 50									13 20
Quakers Yard	d					12 25								12 55									13 25
Aberdare ■	d										12 22									12 52			
Cwmbach	d										12 25									12 55			
Fernhill	d										12 28									12 58			
Mountain Ash	a										12 31									13 01			
	d										12 34									13 04			
Penrhiwceiber	d										12 37									13 07			
Abercynon	d					12 29					12 43			12 59						13 13			13 29
Pontypridd ■	a					12 37				12 48	12 53			13 07				13 17		13 23			13 37
	d					12 39				12 48	12 54			13 09				13 18		13 24			13 39
Trefforest	d					12 42				12 51	12 57			13 12				13 21		13 27			13 42
Trefforest Estate	d					12 46								13 16									13 46
Taffs Well ■	d					12 50				12 58	13 04			13 20				13 28		13 34			13 50
Radyr ■	a					12 53				13 01	13 07			13 23				13 31		13 37			13 53
	d					12 53		13 04		13 01	13 07			13 23			13 34	13 31		13 37			13 53
Danescourt	d							13 08									13 38						
Fairwater	d							13 10									13 40						
Waun-gron Park	d							13 12									13 42						
Ninian Park	d							13 15									13 45						
Llandaf	d					12 56				13 04	13 10			13 26				13 34		13 40			13 56
Cathays	d					13 01				13 09	13 15			13 31				13 39		13 45			14 01
Rhymney ■	d												12 29										
Pontlottyn	d												12 32										
Tir-phil	d												12 36										
Brithdir	d												12 39										
Bargoed	a												12 42										
	d			12 17			12 32						12 47			13 02					13 17		
Gilfach Fargoed	d			12 19																	13 19		
Pengam	d			12 22			12 37						12 52			13 07					13 22		
Hengoed	d			12 25			12 40						12 55			13 10					13 25		
Ystrad Mynach ■	d			12 28			12 43						12 58			13 13					13 28		
Llanbradach	d			12 33			12 48						13 03			13 18					13 33		
Aber	d			12 37			12 52						13 07			13 22					13 37		
Caerphilly ■	d			12 40			12 55						13 10			13 25					13 40		
Lisvane & Thornhill	d			12 44			12 59						13 14			13 29					13 44		
Llanishen	d			12 46			13 01						13 16			13 31					13 46		
Heath High Level	d			12 49			13 04						13 19			13 34					13 49		
Coryton	d																						
Whitchurch (Cardiff)	d																						
Rhiwbina	d																						
Birchgrove	d																						
Ty Glas	d																						
Heath Low Level	d																						
Cardiff Queen Street ■	a			12 54		13 04	13 09			13 14	13 19		13 24	13 34		13 39		13 44		13 49	13 54		14 04
	d	12 48		12 56	13 00	13 06	13 11		13 12	13 16	13 21	13 24	13 26	13 36	13 36	13 41		13 46	13 48	13 51	13 56	14 00	14 06
Cardiff Bay	a	12 52			13 04				13 16			13 28			13 40				13 52			14 04	
Cardiff Central ■	a			12 59		13 09	13 14	13 20		13 22	13 24		13 29	13 39		13 44	13 50	13 52		13 54	13 59		14 09
	d		12 55	13 01		13 10	13 16	13 21			13 25		13 31	13 41		13 46	13 51			13 55	14 01		14 10
Grangetown	d		12 59	13 05		13 14	13 20				13 29		13 35	13 45		13 50				13 59	14 05		14 14
Dingle Road	d			13 11			13 26						13 41			13 56					14 11		
Penarth	a			13 16			13 31						13 46			14 01					14 16		
Cogan	d		13 03			13 18					13 33			13 48						14 03			14 18
Eastbrook	d		13 05			13 20					13 35			13 51						14 05			14 20
Dinas Powys	d		13 07			13 22					13 37			13 53						14 07			14 22
Cadoxton	d		13 12			13 27					13 42			13 57						14 12			14 27
Barry Docks	d		13 15			13 30					13 45			14 00						14 15			14 30
Barry ■	d		13 19			13 34					13 49			14 05						14 19			14 34
Barry Island	a		13 25			13 40					13 55									14 25			14 40
Rhoose Cardiff Int Airport ✈	d													14 12									
Llantwit Major	d													14 22									
Bridgend	a													14 39									

Table 130

Mondays to Fridays
until 03 September

Treherbert, Aberdare, Merthyr, Pontypridd, Rhymney and Coryton - Cardiff, Penarth, Barry, Barry Island and Bridgend

		AW	AW	AW	AW	AW	AW	AW	AW	AW	AW	AW	AW	AW	AW	AW	AW	AW	AW	AW	AW	AW	AW
Treherbert	d				13 17								13 47										
Ynyswen	d				13 19								13 49										
Treorchy	d				13 21								13 51										
Ton Pentre	d				13 23								13 53										
Ystrad Rhondda	a				13 26								13 56										
	d				13 28								13 58										
Llwynypia	d				13 30								14 00										
Tonypandy	d				13 33								14 03										
Dinas Rhondda	d				13 35								14 05										
Porth	a				13 38								14 08										
	d				13 39								14 09										
Trehafod	d				13 42								14 12										
Merthyr Tydfil	d								13 38									14 08					
Pentre-bach	d								13 42									14 12					
Troed Y Rhiw	d								13 45									14 15					
Merthyr Vale	a								13 48									14 18					
	d								13 50									14 20					
Quakers Yard	d								13 55									14 25					
Aberdare ■	d														13 52							14 22	
Cwmbach	d														13 55							14 25	
Fernhill	d														13 58							14 28	
Mountain Ash	a														14 01							14 31	
	d														14 04							14 34	
Penrhiwceiber	d														14 07							14 37	
Abercynon	d					13 45			13 59						14 13			14 29				14 43	
Pontypridd ■	a				13 47	13 53			14 07				14 17		14 23			14 37				14 53	
	d				13 48	13 54			14 09				14 18		14 24			14 39				14 54	
Trefforest	d				13 51	13 57			14 12				14 21		14 27			14 42				14 57	
Trefforest Estate	d								14 16									14 46					
Taffs Well ■	d				13 58	14 04			14 20				14 28		14 34			14 50				15 04	
Radyr ■	a				14 01	14 07			14 23				14 31		14 37			14 53				15 07	
	d		14 04		14 01	14 07			14 23			14 34	14 31		14 37			14 53		15 04		15 07	
Danescourt	d		14 08									14 38								15 08			
Fairwater	d		14 10									14 40								15 10			
Waun-gron Park	d		14 12									14 42								15 12			
Ninian Park	d		14 15									14 45								15 15			
Llandaf	d				14 04	14 10			14 26				14 34		14 40			14 56				15 10	
Cathays	d				14 09	14 15			14 31				14 39		14 45			15 01				15 15	
Rhymney ■	d							13 29															
Pontlottyn	d							13 32															
Tir-phil	d							13 36															
Brithdir	d							13 39															
Bargoed	a							13 42															
	d	13 32						13 47			14 02					14 17			14 32				
Gilfach Fargoed	d															14 19							
Pengam	d	13 37						13 52			14 07					14 22			14 37				
Hengoed	d	13 40						13 55			14 10					14 25			14 40				
Ystrad Mynach ■	d	13 43						13 58			14 13					14 28			14 43				
Llanbradach	d	13 48						14 03			14 18					14 33			14 48				
Aber	d	13 52						14 07			14 22					14 37			14 52				
Caerphilly ■	d	13 55						14 10			14 25					14 40			14 55				
Lisvane & Thornhill	d	13 59						14 14			14 29					14 44			14 59				
Llanishen	d	14 01						14 16			14 31					14 46			15 01				
Heath High Level	d	14 04						14 19			14 34					14 49			15 04				
Coryton	d																						
Whitchurch (Cardiff)	d																						
Rhiwbina	d																						
Birchgrove	d																						
Ty Glas	d																						
Heath Low Level	d																						
Cardiff Queen Street ■	a	14 09			14 14	14 19		14 24	14 34		14 39		14 44		14 49	14 54		15 04	15 09			15 19	
	d	14 11		14 12	14 16	14 21	14 24	14 26	14 36	14 36	14 41		14 46	14 48	14 51	14 56	15 00	15 06	15 11		15 12	15 21	15 24
Cardiff Bay	a			14 16			14 28			14 40				14 52			15 04				15 16		15 28
Cardiff Central ■	a	14 14	14 20		14 22	14 24		14 29	14 39		14 44	14 50	14 52		14 54	14 59		15 09	15 14	15 20		15 24	
	d	14 16	14 21			14 25		14 31	14 41		14 46	14 51			14 55	15 01		15 10	15 16	15 21		15 25	
Grangetown	d	14 20				14 29		14 35	14 45		14 50				14 59	15 05		15 14	15 20			15 29	
Dingle Road	d	14 26						14 41			14 56					15 11			15 26				
Penarth	a	14 31						14 46			15 01					15 16			15 31				
Cogan	d					14 33			14 48						15 03			15 18				15 33	
Eastbrook	d					14 35			14 51						15 05			15 20				15 35	
Dinas Powys	d					14 37			14 53						15 07			15 22				15 37	
Cadoxton	d					14 42			14 57						15 12			15 27				15 42	
Barry Docks	d					14 45			15 00						15 15			15 30				15 45	
Barry ■	d					14 49			15 05						15 19			15 34				15 49	
Barry Island	a					14 55									15 25			15 40				15 55	
Rhoose Cardiff Int Airport ✈	d								15 12														
Llantwit Major	d								15 22														
Bridgend	a								15 39														

Table 130

Mondays to Fridays

until 03 September

Treherbert, Aberdare, Merthyr, Pontypridd, Rhymney and Coryton - Cardiff, Penarth, Barry, Barry Island and Bridgend

Station		AW		AW	AW	AW	AW	AW	AW	AW	AW	AW	AW		AW	AW	AW	AW	AW	AW	AW	AW	AW	AW	AW
Treherbert	d			14 17					14 47										15 15						
Ynyswen	d			14 19					14 49										15 17						
Treorchy	d			14 21					14 51										15 21						
Ton Pentre	d			14 23					14 53										15 23						
Ystrad Rhondda	a			14 26					14 56										15 26						
	d			14 28					14 58										15 28						
Llwynypia	d			14 30					15 00										15 30						
Tonypandy	d			14 33					15 03										15 33						
Dinas Rhondda	d			14 35					15 05										15 35						
Porth	a			14 38					15 08										15 38						
	d			14 52					15 09										15 39						
Trehafod	d			14 55					15 12										15 42						
Merthyr Tydfil	d				14 38										15 08								15 38		
Pentre-bach	d				14 42										15 12								15 42		
Troed Y Rhiw	d				14 45										15 15								15 45		
Merthyr Vale	a				14 48										15 18								15 48		
	d				14 50										15 20								15 50		
Quakers Yard	d				14 55										15 25								15 55		
Aberdare [3]	d										14 52									15 22					
Cwmbach	d										14 55									15 25					
Fernhill	d										14 58									15 28					
Mountain Ash	a										15 01									15 31					
	d										15 04									15 34					
Penrhiwceiber	d										15 07									15 37					
Abercynon	d				14 59						15 13				15 29					15 43			15 59		
Pontypridd [3]	a			15 00	15 07				15 17		15 23				15 37				15 47	15 53			16 08		
	d			15 04	15 09				15 18		15 24				15 39				15 48	15 54			16 09		
Trefforest	d			15 07	15 12				15 21		15 27				15 42				15 51	15 57			16 12		
Trefforest Estate	d				15 16										15 46								16 16		
Taffs Well [3]	d			15 13	15 20				15 28		15 34				15 50				15 58	16 04			16 20		
Radyr [3]	a			15 17	15 23				15 31		15 37				15 53				16 01	16 07			16 23		
	d			15 17	15 23			15 34	15 31		15 37				15 53		16 04		16 01	16 07			16 23		
Danescourt	d							15 38									16 08								
Fairwater	d							15 40									16 10								
Waun-gron Park	d							15 42									16 12								
Ninian Park	d							15 45									16 15								
Llandaf	d				15 26				15 34		15 40				15 56				16 04	16 10			16 26		
Cathays	d				15 31				15 39		15 45				16 01				16 09	16 15			16 31		
Rhymney [3]	d	14 29																				15 29			
Pontlottyn	d	14 32																				15 32			
Tir-phil	d	14 36																				15 36			
Brithdir	d	14 39																				15 39			
Bargoed	a	14 42																				15 42			
	d	14 47					15 02						15 17			15 32						15 47			16 02
Gilfach Fargoed	d												15 19												
Pengam	d	14 52					15 07						15 22			15 37						15 52			16 07
Hengoed	d	14 55					15 10						15 25			15 40						15 55			16 10
Ystrad Mynach [3]	d	14 58					15 13						15 28			15 43						15 58			16 13
Llanbradach	d	15 03					15 18						15 33			15 48						16 03			16 18
Aber	d	15 07					15 22						15 37			15 52						16 07			16 22
Caerphilly [3]	d	15 10					15 25						15 40			15 55						16 10			16 25
Lisvane & Thornhill	d	15 14					15 29						15 44			15 59						16 14			16 29
Llanishen	d	15 16					15 31						15 46			16 01						16 16			16 31
Heath High Level	d	15 19					15 34						15 49			16 04						16 19			16 34
Coryton	d																								
Whitchurch (Cardiff)	d																								
Rhiwbina	d																								
Birchgrove	d																								
Ty Glas	d																								
Heath Low Level	d																								
Cardiff Queen Street [3]	a	15 24			15 34		15 39		15 44		15 49	15 54			16 04	16 09			16 14	16 19		16 24	16 34		16 39
	d	15 26			15 36	15 36	15 41		15 46	15 48	15 51	15 56	16 00		16 06	16 11		16 12	16 16	16 21	16 24	16 26	16 36	16 36	16 41
Cardiff Bay	a					15 40				15 52			16 04					16 16			16 28			16 40	
Cardiff Central [7]	a	15 29		15 34	15 39		15 44	15 50	15 52		15 54	15 59			16 09	16 14	16 20		16 22	16 24		16 32	16 39		16 44
	d	15 31			15 41		15 46	15 51			15 55	16 01			16 10	16 16	16 21			16 25			16 41		16 46
Grangetown	d	15 35			15 45		15 50				15 59	16 05			16 14	16 20				16 29			16 45		16 50
Dingle Road	d	15 41					15 56					16 11				16 26									16 56
Penarth	a	15 46					16 01					16 16				16 31									17 01
Cogan	d				15 48						16 03				16 18					16 33			16 48		
Eastbrook	d				15 51						16 05				16 20					16 35			16 51		
Dinas Powys	d				15 53						16 07				16 22					16 37			16 53		
Cadoxton	d				15 57						16 12				16 27					16 42			16 57		
Barry Docks	d				16 00						16 15				16 30					16 45			17 00		
Barry [3]	d				16 05						16 19				16 34					16 49			17 05		
Barry Island	a										16 25				16 40					16 55					
Rhoose Cardiff Int Airport ✈	d				16 12																		17 12		
Llantwit Major	d				16 22																		17 22		
Bridgend	a				16 39																		17 39		

Table 130

Mondays to Fridays

until 03 September

Treherbert, Aberdare, Merthyr, Pontypridd, Rhymney and Coryton - Cardiff, Penarth, Barry, Barry Island and Bridgend

Station		AW	AW	AW	AW	AW	AW	AW		AW	AW	AW	AW	AW	AW	AW	AW	AW		AW	AW	AW	AW	AW	AW
Treherbert	d		15 47										16 17								16 47				
Ynyswen	d		15 49										16 19								16 49				
Treorchy	d		15 51										16 21								16 51				
Ton Pentre	d		15 53										16 23								16 53				
Ystrad Rhondda	a		15 56										16 26								16 56				
	d		15 58										16 28								16 58				
Llwynypia	d		16 00										16 30								17 00				
Tonypandy	d		16 03										16 33								17 03				
Dinas Rhondda	d		16 05										16 35								17 05				
Porth	a		16 08										16 38								17 08				
	d		16 09										16 39								17 09				
Trehafod	d		16 12										16 42								17 12				
Merthyr Tydfil	d							16 08									16 38								
Pentre-bach	d							16 12									16 42								
Troed Y Rhiw	d							16 15									16 45								
Merthyr Vale	a							16 18									16 48								
	d							16 20									16 50								
Quakers Yard	d							16 25									16 55								
Aberdare [3]	d				15 52									16 22									16 52		
Cwmbach	d				15 55									16 25									16 55		
Fernhill	d				15 58									16 28									16 58		
Mountain Ash	a				16 01									16 31									17 01		
	d				16 04									16 34									17 04		
Penrhiwceiber	d				16 07									16 37									17 07		
Abercynon	d				16 13			16 29						16 43			16 59						17 13		
Pontypridd [3]	a		16 17		16 23			16 37					16 47	16 53			17 07				17 17		17 23		
	d		16 18		16 24			16 39					16 48	16 54			17 09				17 18		17 24		
Trefforest	d		16 21		16 27			16 42					16 51	16 57			17 12				17 21		17 27		
Trefforest Estate	d							16 46									17 16								
Taffs Well [3]	d		16 28		16 34			16 50					16 58	17 04			17 20				17 28		17 34		
Radyr [3]	a		16 31		16 37			16 53					17 01	17 07			17 23				17 31		17 37		
	d	16 34	16 31		16 37			16 53			17 04		17 01	17 07			17 23	17 34			17 31		17 37		
Danescourt	d	16 38									17 08							17 38							
Fairwater	d	16 40									17 10							17 40							
Waun-gron Park	d	16 42									17 12							17 42							
Ninian Park	d	16 45									17 15							17 45							
Llandaf	d		16 34		16 40			16 56					17 04	17 10			17 26				17 34		17 40		
Cathays	d		16 39		16 45			17 01					17 09	17 15			17 31				17 39		17 45		
Rhymney [3]	d															16 29									
Pontlottyn	d															16 32									
Tir-phil	d															16 36									
Brithdir	d															16 39									
Bargoed	a															16 42									
	d					16 17				16 32						16 47								17 17	
Gilfach Fargoed	d					16 19																		17 19	
Pengam	d					16 22				16 37						16 52								17 22	
Hengoed	d					16 25				16 40						16 55								17 25	
Ystrad Mynach [3]	d					16 28				16 43						16 58								17 28	
Llanbradach	d					16 33				16 48						17 03								17 33	
Aber	d					16 37				16 52						17 07								17 37	
Caerphilly [3]	d					16 40				16 55						17 10								17 40	
Lisvane & Thornhill	d					16 44				16 59						17 14								17 44	
Llanishen	d					16 46				17 01						17 16								17 46	
Heath High Level	d					16 49				17 04						17 19								17 49	
Coryton	d																								
Whitchurch (Cardiff)	d																								
Rhiwbina	d																								
Birchgrove	d																								
Ty Glas	d																								
Heath Low Level	d																								
Cardiff Queen Street [3]	a		16 44		16 49	16 54		17 04		17 09			17 14	17 19		17 24	17 34				17 44		17 49	17 54	
	d		16 46	16 48	16 51	16 56	17 00	17 06		17 11		17 12	17 16	17 21	17 24	17 26	17 36			17 36	17 46	17 48	17 51	17 56	18 00
Cardiff Bay	a			16 52			17 04					17 16			17 28					17 40		17 52			18 04
Cardiff Central [7]	a	16 50	16 52		16 54	16 59		17 09		17 14	17 20		17 22	17 24		17 29	17 39	17 50			17 52		17 54	17 59	
	d	16 51			16 55	17 01		17 10		17 16	17 21			17 25		17 31	17 41	17 51					17 55	18 01	
Grangetown	d				16 59	17 05		17 14		17 20				17 29		17 35	17 45						17 59	18 05	
Dingle Road	d					17 11				17 26						17 41								18 11	
Penarth	a					17 16				17 31						17 46								18 16	
Cogan	d				17 03			17 18						17 33			17 48						18 03		
Eastbrook	d				17 05			17 20						17 35			17 51						18 05		
Dinas Powys	d				17 07			17 22						17 37			17 53						18 07		
Cadoxton	d				17 12			17 27						17 42			17 57						18 12		
Barry Docks	d				17 15			17 30						17 45			18 00						18 15		
Barry [3]	d				17 19			17 34						17 49			18 05						18 19		
Barry Island	a				17 25			17 40						17 55									18 25		
Rhoose Cardiff Int Airport ✈	d																18 12								
Llantwit Major	d																18 22								
Bridgend	a																18 39								

Treherbert, Aberdare, Merthyr, Pontypridd, Rhymney and Coryton - Cardiff, Penarth, Barry, Barry Island and Bridgend

		AW	AW	AW		AW	AW	AW	AW	AW	AW	AW	AW	AW		AW	AW	AW	AW	AW	AW	AW	AW	AW
Treherbert	d						17 17							17 47										18 17
Ynyswen	d						17 19							17 49										18 19
Treorchy	d						17 21							17 51										18 21
Ton Pentre	d						17 23							17 53										18 23
Ystrad Rhondda	a						17 26							17 56										18 26
	d						17 28							17 58										18 28
Llwynypia	d						17 30							18 00										18 30
Tonypandy	d						17 33							18 03										18 33
Dinas Rhondda	d						17 35							18 05										18 35
Porth	a						17 38							18 08										18 38
	d						17 39							18 09										18 39
Trehafod	d						17 42							18 12										18 42
Merthyr Tydfil	d	17 08									17 38										18 08			
Pentre-bach	d	17 12									17 42										18 12			
Troed Y Rhiw	d	17 15									17 45										18 15			
Merthyr Vale	a	17 18									17 48										18 18			
	d	17 20									17 50										18 20			
Quakers Yard	d	17 25									17 55										18 25			
Aberdare ■	d							17 22									17 52							
Cwmbach	d							17 25									17 55							
Fernhill	d							17 28									17 58							
Mountain Ash	a							17 31									18 01							
	d							17 34									18 04							
Penrhiwceiber	d							17 37									18 07							
Abercynon	d	17 29						17 43			17 59						18 13				18 29			
Pontypridd ■	a	17 37					17 47	17 53			18 07			18 17			18 23				18 37			18 47
	d	17 39					17 48	17 54			18 09			18 18			18 24				18 39			18 48
Trefforest	d	17 42					17 51	17 57			18 12			18 21			18 27				18 42			18 51
Trefforest Estate	d	17 46									18 16										18 46			
Taffs Well ■	d	17 50					17 58	18 04			18 20			18 28			18 34				18 50			18 58
Radyr ■	a	17 53					18 01	18 07			18 23			18 31			18 37				18 53			19 01
	d	17 53		18 04			18 01	18 07			18 23	18 34		18 31			18 37				18 53	19 04		19 01
Danescourt	d			18 08								18 38										19 08		
Fairwater	d			18 10								18 40										19 10		
Waun-gron Park	d			18 12								18 42										19 12		
Ninian Park	d			18 15								18 45										19 15		
Llandaf	d	17 56					18 04	18 10			18 26			18 34			18 40				18 56			19 04
Cathays	d	18 01					18 09	18 15			18 31			18 39			18 45				19 01			19 09
Rhymney ■	d									17 29														
Pontlottyn	d									17 32														
Tir-phil	d									17 36														
Brithdir	d									17 39														
Bargoed	a									17 42														
	d		17 32							17 47								18 17						
Gilfach Fargoed	d																	18 19						
Pengam	d		17 37							17 52								18 22						
Hengoed	d		17 40							17 55								18 25						
Ystrad Mynach ■	d		17 43							17 58								18 28						
Llanbradach	d		17 48							18 03								18 33						
Aber	d		17 52							18 07								18 37						
Caerphilly ■	d		17 55							18 10								18 40						
Lisvane & Thornhill	d		17 59							18 14								18 44						
Llanishen	d		18 01							18 16								18 46						
Heath High Level	d		18 04							18 19								18 49						
Coryton	d																		18 45					
Whitchurch (Cardiff)	d																		18 46					
Rhiwbina	d																		18 48					
Birchgrove	d																		18 50					
Ty Glas	d																		18 51					
Heath Low Level	d																		18 54					
Cardiff Queen Street ■	a	18 04	18 09				18 14	18 19		18 24	18 34			18 44			18 49	18 54	18 59		19 04			19 14
	d	18 06	18 11			18 12	18 16	18 21	18 24	18 26	18 36		18 36	18 46		18 48	18 51	18 56	19 01	19 00	19 06		19 12	19 16
Cardiff Bay	a					18 16			18 28				18 40			18 52				19 04			19 16	
Cardiff Central ■	a	18 09	18 14	18 20			18 22	18 24		18 29	18 39	18 50		18 53			18 54	18 59	19 06		19 10	19 22		19 22
	d	18 10	18 16	18 21				18 25		18 31	18 41	18 51					18 55	19 01						
Grangetown	d	18 14	18 20					18 29		18 35	18 45						18 59	19 05						
Dingle Road	d		18 26							18 41								19 11						
Penarth	a		18 31							18 46								19 16						
Cogan	d	18 18						18 33			18 48						19 03							
Eastbrook	d	18 20						18 35			18 51						19 05							
Dinas Powys	d	18 22						18 37			18 53						19 07							
Cadoxton	d	18 27						18 42			18 57						19 12							
Barry Docks	d	18 30						18 45			19 00						19 15							
Barry ■	d	18 34						18 49			19 05						19 19							
Barry Island	a	18 40						18 55									19 25							
Rhoose Cardiff Int Airport ✈	d										19 12													
Llantwit Major	d										19 22													
Bridgend	a										19 39													

Treherbert, Aberdare, Merthyr, Pontypridd, Rhymney and Coryton - Cardiff, Penarth, Barry, Barry Island and Bridgend

		AW	AW	AW	AW	AW	AW	AW	AW	AW		AW	AW	AW	AW	AW	AW	AW	AW	AW		AW	AW	AW	AW
Treherbert	d						18 47								19 17								19 47		
Ynyswen	d						18 49								19 19								19 49		
Treorchy	d						18 51								19 21								19 51		
Ton Pentre	d						18 53								19 23								19 53		
Ystrad Rhondda	a						18 56								19 26								19 56		
	d						18 58								19 28								19 58		
Llwynypia	d						19 00								19 30								20 00		
Tonypandy	d						19 03								19 33								20 03		
Dinas Rhondda	d						19 05								19 35								20 05		
Porth	a						19 08								19 38								20 08		
	d						19 09								19 39								20 09		
Trehafod	d						19 12								19 42								20 12		
Merthyr Tydfil	d				18 38								19 08						19 38						
Pentre-bach	d				18 42								19 12						19 42						
Troed Y Rhiw	d				18 45								19 15						19 45						
Merthyr Vale	a				18 48								19 18						19 48						
	d				18 50								19 20						19 50						
Quakers Yard	d				18 55								19 25						19 55						
Aberdare ■	d	18 22							18 52																19 52
Cwmbach	d	18 25							18 55																19 55
Fernhill	d	18 28							18 58																19 58
Mountain Ash	a	18 31							19 01																20 01
	d	18 34							19 04																20 04
Penrhiwceiber	d	18 37							19 07																20 07
Abercynon	d	18 43			18 59				19 13				19 29				19 43		19 59						20 13
Pontypridd ■	a	18 53			19 07		19 17		19 23				19 37		19 47		19 53		20 07				20 17		20 23
	d	18 54			19 09		19 18		19 24				19 39		19 48		19 54		20 09				20 18		20 24
Trefforest	d	18 57			19 12		19 21		19 27				19 42		19 51		19 57		20 12				20 21		20 27
Trefforest Estate	d				19 16								19 46						20 16						
Taffs Well ■	d	19 04			19 20		19 28		19 34				19 50		19 58		20 04		20 20				20 28		20 34
Radyr ■	a	19 07			19 23		19 31		19 37				19 53		20 01		20 07		20 23				20 31		20 37
	d	19 07			19 23		19 31		19 37				19 53		20 01	20 04	20 07		20 23				20 31		20 37
Danescourt	d															20 08									
Fairwater	d															20 10									
Waun-gron Park	d															20 12									
Ninian Park	d															20 15									
Llandaf	d	19 10			19 26		19 34		19 40				19 56		20 04		20 10		20 26				20 34		20 40
Cathays	d	19 15			19 31		19 39		19 45				20 01		20 09		20 15		20 31				20 39		20 45
Rhymney ■	d																					19 45			
Pontlottyn	d																					19 48			
Tir-phil	d																					19 52			
Brithdir	d																					19 55			
Bargoed	a																					19 58			
	d			18 48																		19 59			
Gilfach Fargoed	d			18 50																		20 01			
Pengam	d			18 53																		20 04			
Hengoed	d			18 56																		20 07			
Ystrad Mynach ■	d			18 59																		20 10			
Llanbradach	d			19 04																		20 15			
Aber	d			19 08																		20 19			
Caerphilly ■	d			19 11						19 40												20 22			
Lisvane & Thornhill	d			19 15						19 44												20 26			
Llanishen	d			19 17						19 46												20 28			
Heath High Level	d			19 20						19 49												20 31			
Coryton	d																								
Whitchurch (Cardiff)	d																								
Rhiwbina	d																								
Birchgrove	d																								
Ty Glas	d																								
Heath Low Level	d																								
Cardiff Queen Street ■	a	19 19		19 24	19 35		19 44		19 49	19 54			20 04		20 14		20 19		20 34			20 39	20 44		20 49
	d	19 21	19 24	19 26	19 36	19 36	19 46	19 48	19 51	19 56		20 00	20 06	20 12	20 16		20 21	20 24	20 36	20 36		20 41	20 46	20 48	20 51
Cardiff Bay	a		19 28			19 40		19 52				20 04		20 16				20 28		20 40				20 52	
Cardiff Central ■	a	19 24		19 29	19 40		19 52		19 57	19 59			20 10		20 20	20 22	20 25		20 39			20 47	20 52		20 57
	d	19 25		19 31	19 41					20 06			20 10				20 31		20 41						21 06
Grangetown	d	19 29		19 35	19 45					20 10			20 14				20 37		20 45						21 10
Dingle Road	d			19 41						20 14							20 41								21 14
Penarth	a			19 46						20 19							20 46								21 19
Cogan	d	19 33			19 48								20 18						20 48						
Eastbrook	d	19 35			19 51								20 20						20 51						
Dinas Powys	d	19 37			19 53								20 22						20 53						
Cadoxton	d	19 42			19 57								20 27						20 57						
Barry Docks	d	19 45			20 00								20 30						21 00						
Barry ■	d	19 49			20 05								20 34						21 05						
Barry Island	a	19 55											20 41												
Rhoose Cardiff Int Airport ✈	d				20 12														21 12						
Llantwit Major	d				20 22														21 22						
Bridgend	a				20 39														21 39						

Table 130

Mondays to Fridays
until 03 September

Treherbert, Aberdare, Merthyr, Pontypridd, Rhymney and Coryton - Cardiff, Penarth, Barry, Barry Island and Bridgend

		AW	AW	AW	AW	AW		AW	AW	AW	AW	AW	AW	AW	AW	AW		AW	AW	AW	AW	AW	AW	AW	AW	AW
Treherbert	d					20 17															21 17					
Ynyswen	d					20 19															21 19					
Treorchy	d					20 21															21 21					
Ton Pentre	d					20 23															21 23					
Ystrad Rhondda	a					20 26															21 26					
	d					20 28															21 28					
Llwynypia	d					20 30															21 30					
Tonypandy	d					20 33															21 33					
Dinas Rhondda	d					20 35															21 35					
Porth	a					20 38															21 38					
	d					20 39															21 39					
Trehafod	d					20 42															21 42					
Merthyr Tydfil	d										20 38													21 38		
Pentre-bach	d										20 42													21 42		
Troed Y Rhiw	d										20 45													21 45		
Merthyr Vale	a										20 48													21 48		
	d										20 50													21 50		
Quakers Yard	d										20 55													21 55		
Aberdare 3	d							20 22							20 52											
Cwmbach	d							20 25							20 55											
Fernhill	d							20 28							20 58											
Mountain Ash	a							20 31							21 01											
	d							20 34							21 04											
Penrhiwceiber	d							20 37							21 07											
Abercynon	d							20 43			20 59				21 13									21 59		
Pontypridd 3	a					20 47		20 53			21 07				21 23						21 47			22 07		
	d					20 48		20 54			21 09				21 24						21 48			22 09		
Trefforest	d					20 51		20 57			21 12				21 27						21 51			22 12		
Trefforest Estate	d										21 16													22 16		
Taffs Well 3	d					20 58		21 04			21 20				21 34						21 58			22 20		
Radyr 3	a					21 01		21 07			21 23				21 37						22 01			22 23		
	d			21 04		21 01		21 07			21 23				21 37				22 04		22 01			22 23		
Danescourt	d			21 08															22 08							
Fairwater	d			21 10															22 10							
Waun-gron Park	d			21 12															22 12							
Ninian Park	d			21 15															22 15							
Llandaf	d					21 04		21 10			21 26				21 40						22 04			22 26		
Cathays	d					21 09		21 15			21 31				21 45						22 09			22 31		
Rhymney 3	d												20 48									21 33				
Pontlottyn	d												20 51									21 36				
Tir-phil	d												20 55									21 40				
Brithdir	d												20 58									21 43				
Bargoed	a												21 01									21 46				
	d												21 02									21 47				
Gilfach Fargoed	d												21 04									21 49				
Pengam	d												21 07									21 52				
Hengoed	d												21 10									21 55				
Ystrad Mynach 3	d												21 13									21 58				
Llanbradach	d												21 18									22 03				
Aber	d												21 22									22 07				
Caerphilly 3	d	20 40											21 25			21 45						22 10				
Lisvane & Thornhill	d	20 44											21 29			21 50						22 14				
Llanishen	d	20 46											21 31			21 52						22 16				
Heath High Level	d	20 49											21 34			21 54						22 19				
Coryton	d																									
Whitchurch (Cardiff)	d																									
Rhiwbina	d																									
Birchgrove	d																									
Ty Glas	d																									
Heath Low Level	d																									
Cardiff Queen Street 3	a	20 54				21 14		21 19			21 34		21 42		21 49	22 00					22 14	22 24		22 34		
	d	20 56	21 00		21 12	21 16		21 21	21 24		21 36	21 36	21 44	21 48	21 51	22 01		22 00		22 12	22 16	22 26	22 24	22 36	22 36	22 48
Cardiff Bay	a		21 04		21 16				21 28			21 40		21 52				22 04		22 16			22 28		22 40	22 52
Cardiff Central 7	a	20 59		21 25		21 22		21 24			21 39		21 47		21 54	22 07			22 20		22 22	22 29		22 39		
	d	21 10								21 31	21 41				21 56	22 10			22 21			22 31		22 41		
Grangetown	d	21 14								21 35	21 45				22 00	22 14						22 35		22 45		
Dingle Road	d									21 41					22 04							22 41				
Penarth	a									21 46					22 07							22 46				
Cogan	d	21 17									21 48					22 18								22 48		
Eastbrook	d	21 20									21 51					22 20								22 51		
Dinas Powys	d	21 22									21 53					22 22								22 53		
Cadoxton	d	21 26									21 57					22 27								22 57		
Barry Docks	d	21 29									22 00					22 30								23 00		
Barry 3	d	21 34									22 05					22 34								23 05		
Barry Island	a	21 40														22 40										
Rhoose Cardiff Int Airport ✈	d										22 12													23 12		
Llantwit Major	d										22 22													23 22		
Bridgend	a										22 39													23 39		

Table 130

Mondays to Fridays
until 03 September

Treherbert, Aberdare, Merthyr, Pontypridd, Rhymney and Coryton - Cardiff, Penarth, Barry, Barry Island and Bridgend

		AW		AW	AW	AW	AW	AW	AW	AW	AW	AW
Treherbert	d											
Ynyswen	d											
Treorchy	d											
Ton Pentre	d											
Ystrad Rhondda	a											
	d											
Llwynypia	d											
Tonypandy	d											
Dinas Rhondda	d											
Porth	a											
	d											
Trehafod	d											
Merthyr Tydfil	d								22 38			
Pentre-bach	d								22 42			
Troed Y Rhiw	d								22 45			
Merthyr Vale	a								22 48			
	d								22 50			
Quakers Yard	d								22 55			
Aberdare 3	d	21 52								22 52		
Cwmbach	d	21 55								22 55		
Fernhill	d	21 58								22 58		
Mountain Ash	a	22 01								23 01		
	d	22 04								23 04		
Penrhiwceiber	d	22 07								23 07		
Abercynon	d	22 14							22 59	23 13		
Pontypridd 3	a	22 24							23 07	23 23		
	d	22 29							23 09			
Trefforest	d	22 32							23 12			
Trefforest Estate	d											
Taffs Well 3	d	22 39							23 20			
Radyr 3	a	22 42							23 23			
	d	22 42					23 10		23 23			
Danescourt	d											
Fairwater	d											
Waun-gron Park	d											
Ninian Park	d											
Llandaf	d	22 45					23 12		23 26			
Cathays	d	22 50					23 16		23 31			
Rhymney 3	d											
Pontlottyn	d											
Tir-phil	d											
Brithdir	d											
Bargoed	a											
	d											
Gilfach Fargoed	d											
Pengam	d											
Hengoed	d											
Ystrad Mynach 3	d											
Llanbradach	d											
Aber	d											
Caerphilly 3	d											
Lisvane & Thornhill	d											
Llanishen	d											
Heath High Level	d											
Coryton	d			22 45								
Whitchurch (Cardiff)	d			22 46								
Rhiwbina	d			22 48								
Birchgrove	d			22 50								
Ty Glas	d			22 51								
Heath Low Level	d			22 54								
Cardiff Queen Street 3	a	22 54		22 59			23 19		23 34			
	d	22 55		23 01	23 00	23 12	23 20	23 24	23 36		23 36	23 48
Cardiff Bay	a				23 04	23 16		23 28			23 40	23 52
Cardiff Central 7	a	23 01		23 06			23 25		23 42			
	d	23 12					23 30					
Grangetown	d	23 16					23 34					
Dingle Road	d	23 20										
Penarth	a	23 25										
Cogan	d						23 37					
Eastbrook	d						23 40					
Dinas Powys	d						23 42					
Cadoxton	d						23 46					
Barry Docks	d						23 49					
Barry 3	d						23 54					
Barry Island	a						23 59					
Rhoose Cardiff Int Airport ✈	d											
Llantwit Major	d											
Bridgend	a											

Table 130

Mondays to Fridays
from 06 September

Treherbert, Aberdare, Merthyr, Pontypridd, Rhymney and Coryton - Cardiff, Penarth, Barry, Barry Island and Bridgend

		AW	AW	AW	AW	AW	AW	AW	AW	AW		AW	AW	AW	AW	AW	AW	AW	AW	AW		AW	AW	AW	AW
Treherbert	d											05 47							06 17						
Ynyswen	d											05 49							06 19						
Treorchy	d											05 51							06 21						
Ton Pentre	d											05 53							06 23						
Ystrad Rhondda	a											05 56							06 26						
	d											05 58							06 28						
Llwynypia	d											06 00							06 30						
Tonypandy	d											06 03							06 33						
Dinas Rhondda	d											06 05							06 35						
Porth	a											06 08							06 38						
	d											06 09							06 39						
Trehafod	d											06 12							06 42						
Merthyr Tydfil	d																								06 38
Pentre-bach	d																								06 42
Troed Y Rhiw	d																								06 45
Merthyr Vale	a																								06 48
	d																								06 50
Quakers Yard	d																								06 55
Aberdare [3]	d																					06 21			
Cwmbach	d																					06 24			
Fernhill	d																					06 28			
Mountain Ash	a																					06 31			
	d																					06 34			
Penrhiwceiber	d																					06 38			
Abercynon	d																					06 44			06 59
Pontypridd [3]	a											06 17							06 47			06 53			07 07
	d				05 24							06 18							06 48			06 54			07 09
Trefforest	d				05 27							06 21							06 51			06 57			07 12
Trefforest Estate	d				05 31							06 25										07 01			07 16
Taffs Well [3]	d				05 34							06 28							06 58	06 53		07 04			07 20
Radyr [3]	a				05 37							06 31							07 01	06 56		07 07			07 23
	d				05 37							06 31							07 01	07 04		07 07			07 23
Danescourt	d																			07 08					
Fairwater	d																			07 10					
Waun-gron Park	d																			07 12					
Ninian Park	d																			07 15					
Llandaf	d				05 40							06 34							07 04			07 10			07 26
Cathays	d				05 45							06 39							07 09			07 15			07 31
Rhymney [3]	d																							06 34	
Pontlottyn	d																							06 37	
Tir-phil	d																							06 41	
Brithdir	d																							06 44	
Bargoed	a																							06 47	
	d																							06 48	
Gilfach Fargoed	d																								
Pengam	d																							06 52	
Hengoed	d																							06 56	
Ystrad Mynach [3]	d																							06 58	
Llanbradach	d																							07 03	
Aber	d																							07 07	
Caerphilly [3]	d							06 10																07 10	
Lisvane & Thornhill	d							06 14																07 14	
Llanishen	d							06 16																07 16	
Heath High Level	d							06 19																07 19	
Coryton	d																								
Whitchurch (Cardiff)	d																								
Rhiwbina	d																								
Birchgrove	d																								
Ty Glas	d																								
Heath Low Level	d																								
Cardiff Queen Street [3]	a				05 48			06 25				06 44							07 14			07 20		07 24	07 35
	d				05 51			06 26	06 36			06 44	06 48		07 00			07 12	07 16			07 21	07 24	07 26	07 36
Cardiff Bay	a								06 40				06 52		07 04			07 16					07 28		
Cardiff Central [7]	a				05 54			06 29				06 48							07 18	07 20		07 24		07 29	07 40
	d	05 20	05 41	05 46	05 55	06 16	06 25	06 41		06 36				06 55		07 01	07 10			07 21		07 25		07 31	07 41
Grangetown	d	05 24	05 45	05 50	05 59	06 20	06 29	06 45		06 40				06 59		07 05	07 14					07 29		07 35	07 45
Dingle Road	d			05 54		06 24				06 44						07 11								07 42	
Penarth	a			06 00		06 29				06 50						07 17								07 47	
Cogan	d	05 28	05 48		06 03		06 33	06 48						07 03			07 18					07 33			07 48
Eastbrook	d	05 30	05 51		06 05		06 35	06 51						07 05			07 20					07 35			07 51
Dinas Powys	d	05 32	05 53		06 07		06 37	06 53						07 07			07 22					07 37			07 53
Cadoxton	d	05 37	05 57		06 12		06 42	06 57						07 12			07 27					07 42			07 57
Barry Docks	d	05 40	06 00		06 15		06 45	07 00						07 15			07 30					07 45			08 00
Barry [3]	d	05 44	06 05		06 19		06 49	07 05						07 19			07 34					07 49			08 05
Barry Island	a	05 51			06 26		06 56							07 26			07 41					07 56			
Rhoose Cardiff Int Airport ✈	d		06 12					07 12																	08 12
Llantwit Major	d		06 22					07 22																	08 22
Bridgend	a		06 40					07 40																	08 40

Table 130

Mondays to Fridays
from 06 September

Treherbert, Aberdare, Merthyr, Pontypridd, Rhymney and Coryton - Cardiff, Penarth, Barry, Barry Island and Bridgend

		AW	AW	AW	AW	AW		AW	AW	AW	AW	AW	AW	AW	AW	AW		AW	AW	AW	AW	AW	AW	AW	AW
Treherbert	d				06 47									07 17									07 45		
Ynyswen	d				06 49									07 19									07 47		
Treorchy	d				06 51									07 21									07 49		
Ton Pentre	d				06 53									07 23									07 51		
Ystrad Rhondda	a				06 56									07 26									07 54		
	d				06 58									07 28									07 58		
Llwynypia	d				07 00									07 30									08 00		
Tonypandy	d				07 03									07 33									08 03		
Dinas Rhondda	d				07 05									07 35									08 05		
Porth	a				07 08									07 38									08 08		
	d				07 09									07 39									08 09		
Trehafod	d				07 12									07 42									08 12		
Merthyr Tydfil	d										07 08								07 38						
Pentre-bach	d										07 12								07 42						
Troed Y Rhiw	d										07 15								07 45						
Merthyr Vale	a										07 18								07 48						
	d										07 20								07 50						
Quakers Yard	d										07 25								07 55						
Aberdare [3]	d							06 51							07 21										07 51
Cwmbach	d							06 54							07 24										07 54
Fernhill	d							06 58							07 28										07 58
Mountain Ash	a							07 01							07 31										08 01
	d							07 04							07 34										08 04
Penrhiwceiber	d							07 08							07 38										08 08
Abercynon	d							07 14			07 29				07 44				07 59						08 14
Pontypridd [3]	a				07 17			07 23			07 37			07 47	07 53				08 07				08 17		08 23
	d				07 18			07 24			07 39			07 48	07 54				08 09				08 18		08 24
Trefforest	d				07 21			07 27			07 42			07 51	07 57				08 12				08 21		08 27
Trefforest Estate	d										07 46								08 16						
Taffs Well [3]	d				07 28			07 34			07 50			07 58	08 04				08 20				08 28		08 34
Radyr [3]	a				07 31			07 37			07 53			08 01	08 07				08 23				08 31		08 37
	d			07 34	07 31			07 37			07 53	08 04		08 01	08 07				08 23			08 34	08 31		08 37
Danescourt	d			07 38								08 08										08 38			
Fairwater	d			07 40								08 10										08 40			
Waun-gron Park	d			07 42								08 12										08 42			
Ninian Park	d			07 45								08 15										08 45			
Llandaf	d				07 34			07 40			07 56			08 04	08 10				08 26				08 34		08 40
Cathays	d				07 39			07 45			08 01			08 09	08 15				08 31				08 39		08 45
Rhymney [3]	d								07 02									07 24			07 44				
Pontlottyn	d								07 05									07 27			07 47				
Tir-phil	d								07 09									07 31			07 51				
Brithdir	d								07 12									07 34			07 54				
Bargoed	a								07 15									07 37			08 00				
	d		07 02						07 17									07 45			08 02				
Gilfach Fargoed	d		07 04						07 19									07 47							
Pengam	d		07 07						07 22									07 50			08 07				
Hengoed	d		07 10						07 25									07 54			08 10				
Ystrad Mynach [3]	d		07 13						07 28									07 57			08 13				
Llanbradach	d		07 18						07 33									08 02			08 18				
Aber	d		07 22						07 37									08 07			08 22				
Caerphilly [3]	d		07 25						07 40									08 10			08 25				
Lisvane & Thornhill	d		07 29						07 44									08 14			08 29				
Llanishen	d		07 31						07 46									08 16			08 31				
Heath High Level	d		07 34						07 49									08 19			08 34				
Coryton	d																								
Whitchurch (Cardiff)	d																								
Rhiwbina	d																								
Birchgrove	d																								
Ty Glas	d																								
Heath Low Level	d																								
Cardiff Queen Street [3]	a		07 39		07 44			07 49	07 54		08 04			08 14	08 19			08 24	08 34		08 39		08 44		08 49
	d	07 36	07 41		07 46	07 48		07 51	07 56	08 00	08 06		08 12	08 16	08 21	08 24		08 26	08 36	08 36	08 41		08 46	08 48	08 51
Cardiff Bay	a	07 40				07 52				08 04			08 16			08 28				08 40				08 52	
Cardiff Central [7]	a		07 44	07 50	07 52			07 54	07 59		08 09	08 20		08 23	08 24			08 29	08 39		08 48	08 50	08 53		08 54
	d		07 46	07 51				07 55	08 01		08 10	08 21			08 25			08 31	08 41			08 51			08 55
Grangetown	d		07 50					07 59	08 05		08 14				08 29			08 35	08 45						08 59
Dingle Road	d		07 56						08 11									08 41							
Penarth	a		08 02						08 17									08 47							
Cogan	d							08 03			08 18				08 33				08 48						09 03
Eastbrook	d							08 05			08 20				08 35				08 51						09 05
Dinas Powys	d							08 07			08 22				08 37				08 53						09 07
Cadoxton	d							08 12			08 27				08 42				08 57						09 12
Barry Docks	d							08 15			08 30				08 45				09 00						09 15
Barry [3]	d							08 19			08 34				08 49				09 05						09 19
Barry Island	a							08 26			08 41				08 56										09 26
Rhoose Cardiff Int Airport ✈	d																		09 12						
Llantwit Major	d																		09 22						
Bridgend	a																		09 40						

Table 130

Mondays to Fridays
from 06 September

Treherbert, Aberdare, Merthyr, Pontypridd, Rhymney and Coryton - Cardiff, Penarth, Barry, Barry Island and Bridgend

		AW	AW	AW	AW	AW	AW	AW	AW	AW	AW	AW	AW	AW	AW	AW	AW	AW	AW	AW	AW	AW
Treherbert	d						08 17							08 47								
Ynyswen	d						08 19							08 49								
Treorchy	d						08 21							08 51								
Ton Pentre	d						08 23							08 53								
Ystrad Rhondda	a						08 26							08 56								
	d						08 28							08 58								
Llwynypia	d						08 30							09 00								
Tonypandy	d						08 33							09 03								
Dinas Rhondda	d						08 35							09 05								
Porth	a						08 38							09 08								
	d						08 39							09 09								
Trehafod	d						08 42							09 12								
Merthyr Tydfil	d		08 08								08 38								09 08			
Pentre-bach	d		08 12								08 42								09 12			
Troed Y Rhiw	d		08 15								08 45								09 15			
Merthyr Vale	a		08 18								08 48								09 18			
	d		08 20								08 50								09 20			
Quakers Yard	d		08 25								08 55								09 25			
Aberdare	d							08 21								08 51						
Cwmbach	d							08 24								08 54						
Fernhill	d							08 28								08 58						
Mountain Ash	a							08 31								09 01						
	d							08 34								09 04						
Penrhiwceiber	d							08 38								09 08						
Abercynon	d		08 29					08 44			08 59					09 14			09 29			
Pontypridd	a		08 37				08 47	08 53			09 07			09 17		09 23			09 37			
	d		08 39				08 48	08 54			09 09			09 18		09 24			09 39			
Trefforest	d		08 42				08 51	08 57			09 12			09 21		09 27			09 42			
Trefforest Estate	d		08 46								09 16								09 46			
Taffs Well	d		08 50				08 58	09 04			09 20			09 28		09 34			09 50			
Radyr	a		08 53				09 01	09 07			09 23			09 31		09 37			09 53			
	d		08 53		09 04		09 01	09 07			09 23	09 34		09 31		09 37			09 53		10 04	
Danescourt	d				09 08							09 38									10 08	
Fairwater	d				09 10							09 40									10 10	
Waun-gron Park	d				09 12							09 42									10 12	
Ninian Park	d				09 15							09 45									10 15	
Llandaf	d		08 56				09 04	09 10			09 26			09 34		09 40			09 56			
Cathays	d		09 01				09 09	09 15			09 31			09 39		09 45			10 01			
Rhymney	d									08 30												
Pontlottyn	d									08 33												
Tir-phil	d									08 37												
Brithdir	d									08 40												
Bargoed	a									08 44												
	d			08 32						08 47										09 25		
Gilfach Fargoed	d																			09 27		
Pengam	d			08 37						08 52										09 30		
Hengoed	d			08 40						08 55										09 33		
Ystrad Mynach	d			08 43						08 58							09 28			09b43		
Llanbradach	d			08 48						09 03							09 33			09 48		
Aber	d			08 52						09 07							09 37			09 52		
Caerphilly	d			08 55						09 10							09 40			09 55		
Lisvane & Thornhill	d			08 59						09 14							09 44			09 59		
Llanishen	d			09 01						09 16							09 46			10 01		
Heath High Level	d			09 04						09 19							09 49			10 04		
Coryton	d																					
Whitchurch (Cardiff)	d																					
Rhiwbina	d																					
Birchgrove	d																					
Ty Glas	d																					
Heath Low Level	d																					
Cardiff Queen Street	a		09 04	09 09			09 14	09 19		09 24	09 34			09 44		09 49	09 54		10 04	10 09		
	d	09 00	09 06	09 11		09 12	09 16	09 21	09 24	09 26	09 36		09 36	09 46	09 48	09 51	09 56	10 00	10 06	10 11		10 12
Cardiff Bay	a	09 04				09 16			09 28				09 40		09 52			10 04				10 16
Cardiff Central	a		09 09	09 14	09 20		09 23	09 24		09 29	09 39	09 50		09 53		09 54	09 59		10 09	10 14	10 20	
	d		09 10	09 16	09 21			09 25		09 31	09 41	09 51				09 55	10 01		10 10	10 16	10 21	
Grangetown	d		09 14	09 20				09 29		09 35	09 45					09 59	10 05		10 14	10 20		
Dingle Road	d			09 26						09 41							10 11			10 26		
Penarth	a			09 32						09 47							10 17			10 32		
Cogan	d		09 18					09 33			09 48					10 03			10 18			
Eastbrook	d		09 20					09 35			09 51					10 05			10 20			
Dinas Powys	d		09 22					09 37			09 53					10 07			10 22			
Cadoxton	d		09 27					09 42			09 57					10 12			10 27			
Barry Docks	d		09 30					09 45			10 00					10 15			10 30			
Barry	d		09 34					09 49			10 05					10 19			10 34			
Barry Island	a		09 41					09 56								10 26			10 41			
Rhoose Cardiff Int Airport ✈	d										10 12											
Llantwit Major	d										10 22											
Bridgend	a										10 40											

b arr. 0936

Table 130

Mondays to Fridays
from 06 September

Treherbert, Aberdare, Merthyr, Pontypridd, Rhymney and Coryton - Cardiff, Penarth, Barry, Barry Island and Bridgend

		AW	AW	AW	AW	AW	AW	AW	AW	AW	AW	AW	AW	AW	AW	AW	AW	AW	AW	AW	AW	AW	AW
Treherbert	d	09 17								09 47												10 17	
Ynyswen	d	09 19								09 49												10 19	
Treorchy	d	09 21								09 51												10 21	
Ton Pentre	d	09 23								09 53												10 23	
Ystrad Rhondda	a	09 26								09 56												10 26	
	d	09 28								09 58												10 28	
Llwynypia	d	09 30								10 00												10 30	
Tonypandy	d	09 33								10 03												10 33	
Dinas Rhondda	d	09 35								10 05												10 35	
Porth	a	09 38								10 08												10 38	
	d	09 39								10 09												10 52	
Trehafod	d	09 42								10 12												10 55	
Merthyr Tydfil	d					09 38							10 04										10 38
Pentre-bach	d					09 42							10 08										10 42
Troed Y Rhiw	d					09 45							10 11										10 45
Merthyr Vale	a					09 48							10 14										10 48
	d					09 50							10 16										10 50
Quakers Yard	d					09 55							10 22										10 55
Aberdare	d		09 21									09 51							10 21				
Cwmbach	d		09 24									09 54							10 24				
Fernhill	d		09 28									09 58							10 28				
Mountain Ash	a		09 31									10 01							10 31				
	d		09 34									10 04							10 34				
Penrhiwceiber	d		09 38									10 08							10 38				
Abercynon	d		09 44			09 59						10 14	10 26						10 44				10 59
Pontypridd	a	09 47	09 53			10 07				10 17		10 23	10 32						10 53			11 00	11 08
	d	09 48	09 54			10 09				10 18		10 24			10 39				10 54			11 04	11 09
Trefforest	d	09 51	09 57			10 12				10 21		10 27			10 42				10 57			11 07	11 12
Trefforest Estate	d					10 16									10 46								11 16
Taffs Well	d	09 58	10 04			10 20				10 28		10 34			10 50				11 04			11 13	11 20
Radyr	a	10 01	10 07			10 23				10 31		10 37			10 53				11 07			11 17	11 23
	d	10 01	10 07			10 23			10 34	10 31		10 37			10 53		11 04		11 07			11 17	11 23
Danescourt	d								10 38								11 08						
Fairwater	d								10 40								11 10						
Waun-gron Park	d								10 42								11 12						
Ninian Park	d								10 45								11 15						
Llandaf	d	10 04	10 10			10 26				10 34		10 40			10 56				11 10				11 26
Cathays	d	10 09	10 15			10 31				10 39		10 45			11 01				11 15				11 31
Rhymney	d				09 29																10 29		
Pontlottyn	d				09 32																10 32		
Tir-phil	d				09 36																10 36		
Brithdir	d				09 39																10 39		
Bargoed	a				09 42																10 42		
	d				09 47			10 02								10 25					10 47		
Gilfach Fargoed	d															10 27							
Pengam	d				09 52			10 07								10 30					10 52		
Hengoed	d				09 55			10 10								10 33					10 55		
Ystrad Mynach	d				09 58			10 13								10b43					10 58		
Llanbradach	d				10 03			10 18								10 48					11 03		
Aber	d				10 07			10 22								10 52					11 07		
Caerphilly	d				10 10			10 25								10 55					11 10		
Lisvane & Thornhill	d				10 14			10 29								10 59					11 14		
Llanishen	d				10 16			10 31								11 01					11 16		
Heath High Level	d				10 19			10 34								11 04					11 19		
Coryton	d																						
Whitchurch (Cardiff)	d																						
Rhiwbina	d																						
Birchgrove	d																						
Ty Glas	d																						
Heath Low Level	d																						
Cardiff Queen Street	a	10 14	10 19		10 24	10 34		10 39		10 44		10 49			11 04	11 09			11 19		11 24		11 34
	d	10 16	10 21	10 24	10 26	10 36	10 36	10 41		10 46	10 48	10 51		11 00	11 06	11 11		11 12	11 21	11 24	11 26		11 36
Cardiff Bay	a			10 28			10 40				10 52			11 04				11 16		11 28			
Cardiff Central	a	10 23	10 24		10 29	10 39		10 44	10 50	10 53		10 54			11 09	11 14	11 20		11 24		11 29	11 34	11 39
	d		10 25		10 31	10 41		10 46	10 51			10 55			11 10	11 16	11 21		11 25		11 31		11 41
Grangetown	d		10 29		10 35	10 45		10 50				10 59			11 14	11 20			11 29		11 35		11 45
Dingle Road	d				10 41			10 56								11 26					11 41		
Penarth	a				10 47			11 02								11 32					11 47		
Cogan	d		10 33			10 48						11 03			11 18				11 33				11 48
Eastbrook	d		10 35			10 51						11 05			11 20				11 35				11 51
Dinas Powys	d		10 37			10 53						11 07			11 22				11 37				11 53
Cadoxton	d		10 42			10 57						11 12			11 27				11 42				11 57
Barry Docks	d		10 45			11 00						11 15			11 30				11 45				12 00
Barry	d		10 49			11 05						11 19			11 34				11 49				12 05
Barry Island	a		10 56									11 26			11 40				11 56				
Rhoose Cardiff Int Airport ✈	d					11 12																	12 12
Llantwit Major	d					11 22																	12 22
Bridgend	a					11 40																	12 40

b arr. 1036

Table 130

Mondays to Fridays
from 06 September

Treherbert, Aberdare, Merthyr, Pontypridd, Rhymney and Coryton - Cardiff, Penarth, Barry, Barry Island and Bridgend

		AW	AW	AW	AW	AW	AW	AW	AW	AW	AW	AW	AW	AW	AW	AW	AW	AW	AW	AW	AW	AW
Treherbert	d				10 47									11 17								11 47
Ynyswen	d				10 49									11 19								11 49
Treorchy	d				10 51									11 21								11 51
Ton Pentre	d				10 53									11 23								11 53
Ystrad Rhondda	a				10 56									11 26								11 56
	d				10 58									11 28								11 58
Llwynypia	d				11 00									11 30								12 00
Tonypandy	d				11 03									11 33								12 03
Dinas Rhondda	d				11 05									11 35								12 05
Porth	a				11 08									11 38								12 08
	d				11 09									11 39								12 09
Trehafod	d				11 12									11 42								12 12
Merthyr Tydfil	d									11 08								11 38				
Pentre-bach	d									11 12								11 42				
Troed Y Rhiw	d									11 15								11 45				
Merthyr Vale	a									11 18								11 48				
	d									11 20								11 50				
Quakers Yard	d									11 25								11 55				
Aberdare [3]	d						10 51								11 21							
Cwmbach	d						10 54								11 24							
Fernhill	d						10 58								11 28							
Mountain Ash	a						11 01								11 31							
	d						11 04								11 34							
Penrhiwceiber	d						11 08								11 38							
Abercynon	d						11 14			11 29					11 44			11 59				
Pontypridd [3]	a				11 17		11 23			11 37				11 47	11 53			12 07				12 17
	d				11 18		11 24			11 39				11 48	11 54			12 09				12 18
Trefforest	d				11 21		11 27			11 42				11 51	11 57			12 12				12 21
Trefforest Estate	d									11 46								12 16				
Taffs Well [3]	d				11 28		11 34			11 50				11 58	12 04			12 20				12 28
Radyr [3]	a				11 31		11 37			11 53				12 01	12 07			12 23				12 31
	d			11 34	11 31		11 37			11 53		12 04		12 01	12 07			12 23			12 34	12 31
Danescourt	d			11 38								12 08									12 38	
Fairwater	d			11 40								12 10									12 40	
Waun-gron Park	d			11 42								12 12									12 42	
Ninian Park	d			11 45								12 15									12 45	
Llandaf	d				11 34		11 40			11 56				12 04	12 10			12 26				12 34
Cathays	d				11 39		11 45			12 01				12 09	12 15			12 31				12 39
Rhymney [3]	d																11 29					
Pontlottyn	d																11 32					
Tir-phil	d																11 36					
Brithdir	d																11 39					
Bargoed	a																11 42					
	d		11 02								11 25						11 47			12 02		
Gilfach Fargoed	d										11 27											
Pengam	d		11 07								11 30						11 52			12 07		
Hengoed	d		11 10								11 33						11 55			12 10		
Ystrad Mynach [3]	d		11 13					11 28			11b43						11 58			12 13		
Llanbradach	d		11 18					11 33			11 48						12 03			12 18		
Aber	d		11 22					11 37			11 52						12 07			12 22		
Caerphilly [3]	d		11 25					11 40			11 55						12 10			12 25		
Lisvane & Thornhill	d		11 29					11 44			11 59						12 14			12 29		
Llanishen	d		11 31					11 46			12 01						12 16			12 31		
Heath High Level	d		11 34					11 49			12 04						12 19			12 34		
Coryton	d																					
Whitchurch (Cardiff)	d																					
Rhiwbina	d																					
Birchgrove	d																					
Ty Glas	d																					
Heath Low Level	d																					
Cardiff Queen Street [3]	a		11 39		11 44		11 49	11 54		12 04	12 09			12 14	12 19		12 24	12 34		12 39		12 44
	d	11 36	11 41		11 46	11 48	11 51	11 56	12 00	12 06	12 11		12 12	12 16	12 21	12 24	12 26	12 36	12 36	12 41		12 46
Cardiff Bay	a	11 40				11 52			12 04				12 16			12 28			12 40			
Cardiff Central [7]	a		11 44	11 50	11 53		11 54	11 59		12 09	12 14	12 20		12 23	12 24		12 29	12 39		12 44	12 50	12 53
	d		11 46	11 51			11 55	12 01		12 10	12 16	12 21			12 25		12 31	12 41		12 46	12 51	
Grangetown	d		11 50				11 59	12 05		12 14	12 20				12 29		12 35	12 45		12 50		
Dingle Road	d		11 56					12 11			12 26						12 41			12 56		
Penarth	a		12 02					12 17			12 32						12 47			13 02		
Cogan	d						12 03			12 18					12 33			12 48				
Eastbrook	d						12 05			12 20					12 35			12 51				
Dinas Powys	d						12 07			12 22					12 37			12 53				
Cadoxton	d						12 12			12 27					12 42			12 57				
Barry Docks	d						12 15			12 30					12 45			13 00				
Barry [3]	d						12 19			12 34					12 49			13 05				
Barry Island	a						12 26			12 41					12 56							
Rhoose Cardiff Int Airport ✈	d																	13 12				
Llantwit Major	d																	13 22				
Bridgend	a																	13 40				

b arr. 1136

Table 130

Mondays to Fridays
from 06 September

Treherbert, Aberdare, Merthyr, Pontypridd, Rhymney and Coryton - Cardiff, Penarth, Barry, Barry Island and Bridgend

		AW	AW	AW	AW	AW	AW	AW	AW	AW	AW	AW	AW	AW	AW	AW	AW	AW	AW	AW	AW	AW	AW
Treherbert	d									12 17								12 47					
Ynyswen	d									12 19								12 49					
Treorchy	d									12 21								12 51					
Ton Pentre	d									12 23								12 53					
Ystrad Rhondda	a									12 26								12 56					
	d									12 28								12 58					
Llwynypia	d									12 30								13 00					
Tonypandy	d									12 33								13 03					
Dinas Rhondda	d									12 35								13 05					
Porth	a									12 38								13 08					
	d									12 39								13 09					
Trehafod	d									12 42								13 12					
Merthyr Tydfil	d					12 08								12 38									13 08
Pentre-bach	d					12 12								12 42									13 12
Troed Y Rhiw	d					12 15								12 45									13 15
Merthyr Vale	a					12 18								12 48									13 18
	d					12 20								12 50									13 20
Quakers Yard	d					12 25								12 55									13 25
Aberdare [3]	d										12 21									12 51			
Cwmbach	d										12 24									12 54			
Fernhill	d										12 28									12 58			
Mountain Ash	a										12 31									13 01			
	d										12 34									13 04			
Penrhiwceiber	d										12 38									13 08			
Abercynon	d					12 29					12 44			12 59						13 14			13 29
Pontypridd [3]	a					12 37				12 48	12 53			13 07				13 17		13 23			13 37
	d					12 39				12 48	12 54			13 09				13 18		13 24			13 39
Trefforest	d					12 42				12 51	12 57			13 12				13 21		13 27			13 42
Trefforest Estate	d					12 46								13 16									13 46
Taffs Well [3]	d					12 50				12 58	13 04			13 20				13 28		13 34			13 50
Radyr [3]	a					12 53				13 01	13 07			13 23				13 31		13 37			13 53
	d					12 53		13 04		13 01	13 07			13 23			13 34	13 31		13 37			13 53
Danescourt	d							13 08									13 38						
Fairwater	d							13 10									13 40						
Waun-gron Park	d							13 12									13 42						
Ninian Park	d							13 15									13 45						
Llandaf	d					12 56				13 04	13 10			13 26				13 34		13 40			13 56
Cathays	d					13 01				13 09	13 15			13 31				13 39		13 45			14 01
Rhymney [3]	d												12 29										
Pontlottyn	d												12 32										
Tir-phil	d												12 36										
Brithdir	d												12 39										
Bargoed	a												12 42										
	d						12 25						12 47			13 02							
Gilfach Fargoed	d						12 27																
Pengam	d						12 30						12 52			13 07							
Hengoed	d						12 33						12 55			13 10							
Ystrad Mynach [3]	d			12 28			12b43						12 58			13 13					13 28		
Llanbradach	d			12 33			12 48						13 03			13 18					13 33		
Aber	d			12 37			12 52						13 07			13 22					13 37		
Caerphilly [3]	d			12 40			12 55						13 10			13 25					13 40		
Lisvane & Thornhill	d			12 44			12 59						13 14			13 29					13 44		
Llanishen	d			12 46			13 01						13 16			13 31					13 46		
Heath High Level	d			12 49			13 04						13 19			13 34					13 49		
Coryton	d																						
Whitchurch (Cardiff)	d																						
Rhiwbina	d																						
Birchgrove	d																						
Ty Glas	d																						
Heath Low Level	d																						
Cardiff Queen Street [3]	a			12 54		13 04	13 09			13 14	13 19		13 24	13 34		13 39		13 44		13 49	13 54		14 04
	d	12 48		12 56	13 00	13 06	13 11		13 12	13 16	13 21	13 24	13 26	13 36	13 36	13 41		13 46	13 48	13 51	13 56	14 00	14 06
Cardiff Bay	a	12 52			13 04				13 16			13 28			13 40				13 52			14 04	
Cardiff Central [7]	a			12 59		13 09	13 14	13 20		13 23	13 24		13 29	13 39		13 44	13 50	13 53		13 54	13 59		14 09
	d		12 55	13 01		13 10	13 16	13 21			13 25		13 31	13 41		13 46	13 51			13 55	14 01		14 10
Grangetown	d		12 59	13 05		13 14	13 20				13 29		13 35	13 45		13 50				13 59	14 05		14 14
Dingle Road	d			13 11			13 26						13 41			13 56					14 11		
Penarth	a			13 17			13 32						13 47			14 02					14 17		
Cogan	d		13 03			13 18					13 33			13 48						14 03			14 18
Eastbrook	d		13 05			13 20					13 35			13 51						14 05			14 20
Dinas Powys	d		13 07			13 22					13 37			13 53						14 07			14 22
Cadoxton	d		13 12			13 27					13 42			13 57						14 12			14 27
Barry Docks	d		13 15			13 30					13 45			14 00						14 15			14 30
Barry [3]	d		13 19			13 34					13 49			14 05						14 19			14 34
Barry Island	a		13 26			13 41					13 56									14 26			14 41
Rhoose Cardiff Int Airport ✈	d													14 12									
Llantwit Major	d													14 22									
Bridgend	a													14 40									

b arr. 1236

Table 130

Mondays to Fridays
from 06 September

Treherbert, Aberdare, Merthyr, Pontypridd, Rhymney and Coryton - Cardiff, Penarth, Barry, Barry Island and Bridgend

		AW	AW	AW	AW	AW		AW	AW	AW	AW	AW	AW	AW	AW	AW		AW	AW	AW	AW	AW	AW	AW	AW
Treherbert	d				13 17									13 47											
Ynyswen	d				13 19									13 49											
Treorchy	d				13 21									13 51											
Ton Pentre	d				13 23									13 53											
Ystrad Rhondda	a				13 26									13 56											
	d				13 28									13 58											
Llwynypia	d				13 30									14 00											
Tonypandy	d				13 33									14 03											
Dinas Rhondda	d				13 35									14 05											
Porth	a				13 38									14 08											
	d				13 39									14 09											
Trehafod	d				13 42									14 12											
Merthyr Tydfil	d									13 38										14 08					
Pentre-bach	d									13 42										14 12					
Troed Y Rhiw	d									13 45										14 15					
Merthyr Vale	a									13 48										14 18					
	d									13 50										14 20					
Quakers Yard	d									13 55										14 25					
Aberdare ■	d															13 51								14 21	
Cwmbach	d															13 54								14 24	
Fernhill	d															13 58								14 28	
Mountain Ash	a															14 01								14 31	
	d															14 04								14 34	
Penrhiwceiber	d															14 08								14 38	
Abercynon	d					13 45				13 59						14 14				14 29				14 44	
Pontypridd ■	a				13 47	13 53				14 07				14 17		14 23				14 37				14 53	
	d				13 48	13 54				14 09				14 18		14 24				14 39				14 54	
Trefforest	d				13 51	13 57				14 12				14 21		14 27				14 42				14 57	
Trefforest Estate	d									14 16										14 46					
Taffs Well ■	d				13 58	14 04				14 20				14 28		14 34				14 50				15 04	
Radyr ■	a				14 01	14 07				14 23				14 31		14 37				14 53				15 07	
	d		14 04		14 01	14 07				14 23			14 34	14 31		14 37				14 53		15 04		15 07	
Danescourt	d		14 08										14 38									15 08			
Fairwater	d		14 10										14 40									15 10			
Waun-gron Park	d		14 12										14 42									15 12			
Ninian Park	d		14 15										14 45									15 15			
Llandaf	d				14 04	14 10				14 26				14 34		14 40				14 56				15 10	
Cathays	d				14 09	14 15				14 31				14 39		14 45				15 01				15 15	
Rhymney ■	d								13 29																
Pontlottyn	d								13 32																
Tir-phil	d								13 36																
Brithdir	d								13 39																
Bargoed	a								13 42																
	d	13 25							13 47			14 02									14 25				
Gilfach Fargoed	d	13 27																			14 27				
Pengam	d	13 30							13 52			14 07									14 30				
Hengoed	d	13 33							13 55			14 10									14 33				
Ystrad Mynach ■	d	13b43							13 58			14 13						14 28			14c43				
Llanbradach	d	13 48							14 03			14 18						14 33			14 48				
Aber	d	13 52							14 07			14 22						14 37			14 52				
Caerphilly ■	d	13 55							14 10			14 25						14 40			14 55				
Lisvane & Thornhill	d	13 59							14 14			14 29						14 44			14 59				
Llanishen	d	14 01							14 16			14 31						14 46			15 01				
Heath High Level	d	14 04							14 19			14 34						14 49			15 04				
Coryton	d																								
Whitchurch (Cardiff)	d																								
Rhiwbina	d																								
Birchgrove	d																								
Ty Glas	d																								
Heath Low Level	d																								
Cardiff Queen Street ■	a	14 09			14 14	14 19			14 24	14 34		14 39		14 44		14 49		14 54		15 04	15 09			15 19	
	d	14 11		14 12	14 16	14 21		14 24	14 26	14 36	14 36	14 41		14 46	14 48	14 51		14 56	15 00	15 06	15 11		15 12	15 21	15 24
Cardiff Bay	a			14 16				14 28			14 40				14 52				15 04				15 16		15 28
Cardiff Central ■	a	14 14	14 20		14 23	14 24			14 29	14 39		14 44	14 50	14 53		14 54		14 59		15 09	15 14	15 20		15 24	
	d	14 16	14 21			14 25			14 31	14 41		14 46	14 51			14 55		15 01		15 10	15 16	15 21		15 25	
Grangetown	d	14 20				14 29			14 35	14 45		14 50				14 59		15 05		15 14	15 20			15 29	
Dingle Road	d	14 26							14 41			14 56						15 11			15 26				
Penarth	a	14 32							14 47			15 02						15 17			15 32				
Cogan	d					14 33				14 48						15 03				15 18				15 33	
Eastbrook	d					14 35				14 51						15 05				15 20				15 35	
Dinas Powys	d					14 37				14 53						15 07				15 22				15 37	
Cadoxton	d					14 42				14 57						15 12				15 27				15 42	
Barry Docks	d					14 45				15 00						15 15				15 30				15 45	
Barry ■	d					14 49				15 05						15 19				15 34				15 49	
Barry Island	a					14 56										15 26				15 41				15 56	
Rhoose Cardiff Int Airport ✈	d									15 12															
Llantwit Major	d									15 22															
Bridgend	a									15 40															

b arr. 1336   c arr. 1436

Table 130

Mondays to Fridays
from 06 September

Treherbert, Aberdare, Merthyr, Pontypridd, Rhymney and Coryton - Cardiff, Penarth, Barry, Barry Island and Bridgend

		AW		AW	AW	AW	AW	AW	AW	AW	AW	AW		AW	AW	AW	AW	AW	AW	AW	AW	AW		AW	AW
Treherbert	d			14 17					14 47									15 15							
Ynyswen	d			14 19					14 49									15 17							
Treorchy	d			14 21					14 51									15 21							
Ton Pentre	d			14 23					14 53									15 23							
Ystrad Rhondda	a			14 26					14 56									15 26							
	d			14 28					14 58									15 28							
Llwynypia	d			14 30					15 00									15 30							
Tonypandy	d			14 33					15 03									15 33							
Dinas Rhondda	d			14 35					15 05									15 35							
Porth	a			14 38					15 08									15 38							
	d			14 52					15 09									15 39							
Trehafod	d			14 55					15 12									15 42							
Merthyr Tydfil	d				14 38									15 08								15 38			
Pentre-bach	d				14 42									15 12								15 42			
Troed Y Rhiw	d				14 45									15 15								15 45			
Merthyr Vale	a				14 48									15 18								15 48			
	d				14 50									15 20								15 50			
Quakers Yard	d				14 55									15 25								15 55			
Aberdare ■	d										14 51								15 21						
Cwmbach	d										14 54								15 24						
Fernhill	d										14 58								15 28						
Mountain Ash	a										15 01								15 31						
	d										15 04								15 34						
Penrhiwceiber	d										15 08								15 38						
Abercynon	d				14 59						15 14			15 29					15 44			15 59			
Pontypridd ■	a			15 00	15 07				15 17		15 23			15 37				15 47	15 53			16 08			
	d			15 04	15 09				15 18		15 24			15 39				15 48	15 54			16 09			
Trefforest	d			15 07	15 12				15 21		15 27			15 42				15 51	15 57			16 12			
Trefforest Estate	d				15 16									15 46								16 16			
Taffs Well ■	d			15 13	15 20				15 28		15 34			15 50				15 58	16 04			16 20			
Radyr ■	a			15 17	15 23				15 31		15 37			15 53				16 01	16 07			16 23			
	d			15 17	15 23			15 34	15 31		15 37			15 53		16 04		16 01	16 07			16 23			
Danescourt	d							15 38								16 08									
Fairwater	d							15 40								16 10									
Waun-gron Park	d							15 42								16 12									
Ninian Park	d							15 45								16 15									
Llandaf	d				15 26				15 34		15 40			15 56				16 04	16 10			16 26			
Cathays	d				15 31				15 39		15 45			16 01				16 09	16 15			16 31			
Rhymney ■	d	14 29																			15 29				
Pontlottyn	d	14 32																			15 32				
Tir-phil	d	14 36																			15 36				
Brithdir	d	14 39																			15 39				
Bargoed	a	14 42																			15 42				
	d	14 47					15 02								15 25						15 47				16 02
Gilfach Fargoed	d														15 27										
Pengam	d	14 52					15 07								15 30						15 52				16 07
Hengoed	d	14 55					15 10								15 33						15 55				16 10
Ystrad Mynach ■	d	14 58					15 13								15b43						15 58				16 13
Llanbradach	d	15 03					15 18								15 48						16 03				16 18
Aber	d	15 07					15 22								15 52						16 07				16 22
Caerphilly ■	d	15 10					15 25								15 55						16 10				16 25
Lisvane & Thornhill	d	15 14					15 29								15 59						16 14				16 29
Llanishen	d	15 16					15 31								16 01						16 16				16 31
Heath High Level	d	15 19					15 34								16 04						16 19				16 34
Coryton	d																								
Whitchurch (Cardiff)	d																								
Rhiwbina	d																								
Birchgrove	d																								
Ty Glas	d																								
Heath Low Level	d																								
Cardiff Queen Street ■	a	15 24			15 34		15 39		15 44		15 49			16 04	16 09			16 14	16 19		16 24	16 34			16 39
	d	15 26			15 36	15 36	15 41		15 46	15 48	15 51	16 00		16 06	16 11		16 12	16 16	16 21	16 24	16 26	16 36		16 36	16 41
Cardiff Bay	a					15 40				15 52		16 04					16 16			16 28				16 40	
Cardiff Central ■	a	15 29		15 34	15 39		15 44	15 50	15 53		15 54			16 09	16 14	16 20		16 23	16 24		16 33	16 39			16 44
	d	15 31			15 41		15 46	15 51			15 55			16 10	16 16	16 21			16 25			16 41			16 46
Grangetown	d	15 35			15 45		15 50				15 59			16 14	16 20				16 29			16 45			16 50
Dingle Road	d	15 41					15 56								16 26										16 56
Penarth	a	15 47					16 02								16 32										17 02
Cogan	d				15 48						16 03			16 18					16 33			16 48			
Eastbrook	d				15 51						16 05			16 20					16 35			16 51			
Dinas Powys	d				15 53						16 07			16 22					16 37			16 53			
Cadoxton	d				15 57						16 12			16 27					16 42			16 57			
Barry Docks	d				16 00						16 15			16 30					16 45			17 00			
Barry ■	d				16 05						16 19			16 34					16 49			17 05			
Barry Island	a										16 26			16 41					16 56						
Rhoose Cardiff Int Airport ✈	d				16 12																	17 12			
Llantwit Major	d				16 22																	17 22			
Bridgend	a				16 40																	17 40			

b arr. 1536

Table 130

Mondays to Fridays

from 06 September

Treherbert, Aberdare, Merthyr, Pontypridd, Rhymney and Coryton - Cardiff, Penarth, Barry, Barry Island and Bridgend

		AW	AW	AW	AW	AW	AW	AW	AW	AW	AW	AW	AW	AW	AW	AW	AW	AW	AW	AW	AW	AW	AW
Treherbert	d		15 47									16 17							16 47				
Ynyswen	d		15 49									16 19							16 49				
Treorchy	d		15 51									16 21							16 51				
Ton Pentre	d		15 53									16 23							16 53				
Ystrad Rhondda	a		15 56									16 26							16 56				
	d		15 58									16 28							16 58				
Llwynypia	d		16 00									16 30							17 00				
Tonypandy	d		16 03									16 33							17 03				
Dinas Rhondda	d		16 05									16 35							17 05				
Porth	a		16 08									16 38							17 08				
	d		16 09									16 39							17 09				
Trehafod	d		16 12									16 42							17 12				
Merthyr Tydfil	d							16 08								16 38							
Pentre-bach	d							16 12								16 42							
Troed Y Rhiw	d							16 15								16 45							
Merthyr Vale	a							16 18								16 48							
	d							16 20								16 50							
Quakers Yard	d							16 25								16 55							
Aberdare ■	d				15 51								16 21								16 51		
Cwmbach	d				15 54								16 24								16 54		
Fernhill	d				15 58								16 28								16 58		
Mountain Ash	a				16 01								16 31								17 01		
	d				16 04								16 34								17 04		
Penrhiwceiber	d				16 08								16 38								17 08		
Abercynon	d				16 14			16 29					16 44			16 59					17 14		
Pontypridd ■	a		16 17		16 23			16 37				16 47	16 53			17 07			17 17		17 23		
	d		16 18		16 24			16 39				16 48	16 54			17 09			17 18		17 24		
Trefforest	d		16 21		16 27			16 42				16 51	16 57			17 12			17 21		17 27		
Trefforest Estate	d							16 46								17 16							
Taffs Well ■	d		16 28		16 34			16 50				16 58	17 04			17 20			17 28		17 34		
Radyr ■	a		16 31		16 37			16 53				17 01	17 07			17 23			17 31		17 37		
	d	16 34	16 31		16 37			16 53		17 04		17 01	17 07			17 23	17 34		17 31		17 37		
Danescourt	d	16 38								17 08							17 38						
Fairwater	d	16 40								17 10							17 40						
Waun-gron Park	d	16 42								17 12							17 42						
Ninian Park	d	16 45								17 15							17 45						
Llandaf	d		16 34		16 40			16 56				17 04	17 10			17 26			17 34		17 40		
Cathays	d		16 39		16 45			17 01				17 09	17 15			17 31			17 39		17 45		
Rhymney ■	d														16 29								
Pontlottyn	d														16 32								
Tir-phil	d														16 36								
Brithdir	d														16 39								
Bargoed	a														16 42								
	d					16 17			16 32						16 47							17 17	
Gilfach Fargoed	d					16 19																17 19	
Pengam	d					16 22			16 37						16 52							17 22	
Hengoed	d					16 25			16 40						16 55							17 25	
Ystrad Mynach ■	d					16 28			16 43						16 58							17 28	
Llanbradach	d					16 33			16 48						17 03							17 33	
Aber	d					16 37			16 52						17 07							17 37	
Caerphilly ■	d					16 40			16 55						17 10							17 40	
Lisvane & Thornhill	d					16 44			16 59						17 14							17 44	
Llanishen	d					16 46			17 01						17 16							17 46	
Heath High Level	d					16 49			17 04						17 19							17 49	
Coryton	d																						
Whitchurch (Cardiff)	d																						
Rhiwbina	d																						
Birchgrove	d																						
Ty Glas	d																						
Heath Low Level	d																						
Cardiff Queen Street ■	a		16 44		16 49	16 54		17 04	17 09			17 14	17 19		17 24	17 34			17 44		17 49	17 54	
	d		16 46	16 48	16 51	16 56	17 00	17 06	17 11		17 12	17 16	17 21	17 24	17 26	17 36		17 36	17 46	17 48	17 51	17 56	18 00
Cardiff Bay	a			16 52			17 04				17 16			17 28				17 40		17 52			18 04
Cardiff Central ■	a	16 50	16 53		16 54	16 59		17 09	17 14	17 20		17 23	17 24		17 29	17 39	17 50		17 53		17 54	17 59	
	d	16 51			16 55	17 01		17 10	17 16	17 21			17 25		17 31	17 41	17 51				17 55	18 01	
Grangetown	d				16 59	17 05		17 14	17 20				17 29		17 35	17 45					17 59	18 05	
Dingle Road	d					17 11			17 26						17 41							18 11	
Penarth	a					17 17			17 32						17 47							18 17	
Cogan	d				17 03			17 18					17 33			17 48					18 03		
Eastbrook	d				17 05			17 20					17 35			17 51					18 05		
Dinas Powys	d				17 07			17 22					17 37			17 53					18 07		
Cadoxton	d				17 12			17 27					17 42			17 57					18 12		
Barry Docks	d				17 15			17 30					17 45			18 00					18 15		
Barry ■	d				17 19			17 34					17 49			18 05					18 19		
Barry Island	a				17 26			17 41					17 56								18 26		
Rhoose Cardiff Int Airport ✈	d															18 12							
Llantwit Major	d															18 22							
Bridgend	a															18 40							

Table 130

Mondays to Fridays

from 06 September

Treherbert, Aberdare, Merthyr, Pontypridd, Rhymney and Coryton - Cardiff, Penarth, Barry, Barry Island and Bridgend

		AW	AW	AW	AW	AW	AW	AW	AW	AW	AW	AW	AW	AW	AW	AW	AW	AW	AW	AW	AW	AW
Treherbert	d					17 17							17 47									18 17
Ynyswen	d					17 19							17 49									18 19
Treorchy	d					17 21							17 51									18 21
Ton Pentre	d					17 23							17 53									18 23
Ystrad Rhondda	a					17 26							17 56									18 26
	d					17 28							17 58									18 28
Llwynypia	d					17 30							18 00									18 30
Tonypandy	d					17 33							18 03									18 33
Dinas Rhondda	d					17 35							18 05									18 35
Porth	a					17 38							18 08									18 38
	d					17 39							18 09									18 39
Trehafod	d					17 42							18 12									18 42
Merthyr Tydfil	d	17 08								17 38									18 08			
Pentre-bach	d	17 12								17 42									18 12			
Troed Y Rhiw	d	17 15								17 45									18 15			
Merthyr Vale	a	17 18								17 48									18 18			
	d	17 20								17 50									18 20			
Quakers Yard	d	17 25								17 55									18 25			
Aberdare ■	d						17 21								17 51							
Cwmbach	d						17 24								17 54							
Fernhill	d						17 28								17 58							
Mountain Ash	a						17 31								18 01							
	d						17 34								18 04							
Penrhiwceiber	d						17 38								18 08							
Abercynon	d	17 29					17 44			17 59					18 14				18 29			
Pontypridd ■	a	17 37				17 47	17 53			18 07			18 17		18 23				18 37			18 47
	d	17 39				17 48	17 54			18 09			18 18		18 24				18 39			18 48
Trefforest	d	17 42				17 51	17 57			18 12			18 21		18 27				18 42			18 51
Trefforest Estate	d	17 46								18 16									18 46			
Taffs Well ■	d	17 50				17 58	18 04			18 20			18 28		18 34				18 50			18 58
Radyr ■	a	17 53				18 01	18 07			18 23			18 31		18 37				18 53			19 01
	d	17 53		18 04		18 01	18 07			18 23	18 34		18 31		18 37				18 53	19 04		19 01
Danescourt	d			18 08							18 38									19 08		
Fairwater	d			18 10							18 40									19 10		
Waun-gron Park	d			18 12							18 42									19 12		
Ninian Park	d			18 15							18 45									19 15		
Llandaf	d	17 56				18 04	18 10			18 26			18 34		18 40				18 56			19 04
Cathays	d	18 01				18 09	18 15			18 31			18 39		18 45				19 01			19 09
Rhymney ■	d								17 29													
Pontlottyn	d								17 32													
Tir-phil	d								17 36													
Brithdir	d								17 39													
Bargoed	a								17 42													
	d		17 32						17 47							18 17						
Gilfach Fargoed	d															18 19						
Pengam	d		17 37						17 52							18 22						
Hengoed	d		17 40						17 55							18 25						
Ystrad Mynach ■	d		17 43						17 58							18 28						
Llanbradach	d		17 48						18 03							18 33						
Aber	d		17 52						18 07							18 37						
Caerphilly ■	d		17 55						18 10							18 40						
Lisvane & Thornhill	d		17 59						18 14							18 44						
Llanishen	d		18 01						18 16							18 46						
Heath High Level	d		18 04						18 19							18 49						
Coryton	d																18 45					
Whitchurch (Cardiff)	d																18 46					
Rhiwbina	d																18 48					
Birchgrove	d																18 50					
Ty Glas	d																18 51					
Heath Low Level	d																18 54					
Cardiff Queen Street ■	a	18 04	18 09			18 14	18 19		18 24	18 34			18 44		18 49	18 54	18 59		19 04			19 14
	d	18 06	18 11		18 12	18 16	18 21	18 24	18 26	18 36		18 36	18 46	18 48	18 51	18 56	19 01	19 00	19 06		19 12	19 16
Cardiff Bay	a				18 16			18 28				18 40		18 52				19 04			19 16	
Cardiff Central ■	a	18 09	18 14	18 20		18 23	18 24		18 29	18 39	18 50		18 53		18 54	18 59	19 07		19 10	19 22		19 23
	d	18 10	18 16	18 21			18 25		18 31	18 41	18 51				18 55	19 01						
Grangetown	d	18 14	18 20				18 29		18 35	18 45					18 59	19 05						
Dingle Road	d		18 26						18 41							19 11						
Penarth	a		18 32						18 47							19 17						
Cogan	d	18 18					18 33			18 48					19 03							
Eastbrook	d	18 20					18 35			18 51					19 05							
Dinas Powys	d	18 22					18 37			18 53					19 07							
Cadoxton	d	18 27					18 42			18 57					19 12							
Barry Docks	d	18 30					18 45			19 00					19 15							
Barry ■	d	18 34					18 49			19 05					19 19							
Barry Island	a	18 41					18 56								19 26							
Rhoose Cardiff Int Airport ✈	d									19 12												
Llantwit Major	d									19 22												
Bridgend	a									19 40												

Table 130

Mondays to Fridays
from 06 September

Treherbert, Aberdare, Merthyr, Pontypridd, Rhymney and Coryton - Cardiff, Penarth, Barry, Barry Island and Bridgend

Station		AW	AW	AW	AW	AW	AW	AW	AW	AW	AW	AW	AW	AW	AW	AW	AW	AW	AW	AW	AW	AW	AW
Treherbert	d						18 47							19 17							19 47		
Ynyswen	d						18 49							19 19							19 49		
Treorchy	d						18 51							19 21							19 51		
Ton Pentre	d						18 53							19 23							19 53		
Ystrad Rhondda	a						18 56							19 26							19 56		
	d						18 58							19 28							19 58		
Llwynypia	d						19 00							19 30							20 00		
Tonypandy	d						19 03							19 33							20 03		
Dinas Rhondda	d						19 05							19 35							20 05		
Porth	a						19 08							19 38							20 08		
	d						19 09							19 39							20 09		
Trehafod	d						19 12							19 42							20 12		
Merthyr Tydfil	d				18 38							19 08						19 38					
Pentre-bach	d				18 42							19 12						19 42					
Troed Y Rhiw	d				18 45							19 15						19 45					
Merthyr Vale	a				18 48							19 18						19 48					
	d				18 50							19 20						19 50					
Quakers Yard	d				18 55							19 25						19 55					
Aberdare [3]	d	18 21							18 51														
Cwmbach	d	18 24							18 54														
Fernhill	d	18 28							18 58														
Mountain Ash	a	18 31							19 01														
	d	18 34							19 04														
Penrhiwceiber	d	18 38							19 08														
Abercynon	d	18 44			18 59				19 14			19 29				19 43		19 59					
Pontypridd [3]	a	18 53			19 07		19 17		19 23			19 37		19 47		19 53		20 07			20 17		
	d	18 54			19 09		19 18		19 24			19 39		19 48		19 54		20 09			20 18		
Trefforest	d	18 57			19 12		19 21		19 27			19 42		19 51		19 57		20 12			20 21		
Trefforest Estate	d				19 16							19 46						20 16					
Taffs Well [3]	d	19 04			19 20		19 28		19 34			19 50		19 58		20 04		20 20			20 28		
Radyr [3]	a	19 07			19 23		19 31		19 37			19 53		20 01		20 07		20 23			20 31		
	d	19 07			19 23		19 31		19 37			19 53		20 01	20 04	20 07		20 23			20 31		
Danescourt	d														20 08								
Fairwater	d														20 10								
Waun-gron Park	d														20 12								
Ninian Park	d														20 15								
Llandaf	d	19 10			19 26		19 34		19 40			19 56		20 04		20 10		20 26			20 34		
Cathays	d	19 15			19 31		19 39		19 45			20 01		20 09		20 15		20 31			20 39		
Rhymney [3]	d																			19 45			
Pontlottyn	d																			19 48			
Tir-phil	d																			19 52			
Brithdir	d																			19 55			
Bargoed	a																			19 58			
	d			18 48																19 59			
Gilfach Fargoed	d			18 50																20 01			
Pengam	d			18 53																20 04			
Hengoed	d			18 56																20 07			
Ystrad Mynach [3]	d			18 59																20 10			
Llanbradach	d			19 04																20 15			
Aber	d			19 08																20 19			
Caerphilly [3]	d			19 11						19 40										20 22			20 40
Lisvane & Thornhill	d			19 15						19 44										20 26			20 44
Llanishen	d			19 17						19 46										20 28			20 46
Heath High Level	d			19 20						19 49										20 31			20 49
Coryton	d																						
Whitchurch (Cardiff)	d																						
Rhiwbina	d																						
Birchgrove	d																						
Ty Glas	d																						
Heath Low Level	d																						
Cardiff Queen Street [3]	a	19 19		19 24	19 35		19 44		19 49	19 54		20 04		20 14		20 19		20 34		20 39	20 44		20 54
	d	19 21	19 24	19 26	19 36	19 36	19 46	19 48	19 51	19 56	20 00	20 06	20 12	20 16		20 21	20 24	20 36	20 36	20 41	20 46	20 48	20 56
Cardiff Bay	a		19 28			19 40		19 52			20 04		20 16				20 28		20 40			20 52	
Cardiff Central [7]	a	19 24		19 29	19 40		19 53		19 57	19 59		20 09		20 21	20 22	20 25		20 39		20 48	20 53		20 59
	d	19 25		19 31	19 41					20 06		20 10				20 31		20 41					21 10
Grangetown	d	19 29		19 35	19 45					20 10		20 14				20 37		20 45					21 14
Dingle Road	d			19 41						20 14						20 41							
Penarth	a			19 47						20 20						20 47							
Cogan	d	19 33			19 48							20 18						20 48					21 17
Eastbrook	d	19 35			19 51							20 20						20 51					21 20
Dinas Powys	d	19 37			19 53							20 22						20 53					21 22
Cadoxton	d	19 42			19 57							20 27						20 57					21 26
Barry Docks	d	19 45			20 00							20 30						21 00					21 29
Barry [3]	d	19 49			20 05							20 34						21 05					21 34
Barry Island	a	19 56										20 41											21 42
Rhoose Cardiff Int Airport ✈	d				20 12													21 12					
Llantwit Major	d				20 22													21 22					
Bridgend	a				20 40													21 40					

Table 130

Mondays to Fridays
from 06 September

Treherbert, Aberdare, Merthyr, Pontypridd, Rhymney and Coryton - Cardiff, Penarth, Barry, Barry Island and Bridgend

Station		AW	AW	AW	AW	AW	AW	AW	AW	AW	AW	AW	AW	AW	AW	AW	AW	AW	AW	AW	AW	AW	AW
Treherbert	d				20 17													21 17					
Ynyswen	d				20 19													21 19					
Treorchy	d				20 21													21 21					
Ton Pentre	d				20 23													21 23					
Ystrad Rhondda	a				20 26													21 26					
	d				20 28													21 28					
Llwynypia	d				20 30													21 30					
Tonypandy	d				20 33													21 33					
Dinas Rhondda	d				20 35													21 35					
Porth	a				20 38													21 38					
	d				20 39													21 39					
Trehafod	d				20 42													21 42					
Merthyr Tydfil	d								20 38											21 38			
Pentre-bach	d								20 42											21 42			
Troed Y Rhiw	d								20 45											21 45			
Merthyr Vale	a								20 48											21 48			
	d								20 50											21 50			
Quakers Yard	d								20 55											21 55			
Aberdare [3]	d					20 21							20 51										21 51
Cwmbach	d					20 24							20 54										21 54
Fernhill	d					20 28							20 58										21 58
Mountain Ash	a					20 31							21 01										22 01
	d					20 34							21 04										22 04
Penrhiwceiber	d					20 38							21 08										22 08
Abercynon	d					20 44			20 59				21 14							21 59			22 14
Pontypridd [3]	a				20 47	20 53			21 07				21 23					21 47		22 07			22 22
	d				20 48	20 54			21 09				21 24					21 48		22 09			22 29
Trefforest	d				20 51	20 57			21 12				21 27					21 51		22 12			22 32
Trefforest Estate	d								21 16											22 16			
Taffs Well [3]	d				20 58	21 04			21 20				21 34					21 58		22 20			22 39
Radyr [3]	a				21 01	21 07			21 23				21 37					22 01		22 23			22 42
	d		21 04		21 01	21 07			21 23				21 37			22 04		22 01		22 23			22 42
Danescourt	d		21 08													22 08							
Fairwater	d		21 10													22 10							
Waun-gron Park	d		21 12													22 12							
Ninian Park	d		21 15													22 15							
Llandaf	d				21 04	21 10			21 26				21 40					22 04		22 26			22 45
Cathays	d				21 09	21 15			21 31				21 45					22 09		22 31			22 50
Rhymney [3]	d										20 48												
Pontlottyn	d										20 51												
Tir-phil	d										20 55												
Brithdir	d										20 58												
Bargoed	a										21 01												
	d										21 02												
Gilfach Fargoed	d										21 04												
Pengam	d										21 07												
Hengoed	d										21 10												
Ystrad Mynach [3]	d										21 13												
Llanbradach	d										21 18												
Aber	d										21 22												
Caerphilly [3]	d										21 25			21 45									
Lisvane & Thornhill	d										21 29			21 50									
Llanishen	d										21 31			21 52									
Heath High Level	d										21 34			21 54									
Coryton	d																						
Whitchurch (Cardiff)	d																						
Rhiwbina	d																						
Birchgrove	d																						
Ty Glas	d																						
Heath Low Level	d																						
Cardiff Queen Street [3]	a				21 14	21 19			21 34		21 42		21 49	22 00				22 14		22 34			22 54
	d	21 00		21 12	21 16	21 21	21 24		21 36	21 36	21 44	21 48	21 51	22 01	22 00		22 12	22 16	22 24	22 36	22 36	22 48	22 55
Cardiff Bay	a	21 04		21 16			21 28			21 40		21 52			22 04		22 16		22 28		22 40	22 52	
Cardiff Central [7]	a		21 25		21 22	21 24			21 39		21 51		21 54	22 07		22 20		22 22		22 39			23 01
	d							21 31	21 41				21 56	22 10		22 21				22 41			23 12
Grangetown	d							21 35	21 45				22 00	22 14						22 45			23 16
Dingle Road	d							21 41					22 04										23 20
Penarth	a							21 47					22 07										23 26
Cogan	d								21 48					22 18						22 48			
Eastbrook	d								21 51					22 20						22 51			
Dinas Powys	d								21 53					22 22						22 53			
Cadoxton	d								21 57					22 27						22 57			
Barry Docks	d								22 00					22 30						23 00			
Barry [3]	d								22 05					22 34						23 05			
Barry Island	a													22 41									
Rhoose Cardiff Int Airport ✈	d								22 12											23 12			
Llantwit Major	d								22 22											23 22			
Bridgend	a								22 40											23 40			

Table 130

Mondays to Fridays
from 06 September

Treherbert, Aberdare, Merthyr, Pontypridd, Rhymney and Coryton - Cardiff, Penarth, Barry, Barry Island and Bridgend

		AW		AW	AW	AW	AW	AW	AW	AW	AW
Treherbert	d										
Ynyswen	d										
Treorchy	d										
Ton Pentre	d										
Ystrad Rhondda	a										
	d										
Llwynypia	d										
Tonypandy	d										
Dinas Rhondda	d										
Porth	a										
	d										
Trehafod	d										
Merthyr Tydfil	d							22 38			
Pentre-bach	d							22 42			
Troed Y Rhiw	d							22 45			
Merthyr Vale	a							22 48			
	d							22 50			
Quakers Yard	d							22 55			
Aberdare ■	d								22 51		
Cwmbach	d								22 54		
Fernhill	d								22 58		
Mountain Ash	a								23 01		
	d								23 04		
Penrhiwceiber	d								23 08		
Abercynon	d							22 59	23 14		
Pontypridd ■	a							23 07	23 22		
	d							23 09			
Trefforest	d							23 12			
Trefforest Estate	d										
Taffs Well ■	d							23 20			
Radyr ■	a							23 23			
	d					23 10		23 23			
Danescourt	d										
Fairwater	d										
Waun-gron Park	d										
Ninian Park	d										
Llandaf	d					23 12		23 26			
Cathays	d					23 16		23 31			
Rhymney ■	d										
Pontlottyn	d										
Tir-phil	d										
Brithdir	d										
Bargoed	a										
	d										
Gilfach Fargoed	d										
Pengam	d										
Hengoed	d										
Ystrad Mynach ■	d										
Llanbradach	d										
Aber	d										
Caerphilly ■	d										
Lisvane & Thornhill	d										
Llanishen	d										
Heath High Level	d										
Coryton	d	22 45									
Whitchurch (Cardiff)	d	22 46									
Rhiwbina	d	22 48									
Birchgrove	d	22 50									
Ty Glas	d	22 51									
Heath Low Level	d	22 54									
Cardiff Queen Street ■	a	22 59				23 19		23 34			
	d	23 01		23 00	23 12	23 20	23 24	23 36		23 36	23 48
Cardiff Bay	a			23 04	23 16		23 28			23 40	23 52
Cardiff Central ■	a	23 07				23 25		23 43			
	d					23 30					
Grangetown	d					23 34					
Dingle Road	d										
Penarth	a										
Cogan	d					23 37					
Eastbrook	d					23 40					
Dinas Powys	d					23 42					
Cadoxton	d					23 46					
Barry Docks	d					23 49					
Barry ■	d					23 54					
Barry Island	a					23 59					
Rhoose Cardiff Int Airport ✈	d										
Llantwit Major	d										
Bridgend	a										

Table 130

Saturdays
until 04 September

Treherbert, Aberdare, Merthyr, Pontypridd, Rhymney and Coryton - Cardiff, Penarth, Barry, Barry Island and Bridgend

		AW	AW	AW	AW	AW	AW	AW	AW	AW		AW	AW	AW	AW	AW	AW	AW	AW	AW		AW	AW	AW	AW
Treherbert	d											05 47							06 17						
Ynyswen	d											05 49							06 19						
Treorchy	d											05 51							06 21						
Ton Pentre	d											05 53							06 23						
Ystrad Rhondda	a											05 56							06 26						
	d											05 58							06 28						
Llwynypia	d											06 00							06 30						
Tonypandy	d											06 03							06 33						
Dinas Rhondda	d											06 05							06 35						
Porth	a											06 08							06 38						
	d											06 09							06 39						
Trehafod	d											06 12							06 42						
Merthyr Tydfil	d																							06 38	
Pentre-bach	d																							06 42	
Troed Y Rhiw	d																							06 45	
Merthyr Vale	a																							06 48	
	d																							06 50	
Quakers Yard	d																							06 55	
Aberdare ■	d																					06 22			
Cwmbach	d																					06 25			
Fernhill	d																					06 28			
Mountain Ash	a																					06 31			
	d																					06 34			
Penrhiwceiber	d																					06 37			
Abercynon	d																					06 43		06 59	
Pontypridd ■	a											06 17							06 47			06 53		07 07	
	d				05 24							06 18							06 48			06 54		07 09	
Trefforest	d				05 27							06 21							06 51			06 57		07 12	
Trefforest Estate	d				05 31							06 25										07 01		07 16	
Taffs Well ■	d				05 34							06 28							06 58	06 53		07 04		07 20	
Radyr ■	a				05 37							06 31							07 01	06 56		07 07		07 23	
	d				05 37							06 31							07 01	07 04		07 07		07 23	
Danescourt	d																			07 08					
Fairwater	d																			07 10					
Waun-gron Park	d																			07 12					
Ninian Park	d																			07 15					
Llandaf	d				05 40							06 34							07 04			07 10		07 26	
Cathays	d				05 45							06 39							07 09			07 15		07 31	
Rhymney ■	d																								
Pontlottyn	d																								
Tir-phil	d																								
Brithdir	d																								
Bargoed	a																								
	d																								
Gilfach Fargoed	d																								
Pengam	d																								
Hengoed	d																								
Ystrad Mynach ■	d																								
Llanbradach	d																								
Aber	d																								
Caerphilly ■	d							06 10																	
Lisvane & Thornhill	d							06 14																	
Llanishen	d							06 16																	
Heath High Level	d							06 19																	
Coryton	d																								
Whitchurch (Cardiff)	d																								
Rhiwbina	d																								
Birchgrove	d																								
Ty Glas	d																								
Heath Low Level	d																								
Cardiff Queen Street ■	a				05 48			06 25				06 44							07 14			07 20		07 35	
	d				05 51			06 26	06 36			06 44	06 48		07 00			07 12	07 16			07 21	07 24	07 36	07 36
Cardiff Bay	a								06 40				06 52		07 04			07 16					07 28		07 40
Cardiff Central ■	a				05 54			06 29				06 48		06 54					07 18	07 20		07 24		07 39	
	d	05 20	05 41	05 46	05 55	06 16	06 25	06 41		06 36				06 55		07 01	07 10			07 21		07 25		07 41	
Grangetown	d	05 24	05 45	05 50	05 59	06 20	06 29	06 45		06 40				06 59		07 05	07 14					07 29		07 45	
Dingle Road	d			05 54		06 24				06 44						07 11									
Penarth	a			05 59		06 28				06 49						07 16									
Cogan	d	05 28	05 48		06 03		06 33	06 48						07 03			07 18					07 33		07 48	
Eastbrook	d	05 30	05 51		06 05		06 35	06 51						07 05			07 20					07 35		07 51	
Dinas Powys	d	05 32	05 53		06 07		06 37	06 53						07 07			07 22					07 37		07 53	
Cadoxton	d	05 37	05 57		06 12		06 42	06 57						07 12			07 27					07 42		07 57	
Barry Docks	d	05 40	06 00		06 15		06 45	07 00						07 15			07 30					07 45		08 00	
Barry ■	d	05 44	06 05		06 19		06 49	07 05						07 19			07 34					07 49		08 05	
Barry Island	a	05 50			06 25		06 55							07 25			07 40					07 55			
Rhoose Cardiff Int Airport ✈	d		06 12					07 12																08 12	
Llantwit Major	d		06 22					07 22																08 22	
Bridgend	a		06 39					07 39																08 39	

Table 130

Saturdays
until 04 September

Treherbert, Aberdare, Merthyr, Pontypridd, Rhymney and Coryton - Cardiff, Penarth, Barry, Barry Island and Bridgend

		AW	AW	AW	AW	AW	AW	AW	AW	AW	AW	AW	AW	AW	AW	AW	AW	AW	AW	AW	AW	AW	AW
Treherbert	d			06 47									07 17								07 45		
Ynyswen	d			06 49									07 19								07 47		
Treorchy	d			06 51									07 21								07 49		
Ton Pentre	d			06 53									07 23								07 51		
Ystrad Rhondda	a			06 56									07 26								07 54		
	d			06 58									07 28								07 58		
Llwynypia	d			07 00									07 30								08 00		
Tonypandy	d			07 03									07 33								08 03		
Dinas Rhondda	d			07 05									07 35								08 05		
Porth	a			07 08									07 38								08 08		
	d			07 09									07 39								08 09		
Trehafod	d			07 12									07 42								08 12		
Merthyr Tydfil	d								07 08								07 38						
Pentre-bach	d								07 12								07 42						
Troed Y Rhiw	d								07 15								07 45						
Merthyr Vale	a								07 18								07 48						
	d								07 20								07 50						
Quakers Yard	d								07 25								07 55						
Aberdare	d					06 52								07 22									07 52
Cwmbach	d					06 55								07 25									07 55
Fernhill	d					06 58								07 28									07 58
Mountain Ash	a					07 01								07 31									08 01
	d					07 04								07 34									08 04
Penrhiwceiber	d					07 07								07 37									08 07
Abercynon	d					07 13			07 29					07 43			07 59						08 13
Pontypridd	a			07 17		07 23			07 37				07 47	07 53			08 07				08 17		08 23
	d			07 18		07 24			07 39				07 48	07 54			08 09				08 18		08 24
Trefforest	d			07 21		07 27			07 42				07 51	07 57			08 12				08 21		08 27
Trefforest Estate	d								07 46								08 16						
Taffs Well	d			07 28		07 34			07 50				07 58	08 04			08 20				08 28		08 34
Radyr	a			07 31		07 37			07 53				08 01	08 07			08 23				08 31		08 37
	d		07 34	07 31		07 37			07 53		08 04		08 01	08 07			08 23			08 34	08 31		08 37
Danescourt	d		07 38								08 08									08 38			
Fairwater	d		07 40								08 10									08 40			
Waun-gron Park	d		07 42								08 12									08 42			
Ninian Park	d		07 45								08 15									08 45			
Llandaf	d			07 34		07 40			07 56				08 04	08 10			08 26				08 34		08 40
Cathays	d			07 39		07 45			08 01				08 09	08 15			08 31				08 39		08 45
Rhymney	d						07 02									07 24			07 44				
Pontlottyn	d						07 05									07 27			07 47				
Tir-phil	d						07 09									07 31			07 51				
Brithdir	d						07 12									07 34			07 54				
Bargoed	a						07 15									07 37			08 00				
	d	07 02					07 17			07 32						07 45			08 02				
Gilfach Fargoed	d	07 04					07 19									07 47							
Pengam	d	07 07					07 22			07 37						07 50			08 07				
Hengoed	d	07 10					07 25			07 40						07 54			08 10				
Ystrad Mynach	d	07 13					07 28			07 43						07 57			08 13				
Llanbradach	d	07 18					07 33			07 48						08 02			08 18				
Aber	d	07 22					07 37			07 52						08 07			08 22				
Caerphilly	d	07 25					07 40			07 55						08 10			08 25				
Lisvane & Thornhill	d	07 29					07 44			07 59						08 14			08 29				
Llanishen	d	07 31					07 46			08 01						08 16			08 31				
Heath High Level	d	07 34					07 49			08 04						08 19			08 34				
Coryton	d																						
Whitchurch (Cardiff)	d																						
Rhiwbina	d																						
Birchgrove	d																						
Ty Glas	d																						
Heath Low Level	d																						
Cardiff Queen Street	a	07 39		07 44		07 49	07 54		08 04	08 09			08 14	08 19		08 24	08 34		08 39		08 44		08 49
	d	07 41		07 46	07 48	07 51	07 56	08 00	08 06	08 11		08 12	08 16	08 21	08 24	08 26	08 36	08 36	08 41		08 46	08 48	08 51
Cardiff Bay	a				07 52			08 04				08 16			08 28			08 40				08 52	
Cardiff Central	a	07 44	07 50	07 52		07 54	07 59		08 09	08 14	08 20		08 22	08 24		08 29	08 39		08 47	08 50	08 52		08 54
	d	07 46	07 51			07 55	08 01		08 10	08 16	08 21			08 25		08 31	08 41			08 51			08 55
Grangetown	d	07 50				07 59	08 05		08 14	08 20				08 29		08 35	08 45						08 59
Dingle Road	d	07 56					08 11			08 26						08 41							
Penarth	a	08 01					08 16			08 31						08 46							
Cogan	d					08 03			08 18					08 33			08 48						09 03
Eastbrook	d					08 05			08 20					08 35			08 51						09 05
Dinas Powys	d					08 07			08 22					08 37			08 53						09 07
Cadoxton	d					08 12			08 27					08 42			08 57						09 12
Barry Docks	d					08 15			08 30					08 45			09 00						09 15
Barry	d					08 19			08 34					08 49			09 05						09 19
Barry Island	a					08 25			08 40					08 55									09 25
Rhoose Cardiff Int Airport ✈	d																09 12						
Llantwit Major	d																09 22						
Bridgend	a																09 39						

Table 130

Saturdays
until 04 September

Treherbert, Aberdare, Merthyr, Pontypridd, Rhymney and Coryton - Cardiff, Penarth, Barry, Barry Island and Bridgend

		AW	AW	AW	AW	AW	AW	AW	AW	AW	AW	AW	AW	AW	AW	AW	AW	AW	AW	AW	AW	AW
Treherbert	d							08 17							08 47							
Ynyswen	d							08 19							08 49							
Treorchy	d							08 21							08 51							
Ton Pentre	d							08 23							08 53							
Ystrad Rhondda	a							08 26							08 56							
	d							08 28							08 58							
Llwynypia	d							08 30							09 00							
Tonypandy	d							08 33							09 03							
Dinas Rhondda	d							08 35							09 05							
Porth	a							08 38							09 08							
	d							08 39							09 09							
Trehafod	d							08 42							09 12							
Merthyr Tydfil	d			08 08								08 38								09 08		
Pentre-bach	d			08 12								08 42								09 12		
Troed Y Rhiw	d			08 15								08 45								09 15		
Merthyr Vale	a			08 18								08 48								09 18		
	d			08 20								08 50								09 20		
Quakers Yard	d			08 25								08 55								09 25		
Aberdare	d								08 22								08 52					
Cwmbach	d								08 25								08 55					
Fernhill	d								08 28								08 58					
Mountain Ash	a								08 31								09 01					
	d								08 34								09 04					
Penrhiwceiber	d								08 37								09 07					
Abercynon	d			08 29					08 43			08 59					09 13			09 29		
Pontypridd	a			08 37				08 47	08 53			09 07			09 17		09 23			09 37		
	d			08 39				08 48	08 54			09 09			09 18		09 24			09 39		
Trefforest	d			08 42				08 51	08 57			09 12			09 21		09 27			09 42		
Trefforest Estate	d			08 46								09 16								09 46		
Taffs Well	d			08 50				08 58	09 04			09 20			09 28		09 34			09 50		
Radyr	a			08 53				09 01	09 07			09 23			09 31		09 37			09 53		
	d			08 53		09 04		09 01	09 07			09 23	09 34		09 31		09 37			09 53		10 04
Danescourt	d					09 08							09 38									10 08
Fairwater	d					09 10							09 40									10 10
Waun-gron Park	d					09 12							09 42									10 12
Ninian Park	d					09 15							09 45									10 15
Llandaf	d			08 56				09 04	09 10			09 26			09 34		09 40			09 56		
Cathays	d			09 01				09 09	09 15			09 31			09 39		09 45			10 01		
Rhymney	d										08 30											
Pontlottyn	d										08 33											
Tir-phil	d										08 37											
Brithdir	d										08 40											
Bargoed	a										08 44											
	d	08 17			08 32						08 47							09 17			09 32	
Gilfach Fargoed	d	08 19																09 19				
Pengam	d	08 22			08 37						08 52							09 22			09 37	
Hengoed	d	08 25			08 40						08 55							09 25			09 40	
Ystrad Mynach	d	08 28			08 43						08 58							09 28			09 43	
Llanbradach	d	08 33			08 48						09 03							09 33			09 48	
Aber	d	08 37			08 52						09 07							09 37			09 52	
Caerphilly	d	08 40			08 55						09 10							09 40			09 55	
Lisvane & Thornhill	d	08 44			08 59						09 14							09 44			09 59	
Llanishen	d	08 46			09 01						09 16							09 46			10 01	
Heath High Level	d	08 49			09 04						09 19							09 49			10 04	
Coryton	d																					
Whitchurch (Cardiff)	d																					
Rhiwbina	d																					
Birchgrove	d																					
Ty Glas	d																					
Heath Low Level	d																					
Cardiff Queen Street	a	08 54		09 04	09 09			09 14	09 19		09 24	09 34			09 44		09 49	09 54		10 04	10 09	
	d	08 56	09 00	09 06	09 11		09 12	09 16	09 21	09 24	09 26	09 36		09 36	09 46	09 48	09 51	09 56	10 00	10 06	10 11	
Cardiff Bay	a		09 04				09 16			09 28				09 40		09 52			10 04			
Cardiff Central	a	08 59		09 09	09 14	09 20		09 22	09 24		09 29	09 39	09 50		09 52		09 54	09 59		10 09	10 14	10 20
	d	09 01		09 10	09 16	09 21			09 25		09 31	09 41	09 51				09 55	10 01		10 10	10 16	10 21
Grangetown	d	09 05		09 14	09 20				09 29		09 35	09 45					09 59	10 05		10 14	10 20	
Dingle Road	d	09 11			09 26						09 41							10 11			10 26	
Penarth	a	09 16			09 31						09 46							10 16			10 31	
Cogan	d			09 18					09 33			09 48					10 03			10 18		
Eastbrook	d			09 20					09 35			09 51					10 05			10 20		
Dinas Powys	d			09 22					09 37			09 53					10 07			10 22		
Cadoxton	d			09 27					09 42			09 57					10 12			10 27		
Barry Docks	d			09 30					09 45			10 00					10 15			10 30		
Barry	d			09 34					09 49			10 05					10 19			10 34		
Barry Island	a			09 40					09 55								10 25			10 40		
Rhoose Cardiff Int Airport ✈	d											10 12										
Llantwit Major	d											10 22										
Bridgend	a											10 39										

Table 130

Saturdays
until 04 September

Treherbert, Aberdare, Merthyr, Pontypridd, Rhymney and Coryton - Cardiff, Penarth, Barry, Barry Island and Bridgend

		AW	AW	AW	AW	AW	AW	AW	AW	AW	AW	AW	AW	AW	AW	AW	AW	AW	AW	AW	AW	AW	AW
Treherbert	d		09 17								09 47												10 17
Ynyswen	d		09 19								09 49												10 19
Treorchy	d		09 21								09 51												10 21
Ton Pentre	d		09 23								09 53												10 23
Ystrad Rhondda	a		09 26								09 56												10 26
	d		09 28								09 58												10 28
Llwynypia	d		09 30								10 00												10 30
Tonypandy	d		09 33								10 03												10 33
Dinas Rhondda	d		09 35								10 05												10 35
Porth	a		09 38								10 08												10 38
	d		09 39								10 09												10 52
Trehafod	d		09 42								10 12												10 55
Merthyr Tydfil	d						09 38							10 04									
Pentre-bach	d						09 42							10 08									
Troed Y Rhiw	d						09 45							10 11									
Merthyr Vale	a						09 48							10 14									
	d						09 50							10 16									
Quakers Yard	d						09 55							10 22									
Aberdare ■3	d			09 22									09 52							10 22			
Cwmbach	d			09 25									09 55							10 25			
Fernhill	d			09 28									09 58							10 28			
Mountain Ash	a			09 31									10 01							10 31			
	d			09 34									10 04							10 34			
Penrhiwceiber	d			09 37									10 07							10 37			
Abercynon	d			09 43			09 59						10 13	10 26						10 43			
Pontypridd ■3	a		09 47	09 53			10 07				10 17		10 23	10 32						10 53			11 00
	d		09 48	09 54			10 09				10 18		10 24			10 39				10 54			11 04
Trefforest	d		09 51	09 57			10 12				10 21		10 27			10 42				10 57			11 07
Trefforest Estate	d						10 16									10 46							
Taffs Well ■3	d		09 58	10 04			10 20				10 28		10 34			10 50				11 04			11 13
Radyr ■3	a		10 01	10 07			10 23				10 31		10 37			10 53				11 07			11 17
	d		10 01	10 07			10 23			10 34	10 31		10 37			10 53		11 04		11 07			11 17
Danescourt	d									10 38								11 08					
Fairwater	d									10 40								11 10					
Waun-gron Park	d									10 42								11 12					
Ninian Park	d									10 45								11 15					
Llandaf	d		10 04	10 10			10 26				10 34		10 40			10 56				11 10			
Cathays	d		10 09	10 15			10 31				10 39		10 45			11 01				11 15			
Rhymney ■3	d					09 29																10 29	
Pontlottyn	d					09 32																10 32	
Tir-phil	d					09 36																10 36	
Brithdir	d					09 39																10 39	
Bargoed	a					09 42																10 42	
	d					09 47			10 02								10 32					10 47	
Gilfach Fargoed	d																						
Pengam	d					09 52			10 07								10 37					10 52	
Hengoed	d					09 55			10 10								10 40					10 55	
Ystrad Mynach ■3	d					09 58			10 13								10 43					10 58	
Llanbradach	d					10 03			10 18								10 48					11 03	
Aber	d					10 07			10 22								10 52					11 07	
Caerphilly ■3	d					10 10			10 25								10 55					11 10	
Lisvane & Thornhill	d					10 14			10 29								10 59					11 14	
Llanishen	d					10 16			10 31								11 01					11 16	
Heath High Level	d					10 19			10 34								11 04					11 19	
Coryton	d																						
Whitchurch (Cardiff)	d																						
Rhiwbina	d																						
Birchgrove	d																						
Ty Glas	d																						
Heath Low Level	d																						
Cardiff Queen Street ■3	a		10 14	10 19		10 24	10 34		10 39		10 44		10 49			11 04	11 09			11 19		11 24	
	d	10 12	10 16	10 21	10 24	10 26	10 36	10 36	10 41		10 46	10 48	10 51		11 00	11 06	11 11		11 12	11 21	11 24	11 26	
Cardiff Bay	a	10 16			10 28			10 40				10 52			11 04				11 16		11 28		
Cardiff Central ■7	a		10 22	10 24		10 29	10 39		10 44	10 50	10 52		10 54			11 09	11 14	11 20		11 24		11 29	11 34
	d			10 25		10 31	10 41		10 46	10 51			10 55			11 10	11 16	11 21		11 25		11 31	
Grangetown	d			10 29		10 35	10 45		10 50				10 59			11 14	11 20			11 29		11 35	
Dingle Road	d					10 41			10 56								11 26					11 41	
Penarth	a					10 46			11 01								11 31					11 46	
Cogan	d			10 33			10 48						11 03			11 18				11 33			
Eastbrook	d			10 35			10 51						11 05			11 20				11 35			
Dinas Powys	d			10 37			10 53						11 07			11 22				11 37			
Cadoxton	d			10 42			10 57						11 12			11 27				11 42			
Barry Docks	d			10 45			11 00						11 15			11 30				11 45			
Barry ■3	d			10 49			11 05						11 19			11 34				11 49			
Barry Island	a			10 55									11 25			11 40				11 55			
Rhoose Cardiff Int Airport ✈	d						11 12																
Llantwit Major	d						11 22																
Bridgend	a						11 39																

Table 130

Saturdays
until 04 September

Treherbert, Aberdare, Merthyr, Pontypridd, Rhymney and Coryton - Cardiff, Penarth, Barry, Barry Island and Bridgend

		AW	AW	AW	AW	AW	AW	AW	AW	AW	AW	AW	AW	AW	AW	AW	AW	AW	AW	AW	AW	AW
Treherbert	d					10 47									11 17							
Ynyswen	d					10 49									11 19							
Treorchy	d					10 51									11 21							
Ton Pentre	d					10 53									11 23							
Ystrad Rhondda	a					10 56									11 26							
	d					10 58									11 28							
Llwynypia	d					11 00									11 30							
Tonypandy	d					11 03									11 33							
Dinas Rhondda	d					11 05									11 35							
Porth	a					11 08									11 38							
	d					11 09									11 39							
Trehafod	d					11 12									11 42							
Merthyr Tydfil	d	10 38									11 08								11 38			
Pentre-bach	d	10 42									11 12								11 42			
Troed Y Rhiw	d	10 45									11 15								11 45			
Merthyr Vale	a	10 48									11 18								11 48			
	d	10 50									11 20								11 50			
Quakers Yard	d	10 55									11 25								11 55			
Aberdare ■3	d							10 52								11 22						
Cwmbach	d							10 55								11 25						
Fernhill	d							10 58								11 28						
Mountain Ash	a							11 01								11 31						
	d							11 04								11 34						
Penrhiwceiber	d							11 07								11 37						
Abercynon	d	10 59						11 13			11 29					11 43			11 59			
Pontypridd ■3	a	11 08				11 17		11 23			11 37				11 47	11 53			12 07			
	d	11 09				11 18		11 24			11 39				11 48	11 54			12 09			
Trefforest	d	11 12				11 21		11 27			11 42				11 51	11 57			12 12			
Trefforest Estate	d	11 16									11 46								12 16			
Taffs Well ■3	d	11 20				11 28		11 34			11 50				11 58	12 04			12 20			
Radyr ■3	a	11 23				11 31		11 37			11 53				12 01	12 07			12 23			
	d	11 23			11 34	11 31		11 37			11 53		12 04		12 01	12 07			12 23			12 34
Danescourt	d				11 38								12 08									12 38
Fairwater	d				11 40								12 10									12 40
Waun-gron Park	d				11 42								12 12									12 42
Ninian Park	d				11 45								12 15									12 45
Llandaf	d	11 26				11 34		11 40			11 56				12 04	12 10			12 26			
Cathays	d	11 31				11 39		11 45			12 01				12 09	12 15			12 31			
Rhymney ■3	d																	11 29				
Pontlottyn	d																	11 32				
Tir-phil	d																	11 36				
Brithdir	d																	11 39				
Bargoed	a																	11 42				
	d			11 02					11 17			11 32						11 47			12 02	
Gilfach Fargoed	d								11 19													
Pengam	d			11 07					11 22			11 37						11 52			12 07	
Hengoed	d			11 10					11 25			11 40						11 55			12 10	
Ystrad Mynach ■3	d			11 13					11 28			11 43						11 58			12 13	
Llanbradach	d			11 18					11 33			11 48						12 03			12 18	
Aber	d			11 22					11 37			11 52						12 07			12 22	
Caerphilly ■3	d			11 25					11 40			11 55						12 10			12 25	
Lisvane & Thornhill	d			11 29					11 44			11 59						12 14			12 29	
Llanishen	d			11 31					11 46			12 01						12 16			12 31	
Heath High Level	d			11 34					11 49			12 04						12 19			12 34	
Coryton	d																					
Whitchurch (Cardiff)	d																					
Rhiwbina	d																					
Birchgrove	d																					
Ty Glas	d																					
Heath Low Level	d																					
Cardiff Queen Street ■3	a	11 34		11 39		11 44		11 49	11 54		12 04	12 09			12 14	12 19		12 24	12 34		12 39	
	d	11 36	11 36	11 41		11 46	11 48	11 51	11 56	12 00	12 06	12 11		12 12	12 16	12 21	12 24	12 26	12 36	12 36	12 41	
Cardiff Bay	a		11 40				11 52			12 04				12 16			12 28			12 40		
Cardiff Central ■7	a	11 39		11 44	11 50	11 52		11 54	11 59		12 09	12 14	12 20		12 22	12 24		12 29	12 39		12 44	12 50
	d	11 41		11 46	11 51			11 55	12 01		12 10	12 16	12 21			12 25		12 31	12 41		12 46	12 51
Grangetown	d	11 45		11 50				11 59	12 05		12 14	12 20				12 29		12 35	12 45		12 50	
Dingle Road	d			11 56					12 11			12 26						12 41			12 56	
Penarth	a			12 01					12 16			12 31						12 46			13 01	
Cogan	d	11 48						12 03			12 18					12 33			12 48			
Eastbrook	d	11 51						12 05			12 20					12 35			12 51			
Dinas Powys	d	11 53						12 07			12 22					12 37			12 53			
Cadoxton	d	11 57						12 12			12 27					12 42			12 57			
Barry Docks	d	12 00						12 15			12 30					12 45			13 00			
Barry ■3	d	12 05						12 19			12 34					12 49			13 05			
Barry Island	a							12 25			12 40					12 55						
Rhoose Cardiff Int Airport ✈	d	12 12																	13 12			
Llantwit Major	d	12 22																	13 22			
Bridgend	a	12 39																	13 39			

Table 130

Saturdays
until 04 September

Treherbert, Aberdare, Merthyr, Pontypridd, Rhymney and Coryton - Cardiff, Penarth, Barry, Barry Island and Bridgend

		AW	AW	AW	AW	AW	AW	AW	AW	AW	AW	AW	AW	AW	AW	AW	AW	AW	AW	AW	AW	AW
Treherbert	d				17 17							17 47									18 17	
Ynyswen	d				17 19							17 49									18 19	
Treorchy	d				17 21							17 51									18 21	
Ton Pentre	d				17 23							17 53									18 23	
Ystrad Rhondda	a				17 26							17 56									18 26	
	d				17 28							17 58									18 28	
Llwynypia	d				17 30							18 00									18 30	
Tonypandy	d				17 33							18 03									18 33	
Dinas Rhondda	d				17 35							18 05									18 35	
Porth	a				17 38							18 08									18 38	
	d				17 39							18 09									18 39	
Trehafod	d				17 42							18 12									18 42	
Merthyr Tydfil	d	17 08							17 38									18 08				
Pentre-bach	d	17 12							17 42									18 12				
Troed Y Rhiw	d	17 15							17 45									18 15				
Merthyr Vale	a	17 18							17 48									18 18				
	d	17 20							17 50									18 20				
Quakers Yard	d	17 25							17 55									18 25				
Aberdare ■	d					17 22								17 52								18 22
Cwmbach	d					17 25								17 55								18 25
Fernhill	d					17 28								17 58								18 28
Mountain Ash	a					17 31								18 01								18 31
	d					17 34								18 04								18 34
Penrhiwceiber	d					17 37								18 07								18 37
Abercynon	d	17 29				17 43			17 59					18 13				18 29				18 43
Pontypridd ■	a	17 37			17 47	17 53			18 07			18 17		18 23				18 37			18 47	18 53
	d	17 39			17 48	17 54			18 09			18 18		18 24				18 39			18 48	18 54
Trefforest	d	17 42			17 51	17 57			18 12			18 21		18 27				18 42			18 51	18 57
Trefforest Estate	d	17 46							18 16									18 46				
Taffs Well ■	d	17 50			17 58	18 04			18 20			18 28		18 34				18 50			18 58	19 04
Radyr ■	a	17 53			18 01	18 07			18 23			18 31		18 37				18 53			19 01	19 07
	d	17 53	18 04		18 01	18 07			18 23	18 34		18 31		18 37				18 53	19 04		19 01	19 07
Danescourt	d		18 08							18 38									19 08			
Fairwater	d		18 10							18 40									19 10			
Waun-gron Park	d		18 12							18 42									19 12			
Ninian Park	d		18 15							18 45									19 15			
Llandaf	d	17 56			18 04	18 10			18 26			18 34		18 40				18 56			19 04	19 10
Cathays	d	18 01			18 09	18 15			18 31			18 39		18 45				19 01			19 09	19 15
Rhymney ■	d							17 29														
Pontlottyn	d							17 32														
Tir-phil	d							17 36														
Brithdir	d							17 39														
Bargoed	a							17 42														
	d							17 47							18 17							
Gilfach Fargoed	d														18 19							
Pengam	d							17 52							18 22							
Hengoed	d							17 55							18 25							
Ystrad Mynach ■	d							17 58							18 28							
Llanbradach	d							18 03							18 33							
Aber	d							18 07							18 37							
Caerphilly ■	d							18 10							18 40							
Lisvane & Thornhill	d							18 14							18 44							
Llanishen	d							18 16							18 46							
Heath High Level	d							18 19							18 49							
Coryton	d															18 45						
Whitchurch (Cardiff)	d															18 46						
Rhiwbina	d															18 48						
Birchgrove	d															18 50						
Ty Glas	d															18 51						
Heath Low Level	d															18 54						
Cardiff Queen Street ■	a	18 04			18 14	18 19		18 24	18 34			18 44		18 49	18 54	18 59		19 04			19 14	19 19
	d	18 06		18 12	18 16	18 21	18 24	18 26	18 36		18 36	18 46	18 48	18 51	18 56	19 01	19 00	19 06		19 12	19 16	19 21
Cardiff Bay	a			18 16			18 28				18 40		18 52				19 04			19 16		
Cardiff Central ■	a	18 09	18 20		18 22	18 24		18 29	18 39	18 50		18 52		18 54	18 59	19 06		19 10	19 22		19 22	19 24
	d	18 10	18 21			18 25		18 31	18 41	18 51				18 55	19 01							19 25
Grangetown	d	18 14				18 29		18 35	18 45					18 59	19 05							19 29
Dingle Road	d							18 41							19 11							
Penarth	a							18 46							19 16							
Cogan	d	18 18				18 33			18 48					19 03								19 33
Eastbrook	d	18 20				18 35			18 51					19 05								19 35
Dinas Powys	d	18 22				18 37			18 53					19 07								19 37
Cadoxton	d	18 27				18 42			18 57					19 12								19 42
Barry Docks	d	18 30				18 45			19 00					19 15								19 45
Barry ■	d	18 34				18 49			19 05					19 19								19 49
Barry Island	a	18 40				18 55								19 25								19 55
Rhoose Cardiff Int Airport ✈	d								19 12													
Llantwit Major	d								19 22													
Bridgend	a								19 39													

Table 130

Saturdays
until 04 September

Treherbert, Aberdare, Merthyr, Pontypridd, Rhymney and Coryton - Cardiff, Penarth, Barry, Barry Island and Bridgend

		AW	AW	AW	AW	AW	AW	AW	AW	AW	AW	AW	AW	AW	AW	AW	AW	AW	AW	AW	AW	AW	AW
Treherbert	d					18 47							19 17							19 47			
Ynyswen	d					18 49							19 19							19 49			
Treorchy	d					18 51							19 21							19 51			
Ton Pentre	d					18 53							19 23							19 53			
Ystrad Rhondda	a					18 56							19 26							19 56			
	d					18 58							19 28							19 58			
Llwynypia	d					19 00							19 30							20 00			
Tonypandy	d					19 03							19 33							20 03			
Dinas Rhondda	d					19 05							19 35							20 05			
Porth	a					19 08							19 38							20 08			
	d					19 09							19 39							20 09			
Trehafod	d					19 12							19 42							20 12			
Merthyr Tydfil	d			18 38							19 08						19 38						
Pentre-bach	d			18 42							19 12						19 42						
Troed Y Rhiw	d			18 45							19 15						19 45						
Merthyr Vale	a			18 48							19 18						19 48						
	d			18 50							19 20						19 50						
Quakers Yard	d			18 55							19 25						19 55						
Aberdare ■	d							18 52														19 52	
Cwmbach	d							18 55														19 55	
Fernhill	d							18 58														19 58	
Mountain Ash	a							19 01														20 01	
	d							19 04														20 04	
Penrhiwceiber	d							19 07														20 07	
Abercynon	d			18 59				19 13			19 29				19 43		19 59					20 13	
Pontypridd ■	a			19 07		19 17		19 23			19 37		19 47		19 53		20 07			20 17		20 23	
	d			19 09		19 18		19 24			19 39		19 48		19 54		20 09			20 18		20 24	
Trefforest	d			19 12		19 21		19 27			19 42		19 51		19 57		20 12			20 21		20 27	
Trefforest Estate	d			19 16							19 46						20 16						
Taffs Well ■	d			19 20		19 28		19 34			19 50		19 58		20 04		20 20			20 28		20 34	
Radyr ■	a			19 23		19 31		19 37			19 53		20 01		20 07		20 23			20 31		20 37	
	d			19 23		19 31		19 37			19 53		20 01	20 04	20 07		20 23			20 31		20 37	
Danescourt	d													20 08									
Fairwater	d													20 10									
Waun-gron Park	d													20 12									
Ninian Park	d													20 15									
Llandaf	d			19 26		19 34		19 40			19 56		20 04		20 10		20 26			20 34		20 40	
Cathays	d			19 31		19 39		19 45			20 01		20 09		20 15		20 31			20 39		20 45	
Rhymney ■	d																		19 45				
Pontlottyn	d																		19 48				
Tir-phil	d																		19 52				
Brithdir	d																		19 55				
Bargoed	a																		19 58				
	d		18 48																19 59				
Gilfach Fargoed	d		18 50																20 01				
Pengam	d		18 53																20 04				
Hengoed	d		18 56																20 07				
Ystrad Mynach ■	d		18 59																20 10				
Llanbradach	d		19 04																20 15				
Aber	d		19 08																20 19				
Caerphilly ■	d		19 11						19 40										20 22				20 40
Lisvane & Thornhill	d		19 15						19 44										20 26				20 44
Llanishen	d		19 17						19 46										20 28				20 46
Heath High Level	d		19 20						19 49										20 31				20 49
Coryton	d																						
Whitchurch (Cardiff)	d																						
Rhiwbina	d																						
Birchgrove	d																						
Ty Glas	d																						
Heath Low Level	d																						
Cardiff Queen Street ■	a		19 24	19 35		19 44		19 49	19 54		20 04		20 14		20 19		20 34		20 39	20 44		20 49	20 54
	d	19 24	19 26	19 36	19 36	19 46	19 48	19 51	19 56	20 00	20 06	20 12	20 16		20 21	20 24	20 36	20 36	20 41	20 46	20 48	20 51	21 00
Cardiff Bay	a	19 28			19 40		19 52			20 04		20 16				20 28		20 40			20 52		
Cardiff Central ■	a		19 29	19 40		19 52		19 57	19 59		20 10		20 20	20 25	20 24		20 39		20 47	20 52		20 57	21 03
	d		19 31	19 41					20 06		20 10				20 31		20 41					21 06	21 10
Grangetown	d		19 35	19 45					20 10		20 14				20 35		20 45					21 10	21 14
Dingle Road	d		19 41						20 14						20 41							21 14	
Penarth	a		19 46						20 19						20 46							21 19	
Cogan	d			19 48							20 18						20 48						21 18
Eastbrook	d			19 51							20 20						20 51						21 20
Dinas Powys	d			19 53							20 22						20 53						21 22
Cadoxton	d			19 57							20 27						20 57						21 27
Barry Docks	d			20 00							20 30						21 00						21 30
Barry ■	d			20 05							20 34						21 05						21 34
Barry Island	a										20 40												21 41
Rhoose Cardiff Int Airport ✈	d			20 12													21 12						
Llantwit Major	d			20 22													21 22						
Bridgend	a			20 39													21 39						

Table 130

Saturdays
until 04 September

Treherbert, Aberdare, Merthyr, Pontypridd, Rhymney and Coryton - Cardiff, Penarth, Barry, Barry Island and Bridgend

		AW	AW	AW	AW	AW		AW	AW	AW	AW	AW	AW	AW	AW	AW		AW	AW	AW	AW	AW	AW	AW	AW
Treherbert	d				20 17															21 17					
Ynyswen	d				20 19															21 19					
Treorchy	d				20 21															21 21					
Ton Pentre	d				20 23															21 23					
Ystrad Rhondda	a				20 26															21 26					
	d				20 28															21 28					
Llwynypia	d				20 30															21 30					
Tonypandy	d				20 33															21 33					
Dinas Rhondda	d				20 35															21 35					
Porth	a				20 38															21 38					
	d				20 39															21 39					
Trehafod	d				20 42															21 42					
Merthyr Tydfil	d									20 38												21 38			
Pentre-bach	d									20 42												21 42			
Troed Y Rhiw	d									20 45												21 45			
Merthyr Vale	a									20 48												21 48			
	d									20 50												21 50			
Quakers Yard	d									20 55												21 55			
Aberdare 3	d					20 22								20 52											21 52
Cwmbach	d					20 25								20 55											21 55
Fernhill	d					20 28								20 58											21 58
Mountain Ash	a					20 31								21 01											22 01
	d					20 34								21 04											22 04
Penrhiwceiber	d					20 37								21 07											22 07
Abercynon	d					20 43				20 59				21 13								21 59			22 14
Pontypridd 3	a				20 47	20 53				21 07				21 23						21 47		22 07			22 23
	d				20 48	20 54				21 09				21 24						21 48		22 09			22 29
Trefforest	d				20 51	20 57				21 12				21 27						21 51		22 12			22 32
Trefforest Estate	d									21 16												22 16			
Taffs Well 3	d				20 58	21 04				21 20				21 34						21 58		22 20			22 39
Radyr 3	a				21 01	21 07				21 23				21 37						22 01		22 23			22 42
	d		21 04		21 01	21 07				21 23				21 37				22 04		22 01		22 23			22 42
Danescourt	d		21 08															22 08							
Fairwater	d		21 10															22 10							
Waun-gron Park	d		21 12															22 12							
Ninian Park	d		21 15															22 15							
Llandaf	d				21 04	21 10				21 26				21 40						22 04		22 26			22 45
Cathays	d				21 09	21 15				21 31				21 45						22 09		22 31			22 50
Rhymney 3	d											20 48													
Pontlottyn	d											20 51													
Tir-phil	d											20 55													
Brithdir	d											20 58													
Bargoed	a											21 01													
	d											21 02													
Gilfach Fargoed	d											21 04													
Pengam	d											21 07													
Hengoed	d											21 10													
Ystrad Mynach 3	d											21 13													
Llanbradach	d											21 18													
Aber	d											21 22													
Caerphilly 3	d											21 25			21 45										
Lisvane & Thornhill	d											21 29			21 50										
Llanishen	d											21 31			21 52										
Heath High Level	d											21 34			21 54										
Coryton	d																								
Whitchurch (Cardiff)	d																								
Rhiwbina	d																								
Birchgrove	d																								
Ty Glas	d																								
Heath Low Level	d																								
Cardiff Queen Street 3	a				21 14	21 19				21 34		21 39		21 49	22 00					22 14		22 34			22 54
	d	21 00		21 12	21 16	21 21		21 24		21 36	21 36	21 44	21 48	21 51	22 01	22 00			22 12	22 16	22 24	22 36	22 36	22 48	22 55
Cardiff Bay	a	21 04		21 16				21 28			21 40		21 52			22 04			22 16		22 28		22 40	22 52	
Cardiff Central 7	a		21 25		21 21	21 24				21 39		21 51		21 57	22 04			22 20		22 22		22 41			23 00
	d								21 32	21 41				22 06	22 10			22 21							23 12
Grangetown	d								21 35	21 45				22 10	22 14										23 16
Dingle Road	d								21 41					22 14											23 20
Penarth	a								21 46					22 19											23 25
Cogan	d									21 48					22 18										
Eastbrook	d									21 51					22 20										
Dinas Powys	d									21 53					22 22										
Cadoxton	d									21 57					22 27										
Barry Docks	d									22 00					22 30										
Barry 3	d									22 05					22 34										
Barry Island	a														22 40										
Rhoose Cardiff Int Airport ✈	d									22 12															
Llantwit Major	d									22 22															
Bridgend	a									22 39															

Table 130

Saturdays
until 04 September

Treherbert, Aberdare, Merthyr, Pontypridd, Rhymney and Coryton - Cardiff, Penarth, Barry, Barry Island and Bridgend

		AW		AW	AW	AW	AW	AW	AW	AW	AW
Treherbert	d										
Ynyswen	d										
Treorchy	d										
Ton Pentre	d										
Ystrad Rhondda	a										
	d										
Llwynypia	d										
Tonypandy	d										
Dinas Rhondda	d										
Porth	a										
	d										
Trehafod	d										
Merthyr Tydfil	d							22 38			
Pentre-bach	d							22 42			
Troed Y Rhiw	d							22 45			
Merthyr Vale	a							22 48			
	d							22 50			
Quakers Yard	d							22 55			
Aberdare 3	d								22 52		
Cwmbach	d								22 55		
Fernhill	d								22 58		
Mountain Ash	a								23 01		
	d								23 04		
Penrhiwceiber	d								23 07		
Abercynon	d							22 59	23 13		
Pontypridd 3	a							23 07	23 23		
	d							23 09			
Trefforest	d							23 12			
Trefforest Estate	d										
Taffs Well 3	d							23 20			
Radyr 3	a							23 23			
	d					23 10		23 23			
Danescourt	d										
Fairwater	d										
Waun-gron Park	d										
Ninian Park	d										
Llandaf	d					23 12		23 26			
Cathays	d					23 16		23 31			
Rhymney 3	d										
Pontlottyn	d										
Tir-phil	d										
Brithdir	d										
Bargoed	a										
	d										
Gilfach Fargoed	d										
Pengam	d										
Hengoed	d										
Ystrad Mynach 3	d										
Llanbradach	d										
Aber	d										
Caerphilly 3	d										
Lisvane & Thornhill	d										
Llanishen	d										
Heath High Level	d										
Coryton	d	22 45									
Whitchurch (Cardiff)	d	22 46									
Rhiwbina	d	22 48									
Birchgrove	d	22 50									
Ty Glas	d	22 51									
Heath Low Level	d	22 54									
Cardiff Queen Street 3	a	22 59				23 19		23 34			
	d	23 01		23 00	23 12	23 20	23 24	23 36		23 36	23 48
Cardiff Bay	a			23 04	23 16		23 28			23 40	23 52
Cardiff Central 7	a	23 06				23 25		23 42			
	d					23 30					
Grangetown	d					23 34					
Dingle Road	d										
Penarth	a										
Cogan	d					23 37					
Eastbrook	d					23 40					
Dinas Powys	d					23 42					
Cadoxton	d					23 46					
Barry Docks	d					23 49					
Barry 3	d					23 54					
Barry Island	a					23 59					
Rhoose Cardiff Int Airport ✈	d										
Llantwit Major	d										
Bridgend	a										

Table 130

Saturdays from 11 September

Treherbert, Aberdare, Merthyr, Pontypridd, Rhymney and Coryton - Cardiff, Penarth, Barry, Barry Island and Bridgend

		AW	AW	AW	AW	AW	AW	AW	AW	AW		AW	AW
Treherbert	d											05 47	
Ynyswen	d											05 49	
Treorchy	d											05 51	
Ton Pentre	d											05 53	
Ystrad Rhondda	a											05 56	
	d											05 58	
Llwynypia	d											06 00	
Tonypandy	d											06 03	
Dinas Rhondda	d											06 05	
Porth	a											06 08	
	d											06 09	
Trehafod	d											06 12	
Merthyr Tydfil	d												
Pentre-bach	d												
Troed Y Rhiw	d												
Merthyr Vale	a												
	d												
Quakers Yard	d												
Aberdare	d												
Cwmbach	d												
Fernhill	d												
Mountain Ash	a												
	d												
Penrhiwceiber	d												
Abercynon	d												
Pontypridd	a											06 17	
	d				05 24							06 18	
Trefforest	d				05 27							06 21	
Trefforest Estate	d				05 31							06 25	
Taffs Well	d				05 34							06 28	
Radyr	a				05 37							06 31	
	d				05 37							06 31	
Danescourt	d												
Fairwater	d												
Waun-gron Park	d												
Ninian Park	d												
Llandaf	d				05 40							06 34	
Cathays	d				05 45							06 39	
Rhymney	d												
Pontlottyn	d												
Tir-phil	d												
Brithdir	d												
Bargoed	a												
	d												
Gilfach Fargoed	d												
Pengam	d												
Hengoed	d												
Ystrad Mynach	d												
Llanbradach	d												
Aber	d												
Caerphilly	d							06 10					
Lisvane & Thornhill	d							06 14					
Llanishen	d							06 16					
Heath High Level	d							06 19					
Coryton	d												
Whitchurch (Cardiff)	d												
Rhiwbina	d												
Birchgrove	d												
Ty Glas	d												
Heath Low Level	d												
Cardiff Queen Street	a				05 48			06 25				06 44	
	d				05 51			06 26	06 36			06 44	06 48
Cardiff Bay	a								06 40				06 52
Cardiff Central	a				05 54			06 29				06 48	
	d	05 20	05 41	05 46	05 55	06 16	06 25	06 41		06 36			
Grangetown	d	05 24	05 45	05 50	05 59	06 20	06 29	06 45		06 40			
Dingle Road	d			05 54		06 24				06 44			
Penarth	a			06 00		06 29				06 50			
Cogan	d	05 28	05 48		06 03		06 33	06 48					
Eastbrook	d	05 30	05 51		06 05		06 35	06 51					
Dinas Powys	d	05 32	05 53		06 07		06 37	06 53					
Cadoxton	d	05 37	05 57		06 12		06 42	06 57					
Barry Docks	d	05 40	06 00		06 15		06 45	07 00					
Barry	d	05 44	06 05		06 19		06 49	07 05					
Barry Island	a	05 51			06 26		06 56						
Rhoose Cardiff Int Airport ✈	d		06 12					07 12					
Llantwit Major	d		06 22					07 22					
Bridgend	a		06 40					07 40					

		AW A	AW B	AW	AW	AW	AW	AW		AW	AW	AW	AW
Treherbert	d							06 17					
Ynyswen	d							06 19					
Treorchy	d							06 21					
Ton Pentre	d							06 23					
Ystrad Rhondda	a							06 26					
	d							06 28					
Llwynypia	d							06 30					
Tonypandy	d							06 33					
Dinas Rhondda	d							06 35					
Porth	a							06 38					
	d							06 39					
Trehafod	d							06 42					
Merthyr Tydfil	d												06 38
Pentre-bach	d												06 42
Troed Y Rhiw	d												06 45
Merthyr Vale	a												06 48
	d												06 50
Quakers Yard	d												06 55
Aberdare	d										06 21		
Cwmbach	d										06 24		
Fernhill	d										06 28		
Mountain Ash	a										06 31		
	d										06 34		
Penrhiwceiber	d										06 38		
Abercynon	d										06 44		06 59
Pontypridd	a							06 47			06 53		07 07
	d							06 48			06 54		07 09
Trefforest	d							06 51			06 57		07 12
Trefforest Estate	d										07 01		07 16
Taffs Well	d							06 58		06 53	07 04		07 20
Radyr	a							07 01		06 56	07 07		07 23
	d							07 01		07 04	07 07		07 23
Danescourt	d									07 08			
Fairwater	d									07 10			
Waun-gron Park	d									07 12			
Ninian Park	d									07 15			
Llandaf	d							07 04			07 10		07 26
Cathays	d							07 09			07 15		07 31
Rhymney	d												
Pontlottyn	d												
Tir-phil	d												
Brithdir	d												
Bargoed	a												
	d												
Gilfach Fargoed	d												
Pengam	d												
Hengoed	d												
Ystrad Mynach	d												
Llanbradach	d												
Aber	d												
Caerphilly	d												
Lisvane & Thornhill	d												
Llanishen	d												
Heath High Level	d												
Coryton	d												
Whitchurch (Cardiff)	d												
Rhiwbina	d												
Birchgrove	d												
Ty Glas	d												
Heath Low Level	d												
Cardiff Queen Street	a							07 14			07 20		07 35
	d			07 00			07 12	07 16			07 21	07 24	07 36
Cardiff Bay	a			07 04			07 16					07 28	
Cardiff Central	a	06 54	06 54					07 18		07 20	07 24		07 39
	d	06 55	06 55		07 01	07 10				07 21	07 25		07 41
Grangetown	d	06 59	06 59		07 05	07 14					07 29		07 45
Dingle Road	d				07 11								
Penarth	a				07 17								
Cogan	d	07 03	07 03			07 18					07 33		07 48
Eastbrook	d	07 05	07 05			07 20					07 35		07 51
Dinas Powys	d	07 07	07 07			07 22					07 37		07 53
Cadoxton	d	07 12	07 12			07 27					07 42		07 57
Barry Docks	d	07 15	07 15			07 30					07 45		08 00
Barry	d	07 19	07 19			07 34					07 49		08 05
Barry Island	a	07 25	07 26			07 41					07 56		
Rhoose Cardiff Int Airport ✈	d												08 12
Llantwit Major	d												08 22
Bridgend	a												08 40

A 11 September

B not 11 September

Table 130

Saturdays from 11 September

Treherbert, Aberdare, Merthyr, Pontypridd, Rhymney and Coryton - Cardiff, Penarth, Barry, Barry Island and Bridgend

		AW	AW	AW	AW	AW		AW	AW	AW	AW	AW	AW
Treherbert	d				06 47								
Ynyswen	d				06 49								
Treorchy	d				06 51								
Ton Pentre	d				06 53								
Ystrad Rhondda	a				06 56								
	d				06 58								
Llwynypia	d				07 00								
Tonypandy	d				07 03								
Dinas Rhondda	d				07 05								
Porth	a				07 08								
	d				07 09								
Trehafod	d				07 12								
Merthyr Tydfil	d										07 08		
Pentre-bach	d										07 12		
Troed Y Rhiw	d										07 15		
Merthyr Vale	a										07 18		
	d										07 20		
Quakers Yard	d										07 25		
Aberdare	d							06 51					
Cwmbach	d							06 54					
Fernhill	d							06 58					
Mountain Ash	a							07 01					
	d							07 04					
Penrhiwceiber	d							07 08					
Abercynon	d							07 14			07 29		
Pontypridd	a				07 17			07 23			07 37		
	d				07 18			07 24			07 39		
Trefforest	d				07 21			07 27			07 42		
Trefforest Estate	d										07 46		
Taffs Well	d				07 28			07 34			07 50		
Radyr	a				07 31			07 37			07 53		
	d			07 34	07 31			07 37			07 53		08 04
Danescourt	d			07 38									08 08
Fairwater	d			07 40									08 10
Waun-gron Park	d			07 42									08 12
Ninian Park	d			07 45									08 15
Llandaf	d				07 34			07 40			07 56		
Cathays	d				07 39			07 45			08 01		
Rhymney	d								07 02				
Pontlottyn	d								07 05				
Tir-phil	d								07 09				
Brithdir	d								07 12				
Bargoed	a								07 15				
	d		07 02						07 17			07 32	
Gilfach Fargoed	d		07 04						07 19				
Pengam	d		07 07						07 22			07 37	
Hengoed	d		07 10						07 25			07 40	
Ystrad Mynach	d		07 13						07 28			07 43	
Llanbradach	d		07 18						07 33			07 48	
Aber	d		07 22						07 37			07 52	
Caerphilly	d		07 25						07 40			07 55	
Lisvane & Thornhill	d		07 29						07 44			07 59	
Llanishen	d		07 31						07 46			08 01	
Heath High Level	d		07 34						07 49			08 04	
Coryton	d												
Whitchurch (Cardiff)	d												
Rhiwbina	d												
Birchgrove	d												
Ty Glas	d												
Heath Low Level	d												
Cardiff Queen Street	a		07 39		07 44			07 49	07 54		08 04	08 09	
	d	07 36	07 41		07 46	07 48		07 51	07 56	08 00	08 06	08 11	
Cardiff Bay	a	07 40				07 52				08 04			
Cardiff Central	a		07 44	07 50	07 53			07 54	07 59		08 09	08 14	08 20
	d		07 46	07 51				07 55	08 01		08 10	08 16	08 21
Grangetown	d		07 50					07 59	08 05		08 14	08 20	
Dingle Road	d		07 56						08 11			08 26	
Penarth	a		08 02						08 17			08 32	
Cogan	d							08 03			08 18		
Eastbrook	d							08 05			08 20		
Dinas Powys	d							08 07			08 22		
Cadoxton	d							08 12			08 27		
Barry Docks	d							08 15			08 30		
Barry	d							08 19			08 34		
Barry Island	a							08 26			08 41		
Rhoose Cardiff Int Airport ✈	d												
Llantwit Major	d												
Bridgend	a												

		AW	AW	AW		AW	AW	AW	AW	AW	AW	AW	AW
Treherbert	d		07 17									07 45	
Ynyswen	d		07 19									07 47	
Treorchy	d		07 21									07 49	
Ton Pentre	d		07 23									07 51	
Ystrad Rhondda	a		07 26									07 54	
	d		07 28									07 58	
Llwynypia	d		07 30									08 00	
Tonypandy	d		07 33									08 03	
Dinas Rhondda	d		07 35									08 05	
Porth	a		07 38									08 08	
	d		07 39									08 09	
Trehafod	d		07 42									08 12	
Merthyr Tydfil	d							07 38					
Pentre-bach	d							07 42					
Troed Y Rhiw	d							07 45					
Merthyr Vale	a							07 48					
	d							07 50					
Quakers Yard	d							07 55					
Aberdare	d			07 21									
Cwmbach	d			07 24									
Fernhill	d			07 28									
Mountain Ash	a			07 31									
	d			07 34									
Penrhiwceiber	d			07 38									
Abercynon	d			07 44				07 59					
Pontypridd	a		07 47	07 53				08 07				08 17	
	d		07 48	07 54				08 09				08 18	
Trefforest	d		07 51	07 57				08 12				08 21	
Trefforest Estate	d							08 16					
Taffs Well	d		07 58	08 04				08 20				08 28	
Radyr	a		08 01	08 07				08 23				08 31	
	d		08 01	08 07				08 23			08 34	08 31	
Danescourt	d										08 38		
Fairwater	d										08 40		
Waun-gron Park	d										08 42		
Ninian Park	d										08 45		
Llandaf	d		08 04	08 10				08 26				08 34	
Cathays	d		08 09	08 15				08 31				08 39	
Rhymney	d						07 24			07 44			
Pontlottyn	d						07 27			07 47			
Tir-phil	d						07 31			07 51			
Brithdir	d						07 34			07 54			
Bargoed	a						07 37			08 00			
	d						07 45			08 02			
Gilfach Fargoed	d						07 47						
Pengam	d						07 50			08 07			
Hengoed	d						07 54			08 10			
Ystrad Mynach	d						07 57			08 13			
Llanbradach	d						08 02			08 18			
Aber	d						08 07			08 22			
Caerphilly	d						08 10			08 25			
Lisvane & Thornhill	d						08 14			08 29			
Llanishen	d						08 16			08 31			
Heath High Level	d						08 19			08 34			
Coryton	d												
Whitchurch (Cardiff)	d												
Rhiwbina	d												
Birchgrove	d												
Ty Glas	d												
Heath Low Level	d												
Cardiff Queen Street	a		08 14	08 19			08 24	08 34		08 39		08 44	
	d	08 12	08 16	08 21		08 24	08 26	08 36	08 36	08 41		08 46	08 48
Cardiff Bay	a	08 16				08 28			08 40				08 52
Cardiff Central	a		08 23	08 24			08 29	08 39		08 48	08 50	08 53	
	d			08 25			08 31	08 41			08 51		
Grangetown	d			08 29			08 35	08 45					
Dingle Road	d						08 41						
Penarth	a						08 47						
Cogan	d			08 33				08 48					
Eastbrook	d			08 35				08 51					
Dinas Powys	d			08 37				08 53					
Cadoxton	d			08 42				08 57					
Barry Docks	d			08 45				09 00					
Barry	d			08 49				09 05					
Barry Island	a			08 56									
Rhoose Cardiff Int Airport ✈	d							09 12					
Llantwit Major	d							09 22					
Bridgend	a							09 40					

Table 130

Saturdays
from 11 September

Treherbert, Aberdare, Merthyr, Pontypridd, Rhymney and Coryton - Cardiff, Penarth, Barry, Barry Island and Bridgend

		AW	AW	AW	AW	AW	AW	AW	AW	AW	AW	AW	AW	AW	AW	AW	AW	AW	AW	AW	AW	AW
Treherbert	d								08 17							08 47						
Ynyswen	d								08 19							08 49						
Treorchy	d								08 21							08 51						
Ton Pentre	d								08 23							08 53						
Ystrad Rhondda	a								08 26							08 56						
	d								08 28							08 58						
Llwynypia	d								08 30							09 00						
Tonypandy	d								08 33							09 03						
Dinas Rhondda	d								08 35							09 05						
Porth	a								08 38							09 08						
	d								08 39							09 09						
Trehafod	d								08 42							09 12						
Merthyr Tydfil	d				08 08								08 38								09 08	
Pentre-bach	d				08 12								08 42								09 12	
Troed Y Rhiw	d				08 15								08 45								09 15	
Merthyr Vale	a				08 18								08 48								09 18	
	d				08 20								08 50								09 20	
Quakers Yard	d				08 25								08 55								09 25	
Aberdare ■	d	07 51								08 21								08 51				
Cwmbach	d	07 54								08 24								08 54				
Fernhill	d	07 58								08 28								08 58				
Mountain Ash	a	08 01								08 31								09 01				
	d	08 04								08 34								09 04				
Penrhiwceiber	d	08 08								08 38								09 08				
Abercynon	d	08 14			08 29					08 44			08 59					09 14			09 29	
Pontypridd ■	a	08 23			08 37				08 47	08 53			09 07			09 17		09 23			09 37	
	d	08 24			08 39				08 48	08 54			09 09			09 18		09 24			09 39	
Trefforest	d	08 27			08 42				08 51	08 57			09 12			09 21		09 27			09 42	
Trefforest Estate	d				08 46								09 16								09 46	
Taffs Well ■	d	08 34			08 50				08 58	09 04			09 20			09 28		09 34			09 50	
Radyr ■	a	08 37			08 53				09 01	09 07			09 23			09 31		09 37			09 53	
	d	08 37			08 53		09 04		09 01	09 07			09 23	09 34		09 31		09 37			09 53	
Danescourt	d						09 08							09 38								
Fairwater	d						09 10							09 40								
Waun-gron Park	d						09 12							09 42								
Ninian Park	d						09 15							09 45								
Llandaf	d	08 40			08 56				09 04	09 10			09 26			09 34		09 40			09 56	
Cathays	d	08 45			09 01				09 09	09 15			09 31			09 39		09 45			10 01	
Rhymney ■	d											08 30										
Pontlottyn	d											08 33										
Tir-phil	d											08 37										
Brithdir	d											08 40										
Bargoed	a											08 44										
	d		08 17			08 32						08 47										09 25
Gilfach Fargoed	d		08 19																			09 27
Pengam	d		08 22			08 37						08 52										09 30
Hengoed	d		08 25			08 40						08 55										09 33
Ystrad Mynach ■	d		08 28			08 43						08 58							09 28			09b43
Llanbradach	d		08 33			08 48						09 03							09 33			09 48
Aber	d		08 37			08 52						09 07							09 37			09 52
Caerphilly ■	d		08 40			08 55						09 10							09 40			09 55
Lisvane & Thornhill	d		08 44			08 59						09 14							09 44			09 59
Llanishen	d		08 46			09 01						09 16							09 46			10 01
Heath High Level	d		08 49			09 04						09 19							09 49			10 04
Coryton	d																					
Whitchurch (Cardiff)	d																					
Rhiwbina	d																					
Birchgrove	d																					
Ty Glas	d																					
Heath Low Level	d																					
Cardiff Queen Street ■	a	08 49	08 54		09 04	09 09			09 14	09 19		09 24	09 34			09 44		09 49	09 54		10 04	10 09
	d	08 51	08 56	09 00	09 06	09 11		09 12	09 16	09 21	09 24	09 26	09 36		09 36	09 46	09 48	09 51	09 56	10 00	10 06	10 11
Cardiff Bay	a			09 04				09 16			09 28				09 40		09 52			10 04		
Cardiff Central ■	a	08 54	08 59		09 09	09 14	09 20		09 23	09 24		09 29	09 39	09 50		09 53		09 54	09 59		10 09	10 14
	d	08 55	09 01		09 10	09 16	09 21			09 25		09 31	09 41	09 51				09 55	10 01		10 10	10 16
Grangetown	d	08 59	09 05		09 14	09 20				09 29		09 35	09 45					09 59	10 05		10 14	10 20
Dingle Road	d		09 11			09 26						09 41							10 11			10 26
Penarth	a		09 17			09 32						09 47							10 17			10 32
Cogan	d	09 03			09 18					09 33			09 48					10 03			10 18	
Eastbrook	d	09 05			09 20					09 35			09 51					10 05			10 20	
Dinas Powys	d	09 07			09 22					09 37			09 53					10 07			10 22	
Cadoxton	d	09 12			09 27					09 42			09 57					10 12			10 27	
Barry Docks	d	09 15			09 30					09 45			10 00					10 15			10 30	
Barry ■	d	09 19			09 34					09 49			10 05					10 19			10 34	
Barry Island	a	09 26			09 41					09 56								10 26			10 41	
Rhoose Cardiff Int Airport ✈	d												10 12									
Llantwit Major	d												10 22									
Bridgend	a												10 40									

b arr. 0936

Table 130

Saturdays
from 11 September

Treherbert, Aberdare, Merthyr, Pontypridd, Rhymney and Coryton - Cardiff, Penarth, Barry, Barry Island and Bridgend

		AW	AW	AW	AW	AW	AW	AW	AW	AW	AW	AW	AW	AW	AW	AW	AW	AW	AW	AW	AW	AW	AW
Treherbert	d			09 17								09 47											
Ynyswen	d			09 19								09 49											
Treorchy	d			09 21								09 51											
Ton Pentre	d			09 23								09 53											
Ystrad Rhondda	a			09 26								09 56											
	d			09 28								09 58											
Llwynypia	d			09 30								10 00											
Tonypandy	d			09 33								10 03											
Dinas Rhondda	d			09 35								10 05											
Porth	a			09 38								10 08											
	d			09 39								10 09											
Trehafod	d			09 42								10 12											
Merthyr Tydfil	d							09 38							10 04								
Pentre-bach	d							09 42							10 08								
Troed Y Rhiw	d							09 45							10 11								
Merthyr Vale	a							09 48							10 14								
	d							09 50							10 16								
Quakers Yard	d							09 55							10 22								
Aberdare ■	d				09 21									09 51							10 21		
Cwmbach	d				09 24									09 54							10 24		
Fernhill	d				09 28									09 58							10 28		
Mountain Ash	a				09 31									10 01							10 31		
	d				09 34									10 04							10 34		
Penrhiwceiber	d				09 38									10 08							10 38		
Abercynon	d				09 44			09 59						10 14	10 26						10 44		
Pontypridd ■	a			09 47	09 53			10 07				10 17		10 23	10 32						10 53		
	d			09 48	09 54			10 09				10 18		10 24			10 39				10 54		
Trefforest	d			09 51	09 57			10 12				10 21		10 27			10 42				10 57		
Trefforest Estate	d							10 16									10 46						
Taffs Well ■	d			09 58	10 04			10 20				10 28		10 34			10 50				11 04		
Radyr ■	a			10 01	10 07			10 23				10 31		10 37			10 53				11 07		
	d	10 04		10 01	10 07			10 23			10 34	10 31		10 37			10 53		11 04		11 07		
Danescourt	d	10 08									10 38								11 08				
Fairwater	d	10 10									10 40								11 10				
Waun-gron Park	d	10 12									10 42								11 12				
Ninian Park	d	10 15									10 45								11 15				
Llandaf	d			10 04	10 10			10 26				10 34		10 40			10 56				11 10		
Cathays	d			10 09	10 15			10 31				10 39		10 45			11 01				11 15		
Rhymney ■	d						09 29																10 29
Pontlottyn	d						09 32																10 32
Tir-phil	d						09 36																10 36
Brithdir	d						09 39																10 39
Bargoed	a						09 42																10 42
	d						09 47			10 02								10 25					10 47
Gilfach Fargoed	d																	10 27					
Pengam	d						09 52			10 07								10 30					10 52
Hengoed	d						09 55			10 10								10 33					10 55
Ystrad Mynach ■	d						09 58			10 13								10b43					10 58
Llanbradach	d						10 03			10 18								10 48					11 03
Aber	d						10 07			10 22								10 52					11 07
Caerphilly ■	d						10 10			10 25								10 55					11 10
Lisvane & Thornhill	d						10 14			10 29								10 59					11 14
Llanishen	d						10 16			10 31								11 01					11 16
Heath High Level	d						10 19			10 34								11 04					11 19
Coryton	d																						
Whitchurch (Cardiff)	d																						
Rhiwbina	d																						
Birchgrove	d																						
Ty Glas	d																						
Heath Low Level	d																						
Cardiff Queen Street ■	a			10 14	10 19		10 24	10 34		10 39		10 44		10 49			11 04	11 09			11 19		11 24
	d		10 12	10 16	10 21	10 24	10 26	10 36	10 36	10 41		10 46	10 48	10 51		11 00	11 06	11 11		11 12	11 21	11 24	11 26
Cardiff Bay	a		10 16			10 28			10 40				10 52			11 04				11 16		11 28	
Cardiff Central ■	a	10 20		10 23	10 24		10 29	10 39		10 44	10 50	10 53		10 54			11 09	11 14	11 20		11 24		11 29
	d	10 21			10 25		10 31	10 41		10 46	10 51			10 55			11 10	11 16	11 21		11 25		11 31
Grangetown	d				10 29		10 35	10 45		10 50				10 59			11 14	11 20			11 29		11 35
Dingle Road	d						10 41			10 56								11 26					11 41
Penarth	a						10 47			11 02								11 32					11 47
Cogan	d				10 33			10 48						11 03			11 18				11 33		
Eastbrook	d				10 35			10 51						11 05			11 20				11 35		
Dinas Powys	d				10 37			10 53						11 07			11 22				11 37		
Cadoxton	d				10 42			10 57						11 12			11 27				11 42		
Barry Docks	d				10 45			11 00						11 15			11 30				11 45		
Barry ■	d				10 49			11 05						11 19			11 34				11 49		
Barry Island	a				10 56									11 26			11 41				11 56		
Rhoose Cardiff Int Airport ✈	d							11 12															
Llantwit Major	d							11 22															
Bridgend	a							11 40															

b arr. 1036

Table 130

Saturdays from 11 September

Treherbert, Aberdare, Merthyr, Pontypridd, Rhymney and Coryton - Cardiff, Penarth, Barry, Barry Island and Bridgend

		AW	AW	AW		AW	AW	AW	AW	AW	AW	AW	AW	AW		AW	AW	AW	AW	AW	AW	AW	AW	AW
Treherbert	d	10 17						10 47										11 17						
Ynyswen	d	10 19						10 49										11 19						
Treorchy	d	10 21						10 51										11 21						
Ton Pentre	d	10 23						10 53										11 23						
Ystrad Rhondda	a	10 26						10 56										11 26						
	d	10 28						10 58										11 28						
Llwynypia	d	10 30						11 00										11 30						
Tonypandy	d	10 33						11 03										11 33						
Dinas Rhondda	d	10 35						11 05										11 35						
Porth	a	10 38						11 08										11 38						
	d	10 52						11 09										11 39						
Trehafod	d	10 55						11 12										11 42						
Merthyr Tydfil	d		10 38										11 08									11 38		
Pentre-bach	d		10 42										11 12									11 42		
Troed Y Rhiw	d		10 45										11 15									11 45		
Merthyr Vale	a		10 48										11 18									11 48		
	d		10 50										11 20									11 50		
Quakers Yard	d		10 55										11 25									11 55		
Aberdare ■	d									10 51									11 21					
Cwmbach	d									10 54									11 24					
Fernhill	d									10 58									11 28					
Mountain Ash	a									11 01									11 31					
	d									11 04									11 34					
Penrhiwceiber	d									11 08									11 38					
Abercynon	d		10 59							11 14			11 29						11 44			11 59		
Pontypridd ■	a	11 00	11 08					11 17		11 23			11 37					11 47	11 53			12 07		
	d	11 04	11 09					11 18		11 24			11 39					11 48	11 54			12 09		
Trefforest	d	11 07	11 12					11 21		11 27			11 42					11 51	11 57			12 12		
Trefforest Estate	d		11 16										11 46									12 16		
Taffs Well ■	d	11 13	11 20					11 28		11 34			11 50					11 58	12 04			12 20		
Radyr ■	a	11 17	11 23					11 31		11 37			11 53					12 01	12 07			12 23		
	d	11 17	11 23				11 34	11 31		11 37			11 53			12 04		12 01	12 07			12 23		
Danescourt	d						11 38									12 08								
Fairwater	d						11 40									12 10								
Waun-gron Park	d						11 42									12 12								
Ninian Park	d						11 45									12 15								
Llandaf	d		11 26					11 34		11 40			11 56					12 04	12 10			12 26		
Cathays	d		11 31					11 39		11 45			12 01					12 09	12 15			12 31		
Rhymney ■	d																				11 29			
Pontlottyn	d																				11 32			
Tir-phil	d																				11 36			
Brithdir	d																				11 39			
Bargoed	a																				11 42			
	d					11 02								11 25							11 47			12 02
Gilfach Fargoed	d													11 27										
Pengam	d					11 07								11 30							11 52			12 07
Hengoed	d					11 10								11 33							11 55			12 10
Ystrad Mynach ■	d					11 13					11 28			11b43							11 58			12 13
Llanbradach	d					11 18					11 33			11 48							12 03			12 18
Aber	d					11 22					11 37			11 52							12 07			12 22
Caerphilly ■	d					11 25					11 40			11 55							12 10			12 25
Lisvane & Thornhill	d					11 29					11 44			11 59							12 14			12 29
Llanishen	d					11 31					11 46			12 01							12 16			12 31
Heath High Level	d					11 34					11 49			12 04							12 19			12 34
Coryton	d																							
Whitchurch (Cardiff)	d																							
Rhiwbina	d																							
Birchgrove	d																							
Ty Glas	d																							
Heath Low Level	d																							
Cardiff Queen Street ■	a		11 34			11 39		11 44		11 49	11 54		12 04	12 09				12 14	12 19		12 24	12 34		12 39
	d		11 36	11 36		11 41		11 46	11 48	11 51	11 56	12 00	12 06	12 11			12 12	12 16	12 21	12 24	12 26	12 36	12 36	12 41
Cardiff Bay	a			11 40					11 52			12 04					12 16			12 28			12 40	
Cardiff Central ■	a	11 34	11 39			11 44	11 50	11 53		11 54	11 59		12 09	12 14		12 20		12 23	12 24		12 29	12 39		12 44
	d		11 41			11 46	11 51			11 55	12 01		12 10	12 16		12 21			12 25		12 31	12 41		12 46
Grangetown	d		11 45			11 50				11 59	12 05		12 14	12 20					12 29		12 35	12 45		12 50
Dingle Road	d					11 56					12 11			12 26							12 41			12 56
Penarth	a					12 02					12 17			12 32							12 47			13 02
Cogan	d		11 48							12 03			12 18						12 33			12 48		
Eastbrook	d		11 51							12 05			12 20						12 35			12 51		
Dinas Powys	d		11 53							12 07			12 22						12 37			12 53		
Cadoxton	d		11 57							12 12			12 27						12 42			12 57		
Barry Docks	d		12 00							12 15			12 30						12 45			13 00		
Barry ■	d		12 05							12 19			12 34						12 49			13 05		
Barry Island	a									12 26			12 41						12 56					
Rhoose Cardiff Int Airport ✈	d		12 12																			13 12		
Llantwit Major	d		12 22																			13 22		
Bridgend	a		12 40																			13 40		

b arr. 1136

Table 130

Saturdays from 11 September

Treherbert, Aberdare, Merthyr, Pontypridd, Rhymney and Coryton - Cardiff, Penarth, Barry, Barry Island and Bridgend

		AW	AW	AW	AW	AW	AW	AW	AW	AW		AW	AW	AW	AW	AW	AW	AW	AW	AW		AW	AW	AW	AW
Treherbert	d		11 47									12 17								12 47					
Ynyswen	d		11 49									12 19								12 49					
Treorchy	d		11 51									12 21								12 51					
Ton Pentre	d		11 53									12 23								12 53					
Ystrad Rhondda	a		11 56									12 26								12 56					
	d		11 58									12 28								12 58					
Llwynypia	d		12 00									12 30								13 00					
Tonypandy	d		12 03									12 33								13 03					
Dinas Rhondda	d		12 05									12 35								13 05					
Porth	a		12 08									12 38								13 08					
	d		12 09									12 39								13 09					
Trehafod	d		12 12									12 42								13 12					
Merthyr Tydfil	d						12 08									12 38									
Pentre-bach	d						12 12									12 42									
Troed Y Rhiw	d						12 15									12 45									
Merthyr Vale	a						12 18									12 48									
	d						12 20									12 50									
Quakers Yard	d						12 25									12 55									
Aberdare ■	d												12 21										12 51		
Cwmbach	d												12 24										12 54		
Fernhill	d												12 28										12 58		
Mountain Ash	a												12 31										13 01		
	d												12 34										13 04		
Penrhiwceiber	d												12 38										13 08		
Abercynon	d						12 29						12 44			12 59							13 14		
Pontypridd ■	a		12 17				12 37					12 48	12 53			13 07				13 17			13 23		
	d		12 18				12 39					12 48	12 54			13 09				13 18			13 24		
Trefforest	d		12 21				12 42					12 51	12 57			13 12				13 21			13 27		
Trefforest Estate	d						12 46									13 16									
Taffs Well ■	d		12 28				12 50					12 58	13 04			13 20				13 28			13 34		
Radyr ■	a		12 31				12 53					13 01	13 07			13 23				13 31			13 37		
	d	12 34	12 31				12 53		13 04			13 01	13 07			13 23			13 34	13 31			13 37		
Danescourt	d	12 38							13 08										13 38						
Fairwater	d	12 40							13 10										13 40						
Waun-gron Park	d	12 42							13 12										13 42						
Ninian Park	d	12 45							13 15										13 45						
Llandaf	d		12 34				12 56					13 04	13 10			13 26				13 34			13 40		
Cathays	d		12 39				13 01					13 09	13 15			13 31				13 39			13 45		
Rhymney ■	d														12 29										
Pontlottyn	d														12 32										
Tir-phil	d														12 36										
Brithdir	d														12 39										
Bargoed	a														12 42										
	d							12 25							12 47			13 02							
Gilfach Fargoed	d							12 27																	
Pengam	d							12 30							12 52			13 07							
Hengoed	d							12 33							12 55			13 10							
Ystrad Mynach ■	d				12 28			12b43							12 58			13 13						13 28	
Llanbradach	d				12 33			12 48							13 03			13 18						13 33	
Aber	d				12 37			12 52							13 07			13 22						13 37	
Caerphilly ■	d				12 40			12 55							13 10			13 25						13 40	
Lisvane & Thornhill	d				12 44			12 59							13 14			13 29						13 44	
Llanishen	d				12 46			13 01							13 16			13 31						13 46	
Heath High Level	d				12 49			13 04							13 19			13 34						13 49	
Coryton	d																								
Whitchurch (Cardiff)	d																								
Rhiwbina	d																								
Birchgrove	d																								
Ty Glas	d																								
Heath Low Level	d																								
Cardiff Queen Street ■	a		12 44		12 54		13 04	13 09				13 14	13 19		13 24	13 34		13 39		13 44			13 49	13 54	
	d		12 46	12 48	12 56	13 00	13 06	13 11		13 12		13 16	13 21	13 24	13 26	13 36	13 36	13 41		13 46		13 48	13 51	13 56	14 00
Cardiff Bay	a			12 52		13 04				13 16				13 28			13 40					13 52			14 04
Cardiff Central ■	a	12 50	12 52		12 59		13 09	13 14	13 20			13 23	13 24		13 29	13 39		13 44	13 50	13 53			13 54	13 59	
	d	12 51	12 55		13 01		13 10	13 16	13 21				13 25		13 31	13 41		13 46	13 51				13 55	14 01	
Grangetown	d		12 59		13 05		13 14	13 20					13 29		13 35	13 45		13 50					13 59	14 05	
Dingle Road	d				13 11			13 26							13 41			13 56						14 11	
Penarth	a				13 17			13 32							13 47			14 02						14 17	
Cogan	d		13 03				13 18						13 33			13 48							14 03		
Eastbrook	d		13 05				13 20						13 35			13 51							14 05		
Dinas Powys	d		13 07				13 22						13 37			13 53							14 07		
Cadoxton	d		13 12				13 27						13 42			13 57							14 12		
Barry Docks	d		13 15				13 30						13 45			14 00							14 15		
Barry ■	d		13 19				13 34						13 49			14 05							14 19		
Barry Island	a		13 26				13 41						13 56										14 26		
Rhoose Cardiff Int Airport ✈	d															14 12									
Llantwit Major	d															14 22									
Bridgend	a															14 40									

b arr. 1236

Table 130

Saturdays
from 11 September

Treherbert, Aberdare, Merthyr, Pontypridd, Rhymney and Coryton - Cardiff, Penarth, Barry, Barry Island and Bridgend

		AW	AW	AW	AW	AW	AW	AW	AW	AW	AW	AW	AW	AW	AW	AW	AW	AW	AW	AW	AW	AW	AW
Treherbert	d					13 17								13 47									
Ynyswen	d					13 19								13 49									
Treorchy	d					13 21								13 51									
Ton Pentre	d					13 23								13 53									
Ystrad Rhondda	a					13 26								13 56									
	d					13 28								13 58									
Llwynypia	d					13 30								14 00									
Tonypandy	d					13 33								14 03									
Dinas Rhondda	d					13 35								14 05									
Porth	a					13 38								14 08									
	d					13 39								14 09									
Trehafod	d					13 42								14 12									
Merthyr Tydfil	d	13 08								13 38									14 08				
Pentre-bach	d	13 12								13 42									14 12				
Troed Y Rhiw	d	13 15								13 45									14 15				
Merthyr Vale	a	13 18								13 48									14 18				
	d	13 20								13 50									14 20				
Quakers Yard	d	13 25								13 55									14 25				
Aberdare ■	d															13 51							14 21
Cwmbach	d															13 54							14 24
Fernhill	d															13 58							14 28
Mountain Ash	a															14 01							14 31
	d															14 04							14 34
Penrhiwceiber	d															14 08							14 38
Abercynon	d	13 29					13 45			13 59						14 14			14 29				14 44
Pontypridd ■	a	13 37				13 47	13 53			14 07				14 17		14 23			14 37				14 53
	d	13 39				13 48	13 54			14 09				14 18		14 24			14 39				14 54
Trefforest	d	13 42				13 51	13 57			14 12				14 21		14 27			14 42				14 57
Trefforest Estate	d	13 46								14 16									14 46				
Taffs Well ■	d	13 50				13 58	14 04			14 20				14 28		14 34			14 50				15 04
Radyr ■	a	13 53				14 01	14 07			14 23				14 31		14 37			14 53				15 07
	d	13 53		14 04		14 01	14 07			14 23			14 34	14 31		14 37			14 53		15 04		15 07
Danescourt	d			14 08									14 38								15 08		
Fairwater	d			14 10									14 40								15 10		
Waun-gron Park	d			14 12									14 42								15 12		
Ninian Park	d			14 15									14 45								15 15		
Llandaf	d	13 56				14 04	14 10			14 26				14 34		14 40			14 56				15 10
Cathays	d	14 01				14 09	14 15			14 31				14 39		14 45			15 01				15 15
Rhymney ■	d								13 29														
Pontlottyn	d								13 32														
Tir-phil	d								13 36														
Brithdir	d								13 39														
Bargoed	a								13 42														
	d		13 25						13 47			14 02								14 25			
Gilfach Fargoed	d		13 27																	14 27			
Pengam	d		13 30						13 52			14 07								14 30			
Hengoed	d		13 33						13 55			14 10								14 33			
Ystrad Mynach ■	d		13b43						13 58			14 13					14 28			14c43			
Llanbradach	d		13 48						14 03			14 18					14 33			14 48			
Aber	d		13 52						14 07			14 22					14 37			14 52			
Caerphilly ■	d		13 55						14 10			14 25					14 40			14 55			
Lisvane & Thornhill	d		13 59						14 14			14 29					14 44			14 59			
Llanishen	d		14 01						14 16			14 31					14 46			15 01			
Heath High Level	d		14 04						14 19			14 34					14 49			15 04			
Coryton	d																						
Whitchurch (Cardiff)	d																						
Rhiwbina	d																						
Birchgrove	d																						
Ty Glas	d																						
Heath Low Level	d																						
Cardiff Queen Street ■	a	14 04	14 09			14 14	14 19		14 24	14 34		14 39		14 44		14 49	14 54		15 04	15 09			15 19
	d	14 06	14 11		14 12	14 16	14 21	14 24	14 26	14 36	14 36	14 41		14 46	14 48	14 51	14 56	15 00	15 06	15 11		15 12	15 21
Cardiff Bay	a				14 16			14 28			14 40				14 52			15 04				15 16	
Cardiff Central ■	a	14 09	14 14	14 20		14 23	14 24		14 29	14 39		14 44	14 50	14 53		14 54	14 59		15 09	15 14	15 20		15 24
	d	14 10	14 16	14 21			14 25		14 31	14 41		14 46	14 51			14 55	15 01		15 10	15 16	15 21		15 25
Grangetown	d	14 14	14 20				14 29		14 35	14 45		14 50				14 59	15 05		15 14	15 20			15 29
Dingle Road	d		14 26						14 41			14 56					15 11			15 26			
Penarth	a		14 32						14 47			15 02					15 17			15 32			
Cogan	d	14 18					14 33			14 48						15 03			15 18				15 33
Eastbrook	d	14 20					14 35			14 51						15 05			15 20				15 35
Dinas Powys	d	14 22					14 37			14 53						15 07			15 22				15 37
Cadoxton	d	14 27					14 42			14 57						15 12			15 27				15 42
Barry Docks	d	14 30					14 45			15 00						15 15			15 30				15 45
Barry ■	d	14 34					14 49			15 05						15 19			15 34				15 49
Barry Island	a	14 41					14 56									15 26			15 41				15 56
Rhoose Cardiff Int Airport ✈	d									15 12													
Llantwit Major	d									15 22													
Bridgend	a									15 40													

b arr. 1336 c arr. 1436

Table 130

Saturdays
from 11 September

Treherbert, Aberdare, Merthyr, Pontypridd, Rhymney and Coryton - Cardiff, Penarth, Barry, Barry Island and Bridgend

		AW	AW	AW	AW	AW	AW	AW	AW	AW	AW	AW	AW	AW	AW	AW	AW	AW	AW	AW	AW	AW
Treherbert	d			14 17					14 47								15 15					
Ynyswen	d			14 19					14 49								15 17					
Treorchy	d			14 21					14 51								15 21					
Ton Pentre	d			14 23					14 53								15 23					
Ystrad Rhondda	a			14 26					14 56								15 26					
	d			14 28					14 58								15 28					
Llwynypia	d			14 30					15 00								15 30					
Tonypandy	d			14 33					15 03								15 33					
Dinas Rhondda	d			14 35					15 05								15 35					
Porth	a			14 38					15 08								15 38					
	d			14 52					15 09								15 39					
Trehafod	d			14 55					15 12								15 42					
Merthyr Tydfil	d				14 38								15 08								15 38	
Pentre-bach	d				14 42								15 12								15 42	
Troed Y Rhiw	d				14 45								15 15								15 45	
Merthyr Vale	a				14 48								15 18								15 48	
	d				14 50								15 20								15 50	
Quakers Yard	d				14 55								15 25								15 55	
Aberdare ■	d										14 51							15 21				
Cwmbach	d										14 54							15 24				
Fernhill	d										14 58							15 28				
Mountain Ash	a										15 01							15 31				
	d										15 04							15 34				
Penrhiwceiber	d										15 08							15 38				
Abercynon	d				14 59						15 14		15 29					15 44			15 59	
Pontypridd ■	a			15 00	15 07				15 17		15 23		15 37				15 47	15 53			16 08	
	d			15 04	15 09				15 18		15 24		15 39				15 48	15 54			16 09	
Trefforest	d			15 07	15 12				15 21		15 27		15 42				15 51	15 57			16 12	
Trefforest Estate	d				15 16								15 46								16 16	
Taffs Well ■	d			15 13	15 20				15 28		15 34		15 50				15 58	16 04			16 20	
Radyr ■	a			15 17	15 23				15 31		15 37		15 53				16 01	16 07			16 23	
	d			15 17	15 23			15 34	15 31		15 37		15 53		16 04		16 01	16 07			16 23	
Danescourt	d							15 38							16 08							
Fairwater	d							15 40							16 10							
Waun-gron Park	d							15 42							16 12							
Ninian Park	d							15 45							16 15							
Llandaf	d				15 26				15 34		15 40		15 56				16 04	16 10			16 26	
Cathays	d				15 31				15 39		15 45		16 01				16 09	16 15			16 31	
Rhymney ■	d		14 29																	15 29		
Pontlottyn	d		14 32																	15 32		
Tir-phil	d		14 36																	15 36		
Brithdir	d		14 39																	15 39		
Bargoed	a		14 42																	15 42		
	d		14 47				15 02							15 25						15 47		
Gilfach Fargoed	d													15 27								
Pengam	d		14 52				15 07							15 30						15 52		
Hengoed	d		14 55				15 10							15 33						15 55		
Ystrad Mynach ■	d		14 58				15 13							15b43						15 58		
Llanbradach	d		15 03				15 18							15 48						16 03		
Aber	d		15 07				15 22							15 52						16 07		
Caerphilly ■	d		15 10				15 25							15 55						16 10		
Lisvane & Thornhill	d		15 14				15 29							15 59						16 14		
Llanishen	d		15 16				15 31							16 01						16 16		
Heath High Level	d		15 19				15 34							16 04						16 19		
Coryton	d																					
Whitchurch (Cardiff)	d																					
Rhiwbina	d																					
Birchgrove	d																					
Ty Glas	d																					
Heath Low Level	d																					
Cardiff Queen Street ■	a		15 24		15 34		15 39		15 44		15 49		16 04	16 09			16 14	16 19		16 24	16 34	
	d	15 24	15 26		15 36	15 36	15 41		15 46	15 48	15 51	16 00	16 06	16 11		16 12	16 16	16 21	16 24	16 26	16 36	16 36
Cardiff Bay	a	15 28				15 40				15 52		16 04				16 16			16 28			16 40
Cardiff Central ■	a		15 29	15 34	15 39		15 44	15 50	15 53		15 54		16 09	16 14	16 20		16 23	16 24		16 33	16 39	
	d		15 31		15 41		15 46	15 51			15 55		16 10	16 16	16 21			16 25			16 41	
Grangetown	d		15 35		15 45		15 50				15 59		16 14	16 20				16 29			16 45	
Dingle Road	d		15 41				15 56							16 26								
Penarth	a		15 47				16 02							16 32								
Cogan	d				15 48						16 03		16 18					16 33			16 48	
Eastbrook	d				15 51						16 05		16 20					16 35			16 51	
Dinas Powys	d				15 53						16 07		16 22					16 37			16 53	
Cadoxton	d				15 57						16 12		16 27					16 42			16 57	
Barry Docks	d				16 00						16 15		16 30					16 45			17 00	
Barry ■	d				16 05						16 19		16 34					16 49			17 05	
Barry Island	a										16 26		16 41					16 56				
Rhoose Cardiff Int Airport ✈	d				16 12																17 12	
Llantwit Major	d				16 22																17 22	
Bridgend	a				16 40																17 40	

b arr. 1536

Table 130

Saturdays from 11 September

Treherbert, Aberdare, Merthyr, Pontypridd, Rhymney and Coryton - Cardiff, Penarth, Barry, Barry Island and Bridgend

		AW	AW	AW	AW	AW	AW	AW	AW	AW	AW	AW	AW	AW	AW	AW	AW	AW	AW	AW	AW	AW	AW
Treherbert	d			15 47									16 17								16 47		
Ynyswen	d			15 49									16 19								16 49		
Treorchy	d			15 51									16 21								16 51		
Ton Pentre	d			15 53									16 23								16 53		
Ystrad Rhondda	a			15 56									16 26								16 56		
	d			15 58									16 28								16 58		
Llwynypia	d			16 00									16 30								17 00		
Tonypandy	d			16 03									16 33								17 03		
Dinas Rhondda	d			16 05									16 35								17 05		
Porth	a			16 08									16 38								17 08		
	d			16 09									16 39								17 09		
Trehafod	d			16 12									16 42								17 12		
Merthyr Tydfil	d								16 08								16 38						
Pentre-bach	d								16 12								16 42						
Troed Y Rhiw	d								16 15								16 45						
Merthyr Vale	a								16 18								16 48						
	d								16 20								16 50						
Quakers Yard	d								16 25								16 55						
Aberdare	d					15 51								16 21									16 51
Cwmbach	d					15 54								16 24									16 54
Fernhill	d					15 58								16 28									16 58
Mountain Ash	a					16 01								16 31									17 01
	d					16 04								16 34									17 04
Penrhiwceiber	d					16 08								16 38									17 08
Abercynon	d					16 14			16 29					16 44			16 59						17 14
Pontypridd	a			16 17		16 23			16 37				16 47	16 53			17 07				17 17		17 23
	d			16 18		16 24			16 39				16 48	16 54			17 09				17 18		17 24
Trefforest	d			16 21		16 27			16 42				16 51	16 57			17 12				17 21		17 27
Trefforest Estate	d								16 46								17 16						
Taffs Well	d			16 28		16 34			16 50				16 58	17 04			17 20				17 28		17 34
Radyr	a			16 31		16 37			16 53				17 01	17 07			17 23				17 31		17 37
	d		16 30	16 31		16 37			16 53		17 04		17 01	17 07			17 23			17 34	17 31		17 37
Danescourt	d		16 34								17 08									17 38			
Fairwater	d		16 36								17 10									17 40			
Waun-gron Park	d		16 38								17 12									17 42			
Ninian Park	d		16 45								17 15									17 45			
Llandaf	d			16 34		16 40			16 56				17 04	17 10			17 26				17 34		17 40
Cathays	d			16 39		16 45			17 01				17 09	17 15			17 31				17 39		17 45
Rhymney	d															16 29							
Pontlottyn	d															16 32							
Tir-phil	d															16 36							
Brithdir	d															16 39							
Bargoed	a															16 42							
	d	16 02					16 17			16 32						16 47			17 02				
Gilfach Fargoed	d						16 19																
Pengam	d	16 07					16 22			16 37						16 52			17 07				
Hengoed	d	16 10					16 25			16 40						16 55			17 10				
Ystrad Mynach	d	16 13					16 28			16 43						16 58			17 13				
Llanbradach	d	16 18					16 33			16 48						17 03			17 18				
Aber	d	16 22					16 37			16 52						17 07			17 22				
Caerphilly	d	16 25					16 40			16 55						17 10			17 25				
Lisvane & Thornhill	d	16 29					16 44			16 59						17 14			17 29				
Llanishen	d	16 31					16 46			17 01						17 16			17 31				
Heath High Level	d	16 34					16 49			17 04						17 19			17 34				
Coryton	d																						
Whitchurch (Cardiff)	d																						
Rhiwbina	d																						
Birchgrove	d																						
Ty Glas	d																						
Heath Low Level	d																						
Cardiff Queen Street	a	16 39		16 44		16 49	16 54		17 04	17 09			17 14	17 19		17 24	17 34		17 39		17 44		17 49
	d	16 41		16 46	16 48	16 51	16 56	17 00	17 06	17 11		17 12	17 16	17 21	17 24	17 26	17 36	17 36	17 41		17 46	17 48	17 51
Cardiff Bay	a				16 52			17 04				17 16			17 28			17 40				17 52	
Cardiff Central	a	16 44	16 50	17 04		16 54	16 59		17 09	17 14	17 20		17 23	17 24		17 29	17 39		17 44	17 50	17 53		17 54
	d	16 46	16 51			16 55	17 01		17 10	17 16	17 21			17 25		17 31	17 41		17 46	17 51			17 55
Grangetown	d	16 50				16 59	17 05		17 14	17 20				17 29		17 35	17 45		17 50				17 59
Dingle Road	d	16 56					17 11			17 26						17 41			17 56				
Penarth	a	17 02					17 17			17 32						17 47			18 02				
Cogan	d					17 03			17 18					17 33			17 48						18 03
Eastbrook	d					17 05			17 20					17 35			17 51						18 05
Dinas Powys	d					17 07			17 22					17 37			17 53						18 07
Cadoxton	d					17 12			17 27					17 42			17 57						18 12
Barry Docks	d					17 15			17 30					17 45			18 00						18 15
Barry	d					17 19			17 34					17 49			18 05						18 19
Barry Island	a					17 26			17 41					17 56									18 26
Rhoose Cardiff Int Airport ✈	d																18 12						
Llantwit Major	d																18 22						
Bridgend	a																18 40						

Table 130

Saturdays from 11 September

Treherbert, Aberdare, Merthyr, Pontypridd, Rhymney and Coryton - Cardiff, Penarth, Barry, Barry Island and Bridgend

		AW	AW	AW	AW	AW	AW	AW	AW	AW	AW	AW	AW	AW	AW	AW	AW	AW	AW	AW	AW	AW
Treherbert	d					17 17							17 47									18 17
Ynyswen	d					17 19							17 49									18 19
Treorchy	d					17 21							17 51									18 21
Ton Pentre	d					17 23							17 53									18 23
Ystrad Rhondda	a					17 26							17 56									18 26
	d					17 28							17 58									18 28
Llwynypia	d					17 30							18 00									18 30
Tonypandy	d					17 33							18 03									18 33
Dinas Rhondda	d					17 35							18 05									18 35
Porth	a					17 38							18 08									18 38
	d					17 39							18 09									18 39
Trehafod	d					17 42							18 12									18 42
Merthyr Tydfil	d		17 08							17 38									18 08			
Pentre-bach	d		17 12							17 42									18 12			
Troed Y Rhiw	d		17 15							17 45									18 15			
Merthyr Vale	a		17 18							17 48									18 18			
	d		17 20							17 50									18 20			
Quakers Yard	d		17 25							17 55									18 25			
Aberdare	d						17 21								17 51							
Cwmbach	d						17 24								17 54							
Fernhill	d						17 28								17 58							
Mountain Ash	a						17 31								18 01							
	d						17 34								18 04							
Penrhiwceiber	d						17 38								18 08							
Abercynon	d		17 29				17 44			17 59					18 14				18 29			
Pontypridd	a		17 37			17 47	17 53			18 07			18 17		18 23				18 37			18 47
	d		17 39			17 48	17 54			18 09			18 18		18 24				18 39			18 48
Trefforest	d		17 42			17 51	17 57			18 12			18 21		18 27				18 42			18 51
Trefforest Estate	d		17 46							18 16									18 46			
Taffs Well	d		17 50			17 58	18 04			18 20			18 28		18 34				18 50			18 58
Radyr	a		17 53			18 01	18 07			18 23			18 31		18 37				18 53			19 01
	d		17 53	18 04		18 01	18 07			18 23	18 34		18 31		18 37				18 53	19 04		19 01
Danescourt	d			18 08							18 38									19 08		
Fairwater	d			18 10							18 40									19 10		
Waun-gron Park	d			18 12							18 42									19 12		
Ninian Park	d			18 15							18 45									19 15		
Llandaf	d		17 56			18 04	18 10			18 26			18 34		18 40				18 56			19 04
Cathays	d		18 01			18 09	18 15			18 31			18 39		18 45				19 01			19 09
Rhymney	d								17 29													
Pontlottyn	d								17 32													
Tir-phil	d								17 36													
Brithdir	d								17 39													
Bargoed	a								17 42													
	d								17 47							18 17						
Gilfach Fargoed	d															18 19						
Pengam	d								17 52							18 22						
Hengoed	d								17 55							18 25						
Ystrad Mynach	d								17 58							18 28						
Llanbradach	d								18 03							18 33						
Aber	d								18 07							18 37						
Caerphilly	d								18 10							18 40						
Lisvane & Thornhill	d								18 14							18 44						
Llanishen	d								18 16							18 46						
Heath High Level	d								18 19							18 49						
Coryton	d																18 45					
Whitchurch (Cardiff)	d																18 46					
Rhiwbina	d																18 48					
Birchgrove	d																18 50					
Ty Glas	d																18 51					
Heath Low Level	d																18 54					
Cardiff Queen Street	a		18 04			18 14	18 19		18 24	18 34			18 44		18 49	18 54	18 59		19 04			19 14
	d	18 00	18 06		18 12	18 16	18 21	18 24	18 26	18 36		18 36	18 46	18 48	18 51	18 56	19 01	19 00	19 06		19 12	19 16
Cardiff Bay	a	18 04			18 16			18 28				18 40		18 52				19 04			19 16	
Cardiff Central	a		18 09	18 20		18 23	18 24		18 29	18 39	18 50		18 53		18 54	18 59	19 07		19 10	19 22		19 23
	d		18 10	18 21			18 25		18 31	18 41	18 51				18 55	19 01						
Grangetown	d		18 14				18 29		18 35	18 45					18 59	19 05						
Dingle Road	d								18 41							19 11						
Penarth	a								18 47							19 17						
Cogan	d		18 18				18 33			18 48					19 03							
Eastbrook	d		18 20				18 35			18 51					19 05							
Dinas Powys	d		18 22				18 37			18 53					19 07							
Cadoxton	d		18 27				18 42			18 57					19 12							
Barry Docks	d		18 30				18 45			19 00					19 15							
Barry	d		18 34				18 49			19 05					19 19							
Barry Island	a		18 41				18 56								19 26							
Rhoose Cardiff Int Airport ✈	d									19 12												
Llantwit Major	d									19 22												
Bridgend	a									19 40												

Table 130

Saturdays
from 11 September

Treherbert, Aberdare, Merthyr, Pontypridd, Rhymney and Coryton - Cardiff, Penarth, Barry, Barry Island and Bridgend

		AW	AW	AW	AW	AW	AW	AW	AW	AW A		AW B	AW	AW	AW	AW	AW	AW	AW	AW		AW	AW	AW	AW
Treherbert	d						18 47									19 17								19 47	
Ynyswen	d						18 49									19 19								19 49	
Treorchy	d						18 51									19 21								19 51	
Ton Pentre	d						18 53									19 23								19 53	
Ystrad Rhondda	a						18 56									19 26								19 56	
	d						18 58									19 28								19 58	
Llwynypia	d						19 00									19 30								20 00	
Tonypandy	d						19 03									19 33								20 03	
Dinas Rhondda	d						19 05									19 35								20 05	
Porth	a						19 08									19 38								20 08	
	d						19 09									19 39								20 09	
Trehafod	d						19 12									19 42								20 12	
Merthyr Tydfil	d				18 38									19 08						19 38					
Pentre-bach	d				18 42									19 12						19 42					
Troed Y Rhiw	d				18 45									19 15						19 45					
Merthyr Vale	a				18 48									19 18						19 48					
	d				18 50									19 20						19 50					
Quakers Yard	d				18 55									19 25						19 55					
Aberdare ■	d	18 21							18 51																
Cwmbach	d	18 24							18 54																
Fernhill	d	18 28							18 58																
Mountain Ash	a	18 31							19 01																
	d	18 34							19 04																
Penrhiwceiber	d	18 38							19 08																
Abercynon	d	18 44			18 59				19 14					19 29				19 43		19 59					
Pontypridd ■	a	18 53			19 07		19 17		19 23					19 37		19 47		19 53		20 07				20 17	
	d	18 54			19 09		19 18		19 24					19 39		19 48		19 54		20 09				20 18	
Trefforest	d	18 57			19 12		19 21		19 27					19 42		19 51		19 57		20 12				20 21	
Trefforest Estate	d				19 16									19 46						20 16					
Taffs Well ■	d	19 04			19 20		19 28		19 34					19 50		19 58		20 04		20 20				20 28	
Radyr ■	a	19 07			19 23		19 31		19 37					19 53		20 01		20 07		20 23				20 31	
	d	19 07			19 23		19 31		19 37					19 53		20 01	20 04	20 07		20 23				20 31	
Danescourt	d																20 08								
Fairwater	d																20 10								
Waun-gron Park	d																20 12								
Ninian Park	d																20 15								
Llandaf	d	19 10			19 26		19 34		19 40					19 56		20 04		20 10		20 26				20 34	
Cathays	d	19 15			19 31		19 39		19 45					20 01		20 09		20 15		20 31				20 39	
Rhymney ■	d																						19 45		
Pontlottyn	d																						19 48		
Tir-phil	d																						19 52		
Brithdir	d																						19 55		
Bargoed	a																						19 58		
	d			18 48																			19 59		
Gilfach Fargoed	d			18 50																			20 01		
Pengam	d			18 53																			20 04		
Hengoed	d			18 56																			20 07		
Ystrad Mynach ■	d			18 59																			20 10		
Llanbradach	d			19 04																			20 15		
Aber	d			19 08																			20 19		
Caerphilly ■	d			19 11						19 40		19 40											20 22		
Lisvane & Thornhill	d			19 15						19 44		19 44											20 26		
Llanishen	d			19 17						19 46		19 46											20 28		
Heath High Level	d			19 20						19 49		19 49											20 31		
Coryton	d																								
Whitchurch (Cardiff)	d																								
Rhiwbina	d																								
Birchgrove	d																								
Ty Glas	d																								
Heath Low Level	d																								
Cardiff Queen Street ■	a	19 19		19 24	19 35		19 44		19 49	19 54		19 54		20 04		20 14		20 19		20 34			20 39	20 44	
	d	19 21	19 24	19 26	19 36	19 36	19 46	19 48	19 51	19 56		19 56	20 00	20 06	20 12	20 16		20 21	20 24	20 36		20 36	20 41	20 46	20 48
Cardiff Bay	a		19 28			19 40		19 52					20 04		20 16				20 28			20 40			20 52
Cardiff Central ■	a	19 24		19 29	19 40		19 53		19 57	19 59		19 59		20 10		20 20	20 25	20 24		20 39			20 48	20 53	
	d	19 25		19 31	19 41					20 06		20 06		20 10				20 31		20 41					
Grangetown	d	19 29		19 35	19 45					20 10		20 10		20 14				20 35		20 45					
Dingle Road	d			19 41						20 14		20 14						20 41							
Penarth	a			19 47						20 19		20 20						20 47							
Cogan	d	19 33			19 48									20 18						20 48					
Eastbrook	d	19 35			19 51									20 20						20 51					
Dinas Powys	d	19 37			19 53									20 22						20 53					
Cadoxton	d	19 42			19 57									20 27						20 57					
Barry Docks	d	19 45			20 00									20 30						21 00					
Barry ■	d	19 49			20 05									20 34						21 05					
Barry Island	a	19 56												20 41											
Rhoose Cardiff Int Airport ✈	d				20 12															21 12					
Llantwit Major	d				20 22															21 22					
Bridgend	a				20 40															21 40					

A 11 September **B** not 11 September

Table 130

Saturdays
from 11 September

Treherbert, Aberdare, Merthyr, Pontypridd, Rhymney and Coryton - Cardiff, Penarth, Barry, Barry Island and Bridgend

		AW	AW	AW	AW	AW		AW	AW	AW	AW	AW	AW	AW	AW	AW		AW	AW	AW	AW	AW	AW	AW	AW
Treherbert	d							20 17														21 17			
Ynyswen	d							20 19														21 19			
Treorchy	d							20 21														21 21			
Ton Pentre	d							20 23														21 23			
Ystrad Rhondda	a							20 26														21 26			
	d							20 28														21 28			
Llwynypia	d							20 30														21 30			
Tonypandy	d							20 33														21 33			
Dinas Rhondda	d							20 35														21 35			
Porth	a							20 38														21 38			
	d							20 39														21 39			
Trehafod	d							20 42														21 42			
Merthyr Tydfil	d											20 38												21 38	
Pentre-bach	d											20 42												21 42	
Troed Y Rhiw	d											20 45												21 45	
Merthyr Vale	a											20 48												21 48	
	d											20 50												21 50	
Quakers Yard	d											20 55												21 55	
Aberdare ■	d	19 51							20 21							20 51									
Cwmbach	d	19 54							20 24							20 54									
Fernhill	d	19 58							20 28							20 58									
Mountain Ash	a	20 01							20 31							21 01									
	d	20 04							20 34							21 04									
Penrhiwceiber	d	20 08							20 38							21 08									
Abercynon	d	20 14							20 44			20 59				21 14								21 59	
Pontypridd ■	a	20 23						20 47	20 53			21 07				21 23						21 47		22 07	
	d	20 24						20 48	20 54			21 09				21 24						21 48		22 09	
Trefforest	d	20 27						20 51	20 57			21 12				21 27						21 51		22 12	
Trefforest Estate	d											21 16												22 16	
Taffs Well ■	d	20 34						20 58	21 04			21 20				21 34						21 58		22 20	
Radyr ■	a	20 37						21 01	21 07			21 23				21 37						22 01		22 23	
	d	20 37			21 04			21 01	21 07			21 23				21 37				22 04		22 01		22 23	
Danescourt	d				21 08															22 08					
Fairwater	d				21 10															22 10					
Waun-gron Park	d				21 12															22 12					
Ninian Park	d				21 15															22 15					
Llandaf	d	20 40						21 04	21 10			21 26				21 40						22 04		22 26	
Cathays	d	20 45						21 09	21 15			21 31				21 45						22 09		22 31	
Rhymney ■	d													20 48											
Pontlottyn	d													20 51											
Tir-phil	d													20 55											
Brithdir	d													20 58											
Bargoed	a													21 01											
	d													21 02											
Gilfach Fargoed	d													21 04											
Pengam	d													21 07											
Hengoed	d													21 10											
Ystrad Mynach ■	d													21 13											
Llanbradach	d													21 18											
Aber	d													21 22											
Caerphilly ■	d		20 40											21 25				21 45							
Lisvane & Thornhill	d		20 44											21 29				21 50							
Llanishen	d		20 46											21 31				21 52							
Heath High Level	d		20 49											21 34				21 54							
Coryton	d																								
Whitchurch (Cardiff)	d																								
Rhiwbina	d																								
Birchgrove	d																								
Ty Glas	d																								
Heath Low Level	d																								
Cardiff Queen Street ■	a	20 49	20 54					21 14	21 19			21 34		21 42		21 49		22 00				22 14		22 34	
	d	20 51	20 56	21 00		21 12		21 16	21 21	21 24		21 36	21 36	21 44	21 48	21 51		22 01	22 00		22 12	22 16	22 24	22 36	22 36
Cardiff Bay	a			21 04		21 16				21 28			21 40		21 52				22 04		22 16		22 28		22 40
Cardiff Central ■	a	20 57	20 59		21 25			21 22	21 24			21 39		21 51		21 57		22 04		22 20		22 22		22 41	
	d	21 06	21 10								21 32	21 41				22 06		22 10		22 21					
Grangetown	d	21 10	21 14								21 35	21 45				22 10		22 14							
Dingle Road	d	21 14									21 41					22 14									
Penarth	a	21 20									21 47					22 17									
Cogan	d		21 18									21 48						22 18							
Eastbrook	d		21 20									21 51						22 20							
Dinas Powys	d		21 22									21 53						22 22							
Cadoxton	d		21 27									21 57						22 27							
Barry Docks	d		21 30									22 00						22 30							
Barry ■	d		21 34									22 05						22 34							
Barry Island	a		21 42															22 41							
Rhoose Cardiff Int Airport ✈	d											22 12													
Llantwit Major	d											22 22													
Bridgend	a											22 40													

Table 130

Saturdays
from 11 September

Treherbert, Aberdare, Merthyr, Pontypridd, Rhymney and Coryton - Cardiff, Penarth, Barry, Barry Island and Bridgend

		AW	AW	AW	AW	AW	AW	AW	AW	AW	AW	AW
Treherbert	d											
Ynyswen	d											
Treorchy	d											
Ton Pentre	d											
Ystrad Rhondda	a											
	d											
Llwynypia	d											
Tonypandy	d											
Dinas Rhondda	d											
Porth	a											
	d											
Trehafod	d											
Merthyr Tydfil	d								22 38			
Pentre-bach	d								22 42			
Troed Y Rhiw	d								22 45			
Merthyr Vale	a								22 48			
	d								22 50			
Quakers Yard	d								22 55			
Aberdare 3	d		21 51							22 51		
Cwmbach	d		21 54							22 54		
Fernhill	d		21 58							22 58		
Mountain Ash	a		22 01							23 01		
	d		22 04							23 04		
Penrhiwceiber	d		22 08							23 08		
Abercynon	d		22 14						22 59	23 14		
Pontypridd 3	a		22 22						23 07	23 22		
	d		22 29						23 09			
Trefforest	d		22 32						23 12			
Trefforest Estate	d											
Taffs Well 3	d		22 39						23 20			
Radyr 3	a		22 42						23 23			
	d		22 42				23 10		23 23			
Danescourt	d											
Fairwater	d											
Waun-gron Park	d											
Ninian Park	d											
Llandaf	d		22 45				23 12		23 26			
Cathays	d		22 50				23 16		23 31			
Rhymney 3	d											
Pontlottyn	d											
Tir-phil	d											
Brithdir	d											
Bargoed	a											
	d											
Gilfach Fargoed	d											
Pengam	d											
Hengoed	d											
Ystrad Mynach 3	d											
Llanbradach	d											
Aber	d											
Caerphilly 3	d											
Lisvane & Thornhill	d											
Llanishen	d											
Heath High Level	d											
Coryton	d			22 45								
Whitchurch (Cardiff)	d			22 46								
Rhiwbina	d			22 48								
Birchgrove	d			22 50								
Ty Glas	d			22 51								
Heath Low Level	d			22 54								
Cardiff Queen Street 3	a		22 54	22 59			23 19		23 34			
	d	22 48	22 55	23 01	23 00	23 12	23 20	23 24	23 36		23 36	23 48
Cardiff Bay	a	22 52			23 04	23 16		23 28			23 40	23 52
Cardiff Central 7	a		23 00	23 07			23 25		23 43			
	d		23 12				23 30					
Grangetown	d		23 16				23 34					
Dingle Road	d		23 20									
Penarth	a		23 26									
Cogan	d						23 37					
Eastbrook	d						23 40					
Dinas Powys	d						23 42					
Cadoxton	d						23 46					
Barry Docks	d						23 49					
Barry 3	d						23 54					
Barry Island	a						00 01					
Rhoose Cardiff Int Airport ✈	d											
Llantwit Major	d											
Bridgend	a											

Table 130

Sundays
until 11 July

Treherbert, Aberdare, Merthyr, Pontypridd, Rhymney and Coryton - Cardiff, Penarth, Barry, Barry Island and Bridgend

		AW	AW	AW	AW	AW	AW	AW	AW	AW	AW	AW	AW	AW	AW	AW	AW	AW	AW	AW	AW	AW	AW
Treherbert	d					08 17																	10 07
Ynyswen	d					08 19																	10 09
Treorchy	d					08 21																	10 11
Ton Pentre	d					08 23																	10 13
Ystrad Rhondda	a					08 26																	10 16
	d					08 28																	10 18
Llwynypia	d					08 30																	10 20
Tonypandy	d					08 33																	10 23
Dinas Rhondda	d					08 35																	10 25
Porth	a					08 38																	10 28
	d					08 39																	10 29
Trehafod	d					08 42																	10 32
Merthyr Tydfil	d															09 38							
Pentre-bach	d															09 42							
Troed Y Rhiw	d															09 45							
Merthyr Vale	a															09 48							
	d															09 50							
Quakers Yard	d															09 55							
Aberdare 3	d																		09 52				
Cwmbach	d																		09 55				
Fernhill	d																		09 58				
Mountain Ash	a																		10 01				
	d																		10 04				
Penrhiwceiber	d																		10 07				
Abercynon	d															09 59			10 13				
Pontypridd 3	a					08 47										10 07			10 23				10 37
	d					08 48										10 09			10 24				10 38
Trefforest	d					08 51										10 12			10 27				10 41
Trefforest Estate	d																						
Taffs Well 3	d					08 58										10 20			10 34				10 48
Radyr 3	a					09 01										10 23			10 37				10 51
	d					09 01										10 23			10 37				10 51
Danescourt	d																						
Fairwater	d																						
Waun-gron Park	d																						
Ninian Park	d																						
Llandaf	d					09 04										10 26			10 40				10 54
Cathays	d					09 09										10 31			10 45				10 59
Rhymney 3	d												09 22										
Pontlottyn	d												09 25										
Tir-phil	d												09 29										
Brithdir	d												09 32										
Bargoed	a												09 35										
	d												09 37										
Gilfach Fargoed	d												09 39										
Pengam	d												09 42										
Hengoed	d												09 45										
Ystrad Mynach 3	d												09 48										
Llanbradach	d												09 53										
Aber	d												09 57										
Caerphilly 3	d												10 00										
Lisvane & Thornhill	d												10 04										
Llanishen	d												10 06										
Heath High Level	d												10 09										
Coryton	d																						
Whitchurch (Cardiff)	d																						
Rhiwbina	d																						
Birchgrove	d																						
Ty Glas	d																						
Heath Low Level	d																						
Cardiff Queen Street 3	a			08 57		09 14							10 14			10 34			10 49				11 02
	d			09 00	09 12	09 16	09 24	09 36	09 48		10 00	10 12	10 16	10 24		10 36	10 36	10 48	10 51	11 00	11 12		11 04
Cardiff Bay	a			09 04	09 16		09 28	09 40	09 52		10 04	10 16		10 28			10 40	10 52		11 04	11 16		
Cardiff Central 7	a					09 18							10 18			10 39			10 54			11 13	11 07
	d	08 25	08 41			09 25				09 55			10 29		10 31	10 41			10 55			11 15	11 25
Grangetown	d	08 29	08 45			09 29				09 59			10 33		10 35	10 45			10 59				11 29
Dingle Road	d														10 41								
Penarth	a														10 44								
Cogan	d	08 33	08 48			09 33				10 03			10 37			10 48			11 03				11 33
Eastbrook	d	08 35	08 51			09 35				10 05			10 39			10 51			11 05				11 35
Dinas Powys	d	08 37	08 53			09 37				10 07			10 41			10 53			11 07				11 37
Cadoxton	d	08 42	08 57			09 42				10 12			10 46			10 57			11 12				11 42
Barry Docks	d	08 45	09 00			09 45				10 15			10 49			11 00			11 15				11 45
Barry 3	d	08 49	09 05			09 49				10 19			10 53			11 06			11 19			11 34	11 49
Barry Island	a	08 55				09 55				10 25			10 59						11 25			11 41	11 55
Rhoose Cardiff Int Airport ✈	d		09 12													11 13							
Llantwit Major	d		09 22													11 23							
Bridgend	a		09 39													11 40							

Table 130

Sundays
until 11 July

Treherbert, Aberdare, Merthyr, Pontypridd, Rhymney and Coryton - Cardiff, Penarth, Barry, Barry Island and Bridgend

Station		AW	AW	AW	AW	AW	AW	AW	AW	AW	AW	AW	AW	AW	AW	AW	AW	AW	AW	AW	AW	AW	AW
Treherbert	d															12 07							
Ynyswen	d															12 09							
Treorchy	d															12 11							
Ton Pentre	d															12 13							
Ystrad Rhondda	a															12 16							
	d															12 18							
Llwynypia	d															12 20							
Tonypandy	d															12 23							
Dinas Rhondda	d															12 25							
Porth	a															12 28							
	d															12 29							
Trehafod	d															12 32							
Merthyr Tydfil	d										11 38												
Pentre-bach	d										11 42												
Troed Y Rhiw	d										11 45												
Merthyr Vale	a										11 48												
	d										11 50												
Quakers Yard	d										11 55												
Aberdare ■	d				10 52																		
Cwmbach	d				10 55																		
Fernhill	d				10 58																		
Mountain Ash	a				11 01																		
	d				11 04																		
Penrhiwceiber	d				11 07																		
Abercynon	d				11 13						11 59												
Pontypridd ■	a				11 23						12 07					12 37							
	d				11 24						12 09					12 38							
Trefforest	d				11 27						12 12					12 41							
Trefforest Estate	d																						
Taffs Well ■	d				11 34						12 20					12 48							
Radyr ■	a				11 37						12 23					12 51							
	d				11 37						12 23					12 51							
Danescourt	d																						
Fairwater	d																						
Waun-gron Park	d																						
Ninian Park	d																						
Llandaf	d				11 40						12 26					12 54							
Cathays	d				11 45						12 31					12 59							
Rhymney ■	d						11 10															13 10	
Pontlottyn	d						11 13															13 13	
Tir-phil	d						11 17															13 17	
Brithdir	d						11 20															13 20	
Bargoed	a						11 23															13 23	
	d						11 25															13 25	
Gilfach Fargoed	d						11 27															13 27	
Pengam	d						11 30															13 30	
Hengoed	d						11 33															13 33	
Ystrad Mynach ■	d						11 36															13 36	
Llanbradach	d						11 41															13 41	
Aber	d						11 45															13 45	
Caerphilly ■	d						11 48															13 48	
Lisvane & Thornhill	d						11 52															13 52	
Llanishen	d						11 54															13 54	
Heath High Level	d						11 57															13 57	
Coryton	d																						
Whitchurch (Cardiff)	d																						
Rhiwbina	d																						
Birchgrove	d																						
Ty Glas	d																						
Heath Low Level	d																						
Cardiff Queen Street ■	a				11 49		12 02				12 34					13 04						14 02	
	d	11 24	11 36	11 48	11 51	12 00	12 04	12 12	12 24		12 36	12 36	12 48		13 00	13 04	13 12	13 24	13 36	13 48	14 00	14 04	14 12
Cardiff Bay	a	11 28	11 40	11 52		12 04		12 16	12 28			12 40	12 52		13 04		13 16	13 28	13 40	13 52	14 04		14 16
Cardiff Central ■	a				11 54		12 07				12 39					13 06						14 07	
	d				12 00		12 25			12 31	12 41			12 56		13 25						14 25	
Grangetown	d				12 04		12 29			12 35	12 45			13 00		13 29						14 29	
Dingle Road	d									12 41													
Penarth	a									12 46													
Cogan	d				12 07		12 33				12 48			13 04		13 33						14 33	
Eastbrook	d				12 10		12 35				12 51			13 06		13 35						14 35	
Dinas Powys	d				12 12		12 37				12 53			13 08		13 37						14 37	
Cadoxton	d				12 16		12 42				12 57			13 13		13 42						14 42	
Barry Docks	d				12 19		12 45				13 00			13 16		13 45						14 45	
Barry ■	d				12 24		12 49				13 05			13 20		13 49						14 49	
Barry Island	a				12 30		12 55							13 26		13 55						14 55	
Rhoose Cardiff Int Airport ✈	d										13 12												
Llantwit Major	d										13 22												
Bridgend	a										13 39												

Table 130

Sundays
until 11 July

Treherbert, Aberdare, Merthyr, Pontypridd, Rhymney and Coryton - Cardiff, Penarth, Barry, Barry Island and Bridgend

Station		AW	AW	AW	AW	AW	AW	AW	AW	AW	AW	AW	AW	AW	AW	AW	AW	AW	AW	AW	AW	AW
Treherbert	d									14 17												
Ynyswen	d									14 19												
Treorchy	d									14 21												
Ton Pentre	d									14 23												
Ystrad Rhondda	a									14 26												
	d									14 28												
Llwynypia	d									14 30												
Tonypandy	d									14 33												
Dinas Rhondda	d									14 35												
Porth	a									14 38												
	d									14 39												
Trehafod	d									14 42												
Merthyr Tydfil	d			13 38																15 38		
Pentre-bach	d			13 42																15 42		
Troed Y Rhiw	d			13 45																15 45		
Merthyr Vale	a			13 48																15 48		
	d			13 50																15 50		
Quakers Yard	d			13 55																15 55		
Aberdare ■	d													14 52								
Cwmbach	d													14 55								
Fernhill	d													14 58								
Mountain Ash	a													15 01								
	d													15 04								
Penrhiwceiber	d													15 07								
Abercynon	d			13 59										15 13						15 59		
Pontypridd ■	a			14 07						14 47				15 23						16 07		
	d			14 09						14 48				15 24						16 09		
Trefforest	d			14 12						14 51				15 27						16 12		
Trefforest Estate	d																					
Taffs Well ■	d			14 20						14 58				15 34						16 20		
Radyr ■	a			14 23						15 01				15 37						16 23		
	d			14 23						15 01				15 37						16 23		
Danescourt	d																					
Fairwater	d																					
Waun-gron Park	d																					
Ninian Park	d																					
Llandaf	d			14 26						15 04				15 40						16 26		
Cathays	d			14 31						15 09				15 45						16 31		
Rhymney ■	d																15 22					
Pontlottyn	d																15 25					
Tir-phil	d																15 29					
Brithdir	d																15 32					
Bargoed	a																15 35					
	d																15 37					
Gilfach Fargoed	d																15 39					
Pengam	d																15 42					
Hengoed	d																15 45					
Ystrad Mynach ■	d																15 48					
Llanbradach	d																15 53					
Aber	d																15 57					
Caerphilly ■	d																16 00					
Lisvane & Thornhill	d																16 04					
Llanishen	d																16 06					
Heath High Level	d																16 09					
Coryton	d																					
Whitchurch (Cardiff)	d																					
Rhiwbina	d																					
Birchgrove	d																					
Ty Glas	d																					
Heath Low Level	d																					
Cardiff Queen Street ■	a			14 34						15 14				15 49			16 14			16 34		
	d	14 24		14 35	14 36	14 48		15 00	15 12	15 16	15 24	15 36	15 48	15 51	16 00	16 12	16 16	16 24		16 36	16 36	16 48
Cardiff Bay	a	14 28			14 40	14 52		15 04	15 16		15 28	15 40	15 52		16 04	16 16		16 28			16 40	16 52
Cardiff Central ■	a			14 38						15 18				15 54			16 18			16 39		
	d		14 31	14 39			14 57			15 25				15 57			16 25		16 31	16 41		
Grangetown	d		14 35	14 43			15 01			15 29				16 01			16 29		16 35	16 45		
Dingle Road	d		14 41																16 41			
Penarth	a		14 46																16 46			
Cogan	d			14 47			15 05			15 33				16 04			16 33			16 48		
Eastbrook	d			14 49			15 07			15 35				16 07			16 35			16 51		
Dinas Powys	d			14 51			15 09			15 37				16 09			16 37			16 53		
Cadoxton	d			14 56			15 14			15 42				16 13			16 42			16 57		
Barry Docks	d			14 59			15 17			15 45				16 16			16 45			17 00		
Barry ■	d			15 03			15 21			15 49				16 21			16 49			17b12		
Barry Island	a						15 27			15 55				16 27			16 55					
Rhoose Cardiff Int Airport ✈	d			15 10																17 19		
Llantwit Major	d			15 20																17 29		
Bridgend	a			15 37																17 46		

b arr. 1704

Table 130

Sundays until 11 July

Treherbert, Aberdare, Merthyr, Pontypridd, Rhymney and Coryton - Cardiff, Penarth, Barry, Barry Island and Bridgend

		AW	AW	AW	AW	AW	AW	AW	AW	AW	AW	AW	AW	AW	AW	AW	AW	AW	AW	AW	AW	AW	AW
Treherbert	d				16 17															18 17			
Ynyswen	d				16 19															18 19			
Treorchy	d				16 21															18 21			
Ton Pentre	d				16 23															18 23			
Ystrad Rhondda	a				16 26															18 26			
	d				16 28															18 28			
Llwynypia	d				16 30															18 30			
Tonypandy	d				16 33															18 33			
Dinas Rhondda	d				16 35															18 35			
Porth	a				16 38															18 38			
	d				16 39															18 39			
Trehafod	d				16 42															18 42			
Merthyr Tydfil	d														17 38								
Pentre-bach	d														17 42								
Troed Y Rhiw	d														17 45								
Merthyr Vale	a														17 48								
	d														17 50								
Quakers Yard	d														17 55								
Aberdare ■	d								16 52												18 52		
Cwmbach	d								16 55												18 55		
Fernhill	d								16 58												18 58		
Mountain Ash	a								17 01												19 01		
	d								17 04												19 04		
Penrhiwceiber	d								17 07												19 07		
Abercynon	d								17 13						17 59						19 13		
Pontypridd ■	a				16 47				17 23						18 07					18 47	19 23		
	d				16 48				17 24						18 09					18 48	19 24		
Trefforest	d				16 51				17 27						18 12					18 51	19 27		
Trefforest Estate	d																						
Taffs Well ■	d				16 58				17 34						18 20					18 58	19 34		
Radyr ■	a				17 01				17 37						18 23					19 01	19 37		
	d				17 01				17 37						18 23					19 01	19 37		
Danescourt	d																						
Fairwater	d																						
Waun-gron Park	d																						
Ninian Park	d																						
Llandaf	d				17 04				17 40						18 26					19 04	19 40		
Cathays	d				17 09				17 45						18 31					19 09	19 45		
Rhymney ■	d											17 22										19 22	
Pontlottyn	d											17 25										19 25	
Tir-phil	d											17 29										19 29	
Brithdir	d											17 32										19 32	
Bargoed	a											17 35										19 35	
	d											17 37										19 37	
Gilfach Fargoed	d											17 39										19 39	
Pengam	d											17 42										19 42	
Hengoed	d											17 45										19 45	
Ystrad Mynach ■	d											17 48										19 48	
Llanbradach	d											17 53										19 53	
Aber	d											17 57										19 57	
Caerphilly ■	d											18 00										20 00	
Lisvane & Thornhill	d											18 04										20 04	
Llanishen	d											18 06										20 06	
Heath High Level	d											18 09										20 09	
Coryton	d																						
Whitchurch (Cardiff)	d																						
Rhiwbina	d																						
Birchgrove	d																						
Ty Glas	d																						
Heath Low Level	d																						
Cardiff Queen Street ■	a				17 14				17 49			18 14			18 34					19 14	19 49	20 14	
	d		17 00	17 12	17 16	17 24	17 36	17 48	17 51	18 00	18 12	18 16	18 24		18 36	18 36	18 48		18 57	19 16	19 51	20 16	
Cardiff Bay	a		17 04	17 16		17 28	17 40	17 52		18 04	18 16		18 28			18 40	18 52		19 00				
Cardiff Central ■	a				17 18				17 54			18 18			18 39				19 03	19 18	19 54	20 18	
	d	16 55			17 25				17 57			18 25		18 31	18 41			18 55		19 25	20 01	20 25	20 31
Grangetown	d	16 59			17 29				18 01			18 29		18 35	18 45			18 59		19 29	20 05	20 29	20 35
Dingle Road	d													18 41									20 41
Penarth	a													18 46									20 46
Cogan	d	17 03			17 33				18 05			18 33			18 48			19 03		19 33	20 09	20 33	
Eastbrook	d	17 05			17 35				18 07			18 35			18 51			19 05		19 35	20 11	20 35	
Dinas Powys	d	17 07			17 37				18 09			18 37			18 53			19 07		19 37	20 13	20 37	
Cadoxton	d	17 12			17 42				18 14			18 42			18 57			19 12		19 42	20 18	20 42	
Barry Docks	d	17 15			17 45				18 17			18 45			19 00			19 15		19 45	20 21	20 45	
Barry ■	d	17 19			17 49				18 21			18 49			19 05			19 19		19 49	20 25	20 49	
Barry Island	a	17 25			17 55				18 27			18 55						19 25		19 55	20 31	20 55	
Rhoose Cardiff Int Airport ✈	d														19 12								
Llantwit Major	d														19 22								
Bridgend	a														19 39								

Table 130

Sundays until 11 July

Treherbert, Aberdare, Merthyr, Pontypridd, Rhymney and Coryton - Cardiff, Penarth, Barry, Barry Island and Bridgend

		AW	AW	AW	AW	AW	AW
Treherbert	d			20 17			
Ynyswen	d			20 19			
Treorchy	d			20 21			
Ton Pentre	d			20 23			
Ystrad Rhondda	a			20 26			
	d			20 28			
Llwynypia	d			20 30			
Tonypandy	d			20 33			
Dinas Rhondda	d			20 35			
Porth	a			20 38			
	d			20 39			
Trehafod	d			20 42			
Merthyr Tydfil	d	19 38					21 38
Pentre-bach	d	19 42					21 42
Troed Y Rhiw	d	19 45					21 45
Merthyr Vale	a	19 48					21 48
	d	19 50					21 50
Quakers Yard	d	19 55					21 55
Aberdare ■	d				20 52		
Cwmbach	d				20 55		
Fernhill	d				20 58		
Mountain Ash	a				21 01		
	d				21 04		
Penrhiwceiber	d				21 07		
Abercynon	d	19 59			21 13		21 59
Pontypridd ■	a	20 07		20 47	21 23		22 07
	d	20 09		20 48	21 24		22 09
Trefforest	d	20 12		20 51	21 27		22 12
Trefforest Estate	d						
Taffs Well ■	d	20 20		20 58	21 34		22 20
Radyr ■	a	20 23		21 01	21 37		22 23
	d	20 23		21 01	21 37		22 23
Danescourt	d						
Fairwater	d						
Waun-gron Park	d						
Ninian Park	d						
Llandaf	d	20 26		21 04	21 40		22 26
Cathays	d	20 31		21 09	21 45		22 31
Rhymney ■	d						
Pontlottyn	d						
Tir-phil	d						
Brithdir	d						
Bargoed	a						
	d						
Gilfach Fargoed	d						
Pengam	d						
Hengoed	d						
Ystrad Mynach ■	d						
Llanbradach	d						
Aber	d						
Caerphilly ■	d						
Lisvane & Thornhill	d						
Llanishen	d						
Heath High Level	d						
Coryton	d						
Whitchurch (Cardiff)	d						
Rhiwbina	d						
Birchgrove	d						
Ty Glas	d						
Heath Low Level	d						
Cardiff Queen Street ■	a	20 34		21 14	21 49		22 34
	d	20 36		21 16	21 51		22 36
Cardiff Bay	a						
Cardiff Central ■	a	20 39		21 18	21 57		22 41
	d	20 41	20 59	21 25		22 25	
Grangetown	d	20 45	21 03	21 29		22 29	
Dingle Road	d						
Penarth	a						
Cogan	d	20 48	21 07	21 33		22 33	
Eastbrook	d	20 51	21 09	21 35		22 35	
Dinas Powys	d	20 53	21 11	21 37		22 37	
Cadoxton	d	20 57	21 16	21 42		22 42	
Barry Docks	d	21 00	21 19	21 45		22 45	
Barry ■	d	21 05	21 23	21 49		22 49	
Barry Island	a		21 29	21 55		22 55	
Rhoose Cardiff Int Airport ✈	d	21 12					
Llantwit Major	d	21 22					
Bridgend	a	21 39					

Table 130

Sundays

18 July to 05 September

Treherbert, Aberdare, Merthyr, Pontypridd, Rhymney and Coryton - Cardiff, Penarth, Barry, Barry Island and Bridgend

		AW	AW	AW	AW	AW	AW	AW	AW	AW	AW	AW	AW	AW	AW	AW	AW	AW	AW	AW	AW	AW	AW
Treherbert	d					08 17																10 07	
Ynyswen	d					08 19																10 09	
Treorchy	d					08 21																10 11	
Ton Pentre	d					08 23																10 13	
Ystrad Rhondda	a					08 26																10 16	
	d					08 28																10 18	
Llwynypia	d					08 30																10 20	
Tonypandy	d					08 33																10 23	
Dinas Rhondda	d					08 35																10 25	
Porth	a					08 38																10 28	
	d					08 39																10 29	
Trehafod	d					08 42																10 32	
Merthyr Tydfil	d															09 38							
Pentre-bach	d															09 42							
Troed Y Rhiw	d															09 45							
Merthyr Vale	a															09 48							
	d															09 50							
Quakers Yard	d															09 55							
Aberdare	d																		09 52				
Cwmbach	d																		09 55				
Fernhill	d																		09 58				
Mountain Ash	a																		10 01				
	d																		10 04				
Penrhiwceiber	d																		10 07				
Abercynon	d															09 59			10 13				
Pontypridd	a					08 47										10 07			10 23			10 37	
	d					08 48										10 09			10 24			10 38	
Trefforest	d					08 51										10 12			10 27			10 41	
Trefforest Estate	d																						
Taffs Well	d					08 58										10 20			10 34			10 48	
Radyr	a					09 01										10 23			10 37			10 51	
	d					09 01										10 23			10 37			10 51	
Danescourt	d																						
Fairwater	d																						
Waun-gron Park	d																						
Ninian Park	d																						
Llandaf	d					09 04										10 26			10 40			10 54	
Cathays	d					09 09										10 31			10 45			10 59	
Rhymney	d												09 22										
Pontlottyn	d												09 25										
Tir-phil	d												09 29										
Brithdir	d												09 32										
Bargoed	a												09 35										
	d												09 37										
Gilfach Fargoed	d												09 39										
Pengam	d												09 42										
Hengoed	d												09 45										
Ystrad Mynach	d												09 48										
Llanbradach	d												09 53										
Aber	d												09 57										
Caerphilly	d												10 00										
Lisvane & Thornhill	d												10 04										
Llanishen	d												10 06										
Heath High Level	d												10 09										
Coryton	d																						
Whitchurch (Cardiff)	d																						
Rhiwbina	d																						
Birchgrove	d																						
Ty Glas	d																						
Heath Low Level	d																						
Cardiff Queen Street	a			08 57		09 14							10 14			10 34			10 49			11 02	
	d			09 00	09 12	09 16	09 24	09 36	09 48		10 00	10 12	10 16	10 24		10 36	10 36	10 48	10 51	11 00		11 04	11 12
Cardiff Bay	a			09 04	09 16		09 28	09 40	09 52		10 04	10 16		10 28			10 40	10 52		11 04			11 16
Cardiff Central	a					09 18							10 18			10 39			10 54		11 11	11 07	
	d	08 25	08 41			09 25				09 55			10 25		10 31	10 41			10 55		11 15	11 25	
Grangetown	d	08 29	08 45			09 29				09 59			10 29		10 35	10 45			10 59			11 29	
Dingle Road	d														10 41								
Penarth	a														10 44								
Cogan	d	08 33	08 48			09 33				10 03			10 33			10 48			11 03			11 33	
Eastbrook	d	08 35	08 51			09 35				10 05			10 35			10 51			11 05			11 35	
Dinas Powys	d	08 37	08 53			09 37				10 07			10 37			10 53			11 07			11 37	
Cadoxton	d	08 42	08 57			09 42				10 12			10 42			10 57			11 12			11 42	
Barry Docks	d	08 45	09 00			09 45				10 15			10 45			11 00			11 15			11 45	
Barry	d	08 49	09 05			09 49				10 19			10 49			11 05			11 19		11 34	11 49	
Barry Island	a	08 55				09 55				10 25			10 55						11 25		11 41	11 55	
Rhoose Cardiff Int Airport ✈	d		09 12													11 12							
Llantwit Major	d		09 22													11 22							
Bridgend	a		09 39													11 39							

Table 130

Sundays

18 July to 05 September

Treherbert, Aberdare, Merthyr, Pontypridd, Rhymney and Coryton - Cardiff, Penarth, Barry, Barry Island and Bridgend

		AW	AW	AW	AW	AW	AW	AW	AW	AW	AW	AW	AW	AW	AW	AW	AW	AW	AW	AW	AW	AW	AW
Treherbert	d															12 07							
Ynyswen	d															12 09							
Treorchy	d															12 11							
Ton Pentre	d															12 13							
Ystrad Rhondda	a															12 16							
	d															12 18							
Llwynypia	d															12 20							
Tonypandy	d															12 23							
Dinas Rhondda	d															12 25							
Porth	a															12 28							
	d															12 29							
Trehafod	d															12 32							
Merthyr Tydfil	d										11 38												
Pentre-bach	d										11 42												
Troed Y Rhiw	d										11 45												
Merthyr Vale	a										11 48												
	d										11 50												
Quakers Yard	d										11 55												
Aberdare	d				10 52																12 52		
Cwmbach	d				10 55																12 55		
Fernhill	d				10 58																12 58		
Mountain Ash	a				11 01																13 01		
	d				11 04																13 04		
Penrhiwceiber	d				11 07																13 07		
Abercynon	d				11 13						11 59										13 13		
Pontypridd	a				11 23						12 07					12 37					13 23		
	d				11 24						12 09					12 38					13 24		
Trefforest	d				11 27						12 12					12 41					13 27		
Trefforest Estate	d																						
Taffs Well	d				11 34						12 20					12 48					13 34		
Radyr	a				11 37						12 23					12 51					13 37		
	d				11 37						12 23					12 51					13 37		
Danescourt	d																						
Fairwater	d																						
Waun-gron Park	d																						
Ninian Park	d																						
Llandaf	d				11 40						12 26					12 54					13 40		
Cathays	d				11 45						12 31					12 59					13 45		
Rhymney	d						11 10																13 10
Pontlottyn	d						11 13																13 13
Tir-phil	d						11 17																13 17
Brithdir	d						11 20																13 20
Bargoed	a						11 23																13 23
	d						11 25																13 25
Gilfach Fargoed	d						11 27																13 27
Pengam	d						11 30																13 30
Hengoed	d						11 33																13 33
Ystrad Mynach	d						11 36																13 36
Llanbradach	d						11 41																13 41
Aber	d						11 45																13 45
Caerphilly	d						11 48																13 48
Lisvane & Thornhill	d						11 52																13 52
Llanishen	d						11 54																13 54
Heath High Level	d						11 57																13 57
Coryton	d																						
Whitchurch (Cardiff)	d																						
Rhiwbina	d																						
Birchgrove	d																						
Ty Glas	d																						
Heath Low Level	d																						
Cardiff Queen Street	a				11 49		12 02				12 34					13 04					13 49		14 02
	d	11 24	11 36	11 48	11 51	12 00	12 04	12 12	12 24		12 36	12 36	12 48		13 00	13 04	13 12	13 24	13 36	13 48	13 51	14 00	14 04
Cardiff Bay	a	11 28	11 40	11 52		12 04		12 16	12 28			12 40	12 52		13 04		13 16	13 28	13 40	13 52		14 04	
Cardiff Central	a				11 54		12 07				12 39					13 06					13 54		14 07
	d				11 55		12 25			12 31	12 41			12 55		13 25					13 55		14 25
Grangetown	d				11 59		12 29			12 35	12 45			12 59		13 29					13 59		14 29
Dingle Road	d									12 41													
Penarth	a									12 46													
Cogan	d				12 03		12 33				12 48			13 03		13 33					14 03		14 33
Eastbrook	d				12 05		12 35				12 51			13 05		13 35					14 05		14 35
Dinas Powys	d				12 07		12 37				12 53			13 07		13 37					14 07		14 37
Cadoxton	d				12 12		12 42				12 57			13 12		13 42					14 12		14 42
Barry Docks	d				12 15		12 45				13 00			13 15		13 45					14 15		14 45
Barry	d				12 19		12 49				13 05			13 19		13 49					14 19		14 49
Barry Island	a				12 25		12 55							13 25		13 55					14 25		14 55
Rhoose Cardiff Int Airport ✈	d										13 12												
Llantwit Major	d										13 22												
Bridgend	a										13 39												

Table 130

Sundays

18 July to 05 September

Treherbert, Aberdare, Merthyr, Pontypridd, Rhymney and Coryton - Cardiff, Penarth, Barry, Barry Island and Bridgend

		AW		AW	AW	AW	AW	AW	AW	AW	AW	AW		AW	AW	AW	AW	AW	AW	AW	AW	AW		AW	AW
Treherbert	d										14 17												
Ynyswen	d										14 19												
Treorchy	d										14 21												
Ton Pentre	d										14 23												
Ystrad Rhondda	a										14 26												
	d										14 28												
Llwynypia	d										14 30												
Tonypandy	d										14 33												
Dinas Rhondda	d										14 35												
Porth	a										14 38												
	d										14 39												
Trehafod	d										14 42												
Merthyr Tydfil	d					13 38																		15 38	
Pentre-bach	d					13 42																		15 42	
Troed Y Rhiw	d					13 45																		15 45	
Merthyr Vale	a					13 48																		15 48	
	d					13 50																		15 50	
Quakers Yard	d					13 55																		15 55	
Aberdare [3]	d																14 52								
Cwmbach	d																14 55								
Fernhill	d																14 58								
Mountain Ash	a																15 01								
	d																15 04								
Penrhiwceiber	d																15 07								
Abercynon	d					13 59											15 13							15 59	
Pontypridd [3]	a					14 07						14 47					15 23							16 07	
	d					14 09						14 48					15 24							16 09	
Trefforest	d					14 12						14 51					15 27							16 12	
Trefforest Estate	d																								
Taffs Well [3]	d					14 20						14 58					15 34							16 20	
Radyr [3]	a					14 23						15 01					15 37							16 23	
	d					14 23						15 01					15 37							16 23	
Danescourt	d																								
Fairwater	d																								
Waun-gron Park	d																								
Ninian Park	d																								
Llandaf	d					14 26						15 04					15 40							16 26	
Cathays	d					14 31						15 09					15 45							16 31	
Rhymney [3]	d																			15 22					
Pontlottyn	d																			15 25					
Tir-phil	d																			15 29					
Brithdir	d																			15 32					
Bargoed	a																			15 35					
	d																			15 37					
Gilfach Fargoed	d																			15 39					
Pengam	d																			15 42					
Hengoed	d																			15 45					
Ystrad Mynach [3]	d																			15 48					
Llanbradach	d																			15 53					
Aber	d																			15 57					
Caerphilly [3]	d																			16 00					
Lisvane & Thornhill	d																			16 04					
Llanishen	d																			16 06					
Heath High Level	d																			16 09					
Coryton	d																								
Whitchurch (Cardiff)	d																								
Rhiwbina	d																								
Birchgrove	d																								
Ty Glas	d																								
Heath Low Level	d																								
Cardiff Queen Street [3]	a					14 34						15 14					15 49			16 14				16 34	
	d	14 12		14 24		14 36	14 36	14 48		15 00	15 12	15 16		15 24	15 36	15 48	15 51	16 00	16 12	16 16	16 24			16 36	16 36
Cardiff Bay	a	14 16		14 28			14 40	14 52		15 04	15 16			15 28	15 40	15 52		16 04	16 16		16 28				16 40
Cardiff Central [7]	a					14 39						15 18					15 54			16 18				16 39	
	d				14 31	14 41			14 55			15 25					15 55			16 25		16 31		16 41	
Grangetown	d				14 35	14 45			14 59			15 29					15 59			16 29		16 35		16 45	
Dingle Road	d				14 41																	16 41			
Penarth	a				14 46																	16 46			
Cogan	d					14 48			15 03			15 33					16 03			16 33				16 48	
Eastbrook	d					14 51			15 05			15 35					16 05			16 35				16 51	
Dinas Powys	d					14 53			15 07			15 37					16 07			16 37				16 53	
Cadoxton	d					14 57			15 12			15 42					16 12			16 42				16 57	
Barry Docks	d					15 00			15 15			15 45					16 15			16 45				17 00	
Barry [3]	d					15 05			15 19			15 49					16 19			16 49				17 05	
Barry Island	a								15 25			15 55					16 25			16 55					
Rhoose Cardiff Int Airport ✈	d					15 12																		17 12	
Llantwit Major	d					15 22																		17 22	
Bridgend	a					15 39																		17 39	

Table 130

Sundays

18 July to 05 September

Treherbert, Aberdare, Merthyr, Pontypridd, Rhymney and Coryton - Cardiff, Penarth, Barry, Barry Island and Bridgend

		AW	AW	AW	AW	AW	AW	AW		AW	AW	AW	AW	AW	AW	AW	AW	AW		AW	AW	AW	AW	AW	AW
Treherbert	d					16 17																	18 17		
Ynyswen	d					16 19																	18 19		
Treorchy	d					16 21																	18 21		
Ton Pentre	d					16 23																	18 23		
Ystrad Rhondda	a					16 26																	18 26		
	d					16 28																	18 28		
Llwynypia	d					16 30																	18 30		
Tonypandy	d					16 33																	18 33		
Dinas Rhondda	d					16 35																	18 35		
Porth	a					16 38																	18 38		
	d					16 39																	18 39		
Trehafod	d					16 42																	18 42		
Merthyr Tydfil	d																17 38								
Pentre-bach	d																17 42								
Troed Y Rhiw	d																17 45								
Merthyr Vale	a																17 48								
	d																17 50								
Quakers Yard	d																17 55								
Aberdare [3]	d										16 52													18 52	
Cwmbach	d										16 55													18 55	
Fernhill	d										16 58													18 58	
Mountain Ash	a										17 01													19 01	
	d										17 04													19 04	
Penrhiwceiber	d										17 07													19 07	
Abercynon	d										17 13						17 59							19 13	
Pontypridd [3]	a					16 47					17 23						18 07						18 47	19 23	
	d					16 48					17 24						18 09						18 48	19 24	
Trefforest	d					16 51					17 27						18 12						18 51	19 27	
Trefforest Estate	d																								
Taffs Well [3]	d					16 58					17 34						18 20						18 58	19 34	
Radyr [3]	a					17 01					17 37						18 23						19 01	19 37	
	d					17 01					17 37						18 23						19 01	19 37	
Danescourt	d																								
Fairwater	d																								
Waun-gron Park	d																								
Ninian Park	d																								
Llandaf	d					17 04					17 40						18 26						19 04	19 40	
Cathays	d					17 09					17 45						18 31						19 09	19 45	
Rhymney [3]	d													17 22											19 22
Pontlottyn	d													17 25											19 25
Tir-phil	d													17 29											19 29
Brithdir	d													17 32											19 32
Bargoed	a													17 35											19 35
	d													17 37											19 37
Gilfach Fargoed	d													17 39											19 39
Pengam	d													17 42											19 42
Hengoed	d													17 45											19 45
Ystrad Mynach [3]	d													17 48											19 48
Llanbradach	d													17 53											19 53
Aber	d													17 57											19 57
Caerphilly [3]	d													18 00											20 00
Lisvane & Thornhill	d													18 04											20 04
Llanishen	d													18 06											20 06
Heath High Level	d													18 09											20 09
Coryton	d																								
Whitchurch (Cardiff)	d																								
Rhiwbina	d																								
Birchgrove	d																								
Ty Glas	d																								
Heath Low Level	d																								
Cardiff Queen Street [3]	a					17 14					17 49			18 14			18 34					18 57	19 14	19 49	20 14
	d	16 48		17 00	17 12	17 16	17 24	17 36		17 48	17 51	18 00	18 12	18 16	18 24		18 36	18 36		18 48		19 00	19 16	19 51	20 16
Cardiff Bay	a	16 52		17 04	17 16		17 28	17 40		17 52		18 04	18 16		18 28			18 40		18 52					
Cardiff Central [7]	a					17 18					17 54			18 18			18 39					19 03	19 18	19 54	20 18
	d		16 55			17 25					17 55			18 25		18 31	18 41				18 55		19 25	19 55	20 25
Grangetown	d		16 59			17 29					17 59			18 29		18 35	18 45				18 59		19 29	19 59	20 29
Dingle Road	d															18 41									
Penarth	a															18 46									
Cogan	d		17 03			17 33					18 03			18 33			18 48				19 03		19 33	20 03	20 33
Eastbrook	d		17 05			17 35					18 05			18 35			18 51				19 05		19 35	20 05	20 35
Dinas Powys	d		17 07			17 37					18 07			18 37			18 53				19 07		19 37	20 07	20 37
Cadoxton	d		17 12			17 42					18 12			18 42			18 57				19 12		19 42	20 12	20 42
Barry Docks	d		17 15			17 45					18 15			18 45			19 00				19 15		19 45	20 15	20 45
Barry [3]	d		17 19			17 49					18 19			18 49			19 05				19 19		19 49	20 19	20 49
Barry Island	a		17 25			17 55					18 25			18 55							19 25		19 55	20 25	20 55
Rhoose Cardiff Int Airport ✈	d																19 12								
Llantwit Major	d																19 22								
Bridgend	a																19 39								

Table 130

Sundays
18 July to 05 September

Treherbert, Aberdare, Merthyr, Pontypridd, Rhymney and Coryton - Cardiff, Penarth, Barry, Barry Island and Bridgend

		AW	AW	AW	AW	AW	AW	AW
Treherbert	d				20 17			
Ynyswen	d				20 19			
Treorchy	d				20 21			
Ton Pentre	d				20 23			
Ystrad Rhondda	a				20 26			
	d				20 28			
Llwynypia	d				20 30			
Tonypandy	d				20 33			
Dinas Rhondda	d				20 35			
Porth	a				20 38			
	d				20 39			
Trehafod	d				20 42			
Merthyr Tydfil	d		19 38					21 38
Pentre-bach	d		19 42					21 42
Troed Y Rhiw	d		19 45					21 45
Merthyr Vale	a		19 48					21 48
	d		19 50					21 50
Quakers Yard	d		19 55					21 55
Aberdare 3	d					20 52		
Cwmbach	d					20 55		
Fernhill	d					20 58		
Mountain Ash	a					21 01		
	d					21 04		
Penrhiwceiber	d					21 07		
Abercynon	d		19 59			21 13		21 59
Pontypridd 3	a		20 07		20 47	21 23		22 07
	d		20 09		20 48	21 24		22 09
Trefforest	d		20 12		20 51	21 27		22 12
Trefforest Estate	d							
Taffs Well 3	d		20 20		20 58	21 34		22 20
Radyr 3	a		20 23		21 01	21 37		22 23
	d		20 23		21 01	21 37		22 23
Danescourt	d							
Fairwater	d							
Waun-gron Park	d							
Ninian Park	d							
Llandaf	d		20 26		21 04	21 40		22 26
Cathays	d		20 31		21 09	21 45		22 31
Rhymney 3	d							
Pontlottyn	d							
Tir-phil	d							
Brithdir	d							
Bargoed	a							
	d							
Gilfach Fargoed	d							
Pengam	d							
Hengoed	d							
Ystrad Mynach 3	d							
Llanbradach	d							
Aber	d							
Caerphilly 3	d							
Lisvane & Thornhill	d							
Llanishen	d							
Heath High Level	d							
Coryton	d							
Whitchurch (Cardiff)	d							
Rhiwbina	d							
Birchgrove	d							
Ty Glas	d							
Heath Low Level	d							
Cardiff Queen Street 3	a		20 34		21 14	21 49		22 34
	d		20 36		21 16	21 51		22 36
Cardiff Bay	a							
Cardiff Central 7	a		20 39		21 18	21 57		22 41
	d	20 31	20 41	20 55	21 25		22 25	
Grangetown	d	20 35	20 45	20 59	21 29		22 29	
Dingle Road	d	20 41						
Penarth	a	20 46						
Cogan	d		20 48	21 03	21 33		22 33	
Eastbrook	d		20 51	21 05	21 35		22 35	
Dinas Powys	d		20 53	21 07	21 37		22 37	
Cadoxton	d		20 57	21 12	21 42		22 42	
Barry Docks	d		21 00	21 15	21 45		22 45	
Barry 3	d		21 05	21 19	21 49		22 49	
Barry Island	a			21 25	21 55		22 55	
Rhoose Cardiff Int Airport ✈	d		21 12					
Llantwit Major	d		21 22					
Bridgend	a		21 39					

Table 130

Sundays
from 12 September

Treherbert, Aberdare, Merthyr, Pontypridd, Rhymney and Coryton - Cardiff, Penarth, Barry, Barry Island and Bridgend

		AW	AW	AW	AW	AW	AW	AW	AW	AW	AW	AW	AW	AW	AW	AW	AW	AW	AW	AW	AW	AW	AW
Treherbert	d						08 17															10 07	
Ynyswen	d						08 19															10 09	
Treorchy	d						08 21															10 11	
Ton Pentre	d						08 23															10 13	
Ystrad Rhondda	a						08 26															10 16	
	d						08 28															10 18	
Llwynypia	d						08 30															10 20	
Tonypandy	d						08 33															10 23	
Dinas Rhondda	d						08 35															10 25	
Porth	a						08 38															10 28	
	d						08 39															10 29	
Trehafod	d						08 42															10 32	
Merthyr Tydfil	d																09 38						
Pentre-bach	d																09 42						
Troed Y Rhiw	d																09 45						
Merthyr Vale	a																09 48						
	d																09 50						
Quakers Yard	d																09 55						
Aberdare 3	d																			09 51			
Cwmbach	d																			09 54			
Fernhill	d																			09 58			
Mountain Ash	a																			10 01			
	d																			10 04			
Penrhiwceiber	d																			10 08			
Abercynon	d																09 59			10 14			
Pontypridd 3	a						08 47										10 07			10 23		10 37	
	d						08 48										10 09			10 24		10 38	
Trefforest	d						08 51										10 12			10 27		10 41	
Trefforest Estate	d																						
Taffs Well 3	d						08 58										10 20			10 34		10 48	
Radyr 3	a						09 01										10 23			10 37		10 51	
	d	23p10					09 01										10 23			10 37		10 51	
Danescourt	d																						
Fairwater	d																						
Waun-gron Park	d																						
Ninian Park	d																						
Llandaf	d	23p12					09 04										10 26			10 40		10 54	
Cathays	d	23p16					09 09										10 31			10 45		10 59	
Rhymney 3	d													09 22									
Pontlottyn	d													09 25									
Tir-phil	d													09 29									
Brithdir	d													09 32									
Bargoed	a													09 35									
	d													09 37									
Gilfach Fargoed	d													09 39									
Pengam	d													09 42									
Hengoed	d													09 45									
Ystrad Mynach 3	d													09 48									
Llanbradach	d													09 53									
Aber	d													09 57									
Caerphilly 3	d													10 00									
Lisvane & Thornhill	d													10 04									
Llanishen	d													10 06									
Heath High Level	d													10 09									
Coryton	d																						
Whitchurch (Cardiff)	d																						
Rhiwbina	d																						
Birchgrove	d																						
Ty Glas	d																						
Heath Low Level	d																						
Cardiff Queen Street 3	a	23p19			08 57		09 14							10 14			10 34			10 49		11 02	
	d	23p20			09 00	09 12	09 16	09 24	09 36	09 48		10 00	10 12	10 16	10 24		10 36	10 36	10 48	10 51	11 00	11 04	11 12
Cardiff Bay	a				09 04	09 16		09 28	09 40	09 52		10 04	10 16		10 28			10 40	10 52		11 04		11 16
Cardiff Central 7	a	23p25					09 18							10 18			10 39			10 54		11 07	
	d	23p30	08 25	08 41			09 25				09 55			10 25		10 31	10 41			10 55		11 25	
Grangetown	d	23p34	08 29	08 45			09 29				09 59			10 29		10 35	10 45			10 59		11 29	
Dingle Road	d															10 41							
Penarth	a															10 44							
Cogan	d	23p37	08 33	08 48			09 33				10 03			10 33			10 48			11 03		11 33	
Eastbrook	d	23p40	08 35	08 51			09 35				10 05			10 35			10 51			11 05		11 35	
Dinas Powys	d	23p42	08 37	08 53			09 37				10 07			10 37			10 53			11 07		11 37	
Cadoxton	d	23p46	08 42	08 57			09 42				10 12			10 42			10 57			11 12		11 42	
Barry Docks	d	23p49	08 45	09 00			09 45				10 15			10 45			11 00			11 15		11 45	
Barry 3	d	23p54	08 49	09 05			09 49				10 19			10 49			11 05			11 19		11 49	
Barry Island	a	00 01	08 56				09 56				10 26			10 55						11 26		11 56	
Rhoose Cardiff Int Airport ✈	d			09 12													11 12						
Llantwit Major	d			09 22													11 22						
Bridgend	a			09 40													11 40						

Table 130

Sundays
from 12 September

Treherbert, Aberdare, Merthyr, Pontypridd, Rhymney and Coryton - Cardiff, Penarth, Barry, Barry Island and Bridgend

		AW	AW	AW	AW	AW	AW	AW	AW	AW	AW	AW	AW	AW	AW	AW	AW	AW	AW	AW	AW	AW	AW
Treherbert	d															12 07							
Ynyswen	d															12 09							
Treorchy	d															12 11							
Ton Pentre	d															12 13							
Ystrad Rhondda	a															12 16							
	d															12 18							
Llwynypia	d															12 20							
Tonypandy	d															12 23							
Dinas Rhondda	d															12 25							
Porth	a															12 28							
	d															12 29							
Trehafod	d															12 32							
Merthyr Tydfil	d										11 38												
Pentre-bach	d										11 42												
Troed Y Rhiw	d										11 45												
Merthyr Vale	a										11 48												
	d										11 50												
Quakers Yard	d										11 55												
Aberdare 3	d				10 51																12 51		
Cwmbach	d				10 54																12 54		
Fernhill	d				10 58																12 58		
Mountain Ash	a				11 01																13 01		
	d				11 04																13 04		
Penrhiwceiber	d				11 08																13 08		
Abercynon	d				11 14						11 59										13 14		
Pontypridd 3	a				11 23						12 07					12 37					13 23		
	d				11 24						12 09					12 38					13 24		
Trefforest	d				11 27						12 12					12 41					13 27		
Trefforest Estate	d																						
Taffs Well 3	d				11 34						12 20					12 48					13 34		
Radyr 3	a				11 37						12 23					12 51					13 37		
	d				11 37						12 23					12 51					13 37		
Danescourt	d																						
Fairwater	d																						
Waun-gron Park	d																						
Ninian Park	d																						
Llandaf	d				11 40						12 26					12 54					13 40		
Cathays	d				11 45						12 31					12 59					13 45		
Rhymney 3	d						11 10																13 10
Pontlottyn	d						11 13																13 13
Tir-phil	d						11 17																13 17
Brithdir	d						11 20																13 20
Bargoed	a						11 23																13 23
	d						11 25																13 25
Gilfach Fargoed	d						11 27																13 27
Pengam	d						11 30																13 30
Hengoed	d						11 33																13 33
Ystrad Mynach 3	d						11 36																13 36
Llanbradach	d						11 41																13 41
Aber	d						11 45																13 45
Caerphilly 3	d						11 48																13 48
Lisvane & Thornhill	d						11 52																13 52
Llanishen	d						11 54																13 54
Heath High Level	d						11 57																13 57
Coryton	d																						
Whitchurch (Cardiff)	d																						
Rhiwbina	d																						
Birchgrove	d																						
Ty Glas	d																						
Heath Low Level	d																						
Cardiff Queen Street 3	a				11 48		12 02				12 34					13 04					13 49		14 02
	d	11 24	11 36	11 48	11 50	12 00	12 04	12 12	12 24		12 36	12 36	12 48		13 00	13 04	13 12	13 24	13 36	13 48	13 51	14 00	14 04
Cardiff Bay	a	11 28	11 40	11 52		12 04		12 16	12 28			12 40	12 52		13 04		13 16	13 28	13 40	13 52		14 04	
Cardiff Central 7	a				11 53		12 07				12 39					13 06					13 54		14 07
	d				11 55		12 25			12 31	12 41			12 55		13 25					13 55		14 25
Grangetown	d				11 59		12 29			12 35	12 45			12 59		13 29					13 59		14 29
Dingle Road	d									12 41													
Penarth	a									12 47													
Cogan	d				12 03		12 33				12 48			13 03		13 33					14 03		14 33
Eastbrook	d				12 05		12 35				12 51			13 05		13 35					14 05		14 35
Dinas Powys	d				12 07		12 37				12 53			13 07		13 37					14 07		14 37
Cadoxton	d				12 12		12 42				12 57			13 12		13 42					14 12		14 42
Barry Docks	d				12 15		12 45				13 00			13 15		13 45					14 15		14 45
Barry 3	d				12 19		12 49				13 05			13 19		13 49					14 19		14 49
Barry Island	a				12 26		12 55							13 26		13 56					14 26		14 55
Rhoose Cardiff Int Airport ✈	d										13 12												
Llantwit Major	d										13 22												
Bridgend	a										13 40												

Table 130

Sundays
from 12 September

Treherbert, Aberdare, Merthyr, Pontypridd, Rhymney and Coryton - Cardiff, Penarth, Barry, Barry Island and Bridgend

		AW	AW	AW	AW	AW	AW	AW	AW	AW	AW	AW	AW	AW	AW	AW	AW	AW	AW	AW	AW	AW
Treherbert	d										14 17											
Ynyswen	d										14 19											
Treorchy	d										14 21											
Ton Pentre	d										14 23											
Ystrad Rhondda	a										14 26											
	d										14 28											
Llwynypia	d										14 30											
Tonypandy	d										14 33											
Dinas Rhondda	d										14 35											
Porth	a										14 38											
	d										14 39											
Trehafod	d										14 42											
Merthyr Tydfil	d				13 38																15 38	
Pentre-bach	d				13 42																15 42	
Troed Y Rhiw	d				13 45																15 45	
Merthyr Vale	a				13 48																15 48	
	d				13 50																15 50	
Quakers Yard	d				13 55																15 55	
Aberdare 3	d														14 51							
Cwmbach	d														14 54							
Fernhill	d														14 58							
Mountain Ash	a														15 01							
	d														15 04							
Penrhiwceiber	d														15 08							
Abercynon	d				13 59										15 14						15 59	
Pontypridd 3	a				14 07						14 47				15 23						16 07	
	d				14 09						14 48				15 24						16 09	
Trefforest	d				14 12						14 51				15 27						16 12	
Trefforest Estate	d																					
Taffs Well 3	d				14 20						14 58				15 34						16 20	
Radyr 3	a				14 23						15 01				15 37						16 23	
	d				14 23						15 01				15 37						16 23	
Danescourt	d																					
Fairwater	d																					
Waun-gron Park	d																					
Ninian Park	d																					
Llandaf	d				14 26						15 04				15 40						16 26	
Cathays	d				14 31						15 09				15 45						16 31	
Rhymney 3	d																	15 22				
Pontlottyn	d																	15 25				
Tir-phil	d																	15 29				
Brithdir	d																	15 32				
Bargoed	a																	15 35				
	d																	15 37				
Gilfach Fargoed	d																	15 39				
Pengam	d																	15 42				
Hengoed	d																	15 45				
Ystrad Mynach 3	d																	15 48				
Llanbradach	d																	15 53				
Aber	d																	15 57				
Caerphilly 3	d																	16 00				
Lisvane & Thornhill	d																	16 04				
Llanishen	d																	16 06				
Heath High Level	d																	16 09				
Coryton	d																					
Whitchurch (Cardiff)	d																					
Rhiwbina	d																					
Birchgrove	d																					
Ty Glas	d																					
Heath Low Level	d																					
Cardiff Queen Street 3	a				14 34						15 14				15 49			16 14			16 34	
	d	14 12	14 24		14 36	14 36	14 48		15 00	15 12	15 16	15 24	15 36	15 48	15 51	16 00	16 12	16 16	16 24		16 36	16 36
Cardiff Bay	a	14 16	14 28			14 40	14 52		15 04	15 16		15 28	15 40	15 52		16 04	16 16		16 28			16 40
Cardiff Central 7	a				14 39						15 18				15 54			16 18			16 39	
	d			14 31	14 41			14 55			15 25				15 55			16 25		16 31	16 41	
Grangetown	d			14 35	14 45			14 59			15 29				15 59			16 29		16 35	16 45	
Dingle Road	d			14 41																16 41		
Penarth	a			14 47																16 47		
Cogan	d				14 48			15 03			15 33				16 03			16 33			16 48	
Eastbrook	d				14 51			15 05			15 35				16 05			16 35			16 51	
Dinas Powys	d				14 53			15 07			15 37				16 07			16 37			16 53	
Cadoxton	d				14 57			15 12			15 42				16 12			16 42			16 57	
Barry Docks	d				15 00			15 15			15 45				16 15			16 45			17 00	
Barry 3	d				15 05			15 19			15 49				16 19			16 49			17 05	
Barry Island	a							15 26			15 56				16 26			16 55				
Rhoose Cardiff Int Airport ✈	d				15 12																17 12	
Llantwit Major	d				15 22																17 22	
Bridgend	a				15 40																17 40	

Table 130

Sundays
from 12 September

Treherbert, Aberdare, Merthyr, Pontypridd, Rhymney and Coryton - Cardiff, Penarth, Barry, Barry Island and Bridgend

		AW	AW	AW	AW	AW	AW	AW		AW	AW	AW	AW	AW	AW	AW	AW	AW		AW	AW	AW	AW	AW	AW
Treherbert	d					16 17																	18 17		
Ynyswen	d					16 19																	18 19		
Treorchy	d					16 21																	18 21		
Ton Pentre	d					16 23																	18 23		
Ystrad Rhondda	a					16 26																	18 26		
	d					16 28																	18 28		
Llwynypia	d					16 30																	18 30		
Tonypandy	d					16 33																	18 33		
Dinas Rhondda	d					16 35																	18 35		
Porth	a					16 38																	18 38		
	d					16 39																	18 39		
Trehafod	d					16 42																	18 42		
Merthyr Tydfil	d																17 38								
Pentre-bach	d																17 42								
Troed Y Rhiw	d																17 45								
Merthyr Vale	a																17 48								
	d																17 50								
Quakers Yard	d																17 55								
Aberdare ■	d										16 51													18 51	
Cwmbach	d										16 54													18 54	
Fernhill	d										16 58													18 58	
Mountain Ash	a										17 01													19 01	
	d										17 04													19 04	
Penrhiwceiber	d										17 08													19 08	
Abercynon	d										17 14						17 59							19 14	
Pontypridd ■	a					16 47					17 23						18 07						18 47	19 23	
	d					16 48					17 24						18 09						18 48	19 24	
Trefforest	d					16 51					17 27						18 12						18 51	19 27	
Trefforest Estate	d																								
Taffs Well ■	d					16 58					17 34						18 20						18 58	19 34	
Radyr ■	a					17 01					17 37						18 23						19 01	19 37	
	d					17 01					17 37						18 23						19 01	19 37	
Danescourt	d																								
Fairwater	d																								
Waun-gron Park	d																								
Ninian Park	d																								
Llandaf	d					17 04					17 40						18 26						19 04	19 40	
Cathays	d					17 09					17 45						18 31						19 09	19 45	
Rhymney ■	d													17 22											19 22
Pontlottyn	d													17 25											19 25
Tir-phil	d													17 29											19 29
Brithdir	d													17 32											19 32
Bargoed	a													17 35											19 35
	d													17 37											19 37
Gilfach Fargoed	d													17 39											19 39
Pengam	d													17 42											19 42
Hengoed	d													17 45											19 45
Ystrad Mynach ■	d													17 48											19 48
Llanbradach	d													17 53											19 53
Aber	d													17 57											19 57
Caerphilly ■	d													18 00											20 00
Lisvane & Thornhill	d													18 04											20 04
Llanishen	d													18 06											20 06
Heath High Level	d													18 09											20 09
Coryton	d																								
Whitchurch (Cardiff)	d																								
Rhiwbina	d																								
Birchgrove	d																								
Ty Glas	d																								
Heath Low Level	d																								
Cardiff Queen Street ■	a					17 14					17 49			18 14			18 34					18 57	19 14	19 49	20 14
	d	16 48		17 00	17 12	17 16	17 24	17 36		17 48	17 51	18 00	18 12	18 16	18 24		18 36	18 36		18 48		19 00	19 16	19 51	20 16
Cardiff Bay	a	16 52		17 04	17 16		17 28	17 40		17 52		18 04	18 16		18 28			18 40		18 52					
Cardiff Central ■	a					17 18					17 54			18 18			18 39					19 03	19 18	19 54	20 18
	d		16 55			17 25					17 55			18 25		18 31	18 41				18 55		19 25	19 55	20 25
Grangetown	d		16 59			17 29					17 59			18 29		18 35	18 45				18 59		19 29	19 59	20 29
Dingle Road	d															18 41									
Penarth	a															18 47									
Cogan	d		17 03			17 33					18 03			18 33			18 48				19 03		19 33	20 03	20 33
Eastbrook	d		17 05			17 35					18 05			18 35			18 51				19 05		19 35	20 05	20 35
Dinas Powys	d		17 07			17 37					18 07			18 37			18 53				19 07		19 37	20 07	20 37
Cadoxton	d		17 12			17 42					18 12			18 42			18 57				19 12		19 42	20 12	20 42
Barry Docks	d		17 15			17 45					18 15			18 45			19 00				19 15		19 45	20 15	20 45
Barry ■	d		17 19			17 49					18 19			18 49			19 05				19 19		19 49	20 19	20 49
Barry Island	a		17 26			17 56					18 26			18 55							19 26		19 56	20 26	20 55
Rhoose Cardiff Int Airport ✈	d																19 12								
Llantwit Major	d																19 22								
Bridgend	a																19 40								

Table 130

Sundays
from 12 September

Treherbert, Aberdare, Merthyr, Pontypridd, Rhymney and Coryton - Cardiff, Penarth, Barry, Barry Island and Bridgend

		AW	AW	AW		AW	AW	AW	AW
Treherbert	d					20 17			
Ynyswen	d					20 19			
Treorchy	d					20 21			
Ton Pentre	d					20 23			
Ystrad Rhondda	a					20 26			
	d					20 28			
Llwynypia	d					20 30			
Tonypandy	d					20 33			
Dinas Rhondda	d					20 35			
Porth	a					20 38			
	d					20 39			
Trehafod	d					20 42			
Merthyr Tydfil	d		19 38						21 38
Pentre-bach	d		19 42						21 42
Troed Y Rhiw	d		19 45						21 45
Merthyr Vale	a		19 48						21 48
	d		19 50						21 50
Quakers Yard	d		19 55						21 55
Aberdare ■	d						20 51		
Cwmbach	d						20 54		
Fernhill	d						20 58		
Mountain Ash	a						21 01		
	d						21 04		
Penrhiwceiber	d						21 08		
Abercynon	d		19 59				21 14		21 59
Pontypridd ■	a		20 07			20 47	21 24		22 07
	d		20 09			20 48	21 24		22 09
Trefforest	d		20 12			20 51	21 27		22 12
Trefforest Estate	d								
Taffs Well ■	d		20 20			20 58	21 34		22 20
Radyr ■	a		20 23			21 01	21 37		22 23
	d		20 23			21 01	21 37		22 23
Danescourt	d								
Fairwater	d								
Waun-gron Park	d								
Ninian Park	d								
Llandaf	d		20 26			21 04	21 40		22 26
Cathays	d		20 31			21 09	21 45		22 31
Rhymney ■	d								
Pontlottyn	d								
Tir-phil	d								
Brithdir	d								
Bargoed	a								
	d								
Gilfach Fargoed	d								
Pengam	d								
Hengoed	d								
Ystrad Mynach ■	d								
Llanbradach	d								
Aber	d								
Caerphilly ■	d								
Lisvane & Thornhill	d								
Llanishen	d								
Heath High Level	d								
Coryton	d								
Whitchurch (Cardiff)	d								
Rhiwbina	d								
Birchgrove	d								
Ty Glas	d								
Heath Low Level	d								
Cardiff Queen Street ■	a		20 34			21 14	21 49		22 34
	d		20 36			21 16	21 51		22 36
Cardiff Bay	a								
Cardiff Central ■	a		20 39			21 18	21 57		22 42
	d	20 31	20 41	20 55		21 25		22 25	
Grangetown	d	20 35	20 45	20 59		21 29		22 29	
Dingle Road	d	20 41							
Penarth	a	20 47							
Cogan	d		20 48	21 03		21 33		22 33	
Eastbrook	d		20 51	21 05		21 35		22 35	
Dinas Powys	d		20 53	21 07		21 37		22 37	
Cadoxton	d		20 57	21 12		21 42		22 42	
Barry Docks	d		21 00	21 15		21 45		22 45	
Barry ■	d		21 05	21 19		21 49		22 49	
Barry Island	a			21 26		21 56		22 56	
Rhoose Cardiff Int Airport ✈	d		21 12						
Llantwit Major	d		21 22						
Bridgend	a		21 40						

Table 130

Mondays to Fridays
until 03 September

Bridgend, Barry Island, Barry, Penarth and Cardiff - Coryton. Rhymney, Pontypridd, Merthyr, Aberdare and Treherbert

Station		AW	AW	AW	AW	AW	AW	AW	AW	AW		AW	AW	AW	AW	AW	AW	AW	AW	AW		AW	AW	AW	AW
Bridgend	d											05 42													
Llantwit Major	d											05 56													
Rhoose Cardiff Int Airport ✈	d											06 06													
Barry Island	d								05 52							06 25									06 55
Barry ■	d								05 57			06 15				06 30									07 00
Barry Docks	d								06 01			06 19				06 34									07 04
Cadoxton	d								06 04			06 22				06 37									07 07
Dinas Powys	d								06 08			06 26				06 41									07 11
Eastbrook	d								06 10			06 28				06 43									07 13
Cogan	d								06 12			06 30				06 45									07 15
Penarth	d						06 02							06 32									07 02		
Dingle Road	d						06 04							06 34									07 04		
Grangetown	d						06 08		06 16			06 34		06 38		06 49							07 08		07 19
Cardiff Central ■	a						06 13		06 21			06 39		06 44		06 54			07 04				07 14		07 24
	d	05 26	05 46		05 56	06 11	06 15	06 19	06 26	06 36		06 41		06 46	06 51	06 56		07 06	07 06			07 11	07 16		07 26
Cardiff Bay	d												06 42				06 54			07 06				07 18	
Cardiff Queen Street ■	a	05 29	05 49		05 59	06 14	06 19	06 24	06 29	06 39		06 44	06 46	06 49	06 54	06 59	06 58	07 09		07 10		07 14	07 19	07 22	07 29
	d	05 30	05 50		06 00	06 15	06 20	06 25	06 30	06 40		06 45		06 50	06 55	07 00		07 10				07 15	07 20		07 30
Heath Low Level	d							06 30							07 00										
Ty Glas	d							06 33							07 03										
Birchgrove	d							06 34							07 04										
Rhiwbina	d							06 36							07 06										
Whitchurch (Cardiff)	d							06 38							07 08										
Coryton	a							06 43							07 13										
Heath High Level	d		05 54				06 25							06 55									07 25		
Llanishen	d		05 57				06 28							06 58									07 28		
Lisvane & Thornhill	d		06 00				06 30							07 00									07 30		
Caerphilly ■	d		06a09				06 36							07 06									07 36		
Aber	d						06 38							07 08									07 38		
Llanbradach	d						06 42							07 12									07 42		
Ystrad Mynach ■	d						06 47							07 17									07 47		
Hengoed	d						06 50							07 20									07 50		
Pengam	d						06 53							07 23									07 53		
Gilfach Fargoed	d																								
Bargoed	a						07 01							07 31									08 01		
	d																								
Brithdir	d																								
Tir-phil	d																								
Pontlottyn	d																								
Rhymney ■	a																								
Cathays	d	05 33			06 03	06 18			06 33	06 43		06 48				07 03		07 13				07 18			07 33
Llandaf	d	05 37			06 07	06 22			06 37	06 47		06 52				07 07		07 17				07 22			07 37
Ninian Park	d																		07 10						
Waun-gron Park	d																		07 13						
Fairwater	d																		07 15						
Danescourt	d																		07 17						
Radyr ■	a	05 39			06 10	06 24			06 40	06 50		06 54				07 10		07 20	07 24			07 25			07 40
	d	05 40			06 10	06 24			06 40	06 50		06 55				07 10		07 20				07 25			07 40
Taffs Well ■	d	05 43			06 14	06 28			06 44	06 54		06 59				07 14		07 24				07 29			07 44
Trefforest Estate	d	05 47			06 18				06 48							07 18									07 48
Trefforest	d	05 52			06 22	06 35			06 52	07 01		07 06				07 22		07 31				07 36			07 52
Pontypridd ■	a	05 55			06 25	06 38			06 55	07 04		07 09				07 25		07 34				07 39			07 55
	d	05 57		06 11	06 27	06 41			06 57	07 06		07 11				07 27		07 36				07 41			07 57
Abercynon	d	06 04		06 19	06 34	06 49			07 04			07 19				07 34						07 49			08 04
Penrhiwceiber	d			06 24		06 54						07 24										07 54			
Mountain Ash	a			06 28		06 58						07 28										07 58			
	d			06 33		07 03						07 33										08 03			
Fernhill	d			06 35		07 05						07 35										08 05			
Cwmbach	d			06 39		07 09						07 39										08 09			
Aberdare ■	a			06 46		07 16						07 46										08 16			
Quakers Yard	d	06 09			06 39				07 09							07 39									08 09
Merthyr Vale	a	06 14			06 44				07 14							07 44									08 14
	d	06 17			06 47				07 17							07 47									08 17
Troed Y Rhiw	d	06 20			06 50				07 20							07 50									08 20
Pentre-bach	d	06 23			06 53				07 23							07 53									08 23
Merthyr Tydfil	a	06 31			07 01				07 31							08 01									08 31
Trehafod	d									07 11								07 41							
Porth	a									07 14								07 44							
	d									07 15								07 45							
Dinas Rhondda	d									07 19								07 49							
Tonypandy	d									07 21								07 51							
Llwynypia	d									07 23								07 53							
Ystrad Rhondda	a									07 26								07 56							
	d									07 29								07 59							
Ton Pentre	d									07 31								08 01							
Treorchy	d									07 34								08 04							
Ynyswen	d									07 37								08 07							
Treherbert	a									07 43								08 13							

Table 130

Mondays to Fridays
until 03 September

Bridgend, Barry Island, Barry, Penarth and Cardiff - Coryton. Rhymney, Pontypridd, Merthyr, Aberdare and Treherbert

Station		AW	AW	AW	AW	AW		AW	AW	AW	AW	AW	AW	AW	AW	AW		AW	AW	AW	AW	AW	AW	AW	AW
Bridgend	d					06 42																			07 42
Llantwit Major	d					06 56																			07 56
Rhoose Cardiff Int Airport ✈	d					07 06																			08 06
Barry Island	d									07 25						07 40				07 55					
Barry ■	d					07 15				07 30						07 45				08 00					08 15
Barry Docks	d					07 19				07 34						07 49				08 04					08 19
Cadoxton	d					07 22				07 37						07 52				08 07					08 22
Dinas Powys	d					07 26				07 41						07 56				08 11					08 26
Eastbrook	d					07 28				07 43						07 58				08 13					08 28
Cogan	d					07 30				07 45						08 00				08 15					08 30
Penarth	d	07 17							07 32			07 47						08 02			08 17				
Dingle Road	d	07 19							07 34			07 49						08 04			08 19				
Grangetown	d	07 23				07 34			07 38	07 49		07 54				08 04		08 08		08 19	08 23				08 34
Cardiff Central ■	a	07 29			07 34	07 39			07 44	07 54		08 00		08 04		08 09		08 14		08 24	08 29			08 34	08 39
	d	07 31		07 36	07 36	07 41			07 46	07 56		08 01	08 06	08 06		08 11		08 16		08 26	08 31		08 36	08 36	08 41
Cardiff Bay	d		07 30					07 42			07 54				08 06				08 18			08 30			
Cardiff Queen Street ■	a	07 34	07 34	07 39		07 44		07 46	07 49	07 59	07 58	08 04	08 09		08 10	08 14		08 19	08 22	08 29	08 34	08 34	08 39		08 44
	d	07 35		07 40		07 45			07 50	08 00		08 05	08 10			08 15		08 20		08 30	08 35		08 40		08 45
Heath Low Level	d																								
Ty Glas	d																								
Birchgrove	d																								
Rhiwbina	d																								
Whitchurch (Cardiff)	d																								
Coryton	a																								
Heath High Level	d	07 40							07 55			08 10						08 25			08 40				
Llanishen	d	07 43							07 58			08 13						08 28			08 43				
Lisvane & Thornhill	d	07 45							08 00			08 15						08 30			08 45				
Caerphilly ■	d	07 51							08 06			08 21						08 36			08 51				
Aber	d	07 53							08 08			08 23						08 38			08 53				
Llanbradach	d	07 57							08 12			08 27						08 42			08 57				
Ystrad Mynach ■	d	08 02							08 17			08 32						08 47			09 02				
Hengoed	d	08 05							08 20			08 35						08 50			09 05				
Pengam	d	08 08							08 23			08 38						08 53			09 08				
Gilfach Fargoed	d											08 41													
Bargoed	a	08 13							08 31			08 48						08 58			09 16				
	d	08 14																08 59							
Brithdir	d	08 18																09 03							
Tir-phil	d	08 21																09 06							
Pontlottyn	d	08 25																09 10							
Rhymney ■	a	08 28																09 16							
Cathays	d			07 43		07 48				08 03			08 13			08 18				08 33			08 43		08 48
Llandaf	d			07 47		07 52				08 07			08 17			08 22				08 37			08 47		08 52
Ninian Park	d				07 40									08 10										08 40	
Waun-gron Park	d				07 43									08 13										08 43	
Fairwater	d				07 45									08 15										08 45	
Danescourt	d				07 47									08 17										08 47	
Radyr ■	a			07 50	07 54	07 55				08 10			08 20	08 24		08 25				08 40			08 50	08 54	08 55
	d			07 50		07 55				08 10			08 20			08 25				08 40			08 50		08 55
Taffs Well ■	d			07 54		07 59				08 14			08 24			08 29				08 44			08 54		08 59
Trefforest Estate	d									08 18										08 48					
Trefforest	d			08 01		08 06				08 23			08 31			08 36				08 52			09 01		09 06
Pontypridd ■	a			08 04		08 09				08 26			08 34			08 39				08 55			09 04		09 09
	d			08 06		08 11				08 27			08 36			08 41				08 57			09 06		09 11
Abercynon	d					08 19				08 34						08 49				09 04					09 19
Penrhiwceiber	d					08 24										08 54									09 24
Mountain Ash	a					08 28										08 58									09 28
	d					08 33										09 03									09 33
Fernhill	d					08 35										09 05									09 35
Cwmbach	d					08 39										09 09									09 39
Aberdare ■	a					08 46										09 16									09 46
Quakers Yard	d									08 39										09 09					
Merthyr Vale	a									08 44										09 14					
	d									08 47										09 17					
Troed Y Rhiw	d									08 50										09 20					
Pentre-bach	d									08 53										09 23					
Merthyr Tydfil	a									09 01										09 31					
Trehafod	d			08 11									08 41										09 11		
Porth	a			08 14									08 44										09 14		
	d			08 15									08 45										09 15		
Dinas Rhondda	d			08 19									08 49										09 19		
Tonypandy	d			08 21									08 51										09 21		
Llwynypia	d			08 23									08 53										09 23		
Ystrad Rhondda	a			08 26									08 56										09 26		
	d			08 29									08 59										09 29		
Ton Pentre	d			08 31									09 01										09 31		
Treorchy	d			08 34									09 04										09 34		
Ynyswen	d			08 37									09 07										09 37		
Treherbert	a			08 43									09 13										09 43		

Table 130

Bridgend, Barry Island, Barry, Penarth and Cardiff - Coryton. Rhymney, Pontypridd, Merthyr, Aberdare and Treherbert

		AW		AW	AW	AW	AW	AW	AW	AW	AW	AW		AW	AW	AW	AW	AW	AW	AW	AW	AW		AW	AW
Bridgend	d																			08 42					
Llantwit Major	d																			08 56					
Rhoose Cardiff Int Airport ✈	d																			09 06					
Barry Island	d				08 25						08 40				08 55										09 25
Barry	d				08 30						08 45				09 00					09 15					09 30
Barry Docks	d				08 34						08 49				09 04					09 19					09 34
Cadoxton	d				08 37						08 52				09 07					09 22					09 37
Dinas Powys	d				08 41						08 56				09 11					09 26					09 41
Eastbrook	d				08 43						08 58				09 13					09 28					09 43
Cogan	d				08 45						09 00				09 15					09 30					09 45
Penarth	d			08 32			08 47									09 17						09 32			
Dingle Road	d			08 34			08 49									09 19						09 34			
Grangetown	d			08 38	08 49		08 53				09 04				09 19	09 23				09 34		09 38			09 49
Cardiff Central	a			08 44	08 54		08 59		09 04		09 09				09 24	09 29			09 34	09 39		09 44			09 54
	d			08 46	08 56		09 01	09 06	09 06		09 11	09 16			09 26	09 31		09 36	09 36	09 41		09 46			09 56
Cardiff Bay	d	08 42				08 54				09 06				09 18			09 30				09 42			09 54	
Cardiff Queen Street	a	08 46		08 49	08 59	08 58	09 04	09 09		09 10	09 14	09 19		09 22	09 29	09 34	09 34	09 39		09 44	09 46	09 49		09 58	09 59
	d			08 50	09 00		09 05	09 10			09 15	09 20			09 30	09 35		09 40		09 45		09 50			10 00
Heath Low Level	d																								
Ty Glas	d																								
Birchgrove	d																								
Rhiwbina	d																								
Whitchurch (Cardiff)	d																								
Coryton	a																								
Heath High Level	d			08 55			09 10					09 25				09 40						09 55			
Llanishen	d			08 58			09 13					09 28				09 43						09 58			
Lisvane & Thornhill	d			09 00			09 15					09 30				09 45						10 00			
Caerphilly	d			09 06			09 21					09 36				09 51						10 06			
Aber	d			09 08			09 23					09 38				09 53						10 08			
Llanbradach	d			09 12			09 27					09 42				09 57						10 12			
Ystrad Mynach	d			09 17			09 32					09 47				10 02						10 17			
Hengoed	d			09 20			09 35					09 50				10 05						10 20			
Pengam	d			09 23			09 38					09 53				10 08						10 23			
Gilfach Fargoed	d						09 41																		
Bargoed	a			09 31			09 48					09 58				10 16						10 31			
	d											09 59													
Brithdir	d											10 03													
Tir-phil	d											10 06													
Pontlottyn	d											10 10													
Rhymney	a											10 16													
Cathays	d				09 03			09 13			09 18				09 33			09 43		09 48					10 03
Llandaf	d				09 07			09 17			09 22				09 37			09 47		09 52					10 07
Ninian Park	d								09 10										09 40						
Waun-gron Park	d								09 13										09 43						
Fairwater	d								09 15										09 45						
Danescourt	d								09 17										09 47						
Radyr	a				09 10			09 20	09 24		09 25				09 40			09 50	09 54	09 55					10 10
	d				09 10			09 20			09 25				09 40			09 50		09 55					10 10
Taffs Well	d				09 14			09 24			09 29				09 44			09 54		09 59					10 14
Trefforest Estate	d				09 18										09 48										10 18
Trefforest	d				09 22			09 31			09 36				09 52			10 01		10 06					10 22
Pontypridd	a				09 25			09 34			09 39				09 55			10 04		10 09					10 30
	d				09 27			09 36			09 41				09 57			10 06		10 11					
Abercynon	d				09 34						09 49				10 04					10 19					
Penrhiwceiber	d										09 54									10 24					
Mountain Ash	a										09 58									10 28					
	d										10 03									10 33					
Fernhill	d										10 05									10 35					
Cwmbach	d										10 09									10 39					
Aberdare	a										10 16									10 46					
Quakers Yard	d				09 39										10 09										
Merthyr Vale	a				09 44										10 14										
	d				09 47										10 17										
Troed Y Rhiw	d				09 50										10 20										
Pentre-bach	d				09 53										10 23										
Merthyr Tydfil	a				10 01										10 31										
Trehafod	d							09 41										10 11							
Porth	a							09 44										10 14							
	d							09 45										10 15							
Dinas Rhondda	d							09 49										10 19							
Tonypandy	d							09 51										10 21							
Llwynypia	d							09 53										10 23							
Ystrad Rhondda	a							09 56										10 26							
	d							09 59										10 29							
Ton Pentre	d							10 01										10 31							
Treorchy	d							10 04										10 34							
Ynyswen	d							10 07										10 37							
Treherbert	a							10 13										10 43							

Table 130

Bridgend, Barry Island, Barry, Penarth and Cardiff - Coryton. Rhymney, Pontypridd, Merthyr, Aberdare and Treherbert

		AW	AW	AW	AW	AW	AW	AW		AW	AW	AW	AW	AW	AW	AW	AW	AW		AW	AW	AW	AW	AW	AW
Bridgend	d															09 42									
Llantwit Major	d															09 56									
Rhoose Cardiff Int Airport ✈	d															10 06									
Barry Island	d						09 40				09 55										10 25				
Barry	d						09 45				10 00					10 15					10 30				
Barry Docks	d						09 49				10 04					10 19					10 34				
Cadoxton	d						09 52				10 07					10 22					10 37				
Dinas Powys	d						09 56				10 11					10 26					10 41				
Eastbrook	d						09 58				10 13					10 28					10 43				
Cogan	d						10 00				10 15					10 30					10 45				
Penarth	d	09 47						10 02				10 17						10 32						10 47	
Dingle Road	d	09 49						10 04				10 19						10 34						10 49	
Grangetown	d	09 53					10 04	10 08			10 19	10 23				10 34		10 38			10 49			10 53	
Cardiff Central	a	09 59		10 04			10 09	10 14			10 24	10 29			10 34	10 42		10 44			10 54			10 59	11 04
	d	10 01	10 06	10 06			10 11	10 16			10 26	10 31		10 36	10 36			10 46		10 51	10 56			11 01	11 06
Cardiff Bay	d				10 06					10 18			10 30				10 42						10 54		
Cardiff Queen Street	a	10 04	10 09		10 10		10 14	10 19		10 22	10 29	10 34	10 34	10 39			10 46	10 49			10 59		10 58	11 04	
	d	10 05	10 10				10 15	10 20			10 30	10 35		10 40				10 50			11 00			11 05	
Heath Low Level	d																								
Ty Glas	d																								
Birchgrove	d																								
Rhiwbina	d																								
Whitchurch (Cardiff)	d																								
Coryton	a																								
Heath High Level	d	10 10						10 25				10 40						10 55						11 10	
Llanishen	d	10 13						10 28				10 43						10 58						11 13	
Lisvane & Thornhill	d	10 15						10 30				10 45						11 00						11 15	
Caerphilly	d	10 21						10 36				10 51						11 06						11 21	
Aber	d	10 23						10 38				10 53						11 08						11 23	
Llanbradach	d	10 27						10 42				10 57						11 12						11 27	
Ystrad Mynach	d	10 32						10 47				11 02						11 17						11 32	
Hengoed	d	10 35						10 50				11 05						11 20						11 35	
Pengam	d	10 38						10 53				11 08						11 23						11 38	
Gilfach Fargoed	d	10 41																						11 41	
Bargoed	a	10 48						10 58				11 16						11 31						11 48	
	d							10 59																	
Brithdir	d							11 03																	
Tir-phil	d							11 06																	
Pontlottyn	d							11 10																	
Rhymney	a							11 16																	
Cathays	d		10 13				10 18				10 33			10 43							11 03				
Llandaf	d		10 17				10 22				10 37			10 47							11 07				
Ninian Park	d			10 10											10 40										11 10
Waun-gron Park	d			10 13											10 43										11 13
Fairwater	d			10 15											10 45										11 15
Danescourt	d			10 17											10 47										11 17
Radyr	a		10 20	10 24			10 25				10 40			10 50	10 54					11 02	11 10				11 24
	d		10 20				10 25				10 40			10 50						11 20	11 10				
Taffs Well	d		10 24				10 29				10 44			10 54						11 24	11 14				
Trefforest Estate	d										10 48										11 18				
Trefforest	d		10 31				10 36				10 52			11 01						11 31	11 22	←			
Pontypridd	a		10 34				10 39				10 55			11 04						11 34	11 25	11 34			
	d		10 36			10 35	10 41				10 57			11 06						11 36	11 27	11 36			
Abercynon	d					10 41	10 49				11 04									→	11 34				
Penrhiwceiber	d						10 54																		
Mountain Ash	a						10 58																		
	d						11 03																		
Fernhill	d						11 05																		
Cwmbach	d						11 09																		
Aberdare	a						11 16																		
Quakers Yard	d					10 45					11 09										11 39				
Merthyr Vale	a					10 50					11 14										11 44				
	d					10 52					11 17										11 47				
Troed Y Rhiw	d					10 55					11 20										11 50				
Pentre-bach	d					10 58					11 23										11 53				
Merthyr Tydfil	a					11 06					11 31										12 01				
Trehafod	d		10 41											11 11								11 41			
Porth	a		10 44											11 14								11 44			
	d		10 45											11 15								11 45			
Dinas Rhondda	d		10 49											11 19								11 49			
Tonypandy	d		10 51											11 21								11 51			
Llwynypia	d		10 53											11 23								11 53			
Ystrad Rhondda	a		10 56											11 26								11 56			
	d		10 59											11 29								11 59			
Ton Pentre	d		11 01											11 31								12 01			
Treorchy	d		11 04											11 34								12 04			
Ynyswen	d		11 07											11 37								12 07			
Treherbert	a		11 13											11 43								12 13			

Table 130

Mondays to Fridays

until 03 September

Bridgend, Barry Island, Barry, Penarth and Cardiff - Coryton. Rhymney, Pontypridd, Merthyr, Aberdare and Treherbert

		AW	AW	AW		AW	AW	AW	AW	AW	AW	AW	AW	AW		AW	AW	AW	AW	AW	AW	AW	AW	AW
Bridgend	d											10 42												
Llantwit Major	d											10 56												
Rhoose Cardiff Int Airport ✈	d											11 06												
Barry Island	d		10 40				10 55									11 25						11 40		
Barry ■	d		10 45				11 00					11 15				11 30						11 45		
Barry Docks	d		10 49				11 04					11 19				11 34						11 49		
Cadoxton	d		10 52				11 07					11 22				11 37						11 52		
Dinas Powys	d		10 56				11 11					11 26				11 41						11 56		
Eastbrook	d		10 58				11 13					11 28				11 43						11 58		
Cogan	d		11 00				11 15					11 30				11 45						12 00		
Penarth	d			11 02				11 17						11 32				11 47					12 02	
Dingle Road	d			11 04				11 19						11 34				11 49					12 04	
Grangetown	d		11 04	11 08			11 19	11 23				11 34		11 38		11 49		11 53				12 04	12 08	
Cardiff Central ■	a		11 09	11 14			11 24	11 29			11 34	11 39		11 44		11 54		12 00		12 04		12 09	12 14	
	d		11 11	11 16			11 26	11 31		11 36	11 36	11 41		11 46		11 56		12 01	12 06	12 06		12 11	12 16	
Cardiff Bay	d	11 06				11 18			11 30				11 42				11 54				12 06			12 18
Cardiff Queen Street ■	a	11 10	11 14	11 19		11 22	11 29	11 34	11 34	11 39		11 44	11 46	11 49		11 59	11 58	12 04	12 09		12 10	12 14	12 19	12 22
	d		11 15	11 20			11 30	11 35		11 40		11 45		11 50		12 00		12 05	12 10			12 15	12 20	
Heath Low Level	d																							
Ty Glas	d																							
Birchgrove	d																							
Rhiwbina	d																							
Whitchurch (Cardiff)	d																							
Coryton	a																							
Heath High Level	d			11 25				11 40						11 55				12 10					12 25	
Llanishen	d			11 28				11 43						11 58				12 13					12 28	
Lisvane & Thornhill	d			11 30				11 45						12 00				12 15					12 30	
Caerphilly ■	d			11 36				11 51						12 06				12 21					12 36	
Aber	d			11 38				11 53						12 08				12 23					12 38	
Llanbradach	d			11 42				11 57						12 12				12 27					12 42	
Ystrad Mynach ■	d			11 47				12 02						12 17				12 32					12 47	
Hengoed	d			11 50				12 05						12 20				12 35					12 50	
Pengam	d			11 53				12 08						12 23				12 38					12 53	
Gilfach Fargoed	d																	12 41						
Bargoed	a			11 58				12 16						12 31				12 48					12 58	
	d			11 59																			12 59	
Brithdir	d			12 03																			13 03	
Tir-phil	d			12 06																			13 06	
Pontlottyn	d			12 10																			13 10	
Rhymney ■	a			12 16																			13 16	
Cathays	d		11 18				11 33			11 43		11 48				12 03			12 13			12 18		
Llandaf	d		11 22				11 37			11 47		11 52				12 07			12 17			12 22		
Ninian Park	d										11 40									12 10				
Waun-gron Park	d										11 43									12 13				
Fairwater	d										11 45									12 15				
Danescourt	d										11 47									12 17				
Radyr ■	a		11 25				11 40			11 50	11 54	11 55				12 10			12 20	12 24		12 25		
	d		11 25				11 40			11 50		11 55				12 10			12 20			12 25		
Taffs Well ■	d		11 29				11 44			11 54		11 59				12 14			12 24			12 29		
Trefforest Estate	d						11 48									12 18								
Trefforest	d		11 36				11 52			12 01		12 06				12 22			12 31			12 36		
Pontypridd ■	a		11 39				11 55			12 04		12 09				12 25			12 34			12 42		
	d		11 41				11 57			12 06		12 11				12 27			12 36					
Abercynon	d		11 49				12 04					12 19				12 34								
Penrhiwceiber	d		11 54									12 24												
Mountain Ash	a		11 58									12 28												
	d		12 03									12 33												
Fernhill	d		12 05									12 35												
Cwmbach	d		12 09									12 39												
Aberdare ■	a		12 16									12 46												
Quakers Yard	d						12 09									12 39								
Merthyr Vale	a						12 14									12 44								
	d						12 17									12 47								
Troed Y Rhiw	d						12 20									12 50								
Pentre-bach	d						12 23									12 53								
Merthyr Tydfil	a						12 31									13 01								
Trehafod	d									12 11									12 41					
Porth	a									12 14									12 44					
	d									12 15									12 45					
Dinas Rhondda	d									12 19									12 49					
Tonypandy	d									12 21									12 51					
Llwynypia	d									12 23									12 53					
Ystrad Rhondda	a									12 26									12 56					
	d									12 29									12 59					
Ton Pentre	d									12 31									13 01					
Treorchy	d									12 34									13 04					
Ynyswen	d									12 37									13 07					
Treherbert	a									12 43									13 13					

Table 130

Mondays to Fridays

until 03 September

Bridgend, Barry Island, Barry, Penarth and Cardiff - Coryton. Rhymney, Pontypridd, Merthyr, Aberdare and Treherbert

		AW	AW	AW	AW	AW	AW	AW	AW	AW		AW	AW	AW	AW	AW	AW	AW	AW	AW		AW	AW	AW	AW
Bridgend	d							11 42																	
Llantwit Major	d							11 56																	
Rhoose Cardiff Int Airport ✈	d							12 06																	
Barry Island	d	11 55										12 25						12 40				12 55			
Barry ■	d	12 00						12 15				12 30						12 45				13 00			
Barry Docks	d	12 04						12 19				12 34						12 49				13 04			
Cadoxton	d	12 07						12 22				12 37						12 52				13 07			
Dinas Powys	d	12 11						12 26				12 41						12 56				13 11			
Eastbrook	d	12 13						12 28				12 43						12 58				13 13			
Cogan	d	12 15						12 30				12 45						13 00				13 15			
Penarth	d		12 17							12 32				12 47					13 02				13 17		
Dingle Road	d		12 19							12 34				12 49					13 04				13 19		
Grangetown	d	12 19	12 23					12 34		12 38		12 49		12 53				13 04	13 08			13 19	13 23		
Cardiff Central ■	a	12 24	12 29			12 34		12 44		12 44		12 54		12 59		13 04		13 09	13 14			13 24	13 29		
	d	12 26	12 31		12 36	12 36	12 41			12 46		12 56		13 01	13 06	13 06		13 11	13 16			13 26	13 31		13 36
Cardiff Bay	d			12 30					12 42				12 54				13 06			13 18				13 30	
Cardiff Queen Street ■	a	12 29	12 34	12 34	12 39		12 44		12 46	12 49		12 59	12 58	13 04	13 09		13 10	13 14	13 19	13 22		13 29	13 34	13 34	13 39
	d	12 30	12 35		12 40		12 45			12 50		13 00		13 05	13 10			13 15	13 20			13 30	13 35		13 40
Heath Low Level	d																								
Ty Glas	d																								
Birchgrove	d																								
Rhiwbina	d																								
Whitchurch (Cardiff)	d																								
Coryton	a																								
Heath High Level	d		12 40							12 55				13 10					13 25				13 40		
Llanishen	d		12 43							12 58				13 13					13 28				13 43		
Lisvane & Thornhill	d		12 45							13 00				13 15					13 30				13 45		
Caerphilly ■	d		12 51							13 06				13 21					13 36				13 51		
Aber	d		12 53							13 08				13 23					13 38				13 53		
Llanbradach	d		12 57							13 12				13 27					13 42				13 57		
Ystrad Mynach ■	d		13 02							13 17				13 32					13 47				14 02		
Hengoed	d		13 05							13 20				13 35					13 50				14 05		
Pengam	d		13 08							13 23				13 38					13 53				14 08		
Gilfach Fargoed	d													13 41											
Bargoed	a		13 16							13 31				13 48					13 58				14 16		
	d																		13 59						
Brithdir	d																		14 03						
Tir-phil	d																		14 06						
Pontlottyn	d																		14 10						
Rhymney ■	a																		14 16						
Cathays	d	12 33			12 43		12 48					13 03			13 13			13 18				13 33			13 43
Llandaf	d	12 37			12 47		12 52					13 07			13 17			13 22				13 37			13 47
Ninian Park	d					12 40										13 10									
Waun-gron Park	d					12 43										13 13									
Fairwater	d					12 45										13 15									
Danescourt	d					12 47										13 17									
Radyr ■	a	12 40			12 50	12 54	12 55					13 10			13 20	13 24		13 25				13 40			13 50
	d	12 40			12 50		12 55					13 10			13 20			13 25				13 40			13 50
Taffs Well ■	d	12 44			12 54		12 59					13 14			13 24			13 29				13 44			13 54
Trefforest Estate	d	12 48										13 18										13 48			
Trefforest	d	12 52			13 01		13 06					13 22			13 31			13 36				13 52			14 01
Pontypridd ■	a	12 55			13 04		13 09					13 25			13 34			13 39				13 55			14 04
	d	12 57			13 06		13 11					13 27			13 36			13 41				13 57			14 06
Abercynon	d	13 04					13 19					13 34						13 49				14 04			
Penrhiwceiber	d						13 24											13 54							
Mountain Ash	a						13 28											13 58							
	d						13 33											14 03							
Fernhill	d						13 35											14 05							
Cwmbach	d						13 39											14 09							
Aberdare ■	a						13 46											14 16							
Quakers Yard	d	13 09										13 39										14 09			
Merthyr Vale	a	13 14										13 44										14 14			
	d	13 17										13 47										14 17			
Troed Y Rhiw	d	13 20										13 50										14 20			
Pentre-bach	d	13 23										13 53										14 23			
Merthyr Tydfil	a	13 31										14 01										14 31			
Trehafod	d				13 11										13 41										14 11
Porth	a				13 14										13 44										14 14
	d				13 15										13 45										14 15
Dinas Rhondda	d				13 19										13 49										14 19
Tonypandy	d				13 21										13 51										14 21
Llwynypia	d				13 23										13 53										14 23
Ystrad Rhondda	a				13 26										13 56										14 26
	d				13 29										13 59										14 29
Ton Pentre	d				13 31										14 01										14 31
Treorchy	d				13 34										14 04										14 34
Ynyswen	d				13 37										14 07										14 37
Treherbert	a				13 43										14 13										14 43

Table 130

Mondays to Fridays
until 03 September

Bridgend, Barry Island, Barry, Penarth and Cardiff - Coryton. Rhymney, Pontypridd, Merthyr, Aberdare and Treherbert

Station		AW	AW	AW	AW	AW	AW	AW	AW	AW	AW	AW	AW	AW	AW	AW	AW	AW	AW	AW	AW	AW	AW
Bridgend	d		12 42																	13 42			
Llantwit Major	d		12 56																	13 56			
Rhoose Cardiff Int Airport ✈	d		13 06																	14 06			
Barry Island	d					13 25						13 40			13 55								
Barry ■	d		13 15			13 30						13 45			14 00					14 15			
Barry Docks	d		13 19			13 34						13 49			14 04					14 19			
Cadoxton	d		13 22			13 37						13 52			14 07					14 22			
Dinas Powys	d		13 26			13 41						13 56			14 11					14 26			
Eastbrook	d		13 28			13 43						13 58			14 13					14 28			
Cogan	d		13 30			13 45						14 00			14 15					14 30			
Penarth	d				13 32			13 47					14 02			14 17						14 32	
Dingle Road	d				13 34			13 49					14 04			14 19						14 34	
Grangetown	d		13 34		13 38	13 49		13 53				14 04	14 08		14 19	14 23				14 34		14 38	
Cardiff Central ■	a	13 34	13 39		13 44	13 54		13 59		14 04		14 09	14 14		14 24	14 29			14 34	14 39		14 44	
	d	13 36	13 41		13 46	13 56		14 01	14 06	14 06		14 11	14 16		14 26	14 31		14 36	14 36	14 41		14 46	14 51
Cardiff Bay	d			13 42			13 54				14 06			14 18			14 30				14 42		
Cardiff Queen Street ■	a		13 44	13 46	13 49	13 59	13 58	14 04	14 09		14 10	14 14	14 19	14 22	14 29	14 34	14 34	14 39		14 44	14 46	14 49	
	d		13 45		13 50	14 00		14 05	14 10			14 15	14 20		14 30	14 35		14 40		14 45		14 50	
Heath Low Level	d																						
Ty Glas	d																						
Birchgrove	d																						
Rhiwbina	d																						
Whitchurch (Cardiff)	d																						
Coryton	a																						
Heath High Level	d				13 55			14 10					14 25			14 40						14 55	
Llanishen	d				13 58			14 13					14 28			14 43						14 58	
Lisvane & Thornhill	d				14 00			14 15					14 30			14 45						15 00	
Caerphilly ■	d				14 06			14 21					14 36			14 51						15 06	
Aber	d				14 08			14 23					14 38			14 53						15 08	
Llanbradach	d				14 12			14 27					14 42			14 57						15 12	
Ystrad Mynach ■	d				14 17			14 32					14 47			15 02						15 17	
Hengoed	d				14 20			14 35					14 50			15 05						15 20	
Pengam	d				14 23			14 38					14 53			15 08						15 23	
Gilfach Fargoed	d							14 41															
Bargoed	a				14 31			14 48					14 58			15 16						15 31	
	d												14 59										
Brithdir	d												15 03										
Tir-phil	d												15 06										
Pontlottyn	d												15 10										
Rhymney ■	a												15 16										
Cathays	d		13 48			14 03			14 13			14 18			14 33			14 43		14 48			
Llandaf	d		13 52			14 07			14 17			14 22			14 37			14 47		14 52			
Ninian Park	d	13 40								14 10									14 40				
Waun-gron Park	d	13 43								14 13									14 43				
Fairwater	d	13 45								14 15									14 45				
Danescourt	d	13 47								14 17									14 47				
Radyr ■	a	13 54	13 55			14 10			14 20	14 24		14 25			14 40			14 50	14 54	14 55			15 08
	d		13 55			14 10			14 20			14 25			14 40			14 50		14 55			15 20
Taffs Well ■	d		13 59			14 14			14 24			14 29			14 44			14 54		14 59			15 24
Trefforest Estate	d					14 18									14 48								
Trefforest	d		14 06			14 22			14 31			14 36			14 52			15 01		15 06			15 31
Pontypridd ■	a		14 09			14 25			14 34			14 39			14 55			15 04		15 09			15 34
	d		14 11			14 27			14 36			14 41			14 57			15 06		15 11			15 36
Abercynon	d		14 19			14 34						14 49			15 04					15 19			→
Penrhiwceiber	d		14 24									14 54								15 24			
Mountain Ash	a		14 28									14 58								15 28			
	d		14 33									15 03								15 33			
Fernhill	d		14 35									15 05								15 35			
Cwmbach	d		14 39									15 09								15 39			
Aberdare ■	a		14 46									15 16								15 46			
Quakers Yard	d					14 39									15 09								
Merthyr Vale	a					14 44									15 14								
	d					14 47									15 17								
Troed Y Rhiw	d					14 50									15 20								
Pentre-bach	d					14 53									15 23								
Merthyr Tydfil	a					15 01									15 31								
Trehafod	d								14 41									15 11					
Porth	a								14 44									15 14					
	d								14 45									15 15					
Dinas Rhondda	d								14 49									15 19					
Tonypandy	d								14 51									15 21					
Llwynypia	d								14 53									15 23					
Ystrad Rhondda	a								14 56									15 26					
	d								14 59									15 29					
Ton Pentre	d								15 01									15 31					
Treorchy	d								15 04									15 34					
Ynyswen	d								15 07									15 37					
Treherbert	a								15 13									15 43					

Table 130

Mondays to Fridays
until 03 September

Bridgend, Barry Island, Barry, Penarth and Cardiff - Coryton. Rhymney, Pontypridd, Merthyr, Aberdare and Treherbert

Station		AW	AW	AW	AW	AW	AW	AW	AW	AW	AW	AW	AW	AW	AW	AW	AW	AW	AW	AW	AW	AW
Bridgend	d															14 42						
Llantwit Major	d															14 56						
Rhoose Cardiff Int Airport ✈	d															15 06						
Barry Island	d	14 25						14 40			14 55								15 25			
Barry ■	d	14 30						14 45			15 00					15 15			15 30			
Barry Docks	d	14 34						14 49			15 04					15 19			15 34			
Cadoxton	d	14 37						14 52			15 07					15 22			15 37			
Dinas Powys	d	14 41						14 56			15 11					15 26			15 41			
Eastbrook	d	14 43						14 58			15 13					15 28			15 43			
Cogan	d	14 45						15 00			15 15					15 30			15 45			
Penarth	d				14 47				15 02			15 17						15 32			15 47	
Dingle Road	d				14 49				15 04			15 19						15 34			15 49	
Grangetown	d	14 49			14 53			15 04	15 08		15 19	15 23				15 34		15 38	15 49		15 53	
Cardiff Central ■	a	14 54			14 59	15 04		15 09	15 14		15 24	15 29			15 34	15 39		15 44	15 54		15 59	
	d	14 56			15 01	15 06		15 11	15 16		15 26	15 31		15 36	15 36	15 41		15 46	15 56		16 01	16 06
Cardiff Bay	d			14 54			15 06			15 18			15 30				15 42			15 54		
Cardiff Queen Street ■	a	14 59		14 58	15 04		15 10	15 14	15 19	15 22	15 29	15 34	15 34	15 39		15 44	15 46	15 49	15 59	15 58	16 04	16 09
	d	15 00			15 05			15 15	15 20		15 30	15 35		15 40		15 45		15 50	16 00		16 05	16 10
Heath Low Level	d																					
Ty Glas	d																					
Birchgrove	d																					
Rhiwbina	d																					
Whitchurch (Cardiff)	d																					
Coryton	a																					
Heath High Level	d				15 10				15 25			15 40						15 55			16 10	
Llanishen	d				15 13				15 28			15 43						15 58			16 13	
Lisvane & Thornhill	d				15 15				15 30			15 45						16 00			16 15	
Caerphilly ■	d				15 21				15 36			15 51						16 06			16 21	
Aber	d				15 23				15 38			15 53						16 08			16 23	
Llanbradach	d				15 27				15 42			15 57						16 12			16 27	
Ystrad Mynach ■	d				15 32				15 47			16 02						16 17			16 32	
Hengoed	d				15 35				15 50			16 05						16 20			16 35	
Pengam	d				15 38				15 53			16 08						16 23			16 38	
Gilfach Fargoed	d				15 41																16 41	
Bargoed	a				15 48				15 58			16 16						16 31			16 48	
	d								15 59													
Brithdir	d								16 03													
Tir-phil	d								16 06													
Pontlottyn	d								16 10													
Rhymney ■	a								16 16													
Cathays	d	15 03						15 18			15 33			15 43		15 48			16 03			16 13
Llandaf	d	15 07						15 22			15 37			15 47		15 52			16 07			16 17
Ninian Park	d					15 10									15 40							
Waun-gron Park	d					15 13									15 43							
Fairwater	d					15 15									15 45							
Danescourt	d					15 17									15 47							
Radyr ■	a	15 10				15 24		15 25			15 40			15 50	15 54	15 55			16 10			16 20
	d	15 10						15 25			15 40			15 50		15 55			16 10			16 20
Taffs Well ■	d	15 14						15 29			15 44			15 54		15 59			16 14			16 24
Trefforest Estate	d	15 18									15 48								16 18			
Trefforest	d	15 22	←					15 36			15 52			16 01		16 06			16 22			16 31
Pontypridd ■	a	15 25	15 34					15 39			15 55			16 04		16 09			16 25			16 34
	d	15 27	15 36					15 41			15 57			16 06		16 11			16 27			16 36
Abercynon	d	15 34						15 49			16 04					16 19			16 34			
Penrhiwceiber	d							15 54								16 24						
Mountain Ash	a							15 58								16 28						
	d							16 03								16 33						
Fernhill	d							16 05								16 35						
Cwmbach	d							16 09								16 39						
Aberdare ■	a							16 16								16 46						
Quakers Yard	d	15 39									16 09								16 39			
Merthyr Vale	a	15 44									16 14								16 44			
	d	15 47									16 17								16 47			
Troed Y Rhiw	d	15 50									16 20								16 50			
Pentre-bach	d	15 53									16 23								16 53			
Merthyr Tydfil	a	16 01									16 31								17 01			
Trehafod	d		15 41											16 11								16 41
Porth	a		15 44											16 14								16 44
	d		15 45											16 15								16 45
Dinas Rhondda	d		15 49											16 19								16 49
Tonypandy	d		15 51											16 21								16 51
Llwynypia	d		15 53											16 23								16 53
Ystrad Rhondda	a		15 56											16 26								16 56
	d		15 59											16 29								16 59
Ton Pentre	d		16 01											16 31								17 01
Treorchy	d		16 04											16 34								17 04
Ynyswen	d		16 07											16 37								17 07
Treherbert	a		16 13											16 43								17 13

Table 130

Mondays to Fridays
until 03 September

Bridgend, Barry Island, Barry, Penarth and Cardiff - Coryton. Rhymney, Pontypridd, Merthyr, Aberdare and Treherbert

		AW	AW	AW	AW	AW	AW	AW		AW	AW	AW	AW	AW	AW	AW	AW	AW		AW	AW	AW	AW	AW	AW
Bridgend	d												15 42												
Llantwit Major	d												15 56												
Rhoose Cardiff Int Airport ✈	d												16 06												
Barry Island	d			15 40			15 55									16 25							16 40		
Barry ■	d			15 45			16 00						16 15			16 30							16 45		
Barry Docks	d			15 49			16 04						16 19			16 34							16 49		
Cadoxton	d			15 52			16 07						16 22			16 37							16 52		
Dinas Powys	d			15 56			16 11						16 26			16 41							16 56		
Eastbrook	d			15 58			16 13						16 28			16 43							16 58		
Cogan	d			16 00			16 15						16 30			16 45							17 00		
Penarth	d				16 02			16 17							16 32									17 02	
Dingle Road	d				16 04			16 19							16 34									17 04	
Grangetown	d			16 04	16 08		16 19	16 23					16 34		16 38	16 49							17 04	17 08	
Cardiff Central ■	a	16 05		16 09	16 14		16 24	16 29				16 34	16 39		16 44	16 54					17 04		17 09	17 14	
	d	16 06		16 11	16 16		16 26	16 31			16 36	16 36	16 41		16 46	16 56		17 01		17 06	17 06		17 11	17 16	
Cardiff Bay	d		16 06			16 18				16 30				16 42			16 54					17 06			17 18
Cardiff Queen Street ■	a		16 10	16 14	16 19	16 22	16 29	16 34		16 34	16 39		16 44	16 46	16 49	16 59	16 58	17 04		17 09		17 10	17 14	17 19	17 22
	d			16 15	16 20		16 30	16 35			16 40		16 45		16 50	17 00		17 05		17 10			17 15	17 20	
Heath Low Level	d																								
Ty Glas	d																								
Birchgrove	d																								
Rhiwbina	d																								
Whitchurch (Cardiff)	d																								
Coryton	a																								
Heath High Level	d				16 25			16 40							16 55			17 10						17 25	
Llanishen	d				16 28			16 43							16 58			17 13						17 28	
Lisvane & Thornhill	d				16 30			16 45							17 00			17 15						17 30	
Caerphilly ■	d				16 36			16 51							17 06			17 21						17 36	
Aber	d				16 38			16 53							17 08			17 23						17 38	
Llanbradach	d				16 42			16 57							17 12			17 27						17 42	
Ystrad Mynach ■	d				16 47			17 02							17 17			17 33						17 47	
Hengoed	d				16 50			17 05							17 20			17 35						17 50	
Pengam	d				16 53			17 08							17 23			17 39						17 53	
Gilfach Fargoed	d																	17 42							
Bargoed	a				16 58			17 16							17 31			17 45						18 01	
	d				16 59													17 47							
Brithdir	d				17 03													17 50							
Tir-phil	d				17 06													17 53							
Pontlottyn	d				17 10													17 58							
Rhymney ■	a				17 16													18 04							
Cathays	d			16 18			16 33				16 43		16 48			17 03				17 13			17 18		
Llandaf	d			16 22			16 37				16 47		16 52			17 07				17 17			17 22		
Ninian Park	d	16 10										16 40									17 10				
Waun-gron Park	d	16 13										16 43									17 13				
Fairwater	d	16 15										16 45									17 15				
Danescourt	d	16 17										16 47									17 17				
Radyr ■	a	16 24		16 25			16 40				16 50	16 54	16 55			17 10				17 20	17 24		17 25		
	d			16 25			16 40				16 50		16 55			17 10				17 20			17 25		
Taffs Well ■	d			16 29			16 44				16 54		16 59			17 14				17 24			17 29		
Trefforest Estate	d						16 48									17 18									
Trefforest	d			16 36			16 52				17 01		17 06			17 22				17 31			17 36		
Pontypridd ■	a			16 39			16 55				17 04		17 09			17 25				17 34			17 39		
	d			16 41			16 57				17 06		17 11			17 27				17 36			17 41		
Abercynon	d			16 49			17 04						17 19			17 34							17 49		
Penrhiwceiber	d			16 54									17 24										17 54		
Mountain Ash	a			16 58									17 28										17 58		
	d			17 03									17 33										18 03		
Fernhill	d			17 05									17 35										18 05		
Cwmbach	d			17 09									17 39										18 09		
Aberdare ■	a			17 16									17 46										18 16		
Quakers Yard	d						17 09									17 39									
Merthyr Vale	a						17 14									17 44									
	d						17 17									17 47									
Troed Y Rhiw	d						17 20									17 50									
Pentre-bach	d						17 23									17 53									
Merthyr Tydfil	a						17 31									18 01									
Trehafod	d										17 11									17 41					
Porth	a										17 14									17 44					
	d										17 15									17 45					
Dinas Rhondda	d										17 19									17 49					
Tonypandy	d										17 21									17 51					
Llwynypia	d										17 23									17 53					
Ystrad Rhondda	a										17 26									17 56					
	d										17 29									17 59					
Ton Pentre	d										17 31									18 01					
Treorchy	d										17 34									18 04					
Ynyswen	d										17 37									18 07					
Treherbert	a										17 43									18 13					

Table 130

Mondays to Fridays
until 03 September

Bridgend, Barry Island, Barry, Penarth and Cardiff - Coryton. Rhymney, Pontypridd, Merthyr, Aberdare and Treherbert

		AW	AW	AW		AW	AW	AW	AW	AW	AW	AW	AW	AW		AW	AW	AW	AW	AW	AW	AW	AW	AW
Bridgend	d							16 42																
Llantwit Major	d							16 56																
Rhoose Cardiff Int Airport ✈	d							17 06																
Barry Island	d	16 55										17 25						17 40			17 55			
Barry ■	d	17 00						17 15				17 30						17 45			18 00			
Barry Docks	d	17 04						17 19				17 34						17 49			18 04			
Cadoxton	d	17 07						17 22				17 37						17 52			18 07			
Dinas Powys	d	17 11						17 26				17 41						17 56			18 11			
Eastbrook	d	17 13						17 28				17 43						17 58			18 13			
Cogan	d	17 15						17 30				17 45						18 00			18 15			
Penarth	d		17 17							17 32			17 47						18 02			18 17		
Dingle Road	d		17 19							17 34			17 49						18 04			18 19		
Grangetown	d	17 19	17 23					17 34		17 38		17 49	17 53					18 04	18 08		18 19	18 23		
Cardiff Central ■	a	17 24	17 29				17 34	17 39		17 44		17 54	17 59			18 04		18 09	18 14		18 24	18 29		
	d	17 26	17 31			17 36	17 36	17 41		17 46		17 56	18 01	18 06		18 06		18 11	18 16		18 26	18 31		18 36
Cardiff Bay	d			17 30					17 42		17 54						18 06			18 18			18 30	
Cardiff Queen Street ■	a	17 29	17 34	17 34		17 39		17 44	17 46	17 49	17 58	17 59	18 04	18 09			18 10	18 14	18 19	18 22	18 29	18 34	18 34	18 38
	d	17 30	17 35			17 40		17 45		17 50		18 00	18 05	18 10				18 15	18 20		18 30	18 35		18 40
Heath Low Level	d																							
Ty Glas	d																							
Birchgrove	d																							
Rhiwbina	d																							
Whitchurch (Cardiff)	d																							
Coryton	a																							
Heath High Level	d		17 40							17 55			18 10						18 25			18 40		
Llanishen	d		17 43							17 59			18 13						18 28			18 43		
Lisvane & Thornhill	d		17 45							18 02			18 15						18 30			18 45		
Caerphilly ■	d		17 51							18 07			18 21						18 36			18 51		
Aber	d		17 53							18 10			18 23						18 38			18 53		
Llanbradach	d		17 57							18 14			18 27						18 42			18 57		
Ystrad Mynach ■	d		18 02							18 20			18 32						18a51			19 02		
Hengoed	d		18 05							18 23			18 35									19 05		
Pengam	d		18 08							18 27			18 38									19 08		
Gilfach Fargoed	d		18 11							18 30			18 41									19 11		
Bargoed	a		18 14							18 34			18 48									19 14		
	d		18 16							18 44												19 16		
Brithdir	d		18 20							18 48												19 20		
Tir-phil	d		18 23							18 51												19 23		
Pontlottyn	d		18 27							18 55												19 27		
Rhymney ■	a		18 33							19 01												19 33		
Cathays	d	17 33				17 43		17 48				18 03		18 13				18 18			18 33			18 43
Llandaf	d	17 37				17 47		17 52				18 07		18 17				18 22			18 37			18 47
Ninian Park	d						17 40									18 10								
Waun-gron Park	d						17 43									18 13								
Fairwater	d						17 45									18 15								
Danescourt	d						17 47									18 17								
Radyr ■	a	17 40				17 50	17 54	17 55				18 10		18 20		18 24		18 25			18 40			18 50
	d	17 40				17 50		17 55				18 10		18 20				18 25			18 40			18 50
Taffs Well ■	d	17 44				17 54		17 59				18 14		18 24				18 29			18 44			18 54
Trefforest Estate	d	17 48										18 18									18 48			
Trefforest	d	17 52				18 01		18 06				18 22		18 31				18 36			18 52			19 01
Pontypridd ■	a	17 55				18 04		18 09				18 25		18 34				18 42			18 55			19 04
	d	17 57				18 06		18 11				18 27		18 36							18 57			19 06
Abercynon	d	18 04						18 19				18 34									19 04			
Penrhiwceiber	d							18 24																
Mountain Ash	a							18 28																
	d							18 33																
Fernhill	d							18 35																
Cwmbach	d							18 39																
Aberdare ■	a							18 46																
Quakers Yard	d	18 09										18 39									19 09			
Merthyr Vale	a	18 14										18 44									19 14			
	d	18 17										18 47									19 17			
Troed Y Rhiw	d	18 20										18 50									19 20			
Pentre-bach	d	18 23										18 53									19 23			
Merthyr Tydfil	a	18 31										19 01									19 31			
Trehafod	d					18 11								18 41										19 11
Porth	a					18 14								18 44										19 14
	d					18 15								18 45										19 15
Dinas Rhondda	d					18 19								18 49										19 19
Tonypandy	d					18 21								18 51										19 21
Llwynypia	d					18 23								18 53										19 23
Ystrad Rhondda	a					18 26								18 56										19 26
	d					18 29								18 59										19 29
Ton Pentre	d					18 31								19 01										19 31
Treorchy	d					18 34								19 04										19 34
Ynyswen	d					18 37								19 07										19 37
Treherbert	a					18 43								19 13										19 43

Bridgend, Barry Island, Barry, Penarth and Cardiff - Coryton. Rhymney, Pontypridd, Merthyr, Aberdare and Treherbert

		AW	AW	AW	AW	AW	AW	AW	AW	AW	AW	AW	AW	AW	AW	AW	AW	AW	AW	AW	AW	AW	AW
Bridgend	d		17 42														18 42						
Llantwit Major	d		17 56														18 56						
Rhoose Cardiff Int Airport ✈	d		18 06														19 06						
Barry Island	d				18 25						18 40		18 55								19 25		
Barry ■	d		18 15		18 30						18 45		19 00				19 15				19 30		
Barry Docks	d		18 19		18 34						18 49		19 04				19 19				19 34		
Cadoxton	d		18 22		18 37						18 52		19 07				19 22				19 37		
Dinas Powys	d		18 26		18 41						18 56		19 11				19 26				19 41		
Eastbrook	d		18 28		18 43						18 58		19 13				19 28				19 43		
Cogan	d		18 30		18 45						19 00		19 15				19 30				19 45		
Penarth	d			18 32				18 47						19 17								19 47	
Dingle Road	d			18 34				18 49						19 19								19 49	
Grangetown	d		18 34	18 38	18 49			18 53			19 04		19 19	19 23			19 34				19 49	19 54	
Cardiff Central ■	a	18 34	18 39	18 45	18 55			18 59			19 09		19 24	19 29		19 34	19 39				19 56	19 59	
	d	18 36	18 41					19 01	19 06		19 11		19 26	19 31		19 36	19 41		19 51		20 01	20 06	
Cardiff Bay	d					18 42	18 54			19 06		19 18			19 30			19 42		19 54			20 06
Cardiff Queen Street ■	a		18 44			18 46	18 58	19 04	19 09	19 10	19 14	19 22	19 29	19 34	19 34		19 44	19 46	19 54	19 58	20 04	20 09	20 10
	d		18 50					19 05	19 10		19 15		19 30	19 35			19 45		19 55		20 05	20 10	
Heath Low Level	d																		20 00				
Ty Glas	d																		20 03				
Birchgrove	d																		20 04				
Rhiwbina	d																		20 06				
Whitchurch (Cardiff)	d																		20 08				
Coryton	a																		20 13				
Heath High Level	d							19 10						19 40							20 10		
Llanishen	d							19 13						19 43							20 13		
Lisvane & Thornhill	d							19 15						19 45							20 15		
Caerphilly ■	d							19a24						19 51							20a28		
Aber	d													19 53									
Llanbradach	d													19 57									
Ystrad Mynach ■	d													20 02									
Hengoed	d													20 05									
Pengam	d													20 08									
Gilfach Fargoed	d													20 11									
Bargoed	a													20 15									
	d													20 16									
Brithdir	d													20 20									
Tir-phil	d													20 23									
Pontlottyn	d													20 27									
Rhymney ■	a													20 33									
Cathays	d		18 52						19 13		19 18		19 33				19 48					20 13	
Llandaf	d		18 56						19 17		19 22		19 37				19 52					20 17	
Ninian Park	d	18 40														19 40							
Waun-gron Park	d	18 43														19 43							
Fairwater	d	18 45														19 45							
Danescourt	d	18 47														19 47							
Radyr ■	a	18 54	18 58						19 20		19 25		19 40			19 54	19 55					20 20	
	d		18 58						19 20		19 25		19 40				19 55					20 20	
Taffs Well ■	d		19 03						19 24		19 29		19 44				19 59					20 24	
Trefforest Estate	d												19 48										
Trefforest	d		19 10						19 31		19 36		19 52				20 06					20 31	
Pontypridd ■	a		19 13						19 34		19 39		19 55				20 09					20 35	
	d		19 14						19 36		19 41		19 57				20 11					20 36	
Abercynon	d		19 21								19 49		20 04				20 21						
Penrhiwceiber	d		19 26								19 54						20 27						
Mountain Ash	a		19 30								19 56						20 30						
	d		19 33								20 03						20 33						
Fernhill	d		19 35								20 05						20 35						
Cwmbach	d		19 39								20 09						20 39						
Aberdare ■	a		19 46								20 16						20 46						
Quakers Yard	d												20 09										
Merthyr Vale	a												20 14										
	d												20 14										
Troed Y Rhiw	d												20 18										
Pentre-bach	d												20 21										
Merthyr Tydfil	a												20 29										
Trehafod	d								19 41													20 41	
Porth	a								19 44													20 44	
	d								19 45													20 45	
Dinas Rhondda	d								19 49													20 49	
Tonypandy	d								19 51													20 51	
Llwynypia	d								19 53													20 53	
Ystrad Rhondda	a								19 56													20 56	
	d								19 59													20 59	
Ton Pentre	d								20 01													21 01	
Treorchy	d								20 04													21 04	
Ynyswen	d								20 07													21 07	
Treherbert	a								20 13													21 13	

Bridgend, Barry Island, Barry, Penarth and Cardiff - Coryton. Rhymney, Pontypridd, Merthyr, Aberdare and Treherbert

		AW	AW	AW	AW	AW	AW	AW	AW	AW	AW	AW	AW	AW	AW	AW	AW	AW	AW	AW	AW	AW	AW
Bridgend	d						19 42													20 42			
Llantwit Major	d						19 56													20 56			
Rhoose Cardiff Int Airport ✈	d						20 06													21 06			
Barry Island	d		19 55												20 55								
Barry ■	d		20 00				20 15								21 00					21 15			
Barry Docks	d		20 04				20 19								21 04					21 19			
Cadoxton	d		20 07				20 22								21 07					21 22			
Dinas Powys	d		20 11				20 26								21 11					21 26			
Eastbrook	d		20 13				20 28								21 13					21 28			
Cogan	d		20 15				20 30								21 15					21 30			
Penarth	d				20 19						20 47								21 20				21 47
Dingle Road	d				20 21						20 49								21 22				21 49
Grangetown	d		20 19		20 24		20 34				20 53				21 19				21 26	21 34			21 53
Cardiff Central ■	a		20 26		20 31	20 34	20 39				20 59				21 24			21 34	21 37	21 39			21 59
	d		20 26		20 32	20 36	20 41		20 51		21 01	21 06			21 26		21 31	21 36		21 41			22 01
Cardiff Bay	d	20 18		20 30				20 42		20 54			21 06	21 18		21 30					21 42	21 54	
Cardiff Queen Street ■	a	20 22	20 29	20 34	20 35		20 44	20 46	20 54	20 58	21 04	21 09	21 10	21 22	21 29	21 34	21 34			21 44	21 46	21 58	22 04
	d		20 30		20 36		20 45		20 55		21 05	21 10			21 30		21 35			21 45			22 05
Heath Low Level	d								21 00														
Ty Glas	d								21 03														
Birchgrove	d								21 04														
Rhiwbina	d								21 06														
Whitchurch (Cardiff)	d								21 08														
Coryton	a								21 13														
Heath High Level	d				20 41						21 10						21 40						22 10
Llanishen	d				20 44						21 13						21 43						22 13
Lisvane & Thornhill	d				20 46						21 15						21 45						22 15
Caerphilly ■	d				20 52						21a34						21 51						22a24
Aber	d				20 54												21 53						
Llanbradach	d				20 58												21 57						
Ystrad Mynach ■	d				21 03												22 02						
Hengoed	d				21 06												22 05						
Pengam	d				21 09												22 08						
Gilfach Fargoed	d				21 12												22 11						
Bargoed	a				21 16												22 15						
	d				21 17												22 16						
Brithdir	d				21 21												22 20						
Tir-phil	d				21 24												22 23						
Pontlottyn	d				21 28												22 27						
Rhymney ■	a				21 34												22 33						
Cathays	d		20 33				20 48					21 13			21 33					21 48			
Llandaf	d		20 37				20 52					21 17			21 37					21 52			
Ninian Park	d					20 40												21 40					
Waun-gron Park	d					20 43												21 43					
Fairwater	d					20 45												21 45					
Danescourt	d					20 47												21 47					
Radyr ■	a		20 40			20 54	20 55					21 20			21 40			21 54		21 55			
	d		20 40				20 55					21 20			21 40					21 55			
Taffs Well ■	d		20 44				20 59					21 24			21 44					21 59			
Trefforest Estate	d		20 48												21 48								
Trefforest	d		20 52				21 06					21 31			21 52					22 06			
Pontypridd ■	a		20 56				21 09					21 34			21 55					22 09			
	d		20 57				21 11					21 36			21 57					22 11			
Abercynon	d		21 04				21 19								22 04					22 19			
Penrhiwceiber	d						21 24													22 24			
Mountain Ash	a						21 28													22 28			
	d						21 29													22 29			
Fernhill	d						21 31													22 31			
Cwmbach	d						21 35													22 35			
Aberdare ■	a						21 42													22 42			
Quakers Yard	d		21 09												22 09								
Merthyr Vale	a		21 14												22 14								
	d		21 14												22 14								
Troed Y Rhiw	d		21 18												22 18								
Pentre-bach	d		21 21												22 21								
Merthyr Tydfil	a		21 29												22 29								
Trehafod	d											21 41											
Porth	a											21 44											
	d											21 45											
Dinas Rhondda	d											21 49											
Tonypandy	d											21 51											
Llwynypia	d											21 53											
Ystrad Rhondda	a											21 56											
	d											21 59											
Ton Pentre	d											22 01											
Treorchy	d											22 04											
Ynyswen	d											22 07											
Treherbert	a											22 13											

Table 130

Mondays to Fridays
until 03 September

Bridgend, Barry Island, Barry, Penarth and Cardiff - Coryton. Rhymney, Pontypridd, Merthyr, Aberdare and Treherbert

		AW		AW	AW	AW	AW	AW	AW	AW	AW	AW		AW	AW	AW	AW	AW	AW	AW	AW	AW			
Bridgend	d								21 42										22 42						
Llantwit Major	d								21 56										22 56						
Rhoose Cardiff Int Airport ✈	d								22 06										23 06						
Barry Island	d					21 55											22 44								
Barry	d					22 00			22 15								22 48		23 15						
Barry Docks	d					22 04			22 19								22 52		23 19						
Cadoxton	d					22 07			22 22								22 55		23 22						
Dinas Powys	d					22 11			22 26								22 59		23 26						
Eastbrook	d					22 13			22 28								23 01		23 28						
Cogan	d					22 15			22 30								23 03		23 30						
Penarth	d							22 19							22 47			23 26							
Dingle Road	d							22 21							22 49			23 28							
Grangetown	d					22 19		22 25	22 34						22 53		23 07	23 32	23 34						
Cardiff Central	a					22 24		22 33	22 39						23 00		23 12	23 38	23 42						
	d	22 06				22 26		22 35	22 41		22 46				23 15		23 26								
Cardiff Bay	d			22 06	22 18		22 30			22 42		22 54		23 06		23 18				23 30	23 42	23 54			
Cardiff Queen Street	a	22 09		22 10	22 22	22 29	22 34	22 38	22 44	22 46	22 49	22 58		23 10	23 18	23 22	23 29			23 34	23 46	23 58			
	d	22 10				22 30		22 39	22 45		22 50				23 19		23 30								
Heath Low Level	d																								
Ty Glas	d																								
Birchgrove	d																								
Rhiwbina	d																								
Whitchurch (Cardiff)	d																								
Coryton	a																								
Heath High Level	d							22 44							23 24										
Llanishen	d							22 47							23 27										
Lisvane & Thornhill	d							22 49							23 29										
Caerphilly	d							22 55							23 35										
Aber	d							22 57							23 37										
Llanbradach	d							23 01							23 41										
Ystrad Mynach	d							23 06							23a50										
Hengoed	d							23 09																	
Pengam	d							23 12																	
Gilfach Fargoed	d							23 15																	
Bargoed	a							23 19																	
	d							23 20																	
Brithdir	d							23 24																	
Tir-phil	d							23 27																	
Pontlottyn	d							23 31																	
Rhymney	a							23 37																	
Cathays	d	22 13				22 33			22 48		22 53						23 33								
Llandaf	d	22 17				22 37			22 52		22 57						23 37								
Ninian Park	d																								
Waun-gron Park	d																								
Fairwater	d																								
Danescourt	d																								
Radyr	a	22 20				22 40			22 55		22 59						23 40								
	d	22 20				22 40			22 55		22 59						23 40								
Taffs Well	d	22 24				22 44			22 59		23 03						23 44								
Trefforest Estate	d					22 48											23 48								
Trefforest	d	22 31				22 52			23 06		23 10						23 52								
Pontypridd	a	22 34				22 55			23 09		23 14						23 58								
	d	22 36				22 57			23 11		23 15														
Abercynon	d					23 04			23 19																
Penrhiwceiber	d								23 24																
Mountain Ash	a								23 28																
	d								23 33																
Fernhill	d								23 35																
Cwmbach	d								23 39																
Aberdare	a								23 46																
Quakers Yard	d					23 09																			
Merthyr Vale	a					23 14																			
	d					23 14																			
Troed Y Rhiw	d					23 18																			
Pentre-bach	d					23 21																			
Merthyr Tydfil	a					23 29																			
Trehafod	d	22 41									23 20														
Porth	a	22 44									23 23														
	d	22 45									23 24														
Dinas Rhondda	d	22 49									23 28														
Tonypandy	d	22 51									23 30														
Llwynypia	d	22 53									23 32														
Ystrad Rhondda	a	22 56									23 35														
	d	22 59									23 38														
Ton Pentre	d	23 01									23 40														
Treorchy	d	23 04									23 43														
Ynyswen	d	23 07									23 46														
Treherbert	a	23 13									23 52														

Table 130

Mondays to Fridays
from 06 September

Bridgend, Barry Island, Barry, Penarth and Cardiff - Coryton. Rhymney, Pontypridd, Merthyr, Aberdare and Treherbert

		AW MX	AW	AW	AW	AW	AW	AW	AW	AW		AW	AW	AW	AW	AW	AW	AW	AW	AW		AW	AW	AW	AW
Bridgend	d												05 42												
Llantwit Major	d												05 56												
Rhoose Cardiff Int Airport ✈	d												06 06												
Barry Island	d	22p44								05 52							06 25								
Barry	d	22p48								05 57			06 15				06 30								
Barry Docks	d	22p52								06 01			06 19				06 34								
Cadoxton	d	22p55								06 04			06 22				06 37								
Dinas Powys	d	22p59								06 08			06 26				06 41								
Eastbrook	d	23p01								06 10			06 28				06 43								
Cogan	d	23p03								06 12			06 30				06 45								
Penarth	d							06 02							06 32									07 02	
Dingle Road	d							06 04							06 34									07 04	
Grangetown	d	23p07						06 08		06 16			06 34		06 38		06 49							07 08	
Cardiff Central	a	23p12						06 13		06 21			06 39		06 44		06 54						07 04	07 14	
	d	23p26	05 26	05 46		05 56	06 11	06 15	06 19	06 26		06 36	06 41		06 46	06 51	06 56		07 06			07 11	07 06	07 16	
Cardiff Bay	d													06 42				06 54		07 06					07 18
Cardiff Queen Street	a	23p29	05 29	05 49		05 59	06 14	06 19	06 24	06 29		06 39	06 44	06 46	06 49	06 54	06 59	06 58	07 09	07 10		07 14		07 19	07 22
	d	23p30	05 30	05 50		06 00	06 15	06 20	06 25	06 30		06 40	06 45		06 50	06 55	07 00		07 10			07 15		07 20	
Heath Low Level	d								06 30							07 00									
Ty Glas	d								06 33							07 03									
Birchgrove	d								06 34							07 04									
Rhiwbina	d								06 36							07 06									
Whitchurch (Cardiff)	d								06 38							07 08									
Coryton	a								06 44							07 14									
Heath High Level	d			05 54				06 25							06 55									07 25	
Llanishen	d			05 57				06 28							06 58									07 28	
Lisvane & Thornhill	d			06 00				06 30							07 00									07 30	
Caerphilly	d			06a09				06 36							07 06									07 36	
Aber	d							06 38							07 08									07 38	
Llanbradach	d							06 42							07 12									07 42	
Ystrad Mynach	d							06 47							07 17									07 47	
Hengoed	d							06 50							07 20									07 50	
Pengam	d							06 53							07 23									07 53	
Gilfach Fargoed	d																								
Bargoed	a							07 02							07 32									08 02	
	d																								
Brithdir	d																								
Tir-phil	d																								
Pontlottyn	d																								
Rhymney	a																								
Cathays	d	23p33	05 33			06 03	06 18			06 33		06 43	06 48				07 03		07 13			07 18			
Llandaf	d	23p37	05 37			06 07	06 22			06 37		06 47	06 52				07 07		07 17			07 22			
Ninian Park	d																						07 10		
Waun-gron Park	d																						07 14		
Fairwater	d																						07 16		
Danescourt	d																						07 19		
Radyr	a	23p40	05 39			06 10	06 24			06 40		06 50	06 54				07 10		07 20			07 25	07 27		
	d	23p40	05 40			06 10	06 24			06 40		06 50	06 55				07 10		07 20			07 25			
Taffs Well	d	23p44	05 43			06 14	06 28			06 44		06 54	06 59				07 14		07 24			07 29			
Trefforest Estate	d	23p48	05 47			06 18				06 48							07 18								
Trefforest	d	23p52	05 52			06 22	06 35			06 52		07 01	07 06				07 22		07 31			07 36			
Pontypridd	a	00 01	05 55			06 25	06 38			06 55		07 04	07 09				07 25		07 34			07 39			
	d		05 57		06 11	06 27	06 41			06 57		07 06	07 11				07 27		07 36			07 41			
Abercynon	d		06 04		06 19	06 34	06 49			07 04			07 19				07 34					07 49			
Penrhiwceiber	d				06 25		06 55						07 25									07 55			
Mountain Ash	a				06 28		06 58						07 28									07 58			
	d				06 34		07 04						07 34									08 04			
Fernhill	d				06 37		07 07						07 37									08 07			
Cwmbach	d				06 41		07 11						07 41									08 11			
Aberdare	a				06 49		07 19						07 49									08 19			
Quakers Yard	d		06 09			06 39				07 09							07 39								
Merthyr Vale	a		06 14			06 44				07 14							07 44								
	d		06 17			06 47				07 17							07 47								
Troed Y Rhiw	d		06 21			06 51				07 21							07 51								
Pentre-bach	d		06 24			06 54				07 24							07 54								
Merthyr Tydfil	a		06 33			07 03				07 33							08 03								
Trehafod	d											07 11							07 41						
Porth	a											07 14							07 44						
	d											07 15							07 45						
Dinas Rhondda	d											07 19							07 49						
Tonypandy	d											07 21							07 51						
Llwynypia	d											07 23							07 53						
Ystrad Rhondda	a											07 26							07 56						
	d											07 29							07 59						
Ton Pentre	d											07 31							08 01						
Treorchy	d											07 34							08 04						
Ynyswen	d											07 37							08 07						
Treherbert	a											07 44							08 14						

Table 130

Mondays to Fridays

from 06 September

Bridgend, Barry Island, Barry, Penarth and Cardiff - Coryton. Rhymney, Pontypridd, Merthyr, Aberdare and Treherbert

Station		AW	AW	AW	AW	AW	AW	AW	AW	AW	AW	AW	AW	AW	AW	AW	AW	AW	AW	AW	AW	AW	AW
Bridgend	d						06 42																
Llantwit Major	d						06 56																
Rhoose Cardiff Int Airport ✈	d						07 06																
Barry Island	d	06 55								07 25						07 40			07 55				
Barry ■	d	07 00					07 15			07 30						07 45			08 00				
Barry Docks	d	07 04					07 19			07 34						07 49			08 04				
Cadoxton	d	07 07					07 22			07 37						07 52			08 07				
Dinas Powys	d	07 11					07 26			07 41						07 56			08 11				
Eastbrook	d	07 13					07 28			07 43						07 58			08 13				
Cogan	d	07 15					07 30			07 45						08 00			08 15				
Penarth	d		07 17							07 32			07 47						08 02			08 17			
Dingle Road	d		07 19							07 34			07 49						08 04			08 19			
Grangetown	d	07 19	07 23				07 34		07 38	07 49		07 54				08 04	08 08		08 19	08 23			
Cardiff Central ■	a	07 24	07 29		07 34		07 39		07 44	07 54		08 00	08 04			08 09	08 14		08 24	08 29		08 34	
	d	07 26	07 31		07 36	07 36	07 41		07 46	07 56		08 01	08 06	08 06		08 11	08 16		08 26	08 31		08 36	08 36
Cardiff Bay	d			07 30				07 42			07 54				08 06			08 18			08 30		
Cardiff Queen Street ■	a	07 29	07 34	07 34		07 39	07 44	07 46	07 49	07 59	07 58	08 04		08 09	08 10	08 14	08 19	08 22	08 29	08 34	08 34		08 39
	d	07 30	07 35			07 40	07 45		07 50	08 00		08 05		08 10		08 15	08 20		08 30	08 35			08 40
Heath Low Level	d																						
Ty Glas	d																						
Birchgrove	d																						
Rhiwbina	d																						
Whitchurch (Cardiff)	d																						
Coryton	a																						
Heath High Level	d		07 40							07 55			08 10						08 25			08 40			
Llanishen	d		07 43							07 58			08 13						08 28			08 43			
Lisvane & Thornhill	d		07 45							08 00			08 15						08 30			08 45			
Caerphilly ■	d		07 51							08 06			08 21						08 36			08 51			
Aber	d		07 53							08 08			08 23						08 38			08 53			
Llanbradach	d		07 57							08 12			08 27						08 42			08 57			
Ystrad Mynach ■	d		08 02							08 17			08 32						08 47			09 07			
Hengoed	d		08 05							08 20			08 35						08 50			09 10			
Pengam	d		08 08							08 23			08 38						08 53			09 13			
Gilfach Fargoed	d												08 41										
Bargoed	a		08 13							08 31			08 49						08 58			09 25			
	d		08 14																08 59						
Brithdir	d		08 18																09 03						
Tir-phil	d		08 21																09 06						
Pontlottyn	d		08 25																09 10						
Rhymney ■	a		08 28																09 17						
Cathays	d	07 33				07 43	07 48			08 03				08 13		08 18			08 33				08 43
Llandaf	d	07 37				07 47	07 52			08 07				08 17		08 22			08 37				08 47
Ninian Park	d				07 40								08 10									08 40	
Waun-gron Park	d				07 44								08 14									08 44	
Fairwater	d				07 46								08 16									08 46	
Danescourt	d				07 49								08 19									08 49	
Radyr ■	a	07 40			07 57	07 50	07 55			08 10			08 27	08 20		08 25			08 40			08 57	08 50
	d	07 40				07 50	07 55			08 10				08 20		08 25			08 40				08 50
Taffs Well ■	d	07 44				07 54	07 59			08 14				08 24		08 29			08 44				08 54
Trefforest Estate	d	07 48								08 18										08 48				
Trefforest	d	07 52				08 01	08 06			08 23				08 31		08 36			08 52				09 01
Pontypridd ■	a	07 55				08 04	08 09			08 26				08 34		08 39			08 55				09 04
	d	07 57				08 06	08 11			08 27				08 36		08 41			08 57				09 06
Abercynon	d	08 04					08 19			08 34						08 49			09 04				
Penrhiwceiber	d						08 25									08 55							
Mountain Ash	a						08 28									08 58							
	d						08 34									09 04							
Fernhill	d						08 37									09 07							
Cwmbach	d						08 41									09 11							
Aberdare ■	a						08 49									09 19							
Quakers Yard	d	08 09								08 39										09 09				
Merthyr Vale	a	08 14								08 44										09 14				
	d	08 17								08 47										09 17				
Troed Y Rhiw	d	08 21								08 51										09 21				
Pentre-bach	d	08 24								08 54										09 24				
Merthyr Tydfil	a	08 33								09 03										09 33				
Trehafod	d					08 11								08 41									09 11
Porth	a					08 14								08 44									09 14
	d					08 15								08 45									09 15
Dinas Rhondda	d					08 19								08 49									09 19
Tonypandy	d					08 21								08 51									09 21
Llwynypia	d					08 23								08 53									09 23
Ystrad Rhondda	a					08 26								08 56									09 26
	d					08 29								08 59									09 29
Ton Pentre	d					08 31								09 01									09 31
Treorchy	d					08 34								09 04									09 34
Ynyswen	d					08 37								09 07									09 37
Treherbert	a					08 44								09 14									09 44

Table 130

Mondays to Fridays

from 06 September

Bridgend, Barry Island, Barry, Penarth and Cardiff - Coryton. Rhymney, Pontypridd, Merthyr, Aberdare and Treherbert

Station		AW	AW	AW	AW	AW	AW	AW	AW	AW	AW	AW	AW	AW	AW	AW	AW	AW	AW	AW	AW	AW
Bridgend	d	07 42																08 42			
Llantwit Major	d	07 56																08 56			
Rhoose Cardiff Int Airport ✈	d	08 06																09 06			
Barry Island	d				08 25						08 40			08 55							
Barry ■	d	08 15			08 30						08 45			09 00					09 15			
Barry Docks	d	08 19			08 34						08 49			09 04					09 19			
Cadoxton	d	08 22			08 37						08 52			09 07					09 22			
Dinas Powys	d	08 26			08 41						08 56			09 11					09 26			
Eastbrook	d	08 28			08 43						08 58			09 13					09 28			
Cogan	d	08 30			08 45						09 00			09 15					09 30			
Penarth	d			08 32			08 47									09 17					09 32	
Dingle Road	d			08 34			08 49									09 19					09 34	
Grangetown	d	08 34		08 38	08 49		08 53				09 04			09 19	09 23				09 34		09 38	
Cardiff Central ■	a	08 39		08 44	08 54		08 59	09 04			09 09			09 24	09 29		09 34		09 39		09 44	
	d	08 41		08 46	08 56		09 01	09 06	09 06		09 11	09 16		09 26	09 31		09 36	09 36	09 41		09 46	
Cardiff Bay	d		08 42			08 54				09 06			09 18			09 30				09 42		09 54
Cardiff Queen Street ■	a	08 44	08 46	08 49	08 59	08 58	09 04		09 09	09 10	09 14	09 19	09 22	09 29	09 34	09 34		09 39	09 44	09 46	09 49	09 58
	d	08 45		08 50	09 00		09 05		09 10		09 15	09 20		09 30	09 35			09 40	09 45		09 50	
Heath Low Level	d																					
Ty Glas	d																					
Birchgrove	d																					
Rhiwbina	d																					
Whitchurch (Cardiff)	d																					
Coryton	a																					
Heath High Level	d			08 55			09 10					09 25			09 40					09 55	
Llanishen	d			08 58			09 13					09 28			09 43					09 58	
Lisvane & Thornhill	d			09 00			09 15					09 30			09 45					10 00	
Caerphilly ■	d			09 06			09 21					09 36			09 51					10 06	
Aber	d			09 08			09 23					09 38			09 53					10 08	
Llanbradach	d			09 12			09 27					09 42			09 57					10 12	
Ystrad Mynach ■	d			09a22			09 32					09 47			10 07					10a22	
Hengoed	d						09 35					09 50			10 10						
Pengam	d						09 38					09 53			10 13						
Gilfach Fargoed	d						09 41															
Bargoed	a						09 49					09 58			10 25						
	d											09 59									
Brithdir	d											10 03									
Tir-phil	d											10 06									
Pontlottyn	d											10 10									
Rhymney ■	a											10 17									
Cathays	d	08 48			09 03				09 13		09 18			09 33				09 43	09 48			
Llandaf	d	08 52			09 07				09 17		09 22			09 37				09 47	09 52			
Ninian Park	d							09 10										09 40					
Waun-gron Park	d							09 14										09 44					
Fairwater	d							09 16										09 46					
Danescourt	d							09 19										09 49					
Radyr ■	a	08 55			09 10			09 27	09 20		09 25			09 40			09 57	09 50	09 55			
	d	08 55			09 10				09 20		09 25			09 40				09 50	09 55			
Taffs Well ■	d	08 59			09 14				09 24		09 29			09 44				09 54	09 59			
Trefforest Estate	d				09 18									09 48							
Trefforest	d	09 06			09 22				09 31		09 36			09 52				10 01	10 06			
Pontypridd ■	a	09 09			09 25				09 34		09 39			09 55				10 04	10 09			
	d	09 11			09 27				09 36		09 41			09 57				10 06	10 11			
Abercynon	d	09 19			09 34						09 49			10 04					10 19			
Penrhiwceiber	d	09 25									09 55								10 25			
Mountain Ash	a	09 28									09 58								10 28			
	d	09 34									10 04								10 34			
Fernhill	d	09 37									10 07								10 37			
Cwmbach	d	09 41									10 11								10 41			
Aberdare ■	a	09 49									10 19								10 49			
Quakers Yard	d				09 39									10 09							
Merthyr Vale	a				09 44									10 14							
	d				09 47									10 17							
Troed Y Rhiw	d				09 51									10 21							
Pentre-bach	d				09 54									10 24							
Merthyr Tydfil	a				10 03									10 33							
Trehafod	d								09 41									10 11				
Porth	a								09 44									10 14				
	d								09 45									10 15				
Dinas Rhondda	d								09 49									10 19				
Tonypandy	d								09 51									10 21				
Llwynypia	d								09 53									10 23				
Ystrad Rhondda	a								09 56									10 26				
	d								09 59									10 29				
Ton Pentre	d								10 01									10 31				
Treorchy	d								10 04									10 34				
Ynyswen	d								10 07									10 37				
Treherbert	a								10 14									10 44				

Table 130

Mondays to Fridays
from 06 September

Bridgend, Barry Island, Barry, Penarth and Cardiff - Coryton. Rhymney, Pontypridd, Merthyr, Aberdare and Treherbert

		AW	AW	AW	AW	AW	AW	AW	AW	AW	AW	AW	AW	AW	AW	AW	AW	AW	AW	AW	AW	AW	AW
Bridgend	d															09 42							
Llantwit Major	d															09 56							
Rhoose Cardiff Int Airport ✈	d															10 06							
Barry Island	d	09 25						09 40			09 55									10 25			
Barry ■	d	09 30						09 45			10 00					10 15				10 30			
Barry Docks	d	09 34						09 49			10 04					10 19				10 34			
Cadoxton	d	09 37						09 52			10 07					10 22				10 37			
Dinas Powys	d	09 41						09 56			10 11					10 26				10 41			
Eastbrook	d	09 43						09 58			10 13					10 28				10 43			
Cogan	d	09 45						10 00			10 15					10 30				10 45			
Penarth	d		09 47						10 02			10 17						10 32					10 47
Dingle Road	d		09 49						10 04			10 19						10 34					10 49
Grangetown	d	09 49	09 53					10 04	10 08		10 19	10 23				10 34		10 38		10 49			10 53
Cardiff Central ■	a	09 54	09 59	10 04				10 09	10 14		10 24	10 29			10 34	10 42		10 44		10 54			10 59
	d	09 56	10 01	10 06	10 06			10 11	10 16		10 26	10 31		10 36	10 36			10 46	10 51	10 56			11 01
Cardiff Bay	d					10 06				10 18			10 30				10 42					10 54	
Cardiff Queen Street ■	a	09 59	10 04		10 09	10 10		10 14	10 19	10 22	10 29	10 34	10 34	10 39			10 46	10 49		10 59		10 58	11 04
	d	10 00	10 05		10 10			10 15	10 20		10 30	10 35		10 40				10 50		11 00			11 05
Heath Low Level	d																						
Ty Glas	d																						
Birchgrove	d																						
Rhiwbina	d																						
Whitchurch (Cardiff)	d																						
Coryton	a																						
Heath High Level	d		10 10						10 25			10 40						10 55					11 10
Llanishen	d		10 13						10 28			10 43						10 58					11 13
Lisvane & Thornhill	d		10 15						10 30			10 45						11 00					11 15
Caerphilly ■	d		10 21						10 36			10 51						11 06					11 21
Aber	d		10 23						10 38			10 53						11 08					11 23
Llanbradach	d		10 27						10 42			10 57						11 12					11 27
Ystrad Mynach ■	d		10 32						10 47			11 07						11a22					11 32
Hengoed	d		10 35						10 50			11 10											11 35
Pengam	d		10 38						10 53			11 13											11 38
Gilfach Fargoed	d		10 41																				11 41
Bargoed	a		10 49						10 58			11 25											11 49
	d								10 59														
Brithdir	d								11 03														
Tir-phil	d								11 06														
Pontlottyn	d								11 10														
Rhymney ■	a								11 17														
Cathays	d	10 03			10 13			10 18			10 33			10 43						11 03			
Llandaf	d	10 07			10 17			10 22			10 37			10 47						11 07			
Ninian Park	d			10 10											10 40								
Waun-gron Park	d			10 14											10 44								
Fairwater	d			10 16											10 46								
Danescourt	d			10 19											10 49								
Radyr ■	a	10 10		10 27	10 20			10 25			10 40			10 50	10 57				11 02	11 10			
	d	10 10			10 20			10 25			10 40			10 50					11 20	11 10			
Taffs Well ■	d	10 14			10 24			10 29			10 44			10 54					11 24	11 14			
Trefforest Estate	d	10 18									10 48									11 18			
Trefforest	d	10 22			10 31			10 36			10 52			11 01					11 31	11 22	←		
Pontypridd ■	a	10 30			10 34			10 39			10 55			11 04					11 34	11 25	11 34		
	d				10 36		10 35	10 41			10 57			11 06					11 36	11 27	11 36		
Abercynon	d						10 41	10 49			11 04								→	11 34			
Penrhiwceiber	d							10 55															
Mountain Ash	a							10 58															
	d							11 04															
Fernhill	d							11 07															
Cwmbach	d							11 11															
Aberdare ■	a							11 19															
Quakers Yard	d						10 45				11 09									11 39			
Merthyr Vale	a						10 50				11 14									11 44			
	d						10 52				11 17									11 47			
Troed Y Rhiw	d						10 56				11 21									11 51			
Pentre-bach	d						10 59				11 24									11 54			
Merthyr Tydfil	a						11 08				11 33									12 03			
Trehafod	d				10 41									11 11							11 41		
Porth	a				10 44									11 14							11 44		
	d				10 45									11 15							11 45		
Dinas Rhondda	d				10 49									11 19							11 49		
Tonypandy	d				10 51									11 21							11 51		
Llwynypia	d				10 53									11 23							11 53		
Ystrad Rhondda	a				10 56									11 26							11 56		
	d				10 59									11 29							11 59		
Ton Pentre	d				11 01									11 31							12 01		
Treorchy	d				11 04									11 34							12 04		
Ynyswen	d				11 07									11 37							12 07		
Treherbert	a				11 14									11 44							12 14		

Table 130

Mondays to Fridays
from 06 September

Bridgend, Barry Island, Barry, Penarth and Cardiff - Coryton. Rhymney, Pontypridd, Merthyr, Aberdare and Treherbert

		AW	AW	AW	AW	AW	AW	AW	AW	AW	AW	AW	AW	AW	AW	AW	AW	AW	AW	AW	AW	AW
Bridgend	d											10 42										
Llantwit Major	d											10 56										
Rhoose Cardiff Int Airport ✈	d											11 06										
Barry Island	d			10 40			10 55								11 25						11 40	
Barry ■	d			10 45			11 00					11 15			11 30						11 45	
Barry Docks	d			10 49			11 04					11 19			11 34						11 49	
Cadoxton	d			10 52			11 07					11 22			11 37						11 52	
Dinas Powys	d			10 56			11 11					11 26			11 41						11 56	
Eastbrook	d			10 58			11 13					11 28			11 43						11 58	
Cogan	d			11 00			11 15					11 30			11 45						12 00	
Penarth	d				11 02			11 17						11 32			11 47					12 02
Dingle Road	d				11 04			11 19						11 34			11 49					12 04
Grangetown	d			11 04	11 08		11 19	11 23				11 34		11 38	11 49		11 53				12 04	12 08
Cardiff Central ■	a	11 04		11 09	11 14		11 24	11 29		11 34		11 39		11 44	11 54		12 00	12 04			12 09	12 14
	d	11 06		11 11	11 16		11 26	11 31		11 36	11 36	11 41		11 46	11 56		12 01	12 06	12 06		12 11	12 16
Cardiff Bay	d		11 06			11 18			11 30				11 42			11 54				12 06		
Cardiff Queen Street ■	a		11 10	11 14	11 19	11 22	11 29	11 34	11 34		11 39	11 44	11 46	11 49	11 59	11 58	12 04		12 09	12 10	12 14	12 19
	d			11 15	11 20		11 30	11 35			11 40	11 45		11 50	12 00		12 05		12 10		12 15	12 20
Heath Low Level	d																					
Ty Glas	d																					
Birchgrove	d																					
Rhiwbina	d																					
Whitchurch (Cardiff)	d																					
Coryton	a																					
Heath High Level	d				11 25			11 40						11 55			12 10					12 25
Llanishen	d				11 28			11 43						11 58			12 13					12 28
Lisvane & Thornhill	d				11 30			11 45						12 00			12 15					12 30
Caerphilly ■	d				11 36			11 51						12 06			12 21					12 36
Aber	d				11 38			11 53						12 08			12 23					12 38
Llanbradach	d				11 42			11 57						12 12			12 27					12 42
Ystrad Mynach ■	d				11 47			12 07						12a22			12 32					12 47
Hengoed	d				11 50			12 10									12 35					12 50
Pengam	d				11 53			12 13									12 38					12 53
Gilfach Fargoed	d																12 41					
Bargoed	a				11 58			12 25									12 49					12 58
	d				11 59																	12 59
Brithdir	d				12 03																	13 03
Tir-phil	d				12 06																	13 06
Pontlottyn	d				12 10																	13 10
Rhymney ■	a				12 17																	13 17
Cathays	d			11 18			11 33				11 43	11 48			12 03				12 13		12 18	
Llandaf	d			11 22			11 37				11 47	11 52			12 07				12 17		12 22	
Ninian Park	d	11 10								11 40								12 10				
Waun-gron Park	d	11 14								11 44								12 14				
Fairwater	d	11 16								11 46								12 16				
Danescourt	d	11 19								11 49								12 19				
Radyr ■	a	11 27		11 25			11 40			11 57	11 50	11 55			12 10			12 27	12 20		12 25	
	d			11 25			11 40				11 50	11 55			12 10				12 20		12 25	
Taffs Well ■	d			11 29			11 44				11 54	11 59			12 14				12 24		12 29	
Trefforest Estate	d						11 48								12 18							
Trefforest	d			11 36			11 52				12 01	12 06			12 22				12 31		12 36	
Pontypridd ■	a			11 39			11 55				12 04	12 09			12 25				12 34		12 42	
	d			11 41			11 57				12 06	12 11			12 27				12 36			
Abercynon	d			11 49			12 04					12 20			12 34							
Penrhiwceiber	d			11 55								12 25										
Mountain Ash	a			11 58								12 28										
	d			12 04								12 34										
Fernhill	d			12 07								12 37										
Cwmbach	d			12 11								12 41										
Aberdare ■	a			12 19								12 49										
Quakers Yard	d						12 09								12 39							
Merthyr Vale	a						12 14								12 44							
	d						12 17								12 47							
Troed Y Rhiw	d						12 21								12 51							
Pentre-bach	d						12 24								12 54							
Merthyr Tydfil	a						12 33								13 03							
Trehafod	d										12 11								12 41			
Porth	a										12 14								12 44			
	d										12 15								12 45			
Dinas Rhondda	d										12 19								12 49			
Tonypandy	d										12 21								12 51			
Llwynypia	d										12 23								12 53			
Ystrad Rhondda	a										12 26								12 56			
	d										12 29								12 59			
Ton Pentre	d										12 31								13 01			
Treorchy	d										12 34								13 04			
Ynyswen	d										12 37								13 07			
Treherbert	a										12 44								13 14			

Bridgend, Barry Island, Barry, Penarth and Cardiff - Coryton. Rhymney, Pontypridd, Merthyr, Aberdare and Treherbert

		AW	AW	AW	AW	AW	AW	AW	AW	AW	AW	AW	AW	AW	AW	AW	AW	AW	AW	AW	AW	AW	AW
Bridgend	d								11 42														
Llantwit Major	d								11 56														
Rhoose Cardiff Int Airport ✈	d								12 06														
Barry Island	d		11 55									12 25						12 40			12 55		
Barry [3]	d		12 00						12 15			12 30						12 45			13 00		
Barry Docks	d		12 04						12 19			12 34						12 49			13 04		
Cadoxton	d		12 07						12 22			12 37						12 52			13 07		
Dinas Powys	d		12 11						12 26			12 41						12 56			13 11		
Eastbrook	d		12 13						12 28			12 43						12 58			13 13		
Cogan	d		12 15						12 30			12 45						13 00			13 15		
Penarth	d			12 17							12 32			12 47					13 02			13 17	
Dingle Road	d			12 19							12 34			12 49					13 04			13 19	
Grangetown	d		12 19	12 23					12 34		12 38	12 49		12 53				13 04	13 08		13 19	13 23	
Cardiff Central [7]	a		12 24	12 29				12 34	12 44		12 44	12 54		12 59	13 04			13 09	13 14		13 24	13 29	
	d		12 26	12 31		12 36	12 41	12 36			12 46	12 56		13 01	13 06	13 06		13 11	13 16		13 26	13 31	
Cardiff Bay	d	12 18			12 30					12 42			12 54				13 06			13 18			13 30
Cardiff Queen Street [3]	a	12 22	12 29	12 34	12 34	12 39	12 44			12 46	12 49	12 59	12 58	13 04		13 09	13 10	13 14	13 19	13 22	13 29	13 34	13 34
	d		12 30	12 35		12 40	12 45				12 50	13 00		13 05		13 10		13 15	13 20		13 30	13 35	
Heath Low Level	d																						
Ty Glas	d																						
Birchgrove	d																						
Rhiwbina	d																						
Whitchurch (Cardiff)	d																						
Coryton	a																						
Heath High Level	d			12 40							12 55			13 10					13 25			13 40	
Llanishen	d			12 43							12 58			13 13					13 28			13 43	
Lisvane & Thornhill	d			12 45							13 00			13 15					13 30			13 45	
Caerphilly [3]	d			12 51							13 06			13 21					13 36			13 51	
Aber	d			12 53							13 08			13 23					13 38			13 53	
Llanbradach	d			12 57							13 12			13 27					13 42			13 57	
Ystrad Mynach [3]	d			13 07							13a22			13 32					13 47			14 07	
Hengoed	d			13 10										13 35					13 50			14 10	
Pengam	d			13 13										13 38					13 53			14 13	
Gilfach Fargoed	d													13 41									
Bargoed	a			13 25										13 49					13 58			14 25	
	d																		13 59				
Brithdir	d																		14 03				
Tir-phil	d																		14 06				
Pontlottyn	d																		14 10				
Rhymney [3]	a																		14 17				
Cathays	d		12 33			12 43	12 48					13 03				13 13		13 18			13 33		
Llandaf	d		12 37			12 47	12 52					13 07				13 17		13 22			13 37		
Ninian Park	d							12 40							13 10								
Waun-gron Park	d							12 44							13 14								
Fairwater	d							12 46							13 16								
Danescourt	d							12 49							13 19								
Radyr [3]	a		12 40			12 50	12 55	12 57				13 10			13 27	13 20		13 25			13 40		
	d		12 40			12 50	12 55					13 10				13 20		13 25			13 40		
Taffs Well [3]	d		12 44			12 54	12 59					13 14				13 24		13 29			13 44		
Trefforest Estate	d		12 48									13 18									13 48		
Trefforest	d		12 52			13 01	13 06					13 22				13 31		13 36			13 52		
Pontypridd [3]	a		12 55			13 04	13 09					13 25				13 34		13 39			13 55		
	d		12 57			13 06	13 11					13 27				13 36		13 41			13 57		
Abercynon	d		13 04				13 19					13 34						13 49			14 04		
Penrhiwceiber	d						13 25											13 55					
Mountain Ash	a						13 28											13 58					
	d						13 34											14 04					
Fernhill	d						13 37											14 07					
Cwmbach	d						13 41											14 11					
Aberdare [3]	a						13 49											14 19					
Quakers Yard	d		13 09									13 39									14 09		
Merthyr Vale	a		13 14									13 44									14 14		
	d		13 17									13 47									14 17		
Troed Y Rhiw	d		13 21									13 51									14 21		
Pentre-bach	d		13 24									13 54									14 24		
Merthyr Tydfil	a		13 33									14 03									14 33		
Trehafod	d					13 11										13 41							
Porth	a					13 14										13 44							
	d					13 15										13 45							
Dinas Rhondda	d					13 19										13 49							
Tonypandy	d					13 21										13 51							
Llwynypia	d					13 23										13 53							
Ystrad Rhondda	a					13 26										13 56							
	d					13 29										13 59							
Ton Pentre	d					13 31										14 01							
Treorchy	d					13 34										14 04							
Ynyswen	d					13 37										14 07							
Treherbert	a					13 43										14 14							

Bridgend, Barry Island, Barry, Penarth and Cardiff - Coryton. Rhymney, Pontypridd, Merthyr, Aberdare and Treherbert

		AW	AW	AW	AW	AW	AW	AW	AW	AW	AW	AW	AW	AW	AW	AW	AW	AW	AW	AW	AW	AW	AW
Bridgend	d			12 42																	13 42		
Llantwit Major	d			12 56																	13 56		
Rhoose Cardiff Int Airport ✈	d			13 06																	14 06		
Barry Island	d						13 25						13 40			13 55							
Barry [3]	d			13 15			13 30						13 45			14 00					14 15		
Barry Docks	d			13 19			13 34						13 49			14 04					14 19		
Cadoxton	d			13 22			13 37						13 52			14 07					14 22		
Dinas Powys	d			13 26			13 41						13 56			14 11					14 26		
Eastbrook	d			13 28			13 43						13 58			14 13					14 28		
Cogan	d			13 30			13 45						14 00			14 15					14 30		
Penarth	d					13 32			13 47					14 02			14 17						14 32
Dingle Road	d					13 34			13 49					14 04			14 19						14 34
Grangetown	d			13 34		13 38	13 49		13 53				14 04	14 08		14 19	14 23				14 34		14 38
Cardiff Central [7]	a	13 34		13 39		13 44	13 54		13 59	14 04			14 09	14 14		14 24	14 29		14 34		14 39		14 44
	d	13 36	13 36	13 41		13 46	13 56		14 01	14 06	14 06		14 11	14 16		14 26	14 31		14 36	14 36	14 41		14 46
Cardiff Bay	d				13 42			13 54				14 06			14 18			14 30				14 42	
Cardiff Queen Street [3]	a		13 39	13 44	13 46	13 49	13 59	13 58	14 04		14 09	14 10	14 14	14 19	14 22	14 29	14 34	14 34		14 39	14 44	14 46	14 49
	d		13 40	13 45		13 50	14 00		14 05		14 10		14 15	14 20		14 30	14 35			14 40	14 45		14 50
Heath Low Level	d																						
Ty Glas	d																						
Birchgrove	d																						
Rhiwbina	d																						
Whitchurch (Cardiff)	d																						
Coryton	a																						
Heath High Level	d					13 55			14 10					14 25			14 40						14 55
Llanishen	d					13 58			14 13					14 28			14 43						14 58
Lisvane & Thornhill	d					14 00			14 15					14 30			14 45						15 00
Caerphilly [3]	d					14 06			14 21					14 36			14 51						15 06
Aber	d					14 08			14 23					14 38			14 53						15 08
Llanbradach	d					14 12			14 27					14 42			14 57						15 12
Ystrad Mynach [3]	d					14a22			14 32					14 47			15 07						15a22
Hengoed	d								14 35					14 50			15 10						
Pengam	d								14 38					14 53			15 13						
Gilfach Fargoed	d								14 41														
Bargoed	a								14 49					14 58			15 25						
	d													14 59									
Brithdir	d													15 03									
Tir-phil	d													15 06									
Pontlottyn	d													15 10									
Rhymney [3]	a													15 17									
Cathays	d		13 43	13 48			14 03				14 13		14 18			14 33				14 43	14 48		
Llandaf	d		13 47	13 52			14 07				14 17		14 22			14 37				14 47	14 52		
Ninian Park	d	13 40								14 10									14 40				
Waun-gron Park	d	13 44								14 14									14 44				
Fairwater	d	13 46								14 16									14 46				
Danescourt	d	13 49								14 19									14 49				
Radyr [3]	a	13 57	13 50	13 55			14 10			14 27	14 20		14 25			14 40			14 57	14 50	14 55		
	d		13 50	13 55			14 10				14 20		14 25			14 40				14 50	14 55		
Taffs Well [3]	d		13 54	13 59			14 14				14 24		14 29			14 44				14 54	14 59		
Trefforest Estate	d						14 18									14 48							
Trefforest	d		14 01	14 06			14 22				14 31		14 36			14 52				15 01	15 06		
Pontypridd [3]	a		14 04	14 09			14 25				14 34		14 39			14 55				15 04	15 09		
	d		14 06	14 11			14 27				14 36		14 41			14 57				15 06	15 11		
Abercynon	d			14 19			14 34						14 49			15 04					15 19		
Penrhiwceiber	d			14 25									14 55								15 25		
Mountain Ash	a			14 28									14 58								15 28		
	d			14 34									15 04								15 34		
Fernhill	d			14 37									15 07								15 37		
Cwmbach	d			14 41									15 11								15 41		
Aberdare [3]	a			14 49									15 19								15 49		
Quakers Yard	d						14 39									15 09							
Merthyr Vale	a						14 44									15 14							
	d						14 47									15 17							
Troed Y Rhiw	d						14 51									15 21							
Pentre-bach	d						14 54									15 24							
Merthyr Tydfil	a						15 03									15 33							
Trehafod	d		14 11								14 41									15 11			
Porth	a		14 14								14 44									15 14			
	d		14 15								14 45									15 15			
Dinas Rhondda	d		14 19								14 49									15 19			
Tonypandy	d		14 21								14 51									15 21			
Llwynypia	d		14 23								14 53									15 23			
Ystrad Rhondda	a		14 26								14 56									15 26			
	d		14 29								14 59									15 29			
Ton Pentre	d		14 31								15 01									15 31			
Treorchy	d		14 34								15 04									15 34			
Ynyswen	d		14 37								15 07									15 37			
Treherbert	a		14 44								15 14									15 44			

Bridgend, Barry Island, Barry, Penarth and Cardiff - Coryton. Rhymney, Pontypridd, Merthyr, Aberdare and Treherbert

Station		AW		AW	AW	AW	AW	AW	AW	AW	AW	AW		AW	AW	AW	AW	AW	AW	AW	AW	AW		AW	AW
Bridgend	d																		14 42						
Llantwit Major	d																		14 56						
Rhoose Cardiff Int Airport ✈	d																		15 06						
Barry Island	d			14 25						14 40				14 55								15 25			
Barry 3	d			14 30						14 45				15 00					15 15			15 30			
Barry Docks	d			14 34						14 49				15 04					15 19			15 34			
Cadoxton	d			14 37						14 52				15 07					15 22			15 37			
Dinas Powys	d			14 41						14 56				15 11					15 26			15 41			
Eastbrook	d			14 43						14 58				15 13					15 28			15 43			
Cogan	d			14 45						15 00				15 15					15 30			15 45			
Penarth	d						14 47				15 02				15 17						15 32				15 47
Dingle Road	d						14 49				15 04				15 19						15 34				15 49
Grangetown	d			14 49			14 53			15 04	15 08			15 19	15 23				15 34		15 38	15 49			15 53
Cardiff Central 7	a			14 54			14 59	15 04		15 09	15 14			15 24	15 29		15 34		15 39		15 44	15 54			15 59
	d	14 51		14 56			15 01	15 06		15 11	15 16			15 26	15 31		15 36	15 36	15 41		15 46	15 56			16 01
Cardiff Bay	d					14 54			15 06			15 18				15 30				15 42				15 54	
Cardiff Queen Street 3	a			14 59		14 58	15 04		15 10	15 14	15 19	15 22		15 29	15 34	15 34		15 39	15 44	15 46	15 49	15 59		15 58	16 04
	d			15 00			15 05			15 15	15 20			15 30	15 35			15 40	15 45		15 50	16 00			16 05
Heath Low Level	d																								
Ty Glas	d																								
Birchgrove	d																								
Rhiwbina	d																								
Whitchurch (Cardiff)	d																								
Coryton	a																								
Heath High Level	d						15 10				15 25				15 40						15 55				16 10
Llanishen	d						15 13				15 28				15 43						15 58				16 13
Lisvane & Thornhill	d						15 15				15 30				15 45						16 00				16 15
Caerphilly 3	d						15 21				15 36				15 51						16 06				16 21
Aber	d						15 23				15 38				15 53						16 08				16 23
Llanbradach	d						15 27				15 42				15 57						16 12				16 27
Ystrad Mynach 3	d						15 32				15 47				16 02						16 17				16 32
Hengoed	d						15 35				15 50				16 05						16 20				16 35
Pengam	d						15 38				15 53				16 08						16 23				16 38
Gilfach Fargoed	d						15 41																		16 41
Bargoed	a						15 49				15 58				16 17						16 32				16 49
	d										15 59														
Brithdir	d										16 03														
Tir-phil	d										16 06														
Pontlottyn	d										16 10														
Rhymney 3	a										16 17														
Cathays	d			15 03						15 18				15 33				15 43	15 48			16 03			
Llandaf	d			15 07						15 22				15 37				15 47	15 52			16 07			
Ninian Park	d							15 10									15 40								
Waun-gron Park	d							15 14									15 44								
Fairwater	d							15 16									15 46								
Danescourt	d							15 19									15 49								
Radyr 3	a	15 08		15 10				15 27		15 25				15 40			15 57	15 50	15 55			16 10			
	d	15 20		15 10						15 25				15 40				15 50	15 55			16 10			
Taffs Well 3	d	15 24		15 14						15 29				15 44				15 54	15 59			16 14			
Trefforest Estate	d			15 18										15 48								16 18			
Trefforest	d	15 31		15 22	←					15 36				15 52				16 01	16 06			16 22			
Pontypridd 3	a	15 34		15 25	15 34					15 39				15 55				16 04	16 09			16 25			
	d	15 36		15 27	15 36					15 41				15 57				16 06	16 11			16 27			
Abercynon	d	→		15 34						15 49				16 04					16 19			16 34			
Penrhiwceiber	d									15 55									16 25						
Mountain Ash	a									15 58									16 28						
	d									16 04									16 34						
Fernhill	d									16 07									16 37						
Cwmbach	d									16 11									16 41						
Aberdare 3	a									16 19									16 49						
Quakers Yard	d			15 39										16 09								16 39			
Merthyr Vale	a			15 44										16 14								16 44			
	d			15 47										16 17								16 47			
Troed Y Rhiw	d			15 51										16 21								16 51			
Pentre-bach	d			15 54										16 24								16 54			
Merthyr Tydfil	a			16 03										16 33								17 03			
Trehafod	d				15 41													16 11							
Porth	a				15 44													16 14							
	d				15 45													16 15							
Dinas Rhondda	d				15 49													16 19							
Tonypandy	d				15 51													16 21							
Llwynypia	d				15 53													16 23							
Ystrad Rhondda	a				15 56													16 26							
	d				15 59													16 29							
Ton Pentre	d				16 01													16 31							
Treorchy	d				16 04													16 34							
Ynyswen	d				16 07													16 37							
Treherbert	a				16 14													16 44							

Bridgend, Barry Island, Barry, Penarth and Cardiff - Coryton. Rhymney, Pontypridd, Merthyr, Aberdare and Treherbert

Station		AW	AW	AW	AW	AW	AW	AW		AW	AW	AW	AW	AW	AW	AW	AW	AW		AW	AW	AW	AW	AW	AW
Bridgend	d													15 42											
Llantwit Major	d													15 56											
Rhoose Cardiff Int Airport ✈	d													16 06											
Barry Island	d				15 40			15 55									16 25							16 40	
Barry 3	d				15 45			16 00						16 15			16 30							16 45	
Barry Docks	d				15 49			16 04						16 19			16 34							16 49	
Cadoxton	d				15 52			16 07						16 22			16 37							16 52	
Dinas Powys	d				15 56			16 11						16 26			16 41							16 56	
Eastbrook	d				15 58			16 13						16 28			16 43							16 58	
Cogan	d				16 00			16 15						16 30			16 45							17 00	
Penarth	d					16 02				16 17						16 32									17 02
Dingle Road	d					16 04				16 19						16 34									17 04
Grangetown	d				16 04	16 08		16 19		16 23				16 34		16 38	16 49							17 04	17 08
Cardiff Central 7	a	16 05			16 09	16 14		16 24		16 29		16 34		16 39		16 44	16 54				17 04			17 09	17 14
	d	16 06	16 06		16 11	16 16		16 26		16 31		16 36	16 36	16 41		16 46	16 56			17 01	17 06	17 06		17 11	17 16
Cardiff Bay	d			16 06			16 18				16 30				16 42			16 54					17 06		
Cardiff Queen Street 3	a		16 09	16 10	16 14	16 19	16 22	16 29		16 34	16 34		16 39	16 44	16 46	16 49	16 59	16 58		17 04		17 09	17 10	17 14	17 19
	d		16 10		16 15	16 20		16 30		16 35			16 40	16 45		16 50	17 00			17 05		17 10		17 15	17 20
Heath Low Level	d																								
Ty Glas	d																								
Birchgrove	d																								
Rhiwbina	d																								
Whitchurch (Cardiff)	d																								
Coryton	a																								
Heath High Level	d					16 25				16 40						16 55				17 10					17 25
Llanishen	d					16 28				16 43						16 58				17 13					17 28
Lisvane & Thornhill	d					16 30				16 45						17 00				17 15					17 30
Caerphilly 3	d					16 36				16 51						17 06				17 21					17 36
Aber	d					16 38				16 53						17 08				17 23					17 38
Llanbradach	d					16 42				16 57						17 12				17 27					17 42
Ystrad Mynach 3	d					16 47				17 02						17 17				17 33					17 47
Hengoed	d					16 50				17 05						17 20				17 35					17 50
Pengam	d					16 53				17 08						17 23				17 39					17 53
Gilfach Fargoed	d																			17 42					
Bargoed	a					16 58				17 17						17 32				17 45					18 02
	d					16 59														17 47					
Brithdir	d					17 03														17 50					
Tir-phil	d					17 06														17 53					
Pontlottyn	d					17 10														17 58					
Rhymney 3	a					17 17														18 05					
Cathays	d		16 13		16 18			16 33					16 43	16 48			17 03					17 13		17 18	
Llandaf	d		16 17		16 22			16 37					16 47	16 52			17 07					17 17		17 22	
Ninian Park	d	16 10										16 40									17 10				
Waun-gron Park	d	16 14										16 44									17 14				
Fairwater	d	16 16										16 46									17 16				
Danescourt	d	16 19										16 49									17 19				
Radyr 3	a	16 27	16 20		16 25			16 40				16 57	16 50	16 55			17 10				17 27	17 20		17 25	
	d		16 20		16 25			16 40					16 50	16 55			17 10					17 20		17 25	
Taffs Well 3	d		16 24		16 29			16 44					16 54	16 59			17 14					17 24		17 29	
Trefforest Estate	d							16 48									17 18								
Trefforest	d		16 31		16 36			16 52					17 01	17 06			17 22					17 31		17 36	
Pontypridd 3	a		16 34		16 39			16 55					17 04	17 09			17 25					17 34		17 39	
	d		16 36		16 41			16 57					17 06	17 11			17 27					17 36		17 41	
Abercynon	d				16 49			17 04						17 19			17 34							17 49	
Penrhiwceiber	d				16 55									17 25										17 55	
Mountain Ash	a				16 58									17 28										17 58	
	d				17 04									17 34										18 04	
Fernhill	d				17 07									17 37										18 07	
Cwmbach	d				17 11									17 41										18 11	
Aberdare 3	a				17 19									17 49										18 19	
Quakers Yard	d							17 09									17 39								
Merthyr Vale	a							17 14									17 44								
	d							17 17									17 47								
Troed Y Rhiw	d							17 21									17 51								
Pentre-bach	d							17 24									17 54								
Merthyr Tydfil	a							17 33									18 03								
Trehafod	d		16 41										17 11									17 41			
Porth	a		16 44										17 14									17 44			
	d		16 45										17 15									17 45			
Dinas Rhondda	d		16 49										17 19									17 49			
Tonypandy	d		16 51										17 21									17 51			
Llwynypia	d		16 53										17 23									17 53			
Ystrad Rhondda	a		16 56										17 26									17 56			
	d		16 59										17 29									17 59			
Ton Pentre	d		17 01										17 31									18 01			
Treorchy	d		17 04										17 34									18 04			
Ynyswen	d		17 07										17 37									18 07			
Treherbert	a		17 14										17 44									18 14			

Table 130

Mondays to Fridays
from 06 September

Bridgend, Barry Island, Barry, Penarth and Cardiff - Coryton. Rhymney, Pontypridd, Merthyr, Aberdare and Treherbert

		AW	AW	AW	AW	AW	AW	AW	AW	AW	AW	AW	AW	AW	AW	AW	AW	AW	AW	AW	AW	AW
Bridgend	d							16 42														
Llantwit Major	d							16 56														
Rhoose Cardiff Int Airport ✈	d							17 06														
Barry Island	d		16 55									17 25					17 40			17 55		
Barry ■	d		17 00					17 15				17 30					17 45			18 00		
Barry Docks	d		17 04					17 19				17 34					17 49			18 04		
Cadoxton	d		17 07					17 22				17 37					17 52			18 07		
Dinas Powys	d		17 11					17 26				17 41					17 56			18 11		
Eastbrook	d		17 13					17 28				17 43					17 58			18 13		
Cogan	d		17 15					17 30				17 45					18 00			18 15		
Penarth	d			17 17						17 32			17 47					18 02			18 17	
Dingle Road	d			17 19						17 34			17 49					18 04			18 19	
Grangetown	d		17 19	17 23				17 34		17 38		17 49	17 53				18 04	18 08		18 19	18 23	
Cardiff Central ■	a		17 24	17 29		17 34		17 39		17 44		17 54	17 59	18 04			18 09	18 14		18 24	18 29	
	d		17 26	17 31		17 36	17 36	17 41		17 46		17 56	18 01	18 06	18 06		18 11	18 16		18 26	18 31	
Cardiff Bay	d	17 18			17 30				17 42		17 54					18 06			18 18			18 30
Cardiff Queen Street ■	a	17 22	17 29	17 34	17 34		17 39	17 44	17 46	17 49	17 58	17 59	18 04		18 09	18 10	18 14	18 19	18 22	18 29	18 34	18 34
	d		17 30	17 35			17 40	17 45		17 50		18 00	18 05		18 10		18 15	18 20		18 30	18 35	
Heath Low Level	d																					
Ty Glas	d																					
Birchgrove	d																					
Rhiwbina	d																					
Whitchurch (Cardiff)	d																					
Coryton	a																					
Heath High Level	d			17 40						17 55			18 10					18 25			18 40	
Llanishen	d			17 43						17 59			18 13					18 28			18 43	
Lisvane & Thornhill	d			17 45						18 02			18 15					18 30			18 45	
Caerphilly ■	d			17 51						18 07			18 21					18 36			18 51	
Aber	d			17 53						18 10			18 23					18 38			18 53	
Llanbradach	d			17 57						18 14			18 27					18 42			18 57	
Ystrad Mynach ■	d			18 02						18 20			18 32					18a52			19 02	
Hengoed	d			18 05						18 23			18 35								19 05	
Pengam	d			18 08						18 27			18 38								19 08	
Gilfach Fargoed	d			18 11						18 30			18 41								19 11	
Bargoed	a			18 14						18 34			18 49								19 14	
	d			18 16						18 44											19 16	
Brithdir	d			18 20						18 48											19 20	
Tir-phil	d			18 23						18 51											19 23	
Pontlottyn	d			18 27						18 55											19 27	
Rhymney ■	a			18 34						19 02											19 34	
Cathays	d		17 33				17 43	17 48				18 03			18 13		18 18			18 33		
Llandaf	d		17 37				17 47	17 52				18 07			18 17		18 22			18 37		
Ninian Park	d					17 40								18 10								
Waun-gron Park	d					17 44								18 14								
Fairwater	d					17 46								18 16								
Danescourt	d					17 49								18 19								
Radyr ■	a		17 40			17 57	17 50	17 55				18 10		18 27	18 20		18 25			18 40		
	d		17 40				17 50	17 55				18 10			18 20		18 25			18 40		
Taffs Well ■	d		17 44				17 54	17 59				18 14			18 24		18 29			18 44		
Trefforest Estate	d		17 48									18 18								18 48		
Trefforest	d		17 52				18 01	18 06				18 22			18 31		18 36			18 52		
Pontypridd ■	a		17 55				18 04	18 09				18 25			18 34		18 42			18 55		
	d		17 57				18 06	18 11				18 27			18 36					18 57		
Abercynon	d		18 04					18 19				18 34								19 04		
Penrhiwceiber	d							18 25														
Mountain Ash	a							18 28														
	d							18 34														
Fernhill	d							18 37														
Cwmbach	d							18 41														
Aberdare ■	a							18 49														
Quakers Yard	d		18 09									18 39								19 09		
Merthyr Vale	a		18 14									18 44								19 14		
	d		18 17									18 47								19 17		
Troed Y Rhiw	d		18 21									18 51								19 21		
Pentre-bach	d		18 24									18 54								19 24		
Merthyr Tydfil	a		18 33									19 02								19 33		
Trehafod	d						18 11								18 41							
Porth	a						18 14								18 44							
	d						18 15								18 45							
Dinas Rhondda	d						18 19								18 49							
Tonypandy	d						18 21								18 51							
Llwynypia	d						18 23								18 53							
Ystrad Rhondda	a						18 26								18 56							
	d						18 29								18 59							
Ton Pentre	d						18 31								19 01							
Treorchy	d						18 34								19 04							
Ynyswen	d						18 37								19 07							
Treherbert	a						18 44								19 14							

Table 130

Mondays to Fridays
from 06 September

Bridgend, Barry Island, Barry, Penarth and Cardiff - Coryton. Rhymney, Pontypridd, Merthyr, Aberdare and Treherbert

		AW	AW	AW	AW	AW	AW	AW	AW	AW	AW	AW	AW	AW	AW	AW	AW	AW	AW	AW	AW	AW	AW
Bridgend	d			17 42														18 42					
Llantwit Major	d			17 56														18 56					
Rhoose Cardiff Int Airport ✈	d			18 06														19 06					
Barry Island	d					18 25						18 40		18 55								19 25	
Barry ■	d			18 15		18 30						18 45		19 00				19 15				19 30	
Barry Docks	d			18 19		18 34						18 49		19 04				19 19				19 34	
Cadoxton	d			18 22		18 37						18 52		19 07				19 22				19 37	
Dinas Powys	d			18 26		18 41						18 56		19 11				19 26				19 41	
Eastbrook	d			18 28		18 43						18 58		19 13				19 28				19 43	
Cogan	d			18 30		18 45						19 00		19 15				19 30				19 45	
Penarth	d				18 32				18 47						19 17								19 47
Dingle Road	d				18 34				18 49						19 19								19 49
Grangetown	d			18 34	18 38	18 49			18 53			19 04		19 19	19 23			19 34				19 49	19 54
Cardiff Central ■	a		18 34	18 39	18 47	18 55			18 59			19 09		19 24	19 29		19 34	19 39				19 56	19 59
	d	18 36	18 36	18 41					19 01	19 06		19 11		19 26	19 31		19 36	19 41		19 51		20 01	20 06
Cardiff Bay	d						18 42	18 54			19 06		19 18			19 30			19 42		19 54		
Cardiff Queen Street ■	a	18 38		18 44			18 46	18 58	19 04	19 09	19 10	19 14	19 22	19 29	19 34	19 34		19 44	19 46	19 54	19 58	20 04	20 09
	d	18 40		18 50					19 05	19 10		19 15		19 30	19 35			19 45		19 55		20 05	20 10
Heath Low Level	d																			20 00			
Ty Glas	d																			20 03			
Birchgrove	d																			20 04			
Rhiwbina	d																			20 06			
Whitchurch (Cardiff)	d																			20 08			
Coryton	a																			20 14			
Heath High Level	d								19 10						19 40							20 10	
Llanishen	d								19 13						19 43							20 13	
Lisvane & Thornhill	d								19 15						19 45							20 15	
Caerphilly ■	d								19a24						19 51							20a28	
Aber	d														19 53								
Llanbradach	d														19 57								
Ystrad Mynach ■	d														20 02								
Hengoed	d														20 05								
Pengam	d														20 08								
Gilfach Fargoed	d														20 11								
Bargoed	a														20 15								
	d														20 16								
Brithdir	d														20 20								
Tir-phil	d														20 23								
Pontlottyn	d														20 27								
Rhymney ■	a														20 34								
Cathays	d	18 43		18 52						19 13		19 18		19 33				19 48					20 13
Llandaf	d	18 47		18 56						19 17		19 22		19 37				19 52					20 17
Ninian Park	d		18 40														19 40						
Waun-gron Park	d		18 44														19 44						
Fairwater	d		18 46														19 46						
Danescourt	d		18 49														19 49						
Radyr ■	a	18 50	18 57	18 58						19 20		19 25		19 40			19 57	19 55					20 20
	d	18 50		18 58						19 20		19 25		19 40				19 55					20 20
Taffs Well ■	d	18 54		19 03						19 24		19 29		19 44				19 59					20 24
Trefforest Estate	d													19 48									
Trefforest	d	19 01		19 10						19 31		19 36		19 52				20 06					20 31
Pontypridd ■	a	19 04		19 13						19 34		19 39		19 55				20 09					20 35
	d	19 06		19 14						19 36		19 41		19 57				20 11					20 36
Abercynon	d			19 21								19 49		20 04				20 21					
Penrhiwceiber	d			19 27								19 55						20 27					
Mountain Ash	a			19 30								19 58						20 31					
	d			19 34								20 04						20 34					
Fernhill	d			19 37								20 07						20 37					
Cwmbach	d			19 41								20 11						20 41					
Aberdare ■	a			19 49								20 19						20 49					
Quakers Yard	d													20 09									
Merthyr Vale	a													20 14									
	d													20 14									
Troed Y Rhiw	d													20 18									
Pentre-bach	d													20 22									
Merthyr Tydfil	a													20 31									
Trehafod	d	19 11								19 41													20 41
Porth	a	19 14								19 44													20 44
	d	19 15								19 45													20 45
Dinas Rhondda	d	19 19								19 49													20 49
Tonypandy	d	19 21								19 51													20 51
Llwynypia	d	19 23								19 53													20 53
Ystrad Rhondda	a	19 26								19 56													20 56
	d	19 29								19 59													20 59
Ton Pentre	d	19 31								20 01													21 01
Treorchy	d	19 34								20 04													21 04
Ynyswen	d	19 37								20 07													21 07
Treherbert	a	19 44								20 14													21 14

Table 130

Mondays to Fridays
from 06 September

Bridgend, Barry Island, Barry, Penarth and Cardiff - Coryton. Rhymney, Pontypridd, Merthyr, Aberdare and Treherbert

		AW	AW	AW	AW	AW		AW	AW	AW	AW	AW	AW	AW	AW	AW		AW	AW	AW	AW	AW	AW	AW	AW
Bridgend	d							19 42														20 42		
Llantwit Major	d							19 56														20 56		
Rhoose Cardiff Int Airport ✈	d							20 06														21 06		
Barry Island	d			19 55														20 55							
Barry [3]	d			20 00					20 15									21 00					21 15		
Barry Docks	d			20 04					20 19									21 04					21 19		
Cadoxton	d			20 07					20 22									21 07					21 22		
Dinas Powys	d			20 11					20 26									21 11					21 26		
Eastbrook	d			20 13					20 28									21 13					21 28		
Cogan	d			20 15					20 30									21 15					21 30		
Penarth	d					20 19							20 47									21 20			
Dingle Road	d					20 21							20 49									21 22			
Grangetown	d			20 19		20 24			20 34				20 53					21 19				21 26	21 34		
Cardiff Central [7]	a			20 26		20 31		20 34	20 39				20 59					21 24			21 34	21 37	21 39		
	d			20 26		20 32		20 36	20 41		20 51		21 01	21 06				21 26		21 31	21 36		21 41		
Cardiff Bay	d	20 06	20 18		20 30					20 42		20 54			21 06	21 18			21 30					21 42	21 54
Cardiff Queen Street [3]	a	20 10	20 22	20 29	20 34	20 35			20 44	20 46	20 54	20 58	21 04	21 09	21 10	21 22		21 29	21 34	21 34			21 44	21 46	21 58
	d			20 30		20 36			20 45		20 55		21 05	21 10				21 30		21 35			21 45		
Heath Low Level	d										21 00														
Ty Glas	d										21 03														
Birchgrove	d										21 04														
Rhiwbina	d										21 06														
Whitchurch (Cardiff)	d										21 08														
Coryton	a										21 14														
Heath High Level	d					20 41							21 10							21 40					
Llanishen	d					20 44							21 13							21 43					
Lisvane & Thornhill	d					20 46							21 15							21 45					
Caerphilly [3]	d					20 52							21a34							21 51					
Aber	d					20 54														21 53					
Llanbradach	d					20 58														21 57					
Ystrad Mynach [3]	d					21 03														22 02					
Hengoed	d					21 06														22 05					
Pengam	d					21 09														22 08					
Gilfach Fargoed	d					21 12														22 11					
Bargoed	a					21 16														22 15					
	d					21 17														22 16					
Brithdir	d					21 21														22 20					
Tir-phil	d					21 24														22 23					
Pontlottyn	d					21 28														22 27					
Rhymney [3]	a					21 35														22 34					
Cathays	d			20 33					20 48					21 13				21 33					21 48		
Llandaf	d			20 37					20 52					21 17				21 37					21 52		
Ninian Park	d							20 40													21 40				
Waun-gron Park	d							20 44													21 44				
Fairwater	d							20 46													21 46				
Danescourt	d							20 49													21 49				
Radyr [3]	a			20 40				20 57	20 55					21 20				21 40			21 57		21 55		
	d			20 40					20 55					21 20				21 40					21 55		
Taffs Well [3]	d			20 44					20 59					21 24				21 44					21 59		
Trefforest Estate	d			20 48														21 48							
Trefforest	d			20 52					21 06					21 31				21 52					22 06		
Pontypridd [3]	a			20 56					21 09					21 34				21 55					22 09		
	d			20 57					21 11					21 36				21 57					22 11		
Abercynon	d			21 04					21 19									22 04					22 19		
Penrhiwceiber	d							21 25														22 25		
Mountain Ash	a							21 28														22 28		
	d							21 29														22 29		
Fernhill	d							21 32														22 32		
Cwmbach	d							21 36														22 36		
Aberdare [3]	a							21 44														22 44		
Quakers Yard	d			21 09														22 09							
Merthyr Vale	a			21 14														22 14							
	d			21 14														22 14							
Troed Y Rhiw	d			21 18														22 18							
Pentre-bach	d			21 22														22 22							
Merthyr Tydfil	a			21 31														22 31							
Trehafod	d												21 41											
Porth	a												21 44											
	d												21 45											
Dinas Rhondda	d												21 49											
Tonypandy	d												21 51											
Llwynypia	d												21 53											
Ystrad Rhondda	a												21 56											
	d												21 59											
Ton Pentre	d												22 01											
Treorchy	d												22 04											
Ynyswen	d												22 07											
Treherbert	a												22 13											

Table 130

Mondays to Fridays
from 06 September

Bridgend, Barry Island, Barry, Penarth and Cardiff - Coryton. Rhymney, Pontypridd, Merthyr, Aberdare and Treherbert

		AW		AW	AW	AW	AW	AW	AW	AW	AW	AW		AW	AW	AW	AW	AW	AW	AW	AW	AW		AW	
Bridgend	d								21 42										22 42					
Llantwit Major	d								21 56										22 56					
Rhoose Cardiff Int Airport ✈	d								22 06										23 06					
Barry Island	d					21 55											22 44							
Barry [3]	d					22 00			22 15								22 48		23 15					
Barry Docks	d					22 04			22 19								22 52		23 19					
Cadoxton	d					22 07			22 22								22 55		23 22					
Dinas Powys	d					22 11			22 26								22 59		23 26					
Eastbrook	d					22 13			22 28								23 01		23 28					
Cogan	d					22 15			22 30								23 03		23 30					
Penarth	d	21 47							22 19							22 47			23 26						
Dingle Road	d	21 49							22 21							22 49			23 28						
Grangetown	d	21 53					22 19		22 25	22 34						22 53		23 07	23 32	23 34					
Cardiff Central [7]	a	21 59					22 24		22 33	22 39						23 00		23 12	23 40	23 42					
	d	22 01		22 06			22 26		22 35	22 41		22 46				23 15		23 26							
Cardiff Bay	d				22 06	22 18		22 30			22 42			22 54	23 06		23 18				23 30	23 42		23 54	
Cardiff Queen Street [3]	a	22 04		22 09	22 10	22 22	22 29	22 34	22 38	22 44	22 46	22 49		22 58	23 10	23 18	23 22	23 29			23 34	23 46		23 58	
	d	22 05		22 10			22 30		22 39	22 45		22 50				23 19		23 30							
Heath Low Level	d																							
Ty Glas	d																							
Birchgrove	d																							
Rhiwbina	d																							
Whitchurch (Cardiff)	d																							
Coryton	a																							
Heath High Level	d	22 10							22 44							23 24									
Llanishen	d	22 13							22 47							23 27									
Lisvane & Thornhill	d	22 15							22 49							23 29									
Caerphilly [3]	d	22a24							22 55							23 35									
Aber	d								22 57							23 37									
Llanbradach	d								23 01							23 41									
Ystrad Mynach [3]	d								23 06							23a51									
Hengoed	d								23 09																
Pengam	d								23 12																
Gilfach Fargoed	d								23 15																
Bargoed	a								23 19																
	d								23 20																
Brithdir	d								23 24																
Tir-phil	d								23 27																
Pontlottyn	d								23 31																
Rhymney [3]	a								23 38																
Cathays	d			22 13			22 33			22 48		22 53						23 33							
Llandaf	d			22 17			22 37			22 52		22 57						23 37							
Ninian Park	d																							
Waun-gron Park	d																							
Fairwater	d																							
Danescourt	d																							
Radyr [3]	a			22 20			22 40			22 55		22 59						23 40							
	d			22 20			22 40			22 55		22 59						23 40							
Taffs Well [3]	d			22 24			22 44			22 59		23 03						23 44							
Trefforest Estate	d						22 48											23 48							
Trefforest	d			22 31			22 52			23 06		23 10						23 52							
Pontypridd [3]	a			22 34			22 55			23 09		23 14						00 01							
	d			22 36			22 57			23 11		23 15													
Abercynon	d						23 04			23 19															
Penrhiwceiber	d									23 25															
Mountain Ash	a									23 28															
	d									23 34															
Fernhill	d									23 37															
Cwmbach	d									23 41															
Aberdare [3]	a									23 49															
Quakers Yard	d						23 09																			
Merthyr Vale	a						23 14																			
	d						23 14																			
Troed Y Rhiw	d						23 18																			
Pentre-bach	d						23 22																			
Merthyr Tydfil	a						23 31																			
Trehafod	d			22 41								23 20													
Porth	a			22 44								23 23													
	d			22 45								23 24													
Dinas Rhondda	d			22 49								23 28													
Tonypandy	d			22 51								23 30													
Llwynypia	d			22 53								23 32													
Ystrad Rhondda	a			22 56								23 35													
	d			22 59								23 38													
Ton Pentre	d			23 01								23 40													
Treorchy	d			23 04								23 43													
Ynyswen	d			23 07								23 46													
Treherbert	a			23 13								23 53													

Table 130

Saturdays
until 04 September

Bridgend, Barry Island, Barry, Penarth and Cardiff - Coryton. Rhymney, Pontypridd, Merthyr, Aberdare and Treherbert

Station		AW	AW	AW	AW	AW	AW	AW	AW	AW	AW	AW	AW	AW	AW	AW	AW	AW	AW	AW	AW	AW	AW
Bridgend	d										05 42												
Llantwit Major	d										05 56												
Rhoose Cardiff Int Airport ✈	d										06 06												
Barry Island	d								05 52						06 25								06 55
Barry [3]	d								05 57		06 15				06 30								07 00
Barry Docks	d								06 01		06 19				06 34								07 04
Cadoxton	d								06 04		06 22				06 37								07 07
Dinas Powys	d								06 08		06 26				06 41								07 11
Eastbrook	d								06 10		06 28				06 43								07 13
Cogan	d								06 12		06 30				06 45								07 15
Penarth	d						06 02						06 32								07 02		
Dingle Road	d						06 04						06 34								07 04		
Grangetown	d						06 08		06 16		06 34		06 38		06 49						07 08		07 19
Cardiff Central [7]	a						06 13		06 21		06 39		06 44		06 54			07 04			07 14		07 24
	d	05 26	05 46		05 56	06 11	06 15	06 19	06 26	06 36	06 41		06 46	06 51	06 56		07 06	07 06		07 11	07 16		07 26
Cardiff Bay	d											06 42				06 54			07 06			07 18	
Cardiff Queen Street [3]	a	05 29	05 49		05 59	06 14	06 19	06 24	06 29	06 39	06 44	06 46	06 49	06 54	06 59	06 58	07 09		07 10	07 14	07 19	07 22	07 29
	d	05 30	05 50		06 00	06 15	06 20	06 25	06 30	06 40	06 45		06 50	06 55	07 00		07 10			07 15	07 20		07 30
Heath Low Level	d							06 30						07 00									
Ty Glas	d							06 33						07 03									
Birchgrove	d							06 34						07 04									
Rhiwbina	d							06 36						07 06									
Whitchurch (Cardiff)	d							06 38						07 08									
Coryton	a							06 43						07 13									
Heath High Level	d		05 54				06 25						06 55								07 25		
Llanishen	d		05 57				06 28						06 58								07 28		
Lisvane & Thornhill	d		06 00				06 30						07 00								07 30		
Caerphilly [3]	d		06a09				06 36						07 06								07 36		
Aber	d						06 38						07 08								07 38		
Llanbradach	d						06 42						07 12								07 42		
Ystrad Mynach [3]	d						06 47						07 17								07 47		
Hengoed	d						06 50						07 20								07 50		
Pengam	d						06 53						07 23								07 53		
Gilfach Fargoed	d																						
Bargoed	a						07 01						07 31								08 01		
	d																						
Brithdir	d																						
Tir-phil	d																						
Pontlottyn	d																						
Rhymney [3]	a																						
Cathays	d	05 33			06 03	06 18			06 33	06 43	06 48				07 03		07 13			07 18			07 33
Llandaf	d	05 37			06 07	06 22			06 37	06 47	06 52				07 07		07 17			07 22			07 37
Ninian Park	d																	07 10					
Waun-gron Park	d																	07 13					
Fairwater	d																	07 15					
Danescourt	d																	07 17					
Radyr [3]	a	05 39			06 10	06 24			06 40	06 50	06 54				07 10		07 20	07 24		07 25			07 40
	d	05 40			06 10	06 24			06 40	06 50	06 55				07 10		07 20			07 25			07 40
Taffs Well [3]	d	05 43			06 14	06 28			06 44	06 54	06 59				07 14		07 24			07 29			07 44
Trefforest Estate	d	05 47			06 18				06 48						07 18								07 48
Trefforest	d	05 52			06 22	06 35			06 52	07 01	07 06				07 22		07 31			07 36			07 52
Pontypridd [3]	a	05 55			06 25	06 38			06 55	07 04	07 09				07 25		07 34			07 39			07 55
	d	05 57		06 11	06 27	06 41			06 57	07 06	07 11				07 27		07 36			07 41			07 57
Abercynon	d	06 04		06 19	06 34	06 49			07 04		07 19				07 34					07 49			08 04
Penrhiwceiber	d			06 24		06 54					07 24									07 54			
Mountain Ash	a			06 28		06 58					07 28									07 58			
	d			06 33		07 03					07 33									08 03			
Fernhill	d			06 35		07 05					07 35									08 05			
Cwmbach	d			06 39		07 09					07 39									08 09			
Aberdare [3]	a			06 46		07 16					07 46									08 16			
Quakers Yard	d	06 09			06 39				07 09						07 39								08 09
Merthyr Vale	a	06 14			06 44				07 14						07 44								08 14
	d	06 17			06 47				07 17						07 47								08 17
Troed Y Rhiw	d	06 20			06 50				07 20						07 50								08 20
Pentre-bach	d	06 23			06 53				07 23						07 53								08 23
Merthyr Tydfil	a	06 31			07 01				07 31						08 01								08 31
Trehafod	d									07 11							07 41						
Porth	a									07 14							07 44						
	d									07 15							07 45						
Dinas Rhondda	d									07 19							07 49						
Tonypandy	d									07 21							07 51						
Llwynypia	d									07 23							07 53						
Ystrad Rhondda	a									07 26							07 56						
	d									07 29							07 59						
Ton Pentre	d									07 31							08 01						
Treorchy	d									07 34							08 04						
Ynyswen	d									07 37							08 07						
Treherbert	a									07 43							08 13						

Table 130

Saturdays
until 04 September

Bridgend, Barry Island, Barry, Penarth and Cardiff - Coryton. Rhymney, Pontypridd, Merthyr, Aberdare and Treherbert

Station		AW	AW	AW	AW	AW	AW	AW	AW	AW	AW	AW	AW	AW	AW	AW	AW	AW	AW	AW	AW	AW	AW
Bridgend	d					06 42																	07 42
Llantwit Major	d					06 56																	07 56
Rhoose Cardiff Int Airport ✈	d					07 06																	08 06
Barry Island	d									07 25					07 40			07 55					
Barry [3]	d					07 15				07 30					07 45			08 00					08 15
Barry Docks	d					07 19				07 34					07 49			08 04					08 19
Cadoxton	d					07 22				07 37					07 52			08 07					08 22
Dinas Powys	d					07 26				07 41					07 56			08 11					08 26
Eastbrook	d					07 28				07 43					07 58			08 13					08 28
Cogan	d					07 30				07 45					08 00			08 15					08 30
Penarth	d	07 17						07 32			07 47					08 02			08 17				
Dingle Road	d	07 19						07 34			07 49					08 04			08 19				
Grangetown	d	07 23				07 34		07 38		07 49	07 53				08 04	08 08		08 19	08 23				08 34
Cardiff Central [7]	a	07 29			07 34	07 39		07 44		07 55	07 59		08 04		08 09	08 14		08 24	08 29			08 34	08 39
	d	07 31		07 36	07 36	07 41		07 46		07 56	08 01	08 06	08 06		08 11	08 16		08 26	08 31		08 36	08 36	08 41
Cardiff Bay	d		07 30				07 42		07 54					08 06			08 18			08 30			
Cardiff Queen Street [3]	a	07 34	07 34	07 39		07 44	07 46	07 49	07 58	07 59	08 04	08 09		08 10	08 14	08 19	08 22	08 29	08 34	08 34	08 39		08 44
	d	07 35		07 40		07 45		07 50		08 00	08 05	08 10			08 15	08 20		08 30	08 35		08 40		08 45
Heath Low Level	d																						
Ty Glas	d																						
Birchgrove	d																						
Rhiwbina	d																						
Whitchurch (Cardiff)	d																						
Coryton	a																						
Heath High Level	d	07 40						07 55			08 10					08 25			08 40				
Llanishen	d	07 43						07 58			08 13					08 28			08 43				
Lisvane & Thornhill	d	07 45						08 00			08 15					08 30			08 45				
Caerphilly [3]	d	07 51						08 06			08 21					08 36			08 51				
Aber	d	07 53						08 08			08 23					08 38			08 53				
Llanbradach	d	07 57						08 12			08 27					08 42			08 57				
Ystrad Mynach [3]	d	08 02						08 17			08 32					08 47			09 02				
Hengoed	d	08 05						08 20			08 35					08 50			09 05				
Pengam	d	08 08						08 23			08 38					08 53			09 08				
Gilfach Fargoed	d										08 41												
Bargoed	a	08 13						08 31			08 48					08 58			09 16				
	d	08 14														08 59							
Brithdir	d	08 18														09 03							
Tir-phil	d	08 21														09 06							
Pontlottyn	d	08 25														09 10							
Rhymney [3]	a	08 28														09 16							
Cathays	d			07 43		07 48				08 03		08 13			08 18			08 33			08 43		08 48
Llandaf	d			07 47		07 52				08 07		08 17			08 22			08 37			08 47		08 52
Ninian Park	d				07 40								08 10									08 40	
Waun-gron Park	d				07 43								08 13									08 43	
Fairwater	d				07 45								08 15									08 45	
Danescourt	d				07 47								08 17									08 47	
Radyr [3]	a			07 50	07 54	07 55				08 10		08 20	08 24		08 25			08 40			08 50	08 54	08 55
	d			07 50		07 55				08 10		08 20			08 25			08 40			08 50		08 55
Taffs Well [3]	d			07 54		07 59				08 14		08 24			08 29			08 44			08 54		08 59
Trefforest Estate	d									08 18								08 48					
Trefforest	d			08 01		08 06				08 22		08 31			08 36			08 52			09 01		09 06
Pontypridd [3]	a			08 04		08 09				08 25		08 34			08 39			08 55			09 04		09 09
	d			08 06		08 11				08 27		08 36			08 41			08 57			09 06		09 11
Abercynon	d					08 19				08 34					08 49			09 04					09 19
Penrhiwceiber	d					08 24									08 54								09 24
Mountain Ash	a					08 28									08 58								09 28
	d					08 33									09 03								09 33
Fernhill	d					08 35									09 05								09 35
Cwmbach	d					08 39									09 09								09 39
Aberdare [3]	a					08 46									09 16								09 46
Quakers Yard	d									08 39								09 09					
Merthyr Vale	a									08 44								09 14					
	d									08 47								09 17					
Troed Y Rhiw	d									08 50								09 20					
Pentre-bach	d									08 53								09 23					
Merthyr Tydfil	a									09 01								09 31					
Trehafod	d			08 11								08 41									09 11		
Porth	a			08 14								08 44									09 14		
	d			08 15								08 45									09 15		
Dinas Rhondda	d			08 19								08 49									09 19		
Tonypandy	d			08 21								08 51									09 21		
Llwynypia	d			08 23								08 53									09 23		
Ystrad Rhondda	a			08 26								08 56									09 26		
	d			08 29								08 59									09 29		
Ton Pentre	d			08 31								09 01									09 31		
Treorchy	d			08 34								09 04									09 34		
Ynyswen	d			08 37								09 07									09 37		
Treherbert	a			08 43								09 13									09 43		

Table 130

Saturdays
until 04 September

Bridgend, Barry Island, Barry, Penarth and Cardiff - Coryton. Rhymney, Pontypridd, Merthyr, Aberdare and Treherbert

		AW	AW	AW	AW	AW	AW	AW	AW	AW	AW	AW	AW	AW	AW	AW	AW	AW	AW	AW	AW	AW
Bridgend	d																	08 42				
Llantwit Major	d																	08 56				
Rhoose Cardiff Int Airport ✈	d																	09 06				
Barry Island	d			08 25						08 40			08 55									09 25
Barry ■	d			08 30						08 45			09 00					09 15				09 30
Barry Docks	d			08 34						08 49			09 04					09 19				09 34
Cadoxton	d			08 37						08 52			09 07					09 22				09 37
Dinas Powys	d			08 41						08 56			09 11					09 26				09 41
Eastbrook	d			08 43						08 58			09 13					09 28				09 43
Cogan	d			08 45						09 00			09 15					09 30				09 45
Penarth	d		08 32			08 47								09 17						09 32		
Dingle Road	d		08 34			08 49								09 19						09 34		
Grangetown	d		08 38	08 49		08 53				09 04			09 19	09 23				09 34		09 38		09 49
Cardiff Central ■	a		08 44	08 54		08 59		09 04		09 09			09 24	09 29			09 34	09 39		09 44		09 54
	d		08 46	08 56		09 01	09 06	09 06		09 11	09 16		09 26	09 31		09 36	09 36	09 41		09 46		09 56
Cardiff Bay	d	08 42			08 54				09 06			09 18			09 30				09 42		09 54	
Cardiff Queen Street ■	a	08 46	08 49	08 59	08 58	09 04	09 09		09 10	09 14	09 19	09 22	09 29	09 34	09 34	09 39		09 44	09 46	09 49	09 58	09 59
	d		08 50	09 00		09 05	09 10			09 15	09 20		09 30	09 35		09 40		09 45		09 50		10 00
Heath Low Level	d																					
Ty Glas	d																					
Birchgrove	d																					
Rhiwbina	d																					
Whitchurch (Cardiff)	d																					
Coryton	a																					
Heath High Level	d		08 55			09 10					09 25			09 40						09 55		
Llanishen	d		08 58			09 13					09 28			09 43						09 58		
Lisvane & Thornhill	d		09 00			09 15					09 30			09 45						10 00		
Caerphilly ■	d		09 06			09 21					09 36			09 51						10 06		
Aber	d		09 08			09 23					09 38			09 53						10 08		
Llanbradach	d		09 12			09 27					09 42			09 57						10 12		
Ystrad Mynach ■	d		09 17			09 32					09 47			10 02						10 17		
Hengoed	d		09 20			09 35					09 50			10 05						10 20		
Pengam	d		09 23			09 38					09 53			10 08						10 23		
Gilfach Fargoed	d					09 41																
Bargoed	a		09 31			09 48					09 58			10 16						10 31		
	d										09 59											
Brithdir	d										10 03											
Tir-phil	d										10 06											
Pontlottyn	d										10 10											
Rhymney ■	a										10 16											
Cathays	d			09 03			09 13			09 18			09 33			09 43		09 48				10 03
Llandaf	d			09 07			09 17			09 22			09 37			09 47		09 52				10 07
Ninian Park	d							09 10									09 40					
Waun-gron Park	d							09 13									09 43					
Fairwater	d							09 15									09 45					
Danescourt	d							09 17									09 47					
Radyr ■	a			09 10			09 20	09 24		09 25			09 40			09 50	09 54	09 55				10 10
	d			09 10			09 20			09 25			09 40			09 50		09 55				10 10
Taffs Well ■	d			09 14			09 24			09 29			09 44			09 54		09 59				10 14
Trefforest Estate	d			09 18									09 48									10 18
Trefforest	d			09 22			09 31			09 36			09 52			10 01		10 06				10 22
Pontypridd ■	a			09 25			09 34			09 39			09 55			10 04		10 09				10 30
	d			09 27			09 36			09 41			09 57			10 06		10 11				
Abercynon	d			09 34						09 49			10 04					10 19				
Penrhiwceiber	d									09 54								10 24				
Mountain Ash	a									09 58								10 28				
	d									10 03								10 33				
Fernhill	d									10 05								10 35				
Cwmbach	d									10 09								10 39				
Aberdare ■	a									10 16								10 46				
Quakers Yard	d			09 39									10 09									
Merthyr Vale	a			09 44									10 14									
	d			09 47									10 17									
Troed Y Rhiw	d			09 50									10 20									
Pentre-bach	d			09 53									10 23									
Merthyr Tydfil	a			10 01									10 31									
Trehafod	d						09 41									10 11						
Porth	a						09 44									10 14						
	d						09 45									10 15						
Dinas Rhondda	d						09 49									10 19						
Tonypandy	d						09 51									10 21						
Llwynypia	d						09 53									10 23						
Ystrad Rhondda	a						09 56									10 26						
	d						09 59									10 29						
Ton Pentre	d						10 01									10 31						
Treorchy	d						10 04									10 34						
Ynyswen	d						10 07									10 37						
Treherbert	a						10 13									10 43						

Table 130

Saturdays
until 04 September

Bridgend, Barry Island, Barry, Penarth and Cardiff - Coryton. Rhymney, Pontypridd, Merthyr, Aberdare and Treherbert

		AW	AW	AW	AW	AW	AW	AW	AW	AW	AW	AW	AW	AW	AW	AW	AW	AW	AW	AW	AW	AW	AW
Bridgend	d														09 42								
Llantwit Major	d														09 56								
Rhoose Cardiff Int Airport ✈	d														10 06								
Barry Island	d						09 40			09 55									10 25				
Barry ■	d						09 45			10 00					10 15				10 30				
Barry Docks	d						09 49			10 04					10 19				10 34				
Cadoxton	d						09 52			10 07					10 22				10 37				
Dinas Powys	d						09 56			10 11					10 26				10 41				
Eastbrook	d						09 58			10 13					10 28				10 43				
Cogan	d						10 00			10 15					10 30				10 45				
Penarth	d	09 47						10 02			10 17						10 32					10 47	
Dingle Road	d	09 49						10 04			10 19						10 34					10 49	
Grangetown	d	09 53					10 04	10 08		10 19	10 23				10 34		10 38		10 49			10 53	
Cardiff Central ■	a	09 59		10 04			10 09	10 14		10 24	10 29			10 34	10 42		10 44		10 54			10 59	11 04
	d	10 01	10 06	10 06			10 11	10 16		10 26	10 31		10 36	10 36			10 46	10 51	10 56			11 01	11 06
Cardiff Bay	d				10 06				10 18			10 30				10 42					10 54		
Cardiff Queen Street ■	a	10 04	10 09		10 10		10 14	10 19	10 22	10 29	10 34	10 34	10 39			10 46	10 49		10 59		10 58	11 04	
	d	10 05	10 10				10 15	10 20		10 30	10 35		10 40				10 50		11 00			11 05	
Heath Low Level	d																						
Ty Glas	d																						
Birchgrove	d																						
Rhiwbina	d																						
Whitchurch (Cardiff)	d																						
Coryton	a																						
Heath High Level	d	10 10						10 25			10 40						10 55					11 10	
Llanishen	d	10 13						10 28			10 43						10 58					11 13	
Lisvane & Thornhill	d	10 15						10 30			10 45						11 00					11 15	
Caerphilly ■	d	10 21						10 36			10 51						11 06					11 21	
Aber	d	10 23						10 38			10 53						11 08					11 23	
Llanbradach	d	10 27						10 42			10 57						11 12					11 27	
Ystrad Mynach ■	d	10 32						10 47			11 02						11 17					11 32	
Hengoed	d	10 35						10 50			11 05						11 20					11 35	
Pengam	d	10 38						10 53			11 08						11 23					11 38	
Gilfach Fargoed	d	10 41																				11 41	
Bargoed	a	10 48						10 58			11 16						11 31					11 48	
	d							10 59															
Brithdir	d							11 03															
Tir-phil	d							11 06															
Pontlottyn	d							11 10															
Rhymney ■	a							11 16															
Cathays	d		10 13				10 18			10 33			10 43						11 03				
Llandaf	d		10 17				10 22			10 37			10 47						11 07				
Ninian Park	d			10 10										10 40									11 10
Waun-gron Park	d			10 13										10 43									11 13
Fairwater	d			10 15										10 45									11 15
Danescourt	d			10 17										10 47									11 17
Radyr ■	a		10 20	10 24			10 25			10 40			10 50	10 54				11 02	11 10				11 24
	d		10 20				10 25			10 40			10 50					11 20	11 10				
Taffs Well ■	d		10 24				10 29			10 44			10 54					11 24	11 14				
Trefforest Estate	d									10 48									11 18				
Trefforest	d		10 31				10 36			10 52			11 01					11 31	11 22	←			
Pontypridd ■	a		10 34				10 39			10 55			11 04					11 34	11 25	11 34			
	d		10 36			10 35	10 41			10 57			11 06					11 36	11 27	11 36			
Abercynon	d					10 41	10 49			11 04								→	11 34				
Penrhiwceiber	d						10 54																
Mountain Ash	a						10 58																
	d						11 03																
Fernhill	d						11 05																
Cwmbach	d						11 09																
Aberdare ■	a						11 16																
Quakers Yard	d					10 45				11 09									11 39				
Merthyr Vale	a					10 50				11 14									11 44				
	d					10 52				11 17									11 47				
Troed Y Rhiw	d					10 55				11 20									11 50				
Pentre-bach	d					10 58				11 23									11 53				
Merthyr Tydfil	a					11 06				11 31									12 01				
Trehafod	d		10 41										11 11							11 41			
Porth	a		10 44										11 14							11 44			
	d		10 45										11 15							11 45			
Dinas Rhondda	d		10 49										11 19							11 49			
Tonypandy	d		10 51										11 21							11 51			
Llwynypia	d		10 53										11 23							11 53			
Ystrad Rhondda	a		10 56										11 26							11 56			
	d		10 59										11 29							11 59			
Ton Pentre	d		11 01										11 31							12 01			
Treorchy	d		11 04										11 34							12 04			
Ynyswen	d		11 07										11 37							12 07			
Treherbert	a		11 13										11 43							12 13			

Table 130

Saturdays until 04 September

Bridgend, Barry Island, Barry, Penarth and Cardiff - Coryton. Rhymney, Pontypridd, Merthyr, Aberdare and Treherbert

		AW	AW	AW	AW	AW	AW	AW	AW	AW	AW	AW	AW	AW	AW	AW	AW	AW	AW	AW	AW	AW
Bridgend	d										10 42											
Llantwit Major	d										10 56											
Rhoose Cardiff Int Airport ✈	d										11 06											
Barry Island	d		10 40			10 55								11 25						11 40		
Barry	d		10 45			11 00					11 15			11 30						11 45		
Barry Docks	d		10 49			11 04					11 19			11 34						11 49		
Cadoxton	d		10 52			11 07					11 22			11 37						11 52		
Dinas Powys	d		10 56			11 11					11 26			11 41						11 56		
Eastbrook	d		10 58			11 13					11 28			11 43						11 58		
Cogan	d		11 00			11 15					11 30			11 45						12 00		
Penarth	d			11 02			11 17						11 32			11 47					12 02	
Dingle Road	d			11 04			11 19						11 34			11 49					12 04	
Grangetown	d		11 04	11 08		11 19	11 23				11 34		11 38	11 49		11 53				12 04	12 08	
Cardiff Central	a		11 09	11 14		11 24	11 29			11 34	11 38		11 44	11 54		11 59		12 04		12 09	12 14	
	d		11 11	11 16		11 26	11 31		11 36	11 36	11 40		11 46	11 56		12 01	12 06	12 06		12 11	12 16	
Cardiff Bay	d	11 06			11 18			11 30				11 42			11 54				12 06			12 18
Cardiff Queen Street	a	11 10	11 14	11 19	11 22	11 29	11 34	11 34	11 39		11 43	11 46	11 49	11 59	11 58	12 04	12 09		12 10	12 14	12 19	12 22
	d		11 15	11 20		11 30	11 35		11 40		11 44		11 50	12 00		12 05	12 10			12 15	12 20	
Heath Low Level	d																					
Ty Glas	d																					
Birchgrove	d																					
Rhiwbina	d																					
Whitchurch (Cardiff)	d																					
Coryton	a																					
Heath High Level	d			11 25			11 40						11 55			12 10					12 25	
Llanishen	d			11 28			11 43						11 58			12 13					12 28	
Lisvane & Thornhill	d			11 30			11 45						12 00			12 15					12 30	
Caerphilly	d			11 36			11 51						12 06			12 21					12 36	
Aber	d			11 38			11 53						12 08			12 23					12 38	
Llanbradach	d			11 42			11 57						12 12			12 27					12 42	
Ystrad Mynach	d			11 47			12 02						12 17			12 32					12 47	
Hengoed	d			11 50			12 05						12 20			12 35					12 50	
Pengam	d			11 53			12 08						12 23			12 38					12 53	
Gilfach Fargoed	d															12 41						
Bargoed	a			11 58			12 16						12 31			12 48					12 58	
	d			11 59																	12 59	
Brithdir	d			12 03																	13 03	
Tir-phil	d			12 06																	13 06	
Pontlottyn	d			12 10																	13 10	
Rhymney	a			12 16																	13 16	
Cathays	d		11 18			11 33			11 43		11 48			12 03			12 13			12 18		
Llandaf	d		11 22			11 37			11 47		11 52			12 07			12 17			12 22		
Ninian Park	d									11 40								12 10				
Waun-gron Park	d									11 43								12 13				
Fairwater	d									11 45								12 15				
Danescourt	d									11 47								12 17				
Radyr	a		11 25			11 40			11 50	11 54	11 54			12 10			12 20	12 24		12 25		
	d		11 25			11 40			11 50		11 55			12 10			12 20			12 25		
Taffs Well	d		11 29			11 44			11 54		11 59			12 14			12 24			12 29		
Trefforest Estate	d					11 48								12 18								
Trefforest	d		11 36			11 52			12 01		12 06			12 22			12 31			12 36		
Pontypridd	a		11 39			11 55			12 04		12 09			12 25			12 34			12 42		
	d		11 41			11 57			12 06		12 11			12 27			12 36					
Abercynon	d		11 49			12 04					12 19			12 34								
Penrhiwceiber	d		11 54								12 24											
Mountain Ash	a		11 58								12 28											
	d		12 03								12 33											
Fernhill	d		12 05								12 35											
Cwmbach	d		12 09								12 39											
Aberdare	a		12 16								12 46											
Quakers Yard	d					12 09								12 39								
Merthyr Vale	a					12 14								12 44								
	d					12 17								12 47								
Troed Y Rhiw	d					12 20								12 50								
Pentre-bach	d					12 23								12 53								
Merthyr Tydfil	a					12 31								13 01								
Trehafod	d								12 11								12 41					
Porth	a								12 14								12 44					
	d								12 15								12 45					
Dinas Rhondda	d								12 19								12 49					
Tonypandy	d								12 21								12 51					
Llwynypia	d								12 23								12 53					
Ystrad Rhondda	a								12 26								12 56					
	d								12 29								12 59					
Ton Pentre	d								12 31								13 01					
Treorchy	d								12 34								13 04					
Ynyswen	d								12 37								13 07					
Treherbert	a								12 43								13 13					

Table 130

Saturdays until 04 September

Bridgend, Barry Island, Barry, Penarth and Cardiff - Coryton. Rhymney, Pontypridd, Merthyr, Aberdare and Treherbert

		AW	AW	AW	AW	AW	AW	AW	AW	AW	AW	AW	AW	AW	AW	AW	AW	AW	AW	AW	AW	AW	AW
Bridgend	d						11 42																
Llantwit Major	d						11 56																
Rhoose Cardiff Int Airport ✈	d						12 06																
Barry Island	d	11 55								12 25						12 40			12 55				
Barry	d	12 00					12 15			12 30						12 45			13 00				
Barry Docks	d	12 04					12 19			12 34						12 49			13 04				
Cadoxton	d	12 07					12 22			12 37						12 52			13 07				
Dinas Powys	d	12 11					12 26			12 41						12 56			13 11				
Eastbrook	d	12 13					12 28			12 43						12 58			13 13				
Cogan	d	12 15					12 30			12 45						13 00			13 15				
Penarth	d		12 17						12 32			12 47					13 02			13 17			
Dingle Road	d		12 19						12 34			12 49					13 04			13 19			
Grangetown	d	12 19	12 23				12 34		12 38	12 49		12 53				13 04	13 08		13 19	13 23			
Cardiff Central	a	12 24	12 29			12 34	12 39		12 44	12 54		12 59		13 04		13 09	13 14		13 24	13 29			13 34
	d	12 26	12 31		12 36	12 36	12 41		12 46	12 56		13 01	13 06	13 06		13 11	13 16		13 26	13 31		13 36	13 36
Cardiff Bay	d			12 30				12 42			12 54				13 06			13 18			13 30		
Cardiff Queen Street	a	12 29	12 34	12 34	12 39		12 44	12 46	12 49	12 59	12 58	13 04	13 09		13 10	13 14	13 19	13 22	13 29	13 34	13 34	13 39	
	d	12 30	12 35		12 40		12 45		12 50	13 00		13 05	13 10			13 15	13 20		13 30	13 35		13 40	
Heath Low Level	d																						
Ty Glas	d																						
Birchgrove	d																						
Rhiwbina	d																						
Whitchurch (Cardiff)	d																						
Coryton	a																						
Heath High Level	d		12 40						12 55			13 10					13 25			13 40			
Llanishen	d		12 43						12 58			13 13					13 28			13 43			
Lisvane & Thornhill	d		12 45						13 00			13 15					13 30			13 45			
Caerphilly	d		12 51						13 06			13 21					13 36			13 51			
Aber	d		12 53						13 08			13 23					13 38			13 53			
Llanbradach	d		12 57						13 12			13 27					13 42			13 57			
Ystrad Mynach	d		13 02						13 17			13 32					13 47			14 02			
Hengoed	d		13 05						13 20			13 35					13 50			14 05			
Pengam	d		13 08						13 23			13 38					13 53			14 08			
Gilfach Fargoed	d											13 41											
Bargoed	a		13 16						13 31			13 48					13 58			14 16			
	d																13 59						
Brithdir	d																14 03						
Tir-phil	d																14 06						
Pontlottyn	d																14 10						
Rhymney	a																14 16						
Cathays	d	12 33			12 43		12 48			13 03			13 13			13 18			13 33			13 43	
Llandaf	d	12 37			12 47		12 52			13 07			13 17			13 22			13 37			13 47	
Ninian Park	d					12 40								13 10									13 40
Waun-gron Park	d					12 43								13 13									13 43
Fairwater	d					12 45								13 15									13 45
Danescourt	d					12 47								13 17									13 47
Radyr	a	12 40			12 50	12 54	12 55			13 10			13 20	13 24		13 25			13 40			13 50	13 54
	d	12 40			12 50		12 55			13 10			13 20			13 25			13 40			13 50	
Taffs Well	d	12 44			12 54		12 59			13 14			13 24			13 29			13 44			13 54	
Trefforest Estate	d	12 48								13 18									13 48				
Trefforest	d	12 52			13 01		13 06			13 22			13 31			13 36			13 52			14 01	
Pontypridd	a	12 55			13 04		13 09			13 25			13 34			13 39			13 55			14 04	
	d	12 57			13 06		13 11			13 27			13 36			13 41			13 57			14 06	
Abercynon	d	13 04					13 19			13 34						13 49			14 04				
Penrhiwceiber	d						13 24									13 54							
Mountain Ash	a						13 28									13 58							
	d						13 33									14 03							
Fernhill	d						13 35									14 05							
Cwmbach	d						13 39									14 09							
Aberdare	a						13 46									14 16							
Quakers Yard	d	13 09								13 39									14 09				
Merthyr Vale	a	13 14								13 44									14 14				
	d	13 17								13 47									14 17				
Troed Y Rhiw	d	13 20								13 50									14 20				
Pentre-bach	d	13 23								13 53									14 23				
Merthyr Tydfil	a	13 31								14 01									14 31				
Trehafod	d				13 11								13 41									14 11	
Porth	a				13 14								13 44									14 14	
	d				13 15								13 45									14 15	
Dinas Rhondda	d				13 19								13 49									14 19	
Tonypandy	d				13 21								13 51									14 21	
Llwynypia	d				13 23								13 53									14 23	
Ystrad Rhondda	a				13 26								13 56									14 26	
	d				13 29								13 59									14 29	
Ton Pentre	d				13 31								14 01									14 31	
Treorchy	d				13 34								14 04									14 34	
Ynyswen	d				13 37								14 07									14 37	
Treherbert	a				13 43								14 13									14 43	

Table 130

Saturdays
until 04 September

Bridgend, Barry Island, Barry, Penarth and Cardiff - Coryton. Rhymney, Pontypridd, Merthyr, Aberdare and Treherbert

		AW	AW	AW	AW	AW		AW	AW	AW	AW	AW	AW	AW	AW	AW		AW	AW	AW	AW	AW	AW	AW	AW
Bridgend	d	12 42																			13 42				
Llantwit Major	d	12 56																			13 56				
Rhoose Cardiff Int Airport ✈	d	13 06																			14 06				
Barry Island	d				13 25							13 40			13 55										14 25
Barry 3	d	13 15			13 30							13 45			14 00						14 15				14 30
Barry Docks	d	13 19			13 34							13 49			14 04						14 19				14 34
Cadoxton	d	13 22			13 37							13 52			14 07						14 22				14 37
Dinas Powys	d	13 26			13 41							13 56			14 11						14 26				14 41
Eastbrook	d	13 28			13 43							13 58			14 13						14 28				14 43
Cogan	d	13 30			13 45							14 00			14 15						14 30				14 45
Penarth	d			13 32				13 47					14 02			14 17							14 32		
Dingle Road	d			13 34				13 49					14 04			14 19							14 34		
Grangetown	d	13 34		13 38	13 49			13 53				14 04	14 08		14 19	14 23					14 34		14 38		14 49
Cardiff Central 7	a	13 39		13 44	13 54			13 59		14 04		14 09	14 14		14 24	14 29				14 34	14 39		14 44		14 54
	d	13 41		13 46	13 56			14 01	14 06	14 06		14 11	14 16		14 26	14 31			14 36	14 36	14 41		14 46	14 51	14 56
Cardiff Bay	d		13 42			13 54					14 06			14 18				14 30				14 42			
Cardiff Queen Street 3	a	13 44	13 46	13 49	13 59	13 58		14 04	14 09		14 10	14 14	14 19	14 22	14 29	14 34		14 34	14 39		14 44	14 46	14 49		14 59
	d	13 45		13 50	14 00			14 05	14 10			14 15	14 20		14 30	14 35			14 40		14 45		14 50		15 00
Heath Low Level	d																								
Ty Glas	d																								
Birchgrove	d																								
Rhiwbina	d																								
Whitchurch (Cardiff)	d																								
Coryton	a																								
Heath High Level	d			13 55				14 10					14 25			14 40							14 55		
Llanishen	d			13 58				14 13					14 28			14 43							14 58		
Lisvane & Thornhill	d			14 00				14 15					14 30			14 45							15 00		
Caerphilly 3	d			14 06				14 21					14 36			14 51							15 06		
Aber	d			14 08				14 23					14 38			14 53							15 08		
Llanbradach	d			14 12				14 27					14 42			14 57							15 12		
Ystrad Mynach 3	d			14 17				14 32					14 47			15 02							15 17		
Hengoed	d			14 20				14 35					14 50			15 05							15 20		
Pengam	d			14 23				14 38					14 53			15 08							15 23		
Gilfach Fargoed	d							14 41																	
Bargoed	a			14 31				14 48					14 58			15 16							15 31		
	d												14 59												
Brithdir	d												15 03												
Tir-phil	d												15 06												
Pontlottyn	d												15 10												
Rhymney 3	a												15 16												
Cathays	d	13 48			14 03				14 13			14 18			14 33				14 43		14 48				15 03
Llandaf	d	13 52			14 07				14 17			14 22			14 37				14 47		14 52				15 07
Ninian Park	d									14 10										14 40					
Waun-gron Park	d									14 13										14 43					
Fairwater	d									14 15										14 45					
Danescourt	d									14 17										14 47					
Radyr 3	a	13 55			14 10				14 20	14 24		14 25			14 40				14 50	14 54	14 55			15 08	15 10
	d	13 55			14 10				14 20			14 25			14 40				14 50		14 55			15 20	15 10
Taffs Well 3	d	13 59			14 14				14 24			14 29			14 44				14 54		14 59			15 24	15 14
Trefforest Estate	d				14 18										14 48										15 18
Trefforest	d	14 06			14 22				14 31			14 36			14 52				15 01		15 06			15 31	15 22
Pontypridd 3	a	14 09			14 25				14 34			14 39			14 55				15 04		15 09			15 34	15 25
	d	14 11			14 27				14 36			14 41			14 57				15 06		15 11			15 36	15 27
Abercynon	d	14 19			14 34							14 49			15 04						15 19			→	15 34
Penrhiwceiber	d	14 24										14 54									15 24				
Mountain Ash	a	14 28										14 58									15 28				
	d	14 33										15 03									15 33				
Fernhill	d	14 35										15 05									15 35				
Cwmbach	d	14 39										15 09									15 39				
Aberdare 3	a	14 46										15 16									15 46				
Quakers Yard	d				14 39										15 09										15 39
Merthyr Vale	a				14 44										15 14										15 44
	d				14 47										15 17										15 47
Troed Y Rhiw	d				14 50										15 20										15 50
Pentre-bach	d				14 53										15 23										15 53
Merthyr Tydfil	a				15 01										15 31										16 01
Trehafod	d								14 41										15 11						
Porth	a								14 44										15 14						
	d								14 45										15 15						
Dinas Rhondda	d								14 49										15 19						
Tonypandy	d								14 51										15 21						
Llwynypia	d								14 53										15 23						
Ystrad Rhondda	a								14 56										15 26						
	d								14 59										15 29						
Ton Pentre	d								15 01										15 31						
Treorchy	d								15 04										15 34						
Ynyswen	d								15 07										15 37						
Treherbert	a								15 13										15 43						

Table 130

Saturdays
until 04 September

Bridgend, Barry Island, Barry, Penarth and Cardiff - Coryton. Rhymney, Pontypridd, Merthyr, Aberdare and Treherbert

		AW		AW	AW	AW	AW	AW	AW	AW	AW	AW		AW	AW	AW	AW	AW	AW	AW	AW	AW		AW	AW
Bridgend	d																14 42								
Llantwit Major	d																14 56								
Rhoose Cardiff Int Airport ✈	d																15 06								
Barry Island	d							14 40			14 55									15 25					
Barry 3	d							14 45			15 00						15 15			15 30					
Barry Docks	d							14 49			15 04						15 19			15 34					
Cadoxton	d							14 52			15 07						15 22			15 37					
Dinas Powys	d							14 56			15 11						15 26			15 41					
Eastbrook	d							14 58			15 13						15 28			15 43					
Cogan	d							15 00			15 15						15 30			15 45					
Penarth	d				14 47				15 02			15 17							15 32			15 47			
Dingle Road	d				14 49				15 04			15 19							15 34			15 49			
Grangetown	d				14 53			15 04	15 08		15 19	15 23					15 34		15 38	15 49		15 53			
Cardiff Central 7	a				14 59	15 04		15 09	15 14		15 24	15 29				15 34	15 39		15 44	15 54		15 59			16 05
	d				15 01	15 06		15 11	15 16		15 26	15 31			15 36	15 36	15 41		15 46	15 56		16 01		16 06	16 06
Cardiff Bay	d			14 54			15 06			15 18				15 30				15 42			15 54				
Cardiff Queen Street 3	a			14 58	15 04		15 10	15 14	15 19	15 22	15 29	15 34		15 34	15 39		15 44	15 46	15 49	15 59	15 58	16 04		16 09	
	d				15 05			15 15	15 20		15 30	15 35			15 40		15 45		15 50	16 00		16 05		16 10	
Heath Low Level	d																								
Ty Glas	d																								
Birchgrove	d																								
Rhiwbina	d																								
Whitchurch (Cardiff)	d																								
Coryton	a																								
Heath High Level	d				15 10				15 25			15 40							15 55			16 10			
Llanishen	d				15 13				15 28			15 43							15 58			16 13			
Lisvane & Thornhill	d				15 15				15 30			15 45							16 00			16 15			
Caerphilly 3	d				15 21				15 36			15 51							16 06			16 21			
Aber	d				15 23				15 38			15 53							16 08			16 23			
Llanbradach	d				15 27				15 42			15 57							16 12			16 27			
Ystrad Mynach 3	d				15 32				15 47			16 02							16 17			16 32			
Hengoed	d				15 35				15 50			16 05							16 20			16 35			
Pengam	d				15 38				15 53			16 08							16 23			16 38			
Gilfach Fargoed	d				15 41																	16 41			
Bargoed	a				15 48				15 58			16 16							16 31			16 48			
	d								15 59																
Brithdir	d								16 03																
Tir-phil	d								16 06																
Pontlottyn	d								16 10																
Rhymney 3	a								16 16																
Cathays	d							15 18			15 33					15 43		15 48			16 03				16 13	
Llandaf	d							15 22			15 37					15 47		15 52			16 07				16 17	
Ninian Park	d					15 10											15 40								16 10
Waun-gron Park	d					15 13											15 43								16 13
Fairwater	d					15 15											15 45								16 15
Danescourt	d					15 17											15 47								16 17
Radyr 3	a					15 24		15 25			15 40					15 50	15 54	15 55			16 10			16 20	16 24
	d							15 25			15 40					15 50		15 55			16 10			16 20	
Taffs Well 3	d							15 29			15 44					15 54		15 59			16 14			16 24	
Trefforest Estate	d										15 48										16 18				
Trefforest	d	←						15 36			15 52					16 01		16 06			16 22			16 31	
Pontypridd 3	a	15 34						15 39			15 55					16 04		16 09			16 25			16 34	
	d	15 36						15 41			15 57					16 06		16 11			16 27			16 36	
Abercynon	d							15 49			16 04							16 19			16 34				
Penrhiwceiber	d							15 54										16 24							
Mountain Ash	a							15 58										16 28							
	d							16 03										16 33							
Fernhill	d							16 05										16 35							
Cwmbach	d							16 09										16 39							
Aberdare 3	a							16 16										16 46							
Quakers Yard	d										16 09										16 39				
Merthyr Vale	a										16 14										16 44				
	d										16 17										16 47				
Troed Y Rhiw	d										16 20										16 50				
Pentre-bach	d										16 23										16 53				
Merthyr Tydfil	a										16 31										17 01				
Trehafod	d	15 41														16 11								16 41	
Porth	a	15 44														16 14								16 44	
	d	15 45														16 15								16 45	
Dinas Rhondda	d	15 49														16 19								16 49	
Tonypandy	d	15 51														16 21								16 51	
Llwynypia	d	15 53														16 23								16 53	
Ystrad Rhondda	a	15 56														16 26								16 56	
	d	15 59														16 29								16 59	
Ton Pentre	d	16 01														16 31								17 01	
Treorchy	d	16 04														16 34								17 04	
Ynyswen	d	16 07														16 37								17 07	
Treherbert	a	16 13														16 43								17 13	

Table 130

Bridgend, Barry Island, Barry, Penarth and Cardiff - Coryton. Rhymney, Pontypridd, Merthyr, Aberdare and Treherbert

		AW	AW	AW	AW	AW	AW	AW	AW	AW	AW	AW	AW	AW	AW	AW	AW	AW	AW	AW	AW	AW	AW
Bridgend	d									15 42												
Llantwit Major	d									15 56												
Rhoose Cardiff Int Airport ✈	d									16 06												
Barry Island	d		15 40			15 55								16 25						16 40			16 55
Barry	d		15 45			16 00					16 15			16 30						16 45			17 00
Barry Docks	d		15 49			16 04					16 19			16 34						16 49			17 04
Cadoxton	d		15 52			16 07					16 22			16 37						16 52			17 07
Dinas Powys	d		15 56			16 11					16 26			16 41						16 56			17 11
Eastbrook	d		15 58			16 13					16 28			16 43						16 58			17 13
Cogan	d		16 00			16 15					16 30			16 45						17 00			17 15
Penarth	d			16 02			16 17						16 32								17 02		
Dingle Road	d			16 04			16 19						16 34								17 04		
Grangetown	d		16 04	16 08		16 19	16 23				16 34		16 38	16 49						17 04	17 08		17 19
Cardiff Central	a		16 09	16 14		16 24	16 29			16 34	16 39		16 44	16 54				17 05		17 09	17 14		17 24
	d		16 11	16 16		16 26	16 31		16 36	16 36	16 41		16 46	16 56		17 01	17 06	17 06		17 11	17 16		17 26
Cardiff Bay	d	16 06			16 18			16 30				16 42			16 54				17 06			17 18	
Cardiff Queen Street	a	16 10	16 14	16 19	16 22	16 29	16 34	16 34	16 39		16 44	16 46	16 49	16 59	16 58	17 04	17 09		17 10	17 14	17 19	17 22	17 29
	d		16 15	16 20		16 30	16 35		16 40		16 45		16 50	17 00		17 05	17 10			17 15	17 20		17 30
Heath Low Level	d																						
Ty Glas	d																						
Birchgrove	d																						
Rhiwbina	d																						
Whitchurch (Cardiff)	d																						
Coryton	a																						
Heath High Level	d			16 25			16 40						16 55			17 10					17 25		
Llanishen	d			16 28			16 43						16 58			17 13					17 28		
Lisvane & Thornhill	d			16 30			16 45						17 00			17 15					17 30		
Caerphilly	d			16 36			16 51						17 06			17 21					17 36		
Aber	d			16 38			16 53						17 08			17 23					17 38		
Llanbradach	d			16 42			16 57						17 12			17 27					17 42		
Ystrad Mynach	d			16 47			17 02						17 17			17 33					17 47		
Hengoed	d			16 50			17 05						17 20			17 35					17 50		
Pengam	d			16 53			17 08						17 23			17 39					17 53		
Gilfach Fargoed	d															17 42							
Bargoed	a			16 58			17 16						17 31			17 45					18 01		
	d			16 59												17 47							
Brithdir	d			17 03												17 50							
Tir-phil	d			17 06												17 53							
Pontlottyn	d			17 10												17 58							
Rhymney	a			17 16												18 04							
Cathays	d		16 18			16 33			16 43		16 48			17 03			17 13			17 18			17 33
Llandaf	d		16 22			16 37			16 47		16 52			17 07			17 17			17 22			17 37
Ninian Park	d									16 40								17 10					
Waun-gron Park	d									16 43								17 13					
Fairwater	d									16 45								17 15					
Danescourt	d									16 47								17 17					
Radyr	a		16 25			16 40			16 50	16 54	16 55			17 10			17 20	17 24		17 25			17 40
	d		16 25			16 40			16 50		16 55			17 10			17 20			17 25			17 40
Taffs Well	d		16 29			16 44			16 54		16 59			17 14			17 24			17 29			17 44
Trefforest Estate	d					16 48								17 18									17 48
Trefforest	d		16 36			16 52			17 01		17 06			17 22			17 31			17 36			17 52
Pontypridd	a		16 39			16 55			17 04		17 09			17 25			17 34			17 39			17 55
	d		16 41			16 57			17 06		17 11			17 27			17 36			17 41			17 57
Abercynon	d		16 49			17 04					17 19			17 34						17 49			18 04
Penrhiwceiber	d		16 54								17 24									17 54			
Mountain Ash	a		16 58								17 28									17 58			
	d		17 03								17 33									18 03			
Fernhill	d		17 05								17 35									18 05			
Cwmbach	d		17 09								17 39									18 09			
Aberdare	a		17 16								17 46									18 16			
Quakers Yard	d					17 09								17 39									18 09
Merthyr Vale	a					17 14								17 44									18 14
	d					17 17								17 47									18 17
Troed Y Rhiw	d					17 20								17 50									18 20
Pentre-bach	d					17 23								17 53									18 23
Merthyr Tydfil	a					17 31								18 01									18 31
Trehafod	d								17 11								17 41						
Porth	a								17 14								17 44						
	d								17 15								17 45						
Dinas Rhondda	d								17 19								17 49						
Tonypandy	d								17 21								17 51						
Llwynypia	d								17 23								17 53						
Ystrad Rhondda	a								17 26								17 56						
	d								17 29								17 59						
Ton Pentre	d								17 31								18 01						
Treorchy	d								17 34								18 04						
Ynyswen	d								17 37								18 07						
Treherbert	a								17 43								18 13						

Table 130

Bridgend, Barry Island, Barry, Penarth and Cardiff - Coryton. Rhymney, Pontypridd, Merthyr, Aberdare and Treherbert

		AW	AW	AW	AW	AW	AW	AW	AW	AW	AW	AW	AW	AW	AW	AW	AW	AW	AW	AW	AW	AW
Bridgend	d					16 42																
Llantwit Major	d					16 56																
Rhoose Cardiff Int Airport ✈	d					17 06																
Barry Island	d								17 25						17 40			17 55				
Barry	d					17 15			17 30						17 45			18 00				
Barry Docks	d					17 19			17 34						17 49			18 04				
Cadoxton	d					17 22			17 37						17 52			18 07				
Dinas Powys	d					17 26			17 41						17 56			18 11				
Eastbrook	d					17 28			17 43						17 58			18 13				
Cogan	d					17 30			17 45						18 00			18 15				
Penarth	d	17 17						17 32			17 47					18 02			18 17			
Dingle Road	d	17 19						17 34			17 49					18 04			18 19			
Grangetown	d	17 23				17 34		17 38	17 49		17 53				18 04	18 08		18 19	18 23			
Cardiff Central	a	17 29			17 34	17 39		17 44	17 54		17 59		18 05		18 10	18 14		18 24	18 29			18 34
	d	17 31		17 36	17 36	17 41		17 46	17 56		18 01	18 06	18 06		18 11	18 16		18 26	18 31		18 36	18 36
Cardiff Bay	d		17 30				17 42			17 54				18 06			18 18			18 30		
Cardiff Queen Street	a	17 34	17 34	17 39		17 44	17 46	17 49	17 59	17 58	18 04	18 09		18 10	18 14	18 19	18 22	18 29	18 34	18 34	18 38	
	d	17 35		17 40		17 45		17 50	18 00		18 05	18 10			18 15	18 20		18 30	18 35		18 40	
Heath Low Level	d																					
Ty Glas	d																					
Birchgrove	d																					
Rhiwbina	d																					
Whitchurch (Cardiff)	d																					
Coryton	a																					
Heath High Level	d	17 40						17 55			18 10					18 25			18 40			
Llanishen	d	17 43						17 59			18 13					18 28			18 43			
Lisvane & Thornhill	d	17 45						18 02			18 15					18 30			18 45			
Caerphilly	d	17 51						18 07			18 21					18 36			18 51			
Aber	d	17 53						18 10			18 23					18 38			18 53			
Llanbradach	d	17 57						18 14			18 27					18 42			18 57			
Ystrad Mynach	d	18 02						18 20			18 32					18a51			19 02			
Hengoed	d	18 05						18 23			18 35								19 05			
Pengam	d	18 08						18 27			18 38								19 08			
Gilfach Fargoed	d	18 11						18 30			18 41								19x11			
Bargoed	a	18 14						18 34			18 48								19 14			
	d	18 16						18 44											19 16			
Brithdir	d	18 20						18 48											19 20			
Tir-phil	d	18 23						18 51											19 23			
Pontlottyn	d	18 27						18 55											19 27			
Rhymney	a	18 33						19 01											19 33			
Cathays	d			17 43		17 48			18 03			18 13			18 18			18 33			18 43	
Llandaf	d			17 47		17 52			18 07			18 17			18 22			18 37			18 47	
Ninian Park	d				17 40								18 10									18 40
Waun-gron Park	d				17 43								18 13									18 43
Fairwater	d				17 45								18 15									18 45
Danescourt	d				17 47								18 17									18 47
Radyr	a			17 50	17 54	17 55			18 10			18 20	18 24		18 25			18 40			18 50	18 54
	d			17 50		17 55			18 10			18 20			18 25			18 40			18 50	
Taffs Well	d			17 54		17 59			18 14			18 24			18 29			18 44			18 54	
Trefforest Estate	d								18 18									18 48				
Trefforest	d			18 01		18 06			18 22			18 31			18 36			18 52			19 01	
Pontypridd	a			18 04		18 09			18 25			18 34			18 42			18 55			19 04	
	d			18 06		18 11			18 27			18 36						18 57			19 06	
Abercynon	d					18 19			18 34									19 04				
Penrhiwceiber	d					18 24																
Mountain Ash	a					18 28																
	d					18 33																
Fernhill	d					18 35																
Cwmbach	d					18 39																
Aberdare	a					18 46																
Quakers Yard	d								18 39									19 09				
Merthyr Vale	a								18 44									19 14				
	d								18 47									19 17				
Troed Y Rhiw	d								18 50									19 20				
Pentre-bach	d								18 53									19 23				
Merthyr Tydfil	a								19 01									19 31				
Trehafod	d			18 11								18 41									19 11	
Porth	a			18 14								18 44									19 14	
	d			18 15								18 45									19 15	
Dinas Rhondda	d			18 19								18 49									19 19	
Tonypandy	d			18 21								18 51									19 21	
Llwynypia	d			18 23								18 53									19 23	
Ystrad Rhondda	a			18 26								18 56									19 26	
	d			18 29								18 59									19 29	
Ton Pentre	d			18 31								19 01									19 31	
Treorchy	d			18 34								19 04									19 34	
Ynyswen	d			18 37								19 07									19 37	
Treherbert	a			18 43								19 13									19 43	

Table 130

Saturdays
until 04 September

Bridgend, Barry Island, Barry, Penarth and Cardiff - Coryton. Rhymney, Pontypridd, Merthyr, Aberdare and Treherbert

		AW	AW	AW	AW	AW	AW	AW	AW	AW	AW	AW	AW	AW	AW	AW	AW	AW	AW	AW	AW	AW	AW
Bridgend	d	17 42														18 42							
Llantwit Major	d	17 56														18 56							
Rhoose Cardiff Int Airport ✈	d	18 06														19 06							
Barry Island	d			18 25						18 40		18 55								19 25			
Barry	d	18 15		18 30						18 45		19 00				19 15				19 30			
Barry Docks	d	18 19		18 34						18 49		19 04				19 19				19 34			
Cadoxton	d	18 22		18 37						18 52		19 07				19 22				19 37			
Dinas Powys	d	18 26		18 41						18 56		19 11				19 26				19 41			
Eastbrook	d	18 28		18 43						18 58		19 13				19 28				19 43			
Cogan	d	18 30		18 45						19 00		19 15				19 30				19 45			
Penarth	d		18 32				18 47						19 17								19 47		
Dingle Road	d		18 34				18 49						19 19								19 49		
Grangetown	d	18 34	18 38	18 49			18 53			19 04		19 19	19 23			19 34				19 49	19 54		
Cardiff Central	a	18 39	18 45	18 55			18 59			19 09		19 24	19 29		19 34	19 39				19 56	19 59		
	d	18 41					19 01	19 06		19 11		19 26	19 31		19 36	19 41		19 51		20 01	20 06		
Cardiff Bay	d				18 42	18 54			19 06		19 18			19 30			19 42		19 54			20 06	20 18
Cardiff Queen Street	a	18 44			18 46	18 58	19 04	19 09	19 10	19 14	19 22	19 29	19 34	19 34		19 44	19 46	19 54	19 58	20 04	20 09	20 10	20 22
	d	18 50					19 05	19 10		19 15		19 30	19 35			19 45		19 55		20 06	20 10		
Heath Low Level	d																	20 00					
Ty Glas	d																	20 03					
Birchgrove	d																	20 04					
Rhiwbina	d																	20 06					
Whitchurch (Cardiff)	d																	20 08					
Coryton	a																	20 13					
Heath High Level	d						19 10						19 40							20 10			
Llanishen	d						19 13						19 43							20 13			
Lisvane & Thornhill	d						19 15						19 45							20 16			
Caerphilly	d						19a24						19 51							20a28			
Aber	d												19 53										
Llanbradach	d												19 57										
Ystrad Mynach	d												20 02										
Hengoed	d												20 05										
Pengam	d												20 08										
Gilfach Fargoed	d												20 11										
Bargoed	a												20 15										
	d												20 16										
Brithdir	d												20 20										
Tir-phil	d												20 23										
Pontlottyn	d												20 27										
Rhymney	a												20 33										
Cathays	d	18 52						19 13		19 18		19 33				19 48					20 13		
Llandaf	d	18 56						19 17		19 22		19 37				19 52					20 17		
Ninian Park	d														19 40								
Waun-gron Park	d														19 43								
Fairwater	d														19 45								
Danescourt	d														19 47								
Radyr	a	18 58						19 20		19 25		19 40			19 54	19 55					20 20		
	d	18 58						19 20		19 25		19 40				19 55					20 20		
Taffs Well	d	19 03						19 24		19 29		19 44				19 59					20 24		
Trefforest Estate	d											19 48											
Trefforest	d	19 10						19 31		19 36		19 52				20 06					20 31		
Pontypridd	a	19 13						19 34		19 39		19 55				20 09					20 35		
	d	19 14						19 36		19 41		19 57				20 11					20 36		
Abercynon	d	19 21								19 49		20 04				20 21							
Penrhiwceiber	d	19 26								19 54						20 27							
Mountain Ash	a	19 30								19 56						20 30							
	d	19 33								20 03						20 33							
Fernhill	d	19 35								20 05						20 35							
Cwmbach	d	19 39								20 09						20 39							
Aberdare	a	19 46								20 16						20 46							
Quakers Yard	d											20 09											
Merthyr Vale	a											20 14											
	d											20 14											
Troed Y Rhiw	d											20 18											
Pentre-bach	d											20 21											
Merthyr Tydfil	a											20 29											
Trehafod	d							19 41													20 41		
Porth	a							19 44													20 44		
	d							19 45													20 45		
Dinas Rhondda	d							19 49													20 49		
Tonypandy	d							19 51													20 51		
Llwynypia	d							19 53													20 53		
Ystrad Rhondda	a							19 56													20 56		
	d							19 59													20 59		
Ton Pentre	d							20 01													21 01		
Treorchy	d							20 04													21 04		
Ynyswen	d							20 07													21 07		
Treherbert	a							20 13													21 13		

Table 130

Saturdays
until 04 September

Bridgend, Barry Island, Barry, Penarth and Cardiff - Coryton. Rhymney, Pontypridd, Merthyr, Aberdare and Treherbert

		AW	AW	AW	AW	AW	AW	AW	AW	AW	AW	AW	AW	AW	AW	AW	AW	AW	AW	AW	AW	AW	AW
Bridgend	d					19 42													20 42				
Llantwit Major	d					19 56													20 56				
Rhoose Cardiff Int Airport ✈	d					20 06													21 06				
Barry Island	d	19 55												20 55									
Barry	d	20 00				20 15								21 00					21 15				
Barry Docks	d	20 04				20 19								21 04					21 19				
Cadoxton	d	20 07				20 22								21 07					21 22				
Dinas Powys	d	20 11				20 26								21 11					21 26				
Eastbrook	d	20 13				20 28								21 13					21 28				
Cogan	d	20 15				20 30								21 15					21 30				
Penarth	d			20 19						20 47								21 20				21 47	
Dingle Road	d			20 21						20 49								21 22				21 49	
Grangetown	d	20 19		20 25		20 34				20 53				21 19				21 26	21 34			21 53	
Cardiff Central	a	20 24		20 30	20 34	20 39				20 59				21 24			21 34	21 37	21 39			21 59	
	d	20 26		20 32	20 36	20 41		20 51		21 01	21 06			21 26		21 31	21 36		21 41			22 01	22 06
Cardiff Bay	d		20 30				20 42		20 54			21 06	21 18		21 30					21 42	21 54		
Cardiff Queen Street	a	20 29	20 34	20 35		20 44	20 46	20 54	20 58	21 04	21 09	21 10	21 22	21 29	21 34	21 34			21 44	21 46	21 58	22 04	22 09
	d	20 30		20 36		20 45		20 55		21 05	21 10			21 30		21 35			21 45			22 05	22 10
Heath Low Level	d							21 00															
Ty Glas	d							21 03															
Birchgrove	d							21 04															
Rhiwbina	d							21 06															
Whitchurch (Cardiff)	d							21 08															
Coryton	a							21 13															
Heath High Level	d			20 41						21 10						21 40						22 10	
Llanishen	d			20 44						21 13						21 43						22 13	
Lisvane & Thornhill	d			20 46						21 15						21 45						22 15	
Caerphilly	d			20 52						21a34						21 51						22a24	
Aber	d			20 54												21 53							
Llanbradach	d			20 58												21 57							
Ystrad Mynach	d			21 03												22 02							
Hengoed	d			21 06												22 05							
Pengam	d			21 09												22 08							
Gilfach Fargoed	d			21 12												22 11							
Bargoed	a			21 16												22 15							
	d			21 17												22 16							
Brithdir	d			21 21												22 20							
Tir-phil	d			21 24												22 23							
Pontlottyn	d			21 28												22 27							
Rhymney	a			21 34												22 33							
Cathays	d	20 33				20 48					21 13			21 33					21 48				22 13
Llandaf	d	20 37				20 52					21 17			21 37					21 52				22 17
Ninian Park	d				20 40												21 40						
Waun-gron Park	d				20 43												21 43						
Fairwater	d				20 45												21 45						
Danescourt	d				20 47												21 47						
Radyr	a	20 40			20 54	20 55					21 20			21 40			21 54		21 55				22 20
	d	20 40				20 55					21 20			21 40					21 55				22 20
Taffs Well	d	20 44				20 59					21 24			21 44					21 59				22 24
Trefforest Estate	d	20 48												21 48									
Trefforest	d	20 52				21 06					21 31			21 52					22 06				22 31
Pontypridd	a	20 55				21 09					21 34			21 55					22 09				22 34
	d	20 57				21 11					21 36			21 57					22 11				22 36
Abercynon	d	21 04				21 19								22 04					22 19				
Penrhiwceiber	d					21 24													22 24				
Mountain Ash	a					21 28													22 28				
	d					21 29													22 29				
Fernhill	d					21 31													22 31				
Cwmbach	d					21 35													22 35				
Aberdare	a					21 42													22 42				
Quakers Yard	d	21 09												22 09									
Merthyr Vale	a	21 14												22 14									
	d	21 14												22 14									
Troed Y Rhiw	d	21 18												22 18									
Pentre-bach	d	21 21												22 21									
Merthyr Tydfil	a	21 29												22 29									
Trehafod	d										21 41												22 41
Porth	a										21 44												22 44
	d										21 45												22 45
Dinas Rhondda	d										21 49												22 49
Tonypandy	d										21 51												22 51
Llwynypia	d										21 53												22 53
Ystrad Rhondda	a										21 56												22 56
	d										21 59												22 59
Ton Pentre	d										22 01												23 01
Treorchy	d										22 04												23 04
Ynyswen	d										22 07												23 07
Treherbert	a										22 13												23 13

Table 130

Saturdays until 04 September

Bridgend, Barry Island, Barry, Penarth and Cardiff - Coryton. Rhymney, Pontypridd, Merthyr, Aberdare and Treherbert

		AW		AW	AW	AW	AW	AW	AW	AW	AW	AW		AW	AW	AW	AW	AW	AW	AW	AW
Bridgend	d							21 42										22 42			
Llantwit Major	d							21 56										22 56			
Rhoose Cardiff Int Airport ✈	d							22 06										23 06			
Barry Island	d				21 55											22 44					
Barry	d				22 00			22 15								22 48		23 15			
Barry Docks	d				22 04			22 19								22 52		23 19			
Cadoxton	d				22 07			22 22								22 55		23 22			
Dinas Powys	d				22 11			22 26								22 59		23 26			
Eastbrook	d				22 13			22 28								23 01		23 28			
Cogan	d				22 15			22 30								23 03		23 30			
Penarth	d						22 20							22 47			23 26				
Dingle Road	d						22 22							22 49			23 28				
Grangetown	d				22 19		22 26	22 34						22 53		23 07	23 32	23 34			
Cardiff Central	a				22 24		22 33	22 39						23 00		23 12	23 40	23 42			
	d				22 26		22 35	22 41		22 46				23 15		23 26					
Cardiff Bay	d	22 06		22 18		22 30			22 42		22 54	23 06			23 18				23 30	23 42	23 54
Cardiff Queen Street	a	22 10		22 22	22 29	22 34	22 38	22 44	22 46	22 49	22 58	23 10		23 18	23 22	23 29			23 34	23 46	23 58
	d				22 30		22 39	22 45		22 50				23 19		23 30					
Heath Low Level	d																				
Ty Glas	d																				
Birchgrove	d																				
Rhiwbina	d																				
Whitchurch (Cardiff)	d																				
Coryton	a																				
Heath High Level	d						22 44							23 24							
Llanishen	d						22 47							23 27							
Lisvane & Thornhill	d						22 49							23 29							
Caerphilly	d						22 55							23 35							
Aber	d						22 57							23 37							
Llanbradach	d						23 01							23 41							
Ystrad Mynach	d						23 06							23a50							
Hengoed	d						23 09														
Pengam	d						23 12														
Gilfach Fargoed	d						23 15														
Bargoed	a						23 19														
	d						23 20														
Brithdir	d						23 24														
Tir-phil	d						23 27														
Pontlottyn	d						23 31														
Rhymney	a						23 37														
Cathays	d				22 33			22 48		22 53						23 33					
Llandaf	d				22 37			22 52		22 57						23 37					
Ninian Park	d																				
Waun-gron Park	d																				
Fairwater	d																				
Danescourt	d																				
Radyr	a				22 40			22 55		22 59						23 40					
	d				22 40			22 55		22 59						23 40					
Taffs Well	d				22 44			22 59		23 03						23 44					
Trefforest Estate	d				22 48											23 48					
Trefforest	d				22 52			23 06		23 10						23 52					
Pontypridd	a				22 55			23 09		23 14						23 58					
	d				22 57			23 11		23 15											
Abercynon	d				23 04			23 19													
Penrhiwceiber	d							23 24													
Mountain Ash	a							23 28													
	d							23 33													
Fernhill	d							23 35													
Cwmbach	d							23 39													
Aberdare	a							23 46													
Quakers Yard	d				23 09																
Merthyr Vale	a				23 14																
	d				23 14																
Troed Y Rhiw	d				23 18																
Pentre-bach	d				23 21																
Merthyr Tydfil	a				23 29																
Trehafod	d									23 20											
Porth	a									23 23											
	d									23 24											
Dinas Rhondda	d									23 28											
Tonypandy	d									23 30											
Llwynypia	d									23 32											
Ystrad Rhondda	a									23 35											
	d									23 38											
Ton Pentre	d									23 40											
Treorchy	d									23 43											
Ynyswen	d									23 46											
Treherbert	a									23 52											

Table 130

Saturdays from 11 September

Bridgend, Barry Island, Barry, Penarth and Cardiff - Coryton. Rhymney, Pontypridd, Merthyr, Aberdare and Treherbert

		AW	AW	AW	AW	AW	AW	AW	AW	AW		AW	AW	AW	AW	AW A	AW	AW	AW	AW		AW	AW	AW	AW
Bridgend	d												05 42												
Llantwit Major	d												05 56												
Rhoose Cardiff Int Airport ✈	d												06 06												
Barry Island	d	22p44								05 52							06 25								
Barry	d	22p48								05 57			06 15				06 30								
Barry Docks	d	22p52								06 01			06 19				06 34								
Cadoxton	d	22p55								06 04			06 22				06 37								
Dinas Powys	d	22p59								06 08			06 26				06 41								
Eastbrook	d	23p01								06 10			06 28				06 43								
Cogan	d	23p03								06 12			06 30				06 45								
Penarth	d							06 02							06 32									07 02	
Dingle Road	d							06 04							06 34									07 04	
Grangetown	d	23p07						06 08		06 16			06 34		06 38		06 49							07 08	
Cardiff Central	a	23p12						06 13		06 21			06 39		06 44		06 54						07 04	07 14	
	d	23p26	05 26	05 46		05 56	06 11	06 15	06 19	06 26		06 36	06 41		06 46	06 51	06 56		07 06			07 11	07 06	07 16	
Cardiff Bay	d													06 42				06 54		07 06					07 18
Cardiff Queen Street	a	23p29	05 29	05 49		05 59	06 14	06 19	06 24	06 29		06 39	06 44	06 46	06 49	06 54	06 59	06 58	07 09	07 10		07 14		07 19	07 22
	d	23p30	05 30	05 50		06 00	06 15	06 20	06 25	06 30		06 40	06 45		06 50	06 55	07 00		07 10			07 15		07 20	
Heath Low Level	d								06 30							07 00									
Ty Glas	d								06 33							07 03									
Birchgrove	d								06 34							07 04									
Rhiwbina	d								06 36							07 06									
Whitchurch (Cardiff)	d								06 38							07 08									
Coryton	a								06 44							07 14									
Heath High Level	d			05 54				06 25							06 55									07 25	
Llanishen	d			05 57				06 28							06 58									07 28	
Lisvane & Thornhill	d			06 00				06 30							07 00									07 30	
Caerphilly	d			06a09				06 36							07 06									07 36	
Aber	d							06 38							07 08									07 38	
Llanbradach	d							06 42							07 12									07 42	
Ystrad Mynach	d							06 47							07 17									07 47	
Hengoed	d							06 50							07 20									07 50	
Pengam	d							06 53							07 23									07 53	
Gilfach Fargoed	d																								
Bargoed	a							07 02							07 32									08 02	
	d																								
Brithdir	d																								
Tir-phil	d																								
Pontlottyn	d																								
Rhymney	a																								
Cathays	d	23p33	05 33			06 03	06 18			06 33		06 43	06 48				07 03		07 13			07 18			
Llandaf	d	23p37	05 37			06 07	06 22			06 37		06 47	06 52				07 07		07 17			07 22			
Ninian Park	d																						07 10		
Waun-gron Park	d																						07 14		
Fairwater	d																						07 16		
Danescourt	d																						07 19		
Radyr	a	23p40	05 39			06 10	06 24			06 40		06 50	06 54				07 10		07 20			07 25	07 27		
	d	23p40	05 40			06 10	06 24			06 40		06 50	06 55				07 10		07 20			07 25			
Taffs Well	d	23p44	05 43			06 14	06 28			06 44		06 54	06 59				07 14		07 24			07 29			
Trefforest Estate	d	23p48	05 47			06 18				06 48							07 18								
Trefforest	d	23p52	05 52			06 22	06 35			06 52		07 01	07 06				07 22		07 31			07 36			
Pontypridd	a	00 01	05 55			06 25	06 38			06 55		07 04	07 09				07 25		07 34			07 39			
	d		05 57		06 11	06 27	06 41			06 57		07 06	07 11				07 27		07 36			07 41			
Abercynon	d		06 04		06 19	06 34	06 49			07 04			07 19				07 34					07 49			
Penrhiwceiber	d				06 24		06 55						07 25									07 55			
Mountain Ash	a				06 28		06 58						07 28									07 58			
	d				06 34		07 04						07 34									08 04			
Fernhill	d				06 37		07 07						07 37									08 07			
Cwmbach	d				06 41		07 11						07 41									08 11			
Aberdare	a				06 49		07 19						07 49									08 19			
Quakers Yard	d		06 09			06 39				07 09							07 39								
Merthyr Vale	a		06 14			06 44				07 14							07 44								
	d		06 17			06 47				07 17							07 47								
Troed Y Rhiw	d		06 21			06 51				07 21							07 51								
Pentre-bach	d		06 24			06 54				07 24							07 54								
Merthyr Tydfil	a		06 33			07 03				07 33							08 03								
Trehafod	d											07 11							07 41						
Porth	a											07 14							07 44						
	d											07 15							07 45						
Dinas Rhondda	d											07 19							07 49						
Tonypandy	d											07 21							07 51						
Llwynypia	d											07 23							07 53						
Ystrad Rhondda	a											07 26							07 56						
	d											07 29							07 59						
Ton Pentre	d											07 31							08 01						
Treorchy	d											07 34							08 04						
Ynyswen	d											07 37							08 07						
Treherbert	a											07 44							08 14						

A not 11 September

Table 130

Saturdays
from 11 September

Bridgend, Barry Island, Barry, Penarth and Cardiff - Coryton. Rhymney, Pontypridd, Merthyr, Aberdare and Treherbert

		AW	AW	AW	AW	AW		AW	AW	AW	AW	AW	AW	AW	AW	AW		AW	AW	AW	AW	AW	AW	AW	AW
Bridgend	d							06 42																	
Llantwit Major	d							06 56																	
Rhoose Cardiff Int Airport ✈	d							07 06																	
Barry Island	d	06 55										07 25						07 40			07 55				
Barry 3	d	07 00						07 15				07 30						07 45			08 00				
Barry Docks	d	07 04						07 19				07 34						07 49			08 04				
Cadoxton	d	07 07						07 22				07 37						07 52			08 07				
Dinas Powys	d	07 11						07 26				07 41						07 56			08 11				
Eastbrook	d	07 13						07 28				07 43						07 58			08 13				
Cogan	d	07 15						07 30				07 45						08 00			08 15				
Penarth	d		07 17						07 32			07 47						08 02			08 17				
Dingle Road	d		07 19						07 34			07 49						08 04			08 19				
Grangetown	d	07 19	07 23					07 34		07 38		07 49	07 53					08 04	08 08		08 19	08 23			
Cardiff Central 7	a	07 24	07 29		07 34			07 39		07 44		07 55	07 59	08 04				08 09	08 14		08 24	08 29		08 34	
	d	07 26	07 31		07 36	07 36		07 41		07 46		07 56	08 01	08 06	08 06			08 11	08 16		08 26	08 31		08 36	08 36
Cardiff Bay	d			07 30					07 42		07 54					08 06				08 18			08 30		
Cardiff Queen Street 3	a	07 29	07 34	07 34		07 39		07 44	07 46	07 49	07 58	07 59	08 04		08 09	08 10		08 14	08 19	08 22	08 29	08 34	08 34		08 39
	d	07 30	07 35			07 40		07 45		07 50		08 00	08 05		08 10			08 15	08 20		08 30	08 35			08 40
Heath Low Level	d																								
Ty Glas	d																								
Birchgrove	d																								
Rhiwbina	d																								
Whitchurch (Cardiff)	d																								
Coryton	a																								
Heath High Level	d		07 40						07 55			08 10						08 25			08 40				
Llanishen	d		07 43						07 58			08 13						08 28			08 43				
Lisvane & Thornhill	d		07 45						08 00			08 15						08 30			08 45				
Caerphilly 3	d		07 51						08 06			08 21						08 36			08 51				
Aber	d		07 53						08 08			08 23						08 38			08 53				
Llanbradach	d		07 57						08 12			08 27						08 42			08 57				
Ystrad Mynach 3	d		08 02						08 17			08 32						08 47			09 07				
Hengoed	d		08 05						08 20			08 35						08 50			09 10				
Pengam	d		08 08						08 23			08 38						08 53			09 13				
Gilfach Fargoed	d											08 41													
Bargoed	a		08 13						08 32			08 49						08 58			09 25				
	d		08 14															08 59							
Brithdir	d		08 18															09 03							
Tir-phil	d		08 21															09 06							
Pontlottyn	d		08 25															09 10							
Rhymney 3	a		08 28															09 17							
Cathays	d	07 33				07 43		07 48				08 03			08 13			08 18			08 33				08 43
Llandaf	d	07 37				07 47		07 52				08 07			08 17			08 22			08 37				08 47
Ninian Park	d				07 40									08 10										08 40	
Waun-gron Park	d				07 44									08 14										08 44	
Fairwater	d				07 46									08 16										08 46	
Danescourt	d				07 49									08 19										08 49	
Radyr 3	a	07 40			07 57	07 50		07 55				08 10		08 27	08 20			08 25			08 40			08 57	08 50
	d	07 40				07 50		07 55				08 10			08 20			08 25			08 40				08 50
Taffs Well 3	d	07 44				07 54		07 59				08 14			08 24			08 29			08 44				08 54
Trefforest Estate	d	07 48										08 18									08 48				
Trefforest	d	07 52				08 01		08 06				08 22			08 31			08 36			08 52				09 01
Pontypridd 3	a	07 55				08 04		08 09				08 25			08 34			08 39			08 55				09 04
	d	07 57				08 06		08 11				08 27			08 36			08 41			08 57				09 06
Abercynon	d	08 04						08 19				08 34						08 49			09 04				
Penrhiwceiber	d							08 25										08 55							
Mountain Ash	a							08 28										08 58							
	d							08 34										09 04							
Fernhill	d							08 37										09 07							
Cwmbach	d							08 41										09 11							
Aberdare 3	a							08 49										09 19							
Quakers Yard	d	08 09										08 39									09 09				
Merthyr Vale	a	08 14										08 44									09 14				
	d	08 17										08 47									09 17				
Troed Y Rhiw	d	08 21										08 51									09 21				
Pentre-bach	d	08 24										08 54									09 24				
Merthyr Tydfil	a	08 33										09 03									09 33				
Trehafod	d					08 11									08 41										09 11
Porth	a					08 14									08 44										09 14
	d					08 15									08 45										09 15
Dinas Rhondda	d					08 19									08 49										09 19
Tonypandy	d					08 21									08 51										09 21
Llwynypia	d					08 23									08 53										09 23
Ystrad Rhondda	a					08 26									08 56										09 26
	d					08 29									08 59										09 29
Ton Pentre	d					08 31									09 01										09 31
Treorchy	d					08 34									09 04										09 34
Ynyswen	d					08 37									09 07										09 37
Treherbert	a					08 44									09 14										09 44

Table 130

Saturdays
from 11 September

Bridgend, Barry Island, Barry, Penarth and Cardiff - Coryton. Rhymney, Pontypridd, Merthyr, Aberdare and Treherbert

		AW		AW	AW	AW	AW	AW	AW	AW	AW	AW		AW	AW	AW	AW	AW	AW	AW	AW	AW		AW	AW
Bridgend	d	07 42																			08 42				
Llantwit Major	d	07 56																			08 56				
Rhoose Cardiff Int Airport ✈	d	08 06																			09 06				
Barry Island	d					08 25						08 40				08 55									
Barry 3	d	08 15				08 30						08 45				09 00					09 15				
Barry Docks	d	08 19				08 34						08 49				09 04					09 19				
Cadoxton	d	08 22				08 37						08 52				09 07					09 22				
Dinas Powys	d	08 26				08 41						08 56				09 11					09 26				
Eastbrook	d	08 28				08 43						08 58				09 13					09 28				
Cogan	d	08 30				08 45						09 00				09 15					09 30				
Penarth	d				08 32			08 47									09 17							09 32	
Dingle Road	d				08 34			08 49									09 19							09 34	
Grangetown	d	08 34			08 38	08 49		08 53				09 04				09 19	09 23				09 34			09 38	
Cardiff Central 7	a	08 39			08 44	08 54		08 59	09 04			09 09				09 24	09 29		09 34		09 39			09 44	
	d	08 41			08 46	08 56		09 01	09 06	09 06		09 11		09 16		09 26	09 31		09 36	09 36	09 41			09 46	
Cardiff Bay	d			08 42			08 54				09 06				09 18			09 30				09 42			09 54
Cardiff Queen Street 3	a	08 44		08 46	08 49	08 59	08 58	09 04		09 09	09 10	09 14		09 19	09 22	09 29	09 34	09 34		09 39	09 44	09 46		09 49	09 58
	d	08 45			08 50	09 00		09 05		09 10		09 15		09 20		09 30	09 35			09 40	09 45			09 50	
Heath Low Level	d																								
Ty Glas	d																								
Birchgrove	d																								
Rhiwbina	d																								
Whitchurch (Cardiff)	d																								
Coryton	a																								
Heath High Level	d				08 55			09 10						09 25			09 40							09 55	
Llanishen	d				08 58			09 13						09 28			09 43							09 58	
Lisvane & Thornhill	d				09 00			09 15						09 30			09 45							10 00	
Caerphilly 3	d				09 06			09 21						09 36			09 51							10 06	
Aber	d				09 08			09 23						09 38			09 53							10 08	
Llanbradach	d				09 12			09 27						09 42			09 57							10 12	
Ystrad Mynach 3	d				09a22			09 32						09 47			10 07							10a22	
Hengoed	d							09 35						09 50			10 10								
Pengam	d							09 38						09 53			10 13								
Gilfach Fargoed	d							09 41																	
Bargoed	a							09 49						09 58			10 25								
	d													09 59											
Brithdir	d													10 03											
Tir-phil	d													10 06											
Pontlottyn	d													10 10											
Rhymney 3	a													10 17											
Cathays	d	08 48				09 03				09 13		09 18				09 33				09 43	09 48				
Llandaf	d	08 52				09 07				09 17		09 22				09 37				09 47	09 52				
Ninian Park	d								09 10										09 40						
Waun-gron Park	d								09 14										09 44						
Fairwater	d								09 16										09 46						
Danescourt	d								09 19										09 49						
Radyr 3	a	08 55				09 10			09 27	09 20		09 25				09 40			09 57	09 50	09 55				
	d	08 55				09 10				09 20		09 25				09 40				09 50	09 55				
Taffs Well 3	d	08 59				09 14				09 24		09 29				09 44				09 54	09 59				
Trefforest Estate	d					09 18										09 48									
Trefforest	d	09 06				09 22				09 31		09 36				09 52				10 01	10 06				
Pontypridd 3	a	09 09				09 25				09 34		09 39				09 55				10 04	10 09				
	d	09 11				09 27				09 36		09 41				09 57				10 06	10 11				
Abercynon	d	09 19				09 34						09 49				10 04					10 19				
Penrhiwceiber	d	09 25										09 55									10 25				
Mountain Ash	a	09 28										09 58									10 28				
	d	09 34										10 04									10 34				
Fernhill	d	09 37										10 07									10 37				
Cwmbach	d	09 41										10 11									10 41				
Aberdare 3	a	09 49										10 19									10 49				
Quakers Yard	d					09 39										10 09									
Merthyr Vale	a					09 44										10 14									
	d					09 47										10 17									
Troed Y Rhiw	d					09 51										10 21									
Pentre-bach	d					09 54										10 24									
Merthyr Tydfil	a					10 03										10 33									
Trehafod	d									09 41										10 11					
Porth	a									09 44										10 14					
	d									09 45										10 15					
Dinas Rhondda	d									09 49										10 19					
Tonypandy	d									09 51										10 21					
Llwynypia	d									09 53										10 23					
Ystrad Rhondda	a									09 56										10 26					
	d									09 59										10 29					
Ton Pentre	d									10 01										10 31					
Treorchy	d									10 04										10 34					
Ynyswen	d									10 07										10 37					
Treherbert	a									10 14										10 44					

Table 130

Saturdays from 11 September

Bridgend, Barry Island, Barry, Penarth and Cardiff - Coryton. Rhymney, Pontypridd, Merthyr, Aberdare and Treherbert

		AW	AW	AW	AW	AW	AW	AW	AW	AW	AW	AW	AW	AW	AW	AW	AW	AW	AW	AW	AW	AW	AW
Bridgend	d															09 42							
Llantwit Major	d															09 56							
Rhoose Cardiff Int Airport ✈	d															10 06							
Barry Island	d	09 25						09 40			09 55									10 25			
Barry ■	d	09 30						09 45			10 00					10 15				10 30			
Barry Docks	d	09 34						09 49			10 04					10 19				10 34			
Cadoxton	d	09 37						09 52			10 07					10 22				10 37			
Dinas Powys	d	09 41						09 56			10 11					10 26				10 41			
Eastbrook	d	09 43						09 58			10 13					10 28				10 43			
Cogan	d	09 45						10 00			10 15					10 30				10 45			
Penarth	d		09 47						10 02			10 17						10 32					10 47
Dingle Road	d		09 49						10 04			10 19						10 34					10 49
Grangetown	d	09 49	09 53					10 04	10 08		10 19	10 23				10 34		10 38		10 49			10 53
Cardiff Central ■	a	09 54	09 59	10 04				10 09	10 14		10 24	10 29			10 34	10 42		10 44		10 54			10 59
	d	09 56	10 01	10 06	10 06			10 11	10 16		10 26	10 31		10 36	10 36			10 46	10 51	10 56			11 01
Cardiff Bay	d					10 06				10 18			10 30				10 42					10 54	
Cardiff Queen Street ■	a	09 59	10 04		10 09	10 10		10 14	10 19	10 22	10 29	10 34	10 34	10 39			10 46	10 49		10 59		10 58	11 04
	d	10 00	10 05		10 10			10 15	10 20		10 30	10 35		10 40				10 50		11 00			11 05
Heath Low Level	d																						
Ty Glas	d																						
Birchgrove	d																						
Rhiwbina	d																						
Whitchurch (Cardiff)	d																						
Coryton	a																						
Heath High Level	d		10 10						10 25			10 40						10 55					11 10
Llanishen	d		10 13						10 28			10 43						10 58					11 13
Lisvane & Thornhill	d		10 15						10 30			10 45						11 00					11 15
Caerphilly ■	d		10 21						10 36			10 51						11 06					11 21
Aber	d		10 23						10 38			10 53						11 08					11 23
Llanbradach	d		10 27						10 42			10 57						11 12					11 27
Ystrad Mynach ■	d		10 32						10 47			11 07						11a22					11 32
Hengoed	d		10 35						10 50			11 10											11 35
Pengam	d		10 38						10 53			11 13											11 38
Gilfach Fargoed	d		10 41																				11 41
Bargoed	a		10 49						10 58			11 25											11 49
	d								10 59														
Brithdir	d								11 03														
Tir-phil	d								11 06														
Pontlottyn	d								11 10														
Rhymney ■	a								11 17														
Cathays	d	10 03			10 13			10 18			10 33			10 43						11 03			
Llandaf	d	10 07			10 17			10 22			10 37			10 47						11 07			
Ninian Park	d			10 10											10 40								
Waun-gron Park	d			10 14											10 44								
Fairwater	d			10 16											10 46								
Danescourt	d			10 19											10 49								
Radyr ■	a	10 10		10 27	10 20			10 25			10 40			10 50	10 57				11 02	11 10			
	d	10 10			10 20			10 25			10 40			10 50					11 20	11 10			
Taffs Well ■	d	10 14			10 24			10 29			10 44			10 54					11 24	11 14			
Trefforest Estate	d	10 18									10 48									11 18			
Trefforest	d	10 22			10 31			10 36			10 52			11 01					11 31	11 22	←		
Pontypridd ■	a	10 30			10 34			10 39			10 55			11 04					11 34	11 25	11 34		
	d				10 36		10 35	10 41			10 57			11 06					11 36	11 27	11 36		
Abercynon	d						10 41	10 49			11 04								→	11 34			
Penrhiwceiber	d							10 55															
Mountain Ash	a							10 58															
	d							11 04															
Fernhill	d							11 07															
Cwmbach	d							11 11															
Aberdare ■	a							11 19															
Quakers Yard	d						10 45				11 09									11 39			
Merthyr Vale	a						10 50				11 14									11 44			
	d						10 52				11 17									11 47			
Troed Y Rhiw	d						10 56				11 21									11 51			
Pentre-bach	d						10 59				11 24									11 54			
Merthyr Tydfil	a						11 08				11 33									12 03			
Trehafod	d				10 41									11 11							11 41		
Porth	a				10 44									11 14							11 44		
	d				10 45									11 15							11 45		
Dinas Rhondda	d				10 49									11 19							11 49		
Tonypandy	d				10 51									11 21							11 51		
Llwynypia	d				10 53									11 23							11 53		
Ystrad Rhondda	a				10 56									11 26							11 56		
	d				10 59									11 29							11 59		
Ton Pentre	d				11 01									11 31							12 01		
Treorchy	d				11 04									11 34							12 04		
Ynyswen	d				11 07									11 37							12 07		
Treherbert	a				11 14									11 44							12 14		

Table 130

Saturdays from 11 September

Bridgend, Barry Island, Barry, Penarth and Cardiff - Coryton. Rhymney, Pontypridd, Merthyr, Aberdare and Treherbert

		AW	AW	AW	AW	AW	AW	AW	AW	AW	AW	AW	AW	AW	AW	AW	AW	AW	AW	AW	AW	AW
Bridgend	d											10 42										
Llantwit Major	d											10 56										
Rhoose Cardiff Int Airport ✈	d											11 06										
Barry Island	d			10 40			10 55								11 25						11 40	
Barry ■	d			10 45			11 00					11 15			11 30						11 45	
Barry Docks	d			10 49			11 04					11 19			11 34						11 49	
Cadoxton	d			10 52			11 07					11 22			11 37						11 52	
Dinas Powys	d			10 56			11 11					11 26			11 41						11 56	
Eastbrook	d			10 58			11 13					11 28			11 43						11 58	
Cogan	d			11 00			11 15					11 30			11 45						12 00	
Penarth	d				11 02			11 17						11 32			11 47					12 02
Dingle Road	d				11 04			11 19						11 34			11 49					12 04
Grangetown	d			11 04	11 08		11 19	11 23				11 34		11 38	11 49		11 53				12 04	12 08
Cardiff Central ■	a	11 04		11 09	11 14		11 24	11 29		11 34		11 38		11 44	11 54		12 00	12 04			12 09	12 14
	d	11 06		11 11	11 16		11 26	11 31		11 36	11 36	11 40		11 46	11 56		12 01	12 06	12 06		12 11	12 16
Cardiff Bay	d		11 06			11 18			11 30				11 42			11 54				12 06		
Cardiff Queen Street ■	a		11 10	11 14	11 19	11 22	11 29	11 34	11 34		11 39	11 43	11 46	11 49	11 59	11 58	12 04		12 09	12 10	12 14	12 19
	d			11 15	11 20		11 30	11 35			11 40	11 44		11 50	12 00		12 05		12 10		12 15	12 20
Heath Low Level	d																					
Ty Glas	d																					
Birchgrove	d																					
Rhiwbina	d																					
Whitchurch (Cardiff)	d																					
Coryton	a																					
Heath High Level	d				11 25			11 40						11 55			12 10					12 25
Llanishen	d				11 28			11 43						11 58			12 13					12 28
Lisvane & Thornhill	d				11 30			11 45						12 00			12 15					12 30
Caerphilly ■	d				11 36			11 51						12 06			12 21					12 36
Aber	d				11 38			11 53						12 08			12 23					12 38
Llanbradach	d				11 42			11 57						12 12			12 27					12 42
Ystrad Mynach ■	d				11 47			12 07						12a22			12 32					12 47
Hengoed	d				11 50			12 10									12 35					12 50
Pengam	d				11 53			12 13									12 38					12 53
Gilfach Fargoed	d																12 41					
Bargoed	a				11 58			12 25									12 49					12 58
	d				11 59																	12 59
Brithdir	d				12 03																	13 03
Tir-phil	d				12 06																	13 06
Pontlottyn	d				12 10																	13 10
Rhymney ■	a				12 17																	13 17
Cathays	d			11 18			11 33				11 43	11 48			12 03				12 13		12 18	
Llandaf	d			11 22			11 37				11 47	11 52			12 07				12 17		12 22	
Ninian Park	d	11 10								11 40								12 10				
Waun-gron Park	d	11 14								11 44								12 14				
Fairwater	d	11 16								11 46								12 16				
Danescourt	d	11 19								11 49								12 19				
Radyr ■	a	11 27		11 25			11 40			11 57	11 50	11 54			12 10			12 27	12 20		12 25	
	d			11 25			11 40				11 50	11 55			12 10				12 20		12 25	
Taffs Well ■	d			11 29			11 44				11 54	11 59			12 14				12 24		12 29	
Trefforest Estate	d						11 48								12 18							
Trefforest	d			11 36			11 52				12 01	12 06			12 22				12 31		12 36	
Pontypridd ■	a			11 39			11 55				12 04	12 09			12 25				12 34		12 42	
	d			11 41			11 57				12 06	12 11			12 27				12 36			
Abercynon	d			11 49			12 04					12 19			12 34							
Penrhiwceiber	d			11 55								12 25										
Mountain Ash	a			11 58								12 28										
	d			12 04								12 34										
Fernhill	d			12 07								12 37										
Cwmbach	d			12 11								12 41										
Aberdare ■	a			12 19								12 49										
Quakers Yard	d						12 09								12 39							
Merthyr Vale	a						12 14								12 44							
	d						12 17								12 47							
Troed Y Rhiw	d						12 21								12 51							
Pentre-bach	d						12 24								12 54							
Merthyr Tydfil	a						12 33								13 03							
Trehafod	d										12 11								12 41			
Porth	a										12 14								12 44			
	d										12 15								12 45			
Dinas Rhondda	d										12 19								12 49			
Tonypandy	d										12 21								12 51			
Llwynypia	d										12 23								12 53			
Ystrad Rhondda	a										12 26								12 56			
	d										12 29								12 59			
Ton Pentre	d										12 31								13 01			
Treorchy	d										12 34								13 04			
Ynyswen	d										12 37								13 07			
Treherbert	a										12 43								13 14			

Table 130

Saturdays
from 11 September

Bridgend, Barry Island, Barry, Penarth and Cardiff - Coryton. Rhymney, Pontypridd, Merthyr, Aberdare and Treherbert

		AW	AW	AW	AW	AW	AW	AW	AW	AW		AW	AW	AW	AW	AW	AW	AW	AW	AW		AW	AW	AW	AW
Bridgend	d							11 42																	
Llantwit Major	d							11 56																	
Rhoose Cardiff Int Airport ✈	d							12 06																	
Barry Island	d		11 55									12 25						12 40				12 55			
Barry ■	d		12 00					12 15				12 30						12 45				13 00			
Barry Docks	d		12 04					12 19				12 34						12 49				13 04			
Cadoxton	d		12 07					12 22				12 37						12 52				13 07			
Dinas Powys	d		12 11					12 26				12 41						12 56				13 11			
Eastbrook	d		12 13					12 28				12 43						12 58				13 13			
Cogan	d		12 15					12 30				12 45						13 00				13 15			
Penarth	d			12 17						12 32				12 47					13 02				13 17		
Dingle Road	d			12 19						12 34				12 49					13 04				13 19		
Grangetown	d		12 19	12 23				12 34		12 38		12 49		12 53				13 04	13 08			13 19	13 23		
Cardiff Central ■	a		12 24	12 29		12 34		12 39		12 44		12 54		12 59	13 04			13 09	13 14			13 24	13 29		13 34
	d		12 26	12 31		12 36	12 36	12 41		12 46		12 56		13 01	13 06	13 06		13 11	13 16			13 26	13 31		13 36
Cardiff Bay	d	12 18			12 30				12 42				12 54				13 06			13 18				13 30	
Cardiff Queen Street ■	a	12 22	12 29	12 34	12 34		12 39	12 44	12 46	12 49		12 59	12 58	13 04		13 09	13 10	13 14	13 19	13 22		13 29	13 34	13 34	
	d		12 30	12 35			12 40	12 45		12 50		13 00		13 05		13 10		13 15	13 20			13 30	13 35		
Heath Low Level	d																								
Ty Glas	d																								
Birchgrove	d																								
Rhiwbina	d																								
Whitchurch (Cardiff)	d																								
Coryton	a																								
Heath High Level	d			12 40						12 55				13 10					13 25				13 40		
Llanishen	d			12 43						12 58				13 13					13 28				13 43		
Lisvane & Thornhill	d			12 45						13 00				13 15					13 30				13 45		
Caerphilly ■	d			12 51						13 06				13 21					13 36				13 51		
Aber	d			12 53						13 08				13 23					13 38				13 53		
Llanbradach	d			12 57						13 12				13 27					13 42				13 57		
Ystrad Mynach ■	d			13 07						13a22				13 32					13 47				14 07		
Hengoed	d			13 10										13 35					13 50				14 10		
Pengam	d			13 13										13 38					13 53				14 13		
Gilfach Fargoed	d													13 41											
Bargoed	a			13 25										13 49					13 58				14 25		
	d																		13 59						
Brithdir	d																		14 03						
Tir-phil	d																		14 06						
Pontlottyn	d																		14 10						
Rhymney ■	a																		14 17						
Cathays	d		12 33				12 43	12 48				13 03				13 13		13 18				13 33			
Llandaf	d		12 37				12 47	12 52				13 07				13 17		13 22				13 37			
Ninian Park	d					12 40									13 10										13 40
Waun-gron Park	d					12 44									13 14										13 44
Fairwater	d					12 46									13 16										13 46
Danescourt	d					12 49									13 19										13 49
Radyr ■	a		12 40			12 57	12 50	12 55				13 10			13 27	13 20		13 25				13 40			13 57
	d		12 40				12 50	12 55				13 10				13 20		13 25				13 40			
Taffs Well ■	d		12 44				12 54	12 59				13 14				13 24		13 29				13 44			
Trefforest Estate	d		12 48									13 18										13 48			
Trefforest	d		12 52				13 01	13 06				13 22				13 31		13 36				13 52			
Pontypridd ■	a		12 55				13 04	13 09				13 25				13 34		13 39				13 55			
	d		12 57				13 06	13 11				13 27				13 36		13 41				13 57			
Abercynon	d		13 04					13 19				13 34						13 49				14 04			
Penrhiwceiber	d							13 25										13 55							
Mountain Ash	a							13 28										13 58							
	d							13 34										14 04							
Fernhill	d							13 37										14 07							
Cwmbach	d							13 41										14 11							
Aberdare ■	a							13 49										14 19							
Quakers Yard	d		13 09									13 39										14 09			
Merthyr Vale	a		13 14									13 44										14 14			
	d		13 17									13 47										14 17			
Troed Y Rhiw	d		13 21									13 51										14 21			
Pentre-bach	d		13 24									13 54										14 24			
Merthyr Tydfil	a		13 33									14 03										14 33			
Trehafod	d						13 11									13 41									
Porth	a						13 14									13 44									
	d						13 15									13 45									
Dinas Rhondda	d						13 19									13 49									
Tonypandy	d						13 21									13 51									
Llwynypia	d						13 23									13 53									
Ystrad Rhondda	a						13 26									13 56									
	d						13 29									13 59									
Ton Pentre	d						13 31									14 01									
Treorchy	d						13 34									14 04									
Ynyswen	d						13 37									14 07									
Treherbert	a						13 44									14 14									

Table 130

Saturdays
from 11 September

Bridgend, Barry Island, Barry, Penarth and Cardiff - Coryton. Rhymney, Pontypridd, Merthyr, Aberdare and Treherbert

		AW	AW	AW	AW	AW		AW	AW	AW	AW	AW	AW	AW	AW	AW		AW	AW	AW	AW	AW	AW	AW	AW
Bridgend	d		12 42																			13 42			
Llantwit Major	d		12 56																			13 56			
Rhoose Cardiff Int Airport ✈	d		13 06																			14 06			
Barry Island	d					13 25							13 40			13 55									
Barry ■	d		13 15			13 30							13 45			14 00						14 15			
Barry Docks	d		13 19			13 34							13 49			14 04						14 19			
Cadoxton	d		13 22			13 37							13 52			14 07						14 22			
Dinas Powys	d		13 26			13 41							13 56			14 11						14 26			
Eastbrook	d		13 28			13 43							13 58			14 13						14 28			
Cogan	d		13 30			13 45							14 00			14 15						14 30			
Penarth	d				13 32				13 47					14 02				14 17						14 32	
Dingle Road	d				13 34				13 49					14 04				14 19						14 34	
Grangetown	d		13 34		13 38	13 49			13 53				14 04	14 08		14 19		14 23				14 34		14 38	
Cardiff Central ■	a		13 39		13 44	13 54			13 59	14 04			14 09	14 14		14 24		14 29		14 34		14 39		14 44	
	d	13 36	13 41		13 46	13 56			14 01	14 06	14 06		14 11	14 16		14 26		14 31		14 36	14 36	14 41		14 46	14 51
Cardiff Bay	d			13 42				13 54				14 06			14 18				14 30				14 42		
Cardiff Queen Street ■	a	13 39	13 44	13 46	13 49	13 59		13 58	14 04		14 09	14 10	14 14	14 19	14 22	14 29		14 34	14 34		14 39	14 44	14 46	14 49	
	d	13 40	13 45		13 50	14 00			14 05		14 10		14 15	14 20		14 30		14 35			14 40	14 45		14 50	
Heath Low Level	d																								
Ty Glas	d																								
Birchgrove	d																								
Rhiwbina	d																								
Whitchurch (Cardiff)	d																								
Coryton	a																								
Heath High Level	d				13 55				14 10					14 25				14 40						14 55	
Llanishen	d				13 58				14 13					14 28				14 43						14 58	
Lisvane & Thornhill	d				14 00				14 15					14 30				14 45						15 00	
Caerphilly ■	d				14 06				14 21					14 36				14 51						15 06	
Aber	d				14 08				14 23					14 38				14 53						15 08	
Llanbradach	d				14 12				14 27					14 42				14 57						15 12	
Ystrad Mynach ■	d				14a22				14 32					14 47				15 07						15a22	
Hengoed	d								14 35					14 50				15 10							
Pengam	d								14 38					14 53				15 13							
Gilfach Fargoed	d								14 41																
Bargoed	a								14 49					14 58				15 25							
	d													14 59											
Brithdir	d													15 03											
Tir-phil	d													15 06											
Pontlottyn	d													15 10											
Rhymney ■	a													15 17											
Cathays	d	13 43	13 48			14 03					14 13		14 18			14 33					14 43	14 48			
Llandaf	d	13 47	13 52			14 07					14 17		14 22			14 37					14 47	14 52			
Ninian Park	d									14 10										14 40					
Waun-gron Park	d									14 14										14 44					
Fairwater	d									14 16										14 46					
Danescourt	d									14 19										14 49					
Radyr ■	a	13 50	13 55			14 10				14 27	14 20		14 25			14 40				14 57	14 50	14 55			15 08
	d	13 50	13 55			14 10					14 20		14 25			14 40					14 50	14 55			15 20
Taffs Well ■	d	13 54	13 59			14 14					14 24		14 29			14 44					14 54	14 59			15 24
Trefforest Estate	d					14 18										14 48									
Trefforest	d	14 01	14 06			14 22					14 31		14 36			14 52					15 01	15 06			15 31
Pontypridd ■	a	14 04	14 09			14 25					14 34		14 39			14 55					15 04	15 09			15 34
	d	14 06	14 11			14 27					14 36		14 41			14 57					15 06	15 11			15 36
Abercynon	d		14 19			14 34							14 49			15 04						15 19			→
Penrhiwceiber	d		14 25										14 55									15 25			
Mountain Ash	a		14 28										14 58									15 28			
	d		14 34										15 04									15 34			
Fernhill	d		14 37										15 07									15 37			
Cwmbach	d		14 41										15 11									15 41			
Aberdare ■	a		14 49										15 19									15 49			
Quakers Yard	d					14 39										15 09									
Merthyr Vale	a					14 44										15 14									
	d					14 47										15 17									
Troed Y Rhiw	d					14 51										15 21									
Pentre-bach	d					14 54										15 24									
Merthyr Tydfil	a					15 03										15 33									
Trehafod	d	14 11									14 41										15 11				
Porth	a	14 14									14 44										15 14				
	d	14 15									14 45										15 15				
Dinas Rhondda	d	14 19									14 49										15 19				
Tonypandy	d	14 21									14 51										15 21				
Llwynypia	d	14 23									14 53										15 23				
Ystrad Rhondda	a	14 26									14 56										15 26				
	d	14 29									14 59										15 29				
Ton Pentre	d	14 31									15 01										15 31				
Treorchy	d	14 34									15 04										15 34				
Ynyswen	d	14 37									15 07										15 37				
Treherbert	a	14 44									15 14										15 44				

Table 130

Saturdays
from 11 September

Bridgend, Barry Island, Barry, Penarth and Cardiff - Coryton. Rhymney, Pontypridd, Merthyr, Aberdare and Treherbert

		AW		AW	AW	AW	AW	AW	AW	AW	AW	AW		AW	AW	AW	AW	AW	AW	AW	AW	AW		AW	AW
Bridgend	d																	14 42							
Llantwit Major	d																	14 56							
Rhoose Cardiff Int Airport ✈	d																	15 06							
Barry Island	d	14 25							14 40			14 55									15 25				
Barry	d	14 30							14 45			15 00						15 15			15 30				
Barry Docks	d	14 34							14 49			15 04						15 19			15 34				
Cadoxton	d	14 37							14 52			15 07						15 22			15 37				
Dinas Powys	d	14 41							14 56			15 11						15 26			15 41				
Eastbrook	d	14 43							14 58			15 13						15 28			15 43				
Cogan	d	14 45							15 00			15 15						15 30			15 45				
Penarth	d					14 47				15 02				15 17						15 32				15 47	
Dingle Road	d					14 49				15 04				15 19						15 34				15 49	
Grangetown	d	14 49				14 53			15 04	15 08		15 19		15 23				15 34		15 38	15 49			15 53	
Cardiff Central	a	14 54				14 59	15 04		15 09	15 14		15 24		15 29		15 34		15 39		15 44	15 54			15 59	16 05
	d	14 56				15 01	15 06		15 11	15 16		15 26		15 31		15 36	15 36	15 41		15 46	15 56			16 01	16 06
Cardiff Bay	d				14 54			15 06			15 18				15 30				15 42			15 54			
Cardiff Queen Street	a	14 59			14 58	15 04		15 10	15 14	15 19	15 22	15 29		15 34	15 34		15 39	15 44	15 46	15 49	15 59	15 58		16 04	
	d	15 00				15 05			15 15	15 20		15 30		15 35			15 40	15 45		15 50	16 00			16 05	
Heath Low Level	d																								
Ty Glas	d																								
Birchgrove	d																								
Rhiwbina	d																								
Whitchurch (Cardiff)	d																								
Coryton	a																								
Heath High Level	d					15 10				15 25				15 40						15 55				16 10	
Llanishen	d					15 13				15 28				15 43						15 58				16 13	
Lisvane & Thornhill	d					15 15				15 30				15 45						16 00				16 15	
Caerphilly	d					15 21				15 36				15 51						16 06				16 21	
Aber	d					15 23				15 38				15 53						16 08				16 23	
Llanbradach	d					15 27				15 42				15 57						16 12				16 27	
Ystrad Mynach	d					15 32				15 47				16 02						16 17				16 32	
Hengoed	d					15 35				15 50				16 05						16 20				16 35	
Pengam	d					15 38				15 53				16 08						16 23				16 38	
Gilfach Fargoed	d					15 41																		16 41	
Bargoed	a					15 49				15 58				16 17						16 32				16 49	
	d									15 59															
Brithdir	d									16 03															
Tir-phil	d									16 06															
Pontlottyn	d									16 10															
Rhymney	a									16 17															
Cathays	d	15 03							15 18			15 33					15 43	15 48			16 03				
Llandaf	d	15 07							15 22			15 37					15 47	15 52			16 07				
Ninian Park	d						15 10									15 40									16 10
Waun-gron Park	d						15 14									15 44									16 13
Fairwater	d						15 16									15 46									16 15
Danescourt	d						15 19									15 49									16 17
Radyr	a	15 10					15 27		15 25			15 40				15 57	15 50	15 55			16 10				16 27
	d	15 10							15 25			15 40					15 50	15 55			16 10				
Taffs Well	d	15 14							15 29			15 44					15 54	15 59			16 14				
Trefforest Estate	d	15 18										15 48									16 18				
Treforest	d	15 22		←					15 36			15 52					16 01	16 06			16 22				
Pontypridd	a	15 25		15 34					15 39			15 55					16 04	16 09			16 25				
	d	15 27		15 36					15 41			15 57					16 06	16 11			16 27				
Abercynon	d	15 34							15 49			16 04						16 19			16 34				
Penrhiwceiber	d								15 55									16 25							
Mountain Ash	a								15 58									16 28							
	d								16 04									16 34							
Fernhill	d								16 07									16 37							
Cwmbach	d								16 11									16 41							
Aberdare	a								16 19									16 49							
Quakers Yard	d	15 39										16 09									16 39				
Merthyr Vale	a	15 44										16 14									16 44				
	d	15 47										16 17									16 47				
Troed Y Rhiw	d	15 51										16 21									16 51				
Pentre-bach	d	15 54										16 24									16 54				
Merthyr Tydfil	a	16 03										16 33									17 03				
Trehafod	d			15 41													16 11								
Porth	a			15 44													16 14								
	d			15 45													16 15								
Dinas Rhondda	d			15 49													16 19								
Tonypandy	d			15 51													16 21								
Llwynypia	d			15 53													16 23								
Ystrad Rhondda	a			15 56													16 26								
	d			15 59													16 29								
Ton Pentre	d			16 01													16 31								
Treorchy	d			16 04													16 34								
Ynyswen	d			16 07													16 37								
Treherbert	a			16 14													16 44								

Table 130

Saturdays
from 11 September

Bridgend, Barry Island, Barry, Penarth and Cardiff - Coryton. Rhymney, Pontypridd, Merthyr, Aberdare and Treherbert

		AW	AW	AW	AW	AW	AW	AW		AW	AW	AW	AW	AW	AW	AW	AW	AW		AW	AW	AW	AW	AW	AW
Bridgend	d												15 42												
Llantwit Major	d												15 56												
Rhoose Cardiff Int Airport ✈	d												16 06												
Barry Island	d			15 40			15 55									16 25							16 40		
Barry	d			15 45			16 00						16 15			16 30							16 45		
Barry Docks	d			15 49			16 04						16 19			16 34							16 49		
Cadoxton	d			15 52			16 07						16 22			16 37							16 52		
Dinas Powys	d			15 56			16 11						16 26			16 41							16 56		
Eastbrook	d			15 58			16 13						16 28			16 43							16 58		
Cogan	d			16 00			16 15						16 30			16 45							17 00		
Penarth	d				16 02			16 17							16 32									17 02	
Dingle Road	d				16 04			16 19							16 34									17 04	
Grangetown	d			16 04	16 08		16 19	16 23					16 34		16 38	16 49							17 04	17 08	
Cardiff Central	a			16 09	16 14		16 24	16 29			16 34		16 39		16 44	16 54				17 05			17 09	17 14	
	d	16 06		16 11	16 16		16 26	16 31			16 36	16 36	16 41		16 46	16 56		17 01		17 06	17 06		17 11	17 16	
Cardiff Bay	d		16 06			16 18				16 30				16 42			16 54					17 06			17 18
Cardiff Queen Street	a	16 09	16 10	16 14	16 19	16 22	16 29	16 34		16 34		16 39	16 44	16 46	16 49	16 59	16 58	17 04			17 09	17 10	17 14	17 19	17 22
	d	16 10		16 15	16 20		16 30	16 35				16 40	16 45		16 50	17 00		17 05			17 10		17 15	17 20	
Heath Low Level	d																								
Ty Glas	d																								
Birchgrove	d																								
Rhiwbina	d																								
Whitchurch (Cardiff)	d																								
Coryton	a																								
Heath High Level	d				16 25			16 40							16 55			17 10						17 25	
Llanishen	d				16 28			16 43							16 58			17 13						17 28	
Lisvane & Thornhill	d				16 30			16 45							17 00			17 15						17 30	
Caerphilly	d				16 36			16 51							17 06			17 21						17 36	
Aber	d				16 38			16 53							17 08			17 23						17 38	
Llanbradach	d				16 42			16 57							17 12			17 27						17 42	
Ystrad Mynach	d				16 47			17 02							17 17			17 33						17 47	
Hengoed	d				16 50			17 05							17 20			17 35						17 50	
Pengam	d				16 53			17 08							17 23			17 39						17 53	
Gilfach Fargoed	d																	17 42							
Bargoed	a				16 58			17 17							17 32			17 45						18 02	
	d				16 59													17 47							
Brithdir	d				17 03													17 50							
Tir-phil	d				17 06													17 53							
Pontlottyn	d				17 10													17 58							
Rhymney	a				17 17													18 05							
Cathays	d	16 13		16 18			16 33					16 43	16 48			17 03					17 13		17 18		
Llandaf	d	16 17		16 22			16 37					16 47	16 52			17 07					17 17		17 22		
Ninian Park	d										16 40									17 10					
Waun-gron Park	d										16 44									17 14					
Fairwater	d										16 46									17 16					
Danescourt	d										16 49									17 19					
Radyr	a	16 20		16 25			16 40				16 57	16 50	16 55			17 10				17 27	17 20		17 25		
	d	16 20		16 25			16 40					16 50	16 55			17 10					17 20		17 25		
Taffs Well	d	16 24		16 29			16 44					16 54	16 59			17 14					17 24		17 29		
Trefforest Estate	d						16 48									17 18									
Treforest	d	16 31		16 36			16 52					17 01	17 06			17 22					17 31		17 36		
Pontypridd	a	16 34		16 39			16 55					17 04	17 09			17 25					17 34		17 39		
	d	16 36		16 41			16 57					17 06	17 11			17 27					17 36		17 41		
Abercynon	d			16 49			17 04						17 19			17 34							17 49		
Penrhiwceiber	d			16 55									17 25										17 55		
Mountain Ash	a			16 58									17 28										17 58		
	d			17 04									17 34										18 04		
Fernhill	d			17 07									17 37										18 07		
Cwmbach	d			17 11									17 41										18 11		
Aberdare	a			17 19									17 49										18 19		
Quakers Yard	d						17 09									17 39									
Merthyr Vale	a						17 14									17 44									
	d						17 17									17 47									
Troed Y Rhiw	d						17 21									17 51									
Pentre-bach	d						17 24									17 54									
Merthyr Tydfil	a						17 33									18 03									
Trehafod	d	16 41										17 11									17 41				
Porth	a	16 44										17 14									17 44				
	d	16 45										17 15									17 45				
Dinas Rhondda	d	16 49										17 19									17 49				
Tonypandy	d	16 51										17 21									17 51				
Llwynypia	d	16 53										17 23									17 53				
Ystrad Rhondda	a	16 56										17 26									17 56				
	d	16 59										17 29									17 59				
Ton Pentre	d	17 01										17 31									18 01				
Treorchy	d	17 04										17 34									18 04				
Ynyswen	d	17 07										17 37									18 07				
Treherbert	a	17 14										17 44									18 14				

Table 130

Saturdays
from 11 September

Bridgend, Barry Island, Barry, Penarth and Cardiff - Coryton. Rhymney, Pontypridd, Merthyr, Aberdare and Treherbert

Station		AW	AW	AW	AW	AW	AW	AW	AW	AW	AW	AW	AW	AW	AW	AW	AW	AW	AW	AW	AW	AW
Bridgend	d						16 42															
Llantwit Major	d						16 56															
Rhoose Cardiff Int Airport ✈	d						17 06															
Barry Island	d	16 55								17 25						17 40			17 55			
Barry 3	d	17 00					17 15			17 30						17 45			18 00			
Barry Docks	d	17 04					17 19			17 34						17 49			18 04			
Cadoxton	d	17 07					17 22			17 37						17 52			18 07			
Dinas Powys	d	17 11					17 26			17 41						17 56			18 11			
Eastbrook	d	17 13					17 28			17 43						17 58			18 13			
Cogan	d	17 15					17 30			17 45						18 00			18 15			
Penarth	d		17 17						17 32			17 47					18 02			18 17		
Dingle Road	d		17 19						17 34			17 49					18 04			18 19		
Grangetown	d	17 19	17 23				17 34		17 38	17 49		17 53				18 04	18 08		18 19	18 23		
Cardiff Central 7	a	17 24	17 29		17 34		17 39		17 44	17 54		17 59	18 05			18 10	18 14		18 24	18 29		
	d	17 26	17 31		17 36	17 36	17 41		17 46	17 56		18 01	18 06	18 06		18 11	18 16		18 26	18 31		18 36
Cardiff Bay	d			17 30				17 42			17 54				18 06			18 18			18 30	
Cardiff Queen Street 3	a	17 29	17 34	17 34		17 39	17 44	17 46	17 49	17 59	17 58	18 04		18 09	18 10	18 14	18 19	18 22	18 29	18 34	18 34	18 38
	d	17 30	17 35			17 40	17 45		17 50	18 00		18 05		18 10		18 15	18 20		18 30	18 35		18 40
Heath Low Level	d																					
Ty Glas	d																					
Birchgrove	d																					
Rhiwbina	d																					
Whitchurch (Cardiff)	d																					
Coryton	a																					
Heath High Level	d		17 40						17 55			18 10					18 25			18 40		
Llanishen	d		17 43						17 59			18 13					18 28			18 43		
Lisvane & Thornhill	d		17 45						18 02			18 15					18 30			18 45		
Caerphilly 3	d		17 51						18 07			18 21					18 36			18 51		
Aber	d		17 53						18 10			18 23					18 38			18 53		
Llanbradach	d		17 57						18 14			18 27					18 42			18 57		
Ystrad Mynach 3	d		18 02						18 20			18 32					18a52			19 02		
Hengoed	d		18 05						18 23			18 35								19 05		
Pengam	d		18 08						18 27			18 38								19 08		
Gilfach Fargoed	d		18 11						18 30			18 41								19 11		
Bargoed	a		18 14						18 34			18 49								19 14		
	d		18 16						18 44											19 16		
Brithdir	d		18 20						18 48											19 20		
Tir-phil	d		18 23						18 51											19 23		
Pontlottyn	d		18 27						18 55											19 27		
Rhymney 3	a		18 34						19 02											19 34		
Cathays	d	17 33				17 43	17 48			18 03				18 13		18 18			18 33			18 43
Llandaf	d	17 37				17 47	17 52			18 07				18 17		18 22			18 37			18 47
Ninian Park	d				17 40								18 10									
Waun-gron Park	d				17 44								18 14									
Fairwater	d				17 46								18 16									
Danescourt	d				17 49								18 19									
Radyr 3	a	17 40			17 57	17 50	17 55			18 10			18 27	18 20		18 25			18 40			18 50
	d	17 40				17 50	17 55			18 10				18 20		18 25			18 40			18 50
Taffs Well 3	d	17 44				17 54	17 59			18 14				18 24		18 29			18 44			18 54
Trefforest Estate	d	17 48								18 18									18 48			
Trefforest	d	17 52				18 01	18 06			18 22				18 31		18 36			18 52			19 01
Pontypridd 3	a	17 55				18 04	18 09			18 25				18 34		18 42			18 55			19 04
	d	17 57				18 06	18 11			18 27				18 36					18 57			19 06
Abercynon	d	18 04					18 19			18 34									19 04			
Penrhiwceiber	d						18 25															
Mountain Ash	a						18 28															
	d						18 34															
Fernhill	d						18 37															
Cwmbach	d						18 41															
Aberdare 3	a						18 49															
Quakers Yard	d	18 09								18 39									19 09			
Merthyr Vale	a	18 14								18 44									19 14			
	d	18 17								18 47									19 17			
Troed Y Rhiw	d	18 21								18 51									19 21			
Pentre-bach	d	18 24								18 54									19 24			
Merthyr Tydfil	a	18 33								19 03									19 33			
Trehafod	d					18 11								18 41								19 11
Porth	a					18 14								18 44								19 14
	d					18 15								18 45								19 15
Dinas Rhondda	d					18 19								18 49								19 19
Tonypandy	d					18 21								18 51								19 21
Llwynypia	d					18 23								18 53								19 23
Ystrad Rhondda	a					18 26								18 56								19 26
	d					18 29								18 59								19 29
Ton Pentre	d					18 31								19 01								19 31
Treorchy	d					18 34								19 04								19 34
Ynyswen	d					18 37								19 07								19 37
Treherbert	a					18 44								19 14								19 44

Table 130

Saturdays
from 11 September

Bridgend, Barry Island, Barry, Penarth and Cardiff - Coryton. Rhymney, Pontypridd, Merthyr, Aberdare and Treherbert

Station		AW	AW	AW A	AW B	AW	AW	AW	AW	AW	AW	AW	AW	AW	AW	AW	AW	AW	AW	AW B	AW	AW	AW
Bridgend	d		17 42															18 42					
Llantwit Major	d		17 56															18 56					
Rhoose Cardiff Int Airport ✈	d		18 06															19 06					
Barry Island	d					18 25						18 40		18 55								19 25	
Barry 3	d		18 15			18 30						18 45		19 00				19 15				19 30	
Barry Docks	d		18 19			18 34						18 49		19 04				19 19				19 34	
Cadoxton	d		18 22			18 37						18 52		19 07				19 22				19 37	
Dinas Powys	d		18 26			18 41						18 56		19 11				19 26				19 41	
Eastbrook	d		18 28			18 43						18 58		19 13				19 28				19 43	
Cogan	d		18 30			18 45						19 00		19 15				19 30				19 45	
Penarth	d			18 32	18 32				18 47						19 17								19 47
Dingle Road	d			18 34	18 34				18 49						19 19								19 49
Grangetown	d		18 34	18 38	18 38	18 49			18 53			19 04		19 19	19 23			19 34				19 49	19 54
Cardiff Central 7	a	18 34	18 39	18 45	18 47	18 55			18 59			19 09		19 24	19 29		19 34	19 39				19 56	19 59
	d	18 36	18 41						19 01	19 06		19 11		19 26	19 31		19 36	19 41		19 51		20 01	20 06
Cardiff Bay	d						18 42	13 54			19 06		19 18			19 30			19 42		19 54		
Cardiff Queen Street 3	a		18 44				18 46	13 58	19 04	19 09	19 10	19 14	19 22	19 29	19 34	19 34		19 44	19 46	19 54	19 58	20 04	20 09
	d		18 50						19 05	19 10		19 15		19 30	19 35			19 45		19 55		20 06	20 10
Heath Low Level	d																			20 00			
Ty Glas	d																			20 03			
Birchgrove	d																			20 04			
Rhiwbina	d																			20 06			
Whitchurch (Cardiff)	d																			20 08			
Coryton	a																			20 14			
Heath High Level	d								19 10						19 40							20 10	
Llanishen	d								19 13						19 43							20 13	
Lisvane & Thornhill	d								19 15						19 45							20 16	
Caerphilly 3	d								19a24						19 51							20a28	
Aber	d														19 53								
Llanbradach	d														19 57								
Ystrad Mynach 3	d														20 02								
Hengoed	d														20 05								
Pengam	d														20 08								
Gilfach Fargoed	d														20 11								
Bargoed	a														20 15								
	d														20 16								
Brithdir	d														20 20								
Tir-phil	d														20 23								
Pontlottyn	d														20 27								
Rhymney 3	a														20 34								
Cathays	d		18 52							19 13		19 18		19 33				19 48					20 13
Llandaf	d		18 56							19 17		19 22		19 37				19 52					20 17
Ninian Park	d	18 40															19 40						
Waun-gron Park	d	18 44															19 44						
Fairwater	d	18 46															19 46						
Danescourt	d	18 49															19 49						
Radyr 3	a	18 57	18 58							19 20		19 25		19 40			19 57	19 55					20 20
	d		18 58							19 20		19 25		19 40				19 55					20 20
Taffs Well 3	d		19 03							19 24		19 29		19 44				19 59					20 24
Trefforest Estate	d													19 48									
Trefforest	d		19 10							19 31		19 36		19 52				20 06					20 31
Pontypridd 3	a		19 13							19 34		19 39		19 55				20 09					20 35
	d		19 14							19 36		19 41		19 57				20 11					20 36
Abercynon	d		19 21									19 49		20 04				20 21					
Penrhiwceiber	d		19 27									19 55						20 27					
Mountain Ash	a		19 30									19 58						20 31					
	d		19 34									20 04						20 34					
Fernhill	d		19 37									20 07						20 37					
Cwmbach	d		19 41									20 11						20 41					
Aberdare 3	a		19 49									20 19						20 49					
Quakers Yard	d													20 09									
Merthyr Vale	a													20 14									
	d													20 14									
Troed Y Rhiw	d													20 18									
Pentre-bach	d													20 22									
Merthyr Tydfil	a													20 31									
Trehafod	d									19 41													20 41
Porth	a									19 44													20 44
	d									19 45													20 45
Dinas Rhondda	d									19 49													20 49
Tonypandy	d									19 51													20 51
Llwynypia	d									19 53													20 53
Ystrad Rhondda	a									19 56													20 56
	d									19 59													20 59
Ton Pentre	d									20 01													21 01
Treorchy	d									20 04													21 04
Ynyswen	d									20 07													21 07
Treherbert	a									20 14													21 14

A 11 September

B rot 11 September

Table 130

Saturdays
from 11 September

Bridgend, Barry Island, Barry, Penarth and Cardiff - Coryton. Rhymney, Pontypridd, Merthyr, Aberdare and Treherbert

		AW	AW	AW	AW	AW		AW	AW	AW	AW	AW	AW	AW	AW	AW		AW	AW	AW	AW	AW	AW	AW	AW
Bridgend	d								19 42													20 42		
Llantwit Major	d								19 56													20 56		
Rhoose Cardiff Int Airport ✈	d								20 06													21 06		
Barry Island	d			19 55														20 55							
Barry 3	d			20 00					20 15									21 00					21 15		
Barry Docks	d			20 04					20 19									21 04					21 19		
Cadoxton	d			20 07					20 22									21 07					21 22		
Dinas Powys	d			20 11					20 26									21 11					21 26		
Eastbrook	d			20 13					20 28									21 13					21 28		
Cogan	d			20 15					20 30									21 15					21 30		
Penarth	d					20 19							20 47									21 20			
Dingle Road	d					20 21							20 49									21 22			
Grangetown	d			20 19		20 25			20 34				20 53					21 19				21 26	21 34		
Cardiff Central 7	a			20 24		20 31		20 34	20 39				20 59					21 24			21 34	21 37	21 39		
	d			20 26		20 31		20 36	20 41		20 51		21 01	21 06				21 26		21 31	21 36		21 41		
Cardiff Bay	d	20 06	20 18		20 30					20 42		20 54			21 06	21 18			21 30					21 42	21 54
Cardiff Queen Street 3	a	20 10	20 22	20 29	20 34	20 35			20 44	20 46	20 54	20 58	21 04	21 09	21 10	21 22		21 29	21 34	21 34			21 44	21 46	21 58
	d			20 30		20 36			20 45		20 55		21 05	21 10				21 30		21 35			21 45		
Heath Low Level	d										21 00														
Ty Glas	d										21 03														
Birchgrove	d										21 04														
Rhiwbina	d										21 06														
Whitchurch (Cardiff)	d										21 08														
Coryton	a										21 14														
Heath High Level	d					20 41							21 10							21 40					
Llanishen	d					20 44							21 13							21 43					
Lisvane & Thornhill	d					20 46							21 15							21 45					
Caerphilly 3	d					20 52							21a34							21 51					
Aber	d					20 54														21 53					
Llanbradach	d					20 58														21 57					
Ystrad Mynach 3	d					21 03														22 02					
Hengoed	d					21 06														22 05					
Pengam	d					21 09														22 08					
Gilfach Fargoed	d					21 12														22 11					
Bargoed	a					21 16														22 15					
	d					21 17														22 16					
Brithdir	d					21 21														22 20					
Tir-phil	d					21 24														22 23					
Pontlottyn	d					21 28														22 27					
Rhymney 3	a					21 35														22 34					
Cathays	d			20 33					20 48					21 13				21 33					21 48		
Llandaf	d			20 37					20 52					21 17				21 37					21 52		
Ninian Park	d							20 40													21 40				
Waun-gron Park	d							20 44													21 44				
Fairwater	d							20 46													21 46				
Danescourt	d							20 49													21 49				
Radyr 3	a			20 40				20 57	20 55					21 20				21 40			21 57		21 55		
	d			20 40					20 55					21 20				21 40					21 55		
Taffs Well 3	d			20 44					20 59					21 24				21 44					21 59		
Trefforest Estate	d			20 48														21 48							
Trefforest	d			20 52					21 06					21 31				21 52					22 06		
Pontypridd 3	a			20 55					21 09					21 34				21 55					22 09		
	d			20 57					21 11					21 36				21 57					22 11		
Abercynon	d			21 04					21 19									22 04					22 19		
Penrhiwceiber	d								21 25														22 25		
Mountain Ash	a								21 28														22 28		
	d								21 29														22 29		
Fernhill	d								21 32														22 32		
Cwmbach	d								21 36														22 36		
Aberdare 3	a								21 44														22 44		
Quakers Yard	d			21 09														22 09							
Merthyr Vale	a			21 14														22 14							
	d			21 14														22 14							
Troed Y Rhiw	d			21 18														22 18							
Pentre-bach	d			21 22														22 22							
Merthyr Tydfil	a			21 31														22 31							
Trehafod	d													21 41											
Porth	a													21 44											
	d													21 45											
Dinas Rhondda	d													21 49											
Tonypandy	d													21 51											
Llwynypia	d													21 53											
Ystrad Rhondda	a													21 56											
	d													21 59											
Ton Pentre	d													22 01											
Treorchy	d													22 04											
Ynyswen	d													22 07											
Treherbert	a													22 14											

Table 130

Saturdays
from 11 September

Bridgend, Barry Island, Barry, Penarth and Cardiff - Coryton. Rhymney, Pontypridd, Merthyr, Aberdare and Treherbert

		AW		AW	AW	AW	AW	AW	AW	AW	AW	AW		AW	AW	AW	AW	AW	AW	AW	AW	AW		AW	
Bridgend	d									21 42										22 42					
Llantwit Major	d									21 56										22 56					
Rhoose Cardiff Int Airport ✈	d									22 06										23 06					
Barry Island	d						21 55											22 44							
Barry 3	d						22 00			22 15								22 48		23 15					
Barry Docks	d						22 04			22 19								22 52		23 19					
Cadoxton	d						22 07			22 22								22 55		23 22					
Dinas Powys	d						22 11			22 26								22 59		23 26					
Eastbrook	d						22 13			22 28								23 01		23 28					
Cogan	d						22 15			22 30								23 03		23 30					
Penarth	d	21 47							22 20							22 47			23 26						
Dingle Road	d	21 49							22 22							22 49			23 28						
Grangetown	d	21 53					22 19		22 26	22 34						22 53		23 07	23 32	23 34					
Cardiff Central 7	a	21 59					22 24		22 33	22 39						23 00		23 12	23 40	23 42					
	d	22 01		22 06			22 26		22 35	22 41		22 46				23 15		23 26							
Cardiff Bay	d				22 06	22 18		22 30			22 42			22 54	23 06		23 18				23 30	23 42		23 54	
Cardiff Queen Street 3	a	22 04		22 09	22 10	22 22	22 29	22 34	22 38	22 44	22 46	22 49		22 58	23 10	23 18	23 22	23 29			23 34	23 46		23 58	
	d	22 05		22 10			22 30		22 39	22 45		22 50				23 19		23 30							
Heath Low Level	d																								
Ty Glas	d																								
Birchgrove	d																								
Rhiwbina	d																								
Whitchurch (Cardiff)	d																								
Coryton	a																								
Heath High Level	d	22 10							22 44							23 24									
Llanishen	d	22 13							22 47							23 27									
Lisvane & Thornhill	d	22 15							22 49							23 29									
Caerphilly 3	d	22a24							22 55							23 35									
Aber	d								22 57							23 37									
Llanbradach	d								23 01							23 41									
Ystrad Mynach 3	d								23 06							23a51									
Hengoed	d								23 09																
Pengam	d								23 12																
Gilfach Fargoed	d								23 15																
Bargoed	a								23 19																
	d								23 20																
Brithdir	d								23 24																
Tir-phil	d								23 27																
Pontlottyn	d								23 31																
Rhymney 3	a								23 38																
Cathays	d			22 13			22 33			22 48		22 53						23 33							
Llandaf	d			22 17			22 37			22 52		22 57						23 37							
Ninian Park	d																								
Waun-gron Park	d																								
Fairwater	d																								
Danescourt	d																								
Radyr 3	a			22 20			22 40			22 55		22 59						23 40							
	d			22 20			22 40			22 55		22 59						23 40							
Taffs Well 3	d			22 24			22 44			22 59		23 03						23 44							
Trefforest Estate	d						22 48											23 48							
Trefforest	d			22 31			22 52			23 06		23 10						23 52							
Pontypridd 3	a			22 34			22 55			23 09		23 14						00 01							
	d			22 36			22 57			23 11		23 15													
Abercynon	d						23 04			23 19															
Penrhiwceiber	d									23 25															
Mountain Ash	a									23 28															
	d									23 34															
Fernhill	d									23 37															
Cwmbach	d									23 41															
Aberdare 3	a									23 49															
Quakers Yard	d						23 09																		
Merthyr Vale	a						23 14																		
	d						23 14																		
Troed Y Rhiw	d						23 18																		
Pentre-bach	d						23 22																		
Merthyr Tydfil	a						23 31																		
Trehafod	d			22 41								23 20													
Porth	a			22 44								23 23													
	d			22 45								23 24													
Dinas Rhondda	d			22 49								23 28													
Tonypandy	d			22 51								23 30													
Llwynypia	d			22 53								23 32													
Ystrad Rhondda	a			22 56								23 35													
	d			22 59								23 38													
Ton Pentre	d			23 01								23 40													
Treorchy	d			23 04								23 43													
Ynyswen	d			23 07								23 46													
Treherbert	a			23 14								23 53													

Table 130

Sundays until 11 July

Bridgend, Barry Island, Barry, Penarth and Cardiff - Coryton. Rhymney, Pontypridd, Merthyr, Aberdare and Treherbert

		AW	AW	AW	AW	AW	AW	AW	AW	AW		AW	AW	AW	AW	AW	AW	AW	AW	AW		AW	AW	AW	AW
Bridgend	d																09 53								
Llantwit Major	d																10 07								
Rhoose Cardiff Int Airport ✈	d																10 17								
Barry Island	d								08 55							09 55							10 30		
Barry [3]	d								09 00							10 00	10 26						10 35		
Barry Docks	d								09 04							10 04	10 30						10 39		
Cadoxton	d								09 07							10 07	10 33						10 42		
Dinas Powys	d								09 11							10 11	10 37						10 46		
Eastbrook	d								09 13							10 13	10 39						10 48		
Cogan	d								09 15							10 15	10 41						10 50		
Penarth	d																							10 51	
Dingle Road	d																							10 53	
Grangetown	d								09 19							10 19	10 45						10 54	10 57	
Cardiff Central [7]	a								09 24							10 24	10 53						11 01	11 03	
	d	08 26	08 41	08 54	09 00				09 41				10 06			10 26						11 00			
Cardiff Bay	d					09 06	09 18	09 30		09 42		09 54		10 06	10 18			10 30	10 42	10 54					11 06
Cardiff Queen Street [3]	a	08 29	08 44	08 57	09 03	09 10	09 22	09 34	09 44	09 46		09 58	10 09	10 10	10 22	10 29		10 34	10 46	10 58		11 03			11 10
	d	08 30	08 45	09 00	09 04				09 45				10 10			10 30						11 04			
Heath Low Level	d																								
Ty Glas	d																								
Birchgrove	d																								
Rhiwbina	d																								
Whitchurch (Cardiff)	d																								
Coryton	a																								
Heath High Level	d												10 15												
Llanishen	d												10 18												
Lisvane & Thornhill	d												10 20												
Caerphilly [3]	d												10 26												
Aber	d												10 28												
Llanbradach	d												10 32												
Ystrad Mynach [3]	d												10 37												
Hengoed	d												10 40												
Pengam	d												10 43												
Gilfach Fargoed	d												10 46												
Bargoed	a												10 49												
	d												10 49												
Brithdir	d												10 53												
Tir-phil	d												10 56												
Pontlottyn	d												11 00												
Rhymney [3]	a												11 07												
Cathays	d	08 33	08 48		09 07				09 48							10 33						11 07			
Llandaf	d	08 37	08 52		09 11				09 52							10 37						11 11			
Ninian Park	d																								
Waun-gron Park	d																								
Fairwater	d																								
Danescourt	d																								
Radyr [3]	a	08 40	08 55		09 14				09 55							10 40						11 14			
	d	08 40	08 55		09 14				09 55							10 40						11 14			
Taffs Well [3]	d	08 44	08 59		09 18				09 59							10 44						11 18			
Trefforest Estate	d																								
Trefforest	d	08 52	09 06		09 25				10 06							10 52						11 25			
Pontypridd [3]	a	08 55	09 09		09 28				10 09							10 55						11 28			
	d	08 57	09 11		09 30				10 11							10 57						11 30			
Abercynon	d	09 04	09 19						10 19							11 04									
Penrhiwceiber	d		09 24						10 24																
Mountain Ash	a		09 28						10 28																
	d		09 31						10 31																
Fernhill	d		09 33						10 33																
Cwmbach	d		09 37						10 37																
Aberdare [3]	a		09 44						10 44																
Quakers Yard	d	09 09														11 09									
Merthyr Vale	a	09 14														11 14									
	d	09 17														11 17									
Troed Y Rhiw	d	09 20														11 20									
Pentre-bach	d	09 23														11 23									
Merthyr Tydfil	a	09 31														11 31									
Trehafod	d				09 35																	11 35			
Porth	a				09 38																	11 38			
	d				09 39																	11 39			
Dinas Rhondda	d				09 43																	11 43			
Tonypandy	d				09 45																	11 45			
Llwynypia	d				09 47																	11 47			
Ystrad Rhondda	a				09 50																	11 50			
	d				09 53																	11 53			
Ton Pentre	d				09 55																	11 55			
Treorchy	d				09 58																	11 58			
Ynyswen	d				10 01																	12 01			
Treherbert	a				10 07																	12 07			

Table 130

Sundays until 11 July

Bridgend, Barry Island, Barry, Penarth and Cardiff - Coryton. Rhymney, Pontypridd, Merthyr, Aberdare and Treherbert

		AW	AW	AW	AW	AW		AW	AW	AW	AW	AW	AW	AW	AW	AW		AW	AW	AW	AW	AW	AW	AW	AW
Bridgend	d											12 00													
Llantwit Major	d											12 14													
Rhoose Cardiff Int Airport ✈	d											12 24													
Barry Island	d			11 07				11 27			11 55					12 35							12 55		
Barry [3]	d			11 12				11 32			12 00	12 33				12 40							13 00		
Barry Docks	d			11 16				11 36			12 04	12 37				12 44							13 04		
Cadoxton	d			11 19				11 39			12 07	12 40				12 47							13 07		
Dinas Powys	d			11 23				11 43			12 11	12 44				12 51							13 11		
Eastbrook	d			11 25				11 45			12 13	12 46				12 53							13 13		
Cogan	d			11 27				11 47			12 15	12 48				12 55							13 15		
Penarth	d														12 49										
Dingle Road	d														12 51										
Grangetown	d			11 31				11 51			12 19	12 52			12 55	12 59							13 19		
Cardiff Central [7]	a			11 36				12 01			12 24	13 00			13 01	13 06							13 24		
	d			11 41				12 06			12 26								13 06				13 41		
Cardiff Bay	d	11 18	11 30		11 42	11 54			12 06	12 18			12 30	12 42				12 54		13 06	13 18	13 30		13 42	13 54
Cardiff Queen Street [3]	a	11 22	11 34	11 44	11 46	11 58		12 09	12 10	12 22	12 29		12 34	12 46				12 58	13 09	13 10	13 22	13 34	13 44	13 46	13 58
	d			11 45				12 10			12 30								13 10				13 45		
Heath Low Level	d																								
Ty Glas	d																								
Birchgrove	d																								
Rhiwbina	d																								
Whitchurch (Cardiff)	d																								
Coryton	a																								
Heath High Level	d							12 15																	
Llanishen	d							12 18																	
Lisvane & Thornhill	d							12 20																	
Caerphilly [3]	d							12 26																	
Aber	d							12 28																	
Llanbradach	d							12 32																	
Ystrad Mynach [3]	d							12 37																	
Hengoed	d							12 40																	
Pengam	d							12 43																	
Gilfach Fargoed	d							12 46																	
Bargoed	a							12 49																	
	d							12 49																	
Brithdir	d							12 53																	
Tir-phil	d							12 56																	
Pontlottyn	d							13 00																	
Rhymney [3]	a							13 07																	
Cathays	d			11 48							12 33								13 13				13 48		
Llandaf	d			11 52							12 37								13 17				13 52		
Ninian Park	d																								
Waun-gron Park	d																								
Fairwater	d																								
Danescourt	d																								
Radyr [3]	a			11 55							12 40								13 20				13 55		
	d			11 55							12 40								13 20				13 55		
Taffs Well [3]	d			11 59							12 44								13 24				13 59		
Trefforest Estate	d																								
Trefforest	d			12 06							12 52								13 31				14 06		
Pontypridd [3]	a			12 09							12 55								13 34				14 09		
	d			12 11							12 57								13 36				14 11		
Abercynon	d			12 19							13 04												14 19		
Penrhiwceiber	d			12 24																			14 24		
Mountain Ash	a			12 28																			14 28		
	d			12 31																			14 31		
Fernhill	d			12 33																			14 33		
Cwmbach	d			12 37																			14 37		
Aberdare [3]	a			12 44																			14 44		
Quakers Yard	d										13 09														
Merthyr Vale	a										13 14														
	d										13 17														
Troed Y Rhiw	d										13 20														
Pentre-bach	d										13 23														
Merthyr Tydfil	a										13 31														
Trehafod	d																		13 41						
Porth	a																		13 44						
	d																		13 45						
Dinas Rhondda	d																		13 49						
Tonypandy	d																		13 51						
Llwynypia	d																		13 53						
Ystrad Rhondda	a																		13 56						
	d																		13 59						
Ton Pentre	d																		14 01						
Treorchy	d																		14 04						
Ynyswen	d																		14 07						
Treherbert	a																		14 13						

Table 130

Sundays until 11 July

Bridgend, Barry Island, Barry, Penarth and Cardiff - Coryton. Rhymney, Pontypridd, Merthyr, Aberdare and Treherbert

		AW		AW	AW	AW	AW	AW	AW	AW	AW	AW		AW	AW	AW	AW	AW	AW	AW	AW	AW		AW	AW
Bridgend	d													14 07											
Llantwit Major	d													14 21											
Rhoose Cardiff Int Airport ✈	d													14 31											
Barry Island	d	13 26				13 55	14 27											14 55			15 27				15 55
Barry [3]	d	13 31				14 00	14 32							14 40				15 00			15 32				16 00
Barry Docks	d	13 35				14 04	14 36							14 44				15 04			15 36				16 04
Cadoxton	d	13 38				14 07	14 39							14 47				15 07			15 39				16 07
Dinas Powys	d	13 42				14 11	14 43							14 51				15 11			15 43				16 11
Eastbrook	d	13 44				14 13	14 45							14 53				15 13			15 45				16 13
Cogan	d	13 46				14 15	14 47							14 55				15 15			15 47				16 15
Penarth	d									14 49															
Dingle Road	d									14 51															
Grangetown	d	13 50				14 19	14 51			14 55				14 59				15 19			15 51				16 19
Cardiff Central [7]	a	13 58				14 24	14 58			15 01				15 07				15 24			16 00				16 24
	d	14 06				14 26						15 06						15 41			16 06				16 26
Cardiff Bay	d			14 06	14 18			14 30	14 42		14 54				15 06	15 18	15 30		15 42	15 54		16 06		16 18	
Cardiff Queen Street [3]	a	14 09		14 10	14 22	14 29		14 34	14 46		14 58	15 09			15 10	15 22	15 34	15 44	15 46	15 58	16 09	16 10		16 22	16 29
	d	14 10				14 30						15 10						15 45			16 10				16 30
Heath Low Level	d																								
Ty Glas	d																								
Birchgrove	d																								
Rhiwbina	d																								
Whitchurch (Cardiff)	d																								
Coryton	a																								
Heath High Level	d	14 15																			16 15				
Llanishen	d	14 18																			16 18				
Lisvane & Thornhill	d	14 20																			16 20				
Caerphilly [3]	d	14 26																			16 26				
Aber	d	14 28																			16 28				
Llanbradach	d	14 32																			16 32				
Ystrad Mynach [3]	d	14 37																			16 37				
Hengoed	d	14 40																			16 40				
Pengam	d	14 43																			16 43				
Gilfach Fargoed	d	14 46																			16 46				
Bargoed	a	14 49																			16 49				
	d	14 49																			16 49				
Brithdir	d	14 53																			16 53				
Tir-phil	d	14 56																			16 56				
Pontlottyn	d	15 00																			17 00				
Rhymney [3]	a	15 07																			17 07				
Cathays	d					14 33						15 13						15 48							16 33
Llandaf	d					14 37						15 17						15 52							16 37
Ninian Park	d																								
Waun-gron Park	d																								
Fairwater	d																								
Danescourt	d																								
Radyr [3]	a					14 40						15 20						15 55							16 40
	d					14 40						15 20						15 55							16 40
Taffs Well [3]	d					14 44						15 24						15 59							16 44
Trefforest Estate	d																								
Trefforest	d					14 52						15 31						16 06							16 52
Pontypridd [3]	a					14 55						15 34						16 09							16 55
	d					14 57						15 36						16 11							16 57
Abercynon	d					15 04												16 19							17 04
Penrhiwceiber	d																	16 24							
Mountain Ash	a																	16 28							
	d																	16 31							
Fernhill	d																	16 33							
Cwmbach	d																	16 37							
Aberdare [3]	a																	16 44							
Quakers Yard	d					15 09																			17 09
Merthyr Vale	a					15 14																			17 14
	d					15 17																			17 17
Troed Y Rhiw	d					15 20																			17 20
Pentre-bach	d					15 23																			17 23
Merthyr Tydfil	a					15 31																			17 31
Trehafod	d											15 41													
Porth	a											15 44													
	d											15 45													
Dinas Rhondda	d											15 49													
Tonypandy	d											15 51													
Llwynypia	d											15 53													
Ystrad Rhondda	a											15 56													
	d											15 59													
Ton Pentre	d											16 01													
Treorchy	d											16 04													
Ynyswen	d											16 07													
Treherbert	a											16 13													

Table 130

Sundays until 11 July

Bridgend, Barry Island, Barry, Penarth and Cardiff - Coryton. Rhymney, Pontypridd, Merthyr, Aberdare and Treherbert

		AW	AW	AW	AW	AW	AW	AW		AW	AW	AW	AW	AW	AW	AW	AW	AW		AW	AW	AW	AW	AW	AW
Bridgend	d	15 54																				17 47			
Llantwit Major	d	16 08																				18 01			
Rhoose Cardiff Int Airport ✈	d	16 18																				18 11			
Barry Island	d		16 27				16 40							16 55			17 27				17 55				
Barry [3]	d	16 27	16 32				16 45							17 00			17 32				18 00	18 20			
Barry Docks	d	16 31	16 36											17 04			17 36				18 04	18 24			
Cadoxton	d	16 34	16 39											17 07			17 39				18 07	18 27			
Dinas Powys	d	16 38	16 43											17 11			17 43				18 11	18 31			
Eastbrook	d	16 40	16 45											17 13			17 45				18 13	18 33			
Cogan	d	16 42	16 47											17 15			17 47				18 15	18 35			
Penarth	d					16 47																			18 51
Dingle Road	d					16 49																			18 53
Grangetown	d	16 46	16 51			16 54								17 19			17 51				18 19	18 39			18 57
Cardiff Central [7]	a	16 54	16 58			17 00	17 02							17 24			18 01				18 24	18 47			19 03
	d						17 04			17 06				17 41			18 06				18 26				
Cardiff Bay	d			16 30	16 42			16 54			17 06	17 18	17 30		17 42	17 54		18 06		18 18			18 30	18 42	
Cardiff Queen Street [3]	a			16 34	16 46			16 58		17 09	17 10	17 22	17 34	17 44	17 46	17 58	18 09	18 10		18 22	18 29		18 34	18 46	
	d									17 10				17 45			18 10				18 30				
Heath Low Level	d																								
Ty Glas	d																								
Birchgrove	d																								
Rhiwbina	d																								
Whitchurch (Cardiff)	d																								
Coryton	a																								
Heath High Level	d																18 15								
Llanishen	d																18 18								
Lisvane & Thornhill	d																18 20								
Caerphilly [3]	d																18 26								
Aber	d																18 28								
Llanbradach	d																18 32								
Ystrad Mynach [3]	d																18 37								
Hengoed	d																18 40								
Pengam	d																18 43								
Gilfach Fargoed	d																18 46								
Bargoed	a																18 49								
	d																18 49								
Brithdir	d																18 53								
Tir-phil	d																18 56								
Pontlottyn	d																19 00								
Rhymney [3]	a																19 07								
Cathays	d									17 13				17 48							18 33				
Llandaf	d									17 17				17 52							18 37				
Ninian Park	d																								
Waun-gron Park	d																								
Fairwater	d																								
Danescourt	d																								
Radyr [3]	a									17 20				17 55							18 40				
	d									17 20				17 55							18 40				
Taffs Well [3]	d									17 24				17 59							18 44				
Trefforest Estate	d																								
Trefforest	d									17 31				18 06							18 52				
Pontypridd [3]	a									17 34				18 09							18 55				
	d									17 36				18 11							18 57				
Abercynon	d													18 19							19 04				
Penrhiwceiber	d													18 24											
Mountain Ash	a													18 28											
	d													18 31											
Fernhill	d													18 33											
Cwmbach	d													18 37											
Aberdare [3]	a													18 44											
Quakers Yard	d																				19 09				
Merthyr Vale	a																				19 14				
	d																				19 17				
Troed Y Rhiw	d																				19 20				
Pentre-bach	d																				19 23				
Merthyr Tydfil	a																				19 31				
Trehafod	d									17 41															
Porth	a									17 44															
	d									17 45															
Dinas Rhondda	d									17 49															
Tonypandy	d									17 51															
Llwynypia	d									17 53															
Ystrad Rhondda	a									17 56															
	d									17 59															
Ton Pentre	d									18 01															
Treorchy	d									18 04															
Ynyswen	d									18 07															
Treherbert	a									18 13															

Table 130

Sundays until 11 July

Bridgend, Barry Island, Barry, Penarth and Cardiff - Coryton. Rhymney, Pontypridd, Merthyr, Aberdare and Treherbert

		AW	AW	AW	AW	AW	AW	AW	AW	AW	AW	AW	AW	AW	AW	AW
Bridgend	d							19 52							21 57	
Llantwit Major	d							20 06							22 11	
Rhoose Cardiff Int Airport ✈	d							20 16							22 21	
Barry Island	d			18 40	18 55	19 27	19 55			20 32		20 55	21 30	21 55		22 55
Barry ■	d			18 44	19 00	19 32	20 00	20 25		20 37		21 00	21 34	22 00	22 30	23 00
Barry Docks	d			18 48	19 04	19 36	20 04	20 29		20 41		21 04	21 38	22 04	22 34	23 04
Cadoxton	d			18 51	19 07	19 39	20 07	20 32		20 44		21 07	21 41	22 07	22 37	23 07
Dinas Powys	d			18 55	19 11	19 43	20 11	20 36		20 48		21 11	21 45	22 11	22 41	23 11
Eastbrook	d			18 57	19 13	19 45	20 13	20 38		20 50		21 13	21 47	22 13	22 43	23 13
Cogan	d			18 59	19 15	19 47	20 15	20 40		20 52		21 15	21 49	22 15	22 45	23 15
Penarth	d								20 47							
Dingle Road	d								20 49							
Grangetown	d			19 03	19 19	19 51	20 19	20 44	20 53	20 56		21 19	21 53	22 19	22 49	23 19
Cardiff Central ■	a			19 10	19 24	19 59	20 24	20 52	21 01	21 02		21 27	21 58	22 27	22 57	23 27
	d		19 06		19 41	20 06	20 26			21 06	21 16		22 06			
Cardiff Bay	d	18 54														
Cardiff Queen Street ■	a	18 57	19 09		19 44	20 09	20 29			21 09	21 19		22 09			
	d	19 00	19 10		19 45	20 10	20 30			21 10	21 20		22 10			
Heath Low Level	d															
Ty Glas	d															
Birchgrove	d															
Rhiwbina	d															
Whitchurch (Cardiff)	d															
Coryton	a															
Heath High Level	d					20 15					21 25					
Llanishen	d					20 18					21 28					
Lisvane & Thornhill	d					20 20					21 30					
Caerphilly ■	d					20 26					21 36					
Aber	d					20 28					21 38					
Llanbradach	d					20 32					21 42					
Ystrad Mynach ■	d					20 37					21 47					
Hengoed	d					20 40					21 50					
Pengam	d					20 43					21 53					
Gilfach Fargoed	d					20 46					21 56					
Bargoed	a					20 49					21 59					
	d					20 49					21 59					
Brithdir	d					20 53					22 03					
Tir-phil	d					20 56					22 06					
Pontlottyn	d					21 00					22 10					
Rhymney ■	a					21 07					22 16					
Cathays	d		19 13		19 48		20 33			21 13			22 13			
Llandaf	d		19 17		19 52		20 37			21 17			22 17			
Ninian Park	d															
Waun-gron Park	d															
Fairwater	d															
Danescourt	d															
Radyr ■	a		19 20		19 55		20 40			21 20			22 20			
	d		19 20		19 55		20 40			21 20			22 20			
Taffs Well ■	d		19 24		19 59		20 44			21 24			22 24			
Trefforest Estate	d															
Trefforest	d		19 31		20 06		20 52			21 31			22 31			
Pontypridd ■	a		19 34		20 09		20 55			21 34			22 34			
	d		19 36		20 11		20 57			21 36			22 36			
Abercynon	d				20 19		21 04									
Penrhiwceiber	d				20 24											
Mountain Ash	a				20 28											
	d				20 31											
Fernhill	d				20 33											
Cwmbach	d				20 37											
Aberdare ■	a				20 44											
Quakers Yard	d						21 09									
Merthyr Vale	a						21 14									
	d						21 17									
Troed Y Rhiw	d						21 20									
Pentre-bach	d						21 23									
Merthyr Tydfil	a						21 31									
Trehafod	d		19 41							21 41			22 41			
Porth	a		19 44							21 44			22 44			
	d		19 45							21 45			22 45			
Dinas Rhondda	d		19 49							21 49			22 49			
Tonypandy	d		19 51							21 51			22 51			
Llwynypia	d		19 53							21 53			22 53			
Ystrad Rhondda	a		19 56							21 56			22 56			
	d		19 59							21 59			22 59			
Ton Pentre	d		20 01							22 01			23 01			
Treorchy	d		20 04							22 04			23 04			
Ynyswen	d		20 07							22 07			23 07			
Treherbert	a		20 13							22 13			23 13			

Table 130

Sundays 18 July to 05 September

Bridgend, Barry Island, Barry, Penarth and Cardiff - Coryton. Rhymney, Pontypridd, Merthyr, Aberdare and Treherbert

		AW	AW	AW	AW	AW	AW	AW	AW	AW	AW	AW	AW	AW	AW	AW	AW	AW	AW	AW	AW	AW	AW
Bridgend	d															09 42							
Llantwit Major	d															09 56							
Rhoose Cardiff Int Airport ✈	d															10 06							
Barry Island	d								08 55						09 55		10 25						
Barry ■	d								09 00						10 00	10 15	10 30						
Barry Docks	d								09 04						10 04	10 19	10 34						
Cadoxton	d								09 07						10 07	10 22	10 37						
Dinas Powys	d								09 11						10 11	10 26	10 41						
Eastbrook	d								09 13						10 13	10 28	10 43						
Cogan	d								09 15						10 15	10 30	10 45						
Penarth	d																			10 47			
Dingle Road	d																			10 49			
Grangetown	d								09 19						10 19	10 34	10 49			10 53			
Cardiff Central ■	a								09 24						10 24	10 42	10 56			10 59			
	d	08 26	08 41	08 54	09 00				09 41			10 06			10 26							11 00	
Cardiff Bay	d					09 06	09 18	09 30		09 42	09 54		10 06	10 18				10 30	10 42		10 54		11 06
Cardiff Queen Street ■	a	08 29	08 44	08 57	09 03	09 10	09 22	09 34	09 44	09 46	09 58	10 09	10 10	10 22	10 29			10 34	10 46		10 58	11 03	11 10
	d	08 30	08 45	09 00	09 04				09 45			10 10			10 30							11 04	
Heath Low Level	d																						
Ty Glas	d																						
Birchgrove	d																						
Rhiwbina	d																						
Whitchurch (Cardiff)	d																						
Coryton	a																						
Heath High Level	d											10 15											
Llanishen	d											10 18											
Lisvane & Thornhill	d											10 20											
Caerphilly ■	d											10 26											
Aber	d											10 28											
Llanbradach	d											10 32											
Ystrad Mynach ■	d											10 37											
Hengoed	d											10 40											
Pengam	d											10 43											
Gilfach Fargoed	d											10 46											
Bargoed	a											10 49											
	d											10 49											
Brithdir	d											10 53											
Tir-phil	d											10 56											
Pontlottyn	d											11 00											
Rhymney ■	a											11 07											
Cathays	d	08 33	08 48		09 07				09 48						10 33							11 07	
Llandaf	d	08 37	08 52		09 11				09 52						10 37							11 11	
Ninian Park	d																						
Waun-gron Park	d																						
Fairwater	d																						
Danescourt	d																						
Radyr ■	a	08 40	08 55		09 14				09 55						10 40							11 14	
	d	08 40	08 55		09 14				09 55						10 40							11 14	
Taffs Well ■	d	08 44	08 59		09 18				09 59						10 44							11 18	
Trefforest Estate	d																						
Trefforest	d	08 52	09 06		09 25				10 06						10 52							11 25	
Pontypridd ■	a	08 55	09 09		09 28				10 09						10 55							11 28	
	d	08 57	09 11		09 30				10 11						10 57							11 30	
Abercynon	d	09 04	09 19						10 19						11 04								
Penrhiwceiber	d		09 24						10 24														
Mountain Ash	a		09 28						10 28														
	d		09 31						10 31														
Fernhill	d		09 33						10 33														
Cwmbach	d		09 37						10 37														
Aberdare ■	a		09 44						10 44														
Quakers Yard	d	09 09													11 09								
Merthyr Vale	a	09 14													11 14								
	d	09 17													11 17								
Troed Y Rhiw	d	09 20													11 20								
Pentre-bach	d	09 23													11 23								
Merthyr Tydfil	a	09 31													11 31								
Trehafod	d				09 35																	11 35	
Porth	a				09 38																	11 38	
	d				09 39																	11 39	
Dinas Rhondda	d				09 43																	11 43	
Tonypandy	d				09 45																	11 45	
Llwynypia	d				09 47																	11 47	
Ystrad Rhondda	a				09 50																	11 50	
	d				09 53																	11 53	
Ton Pentre	d				09 55																	11 55	
Treorchy	d				09 58																	11 58	
Ynyswen	d				10 01																	12 01	
Treherbert	a				10 07																	12 07	

Table 130

Sundays

18 July to 05 September

Bridgend, Barry Island, Barry, Penarth and Cardiff - Coryton. Rhymney, Pontypridd, Merthyr, Aberdare and Treherbert

		AW	AW	AW	AW	AW		AW	AW	AW	AW	AW	AW	AW	AW	AW		AW	AW	AW	AW	AW	AW	AW	AW
Bridgend	d											11 42													
Llantwit Major	d											11 56													
Rhoose Cardiff Int Airport ✈	d											12 06													
Barry Island	d			10 55				11 25			11 55		12 25										12 55		
Barry 3	d			11 00				11 30			12 00	12 15	12 30										13 00		
Barry Docks	d			11 04				11 34			12 04	12 19	12 34										13 04		
Cadoxton	d			11 07				11 37			12 07	12 22	12 37										13 07		
Dinas Powys	d			11 11				11 41			12 11	12 26	12 41										13 11		
Eastbrook	d			11 13				11 43			12 13	12 28	12 43										13 13		
Cogan	d			11 15				11 45			12 15	12 30	12 45										13 15		
Penarth	d															12 47									
Dingle Road	d															12 49									
Grangetown	d			11 19				11 49			12 19	12 34	12 49			12 53							13 19		
Cardiff Central 7	a			11 24				11 57			12 24	12 42	12 56			12 59							13 24		
	d			11 41				12 06			12 26								13 06				13 41		
Cardiff Bay	d	11 18	11 30		11 42	11 54			12 06	12 18				12 30	12 42			12 54		13 06	13 18	13 30		13 42	13 54
Cardiff Queen Street 3	a	11 22	11 34	11 44	11 46	11 58		12 09	12 10	12 22	12 29			12 34	12 46			12 58	13 09	13 10	13 22	13 34	13 44	13 46	13 58
	d			11 45				12 10			12 30								13 10				13 45		
Heath Low Level	d																								
Ty Glas	d																								
Birchgrove	d																								
Rhiwbina	d																								
Whitchurch (Cardiff)	d																								
Coryton	a																								
Heath High Level	d							12 15																	
Llanishen	d							12 18																	
Lisvane & Thornhill	d							12 20																	
Caerphilly 3	d							12 26																	
Aber	d							12 28																	
Llanbradach	d							12 32																	
Ystrad Mynach 3	d							12 37																	
Hengoed	d							12 40																	
Pengam	d							12 43																	
Gilfach Fargoed	d							12 46																	
Bargoed	a							12 49																	
	d							12 49																	
Brithdir	d							12 53																	
Tir-phil	d							12 56																	
Pontlottyn	d							13 00																	
Rhymney 3	a							13 07																	
Cathays	d			11 48							12 33								13 13				13 48		
Llandaf	d			11 52							12 37								13 17				13 52		
Ninian Park	d																								
Waun-gron Park	d																								
Fairwater	d																								
Danescourt	d																								
Radyr 3	a			11 55							12 40								13 20				13 55		
	d			11 55							12 40								13 20				13 55		
Taffs Well 3	d			11 59							12 44								13 24				13 59		
Trefforest Estate	d																								
Trefforest	d			12 06							12 52								13 31				14 06		
Pontypridd 3	a			12 09							12 55								13 34				14 09		
	d			12 11							12 57								13 36				14 11		
Abercynon	d			12 19							13 04												14 19		
Penrhiwceiber	d			12 24																			14 24		
Mountain Ash	a			12 28																			14 28		
	d			12 31																			14 31		
Fernhill	d			12 33																			14 33		
Cwmbach	d			12 37																			14 37		
Aberdare 3	a			12 44																			14 44		
Quakers Yard	d										13 09														
Merthyr Vale	a										13 14														
	d										13 17														
Troed Y Rhiw	d										13 20														
Pentre-bach	d										13 23														
Merthyr Tydfil	a										13 31														
Trehafod	d																		13 41						
Porth	a																		13 44						
	d																		13 45						
Dinas Rhondda	d																		13 49						
Tonypandy	d																		13 51						
Llwynypia	d																		13 53						
Ystrad Rhondda	a																		13 56						
	d																		13 59						
Ton Pentre	d																		14 01						
Treorchy	d																		14 04						
Ynyswen	d																		14 07						
Treherbert	a																		14 13						

Table 130

Sundays

18 July to 05 September

Bridgend, Barry Island, Barry, Penarth and Cardiff - Coryton. Rhymney, Pontypridd, Merthyr, Aberdare and Treherbert

		AW		AW	AW	AW	AW	AW	AW	AW	AW	AW		AW	AW	AW	AW	AW	AW	AW	AW	AW		AW	AW
Bridgend	d						13 42																		
Llantwit Major	d						13 56																		
Rhoose Cardiff Int Airport ✈	d						14 10																		
Barry Island	d	13 25				13 55		14 25										14 55			15 25				15 55
Barry 3	d	13 30				14 00	14 19	14 30										15 00			15 30				16 00
Barry Docks	d	13 34				14 04	14 23	14 34										15 04			15 34				16 04
Cadoxton	d	13 37				14 07	14 26	14 37										15 07			15 37				16 07
Dinas Powys	d	13 41				14 11	14 30	14 41										15 11			15 41				16 11
Eastbrook	d	13 43				14 13	14 32	14 43										15 13			15 43				16 13
Cogan	d	13 45				14 15	14 34	14 45										15 15			15 45				16 15
Penarth	d										14 47														
Dingle Road	d										14 49														
Grangetown	d	13 49				14 19	14 38	14 49			14 53							15 19			15 49				16 19
Cardiff Central 7	a	13 57				14 24	14 46	14 56			14 59							15 24			15 57				16 24
	d	14 06				14 26								15 06				15 41			16 06				16 26
Cardiff Bay	d			14 06	14 18				14 30	14 42		14 54			15 06	15 18	15 30		15 42	15 54		16 06		16 18	
Cardiff Queen Street 3	a	14 09		14 10	14 22	14 29			14 34	14 46		14 58		15 09	15 10	15 22	15 34	15 44	15 46	15 58	16 09	16 10		16 22	16 29
	d	14 10				14 30								15 10				15 45			16 10				16 30
Heath Low Level	d																								
Ty Glas	d																								
Birchgrove	d																								
Rhiwbina	d																								
Whitchurch (Cardiff)	d																								
Coryton	a																								
Heath High Level	d	14 15																			16 15				
Llanishen	d	14 18																			16 18				
Lisvane & Thornhill	d	14 20																			16 20				
Caerphilly 3	d	14 26																			16 26				
Aber	d	14 28																			16 28				
Llanbradach	d	14 32																			16 32				
Ystrad Mynach 3	d	14 37																			16 37				
Hengoed	d	14 40																			16 40				
Pengam	d	14 43																			16 43				
Gilfach Fargoed	d	14 46																			16 46				
Bargoed	a	14 49																			16 49				
	d	14 49																			16 49				
Brithdir	d	14 53																			16 53				
Tir-phil	d	14 56																			16 56				
Pontlottyn	d	15 00																			17 00				
Rhymney 3	a	15 07																			17 07				
Cathays	d					14 33								15 13				15 48							16 33
Llandaf	d					14 37								15 17				15 52							16 37
Ninian Park	d																								
Waun-gron Park	d																								
Fairwater	d																								
Danescourt	d																								
Radyr 3	a					14 40								15 20				15 55							16 40
	d					14 40								15 20				15 55							16 40
Taffs Well 3	d					14 44								15 24				15 59							16 44
Trefforest Estate	d																								
Trefforest	d					14 52								15 31				16 06							16 52
Pontypridd 3	a					14 55								15 34				16 09							16 55
	d					14 57								15 36				16 11							16 57
Abercynon	d					15 04												16 19							17 04
Penrhiwceiber	d																	16 24							
Mountain Ash	a																	16 28							
	d																	16 31							
Fernhill	d																	16 33							
Cwmbach	d																	16 37							
Aberdare 3	a																	16 44							
Quakers Yard	d					15 09																			17 09
Merthyr Vale	a					15 14																			17 14
	d					15 17																			17 17
Troed Y Rhiw	d					15 20																			17 20
Pentre-bach	d					15 23																			17 23
Merthyr Tydfil	a					15 31																			17 31
Trehafod	d													15 41											
Porth	a													15 44											
	d													15 45											
Dinas Rhondda	d													15 49											
Tonypandy	d													15 51											
Llwynypia	d													15 53											
Ystrad Rhondda	a													15 56											
	d													15 59											
Ton Pentre	d													16 01											
Treorchy	d													16 04											
Ynyswen	d													16 07											
Treherbert	a													16 13											

Table 130

Sundays

18 July to 05 September

Bridgend, Barry Island, Barry, Penarth and Cardiff - Coryton. Rhymney, Pontypridd, Merthyr, Aberdare and Treherbert

		AW	AW	AW	AW	AW	AW	AW		AW	AW	AW	AW	AW	AW	AW	AW	AW		AW	AW	AW	AW	AW	AW
Bridgend	d	15 42																				17 42			
Llantwit Major	d	15 56																				17 56			
Rhoose Cardiff Int Airport ✈	d	16 06																				18 06			
Barry Island	d		16 25				16 40							16 55			17 25				17 55		18 25		
Barry 3	d	16 15	16 30				16 45							17 00			17 30				18 00	18 15	18 30		
Barry Docks	d	16 19	16 34											17 04			17 34				18 04	18 19	18 34		
Cadoxton	d	16 22	16 37											17 07			17 37				18 07	18 22	18 37		
Dinas Powys	d	16 26	16 41											17 11			17 41				18 11	18 26	18 41		
Eastbrook	d	16 28	16 43											17 13			17 43				18 13	18 28	18 43		
Cogan	d	16 30	16 45											17 15			17 45				18 15	18 30	18 45		
Penarth	d					16 47																			
Dingle Road	d					16 49																			
Grangetown	d	16 34	16 49			16 53								17 19			17 49				18 19	18 34	18 49		
Cardiff Central 7	a	16 42	16 56			16 59	17 02							17 24			17 57				18 24	18 42	18 56		
	d						17 04			17 06				17 41			18 06				18 26				
Cardiff Bay	d			16 30	16 42			16 54			17 06	17 18	17 30		17 42	17 54		18 06		18 18				18 30	18 42
Cardiff Queen Street 3	a			16 34	16 46			16 58		17 09	17 10	17 22	17 34	17 44	17 46	17 58	18 09	18 10		18 22	18 29			18 34	18 46
	d									17 10				17 45			18 10				18 30				
Heath Low Level	d																								
Ty Glas	d																								
Birchgrove	d																								
Rhiwbina	d																								
Whitchurch (Cardiff)	d																								
Coryton	a																								
Heath High Level	d																18 15								
Llanishen	d																18 18								
Lisvane & Thornhill	d																18 20								
Caerphilly 3	d																18 26								
Aber	d																18 28								
Llanbradach	d																18 32								
Ystrad Mynach 3	d																18 37								
Hengoed	d																18 40								
Pengam	d																18 43								
Gilfach Fargoed	d																18 46								
Bargoed	a																18 49								
	d																18 49								
Brithdir	d																18 53								
Tir-phil	d																18 56								
Pontlottyn	d																19 00								
Rhymney 3	a																19 07								
Cathays	d									17 13				17 48							18 33				
Llandaf	d									17 17				17 52							18 37				
Ninian Park	d																								
Waun-gron Park	d																								
Fairwater	d																								
Danescourt	d																								
Radyr 3	a									17 20				17 55							18 40				
	d									17 20				17 55							18 40				
Taffs Well 3	d									17 24				17 59							18 44				
Trefforest Estate	d																								
Trefforest	d									17 31				18 06							18 52				
Pontypridd 3	a									17 34				18 09							18 55				
	d									17 36				18 11							18 57				
Abercynon	d													18 19							19 04				
Penrhiwceiber	d													18 24											
Mountain Ash	a													18 28											
	d													18 31											
Fernhill	d													18 33											
Cwmbach	d													18 37											
Aberdare 3	a													18 44											
Quakers Yard	d																				19 09				
Merthyr Vale	a																				19 14				
	d																				19 17				
Troed Y Rhiw	d																				19 20				
Pentre-bach	d																				19 23				
Merthyr Tydfil	a																				19 31				
Trehafod	d									17 41															
Porth	a									17 44															
	d									17 45															
Dinas Rhondda	d									17 49															
Tonypandy	d									17 51															
Llwynypia	d									17 53															
Ystrad Rhondda	a									17 56															
	d									17 59															
Ton Pentre	d									18 01															
Treorchy	d									18 04															
Ynyswen	d									18 07															
Treherbert	a									18 13															

Table 130

Sundays

18 July to 05 September

Bridgend, Barry Island, Barry, Penarth and Cardiff - Coryton. Rhymney, Pontypridd, Merthyr, Aberdare and Treherbert

		AW	AW	AW		AW	AW	AW	AW	AW	AW	AW	AW	AW		AW	AW	AW
Bridgend	d								19 42								21 42	
Llantwit Major	d								19 56								21 56	
Rhoose Cardiff Int Airport ✈	d								20 06								22 06	
Barry Island	d					18 55	19 25	19 55		20 25			20 55	21 25		21 55		22 55
Barry 3	d					19 00	19 30	20 00	20 15	20 30			21 00	21 30		22 00	22 15	23 00
Barry Docks	d					19 04	19 34	20 04	20 19	20 34			21 04	21 34		22 04	22 19	23 04
Cadoxton	d					19 07	19 37	20 07	20 22	20 37			21 07	21 37		22 07	22 22	23 07
Dinas Powys	d					19 11	19 41	20 11	20 26	20 41			21 11	21 41		22 11	22 26	23 11
Eastbrook	d					19 13	19 43	20 13	20 28	20 43			21 13	21 43		22 13	22 28	23 13
Cogan	d					19 15	19 45	20 15	20 30	20 45			21 15	21 45		22 15	22 30	23 15
Penarth	d	18 47									20 47							
Dingle Road	d	18 49									20 49							
Grangetown	d	18 53				19 19	19 49	20 19	20 34	20 49	20 53		21 19	21 49		22 19	22 34	23 19
Cardiff Central 7	a	18 59				19 24	19 57	20 24	20 42	20 54	21 01		21 27	21 54		22 27	22 42	23 27
	d			19 06		19 41	20 06	20 26		21 06		21 16		22 06				
Cardiff Bay	d		18 54															
Cardiff Queen Street 3	a		18 57	19 09		19 44	20 09	20 29		21 09		21 19		22 09				
	d		19 00	19 10		19 45	20 10	20 30		21 10		21 20		22 10				
Heath Low Level	d																	
Ty Glas	d																	
Birchgrove	d																	
Rhiwbina	d																	
Whitchurch (Cardiff)	d																	
Coryton	a																	
Heath High Level	d						20 15					21 25						
Llanishen	d						20 18					21 28						
Lisvane & Thornhill	d						20 20					21 30						
Caerphilly 3	d						20 26					21 36						
Aber	d						20 28					21 38						
Llanbradach	d						20 32					21 42						
Ystrad Mynach 3	d						20 37					21 47						
Hengoed	d						20 40					21 50						
Pengam	d						20 43					21 53						
Gilfach Fargoed	d						20 46					21 56						
Bargoed	a						20 49					21 59						
	d						20 49					21 59						
Brithdir	d						20 53					22 03						
Tir-phil	d						20 56					22 06						
Pontlottyn	d						21 00					22 10						
Rhymney 3	a						21 07					22 16						
Cathays	d			19 13		19 48		20 33		21 13				22 13				
Llandaf	d			19 17		19 52		20 37		21 17				22 17				
Ninian Park	d																	
Waun-gron Park	d																	
Fairwater	d																	
Danescourt	d																	
Radyr 3	a			19 20		19 55		20 40		21 20				22 20				
	d			19 20		19 55		20 40		21 20				22 20				
Taffs Well 3	d			19 24		19 59		20 44		21 24				22 24				
Trefforest Estate	d																	
Trefforest	d			19 31		20 06		20 52		21 31				22 31				
Pontypridd 3	a			19 34		20 09		20 55		21 34				22 34				
	d			19 36		20 11		20 57		21 36				22 36				
Abercynon	d					20 19		21 04										
Penrhiwceiber	d					20 24												
Mountain Ash	a					20 28												
	d					20 31												
Fernhill	d					20 33												
Cwmbach	d					20 37												
Aberdare 3	a					20 44												
Quakers Yard	d							21 09										
Merthyr Vale	a							21 14										
	d							21 17										
Troed Y Rhiw	d							21 20										
Pentre-bach	d							21 23										
Merthyr Tydfil	a							21 31										
Trehafod	d			19 41						21 41				22 41				
Porth	a			19 44						21 44				22 44				
	d			19 45						21 45				22 45				
Dinas Rhondda	d			19 49						21 49				22 49				
Tonypandy	d			19 51						21 51				22 51				
Llwynypia	d			19 53						21 53				22 53				
Ystrad Rhondda	a			19 56						21 56				22 56				
	d			19 59						21 59				22 59				
Ton Pentre	d			20 01						22 01				23 01				
Treorchy	d			20 04						22 04				23 04				
Ynyswen	d			20 07						22 07				23 07				
Treherbert	a			20 13						22 13				23 13				

Table 130

Sundays
from 12 September

Bridgend, Barry Island, Barry, Penarth and Cardiff - Coryton. Rhymney, Pontypridd, Merthyr, Aberdare and Treherbert

		AW	AW	AW	AW	AW	AW	AW	AW	AW		AW	AW	AW	AW	AW	AW	AW	AW	AW		AW	AW	AW	AW
Bridgend	d																09 42							
Llantwit Major	d																09 56							
Rhoose Cardiff Int Airport ✈	d																10 06							
Barry Island	d	22p44								08 55							09 55		10 25						
Barry	d	22p48								09 00							10 00	10 15	10 30						
Barry Docks	d	22p52								09 04							10 04	10 19	10 34						
Cadoxton	d	22p55								09 07							10 07	10 22	10 37						
Dinas Powys	d	22p59								09 11							10 11	10 26	10 41						
Eastbrook	d	23p01								09 13							10 13	10 28	10 43						
Cogan	d	23p03								09 15							10 15	10 30	10 45						
Penarth	d																					10 47			
Dingle Road	d																					10 49			
Grangetown	d	23p07								09 19							10 19	10 34	10 49				10 53		
Cardiff Central	a	23p12								09 24							10 24	10 42	10 57				10 59		
	d	23p26	08 26	08 41	08 54	09 00				09 41				10 06			10 26								11 00
Cardiff Bay	d						09 06	09 18	09 30			09 42	09 54		10 06	10 18				10 30		10 42		10 54	
Cardiff Queen Street	a	23p29	08 29	08 44	08 57	09 03	09 10	09 22	09 34	09 44		09 46	09 58	10 09	10 10	10 22	10 29			10 34		10 46		10 58	11 03
	d	23p30	08 30	08 45	09 00	09 04				09 45				10 10			10 30								11 04
Heath Low Level	d																								
Ty Glas	d																								
Birchgrove	d																								
Rhiwbina	d																								
Whitchurch (Cardiff)	d																								
Coryton	a																								
Heath High Level	d													10 15											
Llanishen	d													10 18											
Lisvane & Thornhill	d													10 20											
Caerphilly	d													10 26											
Aber	d													10 28											
Llanbradach	d													10 32											
Ystrad Mynach	d													10 37											
Hengoed	d													10 40											
Pengam	d													10 43											
Gilfach Fargoed	d													10 46											
Bargoed	a													10 49											
	d													10 49											
Brithdir	d													10 53											
Tir-phil	d													10 56											
Pontlottyn	d													11 00											
Rhymney	a													11 07											
Cathays	d	23p33	08 33	08 48		09 07				09 48							10 33								11 07
Llandaf	d	23p37	08 37	08 52		09 11				09 52							10 37								11 11
Ninian Park	d																								
Waun-gron Park	d																								
Fairwater	d																								
Danescourt	d																								
Radyr	a	23p40	08 40	08 55		09 14				09 55							10 40								11 14
	d	23p40	08 40	08 55		09 14				09 55							10 40								11 14
Taffs Well	d	23p44	08 44	08 59		09 18				09 59							10 44								11 18
Trefforest Estate	d	23p48																							
Trefforest	d	23p52	08 52	09 06		09 25				10 06							10 52								11 25
Pontypridd	a	00 01	08 55	09 09		09 28				10 09							10 55								11 28
	d		08 57	09 11		09 30				10 11							10 57								11 30
Abercynon	d		09 04	09 19						10 19							11 04								
Penrhiwceiber	d			09 25						10 25															
Mountain Ash	a			09 28						10 28															
	d			09 31						10 31															
Fernhill	d			09 34						10 34															
Cwmbach	d			09 38						10 38															
Aberdare	a			09 46						10 46															
Quakers Yard	d		09 09														11 09								
Merthyr Vale	a		09 14														11 14								
	d		09 17														11 17								
Troed Y Rhiw	d		09 21														11 21								
Pentre-bach	d		09 24														11 24								
Merthyr Tydfil	a		09 33														11 33								
Trehafod	d					09 35																			11 35
Porth	a					09 38																			11 38
	d					09 39																			11 39
Dinas Rhondda	d					09 43																			11 43
Tonypandy	d					09 45																			11 45
Llwynypia	d					09 47																			11 47
Ystrad Rhondda	a					09 50																			11 50
	d					09 53																			11 53
Ton Pentre	d					09 55																			11 55
Treorchy	d					09 58																			11 58
Ynyswen	d					10 01																			12 01
Treherbert	a					10 08																			12 08

Table 130

Sundays
from 12 September

Bridgend, Barry Island, Barry, Penarth and Cardiff - Coryton. Rhymney, Pontypridd, Merthyr, Aberdare and Treherbert

		AW	AW	AW	AW	AW		AW	AW	AW	AW	AW	AW	AW	AW	AW		AW	AW	AW	AW	AW	AW	AW	AW
Bridgend	d												11 42												
Llantwit Major	d												11 56												
Rhoose Cardiff Int Airport ✈	d												12 06												
Barry Island	d				10 55				11 25			11 55		12 25										12 55	
Barry	d				11 00				11 30			12 00	12 15	12 30										13 00	
Barry Docks	d				11 04				11 34			12 04	12 19	12 34										13 04	
Cadoxton	d				11 07				11 37			12 07	12 22	12 37										13 07	
Dinas Powys	d				11 11				11 41			12 11	12 26	12 41										13 11	
Eastbrook	d				11 13				11 43			12 13	12 28	12 43										13 13	
Cogan	d				11 15				11 45			12 15	12 30	12 45										13 15	
Penarth	d																	12 47							
Dingle Road	d																	12 49							
Grangetown	d				11 19				11 49			12 19	12 34	12 49				12 53						13 19	
Cardiff Central	a				11 24				11 57			12 24	12 43	12 57				12 59						13 24	
	d				11 41				12 06			12 26								13 06				13 41	
Cardiff Bay	d	11 06	11 18	11 30		11 42		11 54		12 06	12 18				12 30	12 42			12 54		13 06	13 18	13 30		13 42
Cardiff Queen Street	a	11 10	11 22	11 34	11 44	11 46		11 58	12 09	12 10	12 22	12 29			12 34	12 46			12 58	13 09	13 10	13 22	13 34	13 44	13 46
	d				11 45				12 10			12 30								13 10				13 45	
Heath Low Level	d																								
Ty Glas	d																								
Birchgrove	d																								
Rhiwbina	d																								
Whitchurch (Cardiff)	d																								
Coryton	a																								
Heath High Level	d								12 15																
Llanishen	d								12 18																
Lisvane & Thornhill	d								12 20																
Caerphilly	d								12 26																
Aber	d								12 28																
Llanbradach	d								12 32																
Ystrad Mynach	d								12 37																
Hengoed	d								12 40																
Pengam	d								12 43																
Gilfach Fargoed	d								12 46																
Bargoed	a								12 49																
	d								12 49																
Brithdir	d								12 53																
Tir-phil	d								12 56																
Pontlottyn	d								13 00																
Rhymney	a								13 07																
Cathays	d				11 48							12 33								13 13				13 48	
Llandaf	d				11 52							12 37								13 17				13 52	
Ninian Park	d																								
Waun-gron Park	d																								
Fairwater	d																								
Danescourt	d																								
Radyr	a				11 55							12 40								13 20				13 55	
	d				11 55							12 40								13 20				13 55	
Taffs Well	d				11 59							12 44								13 24				13 59	
Trefforest Estate	d																								
Trefforest	d				12 06							12 52								13 31				14 06	
Pontypridd	a				12 09							12 55								13 34				14 09	
	d				12 11							12 57								13 36				14 11	
Abercynon	d				12 19							13 04												14 19	
Penrhiwceiber	d				12 25																			14 25	
Mountain Ash	a				12 28																			14 28	
	d				12 31																			14 31	
Fernhill	d				12 34																			14 34	
Cwmbach	d				12 38																			14 38	
Aberdare	a				12 46																			14 46	
Quakers Yard	d											13 09													
Merthyr Vale	a											13 14													
	d											13 17													
Troed Y Rhiw	d											13 21													
Pentre-bach	d											13 24													
Merthyr Tydfil	a											13 33													
Trehafod	d																			13 41					
Porth	a																			13 44					
	d																			13 45					
Dinas Rhondda	d																			13 49					
Tonypandy	d																			13 51					
Llwynypia	d																			13 53					
Ystrad Rhondda	a																			13 56					
	d																			13 59					
Ton Pentre	d																			14 01					
Treorchy	d																			14 04					
Ynyswen	d																			14 07					
Treherbert	a																			14 14					

Table 130

Sundays
from 12 September

Bridgend, Barry Island, Barry, Penarth and Cardiff - Coryton. Rhymney, Pontypridd, Merthyr, Aberdare and Treherbert

		AW		AW	AW	AW	AW	AW	AW	AW	AW	AW		AW	AW	AW	AW	AW	AW	AW	AW	AW		AW	AW
Bridgend	d							13 42																	
Llantwit Major	d							13 56																	
Rhoose Cardiff Int Airport ✈	d							14 06																	
Barry Island	d			13 25			13 55		14 25										14 55			15 25			
Barry ■	d			13 30			14 00	14 15	14 30										15 00			15 30			
Barry Docks	d			13 34			14 04	14 19	14 34										15 04			15 34			
Cadoxton	d			13 37			14 07	14 22	14 37										15 07			15 37			
Dinas Powys	d			13 41			14 11	14 26	14 41										15 11			15 41			
Eastbrook	d			13 43			14 13	14 28	14 43										15 13			15 43			
Cogan	d			13 45			14 15	14 30	14 45										15 15			15 45			
Penarth	d											14 47													
Dingle Road	d											14 49													
Grangetown	d			13 49			14 19	14 34	14 49			14 53							15 19			15 49			
Cardiff Central ■	a			13 57			14 24	14 42	14 57			14 59							15 24			15 57			
	d			14 06			14 26								15 06				15 41			16 06			
Cardiff Bay	d	13 54			14 06	14 18				14 30	14 42			14 54		15 06	15 18	15 30		15 42	15 54			16 06	16 18
Cardiff Queen Street ■	a	13 58		14 09	14 10	14 22	14 29			14 34	14 46			14 58	15 09	15 10	15 22	15 34	15 44	15 46	15 58	16 09		16 10	16 22
	d			14 10			14 30								15 10				15 45			16 10			
Heath Low Level	d																								
Ty Glas	d																								
Birchgrove	d																								
Rhiwbina	d																								
Whitchurch (Cardiff)	d																								
Coryton	a																								
Heath High Level	d			14 15																		16 15			
Llanishen	d			14 18																		16 18			
Lisvane & Thornhill	d			14 20																		16 20			
Caerphilly ■	d			14 26																		16 26			
Aber	d			14 28																		16 28			
Llanbradach	d			14 32																		16 32			
Ystrad Mynach ■	d			14 37																		16 37			
Hengoed	d			14 40																		16 40			
Pengam	d			14 43																		16 43			
Gilfach Fargoed	d			14 46																		16 46			
Bargoed	a			14 49																		16 49			
	d			14 49																		16 49			
Brithdir	d			14 53																		16 53			
Tir-phil	d			14 56																		16 56			
Pontlottyn	d			15 00																		17 00			
Rhymney ■	a			15 07																		17 07			
Cathays	d						14 33								15 13				15 48						
Llandaf	d						14 37								15 17				15 52						
Ninian Park	d																								
Waun-gron Park	d																								
Fairwater	d																								
Danescourt	d																								
Radyr ■	a						14 40								15 20				15 55						
	d						14 40								15 20				15 55						
Taffs Well ■	d						14 44								15 24				15 59						
Trefforest Estate	d																								
Trefforest	d						14 52								15 31				16 06						
Pontypridd ■	a						14 55								15 34				16 09						
	d						14 57								15 36				16 11						
Abercynon	d						15 04												16 19						
Penrhiwceiber	d																		16 25						
Mountain Ash	a																		16 28						
	d																		16 31						
Fernhill	d																		16 34						
Cwmbach	d																		16 38						
Aberdare ■	a																		16 46						
Quakers Yard	d						15 09																		
Merthyr Vale	a						15 14																		
	d						15 17																		
Troed Y Rhiw	d						15 21																		
Pentre-bach	d						15 24																		
Merthyr Tydfil	a						15 33																		
Trehafod	d														15 41										
Porth	a														15 44										
	d														15 45										
Dinas Rhondda	d														15 49										
Tonypandy	d														15 51										
Llwynypia	d														15 53										
Ystrad Rhondda	a														15 56										
	d														15 59										
Ton Pentre	d														16 01										
Treorchy	d														16 04										
Ynyswen	d														16 07										
Treherbert	a														16 14										

Table 130

Sundays
from 12 September

Bridgend, Barry Island, Barry, Penarth and Cardiff - Coryton. Rhymney, Pontypridd, Merthyr, Aberdare and Treherbert

		AW	AW	AW	AW	AW	AW	AW		AW	AW	AW	AW	AW	AW	AW	AW	AW		AW	AW	AW	AW	AW	AW
Bridgend	d		15 42																			17 42			
Llantwit Major	d		15 56																			17 56			
Rhoose Cardiff Int Airport ✈	d		16 06																			18 06			
Barry Island	d	15 55		16 25										16 55			17 25				17 55		18 25		
Barry ■	d	16 00	16 15	16 30										17 00			17 30				18 00	18 15	18 30		
Barry Docks	d	16 04	16 19	16 34										17 04			17 34				18 04	18 19	18 34		
Cadoxton	d	16 07	16 22	16 37										17 07			17 37				18 07	18 22	18 37		
Dinas Powys	d	16 11	16 26	16 41										17 11			17 41				18 11	18 26	18 41		
Eastbrook	d	16 13	16 28	16 43										17 13			17 43				18 13	18 28	18 43		
Cogan	d	16 15	16 30	16 45										17 15			17 45				18 15	18 30	18 45		
Penarth	d						16 47																		
Dingle Road	d						16 49																		
Grangetown	d	16 19	16 34	16 49			16 53							17 19			17 49				18 19	18 34	18 49		
Cardiff Central ■	a	16 24	16 43	16 57			16 59							17 24			17 57				18 24	18 43	18 57		
	d	16 26								17 06				17 41			18 06				18 26				
Cardiff Bay	d				16 30	16 42		16 54			17 06	17 18	17 30		17 42	17 54		18 06		18 18				18 30	18 42
Cardiff Queen Street ■	a	16 29			16 34	16 46		16 58		17 09	17 10	17 22	17 34	17 44	17 46	17 58	18 09	18 10		18 22	18 29			18 34	18 46
	d	16 30								17 10				17 45			18 10				18 30				
Heath Low Level	d																								
Ty Glas	d																								
Birchgrove	d																								
Rhiwbina	d																								
Whitchurch (Cardiff)	d																								
Coryton	a																								
Heath High Level	d																18 15								
Llanishen	d																18 18								
Lisvane & Thornhill	d																18 20								
Caerphilly ■	d																18 26								
Aber	d																18 28								
Llanbradach	d																18 32								
Ystrad Mynach ■	d																18 37								
Hengoed	d																18 40								
Pengam	d																18 43								
Gilfach Fargoed	d																18 46								
Bargoed	a																18 49								
	d																18 49								
Brithdir	d																18 53								
Tir-phil	d																18 56								
Pontlottyn	d																19 00								
Rhymney ■	a																19 07								
Cathays	d	16 33								17 13				17 48							18 33				
Llandaf	d	16 37								17 17				17 52							18 37				
Ninian Park	d																								
Waun-gron Park	d																								
Fairwater	d																								
Danescourt	d																								
Radyr ■	a	16 40								17 20				17 55							18 40				
	d	16 40								17 20				17 55							18 40				
Taffs Well ■	d	16 44								17 24				17 59							18 44				
Trefforest Estate	d																								
Trefforest	d	16 52								17 31				18 06							18 52				
Pontypridd ■	a	16 55								17 34				18 09							18 55				
	d	16 57								17 36				18 11							18 57				
Abercynon	d	17 04												18 19							19 04				
Penrhiwceiber	d													18 25											
Mountain Ash	a													18 28											
	d													18 31											
Fernhill	d													18 34											
Cwmbach	d													18 38											
Aberdare ■	a													18 46											
Quakers Yard	d	17 09																			19 09				
Merthyr Vale	a	17 14																			19 14				
	d	17 17																			19 17				
Troed Y Rhiw	d	17 21																			19 21				
Pentre-bach	d	17 24																			19 24				
Merthyr Tydfil	a	17 33																			19 33				
Trehafod	d									17 41															
Porth	a									17 44															
	d									17 45															
Dinas Rhondda	d									17 49															
Tonypandy	d									17 51															
Llwynypia	d									17 53															
Ystrad Rhondda	a									17 56															
	d									17 59															
Ton Pentre	d									18 01															
Treorchy	d									18 04															
Ynyswen	d									18 07															
Treherbert	a									18 14															

Table 130

Sundays
from 12 September

Bridgend, Barry Island, Barry, Penarth and Cardiff - Coryton. Rhymney, Pontypridd, Merthyr, Aberdare and Treherbert

		AW	AW	AW	AW	AW	AW	AW	AW	AW	AW	AW	AW	AW	AW	AW
Bridgend	d							19 42							21 42	
Llantwit Major	d							19 56							21 56	
Rhoose Cardiff Int Airport ✈	d							20 06							22 06	
Barry Island	d				18 55	19 25	19 55		20 25			20 55	21 25	21 55		22 55
Barry 3	d				19 00	19 30	20 00	20 15	20 30			21 00	21 30	22 00	22 15	23 00
Barry Docks	d				19 04	19 34	20 04	20 19	20 34			21 04	21 34	22 04	22 19	23 04
Cadoxton	d				19 07	19 37	20 07	20 22	20 37			21 07	21 37	22 07	22 22	23 07
Dinas Powys	d				19 11	19 41	20 11	20 26	20 41			21 11	21 41	22 11	22 26	23 11
Eastbrook	d				19 13	19 43	20 13	20 28	20 43			21 13	21 43	22 13	22 28	23 13
Cogan	d				19 15	19 45	20 15	20 30	20 45			21 15	21 45	22 15	22 30	23 15
Penarth	d	18 47								20 47						
Dingle Road	d	18 49								20 49						
Grangetown	d	18 53			19 19	19 49	20 19	20 34	20 49	20 53		21 19	21 49	22 19	22 34	23 19
Cardiff Central 7	a	18 59			19 24	19 57	20 24	20 43	20 54	20 59		21 28	21 54	22 28	22 43	23 28
	d			19 06	19 41	20 06	20 26		21 06		21 16		22 06			
Cardiff Bay	d		18 54													
Cardiff Queen Street 3	a		18 57	19 09	19 44	20 09	20 29		21 09		21 19		22 09			
	d		19 00	19 10	19 45	20 10	20 30		21 10		21 20		22 10			
Heath Low Level	d															
Ty Glas	d															
Birchgrove	d															
Rhiwbina	d															
Whitchurch (Cardiff)	d															
Coryton	a															
Heath High Level	d					20 15					21 25					
Llanishen	d					20 18					21 28					
Lisvane & Thornhill	d					20 20					21 30					
Caerphilly 3	d					20 26					21 36					
Aber	d					20 28					21 38					
Llanbradach	d					20 32					21 42					
Ystrad Mynach 3	d					20 37					21 47					
Hengoed	d					20 40					21 50					
Pengam	d					20 43					21 53					
Gilfach Fargoed	d					20 46					21 56					
Bargoed	a					20 49					21 59					
	d					20 49					21 59					
Brithdir	d					20 53					22 03					
Tir-phil	d					20 56					22 06					
Pontlottyn	d					21 00					22 10					
Rhymney 3	a					21 07					22 17					
Cathays	d			19 13	19 48		20 33		21 13				22 13			
Llandaf	d			19 17	19 52		20 37		21 17				22 17			
Ninian Park	d															
Waun-gron Park	d															
Fairwater	d															
Danescourt	d															
Radyr 3	a			19 20	19 55		20 40		21 20				22 20			
	d			19 20	19 55		20 40		21 20				22 20			
Taffs Well 3	d			19 24	19 59		20 44		21 24				22 24			
Trefforest Estate	d															
Trefforest	d			19 31	20 06		20 52		21 31				22 31			
Pontypridd 3	a			19 34	20 09		20 55		21 34				22 34			
	d			19 36	20 11		20 57		21 36				22 36			
Abercynon	d				20 19		21 04									
Penrhiwceiber	d				20 25											
Mountain Ash	a				20 28											
	d				20 31											
Fernhill	d				20 34											
Cwmbach	d				20 38											
Aberdare 3	a				20 46											
Quakers Yard	d						21 09									
Merthyr Vale	a						21 14									
	d						21 17									
Troed Y Rhiw	d						21 21									
Pentre-bach	d						21 24									
Merthyr Tydfil	a						21 33									
Trehafod	d			19 41					21 41				22 41			
Porth	a			19 44					21 44				22 44			
	d			19 45					21 45				22 45			
Dinas Rhondda	d			19 49					21 49				22 49			
Tonypandy	d			19 51					21 51				22 51			
Llwynypia	d			19 53					21 53				22 53			
Ystrad Rhondda	a			19 56					21 56				22 56			
	d			19 59					21 59				22 59			
Ton Pentre	d			20 01					22 01				23 01			
Treorchy	d			20 04					22 04				23 04			
Ynyswen	d			20 07					22 07				23 07			
Treherbert	a			20 14					22 14				23 14			

Table 130A

Mondays to Saturdays

Rhoose (Cardiff Intl Airport) - Cardiff International Airport

Bus Service

		AW	AW	AW	AW	AW	AW	AW	AW	AW	AW	AW	AW	AW	AW	AW	AW	AW	AW
		🚌	🚌	🚌	🚌	🚌	🚌	🚌	🚌	🚌	🚌	🚌	🚌	🚌	🚌	🚌	🚌	🚌	🚌
Rhoose Cardiff Int Airport	d	06 16	07 16	08 16	09 16	10 16	11 16	12 16	13 16	14 16	15 16	16 16	17 16	18 16	19 16	20 16	21 16	22 16	23 16
Cardiff International Apt	a	06 23	07 23	08 23	09 23	10 23	11 23	12 23	13 23	14 23	15 23	16 23	17 23	18 23	19 23	20 23	21 23	22 23	23 23

Sundays

		AW	AW	AW	AW	AW	AW	AW	AW	AW	AW	AW	AW	AW	AW	AW	AW	AW	AW	AW	AW	AW	AW
			A	B	A	B	A	B		A	B		A	B	A	B			A	B		A	B
		🚌	🚌	🚌	🚌	🚌	🚌	🚌	🚌	🚌	🚌	🚌	🚌	🚌	🚌	🚌	🚌	🚌	🚌	🚌	🚌	🚌	🚌
Rhoose Cardiff Int Airport	d	09 16	10 16	10 21	11 16	11 17	12 16	12 28	13 16	14 16	14 35	15 16	16 16	16 22	17 16	17 23	18 16	19 16	20 16	20 20	21 16	22 16	22 25
Cardiff International Apt	a	09 23	10 23	10 28	11 23	11 24	12 23	12 35	13 23	14 23	14 42	15 23	16 23	16 29	17 23	17 30	18 23	19 23	20 23	20 27	21 23	22 23	22 32

A from 18 July

B until 11 July

Table 130A

Cardiff International Airport - Rhoose (Cardiff Intl Airport)

Bus Service

		AW	AW	AW	AW	AW	AW	AW	AW	AW	AW	AW	AW	AW	AW	AW	AW	AW	AW
Cardiff International Apt	d	05 51	06 51	07 51	08 51	09 51	10 51	11 51	12 51	13 51	14 51	15 51	16 51	17 51	18 51	19 51	20 51	21 51	22 51
Rhoose Cardiff Int Airport	a	05 58	06 58	07 58	08 58	09 58	10 58	11 58	12 58	13 58	14 58	15 58	16 58	17 58	18 58	19 58	20 58	21 58	22 58

Sundays

		AW	AW	AW	AW	AW	AW	AW	AW	AW	AW	AW	AW	AW	AW	AW
Cardiff International Apt	d	08 51	09 51	10 51	11 51	12 51	13 51	14 51	15 51	16 51	17 51	18 51	19 51	20 51	21 51	22 51
Rhoose Cardiff Int Airport	a	08 58	09 58	10 58	11 58	12 58	13 58	14 58	15 58	16 58	17 58	18 58	19 58	20 58	21 58	22 58

Table 131

Cardiff - Crewe, Liverpool and Manchester

		AW MX ◇	AW MX	AW	AW ◇	AW ◇ H	AW ◇ H	AW ◇	AW	AW ◇ H	AW ◇ H	AW ◇ H	AW	AW ◇ H	AW ◇ H	AW ◇ H	GW ◇■ R	AW	AW ◇ H	AW ◇	AW ◇ H	AW ◇ H	GW ◇■ R
Swansea	d							04 36				06 45		07 45		08 55			09 55	09 15		10 55	
Cardiff Central 7	d	21p55	00 30		04 35	05 10	05 40			06 50	07 20	07 50		08 50	09 20	09 50			10 50	08 09	11 20	11 50	
London Paddington 15 ⊖	d																08 22						10 22
Reading 7	d																08 52						10 52
Newport (South Wales)	d	22p11	00 59		04 53	05 28	05 57			07 04	07 34	08 05		09 05	09 34	10 05			11 05		11 34	12 05	
Cwmbran	d	22p23	01 10		05 04	05 38	06 08			07 15	07 45	08 15		09 15	09 45	10 15			11 15		11 45	12 15	
Pontypool and New Inn	d	22p29	01 16		05 10	05 44	06 13				07 49				09 49						11 49		
Abergavenny	d	22p39	01 27		05 19	05 53	06 19			07 28	08 00	08 28		09 28	10 00	10 28			11 28		12 00	12 28	
Hereford 7	a	23p05	01 55		05 44	06 18	06 47			07 52	08 26	08 53		09 53	10 26	10 53	11 44		11 53		12 26	12 53	13 45
	d	23p07			05 48	06 24	06 48			07 55	08 28	08 55		09 55	10 28	10 55			11 55		12 28	12 55	
Leominster	d	23p20			06 02	06 38	07 01			08 08		09 08		10 08		11 08			12 08			13 08	
Ludlow	d	23p32			06 13	06 49	07 12			08 19	08 49	09 19		10 19	10 49	11 19			12 19		12 49	13 19	
Craven Arms	d	23p41			06 21	06 57	07 21	07 54		08 28		09 28		10 28		11 28			12 28	12 37		13 28	
Church Stretton	d	23p51			06 30	07 06	07 30	08 07		08 37		09 37		10 37		11 37			12 37	12 50		13 37	
Shrewsbury	a	00 06			06 44	07 20	07 45	08 22		08 51	09 15	09 51		10 51	11 15	11 51			12 51	13 08	13 15	13 51	
	d	00 07		05 44	06 46	07 24	07 45		08 27	08 53	09 24	09 53	10 26	10 53	11 24	11 53		12 26	12 53		13 24	13 53	
Yorton	d	00x16		05x52					08x34				10x34					12x34					
Wem	d	00 22		05 58	06 57		07 58		08 40				10 40					12 40					
Prees	d	00x26		06x02					08x45				10x44					12x44					
Whitchurch (Shrops)	d	00 34		06 10	07 06		08 07		08 52				10 52					12 52					
Wrenbury	d	00x39		06x16					08x59				10x58					12x58					
Nantwich	d	00 47		06 23	07 16		08 17		09 05				11 05					13 05					
Crewe 10	a	01 02		06 35	07 25		08 26		09 17	09 25		10 26	11 17	11 25		12 25		13 17	13 25			14 26	
Chester	a					08 20					10 20				12 19						14 20		
Llandudno Junction	a					09 14					11 14				13 14						15 13		
Bangor (Gwynedd)	a					09 31					11 38				13 31						15 31		
Holyhead	a					10 05					12 13				14 14						16 14		
Wilmslow	a				07 44		08 45			09 45		10 45		11 45		12 45			13 45			14 45	
Stockport	a				07 54		08 58			09 58		10 58		11 58		12 58			13 58			14 58	
Manchester Piccadilly 10 ⇌	a				08 08		09 15			10 15		11 15		12 15		13 15			14 15			15 15	

		AW	AW ◇ H	AW ◇ H	AW ◇ H	AW	AW ◇ H	AW ◇	AW ■ H	AW ■ H	AW BHX ◇■ ⊠	AW	AW ■ H	AW ■ H	AW ■ H	AW	AW ◇ H	GW ◇■ R	AW ◇	AW ◇
Swansea	d		11 55		12 55		13 55	13 16		14 55			15 55		16 55		17 55			18 21
Cardiff Central 7	d		12 50	13 20	13 50		14 50		15 20	15 50	16 15		16 50	17 20	17 50		18 50		19 34	
London Paddington 15 ⊖	d																	17 22		
Reading 7	d																	17 50		
Newport (South Wales)	d		13 05	13 34	14 05		15 05		15 34	16 05	16 29		17 05	17 34	18 05		19 05		19 48	
Cwmbran	d		13 15	13 45	14 15		15 15		15 44	16 15	16 40		17 15	17 45	18 15		19 15		19 58	
Pontypool and New Inn	d			13 49					15 49	16 21				17 49	18 21				20 03	
Abergavenny	d		13 28	14 00	14 28		15 28		15 59	16 32	16 54		17 28	18 00	18 30		19 28		20 12	
Hereford 7	a		13 53	14 26	14 53		15 53		16 26	16 56			17 53	18 26	18 55		19 54	20 34	20 39	
	d		13 55	14 28	14 55		15 55		16 28	16 56			17 55	18 28	18 56		19 55		20 39	
Leominster	d		14 08		15 08		16 08			17 08			18 08	18 41	19 08		20 09		20 52	
Ludlow	d		14 19	14 49	15 19		16 19		16 49	17 19			18 19	18 52	19 19		20 19		21 03	
Craven Arms	d		14 28		15 28		16 28	16 37		17 28			18 28		19 28		20 28		21 12	21 36
Church Stretton	d		14 37		15 37			16 50		17 38			18 37		19 37		20 37		21 21	21 49
Shrewsbury	a		14 51	15 15	15 51		16 50	17 10	17 15	17 54	18 05		18 51	19 18	19 53		20 51		21 37	22 06
	d	14 26	14 53	15 24	15 53	16 26	16 52		17 24	17 54	18 06	18 26	18 53	19 24	19 54	20 29	20 53		21 39	
Yorton	d	14x34				16x34						18x34				20x39				
Wem	d	14 40				16 40	17 03					18 40				20 44				
Prees	d	14x44				16x44						18x44				20x48				
Whitchurch (Shrops)	d	14 52				16 52						18 52				20 55				
Wrenbury	d	14x58				16x58						18x58				21x01				
Nantwich	d	15 05				17 05						19 05				21 07				
Crewe 10	a	15 17	15 25		16 26	17 17	17 26			18 26	18 42	19 17	19 25		20 26	21 20	21 26			
Chester	a			16 20					18 20		19 06			20 24					22 34	
Llandudno Junction	a			17 14					19 15		19 52			21 25					23 49	
Bangor (Gwynedd)	a			17 36					19 33		20 09			21 42					00 12	
Holyhead	a			18 19					20 14		20 49			22 24					00 53	
Wilmslow	a		15 45		16 45		17 45			18 45			19 45		20 45		21 45			
Stockport	a		15 58		16 58		17 58			18 58			19 58		20 58		21 58			
Manchester Piccadilly 10 ⇌	a		16 15		17 15		18 15			19 15			20 15		21 15		22 15			

For connections from Bristol Temple Meads please refer to Table 132. For connections to Runcorn and Liverpool Lime Street please refer to Table 91

Table 131

Mondays to Fridays

Cardiff - Crewe, Liverpool and Manchester

		AW ◇	GW ◇1 🍽	AW ◇	GW ◇1 🍽	AW ◇
Swansea	d			20 00		
Cardiff Central 7	d	20 17		20 53		21 55
London Paddington 15 ⊖	d		18 22		19 22	
Reading 7	d		18 50		19 52	
Newport (South Wales)	d	20 31		21 10		22 11
Cwmbran	d	20 41		21 21		22 23
Pontypool and New Inn	d	20 47				22 29
Abergavenny	d	20 56		21 34		22 39
Hereford 7	a	21 21	21 31	22 00	22 52	23 05
	d	21 22		22 00		23 07
Leominster	d	21 35		22 14		23 20
Ludlow	d	21 46		22 25		23 32
Craven Arms	d	21 55		22 33		23 41
Church Stretton	d	22 04		22 42		23 51
Shrewsbury	a	22 18		22 57		00 06
	d	22 19		23 06		00 07
Yorton	d	22x27		23x14		00x16
Wem	d	22 32		23 19		00 22
Prees	d	22x36		23x23		00x26
Whitchurch (Shrops)	d	22 43		23 30		00 34
Wrenbury	d	22x49		23x36		00x39
Nantwich	d	22 54		23 42		00 47
Crewe 10	a	23 03		23 53		01 02
Chester	a			00 27		
Llandudno Junction	a					
Bangor (Gwynedd)	a					
Holyhead	a					
Wilmslow	a	23 23				
Stockport	a	23 32				
Manchester Piccadilly 10 🚢	a	23 48				

Saturdays

		AW ◇	AW	AW	AW A	AW ◇ B	AW ◇ 🛒	AW ◇ 🛒	AW	AW ◇ 🛒	AW ◇ 🛒	AW ◇ 🛒
Swansea	d											06 45
Cardiff Central 7	d	21p55	00 30		04 40	04 40	05 20	05 40		06 50	07 20	07 50
London Paddington 15 ⊖	d											
Reading 7	d											
Newport (South Wales)	d	22p11	00 53		04 57	04 57	05 35	05 54		07 04	07 34	08 05
Cwmbran	d	22p23	01 04		05 07	05 07	05 45	06 04		07 15	07 45	08 15
Pontypool and New Inn	d	22p29	01 10		05 13	05 13	05 51	06 10			07 49	
Abergavenny	d	22p39	01 20		05 22	05 22	06 00	06 19		07 28	08 00	08 28
Hereford 7	a	23p05	01 46		05 47	05 47	06 25	06 47		07 52	08 26	08 53
	d	23p07	01 48		05 48	05 48	06 26	06 48		07 55	08 28	08 55
Leominster	d	23p20	02 01		06 02	06 02	06 40	07 01		08 08		09 08
Ludlow	d	23p32	02 13		06 13	06 13	06 51	07 12		08 19	08 49	09 19
Craven Arms	d	23p41	02 22		06 21	06 21	06 59	07 21		08 28		09 28
Church Stretton	d	23p51	02a33		06 30	06 30	07 08	07 30		08 37		09 37
Shrewsbury	a	00 06			06 44	06 44	07 22	07 45		08 51	09 15	09 51
	d	00 07		05 44	06 46	06 46	07 24	07 45	08 26	08 53	09 24	09 53
Yorton	d	00x16		05x52					08x35			
Wem	d	00 22		05 58	06 57	06 57		07 57	08 41			
Prees	d	00x26		06x02					08x45			
Whitchurch (Shrops)	d	00 34		06 10	07 06	07 06		08 06	08 52			
Wrenbury	d	00x39		06x16					08x59			
Nantwich	d	00 47		06 23	07 16	07 16		08 16	09 05			
Crewe 10	a	01 02		06 35	07 25	07 25		08 25	09 17	09 25		10 25
Chester	a						08 19				10 19	
Llandudno Junction	a						09 14				11 14	
Bangor (Gwynedd)	a						09 31				11 36	
Holyhead	a						10 05				12 11	
Wilmslow	a				07 44	07 44		08 45		09 45		10 45
Stockport	a				07 54	07 54		08 58		09 58		10 58
Manchester Piccadilly 10 🚢	a				08 08	08 08		09 14		10 15		11 15

		AW	AW ◇ 🛒	AW ◇ 🛒	AW ◇ 🛒	GW ◇1 🍽	AW	AW ◇ 🛒	AW ◇	AW ◇ 🛒	AW ◇ 🛒
Swansea	d		07 45		08 55			09 55	09 16		10 55
Cardiff Central 7	d		08 50	09 20	09 50			10 50	08 09	11 20	11 50
London Paddington 15 ⊖	d					08 21					
Reading 7	d					08 54					
Newport (South Wales)	d		09 05	09 34	10 05			11 05		11 34	12 05
Cwmbran	d		09 15	09 45	10 15			11 15		11 45	12 15
Pontypool and New Inn	d			09 49						11 49	
Abergavenny	d		09 28	10 00	10 28			11 28		12 00	12 32
Hereford 7	a		09 53	10 26	10 53	11 42		11 53		12 26	12 56
	d		09 55	10 28	10 55			11 55		12 28	12 58
Leominster	d		10 08		11 08			12 08			13 11
Ludlow	d		10 19	10 49	11 19			12 19		12 49	13 22
Craven Arms	d		10 28		11 28			12 28	12 37		13 28
Church Stretton	d		10 37		11 37			12 37	12 50		13 37
Shrewsbury	a		10 51	11 15	11 51			12 51	13 08	13 15	13 54
	d	10 26	10 53	11 24	11 53		12 26	12 53		13 24	13 55
Yorton	d	10x34					12x34				
Wem	d	10 40					12 40				
Prees	d	10x44					12x44				
Whitchurch (Shrops)	d	10 52					12 52				
Wrenbury	d	10x58					12x58				
Nantwich	d	11 05					13 05				
Crewe 10	a	11 17	11 25		12 25		13 17	13 26			14 26
Chester	a			12 19						14 20	
Llandudno Junction	a			13 14						15 13	
Bangor (Gwynedd)	a			13 31						15 31	
Holyhead	a			14 14						16 14	
Wilmslow	a		11 45		12 45			13 45			14 45
Stockport	a		11 58		12 58			13 58			14 58
Manchester Piccadilly 10 🚢	a		12 15		13 15			14 15			15 15

A until 4 September
B from 11 September

For connections from Bristol Temple Meads please refer to Table 132. For connections to Runcorn and Liverpool Lime Street please refer to Table 91

Table 131

Saturdays

Cardiff - Crewe, Liverpool and Manchester

		GW ◇1 🍽	AW	AW ◇ 🛒	AW ◇ 🛒	AW ◇ 🛒	AW	AW ◇ 🛒	AW ◇	AW ■ 🛒	AW ■ 🛒	AW
Swansea	d			11 55		12 55		13 55	13 16		14 55	15 10
Cardiff Central 7	d			12 50	13 20	13 50		14 50		15 20	15 50	16 19
London Paddington 15 ⊖	d	10 21										
Reading 7	d	10 54										
Newport (South Wales)	d			13 05	13 34	14 05		15 05		15 34	16 05	16 34
Cwmbran	d			13 15	13 45	14 15		15 15		15 45	16 15	16 44
Pontypool and New Inn	d				13 49					15 49	16 21	16 50
Abergavenny	d			13 28	14 00	14 28		15 28		16 00	16 30	17a06
Hereford 7	a	13 42		13 53	14 26	14 53		15 53		16 25	16 56	
	d			13 55	14 28	14 55		15 55		16 28	16 56	
Leominster	d			14 08		15 08		16 08			17 08	
Ludlow	d			14 19	14 49	15 19		16 19		16 49	17 19	
Craven Arms	d			14 28		15 28		16 28	16 37		17 28	
Church Stretton	d			14 37		15 37			16 50		17 38	
Shrewsbury	a			14 51	15 15	15 51		16 48	17 10	17 15	17 54	
	d		14 26	14 53	15 24	15 53	16 26	16 50		17 24	17 54	
Yorton	d		14x34				16x34					
Wem	d		14 40				16 40	17 00				
Prees	d		14x44				16x44					
Whitchurch (Shrops)	d		14 52				16 52	17 10				
Wrenbury	d		14x58				16x58					
Nantwich	d		15 05				17 05					
Crewe 10	a		15 17	15 25		16 25	17 17	17 26			18 25	
Chester	a				16 21					18 20		
Llandudno Junction	a				17 14					19 14		
Bangor (Gwynedd)	a				17 36					19 31		
Holyhead	a				18 19					20 16		
Wilmslow	a			15 45		16 45		17 45			18 45	
Stockport	a			15 58		16 58		17 58			18 58	
Manchester Piccadilly 10 🚢	a			16 15		17 15		18 15			19 15	

		AW	AW ■ 🛒	AW ■ 🛒	AW ■ 🛒	GW ◇1 🍽	AW	AW ◇ 🛒	AW ◇	GW ◇1 🍽	AW ◇	AW ◇ B
Swansea	d		15 55		16 55			17 55			18 21	20 00
Cardiff Central 7	d		16 50	17 20	17 50			18 50	19 34			20 53
London Paddington 15 ⊖	d					16 21				18 21		
Reading 7	d					16 54				18 54		
Newport (South Wales)	d		17 05	17 34	18 05			19 05	19 48			21 10
Cwmbran	d		17 15	17 45	18 15			19 15	19 58			21 21
Pontypool and New Inn	d			17 49	18 21				20 03			
Abergavenny	d		17 28	18 00	18 30			19 28	20 12			21 34
Hereford 7	a		17 53	18 26	18 55	19 45		19 53	20 39	21 36		21 58
	d		17 55	18 28	18 57			19 55	20 39			22 00
Leominster	d		18 08	18 41	19 08			20 08	20 53			22 14
Ludlow	d		18 19	18 52	19 19			20 19	21 04			22 25
Craven Arms	d		18 28		19 28			20 28	21 12		21 38	22 33
Church Stretton	d		18 37		19 37			20 37	21 21		21 51	22 42
Shrewsbury	a		18 51	19 18	19 53			20 51	21 37		22 08	22 57
	d	18 26	18 53	19 24	19 54		20 29	20 53	21 37			23 06
Yorton	d	18x34					20x39					23x14
Wem	d	18 40					20 44					23 20
Prees	d	18x44					20x48					23x24
Whitchurch (Shrops)	d	18 52					20 55					23 31
Wrenbury	d	18x58					21x01					23x36
Nantwich	d	19 05					21 07					23 42
Crewe 10	a	19 17	19 25		20 26		21 19	21 27				23 53
Chester	a			20 20					22 31			00 24
Llandudno Junction	a			21 25					23 33			
Bangor (Gwynedd)	a			21 42								
Holyhead	a			22 24								
Wilmslow	a		19 45		20 45			21 45				
Stockport	a		19 58		20 58			21 58				
Manchester Piccadilly 10 🚢	a		20 15		21 15			22 15				

		AW C 🚌	AW ◇ B	AW C 🚌	AW ◇ C	AW
Swansea	d		20 55			
Cardiff Central 7	d		21 49			
London Paddington 15 ⊖	d					
Reading 7	d					
Newport (South Wales)	d	21 20	22 07	22 15		
Cwmbran	d	21 35	22 19	22 30		
Pontypool and New Inn	d		22 24	22 40		
Abergavenny	d	22 00	22 34	22 55		
Hereford 7	a	22 40	22 58	23 35		
	d					
Leominster	d					
Ludlow	d					
Craven Arms	d					
Church Stretton	d					
Shrewsbury	a					
	d				23 11	23 50
Yorton	d				23x19	23x58
Wem	d				23 25	00 04
Prees	d				23x29	00x07
Whitchurch (Shrops)	d				23 36	00 15
Wrenbury	d				23x41	00x20
Nantwich	d				23 47	00 26
Crewe 10	a				23 58	00 38
Chester	a				00 29	
Llandudno Junction	a					
Bangor (Gwynedd)	a					
Holyhead	a					
Wilmslow	a					
Stockport	a					
Manchester Piccadilly 10 🚢	a					

B until 10 July, from 11 September
C from 17 July until 4 September

For connections from Bristol Temple Meads please refer to Table 132. For connections to Runcorn and Liverpool Lime Street please refer to Table 91

Table 131

Cardiff - Crewe, Liverpool and Manchester

Sundays until 11 July

		AW		AW	AW	AW	AW	AW	AW	GW	AW	GW	AW	AW	GW	AW	AW	AW	AW	AW		AW	AW	AW	AW
				◇	◇ H	◇ H	◇ H	◇	◇ H	◇ 1 🍴	◇ H	◇ 1 🍴	■ H	■ H	◇ 1 🍴	■	■ H	■ H	◇	■		■ H	◇	◇	◇
Swansea	d						09 09	11 06			11 17			13 19				15 09	15 04			17 35			
Cardiff Central 7	d				08 30	09 30	10 35		11 35		12 40		13 40	14 55		15 22	15 55	16 40		17 22		18 58	19 40		21 00
London Paddington 15 ⊖	d									09 35		10 42			12 42										
Reading 7	d									10 12		11 21			13 21										
Newport (South Wales)	d				08 49	09 50	10 50		11 54		12 59		13 54	15 14		15 36	16 14	16 54		17 36		19 14	19 55		21 17
Cwmbran	d				08 59	10 00	11 00		12 04		13 09		14 09	15 25		15 46	16 24	17 09		17 46		19 24	20 10		21 30
Pontypool and New Inn	d				09 05	10 06	11 06		12 10				14 15			15 51		17 15					20 16		21 36
Abergavenny	d				09 14	10 16	11 17		12 20		13 23		14 24	15 38		16 01	16 37	17 25		18 00		19 37	20 26		21 46
Hereford 7	a				09 39	10 40	11 43		12 44	12 58	13 47	14 04	14 49	16 02	16 07	16 27	17 02	17 49		18 25		20 02	20 52		22 12
	d				09 43	10 43	11 50		12 57		13 55		14 50	16 04		16 27	17 04	17 53		18 26		20 03	20 54		22 14
Leominster	d				09 57	10 56	12 03		13 10		14 08		15 04			16 40		18 07				20 17	21 08		22 27
Ludlow	d				10 08	11 07	12 14		13 21		14 19		15 15	16 25		16 51	17 26	18 18		18 47		20 28	21 19		22 39
Craven Arms	d				10 16		12 24	14 42			14 28					17 00		18 26	19 00			20 36	21 29		22 48
Church Stretton	d				10 25		12 33	14 55			14 37					17 09		18 35	19 13			20 45	21 38		22 58
Shrewsbury	a	23p49			10 39	11 36	12 48	15 13	13 47		14 51		15 41	16 51		17 23	17 52	18 49	19 29	19 13		20 59	21 55	22 30	23 13
	d	23p50		09 55	10 41	11 37	12 51		13 50		14 53		15 42	16 53		17 30	17 54	18 54		19 32		21 01		22 32	23 19
Yorton	d	23c58				11x45							15x50												23x27
Wem	d	00 04			10 53	11 51							15 56												23 34
Prees	d	00x07				11x55							16x00												23x38
Whitchurch (Shrops)	d	00 15			11 02	12 03							16 08												23 46
Wrenbury	d	00x20				12x08							16x13												23x51
Nantwich	d	00 26			11 11	12 15							16 20												23 59
Crewe 10	a	00 38		10 25	11 22	12 25	13 26		14 22		15 25		16 29	17 25			18 25	19 24				21 35		23 03	00 14
Chester	a															18 25				20 31				23 30	
Llandudno Junction	a															19 22				21 29					
Bangor (Gwynedd)	a															19 45				21 52					
Holyhead	a															20 18				22 38					
Wilmslow	a			10 51	11 40	12 46	13 49		14 46		15 46		16 49	17 45			18 46	19 46				21 57			
Stockport	a			11 01		12 58	14 00		14 58		15 58		16 58	17 58			18 58	19 58				22 06			
Manchester Piccadilly 10	a			11 15	12 02	13 15	14 17		15 15		16 15		17 15	18 15			19 15	20 15				22 24			

		AW
		◇
Swansea	d	21 42
Cardiff Central 7	d	23 00
London Paddington 15 ⊖	d	
Reading 7	d	
Newport (South Wales)	d	23 20
Cwmbran	d	23 29
Pontypool and New Inn	d	23 35
Abergavenny	d	23 45
Hereford 7	a	00 14
	d	
Leominster	d	
Ludlow	d	
Craven Arms	d	
Church Stretton	d	
Shrewsbury	a	
	d	
Yorton	d	
Wem	d	
Prees	d	
Whitchurch (Shrops)	d	
Wrenbury	d	
Nantwich	d	
Crewe 10	a	
Chester	a	
Llandudno Junction	a	
Bangor (Gwynedd)	a	
Holyhead	a	
Wilmslow	a	
Stockport	a	
Manchester Piccadilly 10	a	

c previous night, stops on request

For connections from Bristol Temple Meads please refer to Table 132. For connections to Runcorn and Liverpool Lime Street please refer to Table 91

Table 131

Cardiff - Crewe, Liverpool and Manchester

Sundays 18 July to 05 September

		AW		AW	AW	AW	AW	GW	AW	GW	AW	AW	AW	GW	AW	AW	AW	AW	AW	AW	AW		AW	AW	AW	AW
				◇	◇ H	◇ H	◇ H	◇ 1 🍴	◇ H	◇ 1 🍴	◇	■ H	■ H	◇ 1 🍴	■	■ H	■ H	◇	■	■ H	■ H		◇	◇	◇	◇
Swansea	d								11 32		11 06		13 40				15 25	15 20			17 31					21 52
Cardiff Central 7	d				08 30	09 30	11 35		12 40			13 40	14 50		15 16	15 50	16 40		17 16	17 35	18 40		19 40		21 00	23 00
London Paddington 15 ⊖	d							09 35		10 42				12 42												
Reading 7	d							10 12		11 21				13 21												
Newport (South Wales)	d				08 49	09 50	11 54		12 59			13 58	15 08		15 34	16 08	16 59		17 34	17 53	18 58		19 59		21 19	23 20
Cwmbran	d				08 59	10 00	12 04		13 09			14 09	15 19		15 44	16 24	17 09		17 44	18 04	19 09		20 10		21 30	23 29
Pontypool and New Inn	d				09 05	10 06	12 10					14 15			15 49		17 15			18 10			20 16		21 36	23 35
Abergavenny	d				09 14	10 16	12 20		13 23			14 24	15 33		16 00	16 37	17 25		17 58	18 20	19 22		20 26		21 46	23 45
Hereford 7	a				09 39	10 40	12 44	12 58	13 47	14 04		14 49	15 57	16 07	16 25	17 02	17 49		18 23	18 44	19 47		20 52		22 12	00 14
	d				09 43	10 43	12 57		13 55			14 50	16 04		16 26	17 04	17 53		18 24	18 47	19 49		20 54		22 14	
Leominster	d				09 57	10 56	13 10		14 08			15 04			16 39		18 07			19 03	20 03		21 08		22 27	
Ludlow	d				10 08	11 07	13 21		14 19			15 15	16 25		16 50	17 26	18 18		18 45	19 14	20 14		21 19		22 39	
Craven Arms	d				10 16				14 28		14 42				17 00		18 26	18 58			20 22		21 29		22 48	
Church Stretton	d				10 25				14 37		14 55				17 09		18 35	19 11			20 31		21 38		22 58	
Shrewsbury	a				10 39	11 36	13 47		14 51		15 13	15 41	16 51		17 23	17 52	18 49	19 29	19 12	19 40	20 45		21 55	22 30	23 13	
	d	23p50		09 55	10 41	11 37	13 50		14 53			15 42	16 53		17 30	17 54	18 54		19 32	19 41	20 48			22 32	23 19	
Yorton	d	23b58				11x45						15x50								19x49					23x27	
Wem	d	00 04			10 53	11 51						15 56								19 55					23 34	
Prees	d	00x07				11x55						16x00								19x59					23x38	
Whitchurch (Shrops)	d	00 15			11 02	12 03						16 08								20 06					23 46	
Wrenbury	d	00x20				12x08						16x13								20x11					23x51	
Nantwich	d	00 26			11 11	12 15						16 20								20 18					23 59	
Crewe 10	a	00 38		10 25	11 22	12 25	14 22		15 25			16 29	17 25			18 25	19 24			20 27	21 21			23 03	00 14	
Chester	a														18 25				20 31					23 30		
Llandudno Junction	a														19 22				21 29							
Bangor (Gwynedd)	a														19 45				21 52							
Holyhead	a														20 18				22 38							
Wilmslow	a			10 46	11 43	12 46	14 46		15 46			16 49	17 45			18 46	19 46			20 45	21 46					
Stockport	a			10 58		12 58	14 58		15 58			16 58	17 58			18 58	19 58			20 57	21 58					
Manchester Piccadilly 10	a			11 15	12 05	13 15	15 15		16 15			17 15	18 15			19 15	20 15			21 14	22 15					

Sundays from 12 September

		AW	AW	AW	AW	AW	AW	GW	AW		AW	AW	AW	GW	AW	AW	AW	GW	AW	AW	AW	AW	AW	AW	AW
			◇	◇ H	◇ H	◇ H	◇ H	◇ 1 🍴	◇ H		◇ H	◇ H	◇	◇ 1 🍴	◇ H	■ H	■ H	◇ 1 🍴	■	◇	■ H	■ H	■	■ H	◇ H
Swansea	d											11 32	11 06				13 40					15 33			
Cardiff Central 7	d			08 30		09 30	10 30				11 35	12 40				13 40	14 55		15 22		15 55	16 40	17 14	17 35	
London Paddington 15 ⊖	d							09 35						10 42				12 42							
Reading 7	d							10 11						11 20				13 21							
Newport (South Wales)	d			08 49		09 50	10 45				11 50	12 54				13 54	15 14		15 36		16 14	16 54	17 28	17 53	
Cwmbran	d			08 59		10 00	11 00				12 04	13 09				14 09	15 24		15 46		16 24	17 09	17 38	18 04	
Pontypool and New Inn	d			09 05		10 06	11 06				12 10					14 15			15 52			17 15		18 10	
Abergavenny	d			09 14		10 16	11 17				12 20	13 23				14 24	15 38		16 02		16 37	17 25	17 52	18 20	
Hereford 7	a			09 39		10 40	11 43	12 54			12 44	13 47		14 05		14 49	16 02	16 07	16 27		17 02	17 49	18 17	18 44	
	d			09 43		10 43	11 50				12 57	13 55				14 50	16 04		16 28		17 04	17 53	18 24	18 49	
Leominster	d			09 57		10 56	12 03				13 10	14 08				15 04			16 41			18 07		19 03	
Ludlow	d			10 08		11 07	12 14				13 21	14 19				15 15	16 25		16 52		17 26	18 18	18 45	19 14	
Craven Arms	d			10 16			12 24					14 28	14 42						17 02			18 26			
Church Stretton	d			10 25			12 33					14 37	14 55						17 11			18 35			
Shrewsbury	a			10 39	11 25	11 36	12 48		13 25		13 47	14 51	15 13		15 25	15 41	16 51		17 25	17 33	17 52	18 49	19 11	19 40	19 26
	d	23p50	09 55	10 41	11 27	11 37	12 51		13 27		13 50	14 53			15 27	15 42	16 53		17 30	17 38	17 54	18 54	19 15	19 41	19 28
Yorton	d	23b58				11x45										15x50								19x49	
Wem	d	00 04		10 53		11 51										15 56								19 55	
Prees	d	00x07				11x55										16x00								19x59	
Whitchurch (Shrops)	d	00 15		11 02		12 03										16 08								20 06	
Wrenbury	d	00x20				12x08										16x13								20x11	
Nantwich	d	00 26		11 11		12 15										16 20								20 18	
Crewe 10	a	00 38	10 25	11 22	11 57	12 25	13 26		13 57		14 22	15 25			15 57	16 29	17 25			18 06	18 25	19 24		20 27	20 01
Chester	a																		18 27				20 31		
Llandudno Junction	a																		19 24				21 29		
Bangor (Gwynedd)	a																		19 46				21 52		
Holyhead	a																		20 20				22 38		
Wilmslow	a		10 46	11 40		12 46	13 49				14 46	15 46				16 49	17 45				18 46	19 46		20 45	
Stockport	a		10 58			12 58	14 00				14 58	15 58				16 58	17 58				18 58	19 58		20 57	
Manchester Piccadilly 10	a		11 15	12 02		13 15	14 17				15 15	16 15				17 15	18 15				19 15	20 15		21 14	

b previous night, stops on request

For connections from Bristol Temple Meads please refer to Table 132. For connections to Runcorn and Liverpool Lime Street please refer to Table 91

Table 131

Sundays from 12 September

Cardiff - Crewe, Liverpool and Manchester

		AW	AW	AW	AW	AW
		■	◇	◇	◇	◇
		H				
Swansea	d	17 30				21 52
Cardiff Central 7	d	18 40	19 40		21 04	23 00
London Paddington 15 ⊖	d					
Reading 7	d					
Newport (South Wales)	d	18 54	19 55		21 19	23 20
Cwmbran	d	19 09	20 10		21 30	23 29
Pontypool and New Inn	d		20 16		21 36	23 35
Abergavenny	d	19 22	20 26		21 46	23 45
Hereford 7	a	19 47	20 52		22 12	00 14
	d	19 49	20 54		22 14	
Leominster	d	20 03	21 08		22 27	
Ludlow	d	20 14	21 19		22 39	
Craven Arms	d	20 22	21 29		22 48	
Church Stretton	d	20 31	21 38		22 58	
Shrewsbury	a	20 45	21 55		23 13	
	d	20 48		22 32	23 19	
Yorton	d				23x27	
Wem	d				23 34	
Prees	d				23x38	
Whitchurch (Shrops)	d				23 46	
Wrenbury	d				23x51	
Nantwich	d				23 59	
Crewe 10	a	21 21		23 03	00 14	
Chester	a			23 30		
Llandudno Junction	a					
Bangor (Gwynedd)	a					
Holyhead	a					
Wilmslow	a	21 46				
Stockport	a	21 58				
Manchester Piccadilly 10 ⇌	a	22 15				

For connections from Bristol Temple Meads please refer to Table 132. For connections to Runcorn and Liverpool Lime Street please refer to Table 91

Table 131

Mondays to Fridays

Manchester, Liverpool and Crewe - Cardiff

		AW MX		AW	GW	AW	AW	GW	AW	AW	AW	AW	AW BHX	AW	AW	AW	AW	AW	AW	AW	AW	AW	AW	GW
		◇		◇	◇1 ⊏	◇	◇ H	◇1 ⊏	◇	◇ H	◇ H	◇ H	◇1 ⊠		◇ H	◇	◇ H	◇ H		◇ H	◇ H	◇ H		◇1 ⊏
Manchester Piccadilly 10 ⇌	d											06 30			07 30			08 30		09 30		10 30		
Stockport	d											06 39			07 39			08 39		09 39		10 39		
Wilmslow	d											06 47			07 47			08 47		09 47		10 47		
Holyhead	d										04 25		05 32				06 29				08 05			
Bangor (Gwynedd)	d										04 57		06 02				07 07				09 02			
Llandudno Junction	d										05 15		06 21				07 25				09 25			
Chester	d								05 15		06f20		07 08				08 22				10 22			
Crewe 10	d						04 54			05 55		07 08	07 33	07 40	08 08			09 07	09 26	10 08		11 07	11 26	
Nantwich	d						05 01			06 03				07 46	08 16				09 32				11 32	
Wrenbury	d									06x08				07x52					09x39				11x39	
Whitchurch (Shrops)	d						05 12			06 15				07 59	08 27				09 47				11 47	
Prees	d									06x21				08x05					09x53				11x53	
Wem	d						05 21			06 26				08 11	08 36				09 59				11 59	
Yorton	d									06x31				08x16					10x05				12x05	
Shrewsbury	a						05 33		06 10	06 42	07 17	07 38	08 09	08 28	08 48		09 17	09 38	10 18	10 38	11 17	11 38	12 18	
	d	23p08				05 19	05 40		06 13	06 44	07 19	07 43	08 10		08 50	09 05	09 21	09 39		10 39	11 21	11 39		
Church Stretton	d	23p24				05 36	05 55		06 29	06 59		07 58				09 22		09 55		10 55		11 55		
Craven Arms	d	23p32				05 47	06 03		06 37	07 07		08 06				09 34		10 03		11 03		12 03		
Ludlow	d	23p41					06 11		06 45	07 15	07 47	08 14			09 17		09 47	10 11		11 11	11 47	12 11		
Leominster	d	23p52					06 22		06 56	07 26	07 58	08 25			09 28			10 21		11 21		12 21		
Hereford 7	a	00 07					06 36		07 10	07 42	08 12	08 39			09 42		10 11	10 36		11 36	12 11	12 36		
	d	00 08		05 25	05 34		06 42	06 43	07 13	07 42	08 14	08 42			09 45		10 12	10 38		11 38	12 12	12 38		13 11
Abergavenny	d	00 32		05 49			07 05		07 36	08 05	08 37	09 05			10 08		10 35	11 01		12 01	12 34	13 12		
Pontypool and New Inn	d	00 42		05 59			07 15		07 46		08 46				10 18						12 45			
Cwmbran	d	00 47		06 04			07 20		07 51	08 18	08 52	09 17			10 23		10 48	11 14		12 14	12 50	13 24		
Newport (South Wales)	a	01 00		06 16			07 33		08 01	08 33	09 02	09 34	09 40		10 34		10 57	11 34		12 33	13 00	13 34		
Reading 7	a				08 21			09 14																15 54
London Paddington 15 ⊖	a				08 51			09 47																16 27
Cardiff Central 7	a	01 20		06 33		10 19	07 51		08 17	08 55	09 22	09 53	09 58		10 53	14 15	11 14	11 53		12 53	13 20	13 53		
Swansea	a			07 45		09 08	08 49			09 56		10 55			11 55	13 06		12 55		13 55		14 55		

		AW	AW	AW	AW	AW	GW	AW	AW	AW	AW	AW	AW	AW	AW	AW	AW	AW	AW	AW	AW	AW	AW FO	AW FX
			■	■				■		■		■		■			■		■	■	■			
		◇ H	H	H	◇		◇7 ⊏	H	◇ H	H		H	◇ H	H	◇		H	◇ H	H	H	H			◇
Manchester Piccadilly 10 ⇌	d	11 30		12 30				13 30		14 30		15 30		16 30			17 30		18 30	19 30	20 30	21 35		
Stockport	d	11 39		12 39				13 39		14 39		15 39		16 39			17 40		18 39	19 39	20 39	21 44		
Wilmslow	d	11 47		12 47				13 47		14 47		15 47		16 49			17 48		18 47	19 47	20 47	21 51		
Holyhead	d		10 33						12 38				14 32					16 36						
Bangor (Gwynedd)	d		11 05						13 07				15 02					17 04						
Llandudno Junction	d		11 25						13 25				15 25					17 22						
Chester	d		12 22						14 22				16 22					18 20						
Crewe 10	d	12 07		13 07		13 26		14 07		15 07	15 26	16 08		17 08		17 26	18 12		19 09	20 10	21 12	22 12		
Nantwich	d					13 32					15 32	16 16				17 33	18 20		19 17	20 19	21 20	22 20		
Wrenbury	d					13x39					15x39					17x40			19x22		21x25	22x25		
Whitchurch (Shrops)	d					13 47					15 47	16 27				17 48	18 31		19 30	20 30	21 33	22 33		
Prees	d					13x53					15x53					17x54			19x35		21x39	22x39		
Wem	d					13 59					15 59	16 36				18 00	18 40		19 41	20 39	21 44	22 44		
Yorton	d					14x05					16x05					18x06			19x46		21x49	22x49		
Shrewsbury	a	12 38	13 19	13 38		14 18		14 38	15 17	15 38	16 18	16 48	17 17	17 39		18 18	18 52	19 15	19 56	20 50	21 59	23 00		
	d	12 39	13 21	13 39	14 05			14 39	15 21	15 39		16 50	17 21	17 41	18 05		18 56	19 17	19 58	20 52	22 01		23 08	23 08
Church Stretton	d	12 55		13 55	14 23			14 55		15 55		17 05		17 59	18 23		19 11		20 13	21 07	22 16		23 24	23 24
Craven Arms	d	13 03		14 03	14 36			15 03		16 03		17 13		18 07	18 35		19 19		20 21	21 15	22 24		23 32	23 32
Ludlow	d	13 11	13 47	14 11				15 11	15 47	16 11		17 21	17 47	18 15			19 27	19 45	20 29	21 23	22 32		23 41	23 41
Leominster	d	13 21		14 21				15 21		16 21		17 32		18 26			19 38		20 40	21 34	22 43		23 52	23 52
Hereford 7	a	13 36	14 11	14 36				15 36	16 11	16 36		17 48	18 11	18 40			19 52	20 08	20 58	21 48	23 01		00 07	00 07
	d	13 38	14 12	14 38			15 11	15 38	16 12	16 38		17 51	18 12	18 43			19 54	20 10	21 01	21 20	23 04		00 08	00 08
Abergavenny	d	14 01	14 35	15 01				16 01	16 35	17 01		18 14	18 35	19 06			20 17	20 33	21 24	22 13	23 27		00 32	00 32
Pontypool and New Inn	d		14 45						16 45				18 45					20 43		22 23			00 42	00 42
Cwmbran	d	14 14	14 50	15 14				16 14	16 50	17 14		18 26	18 50	19 18			20 29	20 48	21 36	22 28	23 39		00 47	00 47
Newport (South Wales)	a	14 35	15 00	15 34				16 33	17 00	17 34		18 38	19 00	19 32			20 40	20 58	21 48	22 42	23 50		01 00	01 00
Reading 7	a						18 01																	
London Paddington 15 ⊖	a						18 30																	
Cardiff Central 7	a	14 54	15 20	15 53				16 53	17 17	17 52		18 56	19 21	19 49			20 56	21 19	22 06	23 05	00 15		01 20	01 20
Swansea	a	15 55		16 58	18 06			18 05		18 58		20 04			22 10		22 07		23 15					

For connections from Liverpool Lime Street and Runcorn please refer to Table 91. For connections to Bristol Temple Meads please refer to Table 132

Manchester, Liverpool and Crewe - Cardiff

Mondays to Fridays

		AW ◇
Manchester Piccadilly 10 ⇌	d	22 35
Stockport	d	22 44
Wilmslow	d	22 52
Holyhead	d	
Bangor (Gwynedd)	d	
Llandudno Junction	d	
Chester	d	
Crewe 10	d	23 14
Nantwich	d	23 22
Wrenbury	d	23x27
Whitchurch (Shrops)	d	23 34
Prees	d	23x40
Wem	d	23 45
Yorton	d	23x50
Shrewsbury	a	00 04
	d	
Church Stretton	d	
Craven Arms	d	
Ludlow	d	
Leominster	d	
Hereford 7	a	
	d	
Abergavenny	d	
Pontypool and New Inn	d	
Cwmbran	d	
Newport (South Wales)	a	
Reading 7	a	
London Paddington 15 ⊖	a	
Cardiff Central 7	a	
Swansea	a	

Saturdays

		AW	AW ◇	AW	AW ◇ 🛒	GW ◇1 🍴	AW	AW ◇ 🛒	AW ◇ 🛒	AW ◇ 🛒	AW	AW ◇ 🛒
Manchester Piccadilly 10 ⇌	d									06 30		07 30
Stockport	d									06 39		07 39
Wilmslow	d									06 47		07 47
Holyhead	d								04 25			
Bangor (Gwynedd)	d								04 57			
Llandudno Junction	d								05 15			
Chester	d								06 12			
Crewe 10	d				04 54			05 55		07 09	07 26	08 08
Nantwich	d				05 01			06 03			07 32	08 16
Wrenbury	d							06x08			07x39	
Whitchurch (Shrops)	d				05 12			06 15			07 47	08 27
Prees	d							06x21			07x53	
Wem	d				05 21			06 26			07 59	08 35
Yorton	d							06x31			08x05	
Shrewsbury	a				05 33			06 42	07 17	07 38	08 18	08 48
	d	23p08	05 19		05 40		06 13	06 44	07 19	07 39		08 50
Church Stretton	d	23p24	05 36		05 55		06 29	06 59		07 55		
Craven Arms	d	23p32	05 47		06 03		06 37	07 07		08 03		
Ludlow	d	23p41			06 11		06 45	07 15	07 47	08 11		09 17
Leominster	d	23p52			06 22		06 56	07 26	07 58	08 21		09 28
Hereford 7	a	00 07			06 36		07 10	07 42	08 12	08 36		09 42
	d	00 08		05 42	06 42	07 10	07 13	07 43	08 14	08 38		09 44
Abergavenny	d	00 32		06 07	07 05		07 36	08 06	08 37	09 01		10 07
Pontypool and New Inn	d	00 42		06 18	07 15		07 46		08 46			10 18
Cwmbran	d	00 47		06 23	07 20		07 51	08 18	08 52	09 14		10 22
Newport (South Wales)	a	01 00		06 34	07 37		08 01	08 34	09 01	09 34		10 34
Reading 7	a					09 54						
London Paddington 15 ⊖	a					10 29						
Cardiff Central 7	a	01 20	10 20	06 54	07 55		08 19	08 55	09 22	09 53		10 53
Swansea	a		09 08		08 55			09 56		10 55		11 55

		AW ◇ 🛒	AW ◇	AW ◇ 🛒	AW	AW ◇ 🛒	AW ◇ 🛒	GW ◇1 🍴	AW ◇ 🛒	AW	AW ◇ 🛒
Manchester Piccadilly 10 ⇌	d			08 30		09 30			10 30		11 30
Stockport	d			08 39		09 39			10 39		11 39
Wilmslow	d			08 47		09 47			10 47		11 47
Holyhead	d	06 35					08 20				
Bangor (Gwynedd)	d	07 07					09 02				
Llandudno Junction	d	07 25					09 25				
Chester	d	08 22					10 22				
Crewe 10	d			09 08	09 26	10 08			11 08	11 26	12 08
Nantwich	d				09 32					11 32	
Wrenbury	d				09x39					11x39	
Whitchurch (Shrops)	d				09 47					11 47	
Prees	d				09x53					11x53	
Wem	d				09 59					11 59	
Yorton	d				10x05					12x05	
Shrewsbury	a	09 17		09 38	10 18	10 38	11 17		11 38	12 18	12 38
	d	09 21	09 05	09 39		10 39	11 21		11 39		12 39
Church Stretton	d		09 22	09 55		10 55			11 55		12 55
Craven Arms	d		09 34	10 03		11 03			12 03		13 03
Ludlow	d	09 47		10 11		11 11	11 47		12 11		13 11
Leominster	d			10 21		11 21			12 21		13 21
Hereford 7	a	10 11		10 36		11 36	12 11		12 36		13 36
	d	10 12		10 38		11 38	12 12	12 13	12 38		13 38
Abergavenny	d	10 34		11 01		12 01	12 34		13 01		14 01
Pontypool and New Inn	d						12 45				
Cwmbran	d	10 47		11 14		12 14	12 50		13 14		14 14
Newport (South Wales)	a	10 57		11 34		12 34	13 00		13 34		14 34
Reading 7	a							14 54			
London Paddington 15 ⊖	a							15 29			
Cardiff Central 7	a	11 20	14 15	11 53		12 53	13 20		13 53		14 54
Swansea	a		13 01	12 55		13 55			14 55		15 55

For connections from Liverpool Lime Street and Runcorn please refer to Table 91. For connections to Bristol Temple Meads please refer to Table 132

Table 131

Manchester, Liverpool and Crewe - Cardiff

Saturdays

		AW ■ 🛒	AW ■ 🛒	AW	GW ◇1 🍴	AW ■ 🛒	AW ■ 🛒	AW ■ 🛒	AW	AW ■ 🛒	AW ◇ 🛒	AW ■ 🛒
Manchester Piccadilly 10 ⇌	d		12 30			13 30		14 30		15 30		16 30
Stockport	d		12 39			13 39		14 39		15 39		16 39
Wilmslow	d		12 47			13 47		14 47		15 47		16 47
Holyhead	d	10 33					12 38				14 23	
Bangor (Gwynedd)	d	11 05					13 07				14 54	
Llandudno Junction	d	11 25					13 25				15 17	
Chester	d	12 22					14 22				16 22	
Crewe 10	d		13 08	13 26		14 08		15 07	15 26	16 08		17 08
Nantwich	d			13 33					15 32	16 16		
Wrenbury	d			13x40					15x39			
Whitchurch (Shrops)	d			13 48					15 47	16 27		
Prees	d			13x54					15x53			
Wem	d			14 00					15 59	16 36		
Yorton	d			14x06					16x05			
Shrewsbury	a	13 17	13 38	14 18		14 38	15 17	15 38	16 18	16 48	17 17	17 38
	d	13 21	13 39			14 39	15 21	15 39		16 50	17 21	17 39
Church Stretton	d		13 55			14 55		15 55		17 05		17 55
Craven Arms	d		14 03			15 03		16 03		17 13		18 03
Ludlow	d	13 47	14 11			15 11	15 47	16 11		17 21	17 47	18 11
Leominster	d		14 21			15 21		16 21		17 32		18 21
Hereford 7	a	14 11	14 36			15 36	16 11	16 36		17 48	18 11	18 36
	d	14 12	14 38		15 10	15 38	16 12	16 38		17 51	18 12	18 38
Abergavenny	d	14 34	15 01			16 01	16 35	17 01		18 14	18 35	19 01
Pontypool and New Inn	d	14 45					16 45				18 45	
Cwmbran	d	14 50	15 14			16 14	16 50	17 14		18 26	18 50	19 14
Newport (South Wales)	a	15 00	15 34			16 28	17 00	17 34		18 37	19 00	19 29
Reading 7	a				17 54							
London Paddington 15 ⊖	a				18 29							
Cardiff Central 7	a	15 21	15 53			16 53	17 17	17 54		18 54	19 21	19 46
Swansea	a		16 58			18 04		18 58		20 04		

		AW	AW ■ 🛒	AW ◇ 🛒	AW ◇ 🛒	AW ◇	AW ◇ G	AW ◇ H	AW ◇	AW G	AW H 🚌
Manchester Piccadilly 10 ⇌	d		17 30		18 30	19 30	20 30	20 30	22 35		
Stockport	d		17 40		18 39	19 39	20 39	20 39	22 44		
Wilmslow	d		17 48		18 47	19 47	20 47	20 47	22 52		
Holyhead	d			16 38							
Bangor (Gwynedd)	d			17 07							
Llandudno Junction	d			17 25							
Chester	d			18 22							
Crewe 10	d	17 26	18 12		19 09	20 10	21 11	21 11	23 14		
Nantwich	d	17 32	18 20		19 17	20 19	21 19	21 19	23 22		
Wrenbury	d	17x39			19x22		21x24	21x24	23x27		
Whitchurch (Shrops)	d	17 47	18 31		19 30	20 30	21 30	21 30	23 35		
Prees	d	17x53			19x35		21x36	21x36	23x40		
Wem	d	17 59	18 40		19 41	20 39	21 41	21 41	23 46		
Yorton	d	18x05			19x46		21x46	21x46	23x50		
Shrewsbury	a	18 18	18 52	19 18	19 56	20 50	21 56	21 56	00 04		
	d		18 54	19 20	19 58	20 52	21 56	21 56			
Church Stretton	d		19 09		20 13	21 07	22 12	22 12			
Craven Arms	d		19 17		20 21	21 15	22 20	22 20			
Ludlow	d		19 25	19 48	20 29	21 23	22 28	22 28			
Leominster	d		19 36		20 40	21 34	22 38	22 38			
Hereford 7	a		19 50	20 10	20 54	21 48	22 55	22 55			
	d		19 52	20 12	20 57	21 50	22 56			23 13	23 05
Abergavenny	d		20 15	20 35	21 20	22 13	23 19			23 36	23 45
Pontypool and New Inn	d			20 45		22 23	23 29				23 59
Cwmbran	d		20 27	20 50	21 32	22 28	23 34			23 48	00 10
Newport (South Wales)	a		20 40	21 00	21 43	22 41	23 47			00 03	00 25
Reading 7	a										
London Paddington 15 ⊖	a										
Cardiff Central 7	a		20 56	21 21	22 03	23 05	00 12			00 24	00 55
Swansea	a		22 00		23 07						

G until 10 July, from 11 September

H from 17 July until 4 September

For connections from Liverpool Lime Street and Runcorn please refer to Table 91. For connections to Bristol Temple Meads please refer to Table 132

Table 131

Manchester, Liverpool and Crewe - Cardiff

Sundays until 11 July

		AW	AW	AW	AW	AW	AW	AW	AW	AW	AW	AW	GW	AW	AW	AW	AW	AW	AW	AW	AW
		🚌	◇ 🛒	◇ 🛒	■ 🛒	◇	■ 🛒	◇	■ 🛒	■ 🛒	◇	■ 🛒	◇1 🛒	■ 🛒	■ 🛒	■ 🛒	■ 🛒	◇	◇	◇	
Manchester Piccadilly 10 ⇌	d			09 30	10 30		11 24		13 30	14 30		15 30		16 30	17 30		18 30	19 30		20 30	
Stockport	d			09 39	10 41		11 40		13 40	14 39		15 39		16 39	17 39		18 39	19 39		20 39	
Wilmslow	d			09 47	10 47		11 48		13 47	14 47		15 47		16 47	17 47		18 47	19 47		20 47	
Holyhead	d							10 20								16 25			18 25		
Bangor (Gwynedd)	d							10 59								17 04			19 04		
Llandudno Junction	d							11 22								17 25			19 24		
Chester	d							12 21								18 24			20 27		
Crewe 10	d			10 13	11 11		12 13		14 13	15 10		16 13		17 13	18 13		19 13	20 13	20 54	21 13	23 20
Nantwich	d			10 22										17 21			19 21			21 21	23 28
Wrenbury	d			10x27										17x26			19x26			21x26	23x33
Whitchurch (Shrops)	d			10 35										17 34			19 34			21 35	23 42
Prees	d			10x40										17x39			19x39			21x40	23x47
Wem	d			10 46										17 45			19 45			21 47	23 54
Yorton	d			10x50										17x49			19x49			21x51	23x58
Shrewsbury	a			11 01	11 41		12 43	13 18	14 43	15 45		16 43		18 00	18 43	19 20	20 00	20 43		22 03	00 11
	d	07 50		11 03	11 45	12 07	12 44	13 19	14 44	15 47	16 18	16 44		18 01	18 44	19 21	20 01	20 44		22 04	
Church Stretton	d	08 15		11 19		12 25		13 35	15 00		16 36	17 00				19 37		21 00		22 20	
Craven Arms	d	08 35		11 27		12 36		13 43	15 08		16 47	17 08				19 45		21 08		22 29	
Ludlow	d	08 55		11 36	12 13		13 12	13 51	15 16	16 17		17 16		18 29	19 12	19 53	20 29	21 16		22 37	
Leominster	d	09 20		11 47	12 23		13 22	14 02	15 26	16 28		17 26		18 39		20 04	20 39	21 26		22 49	
Hereford 7	a	09 50		12 02	12 38		13 37	14 16	15 41	16 41		17 41		18 54	19 34	20 18	20 54	21 41		23 03	
	d		10 09	12 03	12 39		13 39	14 19	15 43	16 43		17 42	18 30	18 57	19 36	20 21	20 55	21 43		23 05	
Abergavenny	d		10 33	12 27	13 02		14 02	14 42	16 06	17 07		18 05		19 20	19 59	20 46	21 18	22 06		23 29	
Pontypool and New Inn	d		10 43		13 12			14 52	16 16			18 15				20 56		22 16		23 39	
Cwmbran	d		10 48	12 40	13 17		14 14	14 57	16 21	17 20		18 20		19 33	20 11	21 01	21 31	22 21		23 44	
Newport (South Wales)	a		10 59	12 51	13 28		14 27	15 06	16 31	17 32		18 31		19 43	20 22	21 14	21 43	22 36		23 55	
Reading 7	a												21 19								
London Paddington 15 ⊖	a												22 04								
Cardiff Central 7	a		11 16	13 13	13 44		14 48	15 28	16 52	17 54	22 03	18 50		20 04	20 43	21 36	22 05	23 02		00 20	
Swansea	a				15 29	16 04				19 29	20 15										

Sundays 18 July to 05 September

		AW	AW	XC	AW	AW	AW	AW	AW	AW	AW	AW	AW	AW	AW	GW	AW	AW	AW	AW	AW	AW	AW	AW
		🚌	🚌	◇1 🛒	◇ 🛒	◇	■ 🛒	◇	■ 🛒	◇	■ 🛒	■ 🛒	■ 🛒	◇	■ 🛒	◇1 🛒	■ 🛒	■ 🛒	■ 🛒	■ 🛒	◇	◇	◇	
Manchester Piccadilly 10 ⇌	d			08 27		09 30	10 30		11 24		12 29	13 30	14 30		15 30		16 30	17 30		18 30	19 30		20 30	
Stockport	d			08 36		09 39	10 41		11 40		12 40	13 40	14 39		15 39		16 39	17 39		18 39	19 39		20 39	
Wilmslow	d			08 43		09 47	10 47		11 48		12 48	13 47	14 47		15 47		16 47	17 47		18 47	19 47		20 47	
Holyhead	d									10 20									16 25			18 25		
Bangor (Gwynedd)	d									10 59									17 04			19 04		
Llandudno Junction	d									11 22									17 25			19 24		
Chester	d									12 21									18 24			20 27		
Crewe 10	d			09 05		10 13	11 11		12 13		13 13	14 13	15 10		16 13		17 13	18 13		19 13	20 13	20 54	21 13	23 20
Nantwich	d					10 22					13 21						17 21			19 21			21 21	23 28
Wrenbury	d					10x27					13x26						17x26			19x26			21x26	23x33
Whitchurch (Shrops)	d					10 35					13 34						17 34			19 34			21 35	23 42
Prees	d					10x40					13x39						17x39			19x39			21x40	23x47
Wem	d					10 46					13 45						17 45			19 45			21 47	23 54
Yorton	d					10x50					13x49						17x49			19x49			21x51	23x58
Shrewsbury	a					11 01	11 41		12 43	13 18	13 59	14 43	15 45		16 43		18 00	18 43	19 20	20 00	20 43		22 03	00 11
	d		07 50			11 03	11 45	12 07	12 44	13 19	14 01	14 44	15 47	16 18	16 44		18 01	18 44	19 21	20 01	20 44		22 04	
Church Stretton	d		08 15			11 19		12 25		13 35		15 00		16 36	17 00				19 37		21 00		22 20	
Craven Arms	d		08 35			11 27		12 36		13 43		15 08		16 47	17 08				19 45		21 08		22 29	
Ludlow	d		08 55			11 36	12 13		13 12	13 51	14 28	15 16	16 17		17 16		18 29	19 12	19 53	20 29	21 16		22 37	
Leominster	d		09 20			11 47	12 23		13 22	14 02	14 39	15 26	16 28		17 26		18 39		20 04	20 39	21 26		22 49	
Hereford 7	a		09 50			12 02	12 38		13 37	14 16	14 53	15 41	16 41		17 41		18 54	19 34	20 18	20 54	21 41		23 03	
	d	23p05			10 09	12 03	12 39		13 39	14 19	14 56	15 43	16 43		17 43	18 30	18 57	19 36	20 21	20 55	21 43		23 05	
Abergavenny	d	23p45			10 33	12 27	13 02		14 02	14 42	15 19	16 06	17 07		18 06		19 20	19 59	20 46	21 18	22 06		23 29	
Pontypool and New Inn	d	23p59			10 43		13 12			14 52		16 16			18 16				20 56		22 16		23 39	
Cwmbran	d	00 10			10 48	12 40	13 17		14 14	14 57	15 31	16 21	17 20		18 21		19 33	20 11	21 01	21 31	22 21		23 44	
Newport (South Wales)	a	00 25			10 59	12 54	13 28		14 27	15 13	15 43	16 31	17 36		18 31		19 43	20 22	21 11	21 45	22 36		23 55	
Reading 7	a			11 42												21 19								
London Paddington 15 ⊖	a															22 04								
Cardiff Central 7	a	00 55			11 19	13 19	13 47		14 52	15 37	16 02	16 56	17 57	21 36	18 55		20 08	20 47	21 38	22 07	23 02		00 20	
Swansea	a							16 02					19 06	20 13										

For connections from Liverpool Lime Street and Runcorn please refer to Table 91. For connections to Bristol Temple Meads please refer to Table 132

Table 131

Manchester, Liverpool and Crewe - Cardiff

Sundays from 12 September

		AW	XC	AW	AW	AW	AW	AW	AW	AW	AW	AW	AW	AW	AW	AW	AW	GW	AW	AW	AW	AW
		🚌	◇1 🛒	◇ 🛒	◇	■ D 🛒	◇	■ 🛒	◇ E	◇ 🛒	■ 🛒	■ 🛒	◇ 🛒	■ 🛒	◇	■ 🛒	◇ 🛒	◇1 🛒	■ 🛒	■ 🛒	■ 🛒	◇ 🛒
Manchester Piccadilly 10 ⇌	d		08 26		09 30	10 29		11 30			12 30	13 30		14 30		15 30			16 30	17 30		
Stockport	d		08 35		09 39	10 39		11 40			12 40	13 40		14 39		15 39			16 39	17 39		
Wilmslow	d		08 41		09 47	10 47		11 47			12 48	13 47		14 47		15 47			16 47	17 47		
Holyhead	d								10 20												16 25	
Bangor (Gwynedd)	d								10 59												17 04	
Llandudno Junction	d								11 22												17 25	
Chester	d								12 21												18 24	
Crewe 10	d		09 05		10 13	11 11		12 13		12 50	13 13	14 13	14 50	15 10		16 13	16 50		17 13	18 13		18 50
Nantwich	d				10 22						13 21								17 21			
Wrenbury	d				10x27						13x26								17x26			
Whitchurch (Shrops)	d				10 35						13 34								17 34			
Prees	d				10x40						13x39								17x39			
Wem	d				10 46						13 45								17 45			
Yorton	d				10x50						13x49								17x49			
Shrewsbury	a				11 01	11 41		12 43	13 18	13 20	13 59	14 43	15 20	15 45		16 43	17 20		18 00	18 43	19 20	19 19
	d	07 50			11 03	11 45	12 07	12 44	13 19	13 27	14 01	14 44	15 27	15 47	16 18	16 44	17 27		18 01	18 44	19 21	19 28
Church Stretton	d	08 15			11 19		12 25		13 35			15 00			16 36	17 00					19 37	
Craven Arms	d	08 35			11 27		12 36		13 43			15 08			16 47	17 08					19 45	
Ludlow	d	08 55			11 36	12 13		13 12	13 51		14 28	15 16		16 17		17 16			18 29	19 12	19 53	
Leominster	d	09 20			11 47	12 23		13 22	14 02		14 39	15 26		16 28		17 26			18 39		20 04	
Hereford 7	a	09 50			12 02	12 38		13 37	14 16		14 53	15 41		16 41		17 41			18 54	19 34	20 18	
	d			10 09	12 03	12 39		13 39	14 19		14 56	15 43		16 43		17 43		18 30	18 57	19 36	20 21	
Abergavenny	d			10 33	12 27	13 02		14 02	14 42		15 19	16 06		17 07		18 06			19 20	19 59	20 46	
Pontypool and New Inn	d			10 43		13 12			14 52			16 16				18 16					20 56	
Cwmbran	d			10 48	12 40	13 17		14 14	14 57		15 31	16 21		17 20		18 21			19 33	20 11	21 01	
Newport (South Wales)	a			10 59	12 51	13 28		14 27	15 07		15 44	16 31		17 33		18 31			19 48	20 22	21 14	
Reading 7	a		11 42															21 19				
London Paddington 15 ⊖	a																	22 05				
Cardiff Central 7	a			11 16	13 13	13 44		14 48	15 27		16 04	16 52		17 51	21 36	18 50			20 09	20 43	21 36	
Swansea	a			12 13		15 08	15 59				17 14			19 13	20 16							

		AW	AW	AW	AW	AW	AW
		■ 🛒	◇	◇	◇	◇	
Manchester Piccadilly 10 ⇌	d	18 30	19 30			20 30	
Stockport	d	18 39	19 39			20 39	
Wilmslow	d	18 47	19 47			20 47	
Holyhead	d				18 25		
Bangor (Gwynedd)	d				19 04		
Llandudno Junction	d				19 24		
Chester	d				20 27		
Crewe 10	d	19 13	20 13	20 50	20 54	21 13	23 20
Nantwich	d	19 21				21 21	23 28
Wrenbury	d	19x26				21x26	23x33
Whitchurch (Shrops)	d	19 34				21 35	23 42
Prees	d	19x39				21x40	23x47
Wem	d	19 45				21 47	23 54
Yorton	d	19x49				21x51	23x58
Shrewsbury	a	20 00	20 43	21 20		22 03	00 11
	d	20 01	20 44	21 30		22 04	
Church Stretton	d		21 00			22 20	
Craven Arms	d		21 08			22 29	
Ludlow	d	20 29	21 16			22 37	
Leominster	d	20 39	21 26			22 49	
Hereford 7	a	20 54	21 41			23 03	
	d	20 55	21 43			23 05	
Abergavenny	d	21 18	22 06			23 29	
Pontypool and New Inn	d		22 16			23 39	
Cwmbran	d	21 31	22 21			23 44	
Newport (South Wales)	a	21 45	22 30			23 55	
Reading 7	a						
London Paddington 15 ⊖	a						
Cardiff Central 7	a	22 07	22 56			00 20	
Swansea	a						

Network Diagram for Tables 132, 133 ,134

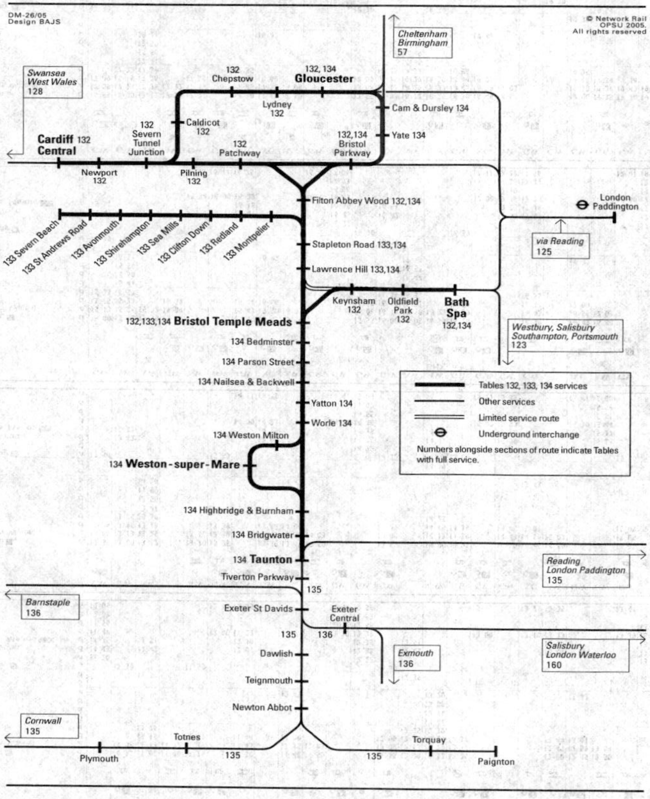

Table 132

Mondays to Fridays

Cardiff - Gloucester, Bristol and Bath Spa

		GW MX	AW MX	AW MX	AW	AW	GW		GW	AW		GW	GW	GW	AW	GW	GW	GW	GW	GW		GW	XC	AW	GW
					◇	◇	◇1		◇1	◇		◇	◇1	◇1		◇1	◇1	◇1 B		◇1		◇	◇1	◇	◇1
						[trolley]	[buffet]		[buffet]	[trolley]			[buffet]	[buffet]		[buffet]	[buffet]	[buffet]		[buffet]		[trolley]		[trolley]	Ø
Cardiff Central 7	d	23p00	23p19	00 30	04 35	05 10	05 15			05 40			05 55		06 12	06 24						06 28	06 40	06 50	06 55
Newport (South Wales)	a	23p16	23p39	00 48	04 51	05 26	05 32			05 56			06 09		06 26	06 37						06 41	06 53	07 02	07 09
	d	23p16	23p40				05 33						06 09		06 28	06 38						06 42	06 55		07 09
Severn Tunnel Jn	d	23p35	23p58												06 38							06 53	07 05		
Caldicot	d		00 01												06 40								07 08		
Chepstow	d		00 10												06 49								07 16		
Lydney	d		00 19												06 58								07 25		
Gloucester 7	a		00 39												07 20								07 44		
Pilning	d																								
Patchway	d	23p49																				07 06			
Bristol Parkway 7	a						05 59						06 29			06 58									07 29
	d																								
Filton Abbey Wood	d	23p52																				07 09			
Bristol Temple Meads 10	a	00 06																				07 18			
	d								05 30			05 44		06 00			06 30	06 40	06 47	07 00		07 23			
Keynsham	d											05 51							06 54						
Oldfield Park	d											05 58							07 01						
Bath Spa 7	a								05 41			06 01		06 11			06 41	06 51	07 04	07 11		07 35			

		GW	XC	AW	AW	GW		GW	GW	GW	XC	AW	GW	GW	GW	SW		GW	GW	GW	GW	GW	XC	AW	GW
										■															
		◇1	◇1		◇	◇1			◇1		◇1	◇	◇1		◇1	◇1			◇1	◇1		◇	◇1	◇	◇1
		[buffet]	[trolley]		[trolley]	[buffet]			Ø	[trolley]		[trolley]	[buffet]		Ø				[buffet]	[buffet]		[trolley]		[trolley]	[buffet]
Cardiff Central 7	d		07 00	07 12	07 20				07 25	07 30	07 45	07 50			07 55			08 00	08 25			08 30	08 45	08 50	
Newport (South Wales)	a		07 13	07 26	07 32				07 39	07 43	07 59	08 03			08 09			08 13	08 39			08 43	08 59	09 03	
	d		07 15	07 27					07 39	07 44	08 02				08 09			08 15	08 39			08 44	09 02		
Severn Tunnel Jn	d		07 25	07 38						07 55								08 25				08 55			
Caldicot	d			07 40																					
Chepstow	d			07 49																					
Lydney	d			07 58																					
Gloucester 7	a			08 20							08 45												09 44		
Pilning	d																								
Patchway	d		07 37															08 40							
Bristol Parkway 7	a								07 59						08 30				08 59						
	d							07 49	08 01					08 19	08 31										
Filton Abbey Wood	d		07 41					07 53		08 09				08 23				08 43				09 09			
Bristol Temple Meads 10	a		07 51					08 01		08 18				08 36				08 53				09 18			
	d	07 30				08 00		08 13		08 23			08 30	08 40		08 51				09 00	09 05	09 23			09 30
Keynsham	d							08 20						08 47		08 58									
Oldfield Park	d							08 27						08 54							09 17				
Bath Spa 7	a	07 41				08 11		08 29		08 35			08 41	08 56		09 05				09 11	09 19	09 34			09 41

		GW		GW	GW	AW	AW	GW	GW	GW	XC	AW		GW	GW	GW	GW	AW	GW	GW	GW	XC		AW	GW
				◇1			◇	◇1	◇1	◇	◇1	◇		◇1		◇1			◇1	◇1	◇	◇1		◇	◇1
				Ø			[trolley]	[buffet]	[buffet]	[trolley]		[trolley]		[buffet]		[buffet]			[buffet]	[buffet]	[trolley]			[trolley]	[buffet]
Cardiff Central 7	d			08 55	09 00	09 12	09 20	09 25		09 30	09 45	09 50				09 55	10 00	10 12	10 25		10 30	10 45		10 50	
Newport (South Wales)	a			09 09	09 13	09 25	09 32	09 39		09 43	09 58	10 03				10 08	10 13	10 25	10 39		10 43	10 58		11 03	
	d			09 09	09 15	09 27		09 39		09 44	10 00					10 09	10 15	10 27	10 39		10 44	11 00			
Severn Tunnel Jn	d				09 25	09 37											10 25	10 38							
Caldicot	d					09 39												10 40							
Chepstow	d					09 48												10 49							
Lydney	d					09 57												10 58							
Gloucester 7	a					10 20					10 42							11 20				11 42			
Pilning	d																								
Patchway	d				09 39												10 39								
Bristol Parkway 7	a			09 30				09 59								10 30			10 59						
	d	09 20													10 22										
Filton Abbey Wood	d	09 23			09 42					10 09					10 25		10 42				11 09				
Bristol Temple Meads 10	a	09 35			09 53					10 18					10 38		10 51				11 18				
	d	09 49							10 00	10 23				10 30	10 49					11 00	11 23				11 30
Keynsham	d	09 56													10 56										
Oldfield Park	d	10 03													11 03										
Bath Spa 7	a	10 05							10 12	10 35				10 41	11 06					11 11	11 35				11 41

B until 2 July, from 6 September

Table 132

Cardiff - Gloucester, Bristol and Bath Spa

		GW	GW	GW	AW	GW	GW	GW		XC	AW	GW	GW	GW	GW	AW	GW	GW		SW	GW	XC	AW	GW	GW
Cardiff Central	d		10 55	11 00	11 20	11 25		11 30		11 45	11 50			11 55	12 00	12 12	12 25				12 30	12 45	12 50		
Newport (South Wales)	a		11 08	11 13	11 32	11 39		11 43		11 58	12 03			12 08	12 13	12 25	12 39				12 43	12 59	13 03		
	d		11 09	11 15		11 39		11 44		12 00				12 09	12 15	12 28	12 39				12 44	13 01			
Severn Tunnel Jn	d			11 25											12 25	12 39									
Caldicot	d															12 42									
Chepstow	d															12 51									
Lydney	d															13 00									
Gloucester	a									12 42						13 20						13 43			
Pilning	d																								
Patchway	d			11 39											12 39										
Bristol Parkway	a		11 30			11 59								12 30			12 59								
	d	11 20											12 22												13 20
Filton Abbey Wood	d	11 23		11 42				12 09					12 25		12 42						13 09				13 23
Bristol Temple Meads	a	11 35		11 51				12 18					12 35		12 51						13 17				13 36
	d	11 49					12 00	12 23				12 30	12 39					13 00		13 10	13 23			13 30	13 49
Keynsham	d	11 56											12 46												13 56
Oldfield Park	d	12 03											12 53												14 03
Bath Spa	a	12 05					12 13	12 35				12 41	12 56					13 11		13 21	13 35			13 41	14 06

		GW	GW	AW		AW	GW	GW	GW	XC	AW	GW	GW	GW		GW	GW	GW	GW	XC	AW	GW	GW	GW
Cardiff Central	d	12 55	13 00	13 12		13 20	13 25		13 30	13 45	13 50			13 55		14 00	14 25		14 30	14 45	14 50			14 55
Newport (South Wales)	a	13 08	13 13	13 25		13 32	13 39		13 43	13 58	14 03			14 08		14 13	14 39		14 43	14 59	15 03			15 08
	d	13 09	13 15	13 28			13 39		13 44	14 00				14 09		14 15	14 39		14 44	15 01				15 09
Severn Tunnel Jn	d		13 25	13 39												14 25								
Caldicot	d			13 41																				
Chepstow	d			13 50																				
Lydney	d			13 59																				
Gloucester	a			14 20						14 42										15 43				
Pilning	d																							
Patchway	d		13 39													14 39								
Bristol Parkway	a	13 30					13 59							14 30			15 00							15 30
	d												14 22										15 20	
Filton Abbey Wood	d		13 42						14 09				14 25			14 42			15 09				15 23	
Bristol Temple Meads	a		13 51						14 19				14 38			14 53			15 18				15 37	
	d							14 00	14 23			14 30	14 48					15 00	15 23			15 30	15 44	
Keynsham	d												14 55										15 51	
Oldfield Park	d												15 02										15 58	
Bath Spa	a							14 11	14 35			14 41	15 04					15 11	15 35			15 41	16 00	

		GW	AW	AW	GW	SW	GW	GW	XC	AW	GW	GW	GW	GW	AW	AW BHX	GW	GW	GW	GW		XC	AW	GW	GW
Cardiff Central	d	15 00	15 12	15 20	15 25			15 30	15 45	15 50			15 55	16 00	16 05	16 15	16 25			16 30		16 45	16 50		
Newport (South Wales)	a	15 13	15 26	15 32	15 39			15 43	15 58	16 03			16 08	16 13	16 18	16 28	16 39			16 43		16 59	17 03		
	d	15 15	15 28		15 39			15 44	16 00				16 09	16 15	16 21		16 39			16 44		17 00			
Severn Tunnel Jn	d	15 25	15 37											16 25	16 33					16 55					
Caldicot	d		15 41												16 35										
Chepstow	d		15 50												16 44										
Lydney	d		15 59												16 53										
Gloucester	a		16 21						16 42						17 15							17 42			
Pilning	d																								
Patchway	d	15 39												16 39											
Bristol Parkway	a				15 59								16 30				16 59								
	d											16 22													17 20
Filton Abbey Wood	d	15 42						16 09				16 25		16 42					16 55	17 09					17 23
Bristol Temple Meads	a	15 51						16 18				16 38		16 51					17 03	17 18					17 37
	d					15 54	16 00	16 23			16 30	16 49						17 00	17 11	17 23				17 30	17 49
Keynsham	d											16 56							17 19						17 56
Oldfield Park	d											17 03							17 26	17 33					18 03
Bath Spa	a					16 05	16 11	16 35			16 41	17 06						17 11	17 29	17 36				17 41	18 06

		GW	GW	AW	AW	GW	GW	GW	XC	AW	GW	GW	GW	GW	AW	GW	GW	XC	AW	GW	GW	GW	GW	GW	AW
Cardiff Central	d	16 55	17 00	17 12	17 20	17 25		17 30	17 45	17 50			17 55	18 00	18 12	18 25	18 30	18 45	18 50			19 00	19 25	19 30	19 34
Newport (South Wales)	a	17 08	17 13	17 25	17 32	17 39		17 43	17 58	18 03			18 08	18 13	18 25	18 39	18 43	18 59	19 03			19 13	19 39	19 42	19 46
	d	17 09	17 15	17 28		17 39		17 44	18 00				18 09	18 15	18 27	18 39	18 44	19 01				19 15	19 39	19 44	
Severn Tunnel Jn	d		17 25	17 39				17 55						18 25	18 38		18 55					19 25			
Caldicot	d			17 41											18 40										
Chepstow	d			17 50											18 49										
Lydney	d			17 59											18 58										
Gloucester	a			18 21					18 42						19 20			19 43							
Pilning	d																								
Patchway	d		17 39											18 39								19 39			
Bristol Parkway	a	17 30				17 59							18 30			18 59							19 59		
	d											18 20									19 20				
Filton Abbey Wood	d		17 42					18 09				18 23		18 42			19 09				19 23	19 42		20 09	
Bristol Temple Meads	a		17 53					18 18			18 28	18 37		18 53			19 18				19 36	19 53		20 18	
	d						18 00	18 23			18 30	18 49					19 23			19 30	19 49			20 23	
Keynsham	d											18 56									19 56				
Oldfield Park	d											19 03									20 03				
Bath Spa	a						18 11	18 34			18 41	19 06					19 35			19 41	20 05			20 35	

Table 132

Cardiff - Gloucester, Bristol and Bath Spa

		XC		GW	GW	GW	AW	GW	GW	AW	XC	AW		GW	GW	GW	SW	GW	XC	XC	AW	GW	GW A	GW B	GW
Cardiff Central	d	19 50				20 00	20 17	20 25	20 30	20 53	21 05	21 12		21 25				21 30	21 40	21 50	21 55		22 00	22 00	
Newport (South Wales)	a	20 03				20 13	20 29	20 38	20 44	21 08	21 18	21 25		21 38				21 43	21 55	22 03	22 09		22 14	22 14	
	d	20 05				20 15		20 39	20 44	21 10	21 20	21 27		21 39				21 44	21 56	22 05			22 16	22 16	
Severn Tunnel Jn	d	20 15				20 25						21 38						21 56					22 34	22 34	
Caldicot	d	20 18										21 40													
Chepstow	d	20 26										21 49													
Lydney	d	20 35										21 58													
Gloucester	a	20 53									22 01	22 22								22 46					
Pilning	d																								
Patchway	d					20 39												22 08					22 48	22 48	
Bristol Parkway	a				20 22			21 00						21 59									22 51	22 51	
	d				20 22			21 01						22 01									22 54	22 58	
Filton Abbey Wood	d				20 25	20 42			21 09									22 12					22 58	23 02	
Bristol Temple Meads	a				20 38	20 53			21 19									22 27	22 29				23 06	23 09	
	d			20 30	20 49				21 23						21 50	22 00	22 25					22 35			23 20
Keynsham	d				20 56											22 07									23 27
Oldfield Park	d				21 03											22 14									23 34
Bath Spa	a			20 41	21 06				21 35						22 01	22 17	22 37					22 46			23 36

		GW	AW FX	AW FO
Cardiff Central	d	23 00	23 19	23 20
Newport (South Wales)	a	23 16	23 39	23 38
	d	23 16	23 40	23 40
Severn Tunnel Jn	d	23 35	23 58	23 58
Caldicot	d		00 01	00 01
Chepstow	d		00 10	00 09
Lydney	d		00 19	00 18
Gloucester	a		00 39	00 39
Pilning	d			
Patchway	d	23 49		
Bristol Parkway	a			
	d			
Filton Abbey Wood	d	23 52		
Bristol Temple Meads	a	00 06		
	d			
Keynsham	d			
Oldfield Park	d			
Bath Spa	a			

Saturdays

		GW	AW	AW		AW	GW	GW	GW	AW		AW	GW	AW	GW	GW	GW	GW	GW	XC		AW	GW	GW	GW
Cardiff Central	d	23p00	23p20	00 30		04 40			04 55	05 20		05 40	05 55	06 12	06 25				06 30	06 40		06 50	06 55		
Newport (South Wales)	a	23p16	23p38	00 48		04 55			05 09	05 33		05 52	06 09	06 25	06 38				06 43	06 53		07 02	07 08		
	d	23p16	23p40	00 53		04 57			05 09				06 09	06 28	06 39				06 44	06 55			07 09		
Severn Tunnel Jn	d	23p35	23p58											06 39					06 55	07 05					
Caldicot	d		00 01											06 41						07 08					
Chepstow	d		00 09											06 50						07 16					
Lydney	d		00 18											06 59						07 25					
Gloucester	a		00 39											07 20						07 44					
Pilning	d																								
Patchway	d	23p49																							
Bristol Parkway	a								05 36				06 29		06 59								07 29		
	d								05 42																
Filton Abbey Wood	d	23p52																	07 09						
Bristol Temple Meads	a	00 06							05 53										07 18						
	d						05 30	05 49	06 00							06 30	06 49	07 00	07 23					07 30	07 49
Keynsham	d							05 56									06 56								07 56
Oldfield Park	d							06 03									07 03								08 03
Bath Spa	a						05 41	06 05	06 11							06 41	07 05	07 11	07 35					07 41	08 05

A from 22 October
B until 21 October

Table 132

Saturdays

Cardiff - Gloucester, Bristol and Bath Spa

		XC	AW	AW	GW	GW	GW	XC	AW	GW	GW	GW	SW	GW	GW	GW	GW	GW	XC	AW	GW	GW	GW
		◇1 ⌶		◇ ⌶	◇1 ⊏	◇1 ⊏	◇	◇1	◇ ⌶	◇1 ⊏		◇1 ⌀	◇1		◇1 ⌀	◇1 ⊏	A	◇	◇1	◇ ⌶	◇1 B ⊏	◇1 A ⊏	
Cardiff Central 7	d	07 00	07 12	07 20	07 25		07 30	07 45	07 50			07 55		08 00	08 25			08 30	08 45	08 50			
Newport (South Wales)	a	07 13	07 25	07 32	07 39		07 43	07 59	08 03			08 08		08 13	08 38			08 43	08 59	09 03			
	d	07 15	07 27		07 39		07 44	08 00				08 09		08 15	08 39			08 44	09 02				
Severn Tunnel Jn	d	07 25	07 38				07 55							08 25				08 55					
Caldicot	d		07 40																				
Chepstow	d		07 49																				
Lydney	d		07 58																				
Gloucester 7	a		08 21					08 46											09 44				
Pilning	d													08 32									
Patchway	d	07 37												08 39									
Bristol Parkway 7	a				07 59							08 30			08 59								
	d										08 19												09 20
Filton Abbey Wood	d	07 41					08 09				08 23			08 42				09 09					09 23
Bristol Temple Meads 10	a	07 51					08 18				08 36			08 52				09 18					09 35
	d					08 00	08 23			08 30	08 40		08 51			09 00	09 09	09 23			09 30	09 30	09 49
Keynsham	d										08 47		08 58				09 17						09 56
Oldfield Park	d										08 54						09 24						10 03
Bath Spa 7	a					08 11	08 35			08 41	08 56		09 05			09 11	09 27	09 35			09 41	09 41	10 05

		GW	GW	AW	AW	GW	GW	GW	XC	AW	GW	GW	GW	AW	GW	GW	GW	XC	AW	GW	GW	GW
		◇1 C ⊏			◇ ⌶	◇1 ⊏	◇1 ⊏	◇ ⌶	◇1	◇ ⌶	◇1 ⊏				◇1 ⊏	◇1 ⊏	◇ ⌶	◇1	◇ ⌶	◇1 ⊏		
Cardiff Central 7	d	08 55	09 00	09 12	09 20	09 25		09 30	09 45	09 50			10 00	10 12	10 25		10 30	10 45	10 50			11 00
Newport (South Wales)	a	09 08	09 13	09 24	09 32	09 39		09 43	09 58	10 03			10 13	10 25	10 39		10 43	10 58	11 03			11 13
	d	09 09	09 15	09 26		09 39		09 44	10 00				10 15	10 27	10 39		10 44	11 00				11 15
Severn Tunnel Jn	d		09 25	09 36									10 25	10 38								11 25
Caldicot	d			09 38										10 40								
Chepstow	d			09 48										10 49								
Lydney	d			09 56										10 58								
Gloucester 7	a			10 21					10 42					11 21				11 42				
Pilning	d																					
Patchway	d		09 39										10 39									11 39
Bristol Parkway 7	a	09 30				09 59									10 59							
	d											10 25									11 20	
Filton Abbey Wood	d		09 42					10 09				10 28	10 42				11 09				11 23	11 42
Bristol Temple Meads 10	a		09 51					10 18				10 39	10 51				11 18				11 35	11 51
	d						10 00	10 23			10 30	10 49				11 00	11 23			11 30	11 49	
Keynsham	d											10 56									11 56	
Oldfield Park	d											11 03									12 03	
Bath Spa 7	a						10 11	10 35			10 41	11 05				11 11	11 35			11 41	12 05	

		AW	GW	GW	GW	XC	AW	GW	GW	GW	AW	GW	GW	SW	GW	XC	AW	GW	GW	GW	AW	AW
		◇ ⌶	◇1 ⊏	◇1 ⊏	◇ ⌶	◇1	◇ ⌶	◇1 ⊏				◇1 ⊏	◇1 ⊏	◇1 ⊏	◇ ⌶	◇1	◇ ⌶	◇1 C ⊏				◇ ⌶
Cardiff Central 7	d	11 20	11 25		11 30	11 45	11 50			12 00	12 12	12 25			12 30	12 45	12 50			13 00	13 12	13 20
Newport (South Wales)	a	11 32	11 39		11 43	11 58	12 03			12 13	12 25	12 39			12 43	12 59	13 03			13 13	13 25	13 32
	d		11 39		11 44	12 00				12 15	12 27	12 39			12 44	13 01				13 15	13 27	
Severn Tunnel Jn	d									12 25	12 38									13 25	13 39	
Caldicot	d										12 40										13 40	
Chepstow	d										12 49										13 49	
Lydney	d										12 58										13 58	
Gloucester 7	a					12 42					13 21					13 42					14 21	
Pilning	d																					
Patchway	d									12 39										13 39		
Bristol Parkway 7	a		11 59									12 59										
	d								12 25										13 20			
Filton Abbey Wood	d				12 09				12 28	12 42					13 09				13 23	13 42		
Bristol Temple Meads 10	a				12 19				12 39	12 51					13 18				13 35	13 51		
	d			12 00	12 23			12 30	12 43				13 00	13 15	13 23			13 30	13 49			
Keynsham	d								12 50										13 56			
Oldfield Park	d								12 57										14 03			
Bath Spa 7	a			12 11	12 35			12 41	13 00				13 11	13 26	13 35			13 41	14 05			

A until 4 September
B from 11 September. The Torbay Express
C from 11 September

Table 132

Saturdays

Cardiff - Gloucester, Bristol and Bath Spa

		GW	GW	GW	XC	AW	GW	GW	GW	GW	GW	GW	XC	AW	GW	GW	GW	AW	AW	GW	SW
		◇1 ⊏	◇1 ⊏	◇	◇1	◇ ⌶	◇1 ⊏	⌶		◇1 ⊏	◇1 ⊏	◇	◇1	◇ ⌶	◇1 ⊏				■ ⌶	◇1 ⊏	◇1
Cardiff Central 7	d	13 25		13 30	13 45	13 50			14 00	14 25		14 30	14 45	14 50			15 00	15 12	15 20	15 25	
Newport (South Wales)	a	13 38		13 43	13 58	14 03			14 13	14 39		14 43	14 59	15 03			15 13	15 25	15 32	15 39	
	d	13 39		13 44	14 00				14 15	14 39		14 44	15 01				15 15	15 27		15 39	
Severn Tunnel Jn	d								14 25								15 25	15 37			
Caldicot	d																	15 39			
Chepstow	d																	15 48			
Lydney	d																	15 57			
Gloucester 7	a				14 42								15 42					16 21			
Pilning	d																				
Patchway	d								14 39								15 39				
Bristol Parkway 7	a	13 59								14 59										15 59	
	d							14 20								15 19					
Filton Abbey Wood	d			14 09				14 25	14 42			15 09				15 22	15 42				
Bristol Temple Meads 10	a			14 18				14 40	14 51			15 18				15 34	15 51				
	d		14 00	14 23			14 30	14 49			15 00	15 23			15 30	15 38					15 54
Keynsham	d							14 56								15 45					
Oldfield Park	d							15 03								15 52					
Bath Spa 7	a		14 11	14 35			14 41	15 05			15 11	15 35			15 41	15 54					16 05

		GW	GW	XC	AW	GW	GW	GW	AW	AW	GW	GW	GW	GW	XC	AW	GW	GW	GW	AW	AW	GW
		◇1 ⊏	◇	◇1	■ ⌶	◇1 ⊏					◇1 C ⊏	◇1 ⊏	■	◇1 D ⊏	◇1	■ ⌶	◇1 ⊏				■ ⌶	◇1 C ⊏
Cardiff Central 7	d		15 30	15 45	15 50			16 00	16 12	16 19	16 25		16 30	16b40	16 45	16 50			17 00	17 12	17 20	17 25
Newport (South Wales)	a		15 43	15 58	16 03			16 13	16 23	16 32	16 39		16 43	16 54	16 59	17 03			17 13	17 27	17 32	17 39
	d		15 44	16 00				16 15	16 27		16 39		16 44	16 55	17 01				17 15	17 27		17 39
Severn Tunnel Jn	d							16 25	16 37				16 55						17 25	17 38		
Caldicot	d								16 39											17 40		
Chepstow	d								16 48											17 49		
Lydney	d								16 57											17 58		
Gloucester 7	a			16 42					17 21						17 42					18 20		
Pilning	d																					
Patchway	d							16 39											17 39			
Bristol Parkway 7	a										16 59			17 15								17 59
	d						16 22											17 20				
Filton Abbey Wood	d		16 09				16 25	16 42					17 09					17 23	17 42			
Bristol Temple Meads 10	a		16 18				16 38	16 51					17 18					17 37	17 51			
	d	16 00	16 23			16 30	16 49					17 00	17 23				17 30	17 49				
Keynsham	d						16 56											17 56				
Oldfield Park	d						17 03											18 03				
Bath Spa 7	a	16 11	16 35			16 41	17 06					17 11	17 35				17 41	18 06				

		GW	GW	GW	XC	AW	GW	GW	GW	AW	GW	GW	GW	XC	AW	GW	GW	GW	GW	GW	GW
		◇1 ⊏	◇	◇1 D ⊏	◇1	■ ⌶	◇1 A ⊏				◇1 C ⊏	◇	◇1 D ⊏	◇1	◇ ⌶	◇1 ⊏			◇1 C ⊏	◇1 D ⊏	◇
Cardiff Central 7	d		17 30	17 40	17 45	17 50			18 00	18 12	18 25	18 30	18 40	18 45	18 50			19 00	19 25	19 25	19 30
Newport (South Wales)	a		17 43	17 54	17 59	18 03			18 13	18 25	18 39	18 43	18 54	18 59	19 03			19 13	19 39	19 39	19 42
	d		17 44	17 55	18 00				18 15	18 27	18 39	18 44	18 55	19 01				19 15	19 39	19 39	19 44
Severn Tunnel Jn	d		17 55						18 25	18 38								19 25			
Caldicot	d									18 40											
Chepstow	d									18 49											
Lydney	d									18 58											
Gloucester 7	a				18 44					19 20				19 42							
Pilning	d																				
Patchway	d								18 39									19 39			
Bristol Parkway 7	a			18 16							18 59		19 15						19 59	20 13	
	d							18 25									19 20				
Filton Abbey Wood	d		18 09					18 28	18 42			19 09					19 24	19 42			20 09
Bristol Temple Meads 10	a		18 18					18 39	18 51			19 18					19 38	19 51			20 18
	d	18 00	18 23				18 30	18 49				19 23				19 30	19 49				20 23
Keynsham	d							18 56									19 56				
Oldfield Park	d							19 03									20 03				
Bath Spa 7	a	18 11	18 35				18 41	19 05				19 35				19 41	20 05				20 35

C until 10 July, from 11 September
D from 17 July until 4 September

Table 132

Cardiff - Gloucester, Bristol and Bath Spa

Saturdays

		AW	GW	GW	GW	XC	GW	XC	AW	GW	GW	AW	GW	SW	XC	AW	GW	GW	AW	GW
		◇	◇■ ⊐			◇■	◇	◇■	◇	◇■ ⊐				■		◇ A	◇■ ⊐			
Cardiff Central ■	d	19 34			19 50	20 00	20 30	20 50	20 53		21 00	21 12			21 30	21 49		22 00	23 20	
Newport (South Wales)	a	19 46			20 03	20 13	20 44	21 03	21 08		21 13	21 25			21 42	22 05		22 14	23 37	
	d				20 05	20 15	20 44	21 05			21 15	21 27			21 44			22 17	23 40	
Severn Tunnel Jn	d				20 15	20 25					21 25	21 38						22 34	23 57	
Caldicot	d					20 28						21 40							23 59	
Chepstow	d					20 36						21 49							00 08	
Lydney	d					20 45						21 58							00 17	
Gloucester ■	a					21 04		21 48				22 19							00 42	
Pilning	d																			
Patchway	d				20 28						21 38							22 48		
Bristol Parkway ■	a																			
	d			20 22																
Filton Abbey Wood	d			20 25	20 39		21 09				21 42							22 52		
Bristol Temple Meads ■	a			20 39	20 48		21 19				21 49				22 25			23 01		
	d		20 33	20 49			21 23			21 47			21 54	22 23			22 33			23 11
Keynsham	d			20 56									21 59							23 18
Oldfield Park	d			21 03									22 06							23 25
Bath Spa ■	a		20 44	21 06			21 35			22 01			22 10	22 34			22 44			23 27

Sundays
until 11 July

		AW	GW	GW	GW	GW	GW	AW	GW	GW	GW	GW	AW	GW	GW	AW	XC	GW	GW	GW	AW	XC	GW
																			■				
		C	◇■ ⊐	◇■ ⊐	◇■ ⊐	◇■ ⊐	◇	◇ ✕	◇■ ⊐		◇■ ⊐	◇	◇ ✕	◇■ ⊐	◇		◇■	◇■ ⊐	◇ ✕	◇■ ⊐	◇ ✕	◇■	◇■ ⊐
Cardiff Central ■	d	23p20		08 00			08 05	08 30	09 05			09 15	09 30		10 08	10 23	10 45		11 08	11 15	11 35	11 45	
Newport (South Wales)	a	23p37		08 16			08 21	08 47	09 18			09 27	09 48		10 20	10 36	10 57		11 20	11 31	11 52	11 57	
	d	23p40		08 18			08 23		09 19			09 29			10 22	10 38	10 59		11 22	11 32		11 59	
Severn Tunnel Jn	d	23p57					08 39					09 46			10 39	10 56			11 39				
Caldicot	d	23p59														10 58							
Chepstow	d	00 08														11 07							
Lydney	d	00 17														11 16							
Gloucester ■	a	00 42														11 42	11 46					12 46	
Pilning	d																						
Patchway	d											09 59											
Bristol Parkway ■	a			08 46					09 46											11 59			
	d																						
Filton Abbey Wood	d						08 54					10 03			10 54				11 54				
Bristol Temple Meads ■	a						09 04					10 13			11 03				12 04				
	d		07 45		08 15	08 45	09 10			09 14	09 55	10 15		10 30	11 10			11 30	12 15				12 30
Keynsham	d						09 17			09 21					11 17								
Oldfield Park	d						09 24			09 29					11 24								
Bath Spa ■	a		07 57		08 26	08 57	09 26			09 32	10 05	10 28		10 42	11 26			11 42	12 26				12 42

		GW	GW	AW	AW	GW	GW	GW	AW	XC	GW	GW	GW	AW	XC	AW	GW	SW	GW	GW	AW	XC	AW
									■							■					■		■
		◇	◇■ ⊐		◇ ✕	◇■ ⊐	◇	◇■ ⊐	✕	◇■	◇■ ⊐	◇	◇■ ⊐		◇■	✕	◇■ ⊐	◇■	◇	◇■ ⊐		◇■	✕
Cardiff Central ■	d	12 08	12 15	12 23	12 40		13 08	13 15	13 40	13 45		14 08	14 15	14 23	14 45	14 55			15 05	15 15	15 22	15 45	15 55
Newport (South Wales)	a	12 20	12 31	12 36	12 57		13 20	13 31	13 52	13 57		14 20	14 31	14 36	14 57	15 12			15 17	15 31	15 34	15 57	16 12
	d	12 22	12 32	12 38			13 22			13 59		14 22	14 32	14 38	14 59				15 19	15 32		15 59	
Severn Tunnel Jn	d	12 39		12 56			13 39					14 39		14 56					15 36				
Caldicot	d			12 58										14 58									
Chepstow	d			13 07										15 07									
Lydney	d			13 16										15 16									
Gloucester ■	a			13 34						14 46				15 37	15 46							16 46	
Pilning	d																						
Patchway	d	12 52																	15 49				
Bristol Parkway ■	a		12 59					13 59					14 59							15 59			
	d																						
Filton Abbey Wood	d	12 57					13 54					14 55							15 53				
Bristol Temple Meads ■	a	13 05					14 04					15 05							16 03				
	d	13 10				13 30	14 15				14 30	15 10					15 30	16 04	16 10				
Keynsham	d	13 17										15 17						16 11					
Oldfield Park	d	13 24										15 24											
Bath Spa ■	a	13 26				13 41	14 26				14 42	15 26					15 42	16 18	16 24				

A until 10 July, from 11 September
C not 23 May

Table 132

Cardiff - Gloucester, Bristol and Bath Spa

Sundays
until 11 July

		GW	GW	GW	GW	AW	GW	GW	AW	XC	AW	GW	GW	GW	GW	AW	GW	GW	XC	GW	GW	GW
									■							■		■				
		◇■ ⊐	◇■ ⊐	◇	◇■ ⊐		◇■ ⊐	◇	✕	◇■			◇■ ⊐	◇	◇■ ⊐		◇■ ⊐		◇■	◇■ ⊐	◇■ ⊐	◇
Cardiff Central ■	d			16 08	16 15	16 22		16 35	16 40	16 45	17 04			17 08	17 15	17 22		17 40	17 45	17 50		18 08
Newport (South Wales)	a			16 20	16 31	16 36		16 47	16 52	16 57	17 21			17 21	17 31	17 34		17 52	17 57	18 03		18 20
	d			16 22	16 32	16 37		16 49		16 59				17 23	17 32			17 54	17 59	18 04		18 22
Severn Tunnel Jn	d			16 39		16 55								17 40								18 39
Caldicot	d					16 58																
Chepstow	d					17 07																
Lydney	d					17 16																
Gloucester ■	a					17 36				17 46									18 46			
Pilning	d																					
Patchway	d																					18 52
Bristol Parkway ■	a				16 59										17 59					18 31		
	d																					
Filton Abbey Wood	d			16 55				17 20						17 55				18 25				18 56
Bristol Temple Meads ■	a			17 06				17 29						18 05				18 33				19 06
	d	16 30	17 00	17 15			17 30	17 40				17 44	18 00	18 10			18 30	18 50			19 00	19 10
Keynsham	d			17 22								17 51		18 17								19 17
Oldfield Park	d			17 29								17 58		18 24								19 24
Bath Spa ■	a	16 41	17 12	17 29			17 42	17 51				18 00	18 12	18 26			18 41	19 01			19 12	19 26

		AW	XC	GW	AW	GW	GW	GW	AW	XC	GW	GW	GW	GW	AW	XC	AW	GW	SW	GW	GW	GW	AW	AW
					■																			
			◇■	◇■ ⊐	✕	◇■ ⊐	◇■ ⊐	◇	◇	◇■	◇■ ⊐		◇■ ⊐	◇		◇■	◇	◇■ ⊐	■	◇■ ⊐		✕		◇
Cardiff Central ■	d	18 23	18 45	18 50	18 58			19 08	19 40	19 45	19 50			20 18	20 23	20 45	21 00	21 05				22 00	22 30	23 00
Newport (South Wales)	a	18 36	18 57	19 03	19 12			19 20	19 53	19 58	20 03			20 30	20 36	20 57	21 13	21 21				22 16	22 47	23 18
	d	18 38	18 59	19 04				19 22		20 00	20 04			20 31	20 38	20 59		21 22				22 18	22 49	
Severn Tunnel Jn	d	18 56						19 40						20 48	20 56							22 35	23 07	
Caldicot	d	18 58													20 58								23 09	
Chepstow	d	19 07													21 07								23 18	
Lydney	d	19 16													21 16								23 27	
Gloucester ■	a	19 38	19 47							20 48					21 40	21 46							23 51	
Pilning	d																							
Patchway	d																					22 48		
Bristol Parkway ■	a			19 31							20 31							21 49						
	d																							
Filton Abbey Wood	d							19 55						21 05								22 52		
Bristol Temple Meads ■	a							20 05						21 13								23 00		
	d					19 30	20 00	20 15				20 50	21 00	21 22					21 35	22 05	22 15	23 10		
Keynsham	d											20 57									22 22			
Oldfield Park	d											21 04									22 29			
Bath Spa ■	a					19 42	20 11	20 26				21 07	21 13	21 33					21 47	22 18	22 31	23 21		

Sundays
18 July to 05 September

		AW	GW	GW	GW	GW	GW	AW	GW	GW	GW	GW	AW	AW	GW	GW	GW	XC	GW	XC	GW	GW	XC
																						■	
			◇■ ⊐	◇■ ⊐	◇■ ⊐	◇■ ⊐	◇	◇ ✕	◇■ ⊐		◇■ ⊐	◇	🚌	◇ ✕	◇■ ⊐	◇■ ⊐	◇	🚌	◇■ ⊐	🚌	◇■ ⊐	◇ ✕	◇■
Cardiff Central ■	d	23p20	07 35				08 05	08 30	08 40			09 15	09 17	09 30	09 45		10 08		10 50			11 08	11 25
Newport (South Wales)	a	23p37	07 51				08 21	08 47	08 56			09 30	09 47	09 48	10 02		10 24		11 12			11 24	11 41
	d	23p40	07 53				08 23		08 58			09 33	09 47		10 03		10 26	10 55	11 13	11 20		11 26	11 43
Severn Tunnel Jn	d	23p57					08 39					09 46	10 12				10 39					11 39	
Caldicot	d	23p59											10 22										
Chepstow	d	00 08											10 37										
Lydney	d	00 17											10 57										
Gloucester ■	a	00 42											11 37					12 10		12 35			12 38
Pilning	d																						
Patchway	d											09 59											
Bristol Parkway ■	a		08 22						09 24						10 23				11 34				
	d																						
Filton Abbey Wood	d						08 54					10 03					10 54					11 54	
Bristol Temple Meads ■	a						09 04					10 13					11 03					12 04	
	d			07 45	08 15	08 45	09 10			09 14	09 48	10 15				10 48	11 10				11 30	12 15	
Keynsham	d						09 17			09 21							11 17						
Oldfield Park	d						09 24			09 29							11 24						
Bath Spa ■	a			07 57	08 26	08 57	09 26			09 32	09 58	10 28				11 00	11 26				11 42	12 26	

Table 132

Cardiff - Gloucester, Bristol and Bath Spa

Sundays from 24 October

		GW	GW	XC	GW	GW	GW	AW		AW	XC	GW	GW	GW	GW	AW	XC	GW		GW	GW	GW	AW	XC	GW
		◇1 ⊏	■	◇1	◇1 ⊏	◇1 ⊏	◇			■ ⊤	◇1	◇1 ⊏	◇1 ⊏	◇1 ⊏	◇	◇	◇1	◇1 ⊏			◇1 ⊏	◇		◇1	◇1 ⊏
Cardiff Central 7	d		17 40	17 45	17 50		18 08	18 23		18 40	18 45	18 50			19 08	19 40	19 45	19 50				20 18	20 23	20 45	20 55
Newport (South Wales)	a		17 52	17 57	18 03		18 20	18 36		18 52	18 57	19 03			19 20	19 53	19 58	20 03				20 30	20 36	20 57	21 08
	d		17 54	17 59	18 04		18 22	18 38			18 59	19 04			19 22		20 00	20 04				20 31	20 38	20 59	21 09
Severn Tunnel Jn	d						18 39	18 56							19 40							20 48	20 56		
Caldicot	d							18 58															20 58		
Chepstow	d							19 07															21 07		
Lydney	d							19 16															21 16		
Gloucester 7	a			18 46				19 38			19 47						20 48						21 40	21 46	
Pilning	d																								
Patchway	d						18 52																		
Bristol Parkway 7	a				18 31							19 31						20 31							21 36
	d																								
Filton Abbey Wood	d		18 25				18 56								19 55							21 05			
Bristol Temple Meads 10	a		18 33				19 06								20 05							21 13			
	d	18 30	18 50			19 00	19 10						19 30	20 00	20 15					20 50	21 00	21 22			
Keynsham	d						19 17													20 57					
Oldfield Park	d						19 24													21 04					
Bath Spa 7	a	18 41	19 01			19 12	19 26						19 42	20 11	20 26					21 07	21 13	21 33			

		AW	SW	GW		GW	GW	AW	AW
		◇	1	◇1 ⊏			⊤		◇
Cardiff Central 7	d	21 04					22 00	22 30	23 00
Newport (South Wales)	a	21 17					22 16	22 47	23 18
	d						22 18	22 49	
Severn Tunnel Jn	d						22 35	23 07	
Caldicot	d							23 09	
Chepstow	d							23 18	
Lydney	d							23 27	
Gloucester 7	a							23 51	
Pilning	d								
Patchway	d						22 48		
Bristol Parkway 7	a								
	d								
Filton Abbey Wood	d						22 52		
Bristol Temple Meads 10	a						23 00		
	d		21 35	22 05		22 15	23 10		
Keynsham	d					22 22			
Oldfield Park	d					22 29			
Bath Spa 7	a		21 47	22 18		22 31	23 21		

Table 132

Bath Spa, Bristol and Gloucester - Cardiff

Mondays to Fridays

		GW	GW MO	GW MX	AW MO	GW	GW MX	GW MX	GW MO	AW MX		GW MX	GW MX	GW MO	XC MX	XC MO	AW	GW	AW	GW		XC	XC	GW	AW
		◇1 A ⊏	◇1 ⊏	◇1 ⊏	◇	◇1 B ⊏	◇1 ⊏	◇1 ⊏	◇1 ⊏	◇		◇1 ⊏	◇1 ⊏	◇1 ⊏	1	1	◇					◇1 ⊤	◇1 ⊤		◇ ⊤
Bath Spa 7	d		23p55	23p55					00s53			01 15		01s23								06 09		06 28	
Oldfield Park	d																							06 31	
Keynsham	d																							06 38	
Bristol Temple Meads 10	a		00 09	00 10					01 05			01 29	01 23	01 36								06 20		06 45	
	d											01 34	01 34		05 19	05 19		05 54		06 19		06 27		06 50	
Filton Abbey Wood	d																	06 01		06 31				07 02	
Bristol Parkway 7	a														05 28	05 28						06 37			
	d	23p17				23p38	00 18	00 24							05 38	05 38						06 40			
Patchway	d																	06 06		06 36					
Pilning	d																								
Gloucester 7	d																		05 50				06 18		
Lydney	d																		06 09				06 37		
Chepstow	d																		06 19				06 46		
Caldicot	d																		06 26				06 55		
Severn Tunnel Jn	d																	06 17	06 29	06 49			06 58	07 14	
Newport (South Wales)	a	23p45			23p55	00 03	00 46	00 52				02s10	02s10		05 58	06 08	06 16	06 29	06 41	07 01			07 09	07 26	07 33
	d	23p45			23p55	00 04	00 48	00 54		01 01		02s12	02s12		06 00	06 10	06 17	06 30	06 44	07 03			07 11	07 28	07 35
Cardiff Central 7	a	00 06			00 20	00 25	01 06	01 12		01 20		02 31	02 31		06 18	06 24	06 33	06 47	07 00	07 20			07 26	07 44	07 51

		GW	XC	AW	GW	GW		GW	SW	GW	GW	GW	AW	AW	GW	AW		GW	GW	XC	GW	GW	GW	GW	GW
		◇1 ⊏	◇1 ⊤	◇					1	◇1 ⊏		◇1 ⊏	◇ ⊤			◇ ⊤		◇1 ⊏		◇1 ⊤	◇ ⊤	◇1 ⊏	◇1 Ø		◇1 Ø
Bath Spa 7	d	06 54				07 07		07 25	07 35		07 48	07 59							08 07		08 21	08 29		08 47	08 57
Oldfield Park	d					07 10		07 28	07 38		07 51								08 10		08 23			08 49	
Keynsham	d					07 17		07 35	07 45		07 58	08 08							08 17		08 33			08 57	
Bristol Temple Meads 10	a	07 07				07 27		07 45	07 52		08 06	08 17							08 29		08 39	08 44		09 05	09 10
	d	07 13			07 19	07 34		07 54			08 10				08 21				08 41		08 54			09 10	
Filton Abbey Wood	d	07 22			07 30	07 43		08 00			08 22				08 30				08 48		09 01			09 22	
Bristol Parkway 7	a				07 33	07 47					08 29								08 52					09 28	
	d				07 40	07 48				08 07								08 40	08 52				09 07		
Patchway	d				07 44			08 05							08 35										
Pilning	d																								
Gloucester 7	d		07 01			08a29								07 58					09a38	08 28					
Lydney	d		07 20											08 17											
Chepstow	d		07 29											08 27											
Caldicot	d		07 38											08 35											
Severn Tunnel Jn	d		07 41		07 56									08 38	08 46										
Newport (South Wales)	a	07 44	07 52		08 08			08 27		08 31				08 50	09 00			09 07		09 12	09 25		09 31		
	d	07 44	07 54	08 01	08 09			08 27		08 31			08 34	08 52	09 02	09 03		09 07		09 14	09 25		09 31		
Cardiff Central 7	a	08 00	08 08	08 17	08 25			08 46		08 48			08 55	09 07	09 23	09 22		09 24		09 30	09 43		09 47		

		AW		AW BHX	AW	GW	GW	GW	XC	GW	GW	GW		GW	AW	GW	GW	GW	XC	GW	GW	GW	GW	AW	GW
		◇ ⊤		◇1 ⊠			◇1 ⊏		◇1 ⊤	◇ ⊤	◇1 ⊏	◇1 ⊏		◇1 ⊏	◇ ⊤		◇1 ⊏	◇	◇1 ⊤	◇1 ⊏	◇ ⊤	◇1 ⊏	◇1 Ø		
Bath Spa 7	d							09 15		09 22	09 30	10 00						10 07		10 24	10 36	11 00			
Oldfield Park	d							09 17										10 10							
Keynsham	d							09 25		09 31								10 17							
Bristol Temple Meads 10	a							09 35		09 39	09 44	10 15						10 29		10 38	10 48	11 15			
	d					09 21		09 41		09 54						10 21		10 41			10 54				11 21
Filton Abbey Wood	d					09 30		09 48		10 00						10 30		10 48			11 00				11 30
Bristol Parkway 7	a							09 52										10 52							
	d						09 40	09 52						10 07			10 40	10 52					11 07		
Patchway	d					09 35										10 35									11 35
Pilning	d																								
Gloucester 7	d				08 58			10a32	09 24									11a36	10 24					10 58	
Lydney	d				09 17																			11 17	
Chepstow	d				09 27																			11 27	
Caldicot	d				09 35																			11 35	
Severn Tunnel Jn	d				09 38	09 46										10 46								11 38	11 46
Newport (South Wales)	a				09 50	09 59	10 04		10 09	10 25				10 31		10 59	11 04		11 11		11 25		11 31	11 50	11 59
	d	09 37		09 41	09 52	10 00	10 04		10 10	10 25				10 31	10 57	11 00	11 04		11 12		11 25		11 31	11 52	12 00
Cardiff Central 7	a	09 53		09 58	10 07	10 18	10 21		10 25	10 43				10 46	11 14	11 22	11 23		11 27		11 43		11 46	12 07	12 18

		GW	GW	XC	GW	GW	SW	GW		GW	AW	AW	GW	AW	GW	GW	XC	GW		GW	GW	GW	AW	GW	GW
		◇1 ⊏		◇1 ⊤	◇1 ⊏	◇ ⊤	◇1	◇1 ⊏		◇1 Ø	◇ ⊤			◇ ⊤	◇1 ⊏	◇	◇1 ⊤	◇1 ⊏		◇ ⊤	◇1 ⊏	◇1 Ø	◇ ⊤		◇1 ⊏
Bath Spa 7	d		11 07		11 24	11 36	11 47	12 00								12 08		12 24		12 36	13 00				
Oldfield Park	d		11 10													12 10									
Keynsham	d		11 17													12 17									
Bristol Temple Meads 10	a		11 29		11 40	11 48	12 05	12 15								12 29		12 39		12 48	13 15				
	d		11 41			11 54							12 21			12 41				12 54				13 21	
Filton Abbey Wood	d		11 48			12 01							12 30			12 48				13 00				13 30	
Bristol Parkway 7	a		11 52													12 52									
	d	11 40	11 52							12 07					12 40	12 52						13 07			13 40
Patchway	d												12 35											13 35	
Pilning	d																								
Gloucester 7	d		12a31	11 24								11 58				13a38	12 24								
Lydney	d											12 17													
Chepstow	d											12 27													
Caldicot	d											12 35													
Severn Tunnel Jn	d											12 38	12 46											13 46	
Newport (South Wales)	a	12 04		12 09		12 25				12 31	12 33	12 50	13 00	13 00	13 04		13 11			13 25		13 31	13 34	13 59	14 04
	d	12 04		12 10		12 25				12 31	12 37	12 52	13 00	13 00	13 04		13 12			13 25		13 31	13 37	14 00	14 04
Cardiff Central 7	a	12 21		12 27		12 43				12 46	12 53	13 07	13 22	13 20	13 22		13 29			13 43		13 46	13 53	14 18	14 22

A MO until 12 July, MO from 13 September

B MO from 19 July until 6 September

Bath Spa, Bristol and Gloucester - Cardiff

		GW	XC	GW	GW	GW	GW	AW	AW	AW	GW	GW	GW	GW	GW	XC	GW	SW	GW	GW	AW	AW	GW	GW	GW
			◇1 ⊼	◇1 ⊡	◇ ⊼	◇1 ⊡	◇1 Ø	◇ ⊼		■ ⊼			◇1 ⊡	◇	◇1 ⊡	◇1 ⊼	◇ ⊼	◇1	◇1 ⊡	◇1 ⊡	⊼		◇1 ⊡		
Bath Spa 7	d	13 19		13 24	13 36	14 00						14 08		14 15	14 24		14 36	14 47	15 00						15 18
Oldfield Park	d	13 21												14 18											15 21
Keynsham	d	13 28												14 25											15 28
Bristol Temple Meads 10	a	13 36		13 41	13 48	14 15								14 35	14 39		14 48	15 05	15 15						15 36
	d	13 41			13 54						14 21			14 41			14 54							15 21	15 41
Filton Abbey Wood	d	13 48			14 00						14 30	14 29		14 48			15 00							15 30	15 48
Bristol Parkway 7	a	13 52										14 37		14 51											15 52
	d						14 07						14 40							15 07			15 40		
Patchway	d										14 35													15 35	
Pilning	d																								
Gloucester 7	d		13 24						13 58							14 24						14 58			
Lydney	d								14 17													15 17			
Chepstow	d								14 27													15 27			
Caldicot	d								14 35													15 35			
Severn Tunnel Jn	d								14 38		14 45											15 38		15 46	
Newport (South Wales)	a		14 09		14 25		14 31		14 50		14 59		15 04			15 12	15 24			15 31	15 34	15 50	16 04	16 06	
	d		14 10		14 25		14 31	14 38	14 52	15 00	15 01		15 04			15 13	15 25			15 31	15 37	15 52	16 04	16 06	
Cardiff Central 7	a		14 27		14 43		14 46	14 54	15 07	15 20	15 24		15 23			15 29	15 43			15 46	15 53	16 10	16 22	16 29	

		XC	GW	GW	GW	GW	AW	AW	GW	GW		XC	GW	GW	GW	GW	AW	AW	GW	GW		GW	GW	XC	GW
		◇1 ⊼	◇1 ⊡	◇ ⊼	◇1 ⊡	◇1 ⊡	■ ⊼	◇ ⊼	◇1 ⊡			◇1 ⊼	◇1 ⊡	■ ⊼	◇1 ⊡	◇1 ⊡	■ ⊼			◇1 ⊡			◇1 ⊡	◇1 ⊼	■ ⊼
Bath Spa 7	d		15 24	15 36	16 00					16 07			16 24	16 36	17 00							17 07	17 24		17 36
Oldfield Park	d									16 10												17 10			
Keynsham	d									16 17												17 17			
Bristol Temple Meads 10	a		15 40	15 48	16 15					16 29			16 39	16 48	17 15							17 29	17 41		17 48
	d			15 54						16 41				16 54					17 21			17 41			17 54
Filton Abbey Wood	d			16 00						16 48				17 00					17 30			17 48			18 00
Bristol Parkway 7	a									16 52												17 52			
	d					16 07			16 40							17 07				17 40					
Patchway	d																		17 35						
Pilning	d																								
Gloucester 7	d	15 24										16 24						16 58						17 27	
Lydney	d																	17 17							
Chepstow	d																	17 27							
Caldicot	d																	17 35							
Severn Tunnel Jn	d													17 14				17 38	17 46						18 14
Newport (South Wales)	a	16 10		16 25		16 31			17 04			17 11		17 25		17 31		17 50	17 59	18 04				18 10	18 25
	d	16 12		16 25		16 31	16 37	17 00	17 04			17 13		17 25		17 31	17 34	17 52	18 00	18 04				18 11	18 25
Cardiff Central 7	a	16 29		16 43		16 46	16 53	17 17	17 22			17 28		17 43		17 46	17 52	18 10	18 18	18 20				18 27	18 43

		GW	GW	AW	AW	AW		GW	GW	GW	GW	XC	GW	GW	AW	GW	AW	GW	GW	GW	XC	GW	GW FX	GW FO	GW FX
		◇1 ⊡	◇1 ⊡	■ ⊼		◇ ⊼			◇1 ⊡		◇1 ⊡	◇1 ⊼	■ ⊼	◇1 ⊡	■ ⊼	◇1 ⊡			◇1 ⊡		◇1 ⊼	◇1 ⊡	◇ ⊼	◇ ⊼	◇1 ⊡
Bath Spa 7	d	18 00								18 07	18 29		18 36	18 59						19 07		19 30	19 36	19 36	
Oldfield Park	d									18 10										19 10					
Keynsham	d									18 17										19 17					
Bristol Temple Meads 10	a	18 15								18 28	18 44		18 49	19 12						19 29		19 43	19 49	19 49	
	d							18 21		18 41			18 54					19 21		19 41				19 54	
Filton Abbey Wood	d							18 30		18 48			19 00					19 30		19 48				20 00	
Bristol Parkway 7	a									18 52										19 52					
	d		18 07						18 40							19 10			19 40						20 07
Patchway	d							18 35										19 35							
Pilning	d																								
Gloucester 7	d				17 59							18 31					18 58				19 28				
Lydney	d				18 18												19 17								
Chepstow	d				18 28												19 27								
Caldicot	d				18 36												19 34								
Severn Tunnel Jn	d				18 39			18 50					19 14				19 37	19 46						20 19	
Newport (South Wales)	a		18 31		18 51			19 06	19 11			19 16	19 25			19 38	19 50	19 59	20 07		20 12			20 30	20 31
	d		18 31	18 40	18 53	19 00		19 06	19 11			19 17	19 25		19 33	19 38	19 52	20 00	20 08		20 14			20 31	20 31
Cardiff Central 7	a		18 48	18 56	19 09	19 21		19 23	19 26			19 33	19 43		19 49	19 53	20 12	20 19	20 22		20 31			20 48	20 45

Bath Spa, Bristol and Gloucester - Cardiff

		GW FO		AW	GW FX	GW	GW	XC	AW	AW	GW	GW		XC	GW	GW	GW	GW	GW	GW	GW	XC FO		XC FX	GW
		◇1 ⊡		■ ⊼			◇1 ⊡	◇1		◇ ⊼	◇1 ⊡	◇		◇1 ⊼	◇1 ⊡	◇ ⊼	◇1 ⊡			◇1 ⊡	◇1 ⊡	◇1 ⊼		◇1 ⊼	◇
Bath Spa 7	d					19 47	19 59					20 11			20 30	20 36	21 00		21 07	21 29					21 36
Oldfield Park	d					19 50						20 13							21 10						
Keynsham	d					19 58						20 20							21 17						
Bristol Temple Meads 10	a					20 05	20 13	20 13				20 29			20 44	20 50	21 15		21 29	21 44					21 49
	d				20 04		20 18	20 15				20 41				20 55	21 18	21 19							21 54
Filton Abbey Wood	d				20 11			20 22				20 48				21 00		21 30							22 00
Bristol Parkway 7	a										20 39	20 52									21 39				
	d	20 07									20 40	20 52									21 40				
Patchway	d							20 25										21 34							22 06
Pilning	d																								
Gloucester 7	d								19 58			21a35		20 24								21 24		21 24	
Lydney	d								20 17													21 43		21 43	
Chepstow	d								20 27													21 52		21 52	
Caldicot	d								20 36													22 01		22 01	
Severn Tunnel Jn	d				20 28			20 37	20 39							21 16		21 46				22 04		22 04	22 18
Newport (South Wales)	a	20 35			20 45			20 47	20 51		21 04			21 08		21 27		21 59			22 03	22 15		22 15	22 37
	d	20 37		20 42	20 46			20 49	20 52	20 58	21 04			21 10		21 27		22 00			22 05	22 17		22 17	22 38
Cardiff Central 7	a	20 51		20 56	21 07			21 02	21 10	21 19	21 19			21 27		21 45		22 18			22 23	22 31		22 35	23 00

		SW	GW	GW	GW	GW FX	GW FO	GW FX	AW	GW	GW	GW FO	GW FX
		◇1	◇1 ⊡		◇1 ⊡	◇1 ⊡	◇	◇			◇1 ⊡	◇1 ⊡	◇1 ⊡
Bath Spa 7	d	21 51	22 13	22 26			22 36	22 36		23 02	23 19	23 49	23 55
Oldfield Park	d			22 28						23 05			
Keynsham	d	21 59		22 35						23 12			
Bristol Temple Meads 10	a	22 06	22 30	22 44			22 48	22 48		23 22	23 33	00 03	00 10
	d						22 54	22 54			23 35		
Filton Abbey Wood	d						23 00	23 00					
Bristol Parkway 7	a												
	d				22 45	22 45							
Patchway	d						23 06	23 06					
Pilning	d												
Gloucester 7	d								23 13				
Lydney	d								23 33				
Chepstow	d								23 42				
Caldicot	d								23 51				
Severn Tunnel Jn	d						23 17	23 17	23 54				
Newport (South Wales)	a				23 18	23 18	23 35	23 34	00 07				
	d				23 18	23 18	23 35	23 35	00 08				
Cardiff Central 7	a				23 39	23 39	23 57	23 57	00 36				

Saturdays

		GW	GW	AW	GW	AW	AW	XC	GW	GW		AW	XC	GW	GW	AW	GW	SW	GW	AW		AW	GW	GW	GW
		◇1 ⊡	◇1 ⊡		◇1 ⊡			◇1 ⊼		◇1		◇ ⊼	◇1 ⊼					1	◇1 ⊡	◇ ⊼					◇1 ⊡
Bath Spa 7	d	23p49			01 13										07 07		07 22	07 35	08 00					08 07	08 24
Oldfield Park	d														07 10		07 25	07 38						08 10	
Keynsham	d														07 17		07 32	07 45						08 17	
Bristol Temple Meads 10	a	00 03			01 27										07 29		07 39	07 53	08 15				08 10	08 29	08 39
	d				01 34				06 50	06 46				07 21	07 41		07 54						08 19	08 41	
Filton Abbey Wood	d								07 02	06 54				07 30	07 48		08 01						08 30	08 48	
Bristol Parkway 7	a									06 58					07 52									08 52	
	d		00 16							07 11					07 52									08 52	
Patchway	d													07 34									08 35		
Pilning	d																								
Gloucester 7	d						05 50	06 15					07 01		08a32							07 58		09 38	
Lydney	d						06 09	06 34					07 20									08 17			
Chepstow	d						06 19	06 43					07 29									08 27			
Caldicot	d						06 27	06 52					07 38									08 35			
Severn Tunnel Jn	d						06 30	06 55	07 14				07 41	07 46								08 38	08 46		
Newport (South Wales)	a		00 38		02s02		06 42	07 06	07 26	07 31			07 52	07 59			08 25					08 50	09 00		
	d		00 38	01 01	02s03	06 38	06 44	07 08	07 28	07 31		07 38	07 54	07 59		08 01	08 25			08 35		08 52	09 00		
Cardiff Central 7	a		00 53	01 20	02 18	06 54	07 00	07 22	07 43	07 48		07 55	08 08	08 18		08 19	08 43			08 55		09 10	09 21		

Table 132

Bath Spa, Bristol and Gloucester - Cardiff

Saturdays

		AW	XC	GW	GW	GW	GW	GW	AW	AW	GW	XC	GW	GW	GW	GW	GW	AW	AW	GW	GW	XC	GW
		◇	◇1	◇		■ 1	◇1	◇1	◇			◇1	◇1	◇	◇1	◇1	◇1		◇		◇	◇1	◇1
						A	B									B	A	B	A				
		trolley	trolley			buffet	buffet	buffet	trolley			trolley	buffet	trolley	buffet	buffet	buffet		trolley			trolley	buffet
Bath Spa [7]	d			08 36	08 47	09 00	09 00						09 24	09 36	10 00						10 07		10 24
Oldfield Park	d				08 49																10 10		
Keynsham	d				08 57																10 17		
Bristol Temple Meads [10]	a			08 47	09 05	09 14	09 15				09 08		09 39	09 48	10 15					10 09	10 29		10 39
	d			08 54							09 21			09 54						10 21	10 41		
Filton Abbey Wood	d			09 00							09 30			10 00						10 30	10 48		
Bristol Parkway [7]	a							09 04													10 52		
	d							09 07								10 07	10 07				10 52		
Patchway	d										09 35									10 35			
Pilning	d																						
Gloucester [7]	d		08 24							08 58		09 24									11a38	10 24	
Lydney	d									09 17													
Chepstow	d									09 27													
Caldicot	d									09 35													
Severn Tunnel Jn	d									09 38	09 46									10 46			
Newport (South Wales)	a		09 07	09 25				09 31		09 50	09 59	10 05		10 25		10 31	10 31			11 00		11 05	
	d	09 02	09 09	09 25				09 31	09 37	09 52	10 00	10 07		10 25		10 31	10 31	10 37	10 37	11 00		11 07	
Cardiff Central [7]	a	09 22	09 23	09 43				09 47	09 53	10 07	10 17	10 21		10 43		10 46	10 47	10 53	10 53	11 22		11 24	

		GW	GW	GW	AW	AW	GW	GW	XC	GW	GW	SW	GW	GW	AW	AW	GW	GW	GW
		◇	◇1	◇1	◇				◇1	◇1	◇	◇1	◇1	◇1	◇			◇	◇1
		trolley	buffet	buffet	trolley				trolley	buffet	trolley		buffet	Ø	trolley				buffet
Bath Spa [7]	d	10 36	11 00					11 07		11 24	11 36	11 47	12 00					12 11	12 24
Oldfield Park	d							11 10										12 14	
Keynsham	d							11 17										12 21	
Bristol Temple Meads [10]	a	10 48	11 15				11 12	11 29		11 39	11 48	12 05	12 15				12 10	12 29	12 39
	d	10 54					11 21	11 41			11 54						12 21	12 41	
Filton Abbey Wood	d	11 00					11 30	11 48			12 00						12 30	12 48	
Bristol Parkway [7]	a			11 04				11 52						12 04				12 52	
	d			11 07				11 52						12 07				12 52	
Patchway	d						11 35										12 35		
Pilning	d																		
Gloucester [7]	d					10 58		12a31	11 24							11 58		13 38	
Lydney	d					11 17										12 17			
Chepstow	d					11 27										12 27			
Caldicot	d					11 35										12 35			
Severn Tunnel Jn	d					11 38	11 46									12 38	12 46		
Newport (South Wales)	a	11 25		11 31		11 50	11 59		12 06		12 25			12 31		12 50	13 00		
	d	11 25		11 31	11 37	11 52	12 00		12 07		12 25			12 31	12 37	12 52	13 00		
Cardiff Central [7]	a	11 43		11 46	11 53	12 07	12 18		12 22		12 43			12 46	12 53	13 07	13 22		

		AW	XC	GW	GW	GW	AW	GW	GW	XC	GW	GW	GW	GW	AW	AW	GW	GW	GW	AW	XC
		◇	◇1	◇	◇1	◇1	◇			◇1	◇1	◇	◇1	◇1	◇			◇	◇1	◇	◇1
		trolley	trolley	trolley	buffet	Ø	trolley			trolley	buffet	trolley	buffet	buffet	trolley				buffet	trolley	trolley
Bath Spa [7]	d			12 36	13 00				13 19		13 24	13 36	14 00					14 07	14 24		
Oldfield Park	d								13 21									14 10			
Keynsham	d								13 28									14 17			
Bristol Temple Meads [10]	a			12 48	13 15			13 09	13 36		13 42	13 48	14 15				14 11	14 29	14 39		
	d			12 54				13 21	13 41			13 54					14 21	14 41			
Filton Abbey Wood	d			13 00				13 30	13 48			14 00					14 30	14 48			
Bristol Parkway [7]	a					13 04			13 52					14 04				14 52			
	d					13 07			13 52					14 07				14 52			
Patchway	d							13 35									14 35				
Pilning	d																				
Gloucester [7]	d		12 24						14a33	13 24						13 58		15a38			14 24
Lydney	d															14 17					
Chepstow	d															14 27					
Caldicot	d															14 35					
Severn Tunnel Jn	d							13 46								14 38	14 46				
Newport (South Wales)	a		13 06	13 25		13 31		13 59		14 05		14 25		14 31		14 50	15 00				15 06
	d	13 00	13 07	13 25		13 31	13 37	14 00		14 07		14 25		14 31	14 38	14 52	15 00			15 00	15 07
Cardiff Central [7]	a	13 20	13 22	13 43		13 47	13 53	14 18		14 21		14 43		14 46	14 54	15 09	15 21			15 21	15 22

A until 4 September

B from 11 September

Table 132

Bath Spa, Bristol and Gloucester - Cardiff

Saturdays

		GW	SW	GW	GW	AW	AW	AW	GW	XC	GW	GW	GW	GW	GW	AW	GW	GW	GW	AW	XC	GW
		◇	◇1	◇1	◇1	■				◇1		◇1	◇	◇1	◇1	■			◇1	■	◇1	◇
						A	B															
				buffet	buffet	trolley				trolley		buffet		buffet	buffet	trolley			buffet	trolley	trolley	
Bath Spa [7]	d	14 36	14 47	15 00							15 18	15 24	15 36	16 00				16 07	16 24			16 36
Oldfield Park	d										15 21							16 10				
Keynsham	d										15 28							16 17				
Bristol Temple Meads [10]	a	14 48	15 05	15 15							15 36	15 41	15 49	16 15				16 29	16 39			16 48
	d	14 54							15 21		15 41		15 54				16 21	16 41				16 54
Filton Abbey Wood	d	15 00							15 30		15 48		16 00				16 30	16 48				17 00
Bristol Parkway [7]	a										15 52							16 52				
	d				15 07						15 52				16 07			16 52				
Patchway	d								15 35								16 35					
Pilning	d								15 41													
Gloucester [7]	d							14 58		15 24	16a32							17 38			16 24	
Lydney	d							15 17														
Chepstow	d							15 27														
Caldicot	d							15 35														
Severn Tunnel Jn	d							15 38	15 46								16 46					17 14
Newport (South Wales)	a	15 25			15 31			15 50	15 59	16 06			16 25		16 31		17 00				17 06	17 25
	d	15 25			15 31	15 37	15 37	15 52	16 00	16 08			16 25		16 31	16 37	17 00			17 00	17 08	17 25
Cardiff Central [7]	a	15 43			15 46	15 53	15 53	16 07	16 18	16 22			16 43		16 47	16 53	17 21			17 17	17 24	17 43

		GW	AW	AW	GW	GW	GW	GW	XC	GW	GW	GW	GW	GW	GW	AW	AW	GW	GW	AW	GW
		◇1	■			◇1	◇1		◇1	◇1			◇1	◇	◇1	■			◇1	◇	◇1
		C			D		A	C		D	C	D			C			D			D
		buffet	trolley			buffet	buffet		trolley	buffet			buffet		buffet	trolley			buffet	trolley	buffet
Bath Spa [7]	d					17 00	17 00				17 07	17 12	17 24	17 36					18 00		
Oldfield Park	d										17 10	17 14									
Keynsham	d										17 17	17 22									
Bristol Temple Meads [10]	a					17 15	17 15				17 29	17 30	17 39	17 48					18 15		
	d				17 10		17 18	17 21			17 41	17 41		17 54				18 13			
Filton Abbey Wood	d				17 21			17 30			17 48	17 48		18 00				18 22			
Bristol Parkway [7]	a										17 52	17 52									
	d	17 07								17 41	17 52	17 52			18 07						18 40
Patchway	d				17 27			17 35										18 27			
Pilning	d																				
Gloucester [7]	d			16 58					17 24		18a32	18a32					17 58				
Lydney	d			17 17													18 17				
Chepstow	d			17 27													18 27				
Caldicot	d			17 35													18 35				
Severn Tunnel Jn	d			17 38	17 41			17 46						18 14			18 38	18 42			
Newport (South Wales)	a	17 30		17 50	17 55			17 59	18 05	18 09				18 25	18 31		18 50	18 55			19 05
	d	17 30	17 34	17 52	17 57			18 00	18 07	18 10				18 25	18 31	18 38	18 52	18 56		19 00	19 05
Cardiff Central [7]	a	17 46	17 54	18 10	18 14			18 18	18 21	18 25				18 43	18 47	18 54	19 10	19 12		19 21	19 22

		GW	GW	GW	GW	XC	GW	GW	AW	GW	AW	GW	GW	XC	GW	GW	GW	GW	GW	GW	GW	GW
					◇1	◇1	■	◇1	■	◇1				◇1	◇1		◇1	◇		◇1	◇1	◇1
		C	B	A						C			A		D	B					C	D
					buffet	trolley		buffet	trolley	buffet				trolley	buffet		buffet			buffet	buffet	buffet
Bath Spa [7]	d		18 07	18 18	18 24		18 36	19 00					19 07			19 07	19 24	19 36	19 47	20 00		
Oldfield Park	d		18 10	18 20									19 10			19 10			19 50			
Keynsham	d		18 17	18 27									19 17			19 17			19 58			
Bristol Temple Meads [10]	a		18 29	18 35	18 39		18 48	19 15					19 29			19 29	19 39	19 48	20 05	20 15		
	d	18 21	18 41	18 41			18 54	19 18				19 21				19 41		19 54		20 15		
Filton Abbey Wood	d	18 30	18 48	18 48			19 00					19 28				19 48		20 00				
Bristol Parkway [7]	a		18 52	18 52												19 52						
	d		18 52	18 52						19 12					19 37	19 52					20 07	20 31
Patchway	d	18 35										19 33										
Pilning	d																					
Gloucester [7]	d		19 38	19 38		18 31					18 58			19 24		20 38						
Lydney	d										19 17											
Chepstow	d										19 27											
Caldicot	d										19 34											
Severn Tunnel Jn	d	18 50									19 37	19 46										
Newport (South Wales)	a	19 06				19 12	19 25		19 29	19 37	19 50	19 59		20 05	20 11			20 25			20 31	21 05
	d	19 06				19 14	19 25		19 31	19 37	19 52	20 00		20 07	20 11			20 25			20 31	21 06
Cardiff Central [7]	a	19 23				19 29	19 42		19 46	19 52	20 11	20 18		20 21	20 27			20 43			20 45	21 20

A until 4 September

B from 11 September

C until 10 July, from 11 September

D from 17 July until 4 September

Bath Spa, Bristol and Gloucester - Cardiff

Saturdays

		AW ■ ⊥	AW	XC ◇1 A ⊥	XC ◇1 B ⊥	AW ◇ ⊥	GW ◇1 A ☕	GW ■	XC ◇1 ⊥	GW ◇1 ☕	GW ◇	GW ◇1 ☕
Bath Spa 7	d							20 18		20 25	20 36	21 00
Oldfield Park	d							20 20				
Keynsham	d							20 27				
Bristol Temple Meads 10	a							20 35		20 40	20 48	21 15
	d			20 21	20 21			20 41			20 54	
Filton Abbey Wood	d			20 28	20 30			20 48			21 00	
Bristol Parkway 7	a							20 52				
	d						20 40	20 52				
Patchway	d			20 32	20 33							
Pilning	d											
Gloucester 7	d		19 58					21 38	20 24			
Lydney	d		20 17									
Chepstow	d		20 27									
Caldicot	d		20 35									
Severn Tunnel Jn	d		20 38	20 45	20 45							
Newport (South Wales)	a		20 50	20 55	20 55		21 04		21 10		21 25	
	d	20 40	20 52	20 57	20 57	21 00	21 04		21 12		21 25	
Cardiff Central 7	a	20 56	21 09	21 11	21 11	21 21	21 22		21 28		21 43	

		GW ◇1 C ☕	AW ◇ ⊥	GW	GW C	GW D	GW ◇1 ☕	GW ◇1 D ☕	XC ◇1 ⊥	GW ◇	SW ◇1
Bath Spa 7	d				21 07	21 10	21 30			21 39	21 51
Oldfield Park	d				21 10	21 13					
Keynsham	d				21 17	21 19					21 59
Bristol Temple Meads 10	a				21 29	21 32	21 45			21 51	22 06
	d			21 28						21 54	
Filton Abbey Wood	d			21 36						22 00	
Bristol Parkway 7	a										
	d	21 07						21 40			
Patchway	d			21 40						22 06	
Pilning	d										
Gloucester 7	d								21 24		
Lydney	d								21 43		
Chepstow	d								21 52		
Caldicot	d								22 01		
Severn Tunnel Jn	d			21 52					22 04	22 18	
Newport (South Wales)	a	21 30		22 08				22 14	22 21	22 36	
	d	21 31	21 44	22 10				22 15	22 22	22 36	
Cardiff Central 7	a	21 47	22 03	22 29				22 35	22 44	22 56	

		GW ◇1 ☕	GW	AW ◇	GW ◇1 C ☕	GW ◇1 D ☕	GW ◇	GW ◇1 ☕	GW	AW ◇ C	GW ◇1 C ☕	AW	GW ◇1 D ☕
Bath Spa 7	d	22 00	22 26				22 36	23 00	23 07				
Oldfield Park	d		22 28						23 10				
Keynsham	d		22 35						23 17				
Bristol Temple Meads 10	a	22 15	22 44				22 50	23 15	23 29				
	d						22 54						
Filton Abbey Wood	d						23 00						
Bristol Parkway 7	a												
	d				22 11	22 37					23 28		23 47
Patchway	d						23 07						
Pilning	d												
Gloucester 7	d											23 09	
Lydney	d											23 28	
Chepstow	d											23 38	
Caldicot	d											23 46	
Severn Tunnel Jn	d						23 18					23 49	
Newport (South Wales)	a				22 46	23 07	23 35				23 58	00 09	00 17
	d			22 42	22 46	23 08	23 36			23 49	23 59	00 10	00 18
Cardiff Central 7	a			23 05	23 06	23 28	23 55			00 12	00 20	00 33	00 39

Sundays until 11 July

		AW E	AW E	GW ◇1 E ☕	GW ◇1 E ☕	AW 🚌	AW ◇ ⊥	GW ◇1 ☕	GW ◇	GW ◇1 ☕	GW	GW ◇1 ☕
Bath Spa 7	d			00 10	01 07					09 49	10 27	10 42
Oldfield Park	d										10 30	
Keynsham	d										10 37	
Bristol Temple Meads 10	a			00 25	01 21				09 38	10 02	10 45	10 56
	d								09 48			
Filton Abbey Wood	d								09 56			
Bristol Parkway 7	a											
	d							09 40				
Patchway	d											
Pilning	d											
Gloucester 7	d		23p09									
Lydney	d		23p28									
Chepstow	d		23p38									
Caldicot	d		23p46									
Severn Tunnel Jn	d		23p49						10 09			
Newport (South Wales)	a		00 09					10 05	10 27			
	d	00 03	00 10			08 45	09 13	10 05	10 28			
Cardiff Central 7	a	00 24	00 33			09 15	09 28	10 23	10 43			

		AW	AW ◇ ⊥	GW ◇1 ☕	AW	GW ■	GW ◇1 ☕	GW ◇1 ☕	GW ◇1 ☕	AW ⊥
Bath Spa 7	d					11 25	11 39		12 39	
Oldfield Park	d					11 28				
Keynsham	d					11 35				
Bristol Temple Meads 10	a					11 43	11 54		12 53	
	d					11 48				
Filton Abbey Wood	d					11 55				
Bristol Parkway 7	a									
	d			11 04				12 04		
Patchway	d					12 00				
Pilning	d									
Gloucester 7	d				10 48					
Lydney	d				11 07					
Chepstow	d				11 17					
Caldicot	d				11 25					
Severn Tunnel Jn	d				11 28	12 11				
Newport (South Wales)	a			11 34	11 46	12 30		12 34		
	d	10 55	11 00	11 34	11 48	12 30		12 36		12 52
Cardiff Central 7	a	11 13	11 16	11 52	12 06	12 45		12 50		13 13

A from 11 September
B until 4 September
C until 10 July, from 11 September
D from 17 July until 4 September
E not 23 May

Table 132

Bath Spa, Bristol and Gloucester - Cardiff

Sundays until 11 July

		AW	GW ◇1 ☕	AW	GW ◇	GW ◇1 ☕	AW ■ ⊥	GW ◇1 ☕	AW	GW ◇	AW	GW ◇1 ☕
Bath Spa 7	d				13 26	13 39				14 25		14 39
Oldfield Park	d				13 29					14 27		
Keynsham	d				13 36					14 35		
Bristol Temple Meads 10	a				13 43	13 54				14 43		14 54
	d				13 48					14 48		
Filton Abbey Wood	d				13 55					14 55		
Bristol Parkway 7	a											
	d		13 04					14 04				
Patchway	d											
Pilning	d											
Gloucester 7	d			12 52							14 31	
Lydney	d			13 12							14 50	
Chepstow	d			13 22							15 00	
Caldicot	d			13 30							15 09	
Severn Tunnel Jn	d			13 33	14 08					15 08	15 12	
Newport (South Wales)	a		13 30	13 51	14 22			14 32		15 27	15 30	
	d	13 29	13 34	13 53	14 23		14 29	14 32	15 07	15 27	15 32	
Cardiff Central 7	a	13 44	13 48	14 11	14 42		14 48	14 50	15 28	15 42	15 53	

		SW ◇1	GW ◇1 ☕	GW ◇	GW ◇1 ☕	GW	AW ■ ⊥	GW ◇	GW ◇1 ☕	GW ◇1 ☕	AW ■ ⊥	AW
Bath Spa 7	d	14 49		15 28	15 39	16 13		16 28	16 39			
Oldfield Park	d					16 16						
Keynsham	d					16 24						
Bristol Temple Meads 10	a	15 02		15 40	15 53	16 31		16 41	16 54			
	d			15 48				16 48				
Filton Abbey Wood	d			15 55				16 55				
Bristol Parkway 7	a											
	d		15 04							17 04		
Patchway	d							17 00				
Pilning	d											
Gloucester 7	d											16 37
Lydney	d											16 56
Chepstow	d											17 07
Caldicot	d											17 13
Severn Tunnel Jn	d			16 08				17 11				17 20
Newport (South Wales)	a		15 32	16 27				17 30		17 34		17 39
	d		15 32	16 27			16 31	17 30		17 34	17 34	17 40
Cardiff Central 7	a		15 50	16 45			16 52	17 47		17 51	17 54	17 59

		GW ■	GW ◇1 ☕	GW	AW ■ ⊥	GW ◇1 ☕	GW ◇	GW ◇1 ☕	GW ◇	GW ◇1 ☕	GW ◇1 ☕
Bath Spa 7	d	17 26	17 43	18 11			18 25	18 39	19 01		19 14
Oldfield Park	d	17 29		18 13					19 03		
Keynsham	d	17 36		18 22					19 11		
Bristol Temple Meads 10	a	17 43	17 57	18 33			18 38	18 53	19 18		19 27
	d	17 48					18 48				
Filton Abbey Wood	d	17 55					18 55				
Bristol Parkway 7	a					18 06				18 06	
	d					18 08				19 04	
Patchway	d										
Pilning	d										
Gloucester 7	d										
Lydney	d										
Chepstow	d										
Caldicot	d										
Severn Tunnel Jn	d	18 08					19 08				
Newport (South Wales)	a	18 27				18 36	19 27			19 32	
	d	18 27			18 32	18 37	19 27			19 32	
Cardiff Central 7	a	18 44			18 50	18 52	19 43			19 51	

		AW ■ ⊥	AW	AW ■ ⊥	GW ◇	GW ◇1 ☕	GW	GW ◇1 ☕	AW ■ ⊥	GW ◇	AW	GW ◇1 ☕
Bath Spa 7	d				19 27	19 39	20 00			20 27		20 39
Oldfield Park	d						20 02					
Keynsham	d						20 11					
Bristol Temple Meads 10	a				19 39	19 53	20 18			20 39		20 54
	d				19 48					20 48		
Filton Abbey Wood	d				19 55					20 55		
Bristol Parkway 7	a							18 06				
	d							20 10				
Patchway	d				20 00							
Pilning	d											
Gloucester 7	d		18 48								20 31	
Lydney	d		19 07								20 50	
Chepstow	d		19 17								21 00	
Caldicot	d		19 25								21 08	
Severn Tunnel Jn	d		19 28		20 11					21 08	21 12	
Newport (South Wales)	a		19 48		20 29			20 37		21 27	21 31	
	d	19 45	19 50	20 23	20 30			20 38	21 14	21 27	21 32	
Cardiff Central 7	a	20 04	20 06	20 43	20 47			20 53	21 36	21 43	21 49	

		SW ◇1	GW ◇1 ☕	GW ◇	GW ◇1 ☕	AW ■ ⊥	GW ◇	GW ◇1 ☕	GW	AW ◇	GW ◇1 ☕	GW ◇	AW	GW ◇1 ☕	GW ◇1 ☕	GW ◇1 ☕	AW ◇
Bath Spa 7	d	20 49		21 07	21 13		21 28	21 39	22 19			22 28		22 43		23 55	
Oldfield Park	d			21 09					22 21								
Keynsham	d	20 57		21 17					22 30								
Bristol Temple Meads 10	a	21 04		21 24	21 29		21 40	21 53	22 37			22 41		22 56		00 09	
	d						21 48					22 48					
Filton Abbey Wood	d						21 57					22 55					
Bristol Parkway 7	a																
	d		21 04								22 04				23 17		
Patchway	d						22 02										
Pilning	d																
Gloucester 7	d												22 33				
Lydney	d												22 52				
Chepstow	d												23 02				
Caldicot	d												23 10				
Severn Tunnel Jn	d						22 13					23 08	23 13				
Newport (South Wales)	a		21 33				22 32				22 40	23 28	23 33		23 45		
	d		21 33			21 43	22 32			22 36	22 40	23 28	23 34		23 45		23 55
Cardiff Central 7	a		21 56			22 05	22 54			23 02	23 02	23 49	23 54		00 06		00 20

Table 132

Bath Spa, Bristol and Gloucester - Cardiff

Sundays — 18 July to 05 September

		AW	GW ◇1 ⊡	GW ◇1 ⊡	AW bus	GW ◇1 ⊡	AW ◇ H	GW ◇	GW ◇1 ⊡	GW ◇1 ⊡		GW	GW ◇1 ⊡	AW	AW ◇ H	AW bus	GW ◇1 ⊡	GW ■	GW ◇1 ⊡	GW ◇1 ⊡		GW ◇1 ⊡	AW	AW	AW bus
Bath Spa 7	d			00 10		01 07			09 49			10 27	10 42					11 25	11 39			12 39			
Oldfield Park	d											10 30						11 28							
Keynsham	d											10 37						11 35							
Bristol Temple Meads 10	a			00 25		01 21		09 38	10 02			10 45	10 56					11 43	11 54			12 53			
	d							09 48										11 48							
Filton Abbey Wood	d							09 56										11 55							
Bristol Parkway 7	a																								
	d		23p47							10 07							11 25			12 26					
Patchway	d																	12 00							
Pilning	d																								
Gloucester 7	d	23p09														09 40									11 42
Lydney	d	23p28														10 20									12 22
Chepstow	d	23p38														10 40									12 42
Caldicot	d	23p46														10 55									12 57
Severn Tunnel Jn	d	23p49						10 09								11 05		12 11							13 07
Newport (South Wales)	a	00 09	00 17					10 23		10 32						11 30	11 48	12 26		12 48					13 32
	d	00 10	00 18		00 25		09 27	10 24		10 32				10 55	11 00	11 30	11 48	12 26		12 48			12 55	13 29	13 32
Cardiff Central 7	a	00 33	00 39		00 55		09 45	10 43		10 50				11 11	11 19	12 00	12 08	12 45		13 08			13 19	13 47	14 02

		XC bus	GW ◇	GW ◇1 ⊡	AW ■ H	XC bus		AW	GW ◇	AW	GW ◇1 ⊡	SW ◇1	AW ■ H	XC ◇1 H	GW ◇	GW ◇1 ⊡		GW	AW ■ H	GW ◇	GW ◇1 ⊡	AW ■ H	GW ■	GW ◇1 ⊡	GW
Bath Spa 7	d		13 26	13 39					14 25		14 39	14 49			15 28	15 39		16 13		16 28	16 39		17 26	17 43	18 11
Oldfield Park	d		13 29						14 27									16 16					17 29		18 13
Keynsham	d		13 36						14 35									16 24					17 36		18 22
Bristol Temple Meads 10	a		13 43	13 54					14 43		14 54	15 02			15 40	15 53		16 31		16 41	16 54		17 43	17 57	18 33
	d		13 48						14 48						15 48					16 48			17 48		
Filton Abbey Wood	d		13 55						14 55						15 55					16 55			17 55		
Bristol Parkway 7	a																								
	d																								
Patchway	d																			17 00					
Pilning	d																								
Gloucester 7	d	12 23				13 30				14 33				15 23											
Lydney	d									14 52															
Chepstow	d									15 02															
Caldicot	d									15 10															
Severn Tunnel Jn	d		14 08						15 08	15 13					16 08					17 11			18 08		
Newport (South Wales)	a	13 38	14 22			14 45			15 23	15 29				16 06	16 23					17 26			18 23		
	d		14 23		14 28			15 13	15 23	15 31			15 43	16 08	16 23				16 31	17 26		17 38	18 23		
Cardiff Central 7	a		14 46		14 52			15 37	15 42	15 52			16 02	16 26	16 45				16 56	17 46		17 57	18 45		

		AW ■ H		GW ◇	GW ◇1 ⊡	GW ◇	GW ◇1 ⊡	AW ■ H	AW	GW ◇1 ⊡	AW ■ H	GW ◇		GW ◇1 ⊡	GW	AW ■ H	GW ◇	AW	GW ◇1 ⊡	SW ◇1	GW ◇	GW ◇1 ⊡		AW ■ H	GW ◇
Bath Spa 7	d			18 25	18 39	19 06	19 14					19 27		19 39	20 06		20 27		20 39	20 49	21 07	21 13			21 28
Oldfield Park	d					19 08									20 08						21 09				
Keynsham	d					19 16									20 16					20 57	21 17				
Bristol Temple Meads 10	a			18 38	18 53	19 23	19 27					19 39		19 53	20 24		20 39		20 54	21 04	21 24	21 29			21 40
	d			18 48								19 48					20 48								21 48
Filton Abbey Wood	d			18 55								19 55					20 55								21 57
Bristol Parkway 7	a																								
	d									19 26															
Patchway	d											20 00													22 02
Pilning	d																								
Gloucester 7	d								18 48									20 31							
Lydney	d								19 07									20 50							
Chepstow	d								19 17									21 00							
Caldicot	d								19 24									21 09							
Severn Tunnel Jn	d			19 08					19 27			20 11					21 08	21 13							22 13
Newport (South Wales)	a			19 23					19 48	19 50		20 27					21 23	21 27							22 32
	d	18 33		19 23				19 45	19 50	19 51	20 23	20 28				21 11	21 23	21 29						21 45	22 32
Cardiff Central 7	a	18 55		19 43				20 08	20 09	20 14	20 47	20 49				21 38	21 44	21 48						22 07	22 54

		GW ◇1 ⊡	GW	AW ◇	GW ◇1 ⊡	GW ◇	AW	GW ◇1 ⊡		GW ◇1 ⊡	AW ◇	GW ◇1 ⊡
Bath Spa 7	d	21 39	22 19			22 28		22 43		23 55		
Oldfield Park	d		22 21									
Keynsham	d		22 30									
Bristol Temple Meads 10	a	21 53	22 37			22 41		22 56		00 09		
	d					22 48						
Filton Abbey Wood	d					22 55						
Bristol Parkway 7	a											
	d				22 30							23 38
Patchway	d											
Pilning	d											
Gloucester 7	d						22 33					
Lydney	d						22 52					
Chepstow	d						23 02					
Caldicot	d						23 10					
Severn Tunnel Jn	d					23 08	23 13					
Newport (South Wales)	a				23 00	23 28	23 33					00 03
	d			22 36	23 00	23 28	23 34				23 55	00 04
Cardiff Central 7	a			23 02	23 21	23 49	23 54				00 20	00 25

Table 132

Bath Spa, Bristol and Gloucester - Cardiff

Sundays — 12 September to 17 October

				AW	AW	GW ◇1 ⊡	GW ◇1 ⊡	AW ◇ H	GW ◇	GW ◇1 ⊡		GW	GW ◇1 ⊡	AW ◇ H	AW	GW ■	GW ◇1 ⊡	GW ◇1 ⊡	GW ◇1 ⊡	AW		AW	AW	GW ◇	GW ◇1 ⊡
Bath Spa 7	d					00 10	01 07			09 38		10 27	10 42			11 25	11 39		12 39					13 26	13 39
Oldfield Park	d											10 30				11 28								13 29	
Keynsham	d											10 37				11 35								13 36	
Bristol Temple Meads 10	a					00 25	01 21		09 38	09 51		10 45	10 56			11 43	11 54		12 53					13 43	13 54
	d								09 48							11 48								13 48	
Filton Abbey Wood	d								09 56							11 55								13 55	
Bristol Parkway 7	a																								
	d																	12 10							
Patchway	d															12 00									
Pilning	d																								
Gloucester 7	d				23p09										10 48								12 30		
Lydney	d				23p28										11 07								12 49		
Chepstow	d				23p38										11 17								12 59		
Caldicot	d				23p46										11 25								13 07		
Severn Tunnel Jn	d				23p49				10 09						11 28	12 11							13 10	14 08	
Newport (South Wales)	a				00 09				10 27						11 46	12 30		12 36					13 32	14 27	
	d			00 03	00 10			09 27	10 28					11 00	11 48	12 30		12 36		12 52		13 29	13 34	14 28	
Cardiff Central 7	a			00 24	00 33			09 42	10 43					11 16	12 06	12 45		12 54		13 13		13 44	13 52	14 51	

		AW ■ H	GW ◇1 ⊡	AW	GW ◇	AW		GW ◇1 ⊡	SW ◇1	GW ◇1 ⊡	AW ■ H	GW ◇	GW ◇1 ⊡	GW	AW ■ H	GW ◇		GW ◇1 ⊡	AW ■ H	AW	GW ◇1 ⊡	GW ■	GW ◇1 ⊡	AW ■ H	GW ◇1 ⊡
Bath Spa 7	d				14 25			14 39	14 49			15 28	15 39	16 01		16 28		16 39				17 26	17 41		
Oldfield Park	d				14 27									16 03								17 29			
Keynsham	d				14 35									16 12								17 36			
Bristol Temple Meads 10	a				14 43			14 54	15 02			15 40	15 53	16 23		16 41		16 54				17 43	17 56		
	d				14 48							15 48				16 48						17 48			
Filton Abbey Wood	d				14 55							15 55				16 55						17 55			
Bristol Parkway 7	a																								
	d		14 10							15 10											17 10				18 10
Patchway	d															17 00									
Pilning	d																								
Gloucester 7	d					14 33														16 37					
Lydney	d					14 52														16 56					
Chepstow	d					15 02														17 07					
Caldicot	d					15 10														17 13					
Severn Tunnel Jn	d				15 08	15 13						16 08				17 11				17 16		18 08			
Newport (South Wales)	a		14 36		15 27	15 31				15 36		16 27				17 30				17 35	17 40	18 27			18 36
	d	14 29	14 36	15 07	15 27	15 33				15 36	15 45	16 27			16 31	17 30			17 34	17 37	17 40	18 27		18 33	18 36
Cardiff Central 7	a	14 48	14 54	15 27	15 42	15 51				15 54	16 04	16 45			16 52	17 47			17 51	17 55	17 57	18 45		18 50	18 54

		GW ◇		GW ◇1 ⊡	GW ◇	GW ◇1 ⊡	GW ◇1 ⊡	AW ■ H	AW	AW ■ H	GW ◇	GW ◇1 ⊡		GW	GW ◇1 ⊡	AW ■ H	GW ◇	AW	GW ◇1 ⊡	SW ◇1	GW ◇1 ⊡	GW ◇		GW ◇1 ⊡	AW ■ H
Bath Spa 7	d	18 25		18 39	19 01	19 08					19 27	19 39		20 00			20 27		20 39	20 49	21 03	21 10			
Oldfield Park	d				19 03									20 02								21 12			
Keynsham	d				19 11									20 11						20 57		21 20			
Bristol Temple Meads 10	a	18 38		18 53	19 18	19 24					19 39	19 53		20 18			20 39		20 54	21 04	21 16	21 27			
	d	18 48									19 48						20 48								
Filton Abbey Wood	d	18 55									19 55						20 55								
Bristol Parkway 7	a																								
	d						19 14								20 10									21 10	
Patchway	d										20 00														
Pilning	d																								
Gloucester 7	d								18 48									20 31							
Lydney	d								19 07									20 50							
Chepstow	d								19 17									21 00							
Caldicot	d								19 28									21 10							
Severn Tunnel Jn	d	19 08							19 31		20 11						21 08	21 13							
Newport (South Wales)	a	19 27					19 41		19 53		20 29				20 36		21 27	21 31						21 36	
	d	19 27					19 41	19 50	19 55	20 23	20 30				20 36	21 14	21 27	21 33						21 36	21 45
Cardiff Central 7	a	19 43					19 59	20 09	20 11	20 43	20 47				20 53	21 36	21 43	21 49						21 58	22 07

		AW ◇	GW ◇	GW ◇1 ⊡	GW ◇1 ⊡	GW	GW ◇	AW		GW ◇1 ⊡	GW ◇1 ⊡	GW ◇1 ⊡	AW ◇
Bath Spa 7	d		21 28	21 39		22 19	22 28			22 43		23 55	
Oldfield Park	d					22 21							
Keynsham	d					22 30							
Bristol Temple Meads 10	a		21 40	21 53		22 37	22 41			22 56		00 09	
	d		21 48				22 48						
Filton Abbey Wood	d		21 57				22 55						
Bristol Parkway 7	a												
	d				22 10						23 17		
Patchway	d		22 02										
Pilning	d												
Gloucester 7	d							22 33					
Lydney	d							22 52					
Chepstow	d							23 02					
Caldicot	d							23 10					
Severn Tunnel Jn	d		22 16				23 08	23 13					
Newport (South Wales)	a		22 36		22 40		23 28	23 33			23 45		
	d	22 31	22 37		22 40		23 28	23 34			23 45		23 55
Cardiff Central 7	a	22 56	22 59		23 02		23 49	23 54			00 06		00 20

b arr. 1627

Table 132

Sundays
from 24 October

Bath Spa, Bristol and Gloucester - Cardiff

		AW	AW	GW	GW	AW	XC	GW	GW	AW	XC	GW	GW	AW	XC	GW	GW	GW	AW	XC	GW
																■					
				◇1 ⊐	◇1 ⊐	◇ ⌶	◇1 ⌶	◇	◇1 ⊐	◇ ⌶	◇1 ⌶		◇1 ⊐		◇1 ⌶		◇1 ⊐	◇1 ⊐		◇1 ⌶	◇1 ⊐
Bath Spa 7	d			00 10	01 07				09 38			10 27	10 42			11 25	11 39				12 39
Oldfield Park	d											10 30				11 28					
Keynsham	d											10 37				11 35					
Bristol Temple Meads 10	a			00 25	01 21				09 51			10 45	10 56			11 43	11 54				12 53
	d						09 30	09 48			10 30				11 30	11 48				12 30	
Filton Abbey Wood	d							09 56								11 55					
Bristol Parkway 7	a						09 38				10 38				11 38					12 38	
	d						09 43				10 43				11 43			12 10		12 43	
Patchway	d															12 00					
Pilning	d																				
Gloucester 7	d		23p09											10 48							
Lydney	d		23p28											11 07							
Chepstow	d		23p38											11 17							
Caldicot	d		23p46											11 25							
Severn Tunnel Jn	d		23p49					10 09						11 28		12 11					
Newport (South Wales)	a		00 09				10 03	10 27			11 07			11 46	12 14	12 30		12 36		13 03	
	d	00 03	00 10			09 27		10 28		11 00				11 48		12 30		12 36	12 52		
Cardiff Central 7	a	00 24	00 33			09 42		10 43		11 16				12 06		12 45		12 54	13 13		

		AW	AW	XC	GW	GW	AW	GW	AW	GW	AW	GW	SW	GW	AW	GW	GW	GW	AW	GW	GW	AW	AW
							■								■				■			■	
				◇1 ⌶	◇	◇1 ⊐	⌶	◇1 ⊐		◇		◇1 ⊐	◇1	◇1 ⊐	⌶	◇	◇1 ⊐		⌶	◇	◇1 ⊐	⌶	
Bath Spa 7	d				13 26	13 39				14 25		14 39	14 49			15 28	15 39	16 01		16 28	16 39		
Oldfield Park	d				13 29					14 27								16 03					
Keynsham	d				13 36					14 35								16 12					
Bristol Temple Meads 10	a				13 43	13 54				14 43		14 54	15 02			15 40	15 53	16 23		16 41	16 54		
	d			13 30	13 48					14 48						15 48				16 48			
Filton Abbey Wood	d				13 55					14 55						15 55				16 55			
Bristol Parkway 7	a			13 38																			
	d			13 43				14 10						15 10									
Patchway	d																			17 00			
Pilning	d																						
Gloucester 7	d		12 30								14 33												16b37
Lydney	d		12 49								14 52												16 56
Chepstow	d		12 59								15 02												17 07
Caldicot	d		13 07								15 10												17 13
Severn Tunnel Jn	d		13 10		14 08					15 08	15 13					16 08				17 11			17 16
Newport (South Wales)	a		13 32	14 03	14 27			14 36		15 27	15 31			15 36		16 27				17 30			17 35
	d	13 29	13 34		14 28		14 29	14 36	15 07	15 27	15 33			15 36	15 45	16 27			16 31	17 30		17 34	17 37
Cardiff Central 7	a	13 44	13 52		14 51		14 48	14 54	15 27	15 42	15 51			15 54	16 04	16 45			16 52	17 47		17 51	17 55

		GW	GW	GW	AW	GW	GW	GW	GW	GW	GW	AW	AW	AW	GW	GW	GW	GW	AW	GW	AW	GW
			■		■							■		■					■			
		◇1 ⊐		◇1 ⊐	⌶	◇1 ⊐	◇	◇1 ⊐	◇	◇1 ⊐	◇1 ⊐	⌶		⌶	◇	◇1 ⊐		◇1 ⊐	⌶	◇		◇1 ⊐
Bath Spa 7	d		17 26	17 41			18 25	18 39	19 01	19 08					19 27	19 39	20 00			20 27		20 39
Oldfield Park	d		17 29						19 03								20 02					
Keynsham	d		17 36						19 11								20 11					
Bristol Temple Meads 10	a		17 43	17 56			18 38	18 53	19 18	19 24					19 39	19 53	20 18			20 39		20 54
	d		17 48				18 48								19 48					20 48		20 55
Filton Abbey Wood	d		17 55				18 55								19 55					20 55		
Bristol Parkway 7	a																					
	d	17 10				18 10					19 14							20 10				
Patchway	d														20 00							
Pilning	d																					
Gloucester 7	d												18 48								20 31	
Lydney	d												19 07								20 50	
Chepstow	d												19 17								21 00	
Caldicot	d												19 28								21 10	
Severn Tunnel Jn	d		18 08				19 08						19 31		20 11					21 08	21 13	
Newport (South Wales)	a	17 40	18 27			18 36	19 27				19 41		19 53		20 29			20 36		21 27	21 31	
	d	17 40	18 27		18 33	18 36	19 27				19 41	19 50	19 55	20 23	20 30			20 36	21 14	21 27	21 33	
Cardiff Central 7	a	17 57	18 45		18 50	18 54	19 43				19 59	20 09	20 11	20 43	20 47			20 53	21 36	21 43	21 49	

		SW	GW	GW	GW	AW	AW	GW	GW	GW	GW	GW	AW	GW	GW	GW	AW
						■											
		◇1	◇1 ⊐	◇	◇1 ⊐	⌶	◇	◇	◇1 ⊐	◇1 ⊐		◇		◇1 ⊐	◇1 ⊐	◇1 ⊐	◇
Bath Spa 7	d	20 49	21 03	21 10				21 28	21 39		22 19	22 28		22 43		23 55	
Oldfield Park	d			21 12							22 21						
Keynsham	d	20 57		21 20							22 30						
Bristol Temple Meads 10	a	21 04	21 16	21 27				21 40	21 53		22 37	22 41		22 56		00 09	
	d							21 48	21 55			22 48					
Filton Abbey Wood	d							21 57				22 55					
Bristol Parkway 7	a																
	d				21 10					22 10					23 17		
Patchway	d							22 02									
Pilning	d																
Gloucester 7	d												22 33				
Lydney	d												22 52				
Chepstow	d												23 02				
Caldicot	d												23 10				
Severn Tunnel Jn	d							22 16				23 08	23 13				
Newport (South Wales)	a				21 36			22 36		22 40		23 28	23 33		23 45		
	d				21 36	21 45	22 31	22 37		22 40		23 28	23 34		23 45		23 55
Cardiff Central 7	a				21 58	22 07	22 56	22 59		23 02		23 49	23 54		00 06		00 20

b arr. 1627

Table 133

Mondays to Fridays

Bristol - Avonmouth and Severn Beach

		GW	GW	GW	GW	GW	GW	GW	GW	GW	GW	GW	GW	GW	GW	GW	GW	GW	GW	GW	GW	GW	GW
Bristol Temple Meads 10	d	05 24	05 48	06 19	06 31	06 50	07 05	07 19	07 46	08 03	08 10	08 36	08 47	09 10	09 16	09 45	10 03	10 34	10 45	11 16	11 45	12 03	12 34
Lawrence Hill	d	05 27		06 22	06 34	06 53	07 07	07 22	07 50	08 05	08 13	08 38		09 13	09 18	09 48		10 36	10 48	11 18	11 48		12 36
Stapleton Road	d	05 29	05 51	06a25	06 36	06a56	07 09	07a24	07a52	08 06	08a16	08 40	08a51	09a15	09 20	09a50	10 06	10 38	10a50	11 20	11a50	12 06	12 38
Montpelier	d	05 33	05 55		06 40		07 14			08 10		08 45			09 24		10 10	10 42		11 24		12 10	12 42
Redland	d	05 35	05 57		06 42		07 16			08 12		08 47			09 26		10 12	10 44		11 26		12 12	12 44
Clifton Down	d	05 38	06 00		06 46		07 19			08 17		08 52			09 29		10 17	10 48		11 29		12 17	12 48
Sea Mills	d	05 42	06 04		06 50		07 23			08 21		08 56			09 33		10 21	10 52		11 33		12 21	12 52
Shirehampton	d	05 45	06 08		06 53		07 26			08 25		08 59			09 37		10 25	10 56		11 37		12 25	12 56
Avonmouth 2	d	05 49	06a13		06 57		07 31			08a30		09a05			09 40		10a30	11a01		11 40		12a30	13a01
St Andrews Road	d	05x52			07x00		07x34								09x44					11x44			
Severn Beach	a	06 01			07 08		07 42								09 53					11 53			

		GW	GW	GW	GW	GW	GW	GW	GW	GW	GW	GW	GW	GW	GW	GW	GW	GW	GW	GW	GW	GW	GW	GW
Bristol Temple Meads 10	d	12 45	13 16	13 45	14 03	14 34	14 45	15 16	15 45	16 03	16 15	16 34	16 45	17 10	17 16	17 45	18 03	18 21	18 48	19 33	19 45	20 34	21 19	22 16
Lawrence Hill	d	12 48	13 18	13 48		14 36	14 48	15 18	15 48	16 05	16 17	16 36	16 48	17 13	17 18	17 48	18 05	18 24	18 51	19 36	19 48	20 36	21 22	22 18
Stapleton Road	d	12a50	13 20	13a50	14 06	14 38	14a50	15 20	15a50	16 06	16a19	16 38	16a50	17a15	17 20	17a50	18 06	18a26	18 53	19 38	19a51	20 38	21a24	22 20
Montpelier	d		13 24		14 10	14 42		15 24		16 10		16 42			17 24		18 10		18 57	19 41		20 42		22 24
Redland	d		13 26		14 12	14 44		15 26		16 12		16 44			17 26		18 12		18 59	19 43		20 44		22 26
Clifton Down	d		13 29		14 17	14 48		15 29		16 17		16 48			17 29		18 17		19 08	19 46		20 48		22 29
Sea Mills	d		13 33		14 21	14 52		15 33		16 21		16 52			17 33		18 21		19 12	19 50		20 52		22 33
Shirehampton	d		13 37		14 25	14 56		15 37		16 25		16 56			17 37		18 25		19 16	19 54		20 56		22 37
Avonmouth 2	d		13 40		14a30	15a01		15 40		16a30		17a01			17 40		18 29		19a21	19a59		20 59		22 40
St Andrews Road	d		13x44					15x44							17x44		18x32					21x02		22x44
Severn Beach	a		13 53					15 53							17 53		18 40					21 11		22 53

Saturdays

		GW	GW	GW	GW	GW	GW	GW	GW 🚌	GW	GW	GW	GW	GW	GW	GW	GW 🚌	GW	GW	GW	GW	GW	GW
Bristol Temple Meads 10	d	06 03	06 34	06 50	07 16	07 46	08 03	08 19		08 34	08 45	09 16	09 21	09 45	10 03	10 21		10 34	10 45	11 16	11 21	11 45	12 03
Lawrence Hill	d		06 36	06 53	07 18	07 50	08 05	08 22		08 36	08 48	09 18		09 48				10 36	10 48	11 18		11 48	
Stapleton Road	d	06 06	06 38	06a56	07 20	07a52	08 06	08a24		08 38	08a50	09 20	09a25	09a50	10 06	10a25		10 38	10a50	11 20	11a25	11a50	12 06
Montpelier	d	06 10	06 42		07 24		08 10			08 42		09 24			10 10			10 42		11 24			12 10
Redland	d	06 12	06 44		07 26		08 12			08 44		09 26			10 12			10 44		11 26			12 12
Clifton Down	d	06 17	06 48		07 29		08 17			08 48		09 29			10 17			10 48		11 29			12 17
Sea Mills	d	06 21	06 52		07 33		08 21			08 52		09 33			10 21			10 52		11 33			12 21
Shirehampton	d	06 25	06 56		07 37		08 25			08 56		09 37			10 25			10 56		11 37			12 25
Avonmouth 2	d	06a30	07a01		07 40		08a30		08 33	09a01		09 40			10a30		10 33	11a01		11 40			12a30
St Andrews Road	d				07x44				08x36			09x44					10x36			11x44			
Severn Beach	a				07 53				08 48			09 53					10 48			11 53			

		GW	GW 🚌	GW	GW	GW	GW	GW	GW	GW	GW 🚌	GW	GW	GW	GW	GW	GW	GW	GW 🚌	GW	GW	GW A	GW
Bristol Temple Meads 10	d	12 21		12 34	12 45	13 16	13 21	13 45	14 03	14 21		14 34	14 45	15 16	15 21	15 45	16 03	16 21		16 34	16 45	17 10	17 16
Lawrence Hill	d			12 36	12 48	13 18		13 48				14 36	14 48	15 18		15 48	16 05			16 36	16 48	⟆	17 18
Stapleton Road	d	12a25		12 38	12a50	13 20	13a25	13a50	14 06	14a25		14 38	14a50	15 20	15a24	15a50	16 06	16a25		16 38	16a50	17a16	17 20
Montpelier	d			12 42		13 24			14 10			14 42		15 24			16 10			16 42			17 24
Redland	d			12 44		13 26			14 12			14 44		15 26			16 12			16 44			17 26
Clifton Down	d			12 48		13 29			14 17			14 48		15 29			16 17			16 48			17 29
Sea Mills	d			12 52		13 33			14 21			14 52		15 33			16 21			16 52			17 33
Shirehampton	d			12 56		13 37			14 25			14 56		15 37			16 25			16 56			17 37
Avonmouth 2	d		12 33	13a01		13 40			14a30		14 33	15a01		15 40			16a30		16 33	17a01			17 40
St Andrews Road	d		12x36			13x44					14x36			15x44					16x36				17x44
Severn Beach	a		12 48			13 53					14 48			15 53					16 48				17 53

		GW B	GW	GW	GW A	GW B	GW	GW	GW	GW	GW	GW
Bristol Temple Meads 10	d	17 21	17 45	18 03	18 13	18 21	18 45	19 03	19 21	19 45	20 34	22 16
Lawrence Hill	d	⟆	17 48	18 05	⟆	⟆	18 48	19 05	19 23	19 48	20 36	22 18
Stapleton Road	d	17a25	17a50	18 06	18a17	18a25	18 50	19 06	19a25	19a50	20 38	22 20
Montpelier	d			18 10				19 10			20 42	22 24
Redland	d			18 12				19 12			20 44	22 26
Clifton Down	d			18 17				19 17			20 48	22 29
Sea Mills	d			18 21				19 21			20 52	22 33
Shirehampton	d			18 25				19 25			20 56	22 37
Avonmouth 2	d			18 29				19 29			20 59	22 40
St Andrews Road	d			18x32				19x32			21x02	22x44
Severn Beach	a			18 40				19 40			21 11	22 53

A from 17 July until 4 September
B until 10 July, from 11 September

Table 133

Bristol - Avonmouth and Severn Beach

Sundays until 05 September

		GW	GW	GW	GW	GW	GW	GW	GW	GW	GW	GW
Bristol Temple Meads 10	d	09 08	10 23	11 23	12 23	13 23	14 23	15 23	16 23	16 53	17 53	18 53
Lawrence Hill	d	09 10	10 25	11 26	12 25	13 25	14 25	15 25	16 25	16 56	17 55	18 56
Stapleton Road	d	09 12	10 27	11 28	12 27	13 27	14 27	15 27	16 27	16 58	17 56	18 58
Montpelier	d	09 16	10 31	11 31	12 31	13 31	14 31	15 31	16 31	17 02	18 00	19 01
Redland	d	09 18	10 33	11 33	12 33	13 33	14 33	15 33	16 33	17 04	18 02	19 03
Clifton Down	d	09 21	10 36	11 36	12 36	13 36	14 36	15 36	16 36	17 06	18 07	19 06
Sea Mills	d	09 25	10 40	11 40	12 40	13 40	14 40	15 40	16 40	17 10	18 11	19 10
Shirehampton	d	09 29	10 43	11 43	12 44	13 44	14 44	15 44	16 44	17 14	18 15	19 14
Avonmouth 2	d	09 33	10 47	11 47	12 48	13 47	14 47	15 47	16 47	17 22	18 19	19 19
St Andrews Road	d	09 36	10 51	11 51	12 51	13 51	14 51	15 51	16 51	17 26	18x22	19 22
Severn Beach	a	09 43	10 58	11 58	12 58	13 58	14 58	15 58	16 58	17 33	18 30	19 29

Sundays from 12 September

		GW	GW	GW	GW	GW	GW	GW	GW	GW	GW
Bristol Temple Meads 10	d	09 08	10 23	11 23	12 23	13 23	14 23	15 23	16 23	16 53	17 53
Lawrence Hill	d	09 10	10 25	11 26	12 25	13 25	14 25	15 25	16 25	16 56	17 55
Stapleton Road	d	09 12	10 27	11 28	12 27	13 27	14 27	15 27	16 27	16 58	17 57
Montpelier	d	09 16	10 31	11 31	12 31	13 31	14 31	15 31	16 31	17 02	18 01
Redland	d	09 18	10 33	11 33	12 33	13 33	14 33	15 33	16 33	17 04	18 03
Clifton Down	d	09 21	10 36	11 36	12 36	13 36	14 36	15 36	16 36	17 06	18 06
Sea Mills	d	09 25	10 40	11 40	12 40	13 40	14 40	15 40	16 40	17 10	18 10
Shirehampton	d	09 29	10 44	11 43	12 44	13 44	14 44	15 44	16 44	17 14	18 14
Avonmouth 2	d	09 33	10a49	11a47	12a49	13a49	14a49	15a49	16a47	17 18	18a17
St Andrews Road	d	09 36								17 21	
Severn Beach	a	09 43								17 28	

Table 133

Mondays to Fridays

Severn Beach and Avonmouth - Bristol

		GW MX	GW	GW	GW	GW	GW	GW	GW	GW	GW	GW	GW	GW	GW	GW	GW	GW	GW	GW	GW	GW	GW	GW
Severn Beach	d		06 03			07 20	07 54					09 54					11 54					13 54		
St Andrews Road	d		06x09			07x26	08x00					10x00					12x00					14x00		
Avonmouth 2	d		06 13	06 32		07 31	08 04		08 38		09 15	10 04		10 35		11 15	12 04		12 35		13 15	14 04		14 35
Shirehampton	d		06 17	06 35		07 34	08 07		08 41		09 18	10 07		10 38		11 18	12 07		12 38		13 18	14 07		14 38
Sea Mills	d		06 21	06 39		07 38	08 11		08 45		09 22	10 11		10 42		11 22	12 11		12 42		13 22	14 11		14 42
Clifton Down	d		06 27	06 45		07 43	08 16		08 52		09 30	10 16		10 48		11 31	12 16		12 47		13 31	14 16		14 48
Redland	d		06 29	06 47		07 46	08 19		08 54		09 33	10 19		10 51		11 34	12 19		12 50		13 34	14 19		14 51
Montpelier	d		06 31	06 49		07 48	08 21		08 56		09 35	10 21		10 53		11 36	12 21		12 52		13 36	14 21		14 53
Stapleton Road	d	23p59	06 36	06 53	07 07	07 52	08 24	08 54	09 01	09 29	09 39	10 24	10 31	10 59	11 29	11 39	12 24	12 32	12 54	13 29	13 39	14 24	14 31	14 59
Lawrence Hill	d	00 01	06 38	06 56	07 09	07 55	08 26	08 56	09 03	09 31	09 41		10 33	11 01	11 31	11 41		12 34	12 56	13 31	13 41		14 33	15 01
Bristol Temple Meads 10	a	00 06	06 41	07 02	07 14	07 58	08 32	09 03	09 09	09 35	09 47	10 31	10 38	11 09	11 35	11 48	12 31	12 39	13 06	13 36	13 48	14 31	14 38	15 09

		GW	GW	GW	GW	GW	GW	GW	GW	GW	GW	GW	GW	GW	GW	GW	GW	GW	GW	GW
Severn Beach	d			15 54						17 54		18 44					21 29		22 54	
St Andrews Road	d			16x00						18x00		18x50					21x35		23x00	
Avonmouth 2	d		15 15	16 04		16 35		17 15		18 04		18 54		19 32	20 02		21 39		23 04	
Shirehampton	d		15 18	16 07		16 38		17 18		18 07		18 58		19 35	20 05		21 43		23 07	
Sea Mills	d		15 22	16 11		16 42		17 22		18 11		19 02		19 39	20 09		21 47		23 11	
Clifton Down	d		15 31	16 16		16 48		17 31		18 16		19 13		19 46	20 14		21 52		23 16	
Redland	d		15 34	16 19		16 51		17 34		18 19		19 15		19 49	20 17		21 54		23 19	
Montpelier	d		15 36	16 21		16 53		17 36		18 21		19 17		19 51	20 19		21 56		23 21	
Stapleton Road	d	15 29	15 39	16 24	16 31	17 00	17 29	17 39	18 19	18 24	18 29	19 22	19 29	19 55	20 23	20 31	22 01	22 17	23 24	23 59
Lawrence Hill	d	15 31	15 41		16 33	17 02	17 31	17 41		18 26	18 31	19 24	19 31	19 57	20 25	20 33	22 03	22 18	23 26	00 01
Bristol Temple Meads 10	a	15 37	15 48	16 31	16 38	17 09	17 37	17 48	18 24	18 34	18 37	19 28	19 36	20 02	20 31	20 38	22 07	22 27	23 32	00 06

Saturdays

		GW	GW	GW	GW	GW	GW 🚌	GW	GW	GW	GW	GW	GW 🚌	GW	GW	GW	GW 🚌	GW	GW	GW	GW	GW	GW 🚌
Severn Beach	d				07 54		08 55			09 54			10 55			11 54	12 55			13 54			14 55
St Andrews Road	d				08x00		09x07			10x00			11x07			12x00	13x07			14x00			15x07
Avonmouth 2	d		06 35	07 15	08 04	08 35	09a10		09 15	10 04		10 35	11a10		11 15	12 04	13a10		13 15	14 04		14 35	15a10
Shirehampton	d		06 38	07 18	08 07	08 38			09 18	10 07		10 38			11 13	12 07			13 18	14 07		14 38	
Sea Mills	d		06 42	07 22	08 11	08 42			09 22	10 11		10 42			11 22	12 11			13 22	14 11		14 42	
Clifton Down	d		06 48	07 31	08 16	08 47			09 30	10 16		10 48			11 31	12 16			13 31	14 16		14 48	
Redland	d		06 50	07 34	08 19	08 50			09 33	10 19		10 51			11 34	12 19			13 34	14 19		14 51	
Montpelier	d		06 52	07 36	08 21	08 52			09 35	10 21		10 53			11 35	12 21			13 36	14 21		14 53	
Stapleton Road	d	23p59	06 55	07 40	08 24	08 54		09 29	09 39	10 24	10 32	10 59		11 29	11 39	12 24		13 27	13 40	14 24	14 31	14 59	
Lawrence Hill	d	00 01	06 57	07 42	08 26	08 56		09 31	09 41		10 34	11 01		11 31	11 41			13 29	13 41		14 33	15 01	
Bristol Temple Meads 10	a	00 06	07 03	07 48	08 32	09 04		09 35	09 47	10 31	10 39	11 09		11 35	11 43	12 31		13 35	13 48	14 31	14 40	15 09	

		GW	GW	GW	GW	GW 🚌	GW	GW	GW	GW	GW	GW	GW A	GW B	GW	GW
Severn Beach	d			15 54		16 55			17 54			18 54	19 47	19 47	21 29	22 54
St Andrews Road	d			16x00		17x07			18x00			19x00	19x53	19x53	21x35	23x00
Avonmouth 2	d		15 15	16 04	16 35	17a10		17 15	18 04			19 04	19 57	19 57	21 39	23 04
Shirehampton	d		15 18	16 07	16 38			17 18	18 07			19 07	20 00	20 00	21 43	23 07
Sea Mills	d		15 22	16 11	16 42			17 22	18 11			19 11	20 04	20 04	21 47	23 11
Clifton Down	d		15 31	16 16	16 47			17 31	18 16			19 29	20 09	20 09	21 52	23 16
Redland	d		15 34	16 19	16 50			17 34	18 19			19 31	20 12	20 12	21 54	23 19
Montpelier	d		15 36	16 21	16 50			17 36	18 21			19 33	20 14	20 14	21 56	23 21
Stapleton Road	d	15 27	15 39	16 24	16 54		17 29	17 39	18 24	18 34	19 30	19 40	20 17	20 20	22 01	23 24
Lawrence Hill	d	15 29	15 41		16 56		17 31	17 41	18 26	18 36	19 32	19 42	20 19	20 22	22 03	23 26
Bristol Temple Meads 10	a	15 34	15 48	16 31	17 06		17 37	17 48	18 31	18 39	19 38	19 46	20 25	20 29	22 09	23 32

Sundays until 05 September

		GW	GW	GW	GW	GW	GW	GW	GW	GW	GW	GW
Severn Beach	d	09 46	11 12	12 12	13 12	14 12	15 12	16 12	17 12	17 42	18 42	19 43
St Andrews Road	d	09 52	11 18	12 18	13 18	14 18	15 18	16 18	17 18	17 48	18x48	19 49
Avonmouth 2	d	09 56	11 22	12 22	13 22	14 22	15 22	16 22	17 22	17 52	18 52	19 53
Shirehampton	d	09 59	11 25	12 25	13 25	14 25	15 25	16 25	17 26	17 56	18 55	19 56
Sea Mills	d	10 03	11 29	12 29	13 29	14 29	15 29	16 29	17 30	18 00	18 59	20 00
Clifton Down	d	10 08	11 37	12 37	13 37	14 37	15 37	16 37	17 35	18 06	19 06	20 05
Redland	d	10 11	11 39	12 39	13 39	14 39	15 39	16 39	17 38	18 09	19 09	20 08
Montpelier	d	10 13	11 41	12 41	13 41	14 41	15 41	16 41	17 40	18 11	19 11	20 10
Stapleton Road	d	10 16	11 46	12 49	13 46	14 48	15 46	16 46	17 44	18 15	19 15	20 16
Lawrence Hill	d	10 18	11 48	12 51	13 48	14 50	15 48	16 48	17 46	18 17	19 17	20 18
Bristol Temple Meads 10	a	10 21	11 53	12 55	13 53	14 54	15 53	16 53	17 50	18 21	19 21	20 21

A until 10 July, from 11 September
B from 17 July until 4 September

Table 133

Sundays
from 12 September

Severn Beach and Avonmouth - Bristol

		GW	GW	GW	GW	GW	GW	GW	GW	GW		GW	GW
Severn Beach	d	09 46								17 42			
St Andrews Road	d	09 52								17 48			
Avonmouth 2	d	09 56	10 52	11 52	12 52	13 52	14 52	15 52	16 52	17 52		18 22	19 22
Shirehampton	d	09 59	10 55	11 55	12 55	13 55	14 55	15 55	16 55	17 56		18 25	19 25
Sea Mills	d	10 03	10 59	11 59	12 59	13 59	14 59	15 59	16 59	18 00		18 29	19 29
Clifton Down	d	10 08	11 04	12 04	13 04	14 04	15 04	16 04	17 07	18 06		18 34	19 34
Redland	d	10 11	11 07	12 07	13 07	14 07	15 07	16 07	17 10	18 09		18 37	19 37
Montpelier	d	10 13	11 09	12 09	13 09	14 09	15 09	16 09	17 12	18 11		18 39	19 39
Stapleton Road	d	10 16	11 13	12 14	13 13	14 13	15 13	16 13	17 16	18 15		18 43	19 43
Lawrence Hill	d	10 18	11 15	12 16	13 15	14 15	15 15	16 15	17 18	18 17		18 45	19 45
Bristol Temple Meads 10	a	10 21	11 20	12 20	13 20	14 20	15 20	16 20	17 22	18 21		18 47	19 49

Table 134

Mondays to Fridays

Gloucester - Taunton

				GW	GW	GW MX	XC MX	XC		GW		GW	GW	GW	XC	GW	GW	GW	GW	GW	GW	GW	XC	GW	GW
				◇■ C ⊡	◇■ D ⊡		◇■	◇■ E ⊼		◇ G		■ H	◇ H	■	◇■ ⊼	◇			◇ ⊼				◇■ ⊼	■ ⊼	
Gloucester 7	d																	06 20		06 42		07 11			
Cam & Dursley	d																	06 35		06 58		07 25			
Yate	d																	06 48		07 12		07 40			
Bristol Parkway 7	a																	06 58		07 23		07 48			
	d						00 02	00 03										06 58		07 25		07 49	07 58		08 12
Filton Abbey Wood	d					23p52												07 02	07 09	07 28		07 53		08 09	08 15
Stapleton Road	d					23p59												07 07		07 33					
Lawrence Hill	d					00 01												07 09		07 35					
Bristol Temple Meads 10	a					00 06	00 17	00 14										07 14	07 18	07 40		08 01	08 08	08 18	08 23
	d			23p35	23p35					05 24		04 41		06 03	06 34	06 26	06 48	07 18				08 13	08 11		08 25
Bedminster	d																06 50				07 53				08 27
Parson Street	d																06 53				07 55				08 29
Nailsea & Backwell	d			23b47	23b47									06 14			07 02	07 28			08 04				08 38
Yatton	d			23b54	23b54							05c02		06 21			07 07	07 34			08 09				08 44
Worle	d			00s01	00s01									06 27			07 12	07 40			08 15				08 50
Weston Milton	d																07 18				08 20				08 55
Weston-super-Mare	a			00s06	00 06					05 43		05 45		06 36		06 47	07 23	07 47			08 26				09 00
	d			00s08	00 08					05 45			05 49			06 51		07 50							09 00
Highbridge & Burnham	d			00 18	00 30					05 55			06 00			07 02		08 01							09 11
Bridgwater	d			00 26	00 45					06 03			06 08			07 10		08 09							09 19
Taunton	a			00 44	01 16					06 16			06 21		07 06	07 23		08 25					08 42		09 33

		GW	XC	GW	GW	GW		XC	GW	GW	GW	XC	GW	GW	XC	GW	GW	GW	XC	GW	XC	GW	GW	GW	XC
			◇■ ⊼			◇■		◇■ ⊼	◇ ⊼			◇■ ⊼			◇■ ⊼	◇ ⊼			◇■ ⊼		◇■ ⊼	◇ ⊼			◇■ ⊼
Gloucester 7	d	07e40									08 42							09 45						10 42	
Cam & Dursley	d	07 54									08 56							09 59						10 56	
Yate	d	08 09									09 10							10 13						11 10	
Bristol Parkway 7	a	08 19									09 19							10 22						11 19	
	d	08 19	08 26					08 58		09 12	09 20	09 26	09 34		09 58		10 12	10 22	10 27		10 58		11 15	11 20	11 28
Filton Abbey Wood	d	08 23		08 43	08 50				09 09		09 23		09 37	09 42		10 09	10 15	10 25		10 42		11 09	11 15	11 23	
Stapleton Road	d				08 54						09 29		09 42					10 31						11 29	
Lawrence Hill	d				08 56						09 31							10 33						11 31	
Bristol Temple Meads 10	a	08 36	08 40	08 53	09 03			09 14	09 18	09 22	09 35	09 39	09 50	09 53	10 08	10 18	10 23	10 38	10 41	10 51	11 12	11 18	11 23	11 35	11 38
	d			08 55		09 13				09 25		09 44		09 55			10 25	10 49	10 44	10 53	11 15	11 23	11 25	11 49	11 44
Bedminster	d									09 28							10 27						11 27		
Parson Street	d			08 57													10 29						11 29		
Nailsea & Backwell	d			09 06						09 38				10 03			10 38			11 03			11 38		
Yatton	d			09 12						09 44				10 08			10 44			11 08			11 44		
Worle	d			09 18						09 50				10 14			10 50			11 14			11 50		
Weston Milton	d									09 55							10 55						11 55		
Weston-super-Mare	a			09 26						10 03				10 22			11 00			11 21	11 32		12 00		
	d			09 29										10 23						11 23	11 37				
Highbridge & Burnham	d			09 40										10 34						11 34					
Bridgwater	d			09 49										10 42						11 42					
Taunton	a		09 15	10 01		09 45						10 16		10 57					11 16	11 57	12 00				12 15

		GW		GW	XC	GW	GW	GW	XC	GW	XC	GW		GW	GW	XC	GW	XC	GW	GW	GW	XC	GW	GW	XC
		◇■ ⊡			◇■ ⊼	◇ ⊼			◇■ ⊼		◇■ ⊼	◇ ⊼				◇■ ⊼		◇■ ⊼	◇ ⊼			◇■ ⊼			◇■ ⊼
Gloucester 7	d							11 45							12 42						13 45				
Cam & Dursley	d							11 59							12 56						13 59				
Yate	d							12 13							13 10						14 13				
Bristol Parkway 7	a							12 22							13 20						14 22				
	d				11 58		12 12	12 22	12 30		12 58			13 12	13 20	13 26		13 59		14 12	14 22	14 29		14 47	14 58
Filton Abbey Wood	d			11 42		12 09	12 15	12 25		12 42		13 09		13 15	13 23		13 42		14 09	14 15	14 25		14 42	14 50	
Stapleton Road	d														13 29						14 31			14 54	
Lawrence Hill	d														13 31						14 33			14 56	
Bristol Temple Meads 10	a			11 51	12 08	12 18	12 23	12 35	12 41	12 51	13 10	13 17		13 23	13 36	13 39	13 51	14 09	14 19	14 23	14 38	14 41	14 53	15 04	15 10
	d	11 47		11 53			12 25		12 44	12 53				13 25		13 44	13 53			14 25	14 48	14 44	14 53		15 13
Bedminster	d						12 27							13 27						14 27					
Parson Street	d						12 29							13 29						14 29					
Nailsea & Backwell	d			12 03			12 38			13 03				13 38			14 03			14 38			15 03		
Yatton	d			12 08			12 44			13 08				13 44			14 08			14 44			15 08		
Worle	d			12 14			12 50			13 14				13 50			14 14			14 50			15 14		
Weston Milton	d						12 55							13 55						14 55					
Weston-super-Mare	a	12 06		12 20			13 00			13 21				14 00			14 21			15 00			15 24		
	d	12 07		12 21						13 23							14 23						15 25		
Highbridge & Burnham	d			12 32						13 34							14 34						15 36		
Bridgwater	d			12 40						13 42							14 42						15 45		
Taunton	a	12 29		12 57					13 16	13 59						14 15	14 55					15 16	16 04		15 44

C MX from 13 July until 15 October
D MX until 9 July
E MO from 25 October
F MO from 13 September
G until 15 November, 22 November, 29 November, 6 December
H MX from 16 November
c arr. 0452
e arr. 0724

Table 134

Gloucester - Taunton

Mondays to Fridays

		GW	GW	GW	XC	GW	XC	GW	GW	GW	XC	GW	GW	GW	XC	GW	GW	GW	GW	XC	GW	GW	XC	GW	GW
		◇			◇1		◇1	◇1	◇		◇1				◇1	◇1	■			◇1			◇1	◇1	■
Gloucester ■7	d			14 42						15 45									16 42						
Cam & Dursley	d			14 56						15 59									16 56						
Yate	d			15 10						16 13									17 10						
Bristol Parkway ■7	a			15 20						16 22									17 20						
	d		15 12	15 20	15 26		15 58			16 22	16 28		16 45		16 58			17 12	17 20	17 26		17 46	18 00		
Filton Abbey Wood	d	15 09	15 15	15 23		15 42			16 09	16 25		16 42	16 48	16 55			17 09	17 15	17 23		17 42	17 49			18 09
Stapleton Road	d			15 29						16 31			16 52						17 29			17 54			
Lawrence Hill	d			15 31						16 33			16 54						17 31			17 56			
Bristol Temple Meads ■10	a	15 18	15 23	15 37	15 40	15 51	16 08	16 15	16 18	16 38	16 41	16 51	16 59	17 03	17 11	17 15	17 18	17 23	17 37	17 40	17 53	18 02	18 10	18 15	18 18
	d		15 25		15 44	15 53		16 18			16 44	16 53			17 14	17 18		17 25		17 44	17 53			18 21	
Bedminster	d		15 27			15 55						16 55						17 27			17 57				
Parson Street	d		15 29			15 57						16 57						17 29			17 59				
Nailsea & Backwell	d		15 38			16 03		16 29				17 03				17 28		17 38			18 07			18 32	
Yatton	d		15 44			16 08		16 36				17 08				17 34		17 44			18 13			18 39	
Worle	d		15 50			16 14		16 43				17 14				17 41		17 50			18 19			18 46	
Weston Milton	d		15 55			16 21						17 22						17 55			18 24				
Weston-super-Mare	a		16 00			16 24		16 50				17 27				17 49		18 00			18 29			18 55	
	d					16 24						17 28									18 29			18 55	
Highbridge & Burnham	d					16 37						17 38									18 40			19 07	
Bridgwater	d					16 45						17 46									18 48			19 15	
Taunton	a				16 15	17 00					17 15	18 01			17 45					18 16	19 08			19 28	

		GW	GW	XC	GW	XC	GW	GW	GW	XC	XC	GW	XC	GW	GW		GW	GW	XC	GW	XC	GW	GW	XC	GW
				◇1		◇1	◇1	◇		FX ◇1	FO ◇1		◇1	◇1	◇				◇1		◇1	◇1	◇	◇1	A
Gloucester ■7	d		17 42						18 42									19 45							
Cam & Dursley	d		17 56						18 56									19 59							
Yate	d		18 10						19 10									20 13							
Bristol Parkway ■7	a		18 20						19 20									20 22							
	d	18 12	18 20	18 29		18 57			19 20	19 29	19 29		19 58				20 11	20 22	20 28		20 58			21 27	
Filton Abbey Wood	d	18 15	18 23		18 42			19 09	19 23			19 42			20 09		20 14	20 25		20 42			21 09		
Stapleton Road	d	18 19	18 29						19 29									20 31							
Lawrence Hill	d		18 31						19 31									20 33							
Bristol Temple Meads ■10	a	18 24	18 37	18 40	18 53	19 07	19 12	19 18	19 36	19 39	19 39	19 53	20 13	20 13	20 18		20 24	20 38	20 41	20 53	21 08	21 15	21 19	21 38	
	d	18 25		18 44	18 55		19 15			19 44	19 44	19 55		20 18					20 47	20 55	21 13	21 18		21 44	21 55
Bedminster	d	18 27			18 57							19 57								20 57					21 57
Parson Street	d	18 29			18 59							19 59								20 59					21 59
Nailsea & Backwell	d	18 38			19 08		19 25					20 08		20 29						21 08		21 27			22 08
Yatton	d	18 44			19 13		19 32					20 13		20 36						21 13		21 34			22 13
Worle	d	19 00			19 19		19 38					20 21		20 44						21 19		21 40			22 19
Weston Milton	d	19 05			19 23		19 43					20 25		20 49						21 23					22 23
Weston-super-Mare	a	19 09			19 28		19 48					20 29		20 53						21 27		21 48			22 27
	d				19 29		19 57					20 30								21 33					22 29
Highbridge & Burnham	d				19 40							20 41								21 44					22 40
Bridgwater	d				19 48							20 49								21 52					22 48
Taunton	a			19 15	20 03		20 21			20 16	20 16	21 10							21 18	22 07	21 44			22 15	23 01

		GW	GW	GW	GW	XC	XC	GW	XC	GW	GW		GW	GW	GW	GW
		B	C	D		◇1 E	◇1 F		◇1	G	H		◇1 A	◇1 I	◇1 D	
Gloucester ■7	d				21 15				22 06							
Cam & Dursley	d				21 29											
Yate	d				21 43											
Bristol Parkway ■7	a				21 52				22 52							
	d				21 52	21 58	21 58		22 52	22 54	22 58					
Filton Abbey Wood	d				21 57			22 12		22 58	23 02					23 52
Stapleton Road	d							22 16								23 59
Lawrence Hill	d							22 18								00 01
Bristol Temple Meads ■10	a				22 10	22 14	22 14	22 27	23 04	23 06	23 09		23 33	23 33	23 33	00 06
	d	21 55	21 55	21 55						23 08	23 12		23 35	23 35	23 35	
Bedminster	d	21 57	21 57	21 57						23 11	23 14					
Parson Street	d	21 59	21 59	21 59						23 14	23 17					
Nailsea & Backwell	d	22 08	22 08	22 08						23 23	23 26		23s47	23s47	23s47	
Yatton	d	22 13	22 13	22 13						23 29	23 32		23s54	23s54	23s54	
Worle	d	22 19	22 19	22 19						23 35	23 38		00s01	00s01	00s01	
Weston Milton	d	22 23	22 23	22 23						23 40	23 43					
Weston-super-Mare	a	22 27	22 27	22 27						23 43	23 46		00s06	00s06	00 06	
	d	22 33	22 33	22 29						23 45			00s08	00s08	00 08	
Highbridge & Burnham	d	22 44	22 44	22 52						23 56			00s18	00 18	00 30	
Bridgwater	d	22 59	22 52	23 07						00 04			00s26	00 26	00 45	
Taunton	a	23 12	23 12	23 35						00s17			00s37	00 44	01 16	

A from 18 October
B from 6 September until 15 October
C from 12 July until 3 September
D until 9 July
E until 3 September
F from 6 September
G from 22 October
H until 21 October
I from 12 July until 15 October

Table 134

Gloucester - Taunton

Saturdays
until 04 September

		GW	GW	GW	XC	GW	GW	XC	GW	GW		GW	GW	GW	GW	XC	GW	GW	GW	XC		GW	XC	GW	GW
		◇1 A	◇1 B		◇1	◇	◇1	◇1		◇				◇		◇1	◇			◇1			◇1	■ 1	◇
Gloucester ■7	d												06 19		07 02				07 40						
Cam & Dursley	d												06 35		07 15				07 54						
Yate	d												06 48		07 30				08 09						
Bristol Parkway ■7	a												06 58		07 39				08 19						
	d				00 02		05 42						06 58		07 40	07 57		08 12	08 19	08 26			08 58		
Filton Abbey Wood	d			23p52									07 02	07 09	07 46		08 09	08 15	08 23			08 42			09 09
Stapleton Road	d			23p59																					
Lawrence Hill	d			00 01																					
Bristol Temple Meads ■10	a	23p33	23p33	00 06	00 16		05 53						07 11	07 18	07 54	08 08	08 18	08 23	08 36	08 38		08 52	09 08	09 14	09 18
	d	23p35	23p35			05 28		06 08	06 18	06 36		06 48	07 18		07 56	08 11		08 25		08 44		08 55		09 15	
Bedminster	d											06 50	07 21					08 27							
Parson Street	d											06 53	07 23					08 29							
Nailsea & Backwell	d	23b47	23b47						06 28			07 01	07 28		08 03			08 38				09 03			
Yatton	d	23b54	23b54						06 34			07 06	07 34		08 08			08 44				09 07			
Worle	d	00s01	00s01						06 40			07 12	07 40		08 14			08 50				09 13			
Weston Milton	d											07 17	07 46					08 55							
Weston-super-Mare	a	00s06	00 06			05 47			06 45	06 55		07 22	07 47		08 23			09 00				09 23			
	d	00s08	00 08			05 49			06 47	06 56			07 50									09 32			
Highbridge & Burnham	d	00 18	00 30			06 00			06 58				08 01									09 44			
Bridgwater	d	00 26	00 45			06 08			07 06				08 09									09 52			
Taunton	a	00 44	01 16			06 21		07 14	07 20	07 24			08 25			08 42				09 15		10 06		09 49	

		GW	GW	XC	GW	XC	GW	GW	GW	XC	GW	GW	XC	GW	GW	GW	XC	GW	XC	GW	GW	GW	GW	XC	GW
				◇1		◇1	◇			◇1	◇1		◇1	◇			◇1		◇1	◇1	◇			◇1	
Gloucester ■7	d		08 42						09 46							10 42							11 46		
Cam & Dursley	d		08 56						10 02							10 56							12 01		
Yate	d		09 11						10 16							11 10							12 16		
Bristol Parkway ■7	a		09 19						10 24							11 19							12 24		
	d	09 12	09 20	09 26		09 59		10 12	10 25	10 31			10 59		11 12	11 20	11 26		11 58			12 12	12 25	12 31	
Filton Abbey Wood	d	09 15	09 23		09 42		10 09	10 15	10 28			10 42		11 09	11 15	11 23		11 42			12 09	12 15	12 28		12 42
Stapleton Road	d		09 29						10 32							11 29							12 32		
Lawrence Hill	d		09 31						10 34							11 31							12 34		
Bristol Temple Meads ■10	a	09 23	09 35	09 38	09 51	10 11	10 18	10 23	10 39	10 42	10 39	10 51	11 11	11 18	11 23	11 35	11 39	11 51	12 08	12 15	12 19	12 23	12 39	12 42	12 51
	d	09 25		09 44	09 55	10 20		10 25		10 44	10 49	10 53	11 14		11 25		11 43	11 53		12 18		12 25		12 44	12 53
Bedminster	d	09 27						10 27							11 27							12 27			
Parson Street	d	09 29						10 29							11 29							12 29			
Nailsea & Backwell	d	09 38			10 03			10 38				11 03			11 38			12 03				12 38			13 03
Yatton	d	09 44			10 08			10 44				11 08			11 44			12 08				12 44			13 08
Worle	d	09 50			10 14			10 50				11 14			11 50			12 14				12 50			13 14
Weston Milton	d	09 55						10 55							11 55							12 55			
Weston-super-Mare	a	10 00			10 22			11 00			11 07	11 21	11 31		12 00			12 22		12 36		13 00			13 22
	d				10 23							11 23	11 39					12 23							13 23
Highbridge & Burnham	d				10 34							11 34						12 34							13 34
Bridgwater	d				10 42							11 42						12 42							13 42
Taunton	a			10 16	10 59	11 01				11 15		11 56	12 00				12 15	12 57						13 15	13 59

		XC		GW	GW	GW	XC	GW	XC	GW	GW	GW	GW		XC	GW	XC	GW	GW	GW	XC	GW	XC	GW	GW
		◇1		◇			◇1		◇1	◇1	◇				◇1		◇1	◇			◇1		◇1	◇1	◇
Gloucester ■7	d					12 42							13 42							14 42					
Cam & Dursley	d					12 56							13 57							14 56					
Yate	d					13 11							14 11							15 10					
Bristol Parkway ■7	a					13 19							14 20							15 18					
	d	12 58			13 12	13 20	13 26		13 59			14 12	14 20		14 28		14 59		15 12	15 19	15 26		15 58		
Filton Abbey Wood	d			13 09	13 15	13 23		13 42			14 09	14 15	14 25			14 42		15 09	15 15	15 22		15 42			16 09
Stapleton Road	d					13 27							14 31							15 27					
Lawrence Hill	d					13 29							14 33							15 29					
Bristol Temple Meads ■10	a	13 08		13 18	13 23	13 35	13 38	13 51	14 10	14 15	14 18	14 23	14 40		14 41	14 51	15 10	15 18	15 23	15 34	15 38	15 51	16 08	16 15	16 18
	d				13 25		13 44	13 53		14 18		14 25	14 49		14 44	14 53	15 13		15 25		15 44	15 53		16 18	
Bedminster	d				13 27							14 27							15 27						
Parson Street	d				13 29							14 29							15 29						
Nailsea & Backwell	d				13 38			14 03				14 38				15 03			15 38			16 03			
Yatton	d				13 44			14 08				14 44				15 08			15 44			16 08			
Worle	d				13 50			14 14				14 50				15 14			15 50			16 14			
Weston Milton	d				13 55							14 55							15 55						
Weston-super-Mare	a				14 00			14 21		14 36		15 00				15 22			16 00			16 22		16 36	
	d							14 23								15 25						16 23			
Highbridge & Burnham	d							14 34								15 36						16 34			
Bridgwater	d							14 42								15 45						16 42			
Taunton	a						14 15	14 59							15 16	16 00	15 44				16 15	16 57			

A from 17 July until 4 September
B until 10 July
b previous night, stops to set down only

Table 134

Gloucester - Taunton

Saturdays
until 04 September

		GW	GW	XC	GW	XC	GW	GW	GW		GW	XC	GW	GW	XC	GW	GW	GW	GW	XC	GW	GW	XC	GW	GW
				◇1 🍴		◇1 🍴	◇1 🛒	■				◇1 🍴	A	B	◇1 🍴	◇1 🛒	◇			◇1 🍴	A	B	◇1 🍴	◇1 🛒	◇
Gloucester 7	d		15 45								16 42								17 46						
Cam & Dursley	d		15 59								16 56								18 01						
Yate	d		16 13								17 10								18 16						
Bristol Parkway 7	a		16 22								17 18								18 24						
	d	16 12	16 22	16 31		16 58			17 12		17 20	17 26			17 58			18 12	18 25	18 31			18 57		
Filton Abbey Wood	d	16 15	16 25		16 42			17 09	17 15		17 23		17 42	17 42			18 09	18 15	18 28		18 42	18 42			19 09
Stapleton Road	d		16 31								17 29								18 34						
Lawrence Hill	d		16 33								17 31								18 36						
Bristol Temple Meads 10	a	16 23	16 38	16 42	16 51	17 10	17 15	17 18	17 23		17 37	17 38	17 51	17 51	18 08	18 15	18 18	18 23	18 39	18 43	18 51	18 51	19 08	19 15	19 18
	d	16 25		16 44	16 53		17 18		17 25			17 44	17 53	17 53		18 18		18 25		18 45	18 53	18 53		19 18	
Bedminster	d	16 27							17 27									18 27							
Parson Street	d	16 29							17 29									18 29							
Nailsea & Backwell	d	16 38			17 03				17 38				18 03	18 03				18 38			19 03	19 03		19 30	
Yatton	d	16 44			17 08				17 44				18 08	18 08				18 44			19 08	19 08		19 37	
Worle	d	16 50			17 14				17 50				18 14	18 14				18 50			19 14	19 14		19 43	
Weston Milton	d	16 55							17 55									18 55			19 20	19 20			
Weston-super-Mare	a	17 00			17 22		17 36		18 00				18 22	18 22		18 36		19 00			19 23	19 23		19 50	
	d				17 27								18 23	18 23		18 40					19 23	19 23			
Highbridge & Burnham	d				17 38								18 34	18 34							19 34	19 34			
Bridgwater	d				17 46								18 42	18 42							19 42	19 42			
Taunton	a			17 17	18 01							18 15	18 56	18 56		19 06				19 16	19 59	19 59			

		GW	GW	XC		GW	GW	XC	GW	GW	GW	GW	GW	XC	GW		GW	XC	GW	XC	GW	GW	XC	GW	XC
				◇1 🍴		A	B	◇1 🍴	◇1 🛒	◇	A	B		◇1 🍴			◇1 🛒	◇1 🍴	◇	◇1 🍴			◇1 🍴	◇1 🛒	◇1 🍴
Gloucester 7	d		18 42										19 45									21 16			22 06
Cam & Dursley	d		18 56										19 59									21 30			
Yate	d		19 11										20 13									21 44			
Bristol Parkway 7	a		19 20										20 22									21 53			22 33
	d	19 19	19 20	19 29				19 58			20 10	20 17	20 22	20 31				20 58		21 25		21 53	21 59		22 35
Filton Abbey Wood	d	19 23	19 24			19 42	19 42			20 09	20 14	20 20	20 25		20 39				21 09		21 42	21 57			
Stapleton Road	d		19 30										20 31												
Lawrence Hill	d		19 32										20 33												
Bristol Temple Meads 10	a	19 31	19 38	19 41		19 51	19 51	20 08	20 15	20 18	20 25	20 29	20 39	20 42	20 48		20 40	21 08	21 19	21 35	21 49	22 05	22 12	22 15	22 46
	d			19 44		19 53	19 53		20 15					20 44			20 55			21 44	21 55			22 17	
Bedminster	d																				21 57				
Parson Street	d																				21 59				
Nailsea & Backwell	d					20 03	20 03										21 04				22 08			22s29	
Yatton	d					20 08	20 08										21 11				22 14			22s36	
Worle	d					20 14	20 14										21 17				22 20			22s42	
Weston Milton	d					20 19	20 19										21 22								
Weston-super-Mare	a					20 23	20 23		20 36								21 26				22 25			22s48	
	d					20 23	20 23		20 38								21 26				22 27			22s49	
Highbridge & Burnham	d					20 34	20 34										21 39				22 38			23s00	
Bridgwater	d					20 42	20 42										21 46				22 46			23s07	
Taunton	a			20 15		20 59	20 59		21 03					21 15			21 58			22 16	22 59			23 18	

		GW
Gloucester 7	d	
Cam & Dursley	d	
Yate	d	
Bristol Parkway 7	a	
	d	
Filton Abbey Wood	d	22 52
Stapleton Road	d	
Lawrence Hill	d	
Bristol Temple Meads 10	a	23 01
	d	
Bedminster	d	
Parson Street	d	
Nailsea & Backwell	d	
Yatton	d	
Worle	d	
Weston Milton	d	
Weston-super-Mare	a	
	d	
Highbridge & Burnham	d	
Bridgwater	d	
Taunton	a	

A from 17 July until 4 September
B until 10 July

Table 134

Gloucester - Taunton

Saturdays
from 11 September

				GW	GW	XC	GW	GW	GW	GW		XC	GW	GW	GW	GW	GW	GW	XC	GW		GW	GW	XC	GW
				◇1 B 🛒		◇1	■1 C	◇ D	◇1 🛒	◇ C		◇1 🍴		◇			◇		◇1 🍴	◇				◇1 🍴	
Gloucester 7	d															06 19		07 02					07 40		
Cam & Dursley	d															06 35		07 15					07 54		
Yate	d															06 48		07 30					08 09		
Bristol Parkway 7	a															06 58		07 39					08 19		
	d					00 02			05 42							06 58		07 40	07 57			08 12	08 19	08 26	
Filton Abbey Wood	d				23p52											07 02	07 09	07 46		08 09		08 15	08 23		08 42
Stapleton Road	d				23p59																				
Lawrence Hill	d				00 01																				
Bristol Temple Meads 10	a			23p33	00 06	00 16			05 53							07 11	07 18	07 54	08 08	08 18		08 23	08 36	08 38	08 52
	d			23p35			04 40	05 28				06 08	06 18	06 36	06 48	07 18		07 56	08 11			08 25		08 44	08 55
Bedminster	d														06 50	07 21						08 27			
Parson Street	d														06 53	07 23						08 29			
Nailsea & Backwell	d			23b47									06 28		07 01	07 28		08 03				08 38			09 03
Yatton	d			23b54			05c01						06 34		07 06	07 34		08 08				08 44			09 07
Worle	d			00s01									06 40		07 12	07 40		08 14				08 50			09 13
Weston Milton	d														07 17	07 46						08 55			
Weston-super-Mare	a			00s06			05 44	05 47					06 45	06 55	07 22	07 47		08 23				09 00			09 23
	d			00s08				05 49		05 49			06 47	06 56		07 50									09 32
Highbridge & Burnham	d			00 18				06 00		06 00			06 58			08 01									09 44
Bridgwater	d			00 26				06 08		06 08			07 06			08 09									09 52
Taunton	a			00 44				06 21		06 21		07 14	07 20	07 24		08 25			08 42					09 15	10 06

		XC	GW	GW	GW	GW	XC	GW	GW	XC	GW	GW	XC	GW	XC	GW	GW	GW	XC	GW	XC	GW	GW	GW	XC
		◇1 🍴	◇1 🛒	◇			◇1 🍴			◇1 🍴	◇ 🍴		◇1 🍴		◇1 🍴	◇ 🍴			◇1 🍴		◇1 🍴	◇ 🍴			◇1 🍴
Gloucester 7	d					08 42		09 46										10 42						11 46	
Cam & Dursley	d					08 56		10 01										10 56						12 01	
Yate	d					09 11		10 16										11 10						12 16	
Bristol Parkway 7	a					09 19		10 24										11 19						12 24	
	d	08 58			09 12	09 20	09 26	10 25		09 58		10 12	10 31		10 59		11 12	11 20	11 26		11 58		12 12	12 25	12 31
Filton Abbey Wood	d			09 09	09 15	09 23		10 28	09 42		10 09	10 15		10 42		11 09	11 15	11 23		11 42		12 09	12 15	12 28	
Stapleton Road	d					09 29		10 32										11 29						12 32	
Lawrence Hill	d					09 31		10 34										11 31						12 34	
Bristol Temple Meads 10	a	09 08	09 15	09 18	09 23	09 35	09 38	10 39	09 51	10 08	10 18	10 23	10 42	10 51	11 10	11 18	11 23	11 35	11 38	11 51	12 08	12 19	12 23	12 39	12 42
	d		09 17		09 25		09 44		09 55			10 25	10 44	10 53	11 14	11 23	11 25		11 44	11 53			12 25		12 44
Bedminster	d				09 27							10 27					11 27						12 27		
Parson Street	d				09 29							10 29					11 29						12 29		
Nailsea & Backwell	d				09 38				10 03			10 38		11 03			11 38			12 03			12 38		
Yatton	d				09 44				10 08			10 44		11 08			11 44			12 08			12 44		
Worle	d				09 50				10 14			10 50		11 14			11 50			12 14			12 50		
Weston Milton	d				09 55							10 55					11 55						12 55		
Weston-super-Mare	a				10 00				10 22			11 00		11 21	11 31		12 00			12 22			13 00		
	d								10 23					11 23	11 39					12 23					
Highbridge & Burnham	d								10 34					11 34						12 34					
Bridgwater	d								10 42					11 42						12 42					
Taunton	a		09 50				10 16		10 59				11 15	11 56	11 59				12 15	12 57					13 15

		GW	XC	GW	GW	GW	XC	GW	XC	GW	GW	GW		XC	GW	XC	GW	GW	GW	XC	GW	XC		GW	GW
			◇1 🍴	◇ 🍴			◇1 🍴		◇1 🍴	◇		🍴		◇1 🍴		◇1 🍴	◇			◇1 🍴		◇1 🍴		◇	
Gloucester 7	d					12 42						13 42							14 42						
Cam & Dursley	d					12 56						13 57							14 56						
Yate	d					13 11						14 11							15 10						
Bristol Parkway 7	a					13 19						14 20							15 18						
	d		12 58		13 12	13 20	13 26		13 59		14 12	14 20		14 28		14 59		15 12	15 19	15 26		15 58			16 12
Filton Abbey Wood	d	12 42		13 09	13 15	13 23		13 42		14 09	14 15	14 25			14 42		15 09	15 15	15 22		15 42			16 09	16 15
Stapleton Road	d					13 27						14 31							15 27						
Lawrence Hill	d					13 29						14 33							15 29						
Bristol Temple Meads 10	a	12 51	13 08	13 18	13 23	13 35	13 38	13 51	14 10	14 18	14 23	14 40		14 41	14 51	15 10	15 18	15 23	15 34	15 38	15 51	16 08		16 18	16 23
	d	12 53			13 25		13 44	13 53			14 25			14 44	14 53			15 25		15 44	15 53				16 25
Bedminster	d				13 27						14 27							15 27							16 27
Parson Street	d				13 29						14 29							15 29							16 29
Nailsea & Backwell	d	13 03			13 38			14 03			14 38				15 03			15 38			16 03				16 38
Yatton	d	13 08			13 44			14 08			14 44				15 08			15 44			16 08				16 44
Worle	d	13 14			13 50			14 14			14 50				15 14			15 50			16 14				16 50
Weston Milton	d				13 55						14 55							15 55							16 55
Weston-super-Mare	a	13 22			14 00			14 21			15 00				15 22			16 00			16 22				17 00
	d	13 23						14 23							15 25						16 23				
Highbridge & Burnham	d	13 34						14 34							15 36						16 34				
Bridgwater	d	13 42						14 42							15 45						16 42				
Taunton	a	13 59					14 15	14 59						15 16	16 00					16 15	16 57				

A from 23 October
B from 11 September until 16 October
C from 20 November
D from 11 September until 13 November
b previous night, stops to set down only
c arr. 0451

Table 134

Gloucester - Taunton

Saturdays from 11 September

		GW	XC	GW	XC	GW	GW	GW	XC		GW	XC	GW	GW	GW	GW	XC	GW	XC	GW	GW	GW	GW	XC	GW
			◇1 ✕		◇1 ✕	■			◇1 ✕			◇1 ✕	◇1 A ⊡	◇			◇1 ✕		◇1 ✕	◇1 ⊡	◇			◇1 ✕	
Gloucester 7	d	15 45						16 42								17 46							18 42		
Cam & Dursley	d	15 59						16 56								18 01							18 56		
Yate	d	16 13						17 10								18 16							19 11		
Bristol Parkway 7	a	16 22						17 18								18 24							19 20		
	d	16 22	16 31		16 58		17 12	17 20	17 26			17 58			18 12	18 25	18 31		18 57			19 19	19 20	19 29	
Filton Abbey Wood	d	16 25		16 42		17 09	17 15	17 23			17 42			18 09	18 15	18 28		18 42			19 09	19 23	19 24		19 42
Stapleton Road	d	16 31						17 29								18 34							19 30		
Lawrence Hill	d	16 33						17 31								18 36							19 32		
Bristol Temple Meads 10	a	16 38	16 42	16 51	17 08	17 18	17 23	17 37	17 38		17 51	18 08	18 15	18 18	18 23	18 39	18 42	18 51	19 07	19 15	19 18	19 31	19 38	19 41	19 51
	d		16 44	16 53	17 11		17 25		17 44		17 53		18 18		18 25		18 44	18 53		19 18				19 44	19 53
Bedminster	d						17 27								18 27										
Parson Street	d						17 29								18 29										
Nailsea & Backwell	d			17 03			17 38				18 03				18 38			19 03		19 30					20 03
Yatton	d			17 08			17 44				18 08				18 44			19 08		19 37					20 08
Worle	d			17 14			17 50				18 14				18 50			19 14		19 43					20 14
Weston Milton	d						17 55								18 55			19 20							20 19
Weston-super-Mare	a			17 22			18 00				18 22		18 36		19 00			19 23		19 50					20 23
	d			17 27							18 23		18 40					19 23							20 23
Highbridge & Burnham	d			17 38							18 34							19 34							20 34
Bridgwater	d			17 46							18 42							19 42							20 42
Taunton	a		17 17	18 01	17 42				18 15		18 56		19 06				19 14	19 59						20 15	20 59

		XC	GW	GW		GW	GW	XC	GW	GW	XC	GW	XC	GW	GW		XC	GW	XC	GW
		◇1 ✕	◇1 ⊡	◇				◇1 ✕		◇1 ⊡	◇1 ✕	◇	◇1 ✕				◇1 ✕	◇1 ⊡	◇1 ✕	
Gloucester 7	d						19 45								21 16				22 06	
Cam & Dursley	d						19 59								21 30					
Yate	d						20 13								21 44					
Bristol Parkway 7	a						20 22								21 53				22 33	
	d	19 58				20 17	20 22	20 31			20 58		21 25		21 53		21 59		22 35	
Filton Abbey Wood	d			20 09		20 20	20 25		20 39			21 09		21 42	21 57					22 52
Stapleton Road	d						20 31													
Lawrence Hill	d						20 33													
Bristol Temple Meads 10	a	20 08	20 15	20 18		20 29	20 39	20 42	20 48	20 40	21 08	21 19	21 35	21 49	22 05		22 12	22 15	22 46	23 01
	d		20 15					20 44		20 55	21 13		21 44	21 55				22 17		
Bedminster	d													21 57						
Parson Street	d													21 59						
Nailsea & Backwell	d									21 04				22 08				22s29		
Yatton	d									21 11				22 14				22s36		
Worle	d									21 17				22 20				22s42		
Weston Milton	d									21 22										
Weston-super-Mare	a		20 36							21 26				22 25				22s48		
	d		20 38							21 26				22 27				22s49		
Highbridge & Burnham	d									21 39				22 38				23s00		
Bridgwater	d									21 46				22 46				23s07		
Taunton	a		21 03					21 15		21 58	21 44		22 16	22 59				23 18		

Sundays until 11 July

		GW	GW	GW	GW	XC	GW	GW	XC	GW		GW	GW	XC	GW	GW	XC	GW	GW	GW		XC	GW	GW	XC
		◇	◇	◇		◇1 ✕	◇1 ⊡	◇	◇1 ✕			◇		◇1 ✕	◇1 ⊡		◇1 ✕		◇			◇1 ✕	◇1 ⊡	◇	◇1 ✕
Gloucester 7	d												10 19							12 14					
Cam & Dursley	d												10 32							12 28					
Yate	d												10 46							12 43					
Bristol Parkway 7	a												10 55							12 51					
	d												10 55				12 38			12 57		13 25			14 25
Filton Abbey Wood	d			08 54				10 03				10 54	10 59			11 54			12 57	13 01				13 54	
Stapleton Road	d									10 16															
Lawrence Hill	d									10 18															
Bristol Temple Meads 10	a			09 04			10 02	10 13		10 21		11 03	11 08		11 54	12 04	12 50		13 05	13 09		13 35	13 54	14 04	14 39
	d	07 45	08 28		09 05	09 48	10 03		10 44	10 23			11 10	11 44	11 55		12 53	13 05				13 44	13 55		14 44
Bedminster	d									10 27															
Parson Street	d									10 29															
Nailsea & Backwell	d		08 38		09 13					10 37			11 21		12 07			13 15					14 06		
Yatton	d	07 58	08 43		09 20					10 43			11 26		12 14			13 20					14 12		
Worle	d		08 49		09 26					10 49			11 32		12 18			13 26					14 19		
Weston Milton	d																								
Weston-super-Mare	a	08 07	08 55		09 37					10 54			11 38		12 31			13 31					14 25		
	d	08 08	08 56							10 55			11 39					13 33							
Highbridge & Burnham	d		09 07							11 09			11 49					13 44							
Bridgwater	d	08 24	09 15							11 17			11 57					13 52							
Taunton	a	08 37	09 28			10 19	10 38		11 19	11 31			12 11	12 19			13 25	14 06				14 15			15 15

A The Torbay Express

Table 134

Gloucester - Taunton

Sundays until 11 July

		GW	GW	XC	GW	XC		GW	GW	GW	XC	XC	GW	GW	XC	GW		GW	XC	GW	GW	GW	XC	XC	GW
		◇1 ⊡	◇	◇1 ✕		◇1 ✕			◇		◇1 ✕	◇1 ✕	◇1 ⊡	◇	◇1 ✕			◇	◇1 ✕	◇			◇1 ✕	◇1 ✕	■
Gloucester 7	d									15 13												17 20			
Cam & Dursley	d									15 27												17 34			
Yate	d									15 41												17 49			
Bristol Parkway 7	a									15 49												17 57			
	d			14 58		15 26				15 51	15 58	16 25			16 58				17 25			17 58	18 02	18 25	
Filton Abbey Wood	d		14 55						15 53	15 55				16 55				17 20		17 55		18 01			18 25
Stapleton Road	d																								
Lawrence Hill	d																								
Bristol Temple Meads 10	a	14 54	15 05	15 08		15 38			16 03	16 06	16 10	16 35	16 54	17 06	17 09			17 29	17 35	18 05		18 10	18 13	18 37	18 33
	d	14 55			15 10	15 44		15 55		16 26	16 14	16 44	16 55			17 25			17 44		18 07			18 44	
Bedminster	d				15 13			15 58								17 28									
Parson Street	d							16 00																	
Nailsea & Backwell	d				15 22			16 08		16 36			17 07			17 37					18 17				
Yatton	d				15 28			16 14		16 41			17 13			17 43					18 23				
Worle	d				15 34			16 20		16 47			17 20			17 49					18 29				
Weston Milton	d				15 39					16 53						17 58									
Weston-super-Mare	a				15 42			16 25		16 57			17 26			18 01					18 35				
	d							16 28					17 28								18 36				
Highbridge & Burnham	d							16 40													18 47				
Bridgwater	d							16 48													18 55				
Taunton	a	15 28				16 16		17 03			16 45	17 15	17 50						18 19		19 09			19 15	

		GW		GW	XC	GW	XC	GW	GW	XC	GW	XC		GW	XC	GW	XC	GW	GW	XC	XC	GW	GW	XC	XC
				◇	◇1 ✕	◇1 ⊡	◇1 ✕	◇		◇1 ✕		◇1 ✕		◇1 ⊡	◇1 ✕	◇	◇1 ✕	◇1 ⊡		◇1 ✕	◇1 ✕	◇		◇1 ✕	◇1 ✕
Gloucester 7	d								19 20										21 15		22 06				
Cam & Dursley	d								19 34										21 31						
Yate	d								19 48										21 45						
Bristol Parkway 7	a								19 56										21 53		22 35				
	d				18 58		19 25		19 57	20 02		20 25			20 58		21 25		21 55	22 00	22 36			23 01	23 24
Filton Abbey Wood	d			18 56				19 55	20 00							21 05			21 58			22 52			
Stapleton Road	d										20 16														
Lawrence Hill	d										20 18														
Bristol Temple Meads 10	a			19 06	19 09	19 27	19 35	20 05	20 10	20 14	20 21	20 35		20 54	21 09	21 13	21 35	21 53	22 07	22 11	22 47	23 00		23 13	23 35
	d	19 05				19 30	19 44			20 19	20 25	20 44		20 55			21 44	21 55					23 10		
Bedminster	d	19 08									20 28												23 13		
Parson Street	d	19 10																					23 15		
Nailsea & Backwell	d	19 18				19 39					20 36			21 06				22 06					23 23		
Yatton	d	19 24				19 46					20 42			21 12				22 12					23 29		
Worle	d	19 30				19 52					20 48			21 19				22 19					23 35		
Weston Milton	d	19 34																					23 40		
Weston-super-Mare	a	19 38				20 00				20 36	20 53			21 25				22 26					23 43		
	d	19 40								20 37	20 58			21 26											
Highbridge & Burnham	d	19 51									21 09														
Bridgwater	d	19 59									21 17														
Taunton	a	20 13					20 16			20 58	21 33	21 15		21 49			22 15								

Sundays 18 July to 05 September

		GW	GW	GW	GW	XC	GW	GW	XC	GW		GW	GW	XC	GW	GW	XC	GW	GW	GW		XC	GW	GW	XC
		◇	◇	◇		◇1 ✕	◇1 ⊡	◇	◇1 ✕			◇		◇1 ✕	◇1 ⊡		◇1 ✕		◇			◇1 ✕	◇1 ⊡	◇	◇1 ✕
Gloucester 7	d												10 19							12 14					
Cam & Dursley	d												10 32							12 28					
Yate	d												10 46							12 43					
Bristol Parkway 7	a												10 55							12 51					
	d												10 55				12 25			12 57		13 25			14 25
Filton Abbey Wood	d			08 54				10 03				10 54	10 59			11 54			12 57	13 01				13 54	
Stapleton Road	d									10 16															
Lawrence Hill	d									10 18															
Bristol Temple Meads 10	a			09 04			10 02	10 13		10 21		11 03	11 08		11 54	12 04	12 37		13 05	13 09		13 35	13 54	14 04	14 39
	d	07 45	08 28		09 24	09 48	10 03		10 44	10 23			11 10	11 44	11 55		12 44	13 05				13 44	13 55		14 44
Bedminster	d									10 27															
Parson Street	d									10 29															
Nailsea & Backwell	d		08 38		09 32					10 37			11 21		12 07			13 15					14 06		
Yatton	d	07 58	08 43		09 39					10 43			11 26		12 14			13 20					14 12		
Worle	d		08 49		09 45					10 49			11 32		12 18			13 26					14 19		
Weston Milton	d																								
Weston-super-Mare	a	08 07	08 55		09 56					10 54			11 38		12 31			13 31					14 25		
	d	08 08	08 56							10 55			11 39					13 33							
Highbridge & Burnham	d		09 07							11 09			11 49					13 44							
Bridgwater	d	08 24	09 15							11 17			11 57					13 52							
Taunton	a	08 37	09 28			10 19	10 38		11 19	11 31			12 11	12 19			13 16	14 06				14 15			15 15

Table 134

Gloucester - Taunton

Sundays
18 July to 05 September

		GW	GW	XC	GW	XC	GW	GW	GW	XC	XC	GW	GW	XC	GW	GW	XC	GW	GW	GW	XC	XC	GW
		◇1	◇	◇1		◇1		◇		◇1	◇1	◇1	◇	◇1		◇	◇1	◇			◇1	◇1	
Gloucester 7	d								15 13											17 20			
Cam & Dursley	d								15 27											17 34			
Yate	d								15 41											17 49			
Bristol Parkway 7	a								15 49											17 57			
	d			14 58		15 26			15 51	16 00	16 25			16 58			17 25			17 58	18 02	18 25	
Filton Abbey Wood	d		14 55					15 57	15 58				16 55			17 20		17 54		18 01			18 25
Stapleton Road	d																						
Lawrence Hill	d																						
Bristol Temple Meads 10	a	14 54	15 05	15 08		15 38		16 06	16 09	16 11	16 35	16 54	17 06	17 09		17 29	17 35	18 04		18 10	18 13	18 37	18 33
	d	14 55			15 10	15 44	15 55		16 26	16 14	16 44	16 55			17 25		17 44		18 07			18 44	
Bedminster	d				15 13		15 58								17 28								
Parson Street	d						16 00																
Nailsea & Backwell	d				15 22		16 08		16 36			17 07			17 37				18 17				
Yatton	d				15 28		16 14		16 41			17 13			17 43				18 23				
Worle	d				15 34		16 20		16 47			17 20			17 49				18 29				
Weston Milton	d				15 39				16 53						17 58								
Weston-super-Mare	a				15 42		16 25		16 57			17 26			18 01				18 35				
	d						16 28					17 28							18 36				
Highbridge & Burnham	d						16 40												18 47				
Bridgwater	d						16 48												18 55				
Taunton	a	15 28				16 16	17 03			16 45	17 15	17 50					18 19		19 09			19 15	

		GW	GW	XC	GW	XC	GW	GW	XC	GW	XC	GW	XC	GW	XC	GW	GW	XC	XC	GW	GW	XC	XC
			◇	◇1	◇1	◇1	◇		◇1		◇1	◇1	◇1	◇	◇1	◇1		◇1	◇1	◇		◇1	◇1
Gloucester 7	d							19 20									21 15		22 06				
Cam & Dursley	d							19 34									21 31						
Yate	d							19 48									21 45						
Bristol Parkway 7	a							19 56									21 53		22 35				
	d			18 58		19 25		19 57	20 02		20 25		20 58		21 25		21 55	22 00	22 36			23 01	23 24
Filton Abbey Wood	d		18 56				19 55	20 00						21 05			21 58			22 52			
Stapleton Road	d									20 16													
Lawrence Hill	d									20 18													
Bristol Temple Meads 10	a		19 06	19 09	19 27	19 35	20 05	20 10	20 14	20 21	20 35	20 54	21 09	21 13	21 35	21 53	22 07	22 11	22 47	23 00		23 13	23 35
	d	19 05			19 30	19 44			20 19	20 25	20 44	20 55			21 44	21 55					23 10		
Bedminster	d	19 08								20 28											23 13		
Parson Street	d	19 10																			23 15		
Nailsea & Backwell	d	19 18			19 39					20 36		21 06				22 06					23 23		
Yatton	d	19 24			19 46					20 42		21 12				22 12					23 29		
Worle	d	19 30			19 52					20 48		21 19				22 19					23 35		
Weston Milton	d	19 34																			23 40		
Weston-super-Mare	a	19 38			20 00				20 36	20 53		21 25				22 26					23 43		
	d	19 40							20 37	20 58		21 26											
Highbridge & Burnham	d	19 51								21 09													
Bridgwater	d	19 59								21 17													
Taunton	a	20 13				20 16			20 58	21 33	21 15	21 49			22 15								

Sundays
12 September to 17 October

		GW	GW	GW	GW	XC	GW	GW	GW	XC	GW	GW	XC	GW	GW	XC	GW	GW	GW	XC	GW	GW	XC
		◇	◇	◇		◇1	◇1	◇		◇1	◇		◇1	◇1		◇1		◇		◇1	◇1	◇	◇1
Gloucester 7	d											10 19							12 14				
Cam & Dursley	d											10 32							12 28				
Yate	d											10 46							12 43				
Bristol Parkway 7	a											10 55							12 51				
	d									10 25		10 55	11 29			12 25			12 57	13 25			14 25
Filton Abbey Wood	d			08 54				10 03			10 54	10 59			11 54			12 57	13 01			13 54	
Stapleton Road	d								10 16														
Lawrence Hill	d								10 18														
Bristol Temple Meads 10	a			09 04			09 51	10 13	10 21	10 35	11 03	11 08	11 41	11 54	12 04	12 36		13 05	13 09	13 35	13 54	14 04	14 39
	d	07 45	08 28		09 05	09 48	09 53		10 23	10 44		11 10	11 44	11 55		12 44	13 05			13 44	13 55		14 44
Bedminster	d																						
Parson Street	d																						
Nailsea & Backwell	d		08 38		09 13				10 33			11 21		12 07			13 15				14 06		
Yatton	d	07 58	08 43		09 20				10 38			11 26		12 14			13 20				14 12		
Worle	d		08 49		09 26				10 44			11 32		12 18			13 26				14 19		
Weston Milton	d																						
Weston-super-Mare	a	08 07	08 55		09 37				10 50			11 38		12 31			13 31				14 25		
	d	08 08	08 56						10 55			11 39					13 33						
Highbridge & Burnham	d		09 07						11 09			11 49					13 44						
Bridgwater	d	08 24	09 15						11 17			11 57					13 52						
Taunton	a	08 37	09 28			10 19	10 27		11 31	11 19		12 11	12 16			13 16	14 06			14 15			15 15

Table 134

Gloucester - Taunton

Sundays
12 September to 17 October

		GW	GW	XC	GW	XC	GW	GW	GW	XC	XC	GW	GW	XC	GW	GW	XC	GW	GW	GW	XC	XC	GW
		◇1	◇	◇1		◇1		◇		◇1	◇1	◇1	◇	◇1		◇	◇1	◇			◇1	◇1	
Gloucester 7	d								15 13											17 20			
Cam & Dursley	d								15 27											17 34			
Yate	d								15 41											17 49			
Bristol Parkway 7	a								15 49											17 57			
	d			14 58		15 26			15 51	16 00	16 25			16 58			17 25			17 58	18 02	18 25	
Filton Abbey Wood	d		14 55					15 56	15 58				16 55			17 20		17 54		18 01			18 25
Stapleton Road	d																						
Lawrence Hill	d																						
Bristol Temple Meads 10	a	14 54	15 05	15 08		15 38		16 06	16 09	16 11	16 35	16 54	17 06	17 09		17 29	17 35	18 04		18 10	18 13	18 37	18 33
	d	14 55			15 10	15 44	15 55		16 26	16 14	16 44	16 55			17 25		17 44		18 07			18 44	
Bedminster	d				15 13		15 58								17 28								
Parson Street	d						16 00																
Nailsea & Backwell	d				15 22		16 08		16 36			17 06			17 37				18 17				
Yatton	d				15 28		16 14		16 41			17 12			17 43				18 23				
Worle	d				15 34		16 20		16 47			17 19			17 49				18 29				
Weston Milton	d				15 39				16 53						17 58								
Weston-super-Mare	a				15 42		16 25		16 57			17 25			18 01				18 35				
	d						16 28					17 27							18 36				
Highbridge & Burnham	d						16 40												18 47				
Bridgwater	d						16 48												18 55				
Taunton	a	15 28				16 16	17 03			16 45	17 15	17 49					18 19		19 09			19 15	

		GW	GW	XC	GW	XC	GW	GW	XC	GW	XC	GW	XC	GW	XC	GW	GW	XC	XC	GW	GW	XC	XC
			◇	◇1	◇1	◇1	◇		◇1		◇1	◇1	◇1	◇	◇1	◇1		◇1	◇1	◇		◇1	◇1
Gloucester 7	d							19 20									21 15		22 06				
Cam & Dursley	d							19 34									21 31						
Yate	d							19 48									21 45						
Bristol Parkway 7	a							19 56									21 53		22 35				
	d			18 58		19 25		19 57	20 02		20 25		20 58		21 25		21 55	22 00	22 36			23 01	23 24
Filton Abbey Wood	d		18 56				19 55	20 00						21 05			21 58			22 52			
Stapleton Road	d	18 43								20 16													
Lawrence Hill	d	18 45								20 18													
Bristol Temple Meads 10	a	18 47	19 06	19 09	19 24	19 35	20 05	20 10	20 14	20 21	20 35	20 54	21 09	21 13	21 35	21 53	22 07	22 11	22 47	23 00		23 13	23 35
	d	19 04			19 25	19 44			20 19	20 25	20 44	20 55			21 44	21 55					23 10		
Bedminster	d	19 08								20 28											23 13		
Parson Street	d	19 10																			23 15		
Nailsea & Backwell	d	19 18			19 36					20 36		21 06				22 06					23 23		
Yatton	d	19 24			19 42					20 42		21 12				22 12					23 29		
Worle	d	19 30			19 49					20 48		21 19				22 19					23 35		
Weston Milton	d																				23 40		
Weston-super-Mare	a	19 36			19 56				20 36	20 53		21 25				22 26					23 43		
	d	19 40							20 37	20 58		21 26											
Highbridge & Burnham	d	19 51								21 09													
Bridgwater	d	19 59								21 17													
Taunton	a	20 13				20 16			20 58	21 33	21 15	21 49			22 15								

Sundays
from 24 October

		GW	GW	GW	GW	GW	XC	GW	GW	XC	GW	GW	GW	XC	GW	GW	GW	GW	XC	GW	GW	GW	GW
		◇	◇	◇		🚌	◇1	◇1	◇	◇1		◇		◇1	🚌	◇1			◇1	🚌		◇	◇1
Gloucester 7	d					09 15								10 02	10 23				11 06	12 30			
Cam & Dursley	d					09 45									10 53					13 00			
Yate	d					10 25									11 33					13 40			
Bristol Parkway 7	a					10 45								11 15	11 53				12 19	14 00			
	d													11 29					12 29				
Filton Abbey Wood	d			08 54					10 03			10 54	10 58				11 54	12 06				12 57	
Stapleton Road	d										10 16												
Lawrence Hill	d										10 18												
Bristol Temple Meads 10	a			09 04				09 51	10 13		10 21	11 03	11 07	11 40		11 54	12 04	12 14	12 41			13 05	13 54
	d	07 45	08 28		09 05		09 48	09 53		10 44	10 23		11 09	11 44		11 55			12 44		13 05		13 55
Bedminster	d																						
Parson Street	d																						
Nailsea & Backwell	d		08 38		09 13						10 33		11 20			12 07					13 15		14 06
Yatton	d	07 58	08 43		09 20						10 38		11 25			12 14					13 20		14 12
Worle	d		08 49		09 26						10 44		11 31			12 18					13 26		14 19
Weston Milton	d																						
Weston-super-Mare	a	08 07	08 55		09 37						10 50		11 37			12 31					13 31		14 25
	d	08 08	08 56								10 55		11 38								13 33		
Highbridge & Burnham	d		09 07								11 09		11 48								13 44		
Bridgwater	d	08 24	09 15								11 17		11 56								13 52		
Taunton	a	08 37	09 28				10 19	10 27		11 19	11 31		12 10	12 15					13 16		14 06		

Table 134

Gloucester - Taunton

Sundays from 24 October

		GW	GW	XC	GW	GW		GW	XC	XC	GW	GW	GW	XC	XC	GW		GW	XC	GW	GW	XC	GW	GW	GW
		◇		◇1	◇1	◇			◇1	◇1		◇		◇1	◇1	◇1		◇	◇1		◇	◇1	◇		
Gloucester	d			13 02					14 04				15 13												17 20
Cam & Dursley	d												15 27												17 34
Yate	d												15 41												17 49
Bristol Parkway	a			14 25					15 11				15 49												17 57
	d		14 15	14 30					15 16	15 26			15 51	16 00	16 25				16 58			17 25			17 58
Filton Abbey Wood	d	13 54	14 19			14 55						15 56	15 58					16 55			17 20		17 54		18 01
Stapleton Road	d																								
Lawrence Hill	d																								
Bristol Temple Meads	a	14 04	14 27	14 40	14 54	15 05			15 26	15 38		16 06	16 09	16 11	16 35	16 54		17 06	17 09		17 29	17 35	18 04		18 10
	d			14 44	14 55			15 10		15 44	15 55		16 26	16 14	16 44	16 55				17 25		17 44		18 07	
Bedminster	d							15 13			15 58									17 28					
Parson Street	d										16 00														
Nailsea & Backwell	d							15 22			16 08		16 36			17 06				17 37				18 17	
Yatton	d							15 28			16 14		16 41			17 12				17 43				18 23	
Worle	d							15 34			16 20		16 47			17 19				17 49				18 29	
Weston Milton	d							15 39					16 53							17 58					
Weston-super-Mare	a							15 42			16 25		16 57			17 25				18 01				18 35	
	d										16 28					17 27								18 36	
Highbridge & Burnham	d										16 40													18 47	
Bridgwater	d										16 48													18 55	
Taunton	a			15 15	15 28					16 16	17 03			16 45	17 15	17 49						18 19		19 09	

		XC		XC	GW	GW	GW	XC	GW	XC	GW	GW	XC	GW	XC	GW	XC	GW	XC	GW	GW	XC	XC	GW	GW
		◇1		◇1	■		◇	◇1	◇1	◇1	◇		◇1		◇1	◇1	◇1	◇	◇1	◇1		◇1	◇1	◇	
Gloucester	d											19 20									21 15		22 06		
Cam & Dursley	d											19 34									21 31				
Yate	d											19 48									21 45				
Bristol Parkway	a											19 56									21 53		22 35		
	d	18 02		18 25				18 58		19 25		19 57	20 02		20 25		20 58		21 25		21 55	22 00	22 36		
Filton Abbey Wood	d				18 25		18 56				19 55	20 00						21 05			21 58			22 52	
Stapleton Road	d					18 43																			
Lawrence Hill	d					18 45																			
Bristol Temple Meads	a	18 13		18 37	18 33	18 47	19 06	19 09	19 24	19 35	20 05	20 10	20 14		20 35	20 54	21 09	21 13	21 35	21 53	22 07	22 11	22 47	23 00	
	d			18 44		19 04			19 25	19 44			20 19	20 25	20 44	20 55			21 44	21 55					23 10
Bedminster	d					19 08								20 28											23 13
Parson Street	d					19 10																			23 15
Nailsea & Backwell	d					19 18			19 36					20 36		21 06				22 06					23 23
Yatton	d					19 24			19 42					20 42		21 12				22 12					23 29
Worle	d					19 30			19 49					20 48		21 19				22 19					23 35
Weston Milton	d																								23 40
Weston-super-Mare	a					19 36			19 56				20 36	20 53		21 25				22 26					23 43
	d					19 40							20 37	20 58		21 26									
Highbridge & Burnham	d					19 51								21 09											
Bridgwater	d					19 59								21 17											
Taunton	a			19 15		20 13				20 16			20 58	21 33	21 15	21 49			22 15						

Table 134

Taunton - Gloucester

Mondays to Fridays

		GW	GW		XC	XC	GW	GW	GW	XC		GW	GW	GW	XC	GW	GW	GW	XC	GW		GW	GW	GW	XC
		MO	A		1	◇1	B	C	◇1	◇1			◇1		◇1			◇1	◇1				◇1		◇1
Taunton	d						05 30	05 40				06 02		06 35	06 51			06 54					07 13	07 28	07 51
Bridgwater	d						05 42	05 52				06 13		06 48				07 05					07 23	07 40	
Highbridge & Burnham	d						05 49	05 59				06 20		06 55				07 12					07 31	07 48	
Weston-super-Mare	a						06 00	06 10				06 32		07 06				07 24					07 41	08 00	
	d	23p47	23p56				06 01	06 11	06 20			06 33	06 49	07 08				07 24				07 37	07 49	08 06	
Weston Milton	d	23p50	23p59						06 25			06 36	06 53	07 11								07 40	07 53	08 09	
Worle	d	23p54	00 03				06 07	06 17	06 30			06 41	06 59	07 16				07 32				07 44	07 59	08 15	
Yatton	d	23p59	00 09				06 12	06 22	06 37			06 47	07 06	07 22				07 39				07 49	08 06	08 21	
Nailsea & Backwell	d	00 06	00 15				06 18	06 28	06 44			06 53	07 13	07 28				07 46				07 55	08 13	08 27	
Parson Street	d		00 22									07 00		07 34								08 02		08 36	
Bedminster	d	00 15	00 25									07 03		07 37			←					08 04		08 38	
Bristol Temple Meads	a	00 19	00 31				06 30	06 40	06 55			07 10	07 24	07 43	07 26		07 43	07 58				08 10	08 25	08 46	08 27
	d				05 19	06 27			07 00	07 00		07 19	07 30	07 46	07 30	07 34	07 46	08 00	08 00	08 10		08 21	08 30	08 47	08 30
Lawrence Hill	d											07 22		→			07 50			08 13				→	
Stapleton Road	d											07 24					07 52			08 16					
Filton Abbey Wood	d											07 30				07 43	07 59			08 22		08a30			
Bristol Parkway	a				05 28	06 37				07 08		07 33			07 38	07 47	08 05		08 08	08 29					08 38
	d															07 48									
Yate	d															07 57									
Cam & Dursley	d															08 10									
Gloucester	a															08 29									

		GW	GW	XC	GW	GW		GW	XC	GW	GW	GW	GW	XC	XC	GW		GW	XC	GW	XC	GW	GW	GW	XC
				◇1					◇1			◇1		◇1	◇1	◇			◇1		◇1				◇1
Taunton	d			08 12				08 36	08 51			09 05			09 52					10 07	10 51			11 02	11 17
Bridgwater	d							08 48												10 19				11 14	
Highbridge & Burnham	d							08 56												10 27				11 22	
Weston-super-Mare	a			08 31				09 09				09 28								10 38				11 34	
	d			08 33		08 40		09 10				09 29	09 45							10 39			11 10	11 45	
Weston Milton	d					08 43		09 13															11 13		
Worle	d					08 45		09 18					09 50							10 45			11 18	11 50	
Yatton	d					08 51		09 23				09 40	09 56							10 51			11 23	11 56	
Nailsea & Backwell	d					08 57		09 29				09 46	10 02							10 57			11 29	12 02	
Parson Street	d					09 05		09 36															11 36		
Bedminster	d		←			09 07		09 38			←							←					11 38		
Bristol Temple Meads	a		08 46	08 55		09 16		09 44	09 27		09 44	09 58	10 14		10 26			10 43		11 13	11 24		11 43	12 17	11 53
	d	08 41	08 47	09 00	09 10	09 21		09 45	09 30	09 41	09 45	10 00	10 21	10 00	10 30	10 41		10 45	11 00	11 21	11 30	11 41	11 45	12 21	12 00
Lawrence Hill	d	08 44			09 13			→			09 48							10 48					11 48	→	
Stapleton Road	d		08 51		09 15						09 50							10 50					11 50		
Filton Abbey Wood	d	08 48	08 57		09 22	09a30				09 48	09 56		10a30			10 48		10 56		11a30		11 48	11 56		
Bristol Parkway	a	08 52	09 05	09 08	09 28				09 38	09 52	10 03			10 08	10 38	10 52		11 03	11 08		11 38	11 52	12 03		12 08
	d	08 52								09 52						10 52						11 52			
Yate	d	09 01								10 01						11 01						12 01			
Cam & Dursley	d	09 14								10 14						11 14						12 14			
Gloucester	a	09 33								10 32						11 34						12 31			

		GW	GW	XC	GW	GW	XC	GW	XC	GW	GW		XC	GW	GW	XC	GW	GW	XC	GW	XC	GW	GW	XC	GW
		◇1		◇1	◇		◇1		◇1				◇1			◇1	◇		◇1		◇1			◇1	
Taunton	d	11 26		11 51				12 07	12 51				13 16		13 07	13 54				14 11	14 54			15 12	
Bridgwater	d							12 19							13 19					14 23					
Highbridge & Burnham	d							12 27							13 27					14 31					
Weston-super-Mare	a							12 38							13 38					14 43				15 37	
	d					12 10		12 39			13 10				13 39			14 10		14 45			15 10	15 38	
Weston Milton	d					12 13					13 13							14 13					15 13		
Worle	d					12 18		12 45			13 18				13 45			14 18		14 50			15 18		
Yatton	d					12 23		12 51			13 23				13 51			14 23		14 57			15 23		
Nailsea & Backwell	d					12 29		12 57			13 29				13 57			14 29		15 03			15 29		
Parson Street	d					12 36					13 36							14 36					15 36		
Bedminster	d		←			12 38					13 38							14 38					15 38		
Bristol Temple Meads	a	11 59	12 17	12 24		12 43		13 10	13 24		13 44		13 56		14 12	14 27		14 43		15 17	15 27		15 43	15 57	
	d		12 21	12 30	12 41	12 45	13 00	13 21	13 30	13 41	13 45		14 00		14 21	14 30	14 41	14 45	15 00	15 21	15 30	15 41	15 45	16 00	16 15
Lawrence Hill	d					12 48					13 48							14 48					15 48		16 17
Stapleton Road	d					12 50					13 50							14 50					15 50		16 19
Filton Abbey Wood	d		12a30		12 48	12 56		13a30		13 48	13 56			14 29	14a30		14 48	14 56		15a30		15 48	15 56		16 25
Bristol Parkway	a			12 38	12 52	13 03	13 08		13 38	13 52	14 03		14 08	14 37		14 38	14 51	15 03	15 08		15 38	15 52	16 03	16 08	16 34
	d				12 52					13 52							14 52					15 52			
Yate	d				13 01					14 01							15 01					16 01			
Cam & Dursley	d				13 14					14 14							15 14					16 14			
Gloucester	a				13 31					14 33							15 32					16 32			

A MX until 15 October

B until 9 July, from 18 October

C from 12 July until 15 October

Table 134

Mondays to Fridays

Taunton - Gloucester

		XC	GW	GW	XC	GW	GW	XC	GW	GW	GW	GW	XC	GW	XC	GW	GW	GW	XC	GW	XC	GW	GW	GW
		◇1 ⊼			◇1 ⊼			◇1 ⊼	◇1 ⊐				◇1 ⊼		◇1 ⊼	◇1 ⊐			◇1 ⊼		◇1 ⊼			
Taunton	d	15 51					16 16	16 54				17 05	17 21		17 51					18 08	18 54			19 17
Bridgwater	d						16 28					17 17								18 19				19 30
Highbridge & Burnham	d						16 36					17 25								18 27				19 38
Weston-super-Mare	a						16 48					17 37								18 40				19 50
	d			16 10		16 35	16 51		17 10		17 15	17 38				18 09		18 15		18 42			19 13	20 07
Weston Milton	d			16 13		16 38						17 41								18 43			19 16	
Worle	d			16 18		16 42					17 21	17 45						18 21		18 47			19 21	20 14
Yatton	d			16 23		16 48					17 26	17 51						18 26		18 53			19 26	20 20
Nailsea & Backwell	d			16 29		16 54					17 32	17 57						18 32		18 59			19 32	20 27
Parson Street	d			16 36								18 04								19 07				20 35
Bedminster	d			16 38		17 02						18 06		←						19 09				20 39
Bristol Temple Meads 10	a	16 27		16 43		17 08	17 14	17 27	17 30		17 45	18 15	17 54	18 15	18 24	18 28		18 46		19 18	19 27		19 44	20 45
	d	16 30	16 41	16 45	17 00	17 10	17 21	17 30	17 30	17 41	17 45	18 21	18 00	18 21	18 30	18 30	18 41	18 48	19 00	19 21	19 30	19 41	19 45	
Lawrence Hill	d			16 48		17 13					17 48	→		18 24				18 51		19 23			19 48	
Stapleton Road	d			16 50		17 15					17 50			18 26				18 53		19 25			19 51	
Filton Abbey Wood	d		16 48	16 56		17 21	17a30			17 48	17 56			18a30			18 48			19a30		19 48	19 57	
Bristol Parkway 7	a	16 38	16 52	17 03	17 08	17 27		17 38		17 52	18 03		18 08		18 38		18 52		19 08		19 38	19 52	20 04	
	d		16 52							17 52							18 52					19 52		
Yate	d		17 01							18 01							19 01					20 01		
Cam & Dursley	d		17 14							18 14							19 14					20 14		
Gloucester 7	a		17 33							18 32							19 30					20 32		

		XC	XC	GW	GW	GW	XC	GW	GW	GW	GW	GW	GW	GW	GW	GW	GW
		◇1	◇1	◇		◇1	◇1	1			◇1						
									E	A		A	B	C	C	D	D
						⊐					⊐					═	
Taunton	d		19 51		20 30	21 14	21 18				21 29	21 45	21 45	22 19	22 45	22 46	
Bridgwater	d				20 42						21 39	21 57	21 57	22 31	22 57	23 11	
Highbridge & Burnham	d				20 50						21 46	22 05	22 05	22 39	23 05	23 27	
Weston-super-Mare	a				21 00						21 57	22 15	22 15	22 49	23 15	23 47	
	d				21 02			21 33			22 01	22 30	22 30	22 51	23 17		23 56
Weston Milton	d				21 05			21 37						22 54	23 20		23 59
Worle	d				21 09			21 42			22 07			22 58	23 24		00 03
Yatton	d				21 14			21 49			22 14			23 04	23 30		00 09
Nailsea & Backwell	d				21 20			21 55			22 20			23 10	23 36		00 15
Parson Street	d				21 28									23 17	23 43		00 22
Bedminster	d				21 30									23 20	23 46		00 25
Bristol Temple Meads 10	a		20 25	20 29	21 35	21 47	21 51	22 06			22 32	22 53	22 57	23 31	23 53		00 31
	d	20 00	20 30	20 41			22 00		22 11	22 28							
Lawrence Hill	d																
Stapleton Road	d																
Filton Abbey Wood	d			20 48					22 18	22 35							
Bristol Parkway 7	a	20 08	20 38	20 52			22 08		22 22	22 39							
	d	20 10	20 40	20 52					22 22	22 39							
Yate	d			21 01					22 31	23 01							
Cam & Dursley	d			21 14					22 45	23 36							
Gloucester 7	a	20 38		21 29					23 41	23 53							

Saturdays
until 04 September

		GW	XC	GW	GW	GW	GW	XC	XC	GW	GW	GW	XC	GW	GW	XC	GW	GW	GW	XC	GW	XC	GW
			◇1 ⊼		◇1	◇1 ⊐		◇1 ⊼	◇1 ⊼			◇1 ⊐	◇1 ⊼			◇1 ⊼			◇1 ⊐	◇1 ⊼		◇1 ⊼	
Taunton	d			05 28			06 35		06 51			06 54			07 32	07 51			07 58	08 12		08 51	
Bridgwater	d			05 40			06 48					07 05			07 44				08 09				
Highbridge & Burnham	d			05 48			06 55					07 12			07 52				08 16				
Weston-super-Mare	a			05 59			07 06					07 24			08 03				08 26				
	d	23p56		06 01		06 24	07 08					07 24		07 37	08 06				08 29		08 39		
Weston Milton	d	23p59		06 04			07 11							07 40	08 09								
Worle	d	00 03		06 07		06 32	07 16					07 32		07 44	08 15						08 45		
Yatton	d	00 09		06 12		06 39	07 22					07 39		07 49	08 21				08 40		08 51		
Nailsea & Backwell	d	00 15		06 18		06 45	07 28					07 46		07 55	08 27				08 46		08 57		
Parson Street	d	00 22		06 29			07 35							08 02	08 36								
Bedminster	d	00 25		06 31			07 38				←			08 04	08 38			←					
Bristol Temple Meads 10	a	00 31		06 34		06 56	07 43		07 25		07 43	07 58	07 51	08 10	08 41	08 24		08 41	08 57	08 49	09 08	09 26	
	d		06 27		06 46		07 46	07 00	07 30	07 41	07 46	08 00	08 00	08 19	08 45	08 30	08 41	08 45	09 00	09 00	09 21	09 30	09 41
Lawrence Hill	d						→				07 50			08 22	→			08 48					
Stapleton Road	d										07 52			08 24				08 50			09 25		
Filton Abbey Wood	d				06 54					07 48	07 59			08a30			08 48	08 56			09a30		09 48
Bristol Parkway 7	a		06 36		06 58			07 08	07 38	07 52	08 05		08 08			08 38	08 52	09 03		09 08		09 38	09 52
	d									07 52							08 52						09 52
Yate	d									08 01							09 01						10 01
Cam & Dursley	d									08 14							09 14						10 14
Gloucester 7	a									08 32							09 33						10 32

A until 3 September
B from 6 September until 15 October
C from 18 October
D until 15 October
E from 6 September

Table 134

Saturdays
until 04 September

Taunton - Gloucester

		GW	XC	GW	XC	GW	GW	XC	GW	GW	XC	GW	GW	GW	GW	XC	GW	XC	GW	GW	XC	GW	XC
			◇1 ⊼		◇1 ⊼	◇		◇1 ⊼		◇1 ⊐	◇1 ⊼			◇1 ⊐		◇1 ⊼		◇1 ⊼	◇		◇1 ⊼		◇1 ⊼
Taunton	d			08 58	09 51			10 07	10 11	10 45	10 51				11 07	11 21		11 52				12 07	12 54
Bridgwater	d			09 10					10 23						11 19							12 19	
Highbridge & Burnham	d			09 18					10 31						11 27							12 27	
Weston-super-Mare	a			09 28				10 32	10 39						11 37							12 37	
	d	09 10		09 39			10 10	10 34	10 39				11 10	11 33	11 39					12 10		12 39	
Weston Milton	d	09 13					10 13						11 13							12 13			
Worle	d	09 18		09 45			10 18		10 45				11 18		11 45					12 18		12 45	
Yatton	d	09 23		09 51			10 23		10 51				11 23		11 51					12 23		12 51	
Nailsea & Backwell	d	09 29		09 57			10 29		10 57				11 29		11 57					12 29		12 57	
Parson Street	d	09 36					10 36						11 36							12 36			
Bedminster	d	09 38					10 38						11 38				←			12 38			
Bristol Temple Meads 10	a	09 43		10 09	10 26		10 43	10 52	11 12	11 20	11 26		11 43	11 53	12 10	11 56	12 10	12 25		12 43		13 09	13 27
	d	09 45	10 00	10 21	10 30	10 41	10 45	11 00	11 21	11 30	11 30	11 41	11 45	12 00	12 21	12 00	12 21	12 30	12 41	12 45	13 00	13 21	13 30
Lawrence Hill	d	09 48					10 48						11 48		→					12 48			
Stapleton Road	d	09 50		10 25			10 50		11 25				11 50				12 25			12 50		13 25	
Filton Abbey Wood	d	09 56		10a30		10 48	10 56		11a30			11 48	11 56				12a30		12 48	12 56		13a30	
Bristol Parkway 7	a	10 03	10 08		10 38	10 52	11 03	11 08			11 38	11 52	12 03			12 08		12 38	12 52	13 03	13 08		13 38
	d					10 52						11 52							12 52				
Yate	d					11 01						12 01							13 01				
Cam & Dursley	d					11 14						12 14							13 14				
Gloucester 7	a					11 32						12 31							13 34				

		GW	GW	GW	XC	GW	XC	GW	GW	XC	GW	XC	GW	GW	GW	XC	GW	XC	GW	GW	XC	GW	GW
		◇1 ⊐			◇1 ⊼		◇1 ⊼	◇		◇1 ⊼		◇1 ⊼	◇1 ⊐			◇1 ⊼		◇1 ⊼			◇1 ⊼	A	B
Taunton	d					13 07	13 54				14 07	14 52				15 03	15 07	15 51				16 07	16 07
Bridgwater	d					13 19					14 19						15 19					16 19	16 19
Highbridge & Burnham	d					13 27					14 27						15 27					16 27	16 27
Weston-super-Mare	a					13 37					14 37					15 24	15 37					16 37	16 37
	d	13 01		13 10		13 39			14 10		14 39		15 01		15 10	15 30	15 39			16 10		16 39	16 39
Weston Milton	d			13 13					14 13						15 13					16 13			
Worle	d			13 18		13 45			14 18		14 45				15 18		15 45			16 18		16 45	16 45
Yatton	d			13 23		13 51			14 23		14 51				15 23		15 51			16 23		16 51	16 51
Nailsea & Backwell	d			13 29		13 57			14 29		14 57				15 29		15 57			16 29		16 57	16 57
Parson Street	d			13 36					14 36						15 36					16 36			
Bedminster	d			13 38					14 38						15 38					16 38			
Bristol Temple Meads 10	a	13 21	13 36	13 43		14 11		14 29	14 43		15 10	15 25	15 21		15 43	15 50	16 09	16 25		16 43		17 09	17 09
	d		13 41	13 45	14 00	14 21	14 30	14 41	14 45	15 00	15 21	15 30		15 41	15 45	16 00	16 21	16 30	16 41	16 45	17 00	17 10	17 21
Lawrence Hill	d			13 48					14 48						15 48					16 48			
Stapleton Road	d			13 50		14 25			14 50		15 25				15 50		16 25			16 50		17 16	17 25
Filton Abbey Wood	d		13 48	13 56		14a30		14 48	14 56		15a30			15 48	15 56		16a30		16 48	16 56		17a21	17a30
Bristol Parkway 7	a		13 52	14 03	14 08		14 38	14 52	15 03	15 08		15 38		15 52	16 03	16 08		16 38	16 52	17 03	17 08		
	d		13 52					14 52						15 52					16 52				
Yate	d		14 01					15 01						16 01					17 01				
Cam & Dursley	d		14 14					15 14						16 14					17 14				
Gloucester 7	a		14 33					15 32						16 32					17 33				

		XC	GW	GW	GW	GW	XC	GW	GW	XC	GW	GW	GW	XC	GW	XC	GW	GW	GW	XC	XC	GW	GW
		◇1 ⊼	◇1 ⊐	B	A		◇1 ⊼	A	B	◇1 ⊼	A	B		◇1 ⊼		◇1 ⊼				◇1 ⊼	◇1 ⊼	◇1 ⊐	1
Taunton	d	16 51						17 07	17 07	17 51					18 07	18 54			19 07	19 18	19 49		
Bridgwater	d							17 17	17 17						18 19				19 19				
Highbridge & Burnham	d							17 25	17 25						18 27				19 27				
Weston-super-Mare	a							17 37	17 37						18 37				19 37				
	d		17 01			17 10		17 39	17 39				18 10		18 39			19 10	19 39			20 10	
Weston Milton	d					17 13							18 13					19 13					
Worle	d					17 18		17 45	17 45				18 18		18 45			19 18	19 45				
Yatton	d					17 23		17 51	17 51				18 23		18 51			19 23	19 51				
Nailsea & Backwell	d					17 29		17 57	17 57				18 29		18 57			19 29	19 57				
Parson Street	d					17 36							18 36					19 36					
Bedminster	d					17 38							18 38					19 38					
Bristol Temple Meads 10	a	17 25	17 21			17 43		18 11	18 11	18 27			18 43		19 09	19 27		19 43	20 09	19 55	20 23	20 30	
	d	17 30		17 41	17 41	17 45	18 00	18 13	18 21	18 30	18 41	18 41	18 45	19 00	19 21	19 30	19 41	19 45		20 00	20 30		20 41
Lawrence Hill	d					17 48							18 48					19 48					
Stapleton Road	d					17 50		18 17	18 25				18 50					19 50					
Filton Abbey Wood	d			17 48	17 48	17 56		18a22	18a30		18 48	18 48	18 56		19 28		19 48	19 56					20 48
Bristol Parkway 7	a	17 38		17 52	17 52	18 03	18 08			18 38	18 52	18 52	19 03	19 08		19 38	19 52	20 03		20 08	20 38		20 52
	d			17 52	17 52						18 52	18 52					19 52				20 40		20 52
Yate	d			18 01	18 01						19 01	19 01					20 01						21 01
Cam & Dursley	d			18 14	18 14						19 14	19 14					20 14						21 14
Gloucester 7	a			18 32	18 32						19 33	19 33					20 33				21 08		21 33

A from 17 July until 4 September
B until 10 July

Table 134

Taunton - Gloucester

Saturdays
until 04 September

		GW	GW	GW	GW	GW
			◇1		◇1	
Taunton	d	20 18	21 14		21 29	21 35
Bridgwater	d	20 30			21 40	21 47
Highbridge & Burnham	d	20 38			21 48	21 55
Weston-super-Mare	a	20 49			21 58	22 05
	d	20 52			21 59	22 07
Weston Milton	d	20 55				22 10
Worle	d	21 00				22 14
Yatton	d	21 06			22 09	22 20
Nailsea & Backwell	d	21 12			22 15	22 26
Parson Street	d	21 19				22 33
Bedminster	d	21 22				22 36
Bristol Temple Meads 10	a	21 27	21 47		22 30	22 44
	d	21 28		22 06		
Lawrence Hill	d					
Stapleton Road	d					
Filton Abbey Wood	d	21 36		22 14		
Bristol Parkway 7	a			22 17		
	d			22 18		
Yate	d			22 28		
Cam & Dursley	d			22 43		
Gloucester 7	a			23 01		

Saturdays
from 11 September

		GW	XC	GW	GW	GW	GW	XC	XC	GW	GW	GW	XC	GW	GW	XC	GW	GW	GW	XC	GW	GW	XC
		A	◇1		◇1	◇1		◇1	◇1			◇1	◇1			◇1			◇1	◇1		◇1 B	◇1
Taunton	d			05 28			06 35		06 51			06 54			07 32	07 51			07 58	08 12		08 38	08 51
Bridgwater	d			05 40			06 48					07 05			07 44				08 09				
Highbridge & Burnham	d			05 48			06 55					07 12			07 52				08 16				
Weston-super-Mare	a			05 59			07 06					07 24			08 03				08 26			08 58	
	d	23p56		06 01		06 24	07 08					07 24		07 37	08 06				08 29		08 39	09 02	
Weston Milton	d	23p59		06 04			07 11							07 40	08 09								
Worle	d	00 03		06 07		06 32	07 16					07 32		07 44	08 15						08 45		
Yatton	d	00 09		06 12		06 39	07 22					07 39		07 49	08 21				08 40		08 51		
Nailsea & Backwell	d	00 15		06 18		06 45	07 28					07 46		07 55	08 27				08 46		08 57		
Parson Street	d	00 22		06 29			07 35							08 02	08 36								
Bedminster	d	00 25		06 31			07 38				←			08 04	08 38			←					
Bristol Temple Meads 10	a	00 31		06 34		06 56	07 43		07 25		07 43	07 58		08 10	08 41	08 24		08 41	08 57	08 49	09 08	09 23	09 26
	d		06 27		06 46		07 46	07 00	07 30	07 41	07 46		08 00	08 19	08 45	08 30	08 41	08 45		09 00	09 21		09 30
Lawrence Hill	d						→				07 50			08 22	→			08 48					
Stapleton Road	d										07 52			08 24				08 50			09 25		
Filton Abbey Wood	d				06 54					07 48	07 59			08a30			08 48	08 56			09a30		
Bristol Parkway 7	a		06 36		06 58			07 08	07 38	07 52	08 05		08 08			08 38	08 52	09 03		09 08			09 38
	d									07 52							08 52						
Yate	d									08 01							09 01						
Cam & Dursley	d									08 14							09 14						
Gloucester 7	a									08 32							09 33						

		GW	GW	XC	GW	XC	GW	GW	XC	GW	XC	GW	GW	GW	XC	GW	XC	GW	GW	XC	GW	XC	GW
				◇1		◇1	◇		◇1		◇1				◇1		◇1	◇		◇1		◇1	
Taunton	d				08 58	09 51				10 11	10 51			11 07	11 17		11 51				12 07	12 51	
Bridgwater	d				09 10					10 23				11 19							12 19		
Highbridge & Burnham	d				09 18					10 31				11 27							12 27		
Weston-super-Mare	a				09 28					10 39				11 37							12 37		
	d		09 10		09 39			10 10		10 39			11 10	11 39					12 10		12 39		
Weston Milton	d		09 13					10 13					11 13						12 13				
Worle	d		09 18		09 45			10 18		10 45			11 18	11 45					12 18		12 45		
Yatton	d		09 23		09 51			10 23		10 51			11 23	11 51					12 23		12 51		
Nailsea & Backwell	d		09 29		09 57			10 29		10 57			11 29	11 57					12 29		12 57		
Parson Street	d		09 36					10 36					11 36						12 36				
Bedminster	d		09 38					10 38					11 38			←			12 38				
Bristol Temple Meads 10	a		09 43		10 09	10 26		10 43		11 12	11 26		11 43	12 10	11 55	12 10	12 25		12 43		13 09	13 24	
	d	09 41	09 45	10 00	10 21	10 30	10 41	10 45	11 00	11 21	11 30	11 41	11 45	12 21	12 00	12 21	12 30	12 41	12 45	13 00	13 21	13 30	13 41
Lawrence Hill	d		09 48					10 48					11 48	→					12 48				
Stapleton Road	d		09 50		10 25			10 50		11 25			11 50			12 25			12 50		13 25		
Filton Abbey Wood	d	09 48	09 56		10a30		10 48	10 56		11a30		11 48	11 56			12a30		12 48	12 56		13a30		13 48
Bristol Parkway 7	a	09 52	10 03	10 08		10 38	10 52	11 03	11 08		11 38	11 52	12 03		12 08		12 38	12 52	13 03	13 08		13 38	13 52
	d	09 52					10 52					11 52						12 52					13 52
Yate	d	10 01					11 01					12 01						13 01					14 01
Cam & Dursley	d	10 14					11 14					12 14						13 14					14 14
Gloucester 7	a	10 32					11 32					12 31						13 34					14 33

A from 11 September until 16 October

B The Torbay Express

Table 134

Taunton - Gloucester

Saturdays
from 11 September

		GW	GW	XC	GW	XC	GW	GW	XC	GW	XC	GW	GW	XC	GW	XC	GW	GW	XC	GW	XC	GW	GW
				◇1		◇1	◇		◇1		◇1			◇1		◇1			◇1		◇1		
Taunton	d		13 07	13 16		13 54				14 07	14 52			15 04	15 07	15 51				16 07	16 51		
Bridgwater	d		13 19							14 19					15 19					16 19			
Highbridge & Burnham	d		13 27							14 27					15 27					16 27			
Weston-super-Mare	a		13 37							14 37				15 23	15 37					16 37			
	d	13 10	13 39					14 10		14 39			15 10	15 30	15 39			16 10		16 39			17 10
Weston Milton	d	13 13						14 13					15 13					16 13					17 13
Worle	d	13 18	13 45					14 18		14 45			15 18		15 45			16 18		16 45			17 18
Yatton	d	13 23	13 51					14 23		14 51			15 23		15 51			16 23		16 51			17 23
Nailsea & Backwell	d	13 29	13 57					14 29		14 57			15 29		15 57			16 29		16 57			17 29
Parson Street	d	13 36						14 36					15 36					16 36					17 36
Bedminster	d	13 38			←			14 38					15 38					16 38					17 38
Bristol Temple Meads 10	a	13 43	14 11	13 56	14 11	14 27		14 43		15 10	15 25		15 43	15 49	16 09	16 25		16 43		17 09	17 25		17 43
	d	13 45	14 21	14 00	14 21	14 30	14 41	14 45	15 00	15 21	15 30	15 41	15 45	16 00	16 21	16 30	16 41	16 45	17 00	17 21	17 30	17 41	17 45
Lawrence Hill	d	13 48	→					14 48					15 48					16 48					17 48
Stapleton Road	d	13 50			14 25			14 50		15 25			15 50		16 25			16 50		17 25			17 50
Filton Abbey Wood	d	13 56			14a30		14 48	14 56		15a30		15 48	15 56		16a30		16 48	16 56		17a30		17 48	17 56
Bristol Parkway 7	a	14 03		14 08		14 38	14 52	15 03	15 08		15 38	15 52	16 03	16 08		16 38	16 52	17 03	17 08		17 38	17 52	18 03
	d						14 52					15 52					16 52					17 52	
Yate	d						15 01					16 01					17 01					18 01	
Cam & Dursley	d						15 14					16 14					17 14					18 14	
Gloucester 7	a						15 32					16 32					17 33					18 32	

		XC	GW	XC	GW	GW	XC	GW	XC	GW	GW	XC	GW	XC	GW	GW	GW	GW	GW	GW	GW
		◇1		◇1			◇1		◇1			◇1		◇1	◇1			◇1		◇1	
Taunton	d		17 07	17 51				18 07	18 54				19 07	19 51			20 18	21 14		21 29	21 35
Bridgwater	d		17 17					18 19					19 19				20 30			21 40	21 47
Highbridge & Burnham	d		17 25					18 27					19 27				20 38			21 48	21 55
Weston-super-Mare	a		17 37					18 37					19 37				20 49			21 58	22 05
	d		17 39			18 10		18 39			19 10		19 39		20 10		20 52			21 59	22 07
Weston Milton	d					18 13					19 13						20 55				22 10
Worle	d		17 45			18 18		18 45			19 18		19 45				21 00				22 14
Yatton	d		17 51			18 23		18 51			19 23		19 51				21 06			22 09	22 20
Nailsea & Backwell	d		17 57			18 29		18 57			19 29		19 57				21 12			22 15	22 26
Parson Street	d					18 36					19 36						21 19				22 33
Bedminster	d					18 38					19 38						21 22				22 36
Bristol Temple Meads 10	a		18 11	18 25		18 43		19 09	19 27		19 43		20 09	20 25	20 30		21 27	21 47		22 30	22 44
	d	18 00	18 21	18 30	18 41	18 45	19 00	19 21	19 30	19 41	19 45	20 00		20 30		20 41	21 28		22 06		
Lawrence Hill	d					18 48					19 48										
Stapleton Road	d		18 25			18 50					19 50										
Filton Abbey Wood	d		18a30		18 48	18 56		19a28		19 48	19 56					20 48	21a36		22 14		
Bristol Parkway 7	a	18 08		18 38	18 52	19 03	19 08		19 38	19 52	20 03	20 08		20 38		20 52			22 17		
	d				18 52					19 52				20 40		20 52			22 18		
Yate	d				19 01					20 01						21 01			22 28		
Cam & Dursley	d				19 14					20 14						21 14			22 43		
Gloucester 7	a				19 33					20 33				21 07		21 33			23 01		

Sundays
until 11 July

		GW	XC	XC	GW	GW	GW	GW	XC	GW	GW	XC	GW	XC	XC	GW	GW	XC	XC	GW	XC	XC	GW
		◇1	◇1	◇1	◇		◇1		◇1		◇1	◇1		◇1	◇1	◇1		◇1	◇1		◇1	◇1	◇1
Taunton	d				08 35			10 11	10 51	11 36	11 46	11 51		12 00	12 51		13 11	13 25	13 54		14 10	14 54	
Bridgwater	d				08 47			10 23		11 48							13 23						
Highbridge & Burnham	d				08 55			10 31		11 55							13 30						
Weston-super-Mare	a				09 04			10 41		12 05				12 20			13 41						
	d	08 11			09 07		09 56	10 45		12 07				12 21		12 51	13 43						14 52
Weston Milton	d				09 10					12 10							13 46						
Worle	d	08 18			09 14		10 03	10 51		12 17							13 50						14 59
Yatton	d	08 25			09 20		10 10	10 56		12 23						13 02	13 56						15 06
Nailsea & Backwell	d	08 31			09 26		10 16	11 02		12 29						13 08	14 02						15 12
Parson Street	d																						
Bedminster	d									12 39													
Bristol Temple Meads 10	a	08 42			09 38		10 27	11 15	11 27	12 42	12 23	12 27		12 47	13 24	13 19	14 14	13 57	14 27		14 46	15 27	15 23
	d		08 45	09 30	09 48	09 41		11 23	11 30			12 30	12 41	13 00	13 30			14 00	14 30	14 41	15 00	15 30	
Lawrence Hill	d							11 26															
Stapleton Road	d							11 28															
Filton Abbey Wood	d				09 56	09 48							12 48							14 48			
Bristol Parkway 7	a		08 53	09 38		09 54			11 38			12 38	12 52	13 08	13 38			14 08	14 38	14 52	15 08	15 38	
	d		08 55	09 40		09 54			11 40			12 40	12 52	13 10	13 40			14 10	14 40	14 53	15 10	15 40	
Yate	d					10 03							13 02							15 03			
Cam & Dursley	d					10 17							13 16							15 17			
Gloucester 7	a			10 07		10 33			12 08				13 31							15 35			

Table 134

Taunton - Gloucester

Sundays until 11 July

		XC	GW	XC	GW	GW	XC	GW	XC	GW	GW	XC	GW	GW	XC	GW	GW	XC	GW	XC	GW	XC	XC
		◇1 🛒		◇1 🛒			◇1 🛒	◇1 ☕	◇1 🛒		◇1 ☕	◇1 🛒		◇1 ☕	◇1 🛒			◇1 🛒	◇1 ☕	◇1 🛒	◇	◇1 🛒	◇1 🛒
Taunton	d		15 18	15 54			16 01	16 39	16 54		17 01		17 19	17 46	17 51				18 23	18 52	19 07	19 23	19 54
Bridgwater	d		15 30										17 30						18 34		19 19		
Highbridge & Burnham	d		15 37										17 37						18 41		19 27		
Weston-super-Mare	a		15 47				16 20	17 00			17 22		17 48						18 51		19 40		
	d		15 49			16 14	16 30	17 01		17 07	17 26		17 50				18 16		18 53		19 41		
Weston Milton	d		15 52			16 17				17 10							18 19						
Worle	d		15 56			16 22				17 17			17 56				18 24		19 00		19 47		
Yatton	d		16 02			16 28				17 22	17 36		18 02				18 30		19 06		19 53		
Nailsea & Backwell	d		16 08			16 34				17 28	17 43		18 08				18 36		19 13		19 59		
Parson Street	d					16 41											18 43						
Bedminster	d					16 44				17 39							18 46						
Bristol Temple Meads 10	a		16 20	16 27		16 49	16 53	17 22	17 28	17 42	17 55		18 20	18 25	18 27		18 50		19 24	19 27	20 11	19 55	20 27
	d	16 00		16 30	16 41	16 53	17 00		17 30	17 44	18 00	18 00		18 30	18 30	18 41	18 53	19 00	19 30	19 30		20 00	20 30
Lawrence Hill	d					16 56											18 56						
Stapleton Road	d					16 58											18 58						
Filton Abbey Wood	d				16 48											18 48							
Bristol Parkway 7	a	16 08		16 38	16 52		17 08		17 38			18 08			18 38	18 52		19 08		19 38		20 08	20 38
	d				16 52											18 52							
Yate	d				17 02											19 02							
Cam & Dursley	d				17 16											19 16							
Gloucester 7	a				17 32											19 32							

		GW	GW	GW	GW	XC	GW	GW
			◇1 ☕		◇1 ☕	◇1 🛒		
Taunton	d			20 20	21 23		21 35	
Bridgwater	d			20 32			21 48	
Highbridge & Burnham	d			20 40			21 55	
Weston-super-Mare	a			20 51			22 05	
	d		20 38	20 55			22 07	23 47
Weston Milton	d			20 58			22 10	23 50
Worle	d			21 03				23 54
Yatton	d			21 09			22 18	23 59
Nailsea & Backwell	d			21 15			22 24	00 06
Parson Street	d							
Bedminster	d			21 26			22 34	00 15
Bristol Temple Meads 10	a		20 58	21 29	22 00		22 38	00 19
	d	20 41				22 10		
Lawrence Hill	d							
Stapleton Road	d							
Filton Abbey Wood	d	20 48						
Bristol Parkway 7	a	20 52				22 18		
	d	20 52						
Yate	d	21 02						
Cam & Dursley	d	21 16						
Gloucester 7	a	21 32						

Sundays 18 July to 05 September

		GW	XC	XC	GW	GW	GW	GW	XC	GW	GW	XC	GW	XC	XC	GW	GW	XC	XC	GW	XC	XC	GW
		◇1 ☕	◇1 🛒	◇1 🛒	◇		◇1 ☕		◇1 🛒		◇1 ☕	◇1 🛒		◇1 🛒	◇1 🛒	◇1 ☕		◇1 🛒	◇1 🛒		◇1 🛒	◇1 🛒	◇1 ☕
Taunton	d				08 35			10 11	10 51	11 36	11 46	11 51		12 00	12 51		13 11	13 25	13 54		14 10	14 54	
Bridgwater	d				08 47			10 23		11 48							13 23						
Highbridge & Burnham	d				08 55			10 31		11 55							13 30						
Weston-super-Mare	a				09 04			10 41		12 05				12 20			13 41						
	d	08 11			09 07		10 14	10 45		12 07				12 21		12 51	13 43						14 52
Weston Milton	d				09 10					12 10							13 46						
Worle	d	08 18			09 14		10 21	10 51		12 17							13 50						14 59
Yatton	d	08 25			09 20		10 28	10 56		12 23						13 02	13 56						15 06
Nailsea & Backwell	d	08 31			09 26		10 34	11 02		12 29						13 08	14 02						15 12
Parson Street	d																						
Bedminster	d									12 39													
Bristol Temple Meads 10	a	08 42			09 38		10 45	11 15	11 27	12 42	12 23	12 27		12 47	13 24	13 19	14 14	13 57	14 27		14 46	15 27	15 23
	d		08 45	09 30	09 48	09 41		11 23	11 30			12 30	12 41	13 00	13 30			14 00	14 30	14 41	15 00	15 30	15 30
Lawrence Hill	d							11 26															
Stapleton Road	d							11 28															
Filton Abbey Wood	d				09 56	09 48							12 48							14 48			
Bristol Parkway 7	a		08 53	09 38		09 54			11 38			12 38	12 52	13 08	13 38			14 08	14 38	14 52	15 08	15 38	
	d			09 40		09 54			11 40				12 52							14 53			
Yate	d					10 03							13 02							15 03			
Cam & Dursley	d					10 17							13 16							15 17			
Gloucester 7	a			10 07		10 33			12 08				13 31							15 35			

Table 134

Taunton - Gloucester

Sundays 18 July to 05 September

		XC	GW	XC	GW	GW	XC	GW	XC	GW	GW	XC	GW	GW	XC	GW	GW	XC	GW	XC	GW	XC	XC
		◇1 🛒		◇1 🛒			◇1 🛒	◇1 ☕	◇1 🛒		◇1 ☕	◇1 🛒		◇1 ☕	◇1 🛒			◇1 🛒	◇1 ☕	◇1 🛒	◇	◇1 🛒	◇1 🛒
Taunton	d		15 18	15 54			16 01	16 39	16 54		17 01		17 19	17 46	17 51				18 23	18 52	19 07	19 23	19 54
Bridgwater	d		15 30										17 30						18 34		19 19		
Highbridge & Burnham	d		15 37										17 37						18 41		19 27		
Weston-super-Mare	a		15 47				16 20	17 00			17 22		17 48						18 51		19 40		
	d		15 49			16 14	16 30	17 01		17 07	17 26		17 50				18 16		18 53		19 41		
Weston Milton	d		15 52			16 17				17 10							18 19						
Worle	d		15 56			16 22				17 17			17 56				18 24		19 00		19 47		
Yatton	d		16 02			16 28				17 22	17 36		18 02				18 30		19 06		19 53		
Nailsea & Backwell	d		16 08			16 34				17 28	17 43		18 08				18 36		19 13		19 59		
Parson Street	d					16 41											18 43						
Bedminster	d					16 44				17 39							18 46						
Bristol Temple Meads 10	a		16 20	16 27		16 49	16 53	17 22	17 28	17 42	17 55		18 20	18 25	18 27		18 50		19 24	19 27	20 11	19 55	20 27
	d	16 00		16 30	16 41	16 53	17 00		17 30			18 00			18 30	18 41	18 53	19 00	19 30	19 30		20 00	20 30
Lawrence Hill	d					16 56											18 56						
Stapleton Road	d					16 58											18 58						
Filton Abbey Wood	d				16 48											18 48							
Bristol Parkway 7	a	16 08		16 38	16 52		17 08		17 38			18 08			18 38	18 52		19 08		19 38		20 08	20 38
	d			16 40	16 52											18 52							
Yate	d				17 02											19 02							
Cam & Dursley	d				17 16											19 16							
Gloucester 7	a				17 32											19 32							

		GW	GW	GW	GW	XC	GW	GW
			◇1 ☕		◇1 ☕	◇1 🛒		
Taunton	d			20 20	21 23		21 35	
Bridgwater	d			20 32			21 48	
Highbridge & Burnham	d			20 40			21 55	
Weston-super-Mare	a			20 51			22 05	
	d		20 38	20 55			22 07	23 47
Weston Milton	d			20 58			22 10	23 50
Worle	d			21 03				23 54
Yatton	d			21 09			22 18	23 59
Nailsea & Backwell	d			21 15			22 24	00 06
Parson Street	d							
Bedminster	d			21 26			22 34	00 15
Bristol Temple Meads 10	a		20 58	21 29	22 00		22 38	00 19
	d	20 41				22 10		
Lawrence Hill	d							
Stapleton Road	d							
Filton Abbey Wood	d	20 48						
Bristol Parkway 7	a	20 52				22 18		
	d	20 52				22 20		
Yate	d	21 02						
Cam & Dursley	d	21 16						
Gloucester 7	a	21 32						

Sundays 12 September to 17 October

		GW	XC	GW	GW	GW	XC	GW	XC	GW	GW	XC	GW	XC	XC	GW	GW	XC	XC	GW	XC	XC	GW
		◇1 ☕	◇1 🛒	◇		◇1 ☕	◇1 🛒		◇1 🛒		◇1 ☕	◇1 🛒		◇1 🛒	◇1 🛒	◇1 ☕		◇1 🛒	◇1 🛒		◇1 🛒	◇1 🛒	◇1 ☕
Taunton	d			08 35				10 19	10 51	11 36	11 46	11 51		12 00	12 51		13 11	13 25	13 54			14 54	
Bridgwater	d			08 47				10 31		11 48							13 23						
Highbridge & Burnham	d			08 55				10 39		11 55							13 30						
Weston-super-Mare	a			09 04				10 49		12 05				12 20			13 41						
	d	08 11		09 07		09 56		10 51		12 07				12 21		12 51	13 43						14 52
Weston Milton	d			09 10						12 10							13 46						
Worle	d	08 18		09 14		10 03		10 57		12 17							13 50						14 59
Yatton	d	08 25		09 20		10 10		11 03		12 23						13 02	13 56						15 06
Nailsea & Backwell	d	08 31		09 26		10 16		11 09		12 29						13 08	14 02						15 12
Parson Street	d																						
Bedminster	d									12 39													
Bristol Temple Meads 10	a	08 42		09 38		10 27		11 20	11 27	12 42	12 23	12 27		12 45	13 24	13 19	14 14	13 57	14 27			15 27	15 23
	d		09 15	09 48	09 41	10 30	10 30	11 23	11 30			12 30	12 41	13 00	13 30			14 00	14 30	14 41	15 00	15 30	15 30
Lawrence Hill	d							11 26															
Stapleton Road	d							11 28															
Filton Abbey Wood	d			09a56	09 48								12 48							14 48			
Bristol Parkway 7	a		09 23		09 54		10 38		11 38			12 38	12 52	13 08	13 38			14 08	14 38	14 52	15 08	15 38	
	d		09 25		09 54								12 52							14 53			
Yate	d				10 03								13 02							15 03			
Cam & Dursley	d				10 17								13 16							15 17			
Gloucester 7	a		09 54		10 33								13 31							15 35			

Table 134

Taunton - Gloucester

Sundays

12 September to 17 October

		XC	GW	XC	GW	GW	XC	GW	XC	GW	GW	XC	GW	GW	XC	GW	GW	XC	GW	XC	GW	XC	XC
		◇1 🛒		◇1 🛒			◇1 🛒	◇1 🍽	◇1 🛒		◇1 🍽	◇1 🛒		◇1 🍽	◇1 🛒			◇1 🛒	◇1 🍽	◇1 🛒	◇	◇1 🛒	◇1 🛒
Taunton	d		15 18	15 54			16 01	16 38	16 54		17 03		17 19	17 46	17 51				18 23	18 52	19 07	19 23	19 54
Bridgwater	d		15 30										17 30						18 34		19 19		
Highbridge & Burnham	d		15 37										17 37						18 41		19 27		
Weston-super-Mare	a		15 47				16 20	16 59			17 25		17 48						18 51		19 40		
	d		15 49			16 14	16 30	17 00		17 07	17 26		17 50				18 16		18 53		19 41		
Weston Milton	d		15 52			16 17				17 10							18 19						
Worle	d		15 56			16 22				17 17			17 56				18 24		19 00		19 47		
Yatton	d		16 02			16 28				17 22	17 37		18 02				18 30		19 06		19 53		
Nailsea & Backwell	d		16 08			16 34				17 28	17 44		18 08				18 36		19 13		19 59		
Parson Street	d					16 41											18 43						
Bedminster	d					16 44				17 39							18 46						
Bristol Temple Meads 10	a		16 20	16 27		16 49	16 53	17 21	17 28	17 42	17 55		18 20	18 25	18 27		18 50		19 24	19 27	20 11	19 55	20 27
	d	16 00		16 30	16 41	16 53	17 00	17 30	17 30	17 44	18 00	18 00		18 30	18 30	18 41		19 00	19 30	19 30		20 00	20 30
Lawrence Hill	d					16 56																	
Stapleton Road	d					16 58																	
Filton Abbey Wood	d				16 48											18 48							
Bristol Parkway 7	a	16 08		16 38	16 52		17 08		17 38			18 08			18 38	18 52		19 08		19 38		20 08	20 38
	d	16 10		16 40	16 52		17 10		17 40			18 10			18 40	18 52		19 10		19 40		20 10	20 40
Yate	d				17 02											19 02							
Cam & Dursley	d				17 16											19 16							
Gloucester 7	a				17 32											19 32							

		GW	GW	GW	GW	XC	GW	GW
			◇1 🍽		◇1 🍽	◇1 🛒		
Taunton	d			20 20	21 23		21 35	
Bridgwater	d			20 32			21 48	
Highbridge & Burnham	d			20 40			21 55	
Weston-super-Mare	a			20 51			22 05	
	d		20 38	20 55			22 07	23 47
Weston Milton	d			20 58			22 10	23 50
Worle	d			21 03				23 54
Yatton	d			21 09			22 18	23 59
Nailsea & Backwell	d			21 15			22 24	00 06
Parson Street	d							
Bedminster	d			21 26			22 34	00 15
Bristol Temple Meads 10	a		20 58	21 29	22 00		22 38	00 19
	d	20 41				22 10		
Lawrence Hill	d							
Stapleton Road	d							
Filton Abbey Wood	d	20 48						
Bristol Parkway 7	a	20 52				22 18		
	d	20 52				22 20		
Yate	d	21 02						
Cam & Dursley	d	21 16						
Gloucester 7	a	21 32						

Sundays

from 24 October

		GW	XC	GW	GW	GW	GW	XC	GW	XC	GW	GW	GW	GW	XC	GW	GW	GW	XC	GW	GW	XC	XC
		◇1 🍽	◇1 🛒	◇		◇1 🍽	🚌	◇1 🛒		◇1 🛒			◇1 🍽	🚌	◇1 🛒		◇1 🍽	🚌	◇1 🛒			◇1 🛒	◇1 🛒
Taunton	d			08 35					10 19	10 51		11 36	11 46		11 51				12 51	13 11		13 54	14 54
Bridgwater	d			08 47					10 31			11 48								13 23			
Highbridge & Burnham	d			08 55					10 39			11 55								13 30			
Weston-super-Mare	a			09 04					10 49			12 05								13 41			
	d	08 11		09 07		09 56			10 51			12 07					12 51			13 43			
Weston Milton	d			09 10								12 10								13 46			
Worle	d	08 18		09 14		10 03			10 57			12 17								13 50			
Yatton	d	08 25		09 20		10 10			11 03			12 23					13 02			13 56			
Nailsea & Backwell	d	08 31		09 26		10 16			11 09			12 29					13 08			14 02			
Parson Street	d																						
Bedminster	d											12 39				←							
Bristol Temple Meads 10	a	08 42		09 38		10 27			11 20	11 26		12 42	12 23		12 27	12 42	13 19		13 24	14 14		14 26	15 27
	d		09 30	09 48	09 41			10 30	11 23	11 30	11 35	12 44			12 30	12 44	13 30		13 30		14 41	15 00	15 30
Lawrence Hill	d								11 26			→											
Stapleton Road	d								11 28														
Filton Abbey Wood	d			09 56	09 48						11 42					12 51					14 48		
Bristol Parkway 7	a		09 38		09 52			10 38		11 38	11 46				12 38	12 55			13 38		14 52	15 08	15 38
	d		09 43				10 00	10 43		11 43				11 56	12 43			13 02	13 43		14 53		
Yate	d						10 20							12 16				13 22			15 03		
Cam & Dursley	d						11 00							12 56				14 02			15 17		
Gloucester 7	a		10 57				11 30	11 59		12 58				13 26	13 57			14 32	14 56		15 35		

Table 134

Taunton - Gloucester

Sundays

from 24 October

		GW	XC	GW	XC	GW	GW	XC	GW	XC	GW	GW	XC	GW	GW	XC	GW	GW	XC	GW	XC	GW	XC
		◇1 🍽	◇1 🛒		◇1 🛒			◇1 🛒	◇1 🍽	◇1 🛒		◇1 🍽	◇1 🛒		◇1 🍽	◇1 🛒			◇1 🛒	◇1 🍽	◇1 🛒	◇	◇1 🛒
Taunton	d			15 18	15 54			16 01	16 38	16 54		17 03		17 19	17 46	17 51				18 23	18 52	19 07	19 23
Bridgwater	d			15 30										17 30						18 34		19 19	
Highbridge & Burnham	d			15 37										17 37						18 41		19 27	
Weston-super-Mare	a			15 47				16 20	16 59			17 25		17 48						18 51		19 40	
	d	14 52		15 49			16 14	16 30	17 00		17 07	17 26		17 50				18 16		18 53		19 41	
Weston Milton	d			15 52			16 17				17 10							18 19					
Worle	d	14 59		15 56			16 22				17 17			17 56				18 24		19 00		19 47	
Yatton	d	15 06		16 02			16 28				17 22	17 37		18 02				18 30		19 06		19 53	
Nailsea & Backwell	d	15 12		16 08			16 34				17 28	17 44		18 08				18 36		19 13		19 59	
Parson Street	d						16 41											18 43					
Bedminster	d						16 44				17 39							18 46					
Bristol Temple Meads 10	a	15 23		16 20	16 27		16 49	16 53	17 21	17 28	17 42	17 55		18 20	18 25	18 27		18 50		19 24	19 27	20 11	19 55
	d		16 00		16 30	16 41	16 53	17 00	17 30	17 30	17 44	18 00	18 00		18 30	18 30	18 41		19 00	19 30	19 30		20 00
Lawrence Hill	d						16 56																
Stapleton Road	d						16 58																
Filton Abbey Wood	d					16 48											18 48						
Bristol Parkway 7	a		16 08		16 38	16 52		17 08		17 38			18 08			18 38	18 52		19 08		19 38		20 08
	d					16 52											18 52						
Yate	d					17 02											19 02						
Cam & Dursley	d					17 16											19 16						
Gloucester 7	a					17 32											19 32						

		XC	GW	GW	GW	XC	GW	GW	GW
		◇1 🛒		◇1 🍽		◇1 🛒	◇1 🍽		
Taunton	d	19 54			20 20		21 23	21 35	
Bridgwater	d				20 32			21 48	
Highbridge & Burnham	d				20 40			21 55	
Weston-super-Mare	a				20 51			22 05	
	d			20 38	20 55			22 07	23 47
Weston Milton	d				20 58			22 10	23 50
Worle	d				21 03				23 54
Yatton	d				21 09			22 18	23 59
Nailsea & Backwell	d				21 15			22 24	00 06
Parson Street	d								
Bedminster	d				21 26			22 34	00 15
Bristol Temple Meads 10	a	20 27		20 58	21 29		22 00	22 38	00 19
	d	20 30	20 41			21 39			
Lawrence Hill	d								
Stapleton Road	d								
Filton Abbey Wood	d		20 48						
Bristol Parkway 7	a	20 38	20 52			21 48			
	d	20 40	20 52			21 52			
Yate	d		21 02						
Cam & Dursley	d		21 16						
Gloucester 7	a		21 32						

Route Diagram for Tables 135, 136, 139, 140, 142, 143, 144

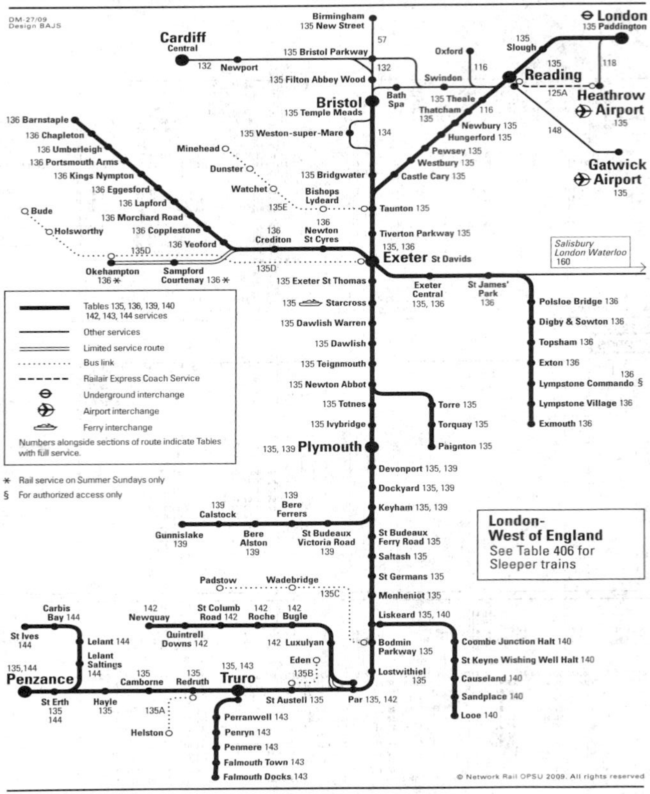

London and Birmingham - Devon and Cornwall

		GW MX	GW MX	GW	GW	GW	GW	GW	GW	XC MO		GW MX	XC MX	GW	GW	GW MO	GW	GW	GW	GW		GW	GW	GW	GW
												■				■									
			◇1			◇1	◇1	◇1		◇1			◇1	1					1	◇		◇	◇	◇	
				A	B	C	D	A												E		F	G	H	
			⊡			⊡	⊡	⊡				sleeper ⊡				sleeper ⊡			⊡						
London Paddington 15 ⊖	d		20p35			21p45	21p45	21p45				23p45				23p50									
Slough 3	d																								
Reading 7	d		21p01			22p11	22p11	22p11				00b37				00u37									
Theale	d																								
Thatcham	d																								
Newbury	d		21p18																						
Hungerford	d																								
Pewsey	d		21p38																						
Westbury	d		21p57									0145													
Castle Cary	d		22p15																						
Birmingham New Street 12	d																								
Cardiff Central 7	d				22p00																				
Newport (South Wales)	d				22p16																				
Swindon	d					22p49	22p49	22p49																	
Bristol Parkway 7	d				22p54																				
Filton Abbey Wood	d				22p58																				
Bath Spa 7	d					23p19	23p19	23p19																	
Bristol Temple Meads 10	d			21p55	23p08	23p35	23p35	23p35								02 55				05 24		05 24	05 24		
Weston-super-Mare	d			22p29	23p45	00s08	00s08	00 08												05 45		05 45	05 45	05 49	
Bridgwater	d			23p07	00 04	00s26	00 26	00 45												06 03		06 03	06 03	06 08	
Taunton	d		22p37	23p37	00s19	00s38	00 45	01 17				02 35								06 18		06 18	06 18	06 22	
Tiverton Parkway	d		22p50	23p52	00s34	00s51	00s58	01 30												06 33		06 33	06 33	06 38	
Exeter St Davids 6	a		23p06	00 11	00 53	01 07	01 14	01 46				03 05				04 05				06 52		06 52	06 52	06 56	
Exmouth	d																								06 46
Exeter Central	d																								07 13
Exeter St Davids 6	d		23p08									04 12				04 35	05 35	06 11		06 53		06 53	06 53	07 01	07 20
Exeter St Thomas	d																05 38	06 14		06 56		06 56	06 56	07 04	07 23
Starcross	d																05 46	06 22		07 05		07 07	07 05	07 12	07 31
Dawlish Warren	d																05 51	06 27		07 10		07 10	07 10	07 17	07 36
Dawlish	d																05 55	06 31		07 14		07 14	07 14	07 21	07 40
Teignmouth	d																06 00	06 36		07 19		07 19	07 19	07 26	07 45
Newton Abbot	a		23p29									04 32				04 55	06 07	06 44		07 26		07 26	07 26	07 33	07 52
	d		23p29						05 42			04 34		07 06		04 56	06 09	06 45		07 26		07 26	07 26	07 34	07 54
Torre	d								05 50					07 15			06 17	06 53							08 02
Torquay	d								05 53					07 20			06 20	06 56							08 05
Paignton	a								06 00					07 29			06 28	07 06							08 14
Totnes	d		23p43																	07 40		07 40	07 40	07 47	
Ivybridge	d																			07 56		07 56	07 56	08 04	
Plymouth	a		00 12									05 13				05 35				08 13		08 13	08 13	08 18	
	d	22p30								05 50		05 50	06 28			06 30			07 02	08 15		08 14	08 15	08 19	
Devonport	d																		07 07			08 18	08 18	08 23	
Dockyard	d																								
Keyham	d																								
St Budeaux Ferry Road	d																								
Saltash	d	22p38																	07 15			08 25	08 25	08 30	
St Germans	d	22p45																	07 22			08 32	08 32	08 37	
Menheniot	d																								
Liskeard 6	d	22p57								06 15		06 15	06 51			07 09			07 34	08 39		08 44	08 44	08 49	
Bodmin Parkway	d	23p11								06 29		06 29	07 03			07 23			07 46	08 51		08 56	08 56	09 01	
Lostwithiel	d	23p16								06 35		06 35	07 09			07 29			07 52	08 56		09 01	09 01	09 06	
Par	d	23p23								06 42		06 42	07 15			07 37			07 59	09 17		09 08	09 08	09 13	
Newquay	a																			10 08					
St Austell	d	23p31								06 50		06 50	07 22			07 45			08 07			09 16	09 16	09 20	
Truro	d	23p49								07 09		07 10	07 39			08 05			08 26			09 34	09 34	09 38	
Redruth	d	00 02								07 23		07 23	07 50			08 19			08 38			09 47	09 47	09 52	
Camborne	d	00 09								07 30		07 30	07 57			08 26			08 46			09 53	09 53	09 58	
Hayle	d	00 16								07 39		07 39	08 05			08 37			08 54			10 00	10 00	10 05	
St Erth	d	00 20								07 44		07 44	08 12		08 28	08 43			08 59			10 08	10 08	10 09	
Penzance	a	00 38								07 57		08 00	08 19		08 40	08 59			09 12			10 19	10 19	10 21	

A MX until 9 July
B MX from 26 October
C MX from 19 October
D MX from 13 July until 15 October
E from 5 July until 3 September
F from 6 September until 15 November, 22 November, 29 November, 6 December
G until 2 July
H MX from 16 November
b stops to pick up only, arr. 0030

For connections from Heathrow Airport, Gatwick Airport and Oxford please refer to Tables 125A, 148 and 116

Table 135

Mondays to Fridays

London and Birmingham - Devon and Cornwall

Station		GW 1 A	XC ◇1	GW	GW ◇	XC ◇1	GW	GW	XC ◇1	GW	GW ◇1	GW	XC ◇1	GW ◇1	GW	GW ◇1 C	GW ◇1 D	GW ◇1 A	GW E	GW	XC ◇1	GW	GW A
London Paddington 15 ⊖	d										07 30			08 18		09 06	09 06	09 06					
Slough 3	d																						
Reading 7	d										07 57			08 48		09u32	09 32	09u32					
Theale	d													08 56									
Thatcham	d													09 04									
Newbury	d													09 12									
Hungerford	d													09 21									
Pewsey	d													09 40									
Westbury	d													10 00									
Castle Cary	d													10 17									
Birmingham New Street 12	d					06 42			07e12				08 12								09 12		
Cardiff Central 7	d											08 00								09 00			
Newport (South Wales)	d											08 15								09 15			
Swindon	d										08 27												
Bristol Parkway 7	d					07 58			08 26				09 26								10 27		
Filton Abbey Wood	d											08 43								09 42			
Bath Spa 7	d										08 57												
Bristol Temple Meads 10	d		06 34		06 26	08 11			08 44		09 13	08 55	09 44							09 55	10 44		
Weston-super-Mare	d				06 51							09 29								10 23			
Bridgwater	d				07 10							09 49								10 42			
Taunton	d		07 08		07 24	08 43			09 17		09 46	10 02	10 18	10 40		10 48	10 48	10 48		10 58	11 18		
Tiverton Parkway	d		07 20		07 39	08 55			09 29				10 30	10 53		11 01	11 01	11 01		11 13	11 30		
Exeter St Davids 6	a		07 34		07 58	09 10			09 43		10 12	10 33	10 46	11 10		11 18	11 18	11 18		11 33	11 46		
Exmouth	d			07 15			08 23			09 23					10 23							11 23	
Exeter Central	d			07 43			08 50			09 50					10 50							11 50	
Exeter St Davids 6	d		07 36	07 50	08 01	09 11	09c16	09 34	09 45	09 56	10 14	10 35	10 48		10 56	11 19	11 19	11 19		11 34	11 48	11 56	
Exeter St Thomas	d			07 53	08 04		09 17			09 59					10 59							11 59	
Starcross	d			08 01			09 25			10 07					11 07							12 07	
Dawlish Warren	d			08 06			09 32			10 12		10 47			11 12							12f23	
Dawlish	d			08 10	08 17		09 36			10 16		10 51			11 16							12 28	
Teignmouth	d			08 15	08 22		09 39			10 21		10 57			11 21							12 33	
Newton Abbot	a		07 56	08 22	08 29		09 46	09 54	10 03	10 31	10 34	11 04	11 08		11 29	11 39	11 39	11 39		11 55	12 07	12 40	
	d		07 57	08 24	08 30		09 48	09 55	10 04	10 39	10 35	11 05	11 09		11 30	11 39	11 39	11 39		11 55	12 08	12 41	
Torre	d			08 32			09 56			10 47		11 14			11 38							12 50	
Torquay	d			08 35		09 41	09 59			10 50		11 18			11 41							12 53	
Paignton	a			08 44		09 46	10 10			10 59		11 27			11 51							13 00	
Totnes	d		08 09		08 43			10 08	10 17		10 49		11 23			11 53	11 53	11 53		12 09	12 22		
Ivybridge	d				09 00			10 25												12 25			
Plymouth	a		08 37		09 14			10 39	10 46		11 17		11 51			12 22	12 22	12 22		12 42	12 50		
	d	08 22			09 17			10 42			11 20							12 28	12 39				
Devonport	d	08 27			09 22																		
Dockyard	d																						
Keyham	d																						
St Budeaux Ferry Road	d							10 48															
Saltash	d	08 35			09 29			10 53										12 38	12 48				
St Germans	d	08 42			09 36			11 00										12 45	12 55				
Menheniot	d																						
Liskeard 6	d	08 54			09 48			11 12			11 43							12 57	13 07				
Bodmin Parkway	d				10 00			11 24			11 56							13 09	13 19				
Lostwithiel	d				10 05			11 29										13 15	13 24				
Par	d	09 14			10 12			11 36			12 07							13 26	13 31				13 37
Newquay	a																	14 26					
St Austell	d	09 22			10 20			11 43			12 15								13 38				13 44
Truro	d	09 40			10 38			12 01			12 32								13 56				14 02
Redruth	d	09 53			10 51			12 14			12 45								14 09				14 15
Camborne	d	10 01			10 57			12 20			12 52								14 15				14 21
Hayle	d	10 09			11 04			12 27											14 22				14 28
St Erth	d	10 14			11b12			12 30			13 03								14 26				14 32
Penzance	a	10 28			11 25			12 42			13 16								14 39				14 45

A from 5 July until 3 September
C until 2 July
D from 6 September
E until 2 July, from 6 September
b arr. 1106
c arr. 0854
e arr. 0652
f arr. 1212

For connections from Heathrow Airport, Gatwick Airport and Oxford please refer to Tables 125A, 148 and 116

Table 135

Mondays to Fridays

London and Birmingham - Devon and Cornwall

Station		GW ◇1	XC ◇1	XC ◇1	GW ◇1	GW	GW	GW ◇1	XC ◇1	GW ◇1	GW	GW ◇1	GW	XC ◇1	GW	GW C	GW D	GW ◇1	GW ◇1	GW	GW	XC ◇1
London Paddington 15 ⊖	d	10 06			10 00			11 06		12 18		12 06						13 06	13 06			
Slough 3	d																					
Reading 7	d	10 32			10 27			11 32		12 48		12 32						13 32	13u32			
Theale	d									12 56												
Thatcham	d									13 04												
Newbury	d									13 12												
Hungerford	d									13 21												
Pewsey	d							12 03		13 40												
Westbury	d							12 22		13 59												
Castle Cary	d							12 39		14 16												
Birmingham New Street 12	d		09 42	10 12					11 12					12 12								13 12
Cardiff Central 7	d																			13 00		
Newport (South Wales)	d																			13 15		
Swindon	d				10 55																	
Bristol Parkway 7	d		10 58	11 28					12 30					13 26								14 29
Filton Abbey Wood	d																			13 42		
Bath Spa 7	d				11 24																	
Bristol Temple Meads 10	d		11 15	11b44	11c47				12 44					13 44						13 53		14 44
Weston-super-Mare	d		11 37		12 07															14 23		
Bridgwater	d																			14 42		
Taunton	d		12 02	12 17	12 29			13 02	13 18	14a39				14 17				14 48	14 48	14 56		15 18
Tiverton Parkway	d		12 14	12 29				13 15	13 30					14 29				15 01	15 01	15 11		15 30
Exeter St Davids 6	a	12 09	12 30	12 43	12 55			13 32	13 46			14 09		14 43				15 17	15 17	15 30		15 46
Exmouth	d					12 23					13 23				14 23							
Exeter Central	d					12 50					13 50				14 50							
Exeter St Davids 6	d	12 09	12 32	12 45	12 56	13e03		13 33	13 48		13 56	14 09		14 45	14 56			15 19	15 19			15 48
Exeter St Thomas	d					13 06					13 59				14 59							
Starcross	d					13 15					14 07				15 07							
Dawlish Warren	d					13 20					14f23				15 12							
Dawlish	d		12 44		13 09	13 24					14 27				15 16							
Teignmouth	d		12 49		13 15	13 29					14 32				15 21							
Newton Abbot	a	12 28	12 55	13 03	13 23	13 36		13 53	14 07		14 40	14 28		15 03	15 29			15 39	15 39			16 07
	d	12 30	12 56	13 04	13 23	13 38		13 54	14 08		14 41	14 30	14 50	15 04	15 30			15 40	15 40		15 58	16 08
Torre	d					13 46					14 49				15 38							
Torquay	d		13 08		13 35	13 49					14 52				15 41							
Paignton	a		13 14		13 43	13 58					15 00				15 51							
Totnes	d			13 17				14 07	14 22				15 02	15 17				15 53	15 53		16 11	16 22
Ivybridge	d												15 19								16 28	
Plymouth	a	13 06		13 43				14 36	14 50			15 06	15 36	15 43				16 22	16 22		16 42	16 50
	d	13 12					13 54					15 12				15 57	15 57		16 31		17 06	
Devonport	d															16 00	16 00				17 09	
Dockyard	d															16x01	16x01				17x10	
Keyham	d															16x03	16x03				17x12	
St Budeaux Ferry Road	d															16 06	16 06				17 15	
Saltash	d						14 03									16 11	16 11				17 20	
St Germans	d						14 10									16 18	16 18				17 27	
Menheniot	d															16x25	16x25				17x34	
Liskeard 6	d	13 35					14 22					15 35				16a31	16 32		16 57		17a40	
Bodmin Parkway	d	13 48					14 34					15 48					16 44		17 09			
Lostwithiel	d						14 39										16 49		17 15			
Par	d	13 59					14 46					15 59					16 56		17 22			
Newquay	a																					
St Austell	d	14 07					14 53					16 07					17 05		17 30			
Truro	d	14 24					15 11					16 24					17 24		17 47			
Redruth	d	14 37					15 24					16 37					17 37		18 00			
Camborne	d	14 45					15 30					16 45					17 43		18 08			
Hayle	d	14 55					15 37										17 50		18 17			
St Erth	d	14 59					15 42					16 56					17 54		18 22			
Penzance	a	15 12					15 54					17 09					18 07		18 35			

C from 5 July until 3 September
D until 2 July, from 6 September
b arr. 1138
c arr. 1140
e arr. 1254
f arr. 1412

For connections from Heathrow Airport, Gatwick Airport and Oxford please refer to Tables 125A, 148 and 116

Table 135

London and Birmingham - Devon and Cornwall

Mondays to Fridays

		XC	GW	GW	GW	GW	XC	GW FO	GW	GW	GW	GW	GW	XC	GW	XC	GW	GW	XC	GW FO	GW FX	GW	GW
		◇1			◇1		◇1	◇					◇1	◇1		◇1	◇1		◇1	◇1	◇1	◇1	
		⊼			⊡⊘		⊼						⊡⊘	⊼		⊼	⊡		⊼	⊡	⊡	⊡	
London Paddington 15 ⊖	d				14 06								15 06				16 06			16 36	16 36	17 06	
Slough 3	d																						
Reading 7	d				14 32								15u32				16 32			17 03	17 03	17 36	
Theale	d																					17 45	
Thatcham	d																					17 55	
Newbury	d																			17 19	17 19	18 02	
Hungerford	d																			17 29	17 29	18 16	
Pewsey	d												16 03							17 44	17 44	18 34	
Westbury	d							15 20					16 23							18 03	18 03	18a52	
Castle Cary	d												16 41							18 21	18 21		
Birmingham New Street 12	d	13b42					14 12							15 12		15 42			16 12				
Cardiff Central 7	d																						
Newport (South Wales)	d																						
Swindon	d																						
Bristol Parkway 7	d	14 58					15 26							16 28		16 58			17 26				
Filton Abbey Wood	d																						
Bath Spa 7	d																						
Bristol Temple Meads 10	d	15 13					15 44							16 44		17 14			17 44				
Weston-super-Mare	d																						
Bridgwater	d																						
Taunton	d	15 46			15 50		16 17	16 24					17 05	17 17		17 46	17 50		18 18	18 43	18 43		
Tiverton Parkway	d	15 58			16 03		16 29						17 18	17 29		17 58	18 03		18 30	18 56	18 56		
Exeter St Davids 6	a	16 13			16 19		16 43	17 01					17 34	17 43		18 13	18 20		18 44	19 13	19 14		
Exmouth	d		15 23			15 53				16 55								17 55					
Exeter Central	d		15 50			16 20			16 46	17 21					17 45			18 23					
Exeter St Davids 6	d		15 56	16 08	16 21	16 26	16 45		16c56	17 26			17 36	17 45	17 50	18 15	18 21	18 28	18 47	19 14			
Exeter St Thomas	d		15 59			16 29			16 59	17 29					17 54			18 31					
Starcross	d		16 07			16 37			17 07	17 37					18 02			18 39					
Dawlish Warren	d		16 12	16 19		16 42			17 12	17e49					18 07			18 44					
Dawlish	d		16 16	16 23		16 46			17 16	17 53					18 11	18 27		18 48					
Teignmouth	d		16 21	16 28		16 51			17 21	17 58					18 16	18 32		18 53					
Newton Abbot	a		16 30	16 35	16 41	16 58	17 03		17 29	18 05			17 56	18 10	18 23	18 38	18 42	19 01	19 06	19 35			
	d		16 30	16 50	16 42	17 00	17 04		17 30	18 09			17 57	18 12	18 25	18 39	18 43	19 10	19 07	19 35			
Torre	d		16 38			17 08			17 38	18 17					18 33			19 18					
Torquay	d		16 41			17 11			17 41	18 20					18 36	18 51		19 21					
Paignton	a		16 51			17 20			17 51	18 30					18 45	18 57		19 30					
Totnes	d			17 04	16 55		17 17						18 10	18 24			18 56		19 20				
Ivybridge	d			17 21													19 12						
Plymouth	a			17 35	17 23		17 43					18 14	18 38	18 51			19 26		19 45	20 13			
	d				17 26						17 55	18 17	18 43	19 00			19 31		19 50				
Devonport	d											18 20											
Dockyard	d											18x21											
Keyham	d											18x23											
St Budeaux Ferry Road	d											18 25											
Saltash	d				17 36						18 03	18 31					19 41						
St Germans	d				17 43							18 38											
Menheniot	d											18x45											
Liskeard 6	d				17 55						18 20	18a53	19 08	19 23			19 57		20 13				
Bodmin Parkway	d				18 07						18 32		19 19	19 35			20 09		20 26				
Lostwithiel	d				18 13						18 37												
Par	d				18 20						18 44		19 30	19 45			20 20		20 36				
Newquay	a																						
St Austell	d				18 28						18 51		19 38	19 52			20 28		20 43				
Truro	d				18 46						19 09		19 58	20 10			20 46		21 00				
Redruth	d				18 58						19 22		20 08	20 25			20 58		21 15				
Camborne	d				19 07						19 28		20 17	20 33			21 07		21 22				
Hayle	d				19 16						19 35												
St Erth	d				19 20						19 40		20 27	20 44			21 17		21 33				22 07
Penzance	a				19 34						19 53		20 41	20 54			21 31		21 42				22 19

b arr. 1331 **c** arr. 1649 **e** arr. 1743

For connections from Heathrow Airport, Gatwick Airport and Oxford please refer to Tables 125A, 148 and 116

Table 135

London and Birmingham - Devon and Cornwall

Mondays to Fridays

		GW	GW	XC	GW	GW	GW	XC	GW FO	GW FX	GW FO	GW FX	GW	GW FX	XC	XC	GW	GW	XC	GW	GW	GW
											2	2										
		◇1		◇1	◇1	◇1	◇1	◇1	◇1	◇1	1	1			◇1	◇1	◇1		◇1	◇1	E	F
		⊡		⊼	⊡	✕⊡	⊡	⊼	⊡	⊡	✕⊡	✕⊡			⊼	⊼	⊡			⊡		
London Paddington 15 ⊖	d	17 03			17 36	18 03	18 06		18 33	18 33	19 03	19 03					19 45			20 35		
Slough 3	d																					
Reading 7	d	17u31			18 03	18u32	18 37		19 01	19 01	19 32	19 32					20 11			21 01		
Theale	d						18 45															
Thatcham	d						18 55															
Newbury	d	17 48			18 19		19 02		19 17	19 17	19 49	19 49					20 27			21 18		
Hungerford	d						19 16		19 27	19 27												
Pewsey	d				18 41		19 34		19 46	19 46							20 47			21 38		
Westbury	d				19 01		19 53		20 05	20 05							21 05			21 57		
Castle Cary	d				19 19				20 22	20 22							21 27			22 15		
Birmingham New Street 12	d			17 12				18 12							19 12	19e42			20 12			
Cardiff Central 7	d																					
Newport (South Wales)	d																					
Swindon	d																					
Bristol Parkway 7	d			18 29				19 29							20 28	20 58			21 27			
Filton Abbey Wood	d																					
Bath Spa 7	d																					
Bristol Temple Meads 10	d			18 44				19b44							20c47	21 13			21g44		21⟆55	21⟆55
Weston-super-Mare	d																				22⟆29	22h33
Bridgwater	d																				22⟆48	22⟆59
Taunton	d	18 52		19 17	19 41	19 48		20 18	20 45	20 45	20 54	20 54			21 19	21 46	21 49		22 17	22 37	23⟆03	23⟆14
Tiverton Parkway	d	19 05		19 29	19 54			20 30	20 58	20 58					21 32	21 58	22 02		22 29	22 50	23⟆18	23⟆29
Exeter St Davids 6	a	19 21		19 43	20 10	20 13		20 44	21 15	21 15	21 21	21 21			21 46	22 13	22 19		22 44	23 06	23⟆37	23⟆48
Exmouth	d		18 55															22 04				
Exeter Central	d		19 21										21 21					22 30				
Exeter St Davids 6	d	19 22	19 28	19 45	20 19	20 16		20 46	21 16		21 22	21 22	21 29		21 48	22 15	22 20	22 37	22 45	23 08		
Exeter St Thomas	d		19 31		20 23								21 32					22 40				
Starcross	d		19 39		20 32								21 40					22 48				
Dawlish Warren	d		19 44		20 36								21 45					22f59				
Dawlish	d		19 48		20 41								21 49					23 03				
Teignmouth	d		19 53		20 47								21 54					23 08				
Newton Abbot	a	19 43	20 00	20 04	20 55	20 35		21 03	21 36		21 43	21 43	22 01		22 05	22 33	22 41	23 15	23 05	23 29		
	d	19 43	20 09	20 06	20 55	20 36		21 05	21 37		21 43	21 43	22 02		22 07	22 34	22 41	23 16	23 05	23 29		
Torre	d		20 17		21 05								22 10					23 24				
Torquay	d		20 20		21 09								22 13					23 27				
Paignton	a		20 29		21 17								22 22					23 37				
Totnes	d	19 57		20 18		20 49		21 18			21 57	21 57			22 20	22 47	22 55		23 18	23 43		
Ivybridge	d																23 10					
Plymouth	a	20 25		20 45		21 17		21 50	22 15		22 25	22 25			22 46	23 12	23 27		23 44	00 12		
	d	20 29		20 52		21 20					22 28			22 30								
Devonport	d																					
Dockyard	d																					
Keyham	d																					
St Budeaux Ferry Road	d																					
Saltash	d	20 39									22 38			22 38								
St Germans	d	20 46									22 45			22 45								
Menheniot	d																					
Liskeard 6	d	20 57		21 15		21 44					22 57			22 57								
Bodmin Parkway	d	21 09		21 28		21 58					23 11			23 11								
Lostwithiel	d			21 33							23 16			23 16								
Par	d	21 20		21 40		22 09					23 23			23 23								
Newquay	a																					
St Austell	d	21 28		21 47		22 17					23 31			23 31								
Truro	d	21 45		22 04		22 35					23 49			23 49								
Redruth	d	21 58		22 15		22 47					00 02			00 02								
Camborne	d			22 23							00 09			00 09								
Hayle	d	22 10		22 31							00 16			00 16								
St Erth	d	22 17		22 35							00 20			00 20								
Penzance	a	22 30		22 45		23 12					00 38			00 38								

E from 18 October
F from 6 September until 15 October
b arr. 1939
c arr. 2041
e arr. 1931
f arr. 2253
g arr. 2138
h arr. 2227

For connections from Heathrow Airport, Gatwick Airport and Oxford please refer to Tables 125A, 148 and 116

Table 135

Mondays to Fridays

London and Birmingham - Devon and Cornwall

		GW	GW	GW	GW	GW	GW	GW FO	GW FX
					◇1	◇1	◇1	R	R
		A	B	C	D	E	B		
London Paddington 15 ⊖	d				21∫45	21∫45	21∫45	23 45	23 45
Slough 3	d								
Reading 7	d				22∫11	22∫11	22∫11	00c37	00e37
Theale	d								
Thatcham	d								
Newbury	d								
Hungerford	d								
Pewsey	d								
Westbury	d							01 37	01f45
Castle Cary	d								
Birmingham New Street 12	d								
Cardiff Central 7	d			22∫00					
Newport (South Wales)	d			22∫16					
Swindon	d				22∫49	22∫49	22∫49		
Bristol Parkway 7	d			22∫54					
Filton Abbey Wood	d			22∫58					
Bath Spa 7	d				23∫19	23∫19	23∫19		
Bristol Temple Meads 10	d	21∫55	21∫55	23∫08	23∫35	23∫35	23∫35		
Weston-super-Mare	d	22b33	22∫29	23∫45	00s08	00s08	00∫08		
Bridgwater	d	22∫52	23∫07	00∫04	00s26	00∫26	00∫45		
Taunton	d	23∫14	23∫37	00s19	00s38	00∫45	01∫17	02 25	02 35
Tiverton Parkway	d	23∫29	23∫52	00s34	00s51	00s58	01∫30		
Exeter St Davids 6	a	23∫48	00∫11	00∫53	01∫07	01∫14	01∫46	02 57	03 05
Exmouth	d								
Exeter Central	d								
Exeter St Davids 6	d							03 00	04 12
Exeter St Thomas	d								
Starcross	d								
Dawlish Warren	d								
Dawlish	d								
Teignmouth	d								
Newton Abbot	a							03 20	04 32
	d							03 22	04 34
Torre	d								
Torquay	d								
Paignton	a								
Totnes	d								
Ivybridge	d								
Plymouth	a							04 01	05 13
	d							05 50	05 50
Devonport	d								
Dockyard	d								
Keyham	d								
St Budeaux Ferry Road	d								
Saltash	d								
St Germans	d								
Menheniot	d								
Liskeard 6	d							06 15	06 15
Bodmin Parkway	d							06 29	06 29
Lostwithiel	d							06 35	06 35
Par	d							06 42	06 42
Newquay	a								
St Austell	d							06 50	06 50
Truro	d							07 10	07 10
Redruth	d							07 23	07 23
Camborne	d							07 30	07 30
Hayle	d							07 39	07 39
St Erth	d							07 44	07 44
Penzance	a							08 00	08 00

A from 12 July until 3 September
B until 9 July
C from 22 October
D from 18 October
E from 12 July until 15 October
b arr. 2227
c stops to pick up only, arr. 0020
e stops to pick up only, arr. 0030
f arr. 0135

For connections from Heathrow Airport, Gatwick Airport and Oxford please refer to Tables 125A, 148 and 116

Table 135

Saturdays
until 04 September

London and Birmingham - Devon and Cornwall

		GW	GW	GW	GW	GW	GW	GW	GW	GW		XC	GW	GW	GW	XC	GW	GW	GW	GW		GW	XC	GW	GW
		R 1 ✕	◇1	B	◇1 C	◇1 B	R					◇1			◇	◇1		◇	◇				◇1	◇	
London Paddington 15 ⊖	d	19p03	20p35		21p45	21p45	23p45																		
Slough 3	d																								
Reading 7	d	19b32	21p01		22p11	22p11	00c37																		
Theale	d																								
Thatcham	d																								
Newbury	d	19p49	21p18																						
Hungerford	d																								
Pewsey	d		21p38																						
Westbury	d		21p57				01 37																		
Castle Cary	d		22p15																						
Birmingham New Street 12	d																						06 42		
Cardiff Central 7	d																								
Newport (South Wales)	d																								
Swindon	d				22p49	22p49																			
Bristol Parkway 7	d																						07 57		
Filton Abbey Wood	d																								
Bath Spa 7	d				23p19	23p19																			
Bristol Temple Meads 10	d			21p55	23p35	23p35									05 28	06 08			06 36				08 11		
Weston-super-Mare	d			22p29	00s08	00∫08									05 49				06 56						
Bridgwater	d			23p07	00∫26	00∫45									06 08										
Taunton	d	20p54	22p37	23p37	00∫45	01∫17	02 25								06 22	07 17			07 25				08 43		
Tiverton Parkway	d		22p50	23p52	00s58	01∫30									06 38	07 29			07 41				08 55		
Exeter St Davids 6	a	21p21	23p06	00∫11	01∫14	01∫46	02 57								06 56	07 43			07 59				09 10		
Exmouth	d																07 15					08 23			
Exeter Central	d																07 43					08 50			
Exeter St Davids 6	d	21p22	23p08				03 00	05 18	05 35	06 11					06 58	07 45	07 50		08 05	08 37		08 56	09 12		
Exeter St Thomas	d							05 21	05 38	06 14					07 01		07 53					08 59			
Starcross	d							05 29	05 46	06 22					07 09		08 01					09 07			
Dawlish Warren	d							05 34	05 51	06 27					07 14		08 06					09e24			
Dawlish	d							05 38	05 55	06 31					07 18		08 10			08 50		09 28			
Teignmouth	d							05 43	06 00	06 36					07 23		08 15			08 55		09 33			
Newton Abbot	a	21p43	23p29				03 20	05 50	06 07	06 44					07 30	08 03	08 22		08 28	09 02		09 40			
	d	21p43	23p29				03 22	05 52	06 09	06 45			07 40		07 31	08 04	08 24		08 29	09 06		09 41			
Torre	d							06 00	06 17	06 53			07 48				08 32					09 50			
Torquay	d							06 03	06 20	06 56			07 51				08 35			09 16		09 53	09 40		
Paignton	a							06 11	06 28	07 06			07 59				08 44			09 25		10 03	09 46		
Totnes	d	21p57	23p43												07 44	08 17			08 42						
Ivybridge	d														08 01				08 58						
Plymouth	a	22p25	00 12				04 01								08 15	08 43			09 12						
	d	22p28					05 50					06 35			08 16			08 58						09 24	09 58
Devonport	d														08 20										10 01
Dockyard	d																								
Keyham	d																								
St Budeaux Ferry Road	d																								
Saltash	d	22p38													08 27									09 34	10 08
St Germans	d	22p45													08 34										10 15
Menheniot	d																								10x22
Liskeard 6	d	22p57					06 15					06 58			08 46			09 22						09 49	10 29
Bodmin Parkway	d	23p11					06 29					07 11			08 58			09 34						10 01	10 41
Lostwithiel	d	23p16					06 35					07 16			09 03									10 08	10 46
Par	d	23p23					06 42					07 26			09 10			09 47						10 15	10a55
Newquay	a											08 25						11 01							
St Austell	d	23p31					06 50								09 17									10 22	
Truro	d	23p49					07 10								09 36									10 39	
Redruth	d	00 02					07 23								09 49									10 52	
Camborne	d	00 09					07 30								09 55									10 59	
Hayle	d	00 16					07 39								10 02									11 10	
St Erth	d	00 20					07 44							08 28	10 07									11 16	
Penzance	a	00 38					08 00							08 40	10 19									11 28	

B until 10 July
C from 17 July until 4 September
b previous night, stops to pick up only
c stops to pick up only, arr. 0020
e arr. 0915

For connections from Heathrow Airport, Gatwick Airport and Oxford please refer to Tables 125A, 148 and 116

Table 135

Saturdays
until 04 September

London and Birmingham - Devon and Cornwall

		GW	XC	GW	GW	GW	GW	GW	XC	GW	GW	GW	XC	XC	GW	GW	XC	XC	GW	GW	GW	GW	XC
			◇1	■ ◇1		■ ◇1			◇1		■ ◇1	■ 1	◇1	◇1		■ 1	◇1	◇1			■ ◇1	■ 1	◇1
											C					E					C		
London Paddington 15 ⊖	d			07 36		07 30					08 35	09 06				10 06					10 35	11 06	
Slough 3	d																						
Reading 7	d			08u06		07 57					09u04	09u33				10u33					11u04	11u33	
Theale	d																						
Thatcham	d																						
Newbury	d										09 21												
Hungerford	d																						
Pewsey	d										09 40										11 36		
Westbury	d										09 58										11 54		
Castle Cary	d										10 15										12 12		
Birmingham New Street 12	d		07b12						08 12				08 42	09 12			09 42	10 12					11 12
Cardiff Central 7	d																						
Newport (South Wales)	d																						
Swindon	d					08 30																	
Bristol Parkway 7	d		08 26						09 26				09 59	10 31			10 59	11 26					12 31
Filton Abbey Wood	d																						
Bath Spa 7	d					09 00																	
Bristol Temple Meads 10	d		08c44			09 15			09e44				10f20	10 44			11 14	11 43					12 44
Weston-super-Mare	d																11g39						
Bridgwater	d																						
Taunton	d		09 17			09 49			10 17		10 37	10 50	11 03	11 17			12 02	12 17			12 35	12 52	13 17
Tiverton Parkway	d		09 29						10 29		10 50	11 03	11 15	11 29			12 14	12 30			12 49		13 29
Exeter St Davids 6	a		09 43	09 52		10 16			10 46		11 06	11 20	11 31	11 43		12 11	12 30	12 45			13 05	13 18	13 43
Exmouth	d				09 23					10 23					11 23					12 23			
Exeter Central	d				09 50			10 30		10 50					11 50					12 50			
Exeter St Davids 6	d	09 28	09 45	09 53	09 56	10 17	10 25	10 35	10 49	10 56	11 08	11 22	11 34	11 46	11 56	12 14	12 33	12 48	12 52	12 56	13 09	13 20	13 46
Exeter St Thomas	d				09 59					10 59					11 59					12 59			
Starcross	d				10 08					11 07					12 07					13 07			
Dawlish Warren	d				10 13			10 47		11 13	11 20				12 13				13 03	13 12			
Dawlish	d				10 18			10 51		11 17	11 25				12 17		12 46		13 07	13 16	13 23		
Teignmouth	d				10 23			10 56		11 23	11 32				12 23		12 52		13 12	13 21	13 29		
Newton Abbot	a	09 48	10 03		10 32	10 38	10 45	11 03	11 08	11 31	11 39	11 43	11 53	12 04	12 31	12 35	12 59	13 07	13 19	13 29	13 36	13 40	14 04
	d	09 49	10 05		10 33	10 38	10 47	11 04	11 10	11 32	11 40	11 44	11 54	12 06	12 32	12 36	13 00	13 09	13 20	13 30	13 38	13 41	14 06
Torre	d				10 41		10 55			11 40					12 40					13 38			
Torquay	d				10 44		10 58	11 14		11 43	11 52				12 43		13 13			13 41	13 51		
Paignton	a				10 54		11 06	11 23		11 53	12 02				12 53		13 20			13 53	14 01		
Totnes	d	10 02	10 17			10 52			11 23			11 58	12 08	12 18				13 22	13 33			13 54	14 18
Ivybridge	d	10 19																	13 49				
Plymouth	a	10 32	10 44	10 51		11 20			11 51			12 26	12 34	12 45		13 14		13 48	14 05			14 22	14 45
	d	10 33		10 53		11 23						12 30	12 38			13 16		13 51				14 26	
Devonport	d																						
Dockyard	d																						
Keyham	d																						
St Budeaux Ferry Road	d	10 39																					
Saltash	d	10 44																					
St Germans	d	10 51																					
Menheniot	d																						
Liskeard 6	d	11 03				11 46						12 53	13 05			13 40		14 15				14 49	
Bodmin Parkway	d	11 15				12 01						13 05	13 20			13 52		14 27				15 02	
Lostwithiel	d	11 20										13 12											
Par	d	11 27		11 35									13 32			14 03		14 38					
Newquay	a			12 44									14 37										
St Austell	d	11 37				12 17						13 23				14 11		14 46				15 17	
Truro	d	11 55				12 34						13 40				14 28		15 04				15 35	
Redruth	d	12 08				12 47						13 53				14 41		15 17				15 47	
Camborne	d	12 14				12 54						14 00				14 48		15 24				15 54	
Hayle	d	12 21										14 10				14 58						16 03	
St Erth	d	12 24				13 06						14 15				15 03		15 36				16 09	
Penzance	a	12 37				13 19						14 29				15 17		15 47				16 24	

C The Torbay Express.
E The Cornish Riviera.**b**arr. 0650
c arr. 0838
e arr. 0938
f arr. 1011
g arr. 1131

For connections from Heathrow Airport, Gatwick Airport and Oxford please refer to Tables 125A, 148 and 116

Table 135

Saturdays
until 04 September

London and Birmingham - Devon and Cornwall

		GW	GW	GW	GW	XC	GW	GW	GW	GW	XC	GW	GW	XC	GW	GW	XC	GW	GW	GW	GW	XC
		■ 1		■ 1		◇1		■ ◇1		■ 1	◇1			◇1		◇1	◇1				◇1	◇1
				A				B														
London Paddington 15 ⊖	d	11 35		12 06				12 35		13 06						14 06					15 06	
Slough 3	d																					
Reading 7	d	12u06		12u33				13u03		13u32						14u33					15u32	
Theale	d																					
Thatcham	d																					
Newbury	d							13 21														
Hungerford	d																					
Pewsey	d							13 41													16 04	
Westbury	d							13 59													16 22	
Castle Cary	d							14 17													16 40	
Birmingham New Street 12	d					12 12					13 12			13 42			14 12					15 12
Cardiff Central 7	d																					
Newport (South Wales)	d																					
Swindon	d																					
Bristol Parkway 7	d					13 26					14 28			14 59			15 26					16 31
Filton Abbey Wood	d																					
Bath Spa 7	d																					
Bristol Temple Meads 10	d					13e44					14 44			15 13			15f44					16 44
Weston-super-Mare	d																					
Bridgwater	d																					
Taunton	d					14 17		14 39		14 48	15 18			15 45		15 49	16 17				17 02	17 18
Tiverton Parkway	d					14 29				15 01	15 30			15 57		16 02					17 15	17 31
Exeter St Davids 6	a	13u53		14 10		14 43		15 04		15 18	15 46			16 12		16 19	16 40				17 32	17 47
Exmouth	d		13 23				14 23						15 23						16 55			
Exeter Central	d		13 50				14 50						15 50					16 48	17 21			
Exeter St Davids 6	d	13u56	14b01	14 12	14 30	14 46	14 56	15 07		15 19	15 49		15 56	16 15		16 21	16 42	16 56	17 24		17 34	17 48
Exeter St Thomas	d		14 04				14 59						15 59					16 59	17 27			
Starcross	d		14 12				15 07						16 07					17 07	17 35			
Dawlish Warren	d		14c24		14 41		15 12	15 20					16 12					17 12	17g47			
Dawlish	d		14 28		14 45		15 16	15 26					16 16					17 16	17 51			
Teignmouth	d		14 33		14 50		15 21	15 32					16 21					17 21	17 56			
Newton Abbot	a		14 41	14 31	14 57	15 04	15 29	15 38		15 43	16 08		16 29	16 34		16 40	17 00	17 29	18 03		17 55	18 08
	d		14 42	14 33	14 59	15 06	15 30	15 39		15 43	16 09	16 18	16 30	16 40		16 42	17 02	17 30	18 09		17 57	18 10
Torre	d		14 50		15 07		15 38						16 38					17 38	18 17			
Torquay	d		14 53		15 10		15 41	15 52					16 41	16 52				17 41	18 20			
Paignton	a		15 01		15 18		15 51	16 02					16 51	16 59				17 51	18 29			
Totnes	d					15 19				15 57	16 23	16 31				16 54	17 14				18 10	18 23
Ivybridge	d											16 47				17 11						
Plymouth	a	14u53		15 10		15 45				16 25	16 49	17 02				17 25	17 40				18 37	18 50
	d	14u56		15 12					16 03	16 28	16 52					17 29	17 42			17 52		18 54
Devonport	d																			17 55		
Dockyard	d																			17x57		
Keyham	d																			17x59		
St Budeaux Ferry Road	d																			18 01		
Saltash	d								16 12											18 06		
St Germans	d								16 19											18 12		
Menheniot	d								16x27											18x19		
Liskeard 6	d			15 36					16 33	16 51	17 16					17 53	18 05			18 26		19 18
Bodmin Parkway	d			15 49					16 45	17 04	17 28					18 04	18 18			18 38		19 30
Lostwithiel	d	15 33							16 50											18 44		
Par	d	15 43		15 59					17a02		17 41					18 16	18 28			18 51		19 41
Newquay	a	16 52									18 45											
St Austell	d			16 07						17 19						18 23	18 34			18 58		19 49
Truro	d			16 25						17 37						18 41	18 52			19 16		20 07
Redruth	d			16 37						17 49						18 53	19 09			19 29		20 20
Camborne	d			16 45						17 57						19 02	19 16			19 35		20 27
Hayle	d									18 06										19 42		
St Erth	d			16 56						18 12					18 32	19 12	19 26			19 46		20 38
Penzance	a			17 13						18 25					18 44	19 25	19 36			19 57		20 49

A The Royal Duchy
B The Torbay Express
b arr. 1354
c arr. 1417
e arr. 1338
f arr. 1538
g arr. 1741

For connections from Heathrow Airport, Gatwick Airport and Oxford please refer to Tables 125A, 148 and 116

Table 135

London and Birmingham - Devon and Cornwall

Saturdays until 04 September

		GW	GW	GW	XC	GW	GW	GW	GW	GW	GW	XC	GW	GW	XC	GW	GW	XC	GW	XC	GW	GW
		1	◇1		◇1			◇1	◇1			◇1		◇1	◇1		◇1	◇1	◇1	◇1		◇1
London Paddington 15 ⊖	d		16 06					17 06	16 30					18 06			19 06		20 06			20 30
Slough 8	d																					
Reading 7	d		16u32					17u32	16 57					18u32			19 32		20 32			20 59
Theale	d																					
Thatcham	d																					
Newbury	d																19 49		20 46			
Hungerford	d																					
Pewsey	d							18 02									20 10		21 06			
Westbury	d							18 21									20 28		21 25			
Castle Cary	d							18 40									20 45		21 43			
Birmingham New Street 12	d				16 12							17 12			18 12			19 12		20 12		
Cardiff Central 7	d																				21 00	
Newport (South Wales)	d																				21 15	
Swindon	d								17 30													21 31
Bristol Parkway 7	d				17 26							18 31			19 29			20 31		21 25		
Filton Abbey Wood	d																				21 42	
Bath Spa 7	d								18 00													22 00
Bristol Temple Meads 10	d				17b44				18 18			18 45			19 44			20 44		21f44	21g55	22 17
Weston-super-Mare	d								18 40												22 27	22s49
Bridgwater	d																				22 46	23s07
Taunton	d		17 49		18 17			19 01	19 06			19 18		19 47	20 17		21 08	21 17	22 06	22 17	22 59	23 19
Tiverton Parkway	d		18 02		18 29			19 14	19 21			19 30			20 29		21 21	21 29	22 19	22 29	23 14	23 32
Exeter St Davids 6	a		18 19		18 43			19 31	19 37			19 44		20 14	20 43		21 38	21 43	22 36	22 44	23 33	23 49
Exmouth	d			17 55									19 38			20 08						
Exeter Central	d			18 21									20 01			20 35						
Exeter St Davids 6	d	17 53	18 20	18 26	18 46	18 56	19 16	19 33	19 38			19 46	20 07	20 15	20 45	20e56	21 38	21 46	22 37	22 46		
Exeter St Thomas	d			18 29			19 19						20 10			20 59						
Starcross	d			18 37			19 27						20 18			21 07						
Dawlish Warren	d	18 04		18 42			19 32						20c32			21 12						
Dawlish	d	18 08		18 46		19 09	19 36						20 36			21 16			22 49			
Teignmouth	d	18 13		18 51		19 14	19 41						20 41			21 21			22 55			
Newton Abbot	a	18 20	18 40	18 59	19 04	19 21	19 48	19 52	19 58			20 04	20 48	20 37	21 03	21 28	21 59	22 05	23 03	23 11		
	d	18 21	18 41	19 01	19 05	19 22	19 50	19 53	19 59			20 06	20 49	20 37	21 05	21 30	21 59	22 10	23 03	23 12		
Torre	d			19 09			19 58		20 09				20 57			21 38						
Torquay	d			19 12		19 32	20 01		20 12				21 00			21 41						
Paignton	a			19 21		19 40	20 09		20 21				21 08			21 48						
Totnes	d	18 34	18 54		19 18			20 06				20 18		20 51	21 17		22 13	22 23	23 17	23 28		
Ivybridge	d	18 50	19 11																			
Plymouth	a	19 04	19 24		19 43			20 33				20 45		21 19	21 44		22 42	22 49	23 48	23 54		
	d	19 07	19 28		19 48						20 42			21 21								
Devonport	d																					
Dockyard	d																					
Keyham	d																					
St Budeaux Ferry Road	d																					
Saltash	d	19 16									20 51											
St Germans	d	19 23									20 58											
Menheniot	d																					
Liskeard 6	d	19 35	19 52		20 11						21 10			21 45								
Bodmin Parkway	d	19 47	20 04		20 24						21 24			22 00								
Lostwithiel	d	19 52			20 29						21 29											
Par	d	19 59	20 15		20 36						21 36			22 10								
Newquay	a																					
St Austell	d	20 06	20 23		20 43						21 44			22 18								
Truro	d	20 25	20 41		21 00						22 03			22 36								
Redruth	d	20 38	20 54		21 12						22 16			22 48								
Camborne	d	20 44	21 02		21 18						22 22			22 57								
Hayle	d				21 26						22 29			23 04								
St Erth	d	20 54	21 14		21 30					22 16	22 32			23 09								
Penzance	a	21 05	21 25		21 43					22 29	22 46			23 24								

b arr. 1738
c arr. 2023
e arr. 2038
f arr. 2135
g arr. 2149

For connections from Heathrow Airport, Gatwick Airport and Oxford please refer to Tables 125A, 148 and 116

Table 135

London and Birmingham - Devon and Cornwall

Saturdays from 11 September

		GW	GW	GW	GW	GW	GW	GW	GW	GW	GW	XC	GW	GW	GW	GW	XC	GW	GW	GW	GW	XC	GW
		1 ✕	◇1	B	◇1 B	◇1 C						◇1			◇ D	◇ E	◇1		◇			◇1	
London Paddington 15 ⊖	d	19p03	20p35		21p45	21p45		23p45															
Slough 8	d																						
Reading 7	d	19p32	21p01		22p11	22p11		00c37															
Theale	d																						
Thatcham	d																						
Newbury	d	19p49	21p18																				
Hungerford	d																						
Pewsey	d		21p38																				
Westbury	d		21p57					01 37															
Castle Cary	d		22p15																				
Birmingham New Street 12	d																					06 42	
Cardiff Central 7	d			22p00																			
Newport (South Wales)	d			22p16																			
Swindon	d				22p49	22p49																	
Bristol Parkway 7	d			22p54																		07 57	
Filton Abbey Wood	d			22p58																			
Bath Spa 7	d				23p19	23p19																	
Bristol Temple Meads 10	d			23p08	23p35	23p35									05 28		06 08		06 36			08 11	
Weston-super-Mare	d			23p45	00s08	00s08									05 49	05 49			06 56				
Bridgwater	d			00 04	00s26	00 26									06 08	06 08							
Taunton	d	20p54	22p37	00s19	00s38	00 45		02 25							06 22	06 22	07 17		07 25			08 43	
Tiverton Parkway	d		22p50	00s34	00s51	00s58									06 38	06 38	07 29		07 41			08 55	
Exeter St Davids 6	a	21p21	23p06	00 53	01 07	01 14		02 57							06 56	06 56	07 43		07 59			09 10	
Exmouth	d																	07 15			08 23		
Exeter Central	d																	07 43			08 50		
Exeter St Davids 6	d	21p22	23p08					03 00	05 18	05 35	06 11				06 58	06 58	07 45	07 50	08 05	08 37	08 56	09 12	
Exeter St Thomas	d								05 21	05 38	06 14				07 01	07 01		07 53	08 08		08 59		
Starcross	d								05 29	05 46	06 22				07 09	07 09		08 01			09 07		
Dawlish Warren	d								05 34	05 51	06 27				07 14	07 14		08 06			09e24		
Dawlish	d								05 38	05 55	06 31				07 18	07 18		08 10	08 20	08 50	09 28		
Teignmouth	d								05 43	06 00	06 36				07 23	07 23		08 15	08 25	08 55	09 33		
Newton Abbot	a	21p43	23p29					03 20	05 50	06 07	06 44				07 30	07 30	08 03	08 22	08 32	09 02	09 40		
	d	21p43	23p29					03 22	05 52	06 09	06 45		07 40		07 31	07 31	08 04	08 24	08 33	09 06	09 41		
Torre	d								06 00	06 17	06 53		07 48					08 32			09 50		
Torquay	d								06 03	06 20	06 56		07 51					08 35		09 16	09 53	09 40	
Paignton	a								06 11	06 28	07 06		07 59					08 44		09 25	10 03	09 46	
Totnes	d	21p57	23p43												07 44	07 44	08 17		08 46				
Ivybridge	d														08 01	08 01			09 03				
Plymouth	a	22p25	00 12					04 01							08 15	08 15	08 43		09 17				
	d	22p28						05 50				06 28			08 16	08 16			09 20				09 51
Devonport	d														08 20	08 20			09 23				09 54
Dockyard	d																						
Keyham	d																						
St Budeaux Ferry Road	d																						
Saltash	d	22p38													08 27	08 27			09 30				10 01
St Germans	d	22p45													08 34	08 34			09 37				10 08
Menheniot	d																						10x15
Liskeard 6	d	22p57						06 15				06 51			08 46	08 46			09 49				10 22
Bodmin Parkway	d	23p11						06 29				07 03			08 58	08 58			10 01				10 34
Lostwithiel	d	23p16						06 35				07 09			09 03	09 03			10 07				10 39
Par	d	23p23					06 09	06 42				07 15			09 10	09 10			10 14				10 46
Newquay	a																						
St Austell	d	23p31					06 16	06 50				07 22			09 17	09 17			10 22				10 54
Truro	d	23p49					06b41	07 10				07 39			09 36	09 36			10 41				11 11
Redruth	d	00 02					06 54	07 23				07 50			09 49	09 49			10 54				11 24
Camborne	d	00 09					07 00	07 30				07 57			09 55	09 55			11 00				11 30
Hayle	d	00 16					07 07	07 39				08 05			10 02	10 02			11 07				11 37
St Erth	d	00 20					07 10	07 44				08 12		08 28	10 07	10 07			11 12				11 44
Penzance	a	00 38					07 23	08 00				08 19		08 40	10 19	10 19			11 24				11 58

B from 23 October
C from 11 September until 16 October
D from 11 September until 13 November
E from 20 November
b arr. 0632
c stops to pick up only, arr. 0020
e arr. 0914

For connections from Heathrow Airport, Gatwick Airport and Oxford please refer to Tables 125A, 148 and 116

London and Birmingham - Devon and Cornwall

		GW	XC	GW	GW	GW	GW	XC	GW	GW	GW	GW	XC	GW	GW	XC	XC	GW	GW	GW	GW	XC	GW
			◇■		◇■			◇■	◇■		◇■		◇■		◇■	◇■	◇■				◇■	◇■	◇■
															B								
			⊼		▭			⊼	▭		▭⊘		⊼		▭⊘	⊼	⊼				▭⊘	⊼	▭
London Paddington ■ ⊖	d				07 30				08 18		09 06				10 06						11 06		12 18
Slough ■	d																						
Reading ■	d				07 57				08 49		09 32				10 32						11 32		12 49
Theale	d								08 58														12 58
Thatcham	d								09 07														13 07
Newbury	d								09 14														13 14
Hungerford	d								09 23														13 23
Pewsey	d								09 41												12 03		13 40
Westbury	d								10 00												12 22		13 59
Castle Cary	d								10 18												12 40		14 16
Birmingham New Street ■	d		07b12					08 12					09 12			09 42	10 12					11 12	
Cardiff Central ■	d																						
Newport (South Wales)	d																						
Swindon	d				08 30																		
Bristol Parkway ■	d		08 26					09 26					10 31			10 59	11 26					12 31	
Filton Abbey Wood	d																						
Bath Spa ■	d				09 00																		
Bristol Temple Meads ■	d		08c44		09 17			09e44					10 44			11 14	11h44					12 44	
Weston-super-Mare	d															11g39							
Bridgwater	d																						
Taunton	d		09 17		09 51			10 17	10 40		10 48		11 17			12 01	12 17				13 02	13 17	14a39
Tiverton Parkway	d		09 29					10 29	10 53		11 01		11 29			12 13	12 29				13 15	13 29	
Exeter St Davids ■	a		09 43		10 17			10 46	11 10		11 18		11 43		12 10	12 27	12 43				13 32	13 43	
Exmouth	d			09 23						10 23				11 23						12 23			
Exeter Central	d			09 50			10 30			10 50				11 50						12 50			
Exeter St Davids ■	d	09 28	09 45	09 56	10 18	10 25	10 35	10 48		10 56	11 20		11 45	11 56	12 10	12 29	12 45		12 52	12 56	13 33	13 45	
Exeter St Thomas	d			09 59						10 59				11 59						12 59			
Starcross	d			10 07						11 07				12 07						13 07			
Dawlish Warren	d			10 12			10 47			11 12				12 12					13 03	13 12			
Dawlish	d			10 16			10 51			11 16				12 16		12 41			13 07	13 16			
Teignmouth	d			10 21			10 56			11 21				12 21		12 46			13 12	13 21			
Newton Abbot	a	09 48	10 03	10 30	10 38	10 45	11 03	11 07		11 29	11 39		12 03	12 29	12 31	12 52	13 03		13 19	13 29	13 52	14 03	
	d	09 49	10 05	10 31	10 39	10 47	11 04	11 08		11 30	11 39		12 05	12 36	12 31	12 53	13 05		13 20	13 30	13 54	14 05	
Torre	d			10 39		10 55				11 38				12 43						13 38			
Torquay	d			10 42		10 58	11 14			11 41				12 46		13 05				13 41			
Paignton	a			10 52		11 06	11 23			11 51				12 56		13 11				13 53			
Totnes	d	10 02	10 17		10 52			11 22			11 53		12 17				13 17		13 33		14 06	14 17	
Ivybridge	d	10 19									12 08								13 49				
Plymouth	a	10 32	10 44		11 20			11 51			12 25		12 44		13 11		13 44		14 05		14 36	14 44	
	d	10 33			11 24							12 30			13 13			13 58					
Devonport	d																						
Dockyard	d																						
Keyham	d																						
St Budeaux Ferry Road	d	10 39																					
Saltash	d	10 44										12 39						14 07					
St Germans	d	10 51										12 46						14 14					
Menheniot	d																						
Liskeard ■	d	11 03			11 47							12 58			13 37			14 26					
Bodmin Parkway	d	11 15			11 59							13 10			13 50			14 38					
Lostwithiel	d	11 20										13 15						14 43					
Par	d	11 27			12 10							13 22			14 01			14 50					
Newquay	a																						
St Austell	d	11 37			12 18							13 29			14 09			14 58					
Truro	d	11 55			12 36							13f54			14 26			15i24					
Redruth	d	12 08			12 48							14 07			14 39			15 36					
Camborne	d	12 14			12 56							14 13			14 47			15 42					
Hayle	d	12 21										14 20			14 57			15 50					
St Erth	d	12 24			13 06							14 24			15 01			15 52					
Penzance	a	12 37			13 20							14 35			15 14			16 07					

B The Cornish Riviera
b arr. 0650
c arr. 0838
e arr. 0938
f arr. 1345
g arr. 1131
h arr. 1138
i arr. 1514

For connections from Heathrow Airport, Gatwick Airport and Oxford please refer to Tables 125A, 148 and 116

London and Birmingham - Devon and Cornwall

		GW	GW	GW	XC	GW	GW	GW	XC	GW	GW	GW	GW	XC	GW	GW	GW	GW	XC	GW	XC	GW
			◇■		◇■			◇■	◇■				◇■	◇■				◇■	◇■	■	◇■	◇■
			A																			
			▭⊘		⊼			▭	⊼				▭	⊼				▭	⊼		⊼	▭
London Paddington ■ ⊖	d		12 06					13 06					14 06					15 06				16 06
Slough ■	d																					
Reading ■	d		12 32					13 32					14 32					15u32				16 32
Theale	d																					
Thatcham	d																					
Newbury	d																					
Hungerford	d																					
Pewsey	d																	16 05				
Westbury	d																	16 23				
Castle Cary	d																	16 41				
Birmingham New Street ■	d				12 12				13 12					14 12					15 12		15 42	
Cardiff Central ■	d																					
Newport (South Wales)	d																					
Swindon	d																					
Bristol Parkway ■	d				13 26				14 28					15 26					16 31		16 58	
Filton Abbey Wood	d																					
Bath Spa ■	d																					
Bristol Temple Meads ■	d				13c44				14 44					15e44					16 44		17 11	
Weston-super-Mare	d																					
Bridgwater	d																					
Taunton	d				14 17			14 48	15 18				15 48	16 17				17 03	17 18		17 43	17 49
Tiverton Parkway	d				14 29			15 01	15 30				16 01	16 29				17 16	17 31		17 55	18 02
Exeter St Davids ■	a		14 10		14 43			15 18	15 46				16 18	16 43				17 33	17 47		18 10	18 19
Exmouth	d	13 23				14 23					15 23					16 55						
Exeter Central	d	13 50				14 50					15 50				16 48	17 21						
Exeter St Davids ■	d	13 56	14 11	14 30	14 45	14 56		15 19	15 48		15 56		16 20	16 45	16 56	17 24		17 35	17 48	17 53	18 11	18 20
Exeter St Thomas	d	13 59				14 59					15 59				16 59	17 27						
Starcross	d	14 07				15 07					16 07				17 07	17 35						
Dawlish Warren	d	14b24		14 41		15 12					16 12				17 12	17f49				18 04		
Dawlish	d	14 28		14 45		15 16					16 16				17 16	17 53				18 08	18 23	
Teignmouth	d	14 33		14 50		15 21					16 21				17 21	17 58				18 13	18 28	
Newton Abbot	a	14 41	14 30	14 57	15 03	15 29		15 40	16 07		16 29		16 39	17 03	17 29	18 05		17 55	18 10	18 20	18 34	18 40
	d	14 42	14 32	14 59	15 05	15 30		15 40	16 08	16 18	16 30		16 41	17 05	17 30	18 09		17 58	18 12	18 21	18 36	18 41
Torre	d	14 50		15 07		15 38					16 38				17 38	18 17						
Torquay	d	14 53		15 10		15 41					16 41				17 41	18 20					18 47	
Paignton	a	15 01		15 18		15 51					16 51				17 51	18 29					18 54	
Totnes	d				15 17			15 54	16 22	16 31			16 53	17 17				18 10	18 25	18 34		18 54
Ivybridge	d									16 47			17 10							18 50		19 11
Plymouth	a		15 09		15 44			16 21	16 50	17 02			17 24	17 44				18 38	18 52	19 04		19 26
	d		15 11				16 03	16 28					17 28				17 52	18 42	19 00	19 07		
Devonport	d																17 55					
Dockyard	d																17x57					
Keyham	d																17x59					
St Budeaux Ferry Road	d																18 01					
Saltash	d						16 12										18 06			19 16		
St Germans	d						16 19										18 12			19 23		
Menheniot	d						16x27										18x19					
Liskeard ■	d		15 35				16 33	16 51					17 52				18 26	19 07	19 24	19 35		
Bodmin Parkway	d		15 48				16 45	17 04					18 03				18 38	19 19	19 36	19 47		
Lostwithiel	d						16 50										18 44			19 52		
Par	d		15 58				16 57						18 15				18 51	19 30	19 47	19 59		
Newquay	a																					
St Austell	d		16 06				17 05	17 19					18 22				18 58	19 38	19 55	20 06		
Truro	d		16 24				17 24	17 37					18 40				19 16	19 58	20 13	20 25		
Redruth	d		16 36				17 37	17 51					18 52				19 29	20 08	20 26	20 38		
Camborne	d		16 45				17 43	17 59					19 01				19 35	20 17	20 33	20 44		
Hayle	d						17 50	18 08									19 42					
St Erth	d		16 55				17 54	18 13				18 32	19 11				19 46	20 28	20 44	20 54		
Penzance	a		17 09				18 07	18 26				18 44	19 24				19 57	20 41	20 55	21 05		

A The Royal Duchy.
b arr. 1412
c arr. 1338
e arr. 1538
f arr. 1741

For connections from Heathrow Airport, Gatwick Airport and Oxford please refer to Tables 125A, 148 and 116

Table 135

London and Birmingham - Devon and Cornwall

Saturdays from 11 September

		GW	XC	GW	GW	GW	GW	GW	XC	GW	GW	XC	GW	GW	XC	XC	GW	XC	GW	GW
			◇1				◇1	◇1 A	◇1		◇1	◇1		◇1	◇1	◇1	◇1	◇1		◇1
London Paddington 15 ⊖	d						17 06	16 30			18 06			19 06			20 06			20 30
Slough 3	d																			
Reading 7	d						17u32	16 57			18 32			19 32			20 32			20 59
Theale	d																			
Thatcham	d																			
Newbury	d													19 49			20 46			
Hungerford	d																			
Pewsey	d						18 03							20 10			21 06			
Westbury	d						18 22							20 28			21 25			
Castle Cary	d						18 41							20 45			21 43			
Birmingham New Street 12	d		16 12						17 12			18 12			19 12	19g42		20 12		
Cardiff Central 7	d																		21 00	
Newport (South Wales)	d																		21 15	
Swindon	d							17 30												21 31
Bristol Parkway 7	d		17 26						18 31			19 29			20 31	20 58		21 25		
Filton Abbey Wood	d																		21 42	
Bath Spa 7	d							18 00												22 00
Bristol Temple Meads 10	d		17b44					18 18	18 44			19 44			20 44	21 13		21h44	21i55	22 17
Weston-super-Mare	d							18 40											22 27	22s49
Bridgwater	d																		22 46	23s07
Taunton	d		18 17				19 02	19 06	19 16		19 47	20 17		21 08	21 17	21 45	22 06	22 17	22 59	23 19
Tiverton Parkway	d		18 29				19 15	19 21	19 28			20 29		21 21	21 29	21 57	22 19	22 29	23 14	23 32
Exeter St Davids 6	a		18 43				19 32	19 37	19 42		20 14	20 43		21 38	21 43	22 12	22 36	22 44	23 33	23 49
Exmouth	d	17 55								19 38			20 08							
Exeter Central	d	18 21								20 01			20 35							
Exeter St Davids 6	d	18 26	18 46	18 56	19 16		19 34	19 38	19 44	20 07	20 15	20 45	20f56	21 38	21 46	22 13	22 37	22 46		
Exeter St Thomas	d	18 29			19 19					20 10			20 59							
Starcross	d	18 37			19 27					20 18			21 07							
Dawlish Warren	d	18 42			19 32					20e32			21 12							
Dawlish	d	18 46		19 09	19 36					20 36			21 16				22 49			
Teignmouth	d	18 51		19 14	19 41					20 41			21 21				22 55			
Newton Abbot	a	18 59	19 04	19 21	19 48		19 53	19 58	20 02	20 48	20 37	21 03	21 28	21 59	22 05	22 31	23 03	23 11		
	d	19 01	19 05	19 22	19 50		19 54	19 59	20 04	20 49	20 37	21 05	21 30	21 59	22 10	22 33	23 03	23 12		
Torre	d	19 09			19 58			20 09		20 57			21 38							
Torquay	d	19 12		19 32	20 01			20 12		21 00			21 41							
Paignton	a	19 21		19 40	20 09			20 21		21 08			21 48							
Totnes	d		19 18				20 07		20 16		20 51	21 17		22 13	22 23	22 45	23 17	23 28		
Ivybridge	d																			
Plymouth	a		19 43				20 35		20 43		21 19	21 44		22 42	22 49	23 12	23 48	23 54		
	d		19 48				20 39		20 58		21 21									
Devonport	d																			
Dockyard	d																			
Keyham	d																			
St Budeaux Ferry Road	d																			
Saltash	d						20 49													
St Germans	d						20 57													
Menheniot	d																			
Liskeard 6	d		20 11				21 08		21 24		21 45									
Bodmin Parkway	d		20 24				21 20		21 36		22 00									
Lostwithiel	d		20 29																	
Par	d		20 36				21 31		21 46		22 10									
Newquay	a																			
St Austell	d		20 43				21 42		21 54		22 18									
Truro	d		21 00				22 02		22c17		22 36									
Redruth	d		21 12				22 12		22 28		22 48									
Camborne	d		21 18						22 35		22 57									
Hayle	d		21 26								23 04									
St Erth	d		21 30			22 16	22 28		22 45		23 09									
Penzance	a		21 43			22 29	22 42		22 55		23 24									

A The Torbay Express
b arr. 1738
c arr. 2210
e arr. 2023
f arr. 2038
g arr. 1933
h arr. 2135
i arr. 2149

For connections from Heathrow Airport, Gatwick Airport and Oxford please refer to Tables 125A, 148 and 116

Table 135

London and Birmingham - Devon and Cornwall

Sundays until 11 July

		GW	XC	GW	GW	GW	GW	XC	GW	GW	GW	GW	XC	GW	GW	GW	XC	GW	GW	GW	GW	XC	GW
					◇		◇	◇1		◇1	◇1		◇1	◇		◇1	◇1		◇1			◇1	
London Paddington 15 ⊖	d									08 00	08 57					09 57			10 57				
Slough 3	d																						
Reading 7	d									08 42	09 32					10 32			11 32				
Theale	d																						
Thatcham	d																						
Newbury	d										09 48												
Hungerford	d																						
Pewsey	d															11 04							
Westbury	d										10 23												
Castle Cary	d															11 34							
Birmingham New Street 12	d																					10e28	
Cardiff Central 7	d																						
Newport (South Wales)	d																						
Swindon	d									09 18													
Bristol Parkway 7	d																					12 38	
Filton Abbey Wood	d																						
Bath Spa 7	d									09 49													
Bristol Temple Meads 10	d				07 45		08 28	09 48		10 03			10 44				11 44					12 53	
Weston-super-Mare	d				08 08		08 56																
Bridgwater	d				08 24		09 15																
Taunton	d				08 39		09 30	10 21		10 39	10 59		11 21			11 57	12 21		12 47			13 25	
Tiverton Parkway	d				08 54		09 45	10 33			11 12		11 34				12 34					13 37	
Exeter St Davids 6	a				09 12		10 04	10 47		11 05	11 29		11 48			12 26	12 48		13 14			13 55	
Exmouth	d																	12 08					
Exeter Central	d											11 20						12 36					
Exeter St Davids 6	d	09 03			09 14	09 53	10 05	10 49	10 54	11 07	11 30	11b35	11 50	12 00	12 08	12 28	12 50	12c54	13 15	13 38		13 57	14 05
Exeter St Thomas	d	09 06				09 56			10 57						12 11			12 57					14 08
Starcross	d	09 14				10 04			11 05						12 19			13 06					14 16
Dawlish Warren	d	09 19				10 09			11 10						12 24			13 11					14 20
Dawlish	d	09 23			09 30	10 13	10 18		11 14	11 20		11 48			12 28			13 15		13 51			14 24
Teignmouth	d	09 28			09 35	10 18	10 23		11 19	11 26		11 53			12 33			13 20		13 56			14 29
Newton Abbot	a	09 35			09 42	10 25	10 30	11 07	11 26	11 32	11 50	12 00	12 08	12 20	12 40	12 48	13 08	13 27	13 35	14 03		14 18	14 36
	d	09 47			09 43	10 35	10 31	11 09	11 28	11 33	11 52	12 01	12 09	12 21	12 41	12 49	13 09	13 28	13 37	14 04		14 20	14 38
Torre	d	09 55				10 43			11 36						12 49			13 36		14 13			14 46
Torquay	d	09 58				10 46			11 39			12 12			12 52			13 39		14 16			14 49
Paignton	a	10 05				10 55			11 46			12 19			12 59			13 46		14 23			14 57
Totnes	d				09 56		10 44	11 21		11 46	12 04		12 23	12 33		13 02	13 23					14 33	
Ivybridge	d				10 12																		
Plymouth	a				10 26		11 12	11 48		12 14	12 32		12 49	13 00		13 31	13 49		14 14			15 01	
	d		09 05	09 15	10 30		11 14			12 15	12 35		12 55			13 34			14 20		14 58		
Devonport	d				10 34																		
Dockyard	d																						
Keyham	d																						
St Budeaux Ferry Road	d			09 22																			
Saltash	d			09 26	10 41		11 23														15 07		
St Germans	d			09 33	10 48		11 30														15 14		
Menheniot	d				10x56		11x38																
Liskeard 6	d		09 31	09 49	11 05		11 44			12 41	12 58		13 18			13 57			14 43		15 26		
Bodmin Parkway	d		09 44	10 01	11 20		11 56			12 53	13 13		13 30			14 09			14 57		15 38		
Lostwithiel	d			10 07	11 25		12 01														15 44		
Par	d		09 57	10 14	11 32		12 08			13 05	13 24		13 40			14 20					15 51		
Newquay	a		11 10													15 25							
St Austell	d			10 21	11 40		12 16			13 12	13 31		13 47						15 12		15 58		
Truro	d			10 40	11 58		12 34			13 31	13 50		14 04						15 31		16 17		
Redruth	d			10 53	12 12		12 47			13 42	14 02		14 16						15 41		16 30		
Camborne	d			10 59	12 18		12 53			13 50	14 11		14 23						15 50		16 36		
Hayle	d			11 06	12 25		13 00														16 43		
St Erth	d			11 10	12 31		13 04			14 03	14 23		14 33						16 00		16 47		
Penzance	a			11 24	12 45		13 18			14 14	14 34		14 43						16 14		16 59		

b arr. 1123
c arr. 1239
e arr. 1021

For connections from Heathrow Airport, Gatwick Airport and Oxford please refer to Tables 125A, 148 and 116

Table 135

London and Birmingham - Devon and Cornwall

		GW	GW	XC	GW	GW	XC	GW	GW	GW	GW	XC	GW	XC	GW	GW	XC	GW	GW	GW	XC	GW	GW
		◇1	◇1	◇1		◇1	◇1		◇1		◇1	◇1		◇1		◇1	◇1		◇1		◇1		◇1
		⊏⊐	⊏⊐	⌶		⊏⊐	⌶		⊏⊐		⊏⊐	⌶		⌶		⊏⊐	⌶		⊏⊐		⌶		⊏⊐
London Paddington 15 ⊖	d	11 37	11 57			12 57			13 00		13 57					14 57			15 57				16 57
Slough 3	d																						
Reading 7	d	12 14	12 32			13 32			13 37		14 32					15 32			16 32				17 32
Theale	d																						
Thatcham	d																						
Newbury	d		12 48								14 48								16 48				
Hungerford	d																						
Pewsey	d	12 45																					
Westbury	d	13 05				14 19													17 24				
Castle Cary	d	13 22									15 35								17 41				
Birmingham New Street 12	d			12 12			13 12					14 12		14h42			15 12				16j12		
Cardiff Central 7	d																						
Newport (South Wales)	d																						
Swindon	d								14 09														
Bristol Parkway 7	d			13 25			14 25					15 26		15 58			16 25				17 25		
Filton Abbey Wood	d																						
Bath Spa 7	d								14 39														
Bristol Temple Meads 10	d			13b44			14 44		14 55			15f44		16 14			16i44				17k44		
Weston-super-Mare	d																						
Bridgwater	d																						
Taunton	d	13 44	13 53	14 17		14 55	15 17		15 29		15 55	16 17		16 46		16 51	17 17		18 06		18 21		18 49
Tiverton Parkway	d		14 07	14 29		15 08	15 29					16 28		16 58		17 04	17 29		18 19		18 33		19 01
Exeter St Davids 6	a	14 11	14 24	14 44		15 24	15 44		15 55		16 22	16 47		17 13		17 20	17 44		18 36		18 48		19 18
Exmouth	d				14 10								16 10									18 10	
Exeter Central	d				14 36								16 36									18 35	
Exeter St Davids 6	d	14 12	14 25	14 45	14c54	15 25	15 45	15 49	15 56	16 05	16 23	16 48	16g54	17 14		17 22	17 45	17 54	18 37		18 49	18l54	19 20
Exeter St Thomas	d				14 57			15 52		16 07			16 57					17 57				18 57	
Starcross	d				15 05			16 00					17 05					18 05				19 05	
Dawlish Warren	d	14 27			15 09			16e11					17 10					18 10				19 10	
Dawlish	d	14 30			15 13			16 15		16 20			17 14	17 26				18 14				19 14	
Teignmouth	d	14 37			15 18			16 20		16 25			17 19	17 31				18 19				19 19	
Newton Abbot	a	14 44	14 49	15 03	15 25	15 46	16 03	16 27	16 18	16 31	16 42	17 07	17 26	17 37		17 41	18 03	18 26	18 58		19 07	19 26	19 39
	d	14 44	14 50	15 04	15 27	15 46	16 04	16 28	16 19	16 31	16 42	17 09	17 28	17 39		17 41	18 04	18 28	18 59		19 09	19 28	19 40
Torre	d				15 35			16 36					17 36					18 36				19 36	
Torquay	d	14 56			15 38			16 39					17 39	17 50				18 39				19 39	
Paignton	a	15 05			15 46			16 46					17 46	17 58				18 46				19 46	
Totnes	d		15 03	15 17		16 00	16 17			16 47	16 58	17 22				17 56	18 17				19 21		19 53
Ivybridge	d									17 03													
Plymouth	a		15 32	15 44		16 29	16 44		16 58	17 17	17 26	17 50				18 23	18 44		19 37		19 48		20 21
	d		15 36			16 35				17 35						18 25	18 55			19 43			20 24
Devonport	d																						
Dockyard	d																						
Keyham	d																						
St Budeaux Ferry Road	d																						
Saltash	d									17 45										19 52			
St Germans	d									17 52										19 59			
Menheniot	d									18x00													
Liskeard 6	d		16 00			16 57				18 06						18 49	19 18			20 11			20 48
Bodmin Parkway	d		16 12			17 09				18 18						19 02	19 30			20 23			21 00
Lostwithiel	d									18 23										20 28			
Par	d		16 23			17 22				18 30						19 13	19 40			20 35			21 12
Newquay	a																						
St Austell	d		16 31			17 28				18 38						19 20	19 51			20 43			21 19
Truro	d		16 48			17 47				18 56						19 38	20 08			21 01			21 36
Redruth	d		17 01			17 59				19 09						19 50	20 19			21 14			21 49
Camborne	d		17 09			18 07				19 15						20 00	20 27			21 20			21 57
Hayle	d									19 22										21 28			
St Erth	d		17 20			18 20				19 25					20 05	20 14	20 37			21 31			22 10
Penzance	a		17 31			18 31				19 39					20 14	20 24	20 47			21 44			22 21

b arr. 1335
c arr. 1440
e arr. 1605
f arr. 1538
g arr. 1639
h arr. 1431
i arr. 1635
j arr. 1600
k arr. 1735
l arr. 1839

For connections from Heathrow Airport, Gatwick Airport and Oxford please refer to Tables 125A, 148 and 116

Table 135

London and Birmingham - Devon and Cornwall

		GW	XC	GW	GW	XC	GW	GW	XC	XC	GW	GW	GW	XC	GW	GW
			◇1		◇1	◇1		◇1	◇1	◇1	◇1		◇1	◇1	◇1	■
			⌶		⊏⊐	⌶		⊏⊐	⌶	⌶	⊏⊐		⊏⊐	⌶	⊏⊐	⊏⊐
London Paddington 15 ⊖	d				17 57			18 57			19 00		19 57		20 57	23 50
Slough 3	d															
Reading 7	d				18 32			19 32			19 37		20 32		21 32	00u37
Theale	d															
Thatcham	d															
Newbury	d				18 48								20 49			
Hungerford	d															
Pewsey	d				19 09								21 09			
Westbury	d				19 28								21 28			
Castle Cary	d							20 29					21 46			
Birmingham New Street 12	d		17b12			18e12			18h42	19i12				20 12		
Cardiff Central 7	d															
Newport (South Wales)	d															
Swindon	d										20 09					
Bristol Parkway 7	d		18 25			19 25			20 02	20 25				21 25		
Filton Abbey Wood	d															
Bath Spa 7	d										20 39					
Bristol Temple Meads 10	d	18 07	18c44			19f44			20 19	20j44	20 55			21 44		02k55
Weston-super-Mare	d	18 36							20 37		21 26					
Bridgwater	d	18 55														
Taunton	d	19 10	19 17		20 02	20 18		20 51	20 59	21 17	21 50		22 06	22 17	22s50	
Tiverton Parkway	d	19 25	19 29		20 16	20 30		21 04	21 12	21 29	22 03		22 19	22 29	23s03	
Exeter St Davids 6	a	19 44	19 48		20 33	20 45		21 21	21 27	21 44	22 19		22 37	22 44	23 19	04 05
Exmouth	d						20 10					21 20				
Exeter Central	d						20 36					21 47				
Exeter St Davids 6	d		19 49	19 54	20 33	20 46	20g54	21 22	21 30	21 45		21 54	22 37	22 45		04 35
Exeter St Thomas	d			19 57			20 57					21 57				
Starcross	d			20 05			21 05					22 05				
Dawlish Warren	d			20 10			21 10					22 10				
Dawlish	d			20 14			21 14	21 36	21 43			22 14				
Teignmouth	d			20 19			21 19	21 42	21 48			22 19				
Newton Abbot	a		20 07	20 26	20 54	21 04	21 26	21 48	21 54	22 03		22 26	22 58	23 04		04 55
	d		20 09	20 28	20 55	21 06	21 28	21 49	21 56	22 04		22 28	22 58	23 06		04 56
Torre	d			20 36			21 36					22 36				
Torquay	d			20 39			21 39		22 07			22 39				
Paignton	a			20 46			21 46		22 11			22 46				
Totnes	d		20 21		21 10	21 18		22 03		22 17			23 11	23 21		
Ivybridge	d															
Plymouth	a		20 48		21 37	21 45		22 31		22 46			23 41	23 59		05 35
	d		20 50		21 40											06 30
Devonport	d															
Dockyard	d															
Keyham	d															
St Budeaux Ferry Road	d															
Saltash	d															
St Germans	d															
Menheniot	d															
Liskeard 6	d		21 13		22 03											07l09
Bodmin Parkway	d		21 25		22 17											07 23
Lostwithiel	d															07 29
Par	d		21 35		22 29											07 37
Newquay	a															
St Austell	d		21 42		22 37											07 45
Truro	d		22 00		22 54											08 05
Redruth	d		22 11		23 07											08 19
Camborne	d		22 21		23 15											08 26
Hayle	d															08 37
St Erth	d		22 31		23 26											08 43
Penzance	a		22 41		23 39											08 59

b arr. 1702
c arr. 1837
e arr. 1800
f arr. 1935
g arr. 2039
h arr. 1831
i arr. 1902
j arr. 2035
k arr. 0155
l arr. 0654

For connections from Heathrow Airport, Gatwick Airport and Oxford please refer to Tables 125A, 148 and 116

Table 135

Sundays

18 July to 05 September

London and Birmingham - Devon and Cornwall

		GW	XC	GW	GW	GW	GW	XC	GW	GW	GW	GW	XC	GW	GW	GW	XC	GW	GW	GW	XC	GW	GW
					◇		◇	◇1		◇1	◇1		◇1	◇		◇1	◇1		◇1		◇1		◇1
London Paddington 15 ⊖	d									08 00	08 57					09 57			10 57				11 37
Slough 3	d																						
Reading 7	d									08 42	09 32					10 32			11 32				12 14
Theale	d																						
Thatcham	d																						
Newbury	d										09 48												
Hungerford	d																						
Pewsey	d															11 04							12 45
Westbury	d										10 23												13 05
Castle Cary	d															11 34							13 22
Birmingham New Street 12	d																				10e28		
Cardiff Central 7	d																						
Newport (South Wales)	d																						
Swindon	d									09 18													
Bristol Parkway 7	d																				12 25		
Filton Abbey Wood	d																						
Bath Spa 7	d									09 49													
Bristol Temple Meads 10	d				07 45		08 28	09 48		10 03			10 44				11 44				12f44		
Weston-super-Mare	d				08 08		08 56																
Bridgwater	d				08 24		09 15																
Taunton	d				08 39		09 30	10 21		10 39	10 59		11 21			11 57	12 21		12 47		13 16		13 44
Tiverton Parkway	d				08 54		09 45	10 33			11 12		11 34				12 34				13 28		
Exeter St Davids 6	a				09 12		10 04	10 47		11 05	11 29		11 48			12 26	12 48		13 14		13 46		14 11
Exmouth	d																	12 08					
Exeter Central	d											11 20						12 36					
Exeter St Davids 6	d	09 03			09 14	09 53	10 05	10 49	10 54	11 07	11 30	11b35	11 50	12 00	12 08	12 28	12 50	12c54	13 15	13 38	13 48	14 05	14 12
Exeter St Thomas	d	09 06				09 56			10 57						12 11			12 57				14 08	
Starcross	d	09 14				10 04			11 05						12 19			13 06				14 16	
Dawlish Warren	d	09 19				10 09			11 10						12 24			13 11				14 20	14 27
Dawlish	d	09 23			09 30	10 13	10 18		11 14	11 20		11 48			12 28			13 15		13 51		14 24	14 30
Teignmouth	d	09 28			09 35	10 18	10 23		11 19	11 26		11 53			12 33			13 20		13 56		14 29	14 37
Newton Abbot	a	09 35			09 42	10 25	10 30	11 07	11 26	11 32	11 50	12 00	12 08	12 20	12 40	12 48	13 08	13 27	13 35	14 03	14 07	14 36	14 44
	d	09 47			09 43	10 35	10 31	11 09	11 28	11 33	11 52	12 01	12 09	12 21	12 41	12 49	13 09	13 28	13 37	14 04	14 09	14 38	14 44
Torre	d	09 55				10 43			11 36						12 49			13 36		14 13		14 46	
Torquay	d	09 58				10 46			11 39			12 12			12 52			13 39		14 16		14 49	14 56
Paignton	a	10 05				10 55			11 46			12 19			12 59			13 46		14 23		14 57	15 05
Totnes	d				09 56		10 44	11 21		11 46	12 04		12 23	12 33		13 02	13 23				14 22		
Ivybridge	d				10 12																		
Plymouth	a				10 26		11 12	11 48		12 14	12 32		12 49	13 00		13 31	13 49		14 14		14 50		
	d		09 05	09 15	10 30		11 14			12 15	12 35		12 55			13 34			14 20				
Devonport	d				10 34																		
Dockyard	d																						
Keyham	d																						
St Budeaux Ferry Road	d			09 22																			
Saltash	d			09 26	10 41		11 23																
St Germans	d			09 33	10 48		11 30																
Menheniot	d				10x56		11x38																
Liskeard 6	d		09 31	09 49	11 05		11 44			12 41	12 58		13 18			13 57			14 43				
Bodmin Parkway	d		09 44	10 01	11 20		11 56			12 53	13 13		13 30			14 09			14 57				
Lostwithiel	d			10 07	11 25		12 01																
Par	d		09 57	10 14	11 32		12 08			13 05	13 24		13 40			14 20							
Newquay	a		11 10													15 25							
St Austell	d			10 21	11 40		12 16			13 12	13 31		13 47						15 12				
Truro	d			10 40	11 58		12 34			13 31	13 50		14 04						15 31				
Redruth	d			10 53	12 12		12 47			13 42	14 02		14 16						15 41				
Camborne	d			10 59	12 18		12 53			13 50	14 11		14 23						15 50				
Hayle	d			11 06	12 25		13 00																
St Erth	d			11 10	12 31		13 04			14 03	14 23		14 33						16 00				
Penzance	a			11 24	12 45		13 18			14 14	14 34		14 43						16 14				

b arr. 1123
c arr. 1239
e arr. 1021
f arr. 1237

For connections from Heathrow Airport, Gatwick Airport and Oxford please refer to Tables 125A, 148 and 116

Table 135

Sundays

18 July to 05 September

London and Birmingham - Devon and Cornwall

		GW	GW	XC	GW	GW	XC	GW	GW	GW	GW	XC	GW	XC	GW	GW	XC	GW	GW	GW	XC	GW	GW
			◇1	◇1		◇1	◇1		◇1		◇1	◇1		◇1		◇1	◇1		◇1		◇1		◇1
London Paddington 15 ⊖	d		11 57			12 57			13 00		13 57					14 57			15 57				16 57
Slough 3	d																						
Reading 7	d		12 32			13 32			13 37		14 32					15 32			16 32				17 32
Theale	d																						
Thatcham	d																						
Newbury	d		12 48								14 48								16 48				
Hungerford	d																						
Pewsey	d																						
Westbury	d					14 19													17 24				
Castle Cary	d										15 35								17 41				
Birmingham New Street 12	d			12 12			13 12					14 12		14h42			15 12				16j12		
Cardiff Central 7	d																						
Newport (South Wales)	d																						
Swindon	d								14 09														
Bristol Parkway 7	d			13 25			14 25					15 26		16 00			16 25				17 25		
Filton Abbey Wood	d																						
Bath Spa 7	d								14 39														
Bristol Temple Meads 10	d			13b44			14 44		14 55			15f44		16 14			16i44				17k44		
Weston-super-Mare	d																						
Bridgwater	d																						
Taunton	d		13 53	14 17		14 55	15 17		15 29		15 55	16 17		16 46		16 51	17 17		18 06		18 21		18 49
Tiverton Parkway	d		14 07	14 29		15 08	15 29					16 28		16 58		17 04	17 29		18 19		18 33		19 01
Exeter St Davids 6	a		14 24	14 44		15 24	15 44		15 55		16 22	16 47		17 13		17 20	17 44		18 36		18 48		19 18
Exmouth	d				14 10								16 10									18 10	
Exeter Central	d				14 36								16 36									18 35	
Exeter St Davids 6	d		14 25	14 45	14c54	15 25	15 45	15 49	15 56	16 05	16 23	16 48	16g54	17 14		17 22	17 45	17 54	18 37		18 49	18l54	19 20
Exeter St Thomas	d				14 57			15 52		16 07			16 57					17 57				18 57	
Starcross	d				15 05			16 00					17 05					18 05				19 05	
Dawlish Warren	d				15 09			16e11					17 10					18 10				19 10	
Dawlish	d				15 13			16 15		16 20			17 14	17 26				18 14				19 14	
Teignmouth	d				15 18			16 20		16 25			17 19	17 31				18 19				19 19	
Newton Abbot	a		14 49	15 03	15 25	15 46	16 03	16 27	16 18	16 31	16 42	17 07	17 26	17 37		17 41	18 03	18 26	18 58		19 07	19 26	19 39
	d		14 50	15 04	15 27	15 46	16 04	16 28	16 19	16 31	16 42	17 09	17 28	17 39		17 41	18 04	18 28	18 59		19 09	19 28	19 40
Torre	d				15 35			16 36					17 36					18 36				19 36	
Torquay	d				15 38			16 39					17 39	17 50				18 39				19 39	
Paignton	a				15 46			16 46					17 46	17 58				18 46				19 46	
Totnes	d		15 03	15 17		16 00	16 17			16 47	16 58	17 22				17 56	18 17				19 21		19 53
Ivybridge	d									17 03													
Plymouth	a		15 32	15 44		16 29	16 44		16 58	17 17	17 26	17 50				18 23	18 44		19 37		19 48		20 21
	d	14 58	15 36			16 35				17 35						18 25	18 55			19 43			20 24
Devonport	d																						
Dockyard	d																						
Keyham	d																						
St Budeaux Ferry Road	d																						
Saltash	d	15 07								17 45										19 52			
St Germans	d	15 14								17 52										19 59			
Menheniot	d									18x00													
Liskeard 6	d	15 26	16 00			16 57				18 06						18 49	19 18			20 11			20 48
Bodmin Parkway	d	15 38	16 12			17 09				18 18						19 02	19 30			20 23			21 00
Lostwithiel	d	15 44								18 23										20 28			
Par	d	15 51	16 23			17 22				18 30						19 13	19 40			20 35			21 12
Newquay	a																						
St Austell	d	15 58	16 31			17 28				18 38						19 20	19 51			20 43			21 19
Truro	d	16 17	16 48			17 47				18 56						19 38	20 08			21 01			21 36
Redruth	d	16 30	17 01			17 59				19 09						19 50	20 19			21 14			21 49
Camborne	d	16 36	17 09			18 07				19 15						20 00	20 27			21 20			21 57
Hayle	d	16 43								19 22										21 28			
St Erth	d	16 47	17 20			18 20				19 25					20 05	20 14	20 37			21 31			22 10
Penzance	a	16 59	17 31			18 31				19 39					20 14	20 24	20 47			21 44			22 21

b arr. 1335
c arr. 1440
e arr. 1605
f arr. 1538
g arr. 1639
h arr. 1431
i arr. 1635
j arr. 1600
k arr. 1735
l arr. 1839

For connections from Heathrow Airport, Gatwick Airport and Oxford please refer to Tables 125A, 148 and 116

Table 135

Sundays

18 July to 05 September

London and Birmingham - Devon and Cornwall

		GW	XC	GW	GW	XC	GW	GW	XC	XC	GW	GW	XC	GW	GW	GW
			◇1 ✕		◇1 ⊡	◇1 ✕		◇1 ⊡	◇1 ✕	◇1 ✕	◇1 ⊡		◇1 ✕	◇1 ⊡	◇1 ⊡	■ ⊡
London Paddington 15 ⊖	d				17 57			18 57			19 00			19 57	20 57	23 50
Slough 3	d															
Reading 7	d				18 32			19 32			19 37			20 32	21 32	00u37
Theale	d															
Thatcham	d															
Newbury	d				18 48									20 49		
Hungerford	d															
Pewsey	d				19 09									21 09		
Westbury	d				19 28									21 28		
Castle Cary	d							20 29						21 46		
Birmingham New Street 12	d		17b12			18e12			18h42	19i12			20 12			
Cardiff Central 7	d															
Newport (South Wales)	d															
Swindon	d										20 09					
Bristol Parkway 7	d		18 25			19 25			20 02	20 25			21 25			
Filton Abbey Wood	d															
Bath Spa 7	d										20 39					
Bristol Temple Meads 10	d	18 07	18c44			19f44			20 19	20j44	20 55		21 44			02k55
Weston-super-Mare	d	18 36							20 37		21 26					
Bridgwater	d	18 55														
Taunton	d	19 10	19 17		20 02	20 18		20 51	20 59	21 17	21 50		22 17	22 06	22s50	
Tiverton Parkway	d	19 25	19 29		20 16	20 30		21 04	21 12	21 29	22 03		22 29	22 19	23s03	
Exeter St Davids 6	a	19 44	19 48		20 33	20 45		21 21	21 27	21 44	22 19		22 44	22 37	23 19	04 05
Exmouth	d						20 10					21 20				
Exeter Central	d						20 36					21 47				
Exeter St Davids 6	d		19 49	19 54	20 33	20 46	20g54	21 22	21 30	21 45		21 54	22 45	22 37		04 35
Exeter St Thomas	d			19 57			20 57					21 57				
Starcross	d			20 05			21 05					22 05				
Dawlish Warren	d			20 10			21 10					22 10				
Dawlish	d			20 14			21 14	21 36	21 43			22 14				
Teignmouth	d			20 19			21 19	21 42	21 48			22 19				
Newton Abbot	a		20 07	20 26	20 54	21 04	21 26	21 48	21 54	22 03		22 26	23 04	22 58		04 55
	d		20 09	20 28	20 55	21 06	21 28	21 49	21 56	22 04		22 28	23 06	22 58		04 56
Torre	d			20 36			21 36					22 36				
Torquay	d			20 39			21 39		22 07			22 39				
Paignton	a			20 46			21 46		22 11			22 46				
Totnes	d		20 21		21 10	21 18		22 03		22 17			23 21	23 11		
Ivybridge	d															
Plymouth	a		20 48		21 37	21 45		22 31		22 46			23 59	23 41		05 35
	d		20 50		21 40											06 30
Devonport	d															
Dockyard	d															
Keyham	d															
St Budeaux Ferry Road	d															
Saltash	d															
St Germans	d															
Menheniot	d															
Liskeard 6	d		21 13		22 03											07l09
Bodmin Parkway	d		21 25		22 17											07 23
Lostwithiel	d															07 29
Par	d		21 35		22 29											07 37
Newquay	a															
St Austell	d		21 42		22 37											07 45
Truro	d		22 00		22 54											08 05
Redruth	d		22 11		23 07											08 19
Camborne	d		22 21		23 15											08 26
Hayle	d															08 37
St Erth	d		22 31		23 26											08 43
Penzance	a		22 41		23 39											08 59

b arr. 1702
c arr. 1837
e arr. 1800
f arr. 1935
g arr. 2039
h arr. 1831
i arr. 1902
j arr. 2035
k arr. 0155
l arr. 0654

For connections from Heathrow Airport, Gatwick Airport and Oxford please refer to Tables 125A, 148 and 116

Table 135

Sundays

12 September to 17 October

London and Birmingham - Devon and Cornwall

		GW	XC	GW	GW	GW	GW	XC	GW	GW	GW	GW	XC	GW	GW	GW	XC	GW	GW	GW	XC	GW	GW
			■	✕	◇		◇	◇1 ✕	◇1 ⊡		◇1 ⊡		◇1 ✕	◇		◇1 ⊡	◇1 ✕		◇1 ⊡		◇1 ✕		◇1 ⊡
London Paddington 15 ⊖	d								07 57		08 57					09 57			10 57				11 27
Slough 3	d																						
Reading 7	d								08 33		09 32					10 32			11 32				12 02
Theale	d																						
Thatcham	d																						
Newbury	d										09 48												
Hungerford	d																						
Pewsey	d															11 04							12 40
Westbury	d										10 23												13 05
Castle Cary	d															11 34							13 22
Birmingham New Street 12	d												09 12				10 12				11 12		
Cardiff Central 7	d																						
Newport (South Wales)	d																						
Swindon	d								09 08														
Bristol Parkway 7	d												10 25				11 29				12 25		
Filton Abbey Wood	d																						
Bath Spa 7	d								09 38														
Bristol Temple Meads 10	d				07 45		08 28	09 48	09 53				10c44				11 44				12f44		
Weston-super-Mare	d				08 08		08 56																
Bridgwater	d				08 24		09 15																
Taunton	d				08 39		09 30	10 21	10 27		10 59		11 21			11 56	12 16		12 47		13 16		13 44
Tiverton Parkway	d				08 54		09 45	10 33	10 41		11 12		11 34				12 28				13 29		13 57
Exeter St Davids 6	a				09 12		10 04	10 47	10 58		11 29		11 48			12 26	12 46		13 14		13 46		14 14
Exmouth	d																	12 08					
Exeter Central	d											11 20						12 36					
Exeter St Davids 6	d	09 03			09 14	09 53	10 05	10 49	11 00	11 05	11 30	11b35	11 50	12 00	12 08	12 28	12 48	12e54	13 15	13 38	13 48	14 05	14 15
Exeter St Thomas	d	09 06				09 56				11 08					12 11			12 57				14 08	
Starcross	d	09 14				10 04				11 16					12 19			13 06				14 16	
Dawlish Warren	d	09 19				10 09				11 21					12 24			13 11				14 20	
Dawlish	d	09 23			09 30	10 13	10 18		11 14	11 25		11 48			12 28			13 15		13 51		14 24	14 30
Teignmouth	d	09 28			09 35	10 18	10 23		11 20	11 30		11 53			12 33			13 20		13 56		14 29	14 36
Newton Abbot	a	09 35			09 42	10 25	10 30	11 07	11 27	11 37	11 50	12 00	12 08	12 20	12 40	12 48	13 09	13 27	13 35	14 03	14 07	14 36	14 44
	d	09 47			09 43	10 35	10 31	11 09	11 27	11 39	11 52	12 01	12 09	12 21	12 41	12 49	13 11	13 28	13 37	14 04	14 09	14 38	14 44
Torre	d	09 55				10 43				11 47					12 49			13 36		14 13		14 46	
Torquay	d	09 58				10 46				11 50		12 12			12 52			13 39		14 16		14 49	14 56
Paignton	a	10 05				10 55				11 57		12 19			12 59			13 46		14 23		14 57	15 05
Totnes	d				09 56		10 44	11 21	11 41		12 04		12 23	12 33		13 02	13 24				14 22		
Ivybridge	d				10 12																		
Plymouth	a				10 26		11 12	11 48	12 09		12 32		12 49	13 00		13 31	13 52		14 14		14 50		
	d		09 05	09 25	10 30		11 14		12 11		12 35		12 55						14 20				
Devonport	d				10 34																		
Dockyard	d																						
Keyham	d																						
St Budeaux Ferry Road	d																						
Saltash	d				10 41		11 23																
St Germans	d				10 48		11 30																
Menheniot	d				10x56		11x38																
Liskeard 6	d		09 30	09 49	11 05		11 44		12 35		12 58		13 18						14 43				
Bodmin Parkway	d		09 43	10 01	11 20		11 56		12 48		13 13		13 30						14 57				
Lostwithiel	d			10 07	11 25		12 01																
Par	d		09 53	10 14	11 32		12 08		12 59		13 24		13 40										
Newquay	a																						
St Austell	d		09 59	10 21	11 40		12 16		13 06		13 31		13 47						15 12				
Truro	d		10 17	10 40	11 58		12 34		13 24		13 50		14 04						15 31				
Redruth	d		10 28	10 53	12 12		12 47		13 36		14 02		14 16						15 41				
Camborne	d		10 34	10 59	12 18		12 53		13 45		14 11		14 23						15 50				
Hayle	d			11 06	12 25		13 00																
St Erth	d		10 44	11 10	12 31		13 04		13 57		14 23		14 33						16 00				
Penzance	a		10 55	11 24	12 45		13 18		14 09		14 34		14 43						16 21				

b arr. 1123
c arr. 1035
e arr. 1239
f arr. 1236

For connections from Heathrow Airport, Gatwick Airport and Oxford please refer to Tables 125A, 148 and 116

Table 135

London and Birmingham - Devon and Cornwall

		GW	GW	XC	GW	GW		XC	GW	GW	GW	GW	XC	GW	XC	GW		GW	XC	GW	GW	GW	XC	GW	GW
		◇1 ⌂	✕	◇1 ✕		◇1 ⌂		◇1 ✕		◇1 ⌂		◇1 ⌂	◇1 ✕		◇1 ✕			◇1 ⌂	◇1 ✕		◇1 ⌂		◇1 ✕		◇1 ⌂
London Paddington 15 ⊖	d	11 57				12 57				13 03		13 57						14 57			15 57				16 57
Slough 3	d																								
Reading 7	d	12 32				13 32				13 37		14 32						15 32			16 32				17 32
Theale	d																								
Thatcham	d																								
Newbury	d	12 48										14 48									16 48				
Hungerford	d																								
Pewsey	d																								
Westbury	d					14 19															17 24				
Castle Cary	d											15 35									17 41				
Birmingham New Street 12	d			12 12				13 12					14 12		14h42				15 12				16j12		
Cardiff Central 7	d																								
Newport (South Wales)	d																								
Swindon	d									14 09															
Bristol Parkway 7	d			13 25				14 25					15 26		16 00				16 25				17 25		
Filton Abbey Wood	d																								
Bath Spa 7	d									14 39															
Bristol Temple Meads 10	d			13b44				14 44		14 55			15f44		16 14				16i44				17k44		
Weston-super-Mare	d																								
Bridgwater	d																								
Taunton	d	13 53		14 17		14 55		15 17		15 29		15 55	16 17		16 46			16 51	17 17		18 06		18 21		18 49
Tiverton Parkway	d			14 29		15 08		15 29					16 28		16 58			17 04	17 29		18 19		18 33		19 01
Exeter St Davids 6	a	14 20		14 44		15 24		15 44		15 55		16 22	16 47		17 13			17 20	17 44		18 36		18 48		19 18
Exmouth	d				14 10									16 10										18 10	
Exeter Central	d				14 36									16 36										18 35	
Exeter St Davids 6	d	14 23		14 45	14c54	15 25		15 45	15 49	15 56	16 05	16 23	16 48	16g54	17 14			17 22	17 45	17 54	18 37		18 49	18l54	19 20
Exeter St Thomas	d				14 57				15 52		16 07			16 57						17 57				18 57	
Starcross	d				15 05				16 00					17 05						18 05				19 05	
Dawlish Warren	d				15 09				16e11					17 10						18 10				19 10	
Dawlish	d				15 13				16 15		16 20			17 14	17 26					18 14				19 14	
Teignmouth	d				15 18				16 20		16 25			17 19	17 31					18 19				19 19	
Newton Abbot	a	14 46		15 03	15 25	15 46		16 03	16 27	16 18	16 31	16 42	17 07	17 26	17 37			17 41	18 03	18 26	18 58		19 07	19 26	19 39
	d	14 48		15 04	15 27	15 46		16 04	16 28	16 19	16 31	16 42	17 09	17 28	17 39			17 41	18 04	18 28	18 59		19 09	19 28	19 40
Torre	d				15 35				16 36					17 36						18 36				19 36	
Torquay	d				15 38				16 39					17 39	17 50					18 39				19 39	
Paignton	a				15 46				16 46					17 46	17 58					18 46				19 46	
Totnes	d	15 00		15 17		16 00		16 17			16 47	16 58	17 22					17 56	18 17				19 21		19 53
Ivybridge	d										17 03														
Plymouth	a	15 29		15 44		16 29		16 44		16 58	17 17	17 26	17 50					18 23	18 44		19 37		19 48		20 21
	d		15 36			16 35					17 35							18 25	18 55			19 43			20 24
Devonport	d																								
Dockyard	d																								
Keyham	d																								
St Budeaux Ferry Road	d																								
Saltash	d		15 45								17 45											19 52			
St Germans	d		15 52								17 52											19 59			
Menheniot	d										18x00														
Liskeard 6	d		16 04			16 57					18 06							18 49	19 18			20 11			20 48
Bodmin Parkway	d		16 17			17 09					18 18							19 02	19 30			20 23			21 00
Lostwithiel	d		16 23								18 23											20 28			
Par	d		16 30			17 22					18 30							19 13	19 40			20 35			21 12
Newquay	a																								
St Austell	d		16 37			17 28					18 38							19 20	19 51			20 43			21 19
Truro	d		16 56			17 47					18 56							19 38	20 08			21 01			21 36
Redruth	d		17 09			17 59					19 09							19 50	20 19			21 14			21 49
Camborne	d		17 15			18 07					19 15							20 00	20 27			21 20			21 57
Hayle	d		17 22								19 22											21 28			
St Erth	d		17 26			18 20					19 25					20 05		20 14	20 37			21 31			22 10
Penzance	a		17 38			18 31					19 39					20 14		20 24	20 47			21 44			22 21

b arr. 1335
c arr. 1440
e arr. 1605
f arr. 1538

g arr. 1639
h arr. 1431
i arr. 1635
j arr. 1600

k arr. 1735
l arr. 1839

For connections from Heathrow Airport, Gatwick Airport and Oxford please refer to Tables 125A, 148 and 116

Table 135

London and Birmingham - Devon and Cornwall

		GW		XC	GW	GW	XC	GW	GW	XC	XC	GW		GW	GW	XC	GW	GW
				◇1 ✕		◇1 ⌂	◇1 ✕		◇1 ⌂	◇1 ✕	◇1 ✕	◇1 ⌂			◇1 ⌂	◇1 ✕	◇1 ⌂	4 🛏 ⌂
London Paddington 15 ⊖	d					17 57			18 57			19 03			19 57		20 57	23 50
Slough 3	d																	
Reading 7	d					18 32			19 32			19 37			20 32		21 32	00u37
Theale	d																	
Thatcham	d																	
Newbury	d					18 48									20 49			
Hungerford	d																	
Pewsey	d					19 09									21 09			
Westbury	d					19 28									21 28			
Castle Cary	d								20 29						21 46			
Birmingham New Street 12	d			17b12			18e12			18h42	19i12					20 12		
Cardiff Central 7	d																	
Newport (South Wales)	d																	
Swindon	d											20 09						
Bristol Parkway 7	d			18 25			19 25			20 02	20 25					21 25		
Filton Abbey Wood	d																	
Bath Spa 7	d											20 39						
Bristol Temple Meads 10	d	18 07		18c44			19f44			20 19	20j44	20 55				21 44		02k55
Weston-super-Mare	d	18 36								20 37		21 26						
Bridgwater	d	18 55																
Taunton	d	19 10		19 17		20 02	20 18		20 51	20 59	21 17	21 50			22 06	22 17	22s50	
Tiverton Parkway	d	19 25		19 29		20 16	20 30		21 04	21 12	21 29	22 03			22 19	22 29	23s03	
Exeter St Davids 6	a	19 44		19 48		20 33	20 45		21 21	21 26	21 44	22 19			22 37	22 44	23 19	04 05
Exmouth	d							20 10						21 20				
Exeter Central	d							20 36						21 47				
Exeter St Davids 6	d			19 49	19 54	20 33	20 46	20g54	21 22	21 30	21 45			21 54	22 37	22 45		04 35
Exeter St Thomas	d				19 57			20 57						21 57				
Starcross	d				20 05			21 05						22 05				
Dawlish Warren	d				20 10			21 10						22 10				
Dawlish	d				20 14			21 14	21 36	21 43				22 14				
Teignmouth	d				20 19			21 19	21 42	21 48				22 19				
Newton Abbot	a			20 07	20 26	20 54	21 04	21 26	21 48	21 54	22 03			22 26	22 58	23 04		04 55
	d			20 09	20 28	20 55	21 06	21 28	21 49	21 56	22 04			22 28	22 58	23 06		04 56
Torre	d				20 36			21 36						22 36				
Torquay	d				20 39			21 39						22 39				
Paignton	a				20 46			21 46						22 46				
Totnes	d			20 21		21 10	21 18		22 03		22 17				23 11	23 21		
Ivybridge	d																	
Plymouth	a			20 48		21 37	21 45		22 31	22 38	22 46				23 41	23 59		05 35
	d			20 50		21 40												06 30
Devonport	d																	
Dockyard	d																	
Keyham	d																	
St Budeaux Ferry Road	d																	
Saltash	d																	
St Germans	d																	
Menheniot	d																	
Liskeard 6	d			21 13		22 03												07l09
Bodmin Parkway	d			21 25		22 17												07 23
Lostwithiel	d																	07 29
Par	d			21 35		22 29												07 37
Newquay	a																	
St Austell	d			21 42		22 37												07 45
Truro	d			22 00		22 54												08 05
Redruth	d			22 11		23 07												08 19
Camborne	d			22 21		23 15												08 26
Hayle	d																	08 37
St Erth	d			22 31		23 26												08 43
Penzance	a			22 41		23 39												08 59

b arr. 1702
c arr. 1837
e arr. 1800
f arr. 1935

g arr. 2039
h arr. 1831
i arr. 1902
j arr. 2035

k arr. 0155
l arr. 0654

For connections from Heathrow Airport, Gatwick Airport and Oxford please refer to Tables 125A, 148 and 116

Table 135

Sundays
from 24 October

London and Birmingham - Devon and Cornwall

		GW	XC	GW	GW	GW	GW	XC	GW	GW	GW	GW	XC	GW	GW	GW	XC	GW	GW	GW	XC	GW	GW
			■		◇		◇	◇■	◇■		◇■		◇■	◇		◇■	◇■		◇■		◇■		◇■
London Paddington ⊖	d								07 57		08 57					09 57			10 57				11 27
Slough	d																						
Reading	d								08 33		09 32					10 32			11 32				12 02
Theale	d																						
Thatcham	d																						
Newbury	d										09 48												
Hungerford	d																						
Pewsey	d															11 04							12 40
Westbury	d										10 23												13 05
Castle Cary	d															11 34							13 22
Birmingham New Street	d																09 12				10 12		
Cardiff Central	d																						
Newport (South Wales)	d																10c52				11g58		
Swindon	d								09 08														
Bristol Parkway	d																11e29				12h29		
Filton Abbey Wood	d																						
Bath Spa	d								09 38														
Bristol Temple Meads	d				07 45		08 28	09 48	09 53				10 44				11 44				12 44		
Weston-super-Mare	d				08 08		08 56																
Bridgwater	d				08 24		09 15																
Taunton	d				08 39		09 30	10 21	10 27		10 59		11 21			11 56	12 17		12 47		13 16		13 44
Tiverton Parkway	d				08 54		09 45	10 33	10 41		11 12		11 34				12 29				13 28		13 57
Exeter St Davids	a				09 12		10 04	10 47	10 58		11 29		11 48			12 26	12 44		13 14		13 46		14 14
Exmouth	d																	12 08					
Exeter Central	d											11 20						12 36					
Exeter St Davids	d	09 03			09 14	09 53	10 05	10 49	11 00	11 05	11 30	11b35	11 50	12 00	12 08	12 28	12 45	12f54	13 15	13 38	13 48	14 05	14 15
Exeter St Thomas	d	09 06				09 56				11 08					12 11			12 57				14 08	
Starcross	d	09 14				10 04				11 16					12 19			13 06				14 16	
Dawlish Warren	d	09 19				10 09				11 21					12 24			13 11				14 20	
Dawlish	d	09 23			09 30	10 13	10 18		11 14	11 25		11 48			12 28			13 15		13 51		14 24	14 30
Teignmouth	d	09 28			09 35	10 18	10 23		11 20	11 30		11 53			12 33			13 20		13 56		14 29	14 36
Newton Abbot	a	09 35			09 42	10 25	10 30	11 07	11 27	11 37	11 50	12 00	12 08	12 20	12 40	12 48	13 03	13 27	13 35	14 03	14 07	14 36	14 44
	d	09 47			09 43	10 35	10 31	11 09	11 27	11 39	11 52	12 01	12 09	12 21	12 41	12 49	13 05	13 28	13 37	14 04	14 09	14 38	14 44
Torre	d	09 55				10 43				11 47					12 49			13 36		14 13		14 46	
Torquay	d	09 58				10 46				11 50		12 12			12 52			13 39		14 16		14 49	14 56
Paignton	a	10 05				10 55				11 57		12 19			12 59			13 46		14 23		14 57	15 05
Totnes	d				09 56		10 44	11 21	11 41		12 04		12 23	12 33		13 02	13 18				14 22		
Ivybridge	d				10 12																		
Plymouth	a				10 26		11 12	11 48	12 09		12 32		12 49	13 00		13 31	13 45		14 14		14 50		
	d		09 05	09 25	10 30		11 14		12 11		12 35		12 55						14 20				
Devonport	d				10 34																		
Dockyard	d																						
Keyham	d																						
St Budeaux Ferry Road	d																						
Saltash	d				10 41		11 23																
St Germans	d				10 48		11 30																
Menheniot	d				10x56		11x38																
Liskeard	d		09 30	09 49	11 05		11 44		12 35		12 58		13 18						14 43				
Bodmin Parkway	d		09 43	10 01	11 20		11 56		12 48		13 13		13 30						14 57				
Lostwithiel	d			10 07	11 25		12 01																
Par	d		09 53	10 14	11 32		12 08		12 59		13 24		13 40										
Newquay	a																						
St Austell	d		09 59	10 21	11 40		12 16		13 06		13 31		13 47						15 12				
Truro	d		10 17	10 40	11 58		12 34		13 24		13 50		14 04						15 31				
Redruth	d		10 28	10 53	12 12		12 47		13 36		14 02		14 16						15 41				
Camborne	d		10 34	10 59	12 18		12 53		13 45		14 11		14 23						15 50				
Hayle	d			11 06	12 25		13 00																
St Erth	d		10 44	11 10	12 31		13 04		13 57		14 23		14 33						16 00				
Penzance	a		10 55	11 24	12 45		13 18		14 09		14 34		14 43						16 21				

b arr. 1123
c arr. 1045
e arr. 1115
f arr. 1239
g arr. 1151
h arr. 1219

For connections from Heathrow Airport, Gatwick Airport and Oxford please refer to Tables 125A, 148 and 116

Table 135

Sundays
from 24 October

London and Birmingham - Devon and Cornwall

		GW	GW	GW	GW	XC	GW	GW	GW	GW	XC	GW	XC	GW	GW	XC	GW	GW	GW	XC	GW	GW	GW
		◇■			◇■	◇■		◇■		◇■	◇■		◇■		◇■	◇■		◇■		◇■		◇■	
London Paddington ⊖	d	11 57			12 57			13 03		13 57					14 57			15 57				16 57	
Slough	d																						
Reading	d	12 32			13 32			13 37		14 32					15 32			16 32				17 32	
Theale	d																						
Thatcham	d																						
Newbury	d	12 48								14 48								16 48					
Hungerford	d																						
Pewsey	d																						
Westbury	d				14 19													17 24					
Castle Cary	d									15 35								17 41					
Birmingham New Street	d					12 12					14 12		14g42			15 12				16i12			
Cardiff Central	d																						
Newport (South Wales)	d					13 58																	
Swindon	d							14 09															
Bristol Parkway	d					14 30					15 26		16 00			16 25				17 25			
Filton Abbey Wood	d																						
Bath Spa	d							14 39															
Bristol Temple Meads	d					14 44		14 55			15e44		16 14			16h44				17j44			18 07
Weston-super-Mare	d																						18 36
Bridgwater	d																						18 55
Taunton	d	13 53			14 55	15 17		15 29		15 55	16 17		16 46		16 51	17 17		18 06		18 21		18 49	19 10
Tiverton Parkway	d				15 08	15 29					16 28		16 58		17 04	17 29		18 19		18 33		19 01	19 25
Exeter St Davids	a	14 20			15 24	15 44		15 55		16 22	16 47		17 13		17 20	17 44		18 36		18 48		19 18	19 44
Exmouth	d		14 10									16 10									18 10		
Exeter Central	d		14 36									16 36									18 35		
Exeter St Davids	d	14 23	14b54		15 25	15 45	15 49	15 56	16 05	16 23	16 48	16f54	17 14		17 22	17 45	17 54	18 37		18 49	18k54	19 20	
Exeter St Thomas	d		14 57				15 52		16 07			16 57					17 57				18 57		
Starcross	d		15 05				16 00					17 05					18 05				19 05		
Dawlish Warren	d		15 09				16c11					17 10					18 10				19 10		
Dawlish	d		15 13				16 15		16 20			17 14	17 26				18 14				19 14		
Teignmouth	d		15 18				16 20		16 25			17 19	17 31				18 19				19 19		
Newton Abbot	a	14 46	15 25		15 46	16 03	16 27	16 18	16 31	16 42	17 07	17 26	17 37		17 41	18 03	18 26	18 58		19 07	19 26	19 39	
	d	14 48	15 27		15 46	16 04	16 28	16 19	16 31	16 42	17 09	17 28	17 39		17 41	18 04	18 28	18 59		19 09	19 28	19 40	
Torre	d		15 35				16 36					17 36					18 36				19 36		
Torquay	d		15 38				16 39					17 39	17 50				18 39				19 39		
Paignton	a		15 46				16 46					17 46	17 58				18 46				19 46		
Totnes	d	15 00			16 00	16 17			16 47	16 58	17 22				17 56	18 17				19 21		19 53	
Ivybridge	d								17 03														
Plymouth	a	15 29			16 29	16 44		16 58	17 17	17 26	17 50				18 23	18 44		19 37		19 48		20 21	
	d			15 36	16 35				17 35						18 25	18 55			19 43			20 24	
Devonport	d																						
Dockyard	d																						
Keyham	d																						
St Budeaux Ferry Road	d																						
Saltash	d			15 45					17 45										19 52				
St Germans	d			15 52					17 52										19 59				
Menheniot	d								18x00														
Liskeard	d			16 04	16 57				18 06						18 49	19 18			20 11			20 48	
Bodmin Parkway	d			16 17	17 09				18 18						19 02	19 30			20 23			21 00	
Lostwithiel	d			16 23					18 23										20 28				
Par	d			16 30	17 22				18 30						19 13	19 40			20 35			21 12	
Newquay	a																						
St Austell	d			16 37	17 28				18 38						19 20	19 51			20 43			21 19	
Truro	d			16 56	17 47				18 56						19 38	20 08			21 01			21 36	
Redruth	d			17 09	17 59				19 09						19 50	20 19			21 14			21 49	
Camborne	d			17 15	18 07				19 15						20 00	20 27			21 20			21 57	
Hayle	d			17 22					19 22										21 28				
St Erth	d			17 26	18 20				19 25					20 05	20 14	20 37			21 31			22 10	
Penzance	a			17 38	18 31				19 39					20 14	20 24	20 47			21 44			22 21	

b arr. 1440
c arr. 1605
e arr. 1538
f arr. 1639
g arr. 1431
h arr. 1635
i arr. 1600
j arr. 1735
k arr. 1839

For connections from Heathrow Airport, Gatwick Airport and Oxford please refer to Tables 125A, 148 and 116

Table 135

Sundays from 24 October

London and Birmingham - Devon and Cornwall

		XC	GW	GW	XC	GW	GW	XC	XC	GW	GW	GW	XC	GW	GW
		◇1		◇1	◇1		◇1	◇1	◇1	◇1		◇1	◇1	◇1	1
London Paddington 15 ⊖	d			17 57			18 57			19 03		19 57		20 57	23 50
Slough 3	d														
Reading 7	d			18 32			19 32			19 37		20 32		21 32	00u37
Theale	d														
Thatcham	d														
Newbury	d			18 48								20 49			
Hungerford	d														
Pewsey	d			19 09								21 09			
Westbury	d			19 28								21 28			
Castle Cary	d						20 29					21 46			
Birmingham New Street 12	d	17b12			18e12			18h42	19i12				20 12		
Cardiff Central 7	d														
Newport (South Wales)	d														
Swindon	d									20 09					
Bristol Parkway 7	d	18 25			19 25			20 02	20 25				21 25		
Filton Abbey Wood	d														
Bath Spa 7	d									20 39					
Bristol Temple Meads 10	d	18c44			19f44			20 19	20j44	20 55			21 44		02k55
Weston-super-Mare	d							20 37		21 26					
Bridgwater	d														
Taunton	d	19 17		20 02	20 18		20 51	20 59	21 17	21 50		22 06	22 17	22s50	
Tiverton Parkway	d	19 29		20 16	20 30		21 04	21 12	21 29	22 03		22 19	22 29	23s03	
Exeter St Davids 6	a	19 48		20 33	20 45		21 21	21 26	21 44	22 19		22 37	22 44	23 19	04 05
Exmouth	d					20 10					21 20				
Exeter Central	d					20 36					21 47				
Exeter St Davids 6	d	19 49	19 54	20 33	20 46	20g54	21 22	21 30	21 45		21 54	22 37	22 45		04 35
Exeter St Thomas	d		19 57			20 57					21 57				
Starcross	d		20 05			21 05					22 05				
Dawlish Warren	d		20 10			21 10					22 10				
Dawlish	d		20 14			21 14	21 36	21 43			22 14				
Teignmouth	d		20 19			21 19	21 42	21 48			22 19				
Newton Abbot	a	20 07	20 26	20 54	21 04	21 26	21 48	21 54	22 03		22 26	22 58	23 04		04 55
	d	20 09	20 28	20 55	21 06	21 28	21 49	21 56	22 04		22 28	22 58	23 06		04 56
Torre	d		20 36			21 36					22 36				
Torquay	d		20 39			21 39					22 39				
Paignton	a		20 46			21 46					22 46				
Totnes	d	20 21		21 10	21 18		22 03		22 17			23 11	23 21		
Ivybridge	d														
Plymouth	a	20 48		21 37	21 45		22 31	22 38	22 46			23 41	23 59		05 35
	d	20 50		21 40											06 30
Devonport	d														
Dockyard	d														
Keyham	d														
St Budeaux Ferry Road	d														
Saltash	d														
St Germans	d														
Menheniot	d														
Liskeard 6	d	21 13		22 03											07l09
Bodmin Parkway	d	21 25		22 17											07 23
Lostwithiel	d														07 29
Par	d	21 35		22 29											07 37
Newquay	a														
St Austell	d	21 42		22 37											07 45
Truro	d	22 00		22 54											08 05
Redruth	d	22 11		23 07											08 19
Camborne	d	22 21		23 15											08 26
Hayle	d														08 37
St Erth	d	22 31		23 26											08 43
Penzance	a	22 41		23 39											08 59

b arr. 1702
c arr. 1837
e arr. 1800
f arr. 1935
g arr. 2039
h arr. 1831
i arr. 1902
j arr. 2035
k arr. 0155
l arr. 0654

For connections from Heathrow Airport, Gatwick Airport and Oxford please refer to Tables 125A, 148 and 116

Table 135

Mondays to Fridays

Cornwall and Devon - Birmingham and London

		XC MX	GW MO	GW MX	GW MO	GW MX	XC MX	GW	GW	GW	GW	XC	GW	GW	GW	GW	GW	GW	XC	XC	GW	GW	GW
		◇1	◇1		1	1	◇1	◇1	◇1	◇1		◇1	◇1	◇1	◇1	◇1			◇1	◇1	◇1		
Penzance	d				21p15	21p45	22p08														05 05	05 21	
St Erth	d				21p25	21p55	22p16																
Hayle	d						22p20															05 31	
Camborne	d				21p38	22p07	22p30															05 40	
Redruth	d				21p45	22p14	22p36														05 25		
Truro	d				22p00	22p27	22p48														05 38	05a56	
St Austell	d				22p18	22p45	23p04														05 55		
Newquay	d																						
Par	d					22p53	23p12																
Lostwithiel	d						23p19																
Bodmin Parkway	d				22p35	23p05	23p26														06 11		
Liskeard 6	d				22p50	23p20	23p39														06 23		
Menheniot	d																						
St Germans	d																						
Saltash	d																						
St Budeaux Ferry Road	d																						
Keyham	d																						
Dockyard	d																						
Devonport	d																						
Plymouth	a				23p15	23p46	00 03														06 49		
	d		19p55		23p20	23p51						05 20		05 30	05 40	05 53			06 25		06 55		
Ivybridge	d																						
Totnes	d				23p48	00 19						05 45		05 57					06 50				
Paignton	d	20p12		23p41													06 09	06 34		07 01			07 09
Torquay	d	20p18		23p46													06 14	06 39		07 07			07 14
Torre	d			23p49													06 17	06 42					07 17
Newton Abbot	a	20p28	20p31	23p57	23p59	00 31						05 56		06 08	06 16	06 28	06 25	06 50	07 01	07 17	07 29		07 24
	d	20p29	20p32	23p58	00 01	00 32						06 03		06 10	06 17	06 30	06 33	06 52	07 03	07 18	07 31		07 34
Teignmouth	d			00 05											06 25		06 40	06 59		07 25			07 41
Dawlish	d			00 10										06 20			06 45	07 04		07 30			07 46
Dawlish Warren	d			00 15													06 50	07c15					07 51
Starcross	d			00 19													06 54	07 19					07 55
Exeter St Thomas	d			00 28													07 02	07 28					08 05
Exeter St Davids 6	a	20p48	20p53	00 34	00 36	00 54						06 21		06 33	06 41	06 50	07 08	07 33	07 21	07 42	07 51		08 10
Exeter Central	a																07 14	07 39					08 16
Exmouth	a																07 43	08 18					
Exeter St Davids 6	d	20p50	20p55		01 27	01 00				05 46	06 00	06 23	06 30	06 35	06 43	06 51			07 23	07 44	07 52		
Tiverton Parkway	d	21p03	21p10							06 02	06 18	06 37		06 50	06 58				07 37	07 57			
Taunton	d	21p18	21p23			01 30				06 17	06 35	06 51	06 54	07 05	07 13	07 17			07 51	08 12	08 18		
Bridgwater	a										06 47		07 05		07 22								
Weston-super-Mare	a										07 06		07 24		07 41					08 31			
Bristol Temple Meads 10	a	21p51	22p00		02 38						07 43	07 26	07 58		08 25				08 27	08 55			
Bath Spa 7	a		22p18										08 11		08 41								
Filton Abbey Wood	a										07 58												
Bristol Parkway 7	a	22p08									08 05	07 38							08 38	09 08			
Swindon	a		22p46			03 15							08 40		09 10								
Newport (South Wales)	a																						
Cardiff Central 7	a																						
Birmingham New Street 12	a	00 10										08 56							09 56	10 26			
Castle Cary	d									06 38				07 27									
Westbury	d							06 08	06 18	07 05				07b51									
Pewsey	d							06 25	06 35	07 22				08 08									
Hungerford	a							06 38	06 53	07 35													
Newbury	a							06 49	07 08	07 46				08 29									
Thatcham	a							06 56	07 15														
Theale	a							07 06	07 25														
Reading 7	a		23p27		04s17	04s02		07 19	07 37	08 06			09 13	08 50	09 44	08 32					09 32		
Slough 3	a																						
London Paddington 15 ⊖	a		00 13		05 06	05 43		07 53	08 09	08 38			09 44	09 21	10 14	09 00					10 02		

b arr. 0745
c arr. 0708

For connections to Oxford, Gatwick Airport and Heathrow Airport please refer to Tables 116, 148 and 125A

Table 135

Mondays to Fridays

Cornwall and Devon - Birmingham and London

		XC	GW	GW	GW	GW	XC	GW	GW	GW	GW	XC	XC	GW	GW	GW	XC	GW	GW	GW	GW	XC	XC	GW
		◇1	◇1	◇1			◇1			◇1		◇1	◇1	◇1 C	◇1 D		◇1	■ 1			◇1	◇1	◇1	
		⊥	⊏	⊏Ø			⊥			⊏Ø		⊥	⊥	⊏	⊏		⊥	⊏			⊏	⊥	⊥	
Penzance	d			05 41		06 00	06 28	06 37		06 48				07 38	07 38		08 28	08 44	08 57				09 40	
St Erth	d					06 08	06 36	06 45		06 58				07 47	07 47		08 36	08 54	09 05				09 48	
Hayle	d					06 11								07 51	07 51								09 52	
Camborne	d			05 59		06 22	06 46			07 09				08 01	08 01		08 46	09 06					10 01	
Redruth	d			06 06		06 28	06 52			07 16				08 08	08 08		08 52	09 13					10 08	
Truro	d			06 18		06 40	07 04			07 28				08 21	08 21		09 04	09 25					10 19	
St Austell	d			06 36		06 57	07 20			07 46				08 38	08 38		09 20	09 43					10 35	
Newquay	d																							
Par	d			06 43		07 04	07 28			07 54				08 46	08 46		09 28	09 50					10 43	
Lostwithiel	d			06 50		07 11				08 01													10 50	
Bodmin Parkway	d			06 57		07 17	07 39			08 07				08 57	08 57		09 39	10 02					10 57	
Liskeard ■	d			07 11		07 30	07 51			08 21				09 11	09 11		09 51	10 15					11 09	
Menheniot	d					07 34																		
St Germans	d			07 22		07 42				08 32				09 22	09 22									
Saltash	d			07 29		07 49				08 39				09 29	09 29									
St Budeaux Ferry Road	d					07 53																		
Keyham	d					07 55																		
Dockyard	d					07 57																		
Devonport	d					07 59																		
Plymouth	a			07 40		08 05	08 20			08 51				09 41	09 41		10 15	10 40					11 39	
	d	07 25		07 48		08 07	08 25			08 55		09 25		09 44	09 44		10 25	10 43				11 25	11 50	
Ivybridge	d					08 22								09 59	09 59									
Totnes	d	07 50		08 15		08 36	08 50			09 22		09 50		10 14	10 14		10 50					11 50	12 15	
Paignton	d		07 40		08 23						09 13		10 06			10 18				11 23				12 13
Torquay	d		07 46		08 28						09 18		10 12			10 23				11 28				12 18
Torre	d		07 50		08 31						09 21					10 26				11 31				12 21
Newton Abbot	a	08 01	07 58	08 26	08 39	08 48	09 01			09 33	09 29	10 01	10 22	10 26	10 26	10 33	11 01			11 39		12 01	12 26	12 30
	d	08 03	08 06	08 28	08 41	08 50	09 03			09 35	09 38	10 03	10 23	10 27	10 27	10 35	11 03			11 41		12 03	12 28	12 31
Teignmouth	d		08 13		08 48	08 57					09 45		10 30	10 35		10 42				11 48				12 38
Dawlish	d		08 19		08 53	09 02					09 50		10 35	10 41		10 47				11 53				12 43
Dawlish Warren	d				08 58						09 54					10 52				11 58				12b54
Starcross	d		08 25		09 02						09 58					10 56				12 02				12 58
Exeter St Thomas	d		08 34		09 11						10 08					11 05				12 11				13 07
Exeter St Davids ■	a	08 21	08 39	08 48	09 15	09 21	09 22			09 55	10 14	10 21	10 47	10 54	10 54	11 11	11 21	11 37		12 16		12 21	12 46	13 13
Exeter Central	a				09 21						10 21					11 21				12 21				13 21
Exmouth	a				09 50						10 50					11 50				12 50				13 50
Exeter St Davids ■	d	08 23	08 40	08 50			09 24		09 33	09 57		10 23	10 49	10 56	10 56		11 23	11 39			11 55	12 23	12 48	
Tiverton Parkway	d	08 37		09 05			09 38		09 50	10 12		10 37	11 02	11 11	11 11		11 37				12 09	12 37	13 02	
Taunton	d	08 51	09 05	09 20			09 52		10 07	10 27		10 51	11 17	11 26	11 26		11 51				12 24	12 51	13 16	
Bridgwater	a								10 19															
Weston-super-Mare	a		09 28						10 38															
Bristol Temple Meads ■	a	09 27	09 58				10 26		11 13			11 24	11 53	11 59	11 59		12 24					13 24	13 56	
Bath Spa ■	a		10 12											12 13	12 13									
Filton Abbey Wood	a								11 30															
Bristol Parkway ■	a	09 38					10 38					11 38	12 08				12 38					13 38	14 08	
Swindon	a		10 40											12 41	12 41									
Newport (South Wales)	a								11 59															
Cardiff Central ■	a								12 18															
Birmingham New Street ■	a	10 56					11 58					12 56	13 26				13 56					14 56	15 26	
Castle Cary	d			09 41																	12 45			
Westbury	d			10 00						11 03											13 05			
Pewsey	d			10 17																	13 21			
Hungerford	a																				13 39			
Newbury	a																				13 49			
Thatcham	a																				13 56			
Theale	a																				14 05			
Reading ■	a		11 08	10 50						11 50				13 09	13 09			13 14			14 15			
Slough ■	a																							
London Paddington ■ ⊖	a		11 38	11 24						12 23				13 38	13 38			13 43			14 44			

C until 3 September

D from 6 September

b arr. 1248

For connections to Oxford, Gatwick Airport and Heathrow Airport please refer to Tables 116, 148 and 125A

Table 135

Mondays to Fridays

Cornwall and Devon - Birmingham and London

		GW	GW	XC	GW	GW	GW	GW	XC	XC	GW	GW	GW	GW	XC	GW	GW	GW	GW	XC	GW	GW	XC
		■ 1	B	◇1		◇1 E	◇1 B		◇1	◇1	◇		◇1		◇1		◇1		◇1	◇1		E	◇1
		✕⊏		⊥		✕⊏	✕⊏		⊥	⊥			⊏		⊥		⊏		⊏	⊥			⊥
Penzance	d	10 00	10 46			10 48					11 41	12 54											
St Erth	d	10 10	10 54			10 57					11 50	13 02											
Hayle	d		10 57			11 01					11 53	13 05											
Camborne	d	10 21	11 07			11 11					12 03	13 15											
Redruth	d	10 28	11 13			11 18					12 09	13 21											
Truro	d	10 41	11 25			11 31					12 22	13 33											
St Austell	d	10 59	11 42			11 48					12 39	13 50											
Newquay	d																						
Par	d	11 07	11 50			11 56					12 45	13 57											
Lostwithiel	d		11 56								12 53	14 04											
Bodmin Parkway	d	11 18	12 02			12 07					12 59	14 10											
Liskeard ■	d	11 31	12 15			12 20					13 12	14 23										16 43	
Menheniot	d										13x16											16x48	
St Germans	d		12 26			12 32					13 24	14 34										16 55	
Saltash	d		12 34			12 39					13 31	14 41										17 04	
St Budeaux Ferry Road	d																					17 08	
Keyham	d																					17x10	
Dockyard	d																					17x12	
Devonport	d																					17 14	
Plymouth	a	11 56	12 46			12 51					13 41	14 51										17 18	
	d	12 00		12 23		12 55	12 55		13 23		13 43	14 54			14 25		15 00	15 08		15 23			
Ivybridge	d	12 15									13 59							15 23					
Totnes	d	12 29		12 49		13 22	13 22		13 49		14 13				14 50		15 27	15 37		15 49			
Paignton	d				12 47			13 13		14 01			14 15	14 22		15 13					16 13		
Torquay	d				12 52			13 18		14 07			14 21	14 27		15 18					16 18		
Torre	d				12 55			13 21						14 30		15 21					16 21		
Newton Abbot	a	12 41		13 01	13 05	13 33	13 33	13 30	14 01	14 17	14 27		14 31	14 38	15 01	15 29	15 38	15 52		16 01	16 29		
	d	12 42		13 03	13 05	13 35	13 35	13 41	14 03	14 18			14 33	14 40	15 03	15 31	15 40			16 03	16 31		
Teignmouth	d				13 13			13 48		14 25			14 40	14 47		15 38					16 38		
Dawlish	d				13 19			13 53		14 30			14 46	14 52		15 43					16 43		
Dawlish Warren	d							13 58						14 57		15b54					16c54		
Starcross	d							14 02						15 01		15 58					16 58		
Exeter St Thomas	d							14 11						15 10		16 07					17 07		
Exeter St Davids ■	a	13 02		13 23	13 33	13 55	13 55	14 16	14 23	14 42			14 59	15 15	15 21	16 13	16 00			16 23	17 13		
Exeter Central	a							14 21						15 21		16 21					17 21		
Exmouth	a							14 50						15 50		16 50					17 51		
Exeter St Davids ■	d	13 04		13 25	13 34	13 57	13 57		14 25	14 44			15 00		15 23		16 00			16 25			16 53
Tiverton Parkway	d	13 19		13 39	13 53				14 39	14 57			15 15		15 37		16 16			16 39			17 07
Taunton	d	13 34		13 54	14 11	14 23	14 23		14 54	15 12			15 30		15 51		16 30		15 23	16 54			17 21
Bridgwater	a				14 45																		
Weston-super-Mare	a				14 50					15 37													
Bristol Temple Meads ■	a			14 27	15 17				15 27	15 57					16 27					17 27			17 54
Bath Spa ■	a																						
Filton Abbey Wood	a				15 30																		
Bristol Parkway ■	a			14 38					15 38	16 08					16 38					17 38			18 08
Swindon	a																						
Newport (South Wales)	a				16 06																		
Cardiff Central ■	a				16 29																		
Birmingham New Street ■	a			15 56					16 58	17 26					17 56					18 55			19 26
Castle Cary	d					14 44	14 44						15 51										
Westbury	d					15 03	15 03												16 06				
Pewsey	d																		16 25				
Hungerford	a																		16 39				
Newbury	a																		16 49				
Thatcham	a																		16 56				
Theale	a																		17 05				
Reading ■	a	14 50				15 50	15 50						16 50				17 50		17 15				
Slough ■	a																						
London Paddington ■ ⊖	a	15 24				16 22	16 22						17 24				18 21		17 54				

B until 2 July, from 6 September

E from 5 July until 3 September

b arr. 1547

c arr. 1647

For connections to Oxford, Gatwick Airport and Heathrow Airport please refer to Tables 116, 148 and 125A

Table 135

Mondays to Fridays

Cornwall and Devon - Birmingham and London

		GW ◇1	XC ◇1	GW	GW	GW ◇1 A	GW ◇1 C	GW	XC ◇1	GW	GW	GW	GW ◇1	GW	XC ◇1	GW	GW FX ◇	GW FO ◇	GW ◇1	GW	GW FX ◇1	GW FO ◇1	GW FX ◇1
Penzance	d	14 00		14 49									16 00				16 44	16 44				17 39	17 39
St Erth	d	14 10		14 57									16 10				16 52	16 52				17 48	17 48
Hayle	d			15 01													16 56	16 56				17 52	17 52
Camborne	d	14 21		15 10									16 21				17 05	17 05				18 02	18 02
Redruth	d	14 28		15 16									16 29				17 11	17 11				18 10	18 10
Truro	d	14 40		15 27									16 41				17 24	17 24				18 23	18 23
St Austell	d	14 58		15 44									16 59				17 41	17 41				18 39	18 39
Newquay	d					15 00																	
Par	d	15 05		15 52		16 00							17 07				17 48	17 48				18 48	18 48
Lostwithiel	d			15 58		16 09							17 14				17 55	17 55					
Bodmin Parkway	d	15 17		16 04		16 15							17 21				18 01	18 01				18 59	18 59
Liskeard 6	d	15 31		16 17		16 28				17 49			17 34				18 14	18 14				19 12	19 12
Menheniot	d			16 21																			
St Germans	d			16 30						18 00							18 25	18 25					
Saltash	d			16 37						18 07							18 32	18 32					
St Budeaux Ferry Road	d			16 41						18 12													
Keyham	d			16 42																			
Dockyard	d			16 45																			
Devonport	d			16 47																			
Plymouth	a	15 56		16 52		16 53				18 19			17 58				18 42	18 42				19 38	19 38
	d	16 00	16 25			16 57	16 57		17 23	18 23		17 46	18 00		18 25		18 44	18 43				19 42	19 42
Ivybridge	d					17 12	17 12					18 01					18 59	18 59					
Totnes	d	16 27	16 50			17 27	17 27		17 49			18 15	18 30		18 50		19 13	19 13				20 09	20 09
Paignton	d				16 55			17 25			17 52			18 35		18 52				19 32			
Torquay	d				17 00			17 30			17 57			18 40		18 57				19 37			
Torre	d				17 03			17 33			18 00			18 43						19 40			
Newton Abbot	a	16 39	17 01		17 11	17 38	17 38	17 41	18 01		18 08	18 27	18 42	18 50	19 01	19 07	19 25	19 25		19 48		20 20	20 20
	d	16 40	17 03		17 13	17 40	17 40	17 43	18 03		18 10	18 28	18 43	18 53	19 03	19 09	19 26	19 26		19 50		20 22	20 22
Teignmouth	d				17 20			17 50			18 17	18 35		19 00		19 16				19 57			
Dawlish	d				17 25			17 55			18 22	18 40		19 05		19 21				20 02			
Dawlish Warren	d				17 30			18 00			18 27	18 44		19b16		19 26				20 07			
Starcross	d				17 34			18 04			18 31			19 20						20 11			
Exeter St Thomas	d				17 43			18 13			18 40			19 29						20 20			
Exeter St Davids 6	a	17 00	17 21		17 50	18 00	18 00	18 18	18 23		18 46	18 56	19 03	19 33	19 21	19 40	19 48	19 48		20 26		20 42	20 42
Exeter Central	a				17 55			18 23			18 53									20 33			
Exmouth	a				18 25			18 52			19 23									21 01			
Exeter St Davids 6	d	17 02	17 23			18 01	18 01		18 25				19 05		19 23			19 48			19 54	20 44	20 44
Tiverton Parkway	d	17 17	17 37			18 16	18 16		18 39				19 20		19 37			20 05			20 09	20 59	20 59
Taunton	d	17 31	17 51			18 30	18 30		18 54				19 35		19 51			20a21			20 24	21 14	21 14
Bridgwater	a																						
Weston-super-Mare	a																						
Bristol Temple Meads 10	a		18 24						19 27						20 25							21 47	21 47
Bath Spa 7	a																					22 01	22 01
Filton Abbey Wood	a																						
Bristol Parkway 7	a		18 38						19 38						20 38								
Swindon	a																						
Newport (South Wales)	a																					22 33	22 33
Cardiff Central 7	a																						
Birmingham New Street 12	a		19 56						20 52						22 09								
Castle Cary	d					18 53	18 53														20 45		
Westbury	d					19 11	19 11												19 17		21 04		
Pewsey	d																		19 34		21 21		
Hungerford	a																		19 51				
Newbury	a					19 45	19 45												20 06		21 42		
Thatcham	a																		20 12				
Theale	a																		20 21				
Reading 7	a	18 49				20 06	20 06						20 50						20 32		21 59	23 06	23 06
Slough 3	a																						
London Paddington 15 ⊖	a	19 24				20 39	20 39						21 21						21 07		22 30	23 42	23 50

A from 5 July until 3 September

C until 2 July, from 6 September

b arr. 1909

For connections to Oxford, Gatwick Airport and Heathrow Airport please refer to Tables 116, 148 and 125A

Table 135

Mondays to Fridays

Cornwall and Devon - Birmingham and London

		GW	XC ◇1	GW FX	GW FO 1	GW FO ◇1	GW	GW B	GW C	GW 1	GW	GW D	GW	GW	GW FX	GW FO	XC ◇1
Penzance	d	19 13		20 16	20 16										21 45	21 45	22 08
St Erth	d	19 21		20 26	20 26										21 55	21 55	22 16
Hayle	d	19 24		20 30	20 30												22 20
Camborne	d	19 34		20 40	20 40										22 07	22 07	22 30
Redruth	d	19 40		20 47	20 47										22 14	22 14	22 36
Truro	d	19 52		21 00	21 00										22 27	22 27	22 48
St Austell	d	20 09		21 17	21 17										22 45	22 45	23 04
Newquay	d																
Par	d	20 16		21 25	21 25										22 53	22 53	23 12
Lostwithiel	d	20 23		21 32	21 32												23 19
Bodmin Parkway	d	20 29		21 38	21 38										23 05	23 05	23 26
Liskeard 6	d	20 43		21 51	21 51										23 20	23 20	23 39
Menheniot	d	20 47															
St Germans	d	20 56		22 02	22 02												
Saltash	d	21 03		22 09	22 09												
St Budeaux Ferry Road	d	21 07															
Keyham	d	21 09															
Dockyard	d	21 11															
Devonport	d	21 13															
Plymouth	a	21 18		22 21	22 21										23 46	23 46	00 03
	d										21 25				23 51	23 51	
Ivybridge	d										21 40						
Totnes	d										21 54				00 19	00 19	
Paignton	d		20 12				20 32			21 31			22 30	23 41			
Torquay	d		20 18				20 37			21 37			22 35	23 46			
Torre	d						20 40			21 41			22 38	23 49			
Newton Abbot	a		20 28				20 48			21 52	22 06		22 46	23 57	00 31	00 31	
	d		20 29				20 50				22 06		22 48	23 58	00 32	00 32	
Teignmouth	d						20 57				22 13		22 55	00 05			
Dawlish	d						21 02				22 18		23 00	00 10			
Dawlish Warren	d						21 07				22 23		23 05	00 15			
Starcross	d						21 11				22 27		23 09	00 19			
Exeter St Thomas	d						21 20				22 36		23 18	00 28			
Exeter St Davids 6	a		20 48				21 28				22 40		23 22	00 34	00 54	00 54	
Exeter Central	a						21 33										
Exmouth	a						22 01										
Exeter St Davids 6	d		20 50					21 11	21 11			21 45			01 00	01 00	
Tiverton Parkway	d		21 03					21 28	21 28			22 02					
Taunton	d		21 18			20 26		21 45	21 45			22 19			01 30	01 30	
Bridgwater	a							21 56	21 56			22 30					
Weston-super-Mare	a							22 15	22 15			22 49					
Bristol Temple Meads 10	a		21 51					22 53	22 57			23 31					
Bath Spa 7	a																
Filton Abbey Wood	a																
Bristol Parkway 7	a		22 08														
Swindon	a														03 15	03 15	
Newport (South Wales)	a																
Cardiff Central 7	a																
Birmingham New Street 12	a		00 10														
Castle Cary	d					20 45											
Westbury	d					21 04											
Pewsey	d					21 21											
Hungerford	a																
Newbury	a					21 42											
Thatcham	a																
Theale	a																
Reading 7	a					21 59									04s02	04s00	
Slough 3	a																
London Paddington 15 ⊖	a					22 30									05 43	05 43	

A from 5 July until 3 September

B until 3 September

C from 6 September until 15 October

D from 18 October

For connections to Oxford, Gatwick Airport and Heathrow Airport please refer to Tables 116, 148 and 125A

Table 135

Saturdays until 04 September

Cornwall and Devon - Birmingham and London

		XC	GW	GW	XC	GW	GW	XC	GW	GW	GW	XC	GW	XC	GW	GW	XC	GW	GW	GW	XC	GW	XC
		◇1		■ 🛏 🍴	◇1			◇1 🛒	◇1 🍴			◇1 🛒	◇1 🍴	◇1 🛒		◇1 🍴⊘	◇1 🛒	◇1 🍴⊘			◇1 🛒		◇1 A 🛒
Penzance	d			21p45	22p08	05 20															06 30	06 37	
St Erth	d			21p55	22p16																06 38	06 45	
Hayle	d				22p20																06 41		
Camborne	d			22p07	22p30	05 37															06 51		
Redruth	d			22p14	22p36	05 43															06 57		
Truro	d			22p27	22p48	05a54															07 09		
St Austell	d			22p45	23p04																07 25		
Newquay	d																						
Par	d			22p53	23p12																07 32		
Lostwithiel	d				23p19																07 39		
Bodmin Parkway	d			23p05	23p26																07 46		
Liskeard 6	d			23p20	23p39																07 58		
Menheniot	d																						
St Germans	d																						
Saltash	d																						
St Budeaux Ferry Road	d																						
Keyham	d																						
Dockyard	d																						
Devonport	d																						
Plymouth	a			23p46	00 03																08 22		
	d			23p51				05 25	05 40			06 25				06 55	07 25	07 47		08 06	08 25		08 40
Ivybridge	d																			08 21			
Totnes	d			00 19				05 50	06 07			06 50					07 50	08 14		08 35	08 50		09 05
Paignton	d	20p12	23p41							06 13	06 34			07 00	07 08				08 06				
Torquay	d	20p18	23p46							06 18	06 39			07 06	07 13				08 11				
Torre	d		23p49							06 21	06 42				07 16				08 14				
Newton Abbot	a	20p28	23p57	00 31				06 01	06 18	06 29	06 50	07 01		07 16	07 24	07 30	08 01	08 26	08 22	08 47	09 01		09 16
	d	20p29	23p58	00 32				06 03	06 20	06 31	06 52	07 03		07 18		07 31	08 03	08 27	08 34	08 48	09 03		09 18
Teignmouth	d		00 05							06 38	06 59			07 25					08 41	08 55			
Dawlish	d		00 10							06 43	07 04			07 30					08 46	09 00			
Dawlish Warren	d		00 15							06 48	07b15								08 51				
Starcross	d		00 19							06 52	07 19								08 55				
Exeter St Thomas	d		00 28							07 01	07 28								09 04				
Exeter St Davids 6	a	20p48	00 34	00 54				06 21	06 40	07 06	07 33	07 21		07 46		07 51	08 21	08 47	09 09	09 16	09 21		09 36
Exeter Central	a									07 14	07 39								09 21				
Exmouth	a									07 43	08 20								09 50				
Exeter St Davids 6	d	20p50		01 00			06 00	06 23	06 41			07 23	07 28	07 48		07 53	08 23	08 49			09 23		09 39
Tiverton Parkway	d	21p03					06 18	06 37	06 56			07 37	07 43				08 37	09 04			09 37		09 52
Taunton	d	21p18		01 30			06 35	06 51	07 11			07 51	07 58	08 12		08 19	08 51	09 19			09 51		10 07
Bridgwater	a						06 47						08 08										
Weston-super-Mare	a						07 06						08 26										10 32
Bristol Temple Meads 10	a	21p51					07 43	07 25				08 24	08 57	08 49			09 26				10 26		10 52
Bath Spa 7	a												09 11										
Filton Abbey Wood	a						07 58																
Bristol Parkway 7	a	22p08					08 05	07 38				08 38		09 08			09 38				10 38		11 08
Swindon	a			03 15									09 39										
Newport (South Wales)	a																						
Cardiff Central 7	a																						
Birmingham New Street 12	a	00 10						08 56				09 56		10 26			10 56				11 56		12 26
Castle Cary	d								07 33									09 40					
Westbury	d								07 56									09 59					
Pewsey	d								08 13									10 16					
Hungerford	a																						
Newbury	a								08 33														
Thatcham	a																						
Theale	a																						
Reading 7	a			04s00					08 52				10 08			09 35		10 51					
Slough 3	a																						
London Paddington 15 ⊖	a			05 43					09 21				10 38			10 08		11 24					

b arr. 0708

For connections to Oxford, Gatwick Airport and Heathrow Airport please refer to Tables 116, 148 and 125A

Table 135

Saturdays until 04 September

Cornwall and Devon - Birmingham and London

		GW	GW	GW	GW	XC	GW	XC	GW	XC	GW	GW	GW	GW	XC	GW	GW	GW	XC	GW	GW	GW	GW
			■ 1 🍴	◇1 🍴		◇1 🛒	■ 1 🍴	◇1 🛒		◇1 🛒	■ 1 B 🍴				◇1 🛒		■ 1 🍴		◇1 🛒			◇1 🍴	■ 1 🍴⊘
Penzance	d		06 50				07 18			08 25	08 39	08 57					09 55						10 59
St Erth	d		07 01				07 30			08 33	08 51	09 05					10 07						11 11
Hayle	d						07 34				08 55						10 11						11 15
Camborne	d		07 12				07 44			08 43	09 05						10 21						11 25
Redruth	d		07 19				07 51			08 50	09 12						10 28						11 32
Truro	d		07 31				08 05			09 02	09 26						10 42						11 46
St Austell	d		07 49				08 22			09 19	09 43						10 59						12 03
Newquay	d														09 27								
Par	d		07 56				08 30			09 26	09 51				10 29		11 07			11 32			
Lostwithiel	d		08 03				08 37													11 39			
Bodmin Parkway	d		08 10				08 43			09 37	10 02				10 42		11 19			11 45			12 20
Liskeard 6	d		08 23				08 56			09 50	10 15				10 55		11 33			11 58			12 33
Menheniot	d																			12x02			
St Germans	d						09 07													12 11			
Saltash	d						09 16													12 18			
St Budeaux Ferry Road	d																						
Keyham	d																						
Dockyard	d																						
Devonport	d																						
Plymouth	a		08 48				09 26			10 18	10 39				11 20		11 59			12 29			12 58
	d		08 52			09 25	09 33			10 25	10 44				11 23		12 00		12 23	12 32			13 00
Ivybridge	d						09 48										12 15			12 47			
Totnes	d		09 19			09 50	10 02			10 50					11 49		12 30		12 49	13 01			13 28
Paignton	d	09 04		09 20	09 30			10 06	10 23				10 56	11 13		12 13		12 35			12 58	13 07	
Torquay	d	09 09		09 27	09 35			10 13	10 28				11 01	11 18		12 18		12 40			13 03	13 15	
Torre	d	09 12			09 38				10 31				11 04	11 21		12 21					13 06		
Newton Abbot	a	09 20	09 30	09 37	09 47	10 01	10 14	10 23	10 38	11 01			11 12	11 29	12 01	12 30	12 41	12 50	13 01	13 13	13 14	13 25	13 40
	d	09 22	09 32	09 39	09 48	10 03	10 15	10 24	10 41	11 03			11 23	11 41	12 03	12 32	12 43	12 52	13 03	13 14	13 21	13 26	13 42
Teignmouth	d	09 29		09 48	09 56			10 33	10 48				11 30	11 48		12 39		12 59			13 28	13 35	
Dawlish	d	09 34		09 55	10 01			10 39	10 53				11 35	11 53		12 44		13 04			13 33	13 43	
Dawlish Warren	d	09b50		10 01	10 06				10 58				11 40	11 58		12c55		13e16			13 38	13f55	
Starcross	d	09 54							11 02				11 44	12 02		12 59					13 42		
Exeter St Thomas	d	10 03							11 12				11 53	12 11		13 08					13 51		
Exeter St Davids 6	a	10 10	09 52	10 13	10 17	10 21	10 35	10 51	11 15	11 21	11 37		11 57	12 16	12 23	13 13	13 03	13 28	13 23	13 35	14 00	14 08	14 01
Exeter Central	a	10 21							11 21					12 21		13 21					14 21		
Exmouth	a	10 50							11 50					12 50		13 50					14 50		
Exeter St Davids 6	d		09 54	10 15		10 23	10 38	10 53		11 24	11 40				12 25		13 05		13 25			14 11	14 04
Tiverton Parkway	d		10 09	10 30		10 37		11 07		11 37					12 39		13 20		13 39				
Taunton	d		10 24	10 45		10 51	11 03	11 21		11 52					12 54		13 35		13 54			14g44	14 30
Bridgwater	a																						
Weston-super-Mare	a																						
Bristol Temple Meads 10	a			11 20		11 26		11 56		12 25					13 27				14 27				
Bath Spa 7	a			11 41																			
Filton Abbey Wood	a																						
Bristol Parkway 7	a					11 38		12 08		12 38					13 38				14 38				
Swindon	a			12 09																			
Newport (South Wales)	a																						
Cardiff Central 7	a																						
Birmingham New Street 12	a					12 56		13 26		13 56					14 56				15 54				
Castle Cary	d						11 24															15 08	
Westbury	d		11 02				11 45															15 28	
Pewsey	d						12 01															15 45	
Hungerford	a																						
Newbury	a																					16 05	
Thatcham	a																						
Theale	a																						
Reading 7	a		11 51	12 48			12 41				13 17						14 52					16 27	15 51
Slough 3	a																						
London Paddington 15 ⊖	a		12 23	13 22			13 14				13 54						15 23					17 06	16 21

B The Cornish Riveira
b arr. 0938
c arr. 1248
e arr. 1308
f arr. 1347
g arr. 1435

For connections to Oxford, Gatwick Airport and Heathrow Airport please refer to Tables 116, 148 and 125A

Table 135

Cornwall and Devon - Birmingham and London

		XC	XC	GW	GW	GW	GW	XC	GW	GW	XC	GW	GW	GW	GW	GW	XC	GW	GW	XC	GW	GW
		◇1	◇1	1			◇1	◇1		1	◇1				◇1		◇1	◇1		◇1		
							B								C							
Penzance	d			11 58	13 00										14 00	14 49						
St Erth	d			12 10	13 08										14 11	14 57						
Hayle	d			12 14	13 11											15 01						
Camborne	d			12 24	13 21										14 22	15 10						
Redruth	d			12 31	13 27										14 29	15 16						
Truro	d			12 45	13 39										14 41	15 28						
St Austell	d			13 02	13 55										14 59	15 45						
Newquay	d									13 14										15 24		
Par	d				14b26					14 16					15 06	15 53				16 28		
Lostwithiel	d				14 32											15 59						
Bodmin Parkway	d			13 19	14 38										15 18	16 05				16 40		
Liskeard 6	d			13 32	14 51										15 34	16 18				16 53		
Menheniot	d															16x22						
St Germans	d				15 02											16 31						
Saltash	d				15 09											16 38						
St Budeaux Ferry Road	d																					
Keyham	d																					
Dockyard	d																					
Devonport	d				15 16																	
Plymouth	a			13 57	15 21					15 03					15 57	16 48				17 18		
	d	13 25		14 00				14 25		15 05	15 25		15 32		16 01		16 25			17 23		17 38
Ivybridge	d												15 47									17 53
Totnes	d	13 50						14 50			15 50		16 01		16 28		16 50			17 49		18 07
Paignton	d		13 47			14 13	14 30		15 13			15 43		16 13				17 03	17 13		17 52	
Torquay	d		13 54			14 18	14 37		15 18			15 48		16 18				17 11	17 18		17 57	
Torre	d					14 21			15 21					16 21					17 21		18 00	
Newton Abbot	a	14 01	14 04	14 35		14 29	14 48	15 01	15 29	15 42	16 01	15 58	16 13	16 29	16 40		17 01	17 21	17 29	18 01	18 08	18 19
	d	14 03	14 06	14 37		14 40	14 50	15 03	15 31	15 44	16 03	16 09		16 31	16 41		17 03	17 22	17 41	18 03	18 10	18 19
Teignmouth	d		14 15			14 48	14 58		15 39			16 16		16 38				17 30	17 49		18 17	18 26
Dawlish	d		14 22			14 53	15 04		15 44			16 21		16 43				17 37	17 54		18 22	18 31
Dawlish Warren	d					14 57	15c17		15e56					16f55				17 42	17 59		18 27	18g47
Starcross	d					15 01			16 01					16 59					18 04		18 31	
Exeter St Thomas	d					15 11			16 10					17 08					18 13		18 40	
Exeter St Davids 6	a	14 21	14 35	14 57		15 15	15 28	15 21	16 14	16 04	16 21	16 34		17 15	17 01		17 21	17 54	18 18	18 23	18 46	18 59
Exeter Central	a					15 21			16 21			16 44		17 21					18 23		18 53	
Exmouth	a					15 50			16 52					17 51					18 52		19 23	
Exeter St Davids 6	d	14 24	14 38	14 59			15 32	15 23		16 06	16 23				17 03		17 23	18 02		18 25		
Tiverton Parkway	d	14 37		15 14				15 37		16 21	16 37				17 17		17 37	18 17		18 39		
Taunton	d	14 52	15 03	15 29			15 57	15 51		16 36	16 51				17 32		17 51	18 32		18 54		
Bridgwater	a																					
Weston-super-Mare	a		15 24																			
Bristol Temple Meads 10	a	15 25	15 50					16 25			17 25						18 27			19 27		
Bath Spa 7	a																					
Filton Abbey Wood	a																					
Bristol Parkway 7	a	15 38	16 08					16 38			17 38						18 38			19 38		
Swindon	a																					
Newport (South Wales)	a																					
Cardiff Central 7	a																					
Birmingham New Street 12	a	16 56	17 26					17 56			18 56						19 56			20 50		
Castle Cary	d						16 19											18 53				
Westbury	d						16 38											19 12				
Pewsey	d						16 53															
Hungerford	a																					
Newbury	a																	19 48				
Thatcham	a																					
Theale	a																					
Reading 7	a			16 50			17 35			17 51					18 49			20 08				
Slough 3	a																					
London Paddington 15 ⊖	a			17 21			18 08			18 23					19 22			20 39				

B The Torbay Express
C The Royal Duchy"
b arr. 1402
c arr. 1509
e arr. 1548
f arr. 1647
g arr. 1835

For connections to Oxford, Gatwick Airport and Heathrow Airport please refer to Tables 116, 148 and 125A

Table 135

Cornwall and Devon - Birmingham and London

		XC	GW	XC	GW	GW	GW	GW	GW	GW	GW	GW	GW	GW	GW	GW	XC	GW	GW	XC	GW
		◇1	◇1	◇1					◇1		◇1						◇			◇1	
Penzance	d		15 51	16 25	16 45						17 39	18 50				19 06				21 32	
St Erth	d		16 02	16 36	16 54						17 49	18 58				19 14				21 42	
Hayle	d				16 58						17 53					19 17					
Camborne	d		16 14	16 47	17 08						18 04					19 27				21 54	
Redruth	d		16 21	16 54	17 15						18 11					19 33				22 01	
Truro	d		16 33	17 06	17 29						18 24					19 45				22 13	
St Austell	d		16 51	17 24	17 45						18 41					20 02				22 31	
Newquay	d								17 18								19 58		21 20		
Par	d		16 58		17 52				18 22		18 49		18 59			20 09	20 56		22 06	22 38	
Lostwithiel	d		17 05		17 58								19 06			20 16		2215	22 15		
Bodmin Parkway	d		17 12	17 40	18 05				18 34		19 00		19 12			20 22	21 09		22 21	22 50	
Liskeard 6	d		17 25	17 53	18 20				18 47		19 13		19 25			20 35	21 22	21 53	22 34	23 03	
Menheniot	d															20x39			22 38		
St Germans	d				18 33								19 36			20 48			22 46		
Saltash	d				18 40								19 43			20 56			22 53		
St Budeaux Ferry Road	d															21 00			22 59		
Keyham	d															21x02			23x01		
Dockyard	d															21x04			23x03		
Devonport	d															21 06			23x05		
Plymouth	a		17 50	18 18	18 51				19 14		19 38		19 55			21 10	21 47	22 18	23 11	23 28	
	d		17 54	18 23			18 42		19 16		19 42					21 15					
Ivybridge	d						18 59									21 30					
Totnes	d		18 21	18 49			19 13				20 09					21 44					
Paignton	d	18 10				18 53		19 21		19 50				20 13	21 13						21 53
Torquay	d	18 17				18 58		19 26		19 55				20 18	21 18						21 58
Torre	d					19 01		19 29						20 21	21 21						22 01
Newton Abbot	a	18 27	18 32	19 01		19 10	19 25	19 38	19 53	20 05	20 20			20 29	21 29	21 56					22 09
	d	18 28	18 34	19 03		19 12	19 26	19 40	19 54	20 07	20 22			20 31	21 31	21 56					22 11
Teignmouth	d					19 19	19 33	19 47		20 14				20 38	21 38	22 03					22 18
Dawlish	d					19 24	19 39	19 52		20 19				20 43	21 43	22 08					22 23
Dawlish Warren	d					19 29		20b06		20 24				20 48	21 48	22 13					22 28
Starcross	d					19 33		20 10						20 52	21 52	22 17					22 32
Exeter St Thomas	d					19 42		20 20						21 01	22 01	22 26					22 41
Exeter St Davids 6	a	18 48	18 54	19 23		19 45	19 52	20 25	20 13	20 36	20 42			21 05	22 05	22 30					22 45
Exeter Central	a							20 33													
Exmouth	a							21 01													
Exeter St Davids 6	d	18 50	18 56	19 25					20 15		20 44										
Tiverton Parkway	d	19 03	19 11								20 59										
Taunton	d	19 18	19 26	19 49					20 42		21 14										
Bridgwater	a																				
Weston-super-Mare	a																				
Bristol Temple Meads 10	a	19 55		20 23							21 47										
Bath Spa 7	a										22 01										
Filton Abbey Wood	a																				
Bristol Parkway 7	a	20 08		20 38																	
Swindon	a										22 29										
Newport (South Wales)	a																				
Cardiff Central 7	a																				
Birmingham New Street 12	a	21 38		22 11																	
Castle Cary	d		19 47																		
Westbury	d		20 06																		
Pewsey	d		20 23																		
Hungerford	a																				
Newbury	a																				
Thatcham	a																				
Theale	a																				
Reading 7	a		20 58						21 58		23 04										
Slough 3	a																				
London Paddington 15 ⊖	a		21 32						22 26		23 38										

b arr. 1956

For connections to Oxford, Gatwick Airport and Heathrow Airport please refer to Tables 116, 148 and 125A

Table 135

Saturdays from 11 September

Cornwall and Devon - Birmingham and London

		XC	GW	GW	XC	GW	GW	XC	GW	GW	GW	XC	GW	XC	GW	GW	GW	XC	GW	GW	GW	XC	GW
		◇1		■ 🛏 ☕	◇1			◇1 ✠	◇1 ☕			◇1 ✠	◇1 ☕	◇1 ✠		◇1 ☕⊘	◇1 C ☕	◇1 ✠	◇1 ☕⊘			◇1 ✠	
Penzance	d			21p45	22p08	05 20																06 30	06 37
St Erth	d			21p55	22p16																	06 38	06 45
Hayle	d				22p20																	06 41	
Camborne	d			22p07	22p30	05 37																06 51	
Redruth	d			22p14	22p36	05 43																06 57	
Truro	d			22p27	22p48	05a54																07 09	
St Austell	d			22p45	23p04																	07 25	
Newquay	d																						
Par	d			22p53	23p12																	07 32	
Lostwithiel	d				23p19																	07 39	
Bodmin Parkway	d			23p05	23p26																	07 46	
Liskeard 6	d			23p20	23p39																	07 58	
Menheniot	d																						
St Germans	d																						
Saltash	d																						
St Budeaux Ferry Road	d																						
Keyham	d																						
Dockyard	d																						
Devonport	d																						
Plymouth	a			23p46	00 03																	08 22	
	d			23p51				05 25	05 40			06 25				06 55		07 25	07 47		08 06	08 25	
Ivybridge	d																				08 21		
Totnes	d			00 19				05 50	06 07			06 50						07 50	08 14		08 35	08 50	
Paignton	d	20p12	23p41							06 13	06 34			07 00	07 08		07 20			08 06			
Torquay	d	20p18	23p46							06 18	06 39			07 06	07 13		07 26			08 11			
Torre	d		23p49							06 21	06 42				07 16		07 30			08 14			
Newton Abbot	a	20p28	23p57	00 31				06 01	06 18	06 29	06 50	07 01		07 16	07 24	07 30	07 39	08 01	08 26	08 22	08 47	09 01	
	d	20p29	23p58	00 32				06 03	06 20	06 31	06 52	07 03		07 18		07 31	07 40	08 03	08 27	08 34	08 48	09 03	
Teignmouth	d		00 05							06 38	06 59			07 25			07 48			08 41	08 55		
Dawlish	d		00 10							06 43	07 04			07 30			07 54			08 46	09 00		
Dawlish Warren	d		00 15							06 48	07b15									08 51			
Starcross	d		00 19							06 52	07 19									08 55			
Exeter St Thomas	d		00 28							07 01	07 28									09 04			
Exeter St Davids 6	a	20p48	00 34	00 54				06 21	06 40	07 06	07 33	07 21		07 46		07 51	08 06	08 21	08 47	09 09	09 16	09 21	
Exeter Central	a									07 14	07 39									09 21			
Exmouth	a									07 43	08 20									09 50			
Exeter St Davids 6	d	20p50		01 00			06 00	06 23	06 41			07 23	07 28	07 48		07 53	08 08	08 23	08 49			09 23	
Tiverton Parkway	d	21p03					06 18	06 37	06 56			07 37	07 43				08 23	08 37	09 04			09 37	
Taunton	d	21p18		01 30			06 35	06 51	07 11			07 51	07 58	08 12		08 19	08 38	08 51	09 19			09 51	
Bridgwater	a						06 47						08 08										
Weston-super-Mare	a						07 06						08 26				08 58						
Bristol Temple Meads 10	a	21p51					07 43	07 25				08 24	08 57	08 49			09 23	09 26				10 26	
Bath Spa 7	a												09 11				09 41						
Filton Abbey Wood	a						07 58																
Bristol Parkway 7	a	22p08					08 05	07 38				08 38		09 08				09 38				10 38	
Swindon	a			03 15									09 39				10 10						
Newport (South Wales)	a																						
Cardiff Central 7	a																						
Birmingham New Street 12	a	00 10						08 56				09 56		10 26				10 56				11 56	
Castle Cary	d								07 33										09 40				
Westbury	d								07 56										09 59				
Pewsey	d								08 13										10 16				
Hungerford	a																						
Newbury	a								08 33														
Thatcham	a																						
Theale	a																						
Reading 7	a			04s00					08 52				10 08			09 35	10 45		10 51				
Slough 3	a																						
London Paddington 15 ⊖	a			05 43					09 21				10 38			10 08	11 14		11 24				

C The Torbay Express

b arr. 0708

For connections to Oxford, Gatwick Airport and Heathrow Airport please refer to Tables 116, 148 and 125A

Table 135

Saturdays from 11 September

Cornwall and Devon - Birmingham and London

		GW	GW	GW	GW	XC	XC	GW	GW	XC	GW	GW	GW	GW	GW	XC	XC	GW	GW	GW	XC	GW	GW
		■ 1 ☕				◇1 ✠	◇1 ✠	◇1 ☕		◇1 ✠	◇1 B ☕				◇1 ☕	◇1 ✠	◇1 ✠		◇1 ☕		◇1 ✠		◇1 ☕⊘
Penzance	d	06 50	07 35					07 59		08 28	08 45	08 57					09 43		10 00	10 36			10 59
St Erth	d	07 01	07 47					08 09		08 36	08 56	09 05					09 51		10 11	10 44			11 09
Hayle	d		07 51					08 13												10 47			
Camborne	d	07 12	08 01					08 23		08 46	09 07						10 01		10 22	10 57			11 20
Redruth	d	07 19	08 08					08 30		08 52	09 14						10 07		10 29	11 03			11 27
Truro	d	07 31	08 21					08 43		09 04	09 26						10 19		10 41	11 15			11 40
St Austell	d	07 49	08 36					09 00		09 20	09 44						10 35		10 59	11 32			11 57
Newquay	d																						
Par	d	07 56	08 45					09 08		09 28	09 51						10 42		11 07	11 39			
Lostwithiel	d	08 03	08 52														10 49			11 46			
Bodmin Parkway	d	08 10	08 58					09 19		09 39	10 03						10 56		11 18	11 52			12 14
Liskeard 6	d	08 23	09 11					09 32		09 51	10 16						11 09		11 31	12 07			12 27
Menheniot	d																			12x11			
St Germans	d		09 22																	12 17			
Saltash	d		09 30																	12 24			
St Budeaux Ferry Road	d																						
Keyham	d																						
Dockyard	d																						
Devonport	d																						
Plymouth	a	08 48	09 41					09 57		10 15	10 40						11 33		11 58	12 37			12 52
	d	08 52				09 25		10 01		10 25	10 44					11 25	11 48		12 00		12 23		12 54
Ivybridge	d							10 16											12 15				
Totnes	d	09 19				09 50		10 30		10 50						11 50	12 13		12 29		12 49		13 21
Paignton	d			09 11	09 30		10 06		10 23				10 56	11 13				12 13				12 43	
Torquay	d			09 16	09 35		10 12		10 28				11 01	11 18				12 18				12 48	
Torre	d			09 19	09 38				10 31				11 04	11 21				12 21					
Newton Abbot	a	09 30		09 27	09 47	10 01	10 22	10 42	10 38	11 01			11 12	11 29		12 01	12 24	12 30	12 41		13 01	12 58	13 34
	d	09 32		09 36	09 48	10 03	10 23	10 43	10 47	11 03			11 23	11 41		12 03	12 25	12 32	12 42		13 03	13 06	13 35
Teignmouth	d			09 43	09 56		10 30		10 54				11 30	11 48				12 39				13 13	
Dawlish	d			09 48	10 01		10 35		10 59				11 35	11 53				12 44				13 18	
Dawlish Warren	d			09 53	10 06				11 04				11 40	11 58				12b55				13 23	
Starcross	d			09 57									11 44	12 02				12 59					
Exeter St Thomas	d			10 06									11 53	12 11				13 08					
Exeter St Davids 6	a	09 52		10 13	10 17	10 21	10 47	11 04	11 15	11 21	11 38		11 57	12 16		12 21	12 44	13 13	13 02		13 23	13 35	13 54
Exeter Central	a			10 21					11 21					12 21				13 21					
Exmouth	a			10 50					11 50					12 50				13 50					
Exeter St Davids 6	d	09 54				10 23	10 49	11 06		11 23	11 40				11 54	12 23	12 48		13 04		13 25		13 56
Tiverton Parkway	d	10 09				10 37	11 02	11 21		11 37					12 09	12 37	13 02		13 19		13 39		
Taunton	d	10 24				10 51	11 17	11 36		11 51					12 24	12 51	13 16		13 34		13 54		14 23
Bridgwater	a																						
Weston-super-Mare	a																						
Bristol Temple Meads 10	a					11 26	11 55			12 25						13 24	13 56				14 27		
Bath Spa 7	a																						
Filton Abbey Wood	a																						
Bristol Parkway 7	a					11 38	12 08			12 38						13 38	14 08				14 38		
Swindon	a																						
Newport (South Wales)	a																						
Cardiff Central 7	a																						
Birmingham New Street 12	a					12 56	13 26			13 56						14 56	15 26				15 55		
Castle Cary	d														12 45								14 44
Westbury	d	11 02													13 05								15 03
Pewsey	d														13 22								
Hungerford	a														13 39								
Newbury	a														13 49								
Thatcham	a														13 56								
Theale	a														14 05								
Reading 7	a	11 51						12 52			13 17				14 19				14 51				15 51
Slough 3	a																						
London Paddington 15 ⊖	a	12 23						13 21			13 46				14 45				15 22				16 23

B The Cornish Riveira

b arr. 1248

For connections to Oxford, Gatwick Airport and Heathrow Airport please refer to Tables 116, 148 and 125A

Table 135

Cornwall and Devon - Birmingham and London

Saturdays
from 11 September

		GW		GW	GW	XC	XC	GW	GW	XC	GW	GW		GW	XC	GW	GW	GW	GW	GW	XC	GW		GW	XC
						◇1	◇1	◇1		◇1		◇1		◇1	◇1				◇1		◇1	◇1			◇1
																			B						
						🛒	🛒	🍴⊘		🛒		🍴		🍴	🛒				🍴		🛒	🍴			🛒
Penzance	d	11 49		13 00															14 00	14 49					
St Erth	d	11 57		13 08															14 11	14 57					
Hayle	d	12 01		13 11																15 01					
Camborne	d	12 10		13 21															14 22	15 10					
Redruth	d	12 16		13 27															14 29	15 16					
Truro	d	12 28		13 39															14 41	15 28					
St Austell	d	12 45		13 55															14 59	15 45					
Newquay	d																								
Par	d	12 53		14 04															15 06	15 53					
Lostwithiel	d	12 59		14 09																15 59					
Bodmin Parkway	d	13 05		14 15															15 18	16 05					
Liskeard 6	d	13 18		14 28															15 34	16 18					
Menheniot	d	13x22																		16x22					
St Germans	d	13 31		14 39																16 31					
Saltash	d	13 40		14 46																16 38					
St Budeaux Ferry Road	d																								
Keyham	d																								
Dockyard	d																								
Devonport	d			14 53																					
Plymouth	a	13 49		14 59															15 57	16 48					
	d					13 25		14 00		14 25		15 04			15 25		15 32		16 01		16 25	16 57			17 23
Ivybridge	d																15 47					17 12			
Totnes	d					13 50				14 50		15 31			15 50		16 01		16 28		16 50	17 27			17 49
Paignton	d				13 13		13 53		14 13		15 13					15 43		16 13						17 13	
Torquay	d				13 18		13 59		14 18		15 18					15 48		16 18						17 18	
Torre	d				13 21				14 21		15 21							16 21						17 21	
Newton Abbot	a				13 29	14 01	14 09	14 35	14 29	15 01	15 29	15 42			16 01	15 58	16 13	16 29	16 40		17 01	17 38		17 29	18 01
	d				13 41	14 03	14 10	14 36	14 40	15 03	15 34	15 44			16 03	16 09		16 31	16 41		17 03	17 40		17 43	18 03
Teignmouth	d				13 48		14 17		14 48		15 42					16 16		16 38						17 50	
Dawlish	d				13 53		14 22		14 53		15 47					16 21		16 43						17 55	
Dawlish Warren	d				13 58				14 57		15b58							16c55						18 00	
Starcross	d				14 02				15 01		16 02							16 59						18 04	
Exeter St Thomas	d				14 11				15 11		16 12							17 08						18 13	
Exeter St Davids 6	a				14 16	14 21	14 34	14 56	15 15	15 21	16 15	16 04			16 21	16 34		17 15	17 01		17 21	18 00		18 18	18 23
Exeter Central	a				14 21				15 21		16 20					16 44		17 21						18 23	
Exmouth	a				14 50				15 50		16 52							17 51						18 52	
Exeter St Davids 6	d					14 24	14 36	14 58		15 23		16 06			16 23				17 03		17 23	18 02			18 25
Tiverton Parkway	d					14 37	14 49	15 13		15 37		16 21			16 37				17 17		17 37	18 17			18 39
Taunton	d					14 52	15 04	15 28		15 51		16 36		15 19	16 51				17 32		17 51	18 32			18 54
Bridgwater	a																								
Weston-super-Mare	a						15 23																		
Bristol Temple Meads 10	a					15 25	15 49			16 25					17 25						18 25				19 27
Bath Spa 7	a																								
Filton Abbey Wood	a																								
Bristol Parkway 7	a					15 38	16 08			16 38					17 38						18 38				19 38
Swindon	a																								
Newport (South Wales)	a																								
Cardiff Central 7	a																								
Birmingham New Street 12	a					16 56	17 26			17 56					18 56						19 56				20 53
Castle Cary	d							15 49														18 53			
Westbury	d													16 08								19 12			
Pewsey	d													16 26											
Hungerford	a													16 42											
Newbury	a													16 53								19 49			
Thatcham	a													16 59											
Theale	a													17 08											
Reading 7	a							16 50				17 53		17 19					18 49			20 07			
Slough 3	a																								
London Paddington 15 ⊖	a							17 21				18 21		17 51					19 22			20 37			

B The Royal Duchy" b arr. 1551 c arr. 1647

For connections to Oxford, Gatwick Airport and Heathrow Airport please refer to Tables 116, 148 and 125A

Table 135

Cornwall and Devon - Birmingham and London

Saturdays
from 11 September

		GW	GW	GW	XC	GW	GW	GW		GW	GW	GW	GW	GW	GW	GW	XC	GW
				◇1	◇1						◇1			1			◇1	
				🍴	🛒						🍴							
Penzance	d			15 51			16 43				17 39	18 50				19 06	21 32	
St Erth	d			16 02			16 51				17 49	18 58				19 14	21 42	
Hayle	d						16 55				17 53					19 17		
Camborne	d			16 14			17 04				18 04					19 27	21 54	
Redruth	d			16 21			17 10				18 11					19 33	22 01	
Truro	d			16 33			17 24				18 24					19 45	22 13	
St Austell	d			16 51			17 39				18 41					20 02	22 31	
Newquay	d																	
Par	d			16 58			17 46				18 49					20 09	22 38	
Lostwithiel	d			17 05			17 52									20 16		
Bodmin Parkway	d			17 12			17 58				19 00					20 22	22 50	
Liskeard 6	d			17 25			18 11				19 13					20 35	23 03	
Menheniot	d															20x39		
St Germans	d						18 25									20 48		
Saltash	d						18 32									20 56		
St Budeaux Ferry Road	d															21 00		
Keyham	d															21x02		
Dockyard	d															21x04		
Devonport	d															21 06		
Plymouth	a			17 50			18 42				19 38					21 10	23 28	
	d		17 38	17 54	18 25		18 44				19 42					21 15		
Ivybridge	d		17 53				18 59									21 30		
Totnes	d		18 07	18 21	18 50		19 13				20 09					21 44		
Paignton	d	17 52				18 53		19 21		19 50			20 13	20 46	21 13			21 53
Torquay	d	17 57				18 58		19 26		19 55			20 18	20 52	21 18			21 58
Torre	d	18 00				19 01		19 29					20 21		21 21			22 01
Newton Abbot	a	18 08	18 19	18 32	19 01	19 10	19 25	19 38		20 05	20 20		20 29	21 02	21 29	21 56		22 09
	d	18 10	18 19	18 34	19 03	19 12	19 26	19 40		20 07	20 22		20 31	21 04	21 31	21 56		22 11
Teignmouth	d	18 17	18 26			19 19	19 33	19 47		20 14			20 38		21 38	22 03		22 18
Dawlish	d	18 22	18 31			19 24	19 38	19 52		20 19			20 43		21 43	22 08		22 23
Dawlish Warren	d	18 27	18b47			19 29		20c06		20 24			20 48		21 48	22 13		22 28
Starcross	d	18 31				19 33		20 10					20 52		21 52	22 17		22 32
Exeter St Thomas	d	18 40				19 42		20 20					21 01		22 01	22 26		22 41
Exeter St Davids 6	a	18 46	18 59	18 54	19 21	19 45	19 50	20 25		20 36	20 42		21 05	21 24	22 05	22 30		22 45
Exeter Central	a	18 53						20 33										
Exmouth	a	19 23						21 01										
Exeter St Davids 6	d			18 56	19 23						20 44							
Tiverton Parkway	d			19 11	19 37						20 59							
Taunton	d			19 26	19 51						21 14							
Bridgwater	a																	
Weston-super-Mare	a																	
Bristol Temple Meads 10	a				20 25						21 47							
Bath Spa 7	a										22 01							
Filton Abbey Wood	a																	
Bristol Parkway 7	a				20 38													
Swindon	a										22 29							
Newport (South Wales)	a																	
Cardiff Central 7	a																	
Birmingham New Street 12	a				22 11													
Castle Cary	d			19 47														
Westbury	d			20 06														
Pewsey	d			20 23														
Hungerford	a																	
Newbury	a																	
Thatcham	a																	
Theale	a																	
Reading 7	a			20 58							23 04							
Slough 3	a																	
London Paddington 15 ⊖	a			21 32							23 38							

b arr. 1835 c arr. 1956

For connections to Oxford, Gatwick Airport and Heathrow Airport please refer to Tables 116, 148 and 125A

Table 135

Cornwall and Devon - Birmingham and London

		GW	GW	GW	GW	XC	GW	GW	XC	XC	GW	GW	GW	XC	GW	GW	XC	GW	XC	XC	GW	GW	XC
		◇	◇1 ☕		◇1 ☕	◇1 🛒		◇1 ☕	◇1 🛒	◇1 🛒	◇1 ☕			◇1 🛒		◇1 ☕	◇1 🛒		◇1 🛒	◇1 🛒		◇1 ☕	◇1 🛒
Penzance	d										08 32	08 45		09 30		09 47						11 00	
St Erth	d										08 41	08 53		09 38		09 59						11 09	
Hayle	d										08 46												
Camborne	d										08 57			09 48		10 11						11 22	
Redruth	d										09 03			09 54		10 17						11 28	
Truro	d										09 17			10 06		10 29						11 42	
St Austell	d										09 33			10 24		10 47						11 58	
Newquay	d																						11 35
Par	d										09 42			10 31		10 54						12 06	
Lostwithiel	d																						
Bodmin Parkway	d										09 53			10 42		11 07						12 18	12 41
Liskeard [6]	d										10 06			10 54		11 20						12 32	12 54
Menheniot	d																						
St Germans	d										10 17												
Saltash	d										10 26												
St Budeaux Ferry Road	d																						
Keyham	d																						
Dockyard	d																						
Devonport	d																						
Plymouth	a										10 36			11 17		11 43						12 57	13 19
	d				08 40	09 25		10 10	10 25		10 40			11 25		11 45	12 00		12 25			13 00	13 23
Ivybridge	d																						
Totnes	d				09 07	09 50		10 40	10 50		11 07			11 50		12 15			12 50			13 28	13 49
Paignton	d						10 10			10 50			11 00		12 01			12 29		12 55	13 04		
Torquay	d						10 15			10 56			11 05		12 06			12 34		13 01	13 09		
Torre	d						10 18						11 08		12 09						13 12		
Newton Abbot	a				09 19	10 01	10 26	10 52	11 01	11 06	11 19		11 16	12 01	12 17	12 27	12 34	12 47	13 01	13 14	13 20	13 39	14 01
	d				09 20	10 03	10 35	10 54	11 03	11 08	11 21		11 28	12 03	12 19	12 29	12 36	12 49	13 03	13 16	13 22	13 41	14 03
Teignmouth	d				09 27		10 42			11 15			11 35		12 26			12 56		13 23	13 29		
Dawlish	d				09 33		10 47			11 20			11 40		12 31			13 01		13 28	13 34		
Dawlish Warren	d						10 52						11 45		12b49			13 06			13 39		
Starcross	d						10 56						11 49		12 53						13 43		
Exeter St Thomas	d						11 07						11 58		13 03						13 52		
Exeter St Davids [6]	a				09 47	10 21	11 10	11 14	11 21	11 30	11 41		12 02	12 21	13 07	12 49	12 55	13 20	13 24	13 39	13 56	14 01	14 23
Exeter Central	a														13 36								
Exmouth	a														14 04								
Exeter St Davids [6]	d	08 01	08 38	09 35	09 48	10 23		11 16	11 23	11 32	11 43			12 23		12 50	12 57		13 26	13 42		14 03	14 25
Tiverton Parkway	d	08 18	08 53	09 53		10 38		11 31	11 37	11 46	11 58			12 37			13 10		13 40	13 55		14 17	14 39
Taunton	d	08 35	09 07	10 11	10 14	10 51		11 46	11 51	12 00	12 13			12 51		13 15	13 25		13 54	14 10		14 32	14 54
Bridgwater	a	08 46		10 23																			
Weston-super-Mare	a	09 04		10 41						12 20													
Bristol Temple Meads [10]	a	09 38		11 15		11 27		12 23	12 27	12 47				13 24			13 57		14 27	14 46			15 27
Bath Spa [7]	a							12 42															
Filton Abbey Wood	a	09 55																					
Bristol Parkway [7]	a					11 38			12 38	13 08				13 38			14 08		14 38	15 08			15 38
Swindon	a							13 10															
Newport (South Wales)	a	10 27																					
Cardiff Central [7]	a	10 43																					
Birmingham New Street [12]	a					13 11			13 50	14 26				14 50			15 27		15 50	16 26			16 50
Castle Cary	d		09 29								12 34												
Westbury	d		09 49		10 53						12 53					13c59							
Pewsey	d		10 06								13 10												
Hungerford	a																						
Newbury	a		10 26		11 26						13 30												
Thatcham	a																						
Theale	a																						
Reading [7]	a		10 47		11 47			13 42			13 48					14 48						15 48	
Slough [3]	a																						
London Paddington [15] ⊖	a		11 24		12 29			14 24			14 30					15 29						16 30	

A not 23 May

b arr. 1235

c arr. 1351

For connections to Oxford, Gatwick Airport and Heathrow Airport please refer to Tables 116, 148 and 125A

Table 135

Cornwall and Devon - Birmingham and London

		GW	GW	GW	GW	XC	XC	GW	GW	GW	XC	GW	GW	GW	GW	GW	XC	GW	GW	GW	XC	GW	XC
		◇1 ☕				◇1 🛒	◇1 🛒		◇1 ☕	◇1 ☕	◇1 🛒	◇1 ☕	◇1 ☕			◇1 ☕	◇1 🛒	◇1 ☕		◇	◇1 🛒	◇1 ☕	◇1 🛒
Penzance	d	11 40		12 02			12 30		12 56						13 50			14 45		15 07	15 30	15 49	
St Erth	d	11 51		12 09			12 40		13 06						14 00			14 55		15 16	15 38	16 00	
Hayle	d						12 44								14 03					15 19			
Camborne	d	12 03		12 25			12 56		13 20						14 13			15 07		15 29	15 51	16 12	
Redruth	d	12 10		12 31			13 02		13 26						14 19			15 14		15 35	15 57	16 19	
Truro	d	12 22		12 43			13 14		13 38						14 32			15 27		15 47	16 09	16 31	
St Austell	d	12 40		13 01			13 31		13 57						14 49			15 44		16 04	16 25	16 49	
Newquay	d																						
Par	d	12 47		13 09			13 38		14 03						14 57			15 52		16 11	16 33	16 55	
Lostwithiel	d			13 16			13 45								15 04					16 18			
Bodmin Parkway	d	12 59		13 19			13 52		14 16						15 10			16 03		16 24	16 44	17 07	
Liskeard [6]	d	13 12		13 33			14 04		14 29						15 24			16 16		16 37	16 56	17 20	
Menheniot	d														15x31								
St Germans	d			13 44											15 39					16 48			
Saltash	d			13 53											15 47					16 57			
St Budeaux Ferry Road	d																						
Keyham	d																						
Dockyard	d																						
Devonport	d																						
Plymouth	a	13 37		14 01			14 28		14 54						15 55			16 41		17 05	17 20	17 42	
	d	13 44		14 06		14 23	14 35		14 55	15 05	15 23		15 40		16 02	16 10	16 25	16 45		17 08	17 26	17 45	
Ivybridge	d			14 21											16 17					17 23			
Totnes	d	14 10		14 35		14 49	15 00		15 25	15 34	15 49		16 08		16 31	16 42	16 50	17 12		17 37	17 52	18 12	
Paignton	d		14 04		14 34			15 01				15 47		16 10					17 04				18 18
Torquay	d		14 09		14 39			15 06				15 53		16 15					17 09				18 24
Torre	d		14 12		14 42							15 58		16 18					17 12				
Newton Abbot	a	14 23	14 20	14 47	14 50	15 01	15 11	15 16	15 37	15 46	16 01	16 06	16 19	16 27	16 43	16 53	17 01	17 24	17 20	17 49	18 02	18 24	18 34
	d	14 24	14 28	14 48	14 53	15 03	15 12	15 17	15 38	15 47	16 03	16 07	16 21	16 29	16 44	16 55	17 03	17 25	17 29	17 51	18 04	18 25	18 35
Teignmouth	d		14 35	14 55	15 00			15 24				16 15		16 36					17 36	17 58			
Dawlish	d		14 40	15 00	15 05			15 29				16 20		16 41					17 41	18 03			
Dawlish Warren	d		14 45					15 33						16 46					17 46				
Starcross	d		14 49					15 37						16 50					17 50				
Exeter St Thomas	d		14 58					15 46						16 59					17 59				
Exeter St Davids [6]	a	14 44	15 02	15 13	15 18	15 23	15 31	15 53	15 58	16 07	16 23	16 34	16 41	17 04	17 07	17 15	17 21	17 45	18 03	18 17	18 22	18 46	18 54
Exeter Central	a				15 34									17 34									
Exmouth	a				16 05									18 04									
Exeter St Davids [6]	d	14 45				15 25	15 33		16 01	16 09	16 25	16 36	16 42			17 17	17 23	17 47		18 36	18 24	18 48	18 56
Tiverton Parkway	d					15 38	15 46		16 16	16 24	16 38		16 58			17 32	17 37	18 02			18 39		19 09
Taunton	d	15 11				15 54	16 01		16 31	16 39	16 54	17 01	17 12			17 46	17 51	18 17		19 07	18 52	19 09	19 23
Bridgwater	a																			19 19			
Weston-super-Mare	a						16 20			17 00		17 22								19 40			
Bristol Temple Meads [10]	a					16 27	16 53			17 22	17 28	17 55				18 25	18 27			20 11	19 27		19 55
Bath Spa [7]	a									17 42		18 12				18 41							
Filton Abbey Wood	a																						
Bristol Parkway [7]	a					16 38	17 08				17 38						18 38				19 38		20 08
Swindon	a									18 10		18 40				19 11							
Newport (South Wales)	a																						
Cardiff Central [7]	a																						
Birmingham New Street [12]	a					17 49	18 27				18 51						19 50				20 50		21 20
Castle Cary	d	15 33											17 34										
Westbury	d	15 50											17 53					18 58					
Pewsey	d	16 08											18 10										
Hungerford	a																						
Newbury	a	16 29											18 30									20 16	
Thatcham	a																						
Theale	a																						
Reading [7]	a	16 47							17 47	18 42		19 12	18 48			19 42		19 43				20 34	
Slough [3]	a																						
London Paddington [15] ⊖	a	17 29							18 29	19 26		19 54	19 29			20 24		20 22				21 12	

For connections to Oxford, Gatwick Airport and Heathrow Airport please refer to Tables 116, 148 and 125A

Table 135

Sundays
until 11 July

Cornwall and Devon - Birmingham and London

		GW	GW	XC	GW	GW	GW	GW	GW	GW	GW	GW	GW	GW	GW
			◇1 ▭	◇1 ✕		◇1 ▭	✕		◇1 ▭			✕			▣ 🛏 ▭
Penzance	d					17 20	17 50				19 00	20 05			21 15
St Erth	d					17 30	17 59				19 09	20 14			21 25
Hayle	d						18 02					20 17			
Camborne	d					17 43	18 11				19 20	20 26			21 38
Redruth	d					17 50	18 17				19 26	20 32			21 45
Truro	d					18 01	18 29				19 38	20 44			22 00
St Austell	d					18 20	18 46				19 55	21 01			22 18
Newquay	d		16 15												
Par	d		17 15			18 27	18 54				20 02	21 09			
Lostwithiel	d		17 24				19 01				20 09				
Bodmin Parkway	d		17 30			18 39	19 08				20 15	21 21			22 35
Liskeard 6	d		17 43			18 52	19 22				20 28	21 35			22 50
Menheniot	d										20x33				
St Germans	d										20 40				
Saltash	d										20 47				
St Budeaux Ferry Road	d						19 43								
Keyham	d														
Dockyard	d														
Devonport	d						19 47				20 55				
Plymouth	a		18 09			19 16	19 50				20 59	22 00			23 15
	d		18 10	18 23		19 20			19 55		21 15				23 20
Ivybridge	d														
Totnes	d		18 40	18 49		19 48					21 42				23 48
Paignton	d	18 25			18 55			19 55		20 55			21 55	23 00	
Torquay	d	18 30			19 00			20 00		21 00			22 00	23 05	
Torre	d				19 03			20 03		21 03			22 03	23 08	
Newton Abbot	a	18 40	18 52	19 01	19 11	19 59		20 11	20 31	21 11	21 54		22 11	23 16	23 59
	d	18 41	18 52	19 03	19 13	20 01		20 13	20 32	21 13	21 55		22 13	23 18	00 01
Teignmouth	d	18 49			19 20			20 20		21 20	22 02		22 20	23 25	
Dawlish	d	18 54			19 25			20 25		21 25	22 07		22 25	23 30	
Dawlish Warren	d	18 58			19 30			20 30		21 30			22 30	23 35	
Starcross	d				19 34			20 34		21 34			22 34	23 39	
Exeter St Thomas	d				19 43			20 43		21 43			22 43	23 48	
Exeter St Davids 6	a	19 10	19 14	19 23	19 47	20 21		20 47	20 53	21 47	22 21		22 47	23 52	00 36
Exeter Central	a	19 36													
Exmouth	a	20 03													
Exeter St Davids 6	d		19 16	19 25		20 22			20 55						01 27
Tiverton Parkway	d		19 31	19 38		20 38			21 10						
Taunton	d		19 45	19 54		20 51			21 23						
Bridgwater	a														
Weston-super-Mare	a														
Bristol Temple Meads 10	a			20 27					22 00						02 38
Bath Spa 7	a								22 18						
Filton Abbey Wood	a														
Bristol Parkway 7	a			20 38											
Swindon	a								22 46						
Newport (South Wales)	a														
Cardiff Central 7	a														
Birmingham New Street 12	a			21 51											
Castle Cary	d		20 07			21 15									
Westbury	d		20 27			21 33									
Pewsey	d					21 51									
Hungerford	a														
Newbury	a					22 11									
Thatcham	a														
Theale	a														
Reading 7	a		21 12			22 29			23 27						04s17
Slough 3	a														
London Paddington 15 ⊖	a		21 53			23 16			00 13						05 06

For connections to Oxford, Gatwick Airport and Heathrow Airport please refer to Tables 116, 148 and 125A

Table 135

Sundays
18 July to 05 September

Cornwall and Devon - Birmingham and London

		GW	GW	GW	GW	XC	GW	GW	XC	XC	GW	GW	GW	XC	GW	GW	XC	GW	XC	XC	GW	GW	XC
		◇	◇1 ▭		◇1 ▭	◇1 ✕		◇1 ▭	◇1 ✕	◇1 ✕	◇1 ▭			◇1 ✕		◇1 ▭	◇1 ✕		◇1 ✕	◇1 ✕		◇1 ▭	◇1 ✕
Penzance	d										08 32	08 45		09 30		09 47						11 00	
St Erth	d										08 41	08 53		09 38		09 59						11 09	
Hayle	d										08 46												
Camborne	d										08 57			09 48		10 11						11 22	
Redruth	d										09 03			09 54		10 17						11 28	
Truro	d										09 17			10 06		10 29						11 42	
St Austell	d										09 33			10 24		10 47						11 58	
Newquay	d																						11 35
Par	d										09 42			10 31		10 54						12 06	
Lostwithiel	d																						
Bodmin Parkway	d										09 53			10 42		11 07						12 18	12 41
Liskeard 6	d										10 06			10 54		11 20						12 32	12 54
Menheniot	d																						
St Germans	d										10 17												
Saltash	d										10 26												
St Budeaux Ferry Road	d																						
Keyham	d																						
Dockyard	d																						
Devonport	d																						
Plymouth	a										10 36			11 17		11 43						12 57	13 19
	d				08 40	09 25		10 10	10 25		10 40			11 25		11 45	12 00		12 25			13 00	13 23
Ivybridge	d																						
Totnes	d				09 07	09 50		10 40	10 50		11 07			11 50		12 15			12 50			13 28	13 49
Paignton	d						10 10			10 50			11 00		12 01			12 29		12 55	13 04		
Torquay	d						10 15			10 56			11 05		12 06			12 34		13 01	13 09		
Torre	d						10 18						11 08		12 09						13 12		
Newton Abbot	a				09 19	10 01	10 26	10 52	11 01	11 06	11 19		11 16	12 01	12 17	12 27	12 34	12 47	13 01	13 14	13 20	13 39	14 01
	d				09 20	10 03	10 35	10 54	11 03	11 08	11 21		11 28	12 03	12 19	12 29	12 36	12 49	13 03	13 16	13 22	13 41	14 03
Teignmouth	d				09 27		10 42			11 15			11 35		12 26			12 56		13 23	13 29		
Dawlish	d				09 33		10 47			11 20			11 40		12 31			13 01		13 28	13 34		
Dawlish Warren	d						10 52						11 45		12b49			13 06			13 39		
Starcross	d						10 56						11 49		12 53						13 43		
Exeter St Thomas	d						11 07						11 58		13 03						13 52		
Exeter St Davids 6	a				09 47	10 21	11 10	11 14	11 21	11 30	11 41		12 02	12 21	13 07	12 49	12 55	13 20	13 24	13 39	13 56	14 01	14 23
Exeter Central	a														13 36								
Exmouth	a														14 04								
Exeter St Davids 6	d	08 01	08 38	09 35	09 48	10 23		11 16	11 23	11 32	11 43			12 23		12 50	12 57		13 26	13 42		14 03	14 25
Tiverton Parkway	d	08 18	08 53	09 53		10 38		11 31	11 37	11 46	11 58			12 37			13 10		13 40	13 55		14 17	14 39
Taunton	d	08 35	09 07	10 11	10 14	10 51		11 46	11 51	12 00	12 13			12 51		13 15	13 25		13 54	14 10		14 32	14 54
Bridgwater	a	08 46		10 23																			
Weston-super-Mare	a	09 04		10 41						12 20													
Bristol Temple Meads 10	a	09 38		11 15		11 27		12 23	12 27	12 47				13 24			13 57		14 27	14 46			15 27
Bath Spa 7	a							12 42															
Filton Abbey Wood	a	09 55																					
Bristol Parkway 7	a					11 38			12 38	13 08				13 38			14 08		14 38	15 08			15 38
Swindon	a							13 10															
Newport (South Wales)	a	10 23																					
Cardiff Central 7	a	10 43																					
Birmingham New Street 12	a					13 11			13 50	14 26				14 50			15 27		15 50	16 26			16 50
Castle Cary	d		09 29								12 34												
Westbury	d		09 49		10 53						12 53					13c59							
Pewsey	d		10 06								13 10												
Hungerford	a																						
Newbury	a		10 26		11 26						13 30												
Thatcham	a																						
Theale	a																						
Reading 7	a		10 47		11 47			13 42			13 48					14 48						15 48	
Slough 3	a																						
London Paddington 15 ⊖	a		11 24		12 29			14 24			14 30					15 29						16 30	

b arr. 1235 c arr. 1351

For connections to Oxford, Gatwick Airport and Heathrow Airport please refer to Tables 116, 148 and 125A

Table 135

Cornwall and Devon - Birmingham and London

		GW	GW	GW	GW	XC	XC	GW	GW	GW	XC	GW	GW	GW	GW	GW	XC	GW	GW	GW	XC	GW	XC
		◇1				◇1	◇1		◇1	◇1	◇1	◇1	◇1			◇1	◇1	◇1		◇	◇1	◇1	◇1
Penzance	d	11 40		12 02			12 30		12 56						13 50			14 45		15 07	15 30	15 49	
St Erth	d	11 51		12 09			12 40		13 06						14 00			14 55		15 16	15 38	16 00	
Hayle	d						12 44								14 03					15 19			
Camborne	d	12 03		12 25			12 56		13 20						14 13			15 07		15 29	15 51	16 12	
Redruth	d	12 10		12 31			13 02		13 26						14 19			15 14		15 35	15 57	16 19	
Truro	d	12 22		12 43			13 14		13 38						14 32			15 27		15 47	16 09	16 31	
St Austell	d	12 40		13 01			13 31		13 57						14 49			15 44		16 04	16 25	16 49	
Newquay	d																						
Par	d	12 47		13 09			13 38		14 03						14 57			15 52		16 11	16 33	16 55	
Lostwithiel	d			13 16			13 45								15 04					16 18			
Bodmin Parkway	d	12 59		13 19			13 52		14 16						15 10			16 03		16 24	16 44	17 07	
Liskeard 8	d	13 12		13 33			14 04		14 29						15 24			16 16		16 37	16 56	17 20	
Menheniot	d														15x31								
St Germans	d			13 44											15 39					16 48			
Saltash	d			13 53											15 47					16 57			
St Budeaux Ferry Road	d																						
Keyham	d																						
Dockyard	d																						
Devonport	d																						
Plymouth	a	13 37		14 01			14 28		14 54						15 55			16 41		17 05	17 20	17 42	
	d	13 44		14 06		14 23	14 35		14 55	15 05	15 23		15 40		16 02	16 10	16 25	16 45		17 08	17 26	17 45	
Ivybridge	d			14 21											16 17					17 23			
Totnes	d	14 10		14 35		14 49	15 00		15 25	15 34	15 49		16 08		16 31	16 42	16 50	17 12		17 37	17 52	18 12	
Paignton	d		14 04		14 34			15 01				15 47		16 10					17 04				18 18
Torquay	d		14 09		14 39			15 06				15 53		16 15					17 09				18 24
Torre	d		14 12		14 42							15 58		16 18					17 12				
Newton Abbot	a	14 23	14 20	14 47	14 50	15 01	15 11	15 16	15 37	15 46	16 01	16 06	16 19	16 27	16 43	16 53	17 01	17 24	17 20	17 49	18 02	18 24	18 34
	d	14 24	14 28	14 48	14 53	15 03	15 12	15 17	15 38	15 47	16 03	16 07	16 21	16 29	16 44	16 55	17 03	17 25	17 29	17 51	18 04	18 25	18 35
Teignmouth	d		14 35	14 55	15 00			15 24				16 15		16 36					17 36	17 58			
Dawlish	d		14 40	15 00	15 05			15 29				16 20		16 41					17 41	18 03			
Dawlish Warren	d		14 45					15 33						16 46					17 46				
Starcross	d		14 49					15 37						16 50					17 50				
Exeter St Thomas	d		14 58					15 46						16 59					17 59				
Exeter St Davids 6	a	14 44	15 02	15 13	15 18	15 23	15 31	15 53	15 58	16 07	16 23	16 34	16 41	17 04	17 07	17 15	17 21	17 45	18 03	18 17	18 22	18 46	18 54
Exeter Central	a				15 34									17 34									
Exmouth	a				16 05									18 04									
Exeter St Davids 6	d	14 45				15 25	15 33		16 01	16 09	16 25	16 36	16 42			17 17	17 23	17 47		18 36	18 24	18 48	18 56
Tiverton Parkway	d					15 38	15 46		16 16	16 24	16 38		16 58			17 32	17 37	18 02			18 39		19 09
Taunton	d	15 11				15 54	16 01		16 31	16 39	16 54	17 01	17 12			17 46	17 51	18 17		19 07	18 52	19 09	19 23
Bridgwater	a																			19 19			
Weston-super-Mare	a						16 20			17 00		17 22								19 40			
Bristol Temple Meads 10	a					16 27	16 53			17 22	17 28	17 55				18 25	18 27			20 11	19 27		19 55
Bath Spa 7	a									17 42		18 12				18 41							
Filton Abbey Wood	a																						
Bristol Parkway 7	a					16 38	17 08				17 38						18 38				19 38		20 08
Swindon	a									18 10		18 40				19 11							
Newport (South Wales)	a																						
Cardiff Central 7	a																						
Birmingham New Street 12	a					17 49	18 27				18 51						19 50				20 50		21 20
Castle Cary	d	15 33											17 34										
Westbury	d	15 50											17 53					18 58					
Pewsey	d	16 08											18 10										
Hungerford	a																						
Newbury	a	16 29											18 30									20 16	
Thatcham	a																						
Theale	a																						
Reading 7	a	16 47							17 47	18 42		19 12	18 48			19 42		19 43				20 34	
Slough 3	a																						
London Paddington 15 ⊖	a	17 29							18 29	19 26		19 54	19 29			20 24		20 22				21 12	

For connections to Oxford, Gatwick Airport and Heathrow Airport please refer to Tables 116, 148 and 125A

Table 135

Sundays
18 July to 05 September

Cornwall and Devon - Birmingham and London

		GW	GW	XC	GW	GW	GW	GW	GW	GW	GW	GW	GW	GW	GW
			◇1	◇1		◇1			◇1						
Penzance	d					17 20	17 50				19 00	20 05			21 15
St Erth	d					17 30	17 59				19 09	20 14			21 25
Hayle	d						18 02					20 17			
Camborne	d					17 43	18 11				19 20	20 26			21 38
Redruth	d					17 50	18 17				19 26	20 32			21 45
Truro	d					18 01	18 29				19 38	20 44			22 00
St Austell	d					18 20	18 46				19 55	21 01			22 18
Newquay	d		16 15												
Par	d		17 15			18 27	18 54				20 02	21 09			
Lostwithiel	d		17 24				19 01				20 09				
Bodmin Parkway	d		17 30			18 39	19 08				20 15	21 21			22 35
Liskeard 8	d		17 43			18 52	19 22				20 28	21 35			22 50
Menheniot	d										20x33				
St Germans	d										20 40				
Saltash	d										20 47				
St Budeaux Ferry Road	d						19 43								
Keyham	d														
Dockyard	d														
Devonport	d						19 47				20 55				
Plymouth	a		18 09			19 16	19 50				20 59	22 00			23 15
	d		18 10	18 23		19 20			19 55		21 15				23 20
Ivybridge	d														
Totnes	d		18 40	18 49		19 48					21 42				23 48
Paignton	d	18 25			18 55			19 55		20 55			21 55	23 00	
Torquay	d	18 30			19 00			20 00		21 00			22 00	23 05	
Torre	d				19 03			20 03		21 03			22 03	23 08	
Newton Abbot	a	18 40	18 52	19 01	19 11	19 59		20 11	20 31	21 11	21 54		22 11	23 16	23 59
	d	18 41	18 52	19 03	19 13	20 01		20 13	20 32	21 13	21 55		22 13	23 18	00 01
Teignmouth	d	18 49			19 20			20 20		21 20	22 02		22 20	23 25	
Dawlish	d	18 54			19 25			20 25		21 25	22 07		22 25	23 30	
Dawlish Warren	d	18 58			19 30			20 30		21 30			22 30	23 35	
Starcross	d				19 34			20 34		21 34			22 34	23 39	
Exeter St Thomas	d				19 43			20 43		21 43			22 43	23 48	
Exeter St Davids 6	a	19 10	19 14	19 23	19 47	20 21		20 47	20 53	21 47	22 21		22 47	23 52	00 36
Exeter Central	a	19 36													
Exmouth	a	20 03													
Exeter St Davids 6	d		19 16	19 25		20 22			20 55						01 27
Tiverton Parkway	d		19 31	19 38		20 38			21 10						
Taunton	d		19 45	19 54		20 51			21 23						
Bridgwater	a														
Weston-super-Mare	a														
Bristol Temple Meads 10	a			20 27					22 00						02 38
Bath Spa 7	a								22 18						
Filton Abbey Wood	a														
Bristol Parkway 7	a			20 38											
Swindon	a								22 46						
Newport (South Wales)	a														
Cardiff Central 7	a														
Birmingham New Street 12	a			21 51											
Castle Cary	d		20 07			21 15									
Westbury	d		20 27			21 33									
Pewsey	d					21 51									
Hungerford	a														
Newbury	a					22 11									
Thatcham	a														
Theale	a														
Reading 7	a		21 12			22 29			23 27						04s17
Slough 3	a														
London Paddington 15 ⊖	a		21 53			23 16			00 13						05 06

For connections to Oxford, Gatwick Airport and Heathrow Airport please refer to Tables 116, 148 and 125A

Table 135

Cornwall and Devon - Birmingham and London

		GW	GW	GW	GW	XC	GW	GW	XC	XC	GW	GW	XC	GW	GW	XC	GW	XC	GW	GW	XC	GW	GW
		◇	◇1 🍽		◇1 🍽	◇1 🛒		◇1 🍽	◇1 🛒	◇1 🛒	◇1 🍽		◇1 🛒		◇1 🍽	◇1 🛒		◇1 🛒		◇1 🍽	◇1 🛒		◇1 🍽
Penzance	d										08 32		09 30		09 47					11 00	11 24	11 45	
St Erth	d										08 42		09 38		09 59					11 10	11 35	11 54	
Hayle	d										08 47												
Camborne	d										08 58		09 48		10 11					11 23	11 46		
Redruth	d										09 04		09 54		10 17					11 29	11 53		
Truro	d										09 17		10 06		10 29					11 42	12 06		
St Austell	d										09 34		10 24		10 47					11 59	12 25		
Newquay	d																						
Par	d										09 42		10 31		10 54					12 06	12 32		
Lostwithiel	d																						
Bodmin Parkway	d										09 54		10 42		11 07					12 19	12 44		
Liskeard 6	d										10 07		10 54		11 20					12 32	12 57		
Menheniot	d																						
St Germans	d										10 18												
Saltash	d										10 27												
St Budeaux Ferry Road	d																						
Keyham	d																						
Dockyard	d																						
Devonport	d																						
Plymouth	a										10 36		11 17		11 43					12 57	13 20		
	d				08 40	09 25		10 10	10 25		10 40		11 25		11 45	12 00		12 25		13 00	13 23		13 44
Ivybridge	d																						
Totnes	d				09 07	09 50		10 40	10 50		11 07		11 50		12 15			12 50		13 29	13 49		14 10
Paignton	d						10 10			10 50		11 00		12 01			12 29		13 04				
Torquay	d						10 15			10 56		11 05		12 06			12 34		13 09				
Torre	d						10 18					11 08		12 09					13 12				
Newton Abbot	a				09 19	10 01	10 26	10 52	11 01	11 06	11 19	11 16	12 01	12 17	12 27	12 34	12 47	13 01	13 20	13 40	14 01		14 23
	d				09 20	10 03	10 35	10 54	11 03	11 08	11 21	11 28	12 03	12 19	12 29	12 36	12 49	13 03	13 22	13 42	14 03		14 24
Teignmouth	d				09 27		10 42			11 15		11 35		12 26			12 56		13 29				
Dawlish	d				09 33		10 47			11 20		11 40		12 31			13 01		13 34				
Dawlish Warren	d						10 52					11 45		12c49			13 06		13 39				
Starcross	d						10 56					11 49		12 53					13 43				
Exeter St Thomas	d						11 07					11 58		13 03					13 52				
Exeter St Davids 6	a				09 47	10 21	11 10	11 14	11 21	11 30	11 41	12 02	12 21	13 07	12 49	12 55	13 20	13 24	13 56	14 02	14 23		14 44
Exeter Central	a													13 36									
Exmouth	a													14 04									
Exeter St Davids 6	d	08 01	08 43	09 35	09 48	10 23		11 16	11 23	11 32	11 43		12 23		12 50	12 57		13 26		14 04	14 25		14 45
Tiverton Parkway	d	08 18	08 58	09 53		10 37		11 31	11 37	11 46	11 58		12 37			13 10		13 40		14 18	14 39		
Taunton	d	08 35	09 12	10b19	10 14	10 51		11 46	11 51	12 00	12 13		12 51		13 15	13 25		13 54		14 33	14 54		15 11
Bridgwater	a	08 46		10 31																			
Weston-super-Mare	a	09 04		10 49						12 20													
Bristol Temple Meads 10	a	09 38		11 20		11 27		12 23	12 27	12 45			13 24			13 57		14 27			15 27		
Bath Spa 7	a							12 42															
Filton Abbey Wood	a	09 55																					
Bristol Parkway 7	a					11 38			12 38	13 08			13 38			14 08		14 38			15 38		
Swindon	a							13 10															
Newport (South Wales)	a	10 27																					
Cardiff Central 7	a	10 43																					
Birmingham New Street 12	a					12 50			13 50	14 26			14 50			15 27		15 50			16 50		
Castle Cary	d		09 34								12 34												15 33
Westbury	d		09 54		10 53						12 53				13e59								15 50
Pewsey	d		10 11								13 10												16 08
Hungerford	a																						
Newbury	a		10 31		11 26						13 30												16 29
Thatcham	a																						
Theale	a																						
Reading 7	a		10 48		11 47			13 42			13 48				14 48					15 49			16 47
Slough 3	a																						
London Paddington 15 ⊖	a		11 29		12 29			14 21			14 29				15 29					16 29			17 29

b arr. 1009 c arr. 1235 e arr. 1351

For connections to Oxford, Gatwick Airport and Heathrow Airport please refer to Tables 116, 148 and 125A

Table 135

Sundays
12 September to 17 October

Cornwall and Devon - Birmingham and London

		GW	GW	GW	XC	XC	GW	GW	GW	XC	GW	GW	GW	GW	GW	XC	GW	GW	GW	XC	GW	XC	GW	GW
					◇1 🛒	◇1 🛒		◇1 🍽	◇1 🍽	◇1 🛒	◇1 🍽	◇1 🍽			◇1 🍽	◇1 🛒	◇1 🍽		◇	◇1 🛒	◇1 🍽	◇1 🛒		◇1 🍽
Penzance	d		12 00			12 30		12 56						13 50			14 45		15 07	15 30				16 10
St Erth	d		12 07			12 40		13 06						14 00			14 55		15 16	15 38				16 21
Hayle	d					12 44								14 03					15 19					
Camborne	d		12 21			12 56		13 20						14 13			15 07		15 29	15 51				16 33
Redruth	d		12 27			13 02		13 26						14 19			15 14		15 35	15 57				16 40
Truro	d		12 39			13 14		13 38						14 32			15 27		15 47	16 09				16 52
St Austell	d		12 57			13 31		13 57						14 49			15 44		16 04	16 25				17 10
Newquay	d																							
Par	d		13 05			13 38		14 03						14 57			15 52		16 11	16 33				17 16
Lostwithiel	d		13 12			13 45								15 04					16 18					
Bodmin Parkway	d		13 19			13 52		14 16						15 10			16 03		16 24	16 44				17 28
Liskeard 6	d		13 33			14 04		14 29						15 24			16 16		16 37	16 56				17 41
Menheniot	d													15x31										
St Germans	d		13 44											15 39					16 48					
Saltash	d		13 53											15 47					16 57					
St Budeaux Ferry Road	d																							
Keyham	d																							
Dockyard	d																							
Devonport	d																							
Plymouth	a		14 01			14 28		14 54						15 55			16 41		17 05	17 20				18 07
	d		14 06		14 23	14 35		14 58	15 05	15 23		15 43		16 02	16 10	16 25	16 45		17 08	17 26	17 46			18 10
Ivybridge	d		14 21											16 17					17 23					
Totnes	d		14 35		14 49	15 00		15 25	15 33	15 49		16 11		16 31	16 42	16 50	17 12		17 37	17 52	18 13			18 38
Paignton	d	14 04		14 34			15 01				15 45		16 10					17 04				18 18	18 25	
Torquay	d	14 09		14 39			15 06				15 51		16 15					17 09				18 24	18 30	
Torre	d	14 12		14 42							15 56		16 18					17 12						
Newton Abbot	a	14 20	14 47	14 50	15 01	15 11	15 16	15 37	15 45	16 01	16 04	16 22	16 27	16 43	16 53	17 01	17 24	17 20	17 49	18 02	18 25	18 34	18 40	18 50
	d	14 28	14 48	14 53	15 03	15 12	15 17	15 38	15 46	16 03	16 05	16 24	16 29	16 44	16 55	17 03	17 25	17 29	17 51	18 04	18 26	18 35	18 41	18 50
Teignmouth	d	14 35	14 55	15 00			15 24				16 13		16 36					17 36	17 58				18 49	
Dawlish	d	14 40	15 00	15 05			15 29				16 18		16 41					17 41	18 03				18 54	
Dawlish Warren	d	14 45					15 33						16 46					17 46					18 58	
Starcross	d	14 49					15 37						16 50					17 50						
Exeter St Thomas	d	14 58					15 46						16 59					17 59						
Exeter St Davids 6	a	15 02	15 13	15 18	15 23	15 31	15 53	15 58	16 06	16 23	16 32	16 44	17 04	17 07	17 15	17 21	17 45	18 03	18 17	18 22	18 47	18 54	19 10	19 14
Exeter Central	a			15 34									17 34										19 36	
Exmouth	a			16 05									18 04										20 03	
Exeter St Davids 6	d				15 25	15 33		16 01	16 08	16 25	16 34	16 45			17 17	17 23	17 47		18 36	18 24	18 49	18 56		19 16
Tiverton Parkway	d				15 38	15 46		16 16	16 23	16 38	16 49	17 01			17 32	17 37	18 02			18 39		19 09		19 31
Taunton	d				15 54	16 01		16 31	16 38	16 54	17 03	17 15			17 46	17 51	18 17		19 07	18 52	19a12	19 23		19 45
Bridgwater	a																		19 19					
Weston-super-Mare	a					16 20			16 59		17 25								19 40					
Bristol Temple Meads 10	a				16 27	16 53			17 21	17 28	17 55				18 25	18 27			20 11	19 27		19 55		
Bath Spa 7	a								17 42		18 12				18 41									
Filton Abbey Wood	a																							
Bristol Parkway 7	a				16 38	17 08				17 38						18 38				19 38		20 08		
Swindon	a								18 10		18 40				19 11									
Newport (South Wales)	a																							
Cardiff Central 7	a																							
Birmingham New Street 12	a				17 49	18 27				18 51						19 50				20 50		21 20		
Castle Cary	d											17 37												20 07
Westbury	d											17 56					18 58							20 27
Pewsey	d											18 13												
Hungerford	a																							
Newbury	a											18 33												
Thatcham	a																							
Theale	a																							
Reading 7	a							17 47	18 42		19 12	18 52			19 42		19 43							21 12
Slough 3	a																							
London Paddington 15 ⊖	a							18 29	19 21		19 59	19 29			20 21		20 29							21 59

For connections to Oxford, Gatwick Airport and Heathrow Airport please refer to Tables 116, 148 and 125A

Table 135

Cornwall and Devon - Birmingham and London

Sundays
12 September to 17 October

		XC ◇1 ✕	GW	GW ◇1	GW	GW ◇1	GW	GW	GW ✕	GW	GW	GW
Penzance	d			17 20				19 00	20 05			21 15
St Erth	d			17 30				19 09	20 14			21 25
Hayle	d								20 17			
Camborne	d			17 43				19 20	20 26			21 38
Redruth	d			17 50				19 26	20 32			21 45
Truro	d			18 01				19 38	20 44			22 00
St Austell	d			18 20				19 55	21 01			22 18
Newquay	d											
Par	d			18 27				20 02	21 09			
Lostwithiel	d							20 09				
Bodmin Parkway	d			18 39				20 15	21 21			22 35
Liskeard 6	d			18 52				20 28	21 35			22 50
Menheniot	d							20x33				
St Germans	d							20 40				
Saltash	d							20 47				
St Budeaux Ferry Road	d											
Keyham	d											
Dockyard	d											
Devonport	d							20 55				
Plymouth	a			19 16				20 59	22 00			23 15
	d	18 23		19 20		19 55		21 15				23 20
Ivybridge	d											
Totnes	d	18 49		19 48				21 42				23 48
Paignton	d		18 55		19 55		20 55			21 55	23 00	
Torquay	d		19 00		20 00		21 00			22 00	23 05	
Torre	d		19 03		20 03		21 03			22 03	23 08	
Newton Abbot	a	19 01	19 11	19 59	20 11	20 31	21 11	21 54		22 11	23 16	23 59
	d	19 03	19 13	20 01	20 13	20 32	21 13	21 55		22 13	23 18	00 01
Teignmouth	d		19 20		20 20		21 20	22 02		22 20	23 25	
Dawlish	d		19 25		20 25		21 25	22 07		22 25	23 30	
Dawlish Warren	d		19 30		20 30		21 30			22 30	23 35	
Starcross	d		19 34		20 34		21 34			22 34	23 39	
Exeter St Thomas	d		19 43		20 43		21 43			22 43	23 48	
Exeter St Davids 6	a	19 23	19 47	20 21	20 47	20 53	21 47	22 21		22 47	23 52	00 36
Exeter Central	a											
Exmouth	a											
Exeter St Davids 6	d	19 25		20 22		20 55						01 27
Tiverton Parkway	d	19 38		20 38		21 10						
Taunton	d	19 54		20 51		21 23						
Bridgwater	a											
Weston-super-Mare	a											
Bristol Temple Meads 10	a	20 27				22 00						02 38
Bath Spa 7	a					22 18						
Filton Abbey Wood	a											
Bristol Parkway 7	a	20 38										
Swindon	a					22 46						
Newport (South Wales)	a											
Cardiff Central 7	a											
Birmingham New Street 12	a	21 51										
Castle Cary	d			21 15								
Westbury	d			21 33								
Pewsey	d			21 51								
Hungerford	a											
Newbury	a			22 11								
Thatcham	a											
Theale	a											
Reading 7	a			22 29		23 27						04s17
Slough 3	a											
London Paddington 15 ⊖	a			23 16		00 13						05 06

For connections to Oxford, Gatwick Airport and Heathrow Airport please refer to Tables 116, 148 and 125A

Table 135

Cornwall and Devon - Birmingham and London

Sundays
from 24 October

		GW ◇	GW ◇1	GW	GW ◇1	XC ◇1 ✕	GW	GW ◇1	XC ◇1 ✕	GW ◇1	GW	XC ◇1 ✕	GW	GW ◇1	GW	XC ◇1 ✕	GW	GW ◇1	XC ◇1 ✕	GW	GW ◇1	GW	GW
Penzance	d									08 32		09 30		09 47				11 00	11 24	11 45			12 00
St Erth	d									08 42		09 38		09 59				11 10	11 35	11 54			12 07
Hayle	d									08 47													
Camborne	d									08 58		09 48		10 11				11 23	11 46				12 21
Redruth	d									09 04		09 54		10 17				11 29	11 53				12 27
Truro	d									09 17		10 06		10 29				11 42	12 06				12 39
St Austell	d									09 34		10 24		10 47				11 59	12 25				12 57
Newquay	d																						
Par	d									09 42		10 31		10 54				12 06	12 32				13 05
Lostwithiel	d																						13 12
Bodmin Parkway	d									09 54		10 42		11 07				12 19	12 44				13 19
Liskeard 6	d									10 07		10 54		11 20				12 32	12 57				13 33
Menheniot	d																						
St Germans	d									10 18													13 44
Saltash	d									10 27													13 53
St Budeaux Ferry Road	d																						
Keyham	d																						
Dockyard	d																						
Devonport	d																						
Plymouth	a									10 36		11 17		11 43				12 57	13 20				14 01
	d				08 40	09 25		10 10	10 25	10 40		11 25		11 45		12 25		13 00	13 23		13 44		14 06
Ivybridge	d																						14 21
Totnes	d				09 07	09 50		10 40	10 50	11 07		11 50		12 15		12 50		13 29	13 49		14 10		14 35
Paignton	d						10 10				11 00		12 01		12 29		13 04					14 04	
Torquay	d						10 15				11 05		12 06		12 34		13 09					14 09	
Torre	d						10 18				11 08		12 09				13 12					14 12	
Newton Abbot	a				09 19	10 01	10 26	10 52	11 01	11 19	11 16	12 01	12 17	12 27	12 47	13 01	13 20	13 40	14 01		14 23	14 20	14 47
	d				09 20	10 03	10 35	10 54	11 03	11 21	11 28	12 03	12 19	12 29	12 49	13 02	13 22	13 42	14 03		14 24	14 28	14 48
Teignmouth	d				09 27		10 42				11 35		12 26		12 56		13 29					14 35	14 55
Dawlish	d				09 33		10 47				11 40		12 31		13 01		13 34					14 40	15 00
Dawlish Warren	d						10 52				11 45		12c49		13 06		13 39					14 45	
Starcross	d						10 56				11 49		12 53				13 43					14 49	
Exeter St Thomas	d						11 07				11 58		13 03				13 52					14 58	
Exeter St Davids 6	a				09 47	10 21	11 10	11 14	11 21	11 41	12 02	12 21	13 07	12 49	13 20	13 24	13 56	14 02	14 23		14 44	15 02	15 13
Exeter Central	a												13 36										
Exmouth	a												14 04										
Exeter St Davids 6	d	08 01	08 43	09 35	09 48	10 23		11 16	11 23	11 43		12 23		12 50		13 26		14 04	14 25		14 45		
Tiverton Parkway	d	08 18	08 58	09 53		10 37		11 31	11 37	11 58		12 37				13 39		14 18	14 39				
Taunton	d	08 35	09 12	10b19	10 14	10 51		11 46	11 51	12 13		12 51		13 15		13 54		14 33	14 54		15 11		
Bridgwater	a	08 46		10 31																			
Weston-super-Mare	a	09 04		10 49																			
Bristol Temple Meads 10	a	09 38		11 20		11 26		12 23	12 27			13 24				14 26			15 27				
Bath Spa 7	a							12 42															
Filton Abbey Wood	a	09 55																					
Bristol Parkway 7	a					11 38			12 38			13 38				15 08			15 38				
Swindon	a							13 10															
Newport (South Wales)	a	10 27				12 14			13 03			14 03											
Cardiff Central 7	a	10 43																					
Birmingham New Street 12	a					13 50			14 53			15 50				16 26			16 50				
Castle Cary	d		09 34							12 34											15 33		
Westbury	d		09 54		10 53					12 53				13e59							15 50		
Pewsey	d		10 11							13 10											16 08		
Hungerford	a																						
Newbury	a		10 31		11 26					13 30											16 29		
Thatcham	a																						
Theale	a																						
Reading 7	a		10 48		11 47			13 42		13 48				14 48				15 49			16 47		
Slough 3	a																						
London Paddington 15 ⊖	a		11 29		12 29			14 21		14 29				15 29				16 29			17 29		

b arr. 1009
c arr. 1235
e arr. 1351

For connections to Oxford, Gatwick Airport and Heathrow Airport please refer to Tables 116, 148 and 125A

Table 135

Cornwall and Devon - Birmingham and London

Sundays
from 24 October

		GW	XC	XC	GW	GW	GW	XC	GW	GW	GW	GW	GW	XC	GW	GW	GW	XC	GW	XC	GW	GW	XC	GW
			◇1 ⌶	◇1 ⌶		◇1 ⊏	◇1 ⊏	◇1 ⌶	◇1 ⊏	◇1 ⊏			◇1 ⊏	◇1 ⌶	◇1 ⊏		◇	◇1 ⌶	◇1 ⊏	◇1 ⌶		◇1 ⊏	◇1 ⌶	
Penzance	d			12 30		12 56						13 50			14 45		15 07	15 30				16 10		
St Erth	d			12 40		13 06						14 00			14 55		15 16	15 38				16 21		
Hayle	d			12 44								14 03					15 19							
Camborne	d			12 56		13 20						14 13			15 07		15 29	15 51				16 33		
Redruth	d			13 02		13 26						14 19			15 14		15 35	15 57				16 40		
Truro	d			13 14		13 38						14 32			15 27		15 47	16 09				16 52		
St Austell	d			13 31		13 57						14 49			15 44		16 04	16 25				17 10		
Newquay	d																							
Par	d			13 38		14 03						14 57			15 52		16 11	16 33				17 16		
Lostwithiel	d			13 45								15 04					16 18							
Bodmin Parkway	d			13 52		14 16						15 10			16 03		16 24	16 44				17 28		
Liskeard 6	d			14 04		14 29						15 24			16 16		16 37	16 56				17 41		
Menheniot	d											15x31												
St Germans	d											15 39					16 48							
Saltash	d											15 47					16 57							
St Budeaux Ferry Road	d																							
Keyham	d																							
Dockyard	d																							
Devonport	d																							
Plymouth	a			14 28		14 54						15 55			16 41		17 05	17 20				18 07		
	d		14 23	14 35		14 58	15 05	15 23		15 43		16 02	16 10	16 25	16 45		17 08	17 26	17 46			18 10	18 23	
Ivybridge	d											16 17					17 23							
Totnes	d		14 49	15 00		15 25	15 33	15 49		16 11		16 31	16 42	16 50	17 12		17 37	17 52	18 13			18 38	18 49	
Paignton	d	14 34			15 01				15 45		16 10					17 04				18 18	18 25			18 55
Torquay	d	14 39			15 06				15 51		16 15					17 09				18 24	18 30			19 00
Torre	d	14 42							15 56		16 18					17 12								19 03
Newton Abbot	a	14 50	15 01	15 11	15 16	15 37	15 45	16 01	16 04	16 22	16 27	16 43	16 53	17 01	17 24	17 20	17 49	18 02	18 25	18 34	18 40	18 50	19 01	19 11
	d	14 53	15 03	15 12	15 17	15 38	15 46	16 03	16 05	16 24	16 29	16 44	16 55	17 03	17 25	17 29	17 51	18 04	18 26	18 35	18 41	18 50	19 03	19 13
Teignmouth	d	15 00			15 24				16 13		16 36					17 36	17 58				18 49			19 20
Dawlish	d	15 05			15 29				16 18		16 41					17 41	18 03				18 54			19 25
Dawlish Warren	d				15 33						16 46					17 46					18 58			19 30
Starcross	d				15 37						16 50					17 50								19 34
Exeter St Thomas	d				15 46						16 59					17 59								19 43
Exeter St Davids 6	a	15 18	15 23	15 31	15 53	15 58	16 06	16 23	16 32	16 44	17 04	17 07	17 15	17 21	17 45	18 03	18 17	18 22	18 47	18 54	19 10	19 14	19 23	19 47
Exeter Central	a	15 34									17 34										19 36			
Exmouth	a	16 05									18 04										20 03			
Exeter St Davids 6	d		15 25	15 33		16 01	16 08	16 25	16 34	16 45			17 17	17 23	17 47		18 36	18 24	18 49	18 56		19 16	19 25	
Tiverton Parkway	d		15 38	15 46		16 16	16 23	16 38	16 49	17 01			17 32	17 37	18 02			18 39		19 09		19 31	19 38	
Taunton	d		15 54	16 01		16 31	16 38	16 54	17 03	17 15			17 46	17 51	18 17		19 07	18 52	19a12	19 23		19 45	19 54	
Bridgwater	a																19 19							
Weston-super-Mare	a			16 20			16 59		17 25								19 40							
Bristol Temple Meads 10	a		16 27	16 53			17 21	17 28	17 55				18 25	18 27			20 11	19 27		19 55			20 27	
Bath Spa 7	a						17 42		18 12				18 41											
Filton Abbey Wood	a																							
Bristol Parkway 7	a		16 38	17 08				17 38						18 38				19 38		20 08			20 38	
Swindon	a						18 10		18 40				19 11											
Newport (South Wales)	a																							
Cardiff Central 7	a																							
Birmingham New Street 12	a		17 49	18 27				18 51						19 50				20 50		21 20			21 51	
Castle Cary	d									17 37												20 07		
Westbury	d									17 56					18 58							20 27		
Pewsey	d									18 13														
Hungerford	a																							
Newbury	a									18 33														
Thatcham	a																							
Theale	a																							
Reading 7	a					17 47	18 42		19 12	18 52			19 42		19 43							21 12		
Slough 3	a																							
London Paddington 15 ⊖	a					18 29	19 21		19 59	19 29			20 21		20 29							21 59		

For connections to Oxford, Gatwick Airport and Heathrow Airport please refer to Tables 116, 148 and 125A

Table 135

Cornwall and Devon - Birmingham and London

Sundays
from 24 October

		GW	GW	GW	GW	GW	GW	GW	GW	GW
		◇1 ⊏		◇1 ⊏			⌶			🛏 ⊏
Penzance	d	17 20				19 00	20 05			21 15
St Erth	d	17 30				19 09	20 14			21 25
Hayle	d						20 17			
Camborne	d	17 43				19 20	20 26			21 38
Redruth	d	17 50				19 26	20 32			21 45
Truro	d	18 01				19 38	20 44			22 00
St Austell	d	18 20				19 55	21 01			22 18
Newquay	d									
Par	d	18 27				20 02	21 09			
Lostwithiel	d					20 09				
Bodmin Parkway	d	18 39				20 15	21 21			22 35
Liskeard 6	d	18 52				20 28	21 35			22 50
Menheniot	d					20x33				
St Germans	d					20 40				
Saltash	d					20 47				
St Budeaux Ferry Road	d									
Keyham	d									
Dockyard	d									
Devonport	d					20 55				
Plymouth	a	19 16				20 59	22 00			23 15
	d	19 20		19 55		21 15				23 20
Ivybridge	d									
Totnes	d	19 48				21 42				23 48
Paignton	d		19 55		20 55			21 55	23 00	
Torquay	d		20 00		21 00			22 00	23 05	
Torre	d		20 03		21 03			22 03	23 08	
Newton Abbot	a	19 59	20 11	20 31	21 11	21 54		22 11	23 16	23 59
	d	20 01	20 13	20 32	21 13	21 55		22 13	23 18	00 01
Teignmouth	d		20 20		21 20	22 02		22 20	23 25	
Dawlish	d		20 25		21 25	22 07		22 25	23 30	
Dawlish Warren	d		20 30		21 30			22 30	23 35	
Starcross	d		20 34		21 34			22 34	23 39	
Exeter St Thomas	d		20 43		21 43			22 43	23 48	
Exeter St Davids 6	a	20 21	20 47	20 53	21 47	22 21		22 47	23 52	00 36
Exeter Central	a									
Exmouth	a									
Exeter St Davids 6	d	20 22		20 55						01 27
Tiverton Parkway	d	20 38		21 10						
Taunton	d	20 51		21 23						
Bridgwater	a									
Weston-super-Mare	a									
Bristol Temple Meads 10	a			22 00						02 38
Bath Spa 7	a			22 18						
Filton Abbey Wood	a									
Bristol Parkway 7	a									
Swindon	a			22 46						
Newport (South Wales)	a									
Cardiff Central 7	a									
Birmingham New Street 12	a									
Castle Cary	d	21 15								
Westbury	d	21 33								
Pewsey	d	21 51								
Hungerford	a									
Newbury	a	22 11								
Thatcham	a									
Theale	a									
Reading 7	a	22 29		23 27						04s17
Slough 3	a									
London Paddington 15 ⊖	a	23 16		00 13						05 06

Table 135A

Redruth - Helston

Bus Service

		GW BHX A	GW BHX	GW BHX	GW BHX	GW BHX	GW BHX	GW BHX	GW BHX	GW BHX	GW BHX	GW BHX	GW BHX	GW BHX	GW BHX
Redruth	d	08 00	09 15	10 15	11 15	12 15	13 15	14 15	15 15	16 15	17 00	18 15	19 15	21 15	23 25
Helston Coinagehall St	a	08 38	09 47	10 47	11 47	12 47	13 47	14 47	15 47	16 47	17 42	18 47	19 47	21 47	23 51

Saturdays

		GW A	GW A	GW	GW	GW	GW	GW	GW	GW	GW	GW	GW	GW	GW
Redruth	d	08 00	09 15	10 15	11 15	12 15	13 15	14 15	15 15	16 15	17 10	18 15	19 15	21 15	23 25
Helston Coinagehall St	a	08 29	09 47	10 47	11 47	12 47	13 47	14 47	15 47	16 47	17 42	18 47	19 47	21 47	23 51

Sundays

		GW	GW	GW	GW	GW
Redruth	d	09 50	11 50	13 50	15 50	17 50
Helston Coinagehall St	a	10 19	12 19	14 19	16 19	18 19

A Operates on School Holidays only

Table 135A

Mondays to Fridays

Helston - Redruth

Bus Service

		GW BHX	GW BHX	GW BHX	GW BHX	GW BHX	GW BHX	GW BHX	GW BHX A	GW BHX	GW BHX B	GW BHX	GW BHX	GW BHX	GW BHX
Helston Coinagehall St	d	07 05	08 06	09 30	10 30	11 30	12 30	13 30	14 30	15 15	16 30	17 30	18 40	19 50	21 50
Redruth	a	07 39	08 55	10 04	11 04	12 04	13 04	14 04	15 04	16 04	17 04	18 04	19 12	20 22	22 22

Saturdays

		GW	GW	GW	GW	GW	GW	GW	GW	GW	GW	GW	GW	GW	GW
Helston Coinagehall St	d	07 05	08 10	09 30	10 30	11 30	12 30	13 30	14 30	15 30	16 30	17 30	18 40	19 50	21 50
Redruth	a	07 39	08 44	10 04	11 04	12 04	13 04	14 04	15 04	16 04	17 04	18 04	19 12	20 22	22 22

Sundays

		GW	GW	GW	GW	GW
Helston Coinagehall St	d	08 50	10 50	12 50	14 50	16 50
Redruth	a	09 21	11 21	13 21	15 21	17 21

A Operates during School Holidays only

B Runs during school holidays only.

Table 135B

Mondays to Fridays

St. Austell - Eden Project

Bus Service

		GW	GW	GW	GW	GW	GW	GW	GW	GW	GW	GW	GW	GW	GW	GW	GW	GW	GW
			BHX	BHX			BHX		BHX	BHX		BHX		BHX		BHX		BHX	
St Austell	d	08 35	08 50	09 30	09 35	10 35	10 40	11 35	11 50	12 30	12 35	13 55	14 35	15 02	15 35	16 10	16 35	16 50	17 35
Eden Project	a	08 57	09 09	09 49	09 57	10 57	10 59	11 57	12 09	12 49	12 57	14 14	14 57	15 21	15 57	16 29	16 57	17 09	17 57

Saturdays

		GW	GW	GW	GW	GW	GW	GW	GW	GW	GW	GW	GW	GW	GW	GW	GW	GW	GW
St Austell	d	08 35	08 50	09 30	09 35	10 35	10 40	11 35	12 05	12 30	12 35	13 35	13 55	14 35	15 02	15 35	15 50	16 35	17 35
Eden Project	a	08 57	09 09	09 49	09 57	10 57	10 59	11 57	12 24	12 49	12 57	13 57	14 14	14 57	15 21	15 57	16 09	16 57	17 57

Sundays

		GW	GW	GW	GW	GW	GW	GW	GW	GW	GW	GW	GW
St Austell	d	08 50	10 35	11 35	11 40	12 30	12 35	13 35	14 35	14 45	15 35	16 25	17 10
Eden Project	a	09 09	10 57	11 57	11 59	12 49	12 57	13 54	14 57	15 04	15 57	16 44	17 29

Table 135B

Mondays to Fridays

Eden Project - St. Austell

Bus Service

		GW	GW	GW	GW	GW	GW	GW	GW	GW	GW	GW	GW	GW	GW	GW	GW	GW
			BHX	BHX			BHX		BHX			BHX		BHX		BHX		
Eden Project	d	09 00	09 10	09 55	10 00	11 00	11 15	12 00	12 10	13 00	14 00	14 25	15 00	15 22	16 00	16 30	17 00	18 00
St Austell	a	09 24	09 29	10 14	10 24	11 24	11 34	12 24	12 29	13 24	14 24	14 44	15 24	15 41	16 24	16 49	17 24	18 24

Saturdays

		GW	GW	GW	GW	GW	GW	GW	GW	GW	GW	GW	GW	GW	GW	GW	GW	GW
Eden Project	d	09 00	09 10	09 55	10 00	11 00	11 15	12 00	13 00	13 15	14 00	14 25	15 00	15 22	16 00	16 25	17 00	18 00
St Austell	a	09 24	09 29	10 14	10 24	11 24	11 34	12 24	13 24	13 34	14 24	14 44	15 24	15 41	16 24	16 44	17 24	18 24

Sundays

		GW	GW	GW	GW	GW	GW	GW	GW	GW	GW	GW	GW
Eden Project	d	09 50	11 00	12 00	13 05	14 00	14 25	15 00	15 15	16 00	16 05	16 50	17 50
St Austell	a	10 09	11 20	12 20	13 24	14 20	14 44	15 20	15 34	16 24	16 24	17 09	18 09

Table 135C

Mondays to Saturdays

Bodmin - Wadebridge and Padstow

Bus Service

		GW	GW	GW	GW	GW BHX	GW	GW	GW	GW	GW	GW BHX	GW	GW BHX	GW
Bodmin Parkway	d	07 25	08 30	09 30	10 30	11 30	12 30	13 30	14 30	15 30	16 30	17 30	18 30	19 30	22 00
Bodmin Mount Folly	a	07 35	08 40	09 40	10 40	11 40	12 40	13 40	14 40	15 40	16 40	17 40	18 40	19 40	22 10
Wadebridge Bus Station	a	07 55	09 00	10 00	11 00	12 00	13 00	14 00	15 00	16 00	17 00	18 00	19 00	20 00	22 30
Padstow Old Rly Station	a	08 27	09 27	10 27	11 27	12 27	13 27	14 27	15 27	16 27	17 27	18 27	19 27	20 27	22 57

Sundays

		GW	GW	GW	GW	GW	GW
Bodmin Parkway	d	09 30	11 30	13 30	15 30	17 30	19 30
Bodmin Mount Folly	a	09 40	11 40	13 40	15 40	17 40	19 40
Wadebridge Bus Station	a	10 00	12 00	14 00	16 00	18 00	20 00
Padstow Old Rly Station	a	10 27	12 27	14 27	16 27	18 27	20 27

Table 135C

Mondays to Saturdays

Padstow and Wadebridge - Bodmin

Bus Service

		GW	GW	GW	GW	GW BHX	GW	GW	GW	GW BHX	GW	GW	GW	GW	GW BHX
Padstow Old Rly Station	d	06 30	07 30	08 30	09 30	10 30	11 30	12 30	13 30	14 30	15 30	16 30	17 30	18 30	20 30
Wadebridge Bus Station	d	06 55	07 55	08 55	09 55	10 55	11 55	12 55	13 55	14 55	15 55	16 55	17 55	18 55	20 55
Bodmin Mount Folly	d	07 15	08 15	09 15	10 15	11 15	12 15	13 15	14 15	15 15	16 15	17 15	18 15	19 15	21 15
Bodmin Parkway	a	07 25	08 25	09 25	10 25	11 25	12 25	13 25	14 25	15 25	16 25	17 25	18 25	19 25	21 25

Sundays

		GW	GW	GW	GW	GW	GW
Padstow Old Rly Station	d	08 30	10 30	12 30	14 30	16 30	18 30
Wadebridge Bus Station	d	08 55	10 55	12 55	14 55	16 55	18 55
Bodmin Mount Folly	d	09 15	11 15	13 15	15 15	17 15	19 15
Bodmin Parkway	a	09 25	11 25	13 25	15 25	17 25	19 25

Table 135D

Mondays to Saturdays

Exeter - Okehampton, Holsworthy and Bude

Bus Service

Exeter St Davids	d
Okehampton West Street	a
Holsworthy Library	a
Holsworthy Cattle Market	a
Bude Strand	a

Sundays

Exeter St Davids	d
Okehampton West Street	a
Holsworthy Library	a
Holsworthy Cattle Market	a
Bude Strand	a

Details of service not available at time of going to press

Table 135D

Mondays to Saturdays

Bude, Holsworthy and Okehampton - Exeter

Bus Service

Bude Strand	d
Holsworthy Church	d
Holsworthy Cattle Market	d
Okehampton West Street	d
Exeter St Davids	a

Sundays

Bude Strand	d
Holsworthy Church	d
Holsworthy Cattle Market	d
Okehampton West Street	d
Exeter St Davids	a

Details of service not available at time of going to press

Table 135E

Mondays to Saturdays

Taunton - Watchet, Dunster and Minehead

Bus Service

Taunton	d
Bishops Lydeard Hithermead	a
Watchet (West Somerset Ry)	a
Dunster Steep	a
Minehead Parade	a
Minehead Butlins	a

Sundays

Taunton	d
Bishops Lydeard Hithermead	a
Watchet (West Somerset Ry)	a
Dunster Steep	a
Minehead Parade	a
Minehead Butlins	a

Details of service not available at time of going to press

Table 135E

Mondays to Saturdays

Minehead, Dunster and Watchet - Taunton

Bus Service

Minehead Butlins	d
Minehead Bancks Street	d
Dunster Steep	d
Watchet (West Somerset Ry)	d
Bishops Lydeard Hithermead	d
Taunton	a

Sundays

Minehead Butlins	d
Minehead Bancks Street	d
Dunster Steep	d
Watchet (West Somerset Ry)	d
Bishops Lydeard Hithermead	d
Taunton	a

Details of service not available at time of going to press

Table 136

Mondays to Fridays

Exmouth - Exeter - Barnstaple

		SW MX ◇1 ☕	GW MO	GW MX	GW	SW 1	GW	GW	SW 1	GW		SW 1	GW	GW	GW	GW	GW	SW ◇1	GW	GW		SW ◇1 ☕	GW	GW	SW ◇1 ☕
Exmouth	d		23p59	00 02			06 12	06 46		07 15			07 53		08 23		08 53		09 23	09 53			10 23	10 53	
Lympstone Village	d		00 03	00 06			06 16	06 50		07 19			07 57		08 27		08 57		09 27	09 57			10 27	10 57	
Lympstone Commando	d		00x04	00x07			06x17	06x53		07x21			07x58		08x29		08x58		09x28				10x28		
Exton	d		00x06	00x09			06x19	06x54		07x22			08x00		08x30		09x00		09x30				10x30		
Topsham	d		00 11	00 14			06 24	06 59		07 29			08 05		08 35		09 05		09 35	10 05			10 35	11 05	
Digby & Sowton	d		00 15	00 19			06 29	07 04		07 33			08 10		08 40		09 10		09 40	10 10			10 40	11 10	
Polsloe Bridge	d		00 19	00 22			06 32	07 07		07 37			08 14		08 44		09 14		09 44				10 44		
St James' Park	d		00 21	00 25			06 35	07 10		07 40			08 17	08 33	08 47		09 17		09 47				10 47		
Exeter Central	a	23p56	00 24	00 27		06 29	06 37	07 12	07 37	07 42		08 12	08 20	08 35	08 49		09 19	09 37	09 50	10 16		10 37	10 49	11 16	11 37
	d	23p57	00 24	00 28		06 32	06 38	07 13	07 39	07 43		08 14	08 24	08 36	08 50	09 06	09 20	09 39	09 50	10 17		10 39	10 50	11 17	11 39
Exeter St Davids 6	a	00 01	00 27	00 31		06 35	06 41	07 16	07 42	07 46		08 17	08 26	08 41	08 54	09 11	09 24	09 42	09 55	10 21		10 42	10 54	11 21	11 42
	d				05 56		06 55	07 20		07 50			08 31		09 16		09 27		09 56	10 27			10 56	11 27	
Newton St Cyres	d																								
Crediton	d				06 07		07 06						08 42				09 38			10 38				11 38	
Yeoford	d				06 13		07 12						08 49				09 44			10 44				11 44	
Sampford Courtenay	d																								
Okehampton	a																								
Copplestone	d				06x18		07x18						08x53				09x49			10x49				11x49	
Morchard Road	d						07x21						08x56				09x52			10x52				11x52	
Lapford	d						07x25																		
Eggesford	d				06 32		07b39						09 11				10 08			11 08				12 08	
Kings Nympton	d						07x44						09x17												
Portsmouth Arms	d						07x49																		
Umberleigh	d				06x47		07x55						09x27				10x23			11x23				12x23	
Chapelton	d						07x59																		
Barnstaple	a				06 59		08 08						09 39				10 35			11 35				12 35	

		GW	GW	SW ◇1 ☕	GW	GW		SW ◇1 ☕	GW	GW	SW ◇1 ☕	GW	GW	SW ◇1 ☕	GW	GW		SW ◇1 ☕	GW	GW	GW	SW ◇1 ☕	GW	GW	GW
Exmouth	d	11 23	11 53		12 23	12 53			13 23	13 53		14 23	14 53		15 23	15 53				16 25	16 55			17 25	17 55
Lympstone Village	d	11 27	11 57		12 27	12 57			13 27	13 57		14 27	14 57		15 27	15 57				16 29	16 59			17 29	18 01
Lympstone Commando	d	11x28			12x28				13x28			14x28			15x28	15x58				16x30	17x00			17x30	18x02
Exton	d	11x30			12x30				13x30			14x30			15x30	16x00				16x32	17x02			17x32	18x04
Topsham	d	11 35	12 05		12 35	13 05			13 35	14 05		14 35	15 05		15 35	16 05				16 37	17 07			17 37	18 09
Digby & Sowton	d	11 40	12 10		12 40	13 10			13 40	14 10		14 40	15 10		15 40	16 10				16 42	17 12			17 42	18 14
Polsloe Bridge	d	11 44			12 44				13 44			14 44			15 44	16 14				16 46	17 15			17 45	18 17
St James' Park	d	11 47			12 47				13 47			14 47			15 47	16 17			16 43	16 48	17 18		17 40	17 48	18 20
Exeter Central	a	11 49	12 16	12 37	12 49	13 16		13 37	13 49	14 16	14 37	14 49	15 16	15 37	15 49	16 19		16 35	16 45	16 51	17 20	17 35	17 42	17 50	18 22
	d	11 50	12 17	12 39	12 50	13 17		13 39	13 50	14 17	14 39	14 50	15 17	15 39	15 50	16 20		16 37	16 46	16 53	17 21	17 36	17 45	17 51	18 23
Exeter St Davids 6	a	11 54	12 21	12 42	12 54	13 21		13 42	13 54	14 21	14 42	14 54	15 21	15 42	15 54	16 25		16 42	16 49	16 56	17 24	17 42	17 48	17 55	18 26
	d	11 56	12 27		13 03	13 27			13 56	14 27		14 56	15 27		15 56	16 26			16 56	16 57	17 26		17 50	17 57	18 28
Newton St Cyres	d																							18x04	
Crediton	d		12 38			13 38				14 38			15 38							17 08				18 11	
Yeoford	d		12 44			13 44				14 44			15 44							17 15				18 17	
Sampford Courtenay	d																								
Okehampton	a																								
Copplestone	d		12x49			13x49				14x49			15x49							17x19				18x22	
Morchard Road	d		12x52			13x52				14x52			15x52							17x22				18x25	
Lapford	d																			17x27				18x29	
Eggesford	d		13 08			14 08				15 08			16 08							17 38				18 41	
Kings Nympton	d					14x15														17x45				18x48	
Portsmouth Arms	d																							18x52	
Umberleigh	d		13x23			14x23				15x23			16x23							17x55				18x59	
Chapelton	d																							19x03	
Barnstaple	a		13 37			14 37				15 35			16 35							18 07				19 13	

		SW ◇1 ☕		GW	GW	GW	SW ◇1 ☕	GW	GW	SW ◇1 ☕	GW	GW		GW	SW ◇1 ☕	GW	GW	SW ◇1 ☕	GW	SW ◇1 ☕
Exmouth	d			18 27		18 55		19 35	20 08					21 04			22 04		23 10	
Lympstone Village	d			18 31		18 59		19 42	20 12					21 08			22 08		23 14	
Lympstone Commando	d					19x00			20x13					21x09			22x09		23x15	
Exton	d					19x02			20x15					21x11			22x11		23x17	
Topsham	d			18 37		19 07		19 49	20 20					21 16			22 16		23 22	
Digby & Sowton	d			18 42		19 12		19 54	20 25					21 21			22 21		23 27	
Polsloe Bridge	d					19 15			20 28					21 24			22 24		23 30	
St James' Park	d					19 18			20 31					21 27			22 27		23 33	
Exeter Central	a	18 38		18 49		19 20	19 38	20 00	20 34	20 39				21 29	21 37		22 29	22 40	23 36	23 56
	d	18 39		18 49	18 58	19 21	19 40	20 01	20 35	20 40	20 55	21 21		21 30	21 39	21 55	22 30	22 42	23 37	23 57
Exeter St Davids 6	a	18 42		18 53	19 02	19 25	19 45	20 05	20 38	20 44	20 58	21 25		21 35	21 44	22 00	22 34	22 45	23 41	00 01
	d			18 57		19 28					21 00	21 29					22 37			
Newton St Cyres	d			19x04							21x07									
Crediton	d			19 11							21 14									
Yeoford	d			19 18							21 20									
Sampford Courtenay	d																			
Okehampton	a																			
Copplestone	d			19x22							21x26									
Morchard Road	d			19x25							21x29									
Lapford	d										21x33									
Eggesford	d			19 42							21 43									
Kings Nympton	d										21x48									
Portsmouth Arms	d										21x53									
Umberleigh	d			19x56							21x59									
Chapelton	d										22x03									
Barnstaple	a			20 08							22 13									

b arr. 0733

For connections at Exeter St Davids please refer to Table 135

Table 136

Saturdays

Exmouth - Exeter - Barnstaple

		SW ◇1 ☕	GW	GW	SW 1	GW	SW 1	GW	SW 1	GW		GW	GW	SW ◇1	GW	GW	GW	SW ◇1 ☕	GW	GW		SW ◇1 ☕	GW	GW	SW ◇1 ☕
Exmouth	d		00 02			06 12		07 15		07 53		08 23	08 53		09 23	09 53			10 23	10 53			11 23	11 53	
Lympstone Village	d		00 06			06 16		07 19		07 57		08 27	08 57		09 27	09 57			10 27	10 57			11 27	11 57	
Lympstone Commando	d		00x07			06x17		07x21		07x58		08x29	08x58		09x28	09x58			10x28	10x58			11x28	11x58	
Exton	d		00x09			06x19		07x22		08x00		08x30	09x00		09x30				10x30				11x30		
Topsham	d		00 14			06 24		07 29		08 05		08 35	09 05		09 35	10 05			10 35	11 05			11 35	12 05	
Digby & Sowton	d		00 19			06 29		07 33		08 10		08 40	09 10		09 40	10 10			10 40	11 10			11 40	12 10	
Polsloe Bridge	d		00 22			06 32		07 37		08 14		08 44	09 14		09 44				10 44				11 44		
St James' Park	d		00 25			06 35		07 40		08 17		08 47	09 17		09 47				10 47				11 47		
Exeter Central	a	23p56	00 27		06 29	06 37	07 37	07 42	08 13	08 20		08 49	09 19	09 37	09 49	10 16		10 37	10 49	11 16		11 37	11 49	12 16	12 37
	d	23p57	00 28		06 32	06 38	07 39	07 43	08 15	08 24		08 50	09 20	09 39	09 50	10 17	10 30	10 39	10 50	11 17		11 39	11 50	12 17	12 39
Exeter St Davids 6	a	00 01	00 31		06 35	06 41	07 42	07 46	08 18	08 27		08 54	09 24	09 42	09 54	10 21	10 33	10 42	10 54	11 21		11 42	11 54	12 21	12 42
	d			05 56		06 50		07 50		08 31		08 56	09 27		09 56	10 27	10 35		10 56	11 27			11 56	12 27	
Newton St Cyres	d																								
Crediton	d			06 07		07 01				08 42			09 38			10 38				11 38				12 38	
Yeoford	d			06 13		07 07				08 49			09 44			10 44				11 44				12 44	
Sampford Courtenay	d																								
Okehampton	a																								
Copplestone	d			06x18		07x12				08x53			09x49			10x49				11x49				12x49	
Morchard Road	d					07x15				08x56			09x52			10x52				11x52				12x52	
Lapford	d					07x19																			
Eggesford	d			06 32		07b39				09 11			10 08			11 08				12 08				13 08	
Kings Nympton	d					07x44				09x17															
Portsmouth Arms	d					07x49																			
Umberleigh	d			06x47		07x55				09x27			10x23			11x23				12x23				13x23	
Chapelton	d					07x59																			
Barnstaple	a			06 59		08 08				09 39			10 35			11 35				12 35				13 37	

		GW	GW	SW ◇1 ☕	GW A	GW B		GW	SW ◇1 ☕	GW	GW	SW ◇1 ☕	GW	GW	SW ◇1 ☕	GW		GW	GW	GW	SW ◇1 ☕	GW	GW	SW ◇1 ☕	GW
Exmouth	d	12 23	12 53		13 23	13 23		13 53		14 23	14 53		15 23	15 53				16 25		16 55		17 25	17 55		18 27
Lympstone Village	d	12 27	12 57		13 27	13 27		13 57		14 27	14 57		15 27	15 57				16 29		16 59		17 29	17 59		18 31
Lympstone Commando	d	12x28	12x58		13x28	13x28		13x58		14x28	14x58		15x28	15x58				16x30		17x00		17x30	18x00		
Exton	d	12x30			13x30	13x30				14x30			15x30	16x00				16x32		17x02		17x32	18x02		
Topsham	d	12 35	13 05		13 35	13 35		14 05		14 35	15 05		15 35	16 05				16 37		17 07		17 37	18 07		18 37
Digby & Sowton	d	12 40	13 10		13 40	13 40		14 10		14 40	15 10		15 40	16 10				16 42		17 12		17 42	18 12		18 42
Polsloe Bridge	d	12 44			13 44	13 44				14 44			15 44	16 14				16 46		17 15		17 45	18 15		
St James' Park	d	12 47			13 47	13 47				14 47			15 47	16 17				16 48	17 05	17 18		17 48	18 18		
Exeter Central	a	12 49	13 16	13 37	13 49	13 49		14 16	14 37	14 49	15 16	15 37	15 49	16 19	16 35			16 51	17 07	17 20	17 37	17 50	18 20	18 35	18 48
	d	12 50	13 17	13 39	13 50	13 50		14 17	14 39	14 50	15 17	15 39	15 50	16 20	16 37	16 48		16 53	17 08	17 21	17 39	17 51	18 21	18 37	18 49
Exeter St Davids 6	a	12 54	13 21	13 42	13 54	13 54		14 21	14 42	14 53	15 21	15 42	15 54	16 25	16 42	16 51		16 56	17 11	17 24	17 42	17 55	18 24	18 42	18 52
	d	12 56	13 27		14 01	13 56		14 27		14 56	15 27		15 56			16 56		16 57		17 24		17 57	18 26		18 57
Newton St Cyres	d																					18x04			19x04
Crediton	d		13 38					14 38			15 38							17 08				18 11			19 11
Yeoford	d		13 44					14 44			15 44							17 15				18 17			19 18
Sampford Courtenay	d																								
Okehampton	a																								
Copplestone	d		13x49					14x49			15x49							17x19				18x22			19x22
Morchard Road	d		13x52					14x52			15x52							17x22				18x25			19x25
Lapford	d																	17x27				18x29			
Eggesford	d		14 08					15 08			16 08							17 38				18 41			19 42
Kings Nympton	d		14x15															17x45				18x48			
Portsmouth Arms	d																					18x52			
Umberleigh	d		14x23					15x23			16x23							17x55				18x59			19x56
Chapelton	d																					19x03			
Barnstaple	a		14 37					15 35			16 35							18 07				19 13			20 08

		GW		SW ◇1 ☕	GW	GW	SW ◇1 ☕	GW	GW	SW ◇1 ☕	GW	SW ◇1 ☕		GW	GW
Exmouth	d	18 55			19 38	20 08			21 04		22 04			23 10	23 43
Lympstone Village	d	18 59			19 42	20 12			21 08		22 08			23 14	23 47
Lympstone Commando	d	19x00				20x13			21x09		22x09			23x15	23x48
Exton	d	19x02				20x15			21x11		22x11			23x17	23x50
Topsham	d	19 07			19 49	20 20			21 16		22 16			23 22	23 55
Digby & Sowton	d	19 12			19 54	20 25			21 21		22 21			23 27	23 59
Polsloe Bridge	d	19 15				20 28			21 24		22 24			23 30	00 03
St James' Park	d	19 18				20 31			21 27		22 27			23 33	00 06
Exeter Central	a	19 20		19 37	20 00	20 34	20 39		21 29	21 37	22 29	22 37		23 35	00 08
	d	19 21		19 39	20 01	20 35	20 40	20 52	21 30	21 39	22 30	22 39		23 36	00 09
Exeter St Davids 6	a	19 25		19 42	20 05	20 38	20 43	20 55	21 34	21 42	22 34	22 42		23 41	00 14
	d				20 07	20 56		21 00							
Newton St Cyres	d							21x07							
Crediton	d							21 14							
Yeoford	d							21 20							
Sampford Courtenay	d														
Okehampton	a														
Copplestone	d							21x26							
Morchard Road	d							21x29							
Lapford	d							21x33							
Eggesford	d							21 43							
Kings Nympton	d							21x48							
Portsmouth Arms	d							21x53							
Umberleigh	d							21x59							
Chapelton	d							22x03							
Barnstaple	a							22 13							

A until 4 September

B from 11 September

b arr. 0728

For connections at Exeter St Davids please refer to Table 135

Table 136

Sundays

Exmouth - Exeter - Barnstaple

		GW	GW	SW	GW	GW	SW	GW	GW	SW		GW	SW	GW	SW	GW	SW	GW	SW	GW		SW	GW	SW	GW
		A		1			◇1			◇1			◇1		◇1		◇1		◇1			◇1		◇1	
Exmouth	d	23p43			09 10	10 03			11 10			12 08		13 10		14 10		15 10		16 10			17 10		18 10
Lympstone Village	d	23p47			09 14	10 07			11 14			12 12		13 14		14 14		15 14		16 14			17 13		18 14
Lympstone Commando	d	23b48			09x15	10x08			11x15			12x13		13x15		14x15		15x15		16x15			17x14		18x15
Exton	d	23b50			09x17	10x10			11x17			12x15		13x17		14x17		15x17		16x17			17x16		18x17
Topsham	d	23p55			09 22	10 15			11 22			12 20		13 22		14 22		15 22		16 22			17 22		18 21
Digby & Sowton	d	23p59			09 27	10 20			11 27			12 25		13 27		14 27		15 27		16 27			17 27		18 26
Polsloe Bridge	d	00 03			09 30	10 23			11 30			12 28		13 30		14 30		15 30		16 30			17 30		18 29
St James' Park	d	00 06			09 33	10 26			11 33			12 31		13 33		14 33		15 33		16 33			17 33		18 32
Exeter Central	a	00 08		08 56	09 36	10 28	10 40		11 35	11 40		12 35	12 40	13 35	13 40	14 35	14 40	15 35	15 40	16 35		16 40	17 35	17 40	18 34
	d	00 09		08 58	09 36	10 29	10 42	11 20	11 35	11 42		12 36	12 42	13 36	13 42	14 36	14 42	15 36	15 42	16 36		16 42	17 36	17 42	18 35
Exeter St Davids ■	a	00 14		09 01	09 40	10 33	10 45	11 23	11 39	11 45		12 39	12 45	13 39	13 45	14 40	14 45	15 39	15 45	16 39		16 45	17 39	17 45	18 39
	d		08 39		09 41			11 35	11 56			12 54		13 56		14 54		16 04		16 54			18 00		18 54
Newton St Cyres	d		08x47		09x49									14x03				16x12							
Crediton	d		08 55		09 57				12 10					14 12				16 19					18c17		
Yeoford	d		09 02		10 04				12 17					14 19				16 26					18 24		
Sampford Courtenay	d																								
Okehampton	a																								
Copplestone	d		09x08		10x08				12x21					14x23				16x31					18x29		
Morchard Road	d		09x11		10x11				12x24					14x26				16x34					18x32		
Lapford	d		09x15		10x16									14x30				16x38					18x37		
Eggesford	d		09 25		10 26				12 37					14 40				16 45					18 46		
Kings Nympton	d		09x31		10x33									14x46				16x53					18x52		
Portsmouth Arms	d				10x37									14x50				16x56					18x57		
Umberleigh	d		09x41		10x43				12x51					14x57				17x04					19x02		
Chapelton	d				10x48									15x01				17x08							
Barnstaple	a		09 52		10 56				13 03					15 10				17 17					19 13		

		SW	GW	SW	GW	SW		SW	GW	GW	GW	SW	GW	GW
		◇1		◇1		◇1		◇1	B	C		◇1		
Exmouth	d		19 10		20 10				21 20	21 20	22 10		23 08	23 59
Lympstone Village	d		19 14		20 14				21 24	21 24	22 14		23 12	00 03
Lympstone Commando	d		19x15		20x15				21x25	21x25	22x15		23x13	00x04
Exton	d		19x17		20x17				21x27	21x27	22x17		23x15	00x06
Topsham	d		19 22		20 22				21 32	21 32	22 23		23 20	00 11
Digby & Sowton	d		19 27		20 27				21 37	21 37	22 28		23 25	00 15
Polsloe Bridge	d		19 30		20 30				21 40	21 40	22 31		23 28	00 19
St James' Park	d		19 33		20 33				21 43	21 44	22 34		23 31	00 21
Exeter Central	a	18 40	19 35	19 40	20 35	20 40		21 40	21 46	21 46	22 36	22 42	23 34	00 24
	d	18 42	19 36	19 42	20 36	20 42		21 42	21 47	21 47	22 37	22 43	23 35	00 24
Exeter St Davids ■	a	18 46	19 39	19 45	20 39	20 45		21 45	21 50	21 50	22 40	22 46	23 38	00 27
	d		19 59		20 54				21 54	21 54				
Newton St Cyres	d		20x06											
Crediton	d		20 16											
Yeoford	d		20 22											
Sampford Courtenay	d													
Okehampton	a													
Copplestone	d		20x27											
Morchard Road	d		20x30											
Lapford	d		20x34											
Eggesford	d		20 44											
Kings Nympton	d		20x50											
Portsmouth Arms	d		20x54											
Umberleigh	d		21x01											
Chapelton	d		21x05											
Barnstaple	a		21 15											

A not 23 May
B until 5 September
C from 12 September
b previous night, stops on request
c arr. 1811

For connections at Exeter St Davids please refer to Table 135

Table 136

Mondays to Fridays

Barnstaple - Exeter - Exmouth

		SW	GW	GW	GW	SW	GW	SW	GW	GW		GW	SW	GW	GW	GW	SW	GW	GW	SW		GW	GW	SW	GW
		◇1				◇1		◇1					◇1				◇1			◇1				◇1	
Barnstaple	d											07 08						08 43				09 43			10 43
Chapelton	d											07x13													
Umberleigh	d											07x17						08x51				09x51			10x51
Portsmouth Arms	d											07x24													
Kings Nympton	d											07x29						09x03							
Eggesford	d											07 38						09 07				10 07			11 07
Lapford	d											07x43						09x14							
Morchard Road	d											07x48						09x17				10x16			11x16
Copplestone	d											07x51						09x22				10x20			11x20
Okehampton	d																								
Sampford Courtenay	d																								
Yeoford	d											07 57						09 25				10 24			11 24
Crediton	d											08 04						09 37				10 37			11 37
Newton St Cyres	d											08x07													
Exeter St Davids ■	a						07 08		07 33	08 10		08 16				09 15		09 48	10 14			10 48	11 11		11 48
	d	05 10	05 44	06 06	06 29	06 40	07 11	07 26	07 36	08 12		08 16	08 26	08 48	08 59	09 18	09 26	09 48	10 18	10 26		10 48	11 18	11 26	11 48
Exeter Central	a	05 13	05 47	06 09	06 32	06 43	07 14	07 29	07 39	08 16		08 20	08 29	08 51	09 04	09 21	09 29	09 51	10 21	10 29		10 51	11 21	11 29	11 51
	d	05 14	05 48	06 10	06 39	06 44	07 15	07 30	07 52	08 17		08 21	08 30	08 52		09 22	09 30	09 52	10 22	10 30		10 52	11 22	11 30	11 52
St James' Park	d			06 12	06 41		07 17		07 54	08a21		08 23		08 54		09 24			10 24				11 24		
Polsloe Bridge	d			06 15	06 44		07 20		07 57			08 27		08 57		09 27			10 27				11 27		
Digby & Sowton	d		05 54	06 19	06 48		07 24		08 01			08 31		09 01		09 31		10 01	10 31			11 01	11 31		12 01
Topsham	d		05 58	06 25	06b58		07 28		08 05			08 35		09 05		09 35		10 05	10 35			11 05	11 35		12 05
Exton	d			06x27	07x01		07x31		08x08			08x38		09x08		09x38			10x38				11x38		
Lympstone Commando	d			06x29	07x03		07x33		08x10			08x40		09x10		09x40			10x40				11x40		
Lympstone Village	d		06 03	06 31	07 06		07 36		08 13			08 43		09 13		09 43		10 11	10 43			11 11	11 43		12 11
Exmouth	a		06 10	06 38	07 11		07 43		08 18			08 48		09 20		09 50		10 19	10 50			11 19	11 50		12 19

		GW	SW	GW	GW	SW		GW	GW	GW	GW	SW	GW	GW	GW	SW		GW	GW	GW	SW	SW	GW	GW	SW
			◇1			◇1						◇1				◇1					◇1	1			◇1
Barnstaple	d			11 43				12 43		13 43			14 43					15 43							
Chapelton	d																								
Umberleigh	d			11x51				12x51		13x51			14x51					15x51							
Portsmouth Arms	d																								
Kings Nympton	d							13x02																	
Eggesford	d			12 07				13 07		14 07			15 07					16 07							
Lapford	d																								
Morchard Road	d			12x16				13x16		14x16			15x16					16x16							
Copplestone	d			12x20				13x20		14x20			15x20					16x20							
Okehampton	d																								
Sampford Courtenay	d																								
Yeoford	d			12 24				13 24		14 24			15 24					16 24							
Crediton	d			12c37				13 37		14 37			15 37					16 37							
Newton St Cyres	d																								
Exeter St Davids ■	a	12 16		12 48	13 13			13 48	14 16	14 48	15 15		15 48		16 13			16 48		17 13			17 50	18 18	
	d	12 18	12 26	12 48	13 18	13 26		13 48	14 18	14 48	15 18	15 26	15 48	16 08	16 18	16 26		16 50	17 10	17 18	17 26	17 46	17 52	18 20	18 26
Exeter Central	a	12 21	12 29	12 51	13 21	13 29		13 51	14 21	14 51	15 21	15 29	15 51	16 11	16 21	16 29		16 53	17 13	17 21	17 29	17 49	17 55	18 23	18 29
	d	12 22	12 30	12 52	13 22	13 30		13 52	14 22	14 52	15 22	15 30	15 52	16 12	16 22	16 30		16 54	17 14	17 22	17 30	17 50	17 56	18 24	18 30
St James' Park	d	12 24			13 24				14 24		15 24			16a16	16 24			16 56	17a18	17 24			17 58	18 26	
Polsloe Bridge	d	12 27			13 27				14 27		15 27				16 27			16 59		17 27			18 01	18 29	
Digby & Sowton	d	12 31		13 01	13 31			14 01	14 31	15 01	15 31		16 01		16 31			17 03		17 31			18 05	18 33	
Topsham	d	12 35		13 05	13 35			14 05	14 35	15 05	15 35		16 05		16 37			17 07		17 37			18 09	18 37	
Exton	d	12x38			13x38				14x38		15x38				16x38			17x10		17x38			18x12	18x38	
Lympstone Commando	d	12x40			13x40				14x40		15x40				16x40			17x12		17x40			18x14	18x40	
Lympstone Village	d	12 43		13 11	13 43			14 11	14 43	15 11	15 43		16 11		16 43			17 15		17 43			18 17	18 43	
Exmouth	a	12 50		13 19	13 50			14 19	14 50	15 19	15 50		16 19		16 50			17 22		17 51			18 25	18 52	

		GW		GW	SW	GW	GW	SW	GW	GW	SW	GW		GW	GW	SW	GW
					◇1			◇1			1					1	
Barnstaple	d	17 08				18 13	19 16							20 24			22 18
Chapelton	d	17x14															22x23
Umberleigh	d	17x18				18x21	19x24							20x32			22x27
Portsmouth Arms	d					18x28											22x34
Kings Nympton	d	17 29				18x33											22x39
Eggesford	d	17 37				18 40	19 40							20 49			22 47
Lapford	d	17 43				18x47											22x52
Morchard Road	d	17x46				18x51	19x49							20x58			22x57
Copplestone	d	17x50				18x55	19x53							21x01			23x00
Okehampton	d																
Sampford Courtenay	d																
Yeoford	d	17 54				18 59	19 58							21 06			23 06
Crediton	d	18e13				19 11	20 06							21 16			23 13
Newton St Cyres	d					19x16	20x09							21x19			23x16
Exeter St Davids ■	a	18 30		18 46		19 25	20 18		20 26			21 28		21 34			23 26
	d	18 32		18 50	19 27	19 32	20 20	20 26	20 30	21 14	21 23	21 30		21 36	22 36	22 57	23 28
Exeter Central	a	18 37		18 53	19 29	19 35	20 25	20 29	20 33	21 19	21 26	21 33		21 41	22 39	23 00	23 31
	d			18 54	19 30	19 36		20 30	20 34		21 29	21 34			22 40	23 01	23 32
St James' Park	d			18 56		19 38			20 36			21 36			22 42		23 34
Polsloe Bridge	d			18 59		19 41			20 39			21 39			22 45		23 37
Digby & Sowton	d			19 03		19 45			20 43			21 43			22 49		23 41
Topsham	d			19 07		19 49			20 47			21 47			22 53		23 45
Exton	d			19x10		19x52			20x49			21x49			22x56		23x47
Lympstone Commando	d			19x12		19x54			20x51			21x51			22x58		23x49
Lympstone Village	d			19 15		19 57			20 54			21 55			23 01		23 52
Exmouth	a			19 23		20 03			21 01			22 01			23 08		23 59

b arr. 0652
c arr. 1232
e arr. 1803

For connections at Exeter St Davids please refer to Table 135

Table 136

For connections at Exeter St Davids please refer to Table 135

Barnstaple - Exeter - Exmouth

Saturdays

		SW	GW	GW	SW	GW	SW	GW	GW	SW		GW	GW	SW	GW	GW	GW	SW	GW	GW		SW	GW	GW	SW
		◇1			◇1		◇1			◇1				◇1				◇1				◇1			◇1
																A	B								
		🛒			🛒		🛒			🛒				🛒				🛒				🛒			🛒
Barnstaple	d								07 08						08 43				09 43				10 43		
Chapelton	d								07x13																
Umberleigh	d								07x17						08x51				09x51				10x51		
Portsmouth Arms	d								07x24																
Kings Nympton	d								07x29						09x03										
Eggesford	d								07 38						09 07				10 07				11 07		
Lapford	d								07x43						09x14										
Morchard Road	d								07x48						09x17				10x16				11x16		
Copplestone	d								07x51						09x22				10x20				11x20		
Okehampton	d																								
Sampford Courtenay	d																								
Yeoford	d								07 57						09 25				10 24				11 24		
Crediton	d								08 04						09 37				10b37				11 37		
Newton St Cyres	d								08x07																
Exeter St Davids ■	a					07 06		07 33	08 16				09 09		09 48	10 10	10 13		10 48	11 15			11 48	12 16	
	d	05 10	05 44	06 29	06 41	07 11	07 26	07 36	08 16	08 26		08 48	09 18	09 26	09 48	10 18	10 18	10 26	10 48	11 18		11 26	11 48	12 18	12 26
Exeter Central	a	05 13	05 47	06 32	06 44	07 14	07 29	07 39	08 20	08 29		08 51	09 21	09 29	09 51	10 21	10 21	10 29	10 51	11 21		11 29	11 51	12 21	12 29
	d	05 14	05 48	06 39	06 45	07 15	07 30	07 52	08 21	08 30		08 52	09 22	09 30	09 52	10 22	10 22	10 30	10 52	11 22		11 30	11 52	12 22	12 30
St James' Park	d			06 41		07 17		07 54	08 23			08 54	09 24		09 55	10 24	10 24			11 24				12 24	
Polsloe Bridge	d			06 44		07 20		07 57	08 27			08 57	09 27		09 58	10 27	10 27			11 27				12 27	
Digby & Sowton	d		05 54	06 48		07 24		08 01	08 31			09 01	09 31		10 01	10 31	10 31		11 01	11 31			12 01	12 31	
Topsham	d		05 58	06 52		07 28		08 05	08 35			09 05	09 35		10 05	10 35	10 35		11 05	11 35			12 05	12 35	
Exton	d			06x54		07x31		08x08	08x38			09x08	09x38		10x08	10x38	10x38			11x38				12x38	
Lympstone Commando	d			06x56		07x33		08x10	08x40			09x10	09x40		10x10	10x40	10x40		11x09	11x40			12x09	12x40	
Lympstone Village	d		06 03	06 59		07 36		08 13	08 43			09 13	09 43		10 11	10 43	10 43		11 11	11 43			12 11	12 43	
Exmouth	a		06 10	07 06		07 43		08 20	08 49			09 20	09 50		10 19	10 50	10 50		11 19	11 50			12 19	12 50	

		GW	GW	SW	GW	GW		GW	SW	GW	GW	SW	GW	GW	GW	SW		GW	GW	GW	GW	SW	GW	GW	SW
				◇1					◇1			◇1				◇1						◇1			◇1
						A		B						B	A										
				🛒					🛒			🛒				🛒						🛒			🛒
Barnstaple	d	11 43			12 43					13 43			14 43						15 43	17 08					
Chapelton	d																			17x14					
Umberleigh	d	11x51			12x51					13x51			14x51						15x51	17x18					
Portsmouth Arms	d																								
Kings Nympton	d				13x02															17x29					
Eggesford	d	12 07			13 07					14 07			15 07						16 07	17 37					
Lapford	d																			17x43					
Morchard Road	d	12x16			13x16					14x16			15x16						16x16	17x46					
Copplestone	d	12x20			13x20					14x20			15x20						16x20	17x50					
Okehampton	d																								
Sampford Courtenay	d																								
Yeoford	d	12 24			13 24					14 24			15 24						16 24	17 54					
Crediton	d	12 37			13 37					14 37			15 37						16 37	18c13					
Newton St Cyres	d																								
Exeter St Davids ■	a	12 48	13 13		13 48	14 00		14 16		14 48	15 15		15 48	16 15	16 14			16 34	16 48	18 30	17 15			18 18	
	d	12 48	13 18	13 26	13 48	14 18		14 18	14 26	14 48	15 18	15 26	15 48	16 17	16 18	16 26		16 41	16 50		17 18	17 26	17 50	18 20	18 26
Exeter Central	a	12 51	13 21	13 29	13 51	14 21		14 21	14 29	14 51	15 21	15 29	15 51	16 20	16 21	16 29		16 44	16 53		17 21	17 29	17 53	18 23	18 29
	d	12 52	13 22	13 30	13 52	14 22		14 22	14 30	14 52	15 22	15 30	15 52	16 21	16 22	16 30			16 54		17 22	17 30	17 54	18 24	18 30
St James' Park	d		13 24			14 24		14 24			15 24		15 57	16 23	16 24				16 56		17 24		17 56	18 26	
Polsloe Bridge	d		13 27			14 27		14 27			15 27			16 26	16 27				16 59		17 27		17 59	18 29	
Digby & Sowton	d	13 01	13 31		14 01	14 31		14 31		15 01	15 31		16 01	16 30	16 31				17 03		17 31		18 03	18 33	
Topsham	d	13 05	13 35		14 05	14 35		14 35		15 05	15 35		16 05	16 37	16 37				17 07		17 37		18 07	18 37	
Exton	d		13x38			14x38		14x38			15x38			16x38	16x38				17x10		17x38		18x10	18x38	
Lympstone Commando	d	13x09	13x40		14x09	14x40		14x40		15x09	15x40		16x09	16x40	16x40				17x12		17x40		18x12	18x40	
Lympstone Village	d	13 11	13 43		14 11	14 43		14 43		15 11	15 43		16 11	16 43	16 43				17 15		17 43		18 15	18 43	
Exmouth	a	13 19	13 50		14 19	14 50		14 50		15 19	15 50		16 19	16 52	16 52				17 22		17 51		18 22	18 52	

		GW		SW	GW	GW	SW	GW	SW	GW	GW	GW		GW	SW	GW
				◇1			◇1		1						1	
				🛒			🛒									
Barnstaple	d				18 13	19 16					20 24	22 18				
Chapelton	d											22x23				
Umberleigh	d				18x21	19x24					20x32	22x27				
Portsmouth Arms	d				18x28							22x34				
Kings Nympton	d				18x33							22x39				
Eggesford	d				18 40	19 40					20 49	22 47				
Lapford	d				18x47							22x52				
Morchard Road	d				18x51	19x49					20x58	22x57				
Copplestone	d				18x55	19x53					21x01	23x00				
Okehampton	d															
Sampford Courtenay	d															
Yeoford	d				18 59	19 58					21 06	23 06				
Crediton	d				19 11	20 06					21 16	23 13				
Newton St Cyres	d				19x16	20x09					21x19	23x16				
Exeter St Davids ■	a	18 46			19 25	20 18		20 25			21 34	23 26				
	d	18 50		19 26	19 32	20 20	20 26	20 30	21 23	21 30	21 36			22 36	22 57	23 06
Exeter Central	a	18 53		19 29	19 35	20 25	20 29	20 33	21 26	21 33	21 41			22 39	23 00	23 09
	d	18 54		19 30	19 36		20 30	20 34	21 29	21 34				22 40	23 01	23 10
St James' Park	d	18 56			19 38			20 36		21 36				22 42		23 12
Polsloe Bridge	d	18 59			19 41			20 39		21 39				22 45		23 15
Digby & Sowton	d	19 03			19 45			20 43		21 43				22 49		23 19
Topsham	d	19 07			19 49			20 47		21 47				22 53		23 23
Exton	d	19x10			19x52			20x49		21x49				22x56		23x25
Lympstone Commando	d	19x12			19x54			20x51		21x51				22x58		23x27
Lympstone Village	d	19 15			19 57			20 54		21 55				23 01		23 31
Exmouth	a	19 23			20 03			21 01		22 01				23 08		23 36

A until 4 September
B from 11 September

b arr. 1032
c arr. 1803

Table 136

Sundays

Barnstaple - Exeter - Exmouth

		GW	SW ◇1	GW	SW ◇1	GW	GW	SW ◇1	GW	SW ◇1	GW	SW ◇1	GW	SW ◇1	GW A	GW B	SW ◇1	GW	SW ◇1	GW	SW ◇1	GW	SW ◇1
Barnstaple	d						10 00				11 10				13~17	13~17				15 17			
Chapelton	d										11x15									15x22			
Umberleigh	d						10x08				11x19				13x25	13x25				15x26			
Portsmouth Arms	d										11x26									15x33			
Kings Nympton	d										11x31									15x38			
Eggesford	d						10 26				11 41				13~42	13~42				15 47			
Lapford	d						10x31				11x46									15x52			
Morchard Road	d						10x35				11x51				13x50	13x50				15x57			
Copplestone	d						10x39				11x54				13x54	13x54				16x00			
Okehampton	d																						
Sampford Courtenay	d																						
Yeoford	d						10 44				12 00				13~59	13~59				16 06			
Crediton	d						10b56				12 08				14~09	14~09				16 17			
Newton St Cyres	d						10x59				12x11									16x21			
Exeter St Davids 6	a						11 12				12 22		13 07		14~21	14~24		15 18		16 30		17 04	
	d	08 25	09 26	09 30	10 26	10 36	11 13	11 26	11 35	12 26	12 33	13 26	13 33	14 26	14~33	14~33	15 26	15 31	16 26	16 33	17 26	17 33	18 26
Exeter Central	a	08 28	09 29	09 33	10 29	10 39	11 16	11 29	11 38	12 29	12 36	13 29	13 36	14 29	14~36	14~36	15 29	15 34	16 29	16 36	17 29	17 34	18 29
	d	08 29	09 30	09 34	10 30	10 40		11 30	11 39	12 30	12 37	13 30	13 37	14 30	14~37	14~37	15 30	15 35	16 30	16 37	17 30	17 35	18 30
St James' Park	d	08 31		09 36		10 42			11 41		12 39		13 39		14~39	14~39		15 37		16 39		17 37	
Polsloe Bridge	d	08 34		09 39		10 45			11 44		12 42		13 42		14~42	14~42		15 42		16 42		17 42	
Digby & Sowton	d	08 38		09 43		10 49			11 48		12 46		13 46		14~46	14~46		15 46		16 46		17 46	
Topsham	d	08 42		09 48		10 53			11 52		12 51		13 51		14~51	14~51		15 50		16 51		17 51	
Exton	d	08x44		09x50		10x55			11x54		12x53		13x53		14x53	14x53		15x53		16x53		17x53	
Lympstone Commando	d	08x46		09x52		10x57			11x56		12x55		13x55		14x55	14x55		15x55		16x55		17x55	
Lympstone Village	d	08 50		09 55		11 01			12 00		12 58		13 59		14~59	14~59		15 59		16 58		17 59	
Exmouth	a	08 54		10 00		11 05			12 04		13 03		14 04		15~04	15~04		16 05		17 03		18 04	

		GW	SW ◇1	GW	SW ◇1	GW	SW 1	GW	GW	SW 1	GW
Barnstaple	d	17 21				19 18			21 30		
Chapelton	d	17x26				19x23					
Umberleigh	d	17x30				19x27			21x38		
Portsmouth Arms	d	17x37				19x34					
Kings Nympton	d	17x42				19x39					
Eggesford	d	17 51				19 48			21 55		
Lapford	d	17x56				19x53					
Morchard Road	d	18x01				19x58					
Copplestone	d	18x04				20x01			22 06		
Okehampton	d										
Sampford Courtenay	d										
Yeoford	d	18 10				20 07			22 10		
Crediton	d	18 19				20 14			22 18		
Newton St Cyres	d	18x23				20x17					
Exeter St Davids 6	a	18 33		19 10		20 30			22 29		
	d	18 33	19 26	19 33	20 26	20 39	21 26	21 33	22 33	23 15	23 26
Exeter Central	a	18 37	19 29	19 36	20 29	20 42	21 29	21 36	22 36	23 18	23 29
	d	18 38	19 30	19 37	20 30	20 43	21 30	21 37	22 37	23 19	23 30
St James' Park	d	18 40		19 39		20 45		21 39	22 39		23 32
Polsloe Bridge	d	18 43		19 42		20 48		21 46	22 42		23 35
Digby & Sowton	d	18 47		19 46		20 52		21 50	22 46		23 39
Topsham	d	18 52		19 51		20 57		21 54	22 51		23 43
Exton	d	18x54		19x53		20x59		21x56	22x54		23x45
Lympstone Commando	d	18x56		19x56		21x01		21x58	22x56		23x47
Lympstone Village	d	19 00		19 59		21 05		22 02	22 58		23 51
Exmouth	a	19 04		20 03		21 11		22 06	23 04		23 55

A until 5 September

B from 12 September

b arr. 1051

Table 139

Mondays to Fridays

Plymouth - Gunnislake

		GW	GW	GW 1	GW ◇ A	GW ◇ B	GW ◇ C	GW 1 D	GW	GW ◇	GW	GW	GW	GW	GW	GW	GW	GW	GW
Plymouth	d	05 06	06 40	07 02	08~14	08~15	08~19	08~22	08 54	09 17	10 42	10 46	12 55	14 54	15 57	16 37	17 06	18 23	21 30
Devonport	d		06 43	07a07	08a18	08a18	08a23	08a27	08 57	09a22		10 49	12 58	14 57	16 00	16 40	17 09	18 26	21 33
Dockyard	d		06x44						08x58			10x50	12x59	14x58	16x01	16x41	17x10	18x27	21x34
Keyham	d		06x46						09x00			10x52	13x01	15x00	16x03	16x43	17x12	18x29	21x36
St Budeaux Ferry Road	a										10 48				16 06		17 15		
St Budeaux Victoria Road	d	05 12	06 49						09 04			10 56	13 05	15 04		16 47		18 33	21 40
Bere Ferrers	d		06 58						09 12			11 04	13 13	15 12		16 55		18 41	21 47
Bere Alston	a	05 25	07 04						09 18			11 10	13 19	15 18		17 01		18 47	21 54
	d	05 27	07 06						09 20			11 12	13 21	15 20		17 03		18 49	21 56
Calstock	d	05 33	07 13						09 27			11 19	13 28	15 27		17 10		18 56	22 03
Gunnislake	a	05 49	07 26						09 40			11 32	13 41	15 40		17 23		19 09	22 16

Saturdays

		GW	GW ◇	GW	GW ◇ E	GW E	GW F	GW	GW	GW	GW	GW	GW	GW	GW
Plymouth	d	06 40	08 16	08 50	09~20	09~51	09~58	10 33	10 46	12 54	14 47	16 40	17 52	18 23	21 30
Devonport	d	06 43	08a20	08 53	09a23	09a54	10a01		10 49	12 57	14 50	16 43	17 55	18 26	21 33
Dockyard	d	06x44		08x54					10x50	12x58	14x51	16x44	17x57	18x27	21x34
Keyham	d	06x46		08x56					10x52	13x00	14x53	16x46	17x59	18x29	21x36
St Budeaux Ferry Road	a							10 39					18 00		
St Budeaux Victoria Road	d	06 49		08 59					10 56	13 04	14 56	16 49		18 33	21 39
Bere Ferrers	d	06 57		09 07					11 04	13 12	15 04	16 57		18 41	21 47
Bere Alston	a	07 03		09 14					11 10	13 18	15 11	17 04		18 47	21 54
	d	07 06		09 16					11 12	13 20	15 13	17 06		18 49	21 56
Calstock	d	07 13		09 23					11 19	13 27	15 20	17 13		18 56	22 03
Gunnislake	a	07 26		09 36					11 32	13 40	15 33	17 26		19 09	22 16

Sundays
until 19 September

		GW	GW G	GW ◇	GW	GW	GW	GW
Plymouth	d	09 09	09~15	10 30	11 17	13 13	15 17	17 41
Devonport	d	09 12		10a34	11 20	13 16	15 20	17 44
Dockyard	d	09x14			11x22	13x18	15x22	17x46
Keyham	d	09x16			11x24	13x20	15x24	17x48
St Budeaux Ferry Road	a		09~21					
St Budeaux Victoria Road	d	09 19			11 27	13 23	15 27	17 51
Bere Ferrers	d	09 27			11 35	13 31	15 35	17 59
Bere Alston	a	09 33			11 41	13 37	15 41	18 05
	d	09 36			11 44	13 40	15 44	18 08
Calstock	d	09 43			11 51	13 47	15 51	18 15
Gunnislake	a	09 55			12 03	13 59	16 03	18 27

Sundays
from 26 September

		GW	GW ◇	GW	GW	GW	GW
Plymouth	d	09 30	10 30	11 40	13 45	15 40	17 45
Devonport	d	09 33	10a34	11 43	13 48	15 43	17 48
Dockyard	d	09x35		11x45	13x50	15x45	17x50
Keyham	d	09x37		11x47	13x52	15x47	17x52
St Budeaux Ferry Road	a						
St Budeaux Victoria Road	d	09 40		11 50	13 55	15 50	17 55
Bere Ferrers	d	09x48		11x58	14x03	15x58	18x03
Bere Alston	a	09 54		12 04	14 09	16 04	18 09
	d	09 57		12 07	14 12	16 07	18 12
Calstock	d	10x04		12x14	14x19	16x14	18x19
Gunnislake	a	10 16		12 26	14 31	16 26	18 31

A from 6 September

B until 2 July

C MX from 16 November

D from 5 July until 3 September

E from 11 September

F until 4 September

G until 5 September

Table 139

Mondays to Fridays

Gunnislake - Plymouth

		GW	GW	GW	GW	GW	GW	GW	GW A	GW	GW	GW
Gunnislake	d	05 50		07 31	09 45	11 37	13 45	15 45		17 29	19 14	22 21
Calstock	d	06 01		07 42	09 56	11 48	13 56	15 56		17 40	19 25	22 32
Bere Alston	a	06 08		07 49	10 03	11 55	14 03	16 03		17 47	19 32	22 39
	d	06 10		07 52	10 05	11 57	14 05	16 05		17 49	19 34	22 41
Bere Ferrers	d	06 16		07 56	10 11	12 03	14 11	16 11		17 55	19 40	22 47
St Budeaux Victoria Road	d	06 24		08 05	10 19	12 11	14 19	16 19		18 03	19 48	22 55
St Budeaux Ferry Road	d		07 53						17 08			
Keyham	d	06 26	07x55	08x07	10x21	12x13	14x21	16x21	17x10	18x05	19x50	22x57
Dockyard	d	06 28	07x57	08x09	10x23	12x15	14x23	16x23	17x12	18x07	19x52	22x59
Devonport	d	06 31	07 59	08 11	10 25	12 17	14 25	16 25	17 14	18 09	19 54	23 01
Plymouth	a	06 35	08 05	08 17	10 30	12 22	14 30	16 30	17 18	18 14	19 59	23 06

Saturdays

		GW	GW	GW	GW	GW B	GW C	GW	GW	GW	GW	GW	GW
Gunnislake	d	07 31	09 45	11 37	13 45			15 45	17 29	19 14		22 21	
Calstock	d	07 42	09 56	11 48	13 56			15 56	17 40	19 25		22 32	
Bere Alston	a	07 49	10 03	11 55	14 03			16 03	17 47	19 32		22 39	
	d	07 52	10 05	11 57	14 05			16 05	17 49	19 34		22 41	
Bere Ferrers	d	07 57	10 10	12 02	14 11			16 11	17 54	19 40		22 47	
St Budeaux Victoria Road	d	08 05	10 19	12 11	14 19			16 19	18 03	19 48		22 55	
St Budeaux Ferry Road	d										21 00		22 59
Keyham	d	08x07	10x21	12x13	14x21			16x21	18x05	19x50	21x02	22x57	23x01
Dockyard	d	08x09	10x23	12x15	14x23			16x23	18x07	19x52	21x04	22x59	23x03
Devonport	d	08 11	10 25	12 17	14 25	14 53	15 16	16 25	18 09	19 54	21 06	23 01	23 05
Plymouth	a	08 16	10 30	12 22	14 30	14 59	15 21	16 30	18 14	19 59	21 10	23 06	23 11

Sundays
until 19 September

		GW	GW	GW	GW	GW	GW D	GW
Gunnislake	d	10 18	12 07	14 05	16 07	18 39		
Calstock	d	10x30	12 19	14 17	16 19	18 51		
Bere Alston	a	10 36	12 25	14 23	16 25	18 57		
	d	10 38	12 27	14 25	16 27	18 59		
Bere Ferrers	d	10x44	12 33	14 31	16 33	19 05		
St Budeaux Victoria Road	d	10 52	12 41	14 39	16 41	19 13		
St Budeaux Ferry Road	d						19 43	
Keyham	d	10x55	12x44	14x42	16x44	19x16		
Dockyard	d	10x57	12x46	14x44	16x46	19x18		
Devonport	d	10 59	12 48	14 46	16 48	19 20	19 47	20 55
Plymouth	a	11 03	12 52	14 50	16 52	19 24	19 50	20 59

Sundays
from 26 September

		GW	GW	GW	GW	GW	GW
Gunnislake	d	10 25	12 45	14 45	16 54	18 39	
Calstock	d	10x37	12x57	14x57	17x06	18x51	
Bere Alston	a	10 43	13 03	15 03	17 12	18 57	
	d	10 45	13 05	15 05	17 14	18 59	
Bere Ferrers	d	10x51	13x11	15x11	17x20	19x05	
St Budeaux Victoria Road	d	10 59	13 19	15 19	17 28	19 13	
St Budeaux Ferry Road	d						
Keyham	d	11x02	13x22	15x22	17x31	19x16	
Dockyard	d	11x04	13x24	15x24	17x33	19x18	
Devonport	d	11 06	13 26	15 26	17 35	19 20	20 55
Plymouth	a	11 10	13 30	15 30	17 39	19 24	20 59

A from 5 July until 3 September
B from 11 September
C until 4 September
D until 5 September

Table 140

Mondays to Fridays

Liskeard - Looe

		GW	GW	GW	GW	GW	GW	GW	GW	GW	GW	GW	GW
Liskeard	d	06 05	07 12	08 33	10 00	11 16	12 14	13 19	14 28	15 40	16 40	18 02	19 18
Coombe Junction Halt	a			08 39	10 06								
	d			08 42	10 09								
St Keyne Wishing Well Halt	d	06x17	07x24	08x48	10x15		12x26	13x31		15x52	16x52	18x14	19x31
Causeland	d	06x21	07x28	08x52	10x19		12x30	13x35		15x56	16x56	18x18	19x33
Sandplace	d	06x24	07x31	08x56	10x22		12x33	13x38		15x59	16x59	18x21	19x38
Looe	a	06 36	07 43	09 04	10 31	11 44	12 45	13 50	14 56	16 11	17 11	18 33	19 48

Saturdays
until 04 September

		GW	GW	GW	GW	GW	GW	GW	GW	GW	GW	GW	GW	GW
Liskeard	d	06 01	07 12	08 33	09 58	11 08	12 12	13 19	14 28	15 42	16 57	18 02	19 22	20 40
Coombe Junction Halt	a			08 39	10 04									
	d			08 42	10 06									
St Keyne Wishing Well Halt	d	06x13	07x24	08x48	10x13		12x24	13x31		15x54	17x10	18x14	19x34	20x52
Causeland	d	06x17	07x28	08x52	10x17		12x28	13x35		15x58	17x13	18x18	19x37	20x55
Sandplace	d	06x20	07x31	08x56	10x20		12x31	13x38		16x01	17x17	18x21	19x42	21x00
Looe	a	06 32	07 43	09 04	10 29	11 36	12 43	13 50	14 56	16 13	17 28	18 33	19 53	21 11

Saturdays
from 11 September

		GW	GW	GW	GW	GW	GW	GW	GW	GW	GW	GW	GW
Liskeard	d	06 01	07 12	08 33	09 58	11 08	12 12	13 24	14 32	15 42	16 57	18 02	19 28
Coombe Junction Halt	a			08 39	10 04								
	d			08 42	10 06								
St Keyne Wishing Well Halt	d	06x13	07x24	08x48	10x13		12x24	13x37		15x54	17x10	18x14	19x41
Causeland	d	06x17	07x28	08x52	10x17		12x28	13x40		15x58	17x13	18x18	19x43
Sandplace	d	06x20	07x31	08x56	10x20		12x31	13x44		16x01	17x17	18x21	19x48
Looe	a	06 32	07 43	09 04	10 29	11 36	12 43	13 55	15 00	16 13	17 28	18 33	19 59

Sundays
until 05 September

		GW	GW	GW	GW	GW	GW	GW	GW
Liskeard	d	10 14	11 26	12 50	14 04	15 07	16 24	18 12	20 16
Coombe Junction Halt	a								
	d								
St Keyne Wishing Well Halt	d	10x27	11x39	13x03	14x17	15x20	16x37	18x25	20x29
Causeland	d	10x30	11x42	13x06	14x20	15x23	16x40	18x28	20x32
Sandplace	d	10x34	11x46	13x10	14x24	15x27	16x44	18x32	20x36
Looe	a	10 43	11 55	13 19	14 33	15 36	16 53	18 41	20 45

No Sunday Service from 12 September

For connections at Liskeard please refer to Table 135

Table 140

Looe - Liskeard

		GW	GW	GW	GW	GW	GW	GW	GW	GW	GW	GW	GW
Looe	d	06 37	07 47	09 09	10 34	11 45	12 46	13 51	14 57	16 12	17 15	18 34	19 52
Sandplace	d	06x42	07x52	09x14	10x39		12x51		15x02		17x20	18x39	19x57
Causeland	d	06x46	07x56	09x18	10x43		12x55		15x06		17x24	18x43	20x01
St Keyne Wishing Well Halt	d	06x49	07x59	09x21	10x46		12x58		15x09		17x27	18x46	20x04
Coombe Junction Halt	a			09 27	10 52								
	d			09 29	10 54								
Liskeard ■6	a	07 05	08 15	09 40	11 05	12 09	13 16	14 15	15 25	16 38	17 43	19 02	20 22

Saturdays
until 04 September

		GW	GW	GW	GW	GW	GW	GW	GW	GW	GW	GW	GW	GW
Looe	d	06 33	07 47	09 09	10 32	11 37	12 44	13 51	14 57	16 14	17 29	18 34	19 54	21 12
Sandplace	d	06x38	07x52	09x14	10x37		12x49		15x02	16x19	17x34	18x39	19x59	21x17
Causeland	d	06x42	07x56	09x18	10x41		12x53		15x06	16x23	17x38	18x43	20x03	21x21
St Keyne Wishing Well Halt	d	06x45	07x59	09x21	10x44		12x56		15x09	16x27	17x42	18x46	20x07	21x25
Coombe Junction Halt	a			09 27	10 50									
	d			09 29	10 52									
Liskeard ■6	a	07 01	08 15	09 40	11 03	12 01	13 12	14 15	15 25	16 44	17 59	19 02	20 22	21 40

Saturdays
from 11 September

		GW	GW	GW	GW	GW	GW	GW	GW	GW	GW	GW	GW
Looe	d	06 33	07 47	09 09	10 32	11 37	12 44	13 56	15 00	16 14	17 29	18 34	20 00
Sandplace	d	06x38	07x52	09x14	10x37		12x49		15x05	16x19	17x34	18x39	20x05
Causeland	d	06x42	07x56	09x18	10x41		12x53		15x09	16x23	17x38	18x43	20x09
St Keyne Wishing Well Halt	d	06x45	07x59	09x21	10x44		12x56		15x12	16x27	17x42	18x46	20x13
Coombe Junction Halt	a			09 27	10 50								
	d			09 29	10 52								
Liskeard ■6	a	07 01	08 15	09 40	11 03	12 01	13 12	14 20	15 29	16 44	17 59	19 02	20 28

Sundays
until 05 September

		GW	GW	GW	GW	GW	GW	GW	GW
Looe	d	10 46	11 58	13 24	14 36	15 39	17 05	18 44	20 51
Sandplace	d	10x51	12x03	13x29	14x41	15x44	17x10	18x49	20x56
Causeland	d	10x55	12x07	13x33	14x45	15x48	17x14	18x53	21x00
St Keyne Wishing Well Halt	d	10x59	12x11	13x37	14x49	15x52	17x18	18x57	21x04
Coombe Junction Halt	a								
	d								
Liskeard ■6	a	11 14	12 26	13 52	15 04	16 07	17 33	19 12	21 19

Table 142

Par - Newquay

		GW	GW	GW	GW	GW	GW	GW	GW	GW	GW	GW
				◇				◇■1				
		A	B	C	D	C	D	C	D			
								⊒				
Par	d	06§01	06§49	09§17	09§17	11§42	12§11	13§26	14§03	16 10	18 29	20 28
Luxulyan	d	06x12	07x00	09x28	09x28	11x53	§	§	14x14	16x21	18x40	20x39
Bugle	d	06x18	07x06	09x34	09x34	11x59	§	§	14x20	16x27	18x46	20x45
Roche	d	06x23	07x11	09x39	09x39	12x04	§	§	14x25	16x32	18x51	20x50
St Columb Road	d	06x34	07x22	09x50	09x50	12x15	§	§	14x36	16x43	19x02	21x01
Quintrell Downs	d	06x42	07x30	09x58	09x58	12x23	12x50	§	14§44	16x51	19x10	21x09
Newquay	a	06§53	07§41	10§08	10§09	12§34	13§01	14§26	14§55	17 02	19 21	21 20

Saturdays
until 04 September

		XC	GW	GW	XC	GW	XC	GW
						■		
		◇■1	◇	◇■1	◇■1	■1	◇■1	
		⊼		⊒	⊼	⊒	⊼	
Par	d	07 26	09 47	11 35	13 32	15 43	17 41	20 21
Luxulyan	d							
Bugle	d							
Roche	d							
St Columb Road	d							
Quintrell Downs	d							
Newquay	a	08 25	11 01	12 44	14 37	16 52	18 45	21 11

Saturdays
from 11 September

		GW	GW	GW	GW	GW	GW	GW
Par	d	06 52	09 18	12 15	14 08	16 10	18 21	20 15
Luxulyan	d	07x03	09x29	12x26		16x21	18x32	20x26
Bugle	d	07x09	09x35	12x32		16x27	18x38	20x32
Roche	d	07x14	09x40	12x37		16x32	18x43	20x37
St Columb Road	d	07x25	09x51	12x48		16x43	18x54	20x48
Quintrell Downs	d	07x33	09x59	12x56		16x51	19x02	20x56
Newquay	a	07 44	10 10	13 07	14 54	17 02	19 13	21 07

Sundays
until 05 September

		GW	XC	GW	GW	GW	GW
			■		◇■1		
					⊒		
Par	d	09 00	09 57	11 56	14 20	16 36	18 45
Luxulyan	d	09x11		12x07			18x56
Bugle	d	09x17		12x18			19x02
Roche	d	09x22		12x23			19x07
St Columb Road	d	09x33		12x34			19x18
Quintrell Downs	d	09x41		12x42			19x26
Newquay	a	09 52	11 10	12 52	15 25	17 30	19 37

A until 3 September
B from 6 September
C from 5 July until 3 September
D until 2 July, from 6 September

No Sunday Service from 12 September

For connections at Par please refer to Table 135

Table 142

Newquay - Par

		GW	GW	GW	GW	GW	GW	GW	GW	GW	GW
		A	B		C	D	D	◇1 C 🍴			
Newquay	d	06ʃ57	07ʃ48	10 13	12ʃ40	13ʃ03	14ʃ58	15ʃ00	17 22	19 25	21 26
Quintrell Downs	d	07ʃ03	07ʃ54	10 19	12ʃ46	13ʃ09	15ʃ04	ʃ	17 28	19 31	21 32
St Columb Road	d	07x11	08x02	10x27	12x54	13x17	15x12	ʃ	17x36		21x40
Roche	d	07x22	08x13	10x38	13x05	13x28	15x23	ʃ	17x47		21x51
Bugle	d	07x27	08x18	10x43	13x10	13x33	15x28	ʃ	17x52		21x56
Luxulyan	d	07x32	08x23	10x48	13x17	13x38	15x33	ʃ	17x57		22x01
Par	a	07ʃ48	08ʃ39	11 02	13ʃ34	13ʃ52	15ʃ47	15ʃ59	18 13	20 11	22 16

Saturdays
until 04 September

		XC	GW	GW	XC	GW	XC	GW
		◇1 🛒	▣ 1 🍴	▣ 1 🍴	◇1 🛒	◇1 🍴	◇	
Newquay	d	09 27	11 22	13 14	15 24	17 18	19 58	21 20
Quintrell Downs	d							
St Columb Road	d							
Roche	d							
Bugle	d							
Luxulyan	d							
Par	a	10 27	12 23	14 15	16 26	18 20	20 55	22 04

Saturdays
from 11 September

		GW	GW	GW	GW	GW	GW	GW
Newquay	d	07 48	10 12	13 09	14 59	17 21	19 19	21 15
Quintrell Downs	d	07 54	10 18	13 15	15 05	17 27	19 25	21 21
St Columb Road	d	08x02	10x26	13x23	15x13	17x35		21x29
Roche	d	08x13	10x37	13x34	15x24	17x46		21x40
Bugle	d	08x18	10x42	13x39	15x29	17x51		21x45
Luxulyan	d	08x23	10x47	13x44	15x34	17x56		21x50
Par	a	08 39	11 01	13 59	15 48	18 10	20 04	22 04

Sundays
until 05 September

		GW	GW	GW	GW	GW
				◇1 🍴		
Newquay	d	09 54	13 00	16 15	17 32	19 40
Quintrell Downs	d	10x00	13x06		17x38	19x46
St Columb Road	d	10x08	13x14		17x46	19x54
Roche	d	10x19	13x25		17x57	20x05
Bugle	d	10x24	13x30		18x02	20x10
Luxulyan	d	10x35	13x35		18x07	20x15
Par	a	10 49	13 50	17 14	18 21	20 30

A until 3 September
B from 6 September
C from 5 July until 3 September
D until 2 July, from 6 September

For connections at Par please refer to Table 135

Table 143

Truro - Falmouth

		GW	GW	GW	GW	GW	GW	GW	GW	GW	GW	GW	GW	GW	GW	GW	GW	GW	GW	GW	GW	GW	GW
Truro	d	06 10	06 37	07 16	07 48	08 20	08 50	09 20	09 50	10 20	10 50	11 20	11 50	12 20	12 50	13 20	13 50	14 20	14 50	15 20	15 50	16 20	16 51
Perranwell	d	06x16	06x43	07x22	07x54	08x26		09x26		10x26		11x26		12x26		13x26		14x26		15x26		16x26	16x57
Penryn	d	06 24	06 51	07 30	08 02	08 34	09 04	09 34	10 04	10 34	11 04	11 34	12 04	12 34	13 04	13 34	14 04	14 34	15 04	15 34	16 04	16 34	17 05
Penmere	d	06 29	06 56	07 35	08 07	08 39	09 09	09 39	10 09	10 39	11 09	11 39	12 09	12 39	13 09	13 39	14 09	14 39	15 09	15 39	16 09	16 39	17 10
Falmouth Town	d	06 32	06 59	07 38	08 10	08 42	09 12	09 42	10 12	10 42	11 12	11 42	12 12	12 42	13 12	13 42	14 12	14 42	15 12	15 42	16 12	16 42	17 13
Falmouth Docks	a	06 34	07 01	07 40	08 12	08 44	09 14	09 44	10 14	10 44	11 14	11 44	12 14	12 44	13 14	13 44	14 14	14 44	15 14	15 44	16 14	16 44	17 15

		GW	GW	GW	GW	GW	GW	GW
Truro	d	17 27	17 58	18 29	19 00	20 01	21 03	22 08
Perranwell	d	17x33	18x04	18x35	19x06	20x07	21x09	22x14
Penryn	d	17 41	18 12	18 43	19 14	20 15	21 17	22 22
Penmere	d	17 46	18 17	18 48	19 19	20 20	21 22	22 27
Falmouth Town	d	17 49	18 20	18 51	19 22	20 23	21 25	22 30
Falmouth Docks	a	17 51	18 22	18 53	19 24	20 25	21 27	22 32

Saturdays

		GW	GW	GW	GW	GW	GW	GW	GW	GW	GW	GW	GW	GW	GW	GW	GW	GW	GW	GW	GW	GW	GW
Truro	d	06 10	06 37	07 17	07 48	08 20	08 50	09 20	09 50	10 20	10 50	11 20	11 50	12 20	12 50	13 20	13 50	14 20	14 50	15 20	15 50	16 20	16 51
Perranwell	d	06x16	06x43	07x22	07x54	08x26		09x26		10x26		11x26		12x26		13x26		14x26		15x26		16x26	16x57
Penryn	d	06 24	06 51	07 30	08 02	08 34	09 04	09 34	10 04	10 34	11 04	11 34	12 04	12 34	13 04	13 34	14 04	14 34	15 04	15 34	16 04	16 34	17 05
Penmere	d	06 29	06 56	07 35	08 07	08 39	09 09	09 39	10 09	10 39	11 09	11 39	12 09	12 39	13 09	13 39	14 09	14 39	15 09	15 39	16 09	16 39	17 10
Falmouth Town	d	06 32	06 59	07 38	08 10	08 42	09 12	09 42	10 12	10 42	11 12	11 42	12 12	12 42	13 12	13 42	14 12	14 42	15 12	15 42	16 12	16 42	17 13
Falmouth Docks	a	06 34	07 01	07 41	08 12	08 44	09 14	09 44	10 14	10 44	11 14	11 44	12 14	12 44	13 14	13 44	14 14	14 44	15 14	15 44	16 14	16 44	17 15

		GW	GW	GW	GW	GW	GW	GW
Truro	d	17 27	17 58	18 29	19 00	20 02	21 03	22 06
Perranwell	d	17x33	18x04	18x35	19x06	20x07	21x09	22x12
Penryn	d	17 41	18 12	18 43	19 14	20 15	21 17	22 20
Penmere	d	17 46	18 17	18 48	19 19	20 20	21 22	22 25
Falmouth Town	d	17 49	18 20	18 51	19 22	20 23	21 25	22 28
Falmouth Docks	a	17 51	18 22	18 53	19 24	20 26	21 27	22 30

Sundays

		GW	GW	GW	GW	GW	GW	GW	GW	GW	GW
Truro	d	10 45	12 15	13 37	14 31	15 35	17 00	18 06	19 48	21 05	22 04
Perranwell	d	10x52	12x22	13x44	14x38	15x42	17x07	18x13	19x55	21x12	22x11
Penryn	d	10 59	12 29	13 51	14 45	15 49	17 14	18 20	20 02	21 19	22 18
Penmere	d	11 03	12 33	13 55	14 49	15 52	17 18	18 24	20 06	21 23	22 22
Falmouth Town	d	11 05	12 35	13 57	14 51	15 55	17 20	18 26	20 08	21 25	22 24
Falmouth Docks	a	11 08	12 38	14 00	14 54	15 58	17 23	18 29	20 11	21 28	22 27

For connections at Truro please refer to Table 135

Table 143

Falmouth - Truro

Mondays to Fridays

		GW	GW	GW	GW	GW	GW	GW	GW	GW	GW	GW	GW	GW	GW	GW	GW	GW	GW	GW	GW	GW	GW
Falmouth Docks	d	06 37	07 17	07 48	08 20	08 50	09 20	09 50	10 20	10 50	11 20	11 50	12 20	12 50	13 20	13 50	14 20	14 50	15 20	15 50	16 20	16 50	17 27
Falmouth Town	d	06 40	07 20	07 51	08 23	08 53	09 23	09 53	10 23	10 53	11 23	11 53	12 23	12 53	13 23	13 53	14 23	14 53	15 23	15 53	16 23	16 53	17 30
Penmere	d	06 43	07 23	07 54	08 26	08 56	09 26	09 56	10 26	10 56	11 26	11 56	12 26	12 56	13 26	13 56	14 26	14 56	15 26	15 56	16 26	16 56	17 33
Penryn	d	06 51	07 31	08 02	08 34	09 04	09 34	10 04	10 34	11 04	11 34	12 04	12 34	13 04	13 34	14 04	14 34	15 04	15 34	16 04	16 34	17 04	17 40
Perranwell	d	06x57	07x37	08x08	08x40		09x40		10x40		11x40		12x40		13x40		14x40		15x40		16x40	17x11	17x48
Truro	a	07 05	07 45	08 16	08 48	09 18	09 48	10 18	10 48	11 18	11 48	12 17	12 48	13 18	13 48	14 18	14 48	15 18	15 48	16 18	16 48	17 19	17 55

		GW	GW	GW	GW	GW	GW	GW
Falmouth Docks	d	17 58	18 29	19 00	19 27	20 29	21 30	22 35
Falmouth Town	d	18 01	18 32	19 03	19 30	20 32	21 33	22 38
Penmere	d	18 04	18 35	19 06	19 33	20 35	21 36	22 41
Penryn	d	18 12	18 43	19 14	19 38	20 40	21 41	22 46
Perranwell	d	18x18	18x49	19x20	19x44	20x46	21x48	22x52
Truro	a	18 26	18 57	19 28	19 53	20 55	21 58	23 02

Saturdays

		GW	GW	GW	GW	GW	GW	GW	GW	GW	GW	GW	GW	GW	GW	GW	GW	GW	GW	GW	GW	GW	GW
Falmouth Docks	d	06 37	07 17	07 48	08 20	08 50	09 20	09 50	10 20	10 50	11 20	11 50	12 20	12 50	13 20	13 50	14 20	14 50	15 20	15 50	16 20	16 51	17 27
Falmouth Town	d	06 40	07 20	07 51	08 23	08 53	09 23	09 53	10 23	10 53	11 23	11 53	12 23	12 53	13 23	13 53	14 23	14 53	15 23	15 53	16 23	16 53	17 30
Penmere	d	06 43	07 23	07 54	08 26	08 56	09 26	09 56	10 26	10 56	11 26	11 56	12 26	12 56	13 26	13 56	14 26	14 56	15 26	15 56	16 26	16 56	17 33
Penryn	d	06 51	07 31	08 02	08 34	09 04	09 34	10 04	10 34	11 04	11 34	12 04	12 34	13 04	13 34	14 04	14 34	15 04	15 34	16 04	16 34	17 04	17 40
Perranwell	d	06x57	07x37	08x08	08x40		09x40		10x40		11x40		12x40		13x40		14x40		15x40		16x40	17x11	17x48
Truro	a	07 05	07 45	08 16	08 48	09 18	09 48	10 18	10 48	11 18	11 48	12 18	12 48	13 18	13 48	14 18	14 48	15 18	15 48	16 18	16 48	17 19	17 55

		GW	GW	GW	GW	GW	GW	GW
Falmouth Docks	d	17 58	18 29	19 00	19 27	20 29	21 30	22 33
Falmouth Town	d	18 01	18 32	19 03	19 30	20 32	21 33	22 36
Penmere	d	18 04	18 35	19 06	19 33	20 35	21 36	22 39
Penryn	d	18 12	18 43	19 14	19 38	20 40	21 41	22 44
Perranwell	d	18x18	18x49	19x20	19x44	20x46	21x48	22x50
Truro	a	18 26	18 57	19 28	19 53	20 55	21 57	23 00

Sundays

		GW	GW	GW	GW	GW A	GW B	GW	GW	GW	GW	GW
Falmouth Docks	d	11 12	12 44	14 03	14 57	16 00	16 22	17 30	18 37	20 15	21 31	22 34
Falmouth Town	d	11 14	12 46	14 05	14 59	16 02	16 24	17 32	18 39	20 17	21 33	22 36
Penmere	d	11 17	12 49	14 08	15 02	16 05	16 27	17 35	18 42	20 20	21 36	22 39
Penryn	d	11 22	12 54	14 13	15 07	16 09	16 31	17 40	18 47	20 25	21 41	22 44
Perranwell	d	11x29	13x01	14x20	15x14	16x16	16x38	17x47	18x54	20x32	21x48	22x51
Truro	a	11 36	13 08	14 27	15 21	16 23	16 45	17 54	19 01	20 39	21 55	23 01

A until 5 September

B from 12 September

Table 144

St. Erth - St. Ives

Mondays to Fridays

		GW	GW	GW	GW	GW	GW	GW	GW	GW	GW	GW	GW	GW	GW	GW	GW	GW	GW	GW	GW	GW	GW
Penzance	d	06 37			08 57																		
St Erth	d	06 45	07 14	08 01	09 05	09 38	10 11	10 41	11 11	11 41	12 11	12 41	13 11	13 41	14 11	14 41	15 11	15 41	16 11	16 41	17 11	17 41	18 11
Lelant Saltings	d				09 09	09 41	10 14	10 44	11 14	11 44	12 14	12 44	13 14	13 44	14 14	14 44	15 14	15 44	16 14		17 14		18 14
Lelant	d	06x48	07x17	08x04	09x11															16x44		17x44	18x15
Carbis Bay	d	06 53	07 22	08 09	09 16	09 47		10 50		11 50		12 50		13 50		14 50		15 50		16 49		17 49	18 20
St Ives	a	06 59	07 27	08 14	09 20	09 52	10 24	10 55	11 24	11 55	12 24	12 55	13 24	13 55	14 24	14 55	15 24	15 55	16 24	16 55	17 24	17 55	18 25

		GW	GW	GW	GW	GW	GW
Penzance	d						
St Erth	d	18 41	19 11	19 41	20 11	20 41	21 36
Lelant Saltings	d		19 14		20 14		21 39
Lelant	d	18x44		19x44		20x44	21x41
Carbis Bay	d	18 49		19 49		20 49	21 46
St Ives	a	18 55	19 25	19 56	20 24	20 55	21 50

Saturdays

		GW	GW	GW	GW	GW	GW	GW	GW	GW	GW	GW	GW	GW	GW	GW	GW	GW	GW	GW	GW	GW	GW
Penzance	d	06 37			08 57																		18 50
St Erth	d	06 45	07 14	08 01	09 05	09 38	10 11	10 41	11 11	11 41	12 11	12 41	13 11	13 41	14 11	14 41	15 11	15 41	16 11	16 41	17 11	17 59	18 58
Lelant Saltings	d				09 09	09 41	10 14	10 44	11 14	11 44	12 14	12 44	13 14	13 44	14 14	14 44	15 14	15 44	16 14	16 44	17 14	18 02	19 02
Lelant	d	06x48	07x17	08x04	09x11															16x46		18x04	19x04
Carbis Bay	d	06 53	07 22	08 09	09 16	09 47		10 50		11 50		12 50		13 50		14 50		15 50		16 51	17 21	18 09	19 09
St Ives	a	06 59	07 27	08 14	09 20	09 52	10 24	10 55	11 24	11 55	12 24	12 55	13 24	13 55	14 24	14 55	15 24	15 55	16 24	16 55	17 26	18 13	19 13

		GW	GW	GW
Penzance	d			
St Erth	d	19 50	20 48	21 46
Lelant Saltings	d	19 53	20 51	21 47
Lelant	d	19x55	20x53	21x49
Carbis Bay	d	20 00	20 58	21 54
St Ives	a	20 04	21 02	22 00

Sundays until 05 September

		GW	GW	GW	GW	GW	GW	GW	GW	GW	GW	GW	GW	GW	GW	GW	GW	GW	GW	GW
Penzance	d	08 45																		
St Erth	d	08 53	09 27	10 00	10 30	11 11	11 41	12 11	12 41	13 11	13 41	14 11	14 41	15 11	15 41	16 11	16 41	17 24	18 24	19 30
Lelant Saltings	d	08 57	09 31	10 04	10 33	11 14	11 44	12 14	12 44	13 14	13 44	14 14	14 44	15 14	15 44	16 14	16 44	17 27	18 27	19 33
Lelant	d	08x59																17x29	18x29	19 35
Carbis Bay	d	09 04			10 39		11 50		12 50		13 50		14 50		15 50		16 50	17 34	18 34	19 40
St Ives	a	09 09	09 41	10 14	10 44	11 24	11 55	12 24	12 55	13 24	13 55	14 24	14 55	15 24	15 55	16 24	16 55	17 39	18 39	19 45

Sundays from 12 September

		GW	GW	GW	GW	GW	GW	GW	GW	GW	GW	GW	GW	GW	GW
Penzance	d	11 45													
St Erth	d	11 54	12 34	13 11	13 41	14 11	14 41	15 11	15 41	16 11	16 41	17 11	17 41	18 30	19 30
Lelant Saltings	d	11 58	12 37	13 14	13 44	14 14	14 44	15 14	15 44	16 14	16 44	17 14	17 44	18 33	19 33
Lelant	d	12x00											17x46	18x35	19x35
Carbis Bay	d	12 05	12 43		13 50		14 50		15 50		16 50		17 51	18 40	19 40
St Ives	a	12 10	12 48	13 24	13 55	14 24	14 55	15 24	15 55	16 24	16 55	17 24	17 56	18 45	19 45

For connections at St Erth please refer to Table 135

Table 144

Mondays to Fridays

St. Ives - St. Erth

		GW	GW	GW	GW	GW	GW	GW	GW	GW	GW	GW	GW	GW	GW	GW	GW	GW	GW	GW	GW	GW	GW
St Ives	d	07 00	07 28	08 15	09 22	09 53	10 25	10 55	11 25	11 55	12 25	12 55	13 25	13 55	14 25	14 55	15 25	15 55	16 25	16 55	17 25	17 55	18 25
Carbis Bay	d	07 03	07 31	08 18	09 25		10 28		11 28		12 28		13 28		14 28		15 28		16 28		17 28		18 28
Lelant	d	07x08	07x36	08x23	09x30																17x33		18x33
Lelant Saltings	d				09 33		10 35		11 35		12 35		13 35	14 05	14 35	15 05	15 35	16 05	16 35	17 05	17 36	18 05	18 36
St Erth	a	07 13	07 41	08 27	09 36	10 05	10 40	11 08	11 39	12 08	12 39	13 08	13 39	14 09	14 39	15 09	15 39	16 09	16 39	17 09	17 39	18 09	18 40
Penzance	a			08 40																			

		GW	GW	GW	GW	GW		GW
St Ives	d	18 55	19 25	19 55	20 25	20 55		21 52
Carbis Bay	d		19 28		20 28			21 55
Lelant	d		19x33		20x33	21x03		22x00
Lelant Saltings	d		19 36	20 05	20 36	21 06		22 03
St Erth	a	19 10	19 40	20 10	20 39	21 09		22 06
Penzance	a							22 19

Saturdays

		GW	GW	GW	GW	GW	GW	GW	GW	GW	GW	GW	GW	GW	GW	GW	GW	GW	GW	GW	GW	GW	GW
St Ives	d	06 59	07 28	08 15	09 22	09 53	10 25	10 55	11 25	11 55	12 25	12 55	13 25	13 55	14 25	14 55	15 25	15 55	16 25	16 57	17 27	18 17	19 25
Carbis Bay	d	07 02	07 31	08 18	09 25		10 28		11 28		12 28		13 28		14 28		15 28		16 28	17 00	17 30	18 20	19 28
Lelant	d	07x07	07x36	08x23	09x30																17x35	18x25	19x33
Lelant Saltings	d				09 33		10 35		11 35		12 35		13 35	14 05	14 35	15 05	15 35	16 05	16 35	17 07	17 38	18 28	19 36
St Erth	a	07 12	07 41	08 27	09 36	10 03	10 39	11 07	11 39	12 08	12 39	13 08	13 39	14 07	14 39	15 09	15 39	16 09	16 39	17 10	17 41	18 31	19 40
Penzance	a			08 40																		18 44	

		GW	GW	GW
St Ives	d	20 10	21 12	22 02
Carbis Bay	d	20 13	21 15	22 05
Lelant	d	20x18	21x20	22x10
Lelant Saltings	d	20 21	21 23	22 13
St Erth	a	20 23	21 25	22 16
Penzance	a			22 29

Sundays
until 05 September

		GW	GW	GW	GW	GW	GW	GW	GW	GW	GW	GW	GW	GW	GW	GW	GW	GW	GW	GW
St Ives	d	09 10	09 42	10 15	10 50	11 25	11 56	12 25	12 56	13 25	13 56	14 25	14 56	15 25	15 56	16 25	16 56	17 40	18 40	19 50
Carbis Bay	d	09 13				11 28		12 28		13 28		14 28		15 28		16 28		17 43	18 43	19 53
Lelant	d	09x18																17x48	18x48	19x58
Lelant Saltings	d	09 21	09 51	10 24	10 59	11 35	12 05	12 35	13 05	13 35	14 05	14 35	15 05	15 35	16 05	16 35	17 05	17 51	18 51	20 01
St Erth	a	09 24	09 53	10 28	11 03	11 39	12 09	12 37	13 09	13 39	14 09	14 39	15 09	15 37	16 07	16 37	17 07	17 53	18 53	20 04
Penzance	a																			20 14

Sundays
from 12 September

		GW	GW	GW	GW	GW	GW	GW	GW	GW	GW	GW	GW	GW	GW
St Ives	d	12 11	12 49	13 25	13 56	14 25	14 56	15 25	15 56	16 25	16 56	17 25	17 57	18 50	19 50
Carbis Bay	d	12 14		13 28		14 28		15 28		16 28		17 28		18 53	19 53
Lelant	d	12x19											18x04	18x58	19x58
Lelant Saltings	d	12 22	12 58	13 35	14 05	14 35	15 05	15 35	16 05	16 35	17 05	17 35	18 07	19 01	20 01
St Erth	a	12 25	13 00	13 39	14 09	14 39	15 09	15 37	16 09	16 39	17 09	17 39	18 11	19 03	20 04
Penzance	a														20 14

Network Diagram for Tables 148, 149

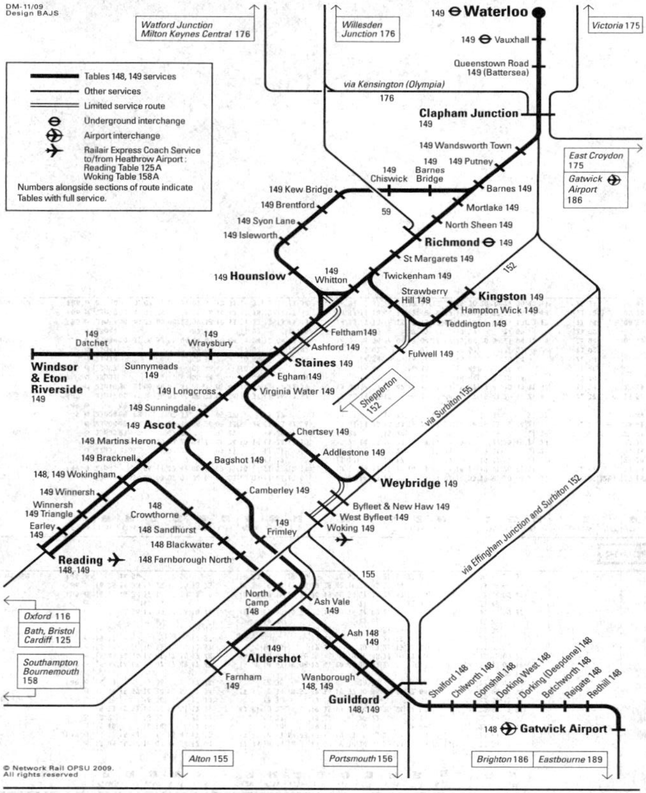

Table 148

Reading - Guildford, Redhill, and Gatwick Airport

Mondays to Fridays

			GW MX [1]	GW MO [1]	GW MX [1]	GW [1]	GW [1]	GW [1]	GW [1]	GW [1]	GW [1]	GW [1]	GW [1]	GW [1]	GW [1]	GW [1]	GW [1]	GW [1]	GW [1]	GW [1]	GW [1]	GW [1]	GW [1]	GW [1]
Reading		d	22p34	23p15	23p34	04 34	05 34	05 51	06 06	06 34	07 04	07 34	08 04	08 20	08 34	09 04	09 34	10 04	10 34	11 04	11 34	12 04	12 34	13 04
Wokingham	149	d	22p43	23p24	23p43	04 43	05 43	06 01	06 16	06 43	07 13	07 43	08 13	08 29	08 43	09 13	09 43	10 13	10 43	11 13	11 43	12 13	12 43	13 13
Crowthorne		d	22p48	23p29	23p48			06 06	06 21		07 18	07 48	08 18	08 34		09 18		10 18		11 18		12 18		13 18
Sandhurst		d	22p52	23p33	23p52			06 10	06 25		07 22	07 52	08 22	08 38		09 22		10 22		11 22		12 22		13 22
Blackwater		d	22p55	23p36	23p55	04 51	05 51	06 13	06 28	06 51	07 25	07 55	08 25	08 41	08 51	09 25	09 51	10 25	10 51	11 25	11 51	12 25	12 51	13 25
Farnborough North		d	23p00	23p41	23p59			06 18	06 33		07 30	08 00	08 30	08 46		09 30		10 30		11 30		12 30		13 30
North Camp		d	23p04	23p45	00 04	04 57	05 57	06 22	06 37	06 57	07 34	08 04	08 34	08 50	09 01	09 34	09 57	10 34	10 57	11 34	11 57	12 34	12 57	13 34
Ash [5]	149	d	23p08	23p49	00 08			06 26	06 41		07 38	08 08	08 38	08 54		09 38		10 38		11 38		12 38		13 38
Wanborough	149	d			00 12			06 30																
Guildford	149	a	23p17	23p58	00 19	05 09	06 09	06 37	06 50	07 08	07 47	08 17	08 47	09 03	09 13	09 47	10 09	10 47	11 08	11 47	12 08	12 47	13 08	13 47
		d	23p18	23p59	00 21	05 10	06 10	06 43	06 57	07 10	07 48	08 18	08 48	09 04	09 13	09 48	10 10	10 48	11 10	11 48	12 10	12 48	13 10	13 48
Shalford		d	23p23					06 48	07a03		07 53		08 53	09a11		09 53		10 53		11 53		12 53		13 53
Chilworth		d	23p27					06 52			07 57		08 57			09 57				11 57				13 57
Gomshall		d	23p34					06 58			08 04		09 04			10 04				12 04				14 04
Dorking West		d	23p41					07 06			08 11		09 11					11 06				13 06		
Dorking Deepdene		d	23p44	00 19	00 37	05 26	06 26	07 08		07 26	08 14	08 35	09 14		09 30	10 11	10 26	11 08	11 26	12 11	12 26	13 08	13 26	14 11
Betchworth		d	23p49					07 13			08 19		09 19					11 13				13 13		
Reigate	186	d	23p54	00 26	00 45	05 34	06 34	07 18		07 34	08 24	08 42	09 24		09 37	10 19	10 34	11 19	11 34	12 19	12 34	13 19	13 34	14 19
Redhill	186	a	23p58	00 30	00 49	05 40	06 39	07 24		07 38	08 30	08 46	09 30		09 42	10 25	10 38	11 25	11 38	12 25	12 38	13 25	13 38	14 25
Gatwick Airport [10]	186	a	00 11	00 41	01 03	05 54	06 56			07 50		09 01			09 59		10 50		11 50		12 50		13 50	

			GW [1]	GW [1]	GW [1]	GW [1]	GW [1]	GW [1]	GW [1]	GW [1]	GW [1]	GW [1]	GW [1]	GW [1]	GW [1]	GW [1]	GW [1]	GW [1]	XC ◇[1]	GW [1]	GW FX [1]	GW FO [1]
Reading		d	13 34	14 04	14 34	15 04	15 28	16 04	16 34	16 50	17 04	17 34	18 04	18 34	19 04	19 34	20 04	20 34	21 34	22b23	22 34	23 34	23 34
Wokingham	149	d	13 43	14 13	14 43	15 13	15 39	16 13	16 43	17 00	17 13	17 43	18 13	18 43	19 13	19 43	20 13	20 43	21 43		22 43	23 43	
Crowthorne		d		14 18		15 18	15 44	16 18		17 06	17 18	17 48	18 18		19 18		20 18		21 48		22 48	23 48	23 48
Sandhurst		d		14 22		15 22	15 48	16 22		17 10	17 22	17 52	18 22		19 22		20 22		21 52		22 52	23 52	23 52
Blackwater		d	13 51	14 25	14 51	15 25	15 51	16 25	16 51	17 13	17 25	17 55	18 25	18 51	19 25	19 51	20 25	20 51	21 55		22 55	23 55	23 55
Farnborough North		d		14 30		15 30		16 30		17 18	17 30	18 00	18 30		19 30		20 30		22 00		23 00	23 59	23 59
North Camp		d	13 57	14 34	14 57	15 34	15 57	16 34	16 57	17 22	17 34	18 04	18 34	18 57	19 34	19 57	20 34	20 57	22 04		23 04	00 04	00 04
Ash [5]	149	d		14 38		15 38		16 38		17 26	17 38	18 08	18 38		19 38		20 38		22 08		23 08	00 08	00 08
Wanborough	149	d						16 42			17 42		18 42									00 12	00 12
Guildford	149	a	14 08	14 47	15 08	15 47	16 08	16 49	17 08	17 35	17 49	18 17	18 49	19 08	19 47	20 08	20 47	21 08	22 17	22 59	23 17	00 19	00 19
		d	14 10	14 48	15 10	15 48	16 10	16 50	17 10	17 40	17 50	18 18	18 51	19 10	19 48	20 10	20 48	21 10	22 18		23 18	00 21	00 21
Shalford		d		14 53		15 53	16 15	16 55		17a48	17 55		18 56		19a55		20 53	21 15	22 23		23 23		
Chilworth		d				15 57		16 59			17 59		19 00				20 58	21 19			23 27		
Gomshall		d				16 04		17 06			18 06		19 06				21 04	21 25			23 34		
Dorking West		d		15 06			16 28	17 13			18 13		19 14				21 12	21 33			23 41		
Dorking Deepdene		d	14 26	15 08	15 26	16 11	16 30	17 16	17 26		18 16	18 35	19 16	19 26		20 26	21 14	21 35	22 37		23 44	00 37	00 37
Betchworth		d		15 13		16 16		17 21			18 21		19 21				21 19	21 40			23 49		
Reigate	186	d	14 34	15 19	15 34	16 21	16 38	17 26	17 34		18 26	18 42	19 26	19 34		20 34	21 24	21 45	22 44		23 54	00 45	00 45
Redhill	186	a	14 38	15 25	15 38	16 27	16 42	17 32	17 38		18 32	18 47	19 32	19 39		20 38	21 30	21 49	22 48		23 58	00 49	00 49
Gatwick Airport [10]	186	a	14 50		15 50		16 59		17 54			19 00		19 55		20 50		22 06	23 06		00 11	01 03	01 03

Saturdays

			GW [1]	GW [1]	GW [1]	GW [1]	GW [1]	GW [1]	GW [1]	GW [1]	GW [1]	GW [1]	GW [1]	GW [1]	GW [1]	GW [1]	GW [1]	GW [1]	GW [1]	GW [1]	GW [1]	GW [1]	GW [1]	GW [1]
Reading		d	22p34	23p34	04 34	05 34	06 04	06 34	07 04	07 34	08 04	08 34	09 04	09 34	10 04	10 34	11 04	11 34	12 04	12 34	13 04	13 34	14 04	14 34
Wokingham	149	d	22p43		04 43	05 43	06 13	06 43	07 13	07 43	08 13	08 43	09 13	09 43	10 13	10 43	11 13	11 43	12 13	12 43	13 13	13 43	14 13	14 43
Crowthorne		d	22p48	23p48			06 18		07 18		08 18		09 18		10 18		11 18		12 18		13 18		14 18	
Sandhurst		d	22p52	23p52			06 22		07 22		08 22		09 22		10 22		11 22		12 22		13 22		14 22	
Blackwater		d	22p55	23p55	04 51	05 51	06 25	06 51	07 25	07 51	08 25	08 51	09 25	09 51	10 25	10 51	11 25	11 51	12 25	12 51	13 25	13 51	14 25	14 51
Farnborough North		d	23p00	23p59			06 30		07 30		08 30		09 30		10 30		11 30		12 30		13 30		14 30	
North Camp		d	23p04	00 04	04 57	05 57	06 34	06 57	07 34	07 57	08 34	08 57	09 34	09 57	10 34	10 57	11 34	11 57	12 34	12 57	13 34	13 57	14 34	14 57
Ash [5]	149	d	23p08	00 08			06 38		07 38		08 38		09 38		10 38		11 38		12 38		13 38		14 38	
Wanborough	149	d		00 12																				
Guildford	149	a	23p17	00 19	05 08	06 08	06 47	07 09	07 47	08 08	08 47	09 08	09 47	10 08	10 47	11 08	11 47	12 08	12 47	13 08	13 47	14 08	14 47	15 08
		d	23p18	00 21	05 10	06 10	06 48	07 10	07 48	08 10	08 48	09 10	09 48	10 10	10 48	11 10	11 48	12 10	12 48	13 10	13 48	14 10	14 48	15 10
Shalford		d	23p23				06 53		07 53		08 53		09 53		10 53		11 53		12 53		13 53		14 53	
Chilworth		d	23p27						07 57				09 57				11 57				13 57			
Gomshall		d	23p34						08 04				10 04				12 04				14 04			
Dorking West		d	23p41				07 06				09 06				11 06				13 06				15 06	
Dorking Deepdene		d	23p44	00 37	05 26	06 26	07 08	07 26	08 11	08 26	09 08	09 26	10 11	10 26	11 08	11 26	12 11	12 26	13 08	13 26	14 11	14 26	15 08	15 26
Betchworth		d	23p49				07 13				09 13				11 13				13 13				15 13	
Reigate	186	d	23p54	00 45	05 34	06 34	07 18	07 34	08 19	08 34	09 18	09 34	10 19	10 34	11 18	11 34	12 19	12 34	13 18	13 34	14 19	14 34	15 18	15 34
Redhill	186	a	23p58	00 49	05 39	06 39	07 25	07 39	08 25	08 38	09 25	09 38	10 25	10 38	11 25	11 38	12 25	12 38	13 25	13 38	14 25	14 38	15 25	15 38
Gatwick Airport [10]	186	a	00 11	01 03	05 58	06 50		07 50		08 50		09 50		10 50		11 50		12 50		13 50		14 50		15 50

b arr. 2216

Table 148

Reading - Guildford, Redhill, and Gatwick Airport

Saturdays

			GW [1]	GW [1]	GW [1]	GW [1]	GW [1]	GW [1]	GW [1]	GW [1]	GW [1]	GW [1]	GW [1]	GW [1]	GW [1]	XC ◇[1]	GW [1]	GW [1]
Reading		d	15 04	15 34	16 04	16 34	17 04	17 34	18 04	18 34	19 04	19 34	20 04	20 34	21 34	22 15	22 34	23 34
Wokingham	149	d	15 13	15 43	16 13	16 43	17 13	17 43	18 13	18 43	19 13	19 43	20 13	20 43	21 43		22 43	
Crowthorne		d	15 18		16 18		17 18		18 18		19 18		20 18		21 48		22 48	23 48
Sandhurst		d	15 22		16 22		17 22		18 22		19 22		20 22		21 52		22 52	23 52
Blackwater		d	15 25	15 51	16 25	16 51	17 25	17 51	18 25	18 51	19 25	19 51	20 25	20 51	21 55		22 55	23 55
Farnborough North		d	15 30		16 30		17 30		18 30		19 30		20 30		22 00		23 00	23 59
North Camp		d	15 34	15 57	16 34	16 57	17 34	17 57	18 34	18 57	19 34	19 57	20 34	20 57	22 04		23 04	00 04
Ash [5]	149	d	15 38		16 38		17 38		18 38		19 38		20 38		22 08		23 08	00 08
Wanborough	149	d																00 12
Guildford	149	a	15 47	16 08	16 47	17 08	17 47	18 08	18 47	19 08	19 47	20 08	20 47	21 08	22 17	22 59	23 17	00 19
		d	15 48	16 10	16 48	17 10	17 48	18 10	18 48	19 10	19 48	20 10	20 48	21 10	22 18		23 18	00 21
Shalford		d	15 53		16 53		17 53		18 53		19 53		20 53	21 15	22 23		23 23	
Chilworth		d	15 57				17 57				19 57			21 19			23 27	
Gomshall		d	16 04				18 04				20 04			21 25			23 34	
Dorking West		d			17 06				19 06				21 06		22 36		23 41	
Dorking Deepdene		d	16 11	16 26	17 08	17 26	18 11	18 26	19 08	19 26	20 11	20 26	21 08	21 33	22 38		23 44	00 37
Betchworth		d			17 13				19 13				21 13		22 43		23 49	
Reigate	186	d	16 19	16 34	17 18	17 34	18 19	18 34	19 18	19 34	20 19	20 34	21 18	21 40	22 48		23 54	00 45
Redhill	186	a	16 25	16 38	17 25	17 38	18 25	18 38	19 25	19 38	20 25	20 38	21 25	21 44	22 52		23 58	00 49
Gatwick Airport [10]	186	a		16 50		17 50		18 50		19 50		20 50		21 59	23 05		00 10	01 02

Sundays

			GW [1]	GW [1]	GW [1]	GW [1]	GW [1]	GW [1]	GW [1]	GW [1]	GW [1]	GW [1]	GW [1]	GW [1]	GW [1]	GW [1]	GW [1]	GW [1]	GW [1]	GW [1]	GW [1]	XC ◇[1]	GW [1]
Reading		d	22p34	23p34	06 03	07 03	08 03	09 03	10 03	11 03	12 03	13 03	14 03	15 03	16 03	17 03	18 03	19 03	20 03	21 03	22 03	22b14	23 15
Wokingham	149	d	22p43		06 11	07 11	08 11	09 11	10 11	11 11	12 11	13 11	14 11	15 11	16 11	17 11	18 11	19 11	20 11	21 11	22 11		23 24
Crowthorne		d	22p48	23p48		07 17		09 17		11 17		13 17		15 17		17 17		19 17		21 17			23 29
Sandhurst		d	22p52	23p52		07 21		09 21		11 21		13 21		15 21		17 21		19 21		21 21			23 33
Blackwater		d	22p55	23p55	06 20	07 24	08 19	09 24	10 19	11 24	12 19	13 24	14 19	15 24	16 19	17 24	18 19	19 24	20 19	21 24	22 19		23 36
Farnborough North		d	23p00	23p59		07 29		09 29		11 29		13 29		15 29		17 29		19 29		21 29			23 41
North Camp		d	23p04	00 04	06 27	07 33	08 26	09 33	10 26	11 33	12 26	13 33	14 26	15 33	16 26	17 33	18 26	19 33	20 26	21 33	22 26		23 45
Ash [5]	149	d	23p08	00 08		07 37		09 37		11 37		13 37		15 37		17 37		19 37		21 37			23 49
Wanborough	149	d		00 12																			
Guildford	149	a	23p17	00 19	06 38	07 46	08 37	09 46	10 37	11 46	12 37	13 46	14 37	15 46	16 37	17 46	18 37	19 46	20 37	21 46	22 37	22 42	23 58
		d	23p18	00 21	06 40	07 47	08 39	09 47	10 39	11 47	12 39	13 47	14 39	15 47	16 39	17 47	18 39	19 47	20 39	21 47	22 39		23 59
Shalford		d	23p23				08 44		10 44		12 44		14 44		16 44		18 44		20 44		22 44		
Chilworth		d	23p27				08 48		10 48		12 48		14 48		16 48		18 48		20 48		22 48		
Gomshall		d	23p34				08 54		10 54		12 54		14 54		16 54		18 54		20 54		22 54		
Dorking West		d	23p41				09 02		11 02		13 02		15 02		17 02		19 02		21 02		23 02		
Dorking Deepdene		d	23p44	00 37	06 57	08 04	09 04	10 04	11 04	12 04	13 04	14 04	15 04	16 04	17 04	18 04	19 04	20 04	21 04	22 04	23 04		00 19
Betchworth		d	23p49				09 09		11 09		13 09		15 09		17 09		19 09		21 09		23 09		
Reigate	186	d	23p54	00 45	07 05	08 13	09 13	10 13	11 13	12 13	13 13	14 13	15 13	16 13	17 13	18 13	19 13	20 13	21 13	22 13	23 13		00 26
Redhill	186	a	23p58	00 49	07 09	08 18	09 18	10 17	11 18	12 17	13 18	14 17	15 18	16 17	17 18	18 17	19 18	20 17	21 18	22 18	23 18		00 30
Gatwick Airport [10]	186	a	00 10	01 02	07 27	08 31	09 31	10 31	11 31	12 31	13 31	14 31	15 31	16 31	17 31	18 31	19 30	20 30	21 30	22 31	23 31		00 41

b arr. 2205

Table 148

Gatwick Airport, Redhill and Guildford - Reading

Mondays to Fridays

		GW MX 1	GW MO 1	GW MX 1	GW 1	GW 1	XC ◇1	GW 1	GW 1	GW 1	GW 1	GW 1	GW 1	GW 1	GW 1	GW 1	GW 1	GW 1	GW 1	GW 1	GW 1	GW 1	GW 1
Gatwick Airport 10	186 d	22p22	23p08	23p18	05 31	05 56			07 00			07 58		09 07			10 03		11 03		12 03		13 03
Redhill	186 d	22p33	23p20	23p28	05 43	06b13		06 24	07 10		07 28	08 08	08 33	09c23		09 34	10 13	10 34	11 13	11 34	12 13	12 34	13 13
Reigate	186 d	22p38	23p23	23p33	05 49	06 18		06 28	07 15		07 32	08 13	08 37	09 28		09 38	10 18	10 38	11 18	11 38	12 18	12 38	13 18
Betchworth	d	22p43						06 33			07 37		08 42			09 43		10 43				12 43	
Dorking Deepdene	d	22p47	23p31	23p40	05 56	06 25		06 37	07 22		07 41	08 20	08 46	09 35		09 47	10 25	10 47	11 25	11 45	12 25	12 47	13 25
Dorking West	d	22p50						06 40			07 44		08 49			09 50		10 50				12 50	
Gomshall	d	22p58						06 48	07 30		07 52		08 57			09 58				11 53			
Chilworth	d	23p04						06 54			07 58		09 03			10 04				11 59			
Shalford	d	23p08						06 58		07 21	08 02		09 07		09 31	10 08		11 03		12 03		13 03	
Guildford	a	23p12	23p50	00 01	06 12	06 41		07 03	07 41	07 25	08 06	08 36	09 11	09 53	09 35	10 12	10 42	11 08	11 42	12 08	12 42	13 08	13 42
	d	23p14	23p52	00 02	06 13	06 43	06 02	07 04	07 43	07 27	08 13	08 38	09 13	09 54	09 37	10 14	10 44	11 09	11 44	12 09	12 44	13 09	13 44
Wanborough	149 d	23p21			06 20			07 12			08 20		09 20										
Ash 5	149 d	23p26	00 01		06 25	06 52		07 16	07 52	07 36	08 25		09 25		09 46	10 23		11 19		12 19		13 19	
North Camp	d	23p30	00 05	00 14	06 29	06 56		07 20	07 56	07 41	08 29	08 50	09 29		09 50	10 27	10 56	11 23	11 56	12 23	12 56	13 23	13 56
Farnborough North	d	23p34	00 09		06 33	07 00		07 24	08 00	07 45	08 33		09 33			10 31		11 27		12 27		13 27	
Blackwater	d	23p38	00 14	00 20	06 37	07 05		07 29	08 05	07 49	08 37	08 56	09 37		09 57	10 36	11 02	11 31	12 02	12 31	13 02	13 31	14 02
Sandhurst	d	23p42	00 16		06 41	07 08		07 32	08 08	07 53	08 41		09 41			10 39		11 35		12 35		13 35	
Crowthorne	d	23p46	00 20		06 45	07 12		07 36	08 12	07 57	08 45		09 45			10 43		11 39		12 39		13 39	
Wokingham	149 d	23p51	00 25	00 29	06 50	07 17		07 41	08 17	08 02	08 50	09 04	09 51		10 05	10 48	11 10	11 44	12 10	12 44	13 10	13 44	14 10
Reading 7	149 a	00 01	00 37	00 39	06 58	07 29	06 31	07 52	08 30	08 17	09 00	09 17	10 01	10 23	10 17	10 59	11 19	11 54	12 19	12 54	13 19	13 54	14 19

		GW 1	GW 1	GW 1	GW 1	GW 1	GW 1	GW 1	GW 1	GW 1	GW 1	GW 1	GW 1	GW 1	GW 1	GW 1	GW 1	GW 1	GW 1	GW 1	GW 1
Gatwick Airport 10	186 d		14 03		15 03		16 03		17 03		18 03			19 16		20 03		21 03		22 22	23 18
Redhill	186 d	13 34	14 13	14 34	15 13	15 29	16 13	16 32	17 13	17 43	18 13		18 43	19 26		20 13	20 34	21 13	21 35	22 33	23 28
Reigate	186 d	13 38	14 18	14 38	15 18	15 34	16 18	16 36	17 18	17 48	18 18		18 47	19 31		20 18	20 40	21 18	21 39	22 38	23 33
Betchworth	d			14 43		15 38		16 41		17 53			18 52				20 45		21 44	22 43	
Dorking Deepdene	d	13 45	14 25	14 47	15 25	15 43	16 25	16 45	17 25	17 57	18 25		18 56	19 38		20 25	20 49	21 25	21 48	22 47	23 40
Dorking West	d			14 50		15 45				18 00			18 59				20 52		21 51	22 50	
Gomshall	d	13 53				15 53		16 53		18 08			19 07				21 00		21 59	22 58	
Chilworth	d	13 59				15 59		16 59		18 14			19 13				21 06		22 05	23 04	
Shalford	d	14 03		15 03		16 03		17 03		18 18		18 05	19 17		20 02		21 10		22 09	23 08	
Guildford	a	14 08	14 42	15 08	15 42	16 08	16 42	17 08	17 43	18 22	18 41	18 12	19 22	19 54	20 06	20 42	21 14	21 42	22 13	23 12	00 01
	d	14 09	14 44	15 09	15 44	16 14	16 44	17 09	17 44	18 24	18 49	18 14	19 36	19 55	20 10	20 43	21 16	21 44	22 15	23 14	00 02
Wanborough	149 d																			23 21	
Ash 5	149 d	14 19		15 19		16 24		17 19	17 54	18 33		18 23	19 46		20 19		21 25		22 23	23 26	
North Camp	d	14 23	14 56	15 23	15 56	16 28	16 56	17 23	17 58	18 38	19 01	18 27	19 50	20 07	20 23	20 55	21 29	21 56	22 27	23 30	00 14
Farnborough North	d	14 27		15 27		16 32		17 27	18 02	18 42		18 31	19 54		20 27		21 33		22 31	23 34	
Blackwater	d	14 31	15 02	15 31	16 02	16 36	17 02	17 31	18 07	18 46	19 07	18 36	19 58	20 14	20 31	21 02	21 38	22 02	22 36	23 38	00 20
Sandhurst	d	14 35		15 35		16 40		17 35		18 51		18 39	20 02		20 35		21 41		22 39	23 42	
Crowthorne	d	14 39		15 39		16 44		17 39		18 59		18 43	20 06		20 39		21 45		22 43	23 46	
Wokingham	149 d	14 44	15 10	15 43	16 10	16 48	17 10	17 44	18 15	19 04	19 15	18 51	20 11	20 22	20 43	21 10	21 50	22 10	22 48	23 51	00 29
Reading 7	149 a	14 55	15 19	15 55	16 24	17 00	17 19	17 54	18 24	19 17	19 25	19 02	20 21	20 32	20 55.	21 19	22 01	22 19	23 01	00 01	00 39

Saturdays

		GW 1	GW 1	GW 1	GW 1	XC ◇1	GW 1	GW 1	GW 1	GW 1	GW 1	GW 1	GW 1	GW 1	GW 1	GW 1	GW 1	GW 1	GW 1	GW 1	GW 1	GW 1	GW 1
Gatwick Airport 10	186 d	22p22	23p18	05 31	06 03			07 03		08 03		09 03		10 03		11 03		12 03		13 03		14 03	
Redhill	186 d	22p33	23p28	05 41	06 13		06 34	07 13	07 34	08 13	08 34	09 13	09 34	10 13	10 34	11 13	11 34	12 13	12 34	13 13	13 34	14 13	14 34
Reigate	186 d	22p38	23p33	05 47	06 18		06 38	07 18	07 38	08 18	08 38	09 18	09 38	10 18	10 38	11 18	11 38	12 18	12 38	13 18	13 38	14 18	14 38
Betchworth	d	22p43					06 43				08 43				10 43				12 43				14 43
Dorking Deepdene	d	22p47	23p40	05 54	06 25		06 47	07 25	07 45	08 25	08 47	09 25	09 45	10 25	10 47	11 25	11 45	12 25	12 47	13 25	13 45	14 25	14 47
Dorking West	d	22p50					06 50				08 50				10 50				12 50				14 50
Gomshall	d	22p58							07 53				09 53				11 53				13 53		
Chilworth	d	23p04							07 59				09 59				11 59				13 59		
Shalford	d	23p08					07 03		08 03		09 03		10 03		11 03		12 03		13 03		14 03		15 03
Guildford	a	23p12	00 01	06 12	06 43		07 08	07 41	08 08	08 42	09 08	09 42	10 08	10 42	11 08	11 42	12 08	12 42	13 08	13 42	14 08	14 42	15 08
	d	23p14	00 02	06 12	06 43	06 09	07 09	07 44	08 09	08 44	09 09	09 44	10 09	10 44	11 09	11 44	12 09	12 44	13 09	13 44	14 09	14 44	15 09
Wanborough	149 d	23p21		06 21																			
Ash 5	149 d	23p26		06 24			07 19		08 19		09 19		10 19		11 19		12 19		13 19		14 19		15 19
North Camp	d	23p30	00 14	06 28	06 55		07 23	07 56	08 23	08 56	09 23	09 56	10 23	10 56	11 23	11 56	12 23	12 56	13 23	13 56	14 23	14 56	15 23
Farnborough North	d	23p34		06 32			07 27		08 27		09 27		10 27		11 27		12 27		13 27		14 27		15 27
Blackwater	d	23p38	00 20	06 38	07 03		07 31	08 02	08 31	09 02	09 31	10 02	10 31	11 02	11 31	12 02	12 31	13 02	13 31	14 02	14 31	15 02	15 31
Sandhurst	d	23p42		06 40			07 35		08 35		09 35		10 35		11 35		12 35		13 35		14 35		15 35
Crowthorne	d	23p46		06 44			07 39		08 39		09 39		10 39		11 39		12 39		13 39		14 39		15 39
Wokingham	149 d	23p51	00 29	06 49	07 11		07 44	08 10	08 44	09 10	09 44	10 10	10 44	11 10	11 44	12 10	12 44	13 10	13 44	14 10	14 44	15 10	15 44
Reading 7	149 a	00 01	00 39	07 03	07 20	06 44	07 54	08 20	08 54	09 22	09 54	10 20	10 54	11 20	11 54	12 20	12 54	13 20	13 54	14 20	14 54	15 20	15 54

b arr. 0607

c arr. 0915

Table 148

Gatwick Airport, Redhill and Guildford - Reading

Saturdays

		GW 1	GW 1	GW 1	GW 1	GW 1	GW 1	GW 1	GW 1	GW 1	GW 1	GW 1	GW 1	GW 1	GW 1	GW 1	GW 1
Gatwick Airport 10	186 d	15 03		16 03		17 03		18 03		19 03		20 03		21 03		22 22	23 18
Redhill	186 d	15 13	15 34	16 13	16 34	17 13	17 34	18 13	18 34	19 13	19 34	20 13	20 34	21 13	21 36	22 33	23 28
Reigate	186 d	15 18	15 38	16 18	16 38	17 18	17 38	18 18	18 38	19 18	19 38	20 18	20 38	21 18	21 40	22 38	23 33
Betchworth	d				16 43				18 43				20 43			22 43	
Dorking Deepdene	d	15 25	15 45	16 25	16 47	17 25	17 45	18 25	18 47	19 25	19 45	20 25	20 47	21 25	21 47	22 47	23 40
Dorking West	d				16 50				18 50				20 50			22 50	
Gomshall	d		15 53				17 53				19 53				21 55	22 58	
Chilworth	d		15 59				17 59				19 59				22 01	23 04	
Shalford	d		16 03		17 03		18 03		19 03		20 03		21 03		22 05	23 08	
Guildford	a	15 42	16 08	16 42	17 08	17 42	18 08	18 42	19 08	19 42	20 08	20 42	21 08	21 43	22 13	23 13	00 01
	d	15 44	16 09	16 44	17 09	17 44	18 09	18 44	19 09	19 44	20 09	20 44	21 09	21 43	22 14	23 14	00 02
Wanborough	149 d															23 22	
Ash 5	149 d		16 19		17 19		18 19		19 19		20 19		21 19		22 24	23 26	
North Camp	d	15 56	16 23	16 56	17 23	17 56	18 23	18 56	19 23	19 56	20 23	20 56	21 23	21 55	22 28	23 30	00 14
Farnborough North	d		16 27		17 27		18 27		19 27		20 27		21 27		22 32	23 34	
Blackwater	d	16 02	16 31	17 02	17 31	18 02	18 31	19 02	19 31	20 02	20 31	21 02	21 31	22 03	22 36	23 39	00 20
Sandhurst	d		16 35		17 35		18 35		19 35		20 35		21 35		22 40	23 42	
Crowthorne	d		16 39		17 39		18 39		19 39		20 39		21 39		22 44	23 46	
Wokingham	149 d	16 10	16 44	17 10	17 44	18 10	18 44	19 10	19 44	20 10	20 44	21 10	21 44	22 11	22 49	23 51	00 29
Reading 7	149 a	16 20	16 54	17 20	17 55	18 20	18 54	19 20	19 54	20 20	20 54	21 20	21 54	22 20	22 58	00 01	00 39

Sundays

		GW 1	GW 1	GW 1	GW 1	GW 1	GW 1	GW 1	GW 1	GW 1	XC ◇1	GW 1	GW 1	GW 1	GW 1	GW 1	GW 1	GW 1	GW 1	GW 1	GW 1	GW 1
Gatwick Airport 10	186 d	22p22	23p18	06 08	07 08	08 08	09 08	10 08	11 08	12 08		13 08	14 08	15 08	16 08	17 08	18 08	19 08	20 08	21 08	22 07	23 08
Redhill	186 d	22p33	23p28	06 21	07 21	08 19	09 20	10 19	11 20	12 19		13 20	14 19	15 20	16 19	17 20	18 19	19 20	20 19	21 19	22 20	23 20
Reigate	186 d	22p38	23p33	06 24	07 24	08 23	09 24	10 23	11 24	12 23		13 24	14 23	15 24	16 23	17 24	18 23	19 24	20 23	21 24	22 23	23 23
Betchworth	d	22p43				08 28		10 28		12 28			14 28		16 28		18 28		20 28		22 28	
Dorking Deepdene	d	22p47	23p40	06 32	07 32	08 31	09 32	10 31	11 32	12 31		13 32	14 31	15 32	16 31	17 32	18 31	19 32	20 31	21 32	22 31	23 31
Dorking West	d	22p50				08 35		10 35		12 35			14 35		16 35		18 35		20 35		22 35	
Gomshall	d	22p58				08 43		10 43		12 43			14 43		16 43		18 43		20 43		22 43	
Chilworth	d	23p04				08 49		10 49		12 49			14 49		16 49		18 49		20 49		22 49	
Shalford	d	23p08				08 53		10 53		12 53			14 53		16 53		18 53		20 53		22 53	
Guildford	a	23p13	00 01	06 49	07 50	08 57	09 52	10 57	11 52	12 57		13 52	14 57	15 52	16 57	17 52	18 57	19 52	20 57	21 52	22 57	23 50
	d	23p14	00 02	06 50	07 52	08 59	09 52	10 59	11 52	12 59	12 14	13 52	14 59	15 52	16 59	17 52	18 59	19 52	20 58	21 52	22 59	23 52
Wanborough	149 d	23p22																				
Ash 5	149 d	23p26			08 02		10 02		12 02			14 02		16 02		18 02		20 02		22 02		00 01
North Camp	d	23p30	00 14	07 02	08 06	09 11	10 06	11 11	12 06	13 11		14 06	15 11	16 06	17 11	18 06	19 11	20 06	21 10	22 06	23 11	00 05
Farnborough North	d	23p34			08 10		10 10		12 10			14 10		16 10		18 10		20 10		22 10		00 09
Blackwater	d	23p39	00 20	07 09	08 14	09 17	10 14	11 18	12 14	13 17		14 14	15 17	16 14	17 17	18 14	19 17	20 14	21 18	22 14	23 17	00 14
Sandhurst	d	23p42			08 18		10 18		12 18			14 18		16 18		18 18		20 18		22 18		00 16
Crowthorne	d	23p46			08 22		10 22		12 22			14 22		16 22		18 22		20 22		22 22		00 20
Wokingham	149 d	23p51	00 29	07 17	08 27	09 25	10 27	11 26	12 27	13 25		14 27	15 25	16 27	17 25	18 27	19 25	20 27	21 26	22 27	23 25	00 25
Reading 7	149 a	00 01	00 39	07 26	08 37	09 36	10 37	11 36	12 37	13 36	12 50	14 37	15 36	16 37	17 36	18 37	19 36	20 37	21 36	22 38	23 25	00 25

Table 149

Mondays to Fridays
24 May to 24 September

London - Hounslow, Richmond, Kingston, Windsor, Weybridge, Ascot, Guildford and Reading

		SW MO 1	SW MO	SW MX 1	SW MX	SW MO 1	SW MX	SW MX 1	SW MX	SW MX	SW MX	SW MO	SW MX 1	SW MO 1	SW MO	SW MX	SW MX	SW	SW	SW 1	SW 1	SW	SW
London Waterloo 15 ⊖	d	22p39	22p50	22p50	22p52	23p09	23p13	23p20	23p22	23p33	23p38			23p39	23p44	23p52	23p58	00 18			05 05		
Vauxhall ⊖	d	22p43	22p54		22p56	23p13	23p17		23p26	23p37				23p43	23p48	23p56	00 02	00 22			05 09		
Queenstown Rd.(Battersea)	d		22p57		22p59				23p29	23p40					23p51	23p59		00 25			05 12		
Clapham Junction 10	d	22p49	23p00	22p58	23p02	23p19	23p23	23p28	23p32	23p43	23p46			23p49	23p54	00 02	00 08	00 28			05 15		
Wandsworth Town	d		23p03		23p05				23p35	23p46					23p57	00 05		00 31			05 18		
Putney	d	22p53	23p06		23p08	23p23	23p27		23p38	23p49				23p53	23p59	00 08	00 12	00 34			05 21		
Barnes	d		23p09		23p12				23p42	23p52					00 03	00 12		00 37			05 24		
Barnes Bridge	d		23p11		23p14				23p44							00 14							
Chiswick	d		23p13		23p17				23p47							00 17							
Kew Bridge	d		23p16		23p20				23p50							00 20							
Brentford	d		23p19		23p23				23p53							00 23							
Syon Lane	d		23p21		23p25				23p55							00 25							
Isleworth	d		23p23		23p27				23p57							00 27							
Hounslow	d		23p26		23p31				00 01							00 31							
Mortlake	d									23p54					00 05			00 39			05 26		
North Sheen	d									23p56					00 07			00 41			05 28		
Richmond ⊖	d	22p59		23p06		23p29	23p33	23p37		23p59	23p54			23p59	00 10		00 18	00 44			05 31		
St Margarets	d									00 01					00 12			00 46			05 33		
Twickenham	a	23p02		23p10		23p32	23p36	23p41		00 03	23p58			00 02	00 14		00 21	00 48			05 35		
	d	23p03		23p10		23p33	23p37	23p41		00 04	23p58			00 03	00 15		00 22	00 49	04 52		05 36		05 53
Strawberry Hill	d									00 07								00s52	04 55				
Fulwell	a																						
Teddington	a									00 10								00s55	04 58				
Hampton Wick	a									00 14								00s58	05 01				
Kingston	a									00 16								01 00	05 03				
Whitton	d						23p40								00 18		00 25				05 39		05 56
Feltham	d	23p09	23p32	23p16	23p36	23p39	23p44	23p48	00 06		00 04			00 09	00 22	00 37	00 29				05 43		06 00
Ashford (Surrey)	d		23p36		23p40		23p48		00 10						00 26	00 41	00 33				05 47		06 04
Staines	d	23p15	23p40	23p23	23p44	23p45	23p52	23p56	00 14		00 11	00 21		00 15	00a30	00a46	00a37			05 23	05 53	05 44	06 08
Wraysbury	d						23p56																06 12
Sunnymeads	d						23p59																06 15
Datchet	d						00 02																06 18
Windsor & Eton Riverside	a						00 06																06 22
Egham	d	23p20	23p45	23p27	23p49	23p50		00 01	00 19		00 15	00s25		00 20						05 27	05 57	05 49	
Virginia Water	a	23p24	23p49	23p31	23p53	23p54		00 05	00 23		00 19	00s30		00 24						05 31	06 01	05 53	
	d	23p24	23p49	23p31	23p53	23p54		00 05	00 23		00 19	00s30		00 24						05 31	06 01	05 53	
Chertsey	d		23p55		23p59				00 29			00s35										05 59	
Addlestone	d		23p58		00 02				00 32			00s38										06 02	
Weybridge	a								00 37													06 07	
Byfleet & New Haw	d		00 02		00 06							00s42											
West Byfleet	d		00 05		00 09							00s45											
Woking	a		00 11		00 18							00 51											
Longcross	d																						
Sunningdale	d	23p29		23p37		23p59		00 11			00 25			00 29						05 37	06 07		
Ascot 3	d	23p34		23p43		00 04		00 15			00 30		00 32	00 34						05 43	06 13		
Bagshot	d												00 38										
Camberley	a												00 44										
Frimley	d												00 48										
Ash Vale	d												00 57										
Aldershot	a												01s02										
	d												01s06										
Ash 5	d																						
Wanborough	d																						
Guildford	a																						
Martins Heron	d	23p38		23p47		00 08		00 19			00 34			00 38						05 47	06 17		
Bracknell	d	23p41		23p50		00 11		00 23			00 37			00 41						05 50	06 20		
Wokingham	d	23p48		23p57		00 18		00 32			00 44			00 48						05 57	06 27		
Winnersh	d	23p51		23p59		00 21		00 36						00 51						06 00	06 30		
Winnersh Triangle	d	23p53		00 01		00 23		00 38						00 53						06 02	06 32		
Earley	d	23p56		00 05		00 26		00 40						00 56						06 05	06 35		
Reading 7	a	00 01		00 10		00 31		00 45			00 52			01 01						06 10	06 40		

Table 149

Mondays to Fridays
24 May to 24 September

London - Hounslow, Richmond, Kingston, Windsor, Weybridge, Ascot, Guildford and Reading

		SW	SW	SW 1	SW 1	SW	SW	SW	SW	SW	SW 1	SW 1	SW	SW	SW	SW	SW	SW 1	SW 1	SW	GW 1 A	SW	SW	SW
London Waterloo 15 ⊖	d	05 33			05 50		05 58	06 03	06 15			06 20	06 22	06 28	06 33		06 45		06 50	06 52		06 58	07 03	07 15
Vauxhall ⊖	d	05 37					06 02	06 07	06 19				06 26	06 32	06 37		06 49			06 56		07 02	07 07	07 19
Queenstown Rd.(Battersea)	d	05 40						06 10	06 22				06 29		06 40		06 52			06 59			07 10	07 22
Clapham Junction 10	d	05 43			05 58		06 08	06 13	06 25			06 28	06 32	06 38	06 43		06 55		06 58	07 02		07 08	07 13	07 25
Wandsworth Town	d	05 46						06 16	06 28				06 35		06 46		06 58			07 05			07 16	07 28
Putney	d	05 49					06 12	06 19	06 31				06 38	06 42	06 49		07 01			07 08		07 12	07 19	07 31
Barnes	d	05 52						06 22	06 35				06 42		06 52		07 05			07 12			07 22	07 35
Barnes Bridge	d												06 44							07 14				
Chiswick	d												06 47							07 17				
Kew Bridge	d												06 50							07 20				
Brentford	d												06 53							07 23				
Syon Lane	d												06 55							07 25				
Isleworth	d												06 57							07 27				
Hounslow	d												07 01			06 48				07 31				
Mortlake	d	05 54						06 24	06 37						06 54		07 07						07 24	07 37
North Sheen	d	05 56						06 26	06 39						06 56		07 09						07 26	07 39
Richmond ⊖	d	05 59			06 06		06 18	06 29	06 42			06 36		06 48	06 59		07 12		07 06			07 18	07 29	07 42
St Margarets	d	06 01						06 31	06 44						07 01		07 14						07 31	07 44
Twickenham	a	06 03			06 10		06 21	06 33	06 46			06 40		06 51	07 03		07 16		07 10			07 21	07 33	07 46
	d	06 05			06 10	06 17	06 22	06 34	06 47			06 40		06 52	07 04		07 17		07 10			07 22	07 34	07 47
Strawberry Hill	d	06 08						06 37							07 07								07 37	
Fulwell	a																							
Teddington	a	06 11						06 40							07 10								07 40	
Hampton Wick	a	06 14						06 44							07 14								07 44	
Kingston	a	06 16						06 46							07 16								07 46	
Whitton	d					06a20	06 25		06 50					06 55		06a53	07 20					07 25		07 50
Feltham	d				06 16		06 29					06 46	07 06	06 59					07 16	07 36		07 29		
Ashford (Surrey)	d						06 33						07 10	07 03						07 40		07 33		
Staines	d		06 14		06 23		06 37			06 44		06 53	07 14	07 07					07 23	07 44		07 37		
Wraysbury	d						06 41							07 11								07 41		
Sunnymeads	d						06 44							07 14								07 44		
Datchet	d						06 47							07 17								07 47		
Windsor & Eton Riverside	a						06 51							07 21								07 51		
Egham	d		06 19		06 27					06 49		06 57	07 19						07 27	07 49				
Virginia Water	a		06 23		06 31					06 53		07 01	07 23						07 31	07 53				
	d		06 23		06 31					06 53		07 01	07 23						07 31	07 53				
Chertsey	d		06 29							06 59			07 29							07 59				
Addlestone	d		06 32							07 02			07 32							08 02				
Weybridge	a		06 37							07 07			07 37							08 07				
Byfleet & New Haw	d																							
West Byfleet	d																							
Woking	a																							
Longcross	d				06 35							07 05							07 35					
Sunningdale	d				06 37							07 07							07 37					
Ascot 3	d			06 23	06 43						06 53	07 13						07 23	07 43					
Bagshot	d			06 29							06 59							07 29						
Camberley	a			06 35							07 05							07 35						
Frimley	d			06 43							07 13							07 43						
Ash Vale	d			06 49							07 19							07 49						
Aldershot	a			06 56							07 26							07 54						
	d			07 08							07 38							08 08						
Ash 5	d			07 15							07 45							08 15						
Wanborough	d			07 18							07 48							08 18						
Guildford	a			07 25							07 55							08 25						
Martins Heron	d				06 47							07 17							07 47					
Bracknell	d				06 50							07 20							07 50					
Wokingham	d				06 57							07 27							07 57		08 17			
Winnersh	d				07 00							07 30							08 00		08 21			
Winnersh Triangle	d				07 02							07 32							08 02					
Earley	d				07 05							07 35							08 05					
Reading 7	a				07 10							07 40							08 10		08 30			

A From Gatwick Airport (Table 148)

Table 149

Mondays to Fridays
24 May to 24 September

London - Hounslow, Richmond, Kingston, Windsor, Weybridge, Ascot, Guildford and Reading

		SW 1	SW	SW 1	SW	SW	SW 1	SW	SW	SW	SW	SW 1	SW	SW	SW	SW 1	SW 1	SW	SW	SW 1	SW
London Waterloo 15 ⊖	d			07 20	07 22	07 28		07 33		07 37	07 45	07 50	07 52	07 58	08 03		08 07	08 10	08 15	08 20	08 22
Vauxhall ⊖	d				07 26	07 32		07 37		07 41	07 49		07 56	08 02	08 07			08 14	08 19		08 26
Queenstown Rd.(Battersea)	d				07 29			07 40		07 44	07 52		07 59		08 10			08 17	08 22		08 29
Clapham Junction 10	d			07 28	07 32	07 38		07 43		07 47	07 55	07 58	08 02	08 08	08 13		08 16	08 20	08 25	08 28	08 32
Wandsworth Town	d				07 35			07 46		07 50	07 58		08 05		08 16			08 23	08 28		08 35
Putney	d				07 38	07 42		07 49		07 53	08 01		08 08	08 12	08 19			08 26	08 31		08 38
Barnes	d				07 42			07 52		07 57	08 05		08 12		08 23			08 27	08 35		08 42
Barnes Bridge	d				07 44					07 59			08 14					08 29			08 44
Chiswick	d				07 47					08 02			08 17					08 32			08 47
Kew Bridge	d				07 50					08 05			08 20					08 35			08 50
Brentford	d				07 53					08 08			08 23					08 38			08 53
Syon Lane	d				07 55					08 10			08 25					08 40			08 55
Isleworth	d				07 57					08 12			08 27					08 42			08 57
Hounslow	d				08 01					08a18			08 31					08 48			09 01
Mortlake	d							07 54			08 07				08 25				08 37		
North Sheen	d							07 56			08 09				08 27				08 39		
Richmond ⊖	d			07 36		07 48	07 54	07 59			08 12	08 06		08 18	08 30		08 24		08 42	08 36	
St Margarets	d							08 01			08 14				08 32				08 44		
Twickenham	a			07 40		07 51	07 57	08 03			08 16	08 10		08 21	08 34		08 28		08 46	08 40	
	d		07 37	07 40		07 52	07 58	08 04	08 07		08 17	08 10		08 22	08 35		08 28		08 47	08 40	
Strawberry Hill	d		07 47					08 07	08 17						08 38						
Fulwell	a																				
Teddington	a		07 50					08 10	08 20						08 41						
Hampton Wick	a		07 52					08 14	08 22						08 44						
Kingston	a		07 54					08 16	08 24						08 46						
Whitton	d					07 55					08 20			08 25				08 53	08 50		
Feltham	d			07 46	08 06	07 59	08 04					08 16	08 36	08 29			08 34			08 46	09 06
Ashford (Surrey)	d				08 10	08 03	08 08						08 40	08 33			08 38				09 10
Staines	d			07 53	08 14	08 07	08 12					08 23	08 44	08 37			08 42			08 53	09 14
Wraysbury	d					08 11								08 41							
Sunnymeads	d					08 14								08 44							
Datchet	d					08 17								08 47							
Windsor & Eton Riverside	a					08 21								08 51							
Egham	d			07 57	08 19		08 16					08 27	08 49				08 47			08 57	09 19
Virginia Water	a			08 01	08 23							08 31	08 53				08 51			09 01	09 23
	d			08 01	08 23							08 31	08 53				08 51			09 01	09 23
Chertsey	d				08 29								08 59								09 29
Addlestone	d				08 32								09 02								09 32
Weybridge	a				08 38								09 08								09 37
Byfleet & New Haw	d																				
West Byfleet	d																				
Woking	a																				
Longcross	d			08 05								08 35					08 54				
Sunningdale	d			08 07								08 37					08 58			09 07	
Ascot 3	d	07 53		08 13			08 26					08 43				08 53	09 02			09 13	
Bagshot	d	07 59					08 32									08 59					
Camberley	a	08 05					08 38									09 05					
Frimley	d	08 13					08 43									09 13					
Ash Vale	d	08 19					08 49									09 19					
Aldershot	a	08 24					08 54									09 25					
	d	08 38					09 08									09 38					
Ash 5	d	08 45					09 15									09 45					
Wanborough	d	08 48					09 18									09 48					
Guildford	a	08 55					09 25									09 55					
Martins Heron	d			08 17								08 47					09 06			09 17	
Bracknell	d			08 20								08 50					09 10			09 20	
Wokingham	d			08 27								08 57					09 17			09 27	
Winnersh	d			08 30								09 00					09 20			09 30	
Winnersh Triangle	d			08 32								09 02					09 22			09 32	
Earley	d			08 35								09 05					09 25			09 35	
Reading 7	a			08 40								09 10					09 30			09 40	

b

Table 149

Mondays to Fridays
24 May to 24 September

London - Hounslow, Richmond, Kingston, Windsor, Weybridge, Ascot, Guildford and Reading

		SW	SW	SW 1	SW 1	SW	SW	SW 1	SW	SW	SW	SW	SW	SW 1	SW 1	SW	SW	SW	SW	SW	SW 1
London Waterloo 15 ⊖	d	08 28	08 33		08 37	08 40	08 43	08 50	08 52	08 58	09 03	09 07	09 15		09 20	09 22	09 28	09 33	09 37	09 45	
Vauxhall ⊖	d	08 32	08 37			08 44	08 47		08 56	09 02	09 07	09 11	09 19			09 26	09 32	09 37	09 41	09 49	
Queenstown Rd.(Battersea)	d		08 40			08 47	08 50		08 59		09 10	09 14	09 22			09 29		09 40	09 44	09 52	
Clapham Junction 10	d	08 38	08 43		08 45	08 50	08 55	08 58	09 02	09 08	09 13	09 17	09 25		09 28	09 32	09 38	09 43	09 47	09 55	
Wandsworth Town	d		08 46			08 53	08 58		09 05		09 16	09 20	09 28			09 35		09 46	09 50	09 58	
Putney	d	08 42	08 49			08 56	09 01		09 08	09 12	09 19	09 23	09 31			09 38	09 42	09 49	09 53	10 01	
Barnes	d		08 52			08 57	09 05		09 12		09 22	09 27	09 35			09 42		09 52	09 57	10 05	
Barnes Bridge	d					08 59			09 14			09 29				09 44			09 59		
Chiswick	d					09 02			09 17			09 32				09 47			10 02		
Kew Bridge	d					09 05			09 20			09 35				09 50			10 05		
Brentford	d					09 08			09 23			09 38				09 53			10 08		
Syon Lane	d					09 10			09 25			09 40				09 55			10 10		
Isleworth	d					09 12			09 27			09 42				09 57			10 12		
Hounslow	d					09 18			09 31			09 48				10 01			10 18		
Mortlake	d		08 54				09 07				09 24		09 37					09 54		10 07	
North Sheen	d		08 56				09 09				09 26		09 39					09 56		10 09	
Richmond ⊖	d	08 48	08 59		08 54		09 12	09 06		09 18	09 29		09 42		09 36		09 48	09 59		10 12	
St Margarets	d		09 01				09 14				09 31		09 44					10 01		10 14	
Twickenham	a	08 51	09 03		08 57		09 16	09 10		09 21	09 33		09 46		09 40		09 51	10 03		10 16	
	d	08 52	09 04		08 58		09 17	09 10		09 22	09 34		09 47		09 40		09 52	10 04		10 17	
Strawberry Hill	d		09 07								09 37							10 07			
Fulwell	a																				
Teddington	a		09 10								09 40							10 10			
Hampton Wick	a		09 14								09 44							10 14			
Kingston	a		09 16								09 46							10 16			
Whitton	d	08 55				09 23	09 20			09 25		09 53	09 50				09 55		10 26	10 20	
Feltham	d	08 59			09 04			09 16	09 36	09 29					09 46	10 06	09 59				
Ashford (Surrey)	d	09 03			09 08				09 40	09 33						10 10	10 03				
Staines	d	09 07			09 12			09 23	09 44	09 37					09 53	10 14	10 07				
Wraysbury	d	09 11								09 41							10 11				
Sunnymeads	d	09 14								09 44							10 14				
Datchet	d	09 17								09 47							10 17				
Windsor & Eton Riverside	a	09 21								09 51							10 21				
Egham	d				09 16			09 27	09 49						09 57	10 19					
Virginia Water	a				09 20			09 31	09 53						10 01	10 23					
	d				09 20			09 31	09 53						10 01	10 23					
Chertsey	d								09 59							10 29					
Addlestone	d								10 02							10 32					
Weybridge	a								10 07							10 37					
Byfleet & New Haw	d																				
West Byfleet	d																				
Woking	a																				
Longcross	d																				
Sunningdale	d				09 26			09 37							10 07						
Ascot 3	d			09 23	09 30			09 43						09 53	10 13						10 23
Bagshot	d			09 29										09 59							10 29
Camberley	a			09 35										10 05							10 35
Frimley	d			09 43										10 13							10 43
Ash Vale	d			09 49										10 19							10 49
Aldershot	a			09 54										10 24							10 54
	d			10 08										10 38							11 08
Ash 5	d			10 15										10 45							11 15
Wanborough	d			10 18										10 48							11 18
Guildford	a			10 25										10 55							11 25
Martins Heron	d				09 34			09 47							10 17						
Bracknell	d				09 38			09 50							10 20						
Wokingham	d				09 47			09 57							10 27						
Winnersh	d							10 00							10 30						
Winnersh Triangle	d							10 02							10 32						
Earley	d							10 05							10 35						
Reading 7	a				09 55			10 10							10 40						

Table 149

Mondays to Fridays

24 May to 24 September

London - Hounslow, Richmond, Kingston, Windsor, Weybridge, Ascot, Guildford and Reading

		SW ■	SW	SW	SW	SW	SW	SW ■	SW ■	SW	SW	SW	SW	SW	SW ■	SW ■	SW	SW	SW
London Waterloo ■15 ⊖	d	09 50	09 52	09 58	10 03	10 07	10 15		10 20	10 22	10 28	10 33	10 37	10 45		10 50	10 52	10 58	11 03
Vauxhall ⊖	d		09 56	10 02	10 07	10 11	10 19			10 26	10 32	10 37	10 41	10 49			10 56	11 02	11 07
Queenstown Rd.(Battersea)	d		09 59		10 10	10 14	10 22			10 29		10 40	10 44	10 52			10 59		11 10
Clapham Junction ■10	d	09 58	10 02	10 08	10 13	10 17	10 25		10 28	10 32	10 38	10 43	10 47	10 55		10 58	11 02	11 08	11 13
Wandsworth Town	d		10 05		10 16	10 20	10 28			10 35		10 46	10 50	10 58			11 05		11 16
Putney	d		10 08	10 12	10 19	10 23	10 31			10 38	10 42	10 49	10 53	11 01			11 08	11 12	11 19
Barnes	d		10 12		10 22	10 27	10 35			10 42		10 52	10 57	11 05			11 12		11 22
Barnes Bridge	d		10 14			10 29				10 44			10 59				11 14		
Chiswick	d		10 17			10 32				10 47			11 02				11 17		
Kew Bridge	d		10 20			10 35				10 50			11 05				11 20		
Brentford	d		10 23			10 38				10 53			11 08				11 23		
Syon Lane	d		10 25			10 40				10 55			11 10				11 25		
Isleworth	d		10 27			10 42				10 57			11 12				11 27		
Hounslow	d		10 31			10 48				11 01			11 18				11 31		
Mortlake	d				10 24		10 37					10 54		11 07					11 24
North Sheen	d				10 26		10 39					10 56		11 09					11 26
Richmond ⊖	d	10 06		10 18	10 29		10 42		10 36		10 48	10 59		11 12		11 06		11 18	11 29
St Margarets	d				10 31		10 44					11 01		11 14					11 31
Twickenham	a	10 10		10 21	10 33		10 46		10 40		10 51	11 03		11 16		11 10		11 21	11 33
	d	10 10		10 22	10 34		10 47		10 40		10 52	11 04		11 17		11 10		11 22	11 34
Strawberry Hill	d				10 37							11 07							11 37
Fulwell	a																		
Teddington	a				10 40							11 10							11 40
Hampton Wick	a				10 44							11 14							11 44
Kingston	a				10 46							11 16							11 46
Whitton	d			10 25		10 56	10 50				10 55		11 23	11 20				11 25	
Feltham	d	10 16	10 36	10 29					10 46	11 06	10 59					11 16	11 36	11 29	
Ashford (Surrey)	d		10 40	10 33						11 10	11 03						11 40	11 33	
Staines	d	10 23	10 44	10 37					10 53	11 14	11 07					11 23	11 44	11 37	
Wraysbury	d			10 41							11 11							11 41	
Sunnymeads	d			10 44							11 14							11 44	
Datchet	d			10 47							11 17							11 47	
Windsor & Eton Riverside	a			10 51							11 21							11 51	
Egham	d	10 27	10 49						10 57	11 19						11 27	11 49		
Virginia Water	a	10 31	10 53						11 01	11 23						11 31	11 53		
	d	10 31	10 53						11 01	11 23						11 31	11 53		
Chertsey	d		10 59							11 29							11 59		
Addlestone	d		11 02							11 32							12 02		
Weybridge	a		11 07							11 37							12 07		
Byfleet & New Haw	d																		
West Byfleet	d																		
Woking	a																		
Longcross	d																		
Sunningdale	d	10 37							11 07							11 37			
Ascot ■	d	10 43						10 53	11 13						11 23	11 43			
Bagshot	d							10 59							11 29				
Camberley	a							11 05							11 35				
Frimley	d							11 13							11 43				
Ash Vale	d							11 19							11 49				
Aldershot	a							11 24							11 54				
	d							11 38							12 08				
Ash ■	d							11 45							12 15				
Wanborough	d							11 48							12 18				
Guildford	a							11 55							12 25				
Martins Heron	d	10 47							11 17							11 47			
Bracknell	d	10 50							11 20							11 50			
Wokingham	d	10 57							11 27							11 57			
Winnersh	d	11 00							11 30							12 00			
Winnersh Triangle	d	11 02							11 32							12 02			
Earley	d	11 05							11 35							12 05			
Reading ■7	a	11 10							11 40							12 10			

Table 149

Mondays to Fridays

24 May to 24 September

London - Hounslow, Richmond, Kingston, Windsor, Weybridge, Ascot, Guildford and Reading

		SW	SW	SW ■	SW ■	SW	SW	SW	SW	SW	SW ■	SW ■	SW	SW	SW	SW	SW ■	SW ■	SW	SW
London Waterloo ■15 ⊖	d	11 07	11 15		11 20	11 22	11 28	11 33	11 37	11 45		11 50	11 52	11 58	12 03	12 07		12 20	12 22	12 28
Vauxhall ⊖	d	11 11	11 19			11 26	11 32	11 37	11 41	11 49			11 56	12 02	12 07	12 11			12 26	12 32
Queenstown Rd.(Battersea)	d	11 14	11 22			11 29		11 40	11 44	11 52			11 59		12 10	12 14			12 29	
Clapham Junction ■10	d	11 17	11 25		11 28	11 32	11 38	11 43	11 47	11 55		11 58	12 02	12 08	12 13	12 17		12 28	12 32	12 38
Wandsworth Town	d	11 20	11 28			11 35		11 46	11 50	11 58			12 05		12 16	12 20			12 35	
Putney	d	11 23	11 31			11 38	11 42	11 49	11 53	12 01			12 08	12 12	12 19	12 23			12 38	12 42
Barnes	d	11 27	11 35			11 42		11 52	11 57	12 05			12 12		12 22	12 27			12 42	
Barnes Bridge	d	11 29				11 44			11 59				12 14			12 29			12 44	
Chiswick	d	11 32				11 47			12 02				12 17			12 32			12 47	
Kew Bridge	d	11 35				11 50			12 05				12 20			12 35			12 50	
Brentford	d	11 38				11 53			12 08				12 23			12 38			12 53	
Syon Lane	d	11 40				11 55			12 10				12 25			12 40			12 55	
Isleworth	d	11 42				11 57			12 12				12 27			12 42			12 57	
Hounslow	d	11 48				12 01			12 18				12 31			12 48			13 01	
Mortlake	d		11 37					11 54		12 07					12 24					
North Sheen	d		11 39					11 56		12 09					12 26					
Richmond ⊖	d		11 42		11 36		11 48	11 59		12 12		12 06		12 18	12 29			12 36		12 48
St Margarets	d		11 44					12 01		12 14					12 31					
Twickenham	a		11 46		11 40		11 51	12 03		12 16		12 10		12 21	12 33			12 40		12 51
	d		11 47		11 40		11 52	12 04		12 17		12 10		12 22	12 34			12 40		12 52
Strawberry Hill	d							12 07							12 37					
Fulwell	a																			
Teddington	a							12 10							12 40					
Hampton Wick	a							12 14							12 44					
Kingston	a							12 16							12 46					
Whitton	d	11 53	11 50				11 55		12 23	12 20				12 25		12 53				12 55
Feltham	d				11 46	12 06	11 59					12 16	12 36	12 29				12 46	13 06	12 59
Ashford (Surrey)	d					12 10	12 03						12 40	12 33					13 10	13 03
Staines	d				11 53	12 14	12 07					12 23	12 44	12 37				12 53	13 14	13 07
Wraysbury	d						12 11							12 41						13 11
Sunnymeads	d						12 14							12 44						13 14
Datchet	d						12 17							12 47						13 17
Windsor & Eton Riverside	a						12 21							12 51						13 21
Egham	d				11 57	12 19						12 27	12 49					12 57	13 19	
Virginia Water	a				12 01	12 23						12 31	12 53					13 01	13 23	
	d				12 01	12 23						12 31	12 53					13 01	13 23	
Chertsey	d					12 29							12 59						13 29	
Addlestone	d					12 32							13 02						13 32	
Weybridge	a					12 37							13 07						13 37	
Byfleet & New Haw	d																			
West Byfleet	d																			
Woking	a																			
Longcross	d																			
Sunningdale	d				12 07							12 37						13 07		
Ascot ■	d			11 53	12 13						12 23	12 43					12 53	13 13		
Bagshot	d			11 59							12 29						12 59			
Camberley	a			12 05							12 35						13 05			
Frimley	d			12 13							12 43						13 13			
Ash Vale	d			12 19							12 49						13 19			
Aldershot	a			12 24							12 54						13 24			
	d			12 38							13 08						13 38			
Ash ■	d			12 45							13 15						13 45			
Wanborough	d			12 48							13 18						13 48			
Guildford	a			12 55							13 25						13 55			
Martins Heron	d				12 17							12 47						13 17		
Bracknell	d				12 20							12 50						13 20		
Wokingham	d				12 27							12 57						13 27		
Winnersh	d				12 30							13 00						13 30		
Winnersh Triangle	d				12 32							13 02						13 32		
Earley	d				12 35							13 05						13 35		
Reading ■7	a				12 40							13 10						13 40		

Table 149

Mondays to Fridays
24 May to 24 September

London - Hounslow, Richmond, Kingston, Windsor, Weybridge, Ascot, Guildford and Reading

Station		SW	SW	SW	SW 1	SW 1	SW	SW	SW	SW	SW	SW 1	SW 1	SW	SW	SW	SW	SW	SW 1	SW 1	SW
London Waterloo 15 ⊖	d	12 33	12 37	12 45		12 50	12 52	12 58	13 03	13 07	13 15		13 20	13 22	13 28	13 33	13 37	13 45		13 50	13 52
Vauxhall ⊖	d	12 37	12 41	12 49			12 56	13 02	13 07	13 11	13 19			13 26	13 32	13 37	13 41	13 49			13 56
Queenstown Rd.(Battersea)	d	12 40	12 44	12 52			12 59		13 10	13 14	13 22			13 29		13 40	13 44	13 52			13 59
Clapham Junction 10	d	12 43	12 47	12 55		12 58	13 02	13 08	13 13	13 17	13 25		13 28	13 32	13 38	13 43	13 47	13 55		13 58	14 02
Wandsworth Town	d	12 46	12 50	12 58			13 05		13 16	13 20	13 28			13 35		13 46	13 50	13 58			14 05
Putney	d	12 49	12 53	13 01			13 08	13 12	13 19	13 23	13 31			13 38	13 42	13 49	13 53	14 01			14 08
Barnes	d	12 52	12 57	13 05			13 12		13 22	13 27	13 35			13 42		13 52	13 57	14 05			14 12
Barnes Bridge	d		12 59				13 14			13 29				13 44			13 59				14 14
Chiswick	d		13 02				13 17			13 32				13 47			14 02				14 17
Kew Bridge	d		13 05				13 20			13 35				13 50			14 05				14 20
Brentford	d		13 08				13 23			13 38				13 53			14 08				14 23
Syon Lane	d		13 10				13 25			13 40				13 55			14 10				14 25
Isleworth	d		13 12				13 27			13 42				13 57			14 12				14 27
Hounslow	d		13 18				13 31			13 48				14 01			14 18				14 31
Mortlake	d	12 54		13 07					13 24		13 37					13 54		14 07			
North Sheen	d	12 56		13 09					13 26		13 39					13 56		14 09			
Richmond ⊖	d	12 59		13 12		13 06		13 18	13 29		13 42		13 36		13 48	13 59		14 12		14 06	
St Margarets	d	13 01		13 14					13 31		13 44					14 01		14 14			
Twickenham	a	13 03		13 16		13 10		13 21	13 33		13 46		13 40		13 51	14 03		14 16		14 10	
	d	13 04		13 17		13 10		13 22	13 34		13 47		13 40		13 52	14 04		14 17		14 10	
Strawberry Hill	d	13 07							13 37							14 07					
Fulwell	a																				
Teddington	a	13 10							13 40							14 10					
Hampton Wick	a	13 14							13 44							14 14					
Kingston	a	13 16							13 46							14 16					
Whitton	d		13 23	13 20				13 25		13 53	13 50				13 55		14 23	14 20			
Feltham	d					13 16	13 36	13 29					13 46	14 06	13 59					14 16	14 36
Ashford (Surrey)	d						13 40	13 33						14 10	14 03						14 40
Staines	d					13 23	13 44	13 37					13 53	14 14	14 07					14 23	14 44
Wraysbury	d							13 41							14 11						
Sunnymeads	d							13 44							14 14						
Datchet	d							13 47							14 17						
Windsor & Eton Riverside	a							13 51							14 21						
Egham	d					13 27	13 49						13 57	14 19						14 27	14 49
Virginia Water	a					13 31	13 53						14 01	14 23						14 31	14 53
	d					13 31	13 53						14 01	14 23						14 31	14 53
Chertsey	d						13 59							14 29							14 59
Addlestone	d						14 02							14 32							15 02
Weybridge	a						14 07							14 37							15 07
Byfleet & New Haw	d																				
West Byfleet	d																				
Woking	a																				
Longcross	d					13 35															
Sunningdale	d					13 37							14 07							14 37	
Ascot 3	d				13 23	13 43						13 53	14 13						14 23	14 43	
Bagshot	d				13 29							13 59							14 29		
Camberley	a				13 35							14 05							14 35		
Frimley	d				13 43							14 13							14 43		
Ash Vale	d				13 49							14 19							14 49		
Aldershot	a				13 54							14 24							14 54		
	d				14 08							14 38							15 08		
Ash 5	d				14 15							14 45							15 15		
Wanborough	d				14 18							14 48							15 18		
Guildford	a				14 25							14 55							15 25		
Martins Heron	d					13 47							14 17							14 47	
Bracknell	d					13 50							14 20							14 50	
Wokingham	d					13 57							14 27							14 57	
Winnersh	d					14 00							14 30							15 00	
Winnersh Triangle	d					14 02							14 32							15 02	
Earley	d					14 05							14 35							15 05	
Reading 7	a					14 10							14 40							15 10	

Table 149

Mondays to Fridays
24 May to 24 September

London - Hounslow, Richmond, Kingston, Windsor, Weybridge, Ascot, Guildford and Reading

Station		SW	SW	SW	SW	SW 1	SW 1	SW	SW	SW	SW	SW	SW 1	SW 1	SW	SW	SW	SW	SW
London Waterloo 15 ⊖	d	13 58	14 03	14 07	14 15		14 20	14 22	14 28	14 33	14 37	14 45		14 50	14 52	14 58	15 03	15 07	15 15
Vauxhall ⊖	d	14 02	14 07	14 11	14 19			14 26	14 32	14 37	14 41	14 49			14 56	15 02	15 07	15 11	15 19
Queenstown Rd.(Battersea)	d		14 10	14 14	14 22			14 29		14 40	14 44	14 52			14 59		15 10	15 14	15 22
Clapham Junction 10	d	14 08	14 13	14 17	14 25		14 28	14 32	14 38	14 43	14 47	14 55		14 58	15 02	15 08	15 13	15 17	15 25
Wandsworth Town	d		14 16	14 20	14 28			14 35		14 46	14 50	14 58			15 05		15 16	15 20	15 28
Putney	d	14 12	14 19	14 23	14 31			14 38	14 42	14 49	14 53	15 01			15 08	15 12	15 19	15 23	15 31
Barnes	d		14 22	14 27	14 35			14 42		14 52	14 57	15 05			15 12		15 22	15 27	15 35
Barnes Bridge	d			14 29				14 44			14 59				15 14			15 29	
Chiswick	d			14 32				14 47			15 02				15 17			15 32	
Kew Bridge	d			14 35				14 50			15 05				15 20			15 35	
Brentford	d			14 38				14 53			15 08				15 23			15 38	
Syon Lane	d			14 40				14 55			15 10				15 25			15 40	
Isleworth	d			14 42				14 57			15 12				15 27			15 42	
Hounslow	d			14 48				15 01			15 18				15 31			15 48	
Mortlake	d		14 24		14 37					14 54		15 07					15 24		15 37
North Sheen	d		14 26		14 39					14 56		15 09					15 26		15 39
Richmond ⊖	d	14 18	14 29		14 42		14 36		14 48	14 59		15 12		15 06		15 18	15 29		15 42
St Margarets	d		14 31		14 44					15 01		15 14					15 31		15 44
Twickenham	a	14 21	14 33		14 46		14 40		14 51	15 03		15 16		15 10		15 21	15 33		15 46
	d	14 22	14 34		14 47		14 40		14 52	15 04		15 17		15 10		15 22	15 34		15 47
Strawberry Hill	d		14 37							15 07							15 37		
Fulwell	a																		
Teddington	a		14 40							15 10							15 40		
Hampton Wick	a		14 44							15 14							15 44		
Kingston	a		14 46							15 16							15 46		
Whitton	d	14 25		14 53	14 50				14 55		15 23	15 20				15 25		15 53	15 50
Feltham	d	14 29					14 46	15 06	14 59					15 16	15 36	15 29			
Ashford (Surrey)	d	14 33						15 10	15 03						15 40	15 33			
Staines	d	14 37					14 53	15 14	15 07					15 23	15 44	15 37			
Wraysbury	d	14 41							15 11							15 41			
Sunnymeads	d	14 44							15 14							15 44			
Datchet	d	14 47							15 17							15 47			
Windsor & Eton Riverside	a	14 51							15 21							15 51			
Egham	d						14 57	15 19						15 27	15 49				
Virginia Water	a						15 01	15 23						15 31	15 53				
	d						15 01	15 23						15 31	15 53				
Chertsey	d							15 29							15 59				
Addlestone	d							15 32							16 02				
Weybridge	a							15 37							16 07				
Byfleet & New Haw	d																		
West Byfleet	d																		
Woking	a																		
Longcross	d																		
Sunningdale	d						15 07							15 37					
Ascot 3	d					14 53	15 13						15 23	15 43					
Bagshot	d					14 59							15 29						
Camberley	a					15 05							15 35						
Frimley	d					15 13							15 43						
Ash Vale	d					15 19							15 49						
Aldershot	a					15 24							15 54						
	d					15 38							16 08						
Ash 5	d					15 45							16 15						
Wanborough	d					15 48							16 18						
Guildford	a					15 55							16 25						
Martins Heron	d						15 17							15 47					
Bracknell	d						15 20							15 50					
Wokingham	d						15 27							15 57					
Winnersh	d						15 30							16 00					
Winnersh Triangle	d						15 32							16 02					
Earley	d						15 35							16 05					
Reading 7	a						15 40							16 10					

Table 149

London - Hounslow, Richmond, Kingston, Windsor, Weybridge, Ascot, Guildford and Reading

		SW [1]	SW [1]	SW	SW	SW	SW	SW	SW [1]	SW [1]	SW	SW	SW	SW [1]	SW [1]	SW	SW	SW [1]	SW	SW
London Waterloo [15] ⊖	d		15 20	15 22	15 28	15 33	15 37	15 45		15 50	15 52	15 58	16 01		16 05	16 07	16 15	16 20	16 22	16 28
Vauxhall ⊖	d			15 26	15 32	15 37	15 41	15 49			15 56	16 02	16 05		16 09	16 11	16 19		16 26	16 32
Queenstown Rd.(Battersea)	d			15 29		15 40	15 44	15 52			15 59		16 08			16 14	16 22		16 29	
Clapham Junction [10]	d		15 28	15 32	15 38	15 43	15 47	15 55		15 58	16 02	16 08	16 11		16 15	16 17	16 25	16 28	16 32	16 38
Wandsworth Town	d			15 35		15 46	15 50	15 58			16 05		16 14			16 20	16 28		16 35	
Putney	d			15 38	15 42	15 49	15 53	16 01			16 08	16 12	16 17			16 23	16 31		16 38	16 42
Barnes	d			15 42		15 52	15 57	16 05			16 12		16 22			16 27	16 35		16 42	
Barnes Bridge	d			15 44			15 59				16 14					16 29			16 44	
Chiswick	d			15 47			16 02				16 17					16 32			16 47	
Kew Bridge	d			15 50			16 05				16 20					16 35			16 50	
Brentford	d			15 53			16 08				16 23					16 38			16 53	
Syon Lane	d			15 55			16 10				16 25					16 40			16 55	
Isleworth	d			15 57			16 12				16 27					16 42			16 57	
Hounslow	d			16 01			16 18				16 31					16 48			17 01	
Mortlake	d					15 54		16 07					16 24				16 37			
North Sheen	d					15 56		16 09					16 26				16 39			
Richmond ⊖	d		15 36		15 48	15 59		16 12		16 06		16 18	16 29		16 23		16 42	16 36		16 48
St Margarets	d					16 01		16 14					16 31				16 44			
Twickenham	a		15 40		15 51	16 03		16 16		16 10		16 21	16 33		16 27		16 46	16 40		16 51
	d		15 40		15 52	16 04		16 17		16 10		16 22	16 34		16 27		16 47	16 40		16 52
Strawberry Hill	d					16 07							16 37							
Fulwell	a																			
Teddington	a					16 10							16 42							
Hampton Wick	a					16 14							16 46							
Kingston	a					16 16							16 48							
Whitton	d				15 55		16 23	16 20				16 25				16 53	16 50			16 55
Feltham	d		15 46	16 06	15 59					16 16	16 36	16 29			16 33			16 46	17 06	16 59
Ashford (Surrey)	d			16 10	16 03						16 40	16 33			16 37				17 10	17 03
Staines	d		15 53	16 14	16 07					16 23	16 44	16 37			16 41			16 53	17 14	17 07
Wraysbury	d				16 11							16 41								17 11
Sunnymeads	d				16 14							16 44								17 14
Datchet	d				16 17							16 47								17 17
Windsor & Eton Riverside	a				16 21							16 51								17 23
Egham	d		15 57	16 19						16 27	16 49				16 46			16 57	17 19	
Virginia Water	a		16 01	16 23						16 31	16 53				16 50			17 01	17 23	
	d		16 01	16 23						16 31	16 53				16 50			17 01	17 23	
Chertsey	d			16 29							16 59								17 29	
Addlestone	d			16 32							17 02								17 32	
Weybridge	a			16 37							17 07								17 40	
Byfleet & New Haw	d																			
West Byfleet	d																			
Woking	a																			
Longcross	d																			
Sunningdale	d		16 07							16 37					16 55			17 07		
Ascot [3]	d	15 53	16 13						16 23	16 43				16 53	17 00			17 13		
Bagshot	d	15 59							16 29					16 59						
Camberley	a	16 05							16 35					17 05						
Frimley	d	16 13							16 43					17 13						
Ash Vale	d	16 19							16 49					17 19						
Aldershot	a	16 24							16 54					17 24						
	d	16 38							17 09					17 38						
Ash [5]	d	16 45							17 15					17 45						
Wanborough	d	16 48							17 18					17 48						
Guildford	a	16 55							17 25					17 55						
Martins Heron	d		16 17							16 47					17 04			17 17		
Bracknell	d		16 20							16 50					17 07			17 20		
Wokingham	d		16 27							16 57					17 17			17 27		
Winnersh	d		16 30							17 00								17 30		
Winnersh Triangle	d		16 32							17 02								17 32		
Earley	d		16 35							17 05								17 35		
Reading [7]	a		16 40							17 10					17 27			17 42		

Table 149

London - Hounslow, Richmond, Kingston, Windsor, Weybridge, Ascot, Guildford and Reading

		SW	SW [1]	SW [1]	SW	SW	SW [1]	SW	SW	SW	SW [1]	SW	SW	SW	SW [1]	SW	SW	SW	SW [1]	SW [1]
London Waterloo [15] ⊖	d	16 31		16 35	16 37	16 45	16 50	16 52	16 58	17 01	17 05	17 07	17 13	17 15	17 20	17 22	17 28	17 31		17 35
Vauxhall ⊖	d	16 35		16 39	16 41	16 49		16 56	17 02	17 05	17 09	17 11	17 17	17 19		17 26	17 32	17 35		17 39
Queenstown Rd.(Battersea)	d	16 38			16 44	16 52		16 59		17 08		17 14		17 22		17 29		17 38		
Clapham Junction [10]	d	16 41		16 45	16 47	16 55	16 58	17 02	17 08	17 11	17 15	17 17	17 23	17 25	17 28	17 32	17 38	17 41		17 45
Wandsworth Town	d	16 44			16 50	16 58		17 05		17 14		17 20		17 28		17 35		17 44		
Putney	d	16 47			16 53	17 01		17 08	17 12	17 17		17 23	17 27	17 31		17 38	17 42	17 47		
Barnes	d	16 52			16 57	17 05		17 12		17 22		17 27		17 35		17 42		17 52		
Barnes Bridge	d				16 59			17 14				17 29				17 44				
Chiswick	d				17 02			17 17				17 32				17 47				
Kew Bridge	d				17 05			17 20				17 35				17 50				
Brentford	d				17 08			17 23				17 38				17 53				
Syon Lane	d				17 10			17 25				17 40				17 55				
Isleworth	d				17 12			17 27				17 42				17 57				
Hounslow	d				17 18			17 31				17 48				18 01				
Mortlake	d	16 54				17 07				17 24				17 37				17 54		
North Sheen	d	16 56				17 09				17 26				17 39				17 56		
Richmond ⊖	d	16 59		16 53		17 12	17 06		17 18	17 29	17 23		17 33	17 42	17 36		17 48	17 59		17 53
St Margarets	d	17 01				17 14				17 31				17 44				18 01		
Twickenham	a	17 03		16 57		17 16	17 10		17 21	17 33	17 27		17 37	17 46	17 40		17 51	18 03		17 57
	d	17 04		16 57		17 17	17 10		17 22	17 34	17 27		17 37	17 47	17 40		17 52	18 04		17 57
Strawberry Hill	d	17 07								17 37			17 41					18 07		
Fulwell	a																			
Teddington	a	17 12								17 42			17 46					18 12		
Hampton Wick	a	17 16								17 46			17 54					18 16		
Kingston	a	17 18								17 48			17 56					18 18		
Whitton	d				17 23	17 20			17 25			17 53		17 50			17 55			
Feltham	d			17 03			17 16	17 36	17 29		17 33				17 46	18 06	17 59			18 03
Ashford (Surrey)	d			17 07				17 40	17 33		17 37					18 10	18 03			18 07
Staines	d			17 11			17 23	17 44	17 37		17 41				17 53	18 14	18 07			18 11
Wraysbury	d								17 41								18 11			
Sunnymeads	d								17 44								18 14			
Datchet	d								17 47								18 17			
Windsor & Eton Riverside	a								17 53								18 23			
Egham	d			17 16			17 27	17 49			17 46				17 57	18 19				18 16
Virginia Water	a			17 20			17 31	17 53			17 50				18 01	18 23				18 20
	d			17 20			17 31	17 53			17 50				18 01	18 23				18 20
Chertsey	d							17 59								18 29				
Addlestone	d							18 02								18 32				
Weybridge	a							18 10								18 40				
Byfleet & New Haw	d																			
West Byfleet	d																			
Woking	a																			
Longcross	d			17 23																
Sunningdale	d			17 27			17 37				17 55				18 07					18 25
Ascot [3]	d		17 23	17 31			17 43				18 00				18 13				18 23	18 30
Bagshot	d		17 29								18 06								18 29	
Camberley	a		17 35								18 12								18 35	
Frimley	d		17 43								18 17								18 43	
Ash Vale	d		17 49								18 24								18 49	
Aldershot	a		17 54								18 31								18 54	
	d		18 08																19 08	
Ash [5]	d		18 15																19 15	
Wanborough	d		18 18																19 18	
Guildford	a		18 25																19 25	
Martins Heron	d			17 35			17 47								18 17					18 34
Bracknell	d			17 39			17 50								18 20					18 37
Wokingham	d			17 47			17 57								18 27					18 47
Winnersh	d						18 00								18 30					
Winnersh Triangle	d						18 02								18 32					
Earley	d						18 05								18 35					
Reading [7]	a			17 58			18 12								18 42					18 57

Table 149

Mondays to Fridays
24 May to 24 September

London - Hounslow, Richmond, Kingston, Windsor, Weybridge, Ascot, Guildford and Reading

		SW	SW	SW	SW 1	SW	SW	SW	SW 1	SW	SW	SW	SW 1	SW	SW	SW	SW 1	SW 1	SW	SW	SW
London Waterloo 15 ⊖	d	17 37	17 43	17 45	17 50	17 52	17 58	18 01	18 05	18 07	18 13	18 15	18 20	18 22	18 28	18 31		18 35	18 37	18 43	18 45
Vauxhall ⊖	d	17 41	17 47	17 49		17 56	18 02	18 05	18 09	18 11	18 17	18 19		18 26	18 32	18 35		18 39	18 41	18 47	18 49
Queenstown Rd.(Battersea)	d	17 44		17 52		17 59		18 08		18 14		18 22		18 29		18 38			18 44		18 52
Clapham Junction 10	d	17 47	17 53	17 55	17 58	18 02	18 08	18 11	18 15	18 17	18 23	18 25	18 28	18 32	18 38	18 41		18 45	18 47	18 53	18 55
Wandsworth Town	d	17 50		17 58		18 05		18 14		18 20		18 28		18 35		18 44			18 50		18 58
Putney	d	17 53	17 57	18 01		18 08	18 12	18 17		18 23	18 27	18 31		18 38	18 42	18 47			18 53	18 57	19 01
Barnes	d	17 57		18 05		18 12		18 22		18 27		18 35		18 42		18 52			18 57		19 05
Barnes Bridge	d	17 59				18 14				18 29				18 44					18 59		
Chiswick	d	18 02				18 17				18 32				18 47					19 02		
Kew Bridge	d	18 05				18 20				18 35				18 50					19 05		
Brentford	d	18 08				18 23				18 38				18 53					19 08		
Syon Lane	d	18 10				18 25				18 40				18 55					19 10		
Isleworth	d	18 12				18 27				18 42				18 57					19 12		
Hounslow	d	18 18				18 31				18 48				19 01					19 18		
Mortlake	d			18 07				18 24				18 37				18 54					19 07
North Sheen	d			18 09				18 26				18 39				18 56					19 09
Richmond ⊖	d		18 03	18 12	18 06		18 18	18 29	18 23		18 33	18 42	18 36		18 48	18 59		18 53		19 03	19 12
St Margarets	d			18 14				18 31				18 44				19 01					19 14
Twickenham	a		18 07	18 16	18 10		18 21	18 33	18 27		18 37	18 46	18 40		18 51	19 03		18 57		19 07	19 16
	d		18 07	18 17	18 10		18 22	18 34	18 27		18 37	18 47	18 40		18 52	19 04		18 57		19 07	19 17
Strawberry Hill	d		18 11					18 37			18 41					19 07				19 11	
Fulwell	a		18 13								18 43									19 13	
Teddington	a							18 42								19 12					
Hampton Wick	a							18 46								19 16					
Kingston	a							18 48								19 18					
Whitton	d	18 23		18 20			18 25			18 53		18 50			18 55				19 23		19 20
Feltham	d				18 16	18 36	18 29		18 33				18 46	19 06	18 59			19 03			
Ashford (Surrey)	d					18 40	18 33		18 37					19 10	19 03			19 07			
Staines	d				18 23	18 44	18 37		18 41				18 53	19 14	19 07			19 11			
Wraysbury	d						18 41								19 11						
Sunnymeads	d						18 44								19 14						
Datchet	d						18 47								19 17						
Windsor & Eton Riverside	a						18 53								19 23						
Egham	d				18 27	18 49			18 46				18 57	19 19				19 16			
Virginia Water	a				18 31	18 53			18 50				19 01	19 23				19 20			
	d				18 31	18 53			18 50				19 01	19 23				19 20			
Chertsey	d					18 59								19 29							
Addlestone	d					19 02								19 32							
Weybridge	a					19 10								19 40							
Byfleet & New Haw	d																				
West Byfleet	d																				
Woking	a																				
Longcross	d				18 35																
Sunningdale	d				18 37				18 55				19 07					19 25			
Ascot 3	d				18 43				19 02				19 13				19 23	19 30			
Bagshot	d								19 08								19 29				
Camberley	a								19 14								19 35				
Frimley	d								19 19								19 43				
Ash Vale	d								19 26								19 49				
Aldershot	a								19 35								19 54				
	d																20 08				
Ash 5	d																20 15				
Wanborough	d																20 18				
Guildford	a																20 25				
Martins Heron	d				18 47								19 17					19 34			
Bracknell	d				18 50								19 20					19 37			
Wokingham	d				18 57								19 27					19 47			
Winnersh	d				19 00								19 30								
Winnersh Triangle	d				19 02								19 32								
Earley	d				19 05								19 35								
Reading 7	a				19 12								19 42					19 57			

Table 149

Mondays to Fridays
24 May to 24 September

London - Hounslow, Richmond, Kingston, Windsor, Weybridge, Ascot, Guildford and Reading

		SW 1	SW	SW	SW	SW 1	SW 1	SW	SW	SW 1	SW	SW	SW	SW	SW	SW 1	SW 1	SW	SW	SW
London Waterloo 15 ⊖	d	18 50	18 52	18 58	19 01		19 05	19 07	19 15	19 20	19 22	19 28	19 33	19 37	19 45		19 50	19 52	19 58	20 03
Vauxhall ⊖	d		18 56	19 02	19 05		19 09	19 11	19 19		19 26	19 32	19 37	19 41	19 49			19 56	20 02	20 07
Queenstown Rd.(Battersea)	d		18 59		19 08			19 14	19 22		19 29		19 40	19 44	19 52			19 59		20 10
Clapham Junction 10	d	18 58	19 02	19 08	19 11		19 15	19 17	19 25	19 28	19 32	19 38	19 43	19 47	19 55		19 58	20 02	20 08	20 13
Wandsworth Town	d		19 05		19 14			19 20	19 28		19 35		19 46	19 50	19 58			20 05		20 16
Putney	d		19 08	19 12	19 17			19 23	19 31		19 38	19 42	19 49	19 53	20 01			20 08	20 12	20 19
Barnes	d		19 12		19 22			19 27	19 35		19 42		19 52	19 57	20 05			20 12		20 22
Barnes Bridge	d		19 14					19 29			19 44			19 59				20 14		
Chiswick	d		19 17					19 32			19 47			20 02				20 17		
Kew Bridge	d		19 20					19 35			19 50			20 05				20 20		
Brentford	d		19 23					19 38			19 53			20 08				20 23		
Syon Lane	d		19 25					19 40			19 55			20 10				20 25		
Isleworth	d		19 27					19 42			19 57			20 12				20 27		
Hounslow	d		19 31					19 48			20 01			20 18				20 31		
Mortlake	d				19 24				19 37				19 54		20 07					20 24
North Sheen	d				19 26				19 39				19 56		20 09					20 26
Richmond ⊖	d	19 06		19 18	19 29		19 23		19 42	19 36		19 48	19 59		20 12		20 06		20 18	20 29
St Margarets	d				19 31				19 44				20 01		20 14					20 31
Twickenham	a	19 10		19 21	19 33		19 27		19 46	19 40		19 51	20 03		20 16		20 10		20 21	20 33
	d	19 10		19 22	19 34		19 27		19 47	19 40		19 52	20 04		20 17		20 10		20 22	20 34
Strawberry Hill	d				19 37								20 07							20 37
Fulwell	a																			
Teddington	a				19 42								20 10							20 40
Hampton Wick	a				19 46								20 14							20 44
Kingston	a				19 48								20 16							20 46
Whitton	d			19 25				19 53	19 50			19 55		20 23	20 20				20 25	
Feltham	d	19 16	19 36	19 29			19 33			19 46	20 06	19 59					20 16	20 36	20 29	
Ashford (Surrey)	d		19 40	19 33			19 37				20 10	20 03						20 40	20 33	
Staines	d	19 23	19 44	19 37			19 41			19 53	20 14	20 07					20 23	20 44	20 37	
Wraysbury	d			19 41								20 11							20 41	
Sunnymeads	d			19 44								20 14							20 44	
Datchet	d			19 47								20 17							20 47	
Windsor & Eton Riverside	a			19 53								20 21							20 51	
Egham	d	19 27	19 49				19 46			19 57	20 19						20 27	20 49		
Virginia Water	a	19 31	19 53				19 50			20 01	20 23						20 31	20 53		
	d	19 31	19 53				19 50			20 01	20 23						20 31	20 53		
Chertsey	d		19 59								20 29							20 59		
Addlestone	d		20 02								20 32							21 02		
Weybridge	a		20 10								20 37							21 07		
Byfleet & New Haw	d																			
West Byfleet	d																			
Woking	a																			
Longcross	d																			
Sunningdale	d	19 37					19 55			20 07							20 37			
Ascot 3	d	19 43				19 53	20 00			20 13						20 23	20 43			
Bagshot	d					19 59										20 29				
Camberley	a					20 05										20 35				
Frimley	d					20 13										20 43				
Ash Vale	d					20 19										20 49				
Aldershot	a					20 24										20 54				
	d					20 38										21 08				
Ash 5	d					20 45										21 15				
Wanborough	d					20 48										21 18				
Guildford	a					20 55										21 25				
Martins Heron	d	19 47					20 04			20 17							20 47			
Bracknell	d	19 50					20 07			20 20							20 50			
Wokingham	d	19 57					20 17			20 27							20 57			
Winnersh	d	20 00								20 30							21 00			
Winnersh Triangle	d	20 02								20 32							21 02			
Earley	d	20 05								20 35							21 05			
Reading 7	a	20 12					20 25			20 40							21 10			

Table 149

Mondays to Fridays
24 May to 24 September

London - Hounslow, Richmond, Kingston, Windsor, Weybridge, Ascot, Guildford and Reading

		SW	SW	SW 1	SW 1	SW	SW	SW	SW	SW	SW 1	SW 1	SW	SW	SW	SW	SW	SW 1	SW
London Waterloo 15 ⊖	d	20 07	20 15		20 20	20 22	20 28	20 33	20 37	20 45		20 50	20 52	20 58	21 03	21 07	21 15	21 20	21 22
Vauxhall ⊖	d	20 11	20 19			20 26	20 32	20 37	20 41	20 49			20 56	21 02	21 07	21 11	21 19		21 26
Queenstown Rd.(Battersea)	d	20 14	20 22			20 29		20 40	20 44	20 52			20 59		21 10	21 14	21 22		21 29
Clapham Junction 10	d	20 17	20 25		20 28	20 32	20 38	20 43	20 47	20 55		20 58	21 02	21 08	21 13	21 17	21 25	21 28	21 32
Wandsworth Town	d	20 20	20 28			20 35		20 46	20 50	20 58			21 05		21 16	21 20	21 28		21 35
Putney	d	20 23	20 31			20 38	20 42	20 49	20 53	21 01			21 08	21 12	21 19	21 23	21 31		21 38
Barnes	d	20 27	20 35			20 42		20 52	20 57	21 05			21 12		21 22	21 27	21 35		21 42
Barnes Bridge	d	20 29				20 44			20 59				21 14			21 29			21 44
Chiswick	d	20 32				20 47			21 02				21 17			21 32			21 47
Kew Bridge	d	20 35				20 50			21 05				21 20			21 35			21 50
Brentford	d	20 38				20 53			21 08				21 23			21 38			21 53
Syon Lane	d	20 40				20 55			21 10				21 25			21 40			21 55
Isleworth	d	20 42				20 57			21 12				21 27			21 42			21 57
Hounslow	d	20 48				21 01			21 18				21 31			21 48			22 01
Mortlake	d		20 37					20 54		21 07					21 24		21 37		
North Sheen	d		20 39					20 56		21 09					21 26		21 39		
Richmond ⊖	d		20 42		20 36		20 48	20 59		21 12		21 06		21 18	21 29		21 42	21 36	
St Margarets	d		20 44					21 01		21 14					21 31		21 44		
Twickenham	a		20 46		20 40		20 51	21 03		21 16		21 10		21 21	21 33		21 46	21 40	
	d		20 47		20 40		20 52	21 04		21 17		21 10		21 22	21 34		21 47	21 40	
Strawberry Hill	d							21 07							21 37				
Fulwell	a																		
Teddington	a							21 10							21 40				
Hampton Wick	a							21 14							21 44				
Kingston	a							21 16							21 46				
Whitton	d	20 53	20 50				20 55		21 23	21 20				21 25		21 53	21 50		
Feltham	d				20 46	21 06	20 59					21 16	21 36	21 29				21 46	22 06
Ashford (Surrey)	d					21 10	21 03						21 40	21 33					22 10
Staines	d				20 53	21 14	21 07					21 23	21 44	21 37				21 53	22 14
Wraysbury	d						21 11							21 41					
Sunnymeads	d						21 14							21 44					
Datchet	d						21 17							21 47					
Windsor & Eton Riverside	a						21 21							21 51					
Egham	d				20 57	21 19						21 27	21 49					21 57	22 19
Virginia Water	a				21 01	21 23						21 31	21 53					22 01	22 23
	d				21 01	21 23						21 31	21 53					22 01	22 23
Chertsey	d					21 29							21 59						22 29
Addlestone	d					21 32							22 02						22 32
Weybridge	a					21 37							22 07						22 37
Byfleet & New Haw	d																		
West Byfleet	d																		
Woking	a																		
Longcross	d																		
Sunningdale	d				21 07							21 37						22 07	
Ascot 3	d			20 53	21 13						21 23	21 43						22 13	
Bagshot	d			20 59							21 29								
Camberley	a			21 05							21 35								
Frimley	d			21 13							21 43								
Ash Vale	d			21 19							21 49								
Aldershot	a			21 24							21 54								
	d			21 38							22 08								
Ash 5	d			21 45							22 15								
Wanborough	d			21 48							22 18								
Guildford	a			21 55							22 25								
Martins Heron	d				21 17							21 47						22 17	
Bracknell	d				21 20							21 50						22 20	
Wokingham	d				21 27							21 57						22 27	
Winnersh	d				21 30							22 00						22 30	
Winnersh Triangle	d				21 32							22 02						22 32	
Earley	d				21 35							22 05						22 35	
Reading 7	a				21 40							22 10						22 40	

Table 149

Mondays to Fridays
24 May to 24 September

London - Hounslow, Richmond, Kingston, Windsor, Weybridge, Ascot, Guildford and Reading

		SW	SW	SW	SW	SW 1	SW 1	SW	SW	SW	SW 1	SW	SW	SW	SW 1	SW 1	SW	SW	SW	SW
London Waterloo 15 ⊖	d	21 28	21 33	21 37	21 45		21 50	21 52	21 58	22 03	22 20	22 22	22 28	22 33		22 50	22 52	22 58	23 03	23 13
Vauxhall ⊖	d	21 32	21 37	21 41	21 49			21 56	22 02	22 07		22 26	22 32	22 37			22 56	23 02	23 07	23 17
Queenstown Rd.(Battersea)	d		21 40	21 44	21 52			21 59		22 10		22 29		22 40			22 59		23 10	
Clapham Junction 10	d	21 38	21 43	21 47	21 55		21 58	22 02	22 08	22 13	22 28	22 32	22 38	22 43		22 58	23 02	23 08	23 13	23 23
Wandsworth Town	d		21 46	21 50	21 58			22 05		22 16		22 35		22 46			23 05		23 16	
Putney	d	21 42	21 49	21 53	22 01			22 08	22 12	22 19		22 38	22 42	22 49			23 08	23 12	23 19	23 27
Barnes	d		21 52	21 57	22 05			22 12		22 22		22 42		22 52			23 12		23 22	
Barnes Bridge	d			21 59				22 14				22 44					23 14			
Chiswick	d			22 02				22 17				22 47					23 17			
Kew Bridge	d			22 05				22 20				22 50					23 20			
Brentford	d			22 08				22 23				22 53					23 23			
Syon Lane	d			22 10				22 25				22 55					23 25			
Isleworth	d			22 12				22 27				22 57					23 27			
Hounslow	d			22 18				22 31				23 01					23 31			
Mortlake	d		21 54		22 07					22 24				22 54					23 24	
North Sheen	d		21 56		22 09					22 26				22 56					23 26	
Richmond ⊖	d	21 48	21 59		22 12		22 06		22 18	22 29	22 36		22 48	22 59		23 06		23 18	23 29	23 33
St Margarets	d		22 01		22 14					22 31				23 01					23 31	
Twickenham	a	21 51	22 03		22 16		22 10		22 21	22 33	22 40		22 51	23 03		23 10		23 21	23 33	23 36
	d	21 52	22 04				22 10		22 22	22 34	22 40		22 52	23 04		23 10		23 22	23 34	23 37
Strawberry Hill	d		22 07							22 37				23 07					23 37	
Fulwell	a																			
Teddington	a		22 10							22 40				23 10					23 40	
Hampton Wick	a		22 14							22 44				23 14					23 44	
Kingston	a		22 16							22 46				23 16					23 46	
Whitton	d	21 55		22 23					22 25				22 55					23 25		23 40
Feltham	d	21 59					22 16	22 36	22 29		22 46	23 06	22 59			23 16	23 36	23 29		23 44
Ashford (Surrey)	d	22 03						22 40	22 33			23 10	23 03				23 40	23 33		23 48
Staines	d	22 07					22 23	22 44	22 37		22 53	23 14	23 07			23 23	23 44	23 37		23 52
Wraysbury	d	22 11							22 41				23 11					23 41		23 56
Sunnymeads	d	22 14							22 44				23 14					23 44		23 59
Datchet	d	22 17							22 47				23 17					23 47		00 02
Windsor & Eton Riverside	a	22 21							22 51				23 21					23 51		00 06
Egham	d						22 27	22 49			22 57	23 19				23 27	23 49			
Virginia Water	a						22 31	22 53			23 01	23 23				23 31	23 53			
	d						22 31	22 53			23 01	23 23				23 31	23 53			
Chertsey	d							22 59				23 29					23 59			
Addlestone	d							23 02				23 32					00 02			
Weybridge	a							23 07				23 37								
Byfleet & New Haw	d																00 06			
West Byfleet	d																00 09			
Woking	a																00 18			
Longcross	d																			
Sunningdale	d						22 37				23 07					23 37				
Ascot 3	d					22 23	22 43				23 13				23 23	23 43				
Bagshot	d					22 29									23 29					
Camberley	a					22 35									23 35					
Frimley	d					22 43									23 43					
Ash Vale	d					22 49									23 49					
Aldershot	a					22 54									23 54					
	d					23 08									23 55					
Ash 5	d					23 15														
Wanborough	d					23 18														
Guildford	a					23 25														
Martins Heron	d						22 47				23 17					23 47				
Bracknell	d						22 50				23 20					23 50				
Wokingham	d						22 57				23 27					23 57				
Winnersh	d						23 00				23 30					23 59				
Winnersh Triangle	d						23 02				23 32					00 01				
Earley	d						23 05				23 35					00 05				
Reading 7	a						23 10				23 40					00 10				

Table 149

Mondays to Fridays

24 May to 24 September

London - Hounslow, Richmond, Kingston, Windsor, Weybridge, Ascot, Guildford and Reading

		SW 1	SW	SW	SW	SW	SW
London Waterloo 15 ⊖	d	23 20	23 22	23 33	23 38	23 52	23 58
Vauxhall ⊖	d		23 26	23 37		23 56	00 02
Queenstown Rd.(Battersea)	d		23 29	23 40		23 59	
Clapham Junction 10	d	23 28	23 32	23 43	23 46	00 02	00 08
Wandsworth Town	d		23 35	23 46		00 05	
Putney	d		23 38	23 49		00 08	00 12
Barnes	d		23 42	23 52		00 12	
Barnes Bridge	d		23 44			00 14	
Chiswick	d		23 47			00 17	
Kew Bridge	d		23 50			00 20	
Brentford	d		23 53			00 23	
Syon Lane	d		23 55			00 25	
Isleworth	d		23 57			00 27	
Hounslow	d		00 01			00 31	
Mortlake	d			23 54			
North Sheen	d			23 56			
Richmond ⊖	d	23 37		23 59	23 54		00 18
St Margarets	d			00 01			
Twickenham	a	23 41		00 03	23 58		00 21
	d	23 41		00 04	23 58		00 22
Strawberry Hill	d			00 07			
Fulwell	a						
Teddington	a			00 10			
Hampton Wick	a			00 14			
Kingston	a			00 16			
Whitton	d						00 25
Feltham	d	23 48	00 06		00 04	00 37	00 29
Ashford (Surrey)	d		00 10			00 41	00 33
Staines	d	23 56	00 14		00 11	00a46	00a37
Wraysbury	d						
Sunnymeads	d						
Datchet	d						
Windsor & Eton Riverside	a						
Egham	d	00 01	00 19		00 15		
Virginia Water	a	00 05	00 23		00 19		
	d	00 05	00 23		00 19		
Chertsey	d		00 29				
Addlestone	d		00 32				
Weybridge	a		00 37				
Byfleet & New Haw	d						
West Byfleet	d						
Woking	a						
Longcross	d						
Sunningdale	d	00 11			00 25		
Ascot 3	d	00 15			00 30		
Bagshot	d						
Camberley	a						
Frimley	d						
Ash Vale	d						
Aldershot	a						
	d						
Ash 5	d						
Wanborough	d						
Guildford	a						
Martins Heron	d	00 19			00 34		
Bracknell	d	00 23			00 37		
Wokingham	d	00 32			00 44		
Winnersh	d	00 36					
Winnersh Triangle	d	00 38					
Earley	d	00 40					
Reading 7	a	00 45			00 52		

Table 149

Mondays to Fridays

27 September to 10 December

London - Hounslow, Richmond, Kingston, Windsor, Weybridge, Ascot, Guildford and Reading

		SW MO 1	SW MO	SW MX 1	SW MX	SW MO 1	SW MX	SW MX 1	SW MX
London Waterloo 15 ⊖	d	22p39	22p50	22p50	22p52	23p09	23p13	23p20	23p22
Vauxhall ⊖	d	22p43	22p54		22p56	23p13	23p17		23p26
Queenstown Rd.(Battersea)	d		22p57		22p59				23p29
Clapham Junction 10	d	22p49	23p00	22p58	23p02	23p19	23p23	23p28	23p32
Wandsworth Town	d		23p03		23p05				23p35
Putney	d	22p53	23p06		23p08	23p23	23p27		23p38
Barnes	d		23p09		23p12				23p42
Barnes Bridge	d		23p11		23p14				23p44
Chiswick	d		23p13		23p17				23p47
Kew Bridge	d		23p16		23p20				23p50
Brentford	d		23p19		23p23				23p53
Syon Lane	d		23p21		23p25				23p55
Isleworth	d		23p23		23p27				23p57
Hounslow	d		23p26		23p31				00 01
Mortlake	d								
North Sheen	d								
Richmond ⊖	d	22p59		23p06		23p29	23p33	23p37	
St Margarets	d								
Twickenham	a	23p02		23p10		23p32	23p36	23p41	
	d	23p03		23p10		23p33	23p37	23p41	
Strawberry Hill	d								
Fulwell	a								
Teddington	a								
Hampton Wick	a								
Kingston	a								
Whitton	d						23p40		
Feltham	d	23p09	23p32	23p16	23p36	23p39	23p44	23p48	00 06
Ashford (Surrey)	d		23p36		23p40		23p48		00 10
Staines	d	23p15	23p40	23p23	23p44	23p45	23p52	23p56	00 14
Wraysbury	d						23p57		
Sunnymeads	d						23p59		
Datchet	d						00 04		
Windsor & Eton Riverside	a						00 09		
Egham	d	23p20	23p45	23p27	23p49	23p50		00 01	00 19
Virginia Water	a	23p24	23p49	23p31	23p53	23p54		00 05	00 23
	d	23p24	23p49	23p31	23p53	23p54		00 05	00 23
Chertsey	d		23p55		23p59				00 29
Addlestone	d		23p58		00 02				00 32
Weybridge	a								00 37
Byfleet & New Haw	d		00 02		00 06				
West Byfleet	d		00 05		00 09				
Woking	a		00 11		00 18				
Longcross	d								
Sunningdale	d	23p29		23p37		23p59		00 11	
Ascot 3	d	23p34		23p43		00 04		00 15	
Bagshot	d								
Camberley	a								
Frimley	d								
Ash Vale	d								
Aldershot	a								
	d								
Ash 5	d								
Wanborough	d								
Guildford	a								
Martins Heron	d	23p38		23p47		00 08		00 19	
Bracknell	d	23p41		23p50		00 11		00 23	
Wokingham	d	23p48		23p57		00 18		00 32	
Winnersh	d	23p51		23p59		00 21		00 36	
Winnersh Triangle	d	23p53		00 02		00 23		00 38	
Earley	d	23p56		00 05		00 26		00 40	
Reading 7	a	00 04		00 13		00 34		00 48	

		SW MX	SW MX	SW MO	SW MX 1	SW MO 1	SW MO	SW MX	SW MX	SW		SW 1	SW 1	SW	SW
London Waterloo 15 ⊖	d	23p33	23p38			23p39	23p44	23p52	23p58	00 18			05 05		
Vauxhall ⊖	d	23p37				23p43	23p48	23p56	00 02	00 22			05 09		
Queenstown Rd.(Battersea)	d	23p40					23p51	23p59		00 25			05 12		
Clapham Junction 10	d	23p43	23p46			23p49	23p54	00 02	00 08	00 28			05 15		
Wandsworth Town	d	23p46					23p57	00 05		00 31			05 18		
Putney	d	23p49				23p53	23p59	00 08	00 12	00 34			05 21		
Barnes	d	23p52					00 03	00 12		00 37			05 24		
Barnes Bridge	d							00 14							
Chiswick	d							00 17							
Kew Bridge	d							00 20							
Brentford	d							00 23							
Syon Lane	d							00 25							
Isleworth	d							00 27							
Hounslow	d							00 31							
Mortlake	d	23p54					00 05			00 39			05 26		
North Sheen	d	23p56					00 07			00 41			05 28		
Richmond ⊖	d	23p59	23p54			23p59	00 10		00 18	00 44			05 31		
St Margarets	d	00 01					00 12			00 46			05 33		
Twickenham	a	00 03	23p58			00 02	00 14		00 21	00 48			05 35		
	d	00 04	23p58			00 03	00 15		00 22	00 49	04 52		05 36		05 53
Strawberry Hill	d	00 07								00s52	04 55				
Fulwell	a														
Teddington	a	00 10								00s55	04 58				
Hampton Wick	a	00 14								00s58	05 01				
Kingston	a	00 16								01 00	05 03				
Whitton	d						00 18		00 25				05 39		05 56
Feltham	d		00 04			00 09	00 22	00 37	00 29				05 43		06 00
Ashford (Surrey)	d						00 26	00 41	00 33				05 47		06 04
Staines	d		00 11	00 21		00 15	00a30	00a46	00a37			05 23	05 53	05 44	06 08
Wraysbury	d														06 13
Sunnymeads	d														06 16
Datchet	d														06 20
Windsor & Eton Riverside	a														06 24
Egham	d		00 15	00s25		00 20						05 27	05 57	05 49	
Virginia Water	a		00 19	00s30		00 24						05 31	06 01	05 53	
	d		00 19	00s30		00 24						05 31	06 01	05 53	
Chertsey	d			00s35										05 59	
Addlestone	d			00s38										06 02	
Weybridge	a													06 07	
Byfleet & New Haw	d			00s42											
West Byfleet	d			00s45											
Woking	a			00 51											
Longcross	d														
Sunningdale	d		00 25			00 29						05 37	06 07		
Ascot 3	d		00 30		00 32	00 34						05 43	06 13		
Bagshot	d				00 38										
Camberley	a				00 44										
Frimley	d				00 48										
Ash Vale	d				00 57										
Aldershot	a				01s02										
	d				01s06										
Ash 5	d														
Wanborough	d														
Guildford	a														
Martins Heron	d		00 34			00 38						05 47	06 17		
Bracknell	d		00 37			00 41						05 50	06 20		
Wokingham	d		00 44			00 48						05 57	06 27		
Winnersh	d					00 51						06 00	06 30		
Winnersh Triangle	d					00 53						06 02	06 32		
Earley	d					00 56						06 05	06 37		
Reading 7	a		00 55			01 04						06 13	06 43		

Table 149

Mondays to Fridays
27 September to 10 December

London - Hounslow, Richmond, Kingston, Windsor, Weybridge, Ascot, Guildford and Reading

		SW	SW	SW 1	SW 1	SW	SW	SW	SW	SW	SW 1	SW 1	SW	SW	SW	SW	SW	SW 1	SW 1	SW	SW	SW	GW 1 A	SW	SW
London Waterloo 15 ⊖	d	05 33			05 50		05 58	06 03	06 15			06 20	06 22	06 28	06 33		06 45		06 50	06 52	06 58	07 03			07 15
Vauxhall ⊖	d	05 37					06 02	06 07	06 19				06 26	06 32	06 37		06 49			06 56	07 02	07 07			07 19
Queenstown Rd.(Battersea)	d	05 40						06 10	06 22				06 29		06 40		06 52			06 59		07 10			07 22
Clapham Junction 10	d	05 43			05 58		06 08	06 13	06 25			06 28	06 32	06 38	06 43		06 55		06 58	07 02	07 08	07 13			07 25
Wandsworth Town	d	05 46						06 16	06 28				06 35		06 46		06 58			07 05		07 16			07 28
Putney	d	05 49					06 12	06 19	06 31				06 38	06 42	06 49		07 01			07 08	07 12	07 19			07 31
Barnes	d	05 52						06 22	06 35				06 42		06 52		07 05			07 12		07 22			07 35
Barnes Bridge	d												06 44							07 14					
Chiswick	d												06 47							07 17					
Kew Bridge	d												06 50							07 20					
Brentford	d												06 53							07 23					
Syon Lane	d												06 55							07 25					
Isleworth	d												06 57							07 27					
Hounslow	d												07 01			06 48				07 31					
Mortlake	d	05 54						06 24	06 37						06 54		07 07					07 24			07 37
North Sheen	d	05 56						06 26	06 39						06 56		07 09					07 26			07 39
Richmond ⊖	d	05 59			06 06		06 18	06 29	06 42			06 36		06 48	06 59		07 12		07 06		07 18	07 29			07 42
St Margarets	d	06 01						06 31	06 44						07 01		07 14					07 31			07 44
Twickenham	a	06 03			06 10		06 21	06 33	06 46			06 40		06 51	07 03		07 16		07 10		07 21	07 33			07 46
	d	06 05			06 10	06 17	06 22	06 34	06 47			06 40		06 52	07 04		07 17		07 10		07 22	07 34		07 37	07 47
Strawberry Hill	d	06 08						06 37							07 07							07 37		07 47	
Fulwell	a																								
Teddington	a	06 11						06 40							07 10							07 40		07 50	
Hampton Wick	a	06 14						06 44							07 14							07 44		07 52	
Kingston	a	06 16						06 46							07 16							07 46		07 54	
Whitton	d					06a20	06 25		06 50					06 55		06 53	07 20				07 25				07 50
Feltham	d				06 16		06 29					06 46	07 06	06 59					07 16	07 36	07 29				
Ashford (Surrey)	d						06 33						07 10	07 03						07 40	07 33				
Staines	d		06 14		06 23		06 37			06 44		06 53	07 14	07 07					07 23	07 44	07 37				
Wraysbury	d						06 42							07 12							07 42				
Sunnymeads	d						06 45							07 15							07 45				
Datchet	d						06 49							07 19							07 49				
Windsor & Eton Riverside	a						06 54							07 24							07 54				
Egham	d		06 19		06 27					06 49		06 57	07 19						07 27	07 49					
Virginia Water	a		06 23		06 31					06 53		07 01	07 23						07 31	07 53					
	d		06 23		06 31					06 53		07 01	07 23						07 31	07 53					
Chertsey	d		06 29							06 59			07 29							07 59					
Addlestone	d		06 32							07 02			07 32							08 02					
Weybridge	a		06 37							07 07			07 37							08 07					
Byfleet & New Haw	d																								
West Byfleet	d																								
Woking	a																								
Longcross	d				06 35							07 05							07 35						
Sunningdale	d				06 37							07 07							07 37						
Ascot 3	d			06 23	06 43						06 53	07 13						07 23	07 43						
Bagshot	d			06 29							06 59							07 29							
Camberley	a			06 35							07 05							07 35							
Frimley	d			06 43							07 13							07 43							
Ash Vale	d			06 49							07 19							07 49							
Aldershot	a			06 56							07 26							07 54							
	d			07 08							07 38							08 08							
Ash 5	d			07 15							07 45							08 15							
Wanborough	d			07 18							07 48							08 18							
Guildford	a			07 25							07 55							08 25							
Martins Heron	d				06 47							07 17							07 47						
Bracknell	d				06 50							07 20							07 50						
Wokingham	d				06 57							07 27							07 57				08 17		
Winnersh	d				07 00							07 30							08 00				08 21		
Winnersh Triangle	d				07 02							07 32							08 02						
Earley	d				07 07							07 37							08 07						
Reading 7	a				07 13							07 43							08 13				08 30		

A From Gatwick Airport (Table 148)

Table 149

Mondays to Fridays
27 September to 10 December

London - Hounslow, Richmond, Kingston, Windsor, Weybridge, Ascot, Guildford and Reading

		SW 1	SW 1	SW	SW	SW 1	SW	SW	SW	SW	SW 1	SW	SW	SW	SW 1	SW 1	SW	SW	SW 1	SW
London Waterloo 15 ⊖	d		07 20	07 22	07 28		07 33		07 37	07 45	07 50	07 52	07 58	08 03		08 07	08 10	08 15	08 20	08 22
Vauxhall ⊖	d			07 26	07 32		07 37		07 41	07 49		07 56	08 02	08 07			08 14	08 19		08 26
Queenstown Rd.(Battersea)	d			07 29			07 40		07 44	07 52		07 59		08 10			08 17	08 22		08 29
Clapham Junction 10	d		07 28	07 32	07 38		07 43		07 47	07 55	07 58	08 02	08 08	08 13		08 16	08 20	08 25	08 28	08 32
Wandsworth Town	d			07 35			07 46		07 50	07 58		08 05		08 16			08 23	08 28		08 35
Putney	d			07 38	07 42		07 49		07 53	08 01		08 08	08 12	08 19			08 26	08 31		08 38
Barnes	d			07 42			07 52		07 57	08 05		08 12		08 23			08 27	08 35		08 42
Barnes Bridge	d			07 44					07 59			08 14					08 29			08 44
Chiswick	d			07 47					08 02			08 17					08 32			08 47
Kew Bridge	d			07 50					08 05			08 20					08 35			08 50
Brentford	d			07 53					08 08			08 23					08 38			08 53
Syon Lane	d			07 55					08 10			08 25					08 40			08 55
Isleworth	d			07 57					08 12			08 27					08 42			08 57
Hounslow	d			08 01					08a18			08 31					08 48			09 01
Mortlake	d						07 54			08 07				08 25				08 37		
North Sheen	d						07 56			08 09				08 27				08 39		
Richmond ⊖	d		07 36		07 48	07 54	07 59			08 12	08 06		08 18	08 30		08 24		08 42	08 36	
St Margarets	d						08 01			08 14				08 32				08 44		
Twickenham	a		07 40		07 51	07 57	08 03			08 16	08 10		08 21	08 34		08 28		08 46	08 40	
	d		07 40		07 52	07 58	08 04	08 07		08 17	08 10		08 22	08 35		08 28		08 47	08 40	
Strawberry Hill	d						08 07	08 17						08 38						
Fulwell	a																			
Teddington	a						08 10	08 20						08 41						
Hampton Wick	a						08 14	08 22						08 44						
Kingston	a						08 16	08 24						08 46						
Whitton	d				07 55					08 20			08 25				08 53	08 50		
Feltham	d		07 46	08 06	07 59	08 04					08 16	08 36	08 29			08 34			08 46	09 06
Ashford (Surrey)	d			08 10	08 03	08 08						08 40	08 33			08 38				09 10
Staines	d		07 53	08 14	08 07	08 12					08 23	08 44	08 37			08 42			08 53	09 14
Wraysbury	d				08 12								08 42							
Sunnymeads	d				08 15								08 45							
Datchet	d				08 19								08 49							
Windsor & Eton Riverside	a				08 24								08 54							
Egham	d		07 57	08 19		08 16					08 27	08 49				08 47			08 57	09 19
Virginia Water	a		08 01	08 23							08 31	08 53				08 51			09 01	09 23
	d		08 01	08 23							08 31	08 53				08 51			09 01	09 23
Chertsey	d			08 29								08 59								09 29
Addlestone	d			08 32								09 02								09 32
Weybridge	a			08 38								09 08								09 37
Byfleet & New Haw	d																			
West Byfleet	d																			
Woking	a																			
Longcross	d		08 05								08 35					08 54				
Sunningdale	d		08 07								08 37					08 58			09 07	
Ascot 3	d	07 53	08 13			08 26					08 43				08 53	09 02			09 13	
Bagshot	d	07 59				08 32									08 59					
Camberley	a	08 05				08 38									09 05					
Frimley	d	08 13				08 43									09 13					
Ash Vale	d	08 19				08 49									09 19					
Aldershot	a	08 24				08 54									09 25					
	d	08 38				09 08									09 38					
Ash 5	d	08 45				09 15									09 45					
Wanborough	d	08 48				09 18									09 48					
Guildford	a	08 55				09 25									09 55					
Martins Heron	d		08 17								08 47					09 06			09 17	
Bracknell	d		08 20								08 50					09 10			09 20	
Wokingham	d		08 27								08 57					09 17			09 27	
Winnersh	d		08 30								09 00					09 20			09 30	
Winnersh Triangle	d		08 32								09 02					09 22			09 32	
Earley	d		08 37								09 07					09 27			09 37	
Reading 7	a		08 43								09 13					09 33			09 43	

Table 149

Mondays to Fridays
27 September to 10 December

London - Hounslow, Richmond, Kingston, Windsor, Weybridge, Ascot, Guildford and Reading

		SW	SW	SW ■1	SW ■1	SW	SW	SW ■1	SW	SW	SW	SW	SW	SW ■1	SW ■1	SW	SW	SW	SW	SW	SW ■1
London Waterloo 15 ⊖	d	08 28	08 33		08 37	08 40	08 43	08 50	08 52	08 58	09 03	09 07	09 15		09 20	09 22	09 28	09 33	09 37	09 45	
Vauxhall ⊖	d	08 32	08 37			08 44	08 47		08 56	09 02	09 07	09 11	09 19			09 26	09 32	09 37	09 41	09 49	
Queenstown Rd.(Battersea)	d		08 40			08 47	08 50		08 59		09 10	09 14	09 22			09 29		09 40	09 44	09 52	
Clapham Junction 10	d	08 38	08 43		08 45	08 50	08 55	08 58	09 02	09 08	09 13	09 17	09 25		09 28	09 32	09 38	09 43	09 47	09 55	
Wandsworth Town	d		08 46			08 53	08 58		09 05		09 16	09 20	09 28			09 35		09 46	09 50	09 58	
Putney	d	08 42	08 49			08 56	09 01		09 08	09 12	09 19	09 23	09 31			09 38	09 42	09 49	09 53	10 01	
Barnes	d		08 52			08 57	09 05		09 12		09 22	09 27	09 35			09 42		09 52	09 57	10 05	
Barnes Bridge	d					08 59			09 14			09 29				09 44			09 59		
Chiswick	d					09 02			09 17			09 32				09 47			10 02		
Kew Bridge	d					09 05			09 20			09 35				09 50			10 05		
Brentford	d					09 08			09 23			09 38				09 53			10 08		
Syon Lane	d					09 10			09 25			09 40				09 55			10 10		
Isleworth	d					09 12			09 27			09 42				09 57			10 12		
Hounslow	d					09 18			09 31			09 48				10 01			10 18		
Mortlake	d		08 54				09 07				09 24		09 37					09 54		10 07	
North Sheen	d		08 56				09 09				09 26		09 39					09 56		10 09	
Richmond ⊖	d	08 48	08 59		08 54		09 12	09 06		09 18	09 29		09 42		09 36		09 48	09 59		10 12	
St Margarets	d		09 01				09 14				09 31		09 44					10 01		10 14	
Twickenham	a	08 51	09 03		08 57		09 16	09 10		09 21	09 33		09 46		09 40		09 51	10 03		10 16	
	d	08 52	09 04		08 58		09 17	09 10		09 22	09 34		09 47		09 40		09 52	10 04		10 17	
Strawberry Hill	d		09 07								09 37							10 07			
Fulwell	a																				
Teddington	a		09 10								09 40							10 10			
Hampton Wick	a		09 14								09 44							10 14			
Kingston	a		09 16								09 46							10 16			
Whitton	d	08 55				09 23	09 20			09 25		09 53	09 50				09 55		10 26	10 20	
Feltham	d	08 59			09 04			09 16	09 36	09 29					09 46	10 06	09 59				
Ashford (Surrey)	d	09 03			09 08				09 40	09 33						10 10	10 03				
Staines	d	09 07			09 12			09 23	09 44	09 37					09 53	10 14	10 07				
Wraysbury	d	09 12								09 42							10 12				
Sunnymeads	d	09 15								09 45							10 15				
Datchet	d	09 19								09 49							10 19				
Windsor & Eton Riverside	a	09 24								09 54							10 24				
Egham	d				09 16			09 27	09 49						09 57	10 19					
Virginia Water	a				09 20			09 31	09 53						10 01	10 23					
	d				09 20			09 31	09 53						10 01	10 23					
Chertsey	d								09 59							10 29					
Addlestone	d								10 02							10 32					
Weybridge	a								10 07							10 37					
Byfleet & New Haw	d																				
West Byfleet	d																				
Woking	a																				
Longcross	d																				
Sunningdale	d				09 26			09 37							10 07						
Ascot 3	d			09 23	09 30			09 43						09 53	10 13						10 23
Bagshot	d			09 29										09 59							10 29
Camberley	a			09 35										10 05							10 35
Frimley	d			09 43										10 13							10 43
Ash Vale	d			09 49										10 19							10 49
Aldershot	a			09 54										10 24							10 54
	d			10 08										10 38							11 08
Ash 5	d			10 15										10 45							11 15
Wanborough	d			10 18										10 48							11 18
Guildford	a			10 25										10 55							11 25
Martins Heron	d				09 34			09 47							10 17						
Bracknell	d				09 38			09 50							10 20						
Wokingham	d				09 47			09 57							10 27						
Winnersh	d							10 00							10 30						
Winnersh Triangle	d							10 02							10 32						
Earley	d							10 07							10 37						
Reading 7	a				09 58			10 13							10 43						

Table 149

Mondays to Fridays
27 September to 10 December

London - Hounslow, Richmond, Kingston, Windsor, Weybridge, Ascot, Guildford and Reading

		SW ■1	SW	SW	SW	SW	SW	SW ■1	SW ■1	SW	SW	SW	SW	SW	SW ■1	SW ■1	SW	SW	SW
London Waterloo 15 ⊖	d	09 50	09 52	09 58	10 03	10 07	10 15		10 20	10 22	10 28	10 33	10 37	10 45		10 50	10 52	10 58	11 03
Vauxhall ⊖	d		09 56	10 02	10 07	10 11	10 19			10 26	10 32	10 37	10 41	10 49			10 56	11 02	11 07
Queenstown Rd.(Battersea)	d		09 59		10 10	10 14	10 22			10 29		10 40	10 44	10 52			10 59		11 10
Clapham Junction 10	d	09 58	10 02	10 08	10 13	10 17	10 25		10 28	10 32	10 38	10 43	10 47	10 55		10 58	11 02	11 08	11 13
Wandsworth Town	d		10 05		10 16	10 20	10 28			10 35		10 46	10 50	10 58			11 05		11 16
Putney	d		10 08	10 12	10 19	10 23	10 31			10 38	10 42	10 49	10 53	11 01			11 08	11 12	11 19
Barnes	d		10 12		10 22	10 27	10 35			10 42		10 52	10 57	11 05			11 12		11 22
Barnes Bridge	d		10 14			10 29				10 44			10 59				11 14		
Chiswick	d		10 17			10 32				10 47			11 02				11 17		
Kew Bridge	d		10 20			10 35				10 50			11 05				11 20		
Brentford	d		10 23			10 38				10 53			11 08				11 23		
Syon Lane	d		10 25			10 40				10 55			11 10				11 25		
Isleworth	d		10 27			10 42				10 57			11 12				11 27		
Hounslow	d		10 31			10 48				11 01			11 18				11 31		
Mortlake	d				10 24		10 37					10 54		11 07					11 24
North Sheen	d				10 26		10 39					10 56		11 09					11 26
Richmond ⊖	d	10 06		10 18	10 29		10 42		10 36		10 48	10 59		11 12		11 06		11 18	11 29
St Margarets	d				10 31		10 44					11 01		11 14					11 31
Twickenham	a	10 10		10 21	10 33		10 46		10 40		10 51	11 03		11 16		11 10		11 21	11 33
	d	10 10		10 22	10 34		10 47		10 40		10 52	11 04		11 17		11 10		11 22	11 34
Strawberry Hill	d				10 37							11 07							11 37
Fulwell	a																		
Teddington	a				10 40							11 10							11 40
Hampton Wick	a				10 44							11 14							11 44
Kingston	a				10 46							11 16							11 46
Whitton	d			10 25		10 56	10 50				10 55		11 23	11 20				11 25	
Feltham	d	10 16	10 36	10 29					10 46	11 06	10 59					11 16	11 36	11 29	
Ashford (Surrey)	d		10 40	10 33						11 10	11 03						11 40	11 33	
Staines	d	10 23	10 44	10 37					10 53	11 14	11 07					11 23	11 44	11 37	
Wraysbury	d			10 42							11 12							11 42	
Sunnymeads	d			10 45							11 15							11 45	
Datchet	d			10 49							11 19							11 49	
Windsor & Eton Riverside	a			10 54							11 24							11 54	
Egham	d	10 27	10 49						10 57	11 19						11 27	11 49		
Virginia Water	a	10 31	10 53						11 01	11 23						11 31	11 53		
	d	10 31	10 53						11 01	11 23						11 31	11 53		
Chertsey	d		10 59							11 29							11 59		
Addlestone	d		11 02							11 32							12 02		
Weybridge	a		11 07							11 37							12 07		
Byfleet & New Haw	d																		
West Byfleet	d																		
Woking	a																		
Longcross	d																		
Sunningdale	d	10 37							11 07							11 37			
Ascot 3	d	10 43						10 53	11 13						11 23	11 43			
Bagshot	d							10 59							11 29				
Camberley	a							11 05							11 35				
Frimley	d							11 13							11 43				
Ash Vale	d							11 19							11 49				
Aldershot	a							11 24							11 54				
	d							11 38							12 08				
Ash 5	d							11 45							12 15				
Wanborough	d							11 48							12 18				
Guildford	a							11 55							12 25				
Martins Heron	d	10 47							11 17							11 47			
Bracknell	d	10 50							11 20							11 50			
Wokingham	d	10 57							11 27							11 57			
Winnersh	d	11 00							11 30							12 00			
Winnersh Triangle	d	11 02							11 32							12 02			
Earley	d	11 07							11 37							12 07			
Reading 7	a	11 13							11 43							12 13			

Table 149

Mondays to Fridays

27 September to 10 December

London - Hounslow, Richmond, Kingston, Windsor, Weybridge, Ascot, Guildford and Reading

		SW	SW	SW 1	SW 1	SW	SW	SW	SW	SW	SW 1	SW 1	SW	SW	SW	SW	SW 1	SW 1	SW	SW
London Waterloo 15 ⊖	d	11 07	11 15		11 20	11 22	11 28	11 33	11 37	11 45		11 50	11 52	11 58	12 03	12 07		12 20	12 22	12 28
Vauxhall ⊖	d	11 11	11 19			11 26	11 32	11 37	11 41	11 49			11 56	12 02	12 07	12 11			12 26	12 32
Queenstown Rd.(Battersea)	d	11 14	11 22			11 29		11 40	11 44	11 52			11 59		12 10	12 14			12 29	
Clapham Junction 10	d	11 17	11 25		11 28	11 32	11 38	11 43	11 47	11 55		11 58	12 02	12 08	12 13	12 17		12 28	12 32	12 38
Wandsworth Town	d	11 20	11 28			11 35		11 46	11 50	11 58			12 05		12 16	12 20			12 35	
Putney	d	11 23	11 31			11 38	11 42	11 49	11 53	12 01			12 08	12 12	12 19	12 23			12 38	12 42
Barnes	d	11 27	11 35			11 42		11 52	11 57	12 05			12 12		12 22	12 27			12 42	
Barnes Bridge	d	11 29				11 44			11 59				12 14			12 29			12 44	
Chiswick	d	11 32				11 47			12 02				12 17			12 32			12 47	
Kew Bridge	d	11 35				11 50			12 05				12 20			12 35			12 50	
Brentford	d	11 38				11 53			12 08				12 23			12 38			12 53	
Syon Lane	d	11 40				11 55			12 10				12 25			12 40			12 55	
Isleworth	d	11 42				11 57			12 12				12 27			12 42			12 57	
Hounslow	d	11 48				12 01			12 18				12 31			12 48			13 01	
Mortlake	d		11 37					11 54		12 07					12 24					
North Sheen	d		11 39					11 56		12 09					12 26					
Richmond ⊖	d		11 42		11 36		11 48	11 59		12 12		12 06		12 18	12 29			12 36		12 48
St Margarets	d		11 44					12 01		12 14					12 31					
Twickenham	a		11 46		11 40		11 51	12 03		12 16		12 10		12 21	12 33			12 40		12 51
	d		11 47		11 40		11 52	12 04		12 17		12 10		12 22	12 34			12 40		12 52
Strawberry Hill	d							12 07							12 37					
Fulwell	a																			
Teddington	a							12 10							12 40					
Hampton Wick	a							12 14							12 44					
Kingston	a							12 16							12 46					
Whitton	d	11 53	11 50				11 55		12 23	12 20				12 25		12 53				12 55
Feltham	d				11 46	12 06	11 59					12 16	12 36	12 29				12 46	13 06	12 59
Ashford (Surrey)	d					12 10	12 03						12 40	12 33					13 10	13 03
Staines	d				11 53	12 14	12 07					12 23	12 44	12 37				12 53	13 14	13 07
Wraysbury	d						12 12							12 42						13 12
Sunnymeads	d						12 15							12 45						13 15
Datchet	d						12 19							12 49						13 19
Windsor & Eton Riverside	a						12 24							12 54						13 24
Egham	d				11 57	12 19						12 27	12 49					12 57	13 19	
Virginia Water	a				12 01	12 23						12 31	12 53					13 01	13 23	
	d				12 01	12 23						12 31	12 53					13 01	13 23	
Chertsey	d					12 29							12 59						13 29	
Addlestone	d					12 32							13 02						13 32	
Weybridge	a					12 37							13 07						13 37	
Byfleet & New Haw	d																			
West Byfleet	d																			
Woking	a																			
Longcross	d																			
Sunningdale	d				12 07							12 37						13 07		
Ascot 3	d			11 53	12 13						12 23	12 43					12 53	13 13		
Bagshot	d			11 59							12 29						12 59			
Camberley	a			12 05							12 35						13 05			
Frimley	d			12 13							12 43						13 13			
Ash Vale	d			12 19							12 49						13 19			
Aldershot	a			12 24							12 54						13 24			
	d			12 38							13 08						13 38			
Ash 5	d			12 45							13 15						13 45			
Wanborough	d			12 48							13 18						13 48			
Guildford	a			12 55							13 25						13 55			
Martins Heron	d				12 17							12 47						13 17		
Bracknell	d				12 20							12 50						13 20		
Wokingham	d				12 27							12 57						13 27		
Winnersh	d				12 30							13 00						13 30		
Winnersh Triangle	d				12 32							13 02						13 32		
Earley	d				12 37							13 07						13 37		
Reading 7	a				12 43							13 13						13 43		

Table 149

Mondays to Fridays

27 September to 10 December

London - Hounslow, Richmond, Kingston, Windsor, Weybridge, Ascot, Guildford and Reading

		SW	SW	SW	SW 1	SW 1	SW	SW	SW	SW	SW	SW 1	SW 1	SW	SW	SW	SW	SW	SW 1	SW 1	SW
London Waterloo 15 ⊖	d	12 33	12 37	12 45		12 50	12 52	12 58	13 03	13 07	13 15		13 20	13 22	13 28	13 33	13 37	13 45		13 50	13 52
Vauxhall ⊖	d	12 37	12 41	12 49			12 56	13 02	13 07	13 11	13 19			13 26	13 32	13 37	13 41	13 49			13 56
Queenstown Rd.(Battersea)	d	12 40	12 44	12 52			12 59		13 10	13 14	13 22			13 29		13 40	13 44	13 52			13 59
Clapham Junction 10	d	12 43	12 47	12 55		12 58	13 02	13 08	13 13	13 17	13 25		13 28	13 32	13 38	13 43	13 47	13 55		13 58	14 02
Wandsworth Town	d	12 46	12 50	12 58			13 05		13 16	13 20	13 28			13 35		13 46	13 50	13 58			14 05
Putney	d	12 49	12 53	13 01			13 08	13 12	13 19	13 23	13 31			13 38	13 42	13 49	13 53	14 01			14 08
Barnes	d	12 52	12 57	13 05			13 12		13 22	13 27	13 35			13 42		13 52	13 57	14 05			14 12
Barnes Bridge	d		12 59				13 14			13 29				13 44			13 59				14 14
Chiswick	d		13 02				13 17			13 32				13 47			14 02				14 17
Kew Bridge	d		13 05				13 20			13 35				13 50			14 05				14 20
Brentford	d		13 08				13 23			13 38				13 53			14 08				14 23
Syon Lane	d		13 10				13 25			13 40				13 55			14 10				14 25
Isleworth	d		13 12				13 27			13 42				13 57			14 12				14 27
Hounslow	d		13 18				13 31			13 48				14 01			14 18				14 31
Mortlake	d	12 54		13 07					13 24		13 37					13 54		14 07			
North Sheen	d	12 56		13 09					13 26		13 39					13 56		14 09			
Richmond ⊖	d	12 59		13 12		13 06		13 18	13 29		13 42		13 36		13 48	13 59		14 12		14 06	
St Margarets	d	13 01		13 14					13 31		13 44					14 01		14 14			
Twickenham	a	13 03		13 16		13 10		13 21	13 33		13 46		13 40		13 51	14 03		14 16		14 10	
	d	13 04		13 17		13 10		13 22	13 34		13 47		13 40		13 52	14 04		14 17		14 10	
Strawberry Hill	d	13 07							13 37							14 07					
Fulwell	a																				
Teddington	a	13 10							13 40							14 10					
Hampton Wick	a	13 14							13 44							14 14					
Kingston	a	13 16							13 46							14 16					
Whitton	d		13 23	13 20				13 25		13 53	13 50				13 55		14 23	14 20			
Feltham	d					13 16	13 36	13 29					13 46	14 06	13 59					14 16	14 36
Ashford (Surrey)	d						13 40	13 33						14 10	14 03						14 40
Staines	d					13 23	13 44	13 37					13 53	14 14	14 07					14 23	14 44
Wraysbury	d							13 42							14 12						
Sunnymeads	d							13 45							14 15						
Datchet	d							13 49							14 19						
Windsor & Eton Riverside	a							13 54							14 24						
Egham	d					13 27	13 49						13 57	14 19						14 27	14 49
Virginia Water	a					13 31	13 53						14 01	14 23						14 31	14 53
	d					13 31	13 53						14 01	14 23						14 31	14 53
Chertsey	d						13 59							14 29							14 59
Addlestone	d						14 02							14 32							15 02
Weybridge	a						14 07							14 37							15 07
Byfleet & New Haw	d																				
West Byfleet	d																				
Woking	a																				
Longcross	d					13 35															
Sunningdale	d					13 37							14 07							14 37	
Ascot 3	d				13 23	13 43						13 53	14 13						14 23	14 43	
Bagshot	d				13 29							13 59							14 29		
Camberley	a				13 35							14 05							14 35		
Frimley	d				13 43							14 13							14 43		
Ash Vale	d				13 49							14 19							14 49		
Aldershot	a				13 54							14 24							14 54		
	d				14 08							14 38							15 08		
Ash 5	d				14 15							14 45							15 15		
Wanborough	d				14 18							14 48							15 18		
Guildford	a				14 25							14 55							15 25		
Martins Heron	d					13 47							14 17							14 47	
Bracknell	d					13 50							14 20							14 50	
Wokingham	d					13 57							14 27							14 57	
Winnersh	d					14 00							14 30							15 00	
Winnersh Triangle	d					14 02							14 32							15 02	
Earley	d					14 07							14 37							15 07	
Reading 7	a					14 13							14 43							15 13	

Table 149

Mondays to Fridays
27 September to 10 December

London - Hounslow, Richmond, Kingston, Windsor, Weybridge, Ascot, Guildford and Reading

		SW	SW	SW	SW	SW 1	SW 1	SW	SW	SW	SW	SW	SW 1	SW 1	SW	SW	SW	SW	SW
London Waterloo 15 ⊖	d	13 58	14 03	14 07	14 15		14 20	14 22	14 28	14 33	14 37	14 45		14 50	14 52	14 58	15 03	15 07	15 15
Vauxhall ⊖	d	14 02	14 07	14 11	14 19			14 26	14 32	14 37	14 41	14 49			14 56	15 02	15 07	15 11	15 19
Queenstown Rd.(Battersea)	d		14 10	14 14	14 22			14 29		14 40	14 44	14 52			14 59		15 10	15 14	15 22
Clapham Junction 10	d	14 08	14 13	14 17	14 25		14 28	14 32	14 38	14 43	14 47	14 55		14 58	15 02	15 08	15 13	15 17	15 25
Wandsworth Town	d		14 16	14 20	14 28			14 35		14 46	14 50	14 58			15 05		15 16	15 20	15 28
Putney	d	14 12	14 19	14 23	14 31			14 38	14 42	14 49	14 53	15 01			15 08	15 12	15 19	15 23	15 31
Barnes	d		14 22	14 27	14 35			14 42		14 52	14 57	15 05			15 12		15 22	15 27	15 35
Barnes Bridge	d			14 29				14 44			14 59				15 14			15 29	
Chiswick	d			14 32				14 47			15 02				15 17			15 32	
Kew Bridge	d			14 35				14 50			15 05				15 20			15 35	
Brentford	d			14 38				14 53			15 08				15 23			15 38	
Syon Lane	d			14 40				14 55			15 10				15 25			15 40	
Isleworth	d			14 42				14 57			15 12				15 27			15 42	
Hounslow	d			14 48				15 01			15 18				15 31			15 48	
Mortlake	d		14 24		14 37					14 54		15 07					15 24		15 37
North Sheen	d		14 26		14 39					14 56		15 09					15 26		15 39
Richmond ⊖	d	14 18	14 29		14 42		14 36		14 48	14 59		15 12		15 06		15 18	15 29		15 42
St Margarets	d		14 31		14 44					15 01		15 14					15 31		15 44
Twickenham	a	14 21	14 33		14 46		14 40		14 51	15 03		15 16		15 10		15 21	15 33		15 46
	d	14 22	14 34		14 47		14 40		14 52	15 04		15 17		15 10		15 22	15 34		15 47
Strawberry Hill	d		14 37							15 07							15 37		
Fulwell	a																		
Teddington	a		14 40							15 10							15 40		
Hampton Wick	a		14 44							15 14							15 44		
Kingston	a		14 46							15 16							15 46		
Whitton	d	14 25		14 53	14 50				14 55		15 23	15 20				15 25		15 53	15 50
Feltham	d	14 29					14 46	15 06	14 59					15 16	15 36	15 29			
Ashford (Surrey)	d	14 33						15 10	15 03						15 40	15 33			
Staines	d	14 37					14 53	15 14	15 07					15 23	15 44	15 37			
Wraysbury	d	14 42							15 12							15 42			
Sunnymeads	d	14 45							15 15							15 45			
Datchet	d	14 49							15 19							15 49			
Windsor & Eton Riverside	a	14 54							15 24							15 54			
Egham	d						14 57	15 19						15 27	15 49				
Virginia Water	a						15 01	15 23						15 31	15 53				
	d						15 01	15 23						15 31	15 53				
Chertsey	d							15 29							15 59				
Addlestone	d							15 32							16 02				
Weybridge	a							15 37							16 07				
Byfleet & New Haw	d																		
West Byfleet	d																		
Woking	a																		
Longcross	d																		
Sunningdale	d						15 07							15 37					
Ascot 3	d					14 53	15 13						15 23	15 43					
Bagshot	d					14 59							15 29						
Camberley	a					15 05							15 35						
Frimley	d					15 13							15 43						
Ash Vale	d					15 19							15 49						
Aldershot	a					15 24							15 54						
	d					15 38							16 08						
Ash 5	d					15 45							16 15						
Wanborough	d					15 48							16 18						
Guildford	a					15 55							16 25						
Martins Heron	d						15 17							15 47					
Bracknell	d						15 20							15 50					
Wokingham	d						15 27							15 57					
Winnersh	d						15 30							16 00					
Winnersh Triangle	d						15 32							16 02					
Earley	d						15 37							16 07					
Reading 7	a						15 43							16 13					

Table 149

Mondays to Fridays
27 September to 10 December

London - Hounslow, Richmond, Kingston, Windsor, Weybridge, Ascot, Guildford and Reading

		SW 1	SW 1	SW	SW	SW	SW	SW	SW 1	SW 1	SW	SW	SW	SW 1	SW 1	SW	SW	SW 1	SW	SW
London Waterloo 15 ⊖	d		15 20	15 22	15 28	15 33	15 37	15 45		15 50	15 52	15 58	16 01		16 05	16 07	16 15	16 20	16 22	16 28
Vauxhall ⊖	d			15 26	15 32	15 37	15 41	15 49			15 56	16 02	16 05		16 09	16 11	16 19		16 26	16 32
Queenstown Rd.(Battersea)	d			15 29		15 40	15 44	15 52			15 59		16 08			16 14	16 22		16 29	
Clapham Junction 10	d		15 28	15 32	15 38	15 43	15 47	15 55		15 58	16 02	16 08	16 11		16 15	16 17	16 25	16 28	16 32	16 38
Wandsworth Town	d			15 35		15 46	15 50	15 58			16 05		16 14			16 20	16 28		16 35	
Putney	d			15 38	15 42	15 49	15 53	16 01			16 08	16 12	16 17			16 23	16 31		16 38	16 42
Barnes	d			15 42		15 52	15 57	16 05			16 12		16 22			16 27	16 35		16 42	
Barnes Bridge	d			15 44			15 59				16 14					16 29			16 44	
Chiswick	d			15 47			16 02				16 17					16 32			16 47	
Kew Bridge	d			15 50			16 05				16 20					16 35			16 50	
Brentford	d			15 53			16 08				16 23					16 38			16 53	
Syon Lane	d			15 55			16 10				16 25					16 40			16 55	
Isleworth	d			15 57			16 12				16 27					16 42			16 57	
Hounslow	d			16 01			16 18				16 31					16 48			17 01	
Mortlake	d					15 54		16 07					16 24				16 37			
North Sheen	d					15 56		16 09					16 26				16 39			
Richmond ⊖	d		15 36		15 48	15 59		16 12		16 06		16 18	16 29		16 23		16 42	16 36		16 48
St Margarets	d					16 01		16 14					16 31				16 44			
Twickenham	a		15 40		15 51	16 03		16 16		16 10		16 21	16 33		16 27		16 46	16 40		16 51
	d		15 40		15 52	16 04		16 17		16 10		16 22	16 34		16 27		16 47	16 40		16 52
Strawberry Hill	d					16 07							16 37							
Fulwell	a																			
Teddington	a					16 10							16 42							
Hampton Wick	a					16 14							16 46							
Kingston	a					16 16							16 48							
Whitton	d				15 55		16 23	16 20				16 25				16 53	16 50			16 55
Feltham	d		15 46	16 06	15 59					16 16	16 36	16 29			16 33			16 46	17 06	16 59
Ashford (Surrey)	d			16 10	16 03						16 40	16 33			16 37				17 10	17 03
Staines	d		15 53	16 14	16 07					16 23	16 44	16 37			16 41			16 53	17 14	17 07
Wraysbury	d				16 12							16 42								17 12
Sunnymeads	d				16 15							16 45								17 15
Datchet	d				16 19							16 49								17 19
Windsor & Eton Riverside	a				16 24							16 54								17 26
Egham	d		15 57	16 19						16 27	16 49				16 46			16 57	17 19	
Virginia Water	a		16 01	16 23						16 31	16 53				16 50			17 01	17 23	
	d		16 01	16 23						16 31	16 53				16 50			17 01	17 23	
Chertsey	d			16 29							16 59								17 29	
Addlestone	d			16 32							17 02								17 32	
Weybridge	a			16 37							17 07								17 40	
Byfleet & New Haw	d																			
West Byfleet	d																			
Woking	a																			
Longcross	d																			
Sunningdale	d		16 07							16 37					16 55			17 07		
Ascot 3	d	15 53	16 13						16 23	16 43				16 53	17 00			17 13		
Bagshot	d	15 59							16 29					16 59						
Camberley	a	16 05							16 35					17 05						
Frimley	d	16 13							16 43					17 13						
Ash Vale	d	16 19							16 49					17 19						
Aldershot	a	16 24							16 54					17 24						
	d	16 38							17 09					17 38						
Ash 5	d	16 45							17 15					17 45						
Wanborough	d	16 48							17 18					17 48						
Guildford	a	16 55							17 25					17 55						
Martins Heron	d		16 17							16 47					17 04			17 17		
Bracknell	d		16 20							16 50					17 07			17 20		
Wokingham	d		16 27							16 57					17 17			17 27		
Winnersh	d		16 30							17 00								17 30		
Winnersh Triangle	d		16 32							17 02								17 32		
Earley	d		16 35							17 07								17 37		
Reading 7	a		16 43							17 13					17 30			17 45		

London - Hounslow, Richmond, Kingston, Windsor, Weybridge, Ascot, Guildford and Reading

		SW	SW [1]	SW [1]	SW	SW	SW [1]	SW	SW	SW	SW [1]	SW	SW	SW	SW [1]	SW	SW	SW	SW [1]	SW [1]
London Waterloo [15] ⊖	d	16 31		16 35	16 37	16 45	16 50	16 52	16 58	17 01	17 05	17 07	17 13	17 15	17 20	17 22	17 28	17 31		17 35
Vauxhall ⊖	d	16 35		16 39	16 41	16 49		16 56	17 02	17 05	17 09	17 11	17 17	17 19		17 26	17 32	17 35		17 39
Queenstown Rd.(Battersea)	d	16 38			16 44	16 52		16 59		17 08		17 14		17 22		17 29		17 38		
Clapham Junction [10]	d	16 41		16 45	16 47	16 55	16 58	17 02	17 08	17 11	17 15	17 17	17 23	17 25	17 28	17 32	17 38	17 41		17 45
Wandsworth Town	d	16 44			16 50	16 58		17 05		17 14		17 20		17 28		17 35		17 44		
Putney	d	16 47			16 53	17 01		17 08	17 12	17 17		17 23	17 27	17 31		17 38	17 42	17 47		
Barnes	d	16 52			16 57	17 05		17 12		17 22		17 27		17 35		17 42		17 52		
Barnes Bridge	d				16 59			17 14				17 29				17 44				
Chiswick	d				17 02			17 17				17 32				17 47				
Kew Bridge	d				17 05			17 20				17 35				17 50				
Brentford	d				17 08			17 23				17 38				17 53				
Syon Lane	d				17 10			17 25				17 40				17 55				
Isleworth	d				17 12			17 27				17 42				17 57				
Hounslow	d				17 18			17 31				17 48				18 01				
Mortlake	d	16 54				17 07				17 24				17 37				17 54		
North Sheen	d	16 56				17 09				17 26				17 39				17 56		
Richmond ⊖	d	16 59		16 53		17 12	17 06		17 18	17 29	17 23		17 33	17 42	17 36		17 48	17 59		17 53
St Margarets	d	17 01				17 14				17 31				17 44				18 01		
Twickenham	a	17 03		16 57		17 16	17 10		17 21	17 33	17 27		17 37	17 46	17 40		17 51	18 03		17 57
	d	17 04		16 57		17 17	17 10		17 22	17 34	17 27		17 37	17 47	17 40		17 52	18 04		17 57
Strawberry Hill	d	17 07								17 37			17 41					18 07		
Fulwell	a																			
Teddington	a	17 12								17 42			17 46					18 12		
Hampton Wick	a	17 16								17 46			17 54					18 16		
Kingston	a	17 18								17 48			17 56					18 18		
Whitton	d				17 23	17 20			17 25			17 53		17 50			17 55			
Feltham	d			17 03			17 16	17 36	17 29		17 33				17 46	18 06	17 59			18 03
Ashford (Surrey)	d			17 07				17 40	17 33		17 37					18 10	18 03			18 07
Staines	d			17 11			17 23	17 44	17 37		17 41				17 53	18 14	18 07			18 11
Wraysbury	d								17 42								18 12			
Sunnymeads	d								17 45								18 15			
Datchet	d								17 49								18 19			
Windsor & Eton Riverside	a								17 56								18 26			
Egham	d			17 16			17 27	17 49			17 46				17 57	18 19				18 16
Virginia Water	a			17 20			17 31	17 53			17 50				18 01	18 23				18 20
	d			17 20			17 31	17 53			17 50				18 01	18 23				18 20
Chertsey	d							17 59								18 29				
Addlestone	d							18 02								18 32				
Weybridge	a							18 10								18 40				
Byfleet & New Haw	d																			
West Byfleet	d																			
Woking	a																			
Longcross	d			17 23																
Sunningdale	d			17 27			17 37				17 55				18 07					18 25
Ascot [3]	d		17 23	17 31			17 43				18 00				18 13				18 23	18 30
Bagshot	d		17 29								18 06								18 29	
Camberley	a		17 35								18 12								18 35	
Frimley	d		17 43								18 17								18 43	
Ash Vale	d		17 49								18 24								18 49	
Aldershot	a		17 54								18 32								18 54	
	d		18 08																19 08	
Ash [5]	d		18 15																19 15	
Wanborough	d		18 18																19 18	
Guildford	a		18 25																19 25	
Martins Heron	d			17 35			17 47								18 17					18 34
Bracknell	d			17 39			17 50								18 20					18 37
Wokingham	d			17 47			17 57								18 27					18 47
Winnersh	d						18 00								18 30					
Winnersh Triangle	d						18 02								18 32					
Earley	d						18 07								18 37					
Reading [7]	a			18 01			18 15								18 45					19 00

London - Hounslow, Richmond, Kingston, Windsor, Weybridge, Ascot, Guildford and Reading

		SW	SW	SW	SW [1]	SW	SW	SW	SW [1]	SW	SW	SW	SW [1]	SW	SW	SW	SW [1]	SW [1]	SW	SW	SW
London Waterloo [15] ⊖	d	17 37	17 43	17 45	17 50	17 52	17 58	18 01	18 05	18 07	18 13	18 15	18 20	18 22	18 28	18 31		18 35	18 37	18 43	18 45
Vauxhall ⊖	d	17 41	17 47	17 49		17 56	18 02	18 05	18 09	18 11	18 17	18 19		18 26	18 32	18 35		18 39	18 41	18 47	18 49
Queenstown Rd.(Battersea)	d	17 44		17 52		17 59		18 08		18 14		18 22		18 29		18 38			18 44		18 52
Clapham Junction [10]	d	17 47	17 53	17 55	17 58	18 02	18 08	18 11	18 15	18 17	18 23	18 25	18 28	18 32	18 38	18 41		18 45	18 47	18 53	18 55
Wandsworth Town	d	17 50		17 58		18 05		18 14		18 20		18 28		18 35		18 44			18 50		18 58
Putney	d	17 53	17 57	18 01		18 08	18 12	18 17		18 23	18 27	18 31		18 38	18 42	18 47			18 53	18 57	19 01
Barnes	d	17 57		18 05		18 12		18 22		18 27		18 35		18 42		18 52			18 57		19 05
Barnes Bridge	d	17 59				18 14				18 29				18 44					18 59		
Chiswick	d	18 02				18 17				18 32				18 47					19 02		
Kew Bridge	d	18 05				18 20				18 35				18 50					19 05		
Brentford	d	18 08				18 23				18 38				18 53					19 08		
Syon Lane	d	18 10				18 25				18 40				18 55					19 10		
Isleworth	d	18 12				18 27				18 42				18 57					19 12		
Hounslow	d	18 18				18 31				18 48				19 01					19 18		
Mortlake	d			18 07				18 24				18 37				18 54					19 07
North Sheen	d			18 09				18 26				18 39				18 56					19 09
Richmond ⊖	d		18 03	18 12	18 06		18 18	18 29	18 23		18 33	18 42	18 36		18 48	18 59		18 53		19 03	19 12
St Margarets	d			18 14				18 31				18 44				19 01					19 14
Twickenham	a		18 07	18 16	18 10		18 21	18 33	18 27		18 37	18 46	18 40		18 51	19 03		18 57		19 07	19 16
	d		18 07	18 17	18 10		18 22	18 34	18 27		18 37	18 47	18 40		18 52	19 04		18 57		19 07	19 17
Strawberry Hill	d		18 11					18 37			18 41					19 07				19 11	
Fulwell	a		18 13								18 43									19 13	
Teddington	a							18 42								19 12					
Hampton Wick	a							18 46								19 16					
Kingston	a							18 48								19 18					
Whitton	d	18 23		18 20			18 25			18 53		18 50			18 55				19 23		19 20
Feltham	d				18 16	18 36	18 29		18 33				18 46	19 06	18 59			19 03			
Ashford (Surrey)	d					18 40	18 33		18 37					19 10	19 03			19 07			
Staines	d				18 23	18 44	18 37		18 41				18 53	19 14	19 07			19 11			
Wraysbury	d						18 42								19 12						
Sunnymeads	d						18 45								19 15						
Datchet	d						18 49								19 19						
Windsor & Eton Riverside	a						18 56								19 26						
Egham	d				18 27	18 49			18 46				18 57	19 19				19 16			
Virginia Water	a				18 31	18 53			18 50				19 01	19 23				19 20			
	d				18 31	18 53			18 50				19 01	19 23				19 20			
Chertsey	d					18 59								19 29							
Addlestone	d					19 02								19 32							
Weybridge	a					19 10								19 40							
Byfleet & New Haw	d																				
West Byfleet	d																				
Woking	a																				
Longcross	d				18 35																
Sunningdale	d				18 37				18 55				19 07					19 25			
Ascot [3]	d				18 43				19 02				19 13				19 23	19 30			
Bagshot	d								19 08								19 29				
Camberley	a								19 14								19 35				
Frimley	d								19 19								19 43				
Ash Vale	d								19 26								19 49				
Aldershot	a								19 36								19 54				
	d																20 08				
Ash [5]	d																20 15				
Wanborough	d																20 18				
Guildford	a																20 25				
Martins Heron	d				18 47								19 17					19 34			
Bracknell	d				18 50								19 20					19 37			
Wokingham	d				18 57								19 27					19 47			
Winnersh	d				19 00								19 30								
Winnersh Triangle	d				19 02								19 32								
Earley	d				19 07								19 37								
Reading [7]	a				19 15								19 45					20 00			

Table 149

Mondays to Fridays

27 September to 10 December

London - Hounslow, Richmond, Kingston, Windsor, Weybridge, Ascot, Guildford and Reading

		SW 1	SW	SW	SW	SW 1	SW 1	SW	SW	SW 1	SW	SW	SW	SW	SW	SW 1	SW 1	SW	SW	SW
London Waterloo 15	⊖ d	18 50	18 52	18 58	19 01		19 05	19 07	19 15	19 20	19 22	19 28	19 33	19 37	19 45		19 50	19 52	19 58	20 03
Vauxhall	⊖ d		18 56	19 02	19 05		19 09	19 11	19 19		19 26	19 32	19 37	19 41	19 49			19 56	20 02	20 07
Queenstown Rd.(Battersea)	d		18 59		19 08			19 14	19 22		19 29		19 40	19 44	19 52			19 59		20 10
Clapham Junction 10	d	18 58	19 02	19 08	19 11		19 15	19 17	19 25	19 28	19 32	19 38	19 43	19 47	19 55		19 58	20 02	20 08	20 13
Wandsworth Town	d		19 05		19 14			19 20	19 28		19 35		19 46	19 50	19 58			20 05		20 16
Putney	d		19 08	19 12	19 17			19 23	19 31		19 38	19 42	19 49	19 53	20 01			20 08	20 12	20 19
Barnes	d		19 12		19 22			19 27	19 35		19 42		19 52	19 57	20 05			20 12		20 22
Barnes Bridge	d		19 14					19 29			19 44			19 59				20 14		
Chiswick	d		19 17					19 32			19 47			20 02				20 17		
Kew Bridge	d		19 20					19 35			19 50			20 05				20 20		
Brentford	d		19 23					19 38			19 53			20 08				20 23		
Syon Lane	d		19 25					19 40			19 55			20 10				20 25		
Isleworth	d		19 27					19 42			19 57			20 12				20 27		
Hounslow	d		19 31					19 48			20 01			20 18				20 31		
Mortlake	d				19 24				19 37				19 54		20 07					20 24
North Sheen	d				19 26				19 39				19 56		20 09					20 26
Richmond	⊖ d	19 06		19 18	19 29		19 23		19 42	19 36		19 48	19 59		20 12		20 06		20 18	20 29
St Margarets	d				19 31				19 44				20 01		20 14					20 31
Twickenham	a	19 10		19 21	19 33		19 27		19 46	19 40		19 51	20 03		20 16		20 10		20 21	20 33
	d	19 10		19 22	19 34		19 27		19 47	19 40		19 52	20 04		20 17		20 10		20 22	20 34
Strawberry Hill	d				19 37								20 07							20 37
Fulwell	a																			
Teddington	a				19 42								20 10							20 40
Hampton Wick	a				19 46								20 14							20 44
Kingston	a				19 48								20 16							20 46
Whitton	d			19 25				19 53	19 50			19 55		20 23	20 20				20 25	
Feltham	d	19 16	19 36	19 29			19 33			19 46	20 06	19 59					20 16	20 36	20 29	
Ashford (Surrey)	d		19 40	19 33			19 37				20 10	20 03						20 40	20 33	
Staines	d	19 23	19 44	19 37			19 41			19 53	20 14	20 07					20 23	20 44	20 37	
Wraysbury	d			19 42								20 12							20 42	
Sunnymeads	d			19 45								20 15							20 45	
Datchet	d			19 49								20 19							20 49	
Windsor & Eton Riverside	a			19 56								20 24							20 54	
Egham	d	19 27	19 49				19 46			19 57	20 19						20 27	20 49		
Virginia Water	a	19 31	19 53				19 50			20 01	20 23						20 31	20 53		
	d	19 31	19 53				19 50			20 01	20 23						20 31	20 53		
Chertsey	d		19 59								20 29							20 59		
Addlestone	d		20 02								20 32							21 02		
Weybridge	a		20 10								20 37							21 07		
Byfleet & New Haw	d																			
West Byfleet	d																			
Woking	a																			
Longcross	d																			
Sunningdale	d	19 37					19 55			20 07							20 37			
Ascot 3	d	19 43				19 53	20 00			20 13						20 23	20 43			
Bagshot	d					19 59										20 29				
Camberley	a					20 05										20 35				
Frimley	d					20 13										20 43				
Ash Vale	d					20 19										20 49				
Aldershot	a					20 24										20 54				
	d					20 38										21 08				
Ash 5	d					20 45										21 15				
Wanborough	d					20 48										21 18				
Guildford	a					20 55										21 25				
Martins Heron	d	19 47					20 04			20 17							20 47			
Bracknell	d	19 50					20 07			20 20							20 50			
Wokingham	d	19 57					20 17			20 27							20 57			
Winnersh	d	20 00								20 30							21 00			
Winnersh Triangle	d	20 02								20 32							21 02			
Earley	d	20 07								20 37							21 07			
Reading 7	a	20 15					20 28			20 43							21 13			

Table 149

Mondays to Fridays

27 September to 10 December

London - Hounslow, Richmond, Kingston, Windsor, Weybridge, Ascot, Guildford and Reading

		SW	SW	SW 1	SW 1	SW	SW	SW	SW	SW	SW 1	SW 1	SW	SW	SW	SW	SW	SW 1	SW
London Waterloo 15	⊖ d	20 07	20 15		20 20	20 22	20 28	20 33	20 37	20 45		20 50	20 52	20 58	21 03	21 07	21 15	21 20	21 22
Vauxhall	⊖ d	20 11	20 19			20 26	20 32	20 37	20 41	20 49			20 56	21 02	21 07	21 11	21 19		21 26
Queenstown Rd.(Battersea)	d	20 14	20 22			20 29		20 40	20 44	20 52			20 59		21 10	21 14	21 22		21 29
Clapham Junction 10	d	20 17	20 25		20 28	20 32	20 38	20 43	20 47	20 55		20 58	21 02	21 08	21 13	21 17	21 25	21 28	21 32
Wandsworth Town	d	20 20	20 28			20 35		20 46	20 50	20 58			21 05		21 16	21 20	21 28		21 35
Putney	d	20 23	20 31			20 38	20 42	20 49	20 53	21 01			21 08	21 12	21 19	21 23	21 31		21 38
Barnes	d	20 27	20 35			20 42		20 52	20 57	21 05			21 12		21 22	21 27	21 35		21 42
Barnes Bridge	d	20 29				20 44			20 59				21 14			21 29			21 44
Chiswick	d	20 32				20 47			21 02				21 17			21 32			21 47
Kew Bridge	d	20 35				20 50			21 05				21 20			21 35			21 50
Brentford	d	20 38				20 53			21 08				21 23			21 38			21 53
Syon Lane	d	20 40				20 55			21 10				21 25			21 40			21 55
Isleworth	d	20 42				20 57			21 12				21 27			21 42			21 57
Hounslow	d	20 48				21 01			21 18				21 31			21 48			22 01
Mortlake	d		20 37					20 54		21 07					21 24		21 37		
North Sheen	d		20 39					20 56		21 09					21 26		21 39		
Richmond	⊖ d		20 42		20 36		20 48	20 59		21 12		21 06		21 18	21 29		21 42	21 36	
St Margarets	d		20 44					21 01		21 14					21 31		21 44		
Twickenham	a		20 46		20 40		20 51	21 03		21 16		21 10		21 21	21 33		21 46	21 40	
	d		20 47		20 40		20 52	21 04		21 17		21 10		21 22	21 34		21 47	21 40	
Strawberry Hill	d							21 07							21 37				
Fulwell	a																		
Teddington	a							21 10							21 40				
Hampton Wick	a							21 14							21 44				
Kingston	a							21 16							21 46				
Whitton	d	20 53	20 50				20 55		21 23	21 20				21 25		21 53	21 50		
Feltham	d				20 46	21 06	20 59					21 16	21 36	21 29				21 46	22 06
Ashford (Surrey)	d					21 10	21 03						21 40	21 33					22 10
Staines	d				20 53	21 14	21 07					21 23	21 44	21 37				21 53	22 14
Wraysbury	d						21 12							21 42					
Sunnymeads	d						21 15							21 45					
Datchet	d						21 19							21 49					
Windsor & Eton Riverside	a						21 24							21 54					
Egham	d				20 57	21 19						21 27	21 49					21 57	22 19
Virginia Water	a				21 01	21 23						21 31	21 53					22 01	22 23
	d				21 01	21 23						21 31	21 53					22 01	22 23
Chertsey	d					21 29							21 59						22 29
Addlestone	d					21 32							22 02						22 32
Weybridge	a					21 37							22 07						22 37
Byfleet & New Haw	d																		
West Byfleet	d																		
Woking	a																		
Longcross	d																		
Sunningdale	d				21 07							21 37						22 07	
Ascot 3	d			20 53	21 13						21 23	21 43						22 13	
Bagshot	d			20 59							21 29								
Camberley	a			21 05							21 35								
Frimley	d			21 13							21 43								
Ash Vale	d			21 19							21 49								
Aldershot	a			21 24							21 54								
	d			21 38							22 08								
Ash 5	d			21 45							22 15								
Wanborough	d			21 48							22 18								
Guildford	a			21 55							22 25								
Martins Heron	d				21 17							21 47						22 17	
Bracknell	d				21 20							21 50						22 20	
Wokingham	d				21 27							21 57						22 27	
Winnersh	d				21 30							22 00						22 30	
Winnersh Triangle	d				21 32							22 02						22 32	
Earley	d				21 37							22 07						22 37	
Reading 7	a				21 43							22 13						22 43	

Table 149

Mondays to Fridays
27 September to 10 December

London - Hounslow, Richmond, Kingston, Windsor, Weybridge, Ascot, Guildford and Reading

		SW	SW	SW	SW	SW 1	SW 1	SW	SW	SW	SW 1	SW	SW	SW	SW 1	SW 1	SW	SW	SW	SW
London Waterloo 15 ⊖	d	21 28	21 33	21 37	21 45		21 50	21 52	21 58	22 03	22 20	22 22	22 28	22 33		22 50	22 52	22 58	23 03	23 13
Vauxhall ⊖	d	21 32	21 37	21 41	21 49			21 56	22 02	22 07		22 26	22 32	22 37			22 56	23 02	23 07	23 17
Queenstown Rd.(Battersea)	d		21 40	21 44	21 52			21 59		22 10		22 29		22 40			22 59		23 10	
Clapham Junction 10	d	21 38	21 43	21 47	21 55		21 58	22 02	22 08	22 13	22 28	22 32	22 38	22 43		22 58	23 02	23 08	23 13	23 23
Wandsworth Town	d		21 46	21 50	21 58			22 05		22 16		22 35		22 46			23 05		23 16	
Putney	d	21 42	21 49	21 53	22 01			22 08	22 12	22 19		22 38	22 42	22 49			23 08	23 12	23 19	23 27
Barnes	d		21 52	21 57	22 05			22 12		22 22		22 42		22 52			23 12		23 22	
Barnes Bridge	d			21 59				22 14				22 44					23 14			
Chiswick	d			22 02				22 17				22 47					23 17			
Kew Bridge	d			22 05				22 20				22 50					23 20			
Brentford	d			22 08				22 23				22 53					23 23			
Syon Lane	d			22 10				22 25				22 55					23 25			
Isleworth	d			22 12				22 27				22 57					23 27			
Hounslow	d			22 18				22 31				23 01					23 31			
Mortlake	d		21 54		22 07					22 24				22 54					23 24	
North Sheen	d		21 56		22 09					22 26				22 56					23 26	
Richmond ⊖	d	21 48	21 59		22 12		22 06		22 18	22 29	22 36		22 48	22 59		23 06		23 18	23 29	23 33
St Margarets	d		22 01		22 14					22 31				23 01					23 31	
Twickenham	a	21 51	22 03		22 16		22 10		22 21	22 33	22 40		22 51	23 03		23 10		23 21	23 33	23 36
	d	21 52	22 04				22 10		22 22	22 34	22 40		22 52	23 04		23 10		23 22	23 34	23 37
Strawberry Hill	d		22 07							22 37				23 07					23 37	
Fulwell	a																			
Teddington	a		22 10							22 40				23 10					23 40	
Hampton Wick	a		22 14							22 44				23 14					23 44	
Kingston	a		22 16							22 46				23 16					23 46	
Whitton	d	21 55		22 23					22 25				22 55					23 25		23 40
Feltham	d	21 59					22 16	22 36	22 29		22 46	23 06	22 59			23 16	23 36	23 29		23 44
Ashford (Surrey)	d	22 03						22 40	22 33			23 10	23 03				23 40	23 33		23 48
Staines	d	22 07					22 23	22 44	22 37		22 53	23 14	23 07			23 23	23 44	23 37		23 52
Wraysbury	d	22 12							22 42				23 12					23 42		23 57
Sunnymeads	d	22 15							22 45				23 15					23 45		23 59
Datchet	d	22 19							22 49				23 19					23 49		00 04
Windsor & Eton Riverside	a	22 24							22 56				23 24					23 54		00 09
Egham	d						22 27	22 49			22 57	23 19				23 27	23 49			
Virginia Water	a						22 31	22 53			23 01	23 23				23 31	23 53			
	d						22 31	22 53			23 01	23 23				23 31	23 53			
Chertsey	d							22 59				23 29					23 59			
Addlestone	d							23 02				23 32					00 02			
Weybridge	a							23 07				23 37								
Byfleet & New Haw	d																00 06			
West Byfleet	d																00 09			
Woking	a																00 18			
Longcross	d																			
Sunningdale	d						22 37				23 07					23 37				
Ascot 3	d					22 23	22 43				23 13				23 23	23 43				
Bagshot	d					22 29									23 29					
Camberley	a					22 35									23 35					
Frimley	d					22 43									23 43					
Ash Vale	d					22 49									23 49					
Aldershot	a					22 54									23 54					
	d					23 08									23 55					
Ash 5	d					23 15														
Wanborough	d					23 18														
Guildford	a					23 25														
Martins Heron	d						22 47				23 17					23 47				
Bracknell	d						22 50				23 20					23 50				
Wokingham	d						22 57				23 27					23 57				
Winnersh	d						23 00				23 30					23 59				
Winnersh Triangle	d						23 02				23 32					00 02				
Earley	d						23 06				23 37					00 05				
Reading 7	a						23 13				23 43					00 13				

Table 149

Mondays to Fridays
27 September to 10 December

London - Hounslow, Richmond, Kingston, Windsor, Weybridge, Ascot, Guildford and Reading

		SW 1	SW	SW	SW	SW	SW
London Waterloo 15 ⊖	d	23 20	23 22	23 33	23 38	23 52	23 58
Vauxhall ⊖	d		23 26	23 37		23 56	00 02
Queenstown Rd.(Battersea)	d		23 29	23 40		23 59	
Clapham Junction 10	d	23 28	23 32	23 43	23 46	00 02	00 08
Wandsworth Town	d		23 35	23 46		00 05	
Putney	d		23 38	23 49		00 08	00 12
Barnes	d		23 42	23 52		00 12	
Barnes Bridge	d		23 44			00 14	
Chiswick	d		23 47			00 17	
Kew Bridge	d		23 50			00 20	
Brentford	d		23 53			00 23	
Syon Lane	d		23 55			00 25	
Isleworth	d		23 57			00 27	
Hounslow	d		00 01			00 31	
Mortlake	d			23 54			
North Sheen	d			23 56			
Richmond ⊖	d	23 37		23 59	23 54		00 18
St Margarets	d			00 01			
Twickenham	a	23 41		00 03	23 58		00 21
	d	23 41		00 04	23 58		00 22
Strawberry Hill	d			00 07			
Fulwell	a						
Teddington	a			00 10			
Hampton Wick	a			00 14			
Kingston	a			00 16			
Whitton	d						00 25
Feltham	d	23 48	00 06		00 04	00 37	00 29
Ashford (Surrey)	d		00 10			00 41	00 33
Staines	d	23 56	00 14		00 11	00a46	00a37
Wraysbury	d						
Sunnymeads	d						
Datchet	d						
Windsor & Eton Riverside	a						
Egham	d	00 01	00 19		00 15		
Virginia Water	a	00 05	00 23		00 19		
	d	00 05	00 23		00 19		
Chertsey	d		00 29				
Addlestone	d		00 32				
Weybridge	a		00 37				
Byfleet & New Haw	d						
West Byfleet	d						
Woking	a						
Longcross	d						
Sunningdale	d	00 11			00 25		
Ascot 3	d	00 15			00 30		
Bagshot	d						
Camberley	a						
Frimley	d						
Ash Vale	d						
Aldershot	a						
	d						
Ash 5	d						
Wanborough	d						
Guildford	a						
Martins Heron	d	00 19			00 34		
Bracknell	d	00 23			00 37		
Wokingham	d	00 32			00 44		
Winnersh	d	00 36					
Winnersh Triangle	d	00 38					
Earley	d	00 40					
Reading 7	a	00 48			00 55		

Table 149

Saturdays
29 May to 25 September

London - Hounslow, Richmond, Kingston, Windsor, Weybridge, Ascot, Guildford and Reading

		SW 1	SW	SW	SW 1	SW	SW	SW	SW		SW	SW	SW	SW 1	SW 1	SW 1	SW	SW	SW	SW	SW 1	SW	SW	SW	SW
London Waterloo 15 ⊖	d	22p50	22p52	23p13	23p20	23p22	23p33	23p38	23p52		23p58	00 18				05 05				05 33	05 50	05 58	06 03		
Vauxhall ⊖	d		22p56	23p17		23p26	23p37		23p56		00 02	00 22				05 09				05 37		06 02	06 07		
Queenstown Rd.(Battersea)	d		22p59			23p29	23p40		23p59			00 25				05 12				05 40			06 10		
Clapham Junction 10	d	22p58	23p02	23p23	23p28	23p32	23p43	23p46	00 02		00 08	00 28				05 15				05 43	05 58	06 08	06 13		
Wandsworth Town	d		23p05			23p35	23p46		00 05			00 31				05 18				05 46			06 16		
Putney	d		23p08	23p27		23p38	23p49		00 08		00 12	00 34				05 21				05 49		06 12	06 19		
Barnes	d		23p12			23p42	23p52		00 12			00 37				05 24				05 52			06 22		
Barnes Bridge	d		23p14			23p44			00 14																
Chiswick	d		23p17			23p47			00 17																
Kew Bridge	d		23p20			23p50			00 20																
Brentford	d		23p23			23p53			00 23																
Syon Lane	d		23p25			23p55			00 25																
Isleworth	d		23p27			23p57			00 27																
Hounslow	d		23p31			00 01			00 31																
Mortlake	d						23p54					00 39				05 26				05 54			06 24		
North Sheen	d						23p56					00 41				05 28				05 56			06 26		
Richmond ⊖	d	23p06		23p33	23p37		23p59	23p54			00 18	00 44				05 31				05 59	06 06	06 18	06 29		
St Margarets	d						00 01					00 46				05 33				06 01			06 31		
Twickenham	a	23p10		23p36	23p41		00 03	23p58			00 21	00 48				05 35				06 03	06 10	06 21	06 33		
	d	23p10		23p37	23p41		00 04	23p58			00 22	00 49	04 52			05 36	05 38		05 53	06 04	06 10	06 22	06 34		
Strawberry Hill	d						00 07					00s52	04 55							06 07			06 37		
Fulwell	a																								
Teddington	a						00 10					00s55	04 58							06 10			06 40		
Hampton Wick	a						00 14					00s58	05 01							06 14			06 44		
Kingston	a						00 16					01 00	05 03							06 16			06 46		
Whitton	d			23p40							00 25					05 39	05a41		05 56			06 25			
Feltham	d	23p16	23p36	23p44	23p48	00 06		00 04	00 37		00 29					05 43			06 00		06 16	06 29			
Ashford (Surrey)	d		23p40	23p48		00 10			00 41		00 33					05 47			06 04			06 33			
Staines	d	23p23	23p44	23p52	23p56	00 14		00 11	00a46		00a37				05 23	05 53		05 44	06 08		06 23	06 37		06 16	06 44
Wraysbury	d			23p56															06 12			06 41			
Sunnymeads	d			23p59															06 15			06 44			
Datchet	d			00 02															06 18			06 47			
Windsor & Eton Riverside	a			00 06															06 22			06 51			
Egham	d	23p27	23p49		00 01	00 19		00 15							05 27	05 57		05 49			06 27			06 20	06 49
Virginia Water	a	23p31	23p53		00 05	00 23		00 19							05 31	06 01		05 53			06 31			06 25	06 53
	d	23p31	23p53		00 05	00 23		00 19							05 31	06 01		05 53			06 31			06 25	06 53
Chertsey	d		23p59			00 29												05 59						06 30	06 59
Addlestone	d		00 02			00 32												06 02						06 33	07 02
Weybridge	a					00 37												06 07						06 38	07 07
Byfleet & New Haw	d		00 06																						
West Byfleet	d		00 09																						
Woking	a		00 18																						
Longcross	d																								
Sunningdale	d	23p37			00 11			00 25							05 37	06 07					06 37				
Ascot 3	d	23p43			00 15			00 30						00 32	05 43	06 13					06 43				
Bagshot	d													00 38											
Camberley	a													00 44											
Frimley	d													00 48											
Ash Vale	d													00 57											
Aldershot	a													01s02											
	d													01s06											
Ash 5	d																								
Wanborough	d																								
Guildford	a																								
Martins Heron	d	23p47			00 19			00 34							05 47	06 17					06 47				
Bracknell	d	23p50			00 23			00 37							05 50	06 20					06 50				
Wokingham	d	23p57			00 32			00 44							05 57	06 27					06 57				
Winnersh	d	23p59			00 36										06 00	06 30					07 00				
Winnersh Triangle	d	00 01			00 38										06 02	06 32					07 02				
Earley	d	00 05			00 40										06 05	06 35					07 05				
Reading 7	a	00 10			00 45			00 52							06 10	06 40					07 10				

Table 149

Saturdays
29 May to 25 September

London - Hounslow, Richmond, Kingston, Windsor, Weybridge, Ascot, Guildford and Reading

		SW 1	SW 1	SW		SW		SW	SW 1	SW		SW	SW	SW	SW 1	SW 1		SW		SW	SW	SW	SW	SW 1	SW 1
London Waterloo 15 ⊖	d		06 20	06 22		06 28		06 33	06 50	06 52		06 58	07 03	07 15		07 20		07 22		07 28	07 33	07 37	07 45		07 50
Vauxhall ⊖	d			06 26		06 32		06 37		06 56		07 02	07 07	07 19				07 26		07 32	07 37	07 41	07 49		
Queenstown Rd.(Battersea)	d			06 29				06 40		06 59			07 10	07 22				07 29			07 40	07 44	07 52		
Clapham Junction 10	d		06 28	06 32		06 38		06 43	06 58	07 02		07 08	07 13	07 25		07 28		07 32		07 38	07 43	07 47	07 55		07 58
Wandsworth Town	d			06 35				06 46		07 05			07 16	07 28				07 35			07 46	07 50	07 58		
Putney	d			06 38		06 42		06 49		07 08		07 12	07 19	07 31				07 38		07 42	07 49	07 53	08 01		
Barnes	d			06 42				06 52		07 12			07 22	07 35				07 42			07 52	07 57	08 05		
Barnes Bridge	d			06 44						07 14								07 44				07 59			
Chiswick	d			06 47						07 17								07 47				08 02			
Kew Bridge	d			06 50						07 20								07 50				08 05			
Brentford	d			06 53						07 23								07 53				08 08			
Syon Lane	d			06 55						07 25								07 55				08 10			
Isleworth	d			06 57						07 27								07 57				08 12			
Hounslow	d			07 01						07 31								08 01				08 18			
Mortlake	d							06 54					07 24	07 37							07 54		08 07		
North Sheen	d							06 56					07 26	07 39							07 56		08 09		
Richmond ⊖	d		06 36			06 48		06 59	07 06			07 18	07 29	07 42		07 36				07 48	07 59		08 12		08 06
St Margarets	d							07 01					07 31	07 44							08 01		08 14		
Twickenham	a		06 40			06 51		07 03	07 10			07 21	07 33	07 46		07 40				07 51	08 03		08 16		08 10
	d		06 40			06 52		07 04	07 10			07 22	07 34	07 47		07 40				07 52	08 04		08 17		08 10
Strawberry Hill	d							07 07					07 37								08 07				
Fulwell	a																								
Teddington	a							07 10					07 40								08 10				
Hampton Wick	a							07 14					07 44								08 14				
Kingston	a							07 16					07 46								08 16				
Whitton	d					06 55						07 25		07 50						07 55		08 23	08 20		
Feltham	d		06 46	07 06		06 59			07 16	07 36		07 29				07 46		08 06		07 59					08 16
Ashford (Surrey)	d			07 10		07 03				07 40		07 33						08 10		08 03					
Staines	d		06 53	07 14		07 07			07 23	07 44		07 37				07 53		08 14		08 07					08 23
Wraysbury	d					07 11						07 41								08 11					
Sunnymeads	d					07 14						07 44								08 14					
Datchet	d					07 17						07 47								08 17					
Windsor & Eton Riverside	a					07 21						07 51								08 21					
Egham	d		06 57	07 19					07 27	07 49						07 57		08 19							08 27
Virginia Water	a		07 01	07 23					07 31	07 53						08 01		08 23							08 31
	d		07 01	07 23					07 31	07 53						08 01		08 23							08 31
Chertsey	d			07 29						07 59								08 29							
Addlestone	d			07 32						08 02								08 32							
Weybridge	a			07 37						08 07								08 37							
Byfleet & New Haw	d																								
West Byfleet	d																								
Woking	a																								
Longcross	d																								
Sunningdale	d		07 07						07 37							08 07									08 37
Ascot 3	d	06 53	07 13						07 43						07 53	08 13								08 23	08 43
Bagshot	d	06 59													07 59									08 29	
Camberley	a	07 05													08 05									08 35	
Frimley	d	07 13													08 13									08 43	
Ash Vale	d	07 19													08 19									08 49	
Aldershot	a	07 24													08 24									08 54	
	d	07 38													08 38									09 08	
Ash 5	d	07 45													08 45									09 15	
Wanborough	d	07 48													08 48									09 18	
Guildford	a	07 55													08 55									09 25	
Martins Heron	d		07 17						07 47							08 17									08 47
Bracknell	d		07 20						07 50							08 20									08 50
Wokingham	d		07 27						07 57							08 27									08 57
Winnersh	d		07 30						08 00							08 30									09 00
Winnersh Triangle	d		07 32						08 02							08 32									09 02
Earley	d		07 35						08 05							08 35									09 05
Reading 7	a		07 40						08 10							08 40									09 10

Table 149

Saturdays

29 May to 25 September

London - Hounslow, Richmond, Kingston, Windsor, Weybridge, Ascot, Guildford and Reading

		SW	SW	SW	SW	SW	SW 1	SW 1	SW	SW	SW	SW	SW	SW 1	SW 1	SW	SW	SW	SW
London Waterloo 15 ⊖	d	07 52	07 58	08 03	08 07	08 15		08 20	08 22	08 28	08 33	08 37	08 45		08 50	08 52	08 58	09 03	09 07
Vauxhall ⊖	d	07 56	08 02	08 07	08 11	08 19			08 26	08 32	08 37	08 41	08 49			08 56	09 02	09 07	09 11
Queenstown Rd.(Battersea)	d	07 59		08 10	08 14	08 22			08 29		08 40	08 44	08 52			08 59		09 10	09 14
Clapham Junction 10	d	08 02	08 08	08 13	08 17	08 25		08 28	08 32	08 38	08 43	08 47	08 55		08 58	09 02	09 08	09 13	09 17
Wandsworth Town	d	08 05		08 16	08 20	08 28			08 35		08 46	08 50	08 58			09 05		09 16	09 20
Putney	d	08 08	08 12	08 19	08 23	08 31			08 38	08 42	08 49	08 53	09 01			09 08	09 12	09 19	09 23
Barnes	d	08 12		08 22	08 27	08 35			08 42		08 52	08 57	09 05			09 12		09 22	09 27
Barnes Bridge	d	08 14			08 29				08 44			08 59				09 14			09 29
Chiswick	d	08 17			08 32				08 47			09 02				09 17			09 32
Kew Bridge	d	08 20			08 35				08 50			09 05				09 20			09 35
Brentford	d	08 23			08 38				08 53			09 08				09 23			09 38
Syon Lane	d	08 25			08 40				08 55			09 10				09 25			09 40
Isleworth	d	08 27			08 42				08 57			09 12				09 27			09 42
Hounslow	d	08 31			08 48				09 01			09 18				09 31			09 48
Mortlake	d			08 24		08 37					08 54		09 07					09 24	
North Sheen	d			08 26		08 39					08 56		09 09					09 26	
Richmond ⊖	d		08 18	08 29		08 42		08 36		08 48	08 59		09 12		09 06		09 18	09 29	
St Margarets	d			08 31		08 44					09 01		09 14					09 31	
Twickenham	a		08 21	08 33		08 46		08 40		08 51	09 03		09 16		09 10		09 21	09 33	
	d		08 22	08 34		08 47		08 40		08 52	09 04		09 17		09 10		09 22	09 34	
Strawberry Hill	d			08 37							09 07							09 37	
Fulwell	a																		
Teddington	a			08 40							09 10							09 40	
Hampton Wick	a			08 44							09 14							09 44	
Kingston	a			08 46							09 16							09 46	
Whitton	d		08 25		08 53	08 50				08 55		09 23	09 20				09 25		09 53
Feltham	d	08 36	08 29					08 46	09 06	08 59					09 16	09 36	09 29		
Ashford (Surrey)	d	08 40	08 33						09 10	09 03						09 40	09 33		
Staines	d	08 44	08 37					08 53	09 14	09 07					09 23	09 44	09 37		
Wraysbury	d		08 41							09 11							09 41		
Sunnymeads	d		08 44							09 14							09 44		
Datchet	d		08 47							09 17							09 47		
Windsor & Eton Riverside	a		08 51							09 21							09 51		
Egham	d	08 49						08 57	09 19						09 27	09 49			
Virginia Water	a	08 53						09 01	09 23						09 31	09 53			
	d	08 53						09 01	09 23						09 31	09 53			
Chertsey	d	08 59							09 29							09 59			
Addlestone	d	09 02							09 32							10 02			
Weybridge	a	09 07							09 37							10 07			
Byfleet & New Haw	d																		
West Byfleet	d																		
Woking	a																		
Longcross	d																		
Sunningdale	d							09 07							09 37				
Ascot 3	d						08 53	09 13						09 23	09 43				
Bagshot	d						08 59							09 29					
Camberley	a						09 05							09 35					
Frimley	d						09 13							09 43					
Ash Vale	d						09 19							09 49					
Aldershot	a						09 24							09 54					
	d						09 38							10 08					
Ash 5	d						09 45							10 15					
Wanborough	d						09 48							10 18					
Guildford	a						09 55							10 25					
Martins Heron	d							09 17							09 47				
Bracknell	d							09 20							09 50				
Wokingham	d							09 27							09 57				
Winnersh	d							09 30							10 00				
Winnersh Triangle	d							09 32							10 02				
Earley	d							09 35							10 05				
Reading 7	a							09 40							10 10				

Table 149

Saturdays

29 May to 25 September

London - Hounslow, Richmond, Kingston, Windsor, Weybridge, Ascot, Guildford and Reading

		SW	SW 1	SW 1	SW	SW	SW	SW	SW	SW 1	SW 1	SW	SW	SW	SW	SW	SW 1	SW 1	SW	SW
London Waterloo 15 ⊖	d	09 15		09 20	09 22	09 28	09 33	09 37	09 45		09 50	09 52	09 58	10 03	10 07	10 15		10 20	10 22	10 28
Vauxhall ⊖	d	09 19			09 26	09 32	09 37	09 41	09 49			09 56	10 02	10 07	10 11	10 19			10 26	10 32
Queenstown Rd.(Battersea)	d	09 22			09 29		09 40	09 44	09 52			09 59		10 10	10 14	10 22			10 29	
Clapham Junction 10	d	09 25		09 28	09 32	09 38	09 43	09 47	09 55		09 58	10 02	10 08	10 13	10 17	10 25		10 28	10 32	10 38
Wandsworth Town	d	09 28			09 35		09 46	09 50	09 58			10 05		10 16	10 20	10 28			10 35	
Putney	d	09 31			09 38	09 42	09 49	09 53	10 01			10 08	10 12	10 19	10 23	10 31			10 38	10 42
Barnes	d	09 35			09 42		09 52	09 57	10 05			10 12		10 22	10 27	10 35			10 42	
Barnes Bridge	d				09 44			09 59				10 14			10 29				10 44	
Chiswick	d				09 47			10 02				10 17			10 32				10 47	
Kew Bridge	d				09 50			10 05				10 20			10 35				10 50	
Brentford	d				09 53			10 08				10 23			10 38				10 53	
Syon Lane	d				09 55			10 10				10 25			10 40				10 55	
Isleworth	d				09 57			10 12				10 27			10 42				10 57	
Hounslow	d				10 01			10 18				10 31			10 48				11 01	
Mortlake	d	09 37					09 54		10 07					10 24		10 37				
North Sheen	d	09 39					09 56		10 09					10 26		10 39				
Richmond ⊖	d	09 42		09 36		09 48	09 59		10 12		10 06		10 18	10 29		10 42		10 36		10 48
St Margarets	d	09 44					10 01		10 14					10 31		10 44				
Twickenham	a	09 46		09 40		09 51	10 03		10 16		10 10		10 21	10 33		10 46		10 40		10 51
	d	09 47		09 40		09 52	10 04		10 17		10 10		10 22	10 34		10 47		10 40		10 52
Strawberry Hill	d						10 07							10 37						
Fulwell	a																			
Teddington	a						10 10							10 40						
Hampton Wick	a						10 14							10 44						
Kingston	a						10 16							10 46						
Whitton	d	09 50				09 55		10 23	10 20				10 25		10 53	10 50				10 55
Feltham	d			09 46	10 06	09 59					10 16	10 36	10 29					10 46	11 06	10 59
Ashford (Surrey)	d				10 10	10 03						10 40	10 33						11 10	11 03
Staines	d			09 53	10 14	10 07					10 23	10 44	10 37					10 53	11 14	11 07
Wraysbury	d					10 11							10 41							11 11
Sunnymeads	d					10 14							10 44							11 14
Datchet	d					10 17							10 47							11 17
Windsor & Eton Riverside	a					10 21							10 51							11 21
Egham	d			09 57	10 19						10 27	10 49						10 57	11 19	
Virginia Water	a			10 01	10 23						10 31	10 53						11 01	11 23	
	d			10 01	10 23						10 31	10 53						11 01	11 23	
Chertsey	d				10 29							10 59							11 29	
Addlestone	d				10 32							11 02							11 32	
Weybridge	a				10 37							11 07							11 37	
Byfleet & New Haw	d																			
West Byfleet	d																			
Woking	a																			
Longcross	d																			
Sunningdale	d			10 07							10 37							11 07		
Ascot 3	d		09 53	10 13						10 23	10 43						10 53	11 13		
Bagshot	d		09 59							10 29							10 59			
Camberley	a		10 05							10 35							11 05			
Frimley	d		10 13							10 43							11 13			
Ash Vale	d		10 19							10 49							11 19			
Aldershot	a		10 24							10 54							11 24			
	d		10 38							11 08							11 38			
Ash 5	d		10 45							11 15							11 45			
Wanborough	d		10 48							11 18							11 48			
Guildford	a		10 55							11 25							11 55			
Martins Heron	d			10 17							10 47							11 17		
Bracknell	d			10 20							10 50							11 20		
Wokingham	d			10 27							10 57							11 27		
Winnersh	d			10 30							11 00							11 30		
Winnersh Triangle	d			10 32							11 02							11 32		
Earley	d			10 35							11 05							11 35		
Reading 7	a			10 40							11 10							11 40		

Table 149

Saturdays
29 May to 25 September

London - Hounslow, Richmond, Kingston, Windsor, Weybridge, Ascot, Guildford and Reading

Station		SW	SW	SW	SW ■1	SW ■1	SW	SW	SW	SW	SW	SW ■1	SW ■1	SW	SW	SW	SW	SW	SW ■1	SW ■1
London Waterloo [15] ⊖	d	10 33	10 37	10 45		10 50	10 52	10 58	11 03	11 07	11 15		11 20	11 22	11 28	11 33	11 37	11 45		11 50
Vauxhall ⊖	d	10 37	10 41	10 49			10 56	11 02	11 07	11 11	11 19			11 26	11 32	11 37	11 41	11 49		
Queenstown Rd.(Battersea)	d	10 40	10 44	10 52			10 59		11 10	11 14	11 22			11 29		11 40	11 44	11 52		
Clapham Junction [10]	d	10 43	10 47	10 55		10 58	11 02	11 08	11 13	11 17	11 25		11 28	11 32	11 38	11 43	11 47	11 55		11 58
Wandsworth Town	d	10 46	10 50	10 58			11 05		11 16	11 20	11 28			11 35		11 46	11 50	11 58		
Putney	d	10 49	10 53	11 01			11 08	11 12	11 19	11 23	11 31			11 38	11 42	11 49	11 53	12 01		
Barnes	d	10 52	10 57	11 05			11 12		11 22	11 27	11 35			11 42		11 52	11 57	12 05		
Barnes Bridge	d		10 59				11 14			11 29				11 44			11 59			
Chiswick	d		11 02				11 17			11 32				11 47			12 02			
Kew Bridge	d		11 05				11 20			11 35				11 50			12 05			
Brentford	d		11 08				11 23			11 38				11 53			12 08			
Syon Lane	d		11 10				11 25			11 40				11 55			12 10			
Isleworth	d		11 12				11 27			11 42				11 57			12 12			
Hounslow	d		11 18				11 31			11 48				12 01			12 18			
Mortlake	d	10 54		11 07					11 24		11 37					11 54		12 07		
North Sheen	d	10 56		11 09					11 26		11 39					11 56		12 09		
Richmond ⊖	d	10 59		11 12		11 06		11 18	11 29		11 42		11 36		11 48	11 59		12 12		12 06
St Margarets	d	11 01		11 14					11 31		11 44					12 01		12 14		
Twickenham	a	11 03		11 16		11 10		11 21	11 33		11 46		11 40		11 51	12 03		12 16		12 10
	d	11 04		11 17		11 10		11 22	11 34		11 47		11 40		11 52	12 04		12 17		12 10
Strawberry Hill	d	11 07							11 37							12 07				
Fulwell	a																			
Teddington	a	11 10							11 40							12 10				
Hampton Wick	a	11 14							11 44							12 14				
Kingston	a	11 16							11 46							12 16				
Whitton	d		11 23	11 20				11 25		11 53	11 50				11 55		12 23	12 20		
Feltham	d					11 16	11 36	11 29					11 46	12 06	11 59					12 16
Ashford (Surrey)	d						11 40	11 33						12 10	12 03					
Staines	d					11 23	11 44	11 37					11 53	12 14	12 07					12 23
Wraysbury	d							11 41							12 11					
Sunnymeads	d							11 44							12 14					
Datchet	d							11 47							12 17					
Windsor & Eton Riverside	a							11 51							12 21					
Egham	d					11 27	11 49						11 57	12 19						12 27
Virginia Water	a					11 31	11 53						12 01	12 23						12 31
	d					11 31	11 53						12 01	12 23						12 31
Chertsey	d						11 59							12 29						
Addlestone	d						12 02							12 32						
Weybridge	a						12 07							12 37						
Byfleet & New Haw	d																			
West Byfleet	d																			
Woking	a																			
Longcross	d																			
Sunningdale	d					11 37							12 07							12 37
Ascot [3]	d				11 23	11 43						11 53	12 13						12 23	12 43
Bagshot	d				11 29							11 59							12 29	
Camberley	a				11 35							12 05							12 35	
Frimley	d				11 43							12 13							12 43	
Ash Vale	d				11 49							12 19							12 49	
Aldershot	a				11 54							12 24							12 54	
	d				12 08							12 38							13 08	
Ash [5]	d				12 15							12 45							13 15	
Wanborough	d				12 18							12 48							13 18	
Guildford	a				12 25							12 55							13 25	
Martins Heron	d					11 47							12 17							12 47
Bracknell	d					11 50							12 20							12 50
Wokingham	d					11 57							12 27							12 57
Winnersh	d					12 00							12 30							13 00
Winnersh Triangle	d					12 02							12 32							13 02
Earley	d					12 05							12 35							13 05
Reading [7]	a					12 10							12 40							13 10

Table 149

Saturdays
29 May to 25 September

London - Hounslow, Richmond, Kingston, Windsor, Weybridge, Ascot, Guildford and Reading

Station		SW	SW	SW	SW	SW	SW ■1	SW ■1	SW	SW	SW	SW	SW	SW ■1	SW ■1	SW	SW	SW	SW	SW
London Waterloo [15] ⊖	d	11 52	11 58	12 03	12 07	12 15		12 20	12 22	12 28	12 33	12 37	12 45		12 50	12 52	12 58	13 03	13 07	13 15
Vauxhall ⊖	d	11 56	12 02	12 07	12 11	12 19			12 26	12 32	12 37	12 41	12 49			12 56	13 02	13 07	13 11	13 19
Queenstown Rd.(Battersea)	d	11 59		12 10	12 14	12 22			12 29		12 40	12 44	12 52			12 59		13 10	13 14	13 22
Clapham Junction [10]	d	12 02	12 08	12 13	12 17	12 25		12 28	12 32	12 38	12 43	12 47	12 55		12 58	13 02	13 08	13 13	13 17	13 25
Wandsworth Town	d	12 05		12 16	12 20	12 28			12 35		12 46	12 50	12 58			13 05		13 16	13 20	13 28
Putney	d	12 08	12 12	12 19	12 23	12 31			12 38	12 42	12 49	12 53	13 01			13 08	13 12	13 19	13 23	13 31
Barnes	d	12 12		12 22	12 27	12 35			12 42		12 52	12 57	13 05			13 12		13 22	13 27	13 35
Barnes Bridge	d	12 14			12 29				12 44			12 59				13 14			13 29	
Chiswick	d	12 17			12 32				12 47			13 02				13 17			13 32	
Kew Bridge	d	12 20			12 35				12 50			13 05				13 20			13 35	
Brentford	d	12 23			12 38				12 53			13 08				13 23			13 38	
Syon Lane	d	12 25			12 40				12 55			13 10				13 25			13 40	
Isleworth	d	12 27			12 42				12 57			13 12				13 27			13 42	
Hounslow	d	12 31			12 48				13 01			13 18				13 31			13 48	
Mortlake	d			12 24		12 37					12 54		13 07					13 24		13 37
North Sheen	d			12 26		12 39					12 56		13 09					13 26		13 39
Richmond ⊖	d		12 18	12 29		12 42		12 36		12 48	12 59		13 12		13 06		13 18	13 29		13 42
St Margarets	d			12 31		12 44					13 01		13 14					13 31		13 44
Twickenham	a		12 21	12 33		12 46		12 40		12 51	13 03		13 16		13 10		13 21	13 33		13 46
	d		12 22	12 34		12 47		12 40		12 52	13 04		13 17		13 10		13 22	13 34		13 47
Strawberry Hill	d			12 37							13 07							13 37		
Fulwell	a																			
Teddington	a			12 40							13 10							13 40		
Hampton Wick	a			12 44							13 14							13 44		
Kingston	a			12 46							13 16							13 46		
Whitton	d		12 25		12 53	12 50				12 55		13 23	13 20				13 25		13 53	13 50
Feltham	d	12 36	12 29					12 46	13 06	12 59					13 16	13 36	13 29			
Ashford (Surrey)	d	12 40	12 33						13 10	13 03						13 40	13 33			
Staines	d	12 44	12 37					12 53	13 14	13 07					13 23	13 44	13 37			
Wraysbury	d		12 41							13 11							13 41			
Sunnymeads	d		12 44							13 14							13 44			
Datchet	d		12 47							13 17							13 47			
Windsor & Eton Riverside	a		12 51							13 21							13 51			
Egham	d	12 49						12 57	13 19						13 27	13 49				
Virginia Water	a	12 53						13 01	13 23						13 31	13 53				
	d	12 53						13 01	13 23						13 31	13 53				
Chertsey	d	12 59							13 29							13 59				
Addlestone	d	13 02							13 32							14 02				
Weybridge	a	13 07							13 37							14 07				
Byfleet & New Haw	d																			
West Byfleet	d																			
Woking	a																			
Longcross	d																			
Sunningdale	d							13 07							13 37					
Ascot [3]	d						12 53	13 13						13 23	13 43					
Bagshot	d						12 59							13 29						
Camberley	a						13 05							13 35						
Frimley	d						13 13							13 43						
Ash Vale	d						13 19							13 49						
Aldershot	a						13 24							13 54						
	d						13 38							14 08						
Ash [5]	d						13 45							14 15						
Wanborough	d						13 48							14 18						
Guildford	a						13 55							14 25						
Martins Heron	d							13 17							13 47					
Bracknell	d							13 20							13 50					
Wokingham	d							13 27							13 57					
Winnersh	d							13 30							14 00					
Winnersh Triangle	d							13 32							14 02					
Earley	d							13 35							14 05					
Reading [7]	a							13 40							14 10					

Table 149

Saturdays

29 May to 25 September

London - Hounslow, Richmond, Kingston, Windsor, Weybridge, Ascot, Guildford and Reading

		SW 1	SW 1	SW	SW	SW	SW	SW	SW 1	SW 1	SW	SW	SW	SW	SW	SW 1	SW 1	SW	SW	SW
London Waterloo 15 ⊖	d		13 20	13 22	13 28	13 33	13 37	13 45		13 50	13 52	13 58	14 03	14 07	14 15		14 20	14 22	14 28	14 33
Vauxhall ⊖	d			13 26	13 32	13 37	13 41	13 49			13 56	14 02	14 07	14 11	14 19			14 26	14 32	14 37
Queenstown Rd.(Battersea)	d			13 29		13 40	13 44	13 52			13 59		14 10	14 14	14 22			14 29		14 40
Clapham Junction 10	d		13 28	13 32	13 38	13 43	13 47	13 55		13 58	14 02	14 08	14 13	14 17	14 25		14 28	14 32	14 38	14 43
Wandsworth Town	d			13 35		13 46	13 50	13 58			14 05		14 16	14 20	14 28			14 35		14 46
Putney	d			13 38	13 42	13 49	13 53	14 01			14 08	14 12	14 19	14 23	14 31			14 38	14 42	14 49
Barnes	d			13 42		13 52	13 57	14 05			14 12		14 22	14 27	14 35			14 42		14 52
Barnes Bridge	d			13 44			13 59				14 14			14 29				14 44		
Chiswick	d			13 47			14 02				14 17			14 32				14 47		
Kew Bridge	d			13 50			14 05				14 20			14 35				14 50		
Brentford	d			13 53			14 08				14 23			14 38				14 53		
Syon Lane	d			13 55			14 10				14 25			14 40				14 55		
Isleworth	d			13 57			14 12				14 27			14 42				14 57		
Hounslow	d			14 01			14 18				14 31			14 48				15 01		
Mortlake	d					13 54		14 07					14 24		14 37					14 54
North Sheen	d					13 56		14 09					14 26		14 39					14 56
Richmond ⊖	d		13 36		13 48	13 59		14 12		14 06		14 18	14 29		14 42		14 36		14 48	14 59
St Margarets	d					14 01		14 14					14 31		14 44					15 01
Twickenham	a		13 40		13 51	14 03		14 16		14 10		14 21	14 33		14 46		14 40		14 51	15 03
	d		13 40		13 52	14 04		14 17		14 10		14 22	14 34		14 47		14 40		14 52	15 04
Strawberry Hill	d					14 07							14 37							15 07
Fulwell	a																			
Teddington	a					14 10							14 40							15 10
Hampton Wick	a					14 14							14 44							15 14
Kingston	a					14 16							14 46							15 16
Whitton	d				13 55		14 23	14 20				14 25		14 53	14 50				14 55	
Feltham	d		13 46	14 06	13 59					14 16	14 36	14 29					14 46	15 06	14 59	
Ashford (Surrey)	d			14 10	14 03						14 40	14 33						15 10	15 03	
Staines	d		13 53	14 14	14 07					14 23	14 44	14 37					14 53	15 14	15 07	
Wraysbury	d				14 11							14 41							15 11	
Sunnymeads	d				14 14							14 44							15 14	
Datchet	d				14 17							14 47							15 17	
Windsor & Eton Riverside	a				14 21							14 51							15 22	
Egham	d		13 57	14 19						14 27	14 49						14 57	15 19		
Virginia Water	a		14 01	14 23						14 31	14 53						15 01	15 23		
	d		14 01	14 23						14 31	14 53						15 01	15 23		
Chertsey	d			14 29							14 59							15 29		
Addlestone	d			14 32							15 02							15 32		
Weybridge	a			14 37							15 07							15 37		
Byfleet & New Haw	d																			
West Byfleet	d																			
Woking	a																			
Longcross	d																			
Sunningdale	d		14 07							14 37							15 07			
Ascot 3	d	13 53	14 13						14 23	14 43						14 53	15 13			
Bagshot	d	13 59							14 29							14 59				
Camberley	a	14 05							14 35							15 05				
Frimley	d	14 13							14 43							15 13				
Ash Vale	d	14 19							14 49							15 19				
Aldershot	a	14 24							14 54							15 24				
	d	14 38							15 08							15 38				
Ash 5	d	14 45							15 15							15 45				
Wanborough	d	14 48							15 18							15 48				
Guildford	a	14 55							15 25							15 55				
Martins Heron	d		14 17							14 47							15 17			
Bracknell	d		14 20							14 50							15 20			
Wokingham	d		14 27							14 57							15 27			
Winnersh	d		14 30							15 00							15 30			
Winnersh Triangle	d		14 32							15 02							15 32			
Earley	d		14 35							15 05							15 35			
Reading 7	a		14 40							15 10							15 40			

Table 149

Saturdays

29 May to 25 September

London - Hounslow, Richmond, Kingston, Windsor, Weybridge, Ascot, Guildford and Reading

		SW	SW	SW 1	SW 1	SW	SW	SW	SW	SW	SW 1	SW 1	SW	SW	SW	SW	SW	SW 1	SW 1	SW
London Waterloo 15 ⊖	d	14 37	14 45		14 50	14 52	14 58	15 03	15 07	15 15		15 20	15 22	15 28	15 33	15 37	15 45		15 50	15 52
Vauxhall ⊖	d	14 41	14 49			14 56	15 02	15 07	15 11	15 19			15 26	15 32	15 37	15 41	15 49			15 56
Queenstown Rd.(Battersea)	d	14 44	14 52			14 59		15 10	15 14	15 22			15 29		15 40	15 44	15 52			15 59
Clapham Junction 10	d	14 47	14 55		14 58	15 02	15 08	15 13	15 17	15 25		15 28	15 32	15 38	15 43	15 47	15 55		15 58	16 02
Wandsworth Town	d	14 50	14 58			15 05		15 16	15 20	15 28			15 35		15 46	15 50	15 58			16 05
Putney	d	14 53	15 01			15 08	15 12	15 19	15 23	15 31			15 38	15 42	15 49	15 53	16 01			16 08
Barnes	d	14 57	15 05			15 12		15 22	15 27	15 35			15 42		15 52	15 57	16 05			16 12
Barnes Bridge	d	14 59				15 14			15 29				15 44			15 59				16 14
Chiswick	d	15 02				15 17			15 32				15 47			16 02				16 17
Kew Bridge	d	15 05				15 20			15 35				15 50			16 05				16 20
Brentford	d	15 08				15 23			15 38				15 53			16 08				16 23
Syon Lane	d	15 10				15 25			15 40				15 55			16 10				16 25
Isleworth	d	15 12				15 27			15 42				15 57			16 12				16 27
Hounslow	d	15 18				15 31			15 48				16 01			16 18				16 31
Mortlake	d		15 07					15 24		15 37					15 54		16 07			
North Sheen	d		15 09					15 26		15 39					15 56		16 09			
Richmond ⊖	d		15 12		15 06		15 18	15 29		15 42		15 36		15 48	15 59		16 12		16 06	
St Margarets	d		15 14					15 31		15 44					16 01		16 14			
Twickenham	a		15 16		15 10		15 21	15 33		15 46		15 40		15 51	16 03		16 16		16 10	
	d		15 17		15 10		15 22	15 34		15 47		15 40		15 52	16 04		16 17		16 10	
Strawberry Hill	d							15 37							16 07					
Fulwell	a																			
Teddington	a							15 40							16 10					
Hampton Wick	a							15 44							16 14					
Kingston	a							15 46							16 16					
Whitton	d	15 23	15 20				15 25		15 53	15 50				15 55		16 23	16 20			
Feltham	d				15 16	15 36	15 29					15 46	16 06	15 59					16 16	16 36
Ashford (Surrey)	d					15 40	15 33						16 10	16 03						16 40
Staines	d				15 23	15 44	15 37					15 53	16 14	16 07					16 23	16 44
Wraysbury	d						15 41							16 11						
Sunnymeads	d						15 44							16 14						
Datchet	d						15 47							16 17						
Windsor & Eton Riverside	a						15 51							16 21						
Egham	d				15 27	15 49						15 57	16 19						16 27	16 49
Virginia Water	a				15 31	15 53						16 01	16 23						16 31	16 53
	d				15 31	15 53						16 01	16 23						16 31	16 53
Chertsey	d					15 59							16 29							16 59
Addlestone	d					16 02							16 32							17 02
Weybridge	a					16 07							16 42							17 07
Byfleet & New Haw	d																			
West Byfleet	d																			
Woking	a																			
Longcross	d																			
Sunningdale	d				15 37							16 07							16 37	
Ascot 3	d			15 23	15 43						15 53	16 13						16 23	16 43	
Bagshot	d			15 29							15 59							16 29		
Camberley	a			15 35							16 05							16 35		
Frimley	d			15 43							16 13							16 43		
Ash Vale	d			15 49							16 19							16 49		
Aldershot	a			15 54							16 24							16 54		
	d			16 08							16 38							17 08		
Ash 5	d			16 15							16 45							17 15		
Wanborough	d			16 18							16 48							17 18		
Guildford	a			16 25							16 55							17 25		
Martins Heron	d				15 47							16 17							16 47	
Bracknell	d				15 50							16 20							16 50	
Wokingham	d				15 57							16 27							16 57	
Winnersh	d				16 00							16 30							17 00	
Winnersh Triangle	d				16 02							16 32							17 02	
Earley	d				16 05							16 35							17 05	
Reading 7	a				16 10							16 40							17 10	

Table 149

Saturdays
29 May to 25 September

London - Hounslow, Richmond, Kingston, Windsor, Weybridge, Ascot, Guildford and Reading

		SW	SW	SW	SW	SW ■1	SW ■1	SW	SW	SW	SW	SW	SW ■1	SW ■1	SW	SW	SW	SW	SW	SW ■1
London Waterloo ■15 ⊖	d	15 58	16 03	16 07	16 15		16 20	16 22	16 28	16 33	16 37	16 45		16 50	16 52	16 58	17 03	17 07	17 15	
Vauxhall ⊖	d	16 02	16 07	16 11	16 19			16 26	16 32	16 37	16 41	16 49			16 56	17 02	17 07	17 11	17 19	
Queenstown Rd.(Battersea)	d		16 10	16 14	16 22			16 29		16 40	16 44	16 52			16 59		17 10	17 14	17 22	
Clapham Junction ■10	d	16 08	16 13	16 17	16 25		16 28	16 32	16 38	16 43	16 47	16 55		16 58	17 02	17 08	17 13	17 17	17 25	
Wandsworth Town	d		16 16	16 20	16 28			16 35		16 46	16 50	16 58			17 05		17 16	17 20	17 28	
Putney	d	16 12	16 19	16 23	16 31			16 38	16 42	16 49	16 53	17 01			17 08	17 12	17 19	17 23	17 31	
Barnes	d		16 22	16 27	16 35			16 42		16 52	16 57	17 05			17 12		17 22	17 27	17 35	
Barnes Bridge	d			16 29				16 44			16 59				17 14			17 29		
Chiswick	d			16 32				16 47			17 02				17 17			17 32		
Kew Bridge	d			16 35				16 50			17 05				17 20			17 35		
Brentford	d			16 38				16 53			17 08				17 23			17 38		
Syon Lane	d			16 40				16 55			17 10				17 25			17 40		
Isleworth	d			16 42				16 57			17 12				17 27			17 42		
Hounslow	d			16 48				17 01			17 18				17 31			17 48		
Mortlake	d		16 24		16 37					16 54		17 07					17 24		17 37	
North Sheen	d		16 26		16 39					16 56		17 09					17 26		17 39	
Richmond ⊖	d	16 18	16 29		16 42		16 36		16 48	16 59		17 12		17 06		17 18	17 29		17 42	
St Margarets	d		16 31		16 44					17 01		17 14					17 31		17 44	
Twickenham	a	16 21	16 33		16 46		16 40		16 51	17 03		17 16		17 10		17 21	17 33		17 46	
	d	16 22	16 34		16 47		16 40		16 52	17 04		17 17		17 10		17 22	17 34		17 47	
Strawberry Hill	d		16 37							17 07							17 37			
Fulwell	a																			
Teddington	a		16 40							17 10							17 40			
Hampton Wick	a		16 44							17 14							17 44			
Kingston	a		16 46							17 16							17 46			
Whitton	d	16 25		16 53	16 50				16 55		17 23	17 20				17 25		17 53	17 50	
Feltham	d	16 29					16 46	17 06	16 59					17 16	17 36	17 29				
Ashford (Surrey)	d	16 33						17 10	17 03						17 40	17 33				
Staines	d	16 37					16 53	17 14	17 07					17 23	17 44	17 37				
Wraysbury	d	16 41							17 11							17 41				
Sunnymeads	d	16 44							17 14							17 44				
Datchet	d	16 47							17 17							17 47				
Windsor & Eton Riverside	a	16 51							17 21							17 51				
Egham	d						16 57	17 19						17 27	17 49					
Virginia Water	a						17 01	17 23						17 31	17 53					
	d						17 01	17 23						17 31	17 53					
Chertsey	d							17 29							17 59					
Addlestone	d							17 32							18 02					
Weybridge	a							17 37							18 07					
Byfleet & New Haw	d																			
West Byfleet	d																			
Woking	a																			
Longcross	d																			
Sunningdale	d						17 07							17 37						
Ascot ■3	d					16 53	17 13						17 23	17 43						17 53
Bagshot	d					16 59							17 29							17 59
Camberley	a					17 05							17 35							18 05
Frimley	d					17 13							17 43							18 13
Ash Vale	d					17 19							17 49							18 19
Aldershot	a					17 24							17 54							18 24
	d					17 38							18 08							18 38
Ash ■5	d					17 45							18 15							18 45
Wanborough	d					17 48							18 18							18 48
Guildford	a					17 55							18 25							18 55
Martins Heron	d						17 17							17 47						
Bracknell	d						17 20							17 50						
Wokingham	d						17 27							17 57						
Winnersh	d						17 30							18 00						
Winnersh Triangle	d						17 32							18 02						
Earley	d						17 35							18 05						
Reading ■7	a						17 40							18 10						

Table 149

Saturdays
29 May to 25 September

London - Hounslow, Richmond, Kingston, Windsor, Weybridge, Ascot, Guildford and Reading

		SW ■1	SW	SW	SW	SW	SW	SW ■1	SW ■1	SW	SW	SW	SW	SW	SW ■1	SW ■1	SW	SW	SW
London Waterloo ■15 ⊖	d	17 20	17 22	17 28	17 33	17 37	17 45		17 50	17 52	17 58	18 03	18 07	18 15		18 20	18 22	18 28	18 33
Vauxhall ⊖	d		17 26	17 32	17 37	17 41	17 49			17 56	18 02	18 07	18 11	18 19			18 26	18 32	18 37
Queenstown Rd.(Battersea)	d		17 29		17 40	17 44	17 52			17 59		18 10	18 14	18 22			18 29		18 40
Clapham Junction ■10	d	17 28	17 32	17 38	17 43	17 47	17 55		17 58	18 02	18 08	18 13	18 17	18 25		18 28	18 32	18 38	18 43
Wandsworth Town	d		17 35		17 46	17 50	17 58			18 05		18 16	18 20	18 28			18 35		18 46
Putney	d		17 38	17 42	17 49	17 53	18 01			18 08	18 12	18 19	18 23	18 31			18 38	18 42	18 49
Barnes	d		17 42		17 52	17 57	18 05			18 12		18 22	18 27	18 35			18 42		18 52
Barnes Bridge	d		17 44			17 59				18 14			18 29				18 44		
Chiswick	d		17 47			18 02				18 17			18 32				18 47		
Kew Bridge	d		17 50			18 05				18 20			18 35				18 50		
Brentford	d		17 53			18 08				18 23			18 38				18 53		
Syon Lane	d		17 55			18 10				18 25			18 40				18 55		
Isleworth	d		17 57			18 12				18 27			18 42				18 57		
Hounslow	d		18 01			18 18				18 31			18 48				19 01		
Mortlake	d				17 54		18 07					18 24		18 37					18 54
North Sheen	d				17 56		18 09					18 26		18 39					18 56
Richmond ⊖	d	17 36		17 48	17 59		18 12		18 06		18 18	18 29		18 42		18 36		18 48	18 59
St Margarets	d				18 01		18 14					18 31		18 44					19 01
Twickenham	a	17 40		17 51	18 03		18 16		18 10		18 21	18 33		18 46		18 40		18 51	19 03
	d	17 40		17 52	18 04		18 17		18 10		18 22	18 34		18 47		18 40		18 52	19 04
Strawberry Hill	d				18 07							18 37							19 07
Fulwell	a																		
Teddington	a				18 10							18 40							19 10
Hampton Wick	a				18 14							18 44							19 14
Kingston	a				18 16							18 46							19 16
Whitton	d			17 55		18 23	18 20				18 25		18 53	18 50				18 55	
Feltham	d	17 46	18 06	17 59					18 16	18 36	18 29					18 46	19 06	18 59	
Ashford (Surrey)	d		18 10	18 03						18 40	18 33						19 10	19 03	
Staines	d	17 53	18 14	18 07					18 23	18 44	18 37					18 53	19 14	19 07	
Wraysbury	d			18 11							18 41							19 11	
Sunnymeads	d			18 14							18 44							19 14	
Datchet	d			18 17							18 47							19 17	
Windsor & Eton Riverside	a			18 21							18 51							19 21	
Egham	d	17 57	18 19						18 27	18 49						18 57	19 19		
Virginia Water	a	18 01	18 23						18 31	18 53						19 01	19 23		
	d	18 01	18 23						18 31	18 53						19 01	19 23		
Chertsey	d		18 29							18 59							19 29		
Addlestone	d		18 32							19 02							19 32		
Weybridge	a		18 37							19 07							19 37		
Byfleet & New Haw	d																		
West Byfleet	d																		
Woking	a																		
Longcross	d																		
Sunningdale	d	18 07							18 37							19 07			
Ascot ■3	d	18 13						18 23	18 43						18 53	19 13			
Bagshot	d							18 29							18 59				
Camberley	a							18 35							19 05				
Frimley	d							18 43							19 13				
Ash Vale	d							18 49							19 19				
Aldershot	a							18 54							19 24				
	d							19 08							19 38				
Ash ■5	d							19 15							19 45				
Wanborough	d							19 18							19 48				
Guildford	a							19 25							19 55				
Martins Heron	d	18 17							18 47							19 17			
Bracknell	d	18 20							18 50							19 20			
Wokingham	d	18 27							18 57							19 27			
Winnersh	d	18 30							19 00							19 30			
Winnersh Triangle	d	18 32							19 02							19 32			
Earley	d	18 35							19 05							19 35			
Reading ■7	a	18 40							19 10							19 40			

Table 149

Saturdays
29 May to 25 September

London - Hounslow, Richmond, Kingston, Windsor, Weybridge, Ascot, Guildford and Reading

		SW	SW	SW 1	SW 1	SW	SW	SW	SW	SW	SW 1	SW 1	SW	SW	SW	SW	SW	SW 1	SW 1	SW
London Waterloo 15 ⊖	d	18 37	18 45		18 50	18 52	18 58	19 03	19 07	19 15		19 20	19 22	19 28	19 33	19 37	19 45		19 50	19 52
Vauxhall ⊖	d	18 41	18 49			18 56	19 02	19 07	19 11	19 19			19 26	19 32	19 37	19 41	19 49			19 56
Queenstown Rd.(Battersea)	d	18 44	18 52			18 59		19 10	19 14	19 22			19 29		19 40	19 44	19 52			19 59
Clapham Junction 10	d	18 47	18 55		18 58	19 02	19 08	19 13	19 17	19 25		19 28	19 32	19 38	19 43	19 47	19 55		19 58	20 02
Wandsworth Town	d	18 50	18 58			19 05		19 16	19 20	19 28			19 35		19 46	19 50	19 58			20 05
Putney	d	18 53	19 01			19 08	19 12	19 19	19 23	19 31			19 38	19 42	19 49	19 53	20 01			20 08
Barnes	d	18 57	19 05			19 12		19 22	19 27	19 35			19 42		19 52	19 57	20 05			20 12
Barnes Bridge	d	18 59				19 14			19 29				19 44			19 59				20 14
Chiswick	d	19 02				19 17			19 32				19 47			20 02				20 17
Kew Bridge	d	19 05				19 20			19 35				19 50			20 05				20 20
Brentford	d	19 08				19 23			19 38				19 53			20 08				20 23
Syon Lane	d	19 10				19 25			19 40				19 55			20 10				20 25
Isleworth	d	19 12				19 27			19 42				19 57			20 12				20 27
Hounslow	d	19 18				19 31			19 48				20 01			20 18				20 31
Mortlake	d		19 07					19 24		19 37					19 54		20 07			
North Sheen	d		19 09					19 26		19 39					19 56		20 09			
Richmond ⊖	d		19 12		19 06		19 18	19 29		19 42		19 36		19 48	19 59		20 12		20 06	
St Margarets	d		19 14					19 31		19 44					20 01		20 14			
Twickenham	a		19 16		19 10		19 21	19 33		19 46		19 40		19 51	20 03		20 16		20 10	
	d		19 17		19 10		19 22	19 34		19 47		19 40		19 52	20 04		20 17		20 10	
Strawberry Hill	d							19 37							20 07					
Fulwell	a																			
Teddington	a							19 40							20 10					
Hampton Wick	a							19 44							20 14					
Kingston	a							19 46							20 16					
Whitton	d	19 23	19 20				19 25		19 53	19 50				19 55		20 23	20 20			
Feltham	d				19 16	19 36	19 29					19 46	20 06	19 59					20 16	20 36
Ashford (Surrey)	d					19 40	19 33						20 10	20 03						20 40
Staines	d				19 23	19 44	19 37					19 53	20 14	20 07					20 23	20 44
Wraysbury	d						19 41							20 11						
Sunnymeads	d						19 44							20 14						
Datchet	d						19 47							20 17						
Windsor & Eton Riverside	a						19 51							20 21						
Egham	d				19 27	19 49						19 57	20 19						20 27	20 49
Virginia Water	a				19 31	19 53						20 01	20 23						20 31	20 53
	d				19 31	19 53						20 01	20 23						20 31	20 53
Chertsey	d					19 59							20 29							20 59
Addlestone	d					20 02							20 32							21 02
Weybridge	a					20 07							20 37							21 07
Byfleet & New Haw	d																			
West Byfleet	d																			
Woking	a																			
Longcross	d																			
Sunningdale	d				19 37							20 07							20 37	
Ascot 3	d			19 23	19 43						19 53	20 13						20 23	20 43	
Bagshot	d			19 29							19 59							20 29		
Camberley	a			19 35							20 05							20 35		
Frimley	d			19 43							20 13							20 43		
Ash Vale	d			19 49							20 19							20 49		
Aldershot	a			19 54							20 24							20 54		
	d			20 08							20 38							21 08		
Ash 5	d			20 15							20 45							21 15		
Wanborough	d			20 18							20 48							21 18		
Guildford	a			20 25							20 55							21 25		
Martins Heron	d				19 47							20 17							20 47	
Bracknell	d				19 50							20 20							20 50	
Wokingham	d				19 57							20 27							20 57	
Winnersh	d				20 00							20 30							21 00	
Winnersh Triangle	d				20 02							20 32							21 02	
Earley	d				20 05							20 35							21 05	
Reading 7	a				20 10							20 40							21 10	

Table 149

Saturdays
29 May to 25 September

London - Hounslow, Richmond, Kingston, Windsor, Weybridge, Ascot, Guildford and Reading

		SW	SW	SW	SW	SW 1	SW 1	SW	SW	SW	SW	SW	SW 1	SW 1	SW	SW	SW	SW	SW	SW 1	SW
London Waterloo 15 ⊖	d	19 58	20 03	20 07	20 15		20 20	20 22	20 28	20 33	20 37	20 45		20 50	20 52	20 58	21 03	21 07	21 15	21 20	21 22
Vauxhall ⊖	d	20 02	20 07	20 11	20 19			20 26	20 32	20 37	20 41	20 49			20 56	21 02	21 07	21 11	21 19		21 26
Queenstown Rd.(Battersea)	d		20 10	20 14	20 22			20 29		20 40	20 44	20 52			20 59		21 10	21 14	21 22		21 29
Clapham Junction 10	d	20 08	20 13	20 17	20 25		20 28	20 32	20 38	20 43	20 47	20 55		20 58	21 02	21 08	21 13	21 17	21 25	21 28	21 32
Wandsworth Town	d		20 16	20 20	20 28			20 35		20 46	20 50	20 58			21 05		21 16	21 20	21 28		21 35
Putney	d	20 12	20 19	20 23	20 31			20 38	20 42	20 49	20 53	21 01			21 08	21 12	21 19	21 23	21 31		21 38
Barnes	d		20 22	20 27	20 35			20 42		20 52	20 57	21 05			21 12		21 22	21 27	21 35		21 42
Barnes Bridge	d			20 29				20 44			20 59				21 14			21 29			21 44
Chiswick	d			20 32				20 47			21 02				21 17			21 32			21 47
Kew Bridge	d			20 35				20 50			21 05				21 20			21 35			21 50
Brentford	d			20 38				20 53			21 08				21 23			21 38			21 53
Syon Lane	d			20 40				20 55			21 10				21 25			21 40			21 55
Isleworth	d			20 42				20 57			21 12				21 27			21 42			21 57
Hounslow	d			20 48				21 01			21 18				21 31			21 48			22 01
Mortlake	d		20 24		20 37					20 54		21 07					21 24		21 37		
North Sheen	d		20 26		20 39					20 56		21 09					21 26		21 39		
Richmond ⊖	d	20 18	20 29		20 42		20 36		20 48	20 59		21 12		21 06		21 18	21 29		21 42	21 36	
St Margarets	d		20 31		20 44					21 01		21 14					21 31		21 44		
Twickenham	a	20 21	20 33		20 46		20 40		20 51	21 03		21 16		21 10		21 21	21 33		21 46	21 40	
	d	20 22	20 34		20 47		20 40		20 52	21 04		21 17		21 10		21 22	21 34		21 47	21 40	
Strawberry Hill	d		20 37							21 07							21 37				
Fulwell	a																				
Teddington	a		20 40							21 10							21 40				
Hampton Wick	a		20 44							21 14							21 44				
Kingston	a		20 46							21 16							21 46				
Whitton	d	20 25		20 53	20 50				20 55		21 23	21 20				21 25		21 53	21 50		
Feltham	d	20 29					20 46	21 06	20 59					21 16	21 36	21 29				21 46	22 06
Ashford (Surrey)	d	20 33						21 10	21 03						21 40	21 33					22 10
Staines	d	20 37					20 53	21 14	21 07					21 23	21 44	21 37				21 53	22 14
Wraysbury	d	20 41							21 11							21 41					
Sunnymeads	d	20 44							21 14							21 44					
Datchet	d	20 47							21 17							21 47					
Windsor & Eton Riverside	a	20 51							21 21							21 51					
Egham	d						20 57	21 19						21 27	21 49					21 57	22 19
Virginia Water	a						21 01	21 23						21 31	21 53					22 01	22 23
	d						21 01	21 23						21 31	21 53					22 01	22 23
Chertsey	d							21 29							21 59						22 29
Addlestone	d							21 32							22 02						22 32
Weybridge	a							21 37							22 07						22 37
Byfleet & New Haw	d																				
West Byfleet	d																				
Woking	a																				
Longcross	d																				
Sunningdale	d						21 07							21 37						22 07	
Ascot 3	d					20 53	21 13						21 23	21 43						22 13	
Bagshot	d					20 59							21 29								
Camberley	a					21 05							21 35								
Frimley	d					21 13							21 43								
Ash Vale	d					21 19							21 49								
Aldershot	a					21 24							21 54								
	d					21 38							22 08								
Ash 5	d					21 45							22 15								
Wanborough	d					21 48							22 18								
Guildford	a					21 55							22 25								
Martins Heron	d						21 17							21 47						22 17	
Bracknell	d						21 20							21 50						22 20	
Wokingham	d						21 27							21 57						22 27	
Winnersh	d						21 30							22 00						22 30	
Winnersh Triangle	d						21 32							22 02						22 32	
Earley	d						21 35							22 05						22 35	
Reading 7	a						21 40							22 10						22 40	

London - Hounslow, Richmond, Kingston, Windsor, Weybridge, Ascot, Guildford and Reading

		SW	SW	SW	SW	SW 1	SW 1	SW	SW	SW	SW 1	SW	SW	SW	SW 1	SW 1	SW	SW
London Waterloo 15 ⊖	d	21 28	21 33	21 37	21 45		21 50	21 52	21 58	22 03	22 20	22 22	22 28	22 33		22 50	22 52	22 58
Vauxhall ⊖	d	21 32	21 37	21 41	21 49			21 56	22 02	22 07		22 26	22 32	22 37			22 56	23 02
Queenstown Rd.(Battersea)	d		21 40	21 44	21 52			21 59		22 10		22 29		22 40			22 59	
Clapham Junction 10	d	21 38	21 43	21 47	21 55		21 58	22 02	22 08	22 13	22 28	22 32	22 38	22 43		22 58	23 02	23 08
Wandsworth Town	d		21 46	21 50	21 58			22 05		22 16		22 35		22 46			23 05	
Putney	d	21 42	21 49	21 53	22 01			22 08	22 12	22 19		22 38	22 42	22 49			23 08	23 12
Barnes	d		21 52	21 57	22 05			22 12		22 22		22 42		22 52			23 12	
Barnes Bridge	d			21 59				22 14				22 44					23 14	
Chiswick	d			22 02				22 17				22 47					23 17	
Kew Bridge	d			22 05				22 20				22 50					23 20	
Brentford	d			22 08				22 23				22 53					23 23	
Syon Lane	d			22 10				22 25				22 55					23 25	
Isleworth	d			22 12				22 27				22 57					23 27	
Hounslow	d			22 18				22 31				23 01					23 31	
Mortlake	d		21 54		22 07					22 24				22 54				
North Sheen	d		21 56		22 09					22 26				22 56				
Richmond ⊖	d	21 48	21 59		22 12		22 06		22 18	22 29	22 36		22 48	22 59		23 06		23 18
St Margarets	d		22 01		22 14					22 31				23 01				
Twickenham	a	21 51	22 03		22 16		22 10		22 21	22 33	22 40		22 51	23 03		23 10		23 21
	d	21 52	22 04				22 10		22 22	22 34	22 40		22 52	23 04		23 10		23 22
Strawberry Hill	d		22 07							22 37				23 07				
Fulwell	a																	
Teddington	a		22 10							22 40				23 10				
Hampton Wick	a		22 14							22 44				23 14				
Kingston	a		22 16							22 46				23 16				
Whitton	d	21 55		22 23					22 25				22 55					23 25
Feltham	d	21 59					22 16	22 36	22 29		22 46	23 06	22 59			23 16	23 36	23 29
Ashford (Surrey)	d	22 03						22 40	22 33			23 10	23 03				23 40	23 33
Staines	d	22 07					22 23	22 44	22 37		22 53	23 14	23 07			23 23	23 44	23 37
Wraysbury	d	22 11							22 41				23 11					23 41
Sunnymeads	d	22 14							22 44				23 14					23 44
Datchet	d	22 17							22 47				23 17					23 47
Windsor & Eton Riverside	a	22 21							22 51				23 21					23 51
Egham	d						22 27	22 49			22 57	23 19				23 27	23 49	
Virginia Water	a						22 31	22 53			23 01	23 23				23 31	23 53	
	d						22 31	22 53			23 01	23 23				23 31	23 53	
Chertsey	d							22 59				23 29					23 59	
Addlestone	d							23 02				23 32					00 02	
Weybridge	a							23 07				23 37						
Byfleet & New Haw	d																00 06	
West Byfleet	d																00 09	
Woking	a																00 20	
Longcross	d																	
Sunningdale	d						22 37				23 07					23 37		
Ascot 3	d					22 23	22 43				23 13				23 23	23 43		
Bagshot	d					22 29									23 29			
Camberley	a					22 35									23 35			
Frimley	d					22 43									23 43			
Ash Vale	d					22 49									23 49			
Aldershot	a					22 54									23 54			
	d					23 08												
Ash 5	d					23 15												
Wanborough	d					23 18												
Guildford	a					23 25												
Martins Heron	d						22 47				23 17					23 47		
Bracknell	d						22 50				23 20					23 50		
Wokingham	d						22 57				23 27					23 57		
Winnersh	d						23 00				23 30					23 59		
Winnersh Triangle	d						23 02				23 32					00 01		
Earley	d						23 05				23 35					00 05		
Reading 7	a						23 10				23 40					00 10		

London - Hounslow, Richmond, Kingston, Windsor, Weybridge, Ascot, Guildford and Reading

		SW	SW	SW 1	SW	SW	SW	SW	SW
London Waterloo 15 ⊖	d	23 03	23 13	23 20	23 22	23 33	23 38	23 52	23 58
Vauxhall ⊖	d	23 07	23 17		23 26	23 37		23 56	00 02
Queenstown Rd.(Battersea)	d	23 10			23 29	23 40		23 59	
Clapham Junction 10	d	23 13	23 23	23 28	23 32	23 43	23 46	00 02	00 08
Wandsworth Town	d	23 16			23 35	23 46		00 05	
Putney	d	23 19	23 27		23 38	23 49		00 08	00 12
Barnes	d	23 22			23 42	23 52		00 12	
Barnes Bridge	d				23 44			00 14	
Chiswick	d				23 47			00 17	
Kew Bridge	d				23 50			00 20	
Brentford	d				23 53			00 23	
Syon Lane	d				23 55			00 25	
Isleworth	d				23 57			00 27	
Hounslow	d				00 01			00 31	
Mortlake	d	23 24				23 54			
North Sheen	d	23 26				23 56			
Richmond ⊖	d	23 29	23 33	23 37		23 59	23 54		00 18
St Margarets	d	23 31				00 01			
Twickenham	a	23 33	23 37	23 41		00 04	23 58		00 21
	d	23 34	23 37	23 41		00 04	23 58		00 22
Strawberry Hill	d	23 37				00 07			
Fulwell	a								
Teddington	a	23 40				00 11			
Hampton Wick	a	23 44				00 14			
Kingston	a	23 46				00 16			
Whitton	d		23 40						00 25
Feltham	d		23 44	23 48	00 06		00 04	00 36	00 29
Ashford (Surrey)	d		23 48		00 10			00 40	00 33
Staines	d		23 52	23 56	00 14		00 11	00a46	00a37
Wraysbury	d		23 56						
Sunnymeads	d		23 59						
Datchet	d		00 02						
Windsor & Eton Riverside	a		00 06						
Egham	d			00 01	00 19		00 15		
Virginia Water	a			00 05	00 23		00 19		
	d			00 05	00 23		00 19		
Chertsey	d				00 29				
Addlestone	d				00 32				
Weybridge	a				00 37				
Byfleet & New Haw	d								
West Byfleet	d								
Woking	a								
Longcross	d								
Sunningdale	d			00 11			00 25		
Ascot 3	d			00 15			00 30		
Bagshot	d								
Camberley	a								
Frimley	d								
Ash Vale	d								
Aldershot	a								
	d								
Ash 5	d								
Wanborough	d								
Guildford	a								
Martins Heron	d			00 19			00 34		
Bracknell	d			00 23			00 37		
Wokingham	d			00 32			00 44		
Winnersh	d			00 36					
Winnersh Triangle	d			00 38					
Earley	d			00 40					
Reading 7	a			00 45			00 52		

Table 149

Saturdays from 02 October

London - Hounslow, Richmond, Kingston, Windsor, Weybridge, Ascot, Guildford and Reading

		SW ■	SW	SW	SW ■	SW	SW	SW	SW	SW	SW	SW	SW ■	SW ■	SW ■	SW	SW	SW	SW	SW ■	SW	SW	SW	SW
London Waterloo ■ ⊖	d	22p50	22p52	23p13	23p20	23p22	23p33	23p38	23p52	23p58	00 18				05 05				05 33	05 50	05 58	06 03		
Vauxhall ⊖	d		22p56	23p17		23p26	23p37		23p56	00 02	00 22				05 09				05 37		06 02	06 07		
Queenstown Rd.(Battersea)	d		22p59			23p29	23p40		23p59		00 25				05 12				05 40			06 10		
Clapham Junction ■	d	22p58	23p02	23p23	23p28	23p32	23p43	23p46	00 02	00 08	00 28				05 15				05 43	05 58	06 08	06 13		
Wandsworth Town	d		23p05			23p35	23p46		00 05		00 31				05 18				05 46			06 16		
Putney	d		23p08	23p27		23p38	23p49		00 08	00 12	00 34				05 21				05 49		06 12	06 19		
Barnes	d		23p12			23p42	23p52		00 12		00 37				05 24				05 52			06 22		
Barnes Bridge	d		23p14			23p44			00 14															
Chiswick	d		23p17			23p47			00 17															
Kew Bridge	d		23p20			23p50			00 20															
Brentford	d		23p23			23p53			00 23															
Syon Lane	d		23p25			23p55			00 25															
Isleworth	d		23p27			23p57			00 27															
Hounslow	d		23p31			00 01			00 31															
Mortlake	d						23p54				00 39				05 26				05 54			06 24		
North Sheen	d						23p56				00 41				05 28				05 56			06 26		
Richmond ⊖	d	23p06		23p33	23p37		23p59	23p54		00 18	00 44				05 31				05 59	06 06	06 18	06 29		
St Margarets	d						00 01				00 46				05 33				06 01			06 31		
Twickenham	a	23p10		23p36	23p41		00 03	23p58		00 21	00 48				05 35				06 03	06 10	06 21	06 33		
	d	23p10		23p37	23p41		00 04	23p58		00 22	00 49	04 52			05 36	05 38		05 53	06 04	06 10	06 22	06 34		
Strawberry Hill	d						00 07				00s52	04 55							06 07			06 37		
Fulwell	a																							
Teddington	a						00 10				00s55	04 58							06 10			06 40		
Hampton Wick	a						00 14				00s58	05 01							06 14			06 44		
Kingston	a						00 16				01 00	05 03							06 16			06 46		
Whitton	d			23p40						00 25					05 39	05a41		05 56			06 25			
Feltham	d	23p16	23p36	23p44	23p48	00 06		00 04	00 37	00 29					05 43			06 00		06 16	06 29			
Ashford (Surrey)	d		23p40	23p48		00 10			00 41	00 33					05 47			06 04			06 33			
Staines	d	23p23	23p44	23p52	23p56	00 14		00 11	00a46	00a37				05 23	05 53		05 44	06 08		06 23	06 37		06 16	06 44
Wraysbury	d			23p57														06 13			06 42			
Sunnymeads	d			23p59														06 16			06 45			
Datchet	d			00 04														06 20			06 49			
Windsor & Eton Riverside	a			00 09														06 24			06 54			
Egham	d	23p27	23p49		00 01	00 19		00 15						05 27	05 57		05 49			06 27			06 20	06 49
Virginia Water	a	23p31	23p53		00 05	00 23		00 19						05 31	06 01		05 53			06 31			06 25	06 53
	d	23p31	23p53		00 05	00 23		00 19						05 31	06 01		05 53			06 31			06 25	06 53
Chertsey	d		23p59			00 29											05 59						06 30	06 59
Addlestone	d		00 02			00 32											06 02						06 33	07 02
Weybridge	a					00 37											06 07						06 38	07 07
Byfleet & New Haw	d		00 06																					
West Byfleet	d		00 09																					
Woking	a		00 18																					
Longcross	d																							
Sunningdale	d	23p37			00 11			00 25						05 37	06 07					06 37				
Ascot ■	d	23p43			00 15			00 30					00 32	05 43	06 13					06 43				
Bagshot	d												00 38											
Camberley	a												00 44											
Frimley	d												00 48											
Ash Vale	d												00 57											
Aldershot	a												01s02											
	d												01s06											
Ash ■	d																							
Wanborough	d																							
Guildford	a																							
Martins Heron	d	23p47			00 19			00 34						05 47	06 17					06 47				
Bracknell	d	23p50			00 23			00 37						05 50	06 20					06 50				
Wokingham	d	23p57			00 32			00 44						05 57	06 27					06 57				
Winnersh	d	23p59			00 36									06 00	06 30					07 00				
Winnersh Triangle	d	00 02			00 38									06 02	06 32					07 02				
Earley	d	00 05			00 40									06 07	06 35					07 07				
Reading ■	a	00 13			00 48			00 55						06 13	06 43					07 13				

Table 149

Saturdays from 02 October

London - Hounslow, Richmond, Kingston, Windsor, Weybridge, Ascot, Guildford and Reading

		SW ■	SW ■	SW	SW	SW	SW ■	SW	SW	SW	SW	SW ■	SW ■	SW	SW	SW	SW	SW	SW ■	SW ■
London Waterloo ■ ⊖	d		06 20	06 22	06 28	06 33	06 50	06 52	06 58	07 03	07 15		07 20	07 22	07 28	07 33	07 37	07 45		07 50
Vauxhall ⊖	d			06 26	06 32	06 37		06 56	07 02	07 07	07 19			07 26	07 32	07 37	07 41	07 49		
Queenstown Rd.(Battersea)	d			06 29		06 40		06 59		07 10	07 22			07 29		07 40	07 44	07 52		
Clapham Junction ■	d		06 28	06 32	06 38	06 43	06 58	07 02	07 08	07 13	07 25		07 28	07 32	07 38	07 43	07 47	07 55		07 58
Wandsworth Town	d			06 35		06 46		07 05		07 16	07 28			07 35		07 46	07 50	07 58		
Putney	d			06 38	06 42	06 49		07 08	07 12	07 19	07 31			07 38	07 42	07 49	07 53	08 01		
Barnes	d			06 42		06 52		07 12		07 22	07 35			07 42		07 52	07 57	08 05		
Barnes Bridge	d			06 44				07 14						07 44			07 59			
Chiswick	d			06 47				07 17						07 47			08 02			
Kew Bridge	d			06 50				07 20						07 50			08 05			
Brentford	d			06 53				07 23						07 53			08 08			
Syon Lane	d			06 55				07 25						07 55			08 10			
Isleworth	d			06 57				07 27						07 57			08 12			
Hounslow	d			07 01				07 31						08 01			08 18			
Mortlake	d					06 54				07 24	07 37					07 54		08 07		
North Sheen	d					06 56				07 26	07 39					07 56		08 09		
Richmond ⊖	d		06 36		06 48	06 59	07 06		07 18	07 29	07 42		07 36		07 48	07 59		08 12		08 06
St Margarets	d					07 01				07 31	07 44					08 01		08 14		
Twickenham	a		06 40		06 51	07 03	07 10		07 21	07 33	07 46		07 40		07 51	08 03		08 16		08 10
	d		06 40		06 52	07 04	07 10		07 22	07 34	07 47		07 40		07 52	08 04		08 17		08 10
Strawberry Hill	d					07 07				07 37						08 07				
Fulwell	a																			
Teddington	a					07 10				07 40						08 10				
Hampton Wick	a					07 14				07 44						08 14				
Kingston	a					07 16				07 46						08 16				
Whitton	d				06 55				07 25		07 50				07 55		08 23	08 20		
Feltham	d		06 46	07 06	06 59		07 16	07 36	07 29				07 46	08 06	07 59					08 16
Ashford (Surrey)	d			07 10	07 03			07 40	07 33					08 10	08 03					
Staines	d		06 53	07 14	07 07		07 23	07 44	07 37				07 53	08 14	08 07					08 23
Wraysbury	d				07 12				07 42						08 12					
Sunnymeads	d				07 15				07 45						08 15					
Datchet	d				07 19				07 49						08 19					
Windsor & Eton Riverside	a				07 24				07 54						08 24					
Egham	d		06 57	07 19			07 27	07 49					07 57	08 19						08 27
Virginia Water	a		07 01	07 23			07 31	07 53					08 01	08 23						08 31
	d		07 01	07 23			07 31	07 53					08 01	08 23						08 31
Chertsey	d			07 29				07 59						08 29						
Addlestone	d			07 32				08 02						08 32						
Weybridge	a			07 37				08 07						08 37						
Byfleet & New Haw	d																			
West Byfleet	d																			
Woking	a																			
Longcross	d																			
Sunningdale	d		07 07				07 37						08 07							08 37
Ascot ■	d	06 53	07 13				07 43					07 53	08 13						08 23	08 43
Bagshot	d	06 59										07 59							08 29	
Camberley	a	07 05										08 05							08 35	
Frimley	d	07 13										08 13							08 43	
Ash Vale	d	07 19										08 19							08 49	
Aldershot	a	07 24										08 24							08 54	
	d	07 38										08 38							09 08	
Ash ■	d	07 45										08 45							09 15	
Wanborough	d	07 48										08 48							09 18	
Guildford	a	07 55										08 55							09 25	
Martins Heron	d		07 17				07 47						08 17							08 47
Bracknell	d		07 20				07 50						08 20							08 50
Wokingham	d		07 27				07 57						08 27							08 57
Winnersh	d		07 30				08 00						08 30							09 00
Winnersh Triangle	d		07 32				08 02						08 32							09 02
Earley	d		07 37				08 07						08 37							09 07
Reading ■	a		07 43				08 13						08 43							09 13

Table 149

London - Hounslow, Richmond, Kingston, Windsor, Weybridge, Ascot, Guildford and Reading

		SW	SW	SW	SW	SW	SW 1	SW 1	SW	SW	SW	SW	SW	SW 1	SW 1	SW	SW	SW	SW
London Waterloo 15 ⊖	d	07 52	07 58	08 03	08 07	08 15		08 20	08 22	08 28	08 33	08 37	08 45		08 50	08 52	08 58	09 03	09 07
Vauxhall ⊖	d	07 56	08 02	08 07	08 11	08 19			08 26	08 32	08 37	08 41	08 49			08 56	09 02	09 07	09 11
Queenstown Rd.(Battersea)	d	07 59		08 10	08 14	08 22			08 29		08 40	08 44	08 52			08 59		09 10	09 14
Clapham Junction 10	d	08 02	08 08	08 13	08 17	08 25		08 28	08 32	08 38	08 43	08 47	08 55		08 58	09 02	09 08	09 13	09 17
Wandsworth Town	d	08 05		08 16	08 20	08 28			08 35		08 46	08 50	08 58			09 05		09 16	09 20
Putney	d	08 08	08 12	08 19	08 23	08 31			08 38	08 42	08 49	08 53	09 01			09 08	09 12	09 19	09 23
Barnes	d	08 12		08 22	08 27	08 35			08 42		08 52	08 57	09 05			09 12		09 22	09 27
Barnes Bridge	d	08 14			08 29				08 44			08 59				09 14			09 29
Chiswick	d	08 17			08 32				08 47			09 02				09 17			09 32
Kew Bridge	d	08 20			08 35				08 50			09 05				09 20			09 35
Brentford	d	08 23			08 38				08 53			09 08				09 23			09 38
Syon Lane	d	08 25			08 40				08 55			09 10				09 25			09 40
Isleworth	d	08 27			08 42				08 57			09 12				09 27			09 42
Hounslow	d	08 31			08 48				09 01			09 18				09 31			09 48
Mortlake	d			08 24		08 37					08 54		09 07					09 24	
North Sheen	d			08 26		08 39					08 56		09 09					09 26	
Richmond ⊖	d		08 18	08 29		08 42		08 36		08 48	08 59		09 12		09 06		09 18	09 29	
St Margarets	d			08 31		08 44					09 01		09 14					09 31	
Twickenham	a		08 21	08 33		08 46		08 40		08 51	09 03		09 16		09 10		09 21	09 33	
	d		08 22	08 34		08 47		08 40		08 52	09 04		09 17		09 10		09 22	09 34	
Strawberry Hill	d			08 37							09 07							09 37	
Fulwell	a																		
Teddington	a			08 40							09 10							09 40	
Hampton Wick	a			08 44							09 14							09 44	
Kingston	a			08 46							09 16							09 46	
Whitton	d		08 25		08 53	08 50				08 55		09 23	09 20				09 25		09 53
Feltham	d	08 36	08 29					08 46	09 06	08 59					09 16	09 36	09 29		
Ashford (Surrey)	d	08 40	08 33						09 10	09 03						09 40	09 33		
Staines	d	08 44	08 37					08 53	09 14	09 07					09 23	09 44	09 37		
Wraysbury	d		08 42							09 12							09 42		
Sunnymeads	d		08 45							09 15							09 45		
Datchet	d		08 49							09 19							09 49		
Windsor & Eton Riverside	a		08 54							09 24							09 54		
Egham	d	08 49						08 57	09 19						09 27	09 49			
Virginia Water	a	08 53						09 01	09 23						09 31	09 53			
	d	08 53						09 01	09 23						09 31	09 53			
Chertsey	d	08 59							09 29							09 59			
Addlestone	d	09 02							09 32							10 02			
Weybridge	a	09 07							09 37							10 07			
Byfleet & New Haw	d																		
West Byfleet	d																		
Woking	a																		
Longcross	d																		
Sunningdale	d							09 07							09 37				
Ascot 3	d						08 53	09 13						09 23	09 43				
Bagshot	d						08 59							09 29					
Camberley	a						09 05							09 35					
Frimley	d						09 13							09 43					
Ash Vale	d						09 19							09 49					
Aldershot	a						09 24							09 54					
	d						09 38							10 08					
Ash 5	d						09 45							10 15					
Wanborough	d						09 48							10 18					
Guildford	a						09 55							10 25					
Martins Heron	d							09 17							09 47				
Bracknell	d							09 20							09 50				
Wokingham	d							09 27							09 57				
Winnersh	d							09 30							10 00				
Winnersh Triangle	d							09 32							10 02				
Earley	d							09 37							10 07				
Reading 7	a							09 43							10 13				

Table 149

London - Hounslow, Richmond, Kingston, Windsor, Weybridge, Ascot, Guildford and Reading

		SW	SW 1	SW 1	SW	SW	SW	SW	SW	SW 1	SW 1	SW	SW	SW	SW	SW	SW 1	SW 1	SW	SW
London Waterloo 15 ⊖	d	09 15		09 20	09 22	09 28	09 33	09 37	09 45		09 50	09 52	09 58	10 03	10 07	10 15		10 20	10 22	10 28
Vauxhall ⊖	d	09 19			09 26	09 32	09 37	09 41	09 49			09 56	10 02	10 07	10 11	10 19			10 26	10 32
Queenstown Rd.(Battersea)	d	09 22			09 29		09 40	09 44	09 52			09 59		10 10	10 14	10 22			10 29	
Clapham Junction 10	d	09 25		09 28	09 32	09 38	09 43	09 47	09 55		09 58	10 02	10 08	10 13	10 17	10 25		10 28	10 32	10 38
Wandsworth Town	d	09 28			09 35		09 46	09 50	09 58			10 05		10 16	10 20	10 28			10 35	
Putney	d	09 31			09 38	09 42	09 49	09 53	10 01			10 08	10 12	10 19	10 23	10 31			10 38	10 42
Barnes	d	09 35			09 42		09 52	09 57	10 05			10 12		10 22	10 27	10 35			10 42	
Barnes Bridge	d				09 44			09 59				10 14			10 29				10 44	
Chiswick	d				09 47			10 02				10 17			10 32				10 47	
Kew Bridge	d				09 50			10 05				10 20			10 35				10 50	
Brentford	d				09 53			10 08				10 23			10 38				10 53	
Syon Lane	d				09 55			10 10				10 25			10 40				10 55	
Isleworth	d				09 57			10 12				10 27			10 42				10 57	
Hounslow	d				10 01			10 18				10 31			10 48				11 01	
Mortlake	d	09 37					09 54		10 07					10 24		10 37				
North Sheen	d	09 39					09 56		10 09					10 26		10 39				
Richmond ⊖	d	09 42		09 36		09 48	09 59		10 12		10 06		10 18	10 29		10 42		10 36		10 48
St Margarets	d	09 44					10 01		10 14					10 31		10 44				
Twickenham	a	09 46		09 40		09 51	10 03		10 16		10 10		10 21	10 33		10 46		10 40		10 51
	d	09 47		09 40		09 52	10 04		10 17		10 10		10 22	10 34		10 47		10 40		10 52
Strawberry Hill	d						10 07							10 37						
Fulwell	a																			
Teddington	a						10 10							10 40						
Hampton Wick	a						10 14							10 44						
Kingston	a						10 16							10 46						
Whitton	d	09 50				09 55		10 23	10 20				10 25		10 53	10 50				10 55
Feltham	d			09 46	10 06	09 59					10 16	10 36	10 29					10 46	11 06	10 59
Ashford (Surrey)	d				10 10	10 03						10 40	10 33						11 10	11 03
Staines	d			09 53	10 14	10 07					10 23	10 44	10 37					10 53	11 14	11 07
Wraysbury	d					10 12							10 42							11 12
Sunnymeads	d					10 15							10 45							11 15
Datchet	d					10 19							10 49							11 19
Windsor & Eton Riverside	a					10 24							10 54							11 24
Egham	d			09 57	10 19						10 27	10 49						10 57	11 19	
Virginia Water	a			10 01	10 23						10 31	10 53						11 01	11 23	
	d			10 01	10 23						10 31	10 53						11 01	11 23	
Chertsey	d				10 29							10 59							11 29	
Addlestone	d				10 32							11 02							11 32	
Weybridge	a				10 37							11 07							11 37	
Byfleet & New Haw	d																			
West Byfleet	d																			
Woking	a																			
Longcross	d																			
Sunningdale	d			10 07							10 37							11 07		
Ascot 3	d		09 53	10 13						10 23	10 43						10 53	11 13		
Bagshot	d		09 59							10 29							10 59			
Camberley	a		10 05							10 35							11 05			
Frimley	d		10 13							10 43							11 13			
Ash Vale	d		10 19							10 49							11 19			
Aldershot	a		10 24							10 54							11 24			
	d		10 38							11 08							11 38			
Ash 5	d		10 45							11 15							11 45			
Wanborough	d		10 48							11 18							11 48			
Guildford	a		10 55							11 25							11 55			
Martins Heron	d			10 17							10 47							11 17		
Bracknell	d			10 20							10 50							11 20		
Wokingham	d			10 27							10 57							11 27		
Winnersh	d			10 30							11 00							11 30		
Winnersh Triangle	d			10 32							11 02							11 32		
Earley	d			10 37							11 07							11 37		
Reading 7	a			10 43							11 13							11 43		

Saturdays
from 02 October

London - Hounslow, Richmond, Kingston, Windsor, Weybridge, Ascot, Guildford and Reading

		SW	SW	SW	SW ■	SW ■	SW	SW	SW	SW	SW	SW ■	SW ■	SW	SW	SW	SW	SW	SW ■	SW ■
London Waterloo ■ ⊖	d	10 33	10 37	10 45		10 50	10 52	10 58	11 03	11 07	11 15		11 20	11 22	11 28	11 33	11 37	11 45		11 50
Vauxhall ⊖	d	10 37	10 41	10 49			10 56	11 02	11 07	11 11	11 19			11 26	11 32	11 37	11 41	11 49		
Queenstown Rd.(Battersea)	d	10 40	10 44	10 52			10 59		11 10	11 14	11 22			11 29		11 40	11 44	11 52		
Clapham Junction ■	d	10 43	10 47	10 55		10 58	11 02	11 08	11 13	11 17	11 25		11 28	11 32	11 38	11 43	11 47	11 55		11 58
Wandsworth Town	d	10 46	10 50	10 58			11 05		11 16	11 20	11 28			11 35		11 46	11 50	11 58		
Putney	d	10 49	10 53	11 01			11 08	11 12	11 19	11 23	11 31			11 38	11 42	11 49	11 53	12 01		
Barnes	d	10 52	10 57	11 05			11 12		11 22	11 27	11 35			11 42		11 52	11 57	12 05		
Barnes Bridge	d		10 59				11 14			11 29				11 44			11 59			
Chiswick	d		11 02				11 17			11 32				11 47			12 02			
Kew Bridge	d		11 05				11 20			11 35				11 50			12 05			
Brentford	d		11 08				11 23			11 38				11 53			12 08			
Syon Lane	d		11 10				11 25			11 40				11 55			12 10			
Isleworth	d		11 12				11 27			11 42				11 57			12 12			
Hounslow	d		11 18				11 31			11 48				12 01			12 18			
Mortlake	d	10 54		11 07					11 24		11 37					11 54		12 07		
North Sheen	d	10 56		11 09					11 26		11 39					11 56		12 09		
Richmond ⊖	d	10 59		11 12		11 06		11 18	11 29		11 42		11 36		11 48	11 59		12 12		12 06
St Margarets	d	11 01		11 14					11 31		11 44					12 01		12 14		
Twickenham	a	11 03		11 16		11 10		11 21	11 33		11 46		11 40		11 51	12 03		12 16		12 10
	d	11 04		11 17		11 10		11 22	11 34		11 47		11 40		11 52	12 04		12 17		12 10
Strawberry Hill	d	11 07							11 37							12 07				
Fulwell	a																			
Teddington	a	11 10							11 40							12 10				
Hampton Wick	a	11 14							11 44							12 14				
Kingston	a	11 16							11 46							12 16				
Whitton	d		11 23	11 20				11 25		11 53	11 50				11 55		12 23	12 20		
Feltham	d					11 16	11 36	11 29					11 46	12 06	11 59					12 16
Ashford (Surrey)	d						11 40	11 33						12 10	12 03					
Staines	d					11 23	11 44	11 37					11 53	12 14	12 07					12 23
Wraysbury	d							11 42							12 12					
Sunnymeads	d							11 45							12 15					
Datchet	d							11 49							12 19					
Windsor & Eton Riverside	a							11 54							12 24					
Egham	d					11 27	11 49						11 57	12 19						12 27
Virginia Water	a					11 31	11 53						12 01	12 23						12 31
	d					11 31	11 53						12 01	12 23						12 31
Chertsey	d						11 59							12 29						
Addlestone	d						12 02							12 32						
Weybridge	a						12 07							12 37						
Byfleet & New Haw	d																			
West Byfleet	d																			
Woking	a																			
Longcross	d																			
Sunningdale	d					11 37							12 07							12 37
Ascot ■	d				11 23	11 43						11 53	12 13						12 23	12 43
Bagshot	d				11 29							11 59							12 29	
Camberley	a				11 35							12 05							12 35	
Frimley	d				11 43							12 13							12 43	
Ash Vale	d				11 49							12 19							12 49	
Aldershot	a				11 54							12 24							12 54	
	d				12 08							12 38							13 08	
Ash ■	d				12 15							12 45							13 15	
Wanborough	d				12 18							12 48							13 18	
Guildford	a				12 25							12 55							13 25	
Martins Heron	d					11 47							12 17							12 47
Bracknell	d					11 50							12 20							12 50
Wokingham	d					11 57							12 27							12 57
Winnersh	d					12 00							12 30							13 00
Winnersh Triangle	d					12 02							12 32							13 02
Earley	d					12 07							12 37							13 07
Reading ■	a					12 13							12 43							13 13

Saturdays
from 02 October

London - Hounslow, Richmond, Kingston, Windsor, Weybridge, Ascot, Guildford and Reading

		SW	SW	SW	SW	SW	SW ■	SW ■	SW	SW	SW	SW	SW	SW ■	SW ■	SW	SW	SW	SW	SW
London Waterloo ■ ⊖	d	11 52	11 58	12 03	12 07	12 15		12 20	12 22	12 28	12 33	12 37	12 45		12 50	12 52	12 58	13 03	13 07	13 15
Vauxhall ⊖	d	11 56	12 02	12 07	12 11	12 19			12 26	12 32	12 37	12 41	12 49			12 56	13 02	13 07	13 11	13 19
Queenstown Rd.(Battersea)	d	11 59		12 10	12 14	12 22			12 29		12 40	12 44	12 52			12 59		13 10	13 14	13 22
Clapham Junction ■	d	12 02	12 08	12 13	12 17	12 25		12 28	12 32	12 38	12 43	12 47	12 55		12 58	13 02	13 08	13 13	13 17	13 25
Wandsworth Town	d	12 05		12 16	12 20	12 28			12 35		12 46	12 50	12 58			13 05		13 16	13 20	13 28
Putney	d	12 08	12 12	12 19	12 23	12 31			12 38	12 42	12 49	12 53	13 01			13 08	13 12	13 19	13 23	13 31
Barnes	d	12 12		12 22	12 27	12 35			12 42		12 52	12 57	13 05			13 12		13 22	13 27	13 35
Barnes Bridge	d	12 14			12 29				12 44			12 59				13 14			13 29	
Chiswick	d	12 17			12 32				12 47			13 02				13 17			13 32	
Kew Bridge	d	12 20			12 35				12 50			13 05				13 20			13 35	
Brentford	d	12 23			12 38				12 53			13 08				13 23			13 38	
Syon Lane	d	12 25			12 40				12 55			13 10				13 25			13 40	
Isleworth	d	12 27			12 42				12 57			13 12				13 27			13 42	
Hounslow	d	12 31			12 48				13 01			13 18				13 31			13 48	
Mortlake	d			12 24		12 37					12 54		13 07					13 24		13 37
North Sheen	d			12 26		12 39					12 56		13 09					13 26		13 39
Richmond ⊖	d		12 18	12 29		12 42		12 36		12 48	12 59		13 12		13 06		13 18	13 29		13 42
St Margarets	d			12 31		12 44					13 01		13 14					13 31		13 44
Twickenham	a		12 21	12 33		12 46		12 40		12 51	13 03		13 16		13 10		13 21	13 33		13 46
	d		12 22	12 34		12 47		12 40		12 52	13 04		13 17		13 10		13 22	13 34		13 47
Strawberry Hill	d			12 37							13 07							13 37		
Fulwell	a																			
Teddington	a			12 40							13 10							13 40		
Hampton Wick	a			12 44							13 14							13 44		
Kingston	a			12 46							13 16							13 46		
Whitton	d		12 25		12 53	12 50				12 55		13 23	13 20				13 25		13 53	13 50
Feltham	d	12 36	12 29					12 46	13 06	12 59					13 16	13 36	13 29			
Ashford (Surrey)	d	12 40	12 33						13 10	13 03						13 40	13 33			
Staines	d	12 44	12 37					12 53	13 14	13 07					13 23	13 44	13 37			
Wraysbury	d		12 42							13 12							13 42			
Sunnymeads	d		12 45							13 15							13 45			
Datchet	d		12 49							13 19							13 49			
Windsor & Eton Riverside	a		12 54							13 24							13 54			
Egham	d	12 49						12 57	13 19						13 27	13 49				
Virginia Water	a	12 53						13 01	13 23						13 31	13 53				
	d	12 53						13 01	13 23						13 31	13 53				
Chertsey	d	12 59							13 29							13 59				
Addlestone	d	13 02							13 32							14 02				
Weybridge	a	13 07							13 37							14 07				
Byfleet & New Haw	d																			
West Byfleet	d																			
Woking	a																			
Longcross	d																			
Sunningdale	d							13 07							13 37					
Ascot ■	d						12 53	13 13						13 23	13 43					
Bagshot	d						12 59							13 29						
Camberley	a						13 05							13 35						
Frimley	d						13 13							13 43						
Ash Vale	d						13 19							13 49						
Aldershot	a						13 24							13 54						
	d						13 38							14 08						
Ash ■	d						13 45							14 15						
Wanborough	d						13 48							14 18						
Guildford	a						13 55							14 25						
Martins Heron	d							13 17							13 47					
Bracknell	d							13 20							13 50					
Wokingham	d							13 27							13 57					
Winnersh	d							13 30							14 00					
Winnersh Triangle	d							13 32							14 02					
Earley	d							13 37							14 07					
Reading ■	a							13 43							14 13					

Table 149

Saturdays from 02 October

London - Hounslow, Richmond, Kingston, Windsor, Weybridge, Ascot, Guildford and Reading

		SW 1	SW 1	SW	SW	SW	SW	SW	SW 1	SW 1	SW	SW	SW	SW	SW	SW 1	SW 1	SW	SW	SW
London Waterloo 15 ⊖	d		13 20	13 22	13 28	13 33	13 37	13 45		13 50	13 52	13 58	14 03	14 07	14 15		14 20	14 22	14 28	14 33
Vauxhall ⊖	d			13 26	13 32	13 37	13 41	13 49			13 56	14 02	14 07	14 11	14 19			14 26	14 32	14 37
Queenstown Rd.(Battersea)	d			13 29		13 40	13 44	13 52			13 59		14 10	14 14	14 22			14 29		14 40
Clapham Junction 10	d		13 28	13 32	13 38	13 43	13 47	13 55		13 58	14 02	14 08	14 13	14 17	14 25		14 28	14 32	14 38	14 43
Wandsworth Town	d			13 35		13 46	13 50	13 58			14 05		14 16	14 20	14 28			14 35		14 46
Putney	d			13 38	13 42	13 49	13 53	14 01			14 08	14 12	14 19	14 23	14 31			14 38	14 42	14 49
Barnes	d			13 42		13 52	13 57	14 05			14 12		14 22	14 27	14 35			14 42		14 52
Barnes Bridge	d			13 44			13 59				14 14			14 29				14 44		
Chiswick	d			13 47			14 02				14 17			14 32				14 47		
Kew Bridge	d			13 50			14 05				14 20			14 35				14 50		
Brentford	d			13 53			14 08				14 23			14 38				14 53		
Syon Lane	d			13 55			14 10				14 25			14 40				14 55		
Isleworth	d			13 57			14 12				14 27			14 42				14 57		
Hounslow	d			14 01			14 18				14 31			14 48				15 01		
Mortlake	d					13 54		14 07					14 24		14 37					14 54
North Sheen	d					13 56		14 09					14 26		14 39					14 56
Richmond ⊖	d		13 36		13 48	13 59		14 12		14 06		14 18	14 29		14 42		14 36		14 48	14 59
St Margarets	d					14 01		14 14					14 31		14 44					15 01
Twickenham	a		13 40		13 51	14 03		14 16		14 10		14 21	14 33		14 46		14 40		14 51	15 03
	d		13 40		13 52	14 04		14 17		14 10		14 22	14 34		14 47		14 40		14 52	15 04
Strawberry Hill	d					14 07							14 37							15 07
Fulwell	a																			
Teddington	a					14 10							14 40							15 10
Hampton Wick	a					14 14							14 44							15 14
Kingston	a					14 16							14 46							15 16
Whitton	d				13 55		14 23	14 20				14 25		14 53	14 50				14 55	
Feltham	d		13 46	14 06	13 59					14 16	14 36	14 29					14 46	15 06	14 59	
Ashford (Surrey)	d			14 10	14 03						14 40	14 33						15 10	15 03	
Staines	d		13 53	14 14	14 07					14 23	14 44	14 37					14 53	15 14	15 07	
Wraysbury	d				14 12							14 42							15 12	
Sunnymeads	d				14 15							14 45							15 15	
Datchet	d				14 19							14 49							15 19	
Windsor & Eton Riverside	a				14 24							14 54							15 24	
Egham	d		13 57	14 19						14 27	14 49						14 57	15 19		
Virginia Water	a		14 01	14 23						14 31	14 53						15 01	15 23		
	d		14 01	14 23						14 31	14 53						15 01	15 23		
Chertsey	d			14 29							14 59							15 29		
Addlestone	d			14 32							15 02							15 32		
Weybridge	a			14 37							15 07							15 37		
Byfleet & New Haw	d																			
West Byfleet	d																			
Woking	a																			
Longcross	d																			
Sunningdale	d		14 07							14 37							15 07			
Ascot 3	d	13 53	14 13						14 23	14 43						14 53	15 13			
Bagshot	d	13 59							14 29							14 59				
Camberley	a	14 05							14 35							15 05				
Frimley	d	14 13							14 43							15 13				
Ash Vale	d	14 19							14 49							15 19				
Aldershot	a	14 24							14 54							15 24				
	d	14 38							15 08							15 38				
Ash 5	d	14 45							15 15							15 45				
Wanborough	d	14 48							15 18							15 48				
Guildford	a	14 55							15 25							15 55				
Martins Heron	d		14 17							14 47							15 17			
Bracknell	d		14 20							14 50							15 20			
Wokingham	d		14 27							14 57							15 27			
Winnersh	d		14 30							15 00							15 30			
Winnersh Triangle	d		14 32							15 02							15 32			
Earley	d		14 37							15 07							15 37			
Reading 7	a		14 43							15 13							15 43			

Table 149

Saturdays from 02 October

London - Hounslow, Richmond, Kingston, Windsor, Weybridge, Ascot, Guildford and Reading

		SW	SW	SW 1	SW 1	SW	SW	SW	SW	SW	SW 1	SW 1	SW	SW	SW	SW	SW	SW 1	SW 1	SW
London Waterloo 15 ⊖	d	14 37	14 45		14 50	14 52	14 58	15 03	15 07	15 15		15 20	15 22	15 28	15 33	15 37	15 45		15 50	15 52
Vauxhall ⊖	d	14 41	14 49			14 56	15 02	15 07	15 11	15 19			15 26	15 32	15 37	15 41	15 49			15 56
Queenstown Rd.(Battersea)	d	14 44	14 52			14 59		15 10	15 14	15 22			15 29		15 40	15 44	15 52			15 59
Clapham Junction 10	d	14 47	14 55		14 58	15 02	15 08	15 13	15 17	15 25		15 28	15 32	15 38	15 43	15 47	15 55		15 58	16 02
Wandsworth Town	d	14 50	14 58			15 05		15 16	15 20	15 28			15 35		15 46	15 50	15 58			16 05
Putney	d	14 53	15 01			15 08	15 12	15 19	15 23	15 31			15 38	15 42	15 49	15 53	16 01			16 08
Barnes	d	14 57	15 05			15 12		15 22	15 27	15 35			15 42		15 52	15 57	16 05			16 12
Barnes Bridge	d	14 59				15 14			15 29				15 44			15 59				16 14
Chiswick	d	15 02				15 17			15 32				15 47			16 02				16 17
Kew Bridge	d	15 05				15 20			15 35				15 50			16 05				16 20
Brentford	d	15 08				15 23			15 38				15 53			16 08				16 23
Syon Lane	d	15 10				15 25			15 40				15 55			16 10				16 25
Isleworth	d	15 12				15 27			15 42				15 57			16 12				16 27
Hounslow	d	15 18				15 31			15 48				16 01			16 18				16 31
Mortlake	d		15 07					15 24		15 37					15 54		16 07			
North Sheen	d		15 09					15 26		15 39					15 56		16 09			
Richmond ⊖	d		15 12		15 06		15 18	15 29		15 42		15 36		15 48	15 59		16 12		16 06	
St Margarets	d		15 14					15 31		15 44					16 01		16 14			
Twickenham	a		15 16		15 10		15 21	15 33		15 46		15 40		15 51	16 03		16 16		16 10	
	d		15 17		15 10		15 22	15 34		15 47		15 40		15 52	16 04		16 17		16 10	
Strawberry Hill	d							15 37							16 07					
Fulwell	a																			
Teddington	a							15 40							16 10					
Hampton Wick	a							15 44							16 14					
Kingston	a							15 46							16 16					
Whitton	d	15 23	15 20				15 25		15 53	15 50				15 55		16 23	16 20			
Feltham	d				15 16	15 36	15 29					15 46	16 06	15 59					16 16	16 36
Ashford (Surrey)	d					15 40	15 33						16 10	16 03						16 40
Staines	d				15 23	15 44	15 37					15 53	16 14	16 07					16 23	16 44
Wraysbury	d						15 42							16 12						
Sunnymeads	d						15 45							16 15						
Datchet	d						15 49							16 19						
Windsor & Eton Riverside	a						15 54							16 24						
Egham	d				15 27	15 49						15 57	16 19						16 27	16 49
Virginia Water	a				15 31	15 53						16 01	16 23						16 31	16 53
	d				15 31	15 53						16 01	16 23						16 31	16 53
Chertsey	d					15 59							16 29							16 59
Addlestone	d					16 02							16 32							17 02
Weybridge	a					16 07							16 42							17 07
Byfleet & New Haw	d																			
West Byfleet	d																			
Woking	a																			
Longcross	d																			
Sunningdale	d				15 37							16 07							16 37	
Ascot 3	d			15 23	15 43						15 53	16 13						16 23	16 43	
Bagshot	d			15 29							15 59							16 29		
Camberley	a			15 35							16 05							16 35		
Frimley	d			15 43							16 13							16 43		
Ash Vale	d			15 49							16 19							16 49		
Aldershot	a			15 54							16 24							16 54		
	d			16 08							16 38							17 08		
Ash 5	d			16 15							16 45							17 15		
Wanborough	d			16 18							16 48							17 18		
Guildford	a			16 25							16 55							17 25		
Martins Heron	d				15 47							16 17							16 47	
Bracknell	d				15 50							16 20							16 50	
Wokingham	d				15 57							16 27							16 57	
Winnersh	d				16 00							16 30							17 00	
Winnersh Triangle	d				16 02							16 32							17 02	
Earley	d				16 07							16 37							17 07	
Reading 7	a				16 13							16 43							17 13	

Table 149

Saturdays
from 02 October

London - Hounslow, Richmond, Kingston, Windsor, Weybridge, Ascot, Guildford and Reading

		SW	SW	SW	SW	SW 1	SW 1	SW	SW	SW	SW	SW	SW 1	SW 1	SW	SW	SW	SW	SW	SW 1
London Waterloo 15 ⊖	d	15 58	16 03	16 07	16 15		16 20	16 22	16 28	16 33	16 37	16 45		16 50	16 52	16 58	17 03	17 07	17 15	
Vauxhall ⊖	d	16 02	16 07	16 11	16 19			16 26	16 32	16 37	16 41	16 49			16 56	17 02	17 07	17 11	17 19	
Queenstown Rd.(Battersea)	d		16 10	16 14	16 22			16 29		16 40	16 44	16 52			16 59		17 10	17 14	17 22	
Clapham Junction 10	d	16 08	16 13	16 17	16 25		16 28	16 32	16 38	16 43	16 47	16 55		16 58	17 02	17 08	17 13	17 17	17 25	
Wandsworth Town	d		16 16	16 20	16 28			16 35		16 46	16 50	16 58			17 05		17 16	17 20	17 28	
Putney	d	16 12	16 19	16 23	16 31			16 38	16 42	16 49	16 53	17 01			17 08	17 12	17 19	17 23	17 31	
Barnes	d		16 22	16 27	16 35			16 42		16 52	16 57	17 05			17 12		17 22	17 27	17 35	
Barnes Bridge	d			16 29				16 44			16 59				17 14			17 29		
Chiswick	d			16 32				16 47			17 02				17 17			17 32		
Kew Bridge	d			16 35				16 50			17 05				17 20			17 35		
Brentford	d			16 38				16 53			17 08				17 23			17 38		
Syon Lane	d			16 40				16 55			17 10				17 25			17 40		
Isleworth	d			16 42				16 57			17 12				17 27			17 42		
Hounslow	d			16 48				17 01			17 18				17 31			17 48		
Mortlake	d		16 24		16 37					16 54		17 07					17 24		17 37	
North Sheen	d		16 26		16 39					16 56		17 09					17 26		17 39	
Richmond ⊖	d	16 18	16 29		16 42		16 36		16 48	16 59		17 12		17 06		17 18	17 29		17 42	
St Margarets	d		16 31		16 44					17 01		17 14					17 31		17 44	
Twickenham	a	16 21	16 33		16 46		16 40		16 51	17 03		17 16		17 10		17 21	17 33		17 46	
	d	16 22	16 34		16 47		16 40		16 52	17 04		17 17		17 10		17 22	17 34		17 47	
Strawberry Hill	d		16 37							17 07							17 37			
Fulwell	a																			
Teddington	a		16 40							17 10							17 40			
Hampton Wick	a		16 44							17 14							17 44			
Kingston	a		16 46							17 16							17 46			
Whitton	d	16 25		16 53	16 50				16 55		17 23	17 20				17 25		17 53	17 50	
Feltham	d	16 29					16 46	17 06	16 59					17 16	17 36	17 29				
Ashford (Surrey)	d	16 33						17 10	17 03						17 40	17 33				
Staines	d	16 37					16 53	17 14	17 07					17 23	17 44	17 37				
Wraysbury	d	16 42							17 12							17 42				
Sunnymeads	d	16 45							17 15							17 45				
Datchet	d	16 49							17 19							17 49				
Windsor & Eton Riverside	a	16 54							17 24							17 54				
Egham	d						16 57	17 19						17 27	17 49					
Virginia Water	a						17 01	17 23						17 31	17 53					
	d						17 01	17 23						17 31	17 53					
Chertsey	d							17 29							17 59					
Addlestone	d							17 32							18 02					
Weybridge	a							17 37							18 07					
Byfleet & New Haw	d																			
West Byfleet	d																			
Woking	a																			
Longcross	d																			
Sunningdale	d						17 07							17 37						
Ascot 3	d					16 53	17 13						17 23	17 43						17 53
Bagshot	d					16 59							17 29							17 59
Camberley	a					17 05							17 35							18 05
Frimley	d					17 13							17 43							18 13
Ash Vale	d					17 19							17 49							18 19
Aldershot	a					17 24							17 54							18 24
	d					17 38							18 08							18 38
Ash 5	d					17 45							18 15							18 45
Wanborough	d					17 48							18 18							18 48
Guildford	a					17 55							18 25							18 55
Martins Heron	d						17 17							17 47						
Bracknell	d						17 20							17 50						
Wokingham	d						17 27							17 57						
Winnersh	d						17 30							18 00						
Winnersh Triangle	d						17 32							18 02						
Earley	d						17 37							18 07						
Reading 7	a						17 43							18 13						

Table 149

Saturdays
from 02 October

London - Hounslow, Richmond, Kingston, Windsor, Weybridge, Ascot, Guildford and Reading

		SW 1	SW	SW	SW	SW	SW	SW 1	SW 1	SW	SW	SW	SW	SW	SW 1	SW 1	SW	SW	SW
London Waterloo 15 ⊖	d	17 20	17 22	17 28	17 33	17 37	17 45		17 50	17 52	17 58	18 03	18 07	18 15		18 20	18 22	18 28	18 33
Vauxhall ⊖	d		17 26	17 32	17 37	17 41	17 49			17 56	18 02	18 07	18 11	18 19			18 26	18 32	18 37
Queenstown Rd.(Battersea)	d		17 29		17 40	17 44	17 52			17 59		18 10	18 14	18 22			18 29		18 40
Clapham Junction 10	d	17 28	17 32	17 38	17 43	17 47	17 55		17 58	18 02	18 08	18 13	18 17	18 25		18 28	18 32	18 38	18 43
Wandsworth Town	d		17 35		17 46	17 50	17 58			18 05		18 16	18 20	18 28			18 35		18 46
Putney	d		17 38	17 42	17 49	17 53	18 01			18 08	18 12	18 19	18 23	18 31			18 38	18 42	18 49
Barnes	d		17 42		17 52	17 57	18 05			18 12		18 22	18 27	18 35			18 42		18 52
Barnes Bridge	d		17 44			17 59				18 14			18 29				18 44		
Chiswick	d		17 47			18 02				18 17			18 32				18 47		
Kew Bridge	d		17 50			18 05				18 20			18 35				18 50		
Brentford	d		17 53			18 08				18 23			18 38				18 53		
Syon Lane	d		17 55			18 10				18 25			18 40				18 55		
Isleworth	d		17 57			18 12				18 27			18 42				18 57		
Hounslow	d		18 01			18 18				18 31			18 48				19 01		
Mortlake	d				17 54		18 07					18 24		18 37					18 54
North Sheen	d				17 56		18 09					18 26		18 39					18 56
Richmond ⊖	d	17 36		17 48	17 59		18 12		18 06		18 18	18 29		18 42		18 36		18 48	18 59
St Margarets	d				18 01		18 14					18 31		18 44					19 01
Twickenham	a	17 40		17 51	18 03		18 16		18 10		18 21	18 33		18 46		18 40		18 51	19 03
	d	17 40		17 52	18 04		18 17		18 10		18 22	18 34		18 47		18 40		18 52	19 04
Strawberry Hill	d				18 07							18 37							19 07
Fulwell	a																		
Teddington	a				18 10							18 40							19 10
Hampton Wick	a				18 14							18 44							19 14
Kingston	a				18 16							18 46							19 16
Whitton	d			17 55		18 23	18 20				18 25		18 53	18 50				18 55	
Feltham	d	17 46	18 06	17 59					18 16	18 36	18 29					18 46	19 06	18 59	
Ashford (Surrey)	d		18 10	18 03						18 40	18 33						19 10	19 03	
Staines	d	17 53	18 14	18 07					18 23	18 44	18 37					18 53	19 14	19 07	
Wraysbury	d			18 12							18 42							19 12	
Sunnymeads	d			18 15							18 45							19 15	
Datchet	d			18 19							18 49							19 19	
Windsor & Eton Riverside	a			18 24							18 54							19 24	
Egham	d	17 57	18 19						18 27	18 49						18 57	19 19		
Virginia Water	a	18 01	18 23						18 31	18 53						19 01	19 23		
	d	18 01	18 23						18 31	18 53						19 01	19 23		
Chertsey	d		18 29							18 59							19 29		
Addlestone	d		18 32							19 02							19 32		
Weybridge	a		18 37							19 07							19 37		
Byfleet & New Haw	d																		
West Byfleet	d																		
Woking	a																		
Longcross	d																		
Sunningdale	d	18 07							18 37							19 07			
Ascot 3	d	18 13						18 23	18 43						18 53	19 13			
Bagshot	d							18 29							18 59				
Camberley	a							18 35							19 05				
Frimley	d							18 43							19 13				
Ash Vale	d							18 49							19 19				
Aldershot	a							18 54							19 24				
	d							19 08							19 38				
Ash 5	d							19 15							19 45				
Wanborough	d							19 18							19 48				
Guildford	a							19 25							19 55				
Martins Heron	d	18 17							18 47							19 17			
Bracknell	d	18 20							18 50							19 20			
Wokingham	d	18 27							18 57							19 27			
Winnersh	d	18 30							19 00							19 30			
Winnersh Triangle	d	18 32							19 02							19 32			
Earley	d	18 37							19 07							19 37			
Reading 7	a	18 43							19 13							19 43			

Table 149

Saturdays from 02 October

London - Hounslow, Richmond, Kingston, Windsor, Weybridge, Ascot, Guildford and Reading

		SW	SW	SW 1	SW 1	SW	SW	SW	SW	SW	SW 1	SW 1	SW	SW	SW	SW	SW	SW 1	SW 1	SW
London Waterloo 15 ⊖	d	18 37	18 45		18 50	18 52	18 58	19 03	19 07	19 15		19 20	19 22	19 28	19 33	19 37	19 45		19 50	19 52
Vauxhall ⊖	d	18 41	18 49			18 56	19 02	19 07	19 11	19 19			19 26	19 32	19 37	19 41	19 49			19 56
Queenstown Rd.(Battersea)	d	18 44	18 52			18 59		19 10	19 14	19 22			19 29		19 40	19 44	19 52			19 59
Clapham Junction 10	d	18 47	18 55		18 58	19 02	19 08	19 13	19 17	19 25		19 28	19 32	19 38	19 43	19 47	19 55		19 58	20 02
Wandsworth Town	d	18 50	18 58			19 05		19 16	19 20	19 28			19 35		19 46	19 50	19 58			20 05
Putney	d	18 53	19 01			19 08	19 12	19 19	19 23	19 31			19 38	19 42	19 49	19 53	20 01			20 08
Barnes	d	18 57	19 05			19 12		19 22	19 27	19 35			19 42		19 52	19 57	20 05			20 12
Barnes Bridge	d	18 59				19 14			19 29				19 44			19 59				20 14
Chiswick	d	19 02				19 17			19 32				19 47			20 02				20 17
Kew Bridge	d	19 05				19 20			19 35				19 50			20 05				20 20
Brentford	d	19 08				19 23			19 38				19 53			20 08				20 23
Syon Lane	d	19 10				19 25			19 40				19 55			20 10				20 25
Isleworth	d	19 12				19 27			19 42				19 57			20 12				20 27
Hounslow	d	19 18				19 31			19 48				20 01			20 18				20 31
Mortlake	d		19 07					19 24		19 37					19 54		20 07			
North Sheen	d		19 09					19 26		19 39					19 56		20 09			
Richmond ⊖	d		19 12		19 06		19 18	19 29		19 42		19 36		19 48	19 59		20 12		20 06	
St Margarets	d		19 14					19 31		19 44					20 01		20 14			
Twickenham	a		19 16		19 10		19 21	19 33		19 46		19 40		19 51	20 03		20 16		20 10	
	d		19 17		19 10		19 22	19 34		19 47		19 40		19 52	20 04		20 17		20 10	
Strawberry Hill	d							19 37							20 07					
Fulwell	a																			
Teddington	a							19 40							20 10					
Hampton Wick	a							19 44							20 14					
Kingston	a							19 46							20 16					
Whitton	d	19 23	19 20				19 25		19 53	19 50				19 55		20 23	20 20			
Feltham	d				19 16	19 36	19 29					19 46	20 06	19 59					20 16	20 36
Ashford (Surrey)	d					19 40	19 33						20 10	20 03						20 40
Staines	d				19 23	19 44	19 37					19 53	20 14	20 07					20 23	20 44
Wraysbury	d						19 42							20 12						
Sunnymeads	d						19 45							20 15						
Datchet	d						19 49							20 19						
Windsor & Eton Riverside	a						19 54							20 24						
Egham	d				19 27	19 49						19 57	20 19						20 27	20 49
Virginia Water	a				19 31	19 53						20 01	20 23						20 31	20 53
	d				19 31	19 53						20 01	20 23						20 31	20 53
Chertsey	d					19 59							20 29							20 59
Addlestone	d					20 02							20 32							21 02
Weybridge	a					20 07							20 37							21 07
Byfleet & New Haw	d																			
West Byfleet	d																			
Woking	a																			
Longcross	d																			
Sunningdale	d				19 37							20 07							20 37	
Ascot 3	d			19 23	19 43						19 53	20 13						20 23	20 43	
Bagshot	d			19 29							19 59							20 29		
Camberley	a			19 35							20 05							20 35		
Frimley	d			19 43							20 13							20 43		
Ash Vale	d			19 49							20 19							20 49		
Aldershot	a			19 54							20 24							20 54		
	d			20 08							20 38							21 08		
Ash 5	d			20 15							20 45							21 15		
Wanborough	d			20 18							20 48							21 18		
Guildford	a			20 25							20 55							21 25		
Martins Heron	d				19 47							20 17							20 47	
Bracknell	d				19 50							20 20							20 50	
Wokingham	d				19 57							20 27							20 57	
Winnersh	d				20 00							20 30							21 00	
Winnersh Triangle	d				20 02							20 32							21 02	
Earley	d				20 07							20 37							21 07	
Reading 7	a				20 13							20 43							21 13	

Table 149

Saturdays from 02 October

London - Hounslow, Richmond, Kingston, Windsor, Weybridge, Ascot, Guildford and Reading

		SW	SW	SW	SW	SW 1	SW 1	SW	SW	SW	SW	SW	SW 1	SW 1	SW	SW	SW	SW	SW	SW 1	SW
London Waterloo 15 ⊖	d	19 58	20 03	20 07	20 15		20 20	20 22	20 28	20 33	20 37	20 45		20 50	20 52	20 58	21 03	21 07	21 15	21 20	21 22
Vauxhall ⊖	d	20 02	20 07	20 11	20 19			20 26	20 32	20 37	20 41	20 49			20 56	21 02	21 07	21 11	21 19		21 26
Queenstown Rd.(Battersea)	d		20 10	20 14	20 22			20 29		20 40	20 44	20 52			20 59		21 10	21 14	21 22		21 29
Clapham Junction 10	d	20 08	20 13	20 17	20 25		20 28	20 32	20 38	20 43	20 47	20 55		20 58	21 02	21 08	21 13	21 17	21 25	21 28	21 32
Wandsworth Town	d		20 16	20 20	20 28			20 35		20 46	20 50	20 58			21 05		21 16	21 20	21 28		21 35
Putney	d	20 12	20 19	20 23	20 31			20 38	20 42	20 49	20 53	21 01			21 08	21 12	21 19	21 23	21 31		21 38
Barnes	d		20 22	20 27	20 35			20 42		20 52	20 57	21 05			21 12		21 22	21 27	21 35		21 42
Barnes Bridge	d			20 29				20 44			20 59				21 14			21 29			21 44
Chiswick	d			20 32				20 47			21 02				21 17			21 32			21 47
Kew Bridge	d			20 35				20 50			21 05				21 20			21 35			21 50
Brentford	d			20 38				20 53			21 08				21 23			21 38			21 53
Syon Lane	d			20 40				20 55			21 10				21 25			21 40			21 55
Isleworth	d			20 42				20 57			21 12				21 27			21 42			21 57
Hounslow	d			20 48				21 01			21 18				21 31			21 48			22 01
Mortlake	d		20 24		20 37					20 54		21 07					21 24		21 37		
North Sheen	d		20 26		20 39					20 56		21 09					21 26		21 39		
Richmond ⊖	d	20 18	20 29		20 42		20 36		20 48	20 59		21 12		21 06		21 18	21 29		21 42	21 36	
St Margarets	d		20 31		20 44					21 01		21 14					21 31		21 44		
Twickenham	a	20 21	20 33		20 46		20 40		20 51	21 03		21 16		21 10		21 21	21 33		21 46	21 40	
	d	20 22	20 34		20 47		20 40		20 52	21 04		21 17		21 10		21 22	21 34		21 47	21 40	
Strawberry Hill	d		20 37							21 07							21 37				
Fulwell	a																				
Teddington	a		20 40							21 10							21 40				
Hampton Wick	a		20 44							21 14							21 44				
Kingston	a		20 46							21 16							21 46				
Whitton	d	20 25		20 53	20 50				20 55		21 23	21 20				21 25		21 53	21 50		
Feltham	d	20 29					20 46	21 06	20 59					21 16	21 36	21 29				21 46	22 06
Ashford (Surrey)	d	20 33						21 10	21 03						21 40	21 33					22 10
Staines	d	20 37					20 53	21 14	21 07					21 23	21 44	21 37				21 53	22 14
Wraysbury	d	20 42							21 12							21 42					
Sunnymeads	d	20 45							21 15							21 45					
Datchet	d	20 49							21 19							21 49					
Windsor & Eton Riverside	a	20 54							21 24							21 54					
Egham	d						20 57	21 19						21 27	21 49					21 57	22 19
Virginia Water	a						21 01	21 23						21 31	21 53					22 01	22 23
	d						21 01	21 23						21 31	21 53					22 01	22 23
Chertsey	d							21 29							21 59						22 29
Addlestone	d							21 32							22 02						22 32
Weybridge	a							21 37							22 07						22 37
Byfleet & New Haw	d																				
West Byfleet	d																				
Woking	a																				
Longcross	d																				
Sunningdale	d						21 07							21 37						22 07	
Ascot 3	d					20 53	21 13						21 23	21 43						22 13	
Bagshot	d					20 59							21 29								
Camberley	a					21 05							21 35								
Frimley	d					21 13							21 43								
Ash Vale	d					21 19							21 49								
Aldershot	a					21 24							21 54								
	d					21 38							22 08								
Ash 5	d					21 45							22 15								
Wanborough	d					21 48							22 18								
Guildford	a					21 55							22 25								
Martins Heron	d						21 17							21 47						22 17	
Bracknell	d						21 20							21 50						22 20	
Wokingham	d						21 27							21 57						22 27	
Winnersh	d						21 30							22 00						22 30	
Winnersh Triangle	d						21 32							22 02						22 32	
Earley	d						21 37							22 07						22 37	
Reading 7	a						21 43							22 13						22 43	

Table 149

Saturdays
from 02 October

London - Hounslow, Richmond, Kingston, Windsor, Weybridge, Ascot, Guildford and Reading

		SW	SW	SW	SW	SW	SW	SW	SW	SW	SW	SW	SW	SW	SW	SW	SW	SW	SW
						■	■				■					■	■		
London Waterloo ■ ⊖	d	21 28	21 33	21 37	21 45		21 50	21 52	21 58	22 03	22 20	22 22	22 27	22 28	22 33		22 50	22 52	22 58
Vauxhall ⊖	d	21 32	21 37	21 41	21 49			21 56	22 02	22 07		22 26	22 31	22 32	22 37			22 56	23 02
Queenstown Rd.(Battersea)	d		21 40	21 44	21 52			21 59		22 10		22 29			22 40			22 59	
Clapham Junction ■	d	21 38	21 43	21 47	21 55		21 58	22 02	22 08	22 13	22 28	22 32		22 38	22 43		22 58	23 02	23 08
Wandsworth Town	d		21 46	21 50	21 58			22 05		22 16		22 35			22 46			23 05	
Putney	d	21 42	21 49	21 53	22 01			22 08	22 12	22 19		22 38		22 42	22 49			23 08	23 12
Barnes	d		21 52	21 57	22 05			22 12		22 22		22 42			22 52			23 12	
Barnes Bridge	d			21 59				22 14				22 44						23 14	
Chiswick	d			22 02				22 17				22 47						23 17	
Kew Bridge	d			22 05				22 20				22 50						23 20	
Brentford	d			22 08				22 23				22 53						23 23	
Syon Lane	d			22 10				22 25				22 55						23 25	
Isleworth	d			22 12				22 27				22 57						23 27	
Hounslow	d			22 18				22 31				23 01						23 31	
Mortlake	d		21 54		22 07					22 24					22 54				
North Sheen	d		21 56		22 09					22 26					22 56				
Richmond ⊖	d	21 48	21 59		22 12		22 06		22 18	22 29	22 36			22 48	22 59		23 06		23 18
St Margarets	d		22 01		22 14					22 31					23 01				
Twickenham	a	21 51	22 03		22 16		22 10		22 21	22 33	22 40		23 12	22 51	23 03		23 10		23 21
	d	21 52	22 04				22 10		22 22	22 34	22 40		23 13	22 52	23 04		23 10		23 22
Strawberry Hill	d		22 07							22 37					23 07				
Fulwell	a																		
Teddington	a		22 10							22 40					23 10				
Hampton Wick	a		22 14							22 44					23 14				
Kingston	a		22 16							22 46					23 16				
Whitton	d	21 55		22 23					22 25					22 55					23 25
Feltham	d	21 59					22 16	22 36	22 29		22 46	23 06		22 59			23 16	23 36	23 29
Ashford (Surrey)	d	22 03						22 40	22 33			23 10		23 03				23 40	23 33
Staines	d	22 07					22 23	22 44	22 37		22 53	23 14		23 07			23 23	23 44	23 37
Wraysbury	d	22 12							22 42					23 12					23 42
Sunnymeads	d	22 15							22 45					23 15					23 45
Datchet	d	22 19							22 49					23 19					23 49
Windsor & Eton Riverside	a	22 24							22 56					23 24					23 54
Egham	d						22 27	22 49			22 57	23 19					23 27	23 49	
Virginia Water	a						22 31	22 53			23 01	23 23					23 31	23 53	
	d						22 31	22 53			23 01	23 23					23 31	23 53	
Chertsey	d							22 59				23 29						23 59	
Addlestone	d							23 02				23 32						00 02	
Weybridge	a							23 07				23 37							
Byfleet & New Haw	d																	00 06	
West Byfleet	d																	00 09	
Woking	a																	00 20	
Longcross	d																		
Sunningdale	d						22 37				23 07						23 37		
Ascot ■	d					22 23	22 43				23 13					23 23	23 43		
Bagshot	d					22 29										23 29			
Camberley	a					22 35										23 35			
Frimley	d					22 43										23 43			
Ash Vale	d					22 49										23 49			
Aldershot	a					22 54										23 54			
	d					23 08													
Ash ■	d					23 15													
Wanborough	d					23 18													
Guildford	a					23 25													
Martins Heron	d						22 47				23 17						23 47		
Bracknell	d						22 50				23 20						23 50		
Wokingham	d						22 57				23 27						23 57		
Winnersh	d						23 00				23 30						23 59		
Winnersh Triangle	d						23 02				23 32						00 01		
Earley	d						23 05				23 37						00 05		
Reading ■	a						23 13				23 43						00 13		

Table 149

Saturdays
from 02 October

London - Hounslow, Richmond, Kingston, Windsor, Weybridge, Ascot, Guildford and Reading

		SW	SW	SW	SW	SW	SW	SW	SW
				■					
London Waterloo ■ ⊖	d	23 03	23 13	23 20	23 22	23 33	23 38	23 52	23 58
Vauxhall ⊖	d	23 07	23 17		23 26	23 37		23 56	00 02
Queenstown Rd.(Battersea)	d	23 10			23 29	23 40		23 59	
Clapham Junction ■	d	23 13	23 23	23 28	23 32	23 43	23 46	00 02	00 08
Wandsworth Town	d	23 16			23 35	23 46		00 05	
Putney	d	23 19	23 27		23 38	23 49		00 08	00 12
Barnes	d	23 22			23 42	23 52		00 12	
Barnes Bridge	d				23 44			00 14	
Chiswick	d				23 47			00 17	
Kew Bridge	d				23 50			00 20	
Brentford	d				23 53			00 23	
Syon Lane	d				23 55			00 25	
Isleworth	d				23 57			00 27	
Hounslow	d				00 01			00 31	
Mortlake	d	23 24				23 54			
North Sheen	d	23 26				23 56			
Richmond ⊖	d	23 29	23 33	23 37		23 59	23 54		00 18
St Margarets	d	23 31				00 01			
Twickenham	a	23 33	23 37	23 41		00 04	23 58		00 21
	d	23 34	23 37	23 41		00 04	23 58		00 22
Strawberry Hill	d	23 37				00 07			
Fulwell	a								
Teddington	a	23 40				00 11			
Hampton Wick	a	23 44				00 14			
Kingston	a	23 46				00 16			
Whitton	d		23 40						00 25
Feltham	d		23 44	23 48	00 06		00 04	00 36	00 29
Ashford (Surrey)	d		23 48		00 10			00 40	00 33
Staines	d		23 52	23 56	00 14		00 11	00a46	00a37
Wraysbury	d		23 57						
Sunnymeads	d		23 59						
Datchet	d		00 04						
Windsor & Eton Riverside	a		00 09						
Egham	d			00 01	00 19		00 15		
Virginia Water	a			00 05	00 23		00 19		
	d			00 05	00 23		00 19		
Chertsey	d				00 29				
Addlestone	d				00 32				
Weybridge	a				00 37				
Byfleet & New Haw	d								
West Byfleet	d								
Woking	a								
Longcross	d								
Sunningdale	d			00 11			00 25		
Ascot ■	d			00 15			00 30		
Bagshot	d								
Camberley	a								
Frimley	d								
Ash Vale	d								
Aldershot	a								
	d								
Ash ■	d								
Wanborough	d								
Guildford	a								
Martins Heron	d			00 19			00 34		
Bracknell	d			00 23			00 37		
Wokingham	d			00 32			00 44		
Winnersh	d			00 36					
Winnersh Triangle	d			00 38					
Earley	d			00 40					
Reading ■	a			00 48			00 55		

Table 149

Sundays
until 19 September

London - Hounslow, Richmond, Kingston, Windsor, Weybridge, Ascot, Guildford and Reading

		SW [1]	SW	SW	SW [1]	SW	SW	SW	SW	SW	SW
London Waterloo [15] ⊖	d	22p50	22p52	23p13	23p20	23p22	23p33	23p38	23p52	23p58	00 18
Vauxhall ⊖	d		22p56	23p17		23p26	23p37		23p56	00 02	00 22
Queenstown Rd.(Battersea)	d		22p59			23p29	23p40		23p59		00 25
Clapham Junction [10]	d	22p58	23p02	23p23	23p28	23p32	23p43	23p46	00 02	00 08	00 28
Wandsworth Town	d		23p05			23p35	23p46		00 05		00 31
Putney	d		23p08	23p27		23p38	23p49		00 08	00 12	00 34
Barnes	d		23p12			23p42	23p52		00 12		00 37
Barnes Bridge	d		23p14			23p44			00 14		
Chiswick	d		23p17			23p47			00 17		
Kew Bridge	d		23p20			23p50			00 20		
Brentford	d		23p23			23p53			00 23		
Syon Lane	d		23p25			23p55			00 25		
Isleworth	d		23p27			23p57			00 27		
Hounslow	d		23p31			00 01			00 31		
Mortlake	d						23p54				00 39
North Sheen	d						23p56				00 41
Richmond ⊖	d	23p06		23p33	23p37		23p59	23p54		00 18	00 44
St Margarets	d						00 01				00 46
Twickenham	a	23p10		23p37	23p41		00 04	23p58		00 21	00 48
	d	23p10		23p37	23p41		00 04	23p58		00 22	00 49
Strawberry Hill	d						00 07				00s52
Fulwell	a										
Teddington	a						00 11				00s55
Hampton Wick	a						00 14				00s58
Kingston	a						00 06				01 00
Whitton	d			23p40						00 25	
Feltham	d	23p16	23p36	23p44	23p48	00 06		00 04	00 36	00 29	
Ashford (Surrey)	d		23p40	23p48		00 10			00 40	00 33	
Staines	d	23p23	23p44	23p52	23p56	00 14		00 11	00a46	00a37	
Wraysbury	d			23p56							
Sunnymeads	d			23p59							
Datchet	d			00 02							
Windsor & Eton Riverside	a			00 06							
Egham	d	23p27	23p49		00 01	00 19		00 15			
Virginia Water	a	23p31	23p53		00 05	00 23		00 19			
	d	23p31	23p53		00 05	00 23		00 19			
Chertsey	d		23p59			00 29					
Addlestone	d		00 02			00 32					
Weybridge	a										
Byfleet & New Haw	d		00 06								
West Byfleet	d		00 09								
Woking	a		00 20								
Longcross	d										
Sunningdale	d	23p37			00 11			00 25			
Ascot [3]	d	23p43			00 15			00 30			
Bagshot	d										
Camberley	a										
Frimley	d										
Ash Vale	d										
Aldershot	a										
	d										
Ash [5]	d										
Wanborough	d										
Guildford	a										
Martins Heron	d	23p47			00 19			00 34			
Bracknell	d	23p50			00 23			00 37			
Wokingham	d	23p57			00 32			00 44			
Winnersh	d	23p59			00 36						
Winnersh Triangle	d	00 01			00 38						
Earley	d	00 05			00 40						
Reading [7]	a	00 10			00 45			00 52			

		SW [1]	SW	SW	SW	SW	SW [1]	SW	SW	SW
London Waterloo [15] ⊖	d		06 14	06 18		06 44	07 09	07 14		07 44
Vauxhall ⊖	d		06 18	06 22		06 48	07 13	07 18		07 48
Queenstown Rd.(Battersea)	d		06 21			06 51		07 21		07 51
Clapham Junction [10]	d		06 24			06 54	07 19	07 24		07 54
Wandsworth Town	d		06 27			06 57		07 27		07 57
Putney	d		06 30			07 00	07 23	07 30		08 00
Barnes	d		06 33			07 03		07 33		08 03
Barnes Bridge	d									
Chiswick	d									
Kew Bridge	d									
Brentford	d									
Syon Lane	d									
Isleworth	d									
Hounslow	d									
Mortlake	d		06 35			07 05		07 35		08 05
North Sheen	d		06 37			07 07		07 37		08 07
Richmond ⊖	d		06 40			07 10	07 29	07 40		08 10
St Margarets	d		06 42			07 12		07 42		08 12
Twickenham	a		06 44	07 02		07 14	07 32	07 44		08 14
	d		06 45	07 03		07 15	07 33	07 45		08 15
Strawberry Hill	d		06 49					07 49		
Fulwell	a									
Teddington	a		06 52					07 52		
Hampton Wick	a		06 57					07 57		
Kingston	a		06 59					07 59		
Whitton	d					07 18				08 18
Feltham	d					07 22	07 39			08 22
Ashford (Surrey)	d					07 26				08 26
Staines	d				06 32	07 30	07 45		07 40	08 30
Wraysbury	d					07 34				08 34
Sunnymeads	d					07 37				08 37
Datchet	d					07 40				08 40
Windsor & Eton Riverside	a					07 44				08 44
Egham	d				06 36		07 50		07 45	
Virginia Water	a				06 41		07 54		07 49	
	d				06 41		07 54		07 49	
Chertsey	d				06 46				07 55	
Addlestone	d				06 49				07 58	
Weybridge	a				06 53					
Byfleet & New Haw	d								08 02	
West Byfleet	d								08 05	
Woking	a								08 11	
Longcross	d									
Sunningdale	d						07 59			
Ascot [3]	d	00 32					08 04			
Bagshot	d	00 38								
Camberley	a	00 44								
Frimley	d	00 48								
Ash Vale	d	00 57								
Aldershot	a	01s02								
	d	01s06								
Ash [5]	d									
Wanborough	d									
Guildford	a									
Martins Heron	d						08 08			
Bracknell	d						08 11			
Wokingham	d						08 18			
Winnersh	d						08 21			
Winnersh Triangle	d						08 23			
Earley	d						08 26			
Reading [7]	a						08 31			

Table 149

Sundays
until 19 September

London - Hounslow, Richmond, Kingston, Windsor, Weybridge, Ascot, Guildford and Reading

		SW	SW [1]	SW [1]	SW [1]	SW	SW [1]	SW [1]	SW	SW	SW [1]
London Waterloo [15] ⊖	d	07 50			08 09	08 14		08 39	08 44	08 50	09 09
Vauxhall ⊖	d	07 54			08 13	08 18		08 43	08 48	08 54	09 13
Queenstown Rd.(Battersea)	d	07 57				08 21			08 51	08 57	
Clapham Junction [10]	d	08 00			08 19	08 24		08 49	08 54	09 00	09 19
Wandsworth Town	d	08 03				08 27			08 57	09 03	
Putney	d	08 06			08 23	08 30		08 53	09 00	09 06	09 23
Barnes	d	08 09				08 33			09 03	09 09	
Barnes Bridge	d	08 11								09 11	
Chiswick	d	08 13								09 13	
Kew Bridge	d	08 16								09 16	
Brentford	d	08 19								09 19	
Syon Lane	d	08 21								09 21	
Isleworth	d	08 23								09 23	
Hounslow	d	08 26								09 26	
Mortlake	d					08 35			09 05		
North Sheen	d					08 37			09 07		
Richmond ⊖	d				08 29	08 40		08 59	09 10		09 29
St Margarets	d					08 42			09 12		
Twickenham	a				08 32	08 44		09 02	09 14		09 32
	d				08 33	08 45		09 03	09 15		09 33
Strawberry Hill	d					08 49					
Fulwell	a										
Teddington	a					08 52					
Hampton Wick	a					08 57					
Kingston	a					08 59					
Whitton	d								09 18		
Feltham	d	08 32			08 39			09 09	09 22	09 32	09 39
Ashford (Surrey)	d	08 36							09 26	09 36	
Staines	d	08 40		08 15	08 45			09 15	09 30	09 40	09 45
Wraysbury	d								09 34		
Sunnymeads	d								09 37		
Datchet	d								09 40		
Windsor & Eton Riverside	a								09 44		
Egham	d	08 45		08 20	08 50			09 20		09 45	09 50
Virginia Water	a	08 49		08 24	08 54			09 24		09 49	09 54
	d	08 49		08 24	08 54			09 24		09 49	09 54
Chertsey	d	08 55								09 55	
Addlestone	d	08 58								09 58	
Weybridge	a										
Byfleet & New Haw	d	09 02								10 02	
West Byfleet	d	09 05								10 05	
Woking	a	09 11								10 11	
Longcross	d										
Sunningdale	d			08 29	08 59			09 29			09 59
Ascot [3]	d		08 13	08 34	09 04		09 13	09 34			10 04
Bagshot	d		08 19				09 19				
Camberley	a		08 25				09 25				
Frimley	d		08 29				09 29				
Ash Vale	d		08 36				09 36				
Aldershot	a		08 41				09 41				
	d		08 48				09 48				
Ash [5]	d		08 55				09 55				
Wanborough	d		08 58				09 58				
Guildford	a		09 05				10 05				
Martins Heron	d			08 38	09 08			09 38			10 08
Bracknell	d			08 41	09 11			09 41			10 11
Wokingham	d			08 48	09 18			09 48			10 18
Winnersh	d			08 51	09 21			09 51			10 21
Winnersh Triangle	d			08 53	09 23			09 53			10 23
Earley	d			08 56	09 26			09 56			10 26
Reading [7]	a			09 01	09 31			10 01			10 31

		SW	SW	SW [1]	SW [1]	SW	SW	SW [1]	SW	SW
London Waterloo [15] ⊖	d	09 14	09 25		09 39	09 44	09 50	10 09	10 14	10 25
Vauxhall ⊖	d	09 18	09 29		09 43	09 48	09 54	10 13	10 18	10 29
Queenstown Rd.(Battersea)	d	09 21				09 51	09 57		10 21	
Clapham Junction [10]	d	09 24	09 35		09 49	09 54	10 00	10 19	10 24	10 35
Wandsworth Town	d	09 27				09 57	10 03		10 27	
Putney	d	09 30	09 39		09 53	10 00	10 06	10 23	10 30	10 39
Barnes	d	09 33				10 03	10 09		10 33	
Barnes Bridge	d						10 11			
Chiswick	d						10 13			
Kew Bridge	d						10 16			
Brentford	d						10 19			
Syon Lane	d						10 21			
Isleworth	d						10 23			
Hounslow	d						10 26			
Mortlake	d	09 35				10 05			10 35	
North Sheen	d	09 37				10 07			10 37	
Richmond ⊖	d	09 40	09 45		09 59	10 10		10 29	10 40	10 45
St Margarets	d	09 42				10 12			10 42	
Twickenham	a	09 44	09 48		10 02	10 14		10 32	10 44	10 48
	d	09 45	09 49		10 03	10 15		10 33	10 45	10 49
Strawberry Hill	d	09 49							10 49	
Fulwell	a									
Teddington	a	09 52							10 52	
Hampton Wick	a	09 57							10 57	
Kingston	a	09 59							10 59	
Whitton	d		09 52			10 18				10 52
Feltham	d		09 56		10 09	10 22	10 32	10 39		10 56
Ashford (Surrey)	d		10 00			10 26	10 36			11 00
Staines	d		10 04		10 15	10 30	10 40	10 45		11 04
Wraysbury	d					10 34				
Sunnymeads	d					10 37				
Datchet	d		10 12			10 40				11 12
Windsor & Eton Riverside	a		10 16			10 44				11 16
Egham	d				10 20		10 45	10 50		
Virginia Water	a				10 24		10 49	10 54		
	d				10 24		10 49	10 54		
Chertsey	d						10 55			
Addlestone	d						10 58			
Weybridge	a									
Byfleet & New Haw	d						11 02			
West Byfleet	d						11 05			
Woking	a						11 11			
Longcross	d									
Sunningdale	d				10 29			10 59		
Ascot [3]	d			10 13	10 34			11 04		
Bagshot	d			10 19						
Camberley	a			10 25						
Frimley	d			10 28						
Ash Vale	d			10 35						
Aldershot	a			10 41						
	d			10 48						
Ash [5]	d			10 55						
Wanborough	d			10 58						
Guildford	a			11 05						
Martins Heron	d				10 38			11 08		
Bracknell	d				10 41			11 11		
Wokingham	d				10 48			11 18		
Winnersh	d				10 51			11 21		
Winnersh Triangle	d				10 53			11 23		
Earley	d				10 56			11 26		
Reading [7]	a				11 01			11 31		

Table 149

Sundays until 19 September

London - Hounslow, Richmond, Kingston, Windsor, Weybridge, Ascot, Guildford and Reading

		SW ■	SW ■	SW	SW	SW ■	SW	SW	SW ■	SW ■	SW	SW	SW ■	SW	SW	SW ■	SW ■	SW	SW	SW ■
London Waterloo ■ ⊖	d		10 39	10 44	10 50	11 09	11 14	11 25		11 39	11 44	11 50	12 09	12 14	12 25		12 39	12 44	12 50	13 09
Vauxhall ⊖	d		10 43	10 48	10 54	11 13	11 19	11 29		11 43	11 48	11 54	12 13	12 19	12 29		12 43	12 48	12 54	13 13
Queenstown Rd.(Battersea)	d			10 51	10 57		11 22				11 51	11 57		12 22				12 51	12 57	
Clapham Junction ■	d		10 49	10 54	11 00	11 19	11 25	11 35		11 49	11 54	12 00	12 19	12 25	12 35		12 49	12 54	13 00	13 19
Wandsworth Town	d			10 57	11 03		11 28				11 57	12 03		12 28				12 57	13 03	
Putney	d		10 53	11 00	11 06	11 23	11 31	11 39		11 53	12 00	12 06	12 23	12 31	12 39		12 53	13 00	13 06	13 23
Barnes	d			11 03	11 09		11 34				12 03	12 09		12 34				13 03	13 09	
Barnes Bridge	d				11 11							12 11							13 11	
Chiswick	d				11 13							12 13							13 13	
Kew Bridge	d				11 16							12 16							13 16	
Brentford	d				11 19							12 19							13 19	
Syon Lane	d				11 21							12 21							13 21	
Isleworth	d				11 23							12 23							13 23	
Hounslow	d				11 26							12 26							13 26	
Mortlake	d			11 05			11 36				12 05			12 36				13 05		
North Sheen	d			11 07			11 38				12 07			12 38				13 07		
Richmond ⊖	d		10 59	11 10		11 29	11 41	11 45		11 59	12 10		12 29	12 41	12 45		12 59	13 10		13 29
St Margarets	d			11 12			11 43				12 12			12 43				13 12		
Twickenham	a		11 02	11 14		11 32	11 45	11 48		12 02	12 14		12 32	12 45	12 48		13 02	13 14		13 32
	d		11 03	11 15		11 33	11 46	11 49		12 03	12 15		12 33	12 46	12 49		13 03	13 15		13 33
Strawberry Hill	d						11 50							12 50						
Fulwell	a																			
Teddington	a						11 53							12 53						
Hampton Wick	a						11 57							12 57						
Kingston	a						11 59							12 59						
Whitton	d			11 18				11 52			12 18				12 52			13 18		
Feltham	d		11 09	11 22	11 32	11 39		11 56		12 09	12 22	12 32	12 39		12 56		13 09	13 22	13 32	13 39
Ashford (Surrey)	d			11 26	11 36			12 00			12 26	12 36			13 00			13 26	13 36	
Staines	d		11 15	11 30	11 40	11 45		12 04		12 15	12 30	12 40	12 45		13 04		13 15	13 30	13 40	13 45
Wraysbury	d			11 34							12 34							13 34		
Sunnymeads	d			11 37							12 37							13 37		
Datchet	d			11 40				12 12			12 40				13 12			13 40		
Windsor & Eton Riverside	a			11 44				12 16			12 44				13 16			13 44		
Egham	d		11 20		11 45	11 50				12 20		12 45	12 50				13 20		13 45	13 50
Virginia Water	a		11 24		11 49	11 54				12 24		12 49	12 54				13 24		13 49	13 54
	d		11 24		11 49	11 54				12 24		12 49	12 54				13 24		13 49	13 54
Chertsey	d				11 55							12 55							13 55	
Addlestone	d				11 58							12 58							13 58	
Weybridge	a																			
Byfleet & New Haw	d				12 02							13 02							14 02	
West Byfleet	d				12 05							13 05							14 05	
Woking	a				12 11							13 11							14 11	
Longcross	d																			
Sunningdale	d		11 29			11 59				12 29			12 59				13 29			13 59
Ascot ■	d	11 13	11 34			12 04			12 13	12 34			13 04			13 13	13 34			14 04
Bagshot	d	11 19							12 19							13 19				
Camberley	a	11 25							12 25							13 25				
Frimley	d	11 29							12 29							13 29				
Ash Vale	d	11 36							12 36							13 36				
Aldershot	a	11 41							12 41							13 41				
	d	11 48							12 48							13 48				
Ash ■	d	11 55							12 55							13 55				
Wanborough	d	11 58							12 58							13 58				
Guildford	a	12 05							13 05							14 05				
Martins Heron	d		11 38			12 08				12 38			13 08				13 38			14 08
Bracknell	d		11 41			12 11				12 41			13 11				13 41			14 11
Wokingham	d		11 48			12 18				12 48			13 18				13 48			14 18
Winnersh	d		11 51			12 21				12 51			13 21				13 51			14 21
Winnersh Triangle	d		11 53			12 23				12 53			13 23				13 53			14 23
Earley	d		11 56			12 26				12 56			13 26				13 56			14 26
Reading ■	a		12 01			12 31				13 01			13 31				14 01			14 31

Table 149

Sundays until 19 September

London - Hounslow, Richmond, Kingston, Windsor, Weybridge, Ascot, Guildford and Reading

		SW	SW	SW ■	SW ■	SW	SW	SW	SW ■	SW	SW	SW ■	SW ■	SW	SW	SW	SW ■	SW	SW	SW ■
London Waterloo ■ ⊖	d	13 14	13 25		13 39	13 44	13 50	13 56	14 09	14 14	14 25		14 39	14 44	14 50	14 56	15 09	15 14	15 25	
Vauxhall ⊖	d	13 18	13 29		13 43	13 48	13 54	14 00	14 13	14 18	14 29		14 43	14 48	14 54	15 00	15 13	15 18	15 29	
Queenstown Rd.(Battersea)	d	13 21				13 51	13 57	14 03		14 21				14 51	14 57	15 03		15 21		
Clapham Junction ■	d	13 24	13 35		13 49	13 54	14 00	14 06	14 19	14 24	14 35		14 49	14 54	15 00	15 06	15 19	15 24	15 35	
Wandsworth Town	d	13 27				13 57	14 03	14 09		14 27				14 57	15 03	15 09		15 27		
Putney	d	13 30	13 39		13 53	14 00	14 06	14 12	14 23	14 30	14 39		14 53	15 00	15 06	15 12	15 23	15 30	15 39	
Barnes	d	13 33				14 03	14 09	14 15		14 33				15 03	15 09	15 15		15 33		
Barnes Bridge	d						14 11								15 11					
Chiswick	d						14 13								15 13					
Kew Bridge	d						14 16								15 16					
Brentford	d						14 19								15 19					
Syon Lane	d						14 21								15 21					
Isleworth	d						14 23								15 23					
Hounslow	d						14 26								15 26					
Mortlake	d	13 35				14 05		14 17		14 35				15 05		15 17		15 35		
North Sheen	d	13 37				14 07		14 19		14 37				15 07		15 19		15 37		
Richmond ⊖	d	13 40	13 45		13 59	14 10		14 22	14 29	14 40	14 45		14 59	15 10		15 22	15 29	15 40	15 45	
St Margarets	d	13 42				14 12		14 24		14 42				15 12		15 24		15 42		
Twickenham	a	13 44	13 48		14 02	14 14		14 26	14 32	14 44	14 48		15 02	15 14		15 26	15 32	15 44	15 48	
	d	13 45	13 49		14 03	14 15		14 27	14 33	14 45	14 49		15 03	15 15		15 27	15 33	15 45	15 49	
Strawberry Hill	d	13 49						14 30		14 49						15 30		15 49		
Fulwell	a																			
Teddington	a	13 52						14 33		14 52						15 33		15 52		
Hampton Wick	a	13 57						14 36		14 57						15 36		15 57		
Kingston	a	13 59						14 38		14 59						15 38		15 59		
Whitton	d		13 52			14 18					14 52			15 18					15 52	
Feltham	d		13 56		14 09	14 22	14 32		14 39		14 56		15 09	15 22	15 32		15 39		15 56	
Ashford (Surrey)	d		14 00			14 26	14 36				15 00			15 26	15 36				16 00	
Staines	d		14 04		14 15	14 30	14 40		14 45		15 04		15 15	15 30	15 40		15 45		16 04	
Wraysbury	d					14 34								15 34						
Sunnymeads	d					14 37								15 37						
Datchet	d		14 12			14 40					15 12			15 40					16 12	
Windsor & Eton Riverside	a		14 16			14 44					15 16			15 44					16 16	
Egham	d				14 20		14 45		14 50				15 20		15 45		15 50			
Virginia Water	a				14 24		14 49		14 54				15 24		15 49		15 54			
	d				14 24		14 49		14 54				15 24		15 49		15 54			
Chertsey	d						14 55								15 55					
Addlestone	d						14 58								15 58					
Weybridge	a																			
Byfleet & New Haw	d						15 02								16 02					
West Byfleet	d						15 05								16 05					
Woking	a						15 11								16 11					
Longcross	d																			
Sunningdale	d				14 29				14 59				15 29				15 59			
Ascot ■	d			14 13	14 34				15 04			15 13	15 34				16 04			16 13
Bagshot	d			14 19								15 19								16 19
Camberley	a			14 25								15 25								16 25
Frimley	d			14 29								15 29								16 29
Ash Vale	d			14 36								15 36								16 36
Aldershot	a			14 41								15 41								16 41
	d			14 48								15 48								16 48
Ash ■	d			14 55								15 55								16 55
Wanborough	d			14 58								15 58								16 58
Guildford	a			15 05								16 05								17 05
Martins Heron	d				14 38				15 08				15 38				16 08			
Bracknell	d				14 41				15 11				15 41				16 11			
Wokingham	d				14 48				15 18				15 48				16 18			
Winnersh	d				14 51				15 21				15 51				16 21			
Winnersh Triangle	d				14 53				15 23				15 53				16 23			
Earley	d				14 56				15 26				15 56				16 26			
Reading ■	a				15 01				15 31				16 01				16 31			

Table 149

Sundays until 19 September

London - Hounslow, Richmond, Kingston, Windsor, Weybridge, Ascot, Guildford and Reading

		SW [1]	SW	SW	SW	SW [1]	SW	SW	SW [1]	SW [1]	SW	SW	SW	SW [1]	SW	SW	SW [1]	SW [1]	SW	SW
London Waterloo [15] ⊖	d	15 39	15 44	15 50	15 56	16 09	16 14	16 25		16 39	16 44	16 50	16 56	17 09	17 14	17 25		17 39	17 44	17 50
Vauxhall ⊖	d	15 43	15 48	15 54	16 00	16 13	16 18	16 29		16 43	16 48	16 54	17 00	17 13	17 18	17 29		17 43	17 48	17 54
Queenstown Rd.(Battersea)	d		15 51	15 57	16 03		16 21				16 51	16 57	17 03		17 21				17 51	17 57
Clapham Junction [10]	d	15 49	15 54	16 00	16 06	16 19	16 24	16 35		16 49	16 54	17 00	17 06	17 19	17 24	17 35		17 49	17 54	18 00
Wandsworth Town	d		15 57	16 03	16 09		16 27				16 57	17 03	17 09		17 27				17 57	18 03
Putney	d	15 53	16 00	16 06	16 12	16 23	16 30	16 39		16 53	17 00	17 06	17 12	17 23	17 30	17 39		17 53	18 00	18 06
Barnes	d		16 03	16 09	16 15		16 33				17 03	17 09	17 15		17 33				18 03	18 09
Barnes Bridge	d			16 11								17 11								18 11
Chiswick	d			16 13								17 13								18 13
Kew Bridge	d			16 16								17 16								18 16
Brentford	d			16 19								17 19								18 19
Syon Lane	d			16 21								17 21								18 21
Isleworth	d			16 23								17 23								18 23
Hounslow	d			16 26								17 26								18 26
Mortlake	d		16 05		16 17		16 35				17 05		17 17		17 35				18 05	
North Sheen	d		16 07		16 19		16 37				17 07		17 19		17 37				18 07	
Richmond ⊖	d	15 59	16 10		16 22	16 29	16 40	16 45		16 59	17 10		17 22	17 29	17 40	17 45		17 59	18 10	
St Margarets	d		16 12		16 24		16 42				17 12		17 24		17 42				18 12	
Twickenham	a	16 02	16 14		16 26	16 32	16 44	16 48		17 02	17 14		17 26	17 32	17 44	17 48		18 02	18 14	
	d	16 03	16 15		16 27	16 33	16 45	16 49		17 03	17 15		17 27	17 33	17 45	17 49		18 03	18 15	
Strawberry Hill	d				16 30		16 49						17 30		17 49					
Fulwell	a																			
Teddington	a				16 33		16 52						17 33		17 52					
Hampton Wick	a				16 36		16 57						17 36		17 57					
Kingston	a				16 38		16 59						17 38		17 59					
Whitton	d		16 18					16 52			17 18					17 52			18 18	
Feltham	d	16 09	16 22	16 32		16 39		16 56		17 09	17 22	17 32		17 39		17 56		18 09	18 22	18 32
Ashford (Surrey)	d		16 26	16 36				17 00			17 26	17 36				18 00			18 26	18 36
Staines	d	16 15	16 30	16 40		16 45		17 04		17 15	17 30	17 40		17 45		18 04		18 15	18 30	18 40
Wraysbury	d		16 34								17 34								18 34	
Sunnymeads	d		16 37								17 37								18 37	
Datchet	d		16 40					17 12			17 40					18 12			18 40	
Windsor & Eton Riverside	a		16 44					17 16			17 44					18 16			18 44	
Egham	d	16 20		16 45		16 50				17 20		17 45		17 50				18 20		18 45
Virginia Water	a	16 24		16 49		16 54				17 24		17 49		17 54				18 24		18 49
	d	16 24		16 49		16 54				17 24		17 49		17 54				18 24		18 49
Chertsey	d			16 55								17 55								18 55
Addlestone	d			16 58								17 58								18 58
Weybridge	a																			
Byfleet & New Haw	d			17 02								18 02								19 02
West Byfleet	d			17 05								18 05								19 05
Woking	a			17 11								18 11								19 11
Longcross	d																			
Sunningdale	d	16 29				16 59				17 29				17 59				18 29		
Ascot [3]	d	16 34				17 04			17 13	17 34				18 04			18 13	18 34		
Bagshot	d								17 19								18 19			
Camberley	a								17 25								18 25			
Frimley	d								17 29								18 29			
Ash Vale	d								17 36								18 36			
Aldershot	a								17 41								18 41			
	d								17 48								18 48			
Ash [5]	d								17 55								18 55			
Wanborough	d								17 58								18 58			
Guildford	a								18 05								19 05			
Martins Heron	d	16 38				17 08				17 38				18 08				18 38		
Bracknell	d	16 41				17 11				17 41				18 11				18 41		
Wokingham	d	16 48				17 18				17 48				18 18				18 48		
Winnersh	d	16 51				17 21				17 51				18 21				18 51		
Winnersh Triangle	d	16 53				17 23				17 53				18 23				18 53		
Earley	d	16 56				17 26				17 56				18 26				18 56		
Reading [7]	a	17 01				17 31				18 01				18 31				19 01		

Table 149

Sundays until 19 September

London - Hounslow, Richmond, Kingston, Windsor, Weybridge, Ascot, Guildford and Reading

		SW	SW [1]	SW	SW	SW [1]	SW [1]	SW	SW	SW	SW [1]	SW	SW	SW [1]	SW [1]	SW	SW	SW	SW [1]	SW
London Waterloo [15] ⊖	d	17 56	18 09	18 14	18 25		18 39	18 44	18 50	18 56	19 09	19 14	19 25		19 39	19 44	19 50	19 56	20 09	20 14
Vauxhall ⊖	d	18 00	18 13	18 18	18 29		18 43	18 48	18 54	19 00	19 13	19 18	19 29		19 43	19 48	19 54	20 00	20 13	20 18
Queenstown Rd.(Battersea)	d	18 03		18 21				18 51	18 57	19 03		19 21				19 51	19 57	20 03		20 21
Clapham Junction [10]	d	18 06	18 19	18 24	18 35		18 49	18 54	19 00	19 06	19 19	19 24	19 35		19 49	19 54	20 00	20 06	20 19	20 24
Wandsworth Town	d	18 09		18 27				18 57	19 03	19 09		19 27				19 57	20 03	20 09		20 27
Putney	d	18 12	18 23	18 30	18 39		18 53	19 00	19 06	19 12	19 23	19 30	19 39		19 53	20 00	20 06	20 12	20 23	20 30
Barnes	d	18 15		18 33				19 03	19 09	19 15		19 33				20 03	20 09	20 15		20 33
Barnes Bridge	d								19 11								20 11			
Chiswick	d								19 13								20 13			
Kew Bridge	d								19 16								20 16			
Brentford	d								19 19								20 19			
Syon Lane	d								19 21								20 21			
Isleworth	d								19 23								20 23			
Hounslow	d								19 26								20 26			
Mortlake	d	18 17		18 35				19 05		19 17		19 35				20 05		20 17		20 35
North Sheen	d	18 19		18 37				19 07		19 19		19 37				20 07		20 19		20 37
Richmond ⊖	d	18 22	18 29	18 40	18 45		18 59	19 10		19 22	19 29	19 40	19 45		19 59	20 10		20 22	20 29	20 40
St Margarets	d	18 24		18 42				19 12		19 24		19 42				20 12		20 24		20 42
Twickenham	a	18 26	18 32	18 44	18 48		19 02	19 14		19 26	19 32	19 44	19 48		20 02	20 14		20 26	20 32	20 44
	d	18 27	18 33	18 45	18 49		19 03	19 15		19 27	19 33	19 45	19 49		20 03	20 15		20 27	20 33	20 45
Strawberry Hill	d	18 30		18 49						19 30		19 49						20 30		20 49
Fulwell	a																			
Teddington	a	18 33		18 52						19 33		19 52						20 33		20 52
Hampton Wick	a	18 36		18 57						19 36		19 57						20 36		20 57
Kingston	a	18 38		18 59						19 38		19 59						20 38		20 59
Whitton	d				18 52			19 18					19 52			20 18				
Feltham	d		18 39		18 56		19 09	19 22	19 32		19 39		19 56		20 09	20 22	20 32		20 39	
Ashford (Surrey)	d				19 00			19 26	19 36				20 00			20 26	20 36			
Staines	d		18 45		19 04		19 15	19 30	19 40		19 45		20 04		20 15	20 30	20 40		20 45	
Wraysbury	d							19 34								20 34				
Sunnymeads	d							19 37								20 37				
Datchet	d				19 12			19 40					20 12			20 40				
Windsor & Eton Riverside	a				19 16			19 44					20 16			20 44				
Egham	d		18 50				19 20		19 45		19 50				20 20		20 45		20 50	
Virginia Water	a		18 54				19 24		19 49		19 54				20 24		20 49		20 54	
	d		18 54				19 24		19 49		19 54				20 24		20 49		20 54	
Chertsey	d								19 55								20 55			
Addlestone	d								19 58								20 58			
Weybridge	a																			
Byfleet & New Haw	d								20 02								21 02			
West Byfleet	d								20 05								21 05			
Woking	a								20 11								21 11			
Longcross	d																			
Sunningdale	d		18 59				19 29				19 59				20 29				20 59	
Ascot [3]	d		19 04			19 13	19 34				20 04			20 13	20 34				21 04	
Bagshot	d					19 19								20 19						
Camberley	a					19 25								20 25						
Frimley	d					19 29								20 29						
Ash Vale	d					19 36								20 36						
Aldershot	a					19 41								20 41						
	d					19 48								20 48						
Ash [5]	d					19 55								20 55						
Wanborough	d					19 58								20 58						
Guildford	a					20 05								21 05						
Martins Heron	d		19 08				19 38				20 08				20 38				21 08	
Bracknell	d		19 11				19 41				20 11				20 41				21 11	
Wokingham	d		19 18				19 48				20 18				20 48				21 18	
Winnersh	d		19 21				19 51				20 21				20 51				21 21	
Winnersh Triangle	d		19 23				19 53				20 23				20 53				21 23	
Earley	d		19 26				19 56				20 26				20 56				21 26	
Reading [7]	a		19 31				20 01				20 31				21 01				21 31	

Table 149

Sundays
until 19 September

London - Hounslow, Richmond, Kingston, Windsor, Weybridge, Ascot, Guildford and Reading

		SW 1	SW 1	SW	SW	SW	SW 1	SW	SW 1	SW 1	SW	SW	SW	SW 1	SW	SW 1	SW 1	SW	SW	SW	SW 1
London Waterloo 15 ⊖	d		20 39	20 44	20 50	20 56	21 09	21 14		21 39	21 44	21 50	21 56	22 09	22 14		22 39	22 44	22 50	22 56	23 09
Vauxhall ⊖	d		20 43	20 48	20 54	21 00	21 13	21 18		21 43	21 48	21 54	22 00	22 13	22 18		22 43	22 48	22 54	23 00	23 13
Queenstown Rd.(Battersea)	d			20 51	20 57	21 03		21 21			21 51	21 57	22 03		22 21			22 51	22 57	23 03	
Clapham Junction 10	d		20 49	20 54	21 00	21 06	21 19	21 24		21 49	21 54	22 00	22 06	22 19	22 24		22 49	22 54	23 00	23 06	23 19
Wandsworth Town	d			20 57	21 03	21 09		21 27			21 57	22 03	22 09		22 27			22 57	23 03	23 09	
Putney	d		20 53	21 00	21 06	21 12	21 23	21 30		21 53	22 00	22 06	22 12	22 23	22 30		22 53	23 00	23 06	23 12	23 23
Barnes	d			21 03	21 09	21 15		21 33			22 03	22 09	22 15		22 33			23 03	23 09	23 15	
Barnes Bridge	d				21 11							22 11							23 11		
Chiswick	d				21 13							22 13							23 13		
Kew Bridge	d				21 16							22 16							23 16		
Brentford	d				21 19							22 19							23 19		
Syon Lane	d				21 21							22 21							23 21		
Isleworth	d				21 23							22 23							23 23		
Hounslow	d				21 26							22 26							23 26		
Mortlake	d			21 05		21 17		21 35			22 05		22 17		22 35			23 05		23 17	
North Sheen	d			21 07		21 19		21 37			22 07		22 19		22 37			23 07		23 19	
Richmond ⊖	d		20 59	21 10		21 22	21 29	21 40		21 59	22 10		22 22	22 29	22 40		22 59	23 10		23 22	23 29
St Margarets	d			21 12		21 24		21 42			22 12		22 24		22 42			23 12		23 24	
Twickenham	a		21 02	21 14		21 26	21 32	21 44		22 02	22 14		22 26	22 32	22 44		23 02	23 14		23 26	23 32
	d		21 03	21 15		21 27	21 33	21 45		22 03	22 15		22 27	22 33	22 45		23 03	23 15		23 27	23 33
Strawberry Hill	d					21 30		21 49					22 30		22 49					23 30	
Fulwell	a																				
Teddington	a					21 33		21 52					22 33		22 52					23 33	
Hampton Wick	a					21 36		21 57					22 36		22 57					23 36	
Kingston	a					21 38		21 59					22 38		22 59					23 38	
Whitton	d			21 18							22 18							23 18			
Feltham	d		21 09	21 22	21 32		21 39			22 09	22 22	22 32		22 39			23 09	23 22	23 32		23 39
Ashford (Surrey)	d			21 26	21 36						22 26	22 36						23 26	23 36		
Staines	d		21 15	21 30	21 40		21 45			22 15	22 30	22 40		22 45			23 15	23 30	23 40		23 45
Wraysbury	d			21 34							22 34							23 34			
Sunnymeads	d			21 37							22 37							23 37			
Datchet	d			21 40							22 40							23 40			
Windsor & Eton Riverside	a			21 44							22 44							23 44			
Egham	d		21 20		21 45		21 50			22 20		22 45		22 50			23 20		23 45		23 50
Virginia Water	a		21 24		21 49		21 54			22 24		22 49		22 54			23 24		23 49		23 54
	d		21 24		21 49		21 54			22 24		22 49		22 54			23 24		23 49		23 54
Chertsey	d				21 55							22 55							23 55		
Addlestone	d				21 58							22 58							23 58		
Weybridge	a																				
Byfleet & New Haw	d				22 02							23 02							00 02		
West Byfleet	d				22 05							23 05							00 05		
Woking	a				22 11							23 11							00 11		
Longcross	d																				
Sunningdale	d		21 29				21 59			22 29				22 59			23 29				23 59
Ascot 3	d	21 13	21 34				22 04		22 13	22 34				23 04		23 13	23 34				00 04
Bagshot	d	21 19							22 19							23 19					
Camberley	a	21 25							22 25							23 25					
Frimley	d	21 29							22 29							23 29					
Ash Vale	d	21 36							22 36							23 36					
Aldershot	a	21 41							22 45							23 41					
	d	21 48							22 49							23 42					
Ash 5	d	21 55							22 55												
Wanborough	d	21 58							22 58												
Guildford	a	22 05							23 05												
Martins Heron	d		21 38				22 08			22 38				23 08			23 38				00 08
Bracknell	d		21 41				22 11			22 41				23 11			23 41				00 11
Wokingham	d		21 48				22 18			22 48				23 18			23 48				00 18
Winnersh	d		21 51				22 21			22 51				23 21			23 51				00 21
Winnersh Triangle	d		21 53				22 23			22 53				23 23			23 53				00 23
Earley	d		21 56				22 26			22 56				23 26			23 56				00 26
Reading 7	a		22 01				22 31			23 01				23 31			00 01				00 31

Table 149

Sundays
until 19 September

London - Hounslow, Richmond, Kingston, Windsor, Weybridge, Ascot, Guildford and Reading

		SW	SW 1	SW
London Waterloo 15 ⊖	d	23 14	23 39	23 44
Vauxhall ⊖	d	23 18	23 43	23 48
Queenstown Rd.(Battersea)	d	23 21		23 51
Clapham Junction 10	d	23 24	23 49	23 54
Wandsworth Town	d	23 27		23 57
Putney	d	23 30	23 53	23 59
Barnes	d	23 33		00 03
Barnes Bridge	d			
Chiswick	d			
Kew Bridge	d			
Brentford	d			
Syon Lane	d			
Isleworth	d			
Hounslow	d			
Mortlake	d	23 35		00 05
North Sheen	d	23 37		00 07
Richmond ⊖	d	23 40	23 59	00 10
St Margarets	d	23 42		00 12
Twickenham	a	23 44	00 02	00 14
	d	23 45	00 03	00 15
Strawberry Hill	d	23 48		
Fulwell	a			
Teddington	a	23 51		
Hampton Wick	a	23 54		
Kingston	a	23 56		
Whitton	d			00 18
Feltham	d		00 09	00 22
Ashford (Surrey)	d			00 26
Staines	d		00 15	00a30
Wraysbury	d			
Sunnymeads	d			
Datchet	d			
Windsor & Eton Riverside	a			
Egham	d		00 20	
Virginia Water	a		00 24	
	d		00 24	
Chertsey	d			
Addlestone	d			
Weybridge	a			
Byfleet & New Haw	d			
West Byfleet	d			
Woking	a			
Longcross	d			
Sunningdale	d		00 29	
Ascot 3	d		00 34	
Bagshot	d			
Camberley	a			
Frimley	d			
Ash Vale	d			
Aldershot	a			
	d			
Ash 5	d			
Wanborough	d			
Guildford	a			
Martins Heron	d		00 38	
Bracknell	d		00 41	
Wokingham	d		00 48	
Winnersh	d		00 51	
Winnersh Triangle	d		00 53	
Earley	d		00 56	
Reading 7	a		01 01	

Table 149

Sundays
from 26 September

London - Hounslow, Richmond, Kingston, Windsor, Weybridge, Ascot, Guildford and Reading

		SW ■1	SW		SW	SW ■1	SW	SW	SW	SW	SW	SW	SW	SW ■1	SW	SW	SW	SW ■1
London Waterloo ■15 ⊖	d	22p50	22p52		23p13	23p20		23p22	23p33	23p38	23p52	23p58	00 18		06 14		06 44	07 09
Vauxhall ⊖	d		22p56		23p17			23p26	23p37		23p56	00 02	00 22		06 18		06 48	07 13
Queenstown Rd.(Battersea)	d		22p59					23p29	23p40		23p59		00 25		06 21		06 51	
Clapham Junction ■10	d	22p58	23p02		23p23	23p28		23p32	23p43	23p46	00 02	00 08	00 28		06 24		06 54	07 19
Wandsworth Town	d		23p05					23p35	23p46		00 05		00 31		06 27		06 57	
Putney	d		23p08		23p27			23p38	23p49		00 08	00 12	00 34		06 30		07 00	07 23
Barnes	d		23p12					23p42	23p52		00 12		00 37		06 33		07 03	
Barnes Bridge	d		23p14					23p44			00 14							
Chiswick	d		23p17					23p47			00 17							
Kew Bridge	d		23p20					23p50			00 20							
Brentford	d		23p23					23p53			00 23							
Syon Lane	d		23p25					23p55			00 25							
Isleworth	d		23p27					23p57			00 27							
Hounslow	d		23p31					00 01			00 31							
Mortlake	d								23p54				00 39		06 35		07 05	
North Sheen	d								23p56				00 41		06 37		07 07	
Richmond ⊖	d	23p06			23p33	23p37			23p59	23p54		00 18	00 44		06 40		07 10	07 29
St Margarets	d								00 01				00 46		06 42		07 12	
Twickenham	a	23p10			23p37	23p41			00 04	23p58		00 21	00 48		06 44		07 14	07 32
	d	23p10			23p37	23p41			00 04	23p58		00 22	00 49		06 45		07 15	07 33
Strawberry Hill	d								00 07				00s52		06 49			
Fulwell	a																	
Teddington	a								00 11				00s55		06 52			
Hampton Wick	a								00 14				00s58		06 57			
Kingston	a								00 16				01 00		06 59			
Whitton	d				23p40							00 25					07 18	
Feltham	d	23p16	23p36		23p44	23p48		00 06		00 04	00 36	00 29					07 22	07 39
Ashford (Surrey)	d		23p40		23p48			00 10			00 40	00 33					07 26	
Staines	d	23p23	23p44		23p52	23p56		00 14		00 11	00a46	00a37				06 32	07 30	07 45
Wraysbury	d				23p57												07 34	
Sunnymeads	d				23p59												07 37	
Datchet	d				00 04												07 40	
Windsor & Eton Riverside	a			6	00 09												07 46	
Egham	d	23p27	23p49			00 01		00 19		00 15						06 36		07 50
Virginia Water	a	23p31	23p53			00 05		00 23		00 19						06 41		07 54
	d	23p31	23p53			00 05		00 23		00 19						06 41		07 54
Chertsey	d		23p59					00 29								06 46		
Addlestone	d		00 02					00 32								06 49		
Weybridge	a															06 53		
Byfleet & New Haw	d		00 06															
West Byfleet	d		00 09															
Woking	a		00 20															
Longcross	d																	
Sunningdale	d	23p37				00 11				00 25								07 59
Ascot ■3	d	23p43				00 15				00 30				00 32				08 04
Bagshot	d													00 38				
Camberley	a													00 44				
Frimley	d													00 48				
Ash Vale	d													00 57				
Aldershot	a													01s02				
	d													01s06				
Ash ■5	d																	
Wanborough	d																	
Guildford	a																	
Martins Heron	d	23p47				00 19				00 34								08 08
Bracknell	d	23p50				00 23				00 37								08 11
Wokingham	d	23p57				00 32				00 44								08 18
Winnersh	d	23p59				00 36												08 21
Winnersh Triangle	d	00 01				00 38												08 23
Earley	d	00 05				00 40												08 26
Reading ■7	a	00 10				00 45				00 55								08 34

Table 149

Sundays
from 26 September

London - Hounslow, Richmond, Kingston, Windsor, Weybridge, Ascot, Guildford and Reading

		SW	SW	SW	SW	SW ■1	SW ■1	SW ■1	SW	SW ■1	SW ■1	SW	SW	SW ■1	SW	SW	SW ■1	SW ■1	SW	SW
London Waterloo ■15 ⊖	d	07 14		07 44	07 50			08 09	08 14		08 39	08 44	08 50	09 09	09 14	09 25		09 39	09 44	09 50
Vauxhall ⊖	d	07 18		07 48	07 54			08 13	08 18		08 43	08 48	08 54	09 13	09 18	09 29		09 43	09 48	09 54
Queenstown Rd.(Battersea)	d	07 21		07 51	07 57				08 21			08 51	08 57		09 21				09 51	09 57
Clapham Junction ■10	d	07 24		07 54	08 00			08 19	08 24		08 49	08 54	09 00	09 19	09 24	09 35		09 49	09 54	10 00
Wandsworth Town	d	07 27		07 57	08 03				08 27			08 57	09 03		09 27				09 57	10 03
Putney	d	07 30		08 00	08 06			08 23	08 30		08 53	09 00	09 06	09 23	09 30	09 39		09 53	10 00	10 06
Barnes	d	07 33		08 03	08 09				08 33			09 03	09 09		09 33				10 03	10 09
Barnes Bridge	d				08 11								09 11							10 11
Chiswick	d				08 13								09 13							10 13
Kew Bridge	d				08 16								09 16							10 16
Brentford	d				08 19								09 19							10 19
Syon Lane	d				08 21								09 21							10 21
Isleworth	d				08 23								09 23							10 23
Hounslow	d				08 26								09 26							10 26
Mortlake	d	07 35		08 05					08 35			09 05			09 35				10 05	
North Sheen	d	07 37		08 07					08 37			09 07			09 37				10 07	
Richmond ⊖	d	07 40		08 10				08 29	08 40		08 59	09 10		09 29	09 40	09 45		09 59	10 10	
St Margarets	d	07 42		08 12					08 42			09 12			09 42				10 12	
Twickenham	a	07 44		08 14				08 32	08 44		09 02	09 14		09 32	09 44	09 48		10 02	10 14	
	d	07 45		08 15				08 33	08 45		09 03	09 15		09 33	09 45	09 49		10 03	10 15	
Strawberry Hill	d	07 49							08 49						09 49					
Fulwell	a																			
Teddington	a	07 52							08 52						09 52					
Hampton Wick	a	07 57							08 57						09 57					
Kingston	a	07 59							08 59						09 59					
Whitton	d			08 18								09 18				09 52			10 18	
Feltham	d			08 22	08 32			08 39			09 09	09 22	09 32	09 39		09 56		10 09	10 22	10 32
Ashford (Surrey)	d			08 26	08 36							09 26	09 36			10 00			10 26	10 36
Staines	d		07 40	08 30	08 40		08 15	08 45			09 15	09 30	09 40	09 45		10 04		10 15	10 30	10 40
Wraysbury	d			08 34								09 34							10 34	
Sunnymeads	d			08 37								09 37							10 37	
Datchet	d			08 40								09 40				10 12			10 40	
Windsor & Eton Riverside	a			08 46								09 46				10 18			10 46	
Egham	d		07 45		08 45		08 20	08 50			09 20		09 45	09 50				10 20		10 45
Virginia Water	a		07 49		08 49		08 24	08 54			09 24		09 49	09 54				10 24		10 49
	d		07 49		08 49		08 24	08 54			09 24		09 49	09 54				10 24		10 49
Chertsey	d		07 55		08 55								09 55							10 55
Addlestone	d		07 58		08 58								09 58							10 58
Weybridge	a																			
Byfleet & New Haw	d		08 02		09 02								10 02							11 02
West Byfleet	d		08 05		09 05								10 05							11 05
Woking	a		08 11		09 11								10 11							11 11
Longcross	d																			
Sunningdale	d						08 29	08 59			09 29			09 59				10 29		
Ascot ■3	d					08 13	08 34	09 04		09 13	09 34			10 04			10 13	10 34		
Bagshot	d					08 19				09 19							10 19			
Camberley	a					08 25				09 25							10 25			
Frimley	d					08 29				09 29							10 28			
Ash Vale	d					08 36				09 36							10 35			
Aldershot	a					08 41				09 41							10 41			
	d					08 48				09 48							10 48			
Ash ■5	d					08 55				09 55							10 55			
Wanborough	d					08 58				09 58							10 58			
Guildford	a					09 05				10 05							11 05			
Martins Heron	d						08 38	09 08			09 38			10 08				10 38		
Bracknell	d						08 41	09 11			09 41			10 11				10 41		
Wokingham	d						08 48	09 18			09 48			10 18				10 48		
Winnersh	d						08 51	09 21			09 51			10 21				10 51		
Winnersh Triangle	d						08 53	09 23			09 53			10 23				10 53		
Earley	d						08 56	09 26			09 56			10 26				10 56		
Reading ■7	a						09 04	09 34			10 04			10 34				11 04		

Table 149

Sundays
from 26 September

London - Hounslow, Richmond, Kingston, Windsor, Weybridge, Ascot, Guildford and Reading

		SW ■	SW	SW	SW ■	SW ■	SW	SW	SW ■	SW	SW	SW ■	SW ■	SW	SW	SW ■	SW	SW	SW ■
London Waterloo [15] ⊖	d	10 09	10 14	10 25		10 39	10 44	10 50	11 09	11 14	11 25		11 39	11 44	11 50	12 09	12 14	12 25	
Vauxhall ⊖	d	10 13	10 18	10 29		10 43	10 48	10 54	11 13	11 19	11 29		11 43	11 48	11 54	12 13	12 19	12 29	
Queenstown Rd.(Battersea)	d		10 21				10 51	10 57		11 22				11 51	11 57		12 22		
Clapham Junction [10]	d	10 19	10 24	10 35		10 49	10 54	11 00	11 19	11 25	11 35		11 49	11 54	12 00	12 19	12 25	12 35	
Wandsworth Town	d		10 27				10 57	11 03		11 28				11 57	12 03		12 28		
Putney	d	10 23	10 30	10 39		10 53	11 00	11 06	11 23	11 31	11 39		11 53	12 00	12 06	12 23	12 31	12 39	
Barnes	d		10 33				11 03	11 09		11 34				12 03	12 09		12 34		
Barnes Bridge	d							11 11							12 11				
Chiswick	d							11 13							12 13				
Kew Bridge	d							11 16							12 16				
Brentford	d							11 19							12 19				
Syon Lane	d							11 21							12 21				
Isleworth	d							11 23							12 23				
Hounslow	d							11 26							12 26				
Mortlake	d		10 35				11 05			11 36				12 05			12 36		
North Sheen	d		10 37				11 07			11 38				12 07			12 38		
Richmond ⊖	d	10 29	10 40	10 45		10 59	11 10		11 29	11 41	11 45		11 59	12 10		12 29	12 41	12 45	
St Margarets	d		10 42				11 12			11 43				12 12			12 43		
Twickenham	a	10 32	10 44	10 48		11 02	11 14		11 32	11 45	11 48		12 02	12 14		12 32	12 45	12 48	
	d	10 33	10 45	10 49		11 03	11 15		11 33	11 46	11 49		12 03	12 15		12 33	12 46	12 49	
Strawberry Hill	d		10 49							11 50							12 50		
Fulwell	a																		
Teddington	a		10 52							11 53							12 53		
Hampton Wick	a		10 57							11 57							12 57		
Kingston	a		10 59							11 59							12 59		
Whitton	d			10 52			11 18				11 52			12 18				12 52	
Feltham	d	10 39		10 56		11 09	11 22	11 32	11 39		11 56		12 09	12 22	12 32	12 39		12 56	
Ashford (Surrey)	d			11 00			11 26	11 36			12 00			12 26	12 36			13 00	
Staines	d	10 45		11 04		11 15	11 30	11 40	11 45		12 04		12 15	12 30	12 40	12 45		13 04	
Wraysbury	d						11 34							12 34					
Sunnymeads	d						11 37							12 37					
Datchet	d			11 12			11 40				12 12			12 40				13 12	
Windsor & Eton Riverside	a			11 18			11 46				12 18			12 46				13 18	
Egham	d	10 50				11 20		11 45	11 50				12 20		12 45	12 50			
Virginia Water	a	10 54				11 24		11 49	11 54				12 24		12 49	12 54			
	d	10 54				11 24		11 49	11 54				12 24		12 49	12 54			
Chertsey	d							11 55							12 55				
Addlestone	d							11 58							12 58				
Weybridge	a																		
Byfleet & New Haw	d							12 02							13 02				
West Byfleet	d							12 05							13 05				
Woking	a							12 11							13 11				
Longcross	d																		
Sunningdale	d	10 59				11 29			11 59				12 29			12 59			
Ascot [3]	d	11 04			11 13	11 34			12 04			12 13	12 34			13 04			13 13
Bagshot	d				11 19							12 19							13 19
Camberley	a				11 25							12 25							13 25
Frimley	d				11 29							12 29							13 29
Ash Vale	d				11 36							12 36							13 36
Aldershot	a				11 41							12 41							13 41
	d				11 48							12 48							13 48
Ash [5]	d				11 55							12 55							13 55
Wanborough	d				11 58							12 58							13 58
Guildford	a				12 05							13 05							14 05
Martins Heron	d	11 08				11 38			12 08				12 38			13 08			
Bracknell	d	11 11				11 41			12 11				12 41			13 11			
Wokingham	d	11 18				11 48			12 18				12 48			13 18			
Winnersh	d	11 21				11 51			12 21				12 51			13 21			
Winnersh Triangle	d	11 23				11 53			12 23				12 53			13 23			
Earley	d	11 26				11 56			12 26				12 56			13 26			
Reading [7]	a	11 34				12 04			12 34				13 04			13 34			

Table 149

Sundays
from 26 September

London - Hounslow, Richmond, Kingston, Windsor, Weybridge, Ascot, Guildford and Reading

		SW ■	SW	SW	SW ■	SW	SW	SW ■	SW ■	SW	SW	SW	SW ■	SW	SW	SW ■	SW ■	SW	SW	SW	SW ■
London Waterloo [15] ⊖	d	12 39	12 44	12 50	13 09	13 14	13 25		13 39	13 44	13 50	13 56	14 09	14 14	14 25		14 39	14 44	14 50	14 56	15 09
Vauxhall ⊖	d	12 43	12 48	12 54	13 13	13 18	13 29		13 43	13 48	13 54	14 00	14 13	14 18	14 29		14 43	14 48	14 54	15 00	15 13
Queenstown Rd.(Battersea)	d		12 51	12 57		13 21				13 51	13 57	14 03		14 21				14 51	14 57	15 03	
Clapham Junction [10]	d	12 49	12 54	13 00	13 19	13 24	13 35		13 49	13 54	14 00	14 06	14 19	14 24	14 35		14 49	14 54	15 00	15 06	15 19
Wandsworth Town	d		12 57	13 03		13 27				13 57	14 03	14 09		14 27				14 57	15 03	15 09	
Putney	d	12 53	13 00	13 06	13 23	13 30	13 39		13 53	14 00	14 06	14 12	14 23	14 30	14 39		14 53	15 00	15 06	15 12	15 23
Barnes	d		13 03	13 09		13 33				14 03	14 09	14 15		14 33				15 03	15 09	15 15	
Barnes Bridge	d			13 11							14 11								15 11		
Chiswick	d			13 13							14 13								15 13		
Kew Bridge	d			13 16							14 16								15 16		
Brentford	d			13 19							14 19								15 19		
Syon Lane	d			13 21							14 21								15 21		
Isleworth	d			13 23							14 23								15 23		
Hounslow	d			13 26							14 26								15 26		
Mortlake	d		13 05			13 35				14 05		14 17		14 35				15 05		15 17	
North Sheen	d		13 07			13 37				14 07		14 19		14 37				15 07		15 19	
Richmond ⊖	d	12 59	13 10		13 29	13 40	13 45		13 59	14 10		14 22	14 29	14 40	14 45		14 59	15 10		15 22	15 29
St Margarets	d		13 12			13 42				14 12		14 24		14 42				15 12		15 24	
Twickenham	a	13 02	13 14		13 32	13 44	13 48		14 02	14 14		14 26	14 32	14 44	14 48		15 02	15 14		15 26	15 32
	d	13 03	13 15		13 33	13 45	13 49		14 03	14 15		14 27	14 33	14 45	14 49		15 03	15 15		15 27	15 33
Strawberry Hill	d					13 49						14 30		14 49						15 30	
Fulwell	a																				
Teddington	a					13 52						14 33		14 52						15 33	
Hampton Wick	a					13 57						14 36		14 57						15 36	
Kingston	a					13 59						14 38		14 59						15 38	
Whitton	d		13 18				13 52			14 18					14 52			15 18			
Feltham	d	13 09	13 22	13 32	13 39		13 56		14 09	14 22	14 32		14 39		14 56		15 09	15 22	15 32		15 39
Ashford (Surrey)	d		13 26	13 36			14 00			14 26	14 36				15 00			15 26	15 36		
Staines	d	13 15	13 30	13 40	13 45		14 04		14 15	14 30	14 40		14 45		15 04		15 15	15 30	15 40		15 45
Wraysbury	d		13 34							14 34								15 34			
Sunnymeads	d		13 37							14 37								15 37			
Datchet	d		13 40				14 12			14 40					15 12			15 40			
Windsor & Eton Riverside	a		13 46				14 18			14 46					15 18			15 46			
Egham	d	13 20		13 45	13 50				14 20		14 45		14 50				15 20		15 45		15 50
Virginia Water	a	13 24		13 49	13 54				14 24		14 49		14 54				15 24		15 49		15 54
	d	13 24		13 49	13 54				14 24		14 49		14 54				15 24		15 49		15 54
Chertsey	d			13 55							14 55								15 55		
Addlestone	d			13 58							14 58								15 58		
Weybridge	a																				
Byfleet & New Haw	d			14 02							15 02								16 02		
West Byfleet	d			14 05							15 05								16 05		
Woking	a			14 11							15 11								16 11		
Longcross	d																				
Sunningdale	d	13 29			13 59				14 29				14 59				15 29				15 59
Ascot [3]	d	13 34			14 04			14 13	14 34				15 04			15 13	15 34				16 04
Bagshot	d							14 19								15 19					
Camberley	a							14 25								15 25					
Frimley	d							14 29								15 29					
Ash Vale	d							14 36								15 36					
Aldershot	a							14 41								15 41					
	d							14 48								15 48					
Ash [5]	d							14 55								15 55					
Wanborough	d							14 58								15 58					
Guildford	a							15 05								16 05					
Martins Heron	d	13 38			14 08				14 38				15 08				15 38				16 08
Bracknell	d	13 41			14 11				14 41				15 11				15 41				16 11
Wokingham	d	13 48			14 18				14 48				15 18				15 48				16 18
Winnersh	d	13 51			14 21				14 51				15 21				15 51				16 21
Winnersh Triangle	d	13 53			14 23				14 53				15 23				15 53				16 23
Earley	d	13 56			14 26				14 56				15 26				15 56				16 26
Reading [7]	a	14 04			14 34				15 04				15 34				16 04				16 34

Table 149

Sundays
from 26 September

London - Hounslow, Richmond, Kingston, Windsor, Weybridge, Ascot, Guildford and Reading

		SW	SW	SW ■	SW ■	SW	SW	SW	SW ■	SW	SW	SW ■	SW ■	SW	SW	SW	SW ■	SW	SW
London Waterloo 15 ⊖	d	15 14	15 25		15 39	15 44	15 50	15 56	16 09	16 14	16 25		16 39	16 44	16 50	16 56	17 09	17 14	17 25
Vauxhall ⊖	d	15 18	15 29		15 43	15 48	15 54	16 00	16 13	16 18	16 29		16 43	16 48	16 54	17 00	17 13	17 18	17 29
Queenstown Rd.(Battersea)	d	15 21				15 51	15 57	16 03		16 21				16 51	16 57	17 03		17 21	
Clapham Junction 10	d	15 24	15 35		15 49	15 54	16 00	16 06	16 19	16 24	16 35		16 49	16 54	17 00	17 06	17 19	17 24	17 35
Wandsworth Town	d	15 27				15 57	16 03	16 09		16 27				16 57	17 03	17 09		17 27	
Putney	d	15 30	15 39		15 53	16 00	16 06	16 12	16 23	16 30	16 39		16 53	17 00	17 06	17 12	17 23	17 30	17 39
Barnes	d	15 33				16 03	16 09	16 15		16 33				17 03	17 09	17 15		17 33	
Barnes Bridge	d						16 11								17 11				
Chiswick	d						16 13								17 13				
Kew Bridge	d						16 16								17 16				
Brentford	d						16 19								17 19				
Syon Lane	d						16 21								17 21				
Isleworth	d						16 23								17 23				
Hounslow	d						16 26								17 26				
Mortlake	d	15 35				16 05		16 17		16 35				17 05		17 17		17 35	
North Sheen	d	15 37				16 07		16 19		16 37				17 07		17 19		17 37	
Richmond ⊖	d	15 40	15 45		15 59	16 10		16 22	16 29	16 40	16 45		16 59	17 10		17 22	17 29	17 40	17 45
St Margarets	d	15 42				16 12		16 24		16 42				17 12		17 24		17 42	
Twickenham	a	15 44	15 48		16 02	16 14		16 26	16 32	16 44	16 48		17 02	17 14		17 26	17 32	17 44	17 48
	d	15 45	15 49		16 03	16 15		16 27	16 33	16 45	16 49		17 03	17 15		17 27	17 33	17 45	17 49
Strawberry Hill	d	15 49						16 30		16 49						17 30		17 49	
Fulwell	a																		
Teddington	a	15 52						16 33		16 52						17 33		17 52	
Hampton Wick	a	15 57						16 36		16 57						17 36		17 57	
Kingston	a	15 59						16 38		16 59						17 38		17 59	
Whitton	d		15 52			16 18					16 52			17 18					17 52
Feltham	d		15 56		16 09	16 22	16 32		16 39		16 56		17 09	17 22	17 32		17 39		17 56
Ashford (Surrey)	d		16 00			16 26	16 36				17 00			17 26	17 36				18 00
Staines	d		16 04		16 15	16 30	16 40		16 45		17 04		17 15	17 30	17 40		17 45		18 04
Wraysbury	d					16 34								17 34					
Sunnymeads	d					16 37								17 37					
Datchet	d		16 12			16 40					17 12			17 40					18 12
Windsor & Eton Riverside	a		16 18			16 46					17 18			17 46					18 18
Egham	d				16 20		16 45		16 50				17 20		17 45		17 50		
Virginia Water	a				16 24		16 49		16 54				17 24		17 49		17 54		
	d				16 24		16 49		16 54				17 24		17 49		17 54		
Chertsey	d						16 55								17 55				
Addlestone	d						16 58								17 58				
Weybridge	a																		
Byfleet & New Haw	d						17 02								18 02				
West Byfleet	d						17 05								18 05				
Woking	a						17 11								18 11				
Longcross	d																		
Sunningdale	d				16 29				16 59				17 29				17 59		
Ascot 3	d			16 13	16 34				17 04			17 13	17 34				18 04		
Bagshot	d			16 19								17 19							
Camberley	a			16 25								17 25							
Frimley	d			16 29								17 29							
Ash Vale	d			16 36								17 36							
Aldershot	a			16 41								17 41							
	d			16 48								17 48							
Ash 5	d			16 55								17 55							
Wanborough	d			16 58								17 58							
Guildford	a			17 05								18 05							
Martins Heron	d				16 38				17 08				17 38				18 08		
Bracknell	d				16 41				17 11				17 41				18 11		
Wokingham	d				16 48				17 18				17 48				18 18		
Winnersh	d				16 51				17 21				17 51				18 21		
Winnersh Triangle	d				16 53				17 23				17 53				18 23		
Earley	d				16 56				17 26				17 56				18 26		
Reading 7	a				17 04				17 34				18 04				18 34		

Table 149

Sundays
from 26 September

London - Hounslow, Richmond, Kingston, Windsor, Weybridge, Ascot, Guildford and Reading

		SW ■	SW ■	SW	SW	SW	SW ■	SW	SW	SW ■	SW ■	SW	SW	SW	SW ■	SW	SW	SW ■	SW ■	SW	SW
London Waterloo 15 ⊖	d		17 39	17 44	17 50	17 56	18 09	18 14	18 25		18 39	18 44	18 50	18 56	19 09	19 14	19 25		19 39	19 44	19 50
Vauxhall ⊖	d		17 43	17 48	17 54	18 00	18 13	18 18	18 29		18 43	18 48	18 54	19 00	19 13	19 18	19 29		19 43	19 48	19 54
Queenstown Rd.(Battersea)	d			17 51	17 57	18 03		18 21				18 51	18 57	19 03		19 21				19 51	19 57
Clapham Junction 10	d		17 49	17 54	18 00	18 06	18 19	18 24	18 35		18 49	18 54	19 00	19 06	19 19	19 24	19 35		19 49	19 54	20 00
Wandsworth Town	d			17 57	18 03	18 09		18 27				18 57	19 03	19 09		19 27				19 57	20 03
Putney	d		17 53	18 00	18 06	18 12	18 23	18 30	18 39		18 53	19 00	19 06	19 12	19 23	19 30	19 39		19 53	20 00	20 06
Barnes	d			18 03	18 09	18 15		18 33				19 03	19 09	19 15		19 33				20 03	20 09
Barnes Bridge	d				18 11								19 11								20 11
Chiswick	d				18 13								19 13								20 13
Kew Bridge	d				18 16								19 16								20 16
Brentford	d				18 19								19 19								20 19
Syon Lane	d				18 21								19 21								20 21
Isleworth	d				18 23								19 23								20 23
Hounslow	d				18 26								19 26								20 26
Mortlake	d			18 05		18 17		18 35				19 05		19 17		19 35				20 05	
North Sheen	d			18 07		18 19		18 37				19 07		19 19		19 37				20 07	
Richmond ⊖	d		17 59	18 10		18 22	18 29	18 40	18 45		18 59	19 10		19 22	19 29	19 40	19 45		19 59	20 10	
St Margarets	d			18 12		18 24		18 42				19 12		19 24		19 42				20 12	
Twickenham	a		18 02	18 14		18 26	18 32	18 44	18 48		19 02	19 14		19 26	19 32	19 44	19 48		20 02	20 14	
	d		18 03	18 15		18 27	18 33	18 45	18 49		19 03	19 15		19 27	19 33	19 45	19 49		20 03	20 15	
Strawberry Hill	d					18 30		18 49						19 30		19 49					
Fulwell	a																				
Teddington	a					18 33		18 52						19 33		19 52					
Hampton Wick	a					18 36		18 57						19 36		19 57					
Kingston	a					18 38		18 59						19 38		19 59					
Whitton	d			18 18					18 52			19 18					19 52			20 18	
Feltham	d		18 09	18 22	18 32		18 39		18 56		19 09	19 22	19 32		19 39		19 56		20 09	20 22	20 32
Ashford (Surrey)	d			18 26	18 36				19 00			19 26	19 36				20 00			20 26	20 36
Staines	d		18 15	18 30	18 40		18 45		19 04		19 15	19 30	19 40		19 45		20 04		20 15	20 30	20 40
Wraysbury	d			18 34								19 34								20 34	
Sunnymeads	d			18 37								19 37								20 37	
Datchet	d			18 40					19 12			19 40					20 12			20 40	
Windsor & Eton Riverside	a			18 46					19 18			19 46					20 18			20 46	
Egham	d		18 20		18 45		18 50				19 20		19 45		19 50				20 20		20 45
Virginia Water	a		18 24		18 49		18 54				19 24		19 49		19 54				20 24		20 49
	d		18 24		18 49		18 54				19 24		19 49		19 54				20 24		20 49
Chertsey	d				18 55								19 55								20 55
Addlestone	d				18 58								19 58								20 58
Weybridge	a																				
Byfleet & New Haw	d				19 02								20 02								21 02
West Byfleet	d				19 05								20 05								21 05
Woking	a				19 11								20 11								21 11
Longcross	d																				
Sunningdale	d		18 29				18 59				19 29				19 59				20 29		
Ascot 3	d	18 13	18 34				19 04			19 13	19 34				20 04			20 13	20 34		
Bagshot	d	18 19								19 19								20 19			
Camberley	a	18 25								19 25								20 25			
Frimley	d	18 29								19 29								20 29			
Ash Vale	d	18 36								19 36								20 36			
Aldershot	a	18 41								19 41								20 41			
	d	18 48								19 48								20 48			
Ash 5	d	18 55								19 55								20 55			
Wanborough	d	18 58								19 58								20 58			
Guildford	a	19 05								20 05								21 05			
Martins Heron	d		18 38				19 08				19 38				20 08				20 38		
Bracknell	d		18 41				19 11				19 41				20 11				20 41		
Wokingham	d		18 48				19 18				19 48				20 18				20 48		
Winnersh	d		18 51				19 21				19 51				20 21				20 51		
Winnersh Triangle	d		18 53				19 23				19 53				20 23				20 53		
Earley	d		18 56				19 26				19 56				20 26				20 56		
Reading 7	a		19 04				19 34				20 04				20 34				21 04		

Table 149

Sundays
from 26 September

London - Hounslow, Richmond, Kingston, Windsor, Weybridge, Ascot, Guildford and Reading

		SW	SW ■	SW	SW ■	SW ■	SW	SW	SW	SW ■	SW	SW ■	SW ■	SW	SW	SW	SW ■	SW	SW ■	SW ■
London Waterloo 15	⊖ d	19 56	20 09	20 14		20 39	20 44	20 50	20 56	21 09	21 14		21 39	21 44	21 50	21 56	22 09	22 14		22 39
Vauxhall	⊖ d	20 00	20 13	20 18		20 43	20 48	20 54	21 00	21 13	21 18		21 43	21 48	21 54	22 00	22 13	22 18		22 43
Queenstown Rd.(Battersea)	d	20 03		20 21			20 51	20 57	21 03		21 21			21 51	21 57	22 03		22 21		
Clapham Junction 10	d	20 06	20 19	20 24		20 49	20 54	21 00	21 06	21 19	21 24		21 49	21 54	22 00	22 06	22 19	22 24		22 49
Wandsworth Town	d	20 09		20 27			20 57	21 03	21 09		21 27			21 57	22 03	22 09		22 27		
Putney	d	20 12	20 23	20 30		20 53	21 00	21 06	21 12	21 23	21 30		21 53	22 00	22 06	22 12	22 23	22 30		22 53
Barnes	d	20 15		20 33			21 03	21 09	21 15		21 33			22 03	22 09	22 15		22 33		
Barnes Bridge	d							21 11							22 11					
Chiswick	d							21 13							22 13					
Kew Bridge	d							21 16							22 16					
Brentford	d							21 19							22 19					
Syon Lane	d							21 21							22 21					
Isleworth	d							21 23							22 23					
Hounslow	d							21 26							22 26					
Mortlake	d	20 17		20 35			21 05		21 17		21 35			22 05		22 17		22 35		
North Sheen	d	20 19		20 37			21 07		21 19		21 37			22 07		22 19		22 37		
Richmond	⊖ d	20 22	20 29	20 40		20 59	21 10		21 22	21 29	21 40		21 59	22 10		22 22	22 29	22 40		22 59
St Margarets	d	20 24		20 42			21 12		21 24		21 42			22 12		22 24		22 42		
Twickenham	a	20 26	20 32	20 44		21 02	21 14		21 26	21 32	21 44		22 02	22 14		22 26	22 32	22 44		23 02
	d	20 27	20 33	20 45		21 03	21 15		21 27	21 33	21 45		22 03	22 15		22 27	22 33	22 45		23 03
Strawberry Hill	d	20 30		20 49					21 30		21 49					22 30		22 49		
Fulwell	a																			
Teddington	a	20 33		20 52					21 33		21 52					22 33		22 52		
Hampton Wick	a	20 36		20 57					21 36		21 57					22 36		22 57		
Kingston	a	20 38		20 59					21 38		21 59					22 38		22 59		
Whitton	d						21 18							22 18						
Feltham	d		20 39			21 09	21 22	21 32		21 39			22 09	22 22	22 32		22 39			23 09
Ashford (Surrey)	d						21 26	21 36						22 26	22 36					
Staines	d		20 45			21 15	21 30	21 40		21 45			22 15	22 30	22 40		22 45			23 15
Wraysbury	d						21 34							22 34						
Sunnymeads	d						21 37							22 37						
Datchet	d						21 40							22 40						
Windsor & Eton Riverside	a						21 46							22 46						
Egham	d		20 50			21 20		21 45		21 50			22 20		22 45		22 50			23 20
Virginia Water	a		20 54			21 24		21 49		21 54			22 24		22 49		22 54			23 24
	d		20 54			21 24		21 49		21 54			22 24		22 49		22 54			23 24
Chertsey	d							21 55							22 55					
Addlestone	d							21 58							22 58					
Weybridge	a																			
Byfleet & New Haw	d							22 02							23 02					
West Byfleet	d							22 05							23 05					
Woking	a							22 11							23 11					
Longcross	d																			
Sunningdale	d		20 59			21 29				21 59			22 29				22 59			23 29
Ascot 3	d		21 04		21 13	21 34				22 04		22 13	22 34				23 04		23 13	23 34
Bagshot	d				21 19							22 19							23 19	
Camberley	a				21 25							22 25							23 25	
Frimley	d				21 29							22 29							23 29	
Ash Vale	d				21 36							22 36							23 36	
Aldershot	a				21 41							22 45							23 41	
	d				21 48							22 49							23 42	
Ash 5	d				21 55							22 55								
Wanborough	d				21 58							22 58								
Guildford	a				22 05							23 05								
Martins Heron	d		21 08			21 38				22 08			22 38				23 08			23 38
Bracknell	d		21 11			21 41				22 11			22 41				23 11			23 41
Wokingham	d		21 18			21 48				22 18			22 48				23 18			23 48
Winnersh	d		21 21			21 51				22 21			22 51				23 21			23 51
Winnersh Triangle	d		21 23			21 53				22 23			22 53				23 23			23 53
Earley	d		21 26			21 56				22 26			22 56				23 26			23 56
Reading 7	a		21 34			22 04				22 34			23 04				23 34			00 04

Table 149

Sundays
from 26 September

London - Hounslow, Richmond, Kingston, Windsor, Weybridge, Ascot, Guildford and Reading

		SW	SW	SW	SW ■	SW	SW ■	SW
London Waterloo 15	⊖ d	22 44	22 50	22 56	23 09	23 14	23 39	23 44
Vauxhall	⊖ d	22 48	22 54	23 00	23 13	23 18	23 43	23 48
Queenstown Rd.(Battersea)	d	22 51	22 57	23 03		23 21		23 51
Clapham Junction 10	d	22 54	23 00	23 06	23 19	23 24	23 49	23 54
Wandsworth Town	d	22 57	23 03	23 09		23 27		23 57
Putney	d	23 00	23 06	23 12	23 23	23 30	23 53	23 59
Barnes	d	23 03	23 09	23 15		23 33		00 03
Barnes Bridge	d		23 11					
Chiswick	d		23 13					
Kew Bridge	d		23 16					
Brentford	d		23 19					
Syon Lane	d		23 21					
Isleworth	d		23 23					
Hounslow	d		23 26					
Mortlake	d	23 05		23 17		23 35		00 05
North Sheen	d	23 07		23 19		23 37		00 07
Richmond	⊖ d	23 10		23 22	23 29	23 40	23 59	00 10
St Margarets	d	23 12		23 24		23 42		00 12
Twickenham	a	23 14		23 26	23 32	23 44	00 02	00 14
	d	23 15		23 27	23 33	23 45	00 03	00 15
Strawberry Hill	d			23 30		23 48		
Fulwell	a							
Teddington	a			23 33		23 51		
Hampton Wick	a			23 36		23 54		
Kingston	a			23 38		23 56		
Whitton	d	23 18						00 18
Feltham	d	23 22	23 32		23 39		00 09	00 22
Ashford (Surrey)	d	23 26	23 36					00 26
Staines	d	23 30	23 40		23 45		00 15	00a30
Wraysbury	d	23 34						
Sunnymeads	d	23 37						
Datchet	d	23 40						
Windsor & Eton Riverside	a	23 46						
Egham	d		23 45		23 50		00 20	
Virginia Water	a		23 49		23 54		00 24	
	d		23 49		23 54		00 24	
Chertsey	d		23 55					
Addlestone	d		23 58					
Weybridge	a							
Byfleet & New Haw	d		00 02					
West Byfleet	d		00 05					
Woking	a		00 11					
Longcross	d							
Sunningdale	d				23 59		00 29	
Ascot 3	d				00 04		00 34	
Bagshot	d							
Camberley	a							
Frimley	d							
Ash Vale	d							
Aldershot	a							
	d							
Ash 5	d							
Wanborough	d							
Guildford	a							
Martins Heron	d				00 08		00 38	
Bracknell	d				00 11		00 41	
Wokingham	d				00 18		00 48	
Winnersh	d				00 21		00 51	
Winnersh Triangle	d				00 23		00 53	
Earley	d				00 26		00 56	
Reading 7	a				00 34		01 04	

Table 149

Mondays to Fridays

24 May to 24 September

Reading, Guildford, Ascot, Weybridge, Windsor, Kingston, Richmond and Hounslow - London

		SW MO	SW MO	SW MX	SW MX ■1	SW MX	SW MO ■1	SW MX ■1	SW	SW	SW	SW	SW	SW	SW	SW	SW	SW ■1	SW ■1	SW
Reading ■7	d				22p42		22p54	23p12										05 42		
Earley	d				22p47		22p59	23p17										05 47		
Winnersh Triangle	d				22p49		23p01	23p19										05 49		
Winnersh	d				22p51		23p03	23p21										05 51		
Wokingham	d				22p56		23p08	23p26										05 56		
Bracknell	d				23p02		23p14	23p32										06 02		
Martins Heron	d				23p05		23p17	23p35										06 05		
Guildford	d																			
Wanborough	d																			
Ash ■5	d																			
Aldershot	a																			
	d																		05 58	
Ash Vale	d																		06 02	
Frimley	d																		06 10	
Camberley	a																		06 14	
	d																		06 18	
Bagshot	d																		06 23	
Ascot ■3	d				23p10		23p22	23p40										06 10	06a30	
Sunningdale	d				23p13		23p25	23p43										06 13		
Longcross	d																			
Woking	d		22p52												05 25					
West Byfleet	d		22p56												05 30					
Byfleet & New Haw	d		23p00												05 33					
Weybridge	d																			
Addlestone	d		23p04												05 37					
Chertsey	d		23p07												05 40					
Virginia Water	a		23p12		23p19		23p30	23p49							05 45			06 19		
	d		23p12		23p19		23p30	23p49							05 54			06 19		
Egham	d		23p16		23p23		23p34	23p53							05 57			06 23		
Windsor & Eton Riverside	d	23p01														05 53				
Datchet	d	23p04														05 56				
Sunnymeads	d	23p07														05 59				
Wraysbury	d	23p10														06 02				
Staines	d	23p16	23p21		23p29		23p39	23p59	04 58			05 37			06 03	06 08		06 29		
Ashford (Surrey)	d	23p19	23p24						05 01			05 40			06 06	06 11				
Feltham	d	23p24	23p29		23p35		23p46	00 05	05 06			05 45			06 11	06 16		06 35		
Whitton	d	23p28							05 10			05 49				06 20	06 20			
Kingston	d					23p29								05 59						06 29
Hampton Wick	d					23p31								06 01						06 31
Teddington	d					23p35								06 05						06 35
Fulwell	d										05 36									
Strawberry Hill	d					23p38					05 38			06 08						06 38
Twickenham	a	23p31		23p33	23p40	23p42	23p51	00 10	05 13		05 42	05 52		06 12		06 23		06 40		06 42
	d	23p32		23p34	23p41	23p43	23p51	00 11	05 13		05 43	05 53		06 13		06 23		06 41		06 43
St Margarets	d	23p34				23p45			05 15		05 45			06 15						06 45
Richmond ⊖	d	23p37			23p45	23p49	23p56	00 15	05 19		05 49	05 58		06 19		06 28		06 45		06 49
North Sheen	d	23p39				23p51			05 21		05 51			06 21						06 51
Mortlake	d	23p42				23p53			05 23		05 53			06 23						06 53
Hounslow	d		23p35							05 31			06 01		06 16		06 31			
Isleworth	d		23p38							05 34			06 04		06 19		06 34			
Syon Lane	d		23p40							05 36			06 06		06 21		06 36			
Brentford	d		23p42							05 39			06 09		06 24		06 39			
Kew Bridge	d		23p45							05 41			06 11		06 26		06 41			
Chiswick	d		23p47							05 44			06 14		06 29		06 44			
Barnes Bridge	d		23p50							05 46			06 16		06 31		06 46			
Barnes	d	23p45	23p53			23p56			05 26	05 49	05 56		06 19	06 26	06 34		06 49			06 56
Putney	d	23p48	23p56			23p59	00 02		05 29	05 52	05 59	06 04	06 22	06 29	06 37	06 34	06 52	06 52		06 59
Wandsworth Town	d	23p51	23p59			00 02			05 32	05 55	06 02		06 25	06 32	06 40		06 55			07 02
Clapham Junction ■10	d	23p54	00 02		23p54	00 05	00 07	00 24	05 35	05 58	06 05	06 09	06 28	06 35	06 43	06 39	06 58	06 56		07 05
Queenstown Rd.(Battersea)	d	23p57	00 05			00 08			05 38	06 01	06 08		06 31	06 38	06 46		07 01			07 08
Vauxhall ⊖	d	23p59	00 08	00 17		00 12	00 12		05 42	06 05	06 12	06 15	06 35	06 42	06 50	06 45	07 05			07 12
London Waterloo ■15 ⊖	a	00 05	00 13	00 23	00 04	00 16	00 17	00 32	05 46	06 09	06 16	06 19	06 39	06 46	06 56	06 49	07 11	07 07		07 18

Table 149

Mondays to Fridays

24 May to 24 September

Reading, Guildford, Ascot, Weybridge, Windsor, Kingston, Richmond and Hounslow - London

		SW	SW	SW	SW	SW ■1	SW	SW	SW	SW	SW ■1	SW	SW	SW ■1	SW	SW	SW	SW	SW ■1	SW	SW
Reading ■7	d					06 12								06 42							
Earley	d					06 17								06 47							
Winnersh Triangle	d					06 19								06 49							
Winnersh	d					06 21								06 51							
Wokingham	d					06 26								06 56							
Bracknell	d					06 32								07 02							
Martins Heron	d					06 35								07 05							
Guildford	d																				
Wanborough	d																				
Ash ■5	d																				
Aldershot	a																				
	d										06 28								07 00		
Ash Vale	d										06 32								07 04		
Frimley	d										06 40								07 10		
Camberley	a										06 44								07 14		
	d										06 47								07 17		
Bagshot	d										06 52								07 22		
Ascot ■3	d					06 40					06 59			07 10					07 29		
Sunningdale	d					06 43					07 02			07 13					07 32		
Longcross	d																				
Woking	d																				
West Byfleet	d																				
Byfleet & New Haw	d																				
Weybridge	d							06 33								07 03					
Addlestone	d							06 37								07 07					
Chertsey	d							06 40								07 10					
Virginia Water	a					06 49		06 45			07 08			07 19		07 15			07 38		
	d					06 49		06 54			07 08			07 19		07 24			07 38		
Egham	d					06 53		06 57			07 12			07 23		07 27			07 42		
Windsor & Eton Riverside	d	06 23							06 53								07 23				
Datchet	d	06 26							06 56								07 26				
Sunnymeads	d	06 29							06 59								07 29				
Wraysbury	d	06 32							07 02								07 32				
Staines	d	06 38	06 33			06 59		07 03	07 08		07 18			07 29		07 33	07 38		07 48		
Ashford (Surrey)	d	06 41	06 36					07 06	07 11		07 21					07 36	07 41		07 51		
Feltham	d	06 46	06 41			07 05		07 11	07 16		07 26			07 35		07 41	07 46		07 56		
Whitton	d	06 50		06 53	06 50				07 20		07 30	07 20					07 50		08 00	07 50	
Kingston	d						06 59								07 29						
Hampton Wick	d						07 01								07 31						
Teddington	d						07 05								07 35						
Fulwell	d									07 12								07 42			
Strawberry Hill	d						07 08			07 14					07 38			07 44			
Twickenham	a	06 53		06 56		07 10	07 12		07 23	07 18	07 33		07 33	07 40	07 42		07 53	07 48	08 03		08 03
	d	06 53		06 58		07 11	07 13		07 23	07 27	07 33		07 34	07 41	07 43		07 53	07 57	08 03		08 04
St Margarets	d			07 00			07 15			07 29					07 45			07 59			
Richmond ⊖	d	06 58		07 04		07 15	07 19		07 28	07 32	07 38			07 45	07 49		07 58	08 02	08 08		
North Sheen	d			07 06			07 21			07 34					07 51			08 04			
Mortlake	d			07 08			07 23			07 37					07 53			08 07			
Hounslow	d		06 46		07 01			07 16				07 31				07 46				08 01	
Isleworth	d		06 49		07 04			07 19				07 34				07 49				08 04	
Syon Lane	d		06 51		07 06			07 21				07 36				07 51				08 06	
Brentford	d		06 54		07 09			07 24				07 39				07 54				08 09	
Kew Bridge	d		06 56		07 11			07 26				07 41				07 56				08 11	
Chiswick	d		06 59		07 14			07 29				07 44				07 59				08 14	
Barnes Bridge	d		07 01		07 16			07 31				07 46				08 01				08 16	
Barnes	d		07 04	07 11	07 19		07 26	07 34		07 40		07 49			07 56	08 04		08 10		08 19	
Putney	d	07 04	07 07	07 14	07 22	07 22	07 29	07 37	07 34	07 43		07 52			07 59	08 07	08 04	08 13		08 22	
Wandsworth Town	d		07 10	07 17	07 25		07 32	07 40		07 46		07 55			08 02	08 10		08 16		08 25	
Clapham Junction ■10	d	07 09	07 13	07 20	07 28	07 26	07 35	07 43	07 39	07 49	07 47	07 58		07 54	08 05	08 13	08 09	08 19	08 17	08 28	
Queenstown Rd.(Battersea)	d		07 16	07 23	07 31		07 38	07 46		07 52		08 01			08 08	08 16		08 22		08 31	
Vauxhall ⊖	d	07 15	07 20	07 27	07 35		07 42	07 50	07 45	07 56	07 53	08 05	08 14		08 12	08 20	08 15	08 26	08 23	08 35	08 44
London Waterloo ■15 ⊖	a	07 21	07 28	07 34	07 43	07 37	07 48	07 58	07 51	08 04	07 59	08 11	08 21	08 06	08 18	08 28	08 21	08 34	08 29	08 43	08 51

Table 149

Mondays to Fridays
24 May to 24 September

Reading, Guildford, Ascot, Weybridge, Windsor, Kingston, Richmond and Hounslow - London

		SW	SW ■	SW	SW ■	SW	SW	SW	SW ■	SW	SW ■	SW ■	SW	SW	SW	SW	SW	SW ■	SW ■	SW
Reading ■	d		07 12		07 24						07 42							08 12		
Earley	d		07 17								07 47							08 17		
Winnersh Triangle	d		07 19								07 49							08 19		
Winnersh	d		07 21								07 51							08 21		
Wokingham	d		07 26		07 33						07 56							08 26		
Bracknell	d		07 32		07 39						08 02							08 32		
Martins Heron	d		07 35		07 42						08 05							08 35		
Guildford	d											07 30							08 00	
Wanborough	d											07 36							08 06	
Ash ■	d											07 40							08 10	
Aldershot	a											07 47							08 17	
	d								07 30			08 00							08 30	
Ash Vale	d								07 34			08 04							08 34	
Frimley	d								07 40			08 10							08 40	
Camberley	a								07 44			08 14							08 44	
	d								07 47			08 18							08 48	
Bagshot	d								07 52			08 23							08 53	
Ascot ■	d		07 40		07 47				07 59		08 10	08a30						08 40	09a00	
Sunningdale	d		07 43		07 50				08 02		08 13							08 43		
Longcross	d										08 16							08 46		
Woking	d																			
West Byfleet	d																			
Byfleet & New Haw	d																			
Weybridge	d					07 33								08 03						
Addlestone	d					07 37								08 07						
Chertsey	d					07 40								08 10						
Virginia Water	a				07 55	07 45			08 08		08 19			08 15				08 49		
	d				07 55	07 51			08 08		08 19			08 24				08 49		
Egham	d		07 50		07 58	07 54			08 12		08 23			08 27				08 53		
Windsor & Eton Riverside	d						07 53								08 23					
Datchet	d						07 56								08 26					
Sunnymeads	d						07 59								08 29					
Wraysbury	d						08 02								08 32					
Staines	d		07 56		08 04	08 00	08 08		08 18		08 29			08 33	08 38			08 59		
Ashford (Surrey)	d					08 03	08 11		08 21					08 36	08 41					
Feltham	d		08 02		08 12	08 08	08 16		08 26		08 35			08 41	08 46			09 05		
Whitton	d						08 20		08 30	08 20					08 50	08 53	08 50			
Kingston	d			07 59									08 29							08 59
Hampton Wick	d			08 01									08 31							09 01
Teddington	d			08 05									08 35							09 05
Fulwell	d							08 12												
Strawberry Hill	d			08 08				08 14					08 38							09 08
Twickenham	a		08 09	08 12	08 17		08 23	08 18	08 33		08 40		08 42		08 53	08 56		09 10		09 12
	d		08 09	08 13	08 18		08 23	08 27	08 33		08 41		08 43		08 53	08 58		09 11		09 13
St Margarets	d			08 15				08 29					08 45			09 00				09 15
Richmond ⊖	d		08 14	08 19	08 24		08 28	08 32	08 38		08 45		08 49		08 58	09 04		09 15		09 19
North Sheen	d			08 21				08 34					08 51			09 06				09 21
Mortlake	d			08 23				08 37					08 53			09 08				09 23
Hounslow	d					08 16				08 31				08 46			09 01			
Isleworth	d					08 19				08 34				08 49			09 04			
Syon Lane	d					08 21				08 36				08 51			09 06			
Brentford	d					08 24				08 39				08 54			09 09			
Kew Bridge	d					08 26				08 41				08 56			09 11			
Chiswick	d					08 29				08 44				08 59			09 14			
Barnes Bridge	d					08 31				08 46				09 01			09 16			
Barnes	d			08 26		08 34		08 40		08 49			08 56	09 04		09 11	09 19			09 26
Putney	d			08 29		08 37	08 34	08 43		08 52			08 59	09 07	09 04	09 14	09 22			09 29
Wandsworth Town	d			08 32		08 40		08 46		08 55			09 02	09 10		09 17	09 25			09 32
Clapham Junction ■■	d		08 22	08 35	08 33	08 43	08 39	08 49	08 47	08 58	08 54		09 05	09 13	09 09	09 20	09 28	09 24		09 35
Queenstown Rd.(Battersea)	d			08 38		08 46		08 52		09 01			09 08	09 16		09 23	09 31			09 38
Vauxhall ⊖	d			08 42	08 38	08 50	08 45	08 56	08 53	09 05			09 12	09 20	09 15	09 27	09 35			09 42
London Waterloo ■■ ⊖	a		08 38	08 49	08 46	08 58	08 51	09 04	09 00	09 13	09 06		09 18	09 28	09 21	09 34	09 43	09 34		09 48

Table 149

Mondays to Fridays
24 May to 24 September

Reading, Guildford, Ascot, Weybridge, Windsor, Kingston, Richmond and Hounslow - London

		SW	SW	SW	SW	SW ■	SW ■	SW	SW	SW	SW	SW	SW ■	SW	SW	SW	SW ■	SW ■	SW	SW	SW
Reading ■	d					08 42							09 12				09 25				
Earley	d					08 47							09 17				09 30				
Winnersh Triangle	d					08 49							09 19				09 32				
Winnersh	d					08 51							09 21				09 34				
Wokingham	d					08 56							09 26				09 39				
Bracknell	d					09 02							09 32				09 46				
Martins Heron	d					09 05							09 35				09 49				
Guildford	d						08 30											09 00			
Wanborough	d						08 36											09 06			
Ash ■	d						08 40											09 10			
Aldershot	a						08 47											09 17			
	d						09 00											09 30			
Ash Vale	d						09 04											09 34			
Frimley	d						09 10											09 40			
Camberley	a						09 14											09 44			
	d						09 18											09 48			
Bagshot	d						09 23											09 53			
Ascot ■	d					09 10	09a30						09 40				09 55	10a00			
Sunningdale	d					09 13							09 43				09 58				
Longcross	d					09 16															
Woking	d																				
West Byfleet	d																				
Byfleet & New Haw	d																				
Weybridge	d	08 33							09 03						09 33						
Addlestone	d	08 37							09 07						09 37						
Chertsey	d	08 40							09 10						09 40						
Virginia Water	a	08 45				09 19			09 15				09 49		09 45		10 03				
	d	08 54				09 19			09 24				09 49		09 54		10 03				
Egham	d	08 57				09 23			09 27				09 53		09 57		10 06				
Windsor & Eton Riverside	d		08 53							09 23						09 53					
Datchet	d		08 56							09 26						09 56					
Sunnymeads	d		08 59							09 29						09 59					
Wraysbury	d		09 02							09 32						10 02					
Staines	d	09 03	09 08			09 29			09 33	09 38			09 59		10 03	10 08	10 14				
Ashford (Surrey)	d	09 06	09 11						09 36	09 41					10 06	10 11					
Feltham	d	09 11	09 16			09 35			09 41	09 46			10 05		10 11	10 16	10 20				
Whitton	d		09 20	09 23	09 20					09 50	09 53	09 50				10 20			10 26	10 20	
Kingston	d							09 29						09 59							
Hampton Wick	d							09 31						10 01							
Teddington	d							09 35						10 05							
Fulwell	d																				
Strawberry Hill	d							09 38						10 08							
Twickenham	a		09 23	09 26		09 40		09 42		09 53	09 56		10 10	10 12		10 23	10 27		10 28		
	d		09 23	09 28		09 41		09 43		09 53	09 58		10 11	10 13		10 23	10 27		10 28		
St Margarets	d			09 30				09 45			10 00			10 15					10 30		
Richmond ⊖	d		09 28	09 34		09 45		09 49		09 58	10 04		10 15	10 19		10 28	10 32		10 34		
North Sheen	d			09 36				09 51			10 06			10 21					10 36		
Mortlake	d			09 38				09 53			10 08			10 23					10 38		
Hounslow	d	09 16			09 31				09 46			10 01			10 16					10 31	
Isleworth	d	09 19			09 34				09 49			10 04			10 19					10 34	
Syon Lane	d	09 21			09 36				09 51			10 06			10 21					10 36	
Brentford	d	09 24			09 39				09 54			10 09			10 24					10 39	
Kew Bridge	d	09 26			09 41				09 56			10 11			10 26					10 41	
Chiswick	d	09 29			09 44				09 59			10 14			10 29					10 44	
Barnes Bridge	d	09 31			09 46				10 01			10 16			10 31					10 46	
Barnes	d	09 34		09 41	09 49			09 56	10 04		10 11	10 19		10 26	10 34				10 41	10 49	
Putney	d	09 37	09 34	09 44	09 52			09 59	10 07	10 04	10 14	10 22		10 29	10 37	10 34			10 44	10 52	
Wandsworth Town	d	09 40		09 47	09 55			10 02	10 10		10 17	10 25		10 32	10 40				10 47	10 55	
Clapham Junction ■■	d	09 43	09 39	09 50	09 58	09 54		10 05	10 13	10 09	10 20	10 28	10 24	10 35	10 43	10 39	10 42		10 50	10 58	
Queenstown Rd.(Battersea)	d	09 46		09 53	10 01			10 08	10 16		10 23	10 31		10 38	10 47				10 53	11 01	
Vauxhall ⊖	d	09 50	09 45	09 57	10 05			10 12	10 20	10 15	10 27	10 35		10 42	10 50	10 45			10 57	11 05	
London Waterloo ■■ ⊖	a	09 58	09 51	10 02	10 11	10 04		10 16	10 26	10 19	10 32	10 41	10 34	10 46	10 56	10 49	10 53		11 02	11 11	

24 May to 24 September

Reading, Guildford, Ascot, Weybridge, Windsor, Kingston, Richmond and Hounslow - London

		SW 1	SW	SW	SW	SW 1	SW 1	SW	SW	SW 1	SW 1	SW	SW	SW	SW	SW	SW 1	SW 1	SW	SW
Reading 7	d	09 42				09 56				10 12							10 42			
Earley	d	09 47				10 01				10 17							10 47			
Winnersh Triangle	d	09 49				10 03				10 19							10 49			
Winnersh	d	09 51				10 05				10 21							10 51			
Wokingham	d	09 56				10 10				10 26							10 56			
Bracknell	d	10 02				10 16				10 32							11 02			
Martins Heron	d	10 05				10 19				10 35							11 05			
Guildford	d						09 30				10 00							10 30		
Wanborough	d						09 36				10 06							10 36		
Ash 5	d						09 40				10 10							10 40		
Aldershot	a						09 47				10 17							10 47		
	d						10 00				10 30							11 00		
Ash Vale	d						10 04				10 34							11 04		
Frimley	d						10 10				10 40							11 10		
Camberley	a						10 14				10 44							11 14		
	d						10 18				10 48							11 18		
Bagshot	d						10 23				10 53							11 23		
Ascot 3	d	10 10				10 25	10a30			10 40	11a00						11 10	11a30		
Sunningdale	d	10 13				10 28				10 43							11 13			
Longcross	d																			
Woking	d																			
West Byfleet	d																			
Byfleet & New Haw	d																			
Weybridge	d			10 03									10 33							11 03
Addlestone	d			10 07									10 37							11 07
Chertsey	d			10 10									10 40							11 10
Virginia Water	a	10 19		10 15		10 33				10 49			10 45				11 19			11 15
	d	10 19		10 24		10 33				10 49			10 54				11 19			11 24
Egham	d	10 23		10 27		10 36				10 53			10 57				11 23			11 27
Windsor & Eton Riverside	d				10 23									10 53						
Datchet	d				10 26									10 56						
Sunnymeads	d				10 29									10 59						
Wraysbury	d				10 32									11 02						
Staines	d	10 29		10 33	10 38	10 44				10 59			11 03	11 08			11 29			11 33
Ashford (Surrey)	d			10 36	10 41								11 06	11 11						11 36
Feltham	d	10 35		10 41	10 46	10 50				11 05			11 11	11 16			11 35			11 41
Whitton	d				10 50			10 56	10 50					11 20	11 23	11 20				
Kingston	d		10 29									10 59							11 29	
Hampton Wick	d		10 31									11 01							11 31	
Teddington	d		10 35									11 05							11 35	
Fulwell	d																			
Strawberry Hill	d		10 38									11 08							11 38	
Twickenham	a	10 40	10 42		10 53	10 57		10 58		11 10		11 12		11 23	11 26		11 40		11 42	
	d	10 41	10 43		10 53	10 57		10 58		11 11		11 13		11 23	11 28		11 41		11 43	
St Margarets	d		10 45					11 00				11 15			11 30				11 45	
Richmond ⊖	d	10 45	10 49		10 58	11 02		11 04		11 15		11 19		11 28	11 34		11 45		11 49	
North Sheen	d		10 51					11 06				11 21			11 36				11 51	
Mortlake	d		10 53					11 08				11 23			11 38				11 53	
Hounslow	d			10 46					11 01				11 16			11 31				11 46
Isleworth	d			10 49					11 04				11 19			11 34				11 49
Syon Lane	d			10 51					11 06				11 21			11 36				11 51
Brentford	d			10 54					11 09				11 24			11 39				11 54
Kew Bridge	d			10 56					11 11				11 26			11 41				11 56
Chiswick	d			10 59					11 14				11 29			11 44				11 59
Barnes Bridge	d			11 01					11 16				11 31			11 46				12 01
Barnes	d		10 56	11 04				11 11	11 19			11 26	11 34		11 41	11 49			11 56	12 04
Putney	d		10 59	11 07	11 04			11 14	11 22			11 29	11 37	11 34	11 44	11 52			11 59	12 07
Wandsworth Town	d		11 02	11 10				11 17	11 25			11 32	11 40		11 47	11 55			12 02	12 10
Clapham Junction 10	d	10 54	11 05	11 13	11 09	11 12		11 20	11 28	11 24		11 35	11 43	11 39	11 50	11 58	11 54		12 05	12 13
Queenstown Rd.(Battersea)	d		11 08	11 17				11 23	11 31			11 38	11 46		11 53	12 01			12 08	12 16
Vauxhall ⊖	d		11 12	11 20	11 15			11 27	11 35			11 42	11 50	11 45	11 57	12 05			12 12	12 20
London Waterloo 15 ⊖	a	11 04	11 16	11 27	11 19	11 25		11 32	11 41	11 34		11 46	11 56	11 49	12 02	12 11	12 04		12 16	12 26

24 May to 24 September

Reading, Guildford, Ascot, Weybridge, Windsor, Kingston, Richmond and Hounslow - London

		SW	SW	SW	SW 1	SW 1	SW	SW	SW	SW	SW 1	SW 1	SW	SW	SW	SW	SW	SW 1	SW 1	SW	SW
Reading 7	d				11 12						11 42							12 12			
Earley	d				11 17						11 47							12 17			
Winnersh Triangle	d				11 19						11 49							12 19			
Winnersh	d				11 21						11 51							12 21			
Wokingham	d				11 26						11 56							12 26			
Bracknell	d				11 32						12 02							12 32			
Martins Heron	d				11 35						12 05							12 35			
Guildford	d					11 00						11 30							12 00		
Wanborough	d					11 06						11 36							12 06		
Ash 5	d					11 10						11 40							12 10		
Aldershot	a					11 17						11 47							12 17		
	d					11 30						12 00							12 30		
Ash Vale	d					11 34						12 04							12 34		
Frimley	d					11 40						12 10							12 40		
Camberley	a					11 44						12 14							12 44		
	d					11 48						12 18							12 48		
Bagshot	d					11 53						12 23							12 53		
Ascot 3	d				11 40	12a00					12 10	12a30						12 40	13a00		
Sunningdale	d				11 43						12 13							12 43			
Longcross	d																				
Woking	d																				
West Byfleet	d																				
Byfleet & New Haw	d																				
Weybridge	d													12 03							12 33
Addlestone	d													12 07							12 37
Chertsey	d													12 10							12 40
Virginia Water	a				11 49						12 19			12 15				12 49			12 45
	d				11 49						12 19			12 24				12 49			12 54
Egham	d				11 53						12 23			12 27				12 53			12 57
Windsor & Eton Riverside	d	11 23						11 53							12 23						
Datchet	d	11 26						11 56							12 26						
Sunnymeads	d	11 29						11 59							12 29						
Wraysbury	d	11 32						12 02							12 32						
Staines	d	11 38			11 59			12 08			12 29			12 33	12 38			12 59			13 03
Ashford (Surrey)	d	11 41						12 11						12 36	12 41						13 06
Feltham	d	11 46			12 05			12 16			12 35			12 41	12 46			13 05			13 11
Whitton	d	11 50	11 53	11 50				12 20	12 23	12 20					12 50	12 53					
Kingston	d						11 59						12 29							12 59	
Hampton Wick	d						12 01						12 31							13 01	
Teddington	d						12 05						12 35							13 05	
Fulwell	d																				
Strawberry Hill	d						12 08						12 38							13 08	
Twickenham	a	11 53	11 56		12 10		12 12	12 23	12 26		12 40		12 42		12 53	12 56		13 10		13 12	
	d	11 53	11 58		12 11		12 13	12 23	12 28		12 41		12 43		12 53	12 58		13 11		13 13	
St Margarets	d		12 00				12 15		12 30				12 45			13 00				13 15	
Richmond ⊖	d	11 58	12 04		12 15		12 19	12 28	12 34		12 45		12 49		12 58	13 04		13 15		13 19	
North Sheen	d		12 06				12 21		12 36				12 51			13 06				13 21	
Mortlake	d		12 08				12 23		12 38				12 53			13 08				13 23	
Hounslow	d			12 01						12 31				12 46							13 16
Isleworth	d			12 04						12 34				12 49							13 19
Syon Lane	d			12 06						12 36				12 51							13 21
Brentford	d			12 09						12 39				12 54							13 24
Kew Bridge	d			12 11						12 41				12 56							13 26
Chiswick	d			12 14						12 44				12 59							13 29
Barnes Bridge	d			12 16						12 46				13 01							13 31
Barnes	d		12 11	12 19			12 26		12 41	12 49			12 56	13 04		13 11				13 26	13 34
Putney	d	12 04	12 14	12 22			12 29	12 34	12 44	12 52			12 59	13 07	13 04	13 14				13 29	13 37
Wandsworth Town	d		12 17	12 25			12 32		12 47	12 55			13 02	13 10		13 17				13 32	13 40
Clapham Junction 10	d	12 09	12 20	12 28	12 25		12 35	12 39	12 50	12 58	12 54		13 05	13 13	13 09	13 20		13 24		13 35	13 43
Queenstown Rd.(Battersea)	d		12 23	12 31			12 38		12 53	13 01			13 08	13 16		13 23				13 38	13 46
Vauxhall ⊖	d	12 15	12 27	12 35			12 42	12 45	12 57	13 05			13 12	13 20	13 15	13 27				13 42	13 50
London Waterloo 15 ⊖	a	12 19	12 32	12 41	12 34		12 46	12 49	13 02	13 11	13 04		13 16	13 26	13 19	13 32		13 34		13 46	13 56

Reading, Guildford, Ascot, Weybridge, Windsor, Kingston, Richmond and Hounslow - London

		SW	SW	SW	SW 1	SW 1	SW	SW	SW	SW	SW	SW 1	SW 1	SW	SW	SW	SW	SW	SW 1	SW 1
Reading 7	d				12 42							13 12							13 42	
Earley	d				12 47							13 17							13 47	
Winnersh Triangle	d				12 49							13 19							13 49	
Winnersh	d				12 51							13 21							13 51	
Wokingham	d				12 56							13 26							13 56	
Bracknell	d				13 02							13 32							14 02	
Martins Heron	d				13 05							13 35							14 05	
Guildford	d					12 30							13 00							13 30
Wanborough	d					12 36							13 06							13 36
Ash 5	d					12 40							13 10							13 40
Aldershot	a					12 47							13 17							13 47
	d					13 00							13 30							14 00
Ash Vale	d					13 04							13 34							14 04
Frimley	d					13 10							13 40							14 10
Camberley	a					13 14							13 44							14 14
	d					13 18							13 48							14 18
Bagshot	d					13 23							13 53							14 23
Ascot 3	d				13 10	13a30						13 40	14a00						14 10	14a30
Sunningdale	d				13 13							13 43							14 13	
Longcross	d				13 16															
Woking	d																			
West Byfleet	d																			
Byfleet & New Haw	d																			
Weybridge	d							13 03							13 33					
Addlestone	d							13 07							13 37					
Chertsey	d							13 10							13 40					
Virginia Water	a				13 19			13 15				13 49			13 45				14 19	
	d				13 19			13 24				13 49			13 54				14 19	
Egham	d				13 23			13 27				13 53			13 57				14 23	
Windsor & Eton Riverside	d	12 53							13 23							13 53				
Datchet	d	12 56							13 26							13 56				
Sunnymeads	d	12 59							13 29							13 59				
Wraysbury	d	13 02							13 32							14 02				
Staines	d	13 08			13 29			13 33	13 38			13 59			14 03	14 08			14 29	
Ashford (Surrey)	d	13 11						13 36	13 41						14 06	14 11				
Feltham	d	13 16			13 35			13 41	13 46			14 05			14 11	14 16			14 35	
Whitton	d	13 20	13 23	13 20					13 50	13 53	13 50					14 20	14 23	14 20		
Kingston	d						13 29							13 59						
Hampton Wick	d						13 31							14 01						
Teddington	d						13 35							14 05						
Fulwell	d																			
Strawberry Hill	d						13 38							14 08						
Twickenham	a	13 23	13 26		13 40		13 42		13 53	13 56		14 10		14 12		14 23	14 26		14 40	
	d	13 23	13 28		13 41		13 43		13 53	13 58		14 11		14 13		14 23	14 28		14 41	
St Margarets	d		13 30				13 45			14 00				14 15			14 30			
Richmond ⊖	d	13 28	13 34		13 45		13 49		13 58	14 04		14 15		14 19		14 28	14 34		14 45	
North Sheen	d		13 36				13 51			14 06				14 21			14 36			
Mortlake	d		13 38				13 53			14 08				14 23			14 38			
Hounslow	d			13 31				13 46			14 01				14 16			14 31		
Isleworth	d			13 34				13 49			14 04				14 19			14 34		
Syon Lane	d			13 36				13 51			14 06				14 21			14 36		
Brentford	d			13 39				13 54			14 09				14 24			14 39		
Kew Bridge	d			13 41				13 56			14 11				14 26			14 41		
Chiswick	d			13 44				13 59			14 14				14 29			14 44		
Barnes Bridge	d			13 46				14 01			14 16				14 31			14 46		
Barnes	d		13 41	13 49			13 56	14 04		14 11	14 19			14 26	14 34		14 41	14 49		
Putney	d	13 34	13 44	13 52			13 59	14 07	14 04	14 14	14 22			14 29	14 37	14 34	14 44	14 52		
Wandsworth Town	d		13 47	13 55			14 02	14 10		14 17	14 25			14 32	14 40		14 47	14 55		
Clapham Junction 10	d	13 39	13 50	13 58	13 54		14 05	14 13	14 09	14 20	14 28	14 24		14 35	14 43	14 39	14 50	14 58	14 54	
Queenstown Rd.(Battersea)	d		13 53	14 01			14 08	14 16		14 23	14 31			14 38	14 46		14 53	15 01		
Vauxhall ⊖	d	13 45	13 57	14 05			14 12	14 20	14 15	14 27	14 35			14 42	14 50	14 45	14 57	15 05		
London Waterloo 15 ⊖	a	13 49	14 02	14 11	14 04		14 16	14 26	14 19	14 32	14 41	14 34		14 46	14 56	14 49	15 02	15 11	15 04	

Reading, Guildford, Ascot, Weybridge, Windsor, Kingston, Richmond and Hounslow - London

		SW	SW	SW	SW	SW	SW 1	SW 1	SW	SW	SW	SW	SW	SW 1	SW 1	SW	SW	SW	SW	SW
Reading 7	d						14 12							14 42						
Earley	d						14 17							14 47						
Winnersh Triangle	d						14 19							14 49						
Winnersh	d						14 21							14 51						
Wokingham	d						14 26							14 56						
Bracknell	d						14 32							15 02						
Martins Heron	d						14 35							15 05						
Guildford	d							14 00							14 30					
Wanborough	d							14 06							14 36					
Ash 5	d							14 10							14 40					
Aldershot	a							14 17							14 47					
	d							14 30							15 00					
Ash Vale	d							14 34							15 04					
Frimley	d							14 40							15 10					
Camberley	a							14 44							15 14					
	d							14 48							15 18					
Bagshot	d							14 53							15 23					
Ascot 3	d						14 40	15a00						15 10	15a30					
Sunningdale	d						14 43							15 13						
Longcross	d																			
Woking	d																			
West Byfleet	d																			
Byfleet & New Haw	d																			
Weybridge	d		14 03							14 33							15 03			
Addlestone	d		14 07							14 37							15 07			
Chertsey	d		14 10							14 40							15 10			
Virginia Water	a		14 15				14 49			14 45				15 19			15 15			
	d		14 24				14 49			14 54				15 19			15 24			
Egham	d		14 27				14 53			14 57				15 23			15 27			
Windsor & Eton Riverside	d			14 23							14 53							15 23		
Datchet	d			14 26							14 56							15 26		
Sunnymeads	d			14 29							14 59							15 29		
Wraysbury	d			14 32							15 02							15 32		
Staines	d		14 33	14 38			14 59			15 03	15 08			15 29			15 33	15 38		
Ashford (Surrey)	d		14 36	14 41						15 06	15 11						15 36	15 41		
Feltham	d		14 41	14 46			15 05			15 11	15 16			15 35			15 41	15 46		
Whitton	d			14 50	14 53	14 50					15 20	15 23	15 20					15 50	15 53	15 50
Kingston	d	14 29							14 59							15 29				
Hampton Wick	d	14 31							15 01							15 31				
Teddington	d	14 35							15 05							15 35				
Fulwell	d																			
Strawberry Hill	d	14 38							15 08							15 38				
Twickenham	a	14 42		14 53	14 56		15 10		15 12		15 23	15 26		15 40		15 42		15 53	15 56	
	d	14 43		14 53	14 58		15 11		15 13		15 23	15 28		15 41		15 43		15 53	15 58	
St Margarets	d	14 45			15 00				15 15			15 30				15 45			16 00	
Richmond ⊖	d	14 49		14 58	15 04		15 15		15 19		15 28	15 34		15 45		15 49		15 58	16 04	
North Sheen	d	14 51			15 06				15 21			15 36				15 51			16 06	
Mortlake	d	14 53			15 08				15 23			15 38				15 53			16 08	
Hounslow	d		14 46			15 01				15 16			15 31				15 46			16 01
Isleworth	d		14 49			15 04				15 19			15 34				15 49			16 04
Syon Lane	d		14 51			15 06				15 21			15 36				15 51			16 06
Brentford	d		14 54			15 09				15 24			15 39				15 54			16 09
Kew Bridge	d		14 56			15 11				15 26			15 41				15 56			16 11
Chiswick	d		14 59			15 14				15 29			15 44				15 59			16 14
Barnes Bridge	d		15 01			15 16				15 31			15 46				16 01			16 16
Barnes	d	14 56	15 04		15 11	15 19			15 26	15 34		15 41	15 49			15 56	16 04		16 11	16 19
Putney	d	14 59	15 07	15 04	15 14	15 22			15 29	15 37	15 34	15 44	15 52			15 59	16 07	16 04	16 14	16 22
Wandsworth Town	d	15 02	15 10		15 17	15 25			15 32	15 40		15 47	15 55			16 02	16 10		16 17	16 25
Clapham Junction 10	d	15 05	15 13	15 09	15 20	15 28	15 24		15 35	15 43	15 39	15 50	15 58	15 54		16 05	16 13	16 09	16 20	16 28
Queenstown Rd.(Battersea)	d	15 08	15 16		15 23	15 31			15 38	15 46		15 53	16 01			16 08	16 16		16 23	16 31
Vauxhall ⊖	d	15 12	15 20	15 15	15 27	15 35			15 42	15 50	15 45	15 57	16 05			16 12	16 20	16 15	16 27	16 35
London Waterloo 15 ⊖	a	15 16	15 26	15 19	15 32	15 41	15 34		15 46	15 56	15 49	16 02	16 11	16 05		16 19	16 26	16 19	16 32	16 41

Table 149

Mondays to Fridays

24 May to 24 September

Reading, Guildford, Ascot, Weybridge, Windsor, Kingston, Richmond and Hounslow - London

			SW	SW	SW	SW	SW	SW	GW	SW		SW	SW	SW	SW	SW	SW	SW		SW		SW	SW	SW	SW
			1	1					1 A			1	1									1	1		
Reading 7	d		15 12						15 28			15 42										16 12			
Earley	d		15 17									15 47										16 17			
Winnersh Triangle	d		15 19									15 49										16 19			
Winnersh	d		15 21						15 35			15 51										16 21			
Wokingham	d		15 26						15a38			15 56										16 26			
Bracknell	d		15 32									16 02										16 32			
Martins Heron	d		15 35									16 05										16 35			
Guildford	d			15 00									15 30										16 00		
Wanborough	d			15 06									15 36										16 06		
Ash 5	d			15 10									15 40										16 10		
Aldershot	a			15 17									15 47										16 17		
	d			15 30									16 00										16 30		
Ash Vale	d			15 34									16 04										16 34		
Frimley	d			15 40									16 10										16 40		
Camberley	a			15 44									16 14										16 44		
	d			15 48									16 18										16 48		
Bagshot	d			15 53									16 23										16 53		
Ascot 5	d		15 40	16a00								16 10	16a30									16 40	17a00		
Sunningdale	d		15 43									16 13										16 43			
Longcross	d																								
Woking	d																								
West Byfleet	d																								
Byfleet & New Haw	d																								
Weybridge	d					15 33									16 03										16 33
Addlestone	d					15 37									16 07										16 37
Chertsey	d					15 40									16 10										16 40
Virginia Water	a		15 49			15 45						16 19			16 15							16 49			16 45
	d		15 49			15 54						16 19			16 24							16 49			16 54
Egham	d		15 53			15 57						16 23			16 27							16 53			16 57
Windsor & Eton Riverside	d						15 53										16 23								
Datchet	d						15 56										16 26								
Sunnymeads	d						15 59										16 29								
Wraysbury	d						16 02										16 32								
Staines	d		15 59			16 03	16 08					16 29			16 33		16 38					16 59			17 03
Ashford (Surrey)	d					16 06	16 11								16 36		16 41								17 06
Feltham	d		16 05			16 11	16 16					16 35			16 41		16 46					17 05			17 11
Whitton	d						16 20	16 23		16 20							16 50	16 53		16 50					
Kingston	d				15 59									16 29										16 59	
Hampton Wick	d				16 01									16 31										17 01	
Teddington	d				16 05									16 35										17 05	
Fulwell	d																								
Strawberry Hill	d				16 08									16 38										17 08	
Twickenham	a		16 10		16 12		16 23	16 26				16 40		16 42			16 53	16 56				17 10		17 12	
	d		16 11		16 13		16 23	16 28				16 41		16 43		16 50	16 53	16 58				17 11		17 13	
St Margarets	d				16 15			16 30						16 45				17 00						17 15	
Richmond ⊖	d		16 15		16 19		16 28	16 34				16 45		16 49			16 58	17 04				17 15		17 19	
North Sheen	d				16 21			16 36						16 51				17 06						17 21	
Mortlake	d				16 23			16 38						16 53				17 08						17 23	
Hounslow	d					16 16				16 31					16 46					17 01					17 16
Isleworth	d					16 19				16 34					16 49					17 04					17 19
Syon Lane	d					16 21				16 36					16 51					17 06					17 21
Brentford	d					16 24				16 39					16 54					17 09					17 24
Kew Bridge	d					16 26				16 41					16 56					17 11					17 26
Chiswick	d					16 29				16 44					16 59					17 14					17 29
Barnes Bridge	d					16 31				16 46					17 01					17 16					17 31
Barnes	d				16 26	16 34		16 41		16 49				16 56	17 04			17 11		17 19				17 26	17 34
Putney	d				16 29	16 37	16 34	16 44		16 52				16 59	17 07		17 05	17 14		17 22				17 29	17 37
Wandsworth Town	d				16 32	16 40		16 47		16 55				17 02	17 10			17 17		17 25				17 32	17 40
Clapham Junction 10	d		16 24		16 35	16 43	16 39	16 50		16 58		16 54		17 05	17 13	17 09	17 09	17 20		17 28		17 24		17 35	17 43
Queenstown Rd.(Battersea)	d				16 38	16 46		16 53		17 01				17 08	17 16			17 23		17 31				17 38	17 46
Vauxhall ⊖	d				16 42	16 50	16 45	16 57		17 05				17 12	17 20		17 15	17 27		17 35				17 42	17 50
London Waterloo 15 ⊖	a		16 34		16 49	16 56	16 49	17 02		17 11		17 04		17 19	17 26	17 24	17 19	17 32		17 41		17 35		17 49	17 56

A To Gatwick Airport (Table 148)

Table 149

Mondays to Fridays

24 May to 24 September

Reading, Guildford, Ascot, Weybridge, Windsor, Kingston, Richmond and Hounslow - London

		SW	SW	SW				SW	SW	SW	SW	SW	SW	SW			SW	SW	SW	SW	SW	SW	SW	SW	
								1	1								1	1	1						
Reading 7	d							16 42									17 12	17 22							
Earley	d							16 47									17 17	17 27							
Winnersh Triangle	d							16 49									17 19	17 29							
Winnersh	d							16 51									17 21	17 31							
Wokingham	d							16 56									17 26	17 36							
Bracknell	d							17 02									17 32	17 42							
Martins Heron	d							17 05									17 35	17 45							
Guildford	d								16 30										17 00						
Wanborough	d								16 36										17 06						
Ash 5	d								16 40										17 10						
Aldershot	a								16 47										17 17						
	d								17 00										17 30						
Ash Vale	d								17 04										17 34						
Frimley	d								17 10										17 40						
Camberley	a								17 14										17 44						
	d								17 18										17 48						
Bagshot	d								17 23										17 53						
Ascot 5	d							17 10	17a30								17 40	17b55	18a00						
Sunningdale	d							17 13									17 43	17 58							
Longcross	d							17 16																	
Woking	d																								
West Byfleet	d																								
Byfleet & New Haw	d																								
Weybridge	d										17 03										17 37				
Addlestone	d										17 07										17 41				
Chertsey	d										17 10										17 44				
Virginia Water	a							17 19			17 15						17 49	18 03			17 49				
	d							17 19			17 24						17 49	18 03			17 54				
Egham	d							17 23			17 27						17 53	18 06			17 57				
Windsor & Eton Riverside	d	16 53										17 23										17 53			
Datchet	d	16 56										17 26										17 56			
Sunnymeads	d	16 59										17 29										17 59			
Wraysbury	d	17 02										17 32										18 02			
Staines	d	17 08						17 29			17 33	17 38					17 59	18 14			18 03	18 08			
Ashford (Surrey)	d	17 11									17 36	17 41									18 06	18 11			
Feltham	d	17 16						17 35			17 41	17 46					18 05	18 20			18 11	18 16			
Whitton	d	17 20	17 23	17 20								17 50	17 53	17 50								18 20	18 23	18 20	
Kingston	d									17 29										17 59					
Hampton Wick	d									17 31										18 01					
Teddington	d									17 35										18 05					
Fulwell	d																								
Strawberry Hill	d									17 38										18 08					
Twickenham	a	17 23	17 26					17 40		17 42		17 53	17 56				18 10			18 12		18 23	18 26		
	d	17 23	17 28					17 41		17 43		17 53	17 58				18 11			18 13		18 23	18 28		
St Margarets	d		17 30							17 45			18 00							18 15			18 30		
Richmond ⊖	d	17 28	17 34					17 45		17 49		17 58	18 04				18 15			18 19		18 28	18 34		
North Sheen	d		17 36							17 51			18 06							18 21			18 36		
Mortlake	d		17 38							17 53			18 08							18 23			18 38		
Hounslow	d			17 31							17 46			18 01				18 26			18 16			18 31	
Isleworth	d			17 34							17 49			18 04							18 19			18 34	
Syon Lane	d			17 36							17 51			18 06							18 21			18 36	
Brentford	d			17 39							17 54			18 09				18 31			18 24			18 39	
Kew Bridge	d			17 41							17 56			18 11							18 26			18 41	
Chiswick	d			17 44							17 59			18 14							18 29			18 44	
Barnes Bridge	d			17 46							18 01			18 16							18 31			18 46	
Barnes	d		17 41	17 49						17 56	18 04		18 11	18 19						18 26	18 34		18 41	18 49	
Putney	d	17 34	17 44	17 52						17 59	18 07	18 04	18 14	18 22				18 39		18 29	18 37	18 34	18 44	18 52	
Wandsworth Town	d		17 47	17 55						18 02	18 10		18 17	18 25						18 32	18 40		18 47	18 55	
Clapham Junction 10	d	17 39	17 50	17 58				17 54		18 05	18 13	18 09	18 20	18 28			18 24	18 44		18 35	18 43	18 39	18 50	18 58	
Queenstown Rd.(Battersea)	d		17 53	18 01						18 08	18 16		18 23	18 31						18 38	18 46		18 53	19 01	
Vauxhall ⊖	d	17 45	17 57	18 05						18 12	18 20	18 15	18 27	18 35						18 42	18 50	18 45	18 57	19 05	
London Waterloo 15 ⊖	a	17 49	18 02	18 11				18 04		18 19	18 26	18 19	18 32	18 41			18 34	18 56		18 49	18 56	18 49	19 02	19 11	

b arr. 1749

Table 149

Mondays to Fridays

24 May to 24 September

Reading, Guildford, Ascot, Weybridge, Windsor, Kingston, Richmond and Hounslow - London

		SW 1	SW 1	SW 1	SW	SW	SW	SW	SW	SW 1	SW 1	SW	SW	SW	SW	SW	SW 1	SW 1	SW 1	SW
Reading 7	d	17 42	17 53							18 12							18 42	18 52		
Earley	d	17 47	17 58							18 17							18 47	18 57		
Winnersh Triangle	d	17 49	18 00							18 19							18 49	18 59		
Winnersh	d	17 51	18 02							18 21							18 51	19 01		
Wokingham	d	17 56	18 07							18 26							18 56	19 06		
Bracknell	d	18 02	18 13							18 32							19 02	19 12		
Martins Heron	d	18 05	18 16							18 35							19 05	19 15		
Guildford	d			17 30							18 00								18 30	
Wanborough	d			17 36							18 06								18 36	
Ash 5	d			17 40							18 10								18 40	
Aldershot	a			17 47							18 17								18 47	
	d			18 00							18 30								19 00	
Ash Vale	d			18 04							18 34								19 04	
Frimley	d			18 10							18 40								19 10	
Camberley	a			18 14							18 44								19 14	
	d			18 18							18 48								19 18	
Bagshot	d			18 23							18 53								19 23	
Ascot 3	d	18 10	18 25	18a30						18 40	19a00						19 10	19a19	19a30	
Sunningdale	d	18 13	18 28							18 43							19 13			
Longcross	d	18 16								18 46							19 16			
Woking	d																			
West Byfleet	d																			
Byfleet & New Haw	d																			
Weybridge	d					18 07							18 37							
Addlestone	d					18 11							18 41							
Chertsey	d					18 14							18 44							
Virginia Water	a	18 19	18 33			18 19				18 49			18 49				19 19			
	d	18 19	18 33			18 24				18 49			18 54				19 19			
Egham	d	18 23	18 37			18 27				18 53			18 57				19 23			
Windsor & Eton Riverside	d						18 23							18 53						
Datchet	d						18 26							18 56						
Sunnymeads	d						18 29							18 59						
Wraysbury	d						18 32							19 02						
Staines	d	18 29	18 44			18 33	18 38			18 59			19 03	19 08			19 29			
Ashford (Surrey)	d					18 36	18 41						19 06	19 11						
Feltham	d	18 35	18 50			18 41	18 46			19 05			19 11	19 16			19 35			
Whitton	d						18 50	18 53	18 50					19 20	19 23	19 20				
Kingston	d				18 29							18 59								19 29
Hampton Wick	d				18 31							19 01								19 31
Teddington	d				18 35							19 05								19 35
Fulwell	d																			
Strawberry Hill	d				18 38							19 08								19 38
Twickenham	a	18 40			18 42		18 53	18 56		19 10		19 12		19 23	19 26		19 40			19 42
	d	18 41			18 43		18 53	18 58		19 11		19 13		19 23	19 28		19 41			19 43
St Margarets	d				18 45			19 00				19 15			19 30					19 45
Richmond ⊖	d	18 45			18 49		18 58	19 04		19 15		19 19		19 28	19 34		19 45			19 49
North Sheen	d				18 51			19 06				19 21			19 36					19 51
Mortlake	d				18 53			19 08				19 23			19 38					19 53
Hounslow	d		18 56			18 46			19 01				19 16			19 31				
Isleworth	d					18 49			19 04				19 19			19 34				
Syon Lane	d					18 51			19 06				19 21			19 36				
Brentford	d		19 01			18 54			19 09				19 24			19 39				
Kew Bridge	d					18 56			19 11				19 26			19 41				
Chiswick	d					18 59			19 14				19 29			19 44				
Barnes Bridge	d					19 01			19 16				19 31			19 46				
Barnes	d				18 56	19 04		19 11	19 19			19 26	19 34		19 41	19 49				19 56
Putney	d		19 09		18 59	19 07	19 04	19 14	19 22			19 29	19 37	19 34	19 44	19 52				19 59
Wandsworth Town	d				19 02	19 10		19 17	19 25			19 32	19 40		19 47	19 55				20 02
Clapham Junction 10	d	18 54	19 14		19 05	19 13	19 09	19 20	19 28	19 24		19 35	19 43	19 39	19 50	19 58	19 54			20 05
Queenstown Rd.(Battersea)	d				19 08	19 16		19 23	19 31			19 38	19 46		19 53	20 01				20 08
Vauxhall ⊖	d				19 12	19 20	19 15	19 27	19 35			19 42	19 50	19 45	19 57	20 05				20 12
London Waterloo 15 ⊖	a	19 04	19 28		19 16	19 26	19 19	19 32	19 41	19 34		19 46	19 56	19 49	20 02	20 09	20 04			20 16

Table 149

Mondays to Fridays

24 May to 24 September

Reading, Guildford, Ascot, Weybridge, Windsor, Kingston, Richmond and Hounslow - London

		SW	SW	SW	SW	SW 1	SW 1	SW	SW	SW	SW	SW	SW 1	SW 1	SW	SW	SW	SW	SW	SW 1
Reading 7	d					19 12							19 42							20 12
Earley	d					19 17							19 47							20 17
Winnersh Triangle	d					19 19							19 49							20 19
Winnersh	d					19 21							19 51							20 21
Wokingham	d					19 26							19 56							20 26
Bracknell	d					19 32							20 02							20 32
Martins Heron	d					19 35							20 05							20 35
Guildford	d						19 00							19 30						
Wanborough	d						19 06							19 36						
Ash 5	d						19 10							19 40						
Aldershot	a						19 17							19 47						
	d						19 30							20 00						
Ash Vale	d						19 34							20 04						
Frimley	d						19 40							20 10						
Camberley	a						19 44							20 14						
	d						19 48							20 18						
Bagshot	d						19 53							20 23						
Ascot 3	d					19 40	20a00						20 10	20a30						20 40
Sunningdale	d					19 43							20 13							20 43
Longcross	d					19 46							20 16							20 46
Woking	d																			
West Byfleet	d																			
Byfleet & New Haw	d																			
Weybridge	d	19 07							19 37							20 03				
Addlestone	d	19 11							19 41							20 07				
Chertsey	d	19 14							19 44							20 10				
Virginia Water	a	19 19				19 49			19 49				20 19			20 15				20 49
	d	19 24				19 49			19 54				20 19			20 24				20 49
Egham	d	19 27				19 53			19 57				20 23			20 27				20 53
Windsor & Eton Riverside	d		19 23							19 53							20 23			
Datchet	d		19 26							19 56							20 26			
Sunnymeads	d		19 29							19 59							20 29			
Wraysbury	d		19 32							20 02							20 32			
Staines	d	19 33	19 38			19 59			20 03	20 08			20 29			20 33	20 38			20 59
Ashford (Surrey)	d	19 36	19 41						20 06	20 11						20 36	20 41			
Feltham	d	19 41	19 46			20 05			20 11	20 16			20 35			20 41	20 46			21 05
Whitton	d		19 50	19 53	19 50					20 20	20 23	20 20					20 50	20 53	20 50	
Kingston	d							19 59							20 29					
Hampton Wick	d							20 01							20 31					
Teddington	d							20 05							20 35					
Fulwell	d																			
Strawberry Hill	d							20 08							20 38					
Twickenham	a		19 53	19 56		20 10		20 12		20 23	20 26		20 40		20 42		20 53	20 56		21 10
	d		19 53	19 58		20 11		20 13		20 23	20 28		20 41		20 43		20 53	20 58		21 11
St Margarets	d			20 00				20 15			20 30				20 45			21 00		
Richmond ⊖	d		19 58	20 04		20 15		20 19		20 28	20 34		20 45		20 49		20 58	21 04		21 15
North Sheen	d			20 06				20 21			20 36				20 51			21 06		
Mortlake	d			20 08				20 23			20 38				20 53			21 08		
Hounslow	d	19 46			20 01				20 16			20 31				20 46			21 01	
Isleworth	d	19 49			20 04				20 19			20 34				20 49			21 04	
Syon Lane	d	19 51			20 06				20 21			20 36				20 51			21 06	
Brentford	d	19 54			20 09				20 24			20 39				20 54			21 09	
Kew Bridge	d	19 56			20 11				20 26			20 41				20 56			21 11	
Chiswick	d	19 59			20 14				20 29			20 44				20 59			21 14	
Barnes Bridge	d	20 01			20 16				20 31			20 46				21 01			21 16	
Barnes	d	20 04		20 11	20 19			20 26	20 34		20 41	20 49			20 56	21 04		21 11	21 19	
Putney	d	20 07	20 04	20 14	20 22			20 29	20 37	20 34	20 44	20 52			20 59	21 07	21 04	21 14	21 22	
Wandsworth Town	d	20 10		20 17	20 25			20 32	20 40		20 47	20 55			21 02	21 10		21 17	21 25	
Clapham Junction 10	d	20 13	20 09	20 20	20 28	20 24		20 35	20 43	20 39	20 50	20 58	20 54		21 05	21 13	21 09	21 20	21 28	21 24
Queenstown Rd.(Battersea)	d	20 16		20 23	20 31			20 38	20 46		20 53	21 01			21 08	21 16		21 23	21 31	
Vauxhall ⊖	d	20 20	20 15	20 27	20 35			20 42	20 50	20 45	20 57	21 05			21 12	21 20	21 15	21 27	21 35	
London Waterloo 15 ⊖	a	20 26	20 19	20 32	20 41	20 34		20 46	20 56	20 49	21 02	21 11	21 04		21 16	21 26	21 19	21 32	21 41	21 34

Table 149

Mondays to Fridays
24 May to 24 September

Reading, Guildford, Ascot, Weybridge, Windsor, Kingston, Richmond and Hounslow - London

		SW [1]	SW	SW	SW	SW	SW	SW [1]	SW	SW	SW	SW	SW	SW [1]	SW [1]	SW	SW	SW	SW
Reading [7]	d							20 42						21 12					
Earley	d							20 47						21 17					
Winnersh Triangle	d							20 49						21 19					
Winnersh	d							20 51						21 21					
Wokingham	d							20 56						21 26					
Bracknell	d							21 02						21 32					
Martins Heron	d							21 05						21 35					
Guildford	d	20 00													21 00				
Wanborough	d	20 06													21 06				
Ash [5]	d	20 10													21 10				
Aldershot	a	20 17													21 17				
	d	20 30													21 30				
Ash Vale	d	20 34													21 34				
Frimley	d	20 40													21 40				
Camberley	a	20 44													21 44				
	d	20 48													21 48				
Bagshot	d	20 53													21 53				
Ascot [3]	d	21a00						21 10						21 40	22a00				
Sunningdale	d							21 13						21 43					
Longcross	d																		
Woking	d																		
West Byfleet	d																		
Byfleet & New Haw	d																		
Weybridge	d			20 33						21 03							21 33		
Addlestone	d			20 37						21 07							21 37		
Chertsey	d			20 40						21 10							21 40		
Virginia Water	a			20 45				21 19		21 15				21 49			21 45		
	d			20 54				21 19		21 24				21 49			21 54		
Egham	d			20 57				21 23		21 27				21 53			21 57		
Windsor & Eton Riverside	d				20 53						21 23							21 53	
Datchet	d				20 56						21 26							21 56	
Sunnymeads	d				20 59						21 29							21 59	
Wraysbury	d				21 02						21 32							22 02	
Staines	d			21 03	21 08			21 29		21 33	21 38			21 59			22 03	22 08	
Ashford (Surrey)	d			21 06	21 11					21 36	21 41						22 06	22 11	
Feltham	d			21 11	21 16			21 35		21 41	21 46			22 05			22 11	22 16	
Whitton	d				21 20	21 23	21 20				21 50	21 53	21 50					22 20	22 23
Kingston	d		20 59						21 29							21 59			
Hampton Wick	d		21 01						21 31							22 01			
Teddington	d		21 05						21 35							22 05			
Fulwell	d																		
Strawberry Hill	d		21 08						21 38							22 08			
Twickenham	a		21 12		21 23	21 26		21 40	21 42		21 53	21 56		22 10		22 12		22 23	22 26
	d		21 13		21 23	21 28		21 41	21 43		21 53	21 58		22 11		22 13		22 23	22 28
St Margarets	d		21 15			21 30			21 45			22 00				22 15			22 30
Richmond ⊖	d		21 19		21 28	21 34		21 45	21 49		21 58	22 04		22 15		22 19		22 28	22 34
North Sheen	d		21 21			21 36			21 51			22 06				22 21			22 36
Mortlake	d		21 23			21 38			21 53			22 08				22 23			22 38
Hounslow	d			21 16			21 31			21 46			22 01				22 16		
Isleworth	d			21 19			21 34			21 49			22 04				22 19		
Syon Lane	d			21 21			21 36			21 51			22 06				22 21		
Brentford	d			21 24			21 39			21 54			22 09				22 24		
Kew Bridge	d			21 26			21 41			21 56			22 11				22 26		
Chiswick	d			21 29			21 44			21 59			22 14				22 29		
Barnes Bridge	d			21 31			21 46			22 01			22 16				22 31		
Barnes	d		21 26	21 34		21 41	21 49		21 56	22 04		22 11	22 19			22 26	22 34		22 41
Putney	d		21 29	21 37	21 34	21 44	21 52		21 59	22 07	22 04	22 14	22 22			22 29	22 37	22 34	22 44
Wandsworth Town	d		21 32	21 40		21 47	21 55		22 02	22 10		22 17	22 25			22 32	22 40		22 47
Clapham Junction [10]	d		21 35	21 43	21 39	21 50	21 58	21 54	22 05	22 13	22 09	22 20	22 28	22 24		22 35	22 43	22 39	22 50
Queenstown Rd.(Battersea)	d		21 38	21 46		21 53	22 01		22 08	22 16		22 23	22 31			22 38	22 46		22 53
Vauxhall ⊖	d		21 42	21 50	21 45	21 57	22 05		22 12	22 20	22 15	22 27	22 35			22 42	22 50	22 45	22 57
London Waterloo [15] ⊖	a		21 46	21 56	21 49	22 02	22 11	22 04	22 16	22 26	22 19	22 32	22 41	22 34		22 46	22 56	22 49	23 02

Table 149

Mondays to Fridays
24 May to 24 September

Reading, Guildford, Ascot, Weybridge, Windsor, Kingston, Richmond and Hounslow - London

		SW [1]	SW	SW	SW	SW [1]	SW [1]	SW	SW	SW	SW	SW	SW [1]	SW	SW [1]	SW [1]	SW
Reading [7]	d	21 42				22 12							22 42		23 12		
Earley	d	21 47				22 17							22 47		23 17		
Winnersh Triangle	d	21 49				22 19							22 49		23 19		
Winnersh	d	21 51				22 21							22 51		23 21		
Wokingham	d	21 56				22 26							22 56		23 26		
Bracknell	d	22 02				22 32							23 02		23 32		
Martins Heron	d	22 05				22 35							23 05		23 35		
Guildford	d						22 00									23 00	
Wanborough	d						22 06									23 06	
Ash [5]	d						22 10									23 10	
Aldershot	a						22 17									23 17	
	d						22 30									23 30	
Ash Vale	d						22 34									23 34	
Frimley	d						22 40									23 40	
Camberley	a						22 44									23 44	
	d						22 48									23 48	
Bagshot	d						22 53									23 53	
Ascot [3]	d	22 10				22 40	23a00						23 10		23 40	00a01	
Sunningdale	d	22 13				22 43							23 13		23 43		
Longcross	d																
Woking	d																
West Byfleet	d																
Byfleet & New Haw	d																
Weybridge	d			22 03					22 33		23 03						23 33
Addlestone	d			22 07					22 37		23 07						23 37
Chertsey	d			22 10					22 40		23 10						23 40
Virginia Water	a	22 19		22 15		22 49			22 45		23 15		23 19		23 49		23 45
	d	22 19		22 24		22 49			22 54		23 24		23 19		23 49		23 54
Egham	d	22 23		22 27		22 53			22 57		23 27		23 23		23 53		23 57
Windsor & Eton Riverside	d				22 23					22 53		23 23					
Datchet	d				22 26					22 56		23 26					
Sunnymeads	d				22 29					22 59		23 29					
Wraysbury	d				22 32					23 02		23 32					
Staines	d	22 29		22 33	22 38	22 59			23 03	23 08	23a32	23a37	23 29		23 59		00a02
Ashford (Surrey)	d			22 36	22 41				23 06	23 11							
Feltham	d	22 35		22 41	22 46	23 05			23 11	23 16			23 35		00 05		
Whitton	d				22 50					23 20							
Kingston	d		22 29					22 59						23 29			
Hampton Wick	d		22 31					23 01						23 31			
Teddington	d		22 35					23 05						23 35			
Fulwell	d																
Strawberry Hill	d		22 38					23 08						23 38			
Twickenham	a	22 40	22 42		22 53	23 10		23 12		23 23			23 40	23 42	00 10		
	d	22 41	22 43		22 53	23 11		23 13		23 23			23 41	23 43	00 11		
St Margarets	d		22 45					23 15						23 45			
Richmond ⊖	d	22 45	22 49		22 58	23 15		23 19		23 28			23 45	23 49	00 15		
North Sheen	d		22 51					23 21						23 51			
Mortlake	d		22 53					23 23						23 53			
Hounslow	d			22 46					23 16								
Isleworth	d			22 49					23 19								
Syon Lane	d			22 51					23 21								
Brentford	d			22 54					23 24								
Kew Bridge	d			22 56					23 26								
Chiswick	d			22 59					23 29								
Barnes Bridge	d			23 01					23 31								
Barnes	d		22 56	23 04				23 26	23 34					23 56			
Putney	d		22 59	23 07	23 04			23 29	23 37	23 34				23 59			
Wandsworth Town	d		23 02	23 10				23 32	23 40					00 02			
Clapham Junction [10]	d	22 54	23 05	23 13	23 09	23 24		23 35	23 43	23 39			23 54	00 05	00 24		
Queenstown Rd.(Battersea)	d		23 08	23 16				23 38	23 46					00 08			
Vauxhall ⊖	d		23 12	23 20	23 15			23 42	23 50	23 45				00 12			
London Waterloo [15] ⊖	a	23 04	23 16	23 26	23 19	23 34		23 46	23 56	23 49			00 04	00 16	00 32		

Reading, Guildford, Ascot, Weybridge, Windsor, Kingston, Richmond and Hounslow - London

		SW MO	SW MO	SW MX	SW MX ■	SW MX	SW MO ■	SW MX ■	SW	SW	SW	SW	SW	SW	SW	SW	SW	SW ■	SW ■	SW
Reading ■	d				22p39		22p54	23p12										05 39		
Earley	d				22p44		22p59	23p17										05 44		
Winnersh Triangle	d				22p46		23p01	23p19										05 46		
Winnersh	d				22p48		23p03	23p21										05 48		
Wokingham	d				22p53		23p08	23p26										05 53		
Bracknell	d				22p59		23p14	23p32										05 59		
Martins Heron	d				23p02		23p17	23p35										06 02		
Guildford	d																			
Wanborough	d																			
Ash ■	d																			
Aldershot	a																			
	d																		05 58	
Ash Vale	d																		06 02	
Frimley	d																		06 10	
Camberley	a																		06 14	
	d																		06 18	
Bagshot	d																		06 23	
Ascot ■	d				23p07		23p22	23p40										06 07	06a30	
Sunningdale	d				23p10		23p25	23p43										06 10		
Longcross	d																			
Woking	d		22p52												05 25					
West Byfleet	d		22p56												05 30					
Byfleet & New Haw	d		23p00												05 33					
Weybridge	d																			
Addlestone	d		23p04												05 37					
Chertsey	d		23p07												05 40					
Virginia Water	a		23p12		23p19		23p30	23p49							05 45			06 19		
	d		23p12		23p19		23p30	23p49							05 54			06 19		
Egham	d		23p16		23p23		23p34	23p53							05 57			06 23		
Windsor & Eton Riverside	d	23p01														05 51				
Datchet	d	23p04														05 55				
Sunnymeads	d	23p07														05 58				
Wraysbury	d	23p10														06 02				
Staines	d	23p16	23p21		23p29		23p39	23p59	04 58			05 37			06 03	06 08		06 29		
Ashford (Surrey)	d	23p19	23p24						05 01			05 40			06 06	06 11				
Feltham	d	23p24	23p29		23p35		23p46	00 05	05 06			05 45			06 11	06 16		06 35		
Whitton	d	23p28							05 10			05 49				06 20	06 20			
Kingston	d					23p29								05 59						06 29
Hampton Wick	d					23p31								06 01						06 31
Teddington	d					23p35								06 05						06 35
Fulwell	d										05 36									
Strawberry Hill	d					23p38					05 38			06 08						06 38
Twickenham	a	23p31			23p40	23p42	23p51	00 10	05 13		05 42	05 52		06 12		06 23		06 40		06 42
	d	23p32			23p41	23p43	23p51	00 11	05 13		05 43	05 53		06 13		06 23		06 41		06 43
St Margarets	d	23p34				23p45			05 15		05 45			06 15						06 45
Richmond ⊖	d	23p37			23p45	23p49	23p56	00 15	05 19		05 49	05 58		06 19		06 28		06 45		06 49
North Sheen	d	23p39				23p51			05 21		05 51			06 21						06 51
Mortlake	d	23p42				23p53			05 23		05 53			06 23						06 53
Hounslow	d		23p35							05 31			06 01		06 16		06 31			
Isleworth	d		23p38							05 34			06 04		06 19		06 34			
Syon Lane	d		23p40							05 36			06 06		06 21		06 36			
Brentford	d		23p42							05 39			06 09		06 24		06 39			
Kew Bridge	d		23p45							05 41			06 11		06 26		06 41			
Chiswick	d		23p47							05 44			06 14		06 29		06 44			
Barnes Bridge	d		23p50							05 46			06 16		06 31		06 46			
Barnes	d	23p45	23p53			23p56			05 26	05 49	05 56		06 19	06 26	06 34		06 49			06 56
Putney	d	23p48	23p56			23p59	00 02		05 29	05 52	05 59	06 04	06 22	06 29	06 37	06 34	06 52	06 52		06 59
Wandsworth Town	d	23p51	23p59			00 02			05 32	05 55	06 02		06 25	06 32	06 40		06 55			07 02
Clapham Junction ■	d	23p54	00 02		23p54	00 05	00 07	00 24	05 35	05 58	06 05	06 09	06 28	06 35	06 43	06 39	06 58	06 56		07 05
Queenstown Rd.(Battersea)	d	23p57	00 05			00 08			05 38	06 01	06 08		06 31	06 38	06 46		07 01			07 08
Vauxhall ⊖	d	23p59	00 08			00 12	00 12		05 42	06 05	06 12	06 15	06 35	06 42	06 50	06 45	07 05			07 12
London Waterloo ■ ⊖	a	00 05	00 13		00 04	00 16	00 17	00 32	05 46	06 09	06 16	06 19	06 39	06 46	06 56	06 49	07 11	07 07		07 18

Table 149

Mondays to Fridays
from 27 September

Reading, Guildford, Ascot, Weybridge, Windsor, Kingston, Richmond and Hounslow - London

		SW	SW	SW	SW	SW ■	SW	SW	SW	SW	SW ■	SW	SW	SW ■	SW	SW	SW	SW	SW ■	SW
Reading ■	d					06 12								06 39						
Earley	d					06 17								06 44						
Winnersh Triangle	d					06 19								06 46						
Winnersh	d					06 21								06 48						
Wokingham	d					06 26								06 53						
Bracknell	d					06 32								06 59						
Martins Heron	d					06 35								07 02						
Guildford	d																			
Wanborough	d																			
Ash ■	d																			
Aldershot	a																			
	d										06 28								06 59	
Ash Vale	d										06 32								07 03	
Frimley	d										06 39								07 09	
Camberley	a										06 43								07 13	
	d										06 44								07 14	
Bagshot	d										06 49								07 19	
Ascot ■	d					06 40					06 56			07 07					07 26	
Sunningdale	d					06 43					06 59			07 10					07 29	
Longcross	d																			
Woking	d																			
West Byfleet	d																			
Byfleet & New Haw	d																			
Weybridge	d							06 33								07 03				
Addlestone	d							06 37								07 07				
Chertsey	d							06 40								07 10				
Virginia Water	a					06 49		06 45			07 08			07 19		07 15			07 38	
	d					06 49		06 54			07 08			07 19		07 24			07 38	
Egham	d					06 53		06 57			07 12			07 23		07 27			07 42	
Windsor & Eton Riverside	d	06 21							06 51								07 21			
Datchet	d	06 25							06 55								07 25			
Sunnymeads	d	06 28							06 58								07 28			
Wraysbury	d	06 32							07 02								07 32			
Staines	d	06 38	06 33			06 59		07 03	07 08		07 18			07 29		07 33	07 38		07 48	
Ashford (Surrey)	d	06 41	06 36					07 06	07 11		07 21					07 36	07 41		07 51	
Feltham	d	06 46	06 41			07 05		07 11	07 16		07 26			07 35		07 41	07 46		07 56	
Whitton	d	06 50		06 53	06 50				07 20		07 30	07 20					07 50		08 00	07 50
Kingston	d						06 59								07 29					
Hampton Wick	d						07 01								07 31					
Teddington	d						07 05								07 35					
Fulwell	d									07 12								07 42		
Strawberry Hill	d						07 08			07 14					07 38			07 44		
Twickenham	a	06 53		06 56		07 10	07 12		07 23	07 18	07 33		07 33	07 40	07 42		07 53	07 48	08 03	
	d	06 53		06 58		07 11	07 13		07 23	07 27	07 33		07 34	07 41	07 43		07 53	07 57	08 03	
St Margarets	d			07 00			07 15			07 29					07 45			07 59		
Richmond ⊖	d	06 58		07 04		07 15	07 19		07 28	07 32	07 38			07 45	07 49		07 58	08 02	08 08	
North Sheen	d			07 06			07 21			07 34					07 51			08 04		
Mortlake	d			07 08			07 23			07 37					07 53			08 07		
Hounslow	d		06 46		07 01			07 16				07 31				07 46				08 01
Isleworth	d		06 49		07 04			07 19				07 34				07 49				08 04
Syon Lane	d		06 51		07 06			07 21				07 36				07 51				08 06
Brentford	d		06 54		07 09			07 24				07 39				07 54				08 09
Kew Bridge	d		06 56		07 11			07 26				07 41				07 56				08 11
Chiswick	d		06 59		07 14			07 29				07 44				07 59				08 14
Barnes Bridge	d		07 01		07 16			07 31				07 46				08 01				08 16
Barnes	d		07 04	07 11	07 19		07 26	07 34		07 40		07 49			07 56	08 04		08 10		08 19
Putney	d	07 04	07 07	07 14	07 22	07 22	07 29	07 37	07 34	07 43		07 52			07 59	08 07	08 04	08 13		08 22
Wandsworth Town	d		07 10	07 17	07 25		07 32	07 40		07 46		07 55			08 02	08 10		08 16		08 25
Clapham Junction ■	d	07 09	07 13	07 20	07 28	07 26	07 35	07 43	07 39	07 49	07 47	07 58		07 54	08 05	08 13	08 09	08 19	08 17	08 28
Queenstown Rd.(Battersea)	d		07 16	07 23	07 31		07 38	07 46		07 52		08 01			08 08	08 16		08 22		08 31
Vauxhall ⊖	d	07 15	07 20	07 27	07 35		07 42	07 50	07 45	07 56	07 53	08 05	08 14		08 12	08 20	08 15	08 26	08 23	08 35
London Waterloo ■ ⊖	a	07 21	07 28	07 34	07 43	07 37	07 48	07 58	07 51	08 04	07 59	08 11	08 21	08 06	08 18	08 28	08 21	08 34	08 29	08 43

Table 149

Mondays to Fridays
from 27 September

Reading, Guildford, Ascot, Weybridge, Windsor, Kingston, Richmond and Hounslow - London

		SW		SW ■	SW	SW ■	SW	SW	SW	SW ■	SW			SW ■	SW ■	SW	SW	SW	SW	SW		SW ■		SW ■	SW
Reading 7	d			07 09		07 24								07 39								08 09			
Earley	d			07 14										07 44								08 14			
Winnersh Triangle	d			07 16										07 46								08 16			
Winnersh	d			07 18										07 48								08 18			
Wokingham	d			07 23		07 33								07 53								08 23			
Bracknell	d			07 29		07 39								07 59								08 29			
Martins Heron	d			07 32		07 42								08 02								08 32			
Guildford	d														07 30									08 00	
Wanborough	d														07 36									08 06	
Ash 5	d														07 40									08 10	
Aldershot	a														07 47									08 17	
	d									07 29					08 00									08 30	
Ash Vale	d									07 33					08 04									08 34	
Frimley	d									07 39					08 10									08 40	
Camberley	a									07 43					08 14									08 44	
	d									07 44					08 18									08 48	
Bagshot	d									07 49					08 23									08 53	
Ascot 3	d			07 37		07 47				07 56				08 07	08a30							08 37		09a00	
Sunningdale	d			07 40		07 50				07 59				08 10								08 40			
Longcross	d													08 13								08 43			
Woking	d																								
West Byfleet	d																								
Byfleet & New Haw	d																								
Weybridge	d						07 33										08 03								
Addlestone	d						07 37										08 07								
Chertsey	d						07 40										08 10								
Virginia Water	a					07 55	07 45			08 08				08 19			08 15					08 49			
	d					07 55	07 51			08 08				08 19			08 24					08 49			
Egham	d			07 50		07 58	07 54			08 12				08 23			08 27					08 53			
Windsor & Eton Riverside	d							07 51										08 21							
Datchet	d							07 55										08 25							
Sunnymeads	d							07 58										08 28							
Wraysbury	d							08 02										08 32							
Staines	d			07 56		08 04	08 00	08 08		08 18				08 29			08 33	08 38				08 59			
Ashford (Surrey)	d						08 03	08 11		08 21							08 36	08 41							
Feltham	d			08 02		08 12	08 08	08 16		08 26				08 35			08 41	08 46				09 05			
Whitton	d							08 20		08 30	08 20							08 50	08 53	08 50					
Kingston	d				07 59											08 29									08 59
Hampton Wick	d				08 01											08 31									09 01
Teddington	d				08 05											08 35									09 05
Fulwell	d								08 12																
Strawberry Hill	d				08 08				08 14							08 38									09 08
Twickenham	a			08 09	08 12	08 17		08 23	08 18	08 33				08 40		08 42		08 53	08 56			09 10			09 12
	d			08 09	08 13	08 18		08 23	08 27	08 33				08 41		08 43		08 53	08 58			09 11			09 13
St Margarets	d				08 15				08 29							08 45			09 00						09 15
Richmond ⊖	d			08 14	08 19	08 24		08 28	08 32	08 38				08 45		08 49		08 58	09 04			09 15			09 19
North Sheen	d				08 21				08 34							08 51			09 06						09 21
Mortlake	d				08 23				08 37							08 53			09 08						09 23
Hounslow	d						08 16				08 31						08 46			09 01					
Isleworth	d						08 19				08 34						08 49			09 04					
Syon Lane	d						08 21				08 36						08 51			09 06					
Brentford	d						08 24				08 39						08 54			09 09					
Kew Bridge	d						08 26				08 41						08 56			09 11					
Chiswick	d						08 29				08 44						08 59			09 14					
Barnes Bridge	d						08 31				08 46						09 01			09 16					
Barnes	d				08 26		08 34		08 40		08 49					08 56	09 04		09 11	09 19					09 26
Putney	d				08 29		08 37	08 34	08 43		08 52					08 59	09 07	09 04	09 14	09 22					09 29
Wandsworth Town	d				08 32		08 40		08 46		08 55					09 02	09 10		09 17	09 25					09 32
Clapham Junction 10	d			08 22	08 35	08 33	08 43	08 39	08 49	08 47	08 58			08 54		09 05	09 13	09 09	09 20	09 28		09 24			09 35
Queenstown Rd.(Battersea)	d				08 38		08 46		08 52		09 01					09 08	09 16		09 23	09 31					09 38
Vauxhall ⊖	d				08 42	08 38	08 50	08 45	08 56	08 53	09 05					09 12	09 20	09 15	09 27	09 35					09 42
London Waterloo 15 ⊖	a			08 38	08 49	08 46	08 58	08 51	09 04	09 00	09 13			09 06		09 18	09 28	09 21	09 34	09 43		09 34			09 48

Table 149

Mondays to Fridays
from 27 September

Reading, Guildford, Ascot, Weybridge, Windsor, Kingston, Richmond and Hounslow - London

		SW	SW	SW	SW		SW ■	SW ■		SW	SW	SW	SW	SW		SW ■	SW	SW		SW	SW ■	SW ■	SW	SW	
Reading 7	d						08 39									09 09					09 22				
Earley	d						08 44									09 14					09 27				
Winnersh Triangle	d						08 46									09 16					09 29				
Winnersh	d						08 48									09 18					09 31				
Wokingham	d						08 53									09 23					09 36				
Bracknell	d						08 59									09 29					09 43				
Martins Heron	d						09 02									09 32					09 46				
Guildford	d							08 30														09 00			
Wanborough	d							08 36														09 06			
Ash 5	d							08 40														09 10			
Aldershot	a							08 47														09 17			
	d							09 00														09 30			
Ash Vale	d							09 04														09 34			
Frimley	d							09 10														09 40			
Camberley	a							09 14														09 44			
	d							09 18														09 48			
Bagshot	d							09 23														09 53			
Ascot 3	d						09 07	09a30								09 37					09 52	10a00			
Sunningdale	d						09 10									09 40					09 55				
Longcross	d						09 13																		
Woking	d																								
West Byfleet	d																								
Byfleet & New Haw	d																								
Weybridge	d	08 33									09 03							09 33							
Addlestone	d	08 37									09 07							09 37							
Chertsey	d	08 40									09 10							09 40							
Virginia Water	a	08 45					09 19				09 15					09 49		09 45			10 03				
	d	08 54					09 19				09 24					09 49		09 54			10 03				
Egham	d	08 57					09 23				09 27					09 53		09 57			10 06				
Windsor & Eton Riverside	d		08 51									09 21								09 51					
Datchet	d		08 55									09 25								09 55					
Sunnymeads	d		08 58									09 28								09 58					
Wraysbury	d		09 02									09 32								10 02					
Staines	d	09 03	09 08				09 29				09 33	09 38				09 59		10 03		10 08	10 14				
Ashford (Surrey)	d	09 06	09 11								09 36	09 41						10 06		10 11					
Feltham	d	09 11	09 16				09 35				09 41	09 46				10 05		10 11		10 16	10 20				
Whitton	d		09 20	09 23	09 20							09 50	09 53	09 50						10 20			10 26	10 20	
Kingston	d									09 29							09 59								
Hampton Wick	d									09 31							10 01								
Teddington	d									09 35							10 05								
Fulwell	d																								
Strawberry Hill	d									09 38							10 08								
Twickenham	a		09 23	09 26			09 40			09 42		09 53	09 56			10 10	10 12			10 23	10 27		10 28		
	d		09 23	09 28			09 41			09 43		09 53	09 58			10 11	10 13			10 23	10 27		10 28		
St Margarets	d			09 30						09 45			10 00				10 15						10 30		
Richmond ⊖	d		09 28	09 34			09 45			09 49		09 58	10 04			10 15	10 19			10 28	10 32		10 34		
North Sheen	d			09 36						09 51			10 06				10 21						10 36		
Mortlake	d			09 38						09 53			10 08				10 23						10 38		
Hounslow	d	09 16			09 31						09 46			10 01				10 16						10 31	
Isleworth	d	09 19			09 34						09 49			10 04				10 19						10 34	
Syon Lane	d	09 21			09 36						09 51			10 06				10 21						10 36	
Brentford	d	09 24			09 39						09 54			10 09				10 24						10 39	
Kew Bridge	d	09 26			09 41						09 56			10 11				10 26						10 41	
Chiswick	d	09 29			09 44						09 59			10 14				10 29						10 44	
Barnes Bridge	d	09 31			09 46						10 01			10 16				10 31						10 46	
Barnes	d	09 34		09 41	09 49					09 56	10 04		10 11	10 19			10 26	10 34					10 41	10 49	
Putney	d	09 37	09 34	09 44	09 52					09 59	10 07	10 04	10 14	10 22			10 29	10 37		10 34			10 44	10 52	
Wandsworth Town	d	09 40		09 47	09 55					10 02	10 10		10 17	10 25			10 32	10 40					10 47	10 55	
Clapham Junction 10	d	09 43	09 39	09 50	09 58		09 54			10 05	10 13	10 09	10 20	10 28		10 24	10 35	10 43		10 39	10 42		10 50	10 58	
Queenstown Rd.(Battersea)	d	09 46		09 53	10 01					10 08	10 16		10 23	10 31			10 38	10 47					10 53	11 01	
Vauxhall ⊖	d	09 50	09 45	09 57	10 05					10 12	10 20	10 15	10 27	10 35			10 42	10 50		10 45			10 57	11 05	
London Waterloo 15 ⊖	a	09 58	09 51	10 02	10 11		10 04			10 16	10 26	10 19	10 32	10 41		10 34	10 46	10 56		10 49	10 53		11 02	11 11	

Reading, Guildford, Ascot, Weybridge, Windsor, Kingston, Richmond and Hounslow - London

		SW ■1	SW	SW	SW	SW ■1	SW ■1	SW	SW	SW ■1	SW ■1	SW	SW	SW	SW	SW	SW ■1	SW ■1	SW	SW
Reading 7	d	09 39				09 53				10 09							10 39			
Earley	d	09 44				09 58				10 14							10 44			
Winnersh Triangle	d	09 46				10 00				10 16							10 46			
Winnersh	d	09 48				10 02				10 18							10 48			
Wokingham	d	09 53				10 07				10 23							10 53			
Bracknell	d	09 59				10 13				10 29							10 59			
Martins Heron	d	10 02				10 16				10 32							11 02			
Guildford	d						09 30				10 00							10 30		
Wanborough	d						09 36				10 06							10 36		
Ash 5	d						09 40				10 10							10 40		
Aldershot	a						09 47				10 17							10 47		
	d						10 00				10 30							11 00		
Ash Vale	d						10 04				10 34							11 04		
Frimley	d						10 10				10 40							11 10		
Camberley	a						10 14				10 44							11 14		
	d						10 18				10 48							11 18		
Bagshot	d						10 23				10 53							11 23		
Ascot 3	d	10 07				10 22	10a30			10 37	11a00						11 07	11a30		
Sunningdale	d	10 10				10 25				10 40							11 10			
Longcross	d																			
Woking	d																			
West Byfleet	d																			
Byfleet & New Haw	d																			
Weybridge	d			10 03									10 33							11 03
Addlestone	d			10 07									10 37							11 07
Chertsey	d			10 10									10 40							11 10
Virginia Water	a	10 19		10 15		10 33				10 49			10 45				11 19			11 15
	d	10 19		10 24		10 33				10 49			10 54				11 19			11 24
Egham	d	10 23		10 27		10 36				10 53			10 57				11 23			11 27
Windsor & Eton Riverside	d				10 21									10 51						
Datchet	d				10 25									10 55						
Sunnymeads	d				10 28									10 58						
Wraysbury	d				10 32									11 02						
Staines	d	10 29		10 33	10 38	10 44				10 59			11 03	11 08			11 29			11 33
Ashford (Surrey)	d			10 36	10 41								11 06	11 11						11 36
Feltham	d	10 35		10 41	10 46	10 50				11 05			11 11	11 16			11 35			11 41
Whitton	d				10 50			10 56	10 50					11 20	11 23	11 20				
Kingston	d		10 29									10 59							11 29	
Hampton Wick	d		10 31									11 01							11 31	
Teddington	d		10 35									11 05							11 35	
Fulwell	d																			
Strawberry Hill	d		10 38									11 08							11 38	
Twickenham	a	10 40	10 42		10 53	10 57		10 58		11 10		11 12		11 23	11 26		11 40		11 42	
	d	10 41	10 43		10 53	10 57		10 58		11 11		11 13		11 23	11 28		11 41		11 43	
St Margarets	d		10 45					11 00				11 15			11 30				11 45	
Richmond ⊖	d	10 45	10 49		10 58	11 02		11 04		11 15		11 19		11 28	11 34		11 45		11 49	
North Sheen	d		10 51					11 06				11 21			11 36				11 51	
Mortlake	d		10 53					11 08				11 23			11 38				11 53	
Hounslow	d			10 46					11 01				11 16			11 31				11 46
Isleworth	d			10 49					11 04				11 19			11 34				11 49
Syon Lane	d			10 51					11 06				11 21			11 36				11 51
Brentford	d			10 54					11 09				11 24			11 39				11 54
Kew Bridge	d			10 56					11 11				11 26			11 41				11 56
Chiswick	d			10 59					11 14				11 29			11 44				11 59
Barnes Bridge	d			11 01					11 16				11 31			11 46				12 01
Barnes	d		10 56	11 04				11 11	11 19			11 26	11 34		11 41	11 49			11 56	12 04
Putney	d		10 59	11 07	11 04			11 14	11 22			11 29	11 37	11 34	11 44	11 52			11 59	12 07
Wandsworth Town	d		11 02	11 10				11 17	11 25			11 32	11 40		11 47	11 55			12 02	12 10
Clapham Junction 10	d	10 54	11 05	11 13	11 09	11 12		11 20	11 28	11 24		11 35	11 43	11 39	11 50	11 58	11 54		12 05	12 13
Queenstown Rd.(Battersea)	d		11 08	11 17				11 23	11 31			11 38	11 46		11 53	12 01			12 08	12 16
Vauxhall ⊖	d		11 12	11 20	11 15			11 27	11 35			11 42	11 50	11 45	11 57	12 05			12 12	12 20
London Waterloo 15 ⊖	a	11 04	11 16	11 27	11 19	11 25		11 32	11 41	11 34		11 46	11 56	11 49	12 02	12 11	12 04		12 16	12 26

Reading, Guildford, Ascot, Weybridge, Windsor, Kingston, Richmond and Hounslow - London

		SW	SW	SW	SW ■1	SW ■1	SW	SW	SW	SW	SW ■1	SW ■1	SW	SW	SW	SW	SW ■1	SW ■1	SW	SW
Reading 7	d				11 09						11 39						12 09			
Earley	d				11 14						11 44						12 14			
Winnersh Triangle	d				11 16						11 46						12 16			
Winnersh	d				11 18						11 48						12 18			
Wokingham	d				11 23						11 53						12 23			
Bracknell	d				11 29						11 59						12 29			
Martins Heron	d				11 32						12 02						12 32			
Guildford	d					11 00						11 30						12 00		
Wanborough	d					11 06						11 36						12 06		
Ash 5	d					11 10						11 40						12 10		
Aldershot	a					11 17						11 47						12 17		
	d					11 30						12 00						12 30		
Ash Vale	d					11 34						12 04						12 34		
Frimley	d					11 40						12 10						12 40		
Camberley	a					11 44						12 14						12 44		
	d					11 48						12 18						12 48		
Bagshot	d					11 53						12 23						12 53		
Ascot 3	d				11 37	12a00					12 07	12a30					12 37	13a00		
Sunningdale	d				11 40						12 10						12 40			
Longcross	d																			
Woking	d																			
West Byfleet	d																			
Byfleet & New Haw	d																			
Weybridge	d													12 03						12 33
Addlestone	d													12 07						12 37
Chertsey	d													12 10						12 40
Virginia Water	a				11 49						12 19			12 15			12 49			12 45
	d				11 49						12 19			12 24			12 49			12 54
Egham	d				11 53						12 23			12 27			12 53			12 57
Windsor & Eton Riverside	d	11 21						11 51							12 21					
Datchet	d	11 25						11 55							12 25					
Sunnymeads	d	11 28						11 58							12 28					
Wraysbury	d	11 32						12 02							12 32					
Staines	d	11 38			11 59			12 08			12 29			12 33	12 38		12 59			13 03
Ashford (Surrey)	d	11 41						12 11						12 36	12 41					13 06
Feltham	d	11 46			12 05			12 16			12 35			12 41	12 46		13 05			13 11
Whitton	d	11 50	11 53	11 50				12 20	12 23	12 20					12 50	12 53				
Kingston	d						11 59						12 29						12 59	
Hampton Wick	d						12 01						12 31						13 01	
Teddington	d						12 05						12 35						13 05	
Fulwell	d																			
Strawberry Hill	d						12 08						12 38						13 08	
Twickenham	a	11 53	11 56		12 10		12 12	12 23	12 26		12 40		12 42		12 53	12 56	13 10		13 12	
	d	11 53	11 58		12 11		12 13	12 23	12 28		12 41		12 43		12 53	12 58	13 11		13 13	
St Margarets	d		12 00				12 15		12 30				12 45			13 00			13 15	
Richmond ⊖	d	11 58	12 04		12 15		12 19	12 28	12 34		12 45		12 49		12 58	13 04	13 15		13 19	
North Sheen	d		12 06				12 21		12 36				12 51			13 06			13 21	
Mortlake	d		12 08				12 23		12 38				12 53			13 08			13 23	
Hounslow	d			12 01						12 31				12 46						13 16
Isleworth	d			12 04						12 34				12 49						13 19
Syon Lane	d			12 06						12 36				12 51						13 21
Brentford	d			12 09						12 39				12 54						13 24
Kew Bridge	d			12 11						12 41				12 56						13 26
Chiswick	d			12 14						12 44				12 59						13 29
Barnes Bridge	d			12 16						12 46				13 01						13 31
Barnes	d		12 11	12 19			12 26		12 41	12 49			12 56	13 04		13 11			13 26	13 34
Putney	d	12 04	12 14	12 22			12 29	12 34	12 44	12 52			12 59	13 07	13 04	13 14			13 29	13 37
Wandsworth Town	d		12 17	12 25			12 32		12 47	12 55			13 02	13 10		13 17			13 32	13 40
Clapham Junction 10	d	12 09	12 20	12 28	12 25		12 35	12 39	12 50	12 58	12 54		13 05	13 13	13 09	13 20	13 24		13 35	13 43
Queenstown Rd.(Battersea)	d		12 23	12 31			12 38		12 53	13 01			13 08	13 16		13 23			13 38	13 46
Vauxhall ⊖	d	12 15	12 27	12 35			12 42	12 45	12 57	13 05			13 12	13 20	13 15	13 27			13 42	13 50
London Waterloo 15 ⊖	a	12 19	12 32	12 41	12 34		12 46	12 49	13 02	13 11	13 04		13 16	13 26	13 19	13 32	13 34		13 46	13 56

Table 149

Mondays to Fridays
from 27 September

Reading, Guildford, Ascot, Weybridge, Windsor, Kingston, Richmond and Hounslow - London

		SW	SW	SW	SW ■	SW ■	SW	SW	SW	SW	SW	SW ■	SW ■	SW	SW	SW	SW	SW	SW ■	SW ■
Reading ■	d				12 39							13 09							13 39	
Earley	d				12 44							13 14							13 44	
Winnersh Triangle	d				12 46							13 16							13 46	
Winnersh	d				12 48							13 18							13 48	
Wokingham	d				12 53							13 23							13 53	
Bracknell	d				12 59							13 29							13 59	
Martins Heron	d				13 02							13 32							14 02	
Guildford	d					12 30							13 00							13 30
Wanborough	d					12 36							13 06							13 36
Ash ■	d					12 40							13 10							13 40
Aldershot	a					12 47							13 17							13 47
	d					13 00							13 30							14 00
Ash Vale	d					13 04							13 34							14 04
Frimley	d					13 10							13 40							14 10
Camberley	a					13 14							13 44							14 14
	d					13 18							13 48							14 18
Bagshot	d					13 23							13 53							14 23
Ascot ■	d				13 07	13a30						13 37	14a00						14 07	14a30
Sunningdale	d				13 10							13 40							14 10	
Longcross	d				13 13															
Woking	d																			
West Byfleet	d																			
Byfleet & New Haw	d																			
Weybridge	d							13 03							13 33					
Addlestone	d							13 07							13 37					
Chertsey	d							13 10							13 40					
Virginia Water	a				13 19			13 15				13 49			13 45				14 19	
	d				13 19			13 24				13 49			13 54				14 19	
Egham	d				13 23			13 27				13 53			13 57				14 23	
Windsor & Eton Riverside	d	12 51							13 21							13 51				
Datchet	d	12 55							13 25							13 55				
Sunnymeads	d	12 58							13 28							13 58				
Wraysbury	d	13 02							13 32							14 02				
Staines	d	13 08			13 29			13 33	13 38			13 59			14 03	14 08			14 29	
Ashford (Surrey)	d	13 11						13 36	13 41						14 06	14 11				
Feltham	d	13 16			13 35			13 41	13 46			14 05			14 11	14 16			14 35	
Whitton	d	13 20	13 23	13 20					13 50	13 53	13 50					14 20	14 23	14 20		
Kingston	d						13 29							13 59						
Hampton Wick	d						13 31							14 01						
Teddington	d						13 35							14 05						
Fulwell	d																			
Strawberry Hill	d						13 38							14 08						
Twickenham	a	13 23	13 26		13 40		13 42		13 53	13 56		14 10		14 12		14 23	14 26		14 40	
	d	13 23	13 28		13 41		13 43		13 53	13 58		14 11		14 13		14 23	14 28		14 41	
St Margarets	d		13 30				13 45			14 00				14 15			14 30			
Richmond ⊖	d	13 28	13 34		13 45		13 49		13 58	14 04		14 15		14 19		14 28	14 34		14 45	
North Sheen	d		13 36				13 51			14 06				14 21			14 36			
Mortlake	d		13 38				13 53			14 08				14 23			14 38			
Hounslow	d			13 31				13 46			14 01				14 16			14 31		
Isleworth	d			13 34				13 49			14 04				14 19			14 34		
Syon Lane	d			13 36				13 51			14 06				14 21			14 36		
Brentford	d			13 39				13 54			14 09				14 24			14 39		
Kew Bridge	d			13 41				13 56			14 11				14 26			14 41		
Chiswick	d			13 44				13 59			14 14				14 29			14 44		
Barnes Bridge	d			13 46				14 01			14 16				14 31			14 46		
Barnes	d		13 41	13 49			13 56	14 04		14 11	14 19			14 26	14 34		14 41	14 49		
Putney	d	13 34	13 44	13 52			13 59	14 07	14 04	14 14	14 22			14 29	14 37	14 34	14 44	14 52		
Wandsworth Town	d		13 47	13 55			14 02	14 10		14 17	14 25			14 32	14 40		14 47	14 55		
Clapham Junction ■	d	13 39	13 50	13 58	13 54		14 05	14 13	14 09	14 20	14 28	14 24		14 35	14 43	14 39	14 50	14 58	14 54	
Queenstown Rd.(Battersea)	d		13 53	14 01			14 08	14 16		14 23	14 31			14 38	14 46		14 53	15 01		
Vauxhall ⊖	d	13 45	13 57	14 05			14 12	14 20	14 15	14 27	14 35			14 42	14 50	14 45	14 57	15 05		
London Waterloo ■ ⊖	a	13 49	14 02	14 11	14 04		14 16	14 26	14 19	14 32	14 41	14 34		14 46	14 56	14 49	15 02	15 11	15 04	

Table 149

Mondays to Fridays
from 27 September

Reading, Guildford, Ascot, Weybridge, Windsor, Kingston, Richmond and Hounslow - London

		SW	SW	SW	SW	SW	SW ■	SW ■	SW	SW	SW	SW	SW	SW ■	SW ■	SW	SW	SW	SW	SW
Reading ■	d						14 09							14 39						
Earley	d						14 14							14 44						
Winnersh Triangle	d						14 16							14 46						
Winnersh	d						14 18							14 48						
Wokingham	d						14 23							14 53						
Bracknell	d						14 29							14 59						
Martins Heron	d						14 32							15 02						
Guildford	d							14 00							14 30					
Wanborough	d							14 06							14 36					
Ash ■	d							14 10							14 40					
Aldershot	a							14 17							14 47					
	d							14 30							15 00					
Ash Vale	d							14 34							15 04					
Frimley	d							14 40							15 10					
Camberley	a							14 44							15 14					
	d							14 48							15 18					
Bagshot	d							14 53							15 23					
Ascot ■	d						14 37	15a00						15 07	15a30					
Sunningdale	d						14 40							15 10						
Longcross	d																			
Woking	d																			
West Byfleet	d																			
Byfleet & New Haw	d																			
Weybridge	d		14 03							14 33							15 03			
Addlestone	d		14 07							14 37							15 07			
Chertsey	d		14 10							14 40							15 10			
Virginia Water	a		14 15				14 49			14 45				15 19			15 15			
	d		14 24				14 49			14 54				15 19			15 24			
Egham	d		14 27				14 53			14 57				15 23			15 27			
Windsor & Eton Riverside	d			14 21							14 51							15 21		
Datchet	d			14 25							14 55							15 25		
Sunnymeads	d			14 28							14 58							15 28		
Wraysbury	d			14 32							15 02							15 32		
Staines	d		14 33	14 38			14 59			15 03	15 08			15 29			15 33	15 38		
Ashford (Surrey)	d		14 36	14 41						15 06	15 11						15 36	15 41		
Feltham	d		14 41	14 46			15 05			15 11	15 16			15 35			15 41	15 46		
Whitton	d			14 50	14 53	14 50					15 20	15 23	15 20					15 50	15 53	15 50
Kingston	d	14 29							14 59							15 29				
Hampton Wick	d	14 31							15 01							15 31				
Teddington	d	14 35							15 05							15 35				
Fulwell	d																			
Strawberry Hill	d	14 38							15 08							15 38				
Twickenham	a	14 42		14 53	14 56		15 10		15 12		15 23	15 26		15 40		15 42		15 53	15 56	
	d	14 43		14 53	14 58		15 11		15 13		15 23	15 28		15 41		15 43		15 53	15 58	
St Margarets	d	14 45			15 00				15 15			15 30				15 45			16 00	
Richmond ⊖	d	14 49		14 58	15 04		15 15		15 19		15 28	15 34		15 45		15 49		15 58	16 04	
North Sheen	d	14 51			15 06				15 21			15 36				15 51			16 06	
Mortlake	d	14 53			15 08				15 23			15 38				15 53			16 08	
Hounslow	d		14 46			15 01				15 16			15 31				15 46			16 01
Isleworth	d		14 49			15 04				15 19			15 34				15 49			16 04
Syon Lane	d		14 51			15 06				15 21			15 36				15 51			16 06
Brentford	d		14 54			15 09				15 24			15 39				15 54			16 09
Kew Bridge	d		14 56			15 11				15 26			15 41				15 56			16 11
Chiswick	d		14 59			15 14				15 29			15 44				15 59			16 14
Barnes Bridge	d		15 01			15 16				15 31			15 46				16 01			16 16
Barnes	d	14 56	15 04		15 11	15 19			15 26	15 34		15 41	15 49			15 56	16 04		16 11	16 19
Putney	d	14 59	15 07	15 04	15 14	15 22			15 29	15 37	15 34	15 44	15 52			15 59	16 07	16 04	16 14	16 22
Wandsworth Town	d	15 02	15 10		15 17	15 25			15 32	15 40		15 47	15 55			16 02	16 10		16 17	16 25
Clapham Junction ■	d	15 05	15 13	15 09	15 20	15 28	15 24		15 35	15 43	15 39	15 50	15 58	15 54		16 05	16 13	16 09	16 20	16 28
Queenstown Rd.(Battersea)	d	15 08	15 16		15 23	15 31			15 38	15 46		15 53	16 01			16 08	16 16		16 23	16 31
Vauxhall ⊖	d	15 12	15 20	15 15	15 27	15 35			15 42	15 50	15 45	15 57	16 05			16 12	16 20	16 15	16 27	16 35
London Waterloo ■ ⊖	a	15 16	15 26	15 19	15 32	15 41	15 34		15 46	15 56	15 49	16 02	16 11	16 05		16 19	16 26	16 19	16 32	16 41

Table 149

Reading, Guildford, Ascot, Weybridge, Windsor, Kingston, Richmond and Hounslow - London

		SW ■	SW ■	SW	SW	SW	SW	GW ■ A	SW		SW ■	SW ■	SW	SW	SW	SW	SW		SW		SW ■	SW ■	SW	SW
Reading ■	d	15 09						15 28			15 39										16 09			
Earley	d	15 14									15 44										16 14			
Winnersh Triangle	d	15 16									15 46										16 16			
Winnersh	d	15 18						15 35			15 48										16 18			
Wokingham	d	15 23						15a38			15 53										16 23			
Bracknell	d	15 29									15 59										16 29			
Martins Heron	d	15 32									16 02										16 32			
Guildford	d		15 00									15 30										16 00		
Wanborough	d		15 06									15 36										16 06		
Ash ■	d		15 10									15 40										16 10		
Aldershot	a		15 17									15 47										16 17		
	d		15 30									16 00										16 30		
Ash Vale	d		15 34									16 04										16 34		
Frimley	d		15 40									16 10										16 40		
Camberley	a		15 44									16 14										16 44		
	d		15 48									16 18										16 48		
Bagshot	d		15 53									16 23										16 53		
Ascot ■	d	15 37	16a00								16 07	16a30									16 37	17a00		
Sunningdale	d	15 40									16 10										16 40			
Longcross	d																							
Woking	d																							
West Byfleet	d																							
Byfleet & New Haw	d																							
Weybridge	d				15 33									16 03										16 33
Addlestone	d				15 37									16 07										16 37
Chertsey	d				15 40									16 10										16 40
Virginia Water	a	15 49			15 45						16 19			16 15							16 49			16 45
	d	15 49			15 54						16 19			16 24							16 49			16 54
Egham	d	15 53			15 57						16 23			16 27							16 53			16 57
Windsor & Eton Riverside	d					15 51										16 21								
Datchet	d					15 55										16 25								
Sunnymeads	d					15 58										16 28								
Wraysbury	d					16 02										16 32								
Staines	d	15 59			16 03	16 08					16 29			16 33		16 38					16 59			17 03
Ashford (Surrey)	d				16 06	16 11								16 36		16 41								17 06
Feltham	d	16 05			16 11	16 16					16 35			16 41		16 46					17 05			17 11
Whitton	d					16 20	16 23		16 20							16 50	16 53		16 50					
Kingston	d			15 59									16 29										16 59	
Hampton Wick	d			16 01									16 31										17 01	
Teddington	d			16 05									16 35										17 05	
Fulwell	d																							
Strawberry Hill	d			16 08									16 38										17 08	
Twickenham	a	16 10		16 12		16 23	16 26				16 40		16 42			16 53	16 56				17 10		17 12	
	d	16 11		16 13		16 23	16 28				16 41		16 43			16 53	16 58				17 11		17 13	
St Margarets	d			16 15			16 30						16 45				17 00						17 15	
Richmond ⊖	d	16 15		16 19		16 28	16 34				16 45		16 49			16 58	17 04				17 15		17 19	
North Sheen	d			16 21			16 36						16 51				17 06						17 21	
Mortlake	d			16 23			16 38						16 53				17 08						17 23	
Hounslow	d				16 16				16 31					16 46					17 01					17 16
Isleworth	d				16 19				16 34					16 49					17 04					17 19
Syon Lane	d				16 21				16 36					16 51					17 06					17 21
Brentford	d				16 24				16 39					16 54					17 09					17 24
Kew Bridge	d				16 26				16 41					16 56					17 11					17 26
Chiswick	d				16 29				16 44					16 59					17 14					17 29
Barnes Bridge	d				16 31				16 46					17 01					17 16					17 31
Barnes	d			16 26	16 34		16 41		16 49				16 56	17 04			17 11		17 19				17 26	17 34
Putney	d			16 29	16 37	16 34	16 44		16 52				16 59	17 07		17 05	17 14		17 22				17 29	17 37
Wandsworth Town	d			16 32	16 40		16 47		16 55				17 02	17 10			17 17		17 25				17 32	17 40
Clapham Junction ■	d	16 24		16 35	16 43	16 39	16 50		16 58		16 54		17 05	17 13		17 09	17 20		17 28		17 24		17 35	17 43
Queenstown Rd.(Battersea)	d			16 38	16 46		16 53		17 01				17 08	17 16			17 23		17 31				17 38	17 46
Vauxhall ⊖	d			16 42	16 50	16 45	16 57		17 05				17 12	17 20		17 15	17 27		17 35				17 42	17 50
London Waterloo ■ ⊖	a	16 34		16 49	16 56	16 49	17 02		17 11		17 04		17 19	17 26		17 19	17 32		17 41		17 35		17 49	17 56

A To Gatwick Airport (Table 148)

Table 149

Reading, Guildford, Ascot, Weybridge, Windsor, Kingston, Richmond and Hounslow - London

		SW	SW	SW			SW	SW ■	SW ■	SW	SW	SW	SW	SW			SW ■	SW ■	SW ■	SW	SW	SW	SW	SW
Reading ■	d							16 41									17 09	17 22						
Earley	d							16 46									17 14	17 27						
Winnersh Triangle	d							16 48									17 16	17 29						
Winnersh	d							16 50									17 18	17 31						
Wokingham	d							16 55									17 23	17 36						
Bracknell	d							17 01									17 29	17 42						
Martins Heron	d							17 04									17 32	17 45						
Guildford	d								16 30										17 00					
Wanborough	d								16 36										17 06					
Ash ■	d								16 40										17 10					
Aldershot	a								16 47										17 17					
	d								17 00										17 30					
Ash Vale	d								17 04										17 34					
Frimley	d								17 10										17 40					
Camberley	a								17 14										17 44					
	d								17 18										17 48					
Bagshot	d								17 23										17 53					
Ascot ■	d							17 09	17a30								17 37	17b55	18a00					
Sunningdale	d							17 12									17 40	17 58						
Longcross	d							17 15																
Woking	d																							
West Byfleet	d																							
Byfleet & New Haw	d																							
Weybridge	d										17 03										17 37			
Addlestone	d										17 07										17 41			
Chertsey	d										17 10										17 44			
Virginia Water	a							17 19			17 15						17 49	18 03			17 49			
	d							17 19			17 24						17 49	18 03			17 54			
Egham	d							17 23			17 27						17 53	18 06			17 57			
Windsor & Eton Riverside	d	16 51										17 21										17 51		
Datchet	d	16 55										17 25										17 55		
Sunnymeads	d	16 58										17 28										17 58		
Wraysbury	d	17 02										17 32										18 02		
Staines	d	17 08						17 29			17 33	17 38					17 59	18 14			18 03	18 08		
Ashford (Surrey)	d	17 11									17 36	17 41									18 06	18 11		
Feltham	d	17 16						17 35			17 41	17 46					18 05	18 20			18 11	18 16		
Whitton	d	17 20	17 23	17 20								17 50	17 53	17 50								18 20	18 23	18 20
Kingston	d									17 29										17 59				
Hampton Wick	d									17 31										18 01				
Teddington	d									17 35										18 05				
Fulwell	d																							
Strawberry Hill	d									17 38										18 08				
Twickenham	a	17 23	17 26				17 37	17 40		17 42		17 53	17 56				18 10			18 12		18 23	18 26	
	d	17 23	17 28				17 37	17 41		17 43		17 53	17 58				18 11			18 13		18 23	18 28	
St Margarets	d		17 30							17 45			18 00							18 15			18 30	
Richmond ⊖	d	17 28	17 34					17 45		17 49		17 58	18 04				18 15			18 19		18 28	18 34	
North Sheen	d		17 36							17 51			18 06							18 21			18 36	
Mortlake	d		17 38							17 53			18 08							18 23			18 38	
Hounslow	d			17 31							17 46			18 01				18 26			18 16			18 31
Isleworth	d			17 34							17 49			18 04							18 19			18 34
Syon Lane	d			17 36							17 51			18 06							18 21			18 36
Brentford	d			17 39							17 54			18 09				18 31			18 24			18 39
Kew Bridge	d			17 41							17 56			18 11							18 26			18 41
Chiswick	d			17 44							17 59			18 14							18 29			18 44
Barnes Bridge	d			17 46							18 01			18 16							18 31			18 46
Barnes	d		17 41	17 49						17 56	18 04		18 11	18 19						18 26	18 34		18 41	18 49
Putney	d	17 34	17 44	17 52						17 59	18 07	18 04	18 14	18 22				18 39		18 29	18 37	18 34	18 44	18 52
Wandsworth Town	d		17 47	17 55						18 02	18 10		18 17	18 25						18 32	18 40		18 47	18 55
Clapham Junction ■	d	17 39	17 50	17 58				17 54		18 05	18 13	18 09	18 20	18 28			18 24	18 44		18 35	18 43	18 39	18 50	18 58
Queenstown Rd.(Battersea)	d		17 53	18 01						18 08	18 16		18 23	18 31						18 38	18 46		18 53	19 01
Vauxhall ⊖	d	17 45	17 57	18 05			18 24			18 12	18 20	18 15	18 27	18 35						18 42	18 50	18 45	18 57	19 05
London Waterloo ■ ⊖	a	17 49	18 02	18 11			18 29	18 04		18 19	18 26	18 19	18 32	18 41			18 34	18 56		18 49	18 56	18 49	19 02	19 11

b arr. 1749

Reading, Guildford, Ascot, Weybridge, Windsor, Kingston, Richmond and Hounslow - London

		SW 1	SW 1	SW 1	SW	SW	SW	SW	SW	SW 1	SW 1	SW	SW	SW	SW	SW	SW 1	SW 1	SW 1	SW
Reading 7	d	17 39	17 53							18 09							18 39	18 52		
Earley	d	17 44	17 58							18 14							18 44	18 57		
Winnersh Triangle	d	17 46	18 00							18 16							18 46	18 59		
Winnersh	d	17 48	18 02							18 18							18 48	19 01		
Wokingham	d	17 53	18 07							18 23							18 53	19 06		
Bracknell	d	17 59	18 13							18 29							18 59	19 12		
Martins Heron	d	18 02	18 16							18 32							19 02	19 15		
Guildford	d			17 30							18 00								18 30	
Wanborough	d			17 36							18 06								18 36	
Ash 5	d			17 40							18 10								18 40	
Aldershot	a			17 47							18 17								18 47	
	d			18 00							18 30								19 00	
Ash Vale	d			18 04							18 34								19 04	
Frimley	d			18 10							18 40								19 10	
Camberley	a			18 14							18 44								19 14	
	d			18 18							18 48								19 18	
Bagshot	d			18 23							18 53								19 23	
Ascot 3	d	18 07	18 25	18a30						18 37	19a00						19 07	19a19	19a30	
Sunningdale	d	18 10	18 28							18 40							19 10			
Longcross	d	18 13								18 43							19 13			
Woking	d																			
West Byfleet	d																			
Byfleet & New Haw	d																			
Weybridge	d					18 07							18 37							
Addlestone	d					18 11							18 41							
Chertsey	d					18 14							18 44							
Virginia Water	a	18 19	18 33			18 19				18 49			18 49				19 19			
	d	18 19	18 33			18 24				18 49			18 54				19 19			
Egham	d	18 23	18 37			18 27				18 53			18 57				19 23			
Windsor & Eton Riverside	d						18 21							18 51						
Datchet	d						18 25							18 55						
Sunnymeads	d						18 28							18 58						
Wraysbury	d						18 32							19 02						
Staines	d	18 29	18 44			18 33	18 38			18 59			19 03	19 08			19 29			
Ashford (Surrey)	d					18 36	18 41						19 06	19 11						
Feltham	d	18 35	18 50			18 41	18 46			19 05			19 11	19 16			19 35			
Whitton	d						18 50	18 53	18 50					19 20	19 23	19 20				
Kingston	d				18 29							18 59								19 29
Hampton Wick	d				18 31							19 01								19 31
Teddington	d				18 35							19 05								19 35
Fulwell	d																			
Strawberry Hill	d				18 38							19 08								19 38
Twickenham	a	18 40			18 42		18 53	18 56		19 10		19 12		19 23	19 26		19 40			19 42
	d	18 41			18 43		18 53	18 58		19 11		19 13		19 23	19 28		19 41			19 43
St Margarets	d				18 45			19 00				19 15			19 30					19 45
Richmond ⊖	d	18 45			18 49		18 58	19 04		19 15		19 19		19 28	19 34		19 45			19 49
North Sheen	d				18 51			19 06				19 21			19 36					19 51
Mortlake	d				18 53			19 08				19 23			19 38					19 53
Hounslow	d		18 56			18 46			19 01				19 16			19 31				
Isleworth	d					18 49			19 04				19 19			19 34				
Syon Lane	d					18 51			19 06				19 21			19 36				
Brentford	d		19 01			18 54			19 09				19 24			19 39				
Kew Bridge	d					18 56			19 11				19 26			19 41				
Chiswick	d					18 59			19 14				19 29			19 44				
Barnes Bridge	d					19 01			19 16				19 31			19 46				
Barnes	d				18 56	19 04		19 11	19 19			19 26	19 34		19 41	19 49				19 56
Putney	d		19 09		18 59	19 07	19 04	19 14	19 22			19 29	19 37	19 34	19 44	19 52				19 59
Wandsworth Town	d				19 02	19 10		19 17	19 25			19 32	19 40		19 47	19 55				20 02
Clapham Junction 10	d	18 54	19 14		19 05	19 13	19 09	19 20	19 28	19 24		19 35	19 43	19 39	19 50	19 58	19 54			20 05
Queenstown Rd.(Battersea)	d				19 08	19 16		19 23	19 31			19 38	19 46		19 53	20 01				20 08
Vauxhall ⊖	d				19 12	19 20	19 15	19 27	19 35			19 42	19 50	19 45	19 57	20 05				20 12
London Waterloo 15 ⊖	a	19 04	19 28		19 16	19 26	19 19	19 32	19 41	19 34		19 46	19 56	19 49	20 02	20 09	20 04			20 16

Reading, Guildford, Ascot, Weybridge, Windsor, Kingston, Richmond and Hounslow - London

		SW	SW	SW	SW	SW 1	SW 1	SW	SW	SW	SW	SW	SW 1	SW 1	SW	SW	SW	SW	SW	SW 1
Reading 7	d					19 09							19 39							20 09
Earley	d					19 14							19 44							20 14
Winnersh Triangle	d					19 16							19 46							20 16
Winnersh	d					19 18							19 48							20 18
Wokingham	d					19 23							19 53							20 23
Bracknell	d					19 29							19 59							20 29
Martins Heron	d					19 32							20 02							20 32
Guildford	d						19 00							19 30						
Wanborough	d						19 06							19 36						
Ash 5	d						19 10							19 40						
Aldershot	a						19 17							19 47						
	d						19 30							20 00						
Ash Vale	d						19 34							20 04						
Frimley	d						19 40							20 10						
Camberley	a						19 44							20 14						
	d						19 48							20 18						
Bagshot	d						19 53							20 23						
Ascot 3	d					19 37	20a00						20 07	20a30						20 37
Sunningdale	d					19 40							20 10							20 40
Longcross	d					19 43							20 13							20 43
Woking	d																			
West Byfleet	d																			
Byfleet & New Haw	d																			
Weybridge	d	19 07							19 37							20 03				
Addlestone	d	19 11							19 41							20 07				
Chertsey	d	19 14							19 44							20 10				
Virginia Water	a	19 19				19 49			19 49				20 19			20 15				20 49
	d	19 24				19 49			19 54				20 19			20 24				20 49
Egham	d	19 27				19 53			19 57				20 23			20 27				20 53
Windsor & Eton Riverside	d		19 21							19 51							20 21			
Datchet	d		19 25							19 55							20 25			
Sunnymeads	d		19 28							19 58							20 28			
Wraysbury	d		19 32							20 02							20 32			
Staines	d	19 33	19 38			19 59			20 03	20 08			20 29			20 33	20 38			20 59
Ashford (Surrey)	d	19 36	19 41						20 06	20 11						20 36	20 41			
Feltham	d	19 41	19 46			20 05			20 11	20 16			20 35			20 41	20 46			21 05
Whitton	d		19 50	19 53	19 50					20 20	20 23	20 20					20 50	20 53	20 50	
Kingston	d							19 59							20 29					
Hampton Wick	d							20 01							20 31					
Teddington	d							20 05							20 35					
Fulwell	d																			
Strawberry Hill	d							20 08							20 38					
Twickenham	a		19 53	19 56		20 10		20 12		20 23	20 26		20 40		20 42		20 53	20 56		21 10
	d		19 53	19 58		20 11		20 13		20 23	20 28		20 41		20 43		20 53	20 58		21 11
St Margarets	d			20 00				20 15			20 30				20 45			21 00		
Richmond ⊖	d		19 58	20 04		20 15		20 19		20 28	20 34		20 45		20 49		20 58	21 04		21 15
North Sheen	d			20 06				20 21			20 36				20 51			21 06		
Mortlake	d			20 08				20 23			20 38				20 53			21 08		
Hounslow	d	19 46			20 01				20 16			20 31				20 46			21 01	
Isleworth	d	19 49			20 04				20 19			20 34				20 49			21 04	
Syon Lane	d	19 51			20 06				20 21			20 36				20 51			21 06	
Brentford	d	19 54			20 09				20 24			20 39				20 54			21 09	
Kew Bridge	d	19 56			20 11				20 26			20 41				20 56			21 11	
Chiswick	d	19 59			20 14				20 29			20 44				20 59			21 14	
Barnes Bridge	d	20 01			20 16				20 31			20 46				21 01			21 16	
Barnes	d	20 04		20 11	20 19			20 26	20 34		20 41	20 49			20 56	21 04		21 11	21 19	
Putney	d	20 07	20 04	20 14	20 22			20 29	20 37	20 34	20 44	20 52			20 59	21 07	21 04	21 14	21 22	
Wandsworth Town	d	20 10		20 17	20 25			20 32	20 40		20 47	20 55			21 02	21 10		21 17	21 25	
Clapham Junction 10	d	20 13	20 09	20 20	20 28	20 24		20 35	20 43	20 39	20 50	20 58	20 54		21 05	21 13	21 09	21 20	21 28	21 24
Queenstown Rd.(Battersea)	d	20 16		20 23	20 31			20 38	20 46		20 53	21 01			21 08	21 16		21 23	21 31	
Vauxhall ⊖	d	20 20	20 15	20 27	20 35			20 42	20 50	20 45	20 57	21 05			21 12	21 20	21 15	21 27	21 35	
London Waterloo 15 ⊖	a	20 26	20 19	20 32	20 41	20 34		20 46	20 56	20 49	21 02	21 11	21 04		21 16	21 26	21 19	21 32	21 41	21 34

Table 149

Mondays to Fridays
from 27 September

Reading, Guildford, Ascot, Weybridge, Windsor, Kingston, Richmond and Hounslow - London

		SW ■	SW	SW	SW	SW	SW	SW ■	SW	SW	SW	SW	SW	SW ■	SW ■	SW	SW	SW	SW
Reading ■	d							20 39						21 09					
Earley	d							20 44						21 14					
Winnersh Triangle	d							20 46						21 16					
Winnersh	d							20 48						21 18					
Wokingham	d							20 53						21 23					
Bracknell	d							20 59						21 29					
Martins Heron	d							21 02						21 32					
Guildford	d	20 00													21 00				
Wanborough	d	20 06													21 06				
Ash ■	d	20 10													21 10				
Aldershot	a	20 17													21 17				
	d	20 30													21 30				
Ash Vale	d	20 34													21 34				
Frimley	d	20 40													21 40				
Camberley	a	20 44													21 44				
	d	20 48													21 48				
Bagshot	d	20 53													21 53				
Ascot ■	d	21a00						21 07						21 37	22a00				
Sunningdale	d							21 10						21 40					
Longcross	d																		
Woking	d																		
West Byfleet	d																		
Byfleet & New Haw	d																		
Weybridge	d			20 33						21 03							21 33		
Addlestone	d			20 37						21 07							21 37		
Chertsey	d			20 40						21 10							21 40		
Virginia Water	a			20 45				21 19		21 15				21 49			21 45		
	d			20 54				21 19		21 24				21 49			21 54		
Egham	d			20 57				21 23		21 27				21 53			21 57		
Windsor & Eton Riverside	d				20 51						21 21							21 51	
Datchet	d				20 55						21 25							21 55	
Sunnymeads	d				20 58						21 28							21 58	
Wraysbury	d				21 02						21 32							22 02	
Staines	d			21 03	21 08			21 29		21 33	21 38			21 59			22 03	22 08	
Ashford (Surrey)	d			21 06	21 11					21 36	21 41						22 06	22 11	
Feltham	d			21 11	21 16			21 35		21 41	21 46			22 05			22 11	22 16	
Whitton	d				21 20	21 23	21 20				21 50	21 53	21 50					22 20	22 23
Kingston	d		20 59						21 29							21 59			
Hampton Wick	d		21 01						21 31							22 01			
Teddington	d		21 05						21 35							22 05			
Fulwell	d																		
Strawberry Hill	d		21 08						21 38							22 08			
Twickenham	a		21 12		21 23	21 26		21 40	21 42		21 53	21 56		22 10		22 12		22 23	22 26
	d		21 13		21 23	21 28		21 41	21 43		21 53	21 58		22 11		22 13		22 23	22 28
St Margarets	d		21 15			21 30			21 45			22 00				22 15			22 30
Richmond	⊖ d		21 19		21 28	21 34		21 45	21 49		21 58	22 04		22 15		22 19		22 28	22 34
North Sheen	d		21 21			21 36			21 51			22 06				22 21			22 36
Mortlake	d		21 23			21 38			21 53			22 08				22 23			22 38
Hounslow	d			21 16			21 31			21 46			22 01				22 16		
Isleworth	d			21 19			21 34			21 49			22 04				22 19		
Syon Lane	d			21 21			21 36			21 51			22 06				22 21		
Brentford	d			21 24			21 39			21 54			22 09				22 24		
Kew Bridge	d			21 26			21 41			21 56			22 11				22 26		
Chiswick	d			21 29			21 44			21 59			22 14				22 29		
Barnes Bridge	d			21 31			21 46			22 01			22 16				22 31		
Barnes	d		21 26	21 34		21 41	21 49		21 56	22 04		22 11	22 19			22 26	22 34		22 41
Putney	d		21 29	21 37	21 34	21 44	21 52		21 59	22 07	22 04	22 14	22 22			22 29	22 37	22 34	22 44
Wandsworth Town	d		21 32	21 40		21 47	21 55		22 02	22 10		22 17	22 25			22 32	22 40		22 47
Clapham Junction ■	d		21 35	21 43	21 39	21 50	21 58	21 54	22 05	22 13	22 09	22 20	22 28	22 24		22 35	22 43	22 39	22 50
Queenstown Rd.(Battersea)	d		21 38	21 46		21 53	22 01		22 08	22 16		22 23	22 31			22 38	22 46		22 53
Vauxhall	⊖ d		21 42	21 50	21 45	21 57	22 05		22 12	22 20	22 15	22 27	22 35			22 42	22 50	22 45	22 57
London Waterloo ■	⊖ a		21 46	21 56	21 49	22 02	22 11	22 04	22 16	22 26	22 19	22 32	22 41	22 34		22 46	22 56	22 49	23 02

Table 149

Mondays to Fridays
from 27 September

Reading, Guildford, Ascot, Weybridge, Windsor, Kingston, Richmond and Hounslow - London

		SW ■	SW	SW	SW	SW ■	SW ■	SW	SW	SW	SW	SW	SW ■	SW	SW ■	SW ■	SW
Reading ■	d	21 39				22 09							22 39		23 12		
Earley	d	21 44				22 14							22 44		23 17		
Winnersh Triangle	d	21 46				22 16							22 46		23 19		
Winnersh	d	21 48				22 18							22 48		23 21		
Wokingham	d	21 53				22 23							22 53		23 26		
Bracknell	d	21 59				22 29							22 59		23 32		
Martins Heron	d	22 02				22 32							23 02		23 35		
Guildford	d						22 00									23 00	
Wanborough	d						22 06									23 06	
Ash ■	d						22 10									23 10	
Aldershot	a						22 17									23 17	
	d						22 30									23 30	
Ash Vale	d						22 34									23 34	
Frimley	d						22 40									23 40	
Camberley	a						22 44									23 44	
	d						22 48									23 48	
Bagshot	d						22 53									23 53	
Ascot ■	d	22 07				22 37	23a00						23 07		23 40	00a01	
Sunningdale	d	22 10				22 40							23 10		23 43		
Longcross	d																
Woking	d																
West Byfleet	d																
Byfleet & New Haw	d																
Weybridge	d			22 03					22 33		23 03						23 33
Addlestone	d			22 07					22 37		23 07						23 37
Chertsey	d			22 10					22 40		23 10						23 40
Virginia Water	a	22 19		22 15		22 49			22 45		23 15		23 19		23 49		23 45
	d	22 19		22 24		22 49			22 54		23 24		23 19		23 49		23 54
Egham	d	22 23		22 27		22 53			22 57		23 27		23 23		23 53		23 57
Windsor & Eton Riverside	d				22 21					22 53		23 23					
Datchet	d				22 25					22 56		23 26					
Sunnymeads	d				22 28					22 59		23 29					
Wraysbury	d				22 32					23 02		23 32					
Staines	d	22 29		22 33	22 38	22 59			23 03	23 08	23a32	23a37	23 29		23 59		00a02
Ashford (Surrey)	d			22 36	22 41				23 06	23 11							
Feltham	d	22 35		22 41	22 46	23 05			23 11	23 16			23 35		00 05		
Whitton	d				22 50					23 20							
Kingston	d		22 29					22 59						23 29			
Hampton Wick	d		22 31					23 01						23 31			
Teddington	d		22 35					23 05						23 35			
Fulwell	d																
Strawberry Hill	d		22 38					23 08						23 38			
Twickenham	a	22 40	22 42		22 53	23 10		23 12		23 23			23 40	23 42	00 10		
	d	22 41	22 43		22 53	23 11		23 13		23 23			23 41	23 43	00 11		
St Margarets	d		22 45					23 15						23 45			
Richmond	⊖ d	22 45	22 49		22 58	23 15		23 19		23 28			23 45	23 49	00 15		
North Sheen	d		22 51					23 21						23 51			
Mortlake	d		22 53					23 23						23 53			
Hounslow	d			22 46					23 16								
Isleworth	d			22 49					23 19								
Syon Lane	d			22 51					23 21								
Brentford	d			22 54					23 24								
Kew Bridge	d			22 56					23 26								
Chiswick	d			22 59					23 29								
Barnes Bridge	d			23 01					23 31								
Barnes	d		22 56	23 04				23 26	23 34					23 56			
Putney	d		22 59	23 07	23 04			23 29	23 37	23 34				23 59			
Wandsworth Town	d		23 02	23 10				23 32	23 40					00 02			
Clapham Junction ■	d	22 54	23 05	23 13	23 09	23 24		23 35	23 43	23 39			23 54	00 05	00 24		
Queenstown Rd.(Battersea)	d		23 08	23 16				23 38	23 46					00 08			
Vauxhall	⊖ d		23 12	23 20	23 15			23 42	23 50	23 45				00 12			
London Waterloo ■	⊖ a	23 04	23 16	23 26	23 19	23 34		23 46	23 56	23 49			00 04	00 16	00 32		

Table 149

Saturdays

29 May to 25 September

Reading, Guildford, Ascot, Weybridge, Windsor, Kingston, Richmond and Hounslow - London

		SW	SW ■	SW	SW ■	SW	SW	SW	SW	SW	SW	SW	SW	SW ■	SW ■	SW	SW	SW	SW ■	SW
Reading ■	d		22p42		23p12									05 42					06 12	
Earley	d		22p47		23p17									05 47					06 17	
Winnersh Triangle	d		22p49		23p19									05 49					06 19	
Winnersh	d		22p51		23p21									05 51					06 21	
Wokingham	d		22p56		23p26									05 56					06 26	
Bracknell	d		23p02		23p32									06 02					06 32	
Martins Heron	d		23p05		23p35									06 05					06 35	
Guildford	d																			
Wanborough	d																			
Ash ■	d																			
Aldershot	a																			
	d														06 00					
Ash Vale	d														06 04					
Frimley	d														06 10					
Camberley	a														06 14					
	d														06 18					
Bagshot	d														06 23					
Ascot ■	d		23p10		23p40									06 10	06a30				06 40	
Sunningdale	d		23p13		23p43									06 13					06 43	
Longcross	d																			
Woking	d										05 25									
West Byfleet	d										05 30									
Byfleet & New Haw	d										05 33									
Weybridge	d																			
Addlestone	d										05 37									
Chertsey	d										05 40									
Virginia Water	a		23p19		23p49						05 45			06 19					06 49	
	d		23p19		23p49						05 54			06 19					06 49	
Egham	d		23p23		23p53						05 57			06 23					06 53	
Windsor & Eton Riverside	d											05 53					06 23			
Datchet	d											05 56					06 26			
Sunnymeads	d											05 59					06 29			
Wraysbury	d											06 02					06 32			
Staines	d		23p29		23p59	04 58		05 37			06 03	06 08		06 29			06 38	06 33	06 59	
Ashford (Surrey)	d					05 01		05 40			06 06	06 11					06 41	06 36		
Feltham	d		23p35		00 05	05 06		05 45			06 11	06 16		06 35			06 46	06 41	07 05	
Whitton	d					05 10		05 49	05 41			06 20					06 50			
Kingston	d			23p29						05 59						06 29				06 59
Hampton Wick	d			23p31						06 01						06 31				07 01
Teddington	d			23p35						06 05						06 35				07 05
Fulwell	d																			
Strawberry Hill	d			23p38			05 38			06 08						06 38				07 08
Twickenham	a	23p33	23p40	23p42	00 10	05 13	05 41	05 52		06 12		06 23	06 33	06 40		06 42	06 53		07 10	07 12
	d	23p34	23p41	23p43	00 11	05 13	05 43	05 53		06 13		06 23	06 34	06 41		06 43	06 53		07 11	07 13
St Margarets	d			23p45		05 15	05 45			06 15						06 45				07 15
Richmond ⊖	d		23p45	23p49	00 15	05 19	05 49	05 58		06 19		06 28		06 45		06 49	06 58		07 15	07 19
North Sheen	d			23p51		05 21	05 51			06 21						06 51				07 21
Mortlake	d			23p53		05 23	05 53			06 23						06 53				07 23
Hounslow	d								05 46		06 16							06 46		
Isleworth	d								05 49		06 19							06 49		
Syon Lane	d								05 51		06 21							06 51		
Brentford	d								05 54		06 24							06 54		
Kew Bridge	d								05 56		06 26							06 56		
Chiswick	d								05 59		06 29							06 59		
Barnes Bridge	d								06 01		06 31							07 01		
Barnes	d			23p56		05 26	05 56		06 04	06 26	06 34					06 56		07 04		07 26
Putney	d			23p59		05 29	05 59	06 04	06 07	06 29	06 37	06 34				06 59	07 04	07 07		07 29
Wandsworth Town	d			00 02		05 32	06 02		06 10	06 32	06 40					07 02		07 10		07 32
Clapham Junction ■	d		23p54	00 05	00 24	05 35	06 05	06 09	06 13	06 35	06 43	06 39		06 54		07 05	07 09	07 13	07 24	07 35
Queenstown Rd.(Battersea)	d			00 08		05 38	06 08		06 16	06 38	06 46					07 08		07 16		07 38
Vauxhall ⊖	d	00 17		00 12		05 42	06 12	06 15	06 20	06 42	06 50	06 45	07 14			07 12	07 15	07 20		07 42
London Waterloo ■ ⊖	a	00 23	00 04	00 16	00 32	05 46	06 16	06 19	06 26	06 46	06 56	06 49	07 19	07 04		07 16	07 19	07 26	07 34	07 46

Table 149

Saturdays

29 May to 25 September

Reading, Guildford, Ascot, Weybridge, Windsor, Kingston, Richmond and Hounslow - London

		SW	SW	SW	SW ■	SW ■	SW	SW	SW	SW	SW	SW ■	SW ■	SW	SW	SW	SW	SW	SW ■	SW ■
Reading ■	d				06 42							07 12							07 42	
Earley	d				06 47							07 17							07 47	
Winnersh Triangle	d				06 49							07 19							07 49	
Winnersh	d				06 51							07 21							07 51	
Wokingham	d				06 56							07 26							07 56	
Bracknell	d				07 02							07 32							08 02	
Martins Heron	d				07 05							07 35							08 05	
Guildford	d					06 30							07 00							07 30
Wanborough	d					06 36							07 06							07 36
Ash ■	d					06 40							07 10							07 40
Aldershot	a					06 47							07 17							07 47
	d					07 00							07 30							08 00
Ash Vale	d					07 04							07 34							08 04
Frimley	d					07 10							07 40							08 10
Camberley	a					07 14							07 44							08 14
	d					07 18							07 48							08 18
Bagshot	d					07 23							07 53							08 23
Ascot ■	d				07 10	07a30						07 40	08a00						08 10	08a30
Sunningdale	d				07 13							07 43							08 13	
Longcross	d																			
Woking	d																			
West Byfleet	d																			
Byfleet & New Haw	d																			
Weybridge	d	06 33						07 03							07 33					
Addlestone	d	06 37						07 07							07 37					
Chertsey	d	06 40						07 10							07 40					
Virginia Water	a	06 45			07 19			07 15				07 49			07 45				08 19	
	d	06 54			07 19			07 24				07 49			07 54				08 19	
Egham	d	06 57			07 23			07 27				07 53			07 57				08 23	
Windsor & Eton Riverside	d		06 53						07 23							07 53				
Datchet	d		06 56						07 26							07 56				
Sunnymeads	d		06 59						07 29							07 59				
Wraysbury	d		07 02						07 32							08 02				
Staines	d	07 03	07 08		07 29			07 33	07 38			07 59			08 03	08 08			08 29	
Ashford (Surrey)	d	07 06	07 11					07 36	07 41						08 06	08 11				
Feltham	d	07 11	07 16		07 35			07 41	07 46			08 05			08 11	08 16			08 35	
Whitton	d		07 20						07 50		07 50					08 20	08 23	08 20		
Kingston	d						07 29							07 59						
Hampton Wick	d						07 31							08 01						
Teddington	d						07 35							08 05						
Fulwell	d																			
Strawberry Hill	d						07 38							08 08						
Twickenham	a		07 23		07 40		07 42		07 53			08 10		08 12		08 23	08 26		08 40	
	d		07 23		07 41		07 43		07 53	07 58		08 11		08 13		08 23	08 28		08 41	
St Margarets	d						07 45			08 00				08 15			08 30			
Richmond ⊖	d		07 28		07 45		07 49		07 58	08 04		08 15		08 19		08 28	08 34		08 45	
North Sheen	d						07 51			08 06				08 21			08 36			
Mortlake	d						07 53			08 08				08 23			08 38			
Hounslow	d	07 16		07 31				07 46			08 01				08 16			08 31		
Isleworth	d	07 19		07 34				07 49			08 04				08 19			08 34		
Syon Lane	d	07 21		07 36				07 51			08 06				08 21			08 36		
Brentford	d	07 24		07 39				07 54			08 09				08 24			08 39		
Kew Bridge	d	07 26		07 41				07 56			08 11				08 26			08 41		
Chiswick	d	07 29		07 44				07 59			08 14				08 29			08 44		
Barnes Bridge	d	07 31		07 46				08 01			08 16				08 31			08 46		
Barnes	d	07 34		07 49			07 56	08 04		08 11	08 19			08 26	08 34		08 41	08 49		
Putney	d	07 37	07 34	07 52			07 59	08 07	08 04	08 14	08 22			08 29	08 37	08 34	08 44	08 52		
Wandsworth Town	d	07 40		07 55			08 02	08 10		08 17	08 25			08 32	08 40		08 47	08 55		
Clapham Junction ■	d	07 43	07 39	07 58	07 54		08 05	08 13	08 09	08 20	08 28	08 24		08 35	08 43	08 39	08 50	08 58	08 54	
Queenstown Rd.(Battersea)	d	07 46		08 01			08 08	08 16		08 23	08 31			08 38	08 46		08 53	09 01		
Vauxhall ⊖	d	07 50	07 45	08 05			08 12	08 20	08 15	08 27	08 35			08 42	08 50	08 45	08 57	09 05		
London Waterloo ■ ⊖	a	07 56	07 49	08 11	08 04		08 16	08 26	08 19	08 32	08 41	08 34		08 46	08 56	08 49	09 02	09 11	09 04	

Table 149

Saturdays
29 May to 25 September

Reading, Guildford, Ascot, Weybridge, Windsor, Kingston, Richmond and Hounslow - London

		SW	SW	SW	SW	SW	SW ■	SW ■	SW	SW	SW	SW	SW	SW ■	SW ■	SW	SW	SW	SW	SW
Reading ■	d						08 12							08 42						
Earley	d						08 17							08 47						
Winnersh Triangle	d						08 19							08 49						
Winnersh	d						08 21							08 51						
Wokingham	d						08 26							08 56						
Bracknell	d						08 32							09 02						
Martins Heron	d						08 35							09 05						
Guildford	d							08 00							08 30					
Wanborough	d							08 06							08 36					
Ash ■	d							08 10							08 40					
Aldershot	a							08 17							08 47					
	d							08 30							09 00					
Ash Vale	d							08 34							09 04					
Frimley	d							08 40							09 10					
Camberley	a							08 44							09 14					
	d							08 48							09 18					
Bagshot	d							08 53							09 23					
Ascot ■	d						08 40	09a00						09 10	09a30					
Sunningdale	d						08 43							09 13						
Longcross	d																			
Woking	d																			
West Byfleet	d																			
Byfleet & New Haw	d																			
Weybridge	d		08 03							08 33							09 03			
Addlestone	d		08 07							08 37							09 07			
Chertsey	d		08 10							08 40							09 10			
Virginia Water	a		08 15				08 49			08 45				09 19			09 15			
	d		08 24				08 49			08 54				09 19			09 24			
Egham	d		08 27				08 53			08 57				09 23			09 27			
Windsor & Eton Riverside	d			08 23							08 53							09 23		
Datchet	d			08 26							08 56							09 26		
Sunnymeads	d			08 29							08 59							09 29		
Wraysbury	d			08 32							09 02							09 32		
Staines	d		08 33	08 38			08 59			09 03	09 08			09 29			09 33	09 38		
Ashford (Surrey)	d		08 36	08 41						09 06	09 11						09 36	09 41		
Feltham	d		08 41	08 46			09 05			09 11	09 16			09 35			09 41	09 46		
Whitton	d			08 50	08 53	08 50					09 20	09 23	09 20					09 50	09 53	09 50
Kingston	d	08 29							08 59							09 29				
Hampton Wick	d	08 31							09 01							09 31				
Teddington	d	08 35							09 05							09 35				
Fulwell	d																			
Strawberry Hill	d	08 38							09 08							09 38				
Twickenham	a	08 42		08 53	08 56		09 10		09 12		09 23	09 26		09 40		09 42		09 53	09 56	
	d	08 43		08 53	08 58		09 11		09 13		09 23	09 28		09 41		09 43		09 53	09 58	
St Margarets	d	08 45			09 00				09 15			09 30				09 45			10 00	
Richmond ⊖	d	08 49		08 58	09 04		09 15		09 19		09 28	09 34		09 45		09 49		09 58	10 04	
North Sheen	d	08 51			09 06				09 21			09 36				09 51			10 06	
Mortlake	d	08 53			09 08				09 23			09 38				09 53			10 08	
Hounslow	d		08 46			09 01				09 16			09 31				09 46			10 01
Isleworth	d		08 49			09 04				09 19			09 34				09 49			10 04
Syon Lane	d		08 51			09 06				09 21			09 36				09 51			10 06
Brentford	d		08 54			09 09				09 24			09 39				09 54			10 09
Kew Bridge	d		08 56			09 11				09 26			09 41				09 56			10 11
Chiswick	d		08 59			09 14				09 29			09 44				09 59			10 14
Barnes Bridge	d		09 01			09 16				09 31			09 46				10 01			10 16
Barnes	d	08 56	09 04		09 11	09 19			09 26	09 34		09 41	09 49			09 56	10 04		10 11	10 19
Putney	d	08 59	09 07	09 04	09 14	09 22			09 29	09 37	09 34	09 44	09 52			09 59	10 07	10 04	10 14	10 22
Wandsworth Town	d	09 02	09 10		09 17	09 25			09 32	09 40		09 47	09 55			10 02	10 10		10 17	10 25
Clapham Junction ■	d	09 05	09 13	09 09	09 20	09 28	09 24		09 35	09 43	09 39	09 50	09 58	09 54		10 05	10 13	10 09	10 20	10 28
Queenstown Rd.(Battersea)	d	09 08	09 16		09 23	09 31			09 38	09 46		09 53	10 01			10 08	10 16		10 23	10 31
Vauxhall ⊖	d	09 12	09 20	09 15	09 27	09 35			09 42	09 50	09 45	09 57	10 05			10 12	10 20	10 15	10 27	10 35
London Waterloo ■ ⊖	a	09 16	09 26	09 19	09 32	09 41	09 34		09 46	09 56	09 49	10 02	10 11	10 04		10 16	10 26	10 19	10 32	10 41

Table 149

Saturdays
29 May to 25 September

Reading, Guildford, Ascot, Weybridge, Windsor, Kingston, Richmond and Hounslow - London

		SW	SW ■	SW ■	SW	SW	SW	SW	SW	SW ■	SW ■	SW	SW	SW	SW	SW	SW ■	SW ■	SW	SW	SW
Reading ■	d		09 12							09 42							10 12				
Earley	d		09 17							09 47							10 17				
Winnersh Triangle	d		09 19							09 49							10 19				
Winnersh	d		09 21							09 51							10 21				
Wokingham	d		09 26							09 56							10 26				
Bracknell	d		09 32							10 02							10 32				
Martins Heron	d		09 35							10 05							10 35				
Guildford	d			09 00							09 30							10 00			
Wanborough	d			09 06							09 36							10 06			
Ash ■	d			09 10							09 40							10 10			
Aldershot	a			09 17							09 47							10 17			
	d			09 30							10 00							10 30			
Ash Vale	d			09 34							10 04							10 34			
Frimley	d			09 40							10 10							10 40			
Camberley	a			09 44							10 14							10 44			
	d			09 48							10 18							10 48			
Bagshot	d			09 53							10 23							10 53			
Ascot ■	d		09 40	10a00						10 10	10a30						10 40	11a00			
Sunningdale	d		09 43							10 13							10 43				
Longcross	d																				
Woking	d																				
West Byfleet	d																				
Byfleet & New Haw	d																				
Weybridge	d					09 33							10 03							10 33	
Addlestone	d					09 37							10 07							10 37	
Chertsey	d					09 40							10 10							10 40	
Virginia Water	a		09 49			09 45				10 19			10 15				10 49			10 45	
	d		09 49			09 54				10 19			10 24				10 49			10 54	
Egham	d		09 53			09 57				10 23			10 27				10 53			10 57	
Windsor & Eton Riverside	d						09 53							10 23							10 53
Datchet	d						09 56							10 26							10 56
Sunnymeads	d						09 59							10 29							10 59
Wraysbury	d						10 02							10 32							11 02
Staines	d		09 59			10 03	10 08			10 29			10 33	10 38			10 59			11 03	11 08
Ashford (Surrey)	d					10 06	10 11						10 36	10 41						11 06	11 11
Feltham	d		10 05			10 11	10 16			10 35			10 41	10 46			11 05			11 11	11 16
Whitton	d						10 20	10 23	10 20					10 50	10 53	10 50					11 20
Kingston	d				09 59							10 29							10 59		
Hampton Wick	d				10 01							10 31							11 01		
Teddington	d				10 05							10 35							11 05		
Fulwell	d																				
Strawberry Hill	d				10 08							10 38							11 08		
Twickenham	a	10 03	10 10		10 12		10 23	10 26		10 40		10 42		10 53	10 56		11 10		11 12		11 23
	d	10 04	10 11		10 13		10 23	10 28		10 41		10 43		10 53	10 58		11 11		11 13		11 23
St Margarets	d				10 15			10 30				10 45			11 00				11 15		
Richmond ⊖	d		10 15		10 19		10 28	10 34		10 45		10 49		10 58	11 04		11 15		11 19		11 28
North Sheen	d				10 21			10 36				10 51			11 06				11 21		
Mortlake	d				10 23			10 38				10 53			11 08				11 23		
Hounslow	d					10 16			10 31				10 46			11 01				11 16	
Isleworth	d					10 19			10 34				10 49			11 04				11 19	
Syon Lane	d					10 21			10 36				10 51			11 06				11 21	
Brentford	d					10 24			10 39				10 54			11 09				11 24	
Kew Bridge	d					10 26			10 41				10 56			11 11				11 26	
Chiswick	d					10 29			10 44				10 59			11 14				11 29	
Barnes Bridge	d					10 31			10 46				11 01			11 16				11 31	
Barnes	d				10 26	10 34		10 41	10 49			10 56	11 04		11 11	11 19			11 26	11 34	
Putney	d				10 29	10 37	10 34	10 44	10 52			10 59	11 07	11 04	11 14	11 22			11 29	11 37	11 34
Wandsworth Town	d				10 32	10 40		10 47	10 55			11 02	11 10		11 17	11 25			11 32	11 40	
Clapham Junction ■	d		10 24		10 35	10 43	10 39	10 50	10 58	10 54		11 05	11 13	11 09	11 20	11 28	11 24		11 35	11 43	11 39
Queenstown Rd.(Battersea)	d				10 38	10 46		10 53	11 01			11 08	11 16		11 23	11 31			11 38	11 46	
Vauxhall ⊖	d	10 44			10 42	10 50	10 45	10 57	11 05			11 12	11 20	11 15	11 27	11 35			11 42	11 50	11 45
London Waterloo ■ ⊖	a	10 49	10 34		10 46	10 56	10 49	11 02	11 11	11 04		11 16	11 26	11 19	11 32	11 41	11 34		11 46	11 56	11 49

Table 149

Saturdays
29 May to 25 September

Reading, Guildford, Ascot, Weybridge, Windsor, Kingston, Richmond and Hounslow - London

		SW	SW	SW ■	SW ■	SW	SW	SW	SW	SW	SW ■	SW ■	SW	SW	SW	SW	SW	SW ■	SW ■
Reading ■	d			10 42							11 12							11 42	
Earley	d			10 47							11 17							11 47	
Winnersh Triangle	d			10 49							11 19							11 49	
Winnersh	d			10 51							11 21							11 51	
Wokingham	d			10 56							11 26							11 56	
Bracknell	d			11 02							11 32							12 02	
Martins Heron	d			11 05							11 35							12 05	
Guildford	d				10 30							11 00							11 30
Wanborough	d				10 36							11 06							11 36
Ash ■	d				10 40							11 10							11 40
Aldershot	a				10 47							11 17							11 47
	d				11 00							11 30							12 00
Ash Vale	d				11 04							11 34							12 04
Frimley	d				11 10							11 40							12 10
Camberley	a				11 14							11 44							12 14
	d				11 18							11 48							12 18
Bagshot	d				11 23							11 53							12 23
Ascot ■	d			11 10	11a30						11 40	12a00						12 10	12a30
Sunningdale	d			11 13							11 43							12 13	
Longcross	d																		
Woking	d																		
West Byfleet	d																		
Byfleet & New Haw	d																		
Weybridge	d						11 03							11 33					
Addlestone	d						11 07							11 37					
Chertsey	d						11 10							11 40					
Virginia Water	a			11 19			11 15				11 49			11 45				12 19	
	d			11 19			11 24				11 49			11 54				12 19	
Egham	d			11 23			11 27				11 53			11 57				12 23	
Windsor & Eton Riverside	d							11 23							11 53				
Datchet	d							11 26							11 56				
Sunnymeads	d							11 29							11 59				
Wraysbury	d							11 32							12 02				
Staines	d			11 29			11 33	11 38			11 59			12 03	12 08			12 29	
Ashford (Surrey)	d						11 36	11 41						12 06	12 11				
Feltham	d			11 35			11 41	11 46			12 05			12 11	12 16			12 35	
Whitton	d	11 23	11 20					11 50	11 53	11 50					12 20	12 23	12 20		
Kingston	d					11 29							11 59						
Hampton Wick	d					11 31							12 01						
Teddington	d					11 35							12 05						
Fulwell	d																		
Strawberry Hill	d					11 38							12 08						
Twickenham	a	11 26		11 40		11 42		11 53	11 56		12 10		12 12		12 23	12 27		12 40	
	d	11 28		11 41		11 43		11 53	11 58		12 11		12 13		12 23	12 28		12 41	
St Margarets	d	11 30				11 45			12 00				12 15			12 30			
Richmond ⊖	d	11 34		11 45		11 49		11 58	12 04		12 15		12 19		12 28	12 34		12 45	
North Sheen	d	11 36				11 51			12 06				12 21			12 36			
Mortlake	d	11 38				11 53			12 08				12 23			12 38			
Hounslow	d		11 31				11 46			12 01				12 16			12 31		
Isleworth	d		11 34				11 49			12 04				12 19			12 34		
Syon Lane	d		11 36				11 51			12 06				12 21			12 36		
Brentford	d		11 39				11 54			12 09				12 24			12 39		
Kew Bridge	d		11 41				11 56			12 11				12 26			12 41		
Chiswick	d		11 44				11 59			12 14				12 29			12 44		
Barnes Bridge	d		11 46				12 01			12 16				12 31			12 46		
Barnes	d	11 41	11 49			11 56	12 04		12 11	12 19			12 26	12 34		12 41	12 49		
Putney	d	11 44	11 52			11 59	12 07	12 04	12 14	12 22			12 29	12 37	12 34	12 44	12 52		
Wandsworth Town	d	11 47	11 55			12 02	12 10		12 17	12 25			12 32	12 40		12 47	12 55		
Clapham Junction ■	d	11 50	11 58	11 54		12 05	12 13	12 09	12 20	12 28	12 24		12 35	12 43	12 39	12 50	12 58	12 54	
Queenstown Rd.(Battersea)	d	11 53	12 01			12 08	12 16		12 23	12 31			12 38	12 46		12 53	13 01		
Vauxhall ⊖	d	11 57	12 05			12 12	12 20	12 15	12 27	12 35			12 42	12 50	12 45	12 57	13 05		
London Waterloo ■ ⊖	a	12 02	12 11	12 04		12 16	12 26	12 19	12 32	12 41	12 34		12 46	12 56	12 49	13 02	13 11	13 04	

Table 149

Saturdays
29 May to 25 September

Reading, Guildford, Ascot, Weybridge, Windsor, Kingston, Richmond and Hounslow - London

		SW	SW	SW	SW	SW	SW ■	SW ■	SW	SW	SW	SW	SW	SW ■	SW ■	SW	SW	SW	SW	SW
Reading ■	d						12 12							12 42						
Earley	d						12 17							12 47						
Winnersh Triangle	d						12 19							12 49						
Winnersh	d						12 21							12 51						
Wokingham	d						12 26							12 56						
Bracknell	d						12 32							13 02						
Martins Heron	d						12 35							13 05						
Guildford	d							12 00							12 30					
Wanborough	d							12 06							12 36					
Ash ■	d							12 10							12 40					
Aldershot	a							12 17							12 47					
	d							12 30							13 00					
Ash Vale	d							12 34							13 04					
Frimley	d							12 40							13 10					
Camberley	a							12 44							13 14					
	d							12 48							13 18					
Bagshot	d							12 53							13 23					
Ascot ■	d						12 40	13a00						13 10	13a30					
Sunningdale	d						12 43							13 13						
Longcross	d																			
Woking	d																			
West Byfleet	d																			
Byfleet & New Haw	d																			
Weybridge	d		12 03							12 33							13 03			
Addlestone	d		12 07							12 37							13 07			
Chertsey	d		12 10							12 40							13 10			
Virginia Water	a		12 15				12 49			12 45				13 19			13 15			
	d		12 24				12 49			12 54				13 19			13 24			
Egham	d		12 27				12 53			12 57				13 23			13 27			
Windsor & Eton Riverside	d			12 23							12 53							13 23		
Datchet	d			12 26							12 56							13 26		
Sunnymeads	d			12 29							12 59							13 29		
Wraysbury	d			12 32							13 02							13 32		
Staines	d		12 33	12 38			12 59			13 03	13 08			13 29			13 33	13 38		
Ashford (Surrey)	d		12 36	12 41						13 06	13 11						13 36	13 41		
Feltham	d		12 41	12 46			13 05			13 11	13 16			13 35			13 41	13 46		
Whitton	d			12 50	12 53	12 50					13 20	13 23	13 20					13 50	13 53	13 50
Kingston	d	12 29							12 59							13 29				
Hampton Wick	d	12 31							13 01							13 31				
Teddington	d	12 35							13 05							13 35				
Fulwell	d																			
Strawberry Hill	d	12 38							13 08							13 38				
Twickenham	a	12 42		12 53	12 56		13 10		13 12		13 23	13 26		13 40		13 42		13 53	13 56	
	d	12 43		12 53	12 58		13 11		13 13		13 23	13 28		13 41		13 43		13 53	13 58	
St Margarets	d	12 45			13 00				13 15			13 30				13 45			14 00	
Richmond ⊖	d	12 49		12 58	13 04		13 15		13 19		13 28	13 34		13 45		13 49		13 58	14 04	
North Sheen	d	12 51			13 06				13 21			13 36				13 51			14 06	
Mortlake	d	12 53			13 08				13 23			13 38				13 53			14 08	
Hounslow	d		12 46			13 01				13 16			13 31				13 46			14 01
Isleworth	d		12 49			13 04				13 19			13 34				13 49			14 04
Syon Lane	d		12 51			13 06				13 21			13 36				13 51			14 06
Brentford	d		12 54			13 09				13 24			13 39				13 54			14 09
Kew Bridge	d		12 56			13 11				13 26			13 41				13 56			14 11
Chiswick	d		12 59			13 14				13 29			13 44				13 59			14 14
Barnes Bridge	d		13 01			13 16				13 31			13 46				14 01			14 16
Barnes	d	12 56	13 04		13 11	13 19			13 26	13 34		13 41	13 49			13 56	14 04		14 11	14 19
Putney	d	12 59	13 07	13 04	13 14	13 22			13 29	13 37	13 34	13 44	13 52			13 59	14 07	14 04	14 14	14 22
Wandsworth Town	d	13 02	13 10		13 17	13 25			13 32	13 40		13 47	13 55			14 02	14 10		14 17	14 25
Clapham Junction ■	d	13 05	13 13	13 09	13 20	13 28	13 24		13 35	13 43	13 39	13 50	13 58	13 54		14 05	14 13	14 09	14 20	14 28
Queenstown Rd.(Battersea)	d	13 08	13 16		13 23	13 31			13 38	13 46		13 53	14 01			14 08	14 16		14 23	14 31
Vauxhall ⊖	d	13 12	13 20	13 15	13 27	13 35			13 42	13 50	13 45	13 57	14 05			14 12	14 20	14 15	14 27	14 35
London Waterloo ■ ⊖	a	13 16	13 26	13 19	13 32	13 41	13 34		13 46	13 56	13 49	14 02	14 11	14 04		14 16	14 26	14 19	14 32	14 41

Table 149

Saturdays

29 May to 25 September

Reading, Guildford, Ascot, Weybridge, Windsor, Kingston, Richmond and Hounslow - London

		SW ■1	SW ■1	SW	SW	SW		SW	SW		SW ■1	SW ■1	SW	SW	SW	SW		SW		SW ■1	SW ■1	SW	SW	SW	SW
Reading ■7	d	13 12									13 42									14 12					
Earley	d	13 17									13 47									14 17					
Winnersh Triangle	d	13 19									13 49									14 19					
Winnersh	d	13 21									13 51									14 21					
Wokingham	d	13 26									13 56									14 26					
Bracknell	d	13 32									14 02									14 32					
Martins Heron	d	13 35									14 05									14 35					
Guildford	d		13 00									13 30									14 00				
Wanborough	d		13 06									13 36									14 06				
Ash ■5	d		13 10									13 40									14 10				
Aldershot	a		13 17									13 47									14 17				
	d		13 30									14 00									14 30				
Ash Vale	d		13 34									14 04									14 34				
Frimley	d		13 40									14 10									14 40				
Camberley	a		13 44									14 14									14 44				
	d		13 48									14 18									14 48				
Bagshot	d		13 53									14 23									14 53				
Ascot ■3	d	13 40	14a00								14 10	14a30								14 40	15a00				
Sunningdale	d	13 43									14 13									14 43					
Longcross	d																								
Woking	d																								
West Byfleet	d																								
Byfleet & New Haw	d																								
Weybridge	d				13 33									14 03									14 33		
Addlestone	d				13 37									14 07									14 37		
Chertsey	d				13 40									14 10									14 40		
Virginia Water	a	13 49			13 45						14 19			14 15						14 49			14 45		
	d	13 49			13 54						14 19			14 24						14 49			14 54		
Egham	d	13 53			13 57						14 23			14 27						14 53			14 57		
Windsor & Eton Riverside	d					13 53									14 23									14 53	
Datchet	d					13 56									14 26									14 56	
Sunnymeads	d					13 59									14 29									14 59	
Wraysbury	d					14 02									14 32									15 02	
Staines	d	13 59			14 03	14 08					14 29			14 33	14 38					14 59			15 03	15 08	
Ashford (Surrey)	d				14 06	14 11								14 36	14 41								15 06	15 11	
Feltham	d	14 05			14 11	14 16					14 35			14 41	14 46					15 05			15 11	15 16	
Whitton	d					14 20		14 23	14 20						14 50	14 53		14 50						15 20	15 23
Kingston	d			13 59									14 29									14 59			
Hampton Wick	d			14 01									14 31									15 01			
Teddington	d			14 05									14 35									15 05			
Fulwell	d																								
Strawberry Hill	d			14 08									14 38									15 08			
Twickenham	a	14 10		14 12		14 23		14 26			14 40		14 42		14 53	14 56				15 10		15 12		15 23	15 26
	d	14 11		14 13		14 23		14 28			14 41		14 43		14 53	14 58				15 11		15 13		15 23	15 28
St Margarets	d			14 15				14 30					14 45			15 00						15 15			15 30
Richmond ⊖	d	14 15		14 19		14 28		14 34			14 45		14 49		14 58	15 04				15 15		15 19		15 28	15 34
North Sheen	d			14 21				14 36					14 51			15 06						15 21			15 36
Mortlake	d			14 23				14 38					14 53			15 08						15 23			15 38
Hounslow	d				14 16				14 31					14 46				15 01					15 16		
Isleworth	d				14 19				14 34					14 49				15 04					15 19		
Syon Lane	d				14 21				14 36					14 51				15 06					15 21		
Brentford	d				14 24				14 39					14 54				15 09					15 24		
Kew Bridge	d				14 26				14 41					14 56				15 11					15 26		
Chiswick	d				14 29				14 44					14 59				15 14					15 29		
Barnes Bridge	d				14 31				14 46					15 01				15 16					15 31		
Barnes	d			14 26	14 34			14 41	14 49				14 56	15 04		15 11		15 19				15 26	15 34		15 41
Putney	d			14 29	14 37	14 34		14 44	14 52				14 59	15 07	15 04	15 14		15 22				15 29	15 37	15 34	15 44
Wandsworth Town	d			14 32	14 40			14 47	14 55				15 02	15 10		15 17		15 25				15 32	15 40		15 47
Clapham Junction ■10	d	14 24		14 35	14 43	14 39		14 50	14 58		14 54		15 05	15 13	15 09	15 20		15 28		15 24		15 35	15 43	15 39	15 50
Queenstown Rd.(Battersea)	d			14 38	14 46			14 53	15 01				15 08	15 16		15 23		15 31				15 38	15 46		15 53
Vauxhall ⊖	d			14 42	14 50	14 45		14 57	15 05				15 12	15 20	15 15	15 27		15 35				15 42	15 50	15 45	15 57
London Waterloo ■15 ⊖	a	14 34		14 46	14 56	14 49		15 02	15 11		15 04		15 16	15 26	15 19	15 32		15 41		15 34		15 46	15 56	15 49	16 02

Table 149

Saturdays

29 May to 25 September

Reading, Guildford, Ascot, Weybridge, Windsor, Kingston, Richmond and Hounslow - London

		SW			SW ■1	SW ■1	SW	SW	SW	SW	SW			SW ■1	SW ■1	SW	SW	SW	SW	SW		SW ■1		SW ■1	SW
Reading ■7	d				14 42									15 12								15 42			
Earley	d				14 47									15 17								15 47			
Winnersh Triangle	d				14 49									15 19								15 49			
Winnersh	d				14 51									15 21								15 51			
Wokingham	d				14 56									15 26								15 56			
Bracknell	d				15 02									15 32								16 02			
Martins Heron	d				15 05									15 35								16 05			
Guildford	d					14 30									15 00									15 30	
Wanborough	d					14 36									15 06									15 36	
Ash ■5	d					14 40									15 10									15 40	
Aldershot	a					14 47									15 17									15 47	
	d					15 00									15 30									16 00	
Ash Vale	d					15 04									15 34									16 04	
Frimley	d					15 10									15 40									16 10	
Camberley	a					15 14									15 44									16 14	
	d					15 18									15 48									16 18	
Bagshot	d					15 23									15 53									16 23	
Ascot ■3	d				15 10	15a30								15 40	16a00							16 10		16a30	
Sunningdale	d				15 13									15 43								16 13			
Longcross	d																								
Woking	d																								
West Byfleet	d																								
Byfleet & New Haw	d																								
Weybridge	d							15 03									15 33								
Addlestone	d							15 07									15 37								
Chertsey	d							15 10									15 40								
Virginia Water	a				15 19			15 15						15 49			15 45					16 19			
	d				15 19			15 24						15 49			15 54					16 19			
Egham	d				15 23			15 27						15 53			15 57					16 23			
Windsor & Eton Riverside	d								15 23									15 53							
Datchet	d								15 26									15 56							
Sunnymeads	d								15 29									15 59							
Wraysbury	d								15 32									16 02							
Staines	d				15 29			15 33	15 38					15 59			16 03	16 08				16 29			
Ashford (Surrey)	d							15 36	15 41								16 06	16 11							
Feltham	d				15 35			15 41	15 46					16 05			16 11	16 16				16 35			
Whitton	d	15 20							15 50	15 53	15 50							16 20	16 23	16 20					
Kingston	d						15 29									15 59									16 29
Hampton Wick	d						15 31									16 01									16 31
Teddington	d						15 35									16 05									16 35
Fulwell	d																								
Strawberry Hill	d						15 38									16 08									16 38
Twickenham	a				15 40		15 42		15 53	15 56				16 10		16 12		16 23	16 26			16 40			16 42
	d				15 41		15 43		15 53	15 58				16 11		16 13		16 23	16 28			16 41			16 43
St Margarets	d						15 45			16 00						16 15			16 30						16 45
Richmond ⊖	d				15 45		15 49		15 58	16 04				16 15		16 19		16 28	16 34			16 45			16 49
North Sheen	d						15 51			16 06						16 21			16 36						16 51
Mortlake	d						15 53			16 08						16 23			16 38						16 53
Hounslow	d	15 31						15 46			16 01						16 16			16 31					
Isleworth	d	15 34						15 49			16 04						16 19			16 34					
Syon Lane	d	15 36						15 51			16 06						16 21			16 36					
Brentford	d	15 39						15 54			16 09						16 24			16 39					
Kew Bridge	d	15 41						15 56			16 11						16 26			16 41					
Chiswick	d	15 44						15 59			16 14						16 29			16 44					
Barnes Bridge	d	15 46						16 01			16 16						16 31			16 46					
Barnes	d	15 49					15 56	16 04		16 11	16 19					16 26	16 34		16 41	16 49					16 56
Putney	d	15 52					15 59	16 07	16 04	16 14	16 22					16 29	16 37	16 34	16 44	16 52					16 59
Wandsworth Town	d	15 55					16 02	16 10		16 17	16 25					16 32	16 40		16 47	16 55					17 02
Clapham Junction ■10	d	15 58			15 54		16 05	16 13	16 09	16 20	16 28			16 24		16 35	16 43	16 39	16 50	16 58		16 54			17 05
Queenstown Rd.(Battersea)	d	16 01					16 08	16 16		16 23	16 31					16 38	16 46		16 53	17 01					17 08
Vauxhall ⊖	d	16 05					16 12	16 20	16 15	16 27	16 35					16 42	16 50	16 45	16 57	17 05					17 12
London Waterloo ■15 ⊖	a	16 11			16 04		16 16	16 26	16 19	16 32	16 41			16 34		16 46	16 56	16 49	17 02	17 11		17 04			17 16

Table 149

Saturdays

29 May to 25 September

Reading, Guildford, Ascot, Weybridge, Windsor, Kingston, Richmond and Hounslow - London

		SW	SW	SW	SW	SW ■	SW ■	SW	SW	SW	SW	SW	SW ■	SW ■	SW	SW	SW	SW	SW	SW ■
Reading 7	d					16 12							16 42							17 12
Earley	d					16 17							16 47							17 17
Winnersh Triangle	d					16 19							16 49							17 19
Winnersh	d					16 21							16 51							17 21
Wokingham	d					16 26							16 56							17 26
Bracknell	d					16 32							17 02							17 32
Martins Heron	d					16 35							17 05							17 35
Guildford	d						16 00							16 30						
Wanborough	d						16 06							16 36						
Ash 5	d						16 10							16 40						
Aldershot	a						16 17							16 47						
	d						16 30							17 00						
Ash Vale	d						16 34							17 04						
Frimley	d						16 40							17 10						
Camberley	a						16 44							17 14						
	d						16 48							17 18						
Bagshot	d						16 53							17 23						
Ascot 3	d					16 40	17a00						17 10	17a30						17 40
Sunningdale	d					16 43							17 13							17 43
Longcross	d																			
Woking	d																			
West Byfleet	d																			
Byfleet & New Haw	d																			
Weybridge	d	16 03							16 33							17 03				
Addlestone	d	16 07							16 37							17 07				
Chertsey	d	16 10							16 40							17 10				
Virginia Water	a	16 15				16 49			16 45				17 19			17 15				17 49
	d	16 24				16 49			16 54				17 19			17 24				17 49
Egham	d	16 27				16 53			16 57				17 23			17 27				17 53
Windsor & Eton Riverside	d		16 23							16 53							17 23			
Datchet	d		16 26							16 56							17 26			
Sunnymeads	d		16 29							16 59							17 29			
Wraysbury	d		16 32							17 02							17 32			
Staines	d	16 33	16 38			16 59			17 03	17 08			17 29			17 33	17 38			17 59
Ashford (Surrey)	d	16 36	16 41						17 06	17 11						17 36	17 41			
Feltham	d	16 41	16 46			17 05			17 11	17 16			17 35			17 41	17 46			18 05
Whitton	d		16 50	16 53	16 50					17 20	17 23	17 20					17 50	17 53	17 50	
Kingston	d							16 59							17 29					
Hampton Wick	d							17 01							17 31					
Teddington	d							17 05							17 35					
Fulwell	d																			
Strawberry Hill	d							17 08							17 38					
Twickenham	a		16 53	16 56		17 10		17 12		17 23	17 26		17 40		17 42		17 53	17 56		18 10
	d		16 53	16 58		17 11		17 13		17 23	17 28		17 41		17 43		17 53	17 58		18 11
St Margarets	d			17 00				17 15			17 30				17 45			18 00		
Richmond ⊖	d		16 58	17 04		17 15		17 19		17 28	17 34		17 45		17 49		17 58	18 04		18 15
North Sheen	d			17 06				17 21			17 36				17 51			18 06		
Mortlake	d			17 08				17 23			17 38				17 53			18 08		
Hounslow	d	16 46			17 01				17 16			17 31				17 46			18 01	
Isleworth	d	16 49			17 04				17 19			17 34				17 49			18 04	
Syon Lane	d	16 51			17 06				17 21			17 36				17 51			18 06	
Brentford	d	16 54			17 09				17 24			17 39				17 54			18 09	
Kew Bridge	d	16 56			17 11				17 26			17 41				17 56			18 11	
Chiswick	d	16 59			17 14				17 29			17 44				17 59			18 14	
Barnes Bridge	d	17 01			17 16				17 31			17 46				18 01			18 16	
Barnes	d	17 04		17 11	17 19			17 26	17 34		17 41	17 49			17 56	18 04		18 11	18 19	
Putney	d	17 07	17 04	17 14	17 22			17 29	17 37	17 34	17 44	17 52			17 59	18 07	18 04	18 14	18 22	
Wandsworth Town	d	17 10		17 17	17 25			17 32	17 40		17 47	17 55			18 02	18 10		18 17	18 25	
Clapham Junction 10	d	17 13	17 09	17 20	17 28	17 24		17 35	17 43	17 39	17 50	17 58	17 54		18 05	18 13	18 09	18 20	18 28	18 24
Queenstown Rd.(Battersea)	d	17 16		17 23	17 31			17 38	17 46		17 53	18 01			18 08	18 16		18 23	18 31	
Vauxhall ⊖	d	17 20	17 15	17 27	17 35			17 42	17 50	17 45	17 57	18 05			18 12	18 20	18 15	18 27	18 35	
London Waterloo 15 ⊖	a	17 26	17 19	17 32	17 41	17 34		17 46	17 56	17 49	18 02	18 11	18 04		18 16	18 26	18 19	18 32	18 41	18 34

Table 149

Saturdays

29 May to 25 September

Reading, Guildford, Ascot, Weybridge, Windsor, Kingston, Richmond and Hounslow - London

		SW ■	SW	SW	SW	SW	SW	SW ■	SW ■	SW	SW	SW	SW	SW	SW ■	SW ■	SW	SW	SW	SW
Reading 7	d							17 42							18 12					
Earley	d							17 47							18 17					
Winnersh Triangle	d							17 49							18 19					
Winnersh	d							17 51							18 21					
Wokingham	d							17 56							18 26					
Bracknell	d							18 02							18 32					
Martins Heron	d							18 05							18 35					
Guildford	d	17 00							17 30							18 00				
Wanborough	d	17 06							17 36							18 06				
Ash 5	d	17 10							17 40							18 10				
Aldershot	a	17 17							17 47							18 17				
	d	17 30							18 00							18 30				
Ash Vale	d	17 34							18 04							18 34				
Frimley	d	17 40							18 10							18 40				
Camberley	a	17 44							18 14							18 44				
	d	17 48							18 18							18 48				
Bagshot	d	17 53							18 23							18 53				
Ascot 3	d	18a00						18 10	18a30						18 40	19a00				
Sunningdale	d							18 13							18 43					
Longcross	d																			
Woking	d																			
West Byfleet	d																			
Byfleet & New Haw	d																			
Weybridge	d			17 33							18 03							18 33		
Addlestone	d			17 37							18 07							18 37		
Chertsey	d			17 40							18 10							18 40		
Virginia Water	a			17 45				18 19			18 15				18 49			18 45		
	d			17 54				18 19			18 24				18 49			18 54		
Egham	d			17 57				18 23			18 27				18 53			18 57		
Windsor & Eton Riverside	d				17 53							18 23							18 53	
Datchet	d				17 56							18 26							18 56	
Sunnymeads	d				17 59							18 29							18 59	
Wraysbury	d				18 02							18 32							19 02	
Staines	d			18 03	18 08			18 29			18 33	18 38			18 59			19 03	19 08	
Ashford (Surrey)	d			18 06	18 11						18 36	18 41						19 06	19 11	
Feltham	d			18 11	18 16			18 35			18 41	18 46			19 05			19 11	19 16	
Whitton	d				18 20	18 23	18 20					18 50	18 53	18 50					19 20	19 23
Kingston	d		17 59							18 29							18 59			
Hampton Wick	d		18 01							18 31							19 01			
Teddington	d		18 05							18 35							19 05			
Fulwell	d																			
Strawberry Hill	d		18 08							18 38							19 08			
Twickenham	a		18 12		18 23	18 26		18 40		18 42		18 53	18 56		19 10		19 12		19 23	19 26
	d		18 13		18 23	18 28		18 41		18 43		18 53	18 58		19 11		19 13		19 23	19 28
St Margarets	d		18 15			18 30				18 45			19 00				19 15			19 30
Richmond ⊖	d		18 19		18 28	18 34		18 45		18 49		18 58	19 04		19 15		19 19		19 28	19 34
North Sheen	d		18 21			18 36				18 51			19 06				19 21			19 36
Mortlake	d		18 23			18 38				18 53			19 08				19 23			19 38
Hounslow	d			18 16			18 31				18 46			19 01				19 16		
Isleworth	d			18 19			18 34				18 49			19 04				19 19		
Syon Lane	d			18 21			18 36				18 51			19 06				19 21		
Brentford	d			18 24			18 39				18 54			19 09				19 24		
Kew Bridge	d			18 26			18 41				18 56			19 11				19 26		
Chiswick	d			18 29			18 44				18 59			19 14				19 29		
Barnes Bridge	d			18 31			18 46				19 01			19 16				19 31		
Barnes	d		18 26	18 34		18 41	18 49			18 56	19 04		19 11	19 19			19 26	19 34		19 41
Putney	d		18 29	18 37	18 34	18 44	18 52			18 59	19 07	19 04	19 14	19 22			19 29	19 37	19 34	19 44
Wandsworth Town	d		18 32	18 40		18 47	18 55			19 02	19 10		19 17	19 25			19 32	19 40		19 47
Clapham Junction 10	d		18 35	18 43	18 39	18 50	18 58	18 54		19 05	19 13	19 09	19 20	19 28	19 24		19 35	19 43	19 39	19 50
Queenstown Rd.(Battersea)	d		18 38	18 46		18 53	19 01			19 08	19 16		19 23	19 31			19 38	19 46		19 53
Vauxhall ⊖	d		18 42	18 50	18 45	18 57	19 05			19 12	19 20	19 15	19 27	19 35			19 42	19 50	19 45	19 57
London Waterloo 15 ⊖	a		18 46	18 56	18 49	19 02	19 11	19 04		19 16	19 26	19 19	19 32	19 41	19 34		19 46	19 56	19 49	20 02

Table 149

Reading, Guildford, Ascot, Weybridge, Windsor, Kingston, Richmond and Hounslow - London

		SW	SW ■	SW ■	SW	SW	SW	SW	SW	SW ■	SW ■	SW	SW	SW	SW	SW	SW ■	SW ■	SW	SW
Reading ■	d		18 42							19 12							19 42			
Earley	d		18 47							19 17							19 47			
Winnersh Triangle	d		18 49							19 19							19 49			
Winnersh	d		18 51							19 21							19 51			
Wokingham	d		18 56							19 26							19 56			
Bracknell	d		19 02							19 32							20 02			
Martins Heron	d		19 05							19 35							20 05			
Guildford	d			18 30							19 00							19 30		
Wanborough	d			18 36							19 06							19 36		
Ash ■	d			18 40							19 10							19 40		
Aldershot	a			18 47							19 17							19 47		
	d			19 00							19 30							20 00		
Ash Vale	d			19 04							19 34							20 04		
Frimley	d			19 10							19 40							20 10		
Camberley	a			19 14							19 44							20 14		
	d			19 18							19 48							20 18		
Bagshot	d			19 23							19 53							20 23		
Ascot ■	d		19 10	19a30						19 40	20a00						20 10	20a30		
Sunningdale	d		19 13							19 43							20 13			
Longcross	d																			
Woking	d																			
West Byfleet	d																			
Byfleet & New Haw	d																			
Weybridge	d					19 03							19 33							20 03
Addlestone	d					19 07							19 37							20 07
Chertsey	d					19 10							19 40							20 10
Virginia Water	a		19 19			19 15				19 49			19 45				20 19			20 15
	d		19 19			19 24				19 49			19 54				20 19			20 24
Egham	d		19 23			19 27				19 53			19 57				20 23			20 27
Windsor & Eton Riverside	d						19 23							19 53						
Datchet	d						19 26							19 56						
Sunnymeads	d						19 29							19 59						
Wraysbury	d						19 32							20 02						
Staines	d		19 29			19 33	19 38			19 59			20 03	20 08			20 29			20 33
Ashford (Surrey)	d					19 36	19 41						20 06	20 11						20 36
Feltham	d		19 35			19 41	19 46			20 05			20 11	20 16			20 35			20 41
Whitton	d	19 20					19 50	19 53	19 50					20 20	20 23	20 20				
Kingston	d				19 29							19 59							20 29	
Hampton Wick	d				19 31							20 01							20 31	
Teddington	d				19 35							20 05							20 35	
Fulwell	d																			
Strawberry Hill	d				19 38							20 08							20 38	
Twickenham	a		19 40		19 42		19 53	19 56		20 10		20 12		20 23	20 26		20 40		20 42	
	d		19 41		19 43		19 53	19 58		20 11		20 13		20 23	20 28		20 41		20 43	
St Margarets	d				19 45			20 00				20 15			20 30				20 45	
Richmond ⊖	d		19 45		19 49		19 58	20 04		20 15		20 19		20 28	20 34		20 45		20 49	
North Sheen	d				19 51			20 06				20 21			20 36				20 51	
Mortlake	d				19 53			20 08				20 23			20 38				20 53	
Hounslow	d	19 31				19 46			20 01				20 16			20 31				20 46
Isleworth	d	19 34				19 49			20 04				20 19			20 34				20 49
Syon Lane	d	19 36				19 51			20 06				20 21			20 36				20 51
Brentford	d	19 39				19 54			20 09				20 24			20 39				20 54
Kew Bridge	d	19 41				19 56			20 11				20 26			20 41				20 56
Chiswick	d	19 44				19 59			20 14				20 29			20 44				20 59
Barnes Bridge	d	19 46				20 01			20 16				20 31			20 46				21 01
Barnes	d	19 49			19 56	20 04		20 11	20 19			20 26	20 34		20 41	20 49			20 56	21 04
Putney	d	19 52			19 59	20 07	20 04	20 14	20 22			20 29	20 37	20 34	20 44	20 52			20 59	21 07
Wandsworth Town	d	19 55			20 02	20 10		20 17	20 25			20 32	20 40		20 47	20 55			21 02	21 10
Clapham Junction ■	d	19 58	19 54		20 05	20 13	20 09	20 20	20 28	20 24		20 35	20 43	20 39	20 50	20 58	20 54		21 05	21 13
Queenstown Rd.(Battersea)	d	20 01			20 08	20 16		20 23	20 31			20 38	20 46		20 53	21 01			21 08	21 16
Vauxhall ⊖	d	20 05			20 12	20 20	20 15	20 27	20 35			20 42	20 50	20 45	20 57	21 05			21 12	21 20
London Waterloo ■ ⊖	a	20 11	20 04		20 16	20 26	20 19	20 32	20 41	20 34		20 46	20 56	20 49	21 02	21 11	21 04		21 16	21 26

Table 149

Reading, Guildford, Ascot, Weybridge, Windsor, Kingston, Richmond and Hounslow - London

		SW	SW	SW	SW ■	SW ■	SW	SW	SW	SW	SW	SW ■	SW	SW	SW	SW	SW	SW ■	SW ■	SW
Reading ■	d				20 12							20 42						21 12		
Earley	d				20 17							20 47						21 17		
Winnersh Triangle	d				20 19							20 49						21 19		
Winnersh	d				20 21							20 51						21 21		
Wokingham	d				20 26							20 56						21 26		
Bracknell	d				20 32							21 02						21 32		
Martins Heron	d				20 35							21 05						21 35		
Guildford	d					20 00													21 00	
Wanborough	d					20 06													21 06	
Ash ■	d					20 10													21 10	
Aldershot	a					20 17													21 17	
	d					20 30													21 30	
Ash Vale	d					20 34													21 34	
Frimley	d					20 40													21 40	
Camberley	a					20 44													21 44	
	d					20 48													21 48	
Bagshot	d					20 53													21 53	
Ascot ■	d				20 40	21a00						21 10						21 40	22a00	
Sunningdale	d				20 43							21 13						21 43		
Longcross	d																			
Woking	d																			
West Byfleet	d																			
Byfleet & New Haw	d																			
Weybridge	d							20 33						21 03						
Addlestone	d							20 37						21 07						
Chertsey	d							20 40						21 10						
Virginia Water	a				20 49			20 45				21 19		21 15				21 49		
	d				20 49			20 54				21 19		21 24				21 49		
Egham	d				20 53			20 57				21 23		21 27				21 53		
Windsor & Eton Riverside	d	20 23							20 53						21 23					
Datchet	d	20 26							20 56						21 26					
Sunnymeads	d	20 29							20 59						21 29					
Wraysbury	d	20 32							21 02						21 32					
Staines	d	20 38			20 59			21 03	21 08			21 29		21 33	21 38			21 59		
Ashford (Surrey)	d	20 41						21 06	21 11					21 36	21 41					
Feltham	d	20 46			21 05			21 11	21 16			21 35		21 41	21 46			22 05		
Whitton	d	20 50	20 53	20 50					21 20	21 23	21 20				21 50	21 53	21 50			
Kingston	d						20 59						21 29							21 59
Hampton Wick	d						21 01						21 31							22 01
Teddington	d						21 05						21 35							22 05
Fulwell	d																			
Strawberry Hill	d						21 08						21 38							22 08
Twickenham	a	20 53	20 56		21 10		21 12		21 23	21 26		21 40	21 42		21 53	21 56		22 10		22 12
	d	20 53	20 58		21 11		21 13		21 23	21 28		21 41	21 43		21 53	21 58		22 11		22 13
St Margarets	d		21 00				21 15			21 30			21 45			22 00				22 15
Richmond ⊖	d	20 58	21 04		21 15		21 19		21 28	21 34		21 45	21 49		21 58	22 04		22 15		22 19
North Sheen	d		21 06				21 21			21 36			21 51			22 06				22 21
Mortlake	d		21 08				21 23			21 38			21 53			22 08				22 23
Hounslow	d			21 01				21 16			21 31			21 46			22 01			
Isleworth	d			21 04				21 19			21 34			21 49			22 04			
Syon Lane	d			21 06				21 21			21 36			21 51			22 06			
Brentford	d			21 09				21 24			21 39			21 54			22 09			
Kew Bridge	d			21 11				21 26			21 41			21 56			22 11			
Chiswick	d			21 14				21 29			21 44			21 59			22 14			
Barnes Bridge	d			21 16				21 31			21 46			22 01			22 16			
Barnes	d		21 11	21 19			21 26	21 34		21 41	21 49		21 56	22 04		22 11	22 19			22 26
Putney	d	21 04	21 14	21 22			21 29	21 37	21 34	21 44	21 52		21 59	22 07	22 04	22 14	22 22			22 29
Wandsworth Town	d		21 17	21 25			21 32	21 40		21 47	21 55		22 02	22 10		22 17	22 25			22 32
Clapham Junction ■	d	21 09	21 20	21 28	21 24		21 35	21 43	21 39	21 50	21 58	21 54	22 05	22 13	22 09	22 20	22 28	22 24		22 35
Queenstown Rd.(Battersea)	d		21 23	21 31			21 38	21 46		21 53	22 01		22 08	22 16		22 23	22 31			22 38
Vauxhall ⊖	d	21 15	21 27	21 35			21 42	21 50	21 45	21 57	22 05		22 12	22 20	22 15	22 27	22 35			22 42
London Waterloo ■ ⊖	a	21 19	21 32	21 41	21 34		21 46	21 56	21 49	22 02	22 11	22 04	22 16	22 26	22 19	22 32	22 41	22 34		22 46

Table 149

Saturdays
29 May to 25 September

Reading, Guildford, Ascot, Weybridge, Windsor, Kingston, Richmond and Hounslow - London

		SW	SW	SW	SW 1	SW	SW	SW	SW 1	SW 1	SW	SW	SW	SW	SW	SW 1	SW	SW 1	SW 1
Reading 7	d				21 42				22 12							22 42		23 12	
Earley	d				21 47				22 17							22 47		23 17	
Winnersh Triangle	d				21 49				22 19							22 49		23 19	
Winnersh	d				21 51				22 21							22 51		23 21	
Wokingham	d				21 56				22 26							22 56		23 26	
Bracknell	d				22 02				22 32							23 02		23 32	
Martins Heron	d				22 05				22 35							23 05		23 35	
Guildford	d									22 00									23 00
Wanborough	d									22 06									23 06
Ash 5	d									22 10									23 10
Aldershot	a									22 17									23 17
	d									22 30									23 30
Ash Vale	d									22 34									23 34
Frimley	d									22 40									23 40
Camberley	a									22 44									23 44
	d									22 48									23 48
Bagshot	d									22 53									23 53
Ascot 3	d				22 10				22 40	23a00						23 10		23 40	00a01
Sunningdale	d				22 13				22 43							23 13		23 43	
Longcross	d																		
Woking	d																		
West Byfleet	d																		
Byfleet & New Haw	d																		
Weybridge	d	21 33					22 03					22 33		23 03					
Addlestone	d	21 37					22 07					22 37		23 07					
Chertsey	d	21 40					22 10					22 40		23 10					
Virginia Water	a	21 45			22 19		22 15		22 49			22 45		23 15		23 19		23 49	
	d	21 54			22 19		22 24		22 49			22 54		23 24		23 19		23 49	
Egham	d	21 57			22 23		22 27		22 53			22 57		23 27		23 23		23 53	
Windsor & Eton Riverside	d		21 53					22 23					22 53		23 23				
Datchet	d		21 56					22 26					22 56		23 26				
Sunnymeads	d		21 59					22 29					22 59		23 29				
Wraysbury	d		22 02					22 32					23 02		23 32				
Staines	d	22 03	22 08		22 29		22 33	22 38	22 59			23 03	23 08	23a32	23a37	23 29		23 59	
Ashford (Surrey)	d	22 06	22 11				22 36	22 41				23 06	23 11						
Feltham	d	22 11	22 16		22 35		22 41	22 46	23 05			23 11	23 16			23 35		00 05	
Whitton	d		22 20	22 23				22 50					23 20						
Kingston	d					22 29					22 59						23 29		
Hampton Wick	d					22 31					23 01						23 31		
Teddington	d					22 35					23 05						23 35		
Fulwell	d																		
Strawberry Hill	d					22 38					23 08						23 38		
Twickenham	a		22 23	22 26	22 40	22 42		22 53	23 10		23 12		23 23			23 40	23 42	00 10	
	d		22 23	22 28	22 41	22 43		22 53	23 11		23 13		23 23			23 41	23 43	00 11	
St Margarets	d			22 30		22 45					23 15						23 45		
Richmond ⊖	d		22 28	22 34	22 45	22 49		22 58	23 15		23 19		23 28			23 45	23 49	00 15	
North Sheen	d			22 36		22 51					23 21						23 51		
Mortlake	d			22 38		22 53					23 23						23 53		
Hounslow	d	22 16					22 46					23 16							
Isleworth	d	22 19					22 49					23 19							
Syon Lane	d	22 21					22 51					23 21							
Brentford	d	22 24					22 54					23 24							
Kew Bridge	d	22 26					22 56					23 26							
Chiswick	d	22 29					22 59					23 29							
Barnes Bridge	d	22 31					23 01					23 31							
Barnes	d	22 34		22 41		22 56	23 04				23 26	23 34					23 56		
Putney	d	22 37	22 34	22 44		22 59	23 07	23 04			23 29	23 37	23 34				23 59		
Wandsworth Town	d	22 40		22 47		23 02	23 10				23 32	23 40					00 02		
Clapham Junction 10	d	22 43	22 39	22 50	22 54	23 05	23 13	23 09	23 24		23 35	23 43	23 39			23 54	00 05	00 24	
Queenstown Rd.(Battersea)	d	22 46		22 53		23 08	23 16				23 38	23 46					00 08		
Vauxhall ⊖	d	22 50	22 45	22 57		23 12	23 20	23 15			23 42	23 50	23 45				00 12		
London Waterloo 15 ⊖	a	22 56	22 49	23 02	23 04	23 17	23 26	23 19	23 34		23 46	23 56	23 49			00 02	00 16	00 33	

Table 149

Saturdays
29 May to 25 September

Reading, Guildford, Ascot, Weybridge, Windsor, Kingston, Richmond and Hounslow - London

		SW
Reading 7	d	
Earley	d	
Winnersh Triangle	d	
Winnersh	d	
Wokingham	d	
Bracknell	d	
Martins Heron	d	
Guildford	d	
Wanborough	d	
Ash 5	d	
Aldershot	a	
	d	
Ash Vale	d	
Frimley	d	
Camberley	a	
	d	
Bagshot	d	
Ascot 3	d	
Sunningdale	d	
Longcross	d	
Woking	d	
West Byfleet	d	
Byfleet & New Haw	d	
Weybridge	d	23 33
Addlestone	d	23 37
Chertsey	d	23 40
Virginia Water	a	23 45
	d	23 54
Egham	d	23 57
Windsor & Eton Riverside	d	
Datchet	d	
Sunnymeads	d	
Wraysbury	d	
Staines	d	00a02
Ashford (Surrey)	d	
Feltham	d	
Whitton	d	
Kingston	d	
Hampton Wick	d	
Teddington	d	
Fulwell	d	
Strawberry Hill	d	
Twickenham	a	
	d	
St Margarets	d	
Richmond ⊖	d	
North Sheen	d	
Mortlake	d	
Hounslow	d	
Isleworth	d	
Syon Lane	d	
Brentford	d	
Kew Bridge	d	
Chiswick	d	
Barnes Bridge	d	
Barnes	d	
Putney	d	
Wandsworth Town	d	
Clapham Junction 10	d	
Queenstown Rd.(Battersea)	d	
Vauxhall ⊖	d	
London Waterloo 15 ⊖	a	

Table 149

Saturdays from 02 October

Reading, Guildford, Ascot, Weybridge, Windsor, Kingston, Richmond and Hounslow - London

		SW	SW [1]	SW	SW [1]	SW	SW	SW	SW	SW	SW	SW	SW	SW [1]	SW [1]	SW	SW	SW	SW [1]	SW
Reading [7]	d		22p39		23p12									05 39					06 09	
Earley	d		22p44		23p17									05 44					06 14	
Winnersh Triangle	d		22p46		23p19									05 46					06 16	
Winnersh	d		22p48		23p21									05 48					06 18	
Wokingham	d		22p53		23p26									05 53					06 23	
Bracknell	d		22p59		23p32									05 59					06 29	
Martins Heron	d		23p02		23p35									06 02					06 32	
Guildford	d																			
Wanborough	d																			
Ash [5]	d																			
Aldershot	a																			
	d														06 00					
Ash Vale	d														06 04					
Frimley	d														06 10					
Camberley	a														06 14					
	d														06 18					
Bagshot	d														06 23					
Ascot [3]	d		23p07		23p40									06 07	06a30				06 37	
Sunningdale	d		23p10		23p43									06 10					06 40	
Longcross	d																			
Woking	d											05 25								
West Byfleet	d											05 30								
Byfleet & New Haw	d											05 33								
Weybridge	d																			
Addlestone	d											05 37								
Chertsey	d											05 40								
Virginia Water	a		23p19		23p49							05 45		06 19					06 49	
	d		23p19		23p49							05 54		06 19					06 49	
Egham	d		23p23		23p53							05 57		06 23					06 53	
Windsor & Eton Riverside	d												05 51				06 21			
Datchet	d												05 55				06 25			
Sunnymeads	d												05 58				06 28			
Wraysbury	d												06 02				06 32			
Staines	d		23p29		23p59	04 58		05 37				06 03	06 08	06 29			06 38	06 33	06 59	
Ashford (Surrey)	d					05 01		05 40				06 06	06 11				06 41	06 36		
Feltham	d		23p35		00 05	05 06		05 45				06 11	06 16	06 35			06 46	06 41	07 05	
Whitton	d					05 10		05 49	05 41				06 20				06 50			
Kingston	d			23p29							05 59					06 29				06 59
Hampton Wick	d			23p31							06 01					06 31				07 01
Teddington	d			23p35							06 05					06 35				07 05
Fulwell	d																			
Strawberry Hill	d			23p38			05 38				06 08					06 38				07 08
Twickenham	a	23p33	23p40	23p42	00 10	05 13	05 41	05 52			06 12		06 23	06 40		06 42	06 53		07 10	07 12
	d	23p34	23p41	23p43	00 11	05 13	05 43	05 53			06 13		06 23	06 41		06 43	06 53		07 11	07 13
St Margarets	d			23p45		05 15	05 45				06 15					06 45				07 15
Richmond ⊖	d		23p45	23p49	00 15	05 19	05 49	05 58			06 19		06 28	06 45		06 49	06 58		07 15	07 19
North Sheen	d			23p51		05 21	05 51				06 21					06 51				07 21
Mortlake	d			23p53		05 23	05 53				06 23					06 53				07 23
Hounslow	d								05 46			06 16						06 46		
Isleworth	d								05 49			06 19						06 49		
Syon Lane	d								05 51			06 21						06 51		
Brentford	d								05 54			06 24						06 54		
Kew Bridge	d								05 56			06 26						06 56		
Chiswick	d								05 59			06 29						06 59		
Barnes Bridge	d								06 01			06 31						07 01		
Barnes	d			23p56		05 26	05 56		06 04		06 26	06 34				06 56		07 04		07 26
Putney	d			23p59		05 29	05 59	06 04	06 07		06 29	06 37	06 34			06 59	07 04	07 07		07 29
Wandsworth Town	d			00 02		05 32	06 02		06 10		06 32	06 40				07 02		07 10		07 32
Clapham Junction [10]	d		23p54	00 05	00 24	05 35	06 05	06 09	06 13		06 35	06 43	06 39	06 54		07 05	07 09	07 13	07 24	07 35
Queenstown Rd.(Battersea)	d			00 08		05 38	06 08		06 16		06 38	06 46				07 08		07 16		07 38
Vauxhall ⊖	d	00 17		00 12		05 42	06 12	06 15	06 20		06 42	06 50	06 45			07 12	07 15	07 20		07 42
London Waterloo [15] ⊖	a	00 23	00 04	00 16	00 32	05 46	06 16	06 19	06 26		06 46	06 56	06 49	07 04		07 16	07 19	07 26	07 34	07 46

Table 149

Saturdays from 02 October

Reading, Guildford, Ascot, Weybridge, Windsor, Kingston, Richmond and Hounslow - London

		SW	SW	SW	SW [1]	SW [1]	SW	SW	SW	SW	SW	SW [1]	SW [1]	SW	SW	SW	SW	SW	SW [1]	SW [1]
Reading [7]	d				06 42							07 09							07 39	
Earley	d				06 47							07 14							07 44	
Winnersh Triangle	d				06 49							07 16							07 46	
Winnersh	d				06 51							07 18							07 48	
Wokingham	d				06 56							07 23							07 53	
Bracknell	d				07 02							07 29							07 59	
Martins Heron	d				07 05							07 32							08 02	
Guildford	d					06 30							07 00							07 30
Wanborough	d					06 36							07 06							07 36
Ash [5]	d					06 40							07 10							07 40
Aldershot	a					06 47							07 17							07 47
	d					07 00							07 30							08 00
Ash Vale	d					07 04							07 34							08 04
Frimley	d					07 10							07 40							08 10
Camberley	a					07 14							07 44							08 14
	d					07 18							07 48							08 18
Bagshot	d					07 23							07 53							08 23
Ascot [3]	d				07 10	07a30						07 37	08a00						08 07	08a30
Sunningdale	d				07 13							07 40							08 10	
Longcross	d																			
Woking	d																			
West Byfleet	d																			
Byfleet & New Haw	d																			
Weybridge	d	06 33						07 03							07 33					
Addlestone	d	06 37						07 07							07 37					
Chertsey	d	06 40						07 10							07 40					
Virginia Water	a	06 45			07 19			07 15				07 49			07 45				08 19	
	d	06 54			07 19			07 24				07 49			07 54				08 19	
Egham	d	06 57			07 23			07 27				07 53			07 57				08 23	
Windsor & Eton Riverside	d		06 51						07 21							07 51				
Datchet	d		06 55						07 25							07 55				
Sunnymeads	d		06 58						07 28							07 58				
Wraysbury	d		07 02						07 32							08 02				
Staines	d	07 03	07 08		07 29			07 33	07 38			07 59			08 03	08 08			08 29	
Ashford (Surrey)	d	07 06	07 11					07 36	07 41						08 06	08 11				
Feltham	d	07 11	07 16		07 35			07 41	07 46			08 05			08 11	08 16			08 35	
Whitton	d		07 20						07 50		07 50					08 20	08 23	08 20		
Kingston	d						07 29							07 59						
Hampton Wick	d						07 31							08 01						
Teddington	d						07 35							08 05						
Fulwell	d																			
Strawberry Hill	d						07 38							08 08						
Twickenham	a		07 23		07 40		07 42		07 53			08 10		08 12		08 23	08 26		08 40	
	d		07 23		07 41		07 43		07 53	07 58		08 11		08 13		08 23	08 28		08 41	
St Margarets	d						07 45			08 00				08 15			08 30			
Richmond ⊖	d		07 28		07 45		07 49		07 58	08 04		08 15		08 19		08 28	08 34		08 45	
North Sheen	d						07 51			08 06				08 21			08 36			
Mortlake	d						07 53			08 08				08 23			08 38			
Hounslow	d	07 16		07 31				07 46			08 01				08 16			08 31		
Isleworth	d	07 19		07 34				07 49			08 04				08 19			08 34		
Syon Lane	d	07 21		07 36				07 51			08 06				08 21			08 36		
Brentford	d	07 24		07 39				07 54			08 09				08 24			08 39		
Kew Bridge	d	07 26		07 41				07 56			08 11				08 26			08 41		
Chiswick	d	07 29		07 44				07 59			08 14				08 29			08 44		
Barnes Bridge	d	07 31		07 46				08 01			08 16				08 31			08 46		
Barnes	d	07 34		07 49			07 56	08 04		08 11	08 19			08 26	08 34		08 41	08 49		
Putney	d	07 37	07 34	07 52			07 59	08 07	08 04	08 14	08 22			08 29	08 37	08 34	08 44	08 52		
Wandsworth Town	d	07 40		07 55			08 02	08 10		08 17	08 25			08 32	08 40		08 47	08 55		
Clapham Junction [10]	d	07 43	07 39	07 58	07 54		08 05	08 13	08 09	08 20	08 28	08 24		08 35	08 43	08 39	08 50	08 58	08 54	
Queenstown Rd.(Battersea)	d	07 46		08 01			08 08	08 16		08 23	08 31			08 38	08 46		08 53	09 01		
Vauxhall ⊖	d	07 50	07 45	08 05			08 12	08 20	08 15	08 27	08 35			08 42	08 50	08 45	08 57	09 05		
London Waterloo [15] ⊖	a	07 56	07 49	08 11	08 04		08 16	08 26	08 19	08 32	08 41	08 34		08 46	08 56	08 49	09 02	09 11	09 04	

Table 149

Saturdays
from 02 October

Reading, Guildford, Ascot, Weybridge, Windsor, Kingston, Richmond and Hounslow - London

		SW	SW	SW	SW	SW	SW 1	SW 1	SW	SW	SW	SW	SW	SW 1	SW 1	SW	SW	SW	SW	SW
Reading 7	d						08 09							08 39						
Earley	d						08 14							08 44						
Winnersh Triangle	d						08 16							08 46						
Winnersh	d						08 18							08 48						
Wokingham	d						08 23							08 53						
Bracknell	d						08 29							08 59						
Martins Heron	d						08 32							09 02						
Guildford	d							08 00							08 30					
Wanborough	d							08 06							08 36					
Ash 5	d							08 10							08 40					
Aldershot	a							08 17							08 47					
	d							08 30							09 00					
Ash Vale	d							08 34							09 04					
Frimley	d							08 40							09 10					
Camberley	a							08 44							09 14					
	d							08 48							09 18					
Bagshot	d							08 53							09 23					
Ascot 3	d						08 37	09a00						09 07	09a30					
Sunningdale	d						08 40							09 10						
Longcross	d																			
Woking	d																			
West Byfleet	d																			
Byfleet & New Haw	d																			
Weybridge	d		08 03							08 33							09 03			
Addlestone	d		08 07							08 37							09 07			
Chertsey	d		08 10							08 40							09 10			
Virginia Water	a		08 15				08 49			08 45				09 19			09 15			
	d		08 24				08 49			08 54				09 19			09 24			
Egham	d		08 27				08 53			08 57				09 23			09 27			
Windsor & Eton Riverside	d			08 21							08 51							09 21		
Datchet	d			08 25							08 55							09 25		
Sunnymeads	d			08 28							08 58							09 28		
Wraysbury	d			08 32							09 02							09 32		
Staines	d		08 33	08 38			08 59			09 03	09 08			09 29			09 33	09 38		
Ashford (Surrey)	d		08 36	08 41						09 06	09 11						09 36	09 41		
Feltham	d		08 41	08 46			09 05			09 11	09 16			09 35			09 41	09 46		
Whitton	d			08 50	08 53	08 50					09 20	09 23	09 20					09 50	09 53	09 50
Kingston	d	08 29							08 59							09 29				
Hampton Wick	d	08 31							09 01							09 31				
Teddington	d	08 35							09 05							09 35				
Fulwell	d																			
Strawberry Hill	d	08 38							09 08							09 38				
Twickenham	a	08 42		08 53	08 56		09 10		09 12		09 23	09 26		09 40		09 42		09 53	09 56	
	d	08 43		08 53	08 58		09 11		09 13		09 23	09 28		09 41		09 43		09 53	09 58	
St Margarets	d	08 45			09 00				09 15			09 30				09 45			10 00	
Richmond ⊖	d	08 49		08 58	09 04		09 15		09 19		09 28	09 34		09 45		09 49		09 58	10 04	
North Sheen	d	08 51			09 06				09 21			09 36				09 51			10 06	
Mortlake	d	08 53			09 08				09 23			09 38				09 53			10 08	
Hounslow	d		08 46			09 01				09 16			09 31				09 46			10 01
Isleworth	d		08 49			09 04				09 19			09 34				09 49			10 04
Syon Lane	d		08 51			09 06				09 21			09 36				09 51			10 06
Brentford	d		08 54			09 09				09 24			09 39				09 54			10 09
Kew Bridge	d		08 56			09 11				09 26			09 41				09 56			10 11
Chiswick	d		08 59			09 14				09 29			09 44				09 59			10 14
Barnes Bridge	d		09 01			09 16				09 31			09 46				10 01			10 16
Barnes	d	08 56	09 04		09 11	09 19			09 26	09 34		09 41	09 49			09 56	10 04		10 11	10 19
Putney	d	08 59	09 07	09 04	09 14	09 22			09 29	09 37	09 34	09 44	09 52			09 59	10 07	10 04	10 14	10 22
Wandsworth Town	d	09 02	09 10		09 17	09 25			09 32	09 40		09 47	09 55			10 02	10 10		10 17	10 25
Clapham Junction 10	d	09 05	09 13	09 09	09 20	09 28	09 24		09 35	09 43	09 39	09 50	09 58	09 54		10 05	10 13	10 09	10 20	10 28
Queenstown Rd.(Battersea)	d	09 08	09 16		09 23	09 31			09 38	09 46		09 53	10 01			10 08	10 16		10 23	10 31
Vauxhall ⊖	d	09 12	09 20	09 15	09 27	09 35			09 42	09 50	09 45	09 57	10 05			10 12	10 20	10 15	10 27	10 35
London Waterloo 15 ⊖	a	09 16	09 26	09 19	09 32	09 41	09 34		09 46	09 56	09 49	10 02	10 11	10 04		10 16	10 26	10 19	10 32	10 41

Table 149

Saturdays
from 02 October

Reading, Guildford, Ascot, Weybridge, Windsor, Kingston, Richmond and Hounslow - London

		SW	SW 1	SW 1	SW	SW	SW	SW	SW	SW	SW 1	SW 1	SW	SW	SW	SW	SW	SW	SW 1	SW 1	SW	SW	SW
Reading 7	d		09 09								09 39								10 09				
Earley	d		09 14								09 44								10 14				
Winnersh Triangle	d		09 16								09 46								10 16				
Winnersh	d		09 18								09 48								10 18				
Wokingham	d		09 23								09 53								10 23				
Bracknell	d		09 29								09 59								10 29				
Martins Heron	d		09 32								10 02								10 32				
Guildford	d			09 00								09 30								10 00			
Wanborough	d			09 06								09 36								10 06			
Ash 5	d			09 10								09 40								10 10			
Aldershot	a			09 17								09 47								10 17			
	d			09 30								10 00								10 30			
Ash Vale	d			09 34								10 04								10 34			
Frimley	d			09 40								10 10								10 40			
Camberley	a			09 44								10 14								10 44			
	d			09 48								10 18								10 48			
Bagshot	d			09 53								10 23								10 53			
Ascot 3	d		09 37	10a00							10 07	10a30							10 37	11a00			
Sunningdale	d		09 40								10 10								10 40				
Longcross	d																						
Woking	d																						
West Byfleet	d																						
Byfleet & New Haw	d																						
Weybridge	d					09 33								10 03								10 33	
Addlestone	d					09 37								10 07								10 37	
Chertsey	d					09 40								10 10								10 40	
Virginia Water	a		09 49			09 45					10 19			10 15					10 49			10 45	
	d		09 49			09 54					10 19			10 24					10 49			10 54	
Egham	d		09 53			09 57					10 23			10 27					10 53			10 57	
Windsor & Eton Riverside	d						09 51								10 21								10 51
Datchet	d						09 55								10 25								10 55
Sunnymeads	d						09 58								10 28								10 58
Wraysbury	d						10 02								10 32								11 02
Staines	d		09 59			10 03	10 08				10 29			10 33	10 38				10 59			11 03	11 08
Ashford (Surrey)	d					10 06	10 11							10 36	10 41							11 06	11 11
Feltham	d		10 05			10 11	10 16				10 35			10 41	10 46				11 05			11 11	11 16
Whitton	d						10 20	10 23	10 20						10 50	10 53	10 50						11 20
Kingston	d				09 59								10 29								10 59		
Hampton Wick	d				10 01								10 31								11 01		
Teddington	d				10 05								10 35								11 05		
Fulwell	d																						
Strawberry Hill	d				10 08								10 38								11 08		
Twickenham	a		10 10		10 12		10 23	10 26			10 40		10 42		10 53	10 56			11 10		11 12		11 23
	d		10 11		10 13		10 23	10 28			10 41		10 43		10 53	10 58			11 11		11 13		11 23
St Margarets	d				10 15			10 30					10 45			11 00					11 15		
Richmond ⊖	d		10 15		10 19		10 28	10 34			10 45		10 49		10 58	11 04			11 15		11 19		11 28
North Sheen	d				10 21			10 36					10 51			11 06					11 21		
Mortlake	d				10 23			10 38					10 53			11 08					11 23		
Hounslow	d					10 16			10 31					10 46			11 01					11 16	
Isleworth	d					10 19			10 34					10 49			11 04					11 19	
Syon Lane	d					10 21			10 36					10 51			11 06					11 21	
Brentford	d					10 24			10 39					10 54			11 09					11 24	
Kew Bridge	d					10 26			10 41					10 56			11 11					11 26	
Chiswick	d					10 29			10 44					10 59			11 14					11 29	
Barnes Bridge	d					10 31			10 46					11 01			11 16					11 31	
Barnes	d				10 26	10 34		10 41	10 49				10 56	11 04		11 11	11 19				11 26	11 34	
Putney	d				10 29	10 37	10 34	10 44	10 52				10 59	11 07	11 04	11 14	11 22				11 29	11 37	11 34
Wandsworth Town	d				10 32	10 40		10 47	10 55				11 02	11 10		11 17	11 25				11 32	11 40	
Clapham Junction 10	d		10 24		10 35	10 43	10 39	10 50	10 58		10 54		11 05	11 13	11 09	11 20	11 28		11 24		11 35	11 43	11 39
Queenstown Rd.(Battersea)	d				10 38	10 46		10 53	11 01				11 08	11 16		11 23	11 31				11 38	11 46	
Vauxhall ⊖	d				10 42	10 50	10 45	10 57	11 05				11 12	11 20	11 15	11 27	11 35				11 42	11 50	11 45
London Waterloo 15 ⊖	a		10 34		10 46	10 56	10 49	11 02	11 11		11 04		11 16	11 26	11 19	11 32	11 41		11 34		11 46	11 56	11 49

Reading, Guildford, Ascot, Weybridge, Windsor, Kingston, Richmond and Hounslow - London

		SW	SW			SW ■	SW ■	SW	SW	SW	SW	SW		SW ■		SW ■	SW	SW	SW	SW	SW		SW ■	SW ■
Reading ■	d					10 39								11 09									11 39	
Earley	d					10 44								11 14									11 44	
Winnersh Triangle	d					10 46								11 16									11 46	
Winnersh	d					10 48								11 18									11 48	
Wokingham	d					10 53								11 23									11 53	
Bracknell	d					10 59								11 29									11 59	
Martins Heron	d					11 02								11 32									12 02	
Guildford	d						10 30									11 00								11 30
Wanborough	d						10 36									11 06								11 36
Ash ■	d						10 40									11 10								11 40
Aldershot	a						10 47									11 17								11 47
	d						11 00									11 30								12 00
Ash Vale	d						11 04									11 34								12 04
Frimley	d						11 10									11 40								12 10
Camberley	a						11 14									11 44								12 14
	d						11 18									11 48								12 18
Bagshot	d						11 23									11 53								12 23
Ascot ■	d					11 07	11a30							11 37		12a00							12 07	12a30
Sunningdale	d					11 10								11 40									12 10	
Longcross	d																							
Woking	d																							
West Byfleet	d																							
Byfleet & New Haw	d																							
Weybridge	d								11 03									11 33						
Addlestone	d								11 07									11 37						
Chertsey	d								11 10									11 40						
Virginia Water	a					11 19			11 15					11 49				11 45					12 19	
	d					11 19			11 24					11 49				11 54					12 19	
Egham	d					11 23			11 27					11 53				11 57					12 23	
Windsor & Eton Riverside	d									11 21									11 51					
Datchet	d									11 25									11 55					
Sunnymeads	d									11 28									11 58					
Wraysbury	d									11 32									12 02					
Staines	d					11 29			11 33	11 38				11 59				12 03	12 08				12 29	
Ashford (Surrey)	d								11 36	11 41								12 06	12 11					
Feltham	d					11 35			11 41	11 46				12 05				12 11	12 16				12 35	
Whitton	d	11 23	11 20							11 50	11 53	11 50							12 20	12 23	12 20			
Kingston	d							11 29									11 59							
Hampton Wick	d							11 31									12 01							
Teddington	d							11 35									12 05							
Fulwell	d																							
Strawberry Hill	d							11 38									12 08							
Twickenham	a	11 26				11 40		11 42		11 53	11 56			12 10			12 12		12 23	12 27			12 40	
	d	11 28				11 41		11 43		11 53	11 58			12 11			12 13		12 23	12 28			12 41	
St Margarets	d	11 30						11 45			12 00						12 15			12 30				
Richmond ⊖	d	11 34				11 45		11 49		11 58	12 04			12 15			12 19		12 28	12 34			12 45	
North Sheen	d	11 36						11 51			12 06						12 21			12 36				
Mortlake	d	11 38						11 53			12 08						12 23			12 38				
Hounslow	d		11 31						11 46			12 01						12 16			12 31			
Isleworth	d		11 34						11 49			12 04						12 19			12 34			
Syon Lane	d		11 36						11 51			12 06						12 21			12 36			
Brentford	d		11 39						11 54			12 09						12 24			12 39			
Kew Bridge	d		11 41						11 56			12 11						12 26			12 41			
Chiswick	d		11 44						11 59			12 14						12 29			12 44			
Barnes Bridge	d		11 46						12 01			12 16						12 31			12 46			
Barnes	d	11 41	11 49					11 56	12 04		12 11	12 19					12 26	12 34		12 41	12 49			
Putney	d	11 44	11 52					11 59	12 07	12 04	12 14	12 22					12 29	12 37	12 34	12 44	12 52			
Wandsworth Town	d	11 47	11 55					12 02	12 10		12 17	12 25					12 32	12 40		12 47	12 55			
Clapham Junction ■	d	11 50	11 58			11 54		12 05	12 13	12 09	12 20	12 28		12 24			12 35	12 43	12 39	12 50	12 58		12 54	
Queenstown Rd.(Battersea)	d	11 53	12 01					12 08	12 16		12 23	12 31					12 38	12 46		12 53	13 01			
Vauxhall ⊖	d	11 57	12 05					12 12	12 20	12 15	12 27	12 35					12 42	12 50	12 45	12 57	13 05			
London Waterloo ■ ⊖	a	12 02	12 11			12 04		12 16	12 26	12 19	12 32	12 41		12 34			12 46	12 56	12 49	13 02	13 11		13 04	

Reading, Guildford, Ascot, Weybridge, Windsor, Kingston, Richmond and Hounslow - London

		SW	SW	SW	SW	SW		SW ■	SW ■	SW		SW	SW	SW	SW		SW ■	SW ■	SW	SW		SW	SW	SW
Reading ■	d							12 09									12 39							
Earley	d							12 14									12 44							
Winnersh Triangle	d							12 16									12 46							
Winnersh	d							12 18									12 48							
Wokingham	d							12 23									12 53							
Bracknell	d							12 29									12 59							
Martins Heron	d							12 32									13 02							
Guildford	d								12 00									12 30						
Wanborough	d								12 06									12 36						
Ash ■	d								12 10									12 40						
Aldershot	a								12 17									12 47						
	d								12 30									13 00						
Ash Vale	d								12 34									13 04						
Frimley	d								12 40									13 10						
Camberley	a								12 44									13 14						
	d								12 48									13 18						
Bagshot	d								12 53									13 23						
Ascot ■	d							12 37	13a00								13 07	13a30						
Sunningdale	d							12 40									13 10							
Longcross	d																							
Woking	d																							
West Byfleet	d																							
Byfleet & New Haw	d																							
Weybridge	d		12 03									12 33								13 03				
Addlestone	d		12 07									12 37								13 07				
Chertsey	d		12 10									12 40								13 10				
Virginia Water	a		12 15					12 49				12 45					13 19			13 15				
	d		12 24					12 49				12 54					13 19			13 24				
Egham	d		12 27					12 53				12 57					13 23			13 27				
Windsor & Eton Riverside	d			12 21									12 51									13 21		
Datchet	d			12 25									12 55									13 25		
Sunnymeads	d			12 28									12 58									13 28		
Wraysbury	d			12 32									13 02									13 32		
Staines	d		12 33	12 38				12 59				13 03	13 08				13 29			13 33		13 38		
Ashford (Surrey)	d		12 36	12 41								13 06	13 11							13 36		13 41		
Feltham	d		12 41	12 46				13 05				13 11	13 16				13 35			13 41		13 46		
Whitton	d			12 50	12 53	12 50							13 20	13 23	13 20							13 50	13 53	13 50
Kingston	d	12 29								12 59									13 29					
Hampton Wick	d	12 31								13 01									13 31					
Teddington	d	12 35								13 05									13 35					
Fulwell	d																							
Strawberry Hill	d	12 38								13 08									13 38					
Twickenham	a	12 42		12 53	12 56			13 10		13 12			13 23	13 26			13 40		13 42			13 53	13 56	
	d	12 43		12 53	12 58			13 11		13 13			13 23	13 28			13 41		13 43			13 53	13 58	
St Margarets	d	12 45			13 00					13 15				13 30					13 45				14 00	
Richmond ⊖	d	12 49		12 58	13 04			13 15		13 19			13 28	13 34			13 45		13 49			13 58	14 04	
North Sheen	d	12 51			13 06					13 21				13 36					13 51				14 06	
Mortlake	d	12 53			13 08					13 23				13 38					13 53				14 08	
Hounslow	d		12 46			13 01						13 16			13 31					13 46				14 01
Isleworth	d		12 49			13 04						13 19			13 34					13 49				14 04
Syon Lane	d		12 51			13 06						13 21			13 36					13 51				14 06
Brentford	d		12 54			13 09						13 24			13 39					13 54				14 09
Kew Bridge	d		12 56			13 11						13 26			13 41					13 56				14 11
Chiswick	d		12 59			13 14						13 29			13 44					13 59				14 14
Barnes Bridge	d		13 01			13 16						13 31			13 46					14 01				14 16
Barnes	d	12 56	13 04		13 11	13 19				13 26		13 34		13 41	13 49				13 56	14 04			14 11	14 19
Putney	d	12 59	13 07	13 04	13 14	13 22				13 29		13 37	13 34	13 44	13 52				13 59	14 07		14 04	14 14	14 22
Wandsworth Town	d	13 02	13 10		13 17	13 25				13 32		13 40		13 47	13 55				14 02	14 10			14 17	14 25
Clapham Junction ■	d	13 05	13 13	13 09	13 20	13 28		13 24		13 35		13 43	13 39	13 50	13 58		13 54		14 05	14 13		14 09	14 20	14 28
Queenstown Rd.(Battersea)	d	13 08	13 16		13 23	13 31				13 38		13 46		13 53	14 01				14 08	14 16			14 23	14 31
Vauxhall ⊖	d	13 12	13 20	13 15	13 27	13 35				13 42		13 50	13 45	13 57	14 05				14 12	14 20		14 15	14 27	14 35
London Waterloo ■ ⊖	a	13 16	13 26	13 19	13 32	13 41		13 34		13 46		13 56	13 49	14 02	14 11		14 04		14 16	14 26		14 19	14 32	14 41

Table 149

Saturdays
from 02 October

Reading, Guildford, Ascot, Weybridge, Windsor, Kingston, Richmond and Hounslow - London

		SW ■	SW ■	SW	SW	SW		SW	SW		SW ■	SW ■	SW	SW	SW	SW		SW		SW ■	SW ■	SW	SW	SW	SW
Reading ■	d	13 09									13 39									14 09					
Earley	d	13 14									13 44									14 14					
Winnersh Triangle	d	13 16									13 46									14 16					
Winnersh	d	13 18									13 48									14 18					
Wokingham	d	13 23									13 53									14 23					
Bracknell	d	13 29									13 59									14 29					
Martins Heron	d	13 32									14 02									14 32					
Guildford	d		13 00									13 30									14 00				
Wanborough	d		13 06									13 36									14 06				
Ash ■	d		13 10									13 40									14 10				
Aldershot	a		13 17									13 47									14 17				
	d		13 30									14 00									14 30				
Ash Vale	d		13 34									14 04									14 34				
Frimley	d		13 40									14 10									14 40				
Camberley	a		13 44									14 14									14 44				
	d		13 48									14 18									14 48				
Bagshot	d		13 53									14 23									14 53				
Ascot ■	d	13 37	14a00								14 07	14a30								14 37	15a00				
Sunningdale	d	13 40									14 10									14 40					
Longcross	d																								
Woking	d																								
West Byfleet	d																								
Byfleet & New Haw	d																								
Weybridge	d				13 33									14 03									14 33		
Addlestone	d				13 37									14 07									14 37		
Chertsey	d				13 40									14 10									14 40		
Virginia Water	a	13 49			13 45						14 19			14 15						14 49			14 45		
	d	13 49			13 54						14 19			14 24						14 49			14 54		
Egham	d	13 53			13 57						14 23			14 27						14 53			14 57		
Windsor & Eton Riverside	d					13 51									14 21									14 51	
Datchet	d					13 55									14 25									14 55	
Sunnymeads	d					13 58									14 28									14 58	
Wraysbury	d					14 02									14 32									15 02	
Staines	d	13 59			14 03	14 08					14 29			14 33	14 38					14 59			15 03	15 08	
Ashford (Surrey)	d				14 06	14 11								14 36	14 41								15 06	15 11	
Feltham	d	14 05			14 11	14 16					14 35			14 41	14 46					15 05			15 11	15 16	
Whitton	d					14 20		14 23	14 20						14 50	14 53		14 50						15 20	15 23
Kingston	d			13 59									14 29									14 59			
Hampton Wick	d			14 01									14 31									15 01			
Teddington	d			14 05									14 35									15 05			
Fulwell	d																								
Strawberry Hill	d			14 08									14 38									15 08			
Twickenham	a	14 10		14 12		14 23		14 26			14 40		14 42		14 53	14 56				15 10		15 12		15 23	15 26
	d	14 11		14 13		14 23		14 28			14 41		14 43		14 53	14 58				15 11		15 13		15 23	15 28
St Margarets	d			14 15				14 30					14 45			15 00						15 15			15 30
Richmond ⊖	d	14 15		14 19		14 28		14 34			14 45		14 49		14 58	15 04				15 15		15 19		15 28	15 34
North Sheen	d			14 21				14 36					14 51			15 06						15 21			15 36
Mortlake	d			14 23				14 38					14 53			15 08						15 23			15 38
Hounslow	d				14 16				14 31					14 46				15 01					15 16		
Isleworth	d				14 19				14 34					14 49				15 04					15 19		
Syon Lane	d				14 21				14 36					14 51				15 06					15 21		
Brentford	d				14 24				14 39					14 54				15 09					15 24		
Kew Bridge	d				14 26				14 41					14 56				15 11					15 26		
Chiswick	d				14 29				14 44					14 59				15 14					15 29		
Barnes Bridge	d				14 31				14 46					15 01				15 16					15 31		
Barnes	d			14 26	14 34			14 41	14 49				14 56	15 04		15 11		15 19				15 26	15 34		15 41
Putney	d			14 29	14 37	14 34		14 44	14 52				14 59	15 07	15 04	15 14		15 22				15 29	15 37	15 34	15 44
Wandsworth Town	d			14 32	14 40			14 47	14 55				15 02	15 10		15 17		15 25				15 32	15 40		15 47
Clapham Junction ■	d	14 24		14 35	14 43	14 39		14 50	14 58		14 54		15 05	15 13	15 09	15 20		15 28		15 24		15 35	15 43	15 39	15 50
Queenstown Rd.(Battersea)	d			14 38	14 46			14 53	15 01				15 08	15 16		15 23		15 31				15 38	15 46		15 53
Vauxhall ⊖	d			14 42	14 50	14 45		14 57	15 05				15 12	15 20	15 15	15 27		15 35				15 42	15 50	15 45	15 57
London Waterloo ■ ⊖	a	14 34		14 46	14 56	14 49		15 02	15 11		15 04		15 16	15 26	15 19	15 32		15 41		15 34		15 46	15 56	15 49	16 02

Table 149

Saturdays
from 02 October

Reading, Guildford, Ascot, Weybridge, Windsor, Kingston, Richmond and Hounslow - London

		SW			SW ■	SW ■	SW	SW	SW	SW	SW			SW ■	SW ■	SW	SW	SW	SW	SW		SW ■		SW ■	SW
Reading ■	d				14 39									15 09								15 39			
Earley	d				14 44									15 14								15 44			
Winnersh Triangle	d				14 46									15 16								15 46			
Winnersh	d				14 48									15 18								15 48			
Wokingham	d				14 53									15 23								15 53			
Bracknell	d				14 59									15 29								15 59			
Martins Heron	d				15 02									15 32								16 02			
Guildford	d					14 30									15 00									15 30	
Wanborough	d					14 36									15 06									15 36	
Ash ■	d					14 40									15 10									15 40	
Aldershot	a					14 47									15 17									15 47	
	d					15 00									15 30									16 00	
Ash Vale	d					15 04									15 34									16 04	
Frimley	d					15 10									15 40									16 10	
Camberley	a					15 14									15 44									16 14	
	d					15 18									15 48									16 18	
Bagshot	d					15 23									15 53									16 23	
Ascot ■	d				15 07	15a30								15 37	16a00							16 07		16a30	
Sunningdale	d				15 10									15 40								16 10			
Longcross	d																								
Woking	d																								
West Byfleet	d																								
Byfleet & New Haw	d																								
Weybridge	d							15 03									15 33								
Addlestone	d							15 07									15 37								
Chertsey	d							15 10									15 40								
Virginia Water	a				15 19			15 15						15 49			15 45					16 19			
	d				15 19			15 24						15 49			15 54					16 19			
Egham	d				15 23			15 27						15 53			15 57					16 23			
Windsor & Eton Riverside	d								15 21									15 51							
Datchet	d								15 25									15 55							
Sunnymeads	d								15 28									15 58							
Wraysbury	d								15 32									16 02							
Staines	d				15 29			15 33	15 38					15 59			16 03	16 08				16 29			
Ashford (Surrey)	d							15 36	15 41								16 06	16 11							
Feltham	d				15 35			15 41	15 46					16 05			16 11	16 16				16 35			
Whitton	d	15 20							15 50	15 53	15 50							16 20	16 23	16 20					
Kingston	d						15 29									15 59									16 29
Hampton Wick	d						15 31									16 01									16 31
Teddington	d						15 35									16 05									16 35
Fulwell	d																								
Strawberry Hill	d						15 38									16 08									16 38
Twickenham	a				15 40		15 42		15 53	15 56				16 10		16 12		16 23	16 26			16 40			16 42
	d				15 41		15 43		15 53	15 58				16 11		16 13		16 23	16 28			16 41			16 43
St Margarets	d						15 45			16 00						16 15			16 30						16 45
Richmond ⊖	d				15 45		15 49		15 58	16 04				16 15		16 19		16 28	16 34			16 45			16 49
North Sheen	d						15 51			16 06						16 21			16 36						16 51
Mortlake	d						15 53			16 08						16 23			16 38						16 53
Hounslow	d	15 31						15 46			16 01						16 16			16 31					
Isleworth	d	15 34						15 49			16 04						16 19			16 34					
Syon Lane	d	15 36						15 51			16 06						16 21			16 36					
Brentford	d	15 39						15 54			16 09						16 24			16 39					
Kew Bridge	d	15 41						15 56			16 11						16 26			16 41					
Chiswick	d	15 44						15 59			16 14						16 29			16 44					
Barnes Bridge	d	15 46						16 01			16 16						16 31			16 46					
Barnes	d	15 49					15 56	16 04		16 11	16 19					16 26	16 34		16 41	16 49					16 56
Putney	d	15 52					15 59	16 07	16 04	16 14	16 22					16 29	16 37	16 34	16 44	16 52					16 59
Wandsworth Town	d	15 55					16 02	16 10		16 17	16 25					16 32	16 40		16 47	16 55					17 02
Clapham Junction ■	d	15 58			15 54		16 05	16 13	16 09	16 20	16 28			16 24		16 35	16 43	16 39	16 50	16 58		16 54			17 05
Queenstown Rd.(Battersea)	d	16 01					16 08	16 16		16 23	16 31					16 38	16 46		16 53	17 01					17 08
Vauxhall ⊖	d	16 05					16 12	16 20	16 15	16 27	16 35					16 42	16 50	16 45	16 57	17 05					17 12
London Waterloo ■ ⊖	a	16 11			16 04		16 16	16 26	16 19	16 32	16 41			16 34		16 46	16 56	16 49	17 02	17 11		17 04			17 16

Table 149

Saturdays
from 02 October

Reading, Guildford, Ascot, Weybridge, Windsor, Kingston, Richmond and Hounslow - London

		SW	SW	SW	SW	SW [1]	SW [1]	SW	SW	SW	SW	SW	SW [1]	SW [1]	SW	SW	SW	SW	SW	SW [1]
Reading [7]	d					16 09							16 39							17 09
Earley	d					16 14							16 44							17 14
Winnersh Triangle	d					16 16							16 46							17 16
Winnersh	d					16 18							16 48							17 18
Wokingham	d					16 23							16 53							17 23
Bracknell	d					16 29							16 59							17 29
Martins Heron	d					16 32							17 02							17 32
Guildford	d						16 00							16 30						
Wanborough	d						16 06							16 36						
Ash [5]	d						16 10							16 40						
Aldershot	a						16 17							16 47						
	d						16 30							17 00						
Ash Vale	d						16 34							17 04						
Frimley	d						16 40							17 10						
Camberley	a						16 44							17 14						
	d						16 48							17 18						
Bagshot	d						16 53							17 23						
Ascot [3]	d					16 37	17a00						17 07	17a30						17 37
Sunningdale	d					16 40							17 10							17 40
Longcross	d																			
Woking	d																			
West Byfleet	d																			
Byfleet & New Haw	d																			
Weybridge	d	16 03							16 33							17 03				
Addlestone	d	16 07							16 37							17 07				
Chertsey	d	16 10							16 40							17 10				
Virginia Water	a	16 15				16 49			16 45				17 19			17 15				17 49
	d	16 24				16 49			16 54				17 19			17 24				17 49
Egham	d	16 27				16 53			16 57				17 23			17 27				17 53
Windsor & Eton Riverside	d		16 21							16 51							17 21			
Datchet	d		16 25							16 55							17 25			
Sunnymeads	d		16 28							16 58							17 28			
Wraysbury	d		16 32							17 02							17 32			
Staines	d	16 33	16 38			16 59			17 03	17 08			17 29			17 33	17 38			17 59
Ashford (Surrey)	d	16 36	16 41						17 06	17 11						17 36	17 41			
Feltham	d	16 41	16 46			17 05			17 11	17 16			17 35			17 41	17 46			18 05
Whitton	d		16 50	16 53	16 50					17 20	17 23	17 20					17 50	17 53	17 50	
Kingston	d							16 59							17 29					
Hampton Wick	d							17 01							17 31					
Teddington	d							17 05							17 35					
Fulwell	d																			
Strawberry Hill	d							17 08							17 38					
Twickenham	a		16 53	16 56		17 10		17 12		17 23	17 26		17 40		17 42		17 53	17 56		18 10
	d		16 53	16 58		17 11		17 13		17 23	17 28		17 41		17 43		17 53	17 58		18 11
St Margarets	d			17 00				17 15			17 30				17 45			18 00		
Richmond ⊖	d		16 58	17 04		17 15		17 19		17 28	17 34		17 45		17 49		17 58	18 04		18 15
North Sheen	d			17 06				17 21			17 36				17 51			18 06		
Mortlake	d			17 08				17 23			17 38				17 53			18 08		
Hounslow	d	16 46			17 01				17 16			17 31				17 46			18 01	
Isleworth	d	16 49			17 04				17 19			17 34				17 49			18 04	
Syon Lane	d	16 51			17 06				17 21			17 36				17 51			18 06	
Brentford	d	16 54			17 09				17 24			17 39				17 54			18 09	
Kew Bridge	d	16 56			17 11				17 26			17 41				17 56			18 11	
Chiswick	d	16 59			17 14				17 29			17 44				17 59			18 14	
Barnes Bridge	d	17 01			17 16				17 31			17 46				18 01			18 16	
Barnes	d	17 04		17 11	17 19			17 26	17 34		17 41	17 49			17 56	18 04		18 11	18 19	
Putney	d	17 07	17 04	17 14	17 22			17 29	17 37	17 34	17 44	17 52			17 59	18 07	18 04	18 14	18 22	
Wandsworth Town	d	17 10		17 17	17 25			17 32	17 40		17 47	17 55			18 02	18 10		18 17	18 25	
Clapham Junction [10]	d	17 13	17 09	17 20	17 28	17 24		17 35	17 43	17 39	17 50	17 58	17 54		18 05	18 13	18 09	18 20	18 28	18 24
Queenstown Rd.(Battersea)	d	17 16		17 23	17 31			17 38	17 46		17 53	18 01			18 08	18 16		18 23	18 31	
Vauxhall ⊖	d	17 20	17 15	17 27	17 35			17 42	17 50	17 45	17 57	18 05			18 12	18 20	18 15	18 27	18 35	
London Waterloo [15] ⊖	a	17 26	17 19	17 32	17 41	17 34		17 46	17 56	17 49	18 02	18 11	18 04		18 16	18 26	18 19	18 32	18 41	18 34

Table 149

Saturdays
from 02 October

Reading, Guildford, Ascot, Weybridge, Windsor, Kingston, Richmond and Hounslow - London

		SW [1]	SW	SW	SW	SW	SW	SW	SW [1]	SW [1]	SW	SW	SW	SW	SW	SW	SW [1]	SW [1]	SW	SW	SW	SW
Reading [7]	d								17 39								18 09					
Earley	d								17 44								18 14					
Winnersh Triangle	d								17 46								18 16					
Winnersh	d								17 48								18 18					
Wokingham	d								17 53								18 23					
Bracknell	d								17 59								18 29					
Martins Heron	d								18 02								18 32					
Guildford	d	17 00								17 30								18 00				
Wanborough	d	17 06								17 36								18 06				
Ash [5]	d	17 10								17 40								18 10				
Aldershot	a	17 17								17 47								18 17				
	d	17 30								18 00								18 30				
Ash Vale	d	17 34								18 04								18 34				
Frimley	d	17 40								18 10								18 40				
Camberley	a	17 44								18 14								18 44				
	d	17 48								18 18								18 48				
Bagshot	d	17 53								18 23								18 53				
Ascot [3]	d	18a00							18 07	18a30							18 37	19a00				
Sunningdale	d								18 10								18 40					
Longcross	d																					
Woking	d																					
West Byfleet	d																					
Byfleet & New Haw	d																					
Weybridge	d			17 33								18 03								18 33		
Addlestone	d			17 37								18 07								18 37		
Chertsey	d			17 40								18 10								18 40		
Virginia Water	a			17 45					18 19			18 15					18 49			18 45		
	d			17 54					18 19			18 24					18 49			18 54		
Egham	d			17 57					18 23			18 27					18 53			18 57		
Windsor & Eton Riverside	d				17 51								18 21								18 51	
Datchet	d				17 55								18 25								18 55	
Sunnymeads	d				17 58								18 28								18 58	
Wraysbury	d				18 02								18 32								19 02	
Staines	d			18 03	18 08				18 29			18 33	18 38				18 59			19 03	19 08	
Ashford (Surrey)	d			18 06	18 11							18 36	18 41							19 06	19 11	
Feltham	d			18 11	18 16				18 35			18 41	18 46				19 05			19 11	19 16	
Whitton	d				18 20	18 23	18 20						18 50	18 53	18 50						19 20	19 23
Kingston	d		17 59								18 29								18 59			
Hampton Wick	d		18 01								18 31								19 01			
Teddington	d		18 05								18 35								19 05			
Fulwell	d																					
Strawberry Hill	d		18 08								18 38								19 08			
Twickenham	a		18 12		18 23	18 26			18 40		18 42		18 53	18 56			19 10		19 12		19 23	19 26
	d		18 13		18 23	18 28			18 41		18 43		18 53	18 58			19 11		19 13		19 23	19 28
St Margarets	d		18 15			18 30					18 45			19 00					19 15			19 30
Richmond ⊖	d		18 19		18 28	18 34			18 45		18 49		18 58	19 04			19 15		19 19		19 28	19 34
North Sheen	d		18 21			18 36					18 51			19 06					19 21			19 36
Mortlake	d		18 23			18 38					18 53			19 08					19 23			19 38
Hounslow	d			18 16			18 31					18 46			19 01					19 16		
Isleworth	d			18 19			18 34					18 49			19 04					19 19		
Syon Lane	d			18 21			18 36					18 51			19 06					19 21		
Brentford	d			18 24			18 39					18 54			19 09					19 24		
Kew Bridge	d			18 26			18 41					18 56			19 11					19 26		
Chiswick	d			18 29			18 44					18 59			19 14					19 29		
Barnes Bridge	d			18 31			18 46					19 01			19 16					19 31		
Barnes	d		18 26	18 34		18 41	18 49				18 56	19 04		19 11	19 19				19 26	19 34		19 41
Putney	d		18 29	18 37	18 34	18 44	18 52				18 59	19 07	19 04	19 14	19 22				19 29	19 37	19 34	19 44
Wandsworth Town	d		18 32	18 40		18 47	18 55				19 02	19 10		19 17	19 25				19 32	19 40		19 47
Clapham Junction [10]	d		18 35	18 43	18 39	18 50	18 58		18 54		19 05	19 13	19 09	19 20	19 28		19 24		19 35	19 43	19 39	19 50
Queenstown Rd.(Battersea)	d		18 38	18 46		18 53	19 01				19 08	19 16		19 23	19 31				19 38	19 46		19 53
Vauxhall ⊖	d		18 42	18 50	18 45	18 57	19 05				19 12	19 20	19 15	19 27	19 35				19 42	19 50	19 45	19 57
London Waterloo [15] ⊖	a		18 46	18 56	18 49	19 02	19 11		19 04		19 16	19 26	19 19	19 32	19 41		19 34		19 46	19 56	19 49	20 02

Table 149

Saturdays
from 02 October

Reading, Guildford, Ascot, Weybridge, Windsor, Kingston, Richmond and Hounslow - London

		SW	SW	SW 1	SW 1	SW	SW	SW	SW	SW	SW	SW 1	SW 1	SW	SW	SW	SW	SW	SW	SW 1	SW 1	SW	SW
Reading 7	d			18 39								19 09								19 39			
Earley	d			18 44								19 14								19 44			
Winnersh Triangle	d			18 46								19 16								19 46			
Winnersh	d			18 48								19 18								19 48			
Wokingham	d			18 53								19 23								19 53			
Bracknell	d			18 59								19 29								19 59			
Martins Heron	d			19 02								19 32								20 02			
Guildford	d				18 30								19 00								19 30		
Wanborough	d				18 36								19 06								19 36		
Ash 5	d				18 40								19 10								19 40		
Aldershot	a				18 47								19 17								19 47		
	d				19 00								19 30								20 00		
Ash Vale	d				19 04								19 34								20 04		
Frimley	d				19 10								19 40								20 10		
Camberley	a				19 14								19 44								20 14		
	d				19 18								19 48								20 18		
Bagshot	d				19 23								19 53								20 23		
Ascot 3	d			19 07	19a30							19 37	20a00							20 07	20a30		
Sunningdale	d			19 10								19 40								20 10			
Longcross	d																						
Woking	d																						
West Byfleet	d																						
Byfleet & New Haw	d																						
Weybridge	d						19 03								19 33								20 03
Addlestone	d						19 07								19 37								20 07
Chertsey	d						19 10								19 40								20 10
Virginia Water	a			19 19			19 15					19 49			19 45					20 19			20 15
	d			19 19			19 24					19 49			19 54					20 19			20 24
Egham	d			19 23			19 27					19 53			19 57					20 23			20 27
Windsor & Eton Riverside	d							19 21								19 51							
Datchet	d							19 25								19 55							
Sunnymeads	d							19 28								19 58							
Wraysbury	d							19 32								20 02							
Staines	d			19 29			19 33	19 38				19 59			20 03	20 08				20 29			20 33
Ashford (Surrey)	d						19 36	19 41							20 06	20 11							20 36
Feltham	d			19 35			19 41	19 46				20 05			20 11	20 16				20 35			20 41
Whitton	d	19 20						19 50	19 53	19 50						20 20	20 23	20 20					
Kingston	d					19 29								19 59								20 29	
Hampton Wick	d					19 31								20 01								20 31	
Teddington	d					19 35								20 05								20 35	
Fulwell	d																						
Strawberry Hill	d					19 38								20 08								20 38	
Twickenham	a			19 40		19 42		19 53	19 56			20 10		20 12		20 23	20 26			20 40		20 42	
	d			19 41		19 43		19 53	19 58			20 11		20 13		20 23	20 28			20 41		20 43	
St Margarets	d					19 45			20 00					20 15			20 30					20 45	
Richmond ⊖	d			19 45		19 49		19 58	20 04			20 15		20 19		20 28	20 34			20 45		20 49	
North Sheen	d					19 51			20 06					20 21			20 36					20 51	
Mortlake	d					19 53			20 08					20 23			20 38					20 53	
Hounslow	d	19 31					19 46			20 01					20 16			20 31					20 46
Isleworth	d	19 34					19 49			20 04					20 19			20 34					20 49
Syon Lane	d	19 36					19 51			20 06					20 21			20 36					20 51
Brentford	d	19 39					19 54			20 09					20 24			20 39					20 54
Kew Bridge	d	19 41					19 56			20 11					20 26			20 41					20 56
Chiswick	d	19 44					19 59			20 14					20 29			20 44					20 59
Barnes Bridge	d	19 46					20 01			20 16					20 31			20 46					21 01
Barnes	d	19 49				19 56	20 04		20 11	20 19				20 26	20 34		20 41	20 49				20 56	21 04
Putney	d	19 52				19 59	20 07	20 04	20 14	20 22				20 29	20 37	20 34	20 44	20 52				20 59	21 07
Wandsworth Town	d	19 55				20 02	20 10		20 17	20 25				20 32	20 40		20 47	20 55				21 02	21 10
Clapham Junction 10	d	19 58		19 54		20 05	20 13	20 09	20 20	20 28		20 24		20 35	20 43	20 39	20 50	20 58		20 54		21 05	21 13
Queenstown Rd.(Battersea)	d	20 01				20 08	20 16		20 23	20 31				20 38	20 46		20 53	21 01				21 08	21 16
Vauxhall ⊖	d	20 05				20 12	20 20	20 15	20 27	20 35				20 42	20 50	20 45	20 57	21 05				21 12	21 20
London Waterloo 15 ⊖	a	20 11		20 04		20 16	20 26	20 19	20 32	20 41		20 34		20 46	20 56	20 49	21 02	21 11		21 04		21 16	21 26

Table 149

Saturdays
from 02 October

Reading, Guildford, Ascot, Weybridge, Windsor, Kingston, Richmond and Hounslow - London

		SW	SW	SW	SW 1	SW 1	SW	SW	SW	SW	SW	SW 1	SW	SW	SW	SW	SW	SW 1	SW 1	SW
Reading 7	d				20 09							20 39						21 09		
Earley	d				20 14							20 44						21 14		
Winnersh Triangle	d				20 16							20 46						21 16		
Winnersh	d				20 18							20 48						21 18		
Wokingham	d				20 23							20 53						21 23		
Bracknell	d				20 29							20 59						21 29		
Martins Heron	d				20 32							21 02						21 32		
Guildford	d					20 00													21 00	
Wanborough	d					20 06													21 06	
Ash 5	d					20 10													21 10	
Aldershot	a					20 17													21 17	
	d					20 30													21 30	
Ash Vale	d					20 34													21 34	
Frimley	d					20 40													21 40	
Camberley	a					20 44													21 44	
	d					20 48													21 48	
Bagshot	d					20 53													21 53	
Ascot 3	d				20 37	21a00						21 07						21 37	22a00	
Sunningdale	d				20 40							21 10						21 40		
Longcross	d																			
Woking	d																			
West Byfleet	d																			
Byfleet & New Haw	d																			
Weybridge	d							20 33						21 03						
Addlestone	d							20 37						21 07						
Chertsey	d							20 40						21 10						
Virginia Water	a				20 49			20 45				21 19		21 15				21 49		
	d				20 49			20 54				21 19		21 24				21 49		
Egham	d				20 53			20 57				21 23		21 27				21 53		
Windsor & Eton Riverside	d	20 21							20 51						21 21					
Datchet	d	20 25							20 55						21 25					
Sunnymeads	d	20 28							20 58						21 28					
Wraysbury	d	20 32							21 02						21 32					
Staines	d	20 38			20 59			21 03	21 08			21 29		21 33	21 38			21 59		
Ashford (Surrey)	d	20 41						21 06	21 11					21 36	21 41					
Feltham	d	20 46			21 05			21 11	21 16			21 35		21 41	21 46			22 05		
Whitton	d	20 50	20 53	20 50					21 20	21 23	21 20				21 50	21 53	21 50			
Kingston	d						20 59						21 29							21 59
Hampton Wick	d						21 01						21 31							22 01
Teddington	d						21 05						21 35							22 05
Fulwell	d																			
Strawberry Hill	d						21 08						21 38							22 08
Twickenham	a	20 53	20 56		21 10		21 12		21 23	21 26		21 40	21 42		21 53	21 56		22 10		22 12
	d	20 53	20 58		21 11		21 13		21 23	21 28		21 41	21 43		21 53	21 58		22 11		22 13
St Margarets	d		21 00				21 15			21 30			21 45			22 00				22 15
Richmond ⊖	d	20 58	21 04		21 15		21 19		21 28	21 34		21 45	21 49		21 58	22 04		22 15		22 19
North Sheen	d		21 06				21 21			21 36			21 51			22 06				22 21
Mortlake	d		21 08				21 23			21 38			21 53			22 08				22 23
Hounslow	d			21 01				21 16			21 31			21 46			22 01			
Isleworth	d			21 04				21 19			21 34			21 49			22 04			
Syon Lane	d			21 06				21 21			21 36			21 51			22 06			
Brentford	d			21 09				21 24			21 39			21 54			22 09			
Kew Bridge	d			21 11				21 26			21 41			21 56			22 11			
Chiswick	d			21 14				21 29			21 44			21 59			22 14			
Barnes Bridge	d			21 16				21 31			21 46			22 01			22 16			
Barnes	d		21 11	21 19			21 26	21 34		21 41	21 49		21 56	22 04		22 11	22 19			22 26
Putney	d	21 04	21 14	21 22			21 29	21 37	21 34	21 44	21 52		21 59	22 07	22 04	22 14	22 22			22 29
Wandsworth Town	d		21 17	21 25			21 32	21 40		21 47	21 55		22 02	22 10		22 17	22 25			22 32
Clapham Junction 10	d	21 09	21 20	21 28	21 24		21 35	21 43	21 39	21 50	21 58	21 54	22 05	22 13	22 09	22 20	22 28	22 24		22 35
Queenstown Rd.(Battersea)	d		21 23	21 31			21 38	21 46		21 53	22 01		22 08	22 16		22 23	22 31			22 38
Vauxhall ⊖	d	21 15	21 27	21 35			21 42	21 50	21 45	21 57	22 05		22 12	22 20	22 15	22 27	22 35			22 42
London Waterloo 15 ⊖	a	21 19	21 32	21 41	21 34		21 46	21 56	21 49	22 02	22 11	22 04	22 16	22 26	22 19	22 32	22 41	22 34		22 46

Table 149

Saturdays from 02 October

Reading, Guildford, Ascot, Weybridge, Windsor, Kingston, Richmond and Hounslow - London

		SW	SW	SW	SW	SW ■	SW	SW	SW	SW ■	SW ■	SW	SW	SW	SW	SW	SW ■	SW	SW ■	SW ■
Reading ■	d					21 39				22 09							22 39		23 12	
Earley	d					21 44				22 14							22 44		23 17	
Winnersh Triangle	d					21 46				22 16							22 46		23 19	
Winnersh	d					21 48				22 18							22 48		23 21	
Wokingham	d					21 53				22 23							22 53		23 26	
Bracknell	d					21 59				22 29							22 59		23 32	
Martins Heron	d					22 02				22 32							23 02		23 35	
Guildford	d										22 00									23 00
Wanborough	d										22 06									23 06
Ash ■	d										22 10									23 10
Aldershot	a										22 17									23 17
	d										22 30									23 30
Ash Vale	d										22 34									23 34
Frimley	d										22 40									23 40
Camberley	a										22 44									23 44
	d										22 48									23 48
Bagshot	d										22 53									23 53
Ascot ■	d					22 07				22 37	23a00						23 07		23 40	00a01
Sunningdale	d					22 10				22 40							23 10		23 43	
Longcross	d																			
Woking	d																			
West Byfleet	d																			
Byfleet & New Haw	d																			
Weybridge	d	21 33						22 03					22 33		23 03					
Addlestone	d	21 37						22 07					22 37		23 07					
Chertsey	d	21 40						22 10					22 40		23 10					
Virginia Water	a	21 45				22 19		22 15		22 49			22 45		23 15		23 19		23 49	
	d	21 54				22 19		22 24		22 49			22 54		23 24		23 19		23 49	
Egham	d	21 57				22 23		22 27		22 53			22 57		23 27		23 23		23 53	
Windsor & Eton Riverside	d		21 51						22 21					22 53		23 23				
Datchet	d		21 55						22 25					22 56		23 26				
Sunnymeads	d		21 58						22 28					22 59		23 29				
Wraysbury	d		22 02						22 32					23 02		23 32				
Staines	d	22 03	22 08			22 29		22 33	22 38	22 59			23 03	23 08	23a32	23a37	23 29		23 59	
Ashford (Surrey)	d	22 06	22 11					22 36	22 41				23 06	23 11						
Feltham	d	22 11	22 16			22 35		22 41	22 46	23 05			23 11	23 16			23 35		00 05	
Whitton	d		22 20	22 23					22 50					23 20						
Kingston	d						22 29					22 59						23 29		
Hampton Wick	d						22 31					23 01						23 31		
Teddington	d						22 35					23 05						23 35		
Fulwell	d																			
Strawberry Hill	d						22 38					23 08						23 38		
Twickenham	a		22 23	22 26	22 33	22 40	22 42		22 53	23 10		23 12		23 23			23 40	23 42	00 10	
	d		22 23	22 28	22 34	22 41	22 43		22 53	23 11		23 13		23 23			23 41	23 43	00 11	
St Margarets	d			22 30			22 45					23 15						23 45		
Richmond ⊖	d		22 28	22 34		22 45	22 49		22 58	23 15		23 19		23 28			23 45	23 49	00 15	
North Sheen	d			22 36			22 51					23 21						23 51		
Mortlake	d			22 38			22 53					23 23						23 53		
Hounslow	d	22 16						22 46					23 16							
Isleworth	d	22 19						22 49					23 19							
Syon Lane	d	22 21						22 51					23 21							
Brentford	d	22 24						22 54					23 24							
Kew Bridge	d	22 26						22 56					23 26							
Chiswick	d	22 29						22 59					23 29							
Barnes Bridge	d	22 31						23 01					23 31							
Barnes	d	22 34		22 41			22 56	23 04				23 26	23 34					23 56		
Putney	d	22 37	22 34	22 44			22 59	23 07	23 04			23 29	23 37	23 34				23 59		
Wandsworth Town	d	22 40		22 47			23 02	23 10				23 32	23 40					00 02		
Clapham Junction ■	d	22 43	22 39	22 50		22 54	23 05	23 13	23 09	23 24		23 35	23 43	23 39			23 54	00 05	00 24	
Queenstown Rd.(Battersea)	d	22 46		22 53			23 08	23 16				23 38	23 46					00 08		
Vauxhall ⊖	d	22 50	22 45	22 57	23 14		23 12	23 20	23 15			23 42	23 50	23 45				00 12		
London Waterloo ■ ⊖	a	22 56	22 49	23 02	23 19	23 04	23 17	23 26	23 19	23 34		23 46	23 56	23 49			00 02	00 16	00 33	

Table 149

Saturdays from 02 October

Reading, Guildford, Ascot, Weybridge, Windsor, Kingston, Richmond and Hounslow - London

		SW
Reading ■	d	
Earley	d	
Winnersh Triangle	d	
Winnersh	d	
Wokingham	d	
Bracknell	d	
Martins Heron	d	
Guildford	d	
Wanborough	d	
Ash ■	d	
Aldershot	a	
	d	
Ash Vale	d	
Frimley	d	
Camberley	a	
	d	
Bagshot	d	
Ascot ■	d	
Sunningdale	d	
Longcross	d	
Woking	d	
West Byfleet	d	
Byfleet & New Haw	d	
Weybridge	d	23 33
Addlestone	d	23 37
Chertsey	d	23 40
Virginia Water	a	23 45
	d	23 54
Egham	d	23 57
Windsor & Eton Riverside	d	
Datchet	d	
Sunnymeads	d	
Wraysbury	d	
Staines	d	00a02
Ashford (Surrey)	d	
Feltham	d	
Whitton	d	
Kingston	d	
Hampton Wick	d	
Teddington	d	
Fulwell	d	
Strawberry Hill	d	
Twickenham	a	
	d	
St Margarets	d	
Richmond ⊖	d	
North Sheen	d	
Mortlake	d	
Hounslow	d	
Isleworth	d	
Syon Lane	d	
Brentford	d	
Kew Bridge	d	
Chiswick	d	
Barnes Bridge	d	
Barnes	d	
Putney	d	
Wandsworth Town	d	
Clapham Junction ■	d	
Queenstown Rd.(Battersea)	d	
Vauxhall ⊖	d	
London Waterloo ■ ⊖	a	

Table 149

Sundays
until 19 September

Reading, Guildford, Ascot, Weybridge, Windsor, Kingston, Richmond and Hounslow - London

		SW	SW 1	SW	SW 1	SW	SW	SW	SW 1	SW	SW	SW	SW 1	SW	SW 1	SW 1	SW	SW	SW 1
Reading 7	d		22p42		23p12								07 54		08 24				08 54
Earley	d		22p47		23p17								07 59		08 29				08 59
Winnersh Triangle	d		22p49		23p19								08 01		08 31				09 01
Winnersh	d		22p51		23p21								08 03		08 33				09 03
Wokingham	d		22p56		23p26								08 08		08 38				09 08
Bracknell	d		23p02		23p32								08 14		08 44				09 14
Martins Heron	d		23p05		23p35								08 17		08 47				09 17
Guildford	d								07 17							08 17			
Wanborough	d								07 23							08 23			
Ash 5	d								07 27							08 27			
Aldershot	a								07 34							08 34			
	d								07 40							08 40			
Ash Vale	d								07 45							08 45			
Frimley	d								07 51							08 51			
Camberley	a								07 55							08 55			
	d								07 55							08 55			
Bagshot	d								08 01							09 01			
Ascot 3	d		23p10		23p40				08a07				08 22		08 52	09a07			09 22
Sunningdale	d		23p13		23p43								08 25		08 55				09 25
Longcross	d																		
Woking	d											07 52						08 52	
West Byfleet	d											07 56						08 56	
Byfleet & New Haw	d											08 00						09 00	
Weybridge	d							07 00											
Addlestone	d							07 04				08 04						09 04	
Chertsey	d							07 07				08 07						09 07	
Virginia Water	a		23p19		23p49			07 12				08 12	08 30		09 00			09 12	09 30
	d		23p19		23p49			07 12				08 12	08 30		09 00			09 12	09 30
Egham	d		23p23		23p53			07 16				08 16	08 34		09 04			09 16	09 34
Windsor & Eton Riverside	d						07 01				08 01						09 01		
Datchet	d						07 04				08 04						09 04		
Sunnymeads	d						07 07				08 07						09 07		
Wraysbury	d						07 10				08 10						09 10		
Staines	d		23p29		23p59		07 16	07 21			08 16	08 21	08 39		09 09		09 16	09 21	09 39
Ashford (Surrey)	d						07 19	07 24			08 19	08 24					09 19	09 24	
Feltham	d		23p35		00 05		07 24	07 29			08 24	08 29	08 46		09 16		09 24	09 29	09 46
Whitton	d						07 28				08 28						09 28		
Kingston	d			23p29		06 49				07 49				08 49					
Hampton Wick	d			23p31		06 51				07 51				08 51					
Teddington	d			23p35		06 56				07 56				08 56					
Fulwell	d																		
Strawberry Hill	d			23p38		06 59				07 59				08 59					
Twickenham	a	23p33	23p40	23p42	00 10	07 02	07 31			08 02	08 31		08 51	09 02	09 21		09 31		09 51
	d	23p34	23p41	23p43	00 11	07 03	07 32			08 03	08 32		08 51	09 03	09 21		09 32		09 51
St Margarets	d			23p45		07 05	07 34			08 05	08 34			09 05			09 34		
Richmond ⊖	d		23p45	23p49	00 15	07 09	07 37			08 09	08 37		08 56	09 09	09 26		09 37		09 56
North Sheen	d			23p51		07 11	07 39			08 11	08 39			09 11			09 39		
Mortlake	d			23p53		07 13	07 42			08 13	08 42			09 13			09 42		
Hounslow	d							07 35				08 35						09 35	
Isleworth	d							07 38				08 38						09 38	
Syon Lane	d							07 40				08 40						09 40	
Brentford	d							07 42				08 42						09 42	
Kew Bridge	d							07 45				08 45						09 45	
Chiswick	d							07 47				08 47						09 47	
Barnes Bridge	d							07 50				08 50						09 50	
Barnes	d			23p56		07 16	07 45	07 53		08 16	08 45	08 53		09 16			09 45	09 53	
Putney	d			23p59		07 19	07 48	07 56		08 19	08 48	08 56	09 02	09 19	09 32		09 48	09 56	10 02
Wandsworth Town	d			00 02		07 22	07 51	07 59		08 22	08 51	08 59		09 22			09 51	09 59	
Clapham Junction 10	d		23p54	00 05	00 24	07 25	07 54	08 02		08 25	08 54	09 02	09 07	09 25	09 37		09 54	10 02	10 07
Queenstown Rd.(Battersea)	d			00 08		07 28	07 57	08 05		08 28	08 57	09 05		09 28			09 57	10 05	
Vauxhall ⊖	d	00 19		00 12		07 32	08 00	08 08		08 32	09 00	09 08	09 12	09 32	09 42		10 00	10 08	10 12
London Waterloo 15 ⊖	a	00 24	00 02	00 16	00 33	07 41	08 10	08 13		08 41	09 10	09 13	09 23	09 41	09 53		10 10	10 13	10 23

Table 149

Sundays
until 19 September

Reading, Guildford, Ascot, Weybridge, Windsor, Kingston, Richmond and Hounslow - London

		SW	SW 1	SW 1	SW	SW	SW 1	SW	SW	SW 1	SW 1	SW	SW	SW 1	SW	SW	SW 1	SW 1	SW	SW
Reading 7	d		09 24				09 54			10 24				10 54			11 24			
Earley	d		09 29				09 59			10 29				10 59			11 29			
Winnersh Triangle	d		09 31				10 01			10 31				11 01			11 31			
Winnersh	d		09 33				10 03			10 33				11 03			11 33			
Wokingham	d		09 38				10 08			10 38				11 08			11 38			
Bracknell	d		09 44				10 14			10 44				11 14			11 44			
Martins Heron	d		09 47				10 17			10 47				11 17			11 47			
Guildford	d			09 17							10 17							11 17		
Wanborough	d			09 23							10 23							11 23		
Ash 5	d			09 27							10 27							11 27		
Aldershot	a			09 34							10 34							11 34		
	d			09 40							10 40							11 40		
Ash Vale	d			09 45							10 45							11 45		
Frimley	d			09 51							10 51							11 51		
Camberley	a			09 55							10 55							11 55		
	d			09 55							10 55							11 55		
Bagshot	d			10 01							11 01							12 01		
Ascot 3	d		09 52	10a07			10 22			10 52	11a07			11 22			11 52	12a07		
Sunningdale	d		09 55				10 25			10 55				11 25			11 55			
Longcross	d																			
Woking	d					09 52							10 52							11 52
West Byfleet	d					09 56							10 56							11 56
Byfleet & New Haw	d					10 00							11 00							12 00
Weybridge	d																			
Addlestone	d					10 04							11 04							12 04
Chertsey	d					10 07							11 07							12 07
Virginia Water	a		10 00			10 12	10 30			11 00			11 12	11 30			12 00			12 12
	d		10 00			10 12	10 30			11 00			11 12	11 30			12 00			12 12
Egham	d		10 04			10 16	10 34			11 04			11 16	11 34			12 04			12 16
Windsor & Eton Riverside	d				10 01			10 34				11 01			11 34				12 01	
Datchet	d				10 04			10 37				11 04			11 37				12 04	
Sunnymeads	d				10 07							11 07							12 07	
Wraysbury	d				10 10							11 10							12 10	
Staines	d		10 09		10 16	10 21	10 39	10 45		11 09		11 16	11 21	11 39	11 45		12 09		12 16	12 21
Ashford (Surrey)	d				10 19	10 24		10 48				11 19	11 24		11 48				12 19	12 24
Feltham	d		10 16		10 24	10 29	10 46	10 53		11 16		11 24	11 29	11 46	11 53		12 16		12 24	12 29
Whitton	d				10 28			10 57				11 28			11 57				12 28	
Kingston	d	09 49							10 49							11 49				
Hampton Wick	d	09 51							10 51							11 51				
Teddington	d	09 56							10 56							11 56				
Fulwell	d																			
Strawberry Hill	d	09 59							10 59							11 59				
Twickenham	a	10 02	10 21		10 31		10 51	11 00	11 02	11 21		11 31		11 51	12 00	12 02	12 21		12 31	
	d	10 03	10 21		10 32		10 51	11 01	11 03	11 21		11 32		11 51	12 01	12 03	12 21		12 32	
St Margarets	d	10 05			10 34				11 05			11 34				12 05			12 34	
Richmond ⊖	d	10 09	10 26		10 37		10 56	11 05	11 09	11 26		11 37		11 56	12 05	12 09	12 26		12 37	
North Sheen	d	10 11			10 39				11 11			11 39				12 11			12 39	
Mortlake	d	10 13			10 42				11 13			11 42				12 13			12 42	
Hounslow	d					10 35							11 35							12 35
Isleworth	d					10 38							11 38							12 38
Syon Lane	d					10 40							11 40							12 40
Brentford	d					10 42							11 42							12 42
Kew Bridge	d					10 45							11 45							12 45
Chiswick	d					10 47							11 47							12 47
Barnes Bridge	d					10 50							11 50							12 50
Barnes	d	10 16			10 45	10 53			11 16			11 45	11 53			12 16			12 45	12 53
Putney	d	10 19	10 32		10 48	10 56	11 02	11 14	11 19	11 32		11 48	11 56	12 02	12 14	12 19	12 32		12 48	12 56
Wandsworth Town	d	10 22			10 51	10 59			11 22			11 51	11 59			12 22			12 51	12 59
Clapham Junction 10	d	10 25	10 37		10 53	11 02	11 07	11 18	11 25	11 37		11 53	12 02	12 07	12 18	12 25	12 37		12 53	13 02
Queenstown Rd.(Battersea)	d	10 28			10 57	11 05			11 28			11 57	12 05			12 28			12 57	13 05
Vauxhall ⊖	d	10 32	10 42		11 00	11 08	11 12	11 24	11 32	11 42		12 00	12 08	12 12	12 24	12 32	12 42		13 00	13 08
London Waterloo 15 ⊖	a	10 41	10 53		11 10	11 13	11 23	11 34	11 41	11 53		12 10	12 13	12 23	12 34	12 41	12 53		13 10	13 13

Table 149

Reading, Guildford, Ascot, Weybridge, Windsor, Kingston, Richmond and Hounslow - London

		SW ■	SW	SW	SW ■	SW ■	SW	SW	SW	SW ■	SW	SW	SW ■	SW ■	SW	SW	SW	SW ■	SW	SW
Reading ■7	d	11 54			12 24					12 54			13 24					13 54		
Earley	d	11 59			12 29					12 59			13 29					13 59		
Winnersh Triangle	d	12 01			12 31					13 01			13 31					14 01		
Winnersh	d	12 03			12 33					13 03			13 33					14 03		
Wokingham	d	12 08			12 38					13 08			13 38					14 08		
Bracknell	d	12 14			12 44					13 14			13 44					14 14		
Martins Heron	d	12 17			12 47					13 17			13 47					14 17		
Guildford	d					12 17								13 17						
Wanborough	d					12 23								13 23						
Ash ■5	d					12 27								13 27						
Aldershot	a					12 34								13 34						
	d					12 40								13 40						
Ash Vale	d					12 45								13 45						
Frimley	d					12 51								13 51						
Camberley	a					12 55								13 55						
	d					12 55								13 55						
Bagshot	d					13 01								14 01						
Ascot ■3	d	12 22			12 52	13a07				13 22			13 52	14a07				14 22		
Sunningdale	d	12 25			12 55					13 25			13 55					14 25		
Longcross	d																			
Woking	d								12 52								13 52			
West Byfleet	d								12 56								13 56			
Byfleet & New Haw	d								13 00								14 00			
Weybridge	d																			
Addlestone	d								13 04								14 04			
Chertsey	d								13 07								14 07			
Virginia Water	a	12 30			13 00				13 12	13 30			14 00				14 12	14 30		
	d	12 30			13 00				13 12	13 30			14 00				14 12	14 30		
Egham	d	12 34			13 04				13 16	13 34			14 04				14 16	14 34		
Windsor & Eton Riverside	d		12 34					13 01			13 34					14 01			14 34	
Datchet	d		12 37					13 04			13 37					14 04			14 37	
Sunnymeads	d							13 07								14 07				
Wraysbury	d							13 10								14 10				
Staines	d	12 39	12 45		13 09			13 16	13 21	13 39	13 45		14 09			14 16	14 21	14 39	14 45	
Ashford (Surrey)	d		12 48					13 19	13 24		13 48					14 19	14 24		14 48	
Feltham	d	12 46	12 53		13 16			13 24	13 29	13 46	13 53		14 16			14 24	14 29	14 46	14 53	
Whitton	d		12 57					13 28			13 57					14 28			14 57	
Kingston	d			12 49			13 11					13 49			14 11					14 49
Hampton Wick	d			12 51			13 13					13 51			14 13					14 51
Teddington	d			12 56			13 16					13 56			14 16					14 56
Fulwell	d																			
Strawberry Hill	d			12 59			13 19					13 59			14 19					14 59
Twickenham	a	12 51	13 00	13 02	13 21		13 22	13 31		13 51	14 00	14 02	14 21		14 22	14 31		14 51	15 00	15 02
	d	12 51	13 01	13 03	13 21		13 23	13 32		13 51	14 01	14 03	14 21		14 23	14 32		14 51	15 01	15 03
St Margarets	d			13 05			13 25	13 34				14 05			14 25	14 34				15 05
Richmond ⊖	d	12 56	13 05	13 09	13 26		13 29	13 37		13 56	14 05	14 09	14 26		14 29	14 37		14 56	15 05	15 09
North Sheen	d			13 11			13 31	13 39				14 11			14 31	14 39				15 11
Mortlake	d			13 13			13 33	13 42				14 13			14 33	14 42				15 13
Hounslow	d								13 35								14 35			
Isleworth	d								13 38								14 38			
Syon Lane	d								13 40								14 40			
Brentford	d								13 42								14 42			
Kew Bridge	d								13 45								14 45			
Chiswick	d								13 47								14 47			
Barnes Bridge	d								13 50								14 50			
Barnes	d			13 16			13 36	13 45	13 53			14 16			14 36	14 45	14 53			15 16
Putney	d	13 02	13 14	13 19	13 32		13 39	13 48	13 56	14 02	14 14	14 19	14 32		14 39	14 48	14 56	15 02	15 14	15 19
Wandsworth Town	d			13 22			13 42	13 51	13 59			14 22			14 42	14 51	14 59			15 22
Clapham Junction ■10	d	13 07	13 18	13 25	13 37		13 45	13 54	14 02	14 07	14 18	14 25	14 37		14 45	14 54	15 02	15 07	15 18	15 25
Queenstown Rd.(Battersea)	d			13 28			13 48	13 57	14 05			14 28			14 48	14 57	15 05			15 28
Vauxhall ⊖	d	13 12	13 24	13 32	13 42		13 52	14 00	14 08	14 12	14 24	14 32	14 42		14 52	15 00	15 08	15 12	15 24	15 32
London Waterloo ■15 ⊖	a	13 23	13 34	13 41	13 53		14 00	14 10	14 13	14 23	14 34	14 41	14 53		15 00	15 05	15 13	15 18	15 29	15 36

Table 149

Reading, Guildford, Ascot, Weybridge, Windsor, Kingston, Richmond and Hounslow - London

		SW ■	SW ■	SW	SW	SW	SW ■	SW	SW	SW ■	SW ■	SW	SW	SW	SW ■	SW	SW	SW ■	SW ■	SW	SW
Reading ■7	d	14 24					14 54			15 24					15 54			16 24			
Earley	d	14 29					14 59			15 29					15 59			16 29			
Winnersh Triangle	d	14 31					15 01			15 31					16 01			16 31			
Winnersh	d	14 33					15 03			15 33					16 03			16 33			
Wokingham	d	14 38					15 08			15 38					16 08			16 38			
Bracknell	d	14 44					15 14			15 44					16 14			16 44			
Martins Heron	d	14 47					15 17			15 47					16 17			16 47			
Guildford	d		14 17								15 17								16 17		
Wanborough	d		14 23								15 23								16 23		
Ash ■5	d		14 27								15 27								16 27		
Aldershot	a		14 34								15 34								16 34		
	d		14 40								15 40								16 40		
Ash Vale	d		14 45								15 45								16 45		
Frimley	d		14 51								15 51								16 51		
Camberley	a		14 55								15 55								16 55		
	d		14 55								15 55								16 55		
Bagshot	d		15 01								16 01								17 01		
Ascot ■3	d	14 52	15a07				15 22			15 52	16a07				16 22			16 52	17a07		
Sunningdale	d	14 55					15 25			15 55					16 25			16 55			
Longcross	d																				
Woking	d					14 52								15 52							
West Byfleet	d					14 56								15 56							
Byfleet & New Haw	d					15 00								16 00							
Weybridge	d																				
Addlestone	d					15 04								16 04							
Chertsey	d					15 07								16 07							
Virginia Water	a	15 00				15 12	15 30			16 00				16 12	16 30			17 00			
	d	15 00				15 12	15 30			16 00				16 12	16 30			17 00			
Egham	d	15 04				15 16	15 34			16 04				16 16	16 34			17 04			
Windsor & Eton Riverside	d				15 01			15 34					16 01			16 34					17 01
Datchet	d				15 04			15 37					16 04			16 37					17 04
Sunnymeads	d				15 07								16 07								17 07
Wraysbury	d				15 10								16 10								17 10
Staines	d	15 09			15 16	15 21	15 39	15 45		16 09			16 16	16 21	16 39	16 45		17 09			17 16
Ashford (Surrey)	d				15 19	15 24		15 48					16 19	16 24		16 48					17 19
Feltham	d	15 16			15 24	15 29	15 46	15 53		16 16			16 24	16 29	16 46	16 53		17 16			17 24
Whitton	d				15 28			15 57					16 28			16 57					17 28
Kingston	d			15 11					15 49			16 11					16 49			17 11	
Hampton Wick	d			15 13					15 51			16 13					16 51			17 13	
Teddington	d			15 16					15 56			16 16					16 56			17 16	
Fulwell	d																				
Strawberry Hill	d			15 19					15 59			16 19					16 59			17 19	
Twickenham	a	15 21		15 22	15 31		15 51	16 00	16 02	16 21		16 22	16 31		16 51	17 00	17 02	17 21		17 22	17 31
	d	15 21		15 23	15 32		15 51	16 01	16 03	16 21		16 23	16 32		16 51	17 01	17 03	17 21		17 23	17 32
St Margarets	d			15 25	15 34				16 05			16 25	16 34				17 05			17 25	17 34
Richmond ⊖	d	15 26		15 29	15 37		15 56	16 05	16 09	16 26		16 29	16 37		16 56	17 05	17 09	17 26		17 29	17 37
North Sheen	d			15 31	15 39				16 11			16 31	16 39				17 11			17 31	17 39
Mortlake	d			15 33	15 42				16 13			16 33	16 42				17 13			17 33	17 42
Hounslow	d					15 35								16 35							
Isleworth	d					15 38								16 38							
Syon Lane	d					15 40								16 40							
Brentford	d					15 42								16 42							
Kew Bridge	d					15 45								16 45							
Chiswick	d					15 47								16 47							
Barnes Bridge	d					15 50								16 50							
Barnes	d			15 36	15 45	15 53			16 16			16 36	16 45	16 53			17 16			17 36	17 45
Putney	d	15 32		15 39	15 48	15 56	16 02	16 14	16 19	16 32		16 39	16 48	16 56	17 02	17 14	17 19	17 32		17 39	17 48
Wandsworth Town	d			15 42	15 51	15 59			16 22			16 42	16 51	16 59			17 22			17 42	17 51
Clapham Junction ■10	d	15 37		15 45	15 54	16 02	16 07	16 18	16 25	16 37		16 45	16 54	17 02	17 07	17 18	17 25	17 37		17 45	17 54
Queenstown Rd.(Battersea)	d			15 48	15 57	16 05			16 28			16 48	16 57	17 05			17 28			17 48	17 57
Vauxhall ⊖	d	15 42		15 52	16 00	16 08	16 12	16 24	16 32	16 42		16 52	17 00	17 08	17 12	17 24	17 32	17 42		17 52	18 00
London Waterloo ■15 ⊖	a	15 48		16 00	16 05	16 13	16 18	16 29	16 36	16 48		17 00	17 05	17 13	17 18	17 29	17 36	17 48		18 00	18 05

Table 149

Sundays until 19 September

Reading, Guildford, Ascot, Weybridge, Windsor, Kingston, Richmond and Hounslow - London

		SW	SW ■	SW	SW	SW ■	SW ■	SW	SW	SW	SW ■	SW	SW	SW ■	SW ■	SW	SW	SW	SW ■
Reading	d		16 54			17 24					17 54			18 24					18 54
Earley	d		16 59			17 29					17 59			18 29					18 59
Winnersh Triangle	d		17 01			17 31					18 01			18 31					19 01
Winnersh	d		17 03			17 33					18 03			18 33					19 03
Wokingham	d		17 08			17 38					18 08			18 38					19 08
Bracknell	d		17 14			17 44					18 14			18 44					19 14
Martins Heron	d		17 17			17 47					18 17			18 47					19 17
Guildford	d						17 17								18 17				
Wanborough	d						17 23								18 23				
Ash	d						17 27								18 27				
Aldershot	a						17 34								18 34				
	d						17 40								18 40				
Ash Vale	d						17 45								18 45				
Frimley	d						17 51								18 51				
Camberley	a						17 55								18 55				
	d						17 55								18 55				
Bagshot	d						18 01								19 01				
Ascot	d		17 22			17 52	18a07				18 22			18 52	19a07				19 22
Sunningdale	d		17 25			17 55					18 25			18 55					19 25
Longcross	d																		
Woking	d	16 52								17 52								18 52	
West Byfleet	d	16 56								17 56								18 56	
Byfleet & New Haw	d	17 00								18 00								19 00	
Weybridge	d																		
Addlestone	d	17 04								18 04								19 04	
Chertsey	d	17 07								18 07								19 07	
Virginia Water	a	17 12	17 30			18 00				18 12	18 30			19 00				19 12	19 30
	d	17 12	17 30			18 00				18 12	18 30			19 00				19 12	19 30
Egham	d	17 16	17 34			18 04				18 16	18 34			19 04				19 16	19 34
Windsor & Eton Riverside	d			17 34					18 01			18 34					19 01		
Datchet	d			17 37					18 04			18 37					19 04		
Sunnymeads	d								18 07								19 07		
Wraysbury	d								18 10								19 10		
Staines	d	17 21	17 39	17 45		18 09			18 16	18 21	18 39	18 45		19 09			19 16	19 21	19 39
Ashford (Surrey)	d	17 24		17 48					18 19	18 24		18 48					19 19	19 24	
Feltham	d	17 29	17 46	17 53		18 16			18 24	18 29	18 46	18 53		19 16			19 24	19 29	19 46
Whitton	d			17 57					18 28			18 57					19 28		
Kingston	d				17 49			18 11					18 49			19 11			
Hampton Wick	d				17 51			18 13					18 51			19 13			
Teddington	d				17 56			18 16					18 56			19 16			
Fulwell	d																		
Strawberry Hill	d				17 59			18 19					18 59			19 19			
Twickenham	a		17 51	18 00	18 02	18 21		18 22	18 31		18 51	19 00	19 02	19 21		19 22	19 31		19 51
	d		17 51	18 01	18 03	18 21		18 23	18 32		18 51	19 01	19 03	19 21		19 23	19 32		19 51
St Margarets	d				18 05			18 25	18 34				19 05			19 25	19 34		
Richmond ⊖	d		17 56	18 05	18 09	18 26		18 29	18 37		18 56	19 05	19 09	19 26		19 29	19 37		19 56
North Sheen	d				18 11			18 31	18 39				19 11			19 31	19 39		
Mortlake	d				18 13			18 33	18 42				19 13			19 33	19 42		
Hounslow	d	17 35								18 35								19 35	
Isleworth	d	17 38								18 38								19 38	
Syon Lane	d	17 40								18 40								19 40	
Brentford	d	17 42								18 42								19 42	
Kew Bridge	d	17 45								18 45								19 45	
Chiswick	d	17 47								18 47								19 47	
Barnes Bridge	d	17 50								18 50								19 50	
Barnes	d	17 53			18 16			18 36	18 45	18 53			19 16			19 36	19 45	19 53	
Putney	d	17 56	18 02	18 14	18 19	18 32		18 39	18 48	18 56	19 02	19 14	19 19	19 32		19 39	19 48	19 56	20 02
Wandsworth Town	d	17 59			18 22			18 42	18 51	18 59			19 22			19 42	19 51	19 59	
Clapham Junction	d	18 02	18 07	18 18	18 25	18 37		18 45	18 54	19 02	19 07	19 18	19 25	19 37		19 45	19 54	20 02	20 07
Queenstown Rd.(Battersea)	d	18 05			18 28			18 48	18 57	19 05			19 28			19 48	19 57	20 05	
Vauxhall ⊖	d	18 08	18 12	18 24	18 32	18 42		18 52	19 00	19 08	19 12	19 24	19 32	19 42		19 52	20 00	20 08	20 12
London Waterloo ⊖	a	18 13	18 18	18 29	18 36	18 48		19 00	19 05	19 13	19 18	19 29	19 36	19 48		20 00	20 05	20 13	20 18

Table 149

Sundays until 19 September

Reading, Guildford, Ascot, Weybridge, Windsor, Kingston, Richmond and Hounslow - London

		SW	SW	SW ■	SW ■	SW	SW	SW	SW ■	SW	SW	SW ■	SW ■	SW	SW	SW	SW ■	SW	SW ■	SW ■	SW
Reading	d			19 24					19 54			20 24					20 54		21 24		
Earley	d			19 29					19 59			20 29					20 59		21 29		
Winnersh Triangle	d			19 31					20 01			20 31					21 01		21 31		
Winnersh	d			19 33					20 03			20 33					21 03		21 33		
Wokingham	d			19 38					20 08			20 38					21 08		21 38		
Bracknell	d			19 44					20 14			20 44					21 14		21 44		
Martins Heron	d			19 47					20 17			20 47					21 17		21 47		
Guildford	d				19 17								20 17							21 17	
Wanborough	d				19 23								20 23							21 23	
Ash	d				19 27								20 27							21 27	
Aldershot	a				19 34								20 34							21 34	
	d				19 40								20 40							21 40	
Ash Vale	d				19 45								20 45							21 45	
Frimley	d				19 51								20 51							21 51	
Camberley	a				19 55								20 55							21 55	
	d				19 55								20 55							21 55	
Bagshot	d				20 01								21 01							22 01	
Ascot	d			19 52	20a07				20 22			20 52	21a07				21 22		21 52	22a07	
Sunningdale	d			19 55					20 25			20 55					21 25		21 55		
Longcross	d																				
Woking	d							19 52								20 52					
West Byfleet	d							19 56								20 56					
Byfleet & New Haw	d							20 00								21 00					
Weybridge	d																				
Addlestone	d							20 04								21 04					
Chertsey	d							20 07								21 07					
Virginia Water	a			20 00				20 12	20 30			21 00				21 12	21 30		22 00		
	d			20 00				20 12	20 30			21 00				21 12	21 30		22 00		
Egham	d			20 04				20 16	20 34			21 04				21 16	21 34		22 04		
Windsor & Eton Riverside	d	19 34					20 01			20 34					21 01						
Datchet	d	19 37					20 04			20 37					21 04						
Sunnymeads	d						20 07								21 07						
Wraysbury	d						20 10								21 10						
Staines	d	19 45		20 09			20 16	20 21	20 39	20 45		21 09			21 16	21 21	21 39		22 09		
Ashford (Surrey)	d	19 48					20 19	20 24		20 48					21 19	21 24					
Feltham	d	19 53		20 16			20 24	20 29	20 46	20 53		21 16			21 24	21 29	21 46		22 16		
Whitton	d	19 57					20 28			20 57					21 28						
Kingston	d		19 49			20 11					20 49			21 11				21 49			22 11
Hampton Wick	d		19 51			20 13					20 51			21 13				21 51			22 13
Teddington	d		19 56			20 16					20 56			21 16				21 56			22 16
Fulwell	d																				
Strawberry Hill	d		19 59			20 19					20 59			21 19				21 59			22 19
Twickenham	a	20 00	20 02	20 21		20 22	20 31		20 51	21 00	21 02	21 21		21 22	21 31		21 51	22 02	22 21		22 22
	d	20 01	20 03	20 21		20 23	20 32		20 51	21 01	21 03	21 21		21 23	21 32		21 51	22 03	22 21		22 23
St Margarets	d		20 05			20 25	20 34				21 05			21 25	21 34			22 05			22 25
Richmond ⊖	d	20 05	20 09	20 26		20 29	20 37		20 56	21 05	21 09	21 26		21 29	21 37		21 56	22 09	22 26		22 29
North Sheen	d		20 11			20 31	20 39				21 11			21 31	21 39			22 11			22 31
Mortlake	d		20 13			20 33	20 42				21 13			21 33	21 42			22 13			22 33
Hounslow	d							20 35								21 35					
Isleworth	d							20 38								21 38					
Syon Lane	d							20 40								21 40					
Brentford	d							20 42								21 42					
Kew Bridge	d							20 45								21 45					
Chiswick	d							20 47								21 47					
Barnes Bridge	d							20 50								21 50					
Barnes	d		20 16			20 36	20 45	20 53			21 16			21 36	21 45	21 53		22 16			22 36
Putney	d	20 14	20 19	20 32		20 39	20 48	20 56	21 02	21 14	21 19	21 32		21 39	21 48	21 56	22 02	22 19	22 32		22 39
Wandsworth Town	d		20 22			20 42	20 51	20 59			21 22			21 42	21 51	21 59		22 22			22 42
Clapham Junction	d	20 18	20 25	20 37		20 45	20 54	21 02	21 07	21 18	21 25	21 37		21 45	21 54	22 02	22 07	22 25	22 37		22 45
Queenstown Rd.(Battersea)	d		20 28			20 48	20 57	21 05			21 28			21 48	21 57	22 05		22 28			22 48
Vauxhall ⊖	d	20 24	20 32	20 42		20 52	21 00	21 08	21 12	21 24	21 32	21 42		21 52	22 00	22 08	22 12	22 32	22 42		22 52
London Waterloo ⊖	a	20 29	20 36	20 48		21 00	21 05	21 13	21 18	21 29	21 36	21 48		22 00	22 05	22 13	22 18	22 36	22 48		23 00

Table 149

Sundays until 19 September

Reading, Guildford, Ascot, Weybridge, Windsor, Kingston, Richmond and Hounslow - London

		SW	SW	SW ■	SW	SW ■	SW ■	SW	SW	SW	SW ■
Reading 7	d			21 54		22 24					22 54
Earley	d			21 59		22 29					22 59
Winnersh Triangle	d			22 01		22 31					23 01
Winnersh	d			22 03		22 33					23 03
Wokingham	d			22 08		22 38					23 08
Bracknell	d			22 14		22 44					23 14
Martins Heron	d			22 17		22 47					23 17
Guildford	d						22 17				
Wanborough	d						22 23				
Ash 5	d						22 27				
Aldershot	a						22 34				
	d						22 40				
Ash Vale	d						22 45				
Frimley	d						22 51				
Camberley	a						22 55				
	d						22 55				
Bagshot	d						23 01				
Ascot 3	d			22 22		22 52	23a07				23 22
Sunningdale	d			22 25		22 55					23 25
Longcross	d										
Woking	d		21 52							22 52	
West Byfleet	d		21 56							22 56	
Byfleet & New Haw	d		22 00							23 00	
Weybridge	d										
Addlestone	d		22 04							23 04	
Chertsey	d		22 07							23 07	
Virginia Water	a		22 12	22 30		23 00				23 12	23 30
	d		22 12	22 30		23 00				23 12	23 30
Egham	d		22 16	22 34		23 04				23 16	23 34
Windsor & Eton Riverside	d	22 01							23 01		
Datchet	d	22 04							23 04		
Sunnymeads	d	22 07							23 07		
Wraysbury	d	22 10							23 10		
Staines	d	22 16	22 21	22 39		23 09			23 16	23 21	23 39
Ashford (Surrey)	d	22 19	22 24						23 19	23 24	
Feltham	d	22 24	22 29	22 46		23 16			23 24	23 29	23 46
Whitton	d	22 28							23 28		
Kingston	d				22 49			23 11			
Hampton Wick	d				22 51			23 13			
Teddington	d				22 56			23 16			
Fulwell	d										
Strawberry Hill	d				22 59			23 19			
Twickenham	a	22 31		22 51	23 02	23 21		23 22	23 31		23 51
	d	22 32		22 51	23 03	23 21		23 23	23 32		23 51
St Margarets	d	22 34			23 05			23 25	23 34		
Richmond ⊖	d	22 37		22 56	23 09	23 26		23 29	23 37		23 56
North Sheen	d	22 39			23 11			23 31	23 39		
Mortlake	d	22 42			23 13			23 33	23 42		
Hounslow	d		22 35							23 35	
Isleworth	d		22 38							23 38	
Syon Lane	d		22 40							23 40	
Brentford	d		22 42							23 42	
Kew Bridge	d		22 45							23 45	
Chiswick	d		22 47							23 47	
Barnes Bridge	d		22 50							23 50	
Barnes	d	22 45	22 53		23 16			23 36	23 45	23 53	
Putney	d	22 48	22 56	23 02	23 19	23 32		23 39	23 48	23 56	00 02
Wandsworth Town	d	22 51	22 59		23 22			23 42	23 51	23 59	
Clapham Junction 10	d	22 54	23 02	23 07	23 25	23 37		23 45	23 54	00 02	00 07
Queenstown Rd.(Battersea)	d	22 57	23 05		23 28			23 48	23 57	00 05	
Vauxhall ⊖	d	23 00	23 08	23 12	23 32	23 42		23 52	23 59	00 08	00 12
London Waterloo 15 ⊖	a	23 05	23 13	23 18	23 36	23 48		23 59	00 05	00 13	00 17

Table 149

Sundays from 26 September

Reading, Guildford, Ascot, Weybridge, Windsor, Kingston, Richmond and Hounslow - London

		SW	SW ■	SW	SW ■	SW	SW	SW	SW ■	SW	SW	SW	SW	SW ■	SW	SW ■	SW ■	SW	SW
Reading 7	d		22p39		23p12									07 51		08 21			
Earley	d		22p44		23p17									07 56		08 26			
Winnersh Triangle	d		22p46		23p19									07 58		08 28			
Winnersh	d		22p48		23p21									08 00		08 30			
Wokingham	d		22p53		23p26									08 05		08 35			
Bracknell	d		22p59		23p32									08 11		08 41			
Martins Heron	d		23p02		23p35									08 14		08 44			
Guildford	d								07 17								08 17		
Wanborough	d								07 23								08 23		
Ash 5	d								07 27								08 27		
Aldershot	a								07 34								08 34		
	d								07 40								08 40		
Ash Vale	d								07 45								08 45		
Frimley	d								07 51								08 51		
Camberley	a								07 55								08 55		
	d								07 55								08 55		
Bagshot	d								08 01								09 01		
Ascot 3	d		23p07		23p40				08a07					08 19		08 49	09a07		
Sunningdale	d		23p10		23p43									08 22		08 52			
Longcross	d																		
Woking	d												07 52						08 52
West Byfleet	d												07 56						08 56
Byfleet & New Haw	d												08 00						09 00
Weybridge	d							07 00											
Addlestone	d							07 04					08 04						09 04
Chertsey	d							07 07					08 07						09 07
Virginia Water	a		23p19		23p49			07 12					08 12	08 30		09 00			09 12
	d		23p19		23p49			07 12					08 12	08 30		09 00			09 12
Egham	d		23p23		23p53			07 16					08 16	08 34		09 04			09 16
Windsor & Eton Riverside	d						06 59					07 59						08 59	
Datchet	d						07 02					08 02						09 02	
Sunnymeads	d						07 05					08 05						09 05	
Wraysbury	d						07 08					08 08						09 08	
Staines	d		23p29		23p59		07 16	07 21				08 16	08 21	08 39		09 09		09 16	09 21
Ashford (Surrey)	d						07 19	07 24				08 19	08 24					09 19	09 24
Feltham	d		23p35		00 05		07 24	07 29				08 24	08 29	08 46		09 16		09 24	09 29
Whitton	d						07 28					08 28						09 28	
Kingston	d			23p29		06 49					07 49				08 49				
Hampton Wick	d			23p31		06 51					07 51				08 51				
Teddington	d			23p35		06 56					07 56				08 56				
Fulwell	d																		
Strawberry Hill	d			23p38		06 59					07 59				08 59				
Twickenham	a	23p33	23p40	23p42	00 10	07 02	07 31			07 44	08 02	08 31		08 51	09 02	09 21		09 31	
	d	23p34	23p41	23p43	00 11	07 03	07 32			07 45	08 03	08 32		08 51	09 03	09 21		09 32	
St Margarets	d			23p45		07 05	07 34				08 05	08 34			09 05			09 34	
Richmond ⊖	d		23p45	23p49	00 15	07 09	07 37				08 09	08 37		08 56	09 09	09 26		09 37	
North Sheen	d			23p51		07 11	07 39				08 11	08 39			09 11			09 39	
Mortlake	d			23p53		07 13	07 42				08 13	08 42			09 13			09 42	
Hounslow	d							07 35					08 35						09 35
Isleworth	d							07 38					08 38						09 38
Syon Lane	d							07 40					08 40						09 40
Brentford	d							07 42					08 42						09 42
Kew Bridge	d							07 45					08 45						09 45
Chiswick	d							07 47					08 47						09 47
Barnes Bridge	d							07 50					08 50						09 50
Barnes	d			23p56		07 16	07 45	07 53			08 16	08 45	08 53		09 16			09 45	09 53
Putney	d			23p59		07 19	07 48	07 56			08 19	08 48	08 56	09 02	09 19	09 32		09 48	09 56
Wandsworth Town	d			00 02		07 22	07 51	07 59			08 22	08 51	08 59		09 22			09 51	09 59
Clapham Junction 10	d		23p54	00 05	00 24	07 25	07 54	08 02			08 25	08 54	09 02	09 07	09 25	09 37		09 54	10 02
Queenstown Rd.(Battersea)	d			00 08		07 28	07 57	08 05			08 28	08 57	09 05		09 28			09 57	10 05
Vauxhall ⊖	d	00 19		00 12		07 32	08 00	08 08		08 29	08 32	09 00	09 08	09 12	09 32	09 42		10 00	10 08
London Waterloo 15 ⊖	a	00 24	0002	00 16	00 33	07 41	08 10	08 13		08 39	08 41	09 10	09 13	09 23	09 41	09 53		10 10	10 13

Table 149

Sundays
from 26 September

Reading, Guildford, Ascot, Weybridge, Windsor, Kingston, Richmond and Hounslow - London

		SW ■1	SW	SW ■1	SW ■1	SW	SW	SW ■1	SW	SW	SW ■1	SW ■1	SW	SW	SW ■1	SW	SW	SW ■1	SW ■1	SW	SW
Reading ■7	d	08 51		09 21				09 51			10 21				10 51			11 21			
Earley	d	08 56		09 26				09 56			10 26				10 56			11 26			
Winnersh Triangle	d	08 58		09 28				09 58			10 28				10 58			11 28			
Winnersh	d	09 00		09 30				10 00			10 30				11 00			11 30			
Wokingham	d	09 05		09 35				10 05			10 35				11 05			11 35			
Bracknell	d	09 11		09 41				10 11			10 41				11 11			11 41			
Martins Heron	d	09 14		09 44				10 14			10 44				11 14			11 44			
Guildford	d				09 17							10 17							11 17		
Wanborough	d				09 23							10 23							11 23		
Ash ■5	d				09 27							10 27							11 27		
Aldershot	a				09 34							10 34							11 34		
	d				09 40							10 40							11 40		
Ash Vale	d				09 45							10 45							11 45		
Frimley	d				09 51							10 51							11 51		
Camberley	a				09 55							10 55							11 55		
	d				09 55							10 55							11 55		
Bagshot	d				10 01							11 01							12 01		
Ascot ■3	d	09 19		09 49	10a07			10 19			10 49	11a07			11 19			11 49	12a07		
Sunningdale	d	09 22		09 52				10 22			10 52				11 22			11 52			
Longcross	d																				
Woking	d						09 52							10 52							11 52
West Byfleet	d						09 56							10 56							11 56
Byfleet & New Haw	d						10 00							11 00							12 00
Weybridge	d																				
Addlestone	d						10 04							11 04							12 04
Chertsey	d						10 07							11 07							12 07
Virginia Water	a	09 30		10 00			10 12	10 30			11 00			11 12	11 30			12 00			12 12
	d	09 30		10 00			10 12	10 30			11 00			11 12	11 30			12 00			12 12
Egham	d	09 34		10 04			10 16	10 34			11 04			11 16	11 34			12 04			12 16
Windsor & Eton Riverside	d					09 59			10 32				10 59			11 32				11 59	
Datchet	d					10 02			10 35				11 02			11 35				12 02	
Sunnymeads	d					10 05							11 05							12 05	
Wraysbury	d					10 08							11 08							12 08	
Staines	d	09 39		10 09		10 16	10 21	10 39	10 45		11 09		11 16	11 21	11 39	11 45		12 09		12 16	12 21
Ashford (Surrey)	d					10 19	10 24		10 48				11 19	11 24		11 48				12 19	12 24
Feltham	d	09 46		10 16		10 24	10 29	10 46	10 53		11 16		11 24	11 29	11 46	11 53		12 16		12 24	12 29
Whitton	d					10 28			10 57				11 28			11 57				12 28	
Kingston	d		09 49							10 49							11 49				
Hampton Wick	d		09 51							10 51							11 51				
Teddington	d		09 56							10 56							11 56				
Fulwell	d																				
Strawberry Hill	d		09 59							10 59							11 59				
Twickenham	a	09 51	10 02	10 21		10 31		10 51	11 00	11 02	11 21		11 31		11 51	12 00	12 02	12 21		12 31	
	d	09 51	10 03	10 21		10 32		10 51	11 01	11 03	11 21		11 32		11 51	12 01	12 03	12 21		12 32	
St Margarets	d		10 05			10 34				11 05			11 34				12 05			12 34	
Richmond ⊖	d	09 56	10 09	10 26		10 37		10 56	11 05	11 09	11 26		11 37		11 56	12 05	12 09	12 26		12 37	
North Sheen	d		10 11			10 39				11 11			11 39				12 11			12 39	
Mortlake	d		10 13			10 42				11 13			11 42				12 13			12 42	
Hounslow	d						10 35							11 35							12 35
Isleworth	d						10 38							11 38							12 38
Syon Lane	d						10 40							11 40							12 40
Brentford	d						10 42							11 42							12 42
Kew Bridge	d						10 45							11 45							12 45
Chiswick	d						10 47							11 47							12 47
Barnes Bridge	d						10 50							11 50							12 50
Barnes	d		10 16			10 45	10 53			11 16			11 45	11 53			12 16			12 45	12 53
Putney	d	10 02	10 19	10 32		10 48	10 56	11 02	11 14	11 19	11 32		11 48	11 56	12 02	12 14	12 19	12 32		12 48	12 56
Wandsworth Town	d		10 22			10 51	10 59			11 22			11 51	11 59			12 22			12 51	12 59
Clapham Junction ■10	d	10 07	10 25	10 37		10 53	11 02	11 07	11 18	11 25	11 37		11 53	12 02	12 07	12 18	12 25	12 37		12 53	13 02
Queenstown Rd.(Battersea)	d		10 28			10 57	11 05			11 28			11 57	12 05			12 28			12 57	13 05
Vauxhall ⊖	d	10 12	10 32	10 42		11 00	11 08	11 12	11 24	11 32	11 42		12 00	12 08	12 12	12 24	12 32	12 42		13 00	13 08
London Waterloo ■15 ⊖	a	10 23	10 41	10 53		11 10	11 13	11 23	11 34	11 41	11 53		12 10	12 13	12 23	12 34	12 41	12 53		13 10	13 13

Table 149

Sundays
from 26 September

Reading, Guildford, Ascot, Weybridge, Windsor, Kingston, Richmond and Hounslow - London

		SW ■1	SW	SW	SW ■1	SW ■1	SW	SW	SW	SW ■1	SW	SW	SW ■1	SW ■1	SW	SW	SW	SW ■1	SW
Reading ■7	d	11 51			12 21					12 51			13 21					13 51	
Earley	d	11 56			12 26					12 56			13 26					13 56	
Winnersh Triangle	d	11 58			12 28					12 58			13 28					13 58	
Winnersh	d	12 00			12 30					13 00			13 30					14 00	
Wokingham	d	12 05			12 35					13 05			13 35					14 05	
Bracknell	d	12 11			12 41					13 11			13 41					14 11	
Martins Heron	d	12 14			12 44					13 14			13 44					14 14	
Guildford	d					12 17								13 17					
Wanborough	d					12 23								13 23					
Ash ■5	d					12 27								13 27					
Aldershot	a					12 34								13 34					
	d					12 40								13 40					
Ash Vale	d					12 45								13 45					
Frimley	d					12 51								13 51					
Camberley	a					12 55								13 55					
	d					12 55								13 55					
Bagshot	d					13 01								14 01					
Ascot ■3	d	12 19			12 49	13a07				13 19			13 49	14a07				14 19	
Sunningdale	d	12 22			12 52					13 22			13 52					14 22	
Longcross	d																		
Woking	d								12 52								13 52		
West Byfleet	d								12 56								13 56		
Byfleet & New Haw	d								13 00								14 00		
Weybridge	d																		
Addlestone	d								13 04								14 04		
Chertsey	d								13 07								14 07		
Virginia Water	a	12 30			13 00				13 12	13 30			14 00				14 12	14 30	
	d	12 30			13 00				13 12	13 30			14 00				14 12	14 30	
Egham	d	12 34			13 04				13 16	13 34			14 04				14 16	14 34	
Windsor & Eton Riverside	d		12 32					12 59			13 32					13 59			14 32
Datchet	d		12 35					13 02			13 35					14 02			14 35
Sunnymeads	d							13 05								14 05			
Wraysbury	d							13 08								14 08			
Staines	d	12 39	12 45		13 09			13 16	13 21	13 39	13 45		14 09			14 16	14 21	14 39	14 45
Ashford (Surrey)	d		12 48					13 19	13 24		13 48					14 19	14 24		14 48
Feltham	d	12 46	12 53		13 16			13 24	13 29	13 46	13 53		14 16			14 24	14 29	14 46	14 53
Whitton	d		12 57					13 28			13 57					14 28			14 57
Kingston	d			12 49			13 11					13 49			14 11				
Hampton Wick	d			12 51			13 13					13 51			14 13				
Teddington	d			12 56			13 16					13 56			14 16				
Fulwell	d																		
Strawberry Hill	d			12 59			13 19					13 59			14 19				
Twickenham	a	12 51	13 00	13 02	13 21		13 22	13 31		13 51	14 00	14 02	14 21		14 22	14 31		14 51	15 00
	d	12 51	13 01	13 03	13 21		13 23	13 32		13 51	14 01	14 03	14 21		14 23	14 32		14 51	15 01
St Margarets	d			13 05			13 25	13 34				14 05			14 25	14 34			
Richmond ⊖	d	12 56	13 05	13 09	13 26		13 29	13 37		13 56	14 05	14 09	14 26		14 29	14 37		14 56	15 05
North Sheen	d			13 11			13 31	13 39				14 11			14 31	14 39			
Mortlake	d			13 13			13 33	13 42				14 13			14 33	14 42			
Hounslow	d								13 35								14 35		
Isleworth	d								13 38								14 38		
Syon Lane	d								13 40								14 40		
Brentford	d								13 42								14 42		
Kew Bridge	d								13 45								14 45		
Chiswick	d								13 47								14 47		
Barnes Bridge	d								13 50								14 50		
Barnes	d			13 16			13 36	13 45	13 53			14 16			14 36	14 45	14 53		
Putney	d	13 02	13 14	13 19	13 32		13 39	13 48	13 56	14 02	14 14	14 19	14 32		14 39	14 48	14 56	15 02	15 14
Wandsworth Town	d			13 22			13 42	13 51	13 59			14 22			14 42	14 51	14 59		
Clapham Junction ■10	d	13 07	13 18	13 25	13 37		13 45	13 54	14 02	14 07	14 18	14 25	14 37		14 45	14 54	15 02	15 07	15 18
Queenstown Rd.(Battersea)	d			13 28			13 48	13 57	14 05			14 28			14 48	14 57	15 05		
Vauxhall ⊖	d	13 12	13 24	13 32	13 42		13 52	14 00	14 08	14 12	14 24	14 32	14 42		14 52	15 00	15 08	15 12	15 24
London Waterloo ■15 ⊖	a	13 23	13 34	13 41	13 53		14 00	14 10	14 13	14 23	14 34	14 41	14 53		15 00	15 05	15 13	15 18	15 29

Table 149

Sundays from 26 September

Reading, Guildford, Ascot, Weybridge, Windsor, Kingston, Richmond and Hounslow - London

		SW	SW ■	SW ■	SW	SW	SW	SW ■	SW	SW	SW ■	SW ■	SW	SW	SW	SW ■	SW	SW	SW ■	SW ■	SW
Reading ■	d		14 21					14 51			15 21					15 51			16 21		
Earley	d		14 26					14 56			15 26					15 56			16 26		
Winnersh Triangle	d		14 28					14 58			15 28					15 58			16 28		
Winnersh	d		14 30					15 00			15 30					16 00			16 30		
Wokingham	d		14 35					15 05			15 35					16 05			16 35		
Bracknell	d		14 41					15 11			15 41					16 11			16 41		
Martins Heron	d		14 44					15 14			15 44					16 14			16 44		
Guildford	d			14 17								15 17								16 17	
Wanborough	d			14 23								15 23								16 23	
Ash ■	d			14 27								15 27								16 27	
Aldershot	a			14 34								15 34								16 34	
	d			14 40								15 40								16 40	
Ash Vale	d			14 45								15 45								16 45	
Frimley	d			14 51								15 51								16 51	
Camberley	a			14 55								15 55								16 55	
	d			14 55								15 55								16 55	
Bagshot	d			15 01								16 01								17 01	
Ascot ■	d		14 49	15a07				15 19			15 49	16a07				16 19			16 49	17a07	
Sunningdale	d		14 52					15 22			15 52					16 22			16 52		
Longcross	d																				
Woking	d						14 52								15 52						
West Byfleet	d						14 56								15 56						
Byfleet & New Haw	d						15 00								16 00						
Weybridge	d																				
Addlestone	d						15 04								16 04						
Chertsey	d						15 07								16 07						
Virginia Water	a		15 00				15 12	15 30			16 00				16 12	16 30			17 00		
	d		15 00				15 12	15 30			16 00				16 12	16 30			17 00		
Egham	d		15 04				15 16	15 34			16 04				16 16	16 34			17 04		
Windsor & Eton Riverside	d					14 59			15 32					15 59			16 32				
Datchet	d					15 02			15 35					16 02			16 35				
Sunnymeads	d					15 05								16 05							
Wraysbury	d					15 08								16 08							
Staines	d		15 09			15 16	15 21	15 39	15 45		16 09			16 16	16 21	16 39	16 45		17 09		
Ashford (Surrey)	d					15 19	15 24		15 48					16 19	16 24		16 48				
Feltham	d		15 16			15 24	15 29	15 46	15 53		16 16			16 24	16 29	16 46	16 53		17 16		
Whitton	d					15 28			15 57					16 28			16 57				
Kingston	d	14 49			15 11					15 49			16 11					16 49			17 11
Hampton Wick	d	14 51			15 13					15 51			16 13					16 51			17 13
Teddington	d	14 56			15 16					15 56			16 16					16 56			17 16
Fulwell	d																				
Strawberry Hill	d	14 59			15 19					15 59			16 19					16 59			17 19
Twickenham	a	15 02	15 21		15 22	15 31		15 51	16 00	16 02	16 21		16 22	16 31		16 51	17 00	17 02	17 21		17 22
	d	15 03	15 21		15 23	15 32		15 51	16 01	16 03	16 21		16 23	16 32		16 51	17 01	17 03	17 21		17 23
St Margarets	d	15 05			15 25	15 34				16 05			16 25	16 34				17 05			17 25
Richmond ⊖	d	15 09	15 26		15 29	15 37		15 56	16 05	16 09	16 26		16 29	16 37		16 56	17 05	17 09	17 26		17 29
North Sheen	d	15 11			15 31	15 39				16 11			16 31	16 39				17 11			17 31
Mortlake	d	15 13			15 33	15 42				16 13			16 33	16 42				17 13			17 33
Hounslow	d						15 35								16 35						
Isleworth	d						15 38								16 38						
Syon Lane	d						15 40								16 40						
Brentford	d						15 42								16 42						
Kew Bridge	d						15 45								16 45						
Chiswick	d						15 47								16 47						
Barnes Bridge	d						15 50								16 50						
Barnes	d	15 16			15 36	15 45	15 53			16 16			16 36	16 45	16 53			17 16			17 36
Putney	d	15 19	15 32		15 39	15 48	15 56	16 02	16 14	16 19	16 32		16 39	16 48	16 56	17 02	17 14	17 19	17 32		17 39
Wandsworth Town	d	15 22			15 42	15 51	15 59			16 22			16 42	16 51	16 59			17 22			17 42
Clapham Junction ■	d	15 25	15 37		15 45	15 54	16 02	16 07	16 18	16 25	16 37		16 45	16 54	17 02	17 07	17 18	17 25	17 37		17 45
Queenstown Rd.(Battersea)	d	15 28			15 48	15 57	16 05			16 28			16 48	16 57	17 05			17 28			17 48
Vauxhall ⊖	d	15 32	15 42		15 52	16 00	16 08	16 12	16 24	16 32	16 42		16 52	17 00	17 08	17 12	17 24	17 32	17 42		17 52
London Waterloo ■ ⊖	a	15 36	15 48		16 00	16 05	16 13	16 18	16 29	16 36	16 48		17 00	17 05	17 13	17 18	17 29	17 36	17 48		18 00

Table 149

Sundays from 26 September

Reading, Guildford, Ascot, Weybridge, Windsor, Kingston, Richmond and Hounslow - London

		SW	SW	SW ■	SW	SW	SW ■	SW ■	SW	SW	SW	SW ■	SW	SW	SW ■	SW ■	SW	SW	SW
Reading ■	d			16 51			17 21					17 51			18 21				
Earley	d			16 56			17 26					17 56			18 26				
Winnersh Triangle	d			16 58			17 28					17 58			18 28				
Winnersh	d			17 00			17 30					18 00			18 30				
Wokingham	d			17 05			17 35					18 05			18 35				
Bracknell	d			17 11			17 41					18 11			18 41				
Martins Heron	d			17 14			17 44					18 14			18 44				
Guildford	d							17 17								18 17			
Wanborough	d							17 23								18 23			
Ash ■	d							17 27								18 27			
Aldershot	a							17 34								18 34			
	d							17 40								18 40			
Ash Vale	d							17 45								18 45			
Frimley	d							17 51								18 51			
Camberley	a							17 55								18 55			
	d							17 55								18 55			
Bagshot	d							18 01								19 01			
Ascot ■	d			17 19			17 49	18a07				18 19			18 49	19a07			
Sunningdale	d			17 22			17 52					18 22			18 52				
Longcross	d																		
Woking	d		16 52								17 52								18 52
West Byfleet	d		16 56								17 56								18 56
Byfleet & New Haw	d		17 00								18 00								19 00
Weybridge	d																		
Addlestone	d		17 04								18 04								19 04
Chertsey	d		17 07								18 07								19 07
Virginia Water	a		17 12	17 30			18 00				18 12	18 30			19 00				19 12
	d		17 12	17 30			18 00				18 12	18 30			19 00				19 12
Egham	d		17 16	17 34			18 04				18 16	18 34			19 04				19 16
Windsor & Eton Riverside	d	16 59			17 32					17 59			18 32					18 59	
Datchet	d	17 02			17 35					18 02			18 35					19 02	
Sunnymeads	d	17 05								18 05								19 05	
Wraysbury	d	17 08								18 08								19 08	
Staines	d	17 16	17 21	17 39	17 45		18 09			18 16	18 21	18 39	18 45		19 09			19 16	19 21
Ashford (Surrey)	d	17 19	17 24		17 48					18 19	18 24		18 48					19 19	19 24
Feltham	d	17 24	17 29	17 46	17 53		18 16			18 24	18 29	18 46	18 53		19 16			19 24	19 29
Whitton	d	17 28			17 57					18 28			18 57					19 28	
Kingston	d					17 49			18 11					18 49			19 11		
Hampton Wick	d					17 51			18 13					18 51			19 13		
Teddington	d					17 56			18 16					18 56			19 16		
Fulwell	d																		
Strawberry Hill	d					17 59			18 19					18 59			19 19		
Twickenham	a	17 31		17 51	18 00	18 02	18 21		18 22	18 31		18 51	19 00	19 02	19 21		19 22	19 31	
	d	17 32		17 51	18 01	18 03	18 21		18 23	18 32		18 51	19 01	19 03	19 21		19 23	19 32	
St Margarets	d	17 34				18 05			18 25	18 34				19 05			19 25	19 34	
Richmond ⊖	d	17 37		17 56	18 05	18 09	18 26		18 29	18 37		18 56	19 05	19 09	19 26		19 29	19 37	
North Sheen	d	17 39				18 11			18 31	18 39				19 11			19 31	19 39	
Mortlake	d	17 42				18 13			18 33	18 42				19 13			19 33	19 42	
Hounslow	d		17 35								18 35								19 35
Isleworth	d		17 38								18 38								19 38
Syon Lane	d		17 40								18 40								19 40
Brentford	d		17 42								18 42								19 42
Kew Bridge	d		17 45								18 45								19 45
Chiswick	d		17 47								18 47								19 47
Barnes Bridge	d		17 50								18 50								19 50
Barnes	d	17 45	17 53			18 16			18 36	18 45	18 53			19 16			19 36	19 45	19 53
Putney	d	17 48	17 56	18 02	18 14	18 19	18 32		18 39	18 48	18 56	19 02	19 14	19 19	19 32		19 39	19 48	19 56
Wandsworth Town	d	17 51	17 59			18 22			18 42	18 51	18 59			19 22			19 42	19 51	19 59
Clapham Junction ■	d	17 54	18 02	18 07	18 18	18 25	18 37		18 45	18 54	19 02	19 07	19 18	19 25	19 37		19 45	19 54	20 02
Queenstown Rd.(Battersea)	d	17 57	18 05			18 28			18 48	18 57	19 05			19 28			19 48	19 57	20 05
Vauxhall ⊖	d	18 00	18 08	18 12	18 24	18 32	18 42		18 52	19 00	19 08	19 12	19 24	19 32	19 42		19 52	20 00	20 08
London Waterloo ■ ⊖	a	18 05	18 13	18 18	18 29	18 36	18 48		19 00	19 05	19 13	19 18	19 29	19 36	19 48		20 00	20 05	20 13

Table 149

Sundays from 26 September

Reading, Guildford, Ascot, Weybridge, Windsor, Kingston, Richmond and Hounslow - London

		SW 1	SW	SW	SW 1	SW 1	SW	SW	SW	SW 1	SW	SW	SW 1	SW 1	SW	SW	SW	SW 1	SW	SW 1	SW 1
Reading 7	d	18 51			19 21					19 51			20 21					20 51		21 21	
Earley	d	18 56			19 26					19 56			20 26					20 56		21 26	
Winnersh Triangle	d	18 58			19 28					19 58			20 28					20 58		21 28	
Winnersh	d	19 00			19 30					20 00			20 30					21 00		21 30	
Wokingham	d	19 05			19 35					20 05			20 35					21 05		21 35	
Bracknell	d	19 11			19 41					20 11			20 41					21 11		21 41	
Martins Heron	d	19 14			19 44					20 14			20 44					21 14		21 44	
Guildford	d					19 17								20 17							21 17
Wanborough	d					19 23								20 23							21 23
Ash 5	d					19 27								20 27							21 27
Aldershot	a					19 34								20 34							21 34
	d					19 40								20 40							21 40
Ash Vale	d					19 45								20 45							21 45
Frimley	d					19 51								20 51							21 51
Camberley	a					19 55								20 55							21 55
	d					19 55								20 55							21 55
Bagshot	d					20 01								21 01							22 01
Ascot 3	d	19 19			19 49	20a07				20 19			20 49	21a07				21 19		21 49	22a07
Sunningdale	d	19 22			19 52					20 22			20 52					21 22		21 52	
Longcross	d																				
Woking	d								19 52								20 52				
West Byfleet	d								19 56								20 56				
Byfleet & New Haw	d								20 00								21 00				
Weybridge	d																				
Addlestone	d								20 04								21 04				
Chertsey	d								20 07								21 07				
Virginia Water	a	19 30			20 00				20 12	20 30			21 00				21 12	21 30		22 00	
	d	19 30			20 00				20 12	20 30			21 00				21 12	21 30		22 00	
Egham	d	19 34			20 04				20 16	20 34			21 04				21 16	21 34		22 04	
Windsor & Eton Riverside	d		19 32					19 59			20 32					20 59					
Datchet	d		19 35					20 02			20 35					21 02					
Sunnymeads	d							20 05								21 05					
Wraysbury	d							20 08								21 08					
Staines	d	19 39	19 45		20 09			20 16	20 21	20 39	20 45		21 09			21 16	21 21	21 39		22 09	
Ashford (Surrey)	d		19 48					20 19	20 24		20 48					21 19	21 24				
Feltham	d	19 46	19 53		20 16			20 24	20 29	20 46	20 53		21 16			21 24	21 29	21 46		22 16	
Whitton	d		19 57					20 28			20 57					21 28					
Kingston	d			19 49			20 11					20 49			21 11				21 49		
Hampton Wick	d			19 51			20 13					20 51			21 13				21 51		
Teddington	d			19 56			20 16					20 56			21 16				21 56		
Fulwell	d																				
Strawberry Hill	d			19 59			20 19					20 59			21 19				21 59		
Twickenham	a	19 51	20 00	20 02	20 21		20 22	20 31		20 51	21 00	21 02	21 21		21 22	21 31		21 51	22 02	22 21	
	d	19 51	20 01	20 03	20 21		20 23	20 32		20 51	21 01	21 03	21 21		21 23	21 32		21 51	22 03	22 21	
St Margarets	d			20 05			20 25	20 34				21 05			21 25	21 34			22 05		
Richmond ⊖	d	19 56	20 05	20 09	20 26		20 29	20 37		20 56	21 05	21 09	21 26		21 29	21 37		21 56	22 09	22 26	
North Sheen	d			20 11			20 31	20 39				21 11			21 31	21 39			22 11		
Mortlake	d			20 13			20 33	20 42				21 13			21 33	21 42			22 13		
Hounslow	d								20 35								21 35				
Isleworth	d								20 38								21 38				
Syon Lane	d								20 40								21 40				
Brentford	d								20 42								21 42				
Kew Bridge	d								20 45								21 45				
Chiswick	d								20 47								21 47				
Barnes Bridge	d								20 50								21 50				
Barnes	d			20 16			20 36	20 45	20 53			21 16			21 36	21 45	21 53		22 16		
Putney	d	20 02	20 14	20 19	20 32		20 39	20 48	20 56	21 02	21 14	21 19	21 32		21 39	21 48	21 56	22 02	22 19	22 32	
Wandsworth Town	d			20 22			20 42	20 51	20 59			21 22			21 42	21 51	21 59		22 22		
Clapham Junction 10	d	20 07	20 18	20 25	20 37		20 45	20 54	21 02	21 07	21 18	21 25	21 37		21 45	21 54	22 02	22 07	22 25	22 37	
Queenstown Rd.(Battersea)	d			20 28			20 48	20 57	21 05			21 28			21 48	21 57	22 05		22 28		
Vauxhall ⊖	d	20 12	20 24	20 32	20 42		20 52	21 00	21 08	21 12	21 24	21 32	21 42		21 52	22 00	22 08	22 12	22 32	22 42	
London Waterloo 15 ⊖	a	20 18	20 29	20 36	20 48		21 00	21 05	21 13	21 18	21 29	21 36	21 48		22 00	22 05	22 13	22 18	22 36	22 48	

Table 149

Sundays from 26 September

Reading, Guildford, Ascot, Weybridge, Windsor, Kingston, Richmond and Hounslow - London

		SW	SW	SW	SW 1	SW	SW 1	SW 1	SW	SW	SW	SW 1
Reading 7	d				21 51		22 21					22 54
Earley	d				21 56		22 26					22 59
Winnersh Triangle	d				21 58		22 28					23 01
Winnersh	d				22 00		22 30					23 03
Wokingham	d				22 05		22 35					23 08
Bracknell	d				22 11		22 41					23 14
Martins Heron	d				22 14		22 44					23 17
Guildford	d							22 17				
Wanborough	d							22 23				
Ash 5	d							22 27				
Aldershot	a							22 34				
	d							22 40				
Ash Vale	d							22 45				
Frimley	d							22 51				
Camberley	a							22 55				
	d							22 55				
Bagshot	d							23 01				
Ascot 3	d				22 19		22 49	23a07				23 22
Sunningdale	d				22 22		22 52					23 25
Longcross	d											
Woking	d			21 52							22 52	
West Byfleet	d			21 56							22 56	
Byfleet & New Haw	d			22 00							23 00	
Weybridge	d											
Addlestone	d			22 04							23 04	
Chertsey	d			22 07							23 07	
Virginia Water	a			22 12	22 30		23 00				23 12	23 30
	d			22 12	22 30		23 00				23 12	23 30
Egham	d			22 16	22 34		23 04				23 16	23 34
Windsor & Eton Riverside	d		21 59							23 01		
Datchet	d		22 02							23 04		
Sunnymeads	d		22 05							23 07		
Wraysbury	d		22 08							23 10		
Staines	d		22 16	22 21	22 39		23 09			23 16	23 21	23 39
Ashford (Surrey)	d		22 19	22 24						23 19	23 24	
Feltham	d		22 24	22 29	22 46		23 16			23 24	23 29	23 46
Whitton	d		22 28							23 28		
Kingston	d	22 11				22 49			23 11			
Hampton Wick	d	22 13				22 51			23 13			
Teddington	d	22 16				22 56			23 16			
Fulwell	d											
Strawberry Hill	d	22 19				22 59			23 19			
Twickenham	a	22 22	22 31		22 51	23 02	23 21		23 22	23 31		23 51
	d	22 23	22 32		22 51	23 03	23 21		23 23	23 32		23 51
St Margarets	d	22 25	22 34			23 05			23 25	23 34		
Richmond ⊖	d	22 29	22 37		22 56	23 09	23 26		23 29	23 37		23 56
North Sheen	d	22 31	22 39			23 11			23 31	23 39		
Mortlake	d	22 33	22 42			23 13			23 33	23 42		
Hounslow	d			22 35							23 35	
Isleworth	d			22 38							23 38	
Syon Lane	d			22 40							23 40	
Brentford	d			22 42							23 42	
Kew Bridge	d			22 45							23 45	
Chiswick	d			22 47							23 47	
Barnes Bridge	d			22 50							23 50	
Barnes	d	22 36	22 45	22 53		23 16			23 36	23 45	23 53	
Putney	d	22 39	22 48	22 56	23 02	23 19	23 32		23 39	23 48	23 56	00 02
Wandsworth Town	d	22 42	22 51	22 59		23 22			23 42	23 51	23 59	
Clapham Junction 10	d	22 45	22 54	23 02	23 07	23 25	23 37		23 45	23 54	00 02	00 07
Queenstown Rd.(Battersea)	d	22 48	22 57	23 05		23 28			23 48	23 57	00 05	
Vauxhall ⊖	d	22 52	23 00	23 08	23 12	23 32	23 42		23 52	23 59	00 08	00 12
London Waterloo 15 ⊖	a	23 00	23 05	23 13	23 18	23 36	23 48		23 59	00 05	00 13	00 17

Network Diagram for Table 152

DM-12/09
Design BAJS

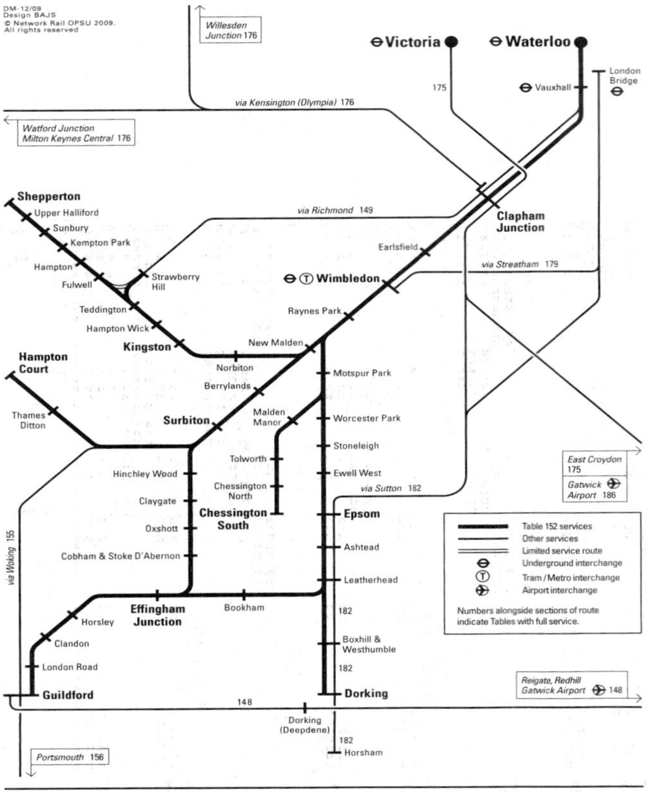

Table 152

Mondays to Fridays
24 May to 24 September

London - Chessington South, Dorking, Guildford, Shepperton and Hampton Court

		SW MX	SW MO	SW MX	SW MO	SW MX	SW MX	SW MX	SW MO	SW MX
London Waterloo 15 ⊖	d	23p03	23p00	23p09	23p10	23p12	23p27	23p30	23p32	23p33
Vauxhall ⊖	d	23p07	23p04	23p13	23p14	23p16	23p31	23p34	23p36	23p37
Clapham Junction 10	d	23p12	23p09	23p18	23p19	23p21	23p36	23p39	23p41	
Earlsfield	d	23p15	23p12	23p21	23p22	23p24	23p39	23p42	23p44	
Wimbledon 6 ⊖	d	23p19	23p16	23p25	23p26	23p28	23p43	23p46	23p48	
Raynes Park 6	d			23p28		23p31	23p46	23p49	23p52	
Motspur Park	d			23p31					23p55	
Malden Manor	d									
Tolworth	d									
Chessington North	d									
Chessington South	a									
Worcester Park	d			23p33					23p57	
Stoneleigh	d			23p36					23p57	
Ewell West	d			23p39					00 03	
Epsom 3	a			23p42					00 06	
	d			23p47						
Ashtead	d			23p51						
Leatherhead	d			23p54						
Boxhill & Westhumble	d			23p59						
Dorking 4	a			00 01						
New Malden 6	d					23p34	23p49	23p52		
Norbiton	d					23p37	23p52			
Kingston	a					23p40	23p55			00 16
	d					23p40	23p55			
Hampton Wick	d					23p42	23p57			
Teddington	d					23p45	23p59			
Strawberry Hill	a						00 03			
Fulwell	d					23p49				
Hampton	d					23p53				
Kempton Park	d					23p56				
Sunbury	d					23p58				
Upper Halliford	d					23p59				
Shepperton	a					00 03				
Berrylands	d							23p54		
Surbiton 6	d	23p27	23p32		23p35			23p59		
Thames Ditton	d							00 03		
Hampton Court	a							00 06		
Hinchley Wood	d	23p31	23p36							
Claygate	d	23p34	23p39							
Oxshott	d	23p37	23p42							
Cobham & Stoke D'abernon	d	23p41	23p46							
Bookham	d									
Effingham Junction 6	d	23p45	23p50							
Horsley	d	23p48	23p53							
Clandon	d	23p53	23p58							
London Road (Guildford)	d	23p58	00 03							
Guildford	a	00 02	00 07		00 13					

		SW MO 1	SW MX	SW MX	SW MX	SW MO	SW MX	SW MX	SW	SW MX	SW 1	SW	SW 1	SW
London Waterloo 15 ⊖	d	23p40	23p42	23p50	23p57	00 01	00 09	00 15	00 18	00 27	05 00	05 12	05 20	05 33
Vauxhall ⊖	d	23p44	23p46	23p54	00 01	00 04	00 13	00 19	00 22	00 31	05 04	05 16	05 24	05 37
Clapham Junction 10	d	23p49	23p51	23p58	00 06	00 09	00 18	00 24		00 36	05 09	05 21	05 29	
Earlsfield	d	23p52	23p54	00 02	00 09	00 12	00 21	00 27		00s39	05 12	05 24	05 32	
Wimbledon 6 ⊖	d	23p56	23p58	00 06	00 13	00 16	00 25	00 31		00 43	05 16	05 28	05 36	
Raynes Park 6	d		00 01		00 16	00 19		00 34		00 46		05 31		
Motspur Park	d		00 04					00 37						
Malden Manor	d													
Tolworth	d													
Chessington North	d													
Chessington South	a													
Worcester Park	d		00 06					00 39						
Stoneleigh	d		00 09					00 42						
Ewell West	d		00 12					00 45						
Epsom 3	a		00 15					00 48						
	d		00 19											
Ashtead	d		00 23											
Leatherhead	d		00 26											
Boxhill & Westhumble	d													
Dorking 4	a													
New Malden 6	d				00 19	00 22				00 49		05 34		
Norbiton	d				00 22							05 37		
Kingston	a				00 25				01 00			05 40		06 16
	d				00 25							05 40		06 19
Hampton Wick	d				00 27							05 42		
Teddington	d				00 30							05 45		
Strawberry Hill	a													
Fulwell	d				00 34							05 49		
Hampton	d				00 38							05 53		
Kempton Park	d				00 41									
Sunbury	d				00 43							05 58		
Upper Halliford	d				00 45							06 00		
Shepperton	a				00 48							06 03		
Berrylands	d					00 25				00s51				
Surbiton 6	d	00 05		00 14		00 31	00 33			00a55	05 24		05 44	
Thames Ditton	d													
Hampton Court	a													
Hinchley Wood	d			00 18		00 35								
Claygate	d			00 21		00 38								
Oxshott	d			00 24		00 41								
Cobham & Stoke D'abernon	d			00 28		00 45								
Bookham	d		00 31											
Effingham Junction 6	d		00 37	00 32		00 49								
Horsley	d		00 40	00 35		00 52								
Clandon	d		00 45	00 40		00 57								
London Road (Guildford)	d		00 50	00 45		01 02								
Guildford	a		00 54	00 49		01 06	01 06				05 59		06 21	

Table 152

Mondays to Fridays
24 May to 24 September

London - Chessington South, Dorking, Guildford, Shepperton and Hampton Court

		SW	SW	SW	SW	SW		SW	SW	SW	SW	SW	SW	SW	SW	SW		SW	SW	SW	SW	SW ■	SW	SW	SW
London Waterloo ■ ⊖	d	05 47		05 50	06 03	06 03		06 06	06 12		06 16	06 20	06 24	06 27	06 33	06 33		06 36	06 39	06 42	06 46	06 53	06 50	06 54	06 57
Vauxhall ⊖	d	05 51		05 54	06 07	06 07		06 10	06 16		06 20	06 24	06 28	06 31	06 37	06 37		06 40	06 43	06 46	06 50		06 54	06 58	07 01
Clapham Junction ■	d	05 56		05 59	06 12			06 15	06 21		06 25	06 29	06 33	06 36	06 42			06 45	06 48	06 51	06 55	07u00	06 59	07 03	07 06
Earlsfield	d	05 59		06 02	06 15			06 18	06 24		06 28	06 32	06 36	06 39	06 45			06 48	06 51	06 54	06 58		07 02	07 06	07 09
Wimbledon ■ ⊖	d	06 03	05 49	06 06	06 19			06 22	06 28	06 16	06 32	06 36	06 40	06 43	06 49			06 52	06 55	06 58	07 02		07 06	07 10	07 13
Raynes Park ■	d	06 06						06 25	06 31	06 19	06 35		06 43	06 46				06 55	06 58	07 01	07 05			07 13	07 16
Motspur Park	d	06 09								06 21	06 38		06 46								07 08			07 16	
Malden Manor	d									06 25	06 41										07 11				
Tolworth	d									06 27	06 44										07 14				
Chessington North	d									06 30	06 47										07 17				
Chessington South	a									06 32	06 49										07 19				
Worcester Park	d	06 11											06 48						07 02					07 18	
Stoneleigh	d	06 14											06 51						07 05					07 21	
Ewell West	d	06 17											06 54						07 08					07 24	
Epsom ■	a	06 20											06 57						07 11					07 27	
	d	06 21											06 58						07 12					07 28	
Ashtead	d	06 25											07 02						07 16					07 32	
Leatherhead	d	06 28											07 05						07 19					07 35	
Boxhill & Westhumble	d																								
Dorking ■	a												07 11											07 41	
New Malden ■	d							06 28	06 34					06 49				06 58		07 04					07 19
Norbiton	d								06 37					06 52						07 07					07 22
Kingston	a					06 46			06 40					06 55		07 16				07 10					07 25
	d					06 49			06 40					06 59		07 19				07 10					07 29
Hampton Wick	d								06 42					07 01						07 12					07 31
Teddington	d								06 45					07 05						07 15					07 35
Strawberry Hill	a													07 08											07 38
Fulwell	d								06 49											07 19					
Hampton	d								06 53											07 23					
Kempton Park	d																								
Sunbury	d								06 58											07 28					
Upper Halliford	d								07 00											07 30					
Shepperton	a								07 03											07 33					
Berrylands	d							06 30										07 00							
Surbiton ■	d		05 57	06 14	06 27			06 35				06 44			06 57			07 05				07 11	07 14		
Thames Ditton	d							06 39										07 09							
Hampton Court	a							06 42										07 12							
Hinchley Wood	d		06 01		06 31										07 01										
Claygate	d		06 04		06 34										07 04										
Oxshott	d		06 07		06 37										07 07										
Cobham & Stoke D'abernon	d		06 11		06 41										07 11										
Bookham	d	06 33																	07 24						
Effingham Junction ■	d	06 37	06 15		06 45										07 15				07a28						
Horsley	d		06 18		06 48										07 18										
Clandon	d		06 23		06 53										07 23										
London Road (Guildford)	d	06 46	06 28		06 58										07 28										
Guildford	a	06 50	06 32		07 02							07 20			07 32								07 47		

Table 152

Mondays to Fridays
24 May to 24 September

London - Chessington South, Dorking, Guildford, Shepperton and Hampton Court

		SW		SW	SW	SW	SW	SW	SW ■	SW	SW	SW		SW	SW	SW	SW	SW	SW	SW ■	SW	SW		SW	SW
London Waterloo ■ ⊖	d	07 03		07 03	07 06	07 09	07 12	07 16	07 23	07 20	07 24	07 27		07 33	07 33	07 36	07 39	07 42	07 46	07 53	07 50	07 54		07 57	08 03
Vauxhall ⊖	d	07 07		07 07	07 10	07 13	07 16	07 20		07 24	07 28	07 31		07 37	07 37	07 40	07 43	07 46	07 50		07 54	07 58		08 01	08 07
Clapham Junction ■	d	07 12			07 15	07 18	07 21	07 25	07u30	07 29	07 33	07 36		07 42		07 45	07 48	07 51	07 55	08u00	07 59	08 03		08 06	08 12
Earlsfield	d	07 15			07 18	07 21	07 24	07 28		07 32	07 36	07 39		07 45		07 48	07 51	07 54	07 58		08 02	08 06		08 09	08 15
Wimbledon ■ ⊖	d	07 19			07 22	07 25	07 28	07 32		07 36	07 40	07 43		07 49		07 52	07 55	07 58	08 02		08 06	08 10		08 13	08 19
Raynes Park ■	d				07 25	07 28	07 31	07 35			07 43	07 46				07 55	07 58	08 01	08 05			08 13		08 16	
Motspur Park	d					07 31		07 38			07 46						08 01		08 08			08 16			
Malden Manor	d							07 41											08 11						
Tolworth	d							07 44											08 14						
Chessington North	d							07 47											08 17						
Chessington South	a							07 49											08 19						
Worcester Park	d					07 33					07 48						08 03					08 18			
Stoneleigh	d					07 36					07 51						08 06					08 21			
Ewell West	d					07 39					07 54						08 09					08 24			
Epsom ■	a					07 42					07 58						08 13					08 27			
	d										07 58						08 17					08 28			
Ashtead	d										08 02						08 21					08 32			
Leatherhead	d										08 05						08 24					08 35			
Boxhill & Westhumble	d																								
Dorking ■	a										08 12											08 41			
New Malden ■	d				07 28		07 34					07 49				07 58		08 04						08 19	
Norbiton	d						07 37					07 52						08 07						08 22	
Kingston	a			07 46			07 40					07 55			08 16			08 10						08 25	
	d			07 49			07 40					07 59			08 19			08 10						08 29	
Hampton Wick	d						07 42					08 01						08 12						08 31	
Teddington	d						07 45					08 05						08 15						08 35	
Strawberry Hill	a											08 08												08 38	
Fulwell	d						07 49											08 19							
Hampton	d						07 53											08 23							
Kempton Park	d						07 56											08 26							
Sunbury	d						07 58											08 28							
Upper Halliford	d						08 00											08 30							
Shepperton	a						08 03											08 33							
Berrylands	d				07 30											08 00									
Surbiton ■	d	07 27			07 35				07 41	07 44				07 57		08 05				08 11	08 14				08 27
Thames Ditton	d				07 39											08 09									
Hampton Court	a				07 42											08 12									
Hinchley Wood	d	07 31												08 01											08 31
Claygate	d	07 34												08 04											08 34
Oxshott	d	07 37												08 07											08 37
Cobham & Stoke D'abernon	d	07 41												08 11											08 41
Bookham	d																08 29								
Effingham Junction ■	d	07 45												08 15			08 33								08 45
Horsley	d	07 48												08 18			08 36								08 48
Clandon	d	07 53												08 23			08 41								08 53
London Road (Guildford)	d	07 58												08 28			08 46								08 58
Guildford	a	08 02												08 32			08 50				08 50				09 04

London - Chessington South, Dorking, Guildford, Shepperton and Hampton Court

		SW	SW	SW	SW	SW	SW 1	SW	SW	SW	SW	SW	SW	SW	SW	SW	SW 1	SW	SW	SW	SW	SW	SW
London Waterloo 15 ⊖	d	08 03	08 06	08 09	08 12	08 16	08 23	08 20	08 24	08 27	08 33	08 33	08 36	08 39	08 42	08 46	08 53	08 50	08 54	08 57	09 03	09 03	09 06
Vauxhall ⊖	d	08 07	08 10	08 13	08 16	08 20		08 24	08 28	08 31	08 37	08 37	08 40	08 43	08 46	08 50		08 54	08 58	09 01	09 07	09 07	09 10
Clapham Junction 10	d		08 15	08 18	08 21	08 25		08 29	08 33	08 36	08 42		08 45	08 48	08 51	08 55	09u00	08 59	09 03	09 06	09 12		09 15
Earlsfield	d		08 18	08 21	08 24	08 28		08 32	08 36	08 39	08 45		08 48	08 51	08 54	08 58		09 02	09 06	09 09	09 15		09 18
Wimbledon 6 ⊖	d		08 22	08 25	08 28	08 32		08 36	08 40	08 43	08 49		08 52	08 55	08 58	09 02		09 06	09 10	09 13	09 19		09 22
Raynes Park 6	d		08 25	08 28	08 31	08 35			08 43	08 46			08 55	08 58	09 01	09 05			09 13	09 16			09 25
Motspur Park	d			08 31		08 38			08 46					09 01		09 08			09 16				
Malden Manor	d					08 41										09 11							
Tolworth	d					08 44										09 14							
Chessington North	d					08 47										09 17							
Chessington South	a					08 49										09 19							
Worcester Park	d			08 33					08 48					09 03					09 18				
Stoneleigh	d			08 36					08 51					09 06					09 21				
Ewell West	d			08 39					08 54					09 09					09 24				
Epsom 3	a			08 42					08 57					09 16					09 27				
	d			08 47					08 58					09 17					09 28				
Ashtead	d			08 51					09 02					09 21					09 32				
Leatherhead	d			08 54					09 05					09 24					09 35				
Boxhill & Westhumble	d																						
Dorking 4	a								09 11										09 41				
New Malden 6	d		08 28		08 34					08 49			08 58		09 04					09 19			09 28
Norbiton	d				08 37					08 52					09 07					09 22			
Kingston	a	08 46			08 39					08 55		09 16			09 10					09 25		09 46	
	d	08 49			08 40					08 59		09 19			09 10					09 29		09 49	
Hampton Wick	d				08 42					09 01					09 12					09 31			
Teddington	d				08 45					09 05					09 15					09 35			
Strawberry Hill	a									09 08										09 38			
Fulwell	d				08 49										09 19								
Hampton	d				08 53										09 23								
Kempton Park	d				08 56										09 26								
Sunbury	d				08 58										09 28								
Upper Halliford	d				09 00										09 30								
Shepperton	a				09 04										09 33								
Berrylands	d		08 30										09 00										09 30
Surbiton 6	d		08 35				08 41	08 44			08 57		09 05				09 11	09 14			09 27		09 35
Thames Ditton	d		08 39										09 09										09 39
Hampton Court	a		08 42										09 12										09 42
Hinchley Wood	d										09 01										09 31		
Claygate	d										09 04										09 34		
Oxshott	d										09 07										09 37		
Cobham & Stoke D'abernon	d										09 11										09 41		
Bookham	d			08 59										09 29									
Effingham Junction 6	d			09 03							09 15			09 33							09 45		
Horsley	d			09 06							09 18			09 36							09 48		
Clandon	d			09 11							09 23			09 41							09 53		
London Road (Guildford)	d			09 16							09 28			09 46							09 58		
Guildford	a			09 20							09 32			09 50							10 02		

London - Chessington South, Dorking, Guildford, Shepperton and Hampton Court

		SW	SW	SW	SW 1	SW	SW	SW	SW	SW	SW	SW	SW	SW	SW 1	SW	SW	SW	SW	SW	SW	SW
London Waterloo 15 ⊖	d	09 09	09 12	09 16	09 23	09 20	09 24	09 27	09 33	09 33	09 36	09 39	09 42	09 46	09 53	09 50	09 54	09 57	10 03	10 03	10 06	10 09
Vauxhall ⊖	d	09 13	09 16	09 20		09 24	09 28	09 31	09 37	09 37	09 40	09 43	09 46	09 50		09 54	09 58	10 01	10 07	10 07	10 10	10 13
Clapham Junction 10	d	09 18	09 21	09 25		09 29	09 33	09 36	09 42		09 45	09 48	09 51	09 55	10u00	09 59	10 03	10 06	10 12		10 15	10 18
Earlsfield	d	09 21	09 24	09 28		09 32	09 36	09 39	09 45		09 48	09 51	09 54	09 58		10 02	10 06	10 09	10 15		10 18	10 21
Wimbledon 6 ⊖	d	09 25	09 28	09 32		09 36	09 40	09 43	09 49		09 52	09 55	09 58	10 02		10 06	10 10	10 13	10 19		10 22	10 25
Raynes Park 6	d	09 28	09 31	09 35			09 43	09 46			09 55	09 58	10 01	10 05			10 13	10 16			10 25	10 28
Motspur Park	d	09 31		09 38			09 46					10 01		10 08			10 16					10 31
Malden Manor	d			09 41										10 11								
Tolworth	d			09 44										10 14								
Chessington North	d			09 47										10 17								
Chessington South	a			09 49										10 19								
Worcester Park	d	09 33					09 48					10 03					10 18					10 33
Stoneleigh	d	09 36					09 51					10 06					10 21					10 36
Ewell West	d	09 39					09 54					10 09					10 24					10 39
Epsom 3	a	09 42					09 57					10 16					10 27					10 46
	d	09 47					09 58					10 17					10 28					10 47
Ashtead	d	09 51					10 02					10 21					10 32					10 51
Leatherhead	d	09 54					10 05					10 24					10 35					10 54
Boxhill & Westhumble	d																					
Dorking 4	a						10 11										10 41					
New Malden 6	d		09 34					09 49			09 58		10 04					10 19			10 28	
Norbiton	d		09 37					09 52					10 07					10 22				
Kingston	a		09 40					09 55		10 16			10 10					10 25		10 46		
	d		09 40					09 59		10 19			10 10					10 29		10 49		
Hampton Wick	d		09 42					10 01					10 12					10 31				
Teddington	d		09 45					10 05					10 15					10 35				
Strawberry Hill	a							10 08										10 38				
Fulwell	d		09 49										10 19									
Hampton	d		09 53										10 23									
Kempton Park	d		09 56										10 26									
Sunbury	d		09 58										10 28									
Upper Halliford	d		10 00										10 30									
Shepperton	a		10 03										10 33									
Berrylands	d										10 00										10 30	
Surbiton 6	d				09 41	09 44			09 57		10 05				10 11	10 14			10 27		10 35	
Thames Ditton	d										10 09										10 39	
Hampton Court	a										10 12										10 42	
Hinchley Wood	d								10 01										10 31			
Claygate	d								10 04										10 34			
Oxshott	d								10 07										10 37			
Cobham & Stoke D'abernon	d								10 11										10 41			
Bookham	d	09 59										10 29										10 59
Effingham Junction 6	d	10 03							10 15			10 33							10 45			11 03
Horsley	d	10 06							10 18			10 36							10 48			11 06
Clandon	d	10 11							10 23			10 41							10 53			11 11
London Road (Guildford)	d	10 16							10 28			10 46							10 58			11 16
Guildford	a	10 20							10 32			10 50							11 02			11 20

Table 152

Mondays to Fridays
24 May to 24 September

London - Chessington South, Dorking, Guildford, Shepperton and Hampton Court

		SW	SW	SW 1	SW	SW	SW	SW	SW	SW	SW	SW	SW	SW 1	SW	SW	SW	SW	SW	SW	SW	SW	SW
London Waterloo 15 ⊖	d	10 12	10 16	10 23	10 20	10 24	10 27	10 33	10 33	10 36	10 39	10 42	10 46	10 53	10 50	10 54	10 57	11 03	11 03	11 06	11 09	11 12	11 16
Vauxhall ⊖	d	10 16	10 20		10 24	10 28	10 31	10 37	10 37	10 40	10 43	10 46	10 50		10 54	10 58	11 01	11 07	11 07	11 10	11 13	11 16	11 20
Clapham Junction 10	d	10 21	10 25		10 29	10 33	10 36	10 42		10 45	10 48	10 51	10 55	11u00	10 59	11 03	11 06	11 12		11 15	11 18	11 21	11 25
Earlsfield	d	10 24	10 28		10 32	10 36	10 39	10 45		10 48	10 51	10 54	10 58		11 02	11 06	11 09	11 15		11 18	11 21	11 24	11 28
Wimbledon 6 ⊖	d	10 28	10 32		10 36	10 40	10 43	10 49		10 52	10 55	10 58	11 02		11 06	11 10	11 13	11 19		11 22	11 25	11 28	11 32
Raynes Park 6	d	10 31	10 35			10 43	10 46			10 55	10 58	11 01	11 05			11 13	11 16			11 25	11 28	11 31	11 35
Motspur Park	d		10 38			10 46					11 01		11 08			11 16					11 31		11 38
Malden Manor	d		10 41										11 11										11 41
Tolworth	d		10 44										11 14										11 44
Chessington North	d		10 47										11 17										11 47
Chessington South	a		10 49										11 19										11 49
Worcester Park	d					10 48					11 03					11 18					11 33		
Stoneleigh	d					10 51					11 06					11 21					11 36		
Ewell West	d					10 54					11 09					11 24					11 39		
Epsom 3	a					10 57					11 16					11 27					11 46		
	d					10 58					11 17					11 28					11 47		
Ashtead	d					11 02					11 21					11 32					11 51		
Leatherhead	d					11 05					11 24					11 35					11 54		
Boxhill & Westhumble	d																						
Dorking 4	a					11 11										11 41							
New Malden 6	d	10 34					10 49			10 58		11 04					11 19			11 28		11 34	
Norbiton	d	10 37					10 52					11 07					11 22					11 37	
Kingston	a	10 40					10 55		11 16			11 10					11 25		11 46			11 40	
	d	10 40					10 59		11 19			11 10					11 29		11 49			11 40	
Hampton Wick	d	10 42					11 01					11 12					11 31					11 42	
Teddington	d	10 45					11 05					11 15					11 35					11 45	
Strawberry Hill	a						11 08										11 38						
Fulwell	d	10 49										11 19										11 49	
Hampton	d	10 53										11 23										11 53	
Kempton Park	d	10 56										11 26										11 56	
Sunbury	d	10 58										11 28										11 58	
Upper Halliford	d	11 00										11 30										12 00	
Shepperton	a	11 03										11 33										12 03	
Berrylands	d									11 00										11 30			
Surbiton 6	d			10 41	10 44			10 57		11 05				11 11	11 14			11 27		11 35			
Thames Ditton	d									11 09										11 39			
Hampton Court	a									11 12										11 42			
Hinchley Wood	d							11 01										11 31					
Claygate	d							11 04										11 34					
Oxshott	d							11 07										11 37					
Cobham & Stoke D'abernon	d							11 11										11 41					
Bookham	d										11 29										11 59		
Effingham Junction 6	d							11 15			11 33							11 45			12 03		
Horsley	d							11 18			11 36							11 48			12 06		
Clandon	d							11 23			11 41							11 53			12 11		
London Road (Guildford)	d							11 28			11 46							11 58			12 16		
Guildford	a							11 32			11 50							12 02			12 20		

Table 152

Mondays to Fridays
24 May to 24 September

London - Chessington South, Dorking, Guildford, Shepperton and Hampton Court

		SW 1	SW	SW	SW	SW	SW	SW	SW	SW	SW	SW 1	SW	SW	SW	SW	SW	SW	SW	SW	SW	SW 1	SW
London Waterloo 15 ⊖	d	11 23	11 20	11 24	11 27	11 33	11 33	11 36	11 39	11 42	11 46	11 53	11 50	11 54	11 57	12 03	12 03	12 06	12 09	12 12	12 16	12 23	12 20
Vauxhall ⊖	d		11 24	11 28	11 31	11 37	11 37	11 40	11 43	11 46	11 50		11 54	11 58	12 01	12 07	12 07	12 10	12 13	12 16	12 20		12 24
Clapham Junction 10	d		11 29	11 33	11 36	11 42		11 45	11 48	11 51	11 55	12u00	11 59	12 03	12 06	12 12		12 15	12 18	12 21	12 25		12 29
Earlsfield	d		11 32	11 36	11 39	11 45		11 48	11 51	11 54	11 58		12 02	12 06	12 09	12 15		12 18	12 21	12 24	12 28		12 32
Wimbledon 6 ⊖	d		11 36	11 40	11 43	11 49		11 52	11 55	11 58	12 02		12 06	12 10	12 13	12 19		12 22	12 25	12 28	12 32		12 36
Raynes Park 6	d			11 43	11 46			11 55	11 58	12 01	12 05			12 13	12 16			12 25	12 28	12 31	12 35		
Motspur Park	d			11 46					12 01		12 08			12 16					12 31		12 38		
Malden Manor	d										12 11										12 41		
Tolworth	d										12 14										12 44		
Chessington North	d										12 17										12 47		
Chessington South	a										12 19										12 49		
Worcester Park	d			11 48					12 03					12 18					12 33				
Stoneleigh	d			11 51					12 06					12 21					12 36				
Ewell West	d			11 54					12 09					12 24					12 39				
Epsom 3	a			11 57					12 16					12 27					12 46				
	d			11 58					12 17					12 28					12 47				
Ashtead	d			12 02					12 21					12 32					12 51				
Leatherhead	d			12 05					12 24					12 35					12 54				
Boxhill & Westhumble	d																						
Dorking 4	a			12 11										12 41									
New Malden 6	d				11 49			11 58		12 04					12 19			12 28		12 34			
Norbiton	d				11 52					12 07					12 22					12 37			
Kingston	a				11 55		12 16			12 10					12 25		12 46			12 40			
	d				11 59		12 19			12 10					12 29		12 49			12 40			
Hampton Wick	d				12 01					12 12					12 31					12 42			
Teddington	d				12 05					12 15					12 35					12 45			
Strawberry Hill	a				12 08										12 38								
Fulwell	d									12 19										12 49			
Hampton	d									12 23										12 53			
Kempton Park	d									12 26										12 56			
Sunbury	d									12 28										12 58			
Upper Halliford	d									12 30										13 00			
Shepperton	a									12 33										13 03			
Berrylands	d							12 00										12 30					
Surbiton 6	d	11 41	11 44			11 57		12 05				12 11	12 14			12 27		12 35				12 41	12 44
Thames Ditton	d							12 09										12 39					
Hampton Court	a							12 12										12 42					
Hinchley Wood	d					12 01										12 31							
Claygate	d					12 04										12 34							
Oxshott	d					12 07										12 37							
Cobham & Stoke D'abernon	d					12 11										12 41							
Bookham	d								12 29										12 59				
Effingham Junction 6	d					12 15			12 33							12 45			13 03				
Horsley	d					12 18			12 36							12 48			13 06				
Clandon	d					12 23			12 41							12 53			13 11				
London Road (Guildford)	d					12 28			12 46							12 58			13 16				
Guildford	a					12 32			12 50							13 02			13 20				

Table 152

Mondays to Fridays

24 May to 24 September

London - Chessington South, Dorking, Guildford, Shepperton and Hampton Court

		SW	SW	SW	SW	SW	SW	SW	SW	SW 1	SW	SW	SW	SW	SW	SW	SW	SW	SW	SW 1	SW	SW
London Waterloo 15 ⊖	d	12 24	12 27	12 33	12 33	12 36	12 39	12 42	12 46	12 53	12 50	12 54	12 57	13 03	13 03	13 06	13 09	13 12	13 16	13 23	13 20	13 24
Vauxhall ⊖	d	12 28	12 31	12 37	12 37	12 40	12 43	12 46	12 50		12 54	12 58	13 01	13 07	13 07	13 10	13 13	13 16	13 20		13 24	13 28
Clapham Junction 10	d	12 33	12 36	12 42		12 45	12 48	12 51	12 55	13u00	12 59	13 03	13 06	13 12		13 15	13 18	13 21	13 25		13 29	13 33
Earlsfield	d	12 36	12 39	12 45		12 48	12 51	12 54	12 58		13 02	13 06	13 09	13 15		13 18	13 21	13 24	13 28		13 32	13 36
Wimbledon 6 ⊖ ⇌	d	12 40	12 43	12 49		12 52	12 55	12 58	13 02		13 06	13 10	13 13	13 19		13 22	13 25	13 28	13 32		13 36	13 40
Raynes Park 6	d	12 43	12 46			12 55	12 58	13 01	13 05			13 13	13 16			13 25	13 28	13 31	13 35			13 43
Motspur Park	d	12 46					13 01		13 08			13 16					13 31		13 38			13 46
Malden Manor	d								13 11										13 41			
Tolworth	d								13 14										13 44			
Chessington North	d								13 17										13 47			
Chessington South	a								13 19										13 49			
Worcester Park	d	12 48					13 03					13 18					13 33					13 48
Stoneleigh	d	12 51					13 06					13 21					13 36					13 51
Ewell West	d	12 54					13 09					13 24					13 39					13 54
Epsom 3	a	12 57					13 16					13 27					13 46					13 57
	d	12 58					13 17					13 28					13 47					13 58
Ashtead	d	13 02					13 21					13 32					13 51					14 02
Leatherhead	d	13 05					13 24					13 35					13 54					14 05
Boxhill & Westhumble	d																					
Dorking 4	a	13 11										13 41										14 11
New Malden 6	d		12 49			12 58		13 04					13 19			13 28		13 34				
Norbiton	d		12 52					13 07					13 22					13 37				
Kingston	a		12 55		13 16			13 10					13 25		13 46			13 40				
	d		12 59		13 19			13 10					13 29		13 49			13 40				
Hampton Wick	d		13 01					13 12					13 31					13 42				
Teddington	d		13 05					13 15					13 35					13 45				
Strawberry Hill	a		13 08										13 38									
Fulwell	d							13 19										13 49				
Hampton	d							13 23										13 53				
Kempton Park	d							13 26										13 56				
Sunbury	d							13 28										13 58				
Upper Halliford	d							13 30										14 00				
Shepperton	a							13 33										14 03				
Berrylands	d					13 00										13 30						
Surbiton 6	d			12 57		13 05				13 11	13 14			13 27		13 35				13 41	13 44	
Thames Ditton	d					13 09										13 39						
Hampton Court	a					13 12										13 42						
Hinchley Wood	d			13 01										13 31								
Claygate	d			13 04										13 34								
Oxshott	d			13 07										13 37								
Cobham & Stoke D'abernon	d			13 11										13 41								
Bookham	d						13 29										13 59					
Effingham Junction 6	d			13 15			13 33							13 45			14 03					
Horsley	d			13 18			13 36							13 48			14 06					
Clandon	d			13 23			13 41							13 53			14 11					
London Road (Guildford)	d			13 28			13 46							13 58			14 16					
Guildford	a			13 32			13 50							14 02			14 20					

Table 152

Mondays to Fridays

24 May to 24 September

London - Chessington South, Dorking, Guildford, Shepperton and Hampton Court

		SW	SW	SW	SW	SW	SW	SW	SW 1	SW	SW	SW	SW	SW	SW	SW	SW	SW	SW 1	SW	SW	SW	SW
London Waterloo 15 ⊖	d	13 27	13 33	13 33	13 36	13 39	13 42	13 46	13 53	13 50	13 54	13 57	14 03	14 03	14 06	14 09	14 12	14 16	14 23	14 20	14 24	14 27	14 33
Vauxhall ⊖	d	13 31	13 37	13 37	13 40	13 43	13 46	13 50		13 54	13 58	14 01	14 07	14 07	14 10	14 13	14 16	14 20		14 24	14 28	14 31	14 37
Clapham Junction 10	d	13 36	13 42		13 45	13 48	13 51	13 55	14u00	13 59	14 03	14 06	14 12		14 15	14 18	14 21	14 25		14 29	14 33	14 36	14 42
Earlsfield	d	13 39	13 45		13 48	13 51	13 54	13 58		14 02	14 06	14 09	14 15		14 18	14 21	14 24	14 28		14 32	14 36	14 39	14 45
Wimbledon 6 ⊖ ⇌	d	13 43	13 49		13 52	13 55	13 58	14 02		14 06	14 10	14 13	14 19		14 22	14 25	14 28	14 32		14 36	14 40	14 43	14 49
Raynes Park 6	d	13 46			13 55	13 58	14 01	14 05			14 13	14 14			14 25	14 28	14 31	14 35			14 43	14 46	
Motspur Park	d					14 01		14 08			14 16					14 31		14 38			14 46		
Malden Manor	d							14 11										14 41					
Tolworth	d							14 14										14 44					
Chessington North	d							14 17										14 47					
Chessington South	a							14 19										14 49					
Worcester Park	d					14 03					14 18					14 33					14 48		
Stoneleigh	d					14 06					14 21					14 36					14 51		
Ewell West	d					14 09					14 24					14 39					14 54		
Epsom 3	a					14 16					14 27					14 46					14 57		
	d					14 17					14 28					14 47					14 58		
Ashtead	d					14 21					14 32					14 51					15 02		
Leatherhead	d					14 24					14 35					14 54					15 05		
Boxhill & Westhumble	d																						
Dorking 4	a										14 41										15 11		
New Malden 6	d	13 49			13 58		14 04					14 18			14 28		14 34					14 49	
Norbiton	d	13 52					14 07					14 20					14 37					14 52	
Kingston	a	13 55		14 16			14 10					14 24		14 46			14 40					14 55	
	d	13 59		14 19			14 10					14 29		14 49			14 40					14 59	
Hampton Wick	d	14 01					14 12					14 31					14 42					15 01	
Teddington	d	14 05					14 15					14 35					14 45					15 05	
Strawberry Hill	a	14 08										14 38										15 08	
Fulwell	d						14 19										14 49						
Hampton	d						14 23										14 53						
Kempton Park	d						14 26										14 56						
Sunbury	d						14 28										14 58						
Upper Halliford	d						14 30										15 00						
Shepperton	a						14 33										15 03						
Berrylands	d				14 00										14 30								
Surbiton 6	d		13 57		14 05				14 11	14 14			14 27		14 35				14 41	14 44			14 57
Thames Ditton	d				14 09										14 39								
Hampton Court	a				14 12										14 42								
Hinchley Wood	d		14 01										14 31										15 01
Claygate	d		14 04										14 34										15 04
Oxshott	d		14 07										14 37										15 07
Cobham & Stoke D'abernon	d		14 11										14 41										15 11
Bookham	d					14 29										14 59							
Effingham Junction 6	d		14 15			14 33							14 45			15 03							15 15
Horsley	d		14 18			14 36							14 48			15 06							15 18
Clandon	d		14 23			14 41							14 53			15 11							15 23
London Road (Guildford)	d		14 28			14 46							14 58			15 16							15 28
Guildford	a		14 32			14 50							15 02			15 20							15 32

Table 152

Mondays to Fridays
24 May to 24 September

London - Chessington South, Dorking, Guildford, Shepperton and Hampton Court

		SW	SW	SW	SW	SW	SW 1	SW	SW	SW	SW	SW	SW	SW	SW	SW	SW 1	SW	SW	SW	SW	SW
London Waterloo 15 ⊖	d	14 33	14 36	14 39	14 42	14 46	14 53	14 50	14 54	14 57	15 03	15 03	15 06	15 09	15 12	15 16	15 23	15 20	15 24	15 27	15 33	15 33
Vauxhall ⊖	d	14 37	14 40	14 43	14 46	14 50		14 54	14 58	15 01	15 07	15 07	15 10	15 13	15 16	15 20		15 24	15 28	15 31	15 37	15 37
Clapham Junction 10	d		14 45	14 48	14 51	14 55	15u00	14 59	15 03	15 06	15 12		15 15	15 18	15 21	15 25		15 29	15 33	15 36	15 42	
Earlsfield	d		14 48	14 51	14 54	14 58		15 02	15 06	15 09	15 15		15 18	15 21	15 24	15 28		15 32	15 36	15 39	15 45	
Wimbledon 6 ⊖	d		14 52	14 55	14 58	15 02		15 06	15 10	15 13	15 19		15 22	15 25	15 28	15 32		15 36	15 40	15 43	15 49	
Raynes Park 6	d		14 55	14 58	15 01	15 05			15 13	15 16			15 25	15 28	15 31	15 35			15 43	15 46		
Motspur Park	d			15 01		15 08			15 16					15 31		15 38			15 46			
Malden Manor	d					15 11										15 41						
Tolworth	d					15 14										15 44						
Chessington North	d					15 17										15 47						
Chessington South	a					15 19										15 49						
Worcester Park	d			15 03					15 18					15 33					15 48			
Stoneleigh	d			15 06					15 21					15 36					15 51			
Ewell West	d			15 09					15 24					15 39					15 54			
Epsom 3	a			15 16					15 27					15 46					15 57			
	d			15 17					15 28					15 47					15 58			
Ashtead	d			15 21					15 32					15 51					16 02			
Leatherhead	d			15 24					15 35					15 54					16 05			
Boxhill & Westhumble	d																					
Dorking 4	a								15 41										16 11			
New Malden 6	d		14 58		15 04					15 19			15 28		15 34					15 49		
Norbiton	d				15 07					15 22					15 37					15 52		
Kingston	a	15 16			15 10					15 25		15 46			15 40					15 55		16 16
	d	15 19			15 10					15 29		15 49			15 40					15 59		16 19
Hampton Wick	d				15 12					15 31					15 42					16 01		
Teddington	d				15 15					15 35					15 45					16 05		
Strawberry Hill	a									15 38										16 08		
Fulwell	d				15 19										15 49							
Hampton	d				15 23										15 53							
Kempton Park	d				15 26										15 56							
Sunbury	d				15 28										15 58							
Upper Halliford	d				15 30										16 00							
Shepperton	a				15 33										16 03							
Berrylands	d		15 00										15 30									
Surbiton 6	d		15 05				15 11	15 14			15 27		15 35				15 41	15 44			15 57	
Thames Ditton	d		15 09										15 39									
Hampton Court	a		15 12										15 42									
Hinchley Wood	d										15 31										16 01	
Claygate	d										15 34										16 04	
Oxshott	d										15 37										16 07	
Cobham & Stoke D'abernon	d										15 41										16 11	
Bookham	d			15 29										15 59								
Effingham Junction 6	d			15 33							15 45			16 03							16 15	
Horsley	d			15 36							15 48			16 06							16 18	
Clandon	d			15 41							15 53			16 11							16 23	
London Road (Guildford)	d			15 46							15 58			16 16							16 28	
Guildford	a			15 50							16 02			16 20							16 32	

Table 152

Mondays to Fridays
24 May to 24 September

London - Chessington South, Dorking, Guildford, Shepperton and Hampton Court

		SW	SW	SW	SW	SW 1	SW	SW	SW	SW	SW	SW	SW	SW	SW	SW	SW 1	SW	SW	SW	SW	SW	SW
London Waterloo 15 ⊖	d	15 36	15 39	15 42	15 46	15 53	15 50	15 54	15 57	16 01	16 03	16 06	16 09	16 12	16 16	16 24	16 25	16 20	16 27	16 31	16 33	16 36	16 39
Vauxhall ⊖	d	15 40	15 43	15 46	15 50		15 54	15 58	16 01	16 05	16 07	16 10	16 13	16 16	16 20	16 28		16 24	16 31	16 35	16 37	16 40	16 43
Clapham Junction 10	d	15 45	15 48	15 51	15 55	16u00	15 59	16 03	16 06		16 12	16 15	16 18	16 21	16 25	16 33		16 29	16 36		16 42	16 45	16 48
Earlsfield	d	15 48	15 51	15 54	15 58		16 02	16 06	16 09		16 15	16 18	16 21	16 24	16 28	16 36		16 32	16 39		16 45	16 48	16 51
Wimbledon 6 ⊖	d	15 52	15 55	15 58	16 02		16 06	16 10	16 13		16 19	16 22	16 25	16 28	16 32	16 40		16 36	16 43		16 49	16 52	16 55
Raynes Park 6	d	15 55	15 58	16 01	16 05			16 13	16 16			16 25	16 28	16 31	16 35	16 43			16 46			16 55	16 58
Motspur Park	d		16 01		16 08			16 16					16 31		16 38	16 46							17 01
Malden Manor	d				16 11										16 41								
Tolworth	d				16 14										16 44								
Chessington North	d				16 17										16 47								
Chessington South	a				16 19										16 51								
Worcester Park	d		16 03					16 18					16 33			16 48							17 03
Stoneleigh	d		16 06					16 21					16 36			16 51							17 06
Ewell West	d		16 09					16 24					16 39			16 54							17 09
Epsom 3	a		16 15					16 27					16 46			16 57							17 12
	d		16 17					16 28					16 47			16 58							17 17
Ashtead	d		16 21					16 32					16 51			17 02							17 21
Leatherhead	d		16 24					16 35					16 54			17 05							17 24
Boxhill & Westhumble	d															17 10							
Dorking 4	a							16 41								17 14							
New Malden 6	d	15 58		16 04					16 19			16 28		16 34					16 49			16 58	
Norbiton	d			16 07					16 22					16 37					16 52				
Kingston	a			16 10					16 25	16 48				16 40					16 55	17 18			
	d			16 10					16 29	16 49				16 40					16 59	17 19			
Hampton Wick	d			16 12					16 31					16 42					17 01				
Teddington	d			16 15					16 35					16 45					17 05				
Strawberry Hill	a								16 38										17 08				
Fulwell	d			16 19										16 49									
Hampton	d			16 23										16 53									
Kempton Park	d			16 26										16 56									
Sunbury	d			16 28										16 58									
Upper Halliford	d			16 30										17 00									
Shepperton	a			16 33										17 05									
Berrylands	d	16 00										16 30										17 00	
Surbiton 6	d	16 05				16 11	16 14				16 27	16 35					16 41	16 44			16 57	17 05	
Thames Ditton	d	16 09										16 39										17 09	
Hampton Court	a	16 12										16 44										17 14	
Hinchley Wood	d										16 31										17 01		
Claygate	d										16 34										17 04		
Oxshott	d										16 37										17 07		
Cobham & Stoke D'abernon	d										16 41										17 11		
Bookham	d		16 29										16 59										17 29
Effingham Junction 6	d		16 33								16 45		17 03								17 15		17 33
Horsley	d		16 36								16 48		17 06								17 18		17 36
Clandon	d		16 41								16 53		17 11								17 23		17 41
London Road (Guildford)	d		16 46								16 58		17 16								17 28		17 46
Guildford	a		16 50								17 04		17 22								17 34		17 52

Table 152

Mondays to Fridays

24 May to 24 September

London - Chessington South, Dorking, Guildford, Shepperton and Hampton Court

		SW	SW	SW	SW	SW	SW	SW 1	SW	SW	SW	SW	SW	SW	SW	SW	SW	SW	SW	SW 1	SW	SW	SW
London Waterloo ⊖	d	16 42	16 46	16 50	16 54	16 57	17 01	17 02	17 02	17 06	17 09	17 12	17 13	17 16	17 20	17 24	17 27	17 30	17 31	17 32	17 32	17 36	17 39
Vauxhall ⊖	d	16 46	16 50	16 54	16 58	17 01	17 05		17 07	17 10	17 13	17 16	17 17	17 20	17 24	17 28	17 31	17 34	17 35		17 37	17 40	17 43
Clapham Junction	d	16 51	16 55	16 59	17 03	17 06			17 12	17 15	17 18	17 22		17 25	17 29	17 33	17 36	17 39			17 42	17 45	17 48
Earlsfield	d	16 54	16 58	17 02	17 06	17 09			17 15	17 18	17 21	17 25		17 28	17 32	17 36	17 39	17 42			17 45	17 48	17 51
Wimbledon ⊖	d	16 58	17 02	17 06	17 10	17 13			17 19	17 22	17 25	17 29		17 32	17 36	17 40	17 43	17 46			17 49	17 52	17 55
Raynes Park	d	17 01	17 05		17 13	17 16				17 25	17 28	17 32		17 35		17 43	17 46	17 49				17 55	17 58
Motspur Park	d		17 08		17 16						17 31			17 38				17 52					18 01
Malden Manor	d		17 11											17 41									
Tolworth	d		17 14											17 44									
Chessington North	d		17 17											17 47									
Chessington South	a		17 21											17 51									
Worcester Park	d				17 18						17 33					17 47		17 54					18 03
Stoneleigh	d				17 21						17 36							17 57					18 06
Ewell West	d				17 24						17 39							18 00					18 09
Epsom	a				17 27						17 42					17 54		18 07					18 20
	d				17 28						17 47					17 54							18 21
Ashtead	d				17 32						17 51					17 58							18 25
Leatherhead	d				17 35						17 54					18 01							18 28
Boxhill & Westhumble	d				17 40											18 06							
Dorking	a				17 44											18 11							
New Malden	d	17 04				17 19				17 28		17 35					17 49					17 58	
Norbiton	d	17 07				17 22						17 38					17 52						
Kingston	a	17 10				17 25	17 48					17 41	17 56				17 55		18 18				
	d	17 10				17 29	17 49					17 41	17 58				17 59		18 19				
Hampton Wick	d	17 12				17 31						17 43					18 01						
Teddington	d	17 15				17 35						17 46					18 05						
Strawberry Hill	a					17 38											18 08						
Fulwell	d	17 19										17 50											
Hampton	d	17 23										17 54											
Kempton Park	d	17 26										17 57											
Sunbury	d	17 28										17 59											
Upper Halliford	d	17 30										18 01											
Shepperton	a	17 35										18 06											
Berrylands	d									17 30												18 00	
Surbiton	d			17 14				17 18	17 27	17 35					17 44					17 48	17 57	18 05	
Thames Ditton	d									17 39												18 09	
Hampton Court	a									17 44												18 14	
Hinchley Wood	d								17 31												18 05		
Claygate	d								17 34												18 08		
Oxshott	d								17 37												18 11		
Cobham & Stoke D'abernon	d								17 41												18 15		
Bookham	d										17 59												18 34
Effingham Junction	d								17 45		18a05										18 20		18a44
Horsley	d								17 48												18 22		
Clandon	d								17 53												18 27		
London Road (Guildford)	d								17 58												18 32		
Guildford	a							17 56	18 04											18 29	18 38		

Table 152

Mondays to Fridays

24 May to 24 September

London - Chessington South, Dorking, Guildford, Shepperton and Hampton Court

		SW	SW	SW	SW	SW	SW	SW	SW	SW 1	SW	SW	SW	SW	SW	SW	SW	SW	SW	SW	SW	SW
London Waterloo ⊖	d	17 43	17 42	17 46	17 50	17 54	17 57	18 00	18 01	18 02	18 02	18 06	18 09	18 13	18 12	18 16	18 20	18 24	18 27	18 30	18 31	18 32
Vauxhall ⊖	d	17 47	17 46	17 50	17 54	17 58	18 01	18 04	18 05		18 07	18 10	18 13	18 17	18 16	18 20	18 24	18 28	18 31	18 34	18 35	18 37
Clapham Junction	d	17 53	17 52	17 55	17 59	18 03	18 06	18 09			18 12	18 15	18 18	18 23	18 22	18 25	18 29	18 33	18 36	18 39		18 42
Earlsfield	d		17 55	17 58	18 02	18 06	18 09	18 12			18 15	18 18	18 21		18 25	18 28	18 32	18 36	18 39	18 42		18 45
Wimbledon ⊖	d		17 59	18 02	18 06	18 10	18 13	18 16			18 19	18 22	18 25		18 29	18 32	18 36	18 40	18 43	18 46		18 49
Raynes Park	d		18 02	18 05		18 13	18 16	18 19				18 25	18 28		18 32	18 35		18 43	18 46	18 49		
Motspur Park	d			18 08				18 22					18 31			18 38				18 52		
Malden Manor	d			18 11												18 41						
Tolworth	d			18 14												18 44						
Chessington North	d			18 17												18 47						
Chessington South	a			18 21												18 51						
Worcester Park	d					18 17		18 24					18 33					18 47		18 54		
Stoneleigh	d							18 27					18 36							18 57		
Ewell West	d							18 30					18 39							19 00		
Epsom	a					18 24		18 35					18 46					18 54		19 07		
	d					18 24							18 47					18 54				
Ashtead	d					18 28							18 51					18 58				
Leatherhead	d					18 31							18 54					19 01				
Boxhill & Westhumble	d					18 36												19 06				
Dorking	a					18 41												19 11				
New Malden	d		18 05				18 19					18 28			18 35				18 49			
Norbiton	d		18 08				18 22								18 38				18 52			
Kingston	a		18 11				18 25		18 48						18 41				18 55		19 18	
	d		18 11				18 29		18 49						18 41				18 59		19 19	
Hampton Wick	d		18 13				18 31								18 43				19 01			
Teddington	d		18 16				18 35								18 46				19 05			
Strawberry Hill	a	18 11					18 38							18 41					19 08			
Fulwell	d	18 13	18 20											18 43	18 50							
Hampton	d	18 17	18 24											18 47	18 54							
Kempton Park	d		18 27												18 57							
Sunbury	d	18 21	18 29											18 51	18 59							
Upper Halliford	d	18 23	18 31											18 53	19 01							
Shepperton	a	18 28	18 40											18 58	19 10							
Berrylands	d											18 30										
Surbiton	d				18 14					18 18	18 27	18 35					18 44					18 57
Thames Ditton	d											18 39										
Hampton Court	a											18 44										
Hinchley Wood	d										18 35											19 01
Claygate	d										18 38											19 04
Oxshott	d										18 41											19 07
Cobham & Stoke D'abernon	d										18 45											19 11
Bookham	d												18 59									
Effingham Junction	d										18 50		19 03									19 15
Horsley	d										18 52		19 06									19 18
Clandon	d										18 57		19 11									19 23
London Road (Guildford)	d										19 02		19 16									19 28
Guildford	a										19 08		19 22									19 34

Table 152

Mondays to Fridays
24 May to 24 September

London - Chessington South, Dorking, Guildford, Shepperton and Hampton Court

		SW	SW	SW	SW	SW	SW	SW	SW	SW	SW	SW	SW ■	SW	SW	SW	SW	SW	SW	SW	SW	SW	SW
London Waterloo 15 ⊖	d	18 36	18 39	18 43	18 42	18 46	18 48	18 50	18 54	18 57	19 00	19 01	19 02	19 02	19 06	19 09	19 12	19 16	19 20	19 23	19 24	19 27	19 33
Vauxhall ⊖	d	18 40	18 43	18 47	18 46	18 50		18 54	18 58	19 01	19 04	19 05		19 07	19 10	19 13	19 16	19 20	19 24		19 28	19 31	19 37
Clapham Junction 10	d	18 45	18 48	18 53	18 52	18 55		18 59	19 03	19 06	19 09			19 12	19 15	19 18	19 22	19 25	19 29		19 33	19 36	19 42
Earlsfield	d	18 48	18 51		18 55	18 58		19 02	19 06	19 09	19 12			19 15	19 18	19 21	19 25	19 28	19 32		19 36	19 39	19 45
Wimbledon 6 ⊖	d	18 52	18 55		18 59	19 02		19 06	19 10	19 13	19 16			19 19	19 22	19 25	19 29	19 32	19 36		19 40	19 43	19 49
Raynes Park 6	d	18 55	18 58		19 02	19 05			19 13	19 16	19 19				19 25	19 28	19 32	19 35			19 43	19 46	
Motspur Park	d		19 01			19 08					19 22					19 31		19 38			19 46		
Malden Manor	d					19 11												19 41					
Tolworth	d					19 14												19 44					
Chessington North	d					19 17												19 47					
Chessington South	a					19 21												19 49					
Worcester Park	d		19 03						19 17		19 24					19 33					19 48		
Stoneleigh	d		19 06								19 27					19 36					19 51		
Ewell West	d		19 09								19 30					19 39					19 54		
Epsom 3	a		19 12						19 24		19 35					19 43					19 57		
	d		19 17						19 24							19 47					19 58		
Ashtead	d		19 21						19 28							19 51					20 02		
Leatherhead	d		19 24						19 31							19 54					20 05		
Boxhill & Westhumble	d								19 36												20 10		
Dorking 4	a								19 41												20 12		
New Malden 6	d	18 58			19 05					19 19					19 28		19 35					19 49	
Norbiton	d				19 08					19 22							19 38					19 52	
Kingston	a				19 11					19 25		19 48					19 41					19 55	
	d				19 11					19 29		19 49					19 41					19 59	
Hampton Wick	d				19 13					19 31							19 43					20 01	
Teddington	d				19 16					19 35							19 46					20 05	
Strawberry Hill	a			19 11						19 38												20 08	
Fulwell	d			19 13	19 20												19 50						
Hampton	d			19 17	19 24												19 54						
Kempton Park	d				19 27												19 57						
Sunbury	d			19 21	19 29												19 59						
Upper Halliford	d			19 23	19 31												20 01						
Shepperton	a			19 28	19 37												20 04						
Berrylands	d	19 00													19 30								
Surbiton 6	d	19 05					19 06	19 14					19 18	19 27	19 35				19 44	19a39			19 57
Thames Ditton	d	19 09													19 39								
Hampton Court	a	19 14													19 42								
Hinchley Wood	d						19 10							19 31									20 01
Claygate	d						19 13							19 34									20 04
Oxshott	d						19 16							19 37									20 07
Cobham & Stoke D'abernon	d						19 20							19 41									20 11
Bookham	d		19 29													19 59							
Effingham Junction 6	d		19 33				19 24							19 45		20 03							20 15
Horsley	d		19 36				19 27							19 48		20 06							20 18
Clandon	d		19 41				19 32							19 53		20 11							20 23
London Road (Guildford)	d		19 46				19 37							19 58		20 16							20 28
Guildford	a		19 52				19 43							20 02		20 20							20 32

Table 152

Mondays to Fridays
24 May to 24 September

London - Chessington South, Dorking, Guildford, Shepperton and Hampton Court

		SW	SW	SW	SW	SW	SW ■	SW	SW	SW	SW	SW	SW	SW	SW	SW	SW ■	SW	SW	SW	SW	SW
London Waterloo 15 ⊖	d	19 33	19 36	19 39	19 42	19 46	19 53	19 50	19 54	19 57	20 03	20 03	20 06	20 09	20 12	20 16	20 23	20 20	20 24	20 27	20 33	20 33
Vauxhall ⊖	d	19 37	19 40	19 43	19 46	19 50		19 54	19 58	20 01	20 07	20 07	20 10	20 13	20 16	20 20		20 24	20 28	20 31	20 37	20 37
Clapham Junction 10	d		19 45	19 48	19 51	19 55	20u00	19 59	20 03	20 06	20 12		20 15	20 18	20 21	20 25		20 29	20 33	20 36	20 42	
Earlsfield	d		19 48	19 51	19 54	19 58		20 02	20 06	20 09	20 15		20 18	20 21	20 24	20 28		20 32	20 36	20 39	20 45	
Wimbledon 6 ⊖	d		19 52	19 55	19 58	20 02		20 06	20 10	20 13	20 19		20 22	20 25	20 28	20 32		20 36	20 40	20 43	20 49	
Raynes Park 6	d		19 55	19 58	20 01	20 05			20 13	20 16			20 25	20 28	20 31	20 35			20 43	20 46		
Motspur Park	d			20 01		20 08			20 16					20 31		20 38			20 46			
Malden Manor	d					20 11										20 41						
Tolworth	d					20 14										20 44						
Chessington North	d					20 17										20 47						
Chessington South	a					20 19										20 49						
Worcester Park	d			20 03					20 18					20 33					20 48			
Stoneleigh	d			20 06					20 21					20 36					20 51			
Ewell West	d			20 09					20 24					20 39					20 54			
Epsom 3	a			20 16					20 27					20 42					20 57			
	d			20 17										20 47								
Ashtead	d			20 21										20 51								
Leatherhead	d			20 24										20 54								
Boxhill & Westhumble	d													20 59								
Dorking 4	a													21 01								
New Malden 6	d		19 58		20 04					20 19			20 28		20 34					20 49		
Norbiton	d				20 07					20 22					20 37					20 52		
Kingston	a	20 16			20 10					20 25		20 46			20 40					20 55		21 16
	d	20 19			20 10					20 29		20 49			20 40					20 59		21 19
Hampton Wick	d				20 12					20 31					20 42					21 01		
Teddington	d				20 15					20 35					20 45					21 05		
Strawberry Hill	a									20 38										21 08		
Fulwell	d				20 19										20 49							
Hampton	d				20 23										20 53							
Kempton Park	d				20 26										20 56							
Sunbury	d				20 28										20 58							
Upper Halliford	d				20 30										21 00							
Shepperton	a				20 33										21 03							
Berrylands	d		20 00										20 30									
Surbiton 6	d		20 05				20 11	20 14			20 27		20 35				20 41	20 44			20 57	
Thames Ditton	d		20 09										20 39									
Hampton Court	a		20 12										20 42									
Hinchley Wood	d										20 31										21 01	
Claygate	d										20 34										21 04	
Oxshott	d										20 37										21 07	
Cobham & Stoke D'abernon	d										20 41										21 11	
Bookham	d			20 29																		
Effingham Junction 6	d			20 33							20 45										21 15	
Horsley	d			20 36							20 48										21 18	
Clandon	d			20 41							20 53										21 23	
London Road (Guildford)	d			20 46							20 58										21 28	
Guildford	a			20 50							21 02										21 32	

Table 152

Mondays to Fridays
24 May to 24 September

London - Chessington South, Dorking, Guildford, Shepperton and Hampton Court

Station		SW	SW	SW	SW	SW 1	SW	SW	SW	SW	SW	SW	SW	SW 1	SW	SW	SW	SW	SW	SW	SW	SW	SW
London Waterloo 15 ⊖	d	20 36	20 39	20 42	20 46	20 53	20 50	20 54	20 57	21 03	21 03	21 09	21 12	21 23	21 20	21 24	21 27	21 33	21 33	21 36	21 39	21 42	21 46
Vauxhall ⊖	d	20 40	20 43	20 46	20 50		20 54	20 58	21 01	21 07	21 07	21 13	21 16		21 24	21 28	21 31	21 37	21 37	21 40	21 43	21 46	21 50
Clapham Junction 10	d	20 45	20 48	20 51	20 55	21u00	20 59	21 03	21 06	21 12		21 18	21 21		21 29	21 33	21 36	21 42		21 45	21 48	21 51	21 55
Earlsfield	d	20 48	20 51	20 54	20 58		21 02	21 06	21 09	21 15		21 21	21 24		21 32	21 36	21 39	21 45		21 48	21 51	21 54	21 58
Wimbledon 6 ⊖	d	20 52	20 55	20 58	21 02		21 06	21 10	21 13	21 19		21 25	21 28		21 36	21 40	21 43	21 49		21 52	21 55	21 58	22 02
Raynes Park 6	d	20 55	20 58	21 01	21 05			21 13	21 16			21 28	21 31			21 43	21 46			21 55	21 58	22 01	22 05
Motspur Park	d		21 01		21 08			21 16				21 31				21 46					22 01		22 08
Malden Manor	d				21 11																		22 11
Tolworth	d				21 14																		22 14
Chessington North	d				21 17																		22 17
Chessington South	a				21 19																		22 19
Worcester Park	d		21 03					21 18				21 33				21 48					22 03		
Stoneleigh	d		21 06					21 21				21 36				21 51					22 06		
Ewell West	d		21 09					21 24				21 39				21 54					22 09		
Epsom 3	a		21 12					21 27				21 42				21 57					22 12		
	d		21 17									21 47									22 17		
Ashtead	d		21 21									21 51									22 21		
Leatherhead	d		21 24									21 54									22 24		
Boxhill & Westhumble	d											21 59											
Dorking 4	a											22 01											
New Malden 6	d	20 58		21 04					21 19				21 34				21 49			21 58		22 04	
Norbiton	d			21 07					21 22				21 37				21 52					22 07	
Kingston	a			21 10					21 25		21 46		21 40				21 55		22 16			22 10	
	d			21 10					21 29		21 49		21 40				21 59		22 19			22 10	
Hampton Wick	d			21 12					21 31				21 42				22 01					22 12	
Teddington	d			21 15					21 35				21 45				22 05					22 15	
Strawberry Hill	a								21 38								22 08						
Fulwell	d			21 19									21 49									22 19	
Hampton	d			21 23									21 53									22 23	
Kempton Park	d			21 26									21 56									22 26	
Sunbury	d			21 28									21 58									22 28	
Upper Halliford	d			21 30									22 00									22 30	
Shepperton	a			21 33									22 03									22 33	
Berrylands	d	21 00																		22 00			
Surbiton 6	d	21 05				21 11	21 14			21 27				21 41	21 44			21 57		22 05			
Thames Ditton	d	21 09																		22 09			
Hampton Court	a	21 12																		22 12			
Hinchley Wood	d									21 31								22 01					
Claygate	d									21 34								22 04					
Oxshott	d									21 37								22 07					
Cobham & Stoke D'abernon	d									21 41								22 11					
Bookham	d		21 29																		22 29		
Effingham Junction 6	d		21 33							21 45								22 15			22 33		
Horsley	d		21 36							21 48								22 18			22 36		
Clandon	d		21 41							21 53								22 23			22 41		
London Road (Guildford)	d		21 46							21 58								22 28			22 46		
Guildford	a		21 50							22 02								22 32			22 50		

Table 152

Mondays to Fridays
24 May to 24 September

London - Chessington South, Dorking, Guildford, Shepperton and Hampton Court

Station		SW 1	SW	SW	SW	SW	SW	SW	SW	SW 1	SW	SW	SW	SW	SW	SW	SW	SW 1	SW	SW	SW	SW	SW
London Waterloo 15 ⊖	d	21 53	21 50	21 54	21 57	22 03	22 03	22 09	22 12	22 23	22 20	22 27	22 33	22 33	22 36	22 39	22 42	22 53	22 50	22 57	23 00	23 03	23 03
Vauxhall ⊖	d		21 54	21 58	22 01	22 07	22 07	22 13	22 16		22 24	22 31	22 37	22 37	22 40	22 43	22 46		22 54	23 01	23 04	23 07	23 07
Clapham Junction 10	d	22u00	21 59	22 03	22 06	22 12		22 18	22 21	22u30	22 29	22 36	22 42		22 45	22 48	22 51	23u00	22 59	23 06	23 09	23 12	
Earlsfield	d		22 02	22 06	22 09	22 15		22 21	22 24		22 32	22 39	22 45		22 48	22 51	22 54		23 02	23 09	23 12	23 15	
Wimbledon 6 ⊖	d		22 06	22 10	22 13	22 19		22 25	22 28		22 36	22 43	22 49		22 52	22 55	22 58		23 06	23 13	23 16	23 19	
Raynes Park 6	d			22 13	22 16			22 28	22 31			22 46			22 55	22 58	23 01			23 16	23 19		
Motspur Park	d			22 16				22 31								23 01					23 22		
Malden Manor	d																				23 25		
Tolworth	d																				23 28		
Chessington North	d																				23 31		
Chessington South	a																				23 33		
Worcester Park	d			22 18				22 33								23 03							
Stoneleigh	d			22 21				22 36								23 06							
Ewell West	d			22 24				22 39								23 09							
Epsom 3	a			22 27				22 42								23 12							
	d							22 47								23 17							
Ashtead	d							22 51								23 21							
Leatherhead	d							22 54								23 24							
Boxhill & Westhumble	d							22 59															
Dorking 4	a							23 01															
New Malden 6	d				22 19				22 34			22 49			22 58		23 04			23 19			
Norbiton	d				22 22				22 37			22 52					23 07			23 22			
Kingston	a				22 25		22 46		22 40			22 55		23 16			23 10			23 25			23 46
	d				22 29		22 49		22 40			22 59		23 19			23 10			23 29			23 49
Hampton Wick	d				22 31				22 42			23 01					23 12			23 31			
Teddington	d				22 35				22 45			23 05					23 15			23 35			
Strawberry Hill	a				22 38							23 08								23 38			
Fulwell	d								22 49								23 19						
Hampton	d								22 53								23 23						
Kempton Park	d								22 56								23 26						
Sunbury	d								22 58								23 28						
Upper Halliford	d								23 00								23 30						
Shepperton	a								23 03								23 33						
Berrylands	d														23 00								
Surbiton 6	d	22 11	22 14			22 27				22 41	22 44		22 57		23 05			23 11	23 14			23 27	
Thames Ditton	d														23 09								
Hampton Court	a														23 12								
Hinchley Wood	d					22 31							23 01									23 31	
Claygate	d					22 34							23 04									23 34	
Oxshott	d					22 37							23 07									23 37	
Cobham & Stoke D'abernon	d					22 41							23 11									23 41	
Bookham	d															23 29							
Effingham Junction 6	d					22 45							23 15			23 33						23 45	
Horsley	d					22 48							23 18			23 36						23 48	
Clandon	d					22 53							23 23			23 41						23 53	
London Road (Guildford)	d					22 58							23 28			23 46						23 58	
Guildford	a		22 47			23 06							23 32			23 54						00 02	

Table 152

Mondays to Fridays
24 May to 24 September

London - Chessington South, Dorking, Guildford, Shepperton and Hampton Court

		SW	SW	SW	SW	SW	SW	SW	SW	SW
London Waterloo 15 ⊖	d	23 09	23 12	23 20	23 27	23 30	23 33	23 42	23 50	23 57
Vauxhall ⊖	d	23 13	23 16	23 24	23 31	23 34	23 37	23 46	23 54	00 01
Clapham Junction 10	d	23 18	23 21	23 29	23 36	23 39		23 51	23 58	00 06
Earlsfield	d	23 21	23 24	23 32	23 39	23 42		23 54	00 02	00 09
Wimbledon 6 ⊖	d	23 25	23 28	23 36	23 43	23 46		23 58	00 06	00 13
Raynes Park 6	d	23 28	23 31		23 46	23 49		00 01		00 16
Motspur Park	d	23 31						00 04		
Malden Manor	d									
Tolworth	d									
Chessington North	d									
Chessington South	a									
Worcester Park	d	23 33						00 06		
Stoneleigh	d	23 36						00 09		
Ewell West	d	23 39						00 12		
Epsom 3	a	23 42						00 15		
	d	23 47						00 19		
Ashtead	d	23 51						00 23		
Leatherhead	d	23 54						00 26		
Boxhill & Westhumble	d	23 59								
Dorking 4	a	00 01								
New Malden 6	d		23 34		23 49	23 52				00 19
Norbiton	d		23 37		23 52					00 22
Kingston	a		23 40		23 55		00 16			00 25
	d		23 40		23 55					00 25
Hampton Wick	d		23 42		23 57					00 27
Teddington	d		23 45		23 59					00 30
Strawberry Hill	a				00 03					
Fulwell	d		23 49							00 34
Hampton	d		23 53							00 38
Kempton Park	d		23 56							00 41
Sunbury	d		23 58							00 43
Upper Halliford	d		23 59							00 45
Shepperton	a		00 03							00 48
Berrylands	d					23 54				
Surbiton 6	d			23 44		23 59			00 14	
Thames Ditton	d					00 03				
Hampton Court	a					00 06				
Hinchley Wood	d								00 18	
Claygate	d								00 21	
Oxshott	d								00 24	
Cobham & Stoke D'abernon	d								00 28	
Bookham	d							00 31		
Effingham Junction 6	d							00 37	00 32	
Horsley	d							00 40	00 35	
Clandon	d							00 45	00 40	
London Road (Guildford)	d							00 50	00 45	
Guildford	a							00 54	00 49	

Table 152

Mondays to Fridays
from 27 September

London - Chessington South, Dorking, Guildford, Shepperton and Hampton Court

		SW MX	SW MO	SW MX	SW MO	SW MX	SW MX	SW MX	SW MO	SW MX	SW MO 1	SW MX	SW MX	SW MX	SW MO	SW MX	SW MX	SW	SW MX	SW 1	SW	SW 1	SW
London Waterloo 15 ⊖	d	23p03	23p00	23p09	23p10	23p12	23p27	23p30	23p32	23p33	23p40	23p42	23p50	23p57	00 01	00 09	00 15	00 18	00 27	05 00	05 12	05 20	05 33
Vauxhall ⊖	d	23p07	23p04	23p13	23p14	23p16	23p31	23p34	23p36	23p37	23p44	23p46	23p54	00 01	00 04	00 13	00 19	00 22	00 31	05 04	05 16	05 24	05 37
Clapham Junction 10	d	23p12	23p09	23p18	23p19	23p21	23p36	23p39	23p41		23p49	23p51	23p58	00 06	00 09	00 18	00 24		00 36	05 09	05 21	05 29	
Earlsfield	d	23p15	23p12	23p21	23p22	23p24	23p39	23p42	23p44		23p52	23p54	00 02	00 09	00 12	00 21	00 27		00s39	05 12	05 24	05 32	
Wimbledon 6 ⊖	d	23p19	23p16	23p25	23p26	23p28	23p43	23p46	23p48		23p56	23p58	00 06	00 13	00 16	00 25	00 31		00 43	05 16	05 28	05 36	
Raynes Park 6	d			23p28		23p31	23p46	23p49	23p52			00 01		00 16	00 19		00 34		00 46		05 31		
Motspur Park	d			23p31					23p55			00 04					00 37						
Malden Manor	d																						
Tolworth	d																						
Chessington North	d																						
Chessington South	a																						
Worcester Park	d			23p33					23p57			00 06					00 39						
Stoneleigh	d			23p36					23p57			00 09					00 42						
Ewell West	d			23p39					00 03			00 12					00 45						
Epsom 3	a			23p42					00 06			00 15					00 48						
	d			23p47								00 19											
Ashtead	d			23p51								00 23											
Leatherhead	d			23p54								00 26											
Boxhill & Westhumble	d			23p59																			
Dorking 4	a			00 03																			
New Malden 6	d					23p34	23p49	23p52						00 19	00 22				00 49		05 34		
Norbiton	d					23p37	23p52							00 22							05 37		
Kingston	a					23p40	23p55			00 16				00 25				01 00			05 40		06 16
	d					23p40	23p55							00 25							05 40		06 19
Hampton Wick	d					23p42	23p57							00 27							05 42		
Teddington	d					23p45	23p59							00 30							05 45		
Strawberry Hill	a						00 03																
Fulwell	d					23p49								00 34							05 49		
Hampton	d					23p53								00 38							05 53		
Kempton Park	d					23p56								00 41									
Sunbury	d					23p58								00 43							05 58		
Upper Halliford	d					23p59								00 45							06 00		
Shepperton	a					00 05								00 50							06 05		
Berrylands	d							23p54							00 25				00s51				
Surbiton 6	d	23p27	23p32		23p35			23p59			00 05		00 14		00 31	00 33			00a55	05 24		05 44	
Thames Ditton	d							00 03															
Hampton Court	a							00 06															
Hinchley Wood	d	23p31	23p36										00 18		00 35								
Claygate	d	23p34	23p39										00 21		00 38								
Oxshott	d	23p37	23p42										00 24		00 41								
Cobham & Stoke D'abernon	d	23p41	23p46										00 28		00 45								
Bookham	d											00 31											
Effingham Junction 6	d	23p45	23p50									00 37	00 32		00 49								
Horsley	d	23p48	23p53									00 40	00 35		00 52								
Clandon	d	23p53	23p58									00 45	00 40		00 57								
London Road (Guildford)	d	23p58	00 03									00 50	00 45		01 02								
Guildford	a	00 05	00 10		00 13							00 57	00 52		01 09	01 06				05 59		06 21	

Table 152

Mondays to Fridays
from 27 September

London - Chessington South, Dorking, Guildford, Shepperton and Hampton Court

		SW	SW	SW	SW	SW		SW	SW	SW	SW	SW	SW	SW	SW	SW		SW	SW	SW	SW	SW [1]	SW	SW	SW
London Waterloo ⊖	d	05 47		05 50	06 03	06 03		06 06	06 12		06 16	06 20	06 24	06 27	06 33	06 33		06 36	06 39	06 42	06 46	06 53	06 50	06 54	06 57
Vauxhall ⊖	d	05 51		05 54	06 07	06 07		06 10	06 16		06 20	06 24	06 28	06 31	06 37	06 37		06 40	06 43	06 46	06 50		06 54	06 58	07 01
Clapham Junction	d	05 56		05 59	06 12			06 15	06 21		06 25	06 29	06 33	06 36	06 42			06 45	06 48	06 51	06 55	07u00	06 59	07 03	07 06
Earlsfield	d	05 59		06 02	06 15			06 18	06 24		06 28	06 32	06 36	06 39	06 45			06 48	06 51	06 54	06 58		07 02	07 06	07 09
Wimbledon ⊖	d	06 03	05 49	06 06	06 19			06 22	06 28	06 16	06 32	06 36	06 40	06 43	06 49			06 52	06 55	06 58	07 02		07 06	07 10	07 13
Raynes Park	d	06 06						06 25	06 31	06 19	06 35		06 43	06 46				06 55	06 58	07 01	07 05			07 13	07 16
Motspur Park	d	06 09								06 21	06 38		06 46								07 08			07 16	
Malden Manor	d									06 25	06 41										07 11				
Tolworth	d									06 27	06 44										07 14				
Chessington North	d									06 30	06 47										07 17				
Chessington South	a									06 32	06 49										07 19				
Worcester Park	d	06 11											06 48						07 02					07 18	
Stoneleigh	d	06 14											06 51						07 05					07 21	
Ewell West	d	06 17											06 54						07 08					07 24	
Epsom	a	06 20											06 57						07 11					07 27	
	d	06 21											06 58						07 12					07 28	
Ashtead	d	06 25											07 02						07 16					07 32	
Leatherhead	d	06 28											07 05						07 19					07 35	
Boxhill & Westhumble	d																								
Dorking	a												07 13											07 43	
New Malden	d							06 28	06 34					06 49				06 58		07 04					07 19
Norbiton	d								06 37					06 52						07 07					07 22
Kingston	a					06 46			06 40					06 55		07 16				07 10					07 25
	d					06 49			06 40					06 59		07 19				07 10					07 29
Hampton Wick	d								06 42					07 01						07 12					07 31
Teddington	d								06 45					07 05						07 15					07 35
Strawberry Hill	a													07 08											07 38
Fulwell	d								06 49											07 19					
Hampton	d								06 53											07 23					
Kempton Park	d																								
Sunbury	d								06 58											07 28					
Upper Halliford	d								07 00											07 30					
Shepperton	a								07 05											07 35					
Berrylands	d							06 30										07 00							
Surbiton	d		05 57	06 14	06 27			06 35				06 44			06 57			07 05				07 11	07 14		
Thames Ditton	d							06 39										07 09							
Hampton Court	a							06 42										07 12							
Hinchley Wood	d		06 01		06 31										07 01										
Claygate	d		06 04		06 34										07 04										
Oxshott	d		06 07		06 37										07 07										
Cobham & Stoke D'abernon	d		06 11		06 41										07 11										
Bookham	d	06 33																	07 24						
Effingham Junction	d	06 37	06 15		06 45										07 15				07a28						
Horsley	d		06 18		06 48										07 18										
Clandon	d		06 23		06 53										07 23										
London Road (Guildford)	d	06 46	06 28		06 58										07 28										
Guildford	a	06 53	06 35		07 05							07 20			07 35								07 47		

Table 152

Mondays to Fridays
from 27 September

London - Chessington South, Dorking, Guildford, Shepperton and Hampton Court

		SW		SW	SW	SW	SW	SW	SW [1]	SW	SW	SW		SW	SW	SW	SW	SW	SW	SW [1]	SW	SW		SW	SW
London Waterloo ⊖	d	07 03		07 03	07 06	07 09	07 12	07 16	07 23	07 20	07 24	07 27		07 33	07 33	07 36	07 39	07 42	07 46	07 53	07 50	07 54		07 57	08 03
Vauxhall ⊖	d	07 07		07 07	07 10	07 13	07 16	07 20		07 24	07 28	07 31		07 37	07 37	07 40	07 43	07 46	07 50		07 54	07 58		08 01	08 07
Clapham Junction	d	07 12			07 15	07 18	07 21	07 25	07u30	07 29	07 33	07 36		07 42		07 45	07 48	07 51	07 55	08u00	07 59	08 03		08 06	08 12
Earlsfield	d	07 15			07 18	07 21	07 24	07 28		07 32	07 36	07 39		07 45		07 48	07 51	07 54	07 58		08 02	08 06		08 09	08 15
Wimbledon ⊖	d	07 19			07 22	07 25	07 28	07 32		07 36	07 40	07 43		07 49		07 52	07 55	07 58	08 02		08 06	08 10		08 13	08 19
Raynes Park	d				07 25	07 28	07 31	07 35			07 43	07 46				07 55	07 58	08 01	08 05			08 13		08 16	
Motspur Park	d					07 31		07 38			07 46						08 01		08 08			08 16			
Malden Manor	d							07 41											08 11						
Tolworth	d							07 44											08 14						
Chessington North	d							07 47											08 17						
Chessington South	a							07 49											08 19						
Worcester Park	d					07 33					07 48						08 03					08 18			
Stoneleigh	d					07 36					07 51						08 06					08 21			
Ewell West	d					07 39					07 54						08 09					08 24			
Epsom	a					07 42					07 58						08 13					08 27			
	d										07 58						08 17					08 28			
Ashtead	d										08 02						08 21					08 32			
Leatherhead	d										08 05						08 24					08 35			
Boxhill & Westhumble	d																								
Dorking	a										08 14											08 43			
New Malden	d				07 28		07 34					07 49				07 58		08 04						08 19	
Norbiton	d						07 37					07 52						08 07						08 22	
Kingston	a			07 46			07 40					07 55			08 16			08 10						08 25	
	d			07 49			07 40					07 59			08 19			08 10						08 29	
Hampton Wick	d						07 42					08 01						08 12						08 31	
Teddington	d						07 45					08 05						08 15						08 35	
Strawberry Hill	a											08 08												08 38	
Fulwell	d						07 49											08 19							
Hampton	d						07 53											08 23							
Kempton Park	d						07 56											08 26							
Sunbury	d						07 58											08 28							
Upper Halliford	d						08 00											08 30							
Shepperton	a						08 05											08 35							
Berrylands	d				07 30											08 00									
Surbiton	d	07 27			07 35				07 41	07 44				07 57		08 05				08 11	08 14				08 27
Thames Ditton	d				07 39											08 09									
Hampton Court	a				07 42											08 12									
Hinchley Wood	d	07 31												08 01											08 31
Claygate	d	07 34												08 04											08 34
Oxshott	d	07 37												08 07											08 37
Cobham & Stoke D'abernon	d	07 41												08 11											08 41
Bookham	d																08 29								
Effingham Junction	d	07 45												08 15			08 33								08 45
Horsley	d	07 48												08 18			08 36								08 48
Clandon	d	07 53												08 23			08 41								08 53
London Road (Guildford)	d	07 58												08 28			08 46								08 58
Guildford	a	08 05												08 35			08 53				08 50				09 07

Table 152

Mondays to Fridays

from 27 September

London - Chessington South, Dorking, Guildford, Shepperton and Hampton Court

		SW	SW	SW	SW	SW	SW [1]	SW	SW	SW	SW	SW	SW	SW	SW	SW	SW [1]	SW	SW	SW	SW	SW	SW
London Waterloo [15] ⊖	d	08 03	08 06	08 09	08 12	08 16	08 23	08 20	08 24	08 27	08 33	08 33	08 36	08 39	08 42	08 46	08 53	08 50	08 54	08 57	09 03	09 03	09 06
Vauxhall ⊖	d	08 07	08 10	08 13	08 16	08 20		08 24	08 28	08 31	08 37	08 37	08 40	08 43	08 46	08 50		08 54	08 58	09 01	09 07	09 07	09 10
Clapham Junction [10]	d		08 15	08 18	08 21	08 25		08 29	08 33	08 36	08 42		08 45	08 48	08 51	08 55	09u00	08 59	09 03	09 06	09 12		09 15
Earlsfield	d		08 18	08 21	08 24	08 28		08 32	08 36	08 39	08 45		08 48	08 51	08 54	08 58		09 02	09 06	09 09	09 15		09 18
Wimbledon [6] ⊖	d		08 22	08 25	08 28	08 32		08 36	08 40	08 43	08 49		08 52	08 55	08 58	09 02		09 06	09 10	09 13	09 19		09 22
Raynes Park [6]	d		08 25	08 28	08 31	08 35			08 43	08 46			08 55	08 58	09 01	09 05			09 13	09 16			09 25
Motspur Park	d			08 31		08 38			08 46					09 01		09 08			09 16				
Malden Manor	d					08 41										09 11							
Tolworth	d					08 44										09 14							
Chessington North	d					08 47										09 17							
Chessington South	a					08 49										09 19							
Worcester Park	d			08 33					08 48					09 03					09 18				
Stoneleigh	d			08 36					08 51					09 06					09 21				
Ewell West	d			08 39					08 54					09 09					09 24				
Epsom [3]	a			08 42					08 57					09 16					09 27				
	d			08 47					08 58					09 17					09 28				
Ashtead	d			08 51					09 02					09 21					09 32				
Leatherhead	d			08 54					09 05					09 24					09 35				
Boxhill & Westhumble	d																						
Dorking [4]	a								09 13										09 43				
New Malden [6]	d		08 28		08 34					08 49			08 58		09 04					09 19			09 28
Norbiton	d				08 37					08 52					09 07					09 22			
Kingston	a	08 46			08 39					08 55		09 16			09 10					09 25		09 46	
	d	08 49			08 40					08 59		09 19			09 10					09 29		09 49	
Hampton Wick	d				08 42					09 01					09 12					09 31			
Teddington	d				08 45					09 05					09 15					09 35			
Strawberry Hill	a									09 08										09 38			
Fulwell	d				08 49										09 19								
Hampton	d				08 53										09 23								
Kempton Park	d				08 56										09 26								
Sunbury	d				08 58										09 28								
Upper Halliford	d				09 00										09 30								
Shepperton	a				09 06										09 35								
Berrylands	d		08 30										09 00										09 30
Surbiton [6]	d		08 35				08 41	08 44			08 57		09 05				09 11	09 14			09 27		09 35
Thames Ditton	d		08 39										09 09										09 39
Hampton Court	a		08 42										09 12										09 42
Hinchley Wood	d										09 01										09 31		
Claygate	d										09 04										09 34		
Oxshott	d										09 07										09 37		
Cobham & Stoke D'abernon	d										09 11										09 41		
Bookham	d			08 59										09 29									
Effingham Junction [6]	d			09 03							09 15			09 33							09 45		
Horsley	d			09 06							09 18			09 36							09 48		
Clandon	d			09 11							09 23			09 41							09 53		
London Road (Guildford)	d			09 16							09 28			09 46							09 58		
Guildford	a			09 23							09 35			09 53							10 05		

Table 152

Mondays to Fridays

from 27 September

London - Chessington South, Dorking, Guildford, Shepperton and Hampton Court

		SW	SW	SW	SW [1]	SW	SW	SW	SW	SW	SW	SW	SW	SW	SW [1]	SW	SW	SW	SW	SW	SW	SW
London Waterloo [15] ⊖	d	09 09	09 12	09 16	09 23	09 20	09 24	09 27	09 33	09 33	09 36	09 39	09 42	09 46	09 53	09 50	09 54	09 57	10 03	10 03	10 06	10 09
Vauxhall ⊖	d	09 13	09 16	09 20		09 24	09 28	09 31	09 37	09 37	09 40	09 43	09 46	09 50		09 54	09 58	10 01	10 07	10 07	10 10	10 13
Clapham Junction [10]	d	09 18	09 21	09 25		09 29	09 33	09 36	09 42		09 45	09 48	09 51	09 55	10u00	09 59	10 03	10 06	10 12		10 15	10 18
Earlsfield	d	09 21	09 24	09 28		09 32	09 36	09 39	09 45		09 48	09 51	09 54	09 58		10 02	10 06	10 09	10 15		10 18	10 21
Wimbledon [6] ⊖	d	09 25	09 28	09 32		09 36	09 40	09 43	09 49		09 52	09 55	09 58	10 02		10 06	10 10	10 13	10 19		10 22	10 25
Raynes Park [6]	d	09 28	09 31	09 35			09 43	09 46			09 55	09 58	10 01	10 05			10 13	10 16			10 25	10 28
Motspur Park	d	09 31		09 38			09 46					10 01		10 08			10 16					10 31
Malden Manor	d			09 41										10 11								
Tolworth	d			09 44										10 14								
Chessington North	d			09 47										10 17								
Chessington South	a			09 49										10 19								
Worcester Park	d	09 33					09 48					10 03					10 18					10 33
Stoneleigh	d	09 36					09 51					10 06					10 21					10 36
Ewell West	d	09 39					09 54					10 09					10 24					10 39
Epsom [3]	a	09 42					09 57					10 16					10 27					10 46
	d	09 47					09 58					10 17					10 28					10 47
Ashtead	d	09 51					10 02					10 21					10 32					10 51
Leatherhead	d	09 54					10 05					10 24					10 35					10 54
Boxhill & Westhumble	d																					
Dorking [4]	a						10 13										10 43					
New Malden [6]	d		09 34					09 49			09 58		10 04					10 19			10 28	
Norbiton	d		09 37					09 52					10 07					10 22				
Kingston	a		09 40					09 55		10 16			10 10					10 25		10 46		
	d		09 40					09 59		10 19			10 10					10 29		10 49		
Hampton Wick	d		09 42					10 01					10 12					10 31				
Teddington	d		09 45					10 05					10 15					10 35				
Strawberry Hill	a							10 08										10 38				
Fulwell	d		09 49										10 19									
Hampton	d		09 53										10 23									
Kempton Park	d		09 56										10 26									
Sunbury	d		09 58										10 28									
Upper Halliford	d		10 00										10 30									
Shepperton	a		10 05										10 35									
Berrylands	d										10 00										10 30	
Surbiton [6]	d				09 41	09 44			09 57		10 05				10 11	10 14			10 27		10 35	
Thames Ditton	d										10 09										10 39	
Hampton Court	a										10 12										10 42	
Hinchley Wood	d								10 01										10 31			
Claygate	d								10 04										10 34			
Oxshott	d								10 07										10 37			
Cobham & Stoke D'abernon	d								10 11										10 41			
Bookham	d	09 59										10 29										10 59
Effingham Junction [6]	d	10 03							10 15			10 33							10 45			11 03
Horsley	d	10 06							10 18			10 36							10 48			11 06
Clandon	d	10 11							10 23			10 41							10 53			11 11
London Road (Guildford)	d	10 16							10 28			10 46							10 58			11 16
Guildford	a	10 23							10 35			10 53							11 05			11 23

Table 152

Mondays to Fridays
from 27 September

London - Chessington South, Dorking, Guildford, Shepperton and Hampton Court

		SW	SW	SW 1	SW	SW	SW	SW	SW	SW	SW	SW	SW	SW 1	SW	SW	SW	SW	SW	SW	SW	SW	SW
London Waterloo 15 ⊖	d	10 12	10 16	10 23	10 20	10 24	10 27	10 33	10 33	10 36	10 39	10 42	10 46	10 53	10 50	10 54	10 57	11 03	11 03	11 06	11 09	11 12	11 16
Vauxhall ⊖	d	10 16	10 20		10 24	10 28	10 31	10 37	10 37	10 40	10 43	10 46	10 50		10 54	10 58	11 01	11 07	11 07	11 10	11 13	11 16	11 20
Clapham Junction 10	d	10 21	10 25		10 29	10 33	10 36	10 42		10 45	10 48	10 51	10 55	11u00	10 59	11 03	11 06	11 12		11 15	11 18	11 21	11 25
Earlsfield	d	10 24	10 28		10 32	10 36	10 39	10 45		10 48	10 51	10 54	10 58		11 02	11 06	11 09	11 15		11 18	11 21	11 24	11 28
Wimbledon 6 ⊖	d	10 28	10 32		10 36	10 40	10 43	10 49		10 52	10 55	10 58	11 02		11 06	11 10	11 13	11 19		11 22	11 25	11 28	11 32
Raynes Park 6	d	10 31	10 35			10 43	10 46			10 55	10 58	11 01	11 05			11 13	11 16			11 25	11 28	11 31	11 35
Motspur Park	d		10 38			10 46					11 01		11 08			11 16					11 31		11 38
Malden Manor	d		10 41										11 11										11 41
Tolworth	d		10 44										11 14										11 44
Chessington North	d		10 47										11 17										11 47
Chessington South	a		10 49										11 19										11 49
Worcester Park	d					10 48					11 03					11 18					11 33		
Stoneleigh	d					10 51					11 06					11 21					11 36		
Ewell West	d					10 54					11 09					11 24					11 39		
Epsom 3	a					10 57					11 16					11 27					11 46		
	d					10 58					11 17					11 28					11 47		
Ashtead	d					11 02					11 21					11 32					11 51		
Leatherhead	d					11 05					11 24					11 35					11 54		
Boxhill & Westhumble	d																						
Dorking 4	a					11 13										11 43							
New Malden 6	d	10 34					10 49			10 58		11 04					11 19			11 28		11 34	
Norbiton	d	10 37					10 52					11 07					11 22					11 37	
Kingston	a	10 40					10 55		11 16			11 10					11 25		11 46			11 40	
	d	10 40					10 59		11 19			11 10					11 29		11 49			11 40	
Hampton Wick	d	10 42					11 01					11 12					11 31					11 42	
Teddington	d	10 45					11 05					11 15					11 35					11 45	
Strawberry Hill	a						11 08										11 38						
Fulwell	d	10 49										11 19										11 49	
Hampton	d	10 53										11 23										11 53	
Kempton Park	d	10 56										11 26										11 56	
Sunbury	d	10 58										11 28										11 58	
Upper Halliford	d	11 00										11 30										12 00	
Shepperton	a	11 05										11 35										12 05	
Berrylands	d									11 00										11 30			
Surbiton 6	d			10 41	10 44			10 57		11 05				11 11	11 14			11 27		11 35			
Thames Ditton	d									11 09										11 39			
Hampton Court	a									11 12										11 42			
Hinchley Wood	d							11 01										11 31					
Claygate	d							11 04										11 34					
Oxshott	d							11 07										11 37					
Cobham & Stoke D'abernon	d							11 11										11 41					
Bookham	d										11 29										11 59		
Effingham Junction 6	d							11 15			11 33							11 45			12 03		
Horsley	d							11 18			11 36							11 48			12 06		
Clandon	d							11 23			11 41							11 53			12 11		
London Road (Guildford)	d							11 28			11 46							11 58			12 16		
Guildford	a							11 35			11 53							12 05			12 23		

Table 152

Mondays to Fridays
from 27 September

London - Chessington South, Dorking, Guildford, Shepperton and Hampton Court

		SW 1	SW	SW	SW	SW	SW	SW	SW	SW	SW	SW 1	SW	SW	SW	SW	SW	SW	SW	SW	SW	SW 1	SW
London Waterloo 15 ⊖	d	11 23	11 20	11 24	11 27	11 33	11 33	11 36	11 39	11 42	11 46	11 53	11 50	11 54	11 57	12 03	12 03	12 06	12 09	12 12	12 16	12 23	12 20
Vauxhall ⊖	d		11 24	11 28	11 31	11 37	11 37	11 40	11 43	11 46	11 50		11 54	11 58	12 01	12 07	12 07	12 10	12 13	12 16	12 20		12 24
Clapham Junction 10	d		11 29	11 33	11 36	11 42		11 45	11 48	11 51	11 55	12u00	11 59	12 03	12 06	12 12		12 15	12 18	12 21	12 25		12 29
Earlsfield	d		11 32	11 36	11 39	11 45		11 48	11 51	11 54	11 58		12 02	12 06	12 09	12 15		12 18	12 21	12 24	12 28		12 32
Wimbledon 6 ⊖	d		11 36	11 40	11 43	11 49		11 52	11 55	11 58	12 02		12 06	12 10	12 13	12 19		12 22	12 25	12 28	12 32		12 36
Raynes Park 6	d			11 43	11 46			11 55	11 58	12 01	12 05			12 13	12 16			12 25	12 28	12 31	12 35		
Motspur Park	d			11 46					12 01		12 08			12 16					12 31		12 38		
Malden Manor	d										12 11										12 41		
Tolworth	d										12 14										12 44		
Chessington North	d										12 17										12 47		
Chessington South	a										12 19										12 49		
Worcester Park	d			11 48					12 03					12 18					12 33				
Stoneleigh	d			11 51					12 06					12 21					12 36				
Ewell West	d			11 54					12 09					12 24					12 39				
Epsom 3	a			11 57					12 16					12 27					12 46				
	d			11 58					12 17					12 28					12 47				
Ashtead	d			12 02					12 21					12 32					12 51				
Leatherhead	d			12 05					12 24					12 35					12 54				
Boxhill & Westhumble	d																						
Dorking 4	a			12 13										12 43									
New Malden 6	d				11 49			11 58		12 04					12 19			12 28		12 34			
Norbiton	d				11 52					12 07					12 22					12 37			
Kingston	a				11 55		12 16			12 10					12 25		12 46			12 40			
	d				11 59		12 19			12 10					12 29		12 49			12 40			
Hampton Wick	d				12 01					12 12					12 31					12 42			
Teddington	d				12 05					12 15					12 35					12 45			
Strawberry Hill	a				12 08										12 38								
Fulwell	d									12 19										12 49			
Hampton	d									12 23										12 53			
Kempton Park	d									12 26										12 56			
Sunbury	d									12 28										12 58			
Upper Halliford	d									12 30										13 00			
Shepperton	a									12 35										13 05			
Berrylands	d							12 00										12 30					
Surbiton 6	d	11 41	11 44			11 57		12 05				12 11	12 14			12 27		12 35				12 41	12 44
Thames Ditton	d							12 09										12 39					
Hampton Court	a							12 12										12 42					
Hinchley Wood	d					12 01										12 31							
Claygate	d					12 04										12 34							
Oxshott	d					12 07										12 37							
Cobham & Stoke D'abernon	d					12 11										12 41							
Bookham	d								12 29										12 59				
Effingham Junction 6	d					12 15			12 33							12 45			13 03				
Horsley	d					12 18			12 36							12 48			13 06				
Clandon	d					12 23			12 41							12 53			13 11				
London Road (Guildford)	d					12 28			12 46							12 58			13 16				
Guildford	a					12 35			12 53							13 05			13 23				

Table 152

Mondays to Fridays
from 27 September

London - Chessington South, Dorking, Guildford, Shepperton and Hampton Court

		SW	SW	SW	SW	SW	SW	SW	SW	SW 1	SW	SW	SW	SW	SW	SW	SW	SW	SW	SW 1	SW	SW
London Waterloo 15 ⊖	d	12 24	12 27	12 33	12 33	12 36	12 39	12 42	12 46	12 53	12 50	12 54	12 57	13 03	13 03	13 06	13 09	13 12	13 16	13 23	13 20	13 24
Vauxhall ⊖	d	12 28	12 31	12 37	12 37	12 40	12 43	12 46	12 50		12 54	12 58	13 01	13 07	13 07	13 10	13 13	13 16	13 20		13 24	13 28
Clapham Junction 10	d	12 33	12 36	12 42		12 45	12 48	12 51	12 55	13u00	12 59	13 03	13 06	13 12		13 15	13 18	13 21	13 25		13 29	13 33
Earlsfield	d	12 36	12 39	12 45		12 48	12 51	12 54	12 58		13 02	13 06	13 09	13 15		13 18	13 21	13 24	13 28		13 32	13 36
Wimbledon 6 ⊖	d	12 40	12 43	12 49		12 52	12 55	12 58	13 02		13 06	13 10	13 13	13 19		13 22	13 25	13 28	13 32		13 36	13 40
Raynes Park 6	d	12 43	12 46			12 55	12 58	13 01	13 05			13 13	13 16			13 25	13 28	13 31	13 35			13 43
Motspur Park	d	12 46					13 01		13 08			13 16					13 31		13 38			13 46
Malden Manor	d								13 11										13 41			
Tolworth	d								13 14										13 44			
Chessington North	d								13 17										13 47			
Chessington South	a								13 19										13 49			
Worcester Park	d	12 48					13 03					13 18					13 33					13 48
Stoneleigh	d	12 51					13 06					13 21					13 36					13 51
Ewell West	d	12 54					13 09					13 24					13 39					13 54
Epsom 3	a	12 57					13 16					13 27					13 46					13 57
	d	12 58					13 17					13 28					13 47					13 58
Ashtead	d	13 02					13 21					13 32					13 51					14 02
Leatherhead	d	13 05					13 24					13 35					13 54					14 05
Boxhill & Westhumble	d																					
Dorking 4	a	13 13										13 43										14 13
New Malden 6	d		12 49			12 58		13 04					13 19			13 28		13 34				
Norbiton	d		12 52					13 07					13 22					13 37				
Kingston	a		12 55		13 16			13 10					13 25		13 46			13 40				
	d		12 59		13 19			13 10					13 29		13 49			13 40				
Hampton Wick	d		13 01					13 12					13 31					13 42				
Teddington	d		13 05					13 15					13 35					13 45				
Strawberry Hill	a		13 08										13 38									
Fulwell	d							13 19										13 49				
Hampton	d							13 23										13 53				
Kempton Park	d							13 26										13 56				
Sunbury	d							13 28										13 58				
Upper Halliford	d							13 30										14 00				
Shepperton	a							13 35										14 05				
Berrylands	d					13 00										13 30						
Surbiton 6	d			12 57		13 05				13 11	13 14			13 27		13 35				13 41	13 44	
Thames Ditton	d					13 09										13 39						
Hampton Court	a					13 12										13 42						
Hinchley Wood	d			13 01										13 31								
Claygate	d			13 04										13 34								
Oxshott	d			13 07										13 37								
Cobham & Stoke D'abernon	d			13 11										13 41								
Bookham	d						13 29										13 59					
Effingham Junction 6	d			13 15			13 33							13 45			14 03					
Horsley	d			13 18			13 36							13 48			14 06					
Clandon	d			13 23			13 41							13 53			14 11					
London Road (Guildford)	d			13 28			13 46							13 58			14 16					
Guildford	a			13 35			13 53							14 05			14 23					

Table 152

Mondays to Fridays
from 27 September

London - Chessington South, Dorking, Guildford, Shepperton and Hampton Court

		SW	SW	SW	SW	SW	SW	SW	SW 1	SW	SW	SW	SW	SW	SW	SW	SW	SW	SW 1	SW	SW	SW	SW
London Waterloo 15 ⊖	d	13 27	13 33	13 33	13 36	13 39	13 42	13 46	13 53	13 50	13 54	13 57	14 03	14 03	14 06	14 09	14 12	14 16	14 23	14 20	14 24	14 27	14 33
Vauxhall ⊖	d	13 31	13 37	13 37	13 40	13 43	13 46	13 50		13 54	13 58	14 01	14 07	14 07	14 10	14 13	14 16	14 20		14 24	14 28	14 31	14 37
Clapham Junction 10	d	13 36	13 42		13 45	13 48	13 51	13 55	14u00	13 59	14 03	14 06	14 12		14 15	14 18	14 21	14 25		14 29	14 33	14 36	14 42
Earlsfield	d	13 39	13 45		13 48	13 51	13 54	13 58		14 02	14 06	14 09	14 15		14 18	14 21	14 24	14 28		14 32	14 36	14 39	14 45
Wimbledon 6 ⊖	d	13 43	13 49		13 52	13 55	13 58	14 02		14 06	14 10	14 13	14 19		14 22	14 25	14 28	14 32		14 36	14 40	14 43	14 49
Raynes Park 6	d	13 46			13 55	13 58	14 01	14 05			14 13	14 14			14 25	14 28	14 31	14 35			14 43	14 46	
Motspur Park	d					14 01		14 08			14 16					14 31		14 38			14 46		
Malden Manor	d							14 11										14 41					
Tolworth	d							14 14										14 44					
Chessington North	d							14 17										14 47					
Chessington South	a							14 19										14 49					
Worcester Park	d					14 03					14 18					14 33					14 48		
Stoneleigh	d					14 06					14 21					14 36					14 51		
Ewell West	d					14 09					14 24					14 39					14 54		
Epsom 3	a					14 16					14 27					14 46					14 57		
	d					14 17					14 28					14 47					14 58		
Ashtead	d					14 21					14 32					14 51					15 02		
Leatherhead	d					14 24					14 35					14 54					15 05		
Boxhill & Westhumble	d																						
Dorking 4	a										14 43										15 13		
New Malden 6	d	13 49			13 58		14 04					14 18			14 28		14 34					14 49	
Norbiton	d	13 52					14 07					14 20					14 37					14 52	
Kingston	a	13 55		14 16			14 10					14 24		14 46			14 40					14 55	
	d	13 59		14 19			14 10					14 29		14 49			14 40					14 59	
Hampton Wick	d	14 01					14 12					14 31					14 42					15 01	
Teddington	d	14 05					14 15					14 35					14 45					15 05	
Strawberry Hill	a	14 08										14 38										15 08	
Fulwell	d						14 19										14 49						
Hampton	d						14 23										14 53						
Kempton Park	d						14 26										14 56						
Sunbury	d						14 28										14 58						
Upper Halliford	d						14 30										15 00						
Shepperton	a						14 35										15 05						
Berrylands	d				14 00										14 30								
Surbiton 6	d		13 57		14 05				14 11	14 14			14 27		14 35				14 41	14 44			14 57
Thames Ditton	d				14 09										14 39								
Hampton Court	a				14 12										14 42								
Hinchley Wood	d		14 01										14 31										15 01
Claygate	d		14 04										14 34										15 04
Oxshott	d		14 07										14 37										15 07
Cobham & Stoke D'abernon	d		14 11										14 41										15 11
Bookham	d					14 29										14 59							
Effingham Junction 6	d		14 15			14 33							14 45			15 03							15 15
Horsley	d		14 18			14 36							14 48			15 06							15 18
Clandon	d		14 23			14 41							14 53			15 11							15 23
London Road (Guildford)	d		14 28			14 46							14 58			15 16							15 28
Guildford	a		14 35			14 53							15 05			15 23							15 35

Table 152

Mondays to Fridays
from 27 September

London - Chessington South, Dorking, Guildford, Shepperton and Hampton Court

		SW	SW	SW	SW	SW	SW ■	SW	SW	SW	SW	SW	SW	SW	SW	SW	SW ■	SW	SW	SW	SW	SW
London Waterloo ⊖	d	14 33	14 36	14 39	14 42	14 46	14 53	14 50	14 54	14 57	15 03	15 03	15 06	15 09	15 12	15 16	15 23	15 20	15 24	15 27	15 33	15 33
Vauxhall ⊖	d	14 37	14 40	14 43	14 46	14 50		14 54	14 58	15 01	15 07	15 07	15 10	15 13	15 16	15 20		15 24	15 28	15 31	15 37	15 37
Clapham Junction	d		14 45	14 48	14 51	14 55	15u00	14 59	15 03	15 06	15 12		15 15	15 18	15 21	15 25		15 29	15 33	15 36	15 42	
Earlsfield	d		14 48	14 51	14 54	14 58		15 02	15 06	15 09	15 15		15 18	15 21	15 24	15 28		15 32	15 36	15 39	15 45	
Wimbledon ⊖	d		14 52	14 55	14 58	15 02		15 06	15 10	15 13	15 19		15 22	15 25	15 28	15 32		15 36	15 40	15 43	15 49	
Raynes Park	d		14 55	14 58	15 01	15 05			15 13	15 16			15 25	15 28	15 31	15 35			15 43	15 46		
Motspur Park	d			15 01		15 08			15 16					15 31		15 38			15 46			
Malden Manor	d					15 11										15 41						
Tolworth	d					15 14										15 44						
Chessington North	d					15 17										15 47						
Chessington South	a					15 19										15 49						
Worcester Park	d			15 03					15 18					15 33					15 48			
Stoneleigh	d			15 06					15 21					15 36					15 51			
Ewell West	d			15 09					15 24					15 39					15 54			
Epsom	a			15 16					15 27					15 46					15 57			
	d			15 17					15 28					15 47					15 58			
Ashtead	d			15 21					15 32					15 51					16 02			
Leatherhead	d			15 24					15 35					15 54					16 05			
Boxhill & Westhumble	d																					
Dorking	a								15 43										16 13			
New Malden	d		14 58		15 04					15 19			15 28		15 34					15 49		
Norbiton	d				15 07					15 22					15 37					15 52		
Kingston	a	15 16			15 10					15 25		15 46			15 40					15 55		16 16
	d	15 19			15 10					15 29		15 49			15 40					15 59		16 19
Hampton Wick	d				15 12					15 31					15 42					16 01		
Teddington	d				15 15					15 35					15 45					16 05		
Strawberry Hill	a									15 38										16 08		
Fulwell	d				15 19										15 49							
Hampton	d				15 23										15 53							
Kempton Park	d				15 26										15 56							
Sunbury	d				15 28										15 58							
Upper Halliford	d				15 30										16 00							
Shepperton	a				15 35										16 05							
Berrylands	d		15 00										15 30									
Surbiton	d		15 05				15 11	15 14			15 27		15 35				15 41	15 44			15 57	
Thames Ditton	d		15 09										15 39									
Hampton Court	a		15 12										15 42									
Hinchley Wood	d										15 31										16 01	
Claygate	d										15 34										16 04	
Oxshott	d										15 37										16 07	
Cobham & Stoke D'abernon	d										15 41										16 11	
Bookham	d			15 29										15 59								
Effingham Junction	d			15 33							15 45			16 03							16 15	
Horsley	d			15 36							15 48			16 06							16 18	
Clandon	d			15 41							15 53			16 11							16 23	
London Road (Guildford)	d			15 46							15 58			16 16							16 28	
Guildford	a			15 53							16 05			16 23							16 35	

Table 152

Mondays to Fridays
from 27 September

London - Chessington South, Dorking, Guildford, Shepperton and Hampton Court

		SW	SW	SW	SW	SW ■	SW	SW	SW	SW	SW	SW	SW	SW	SW	SW	SW ■	SW	SW	SW	SW	SW	SW
London Waterloo ⊖	d	15 36	15 39	15 42	15 46	15 53	15 50	15 54	15 57	16 01	16 03	16 06	16 09	16 12	16 16	16 24	16 25	16 20	16 27	16 31	16 33	16 36	16 39
Vauxhall ⊖	d	15 40	15 43	15 46	15 50		15 54	15 58	16 01	16 05	16 07	16 10	16 13	16 16	16 20	16 28		16 24	16 31	16 35	16 37	16 40	16 43
Clapham Junction	d	15 45	15 48	15 51	15 55	16u00	15 59	16 03	16 06		16 12	16 15	16 18	16 21	16 25	16 33		16 29	16 36		16 42	16 45	16 48
Earlsfield	d	15 48	15 51	15 54	15 58		16 02	16 06	16 09		16 15	16 18	16 21	16 24	16 28	16 36		16 32	16 39		16 45	16 48	16 51
Wimbledon ⊖	d	15 52	15 55	15 58	16 02		16 06	16 10	16 13		16 19	16 22	16 25	16 28	16 32	16 40		16 36	16 43		16 49	16 52	16 55
Raynes Park	d	15 55	15 58	16 01	16 05			16 13	16 16			16 25	16 28	16 31	16 35	16 43			16 46			16 55	16 58
Motspur Park	d		16 01		16 08			16 16					16 31		16 38	16 46							17 01
Malden Manor	d				16 11										16 41								
Tolworth	d				16 14										16 44								
Chessington North	d				16 17										16 47								
Chessington South	a				16 19										16 51								
Worcester Park	d		16 03					16 18					16 33			16 48							17 03
Stoneleigh	d		16 06					16 21					16 36			16 51							17 06
Ewell West	d		16 09					16 24					16 39			16 54							17 09
Epsom	a		16 15					16 27					16 46			16 57							17 12
	d		16 17					16 28					16 47			16 58							17 17
Ashtead	d		16 21					16 32					16 51			17 02							17 21
Leatherhead	d		16 24					16 35					16 54			17 05							17 24
Boxhill & Westhumble	d															17 10							
Dorking	a							16 43								17 16							
New Malden	d	15 58		16 04					16 19			16 28		16 34					16 49			16 58	
Norbiton	d			16 07					16 22					16 37					16 52				
Kingston	a			16 10					16 25	16 48				16 40					16 55	17 18			
	d			16 10					16 29	16 49				16 40					16 59	17 19			
Hampton Wick	d			16 12					16 31					16 42					17 01				
Teddington	d			16 15					16 35					16 45					17 05				
Strawberry Hill	a								16 38										17 08				
Fulwell	d			16 19										16 49									
Hampton	d			16 23										16 53									
Kempton Park	d			16 26										16 56									
Sunbury	d			16 28										16 58									
Upper Halliford	d			16 30										17 00									
Shepperton	a			16 35										17 07									
Berrylands	d	16 00										16 30										17 00	
Surbiton	d	16 05				16 11	16 14				16 27	16 35					16 41	16 44			16 57	17 05	
Thames Ditton	d	16 09										16 39										17 09	
Hampton Court	a	16 12										16 44										17 14	
Hinchley Wood	d										16 31										17 01		
Claygate	d										16 34										17 04		
Oxshott	d										16 37										17 07		
Cobham & Stoke D'abernon	d										16 41										17 11		
Bookham	d		16 29										16 59										17 29
Effingham Junction	d		16 33								16 45		17 03								17 15		17 33
Horsley	d		16 36								16 48		17 06								17 18		17 36
Clandon	d		16 41								16 53		17 11								17 23		17 41
London Road (Guildford)	d		16 46								16 58		17 16								17 28		17 46
Guildford	a		16 53								17 07		17 25								17 37		17 55

Table 152

Mondays to Fridays
from 27 September

London - Chessington South, Dorking, Guildford, Shepperton and Hampton Court

		SW	SW	SW	SW	SW	SW	SW ■1	SW	SW	SW	SW	SW	SW	SW	SW	SW	SW	SW	SW ■1	SW	SW	SW
London Waterloo ■15 ⊖	d	16 42	16 46	16 50	16 54	16 57	17 01	17 02	17 02	17 06	17 09	17 12	17 13	17 16	17 20	17 24	17 27	17 30	17 31	17 32	17 32	17 36	17 39
Vauxhall ⊖	d	16 46	16 50	16 54	16 58	17 01	17 05		17 07	17 10	17 13	17 16	17 17	17 20	17 24	17 28	17 31	17 34	17 35		17 37	17 40	17 43
Clapham Junction ■10	d	16 51	16 55	16 59	17 03	17 06			17 12	17 15	17 18	17 22		17 25	17 29	17 33	17 36	17 39			17 42	17 45	17 48
Earlsfield	d	16 54	16 58	17 02	17 06	17 09			17 15	17 18	17 21	17 25		17 28	17 32	17 36	17 39	17 42			17 45	17 48	17 51
Wimbledon ■ ⊖ ⛴	d	16 58	17 02	17 06	17 10	17 13			17 19	17 22	17 25	17 29		17 32	17 36	17 40	17 43	17 46			17 49	17 52	17 55
Raynes Park ■	d	17 01	17 05		17 13	17 16				17 25	17 28	17 32		17 35		17 43	17 46	17 49				17 55	17 58
Motspur Park	d		17 08		17 16						17 31			17 38				17 52					18 01
Malden Manor	d		17 11											17 41									
Tolworth	d		17 14											17 44									
Chessington North	d		17 17											17 47									
Chessington South	a		17 21											17 51									
Worcester Park	d				17 18						17 33					17 47		17 54					18 03
Stoneleigh	d				17 21						17 36							17 57					18 06
Ewell West	d				17 24						17 39							18 00					18 09
Epsom ■	a				17 27						17 42					17 54		18 07					18 20
	d				17 28						17 47					17 54							18 21
Ashtead	d				17 32						17 51					17 58							18 25
Leatherhead	d				17 35						17 54					18 01							18 28
Boxhill & Westhumble	d				17 40											18 06							
Dorking ■	a				17 46											18 13							
New Malden ■	d	17 04				17 19				17 28		17 35					17 49					17 58	
Norbiton	d	17 07				17 22						17 38					17 52						
Kingston	a	17 10				17 25	17 48					17 41	17 56				17 55		18 18				
	d	17 10				17 29	17 49					17 41	17 58				17 59		18 19				
Hampton Wick	d	17 12				17 31						17 43					18 01						
Teddington	d	17 15				17 35						17 46					18 05						
Strawberry Hill	a					17 38											18 08						
Fulwell	d	17 19										17 50											
Hampton	d	17 23										17 54											
Kempton Park	d	17 26										17 57											
Sunbury	d	17 28										17 59											
Upper Halliford	d	17 30										18 01											
Shepperton	a	17 37										18 08											
Berrylands	d									17 30												18 00	
Surbiton ■	d			17 14				17 18	17 27	17 35					17 44					17 48	17 57	18 05	
Thames Ditton	d									17 39												18 09	
Hampton Court	a									17 44												18 14	
Hinchley Wood	d								17 31												18 05		
Claygate	d								17 34												18 08		
Oxshott	d								17 37												18 11		
Cobham & Stoke D'abernon	d								17 41												18 15		
Bookham	d										17 59												18 34
Effingham Junction ■	d								17 45		18a05										18 20		18a44
Horsley	d								17 48												18 22		
Clandon	d								17 53												18 27		
London Road (Guildford)	d								17 58												18 32		
Guildford	a							17 56	18 07											18 29	18 41		

Table 152

Mondays to Fridays
from 27 September

London - Chessington South, Dorking, Guildford, Shepperton and Hampton Court

		SW	SW	SW	SW	SW	SW	SW	SW	SW ■1	SW	SW	SW	SW	SW	SW	SW	SW	SW	SW	SW	SW
London Waterloo ■15 ⊖	d	17 43	17 42	17 46	17 50	17 54	17 57	18 00	18 01	18 02	18 02	18 06	18 09	18 13	18 12	18 16	18 20	18 24	18 27	18 30	18 31	18 32
Vauxhall ⊖	d	17 47	17 46	17 50	17 54	17 58	18 01	18 04	18 05		18 07	18 10	18 13	18 17	18 16	18 20	18 24	18 28	18 31	18 34	18 35	18 37
Clapham Junction ■10	d	17 53	17 52	17 55	17 59	18 03	18 06	18 09			18 12	18 15	18 18	18 23	18 22	18 25	18 29	18 33	18 36	18 39		18 42
Earlsfield	d		17 55	17 58	18 02	18 06	18 09	18 12			18 15	18 18	18 21		18 25	18 28	18 32	18 36	18 39	18 42		18 45
Wimbledon ■ ⊖ ⛴	d		17 59	18 02	18 06	18 10	18 13	18 16			18 19	18 22	18 25		18 29	18 32	18 36	18 40	18 43	18 46		18 49
Raynes Park ■	d		18 02	18 05		18 13	18 16	18 19				18 25	18 28		18 32	18 35		18 43	18 46	18 49		
Motspur Park	d			18 08				18 22					18 31			18 38				18 52		
Malden Manor	d			18 11												18 41						
Tolworth	d			18 14												18 44						
Chessington North	d			18 17												18 47						
Chessington South	a			18 21												18 51						
Worcester Park	d					18 17		18 24					18 33					18 47		18 54		
Stoneleigh	d							18 27					18 36							18 57		
Ewell West	d							18 30					18 39							19 00		
Epsom ■	a					18 24		18 35					18 46					18 54		19 07		
	d					18 24							18 47					18 54				
Ashtead	d					18 28							18 51					18 58				
Leatherhead	d					18 31							18 54					19 01				
Boxhill & Westhumble	d					18 36												19 06				
Dorking ■	a					18 43												19 13				
New Malden ■	d		18 05				18 19					18 28			18 35				18 49			
Norbiton	d		18 08				18 22								18 38				18 52			
Kingston	a		18 11				18 25		18 48						18 41				18 55		19 18	
	d		18 11				18 29		18 49						18 41				18 59		19 19	
Hampton Wick	d		18 13				18 31								18 43				19 01			
Teddington	d		18 16				18 35								18 46				19 05			
Strawberry Hill	a	18 11					18 38							18 41					19 08			
Fulwell	d	18 13	18 20											18 43	18 50							
Hampton	d	18 17	18 24											18 47	18 54							
Kempton Park	d		18 27												18 57							
Sunbury	d	18 21	18 29											18 51	18 59							
Upper Halliford	d	18 23	18 31											18 53	19 01							
Shepperton	a	18 30	18 40											19 00	19 10							
Berrylands	d											18 30										
Surbiton ■	d				18 14					18 18	18 27	18 35					18 44					18 57
Thames Ditton	d											18 39										
Hampton Court	a											18 44										
Hinchley Wood	d										18 35											19 01
Claygate	d										18 38											19 04
Oxshott	d										18 41											19 07
Cobham & Stoke D'abernon	d										18 45											19 11
Bookham	d												18 59									
Effingham Junction ■	d										18 50		19 03									19 15
Horsley	d										18 52		19 06									19 18
Clandon	d										18 57		19 11									19 23
London Road (Guildford)	d										19 02		19 16									19 28
Guildford	a										19 11		19 25									19 37

Table 152

London - Chessington South, Dorking, Guildford, Shepperton and Hampton Court

		SW	SW	SW	SW	SW	SW	SW	SW	SW	SW	SW	SW 1	SW	SW	SW	SW	SW	SW	SW	SW	SW	SW
London Waterloo 15 ⊖	d	18 36	18 39	18 43	18 42	18 46	18 48	18 50	18 54	18 57	19 00	19 01	19 02	19 02	19 06	19 09	19 12	19 16	19 20	19 23	19 24	19 27	19 33
Vauxhall ⊖	d	18 40	18 43	18 47	18 46	18 50		18 54	18 58	19 01	19 04	19 05		19 07	19 10	19 13	19 16	19 20	19 24		19 28	19 31	19 37
Clapham Junction 10	d	18 45	18 48	18 53	18 52	18 55		18 59	19 03	19 06	19 09			19 12	19 15	19 18	19 22	19 25	19 29		19 33	19 36	19 42
Earlsfield	d	18 48	18 51		18 55	18 58		19 02	19 06	19 09	19 12			19 15	19 18	19 21	19 25	19 28	19 32		19 36	19 39	19 45
Wimbledon 8 ⊖ 🚋	d	18 52	18 55		18 59	19 02		19 06	19 10	19 13	19 16			19 19	19 22	19 25	19 29	19 32	19 36		19 40	19 43	19 49
Raynes Park 6	d	18 55	18 58		19 02	19 05			19 13	19 16	19 19				19 25	19 28	19 32	19 35			19 43	19 46	
Motspur Park	d		19 01			19 08					19 22					19 31		19 38			19 46		
Malden Manor	d					19 11												19 41					
Tolworth	d					19 14												19 44					
Chessington North	d					19 17												19 47					
Chessington South	a					19 21												19 49					
Worcester Park	d		19 03						19 17		19 24					19 33					19 48		
Stoneleigh	d		19 06								19 27					19 36					19 51		
Ewell West	d		19 09								19 30					19 39					19 54		
Epsom 3	a		19 12						19 24		19 35					19 43					19 57		
	d		19 17						19 24							19 47					19 58		
Ashtead	d		19 21						19 28							19 51					20 02		
Leatherhead	d		19 24						19 31							19 54					20 05		
Boxhill & Westhumble	d								19 36												20 10		
Dorking 4	a								19 43												20 14		
New Malden 6	d	18 58			19 05					19 19					19 28		19 35					19 49	
Norbiton	d				19 08					19 22							19 38					19 52	
Kingston	a				19 11					19 25		19 48					19 41					19 55	
	d				19 11					19 29		19 49					19 41					19 59	
Hampton Wick	d				19 13					19 31							19 43					20 01	
Teddington	d				19 16					19 35							19 46					20 05	
Strawberry Hill	a			19 11						19 38												20 08	
Fulwell	d			19 13	19 20												19 50						
Hampton	d			19 17	19 24												19 54						
Kempton Park	d				19 27												19 57						
Sunbury	d			19 21	19 29												19 59						
Upper Halliford	d			19 23	19 31												20 01						
Shepperton	a			19 30	19 39												20 06						
Berrylands	d	19 00													19 30								
Surbiton 6	d	19 05					19 06	19 14					19 18	19 27	19 35				19 44	19a39			19 57
Thames Ditton	d	19 09													19 39								
Hampton Court	a	19 14													19 42								
Hinchley Wood	d						19 10							19 31									20 01
Claygate	d						19 13							19 34									20 04
Oxshott	d						19 16							19 37									20 07
Cobham & Stoke D'abernon	d						19 20							19 41									20 11
Bookham	d		19 29													19 59							
Effingham Junction 6	d		19 33				19 24							19 45		20 03							20 15
Horsley	d		19 36				19 27							19 48		20 06							20 18
Clandon	d		19 41				19 32							19 53		20 11							20 23
London Road (Guildford)	d		19 46				19 37							19 58		20 16							20 28
Guildford	a		19 55				19 46							20 05		20 23							20 35

Table 152

London - Chessington South, Dorking, Guildford, Shepperton and Hampton Court

		SW	SW	SW	SW	SW	SW 1	SW	SW	SW	SW	SW	SW	SW	SW	SW	SW 1	SW	SW	SW	SW	SW
London Waterloo 15 ⊖	d	19 33	19 36	19 39	19 42	19 46	19 53	19 50	19 54	19 57	20 03	20 03	20 06	20 09	20 12	20 16	20 23	20 20	20 24	20 27	20 33	20 33
Vauxhall ⊖	d	19 37	19 40	19 43	19 46	19 50		19 54	19 58	20 01	20 07	20 07	20 10	20 13	20 16	20 20		20 24	20 28	20 31	20 37	20 37
Clapham Junction 10	d		19 45	19 48	19 51	19 55	20u00	19 59	20 03	20 06	20 12		20 15	20 18	20 21	20 25		20 29	20 33	20 36	20 42	
Earlsfield	d		19 48	19 51	19 54	19 58		20 02	20 06	20 09	20 15		20 18	20 21	20 24	20 28		20 32	20 36	20 39	20 45	
Wimbledon 8 ⊖ 🚋	d		19 52	19 55	19 58	20 02		20 06	20 10	20 13	20 19		20 22	20 25	20 28	20 32		20 36	20 40	20 43	20 49	
Raynes Park 6	d		19 55	19 58	20 01	20 05			20 13	20 16			20 25	20 28	20 31	20 35			20 43	20 46		
Motspur Park	d			20 01		20 08			20 16					20 31		20 38			20 46			
Malden Manor	d					20 11										20 41						
Tolworth	d					20 14										20 44						
Chessington North	d					20 17										20 47						
Chessington South	a					20 19										20 49						
Worcester Park	d			20 03					20 18					20 33					20 48			
Stoneleigh	d			20 06					20 21					20 36					20 51			
Ewell West	d			20 09					20 24					20 39					20 54			
Epsom 3	a			20 16					20 27					20 42					20 57			
	d			20 17										20 47								
Ashtead	d			20 21										20 51								
Leatherhead	d			20 24										20 54								
Boxhill & Westhumble	d													20 59								
Dorking 4	a													21 03								
New Malden 6	d		19 58		20 04					20 19			20 28		20 34					20 49		
Norbiton	d				20 07					20 22					20 37					20 52		
Kingston	a	20 16			20 10					20 25		20 46			20 40					20 55		21 16
	d	20 19			20 10					20 29		20 49			20 40					20 59		21 19
Hampton Wick	d				20 12					20 31					20 42					21 01		
Teddington	d				20 15					20 35					20 45					21 05		
Strawberry Hill	a									20 38										21 08		
Fulwell	d				20 19										20 49							
Hampton	d				20 23										20 53							
Kempton Park	d				20 26										20 56							
Sunbury	d				20 28										20 58							
Upper Halliford	d				20 30										21 00							
Shepperton	a				20 35										21 05							
Berrylands	d		20 00										20 30									
Surbiton 6	d		20 05				20 11	20 14			20 27		20 35				20 41	20 44			20 57	
Thames Ditton	d		20 09										20 39									
Hampton Court	a		20 12										20 42									
Hinchley Wood	d										20 31										21 01	
Claygate	d										20 34										21 04	
Oxshott	d										20 37										21 07	
Cobham & Stoke D'abernon	d										20 41										21 11	
Bookham	d			20 29																		
Effingham Junction 6	d			20 33							20 45										21 15	
Horsley	d			20 36							20 48										21 18	
Clandon	d			20 41							20 53										21 23	
London Road (Guildford)	d			20 46							20 58										21 28	
Guildford	a			20 53							21 05										21 35	

Table 152

Mondays to Fridays
from 27 September

London - Chessington South, Dorking, Guildford, Shepperton and Hampton Court

		SW	SW	SW	SW	SW [1]	SW	SW	SW	SW	SW	SW	SW	SW [1]	SW	SW	SW	SW	SW	SW	SW	SW	SW
London Waterloo [15] ⊖	d	20 36	20 39	20 42	20 46	20 53	20 50	20 54	20 57	21 03	21 03	21 09	21 12	21 23	21 20	21 24	21 27	21 33	21 33	21 36	21 39	21 42	21 46
Vauxhall ⊖	d	20 40	20 43	20 46	20 50		20 54	20 58	21 01	21 07	21 07	21 13	21 16		21 24	21 28	21 31	21 37	21 37	21 40	21 43	21 46	21 50
Clapham Junction [10]	d	20 45	20 48	20 51	20 55	21u00	20 59	21 03	21 06	21 12		21 18	21 21		21 29	21 33	21 36	21 42		21 45	21 48	21 51	21 55
Earlsfield	d	20 48	20 51	20 54	20 58		21 02	21 06	21 09	21 15		21 21	21 24		21 32	21 36	21 39	21 45		21 48	21 51	21 54	21 58
Wimbledon [6] ⊖	d	20 52	20 55	20 58	21 02		21 06	21 10	21 13	21 19		21 25	21 28		21 36	21 40	21 43	21 49		21 52	21 55	21 58	22 02
Raynes Park [6]	d	20 55	20 58	21 01	21 05			21 13	21 16			21 28	21 31			21 43	21 46			21 55	21 58	22 01	22 05
Motspur Park	d		21 01		21 08			21 16				21 31				21 46					22 01		22 08
Malden Manor	d				21 11																		22 11
Tolworth	d				21 14																		22 14
Chessington North	d				21 17																		22 17
Chessington South	a				21 19																		22 19
Worcester Park	d		21 03					21 18				21 33				21 48					22 03		
Stoneleigh	d		21 06					21 21				21 36				21 51					22 06		
Ewell West	d		21 09					21 24				21 39				21 54					22 09		
Epsom [3]	a		21 12					21 27				21 42				21 57					22 12		
	d		21 17									21 47									22 17		
Ashtead	d		21 21									21 51									22 21		
Leatherhead	d		21 24									21 54									22 24		
Boxhill & Westhumble	d											21 59											
Dorking [4]	a											22 03											
New Malden [6]	d	20 58		21 04					21 19				21 34				21 49			21 58		22 04	
Norbiton	d			21 07					21 22				21 37				21 52					22 07	
Kingston	a			21 10					21 25		21 46		21 40				21 55		22 16			22 10	
	d			21 10					21 29		21 49		21 40				21 59		22 19			22 10	
Hampton Wick	d			21 12					21 31				21 42				22 01					22 12	
Teddington	d			21 15					21 35				21 45				22 05					22 15	
Strawberry Hill	a								21 38								22 08						
Fulwell	d			21 19									21 49									22 19	
Hampton	d			21 23									21 53									22 23	
Kempton Park	d			21 26									21 56									22 26	
Sunbury	d			21 28									21 58									22 28	
Upper Halliford	d			21 30									22 00									22 30	
Shepperton	a			21 35									22 05									22 35	
Berrylands	d	21 00																		22 00			
Surbiton [6]	d	21 05				21 11	21 14			21 27				21 41	21 44			21 57		22 05			
Thames Ditton	d	21 09																		22 09			
Hampton Court	a	21 12																		22 12			
Hinchley Wood	d									21 31								22 01					
Claygate	d									21 34								22 04					
Oxshott	d									21 37								22 07					
Cobham & Stoke D'abernon	d									21 41								22 11					
Bookham	d		21 29																		22 29		
Effingham Junction [6]	d		21 33							21 45								22 15			22 33		
Horsley	d		21 36							21 48								22 18			22 36		
Clandon	d		21 41							21 53								22 23			22 41		
London Road (Guildford)	d		21 46							21 58								22 28			22 46		
Guildford	a		21 53							22 05								22 35			22 53		

Table 152

Mondays to Fridays
from 27 September

London - Chessington South, Dorking, Guildford, Shepperton and Hampton Court

		SW [1]	SW	SW	SW	SW	SW	SW	SW	SW [1]	SW	SW	SW	SW	SW	SW	SW	SW [1]	SW	SW	SW	SW	SW
London Waterloo [15] ⊖	d	21 53	21 50	21 54	21 57	22 03	22 03	22 09	22 12	22 23	22 20	22 27	22 33	22 33	22 36	22 39	22 42	22 53	22 50	22 57	23 00	23 03	23 03
Vauxhall ⊖	d		21 54	21 58	22 01	22 07	22 07	22 13	22 16		22 24	22 31	22 37	22 37	22 40	22 43	22 46		22 54	23 01	23 04	23 07	23 07
Clapham Junction [10]	d	22u00	21 59	22 03	22 06	22 12		22 18	22 21	22u30	22 29	22 36	22 42		22 45	22 48	22 51	23u00	22 59	23 06	23 09	23 12	
Earlsfield	d		22 02	22 06	22 09	22 15		22 21	22 24		22 32	22 39	22 45		22 48	22 51	22 54		23 02	23 09	23 12	23 15	
Wimbledon [6] ⊖	d		22 06	22 10	22 13	22 19		22 25	22 28		22 36	22 43	22 49		22 52	22 55	22 58		23 06	23 13	23 16	23 19	
Raynes Park [6]	d			22 13	22 16			22 28	22 31			22 46			22 55	22 58	23 01			23 16	23 19		
Motspur Park	d			22 16				22 31								23 01					23 22		
Malden Manor	d																				23 25		
Tolworth	d																				23 28		
Chessington North	d																				23 31		
Chessington South	a																				23 33		
Worcester Park	d			22 18				22 33								23 03							
Stoneleigh	d			22 21				22 36								23 06							
Ewell West	d			22 24				22 39								23 09							
Epsom [3]	a			22 27				22 42								23 12							
	d							22 47								23 17							
Ashtead	d							22 51								23 21							
Leatherhead	d							22 54								23 24							
Boxhill & Westhumble	d							22 59															
Dorking [4]	a							23 03															
New Malden [6]	d				22 19				22 34			22 49			22 58		23 04			23 19			
Norbiton	d				22 22				22 37			22 52					23 07			23 22			
Kingston	a				22 25		22 46		22 40			22 55		23 16			23 10			23 25			23 46
	d				22 29		22 49		22 40			22 59		23 19			23 10			23 29			23 49
Hampton Wick	d				22 31				22 42			23 01					23 12			23 31			
Teddington	d				22 35				22 45			23 05					23 15			23 35			
Strawberry Hill	a				22 38							23 08								23 38			
Fulwell	d								22 49								23 19						
Hampton	d								22 53								23 23						
Kempton Park	d								22 56								23 26						
Sunbury	d								22 58								23 28						
Upper Halliford	d								23 00								23 30						
Shepperton	a								23 05								23 35						
Berrylands	d														23 00								
Surbiton [6]	d	22 11	22 14			22 27				22 41	22 44		22 57		23 05			23 11	23 14			23 27	
Thames Ditton	d														23 09								
Hampton Court	a														23 12								
Hinchley Wood	d					22 31							23 01									23 31	
Claygate	d					22 34							23 04									23 34	
Oxshott	d					22 37							23 07									23 37	
Cobham & Stoke D'abernon	d					22 41							23 11									23 41	
Bookham	d															23 29							
Effingham Junction [6]	d					22 45							23 15			23 33						23 45	
Horsley	d					22 48							23 18			23 36						23 48	
Clandon	d					22 53							23 23			23 41						23 53	
London Road (Guildford)	d					22 58							23 28			23 46						23 58	
Guildford	a		22 47			23 06							23 35			23 54						00 05	

Table 152

London - Chessington South, Dorking, Guildford, Shepperton and Hampton Court

		SW	SW	SW	SW	SW	SW	SW	SW	SW
London Waterloo 15 ⊖	d	23 09	23 12	23 20	23 27	23 30	23 33	23 42	23 50	23 57
Vauxhall ⊖	d	23 13	23 16	23 24	23 31	23 34	23 37	23 46	23 54	00 01
Clapham Junction 10	d	23 18	23 21	23 29	23 36	23 39		23 51	23 58	00 06
Earlsfield	d	23 21	23 24	23 32	23 39	23 42		23 54	00 02	00 09
Wimbledon 6 ⊖ ⇌	d	23 25	23 28	23 36	23 43	23 46		23 58	00 06	00 13
Raynes Park 6	d	23 28	23 31		23 46	23 49		00 01		00 16
Motspur Park	d	23 31						00 04		
Malden Manor	d									
Tolworth	d									
Chessington North	d									
Chessington South	a									
Worcester Park	d	23 33						00 06		
Stoneleigh	d	23 36						00 09		
Ewell West	d	23 39						00 12		
Epsom 3	a	23 42						00 15		
	d	23 47						00 19		
Ashtead	d	23 51						00 23		
Leatherhead	d	23 54						00 26		
Boxhill & Westhumble	d	23 59								
Dorking 4	a	00 03								
New Malden 6	d		23 34		23 49	23 52				00 19
Norbiton	d		23 37		23 52					00 22
Kingston	a		23 40		23 55		00 16			00 25
	d		23 40		23 55					00 25
Hampton Wick	d		23 42		23 57					00 27
Teddington	d		23 45		23 59					00 30
Strawberry Hill	a				00 03					
Fulwell	d		23 49							00 34
Hampton	d		23 53							00 38
Kempton Park	d		23 56							00 41
Sunbury	d		23 58							00 43
Upper Halliford	d		23 59							00 45
Shepperton	a		00 05							00 50
Berrylands	d					23 54				
Surbiton 6	d			23 44		23 59			00 14	
Thames Ditton	d					00 03				
Hampton Court	a					00 06				
Hinchley Wood	d								00 18	
Claygate	d								00 21	
Oxshott	d								00 24	
Cobham & Stoke D'abernon	d								00 28	
Bookham	d							00 31		
Effingham Junction 6	d							00 37	00 32	
Horsley	d							00 40	00 35	
Clandon	d							00 45	00 40	
London Road (Guildford)	d							00 50	00 45	
Guildford	a							00 57	00 52	

Table 152

London - Chessington South, Dorking, Guildford, Shepperton and Hampton Court

		SW	SW	SW	SW	SW	SW	SW	SW	SW
London Waterloo 15 ⊖	d	23p03	23p09	23p12	23p27	23p30	23p33	23p42	23p50	23p57
Vauxhall ⊖	d	23p07	23p13	23p16	23p31	23p34	23p37	23p46	23p54	00 01
Clapham Junction 10	d	23p12	23p18	23p21	23p36	23p39		23p51	23p58	00 06
Earlsfield	d	23p15	23p21	23p24	23p39	23p42		23p54	00 02	00 09
Wimbledon 6 ⊖ ⇌	d	23p19	23p25	23p28	23p43	23p46		23p58	00 06	00 13
Raynes Park 6	d		23p28	23p31	23p46	23p49		00 01		00 16
Motspur Park	d		23p31					00 04		
Malden Manor	d									
Tolworth	d									
Chessington North	d									
Chessington South	a									
Worcester Park	d		23p33					00 06		
Stoneleigh	d		23p36					00 09		
Ewell West	d		23p39					00 12		
Epsom 3	a		23p42					00 15		
	d		23p47					00 19		
Ashtead	d		23p51					00 23		
Leatherhead	d		23p54					00 26		
Boxhill & Westhumble	d		23p59							
Dorking 4	a		00 01							
New Malden 6	d			23p34	23p49	23p52				00 19
Norbiton	d			23p37	23p52					00 22
Kingston	a			23p40	23p55		00 16			00 25
	d			23p40	23p55					00 25
Hampton Wick	d			23p42	23p57					00 27
Teddington	d			23p45	23p59					00 30
Strawberry Hill	a				00 03					
Fulwell	d			23p49						00 34
Hampton	d			23p53						00 38
Kempton Park	d			23p56						00 41
Sunbury	d			23p58						00 43
Upper Halliford	d			23p59						00 45
Shepperton	a			00 03						00 48
Berrylands	d					23p54				
Surbiton 6	d	23p27				23p59			00 14	
Thames Ditton	d					00 03				
Hampton Court	a					00 06				
Hinchley Wood	d	23p31							00 18	
Claygate	d	23p34							00 21	
Oxshott	d	23p37							00 24	
Cobham & Stoke D'abernon	d	23p41							00 28	
Bookham	d							00 31		
Effingham Junction 6	d	23p45						00 37	00 32	
Horsley	d	23p48						00 40	00 35	
Clandon	d	23p53						00 45	00 40	
London Road (Guildford)	d	23p58						00 50	00 45	
Guildford	a	00 02						00 54	00 49	

		SW	SW	SW	SW	SW	SW 1	SW	SW 1	SW	SW	SW	SW	SW
London Waterloo 15 ⊖	d	00 09	00 15	00 18	00 27	00 42	05 00	05 12	05 20	05 33	05 50	06 03	06 06	06 12
Vauxhall ⊖	d	00 13	00 19	00 22	00 31	00 46	05 04	05 16	05 24	05 37	05 54	06 07	06 10	06 16
Clapham Junction 10	d	00 18	00 24		00 36	00 51	05 09	05 21	05 29		05 59		06 15	06 21
Earlsfield	d	00 21	00 27		00s39		05 12	05 24	05 32		06 02		06 18	06 24
Wimbledon 6 ⊖ ⇌	d	00 25	00 31		00 43	01b05	05 16	05 28	05 36		06 06		06 22	06 28
Raynes Park 6	d		00 34		00 46	01 08		05 31					06 25	06 31
Motspur Park	d		00 37											
Malden Manor	d													
Tolworth	d													
Chessington North	d													
Chessington South	a													
Worcester Park	d		00 39											
Stoneleigh	d		00 42											
Ewell West	d		00 45											
Epsom 3	a		00 48											
	d													
Ashtead	d													
Leatherhead	d													
Boxhill & Westhumble	d													
Dorking 4	a													
New Malden 6	d				00 49	01 11		05 34					06 28	06 34
Norbiton	d					01 14		05 37						06 37
Kingston	a			01 00		01 17		05 40		06 16		06 46		06 40
	d					01 17		05 40		06 19		06 49		06 40
Hampton Wick	d					01s19		05 42						06 42
Teddington	d					01s22		05 45						06 45
Strawberry Hill	a					01 28								
Fulwell	d							05 49						06 49
Hampton	d							05 53						06 53
Kempton Park	d							05 56						06 56
Sunbury	d							05 58						06 58
Upper Halliford	d							06 00						07 00
Shepperton	a							06 03						07 03
Berrylands	d				00s51								06 30	
Surbiton 6	d	00 33			00a55		05 24		05 44		06 14		06 35	
Thames Ditton	d												06 39	
Hampton Court	a												06 42	
Hinchley Wood	d													
Claygate	d													
Oxshott	d													
Cobham & Stoke D'abernon	d													
Bookham	d													
Effingham Junction 6	d													
Horsley	d													
Clandon	d													
London Road (Guildford)	d													
Guildford	a	01 06					05 59		06 23					

b arr. 0056

Table 152

Saturdays

29 May to 25 September

London - Chessington South, Dorking, Guildford, Shepperton and Hampton Court

		SW	SW	SW	SW	SW	SW	SW	SW	SW	SW 1	SW	SW	SW	SW	SW	SW	SW	SW	SW 1	SW	SW	SW
London Waterloo 15 ⊖	d	06 16	06 20	06 27	06 33	06 33	06 36	06 39	06 42	06 46	06 53	06 50	06 57	07 03	07 03	07 06	07 09	07 12	07 16	07 23	07 20	07 24	07 27
Vauxhall ⊖	d	06 20	06 24	06 31	06 37	06 37	06 40	06 43	06 46	06 50		06 54	07 01	07 07	07 07	07 10	07 13	07 16	07 20		07 24	07 28	07 31
Clapham Junction 10	d	06 25	06 29	06 36	06 42		06 45	06 48	06 51	06 55	07u00	06 59	07 06	07 12		07 15	07 18	07 21	07 25	07u30	07 29	07 33	07 36
Earlsfield	d	06 28	06 32	06 39	06 45		06 48	06 51	06 54	06 58		07 02	07 09	07 15		07 18	07 21	07 24	07 28		07 32	07 36	07 39
Wimbledon 6 ⊖	d	06 32	06 36	06 43	06 49		06 52	06 55	06 58	07 02		07 06	07 13	07 19		07 22	07 25	07 28	07 32		07 36	07 40	07 43
Raynes Park 6	d	06 35		06 46			06 55	06 58	07 01	07 05			07 16			07 25	07 28	07 31	07 35			07 43	07 46
Motspur Park	d	06 38						07 01		07 08							07 31		07 38			07 46	
Malden Manor	d	06 41								07 11									07 41				
Tolworth	d	06 44								07 14									07 44				
Chessington North	d	06 47								07 17									07 47				
Chessington South	a	06 49								07 19									07 49				
Worcester Park	d							07 03									07 33					07 48	
Stoneleigh	d							07 06									07 36					07 51	
Ewell West	d							07 09									07 39					07 54	
Epsom 3	a							07 16									07 46					07 57	
	d							07 17									07 47					07 58	
Ashtead	d							07 21									07 51					08 02	
Leatherhead	d							07 24									07 54					08 05	
Boxhill & Westhumble	d																						
Dorking 4	a																					08 11	
New Malden 6	d			06 49			06 58		07 04				07 19			07 28		07 34					07 49
Norbiton	d			06 52					07 07				07 22					07 37					07 52
Kingston	a			06 55		07 16			07 10				07 25		07 46			07 40					07 55
	d			06 59		07 19			07 10				07 29		07 49			07 40					07 59
Hampton Wick	d			07 01					07 12				07 31					07 42					08 01
Teddington	d			07 05					07 15				07 35					07 45					08 05
Strawberry Hill	a			07 08									07 38										08 08
Fulwell	d								07 19									07 49					
Hampton	d								07 23									07 53					
Kempton Park	d								07 26									07 56					
Sunbury	d								07 28									07 58					
Upper Halliford	d								07 30									08 00					
Shepperton	a								07 33									08 03					
Berrylands	d						07 00									07 30							
Surbiton 6	d		06 44		06 57		07 05				07 11	07 14		07 27		07 35				07 41	07 44		
Thames Ditton	d						07 09									07 39							
Hampton Court	a						07 12									07 42							
Hinchley Wood	d				07 01									07 31									
Claygate	d				07 04									07 34									
Oxshott	d				07 07									07 37									
Cobham & Stoke D'abernon	d				07 11									07 41									
Bookham	d							07 29									07 59						
Effingham Junction 6	d				07 15			07 33						07 45			08 03						
Horsley	d				07 18			07 36						07 48			08 06						
Clandon	d				07 23			07 41						07 53			08 11						
London Road (Guildford)	d				07 28			07 46						07 58			08 16						
Guildford	a				07 32			07 50						08 02			08 20						

Table 152

Saturdays

29 May to 25 September

London - Chessington South, Dorking, Guildford, Shepperton and Hampton Court

		SW	SW	SW	SW	SW	SW	SW 1	SW	SW	SW	SW	SW	SW	SW	SW	SW	SW 1	SW	SW	SW	SW
London Waterloo 15 ⊖	d	07 33	07 33	07 36	07 39	07 42	07 46	07 53	07 50	07 54	07 57	08 03	08 03	08 06	08 09	08 12	08 16	08 23	08 20	08 24	08 27	08 33
Vauxhall ⊖	d	07 37	07 37	07 40	07 43	07 46	07 50		07 54	07 58	08 01	08 07	08 07	08 10	08 13	08 16	08 20		08 24	08 28	08 31	08 37
Clapham Junction 10	d	07 42		07 45	07 48	07 51	07 55	08u00	07 59	08 03	08 06	08 12		08 15	08 18	08 21	08 25		08 29	08 33	08 36	08 42
Earlsfield	d	07 45		07 48	07 51	07 54	07 58		08 02	08 06	08 09	08 15		08 18	08 21	08 24	08 28		08 32	08 36	08 39	08 45
Wimbledon 6 ⊖	d	07 49		07 52	07 55	07 58	08 02		08 06	08 10	08 13	08 19		08 22	08 25	08 28	08 32		08 36	08 40	08 43	08 49
Raynes Park 6	d			07 55	07 58	08 01	08 05			08 13	08 16			08 25	08 28	08 31	08 35			08 43	08 46	
Motspur Park	d				08 01		08 08			08 16					08 31		08 38			08 46		
Malden Manor	d						08 11										08 41					
Tolworth	d						08 14										08 44					
Chessington North	d						08 17										08 47					
Chessington South	a						08 19										08 49					
Worcester Park	d				08 03					08 18					08 33					08 48		
Stoneleigh	d				08 06					08 21					08 36					08 51		
Ewell West	d				08 09					08 24					08 39					08 54		
Epsom 3	a				08 16					08 27					08 46					08 57		
	d				08 17					08 28					08 47					08 58		
Ashtead	d				08 21					08 32					08 51					09 02		
Leatherhead	d				08 24					08 35					08 54					09 05		
Boxhill & Westhumble	d																					
Dorking 4	a									08 41										09 11		
New Malden 6	d			07 58		08 04					08 19			08 28		08 34					08 49	
Norbiton	d					08 07					08 22					08 37					08 52	
Kingston	a		08 16			08 10					08 25		08 46			08 40					08 55	
	d		08 19			08 10					08 29		08 49			08 40					08 59	
Hampton Wick	d					08 12					08 31					08 42					09 01	
Teddington	d					08 15					08 35					08 45					09 05	
Strawberry Hill	a										08 38										09 08	
Fulwell	d					08 19										08 49						
Hampton	d					08 23										08 53						
Kempton Park	d					08 26										08 56						
Sunbury	d					08 28										08 58						
Upper Halliford	d					08 30										09 00						
Shepperton	a					08 33										09 03						
Berrylands	d			08 00										08 30								
Surbiton 6	d	07 57		08 05				08 11	08 14			08 27		08 35				08 41	08 44			08 57
Thames Ditton	d			08 09										08 39								
Hampton Court	a			08 12										08 42								
Hinchley Wood	d	08 01										08 31										09 01
Claygate	d	08 04										08 34										09 04
Oxshott	d	08 07										08 37										09 07
Cobham & Stoke D'abernon	d	08 11										08 41										09 11
Bookham	d				08 29										08 59							
Effingham Junction 6	d	08 15			08 33							08 45			09 03							09 15
Horsley	d	08 18			08 36							08 48			09 06							09 18
Clandon	d	08 23			08 41							08 53			09 11							09 23
London Road (Guildford)	d	08 28			08 46							08 58			09 16							09 28
Guildford	a	08 32			08 50							09 02			09 20							09 32

Table 152

Saturdays

29 May to 25 September

London - Chessington South, Dorking, Guildford, Shepperton and Hampton Court

		SW	SW	SW	SW	SW	SW ■	SW	SW	SW	SW	SW	SW	SW	SW	SW	SW ■	SW	SW	SW	SW	SW	SW
London Waterloo ⊖	d	08 33	08 36	08 39	08 42	08 46	08 53	08 50	08 54	08 57	09 03	09 03	09 06	09 09	09 12	09 16	09 23	09 20	09 24	09 27	09 33	09 33	09 36
Vauxhall ⊖	d	08 37	08 40	08 43	08 46	08 50		08 54	08 58	09 01	09 07	09 07	09 10	09 13	09 16	09 20		09 24	09 28	09 31	09 37	09 37	09 40
Clapham Junction	d		08 45	08 48	08 51	08 55	09u00	08 59	09 03	09 06	09 12		09 15	09 18	09 21	09 25		09 29	09 33	09 36	09 42		09 45
Earlsfield	d		08 48	08 51	08 54	08 58		09 02	09 06	09 09	09 15		09 18	09 21	09 24	09 28		09 32	09 36	09 39	09 45		09 48
Wimbledon ⊖	d		08 52	08 55	08 58	09 02		09 06	09 10	09 13	09 19		09 22	09 25	09 28	09 32		09 36	09 40	09 43	09 49		09 52
Raynes Park	d		08 55	08 58	09 01	09 05			09 13	09 16			09 25	09 28	09 31	09 35			09 43	09 46			09 55
Motspur Park	d			09 01		09 08			09 16					09 31		09 38			09 46				
Malden Manor	d					09 11										09 41							
Tolworth	d					09 14										09 44							
Chessington North	d					09 17										09 47							
Chessington South	a					09 19										09 49							
Worcester Park	d			09 03					09 18					09 33					09 48				
Stoneleigh	d			09 06					09 21					09 36					09 51				
Ewell West	d			09 09					09 24					09 39					09 54				
Epsom	a			09 16					09 27					09 46					09 57				
	d			09 17					09 28					09 47					09 58				
Ashtead	d			09 21					09 32					09 51					10 02				
Leatherhead	d			09 24					09 35					09 54					10 05				
Boxhill & Westhumble	d																						
Dorking	a								09 41										10 11				
New Malden	d		08 58		09 04					09 19			09 28		09 34					09 49			09 58
Norbiton	d				09 07					09 22					09 37					09 52			
Kingston	a	09 16			09 10					09 25		09 46			09 40					09 55		10 16	
	d	09 19			09 10					09 29		09 49			09 40					09 59		10 19	
Hampton Wick	d				09 12					09 31					09 42					10 01			
Teddington	d				09 15					09 35					09 45					10 05			
Strawberry Hill	a									09 38										10 08			
Fulwell	d				09 19										09 49								
Hampton	d				09 23										09 53								
Kempton Park	d				09 26										09 56								
Sunbury	d				09 28										09 58								
Upper Halliford	d				09 30										10 00								
Shepperton	a				09 33										10 03								
Berrylands	d		09 00										09 30										10 00
Surbiton	d		09 05				09 11	09 14			09 27		09 35				09 41	09 44			09 57		10 05
Thames Ditton	d		09 09										09 39										10 09
Hampton Court	a		09 12										09 42										10 12
Hinchley Wood	d										09 31										10 01		
Claygate	d										09 34										10 04		
Oxshott	d										09 37										10 07		
Cobham & Stoke D'abernon	d										09 41										10 11		
Bookham	d			09 29										09 59									
Effingham Junction	d			09 33							09 45			10 03							10 15		
Horsley	d			09 36							09 48			10 06							10 18		
Clandon	d			09 41							09 53			10 11							10 23		
London Road (Guildford)	d			09 46							09 58			10 16							10 28		
Guildford	a			09 50							10 02			10 20							10 32		

Table 152

Saturdays

29 May to 25 September

London - Chessington South, Dorking, Guildford, Shepperton and Hampton Court

		SW	SW	SW	SW ■	SW	SW	SW	SW	SW	SW	SW	SW	SW	SW ■	SW	SW	SW	SW	SW	SW	SW
London Waterloo ⊖	d	09 39	09 42	09 46	09 53	09 50	09 54	09 57	10 03	10 03	10 06	10 09	10 12	10 16	10 23	10 20	10 24	10 27	10 33	10 33	10 36	10 39
Vauxhall ⊖	d	09 43	09 46	09 50		09 54	09 58	10 01	10 07	10 07	10 10	10 13	10 16	10 20		10 24	10 28	10 31	10 37	10 37	10 40	10 43
Clapham Junction	d	09 48	09 51	09 55	10u00	09 59	10 03	10 06	10 12		10 15	10 18	10 21	10 25		10 29	10 33	10 36	10 42		10 45	10 48
Earlsfield	d	09 51	09 54	09 58		10 02	10 06	10 09	10 15		10 18	10 21	10 24	10 28		10 32	10 36	10 39	10 45		10 48	10 51
Wimbledon ⊖	d	09 55	09 58	10 02		10 06	10 10	10 13	10 19		10 22	10 25	10 28	10 32		10 36	10 40	10 43	10 49		10 52	10 55
Raynes Park	d	09 58	10 01	10 05			10 13	10 16			10 25	10 28	10 31	10 35			10 43	10 46			10 55	10 58
Motspur Park	d	10 01		10 08			10 16					10 31		10 38			10 46					11 01
Malden Manor	d			10 11										10 41								
Tolworth	d			10 14										10 44								
Chessington North	d			10 17										10 47								
Chessington South	a			10 19										10 49								
Worcester Park	d	10 03					10 18					10 33					10 48					11 03
Stoneleigh	d	10 06					10 21					10 36					10 51					11 06
Ewell West	d	10 09					10 24					10 39					10 54					11 09
Epsom	a	10 16					10 27					10 46					10 57					11 16
	d	10 17					10 28					10 47					10 58					11 17
Ashtead	d	10 21					10 32					10 51					11 02					11 21
Leatherhead	d	10 24					10 35					10 54					11 05					11 24
Boxhill & Westhumble	d																					
Dorking	a						10 41										11 11					
New Malden	d		10 04					10 19			10 28		10 34					10 49			10 58	
Norbiton	d		10 07					10 22					10 37					10 52				
Kingston	a		10 10					10 25		10 46			10 40					10 55		11 16		
	d		10 10					10 29		10 49			10 40					10 59		11 19		
Hampton Wick	d		10 12					10 31					10 42					11 01				
Teddington	d		10 15					10 35					10 45					11 05				
Strawberry Hill	a							10 38										11 08				
Fulwell	d		10 19										10 49									
Hampton	d		10 23										10 53									
Kempton Park	d		10 26										10 56									
Sunbury	d		10 28										10 58									
Upper Halliford	d		10 30										11 00									
Shepperton	a		10 33										11 03									
Berrylands	d										10 30										11 00	
Surbiton	d				10 11	10 14			10 27		10 35				10 41	10 44			10 57		11 05	
Thames Ditton	d										10 39										11 09	
Hampton Court	a										10 42										11 12	
Hinchley Wood	d								10 31										11 01			
Claygate	d								10 34										11 04			
Oxshott	d								10 37										11 07			
Cobham & Stoke D'abernon	d								10 41										11 11			
Bookham	d	10 29										10 59										11 29
Effingham Junction	d	10 33							10 45			11 03							11 15			11 33
Horsley	d	10 36							10 48			11 06							11 18			11 36
Clandon	d	10 41							10 53			11 11							11 23			11 41
London Road (Guildford)	d	10 46							10 58			11 16							11 28			11 46
Guildford	a	10 50							11 02			11 20							11 32			11 50

Table 152

Saturdays

29 May to 25 September

London - Chessington South, Dorking, Guildford, Shepperton and Hampton Court

Station		SW	SW	SW 1	SW	SW	SW	SW	SW	SW	SW	SW	SW	SW 1	SW	SW	SW	SW	SW	SW	SW	SW	SW
London Waterloo ⊖	d	10 42	10 46	10 53	10 50	10 54	10 57	11 03	11 03	11 06	11 09	11 12	11 16	11 23	11 20	11 24	11 27	11 33	11 33	11 36	11 39	11 42	11 46
Vauxhall ⊖	d	10 46	10 50		10 54	10 58	11 01	11 07	11 07	11 10	11 13	11 16	11 20		11 24	11 28	11 31	11 37	11 37	11 40	11 43	11 46	11 50
Clapham Junction	d	10 51	10 55	11u00	10 59	11 03	11 06	11 12		11 15	11 18	11 21	11 25		11 29	11 33	11 36	11 42		11 45	11 48	11 51	11 55
Earlsfield	d	10 54	10 58		11 02	11 06	11 09	11 15		11 18	11 21	11 24	11 28		11 32	11 36	11 39	11 45		11 48	11 51	11 54	11 58
Wimbledon ⊖	d	10 58	11 02		11 06	11 10	11 13	11 19		11 22	11 25	11 28	11 32		11 36	11 40	11 43	11 49		11 52	11 55	11 58	12 02
Raynes Park	d	11 01	11 05			11 13	11 16			11 25	11 28	11 31	11 35			11 43	11 46			11 55	11 58	12 01	12 05
Motspur Park	d		11 08			11 16					11 31		11 38			11 46					12 01		12 08
Malden Manor	d		11 11										11 41										12 11
Tolworth	d		11 14										11 44										12 14
Chessington North	d		11 17										11 47										12 17
Chessington South	a		11 19										11 49										12 19
Worcester Park	d					11 18					11 33					11 48					12 03		
Stoneleigh	d					11 21					11 36					11 51					12 06		
Ewell West	d					11 24					11 39					11 54					12 09		
Epsom	a					11 27					11 46					11 57					12 16		
	d					11 28					11 47					11 58					12 17		
Ashtead	d					11 32					11 51					12 02					12 21		
Leatherhead	d					11 35					11 54					12 05					12 24		
Boxhill & Westhumble	d																						
Dorking	a					11 41										12 11							
New Malden	d	11 04					11 19			11 28		11 34					11 49			11 58		12 04	
Norbiton	d	11 07					11 22					11 37					11 52					12 07	
Kingston	a	11 10					11 25		11 46			11 40					11 55		12 16			12 10	
	d	11 10					11 29		11 49			11 40					11 59		12 19			12 10	
Hampton Wick	d	11 12					11 31					11 42					12 01					12 12	
Teddington	d	11 15					11 35					11 45					12 05					12 15	
Strawberry Hill	a						11 38										12 08						
Fulwell	d	11 19										11 49										12 19	
Hampton	d	11 23										11 53										12 23	
Kempton Park	d	11 26										11 56										12 26	
Sunbury	d	11 28										11 58										12 28	
Upper Halliford	d	11 30										12 00										12 30	
Shepperton	a	11 33										12 03										12 33	
Berrylands	d									11 30										12 00			
Surbiton	d			11 11	11 14			11 27		11 35				11 41	11 44			11 57		12 05			
Thames Ditton	d									11 39										12 09			
Hampton Court	a									11 42										12 12			
Hinchley Wood	d							11 31										12 01					
Claygate	d							11 34										12 04					
Oxshott	d							11 37										12 07					
Cobham & Stoke D'abernon	d							11 41										12 11					
Bookham	d										11 59										12 29		
Effingham Junction	d							11 45			12 03							12 15			12 33		
Horsley	d							11 48			12 06							12 18			12 36		
Clandon	d							11 53			12 11							12 23			12 41		
London Road (Guildford)	d							11 58			12 16							12 28			12 46		
Guildford	a							12 02			12 20							12 32			12 50		

Table 152

Saturdays

29 May to 25 September

London - Chessington South, Dorking, Guildford, Shepperton and Hampton Court

Station		SW 1	SW	SW	SW	SW	SW	SW	SW	SW	SW	SW 1	SW	SW	SW	SW	SW	SW	SW	SW	SW	SW 1	SW
London Waterloo ⊖	d	11 53	11 50	11 54	11 57	12 03	12 03	12 06	12 09	12 12	12 16	12 23	12 20	12 24	12 27	12 33	12 33	12 36	12 39	12 42	12 46	12 53	12 50
Vauxhall ⊖	d		11 54	11 58	12 01	12 07	12 07	12 10	12 13	12 16	12 20		12 24	12 28	12 31	12 37	12 37	12 40	12 43	12 46	12 50		12 54
Clapham Junction	d	12u00	11 59	12 03	12 06	12 12		12 15	12 18	12 21	12 25		12 29	12 33	12 36	12 42		12 45	12 48	12 51	12 55	13u00	12 59
Earlsfield	d		12 02	12 06	12 09	12 15		12 18	12 21	12 24	12 28		12 32	12 36	12 39	12 45		12 48	12 51	12 54	12 58		13 02
Wimbledon ⊖	d		12 06	12 10	12 13	12 19		12 22	12 25	12 28	12 32		12 36	12 40	12 43	12 49		12 52	12 55	12 58	13 02		13 06
Raynes Park	d			12 13	12 16			12 25	12 28	12 31	12 35			12 43	12 46			12 55	12 58	13 01	13 05		
Motspur Park	d			12 16					12 31		12 38			12 46					13 01		13 08		
Malden Manor	d										12 41										13 11		
Tolworth	d										12 44										13 14		
Chessington North	d										12 47										13 17		
Chessington South	a										12 49										13 19		
Worcester Park	d			12 18					12 33					12 48					13 03				
Stoneleigh	d			12 21					12 36					12 51					13 06				
Ewell West	d			12 24					12 39					12 54					13 09				
Epsom	a			12 27					12 46					12 57					13 16				
	d			12 28					12 47					12 58					13 17				
Ashtead	d			12 32					12 51					13 02					13 21				
Leatherhead	d			12 35					12 54					13 05					13 24				
Boxhill & Westhumble	d																						
Dorking	a			12 41										13 11									
New Malden	d				12 19			12 28		12 34					12 49			12 58		13 04			
Norbiton	d				12 22					12 37					12 52					13 07			
Kingston	a				12 25		12 46			12 40					12 55		13 16			13 10			
	d				12 29		12 49			12 40					12 59		13 19			13 10			
Hampton Wick	d				12 31					12 42					13 01					13 12			
Teddington	d				12 35					12 45					13 05					13 15			
Strawberry Hill	a				12 38										13 08								
Fulwell	d									12 49										13 19			
Hampton	d									12 53										13 23			
Kempton Park	d									12 56										13 26			
Sunbury	d									12 58										13 28			
Upper Halliford	d									13 00										13 30			
Shepperton	a									13 03										13 33			
Berrylands	d							12 30										13 00					
Surbiton	d	12 11	12 14			12 27		12 35				12 41	12 44			12 57		13 05				13 11	13 14
Thames Ditton	d							12 39										13 09					
Hampton Court	a							12 42										13 12					
Hinchley Wood	d					12 31										13 01							
Claygate	d					12 34										13 04							
Oxshott	d					12 37										13 07							
Cobham & Stoke D'abernon	d					12 41										13 11							
Bookham	d								12 59										13 29				
Effingham Junction	d					12 45			13 03							13 15			13 33				
Horsley	d					12 48			13 06							13 18			13 36				
Clandon	d					12 53			13 11							13 23			13 41				
London Road (Guildford)	d					12 58			13 16							13 28			13 46				
Guildford	a					13 02			13 20							13 32			13 50				

Table 152

Saturdays
29 May to 25 September

London - Chessington South, Dorking, Guildford, Shepperton and Hampton Court

		SW	SW	SW	SW	SW	SW	SW	SW	SW ■1	SW	SW	SW	SW	SW	SW	SW	SW	SW	SW ■1	SW	SW
London Waterloo ⊖	d	12 54	12 57	13 03	13 03	13 06	13 09	13 12	13 16	13 23	13 20	13 24	13 27	13 33	13 33	13 36	13 39	13 42	13 46	13 53	13 50	13 54
Vauxhall ⊖	d	12 58	13 01	13 07	13 07	13 10	13 13	13 16	13 20		13 24	13 28	13 31	13 37	13 37	13 40	13 43	13 46	13 50		13 54	13 58
Clapham Junction	d	13 03	13 06	13 12		13 15	13 18	13 21	13 25		13 29	13 33	13 36	13 42		13 45	13 48	13 51	13 55	14u00	13 59	14 03
Earlsfield	d	13 06	13 09	13 15		13 18	13 21	13 24	13 28		13 32	13 36	13 39	13 45		13 48	13 51	13 54	13 58		14 02	14 06
Wimbledon ⊖	d	13 10	13 13	13 19		13 22	13 25	13 28	13 32		13 36	13 40	13 43	13 49		13 52	13 55	13 58	14 02		14 06	14 10
Raynes Park	d	13 13	13 16			13 25	13 28	13 31	13 35			13 43	13 46			13 55	13 58	14 01	14 05			14 13
Motspur Park	d	13 16					13 31		13 38			13 46					14 01		14 08			14 16
Malden Manor	d								13 41										14 11			
Tolworth	d								13 44										14 14			
Chessington North	d								13 47										14 17			
Chessington South	a								13 49										14 19			
Worcester Park	d	13 18					13 33					13 48					14 03					14 18
Stoneleigh	d	13 21					13 36					13 51					14 06					14 21
Ewell West	d	13 24					13 39					13 54					14 09					14 24
Epsom	a	13 27					13 46					13 57					14 16					14 27
	d	13 28					13 47					13 58					14 17					14 28
Ashtead	d	13 32					13 51					14 02					14 21					14 32
Leatherhead	d	13 35					13 54					14 05					14 24					14 35
Boxhill & Westhumble	d																					
Dorking	a	13 41										14 11										14 41
New Malden	d		13 19			13 28		13 34					13 49			13 58		14 04				
Norbiton	d		13 22					13 37					13 52					14 07				
Kingston	a		13 25		13 46			13 40					13 55		14 16			14 10				
	d		13 29		13 49			13 40					13 59		14 19			14 10				
Hampton Wick	d		13 31					13 42					14 01					14 12				
Teddington	d		13 35					13 45					14 05					14 15				
Strawberry Hill	a		13 38										14 08									
Fulwell	d							13 49										14 19				
Hampton	d							13 53										14 23				
Kempton Park	d							13 56										14 26				
Sunbury	d							13 58										14 28				
Upper Halliford	d							14 00										14 30				
Shepperton	a							14 03										14 33				
Berrylands	d					13 30										14 00						
Surbiton	d			13 27		13 35				13 41	13 44			13 57		14 05				14 11	14 14	
Thames Ditton	d					13 39										14 09						
Hampton Court	a					13 42										14 12						
Hinchley Wood	d			13 31										14 01								
Claygate	d			13 34										14 04								
Oxshott	d			13 37										14 07								
Cobham & Stoke D'abernon	d			13 41										14 11								
Bookham	d						13 59										14 29					
Effingham Junction	d			13 45			14 03							14 15			14 33					
Horsley	d			13 48			14 06							14 18			14 36					
Clandon	d			13 53			14 11							14 23			14 41					
London Road (Guildford)	d			13 58			14 16							14 28			14 46					
Guildford	a			14 02			14 20							14 32			14 50					

Table 152

Saturdays
29 May to 25 September

London - Chessington South, Dorking, Guildford, Shepperton and Hampton Court

		SW	SW	SW	SW	SW	SW	SW	SW ■1	SW	SW	SW	SW	SW	SW	SW	SW	SW	SW ■1	SW	SW	SW	SW
London Waterloo ⊖	d	13 57	14 03	14 03	14 06	14 09	14 12	14 16	14 23	14 20	14 24	14 27	14 33	14 33	14 36	14 39	14 42	14 46	14 53	14 50	14 54	14 57	15 03
Vauxhall ⊖	d	14 01	14 07	14 07	14 10	14 13	14 16	14 20		14 24	14 28	14 31	14 37	14 37	14 40	14 43	14 46	14 50		14 54	14 58	15 01	15 07
Clapham Junction	d	14 06	14 12		14 15	14 18	14 21	14 25		14 29	14 33	14 36	14 42		14 45	14 48	14 51	14 55	15u00	14 59	15 03	15 06	15 12
Earlsfield	d	14 09	14 15		14 18	14 21	14 24	14 28		14 32	14 36	14 39	14 45		14 48	14 51	14 54	14 58		15 02	15 06	15 09	15 15
Wimbledon ⊖	d	14 13	14 19		14 22	14 25	14 28	14 32		14 36	14 40	14 43	14 49		14 52	14 55	14 58	15 02		15 06	15 10	15 13	15 19
Raynes Park	d	14 16			14 25	14 28	14 31	14 35			14 43	14 46			14 55	14 58	15 01	15 05			15 13	15 16	
Motspur Park	d					14 31		14 38			14 46					15 01		15 08			15 16		
Malden Manor	d							14 41										15 11					
Tolworth	d							14 44										15 14					
Chessington North	d							14 47										15 17					
Chessington South	a							14 49										15 19					
Worcester Park	d					14 33					14 48					15 03					15 18		
Stoneleigh	d					14 36					14 51					15 06					15 21		
Ewell West	d					14 39					14 54					15 09					15 24		
Epsom	a					14 46					14 57					15 16					15 27		
	d					14 47					14 58					15 17					15 28		
Ashtead	d					14 51					15 02					15 21					15 32		
Leatherhead	d					14 54					15 05					15 24					15 35		
Boxhill & Westhumble	d																						
Dorking	a										15 11										15 41		
New Malden	d	14 19			14 28		14 34					14 49			14 58		15 04					15 19	
Norbiton	d	14 22					14 37					14 52					15 07					15 22	
Kingston	a	14 25		14 46			14 40					14 55		15 16			15 10					15 25	
	d	14 29		14 49			14 40					14 59		15 19			15 10					15 29	
Hampton Wick	d	14 31					14 42					15 01					15 12					15 31	
Teddington	d	14 35					14 45					15 05					15 15					15 35	
Strawberry Hill	a	14 38										15 08										15 38	
Fulwell	d						14 49										15 19						
Hampton	d						14 53										15 23						
Kempton Park	d						14 56										15 26						
Sunbury	d						14 58										15 28						
Upper Halliford	d						15 00										15 30						
Shepperton	a						15 03										15 33						
Berrylands	d				14 30										15 00								
Surbiton	d		14 27		14 35				14 41	14 44			14 57		15 05				15 11	15 14			15 27
Thames Ditton	d				14 39										15 09								
Hampton Court	a				14 42										15 12								
Hinchley Wood	d		14 31										15 01										15 31
Claygate	d		14 34										15 04										15 34
Oxshott	d		14 37										15 07										15 37
Cobham & Stoke D'abernon	d		14 41										15 11										15 41
Bookham	d					14 59										15 29							
Effingham Junction	d		14 45			15 03							15 15			15 33							15 45
Horsley	d		14 48			15 06							15 18			15 36							15 48
Clandon	d		14 53			15 11							15 23			15 41							15 53
London Road (Guildford)	d		14 58			15 16							15 28			15 46							15 58
Guildford	a		15 02			15 20							15 32			15 50							16 02

Table 152

Saturdays
29 May to 25 September

London - Chessington South, Dorking, Guildford, Shepperton and Hampton Court

		SW	SW	SW	SW	SW	SW ■	SW	SW	SW	SW	SW	SW	SW	SW	SW	SW ■	SW	SW	SW	SW	SW
London Waterloo ⊖	d	15 03	15 06	15 09	15 12	15 16	15 23	15 20	15 24	15 27	15 33	15 33	15 36	15 39	15 42	15 46	15 53	15 50	15 54	15 57	16 03	16 03
Vauxhall ⊖	d	15 07	15 10	15 13	15 16	15 20		15 24	15 28	15 31	15 37	15 37	15 40	15 43	15 46	15 50		15 54	15 58	16 01	16 07	16 07
Clapham Junction	d		15 15	15 18	15 21	15 25		15 29	15 33	15 36	15 42		15 45	15 48	15 51	15 55	16u00	15 59	16 03	16 06	16 12	
Earlsfield	d		15 18	15 21	15 24	15 28		15 32	15 36	15 39	15 45		15 48	15 51	15 54	15 58		16 02	16 06	16 09	16 15	
Wimbledon ⊖	d		15 22	15 25	15 28	15 32		15 36	15 40	15 43	15 49		15 52	15 55	15 58	16 02		16 06	16 10	16 13	16 19	
Raynes Park	d		15 25	15 28	15 31	15 35			15 43	15 46			15 55	15 58	16 01	16 05			16 13	16 16		
Motspur Park	d			15 31		15 38			15 46					16 01		16 08			16 16			
Malden Manor	d					15 41										16 11						
Tolworth	d					15 44										16 14						
Chessington North	d					15 47										16 17						
Chessington South	a					15 49										16 19						
Worcester Park	d			15 33					15 48					16 03					16 18			
Stoneleigh	d			15 36					15 51					16 06					16 21			
Ewell West	d			15 39					15 54					16 09					16 24			
Epsom	a			15 46					15 57					16 16					16 27			
	d			15 47					15 58					16 17					16 28			
Ashtead	d			15 51					16 02					16 21					16 32			
Leatherhead	d			15 54					16 05					16 24					16 35			
Boxhill & Westhumble	d																					
Dorking	a								16 11										16 41			
New Malden	d		15 28		15 34					15 49			15 58		16 04					16 19		
Norbiton	d				15 37					15 52					16 07					16 22		
Kingston	a	15 46			15 40					15 55		16 16			16 10					16 25		16 46
	d	15 49			15 40					15 59		16 19			16 10					16 29		16 49
Hampton Wick	d				15 42					16 01					16 12					16 31		
Teddington	d				15 45					16 05					16 15					16 35		
Strawberry Hill	a									16 08										16 38		
Fulwell	d				15 49										16 19							
Hampton	d				15 53										16 23							
Kempton Park	d				15 56										16 26							
Sunbury	d				15 58										16 28							
Upper Halliford	d				16 00										16 30							
Shepperton	a				16 03										16 33							
Berrylands	d		15 30										16 00									
Surbiton	d		15 35				15 41	15 44			15 57		16 05				16 11	16 14			16 27	
Thames Ditton	d		15 39										16 09									
Hampton Court	a		15 42										16 12									
Hinchley Wood	d										16 01										16 31	
Claygate	d										16 04										16 34	
Oxshott	d										16 07										16 37	
Cobham & Stoke D'abernon	d										16 11										16 41	
Bookham	d			15 59										16 29								
Effingham Junction	d			16 03							16 15			16 33							16 45	
Horsley	d			16 06							16 18			16 36							16 48	
Clandon	d			16 11							16 23			16 41							16 53	
London Road (Guildford)	d			16 16							16 28			16 46							16 58	
Guildford	a			16 20							16 32			16 50							17 02	

Table 152

Saturdays
29 May to 25 September

London - Chessington South, Dorking, Guildford, Shepperton and Hampton Court

		SW	SW	SW	SW	SW ■	SW	SW	SW	SW	SW	SW	SW	SW	SW	SW ■	SW	SW	SW	SW	SW	SW	SW
London Waterloo ⊖	d	16 06	16 09	16 12	16 16	16 23	16 20	16 24	16 27	16 33	16 33	16 36	16 39	16 42	16 46	16 53	16 50	16 54	16 57	17 03	17 03	17 06	17 09
Vauxhall ⊖	d	16 10	16 13	16 16	16 20		16 24	16 28	16 31	16 37	16 37	16 40	16 43	16 46	16 50		16 54	16 58	17 01	17 07	17 07	17 10	17 13
Clapham Junction	d	16 15	16 18	16 21	16 25		16 29	16 33	16 36	16 42		16 45	16 48	16 51	16 55	17u00	16 59	17 03	17 06	17 12		17 15	17 18
Earlsfield	d	16 18	16 21	16 24	16 28		16 32	16 36	16 39	16 45		16 48	16 51	16 54	16 58		17 02	17 06	17 09	17 15		17 18	17 21
Wimbledon ⊖	d	16 22	16 25	16 28	16 32		16 36	16 40	16 43	16 49		16 52	16 55	16 58	17 02		17 06	17 10	17 13	17 19		17 22	17 25
Raynes Park	d	16 25	16 28	16 31	16 35			16 43	16 46			16 55	16 58	17 01	17 05			17 13	17 16			17 25	17 28
Motspur Park	d		16 31		16 38			16 46					17 01		17 08			17 16					17 31
Malden Manor	d				16 41										17 11								
Tolworth	d				16 44										17 14								
Chessington North	d				16 47										17 17								
Chessington South	a				16 49										17 19								
Worcester Park	d		16 33					16 48					17 03					17 18					17 33
Stoneleigh	d		16 36					16 51					17 06					17 21					17 36
Ewell West	d		16 39					16 54					17 09					17 24					17 39
Epsom	a		16 46					16 57					17 16					17 27					17 46
	d		16 47					16 58					17 17					17 28					17 47
Ashtead	d		16 51					17 02					17 21					17 32					17 51
Leatherhead	d		16 54					17 05					17 24					17 35					17 54
Boxhill & Westhumble	d																						
Dorking	a							17 11										17 41					
New Malden	d	16 28		16 34					16 49			16 58		17 04					17 19			17 28	
Norbiton	d			16 37					16 52					17 07					17 22				
Kingston	a			16 40					16 55		17 16			17 10					17 25		17 46		
	d			16 40					16 59		17 19			17 10					17 29		17 49		
Hampton Wick	d			16 42					17 01					17 12					17 31				
Teddington	d			16 45					17 05					17 15					17 35				
Strawberry Hill	a								17 08										17 38				
Fulwell	d			16 49										17 19									
Hampton	d			16 53										17 23									
Kempton Park	d			16 56										17 26									
Sunbury	d			16 58										17 28									
Upper Halliford	d			17 00										17 30									
Shepperton	a			17 03										17 33									
Berrylands	d	16 30										17 00										17 30	
Surbiton	d	16 35				16 41	16 44			16 57		17 05				17 11	17 14			17 27		17 35	
Thames Ditton	d	16 39										17 09										17 39	
Hampton Court	a	16 42										17 12										17 42	
Hinchley Wood	d									17 01										17 31			
Claygate	d									17 04										17 34			
Oxshott	d									17 07										17 37			
Cobham & Stoke D'abernon	d									17 11										17 41			
Bookham	d		16 59										17 29										17 59
Effingham Junction	d		17 03							17 15			17 33							17 45			18 03
Horsley	d		17 06							17 18			17 36							17 48			18 06
Clandon	d		17 11							17 23			17 41							17 53			18 11
London Road (Guildford)	d		17 16							17 28			17 46							17 58			18 16
Guildford	a		17 20							17 32			17 50							18 02			18 20

Table 152

Saturdays

29 May to 25 September

London - Chessington South, Dorking, Guildford, Shepperton and Hampton Court

		SW	SW	SW 1	SW	SW	SW	SW	SW	SW	SW	SW	SW	SW 1	SW	SW	SW	SW	SW	SW	SW	SW	SW
London Waterloo 15 ⊖	d	17 12	17 16	17 23	17 20	17 24	17 27	17 33	17 33	17 36	17 39	17 42	17 46	17 53	17 50	17 54	17 57	18 03	18 03	18 06	18 09	18 12	18 16
Vauxhall ⊖	d	17 16	17 20		17 24	17 28	17 31	17 37	17 37	17 40	17 43	17 46	17 50		17 54	17 58	18 01	18 07	18 07	18 10	18 13	18 16	18 20
Clapham Junction 10	d	17 21	17 25		17 29	17 33	17 36	17 42		17 45	17 48	17 51	17 55	18u00	17 59	18 03	18 06	18 12		18 15	18 18	18 21	18 25
Earlsfield	d	17 24	17 28		17 32	17 36	17 39	17 45		17 48	17 51	17 54	17 58		18 02	18 06	18 09	18 15		18 18	18 21	18 24	18 28
Wimbledon 6 ⊖	d	17 28	17 32		17 36	17 40	17 43	17 49		17 52	17 55	17 58	18 02		18 06	18 10	18 13	18 19		18 22	18 25	18 28	18 32
Raynes Park 6	d	17 31	17 35			17 43	17 46			17 55	17 58	18 01	18 05			18 13	18 16			18 25	18 28	18 31	18 35
Motspur Park	d		17 38			17 46					18 01		18 08			18 16					18 31		18 38
Malden Manor	d		17 41										18 11										18 41
Tolworth	d		17 44										18 14										18 44
Chessington North	d		17 47										18 17										18 47
Chessington South	a		17 49										18 19										18 49
Worcester Park	d					17 48					18 03					18 18					18 33		
Stoneleigh	d					17 51					18 06					18 21					18 36		
Ewell West	d					17 54					18 09					18 24					18 39		
Epsom 3	a					17 57					18 16					18 27					18 46		
	d					17 58					18 17					18 28					18 47		
Ashtead	d					18 02					18 21					18 32					18 51		
Leatherhead	d					18 05					18 24					18 35					18 54		
Boxhill & Westhumble	d																						
Dorking 4	a					18 11										18 41							
New Malden 6	d	17 34					17 49			17 58		18 04					18 19			18 28		18 34	
Norbiton	d	17 37					17 52					18 07					18 22					18 37	
Kingston	a	17 40					17 55		18 16			18 10					18 25		18 46			18 40	
	d	17 40					17 59		18 19			18 10					18 29		18 49			18 40	
Hampton Wick	d	17 42					18 01					18 12					18 31					18 42	
Teddington	d	17 45					18 05					18 15					18 35					18 45	
Strawberry Hill	a						18 08										18 38						
Fulwell	d	17 49										18 19										18 49	
Hampton	d	17 53										18 23										18 53	
Kempton Park	d	17 56										18 26										18 56	
Sunbury	d	17 58										18 28										18 58	
Upper Halliford	d	18 00										18 30										19 00	
Shepperton	a	18 03										18 33										19 03	
Berrylands	d									18 00										18 30			
Surbiton 6	d			17 41	17 44			17 57		18 05				18 11	18 14			18 27		18 35			
Thames Ditton	d									18 09										18 39			
Hampton Court	a									18 12										18 42			
Hinchley Wood	d							18 01										18 31					
Claygate	d							18 04										18 34					
Oxshott	d							18 07										18 37					
Cobham & Stoke D'abernon	d							18 11										18 41					
Bookham	d										18 29										18 59		
Effingham Junction 6	d							18 15			18 33							18 45			19 03		
Horsley	d							18 18			18 36							18 48			19 06		
Clandon	d							18 23			18 41							18 53			19 11		
London Road (Guildford)	d							18 28			18 46							18 58			19 16		
Guildford	a							18 32			18 50							19 02			19 20		

Table 152

Saturdays

29 May to 25 September

London - Chessington South, Dorking, Guildford, Shepperton and Hampton Court

		SW 1	SW	SW	SW	SW	SW	SW	SW	SW	SW	SW 1	SW	SW	SW	SW	SW	SW	SW	SW	SW	SW 1
London Waterloo 15 ⊖	d	18 23	18 20	18 24	18 27	18 33	18 33	18 36	18 39	18 42	18 46	18 53	18 50	18 54	18 57	19 03	19 03	19 06	19 09	19 12	19 16	19 23
Vauxhall ⊖	d		18 24	18 28	18 31	18 37	18 37	18 40	18 43	18 46	18 50		18 54	18 58	19 01	19 07	19 07	19 10	19 13	19 16	19 20	
Clapham Junction 10	d		18 29	18 33	18 36	18 42		18 45	18 48	18 51	18 55	19u00	18 59	19 03	19 06	19 12		19 15	19 18	19 21	19 25	
Earlsfield	d		18 32	18 36	18 39	18 45		18 48	18 51	18 54	18 58		19 02	19 06	19 09	19 15		19 18	19 21	19 24	19 28	
Wimbledon 6 ⊖	d		18 36	18 40	18 43	18 49		18 52	18 55	18 58	19 02		19 06	19 10	19 13	19 19		19 22	19 25	19 28	19 32	
Raynes Park 6	d			18 43	18 46			18 55	18 58	19 01	19 05			19 13	19 16			19 25	19 28	19 31	19 35	
Motspur Park	d			18 46					19 01		19 08			19 16					19 31		19 38	
Malden Manor	d										19 11										19 41	
Tolworth	d										19 14										19 44	
Chessington North	d										19 17										19 47	
Chessington South	a										19 19										19 49	
Worcester Park	d			18 48					19 03					19 18					19 33			
Stoneleigh	d			18 51					19 06					19 21					19 36			
Ewell West	d			18 54					19 09					19 24					19 39			
Epsom 3	a			18 57					19 12					19 27					19 42			
	d			18 58					19 17					19 28					19 47			
Ashtead	d			19 02					19 21					19 32					19 51			
Leatherhead	d			19 05					19 24					19 35					19 54			
Boxhill & Westhumble	d																					
Dorking 4	a			19 11										19 41								
New Malden 6	d				18 49			18 58		19 04					19 19			19 28		19 34		
Norbiton	d				18 52					19 07					19 22					19 37		
Kingston	a				18 55		19 16			19 10					19 25		19 46			19 40		
	d				18 59		19 19			19 10					19 29		19 49			19 40		
Hampton Wick	d				19 01					19 12					19 31					19 42		
Teddington	d				19 05					19 15					19 35					19 45		
Strawberry Hill	a				19 08										19 38							
Fulwell	d									19 19										19 49		
Hampton	d									19 23										19 53		
Kempton Park	d									19 26										19 56		
Sunbury	d									19 28										19 58		
Upper Halliford	d									19 30										20 00		
Shepperton	a									19 33										20 03		
Berrylands	d							19 00										19 30				
Surbiton 6	d	18 41	18 44			18 57		19 05				19 11	19 14			19 27		19 35				19 41
Thames Ditton	d							19 09										19 39				
Hampton Court	a							19 12										19 42				
Hinchley Wood	d					19 01										19 31						
Claygate	d					19 04										19 34						
Oxshott	d					19 07										19 37						
Cobham & Stoke D'abernon	d					19 11										19 41						
Bookham	d								19 29										19 59			
Effingham Junction 6	d					19 15			19 33							19 45			20 03			
Horsley	d					19 18			19 36							19 48			20 06			
Clandon	d					19 23			19 41							19 53			20 11			
London Road (Guildford)	d					19 28			19 46							19 58			20 16			
Guildford	a					19 32			19 50							20 02			20 20			

Table 152

Saturdays

29 May to 25 September

London - Chessington South, Dorking, Guildford, Shepperton and Hampton Court

		SW	SW	SW	SW	SW	SW	SW	SW	SW	SW 1	SW	SW	SW	SW	SW	SW	SW	SW	SW	SW 1	SW	SW
London Waterloo 15 ⊖	d	19 20	19 24	19 27	19 33	19 33	19 36	19 39	19 42	19 46	19 53	19 50	19 54	19 57	20 03	20 03	20 06	20 09	20 12	20 16	20 23	20 20	20 24
Vauxhall ⊖	d	19 24	19 28	19 31	19 37	19 37	19 40	19 43	19 46	19 50		19 54	19 58	20 01	20 07	20 07	20 10	20 13	20 16	20 20		20 24	20 28
Clapham Junction 10	d	19 29	19 33	19 36	19 42		19 45	19 48	19 51	19 55	20u00	19 59	20 03	20 06	20 12		20 15	20 18	20 21	20 25		20 29	20 33
Earlsfield	d	19 32	19 36	19 39	19 45		19 48	19 51	19 54	19 58		20 02	20 06	20 09	20 15		20 18	20 21	20 24	20 28		20 32	20 36
Wimbledon 6 ⊖ ⇌	d	19 36	19 40	19 43	19 49		19 52	19 55	19 58	20 02		20 06	20 10	20 13	20 19		20 22	20 25	20 28	20 32		20 36	20 40
Raynes Park 6	d		19 43	19 46			19 55	19 58	20 01	20 05			20 13	20 16			20 25	20 28	20 31	20 35			20 43
Motspur Park	d		19 46					20 01		20 08			20 16					20 31		20 38			20 46
Malden Manor	d									20 11										20 41			
Tolworth	d									20 14										20 44			
Chessington North	d									20 17										20 47			
Chessington South	a									20 19										20 49			
Worcester Park	d		19 48					20 03					20 18					20 33					20 48
Stoneleigh	d		19 51					20 06					20 21					20 36					20 51
Ewell West	d		19 54					20 09					20 24					20 39					20 54
Epsom 3	a		19 57					20 12					20 27					20 42					20 57
	d		19 58					20 17										20 47					
Ashtead	d		20 02					20 21										20 51					
Leatherhead	d		20 05					20 24										20 54					
Boxhill & Westhumble	d																						
Dorking 4	a		20 11															21 00					
New Malden 6	d			19 49			19 58		20 04					20 19			20 28		20 34				
Norbiton	d			19 52					20 07					20 22					20 37				
Kingston	a			19 55		20 16			20 10					20 25		20 46			20 40				
	d			19 59		20 19			20 10					20 29		20 49			20 40				
Hampton Wick	d			20 01					20 12					20 31					20 42				
Teddington	d			20 05					20 15					20 35					20 45				
Strawberry Hill	a			20 08										20 38									
Fulwell	d								20 19										20 49				
Hampton	d								20 23										20 53				
Kempton Park	d								20 26										20 56				
Sunbury	d								20 28										20 58				
Upper Halliford	d								20 30										21 00				
Shepperton	a								20 33										21 03				
Berrylands	d						20 00										20 30						
Surbiton 6	d	19 44			19 57		20 05				20 11	20 14			20 27		20 35				20 41	20 44	
Thames Ditton	d						20 09										20 39						
Hampton Court	a						20 12										20 42						
Hinchley Wood	d				20 01										20 31								
Claygate	d				20 04										20 34								
Oxshott	d				20 07										20 37								
Cobham & Stoke D'abernon	d				20 11										20 41								
Bookham	d							20 29															
Effingham Junction 6	d				20 15			20 33							20 45								
Horsley	d				20 18			20 36							20 48								
Clandon	d				20 23			20 41							20 53								
London Road (Guildford)	d				20 28			20 46							20 58								
Guildford	a				20 32			20 50							21 02								

Table 152

Saturdays

29 May to 25 September

London - Chessington South, Dorking, Guildford, Shepperton and Hampton Court

		SW	SW	SW	SW	SW	SW	SW	SW 1	SW	SW	SW	SW	SW	SW	SW	SW 1	SW	SW	SW	SW	SW
London Waterloo 15 ⊖	d	20 27	20 33	20 33	20 36	20 39	20 42	20 46	20 53	20 50	20 54	20 57	21 03	21 03	21 09	21 12	21 23	21 20	21 24	21 27	21 33	21 33
Vauxhall ⊖	d	20 31	20 37	20 37	20 40	20 43	20 46	20 50		20 54	20 58	21 01	21 07	21 07	21 13	21 16		21 24	21 28	21 31	21 37	21 37
Clapham Junction 10	d	20 36	20 42		20 45	20 48	20 51	20 55	21u00	20 59	21 03	21 06	21 12		21 18	21 21		21 29	21 33	21 36	21 42	
Earlsfield	d	20 39	20 45		20 48	20 51	20 54	20 58		21 02	21 06	21 09	21 15		21 21	21 24		21 32	21 36	21 39	21 45	
Wimbledon 6 ⊖ ⇌	d	20 43	20 49		20 52	20 55	20 58	21 02		21 06	21 10	21 13	21 19		21 25	21 28		21 36	21 40	21 43	21 49	
Raynes Park 6	d	20 46			20 55	20 58	21 01	21 05			21 13	21 16			21 28	21 31			21 43	21 46		
Motspur Park	d					21 01		21 08			21 16				21 31				21 46			
Malden Manor	d							21 11														
Tolworth	d							21 14														
Chessington North	d							21 17														
Chessington South	a							21 19														
Worcester Park	d					21 03					21 18				21 33				21 48			
Stoneleigh	d					21 06					21 21				21 36				21 51			
Ewell West	d					21 09					21 24				21 39				21 54			
Epsom 3	a					21 12					21 27				21 42				21 57			
	d					21 17									21 47							
Ashtead	d					21 21									21 51							
Leatherhead	d					21 24									21 54							
Boxhill & Westhumble	d																					
Dorking 4	a														22 00							
New Malden 6	d	20 49			20 58		21 04					21 19				21 34				21 49		
Norbiton	d	20 52					21 07					21 22				21 37				21 52		
Kingston	a	20 55		21 16			21 10					21 25		21 46		21 40				21 55		22 16
	d	20 59		21 19			21 10					21 29		21 49		21 40				21 59		22 19
Hampton Wick	d	21 01					21 12					21 31				21 42				22 01		
Teddington	d	21 05					21 15					21 35				21 45				22 05		
Strawberry Hill	a	21 08										21 38								22 08		
Fulwell	d						21 19									21 49						
Hampton	d						21 23									21 53						
Kempton Park	d						21 26									21 56						
Sunbury	d						21 28									21 58						
Upper Halliford	d						21 30									22 00						
Shepperton	a						21 33									22 03						
Berrylands	d				21 00																	
Surbiton 6	d		20 57		21 05				21 11	21 14			21 27				21 41	21 44			21 57	
Thames Ditton	d				21 09																	
Hampton Court	a				21 12																	
Hinchley Wood	d		21 01										21 31								22 01	
Claygate	d		21 04										21 34								22 04	
Oxshott	d		21 07										21 37								22 07	
Cobham & Stoke D'abernon	d		21 11										21 41								22 11	
Bookham	d					21 29																
Effingham Junction 6	d		21 15			21 33							21 45								22 15	
Horsley	d		21 18			21 36							21 48								22 18	
Clandon	d		21 23			21 41							21 53								22 23	
London Road (Guildford)	d		21 28			21 46							21 58								22 28	
Guildford	a		21 32			21 50							22 02								22 32	

Table 152

Saturdays
29 May to 25 September

London - Chessington South, Dorking, Guildford, Shepperton and Hampton Court

		SW	SW	SW	SW	SW ■	SW	SW	SW	SW	SW	SW	SW	SW ■	SW	SW	SW	SW	SW	SW	SW	SW ■	SW
London Waterloo ■ ⊖	d	21 36	21 39	21 42	21 46	21 53	21 50	21 54	21 57	22 03	22 03	22 09	22 12	22 23	22 20	22 27	22 33	22 33	22 36	22 39	22 42	22 53	22 50
Vauxhall ⊖	d	21 40	21 43	21 46	21 50		21 54	21 58	22 01	22 07	22 07	22 13	22 16		22 24	22 31	22 37	22 37	22 40	22 43	22 46		22 54
Clapham Junction ■	d	21 45	21 48	21 51	21 55	22u00	21 59	22 03	22 06	22 12		22 18	22 21	22u30	22 29	22 36	22 42		22 45	22 48	22 51	23u00	22 59
Earlsfield	d	21 48	21 51	21 54	21 58		22 02	22 06	22 09	22 15		22 21	22 24		22 32	22 39	22 45		22 48	22 51	22 54		23 02
Wimbledon ■ ⊖	d	21 52	21 55	21 58	22 02		22 06	22 10	22 13	22 19		22 25	22 28		22 36	22 43	22 49		22 52	22 55	22 58		23 06
Raynes Park ■	d	21 55	21 58	22 01	22 05			22 13	22 16			22 28	22 31			22 46			22 55	22 58	23 01		
Motspur Park	d		22 01		22 08			22 16				22 31								23 01			
Malden Manor	d				22 11																		
Tolworth	d				22 14																		
Chessington North	d				22 17																		
Chessington South	a				22 19																		
Worcester Park	d		22 03					22 18				22 33								23 03			
Stoneleigh	d		22 06					22 21				22 36								23 06			
Ewell West	d		22 09					22 24				22 39								23 09			
Epsom ■	a		22 12					22 27				22 42								23 12			
	d		22 17									22 47								23 17			
Ashtead	d		22 21									22 51								23 21			
Leatherhead	d		22 24									22 54								23 24			
Boxhill & Westhumble	d																						
Dorking ■	a											23 00											
New Malden ■	d	21 58		22 04					22 19				22 34			22 49			22 58		23 04		
Norbiton	d			22 07					22 22				22 37			22 52					23 07		
Kingston	a			22 10					22 25		22 46		22 40			22 55		23 16			23 10		
	d			22 10					22 29		22 49		22 40			22 59		23 19			23 10		
Hampton Wick	d			22 12					22 31				22 42			23 01					23 12		
Teddington	d			22 15					22 35				22 45			23 05					23 15		
Strawberry Hill	a								22 38							23 08							
Fulwell	d			22 19									22 49								23 19		
Hampton	d			22 23									22 53								23 23		
Kempton Park	d			22 26									22 56								23 26		
Sunbury	d			22 28									22 58								23 28		
Upper Halliford	d			22 30									23 00								23 30		
Shepperton	a			22 33									23 03								23 33		
Berrylands	d	22 00																	23 00				
Surbiton ■	d	22 05				22 11	22 14			22 27				22 41	22 44		22 57		23 05			23 11	23 14
Thames Ditton	d	22 09																	23 09				
Hampton Court	a	22 12																	23 12				
Hinchley Wood	d									22 31							23 01						
Claygate	d									22 34							23 04						
Oxshott	d									22 37							23 07						
Cobham & Stoke D'abernon	d									22 41							23 11						
Bookham	d		22 29																	23 29			
Effingham Junction ■	d		22 33							22 45							23 15			23 33			
Horsley	d		22 36							22 48							23 18			23 36			
Clandon	d		22 41							22 53							23 23			23 41			
London Road (Guildford)	d		22 46							22 58							23 28			23 46			
Guildford	a		22 50				22 47			23 02							23 32			23 54			

Table 152

Saturdays
29 May to 25 September

London - Chessington South, Dorking, Guildford, Shepperton and Hampton Court

		SW	SW	SW	SW	SW	SW	SW	SW	SW	SW	SW	SW	SW
London Waterloo ■ ⊖	d	22 57	23 00	23 03	23 03	23 09	23 12	23 20	23 27	23 30	23 33	23 42	23 50	23 57
Vauxhall ⊖	d	23 01	23 04	23 07	23 07	23 13	23 16	23 24	23 31	23 34	23 37	23 46	23 54	00 01
Clapham Junction ■	d	23 06	23 09	23 12		23 18	23 21	23 29	23 36	23 39		23 51	23 58	00 06
Earlsfield	d	23 09	23 12	23 15		23 21	23 24	23 32	23 39	23 42		23 54	00 02	00 09
Wimbledon ■ ⊖	d	23 13	23 16	23 19		23 25	23 28	23 36	23 43	23 46		23 58	00 06	00 13
Raynes Park ■	d	23 16	23 19			23 28	23 31		23 46	23 49		00 01		00 16
Motspur Park	d		23 22			23 31						00 04		
Malden Manor	d		23 25											
Tolworth	d		23 28											
Chessington North	d		23 31											
Chessington South	a		23 33											
Worcester Park	d					23 33						00 06		
Stoneleigh	d					23 36						00 09		
Ewell West	d					23 39						00 12		
Epsom ■	a					23 42						00 15		
	d					23 47						00 19		
Ashtead	d					23 51						00 23		
Leatherhead	d					23 54						00 26		
Boxhill & Westhumble	d													
Dorking ■	a					00 01								
New Malden ■	d	23 19					23 34		23 49	23 52				00 19
Norbiton	d	23 22					23 37		23 52					00 22
Kingston	a	23 25			23 46		23 40		23 55		00 16			00 25
	d	23 29			23 49		23 40		23 55					00 25
Hampton Wick	d	23 31					23 42		23 57					00 27
Teddington	d	23 35					23 45		23 59					00 30
Strawberry Hill	a	23 38							00 03					
Fulwell	d						23 49							00 34
Hampton	d						23 53							00 38
Kempton Park	d						23 56							00 41
Sunbury	d						23 58							00 43
Upper Halliford	d						23 59							00 45
Shepperton	a						00 03							00 48
Berrylands	d									23 54				
Surbiton ■	d			23 27				23 44		23 59			00 14	
Thames Ditton	d									00 03				
Hampton Court	a									00 06				
Hinchley Wood	d			23 31									00 18	
Claygate	d			23 34									00 21	
Oxshott	d			23 37									00 24	
Cobham & Stoke D'abernon	d			23 41									00 28	
Bookham	d											00 31		
Effingham Junction ■	d			23 45								00 37	00 32	
Horsley	d			23 48								00 40	00 35	
Clandon	d			23 53								00 45	00 40	
London Road (Guildford)	d			23 58								00 50	00 45	
Guildford	a			00 02								00 54	00 49	

Table 152

Saturdays
from 02 October

London - Chessington South, Dorking, Guildford, Shepperton and Hampton Court

		SW	SW	SW	SW	SW	SW	SW	SW	SW	SW	SW	SW	SW	SW	SW [1]	SW	SW [1]	SW	SW	SW	SW	SW
London Waterloo [15] ⊖	d	23p03	23p09	23p12	23p27	23p30	23p33	23p42	23p50	23p57	00 09	00 15	00 18	00 27	00 42	05 00	05 12	05 20	05 33	05 50	06 03	06 06	06 12
Vauxhall ⊖	d	23p07	23p13	23p16	23p31	23p34	23p37	23p46	23p54	00 01	00 13	00 19	00 22	00 31	00 46	05 04	05 16	05 24	05 37	05 54	06 07	06 10	06 16
Clapham Junction [10]	d	23p12	23p18	23p21	23p36	23p39		23p51	23p58	00 06	00 18	00 24		00 36	00 51	05 09	05 21	05 29		05 59		06 15	06 21
Earlsfield	d	23p15	23p21	23p24	23p39	23p42		23p54	00 02	00 09	00 21	00 27		00s39		05 12	05 24	05 32		06 02		06 18	06 24
Wimbledon [6] ⊖	d	23p19	23p25	23p28	23p43	23p46		23p58	00 06	00 13	00 25	00 31		00 43	01b05	05 16	05 28	05 36		06 06		06 22	06 28
Raynes Park [6]	d		23p28	23p31	23p46	23p49		00 01		00 16		00 34		00 46	01 08		05 31					06 25	06 31
Motspur Park	d		23p31					00 04				00 37											
Malden Manor	d																						
Tolworth	d																						
Chessington North	d																						
Chessington South	a																						
Worcester Park	d		23p33					00 06				00 39											
Stoneleigh	d		23p36					00 09				00 42											
Ewell West	d		23p39					00 12				00 45											
Epsom [3]	a		23p42					00 15				00 48											
	d		23p47					00 19															
Ashtead	d		23p51					00 23															
Leatherhead	d		23p54					00 26															
Boxhill & Westhumble	d		23p59																				
Dorking [4]	a		00 03																				
New Malden [6]	d			23p34	23p49	23p52				00 19				00 49	01 11		05 34					06 28	06 34
Norbiton	d			23p37	23p52					00 22					01 14		05 37						06 37
Kingston	a			23p40	23p55		00 16			00 25			01 00		01 17		05 40		06 16		06 46		06 40
	d			23p40	23p55					00 25					01 17		05 40		06 19		06 49		06 40
Hampton Wick	d			23p42	23p57					00 27					01s19		05 42						06 42
Teddington	d			23p45	23p59					00 30					01s22		05 45						06 45
Strawberry Hill	a				00 03										01 28								
Fulwell	d			23p49						00 34							05 49						06 49
Hampton	d			23p53						00 38							05 53						06 53
Kempton Park	d			23p56						00 41							05 56						06 56
Sunbury	d			23p58						00 43							05 58						06 58
Upper Halliford	d			23p59						00 45							06 00						07 00
Shepperton	a			00 05						00 50							06 05						07 05
Berrylands	d					23p54								00s51								06 30	
Surbiton [6]	d	23p27				23p59			00 14		00 33			00a55		05 24		05 44		06 14		06 35	
Thames Ditton	d					00 03																06 39	
Hampton Court	a					00 06																06 42	
Hinchley Wood	d	23p31							00 18														
Claygate	d	23p34							00 21														
Oxshott	d	23p37							00 24														
Cobham & Stoke D'abernon	d	23p41							00 28														
Bookham	d							00 31															
Effingham Junction [6]	d	23p45						00 37	00 32														
Horsley	d	23p48						00 40	00 35														
Clandon	d	23p53						00 45	00 40														
London Road (Guildford)	d	23p58						00 50	00 45														
Guildford	a	00 05						00 57	00 52		01 06					05 59		06 23					

b arr. 0056

Table 152

Saturdays
from 02 October

London - Chessington South, Dorking, Guildford, Shepperton and Hampton Court

		SW	SW	SW	SW	SW	SW	SW	SW	SW	SW [1]	SW	SW	SW	SW	SW	SW	SW	SW	SW [1]	SW	SW	SW
London Waterloo [15] ⊖	d	06 16	06 20	06 27	06 33	06 33	06 36	06 39	06 42	06 46	06 53	06 50	06 57	07 03	07 03	07 06	07 09	07 12	07 16	07 23	07 20	07 24	07 27
Vauxhall ⊖	d	06 20	06 24	06 31	06 37	06 37	06 40	06 43	06 46	06 50		06 54	07 01	07 07	07 07	07 10	07 13	07 16	07 20		07 24	07 28	07 31
Clapham Junction [10]	d	06 25	06 29	06 36	06 42		06 45	06 48	06 51	06 55	07u00	06 59	07 06	07 12		07 15	07 18	07 21	07 25	07u30	07 29	07 33	07 36
Earlsfield	d	06 28	06 32	06 39	06 45		06 48	06 51	06 54	06 58		07 02	07 09	07 15		07 18	07 21	07 24	07 28		07 32	07 36	07 39
Wimbledon [6] ⊖	d	06 32	06 36	06 43	06 49		06 52	06 55	06 58	07 02		07 06	07 13	07 19		07 22	07 25	07 28	07 32		07 36	07 40	07 43
Raynes Park [6]	d	06 35		06 46			06 55	06 58	07 01	07 05			07 16			07 25	07 28	07 31	07 35			07 43	07 46
Motspur Park	d	06 38						07 01		07 08							07 31		07 38			07 46	
Malden Manor	d	06 41								07 11									07 41				
Tolworth	d	06 44								07 14									07 44				
Chessington North	d	06 47								07 17									07 47				
Chessington South	a	06 49								07 19									07 49				
Worcester Park	d							07 03									07 33					07 48	
Stoneleigh	d							07 06									07 36					07 51	
Ewell West	d							07 09									07 39					07 54	
Epsom [3]	a							07 16									07 46					07 57	
	d							07 17									07 47					07 58	
Ashtead	d							07 21									07 51					08 02	
Leatherhead	d							07 24									07 54					08 05	
Boxhill & Westhumble	d																						
Dorking [4]	a																					08 13	
New Malden [6]	d			06 49			06 58		07 04				07 19			07 28		07 34					07 49
Norbiton	d			06 52					07 07				07 22					07 37					07 52
Kingston	a			06 55		07 16			07 10				07 25		07 46			07 40					07 55
	d			06 59		07 19			07 10				07 29		07 49			07 40					07 59
Hampton Wick	d			07 01					07 12				07 31					07 42					08 01
Teddington	d			07 05					07 15				07 35					07 45					08 05
Strawberry Hill	a			07 08									07 38										08 08
Fulwell	d								07 19									07 49					
Hampton	d								07 23									07 53					
Kempton Park	d								07 26									07 56					
Sunbury	d								07 28									07 58					
Upper Halliford	d								07 30									08 00					
Shepperton	a								07 35									08 05					
Berrylands	d						07 00									07 30							
Surbiton [6]	d		06 44		06 57		07 05				07 11	07 14		07 27		07 35				07 41	07 44		
Thames Ditton	d						07 09									07 39							
Hampton Court	a						07 12									07 42							
Hinchley Wood	d				07 01									07 31									
Claygate	d				07 04									07 34									
Oxshott	d				07 07									07 37									
Cobham & Stoke D'abernon	d				07 11									07 41									
Bookham	d							07 29									07 59						
Effingham Junction [6]	d				07 15			07 33						07 45			08 03						
Horsley	d				07 18			07 36						07 48			08 06						
Clandon	d				07 23			07 41						07 53			08 11						
London Road (Guildford)	d				07 28			07 46						07 58			08 16						
Guildford	a				07 35			07 53						08 05			08 23						

Table 152

Saturdays
from 02 October

London - Chessington South, Dorking, Guildford, Shepperton and Hampton Court

		SW	SW	SW	SW	SW	SW	SW ■	SW	SW	SW	SW	SW	SW	SW	SW	SW	SW ■	SW	SW	SW	SW
London Waterloo ⊖	d	07 33	07 33	07 36	07 39	07 42	07 46	07 53	07 50	07 54	07 57	08 03	08 03	08 06	08 09	08 12	08 16	08 23	08 20	08 24	08 27	08 33
Vauxhall ⊖	d	07 37	07 37	07 40	07 43	07 46	07 50		07 54	07 58	08 01	08 07	08 07	08 10	08 13	08 16	08 20		08 24	08 28	08 31	08 37
Clapham Junction	d	07 42		07 45	07 48	07 51	07 55	08u00	07 59	08 03	08 06	08 12		08 15	08 18	08 21	08 25		08 29	08 33	08 36	08 42
Earlsfield	d	07 45		07 48	07 51	07 54	07 58		08 02	08 06	08 09	08 15		08 18	08 21	08 24	08 28		08 32	08 36	08 39	08 45
Wimbledon ⊖	d	07 49		07 52	07 55	07 58	08 02		08 06	08 10	08 13	08 19		08 22	08 25	08 28	08 32		08 36	08 40	08 43	08 49
Raynes Park	d			07 55	07 58	08 01	08 05			08 13	08 16			08 25	08 28	08 31	08 35			08 43	08 46	
Motspur Park	d				08 01		08 08			08 16					08 31		08 38			08 46		
Malden Manor	d						08 11										08 41					
Tolworth	d						08 14										08 44					
Chessington North	d						08 17										08 47					
Chessington South	a						08 19										08 49					
Worcester Park	d				08 03					08 18					08 33					08 48		
Stoneleigh	d				08 06					08 21					08 36					08 51		
Ewell West	d				08 09					08 24					08 39					08 54		
Epsom	a				08 16					08 27					08 46					08 57		
	d				08 17					08 28					08 47					08 58		
Ashtead	d				08 21					08 32					08 51					09 02		
Leatherhead	d				08 24					08 35					08 54					09 05		
Boxhill & Westhumble	d																					
Dorking	a									08 43										09 13		
New Malden	d			07 58		08 04					08 19			08 28		08 34					08 49	
Norbiton	d					08 07					08 22					08 37					08 52	
Kingston	a		08 16			08 10					08 25		08 46			08 40					08 55	
	d		08 19			08 10					08 29		08 49			08 40					08 59	
Hampton Wick	d					08 12					08 31					08 42					09 01	
Teddington	d					08 15					08 35					08 45					09 05	
Strawberry Hill	a										08 38										09 08	
Fulwell	d					08 19										08 49						
Hampton	d					08 23										08 53						
Kempton Park	d					08 26										08 56						
Sunbury	d					08 28										08 58						
Upper Halliford	d					08 30										09 00						
Shepperton	a					08 35										09 05						
Berrylands	d			08 00										08 30								
Surbiton	d	07 57		08 05				08 11	08 14			08 27		08 35				08 41	08 44			08 57
Thames Ditton	d			08 09										08 39								
Hampton Court	a			08 12										08 42								
Hinchley Wood	d	08 01										08 31										09 01
Claygate	d	08 04										08 34										09 04
Oxshott	d	08 07										08 37										09 07
Cobham & Stoke D'abernon	d	08 11										08 41										09 11
Bookham	d				08 29										08 59							
Effingham Junction	d	08 15			08 33							08 45			09 03							09 15
Horsley	d	08 18			08 36							08 48			09 06							09 18
Clandon	d	08 23			08 41							08 53			09 11							09 23
London Road (Guildford)	d	08 28			08 46							08 58			09 16							09 28
Guildford	a	08 35			08 53							09 05			09 23							09 35

Table 152

Saturdays
from 02 October

London - Chessington South, Dorking, Guildford, Shepperton and Hampton Court

		SW	SW	SW	SW	SW	SW ■	SW	SW	SW	SW	SW	SW	SW	SW	SW	SW ■	SW	SW	SW	SW	SW	SW
London Waterloo ⊖	d	08 33	08 36	08 39	08 42	08 46	08 53	08 50	08 54	08 57	09 03	09 03	09 06	09 09	09 12	09 16	09 23	09 20	09 24	09 27	09 33	09 33	09 36
Vauxhall ⊖	d	08 37	08 40	08 43	08 46	08 50		08 54	08 58	09 01	09 07	09 07	09 10	09 13	09 16	09 20		09 24	09 28	09 31	09 37	09 37	09 40
Clapham Junction	d		08 45	08 48	08 51	08 55	09u00	08 59	09 03	09 06	09 12		09 15	09 18	09 21	09 25		09 29	09 33	09 36	09 42		09 45
Earlsfield	d		08 48	08 51	08 54	08 58		09 02	09 06	09 09	09 15		09 18	09 21	09 24	09 28		09 32	09 36	09 39	09 45		09 48
Wimbledon ⊖	d		08 52	08 55	08 58	09 02		09 06	09 10	09 13	09 19		09 22	09 25	09 28	09 32		09 36	09 40	09 43	09 49		09 52
Raynes Park	d		08 55	08 58	09 01	09 05			09 13	09 16			09 25	09 28	09 31	09 35			09 43	09 46			09 55
Motspur Park	d			09 01		09 08			09 16					09 31		09 38			09 46				
Malden Manor	d					09 11										09 41							
Tolworth	d					09 14										09 44							
Chessington North	d					09 17										09 47							
Chessington South	a					09 19										09 49							
Worcester Park	d			09 03					09 18					09 33					09 48				
Stoneleigh	d			09 06					09 21					09 36					09 51				
Ewell West	d			09 09					09 24					09 39					09 54				
Epsom	a			09 16					09 27					09 46					09 57				
	d			09 17					09 28					09 47					09 58				
Ashtead	d			09 21					09 32					09 51					10 02				
Leatherhead	d			09 24					09 35					09 54					10 05				
Boxhill & Westhumble	d																						
Dorking	a								09 43										10 13				
New Malden	d		08 58		09 04					09 19			09 28		09 34					09 49			09 58
Norbiton	d				09 07					09 22					09 37					09 52			
Kingston	a	09 16			09 10					09 25		09 46			09 40					09 55		10 16	
	d	09 19			09 10					09 29		09 49			09 40					09 59		10 19	
Hampton Wick	d				09 12					09 31					09 42					10 01			
Teddington	d				09 15					09 35					09 45					10 05			
Strawberry Hill	a									09 38										10 08			
Fulwell	d				09 19										09 49								
Hampton	d				09 23										09 53								
Kempton Park	d				09 26										09 56								
Sunbury	d				09 28										09 58								
Upper Halliford	d				09 30										10 00								
Shepperton	a				09 35										10 05								
Berrylands	d		09 00										09 30										10 00
Surbiton	d		09 05				09 11	09 14			09 27		09 35				09 41	09 44			09 57		10 05
Thames Ditton	d		09 09										09 39										10 09
Hampton Court	a		09 12										09 42										10 12
Hinchley Wood	d										09 31										10 01		
Claygate	d										09 34										10 04		
Oxshott	d										09 37										10 07		
Cobham & Stoke D'abernon	d										09 41										10 11		
Bookham	d			09 29										09 59									
Effingham Junction	d			09 33							09 45			10 03							10 15		
Horsley	d			09 36							09 48			10 06							10 18		
Clandon	d			09 41							09 53			10 11							10 23		
London Road (Guildford)	d			09 46							09 58			10 16							10 28		
Guildford	a			09 53							10 05			10 23							10 35		

Table 152

Saturdays from 02 October

London - Chessington South, Dorking, Guildford, Shepperton and Hampton Court

		SW	SW	SW	SW ■	SW	SW	SW	SW	SW	SW	SW	SW	SW	SW ■	SW	SW	SW	SW	SW	SW	SW
London Waterloo ⊖	d	09 39	09 42	09 46	09 53	09 50	09 54	09 57	10 03	10 03	10 06	10 09	10 12	10 16	10 23	10 20	10 24	10 27	10 33	10 33	10 36	10 39
Vauxhall ⊖	d	09 43	09 46	09 50		09 54	09 58	10 01	10 07	10 07	10 10	10 13	10 16	10 20		10 24	10 28	10 31	10 37	10 37	10 40	10 43
Clapham Junction	d	09 48	09 51	09 55	10u00	09 59	10 03	10 06	10 12		10 15	10 18	10 21	10 25		10 29	10 33	10 36	10 42		10 45	10 48
Earlsfield	d	09 51	09 54	09 58		10 02	10 06	10 09	10 15		10 18	10 21	10 24	10 28		10 32	10 36	10 39	10 45		10 48	10 51
Wimbledon ⊖	d	09 55	09 58	10 02		10 06	10 10	10 13	10 19		10 22	10 25	10 28	10 32		10 36	10 40	10 43	10 49		10 52	10 55
Raynes Park	d	09 58	10 01	10 05			10 13	10 16			10 25	10 28	10 31	10 35			10 43	10 46			10 55	10 58
Motspur Park	d	10 01		10 08			10 16					10 31		10 38			10 46					11 01
Malden Manor	d			10 11										10 41								
Tolworth	d			10 14										10 44								
Chessington North	d			10 17										10 47								
Chessington South	a			10 19										10 49								
Worcester Park	d	10 03					10 18					10 33					10 48					11 03
Stoneleigh	d	10 06					10 21					10 36					10 51					11 06
Ewell West	d	10 09					10 24					10 39					10 54					11 09
Epsom	a	10 16					10 27					10 46					10 57					11 16
	d	10 17					10 28					10 47					10 58					11 17
Ashtead	d	10 21					10 32					10 51					11 02					11 21
Leatherhead	d	10 24					10 35					10 54					11 05					11 24
Boxhill & Westhumble	d																					
Dorking	a						10 43										11 13					
New Malden	d		10 04					10 19			10 28		10 34					10 49			10 58	
Norbiton	d		10 07					10 22					10 37					10 52				
Kingston	a		10 10					10 25		10 46			10 40					10 55		11 16		
	d		10 10					10 29		10 49			10 40					10 59		11 19		
Hampton Wick	d		10 12					10 31					10 42					11 01				
Teddington	d		10 15					10 35					10 45					11 05				
Strawberry Hill	a							10 38										11 08				
Fulwell	d		10 19										10 49									
Hampton	d		10 23										10 53									
Kempton Park	d		10 26										10 56									
Sunbury	d		10 28										10 58									
Upper Halliford	d		10 30										11 00									
Shepperton	a		10 35										11 05									
Berrylands	d										10 30										11 00	
Surbiton	d				10 11	10 14			10 27		10 35				10 41	10 44			10 57		11 05	
Thames Ditton	d										10 39										11 09	
Hampton Court	a										10 42										11 12	
Hinchley Wood	d								10 31										11 01			
Claygate	d								10 34										11 04			
Oxshott	d								10 37										11 07			
Cobham & Stoke D'abernon	d								10 41										11 11			
Bookham	d	10 29										10 59										11 29
Effingham Junction	d	10 33							10 45			11 03							11 15			11 33
Horsley	d	10 36							10 48			11 06							11 18			11 36
Clandon	d	10 41							10 53			11 11							11 23			11 41
London Road (Guildford)	d	10 46							10 58			11 16							11 28			11 46
Guildford	a	10 53							11 05			11 23							11 35			11 53

Table 152

Saturdays from 02 October

London - Chessington South, Dorking, Guildford, Shepperton and Hampton Court

		SW	SW	SW ■	SW	SW	SW	SW	SW	SW	SW	SW	SW	SW ■	SW	SW	SW	SW	SW	SW	SW	SW	SW
London Waterloo ⊖	d	10 42	10 46	10 53	10 50	10 54	10 57	11 03	11 03	11 06	11 09	11 12	11 16	11 23	11 20	11 24	11 27	11 33	11 33	11 36	11 39	11 42	11 46
Vauxhall ⊖	d	10 46	10 50		10 54	10 58	11 01	11 07	11 07	11 10	11 13	11 16	11 20		11 24	11 28	11 31	11 37	11 37	11 40	11 43	11 46	11 50
Clapham Junction	d	10 51	10 55	11u00	10 59	11 03	11 06	11 12		11 15	11 18	11 21	11 25		11 29	11 33	11 36	11 42		11 45	11 48	11 51	11 55
Earlsfield	d	10 54	10 58		11 02	11 06	11 09	11 15		11 18	11 21	11 24	11 28		11 32	11 36	11 39	11 45		11 48	11 51	11 54	11 58
Wimbledon ⊖	d	10 58	11 02		11 06	11 10	11 13	11 19		11 22	11 25	11 28	11 32		11 36	11 40	11 43	11 49		11 52	11 55	11 58	12 02
Raynes Park	d	11 01	11 05			11 13	11 16			11 25	11 28	11 31	11 35			11 43	11 46			11 55	11 58	12 01	12 05
Motspur Park	d		11 08			11 16					11 31		11 38			11 46					12 01		12 08
Malden Manor	d		11 11										11 41										12 11
Tolworth	d		11 14										11 44										12 14
Chessington North	d		11 17										11 47										12 17
Chessington South	a		11 19										11 49										12 19
Worcester Park	d					11 18					11 33					11 48					12 03		
Stoneleigh	d					11 21					11 36					11 51					12 06		
Ewell West	d					11 24					11 39					11 54					12 09		
Epsom	a					11 27					11 46					11 57					12 16		
	d					11 28					11 47					11 58					12 17		
Ashtead	d					11 32					11 51					12 02					12 21		
Leatherhead	d					11 35					11 54					12 05					12 24		
Boxhill & Westhumble	d																						
Dorking	a					11 43										12 13							
New Malden	d	11 04					11 19			11 28		11 34					11 49			11 58		12 04	
Norbiton	d	11 07					11 22					11 37					11 52					12 07	
Kingston	a	11 10					11 25		11 46			11 40					11 55		12 16			12 10	
	d	11 10					11 29		11 49			11 40					11 59		12 19			12 10	
Hampton Wick	d	11 12					11 31					11 42					12 01					12 12	
Teddington	d	11 15					11 35					11 45					12 05					12 15	
Strawberry Hill	a						11 38										12 08						
Fulwell	d	11 19										11 49										12 19	
Hampton	d	11 23										11 53										12 23	
Kempton Park	d	11 26										11 56										12 26	
Sunbury	d	11 28										11 58										12 28	
Upper Halliford	d	11 30										12 00										12 30	
Shepperton	a	11 35										12 05										12 35	
Berrylands	d									11 30										12 00			
Surbiton	d			11 11	11 14			11 27		11 35				11 41	11 44			11 57		12 05			
Thames Ditton	d									11 39										12 09			
Hampton Court	a									11 42										12 12			
Hinchley Wood	d							11 31										12 01					
Claygate	d							11 34										12 04					
Oxshott	d							11 37										12 07					
Cobham & Stoke D'abernon	d							11 41										12 11					
Bookham	d										11 59										12 29		
Effingham Junction	d							11 45			12 03							12 15			12 33		
Horsley	d							11 48			12 06							12 18			12 36		
Clandon	d							11 53			12 11							12 23			12 41		
London Road (Guildford)	d							11 58			12 16							12 28			12 46		
Guildford	a							12 05			12 23							12 35			12 53		

Saturdays
from 02 October

London - Chessington South, Dorking, Guildford, Shepperton and Hampton Court

		SW 1	SW	SW	SW	SW		SW	SW	SW	SW	SW	SW 1	SW	SW	SW		SW	SW	SW	SW	SW	SW	SW 1	SW
London Waterloo 15 ⊖	d	11 53	11 50	11 54	11 57	12 03		12 03	12 06	12 09	12 12	12 16	12 23	12 20	12 24	12 27		12 33	12 33	12 36	12 39	12 42	12 46	12 53	12 50
Vauxhall ⊖	d		11 54	11 58	12 01	12 07		12 07	12 10	12 13	12 16	12 20		12 24	12 28	12 31		12 37	12 37	12 40	12 43	12 46	12 50		12 54
Clapham Junction 10	d	12u00	11 59	12 03	12 06	12 12			12 15	12 18	12 21	12 25		12 29	12 33	12 36		12 42		12 45	12 48	12 51	12 55	13u00	12 59
Earlsfield	d		12 02	12 06	12 09	12 15			12 18	12 21	12 24	12 28		12 32	12 36	12 39		12 45		12 48	12 51	12 54	12 58		13 02
Wimbledon 6 ⊖	d		12 06	12 10	12 13	12 19			12 22	12 25	12 28	12 32		12 36	12 40	12 43		12 49		12 52	12 55	12 58	13 02		13 06
Raynes Park 6	d			12 13	12 16				12 25	12 28	12 31	12 35			12 43	12 46				12 55	12 58	13 01	13 05		
Motspur Park	d			12 16						12 31		12 38			12 46						13 01		13 08		
Malden Manor	d											12 41											13 11		
Tolworth	d											12 44											13 14		
Chessington North	d											12 47											13 17		
Chessington South	a											12 49											13 19		
Worcester Park	d			12 18						12 33					12 48						13 03				
Stoneleigh	d			12 21						12 36					12 51						13 06				
Ewell West	d			12 24						12 39					12 54						13 09				
Epsom 3	a			12 27						12 46					12 57						13 16				
	d			12 28						12 47					12 58						13 17				
Ashtead	d			12 32						12 51					13 02						13 21				
Leatherhead	d			12 35						12 54					13 05						13 24				
Boxhill & Westhumble	d																								
Dorking 4	a			12 43											13 13										
New Malden 6	d				12 19				12 28		12 34					12 49				12 58		13 04			
Norbiton	d				12 22						12 37					12 52						13 07			
Kingston	a				12 25			12 46			12 40					12 55			13 16			13 10			
	d				12 29			12 49			12 40					12 59			13 19			13 10			
Hampton Wick	d				12 31						12 42					13 01						13 12			
Teddington	d				12 35						12 45					13 05						13 15			
Strawberry Hill	a				12 38											13 08									
Fulwell	d										12 49											13 19			
Hampton	d										12 53											13 23			
Kempton Park	d										12 56											13 26			
Sunbury	d										12 58											13 28			
Upper Halliford	d										13 00											13 30			
Shepperton	a										13 05											13 35			
Berrylands	d								12 30											13 00					
Surbiton 6	d	12 11	12 14			12 27			12 35				12 41	12 44				12 57		13 05				13 11	13 14
Thames Ditton	d								12 39											13 09					
Hampton Court	a								12 42											13 12					
Hinchley Wood	d					12 31												13 01							
Claygate	d					12 34												13 04							
Oxshott	d					12 37												13 07							
Cobham & Stoke D'abernon	d					12 41												13 11							
Bookham	d									12 59											13 29				
Effingham Junction 6	d					12 45				13 03								13 15			13 33				
Horsley	d					12 48				13 06								13 18			13 36				
Clandon	d					12 53				13 11								13 23			13 41				
London Road (Guildford)	d					12 58				13 16								13 28			13 46				
Guildford	a					13 05				13 23								13 35			13 53				

Saturdays
from 02 October

London - Chessington South, Dorking, Guildford, Shepperton and Hampton Court

		SW		SW	SW	SW	SW	SW	SW	SW	SW 1	SW		SW	SW	SW	SW	SW	SW	SW	SW	SW 1		SW	SW
London Waterloo 15 ⊖	d	12 54		12 57	13 03	13 03	13 06	13 09	13 12	13 16	13 23	13 20		13 24	13 27	13 33	13 33	13 36	13 39	13 42	13 46	13 53		13 50	13 54
Vauxhall ⊖	d	12 58		13 01	13 07	13 07	13 10	13 13	13 16	13 20		13 24		13 28	13 31	13 37	13 37	13 40	13 43	13 46	13 50			13 54	13 58
Clapham Junction 10	d	13 03		13 06	13 12		13 15	13 18	13 21	13 25		13 29		13 33	13 36	13 42		13 45	13 48	13 51	13 55	14u00		13 59	14 03
Earlsfield	d	13 06		13 09	13 15		13 18	13 21	13 24	13 28		13 32		13 36	13 39	13 45		13 48	13 51	13 54	13 58			14 02	14 06
Wimbledon 6 ⊖	d	13 10		13 13	13 19		13 22	13 25	13 28	13 32		13 36		13 40	13 43	13 49		13 52	13 55	13 58	14 02			14 06	14 10
Raynes Park 6	d	13 13		13 16			13 25	13 28	13 31	13 35				13 43	13 46			13 55	13 58	14 01	14 05				14 13
Motspur Park	d	13 16						13 31		13 38				13 46					14 01		14 08				14 16
Malden Manor	d									13 41											14 11				
Tolworth	d									13 44											14 14				
Chessington North	d									13 47											14 17				
Chessington South	a									13 49											14 19				
Worcester Park	d	13 18						13 33						13 48					14 03						14 18
Stoneleigh	d	13 21						13 36						13 51					14 06						14 21
Ewell West	d	13 24						13 39						13 54					14 09						14 24
Epsom 3	a	13 27						13 46						13 57					14 16						14 27
	d	13 28						13 47						13 58					14 17						14 28
Ashtead	d	13 32						13 51						14 02					14 21						14 32
Leatherhead	d	13 35						13 54						14 05					14 24						14 35
Boxhill & Westhumble	d																								
Dorking 4	a	13 43												14 13											14 43
New Malden 6	d			13 19			13 28		13 34						13 49			13 58		14 04					
Norbiton	d			13 22					13 37						13 52					14 07					
Kingston	a			13 25		13 46			13 40						13 55		14 16			14 10					
	d			13 29		13 49			13 40						13 59		14 19			14 10					
Hampton Wick	d			13 31					13 42						14 01					14 12					
Teddington	d			13 35					13 45						14 05					14 15					
Strawberry Hill	a			13 38											14 08										
Fulwell	d								13 49											14 19					
Hampton	d								13 53											14 23					
Kempton Park	d								13 56											14 26					
Sunbury	d								13 58											14 28					
Upper Halliford	d								14 00											14 30					
Shepperton	a								14 05											14 35					
Berrylands	d						13 30											14 00							
Surbiton 6	d				13 27		13 35				13 41	13 44				13 57		14 05				14 11		14 14	
Thames Ditton	d						13 39											14 09							
Hampton Court	a						13 42											14 12							
Hinchley Wood	d				13 31											14 01									
Claygate	d				13 34											14 04									
Oxshott	d				13 37											14 07									
Cobham & Stoke D'abernon	d				13 41											14 11									
Bookham	d							13 59											14 29						
Effingham Junction 6	d				13 45			14 03								14 15			14 33						
Horsley	d				13 48			14 06								14 18			14 36						
Clandon	d				13 53			14 11								14 23			14 41						
London Road (Guildford)	d				13 58			14 16								14 28			14 46						
Guildford	a				14 05			14 23								14 35			14 53						

Table 152

Saturdays
from 02 October

London - Chessington South, Dorking, Guildford, Shepperton and Hampton Court

		SW	SW	SW	SW	SW	SW	SW		SW 1	SW	SW	SW	SW	SW	SW	SW	SW		SW	SW 1	SW	SW	SW	SW
London Waterloo 15 ⊖	d	13 57	14 03	14 03	14 06	14 09	14 12	14 16		14 23	14 20	14 24	14 27	14 33	14 33	14 36	14 39	14 42		14 46	14 53	14 50	14 54	14 57	15 03
Vauxhall ⊖	d	14 01	14 07	14 07	14 10	14 13	14 16	14 20			14 24	14 28	14 31	14 37	14 37	14 40	14 43	14 46		14 50		14 54	14 58	15 01	15 07
Clapham Junction 10	d	14 06	14 12		14 15	14 18	14 21	14 25			14 29	14 33	14 36	14 42		14 45	14 48	14 51		14 55	15u00	14 59	15 03	15 06	15 12
Earlsfield	d	14 09	14 15		14 18	14 21	14 24	14 28			14 32	14 36	14 39	14 45		14 48	14 51	14 54		14 58		15 02	15 06	15 09	15 15
Wimbledon 6 ⊖	d	14 13	14 19		14 22	14 25	14 28	14 32			14 36	14 40	14 43	14 49		14 52	14 55	14 58		15 02		15 06	15 10	15 13	15 19
Raynes Park 6	d	14 16			14 25	14 28	14 31	14 35				14 43	14 46			14 55	14 58	15 01		15 05			15 13	15 16	
Motspur Park	d					14 31		14 38				14 46					15 01			15 08			15 16		
Malden Manor	d							14 41												15 11					
Tolworth	d							14 44												15 14					
Chessington North	d							14 47												15 17					
Chessington South	a							14 49												15 19					
Worcester Park	d					14 33						14 48					15 03						15 18		
Stoneleigh	d					14 36						14 51					15 06						15 21		
Ewell West	d					14 39						14 54					15 09						15 24		
Epsom 3	a					14 46						14 57					15 16						15 27		
	d					14 47						14 58					15 17						15 28		
Ashtead	d					14 51						15 02					15 21						15 32		
Leatherhead	d					14 54						15 05					15 24						15 35		
Boxhill & Westhumble	d																								
Dorking 4	a											15 13											15 43		
New Malden 6	d	14 19			14 28		14 34						14 49			14 58		15 04						15 19	
Norbiton	d	14 22					14 37						14 52					15 07						15 22	
Kingston	a	14 25		14 46			14 40						14 55		15 16			15 10						15 25	
	d	14 29		14 49			14 40						14 59		15 19			15 10						15 29	
Hampton Wick	d	14 31					14 42						15 01					15 12						15 31	
Teddington	d	14 35					14 45						15 05					15 15						15 35	
Strawberry Hill	a	14 38											15 08											15 38	
Fulwell	d						14 49											15 19							
Hampton	d						14 53											15 23							
Kempton Park	d						14 56											15 26							
Sunbury	d						14 58											15 28							
Upper Halliford	d						15 00											15 30							
Shepperton	a						15 05											15 35							
Berrylands	d				14 30											15 00									
Surbiton 6	d		14 27		14 35					14 41	14 44			14 57		15 05					15 11	15 14			15 27
Thames Ditton	d				14 39											15 09									
Hampton Court	a				14 42											15 12									
Hinchley Wood	d		14 31											15 01											15 31
Claygate	d		14 34											15 04											15 34
Oxshott	d		14 37											15 07											15 37
Cobham & Stoke D'abernon	d		14 41											15 11											15 41
Bookham	d					14 59											15 29								
Effingham Junction 6	d		14 45			15 03								15 15			15 33								15 45
Horsley	d		14 48			15 06								15 18			15 36								15 48
Clandon	d		14 53			15 11								15 23			15 41								15 53
London Road (Guildford)	d		14 58			15 16								15 28			15 46								15 58
Guildford	a		15 05			15 23								15 35			15 53								16 05

Table 152

Saturdays
from 02 October

London - Chessington South, Dorking, Guildford, Shepperton and Hampton Court

		SW	SW	SW		SW	SW	SW 1	SW	SW	SW	SW	SW	SW		SW	SW	SW	SW 1	SW	SW	SW	SW	SW	
London Waterloo 15 ⊖	d	15 03	15 06	15 09		15 12	15 16	15 23	15 20	15 24	15 27	15 33	15 33	15 36		15 39	15 42	15 46	15 53	15 50	15 54	15 57	16 03	16 03	
Vauxhall ⊖	d	15 07	15 10	15 13		15 16	15 20		15 24	15 28	15 31	15 37	15 37	15 40		15 43	15 46	15 50		15 54	15 58	16 01	16 07	16 07	
Clapham Junction 10	d		15 15	15 18		15 21	15 25		15 29	15 33	15 36	15 42		15 45		15 48	15 51	15 55	16u00	15 59	16 03	16 06	16 12		
Earlsfield	d		15 18	15 21		15 24	15 28		15 32	15 36	15 39	15 45		15 48		15 51	15 54	15 58		16 02	16 06	16 09	16 15		
Wimbledon 6 ⊖	d		15 22	15 25		15 28	15 32		15 36	15 40	15 43	15 49		15 52		15 55	15 58	16 02		16 06	16 10	16 13	16 19		
Raynes Park 6	d		15 25	15 28		15 31	15 35			15 43	15 46			15 55		15 58	16 01	16 05			16 13	16 16			
Motspur Park	d			15 31			15 38			15 46						16 01		16 08			16 16				
Malden Manor	d						15 41											16 11							
Tolworth	d						15 44											16 14							
Chessington North	d						15 47											16 17							
Chessington South	a						15 49											16 19							
Worcester Park	d			15 33						15 48						16 03					16 18				
Stoneleigh	d			15 36						15 51						16 06					16 21				
Ewell West	d			15 39						15 54						16 09					16 24				
Epsom 3	a			15 46						15 57						16 16					16 27				
	d			15 47						15 58						16 17					15 28				
Ashtead	d			15 51						16 02						16 21					16 32				
Leatherhead	d			15 54						16 05						16 24					16 35				
Boxhill & Westhumble	d																								
Dorking 4	a									16 13											16 43				
New Malden 6	d		15 28			15 34					15 49			15 58			16 04					16 19			
Norbiton	d					15 37					15 52						16 07					16 22			
Kingston	a	15 46				15 40					15 55		16 16				16 10					16 25		16 46	
	d	15 49				15 40					15 59		16 19				16 10					16 29		16 49	
Hampton Wick	d					15 42					16 01						16 12					16 31			
Teddington	d					15 45					16 05						16 15					16 35			
Strawberry Hill	a										16 08											16 38			
Fulwell	d					15 49											16 19								
Hampton	d					15 53											16 23								
Kempton Park	d					15 56											16 26								
Sunbury	d					15 58											16 28								
Upper Halliford	d					16 00											16 30								
Shepperton	a					16 05											16 35								
Berrylands	d		15 30											16 00											
Surbiton 6	d		15 35					15 41	15 44			15 57		16 05					16 11	16 14			16 27		
Thames Ditton	d		15 39											16 09											
Hampton Court	a		15 42											16 12											
Hinchley Wood	d											16 01											16 31		
Claygate	d											16 04											16 34		
Oxshott	d											16 07											16 37		
Cobham & Stoke D'abernon	d											16 11											16 41		
Bookham	d			15 59												16 29									
Effingham Junction 6	d			16 03								16 15				16 33							16 45		
Horsley	d			16 06								16 18				16 36							16 48		
Clandon	d			16 11								16 23				16 41							16 53		
London Road (Guildford)	d			16 16								16 28				16 46							16 58		
Guildford	a			16 23								16 35				16 53							17 05		

Table 152

Saturdays
from 02 October

London - Chessington South, Dorking, Guildford, Shepperton and Hampton Court

		SW	SW	SW	SW	SW 1	SW	SW	SW	SW	SW	SW	SW	SW	SW	SW 1	SW	SW	SW	SW	SW	SW	SW
London Waterloo ⊖	d	16 06	16 09	16 12	16 16	16 23	16 20	16 24	16 27	16 33	16 33	16 36	16 39	16 42	16 46	16 53	16 50	16 54	16 57	17 03	17 03	17 06	17 09
Vauxhall ⊖	d	16 10	16 13	16 16	16 20		16 24	16 28	16 31	16 37	16 37	16 40	16 43	16 46	16 50		16 54	16 58	17 01	17 07	17 07	17 10	17 13
Clapham Junction	d	16 15	16 18	16 21	16 25		16 29	16 33	16 36	16 42		16 45	16 48	16 51	16 55	17u00	16 59	17 03	17 06	17 12		17 15	17 18
Earlsfield	d	16 18	16 21	16 24	16 28		16 32	16 36	16 39	16 45		16 48	16 51	16 54	16 58		17 02	17 06	17 09	17 15		17 18	17 21
Wimbledon ⊖	d	16 22	16 25	16 28	16 32		16 36	16 40	16 43	16 49		16 52	16 55	16 58	17 02		17 06	17 10	17 13	17 19		17 22	17 25
Raynes Park	d	16 25	16 28	16 31	16 35			16 43	16 46			16 55	16 58	17 01	17 05			17 13	17 16			17 25	17 28
Motspur Park	d		16 31		16 38			16 46					17 01		17 08			17 16					17 31
Malden Manor	d				16 41										17 11								
Tolworth	d				16 44										17 14								
Chessington North	d				16 47										17 17								
Chessington South	a				16 49										17 19								
Worcester Park	d		16 33					16 48					17 03					17 18					17 33
Stoneleigh	d		16 36					16 51					17 06					17 21					17 36
Ewell West	d		16 39					16 54					17 09					17 24					17 39
Epsom	a		16 46					16 57					17 16					17 27					17 46
	d		16 47					16 58					17 17					17 28					17 47
Ashtead	d		16 51					17 02					17 21					17 32					17 51
Leatherhead	d		16 54					17 05					17 24					17 35					17 54
Boxhill & Westhumble	d																						
Dorking	a							17 13										17 43					
New Malden	d	16 28		16 34					16 49			16 58		17 04					17 19			17 28	
Norbiton	d			16 37					16 52					17 07					17 22				
Kingston	a			16 40					16 55		17 16			17 10					17 25		17 46		
	d			16 40					16 59		17 19			17 10					17 29		17 49		
Hampton Wick	d			16 42					17 01					17 12					17 31				
Teddington	d			16 45					17 05					17 15					17 35				
Strawberry Hill	a								17 08										17 38				
Fulwell	d			16 49										17 19									
Hampton	d			16 53										17 23									
Kempton Park	d			16 56										17 26									
Sunbury	d			16 58										17 28									
Upper Halliford	d			17 00										17 30									
Shepperton	a			17 05										17 35									
Berrylands	d	16 30										17 00										17 30	
Surbiton	d	16 35				16 41	16 44			16 57		17 05				17 11	17 14			17 27		17 35	
Thames Ditton	d	16 39										17 09										17 39	
Hampton Court	a	16 42										17 12										17 42	
Hinchley Wood	d									17 01										17 31			
Claygate	d									17 04										17 34			
Oxshott	d									17 07										17 37			
Cobham & Stoke D'abernon	d									17 11										17 41			
Bookham	d		16 59										17 29										17 59
Effingham Junction	d		17 03							17 15			17 33							17 45			18 03
Horsley	d		17 06							17 18			17 36							17 48			18 06
Clandon	d		17 11							17 23			17 41							17 53			18 11
London Road (Guildford)	d		17 16							17 28			17 46							17 58			18 16
Guildford	a		17 23							17 35			17 53							18 05			18 23

Table 152

Saturdays
from 02 October

London - Chessington South, Dorking, Guildford, Shepperton and Hampton Court

		SW	SW	SW 1	SW	SW	SW	SW	SW	SW	SW	SW	SW	SW 1	SW	SW	SW	SW	SW	SW	SW	SW	SW
London Waterloo ⊖	d	17 12	17 16	17 23	17 20	17 24	17 27	17 33	17 33	17 36	17 39	17 42	17 46	17 53	17 50	17 54	17 57	18 03	18 03	18 06	18 09	18 12	18 16
Vauxhall ⊖	d	17 16	17 20		17 24	17 28	17 31	17 37	17 37	17 40	17 43	17 46	17 50		17 54	17 58	18 01	18 07	18 07	18 10	18 13	18 16	18 20
Clapham Junction	d	17 21	17 25		17 29	17 33	17 36	17 42		17 45	17 48	17 51	17 55	18u00	17 59	18 03	18 06	18 12		18 15	18 18	18 21	18 25
Earlsfield	d	17 24	17 28		17 32	17 36	17 39	17 45		17 48	17 51	17 54	17 58		18 02	18 06	18 09	18 15		18 18	18 21	18 24	18 28
Wimbledon ⊖	d	17 28	17 32		17 36	17 40	17 43	17 49		17 52	17 55	17 58	18 02		18 06	18 10	18 13	18 19		18 22	18 25	18 28	18 32
Raynes Park	d	17 31	17 35			17 43	17 46			17 55	17 58	18 01	18 05			18 13	18 16			18 25	18 28	18 31	18 35
Motspur Park	d		17 38			17 46					18 01		18 08			18 16					18 31		18 38
Malden Manor	d		17 41										18 11										18 41
Tolworth	d		17 44										18 14										18 44
Chessington North	d		17 47										18 17										18 47
Chessington South	a		17 49										18 19										18 49
Worcester Park	d					17 48					18 03					18 18					18 33		
Stoneleigh	d					17 51					18 06					18 21					18 36		
Ewell West	d					17 54					18 09					18 24					18 39		
Epsom	a					17 57					18 16					18 27					18 46		
	d					17 58					18 17					18 28					18 47		
Ashtead	d					18 02					18 21					18 32					18 51		
Leatherhead	d					18 05					18 24					18 35					18 54		
Boxhill & Westhumble	d																						
Dorking	a					18 13										18 43							
New Malden	d	17 34					17 49			17 58		18 04					18 19			18 28		18 34	
Norbiton	d	17 37					17 52					18 07					18 22					18 37	
Kingston	a	17 40					17 55		18 16			18 10					18 25		18 46			18 40	
	d	17 40					17 59		18 19			18 10					18 29		18 49			18 40	
Hampton Wick	d	17 42					18 01					18 12					18 31					18 42	
Teddington	d	17 45					18 05					18 15					18 35					18 45	
Strawberry Hill	a						18 08										18 38						
Fulwell	d	17 49										18 19										18 49	
Hampton	d	17 53										18 23										18 53	
Kempton Park	d	17 56										18 26										18 56	
Sunbury	d	17 58										18 28										18 58	
Upper Halliford	d	18 00										18 30										19 00	
Shepperton	a	18 05										18 35										19 05	
Berrylands	d									18 00										18 30			
Surbiton	d			17 41	17 44			17 57		18 05				18 11	18 14			18 27		18 35			
Thames Ditton	d									18 09										18 39			
Hampton Court	a									18 12										18 42			
Hinchley Wood	d							18 01										18 31					
Claygate	d							18 04										18 34					
Oxshott	d							18 07										18 37					
Cobham & Stoke D'abernon	d							18 11										18 41					
Bookham	d										18 29										18 59		
Effingham Junction	d							18 15			18 33							18 45			19 03		
Horsley	d							18 18			18 36							18 48			19 06		
Clandon	d							18 23			18 41							18 53			19 11		
London Road (Guildford)	d							18 28			18 46							18 58			19 16		
Guildford	a							18 35			18 53							19 05			19 23		

Table 152

Saturdays
from 02 October

London - Chessington South, Dorking, Guildford, Shepperton and Hampton Court

		SW ■	SW	SW	SW	SW	SW	SW	SW	SW	SW	SW ■	SW	SW	SW	SW	SW	SW	SW	SW	SW	SW ■
London Waterloo ■ ⊖	d	18 23	18 20	18 24	18 27	18 33	18 33	18 36	18 39	18 42	18 46	18 53	18 50	18 54	18 57	19 03	19 03	19 06	19 09	19 12	19 16	19 23
Vauxhall ⊖	d		18 24	18 28	18 31	18 37	18 37	18 40	18 43	18 46	18 50		18 54	18 58	19 01	19 07	19 07	19 10	19 13	19 16	19 20	
Clapham Junction ■	d		18 29	18 33	18 36	18 42		18 45	18 48	18 51	18 55	19u00	18 59	19 03	19 06	19 12		19 15	19 18	19 21	19 25	
Earlsfield	d		18 32	18 36	18 39	18 45		18 48	18 51	18 54	18 58		19 02	19 06	19 09	19 15		19 18	19 21	19 24	19 28	
Wimbledon ■ ⊖	d		18 36	18 40	18 43	18 49		18 52	18 55	18 58	19 02		19 06	19 10	19 13	19 19		19 22	19 25	19 28	19 32	
Raynes Park ■	d			18 43	18 46			18 55	18 58	19 01	19 05			19 13	19 16			19 25	19 28	19 31	19 35	
Motspur Park	d			18 46					19 01		19 08			19 16					19 31		19 38	
Malden Manor	d										19 11										19 41	
Tolworth	d										19 14										19 44	
Chessington North	d										19 17										19 47	
Chessington South	a										19 19										19 49	
Worcester Park	d			18 48					19 03					19 18					19 33			
Stoneleigh	d			18 51					19 06					19 21					19 36			
Ewell West	d			18 54					19 09					19 24					19 39			
Epsom ■	a			18 57					19 12					19 27					19 42			
	d			18 58					19 17					19 28					19 47			
Ashtead	d			19 02					19 21					19 32					19 51			
Leatherhead	d			19 05					19 24					19 35					19 54			
Boxhill & Westhumble	d																					
Dorking ■	a			19 13										19 43								
New Malden ■	d				18 49			18 58		19 04					19 19			19 28		19 34		
Norbiton	d				18 52					19 07					19 22					19 37		
Kingston	a				18 55		19 16			19 10					19 25		19 46			19 40		
	d				18 59		19 19			19 10					19 29		19 49			19 40		
Hampton Wick	d				19 01					19 12					19 31					19 42		
Teddington	d				19 05					19 15					19 35					19 45		
Strawberry Hill	a				19 08										19 38							
Fulwell	d									19 19										19 49		
Hampton	d									19 23										19 53		
Kempton Park	d									19 26										19 56		
Sunbury	d									19 28										19 58		
Upper Halliford	d									19 30										20 00		
Shepperton	a									19 35										20 05		
Berrylands	d							19 00										19 30				
Surbiton ■	d	18 41	18 44			18 57		19 05				19 11	19 14			19 27		19 35				19 41
Thames Ditton	d							19 09										19 39				
Hampton Court	a							19 12										19 42				
Hinchley Wood	d					19 01										19 31						
Claygate	d					19 04										19 34						
Oxshott	d					19 07										19 37						
Cobham & Stoke D'abernon	d					19 11										19 41						
Bookham	d								19 29										19 59			
Effingham Junction ■	d					19 15			19 33							19 45			20 03			
Horsley	d					19 18			19 36							19 48			20 06			
Clandon	d					19 23			19 41							19 53			20 11			
London Road (Guildford)	d					19 28			19 46							19 58			20 16			
Guildford	a					19 35			19 53							20 05			20 23			

Table 152

Saturdays
from 02 October

London - Chessington South, Dorking, Guildford, Shepperton and Hampton Court

		SW	SW	SW	SW	SW	SW	SW	SW	SW	SW ■	SW	SW	SW	SW	SW	SW	SW	SW	SW	SW ■	SW	SW
London Waterloo ■ ⊖	d	19 20	19 24	19 27	19 33	19 33	19 36	19 39	19 42	19 46	19 53	19 50	19 54	19 57	20 03	20 03	20 06	20 09	20 12	20 16	20 23	20 20	20 24
Vauxhall ⊖	d	19 24	19 28	19 31	19 37	19 37	19 40	19 43	19 46	19 50		19 54	19 58	20 01	20 07	20 07	20 10	20 13	20 16	20 20		20 24	20 28
Clapham Junction ■	d	19 29	19 33	19 36	19 42		19 45	19 48	19 51	19 55	20u00	19 59	20 03	20 06	20 12		20 15	20 18	20 21	20 25		20 29	20 33
Earlsfield	d	19 32	19 36	19 39	19 45		19 48	19 51	19 54	19 58		20 02	20 06	20 09	20 15		20 18	20 21	20 24	20 28		20 32	20 36
Wimbledon ■ ⊖	d	19 36	19 40	19 43	19 49		19 52	19 55	19 58	20 02		20 06	20 10	20 13	20 19		20 22	20 25	20 28	20 32		20 36	20 40
Raynes Park ■	d		19 43	19 46			19 55	19 58	20 01	20 05			20 13	20 16			20 25	20 28	20 31	20 35			20 43
Motspur Park	d		19 46					20 01		20 08			20 16					20 31		20 38			20 46
Malden Manor	d									20 11										20 41			
Tolworth	d									20 14										20 44			
Chessington North	d									20 17										20 47			
Chessington South	a									20 19										20 49			
Worcester Park	d		19 48					20 03					20 18					20 33					20 48
Stoneleigh	d		19 51					20 06					20 21					20 36					20 51
Ewell West	d		19 54					20 09					20 24					20 39					20 54
Epsom ■	a		19 57					20 12					20 27					20 42					20 57
	d		19 58					20 17										20 47					
Ashtead	d		20 02					20 21										20 51					
Leatherhead	d		20 05					20 24										20 54					
Boxhill & Westhumble	d																						
Dorking ■	a		20 13															21 02					
New Malden ■	d			19 49			19 58		20 04					20 19			20 28		20 34				
Norbiton	d			19 52					20 07					20 22					20 37				
Kingston	a			19 55		20 16			20 10					20 25		20 46			20 40				
	d			19 59		20 19			20 10					20 29		20 49			20 40				
Hampton Wick	d			20 01					20 12					20 31					20 42				
Teddington	d			20 05					20 15					20 35					20 45				
Strawberry Hill	a			20 08										20 38									
Fulwell	d								20 19										20 49				
Hampton	d								20 23										20 53				
Kempton Park	d								20 26										20 56				
Sunbury	d								20 28										20 58				
Upper Halliford	d								20 30										21 00				
Shepperton	a								20 35										21 05				
Berrylands	d						20 00										20 30						
Surbiton ■	d	19 44			19 57		20 05				20 11	20 14			20 27		20 35				20 41	20 44	
Thames Ditton	d						20 09										20 39						
Hampton Court	a						20 12										20 42						
Hinchley Wood	d				20 01										20 31								
Claygate	d				20 04										20 34								
Oxshott	d				20 07										20 37								
Cobham & Stoke D'abernon	d				20 11										20 41								
Bookham	d							20 29															
Effingham Junction ■	d				20 15			20 33							20 45								
Horsley	d				20 18			20 36							20 48								
Clandon	d				20 23			20 41							20 53								
London Road (Guildford)	d				20 28			20 46							20 58								
Guildford	a				20 35			20 53							21 05								

Table 152

Saturdays from 02 October

London - Chessington South, Dorking, Guildford, Shepperton and Hampton Court

		SW	SW	SW	SW	SW	SW	SW	SW 1	SW	SW	SW	SW	SW	SW	SW	SW 1	SW	SW	SW	SW	SW
London Waterloo 15 ⊖	d	20 27	20 33	20 33	20 36	20 39	20 42	20 46	20 53	20 50	20 54	20 57	21 03	21 03	21 09	21 12	21 23	21 20	21 24	21 27	21 33	21 33
Vauxhall ⊖	d	20 31	20 37	20 37	20 40	20 43	20 46	20 50		20 54	20 58	21 01	21 07	21 07	21 13	21 16		21 24	21 28	21 31	21 37	21 37
Clapham Junction 10	d	20 36	20 42		20 45	20 48	20 51	20 55	21u00	20 59	21 03	21 06	21 12		21 18	21 21		21 29	21 33	21 36	21 42	
Earlsfield	d	20 39	20 45		20 48	20 51	20 54	20 58		21 02	21 06	21 09	21 15		21 21	21 24		21 32	21 36	21 39	21 45	
Wimbledon 6 ⊖	d	20 43	20 49		20 52	20 55	20 58	21 02		21 06	21 10	21 13	21 19		21 25	21 28		21 36	21 40	21 43	21 49	
Raynes Park 6	d	20 46			20 55	20 58	21 01	21 05			21 13	21 16			21 28	21 31			21 43	21 46		
Motspur Park	d					21 01		21 08			21 16				21 31				21 46			
Malden Manor	d							21 11														
Tolworth	d							21 14														
Chessington North	d							21 17														
Chessington South	a							21 19														
Worcester Park	d					21 03					21 18				21 33				21 48			
Stoneleigh	d					21 06					21 21				21 36				21 51			
Ewell West	d					21 09					21 24				21 39				21 54			
Epsom 3	a					21 12					21 27				21 42				21 57			
	d					21 17									21 47							
Ashtead	d					21 21									21 51							
Leatherhead	d					21 24									21 54							
Boxhill & Westhumble	d																					
Dorking 4	a														22 02							
New Malden 6	d	20 49			20 58		21 04					21 19				21 34				21 49		
Norbiton	d	20 52					21 07					21 22				21 37				21 52		
Kingston	a	20 55		21 16			21 10					21 25		21 46		21 40				21 55		22 16
	d	20 59		21 19			21 10					21 29		21 49		21 40				21 59		22 19
Hampton Wick	d	21 01					21 12					21 31				21 42				22 01		
Teddington	d	21 05					21 15					21 35				21 45				22 05		
Strawberry Hill	a	21 08										21 38								22 08		
Fulwell	d						21 19									21 49						
Hampton	d						21 23									21 53						
Kempton Park	d						21 26									21 56						
Sunbury	d						21 28									21 58						
Upper Halliford	d						21 30									22 00						
Shepperton	a						21 35									22 05						
Berrylands	d				21 00																	
Surbiton 6	d		20 57		21 05				21 11	21 14			21 27				21 41	21 44			21 57	
Thames Ditton	d				21 09																	
Hampton Court	a				21 12																	
Hinchley Wood	d		21 01										21 31								22 01	
Claygate	d		21 04										21 34								22 04	
Oxshott	d		21 07										21 37								22 07	
Cobham & Stoke D'abernon	d		21 11										21 41								22 11	
Bookham	d					21 29																
Effingham Junction 6	d		21 15			21 33							21 45								22 15	
Horsley	d		21 18			21 36							21 48								22 18	
Clandon	d		21 23			21 41							21 53								22 23	
London Road (Guildford)	d		21 28			21 46							21 58								22 28	
Guildford	a		21 35			21 53							22 05								22 35	

Table 152

Saturdays from 02 October

London - Chessington South, Dorking, Guildford, Shepperton and Hampton Court

		SW	SW	SW	SW	SW 1	SW	SW	SW	SW	SW	SW	SW	SW 1	SW	SW	SW	SW	SW	SW	SW	SW 1	SW
London Waterloo 15 ⊖	d	21 36	21 39	21 42	21 46	21 53	21 50	21 54	21 57	22 03	22 03	22 09	22 12	22 23	22 20	22 27	22 33	22 33	22 36	22 39	22 42	22 53	22 50
Vauxhall ⊖	d	21 40	21 43	21 46	21 50		21 54	21 58	22 01	22 07	22 07	22 13	22 16		22 24	22 31	22 37	22 37	22 40	22 43	22 46		22 54
Clapham Junction 10	d	21 45	21 48	21 51	21 55	22u00	21 59	22 03	22 06	22 12		22 18	22 21	22u30	22 29	22 36	22 42		22 45	22 48	22 51	23u00	22 59
Earlsfield	d	21 48	21 51	21 54	21 58		22 02	22 06	22 09	22 15		22 21	22 24		22 32	22 39	22 45		22 48	22 51	22 54		23 02
Wimbledon 6 ⊖	d	21 52	21 55	21 58	22 02		22 06	22 10	22 13	22 19		22 25	22 28		22 36	22 43	22 49		22 52	22 55	22 58		23 06
Raynes Park 6	d	21 55	21 58	22 01	22 05			22 13	22 16			22 28	22 31			22 46			22 55	22 58	23 01		
Motspur Park	d		22 01		22 08			22 16				22 31								23 01			
Malden Manor	d				22 11																		
Tolworth	d				22 14																		
Chessington North	d				22 17																		
Chessington South	a				22 19																		
Worcester Park	d		22 03					22 18				22 33								23 03			
Stoneleigh	d		22 06					22 21				22 36								23 06			
Ewell West	d		22 09					22 24				22 39								23 09			
Epsom 3	a		22 12					22 27				22 42								23 12			
	d		22 17									22 47								23 17			
Ashtead	d		22 21									22 51								23 21			
Leatherhead	d		22 24									22 54								23 24			
Boxhill & Westhumble	d																						
Dorking 4	a											23 02											
New Malden 6	d	21 58		22 04					22 19				22 34			22 49			22 58		23 04		
Norbiton	d			22 07					22 22				22 37			22 52					23 07		
Kingston	a			22 10					22 25		22 46		22 40			22 55		23 16			23 10		
	d			22 10					22 29		22 49		22 40			22 59		23 19			23 10		
Hampton Wick	d			22 12					22 31				22 42			23 01					23 12		
Teddington	d			22 15					22 35				22 45			23 05					23 15		
Strawberry Hill	a								22 38							23 08							
Fulwell	d			22 19									22 49								23 19		
Hampton	d			22 23									22 53								23 23		
Kempton Park	d			22 26									22 56								23 26		
Sunbury	d			22 28									22 58								23 28		
Upper Halliford	d			22 30									23 00								23 30		
Shepperton	a			22 35									23 05								23 35		
Berrylands	d	22 00																	23 00				
Surbiton 6	d	22 05				22 11	22 14			22 27				22 41	22 44		22 57		23 05			23 11	23 14
Thames Ditton	d	22 09																	23 09				
Hampton Court	a	22 12																	23 12				
Hinchley Wood	d									22 31							23 01						
Claygate	d									22 34							23 04						
Oxshott	d									22 37							23 07						
Cobham & Stoke D'abernon	d									22 41							23 11						
Bookham	d		22 29																	23 29			
Effingham Junction 6	d		22 33							22 45							23 15			23 33			
Horsley	d		22 36							22 48							23 18			23 36			
Clandon	d		22 41							22 53							23 23			23 41			
London Road (Guildford)	d		22 46							22 58							23 28			23 46			
Guildford	a		22 53				22 47			23 05							23 35			23 54			

Table 152

Saturdays
from 02 October

London - Chessington South, Dorking, Guildford, Shepperton and Hampton Court

		SW	SW	SW	SW	SW	SW	SW	SW	SW	SW	SW	SW	SW
London Waterloo ⊖	d	22 57	23 00	23 03	23 03	23 09	23 12	23 20	23 27	23 30	23 33	23 42	23 50	23 57
Vauxhall ⊖	d	23 01	23 04	23 07	23 07	23 13	23 16	23 24	23 31	23 34	23 37	23 46	23 54	00 01
Clapham Junction	d	23 06	23 09	23 12		23 18	23 21	23 29	23 36	23 39		23 51	23 58	00 06
Earlsfield	d	23 09	23 12	23 15		23 21	23 24	23 32	23 39	23 42		23 54	00 02	00 09
Wimbledon ⊖	d	23 13	23 16	23 19		23 25	23 28	23 36	23 43	23 46		23 58	00 06	00 13
Raynes Park	d	23 16	23 19			23 28	23 31		23 46	23 49		00 01		00 16
Motspur Park	d		23 22			23 31						00 04		
Malden Manor	d		23 25											
Tolworth	d		23 28											
Chessington North	d		23 31											
Chessington South	a		23 33											
Worcester Park	d					23 33						00 06		
Stoneleigh	d					23 36						00 09		
Ewell West	d					23 39						00 12		
Epsom	a					23 42						00 15		
	d					23 47						00 19		
Ashtead	d					23 51						00 23		
Leatherhead	d					23 54						00 26		
Boxhill & Westhumble	d													
Dorking	a					00 03								
New Malden	d	23 19					23 34		23 49	23 52				00 19
Norbiton	d	23 22					23 37		23 52					00 22
Kingston	a	23 25			23 46		23 40		23 55		00 16			00 25
	d	23 29			23 49		23 40		23 55					00 25
Hampton Wick	d	23 31					23 42		23 57					00 27
Teddington	d	23 35					23 45		23 59					00 30
Strawberry Hill	a	23 38							00 03					
Fulwell	d						23 49							00 34
Hampton	d						23 53							00 38
Kempton Park	d						23 56							00 41
Sunbury	d						23 58							00 43
Upper Halliford	d						23 59							00 45
Shepperton	a						00 05							00 50
Berrylands	d									23 54				
Surbiton	d			23 27				23 44		23 59			00 14	
Thames Ditton	d									00 03				
Hampton Court	a									00 06				
Hinchley Wood	d			23 31									00 18	
Claygate	d			23 34									00 21	
Oxshott	d			23 37									00 24	
Cobham & Stoke D'abernon	d			23 41									00 28	
Bookham	d											00 31		
Effingham Junction	d			23 45								00 37	00 32	
Horsley	d			23 48								00 40	00 35	
Clandon	d			23 53								00 45	00 40	
London Road (Guildford)	d			23 58								00 50	00 45	
Guildford	a			00 05								00 57	00 52	

Table 152

Sundays
until 19 September

London - Chessington South, Dorking, Guildford, Shepperton and Hampton Court

		SW	SW	SW	SW	SW	SW	SW	SW	SW	SW	SW	SW	SW	SW	SW	SW	SW	SW	SW	SW	SW	SW
London Waterloo ⊖	d	23p03	23p09	23p12	23p27	23p30	23p33	23p42	23p50	23p57	00 09	00 15	00 18	00 27	01 42	06 14	06 18		06 57	07 14		07 10	07 18
Vauxhall ⊖	d	23p07	23p13	23p16	23p31	23p34	23p37	23p46	23p54	00 01	00 13	00 19	00 22	00 31	01 46	06 18	06 22		07 01	07 18		07 14	07 22
Clapham Junction	d	23p12	23p18	23p21	23p36	23p39		23p51	23p58	00 06	00 18	00 24		00 36	01 51		06 27		07 06			07 19	07 27
Earlsfield	d	23p15	23p21	23p24	23p39	23p42		23p54	00 02	00 09	00 21	00 27		00s39					07 09			07 22	07 30
Wimbledon ⊖	d	23p19	23p25	23p28	23p43	23p46		23p58	00 06	00 13	00 25	00 31		00 43	01 57		06 34	06 48	07 13		07 16	07 26	07 34
Raynes Park	d		23p28	23p31	23p46	23p49		00 01		00 16		00 34		00 46	02 00		06 37	06 52	07 16				07 37
Motspur Park	d		23p31					00 04				00 37						06 55					
Malden Manor	d																						
Tolworth	d																						
Chessington North	d																						
Chessington South	a																						
Worcester Park	d		23p33					00 06				00 39						06 57					
Stoneleigh	d		23p36					00 09				00 42						07 00					
Ewell West	d		23p39					00 12				00 45						07 03					
Epsom	a		23p42					00 15				00 48						07 06					
	d		23p47					00 19															
Ashtead	d		23p51					00 23															
Leatherhead	d		23p54					00 26															
Boxhill & Westhumble	d																						
Dorking	a		00 01																				
New Malden	d			23p34	23p49	23p52				00 19				00 49	02 02		06 40		07 19				07 40
Norbiton	d			23p37	23p52					00 22					02 06		06 43						07 43
Kingston	a			23p40	23p55		00 16			00 25			01 00		02 08	06 59	06 46			07 59			07 46
	d			23p40	23p55					00 25					02 09	07 04	06 49			08 04			07 49
Hampton Wick	d			23p42	23p57					00 27					02s11		06 51						07 51
Teddington	d			23p45	23p59					00 30					02s13		06 56						07 56
Strawberry Hill	a				00 03										02s16		06 59						07 59
Fulwell	d			23p49						00 34													
Hampton	d			23p53						00 38													
Kempton Park	d			23p56						00 41													
Sunbury	d			23p58						00 43													
Upper Halliford	d			23p59						00 45													
Shepperton	a			00 03						00 48													
Berrylands	d					23p54								00s51					07 21				
Surbiton	d	23p27				23p59			00 14		00 33			00a55					07 25		07 32	07 35	
Thames Ditton	d					00 03													07 30				
Hampton Court	a					00 06													07 33				
Hinchley Wood	d	23p31							00 18												07 36		
Claygate	d	23p34							00 21												07 39		
Oxshott	d	23p37							00 24												07 42		
Cobham & Stoke D'abernon	d	23p41							00 28												07 46		
Bookham	d							00 31															
Effingham Junction	d	23p45						00 37	00 32												07 50		
Horsley	d	23p48						00 40	00 35												07 53		
Clandon	d	23p53						00 45	00 40												07 58		
London Road (Guildford)	d	23p58						00 50	00 45												08 03		
Guildford	a	00 02						00 54	00 49		01 06										08 07	08 14	

London - Chessington South, Dorking, Guildford, Shepperton and Hampton Court

		SW	SW	SW	SW	SW A	SW	SW	SW	SW	SW	SW	SW	SW	SW	SW	SW	SW	SW	SW	SW	SW	SW
London Waterloo 15 ⊖	d		07 27		07 40	07 48		07 57	08 02		08 14		08 10	08 18	08 21	08 27	08 32	08 40	08 48	08 51	08 57	09 02	09 14
Vauxhall ⊖	d		07 31		07 44	07 52		08 01	08 06		08 18		08 14	08 22	08 25	08 31	08 36	08 44	08 52	08 55	09 01	09 06	09 18
Clapham Junction 10	d		07 36		07 49	07 57		08 06	08 11				08 19	08 27	08 30	08 36	08 41	08 49	08 57	09 00	09 06	09 11	
Earlsfield	d		07 39		07 52	08 00		08 09	08 14				08 22	08 30	08 33	08 39	08 44	08 52	09 00	09 03	09 09	09 14	
Wimbledon 6 ⊖	d	07 18	07 43	07 37	07 56	08 04	07 48	08 13	08 18	08 07		08 16	08 26	08 34	08 37	08 43	08 48	08 56	09 04	09 07	09 13	09 18	
Raynes Park 6	d	07 22	07 46	07 40		08 07	07 52	08 16	08 22	08 10				08 37	08 40	08 46	08 52		09 07	09 10	09 16	09 22	
Motspur Park	d	07 25		07 43			07 55		08 25	08 13					08 43		08 55			09 13		09 25	
Malden Manor	d			07 46						08 16					08 46					09 16			
Tolworth	d			07 49						08 19					08 49					09 19			
Chessington North	d			07 52						08 22					08 52					09 22			
Chessington South	a			07 54						08 24					08 54					09 24			
Worcester Park	d	07 27					07 57		08 27								08 57					09 27	
Stoneleigh	d	07 30					08 00		08 30								09 00					09 30	
Ewell West	d	07 33					08 03		08 33								09 03					09 33	
Epsom 3	a	07 37					08 06		08 36								09 06					09 36	
	d						08 08		08 38								09 08					09 38	
Ashtead	d						08 12		08 42								09 12					09 42	
Leatherhead	d						08 15		08 45								09 15					09 45	
Boxhill & Westhumble	d																						
Dorking 4	a								08 51													09 51	
New Malden 6	d		07 49			08 10		08 19						08 40		08 49			09 10		09 19		
Norbiton	d					08 13								08 43					09 13				
Kingston	a					08 16					08 59			08 46					09 16				09 59
	d					08 16					09 04			08 49					09 16				10 04
Hampton Wick	d					08 18								08 51					09 18				
Teddington	d					08 21								08 56					09 21				
Strawberry Hill	a													08 59									
Fulwell	d					08 25													09 25				
Hampton	d					08 29													09 29				
Kempton Park	d					08 32													09 32				
Sunbury	d					08 34													09 34				
Upper Halliford	d					08 36													09 36				
Shepperton	a					08 39													09 39				
Berrylands	d		07 51					08 21								08 51					09 21		
Surbiton 6	d		07 55		08 05			08 25				08 32	08 35			08 55		09 05			09 25		
Thames Ditton	d		08 00					08 30								09 00					09 30		
Hampton Court	a		08 03					08 33								09 03					09 33		
Hinchley Wood	d											08 36											
Claygate	d											08 39											
Oxshott	d											08 42											
Cobham & Stoke D'abernon	d											08 46											
Bookham	d						08 21										09 21						
Effingham Junction 6	d						08 25					08 50					09 25						
Horsley	d						08 27					08 53					09 27						
Clandon	d						08 32					08 58					09 32						
London Road (Guildford)	d						08 37					09 03					09 37						
Guildford	a				08 40		08 41					09 07	09 10				09 41	09 40					

A not 23 May

Table 152

Sundays
until 19 September

London - Chessington South, Dorking, Guildford, Shepperton and Hampton Court

		SW	SW	SW	SW	SW	SW	SW	SW	SW	SW	SW	SW	SW	SW	SW	SW	SW	SW	SW	SW	SW
London Waterloo 15 ⊖	d		09 10	09 18	09 21	09 27	09 32	09 40	09 48	09 51	09 57	10 02	10 14		10 10	10 18	10 21	10 27	10 32	10 40	10 48	10 51
Vauxhall ⊖	d		09 14	09 22	09 25	09 31	09 36	09 44	09 52	09 55	10 01	10 06	10 18		10 14	10 22	10 25	10 31	10 36	10 44	10 52	10 55
Clapham Junction 10	d		09 19	09 27	09 30	09 36	09 41	09 49	09 57	10 00	10 06	10 11			10 19	10 27	10 30	10 36	10 41	10 49	10 57	11 00
Earlsfield	d		09 22	09 30	09 33	09 39	09 44	09 52	10 00	10 03	10 09	10 14			10 22	10 30	10 33	10 39	10 44	10 52	11 00	11 03
Wimbledon 6 ⊖	d	09 16	09 26	09 34	09 37	09 43	09 48	09 56	10 04	10 07	10 13	10 18		10 16	10 26	10 34	10 37	10 43	10 48	10 56	11 04	11 07
Raynes Park 6	d			09 37	09 40	09 46	09 52		10 07	10 10	10 16	10 22				10 37	10 40	10 46	10 52		11 07	11 10
Motspur Park	d				09 43		09 55			10 13		10 25					10 43		10 55			11 13
Malden Manor	d				09 46					10 16							10 46					11 16
Tolworth	d				09 49					10 19							10 49					11 19
Chessington North	d				09 52					10 22							10 52					11 22
Chessington South	a				09 54					10 24							10 54					11 24
Worcester Park	d						09 57					10 27							10 57			
Stoneleigh	d						10 00					10 30							11 00			
Ewell West	d						10 03					10 33							11 03			
Epsom 3	a						10 06					10 36							11 06			
	d						10 08					10 38							11 08			
Ashtead	d						10 12					10 42							11 12			
Leatherhead	d						10 15					10 45							11 15			
Boxhill & Westhumble	d																					
Dorking 4	a											10 51										
New Malden 6	d			09 40		09 49			10 10		10 19					10 40		10 49			11 10	
Norbiton	d			09 43					10 13							10 43					11 13	
Kingston	a			09 46					10 16				10 59			10 46					11 16	
	d			09 49					10 16				11 04			10 49					11 16	
Hampton Wick	d			09 51					10 18							10 51					11 18	
Teddington	d			09 56					10 21							10 56					11 21	
Strawberry Hill	a			09 59												10 59						
Fulwell	d								10 25												11 25	
Hampton	d								10 29												11 29	
Kempton Park	d								10 32												11 32	
Sunbury	d								10 34												11 34	
Upper Halliford	d								10 36												11 36	
Shepperton	a								10 39												11 39	
Berrylands	d					09 51					10 21							10 51				
Surbiton 6	d	09 32	09 35			09 55		10 05			10 25			10 32	10 35			10 55		11 05		
Thames Ditton	d					10 00					10 30							11 00				
Hampton Court	a					10 03					10 33							11 03				
Hinchley Wood	d	09 36												10 36								
Claygate	d	09 39												10 39								
Oxshott	d	09 42												10 42								
Cobham & Stoke D'abernon	d	09 46												10 46								
Bookham	d						10 21												11 21			
Effingham Junction 6	d	09 50					10 25							10 50					11 25			
Horsley	d	09 53					10 27							10 53					11 27			
Clandon	d	09 58					10 32							10 58					11 32			
London Road (Guildford)	d	10 03					10 37							11 03					11 37			
Guildford	a	10 07	10 10				10 41	10 44						11 07	11 14				11 41	11 44		

		SW	SW	SW	SW	SW	SW	SW	SW	SW	SW	SW	SW	SW	SW	SW	SW	SW	SW	SW	SW	SW	SW
London Waterloo 15 ⊖	d	10 57	11 02	11 14		11 10	11 18	11 21	11 27	11 32	11 40	11 48	11 51	11 57	12 02	12 14		12 10	12 18	12 21	12 27	12 32	12 40
Vauxhall ⊖	d	11 01	11 06	11 19		11 14	11 22	11 25	11 31	11 36	11 44	11 52	11 55	12 01	12 06	12 19		12 14	12 22	12 25	12 31	12 36	12 44
Clapham Junction 10	d	11 06	11 11			11 19	11 27	11 30	11 36	11 41	11 49	11 57	12 00	12 06	12 11			12 19	12 27	12 30	12 36	12 41	12 49
Earlsfield	d	11 09	11 14			11 22	11 30	11 33	11 39	11 44	11 52	12 00	12 03	12 09	12 14			12 22	12 30	12 33	12 39	12 44	12 52
Wimbledon 6 ⊖	d	11 13	11 18		11 16	11 26	11 34	11 37	11 43	11 48	11 56	12 04	12 07	12 13	12 18		12 16	12 26	12 34	12 37	12 43	12 48	12 56
Raynes Park 6	d	11 16	11 22				11 37	11 40	11 46	11 52		12 07	12 10	12 16	12 22				12 37	12 40	12 46	12 52	
Motspur Park	d		11 25					11 43		11 55			12 13		12 25					12 43		12 55	
Malden Manor	d							11 46					12 16							12 46			
Tolworth	d							11 49					12 19							12 49			
Chessington North	d							11 52					12 22							12 52			
Chessington South	a							11 54					12 24							12 54			
Worcester Park	d		11 27							11 57					12 27							12 57	
Stoneleigh	d		11 30							12 00					12 30							13 00	
Ewell West	d		11 33							12 03					12 33							13 03	
Epsom 3	a		11 36							12 06					12 36							13 06	
	d		11 38							12 08					12 38							13 08	
Ashtead	d		11 42							12 12					12 42							13 12	
Leatherhead	d		11 45							12 15					12 45							13 15	
Boxhill & Westhumble	d																						
Dorking 4	a		11 51												12 51								
New Malden 6	d	11 19					11 40		11 49			12 10		12 19					12 40		12 49		
Norbiton	d						11 43					12 13							12 43				
Kingston	a			11 59			11 46					12 16				12 59			12 46				
	d			12 04			11 49					12 16				13 04			12 49				
Hampton Wick	d						11 51					12 18							12 51				
Teddington	d						11 56					12 21							12 56				
Strawberry Hill	a						11 59												12 59				
Fulwell	d											12 25											
Hampton	d											12 29											
Kempton Park	d											12 32											
Sunbury	d											12 34											
Upper Halliford	d											12 36											
Shepperton	a											12 39											
Berrylands	d	11 21							11 51					12 21							12 51		
Surbiton 6	d	11 25			11 32	11 35			11 55		12 05			12 25			12 32	12 35			12 55		13 05
Thames Ditton	d	11 30							12 00					12 30							13 00		
Hampton Court	a	11 33							12 03					12 33							13 03		
Hinchley Wood	d				11 36												12 36						
Claygate	d				11 39												12 39						
Oxshott	d				11 42												12 42						
Cobham & Stoke D'abernon	d				11 46												12 46						
Bookham	d									12 21												13 21	
Effingham Junction 6	d				11 50					12 25							12 50					13 25	
Horsley	d				11 53					12 27							12 53					13 27	
Clandon	d				11 58					12 32							12 58					13 32	
London Road (Guildford)	d				12 03					12 37							13 03					13 37	
Guildford	a				12 07	12 14				12 41	12 44						13 07	13 14				13 41	13 44

Table 152

Sundays until 19 September

London - Chessington South, Dorking, Guildford, Shepperton and Hampton Court

Station		SW	SW	SW	SW	SW	SW	SW	SW	SW	SW	SW	SW	SW	SW	SW	SW	SW	SW	SW	SW	SW
London Waterloo ⊖	d	12 48	12 51	12 57	13 00	13 02	13 10	13 14	13 18	13 21	13 27	13 32	13 40	13 48	13 51	13 56	13 57	14 00	14 02	14 10	14 14	14 18
Vauxhall ⊖	d	12 52	12 55	13 01	13 04	13 06	13 14	13 18	13 22	13 25	13 31	13 36	13 44	13 52	13 55	14 00	14 01	14 04	14 06	14 14	14 18	14 22
Clapham Junction	d	12 57	13 00	13 06	13 09	13 11	13 19		13 27	13 30	13 36	13 41	13 49	13 57	14 00		14 06	14 09	14 11	14 19		14 27
Earlsfield	d	13 00	13 03	13 09	13 12	13 14	13 22		13 30	13 33	13 39	13 44	13 52	14 00	14 03		14 09	14 12	14 14	14 22		14 30
Wimbledon ⊖	d	13 04	13 07	13 13	13 16	13 18	13 26		13 34	13 37	13 43	13 48	13 56	14 04	14 07		14 13	14 16	14 18	14 26		14 34
Raynes Park	d	13 07	13 10	13 16		13 22			13 37	13 40	13 46	13 52		14 07	14 10		14 16		14 22			14 37
Motspur Park	d		13 13			13 25				13 43		13 55			14 13				14 25			
Malden Manor	d		13 16							13 46					14 16							
Tolworth	d		13 19							13 49					14 19							
Chessington North	d		13 22							13 52					14 22							
Chessington South	a		13 24							13 54					14 24							
Worcester Park	d					13 27						13 57							14 27			
Stoneleigh	d					13 30						14 00							14 30			
Ewell West	d					13 33						14 03							14 33			
Epsom	a					13 36						14 06							14 36			
	d					13 38						14 08							14 38			
Ashtead	d					13 42						14 12							14 42			
Leatherhead	d					13 45						14 15							14 45			
Boxhill & Westhumble	d																					
Dorking	a					13 51													14 51			
New Malden	d	13 10		13 19					13 40		13 49			14 10			14 19					14 40
Norbiton	d	13 13							13 43					14 13								14 43
Kingston	a	13 16						13 59	13 46					14 16		14 38					14 59	14 46
	d	13 16						14 04	13 49					14 16							15 04	14 49
Hampton Wick	d	13 18							13 51					14 18								14 51
Teddington	d	13 21							13 56					14 21								14 56
Strawberry Hill	a								13 59													14 59
Fulwell	d	13 25												14 25								
Hampton	d	13 29												14 29								
Kempton Park	d	13 32												14 32								
Sunbury	d	13 34												14 34								
Upper Halliford	d	13 36												14 36								
Shepperton	a	13 39												14 39								
Berrylands	d			13 21							13 51						14 21					
Surbiton	d			13 25	13 32		13 35				13 55		14 05				14 25	14 32		14 35		
Thames Ditton	d			13 30							14 00						14 30					
Hampton Court	a			13 33							14 03						14 33					
Hinchley Wood	d				13 36													14 36				
Claygate	d				13 39													14 39				
Oxshott	d				13 42													14 42				
Cobham & Stoke D'abernon	d				13 46													14 46				
Bookham	d											14 21										
Effingham Junction	d				13 50							14 25						14 50				
Horsley	d				13 53							14 27						14 53				
Clandon	d				13 58							14 32						14 58				
London Road (Guildford)	d				14 03							14 37						15 03				
Guildford	a				14 07		14 14					14 41	14 44					15 07		15 14		

Station		SW	SW	SW	SW	SW	SW	SW	SW	SW	SW	SW	SW	SW	SW	SW	SW	SW	SW	SW	SW	SW	SW
London Waterloo ⊖	d	14 21	14 27	14 32	14 40	14 48	14 51	14 56	14 57	15 00	15 02	15 10	15 14	15 18	15 21	15 27	15 32	15 40	15 48	15 51	15 56	15 57	16 00
Vauxhall ⊖	d	14 25	14 31	14 36	14 44	14 52	14 55	15 00	15 01	15 04	15 06	15 14	15 18	15 22	15 25	15 31	15 36	15 44	15 52	15 55	16 00	16 01	16 04
Clapham Junction	d	14 30	14 36	14 41	14 49	14 57	15 00		15 06	15 09	15 11	15 19		15 27	15 30	15 36	15 41	15 49	15 57	16 00		16 06	16 09
Earlsfield	d	14 33	14 39	14 44	14 52	15 00	15 03		15 09	15 12	15 14	15 22		15 30	15 33	15 39	15 44	15 52	16 00	16 03		16 09	16 12
Wimbledon ⊖	d	14 37	14 43	14 48	14 56	15 04	15 07		15 13	15 16	15 18	15 26		15 34	15 37	15 43	15 48	15 56	16 04	16 07		16 13	16 16
Raynes Park	d	14 40	14 46	14 52		15 07	15 10		15 16		15 22			15 37	15 40	15 46	15 52		16 07	16 10		16 16	
Motspur Park	d	14 43		14 55			15 13				15 25				15 43		15 55			16 13			
Malden Manor	d	14 46					15 16								15 46					16 16			
Tolworth	d	14 49					15 19								15 49					16 19			
Chessington North	d	14 52					15 22								15 52					16 22			
Chessington South	a	14 54					15 24								15 54					16 24			
Worcester Park	d			14 57							15 27						15 57						
Stoneleigh	d			15 00							15 30						16 00						
Ewell West	d			15 03							15 33						16 03						
Epsom	a			15 06							15 36						16 06						
	d			15 08							15 38						16 08						
Ashtead	d			15 12							15 42						16 12						
Leatherhead	d			15 15							15 45						16 15						
Boxhill & Westhumble	d																						
Dorking	a										15 51												
New Malden	d		14 49			15 10			15 19					15 40		15 49			16 10			16 19	
Norbiton	d					15 13								15 43					16 13				
Kingston	a					15 16		15 38					15 59	15 46					16 16		16 38		
	d					15 16							16 04	15 49					16 16				
Hampton Wick	d					15 18								15 51					16 18				
Teddington	d					15 21								15 56					16 21				
Strawberry Hill	a													15 59									
Fulwell	d					15 25													16 25				
Hampton	d					15 29													16 29				
Kempton Park	d					15 32													16 32				
Sunbury	d					15 34													16 34				
Upper Halliford	d					15 36													16 36				
Shepperton	a					15 39													16 39				
Berrylands	d		14 51						15 21							15 51						16 21	
Surbiton	d		14 55		15 05				15 25	15 32		15 35				15 55		16 05				16 25	16 32
Thames Ditton	d		15 00						15 30							16 00						16 30	
Hampton Court	a		15 03						15 33							16 03						16 33	
Hinchley Wood	d									15 36													16 36
Claygate	d									15 39													16 39
Oxshott	d									15 42													16 42
Cobham & Stoke D'abernon	d									15 46													16 46
Bookham	d			15 21													16 21						
Effingham Junction	d			15 25						15 50							16 25						16 50
Horsley	d			15 27						15 53							16 27						16 53
Clandon	d			15 32						15 58							16 32						16 58
London Road (Guildford)	d			15 37						16 03							16 37						17 03
Guildford	a			15 41	15 44					16 07		16 14					16 41	16 44					17 07

Table 152

Sundays until 19 September

London - Chessington South, Dorking, Guildford, Shepperton and Hampton Court

Station		SW	SW	SW	SW	SW	SW	SW	SW	SW	SW	SW	SW	SW	SW	SW	SW	SW	SW	SW	SW	SW	SW
London Waterloo ⊖	d	16 02	16 10	16 14	16 18	16 21	16 27	16 32	16 40	16 48	16 51	16 56	16 57	17 00	17 02	17 10	17 14	17 18	17 21	17 27	17 32	17 40	17 48
Vauxhall ⊖	d	16 06	16 14	16 18	16 22	16 25	16 31	16 36	16 44	16 52	16 55	17 00	17 01	17 04	17 06	17 14	17 18	17 22	17 25	17 31	17 36	17 44	17 52
Clapham Junction	d	16 11	16 19		16 27	16 30	16 36	16 41	16 49	16 57	17 00		17 06	17 09	17 11	17 19		17 27	17 30	17 36	17 41	17 49	17 57
Earlsfield	d	16 14	16 22		16 30	16 33	16 39	16 44	16 52	17 00	17 03		17 09	17 12	17 14	17 22		17 30	17 33	17 39	17 44	17 52	18 00
Wimbledon ⊖	d	16 18	16 26		16 34	16 37	16 43	16 48	16 56	17 04	17 07		17 13	17 16	17 18	17 26		17 34	17 37	17 43	17 48	17 56	18 04
Raynes Park	d	16 22			16 37	16 40	16 46	16 52		17 07	17 10		17 16		17 22			17 37	17 40	17 46	17 52		18 07
Motspur Park	d	16 25				16 43		16 55			17 13				17 25				17 43		17 55		
Malden Manor	d					16 46					17 16								17 46				
Tolworth	d					16 49					17 19								17 49				
Chessington North	d					16 52					17 22								17 52				
Chessington South	a					16 54					17 24								17 54				
Worcester Park	d	16 27						16 57							17 27						17 57		
Stoneleigh	d	16 30						17 00							17 30						18 00		
Ewell West	d	16 33						17 03							17 33						18 03		
Epsom	a	16 36						17 06							17 36						18 06		
	d	16 38						17 08							17 38						18 08		
Ashtead	d	16 42						17 12							17 42						18 12		
Leatherhead	d	16 45						17 15							17 45						18 15		
Boxhill & Westhumble	d																						
Dorking	a	16 51													17 51								
New Malden	d				16 40		16 49			17 10			17 19					17 40		17 49			18 10
Norbiton	d				16 43					17 13								17 43					18 13
Kingston	a			16 59	16 46					17 16		17 38					17 59	17 46					18 16
	d			17 04	16 49					17 16							18 04	17 49					18 16
Hampton Wick	d				16 51					17 18								17 51					18 18
Teddington	d				16 56					17 21								17 56					18 21
Strawberry Hill	a				16 59													17 59					
Fulwell	d									17 25													18 25
Hampton	d									17 29													18 29
Kempton Park	d									17 32													18 32
Sunbury	d									17 34													18 34
Upper Halliford	d									17 36													18 36
Shepperton	a									17 39													18 39
Berrylands	d						16 51						17 21							17 51			
Surbiton	d		16 35				16 55		17 05				17 25	17 32		17 35				17 55		18 05	
Thames Ditton	d						17 00						17 30							18 00			
Hampton Court	a						17 03						17 33							18 03			
Hinchley Wood	d													17 36									
Claygate	d													17 39									
Oxshott	d													17 42									
Cobham & Stoke D'abernon	d													17 46									
Bookham	d							17 21													18 21		
Effingham Junction	d							17 25						17 50							18 25		
Horsley	d							17 27						17 53							18 27		
Clandon	d							17 32						17 58							18 32		
London Road (Guildford)	d							17 37						18 03							18 37		
Guildford	a		17 14					17 41	17 44					18 07		18 14					18 41	18 44	

Station		SW	SW	SW	SW	SW	SW	SW	SW	SW	SW	SW	SW	SW	SW	SW	SW	SW	SW	SW	SW	SW
London Waterloo ⊖	d	17 51	17 56	17 57	18 00	18 02	18 10	18 14	18 18	18 21	18 27	18 32	18 40	18 48	18 51	18 56	18 57	19 00	19 02	19 10	19 14	19 18
Vauxhall ⊖	d	17 55	18 00	18 01	18 04	18 06	18 14	18 18	18 22	18 25	18 31	18 36	18 44	18 52	18 55	19 00	19 01	19 04	19 06	19 14	19 18	19 22
Clapham Junction	d	18 00		18 06	18 09	18 11	18 19		18 27	18 30	18 36	18 41	18 49	18 57	19 00		19 06	19 09	19 11	19 19		19 27
Earlsfield	d	18 03		18 09	18 12	18 14	18 22		18 30	18 33	18 39	18 44	18 52	19 00	19 03		19 09	19 12	19 14	19 22		19 30
Wimbledon ⊖	d	18 07		18 13	18 16	18 18	18 26		18 34	18 37	18 43	18 48	18 56	19 04	19 07		19 13	19 16	19 18	19 26		19 34
Raynes Park	d	18 10		18 16		18 22			18 37	18 40	18 46	18 52		19 07	19 10		19 16		19 22			19 37
Motspur Park	d	18 13				18 25				18 43		18 55			19 13				19 25			
Malden Manor	d	18 16								18 46					19 16							
Tolworth	d	18 19								18 49					19 19							
Chessington North	d	18 22								18 52					19 22							
Chessington South	a	18 24								18 54					19 24							
Worcester Park	d					18 27						18 57							19 27			
Stoneleigh	d					18 30						19 00							19 30			
Ewell West	d					18 33						19 03							19 33			
Epsom	a					18 36						19 06							19 36			
	d					18 38						19 08							19 38			
Ashtead	d					18 42						19 12							19 42			
Leatherhead	d					18 45						19 15							19 45			
Boxhill & Westhumble	d																					
Dorking	a					18 51													19 51			
New Malden	d			18 19					18 40		18 49			19 10			19 19					19 40
Norbiton	d								18 43					19 13								19 43
Kingston	a		18 38					18 59	18 46					19 16		19 38					19 59	19 46
	d							19 04	18 49					19 16							20 04	19 49
Hampton Wick	d								18 51					19 18								19 51
Teddington	d								18 56					19 21								19 56
Strawberry Hill	a								18 59													19 59
Fulwell	d													19 25								
Hampton	d													19 29								
Kempton Park	d													19 32								
Sunbury	d													19 34								
Upper Halliford	d													19 36								
Shepperton	a													19 39								
Berrylands	d			18 21							18 51						19 21					
Surbiton	d			18 25	18 32		18 35				18 55		19 05				19 25	19 32		19 35		
Thames Ditton	d			18 30							19 00						19 30					
Hampton Court	a			18 33							19 03						19 33					
Hinchley Wood	d				18 36													19 36				
Claygate	d				18 39													19 39				
Oxshott	d				18 42													19 42				
Cobham & Stoke D'abernon	d				18 46													19 46				
Bookham	d											19 21										
Effingham Junction	d				18 50							19 25						19 50				
Horsley	d				18 53							19 27						19 53				
Clandon	d				18 58							19 32						19 58				
London Road (Guildford)	d				19 03							19 37						20 03				
Guildford	a				19 07		19 14					19 41	19 44					20 07		20 14		

Table 152

Sundays until 19 September

London - Chessington South, Dorking, Guildford, Shepperton and Hampton Court

		SW	SW	SW	SW	SW	SW	SW	SW	SW	SW	SW	SW	SW	SW	SW	SW	SW	SW	SW	SW	SW	SW
London Waterloo [15] ⊖	d	19 21	19 27	19 32	19 40	19 48	19 56	19 57	20 00	20 02	20 10	20 14	20 18	20 21	20 27	20 32	20 40	20 48	20 56	20 57	21 00	21 02	21 10
Vauxhall ⊖	d	19 25	19 31	19 36	19 44	19 52	20 00	20 01	20 04	20 06	20 14	20 18	20 22	20 25	20 31	20 36	20 44	20 52	21 00	21 01	21 04	21 06	21 14
Clapham Junction [10]	d	19 30	19 36	19 41	19 49	19 57		20 06	20 09	20 11	20 19		20 27	20 30	20 36	20 41	20 49	20 57		21 06	21 09	21 11	21 19
Earlsfield	d	19 33	19 39	19 44	19 52	20 00		20 09	20 12	20 14	20 22		20 30	20 33	20 39	20 44	20 52	21 00		21 09	21 12	21 14	21 22
Wimbledon [6] ⊖	d	19 37	19 43	19 48	19 56	20 04		20 13	20 16	20 18	20 26		20 34	20 37	20 43	20 48	20 56	21 04		21 13	21 16	21 18	21 26
Raynes Park [6]	d	19 40	19 46	19 52		20 07		20 16		20 22			20 37	20 40	20 46	20 52		21 07		21 16		21 22	
Motspur Park	d	19 43		19 55						20 25				20 43		20 55						21 25	
Malden Manor	d	19 46												20 46										
Tolworth	d	19 49												20 49										
Chessington North	d	19 52												20 52										
Chessington South	a	19 54												20 54										
Worcester Park	d			19 57						20 27						20 57						21 27	
Stoneleigh	d			20 00						20 30						21 00						21 30	
Ewell West	d			20 03						20 33						21 03						21 33	
Epsom [3]	a			20 06						20 36						21 06						21 36	
	d			20 08						20 38						21 08						21 38	
Ashtead	d			20 12						20 42						21 12						21 42	
Leatherhead	d			20 15						20 45						21 15						21 45	
Boxhill & Westhumble	d																						
Dorking [4]	a									20 51												21 51	
New Malden [6]	d		19 49			20 10		20 19					20 40		20 49			21 10		21 19			
Norbiton	d					20 13							20 43					21 13					
Kingston	a					20 16	20 38					20 59	20 46					21 16	21 38				
	d					20 16						21 04	20 49					21 16					
Hampton Wick	d					20 18							20 51					21 18					
Teddington	d					20 21							20 56					21 21					
Strawberry Hill	a												20 59										
Fulwell	d					20 25												21 25					
Hampton	d					20 29												21 29					
Kempton Park	d					20 32												21 32					
Sunbury	d					20 34												21 34					
Upper Halliford	d					20 36												21 36					
Shepperton	a					20 39												21 39					
Berrylands	d		19 51					20 21							20 51					21 21			
Surbiton [6]	d		19 55		20 05			20 25	20 32		20 35				20 55		21 05			21 25	21 32		21 35
Thames Ditton	d		20 00					20 30							21 00					21 30			
Hampton Court	a		20 03					20 33							21 03					21 33			
Hinchley Wood	d								20 36												21 36		
Claygate	d								20 39												21 39		
Oxshott	d								20 42												21 42		
Cobham & Stoke D'abernon	d								20 46												21 46		
Bookham	d			20 21												21 21							
Effingham Junction [6]	d			20 25					20 50							21 25					21 50		
Horsley	d			20 27					20 53							21 27					21 53		
Clandon	d			20 32					20 58							21 32					21 58		
London Road (Guildford)	d			20 37					21 03							21 37					22 03		
Guildford	a			20 41	20 44				21 07		21 14					21 41	21 44				22 07		22 14

		SW	SW	SW	SW	SW	SW	SW	SW	SW	SW	SW	SW	SW	SW	SW	SW	SW	SW	SW	SW	SW
London Waterloo [15] ⊖	d	21 14	21 18	21 21	21 32	21 40	21 48	21 56	21 57	22 00	22 02	22 10	22 14	22 18	22 21	22 32	22 40	22 48	22 51	22 56	22 57	23 00
Vauxhall ⊖	d	21 18	21 22	21 25	21 36	21 44	21 52	22 00	22 01	22 04	22 06	22 14	22 18	22 22	22 25	22 36	22 44	22 52	22 55	23 00	23 01	23 04
Clapham Junction [10]	d		21 27	21 30	21 41	21 49	21 57		22 06	22 09	22 11	22 19		22 27	22 30	22 41	22 49	22 57	23 00		23 06	23 09
Earlsfield	d		21 30	21 33	21 44	21 52	22 00		22 09	22 12	22 14	22 22		22 30	22 33	22 44	22 52	23 00	23 03		23 09	23 12
Wimbledon [6] ⊖	d		21 34	21 37	21 48	21 56	22 04		22 13	22 16	22 18	22 26		22 34	22 37	22 48	22 56	23 04	23 07		23 13	23 16
Raynes Park [6]	d		21 37	21 40	21 52		22 07		22 16		22 22			22 37	22 40	22 52		23 07	23 10		23 16	
Motspur Park	d			21 43	21 55						22 25				22 43	22 55			23 13			
Malden Manor	d			21 46											22 46				23 16			
Tolworth	d			21 49											22 49				23 19			
Chessington North	d			21 52											22 52				23 22			
Chessington South	a			21 54											22 54				23 24			
Worcester Park	d				21 57						22 27					22 57						
Stoneleigh	d				22 00						22 30					23 00						
Ewell West	d				22 03						22 33					23 03						
Epsom [3]	a				22 06						22 36					23 06						
	d				22 08						22 38					23 08						
Ashtead	d				22 12						22 42					23 12						
Leatherhead	d				22 15						22 45					23 15						
Boxhill & Westhumble	d																					
Dorking [4]	a										22 51											
New Malden [6]	d		21 40				22 10		22 19					22 40				23 10			23 19	
Norbiton	d		21 43				22 13							22 43				23 13				
Kingston	a	21 59	21 46				22 16	22 38					22 59	22 46				23 16		23 38		
	d	22 04	21 49				22 16						23 04	22 49				23 16				
Hampton Wick	d		21 51				22 18							22 51				23 18				
Teddington	d		21 56				22 21							22 56				23 21				
Strawberry Hill	a		21 59											22 59								
Fulwell	d						22 25											23 25				
Hampton	d						22 29											23 29				
Kempton Park	d						22 32											23 32				
Sunbury	d						22 34											23 34				
Upper Halliford	d						22 36											23 36				
Shepperton	a						22 39											23 39				
Berrylands	d								22 21												23 21	
Surbiton [6]	d					22 05			22 25	22 32		22 35					23 05				23 25	23 32
Thames Ditton	d								22 30												23 30	
Hampton Court	a								22 33												23 33	
Hinchley Wood	d									22 36												23 36
Claygate	d									22 39												23 39
Oxshott	d									22 42												23 42
Cobham & Stoke D'abernon	d									22 46												23 46
Bookham	d				22 21											23 21						
Effingham Junction [6]	d				22 25					22 50						23 25						23 50
Horsley	d				22 27					22 53						23 27						23 53
Clandon	d				22 32					22 58						23 32						23 58
London Road (Guildford)	d				22 37					23 03						23 37						00 03
Guildford	a				22 41	22 44				23 07		23 13				23 41	23 45					00 07

Table 152

Sundays until 19 September

London - Chessington South, Dorking, Guildford, Shepperton and Hampton Court

		SW	SW	SW	SW	SW	SW [1]
London Waterloo [15] ⊖	d	23 02	23 10	23 14	23 18	23 32	23 40
Vauxhall ⊖	d	23 06	23 14	23 18	23 22	23 36	23 44
Clapham Junction [10]	d	23 11	23 19		23 27	23 41	23 49
Earlsfield	d	23 14	23 22		23 30	23 44	23 52
Wimbledon [6] ⊖	d	23 18	23 26		23 34	23 48	23 56
Raynes Park [6]	d	23 22			23 37	23 52	
Motspur Park	d	23 25				23 55	
Malden Manor	d						
Tolworth	d						
Chessington North	d						
Chessington South	a						
Worcester Park	d	23 27				23 57	
Stoneleigh	d	23 30				23 57	
Ewell West	d	23 33				00 03	
Epsom [3]	a	23 36				00 06	
	d						
Ashtead	d						
Leatherhead	d						
Boxhill & Westhumble	d						
Dorking [4]	a						
New Malden [6]	d				23 40		
Norbiton	d				23 43		
Kingston	a			23 56	23 46		
	d				23 47		
Hampton Wick	d				23 49		
Teddington	d				23 51		
Strawberry Hill	a				23 54		
Fulwell	d						
Hampton	d						
Kempton Park	d						
Sunbury	d						
Upper Halliford	d						
Shepperton	a						
Berrylands	d						
Surbiton [6]	d		23 35				00 05
Thames Ditton	d						
Hampton Court	a						
Hinchley Wood	d						
Claygate	d						
Oxshott	d						
Cobham & Stoke D'abernon	d						
Bookham	d						
Effingham Junction [6]	d						
Horsley	d						
Clandon	d						
London Road (Guildford)	d						
Guildford	a		00 13				

Table 152

Sundays
from 26 September

London - Chessington South, Dorking, Guildford, Shepperton and Hampton Court

		SW	SW	SW	SW	SW	SW	SW	SW	SW	SW	SW	SW	SW	SW	SW
London Waterloo 15 ⊖	d	23p03	23p09	23p12	23p27	23p30	23p42	23p50	23p57	00 09	00 15	00 18	00 27	01 42	06 14	06 18
Vauxhall ⊖	d	23p07	23p13	23p16	23p31	23p34	23p46	23p54	00 01	00 13	00 19	00 22	00 31	01 46	06 18	06 22
Clapham Junction 10	d	23p12	23p18	23p21	23p36	23p39	23p51	23p58	00 06	00 18	00 24		00 36	01 51		06 27
Earlsfield	d	23p15	23p21	23p24	23p39	23p42	23p54	00 02	00 09	00 21	00 27		00s39			
Wimbledon 6 ⊖	d	23p19	23p25	23p28	23p43	23p46	23p58	00 06	00 13	00 25	00 31		00 43	01 57		06 34
Raynes Park 6	d		23p28	23p31	23p46	23p49	00 01		00 16		00 34		00 46	02 00		06 37
Motspur Park	d		23p31				00 04				00 37					
Malden Manor	d															
Tolworth	d															
Chessington North	d															
Chessington South	a															
Worcester Park	d		23p33				00 06				00 39					
Stoneleigh	d		23p36				00 09				00 42					
Ewell West	d		23p39				00 12				00 45					
Epsom 3	a		23p42				00 15				00 48					
	d		23p47				00 19									
Ashtead	d		23p51				00 23									
Leatherhead	d		23p54				00 26									
Boxhill & Westhumble	d															
Dorking 4	a		00 03													
New Malden 6	d			23p34	23p49	23p52			00 19				00 49	02 02		06 40
Norbiton	d			23p37	23p52				00 22					02 06		06 43
Kingston	a			23p40	23p55				00 25			01 00		02 08	06 59	06 46
	d			23p40	23p55				00 25					02 09	07 04	06 49
Hampton Wick	d			23p42	23p57				00 27					02s11		06 51
Teddington	d			23p45	23p59				00 30					02s13		06 56
Strawberry Hill	a				00 03									02s16		06 59
Fulwell	d			23p49					00 34							
Hampton	d			23p53					00 38							
Kempton Park	d			23p56					00 41							
Sunbury	d			23p58					00 43							
Upper Halliford	d			23p59					00 45							
Shepperton	a			00 03					00 48							
Berrylands	d					23p54							00s51			
Surbiton 6	d	23p27				23p59		00 14		00 33			00a55			
Thames Ditton	d					00 03										
Hampton Court	a					00 06										
Hinchley Wood	d	23p31						00 18								
Claygate	d	23p34						00 21								
Oxshott	d	23p37						00 24								
Cobham & Stoke D'abernon	d	23p41						00 28								
Bookham	d						00 31									
Effingham Junction 6	d	23p45					00 37	00 32								
Horsley	d	23p48					00 40	00 35								
Clandon	d	23p53					00 45	00 40								
London Road (Guildford)	d	23p58					00 50	00 45								
Guildford	a	00 05					00 57	00 52		01 06						

Table 152

Sundays
from 26 September

London - Chessington South, Dorking, Guildford, Shepperton and Hampton Court

		SW	SW	SW	SW	SW	SW	SW	SW	SW	SW	SW	SW	SW	SW	SW	SW	SW	SW	SW	SW	SW	SW
London Waterloo 15 ⊖	d		06 57	07 14		07 10	07 18		07 27		07 40	07 48		07 57	08 02		08 14		08 10	08 18	08 21	08 27	08 32
Vauxhall ⊖	d		07 01	07 18		07 14	07 22		07 31		07 44	07 52		08 01	08 06		08 18		08 14	08 22	08 25	08 31	08 36
Clapham Junction 10	d		07 06			07 19	07 27		07 36		07 49	07 57		08 06	08 11				08 19	08 27	08 30	08 36	08 41
Earlsfield	d		07 09			07 22	07 30		07 39		07 52	08 00		08 09	08 14				08 22	08 30	08 33	08 39	08 44
Wimbledon 6 ⊖	d	06 48	07 13		07 16	07 26	07 34	07 18	07 43	07 37	07 56	08 04	07 48	08 13	08 18	08 07		08 16	08 26	08 34	08 37	08 43	08 48
Raynes Park 6	d	06 52	07 16				07 37	07 22	07 46	07 40		08 07	07 52	08 16	08 22	08 10				08 37	08 40	08 46	08 52
Motspur Park	d	06 55						07 25		07 43			07 55		08 25	08 13					08 43		08 55
Malden Manor	d									07 46						08 16					08 46		
Tolworth	d									07 49						08 19					08 49		
Chessington North	d									07 52						08 22					08 52		
Chessington South	a									07 54						08 24					08 54		
Worcester Park	d	06 57						07 27					07 57		08 27								08 57
Stoneleigh	d	07 00						07 30					08 00		08 30								09 00
Ewell West	d	07 03						07 33					08 03		08 33								09 03
Epsom 3	a	07 06						07 37					08 06		08 36								09 06
	d												08 08		08 38								09 08
Ashtead	d												08 12		08 42								09 12
Leatherhead	d												08 15		08 45								09 15
Boxhill & Westhumble	d																						
Dorking 4	a														08 53								
New Malden 6	d		07 19				07 40		07 49			08 10		08 19						08 40		08 49	
Norbiton	d						07 43					08 13								08 43			
Kingston	a			07 59			07 46					08 16					08 59			08 46			
	d			08 04			07 49					08 16					09 04			08 49			
Hampton Wick	d						07 51					08 18								08 51			
Teddington	d						07 56					08 21								08 56			
Strawberry Hill	a						07 59													08 59			
Fulwell	d											08 25											
Hampton	d											08 29											
Kempton Park	d											08 32											
Sunbury	d											08 34											
Upper Halliford	d											08 36											
Shepperton	a											08 39											
Berrylands	d		07 21						07 51					08 21								08 51	
Surbiton 6	d		07 25		07 32	07 35			07 55		08 05			08 25				08 32	08 35			08 55	
Thames Ditton	d		07 30						08 00					08 30								09 00	
Hampton Court	a		07 33						08 03					08 33								09 03	
Hinchley Wood	d				07 36													08 36					
Claygate	d				07 39													08 39					
Oxshott	d				07 42													08 42					
Cobham & Stoke D'abernon	d				07 46													08 46					
Bookham	d												08 21										09 21
Effingham Junction 6	d				07 50								08 25					08 50					09 25
Horsley	d				07 53								08 27					08 53					09 27
Clandon	d				07 58								08 32					08 58					09 32
London Road (Guildford)	d				08 03								08 37					09 03					09 37
Guildford	a				08 10	08 14					08 40		08 44					09 10	09 10				09 44

		SW	SW	SW	SW	SW	SW	SW	SW	SW	SW	SW	SW	SW	SW	SW	SW	SW	SW	SW	SW	SW
London Waterloo 15 ⊖	d	08 40	08 48	08 51	08 57	09 02	09 14		09 10	09 18	09 21	09 27	09 32	09 40	09 48	09 51	09 57	10 02	10 14		10 10	10 18
Vauxhall ⊖	d	08 44	08 52	08 55	09 01	09 06	09 18		09 14	09 22	09 25	09 31	09 36	09 44	09 52	09 55	10 01	10 06	10 18		10 14	10 22
Clapham Junction 10	d	08 49	08 57	09 00	09 06	09 11			09 19	09 27	09 30	09 36	09 41	09 49	09 57	10 00	10 06	10 11			10 19	10 27
Earlsfield	d	08 52	09 00	09 03	09 09	09 14			09 22	09 30	09 33	09 39	09 44	09 52	10 00	10 03	10 09	10 14			10 22	10 30
Wimbledon 6 ⊖	d	08 56	09 04	09 07	09 13	09 18		09 16	09 26	09 34	09 37	09 43	09 48	09 56	10 04	10 07	10 13	10 18		10 16	10 26	10 34
Raynes Park 6	d		09 07	09 10	09 16	09 22				09 37	09 40	09 46	09 52		10 07	10 10	10 16	10 22				10 37
Motspur Park	d			09 13		09 25					09 43		09 55			10 13		10 25				
Malden Manor	d			09 16							09 46					10 16						
Tolworth	d			09 19							09 49					10 19						
Chessington North	d			09 22							09 52					10 22						
Chessington South	a			09 24							09 54					10 24						
Worcester Park	d					09 27							09 57					10 27				
Stoneleigh	d					09 30							10 00					10 30				
Ewell West	d					09 33							10 03					10 33				
Epsom 3	a					09 36							10 06					10 36				
	d					09 38							10 08					10 38				
Ashtead	d					09 42							10 12					10 42				
Leatherhead	d					09 45							10 15					10 45				
Boxhill & Westhumble	d																					
Dorking 4	a					09 53												10 53				
New Malden 6	d		09 10		09 19					09 40		09 49			10 10		10 19					10 40
Norbiton	d		09 13							09 43					10 13							10 43
Kingston	a		09 16				09 59			09 46					10 16				10 59			10 46
	d		09 16				10 04			09 49					10 16				11 04			10 49
Hampton Wick	d		09 18							09 51					10 18							10 51
Teddington	d		09 21							09 56					10 21							10 56
Strawberry Hill	a									09 59												10 59
Fulwell	d		09 25												10 25							
Hampton	d		09 29												10 29							
Kempton Park	d		09 32												10 32							
Sunbury	d		09 34												10 34							
Upper Halliford	d		09 36												10 36							
Shepperton	a		09 41												10 41							
Berrylands	d				09 21							09 51					10 21					
Surbiton 6	d	09 05			09 25			09 32	09 35			09 55		10 05			10 25			10 32	10 35	
Thames Ditton	d				09 30							10 00					10 30					
Hampton Court	a				09 33							10 03					10 33					
Hinchley Wood	d							09 36												10 36		
Claygate	d							09 39												10 39		
Oxshott	d							09 42												10 42		
Cobham & Stoke D'abernon	d							09 46												10 46		
Bookham	d												10 21									
Effingham Junction 6	d							09 50					10 25							10 50		
Horsley	d							09 53					10 27							10 53		
Clandon	d							09 58					10 32							10 58		
London Road (Guildford)	d							10 03					10 37							11 03		
Guildford	a	09 40						10 10	10 10				10 44	10 44						11 10	11 14	

Table 152

Sundays from 26 September

London - Chessington South, Dorking, Guildford, Shepperton and Hampton Court

Station		SW	SW	SW	SW	SW	SW	SW		SW	SW	SW	SW	SW	SW	SW	SW	SW		SW	SW	SW	SW	SW	SW
London Waterloo ⊖	d	10 21	10 27	10 32	10 40	10 48	10 51	10 57		11 02	11 14		11 10	11 18	11 21	11 27	11 32	11 40		11 48	11 51	11 57	12 02	12 14	
Vauxhall ⊖	d	10 25	10 31	10 36	10 44	10 52	10 55	11 01		11 06	11 19		11 14	11 22	11 25	11 31	11 36	11 44		11 52	11 55	12 01	12 06	12 19	
Clapham Junction	d	10 30	10 36	10 41	10 49	10 57	11 00	11 06		11 11			11 19	11 27	11 30	11 36	11 41	11 49		11 57	12 00	12 06	12 11		
Earlsfield	d	10 33	10 39	10 44	10 52	11 00	11 03	11 09		11 14			11 22	11 30	11 33	11 39	11 44	11 52		12 00	12 03	12 09	12 14		
Wimbledon ⊖	d	10 37	10 43	10 48	10 56	11 04	11 07	11 13		11 18		11 16	11 26	11 34	11 37	11 43	11 48	11 56		12 04	12 07	12 13	12 18		12 16
Raynes Park	d	10 40	10 46	10 52		11 07	11 10	11 16		11 22				11 37	11 40	11 46	11 52			12 07	12 10	12 16	12 22		
Motspur Park	d	10 43		10 55			11 13			11 25					11 43		11 55				12 13		12 25		
Malden Manor	d	10 46					11 16								11 46						12 16				
Tolworth	d	10 49					11 19								11 49						12 19				
Chessington North	d	10 52					11 22								11 52						12 22				
Chessington South	a	10 54					11 24								11 54						12 24				
Worcester Park	d			10 57						11 27							11 57						12 27		
Stoneleigh	d			11 00						11 30							12 00						12 30		
Ewell West	d			11 03						11 33							12 03						12 33		
Epsom	a			11 06						11 36							12 06						12 36		
	d			11 08						11 38							12 08						12 38		
Ashtead	d			11 12						11 42							12 12						12 42		
Leatherhead	d			11 15						11 45							12 15						12 45		
Boxhill & Westhumble	d																								
Dorking	a									11 53													12 53		
New Malden	d		10 49			11 10		11 19						11 40		11 49				12 10		12 19			
Norbiton	d					11 13								11 43						12 13					
Kingston	a					11 16					11 59			11 46						12 16				12 59	
	d					11 16					12 04			11 49						12 16				13 04	
Hampton Wick	d					11 18								11 51						12 18					
Teddington	d					11 21								11 56						12 21					
Strawberry Hill	a													11 59											
Fulwell	d					11 25														12 25					
Hampton	d					11 29														12 29					
Kempton Park	d					11 32														12 32					
Sunbury	d					11 34														12 34					
Upper Halliford	d					11 36														12 36					
Shepperton	a					11 41														12 41					
Berrylands	d		10 51					11 21								11 51						12 21			
Surbiton	d		10 55		11 05			11 25				11 32	11 35			11 55		12 05				12 25			12 32
Thames Ditton	d		11 00					11 30								12 00						12 30			
Hampton Court	a		11 03					11 33								12 03						12 33			
Hinchley Wood	d											11 36													12 36
Claygate	d											11 39													12 39
Oxshott	d											11 42													12 42
Cobham & Stoke D'abernon	d											11 46													12 46
Bookham	d			11 21													12 21								
Effingham Junction	d			11 25								11 50					12 25								12 50
Horsley	d			11 27								11 53					12 27								12 53
Clandon	d			11 32								11 58					12 32								12 58
London Road (Guildford)	d			11 37								12 03					12 37								13 03
Guildford	a			11 44	11 44							12 10	12 14				12 44	12 44							13 10

Station		SW	SW	SW		SW	SW	SW	SW	SW	SW	SW	SW	SW		SW	SW	SW	SW	SW	SW	SW	SW	SW	
London Waterloo ⊖	d	12 10	12 18	12 21		12 27	12 32	12 40	12 48	12 51	12 57	13 00	13 02	13 10		13 14	13 18	13 21	13 27	13 32	13 40	13 48	13 51	13 56	
Vauxhall ⊖	d	12 14	12 22	12 25		12 31	12 36	12 44	12 52	12 55	13 01	13 04	13 06	13 14		13 18	13 22	13 25	13 31	13 36	13 44	13 52	13 55	14 00	
Clapham Junction	d	12 19	12 27	12 30		12 36	12 41	12 49	12 57	13 00	13 06	13 09	13 11	13 19			13 27	13 30	13 36	13 41	13 49	13 57	14 00		
Earlsfield	d	12 22	12 30	12 33		12 39	12 44	12 52	13 00	13 03	13 09	13 12	13 14	13 22			13 30	13 33	13 39	13 44	13 52	14 00	14 03		
Wimbledon ⊖	d	12 26	12 34	12 37		12 43	12 48	12 56	13 04	13 07	13 13	13 16	13 18	13 26			13 34	13 37	13 43	13 48	13 56	14 04	14 07		
Raynes Park	d		12 37	12 40		12 46	12 52		13 07	13 10	13 16		13 22				13 37	13 40	13 46	13 52		14 07	14 10		
Motspur Park	d			12 43			12 55			13 13			13 25					13 43		13 55			14 13		
Malden Manor	d			12 46						13 16								13 46					14 16		
Tolworth	d			12 49						13 19								13 49					14 19		
Chessington North	d			12 52						13 22								13 52					14 22		
Chessington South	a			12 54						13 24								13 54					14 24		
Worcester Park	d						12 57						13 27							13 57					
Stoneleigh	d						13 00						13 30							14 00					
Ewell West	d						13 03						13 33							14 03					
Epsom	a						13 06						13 36							14 06					
	d						13 08						13 38							14 08					
Ashtead	d						13 12						13 42							14 12					
Leatherhead	d						13 15						13 45							14 15					
Boxhill & Westhumble	d																								
Dorking	a												13 53												
New Malden	d		12 40			12 49			13 10		13 19						13 40		13 49			14 10			
Norbiton	d		12 43						13 13								13 43					14 13			
Kingston	a		12 46						13 16							13 59	13 46					14 16		14 38	
	d		12 49						13 16							14 04	13 49					14 16			
Hampton Wick	d		12 51						13 18								13 51					14 18			
Teddington	d		12 56						13 21								13 56					14 21			
Strawberry Hill	a		12 59														13 59								
Fulwell	d								13 25													14 25			
Hampton	d								13 29													14 29			
Kempton Park	d								13 32													14 32			
Sunbury	d								13 34													14 34			
Upper Halliford	d								13 36													14 36			
Shepperton	a								13 41													14 41			
Berrylands	d					12 51					13 21								13 51						
Surbiton	d	12 35				12 55		13 05			13 25	13 32		13 35					13 55		14 05				
Thames Ditton	d					13 00					13 30								14 00						
Hampton Court	a					13 03					13 33								14 03						
Hinchley Wood	d											13 36													
Claygate	d											13 39													
Oxshott	d											13 42													
Cobham & Stoke D'abernon	d											13 46													
Bookham	d						13 21													14 21					
Effingham Junction	d						13 25					13 50								14 25					
Horsley	d						13 27					13 53								14 27					
Clandon	d						13 32					13 58								14 32					
London Road (Guildford)	d						13 37					14 03								14 37					
Guildford	a	13 14					13 44	13 44				14 10		14 14						14 44	14 44				

Table 152

Sundays from 26 September

London - Chessington South, Dorking, Guildford, Shepperton and Hampton Court

Station		SW	SW	SW	SW	SW	SW	SW	SW	SW		SW	SW	SW	SW	SW	SW	SW	SW	SW		SW	SW	SW	SW
London Waterloo ⊖	d	13 57	14 00	14 02	14 10	14 14	14 18	14 21	14 27	14 32		14 40	14 48	14 51	14 56	14 57	15 00	15 02	15 10	15 14		15 18	15 21	15 27	15 32
Vauxhall ⊖	d	14 01	14 04	14 06	14 14	14 18	14 22	14 25	14 31	14 36		14 44	14 52	14 55	15 00	15 01	15 04	15 06	15 14	15 18		15 22	15 25	15 31	15 36
Clapham Junction	d	14 06	14 09	14 11	14 19		14 27	14 30	14 36	14 41		14 49	14 57	15 00		15 06	15 09	15 11	15 19			15 27	15 30	15 36	15 41
Earlsfield	d	14 09	14 12	14 14	14 22		14 30	14 33	14 39	14 44		14 52	15 00	15 03		15 09	15 12	15 14	15 22			15 30	15 33	15 39	15 44
Wimbledon ⊖	d	14 13	14 16	14 18	14 26		14 34	14 37	14 43	14 48		14 56	15 04	15 07		15 13	15 16	15 18	15 26			15 34	15 37	15 43	15 48
Raynes Park	d	14 16		14 22			14 37	14 40	14 46	14 52			15 07	15 10		15 16		15 22				15 37	15 40	15 46	15 52
Motspur Park	d			14 25				14 43		14 55				15 13				15 25					15 43		15 55
Malden Manor	d							14 46						15 16									15 46		
Tolworth	d							14 49						15 19									15 49		
Chessington North	d							14 52						15 22									15 52		
Chessington South	a							14 54						15 24									15 54		
Worcester Park	d			14 27						14 57								15 27							15 57
Stoneleigh	d			14 30						15 00								15 30							16 00
Ewell West	d			14 33						15 03								15 33							16 03
Epsom	a			14 36						15 06								15 36							16 06
	d			14 38						15 08								15 38							16 08
Ashtead	d			14 42						15 12								15 42							16 12
Leatherhead	d			14 45						15 15								15 45							16 15
Boxhill & Westhumble	d																								
Dorking	a			14 53														15 53							
New Malden	d	14 19					14 40		14 49				15 10			15 19						15 40		15 49	
Norbiton	d						14 43						15 13									15 43			
Kingston	a					14 59	14 46						15 16		15 38					15 59		15 46			
	d					15 04	14 49						15 16							16 04		15 49			
Hampton Wick	d						14 51						15 18									15 51			
Teddington	d						14 56						15 21									15 56			
Strawberry Hill	a						14 59															15 59			
Fulwell	d												15 25												
Hampton	d												15 29												
Kempton Park	d												15 32												
Sunbury	d												15 34												
Upper Halliford	d												15 36												
Shepperton	a												15 41												
Berrylands	d	14 21							14 51							15 21								15 51	
Surbiton	d	14 25	14 32		14 35				14 55			15 05				15 25	15 32		15 35					15 55	
Thames Ditton	d	14 30							15 00							15 30								16 00	
Hampton Court	a	14 33							15 03							15 33								16 03	
Hinchley Wood	d		14 36														15 36								
Claygate	d		14 39														15 39								
Oxshott	d		14 42														15 42								
Cobham & Stoke D'abernon	d		14 46														15 46								
Bookham	d									15 21															16 21
Effingham Junction	d		14 50							15 25							15 50								16 25
Horsley	d		14 53							15 27							15 53								16 27
Clandon	d		14 58							15 32							15 58								16 32
London Road (Guildford)	d		15 03							15 37							16 03								16 37
Guildford	a		15 10		15 14					15 44		15 44					16 10		16 14						16 44

Station		SW	SW	SW	SW	SW		SW	SW	SW	SW	SW	SW	SW	SW	SW		SW	SW	SW	SW	SW	SW	SW	SW
London Waterloo ⊖	d	15 40	15 48	15 51	15 56	15 57		16 00	16 02	16 10	16 14	16 18	16 21	16 27	16 32	16 40		16 48	16 51	16 56	16 57	17 00	17 02	17 10	17 14
Vauxhall ⊖	d	15 44	15 52	15 55	16 00	16 01		16 04	16 06	16 14	16 18	16 22	16 25	16 31	16 36	16 44		16 52	16 55	17 00	17 01	17 04	17 06	17 14	17 18
Clapham Junction	d	15 49	15 57	16 00		16 06		16 09	16 11	16 19		16 27	16 30	16 36	16 41	16 49		16 57	17 00		17 06	17 09	17 11	17 19	
Earlsfield	d	15 52	16 00	16 03		16 09		16 12	16 14	16 22		16 30	16 33	16 39	16 44	16 52		17 00	17 03		17 09	17 12	17 14	17 22	
Wimbledon ⊖	d	15 56	16 04	16 07		16 13		16 16	16 18	16 26		16 34	16 37	16 43	16 48	16 56		17 04	17 07		17 13	17 16	17 18	17 26	
Raynes Park	d		16 07	16 10		16 16			16 22			16 37	16 40	16 46	16 52			17 07	17 10		17 16		17 22		
Motspur Park	d			16 13					16 25				16 43		16 55				17 13				17 25		
Malden Manor	d			16 16									16 46						17 16						
Tolworth	d			16 19									16 49						17 19						
Chessington North	d			16 22									16 52						17 22						
Chessington South	a			16 24									16 54						17 24						
Worcester Park	d								16 27						16 57								17 27		
Stoneleigh	d								16 30						17 00								17 30		
Ewell West	d								16 33						17 03								17 33		
Epsom	a								16 36						17 06								17 36		
	d								16 38						17 08								17 38		
Ashtead	d								16 42						17 12								17 42		
Leatherhead	d								16 45						17 15								17 45		
Boxhill & Westhumble	d																								
Dorking	a								16 53														17 53		
New Malden	d		16 10			16 19						16 40		16 49				17 10			17 19				
Norbiton	d		16 13									16 43						17 13							
Kingston	a		16 16		16 38						16 59	16 46						17 16		17 38					17 59
	d		16 16								17 04	16 49						17 16							18 04
Hampton Wick	d		16 18									16 51						17 18							
Teddington	d		16 21									16 56						17 21							
Strawberry Hill	a											16 59													
Fulwell	d		16 25															17 25							
Hampton	d		16 29															17 29							
Kempton Park	d		16 32															17 32							
Sunbury	d		16 34															17 34							
Upper Halliford	d		16 36															17 36							
Shepperton	a		16 41															17 41							
Berrylands	d					16 21								16 51							17 21				
Surbiton	d	16 05				16 25		16 32		16 35				16 55		17 05					17 25	17 32		17 35	
Thames Ditton	d					16 30								17 00							17 30				
Hampton Court	a					16 33								17 03							17 33				
Hinchley Wood	d							16 36														17 36			
Claygate	d							16 39														17 39			
Oxshott	d							16 42														17 42			
Cobham & Stoke D'abernon	d							16 46														17 46			
Bookham	d														17 21										
Effingham Junction	d							16 50							17 25							17 50			
Horsley	d							16 53							17 27							17 53			
Clandon	d							16 58							17 32							17 58			
London Road (Guildford)	d							17 03							17 37							18 03			
Guildford	a	16 44						17 10		17 14					17 44	17 44						18 10		18 14	

London - Chessington South, Dorking, Guildford, Shepperton and Hampton Court

		SW	SW	SW	SW	SW	SW	SW	SW	SW	SW	SW	SW	SW	SW	SW	SW	SW	SW	SW	SW	SW
London Waterloo 15 ⊖	d	17 18	17 21	17 27	17 32	17 40	17 48	17 51	17 56	17 57	18 00	18 02	18 10	18 14	18 18	18 21	18 27	18 32	18 40	18 48	18 51	18 56
Vauxhall ⊖	d	17 22	17 25	17 31	17 36	17 44	17 52	17 55	18 00	18 01	18 04	18 06	18 14	18 18	18 22	18 25	18 31	18 36	18 44	18 52	18 55	19 00
Clapham Junction 10	d	17 27	17 30	17 36	17 41	17 49	17 57	18 00		18 06	18 09	18 11	18 19		18 27	18 30	18 36	18 41	18 49	18 57	19 00	
Earlsfield	d	17 30	17 33	17 39	17 44	17 52	18 00	18 03		18 09	18 12	18 14	18 22		18 30	18 33	18 39	18 44	18 52	19 00	19 03	
Wimbledon 6 ⊖	d	17 34	17 37	17 43	17 48	17 56	18 04	18 07		18 13	18 16	18 18	18 26		18 34	18 37	18 43	18 48	18 56	19 04	19 07	
Raynes Park 6	d	17 37	17 40	17 46	17 52		18 07	18 10		18 16		18 22			18 37	18 40	18 46	18 52		19 07	19 10	
Motspur Park	d		17 43		17 55			18 13				18 25				18 43		18 55			19 13	
Malden Manor	d		17 46					18 16								18 46					19 16	
Tolworth	d		17 49					18 19								18 49					19 19	
Chessington North	d		17 52					18 22								18 52					19 22	
Chessington South	a		17 54					18 24								18 54					19 24	
Worcester Park	d				17 57							18 27						18 57				
Stoneleigh	d				18 00							18 30						19 00				
Ewell West	d				18 03							18 33						19 03				
Epsom 3	a				18 06							18 36						19 06				
	d				18 08							18 38						19 08				
Ashtead	d				18 12							18 42						19 12				
Leatherhead	d				18 15							18 45						19 15				
Boxhill & Westhumble	d																					
Dorking 4	a											18 53										
New Malden 6	d	17 40		17 49			18 10			18 19					18 40		18 49			19 10		
Norbiton	d	17 43					18 13								18 43					19 13		
Kingston	a	17 46					18 16		18 38					18 59	18 46					19 16		19 38
	d	17 49					18 16							19 04	18 49					19 16		
Hampton Wick	d	17 51					18 18								18 51					19 18		
Teddington	d	17 56					18 21								18 56					19 21		
Strawberry Hill	a	17 59													18 59							
Fulwell	d						18 25													19 25		
Hampton	d						18 29													19 29		
Kempton Park	d						18 32													19 32		
Sunbury	d						18 34													19 34		
Upper Halliford	d						18 36													19 36		
Shepperton	a						18 41													19 41		
Berrylands	d			17 51						18 21							18 51					
Surbiton 6	d			17 55		18 05				18 25	18 32		18 35				18 55		19 05			
Thames Ditton	d			18 00						18 30							19 00					
Hampton Court	a			18 03						18 33							19 03					
Hinchley Wood	d										18 36											
Claygate	d										18 39											
Oxshott	d										18 42											
Cobham & Stoke D'abernon	d										18 46											
Bookham	d				18 21													19 21				
Effingham Junction 6	d				18 25						18 50							19 25				
Horsley	d				18 27						18 53							19 27				
Clandon	d				18 32						18 58							19 32				
London Road (Guildford)	d				18 37						19 03							19 37				
Guildford	a				18 44	18 44					19 10		19 14					19 44	19 44			

		SW	SW	SW	SW	SW	SW	SW	SW	SW	SW	SW	SW	SW	SW	SW	SW	SW	SW	SW	SW	SW	SW
London Waterloo 15 ⊖	d	18 57	19 00	19 02	19 10	19 14	19 18	19 21	19 27	19 32	19 40	19 48	19 56	19 57	20 00	20 02	20 10	20 14	20 18	20 21	20 27	20 32	20 40
Vauxhall ⊖	d	19 01	19 04	19 06	19 14	19 18	19 22	19 25	19 31	19 36	19 44	19 52	20 00	20 01	20 04	20 06	20 14	20 18	20 22	20 25	20 31	20 36	20 44
Clapham Junction 10	d	19 06	19 09	19 11	19 19		19 27	19 30	19 36	19 41	19 49	19 57		20 06	20 09	20 11	20 19		20 27	20 30	20 36	20 41	20 49
Earlsfield	d	19 09	19 12	19 14	19 22		19 30	19 33	19 39	19 44	19 52	20 00		20 09	20 12	20 14	20 22		20 30	20 33	20 39	20 44	20 52
Wimbledon 6 ⊖	d	19 13	19 16	19 18	19 26		19 34	19 37	19 43	19 48	19 56	20 04		20 13	20 16	20 18	20 26		20 34	20 37	20 43	20 48	20 56
Raynes Park 6	d	19 16		19 22			19 37	19 40	19 46	19 52		20 07		20 16		20 22			20 37	20 40	20 46	20 52	
Motspur Park	d			19 25				19 43		19 55						20 25				20 43		20 55	
Malden Manor	d							19 46												20 46			
Tolworth	d							19 49												20 49			
Chessington North	d							19 52												20 52			
Chessington South	a							19 54												20 54			
Worcester Park	d			19 27						19 57						20 27						20 57	
Stoneleigh	d			19 30						20 00						20 30						21 00	
Ewell West	d			19 33						20 03						20 33						21 03	
Epsom 3	a			19 36						20 06						20 36						21 06	
	d			19 38						20 08						20 38						21 08	
Ashtead	d			19 42						20 12						20 42						21 12	
Leatherhead	d			19 45						20 15						20 45						21 15	
Boxhill & Westhumble	d																						
Dorking 4	a			19 53												20 53							
New Malden 6	d	19 19					19 40		19 49			20 10		20 19					20 40		20 49		
Norbiton	d						19 43					20 13							20 43				
Kingston	a					19 59	19 46					20 16	20 38					20 59	20 46				
	d					20 04	19 49					20 16						21 04	20 49				
Hampton Wick	d						19 51					20 18							20 51				
Teddington	d						19 56					20 21							20 56				
Strawberry Hill	a						19 59												20 59				
Fulwell	d											20 25											
Hampton	d											20 29											
Kempton Park	d											20 32											
Sunbury	d											20 34											
Upper Halliford	d											20 36											
Shepperton	a											20 41											
Berrylands	d	19 21							19 51					20 21							20 51		
Surbiton 6	d	19 25	19 32		19 35				19 55		20 05			20 25	20 32		20 35				20 55		21 05
Thames Ditton	d	19 30							20 00					20 30							21 00		
Hampton Court	a	19 33							20 03					20 33							21 03		
Hinchley Wood	d		19 36												20 36								
Claygate	d		19 39												20 39								
Oxshott	d		19 42												20 42								
Cobham & Stoke D'abernon	d		19 46												20 46								
Bookham	d									20 21												21 21	
Effingham Junction 6	d		19 50							20 25					20 50							21 25	
Horsley	d		19 53							20 27					20 53							21 27	
Clandon	d		19 58							20 32					20 58							21 32	
London Road (Guildford)	d		20 03							20 37					21 03							21 37	
Guildford	a		20 10		20 14					20 44	20 44				21 10		21 14					21 44	21 44

Table 152

Sundays
from 26 September

London - Chessington South, Dorking, Guildford, Shepperton and Hampton Court

		SW	SW	SW	SW	SW	SW	SW	SW	SW	SW	SW	SW	SW	SW	SW	SW	SW	SW	SW	SW	SW
London Waterloo 15 ⊖	d	20 48	20 56	20 57	21 00	21 02	21 10	21 14	21 18	21 21	21 32	21 40	21 48	21 56	21 57	22 00	22 02	22 10	22 14	22 18	22 21	22 32
Vauxhall ⊖	d	20 52	21 00	21 01	21 04	21 06	21 14	21 18	21 22	21 25	21 36	21 44	21 52	22 00	22 01	22 04	22 06	22 14	22 18	22 22	22 25	22 36
Clapham Junction 10	d	20 57		21 06	21 09	21 11	21 19		21 27	21 30	21 41	21 49	21 57		22 06	22 09	22 11	22 19		22 27	22 30	22 41
Earlsfield	d	21 00		21 09	21 12	21 14	21 22		21 30	21 33	21 44	21 52	22 00		22 09	22 12	22 14	22 22		22 30	22 33	22 44
Wimbledon 6 ⊖	d	21 04		21 13	21 16	21 18	21 26		21 34	21 37	21 48	21 56	22 04		22 13	22 16	22 18	22 26		22 34	22 37	22 48
Raynes Park 6	d	21 07		21 16		21 22			21 37	21 40	21 52		22 07		22 16		22 22			22 37	22 40	22 52
Motspur Park	d					21 25				21 43	21 55						22 25				22 43	22 55
Malden Manor	d									21 46											22 46	
Tolworth	d									21 49											22 49	
Chessington North	d									21 52											22 52	
Chessington South	a									21 54											22 54	
Worcester Park	d					21 27					21 57						22 27					22 57
Stoneleigh	d					21 30					22 00						22 30					23 00
Ewell West	d					21 33					22 03						22 33					23 03
Epsom 3	a					21 36					22 06						22 36					23 06
	d					21 38					22 08						22 38					23 08
Ashtead	d					21 42					22 12						22 42					23 12
Leatherhead	d					21 45					22 15						22 45					23 15
Boxhill & Westhumble	d																					
Dorking 4	a					21 53											22 53					
New Malden 6	d	21 10		21 19					21 40				22 10		22 19					22 40		
Norbiton	d	21 13							21 43				22 13							22 43		
Kingston	a	21 16	21 38					21 59	21 46				22 16	22 38					22 59	22 46		
	d	21 16						22 04	21 49				22 16						23 04	22 49		
Hampton Wick	d	21 18							21 51				22 18							22 51		
Teddington	d	21 21							21 56				22 21							22 56		
Strawberry Hill	a								21 59											22 59		
Fulwell	d	21 25											22 25									
Hampton	d	21 29											22 29									
Kempton Park	d	21 32											22 32									
Sunbury	d	21 34											22 34									
Upper Halliford	d	21 36											22 36									
Shepperton	a	21 41											22 41									
Berrylands	d			21 21											22 21							
Surbiton 6	d			21 25	21 32		21 35					22 05			22 25	22 32		22 35				
Thames Ditton	d			21 30											22 30							
Hampton Court	a			21 33											22 33							
Hinchley Wood	d				21 36											22 36						
Claygate	d				21 39											22 39						
Oxshott	d				21 42											22 42						
Cobham & Stoke D'abernon	d				21 46											22 46						
Bookham	d										22 21											23 21
Effingham Junction 6	d				21 50						22 25					22 50						23 25
Horsley	d				21 53						22 27					22 53						23 27
Clandon	d				21 58						22 32					22 58						23 32
London Road (Guildford)	d				22 03						22 37					23 03						23 37
Guildford	a				22 10		22 14				22 44	22 44				23 10		23 13				23 44

Table 152

Sundays from 26 September

London - Chessington South, Dorking, Guildford, Shepperton and Hampton Court

		SW	SW	SW	SW	SW	SW	SW	SW	SW		SW	SW	SW 1
London Waterloo ⊖	d	22 40	22 48	22 51	22 56	22 57	23 00	23 02	23 10	23 14		23 18	23 32	23 40
Vauxhall ⊖	d	22 44	22 52	22 55	23 00	23 01	23 04	23 06	23 14	23 18		23 22	23 36	23 44
Clapham Junction	d	22 49	22 57	23 00		23 06	23 09	23 11	23 19			23 27	23 41	23 49
Earlsfield	d	22 52	23 00	23 03		23 09	23 12	23 14	23 22			23 30	23 44	23 52
Wimbledon ⊖	d	22 56	23 04	23 07		23 13	23 16	23 18	23 26			23 34	23 48	23 56
Raynes Park	d		23 07	23 10		23 16		23 22				23 37	23 52	
Motspur Park	d			23 13				23 25					23 55	
Malden Manor	d			23 16										
Tolworth	d			23 19										
Chessington North	d			23 22										
Chessington South	a			23 24										
Worcester Park	d							23 27					23 57	
Stoneleigh	d							23 30					23 57	
Ewell West	d							23 33					00 03	
Epsom	a							23 36					00 06	
	d													
Ashtead	d													
Leatherhead	d													
Boxhill & Westhumble	d													
Dorking	a													
New Malden	d		23 10			23 19						23 40		
Norbiton	d		23 13									23 43		
Kingston	a		23 16		23 38					23 56		23 46		
	d		23 16									23 47		
Hampton Wick	d		23 18									23 49		
Teddington	d		23 21									23 51		
Strawberry Hill	a											23 54		
Fulwell	d		23 25											
Hampton	d		23 29											
Kempton Park	d		23 32											
Sunbury	d		23 34											
Upper Halliford	d		23 36											
Shepperton	a		23 41											
Berrylands	d					23 21								
Surbiton	d	23 05				23 25	23 32		23 35					00 05
Thames Ditton	d					23 30								
Hampton Court	a					23 33								
Hinchley Wood	d						23 36							
Claygate	d						23 39							
Oxshott	d						23 42							
Cobham & Stoke D'abernon	d						23 46							
Bookham	d													
Effingham Junction	d						23 50							
Horsley	d						23 53							
Clandon	d						23 58							
London Road (Guildford)	d						00 03							
Guildford	a	23 45					00 10		00 13					

Table 152

Mondays to Fridays 24 May to 24 September

Hampton Court, Shepperton, Guildford, Dorking and Chessington South - London

		SW MO	SW MX	SW MX 1	SW MX	SW MX	SW MX	SW MO 1	SW MO	SW	
Guildford	d				23p08					04 00	
London Road (Guildford)	d				23p12						
Clandon	d				23p17						
Horsley	d				23p21						
Effingham Junction	d				23p24						
Bookham	d										
Cobham & Stoke d'Abernon	d				23p28						
Oxshott	d				23p31						
Claygate	d				23p34						
Hinchley Wood	d				23p37						
Hampton Court	d								23p45		
Thames Ditton	d								23p47		
Surbiton	d			23p38	23p42			23p46	23p53	04 24	
Berrylands	d								23p55		
Shepperton	d	23p11	23p11								
Upper Halliford	d	23p14	23p14								
Sunbury	d	23p16	23p16								
Kempton Park	d	23p18	23p18								
Hampton	d	23p21	23p21								
Fulwell	d	23p24	23p24								
Strawberry Hill	d					23p37	23p38				
Teddington	d	23p29	23p29			23p41					
Hampton Wick	d	23p31	23p31			23p44					
Kingston	a	23p33	23p33			23p46					
	d	23p34	23p34			23p49					
Norbiton	d	23p36	23p36			23p51					
New Malden	d	23p40	23p40			23p55			23p58		
Dorking	d										
Boxhill & Westhumble	d										
Leatherhead	d										
Ashtead	d										
Epsom	a										
	d										
Ewell West	d										
Stoneleigh	d										
Worcester Park	d										
Chessington South	d										
Chessington North	d										
Tolworth	d										
Malden Manor	d										
Motspur Park	d										
Raynes Park	d	23p43	23p43			23p58			00 01		
Wimbledon ⊖	d	23p47	23p52		23p55	00 05		23p53	00a04	04 32	
Earlsfield	d	23p50	23p55		23p58	00 08					
Clapham Junction-2	d	23p54	23p59	23p55	00 02	00 12		00 01		04 44	
Vauxhall ⊖	d	23p59	00 04		00 07	00 17	00 12				
London Waterloo ⊖	a	00 04	00 11	00 03	00 14	00 23	00 16	00 10		04 53	

		SW	SW	SW	SW	SW	SW	SW	SW	SW		SW	SW	SW	SW
Guildford	d		04 58	05 12						05 38					
London Road (Guildford)	d		05 02							05 42					
Clandon	d		05 07							05 47					
Horsley	d		05 11							05 51					
Effingham Junction	d		05 16							05 54					
Bookham	d		05 19												
Cobham & Stoke d'Abernon	d									05 58					
Oxshott	d									06 01					
Claygate	d									06 04					
Hinchley Wood	d									06 07					
Hampton Court	d								05 54						
Thames Ditton	d								05 56						
Surbiton	d			05 57				06 01	06 02	06 12					
Berrylands	d								06 04						
Shepperton	d				05 23									06 11	
Upper Halliford	d				05 26									06 14	
Sunbury	d				05 28									06 16	
Kempton Park	d														
Hampton	d				05 33									06 21	
Fulwell	d				05 36									06 24	
Strawberry Hill	d	04 55			05 38							06 08	06 08		
Teddington	d	04 59				05 44						06 11		06 29	
Hampton Wick	d	05 01				05 46						06 14		06 31	
Kingston	a	05 03				05 48						06 16		06 33	
	d	05 04				05 49						06 19		06 34	
Norbiton	d	05 06				05 51						06 21		06 36	
New Malden	d	05 10				05 55			06 07			06 25		06 40	
Dorking	d						05 48								
Boxhill & Westhumble	d						05 50								
Leatherhead	d		05 24				05 56								
Ashtead	d		05 28				05 59								
Epsom	a		05 32				06 04								
	d		05 34				06 04								06 18
Ewell West	d		05 37				06 07								06 21
Stoneleigh	d		05 40				06 10								06 24
Worcester Park	d		05 42				06 12								06 27
Chessington South	d														
Chessington North	d														
Tolworth	d														
Malden Manor	d														
Motspur Park	d		05 46				06 16								06 30
Raynes Park	d	05 13	05 49			05 58	06 19		06 10			06 28		06 43	06 34
Wimbledon ⊖	d	05 17	05 53	06 05		06 02	06 23		06 14	06 20		06 32		06 47	06 38
Earlsfield	d	05 21	05 57	06 08		06 05	06 27		06 17	06 24		06 35		06 50	06 42
Clapham Junction-2	d	05 25	06 01	06 12	06 05	06 09	06 31		06 21	06 28		06 39		06 54	06 46
Vauxhall ⊖	d	05 30	06 06	06 17	06 12	06 14	06 36		06 26	06 33		06 44	06 42	06 59	06 51
London Waterloo ⊖	a	05 35	06 11	06 22	06 16	06 19	06 40	06 20	06 31	06 37		06 49	06 46	07 06	06 55

Table 152

Mondays to Fridays
24 May to 24 September

Hampton Court, Shepperton, Guildford, Dorking and Chessington South - London

		SW	SW 1	SW	SW	SW	SW	SW	SW	SW	SW	SW	SW 1	SW	SW	SW	SW	SW	SW	SW	SW	SW	SW 1
Guildford	d	09 58		09 38								10 28		10 08								10 58	
London Road (Guildford)	d	10 02		09 42								10 32		10 12								11 02	
Clandon	d	10 07		09 47								10 37		10 17								11 07	
Horsley	d	10 11		09 51								10 41		10 21								11 11	
Effingham Junction 6	d	10 16		09 54								10 46		10 24								11 16	
Bookham	d	10 19										10 49										11 19	
Cobham & Stoke d'Abernon	d			09 58										10 28									
Oxshott	d			10 01										10 31									
Claygate	d			10 04										10 34									
Hinchley Wood	d			10 07										10 37									
Hampton Court	d									10 24										10 54			
Thames Ditton	d									10 26										10 56			
Surbiton 6	d		10 08	10 12					10 27	10 32			10 38	10 42					10 57	11 02			11 08
Berrylands	d									10 34										11 04			
Shepperton	d							10 11										10 41					
Upper Halliford	d							10 14										10 44					
Sunbury	d							10 16										10 46					
Kempton Park	d							10 18										10 48					
Hampton	d							10 21										10 51					
Fulwell	d							10 24										10 54					
Strawberry Hill	d				10 07	10 08									10 37	10 38							
Teddington	d				10 11			10 29							10 41			10 59					
Hampton Wick	d				10 14			10 31							10 44			11 01					
Kingston	a				10 16			10 33							10 46			11 03					
	d				10 19			10 34							10 49			11 04					
Norbiton	d				10 21			10 36							10 51			11 06					
New Malden 6	d				10 25			10 40		10 37					10 55			11 10		11 07			
Dorking 4	d										10 35										11 05		
Boxhill & Westhumble	d																						
Leatherhead	d	10 24									10 41	10 54									11 11	11 24	
Ashtead	d	10 28									10 44	10 58									11 14	11 28	
Epsom 3	a	10 32									10 49	11 02									11 19	11 32	
	d	10 35									10 50	11 05									11 20	11 35	
Ewell West	d	10 38									10 53	11 08									11 23	11 38	
Stoneleigh	d	10 40									10 55	11 10									11 25	11 40	
Worcester Park	d	10 43									10 58	11 13									11 28	11 43	
Chessington South	d						10 10										10 40						
Chessington North	d						10 12										10 42						
Tolworth	d						10 14										10 44						
Malden Manor	d						10 17										10 47						
Motspur Park	d	10 46					10 20				11 01	11 16					10 50				11 31	11 46	
Raynes Park 6	d	10 49			10 28		10 23	10 43		10 40	11 04	11 19			10 58		10 53	11 13		11 10	11 34	11 49	
Wimbledon 6 ⊖ ⇌	d	10 53		10 20	10 32		10 27	10 47	10 35	10 44	11 08	11 23		10 50	11 02		10 57	11 17	11 05	11 14	11 38	11 53	
Earlsfield	d	10 57		10 24	10 35		10 31	10 50	10 38	10 47	11 12	11 27		10 54	11 05		11 01	11 20	11 08	11 17	11 42	11 57	
Clapham Junction 10	d	11 01		10 28	10 39		10 35	10 54	10 42	10 51	11 16	11 31	10 49	10 58	11 09		11 05	11 24	11 12	11 21	11 46	12 01	
Vauxhall ⊖	d	11 06		10 33	10 44	10 42	10 40	10 59	10 47	10 56	11 21	11 36		11 03	11 14	11 12	11 10	11 29	11 17	11 26	11 51	12 06	
London Waterloo 15 ⊖	a	11 10	10 25	10 37	10 49	10 46	10 45	11 04	10 52	11 01	11 25	11 40	10 57	11 07	11 19	11 16	11 15	11 34	11 22	11 31	11 55	12 10	11 27

Table 152

Mondays to Fridays
24 May to 24 September

Hampton Court, Shepperton, Guildford, Dorking and Chessington South - London

		SW	SW	SW	SW	SW	SW	SW	SW	SW	SW 1	SW	SW	SW	SW	SW	SW	SW	SW	SW	SW 1	SW	SW
Guildford	d	10 38								11 28		11 08								11 58		11 38	
London Road (Guildford)	d	10 42								11 32		11 12								12 02		11 42	
Clandon	d	10 47								11 37		11 17								12 07		11 47	
Horsley	d	10 51								11 41		11 21								12 11		11 51	
Effingham Junction 6	d	10 54								11 46		11 24								12 16		11 54	
Bookham	d									11 49										12 19			
Cobham & Stoke d'Abernon	d	10 58										11 28										11 58	
Oxshott	d	11 01										11 31										12 01	
Claygate	d	11 04										11 34										12 04	
Hinchley Wood	d	11 07										11 37										12 07	
Hampton Court	d							11 24										11 54					
Thames Ditton	d							11 26										11 56					
Surbiton 6	d	11 12					11 27	11 32			11 38	11 42					11 57	12 02			12 08	12 12	
Berrylands	d							11 34										12 04					
Shepperton	d					11 11										11 41							
Upper Halliford	d					11 14										11 44							
Sunbury	d					11 16										11 46							
Kempton Park	d					11 18										11 48							
Hampton	d					11 21										11 51							
Fulwell	d					11 24										11 54							
Strawberry Hill	d		11 07	11 08									11 37	11 38									12 07
Teddington	d		11 11			11 29							11 41			11 59							12 11
Hampton Wick	d		11 14			11 31							11 44			12 01							12 14
Kingston	a		11 16			11 33							11 46			12 03							12 16
	d		11 19			11 34							11 49			12 04							12 19
Norbiton	d		11 21			11 36							11 51			12 06							12 21
New Malden 6	d		11 25			11 40		11 37					11 55			12 10		12 07					12 25
Dorking 4	d								11 35										12 05				
Boxhill & Westhumble	d																						
Leatherhead	d								11 41	11 54									12 11	12 24			
Ashtead	d								11 44	11 58									12 14	12 28			
Epsom 3	a								11 49	12 02									12 19	12 32			
	d								11 50	12 05									12 20	12 35			
Ewell West	d								11 53	12 08									12 23	12 38			
Stoneleigh	d								11 55	12 10									12 25	12 40			
Worcester Park	d								11 58	12 13									12 28	12 43			
Chessington South	d				11 10										11 40								
Chessington North	d				11 12										11 42								
Tolworth	d				11 14										11 44								
Malden Manor	d				11 17										11 47								
Motspur Park	d				11 20				12 01	12 16					11 50				12 31	12 46			
Raynes Park 6	d		11 28		11 23	11 43		11 40	12 04	12 19			11 58		11 53	12 13		12 10	12 34	12 49			12 28
Wimbledon 6 ⊖ ⇌	d	11 20	11 32		11 27	11 47	11 35	11 44	12 08	12 23		11 50	12 02		11 57	12 17	12 05	12 14	12 38	12 53		12 20	12 32
Earlsfield	d	11 24	11 35		11 31	11 50	11 38	11 47	12 12	12 27		11 54	12 05		12 01	12 20	12 08	12 17	12 42	12 57		12 24	12 35
Clapham Junction 10	d	11 28	11 39		11 35	11 54	11 42	11 51	12 16	12 31	11 50	11 58	12 09		12 05	12 24	12 12	12 21	12 46	13 01		12 28	12 39
Vauxhall ⊖	d	11 33	11 44	11 42	11 40	11 59	11 47	11 56	12 21	12 36		12 03	12 14	12 12	12 10	12 29	12 17	12 26	12 51	13 06		12 33	12 44
London Waterloo 15 ⊖	a	11 37	11 49	11 46	11 45	12 04	11 52	12 01	12 25	12 40	11 57	12 07	12 19	12 16	12 15	12 34	12 22	12 31	12 55	13 10	12 27	12 37	12 49

Table 152

Mondays to Fridays
24 May to 24 September

Hampton Court, Shepperton, Guildford, Dorking and Chessington South - London

		SW	SW	SW	SW	SW	SW	SW	SW ■	SW	SW	SW	SW	SW	SW	SW	SW	SW	SW ■	SW	SW	SW
Guildford	d							12 28		12 08								12 58		12 38		
London Road (Guildford)	d							12 32		12 12								13 02		12 42		
Clandon	d							12 37		12 17								13 07		12 47		
Horsley	d							12 41		12 21								13 11		12 51		
Effingham Junction ■	d							12 46		12 24								13 16		12 54		
Bookham	d							12 49										13 19				
Cobham & Stoke d'Abernon	d									12 28										12 58		
Oxshott	d									12 31										13 01		
Claygate	d									12 34										13 04		
Hinchley Wood	d									12 37										13 07		
Hampton Court	d					12 24										12 54						
Thames Ditton	d					12 26										12 56						
Surbiton ■	d				12 27	12 32			12 38	12 42					12 57	13 02			13 08	13 12		
Berrylands	d					12 34										13 04						
Shepperton	d			12 11										12 41								
Upper Halliford	d			12 14										12 44								
Sunbury	d			12 16										12 46								
Kempton Park	d			12 18										12 48								
Hampton	d			12 21										12 51								
Fulwell	d			12 24										12 54								
Strawberry Hill	d	12 08									12 37	12 38									13 07	13 08
Teddington	d			12 29							12 41			12 59							13 11	
Hampton Wick	d			12 31							12 44			13 01							13 14	
Kingston	a			12 33							12 46			13 03							13 16	
	d			12 34							12 49			13 04							13 19	
Norbiton	d			12 36							12 51			13 06							13 21	
New Malden ■	d			12 40		12 37					12 55			13 10		13 07					13 25	
Dorking ■	d						12 35										13 05					
Boxhill & Westhumble	d																					
Leatherhead	d						12 41	12 54									13 11	13 24				
Ashtead	d						12 44	12 58									13 14	13 28				
Epsom ■	a						12 49	13 02									13 19	13 32				
	d						12 50	13 05									13 20	13 35				
Ewell West	d						12 53	13 08									13 23	13 38				
Stoneleigh	d						12 55	13 10									13 25	13 40				
Worcester Park	d						12 58	13 13									13 28	13 43				
Chessington South	d		12 10										12 40									
Chessington North	d		12 12										12 42									
Tolworth	d		12 14										12 44									
Malden Manor	d		12 17										12 47									
Motspur Park	d		12 20				13 01	13 16					12 50				13 31	13 46				
Raynes Park ■	d		12 23	12 43		12 40	13 04	13 19			12 58		12 53	13 13		13 10	13 34	13 49			13 28	
Wimbledon ■ ⊖ ⛴	d		12 27	12 47	12 35	12 44	13 08	13 23		12 50	13 02		12 57	13 17	13 05	13 14	13 38	13 53		13 20	13 32	
Earlsfield	d		12 31	12 50	12 38	12 47	13 12	13 27		12 54	13 05		13 01	13 20	13 08	13 17	13 42	13 57		13 24	13 35	
Clapham Junction ■	d		12 35	12 54	12 42	12 51	13 16	13 31	12 49	12 58	13 09		13 05	13 24	13 12	13 21	13 46	14 01		13 28	13 39	
Vauxhall ⊖	d	12 42	12 40	12 59	12 47	12 56	13 21	13 36		13 03	13 14	13 12	13 10	13 29	13 17	13 26	13 51	14 06		13 33	13 44	13 42
London Waterloo ■ ⊖	a	12 46	12 45	13 04	12 52	13 01	13 25	13 40	12 57	13 07	13 19	13 16	13 15	13 34	13 22	13 31	13 55	14 10	13 25	13 37	13 49	13 46

Table 152

Mondays to Fridays
24 May to 24 September

Hampton Court, Shepperton, Guildford, Dorking and Chessington South - London

		SW	SW	SW	SW	SW	SW	SW ■	SW	SW	SW	SW	SW	SW	SW	SW	SW	SW ■	SW	SW	SW	SW	SW
Guildford	d						13 28		13 08								13 58		13 38				
London Road (Guildford)	d						13 32		13 12								14 02		13 42				
Clandon	d						13 37		13 17								14 07		13 47				
Horsley	d						13 41		13 21								14 11		13 51				
Effingham Junction ■	d						13 46		13 24								14 16		13 54				
Bookham	d						13 49										14 19						
Cobham & Stoke d'Abernon	d								13 28										13 58				
Oxshott	d								13 31										14 01				
Claygate	d								13 34										14 04				
Hinchley Wood	d								13 37										14 07				
Hampton Court	d				13 24										13 54								
Thames Ditton	d				13 26										13 56								
Surbiton ■	d			13 27	13 32			13 38	13 42					13 57	14 02			14 08	14 12				
Berrylands	d				13 34										14 04								
Shepperton	d		13 11										13 41										14 11
Upper Halliford	d		13 14										13 44										14 14
Sunbury	d		13 16										13 46										14 16
Kempton Park	d		13 18										13 48										14 18
Hampton	d		13 21										13 51										14 21
Fulwell	d		13 24										13 54										14 24
Strawberry Hill	d									13 37	13 38									14 07	14 08		
Teddington	d		13 29							13 41			13 59							14 11			14 29
Hampton Wick	d		13 31							13 44			14 01							14 14			14 31
Kingston	a		13 33							13 46			14 03							14 16			14 33
	d		13 34							13 49			14 04							14 19			14 34
Norbiton	d		13 36							13 51			14 06							14 21			14 36
New Malden ■	d		13 40		13 37					13 55			14 10		14 07					14 25			14 40
Dorking ■	d					13 35										14 05							
Boxhill & Westhumble	d																						
Leatherhead	d					13 41	13 54									14 11	14 24						
Ashtead	d					13 44	13 58									14 14	14 28						
Epsom ■	a					13 49	14 02									14 19	14 32						
	d					13 50	14 05									14 20	14 35						
Ewell West	d					13 53	14 08									14 23	14 38						
Stoneleigh	d					13 55	14 10									14 25	14 40						
Worcester Park	d					13 58	14 13									14 28	14 43						
Chessington South	d	13 10										13 40										14 10	
Chessington North	d	13 12										13 42										14 12	
Tolworth	d	13 14										13 44										14 14	
Malden Manor	d	13 17										13 47										14 17	
Motspur Park	d	13 20				14 01	14 16					13 50				14 31	14 46					14 20	
Raynes Park ■	d	13 23	13 43		13 40	14 04	14 19			13 58		13 53	14 13		14 10	14 34	14 49			14 28		14 23	14 43
Wimbledon ■ ⊖ ⛴	d	13 27	13 47	13 35	13 44	14 08	14 23		13 50	14 02		13 57	14 17	14 05	14 14	14 38	14 53		14 20	14 32		14 27	14 47
Earlsfield	d	13 31	13 50	13 38	13 47	14 12	14 27		13 54	14 05		14 01	14 20	14 08	14 17	14 42	14 57		14 24	14 35		14 31	14 50
Clapham Junction ■	d	13 35	13 54	13 42	13 51	14 16	14 31	13 49	13 58	14 09		14 05	14 24	14 12	14 21	14 46	15 01		14 28	14 39		14 35	14 54
Vauxhall ⊖	d	13 40	13 59	13 47	13 56	14 21	14 36		14 03	14 14	14 12	14 10	14 29	14 17	14 26	14 51	15 06		14 33	14 44	14 42	14 40	14 59
London Waterloo ■ ⊖	a	13 45	14 04	13 52	14 01	14 25	14 40	13 57	14 07	14 19	14 16	14 15	14 34	14 22	14 31	14 55	15 10	14 25	14 37	14 49	14 46	14 45	15 04

Table 152

Mondays to Fridays
24 May to 24 September

Hampton Court, Shepperton, Guildford, Dorking and Chessington South - London

		SW	SW	SW		SW	SW ■1	SW	SW	SW	SW	SW	SW	SW		SW	SW	SW ■1	SW	SW	SW	SW	SW	SW	
Guildford	d					14 28		14 08									14 58		14 38						
London Road (Guildford)	d					14 32		14 12									15 02		14 42						
Clandon	d					14 37		14 17									15 07		14 47						
Horsley	d					14 41		14 21									15 11		14 51						
Effingham Junction 6	d					14 46		14 24									15 16		14 54						
Bookham	d					14 49											15 19								
Cobham & Stoke d'Abernon	d							14 28											14 58						
Oxshott	d							14 31											15 01						
Claygate	d							14 34											15 04						
Hinchley Wood	d							14 37											15 07						
Hampton Court	d		14 24											14 54											
Thames Ditton	d		14 26											14 56											
Surbiton 6	d	14 27	14 32				14 38	14 42					14 57	15 02				15 08	15 12					15 27	
Berrylands	d		14 34											15 04											
Shepperton	d											14 41											15 11		
Upper Halliford	d											14 44											15 14		
Sunbury	d											14 46											15 16		
Kempton Park	d											14 48											15 18		
Hampton	d											14 51											15 21		
Fulwell	d											14 54											15 24		
Strawberry Hill	d								14 37	14 38										15 07	15 08				
Teddington	d								14 41			14 59								15 11			15 29		
Hampton Wick	d								14 44			15 01								15 14			15 31		
Kingston	a								14 46			15 03								15 16			15 33		
	d								14 49			15 04								15 19			15 34		
Norbiton	d								14 51			15 06								15 21			15 36		
New Malden 6	d		14 37						14 55			15 10		15 07						15 25			15 40		
Dorking 4	d			14 35												15 05									
Boxhill & Westhumble	d																								
Leatherhead	d			14 41		14 54										15 11	15 24								
Ashtead	d			14 44		14 58										15 14	15 28								
Epsom 3	a			14 49		15 02										15 19	15 32								
	d			14 50		15 05										15 20	15 35								
Ewell West	d			14 53		15 08										15 23	15 38								
Stoneleigh	d			14 55		15 10										15 25	15 40								
Worcester Park	d			14 58		15 13										15 28	15 43								
Chessington South	d										14 40											15 10			
Chessington North	d										14 42											15 12			
Tolworth	d										14 44											15 14			
Malden Manor	d										14 47											15 17			
Motspur Park	d			15 01		15 16					14 50					15 31	15 46					15 20			
Raynes Park 6	d		14 40	15 04		15 19			14 58		14 53	15 13		15 10		15 34	15 49			15 28		15 23	15 43		
Wimbledon 6 ⊖ ⇌	d	14 35	14 44	15 08		15 23		14 50	15 02		14 57	15 17	15 05	15 14		15 38	15 53		15 20	15 32		15 27	15 47	15 35	
Earlsfield	d	14 38	14 47	15 12		15 27		14 54	15 05		15 01	15 20	15 08	15 17		15 42	15 57		15 24	15 35		15 31	15 50	15 38	
Clapham Junction 10	d	14 42	14 51	15 16		15 31	14 49	14 58	15 09		15 05	15 24	15 12	15 21		15 46	16 01		15 28	15 39		15 35	15 54	15 42	
Vauxhall ⊖	d	14 47	14 56	15 21		15 36		15 03	15 14	15 12	15 10	15 29	15 17	15 26		15 51	16 06		15 33	15 44	15 42	15 40	15 59	15 47	
London Waterloo 15 ⊖	a	14 52	15 01	15 25		15 40	14 57	15 07	15 19	15 16	15 15	15 34	15 22	15 31		15 55	16 10	15 25	15 37	15 49	15 46	15 45	16 04	15 52	

Table 152

Mondays to Fridays
24 May to 24 September

Hampton Court, Shepperton, Guildford, Dorking and Chessington South - London

		SW	SW	SW	SW ■1	SW	SW	SW	SW	SW		SW	SW	SW	SW	SW ■1	SW	SW	SW	SW		SW	SW	SW	SW
Guildford	d			15 28		15 08									15 58		15 38								
London Road (Guildford)	d			15 32		15 12									16 02		15 42								
Clandon	d			15 37		15 17									16 07		15 47								
Horsley	d			15 41		15 21									16 11		15 51								
Effingham Junction 6	d			15 46		15 24									16 16		15 54								
Bookham	d			15 49											16 19										
Cobham & Stoke d'Abernon	d					15 28											15 58								
Oxshott	d					15 31											16 01								
Claygate	d					15 34											16 04								
Hinchley Wood	d					15 37											16 07								
Hampton Court	d	15 24											15 54											16 24	
Thames Ditton	d	15 26											15 56											16 26	
Surbiton 6	d	15 32			15 38	15 42						15 57	16 02			16 08	16 12						16 27	16 32	
Berrylands	d	15 34											16 04											16 34	
Shepperton	d									15 41												16 11			
Upper Halliford	d									15 44												16 14			
Sunbury	d									15 46												16 16			
Kempton Park	d									15 48												16 18			
Hampton	d									15 51												16 21			
Fulwell	d									15 54												16 24			
Strawberry Hill	d						15 37	15 38										16 07	16 08						
Teddington	d						15 41			15 59								16 11				16 29			
Hampton Wick	d						15 44			16 01								16 14				16 31			
Kingston	a						15 46			16 03								16 16				16 33			
	d						15 49			16 04								16 19				16 34			
Norbiton	d						15 51			16 06								16 21				16 36			
New Malden 6	d	15 37					15 55			16 10			16 07					16 25				16 40		16 37	
Dorking 4	d		15 35											16 05											16 35
Boxhill & Westhumble	d																								
Leatherhead	d		15 41	15 54										16 11	16 24										16 41
Ashtead	d		15 44	15 58										16 14	16 28										16 44
Epsom 3	a		15 49	16 02										16 19	16 32										16 49
	d		15 50	16 05										16 20	16 35										16 50
Ewell West	d		15 53	16 08										16 23	16 38										16 53
Stoneleigh	d		15 55	16 10										16 25	16 40										16 55
Worcester Park	d		15 58	16 13										16 28	16 43										16 58
Chessington South	d								15 40											16 10					
Chessington North	d								15 42											16 12					
Tolworth	d								15 44											16 14					
Malden Manor	d								15 47											16 17					
Motspur Park	d		16 01	16 16					15 50					16 31	16 46					16 20					17 01
Raynes Park 6	d	15 40	16 04	16 19			15 58		15 53	16 13			16 10	16 34	16 49			16 28		16 23		16 43		16 40	17 04
Wimbledon 6 ⊖ ⇌	d	15 44	16 08	16 23		15 50	16 02		15 57	16 17		16 05	16 14	16 38	16 53		16 20	16 32		16 27		16 47	16 35	16 44	17 08
Earlsfield	d	15 47	16 12	16 27		15 54	16 05		16 01	16 20		16 08	16 17	16 42	16 57		16 24	16 35		16 31		16 50	16 38	16 47	17 12
Clapham Junction 10	d	15 51	16 16	16 31	15 51	15 58	16 09		16 05	16 24		16 12	16 21	16 46	17 01		16 28	16 39		16 35		16 54	16 42	16 51	17 16
Vauxhall ⊖	d	15 56	16 21	16 36		16 03	16 14	16 12	16 10	16 29		16 17	16 26	16 51	17 06		16 33	16 44	16 42	16 40		16 59	16 47	16 56	17 21
London Waterloo 15 ⊖	a	16 01	16 25	16 40	15 58	16 07	16 19	16 19	16 15	16 34		16 22	16 31	16 55	17 10	16 29	16 37	16 49	16 49	16 45		17 05	16 52	17 01	17 25

Table 152

Mondays to Fridays
24 May to 24 September

Hampton Court, Shepperton, Guildford, Dorking and Chessington South - London

		SW	SW ■	SW	SW	SW		SW	SW	SW	SW	SW	SW	SW ■	SW	SW		SW	SW	SW	SW	SW	SW	SW	SW ■
Guildford	d	16 28		16 08									16 58		16 38									17 28	
London Road (Guildford)	d	16 32		16 12									17 02		16 42									17 32	
Clandon	d	16 37		16 17									17 07		16 47									17 37	
Horsley	d	16 41		16 21									17 11		16 51									17 41	
Effingham Junction ■	d	16 46		16 24									17 16		16 54									17 46	
Bookham	d	16 49											17 19											17 49	
Cobham & Stoke d'Abernon	d			16 28											16 58										
Oxshott	d			16 31											17 01										
Claygate	d			16 34											17 04										
Hinchley Wood	d			16 37											17 07										
Hampton Court	d										16 54											17 24			
Thames Ditton	d										16 56											17 26			
Surbiton ■	d		16 38	16 42						16 57	17 02			17 08	17 12						17 27	17 32			17 38
Berrylands	d										17 04											17 34			
Shepperton	d								16 41											17 11					
Upper Halliford	d								16 44											17 14					
Sunbury	d								16 46											17 16					
Kempton Park	d								16 48											17 18					
Hampton	d								16 51											17 21					
Fulwell	d								16 54											17 24					
Strawberry Hill	d				16 37	16 38										17 07		17 08							
Teddington	d				16 43				16 59							17 13				17 29					
Hampton Wick	d				16 46				17 01							17 16				17 31					
Kingston	a				16 48				17 03							17 18				17 33					
	d				16 49				17 04							17 19				17 34					
Norbiton	d				16 51				17 06							17 21				17 36					
New Malden ■	d				16 55				17 10		17 07					17 25				17 40		17 37			
Dorking ■	d											17 05											17 35		
Boxhill & Westhumble	d																								
Leatherhead	d	16 54										17 11	17 24										17 41	17 54	
Ashtead	d	16 58										17 14	17 28										17 44	17 58	
Epsom ■	a	17 02										17 19	17 32										17 49	18 02	
	d	17 05										17 20	17 35										17 50	18 05	
Ewell West	d	17 08										17 23	17 38										17 53	18 08	
Stoneleigh	d	17 10										17 25	17 40										17 55	18 10	
Worcester Park	d	17 13										17 28	17 43										17 58	18 13	
Chessington South	d							16 40											17 10						
Chessington North	d							16 42											17 12						
Tolworth	d							16 44											17 14						
Malden Manor	d							16 47											17 17						
Motspur Park	d	17 16						16 50				17 31	17 46						17 20				18 01	18 16	
Raynes Park ■	d	17 19			16 58			16 53	17 13		17 10	17 34	17 49			17 28			17 23	17 43		17 40	18 04	18 19	
Wimbledon ■ ⊖	d	17 23		16 50	17 02			16 57	17 17	17 05	17 14	17 38	17 53		17 20	17 32			17 27	17 47	17 35	17 44	18 08	18 23	
Earlsfield	d	17 27		16 54	17 05			17 01	17 20	17 08	17 17	17 42	17 57		17 24	17 35			17 31	17 50	17 38	17 47	18 12	18 27	
Clapham Junction ■	d	17 31	16 49	16 58	17 09			17 05	17 24	17 12	17 21	17 46	18 01		17 28	17 39			17 35	17 54	17 42	17 51	18 16	18 31	17 49
Vauxhall ⊖	d	17 36		17 03	17 14	17 12		17 10	17 29	17 17	17 26	17 51	18 06		17 33	17 44		17 42	17 40	17 59	17 47	17 56	18 21	18 36	
London Waterloo ■ ⊖	a	17 40	16 59	17 07	17 19	17 19		17 16	17 35	17 22	17 31	17 55	18 10	17 29	17 37	17 49		17 49	17 45	18 05	17 52	18 01	18 25	18 40	17 59

Table 152

Mondays to Fridays
24 May to 24 September

Hampton Court, Shepperton, Guildford, Dorking and Chessington South - London

		SW		SW	SW	SW	SW	SW	SW	SW	SW	SW		SW ■	SW	SW	SW	SW	SW	SW	SW	SW		SW ■	SW
Guildford	d	17 08										17 58			17 38										18 08
London Road (Guildford)	d	17 12										18 02			17 42										18 12
Clandon	d	17 17										18 07			17 47										18 17
Horsley	d	17 21										18 11			17 51										18 21
Effingham Junction ■	d	17 24										18 16			17 54										18 24
Bookham	d											18 19													
Cobham & Stoke d'Abernon	d	17 28													17 58										18 28
Oxshott	d	17 31													18 01										18 31
Claygate	d	17 34													18 04										18 34
Hinchley Wood	d	17 37													18 07										18 37
Hampton Court	d									17 54											18 24				
Thames Ditton	d									17 56											18 26				
Surbiton ■	d	17 42							17 57	18 02				18 08	18 12					18 27	18 32			18 38	18 42
Berrylands	d									18 04											18 34				
Shepperton	d							17 41											18 11						
Upper Halliford	d							17 44											18 14						
Sunbury	d							17 46											18 16						
Kempton Park	d							17 48											18 18						
Hampton	d							17 51											18 21						
Fulwell	d							17 54											18 24						
Strawberry Hill	d			17 37	17 38	17 41										18 07	18 08								
Teddington	d			17 43		17b52		17 59								18 13			18 29						
Hampton Wick	d			17 46		17 54		18 01								18 16			18 31						
Kingston	a			17 48		17 56		18 03								18 18			18 33						
	d			17 49		17 58		18 04								18 19			18 34						
Norbiton	d			17 51		18 00		18 06								18 21			18 36						
New Malden ■	d			17 55		18 04		18 10		18 07						18 25			18 40		18 37				
Dorking ■	d										18 05											18 35			
Boxhill & Westhumble	d																								
Leatherhead	d										18 11	18 24										18 41			
Ashtead	d										18 14	18 28										18 44			
Epsom ■	a										18 19	18 32										18 49			
	d										18 20	18 35										18 50			
Ewell West	d										18 23	18 38										18 53			
Stoneleigh	d										18 25	18 40										18 55			
Worcester Park	d										18 28	18 43										18 58			
Chessington South	d						17 40											18 10							
Chessington North	d						17 42											18 12							
Tolworth	d						17 44											18 14							
Malden Manor	d						17 47											18 17							
Motspur Park	d						17 50				18 31	18 46						18 20				19 01			
Raynes Park ■	d			17 58		18 07	17 53	18 13		18 10	18 34	18 49				18 28		18 23	18 43		18 40	19 04			
Wimbledon ■ ⊖	d	17 50		18 02		18 11	17 57	18 17	18 05	18 14	18 38	18 53			18 20	18 32		18 27	18 47	18 35	18 44	19 08			18 50
Earlsfield	d	17 54		18 05		18 15	18 01	18 20	18 08	18 17	18 42	18 57			18 24	18 35		18 31	18 50	18 38	18 47	19 12			18 54
Clapham Junction ■	d	17 58		18 09		18 19	18 05	18 24	18 12	18 21	18 46	19 01			18 28	18 39		18 35	18 54	18 42	18 51	19 16		18 49	18 58
Vauxhall ⊖	d	18 03		18 14	18 12	18 24	18 10	18 29	18 17	18 26	18 51	19 06			18 33	18 44	18 42	18 40	18 59	18 47	18 56	19 21			19 03
London Waterloo ■ ⊖	a	18 07		18 19	18 19	18 29	18 15	18 35	18 23	18 31	18 55	19 10		18 29	18 37	18 49	18 49	18 47	19 05	18 52	19 01	19 27		18 57	19 07

b arr. 1746

Hampton Court, Shepperton, Guildford, Dorking and Chessington South - London

		SW	SW	SW	SW	SW	SW	SW		SW	SW ■	SW	SW	SW	SW	SW	SW	SW		SW	SW	SW	SW ■	SW	SW
Guildford	d											18 38										19 28		19 08	
London Road (Guildford)	d											18 42										19 32		19 12	
Clandon	d											18 47										19 37		19 17	
Horsley	d											18 51										19 41		19 21	
Effingham Junction ■	d									18 59		18 54										19 46		19 24	
Bookham	d									19 02												19 49			
Cobham & Stoke d'Abernon	d											18 58												19 28	
Oxshott	d											19 01												19 31	
Claygate	d											19 04												19 34	
Hinchley Wood	d											19 07												19 37	
Hampton Court	d							18 54										19 24							
Thames Ditton	d							18 56										19 26							
Surbiton ■	d						18 57	19 02			19 08	19 12					19 27	19 32					19 38	19 42	
Berrylands	d							19 04										19 34							
Shepperton	d	18 36											19 06												
Upper Halliford	d	18 39											19 09												
Sunbury	d	18 41											19 11												
Kempton Park	d	18 43											19 13												
Hampton	d	18b51											19c21												
Fulwell	d	18 54											19 24												
Strawberry Hill	d		18 37	18 38										19 07	19 08										19 37
Teddington	d	18 59	18 43										19 29	19 13											19 43
Hampton Wick	d	19 01	18 46										19 31	19 16											19 46
Kingston	a	19 03	18 48										19 33	19 18											19 48
	d	19 04	18 49										19 34	19 19											19 49
Norbiton	d	19 06	18 51										19 36	19 21											19 51
New Malden ■	d	19 10	18 55					19 07					19 40	19 25				19 37							19 55
Dorking ■	d					18 50															19 33				
Boxhill & Westhumble	d																								
Leatherhead	d					18 56				19 08											19 39	19 54			
Ashtead	d					18 59				19 12											19 42	19 58			
Epsom ■	a					19 04				19 16											19 47	20 02			
	d					19 05				19 20										19 35	19 50	20 05			
Ewell West	d					19 08				19 23										19 38	19 53	20 08			
Stoneleigh	d					19 10				19 25										19 40	19 55	20 10			
Worcester Park	d					19 13				19 28										19 43	19 58	20 13			
Chessington South	d				18 40											19 10									
Chessington North	d				18 42											19 12									
Tolworth	d				18 44											19 14									
Malden Manor	d				18 47											19 17									
Motspur Park	d				18 50	19 16				19 31						19 20				19 46	20 01	20 16			
Raynes Park ■	d	19 13	18 58		18 53	19 19		19 10		19 34			19 43	19 28		19 23		19 40		19 49	20 04	20 19			19 58
Wimbledon ■ ⊖	d	19 17	19 02		18 57	19 23	19 05	19 14		19 38		19 20	19 47	19 32		19 27	19 35	19 44		19 53	20 08	20 23		19 50	20 02
Earlsfield	d	19 20	19 05		19 01	19 27	19 08	19 17		19 42		19 24	19 50	19 35		19 31	19 38	19 47		19 57	20 12	20 27		19 54	20 05
Clapham Junction ■	d	19 24	19 09		19 05	19 31	19 12	19 21		19 46		19 28	19 54	19 39		19 35	19 42	19 51		20 01	20 16	20 31	19 49	19 58	20 09
Vauxhall ⊖	d	19 29	19 14	19 12	19 10	19 36	19 17	19 26		19 51		19 33	19 59	19 44	19 42	19 40	19 47	19 56		20 06	20 21	20 36		20 03	20 14
London Waterloo ■ ⊖	a	19 34	19 19	19 16	19 14	19 41	19 23	19 31		19 55	19 25	19 37	20 04	19 49	19 46	19 45	19 52	20 01		20 10	20 25	20 41	19 57	20 07	20 19

b arr. 1846

c arr. 1916

Hampton Court, Shepperton, Guildford, Dorking and Chessington South - London

		SW	SW	SW		SW	SW	SW	SW	SW ■	SW	SW	SW	SW		SW	SW	SW	SW	SW ■	SW	SW	SW	SW	
Guildford	d								19 58		19 38										20 08				
London Road (Guildford)	d								20 02		19 42										20 12				
Clandon	d								20 07		19 47										20 17				
Horsley	d								20 11		19 51										20 21				
Effingham Junction ■	d								20 16		19 54										20 24				
Bookham	d								20 19																
Cobham & Stoke d'Abernon	d										19 58										20 28				
Oxshott	d										20 01										20 31				
Claygate	d										20 04										20 34				
Hinchley Wood	d										20 07										20 37				
Hampton Court	d						19 54											20 24							
Thames Ditton	d						19 56											20 26							
Surbiton ■	d					19 57	20 02			20 08	20 12						20 27	20 32		20 38	20 42				
Berrylands	d						20 04											20 34							
Shepperton	d			19 41												20 11									
Upper Halliford	d			19 44												20 14									
Sunbury	d			19 46												20 16									
Kempton Park	d			19 48												20 18									
Hampton	d			19 51												20 21									
Fulwell	d			19 54												20 24									
Strawberry Hill	d	19 38										20 07	20 08									20 37	20 38		
Teddington	d			19 59								20 11				20 29						20 41			
Hampton Wick	d			20 01								20 14				20 31						20 44			
Kingston	a			20 04								20 16				20 33						20 46			
	d			20 04								20 19				20 34						20 49			
Norbiton	d			20 06								20 21				20 36						20 51			
New Malden ■	d			20 10			20 07					20 25				20 40		20 37				20 55			
Dorking ■	d							20 05											20 35						
Boxhill & Westhumble	d																								
Leatherhead	d							20 11	20 24										20 41						
Ashtead	d							20 14	20 28										20 44						
Epsom ■	a							20 19	20 32										20 49						
	d							20 20	20 35										20 50						
Ewell West	d							20 23	20 38										20 53						
Stoneleigh	d							20 25	20 40										20 55						
Worcester Park	d							20 28	20 43										20 58						
Chessington South	d		19 40											20 10										20 40	
Chessington North	d		19 42											20 12										20 42	
Tolworth	d		19 44											20 14										20 44	
Malden Manor	d		19 47											20 17										20 47	
Motspur Park	d		19 50					20 31	20 46					20 20					21 01					20 50	
Raynes Park ■	d		19 53	20 13			20 10	20 34	20 49			20 28		20 23		20 43		20 40	21 04			20 58		20 53	
Wimbledon ■ ⊖	d		19 57	20 17		20 05	20 14	20 38	20 53		20 20	20 32		20 27		20 47	20 35	20 44	21 08		20 50	21 02		20 57	
Earlsfield	d		20 01	20 20		20 08	20 17	20 42	20 57		20 24	20 35		20 31		20 50	20 38	20 47	21 12		20 54	21 05		21 01	
Clapham Junction ■	d		20 05	20 24		20 12	20 21	20 46	21 01		20 28	20 39		20 35		20 54	20 42	20 51	21 16	20 49	20 58	21 09		21 05	
Vauxhall ⊖	d	20 12	20 10	20 29		20 17	20 26	20 51	21 06		20 33	20 44	20 42	20 40		20 59	20 47	20 56	21 21		21 03	21 14	21 12	21 10	
London Waterloo ■ ⊖	a	20 16	20 15	20 35		20 22	20 31	20 55	21 10	20 26	20 38	20 49	20 46	20 46		21 04	20 52	21 01	21 25	20 57	21 07	21 19	21 16	21 15	

Table 152 — **Mondays to Fridays**

24 May to 24 September

Hampton Court, Shepperton, Guildford, Dorking and Chessington South - London

		SW	SW	SW	SW	SW	SW 1	SW	SW	SW	SW	SW	SW	SW	SW	SW	SW 1	SW	SW	SW	SW	SW	SW
Guildford	d					20 46		20 38										21 08					21 46
London Road (Guildford)	d					20 50		20 42										21 12					21 50
Clandon	d					20 55		20 47										21 17					21 55
Horsley	d					20 59		20 51										21 21					21 59
Effingham Junction 6	d					21 03		20 54										21 24					22 03
Bookham	d					21 06																	22 06
Cobham & Stoke d'Abernon	d							20 58										21 28					
Oxshott	d							21 01										21 31					
Claygate	d							21 04										21 34					
Hinchley Wood	d							21 07										21 37					
Hampton Court	d			20 54										21 24									
Thames Ditton	d			20 56										21 26									
Surbiton 6	d		20 57	21 02			21 08	21 12					21 27	21 32			21 38	21 42					
Berrylands	d			21 04										21 34									
Shepperton	d	20 41										21 11										21 41	
Upper Halliford	d	20 44										21 14										21 44	
Sunbury	d	20 46										21 16										21 46	
Kempton Park	d	20 48										21 18										21 48	
Hampton	d	20 51										21 21										21 51	
Fulwell	d	20 54										21 24										21 54	
Strawberry Hill	d								21 07	21 08									21 37	21 38			
Teddington	d	20 59							21 11			21 29							21 41			21 59	
Hampton Wick	d	21 01							21 14			21 31							21 44			22 01	
Kingston	a	21 03							21 16			21 33							21 46			22 03	
	d	21 04							21 19			21 34							21 49			22 04	
Norbiton	d	21 06							21 21			21 36							21 51			22 06	
New Malden 6	d	21 10		21 07					21 25			21 40		21 37					21 55			22 10	
Dorking 4	d															21 35							
Boxhill & Westhumble	d																						
Leatherhead	d					21 11										21 41							22 11
Ashtead	d					21 14										21 44							22 14
Epsom 3	a					21 19										21 49							22 19
	d				21 05	21 20									21 35	21 50							22 20
Ewell West	d				21 08	21 23									21 38	21 53							22 23
Stoneleigh	d				21 10	21 25									21 40	21 55							22 25
Worcester Park	d				21 13	21 28									21 43	21 58							22 28
Chessington South	d										21 10										21 40		
Chessington North	d										21 12										21 42		
Tolworth	d										21 14										21 44		
Malden Manor	d										21 17										21 47		
Motspur Park	d				21 16	21 31					21 20				21 46	22 01					21 50		22 31
Raynes Park 6	d	21 13		21 10	21 19	21 34			21 28		21 23	21 43		21 40	21 49	22 04			21 58		21 53	22 13	22 34
Wimbledon 6 ⊖	d	21 17	21 05	21 14	21 23	21 38		21 20	21 32		21 27	21 47	21 35	21 44	21 53	22 08		21 50	22 02		21 57	22 17	22 38
Earlsfield	d	21 20	21 08	21 17	21 27	21 42		21 24	21 35		21 31	21 50	21 38	21 47	21 57	22 12		21 54	22 05		22 01	22 20	22 42
Clapham Junction 10	d	21 24	21 12	21 21	21 31	21 46		21 28	21 39		21 35	21 54	21 42	21 51	22 01	22 16	21 49	21 58	22 09		22 05	22 24	22 46
Vauxhall ⊖	d	21 29	21 17	21 26	21 36	21 51		21 33	21 44	21 42	21 40	21 59	21 47	21 56	22 06	22 21		22 03	22 14	22 12	22 10	22 29	22 51
London Waterloo 15 ⊖	a	21 34	21 22	21 31	21 40	21 55	21 29	21 37	21 49	21 46	21 45	22 04	21 52	22 01	22 10	22 25	21 57	22 07	22 19	22 16	22 16	22 34	22 55

Table 152 — **Mondays to Fridays**

24 May to 24 September

Hampton Court, Shepperton, Guildford, Dorking and Chessington South - London

		SW	SW 1	SW	SW	SW	SW	SW	SW	SW	SW 1	SW	SW	SW	SW	SW	SW	SW	SW 1	SW	SW	SW	SW
Guildford	d			21 38								22 08	22 20					22 46		22 38	22 55		
London Road (Guildford)	d			21 42								22 12						22 50		22 42			
Clandon	d			21 47								22 17						22 55		22 47			
Horsley	d			21 51								22 21						22 59		22 51			
Effingham Junction 6	d			21 54								22 24						23 03		22 54			
Bookham	d																	23 06					
Cobham & Stoke d'Abernon	d			21 58								22 28								22 58			
Oxshott	d			22 01								22 31								23 01			
Claygate	d			22 04								22 34								23 04			
Hinchley Wood	d			22 07								22 37								23 07			
Hampton Court	d								22 24														
Thames Ditton	d								22 26														
Surbiton 6	d	21 57	22 08	22 12				22 27	22 32		22 38	22 42	22 57						23 08	23 12	23 30		
Berrylands	d								22 34														
Shepperton	d						22 11										22 41						
Upper Halliford	d						22 14										22 44						
Sunbury	d						22 16										22 46						
Kempton Park	d						22 18										22 48						
Hampton	d						22 21										22 51						
Fulwell	d						22 24										22 54						
Strawberry Hill	d				22 07	22 08								22 37	22 38							23 07	23 08
Teddington	d				22 11		22 29							22 41			22 59					23 11	
Hampton Wick	d				22 14		22 31							22 44			23 01					23 14	
Kingston	a				22 16		22 33							22 46			23 03					23 16	
	d				22 19		22 34							22 49			23 04					23 19	
Norbiton	d				22 21		22 36							22 51			23 06					23 21	
New Malden 6	d				22 25		22 40		22 37					22 55			23 10					23 25	
Dorking 4	d									22 35													
Boxhill & Westhumble	d																						
Leatherhead	d									22 41								23 11					
Ashtead	d									22 44								23 14					
Epsom 3	a									22 49								23 19					
	d									22 50								23 20					
Ewell West	d									22 53								23 23					
Stoneleigh	d									22 55								23 25					
Worcester Park	d									22 58								23 28					
Chessington South	d															22 40							
Chessington North	d															22 42							
Tolworth	d															22 44							
Malden Manor	d															22 47							
Motspur Park	d									23 01						22 50		23 31					
Raynes Park 6	d				22 28		22 43		22 40	23 04				22 58		22 53	23 13	23 37				23 28	
Wimbledon 6 ⊖	d	22 05		22 20	22 32		22 47	22 35	22 44	23 08		22 50	23 05	23 02		22 57	23 17	23 41		23 20	23 37	23 32	
Earlsfield	d	22 08		22 24	22 35		22 50	22 38	22 47	23 12		22 54	23 08	23 05		23 01	23 20	23 44		23 24	23 41	23 35	
Clapham Junction 10	d	22 12		22 28	22 39		22 54	22 42	22 51	23 16	22 53	22 58	23 12	23 09		23 05	23 24	23 48		23 28	23 45	23 39	
Vauxhall ⊖	d	22 17		22 33	22 44	22 42	22 59	22 47	22 56	23 21		23 03	23 17	23 14	23 12	23 10	23 29	23 53		23 33	23 50	23 44	23 42
London Waterloo 15 ⊖	a	22 22	22 26	22 39	22 49	22 46	23 04	22 52	23 01	23 27	23 01	23 07	23 23	23 19	23 16	23 15	23 34	23 58	23 27	23 37	23 54	23 49	23 46

Table 152

Mondays to Fridays
24 May to 24 September

Hampton Court, Shepperton, Guildford, Dorking and Chessington South - London

		SW	SW	SN	SW 1	SW	SW	SW	SW
Guildford	d					23 08			
London Road (Guildford)	d					23 12			
Clandon	d					23 17			
Horsley	d					23 21			
Effingham Junction 6	d					23 24			
Bookham	d								
Cobham & Stoke d'Abernon	d					23 28			
Oxshott	d					23 31			
Claygate	d					23 34			
Hinchley Wood	d					23 37			
Hampton Court	d		23 24						
Thames Ditton	d		23 26						
Surbiton 6	d		23 32		23 38	23 42			
Berrylands	d		23 34						
Shepperton	d	23 11							
Upper Halliford	d	23 14							
Sunbury	d	23 16							
Kempton Park	d	23 18							
Hampton	d	23 21							
Fulwell	d	23 24							
Strawberry Hill	d						23 37	23 38	
Teddington	d	23 29					23 41		
Hampton Wick	d	23 31					23 44		
Kingston	a	23 33					23 46		
	d	23 34					23 49		
Norbiton	d	23 36					23 51		
New Malden 6	d	23 40	23 37				23 55		
Dorking 4	d			23 30					
Boxhill & Westhumble	d								
Leatherhead	d			23 36					
Ashtead	d			23 39					
Epsom 3	a			23 45					
	d								
Ewell West	d								
Stoneleigh	d								
Worcester Park	d								
Chessington South	d								23 40
Chessington North	d								23 42
Tolworth	d								23 44
Malden Manor	d								23 47
Motspur Park	d								23 50
Raynes Park 6	d	23 43	23 40				23 58		23 54
Wimbledon 6 ⊖	d	23 52	23a45			23 55	00 05		00a01
Earlsfield	d	23 55				23 58	00 08		
Clapham Junction 10	d	23 59			23 55	00 02	00 12		
Vauxhall ⊖	d	00 04				00 07	00 17	00 12	
London Waterloo 15 ⊖	a	00 11			00 03	00 14	00 23	00 16	

Table 152

Mondays to Fridays
from 27 September

Hampton Court, Shepperton, Guildford, Dorking and Chessington South - London

		SW MO	SW MX	SW MX 1	SW MX	SW MX	SW MX	SW MO 1	SW MO	SW
Guildford	d				23p08					04 00
London Road (Guildford)	d				23p12					
Clandon	d				23p17					
Horsley	d				23p21					
Effingham Junction 6	d				23p24					
Bookham	d									
Cobham & Stoke d'Abernon	d				23p28					
Oxshott	d				23p31					
Claygate	d				23p34					
Hinchley Wood	d				23p37					
Hampton Court	d								23p45	
Thames Ditton	d								23p47	
Surbiton 6	d			23p38	23p42			23p46	23p53	04 24
Berrylands	d								23p55	
Shepperton	d	23p11	23p11							
Upper Halliford	d	23p14	23p14							
Sunbury	d	23p16	23p16							
Kempton Park	d	23p18	23p18							
Hampton	d	23p21	23p21							
Fulwell	d	23p24	23p24							
Strawberry Hill	d					23p37	23p38			
Teddington	d	23p29	23p29			23p41				
Hampton Wick	d	23p31	23p31			23p44				
Kingston	a	23p33	23p33			23p46				
	d	23p34	23p34			23p49				
Norbiton	d	23p36	23p36			23p51				
New Malden 6	d	23p40	23p40			23p55			23p58	
Dorking 4	d									
Boxhill & Westhumble	d									
Leatherhead	d									
Ashtead	d									
Epsom 3	a									
	d									
Ewell West	d									
Stoneleigh	d									
Worcester Park	d									
Chessington South	d									
Chessington North	d									
Tolworth	d									
Malden Manor	d									
Motspur Park	d									
Raynes Park 6	d	23p43	23p43			23p58			00 01	
Wimbledon 6 ⊖	d	23p47	23p52		23p55	00 05		23p53	00a04	04 32
Earlsfield	d	23p50	23p55		23p58	00 08				
Clapham Junction 10	d	23p54	23p59	23p55	00 02	00 12		00 01		04 44
Vauxhall ⊖	d	23p59	00 04		00 07	00 17	00 12			
London Waterloo 15 ⊖	a	00 04	00 11	00 03	00 14	00 23	00 16	00 10		04 53

		SW	SW	SW	SW	SW	SW	SW	SW	SW	SW	SW	SW	SW
Guildford	d		04 58	05 12						05 35				
London Road (Guildford)	d		05 02							05 39				
Clandon	d		05 07							05 44				
Horsley	d		05 11							05 48				
Effingham Junction 6	d		05 16							05 51				
Bookham	d		05 19											
Cobham & Stoke d'Abernon	d									05 55				
Oxshott	d									05 58				
Claygate	d									06 01				
Hinchley Wood	d									06 04				
Hampton Court	d								05 54					
Thames Ditton	d								05 56					
Surbiton 6	d			05 57				06 01	06 02	06 12				
Berrylands	d								06 04					
Shepperton	d				05 23								06 11	
Upper Halliford	d				05 26								06 14	
Sunbury	d				05 28								06 16	
Kempton Park	d													
Hampton	d				05 33								06 21	
Fulwell	d				05 36								06 24	
Strawberry Hill	d	04 55			05 38						06 08	06 08		
Teddington	d	04 59				05 44					06 11		06 29	
Hampton Wick	d	05 01				05 46					06 14		06 31	
Kingston	a	05 03				05 48					06 16		06 33	
	d	05 04				05 49					06 19		06 34	
Norbiton	d	05 06				05 51					06 21		06 36	
New Malden 6	d	05 10				05 55			06 07		06 25		06 40	
Dorking 4	d						05 48							
Boxhill & Westhumble	d						05 50							
Leatherhead	d		05 24				05 56							
Ashtead	d		05 28				05 59							
Epsom 3	a		05 32				06 04							
	d		05 34				06 04							06 18
Ewell West	d		05 37				06 07							06 21
Stoneleigh	d		05 40				06 10							06 24
Worcester Park	d		05 42				06 12							06 27
Chessington South	d													
Chessington North	d													
Tolworth	d													
Malden Manor	d													
Motspur Park	d		05 46				06 16							06 30
Raynes Park 6	d	05 13	05 49			05 58	06 19		06 10		06 28		06 43	06 34
Wimbledon 6 ⊖	d	05 17	05 53	06 05		06 02	06 23		06 14	06 20	06 32		06 47	06 38
Earlsfield	d	05 21	05 57	06 08		06 05	06 27		06 17	06 24	06 35		06 50	06 42
Clapham Junction 10	d	05 25	06 01	06 12	06 05	06 09	06 31		06 21	06 28	06 39		06 54	06 46
Vauxhall ⊖	d	05 30	06 06	06 17	06 12	06 14	06 36		06 26	06 33	06 44	06 42	06 59	06 51
London Waterloo 15 ⊖	a	05 35	06 11	06 22	06 16	06 19	06 40	06 20	06 31	06 37	06 49	06 46	07 06	06 55

Table 152

Mondays to Fridays
from 27 September

Hampton Court, Shepperton, Guildford, Dorking and Chessington South - London

		SW	SW	SW	SW	SW	SW ■	SW	SW	SW	SW	SW	SW	SW	SW	SW	SW ■	SW	SW	SW	SW	SW	SW
Guildford	d	05 58				06 28		06 04										06 34					
London Road (Guildford)	d	06 02				06 32		06 08										06 38					
Clandon	d	06 07				06 37		06 13										06 43					
Horsley	d	06 11				06 41		06 17										06 47					
Effingham Junction ■	d	06 16				06 48		06 21										06 51					
Bookham	d	06 19				06 51																	
Cobham & Stoke d'Abernon	d							06 24										06 54					
Oxshott	d							06 28										06 58					
Claygate	d							06 31										07 01					
Hinchley Wood	d							06 34										07 04					
Hampton Court	d			06 24										06 54									
Thames Ditton	d			06 26										06 56									
Surbiton ■	d		06 28	06 32			06 35	06 42					06 57	07 02			07 08	07 12					
Berrylands	d			06 34										07 04									
Shepperton	d											06 41			07 00							07 11	
Upper Halliford	d											06 44			07 03							07 14	
Sunbury	d											06 46			07 05							07 16	
Kempton Park	d																						
Hampton	d											06 51			07 09							07 21	
Fulwell	d											06 54			07 12							07 24	
Strawberry Hill	d								06 37	06 38					07 14				07 07	07 08			
Teddington	d								06 41			06 59							07 11			07 29	07 20
Hampton Wick	d								06 44			07 01							07 14			07 31	07 22
Kingston	a								06 46			07 03							07 16			07 33	07 24
	d								06 49			07 04							07 19			07 34	07 26
Norbiton	d								06 51			07 06							07 21			07 36	07 28
New Malden ■	d			06 37					06 55			07 10		07 07					07 25			07 40	07 32
Dorking ■	d				06 32											07 02							
Boxhill & Westhumble	d				06 34											07 04							
Leatherhead	d	06 24			06 39	06 56										07 09							
Ashtead	d	06 28			06 43	06 59										07 13							
Epsom ■	a	06 32			06 47	07 04										07 17							
	d	06 34			06 48	07 04										07 18							
Ewell West	d	06 37			06 51	07 07																	
Stoneleigh	d	06 40			06 53	07 10																	
Worcester Park	d	06 42			06 56	07 12										07 25							
Chessington South	d										06 40										07 10		
Chessington North	d										06 42										07 12		
Tolworth	d										06 44										07 14		
Malden Manor	d										06 47										07 17		
Motspur Park	d	06 46			07 00	07 16					06 50										07 20		
Raynes Park ■	d	06 49		06 40	07 04	07 19			06 58		06 54	07 13		07 10		07 31			07 28		07 24	07 43	07 34
Wimbledon ■ ⊖ ⇌	d	06 53	06 35	06 44	07 08	07 23		06 50	07 02		06 58	07 17	07 05	07 14		07 35		07 20	07 32		07 28	07 47	07 38
Earlsfield	d	06 57	06 39	06 47	07 11	07 27		06 54	07 05		07 01	07 20	07 08	07 17		07 38		07 24	07 35		07 31	07 51	07 42
Clapham Junction ■	d	07 01	06 43	06 51	07 15	07 31	06 47	06 58	07 09		07 05	07 24	07 12	07 21	07 49	07 42		07 28	07 39		07 35	07 55	07 46
Vauxhall ⊖	d	07 06	06 48	06 56	07 20	07 36		07 03	07 14	07 12	07 10	07 29	07 17	07 26	07 56	07 47		07 33	07 44	07 42	07 40	08 00	07 51
London Waterloo ■ ⊖	a	07 12	06 52	07 03	07 27	07 42	06 56	07 09	07 21	07 18	07 17	07 36	07 24	07 33	08 04	07 54	07 26	07 39	07 51	07 48	07 47	08 06	07 57

Table 152

Mondays to Fridays
from 27 September

Hampton Court, Shepperton, Guildford, Dorking and Chessington South - London

		SW	SW	SW ■	SW	SW	SW	SW ■	SW	SW	SW	SW	SW	SW	SW	SW	SW	SW ■	SW	SW	SW	SW ■
Guildford	d		06 58						07 04	07 14												
London Road (Guildford)	d		07 02						07 08	07 18												
Clandon	d		07 07						07 13	07 23												
Horsley	d		07 11						07 17	07 27												
Effingham Junction ■	d		07 16						07 21	07 31							07 46					
Bookham	d		07 19														07 49					
Cobham & Stoke d'Abernon	d								07 24	07 34												
Oxshott	d								07 28	07 38												
Claygate	d								07 31	07 41												
Hinchley Wood	d								07 34	07 44												
Hampton Court	d				07 24														07 54			
Thames Ditton	d				07 26														07 56			
Surbiton ■	d			07 27	07 32			07 38	07 42	07 53								07 57	08 02			08 08
Berrylands	d				07 34														08 04			
Shepperton	d					07 30									07 41					08 00		
Upper Halliford	d					07 33									07 44					08 03		
Sunbury	d					07 35									07 46					08 05		
Kempton Park	d																					
Hampton	d					07 39									07 51					08 09		
Fulwell	d					07 42									07 54					08 12		
Strawberry Hill	d					07 44					07 37	07 38	07b47							08 14		
Teddington	d										07 41		07 50		07 59							
Hampton Wick	d										07 44		07 52		08 01							
Kingston	a										07 46		07 54		08 03							
	d										07 49		07 56		08 04							
Norbiton	d										07 51		07 58		08 06							
New Malden ■	d				07 37				07 46		07 55		08 02		08 10				08 07			
Dorking ■	d						07 32														08 02	
Boxhill & Westhumble	d						07 34														08 04	
Leatherhead	d		07 26				07 39										07 56				08 09	
Ashtead	d		07 29				07 43										07 59				08 13	
Epsom ■	a		07 34				07 47										08 04				08 17	
	d	07 22	07 34				07 48									07 52	08 04				08 18	
Ewell West	d	07 25	07 37													07 55	08 07					
Stoneleigh	d	07 27	07 40													07 57	08 10					
Worcester Park	d	07 30	07 43				07 55									08 00	08 13				08 25	
Chessington South	d													07 40								
Chessington North	d													07 42								
Tolworth	d													07 44								
Malden Manor	d													07 47								
Motspur Park	d	07 34	07 46											07 50		08 04	08 16					
Raynes Park ■	d	07 37	07 50		07 40		08 01				07 58		08 04	07 54	08 13	08 07	08 20		08 10		08 31	
Wimbledon ■ ⊖ ⇌	d	07 41	07 54		07 44		08 05		07 51		08 02		08 08	07 58	08 17	08 11	08 24		08 14		08 35	
Earlsfield	d	07 45	07 58		07 48		08 08		07 54		08 05		08 12	08 01	08 21	08 15	08 28		08 18		08 38	
Clapham Junction ■	d	07 49	08 02		07 52	08 19	08 12		07 58		08 09		08 16	08 05	08 25	08 19	08 32		08 22		08 42	
Vauxhall ⊖	d	07 54	08 07		07 57	08 26	08 17		08 03		08 14	08 12	08 21	08 10	08 30	08 24	08 37		08 27	08 56	08 47	
London Waterloo ■ ⊖	a	08 00	08 13	07 49	08 04	08 34	08 24	07 56	08 11	08 13	08 21	08 18	08 27	08 17	08 36	08 30	08 43	08 19	08 33	09 04	08 54	08 26

b arr. 0740

Table 152

Mondays to Fridays
from 27 September

Hampton Court, Shepperton, Guildford, Dorking and Chessington South - London

		SW	SW	SW	SW	SW	SW	SW [1]	SW	SW	SW [1]	SW	SW	SW [1]	SW	SW	SW	SW	SW	SW	SW	SW	SW
Guildford	d	07 34								07 58					08 04						08 20		
London Road (Guildford)	d	07 38								08 02					08 08								
Clandon	d	07 43								08 07					08 13								
Horsley	d	07 47								08 11					08 17								
Effingham Junction [6]	d	07 51								08 16					08 21							08 48	
Bookham	d									08 19												08 51	
Cobham & Stoke d'Abernon	d	07 54													08 24								
Oxshott	d	07 58													08 28								
Claygate	d	08 01													08 31								
Hinchley Wood	d	08 04													08 34								
Hampton Court	d											08 24											08 54
Thames Ditton	d											08 26											08 56
Surbiton [6]	d	08 12						08 19			08 25	08 32		08 38	08 42					08 48	08 57		09 02
Berrylands	d											08 34											09 04
Shepperton	d						08 11												08 41				
Upper Halliford	d						08 14												08 44				
Sunbury	d						08 16												08 46				
Kempton Park	d																						
Hampton	d						08 21												08 51				
Fulwell	d						08 24												08 54				
Strawberry Hill	d		08 07	08 08	08b17											08 38	08 38						
Teddington	d		08 11		08 20		08 29										08 41		08 59				
Hampton Wick	d		08 14		08 22		08 31										08 44		09 01				
Kingston	a		08 16		08 24		08 33										08 46		09 03				
	d		08 19		08 26		08 34										08 49		09 04				
Norbiton	d		08 21		08 28		08 36										08 51		09 06				
New Malden [6]	d	08 16	08 25		08 32		08 40					08 37					08 55		09 10				09 07
Dorking [4]	d												08 31										
Boxhill & Westhumble	d												08 33										
Leatherhead	d									08 25			08 38									08 56	
Ashtead	d									08 28			08 42									08 59	
Epsom [3]	a									08 33			08 46									09 04	
	d								08 22	08 34			08 48									09 04	
Ewell West	d								08 25	08 37			08 51									09 07	
Stoneleigh	d								08 27	08 40			08 54									09 10	
Worcester Park	d								08 30	08 42			08 57									09 12	
Chessington South	d					08 10												08 40					
Chessington North	d					08 12												08 42					
Tolworth	d					08 14												08 44					
Malden Manor	d					08 17												08 47					
Motspur Park	d					08 20			08 34	08 46			09 00					08 50				09 16	
Raynes Park [6]	d		08 28		08 34	08 24	08 43		08 37	08 49		08 40	09 04				08 58	08 54	09 13			09 19	09 10
Wimbledon [6] ⊖ ⛴	d	08 21	08 32		08 38	08 28	08 47		08 41	08 53		08 44	09 08				09 02	08 58	09 17		09 05	09 23	09 14
Earlsfield	d	08 24	08 35		08 42	08 31	08 51		08 45	08 57		08 48	09 12				09 05	09 01	09 20		09 08	09 27	09 17
Clapham Junction [10]	d	08 28	08 39		08 46	08 35	08 55		08 49	09 01		08 52	09 16				09 09	09 05	09 24		09 12	09 31	09 21
Vauxhall ⊖	d	08 33	08 44	08 42	08 51	08 40	09 00		08 54	09 06		08 57	09 21			09 12	09 14	09 10	09 29		09 17	09 36	09 26
London Waterloo [15] ⊖	a	08 40	08 51	08 49	08 57	08 47	09 06	08 36	09 00	09 12	08 46	09 03	09 27	08 59	09 01	09 18	09 21	09 17	09 36	09 06	09 24	09 42	09 33

b arr. 0810

Table 152

Mondays to Fridays
from 27 September

Hampton Court, Shepperton, Guildford, Dorking and Chessington South - London

		SW	SW	SW	SW	SW	SW	SW	SW [1]	SW	SW	SW	SW	SW [1]	SW	SW	SW	SW	SW	SW	SW	SW
Guildford	d	08 34		08 58						08 46			09 28		09 05							
London Road (Guildford)	d	08 38		09 02									09 32		09 09							
Clandon	d	08 43		09 07									09 37		09 14							
Horsley	d	08 47		09 11									09 41		09 18							
Effingham Junction [6]	d	08 51		09 16									09 46		09 21							
Bookham	d			09 19									09 49									
Cobham & Stoke d'Abernon	d	08 54													09 25							
Oxshott	d	08 58													09 28							
Claygate	d	09 01													09 31							
Hinchley Wood	d	09 04													09 34							
Hampton Court	d										09 24										09 54	
Thames Ditton	d										09 26										09 56	
Surbiton [6]	d	09 12							09 19	09 27	09 32			09 38	09 42					09 57	10 02	
Berrylands	d										09 34										10 04	
Shepperton	d							09 11											09 41			
Upper Halliford	d							09 14											09 44			
Sunbury	d							09 16											09 46			
Kempton Park	d							09 18											09 48			
Hampton	d							09 21											09 51			
Fulwell	d							09 24											09 54			
Strawberry Hill	d				09 07	09 08										09 37	09 38					
Teddington	d				09 11			09 29								09 41			09 59			
Hampton Wick	d				09 14			09 31								09 44			10 01			
Kingston	a				09 16			09 33								09 46			10 03			
	d				09 19			09 34								09 49			10 04			
Norbiton	d				09 21			09 36								09 51			10 06			
New Malden [6]	d				09 25			09 40			09 37					09 55			10 10		10 07	
Dorking [4]	d		09 02									09 35										10 05
Boxhill & Westhumble	d		09 04																			
Leatherhead	d		09 09	09 24								09 41	09 54									10 11
Ashtead	d		09 13	09 28								09 45	09 58									10 14
Epsom [3]	a		09 17	09 32								09 49	10 02									10 19
	d		09 18	09 35								09 50	10 05									10 20
Ewell West	d		09 21	09 38								09 53	10 08									10 23
Stoneleigh	d		09 24	09 40								09 55	10 10									10 25
Worcester Park	d		09 27	09 43								09 58	10 13									10 28
Chessington South	d						09 10											09 40				
Chessington North	d						09 12											09 42				
Tolworth	d						09 14											09 44				
Malden Manor	d						09 17											09 47				
Motspur Park	d		09 30	09 46			09 20					10 01	10 16					09 50				10 31
Raynes Park [6]	d		09 34	09 49	09 28		09 24	09 43			09 40	10 04	10 19			09 58		09 53	10 13		10 10	10 34
Wimbledon [6] ⊖ ⛴	d	09 20	09 38	09 53	09 32		09 28	09 47		09 35	09 44	10 08	10 23		09 50	10 02		09 57	10 17	10 05	10 14	10 38
Earlsfield	d	09 24	09 42	09 57	09 35		09 31	09 50		09 38	09 47	10 12	10 27		09 54	10 05		10 01	10 20	10 08	10 17	10 42
Clapham Junction [10]	d	09 28	09 46	10 01	09 39		09 35	09 54		09 42	09 51	10 16	10 31	09 51	09 58	10 09		10 05	10 24	10 12	10 21	10 46
Vauxhall ⊖	d	09 33	09 51	10 06	09 44	09 42	09 40	09 59		09 47	09 56	10 21	10 36		10 03	10 14	10 12	10 10	10 29	10 17	10 26	10 51
London Waterloo [15] ⊖	a	09 39	09 57	10 10	09 51	09 48	09 47	10 04	09 40	09 54	10 01	10 25	10 40	09 59	10 07	10 19	10 16	10 15	10 34	10 22	10 31	10 55

Table 152

Mondays to Fridays

from 27 September

Hampton Court, Shepperton, Guildford, Dorking and Chessington South - London

		SW	SW 1	SW	SW	SW	SW	SW	SW	SW	SW	SW	SW 1	SW	SW	SW	SW	SW	SW	SW	SW	SW	SW 1
Guildford	d	09 58		09 35								10 28		10 05								10 58	
London Road (Guildford)	d	10 02		09 39								10 32		10 09								11 02	
Clandon	d	10 07		09 44								10 37		10 14								11 07	
Horsley	d	10 11		09 48								10 41		10 18								11 11	
Effingham Junction 6	d	10 16		09 51								10 46		10 21								11 16	
Bookham	d	10 19										10 49										11 19	
Cobham & Stoke d'Abernon	d			09 55										10 25									
Oxshott	d			09 58										10 28									
Claygate	d			10 01										10 31									
Hinchley Wood	d			10 04										10 34									
Hampton Court	d									10 24										10 54			
Thames Ditton	d									10 26										10 56			
Surbiton 6	d		10 08	10 12					10 27	10 32			10 38	10 42					10 57	11 02			11 08
Berrylands	d									10 34										11 04			
Shepperton	d							10 11										10 41					
Upper Halliford	d							10 14										10 44					
Sunbury	d							10 16										10 46					
Kempton Park	d							10 18										10 48					
Hampton	d							10 21										10 51					
Fulwell	d							10 24										10 54					
Strawberry Hill	d				10 07	10 08									10 37	10 38							
Teddington	d				10 11			10 29							10 41			10 59					
Hampton Wick	d				10 14			10 31							10 44			11 01					
Kingston	a				10 16			10 33							10 46			11 03					
	d				10 19			10 34							10 49			11 04					
Norbiton	d				10 21			10 36							10 51			11 06					
New Malden 6	d				10 25			10 40		10 37					10 55			11 10		11 07			
Dorking 4	d										10 35										11 05		
Boxhill & Westhumble	d																						
Leatherhead	d	10 24									10 41	10 54									11 11	11 24	
Ashtead	d	10 28									10 44	10 58									11 14	11 28	
Epsom 3	a	10 32									10 49	11 02									11 19	11 32	
	d	10 35									10 50	11 05									11 20	11 35	
Ewell West	d	10 38									10 53	11 08									11 23	11 38	
Stoneleigh	d	10 40									10 55	11 10									11 25	11 40	
Worcester Park	d	10 43									10 58	11 13									11 28	11 43	
Chessington South	d						10 10										10 40						
Chessington North	d						10 12										10 42						
Tolworth	d						10 14										10 44						
Malden Manor	d						10 17										10 47						
Motspur Park	d	10 46					10 20				11 01	11 16					10 50				11 31	11 46	
Raynes Park 6	d	10 49			10 28		10 23	10 43		10 40	11 04	11 19			10 58		10 53	11 13		11 10	11 34	11 49	
Wimbledon 6 ⊖ ⛴	d	10 53		10 20	10 32		10 27	10 47	10 35	10 44	11 08	11 23		10 50	11 02		10 57	11 17	11 05	11 14	11 38	11 53	
Earlsfield	d	10 57		10 24	10 35		10 31	10 50	10 38	10 47	11 12	11 27		10 54	11 05		11 01	11 20	11 08	11 17	11 42	11 57	
Clapham Junction 10	d	11 01		10 28	10 39		10 35	10 54	10 42	10 51	11 16	11 31	10 49	10 58	11 09		11 05	11 24	11 12	11 21	11 46	12 01	
Vauxhall ⊖	d	11 06		10 33	10 44	10 42	10 40	10 59	10 47	10 56	11 21	11 36		11 03	11 14	11 12	11 10	11 29	11 17	11 26	11 51	12 06	
London Waterloo 15 ⊖	a	11 10	10 25	10 37	10 49	10 46	10 45	11 04	10 52	11 01	11 25	11 40	10 57	11 07	11 19	11 16	11 15	11 34	11 22	11 31	11 55	12 10	11 27

Table 152

Mondays to Fridays

from 27 September

Hampton Court, Shepperton, Guildford, Dorking and Chessington South - London

		SW	SW	SW	SW	SW	SW	SW	SW	SW	SW 1	SW	SW	SW	SW	SW	SW	SW	SW	SW	SW 1	SW	SW
Guildford	d	10 35								11 28		11 05								11 58		11 35	
London Road (Guildford)	d	10 39								11 32		11 09								12 02		11 39	
Clandon	d	10 44								11 37		11 14								12 07		11 44	
Horsley	d	10 48								11 41		11 18								12 11		11 48	
Effingham Junction 6	d	10 51								11 46		11 21								12 16		11 51	
Bookham	d									11 49										12 19			
Cobham & Stoke d'Abernon	d	10 55										11 25										11 55	
Oxshott	d	10 58										11 28										11 58	
Claygate	d	11 01										11 31										12 01	
Hinchley Wood	d	11 04										11 34										12 04	
Hampton Court	d							11 24										11 54					
Thames Ditton	d							11 26										11 56					
Surbiton 6	d	11 12					11 27	11 32			11 38	11 42					11 57	12 02			12 08	12 12	
Berrylands	d							11 34										12 04					
Shepperton	d					11 11										11 41							
Upper Halliford	d					11 14										11 44							
Sunbury	d					11 16										11 46							
Kempton Park	d					11 18										11 48							
Hampton	d					11 21										11 51							
Fulwell	d					11 24										11 54							
Strawberry Hill	d		11 07	11 08									11 37	11 38									12 07
Teddington	d		11 11			11 29							11 41			11 59							12 11
Hampton Wick	d		11 14			11 31							11 44			12 01							12 14
Kingston	a		11 16			11 33							11 46			12 03							12 16
	d		11 19			11 34							11 49			12 04							12 19
Norbiton	d		11 21			11 36							11 51			12 06							12 21
New Malden 6	d		11 25			11 40		11 37					11 55			12 10		12 07					12 25
Dorking 4	d								11 35										12 05				
Boxhill & Westhumble	d																						
Leatherhead	d								11 41	11 54									12 11	12 24			
Ashtead	d								11 44	11 58									12 14	12 28			
Epsom 3	a								11 49	12 02									12 19	12 32			
	d								11 50	12 05									12 20	12 35			
Ewell West	d								11 53	12 08									12 23	12 38			
Stoneleigh	d								11 55	12 10									12 25	12 40			
Worcester Park	d								11 58	12 13									12 28	12 43			
Chessington South	d				11 10										11 40								
Chessington North	d				11 12										11 42								
Tolworth	d				11 14										11 44								
Malden Manor	d				11 17										11 47								
Motspur Park	d				11 20				12 01	12 16					11 50				12 31	12 46			
Raynes Park 6	d		11 28		11 23	11 43		11 40	12 04	12 19			11 58		11 53	12 13		12 10	12 34	12 49			12 28
Wimbledon 6 ⊖ ⛴	d	11 20	11 32		11 27	11 47	11 35	11 44	12 08	12 23		11 50	12 02		11 57	12 17	12 05	12 14	12 38	12 53		12 20	12 32
Earlsfield	d	11 24	11 35		11 31	11 50	11 38	11 47	12 12	12 27		11 54	12 05		12 01	12 20	12 08	12 17	12 42	12 57		12 24	12 35
Clapham Junction 10	d	11 28	11 39		11 35	11 54	11 42	11 51	12 16	12 31	11 50	11 58	12 09		12 05	12 24	12 12	12 21	12 46	13 01		12 28	12 39
Vauxhall ⊖	d	11 33	11 44	11 42	11 40	11 59	11 47	11 56	12 21	12 36		12 03	12 14	12 12	12 10	12 29	12 17	12 26	12 51	13 06		12 33	12 44
London Waterloo 15 ⊖	a	11 37	11 49	11 46	11 45	12 04	11 52	12 01	12 25	12 40	11 57	12 07	12 19	12 16	12 15	12 34	12 22	12 31	12 55	13 10	12 27	12 37	12 49

Table 152

Mondays to Fridays
from 27 September

Hampton Court, Shepperton, Guildford, Dorking and Chessington South - London

		SW		SW	SW	SW	SW	SW	SW	SW ■	SW	SW		SW	SW	SW	SW	SW	SW	SW	SW ■	SW		SW	SW
Guildford	d								12 28		12 05									12 58		12 35			
London Road (Guildford)	d								12 32		12 09									13 02		12 39			
Clandon	d								12 37		12 14									13 07		12 44			
Horsley	d								12 41		12 18									13 11		12 48			
Effingham Junction ■	d								12 46		12 21									13 16		12 51			
Bookham	d								12 49											13 19					
Cobham & Stoke d'Abernon	d										12 25											12 55			
Oxshott	d										12 28											12 58			
Claygate	d										12 31											13 01			
Hinchley Wood	d										12 34											13 04			
Hampton Court	d						12 24											12 54							
Thames Ditton	d						12 26											12 56							
Surbiton ■	d					12 27	12 32			12 38	12 42						12 57	13 02			13 08	13 12			
Berrylands	d						12 34											13 04							
Shepperton	d				12 11											12 41									
Upper Halliford	d				12 14											12 44									
Sunbury	d				12 16											12 46									
Kempton Park	d				12 18											12 48									
Hampton	d				12 21											12 51									
Fulwell	d				12 24											12 54									
Strawberry Hill	d	12 08										12 37		12 38										13 07	13 08
Teddington	d				12 29							12 41				12 59								13 11	
Hampton Wick	d				12 31							12 44				13 01								13 14	
Kingston	a				12 33							12 46				13 03								13 16	
	d				12 34							12 49				13 04								13 19	
Norbiton	d				12 36							12 51				13 06								13 21	
New Malden ■	d				12 40		12 37					12 55				13 10		13 07						13 25	
Dorking ■	d							12 35											13 05						
Boxhill & Westhumble	d																								
Leatherhead	d							12 41	12 54										13 11	13 24					
Ashtead	d							12 44	12 58										13 14	13 28					
Epsom ■	a							12 49	13 02										13 19	13 32					
	d							12 50	13 05										13 20	13 35					
Ewell West	d							12 53	13 08										13 23	13 38					
Stoneleigh	d							12 55	13 10										13 25	13 40					
Worcester Park	d							12 58	13 13										13 28	13 43					
Chessington South	d			12 10											12 40										
Chessington North	d			12 12											12 42										
Tolworth	d			12 14											12 44										
Malden Manor	d			12 17											12 47										
Motspur Park	d			12 20				13 01	13 16						12 50				13 31	13 46					
Raynes Park ■	d			12 23	12 43		12 40	13 04	13 19			12 58			12 53	13 13		13 10	13 34	13 49				13 28	
Wimbledon ■ ⊖ ⇌	d			12 27	12 47	12 35	12 44	13 08	13 23		12 50	13 02			12 57	13 17	13 05	13 14	13 38	13 53		13 20		13 32	
Earlsfield	d			12 31	12 50	12 38	12 47	13 12	13 27		12 54	13 05			13 01	13 20	13 08	13 17	13 42	13 57		13 24		13 35	
Clapham Junction ■	d			12 35	12 54	12 42	12 51	13 16	13 31	12 49	12 58	13 09			13 05	13 24	13 12	13 21	13 46	14 01		13 28		13 39	
Vauxhall ⊖	d	12 42		12 40	12 59	12 47	12 56	13 21	13 36		13 03	13 14		13 12	13 10	13 29	13 17	13 26	13 51	14 06		13 33		13 44	13 42
London Waterloo ■ ⊖	a	12 46		12 45	13 04	12 52	13 01	13 25	13 40	12 57	13 07	13 19		13 16	13 15	13 34	13 22	13 31	13 55	14 10	13 25	13 37		13 49	13 46

Table 152

Mondays to Fridays
from 27 September

Hampton Court, Shepperton, Guildford, Dorking and Chessington South - London

		SW	SW	SW	SW	SW	SW	SW ■		SW	SW	SW	SW	SW	SW	SW	SW	SW		SW ■	SW	SW	SW	SW	SW
Guildford	d						13 28			13 05								13 58			13 35				
London Road (Guildford)	d						13 32			13 09								14 02			13 39				
Clandon	d						13 37			13 14								14 07			13 44				
Horsley	d						13 41			13 18								14 11			13 48				
Effingham Junction ■	d						13 46			13 21								14 16			13 51				
Bookham	d						13 49											14 19							
Cobham & Stoke d'Abernon	d									13 25											13 55				
Oxshott	d									13 28											13 58				
Claygate	d									13 31											14 01				
Hinchley Wood	d									13 34											14 04				
Hampton Court	d				13 24											13 54									
Thames Ditton	d				13 26											13 56									
Surbiton ■	d			13 27	13 32			13 38		13 42					13 57	14 02				14 08	14 12				
Berrylands	d				13 34											14 04									
Shepperton	d		13 11											13 41											14 11
Upper Halliford	d		13 14											13 44											14 14
Sunbury	d		13 16											13 46											14 16
Kempton Park	d		13 18											13 48											14 18
Hampton	d		13 21											13 51											14 21
Fulwell	d		13 24											13 54											14 24
Strawberry Hill	d										13 37	13 38										14 07	14 08		
Teddington	d		13 29								13 41			13 59								14 11			14 29
Hampton Wick	d		13 31								13 44			14 01								14 14			14 31
Kingston	a		13 33								13 46			14 03								14 16			14 33
	d		13 34								13 49			14 04								14 19			14 34
Norbiton	d		13 36								13 51			14 06								14 21			14 36
New Malden ■	d		13 40		13 37						13 55			14 10		14 07						14 25			14 40
Dorking ■	d					13 35											14 05								
Boxhill & Westhumble	d																								
Leatherhead	d					13 41	13 54										14 11	14 24							
Ashtead	d					13 44	13 58										14 14	14 28							
Epsom ■	a					13 49	14 02										14 19	14 32							
	d					13 50	14 05										14 20	14 35							
Ewell West	d					13 53	14 08										14 23	14 38							
Stoneleigh	d					13 55	14 10										14 25	14 40							
Worcester Park	d					13 58	14 13										14 28	14 43							
Chessington South	d	13 10											13 40											14 10	
Chessington North	d	13 12											13 42											14 12	
Tolworth	d	13 14											13 44											14 14	
Malden Manor	d	13 17											13 47											14 17	
Motspur Park	d	13 20				14 01	14 16						13 50				14 31	14 46						14 20	
Raynes Park ■	d	13 23	13 43		13 40	14 04	14 19				13 58		13 53	14 13		14 10	14 34	14 49				14 28		14 23	14 43
Wimbledon ■ ⊖ ⇌	d	13 27	13 47	13 35	13 44	14 08	14 23			13 50	14 02		13 57	14 17	14 05	14 14	14 38	14 53			14 20	14 32		14 27	14 47
Earlsfield	d	13 31	13 50	13 38	13 47	14 12	14 27			13 54	14 05		14 01	14 20	14 08	14 17	14 42	14 57			14 24	14 35		14 31	14 50
Clapham Junction ■	d	13 35	13 54	13 42	13 51	14 16	14 31	13 49		13 58	14 09		14 05	14 24	14 12	14 21	14 46	15 01			14 28	14 39		14 35	14 54
Vauxhall ⊖	d	13 40	13 59	13 47	13 56	14 21	14 36			14 03	14 14	14 12	14 10	14 29	14 17	14 26	14 51	15 06			14 33	14 44	14 42	14 40	14 59
London Waterloo ■ ⊖	a	13 45	14 04	13 52	14 01	14 25	14 40	13 57		14 07	14 19	14 16	14 15	14 34	14 22	14 31	14 55	15 10		14 25	14 37	14 49	14 46	14 45	15 04

Hampton Court, Shepperton, Guildford, Dorking and Chessington South - London

		SW	SW	SW	SW	SW 1	SW	SW	SW	SW	SW	SW	SW	SW	SW	SW 1	SW	SW	SW	SW	SW	SW
Guildford	d				14 28		14 05								14 58		14 35					
London Road (Guildford)	d				14 32		14 09								15 02		14 39					
Clandon	d				14 37		14 14								15 07		14 44					
Horsley	d				14 41		14 18								15 11		14 48					
Effingham Junction 6	d				14 46		14 21								15 16		14 51					
Bookham	d				14 49										15 19							
Cobham & Stoke d'Abernon	d						14 25										14 55					
Oxshott	d						14 28										14 58					
Claygate	d						14 31										15 01					
Hinchley Wood	d						14 34										15 04					
Hampton Court	d		14 24										14 54									
Thames Ditton	d		14 26										14 56									
Surbiton 6	d	14 27	14 32			14 38	14 42					14 57	15 02			15 08	15 12					15 27
Berrylands	d		14 34										15 04									
Shepperton	d										14 41										15 11	
Upper Halliford	d										14 44										15 14	
Sunbury	d										14 46										15 16	
Kempton Park	d										14 48										15 18	
Hampton	d										14 51										15 21	
Fulwell	d										14 54										15 24	
Strawberry Hill	d							14 37	14 38									15 07	15 08			
Teddington	d							14 41			14 59							15 11			15 29	
Hampton Wick	d							14 44			15 01							15 14			15 31	
Kingston	a							14 46			15 03							15 16			15 33	
	d							14 49			15 04							15 19			15 34	
Norbiton	d							14 51			15 06							15 21			15 36	
New Malden 6	d		14 37					14 55			15 10		15 07					15 25			15 40	
Dorking 4	d			14 35										15 05								
Boxhill & Westhumble	d																					
Leatherhead	d			14 41	14 54									15 11	15 24							
Ashtead	d			14 44	14 58									15 14	15 28							
Epsom 3	a			14 49	15 02									15 19	15 32							
	d			14 50	15 05									15 20	15 35							
Ewell West	d			14 53	15 08									15 23	15 38							
Stoneleigh	d			14 55	15 10									15 25	15 40							
Worcester Park	d			14 58	15 13									15 28	15 43							
Chessington South	d									14 40										15 10		
Chessington North	d									14 42										15 12		
Tolworth	d									14 44										15 14		
Malden Manor	d									14 47										15 17		
Motspur Park	d			15 01	15 16					14 50				15 31	15 46					15 20		
Raynes Park 6	d		14 40	15 04	15 19			14 58		14 53	15 13		15 10	15 34	15 49			15 28		15 23	15 43	
Wimbledon 6 ⊖	d	14 35	14 44	15 08	15 23		14 50	15 02		14 57	15 17	15 05	15 14	15 38	15 53		15 20	15 32		15 27	15 47	15 35
Earlsfield	d	14 38	14 47	15 12	15 27		14 54	15 05		15 01	15 20	15 08	15 17	15 42	15 57		15 24	15 35		15 31	15 50	15 38
Clapham Junction 10	d	14 42	14 51	15 16	15 31	14 49	14 58	15 09		15 05	15 24	15 12	15 21	15 46	16 01		15 28	15 39		15 35	15 54	15 42
Vauxhall ⊖	d	14 47	14 56	15 21	15 36		15 03	15 14	15 12	15 10	15 29	15 17	15 26	15 51	16 06		15 33	15 44	15 42	15 40	15 59	15 47
London Waterloo 15 ⊖	a	14 52	15 01	15 25	15 40	14 57	15 07	15 19	15 16	15 15	15 34	15 22	15 31	15 55	16 10	15 25	15 37	15 49	15 46	15 45	16 04	15 52

Hampton Court, Shepperton, Guildford, Dorking and Chessington South - London

		SW	SW	SW	SW 1	SW	SW	SW	SW	SW	SW	SW	SW	SW	SW 1	SW	SW	SW	SW	SW	SW	SW	SW
Guildford	d			15 28		15 05								15 58		15 35							
London Road (Guildford)	d			15 32		15 09								16 02		15 39							
Clandon	d			15 37		15 14								16 07		15 44							
Horsley	d			15 41		15 18								16 11		15 48							
Effingham Junction 6	d			15 46		15 21								16 16		15 51							
Bookham	d			15 49										16 19									
Cobham & Stoke d'Abernon	d					15 25										15 55							
Oxshott	d					15 28										15 58							
Claygate	d					15 31										16 01							
Hinchley Wood	d					15 34										16 04							
Hampton Court	d	15 24										15 54										16 24	
Thames Ditton	d	15 26										15 56										16 26	
Surbiton 6	d	15 32			15 38	15 42					15 57	16 02			16 08	16 12					16 27	16 32	
Berrylands	d	15 34										16 04										16 34	
Shepperton	d									15 41										16 11			
Upper Halliford	d									15 44										16 14			
Sunbury	d									15 46										16 16			
Kempton Park	d									15 48										16 18			
Hampton	d									15 51										16 21			
Fulwell	d									15 54										16 24			
Strawberry Hill	d						15 37	15 38									16 07	16 08					
Teddington	d						15 41			15 59							16 11			16 29			
Hampton Wick	d						15 44			16 01							16 14			16 31			
Kingston	a						15 46			16 03							16 16			16 33			
	d						15 49			16 04							16 19			16 34			
Norbiton	d						15 51			16 06							16 21			16 36			
New Malden 6	d	15 37					15 55			16 10		16 07					16 25			16 40		16 37	
Dorking 4	d		15 35										16 05										16 35
Boxhill & Westhumble	d																						
Leatherhead	d		15 41	15 54									16 11	16 24									16 41
Ashtead	d		15 44	15 58									16 14	16 28									16 44
Epsom 3	a		15 49	16 02									16 19	16 32									16 49
	d		15 50	16 05									16 20	16 35									16 50
Ewell West	d		15 53	16 08									16 23	16 38									16 53
Stoneleigh	d		15 55	16 10									16 25	16 40									16 55
Worcester Park	d		15 58	16 13									16 28	16 43									16 58
Chessington South	d								15 40										16 10				
Chessington North	d								15 42										16 12				
Tolworth	d								15 44										16 14				
Malden Manor	d								15 47										16 17				
Motspur Park	d		16 01	16 16					15 50				16 31	16 46					16 20				17 01
Raynes Park 6	d	15 40	16 04	16 19			15 58		15 53	16 13		16 10	16 34	16 49			16 28		16 23	16 43		16 40	17 04
Wimbledon 6 ⊖	d	15 44	16 08	16 23		15 50	16 02		15 57	16 17	16 05	16 14	16 38	16 53		16 20	16 32		16 27	16 47	16 35	16 44	17 08
Earlsfield	d	15 47	16 12	16 27		15 54	16 05		16 01	16 20	16 08	16 17	16 42	16 57		16 24	16 35		16 31	16 50	16 38	16 47	17 12
Clapham Junction 10	d	15 51	16 16	16 31	15 51	15 58	16 09		16 05	16 24	16 12	16 21	16 46	17 01		16 28	16 39		16 35	16 54	16 42	16 51	17 16
Vauxhall ⊖	d	15 56	16 21	16 36		16 03	16 14	16 12	16 10	16 29	16 17	16 26	16 51	17 06		16 33	16 44	16 42	16 40	16 59	16 47	16 56	17 21
London Waterloo 15 ⊖	a	16 01	16 25	16 40	15 58	16 07	16 19	16 19	16 15	16 34	16 22	16 31	16 55	17 10	16 29	16 37	16 49	16 49	16 45	17 05	16 52	17 01	17 25

Table 152

Mondays to Fridays
from 27 September

Hampton Court, Shepperton, Guildford, Dorking and Chessington South - London

		SW	SW 1	SW	SW	SW		SW	SW	SW	SW	SW	SW	SW 1	SW	SW		SW	SW	SW	SW	SW	SW	SW	SW 1
Guildford	d	16 28		16 05									16 58		16 35									17 28	
London Road (Guildford)	d	16 32		16 09									17 02		16 39									17 32	
Clandon	d	16 37		16 14									17 07		16 44									17 37	
Horsley	d	16 41		16 18									17 11		16 48									17 41	
Effingham Junction 6	d	16 46		16 21									17 16		16 51									17 46	
Bookham	d	16 49											17 19											17 49	
Cobham & Stoke d'Abernon	d			16 25											16 55										
Oxshott	d			16 28											16 58										
Claygate	d			16 31											17 01										
Hinchley Wood	d			16 34											17 04										
Hampton Court	d										16 54											17 24			
Thames Ditton	d										16 56											17 26			
Surbiton 6	d		16 38	16 42						16 57	17 02			17 08	17 12						17 27	17 32			17 38
Berrylands	d										17 04											17 34			
Shepperton	d								16 41											17 11					
Upper Halliford	d								16 44											17 14					
Sunbury	d								16 46											17 16					
Kempton Park	d								16 48											17 18					
Hampton	d								16 51											17 21					
Fulwell	d								16 54											17 24					
Strawberry Hill	d				16 37	16 38										17 07		17 08							
Teddington	d				16 43				16 59							17 13				17 29					
Hampton Wick	d				16 46				17 01							17 16				17 31					
Kingston	a				16 48				17 03							17 18				17 33					
	d				16 49				17 04							17 19				17 34					
Norbiton	d				16 51				17 06							17 21				17 36					
New Malden 6	d				16 55				17 10		17 07					17 25				17 40		17 37			
Dorking 4	d											17 05											17 35		
Boxhill & Westhumble	d																								
Leatherhead	d	16 54										17 11	17 24										17 41	17 54	
Ashtead	d	16 58										17 14	17 28										17 44	17 58	
Epsom 3	a	17 02										17 19	17 32										17 49	18 02	
	d	17 05										17 20	17 35										17 50	18 05	
Ewell West	d	17 08										17 23	17 38										17 53	18 08	
Stoneleigh	d	17 10										17 25	17 40										17 55	18 10	
Worcester Park	d	17 13										17 28	17 43										17 58	18 13	
Chessington South	d							16 40											17 10						
Chessington North	d							16 42											17 12						
Tolworth	d							16 44											17 14						
Malden Manor	d							16 47											17 17						
Motspur Park	d	17 16						16 50				17 31	17 46						17 20				18 01	18 16	
Raynes Park 6	d	17 19			16 58			16 53	17 13		17 10	17 34	17 49			17 28			17 23	17 43		17 40	18 04	18 19	
Wimbledon 6 ⊖	d	17 23		16 50	17 02			16 57	17 17	17 05	17 14	17 38	17 53		17 20	17 32			17 27	17 47	17 35	17 44	18 08	18 23	
Earlsfield	d	17 27		16 54	17 05			17 01	17 20	17 08	17 17	17 42	17 57		17 24	17 35			17 31	17 50	17 38	17 47	18 12	18 27	
Clapham Junction 10	d	17 31	16 49	16 58	17 09			17 05	17 24	17 12	17 21	17 46	18 01		17 28	17 39			17 35	17 54	17 42	17 51	18 16	18 31	17 49
Vauxhall ⊖	d	17 36		17 03	17 14	17 12		17 10	17 29	17 17	17 26	17 51	18 06		17 33	17 44		17 42	17 40	17 59	17 47	17 56	18 21	18 36	
London Waterloo 15 ⊖	a	17 40	16 59	17 07	17 19	17 19		17 16	17 35	17 22	17 31	17 55	18 10	17 29	17 37	17 49		17 49	17 45	18 05	17 52	18 01	18 25	18 40	17 59

Table 152

Mondays to Fridays
from 27 September

Hampton Court, Shepperton, Guildford, Dorking and Chessington South - London

		SW		SW	SW	SW	SW	SW	SW	SW	SW	SW		SW 1	SW	SW	SW	SW	SW	SW	SW	SW		SW 1	SW
Guildford	d	17 05										17 58			17 35										18 05
London Road (Guildford)	d	17 09										18 02			17 39										18 09
Clandon	d	17 14										18 07			17 44										18 14
Horsley	d	17 18										18 11			17 48										18 18
Effingham Junction 6	d	17 21										18 16			17 51										18 21
Bookham	d											18 19													
Cobham & Stoke d'Abernon	d	17 25													17 55										18 25
Oxshott	d	17 28													17 58										18 28
Claygate	d	17 31													18 01										18 31
Hinchley Wood	d	17 34													18 04										18 34
Hampton Court	d									17 54											18 24				
Thames Ditton	d									17 56											18 26				
Surbiton 6	d	17 42							17 57	18 02				18 08	18 12					18 27	18 32			18 38	18 42
Berrylands	d									18 04											18 34				
Shepperton	d							17 41											18 11						
Upper Halliford	d							17 44											18 14						
Sunbury	d							17 46											18 16						
Kempton Park	d							17 48											18 18						
Hampton	d							17 51											18 21						
Fulwell	d							17 54											18 24						
Strawberry Hill	d			17 37	17 38	17 41										18 07	18 08								
Teddington	d			17 43		17b52		17 59								18 13			18 29						
Hampton Wick	d			17 46		17 54		18 01								18 16			18 31						
Kingston	a			17 48		17 56		18 03								18 18			18 33						
	d			17 49		17 58		18 04								18 19			18 34						
Norbiton	d			17 51		18 00		18 06								18 21			18 36						
New Malden 6	d			17 55		18 04		18 10		18 07						18 25			18 40		18 37				
Dorking 4	d										18 05											18 35			
Boxhill & Westhumble	d																								
Leatherhead	d										18 11	18 24										18 41			
Ashtead	d										18 14	18 28										18 44			
Epsom 3	a										18 19	18 32										18 49			
	d										18 20	18 35										18 50			
Ewell West	d										18 23	18 38										18 53			
Stoneleigh	d										18 25	18 40										18 55			
Worcester Park	d										18 28	18 43										18 58			
Chessington South	d						17 40											18 10							
Chessington North	d						17 42											18 12							
Tolworth	d						17 44											18 14							
Malden Manor	d						17 47											18 17							
Motspur Park	d						17 50				18 31	18 46						18 20				19 01			
Raynes Park 6	d			17 58		18 07	17 53	18 13		18 10	18 34	18 49				18 28		18 23	18 43		18 40	19 04			
Wimbledon 6 ⊖	d	17 50		18 02		18 11	17 57	18 17	18 05	18 14	18 38	18 53			18 20	18 32		18 27	18 47	18 35	18 44	19 08			18 50
Earlsfield	d	17 54		18 05		18 15	18 01	18 20	18 08	18 17	18 42	18 57			18 24	18 35		18 31	18 50	18 38	18 47	19 12			18 54
Clapham Junction 10	d	17 58		18 09		18 19	18 05	18 24	18 12	18 21	18 46	19 01			18 28	18 39		18 35	18 54	18 42	18 51	19 16		18 49	18 58
Vauxhall ⊖	d	18 03		18 14	18 12	18 24	18 10	18 29	18 17	18 26	18 51	19 06			18 33	18 44	18 42	18 40	18 59	18 47	18 56	19 21			19 03
London Waterloo 15 ⊖	a	18 07		18 19	18 19	18 29	18 15	18 35	18 23	18 31	18 55	19 10		18 29	18 37	18 49	18 49	18 47	19 05	18 52	19 01	19 27		18 57	19 07

b arr. 1746

Table 152

Mondays to Fridays
from 27 September

Hampton Court, Shepperton, Guildford, Dorking and Chessington South - London

		SW	SW	SW	SW	SW	SW	SW	SW	SW ■	SW	SW	SW	SW	SW	SW	SW	SW	SW	SW	SW ■	SW	SW
Guildford	d										18 35									19 28		19 05	
London Road (Guildford)	d										18 39									19 32		19 09	
Clandon	d										18 44									19 37		19 14	
Horsley	d										18 48									19 41		19 18	
Effingham Junction	d								18 59		18 51									19 46		19 21	
Bookham	d								19 02											19 49			
Cobham & Stoke d'Abernon	d										18 55											19 25	
Oxshott	d										18 58											19 28	
Claygate	d										19 01											19 31	
Hinchley Wood	d										19 04											19 34	
Hampton Court	d							18 54									19 24						
Thames Ditton	d							18 56									19 26						
Surbiton	d						18 57	19 02		19 08	19 12					19 27	19 32				19 38	19 42	
Berrylands	d							19 04									19 34						
Shepperton	d	18 36										19 06											
Upper Halliford	d	18 39										19 09											
Sunbury	d	18 41										19 11											
Kempton Park	d	18 43										19 13											
Hampton	d	18b51										19c21											
Fulwell	d	18 54										19 24											
Strawberry Hill	d		18 37	18 38									19 07	19 08									19 37
Teddington	d	18 59	18 43									19 29	19 13										19 43
Hampton Wick	d	19 01	18 46									19 31	19 16										19 46
Kingston	a	19 03	18 48									19 33	19 18										19 48
	d	19 04	18 49									19 34	19 19										19 49
Norbiton	d	19 06	18 51									19 36	19 21										19 51
New Malden	d	19 10	18 55					19 07				19 40	19 25				19 37						19 55
Dorking	d					18 50													19 33				
Boxhill & Westhumble	d																						
Leatherhead	d					18 56			19 08										19 39	19 54			
Ashtead	d					18 59			19 12										19 42	19 58			
Epsom	a					19 04			19 16										19 47	20 02			
	d					19 05			19 20									19 35	19 50	20 05			
Ewell West	d					19 08			19 23									19 38	19 53	20 08			
Stoneleigh	d					19 10			19 25									19 40	19 55	20 10			
Worcester Park	d					19 13			19 28									19 43	19 58	20 13			
Chessington South	d				18 40										19 10								
Chessington North	d				18 42										19 12								
Tolworth	d				18 44										19 14								
Malden Manor	d				18 47										19 17								
Motspur Park	d				18 50	19 16			19 31						19 20			19 46	20 01	20 16			
Raynes Park	d	19 13	18 58		18 53	19 19		19 10	19 34			19 43	19 28		19 23		19 40	19 49	20 04	20 19			19 58
Wimbledon ⊖	d	19 17	19 02		18 57	19 23	19 05	19 14	19 38		19 20	19 47	19 32		19 27	19 35	19 44	19 53	20 08	20 23		19 50	20 02
Earlsfield	d	19 20	19 05		19 01	19 27	19 08	19 17	19 42		19 24	19 50	19 35		19 31	19 38	19 47	19 57	20 12	20 27		19 54	20 05
Clapham Junction	d	19 24	19 09		19 05	19 31	19 12	19 21	19 46		19 28	19 54	19 39		19 35	19 42	19 51	20 01	20 16	20 31	19 49	19 58	20 09
Vauxhall ⊖	d	19 29	19 14	19 12	19 10	19 36	19 17	19 26	19 51		19 33	19 59	19 44	19 42	19 40	19 47	19 56	20 06	20 21	20 36		20 03	20 14
London Waterloo ⊖	a	19 34	19 19	19 16	19 14	19 41	19 23	19 31	19 55	19 25	19 37	20 04	19 49	19 46	19 45	19 52	20 01	20 10	20 25	20 41	19 57	20 07	20 19

b arr. 1846

c arr. 1916

Table 152

Mondays to Fridays
from 27 September

Hampton Court, Shepperton, Guildford, Dorking and Chessington South - London

		SW	SW	SW	SW	SW	SW	SW	SW ■	SW	SW	SW	SW	SW	SW	SW	SW	SW ■	SW	SW	SW	SW
Guildford	d							19 58		19 35									20 05			
London Road (Guildford)	d							20 02		19 39									20 09			
Clandon	d							20 07		19 44									20 14			
Horsley	d							20 11		19 48									20 18			
Effingham Junction	d							20 16		19 51									20 21			
Bookham	d							20 19														
Cobham & Stoke d'Abernon	d									19 55									20 25			
Oxshott	d									19 58									20 28			
Claygate	d									20 01									20 31			
Hinchley Wood	d									20 04									20 34			
Hampton Court	d					19 54										20 24						
Thames Ditton	d					19 56										20 26						
Surbiton	d				19 57	20 02			20 08	20 12					20 27	20 32		20 38	20 42			
Berrylands	d					20 04										20 34						
Shepperton	d			19 41										20 11								
Upper Halliford	d			19 44										20 14								
Sunbury	d			19 46										20 16								
Kempton Park	d			19 48										20 18								
Hampton	d			19 51										20 21								
Fulwell	d			19 54										20 24								
Strawberry Hill	d	19 38									20 07	20 08								20 37	20 38	
Teddington	d			19 59							20 11			20 29						20 41		
Hampton Wick	d			20 01							20 14			20 31						20 44		
Kingston	a			20 04							20 16			20 33						20 46		
	d			20 04							20 19			20 34						20 49		
Norbiton	d			20 06							20 21			20 36						20 51		
New Malden	d			20 10		20 07					20 25			20 40		20 37				20 55		
Dorking	d						20 05										20 35					
Boxhill & Westhumble	d																					
Leatherhead	d						20 11	20 24									20 41					
Ashtead	d						20 14	20 28									20 44					
Epsom	a						20 19	20 32									20 49					
	d						20 20	20 35									20 50					
Ewell West	d						20 23	20 38									20 53					
Stoneleigh	d						20 25	20 40									20 55					
Worcester Park	d						20 28	20 43									20 58					
Chessington South	d		19 40										20 10									20 40
Chessington North	d		19 42										20 12									20 42
Tolworth	d		19 44										20 14									20 44
Malden Manor	d		19 47										20 17									20 47
Motspur Park	d		19 50				20 31	20 46					20 20				21 01					20 50
Raynes Park	d		19 53	20 13		20 10	20 34	20 49			20 28		20 23	20 43		20 40	21 04			20 58		20 53
Wimbledon ⊖	d		19 57	20 17	20 05	20 14	20 38	20 53		20 20	20 32		20 27	20 47	20 35	20 44	21 08		20 50	21 02		20 57
Earlsfield	d		20 01	20 20	20 08	20 17	20 42	20 57		20 24	20 35		20 31	20 50	20 38	20 47	21 12		20 54	21 05		21 01
Clapham Junction	d		20 05	20 24	20 12	20 21	20 46	21 01		20 28	20 39		20 35	20 54	20 42	20 51	21 16	20 49	20 58	21 09		21 05
Vauxhall ⊖	d	20 12	20 10	20 29	20 17	20 26	20 51	21 06		20 33	20 44	20 42	20 40	20 59	20 47	20 56	21 21		21 03	21 14	21 12	21 10
London Waterloo ⊖	a	20 16	20 15	20 35	20 22	20 31	20 55	21 10	20 26	20 38	20 49	20 46	20 46	21 04	20 52	21 01	21 25	20 57	21 07	21 19	21 16	21 15

Table 152

Mondays to Fridays
from 27 September

Hampton Court, Shepperton, Guildford, Dorking and Chessington South - London

		SW	SW	SW	SW	SW	SW [1]	SW	SW	SW		SW	SW	SW	SW	SW	SW	SW [1]	SW	SW		SW	SW	SW	SW
Guildford	d					20 46		20 35											21 05						21 46
London Road (Guildford)	d					20 50		20 39											21 09						21 50
Clandon	d					20 55		20 44											21 14						21 55
Horsley	d					20 59		20 48											21 18						21 59
Effingham Junction [6]	d					21 03		20 51											21 21						22 03
Bookham	d					21 06																			22 06
Cobham & Stoke d'Abernon	d							20 55											21 25						
Oxshott	d							20 58											21 28						
Claygate	d							21 01											21 31						
Hinchley Wood	d							21 04											21 34						
Hampton Court	d			20 54											21 24										
Thames Ditton	d			20 56											21 26										
Surbiton [6]	d		20 57	21 02			21 08	21 12						21 27	21 32			21 38	21 42						
Berrylands	d			21 04											21 34										
Shepperton	d	20 41											21 11											21 41	
Upper Halliford	d	20 44											21 14											21 44	
Sunbury	d	20 46											21 16											21 46	
Kempton Park	d	20 48											21 18											21 48	
Hampton	d	20 51											21 21											21 51	
Fulwell	d	20 54											21 24											21 54	
Strawberry Hill	d								21 07	21 08										21 37		21 38			
Teddington	d	20 59							21 11				21 29							21 41				21 59	
Hampton Wick	d	21 01							21 14				21 31							21 44				22 01	
Kingston	a	21 03							21 16				21 33							21 46				22 03	
	d	21 04							21 19				21 34							21 49				22 04	
Norbiton	d	21 06							21 21				21 36							21 51				22 06	
New Malden [6]	d	21 10		21 07					21 25				21 40		21 37					21 55				22 10	
Dorking [4]	d																21 35								
Boxhill & Westhumble	d																								
Leatherhead	d					21 11											21 41								22 11
Ashtead	d					21 14											21 44								22 14
Epsom [3]	a					21 19											21 49								22 19
	d				21 05	21 20										21 35	21 50								22 20
Ewell West	d				21 08	21 23										21 38	21 53								22 23
Stoneleigh	d				21 10	21 25										21 40	21 55								22 25
Worcester Park	d				21 13	21 28										21 43	21 58								22 28
Chessington South	d											21 10											21 40		
Chessington North	d											21 12											21 42		
Tolworth	d											21 14											21 44		
Malden Manor	d											21 17											21 47		
Motspur Park	d				21 16	21 31						21 20				21 46	22 01						21 50		22 31
Raynes Park [6]	d	21 13		21 10	21 19	21 34			21 28			21 23	21 43		21 40	21 49	22 04			21 58			21 53	22 13	22 34
Wimbledon [6] ⊖	d	21 17	21 05	21 14	21 23	21 38		21 20	21 32			21 27	21 47	21 35	21 44	21 53	22 08		21 50	22 02			21 57	22 17	22 38
Earlsfield	d	21 20	21 08	21 17	21 27	21 42		21 24	21 35			21 31	21 50	21 38	21 47	21 57	22 12		21 54	22 05			22 01	22 20	22 42
Clapham Junction [10]	d	21 24	21 12	21 21	21 31	21 46		21 28	21 39			21 35	21 54	21 42	21 51	22 01	22 16	21 49	21 58	22 09			22 05	22 24	22 46
Vauxhall ⊖	d	21 29	21 17	21 26	21 36	21 51		21 33	21 44	21 42		21 40	21 59	21 47	21 56	22 06	22 21		22 03	22 14		22 12	22 10	22 29	22 51
London Waterloo [15] ⊖	a	21 34	21 22	21 31	21 40	21 55	21 29	21 37	21 49	21 46		21 45	22 04	21 52	22 01	22 10	22 25	21 57	22 07	22 19		22 16	22 16	22 34	22 55

Table 152

Mondays to Fridays
from 27 September

Hampton Court, Shepperton, Guildford, Dorking and Chessington South - London

		SW	SW [1]	SW	SW	SW		SW	SW	SW	SW	SW [1]	SW	SW	SW	SW		SW	SW	SW	SW [1]	SW	SW	SW	SW
Guildford	d			21 35									22 05	22 20						22 46		22 35	22 55		
London Road (Guildford)	d			21 39									22 09							22 50		22 39			
Clandon	d			21 44									22 14							22 55		22 44			
Horsley	d			21 48									22 18							22 59		22 48			
Effingham Junction [6]	d			21 51									22 21							23 03		22 51			
Bookham	d																			23 06					
Cobham & Stoke d'Abernon	d			21 55									22 25									22 55			
Oxshott	d			21 58									22 28									22 58			
Claygate	d			22 01									22 31									23 01			
Hinchley Wood	d			22 04									22 34									23 04			
Hampton Court	d									22 24															
Thames Ditton	d									22 26															
Surbiton [6]	d	21 57	22 08	22 12					22 27	22 32		22 38	22 42	22 57							23 08	23 12	23 30		
Berrylands	d									22 34															
Shepperton	d							22 11											22 41						
Upper Halliford	d							22 14											22 44						
Sunbury	d							22 16											22 46						
Kempton Park	d							22 18											22 48						
Hampton	d							22 21											22 51						
Fulwell	d							22 24											22 54						
Strawberry Hill	d				22 07	22 08									22 37	22 38								23 07	23 08
Teddington	d				22 11			22 29							22 41				22 59					23 11	
Hampton Wick	d				22 14			22 31							22 44				23 01					23 14	
Kingston	a				22 16			22 33							22 46				23 03					23 16	
	d				22 19			22 34							22 49				23 04					23 19	
Norbiton	d				22 21			22 36							22 51				23 06					23 21	
New Malden [6]	d				22 25			22 40		22 37					22 55				23 10					23 25	
Dorking [4]	d										22 35														
Boxhill & Westhumble	d																								
Leatherhead	d										22 41									23 11					
Ashtead	d										22 44									23 14					
Epsom [3]	a										22 49									23 19					
	d										22 50									23 20					
Ewell West	d										22 53									23 23					
Stoneleigh	d										22 55									23 25					
Worcester Park	d										22 58									23 28					
Chessington South	d																	22 40							
Chessington North	d																	22 42							
Tolworth	d																	22 44							
Malden Manor	d																	22 47							
Motspur Park	d										23 01							22 50		23 31					
Raynes Park [6]	d				22 28			22 43		22 40	23 04				22 58			22 53	23 13	23 37				23 28	
Wimbledon [6] ⊖	d	22 05		22 20	22 32			22 47	22 35	22 44	23 08		22 50	23 05	23 02			22 57	23 17	23 41		23 20	23 37	23 32	
Earlsfield	d	22 08		22 24	22 35			22 50	22 38	22 47	23 12		22 54	23 08	23 05			23 01	23 20	23 44		23 24	23 41	23 35	
Clapham Junction [10]	d	22 12		22 28	22 39			22 54	22 42	22 51	23 16	22 53	22 58	23 12	23 09			23 05	23 24	23 48		23 28	23 45	23 39	
Vauxhall ⊖	d	22 17		22 33	22 44	22 42		22 59	22 47	22 56	23 21		23 03	23 17	23 14	23 12		23 10	23 29	23 53		23 33	23 50	23 44	23 42
London Waterloo [15] ⊖	a	22 22	22 26	22 39	22 49	22 46		23 04	22 52	23 01	23 27	23 01	23 07	23 23	23 19	23 16		23 15	23 34	23 58	23 27	23 37	23 54	23 49	23 46

Table 152

Mondays to Fridays
from 27 September

Hampton Court, Shepperton, Guildford, Dorking and Chessington South - London

		SW	SW	SN	SW [1]	SW	SW	SW	SW
Guildford	d					23 08			
London Road (Guildford)	d					23 12			
Clandon	d					23 17			
Horsley	d					23 21			
Effingham Junction [6]	d					23 24			
Bookham	d								
Cobham & Stoke d'Abernon	d					23 28			
Oxshott	d					23 31			
Claygate	d					23 34			
Hinchley Wood	d					23 37			
Hampton Court	d		23 24						
Thames Ditton	d		23 26						
Surbiton [6]	d		23 32		23 38	23 42			
Berrylands	d		23 34						
Shepperton	d	23 11							
Upper Halliford	d	23 14							
Sunbury	d	23 16							
Kempton Park	d	23 18							
Hampton	d	23 21							
Fulwell	d	23 24							
Strawberry Hill	d						23 37	23 38	
Teddington	d	23 29					23 41		
Hampton Wick	d	23 31					23 44		
Kingston	a	23 33					23 46		
	d	23 34					23 49		
Norbiton	d	23 36					23 51		
New Malden [6]	d	23 40	23 37				23 55		
Dorking [4]	d			23 30					
Boxhill & Westhumble	d								
Leatherhead	d			23 36					
Ashtead	d			23 39					
Epsom [3]	a			23 45					
	d								
Ewell West	d								
Stoneleigh	d								
Worcester Park	d								
Chessington South	d								23 40
Chessington North	d								23 42
Tolworth	d								23 44
Malden Manor	d								23 47
Motspur Park	d								23 50
Raynes Park [6]	d	23 43	23 40				23 58		23 54
Wimbledon [6] ⊖ ⛴	d	23 52	23a45			23 55	00 05		00a01
Earlsfield	d	23 55				23 58	00 08		
Clapham Junction [10]	d	23 59			23 55	00 02	00 12		
Vauxhall ⊖	d	00 04				00 07	00 17	00 12	
London Waterloo [15] ⊖	a	00 11			00 03	00 14	00 23	00 16	

Table 152

Saturdays
29 May to 25 September

Hampton Court, Shepperton, Guildford, Dorking and Chessington South - London

		SW	SW [1]	SW	SW	SW	SW	SW	SW	SW
Guildford	d			23p08			04 00		05 12	
London Road (Guildford)	d			23p12						
Clandon	d			23p17						
Horsley	d			23p21						
Effingham Junction [6]	d			23p24						
Bookham	d									
Cobham & Stoke d'Abernon	d			23p28						
Oxshott	d			23p31						
Claygate	d			23p34						
Hinchley Wood	d			23p37						
Hampton Court	d									
Thames Ditton	d									
Surbiton [6]	d		23p38	23p42			04 24		05 57	
Berrylands	d									
Shepperton	d	23p11								
Upper Halliford	d	23p14								
Sunbury	d	23p16								
Kempton Park	d	23p18								
Hampton	d	23p21								
Fulwell	d	23p24								
Strawberry Hill	d				23p37	23p38		04 55		
Teddington	d	23p29			23p41			04 59		
Hampton Wick	d	23p31			23p44			05 01		
Kingston	a	23p33			23p46			05 03		
	d	23p34			23p49			05 04		
Norbiton	d	23p36			23p51			05 06		
New Malden [6]	d	23p40			23p55			05 10		
Dorking [4]	d									
Boxhill & Westhumble	d									
Leatherhead	d									
Ashtead	d									
Epsom [3]	a									
	d									05 35
Ewell West	d									05 38
Stoneleigh	d									05 40
Worcester Park	d									05 43
Chessington South	d									
Chessington North	d									
Tolworth	d									
Malden Manor	d									
Motspur Park	d									05 46
Raynes Park [6]	d	23p43			23p58			05 13		05 49
Wimbledon [6] ⊖ ⛴	d	23p52		23p55	00 05		04 32	05 17	06 05	05 53
Earlsfield	d	23p55		23p58	00 08			05 21	06 08	05 57
Clapham Junction [10]	d	23p59	23p55	00 02	00 12		04 44	05 25	06 12	06 01
Vauxhall ⊖	d	00 04		00 07	00 17	00 12		05 30	06 17	06 06
London Waterloo [15] ⊖	a	00 11	00 03	00 14	00 23	00 16	04 53	05 35	06 22	06 11

		SW	SW	SW	SW	SW	SW	SW	SW	SW	SW	SW	SW	SW
Guildford	d											06 28		
London Road (Guildford)	d											06 32		
Clandon	d											06 37		
Horsley	d											06 41		
Effingham Junction [6]	d											06 46		
Bookham	d											06 49		
Cobham & Stoke d'Abernon	d													
Oxshott	d													
Claygate	d													
Hinchley Wood	d													
Hampton Court	d			05 54						06 24				
Thames Ditton	d			05 56						06 26				
Surbiton [6]	d			06 02					06 27	06 32				
Berrylands	d			06 04						06 34				
Shepperton	d							06 11						
Upper Halliford	d							06 14						
Sunbury	d							06 16						
Kempton Park	d							06 18						
Hampton	d							06 21						
Fulwell	d							06 24						
Strawberry Hill	d	05 38				06 07	06 08						06 37	06 38
Teddington	d		05 44			06 11		06 29					06 41	
Hampton Wick	d		05 46			06 14		06 31					06 44	
Kingston	a		05 48			06 16		06 33					06 46	
	d		05 49			06 19		06 34					06 49	
Norbiton	d		05 51			06 21		06 36					06 51	
New Malden [6]	d		05 55	06 07		06 25		06 40		06 37			06 55	
Dorking [4]	d													
Boxhill & Westhumble	d													
Leatherhead	d											06 54		
Ashtead	d											06 58		
Epsom [3]	a											07 02		
	d				06 05						06 35	07 05		
Ewell West	d				06 08						06 38	07 08		
Stoneleigh	d				06 10						06 40	07 10		
Worcester Park	d				06 13						06 43	07 13		
Chessington South	d													
Chessington North	d													
Tolworth	d													
Malden Manor	d													
Motspur Park	d				06 16						06 46	07 16		
Raynes Park [6]	d		05 58	06 10	06 19	06 28		06 43		06 40	06 49	07 19	06 58	
Wimbledon [6] ⊖ ⛴	d		06 02	06 14	06 23	06 32		06 47	06 35	06 44	06 53	07 23	07 02	
Earlsfield	d		06 05	06 17	06 27	06 35		06 50	06 38	06 47	06 57	07 27	07 05	
Clapham Junction [10]	d		06 09	06 21	06 31	06 39		06 54	06 42	06 51	07 01	07 31	07 09	
Vauxhall ⊖	d	06 12	06 14	06 26	06 36	06 44	06 42	06 59	06 47	06 56	07 06	07 36	07 14	07 12
London Waterloo [15] ⊖	a	06 16	06 19	06 31	06 40	06 49	06 46	07 04	06 52	07 01	07 10	07 40	07 19	07 16

Table 152

Saturdays
29 May to 25 September

Hampton Court, Shepperton, Guildford, Dorking and Chessington South - London

		SW	SW	SW	SW	SW		SW 1	SW	SW	SW	SW	SW	SW	SW	SW		SW 1	SW	SW	SW	SW	SW	SW	SW
Guildford	d					06 58			06 38							07 28			07 08						
London Road (Guildford)	d					07 02			06 42							07 32			07 12						
Clandon	d					07 07			06 47							07 37			07 17						
Horsley	d					07 11			06 51							07 41			07 21						
Effingham Junction 6	d					07 16			06 54							07 46			07 24						
Bookham	d					07 19										07 49									
Cobham & Stoke d'Abernon	d								06 58										07 28						
Oxshott	d								07 01										07 31						
Claygate	d								07 04										07 34						
Hinchley Wood	d								07 07										07 37						
Hampton Court	d				06 54										07 24										07 54
Thames Ditton	d				06 56										07 26										07 56
Surbiton 6	d			06 57	07 02			07 08	07 12					07 27	07 32			07 38	07 42					07 57	08 02
Berrylands	d				07 04										07 34										08 04
Shepperton	d		06 41										07 11										07 41		
Upper Halliford	d		06 44										07 14										07 44		
Sunbury	d		06 46										07 16										07 46		
Kempton Park	d		06 48										07 18										07 48		
Hampton	d		06 51										07 21										07 51		
Fulwell	d		06 54										07 24										07 54		
Strawberry Hill	d									07 07	07 08									07 37	07 38				
Teddington	d		06 59							07 11			07 29							07 41			07 59		
Hampton Wick	d		07 01							07 14			07 31							07 44			08 01		
Kingston	a		07 03							07 16			07 33							07 46			08 03		
	d		07 04							07 19			07 34							07 49			08 04		
Norbiton	d		07 06							07 21			07 36							07 51			08 06		
New Malden 6	d		07 10		07 07					07 25			07 40		07 37					07 55			08 10		08 07
Dorking 4	d																								
Boxhill & Westhumble	d																								
Leatherhead	d					07 24										07 54									
Ashtead	d					07 28										07 58									
Epsom 3	a					07 32										08 02									
	d					07 35										08 05									
Ewell West	d					07 38										08 08									
Stoneleigh	d					07 40										08 10									
Worcester Park	d					07 43										08 13									
Chessington South	d	06 40										07 10										07 40			
Chessington North	d	06 42										07 12										07 42			
Tolworth	d	06 44										07 14										07 44			
Malden Manor	d	06 47										07 17										07 47			
Motspur Park	d	06 50				07 46						07 20				08 16						07 50			
Raynes Park 6	d	06 53	07 13		07 10	07 49				07 28		07 23	07 43		07 40	08 19				07 58		07 53	08 13		08 10
Wimbledon 6 ⊖ ⇌	d	06 57	07 17	07 05	07 14	07 53			07 20	07 32		07 27	07 47	07 35	07 44	08 23			07 50	08 02		07 57	08 17	08 05	08 14
Earlsfield	d	07 01	07 20	07 08	07 17	07 57			07 24	07 35		07 31	07 50	07 38	07 47	08 27			07 54	08 05		08 01	08 20	08 08	08 17
Clapham Junction 10	d	07 05	07 24	07 12	07 21	08 01		07 19	07 28	07 39		07 35	07 54	07 42	07 51	08 31		07 51	07 58	08 09		08 05	08 24	08 12	08 21
Vauxhall ⊖	d	07 10	07 29	07 17	07 26	08 06			07 33	07 44	07 42	07 40	07 59	07 47	07 56	08 36			08 03	08 14	08 12	08 10	08 29	08 17	08 26
London Waterloo 15 ⊖	a	07 15	07 34	07 22	07 31	08 10		07 27	07 37	07 49	07 46	07 45	08 04	07 52	08 01	08 40		07 58	08 07	08 19	08 16	08 15	08 34	08 22	08 31

Table 152

Saturdays
29 May to 25 September

Hampton Court, Shepperton, Guildford, Dorking and Chessington South - London

		SW		SW	SW 1	SW	SW	SW	SW	SW	SW	SW		SW	SW	SW 1	SW	SW	SW	SW	SW	SW		SW	SW
Guildford	d			07 58		07 38									08 28		08 08								
London Road (Guildford)	d			08 02		07 42									08 32		08 12								
Clandon	d			08 07		07 47									08 37		08 17								
Horsley	d			08 11		07 51									08 41		08 21								
Effingham Junction 6	d			08 16		07 54									08 46		08 24								
Bookham	d			08 19											08 49										
Cobham & Stoke d'Abernon	d					07 58											08 28								
Oxshott	d					08 01											08 31								
Claygate	d					08 04											08 34								
Hinchley Wood	d					08 07											08 37								
Hampton Court	d											08 24												08 54	
Thames Ditton	d											08 26												08 56	
Surbiton 6	d				08 08	08 12					08 27	08 32				08 38	08 42					08 57		09 02	
Berrylands	d											08 34												09 04	
Shepperton	d									08 11											08 41				
Upper Halliford	d									08 14											08 44				
Sunbury	d									08 16											08 46				
Kempton Park	d									08 18											08 48				
Hampton	d									08 21											08 51				
Fulwell	d									08 24											08 54				
Strawberry Hill	d						08 07	08 08										08 37	08 38						
Teddington	d						08 11			08 29								08 41			08 59				
Hampton Wick	d						08 14			08 31								08 44			09 01				
Kingston	a						08 16			08 33								08 46			09 03				
	d						08 19			08 34								08 49			09 04				
Norbiton	d						08 21			08 36								08 51			09 06				
New Malden 6	d						08 25			08 40		08 37						08 55			09 10			09 07	
Dorking 4	d	08 05												08 35											09 05
Boxhill & Westhumble	d																								
Leatherhead	d	08 11		08 24										08 41	08 54										09 11
Ashtead	d	08 14		08 28										08 44	08 58										09 14
Epsom 3	a	08 19		08 32										08 49	09 02										09 19
	d	08 20		08 35										08 50	09 05										09 20
Ewell West	d	08 23		08 38										08 53	09 08										09 23
Stoneleigh	d	08 25		08 40										08 55	09 10										09 25
Worcester Park	d	08 28		08 43										08 58	09 13										09 28
Chessington South	d								08 10											08 40					
Chessington North	d								08 12											08 42					
Tolworth	d								08 14											08 44					
Malden Manor	d								08 17											08 47					
Motspur Park	d	08 31		08 46					08 20					09 01	09 16					08 50					09 31
Raynes Park 6	d	08 34		08 49			08 28		08 23	08 43		08 40		09 04	09 19			08 58		08 53	09 13			09 10	09 34
Wimbledon 6 ⊖ ⇌	d	08 38		08 53		08 20	08 32		08 27	08 47	08 35	08 44		09 08	09 23		08 50	09 02		08 57	09 17	09 05		09 14	09 38
Earlsfield	d	08 42		08 57		08 24	08 35		08 31	08 50	08 38	08 47		09 12	09 27		08 54	09 05		09 01	09 20	09 08		09 17	09 42
Clapham Junction 10	d	08 46		09 01		08 28	08 39		08 35	08 54	08 42	08 51		09 16	09 31	08 50	08 58	09 09		09 05	09 24	09 12		09 21	09 46
Vauxhall ⊖	d	08 51		09 06		08 33	08 44	08 42	08 40	08 59	08 47	08 56		09 21	09 36		09 03	09 14	09 12	09 10	09 29	09 17		09 26	09 51
London Waterloo 15 ⊖	a	08 55		09 10	08 25	08 37	08 49	08 46	08 45	09 04	08 52	09 01		09 25	09 40	08 58	09 07	09 19	09 16	09 15	09 34	09 22		09 31	09 55

Saturdays

29 May to 25 September

Hampton Court, Shepperton, Guildford, Dorking and Chessington South - London

		SW	SW ■	SW	SW	SW	SW	SW	SW	SW	SW	SW	SW ■	SW	SW	SW	SW	SW	SW	SW	SW	SW	SW ■
Guildford	d	08 58		08 38								09 28		09 08								09 58	
London Road (Guildford)	d	09 02		08 42								09 32		09 12								10 02	
Clandon	d	09 07		08 47								09 37		09 17								10 07	
Horsley	d	09 11		08 51								09 41		09 21								10 11	
Effingham Junction ■	d	09 16		08 54								09 46		09 24								10 16	
Bookham	d	09 19										09 49										10 19	
Cobham & Stoke d'Abernon	d			08 58										09 28									
Oxshott	d			09 01										09 31									
Claygate	d			09 04										09 34									
Hinchley Wood	d			09 07										09 37									
Hampton Court	d									09 24										09 54			
Thames Ditton	d									09 26										09 56			
Surbiton ■	d		09 08	09 12					09 27	09 32			09 38	09 42					09 57	10 02			10 08
Berrylands	d									09 34										10 04			
Shepperton	d							09 11										09 41					
Upper Halliford	d							09 14										09 44					
Sunbury	d							09 16										09 46					
Kempton Park	d							09 18										09 48					
Hampton	d							09 21										09 51					
Fulwell	d							09 24										09 54					
Strawberry Hill	d				09 07	09 08									09 37	09 38							
Teddington	d				09 11			09 29							09 41			09 59					
Hampton Wick	d				09 14			09 31							09 44			10 01					
Kingston	a				09 16			09 33							09 46			10 03					
	d				09 19			09 34							09 49			10 04					
Norbiton	d				09 21			09 36							09 51			10 06					
New Malden ■	d				09 25			09 40		09 37					09 55			10 10		10 07			
Dorking ■	d										09 35										10 05		
Boxhill & Westhumble	d																						
Leatherhead	d	09 24									09 41	09 54									10 11	10 24	
Ashtead	d	09 28									09 44	09 58									10 14	10 28	
Epsom ■	a	09 32									09 49	10 02									10 19	10 32	
	d	09 35									09 50	10 05									10 20	10 35	
Ewell West	d	09 38									09 53	10 08									10 23	10 38	
Stoneleigh	d	09 40									09 55	10 10									10 25	10 40	
Worcester Park	d	09 43									09 58	10 13									10 28	10 43	
Chessington South	d						09 10										09 40						
Chessington North	d						09 12										09 42						
Tolworth	d						09 14										09 44						
Malden Manor	d						09 17										09 47						
Motspur Park	d	09 46					09 20				10 01	10 16					09 50				10 31	10 46	
Raynes Park ■	d	09 49			09 28		09 23	09 43		09 40	10 04	10 19			09 58		09 53	10 13		10 10	10 34	10 49	
Wimbledon ■ ⊖ ⇌	d	09 53		09 20	09 32		09 27	09 47	09 35	09 44	10 08	10 23		09 50	10 02		09 57	10 17	10 05	10 14	10 38	10 53	
Earlsfield	d	09 57		09 24	09 35		09 31	09 50	09 38	09 47	10 12	10 27		09 54	10 05		10 01	10 20	10 08	10 17	10 42	10 57	
Clapham Junction ■	d	10 01		09 28	09 39		09 35	09 54	09 42	09 51	10 16	10 31	09 49	09 58	10 09		10 05	10 24	10 12	10 21	10 46	11 01	
Vauxhall ⊖	d	10 06		09 33	09 44	09 42	09 40	09 59	09 47	09 56	10 21	10 36		10 03	10 14	10 12	10 10	10 29	10 17	10 26	10 51	11 06	
London Waterloo ■ ⊖	a	10 10	09 25	09 37	09 49	09 46	09 45	10 04	09 52	10 01	10 25	10 40	09 57	10 07	10 19	10 16	10 15	10 34	10 22	10 31	10 55	11 10	10 25

Table 152

Saturdays

29 May to 25 September

Hampton Court, Shepperton, Guildford, Dorking and Chessington South - London

		SW	SW	SW	SW	SW	SW	SW	SW	SW	SW ■	SW	SW	SW	SW	SW	SW	SW	SW	SW	SW ■	SW
Guildford	d	09 38								10 28		10 08								10 58		10 38
London Road (Guildford)	d	09 42								10 32		10 12								11 02		10 42
Clandon	d	09 47								10 37		10 17								11 07		10 47
Horsley	d	09 51								10 41		10 21								11 11		10 51
Effingham Junction ■	d	09 54								10 46		10 24								11 16		10 54
Bookham	d									10 49										11 19		
Cobham & Stoke d'Abernon	d	09 58										10 28										10 58
Oxshott	d	10 01										10 31										11 01
Claygate	d	10 04										10 34										11 04
Hinchley Wood	d	10 07										10 37										11 07
Hampton Court	d							10 24										10 54				
Thames Ditton	d							10 26										10 56				
Surbiton ■	d	10 12					10 27	10 32			10 38	10 42					10 57	11 02			11 08	11 12
Berrylands	d							10 34										11 04				
Shepperton	d					10 11										10 41						
Upper Halliford	d					10 14										10 44						
Sunbury	d					10 16										10 46						
Kempton Park	d					10 18										10 48						
Hampton	d					10 21										10 51						
Fulwell	d					10 24										10 54						
Strawberry Hill	d		10 07	10 08									10 37	10 38								
Teddington	d		10 11			10 29							10 41			10 59						
Hampton Wick	d		10 14			10 31							10 44			11 01						
Kingston	a		10 16			10 33							10 46			11 03						
	d		10 19			10 34							10 49			11 04						
Norbiton	d		10 21			10 36							10 51			11 06						
New Malden ■	d		10 25			10 40		10 37					10 55			11 10		11 07				
Dorking ■	d								10 35										11 05			
Boxhill & Westhumble	d																					
Leatherhead	d								10 41	10 54									11 11	11 24		
Ashtead	d								10 44	10 58									11 14	11 28		
Epsom ■	a								10 49	11 02									11 19	11 32		
	d								10 50	11 05									11 20	11 35		
Ewell West	d								10 53	11 08									11 23	11 38		
Stoneleigh	d								10 55	11 10									11 25	11 40		
Worcester Park	d								10 58	11 13									11 28	11 43		
Chessington South	d				10 10										10 40							
Chessington North	d				10 12										10 42							
Tolworth	d				10 14										10 44							
Malden Manor	d				10 17										10 47							
Motspur Park	d				10 20				11 01	11 16					10 50				11 31	11 46		
Raynes Park ■	d		10 28		10 23	10 43		10 40	11 04	11 19			10 58		10 53	11 13		11 10	11 34	11 49		
Wimbledon ■ ⊖ ⇌	d	10 20	10 32		10 27	10 47	10 35	10 44	11 08	11 23		10 50	11 02		10 57	11 17	11 05	11 14	11 38	11 53		11 20
Earlsfield	d	10 24	10 35		10 31	10 50	10 38	10 47	11 12	11 27		10 54	11 05		11 01	11 20	11 08	11 17	11 42	11 57		11 24
Clapham Junction ■	d	10 28	10 39		10 35	10 54	10 42	10 51	11 16	11 31	10 49	10 58	11 09		11 05	11 24	11 12	11 21	11 46	12 01		11 28
Vauxhall ⊖	d	10 33	10 44	10 42	10 40	10 59	10 47	10 56	11 21	11 36		11 03	11 14	11 12	11 10	11 29	11 17	11 26	11 51	12 06		11 33
London Waterloo ■ ⊖	a	10 37	10 49	10 46	10 45	11 04	10 52	11 01	11 25	11 40	10 57	11 07	11 19	11 16	11 15	11 34	11 22	11 31	11 55	12 10	11 25	11 37

Table 152

Saturdays
29 May to 25 September

Hampton Court, Shepperton, Guildford, Dorking and Chessington South - London

		SW	SW	SW	SW	SW	SW	SW	SW	SW [1]		SW	SW	SW	SW	SW	SW	SW	SW	SW		SW [1]	SW	SW	SW
Guildford	d								11 28			11 08								11 58			11 38		
London Road (Guildford)	d								11 32			11 12								12 02			11 42		
Clandon	d								11 37			11 17								12 07			11 47		
Horsley	d								11 41			11 21								12 11			11 51		
Effingham Junction [6]	d								11 46			11 24								12 16			11 54		
Bookham	d								11 49											12 19					
Cobham & Stoke d'Abernon	d											11 28											11 58		
Oxshott	d											11 31											12 01		
Claygate	d											11 34											12 04		
Hinchley Wood	d											11 37											12 07		
Hampton Court	d						11 24											11 54							
Thames Ditton	d						11 26											11 56							
Surbiton [6]	d					11 27	11 32			11 38		11 42					11 57	12 02				12 08	12 12		
Berrylands	d						11 34											12 04							
Shepperton	d				11 11											11 41									
Upper Halliford	d				11 14											11 44									
Sunbury	d				11 16											11 46									
Kempton Park	d				11 18											11 48									
Hampton	d				11 21											11 51									
Fulwell	d				11 24											11 54									
Strawberry Hill	d	11 07	11 08										11 37	11 38										12 07	12 08
Teddington	d	11 11			11 29								11 41			11 59								12 11	
Hampton Wick	d	11 14			11 31								11 44			12 01								12 14	
Kingston	a	11 16			11 33								11 46			12 03								12 16	
	d	11 19			11 34								11 49			12 04								12 19	
Norbiton	d	11 21			11 36								11 51			12 06								12 21	
New Malden [6]	d	11 25			11 40		11 37						11 55			12 10		12 07						12 25	
Dorking [4]	d							11 35											12 05						
Boxhill & Westhumble	d																								
Leatherhead	d							11 41	11 54										12 11	12 24					
Ashtead	d							11 44	11 58										12 14	12 28					
Epsom [3]	a							11 49	12 02										12 19	12 32					
	d							11 50	12 05										12 20	12 35					
Ewell West	d							11 53	12 08										12 23	12 38					
Stoneleigh	d							11 55	12 10										12 25	12 40					
Worcester Park	d							11 58	12 13										12 28	12 43					
Chessington South	d			11 10											11 40										
Chessington North	d			11 12											11 42										
Tolworth	d			11 14											11 44										
Malden Manor	d			11 17											11 47										
Motspur Park	d			11 20				12 01	12 16						11 50				12 31	12 46					
Raynes Park [6]	d	11 28		11 23	11 43		11 40	12 04	12 19				11 58		11 53	12 13		12 10	12 34	12 49				12 28	
Wimbledon [6] ⊖	d	11 32		11 27	11 47	11 35	11 44	12 08	12 23			11 50	12 02		11 57	12 17	12 05	12 14	12 38	12 53			12 20	12 32	
Earlsfield	d	11 35		11 31	11 50	11 38	11 47	12 12	12 27			11 54	12 05		12 01	12 20	12 08	12 17	12 42	12 57			12 24	12 35	
Clapham Junction [10]	d	11 39		11 35	11 54	11 42	11 51	12 16	12 31	11 49		11 58	12 09		12 05	12 24	12 12	12 21	12 46	13 01			12 28	12 39	
Vauxhall ⊖	d	11 44	11 42	11 40	11 59	11 47	11 56	12 21	12 36			12 03	12 14	12 12	12 10	12 29	12 17	12 26	12 51	13 06			12 33	12 44	12 42
London Waterloo [15] ⊖	a	11 49	11 46	11 45	12 04	11 52	12 01	12 25	12 40	11 57		12 07	12 19	12 16	12 15	12 34	12 22	12 31	12 55	13 10		12 27	12 37	12 49	12 46

Table 152

Saturdays
29 May to 25 September

Hampton Court, Shepperton, Guildford, Dorking and Chessington South - London

		SW	SW	SW	SW	SW		SW	SW [1]	SW	SW	SW	SW	SW	SW	SW		SW	SW	SW [1]	SW	SW	SW	SW	SW
Guildford	d							12 28		12 08									12 58		12 38				
London Road (Guildford)	d							12 32		12 12									13 02		12 42				
Clandon	d							12 37		12 17									13 07		12 47				
Horsley	d							12 41		12 21									13 11		12 51				
Effingham Junction [6]	d							12 46		12 24									13 16		12 54				
Bookham	d							12 49											13 19						
Cobham & Stoke d'Abernon	d									12 28											12 58				
Oxshott	d									12 31											13 01				
Claygate	d									12 34											13 04				
Hinchley Wood	d									12 37											13 07				
Hampton Court	d				12 24											12 54									
Thames Ditton	d				12 26											12 56									
Surbiton [6]	d			12 27	12 32				12 38	12 42					12 57	13 02				13 08	13 12				
Berrylands	d				12 34											13 04									
Shepperton	d		12 11											12 41											13 11
Upper Halliford	d		12 14											12 44											13 14
Sunbury	d		12 16											12 46											13 16
Kempton Park	d		12 18											12 48											13 18
Hampton	d		12 21											12 51											13 21
Fulwell	d		12 24											12 54											13 24
Strawberry Hill	d										12 37	12 38										13 07	13 08		
Teddington	d		12 29								12 41			12 59								13 11			13 29
Hampton Wick	d		12 31								12 44			13 01								13 14			13 31
Kingston	a		12 33								12 46			13 03								13 16			13 33
	d		12 34								12 49			13 04								13 19			13 34
Norbiton	d		12 36								12 51			13 06								13 21			13 36
New Malden [6]	d		12 40		12 37						12 55			13 10		13 07						13 25			13 40
Dorking [4]	d					12 35												13 05							
Boxhill & Westhumble	d																								
Leatherhead	d					12 41		12 54										13 11	13 24						
Ashtead	d					12 44		12 58										13 14	13 28						
Epsom [3]	a					12 49		13 02										13 19	13 32						
	d					12 50		13 05										13 20	13 35						
Ewell West	d					12 53		13 08										13 23	13 38						
Stoneleigh	d					12 55		13 10										13 25	13 40						
Worcester Park	d					12 58		13 13										13 28	13 43						
Chessington South	d	12 10											12 40											13 10	
Chessington North	d	12 12											12 42											13 12	
Tolworth	d	12 14											12 44											13 14	
Malden Manor	d	12 17											12 47											13 17	
Motspur Park	d	12 20				13 01		13 16					12 50					13 31	13 46					13 20	
Raynes Park [6]	d	12 23	12 43		12 40	13 04		13 19			12 58		12 53	13 13		13 10		13 34	13 49			13 28		13 23	13 43
Wimbledon [6] ⊖	d	12 27	12 47	12 35	12 44	13 08		13 23		12 50	13 02		12 57	13 17	13 05	13 14		13 38	13 53		13 20	13 32		13 27	13 47
Earlsfield	d	12 31	12 50	12 38	12 47	13 12		13 27		12 54	13 05		13 01	13 20	13 08	13 17		13 42	13 57		13 24	13 35		13 31	13 50
Clapham Junction [10]	d	12 35	12 54	12 42	12 51	13 16		13 31	12 49	12 58	13 09		13 05	13 24	13 12	13 21		13 46	14 01		13 28	13 39		13 35	13 54
Vauxhall ⊖	d	12 40	12 59	12 47	12 56	13 21		13 36		13 03	13 14	13 12	13 10	13 29	13 17	13 26		13 51	14 06		13 33	13 44	13 42	13 40	13 59
London Waterloo [15] ⊖	a	12 45	13 04	12 52	13 01	13 25		13 40	12 57	13 07	13 19	13 16	13 15	13 34	13 22	13 31		13 55	14 10	13 25	13 37	13 49	13 46	13 45	14 04

Table 152

Hampton Court, Shepperton, Guildford, Dorking and Chessington South - London

		SW		SW	SW	SW	SW 1	SW	SW	SW	SW	SW		SW	SW	SW	SW	SW 1	SW	SW	SW	SW		SW	SW
Guildford	d					13 28		13 08									13 58		13 38						
London Road (Guildford)	d					13 32		13 12									14 02		13 42						
Clandon	d					13 37		13 17									14 07		13 47						
Horsley	d					13 41		13 21									14 11		13 51						
Effingham Junction 6	d					13 46		13 24									14 16		13 54						
Bookham	d					13 49											14 19								
Cobham & Stoke d'Abernon	d							13 28											13 58						
Oxshott	d							13 31											14 01						
Claygate	d							13 34											14 04						
Hinchley Wood	d							13 37											14 07						
Hampton Court	d			13 24											13 54										
Thames Ditton	d			13 26											13 56										
Surbiton 6	d	13 27		13 32			13 38	13 42						13 57	14 02			14 08	14 12						14 27
Berrylands	d			13 34											14 04										
Shepperton	d											13 41												14 11	
Upper Halliford	d											13 44												14 14	
Sunbury	d											13 46												14 16	
Kempton Park	d											13 48												14 18	
Hampton	d											13 51												14 21	
Fulwell	d											13 54												14 24	
Strawberry Hill	d								13 37	13 38										14 07	14 08				
Teddington	d								13 41			13 59								14 11				14 29	
Hampton Wick	d								13 44			14 01								14 14				14 31	
Kingston	a								13 46			14 03								14 16				14 33	
	d								13 49			14 04								14 19				14 34	
Norbiton	d								13 51			14 06								14 21				14 36	
New Malden 6	d			13 37					13 55			14 10			14 07					14 25				14 40	
Dorking 4	d				13 35											14 05									
Boxhill & Westhumble	d																								
Leatherhead	d				13 41	13 54										14 11	14 24								
Ashtead	d				13 44	13 58										14 14	14 28								
Epsom 3	a				13 49	14 02										14 19	14 32								
	d				13 50	14 05										14 20	14 35								
Ewell West	d				13 53	14 08										14 23	14 38								
Stoneleigh	d				13 55	14 10										14 25	14 40								
Worcester Park	d				13 58	14 13										14 28	14 43								
Chessington South	d										13 40											14 10			
Chessington North	d										13 42											14 12			
Tolworth	d										13 44											14 14			
Malden Manor	d										13 47											14 17			
Motspur Park	d				14 01	14 16					13 50					14 31	14 46					14 20			
Raynes Park 6	d			13 40	14 04	14 19			13 58		13 53	14 13			14 10	14 34	14 49			14 28		14 23		14 43	
Wimbledon 6 ⊖	d	13 35		13 44	14 08	14 23		13 50	14 02		13 57	14 17		14 05	14 14	14 38	14 53		14 20	14 32		14 27		14 47	14 35
Earlsfield	d	13 38		13 47	14 12	14 27		13 54	14 05		14 01	14 20		14 08	14 17	14 42	14 57		14 24	14 35		14 31		14 50	14 38
Clapham Junction 10	d	13 42		13 51	14 16	14 31	13 49	13 58	14 09		14 05	14 24		14 12	14 21	14 46	15 01		14 28	14 39		14 35		14 54	14 42
Vauxhall ⊖	d	13 47		13 56	14 21	14 36		14 03	14 14	14 12	14 10	14 29		14 17	14 26	14 51	15 06		14 33	14 44	14 42	14 40		14 59	14 47
London Waterloo 15 ⊖	a	13 52		14 01	14 25	14 40	13 57	14 07	14 19	14 16	14 15	14 34		14 22	14 31	14 55	15 10	14 25	14 37	14 49	14 46	14 45		15 04	14 52

Table 152

Hampton Court, Shepperton, Guildford, Dorking and Chessington South - London

		SW	SW	SW	SW 1	SW	SW	SW		SW	SW	SW	SW	SW	SW	SW 1	SW	SW		SW	SW	SW	SW	SW	SW
Guildford	d			14 28		14 08									14 58		14 38								
London Road (Guildford)	d			14 32		14 12									15 02		14 42								
Clandon	d			14 37		14 17									15 07		14 47								
Horsley	d			14 41		14 21									15 11		14 51								
Effingham Junction 6	d			14 46		14 24									15 16		14 54								
Bookham	d			14 49											15 19										
Cobham & Stoke d'Abernon	d					14 28											14 58								
Oxshott	d					14 31											15 01								
Claygate	d					14 34											15 04								
Hinchley Wood	d					14 37											15 07								
Hampton Court	d	14 24											14 54											15 24	
Thames Ditton	d	14 26											14 56											15 26	
Surbiton 6	d	14 32			14 38	14 42						14 57	15 02			15 08	15 12						15 27	15 32	
Berrylands	d	14 34											15 04											15 34	
Shepperton	d										14 41											15 11			
Upper Halliford	d										14 44											15 14			
Sunbury	d										14 46											15 16			
Kempton Park	d										14 48											15 18			
Hampton	d										14 51											15 21			
Fulwell	d										14 54											15 24			
Strawberry Hill	d						14 37	14 38										15 07		15 08					
Teddington	d						14 41				14 59							15 11				15 29			
Hampton Wick	d						14 44				15 01							15 14				15 31			
Kingston	a						14 46				15 03							15 16				15 33			
	d						14 49				15 04							15 19				15 34			
Norbiton	d						14 51				15 06							15 21				15 36			
New Malden 6	d	14 37					14 55				15 10		15 07					15 25				15 40		15 37	
Dorking 4	d		14 35											15 05											15 35
Boxhill & Westhumble	d																								
Leatherhead	d		14 41	14 54										15 11	15 24										15 41
Ashtead	d		14 44	14 58										15 14	15 28										15 44
Epsom 3	a		14 49	15 02										15 19	15 32										15 49
	d		14 50	15 05										15 20	15 35										15 50
Ewell West	d		14 53	15 08										15 23	15 38										15 53
Stoneleigh	d		14 55	15 10										15 25	15 40										15 55
Worcester Park	d		14 58	15 13										15 28	15 43										15 58
Chessington South	d									14 40											15 10				
Chessington North	d									14 42											15 12				
Tolworth	d									14 44											15 14				
Malden Manor	d									14 47											15 17				
Motspur Park	d		15 01	15 16						14 50				15 31	15 46						15 20				16 01
Raynes Park 6	d	14 40	15 04	15 19			14 58			14 53	15 13		15 10	15 34	15 49			15 28			15 23	15 43		15 40	16 04
Wimbledon 6 ⊖	d	14 44	15 08	15 23		14 50	15 02			14 57	15 17	15 05	15 14	15 38	15 53		15 20	15 32			15 27	15 47	15 35	15 44	16 08
Earlsfield	d	14 47	15 12	15 27		14 54	15 05			15 01	15 20	15 08	15 17	15 42	15 57		15 24	15 35			15 31	15 50	15 38	15 47	16 12
Clapham Junction 10	d	14 51	15 16	15 31	14 49	14 58	15 09			15 05	15 24	15 12	15 21	15 46	16 01		15 28	15 39			15 35	15 54	15 42	15 51	16 16
Vauxhall ⊖	d	14 56	15 21	15 36		15 03	15 14	15 12		15 10	15 29	15 17	15 26	15 51	16 06		15 33	15 44		15 42	15 40	15 59	15 47	15 56	16 21
London Waterloo 15 ⊖	a	15 01	15 25	15 40	14 57	15 07	15 19	15 16		15 15	15 34	15 22	15 31	15 55	16 10	15 25	15 37	15 49		15 46	15 45	16 04	15 52	16 01	16 25

Table 152

Saturdays

29 May to 25 September

Hampton Court, Shepperton, Guildford, Dorking and Chessington South - London

		SW	SW 1	SW		SW	SW	SW	SW	SW	SW	SW	SW	SW 1		SW	SW	SW	SW	SW	SW	SW	SW	SW
Guildford	d	15 28		15 08									15 58			15 38								16 28
London Road (Guildford)	d	15 32		15 12									16 02			15 42								16 32
Clandon	d	15 37		15 17									16 07			15 47								16 37
Horsley	d	15 41		15 21									16 11			15 51								16 41
Effingham Junction 6	d	15 46		15 24									16 16			15 54								16 46
Bookham	d	15 49											16 19											16 49
Cobham & Stoke d'Abernon	d			15 28												15 58								
Oxshott	d			15 31												16 01								
Claygate	d			15 34												16 04								
Hinchley Wood	d			15 37												16 07								
Hampton Court	d										15 54											16 24		
Thames Ditton	d										15 56											16 26		
Surbiton 6	d		15 38	15 42						15 57	16 02			16 08		16 12					16 27	16 32		
Berrylands	d										16 04											16 34		
Shepperton	d								15 41											16 11				
Upper Halliford	d								15 44											16 14				
Sunbury	d								15 46											16 16				
Kempton Park	d								15 48											16 18				
Hampton	d								15 51											16 21				
Fulwell	d								15 54											16 24				
Strawberry Hill	d					15 37	15 38										16 07	16 08						
Teddington	d					15 41			15 59								16 11			16 29				
Hampton Wick	d					15 44			16 01								16 14			16 31				
Kingston	a					15 46			16 03								16 16			16 33				
	d					15 49			16 04								16 19			16 34				
Norbiton	d					15 51			16 06								16 21			16 36				
New Malden 6	d					15 55			16 10		16 07						16 25			16 40		16 37		
Dorking 4	d											16 05											16 35	
Boxhill & Westhumble	d																							
Leatherhead	d	15 54										16 11	16 24										16 41	16 54
Ashtead	d	15 58										16 14	16 28										16 44	16 58
Epsom 3	a	16 02										16 19	16 32										16 49	17 02
	d	16 05										16 20	16 35										16 50	17 05
Ewell West	d	16 08										16 23	16 38										16 53	17 08
Stoneleigh	d	16 10										16 25	16 40										16 55	17 10
Worcester Park	d	16 13										16 28	16 43										16 58	17 13
Chessington South	d							15 40											16 10					
Chessington North	d							15 42											16 12					
Tolworth	d							15 44											16 14					
Malden Manor	d							15 47											16 17					
Motspur Park	d	16 16						15 50				16 31	16 46						16 20				17 01	17 16
Raynes Park 6	d	16 19				15 58		15 53	16 13		16 10	16 34	16 49				16 28		16 23	16 43		16 40	17 04	17 19
Wimbledon 6 ⊖ ⇌	d	16 23		15 50		16 02		15 57	16 17	16 05	16 14	16 38	16 53			16 20	16 32		16 27	16 47	16 35	16 44	17 08	17 23
Earlsfield	d	16 27		15 54		16 05		16 01	16 20	16 08	16 17	16 42	16 57			16 24	16 35		16 31	16 50	16 38	16 47	17 12	17 27
Clapham Junction 10	d	16 31	15 49	15 58		16 09		16 05	16 24	16 12	16 21	16 46	17 01			16 28	16 39		16 35	16 54	16 42	16 51	17 16	17 31
Vauxhall ⊖	d	16 36		16 03		16 14	16 12	16 10	16 29	16 17	16 26	16 51	17 06			16 33	16 44	16 42	16 40	16 59	16 47	16 56	17 21	17 36
London Waterloo 15 ⊖	a	16 40	15 57	16 07		16 19	16 16	16 15	16 34	16 22	16 31	16 55	17 10	16 25		16 37	16 49	16 46	16 45	17 04	16 52	17 01	17 25	17 40

Table 152

Saturdays

29 May to 25 September

Hampton Court, Shepperton, Guildford, Dorking and Chessington South - London

		SW 1	SW	SW	SW	SW	SW	SW	SW	SW		SW	SW 1	SW	SW	SW	SW	SW	SW	SW		SW	SW	SW 1	SW
Guildford	d		16 08									16 58		16 38									17 28		17 08
London Road (Guildford)	d		16 12									17 02		16 42									17 32		17 12
Clandon	d		16 17									17 07		16 47									17 37		17 17
Horsley	d		16 21									17 11		16 51									17 41		17 21
Effingham Junction 6	d		16 24									17 16		16 54									17 46		17 24
Bookham	d											17 19											17 49		
Cobham & Stoke d'Abernon	d		16 28											16 58											17 28
Oxshott	d		16 31											17 01											17 31
Claygate	d		16 34											17 04											17 34
Hinchley Wood	d		16 37											17 07											17 37
Hampton Court	d								16 54											17 24					
Thames Ditton	d								16 56											17 26					
Surbiton 6	d	16 38	16 42					16 57	17 02				17 08	17 12					17 27	17 32				17 38	17 42
Berrylands	d								17 04											17 34					
Shepperton	d						16 41											17 11							
Upper Halliford	d						16 44											17 14							
Sunbury	d						16 46											17 16							
Kempton Park	d						16 48											17 18							
Hampton	d						16 51											17 21							
Fulwell	d						16 54											17 24							
Strawberry Hill	d			16 37	16 38										17 07	17 08									
Teddington	d			16 41			16 59								17 11			17 29							
Hampton Wick	d			16 44			17 01								17 14			17 31							
Kingston	a			16 46			17 03								17 16			17 33							
	d			16 49			17 04								17 19			17 34							
Norbiton	d			16 51			17 06								17 21			17 36							
New Malden 6	d			16 55			17 10		17 07						17 25			17 40		17 37					
Dorking 4	d									17 05												17 35			
Boxhill & Westhumble	d																								
Leatherhead	d									17 11		17 24										17 41	17 54		
Ashtead	d									17 14		17 28										17 44	17 58		
Epsom 3	a									17 19		17 32										17 49	18 02		
	d									17 20		17 35										17 50	18 05		
Ewell West	d									17 23		17 38										17 53	18 08		
Stoneleigh	d									17 25		17 40										17 55	18 10		
Worcester Park	d									17 28		17 43										17 58	18 13		
Chessington South	d					16 40											17 10								
Chessington North	d					16 42											17 12								
Tolworth	d					16 44											17 14								
Malden Manor	d					16 47											17 17								
Motspur Park	d					16 50				17 31		17 46					17 20					18 01	18 16		
Raynes Park 6	d			16 58		16 53	17 13		17 10	17 34		17 49			17 28		17 23	17 43		17 40		18 04	18 19		
Wimbledon 6 ⊖ ⇌	d		16 50	17 02		16 57	17 17	17 05	17 14	17 38		17 53		17 20	17 32		17 27	17 47	17 35	17 44		18 08	18 23		17 50
Earlsfield	d		16 54	17 05		17 01	17 20	17 08	17 17	17 42		17 57		17 24	17 35		17 31	17 50	17 38	17 47		18 12	18 27		17 54
Clapham Junction 10	d	16 49	16 58	17 09		17 05	17 24	17 12	17 21	17 46		18 01		17 28	17 39		17 35	17 54	17 42	17 51		18 16	18 31	17 49	17 58
Vauxhall ⊖	d		17 03	17 14	17 12	17 10	17 29	17 17	17 26	17 51		18 06		17 33	17 44	17 42	17 40	17 59	17 47	17 56		18 21	18 36		18 03
London Waterloo 15 ⊖	a	16 57	17 07	17 19	17 16	17 15	17 34	17 22	17 31	17 55		18 10	17 25	17 37	17 49	17 46	17 45	18 04	17 52	18 01		18 25	18 40	17 57	18 07

Table 152

Saturdays

29 May to 25 September

Hampton Court, Shepperton, Guildford, Dorking and Chessington South - London

		SW	SW	SW	SW	SW		SW	SW	SW	SW 1	SW	SW	SW	SW	SW		SW	SW	SW	SW	SW 1	SW	SW	SW
Guildford	d									17 58		17 38									18 28		18 08		
London Road (Guildford)	d									18 02		17 42									18 32		18 12		
Clandon	d									18 07		17 47									18 37		18 17		
Horsley	d									18 11		17 51									18 41		18 21		
Effingham Junction 6	d									18 16		17 54									18 46		18 24		
Bookham	d									18 19											18 49				
Cobham & Stoke d'Abernon	d											17 58											18 28		
Oxshott	d											18 01											18 31		
Claygate	d											18 04											18 34		
Hinchley Wood	d											18 07											18 37		
Hampton Court	d							17 54											18 24						
Thames Ditton	d							17 56											18 26						
Surbiton 6	d					17 57		18 02			18 08	18 12						18 27	18 32			18 38	18 42		
Berrylands	d							18 04											18 34						
Shepperton	d				17 41											18 11									
Upper Halliford	d				17 44											18 14									
Sunbury	d				17 46											18 16									
Kempton Park	d				17 48											18 18									
Hampton	d				17 51											18 21									
Fulwell	d				17 54											18 24									
Strawberry Hill	d	17 37	17 38										18 07	18 08										18 37	18 38
Teddington	d	17 41			17 59								18 11			18 29								18 41	
Hampton Wick	d	17 44			18 01								18 14			18 31								18 44	
Kingston	a	17 46			18 03								18 16			18 33								18 46	
	d	17 49			18 04								18 19			18 34								18 49	
Norbiton	d	17 51			18 06								18 21			18 36								18 51	
New Malden 6	d	17 55			18 10			18 07					18 25			18 40			18 37					18 55	
Dorking 4	d								18 05											18 35					
Boxhill & Westhumble	d																								
Leatherhead	d								18 11	18 24										18 41	18 54				
Ashtead	d								18 14	18 28										18 44	18 58				
Epsom 3	a								18 19	18 32										18 49	19 02				
	d								18 20	18 35										18 50	19 05				
Ewell West	d								18 23	18 38										18 53	19 08				
Stoneleigh	d								18 25	18 40										18 55	19 10				
Worcester Park	d								18 28	18 43										18 58	19 13				
Chessington South	d			17 40											18 10										
Chessington North	d			17 42											18 12										
Tolworth	d			17 44											18 14										
Malden Manor	d			17 47											18 17										
Motspur Park	d			17 50					18 31	18 46					18 20					19 01	19 16				
Raynes Park 6	d	17 58		17 53	18 13			18 10	18 34	18 49			18 28		18 23	18 43			18 40	19 04	19 19			18 58	
Wimbledon 6 ⊖	d	18 02		17 57	18 17	18 05		18 14	18 38	18 53		18 20	18 32		18 27	18 47		18 35	18 44	19 08	19 23		18 50	19 02	
Earlsfield	d	18 05		18 01	18 20	18 08		18 17	18 42	18 57		18 24	18 35		18 31	18 50		18 38	18 47	19 12	19 27		18 54	19 05	
Clapham Junction 10	d	18 09		18 05	18 24	18 12		18 21	18 46	19 01		18 28	18 39		18 35	18 54		18 42	18 51	19 16	19 31	18 49	18 58	19 09	
Vauxhall ⊖	d	18 14	18 12	18 10	18 29	18 17		18 26	18 51	19 06		18 33	18 44	18 42	18 40	18 59		18 47	18 56	19 21	19 36		19 03	19 14	19 12
London Waterloo 15 ⊖	a	18 19	18 16	18 15	18 34	18 22		18 31	18 55	19 10	18 25	18 37	18 49	18 46	18 45	19 04		18 52	19 01	19 25	19 40	18 57	19 07	19 19	19 16

Table 152

Saturdays

29 May to 25 September

Hampton Court, Shepperton, Guildford, Dorking and Chessington South - London

		SW		SW	SW	SW	SW	SW	SW 1	SW	SW	SW		SW	SW	SW	SW	SW	SW	SW 1	SW	SW		SW	SW
Guildford	d							18 58		18 38									19 28		19 08				
London Road (Guildford)	d							19 02		18 42									19 32		19 12				
Clandon	d							19 07		18 47									19 37		19 17				
Horsley	d							19 11		18 51									19 41		19 21				
Effingham Junction 6	d							19 16		18 54									19 46		19 24				
Bookham	d							19 19											19 49						
Cobham & Stoke d'Abernon	d									18 58											19 28				
Oxshott	d									19 01											19 31				
Claygate	d									19 04											19 34				
Hinchley Wood	d									19 07											19 37				
Hampton Court	d					18 54											19 24								
Thames Ditton	d					18 56											19 26								
Surbiton 6	d				18 57	19 02			19 08	19 12						19 27	19 32			19 38	19 42				
Berrylands	d					19 04											19 34								
Shepperton	d			18 41											19 11										
Upper Halliford	d			18 44											19 14										
Sunbury	d			18 46											19 16										
Kempton Park	d			18 48											19 18										
Hampton	d			18 51											19 21										
Fulwell	d			18 54											19 24										
Strawberry Hill	d										19 07	19 08										19 37		19 38	
Teddington	d			18 59							19 11				19 29							19 41			
Hampton Wick	d			19 01							19 14				19 31							19 44			
Kingston	a			19 03							19 16				19 33							19 46			
	d			19 04							19 19				19 34							19 49			
Norbiton	d			19 06							19 21				19 36							19 51			
New Malden 6	d			19 10		19 07					19 25				19 40		19 37					19 55			
Dorking 4	d						19 05											19 35							
Boxhill & Westhumble	d																								
Leatherhead	d						19 11	19 24										19 41	19 54						
Ashtead	d						19 14	19 28										19 44	19 58						
Epsom 3	a						19 19	19 32										19 49	20 02						
	d						19 20	19 35										19 50	20 05						
Ewell West	d						19 23	19 38										19 53	20 08						
Stoneleigh	d						19 25	19 40										19 55	20 10						
Worcester Park	d						19 28	19 43										19 58	20 13						
Chessington South	d	18 40												19 10											19 40
Chessington North	d	18 42												19 12											19 42
Tolworth	d	18 44												19 14											19 44
Malden Manor	d	18 47												19 17											19 47
Motspur Park	d	18 50					19 31	19 46						19 20				20 01	20 16						19 50
Raynes Park 6	d	18 53		19 13		19 10	19 34	19 49			19 28			19 23	19 43		19 40	20 04	20 19			19 58			19 53
Wimbledon 6 ⊖	d	18 57		19 17	19 05	19 14	19 38	19 53		19 20	19 32			19 27	19 47	19 35	19 44	20 08	20 23		19 50	20 02			19 57
Earlsfield	d	19 01		19 20	19 08	19 17	19 42	19 57		19 24	19 35			19 31	19 50	19 38	19 47	20 12	20 27		19 54	20 05			20 01
Clapham Junction 10	d	19 05		19 24	19 12	19 21	19 46	20 01		19 28	19 39			19 35	19 54	19 42	19 51	20 16	20 31	19 49	19 58	20 09			20 05
Vauxhall ⊖	d	19 10		19 29	19 17	19 26	19 51	20 06		19 33	19 44	19 42		19 40	19 59	19 47	19 56	20 21	20 36		20 03	20 14		20 12	20 10
London Waterloo 15 ⊖	a	19 15		19 34	19 22	19 31	19 55	20 10	19 25	19 37	19 49	19 46		19 45	20 04	19 52	20 01	20 25	20 40	19 57	20 07	20 19		20 16	20 15

Hampton Court, Shepperton, Guildford, Dorking and Chessington South - London

Saturdays
29 May to 25 September

		SW	SW	SW	SW	SW	SW 1	SW	SW	SW	SW	SW	SW	SW	SW	SW 1	SW	SW	SW	SW	SW	SW	SW
Guildford	d					19 58		19 38									20 08						
London Road (Guildford)	d					20 02		19 42									20 12						
Clandon	d					20 07		19 47									20 17						
Horsley	d					20 11		19 51									20 21						
Effingham Junction 6	d					20 16		19 54									20 24						
Bookham	d					20 19																	
Cobham & Stoke d'Abernon	d							19 58									20 28						
Oxshott	d							20 01									20 31						
Claygate	d							20 04									20 34						
Hinchley Wood	d							20 07									20 37						
Hampton Court	d			19 54										20 24									20 54
Thames Ditton	d			19 56										20 26									20 56
Surbiton 6	d		19 57	20 02			20 08	20 12					20 27	20 32		20 38	20 42					20 57	21 02
Berrylands	d			20 04										20 34									21 04
Shepperton	d	19 41										20 11									20 41		
Upper Halliford	d	19 44										20 14									20 44		
Sunbury	d	19 46										20 16									20 46		
Kempton Park	d	19 48										20 18									20 48		
Hampton	d	19 51										20 21									20 51		
Fulwell	d	19 54										20 24									20 54		
Strawberry Hill	d								20 07	20 08								20 37	20 38				
Teddington	d	19 59							20 11			20 29						20 41			20 59		
Hampton Wick	d	20 01							20 14			20 31						20 44			21 01		
Kingston	a	20 03							20 16			20 33						20 46			21 03		
	d	20 04							20 19			20 34						20 49			21 04		
Norbiton	d	20 06							20 21			20 36						20 51			21 06		
New Malden 6	d	20 10		20 07					20 25			20 40		20 37				20 55			21 10		21 07
Dorking 4	d				20 05										20 35								
Boxhill & Westhumble	d																						
Leatherhead	d				20 11	20 24									20 41								
Ashtead	d				20 14	20 28									20 44								
Epsom 3	a				20 19	20 32									20 49								
	d				20 20	20 35									20 50								
Ewell West	d				20 23	20 38									20 53								
Stoneleigh	d				20 25	20 40									20 55								
Worcester Park	d				20 28	20 43									20 58								
Chessington South	d										20 10									20 40			
Chessington North	d										20 12									20 42			
Tolworth	d										20 14									20 44			
Malden Manor	d										20 17									20 47			
Motspur Park	d				20 31	20 46					20 20				21 01					20 50			
Raynes Park 6	d	20 13		20 10	20 34	20 49			20 28		20 23	20 43		20 40	21 04			20 58		20 53	21 13		21 10
Wimbledon 6 ⊖	d	20 17	20 05	20 14	20 38	20 53		20 20	20 32		20 27	20 47	20 35	20 44	21 08		20 50	21 02		20 57	21 17	21 05	21 14
Earlsfield	d	20 20	20 08	20 17	20 42	20 57		20 24	20 35		20 31	20 50	20 38	20 47	21 12		20 54	21 05		21 01	21 20	21 08	21 17
Clapham Junction 10	d	20 24	20 12	20 21	20 46	21 01		20 28	20 39		20 35	20 54	20 42	20 51	21 16	20 49	20 58	21 09		21 05	21 24	21 12	21 21
Vauxhall ⊖	d	20 29	20 17	20 26	20 51	21 06		20 33	20 44	20 42	20 40	20 59	20 47	20 56	21 21		21 03	21 14	21 12	21 10	21 29	21 17	21 26
London Waterloo 15 ⊖	a	20 34	20 22	20 31	20 55	21 10	20 25	20 37	20 49	20 46	20 45	21 04	20 52	21 01	21 25	20 57	21 07	21 19	21 16	21 15	21 34	21 23	21 31

Hampton Court, Shepperton, Guildford, Dorking and Chessington South - London

Saturdays
29 May to 25 September

		SW	SW	SW 1	SW	SW	SW	SW	SW	SW	SW	SW	SW	SW 1	SW	SW	SW	SW	SW	SW	SW	SW 1
Guildford	d		20 46		20 38										21 08					21 46		
London Road (Guildford)	d		20 50		20 42										21 12					21 50		
Clandon	d		20 55		20 47										21 17					21 55		
Horsley	d		20 59		20 51										21 21					21 59		
Effingham Junction 6	d		21 03		20 54										21 24					22 03		
Bookham	d		21 06																	22 06		
Cobham & Stoke d'Abernon	d				20 58										21 28							
Oxshott	d				21 01										21 31							
Claygate	d				21 04										21 34							
Hinchley Wood	d				21 07										21 37							
Hampton Court	d										21 24											
Thames Ditton	d										21 26											
Surbiton 6	d			21 08	21 12					21 27	21 32			21 38	21 42						21 57	22 08
Berrylands	d										21 34											
Shepperton	d								21 11										21 41			
Upper Halliford	d								21 14										21 44			
Sunbury	d								21 16										21 46			
Kempton Park	d								21 18										21 48			
Hampton	d								21 21										21 51			
Fulwell	d								21 24										21 54			
Strawberry Hill	d					21 07	21 08									21 37	21 38					
Teddington	d					21 11			21 29							21 41			21 59			
Hampton Wick	d					21 14			21 31							21 44			22 01			
Kingston	a					21 16			21 33							21 46			22 03			
	d					21 19			21 34							21 49			22 04			
Norbiton	d					21 21			21 36							21 51			22 06			
New Malden 6	d					21 25			21 40		21 37					21 55			22 10			
Dorking 4	d												21 35									
Boxhill & Westhumble	d																					
Leatherhead	d		21 11										21 41							22 11		
Ashtead	d		21 14										21 44							22 14		
Epsom 3	a		21 19										21 49							22 19		
	d	21 05	21 20									21 35	21 50							22 20		
Ewell West	d	21 08	21 23									21 38	21 53							22 23		
Stoneleigh	d	21 10	21 25									21 40	21 55							22 25		
Worcester Park	d	21 13	21 28									21 43	21 58							22 28		
Chessington South	d							21 10										21 40				
Chessington North	d							21 12										21 42				
Tolworth	d							21 14										21 44				
Malden Manor	d							21 17										21 47				
Motspur Park	d	21 16	21 31					21 20				21 46	22 01					21 50		22 31		
Raynes Park 6	d	21 19	21 34			21 28		21 23	21 43		21 40	21 49	22 04			21 58		21 53	22 13	22 34		
Wimbledon 6 ⊖	d	21 23	21 38		21 20	21 32		21 27	21 47	21 35	21 44	21 53	22 08		21 50	22 02		21 57	22 17	22 38	22 05	
Earlsfield	d	21 27	21 42		21 24	21 35		21 31	21 50	21 38	21 47	21 57	22 12		21 54	22 05		22 01	22 20	22 42	22 08	
Clapham Junction 10	d	21 31	21 46		21 28	21 39		21 35	21 54	21 42	21 51	22 01	22 16	21 49	21 58	22 09		22 05	22 24	22 46	22 12	
Vauxhall ⊖	d	21 36	21 51		21 33	21 44	21 42	21 40	21 59	21 47	21 56	22 06	22 21		22 03	22 14	22 12	22 10	22 29	22 51	22 17	
London Waterloo 15 ⊖	a	21 40	21 55	21 29	21 37	21 49	21 46	21 45	22 04	21 52	22 01	22 10	22 25	21 57	22 07	22 19	22 16	22 15	22 34	22 55	22 22	22 27

Table 152

Saturdays

29 May to 25 September

Hampton Court, Shepperton, Guildford, Dorking and Chessington South - London

		SW	SW	SW	SW	SW	SW	SW	SW 1	SW	SW	SW	SW	SW	SW	SW	SW 1	SW	SW	SW	SW	SW	SW
Guildford	d	21 38								22 08	22 20					22 46		22 38	22 55				
London Road (Guildford)	d	21 42								22 12						22 50		22 42					
Clandon	d	21 47								22 17						22 55		22 47					
Horsley	d	21 51								22 21						22 59		22 51					
Effingham Junction 6	d	21 54								22 24						23 03		22 54					
Bookham	d															23 06							
Cobham & Stoke d'Abernon	d	21 58								22 28								22 58					
Oxshott	d	22 01								22 31								23 01					
Claygate	d	22 04								22 34								23 04					
Hinchley Wood	d	22 07								22 37								23 07					
Hampton Court	d						22 24																23 24
Thames Ditton	d						22 26																23 26
Surbiton 6	d	22 12				22 27	22 32		22 38	22 42	22 57						23 08	23 12	23 30				23 32
Berrylands	d						22 34																23 34
Shepperton	d				22 11										22 41							23 11	
Upper Halliford	d				22 14										22 44							23 14	
Sunbury	d				22 16										22 46							23 16	
Kempton Park	d				22 18										22 48							23 18	
Hampton	d				22 21										22 51							23 21	
Fulwell	d				22 24										22 54							23 24	
Strawberry Hill	d		22 07	22 08								22 37	22 38							23 07	23 08		
Teddington	d		22 11		22 29							22 41			22 59					23 11		23 29	
Hampton Wick	d		22 14		22 31							22 44			23 01					23 14		23 31	
Kingston	a		22 16		22 33							22 46			23 03					23 16		23 33	
	d		22 19		22 34							22 49			23 04					23 19		23 34	
Norbiton	d		22 21		22 36							22 51			23 06					23 21		23 36	
New Malden 6	d		22 25		22 40		22 37					22 55			23 10					23 25		23 41	23 37
Dorking 4	d							22 35															
Boxhill & Westhumble	d																						
Leatherhead	d							22 41								23 11							
Ashtead	d							22 44								23 14							
Epsom 3	a							22 49								23 19							
	d							22 50								23 20							
Ewell West	d							22 53								23 23							
Stoneleigh	d							22 55								23 25							
Worcester Park	d							22 58								23 28							
Chessington South	d													22 40									
Chessington North	d													22 42									
Tolworth	d													22 44									
Malden Manor	d													22 47									
Motspur Park	d							23 01						22 50		23 31							
Raynes Park 6	d		22 28		22 43		22 40	23 04				22 58		22 53	23 13	23 37				23 28		23 43	23 40
Wimbledon 6 ⊖ ⇌	d	22 20	22 32		22 47	22 35	22 44	23 08		22 50	23 05	23 02		22 57	23 17	23 41		23 20	23 37	23 32		23 52	23 44
Earlsfield	d	22 24	22 35		22 50	22 38	22 47	23 12		22 54	23 08	23 05		23 01	23 20	23 44		23 24	23 41	23 35		23 55	23 47
Clapham Junction 10	d	22 28	22 39		22 54	22 42	22 51	23 16	22 53	22 58	23 12	23 09		23 05	23 24	23 48		23 28	23 45	23 39		00 04	23 51
Vauxhall ⊖	d	22 33	22 44	22 42	22 59	22 47	22 56	23 21		23 03	23 17	23 14	23 12	23 10	23 29	23 53		23 33	23 50	23 44	23 42	00 09	23 56
London Waterloo 15 ⊖	a	22 39	22 49	22 46	23 04	22 52	23 01	23 25	23 01	23 07	23 22	23 19	23 17	23 15	23 34	23 58	23 28	23 37	23 54	23 49	23 46	00 13	00 02

Table 152

Saturdays

29 May to 25 September

Hampton Court, Shepperton, Guildford, Dorking and Chessington South - London

		SN	SW 1	SW	SW	SW	SW
Guildford	d			23 08			
London Road (Guildford)	d			23 12			
Clandon	d			23 17			
Horsley	d			23 21			
Effingham Junction 6	d			23 24			
Bookham	d						
Cobham & Stoke d'Abernon	d			23 28			
Oxshott	d			23 31			
Claygate	d			23 34			
Hinchley Wood	d			23 37			
Hampton Court	d						
Thames Ditton	d						
Surbiton 6	d		23 38	23 42			
Berrylands	d						
Shepperton	d						
Upper Halliford	d						
Sunbury	d						
Kempton Park	d						
Hampton	d						
Fulwell	d						
Strawberry Hill	d				23 37	23 38	
Teddington	d				23 41		
Hampton Wick	d				23 44		
Kingston	a				23 46		
	d				23 49		
Norbiton	d				23 51		
New Malden 6	d				23 55		
Dorking 4	d	23 30					
Boxhill & Westhumble	d						
Leatherhead	d	23 36					
Ashtead	d	23 39					
Epsom 3	a	23 45					
	d						
Ewell West	d						
Stoneleigh	d						
Worcester Park	d						
Chessington South	d						23 40
Chessington North	d						23 42
Tolworth	d						23 44
Malden Manor	d						23 47
Motspur Park	d						23 50
Raynes Park 6	d				23 58		23 54
Wimbledon 6 ⊖ ⇌	d			23 58	00 07		00a02
Earlsfield	d			00 01	00 10		
Clapham Junction 10	d		23 56	00 07	00 14		
Vauxhall ⊖	d			00 12	00 19	00 12	
London Waterloo 15 ⊖	a		00 04	00 16	00 24	00 16	

Table 152

Saturdays
from 02 October

Hampton Court, Shepperton, Guildford, Dorking and Chessington South - London

		SW	SW 1	SW	SW	SW	SW	SW	SW	SW	SW	SW	SW	SW	SW	SW	SW	SW	SW	SW	SW	SW	SW
Guildford	d			23p08			04 00		05 12												06 28		
London Road (Guildford)	d			23p12																	06 32		
Clandon	d			23p17																	06 37		
Horsley	d			23p21																	06 41		
Effingham Junction 6	d			23p24																	06 46		
Bookham	d																				06 49		
Cobham & Stoke d'Abernon	d			23p28																			
Oxshott	d			23p31																			
Claygate	d			23p34																			
Hinchley Wood	d			23p37																			
Hampton Court	d												05 54						06 24				
Thames Ditton	d												05 56						06 26				
Surbiton 6	d		23p38	23p42			04 24		05 57				06 02					06 27	06 32				
Berrylands	d												06 04						06 34				
Shepperton	d	23p11															06 11						
Upper Halliford	d	23p14															06 14						
Sunbury	d	23p16															06 16						
Kempton Park	d	23p18															06 18						
Hampton	d	23p21															06 21						
Fulwell	d	23p24															06 24						
Strawberry Hill	d				23p37	23p38		04 55			05 38				06 07	06 08						06 37	06 38
Teddington	d	23p29			23p41			04 59				05 44			06 11		06 29					06 41	
Hampton Wick	d	23p31			23p44			05 01				05 46			06 14		06 31					06 44	
Kingston	a	23p33			23p46			05 03				05 48			06 16		06 33					06 46	
	d	23p34			23p49			05 04				05 49			06 19		06 34					06 49	
Norbiton	d	23p36			23p51			05 06				05 51			06 21		06 36					06 51	
New Malden 6	d	23p40			23p55			05 10				05 55	06 07		06 25		06 40		06 37			06 55	
Dorking 4	d																						
Boxhill & Westhumble	d																						
Leatherhead	d																				06 54		
Ashtead	d																				06 58		
Epsom 3	a																				07 02		
	d									05 35				06 05						06 35	07 05		
Ewell West	d									05 38				06 08						06 38	07 08		
Stoneleigh	d									05 40				06 10						06 40	07 10		
Worcester Park	d									05 43				06 13						06 43	07 13		
Chessington South	d																						
Chessington North	d																						
Tolworth	d																						
Malden Manor	d																						
Motspur Park	d									05 46				06 16						06 46	07 16		
Raynes Park 6	d	23p43			23p58			05 13		05 49		05 58	06 10	06 19	06 28		06 43		06 40	06 49	07 19	06 58	
Wimbledon 6 ⊖	d	23p52		23p55	00 05		04 32	05 17	06 05	05 53		06 02	06 14	06 23	06 32		06 47	06 35	06 44	06 53	07 23	07 02	
Earlsfield	d	23p55		23p58	00 08			05 21	06 08	05 57		06 05	06 17	06 27	06 35		06 50	06 38	06 47	06 57	07 27	07 05	
Clapham Junction 10	d	23p59	23p55	00 02	00 12		04 44	05 25	06 12	06 01		06 09	06 21	06 31	06 39		06 54	06 42	06 51	07 01	07 31	07 09	
Vauxhall ⊖	d	00 04		00 07	00 17	00 12		05 30	06 17	06 06	06 12	06 14	06 26	06 36	06 44	06 42	06 59	06 47	06 56	07 06	07 36	07 14	07 12
London Waterloo 15 ⊖	a	00 11	00 03	00 14	00 23	00 16	04 53	05 35	06 22	06 11	06 16	06 19	06 31	06 40	06 49	06 46	07 04	06 52	07 01	07 10	07 40	07 19	07 16

Table 152

Saturdays
from 02 October

Hampton Court, Shepperton, Guildford, Dorking and Chessington South - London

		SW	SW	SW	SW	SW	SW 1	SW	SW	SW	SW	SW	SW	SW	SW	SW 1	SW	SW	SW	SW	SW	SW	SW
Guildford	d					06 58		06 35							07 28		07 05						
London Road (Guildford)	d					07 02		06 39							07 32		07 09						
Clandon	d					07 07		06 44							07 37		07 14						
Horsley	d					07 11		06 48							07 41		07 18						
Effingham Junction 6	d					07 16		06 51							07 46		07 21						
Bookham	d					07 19									07 49								
Cobham & Stoke d'Abernon	d							06 55									07 25						
Oxshott	d							06 58									07 28						
Claygate	d							07 01									07 31						
Hinchley Wood	d							07 04									07 34						
Hampton Court	d				06 54									07 24									07 54
Thames Ditton	d				06 56									07 26									07 56
Surbiton 6	d			06 57	07 02		07 08	07 12					07 27	07 32		07 38	07 42					07 57	08 02
Berrylands	d				07 04									07 34									08 04
Shepperton	d		06 41									07 11									07 41		
Upper Halliford	d		06 44									07 14									07 44		
Sunbury	d		06 46									07 16									07 46		
Kempton Park	d		06 48									07 18									07 48		
Hampton	d		06 51									07 21									07 51		
Fulwell	d		06 54									07 24									07 54		
Strawberry Hill	d								07 07	07 08								07 37	07 38				
Teddington	d		06 59						07 11			07 29						07 41			07 59		
Hampton Wick	d		07 01						07 14			07 31						07 44			08 01		
Kingston	a		07 03						07 16			07 33						07 46			08 03		
	d		07 04						07 19			07 34						07 49			08 04		
Norbiton	d		07 06						07 21			07 36						07 51			08 06		
New Malden 6	d		07 10		07 07				07 25			07 40		07 37				07 55			08 10		08 07
Dorking 4	d																						
Boxhill & Westhumble	d																						
Leatherhead	d					07 24									07 54								
Ashtead	d					07 28									07 58								
Epsom 3	a					07 32									08 02								
	d					07 35									08 05								
Ewell West	d					07 38									08 08								
Stoneleigh	d					07 40									08 10								
Worcester Park	d					07 43									08 13								
Chessington South	d	06 40									07 10									07 40			
Chessington North	d	06 42									07 12									07 42			
Tolworth	d	06 44									07 14									07 44			
Malden Manor	d	06 47									07 17									07 47			
Motspur Park	d	06 50				07 46					07 20				08 16					07 50			
Raynes Park 6	d	06 53	07 13		07 10	07 49			07 28		07 23	07 43		07 40	08 19			07 58		07 53	08 13		08 10
Wimbledon 6 ⊖	d	06 57	07 17	07 05	07 14	07 53		07 20	07 32		07 27	07 47	07 35	07 44	08 23		07 50	08 02		07 57	08 17	08 05	08 14
Earlsfield	d	07 01	07 20	07 08	07 17	07 57		07 24	07 35		07 31	07 50	07 38	07 47	08 27		07 54	08 05		08 01	08 20	08 08	08 17
Clapham Junction 10	d	07 05	07 24	07 12	07 21	08 01	07 19	07 28	07 39		07 35	07 54	07 42	07 51	08 31	07 51	07 58	08 09		08 05	08 24	08 12	08 21
Vauxhall ⊖	d	07 10	07 29	07 17	07 26	08 06		07 33	07 44	07 42	07 40	07 59	07 47	07 56	08 36		08 03	08 14	08 12	08 10	08 29	08 17	08 26
London Waterloo 15 ⊖	a	07 15	07 34	07 22	07 31	08 10	07 30	07 37	07 49	07 46	07 45	08 04	07 52	08 01	08 40	07 58	08 07	08 19	08 16	08 15	08 34	08 22	08 31

Table 152

Saturdays
from 02 October

Hampton Court, Shepperton, Guildford, Dorking and Chessington South - London

		SW		SW	SW 1	SW	SW	SW	SW	SW	SW	SW		SW	SW	SW 1	SW	SW	SW	SW	SW	SW		SW	SW
Guildford	d			07 58		07 35									08 28		08 05								
London Road (Guildford)	d			08 02		07 39									08 32		08 09								
Clandon	d			08 07		07 44									08 37		08 14								
Horsley	d			08 11		07 48									08 41		08 18								
Effingham Junction 6	d			08 16		07 51									08 46		08 21								
Bookham	d			08 19											08 49										
Cobham & Stoke d'Abernon	d					07 55											08 25								
Oxshott	d					07 58											08 28								
Claygate	d					08 01											08 31								
Hinchley Wood	d					08 04											08 34								
Hampton Court	d											08 24												08 54	
Thames Ditton	d											08 26												08 56	
Surbiton 6	d				08 08	08 12					08 27	08 32				08 38	08 42					08 57		09 02	
Berrylands	d											08 34												09 04	
Shepperton	d									08 11											08 41				
Upper Halliford	d									08 14											08 44				
Sunbury	d									08 16											08 46				
Kempton Park	d									08 18											08 48				
Hampton	d									08 21											08 51				
Fulwell	d									08 24											08 54				
Strawberry Hill	d						08 07	08 08										08 37	08 38						
Teddington	d						08 11			08 29								08 41			08 59				
Hampton Wick	d						08 14			08 31								08 44			09 01				
Kingston	a						08 16			08 33								08 46			09 03				
	d						08 19			08 34								08 49			09 04				
Norbiton	d						08 21			08 36								08 51			09 06				
New Malden 6	d						08 25			08 40		08 37						08 55			09 10			09 07	
Dorking 4	d	08 05												08 35											09 05
Boxhill & Westhumble	d																								
Leatherhead	d	08 11		08 24										08 41	08 54										09 11
Ashtead	d	08 14		08 28										08 44	08 58										09 14
Epsom 3	a	08 19		08 32										08 49	09 02										09 19
	d	08 20		08 35										08 50	09 05										09 20
Ewell West	d	08 23		08 38										08 53	09 08										09 23
Stoneleigh	d	08 25		08 40										08 55	09 10										09 25
Worcester Park	d	08 28		08 43										08 58	09 13										09 28
Chessington South	d								08 10											08 40					
Chessington North	d								08 12											08 42					
Tolworth	d								08 14											08 44					
Malden Manor	d								08 17											08 47					
Motspur Park	d	08 31		08 46					08 20					09 01	09 16					08 50					09 31
Raynes Park 6	d	08 34		08 49			08 28		08 23	08 43		08 40		09 04	09 19			08 58		08 53	09 13			09 10	09 34
Wimbledon 6 ⊖ 🚊	d	08 38		08 53		08 20	08 32		08 27	08 47	08 35	08 44		09 08	09 23		08 50	09 02		08 57	09 17	09 05		09 14	09 38
Earlsfield	d	08 42		08 57		08 24	08 35		08 31	08 50	08 38	08 47		09 12	09 27		08 54	09 05		09 01	09 20	09 08		09 17	09 42
Clapham Junction 10	d	08 46		09 01		08 28	08 39		08 35	08 54	08 42	08 51		09 16	09 31	08 50	08 58	09 09		09 05	09 24	09 12		09 21	09 46
Vauxhall ⊖	d	08 51		09 06		08 33	08 44	08 42	08 40	08 59	08 47	08 56		09 21	09 36		09 03	09 14	09 12	09 10	09 29	09 17		09 26	09 51
London Waterloo 15 ⊖	a	08 55		09 10	08 25	08 37	08 49	08 46	08 45	09 04	08 52	09 01		09 25	09 40	08 58	09 07	09 19	09 16	09 15	09 34	09 22		09 31	09 55

Table 152

Saturdays
from 02 October

Hampton Court, Shepperton, Guildford, Dorking and Chessington South - London

		SW	SW 1	SW	SW	SW	SW	SW		SW	SW	SW	SW	SW 1	SW	SW	SW	SW		SW	SW	SW	SW	SW	SW 1
Guildford	d	08 58		08 35									09 28		09 05									09 58	
London Road (Guildford)	d	09 02		08 39									09 32		09 09									10 02	
Clandon	d	09 07		08 44									09 37		09 14									10 07	
Horsley	d	09 11		08 48									09 41		09 18									10 11	
Effingham Junction 6	d	09 16		08 51									09 46		09 21									10 16	
Bookham	d	09 19											09 49											10 19	
Cobham & Stoke d'Abernon	d			08 55											09 25										
Oxshott	d			08 58											09 28										
Claygate	d			09 01											09 31										
Hinchley Wood	d			09 04											09 34										
Hampton Court	d										09 24											09 54			
Thames Ditton	d										09 26											09 56			
Surbiton 6	d		09 08	09 12						09 27	09 32			09 38	09 42						09 57	10 02			10 08
Berrylands	d										09 34											10 04			
Shepperton	d							09 11												09 41					
Upper Halliford	d							09 14												09 44					
Sunbury	d							09 16												09 46					
Kempton Park	d							09 18												09 48					
Hampton	d							09 21												09 51					
Fulwell	d							09 24												09 54					
Strawberry Hill	d				09 07	09 08										09 37	09 38								
Teddington	d				09 11			09 29								09 41				09 59					
Hampton Wick	d				09 14			09 31								09 44				10 01					
Kingston	a				09 16			09 33								09 46				10 03					
	d				09 19			09 34								09 49				10 04					
Norbiton	d				09 21			09 36								09 51				10 06					
New Malden 6	d				09 25			09 40			09 37					09 55				10 10		10 07			
Dorking 4	d											09 35											10 05		
Boxhill & Westhumble	d																								
Leatherhead	d	09 24										09 41	09 54										10 11	10 24	
Ashtead	d	09 28										09 44	09 58										10 14	10 28	
Epsom 3	a	09 32										09 49	10 02										10 19	10 32	
	d	09 35										09 50	10 05										10 20	10 35	
Ewell West	d	09 38										09 53	10 08										10 23	10 38	
Stoneleigh	d	09 40										09 55	10 10										10 25	10 40	
Worcester Park	d	09 43										09 58	10 13										10 28	10 43	
Chessington South	d						09 10											09 40							
Chessington North	d						09 12											09 42							
Tolworth	d						09 14											09 44							
Malden Manor	d						09 17											09 47							
Motspur Park	d	09 46					09 20					10 01	10 16					09 50					10 31	10 46	
Raynes Park 6	d	09 49			09 28		09 23	09 43			09 40	10 04	10 19			09 58		09 53		10 13		10 10	10 34	10 49	
Wimbledon 6 ⊖ 🚊	d	09 53		09 20	09 32		09 27	09 47		09 35	09 44	10 08	10 23		09 50	10 02		09 57		10 17	10 05	10 14	10 38	10 53	
Earlsfield	d	09 57		09 24	09 35		09 31	09 50		09 38	09 47	10 12	10 27		09 54	10 05		10 01		10 20	10 08	10 17	10 42	10 57	
Clapham Junction 10	d	10 01		09 28	09 39		09 35	09 54		09 42	09 51	10 16	10 31	09 49	09 58	10 09		10 05		10 24	10 12	10 21	10 46	11 01	
Vauxhall ⊖	d	10 06		09 33	09 44	09 42	09 40	09 59		09 47	09 56	10 21	10 36		10 03	10 14	10 12	10 10		10 29	10 17	10 26	10 51	11 06	
London Waterloo 15 ⊖	a	10 10	09 25	09 37	09 49	09 46	09 45	10 04		09 52	10 01	10 25	10 40	09 57	10 07	10 19	10 16	10 15		10 34	10 22	10 31	10 55	11 10	10 25

Table 152

Saturdays
from 02 October

Hampton Court, Shepperton, Guildford, Dorking and Chessington South - London

		SW	SW	SW	SW	SW	SW	SW	SW	SW	SW 1	SW	SW	SW	SW	SW	SW	SW	SW	SW	SW 1	SW
Guildford	d	09 35								10 28		10 05								10 58		10 35
London Road (Guildford)	d	09 39								10 32		10 09								11 02		10 39
Clandon	d	09 44								10 37		10 14								11 07		10 44
Horsley	d	09 48								10 41		10 18								11 11		10 48
Effingham Junction 6	d	09 51								10 46		10 21								11 16		10 51
Bookham	d									10 49										11 19		
Cobham & Stoke d'Abernon	d	09 55										10 25										10 55
Oxshott	d	09 58										10 28										10 58
Claygate	d	10 01										10 31										11 01
Hinchley Wood	d	10 04										10 34										11 04
Hampton Court	d							10 24										10 54				
Thames Ditton	d							10 26										10 56				
Surbiton 6	d	10 12					10 27	10 32			10 38	10 42					10 57	11 02			11 08	11 12
Berrylands	d							10 34										11 04				
Shepperton	d					10 11										10 41						
Upper Halliford	d					10 14										10 44						
Sunbury	d					10 16										10 46						
Kempton Park	d					10 18										10 48						
Hampton	d					10 21										10 51						
Fulwell	d					10 24										10 54						
Strawberry Hill	d		10 07	10 08									10 37	10 38								
Teddington	d		10 11			10 29							10 41			10 59						
Hampton Wick	d		10 14			10 31							10 44			11 01						
Kingston	a		10 16			10 33							10 46			11 03						
	d		10 19			10 34							10 49			11 04						
Norbiton	d		10 21			10 36							10 51			11 06						
New Malden 6	d		10 25			10 40		10 37					10 55			11 10		11 07				
Dorking 4	d								10 35										11 05			
Boxhill & Westhumble	d																					
Leatherhead	d								10 41	10 54									11 11	11 24		
Ashtead	d								10 44	10 58									11 14	11 28		
Epsom 3	a								10 49	11 02									11 19	11 32		
	d								10 50	11 05									11 20	11 35		
Ewell West	d								10 53	11 08									11 23	11 38		
Stoneleigh	d								10 55	11 10									11 25	11 40		
Worcester Park	d								10 58	11 13									11 28	11 43		
Chessington South	d				10 10										10 40							
Chessington North	d				10 12										10 42							
Tolworth	d				10 14										10 44							
Malden Manor	d				10 17										10 47							
Motspur Park	d				10 20				11 01	11 16					10 50				11 31	11 46		
Raynes Park 6	d		10 28		10 23	10 43		10 40	11 04	11 19			10 58		10 53	11 13		11 10	11 34	11 49		
Wimbledon 6 ⊖ ⛴	d	10 20	10 32		10 27	10 47	10 35	10 44	11 08	11 23		10 50	11 02		10 57	11 17	11 05	11 14	11 38	11 53		11 20
Earlsfield	d	10 24	10 35		10 31	10 50	10 38	10 47	11 12	11 27		10 54	11 05		11 01	11 20	11 08	11 17	11 42	11 57		11 24
Clapham Junction 10	d	10 28	10 39		10 35	10 54	10 42	10 51	11 16	11 31	10 49	10 58	11 09		11 05	11 24	11 12	11 21	11 46	12 01		11 28
Vauxhall ⊖	d	10 33	10 44	10 42	10 40	10 59	10 47	10 56	11 21	11 36		11 03	11 14	11 12	11 10	11 29	11 17	11 26	11 51	12 06		11 33
London Waterloo 15 ⊖	a	10 37	10 49	10 46	10 45	11 04	10 52	11 01	11 25	11 40	10 57	11 07	11 19	11 16	11 15	11 34	11 22	11 31	11 55	12 10	11 25	11 37

Table 152

Saturdays
from 02 October

Hampton Court, Shepperton, Guildford, Dorking and Chessington South - London

		SW	SW	SW	SW	SW	SW	SW	SW	SW 1	SW	SW	SW	SW	SW	SW	SW	SW	SW	SW 1	SW	SW	SW
Guildford	d								11 28		11 05								11 58		11 35		
London Road (Guildford)	d								11 32		11 09								12 02		11 39		
Clandon	d								11 37		11 14								12 07		11 44		
Horsley	d								11 41		11 18								12 11		11 48		
Effingham Junction 6	d								11 46		11 21								12 16		11 51		
Bookham	d								11 49										12 19				
Cobham & Stoke d'Abernon	d										11 25										11 55		
Oxshott	d										11 28										11 58		
Claygate	d										11 31										12 01		
Hinchley Wood	d										11 34										12 04		
Hampton Court	d						11 24										11 54						
Thames Ditton	d						11 26										11 56						
Surbiton 6	d					11 27	11 32			11 38	11 42					11 57	12 02			12 08	12 12		
Berrylands	d						11 34										12 04						
Shepperton	d				11 11										11 41								
Upper Halliford	d				11 14										11 44								
Sunbury	d				11 16										11 46								
Kempton Park	d				11 18										11 48								
Hampton	d				11 21										11 51								
Fulwell	d				11 24										11 54								
Strawberry Hill	d	11 07	11 08									11 37	11 38									12 07	12 08
Teddington	d	11 11			11 29							11 41			11 59							12 11	
Hampton Wick	d	11 14			11 31							11 44			12 01							12 14	
Kingston	a	11 16			11 33							11 46			12 03							12 16	
	d	11 19			11 34							11 49			12 04							12 19	
Norbiton	d	11 21			11 36							11 51			12 06							12 21	
New Malden 6	d	11 25			11 40		11 37					11 55			12 10		12 07					12 25	
Dorking 4	d							11 35										12 05					
Boxhill & Westhumble	d																						
Leatherhead	d							11 41	11 54									12 11	12 24				
Ashtead	d							11 44	11 58									12 14	12 28				
Epsom 3	a							11 49	12 02									12 19	12 32				
	d							11 50	12 05									12 20	12 35				
Ewell West	d							11 53	12 08									12 23	12 38				
Stoneleigh	d							11 55	12 10									12 25	12 40				
Worcester Park	d							11 58	12 13									12 28	12 43				
Chessington South	d			11 10										11 40									
Chessington North	d			11 12										11 42									
Tolworth	d			11 14										11 44									
Malden Manor	d			11 17										11 47									
Motspur Park	d			11 20				12 01	12 16					11 50				12 31	12 46				
Raynes Park 6	d	11 28		11 23	11 43		11 40	12 04	12 19			11 58		11 53	12 13		12 10	12 34	12 49			12 28	
Wimbledon 6 ⊖ ⛴	d	11 32		11 27	11 47	11 35	11 44	12 08	12 23		11 50	12 02		11 57	12 17	12 05	12 14	12 38	12 53		12 20	12 32	
Earlsfield	d	11 35		11 31	11 50	11 38	11 47	12 12	12 27		11 54	12 05		12 01	12 20	12 08	12 17	12 42	12 57		12 24	12 35	
Clapham Junction 10	d	11 39		11 35	11 54	11 42	11 51	12 16	12 31	11 49	11 58	12 09		12 05	12 24	12 12	12 21	12 46	13 01		12 28	12 39	
Vauxhall ⊖	d	11 44	11 42	11 40	11 59	11 47	11 56	12 21	12 36		12 03	12 14	12 12	12 10	12 29	12 17	12 26	12 51	13 06		12 33	12 44	12 42
London Waterloo 15 ⊖	a	11 49	11 46	11 45	12 04	11 52	12 01	12 25	12 40	11 57	12 07	12 19	12 16	12 15	12 34	12 22	12 31	12 55	13 10	12 27	12 37	12 49	12 46

Table 152

Saturdays from 02 October

Hampton Court, Shepperton, Guildford, Dorking and Chessington South - London

		SW	SW	SW	SW	SW		SW	SW 1	SW	SW	SW	SW	SW	SW	SW		SW	SW	SW 1	SW	SW	SW	SW	SW
Guildford	d							12 28		12 05									12 58		12 35				
London Road (Guildford)	d							12 32		12 09									13 02		12 39				
Clandon	d							12 37		12 14									13 07		12 44				
Horsley	d							12 41		12 18									13 11		12 48				
Effingham Junction 6	d							12 46		12 21									13 16		12 51				
Bookham	d							12 49											13 19						
Cobham & Stoke d'Abernon	d									12 25											12 55				
Oxshott	d									12 28											12 58				
Claygate	d									12 31											13 01				
Hinchley Wood	d									12 34											13 04				
Hampton Court	d				12 24												12 54								
Thames Ditton	d				12 26												12 56								
Surbiton 6	d			12 27	12 32				12 38	12 42						12 57	13 02				13 08	13 12				
Berrylands	d				12 34												13 04								
Shepperton	d		12 11											12 41											13 11
Upper Halliford	d		12 14											12 44											13 14
Sunbury	d		12 16											12 46											13 16
Kempton Park	d		12 18											12 48											13 18
Hampton	d		12 21											12 51											13 21
Fulwell	d		12 24											12 54											13 24
Strawberry Hill	d										12 37	12 38										13 07	13 08		
Teddington	d		12 29								12 41			12 59								13 11			13 29
Hampton Wick	d		12 31								12 44			13 01								13 14			13 31
Kingston	a		12 33								12 46			13 03								13 16			13 33
	d		12 34								12 49			13 04								13 19			13 34
Norbiton	d		12 36								12 51			13 06								13 21			13 36
New Malden 6	d		12 40		12 37						12 55			13 10		13 07						13 25			13 40
Dorking 4	d					12 35												13 05							
Boxhill & Westhumble	d																								
Leatherhead	d					12 41		12 54										13 11	13 24						
Ashtead	d					12 44		12 58										13 14	13 28						
Epsom 3	a					12 49		13 02										13 19	13 32						
	d					12 50		13 05										13 20	13 35						
Ewell West	d					12 53		13 08										13 23	13 38						
Stoneleigh	d					12 55		13 10										13 25	13 40						
Worcester Park	d					12 58		13 13										13 28	13 43						
Chessington South	d	12 10											12 40											13 10	
Chessington North	d	12 12											12 42											13 12	
Tolworth	d	12 14											12 44											13 14	
Malden Manor	d	12 17											12 47											13 17	
Motspur Park	d	12 20				13 01		13 16					12 50					13 31	13 46					13 20	
Raynes Park 6	d	12 23	12 43		12 40	13 04		13 19			12 58		12 53	13 13		13 10		13 34	13 49			13 28		13 23	13 43
Wimbledon 6 ⊖	d	12 27	12 47	12 35	12 44	13 08		13 23		12 50	13 02		12 57	13 17	13 05	13 14		13 38	13 53		13 20	13 32		13 27	13 47
Earlsfield	d	12 31	12 50	12 38	12 47	13 12		13 27		12 54	13 05		13 01	13 20	13 08	13 17		13 42	13 57		13 24	13 35		13 31	13 50
Clapham Junction 10	d	12 35	12 54	12 42	12 51	13 16		13 31	12 49	12 58	13 09		13 05	13 24	13 12	13 21		13 46	14 01		13 28	13 39		13 35	13 54
Vauxhall ⊖	d	12 40	12 59	12 47	12 56	13 21		13 36		13 03	13 14	13 12	13 10	13 29	13 17	13 26		13 51	14 06		13 33	13 44	13 42	13 40	13 59
London Waterloo 15 ⊖	a	12 45	13 04	12 52	13 01	13 25		13 40	12 57	13 07	13 19	13 16	13 15	13 34	13 22	13 31		13 55	14 10	13 25	13 37	13 49	13 46	13 45	14 04

Table 152

Saturdays from 02 October

Hampton Court, Shepperton, Guildford, Dorking and Chessington South - London

		SW		SW	SW	SW	SW 1	SW	SW	SW	SW	SW		SW	SW	SW	SW	SW 1	SW	SW	SW	SW		SW	SW
Guildford	d					13 28		13 05									13 58		13 35						
London Road (Guildford)	d					13 32		13 09									14 02		13 39						
Clandon	d					13 37		13 14									14 07		13 44						
Horsley	d					13 41		13 18									14 11		13 48						
Effingham Junction 6	d					13 46		13 21									14 16		13 51						
Bookham	d					13 49											14 19								
Cobham & Stoke d'Abernon	d							13 25											13 55						
Oxshott	d							13 28											13 58						
Claygate	d							13 31											14 01						
Hinchley Wood	d							13 34											14 04						
Hampton Court	d			13 24											13 54										
Thames Ditton	d			13 26											13 56										
Surbiton 6	d	13 27		13 32			13 38	13 42						13 57	14 02			14 08	14 12						14 27
Berrylands	d			13 34											14 04										
Shepperton	d											13 41												14 11	
Upper Halliford	d											13 44												14 14	
Sunbury	d											13 46												14 16	
Kempton Park	d											13 48												14 18	
Hampton	d											13 51												14 21	
Fulwell	d											13 54												14 24	
Strawberry Hill	d								13 37	13 38										14 07	14 08				
Teddington	d								13 41			13 59								14 11				14 29	
Hampton Wick	d								13 44			14 01								14 14				14 31	
Kingston	a								13 46			14 03								14 16				14 33	
	d								13 49			14 04								14 19				14 34	
Norbiton	d								13 51			14 06								14 21				14 36	
New Malden 6	d			13 37					13 55			14 10			14 07					14 25				14 40	
Dorking 4	d				13 35											14 05									
Boxhill & Westhumble	d																								
Leatherhead	d				13 41	13 54										14 11	14 24								
Ashtead	d				13 44	13 58										14 14	14 28								
Epsom 3	a				13 49	14 02										14 19	14 32								
	d				13 50	14 05										14 20	14 35								
Ewell West	d				13 53	14 08										14 23	14 38								
Stoneleigh	d				13 55	14 10										14 25	14 40								
Worcester Park	d				13 58	14 13										14 28	14 43								
Chessington South	d										13 40											14 10			
Chessington North	d										13 42											14 12			
Tolworth	d										13 44											14 14			
Malden Manor	d										13 47											14 17			
Motspur Park	d				14 01	14 16					13 50					14 31	14 46					14 20			
Raynes Park 6	d			13 40	14 04	14 19			13 58		13 53	14 13			14 10	14 34	14 49			14 28		14 23		14 43	
Wimbledon 6 ⊖	d	13 35		13 44	14 08	14 23		13 50	14 02		13 57	14 17		14 05	14 14	14 38	14 53		14 20	14 32		14 27		14 47	14 35
Earlsfield	d	13 38		13 47	14 12	14 27		13 54	14 05		14 01	14 20		14 08	14 17	14 42	14 57		14 24	14 35		14 31		14 50	14 38
Clapham Junction 10	d	13 42		13 51	14 16	14 31	13 49	13 58	14 09		14 05	14 24		14 12	14 21	14 46	15 01		14 28	14 39		14 35		14 54	14 42
Vauxhall ⊖	d	13 47		13 56	14 21	14 36		14 03	14 14	14 12	14 10	14 29		14 17	14 26	14 51	15 06		14 33	14 44	14 42	14 40		14 59	14 47
London Waterloo 15 ⊖	a	13 52		14 01	14 25	14 40	13 57	14 07	14 19	14 16	14 15	14 34		14 22	14 31	14 55	15 10	14 25	14 37	14 49	14 46	14 45		15 04	14 52

Table 152

Saturdays
from 02 October

Hampton Court, Shepperton, Guildford, Dorking and Chessington South - London

		SW	SW	SW	SW 1	SW	SW	SW	SW	SW	SW	SW	SW	SW	SW 1	SW	SW	SW	SW	SW	SW	SW	SW
Guildford	d			14 28		14 05								14 58		14 35							
London Road (Guildford)	d			14 32		14 09								15 02		14 39							
Clandon	d			14 37		14 14								15 07		14 44							
Horsley	d			14 41		14 18								15 11		14 48							
Effingham Junction 6	d			14 46		14 21								15 16		14 51							
Bookham	d			14 49										15 19									
Cobham & Stoke d'Abernon	d					14 25										14 55							
Oxshott	d					14 28										14 58							
Claygate	d					14 31										15 01							
Hinchley Wood	d					14 34										15 04							
Hampton Court	d	14 24										14 54										15 24	
Thames Ditton	d	14 26										14 56										15 26	
Surbiton 6	d	14 32			14 38	14 42					14 57	15 02			15 08	15 12					15 27	15 32	
Berrylands	d	14 34										15 04										15 34	
Shepperton	d									14 41										15 11			
Upper Halliford	d									14 44										15 14			
Sunbury	d									14 46										15 16			
Kempton Park	d									14 48										15 18			
Hampton	d									14 51										15 21			
Fulwell	d									14 54										15 24			
Strawberry Hill	d						14 37	14 38									15 07	15 08					
Teddington	d						14 41			14 59							15 11			15 29			
Hampton Wick	d						14 44			15 01							15 14			15 31			
Kingston	a						14 46			15 03							15 16			15 33			
	d						14 49			15 04							15 19			15 34			
Norbiton	d						14 51			15 06							15 21			15 36			
New Malden 6	d	14 37					14 55			15 10		15 07					15 25			15 40		15 37	
Dorking 4	d		14 35										15 05										15 35
Boxhill & Westhumble	d																						
Leatherhead	d		14 41	14 54									15 11	15 24									15 41
Ashtead	d		14 44	14 58									15 14	15 28									15 44
Epsom 3	a		14 49	15 02									15 19	15 32									15 49
	d		14 50	15 05									15 20	15 35									15 50
Ewell West	d		14 53	15 08									15 23	15 38									15 53
Stoneleigh	d		14 55	15 10									15 25	15 40									15 55
Worcester Park	d		14 58	15 13									15 28	15 43									15 58
Chessington South	d								14 40										15 10				
Chessington North	d								14 42										15 12				
Tolworth	d								14 44										15 14				
Malden Manor	d								14 47										15 17				
Motspur Park	d		15 01	15 16					14 50				15 31	15 46					15 20				16 01
Raynes Park 6	d	14 40	15 04	15 19			14 58		14 53	15 13		15 10	15 34	15 49			15 28		15 23	15 43		15 40	16 04
Wimbledon 6 ⊖	d	14 44	15 08	15 23		14 50	15 02		14 57	15 17	15 05	15 14	15 38	15 53		15 20	15 32		15 27	15 47	15 35	15 44	16 08
Earlsfield	d	14 47	15 12	15 27		14 54	15 05		15 01	15 20	15 08	15 17	15 42	15 57		15 24	15 35		15 31	15 50	15 38	15 47	16 12
Clapham Junction 10	d	14 51	15 16	15 31	14 49	14 58	15 09		15 05	15 24	15 12	15 21	15 46	16 01		15 28	15 39		15 35	15 54	15 42	15 51	16 16
Vauxhall ⊖	d	14 56	15 21	15 36		15 03	15 14	15 12	15 10	15 29	15 17	15 26	15 51	16 06		15 33	15 44	15 42	15 40	15 59	15 47	15 56	16 21
London Waterloo 15 ⊖	a	15 01	15 25	15 40	14 57	15 07	15 19	15 16	15 15	15 34	15 22	15 31	15 55	16 10	15 25	15 37	15 49	15 46	15 45	16 04	15 52	16 01	16 25

Table 152

Saturdays
from 02 October

Hampton Court, Shepperton, Guildford, Dorking and Chessington South - London

		SW	SW 1	SW	SW	SW	SW	SW	SW	SW	SW	SW	SW 1	SW	SW	SW	SW	SW	SW	SW	SW	SW
Guildford	d	15 28		15 05								15 58		15 35								16 28
London Road (Guildford)	d	15 32		15 09								16 02		15 39								16 32
Clandon	d	15 37		15 14								16 07		15 44								16 37
Horsley	d	15 41		15 18								16 11		15 48								16 41
Effingham Junction 6	d	15 46		15 21								16 16		15 51								16 46
Bookham	d	15 49										16 19										16 49
Cobham & Stoke d'Abernon	d			15 25										15 55								
Oxshott	d			15 28										15 58								
Claygate	d			15 31										16 01								
Hinchley Wood	d			15 34										16 04								
Hampton Court	d									15 54										16 24		
Thames Ditton	d									15 56										16 26		
Surbiton 6	d		15 38	15 42					15 57	16 02			16 08	16 12					16 27	16 32		
Berrylands	d									16 04										16 34		
Shepperton	d							15 41										16 11				
Upper Halliford	d							15 44										16 14				
Sunbury	d							15 46										16 16				
Kempton Park	d							15 48										16 18				
Hampton	d							15 51										16 21				
Fulwell	d							15 54										16 24				
Strawberry Hill	d				15 37	15 38									16 07	16 08						
Teddington	d				15 41			15 59							16 11			16 29				
Hampton Wick	d				15 44			16 01							16 14			16 31				
Kingston	a				15 46			16 03							16 16			16 33				
	d				15 49			16 04							16 19			16 34				
Norbiton	d				15 51			16 06							16 21			16 36				
New Malden 6	d				15 55			16 10		16 07					16 25			16 40		16 37		
Dorking 4	d										16 05										16 35	
Boxhill & Westhumble	d																					
Leatherhead	d	15 54									16 11	16 24									16 41	16 54
Ashtead	d	15 58									16 14	16 28									16 44	16 58
Epsom 3	a	16 02									16 19	16 32									16 49	17 02
	d	16 05									16 20	16 35									16 50	17 05
Ewell West	d	16 08									16 23	16 38									16 53	17 08
Stoneleigh	d	16 10									16 25	16 40									16 55	17 10
Worcester Park	d	16 13									16 28	16 43									16 58	17 13
Chessington South	d						15 40										16 10					
Chessington North	d						15 42										16 12					
Tolworth	d						15 44										16 14					
Malden Manor	d						15 47										16 17					
Motspur Park	d	16 16					15 50				16 31	16 46					16 20				17 01	17 16
Raynes Park 6	d	16 19			15 58		15 53	16 13		16 10	16 34	16 49			16 28		16 23	16 43		16 40	17 04	17 19
Wimbledon 6 ⊖	d	16 23		15 50	16 02		15 57	16 17	16 05	16 14	16 38	16 53		16 20	16 32		16 27	16 47	16 35	16 44	17 08	17 23
Earlsfield	d	16 27		15 54	16 05		16 01	16 20	16 08	16 17	16 42	16 57		16 24	16 35		16 31	16 50	16 38	16 47	17 12	17 27
Clapham Junction 10	d	16 31	15 49	15 58	16 09		16 05	16 24	16 12	16 21	16 46	17 01		16 28	16 39		16 35	16 54	16 42	16 51	17 16	17 31
Vauxhall ⊖	d	16 36		16 03	16 14	16 12	16 10	16 29	16 17	16 26	16 51	17 06		16 33	16 44	16 42	16 40	16 59	16 47	16 56	17 21	17 36
London Waterloo 15 ⊖	a	16 40	15 57	16 07	16 19	16 16	16 15	16 34	16 22	16 31	16 55	17 10	16 25	16 37	16 49	16 46	16 45	17 04	16 52	17 01	17 25	17 40

Table 152

Saturdays
from 02 October

Hampton Court, Shepperton, Guildford, Dorking and Chessington South - London

		SW 1	SW	SW	SW	SW	SW	SW	SW	SW	SW	SW 1	SW	SW	SW	SW	SW	SW	SW	SW	SW	SW 1	SW
Guildford	d		16 05								16 58		16 35								17 28		17 05
London Road (Guildford)	d		16 09								17 02		16 39								17 32		17 09
Clandon	d		16 14								17 07		16 44								17 37		17 14
Horsley	d		16 18								17 11		16 48								17 41		17 18
Effingham Junction 6	d		16 21								17 16		16 51								17 46		17 21
Bookham	d										17 19										17 49		
Cobham & Stoke d'Abernon	d		16 25										16 55										17 25
Oxshott	d		16 28										16 58										17 28
Claygate	d		16 31										17 01										17 31
Hinchley Wood	d		16 34										17 04										17 34
Hampton Court	d								16 54										17 24				
Thames Ditton	d								16 56										17 26				
Surbiton 6	d	16 38	16 42					16 57	17 02			17 08	17 12					17 27	17 32			17 38	17 42
Berrylands	d								17 04										17 34				
Shepperton	d						16 41										17 11						
Upper Halliford	d						16 44										17 14						
Sunbury	d						16 46										17 16						
Kempton Park	d						16 48										17 18						
Hampton	d						16 51										17 21						
Fulwell	d						16 54										17 24						
Strawberry Hill	d			16 37	16 38									17 07	17 08								
Teddington	d			16 41			16 59							17 11			17 29						
Hampton Wick	d			16 44			17 01							17 14			17 31						
Kingston	a			16 46			17 03							17 16			17 33						
	d			16 49			17 04							17 19			17 34						
Norbiton	d			16 51			17 06							17 21			17 36						
New Malden 6	d			16 55			17 10		17 07					17 25			17 40		17 37				
Dorking 4	d									17 05										17 35			
Boxhill & Westhumble	d																						
Leatherhead	d									17 11	17 24									17 41	17 54		
Ashtead	d									17 14	17 28									17 44	17 58		
Epsom 3	a									17 19	17 32									17 49	18 02		
	d									17 20	17 35									17 50	18 05		
Ewell West	d									17 23	17 38									17 53	18 08		
Stoneleigh	d									17 25	17 40									17 55	18 10		
Worcester Park	d									17 28	17 43									17 58	18 13		
Chessington South	d					16 40										17 10							
Chessington North	d					16 42										17 12							
Tolworth	d					16 44										17 14							
Malden Manor	d					16 47										17 17							
Motspur Park	d					16 50				17 31	17 46					17 20				18 01	18 16		
Raynes Park 6	d			16 58		16 53	17 13		17 10	17 34	17 49			17 28		17 23	17 43		17 40	18 04	18 19		
Wimbledon 6 ⊖ ⛴	d		16 50	17 02		16 57	17 17	17 05	17 14	17 38	17 53		17 20	17 32		17 27	17 47	17 35	17 44	18 08	18 23		17 50
Earlsfield	d		16 54	17 05		17 01	17 20	17 08	17 17	17 42	17 57		17 24	17 35		17 31	17 50	17 38	17 47	18 12	18 27		17 54
Clapham Junction 10	d	16 49	16 58	17 09		17 05	17 24	17 12	17 21	17 46	18 01		17 28	17 39		17 35	17 54	17 42	17 51	18 16	18 31	17 49	17 58
Vauxhall ⊖	d		17 03	17 14	17 12	17 10	17 29	17 17	17 26	17 51	18 06		17 33	17 44	17 42	17 40	17 59	17 47	17 56	18 21	18 36		18 03
London Waterloo 15 ⊖	a	16 57	17 07	17 19	17 16	17 15	17 34	17 22	17 31	17 55	18 10	17 25	17 37	17 49	17 46	17 45	18 04	17 52	18 01	18 25	18 40	17 57	18 07

Table 152

Saturdays
from 02 October

Hampton Court, Shepperton, Guildford, Dorking and Chessington South - London

		SW	SW	SW	SW	SW	SW	SW	SW	SW 1	SW	SW	SW	SW	SW	SW	SW	SW	SW	SW 1	SW	SW	SW
Guildford	d								17 58		17 35								18 28		18 05		
London Road (Guildford)	d								18 02		17 39								18 32		18 09		
Clandon	d								18 07		17 44								18 37		18 14		
Horsley	d								18 11		17 48								18 41		18 18		
Effingham Junction 6	d								18 16		17 51								18 46		18 21		
Bookham	d								18 19										18 49				
Cobham & Stoke d'Abernon	d										17 55										18 25		
Oxshott	d										17 58										18 28		
Claygate	d										18 01										18 31		
Hinchley Wood	d										18 04										18 34		
Hampton Court	d						17 54										18 24						
Thames Ditton	d						17 56										18 26						
Surbiton 6	d					17 57	18 02			18 08	18 12					18 27	18 32			18 38	18 42		
Berrylands	d						18 04										18 34						
Shepperton	d				17 41										18 11								
Upper Halliford	d				17 44										18 14								
Sunbury	d				17 46										18 16								
Kempton Park	d				17 48										18 18								
Hampton	d				17 51										18 21								
Fulwell	d				17 54										18 24								
Strawberry Hill	d	17 37	17 38									18 07	18 08									18 37	18 38
Teddington	d	17 41			17 59							18 11			18 29							18 41	
Hampton Wick	d	17 44			18 01							18 14			18 31							18 44	
Kingston	a	17 46			18 03							18 16			18 33							18 46	
	d	17 49			18 04							18 19			18 34							18 49	
Norbiton	d	17 51			18 06							18 21			18 36							18 51	
New Malden 6	d	17 55			18 10		18 07					18 25			18 40		18 37					18 55	
Dorking 4	d							18 05										18 35					
Boxhill & Westhumble	d																						
Leatherhead	d							18 11	18 24									18 41	18 54				
Ashtead	d							18 14	18 28									18 44	18 58				
Epsom 3	a							18 19	18 32									18 49	19 02				
	d							18 20	18 35									18 50	19 05				
Ewell West	d							18 23	18 38									18 53	19 08				
Stoneleigh	d							18 25	18 40									18 55	19 10				
Worcester Park	d							18 28	18 43									18 58	19 13				
Chessington South	d			17 40										18 10									
Chessington North	d			17 42										18 12									
Tolworth	d			17 44										18 14									
Malden Manor	d			17 47										18 17									
Motspur Park	d			17 50				18 31	18 46					18 20				19 01	19 16				
Raynes Park 6	d	17 58		17 53	18 13		18 10	18 34	18 49			18 28		18 23	18 43		18 40	19 04	19 19			18 58	
Wimbledon 6 ⊖ ⛴	d	18 02		17 57	18 17	18 05	18 14	18 38	18 53		18 20	18 32		18 27	18 47	18 35	18 44	19 08	19 23		18 50	19 02	
Earlsfield	d	18 05		18 01	18 20	18 08	18 17	18 42	18 57		18 24	18 35		18 31	18 50	18 38	18 47	19 12	19 27		18 54	19 05	
Clapham Junction 10	d	18 09		18 05	18 24	18 12	18 21	18 46	19 01		18 28	18 39		18 35	18 54	18 42	18 51	19 16	19 31	18 49	18 58	19 09	
Vauxhall ⊖	d	18 14	18 12	18 10	18 29	18 17	18 26	18 51	19 06		18 33	18 44	18 42	18 40	18 59	18 47	18 56	19 21	19 36		19 03	19 14	19 12
London Waterloo 15 ⊖	a	18 19	18 16	18 15	18 34	18 22	18 31	18 55	19 10	18 25	18 37	18 49	18 46	18 45	19 04	18 52	19 01	19 25	19 40	18 57	19 07	19 19	19 16

Table 152

Saturdays
from 02 October

Hampton Court, Shepperton, Guildford, Dorking and Chessington South - London

		SW		SW	SW	SW	SW	SW	SW 1	SW	SW	SW		SW	SW	SW	SW	SW	SW	SW 1	SW	SW		SW	SW
Guildford	d							18 58		18 35									19 28		19 05				
London Road (Guildford)	d							19 02		18 39									19 32		19 09				
Clandon	d							19 07		18 44									19 37		19 14				
Horsley	d							19 11		18 48									19 41		19 18				
Effingham Junction 6	d							19 16		18 51									19 46		19 21				
Bookham	d							19 19											19 49						
Cobham & Stoke d'Abernon	d									18 55											19 25				
Oxshott	d									18 58											19 28				
Claygate	d									19 01											19 31				
Hinchley Wood	d									19 04											19 34				
Hampton Court	d					18 54											19 24								
Thames Ditton	d					18 56											19 26								
Surbiton 6	d				18 57	19 02			19 08	19 12						19 27	19 32			19 38	19 42				
Berrylands	d					19 04											19 34								
Shepperton	d			18 41											19 11										
Upper Halliford	d			18 44											19 14										
Sunbury	d			18 46											19 16										
Kempton Park	d			18 48											19 18										
Hampton	d			18 51											19 21										
Fulwell	d			18 54											19 24										
Strawberry Hill	d										19 07	19 08										19 37		19 38	
Teddington	d			18 59							19 11				19 29							19 41			
Hampton Wick	d			19 01							19 14				19 31							19 44			
Kingston	a			19 03							19 16				19 33							19 46			
	d			19 04							19 19				19 34							19 49			
Norbiton	d			19 06							19 21				19 36							19 51			
New Malden 6	d			19 10		19 07					19 25				19 40		19 37					19 55			
Dorking 4	d						19 05											19 35							
Boxhill & Westhumble	d																								
Leatherhead	d						19 11	19 24										19 41	19 54						
Ashtead	d						19 14	19 28										19 44	19 58						
Epsom 3	a						19 19	19 32										19 49	20 02						
	d						19 20	19 35										19 50	20 05						
Ewell West	d						19 23	19 38										19 53	20 08						
Stoneleigh	d						19 25	19 40										19 55	20 10						
Worcester Park	d						19 28	19 43										19 58	20 13						
Chessington South	d	18 40												19 10											19 40
Chessington North	d	18 42												19 12											19 42
Tolworth	d	18 44												19 14											19 44
Malden Manor	d	18 47												19 17											19 47
Motspur Park	d	18 50					19 31	19 46						19 20				20 01	20 16						19 50
Raynes Park 6	d	18 53		19 13		19 10	19 34	19 49			19 28			19 23	19 43		19 40	20 04	20 19			19 58			19 53
Wimbledon 6 ⊖	d	18 57		19 17	19 05	19 14	19 38	19 53		19 20	19 32			19 27	19 47	19 35	19 44	20 08	20 23		19 50	20 02			19 57
Earlsfield	d	19 01		19 20	19 08	19 17	19 42	19 57		19 24	19 35			19 31	19 50	19 38	19 47	20 12	20 27		19 54	20 05			20 01
Clapham Junction 10	d	19 05		19 24	19 12	19 21	19 46	20 01		19 28	19 39			19 35	19 54	19 42	19 51	20 16	20 31	19 49	19 58	20 09			20 05
Vauxhall ⊖	d	19 10		19 29	19 17	19 26	19 51	20 06		19 33	19 44	19 42		19 40	19 59	19 47	19 56	20 21	20 36		20 03	20 14		20 12	20 10
London Waterloo 15 ⊖	a	19 15		19 34	19 22	19 31	19 55	20 10	19 25	19 37	19 49	19 46		19 45	20 04	19 52	20 01	20 25	20 40	19 57	20 07	20 19		20 16	20 15

Table 152

Saturdays
from 02 October

Hampton Court, Shepperton, Guildford, Dorking and Chessington South - London

		SW	SW	SW	SW	SW	SW 1	SW		SW	SW	SW	SW	SW	SW	SW	SW 1	SW		SW	SW	SW	SW	SW	SW
Guildford	d					19 58		19 35										20 05							
London Road (Guildford)	d					20 02		19 39										20 09							
Clandon	d					20 07		19 44										20 14							
Horsley	d					20 11		19 48										20 18							
Effingham Junction 6	d					20 16		19 51										20 21							
Bookham	d					20 19																			
Cobham & Stoke d'Abernon	d							19 55										20 25							
Oxshott	d							19 58										20 28							
Claygate	d							20 01										20 31							
Hinchley Wood	d							20 04										20 34							
Hampton Court	d			19 54											20 24										20 54
Thames Ditton	d			19 56											20 26										20 56
Surbiton 6	d		19 57	20 02			20 08	20 12						20 27	20 32		20 38	20 42						20 57	21 02
Berrylands	d			20 04											20 34										21 04
Shepperton	d	19 41											20 11										20 41		
Upper Halliford	d	19 44											20 14										20 44		
Sunbury	d	19 46											20 16										20 46		
Kempton Park	d	19 48											20 18										20 48		
Hampton	d	19 51											20 21										20 51		
Fulwell	d	19 54											20 24										20 54		
Strawberry Hill	d									20 07	20 08									20 37	20 38				
Teddington	d	19 59								20 11			20 29							20 41			20 59		
Hampton Wick	d	20 01								20 14			20 31							20 44			21 01		
Kingston	a	20 03								20 16			20 33							20 46			21 03		
	d	20 04								20 19			20 34							20 49			21 04		
Norbiton	d	20 06								20 21			20 36							20 51			21 06		
New Malden 6	d	20 10		20 07						20 25			20 40		20 37					20 55			21 10		21 07
Dorking 4	d				20 05											20 35									
Boxhill & Westhumble	d																								
Leatherhead	d				20 11	20 24										20 41									
Ashtead	d				20 14	20 28										20 44									
Epsom 3	a				20 19	20 32										20 49									
	d				20 20	20 35										20 50									
Ewell West	d				20 23	20 38										20 53									
Stoneleigh	d				20 25	20 40										20 55									
Worcester Park	d				20 28	20 43										20 58									
Chessington South	d											20 10										20 40			
Chessington North	d											20 12										20 42			
Tolworth	d											20 14										20 44			
Malden Manor	d											20 17										20 47			
Motspur Park	d				20 31	20 46						20 20				21 01						20 50			
Raynes Park 6	d	20 13		20 10	20 34	20 49				20 28		20 23	20 43		20 40	21 04				20 58		20 53	21 13		21 10
Wimbledon 6 ⊖	d	20 17	20 05	20 14	20 38	20 53		20 20		20 32		20 27	20 47	20 35	20 44	21 08		20 50		21 02		20 57	21 17	21 05	21 14
Earlsfield	d	20 20	20 08	20 17	20 42	20 57		20 24		20 35		20 31	20 50	20 38	20 47	21 12		20 54		21 05		21 01	21 20	21 08	21 17
Clapham Junction 10	d	20 24	20 12	20 21	20 46	21 01		20 28		20 39		20 35	20 54	20 42	20 51	21 16	20 49	20 58		21 09		21 05	21 24	21 12	21 21
Vauxhall ⊖	d	20 29	20 17	20 26	20 51	21 06		20 33		20 44	20 42	20 40	20 59	20 47	20 56	21 21		21 03		21 14	21 12	21 10	21 29	21 17	21 26
London Waterloo 15 ⊖	a	20 34	20 22	20 31	20 55	21 10	20 25	20 37		20 49	20 46	20 45	21 04	20 52	21 01	21 25	20 57	21 07		21 19	21 16	21 15	21 34	21 23	21 31

Table 152

Saturdays from 02 October

Hampton Court, Shepperton, Guildford, Dorking and Chessington South - London

		SW	SW	SW 1	SW	SW	SW	SW	SW	SW	SW	SW	SW	SW 1	SW	SW	SW	SW	SW	SW	SW	SW 1
Guildford	d		20 46		20 35										21 05					21 46		
London Road (Guildford)	d		20 50		20 39										21 09					21 50		
Clandon	d		20 55		20 44										21 14					21 55		
Horsley	d		20 59		20 48										21 18					21 59		
Effingham Junction 6	d		21 03		20 51										21 21					22 03		
Bookham	d		21 06																	22 06		
Cobham & Stoke d'Abernon	d				20 55										21 25							
Oxshott	d				20 58										21 28							
Claygate	d				21 01										21 31							
Hinchley Wood	d				21 04										21 34							
Hampton Court	d										21 24											
Thames Ditton	d										21 26											
Surbiton 6	d			21 08	21 12					21 27	21 32			21 38	21 42						21 57	22 08
Berrylands	d										21 34											
Shepperton	d								21 11										21 41			
Upper Halliford	d								21 14										21 44			
Sunbury	d								21 16										21 46			
Kempton Park	d								21 18										21 48			
Hampton	d								21 21										21 51			
Fulwell	d								21 24										21 54			
Strawberry Hill	d					21 07	21 08									21 37	21 38					
Teddington	d					21 11			21 29							21 41			21 59			
Hampton Wick	d					21 14			21 31							21 44			22 01			
Kingston	a					21 16			21 33							21 46			22 03			
	d					21 19			21 34							21 49			22 04			
Norbiton	d					21 21			21 36							21 51			22 06			
New Malden 6	d					21 25			21 40		21 37					21 55			22 10			
Dorking 4	d												21 35									
Boxhill & Westhumble	d																					
Leatherhead	d		21 11										21 41							22 11		
Ashtead	d		21 14										21 44							22 14		
Epsom 3	a		21 19										21 49							22 19		
	d	21 05	21 20									21 35	21 50							22 20		
Ewell West	d	21 08	21 23									21 38	21 53							22 23		
Stoneleigh	d	21 10	21 25									21 40	21 55							22 25		
Worcester Park	d	21 13	21 28									21 43	21 58							22 28		
Chessington South	d							21 10										21 40				
Chessington North	d							21 12										21 42				
Tolworth	d							21 14										21 44				
Malden Manor	d							21 17										21 47				
Motspur Park	d	21 16	21 31					21 20				21 46	22 01					21 50		22 31		
Raynes Park 6	d	21 19	21 34			21 28		21 23	21 43		21 40	21 49	22 04			21 58		21 53	22 13	22 34		
Wimbledon 6 ⊖ ⛴	d	21 23	21 38		21 20	21 32		21 27	21 47	21 35	21 44	21 53	22 08		21 50	22 02		21 57	22 17	22 38	22 05	
Earlsfield	d	21 27	21 42		21 24	21 35		21 31	21 50	21 38	21 47	21 57	22 12		21 54	22 05		22 01	22 20	22 42	22 08	
Clapham Junction 10	d	21 31	21 46		21 28	21 39		21 35	21 54	21 42	21 51	22 01	22 16	21 49	21 58	22 09		22 05	22 24	22 46	22 12	
Vauxhall ⊖	d	21 36	21 51		21 33	21 44	21 42	21 40	21 59	21 47	21 56	22 06	22 21		22 03	22 14	22 12	22 10	22 29	22 51	22 17	
London Waterloo 15 ⊖	a	21 40	21 55	21 29	21 37	21 49	21 46	21 45	22 04	21 52	22 01	22 10	22 25	21 57	22 07	22 19	22 16	22 15	22 34	22 55	22 22	22 27

Table 152

Saturdays from 02 October

Hampton Court, Shepperton, Guildford, Dorking and Chessington South - London

		SW	SW	SW	SW	SW	SW	SW	SW 1	SW	SW	SW	SW	SW	SW	SW	SW 1	SW	SW	SW	SW	SW	SW
Guildford	d	21 35								22 05	22 20					22 46		22 35	22 55				
London Road (Guildford)	d	21 39								22 09						22 50		22 39					
Clandon	d	21 44								22 14						22 55		22 44					
Horsley	d	21 48								22 18						22 59		22 48					
Effingham Junction 6	d	21 51								22 21						23 03		22 51					
Bookham	d															23 06							
Cobham & Stoke d'Abernon	d	21 55								22 25								22 55					
Oxshott	d	21 58								22 28								22 58					
Claygate	d	22 01								22 31								23 01					
Hinchley Wood	d	22 04								22 34								23 04					
Hampton Court	d						22 24																23 24
Thames Ditton	d						22 26																23 26
Surbiton 6	d	22 12				22 27	22 32		22 38	22 42	22 57						23 08	23 12	23 30				23 32
Berrylands	d						22 34																23 34
Shepperton	d				22 11										22 41							23 11	
Upper Halliford	d				22 14										22 44							23 14	
Sunbury	d				22 16										22 46							23 16	
Kempton Park	d				22 18										22 48							23 18	
Hampton	d				22 21										22 51							23 21	
Fulwell	d				22 24										22 54							23 24	
Strawberry Hill	d		22 07	22 08								22 37	22 38							23 07	23 08		
Teddington	d		22 11		22 29							22 41			22 59					23 11		23 29	
Hampton Wick	d		22 14		22 31							22 44			23 01					23 14		23 31	
Kingston	a		22 16		22 33							22 46			23 03					23 16		23 33	
	d		22 19		22 34							22 49			23 04					23 19		23 34	
Norbiton	d		22 21		22 36							22 51			23 06					23 21		23 36	
New Malden 6	d		22 25		22 40		22 37					22 55			23 10					23 25		23 41	23 37
Dorking 4	d							22 35															
Boxhill & Westhumble	d																						
Leatherhead	d							22 41								23 11							
Ashtead	d							22 44								23 14							
Epsom 3	a							22 49								23 19							
	d							22 50								23 20							
Ewell West	d							22 53								23 23							
Stoneleigh	d							22 55								23 25							
Worcester Park	d							22 58								23 28							
Chessington South	d													22 40									
Chessington North	d													22 42									
Tolworth	d													22 44									
Malden Manor	d													22 47									
Motspur Park	d							23 01						22 50		23 31							
Raynes Park 6	d		22 28		22 43		22 40	23 04				22 58		22 53	23 13	23 37				23 28		23 43	23 40
Wimbledon 6 ⊖ ⛴	d	22 20	22 32		22 47	22 35	22 44	23 08		22 50	23 05	23 02		22 57	23 17	23 41		23 20	23 37	23 32		23 52	23 44
Earlsfield	d	22 24	22 35		22 50	22 38	22 47	23 12		22 54	23 08	23 05		23 01	23 20	23 44		23 24	23 41	23 35		23 55	23 47
Clapham Junction 10	d	22 28	22 39		22 54	22 42	22 51	23 16	22 53	22 58	23 12	23 09		23 05	23 24	23 48		23 28	23 45	23 39		00 04	23 51
Vauxhall ⊖	d	22 33	22 44	22 42	22 59	22 47	22 56	23 21		23 03	23 17	23 14	23 12	23 10	23 29	23 53		23 33	23 50	23 44	23 42	00 09	23 56
London Waterloo 15 ⊖	a	22 39	22 49	22 46	23 04	22 52	23 01	23 25	23 01	23 07	23 22	23 19	23 17	23 15	23 34	23 58	23 28	23 37	23 54	23 49	23 46	00 13	00 02

Table 152

Saturdays from 02 October

Hampton Court, Shepperton, Guildford, Dorking and Chessington South - London

		SN	SW 1	SW	SW	SW		SW
Guildford	d			23 08				
London Road (Guildford)	d			23 12				
Clandon	d			23 17				
Horsley	d			23 21				
Effingham Junction 6	d			23 24				
Bookham	d							
Cobham & Stoke d'Abernon	d			23 28				
Oxshott	d			23 31				
Claygate	d			23 34				
Hinchley Wood	d			23 37				
Hampton Court	d							
Thames Ditton	d							
Surbiton 6	d		23 38	23 42				
Berrylands	d							
Shepperton	d							
Upper Halliford	d							
Sunbury	d							
Kempton Park	d							
Hampton	d							
Fulwell	d							
Strawberry Hill	d				23 37	23 38		
Teddington	d				23 41			
Hampton Wick	d				23 44			
Kingston	a				23 46			
	d				23 49			
Norbiton	d				23 51			
New Malden 6	d				23 55			
Dorking 4	d	23 30						
Boxhill & Westhumble	d							
Leatherhead	d	23 36						
Ashtead	d	23 39						
Epsom 3	a	23 45						
	d							
Ewell West	d							
Stoneleigh	d							
Worcester Park	d							
Chessington South	d							23 40
Chessington North	d							23 42
Tolworth	d							23 44
Malden Manor	d							23 47
Motspur Park	d							23 50
Raynes Park 6	d				23 58			23 54
Wimbledon 6 ⊖ ⇌	d			23 58	00 07			00a02
Earlsfield	d			00 01	00 10			
Clapham Junction 10	d		23 56	00 07	00 14			
Vauxhall ⊖	d			00 12	00 19	00 12		
London Waterloo 15 ⊖	a		00 04	00 16	00 24	00 16		

Table 152

Sundays until 19 September

Hampton Court, Shepperton, Guildford, Dorking and Chessington South - London

		SW	SW	SW 1	SW	SW	SW	SW	SW	SW		SW	SW
Guildford	d				23p08							06 57	
London Road (Guildford)	d				23p12								
Clandon	d				23p17								
Horsley	d				23p21								
Effingham Junction 6	d				23p24								
Bookham	d												
Cobham & Stoke d'Abernon	d				23p28								
Oxshott	d				23p31								
Claygate	d				23p34								
Hinchley Wood	d				23p37								
Hampton Court	d		23p24										
Thames Ditton	d		23p26										
Surbiton 6	d		23p32	23p38	23p42					07 00		07 30	
Berrylands	d		23p34										
Shepperton	d	23p11											07 11
Upper Halliford	d	23p14											07 14
Sunbury	d	23p16											07 16
Kempton Park	d	23p18											07 18
Hampton	d	23p21											07 21
Fulwell	d	23p24											07 24
Strawberry Hill	d					23p37	23p38	06 49	06 59				
Teddington	d	23p29				23p41		06 55					07 29
Hampton Wick	d	23p31				23p44		06 57					07 31
Kingston	a	23p33				23p46		06 59					07 33
	d	23p34				23p49		07 04					07 34
Norbiton	d	23p36				23p51		07 06					07 36
New Malden 6	d	23p41	23p37			23p55		07 10					07 40
Dorking 4	d												
Boxhill & Westhumble	d												
Leatherhead	d												
Ashtead	d												
Epsom 3	a												
	d												
Ewell West	d												
Stoneleigh	d												
Worcester Park	d												
Chessington South	d												
Chessington North	d												
Tolworth	d												
Malden Manor	d												
Motspur Park	d												
Raynes Park 6	d	23p43	23p40			23p58		07 13					07 43
Wimbledon 6 ⊖ ⇌	d	23p52	23p44		23p58	00 07		07 19		07 08		07 38	07 47
Earlsfield	d	23p55	23p47		00 01	00 10		07 22		07 11		07 41	07 50
Clapham Junction 10	d	00 04	23p51	23p56	00 07	00 14		07 26		07 15		07 45	07 54
Vauxhall ⊖	d	00 09	23p56		00 12	00 19	00 12	07 31	07 32	07 20		07 50	08 02
London Waterloo 15 ⊖	a	00 13	00 02	00 04	00 16	00 24	00 16	07 41	07 41	07 30		08 00	08 07

		SW	SW	SW	SW	SW	SW	SW		SW	SW	SW	SW
Guildford	d			07 27						07 50	07 57		
London Road (Guildford)	d									07 54			
Clandon	d									07 59			
Horsley	d									08 03			
Effingham Junction 6	d									08 06			
Bookham	d												
Cobham & Stoke d'Abernon	d									08 10			
Oxshott	d									08 13			
Claygate	d									08 16			
Hinchley Wood	d									08 19			
Hampton Court	d		07 35					08 05					
Thames Ditton	d		07 37					08 07					
Surbiton 6	d		07 43	08 00				08 13		08 24	08 30		
Berrylands	d		07 45					08 15					
Shepperton	d												08 11
Upper Halliford	d												08 14
Sunbury	d												08 16
Kempton Park	d												08 18
Hampton	d												08 21
Fulwell	d												08 24
Strawberry Hill	d				07 49		07 59						
Teddington	d				07 55								08 29
Hampton Wick	d				07 57								08 31
Kingston	a				07 59								08 33
	d				08 04								08 34
Norbiton	d				08 06								08 36
New Malden 6	d		07 48		08 10			08 18					08 40
Dorking 4	d												
Boxhill & Westhumble	d												
Leatherhead	d												
Ashtead	d												
Epsom 3	a												
	d	07 24				07 54							
Ewell West	d	07 27				07 57							
Stoneleigh	d	07 29				07 59							
Worcester Park	d	07 32				08 02							
Chessington South	d											08 10	
Chessington North	d											08 12	
Tolworth	d											08 14	
Malden Manor	d											08 17	
Motspur Park	d	07 35				08 05						08 20	
Raynes Park 6	d	07 38	07 51		08 13	08 08		08 21				08 24	08 43
Wimbledon 6 ⊖ ⇌	d	07 42	07 55	08 08	08 17	08 12		08 25		08a33	08 38	08 28	08 47
Earlsfield	d	07 46	07 58	08 11	08 20	08 16		08 28			08 41	08 31	08 50
Clapham Junction 10	d	07 50	08 02	08 15	08 24	08 20		08 34			08 45	08 37	08 54
Vauxhall ⊖	d	07 55	08 07	08 20	08 29	08 25	08 32	08 39			08 50	08 42	08 59
London Waterloo 15 ⊖	a	08 04	08 17	08 30	08 39	08 34	08 41	08 47			09 00	08 50	09 07

Table 152

Sundays until 19 September

Hampton Court, Shepperton, Guildford, Dorking and Chessington South - London

		SW	SW	SW	SW	SW		SW	SW	SW	SW	SW	SW	SW	SW	SW		SW	SW	SW	SW	SW	SW	SW	SW
Guildford	d		08 20		08 27						08 50	08 57				09 20			09 27					09 50	09 57
London Road (Guildford)	d		08 24								08 54					09 24								09 54	
Clandon	d		08 29								08 59					09 29								09 59	
Horsley	d		08 33								09 03					09 33								10 03	
Effingham Junction [6]	d		08 36								09 06					09 36								10 06	
Bookham	d		08 39													09 39									
Cobham & Stoke d'Abernon	d										09 10													10 10	
Oxshott	d										09 13													10 13	
Claygate	d										09 16													10 16	
Hinchley Wood	d										09 19													10 19	
Hampton Court	d			08 35						09 05								09 35					10 05		
Thames Ditton	d			08 37						09 07								09 37					10 07		
Surbiton [6]	d			08 43	09 00					09 13	09 24	09 30						09 43	10 00				10 13	10 24	10 30
Berrylands	d			08 45						09 15								09 45					10 15		
Shepperton	d														09 11										
Upper Halliford	d														09 14										
Sunbury	d														09 16										
Kempton Park	d														09 18										
Hampton	d														09 21										
Fulwell	d														09 24										
Strawberry Hill	d							08 49	08 59												09 49	09 59			
Teddington	d							08 55							09 29						09 55				
Hampton Wick	d							08 57							09 31						09 57				
Kingston	a							08 59							09 33						09 59				
	d							09 04							09 34						10 04				
Norbiton	d							09 06							09 36						10 06				
New Malden [6]	d			08 48				09 10		09 18					09 40			09 48			10 10		10 18		
Dorking [4]	d												09 08												
Boxhill & Westhumble	d																								
Leatherhead	d		08 45										09 15			09 45									
Ashtead	d		08 48										09 18			09 48									
Epsom [3]	a		08 53										09 23			09 53									
	d	08 24	08 54										09 24			09 54									
Ewell West	d	08 27	08 57										09 27			09 57									
Stoneleigh	d	08 29	08 59										09 29			09 59									
Worcester Park	d	08 32	09 02										09 32			10 02									
Chessington South	d					08 40								09 10						09 40					
Chessington North	d					08 42								09 12						09 42					
Tolworth	d					08 44								09 14						09 44					
Malden Manor	d					08 47								09 17						09 47					
Motspur Park	d	08 35	09 05			08 50							09 35	09 20		10 05				09 50					
Raynes Park [6]	d	08 38	09 08	08 51		08 54		09 13		09 21			09 38	09 24	09 43	10 08		09 51		09 54	10 13		10 21		
Wimbledon [6]	d	08 42	09 12	08 55	09 08	08 58		09 17		09 25	09a33	09 38	09 42	09 28	09 47	10 12		09 55	10 08	09 58	10 17		10 25	10a33	10 38
Earlsfield	d	08 46	09 16	08 58	09 11	09 01		09 20		09 28		09 41	09 46	09 31	09 50	10 16		09 58	10 11	10 01	10 20		10 28		10 41
Clapham Junction [10]	d	08 50	09 20	09 02	09 15	09 09		09 24		09 33		09 45	09 50	09 36	09 54	10 20		10 02	10 15	10 05	10 24		10 32		10 45
Vauxhall	d	08 55	09 25	09 07	09 20	09 14		09 29	09 32	09 38		09 50	09 55	09 41	09 59	10 25		10 07	10 20	10 10	10 32	10 32	10 37		10 50
London Waterloo [15]	a	09 04	09 34	09 17	09 30	09 20		09 39	09 41	09 47		10 00	10 04	09 50	10 07	10 34		10 17	10 30	10 20	10 39	10 41	10 45		11 00

		SW		SW	SW	SW	SW	SW	SW	SW	SW	SW		SW	SW	SW	SW	SW	SW	SW	SW	SW		SW	SW
Guildford	d					10 20		10 27						10 50	10 57				11 20		11 27				
London Road (Guildford)	d					10 24								10 54					11 24						
Clandon	d					10 29								10 59					11 29						
Horsley	d					10 33								11 03					11 33						
Effingham Junction [6]	d					10 36								11 06					11 36						
Bookham	d					10 39													11 39						
Cobham & Stoke d'Abernon	d													11 10											
Oxshott	d													11 13											
Claygate	d													11 16											
Hinchley Wood	d													11 19											
Hampton Court	d						10 35					11 05								11 35					
Thames Ditton	d						10 37					11 07								11 37					
Surbiton [6]	d						10 43	11 00				11 13		11 24	11 30					11 43	12 00				
Berrylands	d						10 45					11 15								11 45					
Shepperton	d				10 11													11 11							
Upper Halliford	d				10 14													11 14							
Sunbury	d				10 16													11 16							
Kempton Park	d				10 18													11 18							
Hampton	d				10 21													11 21							
Fulwell	d				10 24													11 24							
Strawberry Hill	d									10 49	10 59													11 50	11 59
Teddington	d				10 29					10 55								11 29						11 55	
Hampton Wick	d				10 31					10 57								11 31						11 57	
Kingston	a				10 33					10 59								11 33						11 59	
	d				10 34					11 04								11 34						12 04	
Norbiton	d				10 36					11 06								11 36						12 06	
New Malden [6]	d				10 40		10 48			11 10		11 18						11 40		11 48				12 10	
Dorking [4]	d	10 08														11 08									
Boxhill & Westhumble	d																								
Leatherhead	d	10 15				10 45										11 15			11 45						
Ashtead	d	10 18				10 48										11 18			11 48						
Epsom [3]	a	10 23				10 53										11 23			11 53						
	d	10 24				10 54										11 24			11 54						
Ewell West	d	10 27				10 57										11 27			11 57						
Stoneleigh	d	10 29				10 59										11 29			11 59						
Worcester Park	d	10 32				11 02										11 32			12 02						
Chessington South	d			10 10					10 40								11 10					11 40			
Chessington North	d			10 12					10 42								11 12					11 42			
Tolworth	d			10 14					10 44								11 14					11 44			
Malden Manor	d			10 17					10 47								11 17					11 47			
Motspur Park	d	10 35		10 20		11 05			10 50							11 35	11 20		12 05			11 50			
Raynes Park [6]	d	10 38		10 24	10 43	11 08	10 51		10 54	11 13		11 21				11 38	11 24	11 43	12 08	11 51		11 54		12 13	
Wimbledon [6]	d	10 42		10 28	10 47	11 12	10 55	11 08	10 58	11 17		11 25		11a33	11 38	11 42	11 28	11 47	12 12	11 55	12 08	11 58		12 17	
Earlsfield	d	10 46		10 31	10 50	11 16	10 58	11 11	11 01	11 20		11 28			11 41	11 46	11 31	11 50	12 16	11 58	12 11	12 01		12 20	
Clapham Junction [10]	d	10 50		10 36	10 54	11 20	11 02	11 15	11 05	11 24		11 32			11 45	11 50	11 35	11 54	12 20	12 02	12 15	12 05		12 24	
Vauxhall	d	10 55		10 41	10 59	11 25	11 07	11 20	11 13	11 32	11 32	11 37			11 50	11 55	11 40	11 59	12 25	12 07	12 20	12 13		12 29	12 32
London Waterloo [15]	a	11 03		10 50	11 07	11 34	11 17	11 30	11 20	11 39	11 41	11 47			12 00	12 04	11 50	12 07	12 34	12 17	12 30	12 22		12 39	12 41

Table 152

Sundays until 19 September

Hampton Court, Shepperton, Guildford, Dorking and Chessington South - London

		SW	SW	SW	SW	SW	SW	SW		SW	SW	SW	SW	SW	SW	SW	SW	SW		SW	SW	SW	SW	SW	SW
Guildford	d		11 50	11 57				12 20			12 27					12 50	12 57						13 20		13 27
London Road (Guildford)	d		11 54					12 24								12 54							13 24		
Clandon	d		11 59					12 29								12 59							13 29		
Horsley	d		12 03					12 33								13 03							13 33		
Effingham Junction [6]	d		12 06					12 36								13 06							13 36		
Bookham	d							12 39															13 39		
Cobham & Stoke d'Abernon	d		12 10													13 10									
Oxshott	d		12 13													13 13									
Claygate	d		12 16													13 16									
Hinchley Wood	d		12 19													13 19									
Hampton Court	d	12 05								12 35					13 05									13 35	
Thames Ditton	d	12 07								12 37					13 07									13 37	
Surbiton [6]	d	12 13	12 24	12 30						12 43	13 00				13 13	13 24	13 30							13 43	14 00
Berrylands	d	12 15								12 45					13 15									13 45	
Shepperton	d						12 11														13 11				
Upper Halliford	d						12 14														13 14				
Sunbury	d						12 16														13 16				
Kempton Park	d						12 18														13 18				
Hampton	d						12 21														13 21				
Fulwell	d						12 24														13 24				
Strawberry Hill	d												12 50	12 59								13 19			
Teddington	d						12 29						12 55								13 29				
Hampton Wick	d						12 31						12 57								13 31				
Kingston	a						12 33						12 59								13 33				
	d						12 34						13 04								13 34				
Norbiton	d						12 36						13 06								13 36				
New Malden [6]	d	12 18					12 40			12 48			13 10		13 18						13 40			13 48	
Dorking [4]	d				12 08													13 08							
Boxhill & Westhumble	d																								
Leatherhead	d				12 15			12 45										13 15					13 45		
Ashtead	d				12 18			12 48										13 18					13 48		
Epsom [3]	a				12 23			12 53										13 23					13 53		
	d				12 24			12 54										13 24					13 54		
Ewell West	d				12 27			12 57										13 27					13 57		
Stoneleigh	d				12 29			12 59										13 29					13 59		
Worcester Park	d				12 32			13 02										13 32					14 02		
Chessington South	d					12 10						12 40								13 10					
Chessington North	d					12 12						12 42								13 12					
Tolworth	d					12 14						12 44								13 14					
Malden Manor	d					12 17						12 47								13 17					
Motspur Park	d				12 35	12 20		13 05				12 50						13 35		13 20			14 05		
Raynes Park [6]	d	12 21			12 38	12 24	12 43	13 08		12 51		12 54	13 13		13 21			13 38		13 24	13 43		14 08	13 51	
Wimbledon [6]	d	12 25	12 31	12 38	12 42	12 28	12 47	13 12		12 55	13 08	12 58	13 17		13 25	13 31	13 38	13 42		13 28	13 47		14 12	13 55	14 08
Earlsfield	d	12 28	12 35	12 41	12 46	12 31	12 50	13 16		12 58	13 11	13 01	13 20		13 28	13 35	13 41	13 46		13 31	13 50		14 16	13 58	14 11
Clapham Junction [10]	d	12 32	12 39	12 45	12 50	12 35	12 54	13 20		13 02	13 15	13 05	13 24		13 32	13 39	13 45	13 50		13 35	13 54		14 20	14 02	14 15
Vauxhall	d	12 37	12 44	12 50	12 55	12 40	12 59	13 25		13 07	13 20	13 10	13 29	13 32	13 37	13 44	13 50	13 55		13 40	13 59	13 52	14 25	14 07	14 20
London Waterloo [15]	a	12 47	12 53	13 00	13 04	12 50	13 07	13 34		13 17	13 30	13 20	13 39	13 41	13 47	13 53	14 00	14 04		13 50	14 07	14 00	14 34	14 17	14 30

		SW	SW	SW		SW	SW	SW	SW	SW	SW	SW	SW	SW		SW	SW	SW	SW	SW	SW	SW	SW	SW	
Guildford	d						13 50	13 57					14 20			14 27					14 50	14 57			
London Road (Guildford)	d						13 54						14 24								14 54				
Clandon	d						13 59						14 29								14 59				
Horsley	d						14 03						14 33								15 03				
Effingham Junction [6]	d						14 06						14 36								15 06				
Bookham	d												14 39												
Cobham & Stoke d'Abernon	d						14 10														15 10				
Oxshott	d						14 13														15 13				
Claygate	d						14 16														15 16				
Hinchley Wood	d						14 19														15 19				
Hampton Court	d					14 05								14 35						15 05					
Thames Ditton	d					14 07								14 37						15 07					
Surbiton [6]	d					14 13	14 24	14 30						14 43		15 00				15 13	15 24	15 30			
Berrylands	d					14 15								14 45						15 15					
Shepperton	d										14 11														
Upper Halliford	d										14 14														
Sunbury	d										14 16														
Kempton Park	d										14 18														
Hampton	d										14 21														
Fulwell	d										14 24														
Strawberry Hill	d		13 49	13 59								14 19						14 49	14 59						
Teddington	d		13 55								14 29							14 55							
Hampton Wick	d		13 57								14 31							14 57							
Kingston	a		13 59								14 33							14 59							
	d		14 04								14 34							15 04							
Norbiton	d		14 06								14 36							15 06							
New Malden [6]	d		14 10			14 18					14 40			14 48				15 10		15 18					
Dorking [4]	d								14 08														15 08		
Boxhill & Westhumble	d																								
Leatherhead	d								14 15				14 45										15 15		
Ashtead	d								14 18				14 48										15 18		
Epsom [3]	a								14 23				14 53										15 23		
	d								14 24				14 54										15 24		
Ewell West	d								14 27				14 57										15 27		
Stoneleigh	d								14 29				14 59										15 29		
Worcester Park	d								14 32				15 02										15 32		
Chessington South	d	13 40								14 10							14 40							15 10	
Chessington North	d	13 42								14 12							14 42							15 12	
Tolworth	d	13 44								14 14							14 44							15 14	
Malden Manor	d	13 47								14 17							14 47							15 17	
Motspur Park	d	13 50							14 35	14 20			15 05				14 50						15 35	15 20	
Raynes Park [6]	d	13 54	14 13			14 21			14 38	14 24	14 43		15 08	14 51			14 54	15 13		15 21			15 38	15 24	
Wimbledon [6]	d	13 58	14 17			14 25	14 31	14 38	14 42	14 28	14 47		15 12	14 55		15 08	14 58	15 17		15 25	15 31	15 38	15 42	15 28	
Earlsfield	d	14 01	14 20			14 28	14 35	14 41	14 46	14 31	14 50		15 16	14 58		15 11	15 01	15 20		15 28	15 35	15 41	15 46	15 31	
Clapham Junction [10]	d	14 05	14 24			14 32	14 39	14 45	14 50	14 35	14 54		15 20	15 02		15 15	15 05	15 24		15 32	15 39	15 45	15 50	15 35	
Vauxhall	d	14 10	14 29	14 32		14 37	14 44	14 50	14 55	14 40	14 59	14 52	15 25	15 07		15 20	15 10	15 29	15 32	15 37	15 44	15 50	15 55	15 40	
London Waterloo [15]	a	14 20	14 34	14 41		14 42	14 48	14 55	14 59	14 45	15 04	15 00	15 29	15 12		15 25	15 15	15 34	15 36	15 42	15 48	15 55	15 59	15 45	

Table 152

Sundays
until 19 September

Hampton Court, Shepperton, Guildford, Dorking and Chessington South - London

Station		SW	SW	SW	SW	SW	SW	SW	SW	SW		SW	SW	SW	SW	SW	SW	SW	SW	SW		SW	SW	SW	SW
Guildford	d			15 20		15 27						15 50	15 57					16 20		16 27					
London Road (Guildford)	d			15 24								15 54						16 24							
Clandon	d			15 29								15 59						16 29							
Horsley	d			15 33								16 03						16 33							
Effingham Junction 6	d			15 36								16 06						16 36							
Bookham	d			15 39														16 39							
Cobham & Stoke d'Abernon	d											16 10													
Oxshott	d											16 13													
Claygate	d											16 16													
Hinchley Wood	d											16 19													
Hampton Court	d				15 35					16 05									16 35						17 05
Thames Ditton	d				15 37					16 07									16 37						17 07
Surbiton 6	d				15 43	16 00				16 13		16 24	16 30						16 43	17 00					17 13
Berrylands	d				15 45					16 15									16 45						17 15
Shepperton	d	15 11														16 11									
Upper Halliford	d	15 14														16 14									
Sunbury	d	15 16														16 16									
Kempton Park	d	15 18														16 18									
Hampton	d	15 21														16 21									
Fulwell	d	15 24														16 24									
Strawberry Hill	d		15 19					15 49	15 59								16 19						16 49	16 59	
Teddington	d	15 29						15 55								16 29							16 55		
Hampton Wick	d	15 31						15 57								16 31							16 57		
Kingston	a	15 33						15 59								16 33							16 59		
	d	15 34						16 04								16 34							17 04		
Norbiton	d	15 36						16 06								16 36							17 06		
New Malden 6	d	15 40			15 48			16 10		16 18						16 40			16 48				17 10		17 18
Dorking 4	d													16 08											
Boxhill & Westhumble	d																								
Leatherhead	d			15 45										16 15				16 45							
Ashtead	d			15 48										16 18				16 48							
Epsom 3	a			15 53										16 23				16 53							
	d			15 54										16 24				16 54							
Ewell West	d			15 57										16 27				16 57							
Stoneleigh	d			15 59										16 29				16 59							
Worcester Park	d			16 02										16 32				17 02							
Chessington South	d						15 40								16 10							16 40			
Chessington North	d						15 42								16 12							16 42			
Tolworth	d						15 44								16 14							16 44			
Malden Manor	d						15 47								16 17							16 47			
Motspur Park	d			16 05			15 50							16 35	16 20			17 05				16 50			
Raynes Park 6	d	15 43		16 08	15 51		15 54	16 13		16 21				16 38	16 24	16 43		17 08	16 51			16 54	17 13		17 21
Wimbledon 6 ⊖	d	15 47		16 12	15 55	16 08	15 58	16 17		16 25		16 31	16 38	16 42	16 28	16 47		17 12	16 55	17 08		16 58	17 17		17 25
Earlsfield	d	15 50		16 16	15 58	16 11	16 01	16 20		16 28		16 35	16 41	16 46	16 31	16 50		17 16	16 58	17 11		17 01	17 20		17 28
Clapham Junction 10	d	15 54		16 20	16 02	16 15	16 05	16 24		16 32		16 39	16 45	16 50	16 35	16 54		17 20	17 02	17 15		17 05	17 24		17 32
Vauxhall ⊖	d	15 59	15 52	16 25	16 07	16 20	16 10	16 29	16 32	16 37		16 44	16 50	16 55	16 40	16 59	16 52	17 25	17 07	17 20		17 10	17 29	17 32	17 37
London Waterloo 15 ⊖	a	16 04	16 00	16 29	16 12	16 25	16 15	16 34	16 36	16 42		16 48	16 55	16 59	16 45	17 04	17 00	17 29	17 12	17 25		17 15	17 34	17 36	17 42

Station		SW	SW	SW	SW	SW		SW	SW	SW	SW	SW	SW	SW	SW	SW		SW	SW	SW	SW	SW	SW	SW	SW
Guildford	d	16 50	16 57						17 20		17 27					17 50		17 57					18 20		18 27
London Road (Guildford)	d	16 54							17 24							17 54							18 24		
Clandon	d	16 59							17 29							17 59							18 29		
Horsley	d	17 03							17 33							18 03							18 33		
Effingham Junction 6	d	17 06							17 36							18 06							18 36		
Bookham	d								17 39														18 39		
Cobham & Stoke d'Abernon	d	17 10														18 10									
Oxshott	d	17 13														18 13									
Claygate	d	17 16														18 16									
Hinchley Wood	d	17 19														18 19									
Hampton Court	d									17 35					18 05									18 35	
Thames Ditton	d									17 37					18 07									18 37	
Surbiton 6	d	17 24	17 30							17 43	18 00				18 13	18 24		18 30						18 43	19 00
Berrylands	d									17 45					18 15									18 45	
Shepperton	d					17 11															18 11				
Upper Halliford	d					17 14															18 14				
Sunbury	d					17 16															18 16				
Kempton Park	d					17 18															18 18				
Hampton	d					17 21															18 21				
Fulwell	d					17 24															18 24				
Strawberry Hill	d							17 19					17 49	17 59								18 19			
Teddington	d					17 29							17 55								18 29				
Hampton Wick	d					17 31							17 57								18 31				
Kingston	a					17 33							17 59								18 33				
	d					17 34							18 04								18 34				
Norbiton	d					17 36							18 06								18 36				
New Malden 6	d					17 40				17 48			18 10		18 18						18 40			18 48	
Dorking 4	d			17 08															18 08						
Boxhill & Westhumble	d																								
Leatherhead	d			17 15					17 45										18 15				18 45		
Ashtead	d			17 18					17 48										18 18				18 48		
Epsom 3	a			17 23					17 53										18 23				18 53		
	d			17 24					17 54										18 24				18 54		
Ewell West	d			17 27					17 57										18 27				18 57		
Stoneleigh	d			17 29					17 59										18 29				18 59		
Worcester Park	d			17 32					18 02										18 32				19 02		
Chessington South	d				17 10							17 40								18 10					
Chessington North	d				17 12							17 42								18 12					
Tolworth	d				17 14							17 44								18 14					
Malden Manor	d				17 17							17 47								18 17					
Motspur Park	d			17 35	17 20				18 05			17 50							18 35	18 20			19 05		
Raynes Park 6	d			17 38	17 24	17 43			18 08	17 51		17 54	18 13		18 21				18 38	18 24	18 43		19 08	18 51	
Wimbledon 6 ⊖	d	17 31	17 38	17 42	17 28	17 47			18 12	17 55	18 08	17 58	18 17		18 25	18 31		18 38	18 42	18 28	18 47		19 12	18 55	19 08
Earlsfield	d	17 35	17 41	17 46	17 31	17 50			18 16	17 58	18 11	18 01	18 20		18 28	18 35		18 41	18 46	18 31	18 50		19 16	18 58	19 11
Clapham Junction 10	d	17 39	17 45	17 50	17 35	17 54			18 20	18 02	18 15	18 05	18 24		18 32	18 39		18 45	18 50	18 35	18 54		19 20	19 02	19 15
Vauxhall ⊖	d	17 44	17 50	17 55	17 40	17 59		17 52	18 25	18 07	18 20	18 10	18 29	18 32	18 37	18 44		18 50	18 55	18 40	18 59	18 52	19 25	19 07	19 20
London Waterloo 15 ⊖	a	17 48	17 55	17 59	17 45	18 04		18 00	18 29	18 12	18 25	18 15	18 34	18 36	18 42	18 48		18 55	18 59	18 45	19 04	19 00	19 29	19 12	19 25

Table 152

Sundays
until 19 September

Hampton Court, Shepperton, Guildford, Dorking and Chessington South - London

Station		SW		SW	SW	SW	SW	SW	SW	SW	SW	SW		SW	SW	SW	SW	SW	SW	SW	SW	SW		SW	SW
Guildford	d						18 50	18 57						19 20		19 27					19 50	19 57			
London Road (Guildford)	d						18 54							19 24							19 54				
Clandon	d						18 59							19 29							19 59				
Horsley	d						19 03							19 33							20 03				
Effingham Junction 6	d						19 06							19 36							20 06				
Bookham	d													19 39											
Cobham & Stoke d'Abernon	d						19 10														20 10				
Oxshott	d						19 13														20 13				
Claygate	d						19 16														20 16				
Hinchley Wood	d						19 19														20 19				
Hampton Court	d					19 05									19 35					20 05					
Thames Ditton	d					19 07									19 37					20 07					
Surbiton 6	d					19 13	19 24	19 30							19 43	20 00				20 13	20 24	20 30			
Berrylands	d					19 15									19 45					20 15					
Shepperton	d										19 11														
Upper Halliford	d										19 14														
Sunbury	d										19 16														
Kempton Park	d										19 18														
Hampton	d										19 21														
Fulwell	d										19 24														
Strawberry Hill	d			18 49	18 59							19 19						19 49	19 59						
Teddington	d			18 55							19 29							19 55							
Hampton Wick	d			18 57							19 31							19 57							
Kingston	a			18 59							19 33							19 59							
	d			19 04							19 34							20 04							
Norbiton	d			19 06							19 36							20 06							
New Malden 6	d			19 10		19 18					19 40				19 48			20 10		20 18					
Dorking 4	d								19 08															20 08	
Boxhill & Westhumble	d																								
Leatherhead	d								19 15					19 45										20 15	
Ashtead	d								19 18					19 48										20 18	
Epsom 3	a								19 23					19 53										20 23	
	d								19 24					19 54										20 24	
Ewell West	d								19 27					19 57										20 27	
Stoneleigh	d								19 29					19 59										20 29	
Worcester Park	d								19 32					20 02										20 32	
Chessington South	d	18 40								19 10							19 40								20 10
Chessington North	d	18 42								19 12							19 42								20 12
Tolworth	d	18 44								19 14							19 44								20 14
Malden Manor	d	18 47								19 17							19 47								20 17
Motspur Park	d	18 50							19 35	19 20				20 05			19 50							20 35	20 20
Raynes Park 6	d	18 54		19 13		19 21			19 38	19 24	19 43			20 08	19 51		19 54	20 13		20 21				20 38	20 24
Wimbledon 6 ⊖	d	18 58		19 17		19 25	19 31	19 38	19 42	19 28	19 47			20 12	19 55	20 08	19 58	20 17		20 25	20 31	20 38		20 42	20 28
Earlsfield	d	19 01		19 20		19 28	19 35	19 41	19 46	19 31	19 50			20 16	19 58	20 11	20 01	20 20		20 28	20 35	20 41		20 46	20 31
Clapham Junction 10	d	19 05		19 24		19 32	19 39	19 45	19 50	19 35	19 54			20 20	20 02	20 15	20 05	20 24		20 32	20 39	20 45		20 50	20 35
Vauxhall ⊖	d	19 10		19 29	19 32	19 37	19 44	19 50	19 55	19 40	19 59	19 52		20 25	20 07	20 20	20 10	20 29	20 32	20 37	20 44	20 50		20 55	20 40
London Waterloo 15 ⊖	a	19 15		19 34	19 36	19 42	19 48	19 55	19 59	19 45	20 04	20 00		20 29	20 12	20 25	20 15	20 34	20 36	20 42	20 48	20 55		21 00	20 45

Station		SW	SW	SW	SW	SW	SW	SW		SW	SW	SW	SW	SW	SW	SW	SW	SW		SW	SW	SW	SW	SW	SW
Guildford	d			20 20		20 27					20 50	20 57					21 20			21 27				21 50	21 57
London Road (Guildford)	d			20 24							20 54						21 24							21 54	
Clandon	d			20 29							20 59						21 29							21 59	
Horsley	d			20 33							21 03						21 33							22 03	
Effingham Junction 6	d			20 36							21 06						21 36							22 06	
Bookham	d			20 39													21 39								
Cobham & Stoke d'Abernon	d										21 10													22 10	
Oxshott	d										21 13													22 13	
Claygate	d										21 16													22 16	
Hinchley Wood	d										21 19													22 19	
Hampton Court	d				20 35					21 05								21 35					22 05		
Thames Ditton	d				20 37					21 07								21 37					22 07		
Surbiton 6	d				20 43	21 00				21 13	21 24	21 30						21 43		22 00			22 13	22 24	22 30
Berrylands	d				20 45					21 15								21 45					22 15		
Shepperton	d	20 11													21 11										
Upper Halliford	d	20 14													21 14										
Sunbury	d	20 16													21 16										
Kempton Park	d	20 18													21 18										
Hampton	d	20 21													21 21										
Fulwell	d	20 24													21 24										
Strawberry Hill	d		20 19				20 49	20 59								21 19					21 49	21 59			
Teddington	d	20 29					20 55								21 29						21 55				
Hampton Wick	d	20 31					20 57								21 31						21 57				
Kingston	a	20 33					20 59								21 33						21 59				
	d	20 34					21 04								21 34						22 04				
Norbiton	d	20 36					21 06								21 36						22 06				
New Malden 6	d	20 40			20 48		21 10			21 18					21 40			21 48			22 10		22 18		
Dorking 4	d												21 08												
Boxhill & Westhumble	d																								
Leatherhead	d			20 45									21 15				21 45								
Ashtead	d			20 48									21 18				21 48								
Epsom 3	a			20 53									21 23				21 53								
	d			20 54									21 24				21 54								
Ewell West	d			20 57									21 27				21 57								
Stoneleigh	d			20 59									21 29				21 59								
Worcester Park	d			21 02									21 32				22 02								
Chessington South	d													21 10											
Chessington North	d													21 12											
Tolworth	d													21 14											
Malden Manor	d													21 17											
Motspur Park	d			21 05									21 35	21 20			22 05								
Raynes Park 6	d	20 43		21 08	20 51		21 13			21 21			21 38	21 24	21 43		22 08	21 51			22 13		22 21		
Wimbledon 6 ⊖	d	20 47		21 12	20 55	21 08	21 17			21 25	21 31	21 38	21 42	21 28	21 47		22 12	21 55		22 08	22 17		22 25	22 31	22 38
Earlsfield	d	20 50		21 16	20 58	21 11	21 20			21 28	21 35	21 41	21 46	21 31	21 50		22 16	21 58		22 11	22 20		22 28	22 35	22 41
Clapham Junction 10	d	20 54		21 20	21 02	21 15	21 24			21 32	21 39	21 45	21 50	21 35	21 54		22 20	22 02		22 15	22 24		22 32	22 39	22 45
Vauxhall ⊖	d	20 59	20 52	21 25	21 07	21 20	21 29	21 32		21 37	21 44	21 50	21 55	21 40	21 59	21 52	22 25	22 07		22 20	22 29	22 32	22 37	22 44	22 50
London Waterloo 15 ⊖	a	21 04	21 00	21 29	21 13	21 25	21 35	21 36		21 42	21 48	21 55	22 00	21 45	22 04	22 00	22 29	22 12		22 25	22 35	22 36	22 42	22 48	22 55

Table 152

Sundays until 19 September

Hampton Court, Shepperton, Guildford, Dorking and Chessington South - London

		SW	SW	SW	SW	SW	SW	SW	SW	SW	SW	SW	SW	SW	SW	SW	SW	SW 1	SW
Guildford	d					22 20	22 27				22 50	22 57							
London Road (Guildford)	d					22 24					22 54								
Clandon	d					22 29					22 59								
Horsley	d					22 33					23 03								
Effingham Junction 6	d					22 36					23 06								
Bookham	d					22 39													
Cobham & Stoke d'Abernon	d										23 10								
Oxshott	d										23 13								
Claygate	d										23 16								
Hinchley Wood	d										23 19								
Hampton Court	d									23 05									23 45
Thames Ditton	d									23 07									23 47
Surbiton 6	d						23 00			23 13	23 24	23 30						23 46	23 53
Berrylands	d									23 15									23 55
Shepperton	d			22 11											23 11				
Upper Halliford	d			22 14											23 14				
Sunbury	d			22 16											23 16				
Kempton Park	d			22 18											23 18				
Hampton	d			22 21											23 21				
Fulwell	d			22 24											23 24				
Strawberry Hill	d				22 19			22 49	22 59							23 19			
Teddington	d			22 29				22 55							23 29				
Hampton Wick	d			22 31				22 57							23 31				
Kingston	a			22 33				22 59							23 33				
	d			22 34				23 04							23 34				
Norbiton	d			22 36				23 06							23 36				
New Malden 6	d			22 40				23 10		23 18					23 40				23 58
Dorking 4	d	22 08											23 08						
Boxhill & Westhumble	d																		
Leatherhead	d	22 15				22 45							23 15						
Ashtead	d	22 18				22 48							23 18						
Epsom 3	a	22 23				22 53							23 23						
	d	22 24				22 54							23 24						
Ewell West	d	22 27				22 57							23 27						
Stoneleigh	d	22 29				22 59							23 29						
Worcester Park	d	22 32				23 02							23 32						
Chessington South	d		22 10											23 10			23 40		
Chessington North	d		22 12											23 12			23 42		
Tolworth	d		22 14											23 14			23 44		
Malden Manor	d		22 17											23 17			23 47		
Motspur Park	d	22 35	22 20			23 05							23 35	23 20			23 50		
Raynes Park 6	d	22 38	22 24	22 43		23 08		23 13		23 21			23 38	23 24	23 43		23 54		00 01
Wimbledon 6 ⊖ ⛴	d	22 42	22 28	22 47		23 12	23 08	23 17		23 25	23 31	23 38	23 42	23 28	23 47		23a59	23 53	00a04
Earlsfield	d	22 46	22 31	22 50		23 16	23 11	23 20		23 28	23 35	23 41	23 46	23 31	23 50				
Clapham Junction 10	d	22 50	22 35	22 54		23 20	23 15	23 24		23 32	23 39	23 45	23 50	23 35	23 54			00 01	
Vauxhall ⊖	d	22 55	22 40	22 59	22 52	23 25	23 20	23 29	23 32	23 37	23 44	23 50	23 55	23 40	23 59	23 52			
London Waterloo 15 ⊖	a	23 00	22 45	23 04	23 00	23 29	23 25	23 35	23 36	23 42	23 48	23 55	23 59	23 45	00 04	23 59		00 10	

Table 152

Sundays from 26 September

Hampton Court, Shepperton, Guildford, Dorking and Chessington South - London

		SW	SW	SW 1	SW	SW	SW	SW	SW	SW	SW	SW	SW	SW	SW	SW	SW	SW	SW	SW	SW	SW	SW
Guildford	d				23p08						06 57				07 27					07 48	07 57		
London Road (Guildford)	d				23p12															07 52			
Clandon	d				23p17															07 57			
Horsley	d				23p21															08 01			
Effingham Junction 6	d				23p24															08 04			
Bookham	d																						
Cobham & Stoke d'Abernon	d				23p28															08 08			
Oxshott	d				23p31															08 11			
Claygate	d				23p34															08 14			
Hinchley Wood	d				23p37															08 17			
Hampton Court	d		23p24											07 35					08 05				
Thames Ditton	d		23p26											07 37					08 07				
Surbiton 6	d		23p32	23p38	23p42					07 00	07 30			07 43	08 00				08 13	08 24	08 30		
Berrylands	d		23p34											07 45					08 15				
Shepperton	d	23p11										07 11											08 11
Upper Halliford	d	23p14										07 14											08 14
Sunbury	d	23p16										07 16											08 16
Kempton Park	d	23p18										07 18											08 18
Hampton	d	23p21										07 21											08 21
Fulwell	d	23p24										07 24											08 24
Strawberry Hill	d					23p37	23p38	06 49	06 59							07 49		07 59					
Teddington	d	23p29				23p41		06 55				07 29				07 55							08 29
Hampton Wick	d	23p31				23p44		06 57				07 31				07 57							08 31
Kingston	a	23p33				23p46		06 59				07 33				07 59							08 33
	d	23p34				23p49		07 04				07 34				08 04							08 34
Norbiton	d	23p36				23p51		07 06				07 36				08 06							08 36
New Malden 6	d	23p41	23p37			23p55		07 10				07 40		07 48		08 10			08 18				08 40
Dorking 4	d																						
Boxhill & Westhumble	d																						
Leatherhead	d																						
Ashtead	d																						
Epsom 3	a																						
	d												07 24				07 54						
Ewell West	d												07 27				07 57						
Stoneleigh	d												07 29				07 59						
Worcester Park	d												07 32				08 02						
Chessington South	d																					08 10	
Chessington North	d																					08 12	
Tolworth	d																					08 14	
Malden Manor	d																					08 17	
Motspur Park	d												07 35				08 05					08 20	
Raynes Park 6	d	23p43	23p40			23p58		07 13				07 43	07 38	07 51		08 13	08 08		08 21			08 24	08 43
Wimbledon 6 ⊖ ⛴	d	23p52	23p44		23p58	00 07		07 19		07 08	07 38	07 47	07 42	07 55	08 08	08 17	08 12		08 25	08a33	08 38	08 28	08 47
Earlsfield	d	23p55	23p47		00 01	00 10		07 22		07 11	07 41	07 50	07 46	07 58	08 11	08 20	08 16		08 28		08 41	08 31	08 50
Clapham Junction 10	d	00 04	23p51	23p56	00 07	00 14		07 26		07 15	07 45	07 54	07 50	08 02	08 15	08 24	08 20		08 34		08 45	08 37	08 54
Vauxhall ⊖	d	00 09	23p56		00 12	00 19	00 12	07 31	07 32	07 20	07 50	08 02	07 55	08 07	08 20	08 29	08 25	08 32	08 39		08 50	08 42	08 59
London Waterloo 15 ⊖	a	00 13	00 02	00 04	00 16	00 24	00 16	07 41	07 41	07 30	08 00	08 07	08 04	08 17	08 30	08 39	08 34	08 41	08 47		09 00	08 50	09 07

Table 152

Sundays from 26 September

Hampton Court, Shepperton, Guildford, Dorking and Chessington South - London

Station		SW	SW	SW	SW	SW		SW	SW	SW	SW	SW	SW	SW	SW	SW		SW	SW	SW	SW	SW	SW	SW	SW
Guildford	d		08 18		08 27						08 48	08 57				09 18			09 27					09 48	09 57
London Road (Guildford)	d		08 22								08 52					09 22								09 52	
Clandon	d		08 27								08 57					09 27								09 57	
Horsley	d		08 31								09 01					09 31								10 01	
Effingham Junction	d		08 34								09 04					09 34								10 04	
Bookham	d		08 37													09 37									
Cobham & Stoke d'Abernon	d										09 08													10 08	
Oxshott	d										09 11													10 11	
Claygate	d										09 14													10 14	
Hinchley Wood	d										09 17													10 17	
Hampton Court	d			08 35						09 05								09 35					10 05		
Thames Ditton	d			08 37						09 07								09 37					10 07		
Surbiton	d			08 43	09 00					09 13	09 24	09 30						09 43	10 00				10 13	10 24	10 30
Berrylands	d			08 45						09 15								09 45					10 15		
Shepperton	d														09 11										
Upper Halliford	d														09 14										
Sunbury	d														09 16										
Kempton Park	d														09 18										
Hampton	d														09 21										
Fulwell	d														09 24										
Strawberry Hill	d							08 49	08 59												09 49	09 59			
Teddington	d							08 55							09 29						09 55				
Hampton Wick	d							08 57							09 31						09 57				
Kingston	a							08 59							09 33						09 59				
	d							09 04							09 34						10 04				
Norbiton	d							09 06							09 36						10 06				
New Malden	d			08 48				09 10		09 18					09 40			09 48			10 10		10 18		
Dorking	d												09 08												
Boxhill & Westhumble	d																								
Leatherhead	d		08 45										09 15			09 45									
Ashtead	d		08 48										09 18			09 48									
Epsom	a		08 53										09 23			09 53									
	d	08 24	08 54										09 24			09 54									
Ewell West	d	08 27	08 57										09 27			09 57									
Stoneleigh	d	08 29	08 59										09 29			09 59									
Worcester Park	d	08 32	09 02										09 32			10 02									
Chessington South	d					08 40								09 10						09 40					
Chessington North	d					08 42								09 12						09 42					
Tolworth	d					08 44								09 14						09 44					
Malden Manor	d					08 47								09 17						09 47					
Motspur Park	d	08 35	09 05			08 50							09 35	09 20		10 05				09 50					
Raynes Park	d	08 38	09 08	08 51		08 54		09 13		09 21			09 38	09 24	09 43	10 08		09 51		09 54	10 13		10 21		
Wimbledon ⊖	d	08 42	09 12	08 55	09 08	08 58		09 17		09 25	09a33	09 38	09 42	09 28	09 47	10 12		09 55	10 08	09 58	10 17		10 25	10a33	10 38
Earlsfield	d	08 46	09 16	08 58	09 11	09 01		09 20		09 28		09 41	09 46	09 31	09 50	10 16		09 58	10 11	10 01	10 20		10 28		10 41
Clapham Junction	d	08 50	09 20	09 02	09 15	09 09		09 24		09 33		09 45	09 50	09 36	09 54	10 20		10 02	10 15	10 05	10 24		10 32		10 45
Vauxhall ⊖	d	08 55	09 25	09 07	09 20	09 14		09 29	09 32	09 38		09 50	09 55	09 41	09 59	10 25		10 07	10 20	10 10	10 32	10 32	10 37		10 50
London Waterloo ⊖	a	09 04	09 34	09 17	09 30	09 20		09 39	09 41	09 47		10 00	10 04	09 50	10 07	10 34		10 17	10 30	10 20	10 39	10 41	10 45		11 00

Station		SW		SW	SW	SW	SW	SW	SW	SW	SW	SW		SW	SW	SW	SW	SW	SW	SW	SW	SW		SW	SW
Guildford	d					10 18		10 27						10 48	10 57				11 18		11 27				
London Road (Guildford)	d					10 22								10 52					11 22						
Clandon	d					10 27								10 57					11 27						
Horsley	d					10 31								11 01					11 31						
Effingham Junction	d					10 34								11 04					11 34						
Bookham	d					10 37													11 37						
Cobham & Stoke d'Abernon	d													11 08											
Oxshott	d													11 11											
Claygate	d													11 14											
Hinchley Wood	d													11 17											
Hampton Court	d						10 35					11 05								11 35					
Thames Ditton	d						10 37					11 07								11 37					
Surbiton	d						10 43	11 00				11 13		11 24	11 30					11 43	12 00				
Berrylands	d						10 45					11 15								11 45					
Shepperton	d				10 11													11 11							
Upper Halliford	d				10 14													11 14							
Sunbury	d				10 16													11 16							
Kempton Park	d				10 18													11 18							
Hampton	d				10 21													11 21							
Fulwell	d				10 24													11 24							
Strawberry Hill	d									10 49	10 59													11 50	11 59
Teddington	d				10 29					10 55								11 29						11 55	
Hampton Wick	d				10 31					10 57								11 31						11 57	
Kingston	a				10 33					10 59								11 33						11 59	
	d				10 34					11 04								11 34						12 04	
Norbiton	d				10 36					11 06								11 36						12 06	
New Malden	d				10 40		10 48			11 10		11 18						11 40		11 48				12 10	
Dorking	d	10 08														11 08									
Boxhill & Westhumble	d																								
Leatherhead	d	10 15				10 45										11 15			11 45						
Ashtead	d	10 18				10 48										11 18			11 48						
Epsom	a	10 23				10 53										11 23			11 53						
	d	10 24				10 54										11 24			11 54						
Ewell West	d	10 27				10 57										11 27			11 57						
Stoneleigh	d	10 29				10 59										11 29			11 59						
Worcester Park	d	10 32				11 02										11 32			12 02						
Chessington South	d			10 10					10 40								11 10					11 40			
Chessington North	d			10 12					10 42								11 12					11 42			
Tolworth	d			10 14					10 44								11 14					11 44			
Malden Manor	d			10 17					10 47								11 17					11 47			
Motspur Park	d	10 35		10 20		11 05			10 50							11 35	11 20		12 05			11 50			
Raynes Park	d	10 38		10 24	10 43	11 08	10 51		10 54	11 13		11 21				11 38	11 24	11 43	12 08	11 51		11 54		12 13	
Wimbledon ⊖	d	10 42		10 28	10 47	11 12	10 55	11 08	10 58	11 17		11 25		11a33	11 38	11 42	11 28	11 47	12 12	11 55	12 08	11 58		12 17	
Earlsfield	d	10 46		10 31	10 50	11 16	10 58	11 11	11 01	11 20		11 28			11 41	11 46	11 31	11 50	12 16	11 58	12 11	12 01		12 20	
Clapham Junction	d	10 50		10 36	10 54	11 20	11 02	11 15	11 05	11 24		11 32			11 45	11 50	11 35	11 54	12 20	12 02	12 15	12 05		12 24	
Vauxhall ⊖	d	10 55		10 41	10 59	11 25	11 07	11 20	11 13	11 32	11 32	11 37			11 50	11 55	11 40	11 59	12 25	12 07	12 20	12 13		12 29	12 32
London Waterloo ⊖	a	11 03		10 50	11 07	11 34	11 17	11 30	11 20	11 39	11 41	11 47			12 00	12 04	11 50	12 07	12 34	12 17	12 30	12 22		12 39	12 41

Table 152

Sundays from 26 September

Hampton Court, Shepperton, Guildford, Dorking and Chessington South - London

Station		SW	SW	SW	SW	SW	SW	SW		SW	SW	SW	SW	SW	SW	SW	SW	SW		SW	SW	SW	SW	SW	SW
Guildford	d		11 48	11 57				12 18			12 27					12 48	12 57						13 18		13 27
London Road (Guildford)	d		11 52					12 22								12 52							13 22		
Clandon	d		11 57					12 27								12 57							13 27		
Horsley	d		12 01					12 31								13 01							13 31		
Effingham Junction	d		12 04					12 34								13 04							13 34		
Bookham	d							12 37															13 37		
Cobham & Stoke d'Abernon	d		12 08													13 08									
Oxshott	d		12 11													13 11									
Claygate	d		12 14													13 14									
Hinchley Wood	d		12 17													13 17									
Hampton Court	d	12 05								12 35					13 05									13 35	
Thames Ditton	d	12 07								12 37					13 07									13 37	
Surbiton	d	12 13	12 24	12 30						12 43	13 00				13 13	13 24	13 30							13 43	14 00
Berrylands	d	12 15								12 45					13 15									13 45	
Shepperton	d						12 11														13 11				
Upper Halliford	d						12 14														13 14				
Sunbury	d						12 16														13 16				
Kempton Park	d						12 18														13 18				
Hampton	d						12 21														13 21				
Fulwell	d						12 24														13 24				
Strawberry Hill	d												12 50	12 59								13 19			
Teddington	d						12 29						12 55								13 29				
Hampton Wick	d						12 31						12 57								13 31				
Kingston	a						12 33						12 59								13 33				
	d						12 34						13 04								13 34				
Norbiton	d						12 36						13 06								13 36				
New Malden	d	12 18					12 40			12 48			13 10		13 18						13 40			13 48	
Dorking	d				12 08													13 08							
Boxhill & Westhumble	d																								
Leatherhead	d				12 15			12 45										13 15					13 45		
Ashtead	d				12 18			12 48										13 18					13 48		
Epsom	a				12 23			12 53										13 23					13 53		
	d				12 24			12 54										13 24					13 54		
Ewell West	d				12 27			12 57										13 27					13 57		
Stoneleigh	d				12 29			12 59										13 29					13 59		
Worcester Park	d				12 32			13 02										13 32					14 02		
Chessington South	d					12 10						12 40								13 10					
Chessington North	d					12 12						12 42								13 12					
Tolworth	d					12 14						12 44								13 14					
Malden Manor	d					12 17						12 47								13 17					
Motspur Park	d				12 35	12 20		13 05				12 50						13 35		13 20			14 05		
Raynes Park	d	12 21			12 38	12 24	12 43	13 08		12 51		12 54	13 13		13 21			13 38		13 24	13 43		14 08	13 51	
Wimbledon ⊖	d	12 25	12 31	12 38	12 42	12 28	12 47	13 12		12 55	13 08	12 58	13 17		13 25	13 31	13 38	13 42		13 28	13 47		14 12	13 55	14 08
Earlsfield	d	12 28	12 35	12 41	12 46	12 31	12 50	13 16		12 58	13 11	13 01	13 20		13 28	13 35	13 41	13 46		13 31	13 50		14 16	13 58	14 11
Clapham Junction	d	12 32	12 39	12 45	12 50	12 35	12 54	13 20		13 02	13 15	13 05	13 24		13 32	13 39	13 45	13 50		13 35	13 54		14 20	14 02	14 15
Vauxhall ⊖	d	12 37	12 44	12 50	12 55	12 40	12 59	13 25		13 07	13 20	13 10	13 29	13 32	13 37	13 44	13 50	13 55		13 40	13 59	13 52	14 25	14 07	14 20
London Waterloo ⊖	a	12 47	12 53	13 00	13 04	12 50	13 07	13 34		13 17	13 30	13 20	13 39	13 41	13 47	13 53	14 00	14 04		13 50	14 07	14 00	14 34	14 17	14 30

Station		SW	SW	SW		SW	SW	SW	SW	SW	SW	SW	SW	SW		SW	SW	SW	SW	SW	SW	SW	SW	SW	
Guildford	d						13 48	13 57					14 18			14 27					14 48	14 57			
London Road (Guildford)	d						13 52						14 22								14 52				
Clandon	d						13 57						14 27								14 57				
Horsley	d						14 01						14 31								15 01				
Effingham Junction	d						14 04						14 34								15 04				
Bookham	d												14 37												
Cobham & Stoke d'Abernon	d						14 08														15 08				
Oxshott	d						14 11														15 11				
Claygate	d						14 14														15 14				
Hinchley Wood	d						14 17														15 17				
Hampton Court	d					14 05								14 35						15 05					
Thames Ditton	d					14 07								14 37						15 07					
Surbiton	d					14 13	14 24	14 30						14 43		15 00				15 13	15 24	15 30			
Berrylands	d					14 15								14 45						15 15					
Shepperton	d										14 11														
Upper Halliford	d										14 14														
Sunbury	d										14 16														
Kempton Park	d										14 18														
Hampton	d										14 21														
Fulwell	d										14 24														
Strawberry Hill	d		13 49	13 59								14 19						14 49	14 59						
Teddington	d		13 55								14 29							14 55							
Hampton Wick	d		13 57								14 31							14 57							
Kingston	a		13 59								14 33							14 59							
	d		14 04								14 34							15 04							
Norbiton	d		14 06								14 36							15 06							
New Malden	d		14 10			14 18					14 40			14 48				15 10		15 18					
Dorking	d								14 08														15 08		
Boxhill & Westhumble	d																								
Leatherhead	d								14 15				14 45										15 15		
Ashtead	d								14 18				14 48										15 18		
Epsom	a								14 23				14 53										15 23		
	d								14 24				14 54										15 24		
Ewell West	d								14 27				14 57										15 27		
Stoneleigh	d								14 29				14 59										15 29		
Worcester Park	d								14 32				15 02										15 32		
Chessington South	d	13 40								14 10							14 40							15 10	
Chessington North	d	13 42								14 12							14 42							15 12	
Tolworth	d	13 44								14 14							14 44							15 14	
Malden Manor	d	13 47								14 17							14 47							15 17	
Motspur Park	d	13 50							14 35	14 20			15 05				14 50						15 35	15 20	
Raynes Park	d	13 54	14 13			14 21			14 38	14 24	14 43		15 08	14 51			14 54	15 13		15 21			15 38	15 24	
Wimbledon ⊖	d	13 58	14 17			14 25	14 31	14 38	14 42	14 28	14 47		15 12	14 55		15 08	14 58	15 17		15 25	15 31	15 38	15 42	15 28	
Earlsfield	d	14 01	14 20			14 28	14 35	14 41	14 46	14 31	14 50		15 16	14 58		15 11	15 01	15 20		15 28	15 35	15 41	15 46	15 31	
Clapham Junction	d	14 05	14 24			14 32	14 39	14 45	14 50	14 35	14 54		15 20	15 02		15 15	15 05	15 24		15 32	15 39	15 45	15 50	15 35	
Vauxhall ⊖	d	14 10	14 29	14 32		14 37	14 44	14 50	14 55	14 40	14 59	14 52	15 25	15 07		15 20	15 10	15 29	15 32	15 37	15 44	15 50	15 55	15 40	
London Waterloo ⊖	a	14 20	14 34	14 41		14 42	14 48	14 55	14 59	14 45	15 04	15 00	15 29	15 12		15 25	15 15	15 34	15 36	15 42	15 48	15 55	15 59	15 45	

Table 152

Sundays from 26 September

Hampton Court, Shepperton, Guildford, Dorking and Chessington South - London

		SW	SW	SW	SW	SW	SW	SW	SW	SW	SW	SW	SW	SW	SW	SW	SW	SW	SW	SW	SW	SW	SW
Guildford	d			15 18		15 27					15 48	15 57					16 18		16 27				
London Road (Guildford)	d			15 22							15 52						16 22						
Clandon	d			15 27							15 57						16 27						
Horsley	d			15 31							16 01						16 31						
Effingham Junction [6]	d			15 34							16 04						16 34						
Bookham	d			15 37													16 37						
Cobham & Stoke d'Abernon	d										16 08												
Oxshott	d										16 11												
Claygate	d										16 14												
Hinchley Wood	d										16 17												
Hampton Court	d				15 35					16 05								16 35					17 05
Thames Ditton	d				15 37					16 07								16 37					17 07
Surbiton [6]	d				15 43	16 00				16 13	16 24	16 30						16 43	17 00				17 13
Berrylands	d				15 45					16 15								16 45					17 15
Shepperton	d	15 11													16 11								
Upper Halliford	d	15 14													16 14								
Sunbury	d	15 16													16 16								
Kempton Park	d	15 18													16 18								
Hampton	d	15 21													16 21								
Fulwell	d	15 24													16 24								
Strawberry Hill	d		15 19					15 49	15 59							16 19					16 49	16 59	
Teddington	d	15 29						15 55							16 29						16 55		
Hampton Wick	d	15 31						15 57							16 31						16 57		
Kingston	a	15 33						15 59							16 33						16 59		
	d	15 34						16 04							16 34						17 04		
Norbiton	d	15 36						16 06							16 36						17 06		
New Malden [6]	d	15 40			15 48			16 10		16 18					16 40			16 48			17 10		17 18
Dorking [4]	d												16 08										
Boxhill & Westhumble	d																						
Leatherhead	d			15 45									16 15				16 45						
Ashtead	d			15 48									16 18				16 48						
Epsom [3]	a			15 53									16 23				16 53						
	d			15 54									16 24				16 54						
Ewell West	d			15 57									16 27				16 57						
Stoneleigh	d			15 59									16 29				16 59						
Worcester Park	d			16 02									16 32				17 02						
Chessington South	d						15 40							16 10						16 40			
Chessington North	d						15 42							16 12						16 42			
Tolworth	d						15 44							16 14						16 44			
Malden Manor	d						15 47							16 17						16 47			
Motspur Park	d			16 05			15 50						16 35	16 20			17 05			16 50			
Raynes Park [6]	d	15 43		16 08	15 51		15 54	16 13		16 21			16 38	16 24	16 43		17 08	16 51		16 54	17 13		17 21
Wimbledon [6] ⊖ ⇌	d	15 47		16 12	15 55	16 08	15 58	16 17		16 25	16 31	16 38	16 42	16 28	16 47		17 12	16 55	17 08	16 58	17 17		17 25
Earlsfield	d	15 50		16 16	15 58	16 11	16 01	16 20		16 28	16 35	16 41	16 46	16 31	16 50		17 16	16 58	17 11	17 01	17 20		17 28
Clapham Junction [10]	d	15 54		16 20	16 02	16 15	16 05	16 24		16 32	16 39	16 45	16 50	16 35	16 54		17 20	17 02	17 15	17 05	17 24		17 32
Vauxhall ⊖	d	15 59	15 52	16 25	16 07	16 20	16 10	16 29	16 32	16 37	16 44	16 50	16 55	16 40	16 59	16 52	17 25	17 07	17 20	17 10	17 29	17 32	17 37
London Waterloo [15] ⊖	a	16 04	16 00	16 29	16 12	16 25	16 15	16 34	16 36	16 42	16 48	16 55	16 59	16 45	17 04	17 00	17 29	17 12	17 25	17 15	17 34	17 36	17 42

		SW	SW	SW	SW	SW	SW	SW	SW	SW	SW	SW	SW	SW	SW	SW	SW	SW	SW	SW	SW	SW	SW
Guildford	d	16 48	16 57					17 18		17 27					17 48	17 57					18 18		18 27
London Road (Guildford)	d	16 52						17 22							17 52						18 22		
Clandon	d	16 57						17 27							17 57						18 27		
Horsley	d	17 01						17 31							18 01						18 31		
Effingham Junction [6]	d	17 04						17 34							18 04						18 34		
Bookham	d							17 37													18 37		
Cobham & Stoke d'Abernon	d	17 08													18 08								
Oxshott	d	17 11													18 11								
Claygate	d	17 14													18 14								
Hinchley Wood	d	17 17													18 17								
Hampton Court	d								17 35					18 05								18 35	
Thames Ditton	d								17 37					18 07								18 37	
Surbiton [6]	d	17 24	17 30						17 43	18 00				18 13	18 24	18 30						18 43	19 00
Berrylands	d								17 45					18 15								18 45	
Shepperton	d					17 11													18 11				
Upper Halliford	d					17 14													18 14				
Sunbury	d					17 16													18 16				
Kempton Park	d					17 18													18 18				
Hampton	d					17 21													18 21				
Fulwell	d					17 24													18 24				
Strawberry Hill	d						17 19					17 49	17 59							18 19			
Teddington	d					17 29						17 55							18 29				
Hampton Wick	d					17 31						17 57							18 31				
Kingston	a					17 33						17 59							18 33				
	d					17 34						18 04							18 34				
Norbiton	d					17 36						18 06							18 36				
New Malden [6]	d					17 40			17 48			18 10		18 18					18 40			18 48	
Dorking [4]	d			17 08													18 08						
Boxhill & Westhumble	d																						
Leatherhead	d			17 15				17 45									18 15				18 45		
Ashtead	d			17 18				17 48									18 18				18 48		
Epsom [3]	a			17 23				17 53									18 23				18 53		
	d			17 24				17 54									18 24				18 54		
Ewell West	d			17 27				17 57									18 27				18 57		
Stoneleigh	d			17 29				17 59									18 29				18 59		
Worcester Park	d			17 32				18 02									18 32				19 02		
Chessington South	d				17 10						17 40							18 10					
Chessington North	d				17 12						17 42							18 12					
Tolworth	d				17 14						17 44							18 14					
Malden Manor	d				17 17						17 47							18 17					
Motspur Park	d			17 35	17 20			18 05			17 50						18 35	18 20			19 05		
Raynes Park [6]	d			17 38	17 24	17 43		18 08	17 51		17 54	18 13		18 21			18 38	18 24	18 43		19 08	18 51	
Wimbledon [6] ⊖ ⇌	d	17 31	17 38	17 42	17 28	17 47		18 12	17 55	18 08	17 58	18 17		18 25	18 31	18 38	18 42	18 28	18 47		19 12	18 55	19 08
Earlsfield	d	17 35	17 41	17 46	17 31	17 50		18 16	17 58	18 11	18 01	18 20		18 28	18 35	18 41	18 46	18 31	18 50		19 16	18 58	19 11
Clapham Junction [10]	d	17 39	17 45	17 50	17 35	17 54		18 20	18 02	18 15	18 05	18 24		18 32	18 39	18 45	18 50	18 35	18 54		19 20	19 02	19 15
Vauxhall ⊖	d	17 44	17 50	17 55	17 40	17 59	17 52	18 25	18 07	18 20	18 10	18 29	18 32	18 37	18 44	18 50	18 55	18 40	18 59	18 52	19 25	19 07	19 20
London Waterloo [15] ⊖	a	17 48	17 55	17 59	17 45	18 04	18 00	18 29	18 12	18 25	18 15	18 34	18 36	18 42	18 48	18 55	18 59	18 45	19 04	19 00	19 29	19 12	19 25

Table 152

Sundays from 26 September

Hampton Court, Shepperton, Guildford, Dorking and Chessington South - London

		SW	SW	SW	SW	SW	SW	SW	SW	SW	SW	SW	SW	SW	SW	SW	SW	SW	SW	SW	SW	SW
Guildford	d					18 48	18 57					19 18		19 27					19 48	19 57		
London Road (Guildford)	d					18 52						19 22							19 52			
Clandon	d					18 57						19 27							19 57			
Horsley	d					19 01						19 31							20 01			
Effingham Junction [6]	d					19 04						19 34							20 04			
Bookham	d											19 37										
Cobham & Stoke d'Abernon	d					19 08													20 08			
Oxshott	d					19 11													20 11			
Claygate	d					19 14													20 14			
Hinchley Wood	d					19 17													20 17			
Hampton Court	d				19 05								19 35					20 05				
Thames Ditton	d				19 07								19 37					20 07				
Surbiton [6]	d				19 13	19 24	19 30						19 43	20 00				20 13	20 24	20 30		
Berrylands	d				19 15								19 45					20 15				
Shepperton	d									19 11												
Upper Halliford	d									19 14												
Sunbury	d									19 16												
Kempton Park	d									19 18												
Hampton	d									19 21												
Fulwell	d									19 24												
Strawberry Hill	d		18 49	18 59							19 19					19 49	19 59					
Teddington	d		18 55							19 29						19 55						
Hampton Wick	d		18 57							19 31						19 57						
Kingston	a		18 59							19 33						19 59						
	d		19 04							19 34						20 04						
Norbiton	d		19 06							19 36						20 06						
New Malden [6]	d		19 10		19 18					19 40			19 48			20 10		20 18				
Dorking [4]	d							19 08													20 08	
Boxhill & Westhumble	d																					
Leatherhead	d							19 15				19 45									20 15	
Ashtead	d							19 18				19 48									20 18	
Epsom [3]	a							19 23				19 53									20 23	
	d							19 24				19 54									20 24	
Ewell West	d							19 27				19 57									20 27	
Stoneleigh	d							19 29				19 59									20 29	
Worcester Park	d							19 32				20 02									20 32	
Chessington South	d	18 40							19 10						19 40							20 10
Chessington North	d	18 42							19 12						19 42							20 12
Tolworth	d	18 44							19 14						19 44							20 14
Malden Manor	d	18 47							19 17						19 47							20 17
Motspur Park	d	18 50						19 35	19 20			20 05			19 50						20 35	20 20
Raynes Park [6]	d	18 54	19 13		19 21			19 38	19 24	19 43		20 08	19 51		19 54	20 13		20 21			20 38	20 24
Wimbledon [6] ⊖ ⇌	d	18 58	19 17		19 25	19 31	19 38	19 42	19 28	19 47		20 12	19 55	20 08	19 58	20 17		20 25	20 31	20 38	20 42	20 28
Earlsfield	d	19 01	19 20		19 28	19 35	19 41	19 46	19 31	19 50		20 16	19 58	20 11	20 01	20 20		20 28	20 35	20 41	20 46	20 31
Clapham Junction [10]	d	19 05	19 24		19 32	19 39	19 45	19 50	19 35	19 54		20 20	20 02	20 15	20 05	20 24		20 32	20 39	20 45	20 50	20 35
Vauxhall ⊖	d	19 10	19 29	19 32	19 37	19 44	19 50	19 55	19 40	19 59	19 52	20 25	20 07	20 20	20 10	20 29	20 32	20 37	20 44	20 50	20 55	20 40
London Waterloo [15] ⊖	a	19 15	19 34	19 36	19 42	19 48	19 55	19 59	19 45	20 04	20 00	20 29	20 12	20 25	20 15	20 34	20 36	20 42	20 48	20 55	21 00	20 45

		SW	SW	SW	SW	SW	SW	SW	SW	SW	SW	SW	SW	SW	SW	SW	SW	SW	SW	SW	SW	SW	SW
Guildford	d			20 18		20 27				20 48	20 57					21 18		21 27				21 48	21 57
London Road (Guildford)	d			20 22						20 52						21 22						21 52	
Clandon	d			20 27						20 57						21 27						21 57	
Horsley	d			20 31						21 01						21 31						22 01	
Effingham Junction [6]	d			20 34						21 04						21 34						22 04	
Bookham	d			20 37												21 37							
Cobham & Stoke d'Abernon	d									21 08												22 08	
Oxshott	d									21 11												22 11	
Claygate	d									21 14												22 14	
Hinchley Wood	d									21 17												22 17	
Hampton Court	d				20 35				21 05								21 35				22 05		
Thames Ditton	d				20 37				21 07								21 37				22 07		
Surbiton [6]	d				20 43	21 00			21 13	21 24	21 30						21 43	22 00			22 13	22 24	22 30
Berrylands	d				20 45				21 15								21 45				22 15		
Shepperton	d	20 11												21 11									
Upper Halliford	d	20 14												21 14									
Sunbury	d	20 16												21 16									
Kempton Park	d	20 18												21 18									
Hampton	d	20 21												21 21									
Fulwell	d	20 24												21 24									
Strawberry Hill	d		20 19				20 49	20 59							21 19				21 49	21 59			
Teddington	d	20 29					20 55							21 29					21 55				
Hampton Wick	d	20 31					20 57							21 31					21 57				
Kingston	a	20 33					20 59							21 33					21 59				
	d	20 34					21 04							21 34					22 04				
Norbiton	d	20 36					21 06							21 36					22 06				
New Malden [6]	d	20 40			20 48		21 10		21 18					21 40			21 48		22 10		22 18		
Dorking [4]	d											21 08											
Boxhill & Westhumble	d																						
Leatherhead	d			20 45								21 15				21 45							
Ashtead	d			20 48								21 18				21 48							
Epsom [3]	a			20 53								21 23				21 53							
	d			20 54								21 24				21 54							
Ewell West	d			20 57								21 27				21 57							
Stoneleigh	d			20 59								21 29				21 59							
Worcester Park	d			21 02								21 32				22 02							
Chessington South	d												21 10										
Chessington North	d												21 12										
Tolworth	d												21 14										
Malden Manor	d												21 17										
Motspur Park	d			21 05								21 35	21 20			22 05							
Raynes Park [6]	d	20 43		21 08	20 51		21 13		21 21			21 38	21 24	21 43		22 08	21 51		22 13		22 21		
Wimbledon [6] ⊖ ⇌	d	20 47		21 12	20 55	21 08	21 17		21 25	21 31	21 38	21 42	21 28	21 47		22 12	21 55	22 08	22 17		22 25	22 31	22 38
Earlsfield	d	20 50		21 16	20 58	21 11	21 20		21 28	21 35	21 41	21 46	21 31	21 50		22 16	21 58	22 11	22 20		22 28	22 35	22 41
Clapham Junction [10]	d	20 54		21 20	21 02	21 15	21 24		21 32	21 39	21 45	21 50	21 35	21 54		22 20	22 02	22 15	22 24		22 32	22 39	22 45
Vauxhall ⊖	d	20 59	20 52	21 25	21 07	21 20	21 29	21 32	21 37	21 44	21 50	21 55	21 40	21 59	21 52	22 25	22 07	22 20	22 29	22 32	22 37	22 44	22 50
London Waterloo [15] ⊖	a	21 04	21 00	21 29	21 13	21 25	21 35	21 36	21 42	21 48	21 55	22 00	21 45	22 04	22 00	22 29	22 12	22 25	22 35	22 36	22 42	22 48	22 55

Table 152

Sundays
from 26 September

Hampton Court, Shepperton, Guildford, Dorking and Chessington South - London

		SW	SW	SW	SW	SW	SW	SW	SW	SW	SW	SW	SW	SW	SW	SW	SW	SW 1	SW
Guildford	d					22 20	22 27				22 50	22 57							
London Road (Guildford)	d					22 24					22 54								
Clandon	d					22 29					22 59								
Horsley	d					22 33					23 03								
Effingham Junction 8	d					22 36					23 06								
Bookham	d					22 39													
Cobham & Stoke d'Abernon	d										23 10								
Oxshott	d										23 13								
Claygate	d										23 16								
Hinchley Wood	d										23 19								
Hampton Court	d									23 05									23 45
Thames Ditton	d									23 07									23 47
Surbiton 6	d						23 00			23 13	23 24	23 30						23 46	23 53
Berrylands	d									23 15									23 55
Shepperton	d			22 11											23 11				
Upper Halliford	d			22 14											23 14				
Sunbury	d			22 16											23 16				
Kempton Park	d			22 18											23 18				
Hampton	d			22 21											23 21				
Fulwell	d			22 24											23 24				
Strawberry Hill	d				22 19			22 49	22 59							23 19			
Teddington	d			22 29				22 55							23 29				
Hampton Wick	d			22 31				22 57							23 31				
Kingston	a			22 33				22 59							23 33				
	d			22 34				23 04							23 34				
Norbiton	d			22 36				23 06							23 36				
New Malden 6	d			22 40				23 10		23 18					23 40				23 58
Dorking 4	d	22 08											23 08						
Boxhill & Westhumble	d																		
Leatherhead	d	22 15				22 45							23 15						
Ashtead	d	22 18				22 48							23 18						
Epsom 3	a	22 23				22 53							23 23						
	d	22 24				22 54							23 24						
Ewell West	d	22 27				22 57							23 27						
Stoneleigh	d	22 29				22 59							23 29						
Worcester Park	d	22 32				23 02							23 32						
Chessington South	d		22 10											23 10			23 40		
Chessington North	d		22 12											23 12			23 42		
Tolworth	d		22 14											23 14			23 44		
Malden Manor	d		22 17											23 17			23 47		
Motspur Park	d	22 35	22 20			23 05							23 35	23 20			23 50		
Raynes Park 6	d	22 38	22 24	22 43		23 08		23 13		23 21			23 38	23 24	23 43		23 54		00 01
Wimbledon 6 ⊖ ⇌	d	22 42	22 28	22 47		23 12	23 08	23 17		23 25	23 31	23 38	23 42	23 28	23 47		23a59	23 53	00a04
Earlsfield	d	22 46	22 31	22 50		23 16	23 11	23 20		23 28	23 35	23 41	23 46	23 31	23 50				
Clapham Junction 10	d	22 50	22 35	22 54		23 20	23 15	23 24		23 32	23 39	23 45	23 50	23 35	23 54				
Vauxhall ⊖	d	22 55	22 40	22 59	22 52	23 25	23 20	23 29	23 32	23 37	23 44	23 50	23 55	23 40	23 59	23 52		00 01	
London Waterloo 15 ⊖	a	23 00	22 45	23 04	23 00	23 29	23 25	23 35	23 36	23 42	23 48	23 55	23 59	23 45	00 04	23 59		00 10	

Network Diagram for Tables 155, 156, 157

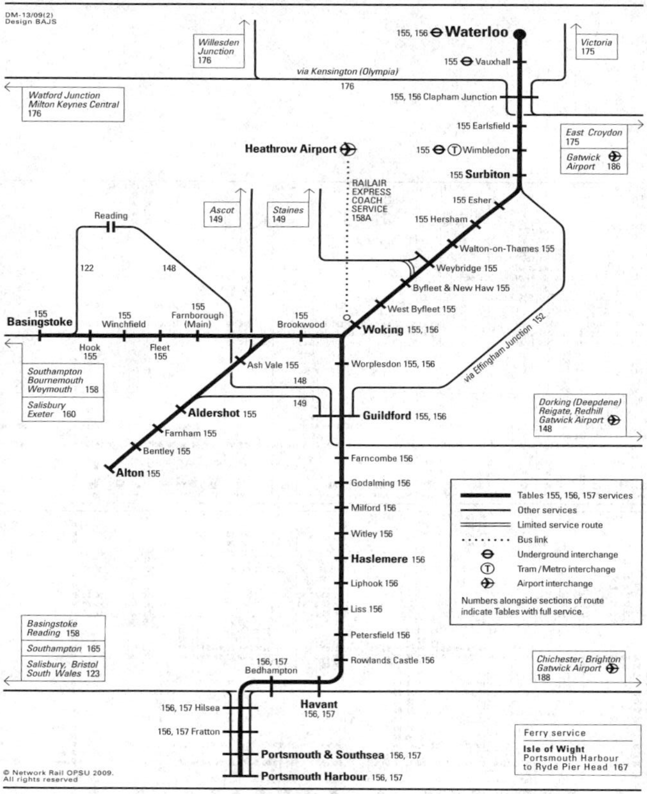

London - Woking, Guildford, Alton and Basingstoke

Station		SW MO [1]	SW MX [1]	SW MO [1]	SW MX [1]	SW MX [1]	SW MO [1]	SW MO	SW MO [1]	SW MX [1]	SW MO [1]	SW MX	SW MX [1]	SW MX [1]	SW MX [1]	SW MO [1]	SW MX [1]	SW MX [1]	SW MX	SW MO [1]	SW	SW [1]	SW [1]	SW ◇[1]
London Waterloo [15] ⊖	d		22p53	23p07	23p12			23p10	23p30	23p35	23p35	23p20	23p39	23p45	23p48	23p40	00 05		00 09	00 50		01 05	05 00	05 30
Vauxhall ⊖	d							23p14				23p24				23p44			00 13			01 09	05 04	
Clapham Junction [10]	d		23b00	23p15	23b19			23p19	23b39	23b43	23b44	23p29	23b46	23b52	23b56	23p49	00u12		00 18	00u57		01 14	05 09	05u37
Earlsfield	d							23p22				23p32				23p52			00 21				05 12	
Wimbledon [6] ⊖	d			23p22				23p26				23p36				23p56	00u18		00 25			01 20	05 16	05 43
Surbiton [6]	d		23p11	23p30	23p30			23p35				23p44			00 10	00 05			00 33				05 24	
Esher	d							23p39				23p48				00 09			00s37				05 28	
Hersham	d							23p42				23p51				00 12			00s40				05 32	
Walton-on-Thames	d				23p37			23p45				23p54			00 17	00 15			00s43				05 35	
Weybridge	d				23p41			23p49				23p57			00 21	00 19			00s47				05 39	
Byfleet & New Haw	d							23p51				00 01				00 21			00s49				05 42	
West Byfleet	d		23p21					23p54				00 03				00 24			00s52				05 45	
Woking	a		23p29	23p42	23p48			23p59	00 01	00 03	00 07	00 08	00 08	00 16	00 27	00 30	00 35		00 57	01 16		01 42	05 50	05 59
	d	23p26	23p30	23p46	23p49		23p49	00 05	00 03	00 05	00 08		00 09	00 17	00 29	00 35	00 36	00 40	00 58	01 18		01 42	05 51	06 01
Worplesdon	d													00 22										
Guildford	a							00 13	00 10					00 28					01 06	01s26			05 59	
Brookwood	d	23p33	23p36	23p52	23p55		23p56								00 35	00 41		00 45						
Ash Vale	d	23p41	23p44			23p49	00 04									00 48		00 53			00 57			
Aldershot	a	23p46	23p49			23p54	00 09									00 53		00 58			01a02			
	d	23p48	23p50			23p55	00 09									00 54		00 59						
Farnham	a	23p54	23p55			00 03	00 15									00 59		01 04			01 11			
	d	23p56	23p56				00 15											01 05						
Bentley	d		00 02				00 23											01s11						
Alton	a	00 07	00 10				00 30											01 18						
Farnborough (Main)	d			23p59	00 03						00 18		00 19		00 42							01s58		
Fleet	d			00 05	00 08						00 24		00 25		00 48									
Winchfield	d			00 10	00 14										00s53									
Hook	d			00 15	00 18										00s58									
Basingstoke	a			00 22	00 25					00 24	00 39		00 36		01 07		00 55					02 12		06 20

Station		SW [1]	SW [1]	SW [1]	SW [1]	SW	SW [1]	SW [1]	SW ◇[1]	SW [1]	SW [1]	SW	SW [1]	SW [1]	SW [1]	SW [1]	SW ◇[1] ☕	SW	SW [1]	SW [1]	SW [1] ☕	SW ◇[1] ☕	SW [1] ☕
London Waterloo [15] ⊖	d		05 20			05 50	06 15	06 12	06 30			06 20	06 45	06 42		06 53	07 10	06 50	07 15	07 12	07 30	07 35	07 39
Vauxhall ⊖	d		05 24			05 54						06 24						06 54					
Clapham Junction [10]	d		05 29			05 59	06u22	06u19	06u37			06 29	06u52	06u49		07u00	07u17	06 59	07u23	07u20			07u46
Earlsfield	d		05 32			06 02						06 32						07 02					
Wimbledon [6] ⊖	d		05 36			06 06						06 36						07 06					
Surbiton [6]	d		05 44			06 14		06 30				06 44		07 00		07 11		07 14		07 31			
Esher	d		05 48			06 18						06 48						07 18					
Hersham	d		05 51			06 21						06 51						07 21					
Walton-on-Thames	d		05 54			06 24		06 37				06 54		07 07				07 24		07 38			
Weybridge	d		05 57			06 27		06 41				06 57		07 11				07 27		07 42			
Byfleet & New Haw	d		06 00			06 30						07 00						07 30					
West Byfleet	d		06 03			06 33						07 03				07 21		07 33					
Woking	a		06 08			06 38	06 41	06 48	06 56			07 07	07 11	07 18		07 26	07 35	07 37	07 42	07 48	07 54	07 58	
	d	06 02	06 11	06 19	06 30		06 43	06 50	06 57		06 58	07 10	07 13	07 19		07 30	07 36	07 39	07 44	07 50	07 55	08 00	
Worplesdon	d		06 16				06 48						07 18						07 49				
Guildford	a		06 21				06 53					07 20	07 23					07 47	07 54		08 03		
Brookwood	d	06 08		06 25	06 36			06 56			07 06			07 25		07 36				07 56			
Ash Vale	d	06 16			06 44					06 49	07 14				07 19	07 44							
Aldershot	a	06 21			06 49					06 56	07 19				07 26	07 49							
	d	06 21			06 50					07 08	07 20				07 38	07 50							
Farnham	a	06 27			06 55						07 25					07 55							
	d	06 27			06 56						07 26					07 56							
Bentley	d	06 34			07 02						07 32					08 02							
Alton	a	06 41			07 10						07 40					08 10							
Farnborough (Main)	d			06 33				07 04						07 33						08 03			08 13
Fleet	d			06 38				07 09						07 38						08 09			08 19
Winchfield	d			06 44				07 15						07 44						08 14			
Hook	d			06 48				07 19						07 48						08 19			
Basingstoke	a			06 58				07 28	07 16					07 56			07 55			08 26		08 19	08 34

b previous night, stops to pick up only

London - Woking, Guildford, Alton and Basingstoke

Station		SW [1]	SW [1]	SW	SW [1]	SW ◇[1] ☕	SW [1]	SW [1]	SW ◇[1] ☕	SW [1]	SW [1]	SW [1]	SW	SW [1]	SW ◇[1] ☕	SW [1]	SW [1] ☕	SW ◇[1] ☕	SW [1]	SW [1]	SW [1]	SW
London Waterloo [15] ⊖	d		07 23	07 20	07 45	07 50	07 42	08 00	08 05		07 53	08 09	07 50	08 15	08 20	08 12	08 30	08 35	08 39		08 23	08 20
Vauxhall ⊖	d			07 24									07 54									08 24
Clapham Junction [10]	d		07u30	07 29	07u52	07u57			08u12		08u00		07 59	08u22	08u27	08u19			08u46			08 29
Earlsfield	d			07 32									08 02									08 32
Wimbledon [6] ⊖	d			07 36									08 06									08 36
Surbiton [6]	d		07 41	07 44			08 00				08 11		08 14			08 30					08 41	08 44
Esher	d			07 48									08 18									08 48
Hersham	d			07 51									08 21									08 51
Walton-on-Thames	d			07 54			08 07						08 24			08 37						08 54
Weybridge	d			07 57			08 11						08 27			08 41						08 57
Byfleet & New Haw	d			08 00									08 30									09 00
West Byfleet	d		07 51	08 03							08 21		08 33								08 51	09 03
Woking	a		07 59	08 08	08 12	08 15	08 18	08 24			08 29	08 33	08 37	08 42	08 46	08 49	08 55	08 58			09 00	09 08
	d		08 00		08 14	08 16	08 19	08 25			08 30	08 35	08 39	08 44	08 46	08 49	08 55	09 00			09 00	
Worplesdon	d				08 19									08 49								
Guildford	a				08 24			08 35					08 50	08 54			09 05					
Brookwood	d		08 06				08 25				08 36					08 55					09 06	
Ash Vale	d	07 49	08 14							08 19	08 44									08 49	09 14	
Aldershot	a	07 54	08 19							08 24	08 49									08 54	09 20	
	d	08 08	08 20							08 38	08 50									09 08	09 20	
Farnham	a		08 25								08 55										09 26	
	d		08 26								08 56										09 26	
Bentley	d		08 32								09 02											
Alton	a		08 39								09 10										09 39	
Farnborough (Main)	d						08 33					08 45				09 03			09 13			
Fleet	d						08 38									09 08			09 19			
Winchfield	d						08 44									09 14						
Hook	d						08 48									09 18						
Basingstoke	a					08 35	08 58		08 47			08 58			09 05	09 28			09 34			

Station		SW [1]	SW ◇[1] ☕	SW [1]	SW [1] ☕	SW ◇[1] ☕	SW [1]	SW [1]	SW [1]	SW	SW [1]	SW ◇[1] ☕	SW [1]	SW [1] ☕	SW ◇[1] ☕	SW [1]	SW [1]	SW [1] A	SW [1] B	SW	SW [1]	SW ◇[1] ☕	SW [1]
London Waterloo [15] ⊖	d	08 45	08 50	08 42	09 00	09 05		08 53	09 09	08 50	09 15	09 20	09 12	09 30	09 35	09 39		09 23	09 23	09 20	09 45	09 50	09 42
Vauxhall ⊖	d									08 54										09 24			
Clapham Junction [10]	d	08u52				09u12		09u00		08 59	09u22	09u27	09u19			09u46				09 29	09u52		
Earlsfield	d									09 02										09 32			
Wimbledon [6] ⊖	d									09 06										09 36			
Surbiton [6]	d			09 00				09 11		09 14			09 30					09 41	09 41	09 44			10 00
Esher	d									09 18										09 48			
Hersham	d									09 21										09 51			
Walton-on-Thames	d			09 07						09 24			09 37							09 54			10 07
Weybridge	d			09 11						09 27			09 41							09 57			10 11
Byfleet & New Haw	d									09 30										10 00			
West Byfleet	d							09 21		09 33								09 51	09 51	10 03			
Woking	a	09 11	09 15	09 18	09 24			09 29	09 33	09 38	09 42	09 45	09 48	09 54	09 58			09 59	09 59	10 08	10 11	10 14	10 18
	d	09 13	09 16	09 19	09 25			09 30	09 35		09 43	09 46	09 49	09 55	10 00			10 00	10 00		10 13	10 16	10 19
Worplesdon	d	09 18																			10 18		
Guildford	a	09 23			09 33						09 52			10 03							10 23		
Brookwood	d			09 25				09 36					09 55					10 06	10 06				10 25
Ash Vale	d						09 19	09 44									09 49	10 14	10 14				
Aldershot	a						09 25	09 49									09 54	10 19	10 19				
	d						09 38	09 50									10 08	10 20	10 20				
Farnham	a							09 55										10 25	10 25				
	d							09 56										10 26	10 26				
Bentley	d							10 02											10b51				
Alton	a							10 10										10 37	10 58				
Farnborough (Main)	d			09 33					09 45				10 03			10 13							10 33
Fleet	d			09 38									10 08			10 19							10 38
Winchfield	d			09 44									10 14										10 44
Hook	d			09 48									10 18										10 48
Basingstoke	a		09 35	09 58		09 47			09 58			10 05	10 28			10 34						10 35	10 58

A until 1 October

B from 4 October

b arr. 1032

London - Woking, Guildford, Alton and Basingstoke

		SW ■ ☕	SW ◇■ ☕	SW ■		SW ■	SW ■	SW	SW ■	SW ◇■ ☕	SW ■	SW ■ ☕	SW ◇■ ☕	SW ■		SW ■	SW ■	SW	SW ■	SW ◇■ ☕	SW ■	SW ■ ☕	SW ◇■ ☕	SW ■	
London Waterloo 15 ⊖	d	10 00	10 05			09 53	10 09	09 50	10 15	10 20	10 12	10 30	10 35	10 39			10 23	10 20	10 45	10 50	10 42	11 00	11 05		
Vauxhall ⊖	d							09 54										10 24							
Clapham Junction 10	d		10u12			10u00		09 59	10u22	10u27	10u19			10u46				10 29	10u52				11u12		
Earlsfield	d							10 02										10 32							
Wimbledon 6 ⊖	d							10 06										10 36							
Surbiton 6	d					10 11		10 14			10 30						10 41	10 44			11 00				
Esher	d							10 18										10 48							
Hersham	d							10 21										10 51							
Walton-on-Thames	d							10 24			10 37							10 54			11 07				
Weybridge	d							10 27			10 41							10 57			11 11				
Byfleet & New Haw	d							10 30										11 00							
West Byfleet	d					10 21		10 33									10 51	11 03							
Woking	a	10 24				10 29	10 33	10 38	10 41	10 45	10 48	10 54	10 58				10 59	11 08	11 11	11 14	11 18	11 24			
	d	10 25				10 30	10 35		10 43	10 46	10 49	10 55	11 00				11 00		11 13	11 16	11 19	11 25			
Worplesdon	d																		11 18						
Guildford	a	10 33							10 50			11 03							11 23			11 33			
Brookwood	d					10 36					10 55						11 06				11 25				
Ash Vale	d			10 19		10 44										10 49	11 14							11 19	
Aldershot	a			10 24		10 49										10 54	11 19							11 24	
	d			10 38		10 50										11 08	11 20							11 38	
Farnham	a					10 55											11 25								
	d					10 56																			
Bentley	d					11 02																			
Alton	a					11 10																			
Farnborough (Main)	d						10 45				11 03			11 13							11 33				
Fleet	d										11 08			11 19							11 38				
Winchfield	d										11 14										11 44				
Hook	d										11 18										11 48				
Basingstoke	a		10 47				10 58			11 05	11 28			11 34						11 35	11 58		11 47		

		SW ■	SW ■	SW	SW ■	SW ◇■ ☕	SW ■	SW ■ ☕	SW ◇■ ☕	SW ■		SW ■	SW ■	SW	SW ■	SW ◇■ ☕	SW ■	SW ■ ☕	SW ◇■ ☕	SW ■		SW ■	SW ■	SW	SW ■
London Waterloo 15 ⊖	d	10 53	11 09	10 50	11 15	11 20	11 12	11 30	11 35	11 39			11 23	11 20	11 45	11 50	11 42	12 00	12 05			11 53	12 09	11 50	12 15
Vauxhall ⊖	d			10 54										11 24										11 54	
Clapham Junction 10	d	11u00		10 59	11u22	11u27	11u19			11u46				11 29	11u52				12u12			12u00		11 59	12u22
Earlsfield	d			11 02										11 32										12 02	
Wimbledon 6 ⊖	d			11 06										11 36										12 06	
Surbiton 6	d	11 11		11 14			11 30						11 41	11 44			12 00					12 11		12 14	
Esher	d			11 18										11 48										12 18	
Hersham	d			11 21										11 51										12 21	
Walton-on-Thames	d			11 24			11 37							11 54			12 07							12 24	
Weybridge	d			11 27			11 41							11 57			12 11							12 27	
Byfleet & New Haw	d			11 30										12 00										12 30	
West Byfleet	d	11 21		11 33									11 51	12 03								12 21		12 33	
Woking	a	11 29	11 33	11 38	11 41	11 45	11 48	11 54	11 58				11 59	12 08	12 11	12 14	12 18	12 24				12 29	12 33	12 38	12 41
	d	11 30	11 35		11 43	11 46	11 49	11 55	12 00				12 00		12 13	12 16	12 19	12 25				12 30	12 35		12 43
Worplesdon	d														12 18										
Guildford	a				11 50			12 03							12 23			12 33							12 50
Brookwood	d	11 36					11 55						12 06				12 25					12 36			
Ash Vale	d	11 44										11 49	12 14							12 19		12 44			
Aldershot	a	11 49										11 54	12 19							12 24		12 49			
	d	11 50										12 08	12 20							12 38		12 50			
Farnham	a	11 55											12 25									12 55			
	d	11 56											12 26									12 56			
Bentley	d	12 02																				13 02			
Alton	a	12 10											12 37									13 10			
Farnborough (Main)	d		11 45				12 03			12 13							12 33						12 45		
Fleet	d						12 08			12 19							12 38								
Winchfield	d						12 14										12 44								
Hook	d						12 18										12 48								
Basingstoke	a		11 58			12 05	12 28			12 34						12 35	12 58		12 47				12 58		

London - Woking, Guildford, Alton and Basingstoke

		SW ◇■ ☕	SW ■	SW ■ ☕	SW ◇■ ☕	SW ■		SW ■	SW ■	SW	SW ■	SW ◇■ ☕	SW ■	SW ■ ☕	SW ◇■ ☕	SW ■		SW ■	SW ■	SW	SW ■	SW ◇■ ☕	SW ■	SW ■ ☕	SW ◇■ ☕
London Waterloo 15 ⊖	d	12 20	12 12	12 30	12 35	12 39			12 23	12 20	12 45	12 50	12 42	13 00	13 05			12 53	13 09	12 50	13 15	13 20	13 12	13 30	13 35
Vauxhall ⊖	d									12 24										12 54					
Clapham Junction 10	d	12u27	12u19			12u46				12 29	12u52				13u12			13u00		12 59	13u22	13u27	13u19		
Earlsfield	d									12 32										13 02					
Wimbledon 6 ⊖	d									12 36										13 06					
Surbiton 6	d		12 30						12 41	12 44			13 00					13 11		13 14			13 30		
Esher	d									12 48										13 18					
Hersham	d									12 51										13 21					
Walton-on-Thames	d		12 37							12 54			13 07							13 24			13 37		
Weybridge	d		12 41							12 57			13 11							13 27			13 41		
Byfleet & New Haw	d									13 00										13 30					
West Byfleet	d								12 51	13 03								13 21		13 33					
Woking	a	12 45	12 48	12 54	12 58				12 59	13 08	13 11	13 14	13 18	13 24				13 29	13 33	13 38	13 41	13 45	13 48	13 54	13 58
	d	12 46	12 49	12 55	13 00				13 00		13 13	13 16	13 19	13 25				13 30	13 35		13 43	13 46	13 49	13 55	14 00
Worplesdon	d										13 18														
Guildford	a			13 03							13 23			13 33							13 50			14 03	
Brookwood	d		12 55						13 06				13 25					13 36					13 55		
Ash Vale	d							12 49	13 14							13 19		13 44							
Aldershot	a							12 54	13 19							13 24		13 49							
	d							13 08	13 20							13 38		13 50							
Farnham	a								13 25									13 55							
	d								13 26									13 56							
Bentley	d																	14 02							
Alton	a								13 37									14 11							
Farnborough (Main)	d		13 03			13 13							13 33						13 45				14 03		
Fleet	d		13 08			13 19							13 38										14 08		
Winchfield	d		13 14										13 44										14 14		
Hook	d		13 18										13 48										14 18		
Basingstoke	a	13 05	13 28			13 34						13 35	13 58		13 47				13 58			14 05	14 28		

		SW ■		SW ■	SW ■	SW	SW ■	SW ◇■ ☕	SW ■	SW ■ ☕	SW ◇■ ☕	SW ■		SW ■	SW ■	SW	SW ■	SW ◇■ ☕	SW ■	SW ■ ☕	SW ◇■ ☕	SW ■		SW ■	SW ■
London Waterloo 15 ⊖	d	13 39			13 23	13 20	13 45	13 50	13 42	14 00	14 05			13 53	14 09	13 50	14 15	14 20	14 12	14 30	14 35	14 39			14 23
Vauxhall ⊖	d					13 24										13 54									
Clapham Junction 10	d	13u46				13 29	13u52				14u12			14u00		13 59	14u22	14u27	14u19			14u46			
Earlsfield	d					13 32										14 02									
Wimbledon 6 ⊖	d					13 36										14 06									
Surbiton 6	d				13 41	13 44			14 00					14 11		14 14			14 30						14 41
Esher	d					13 48										14 18									
Hersham	d					13 51										14 21									
Walton-on-Thames	d					13 54			14 07							14 24			14 37						
Weybridge	d					13 57			14 11							14 27			14 41						
Byfleet & New Haw	d					14 00										14 30									
West Byfleet	d				13 51	14 03								14 21		14 33									14 51
Woking	a				13 59	14 08	14 11	14 14	14 18	14 24				14 29	14 33	14 38	14 41	14 45	14 48	14 54	14 58				14 59
	d				14 00		14 13	14 16	14 19	14 25				14 30	14 35		14 43	14 46	14 49	14 55	15 00				15 00
Worplesdon	d						14 18																		
Guildford	a						14 23			14 33							14 50			15 03					
Brookwood	d				14 06				14 25					14 36					14 55						15 06
Ash Vale	d			13 49	14 14							14 19		14 44										14 49	15 14
Aldershot	a			13 54	14 19							14 24		14 49										14 54	15 19
	d			14 08	14 20							14 38		14 50										15 08	15 20
Farnham	a				14 25									14 55											15 25
	d				14 26									14 56											15 26
Bentley	d													15 02											
Alton	a				14 37									15 10											15 37
Farnborough (Main)	d	14 13							14 33						14 45				15 03			15 13			
Fleet	d	14 19							14 38										15 08			15 19			
Winchfield	d								14 44										15 14						
Hook	d								14 48										15 18						
Basingstoke	a	14 34						14 35	14 58		14 47				14 58			15 05	15 28			15 34			

London - Woking, Guildford, Alton and Basingstoke

Station		SW	SW ■1	SW ◇■1 ⊡	SW ■1	SW ■1 ⊡	SW ◇■1 ⊡	SW ■1	SW ■1	SW ■1	SW	SW ■1	SW ◇■1 ⊡	SW ■1	SW ■1 ⊡	SW ◇■1 ⊡	SW ■1	SW ■1	SW ■1	SW	SW ■1	SW ◇■1 ⊡	SW ■1
London Waterloo ■15 ⊖	d	14 20	14 45	14 50	14 42	15 00	15 05		14 53	15 09	14 50	15 15	15 20	15 12	15 30	15 35	15 39		15 23	15 20	15 45	15 50	15 42
Vauxhall ⊖	d	14 24									14 54									15 24			
Clapham Junction ■10	d	14 29	14u52				15u12		15u00		14 59	15u22	15u27	15u19			15u46			15 29	15u52	15u57	
Earlsfield	d	14 32									15 02									15 32			
Wimbledon ■6 ⊖	d	14 36									15 06									15 36			
Surbiton ■6	d	14 44			15 00				15 11		15 14			15 30					15 41	15 44			16 00
Esher	d	14 48									15 18									15 48			
Hersham	d	14 51									15 21									15 51			
Walton-on-Thames	d	14 54			15 07						15 24			15 37						15 54			16 07
Weybridge	d	14 57			15 11						15 27			15 41						15 57			16 11
Byfleet & New Haw	d	15 00									15 30									16 00			
West Byfleet	d	15 03							15 21		15 33								15 51	16 03			
Woking	a	15 08	15 11	15 14	15 18	15 24			15 29	15 33	15 38	15 41	15 45	15 48	15 54	15 58			15 59	16 08	16 11	16 15	16 18
	d		15 13	15 16	15 19	15 25			15 30	15 35		15 43	15 46	15 49	15 55	16 00			16 00		16 13	16 16	16 19
Worplesdon	d		15 18									15 48											
Guildford	a		15 23			15 33						15 53			16 03						16 20		
Brookwood	d				15 25				15 36					15 55					16 06				16 25
Ash Vale	d							15 19	15 44									15 49	16 14				
Aldershot	a							15 24	15 49									15 54	16 19				
	d							15 38	15 50									16 08	16 20				
Farnham	a								15 55										16 25				
	d								15 56										16 26				
Bentley	d								16 02														
Alton	a								16 10										16 37				
Farnborough (Main)	d				15 33					15 45				16 03			16 13						16 33
Fleet	d				15 38									16 08			16 19						16 38
Winchfield	d				15 44									16 14									16 44
Hook	d				15 48									16 18									16 48
Basingstoke	a			15 35	15 58		15 47			15 58			16 05	16 28			16 34					16 35	16 58

Station		SW ■1 ⊡	SW ◇■1 ⊡	SW ■1	SW ■1	SW ■1	SW	SW ■1	SW ◇■1 ⊡	SW ■1	SW ■1 ⊡	SW ◇■1 ⊡	SW ■1	SW ■1	SW ■1	SW	SW ■1	SW ■1 ⊡	SW ■1	SW ■1 ⊡	SW ■1	SW ■1
London Waterloo ■15 ⊖	d	16 00	16 05		15 53	16 09	15 50	16 15	16 20	16 12	16 30	16 35	16 39		16 25	16 20	16 45	16 50	16 42	17 00		16 55
Vauxhall ⊖	d						15 54									16 24						
Clapham Junction ■10	d		16u12		16u00		15 59	16u22	16u27	16u19			16u46			16 29	16u52	16u57				17u02
Earlsfield	d						16 02									16 32						
Wimbledon ■6 ⊖	d						16 06									16 36						
Surbiton ■6	d				16 11		16 14			16 30					16 41	16 44			17 00			
Esher	d						16 18									16 48						
Hersham	d						16 21									16 51						
Walton-on-Thames	d						16 24			16 37						16 54			17 07			
Weybridge	d						16 27			16 41						16 57			17 11			
Byfleet & New Haw	d						16 30									17 00						
West Byfleet	d				16 21		16 33								16 51	17 03						17 21
Woking	a	16 24			16 29	16 33	16 38	16 41	16 45	16 48	16 54	16u58			16 59	17 10	17 11	17u15	17 18	17 24		17 29
	d	16 25			16 30	16 35		16 43	16 46	16 49	16 54	17u00			17 00		17 13	17u16	17 19	17 25		17 30
Worplesdon	d							16 48												17 30		
Guildford	a	16 33						16 53			17 03						17 20			17 36		
Brookwood	d				16 36					16 55					17 06				17 25			17 36
Ash Vale	d			16 19	16 44									16 49	17 14						17 19	17 44
Aldershot	a			16 24	16 49									16 54	17 19						17 24	17 49
	d			16 38	16 50									17 09	17 20						17 38	17 50
Farnham	a				16 55										17 25							17 55
	d				16 56										17 26							17 56
Bentley	d				17 02										17 32							18 02
Alton	a				17 10										17 41							18 11
Farnborough (Main)	d					16 45				17 03			17 13						17 33			
Fleet	d									17 08			17 19						17 38			
Winchfield	d									17 14									17 44			
Hook	d									17 18									17 48			
Basingstoke	a		16 47			16 58			17 05	17 30			17 34					17 35	18 00			

London - Woking, Guildford, Alton and Basingstoke

Station		SW ■1	SW ■1	SW ■1	SW	SW ■1	SW ◇■1 ⊡	SW ■1	SW ■1	SW ■1	SW ■1	SW ■1 ⊡	SW ■1	SW	SW ■1	SW ■1	SW ◇■1 ⊡	SW ■1	SW ■1	SW ■1	SW	SW ■1	SW ■1
London Waterloo ■15 ⊖	d	17 09	17 12	17 15	16 50	17 02	17 20	17 41		17 25	17 23	17 30	17 39	17 20	17 48	17 32	17 50	17 55	17 53	18 09	17 50	18 12	18 18
Vauxhall ⊖	d				16 54									17 24							17 54		
Clapham Junction ■10	d				16 59									17 29							17 59		
Earlsfield	d				17 02									17 32							18 02		
Wimbledon ■6 ⊖	d				17 06									17 36							18 06		
Surbiton ■6	d				17 14	17 18					17 39			17 44		17 48			18 09		18 14		
Esher	d				17 18	17 22								17 48		17 52					18 18		
Hersham	d				17 21	17 25								17 51		17 55					18 21		
Walton-on-Thames	d				17 24	17 29								17 54		17 59					18 24		
Weybridge	d				17 27	17 33								17 57		18 03					18 27		
Byfleet & New Haw	d				17 30	17 36								18 00		18 06					18 30		
West Byfleet	d				17 33	17 39								18 03		18 09			18 19		18 33		
Woking	a	17 32	17 36	17 38	17 43	17 44	17u44			17 50	17 51	17 54	18 02	18 10	18 11	18 14		18 20	18 23	18 33	18 40		18 42
	d	17 34	17 37	17 40		17 46	17u46			17 51	17 52	17 56	18 04		18 13	18 16		18 21	18 26	18 35			18 43
Worplesdon	d			17 45								18 00				18 21							18 48
Guildford	a			17 51		17 56						18 06				18 29							18 54
Brookwood	d		17 43					18 11			18 00							18 27				18 41	
Ash Vale	d								17 49	18 03								18 35					
Aldershot	a								17 54	18 08								18 40					
	d								18 08	18 09								18 41					
Farnham	a									18 14								18 46					
	d									18 15								18 48					
Bentley	d									18 24								18 54					
Alton	a									18 32								19 03					
Farnborough (Main)	d		17 51					18 19			18 08								18 38			18 48	
Fleet	d		17 56					18 24			18 13								18 44			18 54	
Winchfield	d		18 02					18 30			18 19								18 49			18 59	
Hook	d		18 06					18 34			18 23								18 54			19 04	
Basingstoke	a	17 52	18 16				18 05	18 45			18 32		18 22		18 31		18 37		19 03	18 53		19 16	

Station		SW ◇■1 ⊡	SW ■1	SW ■1	SW ■1	SW ■1	SW ■1	SW ■1 ⊡	SW ■1	SW	SW ■1	SW ◇■1 ⊡	SW ■1	SW ■1	SW ■1 ⊡	SW ◇■1 ⊡	SW ■1	SW ■1	SW	SW ■1	SW ◇■1 ⊡	SW ■1	SW ■1 ⊡
London Waterloo ■15 ⊖	d	18 20	18 02	18 41		18 25	18 23	18 30	18 39	18 20	18 45	18 50	18 32	18 55	19 00	19 05	19 09	19 12	18 50	19 15	19 20	19 02	19 30
Vauxhall ⊖	d									18 24									18 54				
Clapham Junction ■10	d	18u27				18u33			18u46	18 29				19u02		19u12		19u19	18 59	19u22	19u27		
Earlsfield	d									18 32									19 02				
Wimbledon ■6 ⊖	d									18 36									19 06				
Surbiton ■6	d		18 18				18 40			18 44			18 48						19 14			19 18	
Esher	d		18 22							18 48			18 52						19 18			19 22	
Hersham	d		18 25							18 51			18 55						19 21			19 25	
Walton-on-Thames	d		18 29							18 54			18 59						19 24			19 29	
Weybridge	d		18 33							18 57			19 03						19 27			19 33	
Byfleet & New Haw	d		18 36							19 00			19 06						19 30			19 36	
West Byfleet	d		18 39							19 03	19 08		19 09						19 33			19 39	
Woking	a	18 45	18 48			18 52	18 52	18 57	19 05	19 12	19 13	19 17	19 18	19 21	19 24		19 33	19 38	19 42	19 43	19 45	19 48	19 54
	d	18 46				18 53	18 54	18 58	19 06		19 14	19 18	19 20	19 23	19 25		19 35	19 39		19 45	19 46		19 55
Worplesdon	d														19 30								
Guildford	a							19 06			19 23				19 36					19 52			20 03
Brookwood	d			19 13			19 02							19 30				19 45					
Ash Vale	d				18 49	19 05								19 37									
Aldershot	a				18 54	19 10								19 42									
	d				19 08	19 11								19 43									
Farnham	a					19 16								19 48									
	d					19 18								19 49									
Bentley	d					19 24								19 55									
Alton	a					19 33								20 04									
Farnborough (Main)	d			19 20			19 10						19 31				19 45	19 53					
Fleet	d			19 26			19 15						19 37					19 58					
Winchfield	d			19 31			19 21						19 42					20 04					
Hook	d			19 36			19 25						19 47					20 09					
Basingstoke	a	19 05		19 47			19 34		19 28			19 37	20 00			19 47	19 58	20 16			20 06		

London - Woking, Guildford, Alton and Basingstoke

		SW ◇1 ⊏	SW 1	SW 1	SW 1	SW	SW 1	SW ◇1 ⊏	SW 1	SW 1 ⊏	SW ◇1 ⊏	SW 1	SW 1	SW 1	SW	SW 1	SW ◇1 ⊏	SW 1	SW 1 ⊏	SW ◇1 ⊏	SW 1	SW 1
London Waterloo 15 ⊖	d	19 35	19 39		19 25	19 20	19 45	19 50	19 42	20 00	20 05		19 53	20 09	19 50	20 15	20 20	20 12	20 30	20 35	20 39	
Vauxhall ⊖	d					19 24									19 54							
Clapham Junction 10	d		19u46		19u32	19 29	19u52				20u12		20u00		19 59	20u22	20u27	20u19			20u46	
Earlsfield	d					19 32									20 02							
Wimbledon 6 ⊖	d					19 36									20 06							
Surbiton 6	d					19 44			20 00				20 11		20 14			20 30				
Esher	d					19 48									20 18							
Hersham	d					19 51									20 21							
Walton-on-Thames	d					19 54			20 07						20 24			20 37				
Weybridge	d					19 57			20 11						20 27			20 41				
Byfleet & New Haw	d					20 00									20 30							
West Byfleet	d				19 51	20 03							20 21		20 33							
Woking	a	19 58			19 59	20 08	20 11	20 14	20 18	20 24			20 29	20 33	20 38	20 41	20 45	20 48	20 54	20 58		
	d	20 00			20 00		20 13	20 16	20 19	20 25			20 30	20 35		20 43	20 46	20 49	20 55	21 00		
Worplesdon	d						20 18															
Guildford	a						20 23			20 33						20 50			21 03			
Brookwood	d				20 06				20 25				20 36					20 55				
Ash Vale	d			19 49	20 14							20 19	20 44									20 49
Aldershot	a			19 54	20 19							20 24	20 49									20 54
	d			20 08	20 20							20 38	20 50									21 08
Farnham	a				20 25								20 55									
	d				20 26								20 56									
Bentley	d				20 32								21 02									
Alton	a				20 39								21 10									
Farnborough (Main)	d		20 13						20 33					20 45				21 03			21 13	
Fleet	d		20 19						20 38									21 08			21 19	
Winchfield	d								20 44									21 14				
Hook	d								20 48									21 18				
Basingstoke	a		20 34					20 35	20 58		20 47			20 58			21 05	21 28			21 34	

		SW 1	SW	SW 1	SW 1	SW 1 ⊏	SW 1	SW 1	SW ◇1 ⊏	SW	SW 1	SW ◇1 ⊏	SW 1 ⊏	SW ◇1 ⊏	SW 1	SW 1	SW 1	SW	SW 1	SW 1	SW 1	SW 1	SW ◇1 ⊏
London Waterloo 15 ⊖	d	20 23	20 20	20 45	20 42	21 00		20 53	21 05	20 50	21 12	21 20	21 30	21 35	21 39		21 23	21 20	21 45	21 42	22 00	21 53	22 05
Vauxhall ⊖	d		20 24							20 54								21 24					
Clapham Junction 10	d		20 29	20u52				21u00	21u12	20 59	21u19	21u27			21u46			21 29	21u52			22u00	22u12
Earlsfield	d		20 32							21 02								21 32					
Wimbledon 6 ⊖	d		20 36							21 06								21 36					
Surbiton 6	d	20 41	20 44		21 00			21 11		21 14	21 30						21 41	21 44		22 00		22 11	
Esher	d		20 48							21 18								21 48					
Hersham	d		20 51							21 21								21 51					
Walton-on-Thames	d		20 54		21 07					21 24	21 37							21 54		22 07			
Weybridge	d		20 57		21 11					21 27	21 41							21 57		22 11			
Byfleet & New Haw	d		21 00							21 30								22 00					
West Byfleet	d	20 51	21 03					21 21		21 33							21 51	22 03				22 21	
Woking	a	20 59	21 08	21 11	21 18	21 24		21 29	21 31	21 38	21 48	21 45	21 54	21 58			21 59	22 08	22 11	22 18	22 24	22 29	22 31
	d	21 00		21 13	21 19	21 25		21 30	21 32		21 49	21 49	21 55	22 00			22 00		22 13	22 19	22 25	22 30	22 32
Worplesdon	d			21 18															22 18				
Guildford	a			21 23		21 33							22 03						22 23		22 33		
Brookwood	d	21 06			21 25			21 36			21 55						22 06			22 25		22 36	
Ash Vale	d	21 14					21 19	21 44								21 49	22 14					22 44	
Aldershot	a	21 19					21 24	21 49								21 54	22 19					22 50	
	d	21 20					21 38	21 50								22 08	22 20					22 50	
Farnham	a	21 25						21 55									22 25					22 56	
	d	21 26						21 56									22 26					22 56	
Bentley	d	21 32						22 02									22 32					23 02	
Alton	a	21 39						22 10									22 39					23 10	
Farnborough (Main)	d				21 33						22 03				22 13					22 33			
Fleet	d				21 38						22 08				22 19					22 38			
Winchfield	d				21 44						22 14									22 44			
Hook	d				21 48						22 18									22 48			
Basingstoke	a				21 58				21 51		22 28	22 08			22 34					22 58			22 51

Table 155 — Mondays to Fridays

London - Woking, Guildford, Alton and Basingstoke

		SW	SW 1	SW 1 ⊏	SW 1	SW ◇1 ⊏	SW 1	SW 1	SW	SW 1	SW 1	SW 1	SW ◇1	SW	SW 1	SW 1	SW 1	SW	SW 1	SW 1	SW 1	SW 1
London Waterloo 15 ⊖	d	21 50	22 12	22 20	22 30	22 35		22 23	22 20	22 45	22 42	22 53	23 05	22 50	23 15	23 12	23 35	23 20	23 39	23 45	23 48	
Vauxhall ⊖	d	21 54							22 24					22 54				23 24				
Clapham Junction 10	d	21 59	22u19	22u27				22u30	22 29	22u52	22u49	23u00	23u12	22 59	23u22	23u19	23u43	23 29	23u46	23u52	23u56	
Earlsfield	d	22 02							22 32					23 02				23 32				
Wimbledon 6 ⊖	d	22 06							22 36					23 06				23 36				
Surbiton 6	d	22 14	22 30					22 41	22 44		23 00	23 11		23 14		23 30		23 44			00 10	
Esher	d	22 18							22 48					23 18				23 48				
Hersham	d	22 21							22 51					23 21				23 51				
Walton-on-Thames	d	22 24	22 37						22 54		23 07			23 24		23 37		23 54			00 17	
Weybridge	d	22 27	22 41						22 57		23 11			23 27		23 41		23 57			00 21	
Byfleet & New Haw	d	22 30							23 00					23 30				00 01				
West Byfleet	d	22 33						22 51	23 03			23 21		23 33				00 03				
Woking	a	22 37	22 48	22 45	22 54	22 58		22 59	23 08	23 11	23 18	23 29	23 31	23 38	23 41	23 48	00 03	00 08	00 08	00 16	00 27	
	d	22 39	22 49	22 49	22 55	23 00		23 00		23 13	23 19	23 30	23 32		23 43	23 49	00 05		00 09	00 17	00 29	
Worplesdon	d									23 18										00 22		
Guildford	a	22 47			23 03					23 23					23 51					00 28		
Brookwood	d		22 55					23 06			23 25	23 36				23 55					00 35	
Ash Vale	d						22 49	23 14				23 44										23 49
Aldershot	a						22 54	23 19				23 49										23 54
	d						23 08	23 20				23 50										23 55
Farnham	a							23 25				23 55										00 03
	d							23 26				23 56										
Bentley	d							23 32				00 02										
Alton	a							23 39				00 10										
Farnborough (Main)	d		23 03								23 33					00 03			00 19		00 42	
Fleet	d		23 08								23 38					00 08			00 25		00 48	
Winchfield	d		23 14								23 44					00 14					00s53	
Hook	d		23 18								23 48					00 18					00s58	
Basingstoke	a		23 27	23 10							23 57		23 53			00 25	00 24		00 36		01 07	

Saturdays

		SW 1	SW 1	SW 1	SW	SW 1	SW 1	SW 1	SW 1	SW 1	SW 1	SW	SW 1	SW 1	SW 1	SW ◇1	SW 1	SW 1	SW 1	SW 1	SW	SW 1	SW 1
London Waterloo 15 ⊖	d	22p53	23p12	23p35	23p20	23p39	23p45	23p48		00 05		00 09		01 05	05 00	05 30		05 20			05 50	06 15	06 12
Vauxhall ⊖	d				23p24							00 13		01 09	05 04			05 24			05 54		
Clapham Junction 10	d	23b00	23b19	23b43	23p29	23b46	23b52	23b56		00u12		00 18		01 14	05 09	05u37		05 29			05 59	06u22	06u19
Earlsfield	d				23p32							00 21			05 12			05 32			06 02		
Wimbledon 6 ⊖	d				23p36					00u18		00 25		01 20	05 16	05 43		05 36			06 06		
Surbiton 6	d	23p11	23p30		23p44			00 10				00 33		01 29	05 24			05 44			06 14		06 30
Esher	d				23p48							00s37			05 28			05 48			06 18		
Hersham	d				23p51							00s40			05 32			05 51			06 21		
Walton-on-Thames	d		23p37		23p54			00 17				00s43			05 35			05 54			06 24		06 37
Weybridge	d		23p41		23p57			00 21				00s47			05 39			05 57			06 27		06 41
Byfleet & New Haw	d				00 01							00s49			05 42			06 00			06 30		
West Byfleet	d	23p21			00 03							00s52			05 45			06 03			06 33		
Woking	a	23p29	23p48	00 03	00 08	00 08	00 16	00 27		00 35		00 57		01 41	05 50	05 59		06 08			06 38	06 41	06 48
	d	23p30	23p49	00 05		00 09	00 17	00 29		00 36	00 40	00 58		01 42	05 51	06 01	06 02	06 13	06 19	06 30		06 43	06 49
Worplesdon	d						00 22											06 18					
Guildford	a						00 28					01 06			05 59			06 23				06 50	
Brookwood	d	23p36	23p55					00 35			00 45						06 08		06 25	06 36			06 55
Ash Vale	d	23p44							23p49		00 53		00 57				06 16			06 44			
Aldershot	a	23p49							23p54		00 58		01s02				06 21			06 49			
	d	23p50							23p55		00 59		01s06				06 21			06 50			
Farnham	a	23p55							00 03		01 04		01 11				06 27			06 55			
	d	23p56									01 05						06 27			06 56			
Bentley	d	00 02									01s11						06 34			07 02			
Alton	a	00 10									01 18						06 41			07 10			
Farnborough (Main)	d		00 03			00 19		00 42						01s52					06 33				07 03
Fleet	d		00 08			00 25		00 48						01s57					06 38				07 08
Winchfield	d		00 14					00s53											06 43				07 14
Hook	d		00 18					00s58											06 48				07 18
Basingstoke	a		00 25	00 24		00 36		01 07		00 55				02s09		06 20			06 58				07 28

b previous night, stops to pick up only

Table 155

London - Woking, Guildford, Alton and Basingstoke

Saturdays

		SW ◇1	SW 1	SW	SW 1	SW 1	SW 1	SW 1	SW ◇1 ⊏	SW	SW 1	SW 1	SW 1	SW 1	SW ◇1	SW	SW 1	SW 1	SW ◇1 ⊏	SW 1	SW 1	SW ◇1	SW 1
London Waterloo 15 ⊖	d	06 30		06 20	06 45	06 42		06 53	07 10	06 50	07 15	07 12	07 30	07 23	07 35	07 20	07 39	07 45	07 50	07 42	08 00	08 05	
Vauxhall ⊖	d			06 24						06 54						07 24							
Clapham Junction 10	d	06u37		06 29	06u52	06u49		07u00	07u17	06 59	07u23	07u20		07u30		07 29	07u46	07u52	07u57			08u12	
Earlsfield	d			06 32						07 02						07 32							
Wimbledon 6 ⊖	d			06 36						07 06						07 36							
Surbiton 6	d			06 44		07 00		07 11		07 14		07 31		07 41		07 44				08 00			
Esher	d			06 48						07 18						07 48							
Hersham	d			06 51						07 21						07 51							
Walton-on-Thames	d			06 54		07 07				07 24		07 38				07 54				08 07			
Weybridge	d			06 57		07 11				07 27		07 42				07 57				08 11			
Byfleet & New Haw	d			07 00						07 30						08 00							
West Byfleet	d			07 03				07 21		07 33				07 51		08 03							
Woking	a	06 56		07 08	07 11	07 18		07 26	07 35	07 38	07 42	07 48	07 54	07 59	07 58	08 08		08 11	08 15	08 18	08 24		
	d	06 57	07 00		07 13	07 19		07 30	07 36		07 44	07 50	07 55	08 00	08 00			08 13	08 16	08 19	08 25		
Worplesdon	d				07 18													08 18					
Guildford	a				07 23						07 51		08 03					08 23			08 33		
Brookwood	d		07 06			07 25		07 36				07 56		08 06						08 25			
Ash Vale	d		07 14				07 19	07 44						08 14									08 19
Aldershot	a		07 19				07 24	07 49						08 19									08 24
	d		07 20				07 38	07 50						08 20									08 38
Farnham	a		07 25					07 55						08 25									
	d		07 26					07 56						08 26									
Bentley	d		07 32					08 02						08 32									
Alton	a		07 40					08 10						08 39									
Farnborough (Main)	d					07 33						08 03					08 13			08 33			
Fleet	d					07 38						08 09					08 19			08 38			
Winchfield	d					07 44						08 14								08 44			
Hook	d					07 48						08 19								08 48			
Basingstoke	a	07 16				07 58			07 57			08 28			08 20		08 34		08 35	08 58		08 47	

		SW 1	SW 1	SW	SW 1	SW ◇1 ⊏	SW 1	SW 1	SW ◇1 ⊏	SW 1	SW 1	SW 1	SW	SW 1	SW ◇1 ⊏	SW 1	SW 1 ⊏	SW ◇1 ⊏	SW 1	SW 1 A	SW 1 B	SW 1
London Waterloo 15 ⊖	d	07 53	08 09	07 50	08 15	08 20	08 12	08 30	08 35	08 39		08 23	08 20	08 45	08 50	08 42	09 00	09 05		08 53	08 53	09 09
Vauxhall ⊖	d			07 54									08 24									
Clapham Junction 10	d	08u00		07 59	08u22	08u27	08u19			08u46			08 29	08u52				09u12		09u00	09u00	
Earlsfield	d			08 02									08 32									
Wimbledon 6 ⊖	d			08 06									08 36									
Surbiton 6	d	08 11		08 14			08 30					08 41	08 44			09 00				09 11	09 11	
Esher	d			08 18									08 48									
Hersham	d			08 21									08 51									
Walton-on-Thames	d			08 24			08 37						08 54			09 07						
Weybridge	d			08 27			08 41						08 57			09 11						
Byfleet & New Haw	d			08 30									09 00									
West Byfleet	d	08 21		08 33								08 51	09 03							09 21	09 21	
Woking	a	08 29	08 33	08 38	08 41	08 45	08 48	08 54	08 58			08 59	09 08	09 11	09 14	09 18	09 24			09 29	09 29	09 33
	d	08 30	08 35		08 43	08 46	08 49	08 55	09 00			09 00		09 13	09 16	09 19	09 25			09 30	09 30	09 35
Worplesdon	d													09 18								
Guildford	a				08 50			09 03						09 23			09 33					
Brookwood	d	08 36					08 55					09 06				09 25				09 36	09 36	
Ash Vale	d	08 44									08 49	09 14							09 19	09 44	09 44	
Aldershot	a	08 49									08 54	09 19							09 24	09 49	09 49	
	d	08 50									09 08	09 20							09 38	09 50	09 50	
Farnham	a	08 55										09 25								09 55	09 55	
	d	08 56										09 26								09 56	09 56	
Bentley	d	09 02																		10 02	10 02	
Alton	a	09 10										09 37								10 10	10 29	
Farnborough (Main)	d		08 45				09 03			09 13						09 33						09 45
Fleet	d						09 08			09 19						09 38						
Winchfield	d						09 14									09 44						
Hook	d						09 18									09 48						
Basingstoke	a		08 58			09 05	09 28			09 34					09 35	09 58		09 47				09 58

A until 25 September **B** from 2 October

Table 155

London - Woking, Guildford, Alton and Basingstoke

Saturdays

		SW	SW 1	SW ◇1 ⊏	SW 1	SW 1 ⊏	SW ◇1 ⊏	SW 1	SW 1	SW 1	SW	SW 1	SW ◇1 ⊏	SW 1	SW 1 ⊏	SW ◇1 ⊏	SW 1	SW 1	SW 1	SW	SW 1	SW ◇1 ⊏	SW 1
London Waterloo 15 ⊖	d	08 50	09 15	09 20	09 12	09 30	09 35	09 39		09 23	09 20	09 45	09 50	09 42	10 00	10 05		09 53	10 09	09 50	10 15	10 20	10 12
Vauxhall ⊖	d	08 54									09 24									09 54			
Clapham Junction 10	d	08 59	09u22	09u27	09u19			09u46			09 29	09u52				10u12		10u00		09 59	10u22	10u27	10u19
Earlsfield	d	09 02									09 32									10 02			
Wimbledon 6 ⊖	d	09 06									09 36									10 06			
Surbiton 6	d	09 14			09 30					09 41	09 44			10 00				10 11		10 14			10 30
Esher	d	09 18									09 48									10 18			
Hersham	d	09 21									09 51									10 21			
Walton-on-Thames	d	09 24			09 37						09 54			10 07						10 24			10 37
Weybridge	d	09 27			09 41						09 57			10 11						10 27			10 41
Byfleet & New Haw	d	09 30									10 00									10 30			
West Byfleet	d	09 33								09 51	10 03							10 21		10 33			
Woking	a	09 38	09 41	09 45	09 48	09 54	09 58			09 59	10 08	10 11	10 14	10 18	10 24			10 29	10 33	10 38	10 41	10 45	10 48
	d		09 43	09 46	09 49	09 55	10 00			10 00		10 13	10 16	10 19	10 25			10 30	10 35		10 43	10 46	10 49
Worplesdon	d											10 18											
Guildford	a		09 50			10 03						10 23			10 33						10 50		
Brookwood	d				09 55					10 06				10 25				10 36					10 55
Ash Vale	d								09 49	10 14							10 19	10 44					
Aldershot	a								09 54	10 19							10 24	10 49					
	d								10 08	10 20							10 38	10 50					
Farnham	a									10 25								10 55					
	d									10 26								10 56					
Bentley	d																	11 02					
Alton	a									10 37								11 10					
Farnborough (Main)	d				10 03			10 13						10 33					10 45				11 03
Fleet	d				10 08			10 19						10 38									11 08
Winchfield	d				10 14									10 44									11 14
Hook	d				10 18									10 48									11 18
Basingstoke	a			10 05	10 28			10 34					10 35	10 58		10 47			10 58			11 05	11 28

		SW 1 ⊏	SW ◇1 ⊏	SW 1	SW 1	SW 1	SW	SW 1	SW ◇1 ⊏	SW 1	SW 1 ⊏	SW ◇1 ⊏	SW 1	SW 1	SW 1	SW	SW 1	SW ◇1 ⊏	SW 1	SW 1 ⊏	SW ◇1 ⊏	SW 1
London Waterloo 15 ⊖	d	10 30	10 35	10 39		10 23	10 20	10 45	10 50	10 42	11 00	11 05		10 53	11 09	10 50	11 15	11 20	11 12	11 30	11 35	11 39
Vauxhall ⊖	d						10 24									10 54						
Clapham Junction 10	d			10u46			10 29	10u52				11u12		11u00		10 59	11u22	11u27	11u19			11u46
Earlsfield	d						10 32									11 02						
Wimbledon 6 ⊖	d						10 36									11 06						
Surbiton 6	d					10 41	10 44			11 00				11 11		11 14			11 30			
Esher	d						10 48									11 18						
Hersham	d						10 51									11 21						
Walton-on-Thames	d						10 54			11 07						11 24			11 37			
Weybridge	d						10 57			11 11						11 27			11 41			
Byfleet & New Haw	d						11 00									11 30						
West Byfleet	d					10 51	11 03							11 21		11 33						
Woking	a	10 54	10 58			10 59	11 08	11 11	11 14	11 18	11 24			11 29	11 33	11 38	11 41	11 45	11 48	11 54	11 58	
	d	10 55	11 00			11 00		11 13	11 16	11 19	11 25			11 30	11 35		11 43	11 46	11 49	11 55	12 00	
Worplesdon	d							11 18														
Guildford	a	11 03						11 23			11 33						11 50			12 03		
Brookwood	d					11 06				11 25				11 36					11 55			
Ash Vale	d				10 49	11 14							11 19	11 44								
Aldershot	a				10 54	11 19							11 24	11 49								
	d				11 08	11 20							11 38	11 50								
Farnham	a					11 25								11 55								
	d					11 26								11 56								
Bentley	d													12 02								
Alton	a					11 37								12 10								
Farnborough (Main)	d			11 13						11 33					11 45				12 03			12 13
Fleet	d			11 19						11 38									12 08			12 19
Winchfield	d									11 44									12 14			
Hook	d									11 48									12 18			
Basingstoke	a			11 34					11 35	11 58		11 47			11 58			12 05	12 28			12 34

Table 155

Saturdays

London - Woking, Guildford, Alton and Basingstoke

		SW 1	SW 1	SW	SW 1	SW ◇1 🍴	SW 1	SW 1 🍴	SW ◇1 🍴	SW 1		SW 1	SW 1	SW	SW 1	SW ◇1 🍴	SW 1	SW 1 🍴	SW ◇1 🍴	SW 1		SW 1	SW 1	SW	SW 1
London Waterloo 15 ⊖	d		11 23	11 20	11 45	11 50	11 42	12 00	12 05			11 53	12 09	11 50	12 15	12 20	12 12	12 30	12 35	12 39			12 23	12 20	12 45
Vauxhall ⊖	d			11 24										11 54										12 24	
Clapham Junction 10	d			11 29	11u52				12u12			12u00		11 59	12u22	12u27	12u19			12u46				12 29	12u52
Earlsfield	d			11 32										12 02										12 32	
Wimbledon 6 ⊖	d			11 36										12 06										12 36	
Surbiton 6	d		11 41	11 44			12 00					12 11		12 14			12 30						12 41	12 44	
Esher	d			11 48										12 18										12 48	
Hersham	d			11 51										12 21										12 51	
Walton-on-Thames	d			11 54			12 07							12 24			12 37							12 54	
Weybridge	d			11 57			12 11							12 27			12 41							12 57	
Byfleet & New Haw	d			12 00										12 30										13 00	
West Byfleet	d		11 51	12 03								12 21		12 33									12 51	13 03	
Woking	a		11 59	12 08	12 11	12 14	12 18	12 24				12 29	12 33	12 38	12 41	12 45	12 48	12 54	12 58				12 59	13 08	13 11
	d		12 00		12 13	12 16	12 19	12 25				12 30	12 35		12 43	12 46	12 49	12 55	13 00				13 00		13 13
Worplesdon	d				12 18																				13 18
Guildford	a				12 23			12 33							12 50			13 03							13 23
Brookwood	d		12 06				12 25					12 36					12 55						13 06		
Ash Vale	d	11 49	12 14							12 19		12 44										12 49	13 14		
Aldershot	a	11 54	12 19							12 24		12 49										12 54	13 19		
	d	12 08	12 20							12 38		12 50										13 08	13 20		
Farnham	a		12 25									12 55											13 25		
	d		12 26									12 56											13 26		
Bentley	d											13 02													
Alton	a		12 37									13 10											13 37		
Farnborough (Main)	d						12 33						12 45				13 03			13 13					
Fleet	d						12 38										13 08			13 19					
Winchfield	d						12 44										13 14								
Hook	d						12 48										13 18								
Basingstoke	a					12 35	12 58		12 47				12 58			13 05	13 28			13 34					

		SW ◇1 🍴	SW 1	SW 1 🍴	SW ◇1 🍴	SW 1		SW 1	SW 1	SW	SW 1	SW ◇1 🍴	SW 1	SW 1 🍴	SW ◇1 🍴	SW 1		SW 1	SW 1	SW	SW 1	SW ◇1 🍴	SW 1	SW 1 🍴	SW ◇1 🍴
London Waterloo 15 ⊖	d	12 50	12 42	13 00	13 05			12 53	13 09	12 50	13 15	13 20	13 12	13 30	13 35	13 39			13 23	13 20	13 45	13 50	13 42	14 00	14 05
Vauxhall ⊖	d									12 54										13 24					
Clapham Junction 10	d				13u12			13u00		12 59	13u22	13u27	13u19			13u46				13 29	13u52				14u12
Earlsfield	d									13 02										13 32					
Wimbledon 6 ⊖	d									13 06										13 36					
Surbiton 6	d		13 00					13 11		13 14			13 30						13 41	13 44			14 00		
Esher	d									13 18										13 48					
Hersham	d									13 21										13 51					
Walton-on-Thames	d		13 07							13 24			13 37							13 54			14 07		
Weybridge	d		13 11							13 27			13 41							13 57			14 11		
Byfleet & New Haw	d									13 30										14 00					
West Byfleet	d							13 21		13 33									13 51	14 03					
Woking	a	13 14	13 18	13 24				13 29	13 33	13 38	13 41	13 45	13 48	13 54	13 58				13 59	14 08	14 11	14 14	14 18	14 24	
	d	13 16	13 19	13 25				13 30	13 35		13 43	13 46	13 49	13 55	14 00				14 00		14 13	14 16	14 19	14 25	
Worplesdon	d																				14 18				
Guildford	a			13 33							13 50			14 03							14 23			14 33	
Brookwood	d		13 25					13 36					13 55						14 06				14 25		
Ash Vale	d					13 19		13 44										13 49	14 14						
Aldershot	a					13 24		13 49										13 54	14 19						
	d					13 38		13 50										14 08	14 20						
Farnham	a							13 55											14 25						
	d							13 56											14 26						
Bentley	d							14 02																	
Alton	a							14 10											14 37						
Farnborough (Main)	d		13 33						13 45				14 03			14 13							14 33		
Fleet	d		13 38										14 08			14 19							14 38		
Winchfield	d		13 44										14 14										14 44		
Hook	d		13 48										14 18										14 48		
Basingstoke	a	13 35	13 58		13 47				13 58			14 05	14 28			14 34						14 35	14 58		14 47

Table 155

Saturdays

London - Woking, Guildford, Alton and Basingstoke

		SW 1		SW 1	SW 1	SW	SW 1	SW ◇1 🍴	SW 1	SW 1 🍴	SW ◇1 🍴	SW 1		SW 1	SW 1	SW	SW 1	SW ◇1 🍴	SW 1	SW 1 🍴	SW ◇1 🍴	SW 1		SW 1	SW 1
London Waterloo 15 ⊖	d			13 53	14 09	13 50	14 15	14 20	14 12	14 30	14 35	14 39			14 23	14 20	14 45	14 50	14 42	15 00	15 05			14 53	15 09
Vauxhall ⊖	d					13 54										14 24									
Clapham Junction 10	d			14u00		13 59	14u22	14u27	14u19			14u46				14 29	14u52				15u12			15u00	
Earlsfield	d					14 02										14 32									
Wimbledon 6 ⊖	d					14 06										14 36									
Surbiton 6	d			14 11		14 14			14 30						14 41	14 44			15 00					15 11	
Esher	d					14 18										14 48									
Hersham	d					14 21										14 51									
Walton-on-Thames	d					14 24			14 37							14 54			15 07						
Weybridge	d					14 27			14 41							14 57			15 11						
Byfleet & New Haw	d					14 30										15 00									
West Byfleet	d			14 21		14 33									14 51	15 03								15 21	
Woking	a			14 29	14 33	14 38	14 41	14 45	14 48	14 54	14 58				14 59	15 08	15 11	15 14	15 18	15 24				15 29	15 33
	d			14 30	14 35		14 43	14 46	14 49	14 55	15 00				15 00		15 13	15 16	15 19	15 25				15 30	15 35
Worplesdon	d																15 18								
Guildford	a						14 50			15 03							15 23			15 33					
Brookwood	d			14 36					14 55						15 06				15 25					15 36	
Ash Vale	d	14 19		14 44										14 49	15 14							15 19		15 44	
Aldershot	a	14 24		14 49										14 54	15 19							15 24		15 49	
	d	14 38		14 50										15 08	15 20							15 38		15 50	
Farnham	a			14 55											15 25									15 55	
	d			14 56											15 26									15 56	
Bentley	d			15 02																				16 02	
Alton	a			15 10											15 37									16 10	
Farnborough (Main)	d				14 45				15 03			15 13							15 33						15 45
Fleet	d								15 08			15 19							15 38						
Winchfield	d								15 14										15 44						
Hook	d								15 18										15 48						
Basingstoke	a				14 58			15 05	15 28			15 34						15 35	15 58		15 47				15 58

		SW	SW 1	SW ◇1 🍴	SW 1	SW 1 🍴	SW ◇1 🍴	SW 1		SW 1	SW 1	SW	SW 1	SW ◇1 🍴	SW 1	SW 1 🍴	SW ◇1 🍴	SW 1		SW 1	SW 1	SW	SW 1	SW ◇1 🍴	SW 1
London Waterloo 15 ⊖	d	14 50	15 15	15 20	15 12	15 30	15 35	15 39			15 23	15 20	15 45	15 50	15 42	16 00	16 05			15 53	16 09	15 50	16 15	16 20	16 12
Vauxhall ⊖	d	14 54										15 24										15 54			
Clapham Junction 10	d	14 59	15u22	15u27	15u19			15u46				15 29	15u52				16u12			16u00		15 59	16u22	16u27	16u19
Earlsfield	d	15 02										15 32										16 02			
Wimbledon 6 ⊖	d	15 06										15 36										16 06			
Surbiton 6	d	15 14			15 30						15 41	15 44			16 00					16 11		16 14			16 30
Esher	d	15 18										15 48										16 18			
Hersham	d	15 21										15 51										16 21			
Walton-on-Thames	d	15 24			15 37							15 54			16 07							16 24			16 37
Weybridge	d	15 27			15 41							15 57			16 11							16 27			16 41
Byfleet & New Haw	d	15 30										16 00										16 30			
West Byfleet	d	15 33									15 51	16 03								16 21		16 33			
Woking	a	15 38	15 41	15 45	15 48	15 54	15 58				15 59	16 08	16 11	16 14	16 18	16 24				16 29	16 33	16 38	16 41	16 45	16 48
	d		15 43	15 46	15 49	15 55	16 00				16 00		16 13	16 16	16 19	16 25				16 30	16 35		16 43	16 46	16 49
Worplesdon	d												16 18												
Guildford	a		15 50			16 03							16 23			16 33							16 50		
Brookwood	d				15 55						16 06				16 25					16 36					16 55
Ash Vale	d									15 49	16 14							16 19		16 44					
Aldershot	a									15 54	16 19							16 24		16 49					
	d									16 08	16 20							16 38		16 50					
Farnham	a										16 25									16 55					
	d										16 26									16 56					
Bentley	d																			17 02					
Alton	a										16 37									17 10					
Farnborough (Main)	d				16 03			16 13							16 33						16 45				17 03
Fleet	d				16 08			16 19							16 38										17 08
Winchfield	d				16 14										16 44										17 14
Hook	d				16 18										16 48										17 18
Basingstoke	a			16 05	16 28			16 34						16 35	16 58		16 47				16 58			17 05	17 28

London - Woking, Guildford, Alton and Basingstoke

		SW 1 ☕	SW ◇1 ☕	SW 1	SW 1	SW 1	SW	SW 1	SW ◇1 ☕	SW 1	SW 1 ☕	SW ◇1 ☕	SW 1	SW 1	SW 1	SW	SW 1	SW ◇1 ☕	SW 1	SW 1 ☕	SW ◇1 ☕	SW 1
London Waterloo 15 ⊖	d	16 30	16 35	16 39		16 23	16 20	16 45	16 50	16 42	17 00	17 05		16 53	17 09	16 50	17 15	17 20	17 12	17 30	17 35	17 39
Vauxhall ⊖	d						16 24									16 54						
Clapham Junction 10	d			16u46			16 29	16u52				17u12		17u00		16 59	17u22	17u27	17u19			17u46
Earlsfield	d						16 32									17 02						
Wimbledon 6 ⊖	d						16 36									17 06						
Surbiton 6	d					16 41	16 44			17 00				17 11		17 14			17 30			
Esher	d						16 48									17 18						
Hersham	d						16 51									17 21						
Walton-on-Thames	d						16 54			17 07						17 24			17 37			
Weybridge	d						16 57			17 11						17 27			17 41			
Byfleet & New Haw	d						17 00									17 30						
West Byfleet	d					16 51	17 03							17 21		17 33						
Woking	a	16 54	16 58			16 59	17 08	17 11	17 14	17 18	17 24			17 29	17 33	17 38	17 41	17 45	17 48	17 54	17 58	
	d	16 55	17 00			17 00		17 13	17 16	17 19	17 25			17 30	17 35		17 43	17 46	17 49	17 55	18 00	
Worplesdon	d							17 18														
Guildford	a	17 03						17 23			17 33						17 50			18 03		
Brookwood	d					17 06				17 25				17 36					17 55			
Ash Vale	d				16 49	17 14							17 19	17 44								
Aldershot	a				16 54	17 19							17 24	17 49								
	d				17 08	17 20							17 38	17 50								
Farnham	a					17 25								17 55								
	d					17 26								17 56								
Bentley	d					17 32								18 02								
Alton	a					17 39								18 10								
Farnborough (Main)	d			17 13						17 33					17 45				18 03			18 13
Fleet	d			17 19						17 38									18 08			18 19
Winchfield	d									17 44									18 14			
Hook	d									17 48									18 18			
Basingstoke	a			17 34					17 35	17 58		17 47			17 58			18 05	18 28			18 34

		SW 1	SW 1	SW	SW 1	SW ◇1 ☕	SW 1	SW 1 ☕	SW ◇1 ☕	SW 1	SW 1	SW 1	SW	SW 1	SW ◇1 ☕	SW 1	SW 1 ☕	SW ◇1 ☕	SW 1	SW 1	SW 1	SW	SW 1
London Waterloo 15 ⊖	d		17 23	17 20	17 45	17 50	17 42	18 00	18 05		17 53	18 09	17 50	18 15	18 20	18 12	18 30	18 35	18 39		18 23	18 20	18 45
Vauxhall ⊖	d			17 24									17 54									18 24	
Clapham Junction 10	d			17 29	17u52				18u12		18u00		17 59	18u22	18u27	18u19			18u46			18 29	18u52
Earlsfield	d			17 32									18 02									18 32	
Wimbledon 6 ⊖	d			17 36									18 06									18 36	
Surbiton 6	d		17 41	17 44			18 00				18 11		18 14			18 30					18 41	18 44	
Esher	d			17 48									18 18									18 48	
Hersham	d			17 51									18 21									18 51	
Walton-on-Thames	d			17 54			18 07						18 24			18 37						18 54	
Weybridge	d			17 57			18 11						18 27			18 41						18 57	
Byfleet & New Haw	d			18 00									18 30									19 00	
West Byfleet	d		17 51	18 03							18 21		18 33								18 51	19 03	
Woking	a		17 59	18 08	18 11	18 14	18 18	18 24			18 29	18 33	18 38	18 41	18 45	18 48	18 54	18 58			18 59	19 08	19 11
	d		18 00		18 13	18 16	18 19	18 25			18 30	18 35		18 43	18 46	18 49	18 55	19 00			19 00		19 13
Worplesdon	d				18 18																		19 18
Guildford	a				18 23			18 33						18 50			19 03						19 23
Brookwood	d		18 06				18 25				18 36					18 55					19 06		
Ash Vale	d	17 49	18 14							18 19	18 44									18 49	19 14		
Aldershot	a	17 54	18 19							18 24	18 49									18 54	19 19		
	d	18 08	18 20							18 38	18 50									19 08	19 20		
Farnham	a		18 25								18 55										19 25		
	d		18 26								18 56										19 26		
Bentley	d		18 32								19 02										19 32		
Alton	a		18 39								19 10										19 39		
Farnborough (Main)	d						18 33					18 45				19 03			19 13				
Fleet	d						18 38									19 08			19 19				
Winchfield	d						18 44									19 14							
Hook	d						18 48									19 18							
Basingstoke	a					18 35	18 58		18 47			18 58			19 05	19 28			19 34				

Table 155 Saturdays

London - Woking, Guildford, Alton and Basingstoke

		SW ◇1 ☕	SW 1	SW 1 ☕	SW ◇1 ☕	SW 1	SW 1	SW 1	SW	SW 1	SW ◇1 ☕	SW 1	SW 1 ☕	SW ◇1 ☕	SW 1	SW 1	SW 1	SW	SW 1	SW ◇1 ☕	SW 1	SW 1	SW ◇1 ☕
London Waterloo 15 ⊖	d	18 50	18 42	19 00	19 05		18 53	19 09	18 50	19 15	19 20	19 12	19 30	19 35	19 39		19 23	19 20	19 45	19 50	19 42	20 00	20 05
Vauxhall ⊖	d								18 54									19 24					
Clapham Junction 10	d				19u12		19u00		18 59	19u22	19u27	19u19			19u46			19 29	19u52				20u12
Earlsfield	d								19 02									19 32					
Wimbledon 6 ⊖	d								19 06									19 36					
Surbiton 6	d		19 00				19 11		19 14			19 30					19 41	19 44			20 00		
Esher	d								19 18									19 48					
Hersham	d								19 21									19 51					
Walton-on-Thames	d		19 07						19 24			19 37						19 54			20 07		
Weybridge	d		19 11						19 27			19 41						19 57			20 11		
Byfleet & New Haw	d								19 30									20 00					
West Byfleet	d						19 21		19 33								19 51	20 03					
Woking	a	19 15	19 18	19 24			19 29	19 33	19 38	19 41	19 45	19 48	19 54	19 58			19 59	20 08	20 11	20 14	20 18	20 24	
	d	19 16	19 19	19 25			19 30	19 35		19 43	19 46	19 49	19 55	20 00			20 00		20 13	20 16	20 19	20 25	
Worplesdon	d																		20 18				
Guildford	a			19 33						19 50			20 03						20 23			20 33	
Brookwood	d		19 25				19 36					19 55					20 06				20 25		
Ash Vale	d					19 19	19 44									19 49	20 14						
Aldershot	a					19 24	19 49									19 54	20 19						
	d					19 38	19 50									20 08	20 20						
Farnham	a						19 55										20 25						
	d						19 56										20 26						
Bentley	d						20 02										20 32						
Alton	a						20 10										20 39						
Farnborough (Main)	d		19 33					19 45				20 03			20 13						20 33		
Fleet	d		19 38									20 08			20 19						20 38		
Winchfield	d		19 44									20 14									20 44		
Hook	d		19 48									20 18									20 48		
Basingstoke	a	19 35	19 58		19 47			19 58			20 05	20 28			20 34					20 35	20 58		20 47

		SW 1	SW 1	SW 1	SW	SW 1	SW ◇1 ☕	SW 1	SW 1	SW ◇1 ☕	SW 1	SW 1	SW 1	SW	SW 1	SW 1	SW 1	SW 1	SW 1	SW ◇1 ☕	SW	SW 1
London Waterloo 15 ⊖	d		19 53	20 09	19 50	20 15	20 20	20 12	20 30	20 35	20 39		20 23	20 20	20 45	20 42	21 00		20 53	21 05	20 50	21 12
Vauxhall ⊖	d				19 54									20 24							20 54	
Clapham Junction 10	d		20u00		19 59	20u22	20u27	20u19			20u46			20 29	20u52				21u00	21u12	20 59	21u19
Earlsfield	d				20 02									20 32							21 02	
Wimbledon 6 ⊖	d				20 06									20 36							21 06	
Surbiton 6	d		20 11		20 14			20 30					20 41	20 44		21 00			21 11		21 14	21 30
Esher	d				20 18									20 48							21 18	
Hersham	d				20 21									20 51							21 21	
Walton-on-Thames	d				20 24			20 37						20 54		21 07					21 24	21 37
Weybridge	d				20 27			20 41						20 57		21 11					21 27	21 41
Byfleet & New Haw	d				20 30									21 00							21 30	
West Byfleet	d		20 21		20 33								20 51	21 03					21 21		21 33	
Woking	a		20 29	20 33	20 38	20 41	20 45	20 48	20 54	20 58			20 59	21 08	21 11	21 18	21 24		21 29	21 31	21 38	21 48
	d		20 30	20 35		20 43	20 46	20 49	20 55	21 00			21 00		21 13	21 19	21 25		21 30	21 32		21 49
Worplesdon	d														21 18							
Guildford	a					20 50			21 03						21 23		21 33					
Brookwood	d		20 36					20 55					21 06			21 25			21 36			21 55
Ash Vale	d	20 19	20 44									20 49	21 14					21 19	21 44			
Aldershot	a	20 24	20 49									20 54	21 19					21 24	21 49			
	d	20 38	20 50									21 08	21 20					21 38	21 50			
Farnham	a		20 55										21 25						21 55			
	d		20 56										21 26						21 56			
Bentley	d		21 02										21 32						22 02			
Alton	a		21 10										21 39						22 10			
Farnborough (Main)	d			20 45				21 03			21 13					21 33						22 03
Fleet	d							21 08			21 19					21 38						22 08
Winchfield	d							21 14								21 44						22 14
Hook	d							21 18								21 48						22 18
Basingstoke	a			20 58			21 05	21 28			21 34					21 58				21 51		22 25

Table 155

Saturdays

London - Woking, Guildford, Alton and Basingstoke

		SW ◇1 ⊐	SW 1	SW ◇1 ⊐	SW 1	SW 1	SW 1	SW		SW 1	SW 1	SW 1	SW 1	SW ◇1 ⊐	SW	SW 1	SW 1 ⊐	SW 1		SW ◇1 ⊐	SW 1	SW 1	SW	SW 1	SW 1
London Waterloo 15 ⊖	d	21 20	21 30	21 35	21 39		21 23	21 20		21 45	21 42	22 00	21 53	22 05	21 50	22 12	22 20	22 30		22 35		22 23	22 20	22 45	22 42
Vauxhall ⊖	d							21 24							21 54								22 24		
Clapham Junction 10	d	21u27			21u46			21 29		21u52			22u00	22u12	21 59	22u19	22u27					22u30	22 29	22u52	22u49
Earlsfield	d							21 32							22 02								22 32		
Wimbledon 6 ⊖	d							21 36							22 06								22 36		
Surbiton 6	d						21 41	21 44			22 00		22 11		22 14	22 30						22 41	22 44		23 00
Esher	d							21 48							22 18								22 48		
Hersham	d							21 51							22 21								22 51		
Walton-on-Thames	d							21 54			22 07				22 24	22 37							22 54		23 07
Weybridge	d							21 57			22 11				22 27	22 41							22 57		23 11
Byfleet & New Haw	d							22 00							22 30								23 00		
West Byfleet	d						21 51	22 03					22 21		22 33							22 51	23 03		
Woking	a	21 45	21 54	21 58			21 59	22 08		22 11	22 18	22 24	22 29	22 31	22 37	22 48	22 45	22 54		22 58		22 59	23 08	23 11	23 18
	d	21 49	21 55	22 00			22 00			22 13	22 19	22 25	22 30	22 32	22 39	22 49	22 49	22 55		23 00		23 00		23 13	23 19
Worplesdon	d									22 18														23 18	
Guildford	a		22 03							22 23		22 33			22 47			23 03						23 23	
Brookwood	d						22 06				22 25		22 36			22 55						23 06			23 25
Ash Vale	d					21 49	22 14						22 44								22 49	23 14			
Aldershot	a					21 54	22 19						22 50								22 54	23 19			
	d					22 08	22 20						22 50								23 08	23 20			
Farnham	a						22 25						22 56									23 25			
	d						22 26						22 56									23 26			
Bentley	d						22 32						23 02									23 32			
Alton	a						22 39						23 10									23 39			
Farnborough (Main)	d				22 13						22 33					23 03									23 33
Fleet	d				22 19						22 38					23 08									23 38
Winchfield	d										22 44					23 14									23 44
Hook	d										22 48					23 18									23 48
Basingstoke	a	22 09			22 34						22 58			22 51		23 25	23 08								23 55

		SW 1	SW 1	SW ◇1		SW	SW 1	SW 1	SW 1	SW	SW 1	SW 1	SW 1
London Waterloo 15 ⊖	d		22 53	23 05		22 50	23 15	23 12	23 35	23 20	23 39	23 45	23 48
Vauxhall ⊖	d					22 54				23 24			
Clapham Junction 10	d		23u00	23u12		22 59	23u22	23u19	23u42	23 29	23u46	23u52	23u56
Earlsfield	d					23 02				23 32			
Wimbledon 6 ⊖	d					23 06				23 36			
Surbiton 6	d		23 11			23 14		23 30		23 44			00 10
Esher	d					23 18				23 48			
Hersham	d					23 21				23 51			
Walton-on-Thames	d					23 24		23 37		23 54			00 17
Weybridge	d					23 27		23 41		23 57			00 21
Byfleet & New Haw	d					23 30				23 59			
West Byfleet	d		23 21			23 33				00 03			
Woking	a		23 29	23 31		23 38	23 41	23 48	00 03	00 08	00 08	00 16	00 27
	d		23 30	23 32			23 43	23 49	00 05		00 09	00 17	00 29
Worplesdon	d											00 22	
Guildford	a						23 51					00 28	
Brookwood	d		23 36					23 55					00 35
Ash Vale	d		23 44										
Aldershot	a	23 47	23 49										
	d	23 58	23 50										
Farnham	a	00 03	23 55										
	d		23 56										
Bentley	d		00 02										
Alton	a		00 10										
Farnborough (Main)	d							00 03			00 19		00 42
Fleet	d							00 08			00 25		00 48
Winchfield	d							00 14					00s53
Hook	d							00 18					00s58
Basingstoke	a			23 51				00 25	00 24		00 36		01 07

Table 155

Sundays

London - Woking, Guildford, Alton and Basingstoke

		SW 1	SW 1	SW 1	SW	SW 1	SW 1	SW	SW 1	SW 1	SW 1	SW	SW 1	SW 1	SW 1	SW 1	SW 1	SW	SW ◇1	SW	SW	SW 1	SW 1	SW ◇1 ⊐	SW
London Waterloo 15 ⊖	d	22p53	23p12	23p35	23p20	23p39	23p45		23p48	00 05		00 09			01 05			07 10	07 54	07 40		08 00	08 07	08 15	
Vauxhall ⊖	d				23p24							00 13			01 09			07 14		07 44					
Clapham Junction 10	d	23b00	23b19	23b42	23p29	23b46	23b52		23b56	00u12		00 18			01 14			07 19	08u03	07 49		08u09	08 15	08u22	
Earlsfield	d				23p32							00 21						07 22		07 52					
Wimbledon 6 ⊖	d				23p36					00u18		00 25			01 20			07 26		07 56			08 22		
Surbiton 6	d	23p11	23p30		23p44				00 10			00 33						07 35		08 05			08 30		
Esher	d				23p48							00s37						07 39		08 09					
Hersham	d				23p51							00s40						07 42		08 12					
Walton-on-Thames	d		23p37		23p54				00 17			00s43						07 45		08 15					
Weybridge	d		23p41		23p57				00 21			00s47						07 49		08 19					
Byfleet & New Haw	d				23p59			00 07				00s49						07 51		08 21	08 02				
West Byfleet	d	23p21			00 03			00 10				00s52						07 54		08 24	08 05				
Woking	a	23p29	23p48	00 03	00 08	00 08	00 16	00 20	00 27	00 35		00 57			01 42			07 59	08 27	08 29	08 10	08 34	08 42	08 46	<
	d	23p30	23p49	00 05		00 09	00 17		00 29	00 36	00 40	00 58		07 32	01 42	07 46	07 49	08 05	08 28	08 32		08 35	08 46	08 47	08 49
Worplesdon	d						00 22																		
Guildford	a						00 28					01 06		07 39				08 14		08 40		08 43			
Brookwood	d	23p36	23p55						00 35		00 45					07 52	07 56						08 52		08 56
Ash Vale	d	23p44									00 53		00 57				08 04								09 04
Aldershot	a	23p49									00 58		01s02				08 09								09 09
	d	23p50									00 59		01s06				08 09								09 09
Farnham	a	23p55									01 04		01 11				08 15								09 15
	d	23p56									01 05						08 15								09 15
Bentley	d	00 02									01s11						08 24								09 24
Alton	a	00 10									01 18						08 31								09 31
Farnborough (Main)	d		00 03			00 19			00 42						01s58	07 59							08 59		
Fleet	d		00 08			00 25			00 48							08 05							09 05		
Winchfield	d		00 14						00s53							08 10							09 10		
Hook	d		00 18						00s58							08 15							09 15		
Basingstoke	a		00 25	00 24		00 36			01 07	00 55					02 12	08 22			08 46				09 22	09 06	

		SW 1	SW	SW 1	SW ◇1	SW	SW ◇1	SW	SW 1	SW 1	SW ◇1 ⊐	SW 1	SW 1	SW	SW 1	SW ◇1	SW	SW ◇1	SW	SW 1	SW 1	SW ◇1 ⊐	SW 1	SW 1	SW
London Waterloo 15 ⊖	d		08 10	08 30	08 35		08 54	08 40	09 00	09 07	09 15			09 10	09 30	09 35		09 54	09 40	10 00	10 07	10 15			10 10
Vauxhall ⊖	d		08 14					08 44						09 14					09 44						10 14
Clapham Junction 10	d		08 19	08u39	08u45		09u03	08 49	09u09	09 15	09u22			09 19	09u39	09u45		10u03	09 49	10u09	10 15	10u22			10 19
Earlsfield	d		08 22					08 52						09 22					09 52						10 22
Wimbledon 6 ⊖	d		08 26					08 56		09 22				09 26					09 56		10 22				10 26
Surbiton 6	d		08 35					09 05		09 30				09 35					10 05		10 30				10 35
Esher	d		08 39					09 09						09 39					10 09						10 39
Hersham	d		08 42					09 12						09 42					10 12						10 42
Walton-on-Thames	d		08 45					09 15						09 45					10 15						10 45
Weybridge	d		08 49					09 19						09 49					10 19						10 49
Byfleet & New Haw	d		08 51			09 02		09 21						09 51			10 02		10 21						10 51
West Byfleet	d		08 54			09 05		09 24						09 54			10 05		10 24						10 54
Woking	a		08 59	09 03	09 08	09 10	09 27	09 29	09 34	09 42	09 46	<		09 59	10 03	10 08	10 10	10 26	10 29	10 31	10 42	10 45	<		10 59
	d		09 02	09 04	09 09		09 28	09 32	09 35	09 46	09 47	09 49		10 02	10 04	10 09		10 28	10 35	10 32	10 46	10 46	10 49		11 05
Worplesdon	d																								
Guildford	a		09 10	09 12				09 40	09 43					10 10	10 12				10 44	10 40					11 14
Brookwood	d									09 52		09 56									10 52		10 56		
Ash Vale	d	08 36										10 04	09 36										11 04	10 35	
Aldershot	a	08 41										10 09	09 41										11 09	10 41	
	d	08 48										10 09	09 48										11 09	10 48	
Farnham	a											10 15											11 15		
	d											10 15											11 15		
Bentley	d											10 24											11 24		
Alton	a											10 31											11 31		
Farnborough (Main)	d									09 59											10 59				
Fleet	d									10 05											11 05				
Winchfield	d									10 10											11 10				
Hook	d									10 15											11 15				
Basingstoke	a				09 28		09 46			10 22	10 06					10 28		10 46			11 22	11 05			

b previous night, stops to pick up only

Table 155

Sundays

London - Woking, Guildford, Alton and Basingstoke

		SW 1	SW ◇1 ⊥	SW	SW ◇1	SW	SW 1	SW 1	SW ◇1 ⊥	SW 1	SW 1	SW	SW 1 ⊥	SW ◇1 ⊥	SW	SW ◇1 ⊥	SW	SW 1	SW 1	SW ◇1 ⊥	SW 1	SW 1	SW	SW 1 ⊥
London Waterloo 15 ⊖	d	10 30	10 35		10 54	10 40	11 00	11 07	11 15			11 10	11 30	11 35		11 54	11 40	12 00	12 07	12 15			12 10	12 30
Vauxhall ⊖	d					10 44						11 14					11 44						12 14	
Clapham Junction 10	d	10u39	10u45		11u04	10 49	11u09	11 15	11u22			11 19	11u39	11u45		12u04	11 49	12u09	12 15	12u22			12 19	12u39
Earlsfield	d					10 52						11 22					11 52						12 22	
Wimbledon 6 ⊖	d					10 56		11 22				11 26					11 56		12 22				12 26	
Surbiton 6	d					11 05		11 30				11 35					12 05		12 30				12 35	
Esher	d					11 09						11 39					12 09						12 39	
Hersham	d					11 12						11 42					12 12						12 42	
Walton-on-Thames	d					11 15						11 45					12 15						12 45	
Weybridge	d					11 19						11 49					12 19						12 49	
Byfleet & New Haw	d			11 02		11 21						11 51			12 02		12 21						12 51	
West Byfleet	d			11 05		11 24						11 54			12 05		12 24						12 54	
Woking	a	11 01	11 06	11 10	11 26	11 29	11 31	11 42	11 45	<		11 59	12 01	12 06	12 10	12 26	12 29	12 31	12 42	12 45	<		12 59	13 01
	d	11 02	11 07		11 28	11 35	11 32	11 46	11 46	11 49		12 05	12 02	12 07		12 28	12 35	12 32	12 46	12 46	12 49		13 05	13 02
Worplesdon	d																							
Guildford	a	11 10				11 44	11 40					12 14	12 10				12 44	12 40					13 14	13 10
Brookwood	d							11 52		11 56									12 52		12 56			
Ash Vale	d									12 04	11 36										13 04	12 36		
Aldershot	a									12 09	11 41										13 09	12 41		
	d									12 09	11 48										13 09	12 48		
Farnham	a									12 15											13 15			
	d									12 15											13 15			
Bentley	d									12 24											13 24			
Alton	a									12 31											13 31			
Farnborough (Main)	d							11 59											12 59					
Fleet	d							12 05											13 05					
Winchfield	d							12 10											13 10					
Hook	d							12 15											13 15					
Basingstoke	a		11 26		11 46			12 22	12 05					12 26		12 46			13 22	13 05				

		SW ◇1 ⊥	SW	SW ◇1 ⊥	SW	SW 1	SW 1	SW ◇1 ⊥	SW 1	SW 1	SW	SW 1 ⊥	SW ◇1 ⊥	SW	SW ◇1 ⊥	SW	SW 1	SW 1	SW ◇1 ⊥	SW 1	SW 1	SW	SW 1 ⊥	SW ◇1 ⊥	SW
London Waterloo 15 ⊖	d	12 35		12 54	12 40	13 00	13 07	13 15			13 10	13 30	13 35		13 54	13 40	14 00	14 07	14 15			14 10	14 30	14 35	
Vauxhall ⊖	d				12 44						13 14					13 44						14 14			
Clapham Junction 10	d	12u42		13u03	12 49	13u09	13 15	13u22			13 19	13u39	13u42		14u03	13 49	14u09	14 15	14u22			14 19	14u39	14u42	
Earlsfield	d				12 52						13 22					13 52						14 22			
Wimbledon 6 ⊖	d				12 56		13 22				13 26					13 56		14 22				14 26			
Surbiton 6	d				13 05		13 30				13 35					14 05		14 30				14 35			
Esher	d				13 09						13 39					14 09						14 39			
Hersham	d				13 12						13 42					14 12						14 42			
Walton-on-Thames	d				13 15						13 45					14 15						14 45			
Weybridge	d				13 19						13 49					14 19						14 49			
Byfleet & New Haw	d		13 02		13 21						13 51			14 02		14 21						14 51			15 02
West Byfleet	d		13 05		13 24						13 54			14 05		14 24						14 54			15 05
Woking	a	13 06	13 10	13 26	13 29	13 31	13 42	13 45	<		13 59	14 01	14 06	14 10	14 26	14 29	14 31	14 42	14 45			14 59	15 01	15 06	15 10
	d	13 07		13 28	13 35	13 32	13 46	13 46	13 49		14 05	14 02	14 07		14 28	14 35	14 32	14 46	14 46	14 49		15 05	15 02	15 07	
Worplesdon	d																								
Guildford	a				13 44	13 40					14 14	14 10				14 44	14 40					15 14	15 10		
Brookwood	d						13 52		13 56									14 52		14 56					
Ash Vale	d								14 04	13 36										15 04	14 36				
Aldershot	a								14 09	13 41										15 09	14 41				
	d								14 09	13 48										15 09	14 48				
Farnham	a								14 15											15 15					
	d								14 15											15 15					
Bentley	d								14 24											15 24					
Alton	a								14 31											15 31					
Farnborough (Main)	d						13 59											14 59							
Fleet	d						14 05											15 05							
Winchfield	d						14 10											15 10							
Hook	d						14 15											15 15							
Basingstoke	a	13 26		13 46			14 22	14 05					14 26		14 46			15 22	15 05					15 26	

Table 155

Sundays

London - Woking, Guildford, Alton and Basingstoke

		SW ◇1 ⊥	SW	SW 1	SW 1	SW 1	SW ◇1 ⊥	SW 1	SW	SW 1 ⊥	SW ◇1 ⊥	SW	SW 1	SW 1	SW 1	SW ◇1 ⊥	SW	SW 1	SW 1	SW 1	SW ◇1 ⊥	SW	SW 1 ⊥	SW ◇1 ⊥	SW
London Waterloo 15 ⊖	d	14 54	14 40	15 00	15 07		15 15		15 10	15 30	15 35		15 37			15 54	15 40	16 00	16 07		16 15	16 10	16 30	16 35	
Vauxhall ⊖	d		14 44						15 14								15 44					16 14			
Clapham Junction 10	d	15u03	14 49	15u09	15 15		15u22		15 19	15u39	15u42		15 46			16u03	15 49	16u09	16 15		16u22	16 19	16u39	16u42	
Earlsfield	d		14 52						15 22								15 52					16 22			
Wimbledon 6 ⊖	d		14 56		15 22				15 26				15 53				15 56		16 22			16 26			
Surbiton 6	d		15 05		15 30				15 35				16 02				16 05		16 30			16 35			
Esher	d		15 09						15 39								16 09					16 39			
Hersham	d		15 12						15 42								16 12					16 42			
Walton-on-Thames	d		15 15						15 45				16 09				16 15					16 45			
Weybridge	d		15 19						15 49				16 13				16 19					16 49			
Byfleet & New Haw	d		15 21						15 51			16 02					16 21					16 51			17 02
West Byfleet	d		15 24						15 54			16 05					16 24					16 54			17 05
Woking	a	15 26	15 29	15 31	15 42	<	15 45		15 59	16 01	16 06	16 10	16 19	<		16 26	16 29	16 31	16 42	<	16 45	16 59	17 01	17 06	17 10
	d	15 28	15 35	15 32	15 46	15 49	15 46		16 05	16 02	16 07		16 23	16 26		16 28	16 35	16 32	16 46	16 49	16 46	17 05	17 02	17 07	
Worplesdon	d																								
Guildford	a		15 44	15 40					16 14	16 10							16 44	16 40				17 14	17 10		
Brookwood	d				15 52	15 56							16 29	16 33					16 52	16 56					
Ash Vale	d					16 04		15 36						16 41	16 36					17 04					
Aldershot	a					16 09		15 41						16 46	16 41					17 09					
	d					16 09		15 48						16 46	16 48					17 09					
Farnham	a					16 15								16 52						17 15					
	d					16 15								16 56						17 15					
Bentley	d					16 24														17 24					
Alton	a					16 31								17 07						17 31					
Farnborough (Main)	d				15 59								16 36						16 59						
Fleet	d				16 05								16 42						17 05						
Winchfield	d				16 10														17 10						
Hook	d				16 15														17 15						
Basingstoke	a	15 46			16 22		16 05				16 26		16 54			16 46			17 22		17 05			17 26	

		SW 1	SW 1	SW 1	SW ◇1 ⊥	SW	SW 1	SW 1	SW ◇1 ⊥	SW 1	SW	SW 1 ⊥	SW ◇1 ⊥	SW	SW 1	SW 1	SW 1	SW ◇1 ⊥	SW	SW 1	SW 1	SW 1	SW ◇1 ⊥	SW
London Waterloo 15 ⊖	d	16 37			16 54	16 40	17 00	17 07	17 15		17 10	17 30	17 35		17 37			17 54	17 40	18 00	18 07		18 15	18 10
Vauxhall ⊖	d					16 44					17 14								17 44					18 14
Clapham Junction 10	d	16 46			17u03	16 49	17u09	17 15	17u22		17 19	17u39	17u42		17 46			18u03	17 49	18u09	18 15		18u22	18 19
Earlsfield	d					16 52					17 22								17 52					18 22
Wimbledon 6 ⊖	d	16 53				16 56		17 22			17 26				17 53				17 56		18 22			18 26
Surbiton 6	d	17 02				17 05		17 30			17 35				18 02				18 05		18 30			18 35
Esher	d					17 09					17 39								18 09					18 39
Hersham	d					17 12					17 42								18 12					18 42
Walton-on-Thames	d	17 09				17 15					17 45				18 09				18 15					18 45
Weybridge	d	17 13				17 19					17 49				18 13				18 19					18 49
Byfleet & New Haw	d					17 21					17 51			18 02					18 21					18 51
West Byfleet	d					17 24					17 54			18 05					18 24					18 54
Woking	a	17 19	<		17 26	17 29	17 31	17 42	17 45	<	17 59	18 01	18 06	18 10	18 19	<		18 26	18 29	18 31	18 42	<	18 45	18 59
	d	17 23	17 26		17 28	17 35	17 32	17 46	17 46	17 49	18 05	18 02	18 07		18 23	18 26		18 28	18 35	18 32	18 46	18 49	18 46	19 05
Worplesdon	d																							
Guildford	a					17 44	17 40				18 14	18 10							18 44	18 40				19 14
Brookwood	d	17 29	17 33					17 52		17 56					18 29	18 33					18 52	18 56		
Ash Vale	d		17 41	17 36						18 04						18 41	18 36					19 04		
Aldershot	a		17 46	17 41						18 09						18 46	18 41					19 09		
	d		17 46	17 48						18 09						18 46	18 48					19 09		
Farnham	a		17 52							18 15						18 52						19 15		
	d		17 56							18 15						18 56						19 15		
Bentley	d									18 24												19 24		
Alton	a		18 07							18 31						19 07						19 31		
Farnborough (Main)	d	17 36						17 59							18 36						18 59			
Fleet	d	17 42						18 05							18 42						19 05			
Winchfield	d							18 10													19 10			
Hook	d							18 15													19 15			
Basingstoke	a	17 54			17 46			18 22	18 05				18 26		18 54			18 46			19 22		19 05	

Table 155

Sundays

London - Woking, Guildford, Alton and Basingstoke

	SW 1 ⊐	SW ◇1 ⊐	SW	SW 1	SW 1	SW 1	SW ◇1 ⊐	SW	SW 1	SW 1	SW 1	SW ◇1 ⊐
London Waterloo 15 ⊖ d	18 30	18 35		18 37			18 54	18 40	19 00	19 07		19 15
Vauxhall ⊖ d								18 44				
Clapham Junction 10 d	18u39	18u42		18 46			19u03	18 49	19u09	19 15		19u22
Earlsfield d								18 52				
Wimbledon 6 ⊖ d				18 53				18 56		19 22		
Surbiton 6 d				19 02				19 05		19 30		
Esher d								19 09				
Hersham d								19 12				
Walton-on-Thames d				19 09				19 15				
Weybridge d				19 13				19 19				
Byfleet & New Haw d			19 02					19 21				
West Byfleet d			19 05					19 24				
Woking a	19 01	19 06	19 10	19 19	<		19 26	19 29	19 31	19 42	<	19 45
d	19 02	19 07		19 23	19 26		19 28	19 35	19 32	19 46	19 49	19 46
Worplesdon d												
Guildford a	19 10							19 44	19 40			
Brookwood d				19 29	19 33					19 52	19 56	
Ash Vale d					19 41	19 36					20 04	
Aldershot a					19 46	19 41					20 09	
d					19 46	19 48					20 09	
Farnham a					19 52						20 15	
d					19 56						20 15	
Bentley d											20 24	
Alton a					20 07						20 31	
Farnborough (Main) d				19 36						19 59		
Fleet d				19 42						20 05		
Winchfield d										20 10		
Hook d										20 15		
Basingstoke a		19 26		19 54			19 46			20 22		20 05

	SW	SW 1 ⊐	SW ◇1 ⊐	SW	SW 1	SW 1	SW 1	SW ◇1	SW	SW 1	SW 1	SW 1
London Waterloo 15 ⊖ d	19 10	19 30	19 35		19 37			19 54	19 40	20 00	20 07	
Vauxhall ⊖ d	19 14								19 44			
Clapham Junction 10 d	19 19	19u39	19u42		19 46			20u03	19 49	20u09	20 15	
Earlsfield d	19 22								19 52			
Wimbledon 6 ⊖ d	19 26				19 53				19 56		20 22	
Surbiton 6 d	19 35				20 02				20 05		20 30	
Esher d	19 39								20 09			
Hersham d	19 42								20 12			
Walton-on-Thames d	19 45				20 09				20 15			
Weybridge d	19 49				20 13				20 19			
Byfleet & New Haw d	19 51			20 02					20 21			
West Byfleet d	19 54			20 05					20 24			
Woking a	19 59	20 01	20 06	20 10	20 19	<		20 26	20 29	20 31	20 42	<
d	20 05	20 02	20 07		20 23	20 26		20 28	20 35	20 32	20 46	20 49
Worplesdon d												
Guildford a	20 14	20 10							20 44	20 40		
Brookwood d					20 29	20 33					20 52	20 56
Ash Vale d						20 41	20 36					21 04
Aldershot a						20 46	20 41					21 09
d						20 46	20 48					21 09
Farnham a						20 52						21 15
d						20 56						21 15
Bentley d												21 24
Alton a						21 07						21 31
Farnborough (Main) d					20 36						20 59	
Fleet d					20 42						21 05	
Winchfield d											21 10	
Hook d											21 15	
Basingstoke a			20 26		20 54			20 46			21 22	

	SW ◇1 ⊐	SW	SW 1 ⊐	SW ◇1 ⊐	SW	SW 1	SW 1	SW 1	SW ◇1	SW	SW 1	
London Waterloo 15 ⊖ d	20 15	20 10	20 30	20 35		20 37			20 54	20 40	21 00	
Vauxhall ⊖ d		20 14								20 44		
Clapham Junction 10 d	20u22	20 19	20u39	20u42		20 46			21u03	20 49	21u09	
Earlsfield d		20 22								20 52		
Wimbledon 6 ⊖ d		20 26				20 53				20 56		
Surbiton 6 d		20 35				21 02				21 05		
Esher d		20 39								21 09		
Hersham d		20 42								21 12		
Walton-on-Thames d		20 45				21 09				21 15		
Weybridge d		20 49				21 13				21 19		
Byfleet & New Haw d		20 51			21 02					21 21		
West Byfleet d		20 54			21 05					21 24		
Woking a	20 45	20 59	21 01	21 06	21 10	21 19			21 26	21 29	21 31	
d	20 46	21 05	21 02	21 07		21 23	21 26		21 28	21 35	21 32	
Worplesdon d												
Guildford a		21 14	21 10							21 44	21 40	
Brookwood d						21 29	21 33					
Ash Vale d							21 41	21 36				
Aldershot a							21 46	21 41				
d							21 46	21 48				
Farnham a							21 52					
d							21 56					
Bentley d												
Alton a							22 07					
Farnborough (Main) d						21 36						
Fleet d						21 42						
Winchfield d												
Hook d												
Basingstoke a	21 05			21 26		21 54			21 46			

	SW 1	SW 1	SW ◇1 ⊐	SW	SW 1	SW ◇1 ⊐	SW	SW 1	SW 1	SW 1	SW ◇1	SW
London Waterloo 15 ⊖ d	21 07		21 15	21 10	21 30	21 35		21 37			21 54	21 40
Vauxhall ⊖ d				21 14								21 44
Clapham Junction 10 d	21 15		21u22	21 19	21u39	21u42		21 46			22u03	21 49
Earlsfield d				21 22								21 52
Wimbledon 6 ⊖ d	21 22			21 26				21 53				21 56
Surbiton 6 d	21 30			21 35				22 02				22 05
Esher d				21 39								22 09
Hersham d				21 42								22 12
Walton-on-Thames d				21 45				22 09				22 15
Weybridge d				21 49				22 13				22 19
Byfleet & New Haw d				21 51			22 02					22 21
West Byfleet d				21 54			22 05					22 24
Woking a	21 42	<	21 45	21 59	22 01	22 06	22 10	22 19	<		22 26	22 29
d	21 46	21 49	21 46	22 05	22 02	22 07		22 23	22 26		22 28	22 35
Worplesdon d												
Guildford a				22 14	22 10							22 44
Brookwood d	21 52	21 56						22 29	22 33			
Ash Vale d		22 04							22 41	22 36		
Aldershot a		22 09							22 47	22 45		
d		22 09							22 48	22 49		
Farnham a		22 15							22 53			
d		22 15							22 56			
Bentley d		22 24										
Alton a		22 31							23 07			
Farnborough (Main) d	21 59							22 36				
Fleet d	22 05							22 42				
Winchfield d	22 10											
Hook d	22 15											
Basingstoke a	22 22		22 05			22 26		22 54			22 46	

Table 155

Sundays

London - Woking, Guildford, Alton and Basingstoke

	SW 1	SW 1	SW 1	SW 1 ⊐	SW	SW 1	SW	SW 1	SW 1	SW 1	SW ◇1 ⊐	SW
London Waterloo 15 ⊖ d	22 00	22 07		22 15	22 10	22 30		22 37			22 54	22 40
Vauxhall ⊖ d					22 14							22 44
Clapham Junction 10 d	22u09	22 15		22u22	22 19	22u39		22 46			23u03	22 49
Earlsfield d					22 22							22 52
Wimbledon 6 ⊖ d		22 22			22 26			22 53				22 56
Surbiton 6 d		22 30			22 35			23 02				23 05
Esher d					22 39							23 09
Hersham d					22 42							23 12
Walton-on-Thames d					22 45			23 09				23 15
Weybridge d					22 49			23 13				23 19
Byfleet & New Haw d					22 51		23 02					23 21
West Byfleet d					22 54		23 05					23 24
Woking a	22 31	22 42	<	22 45	22 59	23 01	23 10	23 19	<		23 26	23 29
d	22 32	22 46	22 49	22 46	23 05	23 02		23 23	23 26		23 28	23 35
Worplesdon d												
Guildford a	22 40				23 13	23 10						23 45
Brookwood d		22 52	22 56					23 29	23 33			
Ash Vale d			23 04						23 41	23 36		
Aldershot a			23 09						23 46	23 41		
d			23 09						23 48	23 42		
Farnham a			23 15						23 54	23 47		
d			23 15						23 56			
Bentley d			23 24									
Alton a			23 31						00 07			
Farnborough (Main) d		22 59						23 36				
Fleet d		23 05						23 42				
Winchfield d		23 10										
Hook d		23 15										
Basingstoke a		23 22		23 05				23 54			23 46	

	SW 1	SW 1	SW 1	SW	SW 1		SW 1	SW	SW 1			
London Waterloo 15 ⊖ d	23 00	23 07		23 10	23 30		23 35		23 40			
Vauxhall ⊖ d				23 14					23 44			
Clapham Junction 10 d	23u09	23 15		23 19	23u39		23u44		23 49			
Earlsfield d				23 22					23 52			
Wimbledon 6 ⊖ d		23 22		23 26					23 56			
Surbiton 6 d		23 30		23 35					00 05			
Esher d				23 39					00 09			
Hersham d				23 42					00 12			
Walton-on-Thames d				23 45					00 15			
Weybridge d				23 49					00 19			
Byfleet & New Haw d				23 51				00 02	00 21			
West Byfleet d				23 54				00 05	00 24			
Woking a	23 31	23 42	<	23 59	00 01		00 07	00 10	00 30			
d	23 32	23 46	23 49	00 05	00 03		00 08		00 35			
Worplesdon d												
Guildford a	23 40			00 13	00 10							
Brookwood d		23 52	23 56						00 41			
Ash Vale d			00 04						00 48			
Aldershot a			00 09						00 53			
d			00 09						00 54			
Farnham a			00 15						00 59			
d			00 15									
Bentley d			00 23									
Alton a			00 30									
Farnborough (Main) d		23 59					00 18					
Fleet d		00 05					00 24					
Winchfield d		00 10										
Hook d		00 15										
Basingstoke a		00 22					00 39					

Table 155

Mondays to Fridays

Basingstoke, Alton, Guildford and Woking - Waterloo

		SW MX [1]	SW MO [1]	SW MO	SW MX [1]	SW MX [1]	SW MO [1]	SW MX [1]	SW MO ◇[1]	SW MX [1]	SW	SW [1] A	SW [1] B	SW	SW	SW [1]	SW [1] B	SW [1] A	SW	SW [1]	SW [1]	SW ◇[1] ⊏⊐	SW [1]
Basingstoke	d				22p54	23p13			23p44	23p44		04 54	04 54			05 39					05 54	05 59	
Hook	d				23p01					23p51		05 01	05 01								06 01		
Winchfield	d				23p05					23p55		05 05	05 05								06 05		
Fleet	d				23p10					00 02		05 10	05 10			05 50					06 10		
Farnborough (Main)	d				23p16					00 06		05 16	05 16			05 56					06 16		
Alton	d	22p44	22p45														05 42	05 42					
Bentley	d	22p51															05 49	05 49					
Farnham	a	22p56	22p55														05 54	05 54					
	d	22p58	23p00														05 56	05 56					
Aldershot	d	23p04	23p06														06 02	06 02					05 58
Ash Vale	d	23p09	23p11														06 07	06 07					06 02
Brookwood	d	23p16	23p18		23p23					00 13		05 23	05 23				06 14	06 14			06 23		
Guildford	d						23p35	23p39			04 00			05 12						05 50			
Worplesdon	d							23p44						05 17						05 55			
Woking	a	23p21	23p24		23p28	23p33	23p42	23p49	00 02	00 18	04 08	05 28	05 28	05 22		06 05	06 19	06 19		06 00	06 28	06 18	
	d	23p22	23p28	22p52	23p33	23p34	23p45	23p56	00 04	00 20	04 10	05 29	05 29	05 33	05 25	06 06	06 20	06 20	05 43	06 01	06 29	06 19	
West Byfleet	d	23p27		22p56	23p37					00 25				05 37	05 30		06 25	06 25	05 47				
Byfleet & New Haw	d			23p00	23p40									05 40	05 33								
Weybridge	d		23p34		23p43					00 29				05 43					05 51				
Walton-on-Thames	d		23p38		23p47					00 33				05 47					05 55				
Hersham	d				23p49									05 49									
Esher	d				23p52									05 52									
Surbiton [6]	a	23p37	23p45		23p57					00 39	04 24	05 40	05 40	05 56			06 35	06 35	06 01		06 40		
Wimbledon [6] ⊖	a		23p53		00 07					00 47	04 31	05 48	05 48	06 04							06 47		
Earlsfield	a				00 11									06 08									
Clapham Junction [10]	a	23p54	23p59		00 15	23p56	00 04	00 21	00 23	00 53	04 43			06 12		06 25	06 46	06 46		06 20	06 54	06 38	
Vauxhall ⊖	a			00 08	00 20							06 07	06 07	06 17	06 49								
London Waterloo [15] ⊖	a	00 03	00 10	00 13	00 28	00 06	00 14	00 30	00 33	01 02	04 53	06 15	06 12	06 22	06 56	06 34	06 54	06 56	06 20	06 29	07 04	06 49	

		SW	SW [1]	SW [1]	SW [1]	SW [1]	SW ◇[1] ⊏⊐	SW [1]	SW [1] ⊏⊐	SW	SW ◇[1] ⊏⊐	SW [1]	SW [1]	SW [1]	SW [1]	SW ◇[1] ⊏⊐	SW [1]	SW [1]	SW [1] A	SW [1] B	SW [1]	SW [1]	SW [1]
Basingstoke	d					06 23	06 27				06 35			06 42		06 51		06 54					07 06
Hook	d					06 31												07 01					07 13
Winchfield	d					06 35												07 05					07 17
Fleet	d					06 40								06 54				07 10					07 22
Farnborough (Main)	d					06 46								07 00				07 16					07 28
Alton	d			06 12											06 44								
Bentley	d			06 19											06 51								
Farnham	a			06 24											06 56								
	d			06 26											06 58								
Aldershot	d		06 08	06 32				06 28				06 38			07 04				06 59	07 00			
Ash Vale	d			06 37				06 32							07 09				07 03	07 04			
Brookwood	d			06 44		06 53									07 16			07 23					
Guildford	d		06a25		06 24				06 31			06a55					06 53					07 07	
Worplesdon	d				06 30												06 59						
Woking	a			06 49	06 35	06 58	06 46		06 39		06 53			07 10	07 21		07 03	07 28				07 15	
	d	06 04		06 50	06 37	06 59	06 47		06 41	06 32	06 55		06 41	07 11	07 22		07 05	07 29			07 02	07 17	
West Byfleet	d	06 08								06 36			06 46								07 07		
Byfleet & New Haw	d	06 11								06 39			06 49										
Weybridge	d	06 14								06 43			06 52								07 11		
Walton-on-Thames	d	06 18								06 47			06 57								07 16		
Hersham	d	06 20								06 49			07 00								07 19		
Esher	d	06 23								06 52			07 03								07 22		
Surbiton [6]	a	06 27								06 56			07 07								07 26		
Wimbledon [6] ⊖	a	06 35								07 04													
Earlsfield	a	06 39								07 08													
Clapham Junction [10]	a	06 42		07 10	06 58	07 20			07 02	07 12	07 14					07 28	07 24						
Vauxhall ⊖	a	06 47						07 52		07 17									08 22	08 22			
London Waterloo [15] ⊖	a	06 52		07 20	07 08	07 31	07 14	07 59	07 12	07 24	07 24		07 26	07 41	07 51	07 39	07 36	07 59	08 29	08 29	07 49	07 45	08 06

A from 27 September

B until 24 September

Table 155

Mondays to Fridays

Basingstoke, Alton, Guildford and Woking - Waterloo

		SW [1]	SW [1]	SW [1]	SW [1] ⊏⊐	SW [1]	SW ◇[1] ⊏⊐	SW [1]	SW [1] A	SW [1] B	SW [1]	SW ◇[1]	SW [1]	SW [1]	SW [1]	SW [1]	SW [1]	SW [1]	SW [1]	SW [1]	SW ◇[1] ⊏⊐	SW [1]
Basingstoke	d		07 17			07 24	07 29	07b36						07e47						07 52	07 59	08g05
Hook	d					07 31		07 43												07 59		08 12
Winchfield	d					07 35		07 47												08 04		08 16
Fleet	d					07 40		07 52												08 09		08 22
Farnborough (Main)	d					07 46		07 58												08 16		08 28
Alton	d			07 14												07 44						
Bentley	d			07 21												07 51						
Farnham	a			07 26												07 56						
	d			07 28									07 39			07 58						
Aldershot	d			07 34					07 29	07 30			07 46			08 04		08f00				
Ash Vale	d			07 39					07 33	07 34			07 50			08 09		08 04				
Brookwood	d			07 46		07 53							07 57			08 16				08 23		
Guildford	d				07 17										07 45							
Worplesdon	d														07 50							
Woking	a			07 51	07 25	07 58		08 08				07 38	08 03	08 05	07 54	08 21				08 28	08 18	08 38
	d	07 07		07 52	07 26	07 59		08 09			07 32	07 40	08 05	08 06	07 56	08 23			07 47	08 29	08 19	08 39
West Byfleet	d	07 16									07 37		08c16				07 46		07 54			
Byfleet & New Haw	d	07 19											08 19				07 49		07 57			
Weybridge	d	07 22									07 41		08 22				07 52		08 01			
Walton-on-Thames	d	07 27									07 46		08 27				07 57		08 06			
Hersham	d	07 30									07 49		08 30				08 00		08 09			
Esher	d	07 33									07 52		08 33				08 03		08 13			
Surbiton [6]	a	07 37									07 56		08 37				08 07		08 18			
Wimbledon [6] ⊖	a																					
Earlsfield	a																					
Clapham Junction [10]	a																					
Vauxhall ⊖	a								08 52	08 52												
London Waterloo [15] ⊖	a	07 56	08 01	08 22	07 54	08 29	08 14	08 39	09 00	09 00	08 19	08 08	08 59	08 34	08 24	08 52	08 26		08 36	09 00	08 46	09 10

		SW [1]	SW [1]	SW [1]	SW [1] ⊏⊐	SW [1]	SW [1]	SW	SW	SW [1]	SW ◇[1] ⊏⊐	SW [1]	SW ◇[1] ⊏⊐	SW [1]	SW [1]	SW	SW [1]	SW [1]	SW [1]	SW ◇[1] ⊏⊐	SW [1]	SW [1]	SW [1]
Basingstoke	d			08 16						08 24	08 29		08 35	08 42					08 54	08 59		09 17	
Hook	d									08 31									09 01				
Winchfield	d									08 35									09 05				
Fleet	d									08 40				08 53					09 10				
Farnborough (Main)	d									08 46				08 59					09 16			09 31	
Alton	d					08 14									08 44								09 14
Bentley	d					08 21									08 51								09 21
Farnham	a					08 26									08 56								09 26
	d					08 28									08 58								09 28
Aldershot	d					08 34	08h30								09 04		09i00						09 34
Ash Vale	d					08 39	08 34								09 09		09 04						09 39
Brookwood	d					08 46				08 53					09 16				09 23				09 46
Guildford	d	08 03			08 15				08 20			08 31				08 46					09 03		
Worplesdon	d				08 20							08 37				08 51							
Woking	a	08 11		08 34	08 26	08 51			08 30	08 58	08 48	08 41	08 53		09 21	08 59			09 28	09 18	09 11	09 40	09 51
	d	08 12	08 02	08 36	08 27	08 52		08 17	08 32	08 59	08 49	08 43	08 55		09 22	09 02		08 47	09 29	09 19	09 13	09 41	09 52
West Byfleet	d		08 06					08 26	08 36						09 27	09 06		08 54					09 57
Byfleet & New Haw	d							08 29	08 39							09 09		08 57					
Weybridge	d		08 11					08 32	08 43							09 13		09 02	09 36				
Walton-on-Thames	d		08 15					08 36	08 47							09 17		09 07	09 40				
Hersham	d		08 17					08 39	08 49							09 19		09 10					
Esher	d		08 20					08 43	08 52							09 22		09 13					
Surbiton [6]	a		08 24					08 47	08 56	09 10					09 37	09 26		09 18	09 46				10 07
Wimbledon [6] ⊖	a								09 04							09 34							
Earlsfield	a								09 08							09 38							
Clapham Junction [10]	a								09 12			09 03	09 14	09 26	09 50	09 42			09 57	09 38	09 32		
Vauxhall ⊖	a								09 17							09 47							
London Waterloo [15] ⊖	a	08 41	08 46	09 03	08 55	09 21		09 06	09 24	09 29	09 17	09 13	09 25	09 38	09 59	09 54		09 40	10 05	09 51	09 43	10 08	10 25

A from 27 September

B until 24 September

b arr. 0727

c arr. 0810

e arr. 0741

f arr. 0747

g arr. 0758

h arr. 0817

i arr. 0847

Table 155

Basingstoke, Alton, Guildford and Woking - Waterloo

		SW [1] ☕	SW [1]	SW ◇[1] ☕		SW [1]	SW ◇[1] ☕	SW [1]	SW	SW ◇[1] ☕	SW [1] ☕	SW [1]	SW [1] ☕	SW [1]		SW [1]	SW ◇[1] ☕	SW [1]	SW	SW [1]	SW [1]	SW [1] ☕	SW [1]	SW ◇[1] ☕	
Basingstoke	d					09 24	09 31			09 36	09 41					09 54	09 57				10 17				
Hook	d					09 31										10 01									
Winchfield	d					09 35										10 05									
Fleet	d					09 40					09 52					10 10									
Farnborough (Main)	d					09 46					09 58					10 16					10 31				
Alton	d											09 44								10 14					
Bentley	d											09 51								10 21					
Farnham	a											09 56								10 26					
	d											09 58								10 28					
Aldershot	d		09b30									10 04		10c00						10 34			10e30		
Ash Vale	d		09 34									10 09		10 04						10 39			10 34		
Brookwood	d					09 53						10 16				10 23				10 46					
Guildford	d	09 17						09 34					09 47					10 02				10 17			
Worplesdon	d							09 40																	
Woking	a	09 27		09 22		09 58	09 49	09 44		09 54		10 21	09 59			10 28	10 15	10 11		10 51	10 40	10 25		10 20	
	d	09 28		09 24		09 59	09 51	09 46	09 33	09 56		10 22	09 59			10 29	10 17	10 12	10 03	10 52	10 41	10 26		10 21	
West Byfleet	d								09 37			10 27							10 07	10 57					
Byfleet & New Haw	d								09 40										10 10						
Weybridge	d					10 06			09 43							10 36			10 13						
Walton-on-Thames	d					10 10			09 47							10 40			10 17						
Hersham	d								09 49										10 19						
Esher	d								09 52										10 22						
Surbiton [6]	a					10 16			09 56			10 37				10 46			10 26	11 07					
Wimbledon [6] ⊖	a								10 04										10 34						
Earlsfield	a								10 08										10 38						
Clapham Junction [10]	a			09 43			10 10	10 05	10 12	10 15	10 24	10 48				10 57	10 36	10 31	10 42						
Vauxhall ⊖	a								10 17										10 47						
London Waterloo [15] ⊖	a	09 55		09 53		10 35	10 19	10 13	10 22	10 23	10 34	10 57	10 27			11 05	10 49	10 40	10 52	11 27	11 08	10 51		10 49	

		SW [1]	SW ◇[1] ☕	SW [1]	SW ◇[1] ☕	SW	SW [1]	SW [1]	SW [1] ☕	SW [1]		SW [1]	SW ◇[1] ☕	SW [1]	SW	SW [1]	SW [1] ☕	SW [1]	SW [1]	SW ◇[1] ☕		SW [1]	SW ◇[1] ☕	SW [1]	SW
Basingstoke	d	10 24	10 31		10 36		10 41					10 54	10 57			11 17						11 24	11 31		
Hook	d	10 31										11 01										11 31			
Winchfield	d	10 35										11 05										11 35			
Fleet	d	10 40					10 52					11 10										11 40			
Farnborough (Main)	d	10 46					10 58					11 16				11 31						11 46			
Alton	d							10 44										11 15							
Bentley	d							10 51																	
Farnham	a							10 56										11 25							
	d							10 58										11 28							
Aldershot	d							11 04		11f00								11 34	11g30						
Ash Vale	d							11 09		11 04								11 39	11 34						
Brookwood	d	10 53						11 16				11 23						11 46				11 53			
Guildford	d			10 34					10 47					11 02			11 17							11 34	
Worplesdon	d			10 40																				11 40	
Woking	a	10 58	10 49	10 44				11 21	10 57			11 28	11 15	11 11		11 40	11 25	11 51		11 19		11 58	11 49	11 44	
	d	10 59	10 51	10 46		10 33		11 22	10 59			11 29	11 17	11 12	11 03	11 41	11 26	11 52		11 21		11 59	11 51	11 46	11 33
West Byfleet	d					10 37		11 27							11 07			11 57							11 37
Byfleet & New Haw	d					10 40									11 10										11 40
Weybridge	d	11 06				10 43						11 36			11 13							12 06			11 43
Walton-on-Thames	d	11 10				10 47						11 40			11 17							12 10			11 47
Hersham	d					10 49									11 19										11 49
Esher	d					10 52									11 22										11 52
Surbiton [6]	a	11 16				10 56		11 37				11 46			11 26			12 07				12 16			11 56
Wimbledon [6] ⊖	a					11 04									11 34										12 04
Earlsfield	a					11 08									11 38										12 08
Clapham Junction [10]	a			11 05	11 12	11 12	11 23	11 49				11 57	11 36	11 31	11 42									12 05	12 12
Vauxhall ⊖	a					11 17									11 47										12 17
London Waterloo [15] ⊖	a	11 35	11 19	11 13	11 20	11 22	11 34	11 57	11 24			12 06	11 49	11 40	11 52	12 08	11 51	12 27		11 49		12 35	12 19	12 13	12 22

b arr. 0917
c arr. 0947
e arr. 1017
f arr. 1047
g arr. 1117

Table 155

Basingstoke, Alton, Guildford and Woking - Waterloo

		SW ◇[1] ☕	SW [1]	SW [1]	SW [1] ☕	SW [1]		SW [1]	SW ◇[1] ☕	SW [1]	SW	SW [1]	SW [1] ☕	SW [1]	SW ◇[1] ☕	SW [1]		SW ◇[1] ☕	SW [1]	SW [1]	SW	SW ◇[1] ☕	SW [1]	SW [1]	SW [1] ☕
Basingstoke	d	11 36	11 41					11 54	11 57			12 17				12 24		12 31				12 36	12 41		
Hook	d							12 01								12 31									
Winchfield	d							12 05								12 35									
Fleet	d		11 52					12 10								12 40							12 52		
Farnborough (Main)	d		11 58					12 16				12 31				12 46							12 58		
Alton	d			11 44																				12 44	
Bentley	d			11 51																				12 51	
Farnham	a			11 56																				12 56	
	d			11 58															12 28					12 58	
Aldershot	d			12 04		12b00								12c30					12 34					13 04	
Ash Vale	d			12 09		12 04								12 34					12 39					13 09	
Brookwood	d			12 16				12 23								12 53			12 46					13 16	
Guildford	d				11 47					12 02			12 17							12 34					12 47
Worplesdon	d																			12 40					
Woking	a			12 21	11 57			12 28	12 15	12 11		12 40	12 25		12 19	12 58		12 49	12 51	12 44				13 21	12 57
	d			12 22	11 59			12 29	12 17	12 12	12 03	12 41	12 26		12 21	12 59		12 51	12 52	12 46	12 33			13 22	12 59
West Byfleet	d			12 27							12 07								12 57		12 37			13 27	
Byfleet & New Haw	d										12 10										12 40				
Weybridge	d							12 36			12 13					13 06					12 43				
Walton-on-Thames	d							12 40			12 17					13 10					12 47				
Hersham	d										12 19										12 49				
Esher	d										12 22										12 52				
Surbiton [6]	a			12 37				12 46			12 26					13 16			13 07		12 56			13 37	
Wimbledon [6] ⊖	a										12 34										13 04				
Earlsfield	a										12 38										13 08				
Clapham Junction [10]	a	12 12	12 23	12 48				12 57	12 36	12 31	12 42									13 05	13 12	13 12	13 23	13 48	
Vauxhall ⊖	a										12 47										13 17				
London Waterloo [15] ⊖	a	12 20	12 34	12 57	12 23			13 05	12 49	12 40	12 52	13 07	12 51		12 49	13 34		13 19	13 25	13 13	13 22	13 20	13 34	13 57	13 23

		SW [1]		SW [1]	SW ◇[1] ☕	SW [1]	SW	SW [1]	SW [1] ☕	SW [1]	SW [1]	SW ◇[1] ☕		SW [1]	SW ◇[1] ☕	SW [1]	SW	SW ◇[1] ☕	SW [1]	SW [1]	SW [1] ☕	SW [1]		SW [1]	SW ◇[1] ☕
Basingstoke	d			12 54	12 57			13 17						13 24	13 31			13 36	13 41					13 54	13 57
Hook	d			13 01										13 31										14 01	
Winchfield	d			13 05										13 35										14 05	
Fleet	d			13 10										13 40					13 52					14 10	
Farnborough (Main)	d			13 16				13 31						13 46					13 58					14 16	
Alton	d									13 15										13 44					
Bentley	d																			13 51					
Farnham	a									13 25										13 56					
	d									13 28										13 58					
Aldershot	d	13e00								13 34	13f30									14 04		14g00			
Ash Vale	d	13 04								13 39	13 34									14 09		14 04			
Brookwood	d			13 23						13 46				13 53						14 16				14 23	
Guildford	d					13 02			13 17							13 34					13 47				
Worplesdon	d															13 40									
Woking	a			13 28	13 15	13 11		13 40	13 25	13 51		13 19		13 58	13 49	13 44				14 21	13 57			14 28	14 15
	d			13 29	13 17	13 12	13 03	13 41	13 26	13 52		13 21		13 59	13 51	13 46	13 33			14 22	13 59			14 29	14 17
West Byfleet	d						13 07			13 57							13 37			14 27					
Byfleet & New Haw	d						13 10										13 40								
Weybridge	d			13 36			13 13							14 06			13 43							14 36	
Walton-on-Thames	d			13 40			13 17							14 10			13 47							14 40	
Hersham	d						13 19										13 49								
Esher	d						13 22										13 52								
Surbiton [6]	a			13 46			13 26			14 07				14 16			13 56			14 37				14 46	
Wimbledon [6] ⊖	a						13 34										14 04								
Earlsfield	a						13 38										14 08								
Clapham Junction [10]	a			13 57	13 38	13 31	13 42									14 05	14 12	14 12	14 23	14 48				14 57	14 36
Vauxhall ⊖	a						13 47										14 17								
London Waterloo [15] ⊖	a			14 05	13 49	13 40	13 52	14 07	13 51	14 25		13 49		14 35	14 19	14 13	14 22	14 20	14 34	14 57	14 23			15 05	14 49

b arr. 1147
c arr. 1217
e arr. 1247
f arr. 1317
g arr. 1347

Basingstoke, Alton, Guildford and Woking - Waterloo

		SW 1	SW	SW 1	SW 1 ⊡	SW 1	SW 1	SW ◇1 ⊡		SW 1	SW ◇1 ⊡	SW 1	SW	SW ◇1 ⊡	SW 1	SW 1	SW 1 ⊡	SW 1		SW 1	SW ◇1 ⊡	SW 1	SW	SW 1	SW 1 ⊡
Basingstoke	d			14 17						14 24	14 31			14 36	14 41					14 54	14 57			15 17	
Hook	d									14 31										15 01					
Winchfield	d									14 35										15 05					
Fleet	d									14 40					14 52					15 10					
Farnborough (Main)	d			14 31						14 46					14 58					15 16				15 31	
Alton	d					14 15										14 44									
Bentley	d															14 51									
Farnham	a					14 25										14 56									
	d					14 28										14 58									
Aldershot	d					14 34	14b30									15 04		15c00							
Ash Vale	d					14 39	14 34									15 09		15 04							
Brookwood	d					14 46				14 53						15 16				15 23					
Guildford	d	14 02			14 17							14 34					14 47					15 02			15 17
Worplesdon	d											14 40													
Woking	a	14 11		14 40	14 25	14 51		14 19		14 58	14 49	14 44				15 21	14 57			15 28	15 15	15 11		15 40	15 25
	d	14 12	14 03	14 41	14 26	14 52		14 21		14 59	14 51	14 46	14 33			15 22	14 59			15 29	15 17	15 12	15 03	15 41	15 26
West Byfleet	d		14 07			14 57							14 37			15 27							15 07		
Byfleet & New Haw	d		14 10										14 40										15 10		
Weybridge	d		14 13							15 06			14 43							15 36			15 13		
Walton-on-Thames	d		14 17							15 10			14 47							15 40			15 17		
Hersham	d		14 19										14 49										15 19		
Esher	d		14 22										14 52										15 22		
Surbiton 6	a		14 26			15 07				15 16			14 56			15 37				15 46			15 26		
Wimbledon 6 ⊖	a		14 34										15 04										15 34		
Earlsfield	a		14 38										15 08										15 38		
Clapham Junction 10	a	14 31	14 42									15 05	15 12	15 12	15 23	15 50				15 57	15 36	15 31	15 42		
Vauxhall ⊖	a		14 47										15 17										15 47		
London Waterloo 15 ⊖	a	14 40	14 52	15 08	14 51	15 25		14 49		15 35	15 19	15 13	15 22	15 20	15 32	15 58	15 23			16 05	15 49	15 43	15 52	16 07	15 51

		SW 1	SW 1	SW ◇1 ⊡		SW 1	SW ◇1 ⊡	SW 1	SW	SW ◇1 ⊡	SW 1	SW 1	SW 1 ⊡	SW 1		SW 1	SW ◇1 ⊡	SW 1	SW	SW 1	SW 1 ⊡	SW 1	SW 1	SW ◇1 ⊡	
Basingstoke	d					15 24	15 31			15 36	15 41					15 54	15 57			16 17					
Hook	d					15 31										16 01									
Winchfield	d					15 35										16 05									
Fleet	d					15 40					15 52					16 10									
Farnborough (Main)	d					15 46					15 58					16 16				16 31					
Alton	d	15 15										15 44										16 15			
Bentley	d											15 51													
Farnham	a	15 25										15 56										16 25			
	d	15 28										15 58										16 28			
Aldershot	d	15 34	15e30									16 04		16f00								16 34	16g30		
Ash Vale	d	15 39	15 34									16 09		16 04								16 39	16 34		
Brookwood	d	15 46				15 53						16 16				16 23						16 46			
Guildford	d							15 34					15 47					16 00			16 17				
Worplesdon	d							15 40										16 06							
Woking	a	15 51		15 19		15 58	15 49	15 44				16 21	15 57			16 28	16 15	16 11		16 40	16 25	16 51		16 19	
	d	15 52		15 21		15 59	15 51	15 46	15 33			16 22	15 59			16 29	16 17	16 12	16 03	16 41	16 26	16 52		16 21	
West Byfleet	d	15 57							15 37			16 27							16 07			16 57			
Byfleet & New Haw	d								15 40										16 10						
Weybridge	d					16 06			15 43							16 36			16 13						
Walton-on-Thames	d					16 10			15 47							16 40			16 17						
Hersham	d								15 49										16 19						
Esher	d								15 52										16 22						
Surbiton 6	a	16 07				16 16			15 56			16 37				16 46			16 26			17 07			
Wimbledon 6 ⊖	a								16 04										16 34						
Earlsfield	a								16 08										16 38						
Clapham Junction 10	a							16 05	16 12	16 12	16 24	16 48				16 57	16 36	16 31	16 42						
Vauxhall ⊖	a								16 17										16 47						
London Waterloo 15 ⊖	a	16 29		15 49		16 36	16 19	16 13	16 22	16 20	16 34	16 59	16 24			17 08	16 49	16 40	16 52	17 07	16 51	17 29		16 49	

b arr. 1417
c arr. 1447
e arr. 1517
f arr. 1547
g arr. 1617

Basingstoke, Alton, Guildford and Woking - Waterloo

		SW 1	SW ◇1 ⊡	SW 1	SW	SW ◇1 ⊡	SW 1	SW 1	SW 1	SW 1		SW 1	SW ◇1 ⊡	SW 1 ⊡	SW	SW 1	SW 1	SW 1 ⊡	SW 1	SW ◇1 ⊡	SW 1	SW ◇1 ⊡	SW 1	SW	SW ◇1 ⊡
Basingstoke	d	16 24	16 31			16 36	16 41					16 54	16 57				17 17				17 24	17 31			17 36
Hook	d	16 31										17 01									17 31				
Winchfield	d	16 35										17 05									17 35				
Fleet	d	16 40					16 52					17 10									17 40				
Farnborough (Main)	d	16 46					16 58					17 16					17 31				17 46				
Alton	d							16 44								17 14									
Bentley	d							16 51								17 21									
Farnham	a							16 56								17 26									
	d							16 58								17 28									
Aldershot	d							17 04		17b00						17 34			17c30						
Ash Vale	d							17 09		17 04						17 39			17 34						
Brookwood	d	16 53						17 16				17 23				17 46					17 53				
Guildford	d			16 34					16 47					17 00				17 17					17 34		
Worplesdon	d			16 40										17 06									17 40		
Woking	a	16 58	16 49	16 44				17 21	16 57			17 28	17 15	17 11		17 51	17 40	17 25		17 20	17 58	17 49	17 44		
	d	16 59	16 51	16 46	16 33			17 22	16 59			17 29	17 17	17 12	17 03	17 52	17 41	17 26		17 21	17 59	17 51	17 46	17 33	
West Byfleet	d				16 37			17 27							17 07	17 57								17 37	
Byfleet & New Haw	d				16 40										17 10									17 40	
Weybridge	d	17 06			16 43							17 36			17 13						18 06			17 43	
Walton-on-Thames	d	17 10			16 47							17 40			17 17						18 10			17 47	
Hersham	d				16 49										17 19									17 49	
Esher	d				16 52										17 22									17 52	
Surbiton 6	a	17 16			16 56			17 37				17 46			17 26	18 07					18 16			17 56	
Wimbledon 6 ⊖	a				17 04										17 34									18 04	
Earlsfield	a				17 08										17 38									18 08	
Clapham Junction 10	a			17 05	17 12	17 12	17 23	17 48				17 57	17 36	17 31	17 42								18 05	18 12	18 12
Vauxhall ⊖	a				17 17										17 47									18 17	
London Waterloo 15 ⊖	a	17 35	17 19	17 14	17 22	17 20	17 36	17 59	17 27			18 09	17 49	17 43	17 52	18 29	18 08	17 54		17 50	18 38	18 21	18 14	18 23	18 23

		SW 1	SW 1	SW 1	SW 1	SW 1		SW ◇1 ⊡	SW 1 ⊡	SW	SW 1	SW 1	SW 1	SW ◇1 ⊡	SW 1	SW ◇1 ⊡		SW 1	SW	SW ◇1 ⊡	SW 1	SW 1	SW 1	SW 1	SW 1 ⊡
Basingstoke	d	17 41				17 54		17 57				18 17			18 24	18 31				18 36			18 41		
Hook	d					18 01									18 31										
Winchfield	d					18 05									18 35										
Fleet	d	17 52				18 10									18 40								18 52		
Farnborough (Main)	d	17 58				18 16						18 31			18 46								18 58		
Alton	d		17 44								18 14										18 35				
Bentley	d		17 51								18 23										18 42				
Farnham	a		17 56								18 27										18 47				
	d		17 58								18 28										18 58				
Aldershot	d		18 04		18e00						18 34		18f30								19 04	18 38		19g00	
Ash Vale	d		18 09		18 04						18 39		18 34								19 09			19 04	
Brookwood	d		18 16			18 23					18 46				18 53						19 16				
Guildford	d			17 47					18 00									18 34				18a55			18 55
Worplesdon	d								18 06									18 40							
Woking	a		18 21	17 58		18 28		18 15	18 11		18 52	18 40		18 19	18 58	18 49		18 44			19 21				19 03
	d		18 22	17 59		18 29		18 17	18 12	18 03	18 52	18 41		18 21	18 59	18 51		18 46	18 33		19 22				19 05
West Byfleet	d		18 27							18 07	18 57								18 37		19 27				
Byfleet & New Haw	d									18 10									18 40						
Weybridge	d					18 36				18 13					19 06				18 43						
Walton-on-Thames	d					18 40				18 17					19 10				18 47						
Hersham	d									18 19									18 49						
Esher	d									18 22									18 52						
Surbiton 6	a		18 37			18 47				18 26	19 07				19 16				18 56		19 37				
Wimbledon 6 ⊖	a									18 34									19 04						
Earlsfield	a									18 38									19 08						
Clapham Junction 10	a	18 23	18 48			18 58		18 36	18 31	18 42								19 05	19 11	19 12	19 48		19 26		
Vauxhall ⊖	a									18 47									19 16						
London Waterloo 15 ⊖	a	18 34	18 57	18 27		19 06		18 45	18 43	18 52	19 25	19 08		18 47	19 39	19 19		19 13	19 23	19 20	19 57		19 38		19 29

b arr. 1647
c arr. 1717
e arr. 1747
f arr. 1817
g arr. 1847

Basingstoke, Alton, Guildford and Woking - Waterloo

		SW 1	SW ◇1 ☕	SW	SW 1	SW 1	SW 1	SW 1 ☕	SW ◇1 ☕	SW 1	SW ◇1 ☕	SW 1	SW	SW ◇1 ☕	SW 1	SW 1	SW 1	SW 1 ☕	SW 1	SW 1	SW 1	SW
Basingstoke	d	18 54	19 02			19 17				19 24	19 31			19 36			19 41			19 54		
Hook	d	19 01								19 31										20 01		
Winchfield	d	19 05								19 35										20 05		
Fleet	d	19 10								19 40							19 52			20 10		
Farnborough (Main)	d	19 16				19 31				19 46							19 58			20 16		
Alton	d				19 07										19 35							
Bentley	d														19 42							
Farnham	a				19 17										19 47							
	d				19 28										19 58							
Aldershot	d				19 34		19b30								20 04	19 38			20c00			
Ash Vale	d				19 39		19 34								20 09				20 04			
Brookwood	d	19 23			19 46					19 53					20 16					20 23		
Guildford	d							19 21				19 34				19a55		19 46			20 02	
Worplesdon	d											19 40										
Woking	a	19 28	19 20		19 51	19 40		19 28	19 24	19 58	19 49	19 45			20 21			19 57		20 28	20 11	
	d	19 29	19 22	19 03	19 52	19 41		19 30	19 25	19 59	19 51	19 46	19 33		20 22			19 59		20 29	20 12	20 03
West Byfleet	d			19 07	19 57								19 37		20 27							20 07
Byfleet & New Haw	d			19 10									19 40									20 10
Weybridge	d	19 36		19 13						20 06			19 43							20 36		20 13
Walton-on-Thames	d	19 40		19 17						20 10			19 47							20 40		20 17
Hersham	d			19 19									19 49									20 19
Esher	d			19 22									19 52									20 22
Surbiton 6	a	19 46		19 26	20 07					20 16			19 56		20 37					20 46		20 26
Wimbledon 6 ⊖	a			19 34									20 04									20 35
Earlsfield	a			19 38									20 08									20 38
Clapham Junction 10	a	19 57	19 41	19 41								20 05	20 11	20 12	20 48		20 25			20 57	20 31	20 41
Vauxhall ⊖	a			19 46									20 16									20 46
London Waterloo 15 ⊖	a	20 05	19 50	19 52	20 26	20 08		19 59	19 51	20 36	20 19	20 14	20 22	20 20	20 57		20 34	20 24		21 05	20 40	20 52

		SW ◇1 ☕	SW 1	SW 1 ☕	SW 1	SW 1	SW ◇1 ☕	SW 1	SW ◇1 ☕	SW	SW 1	SW 1	SW 1	SW 1	SW 1	SW	SW ◇1 ☕	SW 1	SW 1	SW 1	SW ◇1 ☕	SW 1	SW ◇1
Basingstoke	d	20 09	20 17					20 24	20 36			20 41			20 54		21 09					21 24	21 36
Hook	d							20 31							21 01							21 31	
Winchfield	d							20 35							21 05							21 35	
Fleet	d							20 40				20 52			21 10							21 40	
Farnborough (Main)	d		20 31					20 46				20 58			21 16							21 46	
Alton	d				20 15								20 44						21 15				
Bentley	d												20 51										
Farnham	a				20 25								20 56						21 25				
	d				20 28								20 58						21 28				
Aldershot	d				20 34	20e30							21 04						21 34	21f30			
Ash Vale	d				20 39	20 34							21 09						21 39	21 34			
Brookwood	d				20 46			20 53					21 16		21 23				21 46			21 53	
Guildford	d			20 17							20 39			20 47				21 17					
Worplesdon	d										20 44												
Woking	a	20 29	20 40	20 25	20 51		20 19	20 58			20 52	21 07	21 21	20 56	21 28		21 29	21 25	21 51		21 19	21 58	
	d	20 30	20 41	20 26	20 52		20 21	20 59		20 33	20 53	21 08	21 22	20 59	21 29	21 03	21 30	21 26	21 52		21 21	21 59	
West Byfleet	d				20 57					20 37			21 27			21 07			21 57				
Byfleet & New Haw	d									20 40						21 10							
Weybridge	d							21 06		20 43					21 36	21 13						22 06	
Walton-on-Thames	d							21 10		20 47					21 40	21 17						22 10	
Hersham	d									20 49						21 19							
Esher	d									20 52						21 22							
Surbiton 6	a				21 07			21 16		20 56			21 37		21 46	21 26			22 07			22 16	
Wimbledon 6 ⊖	a									21 05						21 34							
Earlsfield	a									21 08						21 38							
Clapham Junction 10	a	20 52							21 16	21 11	21 12	21 30	21 48		21 57	21 42	21 52						22 14
Vauxhall ⊖	a									21 16						21 47							
London Waterloo 15 ⊖	a	21 00	21 07	20 50	21 29		20 49	21 34	21 24	21 22	21 21	21 38	21 57	21 27	22 05	21 52	22 04	21 50	22 26		21 49	22 34	22 22

b arr. 1917
c arr. 1947
e arr. 2017
f arr. 2117

Basingstoke, Alton, Guildford and Woking - Waterloo

		SW	SW 1	SW 1	SW 1	SW 1	SW 1	SW	SW ◇1 ☕	SW 1	SW 1	SW 1	SW 1	SW	SW ◇1	SW 1	SW 1	SW 1	SW 1	SW 1	SW	SW 1
Basingstoke	d			21 41			21 54		22 09	22b24					22 36			22 41		22 54		23 13
Hook	d						22 01			22 31										23 01		
Winchfield	d						22 05			22 35										23 05		
Fleet	d			21 52			22 10			22 40								22 52		23 10		
Farnborough (Main)	d			21 58			22 16			22 46								22 58		23 16		
Alton	d				21 44						22 15								22 44			
Bentley	d				21 51														22 51			
Farnham	a				21 56						22 25								22 56			
	d				21 58						22 28								22 58			
Aldershot	d				22 04						22 34	22c30					22 38		23 04			
Ash Vale	d				22 09						22 39	22 34							23 09			
Brookwood	d				22 16		22 23			22 53	22 46								23 16	23 23		
Guildford	d		21 39			21 47								22 20		22 39	22a55				22 55	
Worplesdon	d		21 44													22 44						
Woking	a		21 49	22 07	22 21	21 57	22 28		22 28	22 58	22 51		22 19	22 32	22 54	22 49		23 07	23 21	23 28	23 05	23 33
	d	21 33	21 50	22 08	22 22	21 59	22 29	22 03	22 29	22 59	22 52		22 21	22 33	22 55	22 50		23 09	23 22	23 33	23 06	23 34
West Byfleet	d	21 37			22 27			22 07			22 57			22 37					23 27	23 37	23 10	
Byfleet & New Haw	d	21 40						22 10						22 40						23 40	23 13	
Weybridge	d	21 43					22 36	22 13		23 06				22 43						23 43	23 16	
Walton-on-Thames	d	21 47					22 40	22 17		23 10				22 47						23 47	23 20	
Hersham	d	21 49						22 19						22 49						23 49	23 22	
Esher	d	21 52						22 22						22 52						23 52	23 25	
Surbiton 6	a	21 56			22 37		22 46	22 26		23 16	23 07			22 56					23 37	23 57	23 29	
Wimbledon 6 ⊖	a	22 04						22 34						23 04						00 07	23 37	
Earlsfield	a	22 08						22 38						23 08						00 11	23 41	
Clapham Junction 10	a	22 12	22 09	22 28	22 52		22 57	22 42	22 48					23 12	23 14	23 09		23 33	23 54	00 15	23 44	23 56
Vauxhall ⊖	a	22 17						22 47						23 17						00 20	23 49	
London Waterloo 15 ⊖	a	22 22	22 18	22 38	23 01	22 27	23 08	22 52	22 58	23 42	23 27		22 49	23 23	23 23	23 19		23 44	00 03	00 28	23 54	00 06

		SW 1	SW 1	SW 1	SW 1	SW 1
Basingstoke	d				23 44	
Hook	d				23 51	
Winchfield	d				23 55	
Fleet	d				00 02	
Farnborough (Main)	d				00 06	
Alton	d	23 15				23 44
Bentley	d					23 51
Farnham	a	23 25				23 56
	d	23 28				
Aldershot	d	23 34	23e30			
Ash Vale	d	23 39	23 34			
Brookwood	d	23 46			00 13	
Guildford	d			23 39		
Worplesdon	d			23 44		
Woking	a	23 51		23 49	00 18	
	d			23 56	00 20	
West Byfleet	d				00 25	
Byfleet & New Haw	d					
Weybridge	d				00 29	
Walton-on-Thames	d				00 33	
Hersham	d					
Esher	d					
Surbiton 6	a				00 39	
Wimbledon 6 ⊖	a				00 47	
Earlsfield	a					
Clapham Junction 10	a			00 21	00 53	
Vauxhall ⊖	a					
London Waterloo 15 ⊖	a			00 30	01 02	

b arr. 2213
c arr. 2217
e arr. 2317

Table 155

Basingstoke, Alton, Guildford and Woking - Waterloo

		SW ■	SW ■	SW ■	SW ■	SW ■	SW	SW ■ A	SW ■ B	SW	SW	SW ■ A	SW ■ B	SW ◇■ ☕	SW ■	SW ■	SW ■	SW	SW ■ B	SW ■ A	SW ■	SW ◇■ ☕	SW ■
Basingstoke	d		22p54	23p13		23p44		04 54	04 54			05 54	05 54	05 59							06 24	06 31	
Hook	d		23p01			23p51		05 01	05 01			06 01	06 01								06 31		
Winchfield	d		23p05			23p55		05 05	05 05			06 05	06 05								06 35		
Fleet	d		23p10			00 02		05 10	05 10			06 10	06 10								06 40		
Farnborough (Main)	d		23p16			00 06		05 16	05 16			06 16	06 16								06 46		
Alton	d	22p44																	06 14	06 14			
Bentley	d	22p51																	06 21	06 21			
Farnham	a	22p56																	06 26	06 26			
	d	22p58														06 00			06 28	06 28			
Aldershot	d	23p04														06 08	06 00		06 34	06 34			
Ash Vale	d	23p09															06 04		06 39	06 39			
Brookwood	d	23p16	23p23			00 13		05 23	05 23			06 23	06 23						06 46	06 46	06 53		
Guildford	d				23p39		04 00			05 12					06 02	06a25							06 34
Worplesdon	d				23p44					05 17													06 40
Woking	a	23p21	23p28	23p33	23p49	00 18	04 08	05 28	05 28	05 22		06 28	06 28	06 18	06 11				06 51	06 51	06 58	06 49	06 44
	d	23p22	23p33	23p34	23p56	00 20	04 10	05 29	05 29	05 33	05 25	06 29	06 29	06 19	06 13			06 03	06 52	06 52	06 59	06 51	06 46
West Byfleet	d	23p27	23p37			00 25				05 37	05 30							06 07	06 57	06 57			
Byfleet & New Haw	d		23p40							05 40	05 33							06 10					
Weybridge	d		23p43			00 29				05 43		06 36	06 36					06 13			07 06		
Walton-on-Thames	d		23p47			00 33				05 47		06 40	06 40					06 17			07 10		
Hersham	d		23p49							05 49								06 19					
Esher	d		23p52							05 52								06 22					
Surbiton 6	a	23p37	23p57			00 39	04 24	05 40	05 40	05 56		06 46	06 46					06 26	07 07	07 07	07 16		
Wimbledon 6	⊖ a		00 07			00 47	04 31	05 48	05 48	06 04								06 34					
Earlsfield	a		00 11							06 08								06 38					
Clapham Junction 10	a	23p54	00 15	23p56	00 21	00 53	04 43			06 12		06 57	06 57	06 38	06 32			06 42	07 18	07 18			07 05
Vauxhall	⊖ a		00 20					06 07	06 07	06 17	06 49							06 47					
London Waterloo 15	⊖ a	00 03	00 28	00 06	00 30	01 02	04 53	06 15	06 12	06 22	06 56	07 08	07 05	06 49	06 40			06 52	07 27	07 30	07 33	07 19	07 13

		SW	SW ■	SW ■	SW ■	SW ■	SW ■	SW ◇■ ☕	SW ■	SW	SW ◇■ ☕	SW ■	SW ■	SW ■	SW ■	SW ◇■ ☕	SW ■	SW	SW ■	SW ■	SW ■ ☕	SW ■	SW ◇■ ☕
Basingstoke	d		06 40				06 54	06 57			07 09				07 24	07 31			07 42				07 57
Hook	d						07 01								07 31								
Winchfield	d						07 05								07 35								
Fleet	d						07 10								07 40				07 53				
Farnborough (Main)	d						07 16								07 46				07 58				
Alton	d				06 44								07 14							07 44			
Bentley	d				06 51								07 21							07 51			
Farnham	a				06 56								07 26							07 56			
	d				06 58								07 28							07 58			
Aldershot	d			06 38	07 04	07b00						07 08	07 34	07c30						08 04		08e00	
Ash Vale	d				07 09	07 04							07 39	07 34						08 09		08 04	
Brookwood	d				07 16		07 23						07 46		07 53					08 16			
Guildford	d			06a55					07 02			07a25					07 34				07 47		
Worplesdon	d																07 40						
Woking	a		06 58		07 21		07 28	07 15	07 11		07 27		07 51		07 58	07 49	07 44		08 07	08 21	07 57		08 17
	d	06 33	07 00		07 22		07 29	07 17	07 12	07 03	07 29		07 52		07 59	07 51	07 46	07 33	08 09	08 22	07 59		08 18
West Byfleet	d	06 37			07 27					07 07			07 57					07 37		08 27			
Byfleet & New Haw	d	06 40								07 10								07 40					
Weybridge	d	06 43					07 36			07 13					08 06			07 43					
Walton-on-Thames	d	06 47					07 40			07 17					08 10			07 47					
Hersham	d	06 49								07 19								07 49					
Esher	d	06 52								07 22								07 52					
Surbiton 6	a	06 56			07 37		07 46			07 26			08 07		08 16			07 56		08 37			
Wimbledon 6	⊖ a	07 04								07 34								08 04					
Earlsfield	a	07 08								07 38								08 08					
Clapham Junction 10	a	07 12	07 23		07 50		07 57	07 36	07 31	07 42							08 05	08 12	08 30	08 49			08 37
Vauxhall	⊖ a	07 17								07 47								08 17					
London Waterloo 15	⊖ a	07 22	07 31		07 58		08 05	07 49	07 40	07 52	07 53		08 25		08 34	08 19	08 13	08 22	08 38	08 58	08 23		08 49

A from 2 October
B until 25 September
b arr. 0647
c arr. 0717
e arr. 0747

Table 155

Basingstoke, Alton, Guildford and Woking - Waterloo

		SW ■	SW ■	SW	SW ■	SW ■	SW ■	SW ■ ☕	SW ■	SW ◇■ ☕	SW ■	SW ◇■ ☕	SW ■	SW ◇■ ☕	SW	SW ■	SW ■	SW ■ ☕	SW ■	SW ■	SW ◇■ ☕	SW ■
Basingstoke	d	07 54					08 17				08 24	08 31		08 36		08 41				08 54	08 57	
Hook	d	08 01									08 31									09 01		
Winchfield	d	08 05									08 35									09 05		
Fleet	d	08 10									08 40					08 52				09 10		
Farnborough (Main)	d	08 16					08 31				08 46					08 58				09 16		
Alton	d					08 14											08 44					
Bentley	d					08 21											08 51					
Farnham	a					08 26											08 56					
	d					08 28											08 58					
Aldershot	d				08 08	08 34			08b30								09 04		09c00			
Ash Vale	d					08 39			08 34								09 09		09 04			
Brookwood	d	08 23				08 46					08 53						09 16			09 23		
Guildford	d		08 02		08a25			08 17					08 34					08 47				09 02
Worplesdon	d												08 40									
Woking	a	08 28	08 12			08 51	08 40	08 26		08 21	08 58	08 49	08 44				09 21	08 57		09 28	09 15	09 11
	d	08 29	08 13	08 03		08 52	08 41	08 27		08 23	08 59	08 51	08 46		08 33		09 22	08 59		09 29	09 17	09 12
West Byfleet	d			08 07		08 57									08 37		09 27					
Byfleet & New Haw	d			08 10											08 40							
Weybridge	d	08 36		08 13							09 06				08 43					09 36		
Walton-on-Thames	d	08 40		08 17							09 10				08 47					09 40		
Hersham	d			08 19											08 49							
Esher	d			08 22											08 52							
Surbiton 6	a	08 46		08 26		09 07					09 16				08 56		09 37			09 46		
Wimbledon 6	⊖ a			08 34											09 04							
Earlsfield	a			08 38											09 08							
Clapham Junction 10	a	08 57	08 33	08 42									09 05	09 12	09 12	09 23	09 48			09 57	09 36	09 31
Vauxhall	⊖ a			08 47											09 17							
London Waterloo 15	⊖ a	09 05	08 42	08 52		09 25	09 08	08 51		08 49	09 35	09 19	09 13	09 20	09 22	09 34	09 57	09 23		10 05	09 49	09 40

		SW	SW ■	SW ■	SW ■ ☕	SW ■	SW ◇■ ☕	SW ■	SW ◇■ ☕	SW ■	SW ◇■ ☕	SW	SW ■	SW ■	SW ■ ☕	SW ■	SW ◇■ ☕	SW ■	SW ■	SW	SW ■	SW ■	SW ■ ☕
Basingstoke	d			09 17				09 24	09 31		09 36		09 41				09 57	09 54				10 17	
Hook	d							09 31										10 01					
Winchfield	d							09 35										10 05					
Fleet	d							09 40					09 52					10 10					
Farnborough (Main)	d			09 31				09 46					09 58					10 16				10 31	
Alton	d		09 14											09 44							10 14		
Bentley	d		09 21											09 51							10 21		
Farnham	a		09 26											09 56							10 26		
	d		09 28											09 58							10 28		
Aldershot	d		09 34			09e30								10 04		10f00					10 34		
Ash Vale	d		09 39			09 34								10 09		10 04					10 39		
Brookwood	d		09 46					09 53						10 16				10 23			10 46		
Guildford	d				09 17					09 34					09 47				10 02				10 17
Worplesdon	d									09 40													
Woking	a		09 51	09 40	09 25		09 19	09 58	09 49	09 44				10 21	09 57		10 15	10 28	10 11		10 51	10 40	10 25
	d	09 03	09 52	09 41	09 26		09 21	09 59	09 51	09 46		09 33		10 22	09 59		10 17	10 29	10 12	10 03	10 52	10 41	10 26
West Byfleet	d	09 07	09 57									09 37		10 27						10 07	10 57		
Byfleet & New Haw	d	09 10										09 40								10 10			
Weybridge	d	09 13						10 06				09 43						10 36		10 13			
Walton-on-Thames	d	09 17						10 10				09 47						10 40		10 17			
Hersham	d	09 19										09 49								10 19			
Esher	d	09 22										09 52								10 22			
Surbiton 6	a	09 26	10 07					10 16				09 56		10 37				10 46		10 26	11 07		
Wimbledon 6	⊖ a	09 34										10 04								10 34			
Earlsfield	a	09 38										10 08								10 38			
Clapham Junction 10	a	09 42								10 05	10 12	10 12	10 23	10 48			10 36	10 57	10 31	10 42			
Vauxhall	⊖ a	09 47										10 17								10 47			
London Waterloo 15	⊖ a	09 52	10 25	10 07	09 51		09 49	10 35	10 19	10 13	10 20	10 22	10 34	10 57	10 23		10 49	11 05	10 40	10 52	11 25	11 07	10 51

b arr. 0817
c arr. 0847
e arr. 0917
f arr. 0947

Table 155

Saturdays

Basingstoke, Alton, Guildford and Woking - Waterloo

		SW ■	SW ◇■ ⊡	SW ■	SW ◇■ ⊡	SW ■	SW ◇■ ⊡	SW	SW ■	SW ■	SW ■ ⊡	SW ■	SW ■	SW ◇■ ⊡	SW ■	SW	SW ■	SW ■ ⊡	SW ■	SW ■	SW ◇■ ⊡	SW ■
Basingstoke	d			10 24	10 31		10 36		10 41				10 54	10 57			11 17					11 24
Hook	d			10 31									11 01									11 31
Winchfield	d			10 35									11 05									11 35
Fleet	d			10 40					10 52				11 10									11 40
Farnborough (Main)	d			10 46					10 58				11 16				11 31					11 46
Alton	d									10 44									11 15			
Bentley	d									10 51												
Farnham	a									10 56									11 25			
	d									10 58									11 28			
Aldershot	d	10b30								11 04		11c00							11 34	11e30		
Ash Vale	d	10 34								11 09		11 04							11 39	11 34		
Brookwood	d			10 53						11 16			11 23						11 46			11 53
Guildford	d					10 34					10 47				11 02			11 17				
Worplesdon	d					10 40																
Woking	a		10 19	10 58	10 49	10 44				11 21	10 57		11 28	11 15	11 11		11 40	11 25	11 51		11 19	11 58
	d		10 21	10 59	10 51	10 46		10 33		11 22	10 59		11 29	11 17	11 12	11 03	11 41	11 26	11 52		11 21	11 59
West Byfleet	d							10 37		11 27						11 07			11 57			
Byfleet & New Haw	d							10 40								11 10						
Weybridge	d			11 06				10 43					11 36			11 13						12 06
Walton-on-Thames	d			11 10				10 47					11 40			11 17						12 10
Hersham	d							10 49								11 19						
Esher	d							10 52								11 22						
Surbiton 6	a			11 16				10 56		11 37			11 46			11 26			12 07			12 16
Wimbledon 6 ⊖	a							11 04								11 34						
Earlsfield	a							11 08								11 38						
Clapham Junction 10	a					11 05	11 12	11 12	11 23	11 48			11 57	11 36	11 31	11 42						
Vauxhall ⊖	a							11 17								11 47						
London Waterloo 15 ⊖	a		10 49	11 35	11 19	11 13	11 20	11 22	11 34	11 57	11 23		12 05	11 49	11 40	11 52	12 07	11 51	12 27		11 49	12 35

		SW ◇■ ⊡	SW ■	SW ◇■ ⊡	SW	SW ■	SW ■	SW ■ ⊡	SW ■	SW ■	SW ◇■ ⊡	SW ■	SW	SW ■	SW ■ ⊡	SW ■	SW ■	SW ◇■ ⊡	SW ■	SW ◇■ ⊡	SW ■	SW ◇■ ⊡	SW
Basingstoke	d	11 31		11 36		11 41				11 54	11 57			12 17					12 24	12 31		12 36	
Hook	d									12 01									12 31				
Winchfield	d									12 05									12 35				
Fleet	d					11 52				12 10									12 40				
Farnborough (Main)	d					11 58				12 16				12 31					12 46				
Alton	d						11 44									12 15							
Bentley	d						11 51																
Farnham	a						11 56									12 25							
	d						11 58									12 28							
Aldershot	d						12 04		12f00							12 34	12g30						
Ash Vale	d						12 09		12 04							12 39	12 34						
Brookwood	d						12 16			12 23						12 46			12 53				
Guildford	d		11 34					11 47				12 02			12 17						12 34		
Worplesdon	d		11 40																		12 40		
Woking	a	11 49	11 44				12 21	11 57		12 28	12 15	12 11		12 40	12 25	12 51		12 19	12 58	12 49	12 44		
	d	11 51	11 46		11 33		12 22	11 59		12 29	12 17	12 12	12 03	12 41	12 26	12 52		12 21	12 59	12 51	12 46		12 33
West Byfleet	d				11 37		12 27						12 07			12 57							12 37
Byfleet & New Haw	d				11 40								12 10										12 40
Weybridge	d				11 43					12 36			12 13						13 06				12 43
Walton-on-Thames	d				11 47					12 40			12 17						13 10				12 47
Hersham	d				11 49								12 19										12 49
Esher	d				11 52								12 22										12 52
Surbiton 6	a				11 56		12 37			12 46			12 26			13 07			13 16				12 56
Wimbledon 6 ⊖	a				12 04								12 34										13 04
Earlsfield	a				12 08								12 38										13 08
Clapham Junction 10	a		12 05	12 12	12 12	12 23	12 48			12 57	12 36	12 31	12 42								13 05	13 12	13 12
Vauxhall ⊖	a				12 17								12 47										13 17
London Waterloo 15 ⊖	a	12 19	12 13	12 20	12 22	12 34	12 57	12 23		13 05	12 49	12 40	12 52	13 07	12 51	13 25		12 49	13 35	13 19	13 13	13 20	13 22

b arr. 1017
c arr. 1047
e arr. 1117
f arr. 1147
g arr. 1217

Table 155

Saturdays

Basingstoke, Alton, Guildford and Woking - Waterloo

		SW ■	SW ■	SW ■ ⊡	SW ■	SW ■	SW ◇■ ⊡	SW ■	SW	SW ■	SW ■ ⊡	SW ■	SW ■	SW ◇■ ⊡	SW ■	SW ◇■ ⊡	SW ■	SW ◇■ ⊡	SW	SW ■	SW ■	SW ■ ⊡	SW ■
Basingstoke	d	12 41				12 54	12 57			13 17					13 24	13 31		13 36		13 41			
Hook	d					13 01									13 31								
Winchfield	d					13 05									13 35								
Fleet	d	12 52				13 10									13 40					13 52			
Farnborough (Main)	d	12 58				13 16				13 31					13 46					13 58			
Alton	d		12 44									13 15									13 44		
Bentley	d		12 51																		13 51		
Farnham	a		12 56									13 25									13 56		
	d		12 58									13 28									13 58		
Aldershot	d		13 04		13b00							13 34	13c30								14 04		14e00
Ash Vale	d		13 09		13 04							13 39	13 34								14 09		14 04
Brookwood	d		13 16			13 23						13 46			13 53						14 16		
Guildford	d			12 47				13 02			13 17						13 34					13 47	
Worplesdon	d																13 40						
Woking	a		13 21	12 57		13 28	13 15	13 11		13 40	13 25	13 51		13 19	13 58	13 49	13 44				14 21	13 57	
	d		13 22	12 59		13 29	13 17	13 12	13 03	13 41	13 26	13 52		13 21	13 59	13 51	13 46		13 33		14 22	13 59	
West Byfleet	d		13 27						13 07			13 57							13 37		14 27		
Byfleet & New Haw	d								13 10										13 40				
Weybridge	d					13 36			13 13						14 06				13 43				
Walton-on-Thames	d					13 40			13 17						14 10				13 47				
Hersham	d								13 19										13 49				
Esher	d								13 22										13 52				
Surbiton 6	a		13 37			13 46			13 26			14 07			14 16				13 56		14 37		
Wimbledon 6 ⊖	a								13 34										14 04				
Earlsfield	a								13 38										14 08				
Clapham Junction 10	a	13 23	13 48			13 57	13 36	13 31	13 42								14 05	14 12	14 12	14 23	14 48		
Vauxhall ⊖	a								13 47										14 17				
London Waterloo 15 ⊖	a	13 34	13 57	13 23		14 05	13 49	13 40	13 52	14 07	13 51	14 25		13 49	14 35	14 19	14 13	14 20	14 22	14 34	14 57	14 23	

		SW ■	SW ◇■ ⊡	SW ■	SW	SW ■	SW ■ ⊡	SW ■	SW ■	SW ◇■ ⊡	SW ■	SW ◇■ ⊡	SW ■	SW ◇■ ⊡	SW	SW ■	SW ■	SW ■ ⊡	SW ■	SW ■	SW ◇■ ⊡	SW ■
Basingstoke	d	13 54	13 57			14 17					14 24	14 31		14 36		14 41				14 54	14 57	
Hook	d	14 01									14 31									15 01		
Winchfield	d	14 05									14 35									15 05		
Fleet	d	14 10									14 40					14 52				15 10		
Farnborough (Main)	d	14 16				14 31					14 46					14 58				15 16		
Alton	d							14 15									14 44					
Bentley	d																14 51					
Farnham	a							14 25									14 56					
	d							14 28									14 58					
Aldershot	d							14 34	14f30								15 04		15g00			
Ash Vale	d							14 39	14 34								15 09		15 04			
Brookwood	d	14 23						14 46			14 53						15 16			15 23		
Guildford	d			14 02			14 17						14 34					14 47				15 02
Worplesdon	d												14 40									
Woking	a	14 28	14 15	14 11		14 40	14 25	14 51		14 19	14 58	14 49	14 44				15 21	14 57		15 28	15 15	15 11
	d	14 29	14 17	14 12	14 03	14 41	14 26	14 52		14 21	14 59	14 51	14 46		14 33		15 22	14 59		15 29	15 17	15 12
West Byfleet	d				14 07			14 57							14 37		15 27					
Byfleet & New Haw	d				14 10										14 40							
Weybridge	d	14 36			14 13						15 06				14 43					15 36		
Walton-on-Thames	d	14 40			14 17						15 10				14 47					15 40		
Hersham	d				14 19										14 49							
Esher	d				14 22										14 52							
Surbiton 6	a	14 46			14 26			15 07			15 16				14 56		15 37			15 46		
Wimbledon 6 ⊖	a				14 34										15 04							
Earlsfield	a				14 38										15 08							
Clapham Junction 10	a	14 57	14 36	14 31	14 42								15 05	15 12	15 12	15 23	15 48			15 57	15 36	15 31
Vauxhall ⊖	a				14 47										15 17							
London Waterloo 15 ⊖	a	15 05	14 49	14 40	14 52	15 07	14 51	15 25		14 49	15 35	15 19	15 13	15 20	15 22	15 34	15 57	15 23		16 05	15 49	15 40

b arr. 1247
c arr. 1317
e arr. 1347
f arr. 1417
g arr. 1447

Table 155

Basingstoke, Alton, Guildford and Woking - Waterloo

		SW	SW 1	SW 1 ⊐	SW 1	SW 1	SW ◇1 ⊐	SW 1	SW ◇1 ⊐	SW 1	SW ◇1 ⊐	SW	SW 1	SW 1	SW 1 ⊐	SW 1	SW 1	SW ◇1 ⊐	SW 1	SW	SW 1	SW 1 ⊐	SW 1
Basingstoke	d		15 17					15 24	15 31		15 36		15 41				15 54	15 57			16 17		
Hook	d							15 31									16 01						
Winchfield	d							15 35									16 05						
Fleet	d							15 40					15 52				16 10						
Farnborough (Main)	d		15 31					15 46					15 58				16 16				16 31		
Alton	d				15 15									15 44									16 15
Bentley	d													15 51									
Farnham	a				15 25									15 56									16 25
	d				15 28									15 58									16 28
Aldershot	d				15 34	15b30								16 04		16c00							16 34
Ash Vale	d				15 39	15 34								16 09		16 04							16 39
Brookwood	d				15 46			15 53						16 16			16 23						16 46
Guildford	d			15 17						15 34					15 47				16 02			16 17	
Worplesdon	d									15 40													
Woking	a		15 40	15 25	15 51		15 19	15 58	15 49	15 44				16 21	15 57		16 28	16 15	16 11		16 40	16 25	16 51
	d	15 03	15 41	15 26	15 52		15 21	15 59	15 51	15 46		15 33		16 22	15 59		16 29	16 17	16 12	16 03	16 41	16 26	16 52
West Byfleet	d	15 07			15 57							15 37		16 27						16 07			16 57
Byfleet & New Haw	d	15 10										15 40								16 10			
Weybridge	d	15 13						16 06				15 43					16 36			16 13			
Walton-on-Thames	d	15 17						16 10				15 47					16 40			16 17			
Hersham	d	15 19										15 49								16 19			
Esher	d	15 22										15 52								16 22			
Surbiton 6	a	15 26			16 07			16 16				15 56		16 37			16 46			16 26			17 07
Wimbledon 6 ⊖	a	15 34										16 04								16 34			
Earlsfield	a	15 38										16 08								16 38			
Clapham Junction 10	a	15 42								16 05	16 12	16 12	16 23	16 48			16 57	16 36	16 31	16 42			
Vauxhall ⊖	a	15 47										16 17								16 47			
London Waterloo 15 ⊖	a	15 52	16 07	15 51	16 25		15 49	16 35	16 19	16 13	16 20	16 22	16 34	16 57	16 23		17 05	16 49	16 40	16 52	17 07	16 51	17 25

		SW 1	SW ◇1 ⊐	SW 1	SW ◇1 ⊐	SW 1	SW ◇1 ⊐	SW	SW 1	SW 1	SW 1 ⊐	SW 1	SW 1	SW ◇1 ⊐	SW 1	SW	SW 1	SW 1 ⊐	SW 1	SW 1	SW ◇1 ⊐	SW 1
Basingstoke	d			16 24	16 31		16 36		16 41				16 54	16 57			17 17					17 24
Hook	d			16 31									17 01									17 31
Winchfield	d			16 35									17 05									17 35
Fleet	d			16 40					16 52				17 10									17 40
Farnborough (Main)	d			16 46					16 58				17 16				17 31					17 46
Alton	d									16 44									17 15			
Bentley	d									16 51												
Farnham	a									16 56									17 25			
	d									16 58									17 28			
Aldershot	d	16e30								17 04		17f00							17 34	17g30		
Ash Vale	d	16 34								17 09		17 04							17 39	17 34		
Brookwood	d			16 53						17 16			17 23						17 46			17 53
Guildford	d					16 34					16 47				17 02			17 17				
Worplesdon	d					16 40																
Woking	a		16 19	16 58	16 49	16 44				17 21	16 57		17 28	17 15	17 11		17 40	17 25	17 51		17 19	17 58
	d		16 21	16 59	16 51	16 46		16 33		17 22	16 59		17 29	17 17	17 12	17 03	17 41	17 26	17 52		17 21	17 59
West Byfleet	d							16 37		17 27						17 07			17 57			
Byfleet & New Haw	d							16 40								17 10						
Weybridge	d			17 06				16 43					17 36			17 13						18 06
Walton-on-Thames	d			17 10				16 47					17 40			17 17						18 10
Hersham	d							16 49								17 19						
Esher	d							16 52								17 22						
Surbiton 6	a			17 16				16 56		17 37			17 46			17 26			18 07			18 16
Wimbledon 6 ⊖	a							17 04								17 34						
Earlsfield	a							17 08								17 38						
Clapham Junction 10	a					17 05	17 12	17 12	17 23	17 48			17 57	17 36	17 31	17 42						
Vauxhall ⊖	a							17 17								17 47						
London Waterloo 15 ⊖	a		16 49	17 35	17 19	17 13	17 20	17 22	17 34	17 57	17 23		18 05	17 49	17 40	17 52	18 07	17 51	18 25		17 49	18 35

b arr. 1517
c arr. 1547
e arr. 1617
f arr. 1647
g arr. 1717

Table 155

Basingstoke, Alton, Guildford and Woking - Waterloo

		SW ◇1 ⊐	SW 1	SW ◇1 ⊐	SW	SW 1	SW 1	SW 1 ⊐	SW 1	SW 1	SW ◇1 ⊐	SW 1	SW	SW 1	SW 1	SW 1	SW 1	SW ◇1 ⊐	SW 1	SW ◇1 ⊐	SW 1	SW ◇1 ⊐	SW
Basingstoke	d	17 31		17 36		17 41				17 54	17 57			18 17					18 24	18 31		18 36	
Hook	d									18 01									18 31				
Winchfield	d									18 05									18 35				
Fleet	d					17 52				18 10									18 40				
Farnborough (Main)	d					17 58				18 16				18 31					18 46				
Alton	d						17 44									18 15							
Bentley	d						17 51																
Farnham	a						17 56									18 25							
	d						17 58									18 28							
Aldershot	d						18 04		18b00							18 34	18c30						
Ash Vale	d						18 09		18 04							18 39	18 34						
Brookwood	d						18 16			18 23						18 46			18 53				
Guildford	d		17 34					17 47				18 02			18 17						18 34		
Worplesdon	d		17 40																		18 40		
Woking	a	17 49	17 44				18 21	17 57		18 28	18 15	18 11		18 40	18 25	18 51		18 19	18 58	18 49	18 44		
	d	17 51	17 46		17 33		18 22	17 59		18 29	18 17	18 12	18 03	18 41	18 26	18 52		18 21	18 59	18 51	18 46		18 33
West Byfleet	d				17 37		18 27						18 07			18 57							18 37
Byfleet & New Haw	d				17 40								18 10										18 40
Weybridge	d				17 43					18 36			18 13						19 06				18 43
Walton-on-Thames	d				17 47					18 40			18 17						19 10				18 47
Hersham	d				17 49								18 19										18 49
Esher	d				17 52								18 22										18 52
Surbiton 6	a				17 56		18 37			18 46			18 26			19 07			19 16				18 56
Wimbledon 6 ⊖	a				18 04								18 34										19 04
Earlsfield	a				18 08								18 38										19 08
Clapham Junction 10	a		18 05	18 12	18 12	18 23	18 48			18 57	18 36	18 31	18 42								19 05	19 12	19 12
Vauxhall ⊖	a				18 17								18 47										19 17
London Waterloo 15 ⊖	a	18 19	18 13	18 20	18 22	18 34	18 57	18 23		19 05	18 49	18 40	18 52	19 07	18 51	19 25		18 49	19 35	19 19	19 13	19 20	19 22

		SW 1	SW 1	SW 1 ⊐	SW 1	SW 1	SW ◇1 ⊐	SW 1	SW	SW 1	SW 1	SW 1	SW 1	SW ◇1 ⊐	SW 1	SW ◇1 ⊐	SW 1	SW ◇1 ⊐	SW	SW 1	SW 1	SW 1	SW 1
Basingstoke	d	18 41				18 54	18 57			19 17					19 24	19 31		19 36		19 41			
Hook	d					19 01									19 31								
Winchfield	d					19 05									19 35								
Fleet	d	18 52				19 10									19 40					19 52			
Farnborough (Main)	d	18 58				19 16				19 31					19 46					19 58			
Alton	d		18 44									19 15									19 44		
Bentley	d		18 51																		19 51		
Farnham	a		18 56									19 25									19 56		
	d		18 58									19 28									19 58		
Aldershot	d		19 04		19e00							19 34	19f30								20 04		20g00
Ash Vale	d		19 09		19 04							19 39	19 34								20 09		20 04
Brookwood	d		19 16			19 23						19 46			19 53						20 16		
Guildford	d			18 47				19 02			19 17						19 34					19 47	
Worplesdon	d																19 40						
Woking	a		19 21	18 57		19 28	19 15	19 11		19 40	19 25	19 51		19 19	19 58	19 49	19 44				20 21	19 57	
	d		19 22	18 59		19 29	19 17	19 12	19 03	19 41	19 26	19 52		19 21	19 59	19 51	19 46		19 33		20 22	19 59	
West Byfleet	d		19 27						19 07			19 57							19 37		20 27		
Byfleet & New Haw	d								19 10										19 40				
Weybridge	d					19 36			19 13						20 06				19 43				
Walton-on-Thames	d					19 40			19 17						20 10				19 47				
Hersham	d								19 19										19 49				
Esher	d								19 22										19 52				
Surbiton 6	a		19 37			19 46			19 26			20 07			20 16				19 56		20 37		
Wimbledon 6 ⊖	a								19 34										20 04				
Earlsfield	a								19 38										20 08				
Clapham Junction 10	a	19 23	19 48			19 57	19 36	19 31	19 42								20 05	20 12	20 12	20 23	20 48		
Vauxhall ⊖	a								19 47										20 17				
London Waterloo 15 ⊖	a	19 34	19 57	19 23		20 05	19 49	19 40	19 52	20 07	19 51	20 25		19 49	20 35	20 19	20 13	20 20	20 22	20 34	20 57	20 23	

b arr. 1747
c arr. 1817
e arr. 1847
f arr. 1917
g arr. 1947

Table 155

Saturdays

Basingstoke, Alton, Guildford and Woking - Waterloo

		SW 1		SW 1	SW	SW ◇1	SW 1	SW 1	SW 1	SW 1	SW ◇1	SW 1	
Basingstoke	d	19 54				20 09	20 17					20 24	
Hook	d	20 01										20 31	
Winchfield	d	20 05										20 35	
Fleet	d	20 10										20 40	
Farnborough (Main)	d	20 16					20 31					20 46	
Alton	d								20 15				
Bentley	d												
Farnham	a								20 25				
	d								20 28				
Aldershot	d								20 34	20b30			
Ash Vale	d								20 39	20 34			
Brookwood	d	20 23							20 46			20 53	
Guildford	d			20 02				20 17					
Worplesdon	d												
Woking	a	20 28		20 11		20 29	20 40	20 25	20 51		20 19	20 58	
	d	20 29		20 12	20 03	20 30	20 41	20 26	20 52		20 21	20 59	
West Byfleet	d				20 07				20 57				
Byfleet & New Haw	d				20 10								
Weybridge	d	20 36			20 13							21 06	
Walton-on-Thames	d	20 40			20 17							21 10	
Hersham	d				20 19								
Esher	d				20 22								
Surbiton 6	a	20 46			20 26				21 07			21 16	
Wimbledon 6 ⊖	a				20 34								
Earlsfield	a				20 38								
Clapham Junction 10	a	20 57		20 31	20 42	20 52							
Vauxhall ⊖	a				20 47								
London Waterloo 15 ⊖	a	21 05		20 40	20 52	21 04	21 07	20 50	21 29		20 49	21 34	

		SW ◇1	SW	SW 1	SW 1	SW 1	SW 1	SW 1	SW	SW ◇1		SW 1	SW 1
Basingstoke	d	20 36			20 41			20 54		21 09			
Hook	d							21 01					
Winchfield	d							21 05					
Fleet	d				20 52			21 10					
Farnborough (Main)	d				20 58			21 16					
Alton	d					20 44							21 15
Bentley	d					20 51							
Farnham	a					20 56							21 25
	d					20 58							21 28
Aldershot	d					21 04							21 34
Ash Vale	d					21 09							21 39
Brookwood	d					21 16		21 23					21 46
Guildford	d			20 39			20 47					21 17	
Worplesdon	d			20 44									
Woking	a			20 52	21 07	21 21	20 57	21 28		21 29		21 25	21 51
	d		20 33	20 53	21 08	21 22	20 59	21 29	21 03	21 30		21 26	21 52
West Byfleet	d		20 37			21 27			21 07				21 57
Byfleet & New Haw	d		20 40						21 10				
Weybridge	d		20 43					21 36	21 13				
Walton-on-Thames	d		20 47					21 40	21 17				
Hersham	d		20 49						21 19				
Esher	d		20 52						21 22				
Surbiton 6	a		20 56			21 37		21 46	21 26				22 07
Wimbledon 6 ⊖	a		21 04						21 34				
Earlsfield	a		21 08						21 38				
Clapham Junction 10	a	21 16	21 12	21 12	21 30	21 48		21 57	21 42	21 52			
Vauxhall ⊖	a		21 17						21 47				
London Waterloo 15 ⊖	a	21 24	21 23	21 21	21 38	21 57	21 27	22 07	21 52	22 04		21 50	22 27

		SW 1	SW 1	SW ◇1	SW ◇1	SW	SW 1	SW 1		SW 1	SW 1	SW 1	SW
Basingstoke	d	21c24			21 36			21 41				21 54	
Hook	d	21 31										22 01	
Winchfield	d	21 35										22 05	
Fleet	d	21 40						21 52				22 10	
Farnborough (Main)	d	21 46						21 58				22 16	
Alton	d									21 44			
Bentley	d									21 51			
Farnham	a									21 56			
	d									21 58			
Aldershot	d		21e30							22 04			
Ash Vale	d		21 34							22 09			
Brookwood	d	21 53								22 16		22 23	
Guildford	d						21 39				21 49		
Worplesdon	d						21 44						
Woking	a	21 58		21 19			21 49	22 07		22 21	21 57	22 28	
	d	21 59		21 21		21 33	21 50	22 08		22 22	21 59	22 29	22 03
West Byfleet	d					21 37				22 27			22 07
Byfleet & New Haw	d					21 40							22 10
Weybridge	d	22 06				21 43						22 36	22 13
Walton-on-Thames	d	22 10				21 47						22 40	22 17
Hersham	d					21 49							22 19
Esher	d					21 52							22 22
Surbiton 6	a	22 16				21 56				22 37		22 46	22 26
Wimbledon 6 ⊖	a					22 04							22 34
Earlsfield	a					22 08							22 38
Clapham Junction 10	a				22 14	22 12	22 09	22 30		22 52		22 57	22 42
Vauxhall ⊖	a					22 17							22 47
London Waterloo 15 ⊖	a	22 34		21 49	22 22	22 22	22 18	22 38		23 01	22 24	23 05	22 52

		SW ◇1	SW 1	SW 1	SW 1	SW 1		SW	SW ◇1	SW 1	SW 1	SW 1	SW 1
Basingstoke	d	22 09	22f24						22 36			22 41	
Hook	d		22 31										
Winchfield	d		22 35										
Fleet	d		22 40									22 52	
Farnborough (Main)	d		22 46									22 58	
Alton	d			22 15									22 44
Bentley	d												22 51
Farnham	a			22 25									22 56
	d			22 28									22 58
Aldershot	d			22 34	22g30						22 38		23 04
Ash Vale	d			22 39	22 34								23 09
Brookwood	d		22 53	22 46									23 16
Guildford	d							22 20		22 39	22a55		
Worplesdon	d									22 44			
Woking	a	22 28	22 58	22 51		22 19		22 32	22 54	22 49		23 07	23 21
	d	22 29	22 59	22 52		22 21		22 33	22 56	22 50		23 09	23 22
West Byfleet	d			22 57				22 37					23 27
Byfleet & New Haw	d							22 40					
Weybridge	d		23 06					22 43					
Walton-on-Thames	d		23 10					22 47					
Hersham	d							22 49					
Esher	d							22 52					
Surbiton 6	a		23 16	23 07				22 56					23 37
Wimbledon 6 ⊖	a							23 04					
Earlsfield	a							23 08					
Clapham Junction 10	a	22 48						23 12	23 15	23 09		23 33	23 55
Vauxhall ⊖	a							23 17					
London Waterloo 15 ⊖	a	22 57	23 39	23 28		22 49		23 22	23 23	23 18		23 43	00 04

b arr. 2017
c arr. 2116
e arr. 2117
f arr. 2215
g arr. 2217

Table 155

Saturdays

Basingstoke, Alton, Guildford and Woking - Waterloo

		SW 1	SW	SW 1		SW 1	SW 1	SW 1	SW 1	SW 1
Basingstoke	d	22 54		23 14					23 44	
Hook	d	23 01							23 51	
Winchfield	d	23 05							23 55	
Fleet	d	23 10							00 02	
Farnborough (Main)	d	23 16							00 06	
Alton	d					23 15				23 44
Bentley	d									23 51
Farnham	a					23 25				23 56
	d					23 28				
Aldershot	d					23 34	23b30			
Ash Vale	d					23 39	23 34			
Brookwood	d	23 23				23 46			00 13	
Guildford	d		22 55					23 39		
Worplesdon	d							23 44		
Woking	a	23 28	23 05	23 32		23 51		23 49	00 18	
	d	23 33	23 06	23 33				23 56	00 20	
West Byfleet	d	23 37	23 10						00 25	
Byfleet & New Haw	d	23 40	23 13							
Weybridge	d	23 43	23 16						00 29	
Walton-on-Thames	d	23 47	23 20						00 33	
Hersham	d	23 49	23 22							
Esher	d	23 52	23 25							
Surbiton 6	a	23 57	23 29						00 39	
Wimbledon 6 ⊖	a	00 08	23 37						00 47	
Earlsfield	a	00 10	23 41							
Clapham Junction 10	a	00 14	23 44	23 58				00 20	00 53	
Vauxhall ⊖	a	00 20	23 49							
London Waterloo 15 ⊖	a	00 26	23 54	00 10				00 32	01 02	

Sundays

		SW 1	SW 1	SW 1	SW 1	SW 1	SW	SW	SW 1 B	SW 1 C	SW 1	SW ◇1	SW
Basingstoke	d		22p54	23p14		23p44			07 16	07 16		07 20	
Hook	d		23p01			23p51			07 23	07 23			
Winchfield	d		23p05			23p55			07 27	07 27			
Fleet	d		23p10			00 02			07 32	07 32			
Farnborough (Main)	d		23p16			00 06			07 38	07 38			
Alton	d	22p44											
Bentley	d	22p51											
Farnham	a	22p56											
	d	22p58									07 30		
Aldershot	d	23p04									07 36		
Ash Vale	d	23p09									07 41		
Brookwood	d	23p16	23p23			00 13			07 45	07 45	07 48		
Guildford	d				23p39			06 57					07 27
Worplesdon	d				23p44								
Woking	a	23p21	23p28	23p32	23p49	00 18		07 05	07 50	07 50	07 54	07 39	07 35
	d	23p22	23p33	23p33	23p56	00 20	06 36	07 06	07 58	07 58	<	07 40	07 36
West Byfleet	d	23p27	23p37			00 25	06 40	07 10					07 40
Byfleet & New Haw	d		23p40				06 43	07 13					07 43
Weybridge	d		23p43			00 29	06 46	07 16					07 46
Walton-on-Thames	d		23p47			00 33	06 50	07 20					07 50
Hersham	d		23p49				06 52	07 22					07 52
Esher	d		23p52				06 55	07 25					07 55
Surbiton 6	a	23p37	23p57			00 39	06 59	07 29	08 09	08 09			07 59
Wimbledon 6 ⊖	a		00 08			00 47	07 07	07 37	08 19	08 19			08 07
Earlsfield	a		00 10				07 11	07 41					08 11
Clapham Junction 10	a	23p55	00 14	23p58	00 20	00 53	07 15	07 45	08 27	08 27		08 05	08 15
Vauxhall ⊖	a		00 20				07 20	07 50					08 20
London Waterloo 15 ⊖	a	00 04	00 26	00 10	00 32	01 02	07 30	08 00	08 42	08 39		08 19	08 30

			SW 1	SW 1	SW 1	SW	SW	SW 1		SW ◇1	SW 1 B	SW 1 C	SW 1
Basingstoke	d			07 44						08 10	08 16	08 16	
Hook	d										08 23	08 23	
Winchfield	d										08 27	08 27	
Fleet	d										08 32	08 32	
Farnborough (Main)	d										08 38	08 38	
Alton	d												08 15
Bentley	d												08 24
Farnham	a												08 29
	d												08 30
Aldershot	d		07c40		07 48								08 36
Ash Vale	d		07 45										08 41
Brookwood	d										08 45	08 45	08 48
Guildford	d				08a05		07 57	08 05					
Worplesdon	d												
Woking	a			08 02			08 05	08 13		08 28	08 50	08 50	08 54
	d			08 04		07 52	08 06	08 15		08 30	08 58	08 58	<
West Byfleet	d					07 56	08 10						
Byfleet & New Haw	d					08 00	08 13						
Weybridge	d						08 16						
Walton-on-Thames	d						08 20						
Hersham	d						08 22						
Esher	d						08 25						
Surbiton 6	a						08 29				09 09	09 09	
Wimbledon 6 ⊖	a						08 37				09 19	09 19	
Earlsfield	a						08 41						
Clapham Junction 10	a			08 30			08 45	08 40		08 57	09 26	09 26	
Vauxhall ⊖	a						08 50						
London Waterloo 15 ⊖	a			08 42			09 00	08 49		09 09	09 42	09 39	

B from 26 September
C until 19 September
b arr. 2317
c arr. 0734

Table 155

Sundays

Basingstoke, Alton, Guildford and Woking - Waterloo

Station		SW	SW 1	SW 1	SW 1	SW	SW	SW 1	SW ◇1 ☕	SW 1	SW 1	SW
Basingstoke	d				08 44				09 10	09 16		
Hook	d									09 23		
Winchfield	d									09 27		
Fleet	d									09 32		
Farnborough (Main)	d									09 38		
Alton	d										09 15	
Bentley	d										09 24	
Farnham	a										09 29	
	d										09 30	
Aldershot	d			08b40							09 36	
Ash Vale	d			08 45							09 41	
Brookwood	d									09 45	09 48	
Guildford	d	08 27	08 35				08 57	09 05				09 27
Worplesdon	d											
Woking	a	08 35	08 42		09 02		09 05	09 15	09 28	09 50	09 54	09 35
	d	08 36	08 45		09 04	08 52	09 06	09 15	09 30	09 58	<	09 36
West Byfleet	d	08 40				08 56	09 10					09 40
Byfleet & New Haw	d	08 43				09 00	09 13					09 43
Weybridge	d	08 46					09 16					09 46
Walton-on-Thames	d	08 50					09 20					09 50
Hersham	d	08 52					09 22					09 52
Esher	d	08 55					09 25					09 55
Surbiton	a	08 59					09 29			10 09		09 59
Wimbledon	a	09 07					09 37			10 17		10 07
Earlsfield	a	09 11					09 41					10 11
Clapham Junction	a	09 15	09 06		09 30		09 45	09 38	09 57	10 23		10 15
Vauxhall	a	09 20					09 50					10 20
London Waterloo	a	09 30	09 19		09 43		10 00	09 49	10 08	10 38		10 30

Station		SW 1	SW 1	SW 1	SW	SW	SW ◇1 ☕	SW ◇1 ☕	SW 1	SW 1	SW 1	SW
Basingstoke	d			09 44			10 00	10e10		10 16		
Hook	d									10 23		
Winchfield	d									10 27		
Fleet	d									10 32		
Farnborough (Main)	d									10 38		
Alton	d										10 15	
Bentley	d										10 24	
Farnham	a										10 29	
	d										10 30	
Aldershot	d		09c40								10 36	
Ash Vale	d		09 45								10 41	
Brookwood	d									10 45	10 48	
Guildford	d	09 35				09 57			10 05			10 27
Worplesdon	d											
Woking	a	09 42		10 02		10 05	10 19	10 28	10 15	10 50	10 54	10 35
	d	09 45		10 04	09 52	10 06	10 20	10 30	10 15	10 58	<	10 36
West Byfleet	d				09 56	10 10						10 40
Byfleet & New Haw	d				10 00	10 13						10 43
Weybridge	d					10 16						10 46
Walton-on-Thames	d					10 20						10 50
Hersham	d					10 22						10 52
Esher	d					10 25						10 55
Surbiton	a					10 29				11 09		10 59
Wimbledon	a					10 37				11 17		11 07
Earlsfield	a					10 41						11 11
Clapham Junction	a	10 04		10 27		10 45	10 40	10 49	10 35	11 23		11 15
Vauxhall	a					10 50						11 20
London Waterloo	a	10 19		10 42		11 00	10 54	11 04	10 49	11 38		11 30

Station		SW 1 ☕	SW 1	SW 1 ☕	SW	SW	SW ◇1 ☕	SW 1	SW ◇1 ☕	SW 1	SW 1	SW
Basingstoke	d			10 44			11 00		11 10	11 16		
Hook	d									11 23		
Winchfield	d									11 27		
Fleet	d									11 32		
Farnborough (Main)	d									11 38		
Alton	d										11 15	
Bentley	d										11 24	
Farnham	a										11 29	
	d										11 30	
Aldershot	d		10f40								11 36	
Ash Vale	d		10 45								11 41	
Brookwood	d									11 45	11 48	
Guildford	d	10 35				10 57		11 05				11 27
Worplesdon	d											
Woking	a	10 42		11 02		11 05	11 18	11 13	11 28	11 50	11 54	11 35
	d	10 45		11 04	10 52	11 06	11 20	11 15	11 30	11 58	<	11 36
West Byfleet	d				10 56	11 10						11 40
Byfleet & New Haw	d				11 00	11 13						11 43
Weybridge	d					11 16						11 46
Walton-on-Thames	d					11 20						11 50
Hersham	d					11 22						11 52
Esher	d					11 25						11 55
Surbiton	a					11 29				12 09		11 59
Wimbledon	a					11 37				12 17		12 07
Earlsfield	a					11 41						12 11
Clapham Junction	a	11 04		11 27		11 45	11 39	11 34	11 49	12 23		12 15
Vauxhall	a					11 50						12 20
London Waterloo	a	11 19		11 42		12 00	11 54	11 49	12 03	12 39		12 30

Station		SW 1 ☕	SW 1	SW 1 ☕	SW	SW	SW ◇1 ☕	SW ◇1 ☕	SW 1	SW 1	SW 1
Basingstoke	d			11 44			12 00	12h10		12 16	
Hook	d									12 23	
Winchfield	d									12 27	
Fleet	d									12 32	
Farnborough (Main)	d									12 38	
Alton	d										12 15
Bentley	d										12 24
Farnham	a										12 29
	d										12 30
Aldershot	d		11g40								12 36
Ash Vale	d		11 45								12 41
Brookwood	d									12 45	12 48
Guildford	d	11 35				11 57			12 05		
Worplesdon	d										
Woking	a	11 42		12 02		12 05	12 18	12 28	12 13	12 50	12 54
	d	11 45		12 04	11 52	12 06	12 20	12 30	12 15	12 58	<
West Byfleet	d				11 56	12 10					
Byfleet & New Haw	d				12 00	12 13					
Weybridge	d					12 16					
Walton-on-Thames	d					12 20					
Hersham	d					12 22					
Esher	d					12 25					
Surbiton	a					12 29				13 09	
Wimbledon	a					12 37				13 17	
Earlsfield	a					12 41					
Clapham Junction	a	12 04		12 27		12 45	12 39	12 49	12 34	13 23	
Vauxhall	a					12 50					
London Waterloo	a	12 19		12 42		13 00	12 49	13 04	12 49	13 39	

b arr. 0834
c arr. 0934
e arr. 1002
f arr. 1034
g arr. 1134
h arr. 1202

Table 155

Sundays

Basingstoke, Alton, Guildford and Woking - Waterloo

Station		SW	SW 1 ☕	SW 1	SW 1 ☕	SW	SW	SW ◇1 ☕	SW 1	SW ◇1 ☕	SW 1	SW 1
Basingstoke	d				12 44			13 00		13 10	13 16	
Hook	d										13 23	
Winchfield	d										13 27	
Fleet	d										13 32	
Farnborough (Main)	d										13 38	
Alton	d											13 15
Bentley	d											13 24
Farnham	a											13 29
	d											13 30
Aldershot	d			12b40								13 36
Ash Vale	d			12 45								13 41
Brookwood	d										13 45	13 48
Guildford	d	12 27	12 35				12 57		13 05			
Worplesdon	d											
Woking	a	12 35	12 42		13 02		13 05	13 18	13 13	13 28	13 50	13 54
	d	12 36	12 45		13 04	12 52	13 06	13 20	13 15	13 30	13 58	<
West Byfleet	d	12 40				12 56	13 10					
Byfleet & New Haw	d	12 43				13 00	13 13					
Weybridge	d	12 46					13 16					
Walton-on-Thames	d	12 50					13 20					
Hersham	d	12 52					13 22					
Esher	d	12 55					13 25					
Surbiton	a	12 59					13 29				14 09	
Wimbledon	a	13 07					13 37				14 17	
Earlsfield	a	13 11					13 41					
Clapham Junction	a	13 15	13 04		13 27		13 45	13 39	13 34	13 49	14 23	
Vauxhall	a	13 20					13 50					
London Waterloo	a	13 30	13 14		13 37		14 00	13 49	13 44	13 59	14 34	

Station		SW	SW 1 ☕	SW 1	SW 1 ☕	SW 1	SW 1	SW	SW	SW ◇1 ☕	SW ◇1 ☕	SW 1
Basingstoke	d				13 44		13 50			14 00	14e10	
Hook	d											
Winchfield	d											
Fleet	d						14 02					
Farnborough (Main)	d						14 08					
Alton	d					13 45						
Bentley	d											
Farnham	a					13 55						
	d					14 00						
Aldershot	d			13c40		14 06						
Ash Vale	d			13 45		14 11						
Brookwood	d					14 18	14 15					
Guildford	d	13 27	13 35						13 57			14 05
Worplesdon	d											
Woking	a	13 35	13 42		14 02	14 24	14 20		14 05	14 18	14 28	14 13
	d	13 36	13 45		14 04	<	14 28	13 52	14 06	14 20	14 30	14 15
West Byfleet	d	13 40						13 56	14 10			
Byfleet & New Haw	d	13 43						14 00	14 13			
Weybridge	d	13 46					14 34		14 16			
Walton-on-Thames	d	13 50					14 38		14 20			
Hersham	d	13 52							14 22			
Esher	d	13 55							14 25			
Surbiton	a	13 59					14 45		14 29			
Wimbledon	a	14 07					14 53		14 37			
Earlsfield	a	14 11							14 41			
Clapham Junction	a	14 15	14 04		14 27		14 59		14 45	14 39	14 49	14 34
Vauxhall	a	14 20							14 50			
London Waterloo	a	14 30	14 14		14 37		15 10		14 55	14 49	14 59	14 44

Station		SW 1	SW 1	SW	SW 1 ☕	SW 1	SW 1 ☕	SW 1	SW 1	SW	SW	SW ◇1 ☕	SW 1
Basingstoke	d	14 16					14 44	14 50				15 00	
Hook	d	14 23											
Winchfield	d	14 27											
Fleet	d	14 32						15 02					
Farnborough (Main)	d	14 38						15 08					
Alton	d		14 15						14 45				
Bentley	d		14 24										
Farnham	a		14 29						14 55				
	d		14 30						15 00				
Aldershot	d		14 36			14f40			15 06				
Ash Vale	d		14 41			14 45			15 11				
Brookwood	d	14 45	14 48					15 15	15 18				
Guildford	d			14 27	14 35						14 57		15 05
Worplesdon	d												
Woking	a	14 50	14 54	14 35	14 42		15 02	15 20	15 24		15 05	15 18	15 13
	d	14 58	<	14 36	14 45		15 04	15 28	<	14 52	15 06	15 20	15 15
West Byfleet	d			14 40						14 56	15 10		
Byfleet & New Haw	d			14 43						15 00	15 13		
Weybridge	d			14 46				15 34			15 16		
Walton-on-Thames	d			14 50				15 38			15 20		
Hersham	d			14 52							15 22		
Esher	d			14 55							15 25		
Surbiton	a	15 09		14 59				15 45			15 29		
Wimbledon	a	15 17		15 07				15 53			15 37		
Earlsfield	a			15 11							15 41		
Clapham Junction	a	15 23		15 15	15 04		15 27	15 59			15 45	15 39	15 34
Vauxhall	a			15 20							15 50		
London Waterloo	a	15 34		15 25	15 14		15 37	16 10			15 55	15 49	15 44

Station		SW ◇1 ☕	SW 1	SW 1	SW	SW 1 ☕	SW 1	SW 1 ☕	SW 1	SW 1
Basingstoke	d	15 10	15 16					15 44	15 50	
Hook	d		15 23							
Winchfield	d		15 27							
Fleet	d		15 32						16 02	
Farnborough (Main)	d		15 38						16 08	
Alton	d			15 15						15 45
Bentley	d			15 24						
Farnham	a			15 29						15 55
	d			15 30						16 00
Aldershot	d			15 36			15g40			16 06
Ash Vale	d			15 41			15 45			16 11
Brookwood	d		15 45	15 48					16 15	16 18
Guildford	d				15 27	15 35				
Worplesdon	d									
Woking	a	15 28	15 50	15 54	15 35	15 42		16 02	16 20	16 24
	d	15 30	15 58	<	15 36	15 45		16 04	16 28	<
West Byfleet	d				15 40					
Byfleet & New Haw	d				15 43					
Weybridge	d				15 46				16 34	
Walton-on-Thames	d				15 50				16 38	
Hersham	d				15 52					
Esher	d				15 55					
Surbiton	a		16 09		15 59				16 45	
Wimbledon	a		16 17		16 07				16 53	
Earlsfield	a				16 11					
Clapham Junction	a	15 49	16 23		16 15	16 04		16 27	16 59	
Vauxhall	a				16 20					
London Waterloo	a	15 59	16 34		16 25	16 14		16 37	17 10	

b arr. 1234
c arr. 1334
e arr. 1402
f arr. 1434
g arr. 1534

Table 155

Basingstoke, Alton, Guildford and Woking - Waterloo

		SW	SW	SW ◇■ ⊏	SW ◇■ ⊏	SW ■	SW ■	SW ■	SW	SW ■ ⊏	SW	SW ■	SW ■ ⊏	SW ■	SW ■	SW	SW ◇■ ⊏	SW ■	SW ◇■ ⊏		SW ■	SW ■	SW	SW ■ ⊏
Basingstoke	d			16 00	16b10		16 16						16 44	16 50			17 00		17 10		17 16			
Hook	d						16 23														17 23			
Winchfield	d						16 27														17 27			
Fleet	d						16 32							17 02							17 32			
Farnborough (Main)	d						16 38							17 08							17 38			
Alton	d							16 15							16 45							17 15		
Bentley	d							16 24														17 24		
Farnham	a							16 29							16 55							17 29		
	d							16 30							17 00							17 30		
Aldershot	d							16 36				16c40			17 06							17 36		
Ash Vale	d							16 41				16 45			17 11							17 41		
Brookwood	d						16 45	16 48						17 15	17 18						17 45	17 48		
Guildford	d		15 57			16 05			16 27	16 35						16 57		17 05					17 27	17 35
Worplesdon	d																							
Woking	a		16 05	16 18	16 28	16 13	16 50	16 54	16 35	16 42			17 02	17 20	17 24	17 05	17 18	17 13	17 28		17 50	17 54	17 35	17 42
	d	15 52	16 06	16 20	16 30	16 15	16 58	<	16 36	16 45	16 52		17 04	17 28	<	17 06	17 20	17 15	17 30		17 58	<	17 36	17 45
West Byfleet	d	15 56	16 10						16 40		16 56					17 10							17 40	
Byfleet & New Haw	d	16 00	16 13						16 43		17 00					17 13							17 43	
Weybridge	d		16 16						16 46					17 34		17 16							17 46	
Walton-on-Thames	d		16 20						16 50					17 38		17 20							17 50	
Hersham	d		16 22						16 52							17 22							17 52	
Esher	d		16 25						16 55							17 25							17 55	
Surbiton 6	a		16 29				17 09		16 59					17 45		17 29					18 09		17 59	
Wimbledon 6 ⊖	a		16 37				17 17		17 07					17 53		17 37					18 17		18 07	
Earlsfield	a		16 41						17 11							17 41							18 11	
Clapham Junction-2 10	a		16 45	16 39	16 49	16 34	17 23		17 15	17 04			17 27	17 59		17 45	17 39	17 34	17 49		18 23		18 15	18 04
Vauxhall ⊖	a		16 50						17 20							17 50							18 20	
London Waterloo 15 ⊖	a		16 55	16 49	16 59	16 44	17 34		17 25	17 14			17 37	18 10		17 55	17 49	17 44	17 59		18 34		18 25	18 14

		SW	SW ■	SW ■ ⊏	SW ■	SW ■		SW	SW ◇■ ⊏	SW ◇■ ⊏	SW ■	SW ■	SW ■	SW	SW ■ ⊏	SW ■	SW	SW ■	SW ■	SW ■	SW	SW ◇■ ⊏	SW ■	SW ◇■ ⊏
Basingstoke	d			17 44	17 50				18 00	18f10		18 16						18 44	18 50			19 00		19 10
Hook	d											18 23												
Winchfield	d											18 27												
Fleet	d				18 02							18 32							19 02					
Farnborough (Main)	d				18 08							18 38							19 08					
Alton	d					17 45							18 15							18 45				
Bentley	d												18 24											
Farnham	a					17 55							18 29							18 55				
	d					18 00							18 30							19 00				
Aldershot	d		17e40			18 06							18 36			18g40				19 06				
Ash Vale	d		17 45			18 11							18 41			18 45				19 11				
Brookwood	d				18 15	18 18						18 45	18 48						19 15	19 18				
Guildford	d							17 57			18 05			18 27	18 35						18 57		19 05	
Worplesdon	d																							
Woking	a			18 02	18 20	18 24		18 05	18 18	18 28	18 13	18 50	18 54	18 35	18 42			19 02	19 20	19 24	19 05	19 18	19 13	19 28
	d	17 52		18 04	18 28	<		18 06	18 20	18 30	18 15	18 58	<	18 36	18 45		18 52	19 04	19 28	<	19 06	19 20	19 15	19 30
West Byfleet	d	17 56						18 10						18 40			18 56				19 10			
Byfleet & New Haw	d	18 00						18 13						18 43			19 00				19 13			
Weybridge	d				18 34			18 16						18 46					19 34		19 16			
Walton-on-Thames	d				18 38			18 20						18 50					19 38		19 20			
Hersham	d							18 22						18 52							19 22			
Esher	d							18 25						18 55							19 25			
Surbiton 6	a				18 45			18 29				19 09		18 59					19 45		19 29			
Wimbledon 6 ⊖	a				18 53			18 37				19 17		19 07					19 53		19 37			
Earlsfield	a							18 41						19 11							19 41			
Clapham Junction 10	a			18 27	18 59			18 45	18 39	18 49	18 34	19 23		19 15	19 04			19 27	19 59		19 45	19 39	19 34	19 49
Vauxhall ⊖	a							18 50						19 20							19 50			
London Waterloo 15 ⊖	a			18 37	19 10			18 55	18 49	18 59	18 44	19 34		19 25	19 14			19 37	20 10		19 55	19 49	19 44	19 59

b arr. 1602
c arr. 1634
e arr. 1734
f arr. 1802
g arr. 1834

Table 155

Basingstoke, Alton, Guildford and Woking - Waterloo

		SW	SW ■	SW ■	SW	SW ■ ⊏	SW ■	SW ■		SW ■	SW ■	SW		SW ◇■ ⊏	SW ◇■ ⊏	SW ■	SW ■	SW ■	SW	SW ■	SW ■	SW ■		SW ■	SW ■
Basingstoke	d		19 16					19 44		19 50				20 00	20c10		20 16					20 44		20 50	
Hook	d		19 23														20 23								
Winchfield	d		19 27														20 27								
Fleet	d		19 32							20 02							20 32							21 02	
Farnborough (Main)	d		19 38							20 08							20 38							21 08	
Alton	d			19 15							19 45							20 15							20 45
Bentley	d			19 24														20 24							
Farnham	a			19 29							19 55							20 29							20 55
	d			19 30							20 00							20 30							21 00
Aldershot	d			19 36			19b40				20 06							20 36			20e40				21 06
Ash Vale	d			19 41			19 45				20 11							20 41			20 45				21 11
Brookwood	d		19 45	19 48						20 15	20 18						20 45	20 48						21 15	21 18
Guildford	d				19 27	19 35						19 57				20 05			20 27	20 35					
Worplesdon	d																								
Woking	a		19 50	19 54	19 35	19 42		20 02		20 20	20 24	20 05		20 18	20 28	20 13	20 50	20 54	20 35	20 42		21 02		21 20	21 24
	d	19 52	19 58	<	19 36	19 45		20 04		20 28	<	20 06		20 20	20 30	20 15	20 58	<	20 36	20 45		21 04		21 28	
West Byfleet	d	19 56			19 40							20 10							20 40						
Byfleet & New Haw	d	20 00			19 43							20 13							20 43						
Weybridge	d				19 46					20 34		20 16							20 46					21 34	
Walton-on-Thames	d				19 50					20 38		20 20							20 50					21 38	
Hersham	d				19 52							20 22							20 52						
Esher	d				19 55							20 25							20 55						
Surbiton 6	a		20 09		19 59					20 45		20 29					21 09		20 59					21 45	
Wimbledon 6 ⊖	a		20 17		20 07					20 53		20 37					21 17		21 07					21 53	
Earlsfield	a				20 11							20 41							21 11						
Clapham Junction 10	a		20 23		20 15	20 04		20 27		20 59		20 45		20 39	20 49	20 34	21 23		21 15	21 04		21 27		21 59	
Vauxhall ⊖	a				20 20							20 50							21 20						
London Waterloo 15 ⊖	a		20 34		20 25	20 14		20 37		21 10		20 55		20 49	20 59	20 44	21 34		21 25	21 14		21 37		22 10	

		SW	SW	SW ◇■ ⊏	SW ■	SW ◇■ ⊏	SW ■	SW ■	SW	SW ■	SW ■	SW ■	SW ■	SW ■	SW	SW	SW ◇■ ⊏		SW ■	SW ■	SW ■	SW	SW ■	SW ■
Basingstoke	d			21 00		21 10	21 16					21 44	21 50				22g10			22 16				
Hook	d						21 23													22 23				
Winchfield	d						21 27													22 27				
Fleet	d						21 32						22 02							22 32				
Farnborough (Main)	d						21 38						22 08							22 38				
Alton	d							21 15						21 45							22 15			
Bentley	d							21 24													22 24			
Farnham	a							21 29						21 55							22 29			
	d							21 30						22 00							22 30			
Aldershot	d							21 36			21f40			22 06							22 36			22h40
Ash Vale	d							21 41			21 45			22 11							22 41			22 45
Brookwood	d						21 45	21 48					22 15	22 18						22 45	22 48			
Guildford	d		20 57		21 05				21 27	21 35						21 57			22 05			22 27	22 35	
Worplesdon	d																							
Woking	a		21 05	21 18	21 13	21 28	21 50	21 54	21 35	21 42		22 02	22 21	22 24		22 05	22 28		22 13	22 50	22 54	22 35	22 42	
	d	20 52	21 06	21 20	21 15	21 30	21 58	<	21 36	21 45		22 04	22 28	<	21 52	22 06	22 30		22 15	22 58	<	22 36	22 45	
West Byfleet	d	20 56	21 10						21 40						21 56	22 10						22 40		
Byfleet & New Haw	d	21 00	21 13						21 43						22 00	22 13						22 43		
Weybridge	d		21 16						21 46				22 34			22 16						22 46		
Walton-on-Thames	d		21 20						21 50				22 38			22 20						22 50		
Hersham	d		21 22						21 52							22 22						22 52		
Esher	d		21 25						21 55							22 25						22 55		
Surbiton 6	a		21 29				22 09		21 59				22 45			22 29				23 09		22 59		
Wimbledon 6 ⊖	a		21 37				22 17		22 07				22 53			22 37				23 17		23 07		
Earlsfield	a		21 41						22 11							22 41						23 11		
Clapham Junction 10	a		21 45	21 39	21 34	21 49	22 23		22 15	22 04		22 27	22 59			22 45	22 49		22 34	23 23		23 15	23 04	
Vauxhall ⊖	a		21 50						22 20							22 50						23 20		
London Waterloo 15 ⊖	a		21 55	21 49	21 44	21 59	22 34		22 25	22 14		22 37	23 10			22 55	22 59		22 44	23 34		23 25	23 14	

b arr. 1934
c arr. 2002
e arr. 2034
f arr. 2134
g arr. 2203
h arr. 2234

Table 155

Sundays

Basingstoke, Alton, Guildford and Woking - Waterloo

		SW	SW 1	SW 1	SW	SW 1	SW 1	SW 1	SW 1	SW ◇1
Basingstoke	d		22 44					23 16		23 44
Hook	d							23 23		
Winchfield	d							23 27		
Fleet	d							23 32		
Farnborough (Main)	d							23 38		
Alton	d			22 45			23 15			
Bentley	d						23 24			
Farnham	a			22 55			23 29			
	d			23 00			23 30			
Aldershot	d			23 06			23 36			
Ash Vale	d			23 11			23 41			
Brookwood	d			23 18			23 48	23 45		
Guildford	d				22 57	23 05			23 35	
Worplesdon	d									
Woking	a		23 02	23 24	23 05	23 13	23 54	23 50	23 42	00 02
	d	22 52	23 04	23 28	23 06	23 15			23 45	00 04
West Byfleet	d	22 56			23 10					
Byfleet & New Haw	d	23 00			23 13					
Weybridge	d			23 34	23 16					
Walton-on-Thames	d			23 38	23 20					
Hersham	d				23 22					
Esher	d				23 25					
Surbiton 8	a			23 45	23 29					
Wimbledon 8 ⊖	a			23 53	23 37					
Earlsfield	a				23 41					
Clapham Junction 10	a		23 27	23 59	23 45	23 34			00 04	00 23
Vauxhall ⊖	a				23 50					
London Waterloo 15 ⊖	a		23 37	00 10	23 55	23 44			00 14	00 33

Table 156

Mondays to Fridays

London - Guildford, Haslemere and Portsmouth

		SW MX 1	SW MO 1	SW MX 1	SW MO 1	SW MX 1	SW MO 1	SW MX 1	SW MO 1	SW 1	SW 1	SW 1	SW 1	SW 1	SW 1	SW 1	SW 1 ⊡	SW 1	SW 1	SW 1	SW 1 ⊡	SW	SW 1 ⊡
London Waterloo 15 ⊖	d	22p30	22p30	22p45	23p00	23p15	23p30	23p45	00 50		05 00		05 20	06 15	06 45	07 15	07 30	07 45	08 00	08 15	08 [illegible]	[illegible]45	09 00
Clapham Junction 10	d		22b39	22b52	23b09	23b22	23b39	23b52	00u57		05 09		05 29	06u22	06u52	07u23		07u52		08u22		[illegible]52	
Woking	a	22p54	23p01	23p11	23p31	23p41	00 01	00 16	01 16		05 50		06 08	06 41	07 11	07 42	07 54	08 12	08 24	08 42	[illegible]	09 11	09 24
	d	22p55	23p02	23p13	23p32	23p43	00 03	00 17	01 18		05 51		06 11	06 43	07 13	07 44	07 55	08 14	08 25	08 4[illegible]	[illegible]	09 13	09 25
Worplesdon	d			23p18				00 22					06 16	06 48	07 18	07 49		08 19		08 [illegible]		09 18	
Guildford	a	23p03	23p10	23p23	23p40	23p51	00 10	00 28	01s26		05 59		06 21	06 53	07 23	07 54	08 03	08 24	08 35	0[illegible]	[illegible] 05	09 23	09 33
	d	23p04	23p12	23p25	23p42	23p52	00 12	00 30	01s27		06 00	05 15	06 25	06 55	07 25	07 56	08 04	08 26	08 39	[illegible]	[illegible] 07	09 25	09 34
Farncombe	d	23p10		23p31	23p48	23p58		00 36			06 06		06 31	07 01	07 31	08 02		08 32		[illegible]		09 31	
Godalming	d	23p13		23p34	23p51	00 02		00 39			06 09		06 34	07 04	07 34	08 05		08 35		[illegible]05		09 34	
Milford (Surrey)	d			23p38	23p55			00s43			06 13		06 38	07 08	07 38	08 09		08 39		[illegible] 09			
Witley	d			23p42	23p59			00s47			06 18		06 42	07 12	07 42	08 13		08 43		[illegible]9 13			
Haslemere 4	a	23p24	23p26	23p49	00 06	00 12	00 26	00 54			06 24	05 29	06 49	07 19	07 49	08 20	08 24	08 50	08 5[illegible]	09 20	09 24	09 45	09 49
	d	23p25	23p27	23p50	00 07	00 13	00 27	00 54			06 25	05 30	06 55	07 20	07 53	08 30	08 25	08 58	08 [illegible]		09 25	09 55	09 50
Liphook	d			23p55	00 12			00s59			06 30	05 35	07 00	07 25	07 59	08 35		09 03				10 00	
Liss	d			00 01	00 18			01s05			06 36	05 41	07 06	07 31	08 05	08 41		09 09				10 06	
Petersfield	d	23p36	23p38	00 06	00 23	00 24	00 38	01 11			06 41	05 46	07 11	07 36	08 11	08 46	08 36	09 [illegible]			09 36	10 11	10 01
Rowlands Castle	d			00 16	00 33			01s20			06 51	05 56	07 21	07 46	08 21	08 56		09 [illegible]				10 21	
Havant	a	23p48	23p50	00 21	00 38	00 36	00 50	01 25	02s00		06 57	06 01	07 27	07 51	08 26	09 04	08 49	[illegible]	[illegible]9 19		09 49	10 26	10 15
	d	23p49	23p51	00 22	00 39	00 37	00 51	01 26	02s01	04 40	06 58	06 02	07 28	07 52	08 27	09 05	08 50	[illegible]	09 20		09 50	10 27	10 16
Bedhampton	a			00 24	00 41			01s29		04 42	07 00	06 04	07 30	07 54	08 29	09 07		[illegible]32				10 29	
Hilsea	a			00 30				01s34		04 48	07 07	06 10	07 37	08 00	08 35	09 13		[illegible]38				10 36	
Fratton	a	23p58	23p59	00 34	00 49	00 46	01 00	01s38	02s10	04 52	07 11	06 14	07 41	08 04	08 39	09 17	0[illegible]	[illegible]42	09 28		09 59	10 40	10 24
Portsmouth & Southsea	a	00 02	00 04	00 38	00 53	00 50	01 04	01 42	02s14	04 55	07 16	06 18	07 46	08 07	08 43	09 20	[illegible]	09 46	09 32		10 02	10 44	10 28
Portsmouth Harbour	a	00 07	00 09		00 58	00 55	01 09		02 19	04 59	07 20	06 22		08 12	08 48	09 2[illegible]	[illegible]	[illegible]	09 37		10 07		10 33

		SW 1	SW 1 ⊡	SW 1	SW 1 ⊡	SW 1	SW 1 ⊡	SW 1	SW 1 ⊡	SW 1	SW 1 ⊡	SW 1	SW 1 ⊡	SW 1	SW 1 ⊡	SW 1	SW 1 ⊡	SW 1	SW 1 ⊡	SW 1	SW 1 ⊡	SW 1	SW 1 ⊡
London Waterloo 15 ⊖	d	09 15	09 30	09 45	10 00	10 15	10 30	10 45	11 00	11 15	11 30	11 45	12 00	12 15	[illegible]	12 45	13 00	13 15	13 30	13 45	14 00	14 15	14 30
Clapham Junction 10	d	09u22		09u52		10u22		10u52		11u22		11u52		12u2[illegible]		12u52		13u22		13u52		14u22	
Woking	a	09 42	09 54	10 11	10 24	10 41	10 54	11 11	11 24	11 41	11 54	12 11	12 24	12 [illegible]	[illegible]54	13 11	13 24	13 41	13 54	14 11	14 24	14 41	14 54
	d	09 43	09 55	10 13	10 25	10 43	10 55	11 13	11 25	11 43	11 55	12 13	12 25	1[illegible]	[illegible]55	13 13	13 25	13 43	13 55	14 13	14 25	14 43	14 55
Worplesdon	d			10 18				11 18				12 18				13 18				14 18			
Guildford	a	09 52	10 03	10 23	10 33	10 50	11 03	11 23	11 33	11 50	12 03	12 23	12 3[illegible]	[illegible]50	13 03	13 23	13 33	13 50	14 03	14 23	14 33	14 50	15 03
	d	09 54	10 04	10 25	10 34	10 52	11 04	11 25	11 34	11 52	12 04	12 25	12 [illegible]	[illegible]52	13 04	13 25	13 34	13 52	14 04	14 25	14 34	14 52	15 04
Farncombe	d	10 00		10 29		10 58		11 31		11 58		12 31		[illegible]2 58		13 31		13 58		14 31		14 58	
Godalming	d	10 03		10 32		11 01		11 34		12 01		12 34		[illegible]3 01		13 34		14 01		14 34		15 01	
Milford (Surrey)	d	10 07				11 05				12 05				13 05				14 05				15 05	
Witley	d	10 11				11 09				12 09				13 09				14 09				15 09	
Haslemere 4	a	10 19	10 22	10 43	10 48	11 16	11 20	11 45	11 49	12 16	12 20	[illegible]	[illegible]2 49	13 16	13 20	13 45	13 49	14 16	14 20	14 45	14 49	15 16	15 20
	d		10 23	10 55	10 49		11 21	11 55	11 50		12 21	[illegible]	[illegible]2 50		13 21	13 55	13 50		14 21	14 55	14 50		15 21
Liphook	d			11 00				12 00				[illegible]00				14 00				15 00			
Liss	d			11 06				12 06				[illegible]06				14 06				15 06			
Petersfield	d		10 34	11 11	11 00		11 32	12 11	12 01		[illegible]	[illegible]3 11	13 01		13 32	14 11	14 01		14 32	15 11	15 01		15 32
Rowlands Castle	d			11 21				12 21				[illegible]3 21				14 21				15 21			
Havant	a		10 49	11 26	11 14		11 49	12 26	12 15		[illegible]49	13 26	13 15		13 49	14 26	14 15		14 49	15 26	15 14		15 49
	d		10 50	11 27	11 16		11 50	12 27	12 16		[illegible]50	13 27	13 16		13 50	14 27	14 16		14 50	15 27	15 16		15 50
Bedhampton	a			11 29				12 29				13 29				14 29				15 29			
Hilsea	a			11 36				12 36				13 36				14 36				15 36			
Fratton	a		10 59	11 40	11 24		11 59	12 40	12 [illegible]		12 59	13 40	13 24		13 59	14 40	14 24		14 58	15 40	15 24		15 59
Portsmouth & Southsea	a		11 02	11 44	11 28		12 02	12 44	12[illegible]		13 02	13 44	13 28		14 02	14 44	14 28		15 02	15 44	15 28		16 02
Portsmouth Harbour	a		11 07		11 33		12 07		[illegible]		13 07		13 33		14 07		14 33		15 07		15 33		16 07

		SW 1	SW 1 ⊡	SW 1	SW 1 ⊡	SW 1	SW 1 ⊡	SW	SW 1 ⊡	SW 1	SW 1 ⊡	SW 1	SW 1 ⊡	SW 1	SW 1 ⊡	SW 1	SW 1	SW 1 ⊡	SW 1	SW 1 ⊡	SW 1	SW 1 ⊡
London Waterloo 15 ⊖	d	14 45	15 00	15 15	15 30	15 45	16 [illegible]	[illegible]5	16 30	16 45	17 00	17 15	17 30	17 45	18 00	18 15	18 18	18 30	18 45	19 00	19 15	19 30
Clapham Junction 10	d	14u52		15u22		15u52		[illegible]u22		16u52											19u22	
Woking	a	15 11	15 24	15 41	15 54	16 1[illegible]	[illegible]	[illegible]6 41	16 54	17 11	17 24	17 38	17 54				18 42	18 57	19 13	19 24	19 43	19 54
	d	15 13	15 25	15 43	15 55	16 [illegible]	[illegible]25	16 43	16 54	17 13	17 25	17 40	17 56				18 43	18 58	19 14	19 25	19 45	19 55
Worplesdon	d	15 18		15 48		[illegible]		16 48			17 30	17 45	18 00				18 48			19 30		
Guildford	a	15 23	15 33	15 53	16 03	[illegible]	16 33	16 53	17 03	17 20	17 36	17 51	18 06	18 21	18 31	18 52	18 54	19 06	19 23	19 36	19 52	20 03
	d	15 25	15 34	15 55	16 04	[illegible]	16 34	16 55	17 03	17 22	17 37	17 54	18 08	18 23	18 33	18 54	18 57	19 08	19 24	19 37	19 54	20 04
Farncombe	d	15 31		16 01		[illegible]28		17 01		17 28		18 00		18 29			19 03		19 30		20 00	
Godalming	d	15 34		16 04		[illegible]31		17 04		17 31		18 03	18 15	18 32	18 39		19 06	19 14	19 33		20 03	20 11
Milford (Surrey)	d			16 08		16 35		17 08		17 35		18 07		18 36			19 10		19 37		20 07	
Witley	d			16 12		16 39		17 12		17 39		18 11		18 40			19 14		19 41		20 11	
Haslemere 4	a	15 45	15 49	16 [illegible]	[illegible]23	16 46	16 50	17 19	17 23	17 46	17 51	18 18	18 25	18 49	18 51	19 08	19 23	19 25	19 49	19 52	20 18	20 22
	d	15 55	15 50	16[illegible]	[illegible]24	16 55	16 51	17 29	17 24	17 56	17 52	18 31	18 26	18 56	18 52	19 09		19 26	19 57	19 53	20 27	20 22
Liphook	d	16 00		[illegible]		17 00		17 34		18 01		18 36		19 01		19 14			20 02		20 32	
Liss	d	16 06		[illegible]		17 06		17 40		18 07		18 42		19 07		19 20			20 08		20 38	
Petersfield	d	16 11	16 [illegible]	[illegible]45	16 35	17 11	17 02	17 45	17 35	18 12	18 03	18 47	18 37	19 12	19 03	19 25		19 37	20 13	20 04	20 43	20 33
Rowlands Castle	d	16 21		[illegible]55		17 21		17 55		18 22		18 57		19 22		19 35			20 23		20 53	
Havant	a	16 26	[illegible]	17 03	16 49	17 26	17 15	18 03	17 49	18 29	18 19	19 02	18 50	19 29	19 15	19 40		19 50	20 28	20 16	21 00	20 48
	d	16 27	[illegible]	17 04	16 50	17 27	17 16	18 04	17 50	18 30	18 20	19 03	18 51		19 16	19 41		19 51	20 29	20 17		20 49
Bedhampton	a	16 29		17 06		17 29		18 07		18 32		19 06				19 44			20 31			
Hilsea	a	16 36		17 11		17 36		18 12		18 39		19 11				19 49			20 37			
Fratton	a	16 40	[illegible] 24	17 15	16 59	17 40	17 24	18 16	17 59	18 43	18 28	19 15	18 59		19 25	19 55		19 59	20 41	20 25		20 57
Portsmouth & Southsea	a	16 4[illegible]	[illegible]6 28	17 20	17 02	17 44	17 28	18 20	18 02	18 46	18 32		19 03		19 29			20 03	20 44	20 29		21 01
Portsmouth Harbour	a	16 [illegible]	16 33	17 26	17 07		17 35	18 28	18 09		18 39		19 10		19 36			20 10	20 52	20 34		21 06

b previous night, stops to pick u[illegible]

Table 156

London - Guildford, Haslemere and Portsmouth

Mondays to Fridays

Station		SW 1	SW 1 ⊡	SW 1	SW 1 ⊡	SW 1	SW 1 ⊡	SW 1 ⊡	SW 1	SW 1	SW 1	SW 1	SW 1	SW 1
London Waterloo [15] ⊖	d	19 45	20 00	20 15	20 30	20 45	21 00	21 30	21 45	22 00	22 30	22 45	23 15	23 45
Clapham Junction [10]	d	19u52		20u22		20u52			21u52			22u52	23u22	23u52
Woking	a	20 11	20 24	20 41	20 54	21 11	21 24	21 54	22 11	22 24	22 54	23 11	23 41	00 16
	d	20 13	20 25	20 43	20 55	21 13	21 25	21 55	22 13	22 25	22 55	23 13	23 43	00 17
Worplesdon	d	20 18				21 18			22 18			23 18		00 22
Guildford	a	20 23	20 33	20 50	21 03	21 23	21 33	22 03	22 23	22 33	23 03	23 23	23 51	00 28
	d	20 25	20 34	20 52	21 04	21 25	21 34	22 04	22 25	22 34	23 04	23 25	23 52	00 30
Farncombe	d	20 31	20 40	20 58		21 31	21 40	22 10	22 31	22 40	23 10	23 31	23 58	00 36
Godalming	d	20 34	20 43	21 01	21 11	21 34	21 43	22 13	22 34	22 43	23 13	23 34	00 02	00 39
Milford (Surrey)	d	20 38		21 05		21 38			22 38			23 38		00s43
Witley	d	20 42		21 09		21 42			22 42			23 42		00s47
Haslemere [4]	a	20 49	20 54	21 16	21 21	21 49	21 54	22 24	22 49	22 54	23 24	23 49	00 12	00 54
	d	20 59	20 55		21 22	21 59	21 55	22 25	22 59	22 55	23 25	23 50	00 13	00 54
Liphook	d	21 04				22 04			23 04			23 55		00s59
Liss	d	21 10				22 10			23 10			00 01		01s05
Petersfield	d	21 16	21 06		21 33	22 16	22 06	22 36	23 15	23 06	23 36	00 06	00 24	01 11
Rowlands Castle	d	21 25				22 25			23 25			00 16		01s20
Havant	a	21 30	21 18		21 46	22 30	22 18	22 48	23 30	23 18	23 48	00 21	00 36	01 25
	d	21 31	21 19		21 46	22 31	22 19	22 49	23 31	23 19	23 49	00 22	00 37	01 26
Bedhampton	a	21 34				22 34			23 33			00 24		01s29
Hilsea	a	21 41				22 39			23 39			00 30		01s34
Fratton	a	21 45	21 28		21 55	22 43	22 28	22 59	23 43	23 28	23 58	00 34	00 46	01s38
Portsmouth & Southsea	a	21 48	21 32		21 58	22 47	22 32	23 04	23 47	23 32	00 02	00 38	00 50	01 42
Portsmouth Harbour	a		21 37		22 02		22 37	23 08		23 37	00 07		00 55	

Saturdays

Station		SW 1	SW 1	SW 1	SW 1	SW 1	SW 1	SW 1	SW 1	SW 1	SW 1	SW 1	SW 1	SW 1	SW 1	SW 1	SW 1	SW 1	SW 1 ⊡	SW 1	SW 1 ⊡	SW 1	SW 1 ⊡
London Waterloo [15] ⊖	d	22p30	22p45	23p15	23p45		05 00		05 20	06 15	06 45	07 15	07 30	07 45	08 00	08 15	08 30	08 45	09 00	09 15	09 30	09 45	10 00
Clapham Junction [10]	d		22b52	23b22	23b52		05 09		05 29	06u22	06u52	07u23		07u52		08u22		08u52		09u22		09u52	
Woking	a	22p54	23p11	23p41	00 16		05 50		06 08	06 41	07 11	07 42	07 54	08 11	08 24	08 41	08 54	09 11	09 24	09 41	09 54	10 11	10 24
	d	22p55	23p13	23p43	00 17		05 51		06 13	06 43	07 13	07 44	07 55	08 13	08 25	08 43	08 55	09 13	09 25	09 43	09 55	10 13	10 25
Worplesdon	d		23p18		00 22				06 18		07 18			08 18				09 18				10 18	
Guildford	a	23p03	23p23	23p51	00 28		05 59		06 23	06 50	07 23	07 51	08 03	08 23	08 33	08 50	09 03	09 23	09 33	09 50	10 03	10 23	10 33
	d	23p04	23p25	23p52	00 30		06 00	05 15	06 25	06 52	07 25	07 53	08 04	08 25	08 34	08 52	09 04	09 25	09 34	09 52	10 04	10 25	10 34
Farncombe	d	23p10	23p31	23p58	00 36		06 06		06 31	06 58	07 31	07 59		08 31		08 58		09 31		09 58		10 31	
Godalming	d	23p13	23p34	00 02	00 39		06 09		06 34	07 01	07 34	08 02		08 34		09 01		09 34		10 01		10 34	
Milford (Surrey)	d		23p38		00s43		06 13			07 05		08 06				09 05				10 05			
Witley	d		23p42		00s47		06 18			07 09		08 10				09 09				10 09			
Haslemere [4]	a	23p24	23p49	00 12	00 54		06 25	05 29	06 44	07 16	07 44	08 17	08 20	08 45	08 49	09 16	09 20	09 45	09 49	10 16	10 20	10 45	10 49
	d	23p25	23p50	00 13	00 54			05 30	06 45		07 45		08 21	08 55	08 50		09 21	09 55	09 50		10 21	10 55	10 50
Liphook	d		23p55		00s59			05 35	06 50		07 50			09 00				10 00				11 00	
Liss	d		00 01		01s05			05 41	06 56		07 56			09 06				10 06				11 06	
Petersfield	d	23p36	00 06	00 24	01 11			05 46	07 01		08 01		08 32	09 11	09 01		09 32	10 11	10 01		10 32	11 11	11 01
Rowlands Castle	d		00 16		01s20			05 56	07 11		08 11			09 21				10 21				11 21	
Havant	a	23p48	00 21	00 36	01 25			06 01	07 19		08 16		08 49	09 26	09 15		09 49	10 26	10 15		10 49	11 26	11 15
	d	23p49	00 22	00 37	01 26	04 40		06 02	07 20		08 17		08 50	09 27	09 16		09 50	10 27	10 16		10 50	11 27	11 16
Bedhampton	a		00 24		01s29	04 42		06 04	07 22		08 19			09 29				10 29				11 29	
Hilsea	a		00 30		01s34	04 48		06 10	07 27		08 25			09 36				10 36				11 36	
Fratton	a	23p58	00 34	00 46	01s38	04 52		06 14	07 31		08 29		08 59	09 40	09 24		09 59	10 40	10 24		10 59	11 40	11 24
Portsmouth & Southsea	a	00 02	00 38	00 50	01 42	04 55		06 18	07 35		08 32		09 02	09 44	09 28		10 02	10 44	10 28		11 02	11 44	11 28
Portsmouth Harbour	a	00 07		00 55		05 00		06 22	07 40		08 37		09 07		09 33		10 07		10 33		11 07		11 33

Station		SW 1	SW 1 ⊡	SW 1	SW 1 ⊡	SW 1	SW 1 ⊡	SW 1	SW 1 ⊡	SW 1	SW 1 ⊡	SW 1	SW 1 ⊡	SW 1	SW 1 ⊡	SW 1	SW 1 ⊡	SW 1	SW 1 ⊡	SW 1	SW 1 ⊡	SW 1	SW 1 ⊡
London Waterloo [15] ⊖	d	10 15	10 30	10 45	11 00	11 15	11 30	11 45	12 00	12 15	12 30	12 45	13 00	13 15	13 30	13 45	14 00	14 15	14 30	14 45	15 00	15 15	15 30
Clapham Junction [10]	d	10u22		10u52		11u22		11u52		12u22		12u52		13u22		13u52		14u22		14u52		15u22	
Woking	a	10 41	10 54	11 11	11 24	11 41	11 54	12 11	12 24	12 41	12 54	13 11	13 24	13 41	13 54	14 11	14 24	14 41	14 54	15 11	15 24	15 41	15 54
	d	10 43	10 55	11 13	11 25	11 43	11 55	12 13	12 25	12 43	12 55	13 13	13 25	13 43	13 55	14 13	14 25	14 43	14 55	15 13	15 25	15 43	15 55
Worplesdon	d			11 18				12 18				13 18				14 18				15 18			
Guildford	a	10 50	11 03	11 23	11 33	11 50	12 03	12 23	12 33	12 50	13 03	13 23	13 33	13 50	14 03	14 23	14 33	14 50	15 03	15 23	15 33	15 50	16 03
	d	10 52	11 04	11 25	11 34	11 52	12 04	12 25	12 34	12 52	13 04	13 25	13 34	13 52	14 04	14 25	14 34	14 52	15 04	15 25	15 34	15 52	16 04
Farncombe	d	10 58		11 31		11 58		12 31		12 58		13 31		13 58		14 31		14 58		15 31		15 58	
Godalming	d	11 01		11 34		12 01		12 34		13 01		13 34		14 01		14 34		15 01		15 34		16 01	
Milford (Surrey)	d	11 05				12 05				13 05				14 05				15 05				16 05	
Witley	d	11 09				12 09				13 09				14 09				15 09				16 09	
Haslemere [4]	a	11 16	11 20	11 45	11 49	12 16	12 20	12 45	12 49	13 16	13 20	13 45	13 49	14 16	14 20	14 45	14 49	15 16	15 20	15 45	15 49	16 16	16 20
	d		11 21	11 55	11 50		12 21	12 55	12 50		13 21	13 55	13 50		14 21	14 55	14 50		15 21	15 55	15 50		16 21
Liphook	d			12 00				13 00				14 00				15 00				16 00			
Liss	d			12 06				13 06				14 06				15 06				16 06			
Petersfield	d		11 32	12 11	12 01		12 32	13 11	13 01		13 32	14 11	14 01		14 32	15 11	15 01		15 32	16 11	16 01		16 32
Rowlands Castle	d			12 21				13 21				14 21				15 21				16 21			
Havant	a		11 49	12 26	12 15		12 49	13 26	13 15		13 49	14 26	14 15		14 49	15 26	15 14		15 49	16 26	16 15		16 49
	d		11 50	12 27	12 16		12 50	13 27	13 16		13 50	14 27	14 16		14 50	15 27	15 16		15 50	16 27	16 16		16 50
Bedhampton	a			12 29				13 29				14 29				15 29				16 29			
Hilsea	a			12 36				13 36				14 36				15 36				16 36			
Fratton	a		11 59	12 40	12 24		12 59	13 40	13 24		13 59	14 40	14 24		14 59	15 40	15 24		15 59	16 40	16 24		16 59
Portsmouth & Southsea	a		12 02	12 44	12 28		13 02	13 44	13 28		14 02	14 44	14 28		15 02	15 44	15 28		16 02	16 44	16 28		17 02
Portsmouth Harbour	a		12 07		12 33		13 07		13 33		14 07		14 33		15 07		15 33		16 07		16 33		17 07

b previous night, stops to pick up only

Table 156

London - Guildford, Haslemere and Portsmouth

Saturdays

Station		SW 1	SW 1 ⊡	SW 1	SW 1 ⊡	SW 1	SW 1 ⊡	SW 1	SW 1 ⊡	SW 1	SW 1 ⊡	SW 1	SW 1 ⊡	SW 1	SW 1 ⊡	SW 1	SW 1 ⊡	SW 1	SW 1	SW 1	SW 1	SW 1
London Waterloo [15] ⊖	d	15 45	16 00	16 15	16 30	16 45	17 00	17 15	17 30	17 45	18 00	18 15	18 30	18 45	19 00	19 15	19 30	19 45	20 00	20 15	20 30	20 45
Clapham Junction [10]	d	15u52		16u22		16u52		17u22		17u52		18u22		18u52		19u22		19u52		20u22		20u52
Woking	a	16 11	16 24	16 41	16 54	17 11	17 24	17 41	17 54	18 11	18 24	18 41	18 54	19 11	19 24	19 41	19 54	20 11	20 24	20 41	20 54	21 11
	d	16 13	16 25	16 43	16 55	17 13	17 25	17 43	17 55	18 13	18 25	18 43	18 55	19 13	19 25	19 43	19 55	20 13	20 25	20 43	20 55	21 13
Worplesdon	d	16 18				17 18				18 18				19 18				20 18				21 18
Guildford	a	16 23	16 33	16 50	17 03	17 23	17 33	17 50	18 03	18 23	18 33	18 50	19 03	19 23	19 33	19 50	20 03	20 23	20 33	20 50	21 03	21 23
	d	16 25	16 34	16 52	17 04	17 25	17 34	17 52	18 04	18 25	18 34	18 52	19 04	19 25	19 34	19 52	20 04	20 25	20 34	20 52	21 04	21 25
Farncombe	d	16 31		16 58		17 31		17 58		18 31		18 58		19 31		19 58		20 31		20 58		21 31
Godalming	d	16 34		17 01		17 34		18 01		18 34		19 01		19 34		20 01		20 34		21 01		21 34
Milford (Surrey)	d			17 05				18 05				19 05				20 05				21 05		21 38
Witley	d			17 09				18 09				19 09				20 09				21 09		21 42
Haslemere [4]	a	16 45	16 49	17 16	17 20	17 45	17 49	18 16	18 20	18 45	18 49	19 16	19 20	19 45	19 49	20 16	20 20	20 45	20 49	21 16	21 20	21 49
	d	16 55	16 50		17 21	17 55	17 50		18 21	18 55	18 50		19 21	19 55	19 50		20 21	20 55	20 50		21 21	21 59
Liphook	d	17 00				18 00				19 00				20 00				21 00				22 04
Liss	d	17 06				18 06				19 06				20 06				21 06				22 10
Petersfield	d	17 11	17 01		17 32	18 11	18 01		18 32	19 11	19 01		19 32	20 11	20 01		20 32	21 11	21 01		21 32	22 15
Rowlands Castle	d	17 21				18 21				19 21				20 21				21 21				22 25
Havant	a	17 26	17 15		17 49	18 26	18 15		18 49	19 26	19 15		19 49	20 29	20 15		20 49	21 26	21 15		21 45	22 30
	d	17 27	17 16		17 50	18 27	18 16		18 50	19 27	19 16		19 50	20 30	20 16		20 50	21 27	21 16		21 46	22 31
Bedhampton	a	17 29				18 29				19 29				20 32				21 29				22 33
Hilsea	a	17 36				18 36				19 36				20 41				21 36				22 41
Fratton	a	17 40	17 24		17 59	18 40	18 24		18 59	19 40	19 24		19 59	20 45	20 24		20 59	21 40	21 24		21 54	22 45
Portsmouth & Southsea	a	17 44	17 28		18 02	18 44	18 28		19 02	19 44	19 28		20 02	20 48	20 28		21 02	21 43	21 28		21 58	22 49
Portsmouth Harbour	a		17 33		18 07		18 33		19 07		19 33		20 07		20 33		21 07		21 33		22 03	22 53

Station		SW 1	SW 1	SW 1	SW 1	SW 1	SW 1	SW 1	SW 1
London Waterloo [15] ⊖	d	21 00	21 30	21 45	22 00	22 30	22 45	23 15	23 45
Clapham Junction [10]	d			21u52			22u52	23u22	23u52
Woking	a	21 24	21 54	22 11	22 24	22 54	23 11	23 41	00 16
	d	21 25	21 55	22 13	22 25	22 55	23 13	23 43	00 17
Worplesdon	d			22 18			23 18		00 22
Guildford	a	21 33	22 03	22 23	22 33	23 03	23 23	23 51	00 28
	d	21 34	22 04	22 25	22 34	23 04	23 25	23 52	00 29
Farncombe	d	21 40	22 10	22 31	22 40	23 10	23 31	23 58	00 35
Godalming	d	21 43	22 13	22 34	22 43	23 13	23 34	00 02	00 38
Milford (Surrey)	d			22 38			23 38		00s42
Witley	d			22 42			23 42		00s47
Haslemere [4]	a	21 54	22 24	22 49	22 54	23 24	23 49	00 12	00 53
	d	21 55	22 25	22 59	22 55	23 25	23 50	00 13	00 54
Liphook	d			23 04			23 55		00s59
Liss	d			23 10			00 01		01s05
Petersfield	d	22 06	22 36	23 15	23 06	23 36	00 06	00 24	01 10
Rowlands Castle	d			23 25			00 16		01s20
Havant	a	22 18	22 48	23 30	23 18	23 48	00 21	00 36	01 25
	d	22 19	22 49	23 31	23 19	23 49	00 22	00 37	01 26
Bedhampton	a			23 33			00 24		01s28
Hilsea	a			23 41			00 30		01s34
Fratton	a	22 28	22 58	23 45	23 28	23 58	00 34	00 46	01s38
Portsmouth & Southsea	a	22 32	23 02	23 48	23 32	00 02	00 38	00 50	01 42
Portsmouth Harbour	a	22 36	23 08	23 53	23 37	00 07		00 55	

Sundays

Station		SW 1	SW 1	SW 1	SW 1	SW 1	SW 1	SW 1	SW 1	SW 1	SW 1	SW 1	SW 1	SW 1 ⊡	SW 1	SW 1 ⊡	SW 1	SW 1 ⊡	SW 1	SW 1 ⊡	SW 1	SW 1 ⊡	SW 1
London Waterloo [15] ⊖	d	22p30	22p45	23p15	23p45		08 00	08 30	09 00	09 30	10 00	10 30	11 00	11 30	12 00	12 30	13 00	13 30	14 00	14 30	15 00	15 30	16 00
Clapham Junction [10]	d		22b52	23b22	23b52		08u09	08u39	09u09	09u39	10u09	10u39	11u09	11u39	12u09	12u39	13u09	13u39	14u09	14u39	15u09	15u39	16u09
Woking	a	22p54	23p11	23p41	00 16		08 34	09 03	09 34	10 03	10 31	11 01	11 31	12 01	12 31	13 01	13 31	14 01	14 31	15 01	15 31	16 01	16 31
	d	22p55	23p13	23p43	00 17	07 32	08 35	09 04	09 35	10 04	10 32	11 02	11 32	12 02	12 32	13 02	13 32	14 02	14 32	15 02	15 32	16 02	16 32
Worplesdon	d		23p18		00 22																		
Guildford	a	23p03	23p23	23p51	00 28	07 39	08 43	09 12	09 43	10 12	10 40	11 10	11 40	12 10	12 40	13 10	13 40	14 10	14 40	15 10	15 40	16 10	16 40
	d	23p04	23p25	23p52	00 29	07 41	08 45	09 14	09 45	10 14	10 42	11 12	11 42	12 12	12 42	13 12	13 42	14 12	14 42	15 12	15 42	16 12	16 42
Farncombe	d	23p10	23p31	23p58	00 35	07 48	08 53		09 53		10 48		11 48		12 48		13 48		14 48		15 48		16 48
Godalming	d	23p13	23p34	00 02	00 38	07 51	08 56		09 56		10 51		11 51		12 51		13 51		14 51		15 51		16 51
Milford (Surrey)	d		23p38		00s42	07 55	09 00		10 00		10 55		11 55		12 55		13 55		14 55		15 55		16 55
Witley	d		23p42		00s47	07 59	09 04		10 04		10 59		11 59		12 59		13 59		14 59		15 59		16 59
Haslemere [4]	a	23p24	23p49	00 12	00 53	08 06	09 11	09 28	10 11	10 28	11 06	11 26	12 06	12 26	13 06	13 26	14 06	14 26	15 06	15 26	16 06	16 26	17 06
	d	23p25	23p50	00 13	00 54	08 07	09 12	09 29	10 12	10 29	11 07	11 27	12 07	12 27	13 07	13 27	14 07	14 27	15 07	15 27	16 07	16 27	17 07
Liphook	d		23p55		00s59	08 12	09 17		10 17		11 12		12 12		13 12		14 12		15 12		16 12		17 12
Liss	d		00 01		01s05	08 18	09 23		10 23		11 18		12 18		13 18		14 18		15 18		16 18		17 18
Petersfield	d	23p36	00 06	00 24	01 10	08 23	09 28	09 40	10 28	10 40	11 23	11 38	12 23	12 38	13 23	13 38	14 23	14 38	15 23	15 38	16 23	16 38	17 23
Rowlands Castle	d		00 16		01s20	08 33	09 38		10 38		11 33		12 33		13 33		14 33		15 33		16 33		17 33
Havant	a	23p48	00 21	00 36	01 25	08 38	09 44	09 52	10 44	10 52	11 38	11 50	12 38	12 50	13 38	13 50	14 38	14 50	15 38	15 50	16 38	16 50	17 38
	d	23p49	00 22	00 37	01 26	08 39	09 45	09 53	10 45	10 53	11 39	11 51	12 39	12 51	13 39	13 51	14 39	14 51	15 39	15 51	16 39	16 51	17 39
Bedhampton	a		00 24		01s28	08 41	09 47		10 47		11 41		12 41		13 41		14 41		15 41		16 41		17 41
Hilsea	a		00 30		01s34																		
Fratton	a	23p58	00 34	00 46	01s38	08 49	09 55	10 01	10 55	11 01	11 49	12 00	12 49	13 00	13 49	14 00	14 49	15 00	15 49	16 00	16 49	17 00	17 49
Portsmouth & Southsea	a	00 02	00 38	00 50	01 42	08 53	09 59	10 06	10 59	11 05	11 53	12 04	12 53	13 04	13 53	14 04	14 53	15 04	15 54	16 04	16 53	17 04	17 53
Portsmouth Harbour	a	00 07		00 55		08 57	10 04	10 11	11 04	11 11	11 58	12 09	12 58	13 11	13 58	14 11	14 58	15 11	15 58	16 11	16 58	17 11	17 58

b previous night, stops to pick up only

London - Guildford, Haslemere and Portsmouth

		SW 1 ☕	SW 1	SW 1 ☕	SW 1	SW 1 ☕	SW 1	SW 1 ☕	SW 1	SW 1 ☕	SW 1	SW 1	SW 1	SW 1	SW 1	SW 1
London Waterloo 15 ⊖	d	16 30	17 00	17 30	18 00	18 30	19 00	19 30	20 00	20 30	21 00	21 30	22 00	22 30	23 00	23 30
Clapham Junction 10	d	16u39	17u09	17u39	18u09	18u39	19u09	19u39	20u09	20u39	21u09	21u39	22u09	22u39	23u09	23u39
Woking	a	17 01	17 31	18 01	18 31	19 01	19 31	20 01	20 31	21 01	21 31	22 01	22 31	23 01	23 31	00 01
	d	17 02	17 32	18 02	18 32	19 02	19 32	20 02	20 32	21 02	21 32	22 02	22 32	23 02	23 32	00 03
Worplesdon	d															
Guildford	a	17 10	17 40	18 10	18 40	19 10	19 40	20 10	20 40	21 10	21 40	22 10	22 40	23 10	23 40	00 10
	d	17 12	17 42	18 12	18 42	19 12	19 42	20 12	20 42	21 12	21 42	22 12	22 42	23 12	23 42	00 12
Farncombe	d		17 48		18 48		19 48		20 48		21 48		22 48		23 48	
Godalming	d		17 51		18 51		19 51		20 51		21 51		22 51		23 51	
Milford (Surrey)	d		17 55		18 55		19 55		20 55		21 55		22 55		23 55	
Witley	d		17 59		18 59		19 59		20 59		21 59		22 59		23 59	
Haslemere 4	a	17 26	18 06	18 26	19 06	19 26	20 06	20 26	21 06	21 26	22 06	22 26	23 06	23 26	00 06	00 26
	d	17 27	18 07	18 27	19 07	19 27	20 07	20 27	21 07	21 27	22 07	22 27	23 07	23 27	00 07	00 27
Liphook	d		18 12		19 12		20 12		21 12		22 12		23 12		00 12	
Liss	d		18 18		19 18		20 18		21 18		22 18		23 18		00 18	
Petersfield	d	17 38	18 23	18 38	19 23	19 38	20 23	20 38	21 23	21 38	22 23	22 38	23 23	23 38	00 23	00 38
Rowlands Castle	d		18 33		19 33		20 33		21 33		22 33		23 33		00 33	
Havant	a	17 50	18 38	18 50	19 38	19 50	20 38	20 50	21 38	21 50	22 38	22 50	23 38	23 50	00 38	00 50
	d	17 51	18 39	18 51	19 39	19 51	20 39	20 51	21 39	21 51	22 39	22 51	23 39	23 51	00 39	00 51
Bedhampton	a		18 41		19 41		20 41		21 41		22 41		23 41		00 41	
Hilsea	a															
Fratton	a	18 00	18 49	19 00	19 49	20 00	20 49	21 00	21 49	22 00	22 49	23 00	23 49	23 59	00 49	01 00
Portsmouth & Southsea	a	18 04	18 53	19 04	19 53	20 04	20 53	21 04	21 53	22 04	22 53	23 04	23 53	00 04	00 53	01 04
Portsmouth Harbour	a	18 11	18 58	19 11	19 58	20 11	20 58	21 09	21 58	22 11	22 58	23 09	23 58	00 09	00 58	01 09

Portsmouth, Haslemere and Guildford - London

		SW MX 1	SW MO 1	SW MO 1	SW MX 1	SW 1 A	SW 1 B	SW 1 A ☕	SW 1 B ☕	SW 1	SW 1 A	SW 1 B	SW 1 ☕	SW 1 A	SW 1 B	SW 1	SW 1 ☕	SW 1	SW 1	SW 1	SW 1 ☕	SW 1	SW 1 ☕
Portsmouth Harbour	d	22p18	22p32	22p48	23p19	04 25	04 30	05 14	05 19	05 50			06 15				06 42	06 55			07 13	07 29	07 45
Portsmouth & Southsea	d	22p24	22p37	22p53	23p24	04 30	04 35	05 19	05 24	05 55			06 20				06 47	07 00			07 18	07 33	07 50
Fratton	d	22p28	22p41	22p57	23p28	04 34	04 39	05 23	05 28	05 59			06 24				06 51	07 04			07 22	07 37	07 54
Hilsea	d	22p32			23p32	04 38	04 43	05 27	05 32	06 03						06 42		07 08				07 41	
Bedhampton	d	22p37		23p04	23p37	04 43	04 48	05 32	05 37	06 08						06 47		07 13				07 48	
Havant	a	22p39	22p49	23p07	23p39	04 45	04 50	05 35	05 40	06 10			06 33			06 49	06 59	07 15			07 30	07 50	08 03
	d	22p40	22p50	23p07	23p40	04 46	04 51	05 36	05 41	06 11			06 34			06 50	07 00	07 16		07 11	07 32	07 52	08 04
Rowlands Castle	d	22p46		23p13	23p46	04 52	04 57	05 41	05 46	06 16						06 56		07 22				07 57	
Petersfield	d	22p57	23p04	23p24	23p57	05 03	05 08	05 52	05 57	06 29			06 48			07 07	07 14	07 33		07 25	07 46	08 08	08 18
Liss	d	23p02		23p29	00 02	05 08	05 13	05 57	06 02	06 34						07 12	07 20	07 38				08 13	
Liphook	d	23p09		23p36	00 09	05 15	05 20	06 04	06 09	06 41						07 19	07 27	07 45				08 20	
Haslemere 4	a	23p15	23p16	23p41	00 15	05 20	05 25	06 10	06 15	06 46			07 01			07 25	07 33	07 51		07 38	07 59	08 26	08 31
	d	23p15	23p17	23p42	00 15	05 21	05 26	06 11	06 16	06 47	05 57	06 00	07 02	06 27	06 30	07 26	07 35	08 07	07 10	07 40	08 00	08 39	08 32
Witley	d	23p21		23p48	00 21	05 27	05 32				06 03	06 06		06 33	06 36			08 13	07 16	07 46		08 45	
Milford (Surrey)	d	23p25		23p52	00 25	05 31	05 36				06 08	06 11		06 37	06 40			08 17	07 21	07 50		08 49	
Godalming	d	23p29		23p56	00 29	05 35	05 40			06 57	06 12	06 15		06 41	06 44	07 35	07 45	08 21	07 25	07 54		08 53	
Farncombe	d	23p32		23p59	00 32	05 38	05 43			07 00	06 15	06 18		06 44	06 47	07 38		08 25	07 28	07 57		08 57	
Guildford	a	23p37	23p31	00 04	00 37	05 48	05 48	06 29	06 29	07 05	06 23	06 23	07 15	06 52	06 52	07 43	07 52	08 30	07 33	08 02	08 13	09 02	08 46
	d	23p39	23p35	00 05		05 50	05 50	06 31	06 31	07 07	06 24	06 24	07 17	06 53	06 53	07 45	07 54	08 31	07 34	08 03	08 15	09 03	08 54
Worplesdon	d	23p44				05 55	05 55				06 30	06 30		06 59	06 59	07 50		08 37	07 40		08 20		
Woking	a	23p49	23p42	00 13		06 00	06 00	06 39	06 39	07 15	06 35	06 35	07 25	07 03	07 03	07 54		08 41		08 11	08 26	09 11	
	d	23p56	23p45			06 01	06 01	06 41	06 41	07 17	06 37	06 37	07 26	07 05	07 05	07 56		08 43		08 12	08 27	09 13	
Clapham Junction 10	a	00 21	00 04			06 20	06 20	07 02	07 02		06 58	06 58		07 24	07 24			09 03				09 32	
London Waterloo 15 ⊖	a	00 30	00 14			06 29	06 29	07 12	07 12	07 45	07 08	07 08	07 54	07 36	07 36	08 24	08 32	09 13	08 11	08 41	08 55	09 43	09 31

		SW 1 ☕	SW 1	SW 1 ☕	SW 1 ☕	SW 1	SW 1	SW 1 ☕	SW 1 ☕	SW 1	SW 1	SW 1 ☕	SW 1 ☕	SW 1	SW 1	SW 1 ☕	SW 1 ☕	SW 1	SW 1	SW 1 ☕	SW 1 ☕	SW 1	SW 1
Portsmouth Harbour	d	08 15		08 45	09 15	09 18		09 45	10 15			10 45	11 15			11 45	12 15			12 45	13 15		
Portsmouth & Southsea	d	08 20	08 24	08 50	09 20	09 24		09 50	10 20	10 24		10 50	11 20	11 24		11 50	12 20	12 24		12 50	13 20	13 24	
Fratton	d	08 24	08 28	08 54	09 24	09 28		09 54	10 24	10 28		10 54	11 24	11 28		11 54	12 24	12 28		12 54	13 24	13 28	
Hilsea	d		08 32			09 32				10 32				11 32				12 32				13 32	
Bedhampton	d		08 37			09 37				10 37				11 37				12 37				13 37	
Havant	a	08 32	08 40	09 03	09 33	09 39		10 03	10 33	10 39		11 03	11 33	11 39		12 03	12 33	12 39		13 03	13 33	13 39	
	d	08 34	08 40	09 04	09 34	09 40		10 04	10 34	10 40		11 04	11 34	11 40		12 04	12 34	12 40		13 04	13 34	13 40	
Rowlands Castle	d		08 46			09 46				10 46				11 46				12 46				13 46	
Petersfield	d	08 48	08 57	09 18	09 48	09 57		10 18	10 48	10 57		11 18	11 48	11 57		12 18	12 48	12 57		13 18	13 48	13 57	
Liss	d		09 02			10 02				11 02				12 02				13 02				14 02	
Liphook	d		09 09			10 09				11 09				12 09				13 09				14 09	
Haslemere 4	a	09 01	09 15	09 31	10 01	10 15		10 31	11 01	11 15		11 31	12 01	12 15		12 31	13 01	13 15		13 31	14 01	14 15	
	d	09 02	09 15	09 32	10 02	10 15	09 39	10 32	11 02	11 15	10 39	11 32	12 02	12 15	11 39	12 32	13 02	13 15	12 39	13 32	14 02	14 15	13 39
Witley	d						09 45				10 45				11 45				12 45				13 45
Milford (Surrey)	d						09 49				10 49				11 49				12 49				13 49
Godalming	d		09 25			10 25	09 53			11 25	10 53			12 25	11 53			13 25	12 53			14 25	13 53
Farncombe	d		09 28			10 28	09 56			11 28	10 56			12 28	11 56			13 28	12 56			14 28	13 56
Guildford	a	09 15	09 33	09 45	10 15	10 33	10 01	10 46	11 15	11 33	11 01	11 45	12 15	12 33	12 01	12 45	13 15	13 33	13 01	13 45	14 15	14 33	14 01
	d	09 17	09 34	09 47	10 17	10 34	10 02	10 47	11 17	11 34	11 02	11 47	12 17	12 34	12 02	12 47	13 17	13 34	13 02	13 47	14 17	14 34	14 02
Worplesdon	d		09 40			10 40				11 40				12 40				13 40				14 40	
Woking	a	09 27	09 44	09 59	10 25	10 44	10 11	10 57	11 25	11 44	11 11	11 57	12 25	12 44	12 11	12 57	13 25	13 44	13 11	13 57	14 25	14 44	14 11
	d	09 28	09 46	09 59	10 26	10 46	10 12	10 59	11 26	11 46	11 12	11 59	12 26	12 46	12 12	12 59	13 26	13 46	13 12	13 59	14 26	14 46	14 12
Clapham Junction 10	a		10 05			11 05	10 31			12 05	11 31			13 05	12 31			14 05	13 31			15 05	14 31
London Waterloo 15 ⊖	a	09 55	10 13	10 27	10 51	11 13	10 40	11 24	11 51	12 13	11 40	12 23	12 51	13 13	12 40	13 23	13 51	14 13	13 40	14 23	14 51	15 13	14 40

		SW 1 ☕	SW 1 ☕	SW 1	SW 1	SW 1 ☕	SW 1 ☕	SW 1	SW 1	SW 1 ☕	SW 1	SW 1 ☕	SW 1	SW 1 ☕	SW 1 ☕	SW 1	SW 1 ☕	SW 1 ☕	SW 1	SW 1 ☕	SW 1 ☕	SW 1
Portsmouth Harbour	d	13 45	14 15			14 45	15 15			15 45		16 15		16 45	17 15	17 18	17 45	18 15		18 45	19 15	
Portsmouth & Southsea	d	13 50	14 20	14 24		14 50	15 20	15 24		15 50		16 20	16 24	16 50	17 20	17 24	17 50	18 20	18 24	18 50	19 20	19 24
Fratton	d	13 54	14 24	14 28		14 54	15 24	15 28		15 54		16 24	16 28	16 54	17 24	17 28	17 54	18 24	18 28	18 54	19 24	19 28
Hilsea	d			14 32				15 32					16 32			17 32			18 32			19 32
Bedhampton	d			14 37				15 37					16 37			17 37			18 37			19 37
Havant	a	14 03	14 33	14 39		15 03	15 33	15 39		16 03		16 33	16 39	17 03	17 33	17 39	18 03	18 33	18 39	19 03	19 33	19 39
	d	14 04	14 34	14 40		15 04	15 34	15 40		16 04	15 54	16 34	16 40	17 04	17 34	17 40	18 04	18 34	18 40	19 04	19 34	19 40
Rowlands Castle	d			14 46				15 46					16 46			17 46			18 46			19 46
Petersfield	d	14 18	14 48	14 57		15 18	15 48	15 57		16 18	16 10	16 48	16 57	17 18	17 48	17 57	18 18	18 48	18 57	19 18	19 48	19 57
Liss	d			15 02				16 02		16 23			17 02	17 23		18 02			19 02			20 02
Liphook	d			15 09				16 09		16 30			17 09	17 30		18 09			19 09			20 09
Haslemere 4	a	14 31	15 01	15 15		15 31	16 01	16 15		16 36	16 23	17 01	17 15	17 36	18 01	18 15	18 31	19 01	19 15	19 31	20 01	20 15
	d	14 32	15 02	15 15	14 39	15 32	16 02	16 15	15 37	16 37	16 24	17 02	17 15	17 37	18 02	18 15	18 32	19 02	19 15	19 32	20 02	20 15
Witley	d				14 45				15 43	16 43	16 30			17 43			18 38					20 21
Milford (Surrey)	d				14 49				15 47	16 47	16 34			17 47			18 42					20 25
Godalming	d			15 25	14 53			16 25	15 51	16 51	16 38		17 25	17 51		18 25	18 46	19 11	19 25			20 29
Farncombe	d			15 28	14 56			16 28	15 54	16 54	16 41		17 28	17 54		18 28	18 49	19 14	19 28			20 32
Guildford	a	14 45	15 15	15 33	15 01	15 45	16 15	16 33	15 59	16 59	16 46	17 15	17 33	17 59	18 15	18 33	18 54	19 19	19 33	19 45	20 15	20 37
	d	14 47	15 17	15 34	15 02	15 47	16 17	16 34	16 00	17 00	16 47	17 17	17 34	18 00	18 17	18 34	18 55	19 21	19 34	19 46	20 17	20 39
Worplesdon	d			15 40				16 40	16 06	17 06			17 40	18 06		18 40			19 40			20 44
Woking	a	14 57	15 25	15 44	15 11	15 57	16 25	16 44	16 11	17 11	16 57	17 25	17 44	18 11		18 44	19 03	19 28	19 45	19 57	20 25	20 52
	d	14 59	15 26	15 46	15 12	15 59	16 26	16 46	16 12	17 12	16 59	17 26	17 46	18 12		18 46	19 05	19 30	19 46	19 59	20 26	20 53
Clapham Junction 10	a			16 05	15 31			17 05	16 31	17 31			18 05	18 31		19 05			20 05			21 12
London Waterloo 15 ⊖	a	15 23	15 51	16 13	15 43	16 24	16 51	17 14	16 40	17 43	17 27	17 54	18 14	18 43	18 59	19 13	19 29	19 59	20 14	20 24	20 50	21 21

A from 27 September

B until 24 September

Table 156

Portsmouth, Haslemere and Guildford - London

Mondays to Fridays

Station		SW 1	SW 1	SW 1	SW 1	SW 1	SW 1	SW 1	SW 1	SW 1	SW 1
Portsmouth Harbour	d		19 45	20 15	20 18	20 45	21 18	21 28	22 18	22 28	23 19
Portsmouth & Southsea	d		19 50	20 20	20 24	20 50	21 24	21 33	22 24	22 33	23 24
Fratton	d		19 54	20 24	20 28	20 54	21 28	21 37	22 28	22 37	23 28
Hilsea	d				20 32		21 32	21 41	22 32	22 41	23 32
Bedhampton	d				20 37		21 37	21 47	22 37	22 46	23 37
Havant	a		20 03	20 33	20 39	21 03	21 40	21 52	22 39	22 53	23 39
	d		20 04	20 34	20 40	21 04	21 40		22 40		23 40
Rowlands Castle	d				20 46		21 46		22 46		23 46
Petersfield	d		20 18	20 48	20 57	21 18	21 57		22 57		23 57
Liss	d				21 02		22 02		23 02		00 02
Liphook	d				21 09		22 09		23 09		00 09
Haslemere 4	a		20 31	21 01	21 15	21 31	22 15		23 15		00 15
	d	19 39	20 32	21 02	21 15	21 32	22 15		23 15		00 15
Witley	d	19 45			21 21		22 21		23 21		00 21
Milford (Surrey)	d	19 49			21 25		22 25		23 25		00 25
Godalming	d	19 53			21 29		22 29		23 29		00 29
Farncombe	d	19 56			21 32		22 32		23 32		00 32
Guildford	a	20 01	20 45	21 16	21 37	21 45	22 37		23 37		00 37
	d	20 02	20 47	21 17	21 39	21 47	22 39		23 39		
Worplesdon	d				21 44		22 44		23 44		
Woking	a	20 11	20 56	21 25	21 49	21 57	22 49		23 49		
	d	20 12	20 59	21 26	21 50	21 59	22 50		23 56		
Clapham Junction 10	a	20 31			22 09		23 09		00 21		
London Waterloo 15 ⊖	a	20 40	21 27	21 50	22 18	22 27	23 19		00 30		

Saturdays

Station		SW 1	SW 1	SW 1	SW 1	SW 1	SW 1	SW 1	SW 1	SW 1	SW 1	SW 1	SW 1	SW 1	SW 1	SW 1	SW 1	SW 1	SW 1	SW 1	SW 1	SW 1	SW 1
				A	B	A	B			🍴	🍴			🍴	🍴			🍴	🍴			🍴	🍴
Portsmouth Harbour	d	22p18	23p19	04 38	04 43	05 14	05 19	06 19		06 45	07 15			07 45	08 15			08 45	09 15			09 45	10 15
Portsmouth & Southsea	d	22p24	23p24	04 43	04 48	05 19	05 24	06 24		06 50	07 20	07 24		07 50	08 20	08 24		08 50	09 20	09 24		09 50	10 20
Fratton	d	22p28	23p28	04 47	04 52	05 23	05 28	06 28		06 54	07 24	07 28		07 54	08 24	08 28		08 54	09 24	09 28		09 54	10 24
Hilsea	d	22p32	23p32	04 51	04 56	05 27	05 32	06 32				07 32				08 32				09 32			
Bedhampton	d	22p37	23p37	04 56	05 01	05 32	05 37	06 37				07 37				08 37				09 37			
Havant	a	22p39	23p39	04 58	05 03	05 34	05 39	06 40		07 03	07 33	07 39		08 03	08 33	08 39		09 03	09 33	09 39		10 03	10 33
	d	22p40	23p40	04 59	05 04	05 35	05 40	06 41		07 04	07 34	07 40		08 04	08 34	08 40		09 04	09 34	09 40		10 04	10 34
Rowlands Castle	d	22p46	23p46	05 04	05 09	05 41	05 46	06 46				07 46				08 46				09 46			
Petersfield	d	22p57	23p57	05 15	05 20	05 52	05 57	06 57		07 18	07 48	07 57		08 18	08 48	08 57		09 18	09 48	09 57		10 18	10 48
Liss	d	23p02	00 02	05 20	05 25	05 57	06 02	07 02				08 02				09 02				10 02			
Liphook	d	23p09	00 09	05 27	05 32	06 04	06 09	07 09				08 09				09 09				10 09			
Haslemere 4	a	23p15	00 15	05 33	05 38	06 10	06 15	07 15		07 31	08 01	08 15		08 31	09 01	09 15		09 31	10 01	10 15		10 31	11 01
	d	23p15	00 15	05 34	05 39	06 10	06 15	07 15	06 39	07 32	08 02	08 15	07 39	08 32	09 02	09 15	08 39	09 32	10 02	10 15	09 39	10 32	11 02
Witley	d	23p21	00 21	05 40	05 45				06 45				07 45				08 45				09 45		
Milford (Surrey)	d	23p25	00 25	05 44	05 49				06 49				07 49				08 49				09 49		
Godalming	d	23p29	00 29	05 48	05 53	06 20	06 25	07 25	06 53			08 25	07 53			09 25	08 53			10 25	09 53		
Farncombe	d	23p32	00 32	05 51	05 56	06 23	06 28	07 28	06 56			08 28	07 56			09 28	08 56			10 28	09 56		
Guildford	a	23p37	00 37	06 01	06 01	06 33	06 33	07 33	07 01	07 45	08 15	08 33	08 01	08 45	09 15	09 33	09 01	09 45	10 15	10 33	10 01	10 45	11 15
	d	23p39		06 02	06 02	06 34	06 34	07 34	07 02	07 47	08 17	08 34	08 02	08 47	09 17	09 34	09 02	09 47	10 17	10 34	10 02	10 47	11 17
Worplesdon	d	23p44				06 40	06 40	07 40				08 40				09 40				10 40			
Woking	a	23p49		06 11	06 11	06 44	06 44	07 44	07 11	07 57	08 26	08 44	08 12	08 57	09 25	09 44	09 11	09 57	10 25	10 44	10 11	10 57	11 25
	d	23p56		06 13	06 13	06 46	06 46	07 46	07 12	07 59	08 27	08 46	08 13	08 59	09 26	09 46	09 12	09 59	10 26	10 46	10 12	10 59	11 26
Clapham Junction 10	a	00 21		06 32	06 32	07 05	07 05	08 05	07 31			09 05	08 33			10 05	09 31			11 05	10 31		
London Waterloo 15 ⊖	a	00 30		06 40	06 40	07 13	07 13	08 13	07 40	08 23	08 51	09 13	08 42	09 23	09 51	10 13	09 40	10 23	10 51	11 13	10 40	11 23	11 51

Station		SW 1	SW 1	SW 1	SW 1	SW 1	SW 1	SW 1	SW 1	SW 1	SW 1	SW 1	SW 1	SW 1	SW 1	SW 1	SW 1	SW 1	SW 1	SW 1	SW 1	SW 1	SW 1
				🍴	🍴			🍴	🍴			🍴	🍴			🍴	🍴			🍴	🍴		
Portsmouth Harbour	d			10 45	11 15			11 45	12 15			12 45	13 15			13 45	14 15			14 45	15 15		
Portsmouth & Southsea	d	10 24		10 50	11 20	11 24		11 50	12 20	12 24		12 50	13 20	13 24		13 50	14 20	14 24		14 50	15 20	15 24	
Fratton	d	10 28		10 54	11 24	11 28		11 54	12 24	12 28		12 54	13 24	13 28		13 54	14 24	14 28		14 54	15 24	15 28	
Hilsea	d	10 32				11 32				12 32				13 32				14 32				15 32	
Bedhampton	d	10 37				11 37				12 37				13 37				14 37				15 37	
Havant	a	10 39		11 03	11 33	11 39		12 03	12 33	12 39		13 03	13 33	13 39		14 03	14 33	14 39		15 03	15 33	15 39	
	d	10 40		11 04	11 34	11 40		12 04	12 34	12 40		13 04	13 34	13 40		14 04	14 34	14 40		15 04	15 34	15 40	
Rowlands Castle	d	10 46				11 46				12 46				13 46				14 46				15 46	
Petersfield	d	10 57		11 18	11 48	11 57		12 18	12 48	12 57		13 18	13 48	13 57		14 18	14 48	14 57		15 18	15 48	15 57	
Liss	d	11 02				12 02				13 02				14 02				15 02				16 02	
Liphook	d	11 09				12 09				13 09				14 09				15 09				16 09	
Haslemere 4	a	11 15		11 31	12 01	12 15		12 31	13 01	13 15		13 31	14 01	14 15		14 31	15 01	15 15		15 31	16 01	16 15	
	d	11 15	10 39	11 32	12 02	12 15	11 39	12 32	13 02	13 15	12 39	13 32	14 02	14 15	13 39	14 32	15 02	15 15	14 39	15 32	16 02	16 15	15 39
Witley	d		10 45				11 45				12 45				13 45				14 45				15 45
Milford (Surrey)	d		10 49				11 49				12 49				13 49				14 49				15 49
Godalming	d	11 25	10 53			12 25	11 53			13 25	12 53			14 25	13 53			15 25	14 53			16 25	15 53
Farncombe	d	11 28	10 56			12 28	11 56			13 28	12 56			14 28	13 56			15 28	14 56			16 28	15 56
Guildford	a	11 33	11 01	11 45	12 15	12 33	12 01	12 45	13 15	13 33	13 01	13 45	14 15	14 33	14 01	14 45	15 15	15 33	15 01	15 45	16 15	16 33	16 01
	d	11 34	11 02	11 47	12 17	12 34	12 02	12 47	13 17	13 34	13 02	13 47	14 17	14 34	14 02	14 47	15 17	15 34	15 02	15 47	16 17	16 34	16 02
Worplesdon	d	11 40				12 40				13 40				14 40				15 40				16 40	
Woking	a	11 44	11 11	11 57	12 25	12 44	12 11	12 57	13 25	13 44	13 11	13 57	14 25	14 44	14 11	14 57	15 25	15 44	15 11	15 57	16 25	16 44	16 11
	d	11 46	11 12	11 59	12 26	12 46	12 12	12 59	13 26	13 46	13 12	13 59	14 26	14 46	14 12	14 59	15 26	15 46	15 12	15 59	16 26	16 46	16 12
Clapham Junction 10	a	12 05	11 31			13 05	12 31			14 05	13 31			15 05	14 31			16 05	15 31			17 05	16 31
London Waterloo 15 ⊖	a	12 13	11 40	12 23	12 51	13 13	12 40	13 23	13 51	14 13	13 40	14 23	14 51	15 13	14 40	15 23	15 51	16 13	15 40	16 23	16 51	17 13	16 40

A from 2 October

B until 25 September

Table 156

Portsmouth, Haslemere and Guildford - London

Saturdays

Station		SW 1	SW 1	SW 1	SW 1	SW 1	SW 1	SW 1	SW 1	SW 1	SW 1	SW 1	SW 1	SW 1	SW 1	SW 1	SW 1	SW 1	SW 1	SW 1	SW 1	SW 1
		🍴	🍴			🍴				🍴												
Portsmouth Harbour	d	15 45	16 15			16 45		17 18		17 45	18 15			18 45	19 15			19 45	20 15		20 45	21 18
Portsmouth & Southsea	d	15 50	16 20	16 24		16 50	17 10	17 24		17 50	18 20	18 24		18 50	19 20	19 24		19 50	20 20	20 24	20 50	21 24
Fratton	d	15 54	16 24	16 28		16 54	17 14	17 28		17 54	18 24	18 28		18 54	19 24	19 28		19 54	20 24	20 28	20 54	21 28
Hilsea	d			16 32			17 18	17 32				18 32				19 32				20 32		21 32
Bedhampton	d			16 37			17 23	17 37				18 37				19 37				20 37		21 37
Havant	a	16 03	16 33	16 39		17 03	17 25	17 39		18 03	18 33	18 39		19 03	19 33	19 39		20 03	20 33	20 39	21 03	21 39
	d	16 04	16 34	16 40		17 04	17 26	17 40		18 04	18 34	18 40		19 04	19 34	19 40		20 04	20 34	20 40	21 04	21 40
Rowlands Castle	d			16 46			17 32	17 46				18 46				19 46				20 46		21 46
Petersfield	d	16 18	16 48	16 57		17 18	17 43	17 57		18 18	18 48	18 57		19 18	19 48	19 57		20 18	20 48	20 57	21 18	21 57
Liss	d			17 02			17 48	18 02				19 02				20 02				21 02		22 02
Liphook	d			17 09			17 55	18 09				19 09				20 09				21 09		22 09
Haslemere 4	a	16 31	17 01	17 15		17 31	18 01	18 15		18 31	19 01	19 15		19 31	20 01	20 15		20 31	21 01	21 15	21 31	22 15
	d	16 32	17 02	17 15	16 39	17 32	18 02	18 15	17 39	18 32	19 02	19 15	18 39	19 32	20 02	20 15	19 39	20 32	21 02	21 15	21 32	22 15
Witley	d				16 45				17 45				18 45			20 21	19 45			21 21		22 21
Milford (Surrey)	d				16 49				17 49				18 49			20 25	19 49			21 25		22 25
Godalming	d			17 25	16 53			18 25	17 53			19 25	18 53			20 29	19 53			21 29		22 29
Farncombe	d			17 28	16 56			18 28	17 56			19 28	18 56			20 32	19 56			21 32		22 32
Guildford	a	16 45	17 15	17 33	17 01	17 45	18 15	18 33	18 01	18 45	19 15	19 33	19 01	19 45	20 15	20 37	20 01	20 45	21 15	21 37	21 47	22 37
	d	16 47	17 17	17 34	17 02	17 47	18 17	18 34	18 02	18 47	19 17	19 34	19 02	19 47	20 17	20 39	20 02	20 47	21 17	21 39	21 49	22 39
Worplesdon	d			17 40				18 40				19 40				20 44				21 44		22 44
Woking	a	16 57	17 25	17 44	17 11	17 57	18 25	18 44	18 11	18 57	19 25	19 44	19 11	19 57	20 25	20 52	20 11	20 57	21 25	21 49	21 57	22 49
	d	16 59	17 26	17 46	17 12	17 59	18 26	18 46	18 12	18 59	19 26	19 46	19 12	19 59	20 26	20 53	20 12	20 59	21 26	21 50	21 59	22 50
Clapham Junction 10	a			18 05	17 31			19 05	18 31			20 05	19 31			21 12	20 31			22 09		23 09
London Waterloo 15 ⊖	a	17 23	17 51	18 13	17 40	18 23	18 51	19 13	18 40	19 23	19 51	20 13	19 40	20 23	20 50	21 21	20 40	21 27	21 50	22 18	22 24	23 18

Station		SW 1	SW 1
Portsmouth Harbour	d	22 18	23 19
Portsmouth & Southsea	d	22 24	23 24
Fratton	d	22 28	23 28
Hilsea	d	22 32	23 32
Bedhampton	d	22 37	23 37
Havant	a	22 39	23 39
	d	22 40	23 40
Rowlands Castle	d	22 46	23 46
Petersfield	d	22 57	23 57
Liss	d	23 02	00 02
Liphook	d	23 09	00 09
Haslemere 4	a	23 15	00 15
	d	23 15	00 15
Witley	d	23 21	00 21
Milford (Surrey)	d	23 25	00 25
Godalming	d	23 29	00 29
Farncombe	d	23 32	00 32
Guildford	a	23 37	00 37
	d	23 39	
Worplesdon	d	23 44	
Woking	a	23 49	
	d	23 56	
Clapham Junction 10	a	00 20	
London Waterloo 15 ⊖	a	00 32	

Sundays

Station		SW 1	SW 1	SW 1	SW 1	SW 1	SW 1	SW 1	SW 1	SW 1	SW 1	SW 1	SW 1	SW 1	SW 1	SW 1	SW 1	SW 1	SW 1	SW 1	SW 1	SW 1	SW 1
				B	C	B	C		B	C		🍴		🍴		🍴		🍴		🍴		🍴	
Portsmouth Harbour	d	22p18	23p19	06 43	06 48	07 29	07 32	07 48	08 29	08 32	08 48	09 32	09 48	10 32	10 48	11 32	11 48	12 32	12 48	13 32	13 48	14 32	14 48
Portsmouth & Southsea	d	22p24	23p24	06 48	06 53	07 34	07 37	07 53	08 34	08 37	08 53	09 37	09 53	10 37	10 53	11 37	11 53	12 37	12 53	13 37	13 53	14 37	14 53
Fratton	d	22p28	23p28	06 52	06 57	07 38	07 41	07 57	08 38	08 41	08 57	09 41	09 57	10 41	10 57	11 41	11 57	12 41	12 57	13 41	13 57	14 41	14 57
Hilsea	d	22p32	23p32																				
Bedhampton	d	22p37	23p37	06 59	07 04			08 04			09 04		10 04		11 04		12 04		13 04		14 04		15 04
Havant	a	22p39	23p39	07 02	07 07	07 46	07 49	08 07	08 46	08 49	09 07	09 49	10 06	10 49	11 06	11 49	12 07	12 49	13 07	13 49	14 07	14 49	15 07
	d	22p40	23p40	07 02	07 07	07 47	07 50	08 07	08 47	08 50	09 07	09 50	10 07	10 50	11 07	11 50	12 07	12 50	13 07	13 50	14 07	14 50	15 07
Rowlands Castle	d	22p46	23p46	07 08	07 13			08 13			09 13		10 13		11 13		12 13		13 13		14 13		15 13
Petersfield	d	22p57	23p57	07 19	07 24	08 01	08 04	08 24	09 01	09 04	09 24	10 04	10 24	11 04	11 24	12 04	12 24	13 04	13 24	14 04	14 24	15 04	15 24
Liss	d	23p02	00 02	07 24	07 29			08 29			09 29		10 29		11 29		12 29		13 29		14 29		15 29
Liphook	d	23p09	00 09	07 31	07 36			08 36			09 36		10 36		11 36		12 36		13 36		14 36		15 36
Haslemere 4	a	23p15	00 15	07 36	07 41	08 13	08 16	08 41	09 13	09 16	09 41	10 16	10 41	11 16	11 41	12 16	12 41	13 16	13 41	14 16	14 41	15 16	15 41
	d	23p15	00 15	07 37	07 42	08 14	08 17	08 42	09 14	09 17	09 42	10 17	10 42	11 17	11 42	12 17	12 42	13 17	13 42	14 17	14 42	15 17	15 42
Witley	d	23p21	00 21	07 43	07 48			08 48			09 48		10 48		11 48		12 48		13 48		14 48		15 48
Milford (Surrey)	d	23p25	00 25	07 47	07 52			08 52			09 52		10 52		11 52		12 52		13 52		14 52		15 52
Godalming	d	23p29	00 29	07 51	07 56			08 56			09 56		10 56		11 56		12 56		13 56		14 56		15 56
Farncombe	d	23p32	00 32	07 54	07 59			08 59			09 59		10 59		11 59		12 59		13 59		14 59		15 59
Guildford	a	23p37	00 37	08 04	08 04	08 31	08 31	09 04	09 31	09 31	10 04	10 31	11 04	11 31	12 04	12 31	13 04	13 31	14 04	14 31	15 04	15 31	16 04
	d	23p39		08 05	08 05	08 35	08 35	09 05	09 35	09 35	10 05	10 35	11 05	11 35	12 05	12 35	13 05	13 35	14 05	14 35	15 05	15 35	16 05
Worplesdon	d	23p44																					
Woking	a	23p49		08 13	08 13	08 42	08 42	09 15	09 42	09 42	10 15	10 42	11 13	11 42	12 13	12 42	13 13	13 42	14 13	14 42	15 13	15 42	16 13
	d	23p56		08 15	08 15	08 45	08 45	09 15	09 45	09 45	10 15	10 45	11 15	11 45	12 15	12 45	13 15	13 45	14 15	14 45	15 15	15 45	16 15
Clapham Junction 10	a	00 20		08 40	08 40	09 06	09 06	09 38	10 04	10 04	10 35	11 04	11 34	12 04	12 34	13 04	13 34	14 04	14 34	15 04	15 34	16 04	16 34
London Waterloo 15 ⊖	a	00 32		08 49	08 49	09 19	09 19	09 49	10 19	10 19	10 49	11 19	11 49	12 19	12 49	13 14	13 44	14 14	14 44	15 14	15 44	16 14	16 44

B from 26 September

C until 19 September

Table 156

Sundays

Portsmouth, Haslemere and Guildford - London

		SW	SW	SW	SW	SW	SW	SW	SW	SW	SW	SW	SW	SW	SW	SW	SW
		[1]	[1]	[1]	[1]	[1]	[1]	[1]	[1]	[1]	[1]	[1]	[1]	[1]	[1]	[1]	[1]
		⊏		⊏		⊏		⊏									
Portsmouth Harbour	d	15 32	15 48	16 32	16 48	17 32	17 48	18 32	18 48	19 32	19 48	20 32	20 48	21 32	21 48	22 32	22 48
Portsmouth & Southsea	d	15 37	15 53	16 37	16 53	17 37	17 53	18 37	18 53	19 37	19 53	20 37	20 53	21 37	21 53	22 37	22 53
Fratton	d	15 41	15 57	16 41	16 57	17 41	17 57	18 41	18 57	19 41	19 57	20 41	20 57	21 41	21 57	22 41	22 57
Hilsea	d																
Bedhampton	d		16 04		17 04		18 04		19 04		20 04		21 04		22 04		23 04
Havant	a	15 49	16 07	16 49	17 07	17 49	18 07	18 49	19 07	19 49	20 07	20 49	21 07	21 49	22 07	22 49	23 07
	d	15 50	16 07	16 50	17 07	17 50	18 07	18 50	19 07	19 50	20 07	20 50	21 07	21 50	22 07	22 50	23 07
Rowlands Castle	d		16 13		17 13		18 13		19 13		20 13		21 13		22 13		23 13
Petersfield	d	16 04	16 24	17 04	17 24	18 04	18 24	19 04	19 24	20 04	20 24	21 04	21 24	22 04	22 24	23 04	23 24
Liss	d		16 29		17 29		18 29		19 29		20 29		21 29		22 29		23 29
Liphook	d		16 36		17 36		18 36		19 36		20 36		21 36		22 36		23 36
Haslemere [4]	a	16 16	16 41	17 16	17 41	18 16	18 41	19 16	19 41	20 16	20 41	21 16	21 41	22 16	22 41	23 16	23 41
	d	16 17	16 42	17 17	17 42	18 17	18 42	19 17	19 42	20 17	20 42	21 17	21 42	22 17	22 42	23 17	23 42
Witley	d		16 48		17 48		18 48		19 48		20 48		21 48		22 48		23 48
Milford (Surrey)	d		16 52		17 52		18 52		19 52		20 52		21 52		22 52		23 52
Godalming	d		16 56		17 56		18 56		19 56		20 56		21 56		22 56		23 56
Farncombe	d		16 59		17 59		18 59		19 59		20 59		21 59		22 59		23 59
Guildford	a	16 31	17 04	17 31	18 04	18 31	19 04	19 31	20 04	20 31	21 04	21 31	22 04	22 31	23 04	23 31	00 04
	d	16 35	17 05	17 35	18 05	18 35	19 05	19 35	20 05	20 35	21 05	21 35	22 05	22 35	23 05	23 35	00 05
Worplesdon	d																
Woking	a	16 42	17 13	17 42	18 13	18 42	19 13	19 42	20 13	20 42	21 13	21 42	22 13	22 42	23 13	23 42	00 13
	d	16 45	17 15	17 45	18 15	18 45	19 15	19 45	20 15	20 45	21 15	21 45	22 15	22 45	23 15	23 45	
Clapham Junction [10]	a	17 04	17 34	18 04	18 34	19 04	19 34	20 04	20 34	21 04	21 34	22 04	22 34	23 04	23 34	00 04	
London Waterloo [15] ⊖	a	17 14	17 44	18 14	18 44	19 14	19 44	20 14	20 44	21 14	21 44	22 14	22 44	23 14	23 44	00 14	

Table 157

Mondays to Fridays

Havant - Portsmouth Harbour

(Complete service)

		SW	SW	SW	SW	SW	SW	SW	SW	SW	SW	SW	SW	SN	SN	SW	SN	SW	SN	SW	SW	SW	GW	SW
		MX	MO	MO	MX	MX	MX	MO	MO		MX	MO												
		[1]	[1]	[1]	[1]	[1]	[1]	[1]	[1]	[1]	[1]	[1]	[1]	[1]	[1]	[1]	[1]	[1]	[1]	[1]	[1]	[1]		[1]
Havant	d	23p49	23p51			00 22	00 37	00 39	00 51		01 26	02s01	04 40	05 21	05 40	06 02	06 13		06 53		06 58			
Bedhampton	d					00 25		00 41			01s29		04 43			06 05	06 15		06 56		07 01			
Hilsea	d			23p59	00 03	00 30					01s34		04 48			06 10	06 20	06 33	07 01	07 05	07 07	[illegible] 13		07 35
Fratton	d	23p59	00 01	00 04	00 08	00 34	00 47	00 50	01 01	01s05	01s39	02s11	04 52	05 30	05 49	06 15	06 25	06 38	07 05	07 09	07 1[illegible]	[illegible] 17	07 35	07 39
Portsmouth & Southsea	a	00 02	00 04	00 08	00 11	00 38	00 50	00 53	01 04	01s08	01 42	02s14	04 55	05 33	05 52	06 18	06 28	06 44	07 08	07 12	07 [illegible]	07 22	07 38	07 42
	d	00 03	00 05	00 09	00 13		00 51	00 54	01 05	01s09		02s15	04 56	05 33	05 52	06 19	06 28	06 45	07 09	07 13	0[illegible]7		07 39	07 43
Portsmouth Harbour	a	00 07	00 09	00 13	00 16		00 55	00 58	01 09	01 12		02 19	04 59	05 37	05 56	06 22	06 32	06 49	07 12	07 17	[illegible]20		07 45	07 48

		SW	SN	SN	SW	SW	SN	SW	GW	SN	SW	SW	SN	SW	SW	SN	SW	SW	S[illegible]	SW	GW	SN	SN
		[1]	[1]	[1]	[1]	[1]	[1]	[1]	◇	[1]	[1]	[1]	[1]	[1]	[1]	[1]	[1]	[1]		[1]	◇	[1]	◇[1]
														⊏							⊤		
Havant	d	07 28	07 35	07 41	07 52		07 58			08 22	08 27		08 44	08 50		09 01	09 05	09 [illegible]		09 30		09 33	09 46
Bedhampton	d	07 31	07 37		07 55		08 00			08 25	08 30						09 08			09 33		09 36	
Hilsea	d	07 37	07 42		08 00	08 03	08 05	08 09		08 30	08 35	08 45			09 05		09 1[illegible]		09 33	09 38		09 42	
Fratton	d	07 42	07 47	07 50	08 04	08 07	08 10	08 13	08 21	08 34	08 40	08 49	08 53	08 59	09 10	09 13	09 [illegible]	09 29	09 37	09 43	09 42	09 47	09 55
Portsmouth & Southsea	a	07 46	07 50	07 53	08 07	08 11	08 15	08 18	08 24	08 37	08 43	08 52	08 56	09 02	09 13	09 17	09 [illegible]	09 32	09 42	09 46	09 46	09 50	09 58
	d			07 53	08 09	08 13	08 16	08 20	08 25	08 38	08 45	08 54	08 57	09 04	09 14	09 18	[illegible]22	09 34			09 46		09 58
Portsmouth Harbour	a			07 58	08 12	08 16	08 19	08 23	08 30	08 41	08 48	08 58	09 00	09 07	09 18	09 21	[illegible]26	09 37			09 54		10 02

		SW	SW	SN	SW	SW	SW	GW	SN	SN	SW	SW	SN	SW	SW	S[illegible]	GW	SN	SN	SW	SW	SN
								▪														
		[1]	[1]	[1]	[1]	[1]	[1]		[1]	◇[1]	[1]	[1]	[1]	[1]	[1]	[1]	◇	[1]	◇[1]	[1]	[1]	[1]
		⊏			⊏			⊤			⊏			⊏			⊤			⊏		
Havant	d	09 50		10 07	10 16		10 27		10 32	10 46	10 50		11 05	11 [illegible]		11 27		11 32	11 46	11 50		12 05
Bedhampton	d						10 30		10 34							11 30		11 34				
Hilsea	d		10 03			10 33	10 36		10 42			11 03			11 33	11 36		11 42			12 03	
Fratton	d	09 59	10 08	10 16	10 25	10 37	10 40	10 42	10 47	10 55	10 59	11 08	11 14	[illegible] 25	11 37	11 40	11 42	11 47	11 55	11 59	12 08	12 14
Portsmouth & Southsea	a	10 02	10 11	10 19	10 28	10 42	10 44	10 46	10 50	10 58	11 02	11 11	11 [illegible]	[illegible] 28	11 42	11 44	11 46	11 50	11 58	12 02	12 11	12 17
	d	10 04	10 12	10 20	10 29			10 46		10 58	11 04	11 12	11 [illegible]	11 29			11 46		11 58	12 04	12 12	12 17
Portsmouth Harbour	a	10 07	10 18	10 23	10 33			10 54		11 02	11 07	11 18	1[illegible]	11 33			11 54		12 02	12 07	12 18	12 21

		SW	SW	SW	GW	SN	SN	SW	SW	SN	SW	SW	SW	GW	SN	SN	SW	SW	SN	SW	SW	SW	GW
		[1]	[1]	[1]	◇	[1]	◇[1]	[1]	[1]	[1]	[1]	[1]		◇	[1]	◇[1]	[1]	[1]	[1]	[1]	[1]	[1]	◇
		⊏			⊤			⊏			⊏			⊤			⊏			⊏			⊤
Havant	d	12 16		12 27		12 32	12 46	12 50		13 05	13 16		13 27		13 32	13 46	13 50		14 05	14 16		14 27	
Bedhampton	d			12 30		12 34							13 30		13 34							14 30	
Hilsea	d		12 33	12 36		12 42			13 03			[illegible]33	13 36		13 42			14 03			14 33	14 36	
Fratton	d	12 25	12 37	12 40	12 42	12 47	12 55	12 59	13 08	13 14	13 2[illegible]	[illegible]37	13 40	13 42	13 47	13 55	13 59	14 08	14 14	14 25	14 37	14 40	14 42
Portsmouth & Southsea	a	12 28	12 42	12 44	12 46	12 50	12 58	13 02	13 11	13 17	13 [illegible]	13 42	13 44	13 46	13 50	13 58	14 02	14 11	14 17	14 28	14 42	14 44	14 46
	d	12 29			12 46		12 58	13 04	13 12	13 17	1[illegible]9			13 46		13 58	14 04	14 12	14 17	14 29			14 46
Portsmouth Harbour	a	12 33			12 54		13 02	13 07	13 18	13 21	[illegible]33			13 54		14 02	14 07	14 18	14 21	14 33			14 54

		SN	SN	SW	SW	SN	SW	SW	SW	G[illegible]	SN	SN	SW	SW	SN	SN	SW	SW	SW	GW	SN	SN
		[1]	◇[1]	[1]	[1]	[1]	[1]	[1]	[1]	◇	[1]	◇[1]	[1]	[1]	[1]	[1]	[1]	[1]	[1]	◇	[1]	◇[1]
				⊏			⊏			⊤			⊏				⊏			⊤		
Havant	d	14 32	14 47	14 50		15 05	15 16		1[illegible]7		15 32	15 46	15 50		16 02	16 09	16 16		16 27		16 32	16 46
Bedhampton	d	14 34							[illegible]30		15 34				16 04				16 30		16 34	
Hilsea	d	14 42			15 03			15 3[illegible]	[illegible]36		15 42			16 03				16 33	16 36		16 42	
Fratton	d	14 47	14 56	14 59	15 08	15 14	15 25	15 [illegible]	15 40	15 42	15 47	15 55	15 59	16 08	16 12	16 18	16 25	16 37	16 40	16 42	16 47	16 55
Portsmouth & Southsea	a	14 50	14 59	15 02	15 11	15 17	15 28	1[illegible]2	15 44	15 46	15 50	15 58	16 02	16 11	16 15	16 21	16 28	16 40	16 44	16 46	16 50	16 58
	d		14 59	15 04	15 12	15 17	15 29			15 46		15 58	16 04	16 12	16 16	16 22	16 29	16 41	16 45	16 46		16 58
Portsmouth Harbour	a		15 03	15 07	15 18	15 21	15 3[illegible]			15 54		16 02	16 07	16 18	16 21	16 26	16 33	16 44	16 49	16 54		17 02

		SW	SW	SN	SW	SN	SW	[illegible]	SW	SW	GW	SN	SW	SN	SW	SW	SN	SW	SW	SW	SW	SN	GW
		[1]	[1]	[1]	[1]	[1]	[1]	[1]	[1]	[1]	◇	[1]	[1]	◇[1]	[1]	[1]	[1]	[1]	[1]	[1]	[1]	[1]	◇
		⊏					[illegible]				⊤		⊏					⊏					⊤
Havant	d	16 50		17 00	17 04	17 09	[illegible]16			17 27		17 32	17 50	17 54		18 04	18 13	18 20			18 30	18 34	
Bedhampton	d			17 02	17 06					17 30		17 34		17 56		18 07					18 33	18 36	
Hilsea	d		17 03	17 07	17 11				17 33	17 36		17 42		18 01	18 04	18 12			18 33		18 39	18 42	
Fratton	d	16 59	17 08	17 12	17 16	1[illegible]9	17 25	17 32	17 37	17 40	17 42	17 47	17 59	18 06	18 09	18 17	18 22	18 29	18 37	18 40	18 43	18 46	18 48
Portsmouth & Southsea	a	17 02	17 11	17 16	17 20	[illegible]22	17 28	17 35	17 42	17 44	17 46	17 50	18 02	18 09	18 12	18 20	18 25	18 32	18 41	18 43	18 46	18 49	18 52
	d	17 04	17 12	17 16	17 2[illegible]		17 30	17 36			17 46		18 04	18 09	18 14	18 22	18 26	18 33		18 45			18 52
Portsmouth Harbour	a	17 07	17 18	17 20	17 [illegible]		17 35	17 40			17 54		18 09	18 15	18 20	18 28	18 31	18 39		18 51			18 58

		SW	SN	SW	[illegible]W	SN	SW	SW	SW	GW	SN	SW	SN	SW	SW	SN	SW	SW	SW	GW	SW	SN	SW	SN	SW
										▪										▪					
		[1]	◇[1]		◇[1]	[1]	[1]	[1]	[1]		[1]	[1]	◇[1]	[1]	[1]	[1]	[1]	[1]	[1]		[1]	◇[1]	[1]	[1]	[1]
		⊏					⊏			⊤				⊏			⊏			⊤	⊏				⊏
Havant	d	18 51	18 [illegible]		19 03	19 08	19 16				19 33	19 41	19 46	19 51		20 07	20 17		20 29		20 49	20 52		21 10	21 19
Bedhampton	d		[illegible]57		19 06						19 35	19 44							20 32						
Hilsea	d		[illegible]02	19 05	19 11			19 28	19 33		19 43	19 49			20 02			20 33	20 37				21 03		
Fratton	d	19 [illegible]	19 06	19 09	19a15	19 18	19 26	19 33	19 37	19 42	19 47	19a55	19 57	20 00	20 08	20 16	20 26	20 37	20 41	20 42	20 58	21 02	21 08	21 19	21 29
Portsmouth & Southsea	a	19 [illegible]	19 09	19 12		19 21	19 29	19 36	19 42	19 46	19 50		20 01	20 03	20 11	20 19	20 29	20 42	20 44	20 46	21 01	21 06	21 11	21 23	21 32
	d	[illegible]05		19 14		19 21	19 30	19 38		19 46			20 01	20 05	20 12		20 31		20 46	20 46	21 03		21 13	21 23	21 33
Portsmouth Harbour	a	[illegible]10		19 20		19 26	19 36	19 43		19 54			20 07	20 10	20 20		20 34		20 52	20 54	21 06		21 16	21 27	21 37

Table 157

Havant - Portsmouth Harbour
(Complete service)

Mondays to Fridays

		SW 1	GW ◇ ✕	SW 1	SW 1 ⊏	SN ◇1 ✕	SW 1	SN 1	SW 1 ⊏	SW 1	SW 1	SN 1	GW ◇	SW 1 ⊏	SW 1	SN 1	SW 1	SW	SW 1	SW 1	GW ◇	SN 1	SW 1
Havant	d			21 31	21 46	21 49		22 10	22 19		22 31	22 43		22 49	22 59	23 11	23 19			23 31		23 34	23 49
Bedhampton	d			21 34							22 34				23 01					23 34			
Hilsea	d	21 33		21 41			22 03			22 33	22 39							23 24	23 33	23 39			
Fratton	d	21 37	21 42	21 45	21 55	21 58	22 08	22 19	22 29	22 37	22 44	22 52	22 56	23 00		23 20	23 29	23 33	23 37	23 44	23 44	23 47	23 59
Portsmouth & Southsea	a	21 42	21 45	21 48	21 58	22 01	22 11	22 22	22 32	22 42	22 47	22 55	22 59	23 04		23 23	23 32	23 36	23 40	23 47	23 48	23 51	00 02
	d		21 46		21 59	22 02	22 13	22 22	22 33			22 56	22 59	23 05		23 24	23 33	23 36			23 48		00 03
Portsmouth Harbour	a		21 52		22 02	22 05	22 16	22 26	22 37			22 59	23 04	23 08		23 27	23 37	23 40			23 54		00 07

Saturdays

		SW 1	SW 1	SW 1	SW 1	SW 1	SW 1	SW 1	SN 1	SN 1	SN 1	SW 1	SW 1	SN 1	SN 1	SW 1	SN 1	SW 1	SW 1	GW	SN 1	SN 1	SW 1
Havant	d	23p49		00 22	00 37		01 26	04 40	05 34	05 49	05 57	06 02		06 32	06 46		07 04	07 20			07 32	07 46	
Bedhampton	d			00 25			01s29	04 43				06 05		06 34				07 22			07 34		
Hilsea	d		00 03	00 30			01s34	04 48				06 10	06 33	06 42		07 03		07 27	07 33		07 42		08 03
Fratton	d	23p59	00 08	00 34	00 47	01s05	01s39	04 52	05 43	05 58	06 06	06 15	06 37	06 47	06 55	07 08	07 13	07 32	07 37	07 42	07 47	07 55	08 08
Portsmouth & Southsea	a	00 02	00 11	00 38	00 50	01s08	01 42	04 55	05 46	06 01	06 09	06 18	06 42	06 50	06 58	07 11	07 16	07 35	07 42	07 46	07 50	07 58	08 11
	d	00 03	00 13		00 51	01s09		04 57		06 01	06 09	06 19			06 58	07 12	07 16	07 36		07 46		07 59	08 13
Portsmouth Harbour	a	00 07	00 16		00 55	01 12		05 00		06 05	06 16	06 22			07 02	07 16	07 20	07 40		07 52		08 02	08 18

		SN 1	SW 1	SW 1	GW ◇	SN 1	SN 1	SW 1	SW 1	SN 1	SW 1	SW 1	SW 1	GW ◇	SN 1	SN ◇1	SW 1	SW 1	SN 1	SW 1 ⊏	SW 1	SW 1	GW ◇
Havant	d	08 04	08 17			08 32	08 46	08 50		09 04	09 16		09 27		09 32	09 46	09 50		10 07	10 16		10 27	
Bedhampton	d		08 20			08 34							09 30		09 34							10 30	
Hilsea	d		08 25	08 33		08 42			09 04			09 33	09 36		09 42			10 03			10 33	10 36	
Fratton	d	08 13	08 29	08 37	08 42	08 47	08 55	08 59	09 09	09 13	09 25	09 37	09 40	09 42	09 47	09 55	09 59	10 08	10 16	10 25	10 37	10 40	10 42
Portsmouth & Southsea	a	08 16	08 32	08 42	08 46	08 50	08 58	09 02	09 12	09 16	09 28	09 42	09 44	09 46	09 50	09 58	10 02	10 11	10 19	10 28	10 42	10 44	10 46
	d	08 16	08 34		08 46		08 59	09 04	09 13	09 16	09 29			09 46		09 58	10 04	10 12	10 20	10 29			10 46
Portsmouth Harbour	a	08 20	08 37		08 52		09 02	09 07	09 18	09 20	09 33			09 52		10 02	10 07	10 18	10 23	10 33			10 52

		SN 1	SN ◇1	SW 1 ⊏	SW 1	SN 1	SW 1 ⊏	SW 1	SW 1	GW ◇	SN 1	SN ◇1	SW 1 ⊏	SW 1	SN 1	SW 1 ⊏	SW 1	SW 1	GW ◇ ✕	SN 1	SN ◇1	SW 1 ⊏
Havant	d	10 32	10 46	10 50		11 05	11 16		11 27		11 32	11 46	11 50		12 05	12 16		12 27		12 32	12 46	12 50
Bedhampton	d	10 34							11 30		11 34							12 30		12 34		
Hilsea	d	10 43			11 03			11 33	11 36		11 42			12 03			12 33	12 36		12 42		
Fratton	d	10 47	10 55	10 59	11 08	11 14	11 25	11 37	11 40	11 42	11 47	11 55	11 59	12 08	12 14	12 25	12 37	12 40	12 42	12 47	12 55	12 59
Portsmouth & Southsea	a	10 50	10 58	11 02	11 11	11 17	11 28	11 42	11 44	11 46	11 50	11 58	12 02	12 11	12 17	12 28	12 42	12 44	12 46	12 50	12 58	13 02
	d		10 58	11 04	11 12	11 17	11 29			11 46		11 58	12 04	12 12	12 17	12 29			12 46		12 58	13 04
Portsmouth Harbour	a		11 02	11 07	11 18	11 21	11 33			11 52		12 02	12 07	12 18	12 21	12 33			12 51		13 02	13 07

		SW 1	SN 1	SW 1 ⊏	SW 1	SW 1	GW ◇ ✕	SN 1	SN ◇1	SW 1 ⊏	SW 1	SN 1	SW 1 ⊏	SW 1	SW 1	GW ◇ ✕	SN 1	SN ◇1	SW 1 ⊏	SW 1	SN 1	SW 1 ⊏	SW 1
Havant	d		13 05	13 16		13 27		13 32	13 46	13 50		14 05	14 16		14 27		14 32	14 46	14 50		15 05	15 16	
Bedhampton	d					13 30		13 34							14 30		14 34						
Hilsea	d	13 03			13 33	13 36		13 42			14 03			14 33	14 36		14 42			15 03			15 33
Fratton	d	13 08	13 14	13 25	13 37	13 40	13 42	13 47	13 55	13 59	14 08	14 14	14 25	14 37	14 40	14 42	14 47	14 55	14 59	15 08	15 14	15 25	15 37
Portsmouth & Southsea	a	13 11	13 17	13 28	13 42	13 44	13 46	13 50	13 58	14 02	14 11	14 17	14 28	14 42	14 44	14 46	14 50	14 58	15 02	15 11	15 17	15 28	15 42
	d	13 12	13 17	13 29			13 46		13 58	14 04	14 12	14 17	14 29			14 46		14 58	15 04	15 12	15 17	15 29	
Portsmouth Harbour	a	13 18	13 21	13 33			13 51		14 02	14 07	14 18	14 21	14 33			14 51		15 02	15 07	15 18	15 21	15 33	

		SW 1	GW ◇ ✕	SN 1	SN ◇1	SW 1 ⊏	SW 1	SN 1	SW 1 ⊏	SW 1	SW 1	GW ◇	SN 1	SN ◇1	SW 1 ⊏	SW 1	SN 1	SW 1 ⊏	SW 1	SW 1	GW ◇	SN 1
Havant	d	15 27		15 32	15 46	15 50		16 05	16 16		16 27		16 32	16 46	16 50		17 05	17 16		17 27		17 32
Bedhampton	d	15 30		15 34							16 30		16 34							17 30		17 34
Hilsea	d	15 36		15 42			16 03			16 33	16 36		16 42			17 03			17 33	17 36		17 42
Fratton	d	15 40	15 42	15 47	15 55	15 59	16 08	16 14	16 25	16 37	16 40	16 42	16 47	16 55	16 59	17 08	17 14	17 25	17 37	17 40	17 42	17 47
Portsmouth & Southsea	a	15 44	15 46	15 50	15 58	16 02	16 11	16 17	16 28	16 40	16 44	16 46	16 50	16 58	17 02	17 11	17 17	17 28	17 42	17 44	17 46	17 50
	d		15 46		15 58	16 04	16 12	16 17	16 29	16 41		16 46		16 58	17 04	17 12	17 17	17 29			17 46	
Portsmouth Harbour	a		15 51		16 02	16 07	16 18	16 21	16 33	16 44		16 51		17 02	17 07	17 18	17 21	17 33			17 51	

		SN ◇1	SW 1 ⊏	SW 1	SN 1	SW 1 ⊏	SW 1	SW 1	GW ◇	SN 1	SN ◇1	SW 1 ⊏	SW 1	SN 1	SW 1 ⊏	SW 1	SW 1	GW ■	SN 1	SN ◇1	SW 1 ⊏	SW 1	SN 1
Havant	d	17 46	17 50		18 06	18 16		18 27		18 32	18 46	18 50		19 05	19 16		19 27		19 32	19 46	19 50		20 10
Bedhampton	d							18 30		18 34							19 30		19 34				
Hilsea	d			18 03			18 33	18 36		18 42			19 03			19 33	19 36		19 42			20 03	
Fratton	d	17 55	17 59	18 08	18 15	18 25	18 37	18 40	18 42	18 47	18 55	18 59	19 08	19 14	19 25	19 37	19 40	19 42	19 47	19 55	19 59	20 08	20 19
Portsmouth & Southsea	a	17 58	18 02	18 11	18 18	18 28	18 42	18 44	18 46	18 50	18 58	19 02	19 11	19 17	19 28	19 42	19 44	19 46	19 50	19 58	20 02	20 11	20 22
	d	17 58	18 04	18 12	18 19	18 29			18 46		18 58	19 04	19 12	19 17	19 29			19 46		19 58	20 04	20 12	20 22
Portsmouth Harbour	a	18 02	18 07	18 18	18 22	18 33			18 52		19 02	19 07	19 18	19 21	19 33			19 52		20 02	20 07	20 18	20 26

Table 157

Havant - Portsmouth Harbour
(Complete service)

Saturdays

		SW 1 ⊏	SW 1	GW ◇	SW 1	SN ◇1	SW 1 ⊏	SW 1	SN 1	SW 1	SW 1	SW 1	GW ◇	SW 1	SN ◇1	SW 1	SN 1	SW 1	SW 1	GW ◇	SW 1	SN 1	SW 1
Havant	d	20 16			20 30	20 46	20 50		21 10	21 16		21 27		21 46	21 49		22 10	22 19			22 31	22 43	22 49
Bedhampton	d				20 33							21 30									22 34		
Hilsea	d		20 37		20 41			21 03			21 33	21 36				22 03			22 33		22 41		
Fratton	d	20 25	20 41	20 42	20 45	20 55	20 59	21 08	21 19	21 25	21 37	21 40	21 42	21 55	21 59	22 08	22 19	22 29	22 37	22 42	22 45	22 52	22 59
Portsmouth & Southsea	a	20 28	20 44	20 46	20 48	20 58	21 02	21 11	21 22	21 28	21 41	21 43	21 46	21 58	22 02	22 11	22 22	22 32	22 40	22 46	22 49	22 55	23 02
	d	20 29		20 46		20 58	21 04	21 12	21 22	21 29			21 46	22 00	22 03	22 12	22 22	22 33	22 41	22 46	22 50	22 56	23 03
Portsmouth Harbour	a	20 33		20 52		21 02	21 07	21 18	21 26	21 33			21 52	22 03	22 06	22 18	22 26	22 36	22 47	22 52	22 53	22 59	23 08

		SW 1	SN 1	SW 1	SW 1	GW ◇	SW 1	SN 1	SW 1
Havant	d		23 10	23 19			23 31	23 36	23 49
Bedhampton	d						23 34		
Hilsea	d	23 03			23 33		23 41		
Fratton	d	23 08	23 19	23 29	23 37	23 42	23 45	23 48	23 59
Portsmouth & Southsea	a	23 11	23 22	23 32	23 40	23 45	23 48	23 51	00 02
	d	23 12	23 22	23 33		23 46	23 50		00 03
Portsmouth Harbour	a	23 18	23 26	23 37		23 52	23 53		00 07

Sundays

		SW 1	SW 1	SW 1	SW 1	SW 1	SW 1	SN 1	SW 1	SW 1	SN 1 B	SN 1 C	SW 1	SN 1 B	SW 1	SN 1 C	SW 1	SN 1 B	SN 1 C	SW 1	SN 1 B	SW 1	SN 1 C
Havant	d	23p49		00 22	00 37		01 26	07 10			08 09	08 11		08 35	08 39	08 49		09 09	09 11		09 35	09 45	09 49
Bedhampton	d			00 25			01s29							08 37	08 41	08 51					09 37	09 47	09 51
Hilsea	d		00 03	00 30			01s34		07 26	08 00			08 26				09 00			09 26			
Fratton	d	23p59	00 07	00 34	00 47	01s05	01s38	07 19	07 30	08 04	08 18	08 20	08 30	08 45	08 50	08 59	09 04	09 18	09 20	09 30	09 45	09 56	09 59
Portsmouth & Southsea	a	00 02	00 11	00 38	00 50	01s08	01 42	07 22	07 33	08 08	08 21	08 23	08 33	08 48	08 53	09 03	09 08	09 21	09 23	09 33	09 48	09 59	10 03
	d	00 03	00 12		00 51	01s09		07 22		08 09	08 21	08 23		08 49	08 54	09 04	09 09	09 21	09 23		09 49	10 00	10 04
Portsmouth Harbour	a	00 07	00 16		00 55	01 12		07 26		08 13	08 25	08 27		08 52	08 57	09 07	09 13	09 25	09 27		09 52	10 04	10 07

		SW 1	SW 1	SN ◇1 B	SN ◇1 C	SW 1	SN 1 B	SN 1 C	SW 1	SW 1	SW 1	SN ◇1 B	SN ◇1 C	SW 1	GW ◇	SN 1 B	SW 1	SN 1 C	SW 1	SW 1	SN ◇1 B	SN ◇1 C	SW 1
Havant	d	09 53		10 12	10 17		10 35	10 41	10 45	10 53		11 12	11 17			11 35	11 39	11 44	11 51		12 13	12 17	
Bedhampton	d						10 37	10 43	10 47							11 37	11 41	11 46					
Hilsea	d		10 00			10 26					11 00			11 26						12 00			12 26
Fratton	d	10 02	10 05	10 21	10 26	10 30	10 45	10 51	10 56	11 02	11 06	11 21	11 26	11 30	11 42	11 45	11 50	11 54	12 01	12 04	12 22	12 26	12 30
Portsmouth & Southsea	a	10 06	10 10	10 24	10 29	10 33	10 50	10 54	10 59	11 05	11 10	11 24	11 29	11 33	11 45	11 49	11 53	11 57	12 04	12 08	12 25	12 29	12 33
	d	10 08	10 12	10 25	10 30		10 51	10 55	11 00	11 07	11 11	11 25	11 30		11 46	11 50	11 54	11 58	12 05	12 09	12 26	12 30	
Portsmouth Harbour	a	10 11	10 15	10 28	10 35		10 54	10 58	11 04	11 11	11 14	11 28	11 35		11 52	11 53	11 58	12 01	12 09	12 13	12 29	12 35	

		GW ◇ D	GW ◇ E	SW 1	SN 1 B	SN 1 C	SW 1 ⊏	SW 1	SN ◇1 B	SN ◇1 C	SW 1	SN 1 B	SW 1	SN 1 C	SW 1 ⊏	SW 1	SN ◇1 B	SN ◇1 C	SW 1	GW ◇ B ✕	GW ◇ C ✕	SN 1 B
Havant	d			12 39	12 35	12 44	12 51		13 12	13 17		13 35	13 39	13 44	13 51		14 12	14 17				14 35
Bedhampton	d			12 41	12 37	12 46						13 37	13 41	13 46								14 37
Hilsea	d							13 00			13 26					14 00			14 26			
Fratton	d	12 42	12 42	12 50	12b54	12 54	13 01	13 04	13 21	13 26	13 30	13 45	13 50	13 54	14 01	14 04	14 21	14 26	14 30	14 41	14 41	14 45
Portsmouth & Southsea	a	12 45	12 45	12 53	12 57	12 57	13 04	13 08	13 24	13 29	13 33	13 48	13 53	13 57	14 04	14 08	14 24	14 29	14 33	14 44	14 45	14 48
	d	12 45	12 46	12 54	12 58	12 58	13 05	13 09	13 25	13 30		13 49	13 54	13 58	14 05	14 09	14 25	14 30		14 45	14 45	14 49
Portsmouth Harbour	a	12 52	12 52	12 58	13 01	13 01	13 11	13 13	13 28	13 35		13 52	13 58	14 01	14 11	14 13	14 28	14 35		14 50	14 52	14 52

		SW 1	SN 1 C	SW 1 ⊏	SW 1	SN ◇1 B	SN ◇1 C	SW 1	SN 1 B	SW 1	SN 1 C	SW 1 ⊏	SW 1	SN ◇1 B	SN ◇1 C	SW 1	GW ◇ D	GW ◇ F	GW ◇ C	SW 1	SN 1 B	SN 1 C	SW 1 ⊏
Havant	d	14 39	14 44	14 51		15 12	15 17		15 35	15 39	15 44	15 51		16 12	16 17					16 39	16 35	16 44	16 51
Bedhampton	d	14 41	14 46						15 37	15 41	15 46									16 41	16 37	16 46	
Hilsea	d				15 00			15 26					16 00			16 26							
Fratton	d	14 50	14 54	15 01	15 04	15 21	15 26	15 30	15 45	15 50	15 54	16 01	16 04	16 23	16 26	16 30	16 42	16 42	16 42	16 50	16c54	16 54	17 01
Portsmouth & Southsea	a	14 53	14 57	15 04	15 08	15 24	15 29	15 33	15 48	15 54	15 57	16 04	16 08	16 26	16 29	16 33	16 45	16 45	16 46	16 53	16 57	16 57	17 04
	d	14 54	14 58	15 05	15 09	15 25	15 30		15 49	15 54	15 58	16 05	16 09	16 27	16 30		16 46	16 46	16 46	16 54	16 58	16 58	17 05
Portsmouth Harbour	a	14 58	15 01	15 11	15 13	15 28	15 35		15 52	15 58	16 01	16 11	16 13	16 30	16 35		16 53	16 52	16 52	16 58	17 01	17 01	17 11

B until 5 September
C from 12 September
D until 11 July
E from 18 July
F from 18 July until 5 September
b arr. 1246
c arr. 1646

Havant - Portsmouth Harbour
(Complete service)

	SW	SN	SN	SW	GW	SW	SN	SN	SW	SW	SN	SN	SW	GW	GW	SW	SN	SN	SW	SW	SN
	[1]	◇[1]	◇[1]	[1]	◇	[1]	[1]	[1]	[1]	[1]	◇[1]	◇[1]	[1]	◇	◇	[1]	[1]	[1]	[1]	[1]	◇[1]
		A	B				A	B	☕		A	B		C	D		A	B	☕		A
Havant d		17 12	17 17			17 39	17 35	17 44	17 51		18 12	18 17				18 39	18 35	18 44	18 51		19 12
Bedhampton d						17 41	17 37	17 46								18 41	18 37	18 46			
Hilsea d	17 00			17 26						18 00			18 26							19 00	
Fratton d	17 04	17 21	17 26	17 30	17 42	17 50	17b54	17 54	18 01	18 04	18 21	18 26	18 30	18 39	18 42	18 50	18c54	18 54	19 01	19 04	19 21
Portsmouth & Southsea a	17 08	17 24	17 29	17 33	17 45	17 53	17 57	17 57	18 04	18 08	18 24	18 29	18 33	18 42	18 45	18 53	18 57	18 57	19 04	19 08	19 24
d	17 09	17 25	17 30		17 46	17 54	17 58	17 58	18 05	18 09	18 25	18 30		18 43	18 46	18 54	18 58	18 58	19 05	19 09	19 25
Portsmouth Harbour a	17 13	17 28	17 35		17 52	17 58	18 01	18 01	18 11	18 13	18 28	18 35		18 49	18 52	18 58	19 01	19 01	19 11	19 13	19 28

	SN	SW	GW	GW	SW	SN	SN	SW	SW	SN	SN	SW	GW	SN	SW	SN	SW	SW	GW	SN	SN	SW
	◇[1]	[1]	◇	◇	[1]	[1]	[1]	[1]	[1]	◇[1]	◇[1]	[1]	◇	[1]	[1]	[1]	[1]	[1]	■	◇[1]	◇[1]	[1]
	B		E	F		A	B	☕		A	B			A		B	☕			A	B	
Havant d	19 17				19 39	19 35	19 44	19 51		20 12	20 17			20 35	20 39	20 44	20 51			21 12	21 17	
Bedhampton d					19 41	19 37	19 46							20 37	20 41	20 46						
Hilsea d		19 26							20 00			20 26						21 00				21 26
Fratton d	19 26	19 30	19 42	19 42	19 50	19e54	19 54	20 01	20 04	20 21	20 26	20 30	20 42	20 45	20 50	20 54	21 01	21 04	21 10	21 21	21 26	21 30
Portsmouth & Southsea a	19 29	19 33	19 46	19 45	19 53	19 57	19 57	20 04	20 08	20 24	20 29	20 33	20 45	20 48	20 53	20 57	21 04	21 08	21 15	21 24	21 29	21 33
d	19 30		19 46	19 46	19 54	19 58	19 58	20 05	20 09	20 25	20 30		20 46	20 49	20 54	20 58	21 05	21 09	21 15	21 25	21 30	
Portsmouth Harbour a	19 35		19 52	19 52	19 58	20 01	20 01	20 11	20 13	20 28	20 35		20 52	20 52	20 58	21 01	21 09	21 13	21 26	21 28	21 35	

	GW	SN	SW	SN	SW	SW	SN	SN	SW	GW	SN	SW	GW	SN	GW	SW	SW	SW	SN	GW	SW	SW
	◇	[1]	[1]	[1]	[1]	[1]	◇[1]	◇[1]	[1]	◇	[1]	[1]		[1]		[1]	[1]	[1]	◇[1]	◇	[1]	[1]
		A		B	☕		A	B			A		A	B	B							
Havant d		21 35	21 39	21 44	21 51		22 12	22 17			22 35	22 39	22 44	22 44	22 47	22 51			23 22		23 39	23 51
Bedhampton d		21 37	21 41	21 46							22 37	22 41		22 46							23 41	
Hilsea d						22 00			22 26								23 00	23 24				
Fratton d	21 38	21 45	21 50	21 54	22 01	22 04	22 21	22 26	22 30	22 40	22 45	22 50	22 54	22 54	22 57	23 01	23 04	23 29	23 32	23 38	23 50	00 01
Portsmouth & Southsea a	21 41	21 48	21 53	21 57	22 04	22 08	22 24	22 29	22 33	22 43	22 48	22 53	22 57	22 57	23 00	23 04	23 08	23 32	23 35	23 41	23 53	00 04
d	21 41	21 49	21 54	21 58	22 05	22 09	22 25	22 30		22 44	22 49	22 54	22 57	22 58	23 00	23 05	23 09		23 36	23 41	23 54	00 05
Portsmouth Harbour a	21 48	21 52	21 58	22 01	22 11	22 13	22 28	22 35		22 51	22 52	22 58	23 01	23 01	23 04	23 09	23 13		23 39	23 49	23 58	00 09

	SW
	[1]
Havant d	
Bedhampton d	
Hilsea d	23 59
Fratton d	00 04
Portsmouth & Southsea a	00 08
d	00 09
Portsmouth Harbour a	00 13

A until 5 September
B from 12 September
C until 11 July
D from 18 July
E until 11 July, from 12 September
F from 18 July until 5 September
b arr. 1746
c arr. 1846
e arr. 1946

Portsmouth Harbour - Havant
(Complete service)

	SW	SW	SW	SW	SW	SW	SN	SW	SN	SW	GW	SN	SW	SW	SW	SW	SW	SN	SW	SN	GW	SW	GW	SW
	[1]	[1]	[1]	[1]	[1]	[1]	[1]	[1]	◇[1]	[1]	■	[1]	[1]	[1]	[1]	[1]	[1]		[1]	◇[1]	◇	[1]		[1]
	A	B			A ☕	B ☕					🍴		☕						☕		🍴			☕
Portsmouth Harbour d	04 25	04 30	05 00		05 14	05 19	05 33	05 43	05 47	05 50	06 00	06 04	06 15		06 23		06 38		06 42	06 46	06 51	06 55	07 01	07 13
Portsmouth & Southsea a	04 28	04 33	05 03		05 17	05 22	05 36	05 46	05 50	05 53	06 03	06 07	06 18		06 26		06 41		06 45	06 49	06 54	06 58	07 04	07 16
d	04 30	04 35	05 05	05 16	05 19	05 24	05 37	05 48	05 51	05 55	06 04	06 08	06 20	06 23	06 28		06 43		06 47	06 50	06 55	07 00	07 05	07 18
Fratton d	04 34	04 39	05 09	05 20	05 23	05 28	05 41	05 52	05 55	05 59	06 08	06 12	06 24	06 27	06 32		06 47		06 51	06 54	06 59	07 04	07 10	07 22
Hilsea d	04 38	04 43	05 13	05 24	05 27	05 32	05 45	05 56	05 59	06 03				06 31	06 36	06 42	06 51			06 58		07 08		
Bedhampton d	04 43	04 48			05 32	05 37	05 50		06 04	06 08						06 47		06 34		07 03		07 13		
Havant a	04 45	04 50			05 35	05 40	05 52		06 06	06 10		06 20	06 33			06 49		06 37	06 59	07 05		07 15	07 19	07 30

	SN	SW	SW	SW	SW	SW	SN	SW	SN	SW	SW	GW	SN	SW	SW	SN	SW	SN	SW	SW	GW	SN
	[1]	[1]	[1]	[1]	[1]	[1]	[1]	[1]	◇[1]	[1]	[1]	◇	[1]	[1]	[1]	[1]	[1]	◇[1]	[1]	[1]	◇	[1]
					☕					☕		🍴			☕				☕		🍴	
Portsmouth Harbour d	07 20	07 24	07 29		07 45	07 55		08 05	08 10	08 15		08 23	08 29	08 33	08 45	08 51	08 55	09 12	09 15	09 18	09 23	09 29
Portsmouth & Southsea a	07 23	07 27	07 32		07 48	07 58		08 08	08 13	08 18		08 26	08 32	08 36	08 48	08 54	08 58	09 15	09 18	09 22	09 26	09 32
d	07 24	07 29	07 33	07 38	07 50	08 00	08 03	08 10	08 14	08 20	08 24	08 27	08 33	08 38	08 50	08 55	09 00	09 16	09 20	09 24	09 27	09 33
Fratton d	07 28	07 33	07 37	07 43	07 54	08 04	08 07	08 14	08 18	08 24	08 28	08 31	08 37	08 43	08 54	08 59	09 04	09 20	09 24	09 28	09 31	09 37
Hilsea d		07 37	07 41	07 47		08 08	08 11	08 18			08 32			08 47		09 04	09 08			09 32		
Bedhampton d			07 48				08 16				08 37					09 13				09 37		
Havant a	07 36		07 50		08 03		08 18		08 26	08 32	08 40		08 45		09 03	09 15		09 29	09 33	09 39		09 45

	SW	SW	SN	SW	SN	SW	SW	GW	SN	SW	SW	SN	SW	SN	SW	SW	GW	SN	SW	SW	SN
	[1]	[1]	[1]	[1]	◇[1]	[1]	[1]	◇	[1]	[1]	[1]	[1]	[1]	◇[1]	[1]	[1]	◇	[1]	[1]	[1]	[1]
		☕				☕		🍴			☕				☕		🍴			☕	
Portsmouth Harbour d	09 33	09 45		09 55	10 12	10 15		10 23	10 29	10 33	10 45		10 55	11 12	11 15		11 23	11 29		11 45	
Portsmouth & Southsea a	09 36	09 48		09 58	10 15	10 18		10 26	10 32	10 36	10 48		10 58	11 15	11 18		11 26	11 32		11 48	
d	09 38	09 50	09 56	10 00	10 16	10 20	10 24	10 27	10 33	10 38	10 50	10 56	11 00	11 16	11 20	11 24	11 27	11 33	11 38	11 50	11 56
Fratton d	09 43	09 54	10 01	10 04	10 20	10 24	10 28	10 31	10 37	10 43	10 54	11 01	11 04	11 20	11 24	11 28	11 31	11 37	11 43	11 54	12 01
Hilsea d	09 47		10 05	10 08			10 32			10 47		11 05	11 08			11 32			11 47		12 05
Bedhampton d			10 13				10 37					11 13				11 37					12 13
Havant a		10 03	10 15		10 29	10 33	10 39		10 45		11 03	11 15		11 29	11 33	11 39		11 45		12 03	12 15

	SW	SN	SW	SW	GW	SN	SW	SW	SN	SW	SN	SW	SW	GW	SN	SW	SW	SN	SW	SN	SW	SW
	[1]	◇[1]	[1]	[1]	◇	[1]	[1]	[1]	[1]	[1]	◇[1]	[1]	[1]	◇	[1]	[1]	[1]	[1]	[1]	◇[1]	[1]	[1]
			☕		🍴			☕				☕		🍴			☕				☕	
Portsmouth Harbour d	11 55	12 12	12 15		12 23	12 29		12 45		12 55	13 12	13 15		13 23	13 29		13 45		13 55	14 12	14 15	
Portsmouth & Southsea a	11 58	12 15	12 18		12 26	12 32		12 48		12 58	13 15	13 18		13 26	13 32		13 48		13 58	14 15	14 18	
d	12 00	12 16	12 20	12 24	12 27	12 33	12 38	12 50	12 56	13 00	13 16	13 20	13 24	13 27	13 33	13 38	13 50	13 56	14 00	14 16	14 20	14 24
Fratton d	12 04	12 20	12 24	12 28	12 31	12 37	12 43	12 54	13 01	13 04	13 20	13 24	13 28	13 31	13 37	13 43	13 54	14 01	14 04	14 20	14 24	14 28
Hilsea d	12 08			12 32			12 47		13 05	13 08			13 32			13 47		14 05	14 08			14 32
Bedhampton d				12 37					13 13				13 37					14 13				14 37
Havant a		12 29	12 33	12 39		12 45		13 03	13 15		13 29	13 33	13 39		13 45		14 03	14 15		14 29	14 33	14 39

	GW	SN	SW	SW	SN	SW	SN	SW	SW	GW	SN	SW	SW	SN	SW	SN	SW	SW	GW	SN	SW
	■	[1]	[1]	[1]	[1]	[1]	◇[1]	[1]	[1]	■	[1]	[1]	[1]	[1]	[1]	◇[1]	[1]	[1]	■	[1]	[1]
	🍴			☕				☕		🍴			☕				☕		🍴		
Portsmouth Harbour d	14 23	14 29		14 45		14 55	15 12	15 15		15 23	15 29		15 45		15 55	16 12	16 15		16 23	16 29	
Portsmouth & Southsea a	14 26	14 32		14 48		14 58	15 15	15 18		15 26	15 32		15 48		15 58	16 15	16 18		16 26	16 32	
d	14 27	14 33	14 38	14 50	14 56	15 00	15 16	15 20	15 24	15 27	15 33	15 38	15 50	15 56	16 00	16 16	16 20	16 24	16 27	16 33	16 38
Fratton d	14 31	14 37	14 43	14 54	15 01	15 04	15 20	15 24	15 28	15 31	15 37	15 43	15 54	16 01	16 04	16 20	16 24	16 28	16 31	16 37	16 43
Hilsea d			14 47		15 05	15 08			15 32			15 47		16 05	16 08			16 32			16 47
Bedhampton d					15 14				15 37					16 13				16 37			
Havant a		14 45		15 03	15 17		15 29	15 33	15 39		15 45		16 03	16 15		16 29	16 33	16 39		16 45	

	SN	SW	SN	SW	SW	SN	SW	SW	GW	SN	SW	SN	SW	SN	SW	SW	SW	GW	SN	SW	SN	SW
	[1]	[1]	[1]	[1]	[1]	◇[1]	[1]	[1]	◇	[1]	[1]	[1]	[1]	[1]	[1]	[1]	[1]	◇	[1]	[1]	[1]	[1]
		☕					☕		🍴				☕			☕		🍴				☕
Portsmouth Harbour d	16 40	16 45		16 55	17 03	17 12	17 15	17 18	17 23	17 29	17 33		17 45		17 55	18 15		18 23	18 28		18 37	18 45
Portsmouth & Southsea a	16 44	16 48		16 58	17 06	17 15	17 18	17 22	17 26	17 32	17 36		17 48		17 58	18 18		18 26	18 31		18 40	18 48
d	16 46	16 50	16 56	17 00	17 07	17 16	17 20	17 24	17 27	17 33	17 38	17 46	17 50	17 56	18 00	18 20	18 24	18 27	18 32	18 38	18 42	18 50
Fratton d	16 50	16 54	17 01	17 04	17 11	17 20	17 24	17 28	17 31	17 37	17 43	17 50	17 54	18 01	18 04	18 24	18 28	18 31	18 36	18 43	18 46	18 54
Hilsea d	16 54		17 05	17 08	17 15			17 32			17 47	17 54		18 05	18 08		18 32			18 47	18 50	
Bedhampton d			17 14					17 37						18 13			18 37					
Havant a	16 59	17 03	17 17			17 29	17 33	17 39		17 45		17 59	18 03	18 15		18 33	18 39		18 44		18 56	19 03

	SN	SW	SW	SW	GW	SN	SW	SN	SW	SN	SW	SW	SW	GW	SN	SW	SN	SW	SW	SN	SW	GW
	[1]	[1]	[1]	[1]	◇	[1]	[1]	[1]	[1]	[1]	[1]	[1]	[1]	◇	[1]	[1]	[1]	[1]	[1]	[1]	[1]	
			☕																			
Portsmouth Harbour d		18 55	19 15		19 23			19 40	19 45		19 55	20 15	20 18	20 23			20 40	20 45	20 55		21 18	21 23
Portsmouth & Southsea a		18 58	19 18		19 26			19 43	19 48		19 58	20 18	20 22	20 26			20 43	20 48	20 58		21 21	21 26
d	18 56	19 00	19 20	19 24	19 27	19 32	19 38	19 44	19 50	19 56	20 00	20 20	20 24	20 27	20 32	20 38	20 44	20 50	21 00	21 15	21 24	21 27
Fratton d	19 01	19 04	19 24	19 28	19 31	19 36	19 43	19 48	19 54	20 01	20 04	20 24	20 28	20 31	20 36	20 43	20 48	20 54	21 04	21 19	21 28	21 31
Hilsea d	19 05	19 08		19 32			19 47			20 05	20 08		20 32			20 47			21 08	21 23	21 32	
Bedhampton d	19 13			19 37						20 14			20 37							21 28	21 37	
Havant a	19 15		19 33	19 39		19 46		19 56	20 03	20 16		20 33	20 39		20 44		20 56	21 03		21 30	21 40	

A from 27 September
B until 24 September

Table 157

Portsmouth Harbour - Havant
(Complete service)

Mondays to Fridays

		SW 1	SW 1	SN 1	SW 1	SN 1	SW 1	SW 1	SW 1	SN 1	SN 1	SW 1	SW 1
Portsmouth Harbour	d	21 28		21 40	21 55	22 15	22 18	22 28		22 44	23 15	23 19	23 24
Portsmouth & Southsea	a	21 31		21 43	21 58	22 18	22 21	22 31		22 47	23 18	23 22	23 27
	d	21 33	21 38	21 44	22 00	22 19	22 24	22 33	22 38	22 48	23 19	23 24	23 29
Fratton	d	21 37	21 43	21 48	22 04	22 23	22 28	22 37	22 43	22 52	23 23	23 28	23 33
Hilsea	d	21 41	21 47	21 52	22 08	22 27	22 32	22 41	22 47	22 56	23 27	23 32	23 37
Bedhampton	d	21 47		21 57		22 32	22 37	22 46		23 01	23 33	23 37	
Havant	a	21 52		21 59		22 34	22 39	22 53		23 05	23 36	23 39	

Saturdays

		SW 1 A	SW 1 B	SN ◇1	SW 1	SW 1 A	SW 1 B	SW 1	SN 1	GW ◇	SN ◇1	SW 1	SN 1	SW 1	SW 1 🛒	GW	SN 1	SW 1	GW ◇ 🍴	SN ◇1	SW 1 🛒	SW 1	SN 1
Portsmouth Harbour	d	04 38	04 43			05 14	05 19	05 50		06 00	06 12	06 19	06 29		06 45	06 48		06 55	07 05	07 12	07 15		07 29
Portsmouth & Southsea	a	04 41	04 46			05 17	05 22	05 53		06 03	06 15	06 22	06 32		06 48	06 53		06 58	07 08	07 15	07 18		07 32
	d	04 43	04 48	04 56	05 16	05 19	05 24	05 55	05 59	06 04	06 16	06 24	06 33	06 38	06 50	06 54	06 56	07 00	07 09	07 16	07 20	07 24	07 33
Fratton	d	04 47	04 52	05 00	05 20	05 23	05 28	05 59	06 04	06 08	06 20	06 28	06 37	06 43	06 54	06 58	07 01	07 04	07 14	07 20	07 24	07 28	07 37
Hilsea	d	04 51	04 56		05 24	05 27	05 32	06 03	06 08			06 32		06 47			07 05	07 08				07 32	
Bedhampton	d	04 56	05 01			05 32	05 37		06 13			06 37					07 13					07 37	
Havant	a	04 58	05 03	05 08		05 34	05 39		06 15		06 29	06 40	06 45		07 03	07 08	07 15			07 29	07 33	07 39	07 45

		SW 1	SW 1 🛒	SN 1	SW 1	SN ◇1	SW 1 🛒	SW 1	GW ◇ 🍴	SN 1	SW 1	SW 1 🛒	SN 1	SW 1	SN ◇1	SW 1 🛒	SW 1	GW ◇ 🍴	SN 1	SW 1	SW 1 🛒	SN 1	SW 1
Portsmouth Harbour	d		07 45		07 55	08 12	08 15		08 23	08 29		08 45		08 55	09 12	09 15		09 23	09 29		09 45		09 55
Portsmouth & Southsea	a		07 48		07 58	08 15	08 18		08 26	08 32		08 48		08 58	09 15	09 18		09 26	09 32		09 48		09 58
	d	07 38	07 50	07 56	08 00	08 16	08 20	08 24	08 27	08 33	08 38	08 50	08 56	09 00	09 16	09 20	09 24	09 27	09 33	09 38	09 50	09 56	10 00
Fratton	d	07 43	07 54	08 01	08 04	08 20	08 24	08 28	08 31	08 37	08 43	08 54	09 01	09 04	09 20	09 24	09 28	09 31	09 37	09 43	09 54	10 01	10 04
Hilsea	d	07 47		08 05	08 08			08 32			08 47		09 05	09 08			09 32			09 47		10 05	10 08
Bedhampton	d			08 13				08 37					09 13				09 37					10 13	
Havant	a		08 03	08 15		08 29	08 33	08 39		08 45		09 03	09 15		09 29	09 33	09 39		09 45		10 03	10 15	

		SN ◇1	SW 1 🛒	SW 1	GW ◇ 🍴	SN 1	SW 1	SW 1 🛒	SN 1	SW 1	SN ◇1	SW 1 🛒	SW 1	GW ◇ 🍴	SN 1	SW 1	SW 1 🛒	SN 1	SW 1	SN ◇1	SW 1 🛒	SW 1
Portsmouth Harbour	d	10 12	10 15		10 23	10 29		10 45		10 55	11 12	11 15		11 23	11 29		11 45		11 55	12 12	12 15	
Portsmouth & Southsea	a	10 15	10 18		10 26	10 32		10 48		10 58	11 15	11 18		11 26	11 32		11 48		11 58	12 15	12 18	
	d	10 16	10 20	10 24	10 27	10 33	10 38	10 50	10 56	11 00	11 16	11 20	11 24	11 27	11 33	11 38	11 50	11 56	12 00	12 16	12 20	12 24
Fratton	d	10 20	10 24	10 28	10 31	10 37	10 43	10 54	11 01	11 04	11 20	11 24	11 28	11 31	11 37	11 43	11 54	12 01	12 04	12 20	12 24	12 28
Hilsea	d			10 32			10 47		11 05	11 08			11 32			11 47		12 05	12 08			12 32
Bedhampton	d			10 37					11 13				11 37					12 13				12 37
Havant	a	10 29	10 33	10 39		10 45		11 03	11 15		11 29	11 33	11 39		11 45		12 03	12 15		12 29	12 33	12 39

		GW ◇	SN 1	SW 1	SW 1 🛒	SN 1	SW 1	SN ◇1	SW 1 🛒	SW 1	GW ◇	SN 1	SW 1	SW 1 🛒	SN 1	SW 1	SN ◇1	SW 1 🛒	SW 1	GW ◇	SN 1	SW 1	SW 1 🛒
Portsmouth Harbour	d	12 23	12 29		12 45		12 55	13 12	13 15		13 23	13 29		13 45		13 55	14 12	14 15		14 23	14 29		14 45
Portsmouth & Southsea	a	12 26	12 32		12 48		12 58	13 15	13 18		13 26	13 32		13 48		13 58	14 15	14 18		14 26	14 32		14 48
	d	12 27	12 33	12 38	12 50	12 56	13 00	13 16	13 20	13 24	13 27	13 33	13 38	13 50	13 56	14 00	14 16	14 20	14 24	14 27	14 33	14 38	14 50
Fratton	d	12 31	12 37	12 43	12 54	13 01	13 04	13 20	13 24	13 28	13 31	13 37	13 43	13 54	14 01	14 04	14 20	14 24	14 28	14 31	14 37	14 43	14 54
Hilsea	d			12 47		13 05	13 08			13 32			13 47		14 05	14 08			14 32			14 47	
Bedhampton	d					13 13				13 37					14 13				14 37				
Havant	a		12 45		13 03	13 15		13 29	13 33	13 39		13 45		14 03	14 15		14 29	14 33	14 39		14 45		15 03

		SN 1	SW 1	SN ◇1	SW 1 🛒	SW 1	GW ◇	SN 1	SW 1	SW 1 🛒	SN 1	SW 1	SN ◇1	SW 1 🛒	SW 1	GW	SN 1	SW 1	SW 1 🛒	SN 1	SW 1	SW 1
Portsmouth Harbour	d		14 55	15 12	15 15		15 23	15 29		15 45		15 55	16 12	16 15		16 23	16 29		16 45		16 55	
Portsmouth & Southsea	a		14 58	15 15	15 18		15 26	15 32		15 48		15 58	16 15	16 18		16 26	16 32		16 48		16 58	
	d	14 56	15 00	15 16	15 20	15 24	15 27	15 33	15 38	15 50	15 56	16 00	16 16	16 20	16 24	16 27	16 33	16 38	16 50	16 56	17 00	17 10
Fratton	d	15 01	15 04	15 20	15 24	15 28	15 31	15 37	15 43	15 54	16 01	16 04	16 20	16 24	16 28	16 31	16 37	16 43	16 54	17 01	17 04	17 14
Hilsea	d	15 05	15 08			15 32			15 47		16 05	16 08			16 32			16 47		17 05	17 08	17 18
Bedhampton	d	15 14				15 37					16 13				16 37					17 13		17 23
Havant	a	15 17		15 29	15 33	15 39		15 45		16 03	16 15		16 29	16 33	16 39		16 45		17 03	17 15		17 25

		SN ◇1	SW 1	GW ◇	SN 1	SW 1	SW 1 🛒	SN 1	SW 1	SN 1	SW 1	SW 1	GW ◇	SN 1	SW 1	SW 1	SN 1	SW 1	SN 1	SW 1	SW 1	GW ◇	SN 1
Portsmouth Harbour	d	17 12	17 18	17 23	17 29	17 33	17 45		17 55	18 12	18 15		18 23	18 29		18 45		18 55	19 12	19 15		19 23	19 29
Portsmouth & Southsea	a	17 15	17 22	17 26	17 32	17 36	17 48		17 58	18 15	18 18		18 27	18 32		18 48		18 58	19 15	19 18		19 26	19 32
	d	17 16	17 24	17 27	17 33	17 38	17 50	17 56	18 00	18 16	18 20	18 24	18 27	18 33	18 38	18 50	18 56	19 00	19 16	19 20	19 24	19 27	19 33
Fratton	d	17 20	17 28	17 31	17 37	17 43	17 54	18 01	18 04	18 20	18 24	18 28	18 31	18 37	18 43	18 54	19 01	19 04	19 20	19 24	19 28	19 31	19 37
Hilsea	d		17 32			17 47		18 05	18 08			18 32			18 47		19 05	19 08			19 32		
Bedhampton	d		17 37					18 13				18 37					19 13				19 37		
Havant	a	17 29	17 39		17 45		18 03	18 15		18 29	18 33	18 39		18 45		19 03	19 15		19 29	19 33	19 39		19 45

A from 2 October

B until 25 September

Table 157

Portsmouth Harbour - Havant
(Complete service)

Saturdays

		SW 1	SW 1	SN 1	SW 1	SW 1	SW 1	GW ◇	SN 1	SW 1	SN 1	SW 1	SW 1	SN 1	SW 1	SW 1	SN 1	SW 1	SN 1	SW 1	SW 1	SN 1	SN 1
Portsmouth Harbour	d		19 45		19 55	20 15		20 23	20 28		20 40	20 45	20 55	21 11	21 18		21 40	21 55	22 15	22 18		22 44	23 15
Portsmouth & Southsea	a		19 48		19 58	20 18		20 26	20 31		20 43	20 48	20 58	21 14	21 21		21 43	21 58	22 18	22 21		22 47	23 18
	d	19 38	19 50	19 56	20 00	20 20	20 24	20 27	20 32	20 38	20 44	20 50	21 00	21 15	21 24	21 38	21 44	22 00	22 19	22 24	22 38	22 48	23 19
Fratton	d	19 43	19 54	20 01	20 04	20 24	20 28	20 31	20 36	20 43	20 48	20 54	21 04	21 19	21 28	21 43	21 48	22 04	22 23	22 28	22 43	22 52	23 23
Hilsea	d	19 47		20 05	20 08		20 32			20 47			21 08	21 23	21 32	21 47	21 52	22 08	22 27	22 32	22 47	22 56	23 27
Bedhampton	d			20 13			20 37							21 28	21 37		21 57		22 32	22 37		23 01	23 33
Havant	a		20 03	20 15		20 33	20 39		20 44		20 56	21 03		21 30	21 39		21 59		22 34	22 39		23 05	23 36

		SW 1	SW 1
Portsmouth Harbour	d	23 19	23 24
Portsmouth & Southsea	a	23 22	23 28
	d	23 24	23 29
Fratton	d	23 28	23 33
Hilsea	d	23 32	23 37
Bedhampton	d	23 37	
Havant	a	23 39	

Sundays

		SW 1	SW 1 A	SW 1 B	SN 1 C	SN 1 D	SW 1	SW 1 A	SW 1 B	SW 1	SN ◇1	SW 1	SN 1 C	SN 1 D	SW 1	SW 1 A	SW 1 B	SW 1	SN ◇1	SW 1	SN 1 C	GW	SN 1 D
Portsmouth Harbour	d	06 37	06 43	06 48	07 05	07 14	07 17	07 29	07 32		07 43	07 48	08 05	08 14	08 17	08 29	08 32		08 43	08 48	09 05	09 08	09 14
Portsmouth & Southsea	a	06 40	06 46	06 51	07 08	07 17	07 20	07 32	07 35		07 46	07 51	08 08	08 17	08 20	08 32	08 35		08 46	08 51	09 08	09 11	09 17
	d	06 42	06 48	06 53	07 09	07 18	07 22	07 34	07 37	07 42	07 47	07 53	08 09	08 18	08 22	08 34	08 37	08 42	08 47	08 53	09 09	09 12	09 18
Fratton	d	06 46	06 52	06 57	07 13	07 22	07 26	07 38	07 41	07 46	07 51	07 57	08 13	08 22	08 26	08 38	08 41	08 46	08 51	08 57	09 13	09 16	09 22
Hilsea	d	06 50					07 30			07 50					08 30			08 50					
Bedhampton	d		06 59	07 04	07 21	07 30						08 04	08 20	08 30						09 04	09 20		09 30
Havant	a		07 02	07 07	07 24	07 32		07 46	07 49		07 59	08 07	08 23	08 32		08 46	08 49		08 59	09 07	09 23		09 32

		SW 1 🛒	SW 1 🛒	SW 1	SN ◇1	SW 1	SN 1 C	SN 1 D	SW 1 🛒	SW 1 🛒	SW 1	SN ◇1	SW 1	SN 1 C	GW ◇	SN 1 D	SW 1 🛒	SW 1 🛒	SW 1	SN ◇1	SW 1	SN 1 C	SN 1 D
Portsmouth Harbour	d	09 17	09 32		09 43	09 48	10 05	10 14	10 17	10 32		10 43	10 48	11 05	11 08	11 14	11 17	11 32		11 43	11 48	12 05	12 14
Portsmouth & Southsea	a	09 20	09 35		09 46	09 51	10 08	10 17	10 20	10 35		10 46	10 51	11 08	11 11	11 17	11 20	11 35		11 46	11 51	12 08	12 17
	d	09 22	09 37	09 42	09 47	09 53	10 09	10 18	10 22	10 37	10 42	10 47	10 53	11 09	11 12	11 18	11 22	11 37	11 42	11 47	11 53	12 09	12 18
Fratton	d	09 26	09 41	09 46	09 51	09 57	10 13	10 22	10 26	10 41	10 46	10 51	10 57	11 13	11 16	11 22	11 26	11 41	11 46	11 51	11 57	12 13	12 22
Hilsea	d	09 30		09 50					10 30		10 50						11 30		11 50				
Bedhampton	d					10 04	10 20	10 30					11 04	11 20		11 30					12 04	12 20	12 30
Havant	a		09 49		09 59	10 06	10 23	10 32		10 49		10 59	11 06	11 23		11 32		11 49		11 59	12 07	12 23	12 32

		SW 1 🛒	SW 1 🛒	SW 1	SN ◇1	SW 1	SN 1 C	GW ◇	SN 1 D	SW 1	SW 1 🛒	SW 1	SN ◇1	SW 1	SN 1 C	GW ◇	SN 1 D	SW 1	SW 1 🛒	SW 1	SN ◇1	SW 1
Portsmouth Harbour	d	12 17	12 32		12 43	12 48	13 05	13 08	13 14	13 17	13 32		13 43	13 48	14 05	14 08	14 14	14 17	14 32		14 43	14 48
Portsmouth & Southsea	a	12 20	12 35		12 46	12 51	13 08	13 11	13 17	13 20	13 35		13 46	13 51	14 08	14 11	14 17	14 20	14 35		14 46	14 51
	d	12 22	12 37	12 42	12 47	12 53	13 09	13 12	13 18	13 22	13 37	13 42	13 47	13 53	14 09	14 12	14 18	14 22	14 37	14 42	14 47	14 53
Fratton	d	12 26	12 41	12 46	12 51	12 57	13 13	13 16	13 22	13 26	13 41	13 46	13 51	13 57	14 13	14 16	14 22	14 26	14 41	14 46	14 51	14 57
Hilsea	d	12 30		12 50						13 30		13 50						14 30		14 50		
Bedhampton	d					13 04	13 20		13 30					14 04	14 20		14 30					15 04
Havant	a		12 49		12 59	13 07	13 23		13 32		13 49		13 59	14 07	14 23		14 32		14 49		14 59	15 07

		SN 1 C	GW	SN 1 D	SW 1	SW 1 🛒	SW 1	SN ◇1	SW 1	SN 1 C	GW ◇	SN 1 D	SW 1	SW 1 🛒	SW 1	SN ◇1	SW 1	SN 1 C	GW ◇	SN 1 D	SW 1	SW 1 🛒	SW 1
Portsmouth Harbour	d	15 05	15 08	15 14	15 17	15 32		15 43	15 48	16 05	16 08	16 14	16 17	16 32		16 43	16 48	17 05	17 08	17 14	17 17	17 32	
Portsmouth & Southsea	a	15 08	15 11	15 17	15 20	15 35		15 46	15 51	16 08	16 11	16 17	16 20	16 35		16 46	16 51	17 08	17 11	17 17	17 20	17 35	
	d	15 09	15 12	15 18	15 22	15 37	15 42	15 47	15 53	16 09	16 12	16 18	16 22	16 37	16 42	16 47	16 53	17 09	17 12	17 18	17 22	17 37	17 42
Fratton	d	15 13	15 16	15 22	15 26	15 41	15 46	15 51	15 57	16 13	16 16	16 22	16 26	16 41	16 46	16 51	16 57	17 13	17 16	17 22	17 26	17 41	17 46
Hilsea	d				15 30		15 50						16 30		16 50						17 30		17 50
Bedhampton	d	15 20		15 30					16 04	16 20		16 30					17 04	17 20		17 30			
Havant	a	15 23		15 32		15 49		15 59	16 07	16 23		16 32		16 49		16 59	17 07	17 23		17 32		17 49	

A from 26 September

B until 19 September

C until 5 September

D from 12 September

Table 157

Sundays

Portsmouth Harbour - Havant

(Complete service)

		SN	SW	SN	GW	SN	SW	SW	SW	SN	SW	SN	GW	SN	SW	SW	SW	SN	SW	SN	GW	SN
		◇ 1	1	1	◇	1	1	1	1	◇ 1	1	1	◇	1	1	1	1	◇ 1	1	1	◇	1
				A		B						A		B						A		B
Portsmouth Harbour	d	17 43	17 48	18 05	18 08	18 14	18 17	18 32		18 43	18 48	19 05	19 08	19 14	19 17	19 32		19 43	19 48	20 05	20 08	20 14
Portsmouth & Southsea	a	17 46	17 51	18 08	18 11	18 17	18 20	18 35		18 46	18 51	19 08	19 11	19 17	19 20	19 35		19 46	19 51	20 08	20 11	20 17
	d	17 47	17 53	18 09	18 12	18 18	18 22	18 37	18 42	18 47	18 53	19 09	19 12	19 18	19 22	19 37	19 42	19 47	19 53	20 09	20 12	20 18
Fratton	d	17 51	17 57	18 13	18 16	18 22	18 26	18 41	18 46	18 51	18 57	19 13	19 16	19 22	19 26	19 41	19 46	19 51	19 57	20 13	20 16	20 22
Hilsea	d						18 30		18 50						19 30		19 50					
Bedhampton	d		18 04	18 20		18 30					19 04	19 20		19 30					20 04	20 20		20 30
Havant	a	17 59	18 07	18 23		18 32		18 49		18 59	19 07	19 23		19 32		19 49		19 59	20 07	20 23		20 32

		SW	SW	SW	SN	SW	SN	SN	SW	SW	SW	SN	SW	GW	SN	SW	SW	SW	SN	SW	SW
		1	1	1	1	1	1	1	1	1	1	1	1		1	1	1	1	1	1	1
							A	B													
Portsmouth Harbour	d	20 17	20 32		20 43	20 48	21 05	21 14	21 17	21 32		21 43	21 48	22 03	22 14	22 17	22 32		22 43	22 48	23 17
Portsmouth & Southsea	a	20 20	20 35		20 46	20 51	21 08	21 17	21 20	21 35		21 46	21 51	22 11	22 17	22 20	22 35		22 46	22 51	23 20
	d	20 22	20 37	20 42	20 47	20 53	21 09	21 18	21 22	21 37	21 42	21 47	21 53	22 12	22 18	22 22	22 37	22 42	22 47	22 53	23 22
Fratton	d	20 26	20 41	20 46	20 51	20 57	21 13	21 22	21 26	21 41	21 46	21 51	21 57	22 16	22 22	22 26	22 41	22 46	22 51	22 57	23 26
Hilsea	d	20 30		20 50					21 30		21 50					22 30		22 50			23 30
Bedhampton	d					21 04	21 20	21 30					22 04		22 30					23 04	
Havant	a		20 49		20 59	21 07	21 23	21 32		21 49		21 59	22 07		22 32		22 49		22 59	23 07	

A until 5 September

B from 12 September

Network Diagram for Table 158

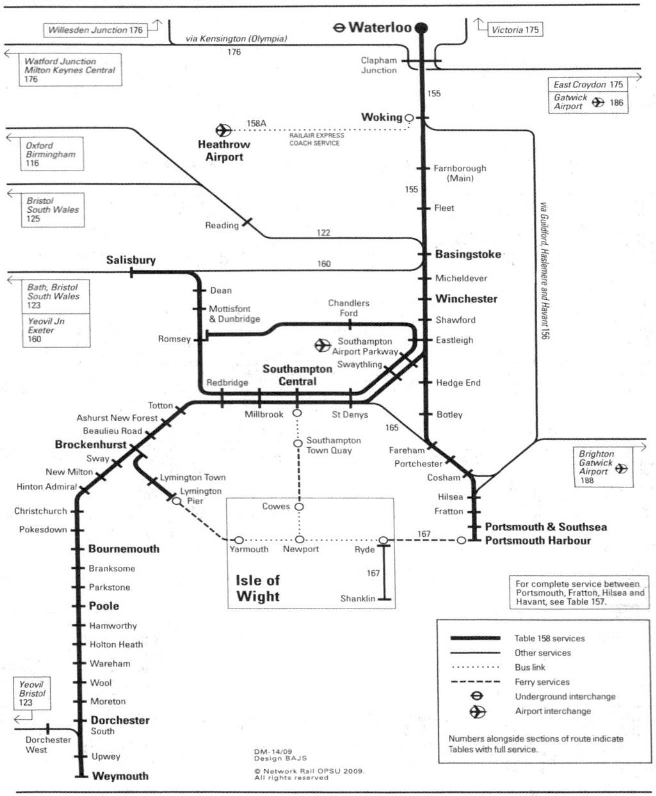

London - Basingstoke, Southampton, Romsey Lymington, Bournemouth and Weymouth

Station		SW MX ◇1 🛒	SW MO ◇1 🛒	SW MO ◇1	SW MO 1	SW MX ◇1 🛒	SW MX 1	SW MX ◇1 🛒	SW MO ◇1 🛒	SW 1	SW MX ◇1	SW MX 1	SW MX 1	SW 1	SW 1	SW 1 C	SW 1 D	SW 1	SW 1		SW 1 C	SW 1 D	SW 1	SW 1
London Waterloo 15 ⊖	d	21p35	21p35	21p54		22p05		22p35	22p54		23p05	23p39	00 05	01 05										
Clapham Junction 10	d		21b42	22b03		22b12			23b03		23b12	23b46	00u12	01 14										
Woking	d	22p00	22p07	22p28		22p32		23p00	23p28		23p32	00 09	00 36	01 42										
Farnborough (Main)	d											00 19		01s58										
Fleet	d											00 25												
Reading 7	d																							
Basingstoke	a		22p26	22p46		22p51			23p46		23p53	00 36	00 55	02s12										
	d		22p28	22p48		22p52			23p48		23p53	00 38	00 57								05 40	05 40		
Micheldever	d			22p58					23p58		00 03										05 50	05 50		
Winchester	d	22p33	22p44	23p08		23p09		23p33	00 08		00 14	00 54	01 13	02s29							05 59	05 59		06 18
Shawford	d																							06 23
Romsey	d						23p07																05 58	
Chandlers Ford	d						23p14																06 06	
Eastleigh 3	a			23p17	>	23p17	23p22		00 18	>	00 22	01 02	01 21	02s38							06 07	06 07	06 11	06 28
	d			23p22	23p26	23p18	23p22		00 22	00 30	00 23	01 03	01 22							06 00	06 08	06 08	06 13	06 29
Hedge End	d				23p32					00s36										06 06				06 35
Botley	d				23p36					00s39										06 10				06 39
Fareham	d				23p44					00s48										06 18				06 50
Portchester	d				23p49					00s53										06 23				06 55
Cosham	d				23p54					00s58										06 28				07 00
Hilsea	a				23p59															06 33				07 05
Fratton	a				00 04					01s05										06 38				07 09
Portsmouth & Southsea	a				00 08					01s08										06 44				07 12
Portsmouth Harbour	a				00 13					01 12										06 49				07 17
Southampton Airport Parkwy ✈	d	22p42	22p53	23p27		23p22	23p26	23p42	00 27		00 27	01 08	01 27	02s43							06 13	06 13	06 17	
Swaythling	d						23p28														06 15	06 15	06 20	
St Denys	d						23p31		00s31		00s31			02s48							06 18	06 18	06 24	
Southampton Central	a	22p49	23p00	23p34		23p29	23p36	23p49	00 36		00 36	01 15	01 36	02 53							06 23	06 23	06 29	
	d	22p51	23p03	23p35		23p31	23p38	23p51	00 37		00 38		01 37								06 25	06 25	06 30	
Millbrook (Hants)	d						23p40																06 33	
Redbridge	d						23p44																06 36	
Romsey	d						23p56																06 44	
Mottisfont & Dunbridge	d						00 01																06 49	
Dean	d						00 07																06 55	
Salisbury	a						00 19																07 07	
Totton	d			23p41		23p36			00s43		00s43		01s43								06 30	06 30		
Ashurst New Forest	d			23p45		23p41															06 35	06 35		
Beaulieu Road	d																							
Brockenhurst 3	a	23p04	23p16	23p53		23p49		00 04	00s53		00s54		01s53								06 43	06 43		
	d	23p05	23p17	23p54		23p50		00 05	00s54		00s55		01s54		05 59			06 16	06 29		06 44	06 44		
Lymington Town	d														06 07				06 37					
Lymington Pier	a														06 10				06 40					
Yarmouth (IOW)	a														*07 15*									
Sway	d			23p59		23p54												06 20			06 48	06 48		
New Milton	d		23p24	00 04		23p59			01s01		01s02		02s01					06 25			06 53	06 53		
Hinton Admiral	d			00 08		00 03												06 29			06 57	06 57		
Christchurch	d			00 13		00 08			01s08		01s09		02s08					06 34			07 02	07 02		
Pokesdown	d			00 16		00 11			01s12		01s12		02s12					06 38			07 06	07 06		
Bournemouth	a	23p25	23p35	00 21		00 15		00 22	01 16		01 16		02 16					06 42			07 10	07 10		
	d	23p29	23p40	00 22		00 17		00 24	01 18		01 18					06 11	06 11	06 44			07 11	07 11		
Branksome	d	23p35	23p45	00 28		00 22		00 29	01s23		01s23					06 16	06 16	06 49			07 16	07 16		
Parkstone (Dorset)	d	23p38	23p48	00 31		00 25		00 32	01s26		01s26					06 19	06 19	06 52			07 19	07 19		
Poole 4	a	23p41	23p51	00 35		00 29		00 36	01 30		01 30					06 23	06 23	06 55			07 23	07 23		
	d	23p42	23p52													06 24	06 24	06 57			07 24	07 24		
Hamworthy	d	23p47	23p57													06 29	06 29	07 02			07 29	07 29		
Holton Heath	d															06 33	06 33	07 06			07 33	07 33		
Wareham	d	23p54	00 04													06 38	06 38	07 11			07 38	07 38		
Wool	d	00 01	00 11													06 44	06 44	07 17			07 44	07 44		
Moreton (Dorset)	d	00 07	00 17													06 50	06 50	07 23			07 50	07 50		
Dorchester South	d	00 14	00 25													06 58	06 58	07 31			07 58	07 58		
Dorchester West	d																							
Upwey	d	00 21	00 32													07 05	07 05	07 38			08 05	08 05		
Weymouth	a	00 25	00 36													07 09	07 14	07 42			08 09	08 14		

C until 24 September

D from 27 September

b previous night, stops to pick up only

London - Basingstoke, Southampton, Romsey Lymington, Bournemouth and Weymouth

Station		GW 🍴	SW 1	SW 1	SW 1	SW 1	GW	SW ◇1	SW 1	SW 1	SW 1	SW 1	GW ◇ 🍴	SW 1	SW ◇1	GW ◇	SW 1	SW 1	SW 1	XC ◇1 🍴	SW 1	SW ◇1 🛒	GW ◇ 🍴	SW 1 🛒	SW 1
London Waterloo 15 ⊖	d							05 30							06 30				06 42			07 35		07 39	
Clapham Junction 10	d							05u37							06u37				06u49					07u46	
Woking	d							06 01						06 19	06 57				07 19			08 00			
Farnborough (Main)	d													06 33					07 33					08 13	
Fleet	d													06 38					07 38					08 19	
Reading 7	d																			07b46					
Basingstoke	a							06 20						06 58	07 16				07 56	08 08		08 19		08 34	
	d							06 21				06 55		07 00	07 18				08 00	08 10		08 20		08 36	
Micheldever	d													07 10					08 10						
Winchester	d							06 38				07 11		07 19	07 34				08 19	08 25		08 37		08 52	
Shawford	d											07 16							08 24					08 57	
Romsey	d										07 07						08 07								
Chandlers Ford	d										07 14						08 14								
Eastleigh 3	a							06 47	06 49		07 20	07 22		07 29	07 43		08 20		08 31			08 47		09 02	
	d			07 02				06 48	06 50		07 21	07 24		07 30	07 44		08 21		08 31			08 48		09 03	
Hedge End	d			07 08										07 36					08 36						
Botley	d			07 12										07 40					08 41						
Fareham	d	06 24		07 20									07 18	07 48					08 50				08 47		
Portchester	d			07 25										07 53					08 55						
Cosham	d			07 29										07 58					09 00						
Hilsea	a			07 35										08 03					09 05						
Fratton	a			07 39										08 07					09 09						
Portsmouth & Southsea	a			07 42										08 11					09 13						
Portsmouth Harbour	a			07 48										08 16					09 18						
Southampton Airport Parkwy ✈	d							06 53			07 25	07 29			07 49		08 25			08 33		08 52		09 08	
Swaythling	d										07 28	07 31					08 28								
St Denys	d										07 31	07 34					08 31								
Southampton Central	a	06 45						07 00			07 36	07 39	07 45		07 57		08 36			08 44		08 59	09 08	09 17	
	d	06 46						07 01		07 18	07 38		07 47		08 00	08 23	08 38			08 46		09 01	09 10	09 30	
Millbrook (Hants)	d									07 20	07 40						08 40								
Redbridge	d									07 24	07 44						08 44								
Romsey	d	07 00							07a03		07 52		08 00			08 35	08 52						09 21		
Mottisfont & Dunbridge	d										07 57						08 57								
Dean	d										08 02						09 02								
Salisbury	a	07 18									08 15		08 20			09 00	09 15						09 40		
Totton	d							07 07		07 27					08 05							09 06		09 35	
Ashurst New Forest	d									07 31														09 40	
Beaulieu Road	d									07 36															
Brockenhurst 3	a							07 17		07 42					08 16					08 59		09 17		09 50	
	d		06 59		07 29	07 59		07 18		07 44					08 17			08 29		09 00	08 59	09 18		10 16	09 29
Lymington Town	d		07 07		07 37	08 07												08 37			09 07				09 37
Lymington Pier	a		07 10		07 40	08 10												08 40			09 10				09 40
Yarmouth (IOW)	a		*08 15*			*09 15*															*09 55*				
Sway	d							07 23		07 48					08 21							09 22		10 20	
New Milton	d							07 28		07 53					08 26							09 27		10 25	
Hinton Admiral	d							07 32		07 57					08 30							09 31		10 29	
Christchurch	d							07 37		08 02					08 35							09 36		10 34	
Pokesdown	d							07 40		08 06					08 39							09 40		10 38	
Bournemouth	a							07 44		08 10					08 43					09 15		09 44		10 42	
	d							07 46		08 11					08 44							09 45		10 43	
Branksome	d							07 51		08 16					08 49							09 50		10 48	
Parkstone (Dorset)	d							07 54		08 19					08 52							09 53		10 51	
Poole 4	a							07 57		08 23					08 56							09 57		10 55	
	d							07 58		08 24					08 57							09 58			
Hamworthy	d							08 03		08 29					09 02							10 03			
Holton Heath	d							08 07		08 33															
Wareham	d							08 12		08 38					09 09							10 10			
Wool	d							08 19		08 44					09 15										
Moreton (Dorset)	d							08 25		08 50					09 21										
Dorchester South	d							08 33		08 58					09 29							10 27			
Dorchester West	d						08 09																		
Upwey	d						08 17	08 40		09 05					09 36										
Weymouth	a						08 23	08 44		09 09					09 40							10 35			

b arr. 0739

London - Basingstoke, Southampton, Romsey Lymington, Bournemouth and Weymouth

		SW	SW	GW	SW	SW	SW	XC	SW	GW	SW	SW	SW	SW	GW	XC	SW	SW	GW	SW	GW	SW
		1	1		◇1	1	1	◇1	◇1	◇	1	◇1	1	1	◇	1	1	1		◇1	◇	1
					☕			🍴	☕	🍴		☕				🍴				☕	🍴	
London Waterloo 15 ⊖	d				08 05		08 09		08 35		08 39	09 05		09 09						09 35		09 39
Clapham Junction 10	d				08u12						08u46	09u12										09u46
Woking	d						08 35		09 00					09 35						10 00		
Farnborough (Main)	d						08 45				09 13			09 45								10 13
Fleet	d										09 19											10 19
Reading 7	d							08 45								09c46						
Basingstoke	a				08 47		08 58	09 08			09 34	09 47		09 58		10 08						10 34
	d				08 49		09 00	09 10			09 36	09 49		10 00		10 10						10 36
Micheldever	d						09 10							10 10								
Winchester	d				09 05		09 19	09 25	09 33		09 52	10 05		10 19		10 25				10 33		10 52
Shawford	d										09 57											10 57
Romsey	d					09 07							10 07									
Chandlers Ford	d					09 14							10 14									
Eastleigh 3	a					09 20	09 27				10 02		10 20	10 27								11 02
	d					09 21	09 28				10 03		10 21	10 28								11 03
Hedge End	d						09 34							10 34								
Botley	d						09 38							10 38								
Fareham	d						09 48			09 47				10 48	10 14						10 47	
Portchester	d						09 53							10 53								
Cosham	d						09 58							10 58								
Hilsea	a						10 03							11 03								
Fratton	a						10 07							11 07								
Portsmouth & Southsea	a						10 11							11 11								
Portsmouth Harbour	a						10 18							11 18								
Southampton Airport Parkwy ✈	d				09 14	09 25		09 33	09 42		10 08	10 14	10 25			10 33				10 42		11 08
Swaythling	d					09 28							10 28									
St Denys	d					09 31							10 31									
Southampton Central	a				09 22	09 36		09 41	09 49	10 08	10 17	10 22	10 36		10 41	10 43				10 49	11 08	11 17
	d				09 24	09 38		09 43	09 51	10 10	10 30	10 24	10 44		10 42	10 45				10 51	11 10	11 30
Millbrook (Hants)	d					09 40							10 48									
Redbridge	d					09 44							10 51									
Romsey	d					09 52				10 21			10 59		10 54						11 21	
Mottisfont & Dunbridge	d					09 57							11 04									
Dean	d					10 02							11 10									
Salisbury	a					10 15				10 40			11 22		11 13						11 40	
Totton	d										10 35											11 35
Ashurst New Forest	d										10 40											11 40
Beaulieu Road	d										10 44											11 44
Brockenhurst 3	a				09 37			09 56	10 04		10 51	10 37				10 58				11 04		11 51
	d	09 59	10 29		09 38			09 57	10 05		11 16	10 38				10 59	10 59	11 29		11 05		12 16
Lymington Town	d	10 07	10 37														11 07	11 37				
Lymington Pier	a	10 10	10 40														11 10	11 40				
Yarmouth (IOW)	a	*11 15*															*11 55*	*12 35*				
Sway	d										11 20											12 20
New Milton	d				09 45						11 25	10 45										12 25
Hinton Admiral	d										11 29											12 29
Christchurch	d				09 52						11 34	10 52										12 34
Pokesdown	d				09 56						11 38	10 56										12 38
Bournemouth	a				10 00			10 12	10 20		11 42	11 00				11 12				11 20		12 42
	d				10 04				10 24		11 43	11 04								11 24		12 43
Branksome	d								10 29		11 48									11 29		12 48
Parkstone (Dorset)	d								10 32		11 51									11 32		12 51
Poole 4	a				10 13				10 36		11 55	11 13								11 36		12 55
	d				10 14				10 37			11 14								11 37		
Hamworthy	d				10 19				10 42			11 19								11 42		
Holton Heath	d				10 23							11 23										
Wareham	d				10 28				10 49			11 28								11 49		
Wool	d				10 35							11 35										
Moreton (Dorset)	d				10 41							11 41										
Dorchester South	d				10b54				11 05			11 49								12 05		
Dorchester West	d			10 46															11 54			
Upwey	d			10 54	11 01							11 55							12 02			
Weymouth	a			11 02	11 06				11 13			12 00							12 08	12 13		

b arr. 1048
c arr. 0939

London - Basingstoke, Southampton, Romsey Lymington, Bournemouth and Weymouth

		SW	SW	SW	XC	SW	SW	GW	SW	GW	SW	SW	SW	SW	XC	SW	SW	GW	SW	GW	SW	SW	SW
		◇1	1	1	◇1	1	◇1	◇	1	◇	1	◇1	1	1	◇1	1	1		◇1	◇	1	◇1	1
		☕			🍴		☕	🍴				☕			🍴				☕	🍴		☕	
London Waterloo 15 ⊖	d	10 05		10 09			10 35		10 39			11 05		11 09					11 35		11 39	12 05	
Clapham Junction 10	d	10u12							10u46			11u12									11u46	12u12	
Woking	d			10 35			11 00							11 35					12 00				
Farnborough (Main)	d			10 45					11 13					11 45							12 13		
Fleet	d								11 19												12 19		
Reading 7	d				10b46										11c46								
Basingstoke	a	10 47		10 58	11 08				11 34			11 47		11 58	12 08						12 34	12 47	
	d	10 49		11 00	11 10				11 36			11 49		12 00	12 10						12 36	12 49	
Micheldever	d			11 10										12 10									
Winchester	d	11 05		11 19	11 25		11 33		11 52			12 05		12 19	12 25				12 33		12 52	13 05	
Shawford	d								11 57												12 57		
Romsey	d		11 07										12 07										13 07
Chandlers Ford	d		11 14										12 14										13 14
Eastleigh 3	a		11 20	11 27					12 02				12 20	12 27							13 02		13 20
	d		11 21	11 28					12 03				12 21	12 28							13 03		13 21
Hedge End	d			11 34										12 34									
Botley	d			11 38										12 38									
Fareham	d			11 48				11 47						12 48						12 47			
Portchester	d			11 53										12 53									
Cosham	d			11 58										12 58									
Hilsea	a			12 03										13 03									
Fratton	a			12 07										13 07									
Portsmouth & Southsea	a			12 11										13 11									
Portsmouth Harbour	a			12 18										13 18									
Southampton Airport Parkwy ✈	d	11 14	11 25		11 33		11 42		12 08			12 14	12 25		12 33				12 42		13 08	13 14	13 25
Swaythling	d		11 28										12 28										13 28
St Denys	d		11 31										12 31										13 31
Southampton Central	a	11 22	11 36		11 43		11 49	12 08	12 17			12 22	12 36		12 41				12 49	13 08	13 17	13 22	13 36
	d	11 24	11 38		11 45		11 51	12 10	12 30	12 26		12 24	12 38		12 43				12 51	13 10	13 30	13 24	13 38
Millbrook (Hants)	d		11 40										12 40										13 40
Redbridge	d		11 44										12 44										13 44
Romsey	d		11 52					12 21		12 39			12 52							13 21			13 52
Mottisfont & Dunbridge	d		11 57										12 57										13 57
Dean	d		12 02										13 02										14 02
Salisbury	a		12 15					12 40		13 02			13 15							13 40			14 15
Totton	d								12 35												13 35		
Ashurst New Forest	d								12 40												13 40		
Beaulieu Road	d																						
Brockenhurst 3	a	11 37			11 58		12 04		12 51			12 37			12 56				13 04		13 51	13 37	
	d	11 38			11 59	11 59	12 05		13 16		12 29	12 38			12 57	12 59	13 29		13 05		14 16	13 38	
Lymington Town	d					12 07					12 37					13 07	13 37						
Lymington Pier	a					12 10					12 40					13 10	13 40						
Yarmouth (IOW)	a					*13 15*										*13 55*	*14 35*						
Sway	d								13 20												14 20		
New Milton	d	11 45							13 25			12 45									14 25	13 45	
Hinton Admiral	d								13 29												14 29		
Christchurch	d	11 52							13 34			12 52									14 34	13 52	
Pokesdown	d	11 56							13 38			12 56									14 38	13 56	
Bournemouth	a	12 00			12 12		12 20		13 42			13 00			13 10				13 20		14 42	14 00	
	d	12 04					12 24		13 43			13 04							13 24		14 43	14 04	
Branksome	d						12 29		13 48										13 29		14 48		
Parkstone (Dorset)	d						12 32		13 51										13 32		14 51		
Poole 4	a	12 13					12 36		13 55			13 13							13 36		14 55	14 13	
	d	12 14					12 37					13 14							13 37			14 14	
Hamworthy	d	12 19					12 42					13 19							13 42			14 19	
Holton Heath	d	12 23										13 23										14 23	
Wareham	d	12 28					12 49					13 28							13 49			14 28	
Wool	d	12 35										13 35										14 35	
Moreton (Dorset)	d	12 41										13 41										14 41	
Dorchester South	d	12 49					13 05					13 49							14 05			14 49	
Dorchester West	d																	13 54					
Upwey	d	12 55										13 55						14 02				14 55	
Weymouth	a	13 00					13 13					14 00						14 09	14 13			15 00	

b arr. 1039
c arr. 1139

London - Basingstoke, Southampton, Romsey Lymington, Bournemouth and Weymouth

		SW	XC	SW	SW	GW	SW	SW	SW	SW	SW	XC	SW	SW	GW	SW	SW	SW	SW	SW	XC	SW
		1	◇1 ⊥	1	◇1 ⊡	◇ ⊥	1	1	◇1 ⊡	1	1	◇1 ⊥	1	◇1 ⊡	■ ⊥	1	1	◇1 ⊡	1	1	◇1 ⊥	1
London Waterloo 15 ⊖	d	12 09			12 35		12 39		13 05		13 09			13 35		13 39		14 05		14 09		
Clapham Junction 10	d						12u46		13u12							13u46		14u12				
Woking	d	12 35			13 00						13 35			14 00						14 35		
Farnborough (Main)	d	12 45					13 13				13 45					14 13				14 45		
Fleet	d						13 19									14 19						
Reading 7	d		12b46									13c46									14e46	
Basingstoke	a	12 58	13 08				13 34		13 47		13 58	14 08				14 34		14 47		14 58	15 08	
	d	13 00	13 10				13 36		13 49		14 00	14 10				14 36		14 49		15 00	15 10	
Micheldever	d	13 10									14 10									15 10		
Winchester	d	13 19	13 25		13 33		13 52		14 05		14 19	14 25		14 33		14 52		15 05		15 19	15 25	
Shawford	d						13 57									14 57						
Romsey	d									14 07									15 07			
Chandlers Ford	d									14 14									15 14			
Eastleigh 8	a	13 27					14 02			14 20	14 27					15 02			15 20	15 27		
	d	13 28					14 03			14 21	14 28					15 03			15 21	15 28		
Hedge End	d	13 34									14 34									15 34		
Botley	d	13 38									14 38									15 38		
Fareham	d	13 48				13 47					14 48				14 47					15 48		
Portchester	d	13 53									14 53									15 53		
Cosham	d	13 58									14 58									15 58		
Hilsea	a	14 03									15 03									16 03		
Fratton	a	14 07									15 07									16 07		
Portsmouth & Southsea	a	14 11									15 11									16 11		
Portsmouth Harbour	a	14 18									15 18									16 18		
Southampton Airport Parkwy ✈	d		13 33		13 42		14 08		14 14	14 25		14 35		14 42		15 08		15 14	15 25		15 33	
Swaythling	d									14 28									15 28			
St Denys	d									14 31									15 31			
Southampton Central	a		13 41		13 49	14 08	14 17		14 22	14 36		14 42		14 49	15 08	15 17		15 22	15 36		15 41	
	d		13 43		13 51	14 10	14 30		14 24	14 38		14 43		14 51	15 10	15 30		15 24	15 38		15 43	
Millbrook (Hants)	d									14 40									15 40			
Redbridge	d									14 44									15 44			
Romsey	d					14 21				14 52					15 21				15 52			
Mottisfont & Dunbridge	d									14 57									15 57			
Dean	d									15 02									16 02			
Salisbury	a					14 40				15 15					15 40				16 15			
Totton	d						14 35									15 35						
Ashurst New Forest	d						14 40									15 40						
Beaulieu Road	d																					
Brockenhurst 3	a		13 56		14 04		14 51		14 37			14 56		15 04		15 51		15 37			15 56	
	d		13 57	13 59	14 05		15 16	14 29	14 38			14 57	14 59	15 05		16 28	15 29	15 38			15 57	15 59
Lymington Town	d			14 07				14 37					15 07				15 37					16 07
Lymington Pier	a			14 10				14 40					15 10				15 40					16 10
Yarmouth (IOW)	a			*15 15*									*15 55*				*16 35*					*17 15*
Sway	d						15 20									16 32						
New Milton	d						15 25		14 45							16 37		15 45				
Hinton Admiral	d						15 29									16 41						
Christchurch	d						15 34		14 52							16 46		15 52				
Pokesdown	d						15 38		14 56							16 50		15 56				
Bournemouth	a		14 10		14 20		15 42		15 00			15 11		15 20		16 54		16 00			16 10	
	d				14 24		15 43		15 04					15 24		16 55		16 04				
Branksome	d				14 29		15 48							15 29		17 00						
Parkstone (Dorset)	d				14 32		15 51							15 32		17 03						
Poole 4	a				14 36		15 55		15 13					15 36		17 07		16 13				
	d				14 37				15 14					15 37				16 14				
Hamworthy	d				14 42				15 19					15 42				16 19				
Holton Heath	d								15 23									16 23				
Wareham	d				14 49				15 28					15 49				16 28				
Wool	d								15 35									16 35				
Moreton (Dorset)	d								15 41									16 41				
Dorchester South	d				15 05				15 49					16 05				16 49				
Dorchester West	d																					
Upwey	d								15 55									16 55				
Weymouth	a				15 13				16 00					16 13				17 00				

b arr. 1239 c arr. 1339 e arr. 1439

London - Basingstoke, Southampton, Romsey Lymington, Bournemouth and Weymouth

		SW	GW	SW	GW	SW	SW	SW	SW	XC	SW	SW	SW	SW	SW	GW	SW	SW	SW	SN	SW	SW	XC
		1		◇1 ⊡	■ ⊥	1	◇1 ⊡	1	1	◇1 ⊥	1	◇1 ⊡	◇1	1	1	■ ⊥	1	1	◇1 ⊡	1	1	1	◇1 ⊥
London Waterloo 15 ⊖	d			14 35		14 39	15 05		15 09			15 35					15 39		16 05			16 09	
Clapham Junction 10	d					14u46	15u12										15u46		16u12				
Woking	d			15 00					15 35			16 00										16 35	
Farnborough (Main)	d					15 13			15 45								16 13					16 45	
Fleet	d					15 19											16 19						
Reading 7	d									15b46													16c46
Basingstoke	a					15 34	15 47		15 58	16 08							16 34		16 47			16 58	17 08
	d					15 36	15 49		16 00	16 10					16 24		16 36		16 49			17 00	17 10
Micheldever	d								16 10													17 10	
Winchester	d			15 33		15 52	16 05		16 19	16 25		16 33		16 38	16 44		16 52		17 05			17 19	17 25
Shawford	d					15 57								16 42			16 57						
Romsey	d							16 07													17 07		
Chandlers Ford	d							16 14													17 14		
Eastleigh 8	a					16 02		16 20	16 27					16 48	16 52		17 02			17 10	17 20	17 27	
	d					16 03		16 21	16 28					16 49	16 54		17 03			17 16	17 21	17 28	
Hedge End	d								16 34						17 00							17 34	
Botley	d								16 38						17 04							17 39	
Fareham	d				15 47				16 48						17 12	16 47						17 48	
Portchester	d								16 53						17 17							17 53	
Cosham	d								16 58						17 22							17 58	
Hilsea	a								17 03													18 04	
Fratton	a								17 07						17 31							18 08	
Portsmouth & Southsea	a								17 11						17 35							18 12	
Portsmouth Harbour	a								17 18						17 40							18 20	
Southampton Airport Parkwy ✈	d			15 42		16 08	16 14	16 25		16 33		16 42		16 53			17 08		17 14		17 25		17 33
Swaythling	d							16 28						16 56							17 28		
St Denys	d							16 31						16 59							17 31		
Southampton Central	a			15 49	16 08	16 17	16 22	16 36		16 41		16 49	>	17 04		17 08	17 17		17 22	17 28	17 36		17 41
	d			15 51	16 10	16 30	16 24	16 38		16 43		16 54	16 56	17 06		17 10	17 30		17 24		17 38		17 43
Millbrook (Hants)	d							16 40													17 40		
Redbridge	d							16 44													17 44		
Romsey	d				16 21			16 52								17 21					17 52		
Mottisfont & Dunbridge	d							16 57													17 57		
Dean	d							17 02													18 02		
Salisbury	a				16 40			17 15								17 40					18 15		
Totton	d					16 35							17 01	17a11			17 35						
Ashurst New Forest	d					16 40							17 06				17 40						
Beaulieu Road	d					16 44											17 44						
Brockenhurst 3	a			16 04		16 51	16 37			16 56		17 07	17 14				17 51		17 37				17 56
	d	16 29		16 05			16 38			16 57	16 59	17 08	17 16					17 29	17 38				17 57
Lymington Town	d	16 37									17 07							17 37					
Lymington Pier	a	16 40									17 10							17 40					
Yarmouth (IOW)	a										*17 55*							*18 45*					
Sway	d						16 43						17 20						17 43				
New Milton	d						16 48						17 25						17 48				
Hinton Admiral	d						16 52						17 29						17 52				
Christchurch	d						16 57						17 34						17 57				
Pokesdown	d						17 00						17 38						18 00				
Bournemouth	a			16 20			17 04			17 10		17 23	17 42						18 04				18 15
	d			16 24			17 07					17 24	17 43						18 09				
Branksome	d			16 29								17 29	17 48										
Parkstone (Dorset)	d			16 32								17 32	17 51										
Poole 4	a			16 36			17 16					17 36	17 55						18 18				
	d			16 37			17 17					17 37							18 19				
Hamworthy	d			16 42			17 22					17 42							18 24				
Holton Heath	d						17 26												18 28				
Wareham	d			16 49			17 31					17 49							18 33				
Wool	d			16 55			17 37					17 55							18 39				
Moreton (Dorset)	d						17 43												18 45				
Dorchester South	d			17 06			17 51					18 06							18 53				
Dorchester West	d		16 58																				
Upwey	d		17 05				17 58												19 00				
Weymouth	a		17 10	17 15			18 02					18 15							19 06				

b arr. 1539 c arr. 1639

Table 158

Mondays to Fridays

London - Basingstoke, Southampton, Romsey Lymington, Bournemouth and Weymouth

		SW ■	SW ■	GW	SW ◇■ ☕	SW ◇■	GW ◇ 🍴	SW ■	SW ■	SW ◇■ ☕	SW ◇■ ☕	SW ■	SW ■	GW ◇	XC ◇■ 🍴	SW ■	SW ■	SW ◇■ ☕	SW ■	GW	SW ◇■ ☕	SW ◇■ ☕	GW ◇ 🍴	SW ■	SW ◇■ ☕
London Waterloo 15 ⊖	d				16 35				16 39	17 05			17 09			17 39					17 35			17 48	18 05
Clapham Junction 10	d								16u46																
Woking	d				17u00								17 34			18 04								18 13	
Farnborough (Main)	d								17 13																
Fleet	d								17 19																
Reading 7	d														17b46										
Basingstoke	a								17 34				17 52		18 08	18 22								18 31	
	d							17 24	17 36				17 54		18 10	18 24								18 33	
Micheldever	d							17 34					18 04			18 34									
Winchester	d				17 33			17 44	17 52	18 00			18 14		18 25	18 44					18 30			18 50	19 00
Shawford	d							17 49					18 18			18 49									
Romsey	d											18 07													
Chandlers Ford	d											18 14													
Eastleigh 3	a							17 54	18 00			18 20	18 24			18 54								18 58	
	d							17 55	18 01			18 21	18 25			18 55								18 59	
Hedge End	d								18 07				18 31			19 01									
Botley	d								18 11				18 35			19 05									
Fareham	d						17 47		18 23				18 45	18 13		19 14							18 47		
Portchester	d								18 28				18 50			19 19									
Cosham	d								18 33				18 55			19 24									
Hilsea	a												19 05			19 28									
Fratton	a								18 40				19 09			19 32									
Portsmouth & Southsea	a								18 43				19 12			19 36									
Portsmouth Harbour	a								18 51				19 20			19 43									
Southampton Airport Parkwy ✈	d				17 42			18 00		18 09		18 26			18 34						18 39			19 03	19 09
Swaythling	d							18 02				18 28												19 06	
St Denys	d							18 05				18 31												19 09	
Southampton Central	a				17 49	>	18 08	18 10		18 16	>	18 36		18 41	18 44						18 46	>	19 08	19 18	19 18
	d				17 53	17 56	18 10			18 21	18 24	18 38		18 42	18 45			18 54			18 51	18 54	19 10		19 19
Millbrook (Hants)	d											18 40													
Redbridge	d											18 44													
Romsey	d						18 21					19 00		18 54									19 21		
Mottisfont & Dunbridge	d											19 05													
Dean	d											19 10													
Salisbury	a						18 40					19 23		19 12									19 40		
Totton	d					18 01					18 29							18 59				18 59			19 25
Ashurst New Forest	d					18 06					18 34							19 04				19 04			
Beaulieu Road	d																								
Brockenhurst 3	a				18 07	18 14					18 42				18 58			19 12				19 12			19 35
	d	17 59	18 29		18 08	18 16					18 43				18 59		18 59	19 13	19 29			19 13			19 36
Lymington Town	d	18 07	18 37														19 07		19 37						
Lymington Pier	a	18 10	18 40														19 10		19 40						
Yarmouth (IOW)	a																*19 55*								
Sway	d					18 20					18 47							19 17				19 17			19 41
New Milton	d					18 25					18 52							19 22				19 22			19 46
Hinton Admiral	d					18 29					18 57							19 26				19 26			19 50
Christchurch	d					18 34					19 01							19 31				19 31			19 55
Pokesdown	d					18 38					19 05							19 35				19 35			19 58
Bournemouth	a				18 22	18 42				18 48	19 09				19 13			19 39			19 20	19 39			20 02
	d				18 24					18 50	19 10							19 40			19 21	19 40			20 07
Branksome	d				18 29					18 55	19 15							19 45			19 26	19 45			20 12
Parkstone (Dorset)	d				18 32					18 58	19 18							19 48			19 29	19 48			20 15
Poole 4	a				18 36					19 02	19 26							19 56			19 33	19 56			20 18
	d				18 37					19 03											19 34				20 19
Hamworthy	d				18 42					19 08											19 39				20 24
Holton Heath	d									19 12															20 28
Wareham	d				18 49					19 17											19 46				20 33
Wool	d									19 23															20 40
Moreton (Dorset)	d									19 30															20 46
Dorchester South	d				19 05					19 38											20 02				20 54
Dorchester West	d			18 58																19 54					
Upwey	d			19 06						19 45										20 01					21 00
Weymouth	a			19 13	19 17					19 51										20 08	20 15				21 07

Table 158

Mondays to Fridays

London - Basingstoke, Southampton, Romsey Lymington, Bournemouth and Weymouth

		SW ■		SW ■	SW ■	XC ◇■ 🍴	SW ◇■ ☕	SW ◇■ ☕	SW ■	SW ■	GW ◇	SW ■		SW ■	SW ◇■ ☕	SW ■	SW ■	XC ◇■ 🍴	SW ■	SW ◇■ ☕	GW ◇	SW ■		GW	SW ■
London Waterloo 15 ⊖	d				18 09		18 35					18 39			19 05		19 09			19 35		19 39			
Clapham Junction 10	d											18u46			19u12							19u46			
Woking	d				18 35							19 06					19 35			20 00					
Farnborough (Main)	d																19 45					20 13			
Fleet	d																					20 19			
Reading 7	d					18b46												19c46							
Basingstoke	a				18 53	19 08						19 28			19 47		19 58	20 09				20 34			
	d				18 55	19 10			19 24			19 30			19 49		20 00	20 10				20 36			
Micheldever	d				19 05							19 40					20 10								
Winchester	d	19 05			19 14	19 25	19 30		19 40			19 49			20 05		20 19	20 25		20 33		20 52			
Shawford	d	19 09			19 19				19 45			19 54					20 24					20 57			
Romsey	d			19 07												20 07									
Chandlers Ford	d			19 14												20 14									
Eastleigh 3	a	19 15		19 20	19 25				19 50			19 59				20 20	20 29					21 02			
	d	19 16		19 21	19 28				19 51			20 00				20 21	20 30					21 03			
Hedge End	d				19 34				19 57								20 36								
Botley	d				19 38				20 01								20 40								
Fareham	d				19 48				20 09		19 47						20 49				20 47				
Portchester	d				19 53												20 54								
Cosham	d				19 58												20 59								
Hilsea	a				20 02												21 03								
Fratton	a				20 06												21 07								
Portsmouth & Southsea	a				20 11												21 11								
Portsmouth Harbour	a				20 20												21 16								
Southampton Airport Parkwy ✈	d	19 20		19 25		19 34	19 39					20 05			20 14	20 25		20 34		20 42		21 08			
Swaythling	d	19 23		19 28												20 28									
St Denys	d	19 26		19 31												20 31									
Southampton Central	a	19 33		19 36		19 41	19 46	>			20 08	20 16			20 22	20 36		20 41		20 49	21 08	21 17			
	d			19 38		19 43	19 51	19 54			20 10	20 30			20 24	20 38		20 43		20 51	21 10			21 20	
Millbrook (Hants)	d			19 40												20 40									
Redbridge	d			19 44												20 44									
Romsey	d			19 52							20 21					20 52					21 21			21 31	
Mottisfont & Dunbridge	d			19 57												20 57									
Dean	d			20 02												21 02									
Salisbury	a			20 15							20 40					21 15					21 40			21 51	
Totton	d							19 59				20 35								20 56					
Ashurst New Forest	d							20 04				20 40													
Beaulieu Road	d											20 44													
Brockenhurst 3	a					19 56		20 12				20 51			20 37			20 58		21 07					
	d					19 57		20 13		19 59		21 16		20 29	20 38			20 59	20 59	21 08					21 29
Lymington Town	d									20 07				20 37					21 07						21 37
Lymington Pier	a									20 10				20 40					21 10						21 40
Yarmouth (IOW)	a													*21 35*											
Sway	d							20 17				21 20													
New Milton	d							20 22				21 25			20 45										
Hinton Admiral	d							20 26				21 29													
Christchurch	d							20 31				21 34			20 52										
Pokesdown	d							20 35				21 38			20 56										
Bournemouth	a					20 12	20 20	20 39				21 42			21 00			21 15		21 22					
	d						20 21	20 40				21 43			21 04					21 27					
Branksome	d						20 26	20 45				21 48								21 32					
Parkstone (Dorset)	d						20 29	20 48				21 51								21 35					
Poole 4	a						20 33	20 56				21 57			21 13					21 38					
	d						20 34								21 15					21 39					
Hamworthy	d						20 39								21 20					21 44					
Holton Heath	d																								
Wareham	d						20 46								21 27					21 51					
Wool	d														21 33					21 58					
Moreton (Dorset)	d														21 39					22 04					
Dorchester South	d						21 02								21 47					22 12					
Dorchester West	d																								
Upwey	d														21 54					22 18					
Weymouth	a						21 13								21 58					22 23					

b arr. 1839

c arr. 1939

Table 158

Mondays to Fridays

London - Basingstoke, Southampton, Romsey Lymington, Bournemouth and Weymouth

		SW	SW	SW	XC	SW	GW	SW	SW	GW	SW	SW	XC	SW	SW	SW	SW	SW	SW	XC	SW	SW	SW	SW
		◇1	1	1	◇1	1		◇1	1		◇1	1	◇1	◇1	1	1	1	◇1	1	◇1	◇1	1	◇1	1
		🛒						🛒			🛒			🛒				🛒			🛒			
London Waterloo 15 ⊖	d	20 05		20 09				20 35	20 39		21 05			21 35		21 39	21 42	22 05			22 35	22 39	23 05	23 39
Clapham Junction 10	d	20u12							20u46		21u12					21u46		22u12				22u46	23u12	23u46
Woking	d			20 35				21 00			21 32			22 00			22 19	22 32			23 00		23 32	00 09
Farnborough (Main)	d			20 45					21 13							22 13	22 33					23 13		00 19
Fleet	d								21 19							22 19	22 38					23 19		00 25
Reading 7	d				20b46								21c46							22e48				
Basingstoke	a	20 47		20 58	21 09				21 34		21 51		22 09			22 34	22 58	22 51		23 12		23 33	23 53	00 36
	d	20 49		21 00	21 10				21 36		21 52		22 10		22 21	22 36	23 00	22 52		23 14		23 34	23 53	00 38
Micheldever	d			21 10					21 46						22 31	22s46	23 10						00 03	
Winchester	d	21 05		21 19	21 25			21 33	21 55		22 09		22 25	22 33	22 40	22 55	23 19	23 09		23 29	23 33	23 51	00 14	00 54
Shawford	d			21 24					22 00						22 45	23 00	23 24					23 55		
Romsey	d		21 07									22 07							23 07					
Chandlers Ford	d		21 14									22 14							23 14					
Eastleigh 3	a		21 20	21 30					22 05	22 05	22 17	22 21			22 50	23 05		23 17	23 22			00 01	00 22	01 02
	d		21 21	21 30					22 06	22 10	22 18	22 22			22 51	23 06		23 18	23 22			00 02	00 23	01 03
Hedge End	d			21 36											22 57		23 36							
Botley	d			21 40											23 01		23 40							
Fareham	d			21 48											23 10		23 48							
Portchester	d			21 53											23 15		23 53							
Cosham	d			21 58											23 20		23 59							
Hilsea	a			22 03											23 24		00 04							
Fratton	a			22 08											23 32		00 08							
Portsmouth & Southsea	a			22 11											23 36		00 11							
Portsmouth Harbour	a			22 16											23 40		00 16							
Southampton Airport Parkwy ✈	d	21 14	21 25		21 34			21 42	22 11		22 22	22 26	22 34	22 42		23 11		23 22	23 26	23 38	23 42	00 06	00 27	01 08
Swaythling	d		21 28									22 28							23 28					
St Denys	d		21 31									22 31							23 31				00s31	
Southampton Central	a	21 24	21 36		21 41			21 49	22 18	22 20	22 29	22 36	22 42	22 49		23 18		23 29	23 36	23 47	23 49	00 13	00 36	01 15
	d	21 24	21 38		21 43			21 51		22 22	22 31	22 38	22 43	22 51				23 31	23 38		23 51		00 38	
Millbrook (Hants)	d		21 40									22 40							23 40					
Redbridge	d		21 44									22 44							23 44					
Romsey	d		21 52							22 33		22a52							23 56					
Mottisfont & Dunbridge	d		21 57																00 01					
Dean	d		22 02																00 07					
Salisbury	a		22 17							22 58									00 19					
Totton	d	21 31									22 36							23 36					00s43	
Ashurst New Forest	d	21 35									22 41							23 41						
Beaulieu Road	d																							
Brockenhurst 3	a	21 43			21 56			22 04			22 49		22 56	23 04				23 49			00 04		00s54	
	d	21 44			21 57	21 59		22 05			22 50		22 59	23 05				23 50			00 05		00s55	
Lymington Town	d					22 07																		
Lymington Pier	a					22 10																		
Yarmouth (IOW)	a					*23 00*																		
Sway	d	21 49									22 54							23 54						
New Milton	d	21 54									22 59							23 59					01s02	
Hinton Admiral	d	21 58									23 03							00 03						
Christchurch	d	22 03									23 08							00 08					01s09	
Pokesdown	d	22 06									23 12							00 11					01s12	
Bournemouth	a	22 10			22 16			22 20			23 16		23 21	23 25				00 15			00 22		01 16	
	d	22 12						22 24			23 17			23 29				00 17			00 24		01 18	
Branksome	d	22 17						22 29			23 22			23 35				00 22			00 29		01s23	
Parkstone (Dorset)	d	22 20						22 32			23 25			23 38				00 25			00 32		01s26	
Poole 4	a	22 23						22 36			23 29			23 41				00 29			00 36		01 30	
	d							22 37						23 42										
Hamworthy	d							22 42						23 47										
Holton Heath	d																							
Wareham	d							22 49						23 54										
Wool	d							22 55						00 01										
Moreton (Dorset)	d							23 01						00 07										
Dorchester South	d							23 09						00 14										
Dorchester West	d						22 54																	
Upwey	d						23 02	23 16						00 21										
Weymouth	a						23 09	23 20						00 25										

b arr. 2039 c arr. 2140 e arr. 2241

Table 158

Saturdays

London - Basingstoke, Southampton, Romsey Lymington, Bournemouth and Weymouth

		SW	SW	SW	SW	SW	SW	SW	SW	SW	SW	SW	SW	SW	SW	SW	SW	GW	SW	SW	SW	SW	GW
		◇1	◇1	1	◇1	◇1	1	1	1	1	1	1	1	1	1	1	1	◇	1	1	1	1	
		🛒	🛒		🛒																		
London Waterloo 15 ⊖	d	21p35	22p05		22p35	23p05		23p39	00 05	01 05													
Clapham Junction 10	d		22b12			23b12		23b46	00u12	01 14													
Woking	d	22p00	22p32		23p00	23p32		00 09	00 36	01 42													
Farnborough (Main)	d							00 19		01s52													
Fleet	d							00 25		01s57													
Reading 7	d																						
Basingstoke	a		22p51			23p53		00 36	00 55	02s09													
	d		22p52			23p53		00 38	00 57	02s10													
Micheldever	d					00 03																	
Winchester	d	22p33	23p09		23p33	00 14		00 54	01 13	02s27													
Shawford	d																						
Romsey	d			23p07													05 58						
Chandlers Ford	d			23p14													06 06						
Eastleigh 3	a		23p17	23p22		00 22		01 02	01 21	02s35							06 11		06 49				
	d		23p18	23p22		00 23	00 30	01 03	01 22	02s36				06 28			06 13		06 50				
Hedge End	d						00s36							06 34									
Botley	d						00s39							06 38									
Fareham	d						00s48							06 48				06 28					
Portchester	d						00s53							06 53									
Cosham	d						00s58							06 58									
Hilsea	a													07 03									
Fratton	a						01s05							07 07									
Portsmouth & Southsea	a						01s08							07 11									
Portsmouth Harbour	a						01 12							07 16									
Southampton Airport Parkwy ✈	d	22p42	23p22	23p26	23p42	00 27		01 08	01 27	02s40							06 17						
Swaythling	d			23p28													06 20						
St Denys	d			23p31		00s31				02s44							06 23						
Southampton Central	a	22p49	23p29	23p36	23p49	00 36		01 15	01 36	02 49							06 28	06 49					
	d	22p51	23p31	23p38	23p51	00 38			01 37							06 25	06 30	06 53					
Millbrook (Hants)	d			23p40													06 32						
Redbridge	d			23p44													06 36						
Romsey	d			23p56													06 44	07 11	07a03				
Mottisfont & Dunbridge	d			00 01													06 49						
Dean	d			00 07													06 54						
Salisbury	a			00 19													07 07	07 29					
Totton	d		23p36			00s43			01s43							06 30							
Ashurst New Forest	d		23p41													06 35							
Beaulieu Road	d																						
Brockenhurst 3	a	23p04	23p49		00 04	00s54			01s53							06 43							
	d	23p05	23p50		00 05	00s55			01s54		05 59		06 16		06 29	06 44				06 59	07 29	07 59	
Lymington Town	d										06 07				06 37					07 07	07 37	08 07	
Lymington Pier	a										06 09				06 39					07 09	07 39	08 09	
Yarmouth (IOW)	a										*07 15*									*08 15*		*09 15*	
Sway	d		23p54										06 20			06 48							
New Milton	d		23p59			01s02			02s01				06 25			06 53							
Hinton Admiral	d		00 03										06 29			06 57							
Christchurch	d		00 08			01s09			02s08				06 34			07 02							
Pokesdown	d		00 11			01s12			02s12				06 38			07 06							
Bournemouth	a	23p25	00 15		00 22	01 16			02 16				06 42			07 10							
	d	23p29	00 17		00 24	01 18						06 11	06 44			07 11							
Branksome	d	23p35	00 22		00 29	01s23						06 16	06 49			07 16							
Parkstone (Dorset)	d	23p38	00 25		00 32	01s26						06 19	06 52			07 19							
Poole 4	a	23p41	00 29		00 36	01 30						06 23	06 55			07 23							
	d	23p42										06 24	06 57			07 24							
Hamworthy	d	23p47										06 29	07 02			07 29							
Holton Heath	d											06 33	07 06			07 33							
Wareham	d	23p54										06 38	07 11			07 38							
Wool	d	00 01										06 44	07 17			07 44							
Moreton (Dorset)	d	00 07										06 50	07 23			07 50							
Dorchester South	d	00 14										06 58	07 31			07 58							
Dorchester West	d																						08 05
Upwey	d	00 21										07 05	07 38			08 05							08 13
Weymouth	a	00 25										07 09	07 42			08 09							08 18

b previous night, stops to pick up only

London - Basingstoke, Southampton, Romsey Lymington, Bournemouth and Weymouth

		SW ◇1	SW 1	SW 1	GW ◇ 🍴	SW 1	SW ◇1	GW ◇	SW 1	SW 1	SW 1	SW 1	XC ◇1 🍴
London Waterloo ⊖	d	05 30					06 30					06 42	
Clapham Junction	d	05u37					06u37					06u49	
Woking	d	06 01				06 19	06 57					07 19	
Farnborough (Main)	d					06 33						07 33	
Fleet	d					06 38						07 38	
Reading 7	d												07b46
Basingstoke	a	06 20				06 58	07 16					07 56	08 08
	d	06 21				07 00	07 18					08 00	08 10
Micheldever	d	06 31				07 10						08 10	
Winchester	d	06 41				07 19	07 34					08 19	08 25
Shawford	d					07 24						08 24	
Romsey	d			07 07							08 07		
Chandlers Ford	d			07 14							08 14		
Eastleigh 3	a	06 50		07 20		07 29	07 42				08 20	08 31	
	d	06 51		07 21		07 30	07 43				08 21	08 31	
Hedge End	d					07 36						08 36	
Botley	d					07 40						08 41	
Fareham	d				07 30	07 48						08 50	
Portchester	d					07 53						08 55	
Cosham	d					07 58						09 00	
Hilsea	a					08 03						09 05	
Fratton	a					08 07						09 09	
Portsmouth & Southsea	a					08 11						09 13	
Portsmouth Harbour	a					08 16						09 18	
Southampton Airport Parkway ✈	d	06 56		07 25			07 48				08 25		08 33
Swaythling	d			07 28							08 28		
St Denys	d			07 31							08 31		
Southampton Central	a	07 03		07 36	07 51		07 56				08 36		08 41
	d	07 05	07 25	07 38	07 54		08 00	08 27		08 22	08 38		08 43
Millbrook (Hants)	d			07 40							08 40		
Redbridge	d			07 44							08 44		
Romsey	d			07 52	08 12			08 38			08 52		
Mottisfont & Dunbridge	d			07 57							08 57		
Dean	d			08 02							09 02		
Salisbury	a			08 15	08 30			09 03			09 15		
Totton	d	07 10	07 30				08 05			08 27			
Ashurst New Forest	d		07 35							08 32			
Beaulieu Road	d									08 36			
Brockenhurst 3	a	07 21	07 43				08 16			08 42			08 56
	d	07 22	07 44				08 17		08 29	08 44			08 58
Lymington Town	d								08 37				
Lymington Pier	a								08 39				
Yarmouth (IOW)	a												
Sway	d	07 26	07 48				08 21			08 48			
New Milton	d	07 31	07 53				08 26			08 53			
Hinton Admiral	d	07 35	07 57				08 30			08 57			
Christchurch	d	07 40	08 02				08 35			09 02			
Pokesdown	d	07 44	08 06				08 39			09 06			
Bournemouth	a	07 48	08 10				08 43			09 10			09 14
	d	07 49	08 11				08 44			09 11			
Branksome	d	07 54	08 16				08 49			09 16			
Parkstone (Dorset)	d	07 57	08 19				08 52			09 19			
Poole 4	a	08 01	08 23				08 56			09 23			
	d	08 02	08 24				08 57			09 24			
Hamworthy	d	08 07	08 29				09 02			09 29			
Holton Heath	d		08 33							09 33			
Wareham	d	08 14	08 38				09 09			09 38			
Wool	d	08 20	08 44				09 15			09 44			
Moreton (Dorset)	d	08 26	08 50				09 21			09 50			
Dorchester South	d	08 34	08 58				09 29			09 58			
Dorchester West	d												
Upwey	d	08 41	09 05				09 36			10 05			
Weymouth	a	08 45	09 09				09 40			10 09			

		SW 1	SW ◇1	GW ◇ 🍴	SW 1	SW 1	SW 1	SW 1	GW	SW ◇1	SW 1	SW 1	XC ◇1 🍴
London Waterloo ⊖	d		07 35		07 39					08 05		08 09	
Clapham Junction	d				07u46					08u12			
Woking	d		08 00									08 35	
Farnborough (Main)	d				08 13							08 45	
Fleet	d				08 19								
Reading 7	d												08c46
Basingstoke	a		08 20		08 34					08 47		08 58	09 08
	d		08 21		08 36					08 49		09 00	09 10
Micheldever	d											09 10	
Winchester	d		08 38		08 52					09 05		09 19	09 25
Shawford	d				08 57								
Romsey	d										09 07		
Chandlers Ford	d										09 14		
Eastleigh 3	a		08 46		09 02						09 20	09 27	
	d		08 47		09 03						09 21	09 28	
Hedge End	d											09 34	
Botley	d											09 38	
Fareham	d			08 47								09 48	
Portchester	d											09 53	
Cosham	d											09 58	
Hilsea	a											10 03	
Fratton	a											10 07	
Portsmouth & Southsea	a											10 11	
Portsmouth Harbour	a											10 18	
Southampton Airport Parkway ✈	d		08 51		09 08					09 14	09 25		09 33
Swaythling	d										09 28		
St Denys	d										09 31		
Southampton Central	a		08 58	09 08	09 17					09 22	09 36		09 40
	d		09 00	09 10	09 30					09 24	09 38		09 43
Millbrook (Hants)	d										09 40		
Redbridge	d										09 44		
Romsey	d			09 21							09 52		
Mottisfont & Dunbridge	d										09 57		
Dean	d										10 02		
Salisbury	a			09 40							10 15		
Totton	d		09 05		09 35								
Ashurst New Forest	d				09 40								
Beaulieu Road	d				09 44								
Brockenhurst 3	a		09 16		09 51					09 37			09 57
	d	08 59	09 17		10 16	09 29	09 59	10 29		09 38			09 58
Lymington Town	d	09 07				09 37	10 07	10 37					
Lymington Pier	a	09 09				09 39	10 09	10 39					
Yarmouth (IOW)	a	*09 55*					*11 15*						
Sway	d		09 21		10 20								
New Milton	d		09 26		10 25					09 45			
Hinton Admiral	d		09 30		10 29								
Christchurch	d		09 35		10 34					09 52			
Pokesdown	d		09 39		10 38					09 56			
Bournemouth	a		09 43		10 42					10 00			10 11
	d		09 44		10 43					10 04			
Branksome	d		09 49		10 48								
Parkstone (Dorset)	d		09 52		10 51								
Poole 4	a		09 56		10 55					10 13			
	d		09 57							10 14			
Hamworthy	d		10 02							10 19			
Holton Heath	d									10 23			
Wareham	d		10 09							10 28			
Wool	d									10 35			
Moreton (Dorset)	d									10 41			
Dorchester South	d		10 27							10 49			
Dorchester West	d								10 38				
Upwey	d								10 49	10 54			
Weymouth	a		10 35						10 56	11 00			

b arr. 0739

c arr. 0839

London - Basingstoke, Southampton, Romsey Lymington, Bournemouth and Weymouth

		SW ◇1 🛒		GW ◇ 🍴	SW 1	SW 1	GW	SW ◇1 🛒	SW 1	SW 1	GW ◇	XC B 1 🍴	
London Waterloo ⊖	d	08 35			08 39			09 05		09 09			
Clapham Junction	d				08u46			09u12					
Woking	d	09 00								09 35			
Farnborough (Main)	d				09 13					09 45			
Fleet	d				09 19								
Reading 7	d											09b46	
Basingstoke	a				09 34			09 47		09 58		10 08	
	d				09 36			09 49		10 00		10 10	
Micheldever	d									10 10			
Winchester	d	09 33			09 52			10 05		10 19		10 25	
Shawford	d				09 57								
Romsey	d								10 07				
Chandlers Ford	d								10 14				
Eastleigh 3	a				10 02				10 20	10 27			
	d				10 03				10 21	10 28			
Hedge End	d									10 34			
Botley	d									10 38			
Fareham	d			09 47						10 48	10 16		
Portchester	d									10 53			
Cosham	d									10 58			
Hilsea	a									11 03			
Fratton	a									11 07			
Portsmouth & Southsea	a									11 11			
Portsmouth Harbour	a									11 18			
Southampton Airport Parkway ✈	d	09 42			10 08			10 14	10 25			10 33	
Swaythling	d								10 28				
St Denys	d								10 31				
Southampton Central	a	09 49		10 08	10 15			10 22	10 36		10 40	10 43	
	d	09 51		10 10	10 30			10 24	10 38		10 42	10 45	
Millbrook (Hants)	d								10 40				
Redbridge	d								10 44				
Romsey	d			10 21					10 59		10 53		
Mottisfont & Dunbridge	d								11 04				
Dean	d								11 10				
Salisbury	a			10 40					11 22		11 13		
Totton	d				10 35								
Ashurst New Forest	d				10 40								
Beaulieu Road	d												
Brockenhurst 3	a	10 04			10 51			10 37				10 58	
	d	10 05			11 16	10 59		10 38				10 59	
Lymington Town	d					11 07							
Lymington Pier	a					11 09							
Yarmouth (IOW)	a					*11 55*							
Sway	d				11 20								
New Milton	d				11 25			10 45					
Hinton Admiral	d				11 29								
Christchurch	d				11 34			10 52					
Pokesdown	d				11 38			10 56					
Bournemouth	a	10 20			11 42			11 00				11 12	
	d	10 24			11 43			11 04					
Branksome	d	10 29			11 48								
Parkstone (Dorset)	d	10 32			11 51								
Poole 4	a	10 36			11 55			11 13					
	d	10 37						11 14					
Hamworthy	d	10 42						11 19					
Holton Heath	d							11 23					
Wareham	d	10 49						11 28					
Wool	d							11 35					
Moreton (Dorset)	d							11 41					
Dorchester South	d	11 05						11 49					
Dorchester West	d						11 30						
Upwey	d							11 55					
Weymouth	a	11 13					11 42	12 00					

		SW 1	GW	SW ◇1 🛒	GW ◇ 🍴	SW 1	SW ◇1 🛒	SW 1	SW 1	XC ◇1 🍴		SW 1	SW ◇1 🛒
London Waterloo ⊖	d			09 35		09 39	10 05		10 09				10 35
Clapham Junction	d					09u46	10u12						
Woking	d			10 00					10 35				11 00
Farnborough (Main)	d					10 13			10 45				
Fleet	d					10 19							
Reading 7	d									10c46			
Basingstoke	a					10 34	10 47		10 58	11 08			
	d					10 36	10 49		11 00	11 10			
Micheldever	d								11 10				
Winchester	d			10 33		10 52	11 05		11 19	11 25			11 33
Shawford	d					10 57							
Romsey	d							11 07					
Chandlers Ford	d							11 14					
Eastleigh 3	a					11 02		11 20	11 27				
	d					11 03		11 21	11 28				
Hedge End	d								11 34				
Botley	d								11 38				
Fareham	d				10 47				11 48				
Portchester	d								11 53				
Cosham	d								11 58				
Hilsea	a								12 03				
Fratton	a								12 07				
Portsmouth & Southsea	a								12 11				
Portsmouth Harbour	a								12 18				
Southampton Airport Parkway ✈	d			10 42		11 08	11 14	11 25		11 33			11 42
Swaythling	d							11 28					
St Denys	d							11 31					
Southampton Central	a			10 49	11 08	11 17	11 22	11 36		11 41			11 49
	d			10 51	11 10	11 30	11 24	11 38		11 43			11 51
Millbrook (Hants)	d							11 40					
Redbridge	d							11 44					
Romsey	d				11 21			11 52					
Mottisfont & Dunbridge	d							11 57					
Dean	d							12 02					
Salisbury	a				11 40			12 15					
Totton	d					11 35							
Ashurst New Forest	d					11 40							
Beaulieu Road	d					11 44							
Brockenhurst 3	a			11 04		11 51	11 37			11 57			12 04
	d	11 29		11 05		12 16	11 38			11 58		11 59	12 05
Lymington Town	d	11 37										12 07	
Lymington Pier	a	11 39										12 09	
Yarmouth (IOW)	a	*12 35*										*13 15*	
Sway	d					12 20							
New Milton	d					12 25	11 45						
Hinton Admiral	d					12 29							
Christchurch	d					12 34	11 52						
Pokesdown	d					12 38	11 56						
Bournemouth	a			11 20		12 42	12 00			12 11			12 20
	d			11 24		12 43	12 04						12 24
Branksome	d			11 29		12 48							12 29
Parkstone (Dorset)	d			11 32		12 51							12 32
Poole 4	a			11 36		12 55	12 13						12 36
	d			11 37			12 14						12 37
Hamworthy	d			11 42			12 19						12 42
Holton Heath	d						12 23						
Wareham	d			11 49			12 28						12 49
Wool	d						12 35						
Moreton (Dorset)	d						12 41						
Dorchester South	d			12 05			12 49						13 05
Dorchester West	d		11 54										
Upwey	d		12 02				12 55						
Weymouth	a		12 08	12 13			13 00						13 13

B until 4 September

b arr. 0939

c arr. 1039

Table 158

Saturdays

London - Basingstoke, Southampton, Romsey Lymington, Bournemouth and Weymouth

Station		GW ◇	SW 1	GW ◇	SW 1	SW ◇1	SW 1	SW 1	XC ◇1	SW 1	SW 1	GW
London Waterloo 15 ⊖	d		10 39			11 05		11 09				
Clapham Junction 10	d		10u46			11u12						
Woking	d							11 35				
Farnborough (Main)	d		11 13					11 45				
Fleet	d		11 19									
Reading 7	d								11b46			
Basingstoke	a		11 34			11 47		11 58	12 08			
	d		11 36			11 49		12 00	12 10			
Micheldever	d							12 10				
Winchester	d		11 52			12 05		12 19	12 25			
Shawford	d		11 57									
Romsey	d						12 07					
Chandlers Ford	d						12 14					
Eastleigh 3	a		12 02				12 20	12 27				
	d		12 03				12 21	12 28				
Hedge End	d							12 34				
Botley	d							12 38				
Fareham	d	11 47						12 48				
Portchester	d							12 53				
Cosham	d							12 58				
Hilsea	a							13 03				
Fratton	a							13 07				
Portsmouth & Southsea	a							13 11				
Portsmouth Harbour	a							13 18				
Southampton Airport Parkwy ✈	d		12 08			12 14	12 25		12 33			
Swaythling	d						12 28					
St Denys	d						12 31					
Southampton Central	a	12 08	12 17			12 22	12 36		12 41			
	d	12 10	12 30	12 27		12 24	12 38		12 43			
Millbrook (Hants)	d						12 40					
Redbridge	d						12 44					
Romsey	d	12 21		12 38			12 52					
Mottisfont & Dunbridge	d						12 57					
Dean	d						13 02					
Salisbury	a	12 40		13 03			13 15					
Totton	d		12 35									
Ashurst New Forest	d		12 40									
Beaulieu Road	d											
Brockenhurst 3	a		12 51			12 37			12 57			
	d		13 16		12 29	12 38			12 58	12 59	13 29	
Lymington Town	d				12 37					13 07	13 37	
Lymington Pier	a				12 39					13 09	13 39	
Yarmouth (IOW)	a									*13 55*	*14 35*	
Sway	d		13 20									
New Milton	d		13 25			12 45						
Hinton Admiral	d		13 29									
Christchurch	d		13 34			12 52						
Pokesdown	d		13 38			12 56						
Bournemouth	a		13 42			13 00			13 11			
	d		13 43			13 04						
Branksome	d		13 48									
Parkstone (Dorset)	d		13 51									
Poole 4	a		13 55			13 13						
	d					13 14						
Hamworthy	d					13 19						
Holton Heath	d					13 23						
Wareham	d					13 28						
Wool	d					13 35						
Moreton (Dorset)	d					13 41						
Dorchester South	d					13 49						
Dorchester West	d											13 54
Upwey	d					13 55						14 02
Weymouth	a					14 00						14 08

Station		SW ◇1	GW ◇	SW 1	SW ◇1	SW 1	SW 1	XC ◇1	SW 1	SW ◇1	GW ◇	SW 1
London Waterloo 15 ⊖	d	11 35		11 39	12 05		12 09			12 35		12 39
Clapham Junction 10	d			11u46	12u12							12u46
Woking	d	12 00					12 35			13 00		
Farnborough (Main)	d			12 13			12 45					13 13
Fleet	d			12 19								13 19
Reading 7	d							12c46				
Basingstoke	a			12 34	12 47		12 58	13 08				13 34
	d			12 36	12 49		13 00	13 10				13 36
Micheldever	d						13 10					
Winchester	d	12 33		12 52	13 05		13 19	13 25		13 33		13 52
Shawford	d			12 57								13 57
Romsey	d					13 07						
Chandlers Ford	d					13 14						
Eastleigh 3	a			13 02		13 20	13 27					14 02
	d			13 03		13 21	13 28					14 03
Hedge End	d						13 34					
Botley	d						13 38					
Fareham	d		12 47				13 48				13 47	
Portchester	d						13 53					
Cosham	d						13 58					
Hilsea	a						14 03					
Fratton	a						14 07					
Portsmouth & Southsea	a						14 11					
Portsmouth Harbour	a						14 18					
Southampton Airport Parkwy ✈	d	12 42		13 08	13 14	13 25		13 33		13 42		14 08
Swaythling	d					13 28						
St Denys	d					13 31						
Southampton Central	a	12 49	13 08	13 17	13 22	13 36		13 41		13 49	14 08	14 17
	d	12 51	13 10	13 30	13 24	13 38		13 43		13 51	14 10	14 30
Millbrook (Hants)	d					13 40						
Redbridge	d					13 44						
Romsey	d		13 21			13 52					14 21	
Mottisfont & Dunbridge	d					13 57						
Dean	d					14 02						
Salisbury	a		13 40			14 15					14 40	
Totton	d			13 35								14 35
Ashurst New Forest	d			13 40								14 40
Beaulieu Road	d			13 44								
Brockenhurst 3	a	13 04		13 51	13 37			13 57		14 04		14 51
	d	13 05		14 16	13 38			13 58	13 59	14 05		15 16
Lymington Town	d								14 07			
Lymington Pier	a								14 09			
Yarmouth (IOW)	a								*15 15*			
Sway	d			14 20								15 20
New Milton	d			14 25	13 45							15 25
Hinton Admiral	d			14 29								15 29
Christchurch	d			14 34	13 52							15 34
Pokesdown	d			14 38	13 56							15 38
Bournemouth	a	13 20		14 42	14 00			14 11		14 20		15 42
	d	13 24		14 43	14 04					14 24		15 43
Branksome	d	13 29		14 48						14 29		15 48
Parkstone (Dorset)	d	13 32		14 51						14 32		15 51
Poole 4	a	13 36		14 55	14 13					14 36		15 55
	d	13 37			14 14					14 37		
Hamworthy	d	13 42			14 19					14 42		
Holton Heath	d				14 23							
Wareham	d	13 49			14 28					14 49		
Wool	d				14 35							
Moreton (Dorset)	d				14 41							
Dorchester South	d	14 05			14 49					15 05		
Dorchester West	d											
Upwey	d				14 55							
Weymouth	a	14 13			15 00					15 13		

b arr. 1139 c arr. 1239

Table 158

Saturdays

London - Basingstoke, Southampton, Romsey Lymington, Bournemouth and Weymouth

Station		SW 1	SW ◇1	SW 1	SW 1	XC ◇1	SW 1	SW ◇1	GW ◇	SW 1	SW 1	SW ◇1
London Waterloo 15 ⊖	d		13 05		13 09			13 35		13 39		14 05
Clapham Junction 10	d		13u12							13u46		14u12
Woking	d				13 35			14 00				
Farnborough (Main)	d				13 45					14 13		
Fleet	d									14 19		
Reading 7	d					13b46						
Basingstoke	a		13 47		13 58	14 08				14 34		14 47
	d		13 49		14 00	14 10				14 36		14 49
Micheldever	d				14 10							
Winchester	d		14 05		14 19	14 25		14 33		14 52		15 05
Shawford	d									14 57		
Romsey	d			14 07								
Chandlers Ford	d			14 14								
Eastleigh 3	a			14 20	14 27					15 02		
	d			14 21	14 28					15 03		
Hedge End	d				14 34							
Botley	d				14 38							
Fareham	d				14 48				14 47			
Portchester	d				14 53							
Cosham	d				14 58							
Hilsea	a				15 03							
Fratton	a				15 07							
Portsmouth & Southsea	a				15 11							
Portsmouth Harbour	a				15 18							
Southampton Airport Parkwy ✈	d		14 14	14 25		14 34		14 42		15 08		15 14
Swaythling	d			14 28								
St Denys	d			14 31								
Southampton Central	a		14 22	14 36		14 41		14 49	15 08	15 17		15 22
	d		14 24	14 38		14 43		14 51	15 10	15 30		15 24
Millbrook (Hants)	d			14 40								
Redbridge	d			14 44								
Romsey	d			14 52					15 21			
Mottisfont & Dunbridge	d			14 57								
Dean	d			15 02								
Salisbury	a			15 15					15 40			
Totton	d									15 35		
Ashurst New Forest	d									15 40		
Beaulieu Road	d									15 44		
Brockenhurst 3	a		14 37			14 57		15 04		15 51		15 37
	d	14 29	14 38			14 58	14 59	15 05		16 16	15 29	15 38
Lymington Town	d	14 37					15 07				15 37	
Lymington Pier	a	14 39					15 09				15 39	
Yarmouth (IOW)	a						*15 55*				*16 35*	
Sway	d									16 20		
New Milton	d		14 45							16 25		15 45
Hinton Admiral	d									16 29		
Christchurch	d		14 52							16 34		15 52
Pokesdown	d		14 56							16 38		15 56
Bournemouth	a		15 00			15 11		15 20		16 42		16 00
	d		15 04					15 24		16 43		16 04
Branksome	d							15 29		16 48		
Parkstone (Dorset)	d							15 32		16 51		
Poole 4	a		15 13					15 36		16 55		16 13
	d		15 14					15 37				16 14
Hamworthy	d		15 19					15 42				16 19
Holton Heath	d		15 23									16 23
Wareham	d		15 28					15 49				16 28
Wool	d		15 35									16 35
Moreton (Dorset)	d		15 41									16 41
Dorchester South	d		15 49					16 05				16 49
Dorchester West	d											
Upwey	d		15 55									16 55
Weymouth	a		16 00					16 13				17 00

Station		SW 1	SW 1	XC ◇1	SW 1	SW 1	GW	SW ◇1	GW ◇	SW 1	SW ◇1
London Waterloo 15 ⊖	d		14 09					14 35		14 39	15 05
Clapham Junction 10	d									14u46	15u12
Woking	d		14 35					15 00			
Farnborough (Main)	d		14 45							15 13	
Fleet	d									15 19	
Reading 7	d			14c46							
Basingstoke	a		14 58	15 08						15 34	15 47
	d		15 00	15 10						15 36	15 49
Micheldever	d		15 10								
Winchester	d		15 19	15 25				15 33		15 52	16 05
Shawford	d									15 57	
Romsey	d	15 07									
Chandlers Ford	d	15 14									
Eastleigh 3	a	15 20	15 27							16 02	
	d	15 21	15 28							16 03	
Hedge End	d		15 34								
Botley	d		15 38								
Fareham	d		15 48						15 47		
Portchester	d		15 53								
Cosham	d		15 58								
Hilsea	a		16 03								
Fratton	a		16 07								
Portsmouth & Southsea	a		16 11								
Portsmouth Harbour	a		16 18								
Southampton Airport Parkwy ✈	d	15 25		15 33				15 42		16 08	16 14
Swaythling	d	15 28									
St Denys	d	15 31									
Southampton Central	a	15 36		15 41				15 49	16 08	16 17	16 22
	d	15 38		15 43				15 51	16 10	16 30	16 24
Millbrook (Hants)	d	15 40									
Redbridge	d	15 44									
Romsey	d	15 52							16 21		
Mottisfont & Dunbridge	d	15 57									
Dean	d	16 02									
Salisbury	a	16 15							16 40		
Totton	d									16 35	
Ashurst New Forest	d									16 40	
Beaulieu Road	d										
Brockenhurst 3	a			15 57				16 04		16 51	16 37
	d			15 58	15 59	16 29		16 05		17 16	16 38
Lymington Town	d				16 07	16 37					
Lymington Pier	a				16 09	16 39					
Yarmouth (IOW)	a				*17 15*						
Sway	d									17 20	
New Milton	d									17 25	16 45
Hinton Admiral	d									17 29	
Christchurch	d									17 34	16 52
Pokesdown	d									17 38	16 56
Bournemouth	a			16 11				16 20		17 42	17 00
	d							16 24		17 43	17 04
Branksome	d							16 29		17 48	
Parkstone (Dorset)	d							16 32		17 51	
Poole 4	a							16 36		17 55	17 13
	d							16 37			17 14
Hamworthy	d							16 42			17 19
Holton Heath	d										17 23
Wareham	d							16 49			17 28
Wool	d										17 35
Moreton (Dorset)	d										17 41
Dorchester South	d							17 05			17 49
Dorchester West	d						16 58				
Upwey	d										17 55
Weymouth	a						17 09	17 13			18 00

b arr. 1339 c arr. 1439

London - Basingstoke, Southampton, Romsey Lymington, Bournemouth and Weymouth

		SW	SW	XC	SW	SW	GW	SW	SW	SW	SW	SW	XC	SW	SW	GW	SW	SW	SW	SW	SW	SW	XC
		1	1	◇1	1	◇1	1	1	1	◇1	1	1	◇1	1	◇1	◇	1	1	1	◇1	1	1	◇1
				⊼		⊡				⊡			⊼		⊡					⊡			⊼
London Waterloo 15 ⊖	d		15 09			15 35		15 39		16 05		16 09			16 35			16 39		17 05		17 09	
Clapham Junction 10	d							15u46		16u12								16u46		17u12			
Woking	d		15 35			16 00						16 35			17 00							17 35	
Farnborough (Main)	d		15 45					16 13				16 45						17 13				17 45	
Fleet	d							16 19										17 19					
Reading 7	d			15b46									16c46										17e46
Basingstoke	a		15 58	16 08				16 34		16 47		16 58	17 08					17 34		17 47		17 58	18 08
	d		16 00	16 10				16 36		16 49		17 00	17 10				17 24	17 36		17 49		18 00	18 10
Micheldever	d		16 10									17 10					17 34					18 10	
Winchester	d		16 19	16 25		16 33		16 52		17 05		17 19	17 25		17 33		17 43	17 52		18 05		18 19	18 25
Shawford	d							16 57									17 48	17 57					
Romsey	d	16 07									17 07										18 07		
Chandlers Ford	d	16 14									17 14										18 14		
Eastleigh 8	a	16 20	16 27					17 02			17 20	17 27					17 53	18 02			18 20	18 27	
	d	16 21	16 28					17 03			17 21	17 28					17 54	18 03			18 21	18 28	
Hedge End	d		16 34									17 34										18 34	
Botley	d		16 38									17 38										18 38	
Fareham	d		16 48				16 47					17 48				17 47						18 48	
Portchester	d		16 53									17 53										18 53	
Cosham	d		16 58									17 58										18 58	
Hilsea	a		17 03									18 03										19 03	
Fratton	a		17 07									18 07										19 07	
Portsmouth & Southsea	a		17 11									18 11										19 11	
Portsmouth Harbour	a		17 18									18 18										19 18	
Southampton Airport Parkway ✈	d	16 25		16 33		16 42		17 08		17 14	17 25		17 33		17 42		17 59	18 08		18 14	18 25		18 33
Swaythling	d	16 28									17 28						18 01				18 28		
St Denys	d	16 31									17 31						18 04				18 31		
Southampton Central	a	16 36		16 41		16 49	17 08	17 17		17 22	17 36		17 41		17 49	18 08	18 10	18 17		18 22	18 36		18 40
	d	16 38		16 43		16 51	17 10	17 30		17 24	17 38		17 43		17 51	18 10		18 30		18 24	18 38		18 43
Millbrook (Hants)	d	16 40									17 40										18 40		
Redbridge	d	16 44									17 44										18 44		
Romsey	d	16 52					17 21				17 52					18 21					19 00		
Mottisfont & Dunbridge	d	16 57									17 57										19 05		
Dean	d	17 02									18 02										19 10		
Salisbury	a	17 15					17 40				18 15					18 40					19 23		
Totton	d							17 35										18 35					
Ashurst New Forest	d							17 40										18 40					
Beaulieu Road	d							17 44															
Brockenhurst 8	a			16 57		17 04		17 51		17 37			17 57		18 04			18 51		18 37			18 57
	d			16 58	16 59	17 05		18 16	17 29	17 38			17 58	17 59	18 05			19 16	18 29	18 38			18 58
Lymington Town	d				17 07				17 37					18 07					18 37				
Lymington Pier	a				17 09				17 39					18 09					18 39				
Yarmouth (IOW)	a				*17 55*				*18 45*														
Sway	d							18 20										19 20					
New Milton	d							18 25		17 45								19 25		18 45			
Hinton Admiral	d							18 29										19 29					
Christchurch	d							18 34		17 52								19 34		18 52			
Pokesdown	d							18 38		17 56								19 38		18 56			
Bournemouth	a			17 11		17 20		18 42		18 00			18 11		18 20			19 42		19 00			19 11
	d					17 24		18 43		18 04					18 24			19 43		19 04			
Branksome	d					17 29		18 48							18 29			19 48					
Parkstone (Dorset)	d					17 32		18 51							18 32			19 51					
Poole 4	a					17 36		18 55		18 13					18 36			19 55		19 13			
	d					17 37				18 14					18 37					19 14			
Hamworthy	d					17 42				18 19					18 42					19 19			
Holton Heath	d									18 23										19 23			
Wareham	d					17 49				18 28					18 49					19 28			
Wool	d									18 35										19 35			
Moreton (Dorset)	d									18 41										19 41			
Dorchester South	d					18 05				18 49					19 05					19 49			
Dorchester West	d																						
Upwey	d									18 55										19 55			
Weymouth	a					18 13				19 00					19 13					20 00			

b arr. 1539 c arr. 1639 e arr. 1739

London - Basingstoke, Southampton, Romsey Lymington, Bournemouth and Weymouth

		GW	SW	SW	GW	SW	GW	SW	SW	SW	SW	XC	SW	SW	GW	SW	SW	SW	SW	SW	XC	SW	SW
		◇	1	1		◇1	◇	1	◇1	1	1	◇1	1	◇1	◇	1	1	◇1	1	1	◇1	1	◇1
						⊡			⊡			⊼		⊡				⊡			⊼		⊡
London Waterloo 15 ⊖	d					17 35		17 39	18 05		18 09			18 35		18 39		19 05		19 09			19 35
Clapham Junction 10	d							17u46	18u12							18u46		19u12					
Woking	d					18 00					18 35			19 00						19 35			20 00
Farnborough (Main)	d							18 13			18 45					19 13				19 45			
Fleet	d							18 19								19 19							
Reading 7	d											18b46									19c46		
Basingstoke	a							18 34	18 47		18 58	19 08				19 34		19 47		19 58	20 08		
	d							18 36	18 49		19 00	19 10				19 36		19 49		20 00	20 10		
Micheldever	d										19 10									20 10			
Winchester	d					18 33		18 52	19 05		19 19	19 25		19 33		19 52		20 05		20 19	20 25		20 33
Shawford	d							18 57								19 57							
Romsey	d									19 07									20 07				
Chandlers Ford	d									19 14									20 14				
Eastleigh 8	a							19 02		19 20	19 27					20 02			20 20	20 27			
	d							19 03		19 21	19 28					20 03			20 21	20 28			
Hedge End	d										19 34									20 34			
Botley	d										19 38									20 38			
Fareham	d	18 15					18 47				19 48				19 47					20 48			
Portchester	d										19 53									20 53			
Cosham	d										19 58									20 58			
Hilsea	a										20 03									21 03			
Fratton	a										20 07									21 07			
Portsmouth & Southsea	a										20 11									21 11			
Portsmouth Harbour	a										20 18									21 18			
Southampton Airport Parkway ✈	d					18 42		19 08	19 14	19 25		19 33		19 42		20 08		20 14	20 25		20 33		20 42
Swaythling	d									19 28									20 28				
St Denys	d									19 31									20 31				
Southampton Central	a	18 43				18 49	19 08	19 17	19 22	19 36		19 41		19 49	20 09	20 17		20 22	20 36		20 41		20 49
	d	18 45				18 51	19 10	19 30	19 24	19 38		19 43		19 51	20 10	20 30		20 24	20 38		20 43		20 51
Millbrook (Hants)	d									19 40									20 40				
Redbridge	d									19 44									20 44				
Romsey	d	18 56					19 21			19 52					20 21				20 52				
Mottisfont & Dunbridge	d									19 57									20 57				
Dean	d									20 02									21 02				
Salisbury	a	19 15					19 40			20 15					20 40				21 15				
Totton	d							19 35								20 35							
Ashurst New Forest	d							19 40								20 40							
Beaulieu Road	d							19 44															
Brockenhurst 8	a					19 04		19 51	19 37			19 57		20 04		20 51		20 37			20 57		21 04
	d		18 59	19 29		19 05		20 16	19 38			19 58	19 59	20 05		21 16	20 29	20 38			20 58	20 59	21 05
Lymington Town	d		19 07	19 37									20 07				20 37					21 07	
Lymington Pier	a		19 09	19 39									20 09				20 39					21 09	
Yarmouth (IOW)	a		*19 55*														*21 35*						
Sway	d							20 20								21 20							
New Milton	d							20 25	19 45							21 25		20 45					
Hinton Admiral	d							20 29								21 29							
Christchurch	d							20 34	19 52							21 34		20 52					
Pokesdown	d							20 38	19 56							21 38		20 56					
Bournemouth	a					19 20		20 42	20 00			20 11		20 20		21 42		21 00			21 11		21 20
	d					19 24		20 43	20 04					20 24		21 43		21 04					21 24
Branksome	d					19 29		20 48						20 29		21 48							21 29
Parkstone (Dorset)	d					19 32		20 51						20 32		21 51							21 32
Poole 4	a					19 36		20 55	20 13					20 36		21 55		21 13					21 36
	d					19 37			20 14					20 37				21 14					21 37
Hamworthy	d					19 42			20 19					20 42				21 19					21 42
Holton Heath	d								20 23														
Wareham	d					19 49			20 28					20 49				21 28					21 49
Wool	d								20 35									21 35					21 55
Moreton (Dorset)	d								20 41									21 41					22 01
Dorchester South	d					20 05			20 49					21 05				21 49					22 09
Dorchester West	d				19 54																		
Upwey	d				20 01				20 55									21 55					22 16
Weymouth	a				20 08	20 13			21 00					21 13				22 00					22 20

b arr. 1839 c arr. 1939

Table 158

Saturdays

London - Basingstoke, Southampton, Romsey Lymington, Bournemouth and Weymouth

		GW	SW	GW	SW	SW	SW	SW	XC	SW	SW	SW	SW
		◇	1		1	◇1	1	1	◇1	1	◇1	1	1
London Waterloo 15 ⊖	d		19 39			20 05		20 09			20 35	20 39	20 42
Clapham Junction 10	d		19u46			20u12						20u46	
Woking	d							20 35			21 00		21 19
Farnborough (Main)	d		20 13					20 45				21 13	21 33
Fleet	d		20 19									21 19	21 38
Reading 7	d								20b46				
Basingstoke	a		20 34			20 47		20 58	21 08			21 34	21 58
	d		20 36			20 49		21 00	21 10			21 36	22 00
Micheldever	d							21 10				21 46	22 10
Winchester	d		20 52			21 05		21 19	21 25		21 33	21 55	22 19
Shawford	d		20 57									22 00	
Romsey	d						21 07						
Chandlers Ford	d						21 14						
Eastleigh 3	a		21 02				21 20	21 27				22 05	
	d		21 03				21 21	21 28				22 06	
Hedge End	d							21 34					22 36
Botley	d							21 38					22 40
Fareham	d	20 47						21 48					22 48
Portchester	d							21 53					22 53
Cosham	d							21 58					22 58
Hilsea	a							22 03					23 03
Fratton	a							22 07					23 07
Portsmouth & Southsea	a							22 11					23 11
Portsmouth Harbour	a							22 18					23 18
Southampton Airport Parkwy ✈	d		21 08			21 14	21 25		21 34		21 42	22 11	
Swaythling	d						21 28						
St Denys	d						21 31						
Southampton Central	a	21 10	21 17			21 22	21 36		21 41		21 49	22 18	
	d	21 10		21 27		21 24	21 38		21 43		21 51		
Millbrook (Hants)	d						21 40						
Redbridge	d						21 44						
Romsey	d	21 21		21 38			21 52						
Mottisfont & Dunbridge	d						21 57						
Dean	d						22 02						
Salisbury	a	21 41		22 03			22 15						
Totton	d					21 29							
Ashurst New Forest	d					21 34							
Beaulieu Road	d												
Brockenhurst 3	a					21 42			21 57		22 04		
	d				21 29	21 43			21 58	21 59	22 05		
Lymington Town	d				21 37					22 07			
Lymington Pier	a				21 39					22 09			
Yarmouth (IOW)	a									*23 00*			
Sway	d					21 47							
New Milton	d					21 52							
Hinton Admiral	d					21 56							
Christchurch	d					22 01							
Pokesdown	d					22 05							
Bournemouth	a					22 09			22 15		22 20		
	d					22 10					22 24		
Branksome	d					22 15					22 29		
Parkstone (Dorset)	d					22 18					22 32		
Poole 4	a					22 23					22 36		
	d										22 37		
Hamworthy	d										22 42		
Holton Heath	d												
Wareham	d										22 49		
Wool	d										22 55		
Moreton (Dorset)	d										23 01		
Dorchester South	d										23 09		
Dorchester West	d												
Upwey	d										23 16		
Weymouth	a										23 20		

		SW	SW	XC	SW	SW	SW	SW	SW	XC	SW	SW
		◇1	1	◇1	◇1	1	1	◇1	1	◇1	◇1	1
London Waterloo 15 ⊖	d	21 05			21 35	21 39	21 42	22 05			22 35	
Clapham Junction 10	d	21u12				21u46		22u12				
Woking	d	21 32			22 00		22 19	22 32			23 00	
Farnborough (Main)	d					22 13	22 33					
Fleet	d					22 19	22 38					
Reading 7	d			21c46						22e48		
Basingstoke	a	21 51		22 08		22 34	22 58	22 51		23 11		
	d	21 52		22 10		22 36	23 00	22 52		23 13		
Micheldever	d					22s46	23 10					
Winchester	d	22 09		22 25	22 33	22 56	23 19	23 09		23 28	23 33	
Shawford	d					23 00	23 24					
Romsey	d		22 07						23 09			23 00
Chandlers Ford	d		22 14						23 16			
Eastleigh 3	a	22 17	22 21			23 06		23 17	23 22			23 35
	d	22 18	22 22			23 07		23 18	23 23			23 37
Hedge End	d						23 36					
Botley	d						23 40					
Fareham	d						23 48					
Portchester	d						23 53					
Cosham	d						23 59					
Hilsea	a						00 04					
Fratton	a						00 08					
Portsmouth & Southsea	a						00 11					
Portsmouth Harbour	a						00 16					
Southampton Airport Parkwy ✈	d	22 22	22 26	22 33	22 42	23 11		23 22	23 27	23 36	23 42	
Swaythling	d		22 29						23 30			
St Denys	d		22 32						23 33			
Southampton Central	a	22 29	22 36	22 41	22 49	23 18		23 29	23 38	23 43	23 49	
	d	22 31	22 38	22 43	22 51			23 31	23 40		23 51	
Millbrook (Hants)	d		22 41						23 42			
Redbridge	d		22 45						23 46			
Romsey	d		22a52						23 57			23a49
Mottisfont & Dunbridge	d								00 02			
Dean	d								00 08			
Salisbury	a								00 20			
Totton	d	22 36						23 36				
Ashurst New Forest	d	22 41						23 41				
Beaulieu Road	d											
Brockenhurst 3	a	22 49		22 57	23 04			23 49			00 04	
	d	22 50		23 00	23 05			23 50			00 05	
Lymington Town	d											
Lymington Pier	a											
Yarmouth (IOW)	a											
Sway	d	22 54						23 54				
New Milton	d	22 59						23 59				
Hinton Admiral	d	23 03						00 03				
Christchurch	d	23 08						00 08				
Pokesdown	d	23 12						00 11				
Bournemouth	a	23 16		23 21	23 25			00 15			00 22	
	d	23 17			23 29			00 17			00 24	
Branksome	d	23 22			23 35			00 23			00 29	
Parkstone (Dorset)	d	23 25			23 38			00 26			00 32	
Poole 4	a	23 29			23 41			00 30			00 36	
	d				23 42							
Hamworthy	d				23 47							
Holton Heath	d											
Wareham	d				23 54							
Wool	d				00 02							
Moreton (Dorset)	d				00 08							
Dorchester South	d				00 15							
Dorchester West	d											
Upwey	d				00 22							
Weymouth	a				00 26							

b arr. 2039 c arr. 2139 e arr. 2241

Table 158

Saturdays

London - Basingstoke, Southampton, Romsey Lymington, Bournemouth and Weymouth

		SW	SW
		◇1	1
London Waterloo 15 ⊖	d	23 05	23 39
Clapham Junction 10	d	23u12	23u46
Woking	d	23 32	00 09
Farnborough (Main)	d		00 19
Fleet	d		00 25
Reading 7	d		
Basingstoke	a	23 51	00 36
	d	23 52	00 38
Micheldever	d	00 02	
Winchester	d	00 12	00 54
Shawford	d		
Romsey	d		
Chandlers Ford	d		
Eastleigh 3	a	00 20	01 02
	d	00 21	01 03
Hedge End	d		
Botley	d		
Fareham	d		
Portchester	d		
Cosham	d		
Hilsea	a		
Fratton	a		
Portsmouth & Southsea	a		
Portsmouth Harbour	a		
Southampton Airport Parkwy ✈	d	00 25	01 08
Swaythling	d		
St Denys	d	00s29	
Southampton Central	a	00 34	01 15
	d	00 36	
Millbrook (Hants)	d		
Redbridge	d		
Romsey	d		
Mottisfont & Dunbridge	d		
Dean	d		
Salisbury	a		
Totton	d	00s42	
Ashurst New Forest	d		
Beaulieu Road	d		
Brockenhurst 3	a	00s52	
	d	00s53	
Lymington Town	d		
Lymington Pier	a		
Sway	d		
New Milton	d	01s00	
Hinton Admiral	d		
Christchurch	d	01s07	
Pokesdown	d	01s11	
Bournemouth	a	01 15	
	d	01 16	
Branksome	d	01s21	
Parkstone (Dorset)	d	01s24	
Poole 4	a	01 29	
	d		
Hamworthy	d		
Holton Heath	d		
Wareham	d		
Wool	d		
Moreton (Dorset)	d		
Dorchester South	d		
Dorchester West	d		
Upwey	d		
Weymouth	a		

London - Basingstoke, Southampton, Romsey Lymington, Bournemouth and Weymouth

		SW	SW	SW	SW	SW	SW	SW	SW	SW	GW	SW	SW	SW	SW	SW	SW	GW	SW	SW	SW	SW	GW
		◇1	◇1	1	◇1	◇1	1	1	1	1		1	1	1	1	1	1	C	1	1	◇1	1	■
		▭	▭		▭																		
London Waterloo 15 ⊖	d	21p35	22p05		22p35	23p05		23p39	00 05												07 54		
Clapham Junction 10	d		22b12			23b12		23b46	00u12												08u03		
Woking	d	22p00	22p32		23p00	23p32		00 09	00 36												08 28		
Farnborough (Main)	d							00 19															
Fleet	d							00 25															
Reading 7	d																						
Basingstoke	a		22p51			23p51		00 36	00 55												08 46		
	d		22p52			23p52		00 38	00 57			07 48									08 48		
Micheldever	d					00 02						07 58									08 58		
Winchester	d	22p33	23p09		23p33	00 12		00 54	01 13			08 08									09 08		
Shawford	d											08 12											
Romsey	d			23p09							08 19									08 35			
Chandlers Ford	d			23p16																08 42			
Eastleigh 3	a		23p17	23p22		00 20		01 02	01 21			08 18	>							08 47	09 18	>	
	d		23p18	23p23		00 21	00 30	01 03	01 22			08 22	08 26							08 54	09 22	09 26	
Hedge End	d						00s36						08 32									09 32	
Botley	d						00s39						08 36									09 36	
Fareham	d						00s48			07 44			08 44									09 44	09 32
Portchester	d						00s53			07 49			08 49									09 49	
Cosham	d						00s58			07 54			08 54									09 54	
Hilsea	a									08 00			09 00									10 00	
Fratton	a						01s05			08 04			09 04									10 04	
Portsmouth & Southsea	a						01s08			08 08			09 08									10 10	
Portsmouth Harbour	a						01 12			08 13			09 13									10 15	
Southampton Airport Parkwy ✈	d	22p42	23p22	23p27	23p42	00 25		01 08	01 27			08 27								08 58	09 27		
Swaythling	d			23p30																09 01			
St Denys	d			23p33		00s29														09 04			
Southampton Central	a	22p49	23p29	23p38	23p49	00 34		01 15	01 36		08 29	08 34								09 09	09 34		09 53
	d	22p51	23p31	23p40	23p51	00 36			01 37		08 31	08 35							09 04	09 10	09 35		09 54
Millbrook (Hants)	d			23p42																09 13			
Redbridge	d			23p46																09 16			
Romsey	d			23p57																09 24			10 05
Mottisfont & Dunbridge	d			00 02																09 29			
Dean	d			00 08																09 35			
Salisbury	a			00 20																09 49			10 24
Totton	d		23p36			00s42			01s43			08 41									09 41		
Ashurst New Forest	d		23p41									08 45									09 45		
Beaulieu Road	d											08 50									09 50		
Brockenhurst 3	a	23p04	23p49		00 04	00s52			01s53			08 56							09 17		09 56		
	d	23p05	23p50		00 05	00s53			01s54			08 57			08 59	09 29	09 59		09 18		09 57		
Lymington Town	d														09 07	09 37	10 07						
Lymington Pier	a														09 09	09 39	10 09						
Yarmouth (IOW)	a															*09 55*							
Sway	d		23p54									09 01									10 01		
New Milton	d		23p59			01s00			02s01			09 06							09 25		10 06		
Hinton Admiral	d		00 03									09 10									10 10		
Christchurch	d		00 08			01s07			02s08			09 15									10 15		
Pokesdown	d		00 11			01s11			02s12			09 19									10 19		
Bournemouth	a	23p25	00 15		00 22	01 15			02 16			09 23							09 35		10 23		
	d	23p29	00 17		00 24	01 16						09 25		08 40					09 40		10 25		
Branksome	d	23p35	00 23		00 29	01s21								08 45					09 45				
Parkstone (Dorset)	d	23p38	00 26		00 32	01s24								08 48					09 48				
Poole 4	a	23p41	00 30		00 36	01 29						09 34		08 51					09 51		10 34		
	d	23p42												08 52					09 52				
Hamworthy	d	23p47												08 57					09 57				
Holton Heath	d																						
Wareham	d	23p54												09 04					10 04				
Wool	d	00 02												09 11					10 11				
Moreton (Dorset)	d	00 08												09 17					10 17				
Dorchester South	d	00 15												09 25					10 25				
Dorchester West	d																	10 13					
Upwey	d	00 22												09 32					10 32				
Weymouth	a	00 26												09 36				10 27	10 36				

C until 5 September

b previous night, stops to pick up only

Table 158

Sundays

London - Basingstoke, Southampton, Romsey Lymington, Bournemouth and Weymouth

		SW	SW		SW	SW	SW	SW	XC	GW	SW	SW	SW	SW	SW	SW	XC	GW	SW	SW	SW	SW	SW	SW
		◇1	1		1	◇1	1	1	◇1	A	◇1	1	1	◇1	1	1	◇1	◇	◇1	1	1	◇1	1	1
									⊼								⊼		▭					
London Waterloo 15 ⊖	d	08 35				08 54					09 35			09 54					10 35			10 54		
Clapham Junction 10	d	08u45				09u03					09u45			10u03					10u45			11u04		
Woking	d	09 09				09 28					10 09			10 28					11 07			11 28		
Farnborough (Main)	d																							
Fleet	d																							
Reading 7	d								09 51								10b51							
Basingstoke	a	09 28				09 46			10 09		10 28			10 46			11 09		11 26			11 46		
	d	09 29				09 48			10 10		10 29			10 48			11 10		11 28			11 48		
Micheldever	d					09 58								10 58								11 58		
Winchester	d	09 46				10 08			10 25		10 46			11 08			11 25		11 44			12 08		
Shawford	d					10 12																12 12		
Romsey	d		09 35									10 35								11 35				
Chandlers Ford	d		09 42									10 42								11 42				
Eastleigh 3	a		09 48			10 18	>					10 48		11 18	>					11 48		12 18	>	
	d		09 54			10 22	10 26					10 54		11 22	11 26					11 54		12 22	12 26	
Hedge End	d						10 32								11 32								12 32	
Botley	d						10 36								11 36								12 36	
Fareham	d						10 44								11 44			11 32					12 44	
Portchester	d						10 49								11 49								12 49	
Cosham	d						10 54								11 54								12 54	
Hilsea	a						11 00								12 00								13 00	
Fratton	a						11 05								12 04								13 04	
Portsmouth & Southsea	a						11 10								12 08								13 08	
Portsmouth Harbour	a			11 14											12 13								13 13	
Southampton Airport Parkwy ✈	d	09 55	09 58			10 27			10 34		10 55	10 58		11 27			11 34		11 53	11 58		12 27		
Swaythling	d		10 01									11 01								12 01				
St Denys	d		10 04									11 04								12 04				
Southampton Central	a	10 02	10 09			10 34			10 42		11 02	11 09		11 34			11 42	11 53	11 59	12 09		12 34		
	d	10 03	10 10			10 35			10 45		11 03	11 10		11 35			11 45	11 54	12 03	12 10		12 35		
Millbrook (Hants)	d		10 13									11 13								12 13				
Redbridge	d		10 16									11 16								12 16				
Romsey	d		10 24									11 24						12 06		12 24				
Mottisfont & Dunbridge	d											11 29												
Dean	d											11 35												
Salisbury	a		10 42									11 48						12 24		12 42				
Totton	d					10 41								11 41								12 41		
Ashurst New Forest	d					10 45								11 45								12 45		
Beaulieu Road	d					10 50								11 50								12 50		
Brockenhurst 3	a	10 17				10 56			11 02		11 17			11 56			12 02		12 16			12 56		
	d	10 18			10 29	10 57		10 59	11 02		11 18		11 29	11 57		11 59	12 03		12 17		12 29	12 57		12 59
Lymington Town	d				10 37			11 07					11 37			12 07					12 37			13 07
Lymington Pier	a				10 39			11 09					11 39			12 09					12 39			13 09
Yarmouth (IOW)	a							*11 55*					*12 35*			*13 15*								*13 55*
Sway	d					11 01								12 01								13 01		
New Milton	d	10 25				11 06					11 25			12 06					12 24			13 06		
Hinton Admiral	d					11 10								12 10								13 10		
Christchurch	d					11 15								12 15								13 15		
Pokesdown	d					11 19								12 19								13 19		
Bournemouth	a	10 35				11 23			11 27		11 35			12 23			12 27		12 35			13 23		
	d	10 40				11 25					11 40			12 25					12 40			13 25		
Branksome	d	10 45									11 45								12 45					
Parkstone (Dorset)	d	10 48									11 48								12 48					
Poole 4	a	10 51				11 34					11 51			12 34					12 51			13 34		
	d	10 52									11 52								12 52					
Hamworthy	d	10 57									11 57								12 57					
Holton Heath	d																							
Wareham	d	11 04									12 04								13 04					
Wool	d	11 11									12 11								13 11					
Moreton (Dorset)	d	11 17									12 17								13 17					
Dorchester South	d	11 25									12 25								13 25					
Dorchester West	d									11 25														
Upwey	d	11 32									12 32								13 32					
Weymouth	a	11 36								11 41	12 36								13 36					

A until 5 September

b arr. 1042

Table 158

Sundays

London - Basingstoke, Southampton, Romsey Lymington, Bournemouth and Weymouth

		XC	GW	SW	SW	SW	SW	SW	SW	XC	GW	SW	SW	SW	SW	SW	SW	XC	GW	SW	GW
		◇1	◇	◇1	1	1	◇1	1	1	◇1	◇	◇1	1	1	◇1	1	1	◇1	◇	1	B
		🍴		🍴			🍴			🍴		🍴			🍴			🍴			
London Waterloo 15 ⊖	d			11 35			11 54					12 35			12 54						
Clapham Junction 10	d			11u45			12u04					12u42			13u03						
Woking	d			12 07			12 28					13 07			13 28						
Farnborough (Main)	d																				
Fleet	d																				
Reading 7	d	11b51								12c51								13e51			
Basingstoke	a	12 09		12 26			12 46			13 09		13 26			13 46			14 09			
	d	12 10		12 28			12 48			13 10		13 28			13 48			14 10			
Micheldever	d						12 58								13 58						
Winchester	d	12 25		12 44			13 08			13 25		13 44			14 08			14 25			
Shawford	d														14 12						
Romsey	d				12 35								13 35								
Chandlers Ford	d				12 42								13 42								
Eastleigh 3	a				12 48		13 18	>					13 48		14 18	>					
	d				12 54		13 22	13 26					13 54		14 22	14 26					
Hedge End	d							13 32								14 32					
Botley	d							13 36								14 36					
Fareham	d		12 32					13 44			13 32					14 44			14 32		
Portchester	d							13 49								14 49					
Cosham	d							13 54								14 54					
Hilsea	a							14 00								15 00					
Fratton	a							14 04								15 04					
Portsmouth & Southsea	a							14 08								15 08					
Portsmouth Harbour	a							14 13								15 13					
Southampton Airport Parkwy ✈	d	12 34		12 53	12 58		13 27			13 34		13 53	13 58		14 27			14 34			
Swaythling	d				13 01								14 01								
St Denys	d				13 04								14 04								
Southampton Central	a	12 42	12 53	13 00	13 09		13 34			13 42	13 53	14 00	14 09		14 34			14 42	14 53		
	d	12 45	12 54	13 03	13 10		13 35			13 45	13 54	14 03	14 10		14 35			14 45	14 54		
Millbrook (Hants)	d				13 13								14 13								
Redbridge	d				13 16								14 16								
Romsey	d		13 06		13 24						14 06		14 24						15 06		
Mottisfont & Dunbridge	d				13 29																
Dean	d				13 35																
Salisbury	a		13 24		13 48						14 24		14 42						15 24		
Totton	d						13 41								14 41						
Ashurst New Forest	d						13 45								14 45						
Beaulieu Road	d						13 50								14 50						
Brockenhurst 3	a	13 02		13 16			13 56			14 01		14 16			14 56			15 02			
	d	13 03		13 17		13 29	13 57		13 59	14 02		14 17		14 29	14 57		14 59	15 03		15 29	
Lymington Town	d					13 37			14 07					14 37			15 07			15 37	
Lymington Pier	a					13 39			14 09					14 39			15 09			15 39	
Yarmouth (IOW)	a					*14 35*			*15 15*								*15 55*				
Sway	d						14 01								15 01						
New Milton	d			13 24			14 06					14 24			15 06						
Hinton Admiral	d						14 10								15 10						
Christchurch	d						14 15								15 15						
Pokesdown	d						14 19								15 19						
Bournemouth	a	13 27		13 35			14 23			14 27		14 35			15 23			15 27			
	d			13 40			14 25					14 40			15 25						
Branksome	d			13 45								14 45									
Parkstone (Dorset)	d			13 48								14 48									
Poole 4	a			13 51			14 34					14 51			15 34						
	d			13 52								14 52									
Hamworthy	d			13 57								14 57									
Holton Heath	d																				
Wareham	d			14 04								15 04									
Wool	d			14 11								15 11									
Moreton (Dorset)	d			14 17								15 17									
Dorchester South	d			14 25								15 25									
Dorchester West	d																				15 36
Upwey	d			14 32								15 32									
Weymouth	a			14 36								15 36									15 49

B until 5 September
b arr. 1142
c arr. 1242
e arr. 1342

Table 158

Sundays

London - Basingstoke, Southampton, Romsey Lymington, Bournemouth and Weymouth

		GW	SW	SW	SW	SW	SW	XC	GW	SW	SW	SW	SW	SW	SW	XC	GW	SW	SW	GW	SW	SW	SW	SW
									A															
			◇1	1	◇1	1	1	◇1		◇1	1	1	◇1	1	1	◇1	◇	◇1	1	◇	1	◇1	1	1
			🍴		🍴			🍴		🍴			🍴			🍴		🍴				🍴		
London Waterloo 15 ⊖	d		13 35		13 54					14 35			14 54					15 35				15 54		15 37
Clapham Junction 10	d		13u42		14u03					14u42			15u03					15u42				16u03		15 46
Woking	d		14 07		14 28					15 07			15 28					16 07				16 28		16 23
Farnborough (Main)	d																							16 36
Fleet	d																							16 42
Reading 7	d							14b51								15c51								
Basingstoke	a		14 26		14 46			15 09		15 26			15 46			16 09		16 26				16 46		16 54
	d		14 28		14 48			15 10		15 28			15 48			16 10		16 28				16 48		
Micheldever	d				14 58								15 58									16 58		
Winchester	d		14 44		15 08			15 25		15 44			16 08			16 25		16 44				17 08		
Shawford	d												16 12											
Romsey	d			14 35							15 35								16 35					
Chandlers Ford	d			14 42							15 42								16 42					
Eastleigh 3	a			14 48	15 18	>					15 48		16 18	>					16 48			17 18	>	
	d			14 54	15 22	15 26					15 54		16 22	16 26					16 54			17 22	17 26	
Hedge End	d					15 32								16 32									17 32	
Botley	d					15 36								16 36									17 36	
Fareham	d					15 44			15 32					16 44			16 32			17 03			17 44	
Portchester	d					15 49								16 49									17 49	
Cosham	d					15 54								16 54									17 54	
Hilsea	a					16 00								17 00									18 00	
Fratton	a					16 04								17 03									18 04	
Portsmouth & Southsea	a					16 08								17 08									18 08	
Portsmouth Harbour	a					16 13								17 13									18 13	
Southampton Airport Parkwy ✈	d		14 53	14 58	15 27			15 34		15 53	15 58		16 27			16 34		16 53	16 58			17 27		
Swaythling	d			15 01							16 01								17 01					
St Denys	d			15 04							16 04								17 04					
Southampton Central	a		15 00	15 09	15 34			15 42	15 53	16 00	16 09		16 34			16 42	16 53	17 00	17 09	17 24		17 34		
	d		15 03	15 10	15 35			15 45	15 54	16 03	16 10		16 35			16 45	16 54	17 03	17 10	17 26		17 35		
Millbrook (Hants)	d			15 13							16 13								17 13					
Redbridge	d			15 16							16 16								17 16					
Romsey	d			15 24					16 06		16 24						17 06		17 24	17 39				
Mottisfont & Dunbridge	d			15 29															17 29					
Dean	d			15 35															17 35					
Salisbury	a			15 48					16 24		16 42						17 24		17 48	18 01				
Totton	d				15 41								16 41									17 41		
Ashurst New Forest	d				15 45								16 45									17 45		
Beaulieu Road	d				15 50								16 50									17 50		
Brockenhurst 3	a		15 16		15 56			16 02		16 16			16 56			17 02		17 16				17 56		
	d		15 17		15 57		15 59	16 03		16 17		16 29	16 57		16 59	17 03		17 17			17 29	17 57		
Lymington Town	d						16 07					16 37			17 07						17 37			
Lymington Pier	a						16 09					16 39			17 09						17 39			
Yarmouth (IOW)	a						*17 15*								*17 55*						*18 45*			
Sway	d				16 01								17 01									18 01		
New Milton	d		15 24		16 06					16 24			17 06					17 24				18 06		
Hinton Admiral	d				16 10								17 10									18 10		
Christchurch	d				16 15								17 15									18 15		
Pokesdown	d				16 19								17 19									18 19		
Bournemouth	a		15 35		16 23			16 27		16 35			17 23			17 27		17 35				18 23		
	d		15 40		16 25					16 40			17 25					17 40				18 25		
Branksome	d		15 45							16 45								17 45						
Parkstone (Dorset)	d		15 48							16 48								17 48						
Poole 4	a		15 51		16 34					16 51			17 34					17 51				18 34		
	d		15 52							16 52								17 52						
Hamworthy	d		15 57							16 57								17 57						
Holton Heath	d																							
Wareham	d		16 04							17 04								18 04						
Wool	d		16 11							17 11								18 11						
Moreton (Dorset)	d		16 17							17 17								18 17						
Dorchester South	d		16 25							17 25								18 25						
Dorchester West	d	16 00																						
Upwey	d	16 09	16 32							17 32								18 32						
Weymouth	a	16 14	16 36							17 36								18 36						

A from 12 September
b arr. 1442
c arr. 1542

Table 158

Sundays

London - Basingstoke, Southampton, Romsey Lymington, Bournemouth and Weymouth

		SW ■	XC ◇■ ⊐P	GW ◇	SW ◇■ ⊐P	SW ■	SW ■	SW ◇■ ⊐P	SW ■	SW ■	SW ■	XC ◇■ ⊐P	GW ◇	SW ■	GW	SW ◇■ ⊐P	SW ■	GW ◇	SW ◇■ ⊐P	SW ■	SW ■	SW ■
London Waterloo 15 ⊖	d				16 35			16 54		16 37						17 35			17 54		17 37	
Clapham Junction 10	d				16u42			17u03		16 46						17u42			18u03		17 46	
Woking	d				17 07			17 28		17 23						18 07			18 28		18 23	
Farnborough (Main)	d									17 36											18 36	
Fleet	d									17 42											18 42	
Reading 7	d		16b51									17c51										
Basingstoke	a		17 09		17 26			17 46		17 54		18 09				18 26			18 46		18 54	
	d		17 10		17 28			17 48				18 10				18 28			18 48			
Micheldever	d							17 58											18 58			
Winchester	d		17 25		17 44			18 08				18 25				18 44			19 08			
Shawford	d							18 12														
Romsey	d					17 35											18 35					
Chandlers Ford	d					17 42											18 42					
Eastleigh 8	a					17 48		18 18	>								18 48		19 18	>		
	d					17 54		18 22	18 26								18 54		19 22	19 26		
Hedge End	d								18 32											19 32		
Botley	d								18 36											19 36		
Fareham	d			17 32					18 44				18 32					19 03		19 44		
Portchester	d								18 49											19 49		
Cosham	d								18 54											19 54		
Hilsea	a								19 00											20 00		
Fratton	a								19 03											20 04		
Portsmouth & Southsea	a								19 08											20 08		
Portsmouth Harbour	a								19 13											20 13		
Southampton Airport Parkway ✈	d		17 34		17 53	17 58		18 27				18 34				18 53	18 58		19 27			
Swaythling	d					18 01											19 01					
St Denys	d					18 04											19 04					
Southampton Central	a		17 40	17 53	18 00	18 09		18 34				18 42	18 53			19 00	19 09	19 25	19 34			
	d		17 45	17 54	18 03	18 10		18 35				18 45	18 54			19 03	19 10	19 30	19 35			
Millbrook (Hants)	d					18 13											19 13					
Redbridge	d					18 16											19 16					
Romsey	d			18 06		18 24							19 06				19 24	19 42				
Mottisfont & Dunbridge	d																19 29					
Dean	d																19 35					
Salisbury	a			18 24		18 42							19 24				19 48	20 00				
Totton	d							18 41											19 41			
Ashurst New Forest	d							18 45											19 45			
Beaulieu Road	d							18 50											19 50			
Brockenhurst 3	a		18 02		18 16			18 56				19 01				19 16			19 56			
	d	17 59	18 03		18 17		18 29	18 57			18 59	19 02		19 29		19 17			19 57			19 59
Lymington Town	d	18 07					18 37				19 07			19 37								20 07
Lymington Pier	a	18 09					18 39				19 09			19 39								20 09
Yarmouth (IOW)	a										*19 55*											
Sway	d							19 01											20 01			
New Milton	d				18 24			19 06								19 24			20 06			
Hinton Admiral	d							19 10											20 10			
Christchurch	d							19 15											20 15			
Pokesdown	d							19 19											20 19			
Bournemouth	a		18 27		18 35			19 23				19 27				19 35			20 23			
	d				18 40			19 25								19 40			20 25			
Branksome	d				18 45											19 45						
Parkstone (Dorset)	d				18 48											19 48						
Poole 4	a				18 51			19 34								19 51			20 34			
	d				18 52											19 52						
Hamworthy	d				18 57											19 57						
Holton Heath	d																					
Wareham	d				19 04											20 04						
Wool	d				19 11											20 11						
Moreton (Dorset)	d				19 17											20 17						
Dorchester South	d				19 25											20 25						
Dorchester West	d														19 47							
Upwey	d				19 32										19 55	20 32						
Weymouth	a				19 36										20 01	20 36						

b arr. 1642 c arr. 1739

Table 158

Sundays

London - Basingstoke, Southampton, Romsey Lymington, Bournemouth and Weymouth

		XC ◇■ ⊐P	GW ◇	SW ◇■ ⊐P	SW ■	SW ■	SW ◇■ ⊐P	SW ■	SW ■	SW ■	XC ◇■ ⊐P	GW ◇	SW ◇■ ⊐P	SW ■	SW ■	SW ◇■	SW ■	SW ■	SW ■	XC ◇■ ⊐P	GW	SW ◇■ ⊐P
London Waterloo 15 ⊖	d			18 35			18 54		18 37				19 35			19 54		19 37				20 35
Clapham Junction 10	d			18u42			19u03		18 46				19u42			20u03		19 46				20u42
Woking	d			19 07			19 28		19 23				20 07			20 28		20 23				21 07
Farnborough (Main)	d								19 36									20 36				
Fleet	d								19 42									20 42				
Reading 7	d	18b51									19c51									20e51		
Basingstoke	a	19 09		19 26			19 46		19 54		20 09		20 26			20 46		20 54		21 09		21 26
	d	19 10		19 28			19 48				20 10		20 28			20 48				21 10		21 28
Micheldever	d						19 58									20 58						
Winchester	d	19 25		19 44			20 08				20 25		20 44			21 08				21 25		21 44
Shawford	d						20 12															
Romsey	d				19 35									20 35								
Chandlers Ford	d				19 42									20 42								
Eastleigh 8	a				19 48		20 18	>						20 48		21 18	>					
	d				19 54		20 22	20 26						20 54		21 22	21 26					
Hedge End	d							20 32									21 32					
Botley	d							20 36									21 36					
Fareham	d		19 32					20 44				20 32					21 44					
Portchester	d							20 49									21 49					
Cosham	d							20 54									21 54					
Hilsea	a							21 00									22 00					
Fratton	a							21 04									22 04					
Portsmouth & Southsea	a							21 08									22 08					
Portsmouth Harbour	a							21 13									22 13					
Southampton Airport Parkway ✈	d	19 34		19 53	19 58		20 27				20 34		20 53	20 58		21 27				21 34		21 53
Swaythling	d				20 01									21 01								
St Denys	d				20 04									21 04								
Southampton Central	a	19 40	19 53	20 00	20 09		20 34				20 43	20 53	21 00	21 09		21 34				21 43		22 00
	d	19 45	19 54	20 03	20 10		20 35				20 45	20 54	21 03	21 10		21 35				21 45		22 03
Millbrook (Hants)	d				20 13									21 13								
Redbridge	d				20 16									21 16								
Romsey	d		20 06		20 24							21 06		21 24								
Mottisfont & Dunbridge	d													21 29								
Dean	d													21 35								
Salisbury	a		20 24		20 42							21 24		21 48								
Totton	d						20 41									21 41						
Ashurst New Forest	d						20 45									21 45						
Beaulieu Road	d						20 50									21 50						
Brockenhurst 3	a	20 02		20 16			20 56				21 02		21 16			21 56				22 02		22 16
	d	20 03		20 17		20 29	20 57			20 59	21 03		21 17		21 29	21 57			21 59	22 03		22 17
Lymington Town	d					20 37				21 07					21 37				22 07			
Lymington Pier	a					20 39				21 09					21 39				22 09			
Yarmouth (IOW)	a					*21 35*													*23 00*			
Sway	d						21 01									22 01						
New Milton	d			20 24			21 06						21 24			22 06						22 24
Hinton Admiral	d						21 10									22 10						
Christchurch	d						21 15									22 15						
Pokesdown	d						21 19									22 19						
Bournemouth	a	20 27		20 35			21 23				21 27		21 35			22 23				22 27		22 35
	d			20 40			21 25						21 40			22 25						22 40
Branksome	d			20 45									21 45									22 45
Parkstone (Dorset)	d			20 48									21 48									22 48
Poole 4	a			20 51			21 34						21 51			22 34						22 51
	d			20 52									21 52									22 52
Hamworthy	d			20 57									21 57									22 57
Holton Heath	d																					
Wareham	d			21 04									22 04									23 04
Wool	d			21 11									22 11									23 11
Moreton (Dorset)	d			21 17									22 17									23 17
Dorchester South	d			21 25									22 25									23 25
Dorchester West	d																				22 53	
Upwey	d			21 32									22 32								23 01	23 32
Weymouth	a			21 36									22 36								23 06	23 36

b arr. 1842 c arr. 1942 e arr. 2042

London - Basingstoke, Southampton, Romsey Lymington, Bournemouth and Weymouth

		SW	SW	SW	SW	XC	GW	SW	SW	SW	SW	SW	SW	SW	SW	SW
		1	◇1	1	1	◇1		◇1	1	◇1	1	1	1	◇1	1	1
						🍴		🍴						🍴		
London Waterloo 15 ⊖	d		20 54		20 37			21 35		21 54		21 37		22 54		22 37
Clapham Junction 10	d		21u03		20 46			21u42		22u03		21 46		23u03		22 46
Woking	d		21 28		21 23			22 07		22 28		22 23		23 28		23 23
Farnborough (Main)	d				21 36							22 36				23 36
Fleet	d				21 42							22 42				23 42
Reading 7	d					21b51										
Basingstoke	a		21 46		21 54	22 11		22 26		22 46		22 54		23 46		23 54
	d		21 48			22 12		22 28		22 48				23 48		
Micheldever	d		21 58							22 58				23 58		
Winchester	d		22 08			22 27		22 44		23 08				00 08		
Shawford	d		22 12													
Romsey	d	21 35							22 35				22 28			
Chandlers Ford	d	21 42							22 42							
Eastleigh 8	a	21 48	22 18	>					22 48	23 17	>		23 19	00 18	>	
	d	21 54	22 22	22 26					22 54	23 22	23 26		23 21	00 22	00 30	
Hedge End	d			22 32							23 32				00s36	
Botley	d			22 36							23 36				00s39	
Fareham	d			22 44			22 32				23 44				00s47	
Portchester	d			22 49							23 49				00s53	
Cosham	d			22 54							23 54				00s57	
Hilsea	a			23 00							23 59					
Fratton	a			23 04							00 04				01s05	
Portsmouth & Southsea	a			23 08							00 08				01s08	
Portsmouth Harbour	a			23 13							00 13				01 12	
Southampton Airport Parkwy ✈	d	21 58	22 27			22 36		22 53	22 58	23 27				00 27		
Swaythling	d	22 01							23 01							
St Denys	d	22 04							23 04					00s31		
Southampton Central	a	22 09	22 34			22 43	22 53	23 00	23 09	23 34				00 36		
	d	22 10	22 35				22 57	23 03	23 10	23 35				00 37		
Millbrook (Hants)	d	22 13							23 13							
Redbridge	d	22 16							23 16							
Romsey	d	22a24					23 09		23 24				23a33			
Mottisfont & Dunbridge	d								23 29							
Dean	d								23 35							
Salisbury	a						23 27		23 51							
Totton	d		22 41							23 41				00s43		
Ashurst New Forest	d		22 45							23 45						
Beaulieu Road	d		22 50													
Brockenhurst 3	a		22 56					23 16		23 53				00s53		
	d		22 57					23 17		23 54				00s54		
Lymington Town	d															
Lymington Pier	a															
Yarmouth (IOW)	a															
Sway	d		23 01							23 59						
New Milton	d		23 06					23 24		00 04				01s01		
Hinton Admiral	d		23 10							00 08						
Christchurch	d		23 15							00 13				01s08		
Pokesdown	d		23 19							00 16				01s12		
Bournemouth	a		23 23					23 35		00 21				01 16		
	d		23 25					23 40		00 22				01 18		
Branksome	d							23 45		00 28				01s23		
Parkstone (Dorset)	d							23 48		00 31				01s26		
Poole 4	a		23 34					23 51		00 35				01 30		
	d							23 52								
Hamworthy	d							23 57								
Holton Heath	d															
Wareham	d							00 04								
Wool	d							00 11								
Moreton (Dorset)	d							00 17								
Dorchester South	d							00 25								
Dorchester West	d															
Upwey	d							00 32								
Weymouth	a							00 36								

b arr. 2142

Weymouth, Bournemouth, Lymington, Romsey, Southampton and Basingstoke - London

		SW MO	SW MO	SW MX	SW MO	SW MX	SW MX	XC	SW	SW	SW	SW	SW	GW	SW	XC	SW	SW	SW	SW	SW	GW
		◇1	1	◇1	1	1	1	◇1	1	◇1	◇1	1	1		1	◇1	◇1	1	◇1	1	1	
										A	B	A	B				A		B			
								🍴		🍴	🍴					🍴	🍴		🍴			
Weymouth	d	20p58		22p10	22p58	23p10								05 33								
Upwey	d	21p02		22p14	23p02	23p14								05 37								
Dorchester West	a													05 44								
Dorchester South	d	21p10		22p22	23p10	23p22																
Moreton (Dorset)	d	21p17		22p28	23p17	23p28																
Wool	d	21p23		22p34	23p23	23p34																
Wareham	d	21p30		22p42	23p30	23p42																
Holton Heath	d																					
Hamworthy	d	21p37		22p48	23p37	23p48																
Poole 4	a	21p41		22p53	23p41	23p53																
	d	21p50		22p54	23p50	23p54				04 57	05 00	05 23	05 26				05 42		05 45			
Parkstone (Dorset)	d	21p54		22p58	23p54					05 01	05 04	05 27	05 30									
Branksome	d	21p57		23p01	23p57					05 04	05 07	05 30	05 33									
Bournemouth	a	22p03		23p07	00 03	00 03				05 09	05 12	05 36	05 38				05 51		05 54			
	d	22p06		23p12						05 12	05 15	05 38	05 40				05 54		05 57			
Pokesdown	d	22p10		23p16						05 16	05 19	05 42	05 44									
Christchurch	d	22p14		23p20						05 20	05 23	05 46	05 48									
Hinton Admiral	d	22p19		23p25								05 51	05 53									
New Milton	d	22p23		23p29						05 27	05 30	05 55	05 57									
Sway	d	22p28		23p34								06 00	06 02									
Yarmouth (IOW)	d																				*04 30*	
Lymington Pier	d																				06 14	
Lymington Town	d																				06 16	
Brockenhurst 3	a	22p33		23p39						05 37	05 37	06 07	06 07				06 12		06 12		06 25	
	d	22p34		23p40						05 38	05 38						06 14		06 14			
Beaulieu Road	d	22p39																				
Ashurst New Forest	d	22p43		23p47																		
Totton	d	22p48		23p52						05 49	05 49									06 12		
Salisbury	d														05 35							06 20
Dean	d														05 47							
Mottisfont & Dunbridge	d														05 53							
Romsey	d														05 58							06 38
Redbridge	d																			06 14		
Millbrook (Hants)	d																			06 17		
Southampton Central	a	22p53		23p57						05 54	05 54						06 27		06 27	06 24		06 49
	d	22p55		23p59				05 15		05 55	05 55					06 15	06 30		06 30	06 35		06 53
St Denys	d			00 04																06 40		
Swaythling	d			00 07																06 43		
Southampton Airport Parkwy ✈	d	23p03		00 10				05 22		06 03	06 03					06 22	06 38		06 38	06 46		
Portsmouth Harbour	d		23p17				23p24		05 00									05 43				
Portsmouth & Southsea	d		23p22				23p29		05 05									05 48				
Fratton	d		23p26				23p33		05 09									05 52				
Hilsea	d		23p30				23p37		05 13									05 56				
Cosham	d		23p35				23p42		05 18									06 03				
Portchester	d		23p40				23p47		05 23									06 08				
Fareham	d		23p46				23p53		05 29									06b19				07 15
Botley	d		23p54				23p59		05 36									06 27				
Hedge End	d		23p58				00 05		05 40									06 31				
Eastleigh 8	a	23p09	00 04	00 14			00 11		05 48	06 07	06 07							06 37		06 49		
	d	23p11					00 19		05 49	06 08	06 08							06 43		06 50		
Chandlers Ford	d														06 06					06 55		
Romsey	a														06 44					07 03		
Shawford	d								05 55									06 49				
Winchester	d	23p23					00a28	05 31	06 01	06 18	06 18					06 31	06 48	06 55	06 48			
Micheldever	d	23p32							06 10									07 04				
Basingstoke	a	23p42						05 46	06 21	06 34	06 34					06 46		07 14				
	d	23p44						05 47		06 35	06 35					06 47		07 17				
Reading 7	a							06 04								07 04						
Fleet	d																					
Farnborough (Main)	d																					
Woking	a	00 02								06 53	06 53											
Clapham Junction 10	a	00 23								07 14	07 14											
London Waterloo 15 ⊖	a	00 33								07 24	07 24						07 47	08 01	07 47			

A from 27 September

B until 24 September

b arr. 0613

Weymouth, Bournemouth, Lymington, Romsey, Southampton and Basingstoke - London

		SW ◇1 A	SW ◇1	SW ◇1 B	SW 1	XC ◇1	SW ◇1 A	SW ◇1	SW ◇1 B	SW 1	SW 1	SW 1	GW ◇	SW ◇1 A	SW ◇1	SW ◇1 B	GW	SW 1	SW 1	XC ◇1	GW	SW 1	SW 1	SW 1
Weymouth	d						05 50		05 55					06 20		06 25	06 40							
Upwey	d						05 54		05 59					06 24		06 29	06 45							
Dorchester West	a																06 52							
Dorchester South	d						06 02		06 07					06 32		06 37								
Moreton (Dorset)	d						06 09		06 14					06 39		06 44								
Wool	d						06 15		06 20					06 45		06 50								
Wareham	d						06 22		06 27					06 52		06 57								
Holton Heath	d						06 26		06 31															
Hamworthy	d						06 31		06 36					06 59		07 04								
Poole 4	a						06 35		06 40					07 03		07 08								
	d	06 08		06 11			06 36		06 41					07 06		07 11								
Parkstone (Dorset)	d	06 12		06 15			06 40		06 45					07 10		07 15								
Branksome	d	06 15		06 18			06 46		06 49					07 14		07 19								
Bournemouth	a	06 23		06 23			06 54		06 54					07 24		07 24								
	d	06 25	06 04	06 25		06 30	06 56	06 34	06 56					07 26	07 04	07 26				07 30				
Pokesdown	d		06 08					06 38							07 08									
Christchurch	d		06 12					06 42							07 12									
Hinton Admiral	d		06 17					06 47							07 17									
New Milton	d		06 21					06 51							07 21									
Sway	d		06 26					06 56							07 26									
Yarmouth (IOW)	d										*05 55*											*06 55*		
Lymington Pier	d										06 44							07 14				07 44		
Lymington Town	d										06 46							07 16				07 46		
Brockenhurst 3	a		06 31			06 46		07 01			06 55				07 31			07 25		07 46		07 55		
	d		06 32			06 49		07 02							07 32					07 49				
Beaulieu Road	d																							
Ashurst New Forest	d		06 40					07 10							07 40									
Totton	d		06 45					07 15							07 45									
Salisbury	d											06 50	07 11								07 36			07 48
Dean	d											07 02												08 00
Mottisfont & Dunbridge	d											07 08												08 06
Romsey	d											07 13	07 30								07 56			08 11
Redbridge	d											07 21												08 21
Millbrook (Hants)	d											07 23												08 24
Southampton Central	a	06 55	06 51	06 55		07 01	07 25	07 20	07 25			07 29	07 41	07 55	07 50	07 55				08 03	08 09			08 27
	d		07 00	<		07 15		07 30	<			07 35	07 42		08 00	<				08 15				08 35
St Denys	d											07 40												08 40
Swaythling	d											07 43												08 43
Southampton Airport Parkwy ✈	d		07 08			07 22		07 38				07 46			08 08					08 22				08 46
Portsmouth Harbour	d				06 23					06 38									07 24				07 55	
Portsmouth & Southsea	d				06 28					06 43									07 29				08 00	
Fratton	d				06 32					06 47									07 33				08 04	
Hilsea	d				06 36					06 51									07 37				08 08	
Cosham	d				06 42					06 58									07 43				08 13	
Portchester	d				06 46					07 03									07 48				08 18	
Fareham	d				06 53					07 11			08 06						07 54				08 24	
Botley	d				07 01					07 25									08 01				08 31	
Hedge End	d				07 05					07 29									08 06				08 36	
Eastleigh 3	a				07 11					07 35		07 49							08 12				08 42	08 49
	d				07 13					07 43		07 50							08 13				08 43	08 50
Chandlers Ford	d											07 55												08 55
Romsey	a											08 03												09 03
Shawford	d									07 49									08 19				08 49	
Winchester	d				07 22	07 31		07 48		07 55					08 18				08 25	08 31			08 54	
Micheldever	d		07 18		07 31					08 02													09 02	
Basingstoke	a				07 41	07 46				08 14					08 34				08 41	08 46			09 15	
	d				07 47	07 47				08 16					08 35				08 42	08 47			09 17	
Reading 7	a					08 04														09 04				
Fleet	d																		08 53					
Farnborough (Main)	d																		08 59				09 31	
Woking	a				08 05					08 34					08 53								09 40	
Clapham Junction 10	a														09 14				09 26					
London Waterloo 15 ⊖	a		08 16		08 34			08 50		09 03					09 25				09 38				10 08	

A from 27 September

B until 24 September

Table 158 — Mondays to Fridays

Weymouth, Bournemouth, Lymington, Romsey, Southampton and Basingstoke - London

		SW 1	SW 1	SW ◇1 A	SW ◇1 B	SW 1	SW ◇1	SW 1	GW ◇	SW 1	XC ◇1	SW ◇1	SW 1	SW 1	SW 1	SW 1	SW ◇1	GW	GW	SW 1	SW 1	XC ◇1
Weymouth	d			06 50	06 55			07 23				07 55					08 20	08 50				
Upwey	d			06 54	06 59			07 27				07 59					08 24	08 55				
Dorchester West	a																	09 02				
Dorchester South	d			07 02	07 07			07 35				08 07					08 33					
Moreton (Dorset)	d			07 09	07 14			07 42				08 14					08 39					
Wool	d			07 15	07 20			07 48				08 20					08 45					
Wareham	d			07 22	07 27			07 55				08 27					08 53					
Holton Heath	d			07 26	07 31			07 59				08 31					08 56					
Hamworthy	d			07 31	07 36			08 04				08 36					09 01					
Poole 4	a			07 35	07 40			08 08				08 40					09 06					
	d		07 20	07 36	07 41		07 55	08 09				08 41				08 50	09 07			09 13		
Parkstone (Dorset)	d		07 24	07 40	07 45		07 59	08 13				08 45				08 54				09 17		
Branksome	d		07 27	07 46	07 49		08 02	08 17				08 49				08 57				09 20		
Bournemouth	a		07 32	07 54	07 54		08 07	08 22				08 54				09 02	09 16			09 25		
	d		07 34	07 59	07 59		08 10	08 23			08 45	08 59				09 05	09 18			09 27		09 45
Pokesdown	d		07 38				08 14	08 27								09 09	09 22			09 30		
Christchurch	d		07 42				08 18	08 31								09 13	09 26			09 34		
Hinton Admiral	d		07 47				08 24	08 36								09 18				09 39		
New Milton	d		07 51				08 29	08 40								09 22	09 33			09 44		
Sway	d		07 56				08 34	08 45								09 27				09 48		
Yarmouth (IOW)	d									*07 55*					*08 35*							
Lymington Pier	d					08 14				08 44					09 14						09 44	
Lymington Town	d					08 16				08 46					09 16						09 46	
Brockenhurst 3	a		08 01	08 14	08 14	08 25	08 39	08 50		08 55	08 58	09 14			09 25	09 32	09 40			09 53	09 55	09 59
	d		08 02	08 15	08 15		08 41				09 00	09 15				09 33	09 41			09 54		10 00
Beaulieu Road	d		08 08																			
Ashurst New Forest	d		08 12				08 48									09 40						
Totton	d		08 17				08 53									09 45						
Salisbury	d								08 32					08 48					09 32			
Dean	d													09 00								
Mottisfont & Dunbridge	d													09 06								
Romsey	d								08 50					09 11					09 50			
Redbridge	d													09 19								
Millbrook (Hants)	d													09 22								
Southampton Central	a		08 22	08 28	08 28		08 58		09 04		09 12	09 28		09 25		09 52	09 55		10 04	10 09		10 12
	d		08 48	08 30	08 30		09 00		09 04		09 15	09 30		09 35		09 55	10 00		10 04			10 15
St Denys	d		08 53											09 40								
Swaythling	d		08 56											09 43								
Southampton Airport Parkway ✈	d		08 59	08 38	08 38		09 08				09 22	09 38		09 46		10 03	10 08					10 22
Portsmouth Harbour	d	08 05											08 55									
Portsmouth & Southsea	d	08 10											09 00									
Fratton	d	08 14											09 04									
Hilsea	d	08 18											09 08									
Cosham	d	08 23											09 13									
Portchester	d	08 28											09 18									
Fareham	d	08 34							09 27				09 24						10 27			
Botley	d	08 42											09 31									
Hedge End	d	08 46											09 36									
Eastleigh 3	a	08 52	09 03										09 42	09 49		10 06						
	d	08 54	09 11										09 43	09 50		10 11						
Chandlers Ford	d													09 55								
Romsey	a													10 03								
Shawford	d		09 17													10 17						
Winchester	d	09 03	09 24	08 48	08 48		09 18				09 31	09 48	09 54			10 24	10 18					10 31
Micheldever	d												10 02									
Basingstoke	a	09 19	09 40				09 35				09 46		10 15			10 40	10 34					10 46
	d		09 41				09 36				09 47		10 17			10 41	10 36					10 47
Reading 7	a										10 04											11 04
Fleet	d		09 52													10 52						
Farnborough (Main)	d		09 58										10 31			10 58						
Woking	a			09 22	09 22		09 54					10 20	10 40									
Clapham Junction 10	a		10 24	09 43	09 43		10 15									11 23	11 12					
London Waterloo 15 ⊖	a		10 34	09 53	09 53		10 23					10 49	11 08			11 34	11 20					

A from 27 September.

B until 24 September.

Table 158

Mondays to Fridays

Weymouth, Bournemouth, Lymington, Romsey, Southampton and Basingstoke - London

		SW ◇1	SW 1	SW 1	SW 1	SW 1	SW ◇1	GW ◇	SW 1	XC ◇1	SW ◇1	SW 1	SW 1	SW 1	SW 1	SW ◇1	GW ◇	SW 1	XC ◇1	GW	SW ◇1	GW	SW 1
Weymouth	d	09 03					09 20				10 03					10 20					11 03	11 10	
Upwey	d						09 24									10 24						11 15	
Dorchester West	a																					11 22	
Dorchester South	d	09 13					09 33				10 13					10 33					11 13		
Moreton (Dorset)	d						09 39									10 39							
Wool	d						09 45									10 45							
Wareham	d	09 28					09 53				10 28					10 53					11 28		
Holton Heath	d						09 56									10 56							
Hamworthy	d	09 35					10 01				10 35					11 01					11 35		
Poole 4	a	09 39					10 06				10 39					11 06					11 39		
	d	09 40				09 50	10 07				10 40				10 50	11 07					11 40		
Parkstone (Dorset)	d	09 44				09 54					10 44				10 54						11 44		
Branksome	d	09 48				09 57					10 48				10 57						11 48		
Bournemouth	a	09 53				10 02	10 17				10 54				11 02	11 17					11 54		
	d	09 55				10 05	10 22			10 45	10 59				11 05	11 22			11 45		11 59		
Pokesdown	d					10 09	10 26								11 09	11 26							
Christchurch	d					10 13	10 30								11 13	11 30							
Hinton Admiral	d					10 18									11 18								
New Milton	d					10 22	10 37								11 22	11 37							
Sway	d					10 27									11 27								
Yarmouth (IOW)	d								*09 55*					*10 35*									
Lymington Pier	d				10 14				10 44					11 14				11 44					
Lymington Town	d				10 16				10 46					11 16				11 46					
Brockenhurst 3	a	10 10			10 25	10 32	10 44		10 55	10 58	11 14			11 25	11 32	11 44		11 55	11 58		12 14		
	d	10 11				10 33	10 45			11 00	11 15				11 33	11 45			12 00		12 15		
Beaulieu Road	d														11 38								
Ashurst New Forest	d					10 40									11 42								
Totton	d					10 45									11 47								
Salisbury	d			09 48				10 30					10 48				11 32			11 39			
Dean	d			10 00									11 00										
Mottisfont & Dunbridge	d			10 06									11 06										
Romsey	d			10 11				10 50					11 11				11 50			12 00			
Redbridge	d			10 19									11 19										
Millbrook (Hants)	d			10 22									11 22										
Southampton Central	a	10 26		10 25		10 53	10 58	11 04		11 12	11 28		11 28		11 53	11 58	12 02		12 12	12 19	12 28		
	d	10 30		10 35		10 55	11 00	11 04		11 15	11 30		11 35		11 55	12 00	12 04		12 15		12 30		
St Denys	d			10 40									11 40										
Swaythling	d			10 43									11 43										
Southampton Airport Parkwy ✈	d	10 38		10 46		11 03	11 08			11 22	11 38		11 46		12 03	12 08			12 22		12 38		
Portsmouth Harbour	d		09 55									10 55											11 55
Portsmouth & Southsea	d		10 00									11 00											12 00
Fratton	d		10 04									11 04											12 04
Hilsea	d		10 08									11 08											12 08
Cosham	d		10 13									11 13											12 13
Portchester	d		10 18									11 18											12 18
Fareham	d		10 24					11 27				11 24					12 27						12 24
Botley	d		10 31									11 31											12 31
Hedge End	d		10 36									11 36											12 36
Eastleigh 3	a		10 42	10 49		11 06						11 42	11 49		12 06								12 42
	d		10 43	10 50		11 11						11 43	11 50		12 11								12 43
Chandlers Ford	d			10 55									11 55										
Romsey	a			11 03									12 03										
Shawford	d					11 17									12 17								
Winchester	d	10 48	10 54			11 24	11 18			11 31	11 48	11 54			12 24	12 18			12 31		12 48		12 54
Micheldever	d		11 02									12 02											13 02
Basingstoke	a		11 15			11 40	11 34			11 46		12 15			12 40	12 34			12 46				13 15
	d		11 17			11 41	11 36			11 47		12 17			12 41	12 36			12 47				13 17
Reading 7	a									12 04									13 04				
Fleet	d					11 52									12 52								
Farnborough (Main)	d		11 31			11 58						12 31			12 58								13 31
Woking	a	11 19	11 40								12 19	12 40									13 19		13 40
Clapham Junction 10	a					12 23	12 12								13 23	13 12							
London Waterloo 15 ⊖	a	11 49	12 08			12 34	12 20				12 49	13 07			13 34	13 20					13 49		14 07

Table 158

Mondays to Fridays

Weymouth, Bournemouth, Lymington, Romsey, Southampton and Basingstoke - London

		SW 1	SW 1	SW 1	SW ◇1	GW ◇	SW 1	XC ◇1	SW ◇1	SW 1	SW 1	SW 1	SW 1	SW ◇1	GW ◇	SW 1	XC ◇1	SW ◇1	GW	SW 1	SW 1	GW ◇
Weymouth	d				11 20				12 03					12 20				13 03	13 10			
Upwey	d				11 24									12 24					13 15			
Dorchester West	a																		13 22			
Dorchester South	d				11 33				12 13					12 33				13 13				
Moreton (Dorset)	d				11 39									12 39								
Wool	d				11 45									12 45								
Wareham	d				11 53				12 28					12 53				13 28				
Holton Heath	d				11 56									12 56								
Hamworthy	d				12 01				12 35					13 01				13 35				
Poole 4	a				12 06				12 39					13 06				13 39				
	d			11 50	12 07				12 40				12 50	13 07				13 40				
Parkstone (Dorset)	d			11 54					12 44				12 54					13 44				
Branksome	d			11 57					12 48				12 57					13 48				
Bournemouth	a			12 02	12 17				12 54				13 02	13 17				13 54				
	d			12 05	12 22			12 45	12 59				13 05	13 22			13 45	13 59				
Pokesdown	d			12 09	12 26								13 09	13 26								
Christchurch	d			12 13	12 30								13 13	13 30								
Hinton Admiral	d			12 18									13 18									
New Milton	d			12 22	12 37								13 22	13 37								
Sway	d			12 27									13 27									
Yarmouth (IOW)	d		*11 15*				*11 55*					*12 35*										
Lymington Pier	d		12 14				12 44					13 14				13 44						
Lymington Town	d		12 16				12 46					13 16				13 46						
Brockenhurst 3	a		12 25	12 32	12 44		12 55	12 58	13 14			13 25	13 32	13 44		13 55	13 58	14 14				
	d			12 33	12 45			13 00	13 15				13 33	13 45			14 00	14 15				
Beaulieu Road	d																					
Ashurst New Forest	d			12 40									13 40									
Totton	d			12 45									13 45									
Salisbury	d	11 48				12 32					12 48				13 32						13 48	13 59
Dean	d	12 00									13 00										14 00	
Mottisfont & Dunbridge	d	12 06									13 06										14 06	
Romsey	d	12 11				12 50					13 11				13 50						14 11	14 20
Redbridge	d	12 19									13 19										14 19	
Millbrook (Hants)	d	12 22									13 22										14 22	
Southampton Central	a	12 25		12 52	12 58	13 04		13 12	13 28		13 25		13 53	13 58	14 04		14 12	14 28			14 25	14 32
	d	12 35		12 55	13 00	13 04		13 15	13 30		13 35		13 55	14 00	14 04		14 15	14 30			14 35	14 34
St Denys	d	12 40									13 40										14 40	
Swaythling	d	12 43									13 43										14 43	
Southampton Airport Parkwy ✈	d	12 46		13 03	13 08			13 22	13 38		13 46		14 03	14 08			14 22	14 38			14 46	
Portsmouth Harbour	d									12 55										13 55		
Portsmouth & Southsea	d									13 00										14 00		
Fratton	d									13 04										14 04		
Hilsea	d									13 08										14 08		
Cosham	d									13 13										14 13		
Portchester	d									13 18										14 18		
Fareham	d					13 27				13 24					14 27					14 24		14 56
Botley	d									13 31										14 31		
Hedge End	d									13 36										14 36		
Eastleigh 3	a	12 49		13 06						13 42	13 49		14 09							14 42	14 49	
	d	12 50		13 11						13 43	13 50		14 11							14 43	14 50	
Chandlers Ford	d	12 55									13 55										14 55	
Romsey	a	13 03									14 03										15 04	
Shawford	d			13 17									14 17									
Winchester	d			13 24	13 18			13 31	13 48	13 54			14 24	14 18			14 31	14 48		14 54		
Micheldever	d									14 02										15 02		
Basingstoke	a			13 40	13 34			13 46		14 15			14 40	14 34			14 46			15 15		
	d			13 41	13 36			13 47		14 17			14 41	14 36			14 47			15 17		
Reading 7	a							14 04									15 04					
Fleet	d			13 52									14 52									
Farnborough (Main)	d			13 58						14 31			14 58							15 31		
Woking	a								14 19	14 40								15 19		15 40		
Clapham Junction 10	a			14 23	14 12								15 23	15 12								
London Waterloo 15 ⊖	a			14 34	14 20				14 49	15 08			15 32	15 20				15 49		16 07		

Table 158

Weymouth, Bournemouth, Lymington, Romsey, Southampton and Basingstoke - London

		SW	SW	SW	GW	SW	XC	SW	SW	SW	SW	SW	SW	GW	SW	XC	SW	GW	SW	SW	SW	SW	SW
		[1]	[1]	◇[1] ⊏⊐	◇ 🛒	[1]	◇[1] 🛒	◇[1] ⊏⊐	[1]	[1]	[1]	[1]	◇[1] ⊏⊐	◇ 🛒	[1]	◇[1] 🛒	◇[1] ⊏⊐		[1]	[1]	[1]	[1]	◇[1] ⊏⊐
Weymouth	d			13 20				14 03					14 20				15 03	15 08					15 20
Upwey	d			13 24									14 24					15 13					15 24
Dorchester West	a																	15 20					
Dorchester South	d			13 33				14 13					14 33				15 13						15 33
Moreton (Dorset)	d			13 39									14 39										15 39
Wool	d			13 45									14 45										15 45
Wareham	d			13 53				14 28					14 53				15 28						15 53
Holton Heath	d			13 56									14 56										15 56
Hamworthy	d			14 01				14 35					15 01				15 35						16 01
Poole [4]	a			14 06				14 39					15 06				15 39						16 06
	d		13 50	14 07				14 40				14 50	15 07				15 40					15 50	16 07
Parkstone (Dorset)	d		13 54					14 44				14 54					15 44					15 54	
Branksome	d		13 57					14 48				14 57					15 48					15 57	
Bournemouth	a		14 02	14 17				14 54				15 02	15 17				15 54					16 02	16 17
	d		14 05	14 22			14 45	14 59				15 05	15 22			15 45	15 59					16 05	16 22
Pokesdown	d		14 09	14 26								15 09	15 26									16 09	16 26
Christchurch	d		14 13	14 30								15 13	15 30									16 13	16 30
Hinton Admiral	d		14 18									15 18										16 18	
New Milton	d		14 22	14 37								15 22	15 37									16 22	16 37
Sway	d		14 27									15 27										16 27	
Yarmouth (IOW)	d	*13 15*				*13 55*					*14 35*												
Lymington Pier	d	14 14				14 44					15 14				15 44						16 14		
Lymington Town	d	14 16				14 46					15 16				15 46						16 16		
Brockenhurst [3]	a	14 25	14 32	14 44		14 55	14 58	15 14			15 25	15 32	15 44		15 55	15 58	16 14				16 25	16 32	16 44
	d		14 33	14 45			15 00	15 15				15 33	15 45			16 00	16 15					16 33	16 45
Beaulieu Road	d																						
Ashurst New Forest	d		14 40									15 40										16 40	
Totton	d		14 45									15 45										16 45	
Salisbury	d				14 32					14 48				15 32						15 48			
Dean	d									15 00										16 00			
Mottisfont & Dunbridge	d									15 06										16 06			
Romsey	d				14 50					15 11				15 50						16 11			
Redbridge	d									15 19										16 19			
Millbrook (Hants)	d									15 22										16 22			
Southampton Central	a		14 53	14 58	15 04		15 12	15 28		15 25		15 51	15 58	16 04		16 12	16 28			16 25		16 51	16 58
	d		14 55	15 00	15 04		15 15	15 30		15 35		15 55	16 00	16 04		16 15	16 30			16 35		16 52	17 00
St Denys	d									15 40										16 40		16 57	
Swaythling	d									15 43										16 43		17 00	
Southampton Airport Parkwy ✈	d		15 03	15 08			15 22	15 38		15 46		16 03	16 08			16 22	16 38			16 46		17 04	17 08
Portsmouth Harbour	d								14 55										15 55				
Portsmouth & Southsea	d								15 00										16 00				
Fratton	d								15 04										16 04				
Hilsea	d								15 08										16 08				
Cosham	d								15 13										16 13				
Portchester	d								15 18										16 18				
Fareham	d				15 27				15 24					16 27					16 24				
Botley	d								15 31										16 31				
Hedge End	d								15 36										16 36				
Eastleigh [3]	a		15 06						15 42	15 49		16 07							16 42	16 49		17 07	
	d		15 11						15 43	15 50		16 11							16 43	16 50		17 11	
Chandlers Ford	d									15 55										16 55			
Romsey	a									16 03										17 03			
Shawford	d		15 17									16 17										17 17	
Winchester	d		15 24	15 18			15 31	15 48	15 54			16 24	16 18			16 31	16 48		16 54			17 24	17 18
Micheldever	d								16 02										17 02				
Basingstoke	a		15 40	15 34			15 46		16 15			16 40	16 34			16 46			17 15			17 40	17 34
	d		15 41	15 36			15 47		16 17			16 41	16 36			16 47			17 17			17 41	17 36
Reading [7]	a						16 04									17 04							
Fleet	d		15 52									16 52										17 52	
Farnborough (Main)	d		15 58						16 31			16 58							17 31			17 58	
Woking	a							16 19	16 40								17 20		17 40				
Clapham Junction [10]	a		16 24	16 12								17 23	17 12									18 23	18 12
London Waterloo [15] ⊖	a		16 34	16 20				16 49	17 07			17 36	17 20				17 50		18 08			18 34	18 23

Table 158

Weymouth, Bournemouth, Lymington, Romsey, Southampton and Basingstoke - London

		GW	SW	XC	SW	SW	SW	SW	SW	SW	SW	SW	GW	SW	XC	SW	SW	SW	SW	SW	SW	GW	GW
		◇ 🛒	[1]	◇[1] 🛒	◇[1] ⊏⊐	[1]	[1]	[1]	[1]	[1]	[1]	◇[1] ⊏⊐	◇ 🛒	[1]	◇[1] 🛒	◇[1] ⊏⊐	[1]	[1]	[1]	[1]	◇[1] ⊏⊐		■ 🛒
Weymouth	d				16 03							16 20				17 04					17 20	17 30	
Upwey	d											16 24									17 24	17 35	
Dorchester West	a																					17 42	
Dorchester South	d				16 13							16 33				17 14					17 33		
Moreton (Dorset)	d											16 39									17 39		
Wool	d											16 45									17 45		
Wareham	d				16 28							16 53				17 29					17 53		
Holton Heath	d											16 56									17 56		
Hamworthy	d				16 35							17 01				17 36					18 01		
Poole [4]	a				16 39							17 06				17 40					18 06		
	d				16 40						16 50	17 07				17 41				17 50	18 07		
Parkstone (Dorset)	d				16 44						16 54					17 45				17 54			
Branksome	d				16 48						16 57					17 49				17 57			
Bournemouth	a				16 54						17 02	17 17				17 54				18 02	18 17		
	d			16 45	16 59						17 05	17 22			17 45	17 59				18 05	18 22		
Pokesdown	d										17 09	17 26								18 09	18 26		
Christchurch	d										17 13	17 30								18 13	18 30		
Hinton Admiral	d										17 18									18 18			
New Milton	d										17 22	17 37								18 22	18 37		
Sway	d										17 27									18 27			
Yarmouth (IOW)	d		*15 55*							*16 35*									*17 15*				
Lymington Pier	d		16 44							17 14				17 44					18 14				
Lymington Town	d		16 46							17 16				17 46					18 16				
Brockenhurst [3]	a		16 55	16 58	17 14					17 25	17 32	17 44		17 55	17 58	18 14			18 25	18 32	18 44		
	d			17 00	17 15				17 20		17 33	17 45			18 00	18 15				18 33	18 45		
Beaulieu Road	d																			18 38			
Ashurst New Forest	d								17 27		17 40									18 42			
Totton	d								17 32		17 45									18 47			
Salisbury	d	16 32					16 45						17 32					17 49					18 34
Dean	d						16 57											18 01					
Mottisfont & Dunbridge	d						17 03											18 07					
Romsey	d	16 50					17 11						17 50					18 12					18 53
Redbridge	d						17 19											18 20					
Millbrook (Hants)	d						17 22											18 23					
Southampton Central	a	17 04		17 12	17 28		17 25		17 41		17 53	17 58	18 04		18 12	18 28		18 26		18 53	18 58		19 04
	d	17 04		17 15	17 30		17 35				17 55	18 00	18 04		18 15	18 30		18 35		18 55	19 00		19 04
St Denys	d						17 40											18 40					
Swaythling	d						17 43											18 43					
Southampton Airport Parkwy ✈	d			17 22	17 38		17 46				18 03	18 08			18 22	18 38		18 46		19 03	19 08		
Portsmouth Harbour	d					16 55		17 03									17 55						
Portsmouth & Southsea	d					17 00		17 07									18 00						
Fratton	d					17 04		17 11									18 04						
Hilsea	d					17 08		17 15									18 08						
Cosham	d					17 13		17 20									18 13						
Portchester	d					17 18		17 25									18 18						
Fareham	d	17 27				17 24		17a30					18 27				18 24						19 27
Botley	d					17 31											18 31						
Hedge End	d					17 36											18 36						
Eastleigh [3]	a					17 42	17 49				18 06						18 42	18 49		19 06			
	d					17 43	17 50				18 11						18 43	18 50		19 11			
Chandlers Ford	d						17 55											18 55					
Romsey	a						18 03											19 04					
Shawford	d										18 17									19 17			
Winchester	d			17 31	17 48	17 54					18 24	18 18			18 31	18 48	18 54			19 24	19 18		
Micheldever	d					18 02											19 02						
Basingstoke	a			17 46		18 15					18 40	18 34			18 46		19 15			19 40	19 34		
	d			17 47		18 17					18 41	18 36			18 47		19 17			19 41	19 36		
Reading [7]	a			18 04											19 04								
Fleet	d										18 52									19 52			
Farnborough (Main)	d					18 31					18 58						19 31			19 58			
Woking	a				18 19	18 40										19 24	19 40						
Clapham Junction [10]	a										19 26	19 12								20 25	20 12		
London Waterloo [15] ⊖	a				18 47	19 08					19 38	19 20				19 51	20 08			20 34	20 20		

Table 158

Weymouth, Bournemouth, Lymington, Romsey, Southampton and Basingstoke - London

		SW		XC	SW	SW	SW	SW	SW	SW	GW	SW		XC	SW	SW	GW	SW	SW	SW	GW	SW		SW	SW
		1		◇1	◇1	1	1	1	1	◇1	■	1		◇1	◇1	1		1	1	◇1	◇	1		1	1
				Ħ	⊏					⊏	Ħ				⊏						Ħ				
Weymouth	d				18 06					18 20					19 06					19 20					
Upwey	d									18 24										19 24					
Dorchester West	a																								
Dorchester South	d				18 16					18 33					19 16					19b38					
Moreton (Dorset)	d									18 39										19 44					
Wool	d									18 45										19 50					
Wareham	d				18 31					18 53					19 31					19 57					
Holton Heath	d									18 56															
Hamworthy	d				18 38					19 01					19 38					20 04					
Poole 4	a				18 42					19 06					19 42					20 08					
	d				18 43				18 50	19 07					19 43				19 50	20 09					
Parkstone (Dorset)	d				18 47				18 54						19 47				19 54						
Branksome	d				18 51				18 57						19 51				19 57						
Bournemouth	a				18 56				19 02	19 17					19 56				20 02	20 18					
	d			18 45	18 59				19 05	19 22				19 45	19 59				20 05	20 22					
Pokesdown	d								19 09	19 26									20 09	20 26					
Christchurch	d								19 13	19 30									20 13	20 30					
Hinton Admiral	d								19 18										20 18						
New Milton	d								19 22	19 37									20 22	20 37					
Sway	d								19 27										20 27						
Yarmouth (IOW)	d	*17 55*						*18 30*										*19 30*							*20 15*
Lymington Pier	d	18 44						19 14				19 44						20 14				20 44			21 14
Lymington Town	d	18 46						19 16				19 46						20 16				20 46			21 16
Brockenhurst 3	a	18 55		18 58	19 14			19 25	19 32	19 44		19 55		19 58	20 14			20 25	20 32	20 44		20 55			21 25
	d			19 00	19 15				19 33	19 45				20 00	20 15				20 33	20 45					
Beaulieu Road	d																								
Ashurst New Forest	d								19 40										20 40						
Totton	d								19 45										20 45						
Salisbury	d						18 49				19 32					19 49	20 13				20 32			20 49	
Dean	d						19 01									20 01								21 01	
Mottisfont & Dunbridge	d						19 07									20 07								21 07	
Romsey	d						19 12				19 50					20 12	20 35				20 50			21 12	
Redbridge	d						19 20									20 20								21 20	
Millbrook (Hants)	d						19 23									20 23								21 23	
Southampton Central	a			19 12	19 28		19 26		19 51	19 58	20 04			20 12	20 28	20 26	20 48		20 51	20 58	21 04			21 26	
	d			19 15	19 30		19 35		19 55	20 00	20 04			20 15	20 30	20 35			20 55	21 00	21 04			21 35	
St Denys	d						19 40									20 40								21 40	
Swaythling	d						19 43									20 43								21 43	
Southampton Airport Parkwy ✈	d			19 22	19 38		19 46		20 03	20 08				20 22	20 38	20 46			21 03	21 08				21 46	
Portsmouth Harbour	d					18 55																			
Portsmouth & Southsea	d					19 00																			
Fratton	d					19 04																			
Hilsea	d					19 08																			
Cosham	d					19 13																			
Portchester	d					19 18																			
Fareham	d					19 24					20 27										21 27				
Botley	d					19 31																			
Hedge End	d					19 36																			
Eastleigh 3	a					19 42	19 49		20 06							20 49			21 06					21 49	
	d					19 43	19 50		20 11							20 50			21 11					21 50	
Chandlers Ford	d						19 55									20 55								21 55	
Romsey	a						20 03									21 03								22 03	
Shawford	d								20 17										21 17						
Winchester	d			19 31	19 48	19 54			20 24	20 18				20 31	20 48				21 24	21 18					
Micheldever	d					20 02																			
Basingstoke	a			19 46		20 15			20 40	20 34				20 46					21 40	21 34					
	d			19 47		20 17			20 41	20 36				20 47					21 41	21 36					
Reading 7	a			20 04										21 04											
Fleet	d								20 52										21 52						
Farnborough (Main)	d					20 31			20 58										21 58						
Woking	a				20 19	20 40			21 07						21 19				22 07						
Clapham Junction 10	a								21 30	21 16									22 28	22 14					
London Waterloo 15 ⊖	a				20 49	21 07			21 38	21 24					21 49				22 38	22 22					

b arr. 1931

Table 158

Weymouth, Bournemouth, Lymington, Romsey, Southampton and Basingstoke - London

		SW	GW	GW	SW	SW	SW	SW		GW	SW	SW	SW
		◇1		◇	1	1	1	1		◇	◇1	1	1
Weymouth	d	20 10	20 21								22 10	23 10	
Upwey	d	20 14	20 26								22 14	23 14	
Dorchester West	a		20 33										
Dorchester South	d	20 22									22 22	23 22	
Moreton (Dorset)	d	20 28									22 28	23 28	
Wool	d	20 34									22 34	23 34	
Wareham	d	20 42									22 42	23 42	
Holton Heath	d												
Hamworthy	d	20 48									22 48	23 48	
Poole 4	a	20 53									22 53	23 53	
	d	20 54									22 54	23 54	
Parkstone (Dorset)	d	20 58									22 58		
Branksome	d	21 01									23 01		
Bournemouth	a	21 07									23 07	00 03	
	d	21 12									23 12		
Pokesdown	d	21 16									23 16		
Christchurch	d	21 20									23 20		
Hinton Admiral	d	21 25									23 25		
New Milton	d	21 29									23 29		
Sway	d	21 34									23 34		
Yarmouth (IOW)	d							*21 15*					
Lymington Pier	d				21 44			22 14					
Lymington Town	d				21 46			22 16					
Brockenhurst 3	a	21 39			21 55			22 25			23 39		
	d	21 40									23 40		
Beaulieu Road	d												
Ashurst New Forest	d	21 47									23 47		
Totton	d	21 52									23 52		
Salisbury	d			21 32			21 49			22 32			
Dean	d						22 01						
Mottisfont & Dunbridge	d						22 07						
Romsey	d			21 50			22 12			22 50			
Redbridge	d						22 20						
Millbrook (Hants)	d						22 23						
Southampton Central	a	21 57		22 02			22 26			23 03	23 57		
	d	22 00		22 04			22 35			23 04	23 59		
St Denys	d						22 40				00 04		
Swaythling	d						22 43				00 07		
Southampton Airport Parkwy ✈	d	22 08					22 46				00 10		
Portsmouth Harbour	d					21 55							23 24
Portsmouth & Southsea	d					22 00							23 29
Fratton	d					22 04							23 33
Hilsea	d					22 08							23 37
Cosham	d					22 13							23 42
Portchester	d					22 18							23 47
Fareham	d					22 24				23 27			23 53
Botley	d					22 31							23 59
Hedge End	d					22 36							00 05
Eastleigh 3	a			22 14		22 43	22 49				00 14		00 11
	d			22 24			22 50						00 19
Chandlers Ford	d						22 55						
Romsey	a						23 03						
Shawford	d												
Winchester	d	22 18											00a28
Micheldever	d												
Basingstoke	a	22 34											
	d	22 36											
Reading 7	a												
Fleet	d												
Farnborough (Main)	d												
Woking	a	22 54											
Clapham Junction 10	a	23 14											
London Waterloo 15 ⊖	a	23 23											

Weymouth, Bournemouth, Lymington, Romsey, Southampton and Basingstoke - London

		SW	SW	SW	XC	SW	XC	SW	SW	SW	XC	GW	XC	GW	SW	SW	SW	SW	SW	SW	SW	GW	GW
		◇1	1	1	◇1	1	◇1	◇1	1	1	◇1		◇1		1	◇1	1	1	1	1	◇1	◇	
					⌶		⌶	⊏			⌶		⌶			⊏					⊏		
Weymouth	d	22p10	23p10											06 40									
Upwey	d	22p14	23p14											06 45									
Dorchester West	a													06 52									
Dorchester South	d	22p22	23p22																				
Moreton (Dorset)	d	22p28	23p28																				
Wool	d	22p34	23p34																				
Wareham	d	22p42	23p42																		06 53		
Holton Heath	d																				06 56		
Hamworthy	d	22p48	23p48																		07 01		
Poole 4	a	22p53	23p53																		07 06		
	d	22p54	23p54					05 28								06 28				06 50	07 07		
Parkstone (Dorset)	d	22p58						05 32								06 32				06 54			
Branksome	d	23p01						05 35								06 35				06 57			
Bournemouth	a	23p07	00 03					05 40								06 40				07 02	07 17		
	d	23p12						05 42			06 25		06 37			06 42				07 05	07 22		
Pokesdown	d	23p16						05 46								06 46				07 09	07 26		
Christchurch	d	23p20						05 50								06 50				07 13	07 30		
Hinton Admiral	d	23p25						05 55								06 55				07 18			
New Milton	d	23p29						05 59								06 59				07 22	07 37		
Sway	d	23p34						06 04								07 04				07 27			
Yarmouth (IOW)	d									*04 30*					*05 55*								
Lymington Pier	d									06 14					06 44				07 14				
Lymington Town	d									06 16					06 46				07 16				
Brockenhurst 3	a	23p39						06 09		06 24	06 38		06 52		06 54	07 09			07 24	07 32	07 44		
	d	23p40						06 10			06 39		06 55			07 10				07 33	07 45		
Beaulieu Road	d																						
Ashurst New Forest	d	23p47						06 17								07 17				07 40			
Totton	d	23p52						06 22	06 12							07 22				07 45			
Salisbury	d					05 35						06 32						06 48				07b24	07 37
Dean	d					05 47												07 00					
Mottisfont & Dunbridge	d					05 53												07 06					
Romsey	d					05 58						06 50						07 11				07 44	07 56
Redbridge	d								06 14									07 19					
Millbrook (Hants)	d								06 18									07 22					
Southampton Central	a	23p57						06 27	06 21		06 52	07 02	07 07			07 27		07 25		07 52	07 58	08 02	08 07
	d	23p59			05 09		06 15	06 30	06 35		06 53	07 05	07 15			07 30		07 35		07 55	08 00	08 04	
St Denys	d	00 04							06 40									07 40					
Swaythling	d	00 07							06 43									07 43					
Southampton Airport Parkwy ✈	d	00 10			05 16		06 22	06 38	06 46		07 01		07 22			07 38		07 46		08 03	08 08		
Portsmouth Harbour	d			23p24													06 55						
Portsmouth & Southsea	d			23p29													07 00						
Fratton	d			23p33													07 04						
Hilsea	d			23p37													07 08						
Cosham	d			23p42													07 13						
Portchester	d			23p47													07 18						
Fareham	d			23p53								07 27					07 24					08 27	
Botley	d			23p59													07 31						
Hedge End	d			00 05													07 36						
Eastleigh 3	a	00 14		00 11				06 41	06 49								07 42	07 49		08 06			
	d			00 19				06 42	06 50								07 43	07 50		08 11			
Chandlers Ford	d					06 06			06 55									07 55					
Romsey	a					06 43			07 03									08 03					
Shawford	d																			08 17			
Winchester	d			00a28	05 25		06 31	06 52			07 09		07 31			07 48	07 54			08 24	08 18		
Micheldever	d																08 02						
Basingstoke	a				05 40		06 46	07 08			07 24		07 46				08 15			08 40	08 34		
	d				05 41		06 47	07 09			07 25		07 47				08 17			08 41	08 36		
Reading 7	a				05 59		07 04				07 42		08 04										
Fleet	d																			08 52			
Farnborough (Main)	d																08 31			08 58			
Woking	a							07 27								08 21	08 40						
Clapham Junction 10	a																			09 23	09 12		
London Waterloo 15 ⊖	a							07 53								08 49	09 08			09 34	09 20		

b arr. 0715

Table 158

Saturdays

Weymouth, Bournemouth, Lymington, Romsey, Southampton and Basingstoke - London

		SW	XC	SW	SW	SW	SW	SW	SW	SW	SW	GW	SW	XC	SW	SW	SW	SW	SW	SW	SW	GW	GW
		1	◇1	◇1	◇1	1	1	1	1	◇1	◇1	◇	1	◇1	◇1	◇1	1	1	1	1	◇1		◇
				A	B					A	B												
			⌶	⊏	⊏					⊏	⊏			⌶	⊏	⊏					⊏		
Weymouth	d			06 50	06 55					07 17	07 20				07 58	08 03					08 20	08 50	
Upwey	d			06 54	06 59					07 21	07 24										08 24	08 55	
Dorchester West	a																					09 02	
Dorchester South	d			07 02	07 07					07 33	07 33				08 08	08 13					08 33		
Moreton (Dorset)	d			07 09	07 14					07 39	07 39										08 39		
Wool	d			07 15	07 20					07 45	07 45										08 45		
Wareham	d			07 22	07 27					07 53	07 53				08 23	08 28					08 53		
Holton Heath	d			07 26	07 31					07 56	07 56										08 56		
Hamworthy	d			07 31	07 36					08 01	08 01				08 30	08 35					09 01		
Poole 4	a			07 35	07 40					08 06	08 06				08 34	08 39					09 07		
	d			07 36	07 41				07 50	08 07	08 07				08 35	08 40				08 50	09 07		
Parkstone (Dorset)	d			07 40	07 45				07 54						08 39	08 44				08 54			
Branksome	d			07 44	07 49				07 57						08 43	08 48				08 57			
Bournemouth	a			07 54	07 54				08 02	08 17	08 17				08 54	08 54				09 02	09 17		
	d		07 45	07 59	07 59				08 05	08 22	08 22			08 45	08 59	08 59				09 05	09 22		
Pokesdown	d								08 09	08 26	08 26									09 09	09 26		
Christchurch	d								08 13	08 30	08 30									09 13	09 30		
Hinton Admiral	d								08 18											09 18			
New Milton	d								08 22	08 37	08 37									09 22	09 37		
Sway	d								08 27											09 27			
Yarmouth (IOW)	d	*06 55*																	*08 35*				
Lymington Pier	d	07 44						08 14					08 44						09 14				
Lymington Town	d	07 46						08 16					08 46						09 16				
Brockenhurst 3	a	07 54	07 58	08 14	08 14			08 24	08 32	08 44	08 44		08 54	08 58	09 14	09 14			09 24	09 32	09 44		
	d		08 00	08 15	08 15				08 33	08 45	08 45			09 00	09 15	09 15				09 33	09 45		
Beaulieu Road	d																			09 38			
Ashurst New Forest	d								08 40											09 42			
Totton	d								08 45											09 47			
Salisbury	d						07 48					08 32						08 48					09 32
Dean	d						08 00											09 00					
Mottisfont & Dunbridge	d						08 06											09 06					
Romsey	d						08 11					08 50						09 11					09 50
Redbridge	d						08 19											09 19					
Millbrook (Hants)	d						08 22											09 22					
Southampton Central	a		08 12	08 28	08 28		08 25		08 52	08 58	08 58	09 02		09 12	09 28	09 28		09 25		09 53	09 58		10 02
	d		08 15	08 30	08 30		08 35		08 55	09 00	09 00	09 04		09 15	09 30	09 30		09 35		09 55	10 00		10 04
St Denys	d						08 40											09 40					
Swaythling	d						08 43											09 43					
Southampton Airport Parkwy ✈	d		08 22	08 38	08 38		08 46		09 03	09 08	09 08			09 22	09 38	09 38		09 46		10 03	10 08		
Portsmouth Harbour	d					07 55											08 55						
Portsmouth & Southsea	d					08 00											09 00						
Fratton	d					08 04											09 04						
Hilsea	d					08 08											09 08						
Cosham	d					08 13											09 13						
Portchester	d					08 18											09 18						
Fareham	d					08 24						09 27					09 24						10 27
Botley	d					08 31											09 31						
Hedge End	d					08 36											09 36						
Eastleigh 3	a					08 42	08 49		09 06								09 42	09 49		10 06			
	d					08 43	08 50		09 11								09 43	09 50		10 11			
Chandlers Ford	d						08 55											09 55					
Romsey	a						09 03											10 03					
Shawford	d								09 17											10 17			
Winchester	d		08 31	08 48	08 48	08 54			09 24	09 18	09 18			09 31	09 48	09 48	09 54			10 24	10 18		
Micheldever	d					09 02											10 02						
Basingstoke	a		08 46			09 15			09 40	09 34	09 34			09 46			10 15			10 40	10 34		
	d		08 47			09 17			09 41	09 36	09 36			09 47			10 17			10 41	10 36		
Reading 7	a		09 04											10 04									
Fleet	d								09 52											10 52			
Farnborough (Main)	d					09 31			09 58								10 31			10 58			
Woking	a			09 19	09 19	09 40									10 19	10 19	10 40						
Clapham Junction 10	a								10 23	10 12	10 12									11 23	11 12		
London Waterloo 15 ⊖	a			09 49	09 49	10 07			10 34	10 20	10 20				10 49	10 49	11 07			11 34	11 20		

A from 2 October. **B** until 25 September.

Table 158

Saturdays

Weymouth, Bournemouth, Lymington, Romsey, Southampton and Basingstoke - London

		SW	XC	SW	SW	SW	SW	SW	SW	GW	SW	XC	SW	SW	SW	SW	SW	SW	GW	SW	XC	GW
		1	◇1	◇1	1	1	1	1	◇1	◇	1	◇1	◇1	1	1	1	1	◇1	◇	1	◇1	
			H	⊐					⊐			H	⊐					⊐	H		H	
Weymouth	d			09 03					09 20				10 03					10 20				
Upwey	d								09 24									10 24				
Dorchester West	a																					
Dorchester South	d			09 13					09 33				10 13					10 33				
Moreton (Dorset)	d								09 39									10 39				
Wool	d								09 45									10 45				
Wareham	d			09 28					09 53				10 28					10 53				
Holton Heath	d								09 56									10 56				
Hamworthy	d			09 35					10 01				10 35					11 01				
Poole 4	a			09 39					10 06				10 39					11 06				
	d			09 40				09 50	10 07				10 40				10 50	11 07				
Parkstone (Dorset)	d			09 44				09 54					10 44				10 54					
Branksome	d			09 48				09 57					10 48				10 57					
Bournemouth	a			09 54				10 02	10 17				10 54				11 02	11 17				
	d		09 45	09 59				10 05	10 22			10 45	10 59				11 05	11 22			11 45	
Pokesdown	d							10 09	10 26								11 09	11 26				
Christchurch	d							10 13	10 30								11 13	11 30				
Hinton Admiral	d							10 18									11 18					
New Milton	d							10 22	10 37								11 22	11 37				
Sway	d							10 27									11 27					
Yarmouth (IOW)	d										*09 55*					*10 35*						
Lymington Pier	d	09 44					10 14				10 44					11 14				11 44		
Lymington Town	d	09 46					10 16				10 46					11 16				11 46		
Brockenhurst 3	a	09 54	09 58	10 14			10 24	10 32	10 44		10 54	10 58	11 14			11 24	11 32	11 44		11 54	11 58	
	d		10 00	10 15				10 33	10 45			11 00	11 15				11 33	11 45			12 00	
Beaulieu Road	d																11 38					
Ashurst New Forest	d							10 40									11 42					
Totton	d							10 45									11 47					
Salisbury	d					09 48				10 32					10 48				11 32			11 39
Dean	d					10 00									11 00							
Mottisfont & Dunbridge	d					10 06									11 06							
Romsey	d					10 11				10 50					11 11				11 50			12 00
Redbridge	d					10 19									11 19							
Millbrook (Hants)	d					10 22									11 22							
Southampton Central	a		10 12	10 28		10 25		10 53	10 58	11 02		11 12	11 28		11 25		11 53	11 58	12 02		12 12	12 20
	d		10 15	10 30		10 35		10 55	11 00	11 04		11 15	11 30		11 35		11 55	12 00	12 04		12 15	
St Denys	d					10 40									11 40							
Swaythling	d					10 43									11 43							
Southampton Airport Parkwy ✈	d		10 22	10 38		10 46		11 03	11 08			11 22	11 38		11 46		12 03	12 08			12 22	
Portsmouth Harbour	d				09 55									10 55								
Portsmouth & Southsea	d				10 00									11 00								
Fratton	d				10 04									11 04								
Hilsea	d				10 08									11 08								
Cosham	d				10 13									11 13								
Portchester	d				10 18									11 18								
Fareham	d				10 24					11 27				11 24					12 27			
Botley	d				10 31									11 31								
Hedge End	d				10 36									11 36								
Eastleigh 3	a				10 42	10 49		11 06						11 42	11 49		12 06					
	d				10 43	10 50		11 11						11 43	11 50		12 11					
Chandlers Ford	d					10 55									11 55							
Romsey	a					11 03									12 03							
Shawford	d							11 17									12 17					
Winchester	d		10 31	10 48	10 54			11 24	11 18			11 31	11 48	11 54			12 24	12 18			12 31	
Micheldever	d				11 02									12 02								
Basingstoke	a		10 46		11 15			11 40	11 34			11 46		12 15			12 40	12 34			12 46	
	d		10 47		11 17			11 41	11 36			11 47		12 17			12 41	12 36			12 47	
Reading 7	a		11 04									12 04									13 04	
Fleet	d							11 52									12 52					
Farnborough (Main)	d				11 31			11 58						12 31			12 58					
Woking	a			11 19	11 40								12 19	12 40								
Clapham Junction 10	a							12 23	12 12								13 23	13 12				
London Waterloo 15 ⊖	a			11 49	12 07			12 34	12 20				12 49	13 07			13 34	13 20				

Table 158

Saturdays

Weymouth, Bournemouth, Lymington, Romsey, Southampton and Basingstoke - London

		SW	GW	SW	SW	SW	SW	SW	GW	SW	XC	SW	SW	SW	SW	SW	SW	GW	SW	XC	SW	GW	SW
		◇1		1	1	1	1	◇1	◇	1	◇1	◇1	1	1	1	1	◇1	◇	1	◇1	◇1		1
		⊐						⊐	H		H	⊐					⊐	H		H	⊐		
Weymouth	d	11 03	11 10					11 20				12 03					12 20				13 03	13 10	
Upwey	d		11 15					11 24									12 24					13 15	
Dorchester West	a		11 23																			13 22	
Dorchester South	d	11 13						11 33				12 13					12 33				13 13		
Moreton (Dorset)	d							11 39									12 39						
Wool	d							11 45									12 45						
Wareham	d	11 28						11 53				12 28					12 53				13 28		
Holton Heath	d							11 56									12 56						
Hamworthy	d	11 35						12 01				12 35					13 01				13 35		
Poole 4	a	11 39						12 06				12 39					13 06				13 39		
	d	11 40					11 50	12 07				12 40				12 50	13 07				13 40		
Parkstone (Dorset)	d	11 44					11 54					12 44				12 54					13 44		
Branksome	d	11 48					11 57					12 48				12 57					13 48		
Bournemouth	a	11 54					12 02	12 17				12 54				13 02	13 17				13 54		
	d	11 59					12 05	12 22			12 45	12 59				13 05	13 22			13 45	13 59		
Pokesdown	d						12 09	12 26								13 09	13 26						
Christchurch	d						12 13	12 30								13 13	13 30						
Hinton Admiral	d						12 18									13 18							
New Milton	d						12 22	12 37								13 22	13 37						
Sway	d						12 27									13 27							
Yarmouth (IOW)	d					*11 15*				*11 55*					*12 35*								
Lymington Pier	d					12 14				12 44					13 14				13 44				
Lymington Town	d					12 16				12 46					13 16				13 46				
Brockenhurst 3	a	12 14				12 24	12 32	12 44		12 54	12 58	13 14			13 24	13 32	13 44		13 54	13 58	14 14		
	d	12 15					12 33	12 45			13 00	13 15				13 33	13 45			14 00	14 15		
Beaulieu Road	d															13 38							
Ashurst New Forest	d						12 40									13 42							
Totton	d						12 45									13 47							
Salisbury	d				11 48				12 32					12 48				13 32					
Dean	d				12 00									13 00									
Mottisfont & Dunbridge	d				12 06									13 06									
Romsey	d				12 11				12 50					13 11				13 50					
Redbridge	d				12 19									13 19									
Millbrook (Hants)	d				12 22									13 22									
Southampton Central	a	12 28			12 25		12 51	12 58	13 02		13 12	13 28		13 25		13 53	13 58	14 02		14 12	14 28		
	d	12 30			12 35		12 55	13 00	13 04		13 15	13 30		13 35		13 55	14 00	14 04		14 15	14 30		
St Denys	d				12 40									13 40									
Swaythling	d				12 43									13 43									
Southampton Airport Parkwy ✈	d	12 38			12 46		13 03	13 08			13 22	13 38		13 46		14 03	14 08			14 22	14 38		
Portsmouth Harbour	d			11 55									12 55										13 55
Portsmouth & Southsea	d			12 00									13 00										14 00
Fratton	d			12 04									13 04										14 04
Hilsea	d			12 08									13 08										14 08
Cosham	d			12 13									13 13										14 13
Portchester	d			12 18									13 18										14 18
Fareham	d			12 24					13 27				13 24					14 27					14 24
Botley	d			12 31									13 31										14 31
Hedge End	d			12 36									13 36										14 36
Eastleigh 3	a			12 42	12 49		13 06						13 42	13 49		14 06							14 42
	d			12 43	12 50		13 11						13 43	13 50		14 11							14 43
Chandlers Ford	d				12 55									13 55									
Romsey	a				13 03									14 03									
Shawford	d						13 17									14 17							
Winchester	d	12 48		12 54			13 24	13 18			13 31	13 48	13 54			14 24	14 18			14 31	14 48		14 54
Micheldever	d			13 02									14 02										15 02
Basingstoke	a			13 15			13 40	13 34			13 46		14 15			14 40	14 34			14 46			15 15
	d			13 17			13 41	13 36			13 47		14 17			14 41	14 36			14 47			15 17
Reading 7	a										14 04									15 04			
Fleet	d						13 52									14 52							
Farnborough (Main)	d			13 31			13 58						14 31			14 58							15 31
Woking	a	13 19		13 40								14 19	14 40								15 19		15 40
Clapham Junction 10	a						14 23	14 12								15 23	15 12						
London Waterloo 15 ⊖	a	13 49		14 07			14 34	14 20				14 49	15 07			15 34	15 20				15 49		16 07

Table 158

Weymouth, Bournemouth, Lymington, Romsey, Southampton and Basingstoke - London

		SW	SW	SW	GW	SW	GW	SW	XC	SW	SW	SW
		1	1	1	◇	◇1 ☕	◇ 🛒	1	◇1 🛒	◇1 ☕	1	1
Weymouth	d					13 20				14 03		
Upwey	d					13 24						
Dorchester West	a											
Dorchester South	d					13 33				14 13		
Moreton (Dorset)	d					13 39						
Wool	d					13 45						
Wareham	d					13 53				14 28		
Holton Heath	d					13 56						
Hamworthy	d					14 01				14 35		
Poole 4	a					14 06				14 39		
	d			13 50		14 07				14 40		
Parkstone (Dorset)	d			13 54						14 44		
Branksome	d			13 57						14 48		
Bournemouth	a			14 02		14 17				14 54		
	d			14 05		14 22			14 45	14 59		
Pokesdown	d			14 09		14 26						
Christchurch	d			14 13		14 30						
Hinton Admiral	d			14 18								
New Milton	d			14 22		14 37						
Sway	d			14 27								
Yarmouth (IOW)	d		*13 15*					*13 55*				
Lymington Pier	d		14 14					14 44				
Lymington Town	d		14 16					14 46				
Brockenhurst 3	a		14 24	14 32		14 44		14 54	14 58	15 14		
	d			14 33		14 45			15 00	15 15		
Beaulieu Road	d											
Ashurst New Forest	d			14 40								
Totton	d			14 45								
Salisbury	d	13 48			13 59		14 32					14 48
Dean	d	14 00										15 00
Mottisfont & Dunbridge	d	14 06										15 06
Romsey	d	14 11			14 19		14 50					15 11
Redbridge	d	14 19										15 19
Millbrook (Hants)	d	14 22										15 22
Southampton Central	a	14 25		14 51	14 32	14 58	15 02		15 12	15 28		15 25
	d	14 35		14 55		15 00	15 04		15 15	15 30		15 35
St Denys	d	14 40										15 40
Swaythling	d	14 43										15 43
Southampton Airport Parkwy ✈	d	14 46		15 03		15 08			15 22	15 38		15 46
Portsmouth Harbour	d										14 55	
Portsmouth & Southsea	d										15 00	
Fratton	d										15 04	
Hilsea	d										15 08	
Cosham	d										15 13	
Portchester	d										15 18	
Fareham	d						15 27				15 24	
Botley	d										15 31	
Hedge End	d										15 36	
Eastleigh 3	a	14 49		15 06							15 42	15 49
	d	14 50		15 11							15 43	15 50
Chandlers Ford	d	14 55										15 55
Romsey	a	15 04										16 03
Shawford	d			15 17								
Winchester	d			15 24		15 18			15 31	15 48	15 54	
Micheldever	d										16 02	
Basingstoke	a			15 40		15 34			15 46		16 15	
	d			15 41		15 36			15 47		16 17	
Reading 7	a								16 05			
Fleet	d			15 52								
Farnborough (Main)	d			15 58							16 31	
Woking	a									16 19	16 40	
Clapham Junction 10	a			16 23		16 12						
London Waterloo 15 ⊖	a			16 34		16 20				16 49	17 07	

		SW	SW	SW	GW	SW	XC	SW	GW	SW	SW	SW
		1	1	◇1 ☕	◇	1	◇1 🛒	◇1 ☕	B	1	1	1
Weymouth	d			14 20				15 03	15 08			
Upwey	d			14 24					15 13			
Dorchester West	a								15 20			
Dorchester South	d			14 33				15 13				
Moreton (Dorset)	d			14 39								
Wool	d			14 45								
Wareham	d			14 53				15 28				
Holton Heath	d			14 56								
Hamworthy	d			15 01				15 35				
Poole 4	a			15 06				15 39				
	d		14 50	15 07				15 40				
Parkstone (Dorset)	d		14 54					15 44				
Branksome	d		14 57					15 48				
Bournemouth	a		15 02	15 17				15 54				
	d		15 05	15 22			15 45	15 59				
Pokesdown	d		15 09	15 26								
Christchurch	d		15 13	15 30								
Hinton Admiral	d		15 18									
New Milton	d		15 22	15 37								
Sway	d		15 27									
Yarmouth (IOW)	d	*14 35*										
Lymington Pier	d	15 14				15 44						16 14
Lymington Town	d	15 16				15 46						16 16
Brockenhurst 3	a	15 24	15 32	15 44		15 54	15 58	16 14				16 24
	d		15 33	15 45			16 00	16 15				
Beaulieu Road	d		15 38									
Ashurst New Forest	d		15 42									
Totton	d		15 47									
Salisbury	d				15 32						15 48	
Dean	d										16 00	
Mottisfont & Dunbridge	d										16 06	
Romsey	d				15 50						16 11	
Redbridge	d										16 19	
Millbrook (Hants)	d										16 22	
Southampton Central	a		15 53	15 58	16 02		16 12	16 28			16 25	
	d		15 55	16 00	16 04		16 15	16 30			16 35	
St Denys	d										16 40	
Swaythling	d										16 43	
Southampton Airport Parkwy ✈	d		16 03	16 08			16 22	16 38			16 46	
Portsmouth Harbour	d									15 55		
Portsmouth & Southsea	d									16 00		
Fratton	d									16 04		
Hilsea	d									16 08		
Cosham	d									16 13		
Portchester	d									16 18		
Fareham	d				16 27					16 24		
Botley	d									16 31		
Hedge End	d									16 36		
Eastleigh 3	a		16 06							16 42	16 49	
	d		16 11							16 43	16 50	
Chandlers Ford	d										16 55	
Romsey	a										17 03	
Shawford	d		16 17									
Winchester	d		16 24	16 18			16 31	16 48		16 54		
Micheldever	d									17 02		
Basingstoke	a		16 40	16 34			16 46			17 15		
	d		16 41	16 36			16 47			17 17		
Reading 7	a						17 04					
Fleet	d		16 52									
Farnborough (Main)	d		16 58							17 31		
Woking	a							17 19		17 40		
Clapham Junction 10	a		17 23	17 12								
London Waterloo 15 ⊖	a		17 34	17 20				17 49		18 07		

B from 11 September

Table 158

Weymouth, Bournemouth, Lymington, Romsey, Southampton and Basingstoke - London

		SW	SW	GW	SW	XC	SW	GW	SW	SW	SW	SW
		1	◇1 ☕	◇	1	◇1 🛒	◇1 ☕	B	1	1	1	1
Weymouth	d		15 20				16 03	16 08				
Upwey	d		15 24					16 13				
Dorchester West	a							16 21				
Dorchester South	d		15 33				16 13					
Moreton (Dorset)	d		15 39									
Wool	d		15 45									
Wareham	d		15 53				16 28					
Holton Heath	d		15 56									
Hamworthy	d		16 01				16 35					
Poole 4	a		16 06				16 39					
	d	15 50	16 07				16 40					16 50
Parkstone (Dorset)	d	15 54					16 44					16 54
Branksome	d	15 57					16 48					16 57
Bournemouth	a	16 02	16 17				16 54					17 02
	d	16 05	16 22			16 45	16 59					17 05
Pokesdown	d	16 09	16 26									17 09
Christchurch	d	16 13	16 30									17 13
Hinton Admiral	d	16 18										17 18
New Milton	d	16 22	16 37									17 22
Sway	d	16 27										17 27
Yarmouth (IOW)	d				*15 55*						*16 35*	
Lymington Pier	d				16 44						17 14	
Lymington Town	d				16 46						17 16	
Brockenhurst 3	a	16 32	16 44		16 54	16 58	17 14				17 24	17 32
	d	16 33	16 45			17 00	17 15					17 33
Beaulieu Road	d											17 38
Ashurst New Forest	d	16 40										17 42
Totton	d	16 45										17 47
Salisbury	d			16 32						16 48		
Dean	d									17 00		
Mottisfont & Dunbridge	d									17 06		
Romsey	d			16 50						17 11		
Redbridge	d									17 19		
Millbrook (Hants)	d									17 22		
Southampton Central	a	16 51	16 58	17 02		17 12	17 28			17 25		17 53
	d	16 55	17 00	17 04		17 15	17 30			17 35		17 55
St Denys	d									17 40		
Swaythling	d									17 43		
Southampton Airport Parkwy ✈	d	17 03	17 08			17 22	17 38			17 46		18 03
Portsmouth Harbour	d								16 55			
Portsmouth & Southsea	d								17 00			
Fratton	d								17 04			
Hilsea	d								17 08			
Cosham	d								17 13			
Portchester	d								17 18			
Fareham	d			17 27					17 24			
Botley	d								17 31			
Hedge End	d								17 36			
Eastleigh 3	a	17 06							17 42	17 49		18 06
	d	17 11							17 43	17 50		18 11
Chandlers Ford	d									17 55		
Romsey	a									18 03		
Shawford	d	17 17										18 17
Winchester	d	17 24	17 18			17 31	17 48		17 54			18 24
Micheldever	d								18 02			
Basingstoke	a	17 40	17 34			17 46			18 15			18 40
	d	17 41	17 36			17 47			18 17			18 41
Reading 7	a					18 04						
Fleet	d	17 52										18 52
Farnborough (Main)	d	17 58							18 31			18 58
Woking	a						18 19		18 40			
Clapham Junction 10	a	18 23	18 12									19 23
London Waterloo 15 ⊖	a	18 34	18 20				18 49		19 07			19 34

		SW	GW	GW	SW	XC	SW	SW	SW	SW	SW	SW
		◇1 ☕	B	◇	1	◇1 🛒	◇1 ☕	1	1	1	1	◇1 ☕
Weymouth	d	16 20	16 55				17 03					17 20
Upwey	d	16 24										17 24
Dorchester West	a		17 06									
Dorchester South	d	16 33					17 13					17 33
Moreton (Dorset)	d	16 39										17 39
Wool	d	16 45										17 45
Wareham	d	16 53					17 28					17 53
Holton Heath	d	16 56										17 56
Hamworthy	d	17 01					17 35					18 01
Poole 4	a	17 06					17 39					18 06
	d	17 07					17 40				17 50	18 07
Parkstone (Dorset)	d						17 44				17 54	
Branksome	d						17 48				17 57	
Bournemouth	a	17 17					17 54				18 02	18 17
	d	17 22				17 45	17 59				18 05	18 22
Pokesdown	d	17 26									18 09	18 26
Christchurch	d	17 30									18 13	18 30
Hinton Admiral	d										18 18	
New Milton	d	17 37									18 22	18 37
Sway	d										18 27	
Yarmouth (IOW)	d									*17 15*		
Lymington Pier	d				17 44					18 14		
Lymington Town	d				17 46					18 16		
Brockenhurst 3	a	17 44			17 54	17 58	18 14			18 24	18 32	18 44
	d	17 45				18 00	18 15				18 33	18 45
Beaulieu Road	d											
Ashurst New Forest	d										18 40	
Totton	d										18 45	
Salisbury	d			17 32					17 48			
Dean	d								18 00			
Mottisfont & Dunbridge	d								18 06			
Romsey	d			17 50					18 11			
Redbridge	d								18 19			
Millbrook (Hants)	d								18 22			
Southampton Central	a	17 58		18 02		18 12	18 28		18 25		18 51	18 58
	d	18 00		18 04		18 15	18 30		18 35		18 55	19 00
St Denys	d								18 40			
Swaythling	d								18 43			
Southampton Airport Parkwy ✈	d	18 08				18 22	18 38		18 46		19 03	19 08
Portsmouth Harbour	d							17 55				
Portsmouth & Southsea	d							18 00				
Fratton	d							18 04				
Hilsea	d							18 08				
Cosham	d							18 13				
Portchester	d							18 18				
Fareham	d			18 27				18 24				
Botley	d							18 31				
Hedge End	d							18 36				
Eastleigh 3	a							18 42	18 49		19 06	
	d							18 43	18 50		19 11	
Chandlers Ford	d								18 55			
Romsey	a								19 04			
Shawford	d										19 17	
Winchester	d	18 18				18 31	18 48	18 54			19 24	19 18
Micheldever	d							19 02				
Basingstoke	a	18 34				18 46		19 15			19 40	19 34
	d	18 36				18 47		19 17			19 41	19 36
Reading 7	a					19 04						
Fleet	d										19 52	
Farnborough (Main)	d							19 31			19 58	
Woking	a						19 19	19 40				
Clapham Junction 10	a	19 12									20 23	20 12
London Waterloo 15 ⊖	a	19 20					19 49	20 07			20 34	20 20

B until 4 September

Table 158

Saturdays

Weymouth, Bournemouth, Lymington, Romsey, Southampton and Basingstoke - London

		GW	GW	SW	XC	SW	SW	SW	SW	SW	SW	GW	SW	XC	GW	SW	SW	SW	SW	SW	GW	SW	SW
			■	1	◇1	◇1	1	1	1	1	◇1	◇	1	◇1		◇1	1	1	1	◇1	◇	1	1
Weymouth	d	17 30				18 03					18 20					19 03				19 20			
Upwey	d	17 35									18 24									19 24			
Dorchester West	a	17 42																					
Dorchester South	d					18 13					18 33					19 13				19 33			
Moreton (Dorset)	d										18 39									19 39			
Wool	d										18 45									19 45			
Wareham	d					18 28					18 53					19 28				19 53			
Holton Heath	d										18 56												
Hamworthy	d					18 35					19 01					19 35				20 01			
Poole 4	a					18 39					19 06					19 39				20 06			
	d					18 40				18 50	19 07					19 40			19 50	20 07			
Parkstone (Dorset)	d					18 44				18 54						19 44			19 54				
Branksome	d					18 48				18 57						19 48			19 57				
Bournemouth	a					18 54				19 02	19 17					19 54			20 02	20 17			
	d				18 45	18 59				19 05	19 22			19 45		19 59			20 05	20 22			
Pokesdown	d									19 09	19 26								20 09	20 26			
Christchurch	d									19 13	19 30								20 13	20 30			
Hinton Admiral	d									19 18									20 18				
New Milton	d									19 22	19 37								20 22	20 37			
Sway	d									19 27									20 27				
Yarmouth (IOW)	d			*17 55*					*18 30*									*19 30*					
Lymington Pier	d			18 44					19 14				19 44					20 14				20 44	
Lymington Town	d			18 46					19 16				19 46					20 16				20 46	
Brockenhurst 3	a			18 54	18 58	19 14			19 24	19 32	19 44		19 54	19 58		20 14		20 24	20 32	20 44		20 54	
	d				19 00	19 15				19 33	19 45			20 00		20 15			20 33	20 45			
Beaulieu Road	d																						
Ashurst New Forest	d									19 40									20 40				
Totton	d									19 45									20 45				
Salisbury	d		18 32					18 48				19 32			19 41		19 48				20 32		20 48
Dean	d							19 00									20 00						21 00
Mottisfont & Dunbridge	d							19 06									20 06						21 06
Romsey	d		18 50					19 11				19 50			20 04		20 11				20 50		21 11
Redbridge	d							19 19									20 19						21 19
Millbrook (Hants)	d							19 22									20 22						21 22
Southampton Central	a		19 02		19 12	19 28		19 25		19 51	19 58	20 02		20 12	20 18	20 28	20 25		20 51	20 58	21 02		21 25
	d		19 04		19 15	19 30		19 35		19 55	20 00	20 04		20 15		20 30	20 35		20 55	21 00	21 04		21 35
St Denys	d							19 40									20 40						21 40
Swaythling	d							19 43									20 43						21 43
Southampton Airport Parkwy ✈	d				19 22	19 38		19 46		20 03	20 08			20 22		20 38	20 46		21 03	21 08			21 46
Portsmouth Harbour	d						18 55																
Portsmouth & Southsea	d						19 00																
Fratton	d						19 04																
Hilsea	d						19 08																
Cosham	d						19 13																
Portchester	d						19 18																
Fareham	d		19 27				19 24					20 27									21 27		
Botley	d						19 31																
Hedge End	d						19 36																
Eastleigh 3	a						19 42	19 49		20 06							20 49		21 06				21 49
	d						19 43	19 50		20 11							20 50		21 11				21 50
Chandlers Ford	d							19 55									20 55						21 55
Romsey	a							20 03									21 03						22 03
Shawford	d									20 17									21 17				
Winchester	d				19 31	19 48	19 54			20 24	20 18			20 31		20 48			21 24	21 18			
Micheldever	d						20 02																
Basingstoke	a				19 46		20 15			20 40	20 34			20 46					21 40	21 34			
	d				19 47		20 17			20 41	20 36			20 47					21 41	21 36			
Reading 7	a				20 04									21 04									
Fleet	d									20 52									21 52				
Farnborough (Main)	d						20 31			20 58									21 58				
Woking	a					20 19	20 40			21 07						21 19			22 07				
Clapham Junction 10	a									21 30	21 16								22 30	22 14			
London Waterloo 15 ⊖	a					20 49	21 07			21 38	21 24					21 49			22 38	22 22			

Table 158

Saturdays

Weymouth, Bournemouth, Lymington, Romsey, Southampton and Basingstoke - London

		SW	SW	GW	GW	SW	SW	SW	SW	GW	SW	SW	SW
		1	◇1		◇	1	1	1	1	◇	1	1	1
Weymouth	d		20 10	20 21							22 10	23 10	
Upwey	d		20 14	20 26							22 14	23 14	
Dorchester West	a			20 33									
Dorchester South	d		20 22								22 22	23 22	
Moreton (Dorset)	d		20 28								22 28	23 28	
Wool	d		20 34								22 34	23 34	
Wareham	d		20 42								22 42	23 42	
Holton Heath	d												
Hamworthy	d		20 48								22 48	23 48	
Poole 4	a		20 53								22 53	23 53	
	d		20 54								22 54	23 54	
Parkstone (Dorset)	d		20 58								22 58		
Branksome	d		21 01								23 01		
Bournemouth	a		21 07								23 07	00 03	
	d		21 12								23 12		
Pokesdown	d		21 16								23 16		
Christchurch	d		21 20								23 20		
Hinton Admiral	d		21 25								23 25		
New Milton	d		21 29								23 29		
Sway	d		21 34								23 34		
Yarmouth (IOW)	d	*20 15*							*21 15*				
Lymington Pier	d	21 14				21 44			22 14				
Lymington Town	d	21 16				21 46			22 16				
Brockenhurst 3	a	21 24	21 39			21 54			22 24		23 39		
	d		21 40								23 40		
Beaulieu Road	d												
Ashurst New Forest	d		21 47								23 47		
Totton	d		21 52								23 52		
Salisbury	d				21 32			21 48		22 32			
Dean	d							22 00					
Mottisfont & Dunbridge	d							22 06					
Romsey	d				21 50			22 11		22 50			
Redbridge	d							22 19					
Millbrook (Hants)	d							22 22					
Southampton Central	a		21 57		22 02			22 25		23 02	23 57		
	d		22 00		22 04			22 35		23 04	23 59		
St Denys	d							22 40			00 04		
Swaythling	d							22 43			00 07		
Southampton Airport Parkwy ✈	d		22 08					22 46			00 10		
Portsmouth Harbour	d						21 55						23 24
Portsmouth & Southsea	d						22 00						23 29
Fratton	d						22 04						23 33
Hilsea	d						22 08						23 37
Cosham	d						22 13						23 42
Portchester	d						22 18						23 47
Fareham	d				22 27		22 24			23 27			23 53
Botley	d						22 31						23 59
Hedge End	d						22 36						00 05
Eastleigh 3	a						22 42	22 49			00 14		00 11
	d							22 50					00 21
Chandlers Ford	d							22 55					
Romsey	a							23 03					
Shawford	d												
Winchester	d		22 18										00a30
Micheldever	d												
Basingstoke	a		22 34										
	d		22 36										
Reading 7	a												
Fleet	d												
Farnborough (Main)	d												
Woking	a		22 54										
Clapham Junction 10	a		23 15										
London Waterloo 15 ⊖	a		23 23										

Table 158

Sundays

Weymouth, Bournemouth, Lymington, Romsey, Southampton and Basingstoke - London

		SW 1	SW 1	SW 1	SW 1	SW ◇1 ☕	SW 1	SW 1	SW ◇1	SW 1	XC ◇1 🛒	SW ◇1 B ☕	SW ◇1 C ☕	SW 1	SW 1 ☕	SW ◇1	SW 1	XC ◇1 🛒	SW 1	SW ◇1 B ☕	SW ◇1 C ☕	SW 1
Weymouth	d	22p10	23p10									07 43	07 48							08 43	08 48	
Upwey	d	22p14	23p14									07 47	07 52							08 47	08 52	
Dorchester West	a																					
Dorchester South	d	22p22	23p22									07 55	08 00							08 55	09 00	
Moreton (Dorset)	d	22p28	23p28									08 02	08 07							09 02	09 07	
Wool	d	22p34	23p34									08 08	08 13							09 08	09 13	
Wareham	d	22p42	23p42									08 15	08 20							09 15	09 20	
Holton Heath	d																					
Hamworthy	d	22p48	23p48									08 22	08 27							09 22	09 27	
Poole 4	a	22p53	23p53									08 26	08 31							09 26	09 31	
	d	22p54	23p54			06 50			07 50			08 27	08 32			08 55				09 27	09 32	
Parkstone (Dorset)	d	22p58				06 54			07 54			08 31	08 36							09 31	09 36	
Branksome	d	23p01				06 57			07 57			08 35	08 40							09 40	09 40	
Bournemouth	a	23p07	00 03			07 02			08 02			08 46	08 46			09 04				09 46	09 46	
	d	23p12				07 06			08 06			08 50	08 50			09 06		09 40		09 50	09 50	
Pokesdown	d	23p16				07 10			08 10							09 10						
Christchurch	d	23p20				07 14			08 14							09 14						
Hinton Admiral	d	23p25				07 19			08 19							09 19						
New Milton	d	23p29				07 23			08 23			09 01	09 01			09 23						
Sway	d	23p34				07 28			08 28							09 28						
Yarmouth (IOW)	d													*08 35*						*s*	*s*	
Lymington Pier	d													09 14					09 44			10 14
Lymington Town	d													09 16					09 46			10 16
Brockenhurst 3	a	23p39				07 33			08 33			09 08	09 08	09 24		09 33		09 53	09 54	10 08	10 08	10 24
	d	23p40				07 34			08 34			09 09	09 09			09 34		09 57		10 09	10 09	
Beaulieu Road	d								08 39							09 39						
Ashurst New Forest	d	23p47				07 43			08 43							09 43						
Totton	d	23p52				07 48			08 48							09 48						
Salisbury	d						08 08			08 20							09 08					
Dean	d						08 20										09 20					
Mottisfont & Dunbridge	d						08 26										09 26					
Romsey	d						08 35			08 39							09 32					
Redbridge	d									08 46							09 39					
Millbrook (Hants)	d									08 50							09 43					
Southampton Central	a	23p57				07 53			08 53	08 52		09 23	09 23			09 53	09 45	10 10		10 23	10 23	
	d	23p59				07 55			08 55	08 59	09 15	09 25	09 25			09 55	09 59	10 15		10 25	10 25	
St Denys	d	00 04								09 04							10 04					
Swaythling	d	00 07								09 07							10 07					
Southampton Airport Parkwy ✈	d	00 10				08 03			09 03	09 10	09 22	09 33	09 33			10 03	10 10	10 22		10 33	10 33	
Portsmouth Harbour	d			23p24	07 17			08 17							09 17							
Portsmouth & Southsea	d			23p29	07 22			08 22							09 22							
Fratton	d			23p33	07 26			08 26							09 26							
Hilsea	d			23p37	07 30			08 30							09 30							
Cosham	d			23p42	07 35			08 35							09 35							
Portchester	d			23p47	07 40			08 40							09 40							
Fareham	d			23p53	07 46			08 46							09 46							
Botley	d			23p59	07 54			08 54							09 54							
Hedge End	d			00 05	07 58			08 58							09 58							
Eastleigh 3	a	00 14		00 11	08 04	08 07		09 04	09 07	09 13					10 04	10 07	10 13					
	d			00 21	08 11	<		09 11	<	09 15					10 11	<	10 15					
Chandlers Ford	d						08 42			09 20							10 20					
Romsey	a						09 24			09 28							10 28					
Shawford	d							09 17														
Winchester	d			00a30	08 23			09 23			09 31	09 42	09 42		10 23			10 31		10 42	10 42	
Micheldever	d				08 32			09 32							10 32							
Basingstoke	a				08 42			09 42			09 46	09 58	09 58		10 42			10 46		10 58	10 58	
	d				08 44			09 44			09 47	10 00	10 00		10 44			10 47		11 00	11 00	
Reading 7	a										10 04							11 04				
Fleet	d																					
Farnborough (Main)	d																					
Woking	a				09 02			10 02				10 19	10 19		11 02					11 18	11 18	
Clapham Junction 10	a				09 30			10 27				10 40	10 40		11 27					11 39	11 39	
London Waterloo 15 ⊖	a				09 43			10 42				10 54	10 54		11 42					11 54	11 54	

B from 26 September.

C until 19 September.

Table 158

Sundays

Weymouth, Bournemouth, Lymington, Romsey, Southampton and Basingstoke - London

		SW 1 ☕	SW ◇1 D ☕	SW 1	GW ◇	XC ◇1 🛒	SW 1	SW ◇1 ☕	SW 1	SW 1 ☕	SW ◇1	SW 1	GW ◇ B	GW ◇ C	XC ◇1 🛒	SW 1	SW ◇1 ☕	GW D	SW 1	SW 1 ☕	SW ◇1 ☕	SW 1	GW ◇	XC ◇1 🛒
Weymouth	d							09 48									10 48	11 10						
Upwey	d							09 52									10 52	11 15						
Dorchester West	a																	11 24						
Dorchester South	d							10 00									11 00							
Moreton (Dorset)	d							10 07									11 07							
Wool	d							10 13									11 13							
Wareham	d							10 20									11 20							
Holton Heath	d																							
Hamworthy	d							10 27									11 27							
Poole 4	a							10 31									11 31							
	d		09 55					10 32			10 55						11 32				11 55			
Parkstone (Dorset)	d							10 36									11 36							
Branksome	d							10 40									11 40							
Bournemouth	a		10 04					10 46			11 04						11 46				12 04			
	d		10 06			10 40		10 50			11 06				11 40		11 50				12 06			12 40
Pokesdown	d		10 10								11 10										12 10			
Christchurch	d		10 14								11 14										12 14			
Hinton Admiral	d		10 19								11 19										12 19			
New Milton	d		10 23					11 01			11 23						12 01				12 23			
Sway	d		10 28								11 28										12 28			
Yarmouth (IOW)	d						*09 55*		*10 35*										*11 15*					
Lymington Pier	d						10 44		11 14							11 44			12 14					
Lymington Town	d						10 46		11 16							11 46			12 16					
Brockenhurst 3	a		10 33			10 53	10 54	11 08	11 24		11 33				11 53	11 54	12 08		12 24		12 33			12 53
	d		10 34			10 57		11 09			11 34				11 57		12 09				12 34			12 57
Beaulieu Road	d		10 39								11 39										12 39			
Ashurst New Forest	d		10 43								11 43										12 43			
Totton	d		10 48								11 48										12 48			
Salisbury	d			10 13	10 32							11 08	11 31	11 32								12 13	12 36	
Dean	d											11 20												
Mottisfont & Dunbridge	d											11 26												
Romsey	d			10 32	10 50							11 32	11 50	11 50								12 32	12 54	
Redbridge	d			10 39								11 39										12 39		
Millbrook (Hants)	d			10 43								11 43										12 43		
Southampton Central	a		10 53	10 45	11 02	11 10		11 23			11 53	11 45	12 02	12 02	12 10		12 23				12 53	12 45	13 06	13 10
	d		10 55	10 59	11 04	11 15		11 25			11 55	11 59	12 02	12 04	12 15		12 25				12 55	12 59	13 08	13 15
St Denys	d			11 04								12 04										13 04		
Swaythling	d			11 07								12 07										13 07		
Southampton Airport Parkwy ✈	d		11 03	11 10		11 22		11 33			12 03	12 10			12 22		12 33				13 03	13 10		13 22
Portsmouth Harbour	d	10 17								11 17										12 17				
Portsmouth & Southsea	d	10 22								11 22										12 22				
Fratton	d	10 26								11 26										12 26				
Hilsea	d	10 30								11 30										12 30				
Cosham	d	10 35								11 35										12 35				
Portchester	d	10 40								11 40										12 40				
Fareham	d	10 46			11 27					11 46			12 27	12 27						12 46			13 34	
Botley	d	10 54								11 54										12 54				
Hedge End	d	10 58								11 58										12 58				
Eastleigh 3	a	11 04	11 07	11 13						12 04	12 07	12 13								13 04	13 07	13 13		
	d	11 11	<	11 15						12 11	<	12 15								13 11	<	13 15		
Chandlers Ford	d			11 20								12 20										13 20		
Romsey	a			11 28								12 28										13 28		
Shawford	d	11 17																		13 17				
Winchester	d	11 23				11 31		11 42		12 23					12 31		12 42			13 23				13 31
Micheldever	d	11 32								12 32										13 32				
Basingstoke	a	11 42				11 46		11 58		12 42					12 46		12 58			13 42				13 46
	d	11 44				11 47		12 00		12 44					12 47		13 00			13 44				13 47
Reading 7	a					12 04									13 04									14 04
Fleet	d																							
Farnborough (Main)	d																							
Woking	a	12 02						12 18		13 02							13 18			14 02				
Clapham Junction 10	a	12 27						12 39		13 27							13 39			14 27				
London Waterloo 15 ⊖	a	12 42						12 49		13 37							13 49			14 37				

B until 11 July

C from 18 July

D until 5 September

Table 158

Sundays

Weymouth, Bournemouth, Lymington, Romsey, Southampton and Basingstoke - London

		SW ■	SW ◇■ 🛒	SW ■	SW ■ 🛒	SW ◇■	SW ■	GW ◇ 🍴	XC ◇■ 🍴	SW ■	SW ◇■ 🛒	SW ■	SW ■ 🛒	SW ◇■	SW ■	GW ◇	SW ■	SW ◇■ 🛒	GW C	GW D	SW ■
Weymouth	d		11 48								12 48							13 48	14 00	14 10	
Upwey	d		11 52								12 52							13 52	14 05	14 15	
Dorchester West	a																		14 12	14 22	
Dorchester South	d		12 00								13 00							14 00			
Moreton (Dorset)	d		12 07								13 07							14 07			
Wool	d		12 13								13 13							14 13			
Wareham	d		12 20								13 20							14 20			
Holton Heath	d																				
Hamworthy	d		12 27								13 27							14 27			
Poole ■4	a		12 31								13 31							14 31			
	d		12 32			12 55					13 32			13 55				14 32			
Parkstone (Dorset)	d		12 36								13 36							14 36			
Branksome	d		12 40								13 40							14 40			
Bournemouth	a		12 46			13 04					13 46			14 04				14 46			
	d		12 50			13 06			13 40		13 50			14 06				14 50			
Pokesdown	d					13 10								14 10							
Christchurch	d					13 14								14 14							
Hinton Admiral	d					13 19								14 19							
New Milton	d		13 01			13 23					14 01			14 23				15 01			
Sway	d					13 28								14 28							
Yarmouth (IOW)	d	*11 55*		*12 35*								*13 15*					*13 55*				*14 35*
Lymington Pier	d	12 44		13 14						13 44		14 14					14 44				15 14
Lymington Town	d	12 46		13 16						13 46		14 16					14 46				15 16
Brockenhurst ■3	a	12 54	13 08	13 24		13 33			13 53	13 54	14 08	14 24		14 33			14 54	15 08			15 24
	d		13 09			13 34			13 57		14 09			14 34				15 09			
Beaulieu Road	d					13 39								14 39							
Ashurst New Forest	d					13 43								14 43							
Totton	d					13 48								14 48							
Salisbury	d						13 08	13 32							14 13	14b48					
Dean	d						13 20														
Mottisfont & Dunbridge	d						13 26														
Romsey	d						13 32	13 50							14 32	15 10					
Redbridge	d						13 39								14 39						
Millbrook (Hants)	d						13 43								14 43						
Southampton Central	a		13 23			13 53	13 45	14 02	14 10		14 23			14 53	14 45	15 20		15 23			
	d		13 25			13 55	13 59	14 04	14 15		14 25			14 55	14 59	15 22		15 25			
St Denys	d						14 04								15 04						
Swaythling	d						14 07								15 07						
Southampton Airport Parkwy ✈	d		13 33			14 03	14 10		14 22		14 33			15 03	15 10			15 33			
Portsmouth Harbour	d				13 17								14 17								
Portsmouth & Southsea	d				13 22								14 22								
Fratton	d				13 26								14 26								
Hilsea	d				13 30								14 30								
Cosham	d				13 35								14 35								
Portchester	d				13 40								14 40								
Fareham	d				13 46			14 26					14 46			15 51					
Botley	d				13 54								14 54								
Hedge End	d				13 58								14 58								
Eastleigh ■3	a				14 04	14 07	14 13						15 04	15 07	15 13						
	d				14 11	<	14 15						15 11	<	15 15						
Chandlers Ford	d						14 20								15 20						
Romsey	a						14 28								15 28						
Shawford	d												15 17								
Winchester	d		13 42		14 23				14 31		14 42		15 23					15 42			
Micheldever	d				14 32								15 32								
Basingstoke	a		13 58		14 42				14 46		14 58		15 42					15 58			
	d		14 00		14 44				14 47		15 00		15 44					16 00			
Reading ■7	a								15 04												
Fleet	d																				
Farnborough (Main)	d																				
Woking	a		14 18		15 02						15 18		16 02					16 18			
Clapham Junction ■10	a		14 39		15 27						15 39		16 27					16 39			
London Waterloo ■15 ⊖	a		14 49		15 37						15 49		16 37					16 49			

C from 12 September
D until 5 September
b arr. 1439

Table 158

Sundays

Weymouth, Bournemouth, Lymington, Romsey, Southampton and Basingstoke - London

		SW ■ 🛒	SW ◇■	SW ■	GW ◇ B	GW ◇ C	XC ◇■ 🍴	SW ■	SW ◇■ 🛒	SW ■	SW ■ 🛒	SW ◇■	SW ■	GW ◇	XC ◇■ 🍴	SW ■	SW ◇■ 🛒	GW B	SW ■	SW ■	SW ◇■	SW ■	GW ◇ E	GW ◇ F
Weymouth	d								14 48								15 48	16 10						
Upwey	d								14 52								15 52	16 15						
Dorchester West	a																	16 22						
Dorchester South	d								15 00								16 00							
Moreton (Dorset)	d								15 07								16 07							
Wool	d								15 13								16 13							
Wareham	d								15 20								16 20							
Holton Heath	d																							
Hamworthy	d								15 27								16 27							
Poole ■4	a								15 31								16 31							
	d		14 55						15 32			15 55					16 32				16 55			
Parkstone (Dorset)	d								15 36								16 36							
Branksome	d								15 40								16 40							
Bournemouth	a		15 04						15 46			16 04					16 46				17 04			
	d		15 06				15 40		15 50			16 06			16 40		16 50				17 06			
Pokesdown	d		15 10									16 10									17 10			
Christchurch	d		15 14									16 14									17 14			
Hinton Admiral	d		15 19									16 19									17 19			
New Milton	d		15 23						16 01			16 23					17 01				17 23			
Sway	d		15 28									16 28									17 28			
Yarmouth (IOW)	d															*15 55*			*16 35*					
Lymington Pier	d							15 44		16 14						16 44			17 14					
Lymington Town	d							15 46		16 16						16 46			17 16					
Brockenhurst ■3	a		15 33				15 53	15 54	16 08	16 24		16 33			16 53	16 54	17 08		17 24		17 33			
	d		15 34				15 57		16 09			16 34			16 57		17 09				17 34			
Beaulieu Road	d		15 39									16 39									17 39			
Ashurst New Forest	d		15 43									16 43									17 43			
Totton	d		15 48									16 48									17 48			
Salisbury	d			15 08	15 32	15 32							16 13	16 32								17 08	17 29	17 32
Dean	d			15 20																		17 20		
Mottisfont & Dunbridge	d			15 26																		17 26		
Romsey	d			15 32	15 50	15 50							16 32	16 50								17 32	17 47	17 50
Redbridge	d			15 39									16 39									17 39		
Millbrook (Hants)	d			15 43									16 43									17 43		
Southampton Central	a		15 53	15 45	16 02	16 02	16 10		16 23			16 53	16 45	17 02	17 10		17 23				17 53	17 45	17 59	18 02
	d		15 55	15 59	16 04	16 03	16 15		16 25			16 55	16 59	17 04	17 15		17 25				17 55	17 59	18 01	18 04
St Denys	d			16 04									17 04									18 04		
Swaythling	d			16 07									17 07									18 07		
Southampton Airport Parkwy ✈	d		16 03	16 10			16 22		16 33			17 03	17 10		17 22		17 33				18 03	18 10		
Portsmouth Harbour	d	15 17									16 17									17 17				
Portsmouth & Southsea	d	15 22									16 22									17 22				
Fratton	d	15 26									16 26									17 26				
Hilsea	d	15 30									16 30									17 30				
Cosham	d	15 35									16 35									17 35				
Portchester	d	15 40									16 40									17 40				
Fareham	d	15 46			16 27	16 27					16 46			17 27						17 46			18 24	18 27
Botley	d	15 54									16 54									17 54				
Hedge End	d	15 58									16 58									17 58				
Eastleigh ■3	a	16 04	16 07	16 13							17 04	17 07	17 13							18 04	18 07	18 13		
	d	16 11	<	16 15							17 11	<	17 15							18 11	<	18 15		
Chandlers Ford	d			16 20									17 20									18 20		
Romsey	a			16 28									17 28									18 28		
Shawford	d										17 17													
Winchester	d	16 23					16 31		16 42		17 23				17 31		17 42			18 23				
Micheldever	d	16 32									17 32									18 32				
Basingstoke	a	16 42					16 46		16 58		17 42				17 46		17 58			18 42				
	d	16 44					16 47		17 00		17 44				17 47		18 00			18 44				
Reading ■7	a						17 04								18 04									
Fleet	d																							
Farnborough (Main)	d																							
Woking	a	17 02							17 18		18 02						18 18			19 02				
Clapham Junction ■10	a	17 27							17 39		18 27						18 39			19 27				
London Waterloo ■15 ⊖	a	17 37							17 49		18 37						18 49			19 37				

B until 5 September
C from 12 September
E until 11 July
F from 18 July

Table 158

Weymouth, Bournemouth, Lymington, Romsey, Southampton and Basingstoke - London

		XC	SW	SW	SW	SW	SW	SW	GW	XC	SW	SW	GW	GW	SW	SW	SW	SW	GW	XC	SW	SW
		◇1 ⟂	1	◇1 ▭	1	1	◇1	1	◇	◇1 ⟂	1	◇1 ▭		◇	1	1	◇1	1	◇	◇1 ⟂	1	◇1 ▭
Weymouth	d			16 48								17 48	17 56									18 48
Upwey	d			16 52								17 52	18 01									18 52
Dorchester West	a												18 08									
Dorchester South	d			17 00								18 00										19 00
Moreton (Dorset)	d			17 07								18 07										19 07
Wool	d			17 13								18 13										19 13
Wareham	d			17 20								18 20										19 20
Holton Heath	d																					
Hamworthy	d			17 27								18 27										19 27
Poole 4	a			17 31								18 31										19 31
	d			17 32			17 55					18 32					18 55					19 32
Parkstone (Dorset)	d			17 36								18 36										19 36
Branksome	d			17 40								18 40										19 40
Bournemouth	a			17 46			18 04					18 46					19 04					19 46
	d	17 40		17 50			18 06			18 40		18 50					19 06			19 40		19 50
Pokesdown	d						18 10										19 10					
Christchurch	d						18 14										19 14					
Hinton Admiral	d						18 19										19 19					
New Milton	d			18 01			18 23					19 01					19 23					20 01
Sway	d						18 28										19 28					
Yarmouth (IOW)	d				*17 15*						*17 55*				*18 30*							
Lymington Pier	d		17 44		18 14						18 44				19 14						19 44	
Lymington Town	d		17 46		18 16						18 46				19 16						19 46	
Brockenhurst 3	a	17 53	17 54	18 08	18 24		18 33			18 53	18 54	19 08			19 24		19 33			19 53	19 54	20 08
	d	17 57		18 09			18 34			18 57		19 09					19 34			19 57		20 09
Beaulieu Road	d						18 39										19 39					
Ashurst New Forest	d						18 43										19 43					
Totton	d						18 48										19 48					
Salisbury	d							18 13	18 32					18 57				19 08	19 32			
Dean	d																	19 20				
Mottisfont & Dunbridge	d																	19 26				
Romsey	d							18 32	18 50					19 15				19 32	19 50			
Redbridge	d							18 39										19 39				
Millbrook (Hants)	d							18 43										19 43				
Southampton Central	a	18 10		18 23			18 53	18 45	19 02	19 10		19 23		19 26			19 53	19 45	20 02	20 10		20 23
	d	18 15		18 25			18 55	18 59	19 04	19 15		19 25		19 27			19 55	19 59	20 04	20 15		20 25
St Denys	d							19 04										20 04				
Swaythling	d							19 07										20 07				
Southampton Airport Parkwy ✈	d	18 22		18 33			19 03	19 10		19 22		19 33					20 03	20 10		20 22		20 33
Portsmouth Harbour	d					18 17										19 17						
Portsmouth & Southsea	d					18 22										19 22						
Fratton	d					18 26										19 26						
Hilsea	d					18 30										19 30						
Cosham	d					18 35										19 35						
Portchester	d					18 40										19 40						
Fareham	d					18 46			19 27					19 49		19 46			20 27			
Botley	d					18 54										19 54						
Hedge End	d					18 58										19 58						
Eastleigh 3	a					19 04	19 07	19 13								20 04	20 07	20 13				
	d					19 11	<	19 15								20 11	<	20 15				
Chandlers Ford	d							19 20										20 20				
Romsey	a							19 28										20 28				
Shawford	d					19 17																
Winchester	d	18 31		18 42		19 23				19 31		19 42				20 23				20 31		20 42
Micheldever	d					19 32										20 32						
Basingstoke	a	18 46		18 58		19 42				19 46		19 58				20 42				20 46		20 58
	d	18 47		19 00		19 44				19 47		20 00				20 44				20 47		21 00
Reading 7	a	19 04								20 04										21 04		
Fleet	d																					
Farnborough (Main)	d																					
Woking	a			19 18		20 02						20 18				21 02						21 18
Clapham Junction 10	a			19 39		20 27						20 39				21 27						21 39
London Waterloo 15 ⊖	a			19 49		20 37						20 49				21 37						21 49

Table 158

Weymouth, Bournemouth, Lymington, Romsey, Southampton and Basingstoke - London

		GW	SW	SW	SW	SW	GW	SW	SW	GW	SW	SW	SW	GW	SW	SW	SW	SW	GW	SW	SW	SW
		7	1	1	◇1	1	◇	1	1		1	◇1	1	◇	1	1	1	◇1	◇	1	1	1
Weymouth	d									20 09		19 58						20 58		21 58	22 58	
Upwey	d									20 14		20 02						21 02		22 02	23 02	
Dorchester West	a									20 21												
Dorchester South	d											20 10						21 10		22 10	23 10	
Moreton (Dorset)	d											20 17						21 17		22 17	23 17	
Wool	d											20 23						21 23		22 23	23 23	
Wareham	d											20 30						21 30		22 30	23 30	
Holton Heath	d																					
Hamworthy	d											20 37						21 37		22 37	23 37	
Poole 4	a											20 41						21 41		22 41	23 41	
	d				19 55							20 50						21 50		22 50	23 50	
Parkstone (Dorset)	d											20 54						21 54		22 54	23 54	
Branksome	d											20 57						21 57		22 57	23 57	
Bournemouth	a				20 04							21 03						22 03		23 03	00 03	
	d				20 06							21 06						22 06		23 06		
Pokesdown	d				20 10							21 10						22 10		23 10		
Christchurch	d				20 14							21 14						22 14		23 14		
Hinton Admiral	d				20 19							21 19						22 19		23 19		
New Milton	d				20 23							21 23						22 23		23 23		
Sway	d				20 28							21 28						22 28		23 28		
Yarmouth (IOW)	d		*19 30*						*20 15*							*21 15*						
Lymington Pier	d		20 14					20 44	21 14						21 44	22 14						
Lymington Town	d		20 16					20 46	21 16						21 46	22 16						
Brockenhurst 3	a		20 24		20 33			20 54	21 24			21 33			21 54	22 24		22 33		23 33		
	d				20 34							21 34						22 34		23 34		
Beaulieu Road	d				20 39							21 39						22 39				
Ashurst New Forest	d				20 43							21 43						22 43		23 43		
Totton	d				20 48							21 48						22 48		23 48		
Salisbury	d	20 00				20 13	20 30						21 08	21b32					22 31			
Dean	d												21 20									
Mottisfont & Dunbridge	d												21 26									
Romsey	d	20 19				20 32	20 48						21 32	21 51					22 50			
Redbridge	d					20 39							21 39									
Millbrook (Hants)	d					20 43							21 43									
Southampton Central	a	20 29			20 53	20 45	20 59					21 53	21 45	22 01				22 53	23 00	23 53		
	d	20 31			20 55	20 59	21 01					21 55	21 59	22 04				22 55	23 02			
St Denys	d					21 04							22 04									
Swaythling	d					21 07							22 07									
Southampton Airport Parkwy ✈	d				21 03	21 10						22 03	22 10					23 03				
Portsmouth Harbour	d			20 17							21 17						22 17					23 17
Portsmouth & Southsea	d			20 22							21 22						22 22					23 22
Fratton	d			20 26							21 26						22 26					23 26
Hilsea	d			20 30							21 30						22 30					23 30
Cosham	d			20 35							21 35						22 35					23 35
Portchester	d			20 40							21 40						22 40					23 40
Fareham	d	20 55		20 46			21 24				21 46			22 27			22 46		23 24			23 46
Botley	d			20 54							21 54						22 54					23 54
Hedge End	d			20 58							21 58						22 58					23 58
Eastleigh 3	a			21 04	21 07	21 13					22 04	22 07	22 13				23 04	23 09				00 04
	d			21 11	<	21 15					22 11	<	22 15					23 11				
Chandlers Ford	d					21 20							22 20									
Romsey	a					21 28							22 31									
Shawford	d			21 17																		
Winchester	d			21 23							22 23							23 23				
Micheldever	d			21 32							22 32							23 32				
Basingstoke	a			21 42							22 42							23 42				
	d			21 44							22 44							23 44				
Reading 7	a																					
Fleet	d																					
Farnborough (Main)	d																					
Woking	a			22 02							23 02							00 02				
Clapham Junction 10	a			22 27							23 27							00 23				
London Waterloo 15 ⊖	a			22 37							23 37							00 33				

b arr. 2127

Table 158A

Mondays to Saturdays

Woking - Heathrow Railair

Express Coach Service

		SW SX	SW SX	SW SX	SW SX	SW	SW	SW	SW SO	SW SX	SW	SW SO	SW SX	SW SO	SW	SW SX	SW SO	SW	SW SX	SW SO	SW	SW SX	SW	SW SO	SW SX
Woking	d		05 20		05 50		06 20		06 50	06 50		07 20	07 20	07 50		07 50	08 20		08 20	08 50		08 50		09 35	09 35
Heathrow Terminal 5 Bus	d		05 45		06 15		06 45		07 15	07 25		07 45	08 05	08 15		08 35	08 45		09 05	09 15		09 35		10 00	10 10
Heathrow Central Bus Stn	a		06 00		06 30		07 00		07 30	07 40		08 00	08 20	08 30		08 50	09 00		09 20	09 30		09 50		10 15	10 25
	d	05 45		06 15		06 45		07 15			07 45				08 30			09 00			09 30		10 00		
Heathrow Terminal 5 Bus	a	06 00		06 30		07 00		07 30			08 00				08 45			09 15			09 45		10 15		
Woking	a	06 30		07 00		07 30		08 05			08 40				09 25			09 55			10 25		10 50		

		SW	SW	SW	SW	SW	SW	SW	SW	SW	SW	SW	SW	SW	SW	SW	SW	SW	SW	SW	SW	SW	SW	SW	SW
Woking	d		10 05		10 35		11 05		11 35		12 05		12 35		13 05		13 35		14 05		14 35		15 05		15 35
Heathrow Terminal 5 Bus	d		10 30		11 00		11 30		12 00		12 30		13 00		13 30		14 00		14 30		15 00		15 30		16 00
Heathrow Central Bus Stn	a		10 45		11 15		11 45		12 15		12 45		13 15		13 45		14 15		14 45		15 15		15 45		16 15
	d	10 30		11 00		11 30		12 00		12 30		13 00		13 30		14 00		14 30		15 00		15 30		16 00	
Heathrow Terminal 5 Bus	a	10 45		11 15		11 45		12 15		12 45		13 15		13 45		14 15		14 45		15 15		15 45		16 15	
Woking	a	11 15		11 45		12 15		12 45		13 15		13 45		14 15		14 45		15 15		15 45		16 15		16 45	

		SW	SW SO	SW SX	SW	SW SO	SW SX	SW	SW SO	SW SX	SW	SW SO	SW SX	SW	SW SO	SW SX	SW	SW	SW	SW SX	SW SO	SW	SW SO	SW SX	SW
Woking	d		16 05	16 05		16 35	16 35		17 05	17 05		17 35	17 35		18 05	18 05		18 35		19 05	19 05		19 35	19 35	
Heathrow Terminal 5 Bus	d		16 30	16 35		17 00	17 10		17 30	17 40		18 00	18 10		18 30	18 40		19 00		19 35	19 30		20 00	20 05	
Heathrow Central Bus Stn	a		16 45	16 50		17 15	17 25		17 45	17 55		18 15	18 25		18 45	18 55		19 15		19 45	19 45		20 15	20 15	
	d	16 30			17 00			17 30			18 00			18 30			19 00		19 30			20 00			20 30
Heathrow Terminal 5 Bus	a	16 45			17 15			17 45			18 15			18 45			19 15		19 45			20 15			20 45
Woking	a	17 25			18 05			18 35			19 05			19 35			19 55		20 15			20 45			21 15

		SW SX	SW SO	SW SX	SW SO	SW	SW SO	SW SX	SW SO	SW SX	SW SO	SW SX	SW SO	SW SX
Woking	d	20 05	20 05	20 35	20 35		21 05	21 05			22 05	22 05		
Heathrow Terminal 5 Bus	d	20 35	20 30	21 05	21 00		21 30	21 35			22 30	22 35		
Heathrow Central Bus Stn	a	20 45	20 45	21 15	21 15		21 45	21 45			22 45	22 45		
	d					21 15			22 15	22 15			23 15	23 15
Heathrow Terminal 5 Bus	a					21 30			22 30	22 30			23 30	23 30
Woking	a					22 00			22 55	23 00			23 55	23 59

Table 158A

Sundays

Woking - Heathrow Railair

Express Coach Service

		SW	SW	SW	SW	SW	SW	SW	SW	SW	SW	SW	SW	SW	SW	SW	SW	SW	SW	SW	SW	SW	SW	SW	SW
Woking	d		06 20		06 50		07 20	07 50		08 20		08 50			09 35		10 05		10 35		11 05		11 35		12 05
Heathrow Terminal 5 Bus	d		06 45		07 15		07 45	08 15		08 45		09 15			10 00		10 30		11 00		11 30		12 00		12 30
Heathrow Central Bus Stn	a		07 00		07 30		08 00	08 30		09 00		09 30			10 15		10 45		11 15		11 45		12 15		12 45
	d	06 45		07 15		07 45			08 30		09 00		09 30	10 00		10 30		11 00		11 30		12 00		12 30	
Heathrow Terminal 5 Bus	a	07 00		07 30		08 00			08 45		09 15		09 45	10 15		10 45		11 15		11 45		12 15		12 45	
Woking	a	07 30		08 00		08 25			09 15		09 45		10 15	10 45		11 15		11 45		12 15		12 45		13 15	

		SW	SW	SW	SW	SW	SW	SW	SW	SW	SW	SW	SW	SW	SW	SW	SW	SW	SW	SW	SW	SW	SW	SW	SW
Woking	d		12 35		13 05		13 35		14 05		14 35		15 05		15 35		16 05		16 35		17 05		17 35		18 05
Heathrow Terminal 5 Bus	d		13 00		13 30		14 00		14 30		15 00		15 30		16 00		16 30		17 00		17 30		18 00		18 30
Heathrow Central Bus Stn	a		13 15		13 45		14 15		14 45		15 15		15 45		16 15		16 45		17 15		17 45		18 15		18 45
	d	13 00		13 30		14 00		14 30		15 00		15 30		16 00		16 30		17 00		17 30		18 00		18 30	
Heathrow Terminal 5 Bus	a	13 15		13 45		14 15		14 45		15 15		15 45		16 15		16 45		17 15		17 45		18 15		18 45	
Woking	a	13 45		14 15		14 45		15 15		15 45		16 15		16 45		17 15		17 45		18 15		18 45		19 15	

		SW	SW	SW	SW	SW	SW	SW	SW	SW	SW	SW	SW	SW	SW
Woking	d		18 35		19 05		19 35		20 05	20 35		21 05		22 05	
Heathrow Terminal 5 Bus	d		19 00		19 30		20 00		20 30	21 00		21 30		22 30	
Heathrow Central Bus Stn	a		19 15		19 45		20 15		20 45	21 15		21 45		22 45	
	d	19 00		19 30		20 00		20 30			21 15		22 15		23 15
Heathrow Terminal 5 Bus	a	19 15		19 45		20 15		20 45			21 30		22 30		23 30
Woking	a	19 45		20 15		20 45		21 15			22 00		23 00		23 59

Network Diagram for Table 160

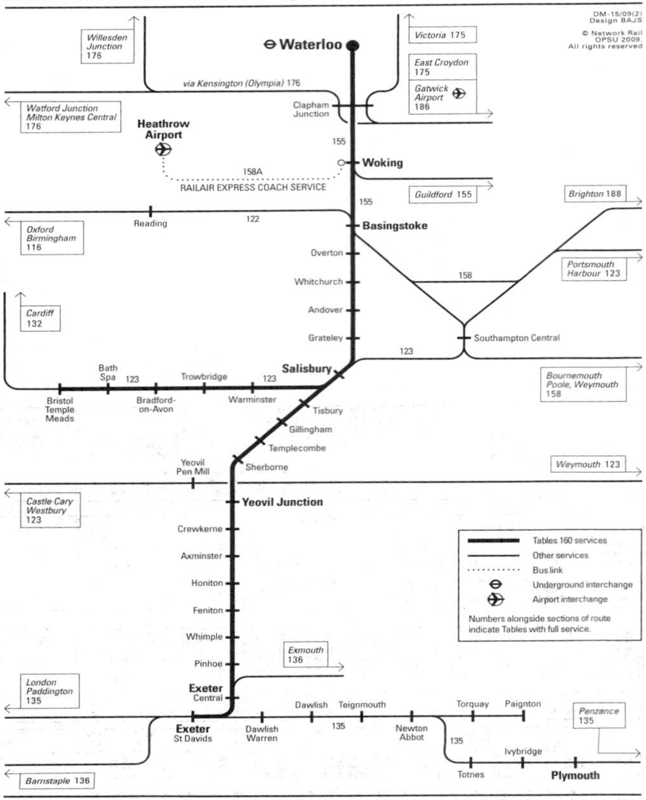

London - Salisbury and Exeter

		SW	SW	SW	SW	SW	SW	SW	SW		SW	SW	SW	SW	SW	SW	SW	SW	SW		SW	SW	SW	SW
		MX	MO	MX	MO																			
		◇1	◇1	1	1	1	1	1	1		◇1	◇1	◇1	◇1	◇1	◇1	◇1	◇1	◇1		◇1	◇1	◇1	◇1
		⊡	⊡										⊡	⊡	⊡	⊡	⊡		⊡		⊡	⊡	⊡	⊡
London Waterloo 15 ⊖	d	20p20	21p15	23p35	23p35								07 10	07 50	08 20	08 50	09 20		09 50		10 20	10 50	11 20	11 50
Clapham Junction 10	d	20b27	21b22	23b43	23b44								07u17	07u57	08u27		09u27				10u27		11u27	
Woking	d	20p46	21p46	00 05	00 08								07 36	08 16	08 46	09 16	09 46		10 16		10 46	11 16	11 46	12 16
Basingstoke	d	21p07	22p07	00 25	00 40							07 22	07 57	08 37	09 07	09 37	10 07		10 37		11 07	11 37	12 07	12 37
Overton	d	21p15		00s34	00s49							07 30	08 05	08 45		09 45			10 45			11 45		12 45
Whitchurch (Hants)	d	21p20		00s39	00s54							07 35	08 10	08 50		09 50			10 50			11 50		12 50
Andover	d	21p29	22p26	00 47	01 02							07 44	08 19	08 59	09 24	09 59	10 24		10 59		11 24	11 59	12 24	12 59
Grateley	d	21p36	22p33	00s55	01s10							07 51	08 26	09 06		10 06			11 06			12 06		13 06
Salisbury	a	21p48	22p45	01 07	01 22							08 03	08 39	09 18	09 43	10 18	10 42	>	11 18		11 42	12 18	12 42	13 19
	d	22p06	22p51					06 08	06 40		07 40	08 08	08 47		09 47		10 47	10 52			11 47		12 47	
Warminster	d								07 00									11 12						
Westbury	d								07 09									11 21						
Trowbridge	d								07 15									11 27						
Bradford-on-Avon	d								07 21									11 33						
Bath Spa 7	a								07 33									11 46						
Bristol Temple Meads 10	a								07 52									12 05						
Tisbury	d	22p24	23p10					06 29			07 59	08 27	09 07		10 07		11 07				12 07		13 07	
Gillingham (Dorset)	a	22p34	23p20					06 39			08 09	08 37	09 17		10 17		11 17				12 17		13 17	
	d	22p35	23p21					06 42			08 11		09 18		10 18		11 18				12 18		13 18	
Templecombe	d	22p42	23p28					06 50			08 19		09 25		10 25		11 25				12 25		13 25	
Sherborne	d	22p50	23p36					06 57			08 26		09 33		10 33		11 33				12 33		13 33	
Yeovil Junction	a	22p55	23p41					07 03			08 32		09 38		10 38		11 38				12 38		13 38	
	d	22p57	23p43				06 15	07 07			08 40		09 40		10 40		11 40				12 40		13 40	
Crewkerne	d	23p06	23p52				06 24	07 16			08 49		09 49		10 49		11 49				12 49		13 49	
Axminster	a	23p19	00 05				06 43	07 35			09 02		10 02		11 02		12 02				13 02		14 02	
	d	23p20	00 06			05 52	06 56	07 36			09 04		10 04		11 04		12 04				13 04		14 04	
Honiton	a	23p31	00 18			06 03	07 07	07 49			09 15		10 15		11 15		12 15				13 15		14 15	
	d	23p32	00 19			06 08	07 12	07 50			09 16		10 16		11 16		12 16				13 16		14 16	
Feniton	d	23p38	00 24			06 13	07 18	07 56			09 21				11 21						13 21			
Whimple	d	23p43	00 29			06 18	07 23	08 01			09 26				11 26						13 26			
Pinhoe	d	23p49					07 30	08 08			09 33		10 28				12 28						14 28	
Exeter Central	a	23p56				06 29	07 37	08 12			09 37		10 37		11 37		12 37				13 37		14 37	
Exeter St Davids 6	a	00 01	00 40			06 35	07 42	08 17			09 42		10 42		11 42		12 42				13 42		14 42	

		SW	SW	SW	SW	SW		SW	SW	SW	SW	SW	SW	SW	SW	SW		SW	SW	SW	SW	SW	SW	SW	SW
		◇1	◇1	◇1	◇1	◇1		◇1	◇1	◇1	◇1	◇1	1	◇1	◇1	◇1		◇1	◇1	◇1	◇1	◇1	◇1	1	1
		⊡		⊡	⊡	⊡		⊡	⊡	⊡	⊡	⊡	⊡	⊡	⊡	⊡		⊡	⊡		⊡	⊡	⊡	⊡	
London Waterloo 15 ⊖	d	12 20		12 50	13 20	13 50		14 20	14 50	15 20	15 50	16 20	16 50	17 20	17 50	18 20		18 50	19 20		19 50	20 20	21 20	22 20	23 35
Clapham Junction 10	d	12u27			13u27			14u27		15u27	15u57	16u27	16u57			18u27			19u27			20u27	21u27	22u27	23u43
Woking	d	12 46		13 16	13 46	14 16		14 46	15 16	15 46	16 16	16 46	17u16	17u46		18 46		19 18	19 46		20 16	20 46	21 49	22 49	00 05
Basingstoke	d	13 07		13 37	14 07	14 37		15 07	15 37	16 07	16 37	17 07	17 37	18 07	18 38	19 07		19 39	20 07		20 37	21 07	22 10	23 10	00 25
Overton	d			13 45		14 45			15 45		16 45	17 15	17 45	18 15	18 47	19 15		19 47	20 15		20 45	21 15	22 18	23 18	00s34
Whitchurch (Hants)	d			13 50		14 50			15 50		16 50	17 20	17 50	18 20	18 52	19 20		19 52	20 20		20 50	21 20	22 23	23 23	00s39
Andover	d	13 24		13 59	14 24	14 59		15 24	15 59	16 24	16 59	17 29	17 59	18 29	19 00	19 29		20 01	20 29		20 59	21 29	22 32	23 32	00 47
Grateley	d			14 06		15 06			16 06		17 06	17 36	18 06	18 36	19 08	19 36		20 08	20 36		21 06	21 36	22 39	23 39	00s55
Salisbury	a	13 43	>	14 20	14 42	15 20		15 42	16 18	16 42	17 18	17 48	18 18	18 48	19 20	19 48		20 22	20 49	>	21 18	21 48	22 55	23 53	01 07
	d	13 47	13 52		14 47	15 23		15 47		16 47	17 23	17 53	18 23	18 53	19 23	19 53			20 53	20 57		22 06	23 03		
Warminster	d		14 12																	21 17					
Westbury	d		14 21																	21 25					
Trowbridge	d		14 27																	21 31					
Bradford-on-Avon	d		14 33																	21 37					
Bath Spa 7	a		14 46																	21 50					
Bristol Temple Meads 10	a		15 05																	22 06					
Tisbury	d	14 07			15 07	15 37		16 07		17 07	17 37	18 08	18 37	19 08	19 37	20 08			21 08			22 24	23s17		
Gillingham (Dorset)	a	14 17			15 17	15 47		16 17		17 17	17 47	18 18	18 47	19 18	19 48	20 18			21 18			22 34	23s27		
	d	14 18			15 18			16 18		17 18		18 19	18 51	19 19	19 51	20 19			21 19			22 35	23s28		
Templecombe	d	14 25			15 25			16 25		17 25		18 27	18 58	19 27	19 58	20 27			21 27			22 42	23s35		
Sherborne	d	14 33			15 33			16 33		17 33		18 34	19 06	19 34	20 06	20 34			21 34			22 50	23s43		
Yeovil Junction	a	14 38			15 38			16 38		17 38		18 40	19 14	19 40	20 14	20 40			21 40			22 55	23 49		
	d	14 40			15 40			16 40		17 40		18 41		19 41		20 41			21 41			22 57			
Crewkerne	d	14 49			15 49			16 49		17 49		18 51		19 51		20 51			21 51			23 06			
Axminster	a	15 02			16 02			17 02		18 02		19 04		20 04		21 04			22 04			23 19			
	d	15 04			16 04			17 04		18 04		19 05		20 05		21 05			22 05			23 20			
Honiton	a	15 15			16 15			17 15		18 15		19 16		20 16		21 16			22 16			23 31			
	d	15 16			16 16			17 16		18 18		19 17		20 17		21 17			22 17			23 32			
Feniton	d	15 21						17 21				19 22				21 22			22 22			23 38			
Whimple	d	15 26						17 26				19 27				21 27			22 27			23 43			
Pinhoe	d				16 28					18 31				20 29					22 34			23 49			
Exeter Central	a	15 37			16 35			17 35		18 38		19 38		20 39		21 37			22 40			23 56			
Exeter St Davids 6	a	15 42			16 42			17 42		18 42		19 45		20 44		21 44			22 45			00 01			

b previous night, stops to pick up only

Table 160

Saturdays

London - Salisbury and Exeter

		SW ◇1 ⊐P	SW 1	SW 1	SW 1	SW 1	SW 1	SW ◇1	SW ◇1		SW ◇1 ⊐P	SW ◇1 ⊐P	SW ◇1 ⊐P	SW ◇1 ⊐P	SW ◇1 ⊐P	SW ◇1	SW ◇1 ⊐P	SW ◇1 ⊐P	SW ◇1 ⊐P		SW ◇1 ⊐P	SW ◇1 ⊐P	SW ◇1 ⊐P	SW ◇1
London Waterloo 15 ⊖	d	20p20	23p35								07 10	07 50	08 20	08 50	09 20		09 50	10 20	10 50		11 20	11 50	12 20	
Clapham Junction 10	d	20b27	23b43								07u17	07u57	08u27		09u27			10u27			11u27		12u27	
Woking	d	20p46	00 05								07 36	08 16	08 46	09 16	09 46		10 16	10 46	11 16		11 46	12 16	12 46	
Basingstoke	d	21p07	00 25						07 22		07 59	08 37	09 07	09 37	10 07		10 37	11 07	11 37		12 07	12 37	13 07	
Overton	d	21p15	00s34						07 30		08 07	08 45		09 45			10 45		11 45			12 45		
Whitchurch (Hants)	d	21p20	00s39						07 35		08 12	08 50		09 50			10 50		11 50			12 50		
Andover	d	21p29	00 47						07 44		08 21	08 59	09 24	09 59	10 24		10 59	11 24	11 59		12 24	12 59	13 24	
Grateley	d	21p36	00s55						07 51		08 28	09 06		10 06			11 06		12 06			13 06		
Salisbury	a	21p48	01 07						08 03		08 42	09 18	09 42	10 18	10 42	>	11 18	11 42	12 18		12 42	13 18	13 42	>
	d	22p06				06 15	06 40	07 45			08 47		09 47		10 47	10 52		11 47			12 47		13 47	13 52
Warminster	d						07 00									11 12								14 12
Westbury	d						07 09									11 21								14 21
Trowbridge	d						07 15									11 27								14 27
Bradford-on-Avon	d						07 21									11 33								14 33
Bath Spa 7	a						07 33									11 46								14 46
Bristol Temple Meads 10	a						07 53									12 05								15 05
Tisbury	d	22p24				06 29		07 59			09 07		10 07		11 07			12 07			13 07		14 07	
Gillingham (Dorset)	a	22p34				06 39		08 09			09 17		10 17		11 17			12 17			13 17		14 17	
	d	22p35				06 42		08 11			09 18		10 18		11 18			12 18			13 18		14 18	
Templecombe	d	22p42				06 50		08 19			09 25		10 25		11 25			12 25			13 25		14 25	
Sherborne	d	22p50				06 57		08 26			09 33		10 33		11 33			12 33			13 33		14 33	
Yeovil Junction	a	22p55				07 03		08 32			09 38		10 38		11 38			12 38			13 38		14 38	
	d	22p57			06 15	07 07		08 40			09 40		10 40		11 40			12 40			13 40		14 40	
Crewkerne	d	23p06			06 24	07 16		08 49			09 49		10 49		11 49			12 49			13 49		14 49	
Axminster	a	23p19			06 43	07 36		09 02			10 02		11 02		12 02			13 02			14 02		15 02	
	d	23p20		05 52	06 56	07 38		09 04			10 04		11 04		12 04			13 04			14 04		15 04	
Honiton	a	23p31		06 03	07 07	07 51		09 15			10 15		11 15		12 15			13 15			14 15		15 15	
	d	23p32		06 08	07 12	07 52		09 16			10 16		11 16		12 16			13 16			14 16		15 16	
Feniton	d	23p38		06 13	07 18	07 57		09 21					11 21					13 21					15 21	
Whimple	d	23p43		06 18	07 23	08 02		09 26					11 26					13 26					15 26	
Pinhoe	d	23p49			07 30	08 09		09 33			10 28				12 28						14 28			
Exeter Central	a	23p56		06 29	07 37	08 13		09 37			10 37		11 37		12 37			13 37			14 37		15 37	
Exeter St Davids 8	a	00 01		06 35	07 42	08 18		09 42			10 42		11 42		12 42			13 42			14 42		15 42	

		SW ◇1 ⊐P	SW ◇1 ⊐P	SW ◇1 ⊐P	SW ◇1 ⊐P	SW ◇1 ⊐P		SW ◇1 ⊐P	SW ◇1 ⊐P	SW ◇1 ⊐P	SW ◇1 ⊐P	SW ◇1 ⊐P	SW ◇1 ⊐P	SW ◇1 ⊐P	SW ◇1 ⊐P	SW ◇1 ⊐P	SW ◇1	SW ◇1 ⊐P	SW ◇1 ⊐P	SW ◇1 ⊐P	SW 1 ⊐P	SW 1		
London Waterloo 15 ⊖	d	12 50	13 20	13 50	14 20	14 50		15 20	15 50	16 20	16 50	17 20	17 50	18 20	18 50	19 20		19 50	20 20	21 20	22 20	23 35		
Clapham Junction 10	d		13u27		14u27			15u27		16u27		17u27		18u27		19u27			20u27	21u27	22u27	23u42		
Woking	d	13 16	13 46	14 16	14 46	15 16		15 46	16 16	16 46	17 16	17 46	18 16	18 46	19 16	19 46		20 16	20 46	21 49	22 49	00 05		
Basingstoke	d	13 37	14 07	14 37	15 07	15 37		16 07	16 37	17 07	17 37	18 07	18 37	19 07	19 37	20 07		20 37	21 07	22 12	23 12	00 25		
Overton	d	13 45		14 45		15 45			16 45		17 45		18 45		19 45			20 45	21 15	22 20	23 20	00s34		
Whitchurch (Hants)	d	13 50		14 50		15 50			16 50		17 50		18 50		19 50			20 50	21 20	22 25	23 25	00s39		
Andover	d	13 59	14 24	14 59	15 24	15 59		16 24	16 59	17 24	17 59	18 24	18 59	19 24	19 59	20 24		20 59	21 29	22 34	23 34	00 47		
Grateley	d	14 06		15 06		16 06			17 06		18 06		19 06		20 06			21 06	21 36	22 41	23 41	00s55		
Salisbury	a	14 18	14 42	15 18	15 42	16 18		16 42	17 18	17 42	18 18	18 43	19 18	19 43	20 18	20 42	>	21 18	21 48	22 53	23 53	01 07		
	d		14 47		15 47			16 47		17 47		18 47		19 47		20 47	20 57		21 53	23 03				
Warminster	d																21 17							
Westbury	d																21 25							
Trowbridge	d																21 31							
Bradford-on-Avon	d																21 37							
Bath Spa 7	a																21 50							
Bristol Temple Meads 10	a																22 06							
Tisbury	d		15 07		16 07			17 07		18 07		19 07		20 07		21 07			22 07	23s17				
Gillingham (Dorset)	a		15 17		16 17			17 17		18 17		19 17		20 17		21 17			22 17	23s27				
	d		15 18		16 18			17 18		18 18		19 18		20 18		21 18			22 18	23s28				
Templecombe	d		15 25		16 25			17 25		18 25		19 25		20 25		21 25			22 25	23s35				
Sherborne	d		15 33		16 33			17 33		18 33		19 33		20 33		21 33			22 33	23s43				
Yeovil Junction	a		15 38		16 38			17 38		18 38		19 38		20 38		21 38			22 40	23 49				
	d		15 40		16 40			17 40		18 40		19 40		20 40		21 40								
Crewkerne	d		15 49		16 49			17 49		18 49		19 49		20 49		21 49								
Axminster	a		16 02		17 02			18 02		19 02		20 02		21 02		22 02								
	d		16 04		17 04			18 04		19 04		20 04		21 04		22 04								
Honiton	a		16 15		17 15			18 15		19 15		20 15		21 15		22 15								
	d		16 16		17 16			18 16		19 16		20 16		21 16		22 16								
Feniton	d				17 21					19 21				21 21		22 21								
Whimple	d				17 26					19 26				21 26		22 26								
Pinhoe	d		16 28					18 28				20 28				22 33								
Exeter Central	a		16 35		17 37			18 35		19 37		20 39		21 37		22 37								
Exeter St Davids 8	a		16 42		17 42			18 42		19 42		20 43		21 42		22 42								

b previous night, stops to pick up only

Table 160

Sundays

London - Salisbury and Exeter

		SW 1	SW 1	SW ◇1	SW ◇1 ⊐P	SW ◇1 ⊐P	SW ◇1 ⊐P	SW ◇1 ⊐P	SW ◇1 ⊐P	SW ◇1		SW ◇1 ⊐P	SW ◇1 ⊐P	SW ◇1 ⊐P	SW ◇1 ⊐P	SW ◇1 ⊐P	SW ◇1 ⊐P	SW ◇1	SW ◇1 ⊐P	SW ◇1 ⊐P		SW ◇1 ⊐P	SW 1 ⊐P	SW 1	
London Waterloo 15 ⊖	d	23p35			08 15	09 15	10 15	11 15	12 15			13 15	14 15	15 15	16 15	17 15	18 15		19 15	20 15		21 15	22 15	23 35	
Clapham Junction 10	d	23b42			08u22	09u22	10u22	11u22	12u22			13u22	14u22	15u22	16u22	17u22	18u22		19u22	20u22		21u22	22u22	23u44	
Woking	d	00 05			08 47	09 47	10 46	11 46	12 46			13 46	14 46	15 46	16 46	17 46	18 46		19 46	20 46		21 46	22 46	00 08	
Basingstoke	d	00 25		08 05	09 08	10 08	11 07	12 07	13 07			14 07	15 07	16 07	17 07	18 07	19 07		20 07	21 07		22 07	23 07	00 40	
Overton	d	00s34		08 13	09 16		11 15		13 15				15 15		17 15		19 15			21 15			23 15	00s49	
Whitchurch (Hants)	d	00s39		08 18	09 21		11 20		13 20				15 20		17 20		19 20			21 20			23 20	00s54	
Andover	d	00 47		08 27	09 30	10 25	11 29	12 24	13 29			14 24	15 29	16 24	17 29	18 24	19 29		20 24	21 29		22 26	23 29	01 02	
Grateley	d	00s55		08 34		10 32		12 31				14 31		16 31		18 31			20 31			22 33	23 36	01s10	
Salisbury	a	01 07		08 46	09 46	10 45	11 45	12 45	13 45	>		14 45	15 45	16 45	17 45	18 45	19 45	>	20 45	21 45		22 45	23 48	01 22	
	d		07 10	08 51	09 51	10 51	11 51	12 51	13 51	13 55		14 51	15 51	16 51	17 51	18 51	19 51	19 55	20 51	21 51		22 51			
Warminster	d									14 15								20 15							
Westbury	d									14 23								20 23							
Trowbridge	d									14 29								20 29							
Bradford-on-Avon	d									14 35								20 35							
Bath Spa 7	a									14 48								20 48							
Bristol Temple Meads 10	a									15 02								21 04							
Tisbury	d		07 24	09 10	10 10	11 10	12 10	13 10	14 10			15 10	16 10	17 10	18 10	19 10	20 10		21 10	22 10		23 10			
Gillingham (Dorset)	a		07 34	09 20	10 20	11 20	12 20	13 20	14 20			15 20	16 20	17 20	18 20	19 20	20 20		21 20	22 20		23 20			
	d		07 35	09 21	10 21	11 21	12 21	13 21	14 21			15 21	16 21	17 21	18 21	19 21	20 21		21 21	22 21		23 21			
Templecombe	d		07 42	09 28	10 28	11 28	12 28	13 28	14 28			15 28	16 28	17 28	18 28	19 28	20 28		21 28	22 28		23 28			
Sherborne	d		07 50	09 36	10 36	11 36	12 36	13 36	14 36			15 36	16 36	17 36	18 36	19 36	20 36		21 36	22 36		23 36			
Yeovil Junction	a		07 55	09 41	10 41	11 41	12 41	13 41	14 41			15 41	16 41	17 41	18 41	19 41	20 41		21 41	22 42		23 41			
	d		07 57	09 43	10 43	11 43	12 43	13 43	14 43			15 43	16 43	17 43	18 43	19 43	20 43		21 43			23 43			
Crewkerne	d		08 06	09 52	10 52	11 52	12 52	13 52	14 52			15 52	16 52	17 52	18 52	19 52	20 52		21 52			23 52			
Axminster	a		08 19	10 05	11 05	12 05	13 05	14 05	15 05			16 05	17 05	18 05	19 05	20 05	21 05		22 05			00 05			
	d		08 20	10 06	11 06	12 06	13 06	14 06	15 06			16 06	17 06	18 06	19 06	20 06	21 06		22 06			00 06			
Honiton	a		08 31	10 18	11 18	12 18	13 18	14 18	15 18			16 18	17 18	18 18	19 18	20 18	21 18		22 18			00 18			
	d		08 35	10 19	11 19	12 19	13 19	14 19	15 19			16 19	17 19	18 19	19 19	20 19	21 19		22 19			00 19			
Feniton	d		08 40		11 24		13 24		15 24				17 24		19 24		21 24		22 24			00 24			
Whimple	d		08 45		11 29		13 29		15 29				17 29		19 29		21 29		22 29			00 29			
Pinhoe	d			10 31		12 31		14 31				16 31		18 31		20 31			22 36						
Exeter Central	a		08 56	10 40	11 40	12 40	13 40	14 40	15 40			16 40	17 40	18 40	19 40	20 40	21 40		22 42						
Exeter St Davids 8	a		09 01	10 45	11 45	12 45	13 45	14 45	15 45			16 45	17 45	18 46	19 45	20 45	21 45		22 46			00 40			

b previous night, stops to pick up only

Table 160

Exeter and Salisbury - London

Mondays to Fridays

		SW MX 1	SW MO 1	SW ◇1 A ☕	SW ◇1 B ☕	SW ◇1 A ☕	SW ◇1 B ☕	SW ◇1 A ☕	SW ◇1 B ☕	SW ◇1 ☕	SW ◇1 ☕	SW ◇1 ☕	SW ◇1 ☕	SW ◇1 ☕	SW ◇1 ☕	SW ◇1 ☕	SW ◇1 ☕	SW ◇1	SW ◇1 ☕	SW ◇1 ☕	SW ◇1 ☕	SW ◇1 ☕
Exeter St Davids 6	d	22p57	23p15								05 10			06 40	07 26		08 26			09 26		10 26
Exeter Central	d	23p01	23p19								05 14			06 44	07 30		08 30			09 30		10 30
Pinhoe	d	23p06									05 19			06 49	07 35		08 35			09 35		
Whimple	d	23p13									05 26			06 56			08 42					10 39
Feniton	d	23p18									05 31			07 01			08 47					10 45
Honiton	a	23p25	23b34								05 38			07 10	07 47		08 54			09 48		10 51
	d	23p32	23b35								05 39	06 19		07 11	07 49		08 55			09 53		10 53
Axminster	a	23p42	23b45								05 49	06 29		07 21	07 59		09 05			10 03		11 03
	d	23p43	23b46								05 52	06 30		07 22	08 00		09 06			10 06		11 06
Crewkerne	d	23p56	00s11								06 05	06 43		07 35	08 13		09 19			10 19		11 19
Yeovil Junction	a	00 04	00s20								06 14	06 52		07 44	08 22		09 27			10 27		11 27
	d	00 09	00s21					05 12	05 15	05 50	06 20	06 53	07 22	07 50	08 29		09 29			10 29		11 29
Sherborne	d							05 18	05 21	05 56	06 26	07 00	07 28	07 56	08 36		09 36			10 36		11 36
Templecombe	d							05 26	05 29	06 04	06 34	07 07	07 36	08 04	08 43		09 43			10 43		11 43
Gillingham (Dorset)	a							05 33	05 36	06 11	06 41	07 14	07 43	08 11	08 50		09 50			10 50		11 50
	d							05 34	05 37	06 12	06 42	07 15	07 44	08 12	08 51	09 18	09 51			10 51		11 51
Tisbury	d							05 44	05 47	06 24	06 52	07 26	07 54	08 22	09 02	09 28	10 02			11 02		12 02
Bristol Temple Meads 10	d																	08 51				
Bath Spa 7	d																	09 07				
Bradford-on-Avon	d																	09 20				
Trowbridge	d																	09 27				
Westbury	d																	09c39				
Warminster	d																	09 46				
Salisbury	a	00 43	00 56					05 59	06 02	06 39	07 07	07 40	08 09	08 37	09 16	09 42	10 16	10 09		11 16		12 16
	d			05 12	05 15	05 40	05 43	06 03	06 06	06 45	07 15	07 45	08 15	08 45	09 21	09 45	10 21	<	10 45	11 21	11 45	12 21
Grateley	d			05 24	05 27	05 52	05 55	06 16	06 19	06 57	07 27	07 57	08 27	08 57		09 57			10 57		11 57	
Andover	d			05 32	05 35	06 00	06 03	06 23	06 26	07 05	07 35	08 05	08 35	09 04	09 38	10 04	10 38		11 04	11 38	12 04	12 38
Whitchurch (Hants)	d			05 40	05 43	06 08	06 11	06 32	06 35	07 13	07 43	08 13	08 43	09 12		10 12			11 12		12 12	
Overton	d			05 46	05 49	06 14	06 17	06 38	06 41	07 19	07 49	08 19	08 49	09 18		10 18			11 18		12 18	
Basingstoke	a			05 58	05 58	06 26	06 26	06 49	06 49	07 28	07 58	08 28	08 58	09 27	09 55	10 27	10 55		11 27	11 55	12 27	12 55
Woking	a			06 18	06 18	06 46	06 46				08 18	08 48	09 18	09 49	10 15	10 49	11 15		11 49	12 15	12 49	13 15
Clapham Junction 10	a			06 38	06 38			07 28	07 28				09 38	10 10	10 36		11 36			12 36		13 38
London Waterloo 15 ⊖	a			06 49	06 49	07 14	07 14	07 39	07 39	08 14	08 46	09 17	09 51	10 19	10 49	11 19	11 49		12 19	12 49	13 19	13 49

		SW ◇1 ☕	SW ◇1 ☕	SW ◇1 ☕	SW ◇1 ☕	SW ◇1 ☕	SW ◇1 ☕	SW ◇1 ☕	SW ◇1 ☕	SW ◇1 ☕	SW ◇1 ☕	SW ◇1	SW ◇1 ☕	SW ◇1 ☕	SW ◇1 ☕	SW ◇1 ☕	SW ◇1 ☕	SW ◇1 ☕	SW ◇1 ☕	SW 1	SW 1	SW 1
Exeter St Davids 6	d		11 26		12 26		13 26		14 26		15 26			16 26		17 26	18 26	19 27	20 26	21 23		22 57
Exeter Central	d		11 30		12 30		13 30		14 30		15 30			16 30		17 30	18 30	19 30	20 30	21 29		23 01
Pinhoe	d		11 35				13 35				15 35					17 35		19 35		21 34		23 06
Whimple	d				12 39				14 39					16 39			18 39		20 39			23 13
Feniton	d				12 45				14 45					16 45			18 45		20 45			23 18
Honiton	a		11 48		12 51		13 48		14 51		15 48			16 51		17 48	18 51	19 49	20 51	21 47		23 25
	d		11 53		12 53		13 53		14 53		15 53			16 53		17 53	18 53	19 53	20 53	21 53		23 32
Axminster	a		12 03		13 03		14 03		15 03		16 03			17 03		18 03	19 03	20 03	21 03	22 03		23 42
	d		12 06		13 06		14 06		15 06		16 06			17 06		18 06	19 06	20 06	21 06	22 06		23 43
Crewkerne	d		12 19		13 19		14 19		15 19		16 19			17 19		18 19	19 19	20 19	21 19	22 19		23 56
Yeovil Junction	a		12 27		13 27		14 27		15 27		16 27			17 27		18 27	19 27	20 27	21 27	22 27		00 04
	d		12 29		13 29		14 29		15 29		16 29			17 29		18 29	19 29	20 29	21 29	22 29		00 09
Sherborne	d		12 36		13 36		14 36		15 36		16 36			17 36		18 36	19 36	20 36	21 36	22 36		
Templecombe	d		12 43		13 43		14 43		15 43		16 43			17 43		18 43	19 43	20 43	21 43	22 47		
Gillingham (Dorset)	a		12 50		13 50		14 50		15 50		16 50			17 50		18 50	19 50	20 50	21 50	22 54		
	d		12 51		13 51		14 51		15 51	16 18	16 51			17 51		18 51	19 51	20 51	21 51	22 55		
Tisbury	d		13 02		14 02		15 02		16 02	16 28	17 02			18 02		19 02	20 02	21 02	22 02	23 05		
Bristol Temple Meads 10	d					13 10						15 54									22 25	
Bath Spa 7	d					13 23						16 07									22 38	
Bradford-on-Avon	d					13 35						16 22									22 51	
Trowbridge	d					13 42						16 28									22 57	
Westbury	d					13 53						16 39									23 08	
Warminster	d					14 00						16 47									23 15	
Salisbury	a		13 16		14 16	14 28	15 16		16 16	16 43	17 16	17 09		18 21		19 23	20 21	21 21	22 16	23 29	23 35	00 43
	d	12 45	13 21	13 45	14 21	14 45	15 21	15 45	16 21	16 48	17 21	<	17 45	18 26	18 45	19 26	20 26	21 26	22 26			
Grateley	d	12 57		13 57		14 57		15 57		17 00			17 57		18 57	19 38	20 38	21 38	22 38			
Andover	d	13 04	13 38	14 04	14 38	15 04	15 38	16 04	16 38	17 07	17 38		18 04	18 43	19 04	19 45	20 45	21 45	22 45			
Whitchurch (Hants)	d	13 12		14 12		15 12		16 12		17 15			18 12		19 12	19 53	20 53	21 53	22 53			
Overton	d	13 18		14 18		15 18		16 18		17 21			18 18		19 18	19 59	20 59	21 59	22 59			
Basingstoke	a	13 27	13 55	14 27	14 55	15 27	15 55	16 28	16 55	17 29	17 55		18 27	19 00	19 28	20 08	21 08	22 07	23 07			
Woking	a	13 49	14 15	14 49	15 15	15 49	16 15	16 49	17 15	17 49	18 15		18 49	19 20	19 49	20 29	21 29	22 28				
Clapham Junction 10	a		14 36		15 36		16 36		17 36		18 36			19 41		20 52	21 52	22 48				
London Waterloo 15 ⊖	a	14 19	14 49	15 19	15 49	16 19	16 49	17 19	17 44	18 21	18 45		19 19	19 50	20 19	21 00	22 04	22 58				

A from 27 September
B until 24 September
b previous night, stops to set down only
c arr. 0933

Table 160

Exeter and Salisbury - London

Saturdays

		SW 1	SW ◇1 A ☕	SW ◇1 B ☕	SW ◇1 A ☕	SW ◇1 B ☕	SW ◇1 A ☕	SW ◇1 B ☕	SW ◇1 ☕	SW ◇1 ☕	SW ◇1 ☕	SW ◇1 ☕	SW ◇1 ☕	SW ◇1 ☕	SW ◇1 ☕	SW ◇1 ☕	SW ◇1	SW ◇1 ☕	SW ◇1 ☕	SW ◇1 ☕	SW ◇1 ☕	SW ◇1 ☕
Exeter St Davids 6	d	22p57								05 10			06 41	07 26		08 26			09 26		10 26	
Exeter Central	d	23p01								05 14			06 45	07 30		08 30			09 30		10 30	
Pinhoe	d	23p06								05 19			06 50	07 35		08 35			09 35			
Whimple	d	23p13								05 26			06 57			08 42					10 39	
Feniton	d	23p18								05 31			07 02			08 47					10 45	
Honiton	a	23p25								05 38			07 11	07 48		08 54			09 48		10 51	
	d	23p32								05 39	06 19		07 13	07 53		08 55			09 53		10 53	
Axminster	a	23p42								05 49	06 29		07 23	08 03		09 05			10 03		11 03	
	d	23p43								05 52	06 30		07 24	08 06		09 06			10 06		11 06	
Crewkerne	d	23p56								06 05	06 43		07 37	08 19		09 19			10 19		11 19	
Yeovil Junction	a	00 04								06 14	06 52		07 45	08 27		09 27			10 27		11 27	
	d	00 09								06 20	06 53		07 50	08 29		09 29			10 29		11 29	
Sherborne	d									06 26	07 00		07 56	08 36		09 36			10 36		11 36	
Templecombe	d									06 34	07 07		08 04	08 43		09 43			10 43		11 43	
Gillingham (Dorset)	a									06 41	07 14		08 11	08 50		09 50			10 50		11 50	
	d									06 42	07 15		08 12	08 51		09 51			10 51		11 51	
Tisbury	d									06 52	07 26		08 22	09 02		10 02			11 02		12 02	
Bristol Temple Meads 10	d																08 51					
Bath Spa 7	d																09 07					
Bradford-on-Avon	d																09 20					
Trowbridge	d																09 27					
Westbury	d																09 39					
Warminster	d																09 46					
Salisbury	a	00 43								07 07	07 40		08 37	09 16		10 16	10 09		11 16		12 16	
	d		05 12	05 15	05 42	05 45	06 18	06 21	06 45	07 21	07 45	08 21	08 45	09 21	09 45	10 21	<	10 45	11 21	11 45	12 21	12 45
Grateley	d		05 24	05 27	05 54	05 57			06 57		07 57		08 57		09 57			10 57		11 57		12 57
Andover	d		05 32	05 35	06 01	06 04	06 35	06 38	07 04	07 38	08 04	08 38	09 04	09 38	10 04	10 38		11 04	11 38	12 04	12 38	13 04
Whitchurch (Hants)	d		05 40	05 43	06 09	06 12			07 12		08 12		09 12		10 12			11 12		12 12		13 12
Overton	d		05 46	05 49	06 15	06 18			07 18		08 18		09 18		10 18			11 18		12 18		13 18
Basingstoke	a		05 58	05 58	06 27	06 27	06 55	06 55	07 27	07 55	08 27	08 55	09 27	09 55	10 27	10 55		11 27	11 55	12 27	12 55	13 27
Woking	a		06 18	06 18	06 49	06 49	07 15	07 15	07 49	08 17	08 49	09 15	09 49	10 15	10 49	11 15		11 49	12 15	12 49	13 15	13 49
Clapham Junction 10	a		06 38	06 38			07 36	07 36		08 37		09 36		10 36		11 36			12 36		13 36	
London Waterloo 15 ⊖	a		06 49	06 49	07 19	07 19	07 49	07 49	08 19	08 49	09 19	09 49	10 19	10 49	11 19	11 49		12 19	12 49	13 19	13 49	14 19

		SW ◇1 ☕	SW ◇1 ☕	SW ◇1 ☕	SW ◇1 ☕	SW ◇1 ☕	SW ◇1 ☕	SW ◇1 ☕	SW ◇1 ☕	SW ◇1 ☕	SW ◇1	SW ◇1 ☕	SW ◇1 ☕	SW ◇1 ☕	SW ◇1 ☕	SW ◇1 ☕	SW ◇1 ☕	SW ◇1 ☕	SW 1	SW 1	SW 1
Exeter St Davids 6	d	11 26		12 26		13 26		14 26		15 26			16 26		17 26	18 26	19 26	20 26	21 23		22 57
Exeter Central	d	11 30		12 30		13 30		14 30		15 30			16 30		17 30	18 30	19 30	20 30	21 29		23 01
Pinhoe	d	11 35				13 35				15 35					17 35		19 35		21 34		23 06
Whimple	d			12 39				14 39					16 39		17 42	18 39		20 39			23 13
Feniton	d			12 45				14 45					16 45		17 47	18 45		20 45			23 18
Honiton	a	11 48		12 51		13 48		14 51		15 48			16 51		17 54	18 51	19 48	20 51	21 47		23 25
	d	11 53		12 53		13 53		14 53		15 53			16 53		17 55	18 53	19 53	20 53	21 53		23 32
Axminster	a	12 03		13 03		14 03		15 03		16 03			17 03		18 05	19 03	20 03	21 03	22 03		23 42
	d	12 06		13 06		14 06		15 06		16 06			17 06		18 06	19 06	20 06	21 06	22 06		23 43
Crewkerne	d	12 19		13 19		14 19		15 19		16 19			17 19		18 19	19 19	20 19	21 19	22 19		23 56
Yeovil Junction	a	12 27		13 27		14 27		15 27		16 27			17 27		18 27	19 27	20 27	21 27	22 27		00 04
	d	12 29		13 29		14 29		15 29		16 29			17 29		18 29	19 29	20 29	21 29	22 29		00 09
Sherborne	d	12 36		13 36		14 36		15 36		16 36			17 36		18 36	19 36	20 36	21 36	22 36		
Templecombe	d	12 43		13 43		14 43		15 43		16 43			17 43		18 43	19 43	20 43	21 43	22 43		
Gillingham (Dorset)	a	12 50		13 50		14 50		15 50		16 50			17 50		18 50	19 50	20 50	21 50	22 50		
	d	12 51		13 51		14 51		15 51		16 51			17 51		18 51	19 51	20 51	21 51	22 51		
Tisbury	d	13 02		14 02		15 02		16 02		17 02			18 02		19 02	20 02	21 02	22 02	23 02		
Bristol Temple Meads 10	d				13 15						15 54									22 23	
Bath Spa 7	d				13 28						16 07									22 36	
Bradford-on-Avon	d				13 40						16 24									22 47	
Trowbridge	d				13 47						16 30									22 53	
Westbury	d				13 54						16 39									23 04	
Warminster	d				14 02						16 47									23 11	
Salisbury	a	13 16		14 16	14 25	15 16		16 16		17 16	17 09		18 16		19 16	20 16	21 16	22 21	23 29	23 34	00 43
	d	13 21	13 45	14 21	14 45	15 21	15 45	16 21	16 45	17 21	<	17 45	18 21	18 45	19 26	20 26	21 26	22 26			
Grateley	d		13 57		14 57		15 57		16 57			17 57		18 57	19 38	20 38	21 38	22 38			
Andover	d	13 38	14 04	14 38	15 04	15 38	16 04	16 38	17 04	17 38		18 04	18 38	19 04	19 45	20 45	21 45	22 45			
Whitchurch (Hants)	d		14 12		15 12		16 12		17 12			18 12		19 12	19 53	20 53	21 53	22 53			
Overton	d		14 18		15 18		16 18		17 18			18 18		19 18	19 59	20 59	21 59	22 59			
Basingstoke	a	13 55	14 27	14 55	15 27	15 55	16 27	16 55	17 27	17 55		18 27	18 55	19 27	20 08	21 08	22 07	23 07			
Woking	a	14 15	14 49	15 15	15 49	16 15	16 49	17 15	17 49	18 15		18 49	19 15	19 49	20 29	21 29	22 28				
Clapham Junction 10	a	14 36		15 36		16 36		17 36		18 36			19 36		20 52	21 52	22 48				
London Waterloo 15 ⊖	a	14 49	15 19	15 49	16 19	16 49	17 19	17 49	18 19	18 49		19 19	19 49	20 19	21 04	22 04	22 57				

A from 2 October
B until 25 September

Table 160

Sundays

Exeter and Salisbury - London

		SW 1	SW ◇1 B	SW ◇1 C	SW ◇1 B	SW ◇1 C	SW ◇1	SW ◇1	SW ◇1	SW ◇1	SW ◇1	SW ◇1	SW ◇1	SW ◇1	SW ◇1	SW ◇1	SW ◇1	SW ◇1	SW ◇1	SW ◇1	SW ◇1	SW ◇1	SW 1
Exeter St Davids 6	d	22p57								09 26	10 26	11 26	12 26	13 26	14 26	15 26		16 26	17 26	18 26	19 26	20 26	
Exeter Central	d	23p01								09 30	10 30	11 30	12 30	13 30	14 30	15 30		16 30	17 30	18 30	19 30	20 30	
Pinhoe	d	23p06								09 35		11 35		13 35		15 35			17 35		19 35		
Whimple	d	23p13								09 42	10 39		12 39		14 39			16 39		18 39		20 39	
Feniton	d	23p18								09 47	10 45		12 45		14 45			16 45		18 45		20 45	
Honiton	a	23p25								09 54	10 51	11 48	12 51	13 48	14 51	15 48		16 51	17 48	18 51	19 48	20 51	
	d	23p32							08 58	09 55	10 53	11 53	12 53	13 53	14 53	15 53		16 53	17 53	18 53	19 53	20 53	
Axminster	a	23p42							09 08	10 05	11 03	12 03	13 03	14 03	15 03	16 03		17 03	18 03	19 03	20 03	21 03	
	d	23p43							09 09	10 09	11 09	12 09	13 09	14 09	15 09	16 09		17 09	18 09	19 09	20 09	21 09	
Crewkerne	d	23p56							09 22	10 22	11 22	12 22	13 22	14 22	15 22	16 22		17 22	18 22	19 22	20 22	21 22	
Yeovil Junction	a	00 04							09 30	10 30	11 30	12 30	13 30	14 30	15 30	16 30		17 30	18 30	19 30	20 30	21 30	
	d	00 09					07 32		09 32	10 32	11 32	12 32	13 32	14 32	15 32	16 32		17 32	18 32	19 32	20 32	21 32	
Sherborne	d						07 39		09 39	10 39	11 39	12 39	13 39	14 39	15 39	16 39		17 39	18 39	19 39	20 39	21 39	
Templecombe	d						07 46		09 46	10 46	11 46	12 46	13 46	14 46	15 46	16 46		17 46	18 46	19 46	20 46	21 46	
Gillingham (Dorset)	a						07 53		09 53	10 53	11 53	12 53	13 53	14 53	15 53	16 53		17 53	18 53	19 53	20 53	21 53	
	d						07 54	08 54	09 54	10 54	11 54	12 54	13 54	14 54	15 54	16 54		17 54	18 54	19 54	20 54	21 54	
Tisbury	d						08 05	09 05	10 05	11 05	12 05	13 05	14 05	15 05	16 05	17 05		18 05	19 05	20 05	21 05	22 05	
Bristol Temple Meads 10	d																16 04						21 35
Bath Spa 7	d																16 20						21 49
Bradford-on-Avon	d																16 31						22 00
Trowbridge	d																16 37						22 06
Westbury	d																16 46						22 15
Warminster	d																16 53						22 22
Salisbury	a	00 43					08 20	09 20	10 20	11 20	12 20	13 20	14 20	15 20	16 20	17 20	17 16	18 20	19 20	20 20	21 20	22 20	22 46
	d		06 42	06 45	07 24	07 27	08 27	09 27	10 27	11 27	12 27	13 27	14 27	15 27	16 27	17 27	<	18 27	19 27	20 27	21 27	22 27	
Grateley	d						08 39	09 39		11 39		13 39		15 39		17 39			19 39		21 39	22 39	
Andover	d		06 59	07 02	07 41	07 44	08 46	09 46	10 44	11 46	12 44	13 46	14 44	15 46	16 44	17 46		18 44	19 46	20 44	21 46	22 46	
Whitchurch (Hants)	d				07 49	07 52	08 54		10 52		12 52		14 52		16 52			18 52		20 52		22 54	
Overton	d				07 55	07 58	09 00		10 58		12 58		14 58		16 58			18 58		20 58		23 00	
Basingstoke	a		07 19	07 19	08 06	08 06	09 08	10 02	11 06	12 02	13 06	14 02	15 06	16 02	17 06	18 02		19 06	20 02	21 06	22 03	23 08	
Woking	a		07 39	07 39	08 28	08 28	09 28	10 28	11 28	12 28	13 28	14 28	15 28	16 28	17 28	18 28		19 28	20 28	21 28	22 28		
Clapham Junction 10	a		08 05	08 05	08 57	08 57	09 57	10 49	11 49	12 49	13 49	14 49	15 49	16 49	17 49	18 49		19 49	20 49	21 49	22 49		
London Waterloo 15 ⊖	a		08 19	08 19	09 09	09 09	10 08	11 04	12 03	13 04	13 59	14 59	15 59	16 59	17 59	18 59		19 59	20 59	21 59	22 59		

		SW 1	SW 1
Exeter St Davids 6	d	21 26	23 15
Exeter Central	d	21 30	23 19
Pinhoe	d	21 35	
Whimple	d	21 42	
Feniton	d	21 47	
Honiton	a	21 54	23s34
	d	21 55	23s35
Axminster	a	22 05	23s45
	d	22 09	23s46
Crewkerne	d	22 22	00s11
Yeovil Junction	a	22 30	00s20
	d	22 32	00s21
Sherborne	d	22 39	
Templecombe	d	22 46	
Gillingham (Dorset)	a	22 53	
	d	22 54	
Tisbury	d	23 05	
Bristol Temple Meads 10	d		
Bath Spa 7	d		
Bradford-on-Avon	d		
Trowbridge	d		
Westbury	d		
Warminster	d		
Salisbury	a	23 19	00 56
	d		
Grateley	d		
Andover	d		
Whitchurch (Hants)	d		
Overton	d		
Basingstoke	a		
Woking	a		
Clapham Junction 10	a		
London Waterloo 15 ⊖	a		

B from 26 September

C until 19 September

Network Diagram for Tables 165, 167

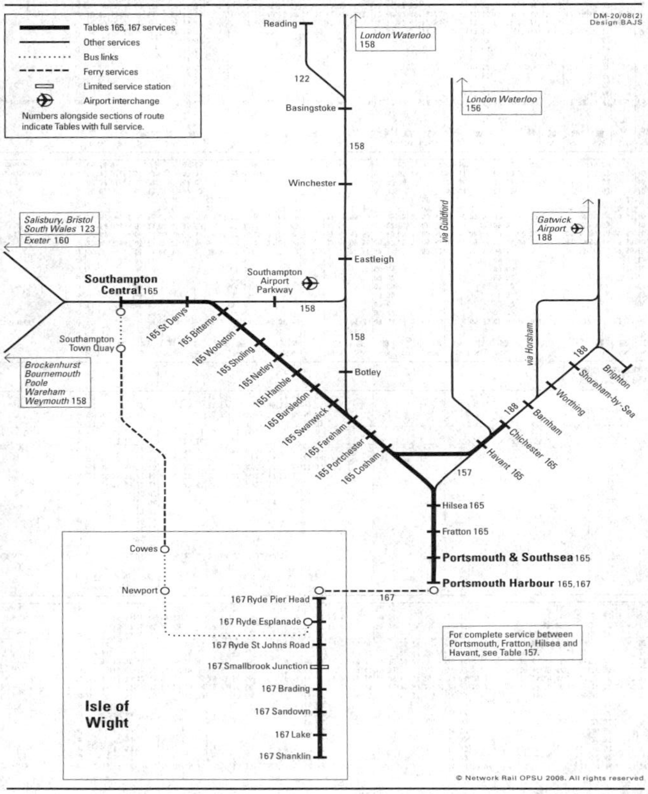

Southampton - Fareham and Portsmouth

		SW MO 1	SW MX 1	SW 1	SN ◇1	SW 1	SN 1	SW 1	SW 1	GW	SW 1	SN ◇1	SW 1	SW 1	SN 1	GW ◇	SW 1	SN ◇1	SW 1	SN 1		SW 1	GW ◇ ⌶	SN ◇1	SW 1
Southampton Central	d				05 48		06 10		06 21	06 53		07 06		07 17	07 33	07 42	07 51	08 10		08 33		08 44	09 04	09 10	
St Denys	d								06 28					07 23			07 57	08 15				08 49			
Bitterne	d								06 30					07 25			08 00					08 52			
Woolston	d				05 57		06 19		06 34			07 15		07 29			08 03					08 55			
Sholing	d								06 36					07 31			08 06					08 58			
Netley	d								06 40					07 35			08 10					09 02			
Hamble	d								06 42					07 37			08 12					09 04			
Bursledon	d								06 45					07 40			08 15					09 07			
Swanwick	d				06 06		06 27		06 49			07 24		07 44	07 51		08 20	08 28		08 50		09 11		09 28	
Fareham	a	23p43	23p48	00s47	06 12		06 33	06 49	06 57	07 14	07 19	07 30	07 46	07 52	07 58	08 05	08 28	08 34	08 50	08 56		09 17	09 27	09 36	09 46
	d	23p44	23p49	00s48	06 13	06 18	06 34	06 50	06 58	07 15	07 20	07 31	07 48	07 53	07 58	08 06	08 29	08 35	08 51	08 57		09 18	09 27	09 37	09 48
Portchester	d	23p49	23p54	00s53	06 18	06 23	06 40	06 55	07 03		07 25	07 36	07 53	07 58			08 34	08 40	08 56			09 23		09 42	09 53
Cosham	d	23p54	23p59	00s58	06 23	06 28	06 44	07 00	07 08	07 23	07 29	07 40	07 58	08 03	08 07	08 14	08 39	08 44	09 01	09 05		09 28	09 35	09 46	09 58
Havant	a				06 37		06 53					07 46			08 13			08 50		09 11				09 53	
Chichester 4	a				06 58		07 07					08 08			08 27			09 11		09 24				10 10	
Hilsea	a	23p59	00 03			06 33		07 05	07 13		07 35		08 03	08 09			08 45		09 05			09 33			10 03
Fratton	a	00 04	00 07	01s05		06 38		07 09	07 17	07 34	07 39		08 07	08 13		08 21	08 49		09 09			09 37	09 42		10 07
Portsmouth & Southsea	a	00 08	00 11	01s08		06 44		07 12	07 22	07 38	07 42		08 11	08 18		08 24	08 52		09 13			09 42	09 46		10 11
Portsmouth Harbour	a	00 13	00 16	01 12		06 49		07 17		07 45	07 48		08 16	08 23		08 30	08 58		09 18				09 54		10 18

		SN 1	SW 1	GW ■ ⌶	SN ◇1	SW 1		SN 1	SW 1	GW ◇ ⌶	SN ◇1	SW 1	SN 1	SW 1	GW ◇ ⌶	SN ◇1		SW 1	SN 1	SW 1	GW ◇ ⌶	SN ◇1	SW 1	SN 1	SW 1
Southampton Central	d	09 33	09 44	10 04	10 13			10 33	10 44	11 04	11 13		11 33	11 44	12 04	12 13			12 33	12 44	13 04	13 13		13 33	13 44
St Denys	d		09 49						10 49					11 49						12 49					13 49
Bitterne	d		09 52						10 52					11 52						12 52					13 52
Woolston	d		09 55						10 55					11 55						12 55					13 55
Sholing	d		09 58						10 58					11 58						12 58					13 58
Netley	d		10 02						11 02					12 02						13 02					14 02
Hamble	d		10 04						11 04					12 04						13 04					14 04
Bursledon	d		10 07						11 07					12 07						13 07					14 07
Swanwick	d	09 50	10 11		10 32			10 50	11 11		11 33		11 50	12 11		12 33			12 50	13 11		13 33		13 50	14 11
Fareham	a	09 56	10 17	10 27	10 38	10 46		10 56	11 17	11 27	11 39	11 46	11 56	12 17	12 27	12 39		12 46	12 56	13 17	13 27	13 39	13 46	13 56	14 17
	d	09 56	10 18	10 27	10 39	10 48		10 57	11 18	11 27	11 40	11 48	11 57	12 18	12 27	12 40		12 48	12 56	13 18	13 27	13 40	13 48	13 56	14 18
Portchester	d		10 23		10 44	10 53			11 23		11 45	11 53		12 23		12 45		12 53		13 23		13 45	13 53		14 23
Cosham	d	10 05	10 28	10 35	10 48	10 58		11 05	11 28	11 35	11 49	11 58	12 05	12 28	12 35	12 49		12 58	13 05	13 28	13 35	13 49	13 58	14 05	14 28
Havant	a	10 11			10 55			11 11			11 55		12 11			12 55			13 11			13 55		14 11	
Chichester 4	a	10 23			11 10			11 24			12 10		12 24			13 10			13 23			14 10		14 23	
Hilsea	a		10 33			11 03			11 33			12 03		12 33				13 03		13 33			14 03		14 33
Fratton	a		10 37	10 42		11 07			11 37	11 42		12 07		12 37	12 42			13 07		13 37	13 42		14 07		14 37
Portsmouth & Southsea	a		10 42	10 46		11 11			11 42	11 46		12 11		12 42	12 46			13 11		13 42	13 46		14 11		14 42
Portsmouth Harbour	a			10 54		11 18				11 54		12 18			12 54			13 18			13 54		14 18		

		GW ◇ ⌶		SN ◇1	SW 1	GW ◇	SN 1	SW 1	GW ◇ ⌶	SN ◇1	SW 1	SN 1		SW 1	GW ◇ ⌶	SN ◇1	SW 1	SW 1	SN 1	SW 1	SW 1	GW ◇ ⌶		SN ◇1	SW 1
Southampton Central	d	14 04		14 13		14 34	14 27	14 44	15 04	15 13		15 33		15 44	16 04	16 12			16 33		16 44	17 04		17 13	
St Denys	d							14 49						15 49							16 49				
Bitterne	d							14 52						15 52							16 52				
Woolston	d							14 55						15 55							16 55				
Sholing	d							14 58						15 58							16 58				
Netley	d							15 02						16 02							17 02				
Hamble	d							15 04						16 04							17 04				
Bursledon	d							15 07						16 07							17 07				
Swanwick	d			14 33				15 11		15 33		15 50		16 11		16 29			16 50		17 11			17 33	
Fareham	a	14 27		14 39	14 46	14 55	14 59	15 17	15 27	15 39	15 46	15 56		16 17	16 27	16 35		16 46	16 56	17 11	17 17	17 27		17 39	17 46
	d	14 27		14 40	14 48	14 56	15 00	15 18	15 27	15 40	15 48	15 57		16 18	16 27	16 36	16 43	16 48	16 57	17 12	17 18	17 27		17 40	17 48
Portchester	d			14 45	14 53			15 23		15 45	15 53			16 23		16 41		16 53		17 17	17 23			17 45	17 53
Cosham	d	14 35		14 49	14 58	15 04		15 28	15 35	15 49	15 58	16 05		16 28	16 35	16 45		16 58	17 05	17 22	17 28	17 35		17 49	17 58
Havant	a			14 55		15 10	15 14			15 57		16 11				16 51	16 55		17 11					17 55	
Chichester 4	a			15 10		15 21	15 25			16 12		16 24				17 08			17 25					18 10	
Hilsea	a				15 03			15 33			16 03			16 33				17 03			17 33				18 04
Fratton	a	14 42			15 07			15 37	15 42		16 07			16 37	16 42			17 07		17 31	17 37	17 42			18 08
Portsmouth & Southsea	a	14 46			15 11			15 42	15 46		16 11			16 40	16 46			17 11		17 35	17 42	17 46			18 12
Portsmouth Harbour	a	14 54			15 18				15 54		16 18			16 44	16 54			17 18		17 40		17 54			18 20

Southampton - Fareham and Portsmouth

		SN 1	SW 1	SW 1	GW ◇ ⌶	SN ◇1	SW 1	SN 1		SW 1	SW 1	GW ■ ⌶	SN ◇1	SW 1	SN 1	SW 1	SW 1	GW ■ ⌶		SN ◇1	SW 1	SN 1	SW 1	GW ◇ ⌶	SN 1
Southampton Central	d	17 33	17 44		18 04	18 11		18 33			18 44	19 04	19 12		19 33		19 44	20 04		20 11		20 33	20 44	21 04	21 13
St Denys	d		17 49								18 49						19 49						20 49		
Bitterne	d		17 52								18 52						19 52						20 52		
Woolston	d		17 55								18 55						19 55						20 55		
Sholing	d		17 58								18 58						19 58						20 58		
Netley	d		18 02								19 02						20 02						21 02		
Hamble	d		18 04								19 04						20 04						21 04		
Bursledon	d		18 07								19 07						20 07						21 07		
Swanwick	d	17 50	18 11			18 28		18 50			19 11		19 29		19 51		20 11			20 28		20 50	21 11		21 33
Fareham	a	17 56	18 17	18 22	18 27	18 34	18 43	18 56		19 13	19 17	19 27	19 35	19 45	19 57	20 09	20 17	20 27		20 34	20 48	20 56	21 17	21 27	21 39
	d	17 56	18 18	18 23	18 27	18 35	18 45	18 56		19 14	19 18	19 27	19 36	19 48	19 57	20 09	20 18	20 27		20 35	20 49	20 57	21 18	21 27	21 40
Portchester	d		18 23	18 28		18 40	18 50			19 19	19 23		19 41	19 53			20 23			20 40	20 54		21 23		21 45
Cosham	d	18 05	18 28	18 33	18 35	18 44	18 55	19 05		19 24	19 28	19 35	19 46	19 58	20 06		20 28			20 44	20 59	21 06	21 28		21 49
Havant	a	18 11				18 50		19 11					19 52		20 12	20 21				20 50		21 12			21 55
Chichester 4	a	18 24				19 05		19 22					20 06		20 24					21 05		21 24			22 06
Hilsea	a		18 33				19 05			19 28	19 33			20 02			20 33				21 03		21 33		
Fratton	a		18 37	18 40	18 48		19 09			19 32	19 37	19 42		20 06			20 37	20 42			21 07		21 37	21 41	
Portsmouth & Southsea	a		18 41	18 43	18 52		19 12			19 36	19 42	19 46		20 11			20 42	20 46			21 11		21 42	21 45	
Portsmouth Harbour	a			18 51	18 58		19 20			19 43		19 54		20 20				20 54			21 16			21 52	

		SW 1	SN ◇1	SW 1		SN ◇1	GW ◇	SN 1	SW 1	GW ◇	SW 1
Southampton Central	d		21 32	21 44		22 13	22 04	22 22	22 44	23 04	
St Denys	d			21 49					22 49		
Bitterne	d			21 52					22 52		
Woolston	d			21 55					22 55		
Sholing	d			21 58					22 58		
Netley	d			22 02					23 02		
Hamble	d			22 04					23 04		
Bursledon	d			22 07					23 07		
Swanwick	d		21 51	22 11		22 30			23 11		
Fareham	a	21 48	21 57	22 17		22 36	22 42	22 59	23 17	23 27	23 48
	d	21 48	21 58	22 18		22 37	22 42	23 00	23 18	23 27	23 49
Portchester	d	21 53	22 03	22 23		22 42			23 23		23 54
Cosham	d	21 58	22 07	22 28		22 47		23 08	23 28		23 59
Havant	a		22 13			22 56		23 14			
Chichester 4	a		22 34			23 11		23 25			
Hilsea	a	22 03		22 33					23 33		00 03
Fratton	a	22 08		22 37			22 56		23 37	23 44	00 07
Portsmouth & Southsea	a	22 11		22 42			22 59		23 40	23 48	00 11
Portsmouth Harbour	a	22 16					23 04			23 54	00 16

Saturdays

		SW 1	SW 1	SW 1	SN ◇1	SW 1	SN 1	SW 1	GW	SN ◇1		SW 1	SN 1	SW 1	GW ◇	SN ◇1	SW 1	SN 1	SW 1	GW ◇		SN ◇1	SW 1	SN 1	SW 1
Southampton Central	d			05 44	06 13		06 33	06 44	07 05	07 13			07 33	07 44	08 04	08 13		08 33	08 44	09 04		09 13		09 33	09 44
St Denys	d			05 49				06 49						07 49					08 49						09 49
Bitterne	d			05 52				06 52						07 52					08 52						09 52
Woolston	d			05 55				06 55						07 55					08 55						09 55
Sholing	d			05 58				06 58						07 58					08 58						09 58
Netley	d			06 02				07 02						08 02					09 02						10 02
Hamble	d			06 04				07 04						08 04					09 04						10 04
Bursledon	d			06 07				07 07						08 07					09 07						10 07
Swanwick	d			06 11	06 33		06 50	07 11		07 33			07 50	08 11		08 33		08 50	09 11			09 33		09 50	10 11
Fareham	a	23p48	00s47	06 17	06 39	06 46	06 56	07 17	07 27	07 39		07 48	07 56	08 17	08 27	08 39	08 48	08 56	09 17	09 27		09 39	09 46	09 56	10 17
	d	23p49	00s48	06 18	06 40	06 48	06 56	07 18	07 27	07 40		07 49	07 56	08 18	08 27	08 40	08 49	08 56	09 18	09 27		09 40	09 48	09 56	10 18
Portchester	d	23p54	00s53	06 23	06 45	06 53		07 23		07 45		07 54		08 23		08 45	08 54		09 23			09 45	09 53		10 23
Cosham	d	23p59	00s58	06 28	06 49	06 58	07 05	07 28	07 35	07 49		07 59	08 05	08 28	08 35	08 49	08 59	09 05	09 28	09 35		09 49	09 58	10 05	10 28
Havant	a				06 55		07 11			07 55			08 11			08 55		09 11				09 55		10 11	
Chichester 4	a				07 10		07 23			08 10			08 23			09 10		09 23				10 10		10 23	
Hilsea	a	00 03		06 33		07 03		07 33				08 03		08 33			09 04		09 33				10 03		10 33
Fratton	a	00 07	01s05	06 37		07 07		07 37	07 42			08 07		08 37	08 42		09 08		09 37	09 42			10 07		10 37
Portsmouth & Southsea	a	00 11	01s08	06 42		07 11		07 42	07 46			08 11		08 42	08 46		09 12		09 42	09 46			10 11		10 42
Portsmouth Harbour	a	00 16	01 12			07 16			07 52			08 18			08 52		09 18			09 52			10 18		

		GW ◇	SN ◇1	SW 1	SN 1	SW 1		GW ◇	SN ◇1	SW 1	SN 1	SW 1	GW ◇ ⌶	SN ◇1	SW 1	SN 1		SW 1	GW ◇ ⌶	SN ◇1	SW 1	SN 1	SW 1	GW ◇ ⌶	SN ◇1
Southampton Central	d	10 04	10 13		10 33	10 44		11 04	11 13		11 33	11 44	12 04	12 13		12 33		12 44	13 04	13 13		13 33	13 44	14 04	14 13
St Denys	d					10 49						11 49						12 49					13 49		
Bitterne	d					10 52						11 52						12 52					13 52		
Woolston	d					10 55						11 55						12 55					13 55		
Sholing	d					10 58						11 58						12 58					13 58		
Netley	d					11 02						12 02						13 02					14 02		
Hamble	d					11 04						12 04						13 04					14 04		
Bursledon	d					11 07						12 07						13 07					14 07		
Swanwick	d		10 33		10 50	11 11			11 33		11 50	12 11		12 33		12 50		13 11		13 33		13 50	14 11		14 33
Fareham	a	10 27	10 39	10 46	10 56	11 17		11 27	11 39	11 46	11 56	12 17	12 27	12 39	12 46	12 56		13 17	13 27	13 39	13 46	13 56	14 17	14 27	14 39
	d	10 27	10 40	10 48	10 56	11 18		11 27	11 40	11 48	11 56	12 18	12 27	12 40	12 48	12 56		13 18	13 27	13 40	13 48	13 56	14 18	14 27	14 40
Portchester	d		10 45	10 53		11 23			11 45	11 53		12 23		12 45	12 53			13 23		13 45	13 53		14 23		14 45
Cosham	d	10 35	10 49	10 58	11 05	11 28		11 35	11 49	11 58	12 05	12 28	12 35	12 49	12 58	13 05		13 28	13 35	13 49	13 58	14 05	14 28	14 35	14 49
Havant	a		10 55		11 11				11 55		12 11			12 55		13 11				13 55		14 11			14 55
Chichester 4	a		11 10		11 23				12 10		12 23			13 10		13 23				14 10		14 23			15 10
Hilsea	a			11 03		11 33				12 03		12 33			13 03			13 33			14 03		14 33		
Fratton	a	10 42		11 07		11 37		11 42		12 07		12 37	12 42		13 07			13 37	13 42		14 07		14 37	14 42	
Portsmouth & Southsea	a	10 46		11 11		11 42		11 46		12 11		12 42	12 46		13 11			13 42	13 46		14 11		14 42	14 46	
Portsmouth Harbour	a	10 52		11 18				11 52		12 18			12 51		13 18				13 51		14 18			14 51	

Table 165

Southampton - Fareham and Portsmouth

Saturdays

	SW	SN	SW	GW	SN	SW	SN	SW	GW	SN	SW	SN	SW	GW	SN	SW	SN	SW	GW	SN	SW
	■	■	■	◇ ⌶	◇■	■	■	■	◇	◇■	■	■	■	◇	◇■	■	■	■	◇	◇■	■
Southampton Central d		14 27	14 44	15 04	15 13		15 33	15 44	16 04	16 13		16 33	16 44	17 04	17 13		17 33	17 44	18 04	18 11	
St Denys d			14 49					15 49					16 49					17 49			
Bitterne d			14 52					15 52					16 52					17 52			
Woolston d			14 55					15 55					16 55					17 55			
Sholing d			14 58					15 58					16 58					17 58			
Netley d			15 02					16 02					17 02					18 02			
Hamble d			15 04					16 04					17 04					18 04			
Bursledon d			15 07					16 07					17 07					18 07			
Swanwick d			15 11		15 33		15 50	16 11		16 33		16 50	17 11		17 33		17 50	18 11		18 28	
Fareham a	14 46	14 59	15 17	15 27	15 39	15 46	15 56	16 17	16 27	16 39	16 46	16 56	17 17	17 27	17 39	17 46	17 56	18 17	18 27	18 34	18 46
d	14 48	15 00	15 18	15 27	15 40	15 48	15 56	16 18	16 27	16 40	16 48	16 56	17 18	17 27	17 40	17 48	17 56	18 18	18 27	18 35	18 48
Portchester d	14 53		15 23		15 45	15 53		16 23		16 45	16 53		17 23		17 45	17 53		18 23		18 40	18 53
Cosham d	14 58		15 28	15 35	15 49	15 58	16 05	16 28	16 35	16 49	16 58	17 05	17 28	17 35	17 49	17 58	18 05	18 28	18 35	18 44	18 58
Havant a		15 14			15 55		16 11			16 55		17 11			17 55		18 11			18 50	
Chichester ■ a		15 25			16 10		16 23			17 10		17 23			18 10		18 23			19 05	
Hilsea a	15 03		15 33			16 03		16 33			17 03		17 33			18 03		18 33			19 03
Fratton a	15 07		15 37	15 42		16 07		16 37	16 42		17 07		17 37	17 42		18 07		18 37	18 42		19 07
Portsmouth & Southsea a	15 11		15 42	15 46		16 11		16 40	16 46		17 11		17 42	17 46		18 11		18 42	18 46		19 11
Portsmouth Harbour a	15 18			15 51		16 18		16 44	16 51		17 18			17 51		18 18			18 52		19 18

	SN	SW	GW	SN	SW	SN	SW	GW	SN	SW	SN	SW	GW	SN	SW	SN	SW	GW	SN	SW	SN	SW
	■	■	▪	◇■	■	■	■	◇	◇■	■	■	■	◇	■	■	■	■	◇	◇■	■	◇■	■
Southampton Central d	18 33	18 44	19 04	19 11		19 33	19 44	20 04	20 11		20 33	20 44	21 04	21 13		21 23	21 44	22 04	22 13		22 33	22 44
St Denys d		18 49					19 49					20 49				21 28	21 49					22 49
Bitterne d		18 52					19 52					20 52					21 52					22 52
Woolston d		18 55					19 55					20 55				21 33	21 55					22 55
Sholing d		18 58					19 58					20 58					21 58					22 58
Netley d		19 02					20 02					21 02				21 37	22 02					23 02
Hamble d		19 04					20 04					21 04					22 04					23 04
Bursledon d		19 07					20 07					21 07					22 07					23 07
Swanwick d	18 50	19 11		19 28		19 50	20 11		20 28		20 50	21 11		21 33		21 45	22 11		22 31		22 50	23 11
Fareham a	18 56	19 17	19 27	19 34	19 46	19 56	20 17	20 27	20 34	20 46	20 56	21 17	21 27	21 39	21 46	21 54	22 17	22 26	22 38	22 46	22 56	23 17
d	18 56	19 18	19 27	19 35	19 48	19 56	20 18	20 27	20 35	20 48	20 56	21 18	21 27	21 40	21 48	21 56	22 18	22 27	22 39	22 48	23 00	23 18
Portchester d		19 23		19 40	19 53		20 23		20 40	20 53		21 23		21 45	21 53	22 01	22 23		22 44	22 53		23 23
Cosham d	19 05	19 28	19 35	19 44	19 58	20 05	20 28		20 44	20 58	21 05	21 28		21 49	21 58	22 06	22 28		22 48	22 58	23 08	23 28
Havant a	19 11			19 51		20 11			20 50		21 11			21 55		22 12			22 54		23 14	
Chichester ■ a	19 23			20 06		20 23			21 05		21 23			22 06		22 33			23 09		23 25	
Hilsea a		19 33			20 03		20 37			21 03		21 33			22 03		22 33			23 03		23 33
Fratton a		19 37	19 42		20 07		20 41	20 42		21 07		21 37	21 42		22 07		22 37	22 42		23 07		23 37
Portsmouth & Southsea a		19 42	19 46		20 11		20 44	20 46		21 11		21 41	21 46		22 11		22 40	22 46		23 11		23 40
Portsmouth Harbour a			19 52		20 18			20 52		21 18			21 52		22 18		22 47	22 52		23 18		

	GW	SW
	◇	■
Southampton Central d	23 04	
St Denys d		
Bitterne d		
Woolston d		
Sholing d		
Netley d		
Hamble d		
Bursledon d		
Swanwick d		
Fareham a	23 27	23 46
d	23 27	23 48
Portchester d		23 53
Cosham d		23 58
Havant a		
Chichester ■ a		
Hilsea a		00 03
Fratton a	23 41	00 07
Portsmouth & Southsea a	23 45	00 11
Portsmouth Harbour a	23 52	00 16

Table 165

Southampton - Fareham and Portsmouth

Sundays

	SW	SW	SW	SW	SW	SW	GW	SW	SW	SW	SW	SW	GW	SW	SW	GW	GW	SW	SW	GW	SW	SW
	■	■	■	■	■	■		■	■	■	■	■	◇	■	■	◇ B	◇ C	■	■	◇	■	■
Southampton Central d			06 35		07 35		08 31	08 35		09 35		10 35	11 04		11 35	12 02	12 04		12 35	13 08		13 35
St Denys d			06 41		07 41			08 41		09 41		10 41			11 41				12 41			13 41
Bitterne d			06 43		07 43			08 43		09 43		10 43			11 43				12 43			13 43
Woolston d			06 47		07 47			08 47		09 47		10 47			11 47				12 47			13 47
Sholing d			06 49		07 49			08 49		09 49		10 49			11 49				12 49			13 49
Netley d			06 53		07 53			08 53		09 53		10 53			11 53				12 53			13 53
Hamble d			06 55		07 55			08 55		09 55		10 55			11 55				12 55			13 55
Bursledon d			06 58		07 58			08 58		09 58		10 58			11 58				12 58			13 58
Swanwick d			07 02		08 02			09 02		10 02		11 02			12 02				13 02			14 02
Fareham a	23p46	00s47	07 09		08 09	08 43	08 51	09 09	09 43	10 09	10 43	11 09	11 27	11 43	12 09	12 26	12 27	12 43	13 09	13 33	13 43	14 09
d	23p48	00s48	07 10	07 44	08 10	08 44	08 52	09 10	09 44	10 10	10 44	11 10	11 27	11 44	12 10	12 27	12 27	12 44	13 10	13 34	13 44	14 10
Portchester d	23p53	00s53	07 15	07 49	08 15	08 49		09 15	09 49	10 15	10 49	11 15		11 49	12 15			12 49	13 15		13 49	14 15
Cosham d	23p58	00s58	07 20	07 54	08 20	08 54	09 00	09 20	09 54	10 20	10 54	11 20	11 35	11 54	12 20	12 35	12 35	12 54	13 20	13 42	13 54	14 20
Havant a							09 11													14 03		
Chichester ■ a							09 22													14 19		
Hilsea a	00 03		07 26	08 00	08 26	09 00		09 26	10 00	10 26	11 00	11 26		12 00	12 26			13 00	13 26		14 00	14 26
Fratton a	00 07	01s05	07 30	08 04	08 30	09 04		09 30	10 04	10 30	11 05	11 30	11 42	12 04	12 30	12 42	12 42	13 04	13 30		14 04	14 30
Portsmouth & Southsea a	00 11	01s08	07 33	08 08	08 33	09 08		09 33	10 10	10 33	11 10	11 33	11 45	12 08	12 33	12 45	12 45	13 08	13 33		14 08	14 33
Portsmouth Harbour a	00 16	01 12		08 13		09 13			10 15		11 14		11 52	12 13		12 52	12 52	13 13			14 13	

	GW	GW	SW	SW	SW	GW	SW	GW	GW	GW	SW	SW	GW	SW	SW	GW	GW	SW	SW	GW	GW	SW
	◇ D ⌶	◇ E ⌶	■	■	■	◇	■	◇ B	◇ F	◇ E	■	■	◇	■	■	◇ B	◇ C	■	■	◇ G	◇ F	■
Southampton Central d	14 04	14 04		14 35		15 22	15 35	16 04	16 04	16 03		16 35	17 04		17 35	18 01	18 04		18 35	19 04	19 04	
St Denys d				14 41			15 41					16 41			17 41				18 41			
Bitterne d				14 43			15 43					16 43			17 43				18 43			
Woolston d				14 47			15 47					16 47			17 47				18 47			
Sholing d				14 49			15 49					16 49			17 49				18 49			
Netley d				14 53			15 53					16 53			17 53				18 53			
Hamble d				14 55			15 55					16 55			17 55				18 55			
Bursledon d				14 58			15 58					16 58			17 58				18 58			
Swanwick d				15 02			16 02					17 02			18 02				19 02			
Fareham a	14 25	14 25	14 43	15 09	15 43	15 50	16 09	16 26	16 27	16 27	16 43	17 09	17 27	17 43	18 09	18 24	18 27	18 43	19 09	19 27	19 27	19 43
d	14 26	14 26	14 44	15 10	15 44	15 51	16 10	16 27	16 27	16 27	16 44	17 10	17 27	17 44	18 10	18 24	18 27	18 44	19 10	19 27	19 27	19 44
Portchester d			14 49	15 15	15 49		16 15				16 49	17 15		17 49	18 15			18 49	19 15			19 49
Cosham d	14 34	14 34	14 54	15 20	15 54	16 01	16 20	16 35	16 35	16 35	16 54	17 20	17 35	17 54	18 20	18 32	18 35	18 54	19 20	19 35	19 35	19 54
Havant a						16 11																
Chichester ■ a						16 22																
Hilsea a			15 00	15 26	16 00		16 26				17 00	17 26		18 00	18 26			19 00	19 26			20 00
Fratton a	14 41	14 41	15 04	15 30	16 04		16 30	16 42	16 42	16 42	17 03	17 30	17 42	18 04	18 30	18 39	18 42	19 03	19 30	19 42	19 42	20 04
Portsmouth & Southsea a	14 44	14 45	15 08	15 33	16 08		16 33	16 45	16 45	16 46	17 08	17 33	17 45	18 08	18 33	18 42	18 45	19 08	19 33	19 46	19 45	20 08
Portsmouth Harbour a	14 50	14 52	15 13		16 13			16 53	16 52	16 52	17 13		17 52	18 13		18 49	18 52	19 13		19 52	19 52	20 13

	GW	SW	GW	SW	GW	SW	GW	SW	SW	GW	SW	SW	GW	SW
	◇	■	◇	■	▪	■	◇	■	■	◇	■	■	◇	■
Southampton Central d	19 27	19 35	20 04		20 31	20 35	21 01		21 35	22 04		22 35	23 02	
St Denys d		19 41				20 41			21 41			22 41		
Bitterne d		19 43				20 43			21 43			22 43		
Woolston d		19 47				20 47			21 47			22 47		
Sholing d		19 49				20 49			21 49			22 49		
Netley d		19 53				20 53			21 53			22 53		
Hamble d		19 55				20 55			21 55			22 55		
Bursledon d		19 58				20 58			21 58			22 58		
Swanwick d		20 02				21 02			22 02			23 02		
Fareham a	19 48	20 09	20 27	20 43	20 54	21 10	21 23	21 43	22 09	22 26	22 43	23 09	23 23	23 43
d	19 49	20 10	20 27	20 44	20 55	21 10	21 24	21 44	22 10	22 27	22 44	23 10	23 24	23 44
Portchester d		20 15		20 49		21 15		21 49	22 15		22 49	23 15		23 49
Cosham d	19 59	20 20		20 54		21 20		21 54	22 20		22 54	23 20		23 54
Havant a	20 10													
Chichester ■ a	20 21													
Hilsea a		20 26		21 00		21 26		22 00	22 26		23 00	23 24		23 59
Fratton a		20 30	20 42	21 04	21 09	21 30	21 37	22 04	22 30	22 40	23 04	23 28	23 37	00 04
Portsmouth & Southsea a		20 33	20 45	21 08	21 15	21 33	21 41	22 08	22 33	22 43	23 08	23 32	23 41	00 08
Portsmouth Harbour a			20 52	21 13	21 26		21 48	22 13		22 51	23 13		23 49	00 13

B until 11 July
C from 18 July
D until 5 September
E from 12 September
F from 18 July until 5 September
G until 11 July, from 12 September

Portsmouth and Fareham - Southampton

Mondays to Fridays

		SW	SN	SW	SW	GW	SN	SW	SW	SN	SW	GW	SN	SN	SW	SW	SN	SW	SW	SN	GW	SW	SW
		1	1	1	1	■ ⊼	1	1	1	1	1	◇ ⊼	1	1	1	1	1	1	1	1	◇ ⊼	1	1
Portsmouth Harbour	d	05 00			05 43	06 00			06 23		06 38	06 51			07 24			07 55	08 05		08 23	08 33	08 55
Portsmouth & Southsea	d	05 05		05 16	05 48	06 04		06 23	06 28		06 43	06 55			07 29	07 38		08 00	08 10		08 27	08 38	09 00
Fratton	d	05 09		05 20	05 52	06 08		06 27	06 32		06 47	06 59			07 33	07 43		08 04	08 14		08 31	08 43	09 04
Hilsea	d	05 13		05 24	05 56			06 31	06 36		06 51				07 37	07 47		08 08	08 18			08 47	09 08
Chichester [4]	d		05 06				06 09			06 26			07 08	07 13			07 52			08 22			
Havant	d		05 17				06 20			06 40			07 19	07 31			08 03			08 37			
Cosham	d	05 18	05 24	05 30	06 03	06 15	06 27	06 36	06 42	06 50	06 58	07 07	07 26	07 38	07 43	07 52	08 09	08 13	08 23	08 45	08 39	08 52	09 13
Portchester	d	05 23	05 28	05 35	06 08			06 41	06 46	06 54	07 03		07 30		07 48	07 57	08 13	08 18	08 28	08 49		08 57	09 18
Fareham	a	05 28	05 33	05 40	06 13	06 23	06 36	06 46	06 51	06 59	07 08	07 17	07 35	07 46	07 53	08 02	08 18	08 23	08 33	08 54	08 46	09 02	09 23
	d	05 29	05 34	05 41	06 19	06 24	06 37	06 47	06 53	07 00	07 11	07 18	07 36	07 47	07 54	08 03	08 19	08 24	08 34	08 55	08 47	09 03	09 24
Swanwick	d		05 40	05 47			06 43	06 53		07 06			07 42	07 53		08 09	08 26			09 01		09 09	
Bursledon	d			05 51				06 57								08 13	08 29					09 13	
Hamble	d			05 54				07 00								08 16	08 32					09 16	
Netley	d		05 46	05 56				07 02					07 48	07 59		08 18	08 34					09 18	
Sholing	d			06 00				07 06								08 22	08 38					09 22	
Woolston	d		05 50	06 02				07 08					07 52	08 04		08 24	08 40					09 24	
Bitterne	d			06 06				07 12								08 28	08 43					09 28	
St Denys	d			06 09				07 15						08 08		08 31	08 46					09 31	
Southampton Central	a		05 59	06 14		06 45	07 02	07 21		07 25		07 45	08 01	08 13		08 38	08 52			09 19	09 08	09 38	

		SN	SN	GW	SW	GW	SW	SN	GW	SN	SW	SW	SN	GW	SN	SW	SW	SN	GW	SN	SW	SW	SN
		◇ 1	1	◇ ⊼	1	◇	1	◇ 1	◇ ⊼	1	1	1	◇ 1	◇ ⊼	1	1	1	◇ 1	◇ ⊼	1	1	1	◇ 1
Portsmouth Harbour	d			09 23	09 33		09 55		10 23		10 33	10 55		11 23			11 55		12 23			12 55	
Portsmouth & Southsea	d			09 27	09 38		10 00		10 27		10 38	11 00		11 27		11 38	12 00		12 27		12 38	13 00	
Fratton	d			09 31	09 43		10 04		10 31		10 43	11 04		11 31		11 43	12 04		12 31		12 43	13 04	
Hilsea	d				09 47		10 08				10 47	11 08				11 47	12 08				12 47	13 08	
Chichester [4]	d	09 08	09 24			09 47		10 06		10 25			11 05		11 25			12 05		12 25			13 05
Havant	d	09 23	09 38			09 59		10 20		10 37			11 19		11 37			12 19		12 37			13 19
Cosham	d	09 29	09 46	09 39	09 52	10 05	10 13	10 28	10 39	10 46	10 52	11 13	11 26	11 39	11 46	11 52	12 13	12 26	12 39	12 46	12 52	13 13	13 26
Portchester	d				09 57		10 18	10 32			10 57	11 18	11 30			11 57	12 18	12 30			12 57	13 18	13 30
Fareham	a	09 37	09 53	09 46	10 02	10 14	10 23	10 37	10 46	10 53	11 02	11 23	11 35	11 46	11 53	12 02	12 23	12 35	12 46	12 53	13 02	13 23	13 35
	d	09 38	09 54	09 47	10 03	10 14	10 24	10 38	10 47	10 54	11 03	11 24	11 36	11 47	11 54	12 03	12 24	12 36	12 47	12 54	13 03	13 24	13 36
Swanwick	d	09 44	10 00		10 09			10 44		11 00	11 09		11 42		12 00	12 09		12 42		13 00	13 09		13 42
Bursledon	d				10 13						11 13					12 13					13 13		
Hamble	d				10 16						11 16					12 16					13 16		
Netley	d				10 18						11 18					12 18					13 18		
Sholing	d				10 22						11 22					12 22					13 22		
Woolston	d				10 24						11 24					12 24					13 24		
Bitterne	d				10 28						11 28					12 28					13 28		
St Denys	d				10 31						11 31					12 31					13 31		
Southampton Central	a	10 01	10 20	10 08	10 38	10 41		11 01	11 08	11 19	11 38		12 01	12 08	12 19	12 38		12 59	13 08	13 19	13 38		13 59

		GW	SN	SW	SW	SN	GW	SN	SW	SW	SN	GW	SN	SW	SW	SN	GW	SN	SW	SW	SW	SN
		◇ ⊼	1	1	1	◇ 1	■ ⊼	1	1	1	◇ 1	■ ⊼	1	1	1	◇ 1	■ ⊼	1	1	1	1	◇ 1
Portsmouth Harbour	d	13 23			13 55		14 23			14 55		15 23			15 55		16 23			16 55	17 03	
Portsmouth & Southsea	d	13 27		13 38	14 00		14 27		14 38	15 00		15 27		15 38	16 00		16 27		16 38	17 00	17 07	
Fratton	d	13 31		13 43	14 04		14 31		14 43	15 04		15 31		15 43	16 04		16 31		16 43	17 04	17 11	
Hilsea	d			13 47	14 08				14 47	15 08				15 47	16 08				16 47	17 08	17 15	
Chichester [4]	d		13 25			14 05		14 25			15 05		15 25			16 05		16 25				17 05
Havant	d		13 37			14 19		14 37			15 19		15 37			16 19		16 37				17 19
Cosham	d	13 39	13 46	13 52	14 13	14 26	14 39	14 46	14 52	15 13	15 26	15 39	15 46	15 52	16 13	16 26	16 39	16 46	16 52	17 13	17 20	17 27
Portchester	d			13 57	14 18	14 30			14 57	15 18	15 30			15 57	16 18	16 30			16 57	17 18	17 25	17 31
Fareham	a	13 46	13 53	14 02	14 23	14 35	14 46	14 53	15 02	15 23	15 35	15 46	15 53	16 02	16 23	16 35	16 46	16 53	17 02	17 23	17 30	17 36
	d	13 47	13 54	14 03	14 24	14 36	14 47	14 54	15 03	15 24	15 36	15 47	15 54	16 03	16 24	16 36	16 47	16 56	17 03	17 24		17 37
Swanwick	d		14 00	14 09		14 42		15 00	15 09		15 42		16 00	16 09		16 42			17 09			17 43
Bursledon	d			14 13					15 13					16 13					17 13			
Hamble	d			14 16					15 16					16 16					17 16			
Netley	d			14 18					15 18					16 18					17 18			17 49
Sholing	d			14 22					15 22					16 22					17 22			
Woolston	d			14 24					15 24					16 24					17 24			17 53
Bitterne	d			14 28					15 28					16 28					17 28			
St Denys	d			14 31					15 31					16 31					17 31			17 58
Southampton Central	a	14 08	14 19	14 39		14 59	15 08	15 19	15 38		15 59	16 08	16 19	16 38		17 01	17 08	17 28	17 38			18 03

Portsmouth and Fareham - Southampton

Mondays to Fridays

		GW	SN	SW	GW	SW	SN	GW	SN	SW	SW	SN	SN	GW	SW	SW	SN	GW	SN	SW	SW	SN	GW
		◇ ⊼	1	1	◇	1	◇ 1	◇ ⊼	1	1	1	◇ 1	1	◇	1	1	◇ 1	◇	1	1	1	◇ 1	
Portsmouth Harbour	d	17 23		17 33		17 55		18 23			18 55			19 23		19 55		20 23			20 55		21 23
Portsmouth & Southsea	d	17 27		17 38		18 00		18 27		18 38	19 00			19 27	19 38	20 00		20 27		20 38	21 00		21 27
Fratton	d	17 31		17 43		18 04		18 31		18 43	19 04			19 31	19 43	20 04		20 31		20 43	21 04		21 31
Hilsea	d			17 47		18 08				18 47	19 08				19 47	20 08				20 47	21 08		
Chichester [4]	d		17 25		17 47		18 05		18 25			19 02	19 20				20 01		20 26			21 05	
Havant	d		17 37		17 58		18 23		18 37			19 20	19 37				20 22		20 37			21 26	
Cosham	d	17 39	17 46	17 52	18 05	18 13	18 29	18 39	18 44	18 52	19 13	19 29	19 46	19 39	19 52	20 13	20 29		20 44	20 52	21 13	21 33	
Portchester	d			17 57		18 18	18 33			18 57	19 18	19 33			19 57	20 18			20 48	20 57	21 18	21 37	
Fareham	a	17 46	17 53	18 02	18 12	18 23	18 38	18 46	18 52	19 02	19 23	19 38	19 54	19 46	20 02	20 23	20 36	20 46	20 53	21 02	21 23	21 42	21 47
	d	17 47	17 54	18 03	18 13	18 24	18 39	18 47	18 53	19 03	19 24	19 39	19 55	19 47	20 03	20 24	20 37	20 47	20 54	21 03	21 24	21 42	21 47
Swanwick	d		18 00	18 09			18 45		18 59	19 09		19 45	20 01		20 09		20 43		21 00	21 09		21 48	
Bursledon	d			18 13						19 13					20 13					21 13			
Hamble	d			18 16						19 16					20 16					21 16			
Netley	d			18 18						19 18					20 18					21 18			
Sholing	d			18 22						19 22					20 22					21 22			
Woolston	d			18 24						19 24					20 24					21 24		21 57	
Bitterne	d			18 28						19 28					20 28					21 28			
St Denys	d			18 31						19 31					20 31					21 31		22 01	
Southampton Central	a	18 08	18 20	18 38	18 41		19 04	19 08	19 20	19 38		20 03	20 18	20 08	20 38		21 01	21 08	21 19	21 38		22 06	22 20

		SN	SW	SW	SW	SN	SW	SW	SW
		1	1	1	1	◇ 1	1	1	1
Portsmouth Harbour	d			21 55					23 24
Portsmouth & Southsea	d		21 38	22 00			22 38		23 29
Fratton	d		21 43	22 04			22 43		23 33
Hilsea	d		21 47	22 08			22 47		23 37
Chichester [4]	d	21 26				22 05			
Havant	d	21 37			21 58	22 26		22 59	
Cosham	d	21 44	21 52	22 13	22 05	22 34	22 52	23 08	23 42
Portchester	d		21 57	22 18			22 57	23 13	23 47
Fareham	a	21 51	22 02	22 23	22 12	22 42	23 02	23 18	23 52
	d	21 52	22 03	22 24		22 43	23 03		23 53
Swanwick	d	21 58	22 09			22 49	23 09		
Bursledon	d		22 13				23 13		
Hamble	d		22 16				23 16		
Netley	d		22 18				23 18		
Sholing	d		22 22				23 22		
Woolston	d		22 24				23 24		
Bitterne	d		22 28				23 28		
St Denys	d		22 31				23 31		
Southampton Central	a	22 16	22 39			23 07	23 39		

Saturdays

		SN	SW	SW	SN	SW	GW	SN	SN	SW	SW	GW	SN	SN	SW	SW	SN	GW	SN	SW	SW	SN	GW
		1	1	1	1	1	◇	1	1	1	1	◇ ⊼	1	1	1	1	1	◇ ⊼	1	1	1	◇ 1	◇ ⊼
Portsmouth Harbour	d					05 50	06 00				06 55	07 05				07 55		08 23			08 55		09 23
Portsmouth & Southsea	d			05 16		05 55	06 04			06 38	07 00	07 09			07 38	08 00		08 27		08 38	09 00		09 27
Fratton	d			05 20		05 59	06 08			06 43	07 04	07 14			07 43	08 04		08 31		08 43	09 04		09 31
Hilsea	d			05 24		06 03				06 47	07 08				07 47	08 08				08 47	09 08		
Chichester [4]	d	05 05			05 28			06 06	06 23				07 07	07 25			08 05		08 25			09 05	
Havant	d	05 16			05 39			06 24	06 37				07 23	07 37			08 20		08 37			09 19	
Cosham	d	05 23	05 09	05 31	05 49	06 08	06 19	06 30	06 46	06 52	07 13	07 21	07 30	07 46	07 52	08 13	08 28	08 39	08 46	08 52	09 13	09 26	09 39
Portchester	d	05 27	05 14	05 35		06 13		06 34		06 57	07 18		07 34		07 57	08 18	08 32			08 57	09 18	09 30	
Fareham	a	05 32	05 19	05 40	05 57	06 18	06 27	06 39	06 53	07 02	07 23	07 29	07 39	07 53	08 02	08 23	08 37	08 46	08 53	09 02	09 23	09 35	09 46
	d	05 33	05 20	05 41	05 58	06 19	06 28	06 40	06 54	07 03	07 24	07 30	07 39	07 54	08 03	08 24	08 38	08 47	08 54	09 03	09 24	09 36	09 47
Swanwick	d	05 39		05 48	06 04			06 46	07 00	07 09			07 45	08 00	08 09		08 44		09 00	09 09		09 42	
Bursledon	d			05 51						07 13					08 13					09 13			
Hamble	d			05 55						07 16					08 16					09 16			
Netley	d	05 45		05 57						07 18					08 18					09 18			
Sholing	d			06 01						07 22					08 22					09 22			
Woolston	d	05 49		06 03						07 24					08 24					09 24			
Bitterne	d			06 06						07 28					08 28					09 28			
St Denys	d			06 09						07 31					08 31					09 31			
Southampton Central	a	05 58		06 14	06 24		06 49	07 05	07 18	07 38		07 51	08 03	08 17	08 38		09 01	09 08	09 19	09 38		09 59	10 08

		SN	SW	GW	SW	SN	GW	SN	SW	SW	SN	GW	SN	SW	SW	SN	GW	SN	SW	SW	SN	GW	SN
		1	1	◇	1	◇ 1	◇ ⊼	1	1	1	◇ 1	◇ ⊼	1	1	1	◇ 1	◇	1	1	1	◇ 1	◇	1
Portsmouth Harbour	d				09 55		10 23			10 55		11 23			11 55		12 23			12 55		13 23	
Portsmouth & Southsea	d		09 38		10 00		10 27		10 38	11 00		11 27		11 38	12 00		12 27		12 38	13 00		13 27	
Fratton	d		09 43		10 04		10 31		10 43	11 04		11 31		11 43	12 04		12 31		12 43	13 04		13 31	
Hilsea	d		09 47		10 08				10 47	11 08				11 47	12 08				12 47	13 08			
Chichester [4]	d	09 25		09 49		10 05		10 25			11 05		11 25			12 05		12 25			13 05		13 25
Havant	d	09 37		10 00		10 19		10 37			11 19		11 37			12 19		12 37			13 19		13 37
Cosham	d	09 46	09 52	10 06	10 13	10 26	10 39	10 46	10 52	11 13	11 26	11 39	11 46	11 52	12 13	12 26	12 39	12 46	12 52	13 13	13 26	13 39	13 46
Portchester	d		09 57		10 18	10 30			10 57	11 18	11 30			11 57	12 18	12 30			12 57	13 18	13 30		
Fareham	a	09 53	10 02	10 15	10 23	10 35	10 46	10 53	11 02	11 23	11 35	11 46	11 53	12 02	12 23	12 35	12 46	12 53	13 02	13 23	13 35	13 46	13 53
	d	09 54	10 03	10 16	10 24	10 36	10 47	10 54	11 03	11 24	11 36	11 47	11 54	12 03	12 24	12 36	12 47	12 54	13 03	13 24	13 36	13 47	13 54
Swanwick	d	10 00	10 09			10 42		11 00	11 09		11 42		12 00	12 09		12 42		13 00	13 09		13 42		14 00
Bursledon	d		10 13						11 13					12 13					13 13				
Hamble	d		10 16						11 16					12 16					13 16				
Netley	d		10 18						11 18					12 18					13 18				
Sholing	d		10 22						11 22					12 22					13 22				
Woolston	d		10 24						11 24					12 24					13 24				
Bitterne	d		10 28						11 28					12 28					13 28				
St Denys	d		10 31						11 31					12 31					13 31				
Southampton Central	a	10 17	10 38	10 40		10 59	11 08	11 19	11 38		11 59	12 08	12 19	12 38		12 59	13 08	13 19	13 38		13 59	14 08	14 19

Table 165

Portsmouth and Fareham - Southampton

Saturdays

		SW	SW	SN	GW	SN	SW	SW	SN	GW	SN	SW	SW	SN	GW	SN	SW	SW	SN	GW	SN	SW
		■	■	◇■	◇	■	■	■	◇■	◇	■	■	■	◇■	▪	■	■	■	◇■	◇	■	■
Portsmouth Harbour	d		13 55		14 23			14 55		15 23			15 55		16 23			16 55		17 23		17 33
Portsmouth & Southsea	d	13 38	14 00		14 27		14 38	15 00		15 27		15 38	16 00		16 27		16 38	17 00		17 27		17 38
Fratton	d	13 43	14 04		14 31		14 43	15 04		15 31		15 43	16 04		16 31		16 43	17 04		17 31		17 43
Hilsea	d	13 47	14 08				14 47	15 08				15 47	16 08				16 47	17 08				17 47
Chichester 4	d			14 05		14 25			15 05		15 25			16 05		16 25			17 05		17 25	
Havant	d			14 19		14 37			15 19		15 37			16 19		16 37			17 19		17 37	
Cosham	d	13 52	14 13	14 26	14 39	14 46	14 52	15 13	15 26	15 39	15 46	15 52	16 13	16 26	16 39	16 46	16 52	17 13	17 26	17 39	17 46	17 52
Portchester	d	13 57	14 18	14 30			14 57	15 18	15 30			15 57	16 18	16 30			16 57	17 18	17 30			17 57
Fareham	a	14 02	14 23	14 35	14 46	14 53	15 02	15 23	15 35	15 46	15 53	16 02	16 23	16 35	16 46	16 53	17 02	17 23	17 35	17 46	17 53	18 02
	d	14 03	14 24	14 36	14 47	14 54	15 03	15 24	15 36	15 47	15 54	16 03	16 24	16 36	16 47	16 54	17 03	17 24	17 36	17 47	17 54	18 03
Swanwick	d	14 09		14 42		15 00	15 09		15 42		16 00	16 09		16 42		17 00	17 09		17 42		18 00	18 09
Bursledon	d	14 13					15 13					16 13					17 13					18 13
Hamble	d	14 16					15 16					16 16					17 16					18 16
Netley	d	14 18					15 18					16 18					17 18					18 18
Sholing	d	14 22					15 22					16 22					17 22					18 22
Woolston	d	14 24					15 24					16 24					17 24					18 24
Bitterne	d	14 28					15 28					16 28					17 28					18 28
St Denys	d	14 31					15 31					16 31					17 31					18 31
Southampton Central	a	14 39		14 59	15 08	15 19	15 38		15 59	16 08	16 19	16 38		16 59	17 08	17 19	17 38		17 59	18 08	18 19	18 38

		GW	SW	SN	GW	SN	SW	SW	SN	GW	SN	SW	SW	SN	GW	SN	SW	SW	SN	SN	SW	SW	SN
		◇	■	◇■	◇	■	■	■	◇■	◇	■	■	■	◇■	◇	■	■	■	◇■	■	■	■	◇■
Portsmouth Harbour	d		17 55		18 23			18 55		19 23			19 55		20 23			20 55				21 55	
Portsmouth & Southsea	d		18 00		18 27		18 38	19 00		19 27		19 38	20 00		20 27		20 38	21 00			21 38	22 00	
Fratton	d		18 04		18 31		18 43	19 04		19 31		19 43	20 04		20 31		20 43	21 04			21 43	22 04	
Hilsea	d		18 08				18 47	19 08				19 47	20 08				20 47	21 08			21 47	22 08	
Chichester 4	d	17 46		18 05		18 25			19 05		19 25			20 05		20 25			21 05	21 28			22 05
Havant	d	18 00		18 19		18 37			19 19		19 37			20 26		20 37			21 23	21 40			22 26
Cosham	d	18 06	18 13	18 26	18 39	18 46	18 52	19 13	19 26	19 39	19 46	19 52	20 13	20 32		20 46	20 52	21 13	21 29	21 47	21 52	22 13	22 34
Portchester	d		18 18	18 30			18 57	19 18	19 30			19 57	20 18	20 36			20 57	21 18	21 33		21 57	22 18	
Fareham	a	18 14	18 23	18 35	18 46	18 53	19 02	19 23	19 35	19 46	19 53	20 02	20 23	20 41	20 45	20 53	21 02	21 23	21 38	21 54	22 02	22 23	22 41
	d	18 15	18 24	18 36	18 47	18 54	19 03	19 24	19 36	19 47	19 54	20 03	20 24	20 42	20 47	20 54	21 03	21 24	21 39	21 55	22 03	22 24	22 42
Swanwick	d			18 42		19 00	19 09		19 42		20 00	20 09		20 48		21 00	21 09		21 45	22 01	22 09		22 48
Bursledon	d						19 13					20 13					21 13				22 13		
Hamble	d						19 16					20 16					21 16				22 16		
Netley	d						19 18					20 18					21 18				22 18		
Sholing	d						19 22					20 22					21 22				22 22		
Woolston	d						19 24					20 24					21 24				22 24		
Bitterne	d						19 28					20 28					21 28				22 28		
St Denys	d						19 31					20 31					21 31				22 31		
Southampton Central	a	18 43		18 59	19 08	19 19	19 38		19 59	20 09	20 19	20 38		21 05	21 10	21 19	21 38		22 02	22 20	22 39		23 05

		SW	SW
		■	■
Portsmouth Harbour	d		23 24
Portsmouth & Southsea	d	22 38	23 29
Fratton	d	22 43	23 33
Hilsea	d	22 47	23 37
Chichester 4	d		
Havant	d		
Cosham	d	22 52	23 42
Portchester	d	22 57	23 47
Fareham	a	23 02	23 52
	d	23 03	23 53
Swanwick	d	23 09	
Bursledon	d	23 13	
Hamble	d	23 16	
Netley	d	23 18	
Sholing	d	23 22	
Woolston	d	23 24	
Bitterne	d	23 28	
St Denys	d	23 31	
Southampton Central	a	23 36	

Table 165

Portsmouth and Fareham - Southampton

Sundays

		SW	SW	SW	SW	SW	GW	SW	SW	SW	SW	GW	SW	SW	GW	SW	SW	GW	SW	SW	GW	SW	SW
		■	■	■	■	■	▪	■ ☕	■	■ ☕	■	◇	■ ☕	■	◇	■ ☕	■	◇	■	■	◇	■	■
Portsmouth Harbour	d	06 37	07 17		08 17		09 08	09 17		10 17		11 08	11 17			12 17		13 08	13 17		14 08	14 17	
Portsmouth & Southsea	d	06 42	07 22	07 42	08 22	08 42	09 12	09 22	09 42	10 22	10 42	11 12	11 22	11 42		12 22	12 42	13 12	13 22	13 42	14 12	14 22	14 42
Fratton	d	06 46	07 26	07 46	08 26	08 46	09 16	09 26	09 46	10 26	10 46	11 16	11 26	11 46		12 26	12 46	13 16	13 26	13 46	14 16	14 26	14 46
Hilsea	d	06 50	07 30	07 50	08 30	08 50		09 30	09 50	10 30	10 50		11 30	11 50		12 30	12 50		13 30	13 50		14 30	14 50
Chichester 4	d														11 54								
Havant	d														12b10								
Cosham	d	06 55	07 35	07 55	08 35	08 55	09 23	09 35	09 55	10 35	10 55	11 23	11 35	11 55	12c23	12 35	12 55	13 23	13 35	13 55	14 23	14 35	14 55
Portchester	d	07 00	07 40	08 00	08 40	09 00		09 40	10 00	10 40	11 00		11 40	12 00		12 40	13 00		13 40	14 00		14 40	15 00
Fareham	a	07 05	07 45	08 05	08 45	09 05	09 31	09 45	10 05	10 45	11 05	11 31	11 45	12 05	12 31	12 45	13 05	13 31	13 45	14 05	14 31	14 45	15 05
	d	07 06	07 46	08 06	08 46	09 06	09 32	09 46	10 06	10 46	11 06	11 32	11 46	12 06	12 32	12 46	13 06	13 32	13 46	14 06	14 32	14 46	15 06
Swanwick	d	07 12		08 12		09 12			10 12		11 12			12 12			13 12			14 12			15 12
Bursledon	d	07 16		08 16		09 16			10 16		11 16			12 16			13 16			14 16			15 16
Hamble	d	07 19		08 19		09 19			10 19		11 19			12 19			13 19			14 19			15 19
Netley	d	07 21		08 21		09 21			10 21		11 21			12 21			13 21			14 21			15 21
Sholing	d	07 25		08 25		09 25			10 25		11 25			12 25			13 25			14 25			15 25
Woolston	d	07 27		08 27		09 27			10 27		11 27			12 27			13 27			14 27			15 27
Bitterne	d	07 31		08 31		09 31			10 31		11 31			12 31			13 31			14 31			15 31
St Denys	d	07 34		08 34		09 34			10 34		11 34			12 34			13 34			14 34			15 34
Southampton Central	a	07 40		08 40		09 40	09 53		10 40		11 40	11 53		12 40	12 53		13 40	13 53		14 40	14 53		15 40

		GW	SW	SW	GW	SW	GW	SW	GW	SW	SW	GW	SW	GW	SW	GW	SW	SW	GW	SW	SW	SW	SW
		▪	■	■	◇	■	◇	■	◇	■	■	◇	■	◇	■	◇	■	■	◇	■	■	■	■
Portsmouth Harbour	d	15 08	15 17		16 08	16 17			17 08	17 17		18 08	18 17			19 08	19 17		20 08	20 17		21 17	
Portsmouth & Southsea	d	15 12	15 22	15 42	16 12	16 22		16 42	17 12	17 22	17 42	18 12	18 22		18 42	19 12	19 22	19 42	20 12	20 22	20 42	21 22	21 42
Fratton	d	15 16	15 26	15 46	16 16	16 26		16 46	17 16	17 26	17 46	18 16	18 26		18 46	19 16	19 26	19 46	20 16	20 26	20 46	21 26	21 46
Hilsea	d		15 30	15 50		16 30		16 50		17 30	17 50		18 30		18 50		19 30	19 50		20 30	20 50	21 30	21 50
Chichester 4	d						16 34							18 34									
Havant	d						16 48							18 48									
Cosham	d	15 23	15 35	15 55	16 23	16 35	16 55	16 59	17 23	17 35	17 55	18 23	18 35	18 55	18 59	19 23	19 35	19 55		20 35	20 55	21 35	21 55
Portchester	d		15 40	16 00		16 40		17 03		17 40	18 00		18 40		19 03		19 40	20 00		20 40	21 00	21 40	22 00
Fareham	a	15 31	15 45	16 05	16 31	16 45	17 02	17 08	17 31	17 45	18 05	18 31	18 45	19 02	19 08	19 31	19 45	20 05	20 31	20 45	21 05	21 45	22 05
	d	15 32	15 46	16 06	16 32	16 46	17 03	17 09	17 32	17 46	18 06	18 32	18 46	19 03	19 09	19 32	19 46	20 06	20 32	20 46	21 06	21 46	22 06
Swanwick	d			16 12				17 16			18 12				19 16			20 12			21 12		22 12
Bursledon	d			16 16				17 19			18 16				19 19			20 16			21 16		22 16
Hamble	d			16 19				17 23			18 19				19 23			20 19			21 19		22 19
Netley	d			16 21				17 25			18 21				19 25			20 21			21 21		22 21
Sholing	d			16 25				17 29			18 25				19 29			20 25			21 25		22 25
Woolston	d			16 27				17 31			18 27				19 31			20 27			21 27		22 27
Bitterne	d			16 31				17 34			18 31				19 34			20 31			21 31		22 31
St Denys	d			16 34				17 38			18 34				19 38			20 34			21 34		22 34
Southampton Central	a	15 53		16 40	16 53		17 24	17 43	17 53		18 40	18 53		19 25	19 43	19 53		20 40	20 53		21 40		22 40

		GW	SW	SW	SW
			■	■	■
Portsmouth Harbour	d	22 03	22 17		23 17
Portsmouth & Southsea	d	22 12	22 22	22 42	23 22
Fratton	d	22 16	22 26	22 46	23 26
Hilsea	d		22 30	22 50	23 30
Chichester 4	d				
Havant	d				
Cosham	d		22 35	22 55	23 35
Portchester	d		22 40	23 00	23 40
Fareham	a	22 31	22 45	23 05	23 45
	d	22 32	22 46	23 06	23 46
Swanwick	d			23 12	
Bursledon	d			23 16	
Hamble	d			23 19	
Netley	d			23 21	
Sholing	d			23 25	
Woolston	d			23 27	
Bitterne	d			23 31	
St Denys	d			23 34	
Southampton Central	a	22 53		23 40	

b arr. 1204

c arr. 1216

Table 167

Mondays to Fridays

To and from the Isle of Wight via Portsmouth and Ryde

		IL	IL	IL	IL	IL	IL	IL	IL	IL	IL	IL	IL	IL	IL	IL	IL	IL	IL	IL	IL	IL	IL
Portsmouth Harbour	d	05 15	05 40	06 15	06 40	07 15	07 40	08 15	08 40	09 15	0940	10 15	10 40	11 15	11 40	12 15	12 40		13 40	14 15		15 15	15 40
Ryde Pier Head	d	05 50	06 08	06 50	07 08	07 50	08 08	08 50	09 08	09 50	10 08	10 50	11 08	11 50	12 08	12 50	13 08	13 50	14 08	14 50	15 08	15 50	16 08
Ryde Esplanade	d	05 52	06 10	06 52	07 10	07 52	08 10	08 52	09 10	09 52	10 10	10 52	11 10	11 52	12 10	12 52	13 10	13 52	14 10	14 52	15 10	15 52	16 10
Ryde St Johns Road	d	05 55	06 13	06 55	07 13	07 55	08 13	08 55	09 13	09 55	10 13	10 55	11 13	11 55	12 13	12 55	13 13	13 55	14 13	14 55	15 13	15 55	16 13
Smallbrook Junction §	d											10 58		11 58	12 16	12 58	13 16			14 58	15 16	15 58	16 16
Brading	d	06 03	06 21	07 03	07 21	08 03	08 21	09 03	09 21	10 03	10 21	11 03	11 21	12 03	12 21	13 03	13 21	14 03	14 21	15 03	15 21	16 03	16 21
Sandown	d	06 08	06 26	07 08	07 26	08 08	08 26	09 08	09 26	10 08	10 26	11 08	11 26	12 08	12 26	13 08	13 26	14 08	14 26	15 08	15 26	16 08	16 26
Lake	d	06 10	06 28	07 10	07 28	08 10	08 28	09 10	09 28	10 10	10 28	11 10	11 28	12 10	12 28	13 10	13 28	14 10	14 28	15 10	15 28	16 10	16 28
Shanklin	a	06 13	06 31	07 13	07 31	08 13	08 31	09 13	09 31	10 13	10 31	11 13	11 31	12 13	12 31	13 13	13 31	14 13	14 31	15 13	15 31	16 13	16 31

		IL	IL	IL	IL	IL	IL	IL	IL	IL	IL	IL
Portsmouth Harbour	d	16 15	16 40	17 15	17 40	18 15		19 15		20 15	21 15	22 15
Ryde Pier Head	d	16 50	17 08	17 50	18 08	18 50	19 08	19 50	20 08	20 45	21 45	22 45
Ryde Esplanade	d	16 52	17 10	17 52	18 10	18 52	19 10	19 52	20 10	20 47	21 47	22 47
Ryde St Johns Road	d	16 55	17 13	17 55	18 13	18 55	19 13	19 55	20 13	20 55	21 50	22a50
Smallbrook Junction §	d											
Brading	d	17 03	17 21	18 03	18 21	19 03	19 21	20 03	20 21	21 03	21 58	
Sandown	d	17 08	17 26	18 08	18 26	19 08	19 26	20 08	20 26	21 07	22 03	
Lake	d	17 10	17 28	18 10	18 28	19 10	19 28	20 10	20 28	21 10	22 05	
Shanklin	a	17 13	17 31	18 13	18 31	19 13	19 31	20 13	20 31	21 13	22 08	

Saturdays

		IL	IL	IL	IL	IL	IL	IL	IL	IL	IL	IL	IL	IL	IL	IL	IL	IL	IL	IL	IL	IL	IL
Portsmouth Harbour	d	05 15		06 15		07 15		08 15	08 40	09 15	09 40	10 15	10 40	11 15	11 40	12 15	12 40	13 15	13 40	14 15	14 40	15 15	15 40
Ryde Pier Head	d	05 50	06 08	06 50	07 08	07 50	08 08	08 50	09 08	09 50	10 08	10 50	11 08	11 50	12 08	12 50	13 08	13 50	14 08	14 50	15 08	15 50	16 08
Ryde Esplanade	d	05 52	06 10	06 52	07 10	07 52	08 10	08 52	09 10	09 52	10 10	10 52	11 10	11 52	12 10	12 52	13 10	13 52	14 10	14 52	15 10	15 52	16 10
Ryde St Johns Road	d	05 55	06 13	06 55	07 13	07 55	08 13	08 55	09 13	09 55	10 13	10 55	11 13	11 55	12 13	12 55	13 13	13 55	14 13	14 55	15 13	15 55	16 13
Smallbrook Junction §	d											10 58		11 58	12 16	12 58	13 16			14 58	15 16	15 58	16 16
Brading	d	06 03	06 21	07 03	07 21	08 03	08 21	09 03	09 21	10 03	10 21	11 03	11 21	12 03	12 21	13 03	13 21	14 03	14 21	15 03	15 21	16 03	16 21
Sandown	d	06 08	06 26	07 08	07 26	08 08	08 26	09 08	09 26	10 08	10 26	11 08	11 26	12 08	12 26	13 08	13 26	14 08	14 26	15 08	15 26	16 08	16 25
Lake	d	06 10	06 28	07 10	07 28	08 10	08 28	09 10	09 28	10 10	10 28	11 10	11 28	12 10	12 28	13 10	13 28	14 10	14 28	15 10	15 28	16 10	16 28
Shanklin	a	06 13	06 31	07 13	07 31	08 13	08 31	09 13	09 31	10 13	10 31	11 13	11 31	12 13	12 31	13 13	13 31	14 13	14 31	15 13	15 31	16 13	16 31

		IL	IL	IL	IL	IL	IL	IL	IL	IL	IL	IL
Portsmouth Harbour	d	16 15	16 40	17 15	17 40	18 15		19 15		20 15	21 15	22 15
Ryde Pier Head	d	16 50	17 08	17 50	18 08	18 50	19 08	19 50	20 08	20 45	21 45	22 45
Ryde Esplanade	d	16 52	17 10	17 52	18 10	18 52	19 10	19 52	20 10	20 47	21 47	22 47
Ryde St Johns Road	d	16 55	17 13	17 55	18 13	18 55	19 13	19 55	20 13	20 55	21 50	22a50
Smallbrook Junction §	d											
Brading	d	17 03	17 21	18 03	18 21	19 03	19 21	20 03	20 21	21 03	21 58	
Sandown	d	17 08	17 26	18 08	18 26	19 08	19 26	20 08	20 26	21 08	22 03	
Lake	d	17 10	17 28	18 10	18 28	19 10	19 28	20 10	20 28	21 10	22 05	
Shanklin	a	17 13	17 31	18 13	18 31	19 13	19 31	20 13	20 31	21 13	22 08	

Sundays

		IL	IL	IL	IL	IL	IL	IL	IL	IL	IL	IL	IL	IL	IL	IL	IL	IL	IL	IL	IL	IL	IL
Portsmouth Harbour	d	06 15	07 15		08 15		09 15	09 40	10 15	10 40	11 15	11 40	12 15	12 40		13 40		14 40	15 15	15 40	16 15	16 40	17 15
Ryde Pier Head	d	06 50	07 50		08 50	09 08	09 50	10 08	10 50	11 08	11 50	12 08	12 50	13 08	13 50	14 08	14 50	15 08	15 50	16 08	16 50	17 08	17 50
Ryde Esplanade	d	06 52	07 52		08 52	09 10	09 52	10 10	10 52	11 10	11 52	12 10	12 52	13 10	13 52	14 10	14 52	15 10	15 52	16 10	16 52	17 10	17 52
Ryde St Johns Road	d	06 55	07 55	08 13	08 55	09 13	09 55	10 13	10 55	11 13	11 55	12 13	12 55	13 13	13 55	14 13	14 55	15 13	15 55	16 13	16 55	17 13	17 55
Smallbrook Junction §	d								10 58		11 58	12 16	12 58	13 16			14 58	15 16	15 58	16 16			
Brading	d	07 03	08 03	08 21	09 03	09 21	10 03	10 21	11 03	11 21	12 03	12 21	13 03	13 21	14 03	14 21	15 03	15 21	16 03	16 21	17 03	17 21	18 03
Sandown	d	07 08	08 08	08 26	09 08	09 26	10 08	10 25	11 08	11 26	12 08	12 26	13 08	13 26	14 08	14 26	15 08	15 26	16 08	16 26	17 08	17 26	18 07
Lake	d	07 10	08 10	08 28	09 10	09 28	10 10	10 28	11 10	11 28	12 10	12 28	13 10	13 28	14 10	14 28	15 10	15 28	16 10	16 28	17 10	17 28	18 10
Shanklin	a	07 13	08 13	08 31	09 13	09 31	10 13	10 31	11 13	11 31	12 13	12 31	13 13	13 31	14 13	14 31	15 13	15 31	16 13	16 31	17 13	17 31	18 13

		IL	IL	IL	IL	IL	IL	IL	IL
Portsmouth Harbour	d	17 40	18 15	18 40	19 15	19 40	20 15	21 15	22 15
Ryde Pier Head	d	18 08	18 50	19 08	19 50	20 08	20 45	21 45	22 45
Ryde Esplanade	d	18 10	18 52	19 10	19 52	20 10	20 47	21 47	22 47
Ryde St Johns Road	d	18 13	18 55	19 13	19 55	20a13	20 50	21 50	22a50
Smallbrook Junction §	d								
Brading	d	18 21	19 03	19 21	20 03		20 58	21 58	
Sandown	d	18 26	19 08	19 26	20 08		21 03	22 02	
Lake	d	18 28	19 10	19 28	20 10		21 05	22 05	
Shanklin	a	18 31	19 13	19 31	20 13		21 08	22 08	

Mondays to Fridays

		IL	IL	IL	IL	IL	IL	IL	IL	IL	IL	IL	IL	IL	IL	IL	IL	IL	IL	IL	IL	IL	IL
Shanklin	d			06 18	06 40	07 18	07 40	08 18	08 40	09 18	09 40	10 18	10 40	11 18	11 40	12 18	12 40	13 18	13 40	14 18	14 40	15 18	15 40
Lake	d			06 21	06 43	07 21	07 43	08 21	08 43	09 21	09 43	10 21	10 43	11 21	11 43	12 21	12 43	13 21	13 43	14 21	14 43	15 21	15 43
Sandown	d			06 25	06 46	07 25	07 46	08 25	08 46	09 25	09 46	10 25	10 46	11 25	11 46	12 25	12 46	13 25	13 46	14 25	14 46	15 25	15 46
Brading	d			06 28	06 50	07 28	07 50	08 28	08 50	09 28	09 50	10 28	10 50	11 28	11 50	12 28	12 50	13 28	13 50	14 28	14 50	15 28	15 50
Smallbrook Junction §	d												10 55		11 55	12 33	12 55	13 33			14 55	15 33	15 55
Ryde St Johns Road	d	05 35	05 57	06 35	06 57	07 35	07 57	08 35	08 57	09 35	09 57	10 35	10 57	11 35	11 57	12 35	12 57	13 35	13 57	14 35	14 57	15 35	15 57
Ryde Esplanade	d	05 38	06 00	06 38	07 00	07 38	08 00	08 38	09 00	09 38	10 00	10 38	11 00	11 38	12 00	12 38	13 00	13 38	14 00	14 39	15 00	15 38	16 00
Ryde Pier Head	a	05 40	06 02	06 40	07 02	07 40	08 02	08 40	09 02	09 40	10 02	10 40	11 02	11 40	12 02	12 40	13 02	13 40	14 02	14 40	15 02	15 40	16 02
Portsmouth Harbour	a	05 45	06 10	06 45	07 10	07 45	08 10	08 45	09 10	09 45	10 10	10 45	11 10	11 45		12 45	13 10		14 10	14 45		15 45	16 10

§ Smallbrook Jn. is only open for access to the I.O.W Steam Railway. For days of operation please enquire locally.

Table 167

Mondays to Fridays

To and from the Isle of Wight via Portsmouth and Ryde

		IL	IL	IL	IL	IL	IL	IL	IL	IL	IL	IL	IL
Shanklin	d	16 18	16 40	17 18	17 40	18 18	18 40	19 18	19 40	20 18	20 34	21 18	22 18
Lake	d	16 21	16 43	17 21	17 43	18 21	18 43	19 21	19 43	20 21	20 37	21 21	22 21
Sandown	d	16 25	16 46	17 25	17 46	18 25	18 46	19 25	19 46	20 25	20 40	21 24	22 24
Brading	d	16 28	16 50	17 28	17 50	18 28	18 50	19 28	19 50	20 28	20 43	21 28	22 28
Smallbrook Junction ‡	d	16 33											
Ryde St Johns Road	d	16 35	16 57	17 35	17 57	18 35	18 57	19 35	19 57	20 35	20a49	21 35	22 35
Ryde Esplanade	d	16 38	17 00	17 38	18 00	18 38	19 00	19 38	20 00	20 38		21 38	22 38
Ryde Pier Head	a	16 40	17 02	17 40	18 02	18 40	19 02	19 40	20 02	20 40		21 40	22 40
Portsmouth Harbour	a	16 45	17 10	17 45	18 10	18 45	19 15	19 45	20 15	20 45		21 45	22 45

Saturdays

		IL	IL	IL	IL	IL	IL	IL	IL	IL	IL	IL	IL	IL	IL	IL	IL	IL	IL	IL	IL	IL	IL
Shanklin	d			06 18	06 40	07 18	07 40	08 18	08 40	09 18	09 40	10 18	10 40	11 18	11 40	12 18	12 40	13 18	13 40	14 18	14 40	15 18	15 40
Lake	d			06 21	06 43	07 21	07 43	08 21	08 43	09 21	09 43	10 21	10 43	11 21	11 43	12 21	12 43	13 21	13 43	14 21	14 43	15 21	15 43
Sandown	d			06 25	06 46	07 25	07 46	08 25	08 46	09 25	09 46	10 25	10 46	11 25	11 46	12 25	12 46	13 25	13 46	14 25	14 46	15 25	15 46
Brading	d			06 28	06 50	07 28	07 50	08 28	08 50	09 28	09 50	10 28	10 50	11 28	11 50	12 28	12 50	13 28	13 50	14 28	14 50	15 28	15 50
Smallbrook Junction ‡	d												10 55		11 55	12 33	12 55	13 33			14 55	15 33	15 55
Ryde St Johns Road	d	05 35	05 57	06 35	06 57	07 35	07 57	08 35	08 57	09 35	09 57	10 35	10 57	11 35	11 57	12 35	12 57	13 35	13 57	14 35	14 57	15 35	15 57
Ryde Esplanade	d	05 38	06 00	06 38	07 00	07 38	08 00	08 38	09 00	09 38	10 00	10 38	11 00	11 38	12 00	12 38	13 00	13 38	14 00	14 39	15 00	15 38	16 00
Ryde Pier Head	a	05 40	06 02	06 40	07 02	07 40	08 02	08 40	09 02	09 40	10 02	10 40	11 02	11 40	12 02	12 40	13 02	13 40	14 02	14 40	15 02	15 40	16 02
Portsmouth Harbour	a	05 45		06 45		07 45		08 45	09 10	09 45	10 10	10 45	11 10	11 45	12 10	12 45	13 10	13 45	14 10	14 45	15 10	15 45	16 10

		IL	IL	IL	IL	IL	IL	IL	IL	IL	IL	IL	IL
Shanklin	d	16 18	16 40	17 18	17 40	18 18	18 40	19 18	19 40	20 18	20 34	21 18	22 18
Lake	d	16 21	16 43	17 21	17 43	18 21	18 43	19 21	19 43	20 21	20 37	21 21	22 21
Sandown	d	16 25	16 46	17 25	17 46	18 25	18 46	19 25	19 46	20 25	20 40	21 25	22 25
Brading	d	16 28	16 50	17 28	17 50	18 28	18 50	19 28	19 50	20 28	20 43	21 28	22 28
Smallbrook Junction ‡	d	16 33											
Ryde St Johns Road	d	16 35	16 57	17 35	17 57	18 35	18 57	19 35	19 57	20 35	20a49	21 35	22 35
Ryde Esplanade	d	16 38	17 00	17 38	18 00	18 38	19 00	19 38	20 00	20 38		21 38	22 38
Ryde Pier Head	a	16 40	17 02	17 40	18 02	18 40	19 02	19 40	20 02	20 40		21 40	22 40
Portsmouth Harbour	a	16 45	17 10	17 45	18 10	18 45	19 15	19 45		20 45		21 45	22 45

Sundays

		IL	IL	IL	IL	IL	IL	IL	IL	IL	IL	IL	IL	IL	IL	IL	IL	IL	IL	IL	IL	IL
Shanklin	d		07 18	08 18	08 40	09 18	09 40	10 18	10 40	11 18	11 40	12 18	12 40	13 18	13 40	14 18	14 40	15 18	15 40	16 18	16 40	17 18
Lake	d		07 21	08 21	08 43	09 21	09 43	10 21	10 43	11 21	11 43	12 21	12 43	13 21	13 43	14 21	14 43	15 21	15 43	16 21	16 43	17 21
Sandown	d		07 25	08 25	08 46	09 25	09 46	10 25	10 46	11 25	11 46	12 25	12 46	13 25	13 46	14 25	14 46	15 25	15 46	16 25	16 46	17 25
Brading	d		07 28	08 28	08 50	09 28	09 50	10 28	10 50	11 28	11 50	12 28	12 50	13 28	13 50	14 28	14 50	15 28	15 50	16 28	16 50	17 28
Smallbrook Junction ‡	d								10 55		11 55	12 33	12 55	13 33			14 55	15 33	15 55	16 33		
Ryde St Johns Road	d	06 35	07 35	08 35	08 57	09 35	09 57	10 35	10 57	11 35	11 57	12 35	12 57	13 35	13 57	14 35	14 57	15 35	15 57	16 35	16 57	17 35
Ryde Esplanade	d	06 38	07 38	08 38	09 00	09 38	10 00	10 38	11 00	11 38	12 00	12 38	13 00	13 38	14 00	14 39	15 00	15 38	16 00	16 38	17 00	17 38
Ryde Pier Head	a	06 40	07 40	08 40	09 02	09 40	10 02	10 40	11 02	11 40	12 02	12 40	13 02	13 40	14 02	14 40	15 02	15 40	16 02	16 40	17 02	17 40
Portsmouth Harbour	a	06 45	07 45	08 45		09 45	10 10	10 45	11 10	11 45	12 10	12 45	13 10		14 10		15 10	15 45	16 10	16 45	17 10	17 45

		IL	IL	IL	IL	IL	IL	IL	IL
Shanklin	d	17 40	18 18	18 40	19 18	19 40	20 18	21 18	22 18
Lake	d	17 43	18 21	18 43	19 21	19 43	20 21	21 21	22 21
Sandown	d	17 46	18 25	18 46	19 25	19 46	20 25	21 25	22 25
Brading	d	17 50	18 28	18 50	19 28	19 50	20 28	21 28	22 28
Smallbrook Junction ‡	d								
Ryde St Johns Road	d	17 57	18 35	18 57	19 35	19 57	20 35	21 35	22 35
Ryde Esplanade	d	18 00	18 38	19 00	19 38	20 00	20 38	21 38	22 38
Ryde Pier Head	a	18 02	18 40	19 02	19 40	20 02	20 40	21 40	22 40
Portsmouth Harbour	a	18 10	18 45	19 10	19 45	20 10	20 45	21 45	22 45

‡ Smallbrook Jn. is only open for access to the I.O.W Steam Railway. For days of operation please enquire locally.

London - East Croydon and Purley

COMPLETE SERVICE

	SN MO	SN MX 1	SN MX	SN MX 1	SN MO	SN MO	SN MX 1	SN MO	SN MO 1	SN MX ◇1	FC	SN 1	SN MX	SN	FC	SN MX	SN	SN ◇1	FC 1	FC 1	SN 1	FC 1
London Victoria 15 ⊖ d				23p47	23p47		23p49	23p49		00 05		00 14		00 17			00 42	01 00			02 00	
Clapham Junction 10 d		23b40		23p53	23p53		23p56	23p56	00 02	00 11		00 20		00 23			00 50	01 08			02 08	
St Pancras International 15 ⊖ d																						
Farringdon 3 ⊖ d																						
City Thameslink 3 d																						
London Blackfriars 3 ⊖ d																						
London Bridge 4 ⊖ d	23p25		23p36			23p39					00 12		00 06		00 42	00 36			01 05	01 35		02 05
Norwood Junction 2 a			23p59			00 02							00 29			00 59						
East Croydon ⇌ a	00 01	00 01	00 03	00 05	00 06	00 08	00 09	00 16	00 22	00 24	00 26	00 31	00 33	00 43	00 56	01 03	01 10	01 21	01 32	02 02	02 21	02 30
South Croydon 4 a			00 06			00 11							00 37									
Purley Oaks a			00 09			00 14							00 40									
Purley 4 a			00 12	00 11		00 17						00 37	00 43					01 27			02 27	

	SN 1	FC	FC 1	SN ◇1	FC 1	FC 1	SN ◇1	FC 1	SN ◇1	FC 1	SN 1	FC 1	SN 1	SN ◇1	SN 1	SN	FC 1	SN ◇1	SN 1	SN	SN ◇1	FC 1
London Victoria 15 ⊖ d	03 00			04 00			05 02		05 32		05 23		05 53	06 02				06 21	06 24	06 15	06 32	
Clapham Junction 10 d	03 08			04 08			05 08		05 38		05 33		05 59	06 08				06 27	06 30	06 23	06 38	
St Pancras International 15 ⊖ d								04 54		05 12		05 32					06 02					06 22
Farringdon 3 ⊖ d								04 59		05 17		05 37					06 07					06 27
City Thameslink 3 d										05 21		05 41					06 11					06 31
London Blackfriars 3 ⊖ d								05 04		05 24		05 44					06 14					06 34
London Bridge 4 ⊖ d		03 05	03 35		04 05	04 35				05 30		05 50			06 08	06 06	06 20					06 42
Norwood Junction 2 a											05 49					06 29						
East Croydon ⇌ a	03 21	03 30	04 00	04 21	04 30	05 00	05 20	05 30	05 48	05 51	05 53	06 04	06 09	06 17	06 22	06 33	06 35	06 38	06 40	06 45	06 48	06 55
South Croydon 4 a											05 56					06 36						
Purley Oaks a																06 39						
Purley 4 a	03 27			04 27			05 25		05 54					06 23		06 42		06 44		06 56	06 54	

	SN ◇1	SN	SN 1	SN 1	SN	FC 1	SN 1	SN 1	SN	SN 1	FC 1	SN ◇1	SN 1	SN	SN 1	SN 1	SN	SN 1	SN 1	FC 1	SN 1
London Victoria 15 ⊖ d	06 47		06 51	06 54	06 44			07 02		07 10		07 17					07 20		07 36		07 40
Clapham Junction 10 d	06 53		06 57	07 00	06 50			07 08		07 16		07 23					07 28		07 42		07 46
St Pancras International 15 ⊖ d						06 38					06 58									07 20	
Farringdon 3 ⊖ d						06 43					07 03									07 25	
City Thameslink 3 d						06 47					07 07									07 29	
London Blackfriars 3 ⊖ d						06 50					07 09									07 32	
London Bridge 4 ⊖ d		06 36				07 00	07 03		06 54		07 16		07 19	07 06	07 25	07 30		07 33		07 42	
Norwood Junction 2 a		06 59							07 17				07 30	07 29	07 36	07 41					
East Croydon ⇌ a	07 03	07 03	07 06	07 10	07 12	07 14	07 16	07 17	07 21	07 26	07 30	07 33	07 34	07 37	07 40	07 45	07 49	07 48	07 52	07 55	07 56
South Croydon 4 a		07 06							07 24					07 40							
Purley Oaks a		07 09							07 28					07 43							
Purley 4 a		07 12						07 23	07 31					07 46			07 55		07 57		

	SN	SN ◇1	SN	SN 1	SN ◇1	SN 1	SN	SN 1	SN ◇1	SN 1	SN ◇1 ⌶	SN 1	FC 1	SN 1	SN	SN ◇1	SN	FC 1	SN 1	SN ◇1	SN 1	SN
London Victoria 15 ⊖ d		07 47			07 52		07 45		08 02		08 07			08 10		08 17				08 21		
Clapham Junction 10 d		07 53			07 58		07 51		08 08		08 13			08 16		08 23				08 27		
St Pancras International 15 ⊖ d													07 48					07 59				
Farringdon 3 ⊖ d													07 53					08 03				
City Thameslink 3 d													07 57					08 07				
London Blackfriars 3 ⊖ d													08 00					08 10				
London Bridge 4 ⊖ d	07 46		07 36	07 53		07 56		08 00		08 02		08 08			08 14		08 06	08 18	08 23		08 25	08 27
Norwood Junction 2 a			07 59			08 07				08 14					08 26		08 29				08 36	
East Croydon ⇌ a	08 00	08 03	08 03	08 06	08 09	08 10	08 12	08 15	08 18	08 18	08 22	08 22	08 25	08 26	08 30	08 33	08 33	08 36	08 37	08 39	08 40	08 42
South Croydon 4 a			08 06				08 15					08 26					08 36					
Purley Oaks a			08 09				08 18										08 39					
Purley 4 a			08 12				08 21			08 24					08 38		08 42					

b previous night, arr. 2333

London - East Croydon and Purley

COMPLETE SERVICE

	SN	SN ◇1 ⌶	SN 1	SN ◇1 ⌶	FC 1	SN 1	SN	SN ◇1 ⌶	SN 1	SN	SN 1	SN	SN ◇1 ⌶	SN 1	SN ◇1 ⌶	SN 1	FC 1	SN 1	SN ◇1 ⌶	SN	SN
London Victoria 15 ⊖ d	08 15	08 32		08 36				08 47			08 53	08 43	09 02		09 06				09 17		
Clapham Junction 10 d	08 23	08 38		08 43				08 53	08b36		08 59	08 51	09 08		09 12				09 23		
St Pancras International 15 ⊖ d					08 20												08 48				
Farringdon 3 ⊖ d					08 25												08 53				
City Thameslink 3 d					08 29												08 57				
London Blackfriars 3 ⊖ d					08 32												09 00				
London Bridge 4 ⊖ d			08 32			08 45	08 47			08 36				09 03		09 08	09 12	09 15		09 06	09 20
Norwood Junction 2 a			08 44			08 56				08 59				09 14				09 26		09 30	09 32
East Croydon ⇌ a	08 44	08 48	08 48	08 52	08 56	08 59	09 02	09 03	09 04	09 06	09 09	09 12	09 18	09 18	09 22	09 22	09 24	09 30	09 33	09 33	09 36
South Croydon 4 a	08 47									09 09		09 15								09 36	
Purley Oaks a	08 50									09 12		09 18								09 39	
Purley 4 a	08 53		08 55			09 05	09 09			09 15		09 21		09 26				09 35		09 42	09 45

	SN ◇1	FC 1	SN 1	SN	SN ◇1 ⌶	SN 1	SN ◇1	FC 1	SN 1	SN 1	SN ◇1 ⌶	SN	SN	FC 1	SN 1	SN	SN ◇1 ⌶	SN 1	SN ◇1 ⌶	SN 1	FC 1	SN 1
London Victoria 15 ⊖ d	09 21		09 23	09 13	09 32		09 36				09 47				09 53	09 43	10 02		10 06			
Clapham Junction 10 d			09 29	09 21	09 38		09 42		09 34		09 53				09 59	09 51	10 08		10 12			
St Pancras International 15 ⊖ d		09 04						09 24						09 40							09 54	
Farringdon 3 ⊖ d		09 09						09 29						09 44							09 59	
City Thameslink 3 d		09 13						09 32						09 47							10 02	
London Blackfriars 3 ⊖ d		09 16						09 34						09 50							10 05	
London Bridge 4 ⊖ d		09 27				09 32		09 42		09 45		09 36	09 50	09 57				10 03		10 08	10 12	10 15
Norwood Junction 2 a						09 44				09 56		09 59	10 02					10 14				10 26
East Croydon ⇌ a	09 37	09 39	09 39	09 42	09 48	09 48	09 52	09 54	09 57	10 00	10 03	10 03	10 06	10 09	10 09	10 12	10 18	10 18	10 22	10 22	10 24	10 30
South Croydon 4 a				09 45					10 01			10 06				10 15						
Purley Oaks a				09 48								10 09				10 18						
Purley 4 a				09 51		09 56				10 05		10 12	10 15			10 21		10 26				10 35

	SN ◇1 ⌶	SN	SN	SN ◇1	FC 1	SN 1	SN	SN ◇1 ⌶	SN 1	SN ◇1 ⌶	FC 1	SN 1	SN 1	SN ◇1 ⌶	SN	SN	FC 1	SN 1	SN	SN ◇1	SN 1	SN ◇1 ⌶
London Victoria 15 ⊖ d	10 17			10 21		10 23	10 13	10 32		10 36				10 47				10 53	10 43	11 02		11 06
Clapham Junction 10 d	10 23					10 29	10 21	10 38		10 42		10 34		10 53				10 59	10 51	11 08		11 12
St Pancras International 15 ⊖ d					10 10						10 24						10 40					
Farringdon 3 ⊖ d					10 14						10 29						10 44					
City Thameslink 3 d					10 17						10 32						10 47					
London Blackfriars 3 ⊖ d					10 20						10 35						10 50					
London Bridge 4 ⊖ d		10 06	10 20		10 27				10 33		10 42		10 45		10 36	10 50	10 57				11 03	
Norwood Junction 2 a		10 29	10 32						10 44				10 56		10 59	11 02					11 14	
East Croydon ⇌ a	10 33	10 33	10 36	10 37	10 39	10 39	10 42	10 48	10 48	10 52	10 54	10 57	11 00	11 03	11 03	11 06	11 09	11 09	11 12	11 18	11 18	11 22
South Croydon 4 a		10 36					10 45					11 01			11 06				11 15			
Purley Oaks a		10 39					10 48								11 09				11 18			
Purley 4 a		10 42	10 45				10 51		10 56				11 05		11 12	11 15			11 21		11 26	

	SN 1	FC 1	SN 1	SN ◇1	SN	SN	SN ◇1	FC 1	SN 1	SN	SN ◇1	SN 1	SN ◇1 ⌶	FC 1	SN 1	SN 1	SN ◇1	SN	SN	FC 1	SN 1
London Victoria 15 ⊖ d				11 17			11 21		11 23	11 13	11 32		11 36				11 47				11 53
Clapham Junction 10 d				11 23					11 29	11 21	11 38		11 42		11 34		11 53				11 59
St Pancras International 15 ⊖ d		10 54						11 10						11 24						11 40	
Farringdon 3 ⊖ d		10 59						11 14						11 29						11 44	
City Thameslink 3 d		11 02						11 17						11 32						11 47	
London Blackfriars 3 ⊖ d		11 05						11 20						11 35						11 50	
London Bridge 4 ⊖ d	11 08	11 12	11 15		11 06	11 20		11 27				11 33		11 42		11 45		11 36	11 50	11 57	
Norwood Junction 2 a			11 26		11 29	11 32						11 44				11 56		11 59	12 02		
East Croydon ⇌ a	11 23	11 24	11 30	11 33	11 33	11 36	11 37	11 39	11 39	11 42	11 48	11 48	11 52	11 54	11 57	12 00	12 03	12 03	12 06	12 09	12 10
South Croydon 4 a					11 36					11 45					12 01			12 06			
Purley Oaks a					11 39					11 48								12 09			
Purley 4 a			11 35		11 42	11 45				11 51		11 56				12 05		12 12	12 15		

b arr. 0817

London - East Croydon and Purley

COMPLETE SERVICE

	SN	SN	SN	SN	SN	FC	SN	SN	SN	SN	SN	FC	SN	SN	SN	SN	SN	FC	SN	SN	SN	SN
		◇1	1	◇1 ⌶	1	1	1	◇1			◇1	1	1		◇1	1	◇1 ⌶	1	1	1	◇1	
London Victoria 15 ⊖ d	11 43	12 02		12 06				12 17			12 21		12 23	12 13	12 32		12 36				12 47	
Clapham Junction 10 d	11 51	12 08		12 12				12 23					12 29	12 21	12 38		12 42		12 34		12 53	
St Pancras International 15 ⊖ d						11 54						12 10						12 24				
Farringdon 3 ⊖ d						11 59						12 14						12 29				
City Thameslink 3 d						12 02						12 17						12 32				
London Blackfriars 3 ⊖ d						12 05						12 20						12 35				
London Bridge 4 ⊖ d			12 03		12 08	12 12	12 15		12 06	12 20		12 27				12 33		12 42		12 45		12 36
Norwood Junction 2 a			12 14				12 26		12 29	12 32						12 46				12 56		12 59
East Croydon a	12 12	12 18	12 18	12 22	12 22	12 24	12 30	12 33	12 33	12 36	12 37	12 39	12 39	12 42	12 48	12 51	12 52	12 54	12 57	13 00	13 03	13 03
South Croydon 4 a	12 15								12 36					12 45					13 01			13 06
Purley Oaks a	12 18								12 39					12 48								13 09
Purley 4 a	12 21		12 26				12 35		12 42	12 45				12 51		12 56				13 05		13 12

	SN	FC	SN	SN	SN	SN	SN	SN	FC	SN	SN	SN	SN	SN	FC	SN	SN	SN	SN	SN	FC
		1	1		◇1	1	◇1 ⌶	1	1	1	◇1			◇1	1	1		◇1 ⌶	1	◇1 ⌶	1
London Victoria 15 ⊖ d			12 53	12 43	13 02		13 06				13 17			13 21		13 23	13 13	13 32		13 36	
Clapham Junction 10 d			12 59	12 51	13 08		13 12				13 23					13 29	13 21	13 38		13 42	
St Pancras International 15 ⊖ d		12 40							12 54						13 10						13 24
Farringdon 3 ⊖ d		12 44							12 59						13 14						13 29
City Thameslink 3 d		12 47							13 02						13 17						13 32
London Blackfriars 3 ⊖ d		12 50							13 05						13 20						13 35
London Bridge 4 ⊖ d	12 50	12 57				13 03		13 08	13 12	13 15		13 06	13 20		13 27				13 33		13 42
Norwood Junction 2 a	13 02					13 14		13 19		13 26		13 29	13 32						13 44		
East Croydon a	13 06	13 09	13 09	13 12	13 18	13 18	13 22	13 23	13 24	13 30	13 33	13 33	13 36	13 37	13 39	13 39	13 42	13 48	13 48	13 52	13 54
South Croydon 4 a				13 15								13 36					13 45				
Purley Oaks a				13 18								13 39					13 48				
Purley 4 a	13 15			13 21		13 26				13 35		13 42	13 45				13 51		13 56		

	SN	SN	SN	SN	SN	FC	SN	SN	SN	SN	SN	SN	FC	SN	SN	SN	SN	SN	FC	SN	SN	SN
	1	1	◇1			1	1		◇1	1	◇1 ⌶	1	1	1	◇1			◇1	1	1		◇1 ⌶
London Victoria 15 ⊖ d			13 47				13 53	13 43	14 02		14 06				14 17			14 21		14 23	14 13	14 32
Clapham Junction 10 d	13 34		13 53				13 59	13 51	14 08		14 12				14 23					14 29	14 21	14 38
St Pancras International 15 ⊖ d						13 40							13 54						14 10			
Farringdon 3 ⊖ d						13 44							13 59						14 14			
City Thameslink 3 d						13 47							14 02						14 17			
London Blackfriars 3 ⊖ d						13 50							14 05						14 20			
London Bridge 4 ⊖ d		13 45		13 36	13 50	13 57				14 03		14 08	14 12	14 15		14 06	14 20		14 27			
Norwood Junction 2 a		13 56		13 59	14 02					14 14		14 19		14 26		14 29	14 32					
East Croydon a	13 57	14 00	14 03	14 03	14 06	14 09	14 09	14 12	14 18	14 18	14 22	14 23	14 24	14 30	14 33	14 33	14 36	14 37	14 39	14 40	14 43	14 48
South Croydon 4 a	14 01			14 06				14 15								14 36					14 46	
Purley Oaks a				14 09				14 18								14 39					14 49	
Purley 4 a		14 05		14 12	14 15			14 21		14 26				14 35		14 42	14 45				14 52	

	SN	SN	FC	SN	SN	SN	SN	SN	FC	SN	SN	SN	SN	SN	SN	FC	SN	SN	SN	SN	SN	FC
	1	◇1 ⌶	1	1	1	◇1			1	1		◇1	1	◇1 ⌶	1	1	1	◇1			◇1	1
London Victoria 15 ⊖ d		14 36				14 47				14 53	14 43	15 02		15 06				15 17			15 21	
Clapham Junction 10 d		14 42		14 34		14 53				14 59	14 51	15 08		15 12				15 23				
St Pancras International 15 ⊖ d			14 24						14 40							14 54						15 10
Farringdon 3 ⊖ d			14 29						14 44							14 59						15 14
City Thameslink 3 d			14 32						14 47							15 02						15 17
London Blackfriars 3 ⊖ d			14 35						14 50							15 05						15 20
London Bridge 4 ⊖ d	14 33		14 42		14 45		14 36	14 50	14 57				15 03		15 08	15 12	15 15		15 06	15 20		15 27
Norwood Junction 2 a	14 44				14 56		14 59	15 02					15 14		15 19		15 26		15 29	15 32		
East Croydon a	14 48	14 52	14 54	14 57	15 00	15 03	15 03	15 06	15 09	15 09	15 12	15 18	15 18	15 22	15 23	15 24	15 30	15 33	15 33	15 36	15 37	15 39
South Croydon 4 a				15 03			15 06				15 15								15 36			
Purley Oaks a							15 09				15 18								15 39			
Purley 4 a	14 56				15 05		15 12	15 18			15 21		15 26				15 35		15 42	15 45		

	SN	SN	SN	SN	SN	SN	FC	SN	SN	SN	SN	SN	FC	SN	SN	SN	SN	SN	SN	FC	SN
	1		◇1	1	◇1 ⌶	1	1	1	1	◇1			1	1		◇1	1	1 ⌶	1	1	1
London Victoria 15 ⊖ d	15 23	15 13	15 32		15 36					15 47				15 53	15 43	16 02		16 06			
Clapham Junction 10 d	15 29	15 21	15 38		15 42			15 34		15 53				15 59	15 51	16 08		16 12			
St Pancras International 15 ⊖ d							15 24						15 40							15 54	
Farringdon 3 ⊖ d							15 29						15 44							15 59	
City Thameslink 3 d							15 32						15 47							16 02	
London Blackfriars 3 ⊖ d							15 35						15 50							16 05	
London Bridge 4 ⊖ d				15 33		15 38	15 42		15 45		15 36	15 50	15 57				16 03		16 08	16 12	16 15
Norwood Junction 2 a				15 44					15 56		15 59	16 02					16 14		16 19		16 26
East Croydon a	15 40	15 43	15 48	15 48	15 52	15 52	15 54	15 57	16 00	16 03	16 03	16 06	16 09	16 09	16 12	16 18	16 18	16 22	16 23	16 24	16 30
South Croydon 4 a	15 43	15 46						16 01			16 06			16 12	16 15						
Purley Oaks a		15 49									16 09				16 18						
Purley 4 a		15 52		15 56					16 05		16 12	16 15			16 21		16 26				16 35

	SN	SN	SN	SN	FC	SN	SN	SN	SN	SN	SN	SN	FC	SN	SN	SN	SN	SN	SN	SN	SN	SN
	◇1 ⌶		1		1	1		◇1 ⌶	1	1 ⌶	1		1	1	◇1 ⌶		1	1	1		1	◇1 ⌶
London Victoria 15 ⊖ d	16 17		16 19			16 23	16 13	16 32		16 36		16 39			16 47		16 49	16 53		16 43		17 02
Clapham Junction 10 d	16 23		16 26			16 29	16 21	16 38		16 42		16 45		16 34	16 53		16 56	16 59		16 51		17 08
St Pancras International 15 ⊖ d					16 10								16 24									
Farringdon 3 ⊖ d					16 14								16 29									
City Thameslink 3 d					16 17								16 33									
London Blackfriars 3 ⊖ d					16 20								16 36									
London Bridge 4 ⊖ d		16 06		16 20	16 27				16 33		16 38		16 43			16 48			16 57		16 59	
Norwood Junction 2 a		16 29		16 32					16 44							17 01					17 10	
East Croydon a	16 33	16 33	16 36	16 36	16 39	16 39	16 42	16 47	16 48	16 52	16 52	16 55	16 59	16 59	17 03	17 05	17 06	17 09	17 09	17 12	17 14	17 17
South Croydon 4 a		16 36				16 42	16 45					16 58		17 02		17 08		17 12		17 19		
Purley Oaks a		16 39					16 48					17 01				17 11				17 22		
Purley 4 a		16 42		16 45			16 51		16 55			17 04				17 14				17 25	17 20	

	SN	SN	FC	SN	SN	SN	SN	SN	SN	SN	SN	FC	SN	SN	SN	SN	SN	SN	SN	SN	SN
	1 ⌶	1	1		1	◇1		1	1	1	1	1	◇1	◇1 ⌶	1		1	1	1	◇1	
London Victoria 15 ⊖ d	17 06			17 09		17 17			17 21	17 23			17 32	17 36		17 39				17 47	
Clapham Junction 10 d	17 12			17 15		17 23			17 27	17 30			17 38	17 42		17 45		17 33		17 53	
St Pancras International 15 ⊖ d			16 46									17 10									
Farringdon 3 ⊖ d			16 51									17 15									
City Thameslink 3 d			16 55									17 19									
London Blackfriars 3 ⊖ d			17 00									17 22									
London Bridge 4 ⊖ d		17 09			17 15		17 17	17 23			17 29				17 42		17 44		17 47		17 49
Norwood Junction 2 a							17 30				17 40										18 01
East Croydon a	17 22	17 22	17 25	17 27	17 29	17 32	17 34	17 35	17 36	17 40	17 44	17 45	17 48	17 51	17 54	17 55	17 57	17 59	17 59	18 02	18 05
South Croydon 4 a				17 30	17 32		17 37									17 58	18 01				18 08
Purley Oaks a				17 33			17 40									18 01					18 11
Purley 4 a				17 36			17 44				17 50					18 04					18 14

	SN	FC	SN	SN	SN	SN	SN	SN	FC	SN	SN	SN	SN	SN	SN	SN	SN	FC	SN	SN	SN	SN
	1	1	1	1	1	◇1	◇1 ⌶	1	1	1		1	◇1			1	1	1	1	1	◇1	1 ⌶
London Victoria 15 ⊖ d	17 49		17 53			18 02	18 06				18 09		18 17				18 19		18 23		18 32	18 36
Clapham Junction 10 d	17 56		18 00			18 08	18 12				18 15		18 23	18 02			18 26		18 30		18 38	18 42
St Pancras International 15 ⊖ d		17 28							17 40									18 08				
Farringdon 3 ⊖ d		17 33							17 45									18 13				
City Thameslink 3 d		17 37							17 49									18 17				
London Blackfriars 3 ⊖ d		17 40							17 52									18 20				
London Bridge 4 ⊖ d				17 57	17 59			18 08		18 12		18 16			18 18	18 23		18 27		18 30		
Norwood Junction 2 a					18 11										18 30					18 41		
East Croydon a	18 05	18 08	18 10	18 11	18 15	18 17	18 22	18 21	18 24	18 24	18 27	18 30	18 33	18 33	18 35	18 36	18 37	18 41	18 40	18 45	18 48	18 52
South Croydon 4 a											18 30	18 33			18 39							
Purley Oaks a											18 33				18 45							
Purley 4 a					18 20						18 36			18 40	18 48		18 42			18 50		

Table 175

Mondays to Fridays

London - East Croydon and Purley

COMPLETE SERVICE

Station		FC 1	SN	SN 1	SN 1	SN ◇1 🍴		SN	SN 1	FC 1	SN 1	SN	SN ◇1 🍴	SN 1	SN 1 🍴	SN 1		FC 1	SN 1	SN ◇1 🍴	SN	FC 1	SN 1	SN	SN ◇1 🍴
London Victoria 15 ⊖	d		18 39			18 47			18 51		18 53	18 45	19 02		19 06				19 10	19 17			19 23	19 15	19 32
Clapham Junction 10	d		18 45		18 34	18 53			18 57		19 00	18 53	19 08		19 12				19 16	19 23			19 29	19 23	19 38
St Pancras International 15 ⊖	d	18 20								18 34								18 54				19 10			
Farringdon 3 ⊖	d	18 25								18 39								18 59				19 14			
City Thameslink 3	d	18 29								18 43								19 03				19 17			
London Blackfriars 3 ⊖	d	18 32								18 46								19 05				19 20			
London Bridge 4 ⊖	d			18 47				18 49		18 57				19 03		19 08		19 12			19 06	19 27			
Norwood Junction 2	a							19 01						19 14							19 29				
East Croydon 🚊	a	18 55	18 57	19 00	19 02	19 02		19 05	19 07	19 10	19 10	19 13	19 18	19 18	19 22	19 22		19 24	19 27	19 33	19 33	19 39	19 39	19 44	19 48
South Croydon 4	a		19 00	19 03				19 08				19 16									19 36			19 47	
Purley Oaks	a		19 03					19 11				19 19									19 39			19 50	
Purley 4	a		19 06					19 14				19 22		19 24					19 33		19 42			19 53	

Station		SN 1		FC 1	SN 1	SN ◇1 🍴	SN	SN 1	FC 1	SN 1	SN	SN ◇1 🍴		SN 1	SN ◇1	FC 1	SN 1	SN ◇1	SN	SN 1	SN 1	SN		SN ◇1	SN 1
London Victoria 15 ⊖	d	19 36			19 40	19 47				19 53	19 45	20 02			20 06		20 10	20 17		20 23		20 15		20 32	
Clapham Junction 10	d	19 42			19 46	19 53				19 59	19 53	20 08			20 12		20 16	20 23		20 29		20 23		20 38	
St Pancras International 15 ⊖	d			19 24					19 40							19 54									
Farringdon 3 ⊖	d			19 29					19 44							19 59									
City Thameslink 3	d			19 32					19 47							20 02									
London Blackfriars 3 ⊖	d			19 35					19 50							20 05									
London Bridge 4 ⊖	d			19 42			19 36	19 52	19 27					20 04		20 12			20 06		20 28				20 34
Norwood Junction 2	a						19 59	20 03						20 16					20 29						20 45
East Croydon 🚊	a	19 52		19 54	19 57	20 03	20 03	20 06	20 09	20 09	20 14	20 19		20 19	20 22	20 24	20 27	20 33	20 33	20 39	20 40	20 44		20 48	20 49
South Croydon 4	a						20 06				20 17								20 36			20 47			
Purley Oaks	a						20 09				20 21								20 39			20 50			
Purley 4	a				20 03		20 12	20 12			20 24						20 33		20 42			20 53			

Station		SN ◇1	FC 1	SN 1	SN	SN ◇1	SN 1	SN 1		SN	SN 1	SN 1	SN ◇1	FC 1	SN 1	SN ◇1	SN	SN 1		SN 1	SN	SN 1	SN ◇1	FC 1	SN 1
London Victoria 15 ⊖	d	20 36		20 40		20 47	20 53			20 45	21 02		21 06		21 10	21 17		21 23			21 15	21 32	21 36		21 40
Clapham Junction 10	d	20 42		20 46		20 53	20 59			20 53	21 08		21 12		21 16	21 23		21 29			21 23	21 38	21 42		21 46
St Pancras International 15 ⊖	d		20 24											20 54										21 24	
Farringdon 3 ⊖	d		20 29											20 59										21 29	
City Thameslink 3	d		20 32											21 02										21 32	
London Blackfriars 3 ⊖	d		20 35											21 05										21 35	
London Bridge 4 ⊖	d		20 42		20 36			20 58				21 04		21 12			21 06			21 26				21 42	
Norwood Junction 2	a				20 59							21 15					21 29			21 37					
East Croydon 🚊	a	20 52	20 54	20 57	21 03	21 03	21 09	21 10		21 14	21 18	21 19	21 22	21 24	21 27	21 33	21 33	21 39		21 41	21 44	21 48	21 52	21 54	21 57
South Croydon 4	a				21 06					21 17							21 36				21 47				
Purley Oaks	a				21 09					21 20							21 39				21 50				
Purley 4	a			21 03	21 12					21 23					21 33		21 42				21 53				22 03

Station		SN ◇1	SN	SN 1		SN	SN ◇1	SN 1	SN ◇1	FC 1	SN 1	SN ◇1	SN	SN 1		SN	SN	SN 1	SN 1	FC 1	SN 1	SN ◇1	SN	SN 1	
London Victoria 15 ⊖	d	21 47		21 53		21 45	22 02		22 06		22 10	22 17		22 23			22 15	22 32	22 36		22 40	22 47		22 53	
Clapham Junction 10	d	21 53		21 59		21 53	22 08		22 12		22 16	22 23		22 29			22 23	22 38	22 42		22 46	22 53		22 59	
St Pancras International 15 ⊖	d									21 54															
Farringdon 3 ⊖	d									21 59															
City Thameslink 3	d									22 02															
London Blackfriars 3 ⊖	d									22 05															
London Bridge 4 ⊖	d		21 36					22 04		22 12			22 08			22 26				22 42			22 38		
Norwood Junction 2	a		21 59					22 15					22 31			22 38							23 01		
East Croydon 🚊	a	22 03	22 03	22 09		22 14	22 18	22 19	22 22	22 24	22 27	22 33	22 35	22 39		22 42	22 44	22 48	22 52	22 54	22 57	23 03	23 05	23 09	
South Croydon 4	a		22 06			22 17							22 38				22 47						23 08		
Purley Oaks	a		22 09			22 20							22 41				22 50						23 11		
Purley 4	a		22 12			22 23					22 33		22 44				22 53				23 03		23 14		

Table 175

Mondays to Fridays

London - East Croydon and Purley

COMPLETE SERVICE

Station		SN 1	SN	SN ◇1	SN ◇1	FC 1	SN 1	SN ◇1	SN	SN 1		SN	SN ◇1	FC 1	SN 1	SN	SN 1	SN 1
London Victoria 15 ⊖	d		22 45	23 02	23 06		23 10	23 17		23 24		23 15	23 32				23 47	23 49
Clapham Junction 10	d		22 53	23 08	23 12		23 16	23 23		23 30		23 23	23 38		23b40		23 53	23 56
St Pancras International 15 ⊖	d																	
Farringdon 3 ⊖	d																	
City Thameslink 3	d																	
London Blackfriars 3 ⊖	d																	
London Bridge 4 ⊖	d	22 56				23 12			23 06					23 42		23 36		
Norwood Junction 2	a	23 07							23 29							23 59		
East Croydon 🚊	a	23 11	23 14	23 19	23 22	23 24	23 27	23 33	23 33	23 40		23 44	23 51	23 56	00 01	00 03	00 05	00 09
South Croydon 4	a		23 17						23 36			23 47				00 06		
Purley Oaks	a		23 20						23 39			23 50				00 09		
Purley 4	a		23 23				23 33		23 42			23 53				00 12	00 11	

Saturdays

Station		SN 1	SN	SN 1	SN 1	SN ◇1	FC	SN 1	SN	SN		FC	SN	SN	SN ◇1	FC 1	FC 1	SN 1	FC 1	SN 1		FC 1	FC 1	SN ◇1	FC 1
London Victoria 15 ⊖	d			23p47	23p49	00 05		00 14		00 17				00 42	01 00			02 00		03 00				04 00	
Clapham Junction 10	d	23c40		23p53	23p56	00 11		00 20		00 23				00 50	01 08			02 08		03 08				04 08	
St Pancras International 15 ⊖	d																								
Farringdon 3 ⊖	d																								
City Thameslink 3	d																								
London Blackfriars 3 ⊖	d																								
London Bridge 4 ⊖	d		23p36				00 12		00 06			00 42	00 36			01 05	01 35		02 05			03 05	03 35		04 05
Norwood Junction 2	a		23p59						00 29				00 59												
East Croydon 🚊	a	00 01	00 03	00 05	00 09	00 24	00 26	00 31	00 33	00 43		00 56	01 03	01 10	01 21	01 32	02 02	02 21	02 30	03 21		03 30	04 00	04 21	04 30
South Croydon 4	a		00 06						00 36																
Purley Oaks	a		00 09						00 39																
Purley 4	a		00 12	00 11				00 37	00 42						01 27			02 27		03 27				04 27	

Station		FC 1	SN ◇1	FC 1	SN ◇1	SN 1		FC 1	SN 1	SN 1	SN 1	FC 1	SN 1	FC 1	SN 1	SN		SN	SN 1	FC 1	SN	SN 1	SN ◇1	SN 1	FC 1
London Victoria 15 ⊖	d		05 02		05 32	05 25			06 02		06 23		06 32						06 53		06 43		07 06		
Clapham Junction 10	d		05 08		05 38	05 31			06 08		06 29		06 38		06 34				06 59		06 51		07 12		
St Pancras International 15 ⊖	d																								
Farringdon 3 ⊖	d																								
City Thameslink 3	d																								
London Blackfriars 3 ⊖	d																								
London Bridge 4 ⊖	d	04 35		05 05				05 52		06 08		06 27		06 42		06 36		06 50		06 57		07 03		07 08	07 12
Norwood Junction 2	a					05 47										06 59		07 02				07 14			
East Croydon 🚊	a	05 00	05 21	05 32	05 48	05 51		06 04	06 18	06 22	06 39	06 39	06 48	06 54	06 57	07 03		07 06	07 09	07 09	07 12	07 18	07 22	07 22	07 24
South Croydon 4	a					05 54									07 01	07 06					07 15				
Purley Oaks	a															07 09					07 18				
Purley 4	a		05 26		05 53				06 23				06 53			07 12		07 15			07 21	07 26			

Station		SN		SN	SN ◇1	SN 1	FC 1	SN	SN ◇1	SN 1	SN ◇1	FC 1		SN 1	SN 1	SN ◇1	SN	SN	SN 1	FC 1	SN	SN ◇1		SN 1	SN ◇1
London Victoria 15 ⊖	d				07 21	07 23		07 13	07 32		07 36					07 47			07 53		07 43	08 02			08 06
Clapham Junction 10	d					07 29		07 21	07 38		07 42			07 34		07 53			07 59		07 51	08 08			08 12
St Pancras International 15 ⊖	d																								
Farringdon 3 ⊖	d																								
City Thameslink 3	d																								
London Blackfriars 3 ⊖	d																								
London Bridge 4 ⊖	d	07 06		07 20			07 27			07 33		07 42			07 45		07 36	07 50		07 57				08 03	
Norwood Junction 2	a	07 29		07 32						07 44					07 56		07 59	08 02						08 14	
East Croydon 🚊	a	07 33		07 36	07 37	07 39	07 39	07 42	07 48	07 48	07 52	07 54		07 57	08 00	08 03	08 03	08 06	08 09	08 09	08 12	08 18		08 18	08 22
South Croydon 4	a	07 36						07 45						08 01			08 06				08 15				
Purley Oaks	a	07 39						07 48									08 09				08 18				
Purley 4	a	07 42		07 45				07 51		07 56					08 05		08 12	08 15			08 21			08 26	

b arr. 2333

c previous night, arr. 2333

Table 175

London - East Croydon and Purley

COMPLETE SERVICE

	SN	FC	SN	SN	SN	SN	SN		SN	FC	SN	SN	SN	SN	FC	SN	SN		SN	SN	SN	SN	FC	SN
	1	1	1	◇1			◇1		1	1		◇1	1	◇1	1	1	1		◇1			1	1	
London Victoria 15 ⊖ d				08 17			08 21		08 23		08 13	08 32		08 36					08 47			08 53		08 43
Clapham Junction 10 d				08 23					08 29		08 21	08 38		08 42		08 34			08 53			08 59		08 51
St Pancras International 15 ⊖ d																								
Farringdon 3 ⊖ d																								
City Thameslink 3 d																								
London Blackfriars 3 ⊖ d																								
London Bridge 4 ⊖ d	08 08	08 12	08 15		08 06	08 20				08 27			08 33		08 42		08 45			08 36	08 50		08 57	
Norwood Junction 2 a			08 26		08 29	08 32							08 44				08 56			08 59	09 02			
East Croydon ⇌ a	08 22	08 24	08 30	08 33	08 33	08 36	08 37		08 39	08 39	08 42	08 48	08 48	08 52	08 54	08 57	09 00		09 03	09 03	09 06	09 09	09 09	09 12
South Croydon 4 a					08 36						08 45					09 01				09 06				09 15
Purley Oaks a					08 39						08 48									09 09				09 18
Purley 4 a			08 35		08 42	08 45					08 51		08 56				09 05			09 12	09 15			09 21

	SN	SN	SN		SN	FC	SN	SN	SN	SN	SN	SN	FC		SN	SN	SN	SN	FC	SN	SN	SN	SN	
	◇1	1	◇1 ⌶		1	1	1	◇1			◇1	1	1			◇1	1	◇1 ⌶	1	1	1	◇1		
London Victoria 15 ⊖ d	09 02		09 06					09 17			09 21	09 23			09 13	09 32		09 36				09 47		
Clapham Junction 10 d	09 08		09 12					09 23				09 29			09 21	09 38		09 42		09 34		09 53		
St Pancras International 15 ⊖ d																								
Farringdon 3 ⊖ d																								
City Thameslink 3 d																								
London Blackfriars 3 ⊖ d																								
London Bridge 4 ⊖ d		09 03			09 08	09 12	09 15		09 06	09 20			09 27				09 33		09 42		09 45		09 36	
Norwood Junction 2 a		09 14					09 26		09 29	09 32							09 44				09 56		09 59	
East Croydon ⇌ a	09 18	09 18	09 22		09 22	09 24	09 30	09 33	09 33	09 36	09 37	09 39	09 39		09 42	09 48	09 48	09 52	09 54	09 57	10 00	10 03	10 03	
South Croydon 4 a									09 36						09 45					10 01			10 06	
Purley Oaks a									09 39						09 48								10 09	
Purley 4 a		09 26					09 35		09 42	09 45					09 51		09 56				10 05		10 12	

	SN	SN	FC	SN	SN	SN	SN	SN	FC		SN	SN	SN	SN	SN	SN	FC	SN	SN		SN	SN	FC	SN
		1	1		◇1 ⌶	1	◇1 ⌶	1	1		1	◇1			◇1	1	1		◇1		1	◇1 ⌶	1	1
London Victoria 15 ⊖ d		09 53		09 43	10 02		10 06					10 17			10 21	10 23		10 13	10 32			10 36		
Clapham Junction 10 d		09 59		09 51	10 08		10 12					10 23				10 29		10 21	10 38			10 42		10 34
St Pancras International 15 ⊖ d																								
Farringdon 3 ⊖ d																								
City Thameslink 3 d																								
London Blackfriars 3 ⊖ d																								
London Bridge 4 ⊖ d	09 50		09 57			10 03		10 08	10 12		10 15		10 06	10 20			10 27				10 33		10 42	
Norwood Junction 2 a	10 02					10 14					10 26		10 29	10 32							10 44			
East Croydon ⇌ a	10 06	10 09	10 09	10 12	10 18	10 18	10 22	10 22	10 24		10 30	10 33	10 33	10 36	10 37	10 39	10 39	10 42	10 48		10 48	10 52	10 54	10 57
South Croydon 4 a				10 15									10 36					10 45						11 01
Purley Oaks a				10 18									10 39					10 48						
Purley 4 a	10 15			10 21		10 26					10 35		10 42	10 45				10 51			10 56			

	SN	SN	SN	SN	SN		FC	SN	SN	SN	SN	SN	FC	SN	SN		SN	SN	SN	SN	FC	SN	SN	SN
	1	◇1			1		1		◇1 ⌶	1	◇1 ⌶	1	1	1	◇1				◇1	1	1		◇1	1
London Victoria 15 ⊖ d		10 47			10 53			10 43	11 02		11 06				11 17				11 21	11 23		11 13	11 32	
Clapham Junction 10 d		10 53			10 59			10 51	11 08		11 12				11 23					11 29		11 21	11 38	
St Pancras International 15 ⊖ d																								
Farringdon 3 ⊖ d																								
City Thameslink 3 d																								
London Blackfriars 3 ⊖ d																								
London Bridge 4 ⊖ d	10 45		10 36	10 50			10 57			11 03		11 08	11 12	11 15			11 06	11 20			11 27			11 33
Norwood Junction 2 a	10 56		10 59	11 02						11 14				11 26			11 29	11 32						11 44
East Croydon ⇌ a	11 00	11 03	11 03	11 06	11 09		11 09	11 12	11 18	11 18	11 22	11 22	11 24	11 30	11 33		11 33	11 36	11 37	11 39	11 39	11 42	11 48	11 48
South Croydon 4 a			11 06					11 15									11 36					11 45		
Purley Oaks a			11 09					11 18									11 39					11 48		
Purley 4 a	11 05		11 12	11 15				11 21		11 26				11 35			11 42	11 45				11 51		11 56

Table 175

Saturdays

London - East Croydon and Purley

COMPLETE SERVICE

	SN		FC	SN	SN	SN	SN	SN	SN	FC	SN		SN	SN	SN	SN	FC	SN	SN	SN	SN		SN	SN
	◇1 ⌶		1	1	1	◇1			1	1			◇1 ⌶	1	◇1 ⌶	1	1	1	◇1				◇1	1
London Victoria 15 ⊖ d	11 36					11 47			11 53		11 43		12 02		12 06				12 17				12 21	12 23
Clapham Junction 10 d	11 42			11 34		11 53			11 59		11 51		12 08		12 12				12 23					12 29
St Pancras International 15 ⊖ d																								
Farringdon 3 ⊖ d																								
City Thameslink 3 d																								
London Blackfriars 3 ⊖ d																								
London Bridge 4 ⊖ d			11 42		11 45		11 36	11 50		11 57				12 03		12 08	12 12	12 15		12 06	12 20			
Norwood Junction 2 a					11 56		11 59	12 02						12 14				12 26		12 29	12 32			
East Croydon ⇌ a	11 52		11 54	11 57	12 00	12 03	12 03	12 06	12 09	12 09	12 12		12 18	12 18	12 22	12 22	12 24	12 30	12 33	12 33	12 36		12 37	12 39
South Croydon 4 a				12 01			12 06				12 15									12 36				
Purley Oaks a							12 09				12 18									12 39				
Purley 4 a					12 05		12 12	12 15			12 21			12 26				12 35		12 42	12 45			

	FC	SN	SN	SN	SN	FC	SN		SN	SN	SN	SN	SN	FC	SN	SN	SN		SN	SN	FC	SN	SN	SN
	1		◇1	1	◇1 ⌶	1	1		1	◇1			1	1		◇1 ⌶	1		◇1 ⌶	1	1	1	◇1	
London Victoria 15 ⊖ d		12 13	12 32		12 36					12 47			12 53		12 43	13 02			13 06				13 17	
Clapham Junction 10 d		12 21	12 38		12 42		12 34			12 53			12 59		12 51	13 08			13 12				13 23	
St Pancras International 15 ⊖ d																								
Farringdon 3 ⊖ d																								
City Thameslink 3 d																								
London Blackfriars 3 ⊖ d																								
London Bridge 4 ⊖ d	12 27			12 33		12 42			12 45		12 36	12 50		12 57			13 03			13 08	13 12	13 15		13 06
Norwood Junction 2 a				12 44					12 56		12 59	13 02					13 14					13 26		13 29
East Croydon ⇌ a	12 39	12 42	12 48	12 48	12 52	12 54	12 57		13 00	13 03	13 03	13 06	13 09	13 09	13 12	13 18	13 18		13 22	13 22	13 24	13 30	13 33	13 33
South Croydon 4 a		12 45					13 01				13 06				13 15									13 36
Purley Oaks a		12 48									13 09				13 18									13 39
Purley 4 a		12 51		12 56					13 05		13 12	13 15			13 21		13 26					13 35		13 42

	SN	SN	SN		FC	SN	SN	SN	SN	FC	SN	SN	SN		SN	SN	SN	FC	SN	SN	SN	SN	SN	
		◇1	1		1		◇1	1	◇1 ⌶	1	1	1	◇1				1	1		◇1 ⌶	1	◇1 ⌶	1	
London Victoria 15 ⊖ d		13 21	13 23			13 13	13 32		13 36				13 47				13 53		13 43	14 02		14 06		
Clapham Junction 10 d			13 29			13 21	13 38		13 42		13 34		13 53				13 59		13 51	14 08		14 12		
St Pancras International 15 ⊖ d																								
Farringdon 3 ⊖ d																								
City Thameslink 3 d																								
London Blackfriars 3 ⊖ d																								
London Bridge 4 ⊖ d	13 20				13 27			13 33		13 42		13 45			13 36	13 50		13 57			14 03		14 08	
Norwood Junction 2 a	13 32							13 44				13 56			13 59	14 02					14 14			
East Croydon ⇌ a	13 36	13 37	13 39		13 39	13 42	13 48	13 48	13 52	13 54	13 57	14 00	14 03		14 03	14 06	14 09	14 09	14 12	14 18	14 18	14 22	14 22	
South Croydon 4 a						13 45					14 01				14 06				14 15					
Purley Oaks a						13 48									14 09				14 18					
Purley 4 a	13 45					13 51		13 56				14 05			14 12	14 15			14 21		14 26			

	FC	SN	SN	SN	SN	SN	SN	FC	SN		SN	SN	SN	FC	SN	SN	SN	SN	SN		SN	FC	SN	SN
	1	1	◇1			◇1	1	1			◇1	1	◇1 ⌶	1	1	1	◇1				1	1		◇1 ⌶
London Victoria 15 ⊖ d			14 17			14 21	14 23		14 13		14 32		14 36				14 47				14 53		14 43	15 02
Clapham Junction 10 d			14 23				14 29		14 21		14 38		14 42		14 34		14 53				14 59		14 51	15 08
St Pancras International 15 ⊖ d																								
Farringdon 3 ⊖ d																								
City Thameslink 3 d																								
London Blackfriars 3 ⊖ d																								
London Bridge 4 ⊖ d	14 12	14 15		14 06	14 20			14 27				14 33		14 42		14 45		14 36	14 50			14 57		
Norwood Junction 2 a		14 26		14 29	14 32							14 44				14 56		14 59	15 02					
East Croydon ⇌ a	14 24	14 30	14 33	14 33	14 36	14 37	14 39	14 39	14 42		14 48	14 48	14 52	14 54	14 57	15 00	15 03	15 03	15 06		15 09	15 09	15 12	15 18
South Croydon 4 a				14 36					14 45						15 01			15 06					15 15	
Purley Oaks a				14 39					14 48									15 09					15 18	
Purley 4 a		14 35		14 42	14 45				14 51			14 56				15 05		15 12	15 15				15 21	

Table 175

London - East Croydon and Purley

COMPLETE SERVICE

Saturdays

	SN 1	SN ◇1 ⊼	SN 1	FC 1	SN 1		SN ◇1	SN	SN	SN ◇1	SN 1	FC 1	SN	SN ◇1	SN 1		SN ◇1 ⊼	FC 1	SN 1	SN 1	SN ◇1	SN	SN	SN 1
London Victoria 15 ⊖ d		15 06					15 17			15 21	15 23		15 13	15 32			15 36				15 47			15 53
Clapham Junction 10 d		15 12					15 23				15 29		15 21	15 38			15 42		15 34		15 53			15 59
St Pancras International 15 ⊖ d																								
Farringdon 3 ⊖ d																								
City Thameslink 3 d																								
London Blackfriars 3 ⊖ d																								
London Bridge 4 ⊖ d	15 03		15 08	15 12	15 15			15 06	15 20			15 27			15 33			15 42		15 45		15 36	15 50	
Norwood Junction 2 a	15 14				15 26			15 29	15 32						15 44					15 56		15 59	16 02	
East Croydon a	15 18	15 22	15 22	15 24	15 30		15 33	15 33	15 36	15 37	15 39	15 39	15 42	15 48	15 48		15 52	15 54	15 57	16 00	16 03	16 03	16 06	16 09
South Croydon 4 a								15 36					15 45						16 01			16 06		
Purley Oaks a								15 39					15 48									16 09		
Purley 4 a	15 26				15 35			15 42	15 45				15 51		15 56					16 05		16 12	16 15	

	FC 1		SN	SN ◇1 ⊼	SN 1	SN ◇1 ⊼	SN 1	FC 1	SN 1	SN ◇1	SN		SN	SN ◇1	SN 1	FC 1	SN	SN ◇1	SN 1	SN ◇1 ⊼	FC 1		SN 1	SN 1
London Victoria 15 ⊖ d			15 43	16 02		16 06				16 17				16 21	16 23		16 13	16 32		16 36				
Clapham Junction 10 d			15 51	16 08		16 12				16 23					16 29		16 21	16 38		16 42			16 34	
St Pancras International 15 ⊖ d																								
Farringdon 3 ⊖ d																								
City Thameslink 3 d																								
London Blackfriars 3 ⊖ d																								
London Bridge 4 ⊖ d	15 57				16 03		16 08	16 12	16 15		16 06		16 20			16 27			16 33		16 42			16 45
Norwood Junction 2 a					16 14				16 26		16 29		16 32						16 44					16 56
East Croydon a	16 09		16 12	16 18	16 18	16 22	16 22	16 24	16 30	16 33	16 33		16 36	16 37	16 39	16 39	16 42	16 48	16 48	16 52	16 54		16 57	17 00
South Croydon 4 a			16 15								16 36						16 45						17 01	
Purley Oaks a			16 18								16 39						16 48							
Purley 4 a			16 21		16 26				16 35		16 42		16 45				16 51		16 56					17 05

	SN ◇1	SN	SN	SN 1	FC 1	SN	SN ◇1 ⊼		SN 1	SN ◇1 ⊼	SN 1	FC 1	SN 1	SN ◇1	SN	SN	SN ◇1		SN 1	FC 1	SN	SN ◇1	SN 1	SN ◇1 ⊼
London Victoria 15 ⊖ d	16 47			16 53		16 43	17 02			17 06				17 17			17 21		17 23		17 13	17 32		17 36
Clapham Junction 10 d	16 53			16 59		16 51	17 08			17 12				17 23					17 29		17 21	17 38		17 42
St Pancras International 15 ⊖ d																								
Farringdon 3 ⊖ d																								
City Thameslink 3 d																								
London Blackfriars 3 ⊖ d																								
London Bridge 4 ⊖ d		16 36	16 50		16 57				17 03		17 08	17 12	17 15		17 06	17 20				17 27			17 33	
Norwood Junction 2 a		16 59	17 02						17 14				17 26		17 29	17 32							17 44	
East Croydon a	17 03	17 03	17 06	17 09	17 09	17 12	17 18		17 18	17 22	17 22	17 24	17 30	17 33	17 33	17 36	17 37		17 39	17 39	17 42	17 48	17 48	17 52
South Croydon 4 a		17 06				17 15									17 36						17 45			
Purley Oaks a		17 09				17 18									17 39						17 48			
Purley 4 a		17 12	17 15			17 21			17 26				17 35		17 42	17 45					17 51		17 56	

	FC 1	SN 1	SN 1		SN ◇1	SN	SN	SN 1	FC 1	SN	SN ◇1 ⊼	SN 1	SN ◇1 ⊼		SN 1	FC 1	SN 1	SN ◇1	SN	SN	SN ◇1	SN 1	FC 1	
London Victoria 15 ⊖ d					17 47			17 53		17 43	18 02		18 06					18 17			18 21	18 23		
Clapham Junction 10 d		17 34			17 53			17 59		17 51	18 08		18 12					18 23				18 29		
St Pancras International 15 ⊖ d																								
Farringdon 3 ⊖ d																								
City Thameslink 3 d																								
London Blackfriars 3 ⊖ d																								
London Bridge 4 ⊖ d	17 42		17 45			17 36	17 50		17 57			18 03			18 08	18 12	18 15		18 06	18 20			18 27	
Norwood Junction 2 a			17 56			17 59	18 02					18 14					18 26		18 29	18 32				
East Croydon a	17 54	17 57	18 00		18 03	18 03	18 06	18 09	18 09	18 12	18 18	18 18	18 22		18 22	18 24	18 30	18 33	18 33	18 36	18 38	18 39	18 39	
South Croydon 4 a		18 01				18 06				18 15									18 36					
Purley Oaks a						18 09				18 18									18 39					
Purley 4 a			18 05			18 12	18 15			18 21		18 26					18 35		18 42	18 45				

Table 175

London - East Croydon and Purley

COMPLETE SERVICE

Saturdays

	SN	SN ◇1	SN 1	SN ◇1 ⊼	FC 1	SN 1	SN 1	SN ◇1	SN		SN	SN 1	FC 1	SN	SN ◇1 ⊼	SN 1	SN ◇1 ⊼	SN 1	FC 1		SN ◇1	SN	SN ◇1	SN 1
London Victoria 15 ⊖ d	18 13	18 32		18 36				18 47				18 53		18 43	19 02		19 06				19 17		19 21	19 23
Clapham Junction 10 d	18 21	18 38		18 42		18 34		18 53				18 59		18 51	19 08		19 12				19 23			19 29
St Pancras International 15 ⊖ d																								
Farringdon 3 ⊖ d																								
City Thameslink 3 d																								
London Blackfriars 3 ⊖ d																								
London Bridge 4 ⊖ d			18 33		18 42		18 45		18 36		18 50		18 57			19 03		19 08	19 12			19 06		
Norwood Junction 2 a			18 44				18 56		18 59		19 02					19 14						19 29		
East Croydon a	18 42	18 48	18 48	18 52	18 54	18 57	19 00	19 03	19 03		19 06	19 09	19 09	19 12	19 18	19 18	19 22	19 22	19 24		19 33	19 33	19 37	19 39
South Croydon 4 a	18 45					19 01			19 06					19 15								19 36		
Purley Oaks a	18 48								19 09					19 18								19 39		
Purley 4 a	18 51		18 56				19 05		19 12		19 15			19 21		19 26						19 42		

	FC 1	SN	SN ◇1	SN 1	SN ◇1		FC 1	SN 1	SN ◇1	SN	SN 1	FC 1	SN	SN ◇1	SN ◇1		SN 1	FC 1	SN 1	SN ◇1	SN	SN ◇1	SN 1	SN
London Victoria 15 ⊖ d		19 15	19 32		19 36				19 47		19 53		19 45	20 02	20 06				20 10	20 17		20 21	20 23	20 15
Clapham Junction 10 d		19 23	19 38		19 42			19 35	19 53		19 59		19 53	20 08	20 12				20 16	20 23			20 29	20 23
St Pancras International 15 ⊖ d																								
Farringdon 3 ⊖ d																								
City Thameslink 3 d																								
London Blackfriars 3 ⊖ d																								
London Bridge 4 ⊖ d	19 27			19 33			19 42			19 36		19 57					20 08	20 12			20 06			
Norwood Junction 2 a				19 44						19 59							20 19				20 29			
East Croydon a	19 39	19 44	19 48	19 49	19 52		19 54	19 57	20 03	20 03	20 09	20 09	20 14	20 19	20 22		20 22	20 24	20 27	20 33	20 33	20 37	20 39	20 44
South Croydon 4 a		19 47								20 06			20 17								20 36			20 47
Purley Oaks a		19 50								20 09			20 20								20 39			20 50
Purley 4 a		19 53		19 57						20 12			20 23						20 33		20 42			20 53

	SN ◇1		SN ◇1	FC 1	SN 1	SN 1	SN ◇1	SN	SN 1	SN	SN ◇1		SN ◇1	SN 1	FC 1	SN 1	SN ◇1	SN	SN 1	SN	SN 1		SN ◇1	FC 1
London Victoria 15 ⊖ d	20 32		20 36		20 40		20 47		20 53	20 45	21 02		21 06			21 10	21 17		21 23	21 15	21 32		21 36	
Clapham Junction 10 d	20 38		20 42		20 46	20 34	20 53		20 59	20 53	21 08		21 12			21 16	21 23		21 29	21 23	21 38		21 42	
St Pancras International 15 ⊖ d																								
Farringdon 3 ⊖ d																								
City Thameslink 3 d																								
London Blackfriars 3 ⊖ d																								
London Bridge 4 ⊖ d				20 42				20 36						21 08	21 12			21 06						21 42
Norwood Junction 2 a								20 59						21 19				21 29						
East Croydon a	20 48		20 52	20 53	20 57	20 59	21 03	21 03	21 09	21 14	21 18		21 22	21 22	21 24	21 27	21 33	21 33	21 39	21 44	21 48		21 52	21 54
South Croydon 4 a								21 06		21 17								21 36		21 47				
Purley Oaks a								21 09		21 20								21 39		21 50				
Purley 4 a					21 03			21 12		21 23						21 33		21 42		21 53				

	SN 1	SN ◇1	SN	SN 1	SN	SN ◇1	SN ◇1		SN 1	FC 1	SN 1	SN ◇1	SN	SN 1	SN	SN 1	SN ◇1		FC 1	SN 1	SN ◇1	SN	SN 1	SN
London Victoria 15 ⊖ d	21 40	21 47		21 53	21 45	22 02	22 06				22 10	22 17		22 23	22 15	22 32	22 36			22 40	22 47		22 53	
Clapham Junction 10 d	21 46	21 53		21 59	21 53	22 08	22 12				22 16	22 23		22 29	22 23	22 38	22 42			22 46	22 53		22 59	
St Pancras International 15 ⊖ d																								
Farringdon 3 ⊖ d																								
City Thameslink 3 d																								
London Blackfriars 3 ⊖ d																								
London Bridge 4 ⊖ d			21 36						22 08	22 12			22 06						22 42			22 36		22 56
Norwood Junction 2 a			21 59						22 19				22 29									22 59		23 07
East Croydon a	21 57	22 03	22 04	22 09	22 14	22 18	22 22		22 22	22 24	22 27	22 33	22 35	22 39	22 44	22 48	22 52		22 54	22 57	23 03	23 03	23 09	23 11
South Croydon 4 a			22 07		22 17								22 38		22 47							23 06		
Purley Oaks a			22 10		22 20								22 41		22 50							23 09		
Purley 4 a	22 03		22 13		22 23						22 33		22 44		22 53					23 03		23 12		

	SN	SN ◇1	SN ◇1		FC 1	SN 1	SN ◇1	SN	SN 1	SN	SN 1	FC 1	SN		SN 1
London Victoria 15 ⊖ d	22 45	23 02	23 06			23 10	23 17		23 24	23 15	23 32				23 49
Clapham Junction 10 d	22 53	23 08	23 12			23 16	23 23		23 30	23 23	23 38				23 56
St Pancras International 15 ⊖ d															
Farringdon 3 ⊖ d															
City Thameslink 3 d															
London Blackfriars 3 ⊖ d															
London Bridge 4 ⊖ d					23 12			23 06				23 42	23 36		
Norwood Junction 2 a								23 29					23 59		
East Croydon a	23 14	23 18	23 22		23 24	23 27	23 33	23 33	23 41	23 44	23 52	23 56	00 03		00 09
South Croydon 4 a	23 17							23 36		23 47			00 06		
Purley Oaks a	23 20							23 39		23 50			00 09		
Purley 4 a	23 23					23 33		23 42		23 53			00 12		

London - East Croydon and Purley

COMPLETE SERVICE

	SN	SN 1	SN ◇1	FC 1	SN 1	SN	SN	FC 1	SN	SN	SN 1	FC 1	SN 1	SN 1	SN 1	SN 1	SN ◇1	SN ◇1	SN ◇1 B	SN 1 B	SN ◇1 C	FC 1 B
London Victoria 15 ⊖ d		23p49	00 05		00 14		00 17			00 42	01 00		02 00	03 00	04 00	05 02	05 47	06 32	07 02		07 02	
Clapham Junction 10 d		23p56	00 11		00 20		00 23			00 50	01 08		02 08	03 08	04 08	05 08	05 53	06 38	07 08		07 08	
St Pancras International 15 ⊖ d																						
Farringdon 3 ⊖ d																						
City Thameslink 3 d																						
London Blackfriars 3 ⊖ d																						
London Bridge 4 ⊖ d	23p36			00 12		00 06		00 42	00 36			01 05								07 05		07 12
Norwood Junction 2 a	23p59					00 29			00 59											07 17		
East Croydon a	00 03	00 09	00 24	00 27	00 31	00 33	00 42	00 56	01 03	01 10	01 21	01 32	02 21	03 21	04 21	05 22	06 05	06 51	07 19	07 21	07 23	07 24
South Croydon 4 a	00 06					00 36																
Purley Oaks a	00 09					00 39																
Purley 4 a	00 12				00 37	00 42					01 27		02 27	03 27	04 27	05 28		06 56	07 25	07 28	07 29	

	FC 1 C	SN ◇1 B	SN 1 C	SN 1 B	SN 1 B	SN ◇1 C	SN 1 C	FC 1 B	FC 1 C	SN	SN	SN ◇1 B	SN 1 B	FC 1 B	SN ◇1 C	FC 1 C	SN	SN ◇1 B	SN	SN ◇1 C	SN ◇1 B	SN 1 C
London Victoria 15 ⊖ d		07 17	07 22	07 25	07 32	07 32	07 34					08 02			08 04			08 17		08 17	08 21	08 22
Clapham Junction 10 d		07 23	07 28	07 31	07 38	07 38	07 41					08 08			08 10			08 23		08 23	08 27	08 28
St Pancras International 15 ⊖ d																						
Farringdon 3 ⊖ d																						
City Thameslink 3 d																						
London Blackfriars 3 ⊖ d																						
London Bridge 4 ⊖ d	07 12							07 42	07 42	07 25	07 39		08 05	08 12		08 12	07 55		08 09			
Norwood Junction 2 a											08 02		08 16						08 32			
East Croydon a	07 26	07 35	07 42	07 42	07 49	07 50	07 53	07 54	07 56	08 02	08 06	08 17	08 20	08 24	08 24	08 27	08 32	08 32	08 36	08 36	08 38	08 42
South Croydon 4 a											08 09								08 39			
Purley Oaks a											08 12								08 42			
Purley 4 a					07 55		07 59				08 15	08 23	08 26		08 30				08 45			

	SN 1 B	SN 1 B	SN ◇1 C	SN 1 C	FC 1 B	FC 1 C	SN	SN ◇1 B 🍴	SN	SN ◇1 C 🍴	SN ◇1 B	SN 1 B	SN ◇1 C	SN ◇1 B	FC 1 B	SN ◇1 C	FC 1 C	SN	SN ◇1 B	SN	SN ◇1 C
London Victoria 15 ⊖ d	08 25	08 32	08 32	08 34				08 47		08 47	09 02		09 02	09 06		09 04			09 17		09 17
Clapham Junction 10 d	08 31	08 38	08 38	08 41				08 53		08 53	09 08		09 08	09 12		09 10			09 23		09 23
St Pancras International 15 ⊖ d																					
Farringdon 3 ⊖ d																					
City Thameslink 3 d																					
London Blackfriars 3 ⊖ d																					
London Bridge 4 ⊖ d					08 42	08 42	08 25		08 39			09 05			09 12		09 12	08 55		09 09	
Norwood Junction 2 a									09 02			09 16								09 32	
East Croydon a	08 42	08 47	08 50	08 53	08 54	08 56	09 00	09 02	09 06	09 06	09 17	09 20	09 21	09 22	09 24	09 24	09 27	09 32	09 32	09 36	09 36
South Croydon 4 a									09 09											09 39	
Purley Oaks a									09 12											09 42	
Purley 4 a		08 53		08 59					09 15		09 23	09 26				09 30				09 45	

	SN ◇1 B	SN 1 C	SN 1 B	SN 1 B	SN ◇1 C	SN ◇1 B	SN 1 C	FC 1 B	FC 1 C	SN	SN ◇1 B 🍴	SN	SN ◇1 C 🍴	SN ◇1 B	SN 1 B	SN ◇1 C 🍴	SN ◇1 B 🍴	FC 1 B	SN ◇1 C 🍴	FC 1 C	SN	SN ◇1 B
London Victoria 15 ⊖ d	09 21	09 22	09 25	09 32	09 32	09 36	09 34				09 47		09 47	10 02		10 02	10 06		10 04			10 17
Clapham Junction 10 d	09 27	09 28	09 31	09 38	09 38	09 42	09 41				09 53		09 53	10 08		10 08	10 12		10 10			10 23
St Pancras International 15 ⊖ d																						
Farringdon 3 ⊖ d																						
City Thameslink 3 d																						
London Blackfriars 3 ⊖ d																						
London Bridge 4 ⊖ d								09 42	09 42	09 25		09 39			10 05			10 12		10 12	09 55	
Norwood Junction 2 a												10 02			10 16							
East Croydon a	09 38	09 42	09 42	09 47	09 50	09 52	09 53	09 54	09 56	10 02	10 02	10 06	10 06	10 17	10 20	10 21	10 22	10 24	10 24	10 27	10 32	10 32
South Croydon 4 a												10 09										
Purley Oaks a												10 12										
Purley 4 a				09 53			09 59					10 15		10 23	10 26				10 30			

B until 5 September

C from 12 September

London - East Croydon and Purley

COMPLETE SERVICE

	SN	SN ◇1 A	SN ◇1 B	SN 1 A	SN 1 B	SN 1 B	SN ◇1 A	SN ◇1 B 🍴	SN 1 A	FC 1 B	FC 1 A	SN	SN ◇1 B 🍴	SN	SN ◇1 A 🍴	SN ◇1 B 🍴	SN 1 B	SN ◇1 A 🍴	SN ◇1 B 🍴	FC 1 B	SN ◇1 A 🍴
London Victoria 15 ⊖ d		10 17	10 21	10 22	10 25	10 32	10 32	10 36	10 34				10 47		10 47	11 02		11 02	11 06		11 04
Clapham Junction 10 d		10 23	10 27	10 28	10 31	10 38	10 38	10 42	10 41				10 53		10 53	11 08		11 08	11 12		11 10
St Pancras International 15 ⊖ d																					
Farringdon 3 ⊖ d																					
City Thameslink 3 d																					
London Blackfriars 3 ⊖ d																					
London Bridge 4 ⊖ d	10 09									10 42	10 42	10 25		10 39			11 05			11 12	
Norwood Junction 2 a	10 32													11 02			11 16				
East Croydon a	10 36	10 36	10 38	10 42	10 42	10 47	10 50	10 52	10 53	10 54	10 56	11 02	11 02	11 06	11 06	11 17	11 20	11 21	11 22	11 24	11 24
South Croydon 4 a	10 39													11 09							
Purley Oaks a	10 42													11 12							
Purley 4 a	10 45					10 53			10 59					11 15		11 23	11 26				11 30

	FC 1 A	SN	SN ◇1 B	SN	SN ◇1 A	SN ◇1 B	SN 1 A	SN 1 B	SN 1 B	SN ◇1 A	SN ◇1 B 🍴	SN 1 A	FC 1 B	FC 1 A	SN	SN ◇1 B 🍴	SN	SN ◇1 A 🍴	SN ◇1 B	SN 1 B	SN ◇1 A 🍴	SN ◇1 B 🍴
London Victoria 15 ⊖ d			11 17		11 17	11 21	11 22	11 25	11 32	11 32	11 36	11 34				11 47		11 47	12 02		12 02	12 06
Clapham Junction 10 d			11 23		11 23	11 27	11 28	11 31	11 38	11 38	11 42	11 41				11 53		11 53	12 08		12 08	12 12
St Pancras International 15 ⊖ d																						
Farringdon 3 ⊖ d																						
City Thameslink 3 d																						
London Blackfriars 3 ⊖ d																						
London Bridge 4 ⊖ d	11 12	10 55		11 09									11 42	11 42	11 25		11 39			12 05		
Norwood Junction 2 a				11 32													12 02			12 16		
East Croydon a	11 27	11 32	11 32	11 36	11 36	11 38	11 42	11 42	11 47	11 50	11 52	11 53	11 54	11 56	12 02	12 02	12 06	12 06	12 17	12 20	12 21	12 22
South Croydon 4 a				11 39													12 09					
Purley Oaks a				11 42													12 12					
Purley 4 a				11 45					11 53			11 59					12 15		12 23	12 26		

	FC 1 B	SN ◇1 A 🍴	FC 1 A	SN	SN ◇1 B	SN	SN ◇1 A	SN ◇1 B	SN 1 A	SN 1 B	SN 1 B	SN ◇1 A	SN ◇1 B 🍴	SN 1 A	FC 1 B	FC 1 A	SN	SN ◇1 B 🍴	SN	SN ◇1 A 🍴	SN ◇1 B	SN 1 B
London Victoria 15 ⊖ d		12 04			12 17		12 17	12 21	12 22	12 25	12 32	12 32	12 36	12 34				12 47		12 47	13 02	
Clapham Junction 10 d		12 10			12 23		12 23	12 27	12 28	12 31	12 38	12 38	12 42	12 41				12 53		12 53	13 08	
St Pancras International 15 ⊖ d																						
Farringdon 3 ⊖ d																						
City Thameslink 3 d																						
London Blackfriars 3 ⊖ d																						
London Bridge 4 ⊖ d	12 12		12 12	11 55		12 09									12 42	12 42	12 25		12 39			13 05
Norwood Junction 2 a						12 32													13 02			13 16
East Croydon a	12 24	12 24	12 27	12 32	12 32	12 36	12 36	12 38	12 42	12 42	12 47	12 50	12 52	12 53	12 54	12 56	13 02	13 02	13 06	13 06	13 17	13 20
South Croydon 4 a						12 39													13 09			
Purley Oaks a						12 42													13 12			
Purley 4 a		12 30				12 45					12 53			12 59					13 15		13 23	13 26

	SN ◇1 A 🍴	SN ◇1 B 🍴	FC 1 B	SN ◇1 A 🍴	FC 1 A	SN	SN ◇1 B	SN	SN ◇1 A	SN ◇1 B	SN 1 A	SN 1 B	SN 1 B	SN ◇1 A	SN ◇1 B 🍴	SN 1 A	FC 1 B	FC 1 A	SN	SN ◇1 B 🍴	SN
London Victoria 15 ⊖ d	13 02	13 06		13 04			13 17		13 17	13 21	13 22	13 25	13 32	13 32	13 36	13 34				13 47	
Clapham Junction 10 d	13 08	13 12		13 10			13 23		13 23	13 27	13 28	13 31	13 38	13 38	13 42	13 41				13 53	
St Pancras International 15 ⊖ d																					
Farringdon 3 ⊖ d																					
City Thameslink 3 d																					
London Blackfriars 3 ⊖ d																					
London Bridge 4 ⊖ d			13 12		13 12	12 55		13 09									13 42	13 42	13 25		13 39
Norwood Junction 2 a								13 32													14 02
East Croydon a	13 21	13 22	13 24	13 24	13 27	13 32	13 32	13 36	13 36	13 38	13 42	13 42	13 47	13 50	13 52	13 53	13 54	13 56	14 02	14 02	14 06
South Croydon 4 a								13 39													14 09
Purley Oaks a								13 42													14 12
Purley 4 a				13 30				13 45					13 53			13 59					14 15

A from 12 September

B until 5 September

Table 175

London - East Croydon and Purley
COMPLETE SERVICE

	SN	SN	SN	SN	SN	FC	SN	FC	SN	SN	SN	SN	SN	SN	SN	SN	SN	SN	SN	FC	FC	SN
	◇1	◇1	1	◇1	◇1	1	◇1	1		◇1		◇1	◇1	1	1	1	◇1	◇1	1	1	1	
	A trolley	B	B	A trolley	B trolley	B	A trolley	A		B		A	B	A	B	B	A	B trolley	A	B	A	
London Victoria 15 ⊖ d	13 47	14 02		14 02	14 06		14 04			14 17		14 17	14 21	14 22	14 25	14 32	14 32	14 36	14 34			
Clapham Junction 10 d	13 53	14 08		14 08	14 12		14 10			14 23		14 23	14 27	14 28	14 31	14 38	14 38	14 42	14 41			
St Pancras International 15 ⊖ d																						
Farringdon 3 ⊖ d																						
City Thameslink 3 d																						
London Blackfriars 3 ⊖ d																						
London Bridge 4 ⊖ d			14 05			14 12		14 12	13 55		14 09									14 42	14 42	14 25
Norwood Junction 2 a			14 16								14 32											
East Croydon a	14 06	14 17	14 20	14 21	14 22	14 24	14 24	14 27	14 32	14 32	14 36	14 36	14 38	14 42	14 42	14 47	14 50	14 52	14 53	14 54	14 56	15 02
South Croydon 4 a											14 39											
Purley Oaks a											14 42											
Purley 4 a		14 23	14 26				14 30				14 45					14 53			14 59			

	SN	SN	SN	SN	SN	SN	SN	FC	SN	FC	SN	SN	SN	SN	SN	SN	SN	SN	SN	SN	SN
	◇1		◇1	◇1	1	◇1	◇1	1	◇1	1		◇1		◇1	◇1	1	1	1	◇1	◇1	1
	B trolley		A trolley	B	B	A trolley	B trolley	B	A trolley	A		B		A	B	A	B	B	A	B trolley	A
London Victoria 15 ⊖ d	14 47		14 47	15 02		15 02	15 06		15 04			15 17		15 17	15 21	15 22	15 25	15 32	15 32	15 36	15 34
Clapham Junction 10 d	14 53		14 53	15 08		15 08	15 12		15 10			15 23		15 23	15 27	15 28	15 31	15 38	15 38	15 42	15 41
St Pancras International 15 ⊖ d																					
Farringdon 3 ⊖ d																					
City Thameslink 3 d																					
London Blackfriars 3 ⊖ d																					
London Bridge 4 ⊖ d		14 39			15 05			15 12		15 12	14 55		15 09								
Norwood Junction 2 a		15 02			15 16								15 32								
East Croydon a	15 02	15 06	15 06	15 17	15 20	15 21	15 22	15 24	15 24	15 27	15 32	15 32	15 36	15 36	15 38	15 42	15 42	15 47	15 50	15 52	15 53
South Croydon 4 a		15 09											15 39								
Purley Oaks a		15 12											15 42								
Purley 4 a		15 15		15 23	15 26				15 30				15 45					15 53			15 59

	FC	FC	SN	SN	SN	SN	SN	SN	SN	SN	FC	SN	FC	SN	SN	SN	SN	SN	SN	SN	SN	SN
	1	1		◇1		◇1	◇1	1	◇1	◇1	1	◇1	1		◇1		◇1	◇1	1	1	1	◇1
	B	A		B trolley		A trolley	B	B	A trolley	B trolley	B	A trolley	A		B		A	B	A	B	B	A
London Victoria 15 ⊖ d				15 47		15 47	16 02		16 02	16 06		16 04			16 17		16 17	16 21	16 22	16 25	16 32	16 32
Clapham Junction 10 d				15 53		15 53	16 08		16 08	16 12		16 10			16 23		16 23	16 27	16 28	16 31	16 38	16 38
St Pancras International 15 ⊖ d																						
Farringdon 3 ⊖ d																						
City Thameslink 3 d																						
London Blackfriars 3 ⊖ d																						
London Bridge 4 ⊖ d	15 42	15 42	15 25		15 39			16 05			16 12		16 12	15 55		16 09						
Norwood Junction 2 a					16 02			16 16								16 32						
East Croydon a	15 54	15 56	16 02	16 02	16 06	16 06	16 17	16 20	16 21	16 22	16 24	16 24	16 27	16 32	16 32	16 36	16 36	16 38	16 42	16 42	16 47	16 50
South Croydon 4 a					16 09											16 39						
Purley Oaks a					16 12											16 42						
Purley 4 a					16 15		16 23	16 26				16 30				16 45					16 53	

	SN	SN	FC	FC	SN	SN	SN	SN	SN	SN	SN	SN	FC	SN	FC	SN	SN	SN	SN	SN	SN	SN
	◇1	1	1	1		◇1		◇1	◇1	1	◇1	◇1	1	◇1	1		◇1		◇1	◇1	1	1
	B trolley	A	B	A		B trolley		A trolley	B	B	A trolley	B trolley	B	A trolley	A		B		A	B	A	B
London Victoria 15 ⊖ d	16 36	16 34				16 47		16 47	17 02		17 02	17 06		17 04			17 17		17 17	17 21	17 22	17 25
Clapham Junction 10 d	16 42	16 41				16 53		16 53	17 08		17 08	17 12		17 10			17 23		17 23	17 27	17 28	17 31
St Pancras International 15 ⊖ d																						
Farringdon 3 ⊖ d																						
City Thameslink 3 d																						
London Blackfriars 3 ⊖ d																						
London Bridge 4 ⊖ d			16 42	16 42	16 25		16 39			17 05			17 12		17 12	16 55		17 09				
Norwood Junction 2 a							17 02			17 16								17 32				
East Croydon a	16 52	16 53	16 54	16 56	17 02	17 02	17 06	17 06	17 17	17 20	17 21	17 22	17 24	17 24	17 27	17 32	17 32	17 36	17 36	17 38	17 42	17 42
South Croydon 4 a							17 09											17 39				
Purley Oaks a							17 12											17 42				
Purley 4 a		16 59					17 15		17 23	17 26				17 30				17 45				

A from 12 September

B until 5 September

Table 175

London - East Croydon and Purley
COMPLETE SERVICE

	SN	SN	SN	SN	FC	FC	SN	SN	SN	SN	SN	SN	SN	SN	FC	SN	FC	SN	SN	SN	SN
	1	◇1	◇1	1	1	1		◇1		◇1	◇1	1	◇1	◇1	1	◇1	1		◇1		◇1
	A	B	A trolley	B	A	B		A trolley		B trolley	A	A	B trolley	A trolley	A	B trolley	B		A		B
London Victoria 15 ⊖ d	17 32	17 32	17 36	17 34				17 47		17 47	18 02		18 02	18 06		18 04			18 17		18 17
Clapham Junction 10 d	17 38	17 38	17 42	17 41				17 53		17 53	18 08		18 08	18 12		18 10			18 23		18 23
St Pancras International 15 ⊖ d																					
Farringdon 3 ⊖ d																					
City Thameslink 3 d																					
London Blackfriars 3 ⊖ d																					
London Bridge 4 ⊖ d					17 42	17 42	17 25		17 39			18 05			18 12		18 12	17 55		18 09	
Norwood Junction 2 a									18 02			18 16								18 32	
East Croydon a	17 47	17 50	17 52	17 53	17 54	17 56	18 02	18 02	18 06	18 06	18 17	18 20	18 21	18 22	18 24	18 24	18 27	18 32	18 32	18 36	18 36
South Croydon 4 a									18 09											18 39	
Purley Oaks a									18 12											18 42	
Purley 4 a	17 53			17 59					18 15		18 23	18 26				18 30				18 45	

	SN	SN	SN	SN	SN	SN	SN	FC	FC	SN	SN	SN	SN	SN	SN	SN	SN	FC	SN	FC	SN	SN
	◇1	1	1	1	◇1	◇1	1	1	1		◇1		◇1	◇1	1	◇1	◇1	1	◇1	1		◇1
	A	B	A	A	B	A trolley	B	A	B		A trolley		B trolley	A	A	B trolley	A trolley	A	B trolley	B		A
London Victoria 15 ⊖ d	18 21	18 22	18 25	18 32	18 32	18 36	18 34				18 47		18 47	19 02		19 02	19 06		19 04			19 17
Clapham Junction 10 d	18 27	18 28	18 31	18 38	18 38	18 42	18 41				18 53		18 53	19 08		19 08	19 12		19 10			19 23
St Pancras International 15 ⊖ d																						
Farringdon 3 ⊖ d																						
City Thameslink 3 d																						
London Blackfriars 3 ⊖ d																						
London Bridge 4 ⊖ d								18 42	18 42	18 25		18 39			19 05			19 12		19 12	18 55	
Norwood Junction 2 a												19 02			19 16							
East Croydon a	18 38	18 42	18 42	18 47	18 50	18 52	18 53	18 54	18 56	19 02	19 02	19 06	19 06	19 17	19 20	19 21	19 22	19 24	19 24	19 27	19 32	19 32
South Croydon 4 a												19 09										
Purley Oaks a												19 12										
Purley 4 a				18 53			18 59					19 15		19 23	19 26				19 30			

	SN	SN	SN	SN	SN	SN	SN	SN	SN	FC	FC	SN	SN	SN	SN	SN	SN	SN	SN	FC	SN
		◇1	◇1	1	1	1	◇1	◇1	1	1	1		◇1		◇1	◇1	1	◇1	◇1	1	◇1
		B	A	B	A	A	B	A	B	A	B		A trolley		B trolley	A	A	B	A	A	B
London Victoria 15 ⊖ d		19 17	19 21	19 22	19 25	19 32	19 32	19 36	19 34				19 47		19 47	20 02		20 02	20 06		20 04
Clapham Junction 10 d		19 23	19 27	19 28	19 31	19 38	19 38	19 42	19 41				19 53		19 53	20 08		20 08	20 12		20 10
St Pancras International 15 ⊖ d																					
Farringdon 3 ⊖ d																					
City Thameslink 3 d																					
London Blackfriars 3 ⊖ d																					
London Bridge 4 ⊖ d	19 09									19 42	19 42	19 25		19 39			20 05			20 12	
Norwood Junction 2 a	19 32													20 02			20 16				
East Croydon a	19 36	19 36	19 38	19 42	19 42	19 47	19 50	19 52	19 53	19 54	19 56	20 02	20 02	20 06	20 06	20 17	20 20	20 21	20 22	20 24	20 24
South Croydon 4 a	19 39													20 09							
Purley Oaks a	19 42													20 12							
Purley 4 a	19 45					19 53			19 59					20 15		20 23	20 26				20 30

	FC	SN	SN	SN	SN	SN	SN	SN	SN	SN	SN	SN	FC	FC	SN	SN	SN	SN	SN	SN	SN	SN
	1		◇1		◇1	◇1	1	1	1	◇1	◇1	1	1	1		◇1		◇1	◇1	1	◇1	◇1
	B		A		B	A	B	A	A	B	A	B	A	B		A		B	A	A	B	A
London Victoria 15 ⊖ d			20 17		20 17	20 21	20 22	20 25	20 32	20 32	20 36	20 34				20 47		20 47	21 02		21 02	21 06
Clapham Junction 10 d			20 23		20 23	20 27	20 28	20 31	20 38	20 38	20 42	20 41				20 53		20 53	21 08		21 08	21 12
St Pancras International 15 ⊖ d																						
Farringdon 3 ⊖ d																						
City Thameslink 3 d																						
London Blackfriars 3 ⊖ d																						
London Bridge 4 ⊖ d	20 12	19 55		20 09									20 42	20 42	20 25		20 39			21 05		
Norwood Junction 2 a				20 32													21 02			21 16		
East Croydon a	20 27	20 32	20 32	20 36	20 36	20 38	20 42	20 42	20 47	20 50	20 52	20 53	20 54	20 56	21 02	21 02	21 06	21 06	21 17	21 20	21 21	21 22
South Croydon 4 a				20 39													21 09					
Purley Oaks a				20 42													21 12					
Purley 4 a				20 45					20 53			20 59					21 15		21 23	21 26		

A until 5 September

B from 12 September

Table 175

London - East Croydon and Purley

COMPLETE SERVICE

Sundays

	FC 1 A	SN ◇1 B	FC 1 B	SN	SN ◇1 A		SN	SN ◇1 B	SN ◇1 A	SN 1 B	SN 1 A	SN 1 A	SN ◇1 B	SN 1 B	FC 1 A		FC 1 B	SN	SN ◇1 A	SN	SN ◇1 B	SN ◇1 A	SN 1 A	FC 1 A
London Victoria 15 ⊖ d		21 04			21 17			21 17	21 21	21 22	21 25	21 32	21 32	21 34					21 47		21 47	22 02		
Clapham Junction 10 d		21 10			21 23			21 23	21 27	21 28	21 31	21 38	21 38	21 41					21 53		21 53	22 08		
St Pancras International 15 ⊖ d																								
Farringdon 3 ⊖ d																								
City Thameslink 3 d																								
London Blackfriars 3 ⊖ d																								
London Bridge 4 ⊖ d	21 12		21 12	20 55			21 09								21 42		21 42	21 25		21 39			22 05	22 12
Norwood Junction 2 a							21 32													22 02			22 16	
East Croydon ⇌ a	21 24	21 24	21 27	21 32	21 32		21 36	21 36	21 38	21 42	21 42	21 47	21 50	21 53	21 54		21 56	22 00	22 02	22 06	22 06	22 17	22 20	22 24
South Croydon 4 a							21 39													22 09				
Purley Oaks a							21 42													22 12				
Purley 4 a		21 30					21 45					21 53		21 59						22 15		22 23	22 26	

	SN ◇1 B		FC 1 B	SN	SN ◇1 A	SN	SN ◇1 B	SN ◇1 A	SN 1 A	SN 1 B	SN 1 A		SN ◇1 B	SN 1 B	FC 1 A	FC 1 B	SN	SN ◇1 A	SN	SN ◇1 B	SN 1		FC 1 A	FC 1 B
London Victoria 15 ⊖ d	22 04				22 17		22 17	22 21	22 25	22 22	22 32		22 32	22 34				22 47		22 47	23 04			
Clapham Junction 10 d	22 10				22 23		22 23	22 27	22 31	22 28	22 38		22 38	22 41				22 53		22 53	23 10			
St Pancras International 15 ⊖ d																								
Farringdon 3 ⊖ d																								
City Thameslink 3 d																								
London Blackfriars 3 ⊖ d																								
London Bridge 4 ⊖ d			22 12	21 55		22 09									22 42	22 42	22 25		22 39				23 12	23 12
Norwood Junction 2 a						22 32													23 02					
East Croydon ⇌ a	22 24		22 27	22 32	22 32	22 36	22 36	22 38	22 42	22 43	22 47		22 50	22 53	22 54	22 56	23 00	23 02	23 06	23 06	23 22		23 24	23 27
South Croydon 4 a						22 39													23 09					
Purley Oaks a						22 42													23 12					
Purley 4 a	22 30					22 45					22 53			22 59					23 15		23 28			

	SN	SN	SN ◇1	SN ◇1	FC 1	SN	SN		SN	SN
London Victoria 15 ⊖ d			23 17	23 32			23 47			23 49
Clapham Junction 10 d			23 23	23 38			23 53			23 56
St Pancras International 15 ⊖ d										
Farringdon 3 ⊖ d										
City Thameslink 3 d										
London Blackfriars 3 ⊖ d										
London Bridge 4 ⊖ d	22 55	23 09			23 42	23 25			23 39	
Norwood Junction 2 a		23 32							00 02	
East Croydon ⇌ a	23 32	23 36	23 37	23 52	23 56	00 01	00 06		00 08	00 16
South Croydon 4 a		23 39							00 11	
Purley Oaks a		23 42							00 14	
Purley 4 a		23 45							00 17	

A until 5 September

B from 12 September

Table 175

Purley and East Croydon - London

COMPLETE SERVICE

Mondays to Fridays

	SN MO 1	SN MX 1	FC 1	SN ◇1	FC 1	SN	SN 1	SN 1	FC 1		SN 1	FC 1	SN 1	FC	SN	FC 1	SN	SN	SN		FC 1	SN 1	SN 1	SN
Purley 4 d	23p50	23p49		00 11			01 22	02 22			03 22		04 22		05 07			05 39				06 00		06 04
Purley Oaks d																		05 42						06 07
South Croydon 4 d																		05 45						06 10
East Croydon ⇌ d	23p56	23p58	00 04	00 17	00 36	00 49	01 28	02 28	02 47		03 28	03 47	04 28	04 47	05 13	05 17	05 34	05 48	05 51		06 02	06 07	06 11	06 13
Norwood Junction 2 d															05 17		05 38		05 55					06 18
London Bridge 4 ⊖ a			00 19		00 52				03 12			04 12			05 41	05 34			06 24		06 15			06 42
London Blackfriars 3 ⊖ a														05 13		05 43					06 24			
City Thameslink 3 a														05 16		05 46					06 26			
Farringdon 3 ⊖ a														05 20		05 50					06 30			
St Pancras International 15 ⊖ a														05 23		05 53					06 33			
Clapham Junction 10 a	00 10	00 11		00 29		01 01	01 40	02 40			03 40		04 47				05 58	06 09				06 18	06 21	
London Victoria 15 ⊖ a	00 18	00 18		00 37		01 09	01 49	02 49			03 49		04 54				06 07	06 18				06 25	06 28	

	SN ◇1	SN	SN 1	SN 1	SN		SN 1	FC 1	SN	SN 1	FC 1	SN	SN 1	SN 1	SN 1		SN 1	FC 1	SN	SN ◇1	SN 1	SN	FC 1	SN
Purley 4 d					06 22		06 26		06 30						06 54		06 59		07b01					07c17
Purley Oaks d					06 25				06 33										07 04					07 20
South Croydon 4 d					06 28				06 36			06 42	06 51						07 07					07 23
East Croydon ⇌ d	06 15	06 17	06 23	06 27	06 31		06 31	06 32	06 39	06 42	06 44	06 45	06 54	06 57	07 00		07 05	07 09	07 10	07 15	07 15	07 18	07 24	07 26
Norwood Junction 2 d					06 37				06 43										07 14					
London Bridge 4 ⊖ a			06 39		06 49			06 46	06 55		06 58		07 11	07 13	07 16			07 23	07 28					
London Blackfriars 3 ⊖ a								06 52			07 04							07 30					07 51	
City Thameslink 3 a								06 54			07 08							07 32					07 56	
Farringdon 3 ⊖ a								06 58			07 12							07 36					08 00	
St Pancras International 15 ⊖ a								07 01			07 15							07 39					08 03	
Clapham Junction 10 a	06 25	06 37		06 38			06 41			06 51		07 05					07 16			07 24	07 27	07 38		07 36
London Victoria 15 ⊖ a	06 32	06 45		06 45			06 48			07 00		07 16					07 25			07 33	07 36	07 48		07 46

	SN 1		SN 1	SN ◇1	SN 1	SN 1	SN 1	SN	SN ◇1	SN 1	SN 1		SN	FC 1	SN	SN 1	SN 1	SN ◇1	SN 1	SN 1	SN 1		SN 1	SN ◇1
Purley 4 d						07 29		07e31							07f47				07 55					
Purley Oaks d								07 34							07 50									
South Croydon 4 d			07 25					07 37							07 53		07 54							
East Croydon ⇌ d	07 27		07 28	07 31	07 32	07 35	07 39	07 40	07 43	07 45	07 46		07 47	07 54	07 56	07 57	07 59	08 01	08 02	08 03	08 05		08 07	08 08
Norwood Junction 2 d								07 44																
London Bridge 4 ⊖ a	07 43		07 47		07 50	07 51		07 58			08 01					08 13	08 17		08 19	08 21	08 23			
London Blackfriars 3 ⊖ a														08 20										
City Thameslink 3 a														08 23										
Farringdon 3 ⊖ a														08 27										
St Pancras International 15 ⊖ a														08 31										
Clapham Junction 10 a				07 40			07 48		07 52	07 55			08 09		08 06			08 10					08 36	08 17
London Victoria 15 ⊖ a				07 49			07 57		08 01	08 04					08 15			08 19						08 26

	SN	SN 1	SN ◇1	SN 1	SN	SN 1	FC 1		SN 1	SN	SN 1	SN 1	SN ◇1	SN 1	SN 1	SN 1	SN		FC 1	SN	SN ◇1	SN 1	SN	SN ◇1
Purley 4 d	08g01					08 15				08h17						08 31				08i33				
Purley Oaks d	08 04									08 20										08 36				
South Croydon 4 d	08 07									08 23		08 26					08 35			08 39		08 42		
East Croydon ⇌ d	08 10	08 11	08 14	08 15	08 18	08 21	08 21		08 25	08 26	08 27	08 29	08 30	08 32	08 33	08 37	08 39		08 39	08 42	08 43	08 45	08 48	08 50
Norwood Junction 2 d	08 14																			08 47				
London Bridge 4 ⊖ a	08 28					08 39			08 41		08 45	08 47		08 54	08 52					09 01				
London Blackfriars 3 ⊖ a							08 53												09 09					
City Thameslink 3 a							08 56												09 12					
Farringdon 3 ⊖ a							09 00												09 16					
St Pancras International 15 ⊖ a							09 03												09 19					
Clapham Junction 10 a		08 20	08 23	08 26	08 38					08 36			08 39			08 47	09 04				08 52	08 55	09 08	09 00
London Victoria 15 ⊖ a		08 29	08 32	08 35	08 48					08 45			08 48			08 58					09 01	09 04	09 18	09 09

b arr. 0655
c arr. 0711
e arr. 0725
f arr. 0741
g arr. 0755
h arr. 0811
i arr. 0827

Table 175

Mondays to Fridays

Purley and East Croydon - London

COMPLETE SERVICE

		SN ■	SN	FC ■	SN ■	SN ■	SN ◇■	SN ■	SN	SN ■	FC ■	SN ■	SN ◇■ 🍴	SN ■	SN	SN	SN ◇■ 🍴	SN ■ 🍴	SN ■	SN	FC ■	SN ■
Purley ■4	d		08b45		08 50				08c56			09 05			09 08	09 14				09 21		
Purley Oaks	d		08 48						08 59						09 11					09 24		
South Croydon ■4	d		08 51			08 54			09 02						09 14					09 27		
East Croydon	d	08 51	08 54	08 54	08 57	08 59	09 01	09 02	09 05	09 08	09 09	09 11	09 14	09 14	09 17	09 20	09 22	09 26	09 29	09 30	09 32	09 33
Norwood Junction ■2	d								09 09							09 25				09 35		
London Bridge ■4 ⊖	a	09 08		09 08	09 13	09 16		09 20	09 23							09 42				10 01	09 46	09 51
London Blackfriars ■3 ⊖	a			09 21							09 37										09 53	
City Thameslink ■3	a			09 25							09 40										09 56	
Farringdon ■3 ⊖	a			09 28							09 44										10 00	
St Pancras International ■15 ⊖	a			09 32							09 47										10 03	
Clapham Junction ■10	a		09 04				09 10			09 34		09 20	09 23	09 26	09 38		09 32	09 35	09 38			
London Victoria ■15 ⊖	a		09 13				09 22					09 29	09 32	09 35	09 48		09 41	09 44	09 48			

		SN ■	SN ◇■ 🍴	SN ◇■	SN ■	SN	FC ■	SN	SN ■	SN ◇■ 🍴	SN	SN ◇■ 🍴	FC ■	SN ■	SN ■	SN ◇■ 🍴	SN ■	SN	FC ■	SN	SN ◇■ 🍴	SN ■	SN ◇■
Purley ■4	d	09 32				09 38		09 45	09 49		09 51			10 02				10 08		10 15		10 19	
Purley Oaks	d					09 41					09 54							10 11					
South Croydon ■4	d					09 44					09 57				10 07			10 14					
East Croydon	d	09 37	09 39	09 43	09 44	09 47	09 47	09 51	09 55	09 55	10 00	10 00	10 02	10 07	10 10	10 11	10 14	10 17	10 17	10 21	10 24	10 25	10 28
Norwood Junction ■2	d	09 42						09 55	10 00		10 05			10 13						10 25		10 30	
London Bridge ■4 ⊖	a	09 56					10 00	10 09	10 13		10 29		10 15	10 25					10 30	10 39		10 43	
London Blackfriars ■3 ⊖	a						10 08						10 23						10 37				
City Thameslink ■3	a						10 10						10 26						10 40				
Farringdon ■3 ⊖	a						10 14						10 30						10 44				
St Pancras International ■15 ⊖	a						10 17						10 33						10 47				
Clapham Junction ■10	a		09 48	09 52	09 55	10 07				10 04		10 09			10 35	10 20	10 25	10 37			10 33		10 37
London Victoria ■15 ⊖	a		09 58	10 00	10 02	10 16				10 11		10 16				10 28	10 35	10 46			10 40		10 44

		SN	FC ■	SN ■	SN ■	SN ◇■	SN ■	SN	FC ■	SN	SN ◇■	SN ■	SN ◇■ 🍴	SN	SN ◇■	FC ■	SN ■	SN ■	SN ◇■	SN ■	SN	FC ■	SN
Purley ■4	d	10 21			10 33			10 38		10 45		10 49		10 51			11 01				11 08		11 15
Purley Oaks	d	10 24						10 41						10 54							11 11		
South Croydon ■4	d	10 27						10 44						10 57				11 07			11 14		
East Croydon	d	10 30	10 32	10 33	10 38	10 41	10 44	10 47	10 47	10 51	10 53	10 55	10 56	11 00	11 00	11 02	11 07	11 11	11 11	11 14	11 17	11 17	11 21
Norwood Junction ■2	d	10 35			10 43					10 55		11 00		11 05			11 13						11 26
London Bridge ■4 ⊖	a	10 59	10 45	10 49	10 55				11 00	11 09		11 13		11 29		11 15	11 25					11 30	11 39
London Blackfriars ■3 ⊖	a		10 52						11 07							11 22						11 37	
City Thameslink ■3	a		10 56						11 10							11 26						11 40	
Farringdon ■3 ⊖	a		11 00						11 14							11 30						11 44	
St Pancras International ■15 ⊖	a		11 03						11 17							11 33						11 47	
Clapham Junction ■10	a					10 50	10 55	11 07			11 02		11 05		11 09			11 33	11 20	11 25	11 37		
London Victoria ■15 ⊖	a					10 57	11 05	11 16			11 09		11 12		11 16				11 27	11 32			

		SN ◇■ 🍴	SN ■	SN ◇■	SN	FC ■	SN ■	SN ■	SN ◇■	SN ■	SN	FC ■	SN	SN ◇■	SN ■	SN ◇■ 🍴	SN	SN ◇■	FC ■	SN ■	SN ■	SN ◇■
Purley ■4	d		11 19		11 21			11 32			11 38		11 45		11 49		11 51			12 02		
Purley Oaks	d				11 24						11 41						11 54					
South Croydon ■4	d				11 27						11 44						11 57				12 07	
East Croydon	d	11 24	11 25	11 28	11 30	11 32	11 33	11 37	11 41	11 44	11 47	11 47	11 51	11 53	11 55	11 56	12 00	12 00	12 02	12 07	12 10	12 11
Norwood Junction ■2	d		11 30		11 35			11 43					11 55		12 00		12 05			12 13		
London Bridge ■4 ⊖	a		11 43		11 59	11 45	11 49	11 55				12 00	12 09		12 13		12 29		12 15	12 25		
London Blackfriars ■3 ⊖	a					11 52						12 07							12 22			
City Thameslink ■3	a					11 56						12 10							12 26			
Farringdon ■3 ⊖	a					12 00						12 14							12 30			
St Pancras International ■15 ⊖	a					12 03						12 17							12 33			
Clapham Junction ■10	a	11 33		11 37					11 50	11 55	12 07			12 02		12 05		12 09			12 34	12 19
London Victoria ■15 ⊖	a	11 40		11 44					11 57	12 02				12 09		12 12		12 18				12 28

b arr. 0839

c arr. 0850

Table 175

Mondays to Fridays

Purley and East Croydon - London

COMPLETE SERVICE

		SN ■	SN	FC ■	SN	SN ◇■ 🍴	SN ■	SN ◇■	SN	FC ■	SN ■	SN ■	SN ◇■	SN ■	SN	FC ■	SN	SN ◇■	SN ■	SN ◇■ 🍴	SN	SN ◇■	FC ■
Purley ■4	d		12 08		12 15		12 19		12 21			12 32			12 38		12 45		12 49		12 51		
Purley Oaks	d		12 11						12 24						12 41						12 54		
South Croydon ■4	d		12 14						12 27						12 44						12 57		
East Croydon	d	12 14	12 17	12 17	12 21	12 24	12 25	12 28	12 30	12 32	12 33	12 37	12 41	12 44	12 47	12 47	12 51	12 53	12 55	12 56	13 00	13 00	13 02
Norwood Junction ■2	d				12 25		12 30		12 35			12 43					12 55		13 00		13 05		
London Bridge ■4 ⊖	a			12 30	12 39		12 43		12 59	12 45	12 49	12 55				13 00	13 09		13 13		13 29		13 15
London Blackfriars ■3 ⊖	a			12 37						12 52						13 07							13 22
City Thameslink ■3	a			12 40						12 56						13 10							13 26
Farringdon ■3 ⊖	a			12 44						13 00						13 14							13 30
St Pancras International ■15 ⊖	a			12 47						13 03						13 17							13 33
Clapham Junction ■10	a	12 25	12 37			12 33		12 37					12 50	12 55	13 07			13 02		13 05		13 09	
London Victoria ■15 ⊖	a	12 32				12 40		12 44					12 57	13 02	13 16			13 09		13 12		13 16	

		SN ■	SN ■	SN ◇■	SN ■	SN	FC ■	SN	SN ◇■ 🍴	SN ■	SN ◇■	SN	FC ■	SN ■	SN ■	SN ◇■	SN ■	SN	FC ■	SN	SN ◇■	SN ■
Purley ■4	d	13 02				13 08		13 15		13 19		13 21			13 32			13 38		13 45		13 49
Purley Oaks	d					13 11						13 24						13 41				
South Croydon ■4	d		13 07			13 14						13 27						13 44				
East Croydon	d	13 07	13 10	13 11	13 14	13 17	13 17	13 21	13 24	13 25	13 28	13 30	13 32	13 33	13 37	13 41	13 44	13 47	13 47	13 51	13 53	13 55
Norwood Junction ■2	d	13 13						13 25		13 30		13 35			13 43					13 55		14 00
London Bridge ■4 ⊖	a	13 25					13 30	13 39		13 43		13 59	13 45	13 49	13 55				14 00	14 09		14 13
London Blackfriars ■3 ⊖	a						13 37						13 52						14 07			
City Thameslink ■3	a						13 40						13 56						14 10			
Farringdon ■3 ⊖	a						13 44						14 00						14 14			
St Pancras International ■15 ⊖	a						13 47						14 03						14 17			
Clapham Junction ■10	a		13 34	13 20	13 25	13 37			13 33		13 37					13 50	13 55	14 07			14 02	
London Victoria ■15 ⊖	a			13 28	13 32				13 40		13 44					13 57	14 02				14 09	

		SN ◇■ 🍴	SN	SN ◇■	FC ■	SN ■	SN ■	SN ◇■	SN ■	SN	FC ■	SN	SN ◇■ 🍴	SN ■	SN ◇■	SN	FC ■	SN ■	SN ■	SN ◇■	SN ■	SN	FC ■
Purley ■4	d		13 51			14 02				14 08		14 15		14 19		14 21			14 32			14 38	
Purley Oaks	d		13 54							14 11						14 24						14 41	
South Croydon ■4	d		13 57				14 07			14 14						14 27						14 44	
East Croydon	d	13 56	14 00	14 00	14 02	14 08	14 10	14 11	14 14	14 17	14 17	14 21	14 24	14 25	14 28	14 30	14 32	14 33	14 37	14 41	14 44	14 47	14 47
Norwood Junction ■2	d		14 05			14 13						14 25		14 30		14 35			14 43				
London Bridge ■4 ⊖	a		14 29		14 15	14 25					14 30	14 39		14 43		14 59	14 45	14 49	14 55				15 00
London Blackfriars ■3 ⊖	a				14 22						14 37						14 52						15 07
City Thameslink ■3	a				14 26						14 40						14 56						15 10
Farringdon ■3 ⊖	a				14 30						14 44						15 00						15 14
St Pancras International ■15 ⊖	a				14 33						14 47						15 03						15 17
Clapham Junction ■10	a	14 05		14 09			14 34	14 20	14 25	14 37			14 33		14 37					14 50	14 55	15 07	
London Victoria ■15 ⊖	a	14 12		14 16				14 27	14 32				14 40		14 44					14 57	15 02	15 16	

		SN	SN ◇■	SN ■	SN ◇■ 🍴	SN	SN ◇■	FC ■	SN ■	SN ■	SN ◇■	SN ■	SN	FC ■	SN	SN ◇■ 🍴	SN ■	SN ◇■	SN	FC ■	SN ■	SN ■	SN ◇■ 🍴
Purley ■4	d	14 45		14 49		14 51			15 02				15 08		15 15		15 19		15 21			15 32	
Purley Oaks	d					14 54							15 11						15 24				
South Croydon ■4	d					14 57				15 07			15 14						15 27				
East Croydon	d	14 51	14 53	14 55	14 56	15 00	15 00	15 02	15 07	15 10	15 11	15 14	15 17	15 17	15 21	15 24	15 25	15 28	15 30	15 32	15 33	15 37	15 41
Norwood Junction ■2	d	14 55		15 00		15 05			15 13						15 25		15 30		15 35			15 43	
London Bridge ■4 ⊖	a	15 09		15 13		15 29		15 15	15 25					15 30	15 39		15 43		15 59	15 45	15 49	15 55	
London Blackfriars ■3 ⊖	a							15 22						15 37						15 52			
City Thameslink ■3	a							15 26						15 40						15 56			
Farringdon ■3 ⊖	a							15 30						15 44						16 00			
St Pancras International ■15 ⊖	a							15 33						15 47						16 03			
Clapham Junction ■10	a		15 02		15 05		15 09			15 34	15 20	15 25	15 37			15 33		15 37					15 50
London Victoria ■15 ⊖	a		15 09		15 12		15 20				15 27	15 32	15 46			15 40		15 44					15 57

Purley and East Croydon - London

COMPLETE SERVICE

	SN 1	SN	FC 1	SN	SN ◇1	SN 1	SN ◇1 ⊥	SN	SN ◇1 ⊥	FC 1	SN 1	SN 1	SN ◇1 ⊥	SN 1	SN	FC 1	SN	SN 1	SN ◇1 ⊥	FC 1	SN
Purley 4 d		15 38		15 45		15 49		15 51			16 02				16 08		16 15	16 18			16 21
Purley Oaks d		15 41						15 54							16 11						16 24
South Croydon 4 d		15 44						15 57				16 07			16 14						16 27
East Croydon ⇌ d	15 44	15 47	15 47	15 51	15 53	15 55	15 56	16 00	16 00	16 02	16 07	16 10	16 11	16 14	16 17	16 17	16 21	16 24	16 26	16 28	16 30
Norwood Junction 2 d				15 55		16 00		16 05			16 13						16 25	16 28			16 35
London Bridge 4 ⊖ a			16 00	16 09		16 13		16 29		16 15	16 25						16 39	16 43			17 00
London Blackfriars 3 ⊖ a			16 07							16 25						16 47				16 55	
City Thameslink 3 a			16 10							16 28						16 54				16 58	
Farringdon 3 ⊖ a			16 13							16 31						16 57				17 01	
St Pancras International 15 ⊖ a			16 17							16 35						17 01				17 05	
Clapham Junction 10 a	15 55	16 07			16 02		16 05		16 09			16 34	16 20	16 25	16 37				16 35		
London Victoria 15 ⊖ a	16 05	16 16			16 09		16 12		16 20				16 27	16 35	16 46				16 42		

	SN ◇1 ⊥	SN 1	SN 1	SN ◇1 ⊥	SN 1	SN	FC 1	SN	SN ◇1	SN 1	SN 1 ⊥	FC 1	SN	SN ◇1	SN 1	FC 1	SN 1	SN ◇1 ⊥	SN 1	SN	SN	FC 1
Purley 4 d			16 34			16 38		16 45		16 49			16 51		17 02					17b08	17 15	
Purley Oaks d						16 41							16 54							17 11		
South Croydon 4 d						16 44							16 57				17 07			17 14		
East Croydon ⇌ d	16 30	16 33	16 40	16 41	16 44	16 47	16 47	16 51	16 53	16 55	16 56	16 57	17 00	17 01	17 07	17 09	17 10	17 12	17 14	17 17	17 21	17 23
Norwood Junction 2 d			16 45					16 55		16 59			17 05		17 12						17 25	
London Bridge 4 ⊖ a		16 47	16 57					17 08		17 14			17 30		17 26	17 27					17 37	
London Blackfriars 3 ⊖ a							17 19					17 25				17 35						17 49
City Thameslink 3 a							17 24					17 28				17 38						17 54
Farringdon 3 ⊖ a							17 27					17 31				17 41						17 57
St Pancras International 15 ⊖ a							17 31					17 35				17 45						18 01
Clapham Junction 10 a	16 39			16 50	16 55	17 07			17 02		17 05			17 10			17 34	17 21	17 25	17 37		
London Victoria 15 ⊖ a	16 46			16 58	17 05	17 16			17 09		17 12			17 17				17 28	17 32	17 48		

	SN 1	SN 1 ⊥	SN	SN ◇1 ⊥	SN 1	SN 1	SN ◇1 ⊥	SN 1	SN 1	SN	FC 1	SN	SN 1	SN	SN 1 ⊥	FC 1	SN ◇1 ⊥	SN	SN 1	SN 1	SN ◇1 ⊥
Purley 4 d	17 19		17 21							17 38		17 45		17 49				17 59			
Purley Oaks d			17 24							17 41								18 02			
South Croydon 4 d			17 27							17 44								18 05			
East Croydon ⇌ d	17 25	17 26	17 30	17 30	17 36	17 38	17 41	17 41	17 44	17 47	17 47	17 51	17 53	17 55	17 56	17 58	18 02	18 08	18 08	18 10	18 12
Norwood Junction 2 d	17 31		17 35					17 45				17 55		17 59				18 12			
London Bridge 4 ⊖ a	17 45		17 59		17 52			17 58			18 13	18 09		18 13				18 26			
London Blackfriars 3 ⊖ a											18 21					18 25					
City Thameslink 3 a											18 24					18 28					
Farringdon 3 ⊖ a											18 27					18 31					
St Pancras International 15 ⊖ a											18 31					18 35					
Clapham Junction 10 a		17 35		17 39		17 47	17 50		17 55	18 07			18 02		18 05		18 13		18 18	18 34	18 21
London Victoria 15 ⊖ a		17 42		17 46		17 54	17 58		18 02	18 16			18 09		18 12		18 20		18 26		18 29

	SN 1	SN	FC 1	SN	SN 1 ⊥	SN 1	SN	SN ◇1 ⊥	FC 1	SN 1	SN 1	SN ◇1 ⊥	SN 1	SN	FC 1	SN 1	SN 1	SN 1	SN 1	SN	SN ◇1	FC 1
Purley 4 d		18 08		18 15		18 19	18 21							18 37			18 49			18 51		
Purley Oaks d		18 11					18 24							18 40						18 54		
South Croydon 4 d		18 14					18 27							18 44						18 57		
East Croydon ⇌ d	18 14	18 17	18 17	18 21	18 25	18 26	18 30	18 30	18 33	18 36	18 40	18 43	18 44	18 47	18 47	18 53	18 55	18 57	18 57	19 00	19 00	19 02
Norwood Junction 2 d				18 29			18 35												19 02	19 05		
London Bridge 4 ⊖ a				18 41			18 59		18 46	18 50					19 00				19 15	19 29		19 15
London Blackfriars 3 ⊖ a			18 51						18 55						19 09							19 22
City Thameslink 3 a			18 54						18 58						19 12							19 26
Farringdon 3 ⊖ a			18 57						19 01						19 15							19 30
St Pancras International 15 ⊖ a			19 01						19 05						19 19							19 33
Clapham Junction 10 a	18 25	18 39			18 34	18 37		18 40			18 49	18 52	18 55	19 08		19 02	19 05	19 08			19 11	
London Victoria 15 ⊖ a	18 32	18 46			18 41	18 44		18 47			18 56	18 59	19 05	19 15		19 09	19 13	19 15			19 18	

b arr. 1656

Purley and East Croydon - London

COMPLETE SERVICE

	SN 1	SN 1	SN ◇1 ⊥	SN 1	SN	FC 1	SN ◇1	SN 1	SN ◇1	SN	FC 1	SN 1	SN 1	SN ◇1	SN 1	SN	FC 1	SN ◇1	SN 1	SN	SN 1	FC 1
Purley 4 d					19 08			19 19		19 21						19 38			19 53	19 51		
Purley Oaks d					19 11					19 24						19 41				19 54		
South Croydon 4 d					19 14					19 27						19 44				19 57		
East Croydon ⇌ d	19 09	19 10	19 12	19 14	19 17	19 17	19 24	19 25	19 29	19 30	19 32	19 33	19 40	19 43	19 44	19 47	19 47	19 54	19 59	20 00	20 01	20 02
Norwood Junction 2 d	19 13									19 35										20 05		
London Bridge 4 ⊖ a	19 25					19 30				19 59	19 45	19 49					20 00			20 29		20 15
London Blackfriars 3 ⊖ a						19 37					19 52						20 07					20 22
City Thameslink 3 a						19 40					19 56						20 10					20 26
Farringdon 3 ⊖ a						19 44					20 00						20 14					20 30
St Pancras International 15 ⊖ a						19 47					20 03						20 17					20 33
Clapham Junction 10 a		19 34	19 21	19 25	19 37		19 33	19 36	19 40				19 49	19 52	19 55	20 07		20 03	20 08		20 11	
London Victoria 15 ⊖ a			19 29	19 32	19 48		19 40	19 43	19 47				19 56	19 59	20 02			20 10	20 15		20 20	

	SN 1	SN ◇1	SN 1	SN	FC 1	SN ◇1	SN 1	SN ◇1	SN	FC 1	SN 1	SN ◇1	SN 1	SN	FC 1	SN 1	SN ◇1	SN 1	SN	SN ◇1	FC 1
Purley 4 d				20 08			20 18		20 22					20 38				20 49	20 51		
Purley Oaks d				20 11					20 25					20 41					20 54		
South Croydon 4 d				20 14					20 28					20 44					20 57		
East Croydon ⇌ d	20 07	20 11	20 14	20 17	20 17	20 24	20 26	20 30	20 31	20 32	20 33	20 41	20 44	20 47	20 47	20 54	20 54	20 57	21 00	21 00	21 02
Norwood Junction 2 d									20 35										21 05		
London Bridge 4 ⊖ a	20 21				20 30				20 59	20 45	20 48				21 00	21 09			21 29		21 15
London Blackfriars 3 ⊖ a					20 37					20 52					21 07						21 22
City Thameslink 3 a					20 40					20 56					21 10						21 26
Farringdon 3 ⊖ a					20 44					21 00					21 14						21 30
St Pancras International 5 ⊖ a					20 47					21 03					21 17						21 33
Clapham Junction 10 a		20 20	20 25	20 37		20 33	20 37	20 40				20 50	20 55	21 07			21 03	21 07		21 11	
London Victoria 15 ⊖ a		20 28	20 32	20 46		20 40	20 44	20 50				20 58	21 05	21 18			21 10	21 15		21 20	

	SN ◇1	SN 1	SN	FC 1	SN ◇1	SN 1	SN	SN ◇1	FC 1	SN 1	SN ◇1	SN 1	SN	SN ◇1	SN 1	SN	SN ◇1	FC 1	SN ◇1	SN 1	SN	SN 1
Purley 4 d			21 08			21 19	21 21						21 38		21 49	21 51					22 08	
Purley Oaks d			21 11				21 24						21 41			21 54					22 11	
South Croydon 4 d			21 14				21 27						21 44			21 57					22 14	
East Croydon ⇌ d	21 10	21 14	21 17	21 17	21 24	21 26	21 30	21 30	21 32	21 33	21 42	21 44	21 47	21 54	21 57	22 00	22 00	22 02	22 10	22 14	22 17	22 17
Norwood Junction 2 d							21 35									22 05						
London Bridge 4 ⊖ a				21 30			21 59		21 45	21 49						22 29		22 17				22 33
London Blackfriars 3 ⊖ a				21 37					21 52													
City Thameslink 3 a				21 40					21 56													
Farringdon 3 ⊖ a				21 44					22 00													
St Pancras International 15 ⊖ a				21 47					22 03													
Clapham Junction 10 a	21 19	21 25	21 37		21 33	21 37		21 40			21 51	21 55	22 07	22 03	22 07		22 10		22 19	22 25	22 37	
London Victoria 15 ⊖ a	21 27	21 35	21 46		21 43	21 45		21 48			21 58	22 05	22 16	22 11	22 14		22 20		22 27	22 35	22 48	

	SN ◇1	SN 1	SN	SN ◇1	FC 1	SN 1	SN ◇1	SN 1	SN	SN ◇1	SN 1	SN ◇1	SN	FC 1	SN 1	SN	SN 1	SN ◇1	FC 1	SN	SN 1
Purley 4 d		22 19	22 21						22 38		22 50		22 52			23 08				23 34	23 49
Purley Oaks d			22 24						22 41				22 55			23 11				23 37	
South Croydon 4 d			22 27						22 44				22 58			23 14				23 40	
East Croydon ⇌ d	22 24	22 25	22 30	22 30	22 32	22 34	22 40	22 44	22 47	22 54	22 56	23 00	23 01	23 02	23 14	23 17	23 20	23 30	23 32	23 43	23 58
Norwood Junction 2 d			22 35										23 06							23a47	
London Bridge 4 ⊖ a			22 59		22 47	22 49							23 30	23 17					23 47		
London Blackfriars 3 ⊖ a																					
City Thameslink 3 a																					
Farringdon 3 ⊖ a																					
St Pancras International 15 ⊖ a																					
Clapham Junction 10 a	22 33	22 37		22 40			22 49	22 55	23 07	23 03	23 06	23 10			23 25	23 37	23 32	23 42			00 11
London Victoria 15 ⊖ a	22 41	22 44		22 50			22 57	23 05	23 18	23 13	23 15	23 20			23 35	23 46	23 40	23 52			00 18

Table 175

Purley and East Croydon - London
COMPLETE SERVICE

		SN 1	FC 1	SN ◇1	FC 1	SN	SN 1	SN 1	FC 1	SN 1		FC 1	SN 1	FC 1	FC 1	FC 1	SN ◇1	SN 1	SN ◇1	FC 1		SN 1	SN	SN ◇1	SN
Purley 4	d	23p49		00 11			01 22	02 22		03 22			04 22				05 58					06 19	06 21		
Purley Oaks	d																						06 24		
South Croydon 4	d																						06 27		
East Croydon	⇌ d	23p58	00 04	00 17	00 36	00 49	01 28	02 28	02 47	03 28		03 47	04 28	04 47	05 17	05 42	06 07	06 10	06 11	06 17		06 25	06 30	06 41	06 43
Norwood Junction 2	d																					06 30	06 35		06 50
London Bridge 4	⊖ a		00 19		00 52				03 12			04 12		05 12	05 42	05 57				06 32		06 43	06 59		07 11
London Blackfriars 3	⊖ a																								
City Thameslink 3	a																								
Farringdon 3	⊖ a																								
St Pancras International 5	⊖ a																								
Clapham Junction 10	a	00 11		00 29		01 01	01 40	02 40		03 40			04 41				06 18	06 34	06 21					06 50	
London Victoria 15	⊖ a	00 18		00 37		01 08	01 49	02 49		03 49			04 49				06 26		06 30					06 57	

		SN	FC 1	SN ◇1	SN 1	SN		SN 1	SN 1	SN ◇1	SN 1	SN	FC 1	SN ◇1	SN 1	SN		SN ◇1	FC 1	SN 1	SN 1	SN ◇1	SN 1	SN	FC 1
Purley 4	d	06 38			06 49	06 51		07 02				07 08			07 19	07 21					07 34			07 38	
Purley Oaks	d	06 41				06 54						07 11				07 24								07 41	
South Croydon 4	d	06 44				06 57			07 07			07 14				07 27								07 44	
East Croydon	⇌ d	06 47	06 47	06 53	06 55	07 00		07 07	07 10	07 11	07 14	07 17	07 17	07 24	07 25	07 30		07 30	07 32	07 33	07 39	07 41	07 44	07 47	07 47
Norwood Junction 2	d				07 00	07 05		07 13							07 30	07 35					07 45				
London Bridge 4	⊖ a		07 02		07 13	07 29		07 25					07 32		07 43	07 59			07 47	07 49	07 57				08 02
London Blackfriars 3	⊖ a																								
City Thameslink 3	a																								
Farringdon 3	⊖ a																								
St Pancras International 15	⊖ a																								
Clapham Junction 10	a	07 07		07 02					07 34	07 20	07 25	07 37		07 33				07 39				07 50	07 55	08 07	
London Victoria 15	⊖ a	07 16		07 09						07 27	07 32	07 46		07 40				07 46				07 57	08 02	08 16	

		SN		SN ◇1	SN 1	SN ◇1	SN	SN ◇1	FC 1	SN 1	SN 1	SN ◇1		SN 1	SN	FC 1	SN	SN ◇1 H	SN 1	SN ◇1	SN	FC 1		SN 1	SN 1
Purley 4	d	07 45			07 49		07 51			08 02					08 08		08 15		08 19		08 21				08 32
Purley Oaks	d						07 54								08 11						08 24				
South Croydon 4	d						07 57				08 07				08 14						08 27				
East Croydon	⇌ d	07 51		07 53	07 55	07 56	08 00	08 00	08 02	08 07	08 10	08 11		08 14	08 17	08 17	08 21	08 24	08 25	08 28	08 30	08 32		08 33	08 37
Norwood Junction 2	d	07 55			08 00		08 05			08 13							08 25		08 30		08 35				08 43
London Bridge 4	⊖ a	08 09			08 13		08 29		08 17	08 25						08 32	08 39		08 43		08 59	08 47		08 49	08 55
London Blackfriars 3	⊖ a																								
City Thameslink 3	a																								
Farringdon 3	⊖ a																								
St Pancras International 15	⊖ a																								
Clapham Junction 10	a			08 02		08 05		08 09			08 34	08 20		08 25	08 37			08 33		08 37					
London Victoria 15	⊖ a			08 09		08 12		08 16				08 27		08 32	08 46			08 40		08 44					

		SN ◇1	SN 1	SN	FC 1	SN	SN ◇1	SN 1		SN ◇1 H	SN	SN ◇1	FC 1	SN 1	SN 1	SN ◇1	SN 1	SN		FC 1	SN	SN ◇1 H	SN 1	SN ◇1 H	SN
Purley 4	d			08 38		08 45		08 49			08 51			09 02				09 08			09 15		09 19		09 21
Purley Oaks	d			08 41							08 54							09 11							09 24
South Croydon 4	d			08 44							08 57				09 07			09 14							09 27
East Croydon	⇌ d	08 41	08 44	08 47	08 47	08 51	08 53	08 55		08 56	09 00	09 00	09 02	09 07	09 10	09 11	09 14	09 17		09 17	09 21	09 24	09 25	09 28	09 30
Norwood Junction 2	d					08 55		09 00			09 05			09 13							09 25		09 30		09 35
London Bridge 4	⊖ a				09 02	09 09		09 13			09 29		09 17	09 25						09 32	09 39		09 43		09 59
London Blackfriars 3	⊖ a																								
City Thameslink 3	a																								
Farringdon 3	⊖ a																								
St Pancras International 5	⊖ a																								
Clapham Junction 10	a	08 50	08 55	09 07			09 02			09 05		09 09			09 34	09 20	09 25	09 37				09 33		09 37	
London Victoria 15	⊖ a	08 57	09 02	09 16			09 09			09 12		09 16				09 27	09 32	09 46				09 40		09 44	

Table 175

Saturdays

Purley and East Croydon - London
COMPLETE SERVICE

		FC 1	SN 1	SN 1		SN ◇1	SN 1	SN	FC 1	SN	SN ◇1	SN 1	SN ◇1 H	SN		SN ◇1	FC 1	SN 1	SN 1	SN ◇1	SN 1	SN	FC 1	SN	
Purley 4	d			09 32				09 38		09 45		09 49		09 51				10 02				10 08		10 15	
Purley Oaks	d							09 41						09 54								10 11			
South Croydon 4	d							09 44						09 57					10 07			10 14			
East Croydon	⇌ d	09 32	09 33	09 37		09 42	09 44	09 47	09 47	09 51	09 53	09 55	09 56	10 00		10 00	10 02	10 07	10 10	10 11	10 14	10 17	10 17	10 21	
Norwood Junction 2	d			09 43						09 55		10 00		10 05				10 13						10 25	
London Bridge 4	⊖ a	09 47	09 49	09 55					10 02	10 09		10 13		10 29			10 17	10 25					10 32	10 39	
London Blackfriars 3	⊖ a																								
City Thameslink 3	a																								
Farringdon 3	⊖ a																								
St Pancras International 15	⊖ a																								
Clapham Junction 10	a					09 51	09 55	10 07			10 02		10 05			10 09			10 34	10 20	10 25	10 37			
London Victoria 15	⊖ a					09 58	10 02	10 16			10 09		10 12			10 16				10 27	10 32	10 46			

		SN ◇1 H	SN 1	SN ◇1 H	SN	FC 1	SN 1	SN 1	SN ◇1	SN ◇1		SN 1	SN	FC 1	SN	SN ◇1	SN 1	SN ◇1 H	SN	SN ◇1		FC 1	SN 1	SN 1	SN ◇1
Purley 4	d		10 19		10 21			10 32					10 38		10 45		10 49		10 51				11 02		
Purley Oaks	d				10 24								10 41						10 54						
South Croydon 4	d				10 27								10 44						10 57					11 07	
East Croydon	⇌ d	10 24	10 25	10 28	10 30	10 32	10 33	10 37	10 38	10 42		10 44	10 47	10 47	10 51	10 53	10 55	10 56	11 00	11 00		11 02	11 07	11 10	11 11
Norwood Junction 2	d		10 30		10 35			10 43							10 55		11 00		11 05				11 13		
London Bridge 4	⊖ a		10 43		10 59	10 47	10 49	10 55						11 02	11 09		11 13		11 29			11 17	11 25		
London Blackfriars 3	⊖ a																								
City Thameslink 3	a																								
Farringdon 3	⊖ a																								
St Pancras International 15	⊖ a																								
Clapham Junction 10	a	10 33		10 37					10 47	10 51		10 55	11 07			11 02		11 05		11 09				11 34	11 20
London Victoria 15	⊖ a	10 40		10 44					10 56	10 59		11 02	11 16			11 09		11 12		11 16					11 27

		SN 1	SN	FC 1	SN	SN ◇1 H		SN 1	SN ◇1 H	SN	FC 1	SN 1	SN 1	SN ◇1	SN 1	SN		FC 1	SN	SN ◇1	SN 1	SN ◇1 H	SN	SN ◇1	FC 1
Purley 4	d		11 08		11 15			11 19		11 21			11 32			11 38			11 45		11 49		11 51		
Purley Oaks	d		11 11							11 24						11 41							11 54		
South Croydon 4	d		11 14							11 27						11 44							11 57		
East Croydon	⇌ d	11 14	11 17	11 17	11 21	11 24		11 25	11 28	11 30	11 32	11 33	11 37	11 41	11 44	11 47		11 47	11 51	11 53	11 55	11 56	12 00	12 00	12 02
Norwood Junction 2	d				11 25			11 30		11 35			11 43						11 55		12 00		12 05		
London Bridge 4	⊖ a			11 32	11 39			11 43		11 59	11 47	11 49	11 55					12 02	12 09		12 13		12 29		12 17
London Blackfriars 3	⊖ a																								
City Thameslink 3	a																								
Farringdon 3	⊖ a																								
St Pancras International 15	⊖ a																								
Clapham Junction 10	a	11 25	11 37			11 33			11 37					11 50	11 55	12 07				12 02		12 05		12 09	
London Victoria 15	⊖ a	11 32	11 46			11 40			11 44					11 57	12 02	12 16				12 09		12 12		12 16	

		SN 1		SN 1	SN ◇1	SN 1	SN	FC 1	SN	SN ◇1 H	SN 1	SN ◇1 H		SN	FC 1	SN 1	SN 1	SN ◇1	SN 1	SN	FC 1	SN		SN ◇1	SN 1
Purley 4	d	12 02					12 08		12 15		12 19			12 21			12 32			12 38		12 45			12 49
Purley Oaks	d						12 11							12 24						12 41					
South Croydon 4	d			12 07			12 14							12 27						12 44					
East Croydon	⇌ d	12 07		12 10	12 11	12 14	12 17	12 17	12 21	12 24	12 25	12 28		12 30	12 32	12 33	12 37	12 41	12 44	12 47	12 47	12 51		12 53	12 55
Norwood Junction 2	d	12 13							12 25		12 30			12 35			12 43					12 55			13 00
London Bridge 4	⊖ a	12 25						12 32	12 39		12 43			12 59	12 47	12 49	12 55				13 02	13 09			13 13
London Blackfriars 3	⊖ a																								
City Thameslink 3	a																								
Farringdon 3	⊖ a																								
St Pancras International 15	⊖ a																								
Clapham Junction 10	a			12 34	12 20	12 25	12 37			12 33		12 37						12 50	12 55	13 07				13 02	
London Victoria 15	⊖ a				12 27	12 32	12 46			12 40		12 44						12 57	13 02	13 16				13 09	

Table 175

Saturdays

Purley and East Croydon - London

COMPLETE SERVICE

	SN ◇1 ✠	SN	SN ◇1	FC 1	SN 1	SN 1	SN ◇1	SN 1	SN	FC 1	SN	SN ◇1 ✠	SN 1	SN ◇1 ✠	SN	FC 1	SN 1	SN 1	SN ◇1	SN 1	SN	FC 1
Purley 4 d		12 51			13 02				13 08		13 15		13 19		13 21			13 32			13 38	
Purley Oaks d		12 54							13 11						13 24						13 41	
South Croydon 4 d		12 57				13 07			13 14						13 27						13 44	
East Croydon ⇌ d	12 56	13 00	13 00	13 02	13 07	13 10	13 11	13 14	13 17	13 17	13 21	13 24	13 25	13 28	13 30	13 32	13 33	13 37	13 41	13 44	13 47	13 47
Norwood Junction 2 d		13 05			13 13						13 25		13 30		13 35			13 43				
London Bridge 4 ⊖ a		13 29		13 17	13 25					13 32	13 39		13 43		13 59	13 47	13 49	13 55				14 02
London Blackfriars 3 ⊖ a																						
City Thameslink 3 a																						
Farringdon 3 ⊖ a																						
St Pancras International 15 ⊖ a																						
Clapham Junction 10 a	13 05		13 09			13 34	13 20	13 25	13 37			13 33		13 37					13 50	13 55	14 07	
London Victoria 15 ⊖ a	13 12		13 16				13 27	13 32	13 46			13 40		13 44					13 57	14 02	14 16	

	SN	SN ◇1	SN 1	SN ◇1 ✠	SN	SN ◇1	FC 1	SN 1	SN 1	SN ◇1	SN 1	SN	FC 1	SN	SN ◇1 ✠	SN 1	SN ◇1 ✠	SN	FC 1	SN 1	SN 1
Purley 4 d	13 45		13 49		13 51			14 02				14 08		14 15		14 19		14 21			14 32
Purley Oaks d					13 54							14 11						14 24			
South Croydon 4 d					13 57				14 07			14 14						14 27			
East Croydon ⇌ d	13 51	13 53	13 55	13 56	14 00	14 00	14 02	14 07	14 10	14 11	14 14	14 17	14 17	14 21	14 24	14 25	14 28	14 30	14 32	14 33	14 37
Norwood Junction 2 d	13 55		14 00		14 05			14 13						14 25		14 30		14 35			14 43
London Bridge 4 ⊖ a	14 09		14 13		14 29		14 17	14 25					14 32	14 39		14 43		14 59	14 47	14 49	14 55
London Blackfriars 3 ⊖ a																					
City Thameslink 3 a																					
Farringdon 3 ⊖ a																					
St Pancras International 15 ⊖ a																					
Clapham Junction 10 a		14 02		14 05		14 09			14 34	14 20	14 25	14 37			14 33		14 37				
London Victoria 15 ⊖ a		14 09		14 12		14 16				14 27	14 32	14 46			14 40		14 44				

	SN ◇1	SN 1	SN	FC 1	SN	SN ◇1	SN 1	SN ◇1 ✠	SN	SN ◇1	FC 1	SN 1	SN 1	SN ◇1	SN 1	SN	FC 1	SN	SN ◇1 ✠	SN 1	SN ◇1 ✠	SN
Purley 4 d			14 38		14 45		14 49		14 51			15 02				15 08		15 15		15 19		15 21
Purley Oaks d			14 41						14 54							15 11						15 24
South Croydon 4 d			14 44						14 57				15 07			15 14						15 27
East Croydon ⇌ d	14 41	14 44	14 47	14 47	14 51	14 53	14 55	14 56	15 00	15 00	15 02	15 07	15 10	15 11	15 14	15 17	15 17	15 21	15 24	15 25	15 28	15 30
Norwood Junction 2 d					14 55		15 00		15 05			15 13						15 25		15 30		15 35
London Bridge 4 ⊖ a				15 02	15 09		15 13		15 29		15 17	15 25					15 32	15 39		15 43		15 59
London Blackfriars 3 ⊖ a																						
City Thameslink 3 a																						
Farringdon 3 ⊖ a																						
St Pancras International 15 ⊖ a																						
Clapham Junction 10 a	14 50	14 55	15 07			15 02		15 05		15 09			15 34	15 20	15 25	15 37			15 33		15 37	
London Victoria 15 ⊖ a	14 57	15 02	15 16			15 09		15 12		15 16				15 27	15 32	15 46			15 40		15 44	

	FC 1	SN 1	SN 1	SN ◇1	SN 1	SN	FC 1	SN	SN ◇1	SN 1	SN ◇1 ✠	SN	SN ◇1	FC 1	SN 1	SN 1	SN ◇1	SN 1	SN	FC 1	SN	SN ◇1 ✠
Purley 4 d			15 32			15 38		15 45		15 49		15 51			16 02				16 08		16 15	
Purley Oaks d						15 41						15 54							16 11			
South Croydon 4 d						15 44						15 57				16 07			16 14			
East Croydon ⇌ d	15 32	15 33	15 37	15 41	15 44	15 47	15 47	15 51	15 53	15 55	15 56	16 00	16 00	16 02	16 07	16 10	16 11	16 14	16 17	16 17	16 21	16 24
Norwood Junction 2 d			15 43					15 55		16 00		16 05			16 13						16 25	
London Bridge 4 ⊖ a	15 47	15 49	15 55				16 02	16 09		16 13		16 29		16 17	16 25					16 32	16 39	
London Blackfriars 3 ⊖ a																						
City Thameslink 3 a																						
Farringdon 3 ⊖ a																						
St Pancras International 15 ⊖ a																						
Clapham Junction 10 a				15 50	15 55	16 07			16 02		16 05		16 09			16 34	16 20	16 25	16 37			16 33
London Victoria 15 ⊖ a				15 57	16 02	16 16			16 09		16 12		16 16				16 27	16 32	16 46			16 40

Table 175

Saturdays

Purley and East Croydon - London

COMPLETE SERVICE

	SN 1	SN ◇1 ✠	SN	FC 1	SN 1	SN 1	SN ◇1	SN 1	SN	FC 1	SN	SN ◇1	SN 1	SN ◇1 ✠	SN	SN ◇1	FC 1	SN 1	SN 1	SN ◇1	SN 1
Purley 4 d	16 19		16 21			16 32			16 38		16 45		16 49		16 51			17 02			
Purley Oaks d			16 24						16 41						16 54						
South Croydon 4 d			16 27						16 44						16 57				17 07		
East Croydon ⇌ d	16 25	16 28	16 30	16 32	16 33	16 37	16 41	16 44	16 47	16 47	16 51	16 53	16 55	16 56	17 00	17 00	17 02	17 07	17 10	17 11	17 14
Norwood Junction 2 d	16 30		16 35			16 43					16 55		17 00		17 05			17 13			
London Bridge 4 ⊖ a	16 43		16 59	16 47	16 49	16 55				17 02	17 09		17 13		17 30		17 17	17 25			
London Blackfriars 3 ⊖ a																					
City Thameslink 3 a																					
Farringdon 3 ⊖ a																					
St Pancras International 15 ⊖ a																					
Clapham Junction 10 a		16 37					16 50	16 55	17 07			17 02		17 05		17 09			17 34	17 20	17 25
London Victoria 15 ⊖ a		16 44					16 57	17 02	17 16			17 09		17 12		17 16				17 28	17 32

	SN	FC 1	SN	SN ◇1 ✠	SN 1	SN ◇1 ✠	SN	FC 1	SN 1	SN 1	SN ◇1	SN 1	SN	FC 1	SN	SN ◇1	SN 1	SN ◇1 ✠	SN	SN ◇1	FC 1	SN 1
Purley 4 d	17 08		17 15		17 19		17 21			17 32			17 38		17 45		17 49		17 51			18 02
Purley Oaks d	17 11						17 24						17 41						17 54			
South Croydon 4 d	17 14						17 27						17 44						17 57			
East Croydon ⇌ d	17 17	17 17	17 21	17 24	17 25	17 28	17 30	17 32	17 33	17 37	17 41	17 44	17 47	17 47	17 51	17 53	17 55	17 56	18 00	18 00	18 02	18 07
Norwood Junction 2 d			17 25		17 30		17 35			17 43					17 55		18 00		18 05			18 13
London Bridge 4 ⊖ a		17 32	17 39		17 43		17 59	17 47	17 49	17 55				18 02	18 09		18 13		18 29		18 17	18 25
London Blackfriars 3 ⊖ a																						
City Thameslink 3 a																						
Farringdon 3 ⊖ a																						
St Pancras International 15 ⊖ a																						
Clapham Junction 10 a	17 38			17 33		17 37					17 50	17 55	18 07			18 02		18 05		18 09		
London Victoria 15 ⊖ a	17 47			17 40		17 44					17 57	18 02	18 16			18 09		18 12		18 16		

	SN 1	SN ◇1	SN 1	SN	FC 1	SN	SN ◇1 ✠	SN 1	SN ◇1 ✠	SN	FC 1	SN 1	SN 1	SN ◇1	SN 1	SN	FC 1	SN	SN ◇1	SN 1	SN ◇1
Purley 4 d				18 08		18 15		18 19		18 21			18 32			18 38		18 45		18 49	
Purley Oaks d				18 11						18 24						18 41					
South Croydon 4 d	18 07			18 14						18 27						18 44					
East Croydon ⇌ d	18 10	18 11	18 14	18 17	18 17	18 21	18 24	18 25	18 28	18 30	18 32	18 33	18 37	18 41	18 44	18 47	18 47	18 51	18 53	18 55	18 56
Norwood Junction 2 d						18 25		18 30		18 35			18 43					18 55		19 00	
London Bridge 4 ⊖ a					18 32	18 39		18 43		18 59	18 47	18 49	18 55				19 02	19 09		19 13	
London Blackfriars 3 ⊖ a																					
City Thameslink 3 a																					
Farringdon 3 ⊖ a																					
St Pancras International 15 ⊖ a																					
Clapham Junction 10 a	18 34	18 20	18 25	18 37			18 33		18 37					18 50	18 55	19 07			19 02		19 05
London Victoria 15 ⊖ a		18 27	18 32	18 46			18 40		18 44					18 57	19 02	19 16			19 09		19 12

	SN	SN ◇1	FC 1	SN 1	SN 1	SN ◇1	SN 1	SN	FC 1	SN ◇1	SN 1	SN ◇1	SN	FC 1	SN 1	SN ◇1	SN 1	SN	FC 1	SN ◇1	SN ◇1	SN 1
Purley 4 d	18 51			19 02				19 08			19 19		19 21					19 38				19 49
Purley Oaks d	18 54							19 11					19 24					19 41				
South Croydon 4 d	18 57				19 07			19 14					19 27					19 44				
East Croydon ⇌ d	19 00	19 00	19 02	19 07	19 10	19 11	19 14	19 17	19 17	19 24	19 25	19 29	19 30	19 32	19 33	19 41	19 44	19 47	19 47	19 53	19 56	19 57
Norwood Junction 2 d	19 05			19 13									19 35									
London Bridge 4 ⊖ a	19 29		19 17	19 25					19 32				19 59	19 47	19 49				20 02			
London Blackfriars 3 ⊖ a																						
City Thameslink 3 a																						
Farringdon 3 ⊖ a																						
St Pancras International 15 ⊖ a																						
Clapham Junction 10 a		19 09			19 34	19 20	19 25	19 37		19 33	19 37	19 40				19 50	19 55	20 07		20 02	20 05	20 08
London Victoria 15 ⊖ a		19 16				19 27	19 32	19 46		19 40	19 44	19 47				19 57	20 02	20 16		20 09	20 12	20 15

Purley and East Croydon - London

COMPLETE SERVICE

		SN	SN 1	FC 1	SN ◇1	SN 1	SN	FC 1	SN ◇1	SN 1	SN	SN ◇1	FC 1	SN 1	SN ◇1	SN 1	SN	FC 1	SN ◇1	SN 1	SN	SN ◇1	FC 1
Purley 4	d	19 51					20 08			20 19	20 21						20 38			20 49	20 51		
Purley Oaks	d	19 54					20 11				20 24						20 41				20 54		
South Croydon 4	d	19 57					20 14				20 27						20 44				20 57		
East Croydon	d	20 00	20 00	20 02	20 11	20 14	20 17	20 17	20 24	20 26	20 30	20 30	20 32	20 33	20 41	20 44	20 47	20 47	20 54	20 56	21 00	21 00	21 02
Norwood Junction 2	d	20 05									20 35										21 05		
London Bridge 4	⊖ a	20 29		20 17				20 32			20 59		20 47	20 49				21 02			21 29		21 17
London Blackfriars 3	⊖ a																						
City Thameslink 3	a																						
Farringdon 3	⊖ a																						
St Pancras International 15	⊖ a																						
Clapham Junction 10	a		20 11		20 20	20 25	20 37		20 33	20 37		20 40			20 50	20 55	21 07		21 03	21 07		21 10	
London Victoria 15	⊖ a		20 20		20 27	20 32	20 46		20 40	20 44		20 50			20 57	21 02	21 16		21 10	21 14		21 17	

		SN ◇1	SN 1	SN	FC 1	SN ◇1	SN 1	SN	SN ◇1	FC 1	SN 1	SN ◇1	SN 1	SN	SN ◇1	SN 1	SN	SN ◇1	FC 1	SN ◇1	SN 1	SN
Purley 4	d			21 08			21 19	21 21						21 38		21 49	21 51					22 08
Purley Oaks	d			21 11				21 24						21 41			21 54					22 11
South Croydon 4	d			21 14				21 27						21 44			21 57					22 14
East Croydon	d	21 11	21 14	21 17	21 17	21 24	21 26	21 30	21 30	21 32	21 33	21 41	21 44	21 47	21 54	21 56	22 00	22 00	22 02	22 11	22 14	22 17
Norwood Junction 2	d							21 35									22 05					
London Bridge 4	⊖ a				21 32			21 59		21 47	21 49						22 29		22 17			
London Blackfriars 3	⊖ a																					
City Thameslink 3	a																					
Farringdon 3	⊖ a																					
St Pancras International 15	⊖ a																					
Clapham Junction 10	a	21 20	21 25	21 37		21 33	21 37		21 40			21 50	21 55	22 07	22 03	22 07		22 10		22 20	22 25	22 37
London Victoria 15	⊖ a	21 27	21 32	21 46		21 40	21 44		21 47			21 57	22 02	22 16	22 10	22 14		22 20		22 28	22 32	22 46

		SN ◇1	SN 1	SN	SN ◇1	FC 1	SN 1	SN ◇1	SN 1	SN	SN 1	SN ◇1	SN	FC 1	SN 1	SN	SN ◇1	FC 1	SN	SN 1
Purley 4	d		22 19	22 21						22 38	22 50		22 52			23 08			23 34	23 49
Purley Oaks	d			22 24						22 41			22 55			23 11			23 37	
South Croydon 4	d			22 27						22 44			22 58			23 14			23 40	
East Croydon	d	22 24	22 26	22 30	22 30	22 32	22 33	22 40	22 44	22 47	22 56	23 00	23 01	23 02	23 14	23 17	23 30	23 32	23 43	23 56
Norwood Junction 2	d			22 35									23 06						23a47	
London Bridge 4	⊖ a			22 59		22 47	22 49						23 30	23 17				23 47		
London Blackfriars 3	⊖ a																			
City Thameslink 3	a																			
Farringdon 3	⊖ a																			
St Pancras International 15	⊖ a																			
Clapham Junction 10	a	22 33	22 37		22 40			22 49	22 55	23 07	23 06	23 10			23 25	23 37	23 42			00 11
London Victoria 15	⊖ a	22 40	22 44		22 50			22 58	23 02	23 18	23 14	23 17			23 32	23 46	23 52			00 18

Sundays

		SN 1	FC 1	SN ◇1	FC 1	SN	SN 1	SN 1	SN 1	SN 1	SN 1	FC 1	SN 1	FC 1	SN	SN	FC 1	SN ◇1 B	SN ◇1 C	SN	SN	SN 1	FC 1 B	SN
Purley 4	d	23p49		00 11			01 37	02 33	03 33	04 33	05 22		05 56			06 38						07 20		
Purley Oaks	d															06 41								
South Croydon 4	d															06 44						07 24		
East Croydon	d	23p56	00 04	00 17	00 36	00 49	01 43	02 40	03 40	04 40	05 28	05 32	06 02	06 32	06 40	06 47	07 02	07 09	07 10	07 14	07 17	07 27	07 33	07 44
Norwood Junction 2	d											05 36		06 36		06 52					07 22			
London Bridge 4	⊖ a		00 19		00 52							05 59		06 59		07 18	07 16			07 49	07 48		07 46	08 19
London Blackfriars 3	⊖ a																							
City Thameslink 3	a																							
Farringdon 3	⊖ a																							
St Pancras International 15	⊖ a																							
Clapham Junction 10	a	00 11		00 28		01 02	01 53	02 52	03 52	04 52	05 48		06 14		07 00			07 18	07 24			07 40		
London Victoria 15	⊖ a	00 18		00 36		01 09	02 05	03 05	04 05	05 05	05 58		06 22		07 08			07 25	07 31			07 48		

B until 5 September

C from 12 September

Purley and East Croydon - London

COMPLETE SERVICE

		SN	SN 1 A	SN 1 B	SN ◇1 B	SN ◇1 A	FC 1 B	FC 1 A	SN ◇1 A ⌶	SN ◇1 B ⌶	SN	SN	SN ◇1 A	SN ◇1 B	SN 1	FC 1 B	FC 1 A	SN 1 A	SN ◇1 A	SN ◇1 B	SN	SN ◇1 A ⌶	SN
Purley 4	d	07 38	07 50	07 49								08 08	08 14	08 19				08 27					08 38
Purley Oaks	d	07 41										08 11											08 41
South Croydon 4	d	07 44										08 14											08 44
East Croydon	d	07 47	07 56	07 58	08 00	08 00	08 02	08 03	08 09	08 10	08 14	08 17	08 21	08 26	08 29	08 32	08 33	08 34	08 39	08 40	08 44	08 46	08 47
Norwood Junction 2	d	07 52										08 22						08 38					08 52
London Bridge 4	⊖ a	08 18					08 16	08 16			08 49	08 48				08 46	08 46	08 51			09 19		09 18
London Blackfriars 3	⊖ a																						
City Thameslink 3	a																						
Farringdon 3	⊖ a																						
St Pancras International 15	⊖ a																						
Clapham Junction 10	a		08 06	08 08	08 11	08 10			08 18	08 24			08 31	08 37	08 41				08 48	08 54		08 55	
London Victoria 15	⊖ a		08 13	08 16	08 18	08 17			08 25	08 31			08 39	08 46	08 48				08 55	09 01		09 02	

		SN 1 A	SN 1 B	SN ◇1 B	SN ◇1 A	FC 1 B	FC 1 A	SN ◇1 A ⌶	SN ◇1 B ⌶	SN ◇1 B ⌶	SN	SN	SN ◇1 A ⌶	SN ◇1 A	SN ◇1 B ⌶	SN 1	FC 1 B	FC 1 A	SN 1 A	SN ◇1 A	SN ◇1 B	SN
Purley 4	d	08 50	08 49									09 08		09 14	09 19				09 27			
Purley Oaks	d											09 11										
South Croydon 4	d											09 14										
East Croydon	d	08 56	08 58	09 00	09 00	09 02	09 03	09 09	09 10	09 13	09 14	09 17	09 17	09 21	09 25	09 29	09 32	09 33	09 34	09 39	09 40	09 44
Norwood Junction 2	d											09 22							09 38			
London Bridge 4	⊖ a					09 16	09 16				09 49	09 48					09 46	09 46	09 51			10 19
London Blackfriars 3	⊖ a																					
City Thameslink 3	a																					
Farringdon 3	⊖ a																					
St Pancras International 15	⊖ a																					
Clapham Junction 10	a	09 06	09 08	09 11	09 10			09 18	09 24	09 27			09 26	09 31	09 37	09 41				09 48	09 54	
London Victoria 15	⊖ a	09 13	09 16	09 18	09 17			09 25	09 31	09 35			09 33	09 39	09 46	09 48				09 55	10 01	

		SN ◇1 A ⌶	SN	SN 1 A	SN 1 B	SN ◇1 B	SN ◇1 A	FC 1 B	FC 1 A	SN ◇1 A ⌶	SN ◇1 B ⌶	SN ◇1 B ⌶	SN	SN	SN ◇1 A ⌶	SN ◇1 A	SN ◇1 B ⌶	SN 1	FC 1 B	FC 1 A	SN 1 A	SN ◇1 A	SN ◇1 B
Purley 4	d		09 38	09 50	09 49									10 08		10 14	10 19				10 27		
Purley Oaks	d		09 41											10 11									
South Croydon 4	d		09 44											10 14									
East Croydon	d	09 46	09 47	09 56	09 58	10 00	10 00	10 02	10 03	10 09	10 10	10 13	10 14	10 17	10 17	10 21	10 25	10 29	10 32	10 33	10 34	10 39	10 40
Norwood Junction 2	d		09 52											10 22							10 38		
London Bridge 4	⊖ a		10 18					10 16	10 16				10 49	10 48					10 46	10 46	10 51		
London Blackfriars 3	⊖ a																						
City Thameslink 3	a																						
Farringdon 3	⊖ a																						
St Pancras International 5	⊖ a																						
Clapham Junction 10	a	09 55		10 06	10 08	10 11	10 10			10 18	10 24	10 27			10 26	10 31	10 37	10 41				10 48	10 54
London Victoria 15	⊖ a	10 02		10 13	10 16	10 18	10 17			10 25	10 31	10 35			10 33	10 39	10 46	10 48				10 55	11 01

		SN	SN ◇1 A ⌶	SN	SN 1 A	SN 1 B	SN ◇1 B	SN ◇1 A	FC 1 B	FC 1 A	SN ◇1 A ⌶	SN ◇1 B ⌶	SN ◇1 B ⌶	SN	SN	SN ◇1 A ⌶	SN ◇1 A ⌶	SN ◇1 B ⌶	SN 1	FC 1 B	FC 1 A	SN 1 A
Purley 4	d			10 38	10 50	10 49									11 08		11 14	11 19				11 27
Purley Oaks	d			10 41											11 11							
South Croydon 4	d			10 44											11 14							
East Croydon	d	10 44	10 46	10 47	10 56	10 58	11 00	11 00	11 02	11 03	11 09	11 10	11 13	11 14	11 17	11 17	11 21	11 25	11 29	11 32	11 33	11 34
Norwood Junction 2	d			10 52											11 22							11 38
London Bridge 4	⊖ a	11 19		11 18					11 16	11 16				11 49	11 48					11 46	11 46	11 51
London Blackfriars 3	⊖ a																					
City Thameslink 3	a																					
Farringdon 3	⊖ a																					
St Pancras International 15	⊖ a																					
Clapham Junction 10	a		10 55		11 06	11 08	11 11	11 10			11 18	11 24	11 27			11 26	11 31	11 37	11 41			
London Victoria 15	⊖ a		11 02		11 13	11 16	11 18	11 17			11 25	11 31	11 35			11 33	11 39	11 46	11 48			

A until 5 September

B from 12 September

Table 175

Sundays

Purley and East Croydon - London

COMPLETE SERVICE

		SN	SN	SN	SN	SN	SN	SN	SN	SN	FC	FC	SN	SN	SN	SN	SN	SN	SN	SN	SN	FC	FC
		◇1 A	◇1 B		◇1 A ⌶		1 A	1 B	◇1 B	◇1 A	1 B	1 A	◇1 A ⌶	◇1 B ⌶	◇1 B ⌶			◇1 A ⌶	◇1 A ⌶	◇1 B ⌶	1	1 B	1 A
Purley 4	d					11 38	11 50	11 49									12 08		12 14	12 19			
Purley Oaks	d					11 41											12 11						
South Croydon 4	d					11 44											12 14						
East Croydon	d	11 39	11 40	11 44	11 46	11 47	11 56	11 58	12 00	12 00	12 02	12 03	12 09	12 10	12 13	12 14	12 17	12 17	12 21	12 25	12 29	12 32	12 33
Norwood Junction 2	d					11 52											12 22						
London Bridge 4	a			12 19		12 18					12 16	12 16				12 49	12 48					12 46	12 46
London Blackfriars 3	a																						
City Thameslink 3	a																						
Farringdon 3	a																						
St Pancras International 15	a																						
Clapham Junction 10	a	11 48	11 54		11 55		12 06	12 08	12 11	12 10			12 18	12 24	12 27			12 26	12 31	12 37	12 41		
London Victoria 15	a	11 55	12 01		12 02		12 13	12 16	12 18	12 17			12 25	12 31	12 35			12 33	12 39	12 46	12 48		

		SN	SN	SN	SN	SN	SN	SN	SN	SN	SN	FC	FC	SN	SN	SN	SN	SN	SN	SN	SN	SN	FC
		1 A	◇1 A	◇1 B		◇1 A ⌶		1 A	1 B	◇1 B	◇1 A	1 B	1 A	◇1 A ⌶	◇1 B ⌶	◇1 B ⌶			◇1 A ⌶	◇1 A ⌶	◇1 B ⌶	1	1 B
Purley 4	d	12 27					12 38	12 50	12 49									13 08		13 14	13 19		
Purley Oaks	d						12 41											13 11					
South Croydon 4	d						12 44											13 14					
East Croydon	d	12 34	12 39	12 40	12 44	12 46	12 47	12 56	12 58	13 00	13 00	13 02	13 03	13 09	13 10	13 13	13 14	13 17	13 17	13 21	13 25	13 29	13 32
Norwood Junction 2	d	12 38					12 52											13 22					
London Bridge 4	a	12 51			13 19		13 18					13 16	13 16				13 49	13 48					13 46
London Blackfriars 3	a																						
City Thameslink 3	a																						
Farringdon 3	a																						
St Pancras International 15	a																						
Clapham Junction 10	a		12 48	12 54		12 55		13 06	13 08	13 11	13 10			13 18	13 24	13 27			13 26	13 31	13 37	13 41	
London Victoria 15	a		12 55	13 01		13 02		13 13	13 16	13 18	13 17			13 25	13 31	13 35			13 33	13 39	13 46	13 48	

		FC	SN	SN	SN	SN	SN	SN	SN	SN	SN	SN	FC	FC	SN	SN	SN	SN	SN	SN	SN	SN
		1 A	1 A	◇1 A	◇1 B		◇1 A ⌶		1 A	1 B	◇1 B	◇1 A	1 B	1 A	◇1 A ⌶	◇1 B ⌶	◇1 B ⌶			◇1 A ⌶	◇1 A ⌶	◇1 B ⌶
Purley 4	d		13 27					13 38	13 50	13 49									14 08		14 14	14 19
Purley Oaks	d							13 41											14 11			
South Croydon 4	d							13 44											14 14			
East Croydon	d	13 33	13 34	13 39	13 40	13 44	13 46	13 47	13 56	13 58	14 00	14 00	14 02	14 03	14 09	14 10	14 13	14 14	14 17	14 17	14 21	14 25
Norwood Junction 2	d		13 38					13 52											14 22			
London Bridge 4	a	13 46	13 51			14 19		14 18					14 16	14 16				14 49	14 48			
London Blackfriars 3	a																					
City Thameslink 3	a																					
Farringdon 3	a																					
St Pancras International 15	a																					
Clapham Junction 10	a			13 48	13 54		13 55		14 06	14 08	14 11	14 10			14 18	14 24	14 27			14 26	14 31	14 37
London Victoria 15	a			13 55	14 01		14 02		14 13	14 16	14 18	14 17			14 25	14 31	14 35			14 33	14 39	14 46

		SN	FC	FC	SN	SN	SN	SN	SN	SN	SN	SN	SN	SN	FC	FC	SN	SN	SN	SN	SN	SN	SN
		1	1 B	1 A	1 A	◇1 A	◇1 B		◇1 A ⌶		1 A	1 B	◇1 B	◇1 A	1 B	1 A	◇1 A ⌶	◇1 B ⌶	◇1 B ⌶			◇1 A ⌶	◇1 A ⌶
Purley 4	d				14 27					14 38	14 50	14 49									15 08		15 14
Purley Oaks	d									14 41											15 11		
South Croydon 4	d									14 44											15 14		
East Croydon	d	14 29	14 32	14 33	14 34	14 39	14 40	14 44	14 46	14 47	14 56	14 58	15 00	15 00	15 02	15 03	15 09	15 10	15 13	15 14	15 17	15 17	15 21
Norwood Junction 2	d				14 38					14 52											15 22		
London Bridge 4	a		14 46	14 46	14 51			15 19		15 18					15 16	15 16				15 49	15 48		
London Blackfriars 3	a																						
City Thameslink 3	a																						
Farringdon 3	a																						
St Pancras International 15	a																						
Clapham Junction 10	a	14 41				14 48	14 54		14 55		15 06	15 08	15 11	15 10			15 18	15 24	15 27			15 26	15 31
London Victoria 15	a	14 48				14 55	15 01		15 02		15 13	15 16	15 18	15 17			15 25	15 31	15 35			15 33	15 39

A until 5 September

B from 12 September

Table 175

Sundays

Purley and East Croydon - London

COMPLETE SERVICE

		SN	SN	FC	FC	SN	SN	SN	SN	SN	SN	SN	SN	SN	SN	FC	FC	SN	SN	SN	SN	SN
		◇1 A ⌶	1	1 A	1 B	1 B	◇1 B	◇1 A		◇1 B ⌶		1 B	1 A	◇1 A	◇1 B	1 A	1 B	◇1 B ⌶	◇1 A ⌶	◇1 A ⌶		
Purley 4	d	15 19				15 27					15 38	15 50	15 49									16 08
Purley Oaks	d										15 41											16 11
South Croydon 4	d										15 44											16 14
East Croydon	d	15 25	15 29	15 32	15 33	15 34	15 39	15 40	15 44	15 46	15 47	15 56	15 58	16 00	16 00	16 02	16 03	16 09	16 10	16 13	16 14	16 17
Norwood Junction 2	d					15 38					15 52											16 22
London Bridge 4	a			15 46	15 46	15 51			16 19		16 18					16 16	16 16				16 49	16 48
London Blackfriars 3	a																					
City Thameslink 3	a																					
Farringdon 3	a																					
St Pancras International 15	a																					
Clapham Junction 10	a	15 37	15 41				15 48	15 54		15 55		16 06	16 08	16 11	16 10			16 18	16 24	16 27		
London Victoria 15	a	15 46	15 48				15 55	16 01		16 02		16 13	16 16	16 18	16 17			16 25	16 31	16 35		

		SN	SN	SN	SN	FC	FC	SN	SN	SN	SN	SN	SN	SN	SN	SN	SN	FC	FC	SN	SN	SN	SN
		◇1 B ⌶	◇1 B ⌶	◇1 A ⌶	1	1 A	1 B	1 B	◇1 B	◇1 A		◇1 B ⌶		1 B	1 A	◇1 A	◇1 B	1 A	1 B	◇1 B ⌶	◇1 A ⌶	◇1 A ⌶	
Purley 4	d		16 14	16 19				16 27					16 38	16 50	16 49								
Purley Oaks	d												16 41										
South Croydon 4	d												16 44										
East Croydon	d	16 17	16 21	16 25	16 29	16 32	16 33	16 34	16 39	16 40	16 44	16 46	16 47	16 56	16 58	17 00	17 00	17 02	17 03	17 09	17 10	17 13	17 14
Norwood Junction 2	d							16 38					16 52										
London Bridge 4	a					16 46	16 46	16 51			17 19		17 18					17 16	17 16				17 49
London Blackfriars 3	a																						
City Thameslink 3	a																						
Farringdon 3	a																						
St Pancras International 15	a																						
Clapham Junction 10	a	16 26	16 31	16 37	16 41				16 48	16 54		16 55		17 06	17 08	17 11	17 10			17 18	17 24	17 27	
London Victoria 15	a	16 33	16 39	16 46	16 48				16 55	17 01		17 02		17 13	17 16	17 18	17 17			17 25	17 31	17 35	

		SN	SN	SN	SN	SN	FC	FC	SN	SN	SN	SN	SN	SN	SN	SN	SN	SN	FC	FC	SN	SN	SN
			◇1 B ⌶	◇1 B ⌶	◇1 A ⌶	1	1 A	1 B	1 B	◇1 B	◇1 A		◇1 B ⌶		1 B	1 A	◇1 A	◇1 B	1 A	1 B	◇1 B ⌶	◇1 A ⌶	◇1 A ⌶
Purley 4	d	17 08		17 14	17 19				17 27					17 38	17 50	17 49							
Purley Oaks	d	17 11												17 41									
South Croydon 4	d	17 14												17 44									
East Croydon	d	17 17	17 17	17 21	17 25	17 29	17 32	17 33	17 34	17 39	17 40	17 44	17 46	17 47	17 56	17 58	18 00	18 00	18 02	18 03	18 09	18 10	18 13
Norwood Junction 2	d	17 22							17 38					17 52									
London Bridge 4	a	17 48					17 46	17 46	17 51			18 19		18 18					18 16	18 16			
London Blackfriars 3	a																						
City Thameslink 3	a																						
Farringdon 3	a																						
St Pancras International 15	a																						
Clapham Junction 10	a		17 26	17 31	17 37	17 41				17 48	17 54		17 55		18 06	18 08	18 11	18 10			18 18	18 24	18 27
London Victoria 15	a		17 33	17 39	17 46	17 48				17 55	18 01		18 02		18 13	18 16	18 18	18 17			18 25	18 31	18 35

		SN	SN	SN	SN	SN	SN	FC	FC	SN	SN	SN	SN	SN	SN	SN	SN	SN	SN	FC	FC	SN
				◇1 B ⌶	◇1 B ⌶	◇1 A ⌶	1	1 A	1 B	1 B	◇1 B	◇1 A		◇1 B		1 B	1 A	◇1 A	◇1 B	1 A	1 B	◇1 B ⌶
Purley 4	d		18 08		18 14	18 19				18 27					18 38	18 50	18 49					
Purley Oaks	d		18 11												18 41							
South Croydon 4	d		18 14												18 44							
East Croydon	d	18 14	18 17	18 17	18 21	18 25	18 29	18 32	18 33	18 34	18 39	18 40	18 44	18 46	18 47	18 56	18 58	19 00	19 00	19 02	19 03	19 09
Norwood Junction 2	d		18 22							18 38					18 52							
London Bridge 4	a	18 49	18 48					18 46	18 46	18 51			19 19		19 18					19 16	19 16	
London Blackfriars 3	a																					
City Thameslink 3	a																					
Farringdon 3	a																					
St Pancras International 15	a																					
Clapham Junction 10	a			18 26	18 31	18 37	18 41				18 48	18 54		18 55		19 06	19 08	19 11	19 10			19 18
London Victoria 15	a			18 33	18 39	18 46	18 48				18 55	19 01		19 02		19 13	19 16	19 18	19 17			19 25

A from 12 September

B until 5 September

Purley and East Croydon - London
COMPLETE SERVICE

		SN	SN	SN	SN	SN	SN	SN	SN	FC	FC	SN	SN	SN	SN	SN	SN	SN	SN	SN	SN	FC	FC
		◇1	◇1			◇1	◇1	◇1	1	1	1	1	◇1	◇1		◇1		1	1	◇1	◇1	1	1
		A	A			B	B	A		A	B	B	B	A		B		B	A	A	B	A	B
Purley 4	d				19 08		19 14	19 19				19 27					19 38	19 50	19 49				
Purley Oaks	d				19 11												19 41						
South Croydon 4	d				19 14												19 44						
East Croydon	d	19 10	19 13	19 14	19 17	19 17	19 21	19 25	19 29	19 32	19 33	19 34	19 39	19 40	19 44	19 46	19 47	19 56	19 58	20 00	20 00	20 02	20 03
Norwood Junction 2	d				19 22							19 38					19 52						
London Bridge 4 ⊖	a			19 49	19 48					19 46	19 46	19 51			20 19		20 18					20 16	20 16
London Blackfriars 3 ⊖	a																						
City Thameslink 3	a																						
Farringdon 3 ⊖	a																						
St Pancras International 15 ⊖	a																						
Clapham Junction 10	a	19 24	19 27			19 26	19 31	19 37	19 41				19 48	19 54		19 55		20 06	20 08	20 11	20 10		
London Victoria 15 ⊖	a	19 31	19 35			19 33	19 39	19 46	19 48				19 55	20 01		20 02		20 13	20 16	20 18	20 17		

		SN	SN	SN	SN	SN	SN	SN	SN	SN	FC	FC	SN	SN	SN	SN	SN	SN	SN	SN	SN	SN
		◇1	◇1	◇1			◇1	◇1	◇1	1	1	1	1	◇1	◇1		◇1		1	1	◇1	◇1
		B	A	A			B	B	A		A	B	B	B	A		B		B	A	A	B
Purley 4	d					20 08		20 14	20 19				20 27					20 38	20 50	20 49		
Purley Oaks	d					20 11												20 41				
South Croydon 4	d					20 14												20 44				
East Croydon	d	20 09	20 10	20 13	20 14	20 17	20 17	20 21	20 25	20 29	20 32	20 33	20 34	20 39	20 40	20 44	20 46	20 47	20 56	20 58	21 00	21 00
Norwood Junction 2	d					20 22							20 38					20 52				
London Bridge 4 ⊖	a				20 49	20 48					20 46	20 46	20 51			21 19		21 18				
London Blackfriars 3 ⊖	a																					
City Thameslink 3	a																					
Farringdon 3 ⊖	a																					
St Pancras International 15 ⊖	a																					
Clapham Junction 10	a	20 18	20 24	20 27			20 26	20 31	20 37	20 41				20 48	20 54		20 55		21 06	21 08	21 11	21 10
London Victoria 15 ⊖	a	20 25	20 31	20 35			20 33	20 39	20 46	20 48				20 55	21 01		21 02		21 13	21 16	21 18	21 17

		FC	FC	SN	SN	SN	SN	SN	SN	SN	SN	SN	FC	FC	SN	SN	SN	SN	SN	SN	SN	SN	SN
		1	1	◇1	◇1	◇1			◇1	◇1	◇1	1	1	1	1	◇1	◇1			1	1	◇1	◇1
		A	B	B	A	A			B	B	A		A	B	B	B	A			B	A	A	B
Purley 4	d							21 08		21 14	21 19				21 27				21 38	21 50	21 49		
Purley Oaks	d							21 11											21 41				
South Croydon 4	d							21 14											21 44				
East Croydon	d	21 02	21 03	21 09	21 10	21 13	21 14	21 17	21 17	21 21	21 25	21 29	21 32	21 33	21 34	21 39	21 40	21 44	21 47	21 56	21 58	22 00	22 00
Norwood Junction 2	d							21 22							21 38				21 52				
London Bridge 4 ⊖	a	21 16	21 16				21 49	21 48					21 46	21 46	21 51			22 19	22 18				
London Blackfriars 3 ⊖	a																						
City Thameslink 3	a																						
Farringdon 3 ⊖	a																						
St Pancras International 15 ⊖	a																						
Clapham Junction 10	a			21 18	21 24	21 27			21 26	21 31	21 37	21 41				21 48	21 54			22 06	22 08	22 11	22 10
London Victoria 15 ⊖	a			21 25	21 31	21 35			21 33	21 39	21 46	21 48				21 55	22 01			22 13	22 16	22 18	22 17

		FC	FC	SN	SN	SN	SN	SN	SN	SN	FC	FC	SN	SN	SN	SN	SN	SN	SN	FC	FC	SN	SN
		1	1	◇1	◇1			◇1	◇1	1	1	1	1			1	1	◇1	◇1	1	1		◇1
		A	B	B	A			B	A		A	B	B			B	A	A	B	A	B		B
Purley 4	d						22 08	22 14	22 18				22 27		22 38	22 50	22 49					23 07	23 14
Purley Oaks	d						22 11								22 41							23 10	
South Croydon 4	d						22 14								22 44							23 13	
East Croydon	d	22 02	22 03	22 09	22 10	22 14	22 17	22 21	22 25	22 29	22 32	22 33	22 34	22 44	22 47	22 56	22 58	23 00	23 00	23 02	23 03	23 16	23 21
Norwood Junction 2	d						22 22						22 38		22 52							23a20	
London Bridge 4 ⊖	a	22 16	22 16			22 49	22 48				22 46	22 46	22 51	23 20	23 18					23 16	23 16		
London Blackfriars 3 ⊖	a																						
City Thameslink 3	a																						
Farringdon 3 ⊖	a																						
St Pancras International 15 ⊖	a																						
Clapham Junction 10	a			22 18	22 24			22 31	22 37	22 41						23 07	23 10	23 12	23 10				23 31
London Victoria 15 ⊖	a			22 25	22 31			22 39	22 46	22 50						23 14	23 16	23 20	23 17				23 38

A from 12 September

B until 5 September

Purley and East Croydon - London
COMPLETE SERVICE

		SN	SN	SN	FC	FC	SN
		◇1		1	1	1	1
		A			A	B	
Purley 4	d	23 18	23 23				23 50
Purley Oaks	d		23 26				
South Croydon 4	d		23 29				
East Croydon	d	23 25	23a31	23 29	23 32	23 33	23 56
Norwood Junction 2	d						
London Bridge 4 ⊖	a				23 46	23 46	
London Blackfriars 3 ⊖	a						
City Thameslink 3	a						
Farringdon 3 ⊖	a						
St Pancras International 15 ⊖	a						
Clapham Junction 10	a	23 37		23 41			00 10
London Victoria 15 ⊖	a	23 46		23 50			00 18

A from 12 September

B until 5 September

Network Diagram for Table 176

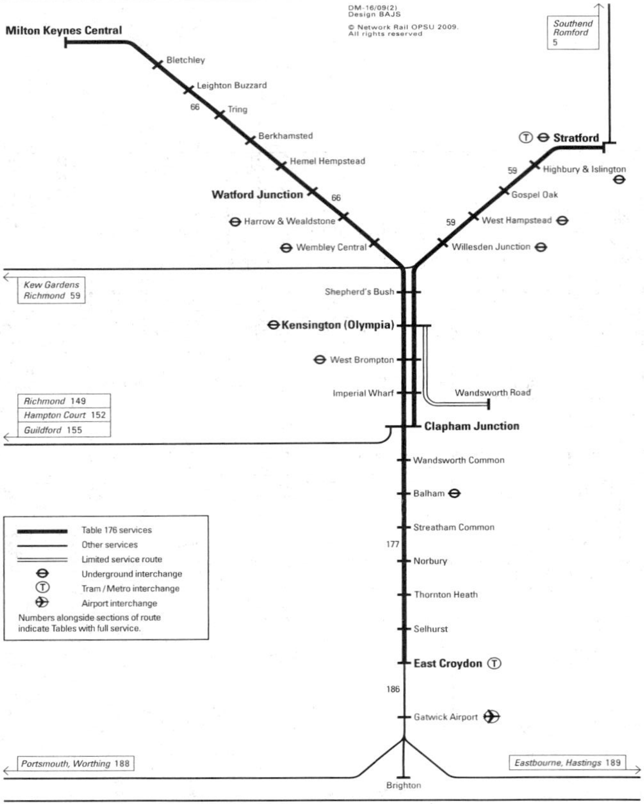

East Croydon, Clapham Junction, Kensington (Olympia) - Watford Junction and Milton Keynes

		SN 1	SN 1	SN 1	LO	LO	SN 1	LO	LO	LO		SN 1	LO	LO	SN	LO	SN 1	SN	LO	SN	LO		SN	LO	SN 1
East Croydon	d														07 47		08 07			08 39					09 08
Selhurst 4	d														07 50		08 13			08 43					09 13
Thornton Heath	d														07 52		08 16			08 46					09 16
Norbury	d														07 55		08 20			08 49					09 19
Streatham Common 4	d														07 58		08 23			08 52					09 21
Balham 4	d		05 25												08 02		08 28			08 58					09 28
Wandsworth Common	d														08 04		08 31			09 00					09 30
Wandsworth Road	d																								
Clapham Junction 10	a		05 29												08 09		08 36			09 04					09 34
	d	05 03	05 30	05 55	06 10	06 30	06 38	06 50	07 10	07 30		07 38	07 50	08 10	08 13	08 30	08 38	08 48	08 50	09 05	09 10		09 24	09 35	09 38
Imperial Wharf	d	05 07	05 39	06 00	06 14	06 34	06 42	06 54	07 14	07 34		07 44	07 54	08 14	08 17	08 34	08 44	08 52	08 54	09 09	09 14		09 28	09 39	09 44
West Brompton	d	05 10	05 41	06 03	06 17	06 37	06 45	06 57	07 17	07 37		07 47	07 57	08 17	08 20	08 37	08 47	08 55	08 57	09 12	09 17		09 31	09 42	09 47
Kensington (Olympia)	d	05 14	05 44	06 07	06 20	06 40	06 49	07 00	07 20	07 40		07 50	08 00	08 20	08 24	08 40	08 50	08 59	09 00	09 15	09 20		09 35	09 45	09 50
Shepherd's Bush	d	05 17	05 47	06 10	06 22	06 42	06 52	07 02	07 22	07 42		07 53	08 02	08 22	08a26	08 42	08 53	09a01	09 02	09a18	09 22		09a37	09 47	09 53
Willesden Jn. High Level	a				06 30	06 50		07 10	07 30	07 50			08 10	08 30		08 50			09 10		09 33			09 57	
West Hampstead	a				06 39	07 00		07 19	07 39	08 03			08 19	08 39		08 59			09 19						
Gospel Oak	a				06 46	07 07		07 26	07 46	08 10			08 26	08 46		09 06			09 26						
Highbury & Islington-I	a				06 57	07 16		07 36	07 56	08 21			08 36	08 56		09 17			09 37						
Stratford	a				07 17	07 36		07 56	08 16	08 41			08 56	09 16		09 36			09 56						
Wembley Central	a		06s00	06 23			07s07					08s08					09s08								10s08
Harrow & Wealdstone	a	05 33	06 07	06 28			07 12					08 13					09 13								10 13
Watford Junction	a	05 40	06 14	06 35			07 19					08 20					09 20								10 20
Hemel Hempstead	a		06 22				07 27					08 28					09 28								10 28
Berkhamsted	a		06 26				07 31					08 32					09 32								10 32
Tring	a		06 33				07 39					08 39					09 39								10 39
Leighton Buzzard	a		06 41				07 50					08 47					09 47								10 47
Bletchley	a		06 48				07 57					08 55					09 55								10 57
Milton Keynes Central 10	a		06 55				08 03					09 01					10 01								11 02

		LO	LO	LO	SN 1	SN		LO	LO	SN 1	LO	LO	SN 1	LO	LO	SN 1		LO	LO	SN 1	LO	LO	SN 1	LO	SN 1
East Croydon	d				10 10					11 11			12 10			13 10				14 10			15 10		16 10
Selhurst 4	d				10 14					11 16			12 14			13 13				14 13			15 13		16 13
Thornton Heath	d				10 16					11 18			12 16			13 16				14 16			15 16		16 16
Norbury	d				10 19					11 21			12 19			13 19				14 19			15 19		16 19
Streatham Common 4	d				10 22					11 24			12 22			13 21				14 21			15 21		16 21
Balham 4	d				10 29					11 28			12 28			13 28				14 28			15 28		16 28
Wandsworth Common	d				10 31					11 30			12 30			13 30				14 30			15 30		16 30
Wandsworth Road	d					10 48																			
Clapham Junction 10	a				10 35					11 33			12 34			13 34				14 34			15 34		16 34
	d	09 50	10 05	10 35	10 38			11 05	11 35	11 38	12 05	12 35	12 38	13 05	13 35	13 38		14 05	14 35	14 38	15 05	15 35	15 38	16 05	16 38
Imperial Wharf	d	09 54	10 09	10 39	10 44			11 09	11 39	11 44	12 09	12 39	12 44	13 09	13 39	13 44		14 09	14 39	14 44	15 09	15 39	15 44	16 09	16 44
West Brompton	d	09 57	10 12	10 42	10 47			11 12	11 42	11 47	12 12	12 42	12 47	13 12	13 42	13 47		14 12	14 42	14 47	15 12	15 42	15 47	16 12	16 47
Kensington (Olympia)	d	10 00	10 15	10 45	10 50	11 11		11 15	11 45	11 50	12 15	12 45	12 50	13 15	13 45	13 50		14 15	14 45	14 50	15 15	15 45	15 50	16 15	16 50
Shepherd's Bush	d	10 02	10 17	10 47	10 53	11 13		11 17	11 47	11 53	12 17	12 47	12 53	13 17	13 47	13 53		14 17	14 47	14 53	15 17	15 47	15 53	16 17	16 53
Willesden Jn. High Level	a	10 12	10 27	10 57				11 27	11 57		12 27	12 57		13 27	13 57			14 27	14 57		15 27	15 57		16 27	
West Hampstead	a																					16 05		16 36	
Gospel Oak	a																					16 12		16 43	
Highbury & Islington-I	a																					16 21		16 52	
Stratford	a																					16 38		17 09	
Wembley Central	a				11s08					12s08			13s08			14s08				15s08			16s08		17s08
Harrow & Wealdstone	a				11 13					12 13			13 13			14 13				15 13			16 13		17 13
Watford Junction	a				11 20					12 20			13 20			14 20				15 20			16 20		17 20
Hemel Hempstead	a				11 28					12 28			13 28			14 28				15 28			16 28		17 28
Berkhamsted	a				11 32					12 32			13 32			14 32				15 32			16 32		17 33
Tring	a				11 39					12 39			13 39			14 39				15 39			16 39		17 38
Leighton Buzzard	a				11 48					12 48			13 48			14 48				15 48			16 47		17 47
Bletchley	a				11 55					12 55			13 55			14 55				15 55			16 55		17 54
Milton Keynes Central 10	a				12 01					13 01			14 01			15 01				16 01			17 00		17 59

Table 176

Mondays to Fridays

East Croydon, Clapham Junction, Kensington (Olympia) - Watford Junction and Milton Keynes

	SN	LO	LO	LO	SN	LO	SN 1	LO	LO	LO	SN 1	LO	LO	LO	SN 1	LO	LO	SN 1	LO	LO	SN 1	LO	LO	SN 1	LO
East Croydon d							17 10				18 10				19 10										
Selhurst 4 d							17 13				18 13				19 13										
Thornton Heath d							17 16				18 16				19 16										
Norbury d							17 19				18 19				19 19										
Streatham Common 4 d							17 21				18 21				19 21										
Balham 4 d							17 28				18 26				19 28										
Wandsworth Common d							17 30				18 28				19 30										
Wandsworth Road d																									
Clapham Junction 10 a							17 34				18 34				19 34										
d	16 48	16 30	16 50	17 10	17 20	17 30	17 38	17 50	18 10	18 30	18 38	18 50	19 05	19 35	19 38	20 05	20 35	20 38	21 05	21 35	21 38	22 05	22 35	22 38	23 05
Imperial Wharf d		16 34	16 54	17 14	17 24	17 34	17 44	17 54	18 14	18 34	18 44	18 54	19 09	19 39	19 44	20 09	20 39	20 44	21 09	21 39	21 44	22 09	22 39	22 44	23 09
West Brompton ⊖ d		16 37	16 57	17 17	17 27	17 37	17 47	17 57	18 17	18 37	18 47	18 57	19 12	19 42	19 47	20 12	20 42	20 47	21 12	21 42	21 47	22 12	22 42	22 47	23 12
Kensington (Olympia) ⊖ d	16a55	16 40	17 00	17 20	17 30	17 40	17 50	18 00	18 20	18 40	18 50	19 00	19 15	19 45	19 50	20 15	20 45	20 50	21 15	21 45	21 50	22 15	22 45	22 50	23 15
Shepherd's Bush ⊖ d		16 42	17 02	17 22	17a32	17 42	17 53	18 02	18 22	18 42	18 53	19 02	19 17	19 47	19 53	20 17	20 47	20 53	21 17	21 47	21 53	22 17	22 47	22 53	23 17
Willesden Jn. High Level ⊖ a		16 50	17 10	17 30		17 50		18 10	18 30	18 52		19 10	19 27	19 57		20 27	20 57		21 27	21 57		22 27	22 57		23 27
West Hampstead ⊖ a		16 59	17 19	17 39		17 59		18 19	18 39			19 19													
Gospel Oak a		17 06	17 26	17 46		18 06		18 26	18 46			19 26													
Highbury & Islington-I ⊖ a		17 16	17 36	17 56		18 16		18 36	18 56			19 36													
Stratford a		17 36	17 56	18 16		18 36		18 56	19 16			19 56													
Wembley Central ⊖ a							18s08				19s08				20s08			21s08							
Harrow & Wealdstone ⊖ a							18 13				19 13				20 13			21 13			22 16			23 16	
Watford Junction a							18 20				19 20				20 20			21 20			23 23			23 23	
Hemel Hempstead a							18 28				19 28				20 28			21 28							
Berkhamsted a							18 32				19 33				20 32			21 32							
Tring a							18 38				19 40				20 39			21 39							
Leighton Buzzard a							18 49				19 51				20 48			21 50							
Bletchley a							18 58				20 00				20 55			21 58							
Milton Keynes Central 10 a							19 03				20 06				21 01			22 05							

Saturdays

	SN 1	SN 1	LO	SN 1	LO	SN 1	LO	LO	SN 1		LO	LO	SN 1	LO	LO	SN 1	LO	LO	SN 1		LO	LO	SN 1	LO
East Croydon d						06 10			07 10				08 10			09 10			10 10				11 10	
Selhurst 4 d						06 13			07 13				08 13			09 13			10 13				11 13	
Thornton Heath d						06 16			07 16				08 16			09 16			10 16				11 16	
Norbury d						06 19			07 19				08 19			09 19			10 19				11 19	
Streatham Common 4 d						06 21			07 21				08 21			09 21			10 21				11 21	
Balham 4 d		05 33				06 28			07 28				08 28			09 28			10 28				11 28	
Wandsworth Common d						06 30			07 30				08 30			09 30			10 30				11 30	
Wandsworth Road d																								
Clapham Junction 10 a		05 37				06 34			07 34				08 34			09 34			10 34				11 34	
d	05 08	05 38	06 05	06 08	06 35	06 38	07 05	07 35	07 38		08 05	08 35	08 38	09 05	09 35	09 38	10 05	10 35	10 38		11 05	11 35	11 38	12 05
Imperial Wharf d	05 12	05 42	06 09	06 15	06 39	06 44	07 09	07 39	07 44		08 09	08 39	08 44	09 09	09 39	09 44	10 09	10 39	10 44		11 09	11 39	11 44	12 09
West Brompton ⊖ d	05 15	05 45	06 12	06 18	06 42	06 47	07 12	07 42	07 47		08 12	08 42	08 47	09 12	09 42	09 47	10 12	10 42	10 47		11 12	11 42	11 47	12 12
Kensington (Olympia) ⊖ d	05 19	05 49	06 15	06 22	06 45	06 50	07 15	07 45	07 50		08 15	08 45	08 50	09 15	09 45	09 50	10 15	10 45	10 50		11 15	11 45	11 50	12 15
Shepherd's Bush ⊖ d	05 22	05 52	06 17	06 25	06 47	06 53	07 17	07 47	07 53		08 17	08 47	08 53	09 17	09 47	09 53	10 17	10 47	10 53		11 17	11 47	11 53	12 17
Willesden Jn. High Level ⊖ a			06 27		06 57		07 28	07 57			08 27	08 57		09 27	09 57		10 27	10 57			11 27	11 57		12 27
West Hampstead ⊖ a																								
Gospel Oak a																								
Highbury & Islington-I ⊖ a																								
Stratford a																								
Wembley Central ⊖ a		06s07		06 38		07s07			08s07				09s07			10s07			11s08				12s07	
Harrow & Wealdstone ⊖ a	05 40	06 12		06 43		07 12			08 12				09 12			10 12			11 13				12 13	
Watford Junction a	05 47	06 19		06 50		07 19			08 19				09 19			10 19			11 20				12 20	
Hemel Hempstead a		06 27				07 27			08 27				09 27			10 27			11 28				12 28	
Berkhamsted a		06 31				07 32			08 31				09 33			10 31			11 33				12 32	
Tring a		06 37				07 39			08 37				09 38			10 37			11 38				12 37	
Leighton Buzzard a		06 46				07 47			08 46				09 47			10 47			11 47				12 47	
Bletchley a		06 54				07 54			08 54				09 54			10 54			11 54				12 54	
Milton Keynes Central 10 a		07 00				08 00			09 00				10 00			11 00			12 00				13 00	

Table 176

Saturdays

East Croydon, Clapham Junction, Kensington (Olympia) - Watford Junction and Milton Keynes

	LO	SN 1	LO	LO	SN 1	LO	LO	SN 1	LO	LO	SN 1	LO	LO	SN 1		LO	LO	SN 1	LO	LO	SN 1	LO	LO	SN 1
East Croydon d		12 10			13 10			14 10			15 10			16 10				17 10			18 10			19 10
Selhurst 4 d		12 13			13 13			14 13			15 13			16 13				17 13			18 13			19 13
Thornton Heath d		12 16			13 16			14 16			15 16			16 16				17 16			18 16			19 16
Norbury d		12 19			13 19			14 19			15 19			16 19				17 19			18 19			19 19
Streatham Common 4 d		12 21			13 21			14 21			15 21			16 21				17 21			18 21			19 21
Balham 4 d		12 28			13 28			14 28			15 28			16 28				17 28			18 28			19 28
Wandsworth Common d		12 30			13 30			14 30			15 30			16 30				17 30			18 30			19 30
Wandsworth Road d																								
Clapham Junction 10 a		12 34			13 34			14 34			15 34			16 34				17 34			18 34			19 34
d	12 35	12 38	13 05	13 35	13 38	14 05	14 35	14 38	15 05	15 35	15 38	16 05	16 35	16 38		17 05	17 35	17 38	18 05	18 35	18 38	19 05	19 35	19 38
Imperial Wharf d	12 39	12 44	13 09	13 39	13 44	14 09	14 39	14 44	15 09	15 39	15 44	16 09	16 39	16 44		17 09	17 39	17 44	18 09	18 39	18 44	19 09	19 39	19 42
West Brompton ⊖ d	12 42	12 47	13 12	13 42	13 47	14 12	14 42	14 47	15 12	15 42	15 47	16 12	16 42	16 47		17 12	17 42	17 47	18 12	18 42	18 47	19 12	19 42	19 45
Kensington (Olympia) ⊖ d	12 45	12 50	13 15	13 45	13 50	14 15	14 45	14 50	15 15	15 45	15 50	16 15	16 45	16 50		17 15	17 45	17 50	18 15	18 45	18 50	19 15	19 45	19 48
Shepherd's Bush ⊖ d	12 47	12 53	13 17	13 47	13 53	14 17	14 47	14 53	15 17	15 47	15 53	16 17	16 47	16 53		17 17	17 47	17 53	18 17	18 47	18 53	19 17	19 47	19 50
Willesden Jn. High Level ⊖ a	12 57		13 27	13 57		14 27	14 57		15 27	15 57		16 27	16 57			17 27	17 57		18 27	18 57		19 27	19 57	
West Hampstead ⊖ a																								
Gospel Oak a																								
Highbury & Islington-I ⊖ a																								
Stratford a																								
Wembley Central ⊖ a		13s07			14s08			15s07			16s07			17s07				18s07			19 08			
Harrow & Wealdstone ⊖ a		13 12			14 13			15 12			16 12			17 12				18 12			19 13			20 08
Watford Junction a		13 19			14 20			15 19			16 19			17 19				18 19			19 21			20 15
Hemel Hempstead a		13 27			14 28			15 27			16 27			17 27				18 27						
Berkhamsted a		13 32			14 32			15 32			16 32			17 32				18 32						
Tring a		13 37			14 37			15 37			16 37			17 37				18 37						
Leighton Buzzard a		13 47			14 47			15 47			16 47			17 46				18 46						
Bletchley a		13 54			14 54			15 54			16 54			17 54				18 54						
Milton Keynes Central 10 a		14 00			15 00			16 00			17 00			18 00				19 00						

	LO		SN 1	LO	LO	LO	SN 1	LO	LO	SN 1	LO
East Croydon d											
Selhurst 4 d											
Thornton Heath d											
Norbury d											
Streatham Common 4 d											
Balham 4 d											
Wandsworth Common d											
Wandsworth Road d											
Clapham Junction 10 a											
d	20 05		20 25	20 35	21 05	21 35	21 38	22 05	22 35	22 38	23 05
Imperial Wharf d	20 09		20 29	20 39	21 09	21 39	21 51	22 09	22 39	22 44	23 09
West Brompton ⊖ d	20 12		20 32	20 42	21 12	21 42	21 54	22 12	22 42	22 47	23 12
Kensington (Olympia) ⊖ d	20 15		20 36	20 45	21 15	21 45	21 57	22 15	22 45	22 50	23 15
Shepherd's Bush ⊖ d	20 17		20 39	20 47	21 17	21 47	22 00	22 17	22 47	22 53	23 17
Willesden Jn. High Level ⊖ a	20 27			20 57	21 27	21 57		22 27	22 57		23 27
West Hampstead ⊖ a											
Gospel Oak a											
Highbury & Islington-I ⊖ a											
Stratford a											
Wembley Central ⊖ a											
Harrow & Wealdstone ⊖ a			21 02				22 20			23 12	
Watford Junction a			21 09				22 27			23 19	
Hemel Hempstead a											
Berkhamsted a											
Tring a											
Leighton Buzzard a											
Bletchley a											
Milton Keynes Central 10 a											

Table 176

East Croydon, Clapham Junction, Kensington (Olympia) - Watford Junction and Milton Keynes

		SN ■	SN ■	LO	SN ■	LO	LO	SN ■	LO	LO		SN ■	LO	LO	SN ■	LO	LO	SN ■	LO	LO		SN ■	LO	LO	SN ■
East Croydon ⇌	d																								
Selhurst ■	d																								
Thornton Heath	d																								
Norbury	d																								
Streatham Common ■	d																								
Balham ■	d																								
Wandsworth Common	d																								
Wandsworth Road	d																								
Clapham Junction ■	a																								
	d	07 24	08 15	08 48	09 15	09 31	09 55	10 15	10 31	10 55		11 15	11 31	11 55	12 05	12 30	12 48	13 05	13 25	13 43		14 05	14 23	14 48	15 05
Imperial Wharf	d	07 28	08 19	08 52	09 19	09 35	09 59	10 19	10 35	10 59		11 19	11 35	11 59	12 09	12 34	12 52	13 09	13 29	13 47		14 09	14 27	14 52	15 09
West Brompton ⊖	d	07 31	08 22	08 55	09 22	09 38	10 02	10 22	10 38	11 02		11 22	11 38	12 02	12 12	12 37	12 55	13 12	13 32	13 50		14 12	14 30	14 55	15 12
Kensington (Olympia) ⊖	d	07 34	08 26	08 58	09 26	09 41	10 05	10 26	10 41	11 05		11 26	11 41	12 05	12 16	12 40	12 58	13 16	13 35	13 53		14 16	14b41	14 58	15 16
Shepherd's Bush ⊖	d	07a36	08 29	09a03	09 29	09a46	10a10	10 29	10a46	11a10		11 29	11a46	12a10	12 19	12a45	13a03	13 19	13a40	13a58		14 19	14a46	15a03	15 19
Willesden Jn. High Level ⊖	a																								
West Hampstead ⊖	a																								
Gospel Oak	a																								
Highbury & Islington-I ⊖	a																								
Stratford	a																								
Wembley Central ⊖	a																								
Harrow & Wealdstone ⊖	a		08 48		09 48			10 48				11 48			12 36			13 36				14 36			15 36
Watford Junction	a		08 56		09 58			10 56				11 56			12 44			13 44				14 44			15 44
Hemel Hempstead	a																								
Berkhamsted	a																								
Tring	a																								
Leighton Buzzard	a																								
Bletchley	a																								
Milton Keynes Central ■	a																								

		LO	LO	SN ■	LO	LO		SN ■	LO	LO	SN ■	LO	LO	SN ■	LO	LO		SN ■	LO	LO	SN ■	LO	LO	SN ■	LO
East Croydon ⇌	d																								
Selhurst ■	d																								
Thornton Heath	d																								
Norbury	d																								
Streatham Common ■	d																								
Balham ■	d																								
Wandsworth Common	d																								
Wandsworth Road	d																								
Clapham Junction ■	a																								
	d	15 26	15 48	16 05	16 30	16 48		17 05	17 25	17 48		18 25	18 48	19 05	19 25	19 48		20 05	20 30	20 48	21 15	21 31	21 55	22 15	22 31
Imperial Wharf	d	15 30	15 52	16 09	16 34	16 52		17 09	17 29	17 52	18 09	18 29	18 52	19 09	19 29	19 52		20 09	20 34	20 52	21 19	21 35	21 59	22 19	22 35
West Brompton ⊖	d	15 33	15 55	16 12	16 37	16 55		17 12	17 32	17 55	18 12	18 32	18 55	19 12	19 32	19 55		20 12	20 37	20 55	21 22	21 38	22 02	22 22	22 38
Kensington (Olympia) ⊖	d	15 36	15 58	16 16	16 40	16 58		17 16	17 35	17 58	18 16	18 35	18 58	19 16	19 35	19 58		20 16	20 40	20 58	21 26	21 41	22 05	22 26	22 41
Shepherd's Bush ⊖	d	15a41	16a03	16 19	16a45	17a03		17 19	17a40	18a03	18 19	18a40	19a03	19 19	19a40	20a03		20 19	20a45	21a03	21 29	21a46	22a10	22 29	22a46
Willesden Jn. High Level ⊖	a																								
West Hampstead ⊖	a																								
Gospel Oak	a																								
Highbury & Islington-I ⊖	a																								
Stratford	a																								
Wembley Central ⊖	a																								
Harrow & Wealdstone ⊖	a			16 36				17 36			18 36			19 36				20 36			21 49			22 48	
Watford Junction	a			16 44				17 44			18 44			19 44				20 44			21 56			22 56	
Hemel Hempstead	a																								
Berkhamsted	a																								
Tring	a																								
Leighton Buzzard	a																								
Bletchley	a																								
Milton Keynes Central ■	a																								

b arr. 1433

Table 176

East Croydon, Clapham Junction, Kensington (Olympia) - Watford Junction and Milton Keynes

		LO	LO
East Croydon ⇌	d		
Selhurst ■	d		
Thornton Heath	d		
Norbury	d		
Streatham Common ■	d		
Balham ■	d		
Wandsworth Common	d		
Wandsworth Road	d		
Clapham Junction ■	a		
	d	22 55	23 31
Imperial Wharf	d	22 59	23 35
West Brompton ⊖	d	23 02	23 38
Kensington (Olympia) ⊖	d	23 05	23 41
Shepherd's Bush ⊖	d	23a10	23a46
Willesden Jn. High Level ⊖	a		
West Hampstead ⊖	a		
Gospel Oak	a		
Highbury & Islington-I ⊖	a		
Stratford	a		
Wembley Central ⊖	a		
Harrow & Wealdstone ⊖	a		
Watford Junction	a		
Hemel Hempstead	a		
Berkhamsted	a		
Tring	a		
Leighton Buzzard	a		
Bletchley	a		
Milton Keynes Central ■	a		

Milton Keynes, Watford Junction, Kensington (Olympia) - Clapham Junction and East Croydon

		SN MX 1	SN MO 1	SN MX 1	LO	SN 1	LO	LO	SN 1	LO		LO	SN 1	LO	LO	SN	LO	SN	LO	SN 1		LO	SN	LO	LO
Milton Keynes Central 10	d	22p11											07 01							08 13					
Bletchley	d	22p15											07 05							08 17					
Leighton Buzzard	d	22p22											07 13							08 24					
Tring	d	22p34											07 22							08 34					
Berkhamsted	d	22p39											07 26							08 39					
Hemel Hempstead	d	22p43											07 31							08 43					
Watford Junction	d	22p53	23p17	23p29		05 54			06 53				07 38							08 51					
Harrow & Wealdstone ⊖	d	23p00	23p23	23p35		06 00			06 59				07 45							08 58					
Wembley Central ⊖	d					06 05			07 04				07u49							09u05					
Stratford 7 ⊖	d							06 21		06 39		06 59		07 19	07 37		07 59		08 19			08 39		08 59	
Highbury & Islington ⊖	d							06 35		06 55		07 15		07 35	07 53		08 15		08 35			08 55		09 15	
Gospel Oak	d							06 48		07 06		07 26		07 46	08 05		08 26		08 46			09 06		09 26	
West Hampstead ⊖	d							06 54		07 12		07 32		07 52	08 11		08 32		08 52			09 12		09 32	
Willesden Jn. High Level ⊖	d				06 08		06 42	07 03		07 22		07 42		08 02	08 20		08 42		09 02			09 22		09 42	10 08
Shepherd's Bush ⊖	d	23p21	23p45	23p54	06 15	06 19	06 49	07 10	07 19	07 29	-	07 49	08 04	08 09	08 27	08 31	08 49	09 06	09 09	09 18	-	09 29	09 42	09 49	10 15
Kensington (Olympia) ⊖	d	23p23	23p48	23p56	06 17	06 22	06 51	07 12	07 22	07 31	-	07 51	08 07	08 11	08 29	08 33	08 51	09 09	09 11	09 21	-	09 31	09 45	09 51	10 17
West Brompton ⊖	d	23p26	23p50	23p59	06 19	06 25	06 54	07 15	07 25	07 34	-	07 54	08 10	08 14	08 32	08 36	08 54	09 12	09 14	09 23	-	09 34	09 48	09 54	10 19
Imperial Wharf	d	23p28	23p53	00 02	06 22	06 27	06 56	07 17	07 27	07 36	-	07 56	08 13	08 16	08 34	08 38	08 56	09 15	09 16	09 26	-	09 36	09 50	09 56	10 22
Clapham Junction 10	a	23p33	23p58	00 07	06 28	06 32	07 02	07 26	07 32	07 45	-	08 05	08 17	08 25	08 43	08 43	09 05	09 19	09 25	09 31	-	09 45	09 55	10 05	10 28
	d	23p40	00 02										08 36							09 34					
Wandsworth Road	a																								
Wandsworth Common	a												08 39							09 37					
Balham 4	a	23p44											08 42							09 41					
Streatham Common 4	a	23p48											08 46							09 45					
Norbury	a	23p51											08 48							09 48					
Thornton Heath	a	23p54											08 51							09 51					
Selhurst 4	a	23p56	00 18										08 54							09 53					
East Croydon	a	00 01	00 22										09 04							09 57					

		SN 1	LO	LO	SN 1	LO		LO	SN 1	SN	LO	LO	SN 1	LO	LO	SN 1		LO	LO	SN 1	LO	LO	SN 1	SN	LO
Milton Keynes Central 10	d	09 13			10 13				11 13				12 13			13 13				14 13			15 13		
Bletchley	d	09 17			10 17				11 17				12 17			13 17				14 17			15 17		
Leighton Buzzard	d	09 24			10 24				11 24				12 24			13 24				14 24			15 24		
Tring	d	09 34			10 34				11 34				12 34			13 34				14 34			15 34		
Berkhamsted	d	09 39			10 39				11 39				12 39			13 39				14 39			15 39		
Hemel Hempstead	d	09 43			10 43				11 43				12 43			13 43				14 43			15 43		
Watford Junction	d	09 51			10 51				11 51				12 51			13 51				14 51			15 51		
Harrow & Wealdstone ⊖	d	09 58			10 59				11 59				12 59			13 59				14 59			15 59		
Wembley Central ⊖	d	10u05			11u04				12u04				13u04			14u04				15u04			16u05		
Stratford 7 ⊖	d																								
Highbury & Islington ⊖	d																								
Gospel Oak	d																								
West Hampstead ⊖	d																								
Willesden Jn. High Level ⊖	d		10 38	11 08		11 38		12 08			12 38	13 08		13 38	14 08			14 38	15 08		15 38	16 08			16 38
Shepherd's Bush ⊖	d	10 21	10 45	11 15	11 19	11 45	-	12 15	12 19	12 29	12 45	13 15	13 19	13 45	14 15	14 19	-	14 45	15 15	15 22	15 45	16 15	16 19	-	16 45
Kensington (Olympia) ⊖	d	10 24	10 47	11 17	11 21	11 47	-	12 17	12 22	12 32	12 47	13 17	13 22	13 47	14 17	14 22	-	14 47	15 17	15 24	15 47	16 17	16 22	16 34	16 47
West Brompton ⊖	d	10 27	10 49	11 19	11 23	11 49	-	12 19	12 25	-	12 49	13 19	13 25	13 49	14 19	14 25	-	14 49	15 19	15 26	15 49	16 19	16 25	16 36	16 49
Imperial Wharf	d	10 29	10 52	11 22	11 26	11 52	-	12 22	12 27	-	12 52	13 22	13 28	13 52	14 22	14 28	-	14 52	15 22	15 29	15 52	16 22	16 27	16 39	16 52
Clapham Junction 10	a	10 34	10 58	11 28	11 30	11 58	-	12 28	12 32	-	12 58	13 28	13 32	13 58	14 28	14 32	-	14 58	15 28	15 33	15 58	16 28	16 32	16 43	16 58
	d	10 34			11 34				12 34				13 34			14 34				15 34			16 34		
Wandsworth Road	a									12 50															
Wandsworth Common	a	10 37			11 37				12 37				13 37			14 37				15 37			16 37		
Balham 4	a	10 40			11 40				12 40				13 40			14 40				15 40			16 40		
Streatham Common 4	a	10 45			11 45				12 45				13 45			14 45				15 45			16 45		
Norbury	a	10 48			11 48				12 48				13 48			14 48				15 48			16 48		
Thornton Heath	a	10 51			11 51				12 51				13 51			14 51				15 51			16 51		
Selhurst 4	a	10 53			11 53				12 53				13 53			14 53				15 53			16 55		
East Croydon	a	10 57			11 57				12 57				13 57			14 57				15 57			16 59		

Table 176 Mondays to Fridays

Milton Keynes, Watford Junction, Kensington (Olympia) - Clapham Junction and East Croydon

		SN		LO	SN 1	LO	SN	LO	LO	SN 1	LO	LO		LO	SN 1	LO	LO	LO	SN 1	LO	LO	SN 1		LO	LO
Milton Keynes Central 10	d				16 13					17 13					18 13				19 15			20 13			
Bletchley	d				16 17					17 17					18 17				19 19			20 17			
Leighton Buzzard	d				16 24					17 24					18 24				19 26			20 24			
Tring	d				16 34					17 34					18 34				19 36			20 34			
Berkhamsted	d				16 39					17 39					18 39				19 41			20 39			
Hemel Hempstead	d				16 43					17 43					18 43				19 45			20 43			
Watford Junction	d				16 51					17 51					18 51				19 54			20 51			
Harrow & Wealdstone ⊖	d				16 59					17 59					18 59				20 01			20 59			
Wembley Central ⊖	d				17u05					18u05					19u05				20u06			21u04			
Stratford 7 ⊖	d			16 19		16 39		16 59	17 19		17 39	17 59		18 19		18 39	18 59								
Highbury & Islington ⊖	d			16 35		16 55		17 15	17 35		17 55.	18 15		18 35		18 55	19 15								
Gospel Oak	d			16 47		17 06		17 26	17 46		18 06	18 26		18 46		19 06	19 26								
West Hampstead ⊖	d			16 53		17 12		17 32	17 52		18 12	18 32		18 52		19 12	19 32								
Willesden Jn. High Level ⊖	d			17 03		17 22		17 42	18 02		18 22	18 42		19 02		19 22	19 41	20 08		20 38	21 08			21 38	22 08
Shepherd's Bush ⊖	d	-		17 10	17 19	17 29	17 45	17 54	18 09	18 19	18 29	18 49	-	19 09	19 18	19 29	19 48	20 15	20 21	20 45	21 15	21 22	-	21 45	22 15
Kensington (Olympia) ⊖	d	17 00		17 12	17 22	17 31	17 47	17 56	18 11	18 22	18 31	18 51	-	19 11	19 20	19 31	19 50	20 17	20 23	20 47	21 17	21 24	-	21 47	22 17
West Brompton ⊖	d	17 02		17 15	17 25	17 34	17 50	17 59	18 14	18 25	18 34	18 54	-	19 14	19 23	19 34	19 52	20 19	20 25	20 49	21 19	21 27	-	21 49	22 19
Imperial Wharf	d	17 05		17 17	17 28	17 36	17 53	18 01	18 16	18 27	18 36	18 56	-	19 16	19 25	19 36	19 55	20 22	20 28	20 52	21 22	21 29	-	21 52	22 22
Clapham Junction 10	a	17 09		17 26	17 32	17 45	17 57	18 06	18 25	18 32	18 45	19 05	-	19 25	19 30	19 45	20 00	20 28	20 33	20 58	21 28	21 34	-	21 58	22 28
	d				17 33		18 02			18 34					19 34										
Wandsworth Road	a																								
Wandsworth Common	a				17 36		18 05			18 37					19 37										
Balham 4	a				17 39		18 08			18 40					19 40										
Streatham Common 4	a				17 46		18 15			18 46					19 45										
Norbury	a				17 48		18 18			18 49					19 48										
Thornton Heath	a				17 51		18 21			18 52					19 51										
Selhurst 4	a				17 54		18 24			18 54					19 53										
East Croydon	a				17 59		18 33			19 02															

		SN 1	LO	SN 1	LO	SN 1	SN 1
Milton Keynes Central 10	d	21 13				22 11	
Bletchley	d	21 17				22 15	
Leighton Buzzard	d	21 24				22 22	
Tring	d	21 34				22 34	
Berkhamsted	d	21 39				22 39	
Hemel Hempstead	d	21 43				22 43	
Watford Junction	d	21 51		22 27		22 53	23 29
Harrow & Wealdstone ⊖	d	21 59		22 33		23 00	23 35
Wembley Central ⊖	d						
Stratford 7 ⊖	d						
Highbury & Islington ⊖	d						
Gospel Oak	d						
West Hampstead ⊖	d						
Willesden Jn. High Level ⊖	d		22 38		23 09		
Shepherd's Bush ⊖	d	22 23	22 45	22 49	23 17	23 21	23 54
Kensington (Olympia) ⊖	d	22 25	22 47	22 51	23 19	23 23	23 56
West Brompton ⊖	d	22 27	22 49	22 54	23 21	23 26	23 59
Imperial Wharf	d	22 30	22 52	22 56	23 24	23 28	00 02
Clapham Junction 10	a	22 34	22 58	23 01	23 30	23 33	00 07
	d					23 40	
Wandsworth Road	a						
Wandsworth Common	a						
Balham 4	a					23 44	
Streatham Common 4	a					23 48	
Norbury	a					23 51	
Thornton Heath	a					23 54	
Selhurst 4	a					23 56	
East Croydon	a					00 01	

Table 176

Saturdays

Milton Keynes, Watford Junction, Kensington (Olympia) - Clapham Junction and East Croydon

		SN 1	SN 1	LO	SN 1	LO	LO	SN 1	LO	LO		SN 1	LO	LO	SN 1	LO	LO	SN 1	LO	LO		SN 1	LO	LO	SN 1
Milton Keynes Central 10	d	22p11										07 13			08 13			09 13				10 13			11 13
Bletchley	d	22p15										07 17			08 17			09 17				10 17			11 17
Leighton Buzzard	d	22p22										07 24			08 24			09 24				10 24			11 24
Tring	d	22p34										07 34			08 34			09 34				10 34			11 34
Berkhamsted	d	22p39										07 39			08 39			09 39				10 39			11 39
Hemel Hempstead	d	22p43										07 43			08 43			09 43				10 43			11 43
Watford Junction	d	22p53	23p29		05 52			06 55				07 52			08 52			09 52				10 52			11 52
Harrow & Wealdstone ⊖	d	23p00	23p35		05 58			07 01				07 59			08 59			09 59				10 59			11 59
Wembley Central ⊖	d							07 06				08u04			09u04			10u04				11u04			12u04
Stratford 7 ⊖	d																								
Highbury & Islington ⊖	d																								
Gospel Oak	d																								
West Hampstead ⊖	d																								
Willesden Jn. High Level ⊖	d			06 08		06 38	07 08		07 38	08 08			08 38	09 08		09 38	10 08		10 38	11 08			11 38	12 08	
Shepherd's Bush ⊖	d	23p21	23p54	06 15	06 20	06 45	07 15	07 20	07 45	08 15		08 20	08 45	09 15	09 20	09 45	10 15	10 20	10 45	11 15		11 20	11 45	12 15	12 20
Kensington (Olympia) ⊖	d	23p23	23p56	06 17	06 23	06 47	07 17	07 23	07 47	08 17		08 23	08 47	09 17	09 23	09 47	10 17	10 23	10 47	11 17		11 23	11 47	12 17	12 23
West Brompton ⊖	d	23p26	23p59	06 19	06 26	06 49	07 19	07 26	07 49	08 19		08 26	08 49	09 19	09 26	09 49	10 19	10 26	10 49	11 19		11 26	11 49	12 19	12 26
Imperial Wharf	d	23p28	00 02	06 22	06 28	06 52	07 22	07 28	07 52	08 22		08 28	08 52	09 22	09 28	09 52	10 22	10 28	10 52	11 22		11 28	11 52	12 22	12 28
Clapham Junction 10	a	23p33	00 07	06 29	06 33	06 59	07 29	07 33	07 59	08 29		08 33	08 59	09 29	09 33	09 59	10 29	10 33	10 59	11 29		11 33	11 59	12 29	12 33
	d	23p40			06 34			07 34				08 34			09 34			10 34				11 34			12 34
Wandsworth Road	a																								
Wandsworth Common	a				06 37			07 37				08 37			09 37			10 37				11 37			12 37
Balham 4	a	23p44			06 40			07 40				08 40			09 40			10 40				11 40			12 40
Streatham Common 4	a	23p48			06 45			07 45				08 45			09 45			10 45				11 45			12 45
Norbury	a	23p51			06 48			07 48				08 48			09 48			10 48				11 48			12 48
Thornton Heath	a	23p54			06 51			07 51				08 51			09 51			10 51				11 51			12 51
Selhurst 4	a	23p56			06 53			07 53				08 53			09 53			10 53				11 53			12 53
East Croydon	a	00 01			06 57			07 57				08 57			09 57			10 57				11 57			12 57

		LO	LO	SN 1	LO	LO		SN 1	LO	LO	SN 1	LO	LO	SN 1	LO	LO		SN 1	LO	LO	SN 1	LO	LO	SN 1	LO
Milton Keynes Central 10	d			12 13				13 13			14 13			15 13				16 13			17 13			18 13	
Bletchley	d			12 17				13 17			14 17			15 17				16 17			17 17			18 17	
Leighton Buzzard	d			12 24				13 24			14 24			15 24				16 24			17 24			18 24	
Tring	d			12 34				13 34			14 34			15 34				16 34			17 34			18 34	
Berkhamsted	d			12 39				13 39			14 39			15 39				16 39			17 39			18 39	
Hemel Hempstead	d			12 43				13 43			14 43			15 43				16 43			17 43			18 43	
Watford Junction	d			12 52				13 52			14 52			15 52				16 52			17 52			18 52	
Harrow & Wealdstone ⊖	d			12 59				13 59			14 59			15 59				16 59			17 59			18 59	
Wembley Central ⊖	d			13u04				14u04			15u04			16u04				17u04			18u04			19u04	
Stratford 7 ⊖	d																								
Highbury & Islington ⊖	d																								
Gospel Oak	d																								
West Hampstead ⊖	d																								
Willesden Jn. High Level ⊖	d	12 38	13 08		13 38	14 08			14 38	15 08		15 38	16 08		16 38	17 08			17 38	18 08		18 38	19 08		19 38
Shepherd's Bush ⊖	d	12 45	13 15	13 20	13 45	14 15		14 20	14 45	15 15	15 20	15 45	16 15	16 20	16 45	17 15		17 20	17 45	18 15	18 20	18 45	19 15	19 20	19 45
Kensington (Olympia) ⊖	d	12 47	13 17	13 23	13 47	14 17		14 23	14 47	15 17	15 23	15 47	16 17	16 23	16 47	17 17		17 23	17 47	18 17	18 23	18 47	19 17	19 23	19 47
West Brompton ⊖	d	12 49	13 19	13 26	13 49	14 19		14 26	14 49	15 19	15 26	15 49	16 19	16 26	16 49	17 19		17 26	17 49	18 19	18 26	18 49	19 19	19 26	19 49
Imperial Wharf	d	12 52	13 22	13 28	13 52	14 22		14 28	14 52	15 22	15 28	15 52	16 22	16 28	16 52	17 22		17 28	17 52	18 22	18 28	18 52	19 22	19 28	19 52
Clapham Junction 10	a	12 59	13 29	13 33	13 59	14 29		14 33	14 59	15 29	15 33	15 59	16 29	16 33	16 59	17 29		17 33	17 59	18 29	18 33	18 59	19 29	19 33	19 59
	d			13 34				14 34			15 34			16 34				17 34			18 34			19 35	
Wandsworth Road	a																								
Wandsworth Common	a			13 37				14 37			15 37			16 37				17 37			18 37			19 38	
Balham 4	a			13 40				14 40			15 40			16 40				17 40			18 40			19 41	
Streatham Common 4	a			13 45				14 45			15 45			16 45				17 45			18 45			19 45	
Norbury	a			13 48				14 48			15 48			16 48				17 48			18 48			19 48	
Thornton Heath	a			13 51				14 51			15 51			16 51				17 51			18 51			19 51	
Selhurst 4	a			13 53				14 53			15 53			16 53				17 53			18 53			19 53	
East Croydon	a			13 57				14 57			15 57			16 57				17 57			18 57			19 57	

Table 176

Saturdays

Milton Keynes, Watford Junction, Kensington (Olympia) - Clapham Junction and East Croydon

		SN 1		LO	SN 1	LO	SN 1	LO	LO	SN 1	LO	LO	SN 1		LO	SN 1
Milton Keynes Central 10	d				19 13											
Bletchley	d				19 17											
Leighton Buzzard	d				19 24											
Tring	d				19 34											
Berkhamsted	d				19 39											
Hemel Hempstead	d				19 43											
Watford Junction	d	19 31			19 51		20 43			21 43			22 48			23 25
Harrow & Wealdstone ⊖	d	19 38			19 58		20 50			21 50			22 55			23 31
Wembley Central ⊖	d	19 43														
Stratford 7 ⊖	d															
Highbury & Islington ⊖	d															
Gospel Oak	d															
West Hampstead ⊖	d															
Willesden Jn. High Level ⊖	d			20 08		20 38		21 08	21 38		22 08	22 40			23 08	
Shepherd's Bush ⊖	d	19 57		20 15	20 20	20 45	21 08	21 15	21 45	22 08	22 15	22 47	23 13		23 15	23 49
Kensington (Olympia) ⊖	d	20 00		20 17	20 23	20 47	21 11	21 17	21 47	22 11	22 17	22 49	23 16		23 17	23 51
West Brompton ⊖	d	20 03		20 19	20 26	20 49	21 14	21 19	21 49	22 14	22 19	22 51	23 19		23 19	23 54
Imperial Wharf	d	20 05		20 22	20 28	20 52	21 16	21 22	21 52	22 16	22 22	22 54	23 21		23 22	23 57
Clapham Junction 10	a	20 10		20 29	20 33	20 59	21 21	21 29	21 59	22 21	22 29	23 01	23 26		23 29	00 02
	d				20 34											
Wandsworth Road	a															
Wandsworth Common	a				20 37											
Balham 4	a				20 40											
Streatham Common 4	a				20 45											
Norbury	a				20 48											
Thornton Heath	a				20 51											
Selhurst 4	a				20 53											
East Croydon	a				20 59											

Sundays

		SN 1	SN 1	SN 1	LO	LO	SN 1	LO	LO	SN 1		LO	LO	SN 1	LO	LO	SN 1	LO	LO	SN 1		LO	LO	SN 1	LO
Milton Keynes Central 10	d																								
Bletchley	d																								
Leighton Buzzard	d																								
Tring	d																								
Berkhamsted	d																								
Hemel Hempstead	d																								
Watford Junction	d	23p25					09 17			10 17				11 17			12 22			13 22				14 22	
Harrow & Wealdstone ⊖	d	23p31					09 23			10 23				11 23			12 29			13 28				14 28	
Wembley Central ⊖	d																								
Stratford 7 ⊖	d																								
Highbury & Islington ⊖	d																								
Gospel Oak	d																								
West Hampstead ⊖	d																								
Willesden Jn. High Level ⊖	d																								
Shepherd's Bush ⊖	d	23p49	07 47	08 50	09 05	09 25	09 45	10 10	10 25	10 45		11 00	11 25	11 45	12 05	12 25	12 45	12 55	13 25	13 45		14 05	14 25	14 45	15 00
Kensington (Olympia) ⊖	d	23p51	07 49	08 53	09 08	09 28	09 48	10 13	10 28	10 48		11 03	11 28	11 48	12 08	12 28	12 48	12 58	13 28	13 48		14 08	14 28	14 48	15 03
West Brompton ⊖	d	23p54	07 51	08 56	09 10	09 30	09 50	10 15	10 30	10 50		11 05	11 30	11 50	12 10	12 30	12 50	13 00	13 30	13 50		14 10	14 30	14 50	15 05
Imperial Wharf	d	23p57	07 54	08 58	09 13	09 33	09 53	10 18	10 33	10 53		11 08	11 33	11 53	12 13	12 33	12 53	13 03	13 33	13 53		14 13	14 33	14 53	15 08
Clapham Junction 10	a	00 02	07 58	09 03	09 18	09 38	09 58	10 23	10 38	10 58		11 13	11 38	11 58	12 18	12 38	12 58	13 08	13 38	13 58		14 18	14 38	14 58	15 13
	d																								
Wandsworth Road	a																								
Wandsworth Common	a																								
Balham 4	a																								
Streatham Common 4	a																								
Norbury	a																								
Thornton Heath	a																								
Selhurst 4	a																								
East Croydon	a																								

Table 176

Sundays

Milton Keynes, Watford Junction, Kensington (Olympia) - Clapham Junction and East Croydon

Station		LO	SN 1	LO	LO	SN 1	LO	LO	SN 1	LO	LO	SN 1	LO	LO	SN 1
Milton Keynes Central 10	d														
Bletchley	d														
Leighton Buzzard	d														
Tring	d														
Berkhamsted	d														
Hemel Hempstead	d														
Watford Junction	d		15 22			16 22			17 22			18 22			19 22
Harrow & Wealdstone ⊖	d		15 28			16 28			17 28			18 28			19 28
Wembley Central ⊖	d														
Stratford 7 ⊖	d														
Highbury & Islington ⊖	d														
Gospel Oak	d														
West Hampstead ⊖	d														
Willesden Jn. High Level ⊖	d														
Shepherd's Bush ⊖	d	15 25	15 45	16 05	16 25	16 45	17 05	17 25	17 45	18 05	18 25	18 45	19 00	19 25	19 45
Kensington (Olympia) ⊖	d	15 28	15 48	16 08	16 28	16 48	17 08	17 28	17 48	18 08	18 28	18 48	19 03	19 28	19 48
West Brompton ⊖	d	15 30	15 50	16 10	16 30	16 50	17 10	17 30	17 50	18 10	18 30	18 50	19 05	19 30	19 50
Imperial Wharf	d	15 33	15 53	16 13	16 33	16 53	17 13	17 33	17 53	18 13	18 33	18 53	19 08	19 33	19 53
Clapham Junction 10	a	15 38	15 58	16 18	16 38	16 58	17 18	17 38	17 58	18 20	18 38	18 58	19 13	19 38	19 58
	d														
Wandsworth Road	a														
Wandsworth Common	a														
Balham 4	a														
Streatham Common 4	a														
Norbury	a														
Thornton Heath	a														
Selhurst 4	a														
East Croydon	a														

Station		LO	LO	SN 1	LO	LO	SN 1	LO	LO
Milton Keynes Central 10	d								
Bletchley	d								
Leighton Buzzard	d								
Tring	d								
Berkhamsted	d								
Hemel Hempstead	d								
Watford Junction	d			20 22			21 17		
Harrow & Wealdstone ⊖	d			20 28			21 23		
Wembley Central ⊖	d								
Stratford 7 ⊖	d								
Highbury & Islington ⊖	d								
Gospel Oak	d								
West Hampstead ⊖	d								
Willesden Jn. High Level ⊖	d								
Shepherd's Bush ⊖	d	20 05	20 25	20 45	21 05	21 25	21 45	22 05	22 25
Kensington (Olympia) ⊖	d	20 08	20 28	20 48	21 08	21 28	21 48	22 08	22 28
West Brompton ⊖	d	20 10	20 30	20 50	21 10	21 30	21 50	22 10	22 30
Imperial Wharf	d	20 13	20 33	20 53	21 13	21 33	21 53	22 13	22 33
Clapham Junction 10	a	20 20	20 38	20 58	21 18	21 38	21 58	22 18	22 38
	d								
Wandsworth Road	a								
Wandsworth Common	a								
Balham 4	a								
Streatham Common 4	a								
Norbury	a								
Thornton Heath	a								
Selhurst 4	a								
East Croydon	a								

Station		SN 1	LO	LO	SN 1
Milton Keynes Central 10	d				
Bletchley	d				
Leighton Buzzard	d				
Tring	d				
Berkhamsted	d				
Hemel Hempstead	d				
Watford Junction	d	22 17			23 17
Harrow & Wealdstone ⊖	d	22 23			23 23
Wembley Central ⊖	d				
Stratford 7 ⊖	d				
Highbury & Islington ⊖	d				
Gospel Oak	d				
West Hampstead ⊖	d				
Willesden Jn. High Level ⊖	d				
Shepherd's Bush ⊖	d	22 45	23 05	23 25	23 45
Kensington (Olympia) ⊖	d	22 48	23 08	23 28	23 48
West Brompton ⊖	d	22 50	23 10	23 30	23 50
Imperial Wharf	d	22 53	23 13	23 33	23 53
Clapham Junction 10	a		23 18		23 58
	d				00 02
Wandsworth Road	a				
Wandsworth Common	a				
Balham 4	a				
Streatham Common 4	a				
Norbury	a				
Thornton Heath	a				
Selhurst 4	a				00 18
East Croydon	a				00 22

Network Diagram for Tables 177, 178, 179, 181, 182 — also 175★

DM-17/10 Design BAJS

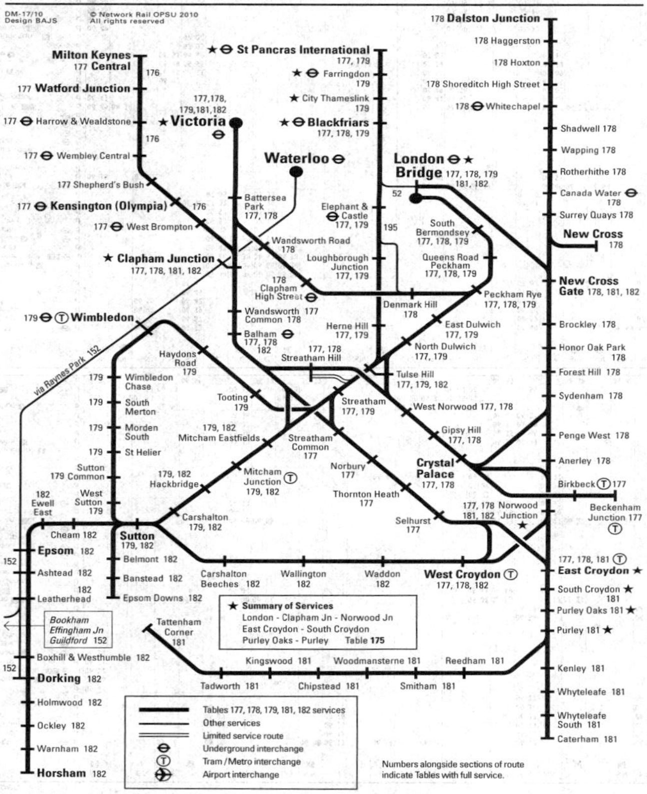

Luton, Milton Keynes and London - East and West Croydon via Tulse Hill - Crystal Palace - Norbury

Local Services

		SN MX 1	SN MO	SN MX	LO MX	SN MX	SN MO	SN MO	SN MX	SN MO	SN MX 1	SN MO	SN MX 1	SN MX	SN MO 1	SN MX ◇1	LO MO	FC	SN 1	SN	LO MX	SN MX	FC MX
London Bridge 4 ⊖	d		23p25			23p36		23p39										00 12				23p48	23p58
South Bermondsey	d		23p29																			23p52	
Queens Rd Peckham	d		23p31																			23p54	
Peckham Rye 4	d		23p34																			23p57	
East Dulwich	d		23p37																			00 01	
North Dulwich	d		23p39																			00 03	
Luton 10	d																						
Luton Airport Parkway 7	d																						
St Pancras International 15 ⊖	d																						
City Thameslink 3	d																						
London Blackfriars 3 ⊖	d																						
Elephant & Castle ⊖	d																						
Loughborough Jn	d																						
Herne Hill 4	d																						
Tulse Hill 3	d		23p42																			00 07	00 10
Streatham 4	d		23p46																				00 14
London Victoria 15 ⊖	d			23p34			23p36		23p37	23p47	23p47	23p49	23p49	23p51		00 05			00 14	00 17			
Battersea Park 4	d			23p38					23p41			23p53		23p55									
Milton Keynes Central	d	22p11																					
Watford Junction	d	22p53													23p17								
Harrow & Wealdstone ⊖	d	23p00													23p23								
Wembley Central ⊖	d																						
Shepherd's Bush ⊖	d	23p21													23p45								
Kensington (Olympia) ⊖	d	23p23													23p48								
West Brompton ⊖	d	23p26													23p50								
Clapham Junction 10	d	23b40		23p42			23p42		23p45	23p53	23p53	23p56	23p56	23p59	00 02	00 11			00 20	00 23			
Wandsworth Common	d			23p45					23p48			23p59		00 02									
Balham 4 ⊖	d	23p44		23p47			23p47		23p51			00 01		00 04						00 28			
Streatham Hill	d						23p50		23p54														
West Norwood 4	d						23p53		23p57													00 10	
Gipsy Hill	d						23p56		23p59													00 13	
Crystal Palace 4	d						23p59		00 03													00 15	
Birkbeck ⇌	d																						
Beckenham Junction 4 ⇌	a																						
Streatham Common 4	d	23p48	23p49	23p51								00 05		00 08						00 32			
Norbury	d	23p51	23p51	23p54								00 08		00 11						00 34			
Thornton Heath	d	23p54	23p54	23p57								00 11		00 14						00 37			
Selhurst 4	d	23p57	23p57	23p59								00 13		00 17	00 19					00 40			
Norwood Junction 2	a				23p50	23p59	00 03	00 02	00 07								00 08				00 20	00 22	
	d				23p50	23p59		00 05	00 09								00 08				00 20		
West Croydon 4 ⇌	a			00 03	00 01				00 14					00 21			00 15				00 27		
East Croydon ⇌	a	00 01	00 01			00 03		00 08		00 06	00 05	00 16	00 09		00 22	00 24		00 26	00 31	00 43			

		SN MX	SN MX	SN	FC	SN ◇1	FC 1	FC 1	SN 1	FC 1	SN 1	FC	FC 1	SN ◇1	FC 1	FC 1	SN ◇1	FC 1	FC 1	FC 1	FC	FC 1	SN 1	SN ◇1
London Bridge 4 ⊖	d	00 06	00 36		00 42		01 05	01 35		02 05		03 05	03 35		04 05	04 35								
South Bermondsey	d																							
Queens Rd Peckham	d																							
Peckham Rye 4	d																							
East Dulwich	d																							
North Dulwich	d																							
Luton 10	d																	04 06	04 34	04 44	05 08	05 24		
Luton Airport Parkway 7	d																	04 08	04 36	04 46	05 10	05 26		
St Pancras International 15 ⊖	d																	04 54	05 12	05 32	05 54	06 02		
City Thameslink 3	d																		05 21	05 41	06 01	06 11		
London Blackfriars 3 ⊖	d																	05 04	05 24	05 44	06 06	06 14		
Elephant & Castle ⊖	d																				06 09			
Loughborough Jn	d																				06 13			
Herne Hill 4	d																				06 16			
Tulse Hill 3	d																				06 22			
Streatham 4	d																				06 25			
London Victoria 15 ⊖	d			00 42		01 00			02 00		03 00			04 00			05 02						05 23	05 32
Battersea Park 4	d			00 46																				
Milton Keynes Central	d																							
Watford Junction	d																							
Harrow & Wealdstone ⊖	d																							
Wembley Central ⊖	d																							
Shepherd's Bush ⊖	d																							
Kensington (Olympia) ⊖	d																							
West Brompton ⊖	d																							
Clapham Junction 10	d			00 50		01 08			02 08		03 08			04 08			05 08						05 33	05 38
Wandsworth Common	d			00 53																				
Balham 4 ⊖	d			00 55																				
Streatham Hill	d																							
West Norwood 4	d																							
Gipsy Hill	d																							
Crystal Palace 4	d																							
Birkbeck ⇌	d																							
Beckenham Junction 4 ⇌	a																							
Streatham Common 4	d			00 59																				
Norbury	d			01 02																				
Thornton Heath	d			01 05																				
Selhurst 4	d			01 07													05 17	05 27						
Norwood Junction 2	a	00 29	00 59																				05 49	
	d	00 30	01 00																				05 50	
West Croydon 4 ⇌	a																							
East Croydon ⇌	a	00 33	01 03	01 10	00 56	01 21	01 32	02 02	02 21	02 30	03 21	03 30	04 00	04 21	04 30	05 00	05 20	05 30	05 51	06 04	06 35	06 35	05 53	05 48

b previous night, arr. 2333

Table 177 Mondays to Fridays

Luton, Milton Keynes and London - East and West Croydon via Tulse Hill - Crystal Palace - Norbury

Local Services

		FC 1	SN	SN	SN 1	SN	SN	SN ◇1	LO	SN 1	SN	SN	LO	SN	LO	SN	SN	SN	SN	SN ◇1	SN 1	SN
London Bridge 4 ⊖	d			05 36		06 00				06 08	06 11	06 19		06 06				06 18				06 30
South Bermondsey	d					06 04					06 15							06 22				06 34
Queens Rd Peckham	d					06 06					06 18							06 24				06 36
Peckham Rye 4	d					06 09					06 20							06 27				06 39
East Dulwich	d					06 12												06 30				06 42
North Dulwich	d					06 14												06 32				06 44
Luton 10	d	05 44																				
Luton Airport Parkway 7	d	05 46																				
St Pancras International 15 ⊖	d	06 22																				
City Thameslink 3	d	06 31																				
London Blackfriars 3 ⊖	d	06 34																				
Elephant & Castle ⊖	d																					
Loughborough Jn	d																					
Herne Hill 4	d																					
Tulse Hill 3	d					06 18												06 36				06 48
Streatham 4	d					06 21												06 39				06 51
London Victoria 15 ⊖	d				05 53		06 00	06 02								06 07	06 15		06 19	06 21	06 24	
Battersea Park 4	d						06 04				06 32					06 11	06 19		06 23			
Milton Keynes Central	d																					
Watford Junction	d																					
Harrow & Wealdstone ⊖	d																					
Wembley Central ⊖	d																					
Shepherd's Bush ⊖	d																					
Kensington (Olympia) ⊖	d																					
West Brompton ⊖	d																					
Clapham Junction 10	d				05 59		06 08	06 08								06 15	06 23		06 27	06 27	06 30	
Wandsworth Common	d						06 11									06 18	06 26		06 30			
Balham 4 ⊖	d						06 13									06 20	06 28		06 32			
Streatham Hill	d															06 23			06 35			
West Norwood 4	d															06 27			06 39			
Gipsy Hill	d											06 41				06 30			06 42			
Crystal Palace 4	d															06 32			06 44			
Birkbeck ⇌	d																					
Beckenham Junction 4 ⇌	a																					
Streatham Common 4	d						06 17										06 32	06 42				
Norbury	d						06 20										06 35	06 45				
Thornton Heath	d						06 23										06 38	06 48				
Selhurst 4	d						06 26										06 41	06 51				
Norwood Junction 2	a			06 00					06 05				06 20	06 29	06 35	06 37						
	d		05 53	06 00					06 05				06 20	06 30	06 35	06 39						
West Croydon 4 ⇌	a		05 57	06 05			06 31		06 13				06 31		06 42	06 44		06 55				
East Croydon ⇌	a	06 55			06 09			06 17		06 22				06 33			06 45			06 38	06 40	

		SN	SN ◇1	SN	SN	SN	FC	FC 1	FC	FC 1	LO	SN	SN	SN 1	LO	SN	SN	SN ◇1	SN	SN	SN 1	SN 1	SN	SN
London Bridge 4 ⊖	d			06 41		06 33						06 36	06 51	07 03					06 48				06 54	06 58
South Bermondsey	d			06 45		06 37													06 52					07 02
Queens Rd Peckham	d			06 48		06 39													06 54					07 04
Peckham Rye 4	d			06 50		06 42													06 57					07 07
East Dulwich	d					06 45													07 00					07 10
North Dulwich	d					06 47													07 02					07 12
Luton 10	d						05 48	06 04	06 06	06 22														
Luton Airport Parkway 7	d						05 50	06 06	06 08	06 24														
St Pancras International 15 ⊖	d						06 34	06 38	06 52	06 58														
City Thameslink 3	d						06 43	06 47	07 01	07 07														
London Blackfriars 3 ⊖	d						06 46	06 50	07 04	07 09														
Elephant & Castle ⊖	d						06 49		07 07															
Loughborough Jn	d						06 53		07 11															
Herne Hill 4	d						06 57		07 16															
Tulse Hill 3	d					06 50	07 02		07 20										07 07					07 16
Streatham 4	d						07 05		07 23										07 10					07 19
London Victoria 15 ⊖	d	06 32	06 32													06 36	06 44	06 47		06 49	06 51	06 54		
Battersea Park 4	d	06 36		07 02												06 40				06 53				
Milton Keynes Central	d																							
Watford Junction	d																							
Harrow & Wealdstone ⊖	d																							
Wembley Central ⊖	d																							
Shepherd's Bush ⊖	d																							
Kensington (Olympia) ⊖	d																							
West Brompton ⊖	d																							
Clapham Junction 10	d	06 40	06 38													06 44	06 50	06 53		06 57	06 57	07 00		
Wandsworth Common	d	06 43														06 47	06 53			07 00				
Balham 4 ⊖	d	06 45														06 49	06 56			07 02				
Streatham Hill	d				06 42											06 53				07 05				
West Norwood 4	d				06 45	06 53										06 56				07 09				
Gipsy Hill	d				06 48	06 56							07 15			06 59				07 12				
Crystal Palace 4	d				06 51	06 59										07 02				07 14				
Birkbeck ⇌	d					07 03																		
Beckenham Junction 4 ⇌	a					07 06																		
Streatham Common 4	d	06 49															07 00		07 13					
Norbury	d	06 52															07 02		07 16					
Thornton Heath	d	06 55															07 05		07 19					
Selhurst 4	d	06 58															07 09		07 21					
Norwood Junction 2	a										06 50	06 59			07 05	07 07							07 17	
	d										06 50	07 00			07 05	07 09							07 18	
West Croydon 4 ⇌	a	07 02									07 01				07 12	07 13			07 25					
East Croydon ⇌	a		06 48					07 14		07 30		07 03		07 16			07 12	07 03			07 06	07 10	07 21	

Table 177

Mondays to Fridays

Luton, Milton Keynes and London - East and West Croydon via Tulse Hill - Crystal Palace - Norbury

Local Services

		SN	SN 1	SN		SN	SN	LO	SN	SN 1	SN	SN 1	SN 1	LO		SN	SN 1	SN	SN ◇1	SN	SN	FC 1	FC 1	FC
London Bridge 4 ⊖	d			07 11			07 03		07 06	07 19	07 21	07 25	07 33								07 16			
South Bermondsey	d			07 15			07 07														07 20			
Queens Rd Peckham	d			07 17			07 09														07 22			
Peckham Rye 4	d			07 20			07 12														07 25			
East Dulwich	d						07 15														07 28			
North Dulwich	d						07 17														07 30			
Luton 10	d																					06 34	06 46	06 36
Luton Airport Parkway 7	d																						06 48	06 38
St Pancras International 15 ⊖	d																					07 06	07 20	07 24
City Thameslink 3	d																					07 15	07 29	07 33
London Blackfriars 3 ⊖	d																					07 18	07 32	07 36
Elephant & Castle ⊖	d																					07 21		07 40
Loughborough Jn	d																					07 25		
Herne Hill 4	d																					07 31		07 46
Tulse Hill 3	d						07 20														07 34	07 37		
Streatham 4	d																				07 37	07 40		
London Victoria 15 ⊖	d	07 00	07 02													07 06	07 10	07 17	07 17	07 20				
Battersea Park 4	d	07 04		07 32												07 10		07 21		07 24				
Milton Keynes Central	d																							
Watford Junction	d																							
Harrow & Wealdstone ⊖	d																							
Wembley Central ⊖	d																							
Shepherd's Bush ⊖	d																							
Kensington (Olympia) ⊖	d																							
West Brompton ⊖	d																							
Clapham Junction 10	d	07 08	07 08													07 14	07 16	07 25	07 23	07 28				
Wandsworth Common	d	07 11														07 17				07 31				
Balham 4 ⊖	d	07 13														07 20		07 29		07 33				
Streatham Hill	d					07 12										07 23		07 32						
West Norwood 4	d					07 15	07 23									07 27		07 38						
Gipsy Hill	d					07 18	07 26				07 45					07 30		07 41						
Crystal Palace 4	d					07 21	07 29									07 32		07 44						
Birkbeck	d						07 33																	
Beckenham Junction 4	a						07 36																	
Streatham Common 4	d	07 18																		07 37	07 41			
Norbury	d	07 21																		07 40	07 43			
Thornton Heath	d	07 24																		07 43	07 46			
Selhurst 4	d	07 27																		07 46	07 50			
Norwood Junction 2	a							07 21	07 29	07 30		07 36		07 36		07 38								
	d							07 21	07 31	07 30		07 36		07 36		07 39								
West Croydon 4	a	07 32						07 31						07 43		07 44					07 55			
East Croydon	a		07 17						07 37	07 34		07 40	07 48				07 26		07 33	07 49			07 55	

		FC 1	SN	SN	SN 1	SN	SN 1	SN	SN	LO	SN	SN	SN 1	SN 1	LO	SN 1	SN	SN 1	SN		SN	FC	FC 1	FC 1
London Bridge 4 ⊖	d		07 29		07 30	07 33		07 41	07 46		07 36	07 51	07 53	08 00		07 56					07 47			
South Bermondsey	d		07 33			07 37		07 45																
Queens Rd Peckham	d		07 35			07 39		07 47																
Peckham Rye 4	d		07 38			07 42		07 50													07 53			
East Dulwich	d		07 41			07 45															07 56			
North Dulwich	d		07 43			07 47															07 58			
Luton 10	d	06 56																				06 50	07 16	07 24
Luton Airport Parkway 7	d																					06 52		07 26
St Pancras International 15 ⊖	d	07 28																				07 32	07 48	07 59
City Thameslink 3	d	07 37																				07 41	07 57	08 07
London Blackfriars 3 ⊖	d	07 40																				07 44	08 00	08 10
Elephant & Castle ⊖	d	07 44																				07 47		
Loughborough Jn	d																					07 51		
Herne Hill 4	d																					07 56		
Tulse Hill 3	d		07 47			07 50															08 02	08 05	08 13	
Streatham 4	d		07 51																		08 05	08 09		
London Victoria 15 ⊖	d			07 30			07 36										07 36	07 40	07 45					
Battersea Park 4	d			07 34				08 02									07 40							
Milton Keynes Central	d																							
Watford Junction	d																							
Harrow & Wealdstone ⊖	d																							
Wembley Central ⊖	d																							
Shepherd's Bush ⊖	d																							
Kensington (Olympia) ⊖	d																							
West Brompton ⊖	d																							
Clapham Junction 10	d			07 38			07 42										07 44	07 46	07 51					
Wandsworth Common	d			07 41													07 47		07 54					
Balham 4 ⊖	d			07 44													07 50		07 57					
Streatham Hill	d																07 53							
West Norwood 4	d					07 53											07 58							
Gipsy Hill	d					07 56						08 15					08 01							
Crystal Palace 4	d					07 59											08 04							
Birkbeck	d					08 03																		
Beckenham Junction 4	a					08 06																		
Streatham Common 4	d			07 48															08 01		08 08			
Norbury	d			07 50															08 03		08 11			
Thornton Heath	d			07 53															08 06		08 14			
Selhurst 4	d			07 56															08 09		08 17			
Norwood Junction 2	a				07 41					07 50	07 59				08 06	08 07	08 08							
	d				07 42					07 50	08 00				08 06	08 07	08 09							
West Croydon 4	a			08 02						08 01					08 13		08 14				08 22			
East Croydon	a				07 45		07 52		08 00		08 03		08 06	08 15		08 10		07 56	08 12				08 25	08 36

Table 177

Mondays to Fridays

Luton, Milton Keynes and London - East and West Croydon via Tulse Hill - Crystal Palace - Norbury

Local Services

		SN ◇1	SN	SN ◇1	SN 1	SN ◇1		SN	SN ◇1 🍴	SN 1	SN	SN	SN	SN	LO	SN		SN	SN	SN 1	SN 1	SN	LO	SN	SN 1
London Bridge 4 ⊖	d				08 02					08 08	08 10		08 03	08 06		08 14		08 06	08 20	08 23	08 25	08 27			
South Bermondsey	d										08 14		08 07	08 11											
Queens Rd Peckham	d										08 16		08 09	08 13											
Peckham Rye 4	d										08 19		08 12	08 16											
East Dulwich	d												08 15	08 19											
North Dulwich	d												08 17	08 21											
Luton 10	d																								
Luton Airport Parkway 7	d																								
St Pancras International 15 ⊖	d																								
City Thameslink 3	d																								
London Blackfriars 3 ⊖	d																								
Elephant & Castle ⊖	d																								
Loughborough Jn	d																								
Herne Hill 4	d																								
Tulse Hill 3	d												08 21	08 25											
Streatham 4	d													08 28											
London Victoria 15 ⊖	d	07 47	07 52	07 52		08 02		08 03	08 07															08 07	08 10
Battersea Park 4	d							08 07			08 32													08 11	
Milton Keynes Central	d																								
Watford Junction	d																								
Harrow & Wealdstone ⊖	d																								
Wembley Central ⊖	d																								
Shepherd's Bush ⊖	d																								
Kensington (Olympia) ⊖	d																								
West Brompton ⊖	d																								
Clapham Junction 10	d	07 53	07 58	07 58		08 08		08 11	08 13															08 15	08 16
Wandsworth Common	d							08 14																08 18	
Balham 4 ⊖	d		08 03					08 16																08 20	
Streatham Hill	d		08 06									08 15												08 23	
West Norwood 4	d		08 09									08 19	08 24											08 28	
Gipsy Hill	d		08 12									08 22	08 27						08 43					08 31	
Crystal Palace 4	d		08 15									08 24	08 29											08 33	
Birkbeck	d												08 33												
Beckenham Junction 4	a												08 37												
Streatham Common 4	d							08 20																	
Norbury	d							08 23																	
Thornton Heath	d							08 26																	
Selhurst 4	d							08 32																	
Norwood Junction 2	a				08 14										08 20	08 26		08 29			08 36		08 36	08 38	
	d				08 14										08 20	08 27		08 30			08 36		08 36	08 39	
West Croydon 4	a							08 36							08 31								08 44	08 44	
East Croydon	a	08 03		08 09	08 18	08 18			08 22	08 22						08 30		08 33		08 37	08 40	08 42			08 26

		SN		SN	FC	FC 1	SN ◇1	SN ◇1	SN	SN 1	SN	SN		SN	SN 1	SN	SN ◇1 🍴	SN	FC 1	FC 1	SN ◇1 🍴	SN		SN	LO
London Bridge 4 ⊖	d			08 17					08 24	08 32								08 33				08 41		08 47	
South Bermondsey	d								08 28									08 37				08 45			
Queens Rd Peckham	d								08 30									08 39				08 48			
Peckham Rye 4	d			08 23					08 33									08 42				08 50			
East Dulwich	d			08 26					08 36									08 45							
North Dulwich	d			08 28					08 38									08 47							
Luton 10	d				07 30	07 48													07 56	08 12					
Luton Airport Parkway 7	d				07 32														07 58	08 14					
St Pancras International 15 ⊖	d				08 12	08 20													08 32	08 48					
City Thameslink 3	d				08 21	08 29													08 41	08 57					
London Blackfriars 3 ⊖	d				08 24	08 32													08 44	09 00					
Elephant & Castle ⊖	d				08 27														08 47						
Loughborough Jn	d				08 31														08 51						
Herne Hill 4	d				08 36														08 57						
Tulse Hill 3	d			08 32	08 40				08 47									08 50	09 01						
Streatham 4	d			08 36	08 44				08 50										09 05						
London Victoria 15 ⊖	d	08 15					08 17	08 21				08 22		08 26		08 31	08 32				08 36				
Battersea Park 4	d	08 19										08 26				08 36						09 02			
Milton Keynes Central	d														07 01										
Watford Junction	d														07 38										
Harrow & Wealdstone ⊖	d														07 45										
Wembley Central ⊖	d														07u49										
Shepherd's Bush ⊖	d														08 04										
Kensington (Olympia) ⊖	d														08 07										
West Brompton ⊖	d														08 10										
Clapham Junction 10	d	08 23					08 23	08 27				08 30		08 33	08b36	08 40	08 38				08 43				
Wandsworth Common	d	08 26										08 33		08 36	08 39	08 43									
Balham 4 ⊖	d	08 28										08 35		08 38	08 42	08 46									
Streatham Hill	d										08 35	08 38													
West Norwood 4	d										08 38	08 42						08 53							
Gipsy Hill	d										08 41	08 45						08 56							
Crystal Palace 4	d										08 44	08 51						08 59							
Birkbeck	d																	09 03							
Beckenham Junction 4	a																	09 06							
Streatham Common 4	d	08 32		08 39										08 42	08 46	08 51									
Norbury	d	08 35		08 41										08 45	08 48	08 54									
Thornton Heath	d	08 38		08 44										08 48	08 51	08 57									
Selhurst 4	d	08 41		08 47										08 51	08 54	09 00									
Norwood Junction 2	a									08 44															08 50
	d									08 45															08 50
West Croydon 4	a			08 52										08 55		09 05									09 01
East Croydon	a	08 44				08 56	08 33	08 39		08 48					09 04		08 48			09 24	08 52			09 02	

b arr. 0817

Luton, Milton Keynes and London - East and West Croydon via Tulse Hill - Crystal Palace - Norbury

Local Services

		SN ■	SN	SN	LO	SN	SN	SN ◇■		SN	SN	SN	SN ■	SN ◇■	SN	FC	FC ■	FC	FC ■	SN	SN ■	SN ■	SN	LO	SN ■
London Bridge ■ ⊖	d	08 45	08 36	08 51								08 48			09 03						09 03	09 08	09 11		09 15
South Bermondsey	d											08 52			09 07								09 15		
Queens Rd Peckham	d											08 54			09 09								09 18		
Peckham Rye ■	d											08 57			09 12								09 20		
East Dulwich	d											09 00			09 15										
North Dulwich	d											09 02			09 17										
Luton ■	d																08 28		08 48						
Luton Airport Parkway ■	d																08 30		08 50						
St Pancras International ■ ⊖	d															08 56	09 04	09 16	09 24						
City Thameslink ■	d															09 05	09 13	09 25	09 32						
London Blackfriars ■ ⊖	d															09 08	09 16	09 28	09 34						
Elephant & Castle ⊖	d															09 12		09 31							
Loughborough Jn	d															09 16		09 35							
Herne Hill ■	d															09 25		09 41							
Tulse Hill ■	d											09 05			09 20	09 31		09 46							
Streatham ■	d											09 09				09 35		09 50							
London Victoria ■ ⊖	d					08 36	08 43	08 47		08 49	08 52		08 53	09 02						09 03					
Battersea Park ■	d					08 40	08 47			08 53	08 56									09 07			09 32		
Milton Keynes Central	d																								
Watford Junction	d																								
Harrow & Wealdstone ⊖	d																								
Wembley Central ⊖	d																								
Shepherd's Bush ⊖	d																								
Kensington (Olympia) ⊖	d																								
West Brompton ⊖	d																								
Clapham Junction ■	d					08 44	08 51	08 53		08 57	09 00		08 59	09 08						09 11					
Wandsworth Common	d					08 47	08 54			09 00	09 03									09 14					
Balham ■ ⊖	d					08 50	08 56			09 02	09 05									09 16					
Streatham Hill	d					08 53				09 05															
West Norwood ■	d					08 57				09 09					09 23										
Gipsy Hill	d			09 15		09 00				09 12					09 26										
Crystal Palace ■	d					09 02				09 14					09 29										
Birkbeck	d														09 33										
Beckenham Junction ■	a														09 36										
Streatham Common ■	d						09 00				09 09	09 13								09 20					
Norbury	d						09 03				09 12	09 15								09 23					
Thornton Heath	d						09 06				09 15	09 18								09 26					
Selhurst ■	d						09 09				09 17	09 21								09 29					
Norwood Junction ■	a	08 56	08 59		09 05	09 07															09 14			09 20	09 26
	d	08 56	09 00		09 05	09 09															09 15			09 20	09 26
West Croydon ■	a				09 12	09 13					09 21	09 25								09 33				09 31	
East Croydon	a	08 59	09 06				09 12	09 03					09 09	09 18			09 39		09 54		09 18	09 22			09 30

		SN	SN	SN		LO	SN	SN ◇■	SN	SN ◇■	SN	SN ◇■	SN	SN		SN ■	SN ■	SN ■	SN ◇■	SN	FC	FC ■	FC ■	SN	
London Bridge ■ ⊖	d	09 06	09 20	09 22										09 18				09 32		09 33					
South Bermondsey	d													09 22						09 37					
Queens Rd Peckham	d													09 24						09 39					
Peckham Rye ■	d													09 27						09 42					
East Dulwich	d													09 30						09 45					
North Dulwich	d													09 32						09 47					
Luton ■	d																				08 54	09 04	09 18		
Luton Airport Parkway ■	d																				08 56	09 06	09 20		
St Pancras International ■ ⊖	d																				09 34	09 40	09 54		
City Thameslink ■	d																				09 43	09 47	10 02		
London Blackfriars ■ ⊖	d																				09 46	09 50	10 05		
Elephant & Castle ⊖	d																				09 49				
Loughborough Jn	d																				09 53				
Herne Hill ■	d																				09 57				
Tulse Hill ■	d													09 35						09 50	10 01				
Streatham ■	d													09 39							10 05				
London Victoria ■ ⊖	d						09 05	09 06	09 13	09 17	09 19	09 21	09 22				09 23		09 32					09 33	
Battersea Park ■	d						09 10		09 17		09 23													09 37	
Milton Keynes Central	d															08 13									
Watford Junction	d															08 51									
Harrow & Wealdstone ⊖	d															08 58									
Wembley Central ⊖	d															09u05									
Shepherd's Bush ⊖	d															09 18									
Kensington (Olympia) ⊖	d															09 21									
West Brompton ⊖	d															09 23									
Clapham Junction ■	d						09 14	09 12	09 21	09 23	09 27		09 30			09 34	09 29		09 38					09 41	
Wandsworth Common	d						09 17		09 24		09 30		09 33			09 37								09 44	
Balham ■ ⊖	d						09 20		09 26		09 32		09 35			09 41								09 46	
Streatham Hill	d						09 23				09 35														
West Norwood ■	d						09 27				09 39									09 53					
Gipsy Hill	d			09 46			09 30				09 42									09 56					
Crystal Palace ■	d						09 32				09b51									09 59					
Birkbeck	d																			10 03					
Beckenham Junction ■	a																			10 06					
Streatham Common ■	d								09 30				09 39	09 42		09 45								09 50	
Norbury	d								09 33				09 42	09 45		09 48								09 53	
Thornton Heath	d								09 36				09 45	09 48		09 51								09 56	
Selhurst ■	d								09 39				09 48	09 51		09 54								09 59	
Norwood Junction ■	a	09 30	09 32			09 35	09 37											09 44							
	d	09 30	09 33			09 35	09 39											09 45							
West Croydon ■	a					09 42	09 43						09 52	09 55										10 03	
East Croydon	a	09 33	09 36					09 22	09 42	09 33		09 37				09 57	09 39	09 48	09 48			10 09	10 24		

b arr. 0945

Table 177 — Mondays to Fridays

Luton, Milton Keynes and London - East and West Croydon via Tulse Hill - Crystal Palace - Norbury

Local Services

		SN	LO	SN ■	SN	SN	SN	LO	SN	SN ◇■		SN	SN ◇■	SN	SN ■	SN	SN	FC	SN ◇■	SN	FC	FC ■	FC ■	SN	SN ■
London Bridge ■ ⊖	d	09 41		09 45	09 36	09 50	09 52										09 48			10 03					10 03
South Bermondsey	d	09 45															09 52			10 07					
Queens Rd Peckham	d	09 48															09 54			10 09					
Peckham Rye ■	d	09 50															09 57			10 12					
East Dulwich	d																10 00			10 15					
North Dulwich	d																10 02			10 17					
Luton ■	d																				09 14	09 34	09 48		
Luton Airport Parkway ■	d																				09 16	09 36	09 50		
St Pancras International ■ ⊖	d																	09 48			10 04	10 10	10 24		
City Thameslink ■	d																	09 57			10 13	10 17	10 32		
London Blackfriars ■ ⊖	d																	10 00			10 16	10 20	10 35		
Elephant & Castle ⊖	d																	10 03			10 19				
Loughborough Jn	d																	10 07			10 23				
Herne Hill ■	d																	10 11			10 27				
Tulse Hill ■	d																10 05	10 16		10 20	10 31				
Streatham ■	d																10 09	10 20			10 35				
London Victoria ■ ⊖	d								09 35	09 36		09 43	09 47	09 49	09 53	09 53			10 02					10 03	
Battersea Park ■	d	10 03							09 40			09 47		09 53										10 07	
Milton Keynes Central	d																								
Watford Junction	d																								
Harrow & Wealdstone ⊖	d																								
Wembley Central ⊖	d																								
Shepherd's Bush ⊖	d																								
Kensington (Olympia) ⊖	d																								
West Brompton ⊖	d																								
Clapham Junction ■	d								09 44	09 42		09 51	09 53	09 57	09 59	10 00			10 08					10 11	
Wandsworth Common	d								09 47			09 54		10 00		10 03								10 14	
Balham ■ ⊖	d								09 50			09 56		10 02		10 05								10 16	
Streatham Hill	d								09 53					10 05											
West Norwood ■	d								09 57					10 10						10 23					
Gipsy Hill	d						10 15		10 00					10 13						10 26					
Crystal Palace ■	d								10 02					10 21						10 29					
Birkbeck	d																			10 33					
Beckenham Junction ■	a																			10 36					
Streatham Common ■	d											10 00				10 09	10 12							10 20	
Norbury	d											10 03				10 12	10 15							10 23	
Thornton Heath	d											10 06				10 15	10 18							10 26	
Selhurst ■	d											10 09				10 18	10 21							10 29	
Norwood Junction ■	a		09 50	09 56	09 59	10 02		10 05	10 07																10 14
	d		09 50	09 56	10 00	10 03		10 05	10 09																10 15
West Croydon ■	a		10 01					10 12	10 13							10 22	10 25							10 33	
East Croydon	a			10 00	10 03	10 06				09 52		10 12	10 03		10 09				10 18			10 39	10 54		10 18

		SN ◇■	SN ■	SN	LO	SN ■	SN	SN	SN	LO	SN	SN	SN ◇■	SN	SN ◇■	SN ■	SN	SN	FC	SN ■	SN ◇■	SN	FC	FC ■	FC
London Bridge ■ ⊖	d		10 08	10 11		10 15	10 06	10 20	10 22									10 18				10 33			
South Bermondsey	d			10 15														10 22				10 37			
Queens Rd Peckham	d			10 18														10 24				10 39			
Peckham Rye ■	d			10 20														10 27				10 42			
East Dulwich	d																	10 30				10 45			
North Dulwich	d																	10 32				10 47			
Luton ■	d																						09 44	10 04	
Luton Airport Parkway ■	d																						09 46	10 06	
St Pancras International ■ ⊖	d																		10 18				10 34	10 40	10 48
City Thameslink ■	d																		10 27				10 43	10 47	10 57
London Blackfriars ■ ⊖	d																		10 30				10 46	10 50	1100
Elephant & Castle ⊖	d																		10 33				10 49		1103
Loughborough Jn	d																		10 37				10 53		1107
Herne Hill ■	d																		10 41				10 57		1111
Tulse Hill ■	d																	10 35	10 46			10 50	11 01		11 16
Streatham ■	d																	10 39	10 50				11 05		11 20
London Victoria ■ ⊖	d	10 06									10 06	10 13	10 17	10 19	10 21	10 23	10 23				10 32				
Battersea Park ■	d			10 32							10 10	10 17		10 23											
Milton Keynes Central	d																			09 13					
Watford Junction	d																			09 51					
Harrow & Wealdstone ⊖	d																			09 58					
Wembley Central ⊖	d																			10u05					
Shepherd's Bush ⊖	d																			10 21					
Kensington (Olympia) ⊖	d																			10 24					
West Brompton ⊖	d																			10 27					
Clapham Junction ■	d	10 12									10 14	10 21	10 23	10 27		10 29	10 30			10 34	10 38				
Wandsworth Common	d										10 17	10 24		10 30			10 33			10 37					
Balham ■ ⊖	d										10 20	10 26		10 32			10 35			10 40					
Streatham Hill	d										10 23			10 35											
West Norwood ■	d										10 27			10 40								10 53			
Gipsy Hill	d								10 45		10 30			10 43								10 56			
Crystal Palace ■	d										10 32			10 51								10 59			
Birkbeck	d																					11 03			
Beckenham Junction ■	a																					11 06			
Streatham Common ■	d											10 30					10 39	10 42		10 45					
Norbury	d											10 33					10 42	10 45		10 48					
Thornton Heath	d											10 36					10 45	10 48		10 51					
Selhurst ■	d											10 39					10 48	10 51		10 54					
Norwood Junction ■	a				10 20	10 26	10 29	10 32		10 35	10 37														
	d				10 20	10 26	10 30	10 33		10 35	10 39														
West Croydon ■	a				10 31					10 42	10 43						10 52	10 55							
East Croydon	a	10 22	10 22			10 30	10 33	10 36				10 42	10 33		10 37	10 39				10 57	10 48			11 09	

Table 177

Mondays to Fridays

Luton, Milton Keynes and London - East and West Croydon via Tulse Hill - Crystal Palace - Norbury

Local Services

		FC 1		SN	SN 1	SN ◇1	SN	LO	SN 1	SN	SN	SN	LO	SN	SN	SN ◇1	SN	SN 1	SN	SN	SN ◇1		SN	FC	FC
London Bridge 4 ⊖	d				10 33		10 41		10 45	10 36	10 50	10 52								10 48			11 03		
South Bermondsey	d						10 45													10 52			11 07		
Queens Rd Peckham	d						10 48													10 54			11 09		
Peckham Rye 4	d						10 50													10 57			11 12		
East Dulwich	d																			11 00			11 15		
North Dulwich	d																			11 02			11 17		
Luton 10	d	10 18																						10 14	
Luton Airport Parkway 7	d	10 20																						10 16	
St Pancras International 15 ⊖	d	10 54																						11 04	11 18
City Thameslink 3	d	11 02																						11 13	11 27
London Blackfriars 3 ⊖	d	11 05																						11 16	11 30
Elephant & Castle ⊖	d																							11 19	11 33
Loughborough Jn	d																							11 23	11 37
Herne Hill 4	d																							11 27	11 41
Tulse Hill 3	d																			11 05			11 20	11 31	11 46
Streatham 4	d																			11 09				11 35	11 50
London Victoria 15 ⊖	d			10 33		10 36								10 36	10 43	10 47	10 49	10 53	10 53		11 02				
Battersea Park 4	d			10 37			11 02							10 40	10 47		10 53								
Milton Keynes Central	d																								
Watford Junction	d																								
Harrow & Wealdstone ⊖	d																								
Wembley Central ⊖	d																								
Shepherd's Bush ⊖	d																								
Kensington (Olympia) ⊖	d																								
West Brompton ⊖	d																								
Clapham Junction 10	d			10 41		10 42								10 44	10 51	10 53	10 57	10 59	11 00		11 08				
Wandsworth Common	d			10 44										10 47	10 54		11 00		11 03						
Balham 4 ⊖	d			10 46										10 50	10 56		11 02		11 05						
Streatham Hill	d													10 53			11 05								
West Norwood 4	d													10 57			11 10						11 23		
Gipsy Hill	d											11 15		11 00			11 13						11 26		
Crystal Palace 4	d													11 02			11 21						11 29		
Birkbeck	d																						11 33		
Beckenham Junction 4	a																						11 36		
Streatham Common 4	d			10 50											11 00				11 09	11 12					
Norbury	d			10 53											11 03				11 12	11 15					
Thornton Heath	d			10 56											11 06				11 15	11 18					
Selhurst 4	d			10 59											11 09				11 18	11 21					
Norwood Junction 2	a				10 44			10 50	10 56	10 59	11 02		11 05	11 07											
	d				10 45			10 50	10 56	11 00	11 03		11 05	11 09											
West Croydon 4	a			11 03				11 01					11 12	11 13					11 22	11 25					
East Croydon	a	11 24			10 48	10 52			11 00	11 03	11 06				11 12	11 03		11 09			11 18				

		FC 1	FC 1	FC	SN	SN 1	SN ◇1	SN 1	SN	LO	SN 1	SN	SN	SN	LO	SN	SN	SN ◇1		SN	SN ◇1	SN 1	SN	SN	SN 1
London Bridge 4 ⊖	d					11 03		11 08	11 11		11 15	11 06	11 20	11 22										11 18	
South Bermondsey	d								11 15															11 22	
Queens Rd Peckham	d								11 18															11 24	
Peckham Rye 4	d								11 20															11 27	
East Dulwich	d																							11 30	
North Dulwich	d																							11 32	
Luton 10	d	10 34	10 48																						
Luton Airport Parkway 7	d	10 36	10 50																						
St Pancras International 15 ⊖	d	11 10	11 24	11 48																					
City Thameslink 3	d	11 17	11 32	11 57																					
London Blackfriars 3 ⊖	d	11 20	11 35	12 00																					
Elephant & Castle ⊖	d			12 03																					
Loughborough Jn	d			12 07																					
Herne Hill 4	d			12 11																					
Tulse Hill 3	d			12 16																				11 35	
Streatham 4	d			12 20																				11 39	
London Victoria 15 ⊖	d				11 03		11 06									11 06	11 13	11 17		11 19	11 21	11 23	11 23		
Battersea Park 4	d				11 07				11 32							11 10	11 17			11 23					
Milton Keynes Central	d																								10 13
Watford Junction	d																								10 51
Harrow & Wealdstone ⊖	d																								10 59
Wembley Central ⊖	d																								11u04
Shepherd's Bush ⊖	d																								11 19
Kensington (Olympia) ⊖	d																								11 21
West Brompton ⊖	d																								11 23
Clapham Junction 10	d				11 11		11 12									11 14	11 21	11 23		11 27		11 29	11 30		11 34
Wandsworth Common	d				11 14											11 17	11 24			11 30			11 33		11 37
Balham 4 ⊖	d				11 16											11 20	11 26			11 32			11 35		11 40
Streatham Hill	d															11 23				11 35					
West Norwood 4	d															11 27				11 40					
Gipsy Hill	d													11 45		11 30				11 43					
Crystal Palace 4	d															11 32				11 51					
Birkbeck	d																								
Beckenham Junction 4	a																								
Streatham Common 4	d				11 20												11 30						11 39	11 42	11 45
Norbury	d				11 23												11 33						11 42	11 45	11 48
Thornton Heath	d				11 26												11 36						11 45	11 48	11 51
Selhurst 4	d				11 29												11 39						11 48	11 51	11 54
Norwood Junction 2	a					11 14				11 20	11 26	11 29	11 32		11 35	11 37									
	d					11 15				11 20	11 26	11 30	11 33		11 35	11 39									
West Croydon 4	a				11 33					11 31					11 42	11 43							11 52	11 55	
East Croydon	a	11 39	11 54	11 54		11 18	11 22	11 23			11 30	11 33	11 36				11 42	11 33			11 37	11 39			11 57

Table 177

Mondays to Fridays

Luton, Milton Keynes and London - East and West Croydon via Tulse Hill - Crystal Palace - Norbury

Local Services

		SN ◇1	SN	FC		FC 1	FC 1	SN	SN 1	SN ◇1	SN	LO	SN 1	SN		SN	SN	LO	SN	SN	SN ◇1	SN	SN 1	SN	
London Bridge 4 ⊖	d		11 33						11 33		11 41		11 45	11 36		11 50	11 52								
South Bermondsey	d		11 37								11 45														
Queens Rd Peckham	d		11 39								11 48														
Peckham Rye 4	d		11 42								11 50														
East Dulwich	d		11 45																						
North Dulwich	d		11 47																						
Luton 10	d			10 44		11 04	11 18																		
Luton Airport Parkway 7	d			10 46		11 06	11 20																		
St Pancras International 15 ⊖	d			11 34		11 40	11 54																		
City Thameslink 3	d			11 43		11 47	12 02																		
London Blackfriars 3 ⊖	d			11 46		11 50	12 05																		
Elephant & Castle ⊖	d			11 49																					
Loughborough Jn	d			11 53																					
Herne Hill 4	d			11 57																					
Tulse Hill 3	d		11 50	12 01																					
Streatham 4	d			12 05																					
London Victoria 15 ⊖	d	11 32						11 33		11 36									11 36	11 43	11 47	11 49	11 53		
Battersea Park 4	d							11 37			12 02								11 40	11 47		11 53			
Milton Keynes Central	d																								
Watford Junction	d																								
Harrow & Wealdstone ⊖	d																								
Wembley Central ⊖	d																								
Shepherd's Bush ⊖	d																								
Kensington (Olympia) ⊖	d																								
West Brompton ⊖	d																								
Clapham Junction 10	d	11 38						11 41		11 42									11 44	11 51	11 53	11 57	11 59	12 00	
Wandsworth Common	d							11 44											11 47	11 54		12 00		12 03	
Balham 4 ⊖	d							11 46											11 50	11 56		12 02		12 05	
Streatham Hill	d																		11 53			12 05			
West Norwood 4	d		11 53																11 57			12 10			
Gipsy Hill	d		11 56														12 15		12 00			12 13			
Crystal Palace 4	d		11 59																12 02			12 21			
Birkbeck	d		12 03																						
Beckenham Junction 4	a		12 06																						
Streatham Common 4	d							11 50												12 00				12 09	
Norbury	d							11 53												12 03				12 12	
Thornton Heath	d							11 56												12 06				12 15	
Selhurst 4	d							11 59												12 09				12 18	
Norwood Junction 2	a								11 44			11 50	11 56	11 59		12 02		12 05	12 07						
	d								11 45			11 50	11 56	12 00		12 03		12 05	12 09						
West Croydon 4	a							12 03				12 01						12 12	12 13					12 22	
East Croydon	a	11 48				12 09	12 24		11 48	11 52			12 00	12 03		12 06				12 12	12 03		12 10		

		SN	SN ◇1	SN	FC	FC 1	FC	FC 1	SN	SN 1	SN ◇1	SN 1	SN	LO	SN 1	SN	SN	SN	LO	SN		SN	SN ◇1	SN	SN ◇1
London Bridge 4 ⊖	d	11 48		12 03						12 03		12 08	12 11		12 15	12 06	12 20	12 22							
South Bermondsey	d	11 52		12 07									12 15												
Queens Rd Peckham	d	11 54		12 09									12 18												
Peckham Rye 4	d	11 57		12 12									12 20												
East Dulwich	d	12 00		12 15																					
North Dulwich	d	12 02		12 17																					
Luton 10	d				11 14	11 34		11 48																	
Luton Airport Parkway 7	d				11 16	11 36		11 50																	
St Pancras International 15 ⊖	d				12 04	12 10	12 18	12 24																	
City Thameslink 3	d				12 13	12 17	12 27	12 32																	
London Blackfriars 3 ⊖	d				12 16	12 20	12 30	12 35																	
Elephant & Castle ⊖	d				12 19		12 33																		
Loughborough Jn	d				12 23		12 37																		
Herne Hill 4	d				12 27		12 41																		
Tulse Hill 3	d	12 05		12 20	12 31		12 46																		
Streatham 4	d	12 09			12 35		12 50																		
London Victoria 15 ⊖	d		12 02						12 03		12 06									12 06		12 13	12 17	12 19	12 21
Battersea Park 4	d								12 07				12 32							12 10		12 17		12 23	
Milton Keynes Central	d																								
Watford Junction	d																								
Harrow & Wealdstone ⊖	d																								
Wembley Central ⊖	d																								
Shepherd's Bush ⊖	d																								
Kensington (Olympia) ⊖	d																								
West Brompton ⊖	d																								
Clapham Junction 10	d		12 08						12 11		12 12									12 14		12 21	12 23	12 27	
Wandsworth Common	d								12 14											12 17		12 24		12 30	
Balham 4 ⊖	d								12 16											12 20		12 26		12 32	
Streatham Hill	d																			12 23				12 35	
West Norwood 4	d			12 23																12 27				12 40	
Gipsy Hill	d			12 26														12 45		12 30				12 43	
Crystal Palace 4	d			12 29																12 32				12 51	
Birkbeck	d			12 33																					
Beckenham Junction 4	a			12 36																					
Streatham Common 4	d	12 12							12 20													12 30			
Norbury	d	12 15							12 23													12 33			
Thornton Heath	d	12 18							12 26													12 36			
Selhurst 4	d	12 21							12 29													12 39			
Norwood Junction 2	a									12 14				12 20	12 26	12 29	12 32		12 35	12 37					
	d									12 15				12 20	12 26	12 30	12 33		12 35	12 39					
West Croydon 4	a	12 25							12 33					12 31					12 42	12 43					
East Croydon	a		12 18			12 39		12 54		12 18	12 22	12 22			12 30	12 33	12 36					12 42	12 33		12 37

Table 177

Luton, Milton Keynes and London - East and West Croydon via Tulse Hill - Crystal Palace - Norbury

Local Services

		SN 1	SN	SN	SN 1	SN ◇1		SN	FC	FC 1	FC	FC 1	SN	SN 1	SN ◇1 ⌶	SN	LO	SN 1	SN	SN	SN	LO	SN	SN	SN ◇1
London Bridge 4 ⊖	d			12 18				12 33						12 33		12 41		12 45	12 36	12 50	12 52				
South Bermondsey	d			12 22				12 37								12 45									
Queens Rd Peckham	d			12 24				12 39								12 48									
Peckham Rye 4	d			12 27				12 42								12 50									
East Dulwich	d			12 30				12 45																	
North Dulwich	d			12 32				12 47																	
Luton 10	d								11 44	12 04		12 18													
Luton Airport Parkway 7	d								11 46	12 06		12 20													
St Pancras International 15 ⊖	d								12 34	12 40	12 48	12 54													
City Thameslink 3	d								12 43	12 47	12 57	13 02													
London Blackfriars 3 ⊖	d								12 46	12 50	13 00	13 05													
Elephant & Castle ⊖	d								12 49		13 03														
Loughborough Jn	d								12 53		13 07														
Herne Hill 4	d								12 57		13 11														
Tulse Hill 3	d			12 35				12 50	13 01		13 16														
Streatham 4	d			12 39					13 05		13 20														
London Victoria 15 ⊖	d	12 23				12 32							12 33		12 36								12 36	12 43	12 47
Battersea Park 4	d												12 37			13 02							12 40	12 47	
Milton Keynes Central	d				11 13																				
Watford Junction	d				11 51																				
Harrow & Wealdstone ⊖	d				11 59																				
Wembley Central ⊖	d				12u04																				
Shepherd's Bush ⊖	d				12 19																				
Kensington (Olympia) ⊖	d				12 22																				
West Brompton ⊖	d				12 25																				
Clapham Junction 10	d	12 29	12 30		12 34	12 38							12 41		12 42								12 44	12 51	12 53
Wandsworth Common	d		12 33		12 37								12 44										12 47	12 54	
Balham 4 ⊖	d		12 35		12 40								12 46										12 50	12 56	
Streatham Hill	d																						12 53		
West Norwood 4	d							12 53															12 57		
Gipsy Hill	d							12 56													13 15		13 00		
Crystal Palace 4	d							12 59															13 02		
Birkbeck ⇌	d							13 03																	
Beckenham Junction 4 ⇌	a							13 06																	
Streatham Common 4	d		12 39	12 42	12 45								12 50											13 00	
Norbury	d		12 42	12 45	12 48								12 53											13 03	
Thornton Heath	d		12 45	12 48	12 51								12 56											13 06	
Selhurst 4	d		12 48	12 51	12 54								12 59											13 09	
Norwood Junction 2	a													12 46			12 50	12 56	12 59	13 02		13 05	13 07		
	d													12 47			12 50	12 56	13 00	13 03		13 05	13 09		
West Croydon 4 ⇌	a		12 52	12 55									13 03				13 01					13 12	13 13		
East Croydon ⇌	a	12 39			12 57	12 48				13 09		13 24		12 51	12 52			13 00	13 03	13 06				13 12	13 03

		SN		SN 1	SN	SN	SN ◇1	SN	FC	FC 1	FC	FC 1		SN 1	SN ◇1 ⌶	SN 1	SN	LO	SN 1	SN	SN	SN		LO	SN
London Bridge 4 ⊖	d					12 48		13 03						13 03		13 08	13 11		13 15	13 06	13 20	13 22			
South Bermondsey	d					12 52		13 07									13 15								
Queens Rd Peckham	d					12 54		13 09									13 18								
Peckham Rye 4	d					12 57		13 12									13 20								
East Dulwich	d					13 00		13 15																	
North Dulwich	d					13 02		13 17																	
Luton 10	d								12 14	12 34		12 48													
Luton Airport Parkway 7	d								12 16	12 36		12 50													
St Pancras International 15 ⊖	d								13 04	13 10	13 18	13 24													
City Thameslink 3	d								13 13	13 17	13 27	13 32													
London Blackfriars 3 ⊖	d								13 16	13 20	13 30	13 35													
Elephant & Castle ⊖	d								13 19		13 33														
Loughborough Jn	d								13 23		13 37														
Herne Hill 4	d								13 27		13 41														
Tulse Hill 3	d					13 05		13 20	13 31		13 46														
Streatham 4	d					13 09			13 35		13 50														
London Victoria 15 ⊖	d	12 49		12 53			13 02								13 06										13 06
Battersea Park 4	d	12 53															13 32								13 10
Milton Keynes Central	d																								
Watford Junction	d																								
Harrow & Wealdstone ⊖	d																								
Wembley Central ⊖	d																								
Shepherd's Bush ⊖	d																								
Kensington (Olympia) ⊖	d																								
West Brompton ⊖	d																								
Clapham Junction 10	d	12 57		12 59	13 00		13 08								13 12										13 14
Wandsworth Common	d	13 00			13 03																				13 17
Balham 4 ⊖	d	13 02			13 05																				13 20
Streatham Hill	d	13 05																							13 23
West Norwood 4	d	13 10						13 23																	13 27
Gipsy Hill	d	13 13						13 26														13 45			13 30
Crystal Palace 4	d	13 21						13 29																	13 32
Birkbeck ⇌	d							13 33																	
Beckenham Junction 4 ⇌	a							13 36																	
Streatham Common 4	d				13 09	13 12																			
Norbury	d				13 12	13 15																			
Thornton Heath	d				13 15	13 18																			
Selhurst 4	d				13 18	13 21																			
Norwood Junction 2	a													13 14		13 19		13 20	13 26	13 29	13 32			13 35	13 37
	d													13 15		13 19		13 20	13 26	13 30	13 33			13 35	13 39
West Croydon 4 ⇌	a				13 22	13 25												13 31						13 42	13 43
East Croydon ⇌	a			13 09			13 18			13 39		13 54		13 18	13 22	13 23			13 30	13 33	13 36				

Table 177

Luton, Milton Keynes and London - East and West Croydon via Tulse Hill - Crystal Palace - Norbury

Local Services

		SN	SN ◇1	SN	SN ◇1	SN	SN	SN 1		SN 1	SN ◇1 ⌶	SN	FC	FC 1	FC	FC 1	SN	SN 1	SN ◇1 ⌶	SN	LO	SN 1	SN	SN	SN
London Bridge 4 ⊖	d						13 18					13 33						13 33		13 41		13 45	13 36	13 50	13 52
South Bermondsey	d						13 22					13 37								13 45					
Queens Rd Peckham	d						13 24					13 39								13 48					
Peckham Rye 4	d						13 27					13 42								13 50					
East Dulwich	d						13 30					13 45													
North Dulwich	d						13 32					13 47													
Luton 10	d												12 44	13 04		13 18									
Luton Airport Parkway 7	d												12 46	13 06		13 20									
St Pancras International 15 ⊖	d												13 34	13 40	13 48	13 54									
City Thameslink 3	d												13 43	13 47	13 57	14 02									
London Blackfriars 3 ⊖	d												13 46	13 50	14 00	14 05									
Elephant & Castle ⊖	d												13 49		14 03										
Loughborough Jn	d												13 53		14 07										
Herne Hill 4	d												13 57		14 11										
Tulse Hill 3	d						13 35					13 50	14 01		14 16										
Streatham 4	d						13 39						14 05		14 20										
London Victoria 15 ⊖	d	13 13	13 17	13 19	13 21	13 23				13 23	13 32						13 33		13 36						
Battersea Park 4	d	13 17		13 23													13 37			14 02					
Milton Keynes Central	d							12 13																	
Watford Junction	d							12 51																	
Harrow & Wealdstone ⊖	d							12 59																	
Wembley Central ⊖	d							13u04																	
Shepherd's Bush ⊖	d							13 19																	
Kensington (Olympia) ⊖	d							13 22																	
West Brompton ⊖	d							13 25																	
Clapham Junction 10	d	13 21	13 23	13 27		13 30		13 34		13 29	13 38						13 41		13 42						
Wandsworth Common	d	13 24		13 30		13 33		13 37									13 44								
Balham 4 ⊖	d	13 26		13 32		13 35		13 40									13 46								
Streatham Hill	d			13 35																					
West Norwood 4	d			13 40								13 53													
Gipsy Hill	d			13 43								13 56													14 15
Crystal Palace 4	d			13 51								13 59													
Birkbeck ⇌	d											14 03													
Beckenham Junction 4 ⇌	a											14 06													
Streatham Common 4	d	13 30				13 39	13 42	13 45									13 50								
Norbury	d	13 33				13 42	13 45	13 48									13 53								
Thornton Heath	d	13 36				13 45	13 48	13 51									13 56								
Selhurst 4	d	13 39				13 48	13 51	13 54									13 59								
Norwood Junction 2	a																	13 44			13 50	13 56	13 59	14 02	
	d																	13 45			13 50	13 56	14 00	14 03	
West Croydon 4 ⇌	a					13 52	13 55										14 03				14 01				
East Croydon ⇌	a	13 42	13 33		13 37			13 57		13 39	13 48			14 09		14 24		13 48	13 52			14 00	14 03	14 06	

		LO	SN	SN		SN ◇1	SN	SN 1	SN	SN	SN ◇1	SN	FC	FC 1	FC		FC 1	SN	SN 1	SN ◇1 ⌶	SN 1	SN	LO	SN 1	SN
London Bridge 4 ⊖	d									13 48		14 03							14 03		14 08	14 11		14 15	14 06
South Bermondsey	d									13 52		14 07										14 15			
Queens Rd Peckham	d									13 54		14 09										14 18			
Peckham Rye 4	d									13 57		14 12										14 20			
East Dulwich	d									14 00		14 15													
North Dulwich	d									14 02		14 17													
Luton 10	d												13 14	13 34			13 48								
Luton Airport Parkway 7	d												13 16	13 36			13 50								
St Pancras International 15 ⊖	d												14 04	14 10	14 18		14 24								
City Thameslink 3	d												14 13	14 17	14 27		14 32								
London Blackfriars 3 ⊖	d												14 16	14 20	14 30		14 35								
Elephant & Castle ⊖	d												14 19		14 33										
Loughborough Jn	d												14 23		14 37										
Herne Hill 4	d												14 27		14 41										
Tulse Hill 3	d									14 05		14 20	14 31		14 46										
Streatham 4	d									14 09			14 35		14 50										
London Victoria 15 ⊖	d		13 36	13 43		13 47	13 49	13 53			14 02							14 03		14 06					
Battersea Park 4	d		13 40	13 47			13 53											14 07				14 32			
Milton Keynes Central	d																								
Watford Junction	d																								
Harrow & Wealdstone ⊖	d																								
Wembley Central ⊖	d																								
Shepherd's Bush ⊖	d																								
Kensington (Olympia) ⊖	d																								
West Brompton ⊖	d																								
Clapham Junction 10	d		13 44	13 51		13 53	13 57	13 59	14 00		14 08							14 11		14 12					
Wandsworth Common	d		13 47	13 54			14 00		14 03									14 14							
Balham 4 ⊖	d		13 50	13 56			14 02		14 05									14 16							
Streatham Hill	d		13 53				14 05																		
West Norwood 4	d		13 57				14 10					14 23													
Gipsy Hill	d		14 00				14 13					14 26													
Crystal Palace 4	d		14 02				14 21					14 29													
Birkbeck ⇌	d											14 33													
Beckenham Junction 4 ⇌	a											14 36													
Streatham Common 4	d			14 00					14 09	14 12								14 20							
Norbury	d			14 03					14 12	14 15								14 23							
Thornton Heath	d			14 06					14 15	14 18								14 26							
Selhurst 4	d			14 09					14 18	14 21								14 29							
Norwood Junction 2	a	14 05	14 07																14 14		14 19		14 20	14 26	14 29
	d	14 05	14 09																14 15		14 19		14 20	14 26	14 30
West Croydon 4 ⇌	a	14 12	14 13						14 22	14 25								14 33					14 31		
East Croydon ⇌	a			14 12		14 03		14 09			14 18			14 39			14 54		14 18	14 22	14 23			14 30	14 33

Table 177

Mondays to Fridays

Luton, Milton Keynes and London - East and West Croydon via Tulse Hill - Crystal Palace - Norbury

Local Services

		SN	SN	LO	SN	SN	SN	SN	SN	SN		SN	SN	SN	SN	SN	FC	FC	FC	FC	SN	SN	SN	SN	LO
							◇1		◇1	1				1	◇1 H			1		1		1	◇1 H		
London Bridge 4 ⊖	d	14 20	14 22										14 18			14 33						14 33		14 41	
South Bermondsey	d												14 22			14 37								14 45	
Queens Rd Peckham	d												14 24			14 39								14 48	
Peckham Rye 4	d												14 27			14 42								14 50	
East Dulwich	d												14 30			14 45									
North Dulwich	d												14 32			14 47									
Luton 10	d																13 44	14 04		14 18					
Luton Airport Parkway 7	d																13 46	14 06		14 20					
St Pancras International 15 ⊖	d																14 34	14 40	14 48	14 54					
City Thameslink 3	d																14 43	14 47	14 57	15 02					
London Blackfriars 3 ⊖	d																14 46	14 50	15 00	15 05					
Elephant & Castle ⊖	d																14 49		15 03						
Loughborough Jn	d																14 53		15 07						
Herne Hill 4	d																14 57		15 11						
Tulse Hill 3	d												14 35			14 50	15 01		15 16						
Streatham 4	d												14 39				15 05		15 20						
London Victoria 15 ⊖	d				14 06	14 13	14 17	14 19	14 21	14 23					14 32						14 33		14 36		
Battersea Park 4	d				14 10	14 17		14 23													14 37			15 02	
Milton Keynes Central	d													13 13											
Watford Junction	d													13 51											
Harrow & Wealdstone ⊖	d													13 59											
Wembley Central ⊖	d													14u04											
Shepherd's Bush ⊖	d													14 19											
Kensington (Olympia) ⊖	d													14 22											
West Brompton ⊖	d													14 25											
Clapham Junction 10	d				14 14	14 21	14 23	14 27		14 29		14 30		14 34	14 38						14 41		14 42		
Wandsworth Common	d				14 17	14 24		14 30				14 33		14 37							14 44				
Balham 4 ⊖	d				14 20	14 26		14 32				14 35		14 40							14 46				
Streatham Hill	d				14 23			14 35																	
West Norwood 4	d				14 27			14 40								14 53									
Gipsy Hill	d		14 45		14 30			14 43								14 56									
Crystal Palace 4	d				14 32			14 51								14 59									
Birkbeck	d															15 03									
Beckenham Junction 4	a															15 06									
Streatham Common 4	d					14 30						14 39	14 42	14 45							14 50				
Norbury	d					14 33						14 42	14 45	14 48							14 53				
Thornton Heath	d					14 36						14 45	14 48	14 51							14 56				
Selhurst 4	d					14 39						14 48	14 51	14 54							14 59				
Norwood Junction 2	a	14 32		14 35	14 37																	14 44			14 50
	d	14 33		14 35	14 39																	14 45			14 50
West Croydon 4	a			14 42	14 43							14 52	14 55								15 03				15 01
East Croydon	a	14 36				14 43	14 33		14 37	14 40				14 57	14 48			15 09		15 24		14 48	14 52		

		SN	SN	SN	SN	LO		SN	SN	SN	SN	SN	SN	SN	SN	SN		FC	FC	FC	SN	SN	SN	SN	SN
		1								◇1		1			◇1				1	1		1	◇1 H	1	
London Bridge 4 ⊖	d	14 45	14 36	14 50	14 52									14 48		15 03						15 03		15 08	15 11
South Bermondsey	d													14 52		15 07									15 15
Queens Rd Peckham	d													14 54		15 09									15 18
Peckham Rye 4	d													14 57		15 12									15 20
East Dulwich	d													15 00		15 15									
North Dulwich	d													15 02		15 17									
Luton 10	d																	14 14	14 34	14 48					
Luton Airport Parkway 7	d																	14 16	14 36	14 50					
St Pancras International 15 ⊖	d																	15 04	15 10	15 24					
City Thameslink 3	d																	15 13	15 17	15 32					
London Blackfriars 3 ⊖	d																	15 16	15 20	15 35					
Elephant & Castle ⊖	d																	15 19							
Loughborough Jn	d																	15 23							
Herne Hill 4	d																	15 27							
Tulse Hill 3	d													15 05		15 20		15 31							
Streatham 4	d													15 09				15 35							
London Victoria 15 ⊖	d							14 36	14 43	14 47	14 49	14 53			15 02						15 03		15 06		
Battersea Park 4	d							14 40	14 47		14 53										15 07				15 32
Milton Keynes Central	d																								
Watford Junction	d																								
Harrow & Wealdstone ⊖	d																								
Wembley Central ⊖	d																								
Shepherd's Bush ⊖	d																								
Kensington (Olympia) ⊖	d																								
West Brompton ⊖	d																								
Clapham Junction 10	d							14 44	14 51	14 53	14 57	14 59	15 00		15 08						15 11		15 12		
Wandsworth Common	d							14 47	14 54		15 00		15 03								15 14				
Balham 4 ⊖	d							14 50	14 56		15 02		15 05								15 16				
Streatham Hill	d							14 53			15 05														
West Norwood 4	d							14 57			15 10					15 23									
Gipsy Hill	d				15 15			15 00			15 13					15 26									
Crystal Palace 4	d							15 02			15 21					15 29									
Birkbeck	d															15 33									
Beckenham Junction 4	a															15 36									
Streatham Common 4	d								15 00				15 09	15 12							15 20				
Norbury	d								15 03				15 12	15 15							15 23				
Thornton Heath	d								15 06				15 15	15 18							15 26				
Selhurst 4	d								15 09				15 18	15 21							15 29				
Norwood Junction 2	a	14 56	14 59	15 02		15 05		15 07														15 14		15 19	
	d	14 56	15 00	15 03		15 05		15 09														15 15		15 19	
West Croydon 4	a					15 12		15 13					15 22	15 25							15 33				
East Croydon	a	15 00	15 03	15 06					15 12	15 03		15 09			15 18				15 39	15 54		15 18	15 22	15 23	

Table 177

Mondays to Fridays

Luton, Milton Keynes and London - East and West Croydon via Tulse Hill - Crystal Palace - Norbury

Local Services

		LO		SN	SN	SN	SN	LO	SN	SN	SN	SN		SN	SN	SN	FC	SN	SN	SN	SN	FC	FC	FC	SN
				1							◇1			◇1				1	1	◇1			1	1	
London Bridge 4 ⊖	d			15 15	15 06	15 20	15 22									15 18					15 33				
South Bermondsey	d															15 22					15 37				
Queens Rd Peckham	d															15 24					15 39				
Peckham Rye 4	d															15 27					15 42				
East Dulwich	d															15 30					15 45				
North Dulwich	d															15 32					15 47				
Luton 10	d																					14 44	15 04	15 18	
Luton Airport Parkway 7	d																					14 46	15 06	15 20	
St Pancras International 15 ⊖	d																15 18					15 34	15 40	15 54	
City Thameslink 3	d																15 27					15 43	15 47	16 02	
London Blackfriars 3 ⊖	d																15 30					15 46	15 50	16 05	
Elephant & Castle ⊖	d																15 33					15 49			
Loughborough Jn	d																15 37					15 53			
Herne Hill 4	d																15 41					15 57			
Tulse Hill 3	d															15 35	15 46				15 50	16 01			
Streatham 4	d															15 39	15 50					16 05			
London Victoria 15 ⊖	d								15 06	15 13	15 17	15 19		15 21	15 23				15 23	15 32					15 33
Battersea Park 4	d								15 10	15 17		15 23													15 37
Milton Keynes Central	d																	14 13							
Watford Junction	d																	14 51							
Harrow & Wealdstone ⊖	d																	14 59							
Wembley Central ⊖	d																	15u04							
Shepherd's Bush ⊖	d																	15 22							
Kensington (Olympia) ⊖	d																	15 24							
West Brompton ⊖	d																	15 26							
Clapham Junction 10	d								15 14	15 21	15 23	15 27			15 30			15 34	15 29	15 38					15 41
Wandsworth Common	d								15 17	15 24		15 30			15 33			15 37							15 44
Balham 4 ⊖	d								15 20	15 26		15 32			15 35			15 40							15 46
Streatham Hill	d								15 23			15 35													
West Norwood 4	d								15 27			15 40									15 53				
Gipsy Hill	d						15 45		15 30			15 43									15 56				
Crystal Palace 4	d								15 32			15 51									15 59				
Birkbeck	d																				16 03				
Beckenham Junction 4	a																				16 06				
Streatham Common 4	d									15 30					15 39	15 42		15 45							15 50
Norbury	d									15 33					15 42	15 45		15 48							15 53
Thornton Heath	d									15 36					15 45	15 48		15 51							15 56
Selhurst 4	d									15 39					15 48	15 51		15 54							15 59
Norwood Junction 2	a	15 20		15 26	15 29	15 32		15 35	15 37																
	d	15 20		15 26	15 30	15 33		15 35	15 39																
West Croydon 4	a	15 31						15 42	15 43						15 52	15 55									16 03
East Croydon	a			15 30	15 33	15 36				15 43	15 33			15 37				15 57	15 40	15 48			16 09	16 24	

		SN	SN	SN	SN	LO	SN	SN		SN	SN	LO	SN	SN	SN	SN	SN	SN	SN	SN	FC	SN	FC	FC	FC
		1	◇1 H	1			1								◇1				1	◇1				1	1
London Bridge 4 ⊖	d	15 33		15 38	15 41		15 45	15 36		15 50	15 52							15 48				16 03			
South Bermondsey	d				15 45													15 52				16 07			
Queens Rd Peckham	d				15 48													15 54				16 09			
Peckham Rye 4	d				15 50													15 57				16 12			
East Dulwich	d																	16 00				16 15			
North Dulwich	d																	16 02				16 17			
Luton 10	d																						15 14	15 34	15 48
Luton Airport Parkway 7	d																						15 16	15 36	15 50
St Pancras International 15 ⊖	d																				15 48		16 04	16 10	16 24
City Thameslink 3	d																				15 57		16 13	16 17	16 33
London Blackfriars 3 ⊖	d																				16 00		16 16	16 20	16 36
Elephant & Castle ⊖	d																				16 03		16 19		
Loughborough Jn	d																				16 07		16 23		
Herne Hill 4	d																				16 11		16 27		
Tulse Hill 3	d																	16 05			16 16	16 20	16 32		
Streatham 4	d																	16 09			16 20		16 36		
London Victoria 15 ⊖	d		15 36										15 36	15 43	15 47	15 49	15 53		15 53	16 02					
Battersea Park 4	d				16 02								15 40	15 47		15 53									
Milton Keynes Central	d																								
Watford Junction	d																								
Harrow & Wealdstone ⊖	d																								
Wembley Central ⊖	d																								
Shepherd's Bush ⊖	d																								
Kensington (Olympia) ⊖	d																								
West Brompton ⊖	d																								
Clapham Junction 10	d		15 42										15 44	15 51	15 53	15 57	16 00		15 59	16 08					
Wandsworth Common	d												15 47	15 54		16 00	16 03								
Balham 4 ⊖	d												15 50	15 56		16 02	16 05								
Streatham Hill	d												15 53			16 05									
West Norwood 4	d												15 57			16 10						16 23			
Gipsy Hill	d										16 15		16 00			16 13						16 26			
Crystal Palace 4	d												16 02			16 21						16 29			
Birkbeck	d																					16 33			
Beckenham Junction 4	a																					16 38			
Streatham Common 4	d													16 00			16 09	16 12							
Norbury	d													16 03			16 12	16 15							
Thornton Heath	d													16 06			16 15	16 18							
Selhurst 4	d													16 09			16 18	16 21							
Norwood Junction 2	a	15 44				15 50	15 56	15 59		16 02		16 05	16 07												
	d	15 45				15 50	15 56	16 00		16 03		16 05	16 09												
West Croydon 4	a					16 01						16 12	16 13				16 22	16 25							
East Croydon	a	15 48	15 52	15 52			16 00	16 03		16 06				16 12	16 03				16 09	16 18				16 39	16 59

Luton, Milton Keynes and London - East and West Croydon via Tulse Hill - Crystal Palace - Norbury

Local Services

Station		SN	SN 1	SN 1 🚌		SN 1	SN	LO	SN 1	SN	SN	SN	LO	SN		SN	SN ◇1 🚌	SN	FC	SN 1	SN	SN 1	SN 1	SN ◇1 🚌	SN
London Bridge 4 ⊖	d		16 03			16 08	16 11		16 15	16 06	16 20	16 22						16 18							16 33
South Bermondsey	d						16 15											16 22							16 37
Queens Rd Peckham	d						16 18											16 24							16 39
Peckham Rye 4	d						16 20											16 27							16 42
East Dulwich	d																	16 30							16 45
North Dulwich	d																	16 32							16 47
Luton 10	d																								
Luton Airport Parkway 7	d																								
St Pancras International 15 ⊖	d																		16 18						
City Thameslink 3	d																		16 27						
London Blackfriars 3 ⊖	d																		16 30						
Elephant & Castle ⊖	d																		16 33						
Loughborough Jn	d																		16 37						
Herne Hill 4	d																		16 41						
Tulse Hill 3	d																	16 35	16 46						16 50
Streatham 4	d																	16 39	16 50						
London Victoria 15 ⊖	d	16 03		16 06										16 07		16 13	16 17				16 19	16 19	16 23	16 32	
Battersea Park 4	d	16 07					16 32							16 11		16 17					16 23				
Milton Keynes Central	d																			15 13					
Watford Junction	d																			15 51					
Harrow & Wealdstone ⊖	d																			15 59					
Wembley Central ⊖	d																			16u05					
Shepherd's Bush ⊖	d																			16 19					
Kensington (Olympia) ⊖	d																			16 22					
West Brompton ⊖	d																			16 25					
Clapham Junction 10	d	16 11		16 12										16 15		16 21	16 23			16 34	16 27	16 26	16 29	16 38	
Wandsworth Common	d	16 14												16 18		16 24				16 37	16 30				
Balham 4 ⊖	d	16 16												16 20		16 26				16 40	16 32				
Streatham Hill	d													16 23							16 35				
West Norwood 4	d													16 27							16 39				16 53
Gipsy Hill	d											16 45		16 30							16 44				16 56
Crystal Palace 4	d													16 32							16 50				16 59
Birkbeck 🚊	d																								17 03
Beckenham Junction 4 🚊	a																								17 08
Streatham Common 4	d	16 20														16 30		16 42		16 45					
Norbury	d	16 23														16 33		16 45		16 48					
Thornton Heath	d	16 26														16 36		16 48		16 51					
Selhurst 4	d	16 29														16 39		16 51		16 56					
Norwood Junction 2	a		16 14			16 19		16 20	16 26	16 29	16 32		16 35	16 37											
	d		16 15			16 19		16 20	16 26	16 30	16 33		16 35	16 39											
West Croydon 4 🚊	a	16 33						16 31					16 42	16 43				16 57							
East Croydon 🚊	a		16 18	16 22		16 23			16 30	16 33	16 36					16 42	16 33			16 59		16 36	16 39	16 47	

Station		FC	FC 1	FC 1	SN	SN 1	SN 1 🚌	SN 1	SN	LO		SN	SN	SN	SN 1	LO	SN	SN	SN	SN ◇1 🚌		SN	SN 1	SN	SN 1
London Bridge 4 ⊖	d					16 33		16 38	16 41			16 36	16 48	16 52	16 57							16 48			
South Bermondsey	d								16 45													16 52			
Queens Rd Peckham	d								16 48													16 54			
Peckham Rye 4	d								16 50													16 57			
East Dulwich	d																					17 00			
North Dulwich	d																					17 02			
Luton 10	d	15 44	16 04	16 14																					
Luton Airport Parkway 7	d	15 46	16 06	16 17																					
St Pancras International 15 ⊖	d	16 34	16 40	16 46																					
City Thameslink 3	d	16 43	16 49	16 55																					
London Blackfriars 3 ⊖	d	16 46	16 52	17 00																					
Elephant & Castle ⊖	d	16 49	16 56	17 04																					
Loughborough Jn	d	16 53	17 00																						
Herne Hill 4	d	16 57	17 06																						
Tulse Hill 3	d	17 02																				17 05			
Streatham 4	d	17 06																				17 09			
London Victoria 15 ⊖	d				16 33		16 36										16 37	16 39	16 43	16 47			16 49	16 52	16 53
Battersea Park 4	d				16 37				17 02								16 41		16 47					16 56	
Milton Keynes Central	d																								
Watford Junction	d																								
Harrow & Wealdstone ⊖	d																								
Wembley Central ⊖	d																								
Shepherd's Bush ⊖	d																								
Kensington (Olympia) ⊖	d																								
West Brompton ⊖	d																								
Clapham Junction 10	d				16 41		16 42										16 45	16 45	16 51	16 53			16 56	17 00	16 59
Wandsworth Common	d				16 44												16 48		16 54					17 03	
Balham 4 ⊖	d				16 46												16 50		16 56					17 06	
Streatham Hill	d																16 53							17 09	
West Norwood 4	d																16 57							17 12	
Gipsy Hill	d													17 15			17 00							17 15	
Crystal Palace 4	d																17 02							17 21	
Birkbeck 🚊	d																								
Beckenham Junction 4 🚊	a																								
Streatham Common 4	d				16 50														17 00			17 12			
Norbury	d				16 53														17 03			17 15			
Thornton Heath	d				16 56														17 06			17 18			
Selhurst 4	d				16 59														17 09			17 21			
Norwood Junction 2	a					16 44				16 50		16 59	17 01			17 05	17 07								
	d					16 45				16 50		17 00	17 02			17 05	17 09								
West Croydon 4 🚊	a				17 03					17 01		17 07				17 12	17 13					17 27			
East Croydon 🚊	a			17 25		16 48	16 52	16 52					17 05		17 09			16 55	17 12	17 03			17 06		17 09

Table 177 — Mondays to Fridays

Luton, Milton Keynes and London - East and West Croydon via Tulse Hill - Crystal Palace - Norbury

Local Services

Station		SN	FC	FC	FC 1	FC 1	SN 1		SN	SN ◇1 🚌	SN	SN 1 🚌	SN 1	SN	SN 1	SN	SN 1	LO	SN	SN	SN	SN 1	LO	SN	SN
London Bridge 4 ⊖	d	16 58					16 59				17 03		17 09	17 11	17 15	17 18			17 05	17 17	17 21	17 23			
South Bermondsey	d	17 02												17 15		17 22									
Queens Rd Peckham	d	17 04												17 18		17 24									
Peckham Rye 4	d	17 07												17 20		17 27									
East Dulwich	d	17 10														17 30									
North Dulwich	d	17 12														17 32									
Luton 10	d			16 16	16 34	16 50																			
Luton Airport Parkway 7	d			16 18	16 36	16 52																			
St Pancras International 15 ⊖	d		16 52	17 02	17 10	17 28																			
City Thameslink 3	d		17 01	17 11	17 19	17 37																			
London Blackfriars 3 ⊖	d		17 04	17 14	17 22	17 40																			
Elephant & Castle ⊖	d		17 08	17 18																					
Loughborough Jn	d		17 12	17 22																					
Herne Hill 4	d		17 16	17 26																					
Tulse Hill 3	d	17 17	17 20	17 31												17 35									
Streatham 4	d		17 24	17 36												17 39									
London Victoria 15 ⊖	d								17 01	17 02		17 06												17 06	17 09
Battersea Park 4	d								17 05					17 32										17 10	
Milton Keynes Central	d																16 13								
Watford Junction	d																16 51								
Harrow & Wealdstone ⊖	d																16 59								
Wembley Central ⊖	d																17u05								
Shepherd's Bush ⊖	d																17 19								
Kensington (Olympia) ⊖	d																17 22								
West Brompton ⊖	d																17 25								
Clapham Junction 10	d								17 09	17 08		17 12					17 33							17 14	17 15
Wandsworth Common	d								17 12								17 36							17 17	
Balham 4 ⊖	d								17 14								17 39							17 19	
Streatham Hill	d																							17 22	
West Norwood 4	d	17 20																						17 27	
Gipsy Hill	d	17 23																			17 46			17 30	
Crystal Palace 4	d	17 26																						17 32	
Birkbeck 🚊	d	17 30																							
Beckenham Junction 4 🚊	a	17 35																							
Streatham Common 4	d								17 18							17 42	17 46								
Norbury	d								17 21							17 44	17 48								
Thornton Heath	d								17 24							17 47	17 51								
Selhurst 4	d								17 27							17 51	17 55								
Norwood Junction 2	a						17 10				17 16							17 20	17 29	17 30			17 35	17 37	
	d						17 11				17 16							17 20	17 30	17 31			17 35	17 39	
West Croydon 4 🚊	a								17 32		17 21					17 57		17 31	17 37				17 42	17 43	
East Croydon 🚊	a				17 45	18 08	17 14			17 17		17 22	17 22		17 29		17 59			17 34		17 35			17 27

Station		SN		SN ◇1	SN 1	SN	SN 1	SN	FC	FC	SN 1	SN	SN ◇1		SN	SN ◇1 🚌	FC 1	FC	SN	SN 1	SN 1	SN 1	SN	SN	LO
London Bridge 4 ⊖	d							17 28			17 29	17 32							17 41	17 42	17 44	17 47	17 48		
South Bermondsey	d							17 32											17 45				17 52		
Queens Rd Peckham	d							17 35											17 47				17 54		
Peckham Rye 4	d							17 37											17 50				17 57		
East Dulwich	d							17 40															18 00		
North Dulwich	d							17 42															18 02		
Luton 10	d									16 46								17 12							
Luton Airport Parkway 7	d									16 48								17 15							
St Pancras International 15 ⊖	d								17 18	17 32							17 40	17 44							
City Thameslink 3	d								17 27	17 41							17 49	17 53							
London Blackfriars 3 ⊖	d								17 30	17 44							17 52	17 56							
Elephant & Castle ⊖	d								17 34	17 48							17 56	18 00							
Loughborough Jn	d								17 38	17 52															
Herne Hill 4	d								17 44	17 57								18 06							
Tulse Hill 3	d							17 46	17 48	18 02													18 05		
Streatham 4	d								17 52	18 06													18 09		
London Victoria 15 ⊖	d	17 13		17 17	17 21	17 22	17 23						17 32		17 33	17 36									
Battersea Park 4	d	17 17				17 26									17 37				18 02						
Milton Keynes Central	d																								
Watford Junction	d																								
Harrow & Wealdstone ⊖	d																								
Wembley Central ⊖	d																								
Shepherd's Bush ⊖	d																							17 45	
Kensington (Olympia) ⊖	d																							17 47	
West Brompton ⊖	d																							17 50	
Clapham Junction 10	d	17 21		17 23	17 27	17 30	17 30						17 38		17 41	17 42								18 02	
Wandsworth Common	d	17 24				17 33									17 44									18 05	
Balham 4 ⊖	d	17 26				17 35									17 46									18 08	
Streatham Hill	d					17 38																			
West Norwood 4	d					17 42		17 49																	
Gipsy Hill	d					17 45		17 52																	
Crystal Palace 4	d					17 48		17 54																	
Birkbeck 🚊	d							17 58																	
Beckenham Junction 4 🚊	a							18 04																	
Streatham Common 4	d	17 30													17 50								18 12	18 15	
Norbury	d	17 33													17 53								18 14	18 18	
Thornton Heath	d	17 36													17 56								18 17	18 21	
Selhurst 4	d	17a40													17 59								18 21	18 26	
Norwood Junction 2	a										17 40	17 45													17 50
	d										17 41	17 46													17 50
West Croydon 4 🚊	a											17 50			18 03								18 27		18 01
East Croydon 🚊	a			17 32	17 36		17 40				17 44		17 48			17 51	18 24			17 54	17 57	17 59		18 33	

Table 177

Mondays to Fridays

Luton, Milton Keynes and London - East and West Croydon via Tulse Hill - Crystal Palace - Norbury

Local Services

		SN	SN	SN	SN 1	LO	SN	SN		SN	SN ◇1	SN 1	SN	SN 1	SN	FC	FC	FC 1	FC 1	FC 1	SN 1	SN	SN ◇1	SN	SN ◇1 H
London Bridge	d	17 36	17 49	17 53	17 57										17 58						17 59	18 02			
South Bermondsey	d														18 02										
Queens Rd Peckham	d														18 04										
Peckham Rye	d														18 07										
East Dulwich	d														18 10										
North Dulwich	d														18 12										
Luton	d																17 18	17 32	17 46	18 00					
Luton Airport Parkway	d																17 20	17 34	17 48	18 02					
St Pancras International	d															17 52	18 04	18 08	18 20	18 34					
City Thameslink	d															18 01	18 13	18 17	18 29	18 43					
London Blackfriars	d															18 04	18 16	18 20	18 32	18 46					
Elephant & Castle	d															18 08	18 20		18 36						
Loughborough Jn	d															18 12	18 24								
Herne Hill	d															18 18	18 28								
Tulse Hill	d														18 17	18 22	18 32								
Streatham	d															18 26	18 36								
London Victoria	d						17 37	17 39		17 45	17 47	17 49	17 52	17 53									18 02	18 03	18 06
Battersea Park	d						17 41			17 49			17 56											18 07	
Milton Keynes Central	d																								
Watford Junction	d																								
Harrow & Wealdstone	d																								
Wembley Central	d																								
Shepherd's Bush	d																								
Kensington (Olympia)	d																								
West Brompton	d																								
Clapham Junction	d						17 45	17 45		17 53	17 53	17 56	18 00	18 00									18 08	18 11	18 12
Wandsworth Common	d						17 48			17 56			18 03											18 14	
Balham	d						17 50			17 58			18 05											18 16	
Streatham Hill	d						17 53						18 08												
West Norwood	d						17 57						18 14		18 20										
Gipsy Hill	d			18 16			18 00						18 17		18 23										
Crystal Palace	d						18 02						18 20		18 26										
Birkbeck	d														18 30										
Beckenham Junction	a														18 35										
Streatham Common	d									18 02														18 20	
Norbury	d									18 05														18 23	
Thornton Heath	d									18 08														18 26	
Selhurst	d									18a12														18 29	
Norwood Junction	a	17 59	18 01			18 06	18 08														18 11	18 15			
	d	18 00	18 02			18 06	18 09														18 11	18 16			
West Croydon	a	18 08				18 12	18 14															18 20		18 34	
East Croydon	a		18 05		18 11			17 55			18 02	18 05		18 10				18 41	18 55	19 10	18 15		18 17		18 22

		SN 1	SN	SN	SN 1		SN 1	SN	SN 1	LO	SN	SN	SN	SN 1	LO	SN	SN	SN	SN ◇1	SN 1	SN	SN 1	SN	SN 1	FC
London Bridge	d	18 08	18 08	18 11	18 12		18 16	18 18			18 06	18 18	18 21	18 23									18 28	18 30	
South Bermondsey	d		18 12	18 15				18 22															18 32		
Queens Rd Peckham	d		18 14	18 18				18 24															18 34		
Peckham Rye	d		18 17	18 20				18 27															18 37		
East Dulwich	d		18 20					18 30															18 40		
North Dulwich	d		18 22					18 32															18 42		
Luton	d																								17 38
Luton Airport Parkway	d																								17 40
St Pancras International	d																								18 24
City Thameslink	d																								18 33
London Blackfriars	d																								18 36
Elephant & Castle	d																								18 40
Loughborough Jn	d																								18 44
Herne Hill	d																								18 48
Tulse Hill	d		18 27					18 35															18 47		18 52
Streatham	d		18 30					18 39																	18 56
London Victoria	d															18 07	18 09	18 13	18 17	18 19	18 23	18 23			
Battersea Park	d			18 32												18 11		18 17			18 27				
Milton Keynes Central	d								17 13																
Watford Junction	d								17 51																
Harrow & Wealdstone	d								17 59																
Wembley Central	d								18u05																
Shepherd's Bush	d								18 19																
Kensington (Olympia)	d								18 22																
West Brompton	d								18 25																
Clapham Junction	d								18 34							18 15	18 15	18 21	18 23	18 26	18 31	18 30			
Wandsworth Common	d								18 37							18 18		18 24			18 34				
Balham	d								18 40							18 20		18 26			18 36				
Streatham Hill	d															18 23					18 39				
West Norwood	d															18 27					18 43		18 50		
Gipsy Hill	d												18 45			18 30					18 46		18 53		
Crystal Palace	d															18 32					18 51		18 56		
Birkbeck	d																						19 00		
Beckenham Junction	a																						19 05		
Streatham Common	d							18 42	18 46									18 30							
Norbury	d							18 44	18 49									18 33							
Thornton Heath	d							18 47	18 52									18 36							
Selhurst	d							18 51	18 56									18a40							
Norwood Junction	a									18 20	18 29	18 30			18 35	18 37								18 41	
	d									18 20	18 32	18 31			18 35	18 39								18 42	
West Croydon	a							18 57		18 31	18 39				18 42	18 44									
East Croydon	a	18 21			18 24		18 30		19 02			18 35		18 36			18 27		18 33	18 37		18 40		18 45	

Table 177

Mondays to Fridays

Luton, Milton Keynes and London - East and West Croydon via Tulse Hill - Crystal Palace - Norbury

Local Services

		SN	SN	SN ◇1	SN 1 H	SN	SN 1	LO	SN	SN		SN	LO	SN	SN	SN	SN ◇1 H	SN	FC	FC 1		SN 1	SN	SN 1	SN
London Bridge	d		18 32			18 41	18 47		18 36	18 49		18 51						18 48							
South Bermondsey	d					18 45												18 52							
Queens Rd Peckham	d					18 48												18 54							
Peckham Rye	d					18 50												18 57							
East Dulwich	d																	19 00							
North Dulwich	d																	19 02							
Luton	d																			18 18					
Luton Airport Parkway	d																			18 20					
St Pancras International	d																		18 38	18 54					
City Thameslink	d																		18 47	19 03					
London Blackfriars	d																		18 50	19 05					
Elephant & Castle	d																		18 54						
Loughborough Jn	d																		18 58						
Herne Hill	d																		19 02						
Tulse Hill	d																	19 05	19 07						
Streatham	d																	19 09	19 11						
London Victoria	d	18 32		18 32	18 36									18 36	18 39	18 45	18 47					18 51	18 52	18 53	19 00
Battersea Park	d	18 36				19 02								18 40		18 49							18 56		19 04
Milton Keynes Central	d																								
Watford Junction	d																								
Harrow & Wealdstone	d																								
Wembley Central	d																								
Shepherd's Bush	d																								
Kensington (Olympia)	d																								
West Brompton	d																								
Clapham Junction	d	18 40		18 38	18 42									18 44	18 45	18 53	18 53					18 57	19 00	19 00	19 08
Wandsworth Common	d	18 43												18 47		18 56							19 03		19 11
Balham	d	18 45												18 49		18 58							19 05		19 14
Streatham Hill	d													18 52									19 08		
West Norwood	d													18 56									19 12		
Gipsy Hill	d											19 15		18 59									19 15		
Crystal Palace	d													19 01									19 21		
Birkbeck	d																								
Beckenham Junction	a																								
Streatham Common	d	18 50														19 02		19 12							19 18
Norbury	d	18 52														19 05		19 15							19 20
Thornton Heath	d	18 55														19 08		19 18							19 23
Selhurst	d	19 00														19 10		19 21							19 27
Norwood Junction	a		18 45					18 50	18 59	19 01			19 05	19 06											
	d		18 46					18 50	19 02	19 02			19 05	19 09											
West Croydon	a	19 04	18 50					19 01	19 09				19 12	19 14				19 27							19 32
East Croydon	a			18 48	18 52		19 00			19 05					18 57	19 13	19 02			19 24		19 07		19 10	

		SN ◇1 H	SN 1	SN 1 H	SN 1	SN	LO	SN	SN	FC	SN	LO	SN	SN	FC	SN 1	FC 1	FC 1	SN 1	SN	SN ◇1 H	SN	SN	SN 1	SN
London Bridge	d		19 03		19 08	19 11		19 06	18 58		19 22			19 08								19 18			
South Bermondsey	d					19 15			19 02					19 12								19 22			
Queens Rd Peckham	d					19 18			19 04					19 14								19 24			
Peckham Rye	d					19 20			19 07					19 17								19 27			
East Dulwich	d								19 10					19 20								19 30			
North Dulwich	d								19 12					19 22								19 32			
Luton	d									18 08					18 22		18 34	18 48							
Luton Airport Parkway	d									18 10					18 25		18 36	18 50							
St Pancras International	d									18 48					19 04		19 10	19 24							
City Thameslink	d									18 57					19 13		19 17	19 32							
London Blackfriars	d									19 00					19 16		19 20	19 35							
Elephant & Castle	d									19 04					19 19										
Loughborough Jn	d									19 08					19 23										
Herne Hill	d									19 12					19 27										
Tulse Hill	d								19 17	19 16				19 27	19 31							19 35			
Streatham	d									19 20					19 35							19 39			
London Victoria	d	19 02		19 06									19 06						19 10	19 15	19 17		19 22	19 23	19 31
Battersea Park	d					19 32							19 10							19 19			19 26		19 35
Milton Keynes Central	d															18 13									
Watford Junction	d															18 51									
Harrow & Wealdstone	d															18 59									
Wembley Central	d															19 05									
Shepherd's Bush	d															19 18									
Kensington (Olympia)	d															19 20									
West Brompton	d															19 23									
Clapham Junction	d	19 08		19 12									19 14			19 34			19 16	19 23	19 23		19 30	19 29	19 39
Wandsworth Common	d												19 17			19 37				19 26			19 33		19 42
Balham	d												19 20			19 40				19 28			19 35		19 44
Streatham Hill	d												19 23										19 38		
West Norwood	d								19 20				19 27	19 30									19 42		
Gipsy Hill	d								19 23		19 45		19 30	19 33									19 45		
Crystal Palace	d								19 26				19 32	19 35									19 51		
Birkbeck	d													19 39											
Beckenham Junction	a													19 43											
Streatham Common	d															19 45				19 32		19 42			19 48
Norbury	d															19 47				19 35		19 45			19 51
Thornton Heath	d															19 50				19 38		19 48			19 54
Selhurst	d															19a53				19 41		19 51			19 57
Norwood Junction	a		19 14				19 20	19 29	19 32			19 35	19 37												
	d		19 15				19 20	19 30	19 33			19 35	19 39												
West Croydon	a						19 31		19 40			19 42	19 44									19 55			20 02
East Croydon	a	19 18	19 18	19 22	19 22			19 33									19 39	19 54	19 27	19 44	19 33			19 39	

Luton, Milton Keynes and London - East and West Croydon via Tulse Hill - Crystal Palace - Norbury

Local Services

		SN		SN ◇1 ✠	SN 1	SN	LO	SN	SN	SN 1	SN	LO	SN	FC	SN	FC	FC 1	FC	FC 1	SN 1	SN	SN ◇1 ✠	SN	SN	SN 1
London Bridge ⊖	d	19 31				19 41		19 28	19 36	19 52	19 54				19 38								19 48		
South Bermondsey	d					19 45		19 32							19 42								19 52		
Queens Rd Peckham	d					19 48		19 34							19 44								19 54		
Peckham Rye	d					19 50		19 37							19 47								19 57		
East Dulwich	d							19 40							19 50								20 00		
North Dulwich	d							19 42							19 52								20 02		
Luton	d															18 54	19 04		19 18						
Luton Airport Parkway	d															18 57	19 06		19 20						
St Pancras International ⊖	d													19 18		19 34	19 40	19 48	19 54						
City Thameslink	d													19 27		19 43	19 47	19 57	20 02						
London Blackfriars ⊖	d													19 30		19 46	19 50	20 00	20 05						
Elephant & Castle ⊖	d													19 33		19 49		20 03							
Loughborough Jn	d													19 37		19 53		20 07							
Herne Hill	d													19 41		19 57		20 11							
Tulse Hill	d							19 46						19 46	19 57	20 01		20 16					20 05		
Streatham	d													19 50		20 05		20 20					20 09		
London Victoria ⊖	d			19 32	19 36								19 36							19 40	19 45	19 47		19 52	19 53
Battersea Park	d					20 02							19 40								19 49			19 56	
Milton Keynes Central	d																								
Watford Junction	d																								
Harrow & Wealdstone ⊖	d																								
Wembley Central ⊖	d																								
Shepherd's Bush ⊖	d																								
Kensington (Olympia) ⊖	d																								
West Brompton ⊖	d																								
Clapham Junction	d			19 38	19 42								19 44							19 46	19 53	19 53		20 00	19 59
Wandsworth Common	d												19 47								19 56			20 03	
Balham ⊖	d												19 50								19 59			20 05	
Streatham Hill	d												19 53											20 08	
West Norwood	d							19 49					19 57		20 00									20 12	
Gipsy Hill	d							19 52			20 16		20 00		20 03									20 15	
Crystal Palace	d							19 54					20 02		20 05									20 21	
Birkbeck	d														20 09										
Beckenham Junction	a														20 13										
Streatham Common	d																				20 03		20 12		
Norbury	d																				20 05		20 15		
Thornton Heath	d																				20 08		20 18		
Selhurst	d																				20 11		20 21		
Norwood Junction	a	19 44					19 50	19 59	19 59	20 03		20 05	20 07												
	d	19 44					19 50	20 02	20 00	20 03		20 05	20 09												
West Croydon	a	19 49					20 01	20 06				20 12	20 13										20 25		
East Croydon	a			19 48	19 52				20 03	20 06							20 09		20 24	19 57	20 14	20 03			20 09

		SN	SN ◇1 ✠	SN	FC	FC 1	SN 1	SN ◇1	SN	LO	SN	SN	SN 1	LO	SN	SN 1	SN		SN ◇1	SN	FC	FC	FC 1	SN	SN 1
London Bridge ⊖	d			20 03			20 04		20 11		20 06	20 22	20 28							20 18					
South Bermondsey	d			20 07					20 15											20 22					
Queens Rd Peckham	d			20 09					20 18											20 24					
Peckham Rye	d			20 12					20 20											20 27					
East Dulwich	d			20 15																20 30					
North Dulwich	d			20 17																20 32					
Luton	d				19 24	19 46																19 50	20 16		
Luton Airport Parkway	d				19 27	19 48																19 52	20 18		
St Pancras International ⊖	d				20 04	20 24															20 18	20 36	20 54		
City Thameslink	d				20 13	20 32															20 27	20 43	21 02		
London Blackfriars ⊖	d				20 16	20 35															20 30	20 46	21 05		
Elephant & Castle ⊖	d				20 19																20 33	20 49			
Loughborough Jn	d				20 23																20 37	20 53			
Herne Hill	d				20 27																20 41	20 57			
Tulse Hill	d			20 20	20 31															20 35	20 46	21 01			
Streatham	d			20 24	20 35															20 39	20 50	21 05			
London Victoria ⊖	d	20 00	20 02					20 06							20 06	20 10	20 15		20 17					20 22	20 23
Battersea Park	d	20 04							20 32						20 10		20 19							20 26	
Milton Keynes Central	d																								
Watford Junction	d																								
Harrow & Wealdstone ⊖	d																								
Wembley Central ⊖	d																								
Shepherd's Bush ⊖	d																								
Kensington (Olympia) ⊖	d																								
West Brompton ⊖	d																								
Clapham Junction	d	20 08	20 08					20 12							20 14	20 16	20 23		20 23					20 30	20 29
Wandsworth Common	d	20 11													20 17		20 26							20 33	
Balham ⊖	d	20 14													20 20		20 28							20 35	
Streatham Hill	d														20 23									20 38	
West Norwood	d														20 27									20 42	
Gipsy Hill	d											20 45			20 30									20 45	
Crystal Palace	d														20 32									20 51	
Birkbeck	d																								
Beckenham Junction	a																								
Streatham Common	d	20 18		20 27													20 32			20 42					
Norbury	d	20 20		20 29													20 35			20 45					
Thornton Heath	d	20 23		20 32													20 38			20 48					
Selhurst	d	20 27		20a35													20 41			20 51					
Norwood Junction	a						20 16			20 21	20 29			20 35	20 37										
	d						20 16			20 21	20 30			20 35	20 39										
West Croydon	a	20 32								20 30				20 42	20 43					20 55					
East Croydon	a		20 19			20 54	20 19	20 22			20 33		20 40			20 27	20 44		20 33				21 24		20 39

Luton, Milton Keynes and London - East and West Croydon via Tulse Hill - Crystal Palace - Norbury

Local Services

		SN	SN ◇1	SN 1		SN ◇1	SN	LO	SN	SN	SN 1	LO	SN	SN 1		SN	SN ◇1	SN	FC	FC 1	SN	SN 1	SN	SN 1
London Bridge ⊖	d			20 34			20 41		20 36	20 52	20 58							20 48						
South Bermondsey	d						20 45											20 52						
Queens Rd Peckham	d						20 48											20 54						
Peckham Rye	d						20 50											20 57						
East Dulwich	d																	21 00						
North Dulwich	d																	21 02						
Luton	d																		20 20	20 46				
Luton Airport Parkway	d																		20 22	20 48				
St Pancras International ⊖	d																		21 06	21 24				
City Thameslink	d																		21 13	21 32				
London Blackfriars ⊖	d																		21 16	21 35				
Elephant & Castle ⊖	d																		21 19					
Loughborough Jn	d																		21 23					
Herne Hill	d																		21 27					
Tulse Hill	d																	21 05	21 31					
Streatham	d																	21 09	21 35					
London Victoria ⊖	d	20 30	20 32			20 36							20 36	20 40		20 45	20 47				20 52	20 53	21 00	21 02
Battersea Park	d	20 34					21 02						20 40			20 49					20 56		21 04	
Milton Keynes Central	d																							
Watford Junction	d																							
Harrow & Wealdstone ⊖	d																							
Wembley Central ⊖	d																							
Shepherd's Bush ⊖	d																							
Kensington (Olympia) ⊖	d																							
West Brompton ⊖	d																							
Clapham Junction	d	20 38	20 38			20 42							20 44	20 46		20 53	20 53				21 00	20 59	21 08	21 08
Wandsworth Common	d	20 41											20 47			20 56					21 03		21 11	
Balham ⊖	d	20 44											20 50			20 58					21 05		21 14	
Streatham Hill	d												20 53								21 08			
West Norwood	d												20 57								21 12			
Gipsy Hill	d									21 15			21 00								21 15			
Crystal Palace	d												21 02								21 21			
Birkbeck	d																							
Beckenham Junction	a																							
Streatham Common	d	20 48														21 02		21 12					21 18	
Norbury	d	20 50														21 05		21 15					21 20	
Thornton Heath	d	20 53														21 08		21 18					21 23	
Selhurst	d	20 57														21 11		21 21					21 27	
Norwood Junction	a			20 45				20 50	20 59			21 05	21 07											
	d			20 45				20 50	21 00			21 05	21 09											
West Croydon	a	21 02						21 01				21 12	21 13					21 25					21 32	
East Croydon	a		20 48	20 49		20 52			21 03		21 10			20 57		21 14	21 03			21 54		21 09		21 18

		SN 1	SN ◇1	SN	LO	SN	SN	LO	SN	SN 1		SN	SN ◇1	SN	FC	FC 1	SN	SN 1	SN 1	SN		SN 1	SN ◇1	SN	LO
London Bridge ⊖	d	21 04		21 11		21 06	21 22							21 18					21 26					21 41	
South Bermondsey	d			21 15										21 22										21 45	
Queens Rd Peckham	d			21 18										21 24										21 48	
Peckham Rye	d			21 20										21 27										21 50	
East Dulwich	d													21 30											
North Dulwich	d													21 32											
Luton	d														20 50	21 16									
Luton Airport Parkway	d														20 52	21 18									
St Pancras International ⊖	d														21 36	21 54									
City Thameslink	d														21 43	22 02									
London Blackfriars ⊖	d														21 46	22 05									
Elephant & Castle ⊖	d														21 49										
Loughborough Jn	d														21 53										
Herne Hill	d														21 57										
Tulse Hill	d													21 35	22 01										
Streatham	d													21 39	22 05										
London Victoria ⊖	d		21 06						21 06	21 10		21 15	21 17				21 22	21 23		21 30		21 32	21 36		
Battersea Park	d			21 32					21 10			21 19					21 26			21 34				22 02	
Milton Keynes Central	d																								
Watford Junction	d																								
Harrow & Wealdstone ⊖	d																								
Wembley Central ⊖	d																								
Shepherd's Bush ⊖	d																								
Kensington (Olympia) ⊖	d																								
West Brompton ⊖	d																								
Clapham Junction	d		21 12						21 14	21 16		21 23	21 23				21 30	21 29		21 38		21 38	21 42		
Wandsworth Common	d								21 17			21 26					21 33			21 41					
Balham ⊖	d								21 20			21 29					21 35			21 44					
Streatham Hill	d								21 23								21 38								
West Norwood	d								21 27								21 42								
Gipsy Hill	d						21 45		21 30								21 45								
Crystal Palace	d								21 32								21 51								
Birkbeck	d																								
Beckenham Junction	a																								
Streatham Common	d											21 33		21 42						21 48					
Norbury	d											21 35		21 45						21 50					
Thornton Heath	d											21 38		21 48						21 53					
Selhurst	d											21 41		21 51						21 57					
Norwood Junction	a	21 15			21 20	21 29		21 35	21 37										21 37						21 50
	d	21 15			21 20	21 30		21 35	21 39										21 38						21 50
West Croydon	a				21 31			21 42	21 43					21 55						22 02					22 01
East Croydon	a	21 19	21 22			21 33				21 27		21 44	21 33			22 24		21 39	21 41			21 48	21 52		

Table 177

Mondays to Fridays

Luton, Milton Keynes and London - East and West Croydon via Tulse Hill - Crystal Palace - Norbury

Local Services

		SN	SN	LO	SN	SN 1		SN	SN ◇1	SN	FC	SN	SN 1	SN	SN ◇1	SN 1		SN ◇1	SN	LO	SN	SN	LO	SN	SN 1
London Bridge	d	21 36	21 52							21 48						22 04			22 11		22 08	22 22			
South Bermondsey	d									21 52									22 15						
Queens Rd Peckham	d									21 54									22 18						
Peckham Rye	d									21 57									22 20						
East Dulwich	d									22 00															
North Dulwich	d									22 02															
Luton	d										21 20														
Luton Airport Parkway	d										21 22														
St Pancras International	d										22 06														
City Thameslink	d										22 13														
London Blackfriars	d										22 16														
Elephant & Castle	d										22 19														
Loughborough Jn	d										22 23														
Herne Hill	d										22 27														
Tulse Hill	d									22 05	22 31														
Streatham	d									22 09	22 35														
London Victoria	d				21 36	21 40		21 45	21 47			21 52	21 53	22 00	22 02			22 06						22 06	22 10
Battersea Park	d				21 40			21 49				21 56		22 04					22 32					22 10	
Milton Keynes Central	d																								
Watford Junction	d																								
Harrow & Wealdstone	d																								
Wembley Central	d																								
Shepherd's Bush	d																								
Kensington (Olympia)	d																								
West Brompton	d																								
Clapham Junction	d				21 44	21 46		21 53	21 53			22 00	21 59	22 08	22 08			22 12						22 14	22 16
Wandsworth Common	d				21 47			21 56				22 03		22 11										22 17	
Balham	d				21 50			21 58				22 05		22 14										22 20	
Streatham Hill	d				21 53							22 08												22 23	
West Norwood	d				21 57							22 12												22 27	
Gipsy Hill	d		22 15		22 00							22 15										22 45		22 30	
Crystal Palace	d				22 02							22 21												22 32	
Birkbeck	d																								
Beckenham Junction	a																								
Streatham Common	d							22 02		22 12				22 18											
Norbury	d							22 05		22 15				22 20											
Thornton Heath	d							22 08		22 18				22 23											
Selhurst	d							22 11		22 21				22 27											
Norwood Junction	a	21 59		22 05	22 07											22 15				22 20	22 31		22 35	22 37	
	d	22 00		22 05	22 09											22 15				22 20	22 32		22 35	22 39	
West Croydon	a			22 12	22 13					22 25				22 32						22 31			22 42	22 43	
East Croydon	a	22 03				21 57		22 14	22 03				22 09		22 18	22 19		22 22			22 35				22 27

		SN		SN ◇1	SN	SN	SN 1	SN	SN	SN 1	SN 1	SN		FC 1	LO	SN	SN	SN 1	SN	SN 1	SN	SN ◇1		SN	SN
London Bridge	d				22 18			22 26				22 41		22 42		22 38	22 52	22 56						22 48	
South Bermondsey	d				22 22							22 45												22 52	
Queens Rd Peckham	d				22 24							22 48												22 54	
Peckham Rye	d				22 27							22 50												22 57	
East Dulwich	d				22 30																			23 00	
North Dulwich	d				22 32																			23 02	
Luton	d																								
Luton Airport Parkway	d																								
St Pancras International	d																								
City Thameslink	d																								
London Blackfriars	d																								
Elephant & Castle	d																								
Loughborough Jn	d																								
Herne Hill	d																								
Tulse Hill	d				22 35																			23 05	
Streatham	d				22 39																			23 09	
London Victoria	d	22 15		22 17		22 22	22 23		22 30	22 32	22 36								22 36	22 40	22 45	22 47			22 52
Battersea Park	d	22 19				22 26			22 34			23 02							22 40		22 49				22 56
Milton Keynes Central	d																								
Watford Junction	d																								
Harrow & Wealdstone	d																								
Wembley Central	d																								
Shepherd's Bush	d																								
Kensington (Olympia)	d																								
West Brompton	d																								
Clapham Junction	d	22 23		22 23		22 30	22 29		22 38	22 38	22 42								22 44	22 46	22 53	22 53			23 00
Wandsworth Common	d	22 26				22 33			22 41										22 47		22 56				23 03
Balham	d	22 28				22 35			22 44										22 50		22 58				23 05
Streatham Hill	d					22 38													22 53						23 08
West Norwood	d					22 42													22 57						23 12
Gipsy Hill	d					22 45											23 15		23 00						23 15
Crystal Palace	d					22 51													23 02						23 21
Birkbeck	d																								
Beckenham Junction	a																								
Streatham Common	d	22 32			22 42				22 48												23 02			23 12	
Norbury	d	22 35			22 45				22 50												23 05			23 15	
Thornton Heath	d	22 38			22 48				22 53												23 08			23 18	
Selhurst	d	22 41			22 51				22 57												23 11			23 21	
Norwood Junction	a							22 38							22 50	23 01		23 07	23 08						
	d							22 38							22 50	23 02		23 07	23 09						
West Croydon	a				22 55				23 02						23 01				23 13					23 25	
East Croydon	a	22 44		22 33			22 39	22 42		22 48	22 52			22 54		23 05		23 11		22 57	23 14	23 03			

Table 177

Mondays to Fridays

Luton, Milton Keynes and London - East and West Croydon via Tulse Hill - Crystal Palace - Norbury

Local Services

		SN 1	SN	SN ◇1	FC	SN ◇1	SN	FC 1		LO	SN	SN	SN 1	SN	SN ◇1	SN	SN 1	SN		SN	SN 1	FC	SN ◇1	SN	FC 1
London Bridge	d				23 02		23 11	23 12			23 06					23 18				23 22		23 28			23 42
South Bermondsey	d						23 15									23 22									
Queens Rd Peckham	d						23 18									23 24									
Peckham Rye	d						23 20									23 27									
East Dulwich	d															23 30									
North Dulwich	d															23 32									
Luton	d																								
Luton Airport Parkway	d																								
St Pancras International	d																								
City Thameslink	d																								
London Blackfriars	d																								
Elephant & Castle	d																								
Loughborough Jn	d																								
Herne Hill	d																								
Tulse Hill	d				23 12											23 35						23 40			
Streatham	d				23 16											23 39						23 44			
London Victoria	d	22 53	23 00	23 02		23 06						23 06	23 10	23 15	23 17			23 22			23 24		23 32	23 34	
Battersea Park	d		23 04				23 32					23 10		23 19				23 26						23 38	
Milton Keynes Central	d																22 11								
Watford Junction	d																22 53								
Harrow & Wealdstone	d																23 00								
Wembley Central	d																								
Shepherd's Bush	d																23 21								
Kensington (Olympia)	d																23 23								
West Brompton	d																23 26								
Clapham Junction	d	22 59	23 08	23 08		23 12						23 14	23 16	23 23	23 23		23b40	23 30			23 30		23 38	23 42	
Wandsworth Common	d		23 11									23 17		23 26				23 33						23 45	
Balham	d		23 14									23 20		23 28			23 44	23 35						23 47	
Streatham Hill	d											23 23						23 38							
West Norwood	d											23 27						23 42							
Gipsy Hill	d											23 30						23 45		23 45					
Crystal Palace	d											23 32						23 51							
Birkbeck	d																								
Beckenham Junction	a																								
Streatham Common	d		23 18											23 32		23 42	23 48							23 51	
Norbury	d		23 20											23 35		23 45	23 51							23 54	
Thornton Heath	d		23 23											23 38		23 48	23 54							23 57	
Selhurst	d		23 27											23 41		23 51	23 57							23 59	
Norwood Junction	a									23 20	23 29	23 37													
	d									23 20	23 30	23 39													
West Croydon	a		23 32							23 31		23 43				23 55								00 03	
East Croydon	a	23 09		23 19		23 22		23 24			23 33		23 27	23 44	23 33		00 01				23 40		23 51		23 56

		LO	SN	SN		SN 1	SN	SN 1	SN	FC
London Bridge	d		23 36				23 48			23 58
South Bermondsey	d						23 52			
Queens Rd Peckham	d						23 54			
Peckham Rye	d						23 57			
East Dulwich	d						00 01			
North Dulwich	d						00 03			
Luton	d									
Luton Airport Parkway	d									
St Pancras International	d									
City Thameslink	d									
London Blackfriars	d									
Elephant & Castle	d									
Loughborough Jn	d									
Herne Hill	d									
Tulse Hill	d						00 07			00 10
Streatham	d									00 14
London Victoria	d			23 37		23 47		23 49	23 51	
Battersea Park	d			23 41					23 55	
Milton Keynes Central	d									
Watford Junction	d									
Harrow & Wealdstone	d									
Wembley Central	d									
Shepherd's Bush	d									
Kensington (Olympia)	d									
West Brompton	d									
Clapham Junction	d			23 45		23 53		23 56	23 59	
Wandsworth Common	d			23 48					00 02	
Balham	d			23 51					00 04	
Streatham Hill	d			23 54						
West Norwood	d			23 57			00 10			
Gipsy Hill	d			23 59			00 13			
Crystal Palace	d			00 03			00 15			
Birkbeck	d									
Beckenham Junction	a									
Streatham Common	d								00 08	
Norbury	d								00 11	
Thornton Heath	d								00 14	
Selhurst	d								00 17	
Norwood Junction	a	23 50	23 59	00 07			00 22			
	d	23 50	23 59	00 09						
West Croydon	a	00 01		00 14					00 21	
East Croydon	a		00 03			00 05		00 09		

b arr. 2333

Luton, Milton Keynes and London - East and West Croydon via Tulse Hill - Crystal Palace - Norbury

Local Services

Station		SN 1	SN	LO	SN	SN	SN 1	SN 1	SN	SN ◇1		FC	SN 1	SN	LO	SN	FC	SN	SN	SN		FC	SN ◇1	FC 1	FC 1
London Bridge 4 ⊖	d			23p36							00 12				23p48	23p58	00 06	00 36			00 42		01 05	01 35
South Bermondsey	d														23p52									
Queens Rd Peckham	d														23p54									
Peckham Rye 4	d														23p57									
East Dulwich	d														00 01									
North Dulwich	d														00 03									
Luton 10	d																							
Luton Airport Parkway 7	d																							
St Pancras International 15 ⊖	d																							
City Thameslink 3	d																							
London Blackfriars 3 ⊖	d																							
Elephant & Castle ⊖	d																							
Loughborough Jn	d																							
Herne Hill 4	d																							
Tulse Hill 3	d														00 07	00 10								
Streatham 4	d															00 14								
London Victoria 15 ⊖	d	23p34			23p37	23p47	23p49	23p51	00 05			00 14	00 17						00 42			01 00		
Battersea Park 4	d	23p38			23p41			23p55											00 46					
Milton Keynes Central	d	22p11																							
Watford Junction	d	22p53																							
Harrow & Wealdstone ⊖	d	23p00																							
Wembley Central ⊖	d																							
Shepherd's Bush ⊖	d	23p21																							
Kensington (Olympia) ⊖	d	23p23																							
West Brompton ⊖	d	23p26																							
Clapham Junction 10	d	23b40	23p42			23p45	23p53	23p56	23p59	00 11			00 20	00 23						00 50			01 08		
Wandsworth Common	d		23p45			23p48			00 02											00 53					
Balham 4 ⊖	d	23p44	23p47			23p51			00 04					00 28						00 55					
Streatham Hill	d				23p54																			
West Norwood 4	d				23p57										00 10									
Gipsy Hill	d				23p59										00 13									
Crystal Palace 4	d				00 03										00 15									
Birkbeck 🚊	d																							
Beckenham Junction 4 🚊	a																							
Streatham Common 4	d	23p48	23p51						00 08					00 32						00 59					
Norbury	d	23p51	23p54						00 11					00 34						01 02					
Thornton Heath	d	23p54	23p57						00 14					00 37						01 05					
Selhurst 4	d	23p57	23p59						00 17					00 40						01 07					
Norwood Junction 2	a			23p50	23p59	00 07									00 20	00 22		00 29	00 59						
	d			23p50	23p59	00 09									00 20			00 30	01 00						
West Croydon 4 🚊	a		00 03	00 01		00 14			00 21						00 27										
East Croydon 🚊	a	00 01			00 03		00 05	00 09		00 24		00 26	00 31	00 43				00 33	01 03	01 10		00 56	01 21	01 32	02 02

Station		SN 1	FC 1	SN 1	FC 1	FC 1		SN ◇1	FC 1	FC 1	SN ◇1	FC 1	SN 1	SN ◇1	FC 1	FC 🚌		SN 1	LO	SN 1	SN	FC 🚌	LO	FC 🚌	FC
London Bridge 4 ⊖	d		02 05		03 05	03 35			04 05	04 35		05 05			05 52					06 08	06 11				06 21
South Bermondsey	d																					06 15				
Queens Rd Peckham	d																					06 18				
Peckham Rye 4	d																					06 20				
East Dulwich	d																							
North Dulwich	d																							
Luton 10	d																							
Luton Airport Parkway 7	d																							
St Pancras International 15 ⊖	d																							
City Thameslink 3	d																							
London Blackfriars 3 ⊖	d															06 00						06 16		06 19	
Elephant & Castle ⊖	d															06 08						06 24		06 27	
Loughborough Jn	d																					06 36			
Herne Hill 4	d															06 16						06 44		06a35	
Tulse Hill 3	d															06a24						06a52			06 31
Streatham 4	d																								06 35
London Victoria 15 ⊖	d	02 00		03 00				04 00			05 02		05 25	05 32				06 02							
Battersea Park 4	d																				06 32				
Milton Keynes Central	d																							
Watford Junction	d																							
Harrow & Wealdstone ⊖	d																							
Wembley Central ⊖	d																							
Shepherd's Bush ⊖	d																							
Kensington (Olympia) ⊖	d																							
West Brompton ⊖	d																							
Clapham Junction 10	d	02 08		03 08				04 08			05 08		05 31	05 38				06 08							
Wandsworth Common	d																							
Balham 4 ⊖	d																							
Streatham Hill	d																							
West Norwood 4	d																							
Gipsy Hill	d																							
Crystal Palace 4	d																							
Birkbeck 🚊	d																							
Beckenham Junction 4 🚊	a																							
Streatham Common 4	d																							
Norbury	d																							
Thornton Heath	d																							
Selhurst 4	d											05 27													
Norwood Junction 2	a												05 47						06 05				06 20		
	d												05 48						06 05				06 20		
West Croydon 4 🚊	a																		06 13				06 31		
East Croydon 🚊	a	02 21	02 30	03 21	03 30	04 00		04 21	04 30	05 00	05 21	05 32	05 51	05 48	06 04			06 18		06 22					

b previous night, arr. 2333

Table 177 — Saturdays

Luton, Milton Keynes and London - East and West Croydon via Tulse Hill - Crystal Palace - Norbury

Local Services

Station		SN 1		SN	SN 1	FC 1	SN 1	SN	LO	FC 🚌	SN	FC 1		SN	FC	FC 🚌	LO	SN	SN	SN 1	SN	SN		FC 1	LO
London Bridge 4 ⊖	d					06 27					06 41	06 42			06 45			06 36	06 50			06 48		06 57	
South Bermondsey	d										06 45											06 52			
Queens Rd Peckham	d										06 48											06 54			
Peckham Rye 4	d										06 50											06 57			
East Dulwich	d																					07 00			
North Dulwich	d																					07 02			
Luton 10	d																							
Luton Airport Parkway 7	d																							
St Pancras International 15 ⊖	d																							
City Thameslink 3	d																							
London Blackfriars 3 ⊖	d									06 37						06 46									
Elephant & Castle ⊖	d									06 45						06 54									
Loughborough Jn	d									06 57						07 06									
Herne Hill 4	d									07a05						07 14									
Tulse Hill 3	d														07 01	07a22						07 05			
Streatham 4	d														07 05							07 09			
London Victoria 15 ⊖	d	06 23		06 23			06 32							06 43						06 53	06 53				
Battersea Park 4	d										07 02			06 47											
Milton Keynes Central	d																							
Watford Junction	d				05 52																				
Harrow & Wealdstone ⊖	d				05 58																				
Wembley Central ⊖	d																							
Shepherd's Bush ⊖	d				06 20																				
Kensington (Olympia) ⊖	d				06 23																				
West Brompton ⊖	d				06 26																				
Clapham Junction 10	d	06 29		06 30	06 34		06 38							06 51						06 59	07 00				
Wandsworth Common	d			06 33	06 37									06 54							07 03				
Balham 4 ⊖	d			06 35	06 40									06 56							07 05				
Streatham Hill	d																							
West Norwood 4	d																							
Gipsy Hill	d																							
Crystal Palace 4	d																							
Birkbeck 🚊	d																							
Beckenham Junction 4 🚊	a																							
Streatham Common 4	d			06 39	06 45									07 00							07 09	07 12			
Norbury	d			06 42	06 48									07 03							07 12	07 15			
Thornton Heath	d			06 45	06 51									07 06							07 15	07 18			
Selhurst 4	d			06 48	06 54									07 09							07 18	07 21			
Norwood Junction 2	a								06 35								06 50	06 59	07 02						07 05
	d							06 33	06 35								06 50	07 00	07 03						07 05
West Croydon 4 🚊	a			06 52					06 42								07 01				07 22	07 25			07 12
East Croydon 🚊	a	06 39			06 57	06 39	06 48	06 36				06 54		07 12				07 03	07 06	07 09				07 09	

Station		SN	SN 1	SN ◇1	FC 🚌	SN 1	SN	FC 1		FC	FC 🚌	LO	SN	SN	FC 1	LO	SN	SN		SN ◇1	SN	SN	SN 1	SN 1	SN ◇1
London Bridge 4 ⊖	d		07 03			07 08	07 11	07 12		07 15			07 06	07 20	07 27							07 18			
South Bermondsey	d						07 15															07 22			
Queens Rd Peckham	d						07 18															07 24			
Peckham Rye 4	d						07 20															07 27			
East Dulwich	d																					07 30			
North Dulwich	d																					07 32			
Luton 10	d																							
Luton Airport Parkway 7	d																							
St Pancras International 15 ⊖	d																							
City Thameslink 3	d																							
London Blackfriars 3 ⊖	d				07 07						07 16														
Elephant & Castle ⊖	d				07 15						07 24														
Loughborough Jn	d				07 27						07 36														
Herne Hill 4	d				07a35						07 44														
Tulse Hill 3	d									07 31	07a52											07 35			
Streatham 4	d									07 35												07 39			
London Victoria 15 ⊖	d			07 06													07 06	07 13		07 21	07 23			07 23	07 32
Battersea Park 4	d						07 32										07 10	07 17							
Milton Keynes Central	d																							
Watford Junction	d																						06 55		
Harrow & Wealdstone ⊖	d																						07 01		
Wembley Central ⊖	d																						07 06		
Shepherd's Bush ⊖	d																						07 20		
Kensington (Olympia) ⊖	d																						07 23		
West Brompton ⊖	d																						07 26		
Clapham Junction 10	d			07 12													07 14	07 21			07 30		07 34	07 29	07 38
Wandsworth Common	d																07 17	07 24			07 33		07 37		
Balham 4 ⊖	d																07 20	07 26			07 35		07 40		
Streatham Hill	d	06 53															07 23								
West Norwood 4	d	06 57															07 27								
Gipsy Hill	d	07 00															07 30								
Crystal Palace 4	d	07 02															07 32								
Birkbeck 🚊	d																							
Beckenham Junction 4 🚊	a																							
Streatham Common 4	d																	07 30			07 39	07 42	07 45		
Norbury	d																	07 33			07 42	07 45	07 48		
Thornton Heath	d																	07 36			07 45	07 48	07 51		
Selhurst 4	d																	07 39			07 48	07 51	07 54		
Norwood Junction 2	a	07 07	07 14									07 20	07 29	07 32		07 35	07 37								
	d	07 09	07 15									07 20	07 30	07 33		07 35	07 39								
West Croydon 4 🚊	a	07 14										07 31				07 42	07 43				07 52	07 55			
East Croydon 🚊	a		07 18	07 22		07 22		07 24					07 33	07 36	07 39			07 42		07 37			07 57	07 39	07 48

Table 177

Luton, Milton Keynes and London - East and West Croydon via Tulse Hill - Crystal Palace - Norbury

Saturdays

Local Services

		SN	SN	SN 1	SN ◇1	FC	SN	FC 1	FC	FC	LO	SN 1	SN	SN	FC 1	LO	SN	SN	SN ◇1	SN	SN 1	SN
London Bridge	d	07 33		07 33			07 41	07 42	07 45			07 45	07 36	07 50	07 57							
South Bermondsey	d	07 37					07 45															
Queens Rd Peckham	d	07 39					07 48															
Peckham Rye	d	07 42					07 50															
East Dulwich	d	07 45																				
North Dulwich	d	07 47																				
Luton	d																					
Luton Airport Parkway	d																					
St Pancras International	d																					
City Thameslink	d																					
London Blackfriars	d					07 37				07 46												
Elephant & Castle	d					07 45				07 54												
Loughborough Jn	d					07 57				08 06												
Herne Hill	d					08a05				08 14												
Tulse Hill	d	07 50							08 01	08a22												
Streatham	d								08 05													
London Victoria	d		07 33		07 36												07 36	07 43	07 47	07 49	07 53	07 53
Battersea Park	d		07 37				08 02										07 40	07 47		07 53		
Milton Keynes Central	d																					
Watford Junction	d																					
Harrow & Wealdstone	d																					
Wembley Central	d																					
Shepherd's Bush	d																					
Kensington (Olympia)	d																					
West Brompton	d																					
Clapham Junction	d		07 41		07 42												07 44	07 51	07 53	07 57	07 59	08 00
Wandsworth Common	d		07 44														07 47	07 54		08 00		08 03
Balham	d		07 46														07 50	07 56		08 02		08 05
Streatham Hill	d																07 53			08 05		
West Norwood	d	07 53															07 57			08 10		
Gipsy Hill	d	07 56															08 00			08 13		
Crystal Palace	d	07 59															08 02			08 21		
Birkbeck	d	08 03																				
Beckenham Junction	a	08 06																				
Streatham Common	d		07 50															08 00				08 09
Norbury	d		07 53															08 03				08 12
Thornton Heath	d		07 56															08 06				08 15
Selhurst	d		07 59															08 09				08 18
Norwood Junction	a			07 44							07 50	07 56	07 59	08 02		08 05	08 07					
	d			07 45							07 50	07 56	08 00	08 03		08 05	08 09					
West Croydon	a		08 03								08 01					08 12	08 13					08 22
East Croydon	a			07 48	07 52			07 54				08 00	08 03	08 06	08 09			08 12	08 03		08 09	

		SN	SN ◇1	SN	SN	SN 1	FC	SN ◇1	SN 1	SN	FC 1	FC	FC	LO	SN 1	SN	SN	SN	FC 1	LO	SN	SN	SN ◇1
London Bridge	d	07 48		08 03		08 03			08 08	08 11	08 12	08 15			08 15	08 06	08 20	08 22	08 27				
South Bermondsey	d	07 52		08 07						08 15													
Queens Rd Peckham	d	07 54		08 09						08 18													
Peckham Rye	d	07 57		08 12						08 20													
East Dulwich	d	08 00		08 15																			
North Dulwich	d	08 02		08 17																			
Luton	d																						
Luton Airport Parkway	d																						
St Pancras International	d																						
City Thameslink	d																						
London Blackfriars	d						08 06						08 16										
Elephant & Castle	d						08 15						08 24										
Loughborough Jn	d						08 27						08 36										
Herne Hill	d						08a35						08 44										
Tulse Hill	d	08 05		08 20								08 31	08a52										
Streatham	d	08 09										08 35											
London Victoria	d		08 02		08 03			08 06													08 06	08 13	08 17
Battersea Park	d				08 07					08 32											08 10	08 17	
Milton Keynes Central	d																						
Watford Junction	d																						
Harrow & Wealdstone	d																						
Wembley Central	d																						
Shepherd's Bush	d																						
Kensington (Olympia)	d																						
West Brompton	d																						
Clapham Junction	d		08 08		08 11			08 12													08 14	08 21	08 23
Wandsworth Common	d				08 14																08 17	08 24	
Balham	d				08 16																08 20	08 26	
Streatham Hill	d																				08 23		
West Norwood	d			08 23																	08 27		
Gipsy Hill	d			08 26														08 45			08 30		
Crystal Palace	d			08 29																	08 32		
Birkbeck	d			08 33																			
Beckenham Junction	a			08 36																			
Streatham Common	d	08 12			08 20																	08 30	
Norbury	d	08 15			08 23																	08 33	
Thornton Heath	d	08 18			08 26																	08 36	
Selhurst	d	08 21			08 29																	08 39	
Norwood Junction	a					08 14								08 20	08 26	08 29	08 32			08 35	08 37		
	d					08 15								08 20	08 26	08 30	08 33			08 35	08 39		
West Croydon	a	08 25			08 33									08 31						08 42	08 43		
East Croydon	a		08 18			08 18		08 22	08 22		08 24				08 30	08 33	08 36		08 39			08 42	08 33

Table 177

Luton, Milton Keynes and London - East and West Croydon via Tulse Hill - Crystal Palace - Norbury

Saturdays

Local Services

		SN	SN ◇1	SN	SN	SN 1	SN 1	SN ◇1	SN	SN	SN 1	SN ◇1	FC	SN	FC 1	FC	FC	LO	SN 1	SN	SN	SN	FC 1
London Bridge	d				08 18				08 33		08 33			08 41	08 42	08 45			08 45	08 36	08 50	08 52	08 57
South Bermondsey	d				08 22				08 37					08 45									
Queens Rd Peckham	d				08 24				08 39					08 48									
Peckham Rye	d				08 27				08 42					08 50									
East Dulwich	d				08 30				08 45														
North Dulwich	d				08 32				08 47														
Luton	d																						
Luton Airport Parkway	d																						
St Pancras International	d																						
City Thameslink	d																						
London Blackfriars	d												08 37				08 46						
Elephant & Castle	d												08 45				08 54						
Loughborough Jn	d												08 57				09 06						
Herne Hill	d												09a05				09 14						
Tulse Hill	d				08 35				08 50							09 01	09a22						
Streatham	d				08 39											09 05							
London Victoria	d	08 19	08 21	08 23			08 23	08 32		08 33		08 36											
Battersea Park	d	08 23								08 37				09 02									
Milton Keynes Central	d					07 13																	
Watford Junction	d					07 52																	
Harrow & Wealdstone	d					07 59																	
Wembley Central	d					08u04																	
Shepherd's Bush	d					08 20																	
Kensington (Olympia)	d					08 23																	
West Brompton	d					08 26																	
Clapham Junction	d	08 27		08 30		08 34	08 29	08 38		08 41		08 42											
Wandsworth Common	d	08 30		08 33		08 37				08 44													
Balham	d	08 32		08 35		08 40				08 46													
Streatham Hill	d	08 35																					
West Norwood	d	08 40							08 53														
Gipsy Hill	d	08 43							08 56													09 15	
Crystal Palace	d	08 51							08 59														
Birkbeck	d								09 03														
Beckenham Junction	a								09 06														
Streatham Common	d			08 39	08 42	08 45				08 50													
Norbury	d			08 42	08 45	08 48				08 53													
Thornton Heath	d			08 45	08 48	08 51				08 56													
Selhurst	d			08 48	08 51	08 54				08 59													
Norwood Junction	a										08 44							08 50	08 56	08 59	09 02		
	d										08 45							08 50	08 56	09 00	09 03		
West Croydon	a			08 52	08 55					09 03								09 01					
East Croydon	a		08 37			08 57	08 39	08 48			08 48	08 52			08 54				09 00	09 03	09 06		09 09

		LO	SN	SN	SN ◇1	SN	SN 1	SN	SN	SN ◇1	SN	SN	SN 1	SN ◇1	FC	SN 1	SN	FC 1	FC	FC	LO	SN 1
London Bridge	d								08 48		09 03		09 03			09 08	09 11	09 12	09 15			09 15
South Bermondsey	d								08 52		09 07						09 15					
Queens Rd Peckham	d								08 54		09 09						09 18					
Peckham Rye	d								08 57		09 12						09 20					
East Dulwich	d								09 00		09 15											
North Dulwich	d								09 02		09 17											
Luton	d																					
Luton Airport Parkway	d																					
St Pancras International	d																					
City Thameslink	d																					
London Blackfriars	d														09 07					09 16		
Elephant & Castle	d														09 15					09 24		
Loughborough Jn	d														09 27					09 36		
Herne Hill	d														09a35					09 44		
Tulse Hill	d								09 05		09 20								09 31	09a52		
Streatham	d								09 09										09 35			
London Victoria	d		08 36	08 43	08 47	08 49	08 53	08 53		09 02		09 03		09 06								
Battersea Park	d		08 40	08 47		08 53						09 07					09 32					
Milton Keynes Central	d																					
Watford Junction	d																					
Harrow & Wealdstone	d																					
Wembley Central	d																					
Shepherd's Bush	d																					
Kensington (Olympia)	d																					
West Brompton	d																					
Clapham Junction	d		08 44	08 51	08 53	08 57	08 59	09 00		09 08		09 11		09 12								
Wandsworth Common	d		08 47	08 54		09 00		09 03				09 14										
Balham	d		08 50	08 56		09 02		09 05				09 16										
Streatham Hill	d		08 53			09 05																
West Norwood	d		08 57			09 10					09 23											
Gipsy Hill	d		09 00			09 13					09 26											
Crystal Palace	d		09 02			09 21					09 29											
Birkbeck	d										09 33											
Beckenham Junction	a										09 36											
Streatham Common	d			09 00				09 09	09 12			09 20										
Norbury	d			09 03				09 12	09 15			09 23										
Thornton Heath	d			09 06				09 15	09 18			09 26										
Selhurst	d			09 09				09 18	09 21			09 29										
Norwood Junction	a	09 05	09 07										09 14								09 20	09 26
	d	09 05	09 09										09 15								09 20	09 26
West Croydon	a	09 12	09 13					09 22	09 25			09 33									09 31	
East Croydon	a			09 12	09 03		09 09			09 18			09 18	09 22		09 22		09 24				09 30

Table 177

Saturdays

Luton, Milton Keynes and London - East and West Croydon via Tulse Hill - Crystal Palace - Norbury

Local Services

		SN	SN	SN	FC ■	LO	SN	SN		SN ◇■	SN	SN ◇■	SN ■	SN	SN	SN ■	SN ◇■	SN		SN	SN ■	FC (bus)	SN ◇■ ⌶	SN	FC ■
London Bridge ■ ⊖	d	09 06	09 20	09 22	09 27										09 18			09 33			09 33			09 41	09 42
South Bermondsey	d														09 22			09 37						09 45	
Queens Rd Peckham	d														09 24			09 39						09 48	
Peckham Rye ■	d														09 27			09 42						09 50	
East Dulwich	d														09 30			09 45							
North Dulwich	d														09 32			09 47							
Luton ■	d																								
Luton Airport Parkway ■	d																								
St Pancras International ■ ⊖	d																								
City Thameslink ■	d																								
London Blackfriars ■ ⊖	d																					09 36			
Elephant & Castle ⊖	d																					09 45			
Loughborough Jn	d																					09 57			
Herne Hill ■	d																					10a05			
Tulse Hill ■	d														09 35			09 50							
Streatham ■	d														09 39										
London Victoria ■ ⊖	d						09 06	09 13		09 17	09 19	09 21	09 23	09 23			09 32			09 33			09 36		
Battersea Park ■	d						09 10	09 17			09 23									09 37				10 02	
Milton Keynes Central	d															08 13									
Watford Junction	d															08 52									
Harrow & Wealdstone ⊖	d															08 59									
Wembley Central ⊖	d															09u04									
Shepherd's Bush ⊖	d															09 20									
Kensington (Olympia) ⊖	d															09 23									
West Brompton ⊖	d															09 26									
Clapham Junction ■	d						09 14	09 21		09 23	09 27		09 29	09 30		09 34	09 38			09 41			09 42		
Wandsworth Common	d						09 17	09 24			09 30			09 33		09 37				09 44					
Balham ■ ⊖	d						09 20	09 26			09 32			09 35		09 40				09 46					
Streatham Hill	d						09 23				09 35														
West Norwood ■	d						09 27				09 40							09 53							
Gipsy Hill	d			09 45			09 30				09 43							09 56							
Crystal Palace ■	d						09 32				09 51							09 59							
Birkbeck	d																	10 03							
Beckenham Junction ■	a																	10 06							
Streatham Common ■	d							09 30						09 39	09 42	09 45				09 50					
Norbury	d							09 33						09 42	09 45	09 48				09 53					
Thornton Heath	d							09 36						09 45	09 48	09 51				09 56					
Selhurst ■	d							09 39						09 48	09 51	09 54				09 59					
Norwood Junction ■	a	09 29	09 32			09 35	09 37														09 44				
	d	09 30	09 33			09 35	09 39														09 45				
West Croydon ■	a					09 42	09 43							09 52	09 55					10 03					
East Croydon	a	09 33	09 36		09 39			09 42		09 33		09 37	09 39			09 57	09 48				09 48		09 52		09 54

Table 177

Saturdays

Luton, Milton Keynes and London - East and West Croydon via Tulse Hill - Crystal Palace - Norbury

Local Services

		FC	FC (bus)	LO		SN ■	SN	SN	SN	FC ■	LO	SN	SN	SN ◇■		SN	SN ■	SN	SN	SN ◇■ ⌶	SN	SN	SN ■	SN ◇■ ⌶
London Bridge ■ ⊖	d	09 45				09 45	09 36	09 50	09 52	09 57									09 48		10 03		10 03	
South Bermondsey	d																		09 52		10 07			
Queens Rd Peckham	d																		09 54		10 09			
Peckham Rye ■	d																		09 57		10 12			
East Dulwich	d																		10 00		10 15			
North Dulwich	d																		10 02		10 17			
Luton ■	d																							
Luton Airport Parkway ■	d																							
St Pancras International ■ ⊖	d																							
City Thameslink ■	d																							
London Blackfriars ■ ⊖	d		09 46																					
Elephant & Castle ⊖	d		09 54																					
Loughborough Jn	d		10 06																					
Herne Hill ■	d		10 14																					
Tulse Hill ■	d	10 01	10a22																10 05		10 20			
Streatham ■	d	10 05																	10 09					
London Victoria ■ ⊖	d											09 36	09 43	09 47		09 49	09 53	09 53		10 02		10 03		10 06
Battersea Park ■	d											09 40	09 47			09 53						10 07		
Milton Keynes Central	d																							
Watford Junction	d																							
Harrow & Wealdstone ⊖	d																							
Wembley Central ⊖	d																							
Shepherd's Bush ⊖	d																							
Kensington (Olympia) ⊖	d																							
West Brompton ⊖	d																							
Clapham Junction ■	d											09 44	09 51	09 53		09 57	09 59	10 00		10 08		10 11		10 12
Wandsworth Common	d											09 47	09 54			10 00		10 03				10 14		
Balham ■ ⊖	d											09 50	09 56			10 02		10 05				10 16		
Streatham Hill	d											09 53				10 05								
West Norwood ■	d											09 57				10 10					10 23			
Gipsy Hill	d								10 15			10 00				10 13					10 26			
Crystal Palace ■	d											10 02				10 21					10 29			
Birkbeck	d																				10 33			
Beckenham Junction ■	a																				10 36			
Streatham Common ■	d												10 00					10 09	10 12			10 20		
Norbury	d												10 03					10 12	10 15			10 23		
Thornton Heath	d												10 06					10 15	10 18			10 26		
Selhurst ■	d												10 09					10 18	10 21			10 29		
Norwood Junction ■	a			09 50		09 56	09 59	10 02			10 05	10 07											10 14	
	d			09 50		09 56	10 00	10 03			10 05	10 09											10 15	
West Croydon ■	a			10 01							10 12	10 13						10 22	10 25			10 33		
East Croydon	a					10 00	10 03	10 06		10 09			10 12	10 03			10 09			10 18			10 18	10 22

		FC (bus)	SN ■	SN	FC ■	FC	FC (bus)	LO	SN ■	SN		SN	SN	FC ■	LO	SN	SN	SN ◇■	SN	SN ◇■		SN	SN	SN ■	SN ■
London Bridge ■ ⊖	d		10 08	10 11	10 12	10 15			10 15	10 06		10 20	10 22	10 27									10 18		
South Bermondsey	d			10 15																			10 22		
Queens Rd Peckham	d			10 18																			10 24		
Peckham Rye ■	d			10 20																			10 27		
East Dulwich	d																						10 30		
North Dulwich	d																						10 32		
Luton ■	d																								
Luton Airport Parkway ■	d																								
St Pancras International ■ ⊖	d																								
City Thameslink ■	d																								
London Blackfriars ■ ⊖	d	10 07					10 16																		
Elephant & Castle ⊖	d	10 15					10 24																		
Loughborough Jn	d	10 27					10 36																		
Herne Hill ■	d	10a35					10 44																		
Tulse Hill ■	d					10 31	10a52																10 35		
Streatham ■	d					10 35																	10 39		
London Victoria ■ ⊖	d															10 06	10 13	10 17	10 19	10 21		10 23			10 23
Battersea Park ■	d			10 32												10 10	10 17		10 23						
Milton Keynes Central	d																							09 13	
Watford Junction	d																							09 52	
Harrow & Wealdstone ⊖	d																							09 59	
Wembley Central ⊖	d																							10u04	
Shepherd's Bush ⊖	d																							10 20	
Kensington (Olympia) ⊖	d																							10 23	
West Brompton ⊖	d																							10 26	
Clapham Junction ■	d															10 14	10 21	10 23	10 27			10 30		10 34	10 29
Wandsworth Common	d															10 17	10 24		10 30			10 33		10 37	
Balham ■ ⊖	d															10 20	10 26		10 32			10 35		10 40	
Streatham Hill	d															10 23			10 35						
West Norwood ■	d															10 27			10 40						
Gipsy Hill	d												10 45			10 30			10 43						
Crystal Palace ■	d															10 32			10 51						
Birkbeck	d																								
Beckenham Junction ■	a																								
Streatham Common ■	d																10 30					10 39	10 42	10 45	
Norbury	d																10 33					10 42	10 45	10 48	
Thornton Heath	d																10 36					10 45	10 48	10 51	
Selhurst ■	d																10 39					10 48	10 51	10 54	
Norwood Junction ■	a							10 20	10 26	10 29		10 32			10 35	10 37									
	d							10 20	10 26	10 30		10 33			10 35	10 39									
West Croydon ■	a							10 31							10 42	10 43						10 52	10 55		
East Croydon	a		10 22		10 24				10 30	10 33		10 36		10 39			10 42	10 33		10 37				10 57	10 39

Table 177

Saturdays

Luton, Milton Keynes and London - East and West Croydon via Tulse Hill - Crystal Palace - Norbury

Local Services

Station		SN ◇1	SN	SN	SN 2	SN ◇1		FC	SN	FC 1	FC	FC	LO	SN 1	SN	SN		SN	FC 1	LO	SN	SN	SN ◇1	SN	SN 1
London Bridge 4 ⊖	d		10 33		10 33				10 41	10 42	10 45			10 45	10 36	10 50		10 52	10 57						
South Bermondsey	d		10 37						10 45																
Queens Rd Peckham	d		10 39						10 48																
Peckham Rye 4	d		10 42						10 50																
East Dulwich	d		10 45																						
North Dulwich	d		10 47																						
Luton 10	d																								
Luton Airport Parkway 7	d																								
St Pancras International 15 ⊖	d																								
City Thameslink 3	d																								
London Blackfriars 3 ⊖	d							10 37				10 46													
Elephant & Castle ⊖	d							10 45				10 54													
Loughborough Jn	d							10 57				11 06													
Herne Hill 4	d							11a05				11 14													
Tulse Hill 3	d		10 50								11 01	11a22													
Streatham 4	d										11 05														
London Victoria 15 ⊖	d	10 32		10 33		10 36															10 36	10 43	10 47	10 49	10 53
Battersea Park 4	d			10 37					11 02												10 40	10 47		10 53	
Milton Keynes Central	d																								
Watford Junction	d																								
Harrow & Wealdstone ⊖	d																								
Wembley Central ⊖	d																								
Shepherd's Bush ⊖	d																								
Kensington (Olympia) ⊖	d																								
West Brompton ⊖	d																								
Clapham Junction 10	d	10 38		10 41		10 42															10 44	10 51	10 53	10 57	10 59
Wandsworth Common	d			10 44																	10 47	10 54		11 00	
Balham 4 ⊖	d			10 46																	10 50	10 56		11 02	
Streatham Hill	d																				10 53			11 05	
West Norwood 4	d		10 53																		10 57			11 10	
Gipsy Hill	d		10 56															11 15			11 00			11 13	
Crystal Palace 4	d		10 59																		11 02			11 21	
Birkbeck	d		11 03																						
Beckenham Junction 4	a		11 06																						
Streatham Common 4	d			10 50																		11 00			
Norbury	d			10 53																		11 03			
Thornton Heath	d			10 56																		11 06			
Selhurst 4	d			10 59																		11 09			
Norwood Junction 2	a				10 44								10 50	10 56	10 59	11 02				11 05	11 07				
	d				10 45								10 50	10 56	11 00	11 03				11 05	11 09				
West Croydon 4	a			11 03									11 01							11 12	11 13				
East Croydon	a	10 48			10 48	10 52				10 54				11 00	11 03	11 06			11 09			11 12	11 03		11 09

Table 177

Saturdays

Luton, Milton Keynes and London - East and West Croydon via Tulse Hill - Crystal Palace - Norbury

Local Services

Station		SN		SN	SN ◇1	SN	SN	SN 1	SN ◇1	FC	SN 1	SN		FC 1	FC	FC	LO	SN 1	SN	SN	SN	FC 1		LO	SN
London Bridge 4 ⊖	d			10 48		11 03		11 03			11 08	11 11		11 12	11 15			11 15	11 06	11 20	11 22	11 27			
South Bermondsey	d			10 52		11 07						11 15													
Queens Rd Peckham	d			10 54		11 09						11 18													
Peckham Rye 4	d			10 57		11 12						11 20													
East Dulwich	d			11 00		11 15																			
North Dulwich	d			11 02		11 17																			
Luton 10	d																								
Luton Airport Parkway 7	d																								
St Pancras International 15 ⊖	d																								
City Thameslink 3	d																								
London Blackfriars 3 ⊖	d									11 07						11 16									
Elephant & Castle ⊖	d									11 15						11 24									
Loughborough Jn	d									11 27						11 36									
Herne Hill 4	d									11a35						11 44									
Tulse Hill 3	d			11 05		11 20									11 31	11a52									
Streatham 4	d			11 09											11 35										
London Victoria 15 ⊖	d	10 53			11 02		11 03		11 06																11 06
Battersea Park 4	d						11 07					11 32													11 10
Milton Keynes Central	d																								
Watford Junction	d																								
Harrow & Wealdstone ⊖	d																								
Wembley Central ⊖	d																								
Shepherd's Bush ⊖	d																								
Kensington (Olympia) ⊖	d																								
West Brompton ⊖	d																								
Clapham Junction 10	d	11 00			11 08		11 11		11 12																11 14
Wandsworth Common	d	11 03					11 14																		11 17
Balham 4 ⊖	d	11 05					11 16																		11 20
Streatham Hill	d																								11 23
West Norwood 4	d					11 23																			11 27
Gipsy Hill	d					11 26															11 45				11 30
Crystal Palace 4	d					11 29																			11 32
Birkbeck	d					11 33																			
Beckenham Junction 4	a					11 36																			
Streatham Common 4	d	11 09		11 12			11 20																		
Norbury	d	11 12		11 15			11 23																		
Thornton Heath	d	11 15		11 18			11 26																		
Selhurst 4	d	11 18		11 21			11 29																		
Norwood Junction 2	a							11 14									11 20	11 26	11 29	11 32				11 35	11 37
	d							11 15									11 20	11 26	11 30	11 33				11 35	11 39
West Croydon 4	a	11 22		11 25			11 33										11 31							11 42	11 43
East Croydon	a				11 18			11 18	11 22		11 22			11 24				11 30	11 33	11 36		11 39			

Table 177

Saturdays

Luton, Milton Keynes and London - East and West Croydon via Tulse Hill - Crystal Palace - Norbury

Local Services

		SN	SN ◇1	SN	SN ◇1	SN 1	SN	SN	SN 1	SN ◇1	SN	SN	SN 1	SN ◇1 ⊼	FC ⊖	SN	FC 1	FC	FC ⊖	LO	SN 1	SN	SN
London Bridge 4 ⊖	d							11 18			11 33		11 33			11 41	11 42	11 45			11 45	11 36	11 50
South Bermondsey	d							11 22			11 37					11 45							
Queens Rd Peckham	d							11 24			11 39					11 48							
Peckham Rye 4	d							11 27			11 42					11 50							
East Dulwich	d							11 30			11 45												
North Dulwich	d							11 32			11 47												
Luton 10	d																						
Luton Airport Parkway 7	d																						
St Pancras International 15 ⊖	d																						
City Thameslink 3	d																						
London Blackfriars 3 ⊖	d														11 37				11 46				
Elephant & Castle ⊖	d														11 45				11 54				
Loughborough Jn	d														11 57				12 06				
Herne Hill 4	d														12a05				12 14				
Tulse Hill 3	d							11 35			11 50							12 01	12a22				
Streatham 4	d							11 39										12 05					
London Victoria 15 ⊖	d	11 13	11 17	11 19	11 21	11 23	11 23			11 32		11 33		11 36									
Battersea Park 4	d	11 17		11 23								11 37				12 02							
Milton Keynes Central	d								10 13														
Watford Junction	d								10 52														
Harrow & Wealdstone ⊖	d								10 59														
Wembley Central ⊖	d								11u04														
Shepherd's Bush ⊖	d								11 20														
Kensington (Olympia) ⊖	d								11 23														
West Brompton ⊖	d								11 26														
Clapham Junction 10	d	11 21	11 23	11 27		11 29	11 30		11 34	11 38		11 41		11 42									
Wandsworth Common	d	11 24		11 30			11 33		11 37			11 44											
Balham 4 ⊖	d	11 26		11 32			11 35		11 40			11 46											
Streatham Hill	d			11 35																			
West Norwood 4	d			11 40							11 53												
Gipsy Hill	d			11 43							11 56												
Crystal Palace 4	d			11 51							11 59												
Birkbeck	d										12 03												
Beckenham Junction 4	a										12 06												
Streatham Common 4	d	11 30					11 39	11 42	11 45			11 50											
Norbury	d	11 33					11 42	11 45	11 48			11 53											
Thornton Heath	d	11 36					11 45	11 48	11 51			11 56											
Selhurst 4	d	11 39					11 48	11 51	11 54			11 59											
Norwood Junction 2	a												11 44							11 50	11 56	11 59	12 02
	d												11 45							11 50	11 56	12 00	12 03
West Croydon 4	a						11 52	11 55				12 03								12 01			
East Croydon	a	11 42	11 33		11 37	11 39			11 57	11 48			11 48	11 52			11 54				12 00	12 03	12 06

Table 177

Saturdays

Luton, Milton Keynes and London - East and West Croydon via Tulse Hill - Crystal Palace - Norbury

Local Services

		SN	FC 1	LO	SN	SN	SN ◇1	SN	SN 1	SN	SN	SN ◇1 ⊼	SN	SN	SN 1	SN ◇1 ⊼	FC ⊖	SN 1	SN	FC 1	FC	FC ⊖
London Bridge 4 ⊖	d	11 52	11 57								11 48		12 03		12 03			12 08	12 11	12 12	12 15	
South Bermondsey	d										11 52		12 07						12 15			
Queens Rd Peckham	d										11 54		12 09						12 18			
Peckham Rye 4	d										11 57		12 12						12 20			
East Dulwich	d										12 00		12 15									
North Dulwich	d										12 02		12 17									
Luton 10	d																					
Luton Airport Parkway 7	d																					
St Pancras International 15 ⊖	d																					
City Thameslink 3	d																					
London Blackfriars 3 ⊖	d																12 07					12 16
Elephant & Castle ⊖	d																12 15					12 24
Loughborough Jn	d																12 27					12 36
Herne Hill 4	d																12a35					12 44
Tulse Hill 3	d										12 05		12 20								12 31	12a52
Streatham 4	d										12 09										12 35	
London Victoria 15 ⊖	d				11 36	11 43	11 47	11 49	11 53	11 53		12 02		12 03		12 06						
Battersea Park 4	d				11 40	11 47		11 53						12 07					12 32			
Milton Keynes Central	d																					
Watford Junction	d																					
Harrow & Wealdstone ⊖	d																					
Wembley Central ⊖	d																					
Shepherd's Bush ⊖	d																					
Kensington (Olympia) ⊖	d																					
West Brompton ⊖	d																					
Clapham Junction 10	d				11 44	11 51	11 53	11 57	11 59	12 00		12 08		12 11		12 12						
Wandsworth Common	d				11 47	11 54		12 00		12 03				12 14								
Balham 4 ⊖	d				11 50	11 56		12 02		12 05				12 16								
Streatham Hill	d				11 53			12 05														
West Norwood 4	d				11 57			12 10					12 23									
Gipsy Hill	d	12 15			12 00			12 13					12 26									
Crystal Palace 4	d				12 02			12 21					12 29									
Birkbeck	d												12 33									
Beckenham Junction 4	a												12 36									
Streatham Common 4	d					12 00				12 09	12 12			12 20								
Norbury	d					12 03				12 12	12 15			12 23								
Thornton Heath	d					12 06				12 15	12 18			12 26								
Selhurst 4	d					12 09				12 18	12 21			12 29								
Norwood Junction 2	a			12 05	12 07										12 14							
	d			12 05	12 09										12 15							
West Croydon 4	a			12 12	12 13					12 22	12 25			12 33								
East Croydon	a		12 09			12 12	12 03		12 09			12 18			12 18	12 22		12 22		12 24		

Table 177

Saturdays

Luton, Milton Keynes and London - East and West Croydon via Tulse Hill - Crystal Palace - Norbury

Local Services

	LO	SN ■1	SN	SN	SN	FC ■1	LO	SN	SN	SN ◇■1	SN	SN ◇■1	SN ■1	SN	SN	SN ■1	SN ◇■1	SN	SN	SN ■1	SN ◇■1 (bus)	FC (bus)
London Bridge [4] ⊖ d		12 15	12 06	12 20	12 22	12 27									12 18			12 33		12 33		
South Bermondsey d															12 22			12 37				
Queens Rd Peckham d															12 24			12 39				
Peckham Rye [4] d															12 27			12 42				
East Dulwich d															12 30			12 45				
North Dulwich d															12 32			12 47				
Luton [10] d																						
Luton Airport Parkway [7] d																						
St Pancras International [15] ⊖ d																						
City Thameslink [3] d																						
London Blackfriars [3] ⊖ d																						12 37
Elephant & Castle ⊖ d																						12 45
Loughborough Jn d																						12 57
Herne Hill [4] d																						13a05
Tulse Hill [3] d															12 35			12 50				
Streatham [4] d															12 39							
London Victoria [15] ⊖ d								12 06	12 13	12 17	12 19	12 21	12 23	12 23			12 32		12 33		12 36	
Battersea Park [4] d								12 10	12 17		12 23								12 37			
Milton Keynes Central d																11 13						
Watford Junction d																11 52						
Harrow & Wealdstone ⊖ d																11 59						
Wembley Central ⊖ d																12u04						
Shepherd's Bush ⊖ d																12 20						
Kensington (Olympia) ⊖ d																12 23						
West Brompton ⊖ d																12 26						
Clapham Junction [10] d								12 14	12 21	12 23	12 27		12 29	12 30		12 34	12 38		12 41		12 42	
Wandsworth Common d								12 17	12 24		12 30			12 33		12 37			12 44			
Balham [4] ⊖ d								12 20	12 26		12 32			12 35		12 40			12 46			
Streatham Hill d								12 23			12 35											
West Norwood [4] d								12 27			12 40							12 53				
Gipsy Hill d					12 45			12 30			12 43							12 56				
Crystal Palace [4] d								12 32			12 51							12 59				
Birkbeck d																		13 03				
Beckenham Junction [4] a																		13 06				
Streatham Common [4] d									12 30					12 39	12 42	12 45			12 50			
Norbury d									12 33					12 42	12 45	12 48			12 53			
Thornton Heath d									12 36					12 45	12 48	12 51			12 56			
Selhurst [4] d									12 39					12 48	12 51	12 54			12 59			
Norwood Junction [2] a	12 20	12 26	12 29	12 32			12 35	12 37												12 44		
d	12 20	12 26	12 30	12 33			12 35	12 39												12 45		
West Croydon [4] a	12 31						12 42	12 43						12 52	12 55				13 03			
East Croydon a		12 30	12 33	12 36		12 39			12 42	12 33		12 37	12 39			12 57	12 48			12 48	12 52	

Table 177

Saturdays

Luton, Milton Keynes and London - East and West Croydon via Tulse Hill - Crystal Palace - Norbury

Local Services

	SN	FC ■1	FC	FC (bus)	LO	SN ■1	SN	SN	SN	FC ■1	LO	SN	SN	SN ◇■1	SN	SN ■1	SN	SN	SN ◇■1 (bus)	SN	SN	SN ■1
London Bridge [4] ⊖ d	12 41	12 42	12 45			12 45	12 36	12 50	12 52	12 57								12 48		13 03		13 03
South Bermondsey d	12 45																	12 52		13 07		
Queens Rd Peckham d	12 48																	12 54		13 09		
Peckham Rye [4] d	12 50																	12 57		13 12		
East Dulwich d																		13 00		13 15		
North Dulwich d																		13 02		13 17		
Luton [10] d																						
Luton Airport Parkway [7] d																						
St Pancras International [15] ⊖ d																						
City Thameslink [3] d																						
London Blackfriars [3] ⊖ d				12 46																		
Elephant & Castle ⊖ d				12 54																		
Loughborough Jn d				13 06																		
Herne Hill [4] d				13 14																		
Tulse Hill [3] d			13 01	13a22														13 05		13 20		
Streatham [4] d			13 05															13 09				
London Victoria [15] ⊖ d												12 36	12 43	12 47	12 49	12 53	12 53		13 02		13 03	
Battersea Park [4] d	13 02											12 40	12 47		12 53						13 07	
Milton Keynes Central d																						
Watford Junction d																						
Harrow & Wealdstone ⊖ d																						
Wembley Central ⊖ d																						
Shepherd's Bush ⊖ d																						
Kensington (Olympia) ⊖ d																						
West Brompton ⊖ d																						
Clapham Junction [10] d												12 44	12 51	12 53	12 57	12 59	13 00		13 08		13 11	
Wandsworth Common d												12 47	12 54		13 00		13 03				13 14	
Balham [4] ⊖ d												12 50	12 56		13 02		13 05				13 16	
Streatham Hill d												12 53			13 05							
West Norwood [4] d												12 57			13 10					13 23		
Gipsy Hill d									13 15			13 00			13 13					13 26		
Crystal Palace [4] d												13 02			13 21					13 29		
Birkbeck d																				13 33		
Beckenham Junction [4] a																				13 36		
Streatham Common [4] d													13 00				13 09	13 12			13 20	
Norbury d													13 03				13 12	13 15			13 23	
Thornton Heath d													13 06				13 15	13 18			13 26	
Selhurst [4] d													13 09				13 18	13 21			13 29	
Norwood Junction [2] a					12 50	12 56	12 59	13 02			13 05	13 07										13 14
d					12 50	12 56	13 00	13 03			13 05	13 09										13 15
West Croydon [4] a					13 01						13 12	13 13					13 22	13 25			13 33	
East Croydon a		12 54				13 00	13 03	13 06		13 09			13 12	13 03		13 09			13 18			13 18

Luton, Milton Keynes and London - East and West Croydon via Tulse Hill - Crystal Palace - Norbury

Local Services

Station		SN ◇1	FC	SN 1	SN	FC 1	FC	FC	LO	SN 1	SN	SN	SN	FC 1	LO	SN	SN	SN ◇1	SN	SN ◇1	SN 1	SN
London Bridge 4 ⊖	d			13 08	13 11	13 12	13 15			13 15	13 06	13 20	13 22	13 27								
South Bermondsey	d				13 15																	
Queens Rd Peckham	d				13 18																	
Peckham Rye 4	d				13 20																	
East Dulwich	d																					
North Dulwich	d																					
Luton 10	d																					
Luton Airport Parkway 7	d																					
St Pancras International 15 ⊖	d																					
City Thameslink 3	d																					
London Blackfriars 3 ⊖	d		13 07					13 16														
Elephant & Castle ⊖	d		13 15					13 24														
Loughborough Jn	d		13 27					13 36														
Herne Hill 4	d		13a35					13 44														
Tulse Hill 3	d						13 31	13a52														
Streatham 4	d						13 35															
London Victoria 15 ⊖	d	13 06														13 06	13 13	13 17	13 19	13 21	13 23	13 23
Battersea Park 4	d				13 32											13 10	13 17		13 23			
Milton Keynes Central	d																					
Watford Junction	d																					
Harrow & Wealdstone ⊖	d																					
Wembley Central ⊖	d																					
Shepherd's Bush ⊖	d																					
Kensington (Olympia) ⊖	d																					
West Brompton ⊖	d																					
Clapham Junction 10	d	13 12														13 14	13 21	13 23	13 27		13 29	13 30
Wandsworth Common	d															13 17	13 24		13 30			13 33
Balham 4 ⊖	d															13 20	13 26		13 32			13 35
Streatham Hill	d															13 23			13 35			
West Norwood 4	d															13 27			13 40			
Gipsy Hill	d												13 45			13 30			13 43			
Crystal Palace 4	d															13 32			13 51			
Birkbeck	d																					
Beckenham Junction 4	a																					
Streatham Common 4	d																13 30					13 39
Norbury	d																13 33					13 42
Thornton Heath	d																13 36					13 45
Selhurst 4	d																13 39					13 48
Norwood Junction 2	a								13 20	13 26	13 29	13 32			13 35	13 37						
	d								13 20	13 26	13 30	13 33			13 35	13 39						
West Croydon 4	a								13 31						13 42	13 43						13 52
East Croydon	a	13 22		13 22		13 24				13 30	13 33	13 36		13 39			13 42	13 33		13 37	13 39	

Luton, Milton Keynes and London - East and West Croydon via Tulse Hill - Crystal Palace - Norbury

Local Services

Station		SN	SN 1	SN ◇1	SN	SN	SN 1	SN ◇1	FC	SN	FC 1	FC	FC	LO	SN 1	SN	SN	SN	FC 1	LO	SN	SN	SN ◇1
London Bridge 4 ⊖	d	13 18			13 33		13 33			13 41	13 42	13 45			13 45	13 36	13 50	13 52	13 57				
South Bermondsey	d	13 22			13 37					13 45													
Queens Rd Peckham	d	13 24			13 39					13 48													
Peckham Rye 4	d	13 27			13 42					13 50													
East Dulwich	d	13 30			13 45																		
North Dulwich	d	13 32			13 47																		
Luton 10	d																						
Luton Airport Parkway 7	d																						
St Pancras International 15 ⊖	d																						
City Thameslink 3	d																						
London Blackfriars 3 ⊖	d								13 37				13 46										
Elephant & Castle ⊖	d								13 45				13 54										
Loughborough Jn	d								13 57				14 06										
Herne Hill 4	d								14a05				14 14										
Tulse Hill 3	d	13 35			13 50							14 01	14a22										
Streatham 4	d	13 39										14 05											
London Victoria 15 ⊖	d			13 32		13 33		13 36													13 36	13 43	13 47
Battersea Park 4	d					13 37				14 02											13 40	13 47	
Milton Keynes Central	d		12 13																				
Watford Junction	d		12 52																				
Harrow & Wealdstone ⊖	d		12 59																				
Wembley Central ⊖	d		13u04																				
Shepherd's Bush ⊖	d		13 20																				
Kensington (Olympia) ⊖	d		13 23																				
West Brompton ⊖	d		13 26																				
Clapham Junction 10	d		13 34	13 38		13 41		13 42													13 44	13 51	13 53
Wandsworth Common	d		13 37			13 44															13 47	13 54	
Balham 4 ⊖	d		13 40			13 46															13 50	13 56	
Streatham Hill	d																				13 53		
West Norwood 4	d				13 53																13 57		
Gipsy Hill	d				13 56													14 15			14 00		
Crystal Palace 4	d				13 59																14 02		
Birkbeck	d				14 03																		
Beckenham Junction 4	a				14 06																		
Streatham Common 4	d	13 42	13 45			13 50																14 00	
Norbury	d	13 45	13 48			13 53																14 03	
Thornton Heath	d	13 48	13 51			13 56																14 06	
Selhurst 4	d	13 51	13 54			13 59																14 09	
Norwood Junction 2	a						13 44							13 50	13 56	13 59	14 02			14 05	14 07		
	d						13 45							13 50	13 56	14 00	14 03			14 05	14 09		
West Croydon 4	a	13 55				14 03								14 01						14 12	14 13		
East Croydon	a		13 57	13 48			13 48	13 52			13 54				14 00	14 03	14 06		14 09			14 12	14 03

Table 177

Saturdays

Luton, Milton Keynes and London - East and West Croydon via Tulse Hill - Crystal Palace - Norbury

Local Services

		SN	SN ■	SN	SN	SN ◇■	SN	SN	SN ■	SN ◇■	FC	SN ■	SN	FC ■	FC	FC	LO	SN ■	SN	SN	SN	FC ■
London Bridge ■ ⊖	d				13 48		14 03		14 03			14 08	14 11	14 12	14 15			14 15	14 06	14 20	14 22	14 27
South Bermondsey	d				13 52		14 07						14 15									
Queens Rd Peckham	d				13 54		14 09						14 18									
Peckham Rye ■	d				13 57		14 12						14 20									
East Dulwich	d				14 00		14 15															
North Dulwich	d				14 02		14 17															
Luton ■	d																					
Luton Airport Parkway ■	d																					
St Pancras International ■ ⊖	d																					
City Thameslink ■	d																					
London Blackfriars ■ ⊖	d										14 07					14 16						
Elephant & Castle ⊖	d										14 15					14 24						
Loughborough Jn	d										14 27					14 36						
Herne Hill ■	d										14a35					14 44						
Tulse Hill ■	d				14 05		14 20								14 31	14a52						
Streatham ■	d				14 09										14 35							
London Victoria ■ ⊖	d	13 49	13 53	13 53		14 02		14 03		14 06												
Battersea Park ■	d	13 53						14 07					14 32									
Milton Keynes Central	d																					
Watford Junction	d																					
Harrow & Wealdstone ⊖	d																					
Wembley Central ⊖	d																					
Shepherd's Bush ⊖	d																					
Kensington (Olympia) ⊖	d																					
West Brompton ⊖	d																					
Clapham Junction ■	d	13 57	13 59	14 00		14 08		14 11		14 12												
Wandsworth Common	d	14 00		14 03				14 14														
Balham ■ ⊖	d	14 02		14 05				14 16														
Streatham Hill	d	14 05																				
West Norwood ■	d	14 10					14 23															
Gipsy Hill	d	14 13					14 26															
Crystal Palace ■	d	14 21					14 29														14 45	
Birkbeck	d						14 33															
Beckenham Junction ■	a						14 36															
Streatham Common ■	d			14 09	14 12			14 20														
Norbury	d			14 12	14 15			14 23														
Thornton Heath	d			14 15	14 18			14 26														
Selhurst ■	d			14 18	14 21			14 29														
Norwood Junction ■	a								14 14								14 20	14 26	14 29	14 32		
	d								14 15								14 20	14 26	14 30	14 33		
West Croydon ■	a			14 22	14 25			14 33									14 31					
East Croydon	a		14 09			14 18			14 18	14 22		14 22		14 24				14 30	14 33	14 36		14 39

Table 177

Saturdays

Luton, Milton Keynes and London - East and West Croydon via Tulse Hill - Crystal Palace - Norbury

Local Services

		LO	SN	SN	SN ◇■	SN	SN ◇■	SN ■	SN	SN	SN ■	SN ◇■	SN	SN	SN ■	SN ◇■	FC	SN	FC ■	FC	FC	LO	SN ■
London Bridge ■ ⊖	d									14 18			14 33		14 33			14 41	14 42	14 45			14 45
South Bermondsey	d									14 22			14 37					14 45					
Queens Rd Peckham	d									14 24			14 39					14 48					
Peckham Rye ■	d									14 27			14 42					14 50					
East Dulwich	d									14 30			14 45										
North Dulwich	d									14 32			14 47										
Luton ■	d																						
Luton Airport Parkway ■	d																						
St Pancras International ■ ⊖	d																						
City Thameslink ■	d																						
London Blackfriars ■ ⊖	d																14 37				14 46		
Elephant & Castle ⊖	d																14 45				14 54		
Loughborough Jn	d																14 57				15 06		
Herne Hill ■	d																15a05				15 14		
Tulse Hill ■	d									14 35			14 50							15 01	15a22		
Streatham ■	d									14 39										15 05			
London Victoria ■ ⊖	d		14 06	14 13	14 17	14 19	14 21	14 23	14 23			14 32		14 33		14 36							
Battersea Park ■	d		14 10	14 17		14 23								14 37				15 02					
Milton Keynes Central	d										13 13												
Watford Junction	d										13 52												
Harrow & Wealdstone ⊖	d										13 59												
Wembley Central ⊖	d										14u04												
Shepherd's Bush ⊖	d										14 20												
Kensington (Olympia) ⊖	d										14 23												
West Brompton ⊖	d										14 26												
Clapham Junction ■	d		14 14	14 21	14 23	14 27		14 29	14 30		14 34	14 38		14 41		14 42							
Wandsworth Common	d		14 17	14 24		14 30			14 33		14 37			14 44									
Balham ■ ⊖	d		14 20	14 26		14 32			14 35		14 40			14 46									
Streatham Hill	d		14 23			14 35																	
West Norwood ■	d		14 27			14 40							14 53										
Gipsy Hill	d		14 30			14 43							14 56										
Crystal Palace ■	d		14 32			14 51							14 59										
Birkbeck	d												15 03										
Beckenham Junction ■	a												15 06										
Streatham Common ■	d			14 30					14 39	14 42	14 45			14 50									
Norbury	d			14 33					14 42	14 45	14 48			14 53									
Thornton Heath	d			14 36					14 45	14 48	14 51			14 56									
Selhurst ■	d			14 39					14 48	14 51	14 54			14 59									
Norwood Junction ■	a	14 35	14 37												14 44							14 50	14 56
	d	14 35	14 39												14 45							14 50	14 56
West Croydon ■	a	14 42	14 43						14 52	14 55				15 03								15 01	
East Croydon	a			14 42	14 33		14 37	14 39			14 57	14 48			14 48	14 52			14 54				15 00

Table 177

Saturdays

Luton, Milton Keynes and London - East and West Croydon via Tulse Hill - Crystal Palace - Norbury

Local Services

		SN	SN	SN	FC	LO		SN	SN	SN	SN	SN	SN	SN	SN	SN		SN	SN	SN	FC	SN	SN	FC	FC
					1					◇1		1			◇1 H				1	◇1 H	=	1		1	
London Bridge	d	14 36	14 50	14 52	14 57									14 48		15 03			15 03			15 08	15 11	15 12	15 15
South Bermondsey	d													14 52		15 07							15 15		
Queens Rd Peckham	d													14 54		15 09							15 18		
Peckham Rye	d													14 57		15 12							15 20		
East Dulwich	d													15 00		15 15									
North Dulwich	d													15 02		15 17									
Luton	d																								
Luton Airport Parkway	d																								
St Pancras International	d																								
City Thameslink	d																								
London Blackfriars	d																				15 07				
Elephant & Castle	d																				15 15				
Loughborough Jn	d																				15 27				
Herne Hill	d																				15a35				
Tulse Hill	d													15 05		15 20									15 31
Streatham	d													15 09											15 35
London Victoria	d							14 36	14 43	14 47	14 49	14 53	14 53		15 02			15 03		15 06					
Battersea Park	d							14 40	14 47		14 53							15 07					15 32		
Milton Keynes Central	d																								
Watford Junction	d																								
Harrow & Wealdstone	d																								
Wembley Central	d																								
Shepherd's Bush	d																								
Kensington (Olympia)	d																								
West Brompton	d																								
Clapham Junction	d							14 44	14 51	14 53	14 57	14 59	15 00		15 08			15 11		15 12					
Wandsworth Common	d							14 47	14 54		15 00		15 03					15 14							
Balham	d							14 50	14 56		15 02		15 05					15 16							
Streatham Hill	d							14 53			15 05														
West Norwood	d							14 57			15 10					15 23									
Gipsy Hill	d			15 15				15 00			15 13					15 26									
Crystal Palace	d							15 02			15 21					15 29									
Birkbeck	d															15 33									
Beckenham Junction	a															15 36									
Streatham Common	d								15 00				15 09	15 12				15 20							
Norbury	d								15 03				15 12	15 15				15 23							
Thornton Heath	d								15 06				15 15	15 18				15 26							
Selhurst	d								15 09				15 18	15 21				15 29							
Norwood Junction	a	14 59	15 02			15 05		15 07											15 14						
	d	15 00	15 03			15 05		15 09											15 15						
West Croydon	a					15 12		15 13					15 22	15 25				15 33							
East Croydon	a	15 03	15 06		15 09				15 12	15 03		15 09			15 18				15 18	15 22		15 22		15 24	

		FC		LO	SN	SN	SN	SN	FC	LO	SN	SN		SN	SN	SN	SN	SN	SN	SN	SN	SN		SN	SN
		=			1				1					◇1		◇1	1			1	◇1				1
London Bridge	d				15 15	15 06	15 20	15 22	15 27										15 18			15 33			15 33
South Bermondsey	d																		15 22			15 37			
Queens Rd Peckham	d																		15 24			15 39			
Peckham Rye	d																		15 27			15 42			
East Dulwich	d																		15 30			15 45			
North Dulwich	d																		15 32			15 47			
Luton	d																								
Luton Airport Parkway	d																								
St Pancras International	d																								
City Thameslink	d																								
London Blackfriars	d	15 16																							
Elephant & Castle	d	15 24																							
Loughborough Jn	d	15 36																							
Herne Hill	d	15 44																							
Tulse Hill	d	15a52																	15 35			15 50			
Streatham	d																		15 39						
London Victoria	d										15 06	15 13		15 17	15 19	15 21	15 23	15 23			15 32			15 33	
Battersea Park	d										15 10	15 17			15 23									15 37	
Milton Keynes Central	d																			14 13					
Watford Junction	d																			14 52					
Harrow & Wealdstone	d																			14 59					
Wembley Central	d																			15u04					
Shepherd's Bush	d																			15 20					
Kensington (Olympia)	d																			15 23					
West Brompton	d																			15 26					
Clapham Junction	d										15 14	15 21		15 23	15 27		15 29	15 30		15 34	15 38			15 41	
Wandsworth Common	d										15 17	15 24			15 30			15 33		15 37				15 44	
Balham	d										15 20	15 26			15 32			15 35		15 40				15 46	
Streatham Hill	d										15 23				15 35										
West Norwood	d										15 27				15 40							15 53			
Gipsy Hill	d							15 45			15 30				15 43							15 56			
Crystal Palace	d										15 32				15 51							15 59			
Birkbeck	d																					16 03			
Beckenham Junction	a																					16 06			
Streatham Common	d											15 30						15 39	15 42	15 45				15 50	
Norbury	d											15 33						15 42	15 45	15 48				15 53	
Thornton Heath	d											15 36						15 45	15 48	15 51				15 56	
Selhurst	d											15 39						15 48	15 51	15 54				15 59	
Norwood Junction	a			15 20	15 26	15 29	15 32			15 35	15 37														15 44
	d			15 20	15 26	15 30	15 33			15 35	15 39														15 45
West Croydon	a			15 31						15 42	15 43							15 52	15 55					16 03	
East Croydon	a				15 30	15 33	15 36		15 39			15 42		15 33		15 37	15 39			15 57	15 48				15 48

Table 177

Saturdays

Luton, Milton Keynes and London - East and West Croydon via Tulse Hill - Crystal Palace - Norbury

Local Services

		SN	FC	SN	FC	FC	FC	LO		SN	SN	SN	SN	FC	LO	SN	SN	SN		SN	SN	SN	SN	SN	SN
		◇1 H	=		1		=			1				1				◇1			1			◇1 H	
London Bridge	d			15 41	15 42	15 45				15 45	15 36	15 50	15 52	15 57									15 48		16 03
South Bermondsey	d			15 45																			15 52		16 07
Queens Rd Peckham	d			15 48																			15 54		16 09
Peckham Rye	d			15 50																			15 57		16 12
East Dulwich	d																						16 00		16 15
North Dulwich	d																						16 02		16 17
Luton	d																								
Luton Airport Parkway	d																								
St Pancras International	d																								
City Thameslink	d																								
London Blackfriars	d		15 37				15 46																		
Elephant & Castle	d		15 45				15 54																		
Loughborough Jn	d		15 57				16 06																		
Herne Hill	d		16a05				16 14																		
Tulse Hill	d					16 01	16a22																16 05		16 20
Streatham	d					16 05																	16 09		
London Victoria	d	15 36														15 36	15 43	15 47		15 49	15 53	15 53		16 02	
Battersea Park	d			16 02												15 40	15 47			15 53					
Milton Keynes Central	d																								
Watford Junction	d																								
Harrow & Wealdstone	d																								
Wembley Central	d																								
Shepherd's Bush	d																								
Kensington (Olympia)	d																								
West Brompton	d																								
Clapham Junction	d	15 42														15 44	15 51	15 53		15 57	15 59	16 00		16 08	
Wandsworth Common	d															15 47	15 54			16 00		16 03			
Balham	d															15 50	15 56			16 02		16 05			
Streatham Hill	d															15 53				16 05					
West Norwood	d															15 57				16 10					16 23
Gipsy Hill	d												16 15			16 00				16 13					16 26
Crystal Palace	d															16 02				16 21					16 29
Birkbeck	d																								16 33
Beckenham Junction	a																								16 36
Streatham Common	d																16 00					16 09	16 12		
Norbury	d																16 03					16 12	16 15		
Thornton Heath	d																16 06					16 15	16 18		
Selhurst	d																16 09					16 18	16 21		
Norwood Junction	a							15 50		15 56	15 59	16 02			16 05	16 07									
	d							15 50		15 56	16 00	16 03			16 05	16 09									
West Croydon	a							16 01							16 12	16 13						16 22	16 25		
East Croydon	a	15 52			15 54					16 00	16 03	16 06		16 09			16 12	16 03			16 09			16 18	

Table 177

Saturdays

Luton, Milton Keynes and London - East and West Croydon via Tulse Hill - Crystal Palace - Norbury

Local Services

		SN	SN	SN	FC	SN	SN	FC	FC	FC	LO	SN	SN	SN	SN	FC	LO	SN	SN	SN	SN	SN
			■	◇■		■		■				■				■				◇■		◇■
London Bridge ⊖	d		16 03			16 08	16 11	16 12	16 15			16 15	16 06	16 20	16 22	16 27						
South Bermondsey	d						16 15															
Queens Rd Peckham	d						16 18															
Peckham Rye	d						16 20															
East Dulwich	d																					
North Dulwich	d																					
Luton	d																					
Luton Airport Parkway	d																					
St Pancras International ⊖	d																					
City Thameslink	d																					
London Blackfriars ⊖	d				16 07					16 16												
Elephant & Castle ⊖	d				16 15					16 24												
Loughborough Jn	d				16 27					16 36												
Herne Hill	d				16a35					16 44												
Tulse Hill	d								16 31	16a52												
Streatham	d								16 35													
London Victoria ⊖	d	16 03		16 06														16 06	16 13	16 17	16 19	16 21
Battersea Park	d	16 07					16 32											16 10	16 17		16 23	
Milton Keynes Central	d																					
Watford Junction	d																					
Harrow & Wealdstone ⊖	d																					
Wembley Central ⊖	d																					
Shepherd's Bush ⊖	d																					
Kensington (Olympia) ⊖	d																					
West Brompton ⊖	d																					
Clapham Junction	d	16 11		16 12														16 14	16 21	16 23	16 27	
Wandsworth Common	d	16 14																16 17	16 24		16 30	
Balham ⊖	d	16 16																16 20	16 26		16 32	
Streatham Hill	d																	16 23			16 35	
West Norwood	d																	16 27			16 40	
Gipsy Hill	d														16 45			16 30			16 43	
Crystal Palace	d																	16 32			16 51	
Birkbeck	d																					
Beckenham Junction	a																					
Streatham Common	d	16 20																	16 30			
Norbury	d	16 23																	16 33			
Thornton Heath	d	16 26																	16 36			
Selhurst	d	16 29																	16 39			
Norwood Junction	a		16 14								16 20	16 26	16 29	16 32			16 35	16 37				
	d		16 15								16 20	16 26	16 30	16 33			16 35	16 39				
West Croydon	a	16 33									16 31						16 42	16 43				
East Croydon	a		16 18	16 22		16 22		16 24				16 30	16 33	16 36		16 39			16 42	16 33		16 37

Table 177

Saturdays

Luton, Milton Keynes and London - East and West Croydon via Tulse Hill - Crystal Palace - Norbury

Local Services

		SN	SN	SN	SN	SN	SN	SN	SN	SN	FC	SN	FC	FC	FC	LO	SN	SN	SN	SN	FC	LO	SN
				■	■	◇■			■	◇■			■				■				■		
London Bridge ⊖	d		16 18				16 33		16 33			16 41	16 42	16 45			16 45	16 36	16 50	16 52	16 57		
South Bermondsey	d		16 22				16 37					16 45											
Queens Rd Peckham	d		16 24				16 39					16 48											
Peckham Rye	d		16 27				16 42					16 50											
East Dulwich	d		16 30				16 45																
North Dulwich	d		16 32				16 47																
Luton	d																						
Luton Airport Parkway	d																						
St Pancras International ⊖	d																						
City Thameslink	d																						
London Blackfriars ⊖	d										16 37				16 46								
Elephant & Castle ⊖	d										16 45				16 54								
Loughborough Jn	d										16 57				17 06								
Herne Hill	d										17a05				17 14								
Tulse Hill	d		16 35				16 50							17 01	17a22								
Streatham	d		16 39											17 05									
London Victoria ⊖	d	16 23			16 23	16 32		16 33		16 36													16 36
Battersea Park	d							16 37				17 02											16 40
Milton Keynes Central	d			15 13																			
Watford Junction	d			15 52																			
Harrow & Wealdstone ⊖	d			15 59																			
Wembley Central ⊖	d			16u04																			
Shepherd's Bush ⊖	d			16 20																			
Kensington (Olympia) ⊖	d			16 23																			
West Brompton ⊖	d			16 26																			
Clapham Junction	d	16 30		16 34	16 29	16 38		16 41		16 42													16 44
Wandsworth Common	d	16 33		16 37				16 44															16 47
Balham ⊖	d	16 35		16 40				16 46															16 50
Streatham Hill	d																						16 53
West Norwood	d						16 53																16 57
Gipsy Hill	d						16 56													17 15			17 00
Crystal Palace	d						16 59																17 02
Birkbeck	d						17 03																
Beckenham Junction	a						17 06																
Streatham Common	d	16 39	16 42	16 45				16 50															
Norbury	d	16 42	16 45	16 48				16 53															
Thornton Heath	d	16 45	16 48	16 51				16 56															
Selhurst	d	16 48	16 51	16 54				16 59															
Norwood Junction	a								16 44							16 50	16 56	16 59	17 02			17 05	17 07
	d								16 45							16 50	16 56	17 00	17 03			17 05	17 09
West Croydon	a	16 52	16 55					17 03								17 01						17 12	17 13
East Croydon	a			16 57	16 39	16 48			16 48	16 52			16 54				17 00	17 03	17 06		17 09		

Table 177 — Saturdays

Luton, Milton Keynes and London - East and West Croydon via Tulse Hill - Crystal Palace - Norbury

Local Services

		SN	SN ◇[1]	SN	SN [1]	SN		SN	SN ◇[1]	SN	SN	SN [1]	SN ◇[1]	FC	SN [1]	SN		FC [1]	FC	FC	LO	SN [1]	SN	SN	SN
London Bridge [4] ⊖	d							16 48		17 03		17 03			17 08	17 11		17 12	17 15			17 15	17 06	17 20	17 22
South Bermondsey	d							16 52		17 07						17 15									
Queens Rd Peckham	d							16 54		17 09						17 18									
Peckham Rye [4]	d							16 57		17 12						17 20									
East Dulwich	d							17 00		17 15															
North Dulwich	d							17 02		17 17															
Luton [10]	d																								
Luton Airport Parkway [7]	d																								
St Pancras International [15] ⊖	d																								
City Thameslink [3]	d																								
London Blackfriars [3] ⊖	d													17 07						17 16					
Elephant & Castle ⊖	d													17 15						17 24					
Loughborough Jn	d													17 27						17 36					
Herne Hill [4]	d													17a35						17 44					
Tulse Hill [3]	d							17 05		17 20									17 31	17a52					
Streatham [4]	d							17 09											17 35						
London Victoria [15] ⊖	d	16 43	16 47	16 49	16 53	16 53			17 02		17 03		17 06												
Battersea Park [4]	d	16 47		16 53							17 07					17 32									
Milton Keynes Central	d																								
Watford Junction	d																								
Harrow & Wealdstone ⊖	d																								
Wembley Central ⊖	d																								
Shepherd's Bush ⊖	d																								
Kensington (Olympia) ⊖	d																								
West Brompton ⊖	d																								
Clapham Junction [10]	d	16 51	16 53	16 57	16 59	17 00			17 08		17 11		17 12												
Wandsworth Common	d	16 54		17 00		17 03					17 14														
Balham [4] ⊖	d	16 56		17 02		17 05					17 16														
Streatham Hill	d			17 05																					
West Norwood [4]	d			17 10						17 23															
Gipsy Hill	d			17 13						17 26															17 45
Crystal Palace [4]	d			17 21						17 29															
Birkbeck	d									17 33															
Beckenham Junction [4]	a									17 36															
Streatham Common [4]	d	17 00				17 09		17 12			17 20														
Norbury	d	17 03				17 12		17 15			17 23														
Thornton Heath	d	17 06				17 15		17 18			17 26														
Selhurst [4]	d	17 09				17 18		17 21			17 29														
Norwood Junction [2]	a											17 14									17 20	17 26	17 29	17 32	
	d											17 15									17 20	17 26	17 30	17 33	
West Croydon [4]	a					17 22		17 25			17 33										17 31				
East Croydon	a	17 12	17 03		17 09				17 18			17 18	17 22		17 22			17 24				17 30	17 33	17 36	

Table 177 — Saturdays

Luton, Milton Keynes and London - East and West Croydon via Tulse Hill - Crystal Palace - Norbury

Local Services

		FC [1]		LO	SN	SN	SN ◇[1]	SN	SN ◇[1]	SN [1]	SN	SN		SN [1]	SN ◇[1]	SN	SN	SN [1]	SN ◇[1]	FC	FC	SN		FC [1]	FC
London Bridge [4] ⊖	d	17 27										17 18				17 33		17 33				17 41		17 42	17 45
South Bermondsey	d											17 22				17 37						17 45			
Queens Rd Peckham	d											17 24				17 39						17 48			
Peckham Rye [4]	d											17 27				17 42						17 50			
East Dulwich	d											17 30				17 45									
North Dulwich	d											17 32				17 47									
Luton [10]	d																								
Luton Airport Parkway [7]	d																								
St Pancras International [15] ⊖	d																								
City Thameslink [3]	d																								
London Blackfriars [3] ⊖	d																			17 37	17 38				
Elephant & Castle ⊖	d																			17 45	17 46				
Loughborough Jn	d																			17 57	17 58				
Herne Hill [4]	d																			18a05	18a06				
Tulse Hill [3]	d											17 35				17 50									18 01
Streatham [4]	d											17 39													18 05
London Victoria [15] ⊖	d				17 06	17 13	17 17	17 19	17 21	17 23	17 23				17 32		17 33		17 36						
Battersea Park [4]	d				17 10	17 17		17 23									17 37					18 02			
Milton Keynes Central	d													16 13											
Watford Junction	d													16 52											
Harrow & Wealdstone ⊖	d													16 59											
Wembley Central ⊖	d													17u04											
Shepherd's Bush ⊖	d													17 20											
Kensington (Olympia) ⊖	d													17 23											
West Brompton ⊖	d													17 26											
Clapham Junction [10]	d				17 14	17 21	17 23	17 27		17 29	17 30			17 34	17 38		17 41		17 42						
Wandsworth Common	d				17 17	17 24		17 30			17 33			17 37			17 44								
Balham [4] ⊖	d				17 20	17 26		17 32			17 35			17 40			17 46								
Streatham Hill	d				17 23			17 35																	
West Norwood [4]	d				17 27			17 40								17 53									
Gipsy Hill	d				17 30			17 43								17 56									
Crystal Palace [4]	d				17 32			17 51								17 59									
Birkbeck	d															18 03									
Beckenham Junction [4]	a															18 06									
Streatham Common [4]	d					17 30					17 39	17 42		17 45			17 50								
Norbury	d					17 33					17 42	17 45		17 48			17 53								
Thornton Heath	d					17 36					17 45	17 48		17 51			17 56								
Selhurst [4]	d					17 39					17 48	17 51		17 54			17 59								
Norwood Junction [2]	a			17 35	17 37													17 44							
	d			17 35	17 39													17 45							
West Croydon [4]	a			17 42	17 43						17 52	17 55					18 03								
East Croydon	a	17 39				17 42	17 33		17 37	17 39				17 57	17 48			17 48	17 52					17 54	

Table 177

Luton, Milton Keynes and London - East and West Croydon via Tulse Hill - Crystal Palace - Norbury

Local Services

		FC	LO	SN	SN	SN	SN	FC		LO	SN	SN	SN	SN	SN	SN	SN	SN		SN	SN	SN	SN	FC	SN
				1				1					◇1		1			◇1				1	◇1		1
London Bridge ⊖	d			17 45	17 36	17 50	17 52	17 57									17 48				18 03	18 03			18 08
South Bermondsey	d																17 52				18 07				
Queens Rd Peckham	d																17 54				18 09				
Peckham Rye	d																17 57				18 12				
East Dulwich	d																18 00				18 15				
North Dulwich	d																18 02				18 17				
Luton	d																								
Luton Airport Parkway	d																								
St Pancras International ⊖	d																								
City Thameslink	d																								
London Blackfriars ⊖	d	17 46																						18 07	
Elephant & Castle ⊖	d	17 54																						18 15	
Loughborough Jn	d	18 06																						18 27	
Herne Hill	d	18 14																						18a35	
Tulse Hill	d	18a22															18 05				18 20				
Streatham	d																18 09								
London Victoria ⊖	d										17 36	17 43	17 47	17 49	17 53	17 53		18 02		18 03			18 06		
Battersea Park	d										17 40	17 47		17 53						18 07					
Milton Keynes Central	d																								
Watford Junction	d																								
Harrow & Wealdstone ⊖	d																								
Wembley Central ⊖	d																								
Shepherd's Bush ⊖	d																								
Kensington (Olympia) ⊖	d																								
West Brompton ⊖	d																								
Clapham Junction	d										17 44	17 51	17 53	17 57	17 59	18 00		18 08		18 11			18 12		
Wandsworth Common	d										17 47	17 54		18 00		18 03				18 14					
Balham ⊖	d										17 50	17 56		18 02		18 05				18 16					
Streatham Hill	d										17 53			18 05											
West Norwood	d										17 57			18 10							18 23				
Gipsy Hill	d						18 15				18 00			18 13							18 26				
Crystal Palace	d										18 02			18 21							18 29				
Birkbeck	d																				18 33				
Beckenham Junction	a																				18 36				
Streatham Common	d											18 00				18 09	18 12			18 20					
Norbury	d											18 03				18 12	18 15			18 23					
Thornton Heath	d											18 06				18 15	18 18			18 26					
Selhurst	d											18 09				18 18	18 21			18 29					
Norwood Junction	a		17 50	17 56	17 59	18 02				18 05	18 07											18 14			
	d		17 50	17 56	18 00	18 03				18 05	18 09											18 15			
West Croydon	a		18 01							18 12	18 13					18 22	18 25			18 33					
East Croydon	a			18 00	18 03	18 06		18 09				18 12	18 03		18 09			18 18				18 18	18 22		18 22

		SN	FC	FC		FC	LO	SN	SN	SN	SN	FC	LO	SN		SN	SN	SN	SN	SN	SN	SN	SN	SN
			1					1				1					◇1		◇1			1	1	◇1
London Bridge ⊖	d	18 11	18 12	18 15				18 15	18 06	18 20	18 22	18 27									18 18			
South Bermondsey	d	18 15																			18 22			
Queens Rd Peckham	d	18 18																			18 24			
Peckham Rye	d	18 20																			18 27			
East Dulwich	d																				18 30			
North Dulwich	d																				18 32			
Luton	d																							
Luton Airport Parkway	d																							
St Pancras International ⊖	d																							
City Thameslink	d																							
London Blackfriars ⊖	d					18 16																		
Elephant & Castle ⊖	d					18 24																		
Loughborough Jn	d					18 36																		
Herne Hill	d					18 44																		
Tulse Hill	d			18 31		18a52															18 35			
Streatham	d			18 35																	18 39			
London Victoria ⊖	d													18 06		18 13	18 17	18 19	18 21	18 23			18 23	18 32
Battersea Park	d	18 32												18 10		18 17		18 23						
Milton Keynes Central	d																					17 13		
Watford Junction	d																					17 52		
Harrow & Wealdstone ⊖	d																					17 59		
Wembley Central ⊖	d																					18u04		
Shepherd's Bush ⊖	d																					18 20		
Kensington (Olympia) ⊖	d																					18 23		
West Brompton ⊖	d																					18 26		
Clapham Junction	d													18 14		18 21	18 23	18 27		18 30		18 34	18 29	18 38
Wandsworth Common	d													18 17		18 24		18 30		18 33		18 37		
Balham ⊖	d													18 20		18 26		18 32		18 35		18 40		
Streatham Hill	d													18 23				18 35						
West Norwood	d													18 27				18 40						
Gipsy Hill	d										18 45			18 30				18 43						
Crystal Palace	d													18 32				18 51						
Birkbeck	d																							
Beckenham Junction	a																							
Streatham Common	d															18 30				18 39	18 42	18 45		
Norbury	d															18 33				18 42	18 45	18 48		
Thornton Heath	d															18 36				18 45	18 48	18 51		
Selhurst	d															18 39				18 48	18 51	18 54		
Norwood Junction	a						18 20	18 26	18 29	18 32			18 35	18 37										
	d						18 20	18 26	18 30	18 33			18 35	18 39										
West Croydon	a						18 31						18 42	18 43						18 52	18 55			
East Croydon	a		18 24					18 30	18 33	18 36		18 39				18 42	18 33		18 38			18 57	18 39	18 48

Table 177

Luton, Milton Keynes and London - East and West Croydon via Tulse Hill - Crystal Palace - Norbury

Local Services

		SN	SN	SN	SN	FC	SN	FC	FC	FC		LO	SN	SN	SN	SN	FC	LO	SN	SN		SN	SN	SN	SN
				1	◇1			1					1				1					◇1			1
London Bridge ⊖	d		18 33	18 33			18 41	18 42	18 45				18 45	18 36	18 50	18 52	18 57						18 48		
South Bermondsey	d		18 37				18 45																18 52		
Queens Rd Peckham	d		18 39				18 48																18 54		
Peckham Rye	d		18 42				18 50																18 57		
East Dulwich	d		18 45																				19 00		
North Dulwich	d		18 47																				19 02		
Luton	d																								
Luton Airport Parkway	d																								
St Pancras International ⊖	d																								
City Thameslink	d																								
London Blackfriars ⊖	d					18 37				18 46															
Elephant & Castle ⊖	d					18 45				18 54															
Loughborough Jn	d					18 57				19 06															
Herne Hill	d					19a05				19 14															
Tulse Hill	d		18 50						19 01	19a22													19 05		
Streatham	d								19 05														19 09		
London Victoria ⊖	d	18 33			18 36														18 36	18 43		18 47		18 53	18 53
Battersea Park	d	18 37					19 02												18 40	18 47				18 57	
Milton Keynes Central	d																								
Watford Junction	d																								
Harrow & Wealdstone ⊖	d																								
Wembley Central ⊖	d																								
Shepherd's Bush ⊖	d																								
Kensington (Olympia) ⊖	d																								
West Brompton ⊖	d																								
Clapham Junction	d	18 41			18 42														18 44	18 51		18 53		19 01	18 59
Wandsworth Common	d	18 44																	18 47	18 54				19 04	
Balham ⊖	d	18 46																	18 50	18 56				19 06	
Streatham Hill	d																		18 53					19 09	
West Norwood	d		18 53																18 57					19 13	
Gipsy Hill	d		18 56													19 15			19 00					19 16	
Crystal Palace	d		18 59																19 02					19 21	
Birkbeck	d		19 03																						
Beckenham Junction	a		19 06																						
Streatham Common	d	18 50																		19 00			19 12		
Norbury	d	18 53																		19 03			19 15		
Thornton Heath	d	18 56																		19 06			19 18		
Selhurst	d	18a58																		19 09			19 21		
Norwood Junction	a			18 44								18 50	18 56	18 59	19 02			19 05	19 07						
	d			18 45								18 50	18 56	19 00	19 03			19 05	19 09						
West Croydon	a											19 01						19 12	19 13				19 25		
East Croydon	a			18 48	18 52			18 54					19 00	19 03	19 06		19 09			19 12		19 03			19 09

Luton, Milton Keynes and London - East and West Croydon via Tulse Hill - Crystal Palace - Norbury

Local Services

Station		SN	SN ◇1	SN	SN 1	SN ◇1		FC 🚌	SN 1	SN	FC 1	FC	FC 🚌	LO	SN	SN		FC 1	LO	SN	SN	SN ◇1	SN	SN 1	SN ◇1
London Bridge 4 ⊖	d			19 03	19 03				19 08	19 11	19 12	19 15			19 06	19 22		19 27					19 18		
South Bermondsey	d			19 07						19 15													19 22		
Queens Rd Peckham	d			19 09						19 18													19 24		
Peckham Rye 4	d			19 12						19 20													19 27		
East Dulwich	d			19 15																			19 30		
North Dulwich	d			19 17																			19 32		
Luton 10	d																								
Luton Airport Parkway 7	d																								
St Pancras International 15 ⊖	d																								
City Thameslink 3	d																								
London Blackfriars 3 ⊖	d							19 07					19 16												
Elephant & Castle ⊖	d							19 15					19 24												
Loughborough Jn	d							19 27					19 36												
Herne Hill 4	d							19a35					19 44												
Tulse Hill 3	d			19 20								19 31	19a53										19 35		
Streatham 4	d											19 35											19 39		
London Victoria 15 ⊖	d	19 01	19 02			19 06														19 06	19 15	19 17			19 21
Battersea Park 4	d	19 05								19 32										19 10	19 19				
Milton Keynes Central	d																							18 13	
Watford Junction	d																							18 52	
Harrow & Wealdstone ⊖	d																							18 59	
Wembley Central ⊖	d																							19u04	
Shepherd's Bush ⊖	d																							19 20	
Kensington (Olympia) ⊖	d																							19 23	
West Brompton ⊖	d																							19 26	
Clapham Junction 10	d	19 09	19 08			19 12														19 14	19 23	19 23		19 35	
Wandsworth Common	d	19 12																		19 17	19 26			19 38	
Balham 4 ⊖	d	19 14																		19 20	19 28			19 41	
Streatham Hill	d																			19 23					
West Norwood 4	d			19 23																19 27					
Gipsy Hill	d			19 26												19 45				19 30					
Crystal Palace 4	d			19 29																19 32					
Birkbeck	d			19 33																					
Beckenham Junction 4	a			19 36																					
Streatham Common 4	d	19 18																			19 32		19 42	19 45	
Norbury	d	19 21																			19 35		19 45	19 48	
Thornton Heath	d	19 24																			19 38		19 48	19 51	
Selhurst 4	d	19 27																			19 41		19 51	19 54	
Norwood Junction 2	a				19 14									19 20	19 29				19 35	19 37					
	d				19 15									19 20	19 30				19 35	19 39					
West Croydon 4	a	19 32												19 31					19 42	19 43			19 55		
East Croydon	a		19 18		19 18	19 22			19 22		19 24				19 33			19 39			19 44	19 33		19 57	19 37

Station		SN		SN 1	SN	SN ◇1	SN	SN 1	SN ◇1	SN	FC 1	FC		FC 🚌	LO	SN	SN	FC 1	LO	SN	SN	SN ◇1		SN	SN
London Bridge 4 ⊖	d						19 33	19 33		19 41	19 42	19 45				19 36	19 52	19 57						19 48	
South Bermondsey	d						19 37			19 45														19 52	
Queens Rd Peckham	d						19 39			19 48														19 54	
Peckham Rye 4	d						19 42			19 50														19 57	
East Dulwich	d						19 45																	20 00	
North Dulwich	d						19 47																	20 02	
Luton 10	d																								
Luton Airport Parkway 7	d																								
St Pancras International 15 ⊖	d																								
City Thameslink 3	d																								
London Blackfriars 3 ⊖	d													19 46											
Elephant & Castle ⊖	d													19 54											
Loughborough Jn	d													20 06											
Herne Hill 4	d													20 14											
Tulse Hill 3	d						19 50					20 01		20a22										20 05	
Streatham 4	d											20 05												20 09	
London Victoria 15 ⊖	d	19 23		19 23	19 31	19 32			19 36											19 36	19 45	19 47			19 53
Battersea Park 4	d	19 27			19 35					20 02										19 40	19 49				19 57
Milton Keynes Central	d																								
Watford Junction	d																								
Harrow & Wealdstone ⊖	d																								
Wembley Central ⊖	d																								
Shepherd's Bush ⊖	d																								
Kensington (Olympia) ⊖	d																								
West Brompton ⊖	d																								
Clapham Junction 10	d	19 31		19 29	19 39	19 38			19 42											19 44	19 53	19 53			20 01
Wandsworth Common	d	19 34			19 42															19 47	19 56				20 04
Balham 4 ⊖	d	19 36			19 44															19 50	19 58				20 06
Streatham Hill	d	19 39																		19 53					20 09
West Norwood 4	d	19 43					19 53													19 57					20 13
Gipsy Hill	d	19 46					19 56										20 15			20 00					20 16
Crystal Palace 4	d	19 51					19 59													20 02					20 21
Birkbeck	d						20 03																		
Beckenham Junction 4	a						20 06																		
Streatham Common 4	d				19 48																20 02			20 12	
Norbury	d				19 51																20 05			20 15	
Thornton Heath	d				19 54																20 08			20 18	
Selhurst 4	d				19 57																20 11			20 21	
Norwood Junction 2	a							19 44							19 50	19 59			20 05	20 07					
	d							19 45							19 50	20 00			20 05	20 09					
West Croydon 4	a				20 02										20 01				20 15	20 15				20 25	
East Croydon	a			19 39		19 48		19 49	19 52		19 54					20 03		20 09			20 14	20 03			

Table 177 Saturdays

Luton, Milton Keynes and London - East and West Croydon via Tulse Hill - Crystal Palace - Norbury

Local Services

Station		SN 1	SN	SN ◇1	SN ◇1	SN 1	SN	FC 1		FC	FC 🚌	LO	SN	SN	LO	SN	SN 1	SN		SN ◇1	SN	SN 1	SN ◇1	SN	SN 1
London Bridge 4 ⊖	d					20 08	20 11	20 12		20 15			20 06	20 22							20 18				
South Bermondsey	d						20 15														20 22				
Queens Rd Peckham	d						20 18														20 24				
Peckham Rye 4	d						20 20														20 27				
East Dulwich	d																				20 30				
North Dulwich	d																				20 32				
Luton 10	d																								
Luton Airport Parkway 7	d																								
St Pancras International 15 ⊖	d																								
City Thameslink 3	d																								
London Blackfriars 3 ⊖	d										20 16														
Elephant & Castle ⊖	d										20 24														
Loughborough Jn	d										20 36														
Herne Hill 4	d										20 44														
Tulse Hill 3	d									20 31	20a52										20 35				
Streatham 4	d									20 35											20 39				
London Victoria 15 ⊖	d	19 53	20 01	20 02	20 06											20 06	20 10	20 15		20 17			20 21	20 23	20 23
Battersea Park 4	d		20 05				20 32									20 10		20 19						20 27	
Milton Keynes Central	d																					19 13			
Watford Junction	d																					19 51			
Harrow & Wealdstone ⊖	d																					19 58			
Wembley Central ⊖	d																								
Shepherd's Bush ⊖	d																					20 20			
Kensington (Olympia) ⊖	d																					20 23			
West Brompton ⊖	d																					20 26			
Clapham Junction 10	d	19 59	20 09	20 08	20 12											20 14	20 16	20 23		20 23		20 34		20 31	20 29
Wandsworth Common	d		20 12													20 17		20 26				20 37		20 34	
Balham 4 ⊖	d		20 14													20 20		20 28				20 40		20 36	
Streatham Hill	d															20 23								20 39	
West Norwood 4	d															20 27								20 43	
Gipsy Hill	d													20 45		20 30								20 46	
Crystal Palace 4	d															20 32								20 51	
Birkbeck	d																								
Beckenham Junction 4	a																								
Streatham Common 4	d		20 18															20 32			20 42	20 45			
Norbury	d		20 21															20 35			20 45	20 48			
Thornton Heath	d		20 24															20 38			20 48	20 51			
Selhurst 4	d		20 27															20 41			20 51	20 55			
Norwood Junction 2	a					20 19						20 20	20 29		20 35	20 37									
	d					20 19						20 20	20 30		20 35	20 39									
West Croydon 4	a		20 32									20 31			20 45	20 45					20 55				
East Croydon	a	20 09		20 19	20 22	20 22		20 24					20 33				20 27	20 44		20 33		20 59	20 37		20 39

Station		SN	SN ◇1	SN ◇1		SN	FC 1	FC	FC 🚌	LO	SN	SN	LO	SN		SN 1	SN	SN ◇1	SN	SN	SN 1	SN	SN ◇1	SN ◇1	
London Bridge 4 ⊖	d					20 41	20 42	20 45			20 36	20 52							20 48						
South Bermondsey	d					20 45													20 52						
Queens Rd Peckham	d					20 48													20 54						
Peckham Rye 4	d					20 50													20 57						
East Dulwich	d																		21 00						
North Dulwich	d																		21 02						
Luton 10	d																								
Luton Airport Parkway 7	d																								
St Pancras International 15 ⊖	d																								
City Thameslink 3	d																								
London Blackfriars 3 ⊖	d								20 46																
Elephant & Castle ⊖	d								20 54																
Loughborough Jn	d								21 06																
Herne Hill 4	d								21 14																
Tulse Hill 3	d							21 01	21a22										21 05						
Streatham 4	d							21 05											21 09						
London Victoria 15 ⊖	d	20 30	20 32	20 36										20 36		20 40	20 45	20 47		20 53	20 53	21 00	21 02	21 06	
Battersea Park 4	d	20 34				21 02								20 40			20 49			20 57		21 04			
Milton Keynes Central	d																								
Watford Junction	d																								
Harrow & Wealdstone ⊖	d																								
Wembley Central ⊖	d																								
Shepherd's Bush ⊖	d																								
Kensington (Olympia) ⊖	d																								
West Brompton ⊖	d																								
Clapham Junction 10	d	20 38	20 38	20 42										20 44		20 46	20 53	20 53		21 01	20 59	21 08	21 08	21 12	
Wandsworth Common	d	20 41												20 47			20 56			21 04		21 11			
Balham 4 ⊖	d	20 44												20 50			20 58			21 06		21 14			
Streatham Hill	d													20 53						21 09					
West Norwood 4	d													20 57						21 13					
Gipsy Hill	d											21 15		21 00						21 16					
Crystal Palace 4	d													21 02						21 21					
Birkbeck	d																								
Beckenham Junction 4	a																								
Streatham Common 4	d	20 48															21 02		21 12			21 18			
Norbury	d	20 51															21 05		21 15			21 20			
Thornton Heath	d	20 54															21 08		21 18			21 23			
Selhurst 4	d	20 58															21 11		21 21			21 26			
Norwood Junction 2	a									20 50	20 59		21 05	21 07											
	d									20 50	21 00		21 05	21 09											
West Croydon 4	a	21 02								21 01			21 15	21 15					21 25			21 32			
East Croydon	a		20 48	20 52			20 53				21 03					20 57	21 14	21 03			21 09		21 18	21 22	

Table 177

Luton, Milton Keynes and London - East and West Croydon via Tulse Hill - Crystal Palace - Norbury

Local Services

Station		SN 1	SN	FC 1	FC	FC bus	LO	SN	SN	LO		SN	SN 1	SN	SN ◇1	SN	SN	SN 1	SN	SN 1		SN ◇1	SN	FC 1	FC
London Bridge 4 ⊖	d	21 08	21 11	21 12	21 15			21 06	21 22							21 18							21 41	21 42	21 45
South Bermondsey	d		21 15													21 22							21 45		
Queens Rd Peckham	d		21 18													21 24							21 48		
Peckham Rye 4	d		21 20													21 27							21 50		
East Dulwich	d															21 30									
North Dulwich	d															21 32									
Luton 10	d																								
Luton Airport Parkway 7	d																								
St Pancras International 15 ⊖	d																								
City Thameslink 3	d																								
London Blackfriars 3 ⊖	d					21 16																			
Elephant & Castle ⊖	d					21 24																			
Loughborough Jn	d					21 36																			
Herne Hill 4	d					21 44																			
Tulse Hill 3	d				21 31	21a52										21 35									22 01
Streatham 4	d				21 35											21 39									22 05
London Victoria 15 ⊖	d											21 06	21 10	21 15	21 17		21 23	21 23	21 30	21 32		21 36			
Battersea Park 4	d		21 32									21 10		21 19			21 27		21 34				22 02		
Milton Keynes Central	d																								
Watford Junction	d																								
Harrow & Wealdstone ⊖	d																								
Wembley Central ⊖	d																								
Shepherd's Bush ⊖	d																								
Kensington (Olympia) ⊖	d																								
West Brompton ⊖	d																								
Clapham Junction 10	d											21 14	21 16	21 23	21 23		21 31	21 29	21 38	21 38		21 42			
Wandsworth Common	d											21 17		21 26			21 34		21 41						
Balham 4 ⊖	d											21 20		21 28			21 36		21 44						
Streatham Hill	d											21 23					21 39								
West Norwood 4	d											21 27					21 43								
Gipsy Hill	d								21 45			21 30					21 46								
Crystal Palace 4	d											21 32					21 51								
Birkbeck	d																								
Beckenham Junction 4	a																								
Streatham Common 4	d													21 32		21 42			21 48						
Norbury	d													21 35		21 45			21 50						
Thornton Heath	d													21 38		21 48			21 53						
Selhurst 4	d													21 41		21 51			21 56						
Norwood Junction 2	a	21 19					21 20	21 29		21 35		21 37													
	d	21 19					21 20	21 30		21 35		21 39													
West Croydon 4	a						21 31			21 45		21 45				21 55			22 02						
East Croydon	a	21 22		21 24				21 33					21 27	21 44	21 33			21 39		21 48		21 52		21 54	

Station		FC bus	LO	SN	SN	LO		SN	SN 1	SN	SN ◇1	SN	SN	SN 1	SN	SN ◇1		SN ◇1	SN 1	SN	FC 1	FC	FC bus	LO	SN
London Bridge 4 ⊖	d			21 36	21 52							21 48							22 08	22 11	22 12	22 15			22 06
South Bermondsey	d											21 52								22 15					
Queens Rd Peckham	d											21 54								22 18					
Peckham Rye 4	d											21 57								22 20					
East Dulwich	d											22 00													
North Dulwich	d											22 02													
Luton 10	d																								
Luton Airport Parkway 7	d																								
St Pancras International 15 ⊖	d																								
City Thameslink 3	d																								
London Blackfriars 3 ⊖	d	21 46																					22 16		
Elephant & Castle ⊖	d	21 54																					22 24		
Loughborough Jn	d	22 06																					22 36		
Herne Hill 4	d	22 14																					22 44		
Tulse Hill 3	d	22a22										22 05										22 31	22a52		
Streatham 4	d											22 09										22 35			
London Victoria 15 ⊖	d							21 36	21 40	21 45	21 47		21 53	21 53	22 00	22 02		22 06							
Battersea Park 4	d							21 40		21 49			21 57		22 04					22 32					
Milton Keynes Central	d																								
Watford Junction	d																								
Harrow & Wealdstone ⊖	d																								
Wembley Central ⊖	d																								
Shepherd's Bush ⊖	d																								
Kensington (Olympia) ⊖	d																								
West Brompton ⊖	d																								
Clapham Junction 10	d							21 44	21 46	21 53	21 53		22 01	21 59	22 08	22 08		22 12							
Wandsworth Common	d							21 47		21 56			22 04		22 11										
Balham 4 ⊖	d							21 50		21 58			22 06		22 14										
Streatham Hill	d							21 53					22 09												
West Norwood 4	d							21 57					22 13												
Gipsy Hill	d				22 15			22 00					22 16												
Crystal Palace 4	d							22 02					22 21												
Birkbeck	d																								
Beckenham Junction 4	a																								
Streatham Common 4	d									22 02		22 12			22 18										
Norbury	d									22 05		22 15			22 20										
Thornton Heath	d									22 08		22 18			22 23										
Selhurst 4	d									22 11		22 21			22 26										
Norwood Junction 2	a		21 50	21 59		22 05		22 08											22 19					22 20	22 29
	d		21 50	22 00		22 05		22 09											22 19					22 20	22 30
West Croydon 4	a		22 01			22 12		22 13				22 25			22 32									22 31	
East Croydon	a			22 04					21 57	22 14	22 03			22 09		22 18		22 22	22 22		22 24				22 35

Table 177

Luton, Milton Keynes and London - East and West Croydon via Tulse Hill - Crystal Palace - Norbury

Local Services

Station		SN		LO	SN	SN 1	SN	SN ◇1	SN	SN	SN 1	SN		SN 1	SN ◇1	SN	FC 1	FC	FC bus	LO	SN	SN		SN	SN
London Bridge 4 ⊖	d	22 22							22 18							22 41	22 42	22 45			22 36	22 52		22 56	
South Bermondsey	d								22 22							22 45									
Queens Rd Peckham	d								22 24							22 48									
Peckham Rye 4	d								22 27							22 50									
East Dulwich	d								22 30																
North Dulwich	d								22 32																
Luton 10	d																								
Luton Airport Parkway 7	d																								
St Pancras International 15 ⊖	d																								
City Thameslink 3	d																								
London Blackfriars 3 ⊖	d																		22 46						
Elephant & Castle ⊖	d																		22 54						
Loughborough Jn	d																		23 06						
Herne Hill 4	d																		23 14						
Tulse Hill 3	d								22 35									23 01	23a22						
Streatham 4	d								22 39									23 05							
London Victoria 15 ⊖	d				22 06	22 10	22 15	22 17		22 23	22 23	22 30		22 32	22 36										22 36
Battersea Park 4	d				22 10		22 19			22 27		22 34				23 02									22 40
Milton Keynes Central	d																								
Watford Junction	d																								
Harrow & Wealdstone ⊖	d																								
Wembley Central ⊖	d																								
Shepherd's Bush ⊖	d																								
Kensington (Olympia) ⊖	d																								
West Brompton ⊖	d																								
Clapham Junction 10	d				22 14	22 16	22 23	22 23		22 31	22 29	22 38		22 38	22 42										22 44
Wandsworth Common	d				22 17		22 26			22 34		22 41													22 47
Balham 4 ⊖	d				22 20		22 28			22 36		22 44													22 50
Streatham Hill	d				22 23					22 39															22 53
West Norwood 4	d				22 27					22 43															22 57
Gipsy Hill	d	22 45			22 30					22 46												23 15			23 00
Crystal Palace 4	d				22 32					22 51															23 02
Birkbeck	d																								
Beckenham Junction 4	a																								
Streatham Common 4	d						22 32		22 42			22 48													
Norbury	d						22 35		22 45			22 50													
Thornton Heath	d						22 38		22 48			22 53													
Selhurst 4	d						22 41		22 51			22 56													
Norwood Junction 2	a			22 35	22 37															22 50	22 59			23 07	23 07
	d			22 35	22 39															22 50	23 00			23 07	23 09
West Croydon 4	a			22 42	22 43				22 55			23 02								23 01					23 13
East Croydon	a					22 27	22 44	22 33			22 39			22 48	22 52		22 54				23 03			23 11	

Station		SN 1	SN	SN ◇1	SN	SN	SN 1	SN		SN ◇1	SN ◇1	SN	FC 1	FC	FC bus	LO	SN	SN		SN 1	SN	SN ◇1	SN	SN	SN
London Bridge 4 ⊖	d				22 48							23 11	23 12	23 15			23 06						23 18	23 22	
South Bermondsey	d				22 52							23 15											23 22		
Queens Rd Peckham	d				22 54							23 18											23 24		
Peckham Rye 4	d				22 57							23 20											23 27		
East Dulwich	d				23 00																		23 30		
North Dulwich	d				23 02																		23 32		
Luton 10	d																								
Luton Airport Parkway 7	d																								
St Pancras International 15 ⊖	d																								
City Thameslink 3	d																								
London Blackfriars 3 ⊖	d														23 16										
Elephant & Castle ⊖	d														23 24										
Loughborough Jn	d														23 36										
Herne Hill 4	d														23 44										
Tulse Hill 3	d				23 05									23 31	23a52								23 35		
Streatham 4	d				23 09									23 35									23 39		
London Victoria 15 ⊖	d	22 40	22 45	22 47		22 53	22 53	23 00		23 02	23 06							23 06		23 10	23 15	23 17			23 22
Battersea Park 4	d		22 49			22 57		23 04				23 32						23 10			23 19				23 26
Milton Keynes Central	d																								
Watford Junction	d																								
Harrow & Wealdstone ⊖	d																								
Wembley Central ⊖	d																								
Shepherd's Bush ⊖	d																								
Kensington (Olympia) ⊖	d																								
West Brompton ⊖	d																								
Clapham Junction 10	d	22 46	22 53	22 53		23 01	22 59	23 08		23 08	23 12							23 14		23 16	23 23	23 23			23 30
Wandsworth Common	d		22 56			23 04		23 11										23 17			23 26				23 33
Balham 4 ⊖	d		22 58			23 06		23 14										23 20			23 28				23 35
Streatham Hill	d					23 09												23 23							23 38
West Norwood 4	d					23 13												23 27							23 42
Gipsy Hill	d					23 16												23 30						23 45	23 45
Crystal Palace 4	d					23 21												23 32							23 51
Birkbeck	d																								
Beckenham Junction 4	a																								
Streatham Common 4	d		23 02		23 12			23 18													23 32		23 42		
Norbury	d		23 05		23 15			23 20													23 35		23 45		
Thornton Heath	d		23 08		23 18			23 23													23 38		23 48		
Selhurst 4	d		23 11		23 21			23 26													23 41		23 51		
Norwood Junction 2	a															23 20	23 29	23 37							
	d															23 20	23 30	23 39							
West Croydon 4	a				23 25			23 32								23 31		23 43					23 55		
East Croydon	a	22 57	23 14	23 03			23 09			23 18	23 22		23 24				23 33			23 27	23 44	23 33			

Table 177

Saturdays

Luton, Milton Keynes and London - East and West Croydon via Tulse Hill - Crystal Palace - Norbury

Local Services

		SN ■	SN ■	SN		FC ■	FC	LO	SN	SN	SN	SN ■	SN
London Bridge ⊖	d					23 42	23 45		23 36		23 48		
South Bermondsey	d										23 52		
Queens Rd Peckham	d										23 54		
Peckham Rye	d										23 57		
East Dulwich	d										00 01		
North Dulwich	d										00 03		
Luton	d												
Luton Airport Parkway	d												
St Pancras International ⊖	d												
City Thameslink	d												
London Blackfriars ⊖	d												
Elephant & Castle ⊖	d												
Loughborough Jn	d												
Herne Hill	d												
Tulse Hill	d						00 01				00 07		
Streatham	d						00 05						
London Victoria ⊖	d	23 24	23 32	23 34						23 37		23 49	23 51
Battersea Park	d			23 38						23 41			23 55
Milton Keynes Central	d												
Watford Junction	d												
Harrow & Wealdstone ⊖	d												
Wembley Central ⊖	d												
Shepherd's Bush ⊖	d												
Kensington (Olympia) ⊖	d												
West Brompton ⊖	d												
Clapham Junction	d	23 30	23 38	23 42						23 45		23 56	23 59
Wandsworth Common	d			23 45						23 48			00 02
Balham ⊖	d			23 47						23 51			00 04
Streatham Hill	d									23 54			
West Norwood	d									23 57	00 10		
Gipsy Hill	d									23 59	00 13		
Crystal Palace	d									00 03	00 15		
Birkbeck	d												
Beckenham Junction	a												
Streatham Common	d			23 51									00 08
Norbury	d			23 54									00 11
Thornton Heath	d			23 57									00 14
Selhurst	d			23 59									00 17
Norwood Junction	a							23 50	23 59	00 07	00 22		
	d							23 50	23 59	00 09			
West Croydon	a			00 03				00 01		00 14			00 21
East Croydon	a	23 41	23 52			23 56			00 03			00 09	

Table 177

Sundays

Luton, Milton Keynes and London - East and West Croydon via Tulse Hill - Crystal Palace - Norbury

Local Services

		SN	FC	LO	SN	SN	SN ■	SN	SN ◇■	FC ■		SN ■	SN
London Bridge ⊖	d		23p45		23p36					00 12			
South Bermondsey	d												
Queens Rd Peckham	d												
Peckham Rye	d												
East Dulwich	d												
North Dulwich	d												
Luton	d												
Luton Airport Parkway	d												
St Pancras International ⊖	d												
City Thameslink	d												
London Blackfriars ⊖	d												
Elephant & Castle ⊖	d												
Loughborough Jn	d												
Herne Hill	d												
Tulse Hill	d		00 01										
Streatham	d		00 05										
London Victoria ⊖	d	23p34				23p37	23p49	23p51	00 05			00 14	00 17
Battersea Park	d	23p38				23p41		23p55					
Milton Keynes Central	d												
Watford Junction	d												
Harrow & Wealdstone ⊖	d												
Wembley Central ⊖	d												
Shepherd's Bush ⊖	d												
Kensington (Olympia) ⊖	d												
West Brompton ⊖	d												
Clapham Junction	d	23p42				23p45	23p56	23p59	00 11			00 20	00 23
Wandsworth Common	d	23p45				23p48		00 02					
Balham ⊖	d	23p47				23p51		00 04					00 27
Streatham Hill	d					23p54							
West Norwood	d					23p57							
Gipsy Hill	d					23p59							
Crystal Palace	d					00 03							
Birkbeck	d												
Beckenham Junction	a												
Streatham Common	d	23p51						00 08					00 31
Norbury	d	23p54						00 11					00 34
Thornton Heath	d	23p57						00 14					00 37
Selhurst	d	23p59						00 17					00 39
Norwood Junction	a			23p50	23p59	00 07							
	d			23p50	23p59	00 09							
West Croydon	a	00 03		00 01		00 14		00 21					
East Croydon	a				00 03		00 09		00 24	00 27		00 31	00 42

		LO	SN	SN	SN	SN	FC ■	SN ■		FC ■	SN ■	SN ■	SN ■
London Bridge ⊖	d		23p48	00 06	00 36		00 42			01 05			
South Bermondsey	d		23p52										
Queens Rd Peckham	d		23p54										
Peckham Rye	d		23p57										
East Dulwich	d		00 01										
North Dulwich	d		00 03										
Luton	d												
Luton Airport Parkway	d												
St Pancras International ⊖	d												
City Thameslink	d												
London Blackfriars ⊖	d												
Elephant & Castle ⊖	d												
Loughborough Jn	d												
Herne Hill	d												
Tulse Hill	d		00 07										
Streatham	d												
London Victoria ⊖	d					00 42		01 00			02 00	03 00	04 00
Battersea Park	d					00 46							
Milton Keynes Central	d												
Watford Junction	d												
Harrow & Wealdstone ⊖	d												
Wembley Central ⊖	d												
Shepherd's Bush ⊖	d												
Kensington (Olympia) ⊖	d												
West Brompton ⊖	d												
Clapham Junction	d					00 50		01 08			02 08	03 08	04 08
Wandsworth Common	d					00 53							
Balham ⊖	d					00 55							
Streatham Hill	d												
West Norwood	d		00 10										
Gipsy Hill	d		00 13										
Crystal Palace	d		00 15										
Birkbeck	d												
Beckenham Junction	a												
Streatham Common	d					00 59							
Norbury	d					01 02							
Thornton Heath	d					01 05							
Selhurst	d					01 07							
Norwood Junction	a	00 20	00 22	00 29	00 59								
	d	00 20		00 30	01 00								
West Croydon	a	00 27											
East Croydon	a			00 33	01 03	01 10	00 56	01 21		01 32	02 21	03 21	04 21

Table 177

Sundays

Luton, Milton Keynes and London - East and West Croydon via Tulse Hill - Crystal Palace - Norbury

Local Services

		SN 1	SN ◇1	SN ◇1	SN	SN ◇1 A	SN ◇1 B	SN 1 A	SN	FC 1 A	FC 1 B	SN ◇1 A	SN	LO	SN 1 B	SN	SN 1 A	SN 1 A	SN ◇1 B	SN 1 B	SN	SN	FC 1 A
London Bridge	d							07 05	07 11	07 12	07 12					07 24					07 25	07 41	07 42
South Bermondsey	d								07 15												07 29	07 45	
Queens Rd Peckham	d								07 18												07 31	07 48	
Peckham Rye	d								07 20												07 34	07 50	
East Dulwich	d																				07 37		
North Dulwich	d																				07 39		
Luton	d																						
Luton Airport Parkway	d																						
St Pancras International	d																						
City Thameslink	d																						
London Blackfriars	d																						
Elephant & Castle	d																						
Loughborough Jn	d																						
Herne Hill	d																						
Tulse Hill	d																				07 42		
Streatham	d																				07 46		
London Victoria	d	05 02	05 47	06 32	06 49	07 02	07 02					07 17	07 19		07 22		07 25	07 32	07 32	07 34			
Battersea Park	d				06 53				07 32				07 23									08 02	
Milton Keynes Central	d																						
Watford Junction	d																						
Harrow & Wealdstone	d																						
Wembley Central	d																						
Shepherd's Bush	d																						
Kensington (Olympia)	d																						
West Brompton	d																						
Clapham Junction	d	05 08	05 53	06 38	06 57	07 08	07 08					07 23	07 27		07 28		07 31	07 38	07 38	07 41			
Wandsworth Common	d				07 00								07 30										
Balham	d				07 02								07 32										
Streatham Hill	d																						
West Norwood	d																						
Gipsy Hill	d																						
Crystal Palace	d																						
Birkbeck	d																						
Beckenham Junction	a																						
Streatham Common	d				07 06								07 36								07 49		
Norbury	d				07 09								07 39								07 51		
Thornton Heath	d				07 12								07 42								07 54		
Selhurst	d				07 15	07 16	07 18						07 45					07 46		07 50	07 58		
Norwood Junction	a							07 17						07 22		07 44							
	d							07 17						07 22		07 48							
West Croydon	a				07 19								07 49	07 30		07 55							
East Croydon	a	05 22	06 05	06 51		07 19	07 23	07 21		07 24	07 26	07 35			07 42		07 42	07 49	07 50	07 53	08 02		07 54

A until 5 September

B from 12 September

Table 177

Sundays

Luton, Milton Keynes and London - East and West Croydon via Tulse Hill - Crystal Palace - Norbury

Local Services

		FC 1 A	LO	SN	SN	SN	SN	SN	SN ◇1 B	SN ◇1 A	SN 1 B	SN	FC 1 B	FC 1 A	LO	SN	SN	SN ◇1 B	SN ◇1 A	SN	SN ◇1 B	SN 1 A
London Bridge	d	07 42			07 39		07 54	07 55			08 05	08 11	08 12	08 12			08 09					
South Bermondsey	d							07 59				08 15										
Queens Rd Peckham	d							08 01				08 18										
Peckham Rye	d							08 04				08 20										
East Dulwich	d							08 07														
North Dulwich	d							08 09														
Luton	d																					
Luton Airport Parkway	d																					
St Pancras International	d																					
City Thameslink	d																					
London Blackfriars	d																					
Elephant & Castle	d																					
Loughborough Jn	d																					
Herne Hill	d																					
Tulse Hill	d							08 12														
Streatham	d							08 16														
London Victoria	d			07 36		07 49			08 02	08 04						08 06		08 17	08 17	08 19	08 21	08 22
Battersea Park	d					07 53						08 32								08 23		
Milton Keynes Central	d																					
Watford Junction	d																					
Harrow & Wealdstone	d																					
Wembley Central	d																					
Shepherd's Bush	d																					
Kensington (Olympia)	d																					
West Brompton	d																					
Clapham Junction	d			07 42		07 57			08 08	08 10						08 12		08 23	08 23	08 27	08 27	08 28
Wandsworth Common	d					08 00														08 30		
Balham	d			07 47		08 02										08 17				08 32		
Streatham Hill	d			07 50												08 20						
West Norwood	d			07 53												08 23						
Gipsy Hill	d			07 56												08 26						
Crystal Palace	d			07 59												08 29						
Birkbeck	d																					
Beckenham Junction	a																					
Streatham Common	d					08 06		08 19												08 36		
Norbury	d					08 09		08 21												08 39		
Thornton Heath	d					08 12		08 24												08 42		
Selhurst	d					08 15		08 27												08 45		
Norwood Junction	a		07 52	08 03	08 02		08 14				08 16				08 22	08 33	08 32					
	d		07 52	08 03	08 03		08 16				08 16				08 22	08 33	08 33					
West Croydon	a		08 00	08 08		08 19	08 24								08 29	08 38				08 49		
East Croydon	a	07 56			08 06			08 32	08 17	08 24	08 20		08 24	08 27			08 36	08 32	08 36		08 38	08 42

A from 12 September

B until 5 September

Luton, Milton Keynes and London - East and West Croydon via Tulse Hill - Crystal Palace - Norbury

Local Services

		SN	SN	SN	SN	SN	SN	SN	FC	FC	FC	LO	SN	SN	SN	SN	SN	SN	SN	SN	SN	SN	SN
				1	1	◇1	1		1	1					◇1	◇1				◇1	◇1	◇1	1
				A	A	B	B		A	B					A	B				B	A	B	A
London Bridge 4	⊖ d	08 24	08 25					08 41	08 42	08 42				08 39				08 54	08 55				09 05
South Bermondsey	d		08 29					08 45											08 59				
Queens Rd Peckham	d		08 31					08 48											09 01				
Peckham Rye 4	d		08 34					08 50											09 04				
East Dulwich	d		08 37																09 07				
North Dulwich	d		08 39																09 09				
Luton 10	d																						
Luton Airport Parkway 7	d																						
St Pancras International 15	⊖ d																						
City Thameslink 3	d																						
London Blackfriars 3	⊖ d										08 49												
Elephant & Castle	⊖ d										08 57												
Loughborough Jn	d										09 09												
Herne Hill 4	d										09 17												
Tulse Hill 3	d		08 42								09a25								09 12				
Streatham 4	d		08 46																09 16				
London Victoria 15	⊖ d			08 25	08 32	08 32	08 34						08 36		08 47	08 47	08 49			09 02	09 02	09 04	
Battersea Park 4	d							09 02									08 53						
Milton Keynes Central	d																						
Watford Junction	d																						
Harrow & Wealdstone	⊖ d																						
Wembley Central	⊖ d																						
Shepherd's Bush	⊖ d																						
Kensington (Olympia)	⊖ d																						
West Brompton	⊖ d																						
Clapham Junction 10	d			08 31	08 38	08 38	08 41						08 42		08 53	08 53	08 57			09 08	09 08	09 10	
Wandsworth Common	d																09 00						
Balham 4	⊖ d												08 47				09 02						
Streatham Hill	d												08 50										
West Norwood 4	d												08 53										
Gipsy Hill	d												08 56										
Crystal Palace 4	d												08 59										
Birkbeck	d																						
Beckenham Junction 4	a																						
Streatham Common 4	d		08 49														09 06		09 19				
Norbury	d		08 51														09 09		09 21				
Thornton Heath	d		08 54														09 12		09 24				
Selhurst 4	d		08 57														09 15		09 27				
Norwood Junction 2	a	08 44										08 52	09 03	09 02				09 14					09 16
	d	08 46										08 52	09 03	09 03				09 16					09 16
West Croydon 4	a	08 54										08 59	09 08				09 19	09 24					
East Croydon	a		09 00	08 42	08 47	08 50	08 53		08 54	08 56				09 06	09 02	09 06			09 32	09 21	09 17	09 24	09 20

A until 5 September **B** from 12 September

Luton, Milton Keynes and London - East and West Croydon via Tulse Hill - Crystal Palace - Norbury

Local Services

		SN	SN	FC	FC	FC	LO	SN	SN	SN	SN	SN	FC	SN	SN	SN	SN	SN	SN	SN	SN	SN
		◇1		1	1					◇1	◇1			◇1	1			1	1	◇1	1	◇1
		A		A	B					A	B			A	B			A	A	B	B	A
London Bridge 4	⊖ d		09 11	09 12	09 12				09 09				09 21			09 24	09 25					
South Bermondsey	d		09 15														09 29					
Queens Rd Peckham	d		09 18														09 31					
Peckham Rye 4	d		09 20														09 34					
East Dulwich	d																09 37					
North Dulwich	d																09 39					
Luton 10	d																					
Luton Airport Parkway 7	d																					
St Pancras International 15	⊖ d																					
City Thameslink 3	d																					
London Blackfriars 3	⊖ d					09 19																
Elephant & Castle	⊖ d					09 27																
Loughborough Jn	d					09 39																
Herne Hill 4	d					09 47																
Tulse Hill 3	d					09a55							09 31				09 42					
Streatham 4	d												09 35				09 46					
London Victoria 15	⊖ d	09 06						09 06		09 17	09 17	09 19		09 21	09 22			09 25	09 32	09 32	09 34	09 36
Battersea Park 4	d		09 32									09 23										
Milton Keynes Central	d																					
Watford Junction	d																					
Harrow & Wealdstone	⊖ d																					
Wembley Central	⊖ d																					
Shepherd's Bush	⊖ d																					
Kensington (Olympia)	⊖ d																					
West Brompton	⊖ d																					
Clapham Junction 10	d	09 12						09 12		09 23	09 23	09 27		09 27	09 28			09 31	09 38	09 38	09 41	09 42
Wandsworth Common	d											09 30										
Balham 4	⊖ d							09 17				09 32										
Streatham Hill	d							09 20														
West Norwood 4	d							09 23														
Gipsy Hill	d							09 26														
Crystal Palace 4	d							09 29														
Birkbeck	d																					
Beckenham Junction 4	a																					
Streatham Common 4	d											09 36					09 49					
Norbury	d											09 39					09 51					
Thornton Heath	d											09 42					09 54					
Selhurst 4	d											09 45					09 57					
Norwood Junction 2	a						09 22	09 33	09 32							09 44						
	d						09 22	09 33	09 33							09 46						
West Croydon 4	a						09 29	09 38				09 49				09 54						
East Croydon	a	09 22		09 24	09 27				09 36	09 32	09 36			09 38	09 42		10 02	09 42	09 47	09 50	09 53	09 52

A until 5 September **B** from 12 September

Table 177

Sundays

Luton, Milton Keynes and London - East and West Croydon via Tulse Hill - Crystal Palace - Norbury

Local Services

		SN	FC	FC	FC	LO	SN	SN	SN	SN	SN	FC	SN	SN	SN	SN	SN	SN	SN	SN	FC	FC	FC
			1	1					◇1	◇1					◇1	◇1	◇1	1	◇1		1	1	
			A	B					A	B					B	A	B	A	A		A	B	
London Bridge 4 ⊖	d	09 41	09 42	09 42				09 39				09 51	09 54	09 55				10 05		10 11	10 12	10 12	
South Bermondsey	d	09 45												09 59						10 15			
Queens Rd Peckham	d	09 48												10 01						10 18			
Peckham Rye 4	d	09 50												10 04						10 20			
East Dulwich	d													10 07									
North Dulwich	d													10 09									
Luton 10	d																						
Luton Airport Parkway 7	d																						
St Pancras International 15 ⊖	d																						
City Thameslink 3	d																						
London Blackfriars 3 ⊖	d				09 49																		10 19
Elephant & Castle ⊖	d				09 57																		10 27
Loughborough Jn	d				10 09																		10 39
Herne Hill 4	d				10 17																		10 47
Tulse Hill 3	d				10a25							10 01		10 12									10a55
Streatham 4	d											10 05		10 16									
London Victoria 15 ⊖	d						09 36		09 47	09 47	09 49				10 02	10 02	10 04		10 06				
Battersea Park 4	d	10 02									09 53									10 32			
Milton Keynes Central	d																						
Watford Junction	d																						
Harrow & Wealdstone ⊖	d																						
Wembley Central ⊖	d																						
Shepherd's Bush ⊖	d																						
Kensington (Olympia) ⊖	d																						
West Brompton ⊖	d																						
Clapham Junction 10	d						09 42		09 53	09 53	09 57				10 08	10 08	10 10		10 12				
Wandsworth Common	d										10 00												
Balham 4 ⊖	d						09 47				10 02												
Streatham Hill	d						09 50																
West Norwood 4	d						09 53																
Gipsy Hill	d						09 56																
Crystal Palace 4	d						09 59																
Birkbeck	d																						
Beckenham Junction 4	a																						
Streatham Common 4	d										10 06			10 19									
Norbury	d										10 09			10 21									
Thornton Heath	d										10 12			10 24									
Selhurst 4	d										10 15			10 27									
Norwood Junction 2	a					09 52	10 03	10 02					10 14					10 16					
	d					09 52	10 03	10 03					10 16					10 16					
West Croydon 4	a					09 59	10 08				10 19		10 24										
East Croydon	a		09 54	09 56				10 06	10 02	10 06				10 32	10 21	10 17	10 24	10 20	10 22		10 24	10 27	

A until 5 September **B** from 12 September

Table 177

Sundays

Luton, Milton Keynes and London - East and West Croydon via Tulse Hill - Crystal Palace - Norbury

Local Services

		LO	SN	SN	SN	SN	SN	FC	SN	SN	SN	SN	SN	SN	SN	SN	SN	SN	FC	FC	FC	LO	SN
					◇1	◇1			◇1	1			1	1	◇1	1	◇1		1	1			
					A	B			A	B			A	A	B	B	A		A	B			
London Bridge 4 ⊖	d			10 09				10 21			10 24	10 25						10 41	10 42	10 42			
South Bermondsey	d											10 29						10 45					
Queens Rd Peckham	d											10 31						10 48					
Peckham Rye 4	d											10 34						10 50					
East Dulwich	d											10 37											
North Dulwich	d											10 39											
Luton 10	d																						
Luton Airport Parkway 7	d																						
St Pancras International 15 ⊖	d																						
City Thameslink 3	d																						
London Blackfriars 3 ⊖	d																				10 49		
Elephant & Castle ⊖	d																				10 57		
Loughborough Jn	d																				11 09		
Herne Hill 4	d																				11 17		
Tulse Hill 3	d							10 31				10 42									11a25		
Streatham 4	d							10 35				10 46											
London Victoria 15 ⊖	d		10 06		10 17	10 17	10 19		10 21	10 22			10 25	10 32	10 32	10 34	10 36						10 36
Battersea Park 4	d						10 23											11 02					
Milton Keynes Central	d																						
Watford Junction	d																						
Harrow & Wealdstone ⊖	d																						
Wembley Central ⊖	d																						
Shepherd's Bush ⊖	d																						
Kensington (Olympia) ⊖	d																						
West Brompton ⊖	d																						
Clapham Junction 10	d		10 12		10 23	10 23	10 27		10 27	10 28			10 31	10 38	10 38	10 41	10 42						10 42
Wandsworth Common	d						10 30																
Balham 4 ⊖	d		10 17				10 32																10 47
Streatham Hill	d		10 20																				10 50
West Norwood 4	d		10 23																				10 53
Gipsy Hill	d		10 26																				10 56
Crystal Palace 4	d		10 29																				10 59
Birkbeck	d																						
Beckenham Junction 4	a																						
Streatham Common 4	d						10 36					10 49											
Norbury	d						10 39					10 51											
Thornton Heath	d						10 42					10 54											
Selhurst 4	d						10 45					10 57											
Norwood Junction 2	a	10 22	10 33	10 32							10 44											10 52	11 03
	d	10 22	10 33	10 33							10 46											10 52	11 03
West Croydon 4	a	10 29	10 38				10 49				10 54											10 59	11 08
East Croydon	a			10 36	10 32	10 36			10 38	10 42		11 02	10 42	10 47	10 50	10 53	10 52		10 54	10 56			

A until 5 September **B** from 12 September

Table 177

Sundays

Luton, Milton Keynes and London - East and West Croydon via Tulse Hill - Crystal Palace - Norbury

Local Services

	SN	SN ◇[1] A 🛒	SN ◇[1] B 🛒	SN	FC	SN	SN	SN ◇[1] B 🛒	SN ◇[1] A 🛒	SN ◇[1] B 🛒	SN [1] A	SN ◇[1] A 🛒	SN	FC [1] A	FC [1] B	FC 🚌	LO	SN	SN	SN ◇[1] A	SN ◇[1] B
London Bridge [4] ⊖ d	10 39				10 51	10 54	10 55				11 05		11 11	11 12	11 12				11 09		
South Bermondsey d							10 59						11 15								
Queens Rd Peckham d							11 01						11 18								
Peckham Rye [4] d							11 04						11 20								
East Dulwich d							11 07														
North Dulwich d							11 09														
Luton [10] d																					
Luton Airport Parkway [7] d																					
St Pancras International [15] ⊖ d																					
City Thameslink [3] d																					
London Blackfriars [3] ⊖ d																11 19					
Elephant & Castle ⊖ d																11 27					
Loughborough Jn d																11 39					
Herne Hill [4] d																11 47					
Tulse Hill [3] d					11 01		11 12									11a55					
Streatham [4] d					11 05		11 16														
London Victoria [15] ⊖ d		10 47	10 47	10 49				11 02	11 02	11 04		11 06						11 06		11 17	11 17
Battersea Park [4] d				10 53									11 32								
Milton Keynes Central d																					
Watford Junction d																					
Harrow & Wealdstone ⊖ d																					
Wembley Central ⊖ d																					
Shepherd's Bush ⊖ d																					
Kensington (Olympia) ⊖ d																					
West Brompton ⊖ d																					
Clapham Junction [10] d		10 53	10 53	10 57				11 08	11 08	11 10		11 12						11 12		11 23	11 23
Wandsworth Common d				11 00																	
Balham [4] ⊖ d				11 02														11 17			
Streatham Hill d																		11 20			
West Norwood [4] d																		11 23			
Gipsy Hill d																		11 26			
Crystal Palace [4] d																		11 29			
Birkbeck 🚊 d																					
Beckenham Junction [4] 🚊 a																					
Streatham Common [4] d				11 06			11 19														
Norbury d				11 09			11 21														
Thornton Heath d				11 12			11 24														
Selhurst [4] d				11 15			11 27														
Norwood Junction [2] a	11 02					11 14					11 16						11 22	11 33	11 32		
d	11 03					11 16					11 16						11 22	11 33	11 33		
West Croydon [4] 🚊 a				11 19		11 24											11 29	11 38			
East Croydon 🚊 a	11 06	11 02	11 06				11 32	11 21	11 17	11 24	11 20	11 22		11 24	11 27				11 36	11 32	11 36

A until 5 September

B from 12 September

Table 177

Sundays

Luton, Milton Keynes and London - East and West Croydon via Tulse Hill - Crystal Palace - Norbury

Local Services

	SN	FC	SN ◇[1] A	SN [1] B	SN	SN	SN [1] A	SN [1] A	SN ◇[1] B	SN [1] B	SN ◇[1] A 🛒	SN	FC [1] A	FC [1] B	FC 🚌	LO	SN	SN	SN ◇[1] A 🛒	SN ◇[1] B 🛒	SN	FC
London Bridge [4] ⊖ d		11 21			11 24	11 25						11 41	11 42	11 42				11 39				11 51
South Bermondsey d						11 29						11 45										
Queens Rd Peckham d						11 31						11 48										
Peckham Rye [4] d						11 34						11 50										
East Dulwich d						11 37																
North Dulwich d						11 39																
Luton [10] d																						
Luton Airport Parkway [7] d																						
St Pancras International [15] ⊖ d																						
City Thameslink [3] d																						
London Blackfriars [3] ⊖ d															11 49							
Elephant & Castle ⊖ d															11 57							
Loughborough Jn d															12 09							
Herne Hill [4] d															12 17							
Tulse Hill [3] d		11 31				11 42									12a25							12 01
Streatham [4] d		11 35				11 46																12 05
London Victoria [15] ⊖ d	11 19		11 21	11 22			11 25	11 32	11 32	11 34	11 36						11 36		11 47	11 47	11 49	
Battersea Park [4] d	11 23											12 02									11 53	
Milton Keynes Central d																						
Watford Junction d																						
Harrow & Wealdstone ⊖ d																						
Wembley Central ⊖ d																						
Shepherd's Bush ⊖ d																						
Kensington (Olympia) ⊖ d																						
West Brompton ⊖ d																						
Clapham Junction [10] d	11 27		11 27	11 28			11 31	11 38	11 38	11 41	11 42						11 42		11 53	11 53	11 57	
Wandsworth Common d	11 30																				12 00	
Balham [4] ⊖ d	11 32																11 47				12 02	
Streatham Hill d																	11 50					
West Norwood [4] d																	11 53					
Gipsy Hill d																	11 56					
Crystal Palace [4] d																	11 59					
Birkbeck 🚊 d																						
Beckenham Junction [4] 🚊 a																						
Streatham Common [4] d	11 36					11 49															12 06	
Norbury d	11 39					11 51															12 09	
Thornton Heath d	11 42					11 54															12 12	
Selhurst [4] d	11 45			11 37		11 57															12 15	
Norwood Junction [2] a					11 44											11 52	12 03	12 02				
d					11 46											11 52	12 03	12 03				
West Croydon [4] 🚊 a	11 49				11 54											11 59	12 08				12 19	
East Croydon 🚊 a			11 38	11 42		12 02	11 42	11 47	11 50	11 53	11 52		11 54	11 56				12 06	12 02	12 06		

A until 5 September

B from 12 September

Table 177

Luton, Milton Keynes and London - East and West Croydon via Tulse Hill - Crystal Palace - Norbury

Local Services

		SN	SN	SN	SN	SN	SN	SN	SN	FC	FC	FC	LO	SN	SN	SN	SN	SN	FC	SN	SN	SN
				◇[1]	◇[1]	◇[1]	[1]	◇[1]		[1]	[1]					◇[1]	◇[1]			◇[1]	[1]	
				A	B	A	B	B		B	A	🚌				B	A			B	A	
				⌶		⌶		⌶														
London Bridge [4] ⊖	d	11 54	11 55				12 05		12 11	12 12	12 12				12 09				12 21			12 25
South Bermondsey	d		11 59						12 15													12 29
Queens Rd Peckham	d		12 01						12 18													12 31
Peckham Rye [4]	d		12 04						12 20													12 34
East Dulwich	d		12 07																			12 37
North Dulwich	d		12 09																			12 39
Luton [10]	d																					
Luton Airport Parkway [7]	d																					
St Pancras International [15] ⊖	d																					
City Thameslink [3]	d																					
London Blackfriars [3] ⊖	d											12 19										
Elephant & Castle ⊖	d											12 27										
Loughborough Jn	d											12 39										
Herne Hill [4]	d											12 47										
Tulse Hill [3]	d		12 12									12a55							12 31			12 42
Streatham [4]	d		12 16																12 35			12 46
London Victoria [15] ⊖	d			12 02	12 02	12 04		12 06						12 06		12 17	12 17	12 19		12 21	12 22	
Battersea Park [4]	d								12 32									12 23				
Milton Keynes Central	d																					
Watford Junction	d																					
Harrow & Wealdstone ⊖	d																					
Wembley Central ⊖	d																					
Shepherd's Bush ⊖	d																					
Kensington (Olympia) ⊖	d																					
West Brompton ⊖	d																					
Clapham Junction [10]	d			12 08	12 08	12 10		12 12						12 12		12 23	12 23	12 27		12 27	12 28	
Wandsworth Common	d																	12 30				
Balham [4] ⊖	d													12 17				12 32				
Streatham Hill	d													12 20								
West Norwood [4]	d													12 23								
Gipsy Hill	d													12 26								
Crystal Palace [4]	d													12 29								
Birkbeck 🚊	d																					
Beckenham Junction [4] 🚊	a																					
Streatham Common [4]	d		12 19															12 36				12 49
Norbury	d		12 21															12 39				12 51
Thornton Heath	d		12 24															12 42				12 54
Selhurst [4]	d		12 27															12 45				12 57
Norwood Junction [2]	a	12 14					12 16						12 22	12 33	12 32							
	d	12 16					12 16						12 22	12 33	12 33							
West Croydon [4] 🚊	a	12 24											12 29	12 38				12 49				
East Croydon 🚊	a		12 32	12 21	12 17	12 24	12 20	12 22		12 24	12 27				12 36	12 32	12 36			12 38	12 42	13 02

A from 12 September
B until 5 September

Table 177

Sundays

Luton, Milton Keynes and London - East and West Croydon via Tulse Hill - Crystal Palace - Norbury

Local Services

		SN	SN	SN	SN	SN	LO	SN	SN	FC	FC	FC	FC	LO	SN	SN	SN	SN	SN	SN	SN	SN	SN
		[1]	[1]	◇[1]	[1]	◇[1]				[1]	[1]						◇[1]	◇[1]			◇[1]	◇[1]	◇[1]
		A	A	B	B	A				A	B	🚌					A	B			B	A	B
						⌶											⌶	⌶			⌶		⌶
London Bridge [4] ⊖	d							12 24	12 41	12 42	12 42		12 51			12 39				12 55			
South Bermondsey	d								12 45											12 59			
Queens Rd Peckham	d								12 48											13 01			
Peckham Rye [4]	d								12 50											13 04			
East Dulwich	d																			13 07			
North Dulwich	d																			13 09			
Luton [10]	d																						
Luton Airport Parkway [7]	d																						
St Pancras International [15] ⊖	d																						
City Thameslink [3]	d																						
London Blackfriars [3] ⊖	d											12 49											
Elephant & Castle ⊖	d											12 57											
Loughborough Jn	d											13 09											
Herne Hill [4]	d											13 17											
Tulse Hill [3]	d											13a25	13 01							13 12			
Streatham [4]	d												13 05							13 16			
London Victoria [15] ⊖	d	12 25	12 32	12 32	12 34	12 36									12 36		12 47	12 47	12 49		13 02	13 02	13 04
Battersea Park [4]	d								13 02										12 53				
Milton Keynes Central	d																						
Watford Junction	d																						
Harrow & Wealdstone ⊖	d																						
Wembley Central ⊖	d																						
Shepherd's Bush ⊖	d																						
Kensington (Olympia) ⊖	d																						
West Brompton ⊖	d																						
Clapham Junction [10]	d	12 31	12 38	12 38	12 41	12 42									12 42		12 53	12 53	12 57		13 08	13 08	13 10
Wandsworth Common	d																		13 00				
Balham [4] ⊖	d														12 47				13 02				
Streatham Hill	d														12 50								
West Norwood [4]	d														12 53								
Gipsy Hill	d														12 56								
Crystal Palace [4]	d														12 59								
Birkbeck 🚊	d																						
Beckenham Junction [4] 🚊	a																						
Streatham Common [4]	d																		13 06	13 19			
Norbury	d																		13 09	13 21			
Thornton Heath	d																		13 12	13 24			
Selhurst [4]	d																		13 15	13 27			
Norwood Junction [2]	a						12 39	12 44						12 53	13 03	13 02							
	d						12 39	12 46						12 53	13 03	13 03							
West Croydon [4] 🚊	a						12 46	12 54						13 00	13 08				13 19				
East Croydon 🚊	a	12 42	12 47	12 50	12 53	12 52				12 54	12 56					13 06	13 02	13 06		13 32	13 21	13 17	13 24

A until 5 September
B from 12 September

Table 177

Sundays

Luton, Milton Keynes and London - East and West Croydon via Tulse Hill - Crystal Palace - Norbury

Local Services

	SN	LO	SN	SN	SN		FC	FC	FC	FC	LO	SN	SN	SN	SN		SN	SN	SN	SN	SN	SN	SN	SN
	◇1			1			1	1						◇1	◇1			◇1	1		1	1	◇1	1
	A			A			A	B						A	B			A	B		A	A	B	B
	⌶								🚌															
London Bridge 4 ⊖ d			12 54	13 05	13 11		13 12	13 12		13 21			13 09							13 25				
South Bermondsey d					13 15															13 29				
Queens Rd Peckham d					13 18															13 31				
Peckham Rye 4 d					13 20															13 34				
East Dulwich d																				13 37				
North Dulwich d																				13 39				
Luton 10 d																								
Luton Airport Parkway 7 d																								
St Pancras International 15 ⊖ d																								
City Thameslink 3 d																								
London Blackfriars 3 ⊖ d									13 19															
Elephant & Castle ⊖ d									13 27															
Loughborough Jn d									13 39															
Herne Hill 4 d									13 47															
Tulse Hill 3 d									13a55	13 31										13 42				
Streatham 4 d										13 35										13 46				
London Victoria 15 ⊖ d	13 06											13 06		13 17	13 17		13 19	13 21	13 22		13 25	13 32	13 32	13 34
Battersea Park 4 d					13 32												13 23							
Milton Keynes Central d																								
Watford Junction d																								
Harrow & Wealdstone ⊖ d																								
Wembley Central ⊖ d																								
Shepherd's Bush ⊖ d																								
Kensington (Olympia) ⊖ d																								
West Brompton ⊖ d																								
Clapham Junction 10 d	13 12											13 12		13 23	13 23		13 27	13 27	13 28		13 31	13 38	13 38	13 41
Wandsworth Common d																	13 30							
Balham 4 ⊖ d												13 17					13 32							
Streatham Hill d												13 20												
West Norwood 4 d												13 23												
Gipsy Hill d												13 26												
Crystal Palace 4 d												13 29												
Birkbeck ⇌ d																								
Beckenham Junction 4 ⇌ a																								
Streatham Common 4 d																	13 36			13 49				
Norbury d																	13 39			13 51				
Thornton Heath d																	13 42			13 54				
Selhurst 4 d																	13 45			13 57				
Norwood Junction 2 a		13 08	13 14	13 16							13 23	13 33	13 32											
d		13 08	13 16	13 16							13 23	13 33	13 33											
West Croydon 4 ⇌ a		13 15	13 24								13 30	13 38					13 49							
East Croydon ⇌ a	13 22			13 20			13 24	13 27					13 36	13 32	13 36			13 38	13 42	14 02	13 42	13 47	13 50	13 53

A until 5 September **B** from 12 September

Table 177

Sundays

Luton, Milton Keynes and London - East and West Croydon via Tulse Hill - Crystal Palace - Norbury

Local Services

	SN		LO	SN	SN	FC	FC	FC	FC	LO	SN		SN	SN	SN	SN	SN	SN	SN	SN	SN		LO	SN
	◇1					1	1							◇1	◇1			◇1	◇1	◇1	◇1			
	A					A	B							A	B			B	A	B	A			
	⌶							🚌						⌶	⌶			⌶		⌶	⌶			
London Bridge 4 ⊖ d				13 24	13 41	13 42	13 42		13 51				13 39				13 55							13 54
South Bermondsey d					13 45												13 59							
Queens Rd Peckham d					13 48												14 01							
Peckham Rye 4 d					13 50												14 04							
East Dulwich d																	14 07							
North Dulwich d																	14 09							
Luton 10 d																								
Luton Airport Parkway 7 d																								
St Pancras International 15 ⊖ d																								
City Thameslink 3 d																								
London Blackfriars 3 ⊖ d								13 49																
Elephant & Castle ⊖ d								13 57																
Loughborough Jn d								14 09																
Herne Hill 4 d								14 17																
Tulse Hill 3 d								14a25	14 01								14 12							
Streatham 4 d									14 05								14 16							
London Victoria 15 ⊖ d	13 36										13 36			13 47	13 47	13 49		14 02	14 02	14 04	14 06			
Battersea Park 4 d					14 02											13 53								
Milton Keynes Central d																								
Watford Junction d																								
Harrow & Wealdstone ⊖ d																								
Wembley Central ⊖ d																								
Shepherd's Bush ⊖ d																								
Kensington (Olympia) ⊖ d																								
West Brompton ⊖ d																								
Clapham Junction 10 d	13 42										13 42			13 53	13 53	13 57		14 08	14 08	14 10	14 12			
Wandsworth Common d																14 00								
Balham 4 ⊖ d											13 47					14 02								
Streatham Hill d											13 50													
West Norwood 4 d											13 53													
Gipsy Hill d											13 56													
Crystal Palace 4 d											13 59													
Birkbeck ⇌ d																								
Beckenham Junction 4 ⇌ a																								
Streatham Common 4 d																14 06	14 19							
Norbury d																14 09	14 21							
Thornton Heath d																14 12	14 24							
Selhurst 4 d																14 15	14 27							
Norwood Junction 2 a			13 38	13 44						13 53	14 03		14 02										14 08	14 14
d			13 38	13 46						13 53	14 03		14 03										14 08	14 16
West Croydon 4 ⇌ a			13 45	13 54						14 00	14 08					14 19							14 15	14 24
East Croydon ⇌ a	13 52					13 54	13 56						14 06	14 02	14 06		14 32	14 21	14 17	14 24	14 22			

A until 5 September **B** from 12 September

Table 177

Sundays

Luton, Milton Keynes and London - East and West Croydon via Tulse Hill - Crystal Palace - Norbury

Local Services

Station		SN ■ A	SN	FC ■ A	FC ■ B	FC	FC	LO	SN	SN	SN ◇■ A	SN ◇■ B	SN	SN ◇■ A	SN ■ B	SN	SN ■ A	SN ■ A	SN ◇■ B	SN ■ B	SN ◇■ A	LO	SN
London Bridge ⊖	d	14 05	14 11	14 12	14 12		14 21			14 09						14 25							14 24
South Bermondsey	d		14 15													14 29							
Queens Rd Peckham	d		14 18													14 31							
Peckham Rye	d		14 20													14 34							
East Dulwich	d															14 37							
North Dulwich	d															14 39							
Luton	d																						
Luton Airport Parkway	d																						
St Pancras International ⊖	d																						
City Thameslink	d																						
London Blackfriars ⊖	d					14 19																	
Elephant & Castle ⊖	d					14 27																	
Loughborough Jn	d					14 39																	
Herne Hill	d					14 47																	
Tulse Hill	d					14a55	14 31									14 42							
Streatham	d						14 35									14 46							
London Victoria ⊖	d								14 06		14 17	14 17	14 19	14 21	14 22		14 25	14 32	14 32	14 34	14 36		
Battersea Park	d		14 32										14 23										
Milton Keynes Central	d																						
Watford Junction	d																						
Harrow & Wealdstone ⊖	d																						
Wembley Central ⊖	d																						
Shepherd's Bush ⊖	d																						
Kensington (Olympia) ⊖	d																						
West Brompton ⊖	d																						
Clapham Junction	d								14 12		14 23	14 23	14 27	14 27	14 28		14 31	14 38	14 38	14 41	14 42		
Wandsworth Common	d												14 30										
Balham ⊖	d								14 17				14 32										
Streatham Hill	d								14 20														
West Norwood	d								14 23														
Gipsy Hill	d								14 26														
Crystal Palace	d								14 29														
Birkbeck	d																						
Beckenham Junction	a																						
Streatham Common	d												14 36			14 49							
Norbury	d												14 39			14 51							
Thornton Heath	d												14 42			14 54							
Selhurst	d												14 45			14 57							
Norwood Junction	a	14 16						14 23	14 33	14 32												14 38	14 44
	d	14 16						14 23	14 33	14 33												14 38	14 46
West Croydon	a							14 30	14 38				14 49									14 45	14 54
East Croydon	a	14 20		14 24	14 27					14 36	14 32	14 36		14 38	14 42	15 02	14 42	14 47	14 50	14 53	14 52		

A until 5 September

B from 12 September

Table 177

Sundays

Luton, Milton Keynes and London - East and West Croydon via Tulse Hill - Crystal Palace - Norbury

Local Services

Station		SN	FC ■ A	FC ■ B	FC	FC	LO	SN	SN	SN ◇■ A	SN ◇■ B	SN	SN	SN ◇■ B	SN ◇■ A	SN ◇■ B	SN ◇■ A	LO	SN	SN ■ A	SN	FC ■ A
London Bridge ⊖	d	14 41	14 42	14 42		14 51			14 39				14 55						14 54	15 05	15 11	15 12
South Bermondsey	d	14 45											14 59								15 15	
Queens Rd Peckham	d	14 48											15 01								15 18	
Peckham Rye	d	14 50											15 04								15 20	
East Dulwich	d												15 07									
North Dulwich	d												15 09									
Luton	d																					
Luton Airport Parkway	d																					
St Pancras International ⊖	d																					
City Thameslink	d																					
London Blackfriars ⊖	d				14 49																	
Elephant & Castle ⊖	d				14 57																	
Loughborough Jn	d				15 09																	
Herne Hill	d				15 17																	
Tulse Hill	d				15a25	15 01							15 12									
Streatham	d					15 05							15 16									
London Victoria ⊖	d							14 36		14 47	14 47	14 49		15 02	15 02	15 04	15 06					
Battersea Park	d	15 02										14 53									15 32	
Milton Keynes Central	d																					
Watford Junction	d																					
Harrow & Wealdstone ⊖	d																					
Wembley Central ⊖	d																					
Shepherd's Bush ⊖	d																					
Kensington (Olympia) ⊖	d																					
West Brompton ⊖	d																					
Clapham Junction	d							14 42		14 53	14 53	14 57		15 08	15 08	15 10	15 12					
Wandsworth Common	d											15 00										
Balham ⊖	d							14 47				15 02										
Streatham Hill	d							14 50														
West Norwood	d							14 53														
Gipsy Hill	d							14 56														
Crystal Palace	d							14 59														
Birkbeck	d																					
Beckenham Junction	a																					
Streatham Common	d											15 06	15 19									
Norbury	d											15 09	15 21									
Thornton Heath	d											15 12	15 24									
Selhurst	d											15 15	15 27									
Norwood Junction	a						14 53	15 03	15 02									15 08	15 14	15 16		
	d						14 53	15 03	15 03									15 08	15 16	15 16		
West Croydon	a						15 00	15 08				15 19						15 15	15 24			
East Croydon	a		14 54	14 56					15 06	15 02	15 06		15 32	15 21	15 17	15 24	15 22			15 20		15 24

A until 5 September

B from 12 September

Table 177

Luton, Milton Keynes and London - East and West Croydon via Tulse Hill - Crystal Palace - Norbury

Local Services

		FC	FC	FC	LO	SN	SN	SN	SN	SN	SN	SN	SN	SN	SN	SN	SN	SN	LO	SN	SN	FC	FC
		■ A	🚌					◇■ B	◇■ A		◇■ B	■ A		■ B	■ B	◇■ A	■ A	◇■ B ⊼				■ B	■ A
London Bridge 4 ⊖	d	15 12		15 21			15 09						15 25							15 24	15 41	15 42	15 42
South Bermondsey	d												15 29								15 45		
Queens Rd Peckham	d												15 31								15 48		
Peckham Rye 4	d												15 34								15 50		
East Dulwich	d												15 37										
North Dulwich	d												15 39										
Luton 10	d																						
Luton Airport Parkway 7	d																						
St Pancras International 15 ⊖	d																						
City Thameslink 3	d																						
London Blackfriars 3 ⊖	d		15 19																				
Elephant & Castle ⊖	d		15 27																				
Loughborough Jn	d		15 39																				
Herne Hill 4	d		15 47																				
Tulse Hill 3	d		15a55	15 31									15 42										
Streatham 4	d			15 35									15 46										
London Victoria 15 ⊖	d					15 06		15 17	15 17	15 19	15 21	15 22		15 25	15 32	15 32	15 34	15 36					
Battersea Park 4	d									15 23											16 02		
Milton Keynes Central	d																						
Watford Junction	d																						
Harrow & Wealdstone ⊖	d																						
Wembley Central ⊖	d																						
Shepherd's Bush ⊖	d																						
Kensington (Olympia) ⊖	d																						
West Brompton ⊖	d																						
Clapham Junction 10	d					15 12		15 23	15 23	15 27	15 27	15 28		15 31	15 38	15 38	15 41	15 42					
Wandsworth Common	d									15 30													
Balham 4 ⊖	d					15 17				15 32													
Streatham Hill	d					15 20																	
West Norwood 4	d					15 23																	
Gipsy Hill	d					15 26																	
Crystal Palace 4	d					15 29																	
Birkbeck 🚊	d																						
Beckenham Junction 4 🚊	a																						
Streatham Common 4	d									15 36			15 49										
Norbury	d									15 39			15 51										
Thornton Heath	d									15 42			15 54										
Selhurst 4	d									15 45			15 57										
Norwood Junction 2	a				15 23	15 33	15 32												15 38	15 44			
	d				15 23	15 33	15 33												15 38	15 46			
West Croydon 4 🚊	a				15 30	15 38				15 49									15 45	15 54			
East Croydon 🚊	a	15 27					15 36	15 32	15 36		15 38	15 42	16 02	15 42	15 47	15 50	15 53	15 52				15 54	15 56

A from 12 September **B** until 5 September

Table 177

Luton, Milton Keynes and London - East and West Croydon via Tulse Hill - Crystal Palace - Norbury

Local Services

		FC	FC	LO	SN	SN	SN	SN	SN	SN	SN	SN	SN	SN	LO	SN	SN	SN	FC	FC	FC	FC	LO
		🚌					◇■ A ⊼	◇■ B ⊼			◇■ B ⊼	◇■ A	◇■ B ⊼	◇■ A ⊼			■ A		■ A	■ B	🚌		
London Bridge 4 ⊖	d		15 51			15 39				15 55						15 54	16 05	16 11	16 12	16 12		16 21	
South Bermondsey	d									15 59								16 15					
Queens Rd Peckham	d									16 01								16 18					
Peckham Rye 4	d									16 04								16 20					
East Dulwich	d									16 07													
North Dulwich	d									16 09													
Luton 10	d																						
Luton Airport Parkway 7	d																						
St Pancras International 15 ⊖	d																						
City Thameslink 3	d																						
London Blackfriars 3 ⊖	d	15 49																			16 19		
Elephant & Castle ⊖	d	15 57																			16 27		
Loughborough Jn	d	16 09																			16 39		
Herne Hill 4	d	16 17																			16 47		
Tulse Hill 3	d	16a25	16 01							16 12											16a55	16 31	
Streatham 4	d		16 05							16 16												16 35	
London Victoria 15 ⊖	d				15 36		15 47	15 47	15 49		16 02	16 02	16 04	16 06									
Battersea Park 4	d								15 53									16 32					
Milton Keynes Central	d																						
Watford Junction	d																						
Harrow & Wealdstone ⊖	d																						
Wembley Central ⊖	d																						
Shepherd's Bush ⊖	d																						
Kensington (Olympia) ⊖	d																						
West Brompton ⊖	d																						
Clapham Junction 10	d				15 42		15 53	15 53	15 57		16 08	16 08	16 10	16 12									
Wandsworth Common	d								16 00														
Balham 4 ⊖	d				15 47				16 02														
Streatham Hill	d				15 50																		
West Norwood 4	d				15 53																		
Gipsy Hill	d				15 56																		
Crystal Palace 4	d				15 59																		
Birkbeck 🚊	d																						
Beckenham Junction 4 🚊	a																						
Streatham Common 4	d								16 06	16 19													
Norbury	d								16 09	16 21													
Thornton Heath	d								16 12	16 24													
Selhurst 4	d								16 15	16 27													
Norwood Junction 2	a			15 53	16 03	16 02									16 08	16 14	16 16						16 23
	d			15 53	16 03	16 03									16 08	16 16	16 16						16 23
West Croydon 4 🚊	a			16 00	16 08				16 19						16 15	16 24							16 30
East Croydon 🚊	a					16 06	16 02	16 06		16 32	16 21	16 17	16 24	16 22			16 20		16 24	16 27			

A until 5 September **B** from 12 September

Table 177

Sundays

Luton, Milton Keynes and London - East and West Croydon via Tulse Hill - Crystal Palace - Norbury

Local Services

Station		SN		SN	SN	SN	SN	SN	SN	SN	SN		SN	SN	SN	LO	SN	SN	FC	FC	FC		FC	LO
					◇1 A	◇1 B		◇1 A	1 B		1 A	1 A		◇1 B	1 B	◇1 A ⊼				1 A	1 B	🚌			
London Bridge 4 ⊖	d			16 09						16 25								16 24	16 41	16 42	16 42			16 51	
South Bermondsey	d									16 29									16 45						
Queens Rd Peckham	d									16 31									16 48						
Peckham Rye 4	d									16 34									16 50						
East Dulwich	d									16 37															
North Dulwich	d									16 39															
Luton 10	d																								
Luton Airport Parkway 7	d																								
St Pancras International 15 ⊖	d																								
City Thameslink 3	d																								
London Blackfriars 3 ⊖	d																					16 49			
Elephant & Castle ⊖	d																					16 57			
Loughborough Jn	d																					17 09			
Herne Hill 4	d																					17 17			
Tulse Hill 3	d									16 42												17a25		17 01	
Streatham 4	d									16 46														17 05	
London Victoria 15 ⊖	d	16 06			16 17	16 17	16 19	16 21	16 22		16 25	16 32		16 32	16 34	16 36									
Battersea Park 4	d						16 23												17 02						
Milton Keynes Central	d																								
Watford Junction	d																								
Harrow & Wealdstone ⊖	d																								
Wembley Central ⊖	d																								
Shepherd's Bush ⊖	d																								
Kensington (Olympia) ⊖	d																								
West Brompton ⊖	d																								
Clapham Junction 10	d	16 12			16 23	16 23	16 27	16 27	16 28		16 31	16 38		16 38	16 41	16 42									
Wandsworth Common	d						16 30																		
Balham 4 ⊖	d	16 17					16 32																		
Streatham Hill	d	16 20																							
West Norwood 4	d	16 23																							
Gipsy Hill	d	16 26																							
Crystal Palace 4	d	16 29																							
Birkbeck 🚊	d																								
Beckenham Junction 4 🚊	a																								
Streatham Common 4	d						16 36			16 49															
Norbury	d						16 39			16 51															
Thornton Heath	d						16 42			16 54															
Selhurst 4	d						16 45			16 57															
Norwood Junction 2	a	16 33		16 32													16 38	16 44							16 53
	d	16 33		16 33													16 38	16 46							16 53
West Croydon 4 🚊	a	16 38					16 49										16 45	16 54							17 00
East Croydon 🚊	a			16 36	16 32	16 36		16 38	16 42	17 02	16 42	16 47		16 50	16 53	16 52				16 54	16 56				

A until 5 September **B** from 12 September

Table 177

Sundays

Luton, Milton Keynes and London - East and West Croydon via Tulse Hill - Crystal Palace - Norbury

Local Services

Station		SN	SN	SN	SN	SN	SN	SN		SN	SN	SN	LO	SN	SN	SN	FC	FC		FC	FC	LO	SN	SN	SN
				◇1 A ⊼	◇1 B ⊼			◇1 B ⊼		◇1 A	◇1 B ⊼	◇1 A ⊼			1 A		1 A	1 B		🚌					◇1 A
London Bridge 4 ⊖	d		16 39				16 55							16 54	17 05	17 11	17 12	17 12			17 21			17 09	
South Bermondsey	d						16 59									17 15									
Queens Rd Peckham	d						17 01									17 18									
Peckham Rye 4	d						17 04									17 20									
East Dulwich	d						17 07																		
North Dulwich	d						17 09																		
Luton 10	d																								
Luton Airport Parkway 7	d																								
St Pancras International 15 ⊖	d																								
City Thameslink 3	d																								
London Blackfriars 3 ⊖	d																			17 19					
Elephant & Castle ⊖	d																			17 27					
Loughborough Jn	d																			17 39					
Herne Hill 4	d																			17 47					
Tulse Hill 3	d						17 12													17a55	17 31				
Streatham 4	d						17 16														17 35				
London Victoria 15 ⊖	d	16 36		16 47	16 47	16 49		17 02		17 02	17 04	17 06											17 06		17 17
Battersea Park 4	d					16 53										17 32									
Milton Keynes Central	d																								
Watford Junction	d																								
Harrow & Wealdstone ⊖	d																								
Wembley Central ⊖	d																								
Shepherd's Bush ⊖	d																								
Kensington (Olympia) ⊖	d																								
West Brompton ⊖	d																								
Clapham Junction 10	d	16 42		16 53	16 53	16 57		17 08		17 08	17 10	17 12											17 12		17 23
Wandsworth Common	d					17 00																			
Balham 4 ⊖	d	16 47				17 02																	17 17		
Streatham Hill	d	16 50																					17 20		
West Norwood 4	d	16 53																					17 23		
Gipsy Hill	d	16 56																					17 26		
Crystal Palace 4	d	16 59																					17 29		
Birkbeck 🚊	d																								
Beckenham Junction 4 🚊	a																								
Streatham Common 4	d					17 06	17 19																		
Norbury	d					17 09	17 21																		
Thornton Heath	d					17 12	17 24																		
Selhurst 4	d					17 15	17 27																		
Norwood Junction 2	a	17 03	17 02										17 08	17 14	17 16							17 23	17 33	17 32	
	d	17 03	17 03										17 08	17 16	17 16							17 23	17 33	17 33	
West Croydon 4 🚊	a	17 08				17 19							17 15	17 24								17 30	17 38		
East Croydon 🚊	a		17 06	17 02	17 06		17 32	17 21		17 17	17 24	17 22			17 20		17 24	17 27						17 36	17 32

A until 5 September **B** from 12 September

Table 177

Sundays

Luton, Milton Keynes and London - East and West Croydon via Tulse Hill - Crystal Palace - Norbury

Local Services

		SN	SN	SN	SN	SN	SN	SN	SN	SN	SN	LO	SN	SN	FC	FC	FC	FC	LO	SN	SN	SN
		◇1		◇1	1		1	1	◇1	1	◇1				1	1						◇1
		A		B	A		B	B	A	A	B				B	A						B
											bike						bus					bike
London Bridge 4 ⊖	d					17 25							17 24	17 41	17 42	17 42		17 51			17 39	
South Bermondsey	d					17 29								17 45								
Queens Rd Peckham	d					17 31								17 48								
Peckham Rye 4	d					17 34								17 50								
East Dulwich	d					17 37																
North Dulwich	d					17 39																
Luton 10	d																					
Luton Airport Parkway 7	d																					
St Pancras International 15 ⊖	d																					
City Thameslink 3	d																					
London Blackfriars 3 ⊖	d																17 49					
Elephant & Castle ⊖	d																17 57					
Loughborough Jn	d																18 09					
Herne Hill 4	d																18 17					
Tulse Hill 3	d					17 42											18a25	18 01				
Streatham 4	d					17 46												18 05				
London Victoria 15 ⊖	d	17 17	17 19	17 21	17 22		17 25	17 32	17 32	17 34	17 36									17 36		17 47
Battersea Park 4	d		17 23											18 02								
Milton Keynes Central	d																					
Watford Junction	d																					
Harrow & Wealdstone ⊖	d																					
Wembley Central ⊖	d																					
Shepherd's Bush ⊖	d																					
Kensington (Olympia) ⊖	d																					
West Brompton ⊖	d																					
Clapham Junction 10	d	17 23	17 27	17 27	17 28		17 31	17 38	17 38	17 41	17 42									17 42		17 53
Wandsworth Common	d		17 30																			
Balham 4 ⊖	d		17 32																	17 47		
Streatham Hill	d																			17 50		
West Norwood 4	d																			17 53		
Gipsy Hill	d																			17 56		
Crystal Palace 4	d																			17 59		
Birkbeck	d																					
Beckenham Junction 4	a																					
Streatham Common 4	d		17 36			17 49																
Norbury	d		17 39			17 51																
Thornton Heath	d		17 42			17 54																
Selhurst 4	d		17 45			17 57																
Norwood Junction 2	a											17 38	17 44						17 53	18 03	18 02	
	d											17 38	17 46						17 53	18 03	18 03	
West Croydon 4	a		17 49									17 45	17 54						18 00	18 08		
East Croydon	a	17 36		17 38	17 42	18 02	17 42	17 47	17 50	17 53	17 52				17 54	17 56					18 06	18 02

A from 12 September

B until 5 September

Table 177

Sundays

Luton, Milton Keynes and London - East and West Croydon via Tulse Hill - Crystal Palace - Norbury

Local Services

		SN	SN	SN	SN	SN	SN	SN	LO	SN	SN	SN	FC	FC	FC	FC	LO	SN	SN	SN	SN	SN	SN
		◇1			◇1	◇1	◇1	◇1			1		1	1						◇1	◇1		◇1
		A			A	B	A	B			B		B	A						B	A		B
		bike			bike		bike	bike							bus								
London Bridge 4 ⊖	d			17 55						17 54	18 05	18 11	18 12	18 12		18 21			18 09				
South Bermondsey	d			17 59								18 15											
Queens Rd Peckham	d			18 01								18 18											
Peckham Rye 4	d			18 04								18 20											
East Dulwich	d			18 07																			
North Dulwich	d			18 09																			
Luton 10	d																						
Luton Airport Parkway 7	d																						
St Pancras International 15 ⊖	d																						
City Thameslink 3	d																						
London Blackfriars 3 ⊖	d														18 19								
Elephant & Castle ⊖	d														18 27								
Loughborough Jn	d														18 39								
Herne Hill 4	d														18 47								
Tulse Hill 3	d			18 12											18a55	18 31							
Streatham 4	d			18 16												18 35							
London Victoria 15 ⊖	d	17 47	17 49		18 02	18 02	18 04	18 06										18 06		18 17	18 17	18 19	18 21
Battersea Park 4	d		17 53									18 32										18 23	
Milton Keynes Central	d																						
Watford Junction	d																						
Harrow & Wealdstone ⊖	d																						
Wembley Central ⊖	d																						
Shepherd's Bush ⊖	d																						
Kensington (Olympia) ⊖	d																						
West Brompton ⊖	d																						
Clapham Junction 10	d	17 53	17 57		18 08	18 08	18 10	18 12										18 12		18 23	18 23	18 27	18 27
Wandsworth Common	d		18 00																			18 30	
Balham 4 ⊖	d		18 02															18 17				18 32	
Streatham Hill	d																	18 20					
West Norwood 4	d																	18 23					
Gipsy Hill	d																	18 26					
Crystal Palace 4	d																	18 29					
Birkbeck	d																						
Beckenham Junction 4	a																						
Streatham Common 4	d		18 06	18 19																		18 36	
Norbury	d		18 09	18 21																		18 39	
Thornton Heath	d		18 12	18 24																		18 42	
Selhurst 4	d		18 15	18 27																		18 45	
Norwood Junction 2	a								18 08	18 14	18 16						18 23	18 33	18 32				
	d								18 08	18 16	18 16						18 23	18 33	18 33				
West Croydon 4	a		18 19						18 15	18 24							18 30	18 38				18 49	
East Croydon	a	18 06		18 32	18 21	18 17	18 24	18 22			18 20		18 24	18 27					18 36	18 32	18 36		18 38

A from 12 September

B until 5 September

Table 177

Sundays

Luton, Milton Keynes and London - East and West Croydon via Tulse Hill - Crystal Palace - Norbury

Local Services

		SN	SN	SN	SN	SN	SN	SN	LO	SN	SN	FC	FC	FC	FC	LO	SN	SN	SN	SN	SN	SN	SN
		■1		■1	■1	◇■1	■1	◇■1				■1	■1						◇■1	◇■1			◇■1
		A		B	B	A	A	B				B	A						B	A			A
								⌶						🚌					⌶	⌶			⌶
London Bridge 4 ⊖	d		18 25							18 24	18 41	18 42	18 42		18 51			18 39				18 55	
South Bermondsey	d		18 29								18 45											18 59	
Queens Rd Peckham	d		18 31								18 48											19 01	
Peckham Rye 4	d		18 34								18 50											19 04	
East Dulwich	d		18 37																			19 07	
North Dulwich	d		18 39																			19 09	
Luton 10	d																						
Luton Airport Parkway 7	d																						
St Pancras International 15 ⊖	d																						
City Thameslink 3	d																						
London Blackfriars 3 ⊖	d													18 49									
Elephant & Castle ⊖	d													18 57									
Loughborough Jn	d													19 09									
Herne Hill 4	d													19 17									
Tulse Hill 3	d		18 42											19a25	19 01							19 12	
Streatham 4	d		18 46												19 05							19 16	
London Victoria 15 ⊖	d	18 22		18 25	18 32	18 32	18 34	18 36									18 36		18 47	18 47	18 49		19 02
Battersea Park 4	d										19 02										18 53		
Milton Keynes Central	d																						
Watford Junction	d																						
Harrow & Wealdstone ⊖	d																						
Wembley Central ⊖	d																						
Shepherd's Bush ⊖	d																						
Kensington (Olympia) ⊖	d																						
West Brompton ⊖	d																						
Clapham Junction 10	d	18 28		18 31	18 38	18 38	18 41	18 42									18 42		18 53	18 53	18 57		19 08
Wandsworth Common	d																				19 00		
Balham 4 ⊖	d																18 47				19 02		
Streatham Hill	d																18 50						
West Norwood 4	d																18 53						
Gipsy Hill	d																18 56						
Crystal Palace 4	d																18 59						
Birkbeck 🚊	d																						
Beckenham Junction 4 🚊	a																						
Streatham Common 4	d		18 49																		19 06	19 19	
Norbury	d		18 51																		19 09	19 21	
Thornton Heath	d		18 54																		19 12	19 24	
Selhurst 4	d		18 57																		19 15	19 27	
Norwood Junction 2	a									18 38	18 44					18 53	19 03	19 02					
	d									18 38	18 46					18 53	19 03	19 03					
West Croydon 4 🚊	a									18 45	18 54					19 00	19 08				19 19		
East Croydon 🚊	a	18 42	19 02	18 42	18 47	18 50	18 53	18 52				18 54	18 56					19 06	19 02	19 06		19 32	19 21

A from 12 September **B** until 5 September

Table 177

Sundays

Luton, Milton Keynes and London - East and West Croydon via Tulse Hill - Crystal Palace - Norbury

Local Services

		SN	SN	SN	LO	SN	SN	SN	FC	FC	FC	FC	LO	SN	SN	SN	SN	SN	SN	SN	SN	SN
		◇■1	◇■1	◇■1			■1		■1	■1						◇■1	◇■1		◇■1	■1		■1
		A	B	A			A		A	B						A	B		A	B		A
			⌶	⌶							🚌											
London Bridge 4 ⊖	d					18 54	19 05	19 11	19 12	19 12		19 21			19 09						19 25	
South Bermondsey	d							19 15													19 29	
Queens Rd Peckham	d							19 18													19 31	
Peckham Rye 4	d							19 20													19 34	
East Dulwich	d																				19 37	
North Dulwich	d																				19 39	
Luton 10	d																					
Luton Airport Parkway 7	d																					
St Pancras International 15 ⊖	d																					
City Thameslink 3	d																					
London Blackfriars 3 ⊖	d										19 19											
Elephant & Castle ⊖	d										19 27											
Loughborough Jn	d										19 39											
Herne Hill 4	d										19 47											
Tulse Hill 3	d										19a55	19 31									19 42	
Streatham 4	d											19 35									19 46	
London Victoria 15 ⊖	d	19 02	19 04	19 06										19 06		19 17	19 17	19 19	19 21	19 22		19 25
Battersea Park 4	d							19 32										19 23				
Milton Keynes Central	d																					
Watford Junction	d																					
Harrow & Wealdstone ⊖	d																					
Wembley Central ⊖	d																					
Shepherd's Bush ⊖	d																					
Kensington (Olympia) ⊖	d																					
West Brompton ⊖	d																					
Clapham Junction 10	d	19 08	19 10	19 12										19 12		19 23	19 23	19 27	19 27	19 28		19 31
Wandsworth Common	d																	19 30				
Balham 4 ⊖	d													19 17				19 32				
Streatham Hill	d													19 20								
West Norwood 4	d													19 23								
Gipsy Hill	d													19 26								
Crystal Palace 4	d													19 29								
Birkbeck 🚊	d																					
Beckenham Junction 4 🚊	a																					
Streatham Common 4	d																	19 36			19 49	
Norbury	d																	19 39			19 51	
Thornton Heath	d																	19 42			19 54	
Selhurst 4	d																	19 45			19 57	
Norwood Junction 2	a				19 08	19 14	19 16						19 23	19 33	19 32							
	d				19 08	19 16	19 16						19 23	19 33	19 33							
West Croydon 4 🚊	a				19 15	19 24							19 30	19 38				19 49				
East Croydon 🚊	a	19 17	19 24	19 22			19 20		19 24	19 27					19 36	19 32	19 36		19 38	19 42	20 02	19 42

A until 5 September **B** from 12 September

Table 177

Sundays

Luton, Milton Keynes and London - East and West Croydon via Tulse Hill - Crystal Palace - Norbury

Local Services

Station		SN 1 A	SN ◇1 B	SN 1 B	SN ◇1 A	LO	SN	SN	FC 1 A	FC 1 B	FC (bus)	FC	LO	SN	SN	SN ◇1 A	SN ◇1 B	SN	SN	SN ◇1 B	SN ◇1 A	SN ◇1 B	SN ◇1 A
London Bridge ⊖	d						19 24	19 41	19 42	19 42		19 51			19 39				19 55				
South Bermondsey	d							19 45											19 59				
Queens Rd Peckham	d							19 48											20 01				
Peckham Rye	d							19 50											20 04				
East Dulwich	d																		20 07				
North Dulwich	d																		20 09				
Luton	d																						
Luton Airport Parkway	d																						
St Pancras International ⊖	d																						
City Thameslink	d																						
London Blackfriars ⊖	d										19 49												
Elephant & Castle ⊖	d										19 57												
Loughborough Jn	d										20 09												
Herne Hill	d										20 17												
Tulse Hill	d										20a25	20 01							20 12				
Streatham	d											20 05							20 16				
London Victoria ⊖	d	19 32	19 32	19 34	19 36									19 36		19 47	19 47	19 49		20 02	20 02	20 04	20 06
Battersea Park	d							20 02										19 53					
Milton Keynes Central	d																						
Watford Junction	d																						
Harrow & Wealdstone ⊖	d																						
Wembley Central ⊖	d																						
Shepherd's Bush ⊖	d																						
Kensington (Olympia) ⊖	d																						
West Brompton ⊖	d																						
Clapham Junction	d	19 38	19 38	19 41	19 42									19 42		19 53	19 53	19 57		20 08	20 08	20 10	20 12
Wandsworth Common	d																	20 00					
Balham ⊖	d													19 47				20 02					
Streatham Hill	d													19 50									
West Norwood	d													19 53									
Gipsy Hill	d													19 56									
Crystal Palace	d													19 59									
Birkbeck	d																						
Beckenham Junction	a																						
Streatham Common	d																	20 06	20 19				
Norbury	d																	20 09	20 21				
Thornton Heath	d																	20 12	20 24				
Selhurst	d																	20 15	20 27				
Norwood Junction	a					19 38	19 44						19 53	20 03	20 02								
	d					19 38	19 46						19 53	20 03	20 03								
West Croydon	a					19 45	19 54						20 00	20 08				20 19					
East Croydon	a	19 47	19 50	19 53	19 52				19 54	19 56					20 06	20 02	20 06		20 32	20 21	20 17	20 24	20 22

A until 5 September **B** from 12 September

Table 177

Sundays

Luton, Milton Keynes and London - East and West Croydon via Tulse Hill - Crystal Palace - Norbury

Local Services

Station		LO	SN	SN 1 A	SN	FC 1 A	FC 1 B	FC (bus)	FC	LO	SN	SN	SN ◇1 A	SN ◇1 B	SN	SN ◇1 A	SN 1 B	SN	SN 1 A	SN 1 A	SN ◇1 B	SN 1 B
London Bridge ⊖	d		19 54	20 05	20 11	20 12	20 12		20 21			20 09						20 25				
South Bermondsey	d				20 15													20 29				
Queens Rd Peckham	d				20 18													20 31				
Peckham Rye	d				20 20													20 34				
East Dulwich	d																	20 37				
North Dulwich	d																	20 39				
Luton	d																					
Luton Airport Parkway	d																					
St Pancras International ⊖	d																					
City Thameslink	d																					
London Blackfriars ⊖	d							20 19														
Elephant & Castle ⊖	d							20 27														
Loughborough Jn	d							20 39														
Herne Hill	d							20 47														
Tulse Hill	d							20a55	20 31									20 42				
Streatham	d								20 35									20 46				
London Victoria ⊖	d										20 06		20 17	20 17	20 19	20 21	20 22		20 25	20 32	20 32	20 34
Battersea Park	d				20 32										20 23							
Milton Keynes Central	d																					
Watford Junction	d																					
Harrow & Wealdstone ⊖	d																					
Wembley Central ⊖	d																					
Shepherd's Bush ⊖	d																					
Kensington (Olympia) ⊖	d																					
West Brompton ⊖	d																					
Clapham Junction	d										20 12		20 23	20 23	20 27	20 27	20 28		20 31	20 38	20 38	20 41
Wandsworth Common	d														20 30							
Balham ⊖	d										20 17				20 32							
Streatham Hill	d										20 20											
West Norwood	d										20 23											
Gipsy Hill	d										20 26											
Crystal Palace	d										20 29											
Birkbeck	d																					
Beckenham Junction	a																					
Streatham Common	d														20 36			20 49				
Norbury	d														20 39			20 51				
Thornton Heath	d														20 42			20 54				
Selhurst	d														20 45			20 57				
Norwood Junction	a	20 08	20 14	20 16						20 23	20 33	20 32										
	d	20 08	20 16	20 16						20 23	20 33	20 33										
West Croydon	a	20 15	20 24							20 30	20 38				20 49							
East Croydon	a			20 20		20 24	20 27					20 36	20 32	20 36		20 38	20 42	21 02	20 42	20 47	20 50	20 53

A until 5 September **B** from 12 September

Table 177

Luton, Milton Keynes and London - East and West Croydon via Tulse Hill - Crystal Palace - Norbury

Local Services

		SN	LO	SN	SN	FC	FC	FC	LO	SN	SN	SN	SN	SN	SN	SN	SN	SN	SN	LO	SN	SN	SN
		◇1				1	1					◇1	◇1			◇1	◇1	◇1	◇1			1	
		A				A	B					A	B			B	A	B	A			A	
London Bridge 4 ⊖	d			20 24	20 41	20 42	20 42	20 51			20 39				20 55						20 54	21 05	21 11
South Bermondsey	d				20 45										20 59								21 15
Queens Rd Peckham	d				20 48										21 01								21 18
Peckham Rye 4	d				20 50										21 04								21 20
East Dulwich	d														21 07								
North Dulwich	d														21 09								
Luton 10	d																						
Luton Airport Parkway 7	d																						
St Pancras International 15 ⊖	d																						
City Thameslink 3	d																						
London Blackfriars 3 ⊖	d																						
Elephant & Castle ⊖	d																						
Loughborough Jn	d																						
Herne Hill 4	d																						
Tulse Hill 3	d							21 01							21 12								
Streatham 4	d							21 05							21 16								
London Victoria 15 ⊖	d	20 36								20 36		20 47	20 47	20 49		21 02	21 02	21 04	21 06				
Battersea Park 4	d				21 02									20 53									21 32
Milton Keynes Central	d																						
Watford Junction	d																						
Harrow & Wealdstone ⊖	d																						
Wembley Central ⊖	d																						
Shepherd's Bush ⊖	d																						
Kensington (Olympia) ⊖	d																						
West Brompton ⊖	d																						
Clapham Junction 10	d	20 42								20 42		20 53	20 53	20 57		21 08	21 08	21 10	21 12				
Wandsworth Common	d													21 00									
Balham 4 ⊖	d									20 47				21 02									
Streatham Hill	d									20 50													
West Norwood 4	d									20 53													
Gipsy Hill	d									20 56													
Crystal Palace 4	d									20 59													
Birkbeck	d																						
Beckenham Junction 4	a																						
Streatham Common 4	d													21 06	21 19								
Norbury	d													21 09	21 21								
Thornton Heath	d													21 12	21 24								
Selhurst 4	d													21 15	21 27								
Norwood Junction 2	a		20 38	20 44					20 53	21 03	21 02									21 08	21 14	21 16	
	d		20 38	20 46					20 53	21 03	21 03									21 08	21 16	21 16	
West Croydon 4	a		20 45	20 54					21 00	21 08				21 19						21 15	21 24		
East Croydon	a	20 52				20 54	20 56				21 06	21 02	21 06		21 32	21 21	21 17	21 24	21 22			21 20	

A until 5 September

B from 12 September

Table 177

Luton, Milton Keynes and London - East and West Croydon via Tulse Hill - Crystal Palace - Norbury

Local Services

		FC	FC	LO	SN	SN	SN	SN	SN	SN	SN	SN	SN	SN	SN	SN	LO	SN	SN	FC	FC	LO	SN
		1	1				◇1	◇1		◇1	1		1	1	◇1	1				1	1		
		A	B				B	A		A	B		A	A	B	B				A	B		
London Bridge 4 ⊖	d	21 12	21 12			21 09						21 25						21 24	21 41	21 42	21 42		
South Bermondsey	d											21 29							21 45				
Queens Rd Peckham	d											21 31							21 48				
Peckham Rye 4	d											21 34							21 50				
East Dulwich	d											21 37											
North Dulwich	d											21 39											
Luton 10	d																						
Luton Airport Parkway 7	d																						
St Pancras International 15 ⊖	d																						
City Thameslink 3	d																						
London Blackfriars 3 ⊖	d																						
Elephant & Castle ⊖	d																						
Loughborough Jn	d																						
Herne Hill 4	d																						
Tulse Hill 3	d											21 42											
Streatham 4	d											21 46											
London Victoria 15 ⊖	d				21 06		21 17	21 17	21 19	21 21	21 22		21 25	21 32	21 32	21 34							21 36
Battersea Park 4	d								21 23										22 02				
Milton Keynes Central	d																						
Watford Junction	d																						
Harrow & Wealdstone ⊖	d																						
Wembley Central ⊖	d																						
Shepherd's Bush ⊖	d																						
Kensington (Olympia) ⊖	d																						
West Brompton ⊖	d																						
Clapham Junction 10	d				21 12		21 23	21 23	21 27	21 27	21 28		21 31	21 38	21 38	21 41							21 42
Wandsworth Common	d								21 30														
Balham 4 ⊖	d				21 17				21 32														21 47
Streatham Hill	d				21 20																		21 50
West Norwood 4	d				21 23																		21 53
Gipsy Hill	d				21 26																		21 56
Crystal Palace 4	d				21 29																		21 59
Birkbeck	d																						
Beckenham Junction 4	a																						
Streatham Common 4	d								21 36			21 49											
Norbury	d								21 39			21 51											
Thornton Heath	d								21 42			21 54											
Selhurst 4	d								21 45			21 57											
Norwood Junction 2	a			21 23	21 33	21 32											21 38	21 44				21 53	22 03
	d			21 23	21 33	21 33											21 38	21 46				21 53	22 03
West Croydon 4	a			21 30	21 38				21 49								21 45	21 54				22 00	22 08
East Croydon	a	21 24	21 27			21 36	21 36	21 32		21 38	21 42	22 00	21 42	21 47	21 50	21 53				21 54	21 56		

A until 5 September

B from 12 September

Table 177

Luton, Milton Keynes and London - East and West Croydon via Tulse Hill - Crystal Palace - Norbury

Local Services

		SN	SN ◇■ A	SN ◇■ B	SN	SN	SN ◇■ A	SN ◇■ B	LO	SN	SN ■ A	SN	FC ■ A	FC ■ B	LO	SN	SN	SN ◇■ B	SN ◇■ A	SN	SN ◇■ A	SN ■ B
London Bridge ■ ⊖	d	21 39				21 55				21 54	22 05	22 11	22 12	22 12			22 09					
South Bermondsey	d					21 59						22 15										
Queens Rd Peckham	d					22 01						22 18										
Peckham Rye ■	d					22 04						22 20										
East Dulwich	d					22 07																
North Dulwich	d					22 09																
Luton ■	d																					
Luton Airport Parkway ■	d																					
St Pancras International ■ ⊖	d																					
City Thameslink ■	d																					
London Blackfriars ■ ⊖	d																					
Elephant & Castle ⊖	d																					
Loughborough Jn	d																					
Herne Hill ■	d																					
Tulse Hill ■	d					22 12																
Streatham ■	d					22 16																
London Victoria ■ ⊖	d		21 47	21 47	21 49		22 02	22 04								22 06		22 17	22 17	22 19	22 21	22 22
Battersea Park ■	d				21 53							22 32								22 23		
Milton Keynes Central	d																					
Watford Junction	d																					
Harrow & Wealdstone ⊖	d																					
Wembley Central ⊖	d																					
Shepherd's Bush ⊖	d																					
Kensington (Olympia) ⊖	d																					
West Brompton ⊖	d																					
Clapham Junction ■	d		21 53	21 53	21 57		22 08	22 10								22 12		22 23	22 23	22 26	22 27	22 28
Wandsworth Common	d				22 00															22 29		
Balham ■ ⊖	d				22 02											22 17				22 32		
Streatham Hill	d															22 20						
West Norwood ■	d															22 23						
Gipsy Hill	d															22 26						
Crystal Palace ■	d															22 29						
Birkbeck	d																					
Beckenham Junction ■	a																					
Streatham Common ■	d				22 06	22 19														22 36		
Norbury	d				22 09	22 21														22 38		
Thornton Heath	d				22 12	22 24														22 41		
Selhurst ■	d				22 15	22 27														22 44		
Norwood Junction ■	a	22 02							22 08	22 14	22 16				22 23	22 33	22 32					
	d	22 03							22 08	22 16	22 16				22 23	22 33	22 33					
West Croydon ■	a				22 19				22 15	22 24					22 30	22 38				22 48		
East Croydon	a	22 06	22 02	22 06		22 32	22 17	22 24			22 20		22 24	22 27			22 36	22 36	22 32		22 38	22 43

A until 5 September

B from 12 September

Table 177

Luton, Milton Keynes and London - East and West Croydon via Tulse Hill - Crystal Palace - Norbury

Local Services

		SN	SN ■ A	SN ■ A	SN ◇■ B	SN ■ B	LO	SN	SN	SN	FC ■ A	FC ■ B	SN ◇■ B	SN ◇■ A	SN	SN	SN ■	LO	SN	SN	SN	FC ■ A	FC ■ B
London Bridge ■ ⊖	d	22 25							22 39	22 41	22 42	22 42				22 55				23 09	23 11	23 12	23 12
South Bermondsey	d	22 29								22 45						22 59					23 15		
Queens Rd Peckham	d	22 31								22 48						23 01					23 18		
Peckham Rye ■	d	22 34								22 50						23 04					23 20		
East Dulwich	d	22 37														23 07							
North Dulwich	d	22 39														23 09							
Luton ■	d																						
Luton Airport Parkway ■	d																						
St Pancras International ■ ⊖	d																						
City Thameslink ■	d																						
London Blackfriars ■ ⊖	d																						
Elephant & Castle ⊖	d																						
Loughborough Jn	d																						
Herne Hill ■	d																						
Tulse Hill ■	d	22 42														23 12							
Streatham ■	d	22 46														23 16							
London Victoria ■ ⊖	d		22 25	22 32	22 32	22 34		22 36					22 47	22 47	22 49		23 04		23 06				
Battersea Park ■	d									23 02					22 53						23 32		
Milton Keynes Central	d																						
Watford Junction	d																						
Harrow & Wealdstone ⊖	d																						
Wembley Central ⊖	d																						
Shepherd's Bush ⊖	d																						
Kensington (Olympia) ⊖	d																						
West Brompton ⊖	d																						
Clapham Junction ■	d		22 31	22 38	22 38	22 41		22 42					22 53	22 53	22 57		23 10		23 12				
Wandsworth Common	d														23 00								
Balham ■ ⊖	d							22 47							23 02				23 17				
Streatham Hill	d							22 50											23 20				
West Norwood ■	d							22 53											23 23				
Gipsy Hill	d							22 56											23 26				
Crystal Palace ■	d							22 59											23 29				
Birkbeck	d																						
Beckenham Junction ■	a																						
Streatham Common ■	d	22 49													23 06	23 19							
Norbury	d	22 51													23 09	23 21							
Thornton Heath	d	22 54													23 12	23 24							
Selhurst ■	d	22 57													23 15	23 27							
Norwood Junction ■	a						22 38	23 03	23 02									23 08	23 33	23 32			
	d						22 38	23 03	23 03									23 08	23 33	23 33			
West Croydon ■	a						22 45	23 08							23 19			23 15	23 38				
East Croydon	a	23 00	22 42	22 47	22 50	22 53			23 06		22 54	22 56	23 06	23 02		23 32	23 22			23 36		23 24	23 27

A until 5 September

B from 12 September

Table 177

Luton, Milton Keynes and London - East and West Croydon via Tulse Hill - Crystal Palace - Norbury

Sundays

Local Services

		SN	SN	SN		SN	LO	SN	SN	FC	SN	SN	SN
		◇1		◇1						1			1
London Bridge 4 ⊖	d					23 25			23 39	23 42			
South Bermondsey	d					23 29							
Queens Rd Peckham	d					23 31							
Peckham Rye 4	d					23 34							
East Dulwich	d					23 37							
North Dulwich	d					23 39							
Luton 10	d												
Luton Airport Parkway 7	d												
St Pancras International 15 ⊖	d												
City Thameslink 3	d												
London Blackfriars 3 ⊖	d												
Elephant & Castle ⊖	d												
Loughborough Jn	d												
Herne Hill 4	d												
Tulse Hill 3	d					23 42							
Streatham 4	d					23 46							
London Victoria 15 ⊖	d	23 17	23 19	23 32				23 36			23 47	23 49	
Battersea Park 4	d		23 23									23 53	
Milton Keynes Central	d												
Watford Junction	d												23 17
Harrow & Wealdstone ⊖	d												23 23
Wembley Central ⊖	d												
Shepherd's Bush ⊖	d												23 45
Kensington (Olympia) ⊖	d												23 48
West Brompton ⊖	d												23 50
Clapham Junction 10	d	23 23	23 27	23 38				23 42			23 53	23 56	00 02
Wandsworth Common	d		23 30									23 59	
Balham 4 ⊖	d		23 32					23 47				00 01	
Streatham Hill	d							23 50					
West Norwood 4	d							23 53					
Gipsy Hill	d							23 56					
Crystal Palace 4	d							23 59					
Birkbeck	d												
Beckenham Junction 4	a												
Streatham Common 4	d		23 36			23 49						00 05	
Norbury	d		23 39			23 51						00 08	
Thornton Heath	d		23 42			23 54						00 11	
Selhurst 4	d		23 45	23 48		23 57						00 13	
Norwood Junction 2	a						23 38	00 03	00 02				
	d						23 38		00 05				
West Croydon 4	a		23 49				23 45						
East Croydon	a	23 37		23 52		00 01			00 08	23 56	00 06	00 16	00 22

Table 177

East and West Croydon, London-Milton Keynes and Luton via Norbury-Crystal Palace-Tulse Hill

Mondays to Fridays

Local Services

		SN MX	SN MX	SN MO	SN MX	FC	SN	FC	SN	SN		SN	FC	SN	FC	SN	FC	SN	SN	FC		SN	FC	LO	SN
				1	1	1	◇1	1		1		1	1	1	1	1				1					
East Croydon	d			23p56	23p58	00 04	00 17	00 36	00 49	01 28		02 28	02 47	03 28	03 47	04 28	04 47		05 13	05 17		05 34			
West Croydon 4	d																							05 39	05 45
Norwood Junction 2	a																		05 17			05 38		05 43	05 50
	d																		05 17			05 38		05 43	05 50
Selhurst 4	d																						05 36		
Thornton Heath	d																						05 38		
Norbury	d																						05 40		
Streatham Common 4	d																						05 43		
Beckenham Junction 4	d																								
Birkbeck	d																								
Crystal Palace 4	d	23p43	23p51																			05 42			
Gipsy Hill	d	23p45																				05 44			
West Norwood 4	d	23p48																				05 47			
Streatham Hill	d	23p52																				05 51			
Balham 4 ⊖	d	23p55																				05 54			
Wandsworth Common	d	23p58																							
Clapham Junction 10	d	00 02		00 11	00 11		00 30		01 01	01 41		02 41		03 41		04 47		05 02				05 59			
West Brompton ⊖	d																								
Kensington (Olympia) ⊖	d																								
Shepherd's Bush ⊖	d																								
Wembley Central ⊖	d																								
Harrow & Wealdstone ⊖	d																								
Watford Junction	d																								
Milton Keynes Central 10	a																								
Battersea Park 4	d	00 05																				06 02			
London Victoria 15 ⊖	a	00 12		00 18	00 18		00 37		01 09	01 49		02 49		03 49		04 54		05 10				06 07			
Streatham 4	d																						05 46		
Tulse Hill 3	d																						05 50		
Herne Hill 4	a																						05 54		
Loughborough Jn	a																								
Elephant & Castle ⊖	a																						06 00		
London Blackfriars 3 ⊖	a																05 13			05 43			06 03		
City Thameslink 3	a																05 16			05 46			06 06		
St Pancras International 15 ⊖	a																05 23			05 53			06 13		
Luton Airport Parkway 7	a																06 10			06 37			06 57		
Luton 10	a																06 12			06 40			07 00		
North Dulwich	d																								
East Dulwich	d																								
Peckham Rye 4	d																								
Queens Rd Peckham	d																								
South Bermondsey	d																								
London Bridge 4 ⊖	a		00 11			00 19		00 52					03 12		04 12				05 41						06 14

		SN	SN	LO	FC	FC		SN	SN	LO	SN	SN	SN	SN	SN	SN		SN	SN	SN	LO	SN	SN	FC	FC
					1				1		1		◇1			1		1	1					1	
East Croydon	d	05 48	05 51		06 02				06 07		06 11	06 13	06 15		06 17	06 23		06 27	06 31				06 31	06 32	
West Croydon 4	d			05 52				06 01		06 09				06 15							06 22	06 26			
Norwood Junction 2	a		05 54	05 58						06 13		06 17		06 19							06 28		06 35		
	d		05 55	05 58						06 13		06 18		06 20						06 23	06 28		06 37		
Selhurst 4	d	05 52				05 56		06 06	06 10						06 20							06 31			
Thornton Heath	d	05 54				05 58		06 08							06 22							06 33			
Norbury	d	05 57				06 00		06 11							06 25							06 36			
Streatham Common 4	d	05 59				06 03		06 13							06 27							06 38			
Beckenham Junction 4	d																								
Birkbeck	d																								
Crystal Palace 4	d		05 59																	06 27					
Gipsy Hill	d		06 01																	06 29					
West Norwood 4	d		06 04																	06 32					
Streatham Hill	d																			06 36					
Balham 4 ⊖	d	06 03						06 17							06 31					06 39		06 42			
Wandsworth Common	d	06 05						06 19							06 33					06 41		06 44			
Clapham Junction 10	d	06 09						06 23	06 18		06 21		06 25		06 37			06 38	06 41	06 45		06 48			
West Brompton ⊖	d																								
Kensington (Olympia) ⊖	d																								
Shepherd's Bush ⊖	d																								
Wembley Central ⊖	d																								
Harrow & Wealdstone ⊖	d																								
Watford Junction	d																								
Milton Keynes Central 10	a																								
Battersea Park 4	d	06 13						06 27							06 41					06 48		06 52			
London Victoria 15 ⊖	a	06 18						06 31	06 25		06 28		06 32		06 45			06 45	06 48	06 53		06 58			
Streatham 4	d					06 06																			06 36
Tulse Hill 3	d		06 07			06 10																			06 40
Herne Hill 4	a					06 14																			06 44
Loughborough Jn	a					06 19																			06 49
Elephant & Castle ⊖	a					06 23																			06 53
London Blackfriars 3 ⊖	a				06 24	06 27																		06 52	06 57
City Thameslink 3	a				06 26	06 32																		06 54	07 02
St Pancras International 15 ⊖	a				06 33	06 39																		07 01	07 09
Luton Airport Parkway 7	a				07 08	07 24																		07 37	07 49
Luton 10	a				07 11	07 26																		07 40	07 54
North Dulwich	d		06 10																						
East Dulwich	d		06 12																						
Peckham Rye 4	d		06 15																						
Queens Rd Peckham	d		06 17																						
South Bermondsey	d		06 20																						
London Bridge 4 ⊖	a		06 24									06 42		06 33		06 39							06 49		

East and West Croydon, London-Milton Keynes and Luton via Norbury-Crystal Palace-Tulse Hill

Local Services

Station		SN		SN	LO	SN 1	SN	FC 1	SN	SN	SN	FC		SN	SN	SN	SN 1	SN	LO	SN 1	SN 1	SN 1		SN	FC 1
East Croydon	d			06 39		06 42		06 44		06 45							06 54			06 57	07 00	07 05			07 09
West Croydon 4	d	06 31			06 39										06 45				06 52					06 58	
Norwood Junction 2	a			06 43	06 43										06 49				06 58						
	d			06 43	06 43									06 47	06 50			06 53	06 58						
Selhurst 4	d	06 35								06 48														07 02	
Thornton Heath	d	06 37								06 50														07 04	
Norbury	d	06 40								06 53														07 07	
Streatham Common 4	d	06 43								06 56														07 10	
Beckenham Junction 4	d																								
Birkbeck	d																								
Crystal Palace 4	d						06 39		06 44					06 51		06 51		06 57							
Gipsy Hill	d						06 41							06 53				06 59							
West Norwood 4	d						06 44							06 56				07 02							
Streatham Hill	d						06 48											07 06							
Balham 4 ⊖	d						06 51			07 00								07 09						07 14	
Wandsworth Common	d									07 02								07 11						07 16	
Clapham Junction 10	d					06 51	06 56			07 06								07 15				07 17		07 20	
West Brompton ⊖	d																								
Kensington (Olympia) ⊖	d																								
Shepherd's Bush ⊖	d																								
Wembley Central ⊖	d																								
Harrow & Wealdstone ⊖	d																								
Watford Junction	d																								
Milton Keynes Central 10	a																								
Battersea Park 4	d									07 09	06 45							07 18						07 23	
London Victoria 15 ⊖	a					07 00	07 05			07 16								07 25				07 25		07 30	
Streatham 4	d	06 46										06 49													
Tulse Hill 3	d	06 50										06 52		07 00											
Herne Hill 4	a											06 56													
Loughborough Jn	a											07 00													
Elephant & Castle ⊖	a											07 05													
London Blackfriars 3 ⊖	a							07 04				07 09													07 30
City Thameslink 3	a							07 08				07 14													07 32
St Pancras International 15 ⊖	a							07 15				07 21													07 39
Luton Airport Parkway 7	a							07 53																	08 09
Luton 10	a							07 56																	08 12
North Dulwich	d	06 53												07 03											
East Dulwich	d	06 55												07 05											
Peckham Rye 4	d	06 59									06 56			07 07											
Queens Rd Peckham	d	07 02									06 59			07 10											
South Bermondsey	d	07 04									07 01			07 12											
London Bridge 4 ⊖	a	07 11		06 55					07 06		07 08			07 19	07 04	07 16	07 11			07 13	07 16				

Station		SN	LO	SN	SN ◇1	SN 1	SN	SN		SN	FC	SN	SN	SN	FC 1	SN	SN	SN 1		SN 1	SN ◇1	SN	LO	SN 1	SN 1
East Croydon	d	07 10			07 15	07 15									07 24	07 26	07 18	07 27		07 28	07 31			07 32	07 35
West Croydon 4	d		07 09	07 13								07 01										07 17	07 22		
Norwood Junction 2	a	07 14	07 13	07 17																		07 21	07 28		
	d	07 14	07 13	07 18																		07 22	07 28		
Selhurst 4	d											07 05					07 21								
Thornton Heath	d											07 07					07 23								
Norbury	d											07 10					07 26								
Streatham Common 4	d											07 13					07 28								
Beckenham Junction 4	d												07 13												
Birkbeck	d												07 16												
Crystal Palace 4	d						07 13	07 14					07 20	07 21								07 26			
Gipsy Hill	d						07 15						07 22									07 28			
West Norwood 4	d						07 18						07 25									07 31			
Streatham Hill	d						07 22															07 35			
Balham 4 ⊖	d						07 25										07 32					07 39			
Wandsworth Common	d						07 27										07 34					07 41			
Clapham Junction 10	d				07 24	07 27	07 31									07 37	07 38				07 41	07 45			
West Brompton ⊖	d																								
Kensington (Olympia) ⊖	d																								
Shepherd's Bush ⊖	d																								
Wembley Central ⊖	d																								
Harrow & Wealdstone ⊖	d																								
Watford Junction	d																								
Milton Keynes Central 10	a																								
Battersea Park 4	d						07 35			07 15							07 42					07 48			
London Victoria 15 ⊖	a				07 33	07 36	07 41									07 46	07 48				07 49	07 57			
Streatham 4	d										07 16	07 19													
Tulse Hill 3	d										07 20	07 24	07 29												
Herne Hill 4	a										07 23				07 40										
Loughborough Jn	a										07 27														
Elephant & Castle ⊖	a										07 31														
London Blackfriars 3 ⊖	a										07 35				07 51										
City Thameslink 3	a										07 38				07 56										
St Pancras International 15 ⊖	a										07 45				08 03										
Luton Airport Parkway 7	a										08 21				08 37										
Luton 10	a										08 24				08 40										
North Dulwich	d											07 27	07 32												
East Dulwich	d											07 29	07 34												
Peckham Rye 4	d									07 26		07 31	07 36												
Queens Rd Peckham	d									07 29		07 34	07 39												
South Bermondsey	d									07 31		07 36	07 41												
London Bridge 4 ⊖	a	07 28		07 32				07 36		07 38		07 43	07 48	07 45				07 43		07 47				07 50	07 51

Table 177 Mondays to Fridays

East and West Croydon, London-Milton Keynes and Luton via Norbury-Crystal Palace-Tulse Hill

Local Services

Station		SN 1	SN	FC		SN	SN	LO	SN ◇1	SN	SN 1	SN 1	SN	SN		SN	SN	SN	SN	SN	FC 1	SN	SN 1	SN 1	
East Croydon	d	07 39					07 40		07 43		07 46	07 45							07 47		07 54	07 56	07 57	07 59	
West Croydon 4	d		07 28			07 31		07 39		07 44			07 34												
Norwood Junction 2	a						07 44	07 43		07 48															
	d						07 44	07 43		07 49															
Selhurst 4	d		07 32			07 35							07 38						07 50						
Thornton Heath	d		07 34			07 37							07 40						07 52						
Norbury	d		07 37			07 40							07 43						07 55						
Streatham Common 4	d		07 40			07 43							07 46						07 58						
Beckenham Junction 4	d																07 42								
Birkbeck	d																07 45								
Crystal Palace 4	d													07 43		07 44	07 49			07 52					
Gipsy Hill	d													07 45			07 51								
West Norwood 4	d													07 48			07 54								
Streatham Hill	d													07 52											
Balham 4 ⊖	d		07 44										07 50	07 55					08 02						
Wandsworth Common	d		07 46										07 52	07 57					08 04						
Clapham Junction 10	d	07 49	07 50						07 52			07 56	07 56	08 01					08 13			08 07			
West Brompton ⊖	d																		08 20						
Kensington (Olympia) ⊖	d																		08 24						
Shepherd's Bush ⊖	d																		08a26						
Wembley Central ⊖	d																								
Harrow & Wealdstone ⊖	d																								
Watford Junction	d																								
Milton Keynes Central 10	a																								
Battersea Park 4	d		07 53										07 59	08 05				07 45							
London Victoria 15 ⊖	a	07 57	08 00						08 01			08 04	08 06	08 11								08 15			
Streatham 4	d			07 38		07 46																			
Tulse Hill 3	d			07 42		07 52											07 59								
Herne Hill 4	a			07 46																					
Loughborough Jn	a			07 50																					
Elephant & Castle ⊖	a			07 54																					
London Blackfriars 3 ⊖	a			07 58																	08 20				
City Thameslink 3	a			08 00																	08 23				
St Pancras International 15 ⊖	a			08 07																	08 31				
Luton Airport Parkway 7	a																				09 00				
Luton 10	a																				09 04				
North Dulwich	d					07 55											08 02								
East Dulwich	d					07 57											08 04								
Peckham Rye 4	d					07 59											08 06	07 56							
Queens Rd Peckham	d					08 02											08 09	07 59							
South Bermondsey	d					08 04											08 11	08 01							
London Bridge 4 ⊖	a					08 11	07 58			08 05	08 01					08 07	08 18	08 08		08 15			08 13	08 17	

Station		SN ◇1	SN	SN	LO	SN 1	SN 1	SN 1	SN ◇1	FC		SN	LO	SN 1	SN	SN	SN ◇1	SN 1	SN	SN 1		SN	SN	SN	SN
East Croydon	d	08 01				08 02	08 03	08 05	08 08			08 10		08 11			08 14	08 15		08 07					
West Croydon 4	d			07 47	07 52								08 09		07 58	08 01			08 05						
Norwood Junction 2	a			07 51	07 58							08 14	08 13												
	d			07 52	07 58							08 14	08 13												
Selhurst 4	d		07 53												08 02	08 05			08 09	08 13					
Thornton Heath	d		07 55												08 04	08 07			08 11	08 16					
Norbury	d		07 58												08 07	08 10			08 14	08 20					
Streatham Common 4	d		08 01												08 10	08 13			08 17	08 23					
Beckenham Junction 4	d																							08 12	
Birkbeck	d																							08 15	
Crystal Palace 4	d			07 56																		08 13	08 15	08 19	
Gipsy Hill	d			07 58																		08 15		08 21	
West Norwood 4	d			08 01																		08 18		08 24	
Streatham Hill	d			08 05																		08 22			
Balham 4 ⊖	d		08 05	08 08											08 14				08 21	08 28		08 25			
Wandsworth Common	d		08 07	08 10											08 16					08 31		08 27			
Clapham Junction 10	d	08 11	08 11	08 14					08 18					08 21	08 20		08 24	08 27	08 26	08 38		08 31			
West Brompton ⊖	d																			08 47					
Kensington (Olympia) ⊖	d																			08 50					
Shepherd's Bush ⊖	d																			08 53					
Wembley Central ⊖	d																			09s08					
Harrow & Wealdstone ⊖	d																			09 13					
Watford Junction	d																			09 20					
Milton Keynes Central 10	a																			10 01					
Battersea Park 4	d		08 15	08 18											08 23							08 35			08 15
London Victoria 15 ⊖	a	08 19	08 21	08 24					08 26					08 29	08 30		08 32	08 35	08 36			08 41			
Streatham 4	d									08 09						08 16									
Tulse Hill 3	d									08 13						08 22								08 28	
Herne Hill 4	a									08 17															
Loughborough Jn	a									08 23															
Elephant & Castle ⊖	a									08 27															
London Blackfriars 3 ⊖	a									08 32															
City Thameslink 3	a									08 35															
St Pancras International 15 ⊖	a									08 43															
Luton Airport Parkway 7	a									09 27															
Luton 10	a									09 32															
North Dulwich	d															08 25								08 31	
East Dulwich	d															08 27								08 33	
Peckham Rye 4	d															08 29								08 35	08 26
Queens Rd Peckham	d															08 32								08 38	08 29
South Bermondsey	d															08 34								08 40	08 31
London Bridge 4 ⊖	a					08 19	08 21	08 23				08 28				08 41							08 37	08 49	08 38

Table 177

Mondays to Fridays

East and West Croydon, London-Milton Keynes and Luton via Norbury-Crystal Palace-Tulse Hill

Local Services

		SN	FC ■	SN ■	SN ■	SN		SN	SN	SN ■	SN ■	SN ◇■	SN	LO	SN ■	SN ■		SN ■	SN	FC	SN	SN	FC ■	LO	SN
East Croydon ⇌	d		08 21	08 21	08 25			08 26	08 18	08 27	08 29	08 30			08 33	08 32		08 37				08 39	08 39		08 42
West Croydon [4] ⇌	d	08 16											08 19	08 23					08 26		08 31			08 39	
Norwood Junction [2]	a	08 20											08 23	08 28										08 43	08 46
	d	08 21											08 25	08 28										08 43	08 47
Selhurst [4]	d								08 21										08 31		08 35	08 43			
Thornton Heath	d								08 23										08 33		08 37	08 46			
Norbury	d								08 26										08 36		08 40	08 49			
Streatham Common [4]	d								08 28										08 38		08 43	08 52			
Beckenham Junction [4] ⇌	d																								
Birkbeck ⇌	d																								
Crystal Palace [4]	d					08 24							08 29												
Gipsy Hill	d												08 31												
West Norwood [4]	d												08 34												
Streatham Hill	d												08 38												
Balham [4] ⊖	d								08 32				08 41						08 43			08 58			
Wandsworth Common	d								08 34				08 43						08 45			09 00			
Clapham Junction [10]	d							08 37	08 38			08 40	08 47					08 48	08 50			09 05			
West Brompton ⊖	d																					09 12			
Kensington (Olympia) ⊖	d																					09 15			
Shepherd's Bush ⊖	d																					09a18			
Wembley Central ⊖	d																								
Harrow & Wealdstone ⊖	d																								
Watford Junction	d																								
Milton Keynes Central [10]	a																								
Battersea Park [4]	d								08 42				08 50						08 53						
London Victoria [15] ⊖	a							08 45	08 48			08 48	08 57					08 58	09 00						
Streatham [4]	d																			08 39	08 50				
Tulse Hill [3]	d		08 36																	08 43	08 54				
Herne Hill [4]	a																			08 46			08 55		
Loughborough Jn	a																			08 50					
Elephant & Castle ⊖	a		08 48																	08 57			09 05		
London Blackfriars [3] ⊖	a		08 53																	09 01			09 09		
City Thameslink [3]	a		08 56																	09 04			09 12		
St Pancras International [15] ⊖	a		09 03																	09 11			09 19		
Luton Airport Parkway [7]	a		09 37																	09 59			09 52		
Luton [10]	a		09 40																	10 04			09 56		
North Dulwich	d																				08 57				
East Dulwich	d																				08 59				
Peckham Rye [4]	d																				09 01				
Queens Rd Peckham	d																				09 04				
South Bermondsey	d																				09 06				
London Bridge [4] ⊖	a	08 35		08 39	08 41	08 47				08 45	08 47				08 52	08 54					09 14				09 01

		SN ◇■ H		SN	SN ■	SN	SN ◇■ H	SN	SN	SN	SN	SN ■		FC ■	SN	SN	SN ■	SN ■	SN ◇■	SN	LO	SN ■		SN	FC
East Croydon ⇌	d	08 43			08 45		08 50					08 51		08 54	08 54	08 48	08 57	08 59	09 01			09 02		09 05	
West Croydon [4] ⇌	d			08 44																08 49	08 52				
Norwood Junction [2]	a			08 49																08 53	08 58			09 09	
	d			08 49																08 54	08 58			09 09	
Selhurst [4]	d															08 51									
Thornton Heath	d															08 53									
Norbury	d															08 56									
Streatham Common [4]	d															08 58									
Beckenham Junction [4] ⇌	d									08 43															
Birkbeck ⇌	d									08 46															
Crystal Palace [4]	d							08 40	08 44	08 50	08 51									08 58					
Gipsy Hill	d							08 43		08 52										09 00					
West Norwood [4]	d							08 46		08 55										09 03					
Streatham Hill	d							08 49												09 07					
Balham [4] ⊖	d							08 55								09 02				09 10					
Wandsworth Common	d							08 57								09 04				09 12					
Clapham Junction [10]	d	08 53			08 56		09 01	09 01							09 04	09 08			09 11	09 16					
West Brompton ⊖	d																								
Kensington (Olympia) ⊖	d																								
Shepherd's Bush ⊖	d																								
Wembley Central ⊖	d																								
Harrow & Wealdstone ⊖	d																								
Watford Junction	d																								
Milton Keynes Central [10]	a																								
Battersea Park [4]	d					08 45		09 05								09 12				09 19					
London Victoria [15] ⊖	a	09 01			09 04		09 09	09 11							09 13	09 18			09 22	09 27					
Streatham [4]	d																								09 08
Tulse Hill [3]	d									08 59															09 16
Herne Hill [4]	a																								09 19
Loughborough Jn	a																								09 23
Elephant & Castle ⊖	a																								09 29
London Blackfriars [3] ⊖	a													09 21											09 33
City Thameslink [3]	a													09 25											09 36
St Pancras International [15] ⊖	a													09 32											09 43
Luton Airport Parkway [7]	a													10 01											10 30
Luton [10]	a													10 04											10 34
North Dulwich	d									09 02															
East Dulwich	d									09 04															
Peckham Rye [4]	d					08 56				09 06															
Queens Rd Peckham	d					08 59				09 09															
South Bermondsey	d					09 01				09 11															
London Bridge [4] ⊖	a			09 04		09 08			09 06	09 20	09 14	09 08					09 13	09 16				09 20		09 23	

Table 177

Mondays to Fridays

East and West Croydon, London-Milton Keynes and Luton via Norbury-Crystal Palace-Tulse Hill

Local Services

		FC ■	LO	SN ■	SN	SN	SN ■	SN ◇■ H		SN ■	SN	SN	SN	SN ◇■ H	SN	SN ■ H	SN	SN ■		SN	SN	LO	SN	SN	FC ■
East Croydon ⇌	d	09 09		09 11			09 08	09 14		09 14				09 22		09 26	09 17	09 29			09 20			09 30	09 32
West Croydon [4] ⇌	d		09 09		08 56	09 01														09 15		09 22			
Norwood Junction [2]	a		09 13																	09 19	09 24	09 28		09 34	
	d		09 13																	09 22	09 25	09 28		09 35	
Selhurst [4]	d				09 01	09 05	09 13										09 21								
Thornton Heath	d				09 03	09 07	09 16										09 23								
Norbury	d				09 06	09 10	09 19										09 26								
Streatham Common [4]	d				09 09	09 13	09 21										09 28								
Beckenham Junction [4] ⇌	d																						09 23		
Birkbeck ⇌	d																						09 26		
Crystal Palace [4]	d										09 13	09 14			09 21					09 26			09 30		
Gipsy Hill	d										09 15									09 28			09 32		
West Norwood [4]	d										09 18									09 31			09 35		
Streatham Hill	d										09 22									09 35					
Balham [4] ⊖	d				09 13		09 28				09 25						09 32			09 41					
Wandsworth Common	d				09 15		09 30				09 27						09 34			09 43					
Clapham Junction [10]	d			09 21	09 19		09 38	09 24		09 27	09 31			09 33		09 36	09 38	09 39		09 47					
West Brompton ⊖	d						09 47																		
Kensington (Olympia) ⊖	d						09 50																		
Shepherd's Bush ⊖	d						09 53																		
Wembley Central ⊖	d						10s08																		
Harrow & Wealdstone ⊖	d						10 13																		
Watford Junction	d						10 20																		
Milton Keynes Central [10]	a						11 02																		
Battersea Park [4]	d				09 22						09 35		09 15				09 42			09 50					
London Victoria [15] ⊖	a			09 29	09 31			09 32		09 35	09 39			09 41		09 44	09 48	09 48		09 58					
Streatham [4]	d					09 20																			
Tulse Hill [3]	d					09 25																	09 39		
Herne Hill [4]	a																								
Loughborough Jn	a																								
Elephant & Castle ⊖	a	09 33																							
London Blackfriars [3] ⊖	a	09 37																							09 53
City Thameslink [3]	a	09 40																							09 56
St Pancras International [15] ⊖	a	09 47																							10 03
Luton Airport Parkway [7]	a	10 21																							10 37
Luton [10]	a	10 24																							10 40
North Dulwich	d					09 28																	09 42		
East Dulwich	d					09 30																	09 44		
Peckham Rye [4]	d					09 32							09 26										09 46		
Queens Rd Peckham	d					09 35							09 29										09 49		
South Bermondsey	d					09 37							09 31										09 51		
London Bridge [4] ⊖	a					09 44						09 37	09 38		09 44						09 42		09 58	10 01	

		SN ■	SN ■	SN ◇■ H		SN	FC	SN	FC	LO	SN ◇■	SN ■	SN	SN	SN		SN	FC ■	SN ◇■ H	SN	SN ◇■ H	SN	SN	LO	SN
East Croydon ⇌	d	09 33	09 37	09 39							09 43	09 44						09 47	09 55	09 47	10 00		09 51		
West Croydon [4] ⇌	d					09 28		09 31		09 39			09 35									09 45		09 52	
Norwood Junction [2]	a		09 41							09 43												09 50	09 55	09 58	
	d		09 42							09 43												09 52	09 55	09 58	
Selhurst [4]	d					09 32		09 35					09 39							09 50					
Thornton Heath	d					09 34		09 37					09 41							09 52					
Norbury	d					09 37		09 40					09 44							09 55					
Streatham Common [4]	d					09 40		09 43					09 47							09 58					
Beckenham Junction [4] ⇌	d																								09 53
Birkbeck ⇌	d																								09 56
Crystal Palace [4]	d													09 43			09b51					09 56			10 00
Gipsy Hill	d													09 46								09 58			10 02
West Norwood [4]	d													09 49								10 01			10 05
Streatham Hill	d													09 52								10 05			
Balham [4] ⊖	d					09 44							09 52	09 56						10 02		10 09			
Wandsworth Common	d					09 46							09 54	09 58						10 04		10 11			
Clapham Junction [10]	d			09 48		09 50					09 53	09 56	09 58	10 02					10 04	10 08	10 09	10 15			
West Brompton ⊖	d																								
Kensington (Olympia) ⊖	d																								
Shepherd's Bush ⊖	d																								
Wembley Central ⊖	d																								
Harrow & Wealdstone ⊖	d																								
Watford Junction	d																								
Milton Keynes Central [10]	a																								
Battersea Park [4]	d					09 53								10 05	09 45					10 11		10 19			
London Victoria [15] ⊖	a			09 58		10 00					10 00	10 02	10 05	10 11					10 11	10 16	10 16	10 24			
Streatham [4]	d						09 38	09 46	09 53																
Tulse Hill [3]	d						09 42	09 54	09 57																10 09
Herne Hill [4]	a						09 46		10 01																
Loughborough Jn	a						09 50		10 04																
Elephant & Castle ⊖	a						09 54		10 08																
London Blackfriars [3] ⊖	a						09 59		10 12									10 08							
City Thameslink [3]	a						10 02		10 15									10 10							
St Pancras International [15] ⊖	a						10 09		10 22									10 17							
Luton Airport Parkway [7]	a						10 59											10 51							
Luton [10]	a						11 04											10 54							
North Dulwich	d							09 57																	10 12
East Dulwich	d							09 59																	10 14
Peckham Rye [4]	d							10 01							09 56										10 16
Queens Rd Peckham	d							10 04							09 59										10 19
South Bermondsey	d							10 06							10 01										10 21
London Bridge [4] ⊖	a	09 51	09 56					10 11							10 06		10 11						10 09		10 26

b arr. 0945

East and West Croydon, London-Milton Keynes and Luton via Norbury-Crystal Palace-Tulse Hill

Local Services

		SN 1	SN	FC 1	SN 1	FC	LO	SN ◇1 ⌶	SN	SN	FC	SN	SN 1	SN 1	SN	SN	SN	FC 1	SN ◇1 ⌶	SN ◇1		SN	SN	SN	LO
East Croydon	d	09 55	10 00	10 02	10 07			10 11					10 10	10 14				10 17	10 24	10 28		10 17		10 21	
West Croydon 4	d						10 09		09 58	10 01		10 04											10 15		10 22
Norwood Junction 2	a	10 00	10 04		10 12		10 13																10 19	10 25	10 28
	d	10 00	10 05		10 13		10 13																10 22	10 25	10 28
Selhurst 4	d								10 02	10 05		10 09	10 14									10 20			
Thornton Heath	d								10 04	10 07		10 11	10 16									10 22			
Norbury	d								10 07	10 10		10 14	10 19									10 25			
Streatham Common 4	d								10 10	10 13		10 17	10 22									10 28			
Beckenham Junction 4	d																								
Birkbeck	d																								
Crystal Palace 4	d														10 13		10 21						10 26		
Gipsy Hill	d														10 15								10 29		
West Norwood 4	d														10 18								10 32		
Streatham Hill	d														10 22								10 35		
Balham 4 ⊖	d								10 14			10 21	10 29		10 25							10 32	10 39		
Wandsworth Common	d								10 16			10 23	10 31		10 27							10 34	10 41		
Clapham Junction 10	d							10 21	10 20			10 27	10 38	10 26	10 31				10 34	10 38		10 38	10 45		
West Brompton ⊖	d												10 47												
Kensington (Olympia) ⊖	d												10 50												
Shepherd's Bush ⊖	d												10 53												
Wembley Central ⊖	d												11s08												
Harrow & Wealdstone ⊖	d												11 13												
Watford Junction	d												11 20												
Milton Keynes Central 10	a												12 01												
Battersea Park 4	d								10 23						10 35	10 15						10 41	10 49		
London Victoria 15 ⊖	a							10 28	10 28			10 34		10 35	10 39				10 40	10 44		10 46	10 53		
Streatham 4	d					10 08				10 16	10 23														
Tulse Hill 3	d					10 12				10 24	10 27														
Herne Hill 4	a					10 16					10 31														
Loughborough Jn	a					10 19					10 34														
Elephant & Castle ⊖	a					10 23					10 38														
London Blackfriars 3 ⊖	a			10 23		10 27					10 42							10 37							
City Thameslink 3	a			10 26		10 30					10 45							10 40							
St Pancras International 15 ⊖	a			10 33		10 37					10 52							10 47							
Luton Airport Parkway 7	a			11 06		11 26												11 21							
Luton 10	a			11 09		11 30												11 24							
North Dulwich	d									10 27															
East Dulwich	d									10 29															
Peckham Rye 4	d									10 31						10 26									
Queens Rd Peckham	d									10 34						10 29									
South Bermondsey	d									10 36						10 31									
London Bridge 4 ⊖	a	10 13	10 29		10 25					10 41						10 36	10 41							10 39	

		SN	SN 1	SN	FC 1	SN 1		FC	SN 1	LO	SN ◇1	SN	SN	FC	SN	SN 1	SN	SN	SN	FC 1	SN ◇1	SN ◇1 ⌶	SN	SN ◇1	SN
East Croydon	d		10 25	10 30	10 32	10 33			10 38		10 41					10 44				10 47	10 53	10 56	10 47	11 00	
West Croydon 4	d									10 39		10 28	10 31		10 34										10 45
Norwood Junction 2	a		10 29	10 34					10 42	10 43															10 49
	d		10 30	10 35					10 43	10 43															10 52
Selhurst 4	d											10 32	10 35		10 39								10 50		
Thornton Heath	d											10 34	10 37		10 41								10 52		
Norbury	d											10 37	10 40		10 44								10 55		
Streatham Common 4	d											10 40	10 43		10 47								10 58		
Beckenham Junction 4	d	10 23																							
Birkbeck	d	10 26																							
Crystal Palace 4	d	10 30															10 43		10 51						10 56
Gipsy Hill	d	10 32															10 45								10 59
West Norwood 4	d	10 35															10 48								11 02
Streatham Hill	d																10 52								11 05
Balham 4 ⊖	d											10 44			10 51		10 55						11 02		11 09
Wandsworth Common	d											10 46			10 53		10 57						11 04		11 11
Clapham Junction 10	d										10 50	10 50			10 57	10 56	11 01				11 03	11 06	11 08	11 10	11 15
West Brompton ⊖	d																								
Kensington (Olympia) ⊖	d																								
Shepherd's Bush ⊖	d																								
Wembley Central ⊖	d																								
Harrow & Wealdstone ⊖	d																								
Watford Junction	d																								
Milton Keynes Central 10	a																								
Battersea Park 4	d											10 53					11 05	10 45					11 11		11 18
London Victoria 15 ⊖	a										10 57	10 58			11 04	11 05	11 09				11 09	11 12	11 16	11 16	11 23
Streatham 4	d							10 38					10 46	10 53											
Tulse Hill 3	d	10 39						10 42					10 54	10 57											
Herne Hill 4	a							10 46						11 01											
Loughborough Jn	a							10 49						11 04											
Elephant & Castle ⊖	a							10 53						11 08											
London Blackfriars 3 ⊖	a				10 52			10 57						11 12						11 07					
City Thameslink 3	a				10 56			11 00						11 15						11 10					
St Pancras International 15 ⊖	a				11 03			11 07						11 22						11 17					
Luton Airport Parkway 7	a				11 37			11 56												11 51					
Luton 10	a				11 40			12 00												11 54					
North Dulwich	d	10 42											10 57												
East Dulwich	d	10 44											10 59												
Peckham Rye 4	d	10 46											11 01					10 56							
Queens Rd Peckham	d	10 49											11 04					10 59							
South Bermondsey	d	10 51											11 06					11 01							
London Bridge 4 ⊖	a	10 56	10 43	10 59		10 49			10 55				11 11					11 06	11 11						

Table 177

Mondays to Fridays

East and West Croydon, London-Milton Keynes and Luton via Norbury-Crystal Palace-Tulse Hill

Local Services

		SN		LO	SN	SN 1	SN	FC 1	SN 1	FC	LO	SN ◇1		SN	SN	FC	SN 1	SN	SN 1	SN	SN	SN	FC 1	SN	SN ◇1 ⌶
East Croydon	d	10 51				10 55	11 00	11 02	11 07			11 11					11 14		11 11				11 17	11 17	11 24
West Croydon 4	d			10 52							11 09			10 58	11 01			11 04							
Norwood Junction 2	a	10 55		10 58		11 00	11 04		11 12		11 13														
	d	10 55		10 58		11 00	11 05		11 13		11 13														
Selhurst 4	d													11 02	11 05			11 09	11 16					11 20	
Thornton Heath	d													11 04	11 07			11 11	11 18					11 22	
Norbury	d													11 07	11 10			11 14	11 21					11 25	
Streatham Common 4	d													11 10	11 13			11 17	11 24					11 28	
Beckenham Junction 4	d				10 53																				
Birkbeck	d				10 56																				
Crystal Palace 4	d				11 00															11 13		11 21			
Gipsy Hill	d				11 02															11 15					
West Norwood 4	d				11 05															11 18					
Streatham Hill	d																			11 22					
Balham 4 ⊖	d													11 14				11 21	11 28	11 25				11 32	
Wandsworth Common	d													11 16				11 23	11 30	11 27				11 34	
Clapham Junction 10	d											11 20		11 20			11 26	11 27	11 38	11 31				11 38	11 33
West Brompton ⊖	d																		11 47						
Kensington (Olympia) ⊖	d																		11 50						
Shepherd's Bush ⊖	d																		11 53						
Wembley Central ⊖	d																		12s08						
Harrow & Wealdstone ⊖	d																		12 13						
Watford Junction	d																		12 20						
Milton Keynes Central 10	a																		13 01						
Battersea Park 4	d													11 23						11 35	11 15			11 41	
London Victoria 15 ⊖	a											11 27		11 28			11 32	11 34		11 39					11 40
Streatham 4	d									11 08					11 16	11 23									
Tulse Hill 3	d				11 09					11 12					11 24	11 27									
Herne Hill 4	a									11 16						11 31									
Loughborough Jn	a									11 19						11 34									
Elephant & Castle ⊖	a									11 23						11 38									
London Blackfriars 3 ⊖	a							11 22		11 27						11 42							11 37		
City Thameslink 3	a							11 26		11 30						11 45							11 40		
St Pancras International 15 ⊖	a							11 33		11 37						11 52							11 47		
Luton Airport Parkway 7	a							12 07		12 26													12 21		
Luton 10	a							12 10		12 30													12 24		
North Dulwich	d				11 12										11 27										
East Dulwich	d				11 14										11 29										
Peckham Rye 4	d				11 16										11 31						11 26				
Queens Rd Peckham	d				11 19										11 34						11 29				
South Bermondsey	d				11 21										11 36						11 31				
London Bridge 4 ⊖	a	11 09			11 26	11 13	11 29		11 25						11 41						11 36	11 41			

		SN ◇1	SN	SN	LO	SN	SN 1	SN		FC 1	SN 1	SN 1	FC	LO	SN ◇1	SN	SN	FC	SN 1	SN	SN	SN	SN	FC 1	SN
East Croydon	d	11 28		11 21			11 25	11 30		11 32	11 33	11 37			11 41				11 44					11 47	11 47
West Croydon 4	d		11 16		11 22									11 39		11 28	11 31			11 34					
Norwood Junction 2	a		11 20	11 26	11 28		11 29	11 34				11 42		11 43											
	d		11 22	11 26	11 28		11 30	11 35				11 43		11 43											
Selhurst 4	d															11 32	11 35			11 39					11 50
Thornton Heath	d															11 34	11 37			11 41					11 52
Norbury	d															11 37	11 40			11 44					11 55
Streatham Common 4	d															11 40	11 43			11 47					11 58
Beckenham Junction 4	d					11 23																			
Birkbeck	d					11 26																			
Crystal Palace 4	d		11 26			11 30															11 43		11 51		
Gipsy Hill	d		11 29			11 32															11 45				
West Norwood 4	d		11 32			11 35															11 48				
Streatham Hill	d		11 35																		11 52				
Balham 4 ⊖	d		11 40													11 44				11 51	11 55				12 02
Wandsworth Common	d		11 42													11 46				11 53	11 57				12 04
Clapham Junction 10	d	11 37	11 46												11 50	11 50			11 56	11 57	12 01				12 08
West Brompton ⊖	d																								
Kensington (Olympia) ⊖	d																								
Shepherd's Bush ⊖	d																								
Wembley Central ⊖	d																								
Harrow & Wealdstone ⊖	d																								
Watford Junction	d																								
Milton Keynes Central 10	a																								
Battersea Park 4	d		11 49													11 53					12 05	11 45			12 11
London Victoria 15 ⊖	a	11 44	11 54												11 57	11 58			12 02	12 04	12 09				
Streatham 4	d												11 38				11 46	11 53							
Tulse Hill 3	d					11 39							11 42				11 54	11 57							
Herne Hill 4	a												11 46					12 01							
Loughborough Jn	a												11 49					12 04							
Elephant & Castle ⊖	a												11 53					12 08							
London Blackfriars 3 ⊖	a									11 52			11 57					12 12						12 07	
City Thameslink 3	a									11 56			12 00					12 15						12 10	
St Pancras International 15 ⊖	a									12 03			12 07					12 22						12 17	
Luton Airport Parkway 7	a									12 37			12 56											12 51	
Luton 10	a									12 40			13 00											12 54	
North Dulwich	d					11 42											11 57								
East Dulwich	d					11 44											11 59								
Peckham Rye 4	d					11 46											12 01					11 56			
Queens Rd Peckham	d					11 49											12 04					11 59			
South Bermondsey	d					11 51											12 06					12 01			
London Bridge 4 ⊖	a			11 39		11 56	11 43	11 59			11 49	11 55					12 11					12 06	12 11		

East and West Croydon, London-Milton Keynes and Luton via Norbury-Crystal Palace-Tulse Hill

Local Services

		SN ◇1	SN ◇1	SN ◇1		SN	SN	LO	SN	SN 1	SN	SN	FC 1	SN 1		FC	SN	FC	LO	SN ◇1	SN 1	SN	SN 1	SN	SN
East Croydon ⇌	d	11 53	11 56	12 00			11 51			11 55		12 00	12 02	12 07						12 11	12 14		12 10		
West Croydon 4 ⇌	d					11 45		11 52			11 58						12 01		12 09			12 04			
Norwood Junction 2	a					11 49	11 55	11 58		12 00		12 04		12 12					12 13						
	d					11 52	11 55	11 58		12 00		12 05		12 13					12 13						
Selhurst 4	d										12 02						12 05					12 09	12 14		
Thornton Heath	d										12 04						12 07					12 11	12 16		
Norbury	d										12 07						12 10					12 14	12 19		
Streatham Common 4	d										12 10						12 13					12 17	12 22		
Beckenham Junction 4 ⇌	d								11 53																
Birkbeck ⇌	d								11 56																
Crystal Palace 4	d					11 56			12 00															12 13	
Gipsy Hill	d					11 59			12 02															12 15	
West Norwood 4	d					12 02			12 05															12 18	
Streatham Hill	d					12 05																		12 22	
Balham 4 ⊖	d					12 09					12 14											12 21	12 28	12 25	
Wandsworth Common	d					12 11					12 16											12 23	12 30	12 27	
Clapham Junction 10	d	12 03	12 06	12 12		12 15					12 20									12 20	12 26	12 27	12 38	12 31	
West Brompton ⊖	d																						12 47		
Kensington (Olympia) ⊖	d																						12 50		
Shepherd's Bush ⊖	d																						12 53		
Wembley Central ⊖	d																						13s08		
Harrow & Wealdstone ⊖	d																						13 13		
Watford Junction	d																						13 20		
Milton Keynes Central 10	a																						14 01		
Battersea Park 4	d					12 18					12 23													12 35	12 15
London Victoria 15 ⊖	a	12 09	12 12	12 18		12 23					12 28									12 28	12 32	12 34		12 39	
Streatham 4	d															12 08	12 16	12 23							
Tulse Hill 3	d								12 09							12 12	12 24	12 27							
Herne Hill 4	a															12 16		12 31							
Loughborough Jn	a															12 19		12 34							
Elephant & Castle ⊖	a															12 23		12 38							
London Blackfriars 3 ⊖	a												12 22			12 27		12 42							
City Thameslink 3	a												12 26			12 30		12 45							
St Pancras International 15 ⊖	a												12 33			12 37		12 52							
Luton Airport Parkway 7	a												13 07			13 26									
Luton 10	a												13 10			13 30									
North Dulwich	d								12 12								12 27								
East Dulwich	d								12 14								12 29								
Peckham Rye 4	d								12 16								12 31								12 26
Queens Rd Peckham	d								12 19								12 34								12 29
South Bermondsey	d								12 21								12 36								12 31
London Bridge 4 ⊖	a						12 09		12 26	12 13		12 29		12 25			12 41								12 36

		SN	FC 1	SN	SN ◇1	SN ◇1	SN	SN	LO	SN		SN 1	SN	FC 1	SN 1	SN 1	FC	LO	SN ◇1	SN	SN	FC	SN 1	SN	SN
East Croydon ⇌	d		12 17	12 17	12 24	12 28		12 21				12 25	12 30	12 32	12 33	12 37			12 41				12 44		
West Croydon 4 ⇌	d						12 15		12 22									12 39		12 28	12 31			12 34	
Norwood Junction 2	a						12 19	12 25	12 28			12 29	12 34			12 42		12 43							
	d						12 22	12 25	12 28			12 30	12 35			12 43		12 43							
Selhurst 4	d			12 20																12 32	12 35			12 39	
Thornton Heath	d			12 22																12 34	12 37			12 41	
Norbury	d			12 25																12 37	12 40			12 44	
Streatham Common 4	d			12 28																12 40	12 43			12 47	
Beckenham Junction 4 ⇌	d									12 23															
Birkbeck ⇌	d									12 26															
Crystal Palace 4	d	12 21					12 26			12 30															12 43
Gipsy Hill	d						12 29			12 32															12 45
West Norwood 4	d						12 32			12 35															12 48
Streatham Hill	d						12 35																		12 52
Balham 4 ⊖	d			12 32			12 39													12 44				12 51	12 55
Wandsworth Common	d			12 34			12 41													12 46				12 53	12 57
Clapham Junction 10	d			12 38	12 33	12 37	12 45												12 50	12 50			12 56	12 57	13 01
West Brompton ⊖	d																								
Kensington (Olympia) ⊖	d																								
Shepherd's Bush ⊖	d																								
Wembley Central ⊖	d																								
Harrow & Wealdstone ⊖	d																								
Watford Junction	d																								
Milton Keynes Central 10	a																								
Battersea Park 4	d			12 41			12 48													12 53					13 05
London Victoria 15 ⊖	a				12 40	12 44	12 53												12 57	12 58			13 02	13 04	13 09
Streatham 4	d																12 38				12 46	12 53			
Tulse Hill 3	d									12 39							12 42				12 54	12 57			
Herne Hill 4	a																12 46					13 01			
Loughborough Jn	a																12 49					13 04			
Elephant & Castle ⊖	a																12 53					13 08			
London Blackfriars 3 ⊖	a		12 37											12 52			12 57					13 12			
City Thameslink 3	a		12 40											12 56			13 00					13 15			
St Pancras International 15 ⊖	a		12 47											13 03			13 07					13 22			
Luton Airport Parkway 7	a		13 21											13 37			13 56								
Luton 10	a		13 24											13 40			14 00								
North Dulwich	d									12 42											12 57				
East Dulwich	d									12 44											12 59				
Peckham Rye 4	d									12 46											13 01				
Queens Rd Peckham	d									12 49											13 04				
South Bermondsey	d									12 51											13 06				
London Bridge 4 ⊖	a	12 41						12 39		12 56		12 43	12 59		12 49	12 55					13 11				

East and West Croydon, London-Milton Keynes and Luton via Norbury-Crystal Palace-Tulse Hill

Local Services

		SN	SN	FC 1	SN ◇1	SN ◇1		SN	SN ◇1	SN	SN	LO	SN	SN 1	SN	SN	FC 1	SN 1	FC	SN	FC	LO	SN ◇1	SN 1	SN
East Croydon ⇌	d			12 47	12 53	12 56		12 47	13 00		12 51			12 55		13 00	13 02	13 07					13 11	13 14	
West Croydon 4 ⇌	d									12 45		12 52			12 58					13 01		13 09			13 04
Norwood Junction 2	a									12 49	12 55	12 58		13 00		13 04		13 12				13 13			
	d									12 52	12 55	12 58		13 00		13 05		13 13				13 13			
Selhurst 4	d							12 50							13 02					13 05					13 09
Thornton Heath	d							12 52							13 04					13 07					13 11
Norbury	d							12 55							13 07					13 10					13 14
Streatham Common 4	d							12 58							13 10					13 13					13 17
Beckenham Junction 4 ⇌	d												12 53												
Birkbeck ⇌	d												12 56												
Crystal Palace 4	d		12 51							12 56			13 00												
Gipsy Hill	d									12 59			13 02												
West Norwood 4	d									13 02			13 05												
Streatham Hill	d									13 05															
Balham 4 ⊖	d							13 02		13 09					13 13										13 21
Wandsworth Common	d							13 04		13 11					13 15										13 23
Clapham Junction 10	d				13 03	13 06		13 08	13 10	13 15					13 20								13 20	13 26	13 27
West Brompton ⊖	d																								
Kensington (Olympia) ⊖	d																								
Shepherd's Bush ⊖	d																								
Wembley Central ⊖	d																								
Harrow & Wealdstone ⊖	d																								
Watford Junction	d																								
Milton Keynes Central 10	a																								
Battersea Park 4	d	12 45						13 11		13 18					13 23										
London Victoria 15 ⊖	a				13 09	13 12		13 16	13 16	13 23					13 28								13 28	13 32	13 34
Streatham 4	d																		13 08	13 16	13 23				
Tulse Hill 3	d												13 09						13 12	13 24	13 27				
Herne Hill 4	a																		13 16		13 31				
Loughborough Jn	a																		13 19		13 34				
Elephant & Castle ⊖	a																		13 23		13 38				
London Blackfriars 3 ⊖	a			13 07													13 22		13 27		13 42				
City Thameslink 3	a			13 10													13 26		13 30		13 45				
St Pancras International 15 ⊖	a			13 17													13 33		13 37		13 52				
Luton Airport Parkway 7	a			13 52													14 07		14 26						
Luton 10	a			13 55													14 10		14 30						
North Dulwich	d												13 12							13 27					
East Dulwich	d												13 14							13 29					
Peckham Rye 4	d	12 56											13 16							13 31					
Queens Rd Peckham	d	12 59											13 19							13 34					
South Bermondsey	d	13 01											13 21							13 36					
London Bridge 4 ⊖	a	13 06	13 11								13 09		13 26	13 13		13 29		13 25		13 41					

		SN 1		SN	SN	SN	FC 1	SN	SN ◇1	SN ◇1	SN	SN		LO	SN	SN 1	SN	FC 1	SN 1	SN 1	FC	LO		SN ◇1	SN
East Croydon ⇌	d	13 10					13 17	13 17	13 24	13 28		13 21				13 25	13 30	13 32	13 33	13 37				13 41	
West Croydon 4 ⇌	d										13 15			13 22								13 39			13 28
Norwood Junction 2	a										13 19	13 25		13 28		13 29	13 34			13 42		13 43			
	d										13 22	13 25		13 28		13 30	13 35			13 43		13 43			
Selhurst 4	d	13 13						13 20																	13 32
Thornton Heath	d	13 16						13 22																	13 34
Norbury	d	13 19						13 25																	13 37
Streatham Common 4	d	13 21						13 28																	13 40
Beckenham Junction 4 ⇌	d														13 23										
Birkbeck ⇌	d														13 26										
Crystal Palace 4	d			13 13		13 21					13 26				13 30										
Gipsy Hill	d			13 15							13 29				13 32										
West Norwood 4	d			13 18							13 32				13 35										
Streatham Hill	d			13 22							13 35														
Balham 4 ⊖	d	13 28		13 25				13 32			13 39														13 44
Wandsworth Common	d	13 30		13 27				13 34			13 41														13 46
Clapham Junction 10	d	13 38		13 31				13 38	13 33	13 37	13 45													13 50	13 50
West Brompton ⊖	d	13 47																							
Kensington (Olympia) ⊖	d	13 50																							
Shepherd's Bush ⊖	d	13 53																							
Wembley Central ⊖	d	14s08																							
Harrow & Wealdstone ⊖	d	14 13																							
Watford Junction	d	14 20																							
Milton Keynes Central 10	a	15 01																							
Battersea Park 4	d			13 35	13 15			13 41			13 48														13 53
London Victoria 15 ⊖	a			13 39					13 40	13 44	13 53													13 57	13 58
Streatham 4	d																				13 38				
Tulse Hill 3	d														13 39						13 42				
Herne Hill 4	a																				13 46				
Loughborough Jn	a																				13 49				
Elephant & Castle ⊖	a																				13 53				
London Blackfriars 3 ⊖	a						13 37											13 52			13 57				
City Thameslink 3	a						13 40											13 56			14 00				
St Pancras International 15 ⊖	a						13 47											14 03			14 07				
Luton Airport Parkway 7	a						14 21											14 37			14 56				
Luton 10	a						14 24											14 40			15 00				
North Dulwich	d														13 42										
East Dulwich	d														13 44										
Peckham Rye 4	d				13 26										13 46										
Queens Rd Peckham	d				13 29										13 49										
South Bermondsey	d				13 31										13 51										
London Bridge 4 ⊖	a				13 36	13 41						13 39			13 56	13 43	13 59		13 49	13 55					

East and West Croydon, London-Milton Keynes and Luton via Norbury-Crystal Palace-Tulse Hill

Local Services

		SN	FC	SN 1	SN	SN	SN	SN	FC 1		SN	SN ◇1	SN ◇1 ⊼	SN ◇1	SN	SN	LO	SN	SN 1	SN	FC 1	SN 1	FC	LO	SN ◇1
East Croydon	d			13 44					13 47		13 47	13 53	13 56	14 00		13 51			13 55	14 00	14 02	14 08			14 11
West Croydon 4	d	13 31			13 34										13 45		13 52							14 09	
Norwood Junction 2	a														13 49	13 55	13 58		14 00	14 04		14 12		14 13	
	d														13 52	13 55	13 58		14 00	14 05		14 13		14 13	
Selhurst 4	d	13 35			13 39						13 50														
Thornton Heath	d	13 37			13 41						13 52														
Norbury	d	13 40			13 44						13 55														
Streatham Common 4	d	13 43			13 47						13 58														
Beckenham Junction 4	d																	13 53							
Birkbeck	d																	13 56							
Crystal Palace 4	d					13 43		13 51							13 56			14 00							
Gipsy Hill	d					13 45									13 59			14 02							
West Norwood 4	d					13 48									14 02			14 05							
Streatham Hill	d					13 52									14 05										
Balham 4 ⊖	d				13 51	13 55					14 02				14 09										
Wandsworth Common	d				13 53	13 57					14 04				14 11										
Clapham Junction 10	d			13 56	13 57	14 01					14 08	14 03	14 06	14 10	14 15										14 20
West Brompton ⊖	d																								
Kensington (Olympia) ⊖	d																								
Shepherd's Bush ⊖	d																								
Wembley Central ⊖	d																								
Harrow & Wealdstone ⊖	d																								
Watford Junction	d																								
Milton Keynes Central 10	a																								
Battersea Park 4	d					14 05	13 45				14 11				14 18										
London Victoria 15 ⊖	a			14 02	14 04	14 09						14 09	14 12	14 16	14 23										14 27
Streatham 4	d	13 46	13 53																				14 08		
Tulse Hill 3	d	13 54	13 57															14 09					14 12		
Herne Hill 4	a		14 01																				14 16		
Loughborough Jn	a		14 04																				14 19		
Elephant & Castle ⊖	a		14 08																				14 23		
London Blackfriars 3 ⊖	a		14 12						14 07												14 22		14 27		
City Thameslink 3	a		14 15						14 10												14 26		14 30		
St Pancras International 15 ⊖	a		14 22						14 17												14 33		14 37		
Luton Airport Parkway 7	a								14 51												15 07		15 26		
Luton 10	a								14 54												15 10		15 30		
North Dulwich	d	13 57																14 12							
East Dulwich	d	13 59																14 14							
Peckham Rye 4	d	14 01					13 56											14 16							
Queens Rd Peckham	d	14 04					13 59											14 19							
South Bermondsey	d	14 06					14 01											14 21							
London Bridge 4 ⊖	a	14 11					14 06	14 11								14 09		14 26	14 13	14 29		14 25			

		SN	SN	FC	SN 1		SN	SN 1	SN	SN	SN	FC 1	SN	SN ◇1 ⊼	SN ◇1		SN	SN	LO	SN	SN 1	SN	FC 1	SN 1	SN 1
East Croydon	d				14 14			14 10				14 17	14 17	14 24	14 28			14 21			14 25	14 30	14 32	14 33	14 37
West Croydon 4	d	13 58	14 01				14 04										14 15		14 22						
Norwood Junction 2	a																14 19	14 25	14 28		14 29	14 34			14 42
	d																14 22	14 25	14 28		14 30	14 35			14 43
Selhurst 4	d	14 02	14 05				14 09	14 13					14 20												
Thornton Heath	d	14 04	14 07				14 11	14 16					14 22												
Norbury	d	14 07	14 10				14 14	14 19					14 25												
Streatham Common 4	d	14 10	14 13				14 17	14 21					14 28												
Beckenham Junction 4	d																			14 23					
Birkbeck	d																			14 26					
Crystal Palace 4	d								14 13		14 21						14 26			14 30					
Gipsy Hill	d								14 15								14 29			14 32					
West Norwood 4	d								14 18								14 32			14 35					
Streatham Hill	d								14 22								14 35								
Balham 4 ⊖	d	14 14					14 21	14 28	14 25				14 32				14 39								
Wandsworth Common	d	14 16					14 23	14 30	14 27				14 34				14 41								
Clapham Junction 10	d	14 20			14 26		14 27	14 38	14 31				14 38	14 33	14 37		14 45								
West Brompton ⊖	d							14 47																	
Kensington (Olympia) ⊖	d							14 50																	
Shepherd's Bush ⊖	d							14 53																	
Wembley Central ⊖	d							15s08																	
Harrow & Wealdstone ⊖	d							15 13																	
Watford Junction	d							15 20																	
Milton Keynes Central 10	a							16 01																	
Battersea Park 4	d	14 23							14 35	14 15			14 41				14 48								
London Victoria 15 ⊖	a	14 28			14 32		14 34		14 39					14 40	14 44		14 53								
Streatham 4	d		14 16	14 23																					
Tulse Hill 3	d		14 24	14 27																14 39					
Herne Hill 4	a			14 31																					
Loughborough Jn	a			14 34																					
Elephant & Castle ⊖	a			14 38																					
London Blackfriars 3 ⊖	a			14 42								14 37											14 52		
City Thameslink 3	a			14 45								14 40											14 56		
St Pancras International 15 ⊖	a			14 52								14 47											15 03		
Luton Airport Parkway 7	a											15 21											15 37		
Luton 10	a											15 24											15 40		
North Dulwich	d		14 27																	14 42					
East Dulwich	d		14 29																	14 44					
Peckham Rye 4	d		14 31							14 26										14 46					
Queens Rd Peckham	d		14 34							14 29										14 49					
South Bermondsey	d		14 36							14 31										14 51					
London Bridge 4 ⊖	a		14 41							14 36	14 41							14 39		14 56	14 43	14 59		14 49	14 55

East and West Croydon, London-Milton Keynes and Luton via Norbury-Crystal Palace-Tulse Hill

Local Services

		FC	LO	SN ◇1	SN	SN	FC	SN 1	SN	SN	SN	SN	FC 1	SN ◇1	SN ◇1 ⊼	SN	SN ◇1	SN	SN	LO		SN	SN 1	SN	FC 1
East Croydon	d			14 41				14 44					14 47	14 53	14 56	14 47	15 00		14 51				14 55	15 00	15 02
West Croydon 4	d		14 39		14 28	14 31			14 34									14 45		14 52					
Norwood Junction 2	a		14 43															14 49	14 55	14 58			15 00	15 04	
	d		14 43															14 52	14 55	14 58			15 00	15 05	
Selhurst 4	d				14 32	14 35			14 39							14 50									
Thornton Heath	d				14 34	14 37			14 41							14 52									
Norbury	d				14 37	14 40			14 44							14 55									
Streatham Common 4	d				14 40	14 43			14 47							14 58									
Beckenham Junction 4	d																					14 53			
Birkbeck	d																					14 56			
Crystal Palace 4	d									14 43		14 51						14 56				15 00			
Gipsy Hill	d									14 45								14 59				15 02			
West Norwood 4	d									14 48								15 02				15 05			
Streatham Hill	d									14 52								15 05							
Balham 4 ⊖	d				14 44				14 51	14 55						15 02		15 09							
Wandsworth Common	d				14 46				14 53	14 57						15 04		15 11							
Clapham Junction 10	d			14 50	14 50			14 56	14 57	15 01				15 03	15 06	15 08	15 10	15 15							
West Brompton ⊖	d																								
Kensington (Olympia) ⊖	d																								
Shepherd's Bush ⊖	d																								
Wembley Central ⊖	d																								
Harrow & Wealdstone ⊖	d																								
Watford Junction	d																								
Milton Keynes Central 10	a																								
Battersea Park 4	d				14 53					15 05	14 45					15 11		15 18							
London Victoria 15 ⊖	a			14 57	14 58			15 02	15 04	15 09				15 09	15 12	15 16	15 20	15 24							
Streatham 4	d	14 38				14 46	14 53																		
Tulse Hill 3	d	14 42				14 54	14 57															15 09			
Herne Hill 4	a	14 46					15 01																		
Loughborough Jn	a	14 49					15 04																		
Elephant & Castle ⊖	a	14 53					15 08																		
London Blackfriars 3 ⊖	a	14 57					15 12						15 07												15 22
City Thameslink 3	a	15 00					15 15						15 10												15 26
St Pancras International 15 ⊖	a	15 07					15 22						15 17												15 33
Luton Airport Parkway 7	a	15 56											15 51												16 06
Luton 10	a	16 00											15 54												16 09
North Dulwich	d					14 57																15 12			
East Dulwich	d					14 59																15 14			
Peckham Rye 4	d					15 01					14 56											15 16			
Queens Rd Peckham	d					15 04					14 59											15 19			
South Bermondsey	d					15 06					15 01											15 21			
London Bridge 4 ⊖	a					15 11					15 06	15 11							15 09			15 26	15 13	15 29	

		SN 1	FC	LO	SN ◇1	SN		SN	FC	SN 1	SN	SN 1	SN	SN	SN	FC 1	SN ◇1 ⊼	SN ◇1	SN	SN	SN	LO	SN	SN 1	SN
East Croydon	d	15 07			15 11					15 14		15 10				15 17	15 24	15 28	15 17		15 21			15 25	15 30
West Croydon 4	d			15 09		14 58		15 01			15 04									15 15		15 22			
Norwood Junction 2	a	15 12		15 13																15 19	15 25	15 28		15 29	15 34
	d	15 13		15 13																15 22	15 25	15 28		15 30	15 35
Selhurst 4	d					15 02		15 05			15 09	15 13							15 20						
Thornton Heath	d					15 04		15 07			15 11	15 16							15 22						
Norbury	d					15 07		15 10			15 14	15 19							15 25						
Streatham Common 4	d					15 10		15 13			15 17	15 21							15 28						
Beckenham Junction 4	d																						15 23		
Birkbeck	d																						15 26		
Crystal Palace 4	d												15 13		15 21					15 26			15 30		
Gipsy Hill	d												15 15							15 29			15 32		
West Norwood 4	d												15 18							15 32			15 35		
Streatham Hill	d												15 22							15 35					
Balham 4 ⊖	d					15 14					15 21	15 28	15 25						15 32	15 39					
Wandsworth Common	d					15 16					15 23	15 30	15 27						15 34	15 41					
Clapham Junction 10	d				15 20	15 20				15 26	15 27	15 38	15 31				15 33	15 38	15 38	15 45					
West Brompton ⊖	d											15 47													
Kensington (Olympia) ⊖	d											15 50													
Shepherd's Bush ⊖	d											15 53													
Wembley Central ⊖	d											16s08													
Harrow & Wealdstone ⊖	d											16 13													
Watford Junction	d											16 20													
Milton Keynes Central 10	a											17 00													
Battersea Park 4	d					15 23							15 35	15 15					15 41	15 49					
London Victoria 15 ⊖	a				15 27	15 28				15 32	15 34		15 39				15 40	15 44	15 46	15 54					
Streatham 4	d		15 08					15 16	15 23																
Tulse Hill 3	d		15 12					15 24	15 27														15 39		
Herne Hill 4	a		15 16						15 31																
Loughborough Jn	a		15 19						15 34																
Elephant & Castle ⊖	a		15 23						15 38																
London Blackfriars 3 ⊖	a		15 27						15 42							15 37									
City Thameslink 3	a		15 30						15 45							15 40									
St Pancras International 15 ⊖	a		15 37						15 52							15 47									
Luton Airport Parkway 7	a		16 30													16 21									
Luton 10	a		16 32													16 24									
North Dulwich	d							15 27															15 42		
East Dulwich	d							15 29															15 44		
Peckham Rye 4	d							15 31						15 26									15 46		
Queens Rd Peckham	d							15 34						15 29									15 49		
South Bermondsey	d							15 36						15 31									15 51		
London Bridge 4 ⊖	a	15 25						15 41						15 36	15 41						15 39		15 56	15 43	15 59

East and West Croydon, London-Milton Keynes and Luton via Norbury-Crystal Palace-Tulse Hill

Local Services

Station		FC ■		SN ■	SN ■	FC	LO	SN ◇■	SN	SN	FC	SN	SN ■	SN	FC ■	SN ◇■	SN	SN	SN ◇■	SN	SN	SN ◇■		SN	SN
East Croydon	d	15 32		15 33	15 37			15 41					15 44		15 47	15 53			15 56	15 47		16 00			15 51
West Croydon	d						15 39		15 28	15 31		15 34												15 45	
Norwood Junction	a				15 42		15 43																	15 49	15 55
	d				15 43		15 43																	15 52	15 55
Selhurst	d								15 32	15 35		15 39								15 50					
Thornton Heath	d								15 34	15 37		15 41								15 52					
Norbury	d								15 37	15 40		15 44								15 55					
Streatham Common	d								15 40	15 43		15 47								15 58					
Beckenham Junction	d																								
Birkbeck	d																								
Crystal Palace	d																15 43	15 51						15 56	
Gipsy Hill	d																15 45							15 59	
West Norwood	d																15 48							16 02	
Streatham Hill	d																15 52				15 56			16 05	
Balham	d								15 44			15 51					15 55			16 02				16 09	
Wandsworth Common	d								15 46			15 53					15 57			16 04				16 11	
Clapham Junction	d							15 50	15 50			15 57	15 56			16 03	16 01		16 06	16 08		16 09		16 15	
West Brompton	d																								
Kensington (Olympia)	d																								
Shepherd's Bush	d																								
Wembley Central	d																								
Harrow & Wealdstone	d																								
Watford Junction	d																								
Milton Keynes Central	a																								
Battersea Park	d								15 53					15 45			16 05			16 11				16 18	
London Victoria	a							15 57	15 58			16 04	16 05			16 09	16 10		16 12	16 16		16 20		16 23	
Streatham	d					15 38				15 46	15 53														
Tulse Hill	d					15 42				15 54	15 57										16 00				
Herne Hill	a					15 46					16 01														
Loughborough Jn	a					15 49					16 04														
Elephant & Castle	a					15 53					16 08														
London Blackfriars	a	15 52				15 57					16 13				16 07										
City Thameslink	a	15 56				16 00					16 16				16 10										
St Pancras International	a	16 03				16 07					16 23				16 17										
Luton Airport Parkway	a	16 37				17 00									16 51										
Luton	a	16 40				17 02									16 54										
North Dulwich	d									15 57											16 03				
East Dulwich	d									15 59											16 05				
Peckham Rye	d									16 01				15 56							16 07				
Queens Rd Peckham	d									16 04				15 59							16 10				
South Bermondsey	d									16 06				16 01							16 12				
London Bridge	a			15 49	15 55					16 11				16 06				16 11			16 17				16 09

Station		LO	SN	SN ■	SN	FC ■	SN ■	FC		LO	SN ◇■	SN	SN	FC	SN	SN ■	SN ■	SN	SN	SN	FC ■	SN ◇■	SN	FC ■	SN ◇■
East Croydon	d			15 55	16 00	16 02	16 07				16 11					16 10	16 14				16 17	16 26	16 17	16 28	16 30
West Croydon	d	15 52								16 09		15 58	16 01		16 04										
Norwood Junction	a	15 58		16 00	16 04		16 12			16 13															
	d	15 58		16 00	16 05		16 13			16 13															
Selhurst	d											16 02	16 05		16 09	16 13							16 20		
Thornton Heath	d											16 04	16 07		16 11	16 16							16 22		
Norbury	d											16 07	16 10		16 14	16 19							16 25		
Streatham Common	d											16 10	16 13		16 17	16 21							16 28		
Beckenham Junction	d		15 53																						
Birkbeck	d		15 56																						
Crystal Palace	d		16 00															16 13		16 21					
Gipsy Hill	d		16 02															16 15							
West Norwood	d		16 05															16 18							
Streatham Hill	d																	16 22							
Balham	d											16 14			16 21	16 28		16 25					16 32		
Wandsworth Common	d											16 16			16 23	16 30		16 27					16 34		
Clapham Junction	d										16 20	16 20			16 27	16 38	16 26	16 31				16 36	16 38		16 40
West Brompton	d															16 47									
Kensington (Olympia)	d															16 50									
Shepherd's Bush	d															16 53									
Wembley Central	d															17s08									
Harrow & Wealdstone	d															17 13									
Watford Junction	d															17 21									
Milton Keynes Central	a															17 59									
Battersea Park	d											16 23						16 35	16 15				16 41		
London Victoria	a										16 27	16 28			16 34		16 35	16 40				16 42	16 46		16 46
Streatham	d							16 08					16 16	16 23											
Tulse Hill	d		16 09					16 12					16 24	16 27							16 33				
Herne Hill	a							16 16						16 31											
Loughborough Jn	a							16 19						16 34											
Elephant & Castle	a							16 23						16 38							16 43				
London Blackfriars	a					16 25		16 29						16 43							16 47			16 55	
City Thameslink	a					16 28		16 32						16 46							16 54			16 58	
St Pancras International	a					16 35		16 39						16 53							17 01			17 05	
Luton Airport Parkway	a					17 09		17 26																17 39	
Luton	a					17 12		17 30													17 34			17 42	
North Dulwich	d		16 12										16 27												
East Dulwich	d		16 14										16 29												
Peckham Rye	d		16 16										16 31						16 26						
Queens Rd Peckham	d		16 19										16 34						16 29						
South Bermondsey	d		16 21										16 36						16 31						
London Bridge	a		16 26	16 13	16 29		16 25						16 41						16 38	16 41					

Table 177 — Mondays to Fridays

East and West Croydon, London-Milton Keynes and Luton via Norbury-Crystal Palace-Tulse Hill

Local Services

Station		SN	SN	LO		SN ■	SN	SN	SN	SN ■	FC	SN	FC	LO	SN ■		SN ◇■	SN	SN ■	SN	FC ■	SN ◇■	SN	SN	SN ■
East Croydon	d		16 21			16 24			16 30	16 33					16 40		16 41		16 44		16 47	16 53			16 56
West Croydon	d	16 15		16 22				16 28				16 31		16 39				16 34							
Norwood Junction	a	16 19	16 25	16 28		16 28			16 34					16 43	16 44										
	d	16 22	16 25	16 28		16 28			16 35					16 43	16 45										
Selhurst	d							16 32				16 35						16 39							
Thornton Heath	d							16 34				16 37						16 41							
Norbury	d							16 37				16 40						16 44							
Streatham Common	d							16 40				16 43						16 47							
Beckenham Junction	d						16 23																		
Birkbeck	d						16 26																		
Crystal Palace	d	16 26					16 30																16 43	16 50	
Gipsy Hill	d	16 29					16 32																16 45		
West Norwood	d	16 32					16 35																16 48		
Streatham Hill	d	16 35																					16 52		
Balham	d	16 39						16 44										16 51					16 55		
Wandsworth Common	d	16 41						16 46										16 53					16 57		
Clapham Junction	d	16 45						16 50									16 50	16 57	16 56			17 03	17 01		17 06
West Brompton	d																								
Kensington (Olympia)	d																								
Shepherd's Bush	d																								
Wembley Central	d																								
Harrow & Wealdstone	d																								
Watford Junction	d																								
Milton Keynes Central	a																								
Battersea Park	d	16 49						16 53												16 45			17 05		
London Victoria	a	16 55						16 58									16 58	17 04	17 05			17 09	17 10		17 12
Streatham	d										16 40	16 46	16 53												
Tulse Hill	d						16 39				16 46	16 53	16 57								17 03				
Herne Hill	a										16 50		17 01												
Loughborough Jn	a										16 53														
Elephant & Castle	a										16 59		17 07								17 14				
London Blackfriars	a										17 03		17 11								17 19				
City Thameslink	a										17 06		17 14								17 24				
St Pancras International	a										17 13		17 21								17 31				
Luton Airport Parkway	a												17 56												
Luton	a												17 59.								18 04				
North Dulwich	d						16 42					16 56													
East Dulwich	d						16 44					16 58													
Peckham Rye	d						16 46					17 00								16 56					
Queens Rd Peckham	d						16 49					17 03								16 59					
South Bermondsey	d						16 51					17 05								17 01					
London Bridge	a		16 39			16 43	16 56		17 00	16 47		17 10			16 57					17 08				17 11	

Station		SN	FC ■	SN ◇■	SN	SN	LO	SN	SN ■	SN		SN	SN ■	FC	SN	FC ■	LO	SN ◇■	SN	SN ■		SN	SN ■	SN	SN
East Croydon	d	16 47	16 57	17 01		16 51			16 55			17 00	17 07			17 09		17 12		17 14			17 10		
West Croydon	d				16 45		16 52			16 56					17 01		17 09		17 12			17 04			
Norwood Junction	a				16 49	16 55	16 58		16 59			17 04	17 11				17 13								
	d				16 52	16 55	16 58		16 59			17 05	17 12				17 13								
Selhurst	d	16 50								17 01					17 05							17 09	17 13		
Thornton Heath	d	16 52								17 03					17 07							17 11	17 16		
Norbury	d	16 55								17 06					17 10							17 14	17 19		
Streatham Common	d	16 58								17 08					17 13							17 17	17 21		
Beckenham Junction	d							16 53																	17 11
Birkbeck	d							16 56																	17 14
Crystal Palace	d				16 56			17 00																17 13	17 18
Gipsy Hill	d				16 59			17 02																17 15	17 20
West Norwood	d				17 02			17 05																17 18	17 23
Streatham Hill	d				17 05																			17 22	
Balham	d	17 02			17 09					17 12												17 21	17 28	17 25	
Wandsworth Common	d	17 04			17 11					17 14												17 23	17 30	17 27	
Clapham Junction	d	17 08		17 11	17 15					17 18								17 22		17 25		17 27	17 38	17 31	
West Brompton	d																						17 47		
Kensington (Olympia)	d																						17 50		
Shepherd's Bush	d																						17 53		
Wembley Central	d																						18s08		
Harrow & Wealdstone	d																						18 13		
Watford Junction	d																						18 20		
Milton Keynes Central	a																						19 03		
Battersea Park	d	17 11			17 18					17 22														17 35	
London Victoria	a	17 16		17 17	17 23					17 26								17 28		17 32		17 34		17 42	
Streatham	d													17 10	17 16										
Tulse Hill	d							17 09						17 16	17 22										17 27
Herne Hill	a													17 20											
Loughborough Jn	a													17 23											
Elephant & Castle	a													17 28											
London Blackfriars	a		17 25											17 31		17 35									
City Thameslink	a		17 28											17 34		17 38									
St Pancras International	a		17 35											17 41		17 45									
Luton Airport Parkway	a		18 09											18 27		18 20									
Luton	a		18 12											18 32		18 23									
North Dulwich	d							17 12							17 25										17 30
East Dulwich	d							17 14							17 27										17 32
Peckham Rye	d							17 16							17 29										17 34
Queens Rd Peckham	d							17 19							17 32										17 37
South Bermondsey	d							17 21							17 34										17 39
London Bridge	a					17 08		17 26	17 14			17 30	17 26		17 39				17 28						17 44

East and West Croydon, London-Milton Keynes and Luton via Norbury-Crystal Palace-Tulse Hill

Local Services

		SN	SN	FC	FC 1	SN 1 ⌶	SN ◇1 ⌶		SN	SN 1	SN 1	SN	SN	LO	SN 1	SN	FC	SN	SN	SN	LO	SN ◇1 ⌶	SN 1	SN	SN 1
East Croydon	d				17 23	17 26	17 30		17 17	17 36	17 38		17 21		17 25				17 30			17 41	17 41		17 44
West Croydon 4	d											17 18		17 22		17 28				17 31	17 39			17 42	
Norwood Junction 2	a											17 22	17 25	17 28	17 30				17 34		17 43		17 45		
	d											17 23	17 25	17 29	17 31			17 32	17 35		17 43		17 45		
Selhurst 4	d								17 20							17 32				17 35					
Thornton Heath	d								17 22							17 34				17 37					
Norbury	d								17 25							17 37				17 40					
Streatham Common 4	d								17 28							17 40				17 43					
Beckenham Junction 4	d																								
Birkbeck	d																								
Crystal Palace 4	d		17 21									17 27						17 36							
Gipsy Hill	d											17 29						17 38							
West Norwood 4	d											17 32						17 42							
Streatham Hill	d											17 36													
Balham 4 ⊖	d								17 32			17 39				17 44									
Wandsworth Common	d								17 34			17 41				17 46									
Clapham Junction 10	d					17 36	17 40		17 38		17 47	17 45				17 50						17 51			17 56
West Brompton ⊖	d																								
Kensington (Olympia) ⊖	d																								
Shepherd's Bush ⊖	d																								
Wembley Central ⊖	d																								
Harrow & Wealdstone ⊖	d																								
Watford Junction	d																								
Milton Keynes Central 10	a																								
Battersea Park 4	d	17 15							17 41			17 48				17 53									
London Victoria 15 ⊖	a					17 42	17 46		17 48		17 54	17 55				17 58						17 58			18 02
Streatham 4	d			17 23													17 40			17 46					
Tulse Hill 3	d			17 27													17 44	17 45		17 54					
Herne Hill 4	a			17 31													17 47								
Loughborough Jn	a			17 34													17 51								
Elephant & Castle ⊖	a			17 38													17 55								
London Blackfriars 3 ⊖	a			17 43	17 49												17 59								
City Thameslink 3	a			17 48	17 54												18 02								
St Pancras International 15 ⊖	a			17 55	18 01												18 09								
Luton Airport Parkway 7	a																18 57								
Luton 10	a				18 34												19 02								
North Dulwich	d																	17 48		17 57					
East Dulwich	d																	17 50		17 59					
Peckham Rye 4	d	17 26																17 53		18 01					
Queens Rd Peckham	d	17 29																17 55		18 04					
South Bermondsey	d	17 31																17 58		18 06					
London Bridge 4 ⊖	a	17 38	17 43							17 52			17 37		17 45			18 02	17 59	18 11			17 58	18 00	

		SN		FC	FC 1	SN	SN 1	SN	SN	SN	SN 1 ⌶	SN	FC 1		SN ◇1 ⌶	SN	LO	SN	SN 1	SN	SN	FC	SN	LO	SN 1
East Croydon	d				17 47	17 51	17 53				17 56	17 47	17 58		18 02			17 55	18 08		18 08				18 10
West Croydon 4	d															17 48	17 52			17 58			18 01	18 09	
Norwood Junction 2	a					17 55										17 54	17 58	17 59			18 12			18 13	
	d					17 55										17 55	17 58	17 59			18 12			18 13	
Selhurst 4	d											17 50								18 02			18 05		18 13
Thornton Heath	d											17 52								18 04			18 07		18 16
Norbury	d											17 55								18 07			18 10		18 19
Streatham Common 4	d											17 58								18 10			18 13		18 21
Beckenham Junction 4	d									17 48															
Birkbeck	d									17 51															
Crystal Palace 4	d							17 44	17 48	17 55						17 59									
Gipsy Hill	d							17 46		17 57						18 01									
West Norwood 4	d							17 49		18 00						18 04									
Streatham Hill	d							17 53								18 08									
Balham 4 ⊖	d							17 56				18 02				18 11				18 14					18 26
Wandsworth Common	d							17 58				18 04				18 13				18 16					18 28
Clapham Junction 10	d						18 03	18 02			18 06	18 08			18 13	18 17			18 19	18 20					18 38
West Brompton ⊖	d																								18 47
Kensington (Olympia) ⊖	d																								18 50
Shepherd's Bush ⊖	d																								18 53
Wembley Central ⊖	d																								19s08
Harrow & Wealdstone ⊖	d																								19 13
Watford Junction	d																								19 21
Milton Keynes Central 10	a																								20 06
Battersea Park 4	d	17 45						18 06				18 11				18 20				18 23					
London Victoria 15 ⊖	a						18 09	18 12			18 12	18 16			18 20	18 25			18 26	18 28					
Streatham 4	d			17 57																		18 10	18 16		
Tulse Hill 3	d			18 01						18 05			18 13									18 16	18 20		
Herne Hill 4	a			18 05																		18 20			
Loughborough Jn	a			18 09																		18 23			
Elephant & Castle ⊖	a			18 13																		18 27			
London Blackfriars 3 ⊖	a			18 17	18 21								18 25									18 31			
City Thameslink 3	a			18 20	18 24								18 28									18 34			
St Pancras International 15 ⊖	a			18 27	18 31								18 35									18 41			
Luton Airport Parkway 7	a												19 09									19 29			
Luton 10	a				19 04								19 12									19 34			
North Dulwich	d									18 08													18 23		
East Dulwich	d									18 10													18 25		
Peckham Rye 4	d	17 57								18 12													18 29		
Queens Rd Peckham	d	17 59								18 15													18 32		
South Bermondsey	d	18 02								18 17													18 34		
London Bridge 4 ⊖	a	18 08				18 09			18 13	18 22								18 13			18 26		18 39		

East and West Croydon, London-Milton Keynes and Luton via Norbury-Crystal Palace-Tulse Hill

Local Services

		SN ◇1 ⌶	SN 1	SN	SN	SN	SN 1 ⌶	SN 1		SN	SN	FC	FC 1	SN	SN	SN ◇1 ⌶	SN	LO	SN	SN	FC 1	SN 1	FC	SN 1	SN
East Croydon	d	18 12	18 14				18 25	18 26					18 17	18 17		18 30			18 21	18 30	18 33	18 36		18 40	
West Croydon 4	d			18 13													18 18	18 22							18 28
Norwood Junction 2	a																18 23	18 28	18 28	18 34					
	d																18 24	18 28	18 29	18 35					
Selhurst 4	d													18 20											18 32
Thornton Heath	d													18 22											18 34
Norbury	d													18 25											18 37
Streatham Common 4	d													18 28											18 40
Beckenham Junction 4	d										18 11														
Birkbeck	d										18 14														
Crystal Palace 4	d									18 13	18 18				18 20		18 28								
Gipsy Hill	d									18 16	18 20						18 30								
West Norwood 4	d									18 19	18 23						18 33								
Streatham Hill	d									18 22							18 37								
Balham 4 ⊖	d									18 29				18 33			18 40								18 44
Wandsworth Common	d									18 31				18 35			18 42								18 46
Clapham Junction 10	d	18 22	18 26				18 34	18 37		18 36				18 39		18 40	18 46							18 49	18 50
West Brompton ⊖	d																								
Kensington (Olympia) ⊖	d																								
Shepherd's Bush ⊖	d																								
Wembley Central ⊖	d																								
Harrow & Wealdstone ⊖	d																								
Watford Junction	d																								
Milton Keynes Central 10	a																								
Battersea Park 4	d				18 15					18 40							18 49								
London Victoria 15 ⊖	a	18 29	18 32				18 41	18 44		18 46				18 46		18 47	18 54							18 56	18 57
Streatham 4	d					18 19						18 23											18 40		
Tulse Hill 3	d					18 24					18 28	18 27	18 38										18 44		
Herne Hill 4	a											18 31											18 47		
Loughborough Jn	a											18 34											18 51		
Elephant & Castle ⊖	a											18 39											18 55		
London Blackfriars 3 ⊖	a											18 43	18 51								18 55		18 59		
City Thameslink 3	a											18 46	18 54								18 58		19 02		
St Pancras International 15 ⊖	a											18 53	19 01								19 05		19 09		
Luton Airport Parkway 7	a											19 35									19 39		19 53		
Luton 10	a											19 40	19 34								19 43		19 58		
North Dulwich	d					18 27					18 31														
East Dulwich	d					18 29					18 33														
Peckham Rye 4	d				18 26	18 32					18 36														
Queens Rd Peckham	d				18 29	18 35					18 38														
South Bermondsey	d				18 31	18 37					18 41														
London Bridge 4 ⊖	a			18 29	18 38	18 42					18 45				18 45				18 41	18 59		18 50			

		SN	FC	LO	SN ◇1 ⌶		SN 1	SN	FC 1	SN 1	SN	SN	SN 1	SN	SN 1		SN	SN	SN ◇1	SN	LO	SN 1	SN	SN	FC 1
East Croydon	d				18 43		18 44		18 47	18 53			18 55	18 47	18 57				19 00			18 57		19 00	19 02
West Croydon 4	d	18 31		18 39																18 47	18 52		18 58		
Norwood Junction 2	a			18 43																18 51	18 58	19 01		19 04	
	d			18 43																18 52	18 58	19 02		19 05	
Selhurst 4	d	18 35												18 51									19 02		
Thornton Heath	d	18 37												18 53									19 04		
Norbury	d	18 40												18 56									19 07		
Streatham Common 4	d	18 43												18 58									19 10		
Beckenham Junction 4	d																	18 44							
Birkbeck	d																	18 47							
Crystal Palace 4	d										18 43	18 51						18 51		18 56					
Gipsy Hill	d										18 45							18 53		18 59					
West Norwood 4	d										18 48							18 56		19 02					
Streatham Hill	d										18 52									19 05					
Balham 4 ⊖	d										18 55			19 02						19 09			19 14		
Wandsworth Common	d										18 57			19 04						19 11			19 16		
Clapham Junction 10	d				18 52		18 56			19 03	19 01		19 06	19 08	19 09				19 12	19 15			19 20		
West Brompton ⊖	d																								
Kensington (Olympia) ⊖	d																								
Shepherd's Bush ⊖	d																								
Wembley Central ⊖	d																								
Harrow & Wealdstone ⊖	d																								
Watford Junction	d																								
Milton Keynes Central 10	a																								
Battersea Park 4	d							18 45			19 05									19 18			19 23		
London Victoria 15 ⊖	a				18 59		19 05			19 09	19 12		19 13	19 15	19 15				19 18	19 25			19 28		
Streatham 4	d	18 46	18 53														18 56								
Tulse Hill 3	d	18 54	18 57														19 00	19b10							
Herne Hill 4	a		19 01																						
Loughborough Jn	a		19 04																						
Elephant & Castle ⊖	a		19 09																						
London Blackfriars 3 ⊖	a		19 14						19 09																19 22
City Thameslink 3	a		19 20						19 12																19 26
St Pancras International 15 ⊖	a		19 27						19 19																19 33
Luton Airport Parkway 7	a								19 57																20 07
Luton 10	a								20 00																20 10
North Dulwich	d	18 57															19 03	19 13							
East Dulwich	d	18 59															19 05	19 15							
Peckham Rye 4	d	19 01						18 57									19 07	19 17							
Queens Rd Peckham	d	19 04						19 00									19 10	19 20							
South Bermondsey	d	19 06						19 02									19 12	19 22							
London Bridge 4 ⊖	a	19 11						19 09				19 13					19 17	19 27				19 15		19 29	

b arr. 1902

East and West Croydon, London-Milton Keynes and Luton via Norbury-Crystal Palace-Tulse Hill

Local Services

		SN 1	FC	SN	LO	SN 1	SN ◇1	SN 1	SN	FC 1	FC		SN ◇1	SN	SN	SN 1	SN	SN ◇1	SN	SN	LO	SN	SN	SN 1	FC 1
East Croydon	d	19 09				19 10	19 12	19 14		19 17			19 24			19 25		19 29	19 17				19 30	19 33	19 32
West Croydon 4	d			19 01	19 09															19 17	19 22				
Norwood Junction 2	a	19 12			19 13															19 21	19 28		19 34		
	d	19 13			19 13															19 22	19 28		19 35		
Selhurst 4	d			19 05		19 13													19 20						
Thornton Heath	d			19 07		19 16													19 22						
Norbury	d			19 10		19 19													19 25						
Streatham Common 4	d			19 13		19 21													19 28						
Beckenham Junction 4	d																					19 25			
Birkbeck	d																					19 28			
Crystal Palace 4	d													19 13	19 21					19 26		19 32			
Gipsy Hill	d													19 15						19 29		19 34			
West Norwood 4	d													19 18						19 32		19 37			
Streatham Hill	d													19 22						19 35					
Balham 4 ⊖	d					19 28								19 25					19 32	19 39					
Wandsworth Common	d					19 30								19 27					19 34	19 41					
Clapham Junction 10	d					19 38	19 22	19 26					19 34	19 31		19 37		19 40	19 38	19 45					
West Brompton ⊖	d					19 47																			
Kensington (Olympia) ⊖	d					19 50																			
Shepherd's Bush ⊖	d					19 53																			
Wembley Central ⊖	d					20s08																			
Harrow & Wealdstone ⊖	d					20 13																			
Watford Junction	d					20 20																			
Milton Keynes Central 10	a					21 01																			
Battersea Park 4	d								19 15					19 35					19 41	19 48					
London Victoria 15 ⊖	a						19 29	19 32					19 40	19 41		19 43		19 47	19 48	19 53					
Streatham 4	d		19 10	19 16							19 21						19 26								
Tulse Hill 3	d		19 14	19 22							19 27						19 31					19 41			
Herne Hill 4	a		19 17								19 31														
Loughborough Jn	a		19 20								19 34														
Elephant & Castle ⊖	a		19 24								19 38														
London Blackfriars 3 ⊖	a		19 28							19 37	19 44														19 52
City Thameslink 3	a		19 32							19 40	19 48														19 56
St Pancras International 15 ⊖	a		19 39							19 47	19 55														20 03
Luton Airport Parkway 7	a		20 26							20 21	20 41														20 37
Luton 10	a		20 30							20 24	20 55														20 40
North Dulwich	d			19 25													19 34					19 44			
East Dulwich	d			19 27													19 36					19 46			
Peckham Rye 4	d			19 29					19 26								19 38					19 48			
Queens Rd Peckham	d			19 32					19 29								19 41					19 51			
South Bermondsey	d			19 34					19 31								19 43					19 53			
London Bridge 4 ⊖	a	19 25		19 41					19 36						19 41		19 51					19 58	19 59	19 49	

		SN 1	SN	FC	SN	LO		SN ◇1	SN 1	FC	SN	SN	SN	FC 1	SN	SN ◇1	SN 1	SN 1	SN	LO	SN	SN	SN	FC 1	FC
East Croydon	d	19 40						19 43	19 44				19 47	19 47		19 54	19 59	20 01					20 00	20 02	
West Croydon 4	d		19 28		19 31	19 39													19 47	19 52		19 58			
Norwood Junction 2	a					19 43													19 51	19 58			20 04		
	d					19 43													19 52	19 58			20 05		
Selhurst 4	d		19 32		19 35								19 50									20 02			
Thornton Heath	d		19 34		19 37								19 52									20 04			
Norbury	d		19 37		19 40								19 55									20 07			
Streatham Common 4	d		19 40		19 43								19 58									20 10			
Beckenham Junction 4	d																				19 54				
Birkbeck	d																				19 57				
Crystal Palace 4	d										19 43				19 51				19 56		20 01				
Gipsy Hill	d										19 45								19 58		20 03				
West Norwood 4	d										19 48								20 01		20 06				
Streatham Hill	d										19 52								20 05						
Balham 4 ⊖	d		19 45								19 55		20 02						20 08			20 14			
Wandsworth Common	d		19 47								19 57		20 04						20 10			20 16			
Clapham Junction 10	d	19 49	19 51					19 52	19 56		20 01		20 08			20 04	20 08	20 11	20 14			20 20			
West Brompton ⊖	d																								
Kensington (Olympia) ⊖	d																								
Shepherd's Bush ⊖	d																								
Wembley Central ⊖	d																								
Harrow & Wealdstone ⊖	d																								
Watford Junction	d																								
Milton Keynes Central 10	a																								
Battersea Park 4	d		19 54								20 05	19 45	20 11						20 18			20 23			
London Victoria 15 ⊖	a	19 56	19 59					19 59	20 02		20 09					20 10	20 15	20 20	20 25			20 28			
Streatham 4	d			19 40	19 46					19 57															20 06
Tulse Hill 3	d			19 44	19 54					20 01											20 11				20 12
Herne Hill 4	a			19 47						20 05															20 16
Loughborough Jn	a			19 50						20 08															20 19
Elephant & Castle ⊖	a			19 54						20 12															20 23
London Blackfriars 3 ⊖	a			19 58						20 16				20 07										20 22	20 27
City Thameslink 3	a			20 02						20 20				20 10										20 26	20 32
St Pancras International 15 ⊖	a			20 09						20 27				20 17										20 33	20 39
Luton Airport Parkway 7	a			20 56										20 51										21 07	21 26
Luton 10	a			21 00										20 54										21 10	21 30
North Dulwich	d				19 57																20 14				
East Dulwich	d				19 59																20 16				
Peckham Rye 4	d				20 01							19 56									20 18				
Queens Rd Peckham	d				20 04							19 59									20 21				
South Bermondsey	d				20 06							20 01									20 23				
London Bridge 4 ⊖	a				20 11							20 06			20 11						20 28		20 29		

East and West Croydon, London-Milton Keynes and Luton via Norbury-Crystal Palace-Tulse Hill

Local Services

		SN	FC		SN 1	LO	SN ◇1	SN 1	SN	SN	FC 1	SN	SN ◇1	SN 1	SN	SN ◇1	SN	LO	SN	SN 1	SN	FC 1		FC	SN
East Croydon	d				20 07		20 11	20 14			20 17		20 24	20 26	20 17	20 30				20 33	20 31	20 32			
West Croydon 4	d	20 01				20 09											20 18	20 22							20 31
Norwood Junction 2	a					20 13											20 22	20 28			20 35				
	d					20 13											20 23	20 28			20 35				
Selhurst 4	d	20 05													20 20										20 35
Thornton Heath	d	20 07													20 22										20 37
Norbury	d	20 10													20 25										20 40
Streatham Common 4	d	20 13													20 28										20 43
Beckenham Junction 4	d																		20 24						
Birkbeck	d																		20 27						
Crystal Palace 4	d								20 13			20 21					20 27		20 31						
Gipsy Hill	d								20 16								20 29		20 33						
West Norwood 4	d								20 19								20 32		20 36						
Streatham Hill	d								20 22								20 36								
Balham 4 ⊖	d								20 25						20 32		20 39								
Wandsworth Common	d								20 27						20 34		20 41								
Clapham Junction 10	d						20 21	20 26	20 31				20 34	20 37	20 38	20 41	20 45								
West Brompton ⊖	d																								
Kensington (Olympia) ⊖	d																								
Shepherd's Bush ⊖	d																								
Wembley Central ⊖	d																								
Harrow & Wealdstone ⊖	d																								
Watford Junction	d																								
Milton Keynes Central 10	a																								
Battersea Park 4	d								20 35	20 15					20 41		20 48								
London Victoria 15 ⊖	a						20 28	20 32	20 39				20 40	20 44	20 46	20 50	20 53								
Streatham 4	d	20 17	20 25																					20 36	20 46
Tulse Hill 3	d	20 24	20 29																20 40					20 42	20 54
Herne Hill 4	a		20 33																					20 46	
Loughborough Jn	a		20 38																					20 49	
Elephant & Castle ⊖	a		20 42																					20 53	
London Blackfriars 3 ⊖	a		20 46								20 37											20 52		20 57	
City Thameslink 3	a		20 50								20 40											20 56		21 02	
St Pancras International 15 ⊖	a		20 57								20 47											21 03		21 09	
Luton Airport Parkway 7	a										21 21											21 37		21 56	
Luton 10	a										21 24											21 40		22 00	
North Dulwich	d	20 27																	20 43						20 57
East Dulwich	d	20 29																	20 45						20 59
Peckham Rye 4	d	20 31								20 26									20 47						21 01
Queens Rd Peckham	d	20 34								20 29									20 50						21 04
South Bermondsey	d	20 36								20 31									20 52						21 06
London Bridge 4 ⊖	a	20 41			20 21					20 36		20 41							20 57	20 48	20 59				21 11

		LO	SN ◇1	SN	SN 1	SN	SN	FC 1		SN	SN 1	SN ◇1	SN 1	SN	SN ◇1	SN	LO	SN	FC	FC 1	FC	SN	SN ◇1	SN	LO
East Croydon	d		20 41		20 44			20 47			20 54	20 54	20 57	20 47	21 00			21 00		21 02			21 10		
West Croydon 4	d	20 39		20 35												20 45	20 52					21 01		21 04	21 09
Norwood Junction 2	a	20 43														20 49	20 58	21 04							21 13
	d	20 43														20 52	20 58	21 05							21 13
Selhurst 4	d			20 39										20 50								21 05		21 09	
Thornton Heath	d			20 41										20 52								21 07		21 11	
Norbury	d			20 44										20 55								21 10		21 14	
Streatham Common 4	d			20 47										20 58								21 13		21 17	
Beckenham Junction 4	d																								
Birkbeck	d																								
Crystal Palace 4	d					20 43				20 51						20 56									
Gipsy Hill	d					20 45										20 59									
West Norwood 4	d					20 48										21 02									
Streatham Hill	d					20 52										21 05									
Balham 4 ⊖	d			20 51		20 55								21 02		21 09								21 21	
Wandsworth Common	d			20 53		20 57								21 04		21 11								21 23	
Clapham Junction 10	d		20 51	20 57	20 57	21 01						21 04	21 08	21 08	21 11	21 15							21 20	21 27	
West Brompton ⊖	d																								
Kensington (Olympia) ⊖	d																								
Shepherd's Bush ⊖	d																								
Wembley Central ⊖	d																								
Harrow & Wealdstone ⊖	d																								
Watford Junction	d																								
Milton Keynes Central 10	a																								
Battersea Park 4	d					21 05	20 45							21 11		21 18									
London Victoria 15 ⊖	a		20 58	21 04	21 05	21 09						21 10	21 15	21 18	21 20	21 23							21 27	21 34	
Streatham 4	d																		20 55		21 06	21 16			
Tulse Hill 3	d																		20 59		21 12	21 24			
Herne Hill 4	a																		21 03		21 16				
Loughborough Jn	a																		21 08		21 19				
Elephant & Castle ⊖	a																		21 12		21 23				
London Blackfriars 3 ⊖	a							21 07											21 16	21 22	21 27				
City Thameslink 3	a							21 10											21 20	21 26	21 32				
St Pancras International 15 ⊖	a							21 17											21 27	21 33	21 39				
Luton Airport Parkway 7	a							21 51												22 07	22 26				
Luton 10	a							21 54												22 10	22 30				
North Dulwich	d																					21 27			
East Dulwich	d																					21 29			
Peckham Rye 4	d						20 56															21 31			
Queens Rd Peckham	d						20 59															21 34			
South Bermondsey	d						21 01															21 36			
London Bridge 4 ⊖	a						21 07			21 13	21 09							21 29				21 41			

Table 177

Mondays to Fridays

East and West Croydon, London-Milton Keynes and Luton via Norbury-Crystal Palace-Tulse Hill

Local Services

		SN ■1	SN	SN		FC ■1	SN	SN ◇■1	SN ■1	SN	SN ◇■1	SN	LO	SN		SN ■1	FC ■1	LO	SN ◇■1	SN	FC	FC	SN	SN	SN ■1
East Croydon	d	21 14				21 17		21 24	21 26	21 17	21 30			21 30		21 33	21 32		21 42						21 44
West Croydon ■4	d											21 18	21 22					21 39					21 31	21 34	
Norwood Junction ■2	a											21 22	21 28	21 34				21 43							
	d											21 23	21 28	21 35				21 43							
Selhurst ■4	d									21 20													21 35	21 39	
Thornton Heath	d									21 22													21 37	21 41	
Norbury	d									21 25													21 40	21 44	
Streatham Common ■4	d									21 28													21 43	21 47	
Beckenham Junction ■4	d																								
Birkbeck	d																								
Crystal Palace ■4	d		21 13				21 21					21 27													
Gipsy Hill	d		21 15									21 29													
West Norwood ■4	d		21 18									21 32													
Streatham Hill	d		21 22									21 36													
Balham ■4 ⊖	d		21 25							21 32		21 39												21 51	
Wandsworth Common	d		21 27							21 34		21 41												21 53	
Clapham Junction ■10	d	21 26	21 31					21 34	21 38	21 38	21 41	21 45							21 51					21 57	21 56
West Brompton ⊖	d																								
Kensington (Olympia) ⊖	d																								
Shepherd's Bush ⊖	d																								
Wembley Central ⊖	d																								
Harrow & Wealdstone ⊖	d																								
Watford Junction	d																								
Milton Keynes Central ■10	a																								
Battersea Park ■4	d		21 35	21 15						21 41		21 48								21 45					
London Victoria ■15 ⊖	a	21 35	21 39					21 43	21 45	21 46	21 48	21 53							21 58					22 04	22 05
Streatham ■4	d																				21 25	21 46	21 50		
Tulse Hill ■3	d																				21 29	21 50	21 54		
Herne Hill ■4	a																				21 33	21 54			
Loughborough Jn	a																				21 38	21 57			
Elephant & Castle ⊖	a																				21 42	22 01			
London Blackfriars ■3 ⊖	a					21 37											21 52				21 46	22 05			
City Thameslink ■3	a					21 40											21 56				21 50	22 10			
St Pancras International ■15 ⊖	a					21 47											22 03				21 57	22 17			
Luton Airport Parkway ■7	a					22 21											22 37					23 01			
Luton ■10	a					22 24											22 40					23 04			
North Dulwich	d																						21 57		
East Dulwich	d																						21 59		
Peckham Rye ■4	d			21 26																21 56			22 01		
Queens Rd Peckham	d			21 29																21 59			22 04		
South Bermondsey	d			21 31																22 01			22 06		
London Bridge ■4 ⊖	a			21 36			21 43							21 59		21 49				22 06			22 11		

		SN	SN	SN ◇■1	SN ■1	SN	SN ◇■1	SN	LO	SN		SN	FC ■1	SN ◇■1	SN	LO	SN ■1	SN	SN	SN ■1		SN	SN ◇■1	SN ■1	SN
East Croydon	d			21 54	21 57	21 47	22 00			22 00			22 02	22 10			22 14			22 17			22 24	22 25	22 17
West Croydon ■4	d							21 48	21 52			22 01			22 04	22 09									
Norwood Junction ■2	a							21 52	21 58	22 04						22 13									
	d							21 53	21 58	22 05						22 13									
Selhurst ■4	d					21 50						22 05			22 09										22 20
Thornton Heath	d					21 52						22 07			22 11										22 22
Norbury	d					21 55						22 10			22 14										22 25
Streatham Common ■4	d					21 58						22 13			22 17										22 28
Beckenham Junction ■4	d																								
Birkbeck	d																								
Crystal Palace ■4	d	21 43	21 51					21 57										22 13				22 21			
Gipsy Hill	d	21 45						21 59										22 15							
West Norwood ■4	d	21 48						22 02										22 18							
Streatham Hill	d	21 52						22 06										22 22							
Balham ■4 ⊖	d	21 55				22 02		22 09							22 21			22 25							22 32
Wandsworth Common	d	21 57				22 04		22 11							22 23			22 27							22 34
Clapham Junction ■10	d	22 01		22 04	22 08	22 08	22 11	22 15						22 20	22 27		22 26	22 31					22 33	22 38	22 38
West Brompton ⊖	d																								
Kensington (Olympia) ⊖	d																								
Shepherd's Bush ⊖	d																								
Wembley Central ⊖	d																								
Harrow & Wealdstone ⊖	d																								
Watford Junction	d																								
Milton Keynes Central ■10	a																								
Battersea Park ■4	d	22 05				22 11		22 18										22 35	22 15						22 41
London Victoria ■15 ⊖	a	22 09		22 11	22 14	22 16	22 20	22 25						22 27	22 34		22 35	22 39					22 41	22 44	22 48
Streatham ■4	d											22 16													
Tulse Hill ■3	d											22 24													
Herne Hill ■4	a																								
Loughborough Jn	a																								
Elephant & Castle ⊖	a																								
London Blackfriars ■3 ⊖	a																								
City Thameslink ■3	a																								
St Pancras International ■15 ⊖	a																								
Luton Airport Parkway ■7	a																								
Luton ■10	a																								
North Dulwich	d											22 27													
East Dulwich	d											22 29													
Peckham Rye ■4	d											22 31							22 26						
Queens Rd Peckham	d											22 34							22 29						
South Bermondsey	d											22 36							22 31						
London Bridge ■4 ⊖	a		22 13							22 29		22 41	22 17						22 36	22 33		22 45			

Table 177

Mondays to Fridays

East and West Croydon, London-Milton Keynes and Luton via Norbury-Crystal Palace-Tulse Hill

Local Services

		SN ◇■1	SN	LO	SN	FC ■1		SN ■1	SN ◇■1	FC	SN	SN	LO	SN ■1	SN	SN		SN	SN ◇■1	SN ■1	SN	SN ◇■1	SN	LO	SN
East Croydon	d	22 30			22 30	22 32		22 34	22 40					22 44					22 54	22 56	22 47	23 00			23 01
West Croydon ■4	d		22 18	22 22							22 31	22 34	22 39										22 48	22 52	
Norwood Junction ■2	a		22 22	22 28	22 34								22 43										22 52	22 58	23 05
	d		22 23	22 28	22 35								22 43										22 53	22 58	23 06
Selhurst ■4	d										22 35	22 39									22 50				
Thornton Heath	d										22 37	22 41									22 52				
Norbury	d										22 40	22 44									22 55				
Streatham Common ■4	d										22 43	22 47									22 58				
Beckenham Junction ■4	d																								
Birkbeck	d																								
Crystal Palace ■4	d		22 27												22 43			22 51					22 57		
Gipsy Hill	d		22 29												22 45								22 59		
West Norwood ■4	d		22 32												22 48								23 02		
Streatham Hill	d		22 36												22 52								23 06		
Balham ■4 ⊖	d		22 39									22 51			22 55						23 02		23 09		
Wandsworth Common	d		22 41									22 53			22 57						23 04		23 11		
Clapham Junction ■10	d	22 41	22 45						22 50			22 57		22 56	23 01				23 04	23 07	23 08	23 11	23 15		
West Brompton ⊖	d																								
Kensington (Olympia) ⊖	d																								
Shepherd's Bush ⊖	d																								
Wembley Central ⊖	d																								
Harrow & Wealdstone ⊖	d																								
Watford Junction	d																								
Milton Keynes Central ■10	a																								
Battersea Park ■4	d		22 48												23 05	22 45					23 11		23 19		
London Victoria ■15 ⊖	a	22 50	22 53						22 57			23 04		23 05	23 10				23 13	23 15	23 18	23 20	23 23		
Streatham ■4	d									22 40	22 46														
Tulse Hill ■3	d									22 43	22 54														
Herne Hill ■4	a																								
Loughborough Jn	a																								
Elephant & Castle ⊖	a																								
London Blackfriars ■3 ⊖	a																								
City Thameslink ■3	a																								
St Pancras International ■15 ⊖	a																								
Luton Airport Parkway ■7	a																								
Luton ■10	a																								
North Dulwich	d										22 57														
East Dulwich	d										22 59														
Peckham Rye ■4	d										23 01					22 56									
Queens Rd Peckham	d										23 04					22 59									
South Bermondsey	d										23 06					23 01									
London Bridge ■4 ⊖	a				22 59	22 47		22 49		22 55	23 11					23 06		23 14							23 30

		SN		FC ■1	SN	SN ■1	SN	SN	SN	SN	SN ■1	SN ◇■1		SN	LO	FC ■1	SN	SN	SN	SN ■1					
East Croydon	d			23 02		23 14			23 17		23 20	23 30				23 32		23 43		23 58					
West Croydon ■4	d	23 01			23 04									23 18	23 22										
Norwood Junction ■2	a													23 22	23 28			23 47							
	d													23 23	23 28										
Selhurst ■4	d	23 05			23 09				23 20		23 24									00 02					
Thornton Heath	d	23 07			23 11				23 22																
Norbury	d	23 10			23 14				23 25																
Streatham Common ■4	d	23 13			23 17				23 28																
Beckenham Junction ■4	d																								
Birkbeck	d																								
Crystal Palace ■4	d						23 13			23 21				23 27			23 43		23 51						
Gipsy Hill	d						23 15							23 29			23 45								
West Norwood ■4	d						23 18							23 32			23 48								
Streatham Hill	d						23 22							23 36			23 52								
Balham ■4 ⊖	d				23 21		23 25		23 32					23 40			23 55								
Wandsworth Common	d				23 23		23 27		23 34					23 42			23 58								
Clapham Junction ■10	d				23 27	23 26	23 31		23 38		23 33	23 42		23 46			00 02			00 11					
West Brompton ⊖	d																								
Kensington (Olympia) ⊖	d																								
Shepherd's Bush ⊖	d																								
Wembley Central ⊖	d																								
Harrow & Wealdstone ⊖	d																								
Watford Junction	d																								
Milton Keynes Central ■10	a																								
Battersea Park ■4	d						23 35	23 15	23 41					23 49			00 05								
London Victoria ■15 ⊖	a				23 34	23 35	23 40		23 46		23 40	23 52		23 54			00 12			00 18					
Streatham ■4	d	23 16																							
Tulse Hill ■3	d	23 24																							
Herne Hill ■4	a																								
Loughborough Jn	a																								
Elephant & Castle ⊖	a																								
London Blackfriars ■3 ⊖	a																								
City Thameslink ■3	a																								
St Pancras International ■15 ⊖	a																								
Luton Airport Parkway ■7	a																								
Luton ■10	a																								
North Dulwich	d	23 27																							
East Dulwich	d	23 29																							
Peckham Rye ■4	d	23 31						23 26																	
Queens Rd Peckham	d	23 34						23 29																	
South Bermondsey	d	23 36						23 31																	
London Bridge ■4 ⊖	a	23 41		23 17				23 36		23 45						23 47			00 11						

Table 177

Saturdays

East and West Croydon, London-Milton Keynes and Luton via Norbury-Crystal Palace-Tulse Hill

Local Services

		SN	SN	SN 1	FC 1	SN ◇1	FC 1	SN	SN 1	SN 1		FC 1	SN 1	FC 1	SN 1	FC 1	FC 1	FC	LO		FC 1	SN	LO	FC (bus)
East Croydon	d			23p58	00 04	00 17	00 36	00 49	01 28	02 28		02 47	03 28	03 47	04 28	04 47	05 17				05 42			
West Croydon 4	d																		05 39				05 52	
Norwood Junction 2	a																		05 43				05 58	
	d																		05 43			05 52	05 58	
Selhurst 4	d																	05 39						
Thornton Heath	d																	05 41						
Norbury	d																	05 43						
Streatham Common 4	d																	05 46						
Beckenham Junction 4	d																							
Birkbeck	d																							
Crystal Palace 4	d	23p43	23p51																			05 56		
Gipsy Hill	d	23p45																				05 59		
West Norwood 4	d	23p48																				06 02		
Streatham Hill	d	23p52																				06 05		
Balham 4 ⊖	d	23p55																				06 09		
Wandsworth Common	d	23p58																				06 11		
Clapham Junction 10	d	00 02		00 11		00 30		01 01	01 41	02 41			03 41		04 41							06 15		
West Brompton ⊖	d																							
Kensington (Olympia) ⊖	d																							
Shepherd's Bush ⊖	d																							
Wembley Central ⊖	d																							
Harrow & Wealdstone ⊖	d																							
Watford Junction	d																							
Milton Keynes Central 10	a																							
Battersea Park 4	d	00 05																				06 18		
London Victoria 15 ⊖	a	00 12		00 18		00 37		01 08	01 49	02 49			03 49		04 49							06 23		
Streatham 4	d																	05 49						
Tulse Hill 3	d																	05 55						06 00
Herne Hill 4	a																							06 08
Loughborough Jn	a																							06 16
Elephant & Castle ⊖	a																							06 28
London Blackfriars 3 ⊖	a																							06 36
City Thameslink 3	a																							
St Pancras International 15 ⊖	a																							
Luton Airport Parkway 7	a																							
Luton 10	a																							
North Dulwich	d																							
East Dulwich	d																							
Peckham Rye 4	d																							
Queens Rd Peckham	d																							
South Bermondsey	d																							
London Bridge 4 ⊖	a		00 11		00 19		00 52					03 12		04 12		05 12	05 42	06 09			05 57			

		SN	FC	SN ◇1	LO	SN ◇1		SN 1	FC 1	SN	LO	SN 1	SN	FC (bus)	SN ◇1	SN		FC	LO	SN	SN	FC 1	SN ◇1	SN	SN
East Croydon	d			06 07		06 11		06 10	06 17			06 25	06 30		06 41					06 43		06 47	06 53	06 47	
West Croydon 4	d				06 09					06 18	06 22								06 39						06 45
Norwood Junction 2	a				06 13					06 22	06 28	06 29	06 34						06 43	06 49					06 52
	d				06 13					06 23	06 28	06 30	06 35			06 41			06 43	06 50					06 53
Selhurst 4	d	06 01	06 09					06 13										06 39						06 50	
Thornton Heath	d	06 03	06 11					06 16										06 41						06 52	
Norbury	d	06 06	06 13					06 19										06 43						06 55	
Streatham Common 4	d	06 08	06 16					06 21										06 46						06 58	
Beckenham Junction 4	d																								
Birkbeck	d																								
Crystal Palace 4	d									06 27						06 45									06 57
Gipsy Hill	d									06 29						06 47									06 59
West Norwood 4	d									06 32						06 50									07 02
Streatham Hill	d									06 36															07 06
Balham 4 ⊖	d	06 12						06 28		06 39														07 02	07 09
Wandsworth Common	d	06 14						06 30		06 41														07 04	07 11
Clapham Junction 10	d	06 18		06 18		06 22		06 38		06 45					06 50								07 03	07 08	07 15
West Brompton ⊖	d							06 47																	
Kensington (Olympia) ⊖	d							06 50																	
Shepherd's Bush ⊖	d							06 53																	
Wembley Central ⊖	d							07s07																	
Harrow & Wealdstone ⊖	d							07 12																	
Watford Junction	d							07 19																	
Milton Keynes Central 10	a							08 00																	
Battersea Park 4	d	06 22								06 48											06 45			07 11	07 18
London Victoria 15 ⊖	a	06 26		06 26		06 30				06 53					06 57								07 09	07 16	07 23
Streatham 4	d		06 19															06 49							
Tulse Hill 3	d		06 23											06 30		06 54		06 57							
Herne Hill 4	a													06 38				07 01							
Loughborough Jn	a													06 46											
Elephant & Castle ⊖	a													06 58											
London Blackfriars 3 ⊖	a													07 06											
City Thameslink 3	a																								
St Pancras International 15 ⊖	a																								
Luton Airport Parkway 7	a																								
Luton 10	a																								
North Dulwich	d															06 57									
East Dulwich	d															06 59									
Peckham Rye 4	d															07 01					06 56				
Queens Rd Peckham	d															07 04					06 59				
South Bermondsey	d															07 06					07 01				
London Bridge 4 ⊖	a		06 35						06 32			06 43	06 59			07 14				07 11	07 06	07 02			

Table 177

Saturdays

East and West Croydon, London-Milton Keynes and Luton via Norbury-Crystal Palace-Tulse Hill

Local Services

		LO		SN 1	SN	SN 1	LO	SN ◇1	SN	FC	SN 1	SN		SN	FC 1	FC (bus)	SN	SN 1	SN ◇1	SN	SN ◇1	SN		LO	SN 1
East Croydon	d			06 55	07 00	07 07		07 11			07 14				07 17			07 10	07 24	07 17	07 30				07 25
West Croydon 4	d	06 52					07 09		06 58			07 15					07 01							07 22	
Norwood Junction 2	a	06 58		07 00	07 04	07 12	07 13					07 19												07 28	07 29
	d	06 58		07 00	07 05	07 13	07 13					07 20										07 23		07 28	07 30
Selhurst 4	d								07 02								07 05	07 13		07 20					
Thornton Heath	d								07 04								07 07	07 16		07 22					
Norbury	d								07 07								07 10	07 19		07 25					
Streatham Common 4	d								07 10								07 13	07 21		07 28					
Beckenham Junction 4	d																								
Birkbeck	d																								
Crystal Palace 4	d																					07 27			
Gipsy Hill	d																					07 29			
West Norwood 4	d																					07 32			
Streatham Hill	d																					07 36			
Balham 4 ⊖	d								07 14									07 28		07 32		07 39			
Wandsworth Common	d								07 16									07 30		07 34		07 41			
Clapham Junction 10	d							07 20	07 20		07 26							07 38	07 33	07 38	07 39	07 45			
West Brompton ⊖	d																	07 47							
Kensington (Olympia) ⊖	d																	07 50							
Shepherd's Bush ⊖	d																	07 53							
Wembley Central ⊖	d																	08s07							
Harrow & Wealdstone ⊖	d																	08 12							
Watford Junction	d																	08 19							
Milton Keynes Central 10	a																	09 00							
Battersea Park 4	d								07 23					07 15						07 41		07 48			
London Victoria 15 ⊖	a							07 27	07 28		07 32								07 40	07 46	07 46	07 53			
Streatham 4	d									07 10							07 16								
Tulse Hill 3	d									07 17						07 20	07 24								
Herne Hill 4	a															07 28									
Loughborough Jn	a															07 36									
Elephant & Castle ⊖	a															07 48									
London Blackfriars 3 ⊖	a															07 56									
City Thameslink 3	a																								
St Pancras International 15 ⊖	a																								
Luton Airport Parkway 7	a																								
Luton 10	a																								
North Dulwich	d																07 27								
East Dulwich	d																07 29								
Peckham Rye 4	d													07 26			07 31								
Queens Rd Peckham	d													07 29			07 34								
South Bermondsey	d													07 31			07 36								
London Bridge 4 ⊖	a			07 13	07 29	07 25				07 30		07 41		07 36	07 32		07 41								07 43

		SN	FC 1	SN 1	LO	SN 1	SN ◇1	SN		FC	SN 1	SN	SN	SN	FC 1	FC (bus)	SN	SN ◇1		SN ◇1	SN	SN ◇1	SN	SN	LO
East Croydon	d	07 30	07 32	07 33		07 39	07 41				07 44				07 47			07 53		07 56	07 47	08 00		07 51	
West Croydon 4	d				07 39			07 28					07 45				07 31								07 52
Norwood Junction 2	a	07 34			07 43	07 44							07 49											07 55	07 58
	d	07 35			07 43	07 45							07 50										07 53	07 55	07 58
Selhurst 4	d							07 32									07 35				07 50				
Thornton Heath	d							07 34									07 37				07 52				
Norbury	d							07 37									07 40				07 55				
Streatham Common 4	d							07 40									07 43				07 58				
Beckenham Junction 4	d																								
Birkbeck	d																								
Crystal Palace 4	d											07 43											07 57		
Gipsy Hill	d											07 45											07 59		
West Norwood 4	d											07 48											08 02		
Streatham Hill	d											07 52											08 06		
Balham 4 ⊖	d							07 44				07 55									08 02		08 09		
Wandsworth Common	d							07 46				07 57									08 04		08 11		
Clapham Junction 10	d						07 50	07 50			07 56	08 01						08 03		08 06	08 08	08 10	08 15		
West Brompton ⊖	d																								
Kensington (Olympia) ⊖	d																								
Shepherd's Bush ⊖	d																								
Wembley Central ⊖	d																								
Harrow & Wealdstone ⊖	d																								
Watford Junction	d																								
Milton Keynes Central 10	a																								
Battersea Park 4	d							07 53				08 05		07 45							08 11		08 18		
London Victoria 15 ⊖	a						07 57	07 58			08 02	08 09						08 09		08 12	08 16	08 16	08 23		
Streatham 4	d									07 40							07 46								
Tulse Hill 3	d									07 47						07 50	07 54								
Herne Hill 4	a															07 58									
Loughborough Jn	a															08 06									
Elephant & Castle ⊖	a															08 18									
London Blackfriars 3 ⊖	a															08 26									
City Thameslink 3	a																								
St Pancras International 15 ⊖	a																								
Luton Airport Parkway 7	a																								
Luton 10	a																								
North Dulwich	d																07 57								
East Dulwich	d																07 59								
Peckham Rye 4	d													07 56			08 01								
Queens Rd Peckham	d													07 59			08 04								
South Bermondsey	d													08 01			08 06								
London Bridge 4 ⊖	a	07 59	07 47	07 49		07 57				08 00			08 11	08 06	08 02		08 11							08 09	

East and West Croydon, London-Milton Keynes and Luton via Norbury-Crystal Palace-Tulse Hill

Local Services

		SN 1	SN	FC 1	SN 1	LO	SN ◇1	SN	FC	SN 1	SN	SN	SN	FC 1	FC (bus)	SN	SN 1	SN ◇1	SN ◇1	SN	SN	SN
East Croydon	d	07 55	08 00	08 02	08 07		08 11			08 14				08 17			08 10	08 24	08 28	08 17		08 21
West Croydon 4	d					08 09		07 58								08 01					08 15	
Norwood Junction 2	a	08 00	08 04		08 12	08 13															08 19	08 25
	d	08 00	08 05		08 13	08 13															08 22	08 25
Selhurst 4	d							08 02								08 05	08 13			08 20		
Thornton Heath	d							08 04								08 07	08 16			08 22		
Norbury	d							08 07								08 10	08 19			08 25		
Streatham Common 4	d							08 10								08 13	08 21			08 28		
Beckenham Junction 4	d																					
Birkbeck	d																					
Crystal Palace 4	d										08 13		08 21								08 26	
Gipsy Hill	d										08 15										08 29	
West Norwood 4	d										08 18										08 32	
Streatham Hill	d										08 22										08 35	
Balham 4	d							08 14			08 25						08 28			08 32	08 39	
Wandsworth Common	d							08 16			08 27						08 30			08 34	08 41	
Clapham Junction 10	d						08 20	08 20		08 26	08 31						08 38	08 33	08 37	08 38	08 45	
West Brompton	d																08 47					
Kensington (Olympia)	d																08 50					
Shepherd's Bush	d																08 53					
Wembley Central	d																09s07					
Harrow & Wealdstone	d																09 12					
Watford Junction	d																09 19					
Milton Keynes Central 10	a																10 00					
Battersea Park 4	d							08 23			08 35	08 15								08 41	08 48	
London Victoria 15	a						08 27	08 28		08 32	08 39							08 40	08 44	08 46	08 53	
Streatham 4	d								08 10							08 16						
Tulse Hill 3	d								08 17						08 20	08 24						
Herne Hill 4	a														08 28							
Loughborough Jn	a														08 36							
Elephant & Castle	a														08 48							
London Blackfriars 3	a														08 56							
City Thameslink 3	a																					
St Pancras International 15	a																					
Luton Airport Parkway 7	a																					
Luton 10	a																					
North Dulwich	d															08 27						
East Dulwich	d															08 29						
Peckham Rye 4	d											08 26				08 31						
Queens Rd Peckham	d											08 29				08 34						
South Bermondsey	d											08 31				08 36						
London Bridge 4	a	08 13	08 29	08 17	08 25				08 30			08 36	08 41	08 32		08 41						08 39

		LO	SN	SN 1	SN	FC 1	SN 1	SN 1	LO	SN ◇1	SN	FC	SN 1	SN	FC 1	FC (bus)	SN	SN	SN	SN	SN ◇1	SN ◇1	SN
East Croydon	d			08 25	08 30	08 32	08 33	08 37		08 41			08 44		08 47						08 53	08 56	08 47
West Croydon 4	d	08 22							08 39		08 28						08 31	08 34					
Norwood Junction 2	a	08 28		08 29	08 34			08 42	08 43														
	d	08 28		08 30	08 35			08 43	08 43														
Selhurst 4	d										08 32						08 35	08 39					08 50
Thornton Heath	d										08 34						08 37	08 41					08 52
Norbury	d										08 37						08 40	08 44					08 55
Streatham Common 4	d										08 40						08 43	08 47					08 58
Beckenham Junction 4	d		08 23																				
Birkbeck	d		08 26																				
Crystal Palace 4	d		08 30																08 43	08 51			
Gipsy Hill	d		08 32																08 45				
West Norwood 4	d		08 35																08 48				
Streatham Hill	d																		08 52				
Balham 4	d										08 44							08 51	08 55				09 02
Wandsworth Common	d										08 46							08 53	08 57				09 04
Clapham Junction 10	d									08 50	08 50		08 56					08 57	09 01		09 03	09 06	09 08
West Brompton	d																						
Kensington (Olympia)	d																						
Shepherd's Bush	d																						
Wembley Central	d																						
Harrow & Wealdstone	d																						
Watford Junction	d																						
Milton Keynes Central 10	a																						
Battersea Park 4	d										08 53			08 45					09 05				09 11
London Victoria 15	a									08 57	08 58		09 02					09 04	09 09		09 09	09 12	09 16
Streatham 4	d											08 40					08 46						
Tulse Hill 3	d		08 39									08 47				08 50	08 54						
Herne Hill 4	a															08 58							
Loughborough Jn	a															09 06							
Elephant & Castle	a															09 18							
London Blackfriars 3	a															09 26							
City Thameslink 3	a																						
St Pancras International 15	a																						
Luton Airport Parkway 7	a																						
Luton 10	a																						
North Dulwich	d		08 42														08 57						
East Dulwich	d		08 44														08 59						
Peckham Rye 4	d		08 46											08 56			09 01						
Queens Rd Peckham	d		08 49											08 59			09 04						
South Bermondsey	d		08 51											09 01			09 06						
London Bridge 4	a		08 56	08 43	08 59	08 47	08 49	08 55				09 00		09 06	09 02		09 11			09 11			

East and West Croydon, London-Milton Keynes and Luton via Norbury-Crystal Palace-Tulse Hill

Local Services

		SN ◇1	SN	SN	LO	SN	SN 1	SN	FC 1	SN 1	LO	SN ◇1	SN	FC	SN 1	SN	FC 1	FC (bus)	SN	SN	SN 1	SN	SN
East Croydon	d	09 00		08 51			08 55	09 00	09 02	09 07		09 11			09 14		09 17				09 10		
West Croydon 4	d		08 45		08 52						09 09		08 58						09 01	09 04			
Norwood Junction 2	a		08 49	08 55	08 58		09 00	09 04		09 12	09 13												
	d		08 52	08 55	08 58		09 00	09 05		09 13	09 13												
Selhurst 4	d												09 02						09 05	09 09	09 13		
Thornton Heath	d												09 04						09 07	09 11	09 16		
Norbury	d												09 07						09 10	09 14	09 19		
Streatham Common 4	d												09 10						09 13	09 17	09 21		
Beckenham Junction 4	d					08 53																	
Birkbeck	d					08 56																	
Crystal Palace 4	d		08 56			09 00																09 13	09 21
Gipsy Hill	d		08 58			09 02																09 15	
West Norwood 4	d		09 01			09 05																09 18	
Streatham Hill	d		09 06																			09 22	
Balham 4	d		09 09										09 14							09 21	09 28	09 25	
Wandsworth Common	d		09 11										09 16							09 23	09 30	09 27	
Clapham Junction 10	d	09 10	09 15									09 20	09 20		09 26					09 27	09 38	09 31	
West Brompton	d																				09 47		
Kensington (Olympia)	d																				09 50		
Shepherd's Bush	d																				09 53		
Wembley Central	d																				10s07		
Harrow & Wealdstone	d																				10 12		
Watford Junction	d																				10 19		
Milton Keynes Central 10	a																				11 00		
Battersea Park 4	d		09 18										09 23			09 15						09 35	
London Victoria 15	a	09 16	09 23									09 27	09 28		09 32					09 34		09 39	
Streatham 4	d													09 10					09 16				
Tulse Hill 3	d					09 09								09 17				09 20	09 24				
Herne Hill 4	a																	09 28					
Loughborough Jn	a																	09 36					
Elephant & Castle	a																	09 48					
London Blackfriars 3	a																	09 56					
City Thameslink 3	a																						
St Pancras International 15	a																						
Luton Airport Parkway 7	a																						
Luton 10	a																						
North Dulwich	d					09 12													09 27				
East Dulwich	d					09 14													09 29				
Peckham Rye 4	d					09 16										09 26			09 31				
Queens Rd Peckham	d					09 19										09 29			09 34				
South Bermondsey	d					09 21										09 31			09 36				
London Bridge 4	a			09 09		09 26	09 13	09 29	09 17	09 25				09 30		09 36	09 32		09 41				09 41

		SN ◇1	SN ◇1	SN	SN	SN	LO	SN	SN 1	SN	SN	FC 1	SN 1	SN 1	LO	FC	SN ◇1	SN 1	SN	FC 1	FC (bus)	SN
East Croydon	d	09 24	09 28	09 17		09 21			09 25		09 30	09 32	09 33	09 37			09 42	09 44		09 47		
West Croydon 4	d				09 15		09 22			09 28					09 39							09 31
Norwood Junction 2	a				09 19	09 25	09 28		09 29		09 34			09 42	09 43							
	d				09 22	09 25	09 28		09 30		09 35			09 43	09 43							
Selhurst 4	d			09 20						09 32												09 35
Thornton Heath	d			09 22						09 34												09 37
Norbury	d			09 25						09 37												09 40
Streatham Common 4	d			09 28						09 40												09 43
Beckenham Junction 4	d							09 23														
Birkbeck	d							09 26														
Crystal Palace 4	d				09 26			09 30														
Gipsy Hill	d				09 29			09 32														
West Norwood 4	d				09 32			09 35														
Streatham Hill	d				09 35																	
Balham 4	d			09 32	09 39					09 44												
Wandsworth Common	d			09 34	09 41					09 46												
Clapham Junction 10	d	09 33	09 37	09 38	09 45					09 50							09 51	09 56				
West Brompton	d																					
Kensington (Olympia)	d																					
Shepherd's Bush	d																					
Wembley Central	d																					
Harrow & Wealdstone	d																					
Watford Junction	d																					
Milton Keynes Central 10	a																					
Battersea Park 4	d			09 41	09 48					09 53									09 45			
London Victoria 15	a	09 40	09 44	09 46	09 53					09 58							09 58	10 02				
Streatham 4	d															09 40						09 46
Tulse Hill 3	d							09 39								09 47					09 50	09 54
Herne Hill 4	a																				09 58	
Loughborough Jn	a																				10 06	
Elephant & Castle	a																				10 18	
London Blackfriars 3	a																				10 26	
City Thameslink 3	a																					
St Pancras International 15	a																					
Luton Airport Parkway 7	a																					
Luton 10	a																					
North Dulwich	d							09 42														09 57
East Dulwich	d							09 44														09 59
Peckham Rye 4	d							09 46											09 56			10 01
Queens Rd Peckham	d							09 49											09 59			10 04
South Bermondsey	d							09 51											10 01			10 06
London Bridge 4	a					09 39		09 56	09 43		09 59	09 47	09 49	09 55		10 00			10 06	10 02		10 11

Table 177

Saturdays

East and West Croydon, London-Milton Keynes and Luton via Norbury-Crystal Palace-Tulse Hill

Local Services

Station		SN	SN	SN	SN ◇1	SN ◇1 trolley	SN	SN ◇1		SN	SN	LO	SN	SN 1	SN	FC 1	SN 1	LO		SN ◇1	SN	FC	SN 1	SN	FC 1
East Croydon	d				09 53	09 56	09 47	10 00			09 51			09 55	10 00	10 02	10 07			10 11			10 14		10 17
West Croydon 4	d	09 34								09 45		09 52						10 09			09 58				
Norwood Junction 2	a									09 49	09 55	09 58		10 00	10 04		10 12	10 13							
	d									09 52	09 55	09 58		10 00	10 05		10 13	10 13							
Selhurst 4	d	09 39					09 50														10 02				
Thornton Heath	d	09 41					09 52														10 04				
Norbury	d	09 44					09 55														10 07				
Streatham Common 4	d	09 47					09 58														10 10				
Beckenham Junction 4	d												09 53												
Birkbeck	d												09 56												
Crystal Palace 4	d		09 43	09 51						09 56			10 00												
Gipsy Hill	d		09 45							09 59			10 02												
West Norwood 4	d		09 48							10 02			10 05												
Streatham Hill	d		09 52							10 05															
Balham 4 ⊖	d	09 51	09 55				10 02			10 09											10 14				
Wandsworth Common	d	09 53	09 57				10 04			10 11											10 16				
Clapham Junction 10	d	09 57	10 01		10 03	10 06	10 08	10 10		10 15										10 20	10 20		10 26		
West Brompton ⊖	d																								
Kensington (Olympia) ⊖	d																								
Shepherd's Bush ⊖	d																								
Wembley Central ⊖	d																								
Harrow & Wealdstone ⊖	d																								
Watford Junction	d																								
Milton Keynes Central 10	a																								
Battersea Park 4	d		10 05				10 11			10 18											10 23			10 15	
London Victoria 15 ⊖	a	10 04	10 09		10 09	10 12	10 16	10 16		10 23										10 27	10 28		10 32		
Streatham 4	d																					10 10			
Tulse Hill 3	d												10 09									10 17			
Herne Hill 4	a																								
Loughborough Jn	a																								
Elephant & Castle ⊖	a																								
London Blackfriars 3 ⊖	a																								
City Thameslink 3	a																								
St Pancras International 15 ⊖	a																								
Luton Airport Parkway 7	a																								
Luton 10	a																								
North Dulwich	d												10 12												
East Dulwich	d												10 14												
Peckham Rye 4	d												10 16											10 26	
Queens Rd Peckham	d												10 19											10 29	
South Bermondsey	d												10 21											10 31	
London Bridge 4 ⊖	a			10 11							10 09		10 26	10 13	10 29	10 17	10 25					10 30		10 36	10 32

Station		FC bus	SN	SN		SN 1	SN	SN	SN ◇1 trolley	SN ◇1 trolley	SN	SN	SN	LO		SN	SN 1	SN	FC 1	SN 1	SN 1	SN ◇1	SN	LO	
East Croydon	d					10 10			10 24	10 28	10 17		10 21				10 25	10 30	10 32	10 33	10 37	10 38			
West Croydon 4	d		10 01	10 04								10 15		10 22									10 28	10 39	
Norwood Junction 2	a											10 19	10 25	10 28			10 29	10 34			10 42			10 43	
	d											10 22	10 25	10 28			10 30	10 35			10 43			10 43	
Selhurst 4	d		10 05	10 09		10 13					10 20												10 32		
Thornton Heath	d		10 07	10 11		10 16					10 22												10 34		
Norbury	d		10 10	10 14		10 19					10 25												10 37		
Streatham Common 4	d		10 13	10 17		10 21					10 28												10 40		
Beckenham Junction 4	d															10 23									
Birkbeck	d															10 26									
Crystal Palace 4	d						10 13	10 21				10 26				10 30									
Gipsy Hill	d						10 15					10 29				10 32									
West Norwood 4	d						10 18					10 32				10 35									
Streatham Hill	d						10 22					10 35													
Balham 4 ⊖	d			10 21		10 28	10 25				10 32	10 39											10 44		
Wandsworth Common	d			10 23		10 30	10 27				10 34	10 41											10 46		
Clapham Junction 10	d			10 27		10 38	10 31		10 33	10 37	10 38	10 45										10 48	10 50		
West Brompton ⊖	d					10 47																			
Kensington (Olympia) ⊖	d					10 50																			
Shepherd's Bush ⊖	d					10 53																			
Wembley Central ⊖	d					11s08																			
Harrow & Wealdstone ⊖	d					11 13																			
Watford Junction	d					11 20																			
Milton Keynes Central 10	a					12 00																			
Battersea Park 4	d						10 35				10 41	10 48											10 53		
London Victoria 15 ⊖	a			10 34			10 39		10 40	10 44	10 46	10 53										10 56	10 58		
Streatham 4	d		10 16																						
Tulse Hill 3	d	10 20	10 24													10 39									
Herne Hill 4	a	10 28																							
Loughborough Jn	a	10 36																							
Elephant & Castle ⊖	a	10 48																							
London Blackfriars 3 ⊖	a	10 56																							
City Thameslink 3	a																								
St Pancras International 15 ⊖	a																								
Luton Airport Parkway 7	a																								
Luton 10	a																								
North Dulwich	d		10 27													10 42									
East Dulwich	d		10 29													10 44									
Peckham Rye 4	d		10 31													10 46									
Queens Rd Peckham	d		10 34													10 49									
South Bermondsey	d		10 36													10 51									
London Bridge 4 ⊖	a		10 41					10 41					10 39			10 56	10 43	10 59	10 47	10 49	10 55				

Table 177

Saturdays

East and West Croydon, London-Milton Keynes and Luton via Norbury-Crystal Palace-Tulse Hill

Local Services

Station		FC	SN ◇1	SN 1	SN	FC 1	FC bus	SN	SN	SN		SN	SN ◇1	SN ◇1 trolley	SN	SN ◇1	SN	SN	LO	SN		SN 1	SN	FC 1	SN 1
East Croydon	d		10 42	10 44		10 47							10 53	10 56	10 47	11 00		10 51				10 55	11 00	11 02	11 07
West Croydon 4	d							10 31	10 34								10 45		10 52						
Norwood Junction 2	a																10 49	10 55	10 58			11 00	11 04		11 12
	d																10 52	10 55	10 58			11 00	11 05		11 13
Selhurst 4	d							10 35	10 39						10 50										
Thornton Heath	d							10 37	10 41						10 52										
Norbury	d							10 40	10 44						10 55										
Streatham Common 4	d							10 43	10 47						10 58										
Beckenham Junction 4	d																			10 53					
Birkbeck	d																			10 56					
Crystal Palace 4	d									10 43		10 51					10 56			11 00					
Gipsy Hill	d									10 45							10 59			11 02					
West Norwood 4	d									10 48							11 02			11 05					
Streatham Hill	d									10 52							11 05								
Balham 4 ⊖	d								10 51	10 55					11 02		11 09								
Wandsworth Common	d								10 53	10 57					11 04		11 11								
Clapham Junction 10	d		10 52	10 56					10 57	11 01			11 03	11 06	11 08	11 10	11 15								
West Brompton ⊖	d																								
Kensington (Olympia) ⊖	d																								
Shepherd's Bush ⊖	d																								
Wembley Central ⊖	d																								
Harrow & Wealdstone ⊖	d																								
Watford Junction	d																								
Milton Keynes Central 10	a																								
Battersea Park 4	d				10 45					11 05					11 11		11 18								
London Victoria 15 ⊖	a		10 59	11 02					11 04	11 09			11 09	11 12	11 16	11 16	11 23								
Streatham 4	d	10 40						10 46																	
Tulse Hill 3	d	10 47					10 50	10 54												11 09					
Herne Hill 4	a						10 58																		
Loughborough Jn	a						11 06																		
Elephant & Castle ⊖	a						11 18																		
London Blackfriars 3 ⊖	a						11 26																		
City Thameslink 3	a																								
St Pancras International 15 ⊖	a																								
Luton Airport Parkway 7	a																								
Luton 10	a																								
North Dulwich	d							10 57												11 12					
East Dulwich	d							10 59												11 14					
Peckham Rye 4	d				10 56			11 01												11 16					
Queens Rd Peckham	d				10 59			11 04												11 19					
South Bermondsey	d				11 01			11 06												11 21					
London Bridge 4 ⊖	a	11 00			11 06	11 02		11 11				11 11						11 09		11 26		11 13	11 29	11 17	11 25

Station		LO	SN ◇1	SN	FC	SN 1		SN	FC 1	FC bus	SN	SN	SN 1	SN	SN	SN ◇1 trolley		SN ◇1 trolley	SN	SN	SN	LO	SN	SN 1	SN
East Croydon	d		11 11			11 14			11 17				11 10			11 24		11 28	11 17		11 21			11 25	11 30
West Croydon 4	d	11 09		10 58							11 01	11 04								11 15		11 22			
Norwood Junction 2	a	11 13																		11 19	11 25	11 28		11 29	11 34
	d	11 13																		11 22	11 25	11 28		11 30	11 35
Selhurst 4	d			11 02							11 05	11 09	11 13						11 20						
Thornton Heath	d			11 04							11 07	11 11	11 16						11 22						
Norbury	d			11 07							11 10	11 14	11 19						11 25						
Streatham Common 4	d			11 10							11 13	11 17	11 21						11 28						
Beckenham Junction 4	d																						11 23		
Birkbeck	d																						11 26		
Crystal Palace 4	d													11 13	11 21					11 26			11 30		
Gipsy Hill	d													11 15						11 29			11 32		
West Norwood 4	d													11 18						11 32			11 35		
Streatham Hill	d													11 22						11 35					
Balham 4 ⊖	d			11 14								11 21	11 28	11 25					11 32	11 39					
Wandsworth Common	d			11 16								11 23	11 30	11 27					11 34	11 41					
Clapham Junction 10	d		11 20	11 20		11 26						11 27	11 38	11 31		11 33		11 37	11 38	11 45					
West Brompton ⊖	d												11 47												
Kensington (Olympia) ⊖	d												11 50												
Shepherd's Bush ⊖	d												11 53												
Wembley Central ⊖	d												12s07												
Harrow & Wealdstone ⊖	d												12 13												
Watford Junction	d												12 20												
Milton Keynes Central 10	a												13 00												
Battersea Park 4	d			11 23				11 15						11 35					11 41	11 48					
London Victoria 15 ⊖	a		11 27	11 28		11 32						11 34		11 39		11 40		11 44	11 46	11 53					
Streatham 4	d				11 10						11 16														
Tulse Hill 3	d				11 17					11 20	11 24												11 39		
Herne Hill 4	a									11 28															
Loughborough Jn	a									11 36															
Elephant & Castle ⊖	a									11 48															
London Blackfriars 3 ⊖	a									11 56															
City Thameslink 3	a																								
St Pancras International 15 ⊖	a																								
Luton Airport Parkway 7	a																								
Luton 10	a																								
North Dulwich	d										11 27												11 42		
East Dulwich	d										11 29												11 44		
Peckham Rye 4	d							11 26			11 31												11 46		
Queens Rd Peckham	d							11 29			11 34												11 49		
South Bermondsey	d							11 31			11 36												11 51		
London Bridge 4 ⊖	a				11 30			11 36	11 32		11 41				11 41						11 39		11 56	11 43	11 59

Table 177

East and West Croydon, London-Milton Keynes and Luton via Norbury-Crystal Palace-Tulse Hill

Local Services

		FC		SN	SN	LO	SN	SN	FC	SN	SN	FC		FC	SN	SN	SN	SN	SN	SN	SN	SN		SN	SN
		1		1	1		◇1			1		1		🚌					◇1	◇1 🚲		◇1			
East Croydon 🚊	d	11 32		11 33	11 37		11 41			11 44		11 47							11 53	11 56	11 47	12 00			11 51
West Croydon 4 🚊	d					11 39		11 28							11 31	11 34								11 45	
Norwood Junction 2	a				11 42	11 43																		11 49	11 55
	d				11 43	11 43																		11 52	11 55
Selhurst 4	d							11 32							11 35	11 39					11 50				
Thornton Heath	d							11 34							11 37	11 41					11 52				
Norbury	d							11 37							11 40	11 44					11 55				
Streatham Common 4	d							11 40							11 43	11 47					11 58				
Beckenham Junction 4 🚊	d																								
Birkbeck 🚊	d																								
Crystal Palace 4	d																11 43	11 51						11 56	
Gipsy Hill	d																11 45							11 59	
West Norwood 4	d																11 48							12 02	
Streatham Hill	d																11 52							12 05	
Balham 4 ⊖	d							11 44								11 51	11 55				12 02			12 09	
Wandsworth Common	d							11 46								11 53	11 57				12 04			12 11	
Clapham Junction 10	d						11 50	11 50		11 56						11 57	12 01		12 03	12 06	12 08	12 10		12 15	
West Brompton ⊖	d																								
Kensington (Olympia) ⊖	d																								
Shepherd's Bush ⊖	d																								
Wembley Central ⊖	d																								
Harrow & Wealdstone ⊖	d																								
Watford Junction	d																								
Milton Keynes Central 10	a																								
Battersea Park 4	d							11 53			11 45						12 05				12 11			12 18	
London Victoria 15 ⊖	a						11 57	11 58		12 02						12 04	12 09		12 09	12 12	12 16	12 16		12 23	
Streatham 4	d								11 40						11 46										
Tulse Hill 3	d								11 47					11 50	11 54										
Herne Hill 4	a													11 58											
Loughborough Jn	a													12 06											
Elephant & Castle ⊖	a													12 18											
London Blackfriars 3 ⊖	a													12 26											
City Thameslink 3	a																								
St Pancras International 15 ⊖	a																								
Luton Airport Parkway 7	a																								
Luton 10	a																								
North Dulwich	d														11 57										
East Dulwich	d														11 59										
Peckham Rye 4	d										11 56				12 01										
Queens Rd Peckham	d										11 59				12 04										
South Bermondsey	d										12 01				12 06										
London Bridge 4 ⊖	a	11 47		11 49	11 55				12 00		12 06	12 02			12 11			12 11							12 09

		LO	SN	SN	SN	FC	SN	LO		SN	SN	FC	SN	SN	FC	FC	SN	SN		SN	SN	SN	SN	SN	SN
				1		1	1			◇1			1		1	🚌				1			◇1 🚲	◇1 🚲	
East Croydon 🚊	d			11 55	12 00	12 02	12 07			12 11			12 14		12 17					12 10			12 24	12 28	12 17
West Croydon 4 🚊	d	11 52						12 09			11 58						12 01	12 04							
Norwood Junction 2	a	11 58		12 00	12 04		12 12	12 13																	
	d	11 58		12 00	12 05		12 13	12 13																	
Selhurst 4	d										12 02						12 05	12 09		12 13					12 20
Thornton Heath	d										12 04						12 07	12 11		12 16					12 22
Norbury	d										12 07						12 10	12 14		12 19					12 25
Streatham Common 4	d										12 10						12 13	12 17		12 21					12 28
Beckenham Junction 4 🚊	d		11 53																						
Birkbeck 🚊	d		11 56																						
Crystal Palace 4	d		12 00																		12 13	12 21			
Gipsy Hill	d		12 02																		12 15				
West Norwood 4	d		12 05																		12 18				
Streatham Hill	d																				12 22				
Balham 4 ⊖	d										12 14							12 21		12 28	12 25				12 32
Wandsworth Common	d										12 16							12 23		12 30	12 27				12 34
Clapham Junction 10	d									12 20	12 20		12 26					12 27		12 38	12 31		12 33	12 37	12 38
West Brompton ⊖	d																			12 47					
Kensington (Olympia) ⊖	d																			12 50					
Shepherd's Bush ⊖	d																			12 53					
Wembley Central ⊖	d																			13s07					
Harrow & Wealdstone ⊖	d																			13 12					
Watford Junction	d																			13 19					
Milton Keynes Central 10	a																			14 00					
Battersea Park 4	d										12 23			12 15							12 35				12 41
London Victoria 15 ⊖	a									12 27	12 28		12 32					12 34			12 39		12 40	12 44	12 46
Streatham 4	d											12 10					12 16								
Tulse Hill 3	d		12 09									12 17				12 20	12 24								
Herne Hill 4	a															12 28									
Loughborough Jn	a															12 36									
Elephant & Castle ⊖	a															12 48									
London Blackfriars 3 ⊖	a															12 56									
City Thameslink 3	a																								
St Pancras International 15 ⊖	a																								
Luton Airport Parkway 7	a																								
Luton 10	a																								
North Dulwich	d		12 12														12 27								
East Dulwich	d		12 14														12 29								
Peckham Rye 4	d		12 16											12 26			12 31								
Queens Rd Peckham	d		12 19											12 29			12 34								
South Bermondsey	d		12 21											12 31			12 36								
London Bridge 4 ⊖	a		12 26	12 13	12 29	12 17	12 25					12 30		12 36	12 32		12 41					12 44			

Table 177

East and West Croydon, London-Milton Keynes and Luton via Norbury-Crystal Palace-Tulse Hill

Local Services

		SN	SN	LO		SN	SN	SN	FC	SN	SN	LO	SN	SN		FC	SN	SN	FC	FC	SN	SN	SN	SN	
							1		1	1	1		◇1				1		1	🚌					
East Croydon 🚊	d		12 21				12 25	12 30	12 32	12 33	12 37		12 41				12 44		12 47						
West Croydon 4 🚊	d	12 15		12 22								12 39		12 28							12 31	12 34			
Norwood Junction 2	a	12 19	12 25	12 28			12 29	12 34			12 42	12 43													
	d	12 22	12 25	12 28			12 30	12 35			12 43	12 43													
Selhurst 4	d													12 32							12 35	12 39			
Thornton Heath	d													12 34							12 37	12 41			
Norbury	d													12 37							12 40	12 44			
Streatham Common 4	d													12 40							12 43	12 47			
Beckenham Junction 4 🚊	d					12 23																			
Birkbeck 🚊	d					12 26																			
Crystal Palace 4	d	12 26				12 30																	12 43	12 51	
Gipsy Hill	d	12 29				12 32																	12 45		
West Norwood 4	d	12 32				12 35																	12 48		
Streatham Hill	d	12 35																					12 52		
Balham 4 ⊖	d	12 39												12 44								12 51	12 55		
Wandsworth Common	d	12 41												12 46								12 53	12 57		
Clapham Junction 10	d	12 45											12 50	12 50			12 56					12 57	13 01		
West Brompton ⊖	d																								
Kensington (Olympia) ⊖	d																								
Shepherd's Bush ⊖	d																								
Wembley Central ⊖	d																								
Harrow & Wealdstone ⊖	d																								
Watford Junction	d																								
Milton Keynes Central 10	a																								
Battersea Park 4	d	12 48												12 53				12 45					13 05		
London Victoria 15 ⊖	a	12 53											12 57	12 58			13 02					13 04	13 09		
Streatham 4	d															12 40					12 46				
Tulse Hill 3	d					12 39										12 47				12 50	12 54				
Herne Hill 4	a																			12 58					
Loughborough Jn	a																			13 06					
Elephant & Castle ⊖	a																			13 18					
London Blackfriars 3 ⊖	a																			13 26					
City Thameslink 3	a																								
St Pancras International 15 ⊖	a																								
Luton Airport Parkway 7	a																								
Luton 10	a																								
North Dulwich	d					12 42															12 57				
East Dulwich	d					12 44															12 59				
Peckham Rye 4	d					12 46												12 56			13 01				
Queens Rd Peckham	d					12 49												12 59			13 04				
South Bermondsey	d					12 51												13 01			13 06				
London Bridge 4 ⊖	a		12 39			12 56	12 43	12 59	12 47	12 49	12 55					13 00		13 06	13 02		13 11			13 11	

		SN	SN	SN	SN	SN	SN	LO	SN	SN		SN	FC	SN	LO	SN	SN	FC	SN	SN		FC	FC	SN	SN
		◇1	◇1 🚲		◇1					1			1	1		◇1			1			1	🚌		
East Croydon 🚊	d	12 53	12 56	12 47	13 00		12 51			12 55		13 00	13 02	13 07		13 11			13 14			13 17			
West Croydon 4 🚊	d					12 45		12 52							13 09		12 58							13 01	13 04
Norwood Junction 2	a					12 49	12 55	12 58		13 00		13 04		13 12	13 13										
	d					12 52	12 55	12 58		13 00		13 05		13 13	13 13										
Selhurst 4	d			12 50													13 02							13 05	13 09
Thornton Heath	d			12 52													13 04							13 07	13 11
Norbury	d			12 55													13 07							13 10	13 14
Streatham Common 4	d			12 58													13 10							13 13	13 17
Beckenham Junction 4 🚊	d								12 53																
Birkbeck 🚊	d								12 56																
Crystal Palace 4	d					12 56			13 00																
Gipsy Hill	d					12 59			13 02																
West Norwood 4	d					13 02			13 05																
Streatham Hill	d					13 05																			
Balham 4 ⊖	d			13 02		13 09											13 14								13 21
Wandsworth Common	d			13 04		13 11											13 16								13 23
Clapham Junction 10	d	13 03	13 06	13 08	13 10	13 15										13 20	13 20		13 26						13 27
West Brompton ⊖	d																								
Kensington (Olympia) ⊖	d																								
Shepherd's Bush ⊖	d																								
Wembley Central ⊖	d																								
Harrow & Wealdstone ⊖	d																								
Watford Junction	d																								
Milton Keynes Central 10	a																								
Battersea Park 4	d			13 11		13 18											13 23			13 15					
London Victoria 15 ⊖	a	13 09	13 12	13 16	13 16	13 23										13 27	13 28		13 32						13 34
Streatham 4	d																	13 10						13 16	
Tulse Hill 3	d								13 09									13 17					13 20	13 24	
Herne Hill 4	a																						13 28		
Loughborough Jn	a																						13 36		
Elephant & Castle ⊖	a																						13 48		
London Blackfriars 3 ⊖	a																						13 56		
City Thameslink 3	a																								
St Pancras International 15 ⊖	a																								
Luton Airport Parkway 7	a																								
Luton 10	a																								
North Dulwich	d								13 12															13 27	
East Dulwich	d								13 14															13 29	
Peckham Rye 4	d								13 16											13 26				13 31	
Queens Rd Peckham	d								13 19											13 29				13 34	
South Bermondsey	d								13 21											13 31				13 36	
London Bridge 4 ⊖	a						13 09		13 26	13 13		13 29	13 17	13 25				13 30		13 36		13 32		13 41	

East and West Croydon, London-Milton Keynes and Luton via Norbury-Crystal Palace-Tulse Hill

Local Services

Station		SN ■	SN	SN	SN ◇■	SN ◇■		SN	SN	SN	LO	SN	SN ■	SN	FC ■	SN ■		SN ■	LO	SN ◇■	SN	FC	SN ■	SN	FC ■
East Croydon	d	13 10			13 24	13 28		13 17		13 21			13 25	13 30	13 32	13 33		13 37		13 41			13 44		13 47
West Croydon	d								13 15		13 22								13 39		13 28				
Norwood Junction	a								13 19	13 25	13 28		13 29	13 34				13 42	13 43						
	d								13 22	13 25	13 28		13 30	13 35				13 43	13 43						
Selhurst	d	13 13						13 20													13 32				
Thornton Heath	d	13 16						13 22													13 34				
Norbury	d	13 19						13 25													13 37				
Streatham Common	d	13 21						13 28													13 40				
Beckenham Junction	d											13 23													
Birkbeck	d											13 26													
Crystal Palace	d		13 13	13 21					13 26			13 30													
Gipsy Hill	d		13 15						13 29			13 32													
West Norwood	d		13 18						13 32			13 35													
Streatham Hill	d		13 22						13 35																
Balham	d	13 28	13 25					13 32	13 39												13 44				
Wandsworth Common	d	13 30	13 27					13 34	13 41												13 46				
Clapham Junction	d	13 38	13 31		13 33	13 37		13 38	13 45											13 50	13 50		13 56		
West Brompton	d	13 47																							
Kensington (Olympia)	d	13 50																							
Shepherd's Bush	d	13 53																							
Wembley Central	d	14s08																							
Harrow & Wealdstone	d	14 13																							
Watford Junction	d	14 20																							
Milton Keynes Central	a	15 00																							
Battersea Park	d		13 35					13 41	13 48												13 53			13 45	
London Victoria	a		13 39		13 40	13 44		13 46	13 53											13 57	13 58		14 02		
Streatham	d																								
Tulse Hill	d											13 39										13 40			
Herne Hill	a																					13 47			
Loughborough Jn	a																								
Elephant & Castle	a																								
London Blackfriars	a																								
City Thameslink	a																								
St Pancras International	a																								
Luton Airport Parkway	a																								
Luton	a																								
North Dulwich	d											13 42													
East Dulwich	d											13 44													
Peckham Rye	d											13 46												13 56	
Queens Rd Peckham	d											13 49												13 59	
South Bermondsey	d											13 51												14 01	
London Bridge	a			13 44						13 39		13 56	13 43	13 59	13 47	13 49		13 55				14 00		14 06	14 02

Station		FC 🚌		SN	SN	SN	SN	SN ◇■	SN ◇■	SN	SN ◇■	SN		SN	LO	SN	SN ■	SN	FC ■	SN ■	LO	SN ◇■		SN	FC
East Croydon	d							13 53	13 56	13 47	14 00			13 51			13 55	14 00	14 02	14 07		14 11			
West Croydon	d			13 31	13 34							13 45			13 52						14 09			13 58	
Norwood Junction	a											13 49		13 55	13 58		14 00	14 04		14 12	14 13				
	d											13 52		13 55	13 58		14 00	14 05		14 13	14 13				
Selhurst	d			13 35	13 39					13 50														14 02	
Thornton Heath	d			13 37	13 41					13 52														14 04	
Norbury	d			13 40	13 44					13 55														14 07	
Streatham Common	d			13 43	13 47					13 58														14 10	
Beckenham Junction	d															13 53									
Birkbeck	d															13 56									
Crystal Palace	d					13 43	13 51					13 56				14 00									
Gipsy Hill	d					13 45						13 59				14 02									
West Norwood	d					13 48						14 02				14 05									
Streatham Hill	d					13 52						14 05													
Balham	d				13 51	13 55				14 02		14 09												14 14	
Wandsworth Common	d				13 53	13 57				14 04		14 11												14 16	
Clapham Junction	d				13 57	14 01		14 03	14 06	14 08	14 10	14 15										14 20		14 20	
West Brompton	d																								
Kensington (Olympia)	d																								
Shepherd's Bush	d																								
Wembley Central	d																								
Harrow & Wealdstone	d																								
Watford Junction	d																								
Milton Keynes Central	a																								
Battersea Park	d					14 05				14 11		14 18												14 23	
London Victoria	a				14 04	14 09		14 09	14 12	14 16	14 16	14 23										14 27		14 28	
Streatham	d			13 46																					
Tulse Hill	d	13 50		13 54												14 09									14 10
Herne Hill	a	13 58																							14 17
Loughborough Jn	a	14 06																							
Elephant & Castle	a	14 18																							
London Blackfriars	a	14 26																							
City Thameslink	a																								
St Pancras International	a																								
Luton Airport Parkway	a																								
Luton	a																								
North Dulwich	d			13 57												14 12									
East Dulwich	d			13 59												14 14									
Peckham Rye	d			14 01												14 16									
Queens Rd Peckham	d			14 04												14 19									
South Bermondsey	d			14 06												14 21									
London Bridge	a			14 11			14 11							14 09		14 26	14 13	14 29	14 17	14 25					14 30

East and West Croydon, London-Milton Keynes and Luton via Norbury-Crystal Palace-Tulse Hill

Local Services

Station		SN ■	SN	FC ■	FC 🚌	SN	SN	SN ■		SN	SN	SN ◇■	SN ◇■	SN	SN	SN	LO	SN		SN ■	SN	FC ■	SN ■	SN ■	LO
East Croydon	d	14 14		14 17				14 10				14 24	14 28	14 17		14 21				14 25	14 30	14 32	14 33	14 37	
West Croydon	d					14 01	14 04								14 15		14 22								14 39
Norwood Junction	a														14 19	14 25	14 28			14 29	14 34			14 42	14 43
	d														14 22	14 25	14 28			14 30	14 35			14 43	14 43
Selhurst	d					14 05	14 09	14 13						14 20											
Thornton Heath	d					14 07	14 11	14 16						14 22											
Norbury	d					14 10	14 14	14 19						14 25											
Streatham Common	d					14 13	14 17	14 21						14 28											
Beckenham Junction	d																	14 23							
Birkbeck	d																	14 26							
Crystal Palace	d									14 13	14 21				14 26			14 30							
Gipsy Hill	d									14 15					14 29			14 32							
West Norwood	d									14 18					14 32			14 35							
Streatham Hill	d									14 22					14 35										
Balham	d						14 21	14 28		14 25				14 32	14 39										
Wandsworth Common	d						14 23	14 30		14 27				14 34	14 41										
Clapham Junction	d	14 26					14 27	14 38		14 31		14 33	14 37	14 38	14 45										
West Brompton	d							14 47																	
Kensington (Olympia)	d							14 50																	
Shepherd's Bush	d							14 53																	
Wembley Central	d							15s07																	
Harrow & Wealdstone	d							15 12																	
Watford Junction	d							15 19																	
Milton Keynes Central	a							16 00																	
Battersea Park	d		14 15							14 35				14 41	14 48										
London Victoria	a	14 32					14 34			14 39		14 40	14 44	14 46	14 53										
Streatham	d					14 16																			
Tulse Hill	d				14 20	14 24												14 39							
Herne Hill	a				14 28																				
Loughborough Jn	a				14 36																				
Elephant & Castle	a				14 48																				
London Blackfriars	a				14 56																				
City Thameslink	a																								
St Pancras International	a																								
Luton Airport Parkway	a																								
Luton	a																								
North Dulwich	d					14 27												14 42							
East Dulwich	d					14 29												14 44							
Peckham Rye	d		14 26			14 31												14 46							
Queens Rd Peckham	d		14 29			14 34												14 49							
South Bermondsey	d		14 31			14 36												14 51							
London Bridge	a		14 36	14 32		14 41					14 44					14 39		14 56		14 43	14 59	14 47	14 49	14 55	

Station		SN ◇■	SN	FC		SN ■	SN	FC ■	FC 🚌	SN	SN	SN	SN	SN ◇■		SN ◇■	SN	SN ◇■	SN	SN	LO	SN	SN ■	SN	
East Croydon	d	14 41				14 44		14 47						14 53		14 56	14 47	15 00		14 51			14 55	15 00	
West Croydon	d		14 28							14 31	14 34								14 45		14 52				
Norwood Junction	a																		14 49	14 55	14 58		15 00	15 04	
	d																		14 52	14 55	14 58		15 00	15 05	
Selhurst	d		14 32							14 35	14 39						14 50								
Thornton Heath	d		14 34							14 37	14 41						14 52								
Norbury	d		14 37							14 40	14 44						14 55								
Streatham Common	d		14 40							14 43	14 47						14 58								
Beckenham Junction	d																					14 53			
Birkbeck	d																					14 56			
Crystal Palace	d											14 43	14 51						14 56			15 00			
Gipsy Hill	d											14 45							14 59			15 02			
West Norwood	d											14 48							15 02			15 05			
Streatham Hill	d											14 52							15 05						
Balham	d		14 44								14 51	14 55					15 02		15 09						
Wandsworth Common	d		14 46								14 53	14 57					15 04		15 11						
Clapham Junction	d	14 50	14 50			14 56					14 57	15 01		15 03		15 06	15 08	15 10	15 15						
West Brompton	d																								
Kensington (Olympia)	d																								
Shepherd's Bush	d																								
Wembley Central	d																								
Harrow & Wealdstone	d																								
Watford Junction	d																								
Milton Keynes Central	a																								
Battersea Park	d		14 53				14 45					15 05					15 11		15 18						
London Victoria	a	14 57	14 58			15 02					15 04	15 09		15 09		15 12	15 16	15 16	15 23						
Streatham	d			14 40						14 46															
Tulse Hill	d			14 47					14 50	14 54												15 09			
Herne Hill	a								14 58																
Loughborough Jn	a								15 06																
Elephant & Castle	a								15 18																
London Blackfriars	a								15 26																
City Thameslink	a																								
St Pancras International	a																								
Luton Airport Parkway	a																								
Luton	a																								
North Dulwich	d									14 57												15 12			
East Dulwich	d									14 59												15 14			
Peckham Rye	d						14 56			15 01												15 16			
Queens Rd Peckham	d						14 59			15 04												15 19			
South Bermondsey	d						15 01			15 06												15 21			
London Bridge	a			15 00			15 06	15 02		15 11			15 11							15 09		15 26	15 13	15 29	

East and West Croydon, London-Milton Keynes and Luton via Norbury-Crystal Palace-Tulse Hill

Local Services

Station		FC [1]	SN [1]	LO	SN ◇[1]	SN	FC	SN [1]	SN	FC [1]	FC 🚌	SN	SN	SN [1]	SN	SN	SN ◇[1] ⊼	SN ◇[1] ⊼	SN	SN	SN	LO	SN
East Croydon 🚋	d	15 02	15 07		15 11			15 14		15 17				15 10			15 24	15 28	15 17		15 21		
West Croydon [4] 🚋	d			15 09		14 58						15 01	15 04							15 15		15 22	
Norwood Junction [2]	a		15 12	15 13																15 19	15 25	15 28	
	d		15 13	15 13																15 22	15 25	15 28	
Selhurst [4]	d					15 02						15 05	15 09	15 13					15 20				
Thornton Heath	d					15 04						15 07	15 11	15 16					15 22				
Norbury	d					15 07						15 10	15 14	15 19					15 25				
Streatham Common [4]	d					15 10						15 13	15 17	15 21					15 28				
Beckenham Junction [4] 🚋	d																						15 23
Birkbeck 🚋	d																						15 26
Crystal Palace [4]	d														15 13	15 21				15 26			15 30
Gipsy Hill	d														15 15					15 29			15 32
West Norwood [4]	d														15 18					15 32			15 35
Streatham Hill	d														15 22					15 35			
Balham [4] ⊖	d					15 14							15 21	15 28	15 25				15 32	15 39			
Wandsworth Common	d					15 16							15 23	15 30	15 27				15 34	15 41			
Clapham Junction [10]	d				15 20	15 20		15 26					15 27	15 38	15 31		15 33	15 37	15 38	15 45			
West Brompton ⊖	d													15 47									
Kensington (Olympia) ⊖	d													15 50									
Shepherd's Bush ⊖	d													15 53									
Wembley Central ⊖	d													16s07									
Harrow & Wealdstone ⊖	d													16 12									
Watford Junction	d													16 19									
Milton Keynes Central [10]	a													17 00									
Battersea Park [4]	d					15 23			15 15						15 35				15 41	15 48			
London Victoria [15] ⊖	a				15 27	15 28		15 32					15 34		15 39		15 40	15 44	15 46	15 53			
Streatham [4]	d						15 10					15 16											
Tulse Hill [3]	d						15 17				15 20	15 24											15 39
Herne Hill [4]	a										15 28												
Loughborough Jn	a										15 36												
Elephant & Castle ⊖	a										15 48												
London Blackfriars [3] ⊖	a										15 56												
City Thameslink [3]	a																						
St Pancras International [15] ⊖	a																						
Luton Airport Parkway [7]	a																						
Luton [10]	a																						
North Dulwich	d											15 27											15 42
East Dulwich	d											15 29											15 44
Peckham Rye [4]	d								15 26			15 31											15 46
Queens Rd Peckham	d								15 29			15 34											15 49
South Bermondsey	d								15 31			15 36											15 51
London Bridge [4] ⊖	a	15 17	15 25				15 30		15 36	15 32		15 41				15 44					15 39		15 56

Station		SN [1]	SN	FC [1]	SN [1]	SN [1]	LO	SN ◇[1]	SN	FC	SN [1]	SN	FC [1]	FC 🚌	SN	SN	SN	SN	SN ◇[1]	SN ◇[1] ⊼	SN	SN ◇[1]	SN
East Croydon 🚋	d	15 25	15 30	15 32	15 33	15 37		15 41			15 44		15 47						15 53	15 56	15 47	16 00	
West Croydon [4] 🚋	d						15 39		15 28						15 31	15 34							15 45
Norwood Junction [2]	a	15 29	15 34			15 42	15 43																15 49
	d	15 30	15 35			15 43	15 43																15 52
Selhurst [4]	d								15 32						15 35	15 39					15 50		
Thornton Heath	d								15 34						15 37	15 41					15 52		
Norbury	d								15 37						15 40	15 44					15 55		
Streatham Common [4]	d								15 40						15 43	15 47					15 58		
Beckenham Junction [4] 🚋	d																						
Birkbeck 🚋	d																						
Crystal Palace [4]	d																15 43	15 51					15 56
Gipsy Hill	d																15 45						15 59
West Norwood [4]	d																15 48						16 02
Streatham Hill	d																15 52						16 05
Balham [4] ⊖	d								15 44							15 51	15 55				16 02		16 09
Wandsworth Common	d								15 46							15 53	15 57				16 04		16 11
Clapham Junction [10]	d							15 50	15 50		15 56					15 57	16 01		16 03	16 06	16 08	16 10	16 15
West Brompton ⊖	d																						
Kensington (Olympia) ⊖	d																						
Shepherd's Bush ⊖	d																						
Wembley Central ⊖	d																						
Harrow & Wealdstone ⊖	d																						
Watford Junction	d																						
Milton Keynes Central [10]	a																						
Battersea Park [4]	d								15 53			15 45					16 05				16 11		16 18
London Victoria [15] ⊖	a							15 57	15 58		16 02					16 04	16 09		16 09	16 12	16 16	16 16	16 23
Streatham [4]	d									15 40					15 46								
Tulse Hill [3]	d									15 47				15 50	15 54								
Herne Hill [4]	a													15 58									
Loughborough Jn	a													16 06									
Elephant & Castle ⊖	a													16 18									
London Blackfriars [3] ⊖	a													16 26									
City Thameslink [3]	a																						
St Pancras International [15] ⊖	a																						
Luton Airport Parkway [7]	a																						
Luton [10]	a																						
North Dulwich	d														15 57								
East Dulwich	d														15 59								
Peckham Rye [4]	d											15 56			16 01								
Queens Rd Peckham	d											15 59			16 04								
South Bermondsey	d											16 01			16 06								
London Bridge [4] ⊖	a	15 43	15 59	15 47	15 49	15 55				16 00		16 06	16 02		16 11			16 11					

East and West Croydon, London-Milton Keynes and Luton via Norbury-Crystal Palace-Tulse Hill

Local Services

Station		SN	LO	SN	SN [1]	SN	FC [1]	SN [1]	LO	SN ◇[1]	SN	FC	SN [1]	SN	FC [1]	FC 🚌	SN	SN	SN [1]	SN	SN	SN ◇[1] ⊼
East Croydon 🚋	d	15 51			15 55	16 00	16 02	16 07		16 11			16 14		16 17				16 10			16 24
West Croydon [4] 🚋	d		15 52						16 09		15 58						16 01	16 04				
Norwood Junction [2]	a	15 55	15 58		16 00	16 04		16 12	16 13													
	d	15 55	15 58		16 00	16 05		16 13	16 13													
Selhurst [4]	d										16 02						16 05	16 09	16 13			
Thornton Heath	d										16 04						16 07	16 11	16 16			
Norbury	d										16 07						16 10	16 14	16 19			
Streatham Common [4]	d										16 10						16 13	16 17	16 21			
Beckenham Junction [4] 🚋	d			15 53																		
Birkbeck 🚋	d			15 56																		
Crystal Palace [4]	d			16 00																16 13	16 21	
Gipsy Hill	d			16 02																16 15		
West Norwood [4]	d			16 05																16 18		
Streatham Hill	d																			16 22		
Balham [4] ⊖	d										16 14							16 21	16 28	16 25		
Wandsworth Common	d										16 16							16 23	16 30	16 27		
Clapham Junction [10]	d									16 20	16 20		16 26					16 27	16 38	16 31		16 33
West Brompton ⊖	d																		16 47			
Kensington (Olympia) ⊖	d																		16 50			
Shepherd's Bush ⊖	d																		16 53			
Wembley Central ⊖	d																		17s07			
Harrow & Wealdstone ⊖	d																		17 12			
Watford Junction	d																		17 19			
Milton Keynes Central [10]	a																		18 00			
Battersea Park [4]	d										16 23			16 15						16 35		
London Victoria [15] ⊖	a									16 27	16 28		16 32					16 34		16 39		16 40
Streatham [4]	d											16 10					16 16					
Tulse Hill [3]	d			16 09								16 17				16 20	16 24					
Herne Hill [4]	a															16 28						
Loughborough Jn	a															16 36						
Elephant & Castle ⊖	a															16 48						
London Blackfriars [3] ⊖	a															16 57						
City Thameslink [3]	a																					
St Pancras International [15] ⊖	a																					
Luton Airport Parkway [7]	a																					
Luton [10]	a																					
North Dulwich	d			16 12													16 27					
East Dulwich	d			16 14													16 29					
Peckham Rye [4]	d			16 16										16 26			16 31					
Queens Rd Peckham	d			16 19										16 29			16 34					
South Bermondsey	d			16 21										16 31			16 36					
London Bridge [4] ⊖	a	16 09		16 26	16 13	16 29	16 17	16 25				16 30		16 36	16 32		16 41				16 41	

Station		SN ◇[1] ⊼	SN	SN	SN	LO	SN	SN [1]	SN	FC [1]	SN [1]	SN [1]	LO	SN ◇[1]	SN	FC	SN [1]	SN	FC [1]	FC 🚌	SN	SN	SN
East Croydon 🚋	d	16 28	16 17		16 21			16 25	16 30	16 32	16 33	16 37		16 41			16 44		16 47				
West Croydon [4] 🚋	d			16 15		16 22							16 39		16 28						16 31	16 34	
Norwood Junction [2]	a			16 19	16 25	16 28		16 29	16 34			16 42	16 43										
	d			16 22	16 25	16 28		16 30	16 35			16 43	16 43										
Selhurst [4]	d		16 20												16 32						16 35	16 39	
Thornton Heath	d		16 22												16 34						16 37	16 41	
Norbury	d		16 25												16 37						16 40	16 44	
Streatham Common [4]	d		16 28												16 40						16 43	16 47	
Beckenham Junction [4] 🚋	d						16 23																
Birkbeck 🚋	d						16 26																
Crystal Palace [4]	d			16 26			16 30																16 43
Gipsy Hill	d			16 29			16 32																16 45
West Norwood [4]	d			16 32			16 35																16 48
Streatham Hill	d			16 35																			16 52
Balham [4] ⊖	d		16 32	16 39											16 44							16 51	16 55
Wandsworth Common	d		16 34	16 41											16 46							16 53	16 57
Clapham Junction [10]	d	16 37	16 38	16 45										16 50	16 50		16 56					16 57	17 01
West Brompton ⊖	d																						
Kensington (Olympia) ⊖	d																						
Shepherd's Bush ⊖	d																						
Wembley Central ⊖	d																						
Harrow & Wealdstone ⊖	d																						
Watford Junction	d																						
Milton Keynes Central [10]	a																						
Battersea Park [4]	d		16 41	16 48											16 53			16 45					17 05
London Victoria [15] ⊖	a	16 44	16 46	16 53										16 57	16 58		17 02					17 04	17 09
Streatham [4]	d															16 40					16 46		
Tulse Hill [3]	d						16 39									16 47				16 50	16 54		
Herne Hill [4]	a																			16 58			
Loughborough Jn	a																			17 06			
Elephant & Castle ⊖	a																			17 18			
London Blackfriars [3] ⊖	a																			17 26			
City Thameslink [3]	a																						
St Pancras International [15] ⊖	a																						
Luton Airport Parkway [7]	a																						
Luton [10]	a																						
North Dulwich	d						16 42														16 57		
East Dulwich	d						16 44														16 59		
Peckham Rye [4]	d						16 46											16 56			17 01		
Queens Rd Peckham	d						16 49											16 59			17 04		
South Bermondsey	d						16 51											17 01			17 06		
London Bridge [4] ⊖	a				16 39		16 56	16 43	16 59	16 47	16 49	16 55				17 00		17 06	17 02		17 11		

East and West Croydon, London-Milton Keynes and Luton via Norbury-Crystal Palace-Tulse Hill

Local Services

Station		SN	SN ◇1	SN ◇1 (trolley)	SN	SN ◇1	SN	SN	LO	SN	SN 1	SN	SN	FC 1	SN 1	LO	SN ◇1	FC	SN 1	SN	FC 1	FC (bus)
East Croydon	d		16 53	16 56	16 47	17 00		16 51			16 55		17 00	17 02	17 07		17 11		17 14		17 17	
West Croydon 4	d						16 45		16 52			16 58				17 09						
Norwood Junction 2	a						16 49	16 55	16 58		17 00		17 04		17 12	17 13						
	d						16 52	16 55	16 58		17 00		17 05		17 13	17 13						
Selhurst 4	d				16 50							17 02										
Thornton Heath	d				16 52							17 04										
Norbury	d				16 55							17 07										
Streatham Common 4	d				16 58							17 10										
Beckenham Junction 4	d									16 53												
Birkbeck	d									16 56												
Crystal Palace 4	d	16 51					16 56			17 00												
Gipsy Hill	d						16 59			17 02												
West Norwood 4	d						17 02			17 05												
Streatham Hill	d						17 05															
Balham 4 ⊖	d				17 02		17 09					17 14										
Wandsworth Common	d				17 04		17 11					17 16										
Clapham Junction 10	d		17 03	17 06	17 08	17 10	17 15					17 20					17 20		17 26			
West Brompton ⊖	d																					
Kensington (Olympia) ⊖	d																					
Shepherd's Bush ⊖	d																					
Wembley Central ⊖	d																					
Harrow & Wealdstone ⊖	d																					
Watford Junction	d																					
Milton Keynes Central 10	a																					
Battersea Park 4	d				17 11		17 18					17 23								17 15		
London Victoria 15 ⊖	a		17 09	17 12	17 16	17 16	17 23					17 28					17 28		17 32			
Streatham 4	d																	17 10				
Tulse Hill 3	d									17 09								17 17				17 20
Herne Hill 4	a																					17 28
Loughborough Jn	a																					17 36
Elephant & Castle ⊖	a																					17 48
London Blackfriars 3 ⊖	a																					17 56
City Thameslink 3	a																					
St Pancras International 15 ⊖	a																					
Luton Airport Parkway 7	a																					
Luton 10	a																					
North Dulwich	d									17 12												
East Dulwich	d									17 14												
Peckham Rye 4	d									17 16										17 26		
Queens Rd Peckham	d									17 19										17 29		
South Bermondsey	d									17 21										17 31		
London Bridge 4 ⊖	a	17 11						17 09		17 26	17 13		17 30	17 17	17 25			17 30		17 36	17 32	

Station		SN	SN	SN 1	SN	SN	SN ◇1 (trolley)	SN ◇1 (trolley)	SN	SN	SN	LO	SN	SN 1	SN	FC 1	SN 1	SN 1	LO	SN ◇1	SN	FC	SN 1
East Croydon	d			17 10			17 24	17 28	17 17		17 21			17 25	17 30	17 32	17 33	17 37		17 41			17 44
West Croydon 4	d	17 01	17 04							17 15		17 22							17 39		17 28		
Norwood Junction 2	a									17 19	17 25	17 28		17 29	17 34			17 42	17 43				
	d									17 22	17 25	17 28		17 30	17 35			17 43	17 43				
Selhurst 4	d	17 05	17 09	17 13					17 20												17 32		
Thornton Heath	d	17 07	17 11	17 16					17 22												17 34		
Norbury	d	17 10	17 14	17 19					17 25												17 37		
Streatham Common 4	d	17 13	17 17	17 21					17 28												17 40		
Beckenham Junction 4	d												17 23										
Birkbeck	d												17 26										
Crystal Palace 4	d				17 13	17 21				17 26			17 30										
Gipsy Hill	d				17 15					17 29			17 32										
West Norwood 4	d				17 18					17 32			17 35										
Streatham Hill	d				17 22					17 35													
Balham 4 ⊖	d		17 21	17 28	17 25				17 33	17 39											17 44		
Wandsworth Common	d		17 23	17 30	17 27				17 35	17 41											17 46		
Clapham Junction 10	d		17 27	17 38	17 32		17 33	17 37	17 39	17 45										17 50	17 50		17 56
West Brompton ⊖	d			17 47																			
Kensington (Olympia) ⊖	d			17 50																			
Shepherd's Bush ⊖	d			17 53																			
Wembley Central ⊖	d			18s07																			
Harrow & Wealdstone ⊖	d			18 12																			
Watford Junction	d			18 19																			
Milton Keynes Central 10	a			19 00																			
Battersea Park 4	d				17 36				17 42	17 48											17 53		
London Victoria 15 ⊖	a		17 34		17 40		17 40	17 44	17 47	17 53										17 57	17 58		18 02
Streatham 4	d	17 16																				17 40	
Tulse Hill 3	d	17 24											17 39									17 47	
Herne Hill 4	a																						
Loughborough Jn	a																						
Elephant & Castle ⊖	a																						
London Blackfriars 3 ⊖	a																						
City Thameslink 3	a																						
St Pancras International 15 ⊖	a																						
Luton Airport Parkway 7	a																						
Luton 10	a																						
North Dulwich	d	17 27											17 42										
East Dulwich	d	17 29											17 44										
Peckham Rye 4	d	17 31											17 46										
Queens Rd Peckham	d	17 34											17 49										
South Bermondsey	d	17 36											17 51										
London Bridge 4 ⊖	a	17 41				17 41					17 39		17 56	17 43	17 59	17 47	17 49	17 55				18 00	

Table 177

Saturdays

East and West Croydon, London-Milton Keynes and Luton via Norbury-Crystal Palace-Tulse Hill

Local Services

Station		SN	FC 1	FC (bus)	SN	SN	SN	SN	SN ◇1	SN ◇1 (trolley)	SN	SN ◇1	SN	SN	LO	SN	SN 1	SN	FC 1	SN 1	LO	SN ◇1	SN
East Croydon	d		17 47						17 53	17 56	17 47	18 00		17 51			17 55	18 00	18 02	18 07		18 11	
West Croydon 4	d				17 31	17 34							17 45		17 52						18 09		17 58
Norwood Junction 2	a												17 49	17 55	17 58		18 00	18 04		18 12	18 13		
	d												17 52	17 55	17 58		18 00	18 05		18 13	18 13		
Selhurst 4	d				17 35	17 39					17 50												18 02
Thornton Heath	d				17 37	17 41					17 52												18 04
Norbury	d				17 40	17 44					17 55												18 07
Streatham Common 4	d				17 43	17 47					17 58												18 10
Beckenham Junction 4	d															17 53							
Birkbeck	d															17 56							
Crystal Palace 4	d						17 43	17 51					17 56			18 00							
Gipsy Hill	d						17 45						17 59			18 02							
West Norwood 4	d						17 48						18 02			18 05							
Streatham Hill	d						17 52						18 05										
Balham 4 ⊖	d					17 51	17 55				18 02		18 09										18 14
Wandsworth Common	d					17 53	17 57				18 04		18 11										18 16
Clapham Junction 10	d					17 57	18 01		18 03	18 06	18 08	18 10	18 15									18 20	18 20
West Brompton ⊖	d																						
Kensington (Olympia) ⊖	d																						
Shepherd's Bush ⊖	d																						
Wembley Central ⊖	d																						
Harrow & Wealdstone ⊖	d																						
Watford Junction	d																						
Milton Keynes Central 10	a																						
Battersea Park 4	d	17 45					18 05				18 11		18 18										18 23
London Victoria 15 ⊖	a					18 04	18 09		18 09	18 12	18 16	18 16	18 23									18 27	18 28
Streatham 4	d				17 46																		
Tulse Hill 3	d			17 50	17 54											18 09							
Herne Hill 4	a			17 58																			
Loughborough Jn	a			18 06																			
Elephant & Castle ⊖	a			18 18																			
London Blackfriars 3 ⊖	a			18 26																			
City Thameslink 3	a																						
St Pancras International 15 ⊖	a																						
Luton Airport Parkway 7	a																						
Luton 10	a																						
North Dulwich	d				17 57											18 12							
East Dulwich	d				17 59											18 14							
Peckham Rye 4	d	17 56			18 01											18 16							
Queens Rd Peckham	d	17 59			18 04											18 19							
South Bermondsey	d	18 01			18 06											18 21							
London Bridge 4 ⊖	a	18 06	18 02		18 11			18 11						18 09		18 26	18 13	18 29	18 17	18 25			

Station		FC	SN 1	SN	FC 1	FC (bus)	SN	SN	SN 1	SN	SN	SN ◇1 (trolley)	SN ◇1 (trolley)	SN	SN	SN	LO	SN	SN 1	SN	FC 1	SN 1
East Croydon	d		18 14		18 17				18 10			18 24	18 28	18 17		18 21			18 25	18 30	18 32	18 33
West Croydon 4	d						18 01	18 04							18 15		18 22					
Norwood Junction 2	a														18 19	18 25	18 28		18 29	18 34		
	d														18 22	18 25	18 28		18 30	18 35		
Selhurst 4	d						18 05	18 09	18 13					18 20								
Thornton Heath	d						18 07	18 11	18 16					18 22								
Norbury	d						18 10	18 14	18 19					18 25								
Streatham Common 4	d						18 13	18 17	18 21					18 28								
Beckenham Junction 4	d																	18 23				
Birkbeck	d																	18 26				
Crystal Palace 4	d									18 13	18 21				18 26			18 30				
Gipsy Hill	d									18 15					18 29			18 32				
West Norwood 4	d									18 18					18 32			18 35				
Streatham Hill	d									18 22					18 35							
Balham 4 ⊖	d							18 21	18 28	18 25				18 32	18 39							
Wandsworth Common	d							18 23	18 30	18 27				18 34	18 41							
Clapham Junction 10	d		18 26					18 27	18 38	18 31		18 33	18 37	18 38	18 45							
West Brompton ⊖	d								18 47													
Kensington (Olympia) ⊖	d								18 50													
Shepherd's Bush ⊖	d								18 53													
Wembley Central ⊖	d								19 08													
Harrow & Wealdstone ⊖	d								19 13													
Watford Junction	d								19a21													
Milton Keynes Central 10	a																					
Battersea Park 4	d			18 15						18 35				18 41	18 48							
London Victoria 15 ⊖	a		18 32					18 34		18 39		18 40	18 44	18 46	18 53							
Streatham 4	d	18 10					18 16															
Tulse Hill 3	d	18 17				18 20	18 24											18 39				
Herne Hill 4	a					18 28																
Loughborough Jn	a					18 36																
Elephant & Castle ⊖	a					18 48																
London Blackfriars 3 ⊖	a					18 56																
City Thameslink 3	a																					
St Pancras International 15 ⊖	a																					
Luton Airport Parkway 7	a																					
Luton 10	a																					
North Dulwich	d						18 27											18 42				
East Dulwich	d						18 29											18 44				
Peckham Rye 4	d			18 26			18 31											18 46				
Queens Rd Peckham	d			18 29			18 34											18 49				
South Bermondsey	d			18 31			18 36											18 51				
London Bridge 4 ⊖	a	18 30		18 36	18 32		18 41				18 41					18 39		18 56	18 43	18 59	18 47	18 49

Table 177

East and West Croydon, London-Milton Keynes and Luton via Norbury-Crystal Palace-Tulse Hill

Local Services

		SN 1	LO	SN ◇1	SN	FC	SN 1	SN		FC 1	FC (bus)	SN	SN	SN	SN	SN ◇1	SN ◇1	SN		SN ◇1	SN	SN	LO	SN	SN 1
East Croydon	d	18 37		18 41			18 44			18 47						18 53	18 56	18 47		19 00		18 51			18 55
West Croydon 4	d		18 39		18 28							18 31	18 34								18 45		18 52		
Norwood Junction 2	a	18 42	18 43																		18 49	18 55	18 58		19 00
	d	18 43	18 43																		18 52	18 55	18 58		19 00
Selhurst 4	d				18 32							18 35	18 39					18 50							
Thornton Heath	d				18 34							18 37	18 41					18 52							
Norbury	d				18 37							18 40	18 44					18 55							
Streatham Common 4	d				18 40							18 43	18 47					18 58							
Beckenham Junction 4	d																							18 53	
Birkbeck	d																							18 56	
Crystal Palace 4	d													18 43	18 51						18 56			19 00	
Gipsy Hill	d													18 45							18 59			19 02	
West Norwood 4	d													18 48							19 02			19 05	
Streatham Hill	d													18 52							19 05				
Balham 4 ⊖	d				18 44								18 51	18 55				19 02			19 09				
Wandsworth Common	d				18 46								18 53	18 57				19 04			19 11				
Clapham Junction 10	d			18 50	18 50		18 56						18 57	19 01		19 03	19 06	19 08		19 10	19 15				
West Brompton ⊖	d																								
Kensington (Olympia) ⊖	d																								
Shepherd's Bush ⊖	d																								
Wembley Central ⊖	d																								
Harrow & Wealdstone ⊖	d																								
Watford Junction	d																								
Milton Keynes Central 10	a																								
Battersea Park 4	d				18 53			18 45						19 05				19 11			19 18				
London Victoria 15 ⊖	a			18 57	18 58		19 02						19 04	19 09		19 09	19 12	19 16		19 16	19 23				
Streatham 4	d					18 40						18 46													
Tulse Hill 3	d					18 47					18 50	18 54												19 09	
Herne Hill 4	a										18 58														
Loughborough Jn	a										19 06														
Elephant & Castle ⊖	a										19 18														
London Blackfriars 3 ⊖	a										19 26														
City Thameslink 3	a																								
St Pancras International 15 ⊖	a																								
Luton Airport Parkway 7	a																								
Luton 10	a																								
North Dulwich	d											18 57												19 12	
East Dulwich	d											18 59												19 14	
Peckham Rye 4	d							18 56				19 01												19 16	
Queens Rd Peckham	d							18 59				19 04												19 19	
South Bermondsey	d							19 01				19 06												19 21	
London Bridge 4 ⊖	a	18 55				19 00		19 06		19 02		19 11			19 11							19 09		19 26	19 13

		SN	FC 1	SN 1		LO	SN ◇1	SN	FC	SN 1	SN	SN	FC 1	SN		FC (bus)	SN	SN 1	SN ◇1	SN 1	SN	SN ◇1	SN	LO	
East Croydon	d	19 00	19 02	19 07			19 11			19 14			19 17					19 10	19 24	19 25	19 17	19 29			
West Croydon 4	d					19 09		18 58									19 01						19 15	19 22	
Norwood Junction 2	a	19 04		19 12		19 13																	19 19	19 28	
	d	19 05		19 13		19 13																	19 22	19 28	
Selhurst 4	d							19 02									19 05	19 13			19 20				
Thornton Heath	d							19 04									19 07	19 16			19 22				
Norbury	d							19 07									19 10	19 19			19 25				
Streatham Common 4	d							19 10									19 13	19 21			19 28				
Beckenham Junction 4	d																								
Birkbeck	d																								
Crystal Palace 4	d										19 13			19 21									19 26		
Gipsy Hill	d										19 15												19 29		
West Norwood 4	d										19 18												19 32		
Streatham Hill	d										19 22												19 35		
Balham 4 ⊖	d							19 14			19 25							19 28			19 32		19 39		
Wandsworth Common	d							19 16			19 27							19 30			19 34		19 41		
Clapham Junction 10	d						19 20	19 20		19 26	19 31							19 38	19 33	19 37	19 38	19 40	19 45		
West Brompton ⊖	d																	19 45							
Kensington (Olympia) ⊖	d																	19 48							
Shepherd's Bush ⊖	d																	19 50							
Wembley Central ⊖	d																								
Harrow & Wealdstone ⊖	d																	20 08							
Watford Junction	d																	20a15							
Milton Keynes Central 10	a																								
Battersea Park 4	d							19 23			19 35	19 15									19 41		19 48		
London Victoria 15 ⊖	a						19 27	19 28		19 32	19 39								19 40	19 44	19 46	19 47	19 53		
Streatham 4	d								19 10								19 16								
Tulse Hill 3	d								19 17							19 20	19 24								
Herne Hill 4	a															19 28									
Loughborough Jn	a															19 36									
Elephant & Castle ⊖	a															19 48									
London Blackfriars 3 ⊖	a															19 56									
City Thameslink 3	a																								
St Pancras International 15 ⊖	a																								
Luton Airport Parkway 7	a																								
Luton 10	a																								
North Dulwich	d																19 27								
East Dulwich	d																19 29								
Peckham Rye 4	d											19 26					19 31								
Queens Rd Peckham	d											19 29					19 34								
South Bermondsey	d											19 31					19 36								
London Bridge 4 ⊖	a	19 29	19 17	19 25					19 30			19 36	19 32	19 41			19 41								

Table 177

East and West Croydon, London-Milton Keynes and Luton via Norbury-Crystal Palace-Tulse Hill

Local Services

		SN	SN	FC 1	SN 1	LO	SN ◇1	SN	FC	SN 1		SN	SN	FC 1	SN	FC (bus)	SN	SN ◇1	SN ◇1	SN 1		SN	SN 1	SN	LO
East Croydon	d		19 30	19 32	19 33		19 41			19 44				19 47				19 53	19 56	19 57		19 47	20 00		
West Croydon 4	d					19 39		19 28									19 31							19 48	19 52
Norwood Junction 2	a		19 34			19 43																		19 52	19 58
	d		19 35			19 43																		19 53	19 58
Selhurst 4	d							19 32									19 35					19 50			
Thornton Heath	d							19 34									19 37					19 52			
Norbury	d							19 37									19 40					19 55			
Streatham Common 4	d							19 40									19 43					19 58			
Beckenham Junction 4	d	19 23																							
Birkbeck	d	19 26																							
Crystal Palace 4	d	19 30										19 43			19 51									19 57	
Gipsy Hill	d	19 32										19 45												19 59	
West Norwood 4	d	19 35										19 48												20 02	
Streatham Hill	d											19 52												20 06	
Balham 4 ⊖	d							19 44				19 55										20 02		20 09	
Wandsworth Common	d							19 46				19 57										20 04		20 11	
Clapham Junction 10	d						19 50	19 50		19 56		20 01						20 03	20 06	20 09		20 08	20 12	20 15	
West Brompton ⊖	d																								
Kensington (Olympia) ⊖	d																								
Shepherd's Bush ⊖	d																								
Wembley Central ⊖	d																								
Harrow & Wealdstone ⊖	d																								
Watford Junction	d																								
Milton Keynes Central 10	a																								
Battersea Park 4	d							19 53				20 05	19 45									20 11		20 18	
London Victoria 15 ⊖	a						19 57	19 58		20 02		20 09						20 09	20 12	20 15		20 16	20 20	20 23	
Streatham 4	d								19 40								19 46								
Tulse Hill 3	d	19 39							19 47							19 50	19 54								
Herne Hill 4	a															19 58									
Loughborough Jn	a															20 06									
Elephant & Castle ⊖	a															20 18									
London Blackfriars 3 ⊖	a															20 26									
City Thameslink 3	a																								
St Pancras International 15 ⊖	a																								
Luton Airport Parkway 7	a																								
Luton 10	a																								
North Dulwich	d	19 42															19 57								
East Dulwich	d	19 44															19 59								
Peckham Rye 4	d	19 46											19 56				20 01								
Queens Rd Peckham	d	19 49											19 59				20 04								
South Bermondsey	d	19 51											20 01				20 06								
London Bridge 4 ⊖	a	19 56	19 59	19 47	19 49				20 00				20 06	20 02	20 11		20 11								

		SN	SN	FC 1	LO	SN ◇1		FC	SN 1	SN	FC 1	FC (bus)	SN	SN	SN	SN		SN ◇1	SN 1	SN	SN ◇1	SN	LO	SN	SN
East Croydon	d		20 00	20 02		20 11			20 14		20 17							20 24	20 26	20 17	20 30				20 30
West Croydon 4	d				20 09								20 01	20 04								20 18	20 22		
Norwood Junction 2	a		20 04		20 13																	20 22	20 28		20 34
	d		20 05		20 13																	20 23	20 28		20 35
Selhurst 4	d												20 05	20 09						20 20					
Thornton Heath	d												20 07	20 11						20 22					
Norbury	d												20 10	20 14						20 25					
Streatham Common 4	d												20 13	20 17						20 28					
Beckenham Junction 4	d	19 53																						20 23	
Birkbeck	d	19 56																						20 26	
Crystal Palace 4	d	20 00													20 13	20 21						20 27		20 30	
Gipsy Hill	d	20 03													20 15							20 29		20 33	
West Norwood 4	d	20 06													20 18							20 32		20 36	
Streatham Hill	d														20 22							20 36			
Balham 4 ⊖	d													20 21	20 25					20 32		20 39			
Wandsworth Common	d													20 23	20 27					20 34		20 41			
Clapham Junction 10	d					20 20			20 26					20 27	20 31			20 33	20 37	20 38	20 41	20 45			
West Brompton ⊖	d																								
Kensington (Olympia) ⊖	d																								
Shepherd's Bush ⊖	d																								
Wembley Central ⊖	d																								
Harrow & Wealdstone ⊖	d																								
Watford Junction	d																								
Milton Keynes Central 10	a																								
Battersea Park 4	d									20 15					20 35					20 41		20 48			
London Victoria 15 ⊖	a					20 27			20 32					20 34	20 39			20 40	20 44	20 46	20 50	20 53			
Streatham 4	d							20 10					20 16												
Tulse Hill 3	d	20 10						20 17				20 20	20 24											20 39	
Herne Hill 4	a											20 28													
Loughborough Jn	a											20 36													
Elephant & Castle ⊖	a											20 48													
London Blackfriars 3 ⊖	a											20 56													
City Thameslink 3	a																								
St Pancras International 15 ⊖	a																								
Luton Airport Parkway 7	a																								
Luton 10	a																								
North Dulwich	d	20 13											20 27											20 42	
East Dulwich	d	20 15											20 29											20 44	
Peckham Rye 4	d	20 17								20 26			20 31											20 46	
Queens Rd Peckham	d	20 20								20 29			20 34											20 49	
South Bermondsey	d	20 22								20 31			20 36											20 51	
London Bridge 4 ⊖	a	20 27	20 29	20 17				20 30		20 36	20 32		20 41			20 41								20 56	20 59

Table 177

Saturdays

East and West Croydon, London-Milton Keynes and Luton via Norbury-Crystal Palace-Tulse Hill

Local Services

Station		FC [1]		SN [1]	LO	SN ◇[1]	FC	SN [1]	SN	FC [1]	FC (bus)	SN		SN	SN	SN	SN ◇[1]	SN [1]	SN	SN ◇[1]	SN	LO		SN	FC [1]
East Croydon	d	20 32		20 33		20 41		20 44		20 47							20 54	20 56	20 47	21 00				21 00	21 02
West Croydon [4]	d				20 39							20 31		20 34							20 48	20 52			
Norwood Junction [2]	a				20 43																20 52	20 58		21 04	
	d				20 43																20 53	20 58		21 05	
Selhurst [4]	d											20 35		20 39					20 50						
Thornton Heath	d											20 37		20 41					20 52						
Norbury	d											20 40		20 44					20 55						
Streatham Common [4]	d											20 43		20 47					20 58						
Beckenham Junction [4]	d																								
Birkbeck	d																								
Crystal Palace [4]	d														20 43	20 51					20 57				
Gipsy Hill	d														20 45						20 59				
West Norwood [4]	d														20 48						21 02				
Streatham Hill	d														20 52						21 06				
Balham [4] ⊖	d													20 51	20 55				21 02		21 09				
Wandsworth Common	d													20 53	20 57				21 04		21 11				
Clapham Junction [10]	d					20 50		20 56						20 57	21 01		21 03	21 07	21 08	21 11	21 15				
West Brompton ⊖	d																								
Kensington (Olympia) ⊖	d																								
Shepherd's Bush ⊖	d																								
Wembley Central ⊖	d																								
Harrow & Wealdstone ⊖	d																								
Watford Junction	d																								
Milton Keynes Central [10]	a																								
Battersea Park [4]	d								20 45						21 05				21 11		21 18				
London Victoria [15] ⊖	a					20 57		21 02						21 04	21 09		21 10	21 14	21 16	21 17	21 23				
Streatham [4]	d						20 40					20 46													
Tulse Hill [3]	d						20 47				20 50	20 54													
Herne Hill [4]	a										20 58														
Loughborough Jn	a										21 06														
Elephant & Castle ⊖	a										21 18														
London Blackfriars [3] ⊖	a										21 26														
City Thameslink [3]	a																								
St Pancras International [15] ⊖	a																								
Luton Airport Parkway [7]	a																								
Luton [10]	a																								
North Dulwich	d											20 57													
East Dulwich	d											20 59													
Peckham Rye [4]	d								20 56			21 01													
Queens Rd Peckham	d								20 59			21 04													
South Bermondsey	d								21 01			21 06													
London Bridge [4] ⊖	a	20 47		20 49			21 00		21 06	21 02		21 11				21 13								21 29	21 17

Station		SN ◇[1]	LO	FC	SN [1]	SN	FC [1]	FC (bus)		SN	SN	SN	SN	SN ◇[1]	SN [1]	SN	SN ◇[1]	SN		LO	SN	FC [1]	SN [1]	LO	SN ◇[1]
East Croydon	d	21 11			21 14		21 17							21 24	21 26	21 17	21 30				21 30	21 32	21 33		21 41
West Croydon [4]	d		21 09							21 01	21 04							21 18		21 22				21 39	
Norwood Junction [2]	a		21 13															21 22		21 28	21 34			21 43	
	d		21 13															21 23		21 28	21 35			21 43	
Selhurst [4]	d									21 05	21 09					21 20									
Thornton Heath	d									21 07	21 11					21 22									
Norbury	d									21 10	21 14					21 25									
Streatham Common [4]	d									21 13	21 17					21 28									
Beckenham Junction [4]	d																								
Birkbeck	d																								
Crystal Palace [4]	d											21 13	21 21					21 27							
Gipsy Hill	d											21 15						21 29							
West Norwood [4]	d											21 18						21 32							
Streatham Hill	d											21 22						21 36							
Balham [4] ⊖	d										21 21	21 25				21 32		21 39							
Wandsworth Common	d										21 23	21 27				21 34		21 41							
Clapham Junction [10]	d	21 20			21 26						21 27	21 31		21 33	21 37	21 38	21 41	21 45							21 50
West Brompton ⊖	d																								
Kensington (Olympia) ⊖	d																								
Shepherd's Bush ⊖	d																								
Wembley Central ⊖	d																								
Harrow & Wealdstone ⊖	d																								
Watford Junction	d																								
Milton Keynes Central [10]	a																								
Battersea Park [4]	d					21 15						21 35				21 41		21 48							
London Victoria [15] ⊖	a	21 27			21 32						21 34	21 39		21 40	21 44	21 46	21 47	21 53							21 57
Streatham [4]	d			21 10						21 16															
Tulse Hill [3]	d			21 17				21 20		21 24															
Herne Hill [4]	a							21 28																	
Loughborough Jn	a							21 36																	
Elephant & Castle ⊖	a							21 48																	
London Blackfriars [3] ⊖	a							21 56																	
City Thameslink [3]	a																								
St Pancras International [15] ⊖	a																								
Luton Airport Parkway [7]	a																								
Luton [10]	a																								
North Dulwich	d									21 27															
East Dulwich	d									21 29															
Peckham Rye [4]	d					21 26				21 31															
Queens Rd Peckham	d					21 29				21 34															
South Bermondsey	d					21 31				21 36															
London Bridge [4] ⊖	a			21 30		21 36	21 32			21 41			21 43								21 59	21 47	21 49		

Table 177

Saturdays

East and West Croydon, London-Milton Keynes and Luton via Norbury-Crystal Palace-Tulse Hill

Local Services

Station		FC	SN [1]	SN		FC (bus)	SN	SN	SN	SN	SN ◇[1]	SN [1]	SN	SN ◇[1]		SN	LO	SN	FC [1]	SN ◇[1]	LO	FC	SN [1]	SN	
East Croydon	d		21 44								21 54	21 56	21 47	22 00				22 00	22 02	22 11			22 14		
West Croydon [4]	d						21 31	21 34								21 48	21 52				22 09				
Norwood Junction [2]	a															21 52	21 58	22 04			22 13				
	d															21 53	21 58	22 05			22 13				
Selhurst [4]	d						21 35	21 39					21 50												
Thornton Heath	d						21 37	21 41					21 52												
Norbury	d						21 40	21 44					21 55												
Streatham Common [4]	d						21 43	21 47					21 58												
Beckenham Junction [4]	d																								
Birkbeck	d																								
Crystal Palace [4]	d								21 43	21 51						21 57									
Gipsy Hill	d								21 45							21 59									
West Norwood [4]	d								21 48							22 02									
Streatham Hill	d								21 52							22 06									
Balham [4] ⊖	d							21 51	21 55				22 02			22 09									
Wandsworth Common	d							21 53	21 57				22 04			22 11									
Clapham Junction [10]	d		21 56					21 57	22 01		22 03	22 07	22 08	22 11		22 15				22 20			22 26		
West Brompton ⊖	d																								
Kensington (Olympia) ⊖	d																								
Shepherd's Bush ⊖	d																								
Wembley Central ⊖	d																								
Harrow & Wealdstone ⊖	d																								
Watford Junction	d																								
Milton Keynes Central [10]	a																								
Battersea Park [4]	d			21 45					22 05				22 11			22 18								22 15	
London Victoria [15] ⊖	a		22 02					22 04	22 09		22 10	22 14	22 16	22 20		22 23				22 28			22 32		
Streatham [4]	d	21 40					21 46															22 10			
Tulse Hill [3]	d	21 47				21 50	21 54															22 17			
Herne Hill [4]	a					21 58																			
Loughborough Jn	a					22 06																			
Elephant & Castle ⊖	a					22 18																			
London Blackfriars [3] ⊖	a					22 26																			
City Thameslink [3]	a																								
St Pancras International [15] ⊖	a																								
Luton Airport Parkway [7]	a																								
Luton [10]	a																								
North Dulwich	d						21 57																		
East Dulwich	d						21 59																		
Peckham Rye [4]	d			21 56			22 01																	22 26	
Queens Rd Peckham	d			21 59			22 04																	22 29	
South Bermondsey	d			22 01			22 06																	22 31	
London Bridge [4] ⊖	a	22 00		22 06			22 11			22 13								22 29	22 17			22 30		22 36	

Station		FC (bus)	SN	SN	SN	SN	SN ◇[1]	SN [1]	SN	SN ◇[1]		SN	LO	SN	FC [1]	SN [1]	SN ◇[1]	LO	FC	SN [1]		SN	FC (bus)	SN	SN
East Croydon	d						22 24	22 26	22 17	22 30				22 30	22 32	22 33	22 40			22 44					
West Croydon [4]	d		22 01	22 04								22 18	22 22					22 39						22 31	22 34
Norwood Junction [2]	a											22 22	22 28	22 34				22 43							
	d											22 23	22 28	22 35				22 43							
Selhurst [4]	d		22 05	22 09					22 20															22 35	22 39
Thornton Heath	d		22 07	22 11					22 22															22 37	22 41
Norbury	d		22 10	22 14					22 25															22 40	22 44
Streatham Common [4]	d		22 13	22 17					22 28															22 43	22 47
Beckenham Junction [4]	d																								
Birkbeck	d																								
Crystal Palace [4]	d				22 13	22 21						22 27													
Gipsy Hill	d				22 15							22 29													
West Norwood [4]	d				22 18							22 32													
Streatham Hill	d				22 22							22 36													
Balham [4] ⊖	d			22 21	22 25				22 32			22 39													22 51
Wandsworth Common	d			22 23	22 27				22 34			22 41													22 53
Clapham Junction [10]	d			22 27	22 31		22 33	22 37	22 38	22 41		22 45					22 50			22 56					22 57
West Brompton ⊖	d																								
Kensington (Olympia) ⊖	d																								
Shepherd's Bush ⊖	d																								
Wembley Central ⊖	d																								
Harrow & Wealdstone ⊖	d																								
Watford Junction	d																								
Milton Keynes Central [10]	a																								
Battersea Park [4]	d				22 35				22 41			22 48										22 45			
London Victoria [15] ⊖	a			22 34	22 39		22 40	22 44	22 46	22 50		22 53					22 58			23 02					23 04
Streatham [4]	d		22 16																22 40					22 46	
Tulse Hill [3]	d	22 20	22 24																22 47				22 50	22 54	
Herne Hill [4]	a	22 28																					22 58		
Loughborough Jn	a	22 36																					23 06		
Elephant & Castle ⊖	a	22 48																					23 18		
London Blackfriars [3] ⊖	a	22 56																					23 26		
City Thameslink [3]	a																								
St Pancras International [15] ⊖	a																								
Luton Airport Parkway [7]	a																								
Luton [10]	a																								
North Dulwich	d		22 27																					22 57	
East Dulwich	d		22 29																					22 59	
Peckham Rye [4]	d		22 31																			22 56		23 01	
Queens Rd Peckham	d		22 34																			22 59		23 04	
South Bermondsey	d		22 36																			23 01		23 06	
London Bridge [4] ⊖	a		22 41			22 43								22 59	22 47	22 49			23 00			23 06		23 11	

Table 177

Saturdays

East and West Croydon, London-Milton Keynes and Luton via Norbury-Crystal Palace-Tulse Hill

Local Services

		SN	SN	SN 1	SN ◇1	SN	SN	LO	SN	SN	FC 1	SN 1	SN	SN	SN	SN	SN	SN ◇1	SN	LO	FC 1	SN	SN
East Croydon	d			22 56	23 00	22 47			23 01		23 02	23 14				23 17		23 30			23 32		23 43
West Croydon 4	d						22 48	22 52		23 01			23 04						23 18	23 22			
Norwood Junction 2	a						22 52	22 58	23 05										23 22	23 28			23 47
	d						22 53	22 58	23 06										23 23	23 28			
Selhurst 4	d					22 50				23 05			23 09			23 20							
Thornton Heath	d					22 52				23 07			23 11			23 22							
Norbury	d					22 55				23 10			23 14			23 25							
Streatham Common 4	d					22 58				23 13			23 17			23 28							
Beckenham Junction 4	d																						
Birkbeck	d																						
Crystal Palace 4	d	22 43	22 51				22 57							23 13			23 21		23 27			23 43	
Gipsy Hill	d	22 45					22 59							23 15					23 29			23 45	
West Norwood 4	d	22 48					23 02							23 18					23 32			23 48	
Streatham Hill	d	22 52					23 06							23 22					23 36			23 52	
Balham 4 ⊖	d	22 55				23 02	23 09						23 21	23 25		23 32			23 40			23 55	
Wandsworth Common	d	22 57				23 04	23 11						23 23	23 27		23 34			23 42			23 57	
Clapham Junction 10	d	23 01		23 07	23 11	23 08	23 15					23 26	23 27	23 31		23 38		23 42	23 46			00 02	
West Brompton ⊖	d																						
Kensington (Olympia) ⊖	d																						
Shepherd's Bush ⊖	d																						
Wembley Central ⊖	d																						
Harrow & Wealdstone ⊖	d																						
Watford Junction	d																						
Milton Keynes Central 10	a																						
Battersea Park 4	d	23 05				23 11	23 18							23 35	23 15	23 41			23 49			00 05	
London Victoria 15 ⊖	a	23 10		23 14	23 17	23 18	23 23					23 32	23 34	23 40		23 46		23 52	23 54			00 10	
Streatham 4	d									23 19													
Tulse Hill 3	d									23 24													
Herne Hill 4	a																						
Loughborough Jn	a																						
Elephant & Castle ⊖	a																						
London Blackfriars 3 ⊖	a																						
City Thameslink 3	a																						
St Pancras International 15 ⊖	a																						
Luton Airport Parkway 7	a																						
Luton 10	a																						
North Dulwich	d									23 27													
East Dulwich	d									23 29													
Peckham Rye 4	d									23 31					23 26								
Queens Rd Peckham	d									23 34					23 29								
South Bermondsey	d									23 36					23 31								
London Bridge 4 ⊖	a		23 13						23 30	23 41	23 17				23 36		23 43				23 47		

		SN	SN 1
East Croydon	d		23 56
West Croydon 4	d		
Norwood Junction 2	a		
	d		
Selhurst 4	d		00 02
Thornton Heath	d		
Norbury	d		
Streatham Common 4	d		
Beckenham Junction 4	d		
Birkbeck	d		
Crystal Palace 4	d	23 51	
Gipsy Hill	d		
West Norwood 4	d		
Streatham Hill	d		
Balham 4 ⊖	d		
Wandsworth Common	d		
Clapham Junction 10	d		00 11
West Brompton ⊖	d		
Kensington (Olympia) ⊖	d		
Shepherd's Bush ⊖	d		
Wembley Central ⊖	d		
Harrow & Wealdstone ⊖	d		
Watford Junction	d		
Milton Keynes Central 10	a		
Battersea Park 4	d		
London Victoria 15 ⊖	a		00 18
Streatham 4	d		
Tulse Hill 3	d		
Herne Hill 4	a		
Loughborough Jn	a		
Elephant & Castle ⊖	a		
London Blackfriars 3 ⊖	a		
City Thameslink 3	a		
St Pancras International 15 ⊖	a		
Luton Airport Parkway 7	a		
Luton 10	a		
North Dulwich	d		
East Dulwich	d		
Peckham Rye 4	d		
Queens Rd Peckham	d		
South Bermondsey	d		
London Bridge 4 ⊖	a	00 11	

Table 177

Sundays

East and West Croydon, London-Milton Keynes and Luton via Norbury-Crystal Palace-Tulse Hill

Local Services

		SN	SN	SN 1	FC 1	SN ◇1	FC 1	SN	SN 1	SN 1	SN 1	SN 1	FC 1	SN 1	FC 1	SN	LO	SN	SN	FC 1	SN ◇1 B	SN	SN ◇1 C
East Croydon	d			23p56	00 04	00 17	00 36	00 49	01 43	02 40	03 40	04 40	05 32	06 02	06 32	06 40		06 47		07 02	07 09		07 10
West Croydon 4	d																06 42						
Norwood Junction 2	a												05 36		06 36		06 47	06 51					
	d												05 36		06 36		06 47	06 52				06 59	
Selhurst 4	d							00 52						06 05		06 43			06 47				
Thornton Heath	d															06 45			06 49				
Norbury	d															06 48			06 52				
Streatham Common 4	d															06 51			06 55				
Beckenham Junction 4	d																						
Birkbeck	d																						
Crystal Palace 4	d	23p43	23p51																			07 05	
Gipsy Hill	d	23p45																				07 07	
West Norwood 4	d	23p48																				07 10	
Streatham Hill	d	23p52																				07 14	
Balham 4 ⊖	d	23p55														06 55						07 17	
Wandsworth Common	d	23p57														06 57							
Clapham Junction 10	d	00 02		00 11		00 29		01 02	01 54	02 53	03 53	04 53		06 14		07 00					07 19	07 22	07 24
West Brompton ⊖	d																						
Kensington (Olympia) ⊖	d																						
Shepherd's Bush ⊖	d																						
Wembley Central ⊖	d																						
Harrow & Wealdstone ⊖	d																						
Watford Junction	d																						
Milton Keynes Central 10	a																						
Battersea Park 4	d	00 05														07 04							
London Victoria 15 ⊖	a	00 10		00 18		00 36		01 09	02 05	03 05	04 05	05 05		06 22		07 08					07 25	07 29	07 31
Streatham 4	d																		06 58				
Tulse Hill 3	d																		07 02				
Herne Hill 4	a																						
Loughborough Jn	a																						
Elephant & Castle ⊖	a																						
London Blackfriars 3 ⊖	a																						
City Thameslink 3	a																						
St Pancras International 15 ⊖	a																						
Luton Airport Parkway 7	a																						
Luton 10	a																						
North Dulwich	d																		07 05				
East Dulwich	d																		07 07				
Peckham Rye 4	d																		07 09				
Queens Rd Peckham	d																		07 12				
South Bermondsey	d																		07 14				
London Bridge 4 ⊖	a		00 11		00 19		00 52						05 59		06 59			07 18	07 19	07 16			

B until 5 September

C from 12 September

Table 177

Sundays

East and West Croydon, London-Milton Keynes and Luton via Norbury-Crystal Palace-Tulse Hill

Local Services

		SN	LO	SN	SN	SN ■	SN	FC ■ A	SN	SN	LO	SN	SN	SN	SN ■ A	SN ■ B	SN ◇■ A	SN ◇■ B	FC ■ B	FC ■ A	SN ◇■ A 🚲	SN	SN
East Croydon 🚊	d			07 14	07 17	07 27		07 33					07 44	07 47	07 56	07 58	08 00	08 00	08 02	08 03	08 09		
West Croydon 4 🚊	d	07 08	07 12				07 22		07 35	07 38	07 42											07 52	08 05
Norwood Junction 2	a		07 17		07 21		07 26		07 39		07 47			07 51								07 56	08 09
	d		07 17		07 22		07 29		07 40		07 47			07 52								07 59	08 10
Selhurst 4	d	07 13		07 17		07 31				07 43			07 47										
Thornton Heath	d	07 15		07 19						07 45			07 49										
Norbury	d	07 18		07 22						07 48			07 52										
Streatham Common 4	d	07 21		07 25						07 51			07 55										
Beckenham Junction 4 🚊	d																						
Birkbeck 🚊	d																						
Crystal Palace 4	d						07 35															08 05	
Gipsy Hill	d						07 37															08 07	
West Norwood 4	d						07 40															08 10	
Streatham Hill	d						07 44															08 14	
Balham 4 ⊖	d	07 25					07 47			07 55												08 17	
Wandsworth Common	d	07 27								07 57													
Clapham Junction 10	d	07 31				07 41	07 52			08 01					08 07	08 09	08 11	08 12			08 19	08 22	
West Brompton ⊖	d																						
Kensington (Olympia) ⊖	d																						
Shepherd's Bush ⊖	d																						
Wembley Central ⊖	d																						
Harrow & Wealdstone ⊖	d																						
Watford Junction	d																						
Milton Keynes Central 10	a																						
Battersea Park 4	d	07 34								08 04		07 45											
London Victoria 15 ⊖	a	07 39				07 48	07 59			08 09					08 13	08 16	08 17	08 18			08 25	08 29	
Streatham 4	d			07 28									07 58										
Tulse Hill 3	d			07 32									08 02										
Herne Hill 4	a																						
Loughborough Jn	a																						
Elephant & Castle ⊖	a																						
London Blackfriars 3 ⊖	a																						
City Thameslink 3	a																						
St Pancras International 15 ⊖	a																						
Luton Airport Parkway 7	a																						
Luton 10	a																						
North Dulwich	d			07 35									08 05										
East Dulwich	d			07 37									08 07										
Peckham Rye 4	d			07 39								07 56	08 09										
Queens Rd Peckham	d			07 42								07 59	08 12										
South Bermondsey	d			07 44								08 01	08 14										
London Bridge 4 ⊖	a			07 49	07 48			07 46	08 01			08 06	08 19	08 18					08 16	08 16			08 31

A until 5 September

B from 12 September

Table 177

Sundays

East and West Croydon, London-Milton Keynes and Luton via Norbury-Crystal Palace-Tulse Hill

Local Services

		SN ◇■ A 🚲	SN	LO	SN	SN	SN	SN ◇■ B	SN ◇■ A	SN ■	FC ■ A	FC ■ B	SN ◇■ B	SN	SN ■ B	SN	SN ◇■ A	LO	SN	SN ◇■ B 🚲	SN	SN
East Croydon 🚊	d	08 10				08 14	08 17	08 21	08 26	08 29	08 32	08 33	08 39		08 34		08 40			08 46		08 44
West Croydon 4 🚊	d		08 08	08 12										08 22		08 35		08 42			08 38	
Norwood Junction 2	a			08 17			08 21							08 26	08 38	08 39		08 47				
	d			08 17			08 22							08 29	08 38	08 40		08 47				
Selhurst 4	d		08 13			08 17				08 33											08 43	08 47
Thornton Heath	d		08 15			08 19															08 45	08 49
Norbury	d		08 18			08 22															08 48	08 52
Streatham Common 4	d		08 21			08 25															08 51	08 55
Beckenham Junction 4 🚊	d																					
Birkbeck 🚊	d																					
Crystal Palace 4	d													08 35								
Gipsy Hill	d													08 37								
West Norwood 4	d													08 40								
Streatham Hill	d													08 44								
Balham 4 ⊖	d		08 25											08 47							08 55	
Wandsworth Common	d		08 27																		08 57	
Clapham Junction 10	d	08 25	08 31					08 32	08 38	08 41			08 49	08 52			08 55			08 55	09 01	
West Brompton ⊖	d																					
Kensington (Olympia) ⊖	d																					
Shepherd's Bush ⊖	d																					
Wembley Central ⊖	d																					
Harrow & Wealdstone ⊖	d																					
Watford Junction	d																					
Milton Keynes Central 10	a																					
Battersea Park 4	d		08 34		08 15														08 45		09 04	
London Victoria 15 ⊖	a	08 31	08 39					08 39	08 46	08 48			08 55	08 59			09 01			09 02	09 09	
Streatham 4	d					08 28																08 58
Tulse Hill 3	d					08 32																09 02
Herne Hill 4	a																					
Loughborough Jn	a																					
Elephant & Castle ⊖	a																					
London Blackfriars 3 ⊖	a																					
City Thameslink 3	a																					
St Pancras International 15 ⊖	a																					
Luton Airport Parkway 7	a																					
Luton 10	a																					
North Dulwich	d					08 35																09 05
East Dulwich	d					08 37																09 07
Peckham Rye 4	d				08 26	08 39													08 56			09 09
Queens Rd Peckham	d				08 29	08 42													08 59			09 12
South Bermondsey	d				08 31	08 44													09 01			09 14
London Bridge 4 ⊖	a				08 36	08 49	08 48				08 46	08 46			08 51	09 01			09 06			09 19

A from 12 September

B until 5 September

East and West Croydon, London-Milton Keynes and Luton via Norbury-Crystal Palace-Tulse Hill

Local Services

		SN	SN 1 A	SN 1 B	SN ◇1 A	SN ◇1 B	FC 1 B	FC 1 A	SN ◇1 A	SN	SN	SN ◇1 B	LO	SN	SN ◇1 A	SN ◇1 B	SN	SN	SN	SN ◇1 A	SN ◇1 B	SN 1	FC 1 B
East Croydon	d	08 47	08 56	08 58	09 00	09 00	09 02	09 03	09 09			09 10			09 17	09 13		09 14	09 17	09 21	09 25	09 29	09 32
West Croydon 4	d									08 52	09 05		09 12				09 08						
Norwood Junction 2	a	08 51								08 56	09 09		09 17						09 21				
	d	08 52								08 59	09 10		09 17						09 22				
Selhurst 4	d																09 13	09 17				09 33	
Thornton Heath	d																09 15	09 19					
Norbury	d																09 18	09 22					
Streatham Common 4	d																09 21	09 25					
Beckenham Junction 4	d																						
Birkbeck	d																						
Crystal Palace 4	d									09 05													
Gipsy Hill	d									09 07													
West Norwood 4	d									09 10													
Streatham Hill	d									09 14													
Balham 4 ⊖	d									09 17							09 25						
Wandsworth Common	d																09 27						
Clapham Junction 10	d		09 07	09 09	09 11	09 12			09 19	09 22		09 25			09 27	09 28	09 31			09 32	09 38	09 41	
West Brompton ⊖	d																						
Kensington (Olympia) ⊖	d																						
Shepherd's Bush ⊖	d																						
Wembley Central ⊖	d																						
Harrow & Wealdstone ⊖	d																						
Watford Junction	d																						
Milton Keynes Central 10	a																						
Battersea Park 4	d													09 15			09 34						
London Victoria 15 ⊖	a		09 13	09 16	09 17	09 18			09 25	09 29		09 31			09 33	09 35	09 39			09 39	09 46	09 48	
Streatham 4	d																	09 28					
Tulse Hill 3	d																	09 32					
Herne Hill 4	a																						
Loughborough Jn	a																						
Elephant & Castle ⊖	a																						
London Blackfriars 3 ⊖	a																						
City Thameslink 3	a																						
St Pancras International 15 ⊖	a																						
Luton Airport Parkway 7	a																						
Luton 10	a																						
North Dulwich	d																	09 35					
East Dulwich	d																	09 37					
Peckham Rye 4	d													09 26				09 39					
Queens Rd Peckham	d													09 29				09 42					
South Bermondsey	d													09 31				09 44					
London Bridge 4 ⊖	a	09 18					09 16	09 16			09 31			09 36				09 49	09 48				09 46

A until 5 September

B from 12 September

East and West Croydon, London-Milton Keynes and Luton via Norbury-Crystal Palace-Tulse Hill

Local Services

		FC 1 A	SN ◇1 A	SN	SN 1 A	SN	SN ◇1 B	LO	SN	SN ◇1 A	SN	SN	SN	SN 1 A	SN 1 B	SN ◇1 A	SN ◇1 B	FC 1 B	FC 1 A	SN ◇1 A	SN	SN
East Croydon	d	09 33	09 39		09 34		09 40			09 46		09 44	09 47	09 56	09 58	10 00	10 00	10 02	10 03	10 09		
West Croydon 4	d			09 22		09 35		09 42			09 38										09 52	10 05
Norwood Junction 2	a			09 26	09 38	09 39		09 47					09 51								09 56	10 09
	d			09 29	09 38	09 40		09 47					09 52								09 59	10 10
Selhurst 4	d										09 43	09 47										
Thornton Heath	d										09 45	09 49										
Norbury	d										09 48	09 52										
Streatham Common 4	d										09 51	09 55										
Beckenham Junction 4	d																					
Birkbeck	d																					
Crystal Palace 4	d			09 35																	10 05	
Gipsy Hill	d			09 37																	10 07	
West Norwood 4	d			09 40																	10 10	
Streatham Hill	d			09 44																	10 14	
Balham 4 ⊖	d			09 47							09 55										10 17	
Wandsworth Common	d										09 57											
Clapham Junction 10	d		09 49	09 52			09 55			09 55	10 01			10 07	10 09	10 11	10 12			10 19	10 22	
West Brompton ⊖	d																					
Kensington (Olympia) ⊖	d																					
Shepherd's Bush ⊖	d																					
Wembley Central ⊖	d																					
Harrow & Wealdstone ⊖	d																					
Watford Junction	d																					
Milton Keynes Central 10	a																					
Battersea Park 4	d								09 45		10 04											
London Victoria 15 ⊖	a		09 55	09 59			10 01			10 02	10 09			10 13	10 16	10 17	10 18			10 25	10 29	
Streatham 4	d											09 58										
Tulse Hill 3	d											10 02										
Herne Hill 4	a																					
Loughborough Jn	a																					
Elephant & Castle ⊖	a																					
London Blackfriars 3 ⊖	a																					
City Thameslink 3	a																					
St Pancras International 15 ⊖	a																					
Luton Airport Parkway 7	a																					
Luton 10	a																					
North Dulwich	d											10 05										
East Dulwich	d											10 07										
Peckham Rye 4	d								09 56			10 09										
Queens Rd Peckham	d								09 59			10 12										
South Bermondsey	d								10 01			10 14										
London Bridge 4 ⊖	a	09 46			09 51	10 01			10 06			10 19	10 18					10 16	10 16			10 31

A until 5 September

B from 12 September

Table 177

Sundays

East and West Croydon, London-Milton Keynes and Luton via Norbury-Crystal Palace-Tulse Hill

Local Services

	SN ◇1 A 🍴	LO	SN	SN ◇1 B 🍴	SN ◇1 A 🍴	SN	SN	SN	SN ◇1 B	SN ◇1 A 🍴	SN 1
East Croydon d	10 10			10 17	10 13		10 14	10 17	10 21	10 25	10 29
West Croydon 4 d		10 12				10 08					
Norwood Junction 2 a		10 17						10 21			
d		10 17						10 22			
Selhurst 4 d						10 13	10 17				10 33
Thornton Heath d						10 15	10 19				
Norbury d						10 18	10 22				
Streatham Common 4 d						10 21	10 25				
Beckenham Junction 4 d											
Birkbeck d											
Crystal Palace 4 d											
Gipsy Hill d											
West Norwood 4 d											
Streatham Hill d											
Balham 4 ⊖ d						10 25					
Wandsworth Common d						10 27					
Clapham Junction 10 d	10 25			10 27	10 28	10 31			10 32	10 38	10 41
West Brompton ⊖ d											
Kensington (Olympia) ⊖ d											
Shepherd's Bush ⊖ d											
Wembley Central ⊖ d											
Harrow & Wealdstone ⊖ d											
Watford Junction d											
Milton Keynes Central 10 a											
Battersea Park 4 d			10 15			10 34					
London Victoria 15 ⊖ a	10 31			10 33	10 35	10 39			10 39	10 46	10 48
Streatham 4 d							10 28				
Tulse Hill 3 d							10 32				
Herne Hill 4 a											
Loughborough Jn a											
Elephant & Castle ⊖ a											
London Blackfriars 3 ⊖ a											
City Thameslink 3 a											
St Pancras International 15 ⊖ a											
Luton Airport Parkway 7 a											
Luton 10 a											
North Dulwich d							10 35				
East Dulwich d							10 37				
Peckham Rye 4 d			10 26				10 39				
Queens Rd Peckham d			10 29				10 42				
South Bermondsey d			10 31				10 44				
London Bridge 4 ⊖ a			10 36				10 49	10 48			

	FC 1 A	FC 1 B	SN ◇1 B	SN	SN 1 B	SN	SN ◇1 A	FC	LO	SN	SN ◇1 B 🍴
East Croydon d	10 32	10 33	10 39		10 34		10 40				10 46
West Croydon 4 d				10 22		10 35			10 42		
Norwood Junction 2 a				10 26	10 38	10 39			10 47		
d				10 29	10 38	10 40			10 47		
Selhurst 4 d											
Thornton Heath d											
Norbury d											
Streatham Common 4 d											
Beckenham Junction 4 d											
Birkbeck d											
Crystal Palace 4 d				10 35							
Gipsy Hill d				10 37							
West Norwood 4 d				10 40							
Streatham Hill d				10 44							
Balham 4 ⊖ d				10 47							
Wandsworth Common d											
Clapham Junction 10 d			10 49	10 52			10 55				10 55
West Brompton ⊖ d											
Kensington (Olympia) ⊖ d											
Shepherd's Bush ⊖ d											
Wembley Central ⊖ d											
Harrow & Wealdstone ⊖ d											
Watford Junction d											
Milton Keynes Central 10 a											
Battersea Park 4 d										10 45	
London Victoria 15 ⊖ a			10 55	10 59			11 01				11 02
Streatham 4 d								10 43			
Tulse Hill 3 d								10 47			
Herne Hill 4 a											
Loughborough Jn a											
Elephant & Castle ⊖ a											
London Blackfriars 3 ⊖ a											
City Thameslink 3 a											
St Pancras International 15 ⊖ a											
Luton Airport Parkway 7 a											
Luton 10 a											
North Dulwich d											
East Dulwich d											
Peckham Rye 4 d										10 56	
Queens Rd Peckham d										10 59	
South Bermondsey d										11 01	
London Bridge 4 ⊖ a	10 46	10 46			10 51	11 01		10 59		11 06	

A from 12 September

B until 5 September

Table 177

Sundays

East and West Croydon, London-Milton Keynes and Luton via Norbury-Crystal Palace-Tulse Hill

Local Services

	SN	SN	SN 1 A	SN 1 B	FC 🚌	SN	SN ◇1 A	SN ◇1 B	FC 1 B	FC 1 A	SN ◇1 A 🍴	SN
East Croydon d		10 47	10 56	10 58		10 44	11 00	11 00	11 02	11 03	11 09	
West Croydon 4 d	10 38											10 52
Norwood Junction 2 a		10 51										10 56
d		10 52										10 59
Selhurst 4 d	10 43					10 47						
Thornton Heath d	10 45					10 49						
Norbury d	10 48					10 52						
Streatham Common 4 d	10 51					10 55						
Beckenham Junction 4 d												
Birkbeck d												
Crystal Palace 4 d												11 05
Gipsy Hill d												11 07
West Norwood 4 d												11 10
Streatham Hill d												11 14
Balham 4 ⊖ d	10 55											11 17
Wandsworth Common d	10 57											
Clapham Junction 10 d	11 01		11 07	11 09			11 11	11 12			11 19	11 22
West Brompton ⊖ d												
Kensington (Olympia) ⊖ d												
Shepherd's Bush ⊖ d												
Wembley Central ⊖ d												
Harrow & Wealdstone ⊖ d												
Watford Junction d												
Milton Keynes Central 10 a												
Battersea Park 4 d	11 04											
London Victoria 15 ⊖ a	11 09		11 13	11 16			11 17	11 18			11 25	11 29
Streatham 4 d						10 58						
Tulse Hill 3 d					10 55	11 02						
Herne Hill 4 a					11 03							
Loughborough Jn a					11 11							
Elephant & Castle ⊖ a					11 23							
London Blackfriars 3 ⊖ a					11 31							
City Thameslink 3 a												
St Pancras International 15 ⊖ a												
Luton Airport Parkway 7 a												
Luton 10 a												
North Dulwich d						11 05						
East Dulwich d						11 07						
Peckham Rye 4 d						11 09						
Queens Rd Peckham d						11 12						
South Bermondsey d						11 14						
London Bridge 4 ⊖ a		11 18				11 19			11 16	11 16		

	SN	SN ◇1 B 🍴	FC	LO	SN	SN ◇1 A 🍴	SN ◇1 B 🍴	SN	SN	SN ◇1 A 🍴
East Croydon d		11 10				11 17	11 13		11 17	11 21
West Croydon 4 d	11 05			11 12				11 08		
Norwood Junction 2 a	11 09			11 17					11 21	
d	11 10			11 17					11 22	
Selhurst 4 d								11 13		
Thornton Heath d								11 15		
Norbury d								11 18		
Streatham Common 4 d								11 21		
Beckenham Junction 4 d										
Birkbeck d										
Crystal Palace 4 d										
Gipsy Hill d										
West Norwood 4 d										
Streatham Hill d										
Balham 4 ⊖ d								11 25		
Wandsworth Common d								11 27		
Clapham Junction 10 d		11 25				11 27	11 28	11 31		11 32
West Brompton ⊖ d										
Kensington (Olympia) ⊖ d										
Shepherd's Bush ⊖ d										
Wembley Central ⊖ d										
Harrow & Wealdstone ⊖ d										
Watford Junction d										
Milton Keynes Central 10 a										
Battersea Park 4 d					11 15			11 34		
London Victoria 15 ⊖ a		11 31				11 33	11 35	11 39		11 39
Streatham 4 d			11 13							
Tulse Hill 3 d			11 17							
Herne Hill 4 a										
Loughborough Jn a										
Elephant & Castle ⊖ a										
London Blackfriars 3 ⊖ a										
City Thameslink 3 a										
St Pancras International 15 ⊖ a										
Luton Airport Parkway 7 a										
Luton 10 a										
North Dulwich d										
East Dulwich d										
Peckham Rye 4 d					11 26					
Queens Rd Peckham d					11 29					
South Bermondsey d					11 31					
London Bridge 4 ⊖ a	11 31		11 29		11 36				11 48	

A until 5 September

B from 12 September

Table 177

Sundays

East and West Croydon, London-Milton Keynes and Luton via Norbury-Crystal Palace-Tulse Hill

Local Services

		SN	FC	SN	SN	FC	FC	SN	SN	SN	SN	SN	FC	LO	SN	SN	SN	SN	SN	SN	FC	SN
		◇1			1	1	1	◇1		1		◇1				◇1			1	1		
		A				A	B	B		B		A				B			B	A		
		🍴	🚌													🍴					🚌	
East Croydon	d	11 25		11 14	11 29	11 32	11 33	11 39		11 34		11 40				11 46		11 47	11 56	11 58		11 44
West Croydon 4	d								11 22		11 35			11 42			11 38					
Norwood Junction 2	a								11 26	11 38	11 39			11 47				11 51				
	d								11 29	11 38	11 40			11 47				11 52				
Selhurst 4	d			11 17	11 33												11 43					11 47
Thornton Heath	d			11 19													11 45					11 49
Norbury	d			11 22													11 48					11 52
Streatham Common 4	d			11 25													11 51					11 55
Beckenham Junction 4	d																					
Birkbeck	d																					
Crystal Palace 4	d								11 35													
Gipsy Hill	d								11 37													
West Norwood 4	d								11 40													
Streatham Hill	d								11 44													
Balham 4 ⊖	d								11 47								11 55					
Wandsworth Common	d																11 57					
Clapham Junction 10	d	11 38			11 41			11 49	11 52			11 55				11 55	12 01		12 07	12 09		
West Brompton ⊖	d																					
Kensington (Olympia) ⊖	d																					
Shepherd's Bush ⊖	d																					
Wembley Central ⊖	d																					
Harrow & Wealdstone ⊖	d																					
Watford Junction	d																					
Milton Keynes Central 10	a																					
Battersea Park 4	d														11 45		12 04					
London Victoria 15 ⊖	a	11 46			11 48			11 55	11 59			12 01				12 02	12 09		12 13	12 16		
Streatham 4	d			11 28									11 43									11 58
Tulse Hill 3	d		11 25	11 32									11 47								11 55	12 02
Herne Hill 4	a		11 33																		12 03	
Loughborough Jn	a		11 41																		12 11	
Elephant & Castle ⊖	a		11 53																		12 23	
London Blackfriars 3 ⊖	a		12 01																		12 31	
City Thameslink 3	a																					
St Pancras International 15 ⊖	a																					
Luton Airport Parkway 7	a																					
Luton 10	a																					
North Dulwich	d			11 35																		12 05
East Dulwich	d			11 37																		12 07
Peckham Rye 4	d			11 39											11 56							12 09
Queens Rd Peckham	d			11 42											11 59							12 12
South Bermondsey	d			11 44											12 01							12 14
London Bridge 4 ⊖	a			11 49		11 46	11 46			11 51	12 01		11 59		12 06			12 18				12 19

A from 12 September

B until 5 September

Table 177

Sundays

East and West Croydon, London-Milton Keynes and Luton via Norbury-Crystal Palace-Tulse Hill

Local Services

		SN	SN	FC	FC	SN	SN	SN	SN	FC	LO	SN	SN	SN	SN	SN	SN	SN	FC	SN	SN	FC	FC
		◇1	◇1	1	1	◇1			◇1				◇1	◇1			◇1	◇1			1	1	1
		A	B	B	A	A			B				A	B			A	B				B	A
						🍴			🍴				🍴	🍴			🍴	🍴	🚌				
East Croydon	d	12 00	12 00	12 02	12 03	12 09			12 10				12 17	12 13		12 17	12 21	12 25		12 14	12 29	12 32	12 33
West Croydon 4	d						11 52	12 05			12 12				12 08								
Norwood Junction 2	a						11 56	12 09			12 16					12 21							
	d						11 59	12 10			12 16					12 22							
Selhurst 4	d														12 13					12 17	12 33		
Thornton Heath	d														12 15					12 19			
Norbury	d														12 18					12 22			
Streatham Common 4	d														12 21					12 25			
Beckenham Junction 4	d																						
Birkbeck	d																						
Crystal Palace 4	d						12 05																
Gipsy Hill	d						12 07																
West Norwood 4	d						12 10																
Streatham Hill	d						12 14																
Balham 4 ⊖	d						12 17								12 25								
Wandsworth Common	d														12 27								
Clapham Junction 10	d	12 11	12 12			12 19	12 22		12 25				12 27	12 28	12 31		12 32	12 38			12 41		
West Brompton ⊖	d																						
Kensington (Olympia) ⊖	d																						
Shepherd's Bush ⊖	d																						
Wembley Central ⊖	d																						
Harrow & Wealdstone ⊖	d																						
Watford Junction	d																						
Milton Keynes Central 10	a																						
Battersea Park 4	d											12 15			12 34								
London Victoria 15 ⊖	a	12 17	12 18			12 25	12 29		12 31				12 33	12 35	12 39		12 39	12 46			12 48		
Streatham 4	d									12 13										12 28			
Tulse Hill 3	d									12 17									12 25	12 32			
Herne Hill 4	a																		12 33				
Loughborough Jn	a																		12 41				
Elephant & Castle ⊖	a																		12 53				
London Blackfriars 3 ⊖	a																		13 01				
City Thameslink 3	a																						
St Pancras International 15 ⊖	a																						
Luton Airport Parkway 7	a																						
Luton 10	a																						
North Dulwich	d																			12 35			
East Dulwich	d																			12 37			
Peckham Rye 4	d											12 26								12 39			
Queens Rd Peckham	d											12 29								12 42			
South Bermondsey	d											12 31								12 44			
London Bridge 4 ⊖	a			12 16	12 16			12 31		12 29		12 36				12 48				12 49		12 46	12 46

A until 5 September

B from 12 September

Table 177

Sundays

East and West Croydon, London-Milton Keynes and Luton via Norbury-Crystal Palace-Tulse Hill

Local Services

		SN ◇1 A	SN	SN 1 A	SN	SN ◇1 B	FC	LO	SN	SN ◇1 A ⌶	SN	SN	SN 1 A	SN 1 B	FC 🚌	SN	SN ◇1 A	SN ◇1 B	FC 1 B	FC 1 A	SN ◇1 A ⌶	SN
East Croydon	d	12 39		12 34		12 40				12 46		12 47	12 56	12 58		12 44	13 00	13 00	13 02	13 03	13 09	
West Croydon 4	d		12 22		12 35			12 42			12 38											12 52
Norwood Junction 2	a		12 26	12 38	12 39			12 46				12 51										12 56
	d		12 29	12 38	12 40			12 46				12 52										12 59
Selhurst 4	d										12 43					12 47						
Thornton Heath	d										12 45					12 49						
Norbury	d										12 48					12 52						
Streatham Common 4	d										12 51					12 55						
Beckenham Junction 4	d																					
Birkbeck	d																					
Crystal Palace 4	d		12 35																			13 05
Gipsy Hill	d		12 37																			13 07
West Norwood 4	d		12 40																			13 10
Streatham Hill	d		12 44																			13 14
Balham 4 ⊖	d		12 47								12 55											13 17
Wandsworth Common	d										12 57											
Clapham Junction 10	d	12 49	12 52			12 55				12 55	13 01		13 07	13 09			13 11	13 12			13 19	13 22
West Brompton ⊖	d																					
Kensington (Olympia) ⊖	d																					
Shepherd's Bush ⊖	d																					
Wembley Central ⊖	d																					
Harrow & Wealdstone ⊖	d																					
Watford Junction	d																					
Milton Keynes Central 10	a																					
Battersea Park 4	d								12 45		13 04											
London Victoria 15 ⊖	a	12 55	12 59			13 01				13 02	13 09		13 13	13 16			13 17	13 18			13 25	13 29
Streatham 4	d						12 43									12 58						
Tulse Hill 3	d						12 47								12 55	13 02						
Herne Hill 4	a														13 03							
Loughborough Jn	a														13 11							
Elephant & Castle ⊖	a														13 23							
London Blackfriars 3 ⊖	a														13 31							
City Thameslink 3	a																					
St Pancras International 15 ⊖	a																					
Luton Airport Parkway 7	a																					
Luton 10	a																					
North Dulwich	d															13 05						
East Dulwich	d															13 07						
Peckham Rye 4	d								12 56							13 09						
Queens Rd Peckham	d								12 59							13 12						
South Bermondsey	d								13 01							13 14						
London Bridge 4 ⊖	a			12 51	13 01		12 59		13 06			13 18				13 19			13 16	13 16		

A until 5 September B from 12 September

Table 177

Sundays

East and West Croydon, London-Milton Keynes and Luton via Norbury-Crystal Palace-Tulse Hill

Local Services

		LO	SN	SN ◇1 A ⌶	FC	LO	SN	SN ◇1 B ⌶	SN ◇1 A ⌶	SN	SN	SN ◇1 B ⌶	SN ◇1 A ⌶	FC 🚌	SN	SN 1	FC 1 A	FC 1 B	SN ◇1 B	SN	LO	SN 1 B	SN
East Croydon	d			13 10				13 17	13 13		13 17	13 21	13 25		13 14	13 29	13 32	13 33	13 39			13 34	
West Croydon 4	d	12 57	13 05			13 12				13 08										13 22	13 27		13 35
Norwood Junction 2	a	13 01	13 09			13 16					13 21									13 26	13 31	13 38	13 39
	d	13 01	13 10			13 16					13 22									13 29	13 31	13 38	13 40
Selhurst 4	d									13 13					13 17	13 33							
Thornton Heath	d									13 15					13 19								
Norbury	d									13 18					13 22								
Streatham Common 4	d									13 21					13 25								
Beckenham Junction 4	d																						
Birkbeck	d																						
Crystal Palace 4	d																			13 35			
Gipsy Hill	d																			13 37			
West Norwood 4	d																			13 40			
Streatham Hill	d																			13 44			
Balham 4 ⊖	d									13 25										13 47			
Wandsworth Common	d									13 27													
Clapham Junction 10	d			13 25				13 27	13 28	13 31		13 32	13 38			13 41			13 49	13 52			
West Brompton ⊖	d																						
Kensington (Olympia) ⊖	d																						
Shepherd's Bush ⊖	d																						
Wembley Central ⊖	d																						
Harrow & Wealdstone ⊖	d																						
Watford Junction	d																						
Milton Keynes Central 10	a																						
Battersea Park 4	d					13 15				13 34													
London Victoria 15 ⊖	a			13 31				13 33	13 35	13 39		13 39	13 46			13 48			13 55	13 59			
Streatham 4	d				13 13										13 28								
Tulse Hill 3	d				13 17									13 25	13 32								
Herne Hill 4	a													13 33									
Loughborough Jn	a													13 41									
Elephant & Castle ⊖	a													13 53									
London Blackfriars 3 ⊖	a													14 01									
City Thameslink 3	a																						
St Pancras International 15 ⊖	a																						
Luton Airport Parkway 7	a																						
Luton 10	a																						
North Dulwich	d														13 35								
East Dulwich	d														13 37								
Peckham Rye 4	d					13 26									13 39								
Queens Rd Peckham	d					13 29									13 42								
South Bermondsey	d					13 31									13 44								
London Bridge 4 ⊖	a		13 31		13 29	13 36					13 48				13 49		13 46	13 46				13 51	14 01

A from 12 September B until 5 September

Table 177

Sundays

East and West Croydon, London-Milton Keynes and Luton via Norbury-Crystal Palace-Tulse Hill

Local Services

		SN ◇1 A	FC	LO	SN	SN ◇1 B 🛒	SN	SN	SN 1 B	SN 1 A	FC 🚌	SN	SN ◇1 B	SN ◇1 A	FC 1 A	FC 1 B	SN ◇1 B 🛒	SN	LO	SN	SN ◇1 A 🛒	FC	LO
East Croydon	d	13 40				13 46		13 47	13 56	13 58		13 44	14 00	14 00	14 02	14 03	14 09				14 10		
West Croydon 4	d			13 42			13 38											13 52	13 57	14 05			14 12
Norwood Junction 2	a			13 46				13 51										13 56	14 01	14 09			14 16
	d			13 46				13 52										13 59	14 01	14 10			14 16
Selhurst 4	d						13 43					13 47											
Thornton Heath	d						13 45					13 49											
Norbury	d						13 48					13 52											
Streatham Common 4	d						13 51					13 55											
Beckenham Junction 4	d																						
Birkbeck	d																						
Crystal Palace 4	d																	14 05					
Gipsy Hill	d																	14 07					
West Norwood 4	d																	14 10					
Streatham Hill	d																	14 14					
Balham 4 ⊖	d						13 55											14 17					
Wandsworth Common	d						13 57																
Clapham Junction 10	d	13 55				13 55	14 01		14 07	14 09			14 11	14 12			14 19	14 22			14 25		
West Brompton ⊖	d																						
Kensington (Olympia) ⊖	d																						
Shepherd's Bush ⊖	d																						
Wembley Central ⊖	d																						
Harrow & Wealdstone ⊖	d																						
Watford Junction	d																						
Milton Keynes Central 10	a																						
Battersea Park 4	d				13 45		14 04																
London Victoria 15 ⊖	a	14 01				14 02	14 09		14 13	14 16			14 17	14 18			14 25	14 29			14 31		
Streatham 4	d		13 43									13 58										14 13	
Tulse Hill 3	d		13 47								13 55	14 02										14 17	
Herne Hill 4	a										14 03												
Loughborough Jn	a										14 11												
Elephant & Castle ⊖	a										14 23												
London Blackfriars 3 ⊖	a										14 31												
City Thameslink 3	a																						
St Pancras International 15 ⊖	a																						
Luton Airport Parkway 7	a																						
Luton 10	a																						
North Dulwich	d											14 05											
East Dulwich	d											14 07											
Peckham Rye 4	d				13 56							14 09											
Queens Rd Peckham	d				13 59							14 12											
South Bermondsey	d				14 01							14 14											
London Bridge 4 ⊖	a		13 59		14 06			14 18				14 19			14 16	14 16				14 31		14 29	

A from 12 September

B until 5 September

Table 177

Sundays

East and West Croydon, London-Milton Keynes and Luton via Norbury-Crystal Palace-Tulse Hill

Local Services

		SN	SN ◇1 A 🛒	SN ◇1 B 🛒	SN	SN	SN ◇1 A 🛒	SN ◇1 B 🛒	FC 🚌	SN	SN 1	FC 1 B	FC 1 A	SN ◇1 A	SN	LO	SN 1 A	SN	SN ◇1 B	FC	LO	SN
East Croydon	d		14 17	14 13		14 17	14 21	14 25		14 14	14 29	14 32	14 33	14 39			14 34		14 40			
West Croydon 4	d				14 08										14 22	14 27		14 35			14 42	
Norwood Junction 2	a					14 21									14 26	14 31	14 38	14 39			14 46	
	d					14 22									14 29	14 31	14 38	14 40			14 46	
Selhurst 4	d				14 13					14 17	14 33											
Thornton Heath	d				14 15					14 19												
Norbury	d				14 18					14 22												
Streatham Common 4	d				14 21					14 25												
Beckenham Junction 4	d																					
Birkbeck	d																					
Crystal Palace 4	d														14 35							
Gipsy Hill	d														14 37							
West Norwood 4	d														14 40							
Streatham Hill	d														14 44							
Balham 4 ⊖	d				14 25										14 47							
Wandsworth Common	d				14 27																	
Clapham Junction 10	d		14 27	14 28	14 31		14 32	14 38			14 41			14 49	14 52				14 55			
West Brompton ⊖	d																					
Kensington (Olympia) ⊖	d																					
Shepherd's Bush ⊖	d																					
Wembley Central ⊖	d																					
Harrow & Wealdstone ⊖	d																					
Watford Junction	d																					
Milton Keynes Central 10	a																					
Battersea Park 4	d	14 15			14 34																	14 45
London Victoria 15 ⊖	a		14 33	14 35	14 39		14 39	14 46			14 48			14 55	14 59				15 01			
Streatham 4	d									14 28										14 43		
Tulse Hill 3	d								14 25	14 32										14 47		
Herne Hill 4	a								14 33													
Loughborough Jn	a								14 41													
Elephant & Castle ⊖	a								14 53													
London Blackfriars 3 ⊖	a								15 01													
City Thameslink 3	a																					
St Pancras International 15 ⊖	a																					
Luton Airport Parkway 7	a																					
Luton 10	a																					
North Dulwich	d									14 35												
East Dulwich	d									14 37												
Peckham Rye 4	d	14 26								14 39												14 56
Queens Rd Peckham	d	14 29								14 42												14 59
South Bermondsey	d	14 31								14 44												15 01
London Bridge 4 ⊖	a	14 36				14 48				14 49		14 46	14 46				14 51	15 01		14 59		15 06

A until 5 September

B from 12 September

East and West Croydon, London-Milton Keynes and Luton via Norbury-Crystal Palace-Tulse Hill

Local Services

Station		SN ◇1 A	SN	SN	SN 1 A	SN 1 B	FC	SN	SN ◇1 A	SN ◇1 B	FC 1 B	FC 1 A	SN ◇1 A	SN	LO	SN	SN ◇1 B	FC	LO	SN	SN ◇1 A	SN ◇1 B	SN
East Croydon	d	14 46		14 47	14 56	14 58		14 44	15 00	15 00	15 02	15 03	15 09				15 10				15 17	15 13	
West Croydon 4	d		14 38											14 52	14 57	15 05			15 12				15 08
Norwood Junction 2	a			14 51										14 56	15 01	15 09			15 16				
	d			14 52										14 59	15 01	15 10			15 16				
Selhurst 4	d		14 43					14 47															15 13
Thornton Heath	d		14 45					14 49															15 15
Norbury	d		14 48					14 52															15 18
Streatham Common 4	d		14 51					14 55															15 21
Beckenham Junction 4	d																						
Birkbeck	d																						
Crystal Palace 4	d													15 05									
Gipsy Hill	d													15 07									
West Norwood 4	d													15 10									
Streatham Hill	d													15 14									
Balham 4 ⊖	d		14 55											15 17									15 25
Wandsworth Common	d		14 57																				15 27
Clapham Junction 10	d	14 55	15 01		15 07	15 09			15 11	15 12			15 19	15 22			15 25				15 27	15 28	15 31
West Brompton ⊖	d																						
Kensington (Olympia) ⊖	d																						
Shepherd's Bush ⊖	d																						
Wembley Central ⊖	d																						
Harrow & Wealdstone ⊖	d																						
Watford Junction	d																						
Milton Keynes Central 10	a																						
Battersea Park 4	d		15 04																	15 15			15 34
London Victoria 15 ⊖	a	15 02	15 09		15 13	15 16			15 17	15 18			15 25	15 29			15 31				15 33	15 35	15 39
Streatham 4	d							14 58										15 13					
Tulse Hill 3	d						14 55	15 02										15 17					
Herne Hill 4	a						15 03																
Loughborough Jn	a						15 11																
Elephant & Castle ⊖	a						15 23																
London Blackfriars 3 ⊖	a						15 31																
City Thameslink 3	a																						
St Pancras International 15 ⊖	a																						
Luton Airport Parkway 7	a																						
Luton 10	a																						
North Dulwich	d							15 05															
East Dulwich	d							15 07															
Peckham Rye 4	d							15 09												15 26			
Queens Rd Peckham	d							15 12												15 29			
South Bermondsey	d							15 14												15 31			
London Bridge 4 ⊖	a			15 18				15 19			15 16	15 16				15 31		15 29		15 36			

A until 5 September

B from 12 September

East and West Croydon, London-Milton Keynes and Luton via Norbury-Crystal Palace-Tulse Hill

Local Services

Station		SN	SN ◇1 A	SN ◇1 B	FC	SN	SN 1	FC 1 B	FC 1 A	SN ◇1 A	SN	LO	SN 1 A	SN	SN ◇1 B	FC	LO	SN	SN ◇1 A	SN	SN	SN 1 A
East Croydon	d	15 17	15 21	15 25		15 14	15 29	15 32	15 33	15 39			15 34		15 40				15 46		15 47	15 56
West Croydon 4	d										15 22	15 27		15 35			15 42			15 38		
Norwood Junction 2	a	15 21									15 26	15 31	15 38	15 39			15 46				15 51	
	d	15 22									15 29	15 31	15 38	15 40			15 46				15 52	
Selhurst 4	d					15 17	15 33													15 43		
Thornton Heath	d					15 19														15 45		
Norbury	d					15 22														15 48		
Streatham Common 4	d					15 25														15 51		
Beckenham Junction 4	d																					
Birkbeck	d																					
Crystal Palace 4	d										15 35											
Gipsy Hill	d										15 37											
West Norwood 4	d										15 40											
Streatham Hill	d										15 44											
Balham 4 ⊖	d										15 47									15 55		
Wandsworth Common	d																			15 57		
Clapham Junction 10	d		15 32	15 38			15 41			15 49	15 52				15 55				15 55	16 01		16 07
West Brompton ⊖	d																					
Kensington (Olympia) ⊖	d																					
Shepherd's Bush ⊖	d																					
Wembley Central ⊖	d																					
Harrow & Wealdstone ⊖	d																					
Watford Junction	d																					
Milton Keynes Central 10	a																					
Battersea Park 4	d																	15 45		16 04		
London Victoria 15 ⊖	a		15 39	15 46			15 48			15 55	15 59				16 01				16 02	16 09		16 13
Streatham 4	d					15 28										15 43						
Tulse Hill 3	d				15 25	15 32										15 47						
Herne Hill 4	a				15 33																	
Loughborough Jn	a				15 41																	
Elephant & Castle ⊖	a				15 53																	
London Blackfriars 3 ⊖	a				16 01																	
City Thameslink 3	a																					
St Pancras International 15 ⊖	a																					
Luton Airport Parkway 7	a																					
Luton 10	a																					
North Dulwich	d					15 35																
East Dulwich	d					15 37																
Peckham Rye 4	d					15 39												15 56				
Queens Rd Peckham	d					15 42												15 59				
South Bermondsey	d					15 44												16 01				
London Bridge 4 ⊖	a	15 48				15 49		15 46	15 46				15 51	16 01		15 59		16 06			16 18	

A until 5 September

B from 12 September

Table 177

Sundays

East and West Croydon, London-Milton Keynes and Luton via Norbury-Crystal Palace-Tulse Hill

Local Services

		SN 1 A	FC	SN	SN ◇1 B	SN ◇1 A	FC 1 A	FC 1 B	SN ◇1 B	SN	LO	SN	SN ◇1 A	FC	LO	SN	SN ◇1 B	SN ◇1 A	SN	SN	SN ◇1 B	SN ◇1 A	FC
East Croydon	d	15 58		15 44	16 00	16 00	16 02	16 03	16 09				16 10				16 17	16 13		16 17	16 21	16 25	
West Croydon 4	d									15 52	15 57	16 05			16 12				16 08				
Norwood Junction 2	a									15 56	16 01	16 09			16 16					16 21			
	d									15 59	16 01	16 10			16 16					16 22			
Selhurst 4	d			15 47															16 13				
Thornton Heath	d			15 49															16 15				
Norbury	d			15 52															16 18				
Streatham Common 4	d			15 55															16 21				
Beckenham Junction 4	d																						
Birkbeck	d																						
Crystal Palace 4	d									16 05													
Gipsy Hill	d									16 07													
West Norwood 4	d									16 10													
Streatham Hill	d									16 14													
Balham 4	d									16 17									16 25				
Wandsworth Common	d																		16 27				
Clapham Junction 10	d	16 09			16 11	16 12			16 19	16 22			16 25				16 27	16 28	16 31		16 32	16 38	
West Brompton	d																						
Kensington (Olympia)	d																						
Shepherd's Bush	d																						
Wembley Central	d																						
Harrow & Wealdstone	d																						
Watford Junction	d																						
Milton Keynes Central 10	a																						
Battersea Park 4	d															16 15			16 34				
London Victoria 15	a	16 16			16 17	16 18			16 25	16 29			16 31				16 33	16 35	16 39		16 39	16 46	
Streatham 4	d			15 58										16 13									
Tulse Hill 3	d		15 55	16 02										16 17									16 25
Herne Hill 4	a		16 03																				16 33
Loughborough Jn	a		16 11																				16 41
Elephant & Castle	a		16 23																				16 53
London Blackfriars 3	a		16 31																				17 01
City Thameslink 3	a																						
St Pancras International 15	a																						
Luton Airport Parkway 7	a																						
Luton 10	a																						
North Dulwich	d			16 05																			
East Dulwich	d			16 07																			
Peckham Rye 4	d			16 09												16 26							
Queens Rd Peckham	d			16 12												16 29							
South Bermondsey	d			16 14												16 31							
London Bridge 4	a			16 19			16 16	16 16				16 31		16 29		16 36				16 48			

A from 12 September

B until 5 September

Table 177

Sundays

East and West Croydon, London-Milton Keynes and Luton via Norbury-Crystal Palace-Tulse Hill

Local Services

		SN	SN 1	FC 1 A	FC 1 B	SN ◇1 B	SN	LO	SN 1 B	SN	SN ◇1 A	FC	LO	SN	SN ◇1 B	SN	SN	SN 1 B	SN 1 A	FC	SN	SN ◇1 B	SN ◇1 A
East Croydon	d	16 14	16 29	16 32	16 33	16 39			16 34		16 40				16 46		16 47	16 56	16 58		16 44	17 00	17 00
West Croydon 4	d						16 22	16 27		16 35			16 42			16 38							
Norwood Junction 2	a						16 26	16 31	16 38	16 39			16 46				16 51						
	d						16 29	16 31	16 38	16 40			16 46				16 52						
Selhurst 4	d	16 17	16 33													16 43					16 47		
Thornton Heath	d	16 19														16 45					16 49		
Norbury	d	16 22														16 48					16 52		
Streatham Common 4	d	16 25														16 51					16 55		
Beckenham Junction 4	d																						
Birkbeck	d																						
Crystal Palace 4	d						16 35																
Gipsy Hill	d						16 37																
West Norwood 4	d						16 40																
Streatham Hill	d						16 44																
Balham 4	d						16 47									16 55							
Wandsworth Common	d															16 57							
Clapham Junction 10	d		16 41			16 49	16 52				16 55				16 55	17 01		17 07	17 09			17 11	17 12
West Brompton	d																						
Kensington (Olympia)	d																						
Shepherd's Bush	d																						
Wembley Central	d																						
Harrow & Wealdstone	d																						
Watford Junction	d																						
Milton Keynes Central 10	a																						
Battersea Park 4	d													16 45		17 04							
London Victoria 15	a		16 48			16 55	16 59				17 01				17 02	17 09		17 13	17 16			17 17	17 18
Streatham 4	d	16 28										16 43									16 58		
Tulse Hill 3	d	16 32										16 47								16 55	17 02		
Herne Hill 4	a																			17 03			
Loughborough Jn	a																			17 11			
Elephant & Castle	a																			17 23			
London Blackfriars 3	a																			17 31			
City Thameslink 3	a																						
St Pancras International 15	a																						
Luton Airport Parkway 7	a																						
Luton 10	a																						
North Dulwich	d	16 35																			17 05		
East Dulwich	d	16 37																			17 07		
Peckham Rye 4	d	16 39												16 56							17 09		
Queens Rd Peckham	d	16 42												16 59							17 12		
South Bermondsey	d	16 44												17 01							17 14		
London Bridge 4	a	16 49		16 46	16 46				16 51	17 01		16 59		17 06			17 18				17 19		

A from 12 September

B until 5 September

Table 177

Sundays

East and West Croydon, London-Milton Keynes and Luton via Norbury-Crystal Palace-Tulse Hill

Local Services

		FC	FC	SN	SN	LO	SN	SN	FC	LO	SN	SN	SN	SN	SN	SN	SN	FC	SN	SN	FC	FC
		1	1	◇1				◇1				◇1	◇1			◇1	◇1			1	1	1
		A	B	B				A				B	A			B	A				A	B
				trolley				trolley				trolley	trolley			trolley	trolley	bus				
East Croydon (tram)	d	17 02	17 03	17 09				17 10				17 17	17 13		17 17	17 21	17 25		17 14	17 29	17 32	17 33
West Croydon [4] (tram)	d				16 52	16 57	17 05			17 12				17 08								
Norwood Junction [2]	a				16 56	17 01	17 09			17 16					17 21							
	d				16 59	17 01	17 10			17 16					17 22							
Selhurst [4]	d													17 13					17 17	17 33		
Thornton Heath	d													17 15					17 19			
Norbury	d													17 18					17 22			
Streatham Common [4]	d													17 21					17 25			
Beckenham Junction [4] (tram)	d																					
Birkbeck (tram)	d																					
Crystal Palace [4]	d				17 05																	
Gipsy Hill	d				17 07																	
West Norwood [4]	d				17 10																	
Streatham Hill	d				17 14																	
Balham [4] ⊖	d				17 17									17 25								
Wandsworth Common	d													17 27								
Clapham Junction [10]	d			17 19	17 22			17 25				17 27	17 28	17 31		17 32	17 38			17 41		
West Brompton ⊖	d																					
Kensington (Olympia) ⊖	d																					
Shepherd's Bush ⊖	d																					
Wembley Central ⊖	d																					
Harrow & Wealdstone ⊖	d																					
Watford Junction	d																					
Milton Keynes Central [10]	a																					
Battersea Park [4]	d										17 15			17 34								
London Victoria [15] ⊖	a			17 25	17 29			17 31				17 33	17 35	17 39		17 39	17 46			17 48		
Streatham [4]	d								17 13										17 28			
Tulse Hill [3]	d								17 17									17 25	17 32			
Herne Hill [4]	a																	17 33				
Loughborough Jn	a																	17 41				
Elephant & Castle ⊖	a																	17 53				
London Blackfriars [3] ⊖	a																	18 01				
City Thameslink [3]	a																					
St Pancras International [15] ⊖	a																					
Luton Airport Parkway [7]	a																					
Luton [10]	a																					
North Dulwich	d																		17 35			
East Dulwich	d																		17 37			
Peckham Rye [4]	d										17 26								17 39			
Queens Rd Peckham	d										17 29								17 42			
South Bermondsey	d										17 31								17 44			
London Bridge [4] ⊖	a	17 16	17 16				17 31		17 29		17 36				17 48				17 49		17 46	17 46

A from 12 September

B until 5 September

Table 177

Sundays

East and West Croydon, London-Milton Keynes and Luton via Norbury-Crystal Palace-Tulse Hill

Local Services

		SN	SN	LO	SN	SN	SN	FC	LO	SN	SN	SN	SN	SN	SN	FC	SN	SN	SN	FC	FC	SN	SN
		◇1			1		◇1				◇1			1	1			◇1	◇1	1	1	◇1	
		A			A		B				A			A	B			A	B	B	A	A	
											trolley					bus						trolley	
East Croydon (tram)	d	17 39			17 34		17 40				17 46		17 47	17 56	17 58		17 44	18 00	18 00	18 02	18 03	18 09	
West Croydon [4] (tram)	d		17 22	17 27		17 35			17 42			17 38											17 52
Norwood Junction [2]	a		17 26	17 31	17 38	17 39			17 46				17 51										17 56
	d		17 29	17 31	17 38	17 40			17 46				17 52										17 59
Selhurst [4]	d											17 43					17 47						
Thornton Heath	d											17 45					17 49						
Norbury	d											17 48					17 52						
Streatham Common [4]	d											17 51					17 55						
Beckenham Junction [4] (tram)	d																						
Birkbeck (tram)	d																						
Crystal Palace [4]	d		17 35																				18 05
Gipsy Hill	d		17 37																				18 07
West Norwood [4]	d		17 40																				18 10
Streatham Hill	d		17 44																				18 14
Balham [4] ⊖	d		17 47									17 55											18 17
Wandsworth Common	d											17 57											
Clapham Junction [10]	d	17 49	17 52				17 55				17 55	18 01		18 07	18 09			18 11	18 12			18 19	18 22
West Brompton ⊖	d																						
Kensington (Olympia) ⊖	d																						
Shepherd's Bush ⊖	d																						
Wembley Central ⊖	d																						
Harrow & Wealdstone ⊖	d																						
Watford Junction	d																						
Milton Keynes Central [10]	a																						
Battersea Park [4]	d									17 45		18 04											
London Victoria [15] ⊖	a	17 55	17 59				18 01				18 02	18 09		18 13	18 16			18 17	18 18			18 25	18 29
Streatham [4]	d							17 43									17 58						
Tulse Hill [3]	d							17 47								17 55	18 02						
Herne Hill [4]	a															18 03							
Loughborough Jn	a															18 11							
Elephant & Castle ⊖	a															18 23							
London Blackfriars [3] ⊖	a															18 31							
City Thameslink [3]	a																						
St Pancras International [15] ⊖	a																						
Luton Airport Parkway [7]	a																						
Luton [10]	a																						
North Dulwich	d																18 05						
East Dulwich	d																18 07						
Peckham Rye [4]	d									17 56							18 09						
Queens Rd Peckham	d									17 59							18 12						
South Bermondsey	d									18 01							18 14						
London Bridge [4] ⊖	a				17 51	18 01		17 59		18 06			18 18				18 19			18 16	18 16		

A until 5 September

B from 12 September

East and West Croydon, London-Milton Keynes and Luton via Norbury-Crystal Palace-Tulse Hill

Local Services

Station	LO	SN	SN ◇1 A ⌶	FC	LO	SN	SN ◇1 B ⌶	SN ◇1 A ⌶	SN	SN	SN ◇1 B ⌶	SN ◇1 A ⌶	FC 🚌	SN	SN 1	FC 1 A	FC 1 B	SN ◇1 B	SN	LO	SN 1 B
East Croydon ⇌ d			18 10				18 17	18 13		18 17	18 21	18 25		18 14	18 29	18 32	18 33	18 39			18 34
West Croydon 4 ⇌ d	17 57	18 05			18 12				18 08										18 22	18 27	
Norwood Junction 2 a	18 01	18 09			18 16					18 21									18 26	18 31	18 38
d	18 01	18 10			18 16					18 22									18 29	18 31	18 38
Selhurst 4 d									18 13					18 17	18 33						
Thornton Heath d									18 15					18 19							
Norbury d									18 18					18 22							
Streatham Common 4 d									18 21					18 25							
Beckenham Junction 4 ⇌ d																					
Birkbeck ⇌ d																					
Crystal Palace 4 d																			18 35		
Gipsy Hill d																			18 37		
West Norwood 4 d																			18 40		
Streatham Hill d																			18 44		
Balham 4 ⊖ d									18 25										18 47		
Wandsworth Common d									18 27												
Clapham Junction 10 d			18 25				18 27	18 28	18 31		18 32	18 38			18 41			18 49	18 52		
West Brompton ⊖ d																					
Kensington (Olympia) ⊖ d																					
Shepherd's Bush ⊖ d																					
Wembley Central ⊖ d																					
Harrow & Wealdstone ⊖ d																					
Watford Junction d																					
Milton Keynes Central 10 a																					
Battersea Park 4 d						18 15			18 34												
London Victoria 15 ⊖ a			18 31				18 33	18 35	18 39		18 39	18 46			18 48			18 55	18 59		
Streatham 4 d				18 13										18 28							
Tulse Hill 3 d				18 17									18 25	18 32							
Herne Hill 4 a													18 33								
Loughborough Jn a													18 41								
Elephant & Castle ⊖ a													18 53								
London Blackfriars 3 ⊖ a													19 01								
City Thameslink 3 a																					
St Pancras International 15 ⊖ a																					
Luton Airport Parkway 7 a																					
Luton 10 a																					
North Dulwich d														18 35							
East Dulwich d														18 37							
Peckham Rye 4 d						18 26								18 39							
Queens Rd Peckham d						18 29								18 42							
South Bermondsey d						18 31								18 44							
London Bridge 4 ⊖ a		18 31		18 29		18 36				18 48				18 49		18 46	18 46				18 51

A from 12 September

B until 5 September

East and West Croydon, London-Milton Keynes and Luton via Norbury-Crystal Palace-Tulse Hill

Local Services

Station	SN	SN ◇1 A	FC	LO	SN	SN ◇1 B	SN	SN	SN 1 B	SN 1 A	FC 🚌	SN	SN ◇1 B	SN ◇1 A	FC 1 A	FC 1 B	SN ◇1 B ⌶	SN	LO	SN	SN ◇1 A ⌶	FC
East Croydon ⇌ d		18 40				18 46		18 47	18 56	18 58		18 44	19 00	19 00	19 02	19 03	19 09				19 10	
West Croydon 4 ⇌ d	18 35			18 42			18 38											18 52	18 57	19 05		
Norwood Junction 2 a	18 39			18 46				18 51										18 56	19 01	19 09		
d	18 40			18 46				18 52										18 59	19 01	19 10		
Selhurst 4 d							18 43					18 47										
Thornton Heath d							18 45					18 49										
Norbury d							18 48					18 52										
Streatham Common 4 d							18 51					18 55										
Beckenham Junction 4 ⇌ d																						
Birkbeck ⇌ d																						
Crystal Palace 4 d																		19 05				
Gipsy Hill d																		19 07				
West Norwood 4 d																		19 10				
Streatham Hill d																		19 14				
Balham 4 ⊖ d							18 55											19 17				
Wandsworth Common d							18 57															
Clapham Junction 10 d		18 55				18 55	19 01		19 07	19 09			19 11	19 12			19 19	19 22			19 25	
West Brompton ⊖ d																						
Kensington (Olympia) ⊖ d																						
Shepherd's Bush ⊖ d																						
Wembley Central ⊖ d																						
Harrow & Wealdstone ⊖ d																						
Watford Junction d																						
Milton Keynes Central 10 a																						
Battersea Park 4 d					18 45		19 04															
London Victoria 15 ⊖ a		19 01				19 02	19 09		19 13	19 16			19 17	19 18			19 25	19 29			19 31	
Streatham 4 d			18 43									18 58										19 13
Tulse Hill 3 d			18 47								18 55	19 02										19 17
Herne Hill 4 a											19 03											
Loughborough Jn a											19 11											
Elephant & Castle ⊖ a											19 23											
London Blackfriars 3 ⊖ a											19 31											
City Thameslink 3 a																						
St Pancras International 15 ⊖ a																						
Luton Airport Parkway 7 a																						
Luton 10 a																						
North Dulwich d												19 05										
East Dulwich d												19 07										
Peckham Rye 4 d					18 56							19 09										
Queens Rd Peckham d					18 59							19 12										
South Bermondsey d					19 01							19 14										
London Bridge 4 ⊖ a	19 01		18 59		19 06			19 18				19 19			19 16	19 16				19 31		19 29

A from 12 September

B until 5 September

Table 177

Sundays

East and West Croydon, London-Milton Keynes and Luton via Norbury-Crystal Palace-Tulse Hill

Local Services

		LO	SN	SN ◇1 A	SN ◇1 B	SN	SN	SN ◇1 A	SN ◇1 B	FC (bus)	SN	SN 1	FC 1 B	FC 1 A	SN ◇1 A	SN	LO	SN 1 A	SN	SN ◇1 B	FC	LO	SN
East Croydon (tram)	d			19 17	19 13		19 17	19 21	19 25		19 14	19 29	19 32	19 33	19 39			19 34		19 40			
West Croydon 4 (tram)	d	19 12				19 08										19 22	19 27		19 35			19 42	
Norwood Junction 2	a	19 16					19 21									19 26	19 31	19 38	19 39			19 46	
	d	19 16					19 22									19 29	19 31	19 38	19 40			19 46	
Selhurst 4	d					19 13					19 17	19 33											
Thornton Heath	d					19 15					19 19												
Norbury	d					19 18					19 22												
Streatham Common 4	d					19 21					19 25												
Beckenham Junction 4 (tram)	d																						
Birkbeck (tram)	d																						
Crystal Palace 4	d															19 35							
Gipsy Hill	d															19 37							
West Norwood 4	d															19 40							
Streatham Hill	d															19 44							
Balham 4 ⊖	d					19 25										19 47							
Wandsworth Common	d					19 27																	
Clapham Junction 10	d			19 27	19 28	19 31		19 32	19 38			19 41			19 49	19 52				19 55			
West Brompton ⊖	d																						
Kensington (Olympia) ⊖	d																						
Shepherd's Bush ⊖	d																						
Wembley Central ⊖	d																						
Harrow & Wealdstone ⊖	d																						
Watford Junction	d																						
Milton Keynes Central 10	a																						
Battersea Park 4	d		19 15			19 34																	19 45
London Victoria 15 ⊖	a			19 33	19 35	19 39		19 39	19 46			19 48			19 55	19 59				20 01			
Streatham 4	d										19 28										19 43		
Tulse Hill 3	d									19 25	19 32										19 47		
Herne Hill 4	a									19 33													
Loughborough Jn	a									19 41													
Elephant & Castle ⊖	a									19 53													
London Blackfriars 3 ⊖	a									20 01													
City Thameslink 3	a																						
St Pancras International 15 ⊖	a																						
Luton Airport Parkway 7	a																						
Luton 10	a																						
North Dulwich	d										19 35												
East Dulwich	d										19 37												
Peckham Rye 4	d		19 26								19 39												19 56
Queens Rd Peckham	d		19 29								19 42												19 59
South Bermondsey	d		19 31								19 44												20 01
London Bridge 4 ⊖	a		19 36				19 48				19 49		19 46	19 46				19 51	20 01		19 59		20 06

A until 5 September **B** from 12 September

Table 177

Sundays

East and West Croydon, London-Milton Keynes and Luton via Norbury-Crystal Palace-Tulse Hill

Local Services

		SN ◇1 A	SN	SN	SN 1 A	SN 1 B	FC (bus)	SN	SN ◇1 A	SN ◇1 B	FC 1 B	FC 1 A	SN ◇1 A	SN	LO	SN	SN ◇1 B	FC	LO	SN	SN ◇1 A	SN ◇1 B
East Croydon (tram)	d	19 46		19 47	19 56	19 58		19 44	20 00	20 00	20 02	20 03	20 09				20 10				20 17	20 13
West Croydon 4 (tram)	d		19 38											19 52	19 57	20 05			20 12			
Norwood Junction 2	a			19 51										19 56	20 01	20 09			20 16			
	d			19 52										19 59	20 01	20 10			20 16			
Selhurst 4	d		19 43					19 47														
Thornton Heath	d		19 45					19 49														
Norbury	d		19 48					19 52														
Streatham Common 4	d		19 51					19 55														
Beckenham Junction 4 (tram)	d																					
Birkbeck (tram)	d																					
Crystal Palace 4	d													20 05								
Gipsy Hill	d													20 07								
West Norwood 4	d													20 10								
Streatham Hill	d													20 14								
Balham 4 ⊖	d		19 55											20 17								
Wandsworth Common	d		19 57																			
Clapham Junction 10	d	19 55	20 01		20 07	20 09			20 11	20 12			20 19	20 22			20 25				20 27	20 28
West Brompton ⊖	d																					
Kensington (Olympia) ⊖	d																					
Shepherd's Bush ⊖	d																					
Wembley Central ⊖	d																					
Harrow & Wealdstone ⊖	d																					
Watford Junction	d																					
Milton Keynes Central 10	a																					
Battersea Park 4	d		20 04																	20 15		
London Victoria 15 ⊖	a	20 02	20 09		20 13	20 16			20 17	20 18			20 25	20 29			20 31				20 33	20 35
Streatham 4	d							19 58										20 13				
Tulse Hill 3	d						19 55	20 02										20 17				
Herne Hill 4	a						20 03															
Loughborough Jn	a						20 11															
Elephant & Castle ⊖	a						20 23															
London Blackfriars 3 ⊖	a						20 31															
City Thameslink 3	a																					
St Pancras International 15 ⊖	a																					
Luton Airport Parkway 7	a																					
Luton 10	a																					
North Dulwich	d							20 05														
East Dulwich	d							20 07														
Peckham Rye 4	d							20 09												20 26		
Queens Rd Peckham	d							20 12												20 29		
South Bermondsey	d							20 14												20 31		
London Bridge 4 ⊖	a			20 18				20 19			20 16	20 16				20 31		20 29		20 36		

A until 5 September **B** from 12 September

Table 177

Sundays

East and West Croydon, London-Milton Keynes and Luton via Norbury-Crystal Palace-Tulse Hill

Local Services

		SN	SN	SN ◇1 A	SN ◇1 B	FC (bus)	SN	SN 1	FC 1 B	FC 1 A	SN ◇1 A	SN	LO	SN 1 A	SN	SN ◇1 B	FC	LO	SN	SN ◇1 A	SN	SN	SN 1 A
East Croydon	d		20 17	20 21	20 25		20 14	20 29	20 32	20 33	20 39			20 34		20 40				20 46		20 47	20 56
West Croydon 4	d	20 08										20 22	20 27		20 35			20 42			20 38		
Norwood Junction 2	a		20 21									20 26	20 31	20 38	20 39			20 46				20 51	
	d		20 22									20 29	20 31	20 38	20 40			20 46				20 52	
Selhurst 4	d	20 13					20 17	20 33													20 43		
Thornton Heath	d	20 15					20 19														20 45		
Norbury	d	20 18					20 22														20 48		
Streatham Common 4	d	20 21					20 25														20 51		
Beckenham Junction 4	d																						
Birkbeck	d																						
Crystal Palace 4	d											20 35											
Gipsy Hill	d											20 37											
West Norwood 4	d											20 40											
Streatham Hill	d											20 44											
Balham 4 ⊖	d	20 25										20 47									20 55		
Wandsworth Common	d	20 27																			20 57		
Clapham Junction 10	d	20 31		20 32	20 38			20 41			20 49	20 52				20 55				20 55	21 01		21 07
West Brompton ⊖	d																						
Kensington (Olympia) ⊖	d																						
Shepherd's Bush ⊖	d																						
Wembley Central ⊖	d																						
Harrow & Wealdstone ⊖	d																						
Watford Junction	d																						
Milton Keynes Central 10	a																						
Battersea Park 4	d	20 34																	20 45		21 04		
London Victoria 15 ⊖	a	20 39		20 39	20 46			20 48			20 55	20 59				21 01				21 02	21 09		21 13
Streatham 4	d						20 28										20 43						
Tulse Hill 3	d					20 25	20 32										20 47						
Herne Hill 4	a					20 33																	
Loughborough Jn	a					20 41																	
Elephant & Castle ⊖	a					20 53																	
London Blackfriars 3 ⊖	a					21 01																	
City Thameslink 3	a																						
St Pancras International 15 ⊖	a																						
Luton Airport Parkway 7	a																						
Luton 10	a																						
North Dulwich	d						20 35																
East Dulwich	d						20 37																
Peckham Rye 4	d						20 39												20 56				
Queens Rd Peckham	d						20 42												20 59				
South Bermondsey	d						20 44												21 01				
London Bridge 4 ⊖	a		20 48				20 49		20 46	20 46				20 51	21 01		20 59		21 06			21 18	

A until 5 September

B from 12 September

Table 177

Sundays

East and West Croydon, London-Milton Keynes and Luton via Norbury-Crystal Palace-Tulse Hill

Local Services

		SN 1 A	FC (bus)	SN	SN ◇1 B	SN ◇1 A	FC 1 A	FC 1 B	SN ◇1 B	SN	LO	SN	SN ◇1 A	FC	LO	SN	SN ◇1 B	SN ◇1 A	SN	SN	SN ◇1 B	SN ◇1 A
East Croydon	d	20 58		20 44	21 00	21 00	21 02	21 03	21 09				21 10				21 17	21 13		21 17	21 21	21 25
West Croydon 4	d									20 52	20 57	21 05			21 12				21 08			
Norwood Junction 2	a									20 56	21 01	21 09			21 16					21 21		
	d									20 59	21 01	21 10			21 16					21 22		
Selhurst 4	d			20 47															21 13			
Thornton Heath	d			20 49															21 15			
Norbury	d			20 52															21 18			
Streatham Common 4	d			20 55															21 21			
Beckenham Junction 4	d																					
Birkbeck	d																					
Crystal Palace 4	d									21 05												
Gipsy Hill	d									21 07												
West Norwood 4	d									21 10												
Streatham Hill	d									21 14												
Balham 4 ⊖	d									21 17									21 25			
Wandsworth Common	d																		21 27			
Clapham Junction 10	d	21 09			21 11	21 12			21 19	21 22			21 25				21 27	21 28	21 31		21 32	21 38
West Brompton ⊖	d																					
Kensington (Olympia) ⊖	d																					
Shepherd's Bush ⊖	d																					
Wembley Central ⊖	d																					
Harrow & Wealdstone ⊖	d																					
Watford Junction	d																					
Milton Keynes Central 10	a																					
Battersea Park 4	d															21 15			21 34			
London Victoria 15 ⊖	a	21 16			21 17	21 18			21 25	21 29			21 31				21 33	21 35	21 39		21 39	21 46
Streatham 4	d			20 58										21 13								
Tulse Hill 3	d		20 55	21 02										21 17								
Herne Hill 4	a		21 03																			
Loughborough Jn	a		21 11																			
Elephant & Castle ⊖	a		21 23																			
London Blackfriars 3 ⊖	a		21 31																			
City Thameslink 3	a																					
St Pancras International 15 ⊖	a																					
Luton Airport Parkway 7	a																					
Luton 10	a																					
North Dulwich	d			21 05																		
East Dulwich	d			21 07																		
Peckham Rye 4	d			21 09												21 26						
Queens Rd Peckham	d			21 12												21 29						
South Bermondsey	d			21 14												21 31						
London Bridge 4 ⊖	a			21 19			21 16	21 16				21 31		21 29		21 36				21 48		

A from 12 September

B until 5 September

Table 177

Sundays

East and West Croydon, London-Milton Keynes and Luton via Norbury-Crystal Palace-Tulse Hill

Local Services

		FC	SN	SN 1	FC 1 A	FC 1 B	SN ◇1 B	SN	LO	SN 1 B	SN	SN ◇1 A	SN	FC	LO	SN	SN	SN 1 B	SN 1 A	FC	SN	SN ◇1 B	SN ◇1 A
East Croydon	d		21 14	21 29	21 32	21 33	21 39			21 34		21 40					21 47	21 56	21 58		21 44	22 00	22 00
West Croydon 4	d							21 22	21 27		21 35		21 38		21 42								
Norwood Junction 2	a							21 26	21 31	21 38	21 39				21 46		21 51						
	d							21 29	21 31	21 38	21 40				21 46		21 52						
Selhurst 4	d		21 17	21 33									21 43								21 47		
Thornton Heath	d		21 19										21 45								21 49		
Norbury	d		21 22										21 48								21 52		
Streatham Common 4	d		21 25										21 51								21 55		
Beckenham Junction 4	d																						
Birkbeck	d																						
Crystal Palace 4	d							21 35															
Gipsy Hill	d							21 37															
West Norwood 4	d							21 40															
Streatham Hill	d							21 44															
Balham 4 ⊖	d							21 47					21 55										
Wandsworth Common	d												21 57										
Clapham Junction 10	d			21 41			21 49	21 52				21 55	22 01					22 07	22 09			22 11	22 12
West Brompton ⊖	d																						
Kensington (Olympia) ⊖	d																						
Shepherd's Bush ⊖	d																						
Wembley Central ⊖	d																						
Harrow & Wealdstone ⊖	d																						
Watford Junction	d																						
Milton Keynes Central 10	a																						
Battersea Park 4	d												22 04			21 45							
London Victoria 15 ⊖	a			21 48			21 55	21 59				22 01	22 09					22 13	22 16			22 17	22 18
Streatham 4	d		21 28											21 43							21 58		
Tulse Hill 3	d	21 25	21 32											21 47						21 55	22 02		
Herne Hill 4	a	21 33																		22 03			
Loughborough Jn	a	21 41																		22 11			
Elephant & Castle ⊖	a	21 53																		22 23			
London Blackfriars 3 ⊖	a	22 01																		22 31			
City Thameslink 3	a																						
St Pancras International 15 ⊖	a																						
Luton Airport Parkway 7	a																						
Luton 10	a																						
North Dulwich	d		21 35																		22 05		
East Dulwich	d		21 37																		22 07		
Peckham Rye 4	d		21 39													21 56					22 09		
Queens Rd Peckham	d		21 42													21 59					22 12		
South Bermondsey	d		21 44													22 01					22 14		
London Bridge 4 ⊖	a		21 49		21 46	21 46				21 51	22 02			21 59		22 06	22 18				22 19		

A from 12 September

B until 5 September

Table 177

Sundays

East and West Croydon, London-Milton Keynes and Luton via Norbury-Crystal Palace-Tulse Hill

Local Services

		FC 1 A	FC 1 B	SN ◇1 B	SN	LO	SN	SN ◇1 A	SN	LO	SN	SN	SN	SN ◇1 B	SN ◇1 A	SN 1	SN	LO	FC 1 A	SN 1 B	FC 1 B	SN	SN
East Croydon	d	22 02	22 03	22 09				22 10				22 14	22 17	22 21	22 25	22 29			22 32	22 34	22 33		
West Croydon 4	d				21 52	21 57	22 05		22 08	22 12							22 22	22 27				22 35	22 38
Norwood Junction 2	a				21 56	22 01	22 09			22 16			22 21				22 26	22 31		22 38		22 39	
	d				21 59	22 01	22 10			22 16			22 22				22 29	22 31		22 38		22 40	
Selhurst 4	d								22 13			22 17				22 33							22 43
Thornton Heath	d								22 15			22 19											22 45
Norbury	d								22 18			22 22											22 48
Streatham Common 4	d								22 21			22 25											22 51
Beckenham Junction 4	d																						
Birkbeck	d																						
Crystal Palace 4	d				22 05												22 35						
Gipsy Hill	d				22 07												22 37						
West Norwood 4	d				22 10												22 40						
Streatham Hill	d				22 14												22 44						
Balham 4 ⊖	d				22 17				22 25								22 47						22 55
Wandsworth Common	d								22 27														22 57
Clapham Junction 10	d			22 19	22 22			22 25	22 31					22 32	22 38	22 41	22 52						23 01
West Brompton ⊖	d																						
Kensington (Olympia) ⊖	d																						
Shepherd's Bush ⊖	d																						
Wembley Central ⊖	d																						
Harrow & Wealdstone ⊖	d																						
Watford Junction	d																						
Milton Keynes Central 10	a																						
Battersea Park 4	d								22 34		22 15												23 04
London Victoria 15 ⊖	a			22 25	22 29			22 31	22 39					22 39	22 46	22 50	22 59						23 09
Streatham 4	d											22 28											
Tulse Hill 3	d											22 32											
Herne Hill 4	a																						
Loughborough Jn	a																						
Elephant & Castle ⊖	a																						
London Blackfriars 3 ⊖	a																						
City Thameslink 3	a																						
St Pancras International 15 ⊖	a																						
Luton Airport Parkway 7	a																						
Luton 10	a																						
North Dulwich	d											22 35											
East Dulwich	d											22 37											
Peckham Rye 4	d										22 26	22 39											
Queens Rd Peckham	d										22 29	22 42											
South Bermondsey	d										22 31	22 44											
London Bridge 4 ⊖	a	22 16	22 16				22 32				22 36	22 49	22 48						22 46	22 51	22 46	23 02	

A from 12 September

B until 5 September

Table 177

Sundays

East and West Croydon, London-Milton Keynes and Luton via Norbury-Crystal Palace-Tulse Hill

Local Services

		LO		SN	SN	SN	SN 1 A	SN 1 B	SN ◇1 A	SN ◇1 B	SN	LO		FC 1 B	FC 1 A	SN	SN	SN ◇1 A	SN	SN ◇1 B	SN 1	SN		FC 1 B	FC 1 A
East Croydon	d				22 44	22 47	22 56	22 58	23 00	23 00				23 02	23 03		23 16	23 21		23 25	23 29			23 32	23 33
West Croydon	d	22 42									22 52	22 57							23 08			23 22			
Norwood Junction	a	22 46				22 51					22 56	23 01					23 20					23 26			
	d	22 46				22 52					22 59	23 01										23 29			
Selhurst	d				22 47		22 59	23 02											23 13		23 33				
Thornton Heath	d				22 49														23 15						
Norbury	d				22 52														23 18						
Streatham Common	d				22 55														23 21						
Beckenham Junction	d																								
Birkbeck	d																								
Crystal Palace	d										23 05											23 35			
Gipsy Hill	d										23 07											23 37			
West Norwood	d										23 10											23 40			
Streatham Hill	d										23 14											23 44			
Balham	d										23 17								23 25			23 47			
Wandsworth Common	d																		23 27						
Clapham Junction	d						23 07	23 10	23 11	23 13	23 22							23 32	23 31	23 38	23 41	23 52			
West Brompton	d																								
Kensington (Olympia)	d																								
Shepherd's Bush	d																								
Wembley Central	d																								
Harrow & Wealdstone	d																								
Watford Junction	d																								
Milton Keynes Central	a																								
Battersea Park	d			22 45												23 15			23 34						
London Victoria	a						23 14	23 16	23 17	23 20	23 29							23 38	23 39	23 46	23 50	23 59			
Streatham	d				22 58																				
Tulse Hill	d				23 02																				
Herne Hill	a																								
Loughborough Jn	a																								
Elephant & Castle	a																								
London Blackfriars	a																								
City Thameslink	a																								
St Pancras International	a																								
Luton Airport Parkway	a																								
Luton	a																								
North Dulwich	d				23 05																				
East Dulwich	d				23 07																				
Peckham Rye	d			22 56	23 09											23 26									
Queens Rd Peckham	d			22 59	23 12											23 29									
South Bermondsey	d			23 01	23 14											23 31									
London Bridge	a			23 06	23 20	23 18								23 16	23 16	23 36								23 46	23 46

		SN	SN 1
East Croydon	d		23 56
West Croydon	d	23 38	
Norwood Junction	a		
	d		
Selhurst	d	23a42	00 01
Thornton Heath	d		
Norbury	d		
Streatham Common	d		
Beckenham Junction	d		
Birkbeck	d		
Crystal Palace	d		
Gipsy Hill	d		
West Norwood	d		
Streatham Hill	d		
Balham	d		
Wandsworth Common	d		
Clapham Junction	d		00 11
West Brompton	d		
Kensington (Olympia)	d		
Shepherd's Bush	d		
Wembley Central	d		
Harrow & Wealdstone	d		
Watford Junction	d		
Milton Keynes Central	a		
Battersea Park	d		
London Victoria	a		00 18
Streatham	d		
Tulse Hill	d		
Herne Hill	a		
Loughborough Jn	a		
Elephant & Castle	a		
London Blackfriars	a		
City Thameslink	a		
St Pancras International	a		
Luton Airport Parkway	a		
Luton	a		
North Dulwich	d		
East Dulwich	d		
Peckham Rye	d		
Queens Rd Peckham	d		
South Bermondsey	d		
London Bridge	a		

A until 5 September

B from 12 September

Table 178

Mondays to Fridays

London Bridge to London Victoria - Croydon and East London Line

		LO MX	SN MX	LO MO	LO MX	SN MX	SN MO	LO MX	FC MX	SN MX		SN MX	FC	SN MX	FC	FC	FC	SE	LO	LO		LO	LO	SN	LO
London Bridge	d		23p22			23p36	23p39		23p55			00 06	00 25	00 36	01 00	03 20	04 20							06 00	
Dalston Junction Stn Ell	d	23p10		23p28	23p30			23p40											05 40			05 50			06 00
Haggerston	d	23p11		23p29	23p31			23p41											05 41			05 51			06 01
Hoxton	d	23p13		23p31	23p33			23p43											05 43			05 53			06 03
Shoreditch High Street	d	23p16		23p34	23p36			23p46											05 46			05 56			06 06
Whitechapel	d	23p18		23p36	23p38			23p48											05 48			05 58			06 08
Shadwell	d	23p20		23p38	23p40			23p50											05 50			06 00			06 10
Wapping	d	23p22		23p40	23p42			23p52											05 52			06 02			06 12
Rotherhithe	d	23p24		23p42	23p44			23p54											05 54			06 04			06 14
Canada Water	d	23p26		23p44	23p46			23p56											05 56			06 06			06 16
Surrey Quays	d	23p27		23p45	23p47			23p57											05 57			06 07			06 17
New Cross Ell	a																					06 13			
New Cross Gate Station Ell	a	23p31		23p49	23p51			00 02											06 01						06 21
	d	23p32		23p50	23p52			00 03											06 02	05 47			05 52		06 22
New Cross Gate	d		23p27			23p41	23p44					00 11		00 41											
Brockley	d	23p34	23p30	23p52	23p54	23p44	23p47	00 04				00 14		00 44					06 04	05 49			05 54		06 24
Honor Oak Park	d	23p37	23p33	23p55	23p57	23p47	23p50	00 07				00 17		00 47					06 07	05 52			05 57		06 27
Forest Hill	d	23p40	23p35	23p58	23p59	23p49	23p52	00 10				00 19		00 49					06 10	05 55			06 00		06 30
Sydenham	d	23p42	23p38	00 01	00 02	23p52	23p55	00 12				00 22		00 52					06 12	05 57			06 02		06 32
Crystal Palace	d		23p43		00a07					00 03													06a07		06a37
Gipsy Hill	d		23p45																						
West Norwood	d		23p48																						
Streatham Hill	d		23p52																						
Balham	d		23p55																						
Wandsworth Common	d		23p58																						
Clapham Junction	d		00 02																						
South Bermondsey	d																							06 04	
Peckham Rye	d																	05 04							
Queens Rd Peckham	d																							06 06	
Denmark Hill	d																	05 07							
London Blackfriars	a								00 10				00 40		01 15	03 35	04 35	05 17							
Clapham High Street	d																								
Wandsworth Road	d																								
Battersea Park	d		00 05																						
London Victoria	a		00 12																						
Penge West	d	23p45		00 03		23p54	23p57	00 15				00 24		00 54					06 15	06 00					
Anerley	d	23p47		00 05		23p56	23p59	00 17				00 26		00 56					06 17	06 02					
Norwood Junction	d	23p50		00 08		23p59	00 05	00 20		00 09		00 30		01 00					06 20	06 05					
West Croydon	a	00 01		00 15				00 27		00 14									06 31	06 13					
East Croydon	a					00 03	00 08					00 33		01 03											

		SE	SN	LO	LO	SN		LO	SN	LO	SE	SN	LO	SN	LO	SN		LO	LO	SN	LO	SE	LO	SN	LO
London Bridge	d		06 06			06 11			06 19			06 30		06 33		06 36				06 41					
Dalston Junction Stn Ell	d				06 10					06 20			06 30		06 35				06 40		06 45				06 50
Haggerston	d				06 11					06 21			06 31		06 36				06 41		06 46				06 51
Hoxton	d				06 13					06 23			06 33		06 38				06 43		06 48				06 53
Shoreditch High Street	d				06 16					06 26			06 36		06 41				06 46		06 51				06 56
Whitechapel	d				06 18					06 28			06 38		06 43				06 48		06 53				06 58
Shadwell	d				06 20					06 30			06 40		06 45				06 50		06 55				07 00
Wapping	d				06 22					06 32			06 42		06 47				06 52		06 57				07 02
Rotherhithe	d				06 24					06 34			06 44		06 49				06 54		06 59				07 04
Canada Water	d				06 26					06 36			06 46		06 51				06 56		07 01				07 06
Surrey Quays	d				06 27					06 37			06 47		06 52				06 57		07 02				07 07
New Cross Ell	a									06 43					06 58										07 13
New Cross Gate Station Ell	a				06 31								06 51						07 01		07 06				
	d			06 07	06 32			06 17					06 52					06 37	07 02		07 07		06 47		
New Cross Gate	d		06 11						06 25							06 41									
Brockley	d		06 14	06 09	06 34			06 19	06 27				06 54			06 44		06 39	07 05		07 09		06 49		
Honor Oak Park	d		06 17	06 12	06 37			06 22	06 30				06 57			06 47		06 42	07 08		07 12		06 52		
Forest Hill	d		06 19	06 15	06 40			06 25	06 33				07 00			06 49		06 45	07 11		07 15		06 55		
Sydenham	d		06 22	06 17	06 42			06 27	06 35				07 02			06 52		06 47	07 13		07 17		06 57		
Crystal Palace	d			06a22					06 39				07a07					06a52			07a22			06 51	
Gipsy Hill	d								06 41															06 53	
West Norwood	d								06 44															06 56	
Streatham Hill	d								06 48																
Balham	d								06 51																
Wandsworth Common	d																								
Clapham Junction	d								06 56																
South Bermondsey	d					06 15						06 34		06 37						06 45					
Peckham Rye	d	06 04									06 30											06 47		07 07	
Queens Rd Peckham	d					06 18						06 36		06 39						06 48				07 10	
Denmark Hill	d	06 07				06 23					06 33									06 53		06 50			
London Blackfriars	a	06 17									06 45														
Clapham High Street	d					06 28														06 58					
Wandsworth Road	d					06 29														06 59					
Battersea Park	d					06 32														07 02					
London Victoria	a					06 36			07 05											07 08		07 04			
Penge West	d		06 24		06 45			06 30								06 54			07 16				07 00		
Anerley	d		06 26		06 47			06 32								06 56			07 18				07 02		
Norwood Junction	d		06 30		06 50			06 35								07 00			07 21				07 05		
West Croydon	a				07 01			06 42											07 31				07 12		
East Croydon	a		06 33													07 03									

Table 178

Mondays to Fridays

London Bridge to London Victoria - Croydon and East London Line

Station		SN		SN	LO	SN	LO	SE	SN	LO	SN	LO		SN	LO	SN	LO	SN	SE	LO	SN	LO		SE	SN
London Bridge 4 ⊖	d	06 51		06 54		06 58			07 03		07 06			07 11				07 21			07 29				07 33
Dalston Junction Stn Ell	d				06 55		07 00			07 05		07 10			07 15		07 20			07 25		07 30			
Haggerston	d				06 56		07 01			07 06		07 11			07 16		07 21			07 26		07 31			
Hoxton	d				06 58		07 03			07 08		07 13			07 18		07 23			07 28		07 33			
Shoreditch High Street	d				07 01		07 06			07 11		07 16			07 21		07 26			07 31		07 36			
Whitechapel	d				07 03		07 08			07 13		07 18			07 23		07 28			07 33		07 38			
Shadwell	d				07 05		07 10			07 15		07 20			07 25		07 30			07 35		07 40			
Wapping	d				07 07		07 12			07 17		07 22			07 27		07 32			07 37		07 42			
Rotherhithe	d				07 09		07 14			07 19		07 24			07 29		07 34			07 39		07 44			
Canada Water	d				07 11		07 16			07 21		07 26			07 31		07 36			07 41		07 46			
Surrey Quays	d				07 12		07 17			07 22		07 27			07 32		07 37			07 42		07 47			
New Cross Ell	a									07 28							07 43								
New Cross Gate Station Ell	a				07 16		07 21					07 31			07 36					07 46		07 51			
	d				07 17		07 22					07 32			07 37					07 47		07 52			
New Cross Gate 4	d	06 56		06 59							07 11							07 26							
Brockley	d	06 59		07 02	07 20		07 24				07 14	07 34			07 39			07 29		07 50		07 54			
Honor Oak Park	d	07 02		07 05	07 23		07 27				07 17	07 37			07 42			07 32		07 53		07 57			
Forest Hill 4	d	07 04		07 07	07 26		07 30				07 19	07 40			07 45			07 34		07 56		08 00			
Sydenham	d	07 07		07 10	07 28		07 32				07 22	07 42			07 47			07 37		07 58		08 02			
Crystal Palace 4	d	07 13					07a37								07a52	07 20		07 43				08a07			
Gipsy Hill	d	07 15														07 22		07 45							
West Norwood 4	d	07 18														07 25		07 48							
Streatham Hill	d	07 22																07 52							
Balham 4 ⊖	d	07 25																07 55							
Wandsworth Common	d	07 27																07 57							
Clapham Junction 10	d	07 31																08 01							
South Bermondsey	d					07 02			07 07					07 15							07 33				07 37
Peckham Rye 4	d							07 02								07 36			07 23					07 34	
Queens Rd Peckham	d					07 04			07 09					07 17		07 39					07 35				07 39
Denmark Hill 4	d							07 05						07 23					07 29					07 37	
London Blackfriars 3 ⊖	a							07 16																07 48	
Clapham High Street ⊖	d													07 28											
Wandsworth Road	d													07 29											
Battersea Park 4	d	07 35												07 32				08 05							
London Victoria 15 ⊖	a	07 41												07 38				08 11	07 42						
Penge West	d			07 12	07 31						07 24	07 45								08 01					
Anerley	d			07 14	07 33						07 26	07 47								08 03					
Norwood Junction 2	d			07 18	07 36						07 31	07 50								08 06					
West Croydon 4	a				07 43							08 01								08 13					
East Croydon	a			07 21							07 37														

Station		LO	SN	LO	SN	LO	SN	LO		SN	SE	LO	SE	LO	SN	LO	SN	SN		SN	LO	SE	LO	SE	SN
London Bridge 4 ⊖	d		07 36		07 41					07 51					08 03		08 06	08 06		08 10					
Dalston Junction Stn Ell	d	07 35		07 40		07 45		07 50				07 55		08 00		08 05					08 10		08 15		
Haggerston	d	07 36		07 41		07 46		07 51				07 56		08 01		08 06					08 11		08 16		
Hoxton	d	07 38		07 43		07 48		07 53				07 58		08 03		08 08					08 13		08 18		
Shoreditch High Street	d	07 41		07 46		07 51		07 56				08 01		08 06		08 11					08 16		08 21		
Whitechapel	d	07 43		07 48		07 53		07 58				08 03		08 08		08 13					08 18		08 23		
Shadwell	d	07 45		07 50		07 55		08 00				08 05		08 10		08 15					08 20		08 25		
Wapping	d	07 47		07 52		07 57		08 02				08 07		08 12		08 17					08 22		08 27		
Rotherhithe	d	07 49		07 54		07 59		08 04				08 09		08 14		08 19					08 24		08 29		
Canada Water	d	07 51		07 56		08 01		08 06				08 11		08 16		08 21					08 26		08 31		
Surrey Quays	d	07 52		07 57		08 02		08 07				08 12		08 17		08 22					08 27		08 32		
New Cross Ell	a	07 58						08 13								08 28									
New Cross Gate Station Ell	a			08 01		08 06						08 16		08 21							08 31		08 36		
	d			08 02		08 07						08 17		08 22							08 32		08 37		
New Cross Gate 4	d		07 41							07 56								08 11							
Brockley	d		07 44	08 04		08 09				07 59		08 20		08 24				08 14			08 34		08 39		
Honor Oak Park	d		07 47	08 07		08 12				08 02		08 23		08 27				08 17			08 37		08 42		
Forest Hill 4	d		07 49	08 10		08 15				08 04		08 26		08 30				08 19			08 40		08 45		
Sydenham	d		07 52	08 12		08 17				08 07		08 28		08 32				08 22			08 42		08 47		
Crystal Palace 4	d					08a22	07 49			08 13				08a37									08a52		08 19
Gipsy Hill	d						07 51			08 15															08 21
West Norwood 4	d						07 54			08 18															08 24
Streatham Hill	d									08 22															
Balham 4 ⊖	d									08 25															
Wandsworth Common	d									08 27															
Clapham Junction 10	d									08 31															
South Bermondsey	d				07 45										08 07		08 11			08 14					
Peckham Rye 4	d						08 06				07 54		08 01									08 13		08 16	08 35
Queens Rd Peckham	d				07 47		08 09								08 09		08 13			08 16					08 38
Denmark Hill 4	d				07 53						07 59		08 04							08 22		08 17		08 19	
London Blackfriars 3 ⊖	a												08 17											08 29	
Clapham High Street ⊖	d				07 58															08 27					
Wandsworth Road	d				07 59															08 29					
Battersea Park 4	d				08 02					08 35										08 32					
London Victoria 15 ⊖	a				08 08					08 41	08 11									08 39		08 29			
Penge West	d		07 54	08 15								08 31						08 24			08 45				
Anerley	d		07 56	08 17								08 33						08 26			08 47				
Norwood Junction 2	d		08 00	08 20								08 36						08 30			08 50				
West Croydon 4	a			08 31								08 44									09 01				
East Croydon	a		08 03															08 33							

Table 178

Mondays to Fridays

London Bridge to London Victoria - Croydon and East London Line

Station		LO	SN	SE		LO	SE 1	LO	SE	SN	SE 1	LO	SN	LO		SN	SE	LO	SN	LO	SN	SE	LO	LO	
London Bridge 4 ⊖	d		08 20							08 33			08 36			08 41					08 51				
Dalston Junction Stn Ell	d	08 20				08 25		08 30				08 35		08 40				08 45		08 50			08 55	09 00	
Haggerston	d	08 21				08 26		08 31				08 36		08 41				08 46		08 51			08 56	09 01	
Hoxton	d	08 23				08 28		08 33				08 38		08 43				08 48		08 53			08 58	09 03	
Shoreditch High Street	d	08 26				08 31		08 36				08 41		08 46				08 51		08 56			09 01	09 06	
Whitechapel	d	08 28				08 33		08 38				08 43		08 48				08 53		08 58			09 03	09 08	
Shadwell	d	08 30				08 35		08 40				08 45		08 50				08 55		09 00			09 05	09 10	
Wapping	d	08 32				08 37		08 42				08 47		08 52				08 57		09 02			09 07	09 12	
Rotherhithe	d	08 34				08 39		08 44				08 49		08 54				08 59		09 04			09 09	09 14	
Canada Water	d	08 36				08 41		08 46				08 51		08 56				09 01		09 06			09 11	09 16	
Surrey Quays	d	08 37				08 42		08 47				08 52		08 57				09 02		09 07			09 12	09 17	
New Cross Ell	a	08 43										08 58								09 13					
New Cross Gate Station Ell	a					08 46		08 51						09 01				09 06					09 16	09 21	
	d					08 47		08 52						09 02				09 07					09 17	09 22	
New Cross Gate 4	d		08 26										08 41								08 57				
Brockley	d		08 29			08 49		08 54					08 44	09 04				09 09			09 00		09 19	09 24	
Honor Oak Park	d		08 32			08 52		08 57					08 47	09 07				09 12			09 03		09 22	09 27	
Forest Hill 4	d		08 34			08 55		09 00					08 49	09 10				09 15			09 05		09 25	09 30	
Sydenham	d		08 37			08 57		09 02					08 52	09 12				09 17			09 08		09 27	09 32	
Crystal Palace 4	d		08 40					09a07										09a22	08 50		09 13			09a37	
Gipsy Hill	d		08 43																08 52		09 15				
West Norwood 4	d		08 46																08 55		09 18				
Streatham Hill	d		08 49																		09 22				
Balham 4 ⊖	d		08 55																		09 25				
Wandsworth Common	d		08 57																		09 27				
Clapham Junction 10	d		09 01																		09 31				
South Bermondsey	d									08 37						08 45									
Peckham Rye 4	d								08 33		08 36						08 44		09 06			08 55			
Queens Rd Peckham	d									08 39						08 48			09 09						
Denmark Hill 4	d			08 26			08 30		08 36		08 39					08 53	08 47					09 02			
London Blackfriars 3 ⊖	a			08 41							08 50						08 58								
Clapham High Street ⊖	d															08 58									
Wandsworth Road	d															08 59									
Battersea Park 4	d		09 05													09 02					09 35				
London Victoria 15 ⊖	a		09 11				08 42		08 49							09 08					09 39	09 11			
Penge West	d					09 00							08 54	09 15									09 30		
Anerley	d					09 02							08 56	09 17									09 32		
Norwood Junction 2	d					09 05							09 00	09 20									09 35		
West Croydon 4	a					09 12								09 31									09 42		
East Croydon	a												09 06												

Station		SE	SN	LO	SN	SE 1	LO	SN	SE	LO		SE	LO	SN	LO	SN	LO	SE	SN	LO		SN	LO	SN	SE
London Bridge 4 ⊖	d		09 03		09 06			09 11						09 22					09 33			09 36		09 41	
Dalston Junction Stn Ell	d			09 05			09 10			09 15			09 20		09 25		09 30			09 35			09 40		
Haggerston	d			09 06			09 11			09 16			09 21		09 26		09 31			09 36			09 41		
Hoxton	d			09 08			09 13			09 18			09 23		09 28		09 33			09 38			09 43		
Shoreditch High Street	d			09 11			09 16			09 21			09 26		09 31		09 36			09 41			09 46		
Whitechapel	d			09 13			09 18			09 23			09 28		09 33		09 38			09 43			09 48		
Shadwell	d			09 15			09 20			09 25			09 30		09 35		09 40			09 45			09 50		
Wapping	d			09 17			09 22			09 27			09 32		09 37		09 42			09 47			09 52		
Rotherhithe	d			09 19			09 24			09 29			09 34		09 39		09 44			09 49			09 54		
Canada Water	d			09 21			09 26			09 31			09 36		09 41		09 46			09 51			09 56		
Surrey Quays	d			09 22			09 27			09 32			09 37		09 42		09 47			09 52			09 57		
New Cross Ell	a			09 28									09 43							09 58					
New Cross Gate Station Ell	a						09 31			09 36					09 46		09 51						10 01		
	d						09 32			09 37					09 47		09 52						10 02		
New Cross Gate 4	d				09 12									09 28								09 41			
Brockley	d				09 14		09 34			09 39				09 30	09 49		09 54					09 44	10 04		
Honor Oak Park	d				09 17		09 37			09 42				09 33	09 52		09 57					09 47	10 07		
Forest Hill 4	d				09 20		09 40			09 45				09 36	09 55		10 00					09 49	10 10		
Sydenham	d				09 22		09 42			09 47				09 38	09 57		10 02					09 52	10 12		
Crystal Palace 4	d									09a52				09 43		09 30	10a07								
Gipsy Hill	d													09 46		09 32									
West Norwood 4	d													09 49		09 35									
Streatham Hill	d													09 52											
Balham 4 ⊖	d													09 56											
Wandsworth Common	d													09 58											
Clapham Junction 10	d													10 02											
South Bermondsey	d		09 07					09 15											09 37					09 45	
Peckham Rye 4	d	09 04				09 09			09 14			09 17				09 46		09 31							09 45
Queens Rd Peckham	d		09 09					09 18								09 49			09 39					09 48	
Denmark Hill 4	d	09 07				09 12		09 23	09 17			09 19						09 34						09 53	09 49
London Blackfriars 3 ⊖	a	09 18				09 26						09 30						09 46							
Clapham High Street ⊖	d							09 28																09 58	
Wandsworth Road	d							09 29																09 59	
Battersea Park 4	d							09 32						10 05										10 03	
London Victoria 15 ⊖	a							09 38	09 29					10 11										10 07	10 00
Penge West	d				09 25		09 45								10 00							09 54	10 15		
Anerley	d				09 27		09 47								10 02							09 56	10 17		
Norwood Junction 2	d				09 30		09 50								10 05							10 00	10 20		
West Croydon 4	a						10 01								10 12								10 31		
East Croydon	a				09 33																	10 03			

London Bridge to London Victoria - Croydon and East London Line

		LO	LO	SN	LO	SN		LO	SN	SE	LO	SN	LO	SN	SE	LO		LO	SN	LO	SN	LO	SN	SE	LO
London Bridge 4 ⊖	d			09 52					10 03			10 06		10 11					10 22				10 33		
Dalston Junction Stn Ell	d	09 45	09 50		09 55			10 00			10 05		10 10			10 15		10 20		10 25		10 30			10 35
Haggerston	d	09 46	09 51		09 56			10 01			10 06		10 11			10 16		10 21		10 26		10 31			10 36
Hoxton	d	09 48	09 53		09 58			10 03			10 08		10 13			10 18		10 23		10 28		10 33			10 38
Shoreditch High Street	d	09 51	09 56		10 01			10 06			10 11		10 16			10 21		10 26		10 31		10 36			10 41
Whitechapel	d	09 53	09 58		10 03			10 08			10 13		10 18			10 23		10 28		10 33		10 38			10 43
Shadwell	d	09 55	10 00		10 05			10 10			10 15		10 20			10 25		10 30		10 35		10 40			10 45
Wapping	d	09 57	10 02		10 07			10 12			10 17		10 22			10 27		10 32		10 37		10 42			10 47
Rotherhithe	d	09 59	10 04		10 09			10 14			10 19		10 24			10 29		10 34		10 39		10 44			10 49
Canada Water	d	10 01	10 06		10 11			10 16			10 21		10 26			10 31		10 36		10 41		10 46			10 51
Surrey Quays	d	10 02	10 07		10 12			10 17			10 22		10 27			10 32		10 37		10 42		10 47			10 52
New Cross Ell	a		10 13								10 28							10 43							10 58
New Cross Gate Station Ell	a	10 06			10 16			10 21					10 31			10 36				10 46		10 51			
	d	10 07			10 17			10 22					10 32			10 37				10 47		10 52			
New Cross Gate 4	d			09 57								10 11							10 27						
Brockley	d	10 09		10 00	10 19			10 24				10 14	10 34			10 39			10 30	10 49		10 54			
Honor Oak Park	d	10 12		10 03	10 22			10 27				10 17	10 37			10 42			10 33	10 52		10 57			
Forest Hill 4	d	10 15		10 05	10 25			10 30				10 19	10 40			10 45			10 35	10 55		11 00			
Sydenham	d	10 17		10 08	10 27			10 32				10 22	10 42			10 47			10 38	10 57		11 02			
Crystal Palace 4	d	10a22		10 13		10 00		10a37								10a52			10 43		10 30	11a07			
Gipsy Hill	d			10 15		10 02													10 45		10 32				
West Norwood 4	d			10 18		10 05													10 48		10 35				
Streatham Hill	d			10 22															10 52						
Balham 4 ⊖	d			10 25															10 55						
Wandsworth Common	d			10 27															10 57						
Clapham Junction 10	d			10 31															11 01						
South Bermondsey	d								10 07					10 15									10 37		
Peckham Rye 4	d					10 16				10 04					10 15						10 46			10 34	
Queens Rd Peckham	d					10 19			10 09					10 18							10 49		10 39		
Denmark Hill 4	d									10 07				10 23	10 19									10 37	
London Blackfriars 3 ⊖	a									10 18														10 48	
Clapham High Street ⊖	d													10 28											
Wandsworth Road	d													10 29											
Battersea Park 4	d			10 35										10 32					11 05						
London Victoria 15 ⊖	a			10 39										10 36	10 28				11 09						
Penge West	d				10 30							10 24	10 45							11 00					
Anerley	d				10 32							10 26	10 47							11 02					
Norwood Junction 2	d				10 35							10 30	10 50							11 05					
West Croydon 4	a				10 42								11 01							11 12					
East Croydon	a											10 33													

		SN		LO	SN	SE	LO	SE	LO	SN	LO	SN		LO	SN	LO	SN	LO	SN	SE	LO	SE		LO	SN
London Bridge 4 ⊖	d	10 36			10 41					10 52					11 03		11 06		11 11						11 22
Dalston Junction Stn Ell	d			10 40			10 45		10 50		10 55			11 00		11 05		11 10			11 15			11 20	
Haggerston	d			10 41			10 46		10 51		10 56			11 01		11 06		11 11			11 16			11 21	
Hoxton	d			10 43			10 48		10 53		10 58			11 03		11 08		11 13			11 18			11 23	
Shoreditch High Street	d			10 46			10 51		10 56		11 01			11 06		11 11		11 16			11 21			11 26	
Whitechapel	d			10 48			10 53		10 58		11 03			11 08		11 13		11 18			11 23			11 28	
Shadwell	d			10 50			10 55		11 00		11 05			11 10		11 15		11 20			11 25			11 30	
Wapping	d			10 52			10 57		11 02		11 07			11 12		11 17		11 22			11 27			11 32	
Rotherhithe	d			10 54			10 59		11 04		11 09			11 14		11 19		11 24			11 29			11 34	
Canada Water	d			10 56			11 01		11 06		11 11			11 16		11 21		11 26			11 31			11 36	
Surrey Quays	d			10 57			11 02		11 07		11 12			11 17		11 22		11 27			11 32			11 37	
New Cross Ell	a								11 13							11 28								11 43	
New Cross Gate Station Ell	a			11 01			11 06				11 16			11 21				11 31			11 36				
	d			11 02			11 07				11 17			11 22				11 32			11 37				
New Cross Gate 4	d	10 41								10 57							11 11								11 27
Brockley	d	10 44		11 04			11 09			11 00	11 19			11 24			11 14	11 34			11 39				11 30
Honor Oak Park	d	10 47		11 07			11 12			11 03	11 22			11 27			11 17	11 37			11 42				11 33
Forest Hill 4	d	10 49		11 10			11 15			11 05	11 25			11 30			11 19	11 40			11 45				11 35
Sydenham	d	10 52		11 12			11 17			11 08	11 27			11 32			11 22	11 42			11 47				11 38
Crystal Palace 4	d						11a22			11 13		11 00		11a37							11a52				11 43
Gipsy Hill	d									11 15		11 02													11 45
West Norwood 4	d									11 18		11 05													11 48
Streatham Hill	d									11 22															11 52
Balham 4 ⊖	d									11 25															11 55
Wandsworth Common	d									11 27															11 57
Clapham Junction 10	d									11 31															12 01
South Bermondsey	d				10 45										11 07				11 15						
Peckham Rye 4	d					10 45		10 50				11 16								11 15		11 20			
Queens Rd Peckham	d				10 48							11 19			11 09				11 18						
Denmark Hill 4	d				10 53	10 49		10 54											11 23	11 19		11 24			
London Blackfriars 3 ⊖	a							11 04														11 34			
Clapham High Street ⊖	d				10 58														11 28						
Wandsworth Road	d				10 59														11 29						
Battersea Park 4	d				11 02					11 35									11 32						12 05
London Victoria 15 ⊖	a				11 06	10 58				11 39									11 36	11 28					12 09
Penge West	d	10 54		11 15							11 30						11 24	11 45							
Anerley	d	10 56		11 17							11 32						11 26	11 47							
Norwood Junction 2	d	11 00		11 20							11 35						11 30	11 50							
West Croydon 4	a			11 31							11 42							12 01							
East Croydon	a	11 03															11 33								

Table 178 Mondays to Fridays

London Bridge to London Victoria - Croydon and East London Line

		LO	SN	LO	SN	LO	SN	LO		SN	SE	LO	SE	LO	SN	LO	SN	LO		SN	LO	SN	LO	SN	SE
London Bridge 4 ⊖	d				11 33		11 36			11 41					11 52					12 03		12 06		12 11	
Dalston Junction Stn Ell	d	11 25		11 30		11 35		11 40				11 45		11 50		11 55		12 00			12 05		12 10		
Haggerston	d	11 26		11 31		11 36		11 41				11 46		11 51		11 56		12 01			12 06		12 11		
Hoxton	d	11 28		11 33		11 38		11 43				11 48		11 53		11 58		12 03			12 08		12 13		
Shoreditch High Street	d	11 31		11 36		11 41		11 46				11 51		11 56		12 01		12 06			12 11		12 16		
Whitechapel	d	11 33		11 38		11 43		11 48				11 53		11 58		12 03		12 08			12 13		12 18		
Shadwell	d	11 35		11 40		11 45		11 50				11 55		12 00		12 05		12 10			12 15		12 20		
Wapping	d	11 37		11 42		11 47		11 52				11 57		12 02		12 07		12 12			12 17		12 22		
Rotherhithe	d	11 39		11 44		11 49		11 54				11 59		12 04		12 09		12 14			12 19		12 24		
Canada Water	d	11 41		11 46		11 51		11 56				12 01		12 06		12 11		12 16			12 21		12 26		
Surrey Quays	d	11 42		11 47		11 52		11 57				12 02		12 07		12 12		12 17			12 22		12 27		
New Cross Ell	a					11 58								12 13							12 28				
New Cross Gate Station Ell	a	11 46		11 51				12 01				12 06				12 16		12 21					12 31		
	d	11 47		11 52				12 02				12 07				12 17		12 22					12 32		
New Cross Gate 4	d						11 41								11 57							12 11			
Brockley	d	11 49		11 54			11 44	12 04				12 09			12 00	12 19		12 24				12 14	12 34		
Honor Oak Park	d	11 52		11 57			11 47	12 07				12 12			12 03	12 22		12 27				12 17	12 37		
Forest Hill 4	d	11 55		12 00			11 49	12 10				12 15			12 05	12 25		12 30				12 19	12 40		
Sydenham	d	11 57		12 02			11 52	12 12				12 17			12 08	12 27		12 32				12 22	12 42		
Crystal Palace 4	d		11 30	12a07								12a22			12 13		12 00	12a37							
Gipsy Hill	d		11 32												12 15		12 02								
West Norwood 4	d		11 35												12 18		12 05								
Streatham Hill	d														12 22										
Balham 4 ⊖	d														12 25										
Wandsworth Common	d														12 27										
Clapham Junction 10	d														12 31										
South Bermondsey	d				11 37					11 45										12 07				12 15	
Peckham Rye 4	d		11 46								11 45		11 50				12 16								12 15
Queens Rd Peckham	d		11 49		11 39					11 48							12 19			12 09				12 18	
Denmark Hill 4	d									11 54	11 49		11 54											12 23	12 19
London Blackfriars 3 ⊖	a												12 04												
Clapham High Street ⊖	d									11 58														12 28	
Wandsworth Road	d									12 00														12 29	
Battersea Park 4	d									12 02					12 35									12 32	
London Victoria 15 ⊖	a									12 07	11 58				12 39									12 36	12 28
Penge West	d	12 00					11 54	12 15								12 30						12 24	12 45		
Anerley	d	12 02					11 56	12 17								12 32						12 26	12 47		
Norwood Junction 2	d	12 05					12 00	12 20								12 35						12 30	12 50		
West Croydon 4	a	12 12						12 31								12 42							13 01		
East Croydon	a						12 03															12 33			

		LO	SE	LO		SN	LO	SN	LO	SN	LO	SN	LO	SN		SE	LO	SE	LO	SN	LO	SN	LO	SN	
London Bridge 4 ⊖	d					12 22				12 33		12 36		12 41						12 52				13 03	
Dalston Junction Stn Ell	d	12 15		12 20			12 25		12 30		12 35		12 40				12 45		12 50		12 55		13 00		
Haggerston	d	12 16		12 21			12 26		12 31		12 36		12 41				12 46		12 51		12 56		13 01		
Hoxton	d	12 18		12 23			12 28		12 33		12 38		12 43				12 48		12 53		12 58		13 03		
Shoreditch High Street	d	12 21		12 26			12 31		12 36		12 41		12 46				12 51		12 56		13 01		13 06		
Whitechapel	d	12 23		12 28			12 33		12 38		12 43		12 48				12 53		12 58		13 03		13 08		
Shadwell	d	12 25		12 30			12 35		12 40		12 45		12 50				12 55		13 00		13 05		13 10		
Wapping	d	12 27		12 32			12 37		12 42		12 47		12 52				12 57		13 02		13 07		13 12		
Rotherhithe	d	12 29		12 34			12 39		12 44		12 49		12 54				12 59		13 04		13 09		13 14		
Canada Water	d	12 31		12 36			12 41		12 46		12 51		12 56				13 01		13 06		13 11		13 16		
Surrey Quays	d	12 32		12 37			12 42		12 47		12 52		12 57				13 02		13 07		13 12		13 17		
New Cross Ell	a			12 43							12 58								13 13						
New Cross Gate Station Ell	a	12 36					12 46		12 51				13 01				13 06				13 16		13 21		
	d	12 37					12 47		12 52				13 02				13 07				13 17		13 22		
New Cross Gate 4	d					12 27						12 41								12 57					
Brockley	d	12 39				12 30	12 49		12 54			12 44	13 04				13 09			13 00	13 19		13 24		
Honor Oak Park	d	12 42				12 33	12 52		12 57			12 47	13 07				13 12			13 03	13 22		13 27		
Forest Hill 4	d	12 45				12 35	12 55		13 00			12 49	13 10				13 15			13 05	13 25		13 30		
Sydenham	d	12 47				12 38	12 57		13 02			12 52	13 12				13 17			13 08	13 27		13 32		
Crystal Palace 4	d	12a52				12 43		12 30	13a07								13a22			13 13		13 00	13a37		
Gipsy Hill	d					12 45		12 32												13 15		13 02			
West Norwood 4	d					12 48		12 35												13 18		13 05			
Streatham Hill	d					12 52														13 22					
Balham 4 ⊖	d					12 55														13 25					
Wandsworth Common	d					12 57														13 27					
Clapham Junction 10	d					13 01														13 31					
South Bermondsey	d									12 37				12 45										13 07	
Peckham Rye 4	d		12 20					12 46								12 45		12 50				13 16			
Queens Rd Peckham	d							12 49		12 39				12 48								13 19		13 09	
Denmark Hill 4	d		12 24											12 53		12 49		12 54							
London Blackfriars 3 ⊖	a		12 34															13 04							
Clapham High Street ⊖	d													12 58											
Wandsworth Road	d													12 59											
Battersea Park 4	d					13 05								13 02						13 35					
London Victoria 15 ⊖	a					13 09								13 06		12 58				13 39					
Penge West	d						13 00					12 54	13 15								13 30				
Anerley	d						13 02					12 56	13 17								13 32				
Norwood Junction 2	d						13 05					13 00	13 20								13 35				
West Croydon 4	a						13 12						13 31								13 42				
East Croydon	a											13 03													

London Bridge to London Victoria - Croydon and East London Line

		LO	SN	LO	SN	SE	LO	SE	LO	SN		LO	SN	LO	SN	LO	SN	LO	SN	SE		LO	SE	LO	SN
London Bridge 4 ⊖	d		13 06		13 11					13 22					13 33		13 36		13 41						13 52
Dalston Junction Stn Ell	d	13 05		13 10			13 15		13 20			13 25		13 30		13 35		13 40				13 45		13 50	
Haggerston	d	13 06		13 11			13 16		13 21			13 26		13 31		13 36		13 41				13 46		13 51	
Hoxton	d	13 08		13 13			13 18		13 23			13 28		13 33		13 38		13 43				13 48		13 53	
Shoreditch High Street	d	13 11		13 16			13 21		13 26			13 31		13 36		13 41		13 46				13 51		13 56	
Whitechapel	d	13 13		13 18			13 23		13 28			13 33		13 38		13 43		13 48				13 53		13 58	
Shadwell	d	13 15		13 20			13 25		13 30			13 35		13 40		13 45		13 50				13 55		14 00	
Wapping	d	13 17		13 22			13 27		13 32			13 37		13 42		13 47		13 52				13 57		14 02	
Rotherhithe	d	13 19		13 24			13 29		13 34			13 39		13 44		13 49		13 54				13 59		14 04	
Canada Water	d	13 21		13 26			13 31		13 36			13 41		13 46		13 51		13 56				14 01		14 06	
Surrey Quays	d	13 22		13 27			13 32		13 37			13 42		13 47		13 52		13 57				14 02		14 07	
New Cross Ell	a	13 28							13 43							13 58								14 13	
New Cross Gate Station Ell	a			13 31			13 36					13 46		13 51				14 01				14 06			
	d			13 32			13 37					13 47		13 52				14 02				14 07			
New Cross Gate 4	d		13 11							13 27							13 41								13 57
Brockley	d		13 14	13 34			13 39			13 30		13 49		13 54			13 44	14 04				14 09			14 00
Honor Oak Park	d		13 17	13 37			13 42			13 33		13 52		13 57			13 47	14 07				14 12			14 03
Forest Hill 4	d		13 19	13 40			13 45			13 35		13 55		14 00			13 49	14 10				14 15			14 05
Sydenham	d		13 22	13 42			13 47			13 38		13 57		14 02			13 52	14 12				14 17			14 08
Crystal Palace 4	d						13a52			13 43			13 30	14a07								14a22			14 13
Gipsy Hill	d									13 45			13 32												14 15
West Norwood 4	d									13 48			13 35												14 18
Streatham Hill	d									13 52															14 22
Balham 4 ⊖	d									13 55															14 25
Wandsworth Common	d									13 57															14 27
Clapham Junction 10	d									14 01															14 31
South Bermondsey	d				13 15										13 37				13 45						
Peckham Rye 4	d					13 15		13 20					13 46							13 45			13 50		
Queens Rd Peckham	d				13 18								13 49		13 39				13 48						
Denmark Hill 4	d				13 23	13 19		13 24											13 53	13 49			13 54		
London Blackfriars 3 ⊖	a							13 34															14 04		
Clapham High Street ⊖	d				13 28														13 58						
Wandsworth Road	d				13 29														13 59						
Battersea Park 4	d				13 32					14 05									14 02						14 35
London Victoria 15 ⊖	a				13 36	13 28				14 09									14 06	13 58					14 39
Penge West	d		13 24	13 45								14 00					13 54	14 15							
Anerley	d		13 26	13 47								14 02					13 56	14 17							
Norwood Junction 2	d		13 30	13 50								14 05					14 00	14 20							
West Croydon 4	a			14 01								14 12						14 31							
East Croydon	a		13 33														14 03								

		LO	SN	LO	SN	LO		SN	LO	SN	SE	LO	SE	LO	SN	LO		SN	LO	SN	LO	SN	LO	SN	SE
London Bridge 4 ⊖	d				14 03			14 06		14 11					14 22					14 33		14 36		14 41	
Dalston Junction Stn Ell	d	13 55		14 00		14 05			14 10			14 15		14 20		14 25			14 30		14 35		14 40		
Haggerston	d	13 56		14 01		14 06			14 11			14 16		14 21		14 26			14 31		14 36		14 41		
Hoxton	d	13 58		14 03		14 08			14 13			14 18		14 23		14 28			14 33		14 38		14 43		
Shoreditch High Street	d	14 01		14 06		14 11			14 16			14 21		14 26		14 31			14 36		14 41		14 46		
Whitechapel	d	14 03		14 08		14 13			14 18			14 23		14 28		14 33			14 38		14 43		14 48		
Shadwell	d	14 05		14 10		14 15			14 20			14 25		14 30		14 35			14 40		14 45		14 50		
Wapping	d	14 07		14 12		14 17			14 22			14 27		14 32		14 37			14 42		14 47		14 52		
Rotherhithe	d	14 09		14 14		14 19			14 24			14 29		14 34		14 39			14 44		14 49		14 54		
Canada Water	d	14 11		14 16		14 21			14 26			14 31		14 36		14 41			14 46		14 51		14 56		
Surrey Quays	d	14 12		14 17		14 22			14 27			14 32		14 37		14 42			14 47		14 52		14 57		
New Cross Ell	a					14 28								14 43							14 58				
New Cross Gate Station Ell	a	14 16		14 21					14 31			14 36				14 46			14 51				15 01		
	d	14 17		14 22					14 32			14 37				14 47			14 52				15 02		
New Cross Gate 4	d							14 11							14 27							14 41			
Brockley	d	14 19		14 24				14 14	14 34			14 39			14 30	14 49			14 54			14 44	15 04		
Honor Oak Park	d	14 22		14 27				14 17	14 37			14 42			14 33	14 52			14 57			14 47	15 07		
Forest Hill 4	d	14 25		14 30				14 19	14 40			14 45			14 35	14 55			15 00			14 49	15 10		
Sydenham	d	14 27		14 32				14 22	14 42			14 47			14 38	14 57			15 02			14 52	15 12		
Crystal Palace 4	d		14 00	14a37								14a52			14 43			14 30	15a07						
Gipsy Hill	d		14 02												14 45			14 32							
West Norwood 4	d		14 05												14 48			14 35							
Streatham Hill	d														14 52										
Balham 4 ⊖	d														14 55										
Wandsworth Common	d														14 57										
Clapham Junction 10	d														15 01										
South Bermondsey	d				14 07					14 15										14 37				14 45	
Peckham Rye 4	d		14 16								14 15		14 20					14 46							14 45
Queens Rd Peckham	d		14 19		14 09					14 18								14 49		14 39				14 48	
Denmark Hill 4	d									14 23	14 19		14 24											14 53	14 49
London Blackfriars 3 ⊖	a												14 34												
Clapham High Street ⊖	d									14 28														14 58	
Wandsworth Road	d									14 29														14 59	
Battersea Park 4	d									14 32					15 05									15 02	
London Victoria 15 ⊖	a									14 36	14 28				15 09									15 06	14 58.
Penge West	d	14 30						14 24	14 45							15 00						14 54	15 15		
Anerley	d	14 32						14 26	14 47							15 02						14 56	15 17		
Norwood Junction 2	d	14 35						14 30	14 50							15 05						15 00	15 20		
West Croydon 4	a	14 42							15 01							15 12							15 31		
East Croydon	a							14 33														15 03			

London Bridge to London Victoria - Croydon and East London Line

		LO		SE	LO	SN	LO	SN	LO	SN	LO	SN		LO	SN	SE	LO	SE	LO	SN	LO	SN		LO	SN
London Bridge 4 ⊖	d					14 52				15 03		15 06			15 11					15 22					15 33
Dalston Junction Stn Ell	d	14 45			14 50		14 55		15 00		15 05			15 10			15 15		15 20		15 25			15 30	
Haggerston	d	14 46			14 51		14 56		15 01		15 06			15 11			15 16		15 21		15 26			15 31	
Hoxton	d	14 48			14 53		14 58		15 03		15 08			15 13			15 18		15 23		15 28			15 33	
Shoreditch High Street	d	14 51			14 56		15 01		15 06		15 11			15 16			15 21		15 26		15 31			15 36	
Whitechapel	d	14 53			14 58		15 03		15 08		15 13			15 18			15 23		15 28		15 33			15 38	
Shadwell	d	14 55			15 00		15 05		15 10		15 15			15 20			15 25		15 30		15 35			15 40	
Wapping	d	14 57			15 02		15 07		15 12		15 17			15 22			15 27		15 32		15 37			15 42	
Rotherhithe	d	14 59			15 04		15 09		15 14		15 19			15 24			15 29		15 34		15 39			15 44	
Canada Water	d	15 01			15 06		15 11		15 16		15 21			15 26			15 31		15 36		15 41			15 46	
Surrey Quays	d	15 02			15 07		15 12		15 17		15 22			15 27			15 32		15 37		15 42			15 47	
New Cross Ell	a				15 13						15 28								15 43						
New Cross Gate Station Ell	a	15 06					15 16		15 21					15 31			15 36				15 46			15 51	
	d	15 07					15 17		15 22					15 32			15 37				15 47			15 52	
New Cross Gate 4	d					14 57						15 11								15 27					
Brockley	d	15 09				15 00	15 19		15 24			15 14		15 34			15 39			15 30	15 49			15 54	
Honor Oak Park	d	15 12				15 03	15 22		15 27			15 17		15 37			15 42			15 33	15 52			15 57	
Forest Hill 4	d	15 15				15 05	15 25		15 30			15 19		15 40			15 45			15 35	15 55			16 00	
Sydenham	d	15 17				15 08	15 27		15 32			15 22		15 42			15 47			15 38	15 57			16 02	
Crystal Palace 4	d	15a22				15 13		15 00	15a37								15a52			15 43		15 30		16a07	
Gipsy Hill	d					15 15		15 02												15 45		15 32			
West Norwood 4	d					15 18		15 05												15 48		15 35			
Streatham Hill	d					15 22														15 52					
Balham 4 ⊖	d					15 25														15 55					
Wandsworth Common	d					15 27														15 57					
Clapham Junction 10	d					15 31														16 01					
South Bermondsey	d									15 07					15 15										15 37
Peckham Rye 4	d			14 50				15 16								15 15		15 20				15 46			
Queens Rd Peckham	d							15 19		15 09					15 18							15 49			15 39
Denmark Hill 4	d			14 54											15 23	15 19		15 24							
London Blackfriars 3 ⊖	a			15 04														15 34							
Clapham High Street ⊖	d														15 28										
Wandsworth Road	d														15 29										
Battersea Park 4	d					15 35									15 32					16 05					
London Victoria 15 ⊖	a					15 39									15 36	15 28.				16 10					
Penge West	d						15 30					15 24		15 45							16 00				
Anerley	d						15 32					15 26		15 47							16 02				
Norwood Junction 2	d						15 35					15 30		15 50							16 05				
West Croydon 4	a						15 42							16 01							16 12				
East Croydon	a											15 33													

		LO	SN	LO	SN	SE	LO	SE		LO	SN	LO	SN	SN	LO	SN	LO	SN		LO	SN	SE	LO	SE 1	LO
London Bridge 4 ⊖	d		15 36		15 41						15 52					16 03		16 06			16 11				
Dalston Junction Stn Ell	d	15 35		15 40			15 45			15 50		15 55			16 00		16 05			16 10			16 15		16 20
Haggerston	d	15 36		15 41			15 46			15 51		15 56			16 01		16 06			16 11			16 16		16 21
Hoxton	d	15 38		15 43			15 48			15 53		15 58			16 03		16 08			16 13			16 18		16 23
Shoreditch High Street	d	15 41		15 46			15 51			15 56		16 01			16 06		16 11			16 16			16 21		16 26
Whitechapel	d	15 43		15 48			15 53			15 58		16 03			16 08		16 13			16 18			16 23		16 28
Shadwell	d	15 45		15 50			15 55			16 00		16 05			16 10		16 15			16 20			16 25		16 30
Wapping	d	15 47		15 52			15 57			16 02		16 07			16 12		16 17			16 22			16 27		16 32
Rotherhithe	d	15 49		15 54			15 59			16 04		16 09			16 14		16 19			16 24			16 29		16 34
Canada Water	d	15 51		15 56			16 01			16 06		16 11			16 16		16 21			16 26			16 31		16 36
Surrey Quays	d	15 52		15 57			16 02			16 07		16 12			16 17		16 22			16 27			16 32		16 37
New Cross Ell	a	15 58								16 13							16 28								16 43
New Cross Gate Station Ell	a			16 01			16 06					16 16			16 21					16 31			16 36		
	d			16 02			16 07					16 17			16 22					16 32			16 37		
New Cross Gate 4	d		15 41								15 57							16 11							
Brockley	d		15 44	16 04			16 09				16 00	16 19			16 24			16 14		16 34			16 39		
Honor Oak Park	d		15 47	16 07			16 12				16 03	16 22			16 27			16 17		16 37			16 42		
Forest Hill 4	d		15 49	16 10			16 15				16 05	16 25			16 30			16 19		16 40			16 45		
Sydenham	d		15 52	16 12			16 17				16 08	16 27			16 32			16 22		16 42			16 47		
Crystal Palace 4	d						16a22				16 13			16 00	16a37								16a52		
Gipsy Hill	d										16 15			16 02											
West Norwood 4	d										16 18			16 05											
Streatham Hill	d										16 22		15 56												
Balham 4 ⊖	d										16 25														
Wandsworth Common	d										16 27														
Clapham Junction 10	d										16 31														
South Bermondsey	d				15 45											16 07					16 15				
Peckham Rye 4	d					15 45		15 50					16 07	16 16								16 15		16 20	
Queens Rd Peckham	d				15 48								16 10	16 19		16 09					16 18				
Denmark Hill 4	d				15 53	15 49		15 54													16 23	16 19		16 24	
London Blackfriars 3 ⊖	a							16 04																16 34	
Clapham High Street ⊖	d				15 58																16 28				
Wandsworth Road	d				15 59																16 29				
Battersea Park 4	d				16 02						16 35										16 32				
London Victoria 15 ⊖	a				16 06	15 58					16 40										16 38	16 28			
Penge West	d		15 54	16 15								16 30						16 24		16 45					
Anerley	d		15 56	16 17								16 32						16 26		16 47					
Norwood Junction 2	d		16 00	16 20								16 35						16 30		16 50					
West Croydon 4	a			16 31								16 42								17 01					
East Croydon	a		16 03															16 33							

London Bridge to London Victoria - Croydon and East London Line

		SN	LO	SN		LO	SN	LO	SN	LO	SN	SE	LO	SE [1]		LO	SN	LO	SN	SN	LO	SE	LO	SN
London Bridge	d	16 22					16 33		16 36		16 41						16 52		16 58					17 05
Dalston Junction Stn Ell	d		16 25			16 30		16 35		16 40			16 45			16 50		16 55			17 00		17 05	
Haggerston	d		16 26			16 31		16 36		16 41			16 46			16 51		16 56			17 01		17 06	
Hoxton	d		16 28			16 33		16 38		16 43			16 48			16 53		16 58			17 03		17 08	
Shoreditch High Street	d		16 31			16 36		16 41		16 46			16 51			16 56		17 01			17 06		17 11	
Whitechapel	d		16 33			16 38		16 43		16 48			16 53			16 58		17 03			17 08		17 13	
Shadwell	d		16 35			16 40		16 45		16 50			16 55			17 00		17 05			17 10		17 15	
Wapping	d		16 37			16 42		16 47		16 52			16 57			17 02		17 07			17 12		17 17	
Rotherhithe	d		16 39			16 44		16 49		16 54			16 59			17 04		17 09			17 14		17 19	
Canada Water	d		16 41			16 46		16 51		16 56			17 01			17 06		17 11			17 16		17 21	
Surrey Quays	d		16 42			16 47		16 52		16 57			17 02			17 07		17 12			17 17		17 22	
New Cross Ell	a							16 58								17 13							17 28	
New Cross Gate Station Ell	a		16 46			16 51				17 01			17 06					17 16			17 21			
	d		16 47			16 52				17 02			17 07					17 17			17 22			
New Cross Gate	d	16 27							16 41								16 57							17 11
Brockley	d	16 30	16 49			16 54			16 44	17 04			17 09				17 00	17 19			17 24			17 14
Honor Oak Park	d	16 33	16 52			16 57			16 47	17 07			17 12				17 03	17 22			17 27			17 17
Forest Hill	d	16 35	16 55			17 00			16 49	17 10			17 15				17 05	17 25			17 30			17 19
Sydenham	d	16 38	16 57			17 02			16 52	17 12			17 17				17 08	17 27			17 32			17 22
Crystal Palace	d	16 43		16 30		17a07							17a22				17 13			17 00	17a37			
Gipsy Hill	d	16 45		16 32													17 15			17 02				
West Norwood	d	16 48		16 35													17 18			17 05				
Streatham Hill	d	16 52															17 22							
Balham	d	16 55															17 25							
Wandsworth Common	d	16 57															17 27							
Clapham Junction	d	17 01															17 31							
South Bermondsey	d						16 37				16 45								17 02					
Peckham Rye	d			16 46								16 45		16 50						17 16		17 02		
Queens Rd Peckham	d			16 49			16 39				16 48								17 04	17 19				
Denmark Hill	d										16 53	16 49		16 54								17 05		
London Blackfriars	a													17 08								17 16		
Clapham High Street	d										16 58													
Wandsworth Road	d										16 59													
Battersea Park	d	17 05									17 02						17 35							
London Victoria	a	17 10									17 08	16 58					17 42							
Penge West	d		17 00						16 54	17 15								17 30						17 24
Anerley	d		17 02						16 56	17 17								17 32						17 26
Norwood Junction	d		17 05						17 00	17 20								17 35						17 30
West Croydon	a		17 12						17 07	17 31								17 42						17 37
East Croydon	a																							

		LO	SN	SE	LO	SN	SE	LO	SN	LO		SN	LO	SN	LO	SN	LO	SN	SE	LO		SE [1]	LO	SN	SN
London Bridge	d		17 11						17 21			17 28				17 36		17 41						17 53	
Dalston Junction Stn Ell	d	17 10			17 15			17 20		17 25			17 30		17 35		17 40			17 45			17 50		
Haggerston	d	17 11			17 16			17 21		17 26			17 31		17 36		17 41			17 46			17 51		
Hoxton	d	17 13			17 18			17 23		17 28			17 33		17 38		17 43			17 48			17 53		
Shoreditch High Street	d	17 16			17 21			17 26		17 31			17 36		17 41		17 46			17 51			17 56		
Whitechapel	d	17 18			17 23			17 28		17 33			17 38		17 43		17 48			17 53			17 58		
Shadwell	d	17 20			17 25			17 30		17 35			17 40		17 45		17 50			17 55			18 00		
Wapping	d	17 22			17 27			17 32		17 37			17 42		17 47		17 52			17 57			18 02		
Rotherhithe	d	17 24			17 29			17 34		17 39			17 44		17 49		17 54			17 59			18 04		
Canada Water	d	17 26			17 31			17 36		17 41			17 46		17 51		17 56			18 01			18 06		
Surrey Quays	d	17 27			17 32			17 37		17 42			17 47		17 52		17 57			18 02			18 07		
New Cross Ell	a							17 43							17 58								18 13		
New Cross Gate Station Ell	a	17 31			17 36					17 46			17 51				18 01			18 06					
	d	17 32			17 37					17 47			17 52				18 02			18 07					
New Cross Gate	d								17 26							17 41								17 58	
Brockley	d	17 34			17 39				17 29	17 49			17 54			17 44	18 04			18 09				18 01	
Honor Oak Park	d	17 37			17 42				17 32	17 52			17 57			17 47	18 07			18 12				18 04	
Forest Hill	d	17 40			17 45				17 34	17 55			18 00			17 49	18 10			18 15				18 06	
Sydenham	d	17 42			17 47				17 37	17 57			18 02			17 52	18 12			18 17				18 09	
Crystal Palace	d				17a52	17 18			17 44				18a07	17 36						18a22				18 13	17 55
Gipsy Hill	d					17 20			17 46					17 38										18 16	17 57
West Norwood	d					17 23			17 49					17 42										18 19	18 00
Streatham Hill	d								17 53															18 22	
Balham	d								17 56															18 29	
Wandsworth Common	d								17 58															18 31	
Clapham Junction	d								18 02															18 36	
South Bermondsey	d		17 15									17 32						17 45							
Peckham Rye	d			17 15		17 34	17 20							17 53					17 45			17 50			18 12
Queens Rd Peckham	d		17 18			17 37						17 35		17 55				17 47							18 15
Denmark Hill	d		17 23	17 19			17 24											17 53	17 49			17 54			
London Blackfriars	a						17 40															18 05			
Clapham High Street	d		17 28															17 58							
Wandsworth Road	d		17 29															17 59							
Battersea Park	d		17 32						18 06									18 02						18 40	
London Victoria	a		17 38	17 28					18 12									18 08	17 59					18 46	
Penge West	d	17 45								18 00						17 54	18 15								
Anerley	d	17 47								18 02						17 56	18 17								
Norwood Junction	d	17 50								18 06						18 00	18 20								
West Croydon	a	18 01								18 12						18 08	18 31								
East Croydon	a																								

Table 178 — Mondays to Fridays

London Bridge to London Victoria - Croydon and East London Line

		LO	SN	LO	LO	SN		LO	SN	SE	LO	SN	SE [1]	LO	SN	LO		SN	LO	LO	SN	LO	SN	SE	LO
London Bridge	d		17 58			18 06			18 11						18 21			18 28			18 36		18 41		
Dalston Junction Stn Ell	d	17 55		18 00	18 05			18 10			18 15			18 20		18 25			18 30	18 35		18 40			18 45
Haggerston	d	17 56		18 01	18 06			18 11			18 16			18 21		18 26			18 31	18 36		18 41			18 46
Hoxton	d	17 58		18 03	18 08			18 13			18 18			18 23		18 28			18 33	18 38		18 43			18 48
Shoreditch High Street	d	18 01		18 06	18 11			18 16			18 21			18 26		18 31			18 36	18 41		18 46			18 51
Whitechapel	d	18 03		18 08	18 13			18 18			18 23			18 28		18 33			18 38	18 43		18 48			18 53
Shadwell	d	18 05		18 10	18 15			18 20			18 25			18 30		18 35			18 40	18 45		18 50			18 55
Wapping	d	18 07		18 12	18 17			18 22			18 27			18 32		18 37			18 42	18 47		18 52			18 57
Rotherhithe	d	18 09		18 14	18 19			18 24			18 29			18 34		18 39			18 44	18 49		18 54			18 59
Canada Water	d	18 11		18 16	18 21			18 26			18 31			18 36		18 41			18 46	18 51		18 56			19 01
Surrey Quays	d	18 12		18 17	18 22			18 27			18 32			18 37		18 42			18 47	18 52		18 57			19 02
New Cross Ell	a				18 28									18 43						18 58					
New Cross Gate Station Ell	a	18 16		18 21				18 31			18 36					18 46			18 51			19 01			19 06
	d	18 17		18 22				18 32			18 37					18 47			18 52			19 02			19 07
New Cross Gate	d					18 11									18 26						18 41				
Brockley	d	18 19		18 24		18 14		18 34			18 39				18 29	18 49			18 54		18 44	19 04			19 09
Honor Oak Park	d	18 22		18 27		18 17		18 37			18 42				18 32	18 52			18 57		18 47	19 07			19 12
Forest Hill	d	18 25		18 30		18 19		18 40			18 45				18 34	18 55			19 00		18 49	19 10			19 15
Sydenham	d	18 27		18 32		18 22		18 42			18 47				18 37	18 57			19 02		18 52	19 12			19 17
Crystal Palace	d			18a37							18a52	18 18			18 43				19a07						19a22
Gipsy Hill	d											18 20			18 45										
West Norwood	d											18 23			18 48										
Streatham Hill	d														18 52										
Balham	d														18 55										
Wandsworth Common	d														18 57										
Clapham Junction	d														19 01										
South Bermondsey	d		18 02						18 15									18 32					18 45		
Peckham Rye	d									18 15		18 36	18 20											18 45	
Queens Rd Peckham	d		18 04						18 18			18 38						18 34					18 48		
Denmark Hill	d								18 23	18 19			18 23										18 53	18 49	
London Blackfriars	a												18 36												
Clapham High Street	d								18 28														18 58		
Wandsworth Road	d								18 29														18 59		
Battersea Park	d								18 32						19 05								19 02		
London Victoria	a								18 39	18 29.					19 12								19 08	18 58	
Penge West	d	18 30				18 24		18 45								19 00					18 54	19 15			
Anerley	d	18 32				18 26		18 47								19 02					18 56	19 17			
Norwood Junction	d	18 35				18 32		18 50								19 05					19 02	19 20			
West Croydon	a	18 42				18 39		19 01								19 12					19 09	19 31			
East Croydon	a																								

		SE		SN	LO	SN	LO	SE	SN	LO	LO	SN		SN	LO	SN	SE	LO	SE	LO	SN	LO		SE	SN
London Bridge	d					18 51			18 58			19 06		19 08		19 11					19 22				19 28
Dalston Junction Stn Ell	d				18 50		18 55			19 00	19 05				19 10			19 15		19 20		19 25			
Haggerston	d				18 51		18 56			19 01	19 06				19 11			19 16		19 21		19 26			
Hoxton	d				18 53		18 58			19 03	19 08				19 13			19 18		19 23		19 28			
Shoreditch High Street	d				18 56		19 01			19 06	19 11				19 16			19 21		19 26		19 31			
Whitechapel	d				18 58		19 03			19 08	19 13				19 18			19 23		19 28		19 33			
Shadwell	d				19 00		19 05			19 10	19 15				19 20			19 25		19 30		19 35			
Wapping	d				19 02		19 07			19 12	19 17				19 22			19 27		19 32		19 37			
Rotherhithe	d				19 04		19 09			19 14	19 19				19 24			19 29		19 34		19 39			
Canada Water	d				19 06		19 11			19 16	19 21				19 26			19 31		19 36		19 41			
Surrey Quays	d				19 07		19 12			19 17	19 22				19 27			19 32		19 37		19 42			
New Cross Ell	a				19 13						19 28									19 43					
New Cross Gate Station Ell	a						19 16			19 21					19 31			19 36				19 46			
	d						19 17			19 22					19 32			19 37				19 47			
New Cross Gate	d					18 56						19 11									19 27				
Brockley	d					18 59	19 19			19 24		19 14			19 34			19 39			19 30	19 49			
Honor Oak Park	d					19 02	19 22			19 27		19 17			19 37			19 42			19 33	19 52			
Forest Hill	d					19 04	19 25			19 30		19 19			19 40			19 45			19 35	19 55			
Sydenham	d					19 07	19 27			19 32		19 22			19 42			19 47			19 38	19 57			
Crystal Palace	d			18 51		19 13				19a37								19a52			19 43				
Gipsy Hill	d			18 53		19 15															19 45				
West Norwood	d			18 56		19 18															19 48				
Streatham Hill	d					19 22															19 52				
Balham	d					19 25															19 55				
Wandsworth Common	d					19 27															19 57				
Clapham Junction	d					19 31															20 01				
South Bermondsey	d								19 02					19 12		19 15									19 32
Peckham Rye	d	18 50		19 17													19 15		19 20						
Queens Rd Peckham	d			19 20					19 04					19 14		19 18									19 34
Denmark Hill	d	18 54						18 59								19 23	19 19		19 24					19 28	
London Blackfriars	a	19 04																	19 34						
Clapham High Street	d															19 28									
Wandsworth Road	d															19 29									
Battersea Park	d					19 35										19 32					20 05				
London Victoria	a					19 41		19 13								19 36	19 28				20 09			19 42	
Penge West	d						19 30					19 24			19 45							20 00			
Anerley	d						19 32					19 26			19 47							20 02			
Norwood Junction	d						19 35		19 33			19 30			19 50							20 05			20 02
West Croydon	a						19 42		19 40						20 01							20 12			20 06
East Croydon	a											19 33													

London Bridge to London Victoria - Croydon and East London Line

		LO	SN	LO	SN	SN	LO	SN	LO	SE	LO	SN	LO	SN	LO	LO	SN	LO	SN	LO	SE	LO	SN
London Bridge 4 ⊖	d				19 36	19 38		19 41				19 54					20 06		20 11				20 22
Dalston Junction Stn Ell	d	19 30		19 35			19 40		19 45		19 50		19 55		20 00	20 05		20 10		20 15		20 20	
Haggerston	d	19 31		19 36			19 41		19 46		19 51		19 56		20 01	20 06		20 11		20 16		20 21	
Hoxton	d	19 33		19 38			19 43		19 48		19 53		19 58		20 03	20 08		20 13		20 18		20 23	
Shoreditch High Street	d	19 36		19 41			19 46		19 51		19 56		20 01		20 06	20 11		20 16		20 21		20 26	
Whitechapel	d	19 38		19 43			19 48		19 53		19 58		20 03		20 08	20 13		20 18		20 23		20 28	
Shadwell	d	19 40		19 45			19 50		19 55		20 00		20 05		20 10	20 15		20 20		20 25		20 30	
Wapping	d	19 42		19 47			19 52		19 57		20 02		20 07		20 12	20 17		20 22		20 27		20 32	
Rotherhithe	d	19 44		19 49			19 54		19 59		20 04		20 09		20 14	20 19		20 24		20 29		20 34	
Canada Water	d	19 46		19 51			19 56		20 01		20 06		20 11		20 16	20 21		20 26		20 31		20 36	
Surrey Quays	d	19 47		19 52			19 57		20 02		20 07		20 12		20 17	20 22		20 27		20 32		20 37	
New Cross Ell	a			19 58							20 13					20 28						20 43	
New Cross Gate Station Ell	a	19 51					20 01		20 06				20 16		20 21			20 31		20 36			
	d	19 52					20 02		20 07				20 17		20 22			20 32		20 37			
New Cross Gate 4	d				19 41							19 59					20 11						20 27
Brockley	d	19 54			19 44		20 05		20 09			20 02	20 19		20 24		20 14	20 34		20 39			20 30
Honor Oak Park	d	19 57			19 47		20 08		20 12			20 05	20 22		20 27		20 17	20 37		20 42			20 33
Forest Hill 4	d	20 00			19 49		20 11		20 15			20 07	20 25		20 30		20 19	20 40		20 45			20 35
Sydenham	d	20 02			19 52		20 13		20 17			20 10	20 27		20 32		20 22	20 42		20 47			20 38
Crystal Palace 4	d	20a07	19 32						20a22			20 13		20 01	20a37					20a52			20 43
Gipsy Hill	d		19 34									20 16		20 03									20 45
West Norwood 4	d		19 37									20 19		20 06									20 48
Streatham Hill	d											20 22											20 52
Balham 4 ⊖	d											20 25											20 55
Wandsworth Common	d											20 27											20 57
Clapham Junction 10	d											20 31											21 01
South Bermondsey	d					19 42		19 45											20 15				
Peckham Rye 4	d		19 48							19 50				20 18							20 20		
Queens Rd Peckham	d		19 51			19 44		19 48						20 21					20 18				
Denmark Hill 4	d							19 53		19 54									20 23		20 24		
London Blackfriars 3 ⊖	a									20 04											20 34		
Clapham High Street ⊖	d							19 58											20 28				
Wandsworth Road	d							19 59											20 29				
Battersea Park 4	d							20 02				20 35							20 32				21 05
London Victoria 15 ⊖	a							20 06				20 39							20 36				21 09
Penge West	d				19 54		20 16						20 30				20 24	20 45					
Anerley	d				19 56		20 18						20 32				20 26	20 47					
Norwood Junction 2	d				20 00		20 21						20 35				20 30	20 50					
West Croydon 4	a						20 30						20 42					21 01					
East Croydon	a				20 03												20 33						

		LO	SN	LO	LO	SN	LO	SN	LO	SE	LO	SN	LO	LO	LO	SN	LO	SN	LO	SE	LO	SN
London Bridge 4 ⊖	d					20 36		20 41				20 52				21 06		21 11				21 22
Dalston Junction Stn Ell	d	20 25		20 30	20 35		20 40		20 45		20 50		20 55	21 00	21 05		21 10		21 15		21 20	
Haggerston	d	20 26		20 31	20 36		20 41		20 46		20 51		20 56	21 01	21 06		21 11		21 16		21 21	
Hoxton	d	20 28		20 33	20 38		20 43		20 48		20 53		20 58	21 03	21 08		21 13		21 18		21 23	
Shoreditch High Street	d	20 31		20 36	20 41		20 46		20 51		20 56		21 01	21 06	21 11		21 16		21 21		21 26	
Whitechapel	d	20 33		20 38	20 43		20 48		20 53		20 58		21 03	21 08	21 13		21 18		21 23		21 28	
Shadwell	d	20 35		20 40	20 45		20 50		20 55		21 00		21 05	21 10	21 15		21 20		21 25		21 30	
Wapping	d	20 37		20 42	20 47		20 52		20 57		21 02		21 07	21 12	21 17		21 22		21 27		21 32	
Rotherhithe	d	20 39		20 44	20 49		20 54		20 59		21 04		21 09	21 14	21 19		21 24		21 29		21 34	
Canada Water	d	20 41		20 46	20 51		20 56		21 01		21 06		21 11	21 16	21 21		21 26		21 31		21 36	
Surrey Quays	d	20 42		20 47	20 52		20 57		21 02		21 07		21 12	21 17	21 22		21 27		21 32		21 37	
New Cross Ell	a				20 58						21 13				21 28						21 43	
New Cross Gate Station Ell	a	20 46		20 51			21 01		21 06				21 16	21 21			21 31		21 36			
	d	20 47		20 52			21 02		21 07				21 17	21 22			21 32		21 37			
New Cross Gate 4	d					20 41						20 57				21 11						21 27
Brockley	d	20 49		20 54		20 44	21 04		21 09			21 00	21 19	21 24		21 14	21 34		21 39			21 30
Honor Oak Park	d	20 52		20 57		20 47	21 07		21 12			21 03	21 22	21 27		21 17	21 37		21 42			21 33
Forest Hill 4	d	20 55		21 00		20 49	21 10		21 15			21 05	21 25	21 30		21 19	21 40		21 45			21 35
Sydenham	d	20 57		21 02		20 52	21 12		21 17			21 08	21 27	21 32		21 22	21 42		21 47			21 38
Crystal Palace 4	d		20 31	21a07					21a22			21 13		21a37					21a52			21 43
Gipsy Hill	d		20 33									21 15										21 45
West Norwood 4	d		20 36									21 18										21 48
Streatham Hill	d											21 22										21 52
Balham 4 ⊖	d											21 25										21 55
Wandsworth Common	d											21 27										21 57
Clapham Junction 10	d											21 31										22 01
South Bermondsey	d							20 45										21 15				
Peckham Rye 4	d		20 47							20 50										21 20		
Queens Rd Peckham	d		20 50					20 48										21 18				
Denmark Hill 4	d							20 53		20 54								21 23		21 23		
London Blackfriars 3 ⊖	a									21 04												
Clapham High Street ⊖	d							20 58										21 28				
Wandsworth Road	d							20 59										21 29				
Battersea Park 4	d							21 02				21 35						21 32				22 05
London Victoria 15 ⊖	a							21 06				21 39						21 36		21 33		22 09
Penge West	d	21 00				20 54	21 15						21 30			21 24	21 45					
Anerley	d	21 02				20 56	21 17						21 32			21 26	21 47					
Norwood Junction 2	d	21 05				21 00	21 20						21 35			21 30	21 50					
West Croydon 4	a	21 12					21 31						21 42				22 01					
East Croydon	a					21 03										21 33						

Table 178

Mondays to Fridays

London Bridge to London Victoria - Croydon and East London Line

		LO	LO	LO	SN	LO	SN	LO	SE	LO	SN	LO	LO	SN	LO	SN	SE	LO	SN	FC	LO	SN	FC
London Bridge 4 ⊖	d				21 36		21 41				21 52			22 08		22 11			22 22	22 25		22 38	22 40
Dalston Junction Stn Ell	d	21 25	21 30	21 35		21 40		21 45		21 50		21 55	22 00		22 10			22 20			22 30		
Haggerston	d	21 26	21 31	21 36		21 41		21 46		21 51		21 56	22 01		22 11			22 21			22 31		
Hoxton	d	21 28	21 33	21 38		21 43		21 48		21 53		21 58	22 03		22 13			22 23			22 33		
Shoreditch High Street	d	21 31	21 36	21 41		21 46		21 51		21 56		22 01	22 06		22 16			22 26			22 36		
Whitechapel	d	21 33	21 38	21 43		21 48		21 53		21 58		22 03	22 08		22 18			22 28			22 38		
Shadwell	d	21 35	21 40	21 45		21 50		21 55		22 00		22 05	22 10		22 20			22 30			22 40		
Wapping	d	21 37	21 42	21 47		21 52		21 57		22 02		22 07	22 12		22 22			22 32			22 42		
Rotherhithe	d	21 39	21 44	21 49		21 54		21 59		22 04		22 09	22 14		22 24			22 34			22 44		
Canada Water	d	21 41	21 46	21 51		21 56		22 01		22 06		22 11	22 16		22 26			22 36			22 46		
Surrey Quays	d	21 42	21 47	21 52		21 57		22 02		22 07		22 12	22 17		22 27			22 37			22 47		
New Cross Ell	a			21 58						22 13								22 43					
New Cross Gate Station Ell	a	21 46	21 51			22 01		22 06				22 16	22 21		22 31						22 51		
	d	21 47	21 52			22 02		22 07				22 17	22 22		22 32						22 52		
New Cross Gate 4	d				21 41						21 57			22 13					22 27			22 43	
Brockley	d	21 49	21 54		21 44	22 04		22 09			22 00	22 19	22 24	22 16	22 34				22 30		22 54	22 46	
Honor Oak Park	d	21 52	21 57		21 47	22 07		22 12			22 03	22 22	22 27	22 19	22 37				22 33		22 57	22 49	
Forest Hill 4	d	21 55	22 00		21 49	22 10		22 15			22 05	22 25	22 30	22 21	22 40				22 35		23 00	22 51	
Sydenham	d	21 57	22 02		21 52	22 12		22 17			22 08	22 27	22 32	22 24	22 42				22 38		23 02	22 54	
Crystal Palace 4	d		22a07					22a22			22 13		22a37						22 43		23a07		
Gipsy Hill	d										22 15								22 45				
West Norwood 4	d										22 18								22 48				
Streatham Hill	d										22 22								22 52				
Balham 4 ⊖	d										22 25								22 55				
Wandsworth Common	d										22 27								22 57				
Clapham Junction 10	d										22 31								23 01				
South Bermondsey	d						21 45									22 15							
Peckham Rye 4	d								21 50								22 20						
Queens Rd Peckham	d						21 48									22 18							
Denmark Hill 4	d						21 53		21 53							22 23	22 23						
London Blackfriars 3 ⊖	a																			22 40			22 55
Clapham High Street ⊖	d						21 58									22 28							
Wandsworth Road	d						21 59									22 29							
Battersea Park 4	d						22 02				22 35					22 32			23 05				
London Victoria 15 ⊖	a						22 06		22 03		22 39					22 36	22 33		23 10				
Penge West	d	22 00			21 54	22 15						22 30		22 26	22 45							22 56	
Anerley	d	22 02			21 56	22 17						22 32		22 28	22 47							22 58	
Norwood Junction 2	d	22 05			22 00	22 20						22 35		22 32	22 50							23 02	
West Croydon 4	a	22 12				22 31						22 42			23 01								
East Croydon	a				22 03									22 35								23 05	

		LO	SN	SE	LO	SN	FC	LO	FC	SN	LO	SN	SE	LO	SN	FC	LO	SN	LO	SN	FC
London Bridge 4 ⊖	d		22 41			22 52	22 55		23 05	23 06		23 11			23 22	23 25		23 36		23 48	23 55
Dalston Junction Stn Ell	d	22 40			22 50			23 00			23 10			23 20			23 30		23 40		
Haggerston	d	22 41			22 51			23 01			23 11			23 21			23 31		23 41		
Hoxton	d	22 43			22 53			23 03			23 13			23 23			23 33		23 43		
Shoreditch High Street	d	22 46			22 56			23 06			23 16			23 26			23 36		23 46		
Whitechapel	d	22 48			22 58			23 08			23 18			23 28			23 38		23 48		
Shadwell	d	22 50			23 00			23 10			23 20			23 30			23 40		23 50		
Wapping	d	22 52			23 02			23 12			23 22			23 32			23 42		23 52		
Rotherhithe	d	22 54			23 04			23 14			23 24			23 34			23 44		23 54		
Canada Water	d	22 56			23 06			23 16			23 26			23 36			23 46		23 56		
Surrey Quays	d	22 57			23 07			23 17			23 27			23 37			23 47		23 57		
New Cross Ell	a				23 13									23 43							
New Cross Gate Station Ell	a	23 01						23 21			23 31						23 51		00 02		
	d	23 02						23 22			23 32						23 52		00 03		
New Cross Gate 4	d					22 57				23 11					23 27			23 41			
Brockley	d	23 04				23 00		23 24		23 14	23 34				23 30		23 54	23 44	00 04		
Honor Oak Park	d	23 07				23 03		23 27		23 17	23 37				23 33		23 57	23 47	00 07		
Forest Hill 4	d	23 10				23 05		23 30		23 19	23 40				23 35		23 59	23 49	00 10		
Sydenham	d	23 12				23 08		23 32		23 22	23 42				23 38		00 02	23 52	00 12		
Crystal Palace 4	d					23 13		23a37							23 43		00a07				
Gipsy Hill	d					23 15									23 45						
West Norwood 4	d					23 18									23 48						
Streatham Hill	d					23 22									23 52						
Balham 4 ⊖	d					23 25									23 55						
Wandsworth Common	d					23 27									23 58						
Clapham Junction 10	d					23 31									00 02						
South Bermondsey	d		22 45									23 15								23 52	
Peckham Rye 4	d			22 50									23 20								
Queens Rd Peckham	d		22 48									23 18								23 54	
Denmark Hill 4	d		22 53	22 53								23 23	23 23								
London Blackfriars 3 ⊖	a						23 10		23 20							23 40					00 10
Clapham High Street ⊖	d		22 58									23 28									
Wandsworth Road	d		22 59									23 29									
Battersea Park 4	d		23 02			23 35						23 32			00 05						
London Victoria 15 ⊖	a		23 06	23 03		23 40						23 37	23 33		00 12						
Penge West	d	23 15								23 24	23 45							23 54	00 15		
Anerley	d	23 17								23 26	23 47							23 56	00 17		
Norwood Junction 2	d	23 20								23 30	23 50							23 59	00 20	00a22	
West Croydon 4	a	23 31									00 01								00 27		
East Croydon	a									23 33								00 03			

London Bridge to London Victoria - Croydon and East London Line

Station		LO	SN	LO	SN	LO	FC 🚌	LO	SN	SN		FC 🚌	SN	FC 🚌	FC 🚌	FC 🚌	FC 🚌	FC 🚌	LO	LO		LO	LO	LO	LO
London Bridge 4 ⊖	d		23p22		23p36		23p55			00 06		00 25	00 36	01 00	02 30	03 20	04 20	05 20							
Dalston Junction Stn ELL	d	23p10		23p30		23p40		00 01											05 40			05 50		06 00	
Haggerston	d	23p11		23p31		23p41		00 02											05 41			05 51		06 01	
Hoxton	d	23p13		23p33		23p43		00 04											05 43			05 53		06 03	
Shoreditch High Street	d	23p16		23p36		23p46		00 07											05 46			05 56		06 06	
Whitechapel	d	23p18		23p38		23p48		00 09											05 48			05 58		06 08	
Shadwell	d	23p20		23p40		23p50		00 11											05 50			06 00		06 10	
Wapping	d	23p22		23p42		23p52		00 13											05 52			06 02		06 12	
Rotherhithe	d	23p24		23p44		23p54		00 15											05 54			06 04		06 14	
Canada Water	d	23p26		23p46		23p56		00 17											05 56			06 06		06 16	
Surrey Quays	d	23p27		23p47		23p57		00 18											05 57			06 07		06 17	
New Cross ELL	a																					06 13			
New Cross Gate Station ELL	a	23p31		23p51		00 02		00 22											06 01					06 21	
	d	23p32		23p52		00 03		00 23											06 02	05 47			05 52	06 22	06 07
New Cross Gate 4	d		23p27		23p41					00 11			00 41												
Brockley	d	23p34	23p30	23p54	23p44	00 04		00 25		00 14			00 44						06 04	05 49			05 54	06 24	06 09
Honor Oak Park	d	23p37	23p33	23p57	23p47	00 07		00 28		00 17			00 47						06 07	05 52			05 57	06 27	06 12
Forest Hill 4	d	23p40	23p35	23p59	23p49	00 10		00 31		00 19			00 49						06 10	05 55			06 00	06 30	06 15
Sydenham	d	23p42	23p38	00 02	23p52	00 12		00 33		00 22			00 52						06 12	05 57			06 02	06 32	06 17
Crystal Palace 4	d		23p43	00a07				00a38	00 03														06a07	06a37	06a22
Gipsy Hill	d		23p45																						
West Norwood 4	d		23p48																						
Streatham Hill	d		23p52																						
Balham 4 ⊖	d		23p55																						
Wandsworth Common	d		23p58																						
Clapham Junction 10	d		00 02																						
South Bermondsey	d																								
Peckham Rye 4	d																								
Queens Rd Peckham	d																								
Denmark Hill 4	d																								
London Blackfriars 3 ⊖	a						00 10					00 40		01 15	02 40	03 35	04 35	05 35							
Clapham High Street ⊖	d																								
Wandsworth Road	d																								
Battersea Park 4	d		00 05																						
London Victoria 15 ⊖	a		00 12																						
Penge West	d	23p45			23p54	00 15				00 24			00 54						06 15	06 00					
Anerley	d	23p47			23p56	00 17				00 26			00 56						06 17	06 02					
Norwood Junction 2	d	23p50			23p59	00 20			00 09	00 30			01 00						06 20	06 05					
West Croydon 4 ⇌	a	00 01				00 27			00 14										06 31	06 13					
East Croydon ⇌	a				00 03					00 33			01 03												

Station		LO	SN	SE	LO	LO		LO	LO	SN	LO	LO	SN	SE	SN	LO		LO	LO	LO	LO	LO	SN	LO	SN
London Bridge 4 ⊖	d		06 11							06 36			06 41										07 06		07 11
Dalston Junction Stn ELL	d	06 10				06 20		06 30	06 35			06 40				06 45			06 50	06 55	07 00	07 05		07 10	
Haggerston	d	06 11				06 21		06 31	06 36			06 41				06 46			06 51	06 56	07 01	07 06		07 11	
Hoxton	d	06 13				06 23		06 33	06 38			06 43				06 48			06 53	06 58	07 03	07 08		07 13	
Shoreditch High Street	d	06 16				06 26		06 36	06 41			06 46				06 51			06 56	07 01	07 06	07 11		07 16	
Whitechapel	d	06 18				06 28		06 38	06 43			06 48				06 53			06 58	07 03	07 08	07 13		07 18	
Shadwell	d	06 20				06 30		06 40	06 45			06 50				06 55			07 00	07 05	07 10	07 15		07 20	
Wapping	d	06 22				06 32		06 42	06 47			06 52				06 57			07 02	07 07	07 12	07 17		07 22	
Rotherhithe	d	06 24				06 34		06 44	06 49			06 54				06 59			07 04	07 09	07 14	07 19		07 24	
Canada Water	d	06 26				06 36		06 46	06 51			06 56				07 01			07 06	07 11	07 16	07 21		07 26	
Surrey Quays	d	06 27				06 37		06 47	06 52			06 57				07 02			07 07	07 12	07 17	07 22		07 27	
New Cross ELL	a					06 43			06 58										07 13			07 28			
New Cross Gate Station ELL	a	06 31						06 51				07 01				07 06				07 16	07 21			07 31	
	d	06 32			06 17			06 52			06 37	07 02				07 07		06 47		07 17	07 22			07 32	
New Cross Gate 4	d									06 41													07 11		
Brockley	d	06 34			06 19			06 54		06 44	06 39	07 04				07 09		06 49		07 19	07 24		07 14	07 34	
Honor Oak Park	d	06 37			06 22			06 57		06 47	06 42	07 07				07 12		06 52		07 22	07 27		07 17	07 37	
Forest Hill 4	d	06 40			06 25			07 00		06 49	06 45	07 10				07 15		06 55		07 25	07 30		07 19	07 40	
Sydenham	d	06 42			06 27			07 02		06 52	06 47	07 12				07 17		06 57		07 27	07 32		07 22	07 42	
Crystal Palace 4	d							07a07			06a52				06 45	07a22					07a37				
Gipsy Hill	d														06 47										
West Norwood 4	d														06 50										
Streatham Hill	d																								
Balham 4 ⊖	d																								
Wandsworth Common	d																								
Clapham Junction 10	d																								
South Bermondsey	d		06 15										06 45												07 15
Peckham Rye 4	d			06 13										06 43	07 01										
Queens Rd Peckham	d		06 18										06 48		07 04										07 18
Denmark Hill 4	d		06 23	06 17									06 53	06 47											07 23
London Blackfriars 3 ⊖	a																								
Clapham High Street ⊖	d		06 28										06 58												07 28
Wandsworth Road	d		06 29										06 59												07 29
Battersea Park 4	d		06 32										07 02												07 32
London Victoria 15 ⊖	a		06 36	06 26									07 06	06 56											07 36
Penge West	d	06 45			06 30					06 54		07 15						07 00		07 30			07 24	07 45	
Anerley	d	06 47			06 32					06 56		07 17						07 02		07 32			07 26	07 47	
Norwood Junction 2	d	06 50			06 35					07 00		07 20						07 05		07 35			07 30	07 50	
West Croydon 4 ⇌	a	07 01			06 42							07 31						07 12		07 42				08 01	
East Croydon ⇌	a									07 03													07 33		

Table 178

Saturdays

London Bridge to London Victoria - Croydon and East London Line

Station		SE		LO	SE	LO	LO	LO	SN	LO	SN	LO		SN	SE	LO	SE	LO	LO	LO	SN	LO		SN	LO
London Bridge 4 ⊖	d								07 33		07 36			07 41							08 03			08 06	
Dalston Junction Stn ELL	d			07 15		07 20	07 25	07 30		07 35		07 40				07 45		07 50	07 55	08 00		08 05			08 10
Haggerston	d			07 16		07 21	07 26	07 31		07 36		07 41				07 46		07 51	07 56	08 01		08 06			08 11
Hoxton	d			07 18		07 23	07 28	07 33		07 38		07 43				07 48		07 53	07 58	08 03		08 08			08 13
Shoreditch High Street	d			07 21		07 26	07 31	07 36		07 41		07 46				07 51		07 56	08 01	08 06		08 11			08 16
Whitechapel	d			07 23		07 28	07 33	07 38		07 43		07 48				07 53		07 58	08 03	08 08		08 13			08 18
Shadwell	d			07 25		07 30	07 35	07 40		07 45		07 50				07 55		08 00	08 05	08 10		08 15			08 20
Wapping	d			07 27		07 32	07 37	07 42		07 47		07 52				07 57		08 02	08 07	08 12		08 17			08 22
Rotherhithe	d			07 29		07 34	07 39	07 44		07 49		07 54				07 59		08 04	08 09	08 14		08 19			08 24
Canada Water	d			07 31		07 36	07 41	07 46		07 51		07 56				08 01		08 06	08 11	08 16		08 21			08 26
Surrey Quays	d			07 32		07 37	07 42	07 47		07 52		07 57				08 02		08 07	08 12	08 17		08 22			08 27
New Cross ELL	a					07 43				07 58								08 13				08 28			
New Cross Gate Station ELL	a			07 36			07 46	07 51				08 01				08 06			08 16	08 21					08 31
	d			07 37			07 47	07 52				08 02				08 07			08 17	08 22					08 32
New Cross Gate 4	d										07 41													08 11	
Brockley	d			07 39			07 49	07 54			07 44	08 04				08 09			08 19	08 24				08 14	08 34
Honor Oak Park	d			07 42			07 52	07 57			07 47	08 07				08 12			08 22	08 27				08 17	08 37
Forest Hill 4	d			07 45			07 55	08 00			07 49	08 10				08 15			08 25	08 30				08 19	08 40
Sydenham	d			07 47			07 57	08 02			07 52	08 12				08 17			08 27	08 32				08 22	08 42
Crystal Palace 4	d			07a52				08a07								08a22				08a37					
Gipsy Hill	d																								
West Norwood 4	d																								
Streatham Hill	d																								
Balham 4 ⊖	d																								
Wandsworth Common	d																								
Clapham Junction 10	d																								
South Bermondsey	d								07 37					07 45							08 07				
Peckham Rye 4	d	07 13			07 17										07 43		07 47								
Queens Rd Peckham	d								07 39					07 48							08 09				
Denmark Hill 4	d	07 17			07 21									07 53	07 47		07 51								
London Blackfriars 3 ⊖	a																								
Clapham High Street ⊖	d													07 58											
Wandsworth Road	d													07 59											
Battersea Park 4	d													08 02											
London Victoria 15 ⊖	a	07 26			07 30									08 06	07 56		08 00								
Penge West	d						08 00				07 54	08 15							08 30					08 24	08 45
Anerley	d						08 02				07 56	08 17							08 32					08 26	08 47
Norwood Junction 2	d						08 05				08 00	08 20							08 35					08 30	08 50
West Croydon 4 ⇌	a						08 12					08 31							08 42						09 01
East Croydon ⇌	a										08 03													08 33	

Station		SN	SE	LO	SE	LO	SN	LO		SN	LO	SN	LO	SN	LO	SN	SE	LO		SE	LO	SN	LO	SN	LO
London Bridge 4 ⊖	d	08 11					08 22					08 33		08 36		08 41						08 52			
Dalston Junction Stn ELL	d			08 15		08 20		08 25			08 30		08 35		08 40			08 45			08 50		08 55		09 00
Haggerston	d			08 16		08 21		08 26			08 31		08 36		08 41			08 46			08 51		08 56		09 01
Hoxton	d			08 18		08 23		08 28			08 33		08 38		08 43			08 48			08 53		08 58		09 03
Shoreditch High Street	d			08 21		08 26		08 31			08 36		08 41		08 46			08 51			08 56		09 01		09 06
Whitechapel	d			08 23		08 28		08 33			08 38		08 43		08 48			08 53			08 58		09 03		09 08
Shadwell	d			08 25		08 30		08 35			08 40		08 45		08 50			08 55			09 00		09 05		09 10
Wapping	d			08 27		08 32		08 37			08 42		08 47		08 52			08 57			09 02		09 07		09 12
Rotherhithe	d			08 29		08 34		08 39			08 44		08 49		08 54			08 59			09 04		09 09		09 14
Canada Water	d			08 31		08 36		08 41			08 46		08 51		08 56			09 01			09 06		09 11		09 16
Surrey Quays	d			08 32		08 37		08 42			08 47		08 52		08 57			09 02			09 07		09 12		09 17
New Cross ELL	a					08 43							08 58								09 13				
New Cross Gate Station ELL	a			08 36				08 46			08 51				09 01			09 06					09 16		09 21
	d			08 37				08 47			08 52				09 02			09 07					09 17		09 22
New Cross Gate 4	d						08 27							08 41								08 57			
Brockley	d			08 39			08 30	08 49			08 54			08 44	09 04			09 09				09 00	09 19		09 24
Honor Oak Park	d			08 42			08 33	08 52			08 57			08 47	09 07			09 12				09 03	09 22		09 27
Forest Hill 4	d			08 45			08 35	08 55			09 00			08 49	09 10			09 15				09 05	09 25		09 30
Sydenham	d			08 47			08 38	08 57			09 02			08 52	09 12			09 17				09 08	09 27		09 32
Crystal Palace 4	d			08a52			08 43			08 30	09a07							09a22				09 13		09 00	09a37
Gipsy Hill	d						08 45			08 32												09 15		09 02	
West Norwood 4	d						08 48			08 35												09 18		09 05	
Streatham Hill	d						08 52															09 22			
Balham 4 ⊖	d						08 55															09 25			
Wandsworth Common	d						08 57															09 27			
Clapham Junction 10	d						09 01															09 31			
South Bermondsey	d	08 15										08 37				08 45									
Peckham Rye 4	d		08 13		08 17					08 46							08 43			08 47				09 16	
Queens Rd Peckham	d	08 18								08 49		08 39				08 48								09 19	
Denmark Hill 4	d	08 23	08 17		08 21											08 53	08 47			08 51					
London Blackfriars 3 ⊖	a																								
Clapham High Street ⊖	d	08 28														08 58									
Wandsworth Road	d	08 29														08 59									
Battersea Park 4	d	08 32					09 05									09 02						09 35			
London Victoria 15 ⊖	a	08 36	08 26		08 30		09 09									09 06	08 56			09 00		09 39			
Penge West	d							09 00						08 54	09 15								09 30		
Anerley	d							09 02						08 56	09 17								09 32		
Norwood Junction 2	d							09 05						09 00	09 20								09 35		
West Croydon 4 ⇌	a							09 12							09 31								09 42		
East Croydon ⇌	a													09 03											

Table 178

London Bridge to London Victoria - Croydon and East London Line

		SN	LO	SN		LO	SN	SE	LO	SE	LO	SN	LO	SN		LO	SN	LO	SN	LO	SN	SE	LO	SE	
London Bridge 4 ⊖	d	09 03		09 06			09 11					09 22					09 33		09 36		09 41				
Dalston Junction Stn ELL	d		09 05			09 10			09 15		09 20		09 25			09 30		09 35		09 40			09 45		
Haggerston	d		09 06			09 11			09 16		09 21		09 26			09 31		09 36		09 41			09 46		
Hoxton	d		09 08			09 13			09 18		09 23		09 28			09 33		09 38		09 43			09 48		
Shoreditch High Street	d		09 11			09 16			09 21		09 26		09 31			09 36		09 41		09 46			09 51		
Whitechapel	d		09 13			09 18			09 23		09 28		09 33			09 38		09 43		09 48			09 53		
Shadwell	d		09 15			09 20			09 25		09 30		09 35			09 40		09 45		09 50			09 55		
Wapping	d		09 17			09 22			09 27		09 32		09 37			09 42		09 47		09 52			09 57		
Rotherhithe	d		09 19			09 24			09 29		09 34		09 39			09 44		09 49		09 54			09 59		
Canada Water	d		09 21			09 26			09 31		09 36		09 41			09 46		09 51		09 56			10 01		
Surrey Quays	d		09 22			09 27			09 32		09 37		09 42			09 47		09 52		09 57			10 02		
New Cross ELL	a		09 28								09 43							09 58							
New Cross Gate Station ELL	a					09 31			09 36				09 46			09 51				10 01			10 06		
	d					09 32			09 37				09 47			09 52				10 02			10 07		
New Cross Gate 4	d			09 11								09 27							09 41						
Brockley	d			09 14		09 34			09 39			09 30	09 49			09 54			09 44	10 04			10 09		
Honor Oak Park	d			09 17		09 37			09 42			09 33	09 52			09 57			09 47	10 07			10 12		
Forest Hill 4	d			09 19		09 40			09 45			09 35	09 55			10 00			09 49	10 10			10 15		
Sydenham	d			09 22		09 42			09 47			09 38	09 57			10 02			09 52	10 12			10 17		
Crystal Palace 4	d								09a52			09 43		09 30		10a07							10a22		
Gipsy Hill	d											09 45		09 32											
West Norwood 4	d											09 48		09 35											
Streatham Hill	d											09 52													
Balham 4 ⊖	d											09 55													
Wandsworth Common	d											09 57													
Clapham Junction 10	d											10 01													
South Bermondsey	d	09 07					09 15										09 37				09 45				
Peckham Rye 4	d							09 13		09 17				09 46								09 43		09 47	
Queens Rd Peckham	d	09 09					09 18							09 49			09 39				09 48				
Denmark Hill 4	d						09 23	09 17		09 21											09 53	09 47		09 51	
London Blackfriars 3 ⊖	a																								
Clapham High Street ⊖	d						09 28														09 58				
Wandsworth Road	d						09 29														09 59				
Battersea Park 4	d						09 32					10 05									10 02				
London Victoria 15 ⊖	a						09 36	09 26.		09 30.		10 09									10 06	09 56		10 00	
Penge West	d			09 24		09 45							10 00						09 54	10 15					
Anerley	d			09 26		09 47							10 02						09 56	10 17					
Norwood Junction 2	d			09 30		09 50							10 05						10 00	10 20					
West Croydon 4	a					10 01							10 12							10 31					
East Croydon	a			09 33															10 03						

		LO	SN	LO	SN	LO	SN	LO	SN	LO		SN	SE	LO	SE	LO	SN	LO	SN	LO		SN	LO	SN	LO
London Bridge 4 ⊖	d		09 52				10 03		10 06			10 11					10 22					10 33		10 36	
Dalston Junction Stn ELL	d	09 50		09 55		10 00		10 05		10 10				10 15		10 20		10 25		10 30			10 35		10 40
Haggerston	d	09 51		09 56		10 01		10 06		10 11				10 16		10 21		10 26		10 31			10 36		10 41
Hoxton	d	09 53		09 58		10 03		10 08		10 13				10 18		10 23		10 28		10 33			10 38		10 43
Shoreditch High Street	d	09 56		10 01		10 06		10 11		10 16				10 21		10 26		10 31		10 36			10 41		10 46
Whitechapel	d	09 58		10 03		10 08		10 13		10 18				10 23		10 28		10 33		10 38			10 43		10 48
Shadwell	d	10 00		10 05		10 10		10 15		10 20				10 25		10 30		10 35		10 40			10 45		10 50
Wapping	d	10 02		10 07		10 12		10 17		10 22				10 27		10 32		10 37		10 42			10 47		10 52
Rotherhithe	d	10 04		10 09		10 14		10 19		10 24				10 29		10 34		10 39		10 44			10 49		10 54
Canada Water	d	10 06		10 11		10 16		10 21		10 26				10 31		10 36		10 41		10 46			10 51		10 56
Surrey Quays	d	10 07		10 12		10 17		10 22		10 27				10 32		10 37		10 42		10 47			10 52		10 57
New Cross ELL	a	10 13						10 28								10 43							10 58		
New Cross Gate Station ELL	a			10 16		10 21				10 31				10 36				10 46		10 51					11 01
	d			10 17		10 22				10 32				10 37				10 47		10 52					11 02
New Cross Gate 4	d		09 57						10 11								10 27							10 41	
Brockley	d		10 00	10 19		10 24			10 14	10 34				10 39			10 30	10 49		10 54				10 44	11 04
Honor Oak Park	d		10 03	10 22		10 27			10 17	10 37				10 42			10 33	10 52		10 57				10 47	11 07
Forest Hill 4	d		10 05	10 25		10 30			10 19	10 40				10 45			10 35	10 55		11 00				10 49	11 10
Sydenham	d		10 08	10 27		10 32			10 22	10 42				10 47			10 38	10 57		11 02				10 52	11 12
Crystal Palace 4	d		10 13		10 00	10a37								10a52			10 43		10 30	11a07					
Gipsy Hill	d		10 15		10 02												10 45		10 32						
West Norwood 4	d		10 18		10 05												10 48		10 35						
Streatham Hill	d		10 22														10 52								
Balham 4 ⊖	d		10 25														10 55								
Wandsworth Common	d		10 27														10 57								
Clapham Junction 10	d		10 31														11 01								
South Bermondsey	d						10 07					10 15										10 37			
Peckham Rye 4	d				10 16								10 13		10 17				10 46						
Queens Rd Peckham	d				10 19		10 09					10 18							10 49			10 39			
Denmark Hill 4	d											10 23	10 17		10 21										
London Blackfriars 3 ⊖	a																								
Clapham High Street ⊖	d											10 28													
Wandsworth Road	d											10 29													
Battersea Park 4	d		10 35									10 32					11 05								
London Victoria 15 ⊖	a		10 39									10 36	10 26		10 30		11 09								
Penge West	d			10 30					10 24	10 45								11 00						10 54	11 15
Anerley	d			10 32					10 26	10 47								11 02						10 56	11 17
Norwood Junction 2	d			10 35					10 30	10 50								11 05						11 00	11 20
West Croydon 4	a			10 42						11 01								11 12							11 31
East Croydon	a								10 33															11 03	

Table 178

London Bridge to London Victoria - Croydon and East London Line

		SN	SE	LO	SE	LO		SN	LO	SN	LO	SN	LO	SN	LO	SN		SE	LO	SE	LO	SN	LO	SN	LO
London Bridge 4 ⊖	d	10 41						10 52				11 03		11 06		11 11						11 22			
Dalston Junction Stn ELL	d			10 45		10 50			10 55		11 00		11 05		11 10				11 15		11 20		11 25		11 30
Haggerston	d			10 46		10 51			10 56		11 01		11 06		11 11				11 16		11 21		11 26		11 31
Hoxton	d			10 48		10 53			10 58		11 03		11 08		11 13				11 18		11 23		11 28		11 33
Shoreditch High Street	d			10 51		10 56			11 01		11 06		11 11		11 16				11 21		11 26		11 31		11 36
Whitechapel	d			10 53		10 58			11 03		11 08		11 13		11 18				11 23		11 28		11 33		11 38
Shadwell	d			10 55		11 00			11 05		11 10		11 15		11 20				11 25		11 30		11 35		11 40
Wapping	d			10 57		11 02			11 07		11 12		11 17		11 22				11 27		11 32		11 37		11 42
Rotherhithe	d			10 59		11 04			11 09		11 14		11 19		11 24				11 29		11 34		11 39		11 44
Canada Water	d			11 01		11 06			11 11		11 16		11 21		11 26				11 31		11 36		11 41		11 46
Surrey Quays	d			11 02		11 07			11 12		11 17		11 22		11 27				11 32		11 37		11 42		11 47
New Cross ELL	a					11 13							11 28								11 43				
New Cross Gate Station ELL	a			11 06					11 16		11 21				11 31				11 36				11 46		11 51
	d			11 07					11 17		11 22				11 32				11 37				11 47		11 52
New Cross Gate 4	d							10 57						11 11								11 27			
Brockley	d			11 09				11 00	11 19		11 24			11 14	11 34				11 39			11 30	11 49		11 54
Honor Oak Park	d			11 12				11 03	11 22		11 27			11 17	11 37				11 42			11 33	11 52		11 57
Forest Hill 4	d			11 15				11 05	11 25		11 30			11 19	11 40				11 45			11 35	11 55		12 00
Sydenham	d			11 17				11 08	11 27		11 32			11 22	11 42				11 47			11 38	11 57		12 02
Crystal Palace 4	d			11a22				11 13		11 00	11a37								11a52			11 43		11 30	12a07
Gipsy Hill	d							11 15		11 02												11 45		11 32	
West Norwood 4	d							11 18		11 05												11 48		11 35	
Streatham Hill	d							11 22														11 52			
Balham 4 ⊖	d							11 25														11 55			
Wandsworth Common	d							11 27														11 57			
Clapham Junction 10	d							11 31														12 01			
South Bermondsey	d	10 45										11 07				11 15									
Peckham Rye 4	d		10 43		10 47					11 16								11 13		11 17				11 46	
Queens Rd Peckham	d	10 48								11 19		11 09				11 18								11 49	
Denmark Hill 4	d	10 53	10 47		10 51											11 23		11 17		11 21					
London Blackfriars 3 ⊖	a																								
Clapham High Street ⊖	d	10 58														11 28									
Wandsworth Road	d	10 59														11 29									
Battersea Park 4	d	11 02						11 35								11 32						12 05			
London Victoria 15 ⊖	a	11 06	10 56		11 00			11 39								11 36		11 26.		11 30		12 09			
Penge West	d								11 30					11 24	11 45								12 00		
Anerley	d								11 32					11 26	11 47								12 02		
Norwood Junction 2	d								11 35					11 30	11 50								12 05		
West Croydon 4	a								11 42						12 01								12 12		
East Croydon	a													11 33											

		SN		LO	SN	LO	SN	SE	LO	SE	LO	SN		LO	SN	LO	SN	LO	SN	LO	SN	SE		LO	SE
London Bridge 4 ⊖	d	11 33			11 36		11 41					11 52					12 03		12 06		12 11				
Dalston Junction Stn ELL	d			11 35		11 40			11 45		11 50			11 55		12 00		12 05		12 10				12 15	
Haggerston	d			11 36		11 41			11 46		11 51			11 56		12 01		12 06		12 11				12 16	
Hoxton	d			11 38		11 43			11 48		11 53			11 58		12 03		12 08		12 13				12 18	
Shoreditch High Street	d			11 41		11 46			11 51		11 56			12 01		12 06		12 11		12 16				12 21	
Whitechapel	d			11 43		11 48			11 53		11 58			12 03		12 08		12 13		12 18				12 23	
Shadwell	d			11 45		11 50			11 55		12 00			12 05		12 10		12 15		12 20				12 25	
Wapping	d			11 47		11 52			11 57		12 02			12 07		12 12		12 17		12 22				12 27	
Rotherhithe	d			11 49		11 54			11 59		12 04			12 09		12 14		12 19		12 24				12 29	
Canada Water	d			11 51		11 56			12 01		12 06			12 11		12 16		12 21		12 26				12 31	
Surrey Quays	d			11 52		11 57			12 02		12 07			12 12		12 17		12 22		12 27				12 32	
New Cross ELL	a			11 58							12 13							12 28							
New Cross Gate Station ELL	a					12 01			12 06					12 16		12 21				12 31				12 36	
	d					12 02			12 07					12 17		12 22				12 32				12 37	
New Cross Gate 4	d				11 41							11 57							12 11						
Brockley	d				11 44	12 04			12 09			12 00		12 19		12 24			12 14	12 34				12 39	
Honor Oak Park	d				11 47	12 07			12 12			12 03		12 22		12 27			12 17	12 37				12 42	
Forest Hill 4	d				11 49	12 10			12 15			12 05		12 25		12 30			12 19	12 40				12 45	
Sydenham	d				11 52	12 12			12 17			12 08		12 27		12 32			12 22	12 42				12 47	
Crystal Palace 4	d								12a22			12 13			12 00	12a37								12a52	
Gipsy Hill	d											12 15			12 02										
West Norwood 4	d											12 18			12 05										
Streatham Hill	d											12 22													
Balham 4 ⊖	d											12 25													
Wandsworth Common	d											12 27													
Clapham Junction 10	d											12 31													
South Bermondsey	d	11 37					11 45										12 07				12 15				
Peckham Rye 4	d							11 43		11 47					12 16							12 13			12 17
Queens Rd Peckham	d	11 39					11 48								12 19		12 09				12 18				
Denmark Hill 4	d						11 53	11 47		11 51											12 23	12 17			12 21
London Blackfriars 3 ⊖	a																								
Clapham High Street ⊖	d						11 58														12 28				
Wandsworth Road	d						11 59														12 29				
Battersea Park 4	d						12 02					12 35									12 32				
London Victoria 15 ⊖	a						12 06	11 56.		12 00		12 39									12 36	12 26			12 30
Penge West	d				11 54	12 15								12 30					12 24	12 45					
Anerley	d				11 56	12 17								12 32					12 26	12 47					
Norwood Junction 2	d				12 00	12 20								12 35					12 30	12 50					
West Croydon 4	a					12 31								12 42						13 01					
East Croydon	a				12 03														12 33						

Table 178

London Bridge to London Victoria - Croydon and East London Line

		LO	SN	LO	SN	LO	SN	LO	SN	LO	SN	SE	LO	SE	LO	SN	LO	SN	LO	SN	LO	SN	LO
London Bridge 4 ⊖	d		12 22				12 33		12 36		12 41					12 52				13 03		13 06	
Dalston Junction Stn Ell	d	12 20		12 25		12 30		12 35		12 40			12 45		12 50		12 55		13 00		13 05		13 10
Haggerston	d	12 21		12 26		12 31		12 36		12 41			12 46		12 51		12 56		13 01		13 06		13 11
Hoxton	d	12 23		12 28		12 33		12 38		12 43			12 48		12 53		12 58		13 03		13 08		13 13
Shoreditch High Street	d	12 26		12 31		12 36		12 41		12 46			12 51		12 56		13 01		13 06		13 11		13 16
Whitechapel	d	12 28		12 33		12 38		12 43		12 48			12 53		12 58		13 03		13 08		13 13		13 18
Shadwell	d	12 30		12 35		12 40		12 45		12 50			12 55		13 00		13 05		13 10		13 15		13 20
Wapping	d	12 32		12 37		12 42		12 47		12 52			12 57		13 02		13 07		13 12		13 17		13 22
Rotherhithe	d	12 34		12 39		12 44		12 49		12 54			12 59		13 04		13 09		13 14		13 19		13 24
Canada Water	d	12 36		12 41		12 46		12 51		12 56			13 01		13 06		13 11		13 16		13 21		13 26
Surrey Quays	d	12 37		12 42		12 47		12 52		12 57			13 02		13 07		13 12		13 17		13 22		13 27
New Cross Ell	a	12 43						12 58							13 13						13 28		
New Cross Gate Station Ell	a			12 46		12 51				13 01			13 06				13 16		13 21				13 31
	d			12 47		12 52				13 02			13 07				13 17		13 22				13 32
New Cross Gate 4	d		12 27						12 41							12 57						13 11	
Brockley	d		12 30	12 49		12 54			12 44	13 04			13 09			13 00	13 19		13 24			13 14	13 34
Honor Oak Park	d		12 33	12 52		12 57			12 47	13 07			13 12			13 03	13 22		13 27			13 17	13 37
Forest Hill 4	d		12 35	12 55		13 00			12 49	13 10			13 15			13 05	13 25		13 30			13 19	13 40
Sydenham	d		12 38	12 57		13 02			12 52	13 12			13 17			13 08	13 27		13 32			13 22	13 42
Crystal Palace 4	d		12 43		12 30	13a07							13a22			13 13		13 00	13a37				
Gipsy Hill	d		12 45		12 32											13 15		13 02					
West Norwood 4	d		12 48		12 35											13 18		13 05					
Streatham Hill	d		12 52													13 22							
Balham 4 ⊖	d		12 55													13 25							
Wandsworth Common	d		12 57													13 27							
Clapham Junction 10	d		13 01													13 31							
South Bermondsey	d						12 37				12 45									13 07			
Peckham Rye 4	d				12 46							12 43		12 47				13 16					
Queens Rd Peckham	d				12 49		12 39				12 48							13 19		13 09			
Denmark Hill 4	d										12 53	12 47		12 51									
London Blackfriars 3 ⊖	a																						
Clapham High Street ⊖	d										12 58												
Wandsworth Road	d										12 59												
Battersea Park 4	d		13 05								13 02					13 35							
London Victoria 15 ⊖	a		13 09								13 06	12 56		13 00		13 39							
Penge West	d			13 00					12 54	13 15							13 30					13 24	13 45
Anerley	d			13 02					12 56	13 17							13 32					13 26	13 47
Norwood Junction 2	d			13 05					13 00	13 20							13 35					13 30	13 50
West Croydon 4	a			13 12						13 31							13 42						14 01
East Croydon	a								13 03													13 33	

		SN	SE	LO	SE	LO	SN	LO	SN	LO	SN	LO	SN	LO	SN	SE	LO	SE	LO	SN	LO	SN
London Bridge 4 ⊖	d	13 11					13 22				13 33		13 36		13 41					13 52		
Dalston Junction Stn Ell	d			13 15		13 20		13 25		13 30		13 35		13 40			13 45		13 50		13 55	
Haggerston	d			13 16		13 21		13 26		13 31		13 36		13 41			13 46		13 51		13 56	
Hoxton	d			13 18		13 23		13 28		13 33		13 38		13 43			13 48		13 53		13 58	
Shoreditch High Street	d			13 21		13 26		13 31		13 36		13 41		13 46			13 51		13 56		14 01	
Whitechapel	d			13 23		13 28		13 33		13 38		13 43		13 48			13 53		13 58		14 03	
Shadwell	d			13 25		13 30		13 35		13 40		13 45		13 50			13 55		14 00		14 05	
Wapping	d			13 27		13 32		13 37		13 42		13 47		13 52			13 57		14 02		14 07	
Rotherhithe	d			13 29		13 34		13 39		13 44		13 49		13 54			13 59		14 04		14 09	
Canada Water	d			13 31		13 36		13 41		13 46		13 51		13 56			14 01		14 06		14 11	
Surrey Quays	d			13 32		13 37		13 42		13 47		13 52		13 57			14 02		14 07		14 12	
New Cross Ell	a					13 43						13 58							14 13			
New Cross Gate Station Ell	a			13 36				13 46		13 51				14 01			14 06				14 16	
	d			13 37				13 47		13 52				14 02			14 07				14 17	
New Cross Gate 4	d						13 27						13 41							13 57		
Brockley	d			13 39			13 30	13 49		13 54			13 44	14 04			14 09			14 00	14 19	
Honor Oak Park	d			13 42			13 33	13 52		13 57			13 47	14 07			14 12			14 03	14 22	
Forest Hill 4	d			13 45			13 35	13 55		14 00			13 49	14 10			14 15			14 05	14 25	
Sydenham	d			13 47			13 38	13 57		14 02			13 52	14 12			14 17			14 08	14 27	
Crystal Palace 4	d			13a52			13 43		13 30	14a07							14a22			14 13		14 00
Gipsy Hill	d						13 45		13 32											14 15		14 02
West Norwood 4	d						13 48		13 35											14 18		14 05
Streatham Hill	d						13 52													14 22		
Balham 4 ⊖	d						13 55													14 25		
Wandsworth Common	d						13 57													14 27		
Clapham Junction 10	d						14 01													14 31		
South Bermondsey	d	13 15									13 37				13 45							
Peckham Rye 4	d		13 13		13 17				13 46							13 43		13 47				14 16
Queens Rd Peckham	d	13 18							13 49		13 39				13 48							14 19
Denmark Hill 4	d	13 23	13 17		13 21										13 53	13 47		13 51				
London Blackfriars 3 ⊖	a																					
Clapham High Street ⊖	d	13 28													13 58							
Wandsworth Road	d	13 29													13 59							
Battersea Park 4	d	13 32					14 05								14 02					14 35		
London Victoria 15 ⊖	a	13 36	13 26		13 30		14 09								14 06	13 56.		14 00		14 39		
Penge West	d							14 00					13 54	14 15							14 30	
Anerley	d							14 02					13 56	14 17							14 32	
Norwood Junction 2	d							14 05					14 00	14 20							14 35	
West Croydon 4	a							14 12						14 31							14 42	
East Croydon	a												14 03									

Table 178

London Bridge to London Victoria - Croydon and East London Line

		LO	SN	LO	SN	LO	SN	SE	LO	SE	LO	SN	LO	SN	LO	SN	LO	SN	LO	SN	SE	LO	SE
London Bridge 4 ⊖	d		14 03		14 06		14 11					14 22				14 33		14 36		14 41			
Dalston Junction Stn Ell	d	14 00		14 05		14 10			14 15		14 20		14 25		14 30		14 35		14 40			14 45	
Haggerston	d	14 01		14 06		14 11			14 16		14 21		14 26		14 31		14 36		14 41			14 46	
Hoxton	d	14 03		14 08		14 13			14 18		14 23		14 28		14 33		14 38		14 43			14 48	
Shoreditch High Street	d	14 06		14 11		14 16			14 21		14 26		14 31		14 36		14 41		14 46			14 51	
Whitechapel	d	14 08		14 13		14 18			14 23		14 28		14 33		14 38		14 43		14 48			14 53	
Shadwell	d	14 10		14 15		14 20			14 25		14 30		14 35		14 40		14 45		14 50			14 55	
Wapping	d	14 12		14 17		14 22			14 27		14 32		14 37		14 42		14 47		14 52			14 57	
Rotherhithe	d	14 14		14 19		14 24			14 29		14 34		14 39		14 44		14 49		14 54			14 59	
Canada Water	d	14 16		14 21		14 26			14 31		14 36		14 41		14 46		14 51		14 56			15 01	
Surrey Quays	d	14 17		14 22		14 27			14 32		14 37		14 42		14 47		14 52		14 57			15 02	
New Cross Ell	a			14 28							14 43						14 58						
New Cross Gate Station Ell	a	14 21				14 31			14 36				14 46		14 51				15 01			15 06	
	d	14 22				14 32			14 37				14 47		14 52				15 02			15 07	
New Cross Gate 4	d				14 11							14 27						14 41					
Brockley	d	14 24			14 14	14 34			14 39			14 30	14 49		14 54			14 44	15 04			15 09	
Honor Oak Park	d	14 27			14 17	14 37			14 42			14 33	14 52		14 57			14 47	15 07			15 12	
Forest Hill 4	d	14 30			14 19	14 40			14 45			14 35	14 55		15 00			14 49	15 10			15 15	
Sydenham	d	14 32			14 22	14 42			14 47			14 38	14 57		15 02			14 52	15 12			15 17	
Crystal Palace 4	d	14a37							14a52			14 43		14 30	15a07							15a22	
Gipsy Hill	d											14 45		14 32									
West Norwood 4	d											14 48		14 35									
Streatham Hill	d											14 52											
Balham 4 ⊖	d											14 55											
Wandsworth Common	d											14 57											
Clapham Junction 10	d											15 01											
South Bermondsey	d		14 07				14 15									14 37				14 45			
Peckham Rye 4	d							14 13		14 17				14 46							14 43		14 47
Queens Rd Peckham	d		14 09				14 18							14 49		14 39				14 48			
Denmark Hill 4	d						14 23	14 17		14 21										14 53	14 47		14 51
London Blackfriars 3 ⊖	a																						
Clapham High Street ⊖	d						14 28													14 58			
Wandsworth Road	d						14 29													14 59			
Battersea Park 4	d						14 32					15 05								15 02			
London Victoria 15 ⊖	a						14 36	14 26		14 30		15 09								15 06	14 56		15 00
Penge West	d				14 24	14 45							15 00					14 54	15 15				
Anerley	d				14 26	14 47							15 02					14 56	15 17				
Norwood Junction 2	d				14 30	14 50							15 05					15 00	15 20				
West Croydon 4	a					15 01							15 12						15 31				
East Croydon	a				14 33													15 03					

		LO	SN	LO	SN	LO	SN	LO	SN	LO	SN	SE	LO	SE	LO	SN	LO	SN	LO	SN	LO	SN	LO
London Bridge 4 ⊖	d		14 52				15 03		15 06		15 11					15 22				15 33		15 36	
Dalston Junction Stn Ell	d	14 50		14 55		15 00		15 05		15 10			15 15		15 20		15 25		15 30		15 35		15 40
Haggerston	d	14 51		14 56		15 01		15 06		15 11			15 16		15 21		15 26		15 31		15 36		15 41
Hoxton	d	14 53		14 58		15 03		15 08		15 13			15 18		15 23		15 28		15 33		15 38		15 43
Shoreditch High Street	d	14 56		15 01		15 06		15 11		15 16			15 21		15 26		15 31		15 36		15 41		15 46
Whitechapel	d	14 58		15 03		15 08		15 13		15 18			15 23		15 28		15 33		15 38		15 43		15 48
Shadwell	d	15 00		15 05		15 10		15 15		15 20			15 25		15 30		15 35		15 40		15 45		15 50
Wapping	d	15 02		15 07		15 12		15 17		15 22			15 27		15 32		15 37		15 42		15 47		15 52
Rotherhithe	d	15 04		15 09		15 14		15 19		15 24			15 29		15 34		15 39		15 44		15 49		15 54
Canada Water	d	15 06		15 11		15 16		15 21		15 26			15 31		15 36		15 41		15 46		15 51		15 56
Surrey Quays	d	15 07		15 12		15 17		15 22		15 27			15 32		15 37		15 42		15 47		15 52		15 57
New Cross Ell	a	15 13						15 28							15 43						15 58		
New Cross Gate Station Ell	a			15 16		15 21				15 31			15 36				15 46		15 51				16 01
	d			15 17		15 22				15 32			15 37				15 47		15 52				16 02
New Cross Gate 4	d		14 57						15 11							15 27						15 41	
Brockley	d		15 00	15 19		15 24			15 14	15 34			15 39			15 30	15 49		15 54			15 44	16 04
Honor Oak Park	d		15 03	15 22		15 27			15 17	15 37			15 42			15 33	15 52		15 57			15 47	16 07
Forest Hill 4	d		15 05	15 25		15 30			15 19	15 40			15 45			15 35	15 55		16 00			15 49	16 10
Sydenham	d		15 08	15 27		15 32			15 22	15 42			15 47			15 38	15 57		16 02			15 52	16 12
Crystal Palace 4	d		15 13		15 00	15a37							15a52			15 43		15 30	16a07				
Gipsy Hill	d		15 15		15 02											15 45		15 32					
West Norwood 4	d		15 18		15 05											15 48		15 35					
Streatham Hill	d		15 22													15 52							
Balham 4 ⊖	d		15 25													15 55							
Wandsworth Common	d		15 27													15 57							
Clapham Junction 10	d		15 31													16 01							
South Bermondsey	d						15 07				15 15									15 37			
Peckham Rye 4	d				15 16							15 13		15 17				15 46					
Queens Rd Peckham	d				15 19		15 09				15 18							15 49		15 39			
Denmark Hill 4	d										15 23	15 17		15 21									
London Blackfriars 3 ⊖	a																						
Clapham High Street ⊖	d										15 28												
Wandsworth Road	d										15 29												
Battersea Park 4	d		15 35								15 32					16 05							
London Victoria 15 ⊖	a		15 39								15 36	15 26		15 30		16 09							
Penge West	d			15 30					15 24	15 45							16 00					15 54	16 15
Anerley	d			15 32					15 26	15 47							16 02					15 56	16 17
Norwood Junction 2	d			15 35					15 30	15 50							16 05					16 00	16 20
West Croydon 4	a			15 42						16 01							16 12						16 31
East Croydon	a								15 33													16 03	

Table 178

Saturdays

London Bridge to London Victoria - Croydon and East London Line

		SN		SE	LO	SE	LO	SN	LO	SN	LO	SN		LO	SN	LO	SN	SE	LO	SE	LO	SN		LO	SN
London Bridge ⊖	d	15 41						15 52				16 03			16 06		16 11					16 22			
Dalston Junction Stn Ell	d				15 45		15 50		15 55		16 00			16 05		16 10			16 15		16 20			16 25	
Haggerston	d				15 46		15 51		15 56		16 01			16 06		16 11			16 16		16 21			16 26	
Hoxton	d				15 48		15 53		15 58		16 03			16 08		16 13			16 18		16 23			16 28	
Shoreditch High Street	d				15 51		15 56		16 01		16 06			16 11		16 16			16 21		16 26			16 31	
Whitechapel	d				15 53		15 58		16 03		16 08			16 13		16 18			16 23		16 28			16 33	
Shadwell	d				15 55		16 00		16 05		16 10			16 15		16 20			16 25		16 30			16 35	
Wapping	d				15 57		16 02		16 07		16 12			16 17		16 22			16 27		16 32			16 37	
Rotherhithe	d				15 59		16 04		16 09		16 14			16 19		16 24			16 29		16 34			16 39	
Canada Water	d				16 01		16 06		16 11		16 16			16 21		16 26			16 31		16 36			16 41	
Surrey Quays	d				16 02		16 07		16 12		16 17			16 22		16 27			16 32		16 37			16 42	
New Cross Ell	a						16 13							16 28							16 43				
New Cross Gate Station Ell	a				16 06				16 16		16 21					16 31			16 36					16 46	
	d				16 07				16 17		16 22					16 32			16 37					16 47	
New Cross Gate	d							15 57							16 11							16 27			
Brockley	d				16 09			16 00	16 19		16 24				16 14	16 34			16 39			16 30		16 49	
Honor Oak Park	d				16 12			16 03	16 22		16 27				16 17	16 37			16 42			16 33		16 52	
Forest Hill	d				16 15			16 05	16 25		16 30				16 19	16 40			16 45			16 35		16 55	
Sydenham	d				16 17			16 08	16 27		16 32				16 22	16 42			16 47			16 38		16 57	
Crystal Palace	d				16a22			16 13		16 00	16a37								16a52			16 43			16 30
Gipsy Hill	d							16 15		16 02												16 45			16 32
West Norwood	d							16 18		16 05												16 48			16 35
Streatham Hill	d							16 22														16 52			
Balham ⊖	d							16 25														16 55			
Wandsworth Common	d							16 27														16 57			
Clapham Junction	d							16 31														17 01			
South Bermondsey	d	15 45										16 07					16 15								
Peckham Rye	d			15 43		15 47				16 16								16 13		16 17					16 46
Queens Rd Peckham	d	15 48								16 19		16 09					16 18								16 49
Denmark Hill	d	15 53		15 47		15 51											16 23	16 17		16 21					
London Blackfriars ⊖	a																								
Clapham High Street ⊖	d	15 58															16 28								
Wandsworth Road	d	15 59															16 29								
Battersea Park	d	16 02						16 35									16 32					17 05			
London Victoria ⊖	a	16 06		15 56		16 00		16 39									16 36	16 26		16 30		17 09			
Penge West	d								16 30						16 24	16 45								17 00	
Anerley	d								16 32						16 26	16 47								17 02	
Norwood Junction	d								16 35						16 30	16 50								17 05	
West Croydon	a								16 42							17 01								17 12	
East Croydon	a														16 33										

		LO	SN	LO	SN	LO	SN	SE		LO	SE	LO	SN	LO	SN	LO	SN	LO		SN	LO	SN	SE	LO	SE
London Bridge ⊖	d		16 33		16 36		16 41						16 52				17 03			17 06		17 11			
Dalston Junction Stn Ell	d	16 30		16 35		16 40				16 45		16 50		16 55		17 00		17 05			17 10			17 15	
Haggerston	d	16 31		16 36		16 41				16 46		16 51		16 56		17 01		17 06			17 11			17 16	
Hoxton	d	16 33		16 38		16 43				16 48		16 53		16 58		17 03		17 08			17 13			17 18	
Shoreditch High Street	d	16 36		16 41		16 46				16 51		16 56		17 01		17 06		17 11			17 16			17 21	
Whitechapel	d	16 38		16 43		16 48				16 53		16 58		17 03		17 08		17 13			17 18			17 23	
Shadwell	d	16 40		16 45		16 50				16 55		17 00		17 05		17 10		17 15			17 20			17 25	
Wapping	d	16 42		16 47		16 52				16 57		17 02		17 07		17 12		17 17			17 22			17 27	
Rotherhithe	d	16 44		16 49		16 54				16 59		17 04		17 09		17 14		17 19			17 24			17 29	
Canada Water	d	16 46		16 51		16 56				17 01		17 06		17 11		17 16		17 21			17 26			17 31	
Surrey Quays	d	16 47		16 52		16 57				17 02		17 07		17 12		17 17		17 22			17 27			17 32	
New Cross Ell	a			16 58								17 13						17 28							
New Cross Gate Station Ell	a	16 51				17 01				17 06				17 16		17 21					17 31			17 36	
	d	16 52				17 02				17 07				17 17		17 22					17 32			17 37	
New Cross Gate	d				16 41								16 57							17 11					
Brockley	d	16 54			16 44	17 04				17 09			17 00	17 19		17 24				17 14	17 34			17 39	
Honor Oak Park	d	16 57			16 47	17 07				17 12			17 03	17 22		17 27				17 17	17 37			17 42	
Forest Hill	d	17 00			16 49	17 10				17 15			17 05	17 25		17 30				17 19	17 40			17 45	
Sydenham	d	17 02			16 52	17 12				17 17			17 08	17 27		17 32				17 22	17 42			17 47	
Crystal Palace	d	17a07								17a22			17 13		17 00	17a37								17a52	
Gipsy Hill	d												17 15		17 02										
West Norwood	d												17 18		17 05										
Streatham Hill	d												17 22												
Balham ⊖	d												17 25												
Wandsworth Common	d												17 27												
Clapham Junction	d												17 32												
South Bermondsey	d		16 37				16 45										17 07					17 15			
Peckham Rye	d							16 43			16 47				17 16								17 13		17 17
Queens Rd Peckham	d		16 39				16 48								17 19		17 09					17 18			
Denmark Hill	d						16 53	16 47			16 51											17 23	17 17		17 21
London Blackfriars ⊖	a																								
Clapham High Street ⊖	d						16 58															17 28			
Wandsworth Road	d						16 59															17 29			
Battersea Park	d						17 02						17 36									17 32			
London Victoria ⊖	a						17 06	16 56			17 00		17 40									17 36	17 26		17 30
Penge West	d				16 54	17 15								17 30						17 24	17 45				
Anerley	d				16 56	17 17								17 32						17 26	17 47				
Norwood Junction	d				17 00	17 20								17 35						17 30	17 50				
West Croydon	a					17 31								17 42							18 01				
East Croydon	a				17 03															17 33					

Table 178

Saturdays

London Bridge to London Victoria - Croydon and East London Line

		LO	SN	LO		SN	LO	SN	LO	SN	LO	SN	SE	LO		SE	LO	SN	LO	SN	LO	SN	LO	SN	
London Bridge ⊖	d		17 22					17 33		17 36		17 41						17 52				18 03		18 06	
Dalston Junction Stn Ell	d	17 20		17 25			17 30		17 35		17 40			17 45			17 50		17 55		18 00		18 05		
Haggerston	d	17 21		17 26			17 31		17 36		17 41			17 46			17 51		17 56		18 01		18 06		
Hoxton	d	17 23		17 28			17 33		17 38		17 43			17 48			17 53		17 58		18 03		18 08		
Shoreditch High Street	d	17 26		17 31			17 36		17 41		17 46			17 51			17 56		18 01		18 06		18 11		
Whitechapel	d	17 28		17 33			17 38		17 43		17 48			17 53			17 58		18 03		18 08		18 13		
Shadwell	d	17 30		17 35			17 40		17 45		17 50			17 55			18 00		18 05		18 10		18 15		
Wapping	d	17 32		17 37			17 42		17 47		17 52			17 57			18 02		18 07		18 12		18 17		
Rotherhithe	d	17 34		17 39			17 44		17 49		17 54			17 59			18 04		18 09		18 14		18 19		
Canada Water	d	17 36		17 41			17 46		17 51		17 56			18 01			18 06		18 11		18 16		18 21		
Surrey Quays	d	17 37		17 42			17 47		17 52		17 57			18 02			18 07		18 12		18 17		18 22		
New Cross Ell	a	17 43							17 58								18 13						18 28		
New Cross Gate Station Ell	a			17 46			17 51				18 01			18 06					18 16		18 21				
	d			17 47			17 52				18 02			18 07					18 17		18 22				
New Cross Gate	d		17 27							17 41								17 57						18 11	
Brockley	d		17 30	17 49			17 54			17 44	18 04			18 09				18 00	18 19		18 24			18 14	
Honor Oak Park	d		17 33	17 52			17 57			17 47	18 07			18 12				18 03	18 22		18 27			18 17	
Forest Hill	d		17 35	17 55			18 00			17 49	18 10			18 15				18 05	18 25		18 30			18 19	
Sydenham	d		17 38	17 57			18 02			17 52	18 12			18 17				18 08	18 27		18 32			18 22	
Crystal Palace	d		17 43			17 30	18a07							18a22				18 13		18 00	18a37				
Gipsy Hill	d		17 45			17 32												18 15		18 02					
West Norwood	d		17 48			17 35												18 18		18 05					
Streatham Hill	d		17 52															18 22							
Balham ⊖	d		17 55															18 25							
Wandsworth Common	d		17 57															18 27							
Clapham Junction	d		18 01															18 31							
South Bermondsey	d							17 37				17 45										18 07			
Peckham Rye	d					17 46							17 43			17 47				18 16					
Queens Rd Peckham	d					17 49		17 39				17 48								18 19		18 09			
Denmark Hill	d											17 53	17 47			17 51									
London Blackfriars ⊖	a																								
Clapham High Street ⊖	d											17 58													
Wandsworth Road	d											17 59													
Battersea Park	d		18 05									18 02						18 35							
London Victoria ⊖	a		18 09									18 06	17 56			18 00		18 39		18 26					
Penge West	d			18 00						17 54	18 15								18 30					18 24	
Anerley	d			18 02						17 56	18 17								18 32					18 26	
Norwood Junction	d			18 05						18 00	18 20								18 35					18 30	
West Croydon	a			18 12							18 31								18 42						
East Croydon	a									18 03														18 33	

		LO	SN	SE	LO	SE	LO	SN	LO	SN		LO	SN	LO	SN	LO	SN	SE	LO	SE		LO	SN	LO	SN
London Bridge ⊖	d		18 11					18 22					18 33		18 36		18 41						18 52		
Dalston Junction Stn Ell	d	18 10			18 15		18 20		18 25			18 30		18 35		18 40			18 45			18 50		18 55	
Haggerston	d	18 11			18 16		18 21		18 26			18 31		18 36		18 41			18 46			18 51		18 56	
Hoxton	d	18 13			18 18		18 23		18 28			18 33		18 38		18 43			18 48			18 53		18 58	
Shoreditch High Street	d	18 16			18 21		18 26		18 31			18 36		18 41		18 46			18 51			18 56		19 01	
Whitechapel	d	18 18			18 23		18 28		18 33			18 38		18 43		18 48			18 53			18 58		19 03	
Shadwell	d	18 20			18 25		18 30		18 35			18 40		18 45		18 50			18 55			19 00		19 05	
Wapping	d	18 22			18 27		18 32		18 37			18 42		18 47		18 52			18 57			19 02		19 07	
Rotherhithe	d	18 24			18 29		18 34		18 39			18 44		18 49		18 54			18 59			19 04		19 09	
Canada Water	d	18 26			18 31		18 36		18 41			18 46		18 51		18 56			19 01			19 06		19 11	
Surrey Quays	d	18 27			18 32		18 37		18 42			18 47		18 52		18 57			19 02			19 07		19 12	
New Cross Ell	a						18 43							18 58								19 13			
New Cross Gate Station Ell	a	18 31			18 36				18 46			18 51				19 01			19 06					19 16	
	d	18 32			18 37				18 47			18 52				19 02			19 07					19 17	
New Cross Gate	d							18 27							18 41								18 57		
Brockley	d	18 34			18 39			18 30	18 49			18 54			18 44	19 04			19 09				19 00	19 19	
Honor Oak Park	d	18 37			18 42			18 33	18 52			18 57			18 47	19 07			19 12				19 03	19 22	
Forest Hill	d	18 40			18 45			18 35	18 55			19 00			18 49	19 10			19 15				19 05	19 25	
Sydenham	d	18 42			18 47			18 38	18 57			19 02			18 52	19 12			19 17				19 08	19 27	
Crystal Palace	d				18a52			18 43		18 30		19a07							19a22				19 13		19 00
Gipsy Hill	d							18 45		18 32													19 15		19 02
West Norwood	d							18 48		18 35													19 18		19 05
Streatham Hill	d							18 52															19 22		
Balham ⊖	d							18 55															19 25		
Wandsworth Common	d							18 57															19 27		
Clapham Junction	d							19 01															19 31		
South Bermondsey	d		18 15										18 37				18 45								
Peckham Rye	d			18 13		18 17				18 46								18 43		18 47					19 16
Queens Rd Peckham	d		18 18							18 49			18 39				18 48								19 19
Denmark Hill	d		18 23	18 17		18 21											18 53	18 47		18 51					
London Blackfriars ⊖	a																								
Clapham High Street ⊖	d		18 28														18 58								
Wandsworth Road	d		18 29														18 59								
Battersea Park	d		18 32					19 05									19 02						19 35		
London Victoria ⊖	a		18 36	18 26		18 30		19 09									19 06	18 56		19 00			19 39		
Penge West	d	18 45							19 00						18 54	19 15								19 30	
Anerley	d	18 47							19 02						18 56	19 17								19 32	
Norwood Junction	d	18 50							19 05						19 00	19 20								19 35	
West Croydon	a	19 01							19 12							19 31								19 42	
East Croydon	a														19 03										

Table 178

London Bridge to London Victoria - Croydon and East London Line

	LO	SN	LO	SN	LO		SN	SE	LO	SE	LO	SN	LO	SN	LO		SN	LO	SN	LO	SN	SE	LO	LO
London Bridge ⊖ d		19 03		19 06			19 11					19 22					19 33		19 36		19 41			
Dalston Junction Stn Ell d	19 00		19 05		19 10				19 15		19 20		19 25		19 30			19 35		19 40			19 45	19 50
Haggerston d	19 01		19 06		19 11				19 16		19 21		19 26		19 31			19 36		19 41			19 46	19 51
Hoxton d	19 03		19 08		19 13				19 18		19 23		19 28		19 33			19 38		19 43			19 48	19 53
Shoreditch High Street d	19 06		19 11		19 16				19 21		19 26		19 31		19 36			19 41		19 46			19 51	19 56
Whitechapel d	19 08		19 13		19 18				19 23		19 28		19 33		19 38			19 43		19 48			19 53	19 58
Shadwell d	19 10		19 15		19 20				19 25		19 30		19 35		19 40			19 45		19 50			19 55	20 00
Wapping d	19 12		19 17		19 22				19 27		19 32		19 37		19 42			19 47		19 52			19 57	20 02
Rotherhithe d	19 14		19 19		19 24				19 29		19 34		19 39		19 44			19 49		19 54			19 59	20 04
Canada Water d	19 16		19 21		19 26				19 31		19 36		19 41		19 46			19 51		19 56			20 01	20 06
Surrey Quays d	19 17		19 22		19 27				19 32		19 37		19 42		19 47			19 52		19 57			20 02	20 07
New Cross Ell a			19 28								19 43							19 58						20 13
New Cross Gate Station Ell a	19 21				19 31				19 36				19 46		19 51					20 01			20 06	
d	19 22				19 32				19 37				19 47		19 52					20 02			20 07	
New Cross Gate d				19 11								19 27							19 41					
Brockley d	19 24			19 14	19 34				19 39			19 30	19 49		19 54				19 44	20 04			20 09	
Honor Oak Park d	19 27			19 17	19 37				19 42			19 33	19 52		19 57				19 47	20 07			20 12	
Forest Hill d	19 30			19 19	19 40				19 45			19 35	19 55		20 00				19 49	20 10			20 15	
Sydenham d	19 32			19 22	19 42				19 47			19 38	19 57		20 02				19 52	20 12			20 17	
Crystal Palace d	19a37								19a52			19 43		19 30	20a07								20a22	
Gipsy Hill d												19 45		19 32										
West Norwood d												19 48		19 35										
Streatham Hill d												19 52												
Balham ⊖ d												19 55												
Wandsworth Common d												19 57												
Clapham Junction d												20 01												
South Bermondsey d		19 07					19 15										19 37				19 45			
Peckham Rye d								19 13		19 17				19 46								19 43		
Queens Rd Peckham d		19 09					19 18							19 49			19 39				19 48			
Denmark Hill d							19 23	19 17		19 21											19 53	19 47		
London Blackfriars ⊖ a																								
Clapham High Street ⊖ d							19 28														19 58			
Wandsworth Road d							19 29														19 59			
Battersea Park d							19 32					20 05									20 02			
London Victoria ⊖ a							19 36	19 26		19 30		20 09									20 06	19 56		
Penge West d				19 24	19 45								20 00						19 54	20 15				
Anerley d				19 26	19 47								20 02						19 56	20 17				
Norwood Junction d				19 30	19 50								20 05						20 00	20 20				
West Croydon a					20 01								20 15							20 31				
East Croydon a				19 33															20 03					

	SN		LO	SN	LO	LO	SN	LO	SN	SE	LO		LO	SN	LO	SN	LO	LO	SN	LO	SN		SE	LO
London Bridge ⊖ d	19 52						20 06		20 11					20 22					20 36		20 41			
Dalston Junction Stn Ell d			19 55		20 00	20 05		20 10			20 15		20 20		20 25		20 30	20 35		20 40				20 45
Haggerston d			19 56		20 01	20 06		20 11			20 16		20 21		20 26		20 31	20 36		20 41				20 46
Hoxton d			19 58		20 03	20 08		20 13			20 18		20 23		20 28		20 33	20 38		20 43				20 48
Shoreditch High Street d			20 01		20 06	20 11		20 16			20 21		20 26		20 31		20 36	20 41		20 46				20 51
Whitechapel d			20 03		20 08	20 13		20 18			20 23		20 28		20 33		20 38	20 43		20 48				20 53
Shadwell d			20 05		20 10	20 15		20 20			20 25		20 30		20 35		20 40	20 45		20 50				20 55
Wapping d			20 07		20 12	20 17		20 22			20 27		20 32		20 37		20 42	20 47		20 52				20 57
Rotherhithe d			20 09		20 14	20 19		20 24			20 29		20 34		20 39		20 44	20 49		20 54				20 59
Canada Water d			20 11		20 16	20 21		20 26			20 31		20 36		20 41		20 46	20 51		20 56				21 01
Surrey Quays d			20 12		20 17	20 22		20 27			20 32		20 37		20 42		20 47	20 52		20 57				21 02
New Cross Ell a						20 28							20 43					20 58						
New Cross Gate Station Ell a			20 16		20 21			20 31			20 36				20 46		20 51			21 01				21 06
d			20 17		20 22			20 32			20 37				20 47		20 52			21 02				21 07
New Cross Gate d	19 57						20 11							20 27					20 41					
Brockley d	20 00		20 19		20 24		20 14	20 34			20 39			20 30	20 49		20 54		20 44	21 04				21 09
Honor Oak Park d	20 03		20 22		20 27		20 17	20 37			20 42			20 33	20 52		20 57		20 47	21 07				21 12
Forest Hill d	20 05		20 25		20 30		20 19	20 40			20 45			20 35	20 55		21 00		20 49	21 10				21 15
Sydenham d	20 08		20 27		20 32		20 22	20 42			20 47			20 38	20 57		21 02		20 52	21 12				21 17
Crystal Palace d	20 13			20 00	20a37						20a52			20 43		20 30	21a07							21a22
Gipsy Hill d	20 15			20 03										20 45		20 33								
West Norwood d	20 18			20 06										20 48		20 36								
Streatham Hill d	20 22													20 52										
Balham ⊖ d	20 25													20 55										
Wandsworth Common d	20 27													20 57										
Clapham Junction d	20 31													21 01										
South Bermondsey d									20 15												20 45			
Peckham Rye d				20 17						20 13						20 46							20 43	
Queens Rd Peckham d				20 20					20 18							20 49					20 48			
Denmark Hill d									20 23	20 17											20 53		20 47	
London Blackfriars ⊖ a																								
Clapham High Street ⊖ d									20 28												20 58			
Wandsworth Road d									20 29												20 59			
Battersea Park d	20 35								20 32					21 05							21 02			
London Victoria ⊖ a	20 39								20 36	20 26				21 09							21 06		20 56	
Penge West d			20 30				20 24	20 45							21 00				20 54	21 15				
Anerley d			20 32				20 26	20 47							21 02				20 56	21 17				
Norwood Junction d			20 35				20 30	20 50							21 05				21 00	21 20				
West Croydon a			20 45					21 01							21 15					21 31				
East Croydon a							20 33												21 03					

Table 178

London Bridge to London Victoria - Croydon and East London Line

	LO	SN	LO	LO	LO	SN	LO		SN	SE	LO	LO	SN	LO	LO	LO	SN		LO	SN	SE	LO	LO	SN
London Bridge ⊖ d		20 52				21 06			21 11				21 22				21 36			21 41				21 52
Dalston Junction Stn Ell d	20 50		20 55	21 00	21 05		21 10				21 15	21 20		21 25	21 30	21 35			21 40			21 45	21 50	
Haggerston d	20 51		20 56	21 01	21 06		21 11				21 16	21 21		21 26	21 31	21 36			21 41			21 46	21 51	
Hoxton d	20 53		20 58	21 03	21 08		21 13				21 18	21 23		21 28	21 33	21 38			21 43			21 48	21 53	
Shoreditch High Street d	20 56		21 01	21 06	21 11		21 16				21 21	21 26		21 31	21 36	21 41			21 46			21 51	21 56	
Whitechapel d	20 58		21 03	21 08	21 13		21 18				21 23	21 28		21 33	21 38	21 43			21 48			21 53	21 58	
Shadwell d	21 00		21 05	21 10	21 15		21 20				21 25	21 30		21 35	21 40	21 45			21 50			21 55	22 00	
Wapping d	21 02		21 07	21 12	21 17		21 22				21 27	21 32		21 37	21 42	21 47			21 52			21 57	22 02	
Rotherhithe d	21 04		21 09	21 14	21 19		21 24				21 29	21 34		21 39	21 44	21 49			21 54			21 59	22 04	
Canada Water d	21 06		21 11	21 16	21 21		21 26				21 31	21 36		21 41	21 46	21 51			21 56			22 01	22 06	
Surrey Quays d	21 07		21 12	21 17	21 22		21 27				21 32	21 37		21 42	21 47	21 52			21 57			22 02	22 07	
New Cross Ell a	21 13				21 28							21 43				21 58							22 13	
New Cross Gate Station Ell a			21 16	21 21			21 31				21 36			21 46	21 51				22 01			22 06		
d			21 17	21 22			21 32				21 37			21 47	21 52				22 02			22 07		
New Cross Gate d		20 57				21 11							21 27				21 41							21 57
Brockley d		21 00	21 19	21 24		21 14	21 34				21 39		21 30	21 49	21 54		21 44		22 04			22 09		22 00
Honor Oak Park d		21 03	21 22	21 27		21 17	21 37				21 42		21 33	21 52	21 57		21 47		22 07			22 12		22 03
Forest Hill d		21 05	21 25	21 30		21 19	21 40				21 45		21 35	21 55	22 00		21 49		22 10			22 15		22 05
Sydenham d		21 08	21 27	21 32		21 22	21 42				21 47		21 38	21 57	22 02		21 52		22 12			22 17		22 08
Crystal Palace d		21 13		21a37							21a52		21 43		22a07							22a22		22 13
Gipsy Hill d		21 15											21 45											22 15
West Norwood d		21 18											21 48											22 18
Streatham Hill d		21 22											21 52											22 22
Balham ⊖ d		21 25											21 55											22 25
Wandsworth Common d		21 27											21 57											22 27
Clapham Junction d		21 31											22 01											22 31
South Bermondsey d									21 15											21 45				
Peckham Rye d										21 13											21 43			
Queens Rd Peckham d									21 18											21 48				
Denmark Hill d									21 23	21 17										21 53	21 47			
London Blackfriars ⊖ a																								
Clapham High Street ⊖ d									21 28											21 58				
Wandsworth Road d									21 29											21 59				
Battersea Park d		21 35							21 32				22 05							22 02				22 35
London Victoria ⊖ a		21 39							21 36	21 26			22 09							22 06	21 56.			22 39
Penge West d			21 30			21 24	21 45							22 00			21 54		22 15					
Anerley d			21 32			21 26	21 47							22 02			21 56		22 17					
Norwood Junction d			21 35			21 30	21 50							22 05			22 00		22 20					
West Croydon a			21 45				22 01							22 12					22 31					
East Croydon a						21 33											22 04							

	LO	LO	SN		LO	SN	SE	LO	SN	LO	SN	LO		SN	SE	LO	SN	LO	SN	LO	SN	
London Bridge ⊖ d			22 06			22 11			22 22		22 36			22 41			22 52		23 06		23 11	
Dalston Junction Stn Ell d	21 55	22 00			22 10			22 20		22 30		22 40				22 50		23 00		23 10		
Haggerston d	21 56	22 01			22 11			22 21		22 31		22 41				22 51		23 01		23 11		
Hoxton d	21 58	22 03			22 13			22 23		22 33		22 43				22 53		23 03		23 13		
Shoreditch High Street d	22 01	22 06			22 16			22 26		22 36		22 46				22 56		23 06		23 16		
Whitechapel d	22 03	22 08			22 18			22 28		22 38		22 48				22 58		23 08		23 18		
Shadwell d	22 05	22 10			22 20			22 30		22 40		22 50				23 00		23 10		23 20		
Wapping d	22 07	22 12			22 22			22 32		22 42		22 52				23 02		23 12		23 22		
Rotherhithe d	22 09	22 14			22 24			22 34		22 44		22 54				23 04		23 14		23 24		
Canada Water d	22 11	22 16			22 26			22 36		22 46		22 56				23 06		23 16		23 26		
Surrey Quays d	22 12	22 17			22 27			22 37		22 47		22 57				23 07		23 17		23 27		
New Cross Ell a								22 43								23 13						
New Cross Gate Station Ell a	22 16	22 21			22 31					22 51		23 01						23 21		23 31		
d	22 17	22 22			22 32					22 52		23 02						23 22		23 32		
New Cross Gate d			22 11						22 27		22 41						22 57		23 11			
Brockley d	22 19	22 24	22 14		22 34				22 30	22 54	22 44	23 04					23 00	23 24	23 14	23 34		
Honor Oak Park d	22 22	22 27	22 17		22 37				22 33	22 57	22 47	23 07					23 03	23 27	23 17	23 37		
Forest Hill d	22 25	22 30	22 19		22 40				22 35	23 00	22 49	23 10					23 05	23 30	23 19	23 40		
Sydenham d	22 27	22 32	22 22		22 42				22 38	23 02	22 52	23 12					23 08	23 32	23 22	23 42		
Crystal Palace d		22a37							22 43	23a07							23 13	23a37				
Gipsy Hill d									22 45								23 15					
West Norwood d									22 48								23 18					
Streatham Hill d									22 52								23 22					
Balham ⊖ d									22 55								23 25					
Wandsworth Common d									22 57								23 27					
Clapham Junction d									23 01								23 31					
South Bermondsey d						22 15								22 45							23 15	
Peckham Rye d							22 13								22 43							
Queens Rd Peckham d						22 18								22 48							23 18	
Denmark Hill d						22 23	22 17							22 53	22 47						23 23	
London Blackfriars ⊖ a																						
Clapham High Street ⊖ d						22 28								22 58							23 28	
Wandsworth Road d						22 29								22 59							23 29	
Battersea Park d						22 32			23 05					23 02			23 35				23 32	
London Victoria ⊖ a						22 36	22 26		23 10					23 06	22 56		23 40				23 37	
Penge West d	22 30		22 24		22 45						22 54	23 15							23 24	23 45		
Anerley d	22 32		22 26		22 47						22 56	23 17							23 26	23 47		
Norwood Junction d	22 35		22 30		22 50						23 00	23 20							23 30	23 50		
West Croydon a	22 42				23 01							23 31								00 01		
East Croydon a			22 35								23 03								23 33			

Table 178

Saturdays

London Bridge to London Victoria - Croydon and East London Line

Station		SE	LO	SN	LO	SN	LO	SN
London Bridge 4 ⊖	d			23 22		23 36		23 48
Dalston Junction Stn Ell	d		23 20		23 30		23 40	
Haggerston	d		23 21		23 31		23 41	
Hoxton	d		23 23		23 33		23 43	
Shoreditch High Street	d		23 26		23 36		23 46	
Whitechapel	d		23 28		23 38		23 48	
Shadwell	d		23 30		23 40		23 50	
Wapping	d		23 32		23 42		23 52	
Rotherhithe	d		23 34		23 44		23 54	
Canada Water	d		23 36		23 46		23 56	
Surrey Quays	d		23 37		23 47		23 57	
New Cross Ell	a		23 43					
New Cross Gate Station Ell	a				23 51		00 02	
	d				23 52		00 03	
New Cross Gate 4	d			23 27		23 41		
Brockley	d			23 30	23 54	23 44	00 04	
Honor Oak Park	d			23 33	23 57	23 47	00 07	
Forest Hill 4	d			23 35	23 59	23 49	00 10	
Sydenham	d			23 38	00 02	23 52	00 12	
Crystal Palace 4	d			23 43	00a07			
Gipsy Hill	d			23 45				
West Norwood 4	d			23 48				
Streatham Hill	d			23 52				
Balham 4 ⊖	d			23 55				
Wandsworth Common	d			23 57				
Clapham Junction 10	d			00 02				
South Bermondsey	d							23 52
Peckham Rye 4	d	23 13						
Queens Rd Peckham	d							23 54
Denmark Hill 4	d	23 17						
London Blackfriars 3 ⊖	a							
Clapham High Street ⊖	d							
Wandsworth Road	d							
Battersea Park 4	d			00 05				
London Victoria 15 ⊖	a	23 26		00 10				
Penge West	d					23 54	00 15	
Anerley	d					23 56	00 17	
Norwood Junction 2	d					23 59	00 20	00a22
West Croydon 4	a						00 27	
East Croydon	a					00 03		

Table 178

Sundays

London Bridge to London Victoria - Croydon and East London Line

Station		LO	SN	LO	SN	LO	LO	SN	SN	SN		FC	FC	LO	LO	SN	SE	LO	SN	LO		SN	SE	SN	LO
												🚌	🚌												
London Bridge 4 ⊖	d		23p22		23p36				00 06	00 36		01 00	06 05			07 11			07 24			07 39		07 41	
Dalston Junction Stn Ell	d	23p10		23p30		23p40	23p45							06 56				07 12		07 26					07 42
Haggerston	d	23p11		23p31		23p41	23p46							06 57				07 13		07 27					07 43
Hoxton	d	23p13		23p33		23p43	23p48							06 59				07 15		07 29					07 45
Shoreditch High Street	d	23p16		23p36		23p46	23p51							07 02				07 18		07 32					07 48
Whitechapel	d	23p18		23p38		23p48	23p53							07 04				07 20		07 34					07 50
Shadwell	d	23p20		23p40		23p50	23p55							07 06				07 22		07 36					07 52
Wapping	d	23p22		23p42		23p52	23p57							07 08				07 24		07 38					07 54
Rotherhithe	d	23p24		23p44		23p54	23p59							07 10				07 26		07 40					07 56
Canada Water	d	23p26		23p46		23p56	00 02							07 12				07 28		07 42					07 58
Surrey Quays	d	23p27		23p47		23p57	00 03							07 13				07 29		07 43					07 59
New Cross Ell	a																								
New Cross Gate Station Ell	a	23p31		23p51		00 02	00 06							07 17				07 33		07 47					08 03
	d	23p32		23p52		00 03	00 07							07 18	07 04			07 34		07 48					08 04
New Cross Gate 4	d		23p27		23p41				00 11	00 41									07 29			07 44			
Brockley	d	23p34	23p30	23p54	23p44	00 04	00 09		00 14	00 44				07 20	07 06			07 36	07 32	07 50		07 47			08 06
Honor Oak Park	d	23p37	23p33	23p57	23p47	00 07	00 12		00 17	00 47				07 23	07 09			07 39	07 35	07 53		07 50			08 09
Forest Hill 4	d	23p40	23p35	23p59	23p49	00 10	00 15		00 19	00 49				07 26	07 12			07 42	07 37	07 56		07 52			08 12
Sydenham	d	23p42	23p38	00 02	23p52	00 12	00 17		00 22	00 52				07 28	07 14			07 44	07 40	07 58		07 55			08 14
Crystal Palace 4	d		23p43	00a07			00a22	00 03						07a33						08a03					
Gipsy Hill	d		23p45																						
West Norwood 4	d		23p48																						
Streatham Hill	d		23p52																						
Balham 4 ⊖	d		23p55																						
Wandsworth Common	d		23p57																						
Clapham Junction 10	d		00 02																						
South Bermondsey	d															07 15								07 45	
Peckham Rye 4	d																07 12						07 42		
Queens Rd Peckham	d															07 18								07 48	
Denmark Hill 4	d															07 23	07 16						07 46	07 53	
London Blackfriars 3 ⊖	a											01 15	06 20												
Clapham High Street ⊖	d															07 28								07 58	
Wandsworth Road	d															07 29								07 59	
Battersea Park 4	d		00 05													07 32								08 02	
London Victoria 15 ⊖	a		00 10													07 36	07 25						07 56	08 06	
Penge West	d	23p45			23p54	00 15			00 24	00 54					07 17			07 47				07 57			08 17
Anerley	d	23p47			23p56	00 17			00 26	00 56					07 19			07 49				07 59			08 19
Norwood Junction 2	d	23p50			23p59	00 20		00 09	00 30	01 00					07 22			07 52	07 48			08 03			08 22
West Croydon 4	a	00 01				00 27		00 14							07 30			08 00	07 55						08 29
East Croydon	a				00 03				00 33	01 03												08 06			

Station		SN	LO	SN	SE	SN		LO	LO	SN	LO	LO	SN	SN	SE	LO		LO	SN	LO	LO	SN	SN	SE	LO
London Bridge 4 ⊖	d	07 54		08 09		08 11				08 24			08 39	08 41					08 54			09 09	09 11		
Dalston Junction Stn Ell	d		07 56					08 12	08 22		08 26	08 37				08 42		08 52		08 56	09 07				09 12
Haggerston	d		07 57					08 13	08 23		08 27	08 38				08 43		08 53		08 57	09 08				09 13
Hoxton	d		07 59					08 15	08 25		08 29	08 40				08 45		08 55		08 59	09 10				09 15
Shoreditch High Street	d		08 02					08 18	08 28		08 32	08 43				08 48		08 58		09 02	09 13				09 18
Whitechapel	d		08 04					08 20	08 30		08 34	08 45				08 50		09 00		09 04	09 15				09 20
Shadwell	d		08 06					08 22	08 32		08 36	08 47				08 52		09 02		09 06	09 17				09 22
Wapping	d		08 08					08 24	08 34		08 38	08 49				08 54		09 04		09 08	09 19				09 24
Rotherhithe	d		08 10					08 26	08 36		08 40	08 51				08 56		09 06		09 10	09 21				09 26
Canada Water	d		08 12					08 28	08 38		08 42	08 53				08 58		09 08		09 12	09 23				09 28
Surrey Quays	d		08 13					08 29	08 39		08 43	08 54				08 59		09 09		09 13	09 24				09 29
New Cross Ell	a								08 45			09 00						09 15			09 30				
New Cross Gate Station Ell	a		08 17					08 33			08 47					09 03				09 17					09 33
	d		08 18					08 34			08 48					09 04				09 18					09 34
New Cross Gate 4	d	07 59		08 14						08 29			08 44						08 59			09 14			
Brockley	d	08 02	08 20	08 17				08 36		08 32	08 50		08 47			09 06			09 02	09 20		09 17			09 36
Honor Oak Park	d	08 05	08 23	08 20				08 39		08 35	08 53		08 50			09 09			09 05	09 23		09 20			09 39
Forest Hill 4	d	08 07	08 26	08 22				08 42		08 37	08 56		08 52			09 12			09 07	09 26		09 22			09 42
Sydenham	d	08 10	08 28	08 25				08 44		08 40	08 58		08 55			09 14			09 10	09 28		09 25			09 44
Crystal Palace 4	d		08a33								09a03									09a33					
Gipsy Hill	d																								
West Norwood 4	d																								
Streatham Hill	d																								
Balham 4 ⊖	d																								
Wandsworth Common	d																								
Clapham Junction 10	d																								
South Bermondsey	d					08 15								08 45									09 15		
Peckham Rye 4	d				08 12										08 42									09 12	
Queens Rd Peckham	d					08 18								08 48									09 18		
Denmark Hill 4	d				08 16	08 23								08 53	08 46								09 23	09 16	
London Blackfriars 3 ⊖	a																								
Clapham High Street ⊖	d					08 28								08 58									09 28		
Wandsworth Road	d					08 29								08 59									09 29		
Battersea Park 4	d					08 32								09 02									09 32		
London Victoria 15 ⊖	a				08 26	08 36								09 06	08 55								09 36	09 25	
Penge West	d			08 27				08 47					08 57			09 17						09 27			09 47
Anerley	d			08 29				08 49					08 59			09 19						09 29			09 49
Norwood Junction 2	d	08 16		08 33				08 52		08 46			09 03			09 22			09 16			09 33			09 52
West Croydon 4	a	08 24						08 59		08 54						09 29			09 24						09 59
East Croydon	a			08 36									09 06									09 36			

Table 178

Sundays

London Bridge to London Victoria - Croydon and East London Line

		LO		SN	LO	LO	SN	SN	SE	LO	LO	SN		LO	LO	SN	SN	SE	LO	LO	SN	LO		LO	SN
London Bridge ⊖	d			09 24			09 39	09 41				09 54				10 09	10 11				10 24				10 39
Dalston Junction Stn Ell	d	09 22			09 26	09 37				09 42	09 52			09 56	10 07				10 12	10 22		10 26		10 37	
Haggerston	d	09 23			09 27	09 38				09 43	09 53			09 57	10 08				10 13	10 23		10 27		10 38	
Hoxton	d	09 25			09 29	09 40				09 45	09 55			09 59	10 10				10 15	10 25		10 29		10 40	
Shoreditch High Street	d	09 28			09 32	09 43				09 48	09 58			10 02	10 13				10 18	10 28		10 32		10 43	
Whitechapel	d	09 30			09 34	09 45				09 50	10 00			10 04	10 15				10 20	10 30		10 34		10 45	
Shadwell	d	09 32			09 36	09 47				09 52	10 02			10 06	10 17				10 22	10 32		10 36		10 47	
Wapping	d	09 34			09 38	09 49				09 54	10 04			10 08	10 19				10 24	10 34		10 38		10 49	
Rotherhithe	d	09 36			09 40	09 51				09 56	10 06			10 10	10 21				10 26	10 36		10 40		10 51	
Canada Water	d	09 38			09 42	09 53				09 58	10 08			10 12	10 23				10 28	10 38		10 42		10 53	
Surrey Quays	d	09 39			09 43	09 54				09 59	10 09			10 13	10 24				10 29	10 39		10 43		10 54	
New Cross Ell	a	09 45				10 00					10 15				10 30					10 45				11 00	
New Cross Gate Station Ell	a				09 47					10 03				10 17					10 33			10 47			
	d				09 48					10 04				10 18					10 34			10 48			
New Cross Gate	d			09 29			09 44					09 59				10 14					10 29				10 44
Brockley	d			09 32	09 50		09 47			10 06		10 02		10 20		10 17			10 36		10 32	10 50			10 47
Honor Oak Park	d			09 35	09 53		09 50			10 09		10 05		10 23		10 20			10 39		10 35	10 53			10 50
Forest Hill	d			09 37	09 56		09 52			10 12		10 07		10 26		10 22			10 42		10 37	10 56			10 52
Sydenham	d			09 40	09 58		09 55			10 14		10 10		10 28		10 25			10 44		10 40	10 58			10 55
Crystal Palace	d				10a03									10a33								11a03			
Gipsy Hill	d																								
West Norwood	d																								
Streatham Hill	d																								
Balham ⊖	d																								
Wandsworth Common	d																								
Clapham Junction	d																								
South Bermondsey	d							09 45									10 15								
Peckham Rye	d								09 42									10 12							
Queens Rd Peckham	d							09 48									10 18								
Denmark Hill	d							09 53	09 46								10 23	10 16							
London Blackfriars ⊖	a																								
Clapham High Street ⊖	d							09 58									10 28								
Wandsworth Road	d							09 59									10 29								
Battersea Park	d							10 02									10 32								
London Victoria ⊖	a							10 06	09 55.								10 36	10 25.							
Penge West	d						09 57			10 17						10 27			10 47						10 57
Anerley	d						09 59			10 19						10 29			10 49						10 59
Norwood Junction	d			09 46			10 03			10 22		10 16				10 33			10 52		10 46				11 03
West Croydon	a			09 54						10 29		10 24							10 59		10 54				
East Croydon	a						10 06									10 36									11 06

		SN	SE	LO	LO	SN	LO	LO		SN	SN	SE	LO	LO	SN	LO	LO	SN		SN	SE	LO	LO	LO	SN
London Bridge ⊖	d	10 41				10 54				11 09	11 11				11 24			11 39		11 41					11 54
Dalston Junction Stn Ell	d			10 42	10 52		10 56	11 07					11 12	11 22		11 26	11 37					11 42	11 48	11 52	
Haggerston	d			10 43	10 53		10 57	11 08					11 13	11 23		11 27	11 38					11 43	11 49	11 53	
Hoxton	d			10 45	10 55		10 59	11 10					11 15	11 25		11 29	11 40					11 45	11 51	11 55	
Shoreditch High Street	d			10 48	10 58		11 02	11 13					11 18	11 28		11 32	11 43					11 48	11 54	11 58	
Whitechapel	d			10 50	11 00		11 04	11 15					11 20	11 30		11 34	11 45					11 50	11 56	12 00	
Shadwell	d			10 52	11 02		11 06	11 17					11 22	11 32		11 36	11 47					11 52	11 58	12 02	
Wapping	d			10 54	11 04		11 08	11 19					11 24	11 34		11 38	11 49					11 54	12 00	12 04	
Rotherhithe	d			10 56	11 06		11 10	11 21					11 26	11 36		11 40	11 51					11 56	12 02	12 06	
Canada Water	d			10 58	11 08		11 12	11 23					11 28	11 38		11 42	11 53					11 58	12 04	12 08	
Surrey Quays	d			10 59	11 09		11 13	11 24					11 29	11 39		11 43	11 54					11 59	12 05	12 09	
New Cross Ell	a				11 15			11 30						11 45			12 00							12 15	
New Cross Gate Station Ell	a			11 03			11 17						11 33			11 47						12 03	12 09		
	d			11 04			11 18						11 34			11 48						12 04	12 10		
New Cross Gate	d					10 59				11 14					11 29			11 44							11 59
Brockley	d			11 06		11 02	11 20			11 17			11 36		11 32	11 50		11 47				12 06	12 12		12 02
Honor Oak Park	d			11 09		11 05	11 23			11 20			11 39		11 35	11 53		11 50				12 09	12 15		12 05
Forest Hill	d			11 12		11 07	11 26			11 22			11 42		11 37	11 56		11 52				12 12	12 18		12 07
Sydenham	d			11 14		11 10	11 28			11 25			11 44		11 40	11 58		11 55				12 14	12 20		12 10
Crystal Palace	d						11a33									12a03							12a25		
Gipsy Hill	d																								
West Norwood	d																								
Streatham Hill	d																								
Balham ⊖	d																								
Wandsworth Common	d																								
Clapham Junction	d																								
South Bermondsey	d	10 45									11 15									11 45					
Peckham Rye	d		10 42									11 12									11 42				
Queens Rd Peckham	d	10 48									11 18									11 48					
Denmark Hill	d	10 53	10 46								11 23	11 16								11 53	11 46				
London Blackfriars ⊖	a																								
Clapham High Street ⊖	d	10 58									11 28									11 58					
Wandsworth Road	d	10 59									11 29									11 59					
Battersea Park	d	11 02									11 32									12 02					
London Victoria ⊖	a	11 06	10 55								11 36	11 25								12 06	11 55.				
Penge West	d			11 17						11 27			11 47					11 57				12 17			
Anerley	d			11 19						11 29			11 49					11 59				12 19			
Norwood Junction	d			11 22		11 16				11 33			11 52		11 46			12 03				12 22			12 16
West Croydon	a			11 29		11 24							11 59		11 54							12 29			12 24
East Croydon	a									11 36								12 06							

Table 178

Sundays

London Bridge to London Victoria - Croydon and East London Line

		LO	LO	LO		SN	SN	SE	LO	LO	LO	SN	LO	LO		LO	SN	SN	SE	LO	LO	LO	SN	LO	
London Bridge ⊖	d					12 09	12 11					12 24					12 39	12 41					12 54		
Dalston Junction Stn Ell	d	11 57	12 03	12 08					12 13	12 18	12 23		12 28	12 33		12 38				12 43	12 48	12 53		12 58	
Haggerston	d	11 58	12 04	12 09					12 14	12 19	12 24		12 29	12 34		12 39				12 44	12 49	12 54		12 59	
Hoxton	d	12 00	12 06	12 11					12 16	12 21	12 26		12 31	12 36		12 41				12 46	12 51	12 56		13 01	
Shoreditch High Street	d	12 03	12 09	12 14					12 19	12 24	12 29		12 34	12 39		12 44				12 49	12 54	12 59		13 04	
Whitechapel	d	12 05	12 11	12 16					12 21	12 26	12 31		12 36	12 41		12 46				12 51	12 56	13 01		13 06	
Shadwell	d	12 07	12 13	12 18					12 23	12 28	12 33		12 38	12 43		12 48				12 53	12 58	13 03		13 08	
Wapping	d	12 09	12 15	12 20					12 25	12 30	12 35		12 40	12 45		12 50				12 55	13 00	13 05		13 10	
Rotherhithe	d	12 11	12 17	12 22					12 27	12 32	12 37		12 42	12 47		12 52				12 57	13 02	13 07		13 12	
Canada Water	d	12 13	12 19	12 24					12 29	12 34	12 39		12 44	12 49		12 54				12 59	13 04	13 09		13 14	
Surrey Quays	d	12 14	12 20	12 25					12 30	12 35	12 40		12 45	12 50		12 55				13 00	13 05	13 10		13 15	
New Cross Ell	a			12 31							12 46					13 01						13 16			
New Cross Gate Station Ell	a	12 18	12 24						12 34	12 39			12 49	12 54						13 04	13 09			13 19	
	d	12 21	12 25						12 35	12 40			12 50	12 55						13 05	13 10			13 20	
New Cross Gate	d					12 14						12 29					12 44						12 59		
Brockley	d	12 23	12 27			12 17			12 37	12 42		12 32	12 52	12 57			12 47			13 07	13 12		13 02	13 22	
Honor Oak Park	d	12 26	12 30			12 20			12 40	12 45		12 35	12 55	13 00			12 50			13 10	13 15		13 05	13 25	
Forest Hill	d	12 29	12 33			12 22			12 43	12 48		12 37	12 58	13 03			12 52			13 13	13 18		13 07	13 28	
Sydenham	d	12 31	12 35			12 25			12 45	12 50		12 40	13 00	13 05			12 55			13 15	13 20		13 10	13 30	
Crystal Palace	d		12a40							12a55				13a10							13a25				
Gipsy Hill	d																								
West Norwood	d																								
Streatham Hill	d																								
Balham ⊖	d																								
Wandsworth Common	d																								
Clapham Junction	d																								
South Bermondsey	d						12 15											12 45							
Peckham Rye	d							12 12											12 42						
Queens Rd Peckham	d						12 18											12 48							
Denmark Hill	d						12 23	12 16										12 53	12 46						
London Blackfriars ⊖	a																								
Clapham High Street ⊖	d						12 28											12 58							
Wandsworth Road	d						12 29											12 59							
Battersea Park	d						12 32											13 02							
London Victoria ⊖	a						12 36	12 25										13 06	12 55						
Penge West	d	12 34				12 27			12 48				13 03				12 57			13 18				13 33	
Anerley	d	12 36				12 29			12 50				13 05				12 59			13 20				13 35	
Norwood Junction	d	12 39				12 33			12 53			12 46	13 08				13 03			13 23			13 16	13 38	
West Croydon	a	12 46							13 00			12 54	13 15							13 30			13 24	13 45	
East Croydon	a					12 36											13 06								

		LO	LO	SN	SN	SE	LO	LO	LO	SN		LO	LO	LO	SN	SN	SE	LO	LO	LO		SN	LO	LO	LO
London Bridge ⊖	d			13 09	13 11					13 24					13 39	13 41						13 54			
Dalston Junction Stn Ell	d	13 03	13 08				13 13	13 18	13 23			13 28	13 33	13 38				13 43	13 48	13 53			13 58	14 03	14 08
Haggerston	d	13 04	13 09				13 14	13 19	13 24			13 29	13 34	13 39				13 44	13 49	13 54			13 59	14 04	14 09
Hoxton	d	13 06	13 11				13 16	13 21	13 26			13 31	13 36	13 41				13 46	13 51	13 56			14 01	14 06	14 11
Shoreditch High Street	d	13 09	13 14				13 19	13 24	13 29			13 34	13 39	13 44				13 49	13 54	13 59			14 04	14 09	14 14
Whitechapel	d	13 11	13 16				13 21	13 26	13 31			13 36	13 41	13 46				13 51	13 56	14 01			14 06	14 11	14 16
Shadwell	d	13 13	13 18				13 23	13 28	13 33			13 38	13 43	13 48				13 53	13 58	14 03			14 08	14 13	14 18
Wapping	d	13 15	13 20				13 25	13 30	13 35			13 40	13 45	13 50				13 55	14 00	14 05			14 10	14 15	14 20
Rotherhithe	d	13 17	13 22				13 27	13 32	13 37			13 42	13 47	13 52				13 57	14 02	14 07			14 12	14 17	14 22
Canada Water	d	13 19	13 24				13 29	13 34	13 39			13 44	13 49	13 54				13 59	14 04	14 09			14 14	14 19	14 24
Surrey Quays	d	13 20	13 25				13 30	13 35	13 40			13 45	13 50	13 55				14 00	14 05	14 10			14 15	14 20	14 25
New Cross Ell	a		13 31						13 46					14 01						14 16					14 31
New Cross Gate Station Ell	a	13 24					13 34	13 39				13 49	13 54					14 04	14 09				14 19	14 24	
	d	13 25					13 35	13 40				13 50	13 55					14 05	14 10				14 20	14 25	
New Cross Gate	d			13 14						13 29					13 44							13 59			
Brockley	d	13 27		13 17			13 37	13 42		13 32		13 52	13 57		13 47			14 07	14 12			14 02	14 22	14 27	
Honor Oak Park	d	13 30		13 20			13 40	13 45		13 35		13 55	14 00		13 50			14 10	14 15			14 05	14 25	14 30	
Forest Hill	d	13 33		13 22			13 43	13 48		13 37		13 58	14 03		13 52			14 13	14 18			14 07	14 28	14 33	
Sydenham	d	13 35		13 25			13 45	13 50		13 40		14 00	14 05		13 55			14 15	14 20			14 10	14 30	14 35	
Crystal Palace	d	13a40						13a55					14a10						14a25					14a40	
Gipsy Hill	d																								
West Norwood	d																								
Streatham Hill	d																								
Balham ⊖	d																								
Wandsworth Common	d																								
Clapham Junction	d																								
South Bermondsey	d				13 15											13 45									
Peckham Rye	d					13 12											13 42								
Queens Rd Peckham	d				13 18											13 48									
Denmark Hill	d				13 23	13 16										13 53	13 46								
London Blackfriars ⊖	a																								
Clapham High Street ⊖	d				13 28											13 58									
Wandsworth Road	d				13 29											13 59									
Battersea Park	d				13 32											14 02									
London Victoria ⊖	a				13 36	13 25										14 06	13 55.								
Penge West	d			13 27			13 48					14 03			13 57			14 18					14 33		
Anerley	d			13 29			13 50					14 05			13 59			14 20					14 35		
Norwood Junction	d			13 33			13 53			13 46		14 08			14 03			14 23				14 16	14 38		
West Croydon	a						14 00			13 54		14 15						14 30				14 24	14 45		
East Croydon	a			13 36											14 06										

London Bridge to London Victoria - Croydon and East London Line

		SN	SN	SE	LO	LO		LO	SN	LO	LO	LO	SN	SN	SE	LO		LO	LO	SN	LO	LO	LO	SN	SN
London Bridge 4 ⊖	d	14 09	14 11						14 24				14 39	14 41						14 54				15 09	15 11
Dalston Junction Stn Ell	d				14 13	14 18		14 23		14 28	14 33	14 38				14 43		14 48	14 53		14 58	15 03	15 08		
Haggerston	d				14 14	14 19		14 24		14 29	14 34	14 39				14 44		14 49	14 54		14 59	15 04	15 09		
Hoxton	d				14 16	14 21		14 26		14 31	14 36	14 41				14 46		14 51	14 56		15 01	15 06	15 11		
Shoreditch High Street	d				14 19	14 24		14 29		14 34	14 39	14 44				14 49		14 54	14 59		15 04	15 09	15 14		
Whitechapel	d				14 21	14 26		14 31		14 36	14 41	14 46				14 51		14 56	15 01		15 06	15 11	15 16		
Shadwell	d				14 23	14 28		14 33		14 38	14 43	14 48				14 53		14 58	15 03		15 08	15 13	15 18		
Wapping	d				14 25	14 30		14 35		14 40	14 45	14 50				14 55		15 00	15 05		15 10	15 15	15 20		
Rotherhithe	d				14 27	14 32		14 37		14 42	14 47	14 52				14 57		15 02	15 07		15 12	15 17	15 22		
Canada Water	d				14 29	14 34		14 39		14 44	14 49	14 54				14 59		15 04	15 09		15 14	15 19	15 24		
Surrey Quays	d				14 30	14 35		14 40		14 45	14 50	14 55				15 00		15 05	15 10		15 15	15 20	15 25		
New Cross Ell	a							14 46				15 01							15 16				15 31		
New Cross Gate Station Ell	a				14 34	14 39				14 49	14 54					15 04		15 09			15 19	15 24			
	d				14 35	14 40				14 50	14 55					15 05		15 10			15 20	15 25			
New Cross Gate 4	d	14 14							14 29				14 44							14 59				15 14	
Brockley	d	14 17			14 37	14 42			14 32	14 52	14 57		14 47			15 07		15 12		15 02	15 22	15 27		15 17	
Honor Oak Park	d	14 20			14 40	14 45			14 35	14 55	15 00		14 50			15 10		15 15		15 05	15 25	15 30		15 20	
Forest Hill 4	d	14 22			14 43	14 48			14 37	14 58	15 03		14 52			15 13		15 18		15 07	15 28	15 33		15 22	
Sydenham	d	14 25			14 45	14 50			14 40	15 00	15 05		14 55			15 15		15 20		15 10	15 30	15 35		15 25	
Crystal Palace 4	d					14a55					15a10							15a25				15a40			
Gipsy Hill	d																								
West Norwood 4	d																								
Streatham Hill	d																								
Balham 4 ⊖	d																								
Wandsworth Common	d																								
Clapham Junction 10	d																								
South Bermondsey	d		14 15											14 45											15 15
Peckham Rye 4	d			14 12											14 42										
Queens Rd Peckham	d		14 18											14 48											15 18
Denmark Hill 4	d		14 23	14 16										14 53	14 46										15 23
London Blackfriars 3 ⊖	a																								
Clapham High Street ⊖	d		14 28											14 58											15 28
Wandsworth Road	d		14 29											14 59											15 29
Battersea Park 4	d		14 32											15 02											15 32
London Victoria 15 ⊖	a		14 36	14 25										15 06	14 55										15 36
Penge West	d	14 27			14 48					15 03			14 57			15 18					15 33			15 27	
Anerley	d	14 29			14 50					15 05			14 59			15 20					15 35			15 29	
Norwood Junction 2	d	14 33			14 53				14 46	15 08			15 03			15 23				15 16	15 38			15 33	
West Croydon 4	a				15 00				14 54	15 15						15 30				15 24	15 45				
East Croydon	a	14 36											15 06											15 36	

		SE		LO	LO	LO	SN	LO	LO	LO	SN	SN		SE	LO	LO	LO	SN	LO	LO	LO	SN		SN	SE
London Bridge 4 ⊖	d						15 24				15 39	15 41						15 54				16 09		16 11	
Dalston Junction Stn Ell	d			15 13	15 18	15 23		15 28	15 33	15 38					15 43	15 48	15 53		15 58	16 03	16 08				
Haggerston	d			15 14	15 19	15 24		15 29	15 34	15 39					15 44	15 49	15 54		15 59	16 04	16 09				
Hoxton	d			15 16	15 21	15 26		15 31	15 36	15 41					15 46	15 51	15 56		16 01	16 06	16 11				
Shoreditch High Street	d			15 19	15 24	15 29		15 34	15 39	15 44					15 49	15 54	15 59		16 04	16 09	16 14				
Whitechapel	d			15 21	15 26	15 31		15 36	15 41	15 46					15 51	15 56	16 01		16 06	16 11	16 16				
Shadwell	d			15 23	15 28	15 33		15 38	15 43	15 48					15 53	15 58	16 03		16 08	16 13	16 18				
Wapping	d			15 25	15 30	15 35		15 40	15 45	15 50					15 55	16 00	16 05		16 10	16 15	16 20				
Rotherhithe	d			15 27	15 32	15 37		15 42	15 47	15 52					15 57	16 02	16 07		16 12	16 17	16 22				
Canada Water	d			15 29	15 34	15 39		15 44	15 49	15 54					15 59	16 04	16 09		16 14	16 19	16 24				
Surrey Quays	d			15 30	15 35	15 40		15 45	15 50	15 55					16 00	16 05	16 10		16 15	16 20	16 25				
New Cross Ell	a					15 46				16 01							16 16				16 31				
New Cross Gate Station Ell	a			15 34	15 39			15 49	15 54						16 04	16 09			16 19	16 24					
	d			15 35	15 40			15 50	15 55						16 05	16 10			16 20	16 25					
New Cross Gate 4	d						15 29				15 44							15 59				16 14			
Brockley	d			15 37	15 42		15 32	15 52	15 57		15 47				16 07	16 12		16 02	16 22	16 27		16 17			
Honor Oak Park	d			15 40	15 45		15 35	15 55	16 00		15 50				16 10	16 15		16 05	16 25	16 30		16 20			
Forest Hill 4	d			15 43	15 48		15 37	15 58	16 03		15 52				16 13	16 18		16 07	16 28	16 33		16 22			
Sydenham	d			15 45	15 50		15 40	16 00	16 05		15 55				16 15	16 20		16 10	16 30	16 35		16 25			
Crystal Palace 4	d				15a55				16a10							16a25				16a40					
Gipsy Hill	d																								
West Norwood 4	d																								
Streatham Hill	d																								
Balham 4 ⊖	d																								
Wandsworth Common	d																								
Clapham Junction 10	d																								
South Bermondsey	d											15 45												16 15	
Peckham Rye 4	d	15 12												15 42											16 12
Queens Rd Peckham	d											15 48												16 18	
Denmark Hill 4	d	15 16										15 53		15 46										16 23	16 16
London Blackfriars 3 ⊖	a																								
Clapham High Street ⊖	d											15 58												16 28	
Wandsworth Road	d											15 59												16 29	
Battersea Park 4	d											16 02												16 32	
London Victoria 15 ⊖	a	15 25										16 06		15 55										16 36	16 25
Penge West	d			15 48				16 03			15 57				16 18				16 33			16 27			
Anerley	d			15 50				16 05			15 59				16 20				16 35			16 29			
Norwood Junction 2	d			15 53			15 46	16 08			16 03				16 23			16 16	16 38			16 33			
West Croydon 4	a			16 00			15 54	16 15							16 30			16 24	16 45						
East Croydon	a										16 06											16 36			

London Bridge to London Victoria - Croydon and East London Line

		LO	LO	LO	SN	LO	LO	LO		SN	SN	SE	LO	LO	LO	SN	LO	LO		LO	SN	SN	SE	LO	LO
London Bridge 4 ⊖	d				16 24					16 39	16 41					16 54					17 09	17 11			
Dalston Junction Stn Ell	d	16 13	16 18	16 23		16 28	16 33	16 38					16 43	16 48	16 53		16 58	17 03		17 08				17 13	17 18
Haggerston	d	16 14	16 19	16 24		16 29	16 34	16 39					16 44	16 49	16 54		16 59	17 04		17 09				17 14	17 19
Hoxton	d	16 16	16 21	16 26		16 31	16 36	16 41					16 46	16 51	16 56		17 01	17 06		17 11				17 16	17 21
Shoreditch High Street	d	16 19	16 24	16 29		16 34	16 39	16 44					16 49	16 54	16 59		17 04	17 09		17 14				17 19	17 24
Whitechapel	d	16 21	16 26	16 31		16 36	16 41	16 46					16 51	16 56	17 01		17 06	17 11		17 16				17 21	17 26
Shadwell	d	16 23	16 28	16 33		16 38	16 43	16 48					16 53	16 58	17 03		17 08	17 13		17 18				17 23	17 28
Wapping	d	16 25	16 30	16 35		16 40	16 45	16 50					16 55	17 00	17 05		17 10	17 15		17 20				17 25	17 30
Rotherhithe	d	16 27	16 32	16 37		16 42	16 47	16 52					16 57	17 02	17 07		17 12	17 17		17 22				17 27	17 32
Canada Water	d	16 29	16 34	16 39		16 44	16 49	16 54					16 59	17 04	17 09		17 14	17 19		17 24				17 29	17 34
Surrey Quays	d	16 30	16 35	16 40		16 45	16 50	16 55					17 00	17 05	17 10		17 15	17 20		17 25				17 30	17 35
New Cross Ell	a			16 46				17 01							17 16					17 31					
New Cross Gate Station Ell	a	16 34	16 39			16 49	16 54						17 04	17 09			17 19	17 24						17 34	17 39
	d	16 35	16 40			16 50	16 55						17 05	17 10			17 20	17 25						17 35	17 40
New Cross Gate 4	d				16 29					16 44						16 59					17 14				
Brockley	d	16 37	16 42		16 32	16 52	16 57			16 47			17 07	17 12		17 02	17 22	17 27			17 17			17 37	17 42
Honor Oak Park	d	16 40	16 45		16 35	16 55	17 00			16 50			17 10	17 15		17 05	17 25	17 30			17 20			17 40	17 45
Forest Hill 4	d	16 43	16 48		16 37	16 58	17 03			16 52			17 13	17 18		17 07	17 28	17 33			17 22			17 43	17 48
Sydenham	d	16 45	16 50		16 40	17 00	17 05			16 55			17 15	17 20		17 10	17 30	17 35			17 25			17 45	17 50
Crystal Palace 4	d		16a55				17a10							17a25				17a40							17a55
Gipsy Hill	d																								
West Norwood 4	d																								
Streatham Hill	d																								
Balham 4 ⊖	d																								
Wandsworth Common	d																								
Clapham Junction 10	d																								
South Bermondsey	d										16 45											17 15			
Peckham Rye 4	d											16 42											17 12		
Queens Rd Peckham	d										16 48											17 18			
Denmark Hill 4	d										16 53	16 46										17 23	17 16		
London Blackfriars 3 ⊖	a																								
Clapham High Street ⊖	d										16 58											17 28			
Wandsworth Road	d										16 59											17 29			
Battersea Park 4	d										17 02											17 32			
London Victoria 15 ⊖	a										17 06	16 55										17 36	17 25		
Penge West	d	16 48				17 03				16 57			17 18				17 33				17 27			17 48	
Anerley	d	16 50				17 05				16 59			17 20				17 35				17 29			17 50	
Norwood Junction 2	d	16 53			16 46	17 08				17 03			17 23			17 16	17 38				17 33			17 53	
West Croydon 4	a	17 00			16 54	17 15							17 30			17 24	17 45							18 00	
East Croydon	a									17 06											17 36				

		LO	SN	LO		LO	LO	SN	SN	SE	LO	LO	LO	SN		LO	LO	LO	SN	SN	SE	LO	LO	LO	
London Bridge 4 ⊖	d		17 24					17 39	17 41					17 54					18 09	18 11					
Dalston Junction Stn Ell	d	17 23		17 28		17 33	17 38				17 43	17 48	17 53			17 58	18 03	18 08				18 13	18 18	18 23	
Haggerston	d	17 24		17 29		17 34	17 39				17 44	17 49	17 54			17 59	18 04	18 09				18 14	18 19	18 24	
Hoxton	d	17 26		17 31		17 36	17 41				17 46	17 51	17 56			18 01	18 06	18 11				18 16	18 21	18 26	
Shoreditch High Street	d	17 29		17 34		17 39	17 44				17 49	17 54	17 59			18 04	18 09	18 14				18 19	18 24	18 29	
Whitechapel	d	17 31		17 36		17 41	17 46				17 51	17 56	18 01			18 06	18 11	18 16				18 21	18 26	18 31	
Shadwell	d	17 33		17 38		17 43	17 48				17 53	17 58	18 03			18 08	18 13	18 18				18 23	18 28	18 33	
Wapping	d	17 35		17 40		17 45	17 50				17 55	18 00	18 05			18 10	18 15	18 20				18 25	18 30	18 35	
Rotherhithe	d	17 37		17 42		17 47	17 52				17 57	18 02	18 07			18 12	18 17	18 22				18 27	18 32	18 37	
Canada Water	d	17 39		17 44		17 49	17 54				17 59	18 04	18 09			18 14	18 19	18 24				18 29	18 34	18 39	
Surrey Quays	d	17 40		17 45		17 50	17 55				18 00	18 05	18 10			18 15	18 20	18 25				18 30	18 35	18 40	
New Cross Ell	a	17 46					18 01						18 16					18 31						18 46	
New Cross Gate Station Ell	a			17 49		17 54					18 04	18 09				18 19	18 24					18 34	18 39		
	d			17 50		17 55					18 05	18 10				18 20	18 25					18 35	18 40		
New Cross Gate 4	d		17 29					17 44						17 59					18 14						
Brockley	d		17 32	17 52		17 57		17 47			18 07	18 12		18 02		18 22	18 27		18 17			18 37	18 42		
Honor Oak Park	d		17 35	17 55		18 00		17 50			18 10	18 15		18 05		18 25	18 30		18 20			18 40	18 45		
Forest Hill 4	d		17 37	17 58		18 03		17 52			18 13	18 18		18 07		18 28	18 33		18 22			18 43	18 48		
Sydenham	d		17 40	18 00		18 05		17 55			18 15	18 20		18 10		18 30	18 35		18 25			18 45	18 50		
Crystal Palace 4	d					18a10						18a25					18a40						18a55		
Gipsy Hill	d																								
West Norwood 4	d																								
Streatham Hill	d																								
Balham 4 ⊖	d																								
Wandsworth Common	d																								
Clapham Junction 10	d																								
South Bermondsey	d								17 45											18 15					
Peckham Rye 4	d									17 42											18 12				
Queens Rd Peckham	d								17 48											18 18					
Denmark Hill 4	d								17 53	17 46										18 23	18 16				
London Blackfriars 3 ⊖	a																								
Clapham High Street ⊖	d								17 58											18 28					
Wandsworth Road	d								17 59											18 29					
Battersea Park 4	d								18 02											18 32					
London Victoria 15 ⊖	a								18 06	17 55										18 36	18 25				
Penge West	d			18 03				17 57			18 18					18 33			18 27			18 48			
Anerley	d			18 05				17 59			18 20					18 35			18 29			18 50			
Norwood Junction 2	d		17 46	18 08				18 03			18 23			18 16		18 38			18 33			18 53			
West Croydon 4	a		17 54	18 15							18 30			18 24		18 45						19 00			
East Croydon	a							18 06											18 36						

Table 178

Sundays

London Bridge to London Victoria - Croydon and East London Line

		SN	LO	LO	LO	SN	SN	SE	LO	LO		LO	SN	LO	LO	LO	SN	SN	SE	LO		LO	LO	SN	LO
London Bridge 4 ⊖	d	18 24				18 39	18 41						18 54				19 09	19 11						19 24	
Dalston Junction Stn Ell	d		18 28	18 33	18 38				18 43	18 48		18 53		18 58	19 03	19 08				19 13		19 18	19 23		19 28
Haggerston	d		18 29	18 34	18 39				18 44	18 49		18 54		18 59	19 04	19 09				19 14		19 19	19 24		19 29
Hoxton	d		18 31	18 36	18 41				18 46	18 51		18 56		19 01	19 06	19 11				19 16		19 21	19 26		19 31
Shoreditch High Street	d		18 34	18 39	18 44				18 49	18 54		18 59		19 04	19 09	19 14				19 19		19 24	19 29		19 34
Whitechapel	d		18 36	18 41	18 46				18 51	18 56		19 01		19 06	19 11	19 16				19 21		19 26	19 31		19 36
Shadwell	d		18 38	18 43	18 48				18 53	18 58		19 03		19 08	19 13	19 18				19 23		19 28	19 33		19 38
Wapping	d		18 40	18 45	18 50				18 55	19 00		19 05		19 10	19 15	19 20				19 25		19 30	19 35		19 40
Rotherhithe	d		18 42	18 47	18 52				18 57	19 02		19 07		19 12	19 17	19 22				19 27		19 32	19 37		19 42
Canada Water	d		18 44	18 49	18 54				18 59	19 04		19 09		19 14	19 19	19 24				19 29		19 34	19 39		19 44
Surrey Quays	d		18 45	18 50	18 55				19 00	19 05		19 10		19 15	19 20	19 25				19 30		19 35	19 40		19 45
New Cross Ell	a				19 01							19 16				19 31							19 46		
New Cross Gate Station Ell	a		18 49	18 54					19 04	19 09				19 19	19 24					19 34		19 39			19 49
	d		18 50	18 55					19 05	19 10				19 20	19 25					19 35		19 40			19 50
New Cross Gate 4	d	18 29				18 44							18 59				19 14							19 29	
Brockley	d	18 32	18 52	18 57		18 47			19 07	19 12			19 02	19 22	19 27		19 17			19 37		19 42		19 32	19 52
Honor Oak Park	d	18 35	18 55	19 00		18 50			19 10	19 15			19 05	19 25	19 30		19 20			19 40		19 45		19 35	19 55
Forest Hill 4	d	18 37	18 58	19 03		18 52			19 13	19 18			19 07	19 28	19 33		19 22			19 43		19 48		19 37	19 58
Sydenham	d	18 40	19 00	19 05		18 55			19 15	19 20			19 10	19 30	19 35		19 25			19 45		19 50		19 40	20 00
Crystal Palace 4	d			19a10						19a25					19a40							19a55			
Gipsy Hill	d																								
West Norwood 4	d																								
Streatham Hill	d																								
Balham 4 ⊖	d																								
Wandsworth Common	d																								
Clapham Junction 10	d																								
South Bermondsey	d						18 45											19 15							
Peckham Rye 4	d							18 42											19 12						
Queens Rd Peckham	d						18 48											19 18							
Denmark Hill 4	d						18 53	18 46										19 23	19 16						
London Blackfriars 3 ⊖	a																								
Clapham High Street ⊖	d						18 58											19 28							
Wandsworth Road	d						18 59											19 29							
Battersea Park 4	d						19 02											19 32							
London Victoria 15 ⊖	a						19 06	18 55										19 36	19 25						
Penge West	d		19 03			18 57			19 18					19 33			19 27			19 48					20 03
Anerley	d		19 05			18 59			19 20					19 35			19 29			19 50					20 05
Norwood Junction 2	d	18 46	19 08			19 03			19 23				19 16	19 38			19 33			19 53				19 46	20 08
West Croydon 4	a	18 54	19 15						19 30				19 24	19 45						20 00				19 54	20 15
East Croydon	a					19 06											19 36								

		LO	LO	SN	SN	SE		LO	LO	LO	SN	LO	LO	LO	SN	SN		SE	LO	LO	LO	SN	LO	LO	LO
London Bridge 4 ⊖	d			19 39	19 41						19 54				20 09	20 11						20 24			
Dalston Junction Stn Ell	d	19 33	19 38					19 43	19 48	19 53		19 58	20 03	20 08					20 13	20 18	20 23		20 28	20 33	20 38
Haggerston	d	19 34	19 39					19 44	19 49	19 54		19 59	20 04	20 09					20 14	20 19	20 24		20 29	20 34	20 39
Hoxton	d	19 36	19 41					19 46	19 51	19 56		20 01	20 06	20 11					20 16	20 21	20 26		20 31	20 36	20 41
Shoreditch High Street	d	19 39	19 44					19 49	19 54	19 59		20 04	20 09	20 14					20 19	20 24	20 29		20 34	20 39	20 44
Whitechapel	d	19 41	19 46					19 51	19 56	20 01		20 06	20 11	20 16					20 21	20 26	20 31		20 36	20 41	20 46
Shadwell	d	19 43	19 48					19 53	19 58	20 03		20 08	20 13	20 18					20 23	20 28	20 33		20 38	20 43	20 48
Wapping	d	19 45	19 50					19 55	20 00	20 05		20 10	20 15	20 20					20 25	20 30	20 35		20 40	20 45	20 50
Rotherhithe	d	19 47	19 52					19 57	20 02	20 07		20 12	20 17	20 22					20 27	20 32	20 37		20 42	20 47	20 52
Canada Water	d	19 49	19 54					19 59	20 04	20 09		20 14	20 19	20 24					20 29	20 34	20 39		20 44	20 49	20 54
Surrey Quays	d	19 50	19 55					20 00	20 05	20 10		20 15	20 20	20 25					20 30	20 35	20 40		20 45	20 50	20 55
New Cross Ell	a		20 01							20 16				20 31							20 46				21 01
New Cross Gate Station Ell	a	19 54						20 04	20 09			20 19	20 24						20 34	20 39			20 49	20 54	
	d	19 55						20 05	20 10			20 20	20 25						20 35	20 40			20 50	20 55	
New Cross Gate 4	d			19 44							19 59				20 14							20 29			
Brockley	d	19 57		19 47				20 07	20 12		20 02	20 22	20 27		20 17				20 37	20 42		20 32	20 52	20 57	
Honor Oak Park	d	20 00		19 50				20 10	20 15		20 05	20 25	20 30		20 20				20 40	20 45		20 35	20 55	21 00	
Forest Hill 4	d	20 03		19 52				20 13	20 18		20 07	20 28	20 33		20 22				20 43	20 48		20 37	20 58	21 03	
Sydenham	d	20 05		19 55				20 15	20 20		20 10	20 30	20 35		20 25				20 45	20 50		20 40	21 00	21 05	
Crystal Palace 4	d	20a10							20a25				20a40							20a55				21a10	
Gipsy Hill	d																								
West Norwood 4	d																								
Streatham Hill	d																								
Balham 4 ⊖	d																								
Wandsworth Common	d																								
Clapham Junction 10	d																								
South Bermondsey	d				19 45											20 15									
Peckham Rye 4	d					19 42												20 12							
Queens Rd Peckham	d				19 48											20 18									
Denmark Hill 4	d				19 53	19 46										20 23		20 16							
London Blackfriars 3 ⊖	a																								
Clapham High Street ⊖	d				19 58											20 28									
Wandsworth Road	d				19 59											20 29									
Battersea Park 4	d				20 02											20 32									
London Victoria 15 ⊖	a				20 06	19 55										20 36		20 25							
Penge West	d			19 57				20 18				20 33			20 27				20 48				21 03		
Anerley	d			19 59				20 20				20 35			20 29				20 50				21 05		
Norwood Junction 2	d			20 03				20 23			20 16	20 38			20 33				20 53			20 46	21 08		
West Croydon 4	a							20 30			20 24	20 45							21 00			20 54	21 15		
East Croydon	a			20 06											20 36										

Table 178

Sundays

London Bridge to London Victoria - Croydon and East London Line

		SN		SN	SE	LO	LO	LO	SN	LO	LO	LO		SN	SN	SE	LO	LO	LO	SN	LO	LO		LO	SN
London Bridge 4 ⊖	d	20 39		20 41					20 54					21 09	21 11					21 24					21 39
Dalston Junction Stn Ell	d					20 43	20 48	20 53		20 58	21 03	21 08					21 13	21 18	21 23		21 28	21 33		21 38	
Haggerston	d					20 44	20 49	20 54		20 59	21 04	21 09					21 14	21 19	21 24		21 29	21 34		21 39	
Hoxton	d					20 46	20 51	20 56		21 01	21 06	21 11					21 16	21 21	21 26		21 31	21 36		21 41	
Shoreditch High Street	d					20 49	20 54	20 59		21 04	21 09	21 14					21 19	21 24	21 29		21 34	21 39		21 44	
Whitechapel	d					20 51	20 56	21 01		21 06	21 11	21 16					21 21	21 26	21 31		21 36	21 41		21 46	
Shadwell	d					20 53	20 58	21 03		21 08	21 13	21 18					21 23	21 28	21 33		21 38	21 43		21 48	
Wapping	d					20 55	21 00	21 05		21 10	21 15	21 20					21 25	21 30	21 35		21 40	21 45		21 50	
Rotherhithe	d					20 57	21 02	21 07		21 12	21 17	21 22					21 27	21 32	21 37		21 42	21 47		21 52	
Canada Water	d					20 59	21 04	21 09		21 14	21 19	21 24					21 29	21 34	21 39		21 44	21 49		21 54	
Surrey Quays	d					21 00	21 05	21 10		21 15	21 20	21 25					21 30	21 35	21 40		21 45	21 50		21 55	
New Cross Ell	a							21 16				21 31							21 46					22 01	
New Cross Gate Station Ell	a					21 04	21 09			21 19	21 24						21 34	21 39			21 49	21 54			
	d					21 05	21 10			21 20	21 25						21 35	21 40			21 50	21 55			
New Cross Gate 4	d	20 44							20 59					21 14						21 29					21 44
Brockley	d	20 47				21 07	21 12		21 02	21 22	21 27			21 17			21 37	21 42		21 32	21 52	21 57			21 47
Honor Oak Park	d	20 50				21 10	21 15		21 05	21 25	21 30			21 20			21 40	21 45		21 35	21 55	22 00			21 50
Forest Hill 4	d	20 52				21 13	21 18		21 07	21 28	21 33			21 22			21 43	21 48		21 37	21 58	22 03			21 52
Sydenham	d	20 55				21 15	21 20		21 10	21 30	21 35			21 25			21 45	21 50		21 40	22 00	22 05			21 55
Crystal Palace 4	d						21a25				21a40							21a55				22a10			
Gipsy Hill	d																								
West Norwood 4	d																								
Streatham Hill	d																								
Balham 4 ⊖	d																								
Wandsworth Common	d																								
Clapham Junction 10	d																								
South Bermondsey	d			20 45											21 15										
Peckham Rye 4	d				20 42											21 12									
Queens Rd Peckham	d			20 48											21 18										
Denmark Hill 4	d			20 53	20 46										21 23	21 16									
London Blackfriars 3 ⊖	a																								
Clapham High Street ⊖	d			20 58											21 28										
Wandsworth Road	d			20 59											21 29										
Battersea Park 4	d			21 02											21 32										
London Victoria 15 ⊖	a			21 06	20 55										21 36	21 25.									
Penge West	d	20 57				21 18				21 33				21 27			21 48				22 03				21 57
Anerley	d	20 59				21 20				21 35				21 29			21 50				22 05				21 59
Norwood Junction 2	d	21 03				21 23			21 16	21 38				21 33			21 53			21 46	22 08				22 03
West Croydon 4	a					21 30			21 24	21 45							22 00			21 54	22 15				
East Croydon	a	21 06												21 36											22 06

		SN	SE	LO	LO	LO	SN	LO		LO	SN	SN	SE	LO	LO	LO	SN	SN		SE	LO	LO	LO	SN	SN
London Bridge 4 ⊖	d	21 41					21 54				22 09	22 11					22 39	22 41						23 09	23 11
Dalston Junction Stn Ell	d			21 43	21 48	21 53		21 58		22 08				22 18	22 28	22 38					22 48	22 58	23 08		
Haggerston	d			21 44	21 49	21 54		21 59		22 09				22 19	22 29	22 39					22 49	22 59	23 09		
Hoxton	d			21 46	21 51	21 56		22 01		22 11				22 21	22 31	22 41					22 51	23 01	23 11		
Shoreditch High Street	d			21 49	21 54	21 59		22 04		22 14				22 24	22 34	22 44					22 54	23 04	23 14		
Whitechapel	d			21 51	21 56	22 01		22 06		22 16				22 26	22 36	22 46					22 56	23 06	23 16		
Shadwell	d			21 53	21 58	22 03		22 08		22 18				22 28	22 38	22 48					22 58	23 08	23 18		
Wapping	d			21 55	22 00	22 05		22 10		22 20				22 30	22 40	22 50					23 00	23 10	23 20		
Rotherhithe	d			21 57	22 02	22 07		22 12		22 22				22 32	22 42	22 52					23 02	23 12	23 22		
Canada Water	d			21 59	22 04	22 09		22 14		22 24				22 34	22 44	22 54					23 04	23 14	23 24		
Surrey Quays	d			22 00	22 05	22 10		22 15		22 25				22 35	22 45	22 55					23 05	23 15	23 25		
New Cross Ell	a					22 16				22 31						23 01							23 31		
New Cross Gate Station Ell	a			22 04	22 09			22 19						22 39	22 49						23 09	23 19			
	d			22 05	22 10			22 20						22 40	22 50						23 10	23 20			
New Cross Gate 4	d						21 59				22 14						22 44							23 14	
Brockley	d			22 07	22 12		22 02	22 22			22 17			22 42	22 52		22 47				23 12	23 22		23 17	
Honor Oak Park	d			22 10	22 15		22 05	22 25			22 20			22 45	22 55		22 50				23 15	23 25		23 20	
Forest Hill 4	d			22 13	22 18		22 07	22 28			22 22			22 48	22 58		22 52				23 18	23 28		23 22	
Sydenham	d			22 15	22 20		22 10	22 30			22 25			22 50	23 00		22 55				23 20	23 30		23 25	
Crystal Palace 4	d				22a25									22a55							23a25				
Gipsy Hill	d																								
West Norwood 4	d																								
Streatham Hill	d																								
Balham 4 ⊖	d																								
Wandsworth Common	d																								
Clapham Junction 10	d																								
South Bermondsey	d	21 45										22 15						22 45							23 15
Peckham Rye 4	d		21 42										22 12							22 42					
Queens Rd Peckham	d	21 48										22 18						22 48							23 18
Denmark Hill 4	d	21 53	21 46									22 23	22 16					22 53		22 46					23 23
London Blackfriars 3 ⊖	a																								
Clapham High Street ⊖	d	21 58										22 28						22 58							23 28
Wandsworth Road	d	21 59										22 29						22 59							23 29
Battersea Park 4	d	22 02										22 32						23 02							23 32
London Victoria 15 ⊖	a	22 06	21 55									22 36	22 25					23 06		22 55					23 37
Penge West	d			22 18				22 33			22 27				23 03		22 57					23 33		23 27	
Anerley	d			22 20				22 35			22 29				23 05		22 59					23 35		23 29	
Norwood Junction 2	d			22 23			22 16	22 38			22 33				23 08		23 03					23 38		23 33	
West Croydon 4	a			22 30			22 24	22 45							23 15							23 45			
East Croydon	a										22 36						23 06							23 36	

Table 178

Sundays

London Bridge to London Victoria - Croydon and East London Line

		SE	LO	SN		LO	SN	SE
London Bridge 4 ⊖	d						23 39	
Dalston Junction Stn Ell	d		23 18			23 28		
Haggerston	d		23 19			23 29		
Hoxton	d		23 21			23 31		
Shoreditch High Street	d		23 24			23 34		
Whitechapel	d		23 26			23 36		
Shadwell	d		23 28			23 38		
Wapping	d		23 30			23 40		
Rotherhithe	d		23 32			23 42		
Canada Water	d		23 34			23 44		
Surrey Quays	d		23 35			23 45		
New Cross Ell	a							
New Cross Gate Station Ell	a		23 39			23 49		
	d		23 40			23 50		
New Cross Gate 4	d						23 44	
Brockley	d		23 42			23 52	23 47	
Honor Oak Park	d		23 45			23 55	23 50	
Forest Hill 4	d		23 48			23 58	23 52	
Sydenham	d		23 50			00 01	23 55	
Crystal Palace 4	d		23a55	23 29				
Gipsy Hill	d							
West Norwood 4	d							
Streatham Hill	d							
Balham 4 ⊖	d							
Wandsworth Common	d							
Clapham Junction 10	d							
South Bermondsey	d							
Peckham Rye 4	d	23 12						23 42
Queens Rd Peckham	d							
Denmark Hill 4	d	23 16						23 46
London Blackfriars 3 ⊖	a							
Clapham High Street ⊖	d							
Wandsworth Road	d							
Battersea Park 4	d							
London Victoria 15 ⊖	a	23 25						23 55
Penge West	d					00 03	23 57	
Anerley	d					00 05	23 59	
Norwood Junction 2	d			23 33		00 08	00 05	
West Croydon 4	a			23 38		00 15		
East Croydon	a						00 08	

Table 178

Mondays to Fridays

East London Line and Croydon-London Victoria to London Bridge

		LO MX	SN MX	LO MX	SN MX	FC	FC	FC	FC	FC		FC	FC	FC	SN	SE	LO	LO	SN	LO	LO		SE		SN
East Croydon	d														05 13				05 51						06 13
West Croydon 4	d	23p22															05 39				05 52				
Norwood Junction 2	d	23p28													05 17		05 43		05 55		05 58				06 18
Anerley	d	23p31													05 20		05 46				06 01				06 21
Penge West	d	23p33													05 22		05 48				06 03				06 23
London Victoria 15 ⊖	d		23p22																						
Battersea Park 4	d		23p26																						
Wandsworth Road	d																								
Clapham High Street ⊖	d																								
London Blackfriars 3 ⊖	d					00 11	00 40	01 10	01 40	02 40		03 10	03 40	04 10		05 28							06 10		
Denmark Hill 4	d															05 39							06 22		
Peckham Rye 4	d				23p57											05 41			06 15				06 25		
Queens Rd Peckham	d																		06 17						
South Bermondsey	d																		06 20						
Clapham Junction 10	d		23p30																						
Wandsworth Common	d		23p33																						
Balham 4 ⊖	d		23p35																						
Streatham Hill	d		23p38																						
West Norwood 4	d		23p42		00 10																				
Gipsy Hill	d		23p45		00 13																				
Crystal Palace 4	d		23p51	23p43	00 15															05 58					
Sydenham	d	23p36	23p54	23p46											05 24		05 51			06 01	06 06				06 25
Forest Hill 4	d	23p38	23p57	23p49											05 27		05 53			06 04	06 08				06 28
Honor Oak Park	d	23p41	23p59	23p51											05 29		05 56			06 06	06 11				06 30
Brockley	d	23p43	00 02	23p54											05 32		05 58			06 09	06 13				06 33
New Cross Gate Station Ell	a																								
	d																								
New Cross Gate 4	d	23p46	00 04	23p56											05 34		06 01			06 11	06 16				06 35
New Cross Ell	d																	06 06							
Surrey Quays	d	23p49		23p59													06 05	06 10		06 15	06 19				
Canada Water	d	23p51		00 02													06 07	06 12		06 17	06 21				
Rotherhithe	d	23p53		00 03													06 08	06 13		06 18	06 23				
Wapping	d	23p54		00 05													06 10	06 15		06 20	06 24				
Shadwell	d	23p56		00 07													06 12	06 17		06 22	06 26				
Whitechapel	d	23p59		00 09													06 14	06 19		06 24	06 29				
Shoreditch High Street	d	00 01		00 11													06 16	06 21		06 26	06 31				
Hoxton	d	00 03		00 13													06 18	06 23		06 28	06 33				
Haggerston	d	00 05		00 15													06 20	06 25		06 30	06 35				
Dalston Junction Stn Ell	a	00 10		00 19													06 25	06 29		06 34	06 40				
London Bridge 4 ⊖	a		00 11			00 26	00 55	01 25	01 55	02 55		03 25	03 55	23 25	05 41				06 24						06 42

		LO	LO	LO	LO	SN	LO	LO	SN	SN	LO	LO	LO	SE	SN	SN	LO	SN	SN	SN	LO	LO	FC 1	SN	SN
East Croydon	d																								
West Croydon 4	d			06 09				06 22	06 31				06 39									06 52		07 01	
Norwood Junction 2	d			06 13				06 28		06 32			06 43						06 47			06 58			07 02
Anerley	d			06 16				06 31		06 35			06 46									07 01			07 05
Penge West	d			06 18				06 33		06 37			06 48									07 03			07 07
London Victoria 15 ⊖	d					06 19										06 41				06 49					
Battersea Park 4	d					06 23										06 45				06 53					
Wandsworth Road	d															06 47									
Clapham High Street ⊖	d															06 49									
London Blackfriars 3 ⊖	d													06 42									06 58		
Denmark Hill 4	d													06 52		06 54							07 09		
Peckham Rye 4	d								06 59					06 55	06 42	06 56			07 07				07 12	07 31	
Queens Rd Peckham	d								07 02							06 59			07 10					07 34	
South Bermondsey	d								07 04							07 01			07 12					07 36	
Clapham Junction-I 10	d					06 27														06 57					
Wandsworth Common	d					06 30														07 00					
Balham 4 ⊖	d					06 32														07 02					
Streatham Hill	d					06 35												06 42		07 05					
West Norwood 4	d					06 39									06 53			06 45		07 09					
Gipsy Hill	d					06 42									06 56			06 48		07 12					
Crystal Palace 4	d		06 13			06 44	06 28					06 41			06 59			06 51		07 14	06 58				
Sydenham	d		06 16	06 21		06 48	06 31	06 36		06 39		06 44	06 51					06 54		07 18	07 01	07 06			07 09
Forest Hill 4	d		06 19	06 23		06 50	06 34	06 38		06 42		06 47	06 54					06 57		07 20	07 04	07 08			07 12
Honor Oak Park	d		06 21	06 26		06 53	06 36	06 41		06 44		06 49	06 56					06 59		07 23	07 06	07 11			07 14
Brockley	d		06 24	06 28		06 55	06 39	06 43		06 47		06 52	06 59					07 02		07 25	07 09	07 13			07 17
New Cross Gate Station Ell	a																								
	d																								
New Cross Gate 4	d		06 26	06 31		06 58	06 41	06 46		06 49		06 54	07 01					07 04		07 28	07 11	07 16			07 19
New Cross Ell	d	06 21			06 36						06 51						07 06								
Surrey Quays	d	06 25	06 30	06 35	06 40		06 45	06 49			06 55	07 00	07 05				07 10				07 15	07 19			
Canada Water	d	06 27	06 32	06 37	06 42		06 47	06 51			06 57	07 02	07 07				07 12				07 17	07 21			
Rotherhithe	d	06 28	06 33	06 38	06 43		06 48	06 53			06 58	07 03	07 09				07 13				07 18	07 23			
Wapping	d	06 30	06 35	06 40	06 45		06 50	06 54			07 00	07 05	07 10				07 15				07 20	07 24			
Shadwell	d	06 32	06 37	06 42	06 47		06 52	06 56			07 02	07 07	07 12				07 17				07 22	07 26			
Whitechapel	d	06 34	06 39	06 44	06 49		06 54	06 59			07 04	07 09	07 15				07 19				07 24	07 29			
Shoreditch High Street	d	06 36	06 41	06 46	06 51		06 56	07 01			07 06	07 11	07 17				07 21				07 26	07 31			
Hoxton	d	06 38	06 43	06 48	06 53		06 58	07 03			07 08	07 13	07 19				07 23				07 28	07 33			
Haggerston	d	06 40	06 45	06 50	06 55		07 00	07 05			07 10	07 15	07 21				07 25				07 30	07 35			
Dalston Junction Stn Ell	a	06 44	06 49	06 55	06 59		07 04	07 10			07 14	07 19	07 26				07 29				07 34	07 40			
London Bridge 4 ⊖	a					07 06			07 11	06 59						07 08		07 16	07 19	07 36				07 43	07 30

East London Line and Croydon-London Victoria to London Bridge

		LO	LO		LO	SN	SN	SN	SN	LO	LO	SN	LO	FC	SN	LO	SN	SN	LO	LO	FC [1]	SN		SN
East Croydon	d																							
West Croydon [4]	d				07 09				07 17				07 22		07 31					07 39				
Norwood Junction [2]	d				07 13				07 22				07 28				07 32			07 43				
Anerley	d				07 16								07 31				07 35			07 46				
Penge West	d				07 18								07 33				07 37			07 48				
London Victoria [15] ⊖	d						07 11					07 17												07 41
Battersea Park [4]	d						07 15					07 21												07 45
Wandsworth Road	d						07 17																	07 47
Clapham High Street ⊖	d						07 19																	07 49
London Blackfriars [3] ⊖	d													07 24							07 40			
Denmark Hill [4]	d						07 24							07 34							07 50			07 54
Peckham Rye [4]	d					07 12	07 26							07 36	07 59			07 36			07 53	07 42		07 56
Queens Rd Peckham	d						07 29								08 02			07 39						07 59
South Bermondsey	d						07 31								08 04			07 41						08 01
Clapham Junction [10]	d											07 25												
Wandsworth Common	d																							
Balham [4] ⊖	d											07 29												
Streatham Hill	d							07 12				07 32												
West Norwood [4]	d					07 23		07 15				07 38										07 53		
Gipsy Hill	d					07 26		07 18				07 41										07 56		
Crystal Palace [4]	d		07 11			07 29		07 21	07 26		07 28	07 44							07 41			07 59		
Sydenham	d		07 14		07 21			07 24			07 31	07 48	07 36				07 39		07 44	07 52				
Forest Hill [4]	d		07 17		07 24			07 27			07 34	07 50	07 38				07 42		07 47	07 54				
Honor Oak Park	d		07 19		07 26			07 29			07 36	07 53	07 41				07 44		07 49	07 57				
Brockley	d		07 22		07 29			07 32			07 39	07 55	07 43				07 47		07 52	07 59				
New Cross Gate Station Ell	a																							
	d																							
New Cross Gate [4]	d		07 24		07 31			07 34			07 41	07 58	07 46				07 49		07 54	08 02				
New Cross Ell	d	07 21								07 36						07 51								
Surrey Quays	d	07 25	07 30		07 35					07 40	07 45		07 49			07 55			08 00	08 05				
Canada Water	d	07 27	07 32		07 37					07 42	07 47		07 51			07 57			08 02	08 07				
Rotherhithe	d	07 28	07 33		07 39					07 43	07 48		07 53			07 58			08 03	08 09				
Wapping	d	07 30	07 35		07 40					07 45	07 50		07 54			08 00			08 05	08 10				
Shadwell	d	07 32	07 37		07 42					07 47	07 52		07 56			08 02			08 07	08 12				
Whitechapel	d	07 34	07 39		07 45					07 49	07 54		07 59			08 04			08 09	08 15				
Shoreditch High Street	d	07 36	07 41		07 47					07 51	07 56		08 01			08 06			08 11	08 17				
Hoxton	d	07 38	07 43		07 49					07 53	07 58		08 03			08 08			08 13	08 19				
Haggerston	d	07 40	07 45		07 51					07 55	08 00		08 05			08 10			08 15	08 21				
Dalston Junction Stn Ell	a	07 44	07 49		07 55					07 59	08 04		08 10			08 14			08 19	08 25				
London Bridge [4] ⊖	a						07 38	07 45				08 07			08 11		07 58	07 48						08 08

		SE	SN	FC	LO	LO	SN	SN			FC	LO	SN	SN	SN	LO	LO	LO	SE	SN		SN	SN	SN	SN
East Croydon	d																								
West Croydon [4]	d		07 47									07 52	08 01					08 09						08 19	
Norwood Junction [2]	d		07 52									07 58		08 02				08 13						08 25	
Anerley	d											08 01		08 05				08 16							
Penge West	d											08 03		08 07				08 18							
London Victoria [15] ⊖	d	07 43						07 52											08 09			08 11			08 22
Battersea Park [4]	d																					08 15			08 26
Wandsworth Road	d																					08 17			
Clapham High Street ⊖	d																					08 19			
London Blackfriars [3] ⊖	d			07 50							07 56														
Denmark Hill [4]	d	07 53		08 00							08 09								08 19			08 24			
Peckham Rye [4]	d	07 56		08 03							08 12		08 29		08 06				08 23	08 12		08 26			
Queens Rd Peckham	d												08 32		08 09							08 29			
South Bermondsey	d												08 34		08 11							08 31			
Clapham Junction [10]	d							07 58																	08 30
Wandsworth Common	d																								08 33
Balham [4] ⊖	d							08 03																	08 35
Streatham Hill	d							08 06															08 15		08 38
West Norwood [4]	d							08 09												08 24			08 19		08 42
Gipsy Hill	d							08 12												08 27			08 22		08 45
Crystal Palace [4]	d		07 56			07 58	07 52	08 15									08 11			08 29			08 24	08 29	08 51
Sydenham	d					08 01	07 56	08 18				08 06		08 09			08 14	08 22					08 28		08 54
Forest Hill [4]	d					08 04	07 58	08 21				08 08		08 12			08 17	08 24					08 30		08 57
Honor Oak Park	d					08 06	08 01	08 23				08 11		08 14			08 19	08 27					08 33		08 59
Brockley	d					08 09	08 03	08 26				08 13		08 17			08 22	08 29					08 35		09 02
New Cross Gate Station Ell	a																								
	d																								
New Cross Gate [4]	d					08 11	08 06	08 28				08 16		08 19			08 24	08 32					08 38		09 04
New Cross Ell	d				08 06											08 21									
Surrey Quays	d				08 10	08 15						08 19				08 25	08 30	08 35							
Canada Water	d				08 12	08 17						08 21				08 27	08 32	08 37							
Rotherhithe	d				08 13	08 18						08 23				08 28	08 33	08 39							
Wapping	d				08 15	08 20						08 24				08 30	08 35	08 40							
Shadwell	d				08 17	08 22						08 26				08 32	08 37	08 42							
Whitechapel	d				08 19	08 24						08 29				08 34	08 39	08 45							
Shoreditch High Street	d				08 21	08 26						08 31				08 36	08 41	08 47							
Hoxton	d				08 23	08 28						08 33				08 38	08 43	08 49							
Haggerston	d				08 25	08 30						08 35				08 40	08 45	08 51							
Dalston Junction Stn Ell	a				08 29	08 34						08 40				08 44	08 49	08 55							
London Bridge [4] ⊖	a						08 15	08 37					08 41	08 31	08 18							08 38	08 47		09 14

East London Line and Croydon-London Victoria to London Bridge

		LO	LO	LO	FC [1]		SN	SN	LO	SN	LO	SN	LO	SE	FC	SN	LO	SN	SN	LO	SN	FC	LO	SN	
East Croydon	d																								
West Croydon [4]	d			08 23			08 31						08 39						08 49				08 52	09 01	
Norwood Junction [2]	d			08 28				08 32					08 43						08 54				08 58		
Anerley	d			08 31				08 35					08 46										09 01		
Penge West	d			08 33				08 37					08 48										09 03		
London Victoria [15] ⊖	d													08 39				08 41			08 49				
Battersea Park [4]	d																	08 45			08 53				
Wandsworth Road	d																	08 47							
Clapham High Street ⊖	d																	08 49							
London Blackfriars [3] ⊖	d				08 28										08 40							08 52			
Denmark Hill [4]	d				08 38									08 48	08 52			08 54				09 02			
Peckham Rye [4]	d				08 41		09 01			08 35				08 51	08 55	08 42		08 56						09 32	
Queens Rd Peckham	d						09 04			08 38								08 59						09 35	
South Bermondsey	d						09 06			08 40								09 01						09 37	
Clapham Junction [10]	d																				08 57				
Wandsworth Common	d																				09 00				
Balham [4] ⊖	d																				09 02				
Streatham Hill	d											08 35									09 05				
West Norwood [4]	d											08 38				08 53					09 09				
Gipsy Hill	d											08 41				08 56					09 12				
Crystal Palace [4]	d		08 28								08 41	08 44				08 59			08 58	08 58	09 14				
Sydenham	d		08 31	08 36				08 39			08 44	08 47	08 51							09 01	09 18		09 06		
Forest Hill [4]	d		08 34	08 38				08 42			08 47	08 50	08 54							09 04	09 20		09 08		
Honor Oak Park	d		08 36	08 41				08 44			08 49	08 52	08 56							09 06	09 23		09 11		
Brockley	d		08 39	08 43				08 47			08 52	08 55	08 59							09 09	09 25		09 13		
New Cross Gate Station Ell	a																								
	d																								
New Cross Gate [4]	d		08 41	08 46				08 49			08 54	08 57	09 01							09 11	09 28		09 16		
New Cross Ell	d	08 36							08 51								09 06								
Surrey Quays	d	08 40	08 45	08 49					08 55		09 00		09 05				09 10			09 15			09 19		
Canada Water	d	08 42	08 47	08 51					08 57		09 02		09 07				09 12			09 17			09 21		
Rotherhithe	d	08 43	08 48	08 53					08 58		09 03		09 09				09 13			09 18			09 23		
Wapping	d	08 45	08 50	08 54					09 00		09 05		09 10				09 15			09 20			09 24		
Shadwell	d	08 47	08 52	08 56					09 02		09 07		09 12				09 17			09 22			09 26		
Whitechapel	d	08 49	08 54	08 59					09 04		09 09		09 15				09 19			09 24			09 29		
Shoreditch High Street	d	08 51	08 56	09 01					09 06		09 11		09 17				09 21			09 26			09 31		
Hoxton	d	08 53	08 58	09 03					09 08		09 13		09 19				09 23			09 28			09 33		
Haggerston	d	08 55	09 00	09 05					09 10		09 15		09 21				09 25			09 30			09 35		
Dalston Junction Stn Ell	a	08 59	09 04	09 10					09 14		09 19		09 25				09 29			09 34			09 40		
London Bridge [4] ⊖	a						09 14	08 58		08 49		09 06						09 08			09 37			09 44	

		SN	SN	LO		LO	LO	SE	SN	SN	FC	LO		SN	SN	SN	LO	LO	SN	SN		LO	SE	SN	SN
East Croydon	d													09 20					09 30						
West Croydon [4]	d						09 09											09 22		09 31					
Norwood Junction [2]	d	09 02					09 13							09 25				09 28	09 35						
Anerley	d	09 05					09 16											09 31	09 38						
Penge West	d	09 07					09 18											09 33	09 40						
London Victoria [15] ⊖	d							09 09		09 11					09 19								09 39		09 41
Battersea Park [4]	d									09 15					09 23										09 45
Wandsworth Road	d									09 17															09 47
Clapham High Street ⊖	d									09 19															09 49
London Blackfriars [3] ⊖	d										09 12														
Denmark Hill [4]	d							09 18		09 24	09 22												09 48		09 54
Peckham Rye [4]	d		09 06					09 21	09 12	09 26	09 25									10 01			09 51	09 42	09 56
Queens Rd Peckham	d		09 09							09 29										10 04					09 59
South Bermondsey	d		09 11							09 31										10 06					10 01
Clapham Junction [10]	d														09 27										
Wandsworth Common	d														09 30										
Balham [4] ⊖	d														09 32										
Streatham Hill	d														09 35										
West Norwood [4]	d								09 23						09 39									09 53	
Gipsy Hill	d								09 26						09 42									09 56	
Crystal Palace [4]	d					09 11			09 29						09b51	09 21	09 28							09 59	
Sydenham	d	09 09				09 14	09 21								09 54	09 24	09 31	09 36	09 42						
Forest Hill [4]	d	09 12				09 17	09 24								09 57	09 27	09 34	09 38	09 45						
Honor Oak Park	d	09 14				09 19	09 26								09 59	09 29	09 36	09 41	09 47						
Brockley	d	09 17				09 22	09 29								10 02	09 32	09 39	09 43	09 50						
New Cross Gate Station Ell	a																								
	d																								
New Cross Gate [4]	d	09 19				09 24	09 31							09 33	10 04	09 34	09 41	09 46	09 52						
New Cross Ell	d			09 21								09 36										09 51			
Surrey Quays	d			09 25		09 30	09 35					09 40					09 45	09 49				09 55			
Canada Water	d			09 27		09 32	09 37					09 42					09 47	09 51				09 57			
Rotherhithe	d			09 28		09 33	09 39					09 43					09 48	09 53				09 58			
Wapping	d			09 30		09 35	09 40					09 45					09 50	09 54				10 00			
Shadwell	d			09 32		09 37	09 42					09 47					09 52	09 56				10 02			
Whitechapel	d			09 34		09 39	09 45					09 49					09 54	09 59				10 04			
Shoreditch High Street	d			09 36		09 41	09 47					09 51					09 56	10 01				10 06			
Hoxton	d			09 38		09 43	09 49					09 53					09 58	10 03				10 08			
Haggerston	d			09 40		09 45	09 51					09 55					10 00	10 05				10 10			
Dalston Junction Stn Ell	a			09 44		09 49	09 55					09 59					10 04	10 10				10 14			
London Bridge [4] ⊖	a	09 29	09 20							09 38				09 42	10 11	09 44			10 01	10 11					10 06

b arr. 0945

Table 178

East London Line and Croydon-London Victoria to London Bridge

		FC	LO	SN	SN	LO	LO	LO	LO	SN	LO	LO	SN	LO	SE	SN	SN	LO	FC	SN	LO	SN	SN
East Croydon	d									10 00												10 30	
West Croydon	d					09 39			09 52				10 01	10 09									
Norwood Junction	d					09 43			09 58	10 05				10 13								10 35	
Anerley	d					09 46			10 01	10 08				10 16								10 38	
Penge West	d					09 48			10 03	10 10				10 18								10 40	
London Victoria	d				09 49										10 09.		10 11						10 19
Battersea Park	d				09 53												10 15						10 23
Wandsworth Road	d																10 17						
Clapham High Street	d																10 19						
London Blackfriars	d	09 42																	10 12				
Denmark Hill	d	09 52													10 18		10 24		10 22				
Peckham Rye	d	09 55		09 46									10 31		10 21	10 12	10 26		10 25	10 16			
Queens Rd Peckham	d			09 49									10 34				10 29			10 19			
South Bermondsey	d			09 51									10 36				10 31			10 21			
Clapham Junction	d				09 57																		10 27
Wandsworth Common	d				10 00																		10 30
Balham	d				10 02																		10 32
Streatham Hill	d				10 05																		10 35
West Norwood	d				10 10											10 23							10 40
Gipsy Hill	d				10 13											10 26							10 43
Crystal Palace	d		09 43		10 21			09 58				10 13				10 29					10 28		10 51
Sydenham	d		09 46		10 24	09 51		10 01	10 06	10 12		10 16		10 21							10 31	10 42	10 54
Forest Hill	d		09 49		10 27	09 53		10 04	10 08	10 15		10 19		10 23							10 34	10 45	10 57
Honor Oak Park	d		09 51		10 29	09 56		10 06	10 11	10 17		10 21		10 26							10 36	10 47	10 59
Brockley	d		09 54		10 32	09 58		10 09	10 13	10 20		10 24		10 28							10 39	10 50	11 02
New Cross Gate Station Ell	a																						
	d																						
New Cross Gate	d		09 56		10 34	10 01		10 11	10 16	10 22		10 26		10 31							10 41	10 52	11 04
New Cross Ell	d						10 06				10 21							10 36					
Surrey Quays	d		10 00			10 05	10 10	10 15	10 19		10 25	10 30		10 35				10 40			10 45		
Canada Water	d		10 02			10 07	10 12	10 17	10 21		10 27	10 32		10 37				10 42			10 47		
Rotherhithe	d		10 03			10 08	10 13	10 18	10 23		10 28	10 33		10 38				10 43			10 48		
Wapping	d		10 05			10 10	10 15	10 20	10 24		10 30	10 35		10 40				10 45			10 50		
Shadwell	d		10 07			10 12	10 17	10 22	10 26		10 32	10 37		10 42				10 47			10 52		
Whitechapel	d		10 09			10 14	10 19	10 24	10 29		10 34	10 39		10 44				10 49			10 54		
Shoreditch High Street	d		10 11			10 16	10 21	10 26	10 31		10 36	10 41		10 46				10 51			10 56		
Hoxton	d		10 13			10 18	10 23	10 28	10 33		10 38	10 43		10 48				10 53			10 58		
Haggerston	d		10 15			10 20	10 25	10 30	10 35		10 40	10 45		10 50				10 55			11 00		
Dalston Junction Stn Ell	a		10 19			10 25	10 29	10 34	10 40		10 44	10 49		10 55				10 59			11 04		
London Bridge	a			09 58	10 41					10 29			10 41				10 36			10 26		10 59	11 11

		SN	LO	LO	LO	LO	SE	SN	SN	FC	SN	SN	LO	LO	LO	SN	SN	SE	SN	LO	SN	FC
East Croydon	d															11 00						
West Croydon	d	10 31	10 22			10 39									10 52		11 01					
Norwood Junction	d		10 28			10 43									10 58	11 05						
Anerley	d		10 31			10 46									11 01	11 08						
Penge West	d		10 33			10 48									11 03	11 10						
London Victoria	d						10 39		10 41			10 49						11 09			11 11	
Battersea Park	d								10 45			10 53									11 15	
Wandsworth Road	d								10 47												11 17	
Clapham High Street	d								10 49												11 19	
London Blackfriars	d									10 42												11 12
Denmark Hill	d						10 48		10 54	10 52								11 18			11 24	11 22
Peckham Rye	d	11 01					10 51	10 42	10 56	10 55	10 46						11 31	11 21	11 12		11 26	11 25
Queens Rd Peckham	d	11 04							10 59		10 49						11 34				11 29	
South Bermondsey	d	11 06							11 01		10 51						11 36				11 31	
Clapham Junction	d											10 57										
Wandsworth Common	d											11 00										
Balham	d											11 02										
Streatham Hill	d											11 05										
West Norwood	d							10 53				11 10							11 23			
Gipsy Hill	d							10 56				11 13							11 26			
Crystal Palace	d				10 43			10 59				11 21		10 58					11 29			
Sydenham	d		10 36		10 46	10 51						11 24		11 01	11 06	11 12						
Forest Hill	d		10 38		10 49	10 53						11 27		11 04	11 08	11 15						
Honor Oak Park	d		10 41		10 51	10 56						11 29		11 06	11 11	11 17						
Brockley	d		10 43		10 54	10 58						11 32		11 09	11 13	11 20						
New Cross Gate Station Ell	a																					
	d																					
New Cross Gate	d		10 46		10 56	11 01						11 34		11 11	11 16	11 22						
New Cross Ell	d			10 51									11 06							11 21		
Surrey Quays	d		10 49	10 55	11 00	11 05							11 10	11 15	11 19					11 25		
Canada Water	d		10 51	10 57	11 02	11 07							11 12	11 17	11 21					11 27		
Rotherhithe	d		10 53	10 58	11 03	11 08							11 13	11 18	11 23					11 28		
Wapping	d		10 54	11 00	11 05	11 10							11 15	11 20	11 24					11 30		
Shadwell	d		10 56	11 02	11 07	11 12							11 17	11 22	11 26					11 32		
Whitechapel	d		10 59	11 04	11 09	11 14							11 19	11 24	11 29					11 34		
Shoreditch High Street	d		11 01	11 06	11 11	11 16							11 21	11 26	11 31					11 36		
Hoxton	d		11 03	11 08	11 13	11 18							11 23	11 28	11 33					11 38		
Haggerston	d		11 05	11 10	11 15	11 20							11 25	11 30	11 35					11 40		
Dalston Junction Stn Ell	a		11 10	11 14	11 19	11 25							11 29	11 34	11 40					11 44		
London Bridge	a	11 11							11 06		10 56	11 41				11 29	11 41				11 36	

Table 178

East London Line and Croydon-London Victoria to London Bridge

		LO	SN	SN	LO	LO	LO	LO	SN	SN	SE	SN	SN	FC	LO	SN	SN	LO	LO	LO	SN	SN
East Croydon	d								11 30												12 00	
West Croydon	d				11 09			11 22		11 31									11 39			12 01
Norwood Junction	d				11 13			11 28	11 35										11 43		12 05	
Anerley	d				11 16			11 31	11 38										11 46		12 08	
Penge West	d				11 18			11 33	11 40										11 48		12 10	
London Victoria	d			11 19							11 39.		11 41				11 49					
Battersea Park	d			11 23									11 45				11 53					
Wandsworth Road	d												11 47									
Clapham High Street	d												11 49									
London Blackfriars	d													11 42								
Denmark Hill	d										11 48		11 54	11 52								
Peckham Rye	d		11 16							12 01	11 51	11 42	11 56	11 55		11 46						12 31
Queens Rd Peckham	d		11 19							12 04			11 59			11 49						12 34
South Bermondsey	d		11 21							12 06			12 01			11 51						12 36
Clapham Junction	d			11 27													11 57					
Wandsworth Common	d			11 30													12 00					
Balham	d			11 32													12 02					
Streatham Hill	d			11 35													12 05					
West Norwood	d			11 40								11 53					12 10					
Gipsy Hill	d			11 43								11 56					12 13					
Crystal Palace	d	11 13		11 51			11 28					11 59			11 43		12 21					
Sydenham	d	11 16		11 54	11 21		11 31	11 36	11 42						11 46		12 24		11 51		12 12	
Forest Hill	d	11 19		11 57	11 23		11 34	11 38	11 45						11 49		12 27		11 53		12 15	
Honor Oak Park	d	11 21		11 59	11 26		11 36	11 41	11 47						11 51		12 29		11 56		12 17	
Brockley	d	11 24		12 02	11 28		11 39	11 43	11 50						11 54		12 32		11 58		12 20	
New Cross Gate Station Ell	a																					
	d																					
New Cross Gate	d	11 26		12 04	11 31		11 41	11 46	11 52						11 56		12 34		12 01		12 22	
New Cross Ell	d					11 36												11 51		12 06		
Surrey Quays	d	11 30			11 35	11 40	11 45	11 49							12 00			11 55	12 05	12 10		
Canada Water	d	11 32			11 37	11 42	11 47	11 51							12 02			11 57	12 07	12 12		
Rotherhithe	d	11 33			11 38	11 43	11 48	11 53							12 03			11 58	12 08	12 13		
Wapping	d	11 35			11 40	11 45	11 50	11 54							12 05			12 00	12 10	12 15		
Shadwell	d	11 37			11 42	11 47	11 52	11 56							12 07			12 02	12 12	12 17		
Whitechapel	d	11 39			11 44	11 49	11 54	11 59							12 09			12 04	12 14	12 19		
Shoreditch High Street	d	11 41			11 46	11 51	11 56	12 01							12 11			12 06	12 16	12 21		
Hoxton	d	11 43			11 48	11 53	11 58	12 03							12 13			12 08	12 18	12 23		
Haggerston	d	11 45			11 50	11 55	12 00	12 05							12 15			12 10	12 20	12 25		
Dalston Junction Stn Ell	a	11 49			11 55	11 59	12 04	12 10							12 19			12 14	12 25	12 29		
London Bridge	a		11 26	12 11					11 59	12 11			12 06			11 56	12 41				12 29	12 41

		LO	LO	LO	LO	LO	SE	SN	SN	FC	SN	SN	LO	LO	LO	SN	SN	SE	SN	SN	FC	LO	LO	LO
East Croydon	d															12 30								
West Croydon	d		11 52			12 09									12 22		12 31							12 39
Norwood Junction	d		11 58			12 13									12 28	12 35								12 43
Anerley	d		12 01			12 16									12 31	12 38								12 46
Penge West	d		12 03			12 18									12 33	12 40								12 48
London Victoria	d						12 09.		12 11			12 19						12 39		12 41				
Battersea Park	d								12 15			12 23								12 45				
Wandsworth Road	d								12 17											12 47				
Clapham High Street	d								12 19											12 49				
London Blackfriars	d									12 12											12 42			
Denmark Hill	d						12 18		12 24	12 22								12 48		12 54	12 52			
Peckham Rye	d						12 21	12 12	12 26	12 25	12 16						13 01	12 51	12 42	12 56	12 55			
Queens Rd Peckham	d								12 29		12 19						13 04			12 59				
South Bermondsey	d								12 31		12 21						13 06			13 01				
Clapham Junction	d											12 27												
Wandsworth Common	d											12 30												
Balham	d											12 32												
Streatham Hill	d											12 35												
West Norwood	d							12 23				12 40							12 53					
Gipsy Hill	d							12 26				12 43							12 56					
Crystal Palace	d	11 58			12 13			12 29				12 51		12 28					12 59				12 43	
Sydenham	d	12 01	12 06		12 16	12 21						12 54		12 31	12 36	12 42							12 46	12 51
Forest Hill	d	12 04	12 08		12 19	12 23						12 57		12 34	12 38	12 45							12 49	12 53
Honor Oak Park	d	12 06	12 11		12 21	12 26						12 59		12 36	12 41	12 47							12 51	12 56
Brockley	d	12 09	12 13		12 24	12 28						13 02		12 39	12 43	12 50							12 54	12 58
New Cross Gate Station Ell	a																							
	d																							
New Cross Gate	d	12 11	12 16		12 26	12 31						13 04		12 41	12 46	12 52							12 56	13 01
New Cross Ell	d			12 21									12 36									12 51		
Surrey Quays	d	12 15	12 19	12 25	12 30	12 35							12 40	12 45	12 49							12 55	13 00	13 05
Canada Water	d	12 17	12 21	12 27	12 32	12 37							12 42	12 47	12 51							12 57	13 02	13 07
Rotherhithe	d	12 18	12 23	12 28	12 33	12 38							12 43	12 48	12 53							12 58	13 03	13 08
Wapping	d	12 20	12 24	12 30	12 35	12 40							12 45	12 50	12 54							13 00	13 05	13 10
Shadwell	d	12 22	12 26	12 32	12 37	12 42							12 47	12 52	12 56							13 02	13 07	13 12
Whitechapel	d	12 24	12 29	12 34	12 39	12 44							12 49	12 54	12 59							13 04	13 09	13 14
Shoreditch High Street	d	12 26	12 31	12 36	12 41	12 46							12 51	12 56	13 01							13 06	13 11	13 16
Hoxton	d	12 28	12 33	12 38	12 43	12 48							12 53	12 58	13 03							13 08	13 13	13 18
Haggerston	d	12 30	12 35	12 40	12 45	12 50							12 55	13 00	13 05							13 10	13 15	13 20
Dalston Junction Stn Ell	a	12 34	12 40	12 44	12 49	12 55							12 59	13 04	13 10							13 14	13 19	13 25
London Bridge	a								12 36		12 26	13 11				12 59	13 11			13 06				

East London Line and Croydon-London Victoria to London Bridge

Station		SN	SN	LO	LO	LO	SN	SN	LO	LO	LO	SE	SN	SN	FC	SN	SN	LO	LO	LO	SN	SN
East Croydon	d						13 00														13 30	
West Croydon	d					12 52		13 01			13 09									13 22		13 31
Norwood Junction	d					12 58	13 05				13 13									13 28	13 35	
Anerley	d					13 01	13 08				13 16									13 31	13 38	
Penge West	d					13 03	13 10				13 18									13 33	13 40	
London Victoria	d		12 49									13 09.		13 11			13 19					
Battersea Park	d		12 53											13 15			13 23					
Wandsworth Road	d													13 17								
Clapham High Street	d													13 19								
London Blackfriars	d														13 12							
Denmark Hill	d											13 18		13 24	13 22							
Peckham Rye	d	12 46						13 31				13 21	13 12	13 26	13 25	13 16						14 01
Queens Rd Peckham	d	12 49						13 34						13 29		13 19						14 04
South Bermondsey	d	12 51						13 36						13 31		13 21						14 06
Clapham Junction	d		12 57														13 27					
Wandsworth Common	d		13 00														13 30					
Balham	d		13 02														13 32					
Streatham Hill	d		13 05														13 35					
West Norwood	d		13 10										13 23				13 40					
Gipsy Hill	d		13 13										13 26				13 43					
Crystal Palace	d		13 21		12 58					13 13			13 29				13 51		13 28			
Sydenham	d		13 24		13 01	13 06	13 12			13 16	13 21						13 54		13 31	13 36	13 42	
Forest Hill	d		13 27		13 04	13 08	13 15			13 19	13 23						13 57		13 34	13 38	13 45	
Honor Oak Park	d		13 29		13 06	13 11	13 17			13 21	13 26						13 59		13 36	13 41	13 47	
Brockley	d		13 32		13 09	13 13	13 20			13 24	13 28						14 02		13 39	13 43	13 50	
New Cross Gate Station Ell	a																					
	d																					
New Cross Gate	d		13 34		13 11	13 16	13 22			13 26	13 31						14 04		13 41	13 46	13 52	
New Cross Ell	d			13 06					13 21									13 36				
Surrey Quays	d			13 10	13 15	13 19			13 25	13 30	13 35							13 40	13 45	13 49		
Canada Water	d			13 12	13 17	13 21			13 27	13 32	13 37							13 42	13 47	13 51		
Rotherhithe	d			13 13	13 18	13 23			13 28	13 33	13 38							13 43	13 48	13 53		
Wapping	d			13 15	13 20	13 24			13 30	13 35	13 40							13 45	13 50	13 54		
Shadwell	d			13 17	13 22	13 26			13 32	13 37	13 42							13 47	13 52	13 56		
Whitechapel	d			13 19	13 24	13 29			13 34	13 39	13 44							13 49	13 54	13 59		
Shoreditch High Street	d			13 21	13 26	13 31			13 36	13 41	13 46							13 51	13 56	14 01		
Hoxton	d			13 23	13 28	13 33			13 38	13 43	13 48							13 53	13 58	14 03		
Haggerston	d			13 25	13 30	13 35			13 40	13 45	13 50							13 55	14 00	14 05		
Dalston Junction Stn Ell	a			13 29	13 34	13 40			13 44	13 49	13 55							13 59	14 04	14 10		
London Bridge	a	12 56	13 41				13 29	13 41						13 36		13 26	14 11				13 59	14 11

Station		LO	LO	LO	SE	SN	SN	LO	FC	SN	SN	LO	LO	SN	SN	LO	SE	SN	SN	FC	LO	SN	SN
East Croydon	d													14 00									
West Croydon	d			13 39									13 52		14 01								
Norwood Junction	d			13 43									13 58	14 05									
Anerley	d			13 46									14 01	14 08									
Penge West	d			13 48									14 03	14 10									
London Victoria	d				13 39		13 41				13 49						14 09	14 11					14 19
Battersea Park	d						13 45				13 53							14 15					14 23
Wandsworth Road	d						13 47											14 17					
Clapham High Street	d						13 49											14 19					
London Blackfriars	d								13 42											14 12			
Denmark Hill	d				13 48		13 54		13 52								14 18	14 24		14 22			
Peckham Rye	d				13 51	13 42	13 56		13 55	13 46					14 31		14 21	14 26	14 12	14 25		14 16	
Queens Rd Peckham	d						13 59			13 49					14 34			14 29				14 19	
South Bermondsey	d						14 01			13 51					14 36			14 31				14 21	
Clapham Junction	d										13 57												14 27
Wandsworth Common	d										14 00												14 30
Balham	d										14 02												14 32
Streatham Hill	d										14 05												14 35
West Norwood	d					13 53					14 10								14 23				14 40
Gipsy Hill	d					13 56					14 13								14 26				14 43
Crystal Palace	d		13 43			13 59					14 21	13 58							14 29		14 13		14 51
Sydenham	d		13 46	13 51							14 24	14 01	14 06	14 12							14 16		14 54
Forest Hill	d		13 49	13 53							14 27	14 04	14 08	14 15							14 19		14 57
Honor Oak Park	d		13 51	13 56							14 29	14 06	14 11	14 17							14 21		14 59
Brockley	d		13 54	13 58							14 32	14 09	14 13	14 20							14 24		15 02
New Cross Gate Station Ell	a																						
	d																						
New Cross Gate	d		13 56	14 01							14 34	14 11	14 16	14 22							14 26		15 04
New Cross Ell	d	13 51						14 06								14 21							
Surrey Quays	d	13 55	14 00	14 05				14 10				14 15	14 19			14 25					14 30		
Canada Water	d	13 57	14 02	14 07				14 12				14 17	14 21			14 27					14 32		
Rotherhithe	d	13 58	14 03	14 08				14 13				14 18	14 23			14 28					14 33		
Wapping	d	14 00	14 05	14 10				14 15				14 20	14 24			14 30					14 35		
Shadwell	d	14 02	14 07	14 12				14 17				14 22	14 26			14 32					14 37		
Whitechapel	d	14 04	14 09	14 14				14 19				14 24	14 29			14 34					14 39		
Shoreditch High Street	d	14 06	14 11	14 16				14 21				14 26	14 31			14 36					14 41		
Hoxton	d	14 08	14 13	14 18				14 23				14 28	14 33			14 38					14 43		
Haggerston	d	14 10	14 15	14 20				14 25				14 30	14 35			14 40					14 45		
Dalston Junction Stn Ell	a	14 14	14 19	14 25				14 29				14 34	14 40			14 44					14 49		
London Bridge	a						14 06			13 56	14 41			14 29	14 41			14 36				14 26	15 11

Table 178 — Mondays to Fridays

East London Line and Croydon-London Victoria to London Bridge

Station		LO	LO	LO	LO	SN	SN	SE	LO	SN	SN	FC	LO	LO	SN	SN	LO	LO	LO	SN	SN	LO
East Croydon	d					14 30														15 00		
West Croydon	d	14 09			14 22		14 31							14 39					14 52		15 01	
Norwood Junction	d	14 13			14 28	14 35								14 43					14 58	15 05		
Anerley	d	14 16			14 31	14 38								14 46					15 01	15 08		
Penge West	d	14 18			14 33	14 40								14 48					15 03	15 10		
London Victoria	d							14 39			14 41					14 49						
Battersea Park	d										14 45					14 53						
Wandsworth Road	d										14 47											
Clapham High Street	d										14 49											
London Blackfriars	d											14 42										
Denmark Hill	d							14 48			14 54	14 52										
Peckham Rye	d						15 01	14 51		14 42	14 56	14 55			14 46						15 31	
Queens Rd Peckham	d						15 04				14 59				14 49						15 34	
South Bermondsey	d						15 06				15 01				14 51						15 36	
Clapham Junction	d															14 57						
Wandsworth Common	d															15 00						
Balham	d															15 02						
Streatham Hill	d															15 05						
West Norwood	d									14 53						15 10						
Gipsy Hill	d									14 56						15 13						
Crystal Palace	d			14 28						14 59			14 43			15 21		14 58				
Sydenham	d	14 21		14 31	14 36	14 42							14 46	14 51		15 24		15 01	15 06	15 12		
Forest Hill	d	14 23		14 34	14 38	14 45							14 49	14 53		15 27		15 04	15 08	15 15		
Honor Oak Park	d	14 26		14 36	14 41	14 47							14 51	14 56		15 29		15 06	15 11	15 17		
Brockley	d	14 28		14 39	14 43	14 50							14 54	14 58		15 32		15 09	15 13	15 20		
New Cross Gate Station Ell	a																					
	d																					
New Cross Gate	d	14 31		14 41	14 46	14 52							14 56	15 01		15 34		15 11	15 16	15 22		
New Cross Ell	d		14 36						14 51								15 06					15 21
Surrey Quays	d	14 35	14 40	14 45	14 49				14 55				15 00	15 05			15 10	15 15	15 19			15 25
Canada Water	d	14 37	14 42	14 47	14 51				14 57				15 02	15 07			15 12	15 17	15 21			15 27
Rotherhithe	d	14 38	14 43	14 48	14 53				14 58				15 03	15 08			15 13	15 18	15 23			15 28
Wapping	d	14 40	14 45	14 50	14 54				15 00				15 05	15 10			15 15	15 20	15 24			15 30
Shadwell	d	14 42	14 47	14 52	14 56				15 02				15 07	15 12			15 17	15 22	15 26			15 32
Whitechapel	d	14 44	14 49	14 54	14 59				15 04				15 09	15 14			15 19	15 24	15 29			15 34
Shoreditch High Street	d	14 46	14 51	14 56	15 01				15 06				15 11	15 16			15 21	15 26	15 31			15 36
Hoxton	d	14 48	14 53	14 58	15 03				15 08				15 13	15 18			15 23	15 28	15 33			15 38
Haggerston	d	14 50	14 55	15 00	15 05				15 10				15 15	15 20			15 25	15 30	15 35			15 40
Dalston Junction Stn Ell	a	14 55	14 59	15 04	15 10				15 14				15 19	15 25			15 29	15 34	15 40			15 44
London Bridge	a					14 59	15 11				15 06				14 56	15 41				15 29	15 41	

Station		SE	SN	SN	FC	LO	SN	LO	LO	SN	LO	LO	SN	SN	LO	SE	SN	SN	FC	LO	SN	LO	SN
East Croydon	d												15 30										
West Croydon	d							15 09				15 22		15 31								15 39	
Norwood Junction	d							15 13				15 28	15 35									15 43	
Anerley	d							15 16				15 31	15 38									15 46	
Penge West	d							15 18				15 33	15 40									15 48	
London Victoria	d	15 09		15 11						15 19						15 39.		15 41					15 49
Battersea Park	d			15 15						15 23								15 45					15 53
Wandsworth Road	d			15 17														15 47					
Clapham High Street	d			15 19														15 49					
London Blackfriars	d				15 12														15 42				
Denmark Hill	d	15 18		15 24	15 22											15 48		15 54	15 52				
Peckham Rye	d	15 21	15 12	15 26	15 25.		15 16							16 01		15 51	15 42	15 56	15 55		15 46		
Queens Rd Peckham	d			15 29			15 19							16 04				15 59			15 49		
South Bermondsey	d			15 31			15 21							16 06				16 01			15 51		
Clapham Junction	d									15 27													15 57
Wandsworth Common	d									15 30													16 00
Balham	d									15 32													16 02
Streatham Hill	d									15 35													16 05
West Norwood	d		15 23							15 40							15 53						16 10
Gipsy Hill	d		15 26							15 43							15 56						16 13
Crystal Palace	d		15 29			15 13				15 51	15 28						15 59			15 43			16 21
Sydenham	d					15 16		15 21		15 54	15 31	15 36	15 42							15 46		15 51	16 24
Forest Hill	d					15 19		15 23		15 57	15 34	15 38	15 45							15 49		15 53	16 27
Honor Oak Park	d					15 21		15 26		15 59	15 36	15 41	15 47							15 51		15 56	16 29
Brockley	d					15 24		15 28		16 02	15 39	15 43	15 50							15 54		15 58	16 32
New Cross Gate Station Ell	a																						
	d																						
New Cross Gate	d					15 26		15 31		16 04	15 41	15 46	15 52							15 56		16 01	16 34
New Cross Ell	d								15 36						15 51								
Surrey Quays	d					15 30		15 35	15 40		15 45	15 49			15 55					16 00		16 05	
Canada Water	d					15 32		15 37	15 42		15 47	15 51			15 57					16 02		16 07	
Rotherhithe	d					15 33		15 38	15 43		15 48	15 53			15 58					16 03		16 08	
Wapping	d					15 35		15 40	15 45		15 50	15 54			16 00					16 05		16 10	
Shadwell	d					15 37		15 42	15 47		15 52	15 56			16 02					16 07		16 12	
Whitechapel	d					15 39		15 44	15 49		15 54	15 59			16 04					16 09		16 14	
Shoreditch High Street	d					15 41		15 46	15 51		15 56	16 01			16 06					16 11		16 16	
Hoxton	d					15 43		15 48	15 53		15 58	16 03			16 08					16 13		16 18	
Haggerston	d					15 45		15 50	15 55		16 00	16 05			16 10					16 15		16 20	
Dalston Junction Stn Ell	a					15 49		15 55	15 59		16 04	16 10			16 14					16 19		16 25	
London Bridge	a			15 36			15 26			16 11			15 59	16 11				16 06			15 56		16 41

Table 178

Mondays to Fridays

East London Line and Croydon-London Victoria to London Bridge

		LO	LO	LO	SN		SN	SN	LO	LO	LO	SE	SN	SN	FC		SN	LO	SN	LO	LO	FC	SN	SN
East Croydon	d				16 00																		16 30	
West Croydon 4	d			15 52			16 01				16 09										16 22			16 31
Norwood Junction 2	d			15 58	16 05						16 13										16 28		16 35	
Anerley	d			16 01	16 08						16 16										16 31		16 38	
Penge West	d			16 03	16 10						16 18										16 33		16 40	
London Victoria 15 ⊖	d											16 09	16 11						16 19					
Battersea Park 4	d												16 15						16 23					
Wandsworth Road	d												16 17											
Clapham High Street ⊖	d												16 19											
London Blackfriars 3 ⊖	d														16 12							16 26		
Denmark Hill 4	d											16 18	16 24		16 22							16 39		
Peckham Rye 4	d						16 31	16 07				16 21	16 26	16 12	16 25		16 16					16 42		17 00
Queens Rd Peckham	d						16 34	16 10					16 29				16 19							17 03
South Bermondsey	d						16 36	16 12					16 31				16 21							17 05
Clapham Junction 10	d																		16 27					
Wandsworth Common	d																		16 30					
Balham 4 ⊖	d																		16 32					
Streatham Hill	d																		16 35					
West Norwood 4	d													16 23					16 39					
Gipsy Hill	d													16 26					16 44					
Crystal Palace 4	d		15 58							16 13				16 29					16 50	16 28				
Sydenham	d		16 01	16 06	16 12					16 16	16 21								16 54	16 31	16 36		16 42	
Forest Hill 4	d		16 04	16 08	16 15					16 19	16 23								16 56	16 34	16 38		16 45	
Honor Oak Park	d		16 06	16 11	16 17					16 21	16 26								16 59	16 36	16 41		16 47	
Brockley	d		16 09	16 13	16 20					16 24	16 28								17 01	16 39	16 43		16 50	
New Cross Gate Station Ell	a																							
	d																							
New Cross Gate 4	d		16 11	16 16	16 22					16 26	16 31								17 04	16 41	16 46		16 52	
New Cross Ell	d	16 06							16 21									16 36						
Surrey Quays	d	16 10	16 15	16 19					16 25	16 30	16 35							16 40		16 45	16 49			
Canada Water	d	16 12	16 17	16 21					16 27	16 32	16 37							16 42		16 47	16 51			
Rotherhithe	d	16 13	16 18	16 23					16 28	16 33	16 38							16 43		16 48	16 53			
Wapping	d	16 15	16 20	16 24					16 30	16 35	16 40							16 45		16 50	16 54			
Shadwell	d	16 17	16 22	16 26					16 32	16 37	16 42							16 47		16 52	16 56			
Whitechapel	d	16 19	16 24	16 29					16 34	16 39	16 44							16 49		16 54	16 59			
Shoreditch High Street	d	16 21	16 26	16 31					16 36	16 41	16 46							16 51		16 56	17 01			
Hoxton	d	16 23	16 28	16 33					16 38	16 43	16 48							16 53		16 58	17 03			
Haggerston	d	16 25	16 30	16 35					16 40	16 45	16 50							16 55		17 00	17 05			
Dalston Junction Stn Ell	a	16 29	16 34	16 40					16 44	16 49	16 55							16 59		17 04	17 10			
London Bridge 4 ⊖	a				16 29		16 41	16 17					16 38				16 26		17 11				17 00	17 10

		LO	SE	FC	SN	SN	LO	LO	SN	LO		SN	LO	SN	SN	LO	SE	SN	FC	LO	LO	LO	SN	SN	SN
East Croydon	d													17 00											
West Croydon 4	d							16 39							17 01	16 52						17 09		17 12	
Norwood Junction 2	d							16 43						17 05		16 58						17 13			
Anerley	d							16 46						17 08		17 01						17 16			
Penge West	d							16 48						17 10		17 03						17 18			
London Victoria 15 ⊖	d		16 39.			16 41						16 52					17 04.						17 11		
Battersea Park 4	d					16 45						16 56											17 15		
Wandsworth Road	d					16 47																	17 17		
Clapham High Street ⊖	d					16 49																	17 19		
London Blackfriars 3 ⊖	d			16 42															17 10						
Denmark Hill 4	d		16 48	16 52		16 54											17 13		17 20				17 24		
Peckham Rye 4	d		16 51	16 55	16 42	16 56			16 46						17 29		17 16	17 07	17 23				17 26		17 16
Queens Rd Peckham	d					16 59			16 49						17 32								17 29		17 19
South Bermondsey	d					17 01			16 51						17 34								17 31		17 21
Clapham Junction 10	d											17 00													
Wandsworth Common	d											17 03													
Balham 4 ⊖	d											17 06													
Streatham Hill	d											17 09													
West Norwood 4	d				16 53							17 12						17 20							
Gipsy Hill	d				16 56							17 15						17 23							
Crystal Palace 4	d				16 59		16 43					17 21	16 58					17 26			17 13				
Sydenham	d						16 46	16 51				17 24	17 01	17 12		17 06					17 16	17 21			
Forest Hill 4	d						16 49	16 53				17 27	17 04	17 15		17 08					17 19	17 23			
Honor Oak Park	d						16 51	16 56				17 29	17 06	17 17		17 11					17 21	17 26			
Brockley	d						16 54	16 58				17 32	17 09	17 20		17 13					17 24	17 28			
New Cross Gate Station Ell	a																								
	d																								
New Cross Gate 4	d						16 56	17 01				17 34	17 11	17 22		17 16					17 26	17 31			
New Cross Ell	d	16 51								17 06										17 21					
Surrey Quays	d	16 55					17 00	17 05		17 10			17 15			17 19				17 25	17 30	17 35			
Canada Water	d	16 57					17 02	17 07		17 12			17 17			17 21				17 27	17 32	17 37			
Rotherhithe	d	16 58					17 03	17 08		17 13			17 18			17 23				17 28	17 33	17 38			
Wapping	d	17 00					17 05	17 10		17 15			17 20			17 24				17 30	17 35	17 40			
Shadwell	d	17 02					17 07	17 12		17 17			17 22			17 26				17 32	17 37	17 42			
Whitechapel	d	17 04					17 09	17 14		17 19			17 24			17 29				17 34	17 39	17 44			
Shoreditch High Street	d	17 06					17 11	17 16		17 21			17 26			17 31				17 36	17 41	17 46			
Hoxton	d	17 08					17 13	17 18		17 23			17 28			17 33				17 38	17 43	17 48			
Haggerston	d	17 10					17 15	17 20		17 25			17 30			17 35				17 40	17 45	17 50			
Dalston Junction Stn Ell	a	17 14					17 19	17 25		17 29			17 34			17 40				17 44	17 49	17 55			
London Bridge 4 ⊖	a					17 08			16 56			17 43		17 30	17 39								17 38	17 28	17 26

Table 178

Mondays to Fridays

East London Line and Croydon-London Victoria to London Bridge

		LO		LO	LO	LO	SN	SN		SN	SN	LO	SN	FC	SE	SN	LO	SN	LO	LO	SN		SN	SE	FC
East Croydon	d							17 30																	
West Croydon 4	d				17 22					17 31							17 39				17 42				
Norwood Junction 2	d				17 29			17 35			17 32						17 43								
Anerley	d				17 32			17 38									17 46								
Penge West	d				17 34			17 40									17 48								
London Victoria 15 ⊖	d						17 22								17 34			17 41					17 52.	17 56	
Battersea Park 4	d						17 26											17 45					17 56		
Wandsworth Road	d																	17 47							
Clapham High Street ⊖	d																	17 49							
London Blackfriars 3 ⊖	d													17 36											18 00
Denmark Hill 4	d													17 47	17 43			17 54						18 06	18 15
Peckham Rye 4	d									18 01	17 53		17 34	17 50	17 46	17 37		17 57						18 09.	18 18.
Queens Rd Peckham	d									18 04	17 55		17 37					17 59							
South Bermondsey	d									18 06	17 58		17 39					18 02							
Clapham Junction 10	d						17 30																18 00		
Wandsworth Common	d						17 33																18 03		
Balham 4 ⊖	d						17 35																18 05		
Streatham Hill	d						17 38																18 08		
West Norwood 4	d						17 42									17 49							18 14		
Gipsy Hill	d						17 45									17 52							18 17		
Crystal Palace 4	d			17 28			17 48					17 42				17 54				17 58			18 20		
Sydenham	d			17 31	17 36		17 54	17 42				17 45					17 51			18 01			18 24		
Forest Hill 4	d			17 34	17 39		17 57	17 45				17 48					17 53			18 04			18 27		
Honor Oak Park	d			17 36	17 41		17 59	17 47				17 50					17 56			18 06			18 29		
Brockley	d			17 39	17 44		18 02	17 50				17 53					17 58			18 09			18 32		
New Cross Gate Station Ell	a																								
	d																								
New Cross Gate 4	d			17 41	17 46		18 04	17 52				17 56					18 01			18 11			18 34		
New Cross Ell	d	17 36				17 51													18 06						
Surrey Quays	d	17 40		17 45	17 50	17 55						18 00					18 05		18 10	18 15					
Canada Water	d	17 42		17 47	17 52	17 57						18 02					18 07		18 12	18 17					
Rotherhithe	d	17 43		17 48	17 53	17 58						18 03					18 08		18 13	18 18					
Wapping	d	17 45		17 50	17 55	18 00						18 05					18 10		18 15	18 20					
Shadwell	d	17 47		17 52	17 57	18 02						18 07					18 12		18 17	18 22					
Whitechapel	d	17 49		17 54	17 59	18 04						18 09					18 14		18 19	18 24					
Shoreditch High Street	d	17 51		17 56	18 01	18 06						18 11					18 16		18 21	18 26					
Hoxton	d	17 53		17 58	18 03	18 08						18 13					18 18		18 23	18 28					
Haggerston	d	17 55		18 00	18 05	18 10						18 15					18 20		18 25	18 30					
Dalston Junction Stn Ell	a	17 59		18 04	18 10	18 14						18 19					18 25		18 29	18 34					
London Bridge 4 ⊖	a						18 13	17 59		18 11	18 02		17 44					18 08			18 00		18 45		

		SN	LO	SN	SN	LO		SN	SN	SN	LO	SE	LO		SN	FC	LO	LO	LO	SN	SN	SN	SN		SN
East Croydon	d																			18 30					
West Croydon 4	d	18 01	17 52							18 13			18 09						18 22		18 31				
Norwood Junction 2	d		17 58	18 04									18 13						18 28	18 35					
Anerley	d		18 01	18 07									18 16						18 31	18 38					
Penge West	d		18 03	18 09									18 18						18 33	18 40					
London Victoria 15 ⊖	d							18 11				18 18			18 23										
Battersea Park 4	d							18 15							18 27										
Wandsworth Road	d							18 17																	
Clapham High Street ⊖	d							18 19																	
London Blackfriars 3 ⊖	d															18 24									
Denmark Hill 4	d							18 24				18 28				18 34									
Peckham Rye 4	d	18 29			18 07			18 26	18 12			18 32				18 38					19 01	18 32	18 36		18 37
Queens Rd Peckham	d	18 32						18 29	18 15												19 04	18 35	18 38		
South Bermondsey	d	18 34						18 31	18 17												19 06	18 37	18 41		
Clapham Junction 10	d														18 31										
Wandsworth Common	d														18 34										
Balham 4 ⊖	d														18 36										
Streatham Hill	d														18 39										
West Norwood 4	d				18 20										18 43										18 50
Gipsy Hill	d				18 23										18 46										18 53
Crystal Palace 4	d				18 26						18 13				18 51			18 28							18 56
Sydenham	d		18 06	18 11							18 16		18 21		18 54			18 31	18 36	18 42					
Forest Hill 4	d		18 08	18 14							18 19		18 23		18 57			18 34	18 38	18 45					
Honor Oak Park	d		18 11	18 16							18 21		18 26		18 59			18 36	18 41	18 47					
Brockley	d		18 13	18 19							18 24		18 28		19 02			18 39	18 43	18 50					
New Cross Gate Station Ell	a																								
	d																								
New Cross Gate 4	d		18 16	18 21							18 26		18 31		19 04			18 41	18 46	18 52					
New Cross Ell	d					18 21											18 36								
Surrey Quays	d		18 19			18 25					18 30		18 35				18 40	18 45	18 49						
Canada Water	d		18 21			18 27					18 32		18 37				18 42	18 47	18 51						
Rotherhithe	d		18 23			18 28					18 33		18 38				18 43	18 48	18 53						
Wapping	d		18 24			18 30					18 35		18 40				18 45	18 50	18 54						
Shadwell	d		18 26			18 32					18 37		18 42				18 47	18 52	18 56						
Whitechapel	d		18 29			18 34					18 39		18 44				18 49	18 54	18 59						
Shoreditch High Street	d		18 31			18 36					18 41		18 46				18 51	18 56	19 01						
Hoxton	d		18 33			18 38					18 43		18 48				18 53	18 58	19 03						
Haggerston	d		18 35			18 40					18 45		18 50				18 55	19 00	19 05						
Dalston Junction Stn Ell	a		18 40			18 44					18 49		18 55				18 59	19 04	19 10						
London Bridge 4 ⊖	a	18 39		18 31				18 38	18 22	18 29					19 13					18 59	19 11	18 42	18 45		

East London Line and Croydon-London Victoria to London Bridge

		LO	SE	SN	FC 1	LO	LO		SN	SN	LO	LO	LO	SN	SN	LO	SE	SN		FC	LO	SN	LO	SN	LO
East Croydon	d									19 00															
West Croydon 4	d						18 39						18 52	19 01									19 09		
Norwood Junction 2	d						18 43			19 05			18 58										19 13		
Anerley	d						18 46			19 08			19 01										19 16		
Penge West	d						18 48			19 10			19 03										19 18		
London Victoria 15	d		18 39	18 41					18 52								19 09	19 11							
Battersea Park 4	d			18 45					18 56									19 15							
Wandsworth Road	d			18 47														19 17							
Clapham High Street	d			18 49														19 19							
London Blackfriars 3	d				18 42															19 12					
Denmark Hill 4	d		18 48	18 54	18 52												19 18	19 24		19 22					
Peckham Rye 4	d		18 51	18 57	18 55									19 29	19 07		19 22	19 26		19 25		19 17		19 17	
Queens Rd Peckham	d			19 00										19 32	19 10			19 29						19 20	
South Bermondsey	d			19 02										19 34	19 12			19 31						19 22	
Clapham Junction 10	d								19 00																
Wandsworth Common	d								19 03																
Balham 4	d								19 05																
Streatham Hill	d								19 08																
West Norwood 4	d								19 12													19 30			
Gipsy Hill	d								19 15													19 33			
Crystal Palace 4	d					18 43			19 21			18 58									19 13	19 35			
Sydenham	d					18 46	18 51		19 24	19 12		19 01	19 06								19 16		19 21		
Forest Hill 4	d					18 49	18 53		19 27	19 15		19 04	19 08								19 19		19 23		
Honor Oak Park	d					18 51	18 56		19 29	19 17		19 06	19 11								19 21		19 26		
Brockley	d					18 54	18 58		19 32	19 20		19 09	19 13								19 24		19 28		
New Cross Gate Station Ell	a																								
	d																								
New Cross Gate 4	d					18 56	19 01		19 34	19 22		19 11	19 16								19 26		19 31		
New Cross Ell	d	18 51									19 06					19 21									19 36
Surrey Quays	d	18 55				19 00	19 05				19 10	19 15	19 19			19 25					19 30		19 35		19 40
Canada Water	d	18 57				19 02	19 07				19 12	19 17	19 21			19 27					19 32		19 37		19 42
Rotherhithe	d	18 58				19 03	19 08				19 13	19 18	19 23			19 28					19 33		19 38		19 43
Wapping	d	19 00				19 05	19 10				19 15	19 20	19 24			19 30					19 35		19 40		19 45
Shadwell	d	19 02				19 07	19 12				19 17	19 22	19 26			19 32					19 37		19 42		19 47
Whitechapel	d	19 04				19 09	19 14				19 19	19 24	19 29			19 34					19 39		19 44		19 49
Shoreditch High Street	d	19 06				19 11	19 16				19 21	19 26	19 31			19 36					19 41		19 46		19 51
Hoxton	d	19 08				19 13	19 18				19 23	19 28	19 33			19 38					19 43		19 48		19 53
Haggerston	d	19 10				19 15	19 20				19 25	19 30	19 35			19 40					19 45		19 50		19 55
Dalston Junction Stn Ell	a	19 14				19 19	19 25				19 29	19 34	19 40			19 44					19 49		19 55		19 59
London Bridge 4	a			19 09					19 41	19 29				19 41	19 17			19 36						19 27	

		LO	SN		SN	LO	LO	SN	SN	LO	LO	SE	SN	FC	SN	LO		SN	LO	LO	SN	SN	SN	LO	LO
East Croydon	d				19 30																	20 00			
West Croydon 4	d					19 22		19 31			19 39									19 52			20 01		
Norwood Junction 2	d				19 35	19 28					19 43									19 58		20 05			
Anerley	d				19 38	19 31					19 46									20 01		20 08			
Penge West	d				19 40	19 33					19 48									20 03		20 10			
London Victoria 15	d		19 22									19 39	19 41								19 52				
Battersea Park 4	d		19 26										19 45								19 56				
Wandsworth Road	d												19 47												
Clapham High Street	d												19 49												
London Blackfriars 3	d													19 42											
Denmark Hill 4	d											19 48	19 54	19 52											
Peckham Rye 4	d							20 01	19 38			19 51	19 56	19 55	19 47			19 48					20 31		
Queens Rd Peckham	d							20 04	19 41				19 59					19 51					20 34		
South Bermondsey	d							20 06	19 43				20 01					19 53					20 36		
Clapham Junction 10	d		19 30																		20 00				
Wandsworth Common	d		19 33																		20 03				
Balham 4	d		19 35																		20 05				
Streatham Hill	d		19 38																		20 08				
West Norwood 4	d		19 42												20 00						20 12				
Gipsy Hill	d		19 45												20 03						20 15				
Crystal Palace 4	d	19 28	19 51							19 43					20 05				19 58		20 21				20 13
Sydenham	d	19 31	19 54		19 42	19 36				19 46	19 51								20 01	20 06	20 24	20 12			20 16
Forest Hill 4	d	19 34	19 57		19 45	19 38				19 49	19 53								20 04	20 08	20 27	20 15			20 19
Honor Oak Park	d	19 36	19 59		19 47	19 41				19 51	19 56								20 06	20 11	20 29	20 17			20 21
Brockley	d	19 39	20 02		19 50	19 43				19 54	19 58								20 09	20 13	20 32	20 20			20 24
New Cross Gate Station Ell	a																								
	d																								
New Cross Gate 4	d	19 41	20 04		19 52	19 46				19 56	20 01								20 11	20 16	20 34	20 22			20 26
New Cross Ell	d						19 51									20 06								20 21	
Surrey Quays	d	19 45				19 49	19 55			20 00	20 05					20 10			20 15	20 19				20 25	20 30
Canada Water	d	19 47				19 51	19 57			20 02	20 07					20 12			20 17	20 21				20 27	20 32
Rotherhithe	d	19 48				19 53	19 58			20 03	20 08					20 13			20 18	20 23				20 28	20 33
Wapping	d	19 50				19 54	20 00			20 05	20 10					20 15			20 20	20 24				20 30	20 35
Shadwell	d	19 52				19 56	20 02			20 07	20 12					20 17			20 22	20 26				20 32	20 37
Whitechapel	d	19 54				19 59	20 04			20 09	20 14					20 19			20 24	20 29				20 34	20 39
Shoreditch High Street	d	19 56				20 01	20 06			20 11	20 16					20 21			20 26	20 31				20 36	20 41
Hoxton	d	19 58				20 03	20 08			20 13	20 18					20 23			20 28	20 33				20 38	20 43
Haggerston	d	20 00				20 05	20 10			20 15	20 20					20 25			20 30	20 35				20 40	20 45
Dalston Junction Stn Ell	a	20 04				20 10	20 14			20 19	20 25					20 29			20 34	20 40				20 44	20 49
London Bridge 4	a		20 11		19 59			20 11	19 51				20 06					19 58			20 41	20 29	20 41		

Table 178

Mondays to Fridays

East London Line and Croydon-London Victoria to London Bridge

		SN	FC		SN	LO	LO	LO	LO	SN	SN		SN	LO	LO	LO	SN	FC	SN	SN		LO	LO	SN	SN
East Croydon	d										20 31													21 00	
West Croydon 4	d					20 09			20 22				20 31			20 39									21 01
Norwood Junction 2	d					20 13			20 28		20 35					20 43								21 05	
Anerley	d					20 16			20 31		20 38					20 46								21 08	
Penge West	d					20 18			20 33		20 40					20 48								21 10	
London Victoria 15	d	20 11								20 22							20 41			20 52					
Battersea Park 4	d	20 15								20 26							20 45			20 56					
Wandsworth Road	d	20 17															20 47								
Clapham High Street	d	20 19															20 49								
London Blackfriars 3	d		20 12															20 42							
Denmark Hill 4	d	20 24	20 22														20 54	20 52							
Peckham Rye 4	d	20 26	20 25		20 18								21 01				20 56	20 55	20 47						21 31
Queens Rd Peckham	d	20 29			20 21								21 04				20 59		20 50						21 34
South Bermondsey	d	20 31			20 23								21 06				21 01		20 52						21 36
Clapham Junction 10	d									20 30										21 00					
Wandsworth Common	d									20 33										21 03					
Balham 4	d									20 35										21 05					
Streatham Hill	d									20 38										21 08					
West Norwood 4	d									20 42										21 12					
Gipsy Hill	d									20 45										21 15					
Crystal Palace 4	d							20 28		20 51					20 43					21 21			20 58		
Sydenham	d					20 21		20 31	20 36	20 54	20 42				20 46	20 51				21 27			21 01	21 12	
Forest Hill 4	d					20 23		20 34	20 38	20 57	20 45				20 49	20 53				21 29			21 04	21 15	
Honor Oak Park	d					20 26		20 36	20 41	20 59	20 47				20 51	20 56				21 32			21 06	21 17	
Brockley	d					20 28		20 39	20 43	21 02	20 50				20 54	20 58				21 34			21 09	21 20	
New Cross Gate Station Ell	a																								
	d																								
New Cross Gate 4	d					20 31		20 41	20 46	21 04	20 52				20 56	21 01				21 37			21 11	21 22	
New Cross Ell	d						20 36							20 51								21 06			
Surrey Quays	d					20 35	20 40	20 45	20 49					20 55	21 00	21 05						21 10	21 15		
Canada Water	d					20 37	20 42	20 47	20 51					20 57	21 02	21 07						21 12	21 17		
Rotherhithe	d					20 38	20 43	20 48	20 53					20 58	21 03	21 08						21 13	21 18		
Wapping	d					20 40	20 45	20 50	20 54					21 00	21 05	21 10						21 15	21 20		
Shadwell	d					20 42	20 47	20 52	20 56					21 02	21 07	21 12						21 17	21 22		
Whitechapel	d					20 44	20 49	20 54	20 59					21 04	21 09	21 14						21 19	21 24		
Shoreditch High Street	d					20 46	20 51	20 56	21 01					21 06	21 11	21 16						21 21	21 26		
Hoxton	d					20 48	20 53	20 58	21 03					21 08	21 13	21 18						21 23	21 28		
Haggerston	d					20 50	20 55	21 00	21 05					21 10	21 15	21 20						21 25	21 30		
Dalston Junction Stn Ell	a					20 55	20 59	21 04	21 10					21 14	21 19	21 25						21 29	21 34		
London Bridge 4	a	20 36			20 28					21 13	20 59		21 11				21 07		20 57	21 43				21 29	21 41

		LO	LO	SN	FC	LO	LO		LO	LO	LO	SN	SN	SN	LO	LO	LO	SN	LO	LO	SE		SN	SN	SN
East Croydon	d												21 30											22 00	
West Croydon 4	d	20 52					21 09				21 22			21 31			21 39								22 01
Norwood Junction 2	d	20 58					21 13				21 28		21 35				21 43							22 05	
Anerley	d	21 01					21 16				21 31		21 38				21 46							22 08	
Penge West	d	21 03					21 18				21 33		21 40				21 48							22 10	
London Victoria 15	d			21 11								21 22						21 41			21 43		21 52		
Battersea Park 4	d			21 15								21 26						21 45					21 56		
Wandsworth Road	d			21 17														21 47							
Clapham High Street	d			21 19														21 49							
London Blackfriars 3	d				21 12																				
Denmark Hill 4	d			21 24	21 22													21 54			21 52				
Peckham Rye 4	d			21 26	21 25									22 01				21 56			21 55				22 31
Queens Rd Peckham	d			21 29										22 04				21 59							22 34
South Bermondsey	d			21 31										22 06				22 01							22 36
Clapham Junction 10	d											21 30											22 00		
Wandsworth Common	d											21 33											22 03		
Balham 4	d											21 35											22 05		
Streatham Hill	d											21 38											22 08		
West Norwood 4	d											21 42											22 12		
Gipsy Hill	d											21 45											22 15		
Crystal Palace 4	d					21 13				21 28		21 51				21 43				21 58			22 21		
Sydenham	d	21 06				21 16	21 21			21 31	21 36	21 54	21 42			21 46	21 51			22 01			22 24	22 12	
Forest Hill 4	d	21 08				21 19	21 23			21 34	21 38	21 57	21 45			21 49	21 53			22 04			22 27	22 15	
Honor Oak Park	d	21 11				21 21	21 26			21 36	21 41	21 59	21 47			21 51	21 56			22 06			22 29	22 17	
Brockley	d	21 13				21 24	21 28			21 39	21 43	22 02	21 50			21 54	21 58			22 09			22 32	22 20	
New Cross Gate Station Ell	a																								
	d																								
New Cross Gate 4	d	21 16				21 26	21 31			21 41	21 46	22 04	21 52			21 56	22 01			22 11			22 34	22 22	
New Cross Ell	d		21 21						21 36						21 51				22 06						
Surrey Quays	d	21 19	21 25			21 30	21 35		21 40	21 45	21 49				21 55	22 00	22 05		22 10	22 15					
Canada Water	d	21 21	21 27			21 32	21 37		21 42	21 47	21 51				21 57	22 02	22 07		22 12	22 17					
Rotherhithe	d	21 23	21 28			21 33	21 38		21 43	21 48	21 53				21 58	22 03	22 08		22 13	22 18					
Wapping	d	21 24	21 30			21 35	21 40		21 45	21 50	21 54				22 00	22 05	22 10		22 15	22 20					
Shadwell	d	21 26	21 32			21 37	21 42		21 47	21 52	21 56				22 02	22 07	22 12		22 17	22 22					
Whitechapel	d	21 29	21 34			21 39	21 44		21 49	21 54	21 59				22 04	22 09	22 14		22 19	22 24					
Shoreditch High Street	d	21 31	21 36			21 41	21 46		21 51	21 56	22 01				22 06	22 11	22 16		22 21	22 26					
Hoxton	d	21 33	21 38			21 43	21 48		21 53	21 58	22 03				22 08	22 13	22 18		22 23	22 28					
Haggerston	d	21 35	21 40			21 45	21 50		21 55	22 00	22 05				22 10	22 15	22 20		22 25	22 30					
Dalston Junction Stn Ell	a	21 40	21 44			21 49	21 55		21 59	22 04	22 10				22 14	22 19	22 25		22 29	22 34					
London Bridge 4	a			21 36								22 13	21 59	22 11				22 06					22 45	22 29	22 41

Table 178

Mondays to Fridays

East London Line and Croydon-London Victoria to London Bridge

		LO		LO	LO	SN	SE	LO	LO	LO	SN	SN	SN		LO	LO	SN	FC	SE	LO	LO	SN	FC	SN	SN
East Croydon	d											22 30												23 01	
West Croydon 4	d	21 52			22 09					22 22			22 31			22 39					22 52				23 01
Norwood Junction 2	d	21 58			22 13					22 28		22 35				22 43					22 58			23 06	
Anerley	d	22 01			22 16					22 31		22 38				22 46					23 01			23 09	
Penge West	d	22 03			22 18					22 33		22 40				22 48					23 03			23 11	
London Victoria 15 ⊖	d					22 11	22 13.				22 22						22 41		22 43			22 52			
Battersea Park 4	d					22 15					22 26						22 45					22 56			
Wandsworth Road	d					22 17											22 47								
Clapham High Street ⊖	d					22 19											22 49								
London Blackfriars 3 ⊖	d																	22 42					22 57		
Denmark Hill 4	d					22 24	22 22										22 54		22 52						
Peckham Rye 4	d					22 26	22 25						23 01				22 56		22 55						23 31
Queens Rd Peckham	d					22 29							23 04				22 59								23 34
South Bermondsey	d					22 31							23 06				23 01								23 36
Clapham Junction 10	d										22 30											23 00			
Wandsworth Common	d										22 33											23 03			
Balham 4 ⊖	d										22 35											23 05			
Streatham Hill	d										22 38											23 08			
West Norwood 4	d										22 42											23 12			
Gipsy Hill	d										22 45											23 15			
Crystal Palace 4	d			22 13					22 28		22 51				22 43							23 21			
Sydenham	d	22 06		22 16	22 21				22 31	22 36	22 54	22 42			22 46	22 51					23 06	23 24		23 13	
Forest Hill 4	d	22 08		22 19	22 23				22 34	22 38	22 57	22 45			22 49	22 53					23 08	23 27		23 16	
Honor Oak Park	d	22 11		22 21	22 26				22 36	22 41	22 59	22 47			22 51	22 56					23 11	23 29		23 18	
Brockley	d	22 13		22 24	22 28				22 39	22 43	23 02	22 50			22 54	22 58					23 13	23 32		23 21	
New Cross Gate Station Ell	a																								
	d																								
New Cross Gate 4	d	22 16		22 26	22 31				22 41	22 46	23 04	22 52			22 56	23 01					23 16	23 34		23 23	
New Cross Ell	d							22 36												23 06					
Surrey Quays	d	22 19		22 30	22 35			22 40	22 45	22 49					23 00	23 05				23 10	23 19				
Canada Water	d	22 21		22 32	22 37			22 42	22 47	22 51					23 02	23 07				23 12	23 21				
Rotherhithe	d	22 23		22 33	22 38			22 43	22 48	22 53					23 03	23 08				23 13	23 23				
Wapping	d	22 24		22 35	22 40			22 45	22 50	22 54					23 05	23 10				23 15	23 24				
Shadwell	d	22 26		22 37	22 42			22 47	22 52	22 56					23 07	23 12				23 17	23 26				
Whitechapel	d	22 29		22 39	22 44			22 49	22 54	22 59					23 09	23 14				23 19	23 29				
Shoreditch High Street	d	22 31		22 41	22 46			22 51	22 56	23 01					23 11	23 16				23 21	23 31				
Hoxton	d	22 33		22 43	22 48			22 53	22 58	23 03					23 13	23 18				23 23	23 33				
Haggerston	d	22 35		22 45	22 50			22 55	23 00	23 05					23 15	23 20				23 25	23 35				
Dalston Junction Stn Ell	a	22 40		22 49	22 54			22 59	23 05	23 10					23 19	23 24				23 29	23 40				
London Bridge 4 ⊖	a					22 36					23 14	22 59	23 11				23 06	22 57				23 45	23 12	23 30	23 41

		LO		SN	FC	LO	SE	LO	SN		FC	FC	LO	SE	SN
East Croydon	d														
West Croydon 4	d							23 22							
Norwood Junction 2	d							23 28							
Anerley	d							23 31							
Penge West	d							23 33							
London Victoria 15 ⊖	d			23 11			23 13		23 22					23 43	
Battersea Park 4	d			23 15					23 26						
Wandsworth Road	d			23 17											
Clapham High Street ⊖	d			23 19											
London Blackfriars 3 ⊖	d				23 12						23 25	23 40			
Denmark Hill 4	d			23 24			23 22							23 52	
Peckham Rye 4	d			23 26			23 25							23 55	23 57
Queens Rd Peckham	d			23 29											
South Bermondsey	d			23 31											
Clapham Junction 10	d								23 30						
Wandsworth Common	d								23 33						
Balham 4 ⊖	d								23 35						
Streatham Hill	d								23 38						
West Norwood 4	d								23 42						00 10
Gipsy Hill	d								23 45						00 13
Crystal Palace 4	d	23 13							23 51				23 43		00 15
Sydenham	d	23 16						23 36	23 54				23 46		
Forest Hill 4	d	23 19						23 38	23 57				23 49		
Honor Oak Park	d	23 21						23 41	23 59				23 51		
Brockley	d	23 24						23 43	00 02				23 54		
New Cross Gate Station Ell	a														
	d														
New Cross Gate 4	d	23 26						23 46	00 04				23 56		
New Cross Ell	d					23 36									
Surrey Quays	d	23 30				23 40		23 49					23 59		
Canada Water	d	23 32				23 42		23 51					00 02		
Rotherhithe	d	23 33				23 43		23 53					00 03		
Wapping	d	23 35				23 45		23 54					00 05		
Shadwell	d	23 37				23 47		23 56					00 07		
Whitechapel	d	23 39				23 49		23 59					00 09		
Shoreditch High Street	d	23 41				23 51		00 01					00 11		
Hoxton	d	23 43				23 53		00 03					00 13		
Haggerston	d	23 45				23 55		00 05					00 15		
Dalston Junction Stn Ell	a	23 49				23 59		00 10					00 19		
London Bridge 4 ⊖	a			23 36	23 27				00 11		23 40	23 54			

Table 178

Saturdays

East London Line and Croydon-London Victoria to London Bridge

		LO	SN	LO	SN	FC	FC	FC	FC	FC		FC	FC	FC	FC	LO	LO	FC	LO	LO	LO	LO		SE	SN
East Croydon	d																								
West Croydon 4	d	23p22														05 39				05 52					06 18
Norwood Junction 2	d	23p28														05 43				05 58					06 23
Anerley	d	23p31														05 46				06 01					
Penge West	d	23p33														05 48				06 03					
London Victoria 15 ⊖	d		23p22																					06 13.	
Battersea Park 4	d		23p26																						
Wandsworth Road	d																								
Clapham High Street ⊖	d																								
London Blackfriars 3 ⊖	d					00 11	00 40	01 10	01 40	03 10		03 40	04 10	04 40	05 10			05 40							
Denmark Hill 4	d																							06 22	
Peckham Rye-I 4	d				23p57																			06 25	
Queens Rd Peckham	d																								
South Bermondsey	d																								
Clapham Junction 10	d		23p30																						
Wandsworth Common	d		23p33																						
Balham 4 ⊖	d		23p35																						
Streatham Hill	d		23p38																						
West Norwood 4	d		23p42		00 10																				
Gipsy Hill	d		23p45		00 13																				
Crystal Palace 4	d		23p51	23p43	00 15														05 58			06 13			06 27
Sydenham	d	23p36	23p54	23p46												05 51			06 01	06 06		06 16			
Forest Hill 4	d	23p38	23p57	23p49												05 53			06 04	06 08		06 19			
Honor Oak Park	d	23p41	23p59	23p51												05 56			06 06	06 11		06 21			
Brockley	d	23p43	00 02	23p54												05 58			06 09	06 13		06 24			
New Cross Gate Station Ell	a																								
	d																								
New Cross Gate 4	d	23p46	00 04	23p56												06 01			06 11	06 16		06 26			
New Cross Ell	d																06 06				06 21				
Surrey Quays	d	23p49		23p59												06 04	06 10		06 15	06 19	06 25	06 30			
Canada Water	d	23p51		00 02												06 06	06 12		06 17	06 21	06 27	06 32			
Rotherhithe	d	23p53		00 03												06 08	06 13		06 18	06 23	06 28	06 33			
Wapping	d	23p54		00 05												06 09	06 15		06 20	06 24	06 30	06 35			
Shadwell	d	23p56		00 07												06 11	06 17		06 22	06 26	06 32	06 37			
Whitechapel	d	23p59		00 09												06 14	06 19		06 24	06 29	06 34	06 39			
Shoreditch High Street	d	00 01		00 11												06 16	06 21		06 26	06 31	06 36	06 41			
Hoxton	d	00 03		00 13												06 18	06 23		06 28	06 33	06 38	06 43			
Haggerston	d	00 05		00 15												06 20	06 25		06 30	06 35	06 40	06 45			
Dalston Junction Stn Ell	a	00 10		00 19												06 25	06 29		06 34	06 40	06 44	06 49			
London Bridge 4 ⊖	a		00 11			00 26	00 55	01 25	01 55	03 25		03 55	04 25	04 55	05 25			05 55							

		LO	LO	LO	LO	SN		LO	SN	SN	SN	LO	LO	SE	SN	LO	LO	LO	LO	SN	SN		SN	LO	SE
East Croydon	d					06 30					06 43									07 00					
West Croydon 4	d	06 09			06 22								06 39		06 45			06 52			07 01				
Norwood Junction 2	d	06 13			06 28	06 35				06 41	06 50		06 43		06 53			06 58		07 05					
Anerley	d	06 16			06 31	06 38							06 46					07 01		07 08					
Penge West	d	06 18			06 33	06 40							06 48					07 03		07 10					
London Victoria 15 ⊖	d								06 41					06 43.									07 11		07 13.
Battersea Park 4	d								06 45														07 15		
Wandsworth Road	d								06 47														07 17		
Clapham High Street ⊖	d								06 49														07 19		
London Blackfriars 3 ⊖	d																								
Denmark Hill 4	d								06 54					06 52									07 24		07 22
Peckham Rye-I 4	d								06 56	07 01				06 55							07 31		07 26		07 25
Queens Rd Peckham	d								06 59	07 04											07 34		07 29		
South Bermondsey	d								07 01	07 06											07 36		07 31		
Clapham Junction 10	d																								
Wandsworth Common	d																								
Balham 4 ⊖	d																								
Streatham Hill	d																								
West Norwood 4	d																								
Gipsy Hill	d																								
Crystal Palace 4	d			06 28								06 43			06 57		06 58							07 13	
Sydenham	d	06 21		06 31	06 36	06 42					06 54	06 46	06 52				07 01	07 06		07 12				07 16	
Forest Hill 4	d	06 23		06 34	06 38	06 45					06 57	06 49	06 54				07 04	07 08		07 15				07 19	
Honor Oak Park	d	06 26		06 36	06 41	06 47					06 59	06 51	06 57				07 06	07 11		07 17				07 21	
Brockley	d	06 28		06 39	06 43	06 50					07 02	06 54	06 59				07 09	07 13		07 20				07 24	
New Cross Gate Station Ell	a																								
	d																								
New Cross Gate 4	d	06 31		06 41	06 46	06 52					07 04	06 56	07 02				07 11	07 16		07 22				07 26	
New Cross Ell	d		06 36					06 51								07 06			07 21						
Surrey Quays	d	06 34	06 40	06 45	06 49			06 55				07 00	07 05			07 10	07 15	07 19	07 25					07 30	
Canada Water	d	06 36	06 42	06 47	06 51			06 57				07 02	07 07			07 12	07 17	07 21	07 27					07 32	
Rotherhithe	d	06 38	06 43	06 48	06 53			06 58				07 03	07 09			07 13	07 18	07 23	07 28					07 33	
Wapping	d	06 39	06 45	06 50	06 54			07 00				07 05	07 10			07 15	07 20	07 24	07 30					07 35	
Shadwell	d	06 41	06 47	06 52	06 56			07 02				07 07	07 12			07 17	07 22	07 26	07 32					07 37	
Whitechapel	d	06 44	06 49	06 54	06 59			07 04				07 09	07 15			07 19	07 24	07 29	07 34					07 39	
Shoreditch High Street	d	06 46	06 51	06 56	07 01			07 06				07 11	07 17			07 21	07 26	07 31	07 36					07 41	
Hoxton	d	06 48	06 53	06 58	07 03			07 08				07 13	07 19			07 23	07 28	07 33	07 38					07 43	
Haggerston	d	06 50	06 55	07 00	07 05			07 10				07 15	07 21			07 25	07 30	07 35	07 40					07 45	
Dalston Junction Stn Ell	a	06 55	06 59	07 04	07 10			07 14				07 19	07 26			07 29	07 34	07 40	07 44					07 49	
London Bridge 4 ⊖	a					06 59			07 06	07 14	07 11									07 29	07 41		07 36		

Table 178

Saturdays

East London Line and Croydon-London Victoria to London Bridge

		LO	LO		LO	LO	SN	SN	LO	LO	LO	SE	SN	SN		LO	SE	SN	LO	LO	SN	SN	LO	LO	SE
East Croydon	d						07 30														08 00				
West Croydon 4	d	07 09				07 22		07 31			07 39									07 52		08 01			
Norwood Junction 2	d	07 13				07 28	07 35				07 43									07 58	08 05				
Anerley	d	07 16				07 31	07 38				07 46									08 01	08 08				
Penge West	d	07 18				07 33	07 40				07 48									08 03	08 10				
London Victoria 15	d											07 39		07 41			07 43	07 49							08 09.
Battersea Park 4	d													07 45				07 53							
Wandsworth Road	d													07 47											
Clapham High Street	d													07 49											
London Blackfriars 3	d																								
Denmark Hill 4	d											07 48		07 54			07 52								08 18
Peckham Rye 4	d							08 01				07 51	07 42	07 56			07 55					08 31			08 21
Queens Rd Peckham	d							08 04						07 59								08 34			
South Bermondsey	d							08 06						08 01								08 36			
Clapham Junction 10	d																	07 57							
Wandsworth Common	d																	08 00							
Balham 4	d																	08 02							
Streatham Hill	d																	08 05							
West Norwood 4	d												07 53					08 10							
Gipsy Hill	d												07 56					08 13							
Crystal Palace 4	d				07 28					07 43			07 59					08 21	07 58					08 13	
Sydenham	d	07 22			07 31	07 36	07 42			07 46	07 52							08 24	08 01	08 06	08 12			08 16	
Forest Hill 4	d	07 24			07 34	07 38	07 45			07 49	07 54							08 27	08 04	08 08	08 15			08 19	
Honor Oak Park	d	07 27			07 36	07 41	07 47			07 51	07 57							08 29	08 06	08 11	08 17			08 21	
Brockley	d	07 29			07 39	07 43	07 50			07 54	07 59							08 32	08 09	08 13	08 20			08 24	
New Cross Gate Station Ell	a																								
	d																								
New Cross Gate 4	d	07 32			07 41	07 46	07 52			07 56	08 02							08 34	08 11	08 16	08 22			08 26	
New Cross Ell	d		07 36						07 51							08 06							08 21		
Surrey Quays	d	07 35	07 40		07 45	07 49			07 55	08 00	08 05					08 10			08 15	08 19			08 25	08 30	
Canada Water	d	07 37	07 42		07 47	07 51			07 57	08 02	08 07					08 12			08 17	08 21			08 27	08 32	
Rotherhithe	d	07 39	07 43		07 48	07 53			07 58	08 03	08 09					08 13			08 18	08 23			08 28	08 33	
Wapping	d	07 40	07 45		07 50	07 54			08 00	08 05	08 10					08 15			08 20	08 24			08 30	08 35	
Shadwell	d	07 42	07 47		07 52	07 56			08 02	08 07	08 12					08 17			08 22	08 26			08 32	08 37	
Whitechapel	d	07 45	07 49		07 54	07 59			08 04	08 09	08 15					08 19			08 24	08 29			08 34	08 39	
Shoreditch High Street	d	07 47	07 51		07 56	08 01			08 06	08 11	08 17					08 21			08 26	08 31			08 36	08 41	
Hoxton	d	07 49	07 53		07 58	08 03			08 08	08 13	08 19					08 23			08 28	08 33			08 38	08 43	
Haggerston	d	07 51	07 55		08 00	08 05			08 10	08 15	08 21					08 25			08 30	08 35			08 40	08 45	
Dalston Junction Stn Ell	a	07 56	07 59		08 04	08 10			08 14	08 19	08 26					08 29			08 34	08 40			08 44	08 49	
London Bridge 4	a						07 59	08 11						08 06				08 41			08 29	08 41			

		LO	SN	SN	SE	SN		LO	LO	LO		SN	SN	LO	LO	LO	SE	SN		SN	LO	SE	SN	SN	LO
East Croydon	d											08 30													
West Croydon 4	d	08 09								08 22			08 31			08 39									
Norwood Junction 2	d	08 13								08 28		08 35				08 43									
Anerley	d	08 16								08 31		08 38				08 46									
Penge West	d	08 18								08 33		08 40				08 48									
London Victoria 15	d		08 11		08 13	08 19											08 39			08 41		08 43		08 49	
Battersea Park 4	d		08 15			08 23														08 45				08 53	
Wandsworth Road	d		08 17																	08 47					
Clapham High Street	d		08 19																	08 49					
London Blackfriars 3	d																								
Denmark Hill 4	d		08 24		08 22												08 48			08 54		08 52			
Peckham Rye 4	d		08 26	08 12	08 25								09 01				08 51	08 42		08 56		08 55	08 46		
Queens Rd Peckham	d		08 29										09 04							08 59			08 49		
South Bermondsey	d		08 31										09 06							09 01			08 51		
Clapham Junction 10	d					08 27																		08 57	
Wandsworth Common	d					08 30																		09 00	
Balham 4	d					08 32																		09 02	
Streatham Hill	d					08 35																		09 05	
West Norwood 4	d			08 23		08 40												08 53						09 10	
Gipsy Hill	d			08 26		08 43												08 56						09 13	
Crystal Palace 4	d			08 29		08 51			08 28						08 43			08 59						09 21	08 58
Sydenham	d	08 22				08 54			08 31	08 36		08 42			08 46	08 52								09 24	09 01
Forest Hill 4	d	08 24				08 57			08 34	08 38		08 45			08 49	08 54								09 27	09 04
Honor Oak Park	d	08 27				08 59			08 36	08 41		08 47			08 51	08 57								09 29	09 06
Brockley	d	08 29				09 02			08 39	08 43		08 50			08 54	08 59								09 32	09 09
New Cross Gate Station Ell	a																								
	d																								
New Cross Gate 4	d	08 32				09 04			08 41	08 46		08 52			08 56	09 02								09 34	09 11
New Cross Ell	d							08 36						08 51							09 06				
Surrey Quays	d	08 35						08 40	08 45	08 49				08 55	09 00	09 05					09 10				09 15
Canada Water	d	08 37						08 42	08 47	08 51				08 57	09 02	09 07					09 12				09 17
Rotherhithe	d	08 39						08 43	08 48	08 53				08 58	09 03	09 09					09 13				09 18
Wapping	d	08 40						08 45	08 50	08 54				09 00	09 05	09 10					09 15				09 20
Shadwell	d	08 42						08 47	08 52	08 56				09 02	09 07	09 12					09 17				09 22
Whitechapel	d	08 45						08 49	08 54	08 59				09 04	09 09	09 15					09 19				09 24
Shoreditch High Street	d	08 47						08 51	08 56	09 01				09 06	09 11	09 17					09 21				09 26
Hoxton	d	08 49						08 53	08 58	09 03				09 08	09 13	09 19					09 23				09 28
Haggerston	d	08 51						08 55	09 00	09 05				09 10	09 15	09 21					09 25				09 30
Dalston Junction Stn Ell	a	08 56						08 59	09 04	09 10				09 14	09 19	09 26					09 29				09 34
London Bridge 4	a		08 36			09 11						08 59	09 11							09 06			08 56	09 41	

Table 178

Saturdays

East London Line and Croydon-London Victoria to London Bridge

		SN	SN		LO	LO	LO	LO	SE	SN	SN	SE	SN	SN	LO		LO	LO	SN	SN	LO	LO	SE	SN	SN
East Croydon	d	09 00																	09 30						
West Croydon 4	d		09 01		08 52			09 09										09 22		09 31					
Norwood Junction 2	d	09 05			08 58			09 13										09 28	09 35						
Anerley	d	09 08			09 01			09 16										09 31	09 38						
Penge West	d	09 10			09 03			09 18										09 33	09 40						
London Victoria 15	d								09 09.		09 11	09 13.		09 19									09 39		09 41
Battersea Park 4	d										09 15			09 23											09 45
Wandsworth Road	d										09 17														09 47
Clapham High Street	d										09 19														09 49
London Blackfriars 3	d																								
Denmark Hill 4	d								09 18		09 24	09 22											09 48		09 54
Peckham Rye 4	d		09 31						09 21	09 12	09 26	09 25	09 16							10 01			09 51	09 42	09 56
Queens Rd Peckham	d		09 34								09 29		09 19							10 04					09 59
South Bermondsey	d		09 36								09 31		09 21							10 06					10 01
Clapham Junction 10	d													09 27											
Wandsworth Common	d													09 30											
Balham 4	d													09 32											
Streatham Hill	d													09 35											
West Norwood 4	d									09 23				09 40										09 53	
Gipsy Hill	d									09 26				09 43										09 56	
Crystal Palace 4	d						09 13			09 29				09 51			09 28					09 43		09 59	
Sydenham	d	09 12			09 06		09 16	09 22						09 54			09 31	09 36	09 42			09 46			
Forest Hill 4	d	09 15			09 08		09 19	09 24						09 57			09 34	09 38	09 45			09 49			
Honor Oak Park	d	09 17			09 11		09 21	09 27						09 59			09 36	09 41	09 47			09 51			
Brockley	d	09 20			09 13		09 24	09 29						10 02			09 39	09 43	09 50			09 54			
New Cross Gate Station Ell	a																								
	d																								
New Cross Gate 4	d	09 22			09 16		09 26	09 32						10 04			09 41	09 46	09 52			09 56			
New Cross Ell	d					09 21									09 36						09 51				
Surrey Quays	d				09 19	09 25	09 30	09 35							09 40		09 45	09 49			09 55	10 00			
Canada Water	d				09 21	09 27	09 32	09 37							09 42		09 47	09 51			09 57	10 02			
Rotherhithe	d				09 23	09 28	09 33	09 39							09 43		09 48	09 53			09 58	10 03			
Wapping	d				09 24	09 30	09 35	09 40							09 45		09 50	09 54			10 00	10 05			
Shadwell	d				09 26	09 32	09 37	09 42							09 47		09 52	09 56			10 02	10 07			
Whitechapel	d				09 29	09 34	09 39	09 45							09 49		09 54	09 59			10 04	10 09			
Shoreditch High Street	d				09 31	09 36	09 41	09 47							09 51		09 56	10 01			10 06	10 11			
Hoxton	d				09 33	09 38	09 43	09 49							09 53		09 58	10 03			10 08	10 13			
Haggerston	d				09 35	09 40	09 45	09 51							09 55		10 00	10 05			10 10	10 15			
Dalston Junction Stn Ell	a				09 40	09 44	09 49	09 56							09 59		10 04	10 10			10 14	10 19			
London Bridge 4	a	09 29	09 41								09 36		09 26	10 11					09 59	10 11					10 06

		LO	LO	SE	SN	SN		LO	LO	SN	SN		LO	LO	LO	SE	SN	SN	SE	SN	SN	LO		LO	SN
East Croydon	d									10 00															10 30
West Croydon 4	d	09 39							09 52		10 01				10 09										
Norwood Junction 2	d	09 43							09 58	10 05					10 13										10 35
Anerley	d	09 46							10 01	10 08					10 16										10 38
Penge West	d	09 48							10 03	10 10					10 18										10 40
London Victoria 15	d			09 43.		09 49										10 09.		10 11	10 13.		10 19				
Battersea Park 4	d					09 53												10 15			10 23				
Wandsworth Road	d																	10 17							
Clapham High Street	d																	10 19							
London Blackfriars 3	d																								
Denmark Hill 4	d			09 52												10 18		10 24	10 22						
Peckham Rye 4	d			09 55	09 46						10 31					10 21	10 12	10 26	10 25	10 16					
Queens Rd Peckham	d				09 49						10 34							10 29		10 19					
South Bermondsey	d				09 51						10 36							10 31		10 21					
Clapham Junction 10	d					09 57															10 27				
Wandsworth Common	d					10 00															10 30				
Balham 4	d					10 02															10 32				
Streatham Hill	d					10 05															10 35				
West Norwood 4	d					10 10											10 23				10 40				
Gipsy Hill	d					10 13											10 26				10 43				
Crystal Palace 4	d					10 21		09 58						10 13			10 29				10 51			10 28	
Sydenham	d	09 51				10 24		10 01	10 06	10 12				10 16	10 21						10 54			10 31	10 42
Forest Hill 4	d	09 53				10 27		10 04	10 08	10 15				10 19	10 23						10 57			10 34	10 45
Honor Oak Park	d	09 56				10 29		10 06	10 11	10 17				10 21	10 26						10 59			10 36	10 47
Brockley	d	09 58				10 32		10 09	10 13	10 20				10 24	10 28						11 02			10 39	10 50
New Cross Gate Station Ell	a																								
	d																								
New Cross Gate 4	d	10 01				10 34		10 11	10 16	10 22				10 26	10 31						11 04			10 41	10 52
New Cross Ell	d		10 06										10 21									10 36			
Surrey Quays	d	10 04	10 10					10 15	10 19				10 25	10 30	10 34							10 40		10 45	
Canada Water	d	10 06	10 12					10 17	10 21				10 27	10 32	10 36							10 42		10 47	
Rotherhithe	d	10 08	10 13					10 18	10 23				10 28	10 33	10 38							10 43		10 48	
Wapping	d	10 09	10 15					10 20	10 24				10 30	10 35	10 39							10 45		10 50	
Shadwell	d	10 11	10 17					10 22	10 26				10 32	10 37	10 41							10 47		10 52	
Whitechapel	d	10 14	10 19					10 24	10 29				10 34	10 39	10 44							10 49		10 54	
Shoreditch High Street	d	10 16	10 21					10 26	10 31				10 36	10 41	10 46							10 51		10 56	
Hoxton	d	10 18	10 23					10 28	10 33				10 38	10 43	10 48							10 53		10 58	
Haggerston	d	10 20	10 25					10 30	10 35				10 40	10 45	10 50							10 55		11 00	
Dalston Junction Stn Ell	a	10 25	10 29					10 34	10 40				10 44	10 49	10 55							10 59		11 04	
London Bridge 4	a				09 56	10 41				10 29	10 41							10 36		10 26	11 11				10 59

East London Line and Croydon-London Victoria to London Bridge

		SN	LO	LO	LO	LO	SE	SN	SN	SE	SN	SN	LO	LO	LO	SN	LO	SN	LO	SE	SN	SN	SE
East Croydon	d															11 00							
West Croydon	d	10 31	10 22			10 39									10 52			11 01					
Norwood Junction	d		10 28			10 43									10 58	11 05							
Anerley	d		10 31			10 46									11 01	11 08							
Penge West	d		10 33			10 48									11 03	11 10							
London Victoria	d						10 39.		10 41	10 43.		10 49								11 09.		11 11	11 13.
Battersea Park	d								10 45			10 53										11 15	
Wandsworth Road	d								10 47													11 17	
Clapham High Street	d								10 49													11 19	
London Blackfriars	d																						
Denmark Hill	d						10 48		10 54	10 52										11 18		11 24	11 22
Peckham Rye	d	11 01					10 51	10 42	10 56	10 55	10 46							11 31		11 21	11 12	11 26	11 25
Queens Rd Peckham	d	11 04							10 59		10 49							11 34				11 29	
South Bermondsey	d	11 06							11 01		10 51							11 36				11 31	
Clapham Junction	d											10 57											
Wandsworth Common	d											11 00											
Balham	d											11 02											
Streatham Hill	d											11 05											
West Norwood	d							10 53				11 10									11 23		
Gipsy Hill	d							10 56				11 13									11 26		
Crystal Palace	d				10 43			10 59				11 21		10 58					11 13		11 29		
Sydenham	d		10 36		10 46	10 51						11 24		11 01	11 06	11 12			11 16				
Forest Hill	d		10 38		10 49	10 53						11 27		11 04	11 08	11 15			11 19				
Honor Oak Park	d		10 41		10 51	10 56						11 29		11 06	11 11	11 17			11 21				
Brockley	d		10 43		10 54	10 58						11 32		11 09	11 13	11 20			11 24				
New Cross Gate Station Ell	a																						
	d																						
New Cross Gate	d		10 46		10 56	11 01						11 34		11 11	11 16	11 22			11 26				
New Cross Ell	d			10 51									11 06				11 21						
Surrey Quays	d		10 49	10 55	11 00	11 04							11 10	11 15	11 19		11 25		11 30				
Canada Water	d		10 51	10 57	11 02	11 06							11 12	11 17	11 21		11 27		11 32				
Rotherhithe	d		10 53	10 58	11 03	11 08							11 13	11 18	11 23		11 28		11 33				
Wapping	d		10 54	11 00	11 05	11 09							11 15	11 20	11 24		11 30		11 35				
Shadwell	d		10 56	11 02	11 07	11 11							11 17	11 22	11 26		11 32		11 37				
Whitechapel	d		10 59	11 04	11 09	11 14							11 19	11 24	11 29		11 34		11 39				
Shoreditch High Street	d		11 01	11 06	11 11	11 16							11 21	11 26	11 31		11 36		11 41				
Hoxton	d		11 03	11 08	11 13	11 18							11 23	11 28	11 33		11 38		11 43				
Haggerston	d		11 05	11 10	11 15	11 20							11 25	11 30	11 35		11 40		11 45				
Dalston Junction Stn Ell	a		11 10	11 14	11 19	11 25							11 29	11 34	11 40		11 44		11 49				
London Bridge	a	11 11							11 06		10 56	11 41				11 29		11 41				11 36	

		SN	LO	SN	LO	LO	LO	SN	SN	LO	LO	LO	SE	LO	SN	SN	SE	SN	SN	LO	LO	SN	SN
East Croydon	d							11 30														12 00	
West Croydon	d		11 09				11 22		11 31			11 39									11 52		12 01
Norwood Junction	d		11 13				11 28	11 35				11 43									11 58	12 05	
Anerley	d		11 16				11 31	11 38				11 46									12 01	12 08	
Penge West	d		11 18				11 33	11 40				11 48									12 03	12 10	
London Victoria	d			11 19									11 39			11 41	11 43.		11 49				
Battersea Park	d			11 23												11 45			11 53				
Wandsworth Road	d															11 47							
Clapham High Street	d															11 49							
London Blackfriars	d																						
Denmark Hill	d												11 48			11 54	11 52						
Peckham Rye	d	11 16							12 01				11 51		11 42	11 56	11 55	11 46					12 31
Queens Rd Peckham	d	11 19							12 04							11 59		11 49					12 34
South Bermondsey	d	11 21							12 06							12 01		11 51					12 36
Clapham Junction	d			11 27															11 57				
Wandsworth Common	d			11 30															12 00				
Balham	d			11 32															12 02				
Streatham Hill	d			11 35															12 05				
West Norwood	d			11 40											11 53				12 10				
Gipsy Hill	d			11 43											11 56				12 13				
Crystal Palace	d			11 51		11 28					11 43				11 59				12 21	11 58			
Sydenham	d		11 21	11 54		11 31	11 36	11 42			11 46	11 51							12 24	12 01	12 06	12 12	
Forest Hill	d		11 23	11 57		11 34	11 38	11 45			11 49	11 53							12 27	12 04	12 08	12 15	
Honor Oak Park	d		11 26	11 59		11 36	11 41	11 47			11 51	11 56							12 29	12 06	12 11	12 17	
Brockley	d		11 28	12 02		11 39	11 43	11 50			11 54	11 58							12 32	12 09	12 13	12 20	
New Cross Gate Station Ell	a																						
	d																						
New Cross Gate	d		11 31	12 04		11 41	11 46	11 52			11 56	12 01							12 34	12 11	12 16	12 22	
New Cross Ell	d				11 36					11 51				12 06									
Surrey Quays	d		11 34		11 40	11 45	11 49			11 55	12 00	12 04		12 10						12 15	12 19		
Canada Water	d		11 36		11 42	11 47	11 51			11 57	12 02	12 06		12 12						12 17	12 21		
Rotherhithe	d		11 38		11 43	11 48	11 53			11 58	12 03	12 08		12 13						12 18	12 23		
Wapping	d		11 39		11 45	11 50	11 54			12 00	12 05	12 09		12 15						12 20	12 24		
Shadwell	d		11 41		11 47	11 52	11 56			12 02	12 07	12 11		12 17						12 22	12 26		
Whitechapel	d		11 44		11 49	11 54	11 59			12 04	12 09	12 14		12 19						12 24	12 29		
Shoreditch High Street	d		11 46		11 51	11 56	12 01			12 06	12 11	12 16		12 21						12 26	12 31		
Hoxton	d		11 48		11 53	11 58	12 03			12 08	12 13	12 18		12 23						12 28	12 33		
Haggerston	d		11 50		11 55	12 00	12 05			12 10	12 15	12 20		12 25						12 30	12 35		
Dalston Junction Stn Ell	a		11 55		11 59	12 04	12 10			12 14	12 19	12 25		12 29						12 34	12 40		
London Bridge	a	11 26		12 11				11 59	12 11							12 06		11 56	12 44			12 29	12 41

Table 178

Saturdays

East London Line and Croydon-London Victoria to London Bridge

		LO	LO	LO	LO	SE	SN	SN	SE	SN	SN	LO	LO	SN	SN	LO	LO	LO	SE	SN	SN	SE	SN
East Croydon	d													12 30									
West Croydon	d			12 09									12 22		12 31			12 39					
Norwood Junction	d			12 13									12 28	12 35				12 43					
Anerley	d			12 16									12 31	12 38				12 46					
Penge West	d			12 18									12 33	12 40				12 48					
London Victoria	d					12 09.		12 11	12 13.		12 19								12 39.		12 41	12 43.	
Battersea Park	d							12 15			12 23										12 45		
Wandsworth Road	d							12 17													12 47		
Clapham High Street	d							12 19													12 49		
London Blackfriars	d																						
Denmark Hill	d					12 18		12 24	12 22										12 48		12 54	12 52	
Peckham Rye	d					12 21	12 12	12 26	12 25	12 16					13 01				12 51	12 42	12 56	12 55	12 46
Queens Rd Peckham	d							12 29		12 19					13 04						12 59		12 49
South Bermondsey	d							12 31		12 21					13 06						13 01		12 51
Clapham Junction	d										12 27												
Wandsworth Common	d										12 30												
Balham	d										12 32												
Streatham Hill	d										12 35												
West Norwood	d						12 23				12 40									12 53			
Gipsy Hill	d						12 26				12 43									12 56			
Crystal Palace	d		12 13				12 29				12 51	12 28					12 43			12 59			
Sydenham	d		12 16	12 21							12 54	12 31	12 36	12 42			12 46	12 51					
Forest Hill	d		12 19	12 23							12 57	12 34	12 38	12 45			12 49	12 53					
Honor Oak Park	d		12 21	12 26							12 59	12 36	12 41	12 47			12 51	12 56					
Brockley	d		12 24	12 28							13 02	12 39	12 43	12 50			12 54	12 58					
New Cross Gate Station Ell	a																						
	d																						
New Cross Gate	d		12 26	12 31							13 04	12 41	12 46	12 52			12 56	13 01					
New Cross Ell	d	12 21			12 36											12 51							
Surrey Quays	d	12 25	12 30	12 34	12 40							12 45	12 49			12 55	13 00	13 04					
Canada Water	d	12 27	12 32	12 36	12 42							12 47	12 51			12 57	13 02	13 06					
Rotherhithe	d	12 28	12 33	12 38	12 43							12 48	12 53			12 58	13 03	13 08					
Wapping	d	12 30	12 35	12 39	12 45							12 50	12 54			13 00	13 05	13 09					
Shadwell	d	12 32	12 37	12 41	12 47							12 52	12 56			13 02	13 07	13 11					
Whitechapel	d	12 34	12 39	12 44	12 49							12 54	12 59			13 04	13 09	13 14					
Shoreditch High Street	d	12 36	12 41	12 46	12 51							12 56	13 01			13 06	13 11	13 16					
Hoxton	d	12 38	12 43	12 48	12 53							12 58	13 03			13 08	13 13	13 18					
Haggerston	d	12 40	12 45	12 50	12 55							13 00	13 05			13 10	13 15	13 20					
Dalston Junction Stn Ell	a	12 44	12 49	12 55	12 59							13 04	13 10			13 14	13 19	13 25					
London Bridge	a							12 36		12 26	13 11			12 59	13 11						13 06		12 56

		LO	SN	LO	LO	LO	LO	SN	SN	LO	LO	SE	SN	SN	SE	SN	SN	LO	LO	SN	SN
East Croydon	d							13 00												13 30	
West Croydon	d				12 52				13 01	13 09									13 22		13 31
Norwood Junction	d				12 58			13 05		13 13									13 28	13 35	
Anerley	d				13 01			13 08		13 16									13 31	13 38	
Penge West	d				13 03			13 10		13 18									13 33	13 40	
London Victoria	d		12 49									13 09.		13 11	13 13.		13 19				
Battersea Park	d		12 53											13 15			13 23				
Wandsworth Road	d													13 17							
Clapham High Street	d													13 19							
London Blackfriars	d																				
Denmark Hill	d											13 18		13 24	13 22						
Peckham Rye	d								13 31			13 21	13 12	13 26	13 25	13 16					14 01
Queens Rd Peckham	d								13 34					13 29		13 19					14 04
South Bermondsey	d								13 36					13 31		13 21					14 06
Clapham Junction	d		12 57														13 27				
Wandsworth Common	d		13 00														13 30				
Balham	d		13 02														13 32				
Streatham Hill	d		13 05														13 35				
West Norwood	d		13 10										13 23				13 40				
Gipsy Hill	d		13 13										13 26				13 43				
Crystal Palace	d		13 21	12 58			13 13						13 29				13 51	13 28			
Sydenham	d		13 24	13 01	13 06		13 16	13 12		13 21							13 54	13 31	13 36	13 42	
Forest Hill	d		13 27	13 04	13 08		13 19	13 15		13 23							13 57	13 34	13 38	13 45	
Honor Oak Park	d		13 29	13 06	13 11		13 21	13 17		13 26							13 59	13 36	13 41	13 47	
Brockley	d		13 32	13 09	13 13		13 24	13 20		13 28							14 02	13 39	13 43	13 50	
New Cross Gate Station Ell	a																				
	d																				
New Cross Gate	d		13 34	13 11	13 16		13 26	13 22		13 31							14 04	13 41	13 46	13 52	
New Cross Ell	d	13 06				13 21					13 36										
Surrey Quays	d	13 10		13 15	13 19	13 25	13 30			13 34	13 40							13 45	13 49		
Canada Water	d	13 12		13 17	13 21	13 27	13 32			13 36	13 42							13 47	13 51		
Rotherhithe	d	13 13		13 18	13 23	13 28	13 33			13 38	13 43							13 48	13 53		
Wapping	d	13 15		13 20	13 24	13 30	13 35			13 39	13 45							13 50	13 54		
Shadwell	d	13 17		13 22	13 26	13 32	13 37			13 41	13 47							13 52	13 56		
Whitechapel	d	13 19		13 24	13 29	13 34	13 39			13 44	13 49							13 54	13 59		
Shoreditch High Street	d	13 21		13 26	13 31	13 36	13 41			13 46	13 51							13 56	14 01		
Hoxton	d	13 23		13 28	13 33	13 38	13 43			13 48	13 53							13 58	14 03		
Haggerston	d	13 25		13 30	13 35	13 40	13 45			13 50	13 55							14 00	14 05		
Dalston Junction Stn Ell	a	13 29		13 34	13 40	13 44	13 49			13 55	13 59							14 04	14 10		
London Bridge	a		13 44					13 29	13 41					13 36		13 26	14 11			13 59	14 11

Table 178

East London Line and Croydon-London Victoria to London Bridge

Station		LO	LO	LO	SE	SN	SN	SE	SN	SN	LO	LO	LO	SN	SN	LO	LO	SE	SN	SN	SE	SN	SN
East Croydon	d													14 00									
West Croydon	d			13 39									13 52		14 01								
Norwood Junction	d			13 43									13 58	14 05									
Anerley	d			13 46									14 01	14 08									
Penge West	d			13 48									14 03	14 10									
London Victoria	d				13 39		13 41	13 43		13 49								14 09		14 11	14 13		14 19
Battersea Park	d						13 45			13 53										14 15			14 23
Wandsworth Road	d						13 47													14 17			
Clapham High Street	d						13 49													14 19			
London Blackfriars	d																						
Denmark Hill	d				13 48		13 54	13 52										14 18		14 24	14 22		
Peckham Rye	d				13 51	13 42	13 56	13 55	13 46						14 31			14 21	14 12	14 26	14 25	14 16	
Queens Rd Peckham	d						13 59		13 49						14 34					14 29		14 19	
South Bermondsey	d						14 01		13 51						14 36					14 31		14 21	
Clapham Junction	d									13 57													14 27
Wandsworth Common	d									14 00													14 30
Balham	d									14 02													14 32
Streatham Hill	d									14 05													14 35
West Norwood	d					13 53				14 10									14 23				14 40
Gipsy Hill	d					13 56				14 13									14 26				14 43
Crystal Palace	d		13 43			13 59				14 21		13 58					14 13		14 29				14 51
Sydenham	d		13 46	13 51						14 24		14 01	14 06	14 12			14 16						14 54
Forest Hill	d		13 49	13 53						14 27		14 04	14 08	14 15			14 19						14 57
Honor Oak Park	d		13 51	13 56						14 29		14 06	14 11	14 17			14 21						14 59
Brockley	d		13 54	13 58						14 32		14 09	14 13	14 20			14 24						15 02
New Cross Gate Station ELL	a																						
	d																						
New Cross Gate	d		13 56	14 01						14 34		14 11	14 16	14 22			14 26						15 04
New Cross ELL	d	13 51									14 06					14 21							
Surrey Quays	d	13 55	14 00	14 04							14 10	14 15	14 19			14 25	14 30						
Canada Water	d	13 57	14 02	14 06							14 12	14 17	14 21			14 27	14 32						
Rotherhithe	d	13 58	14 03	14 08							14 13	14 18	14 23			14 28	14 33						
Wapping	d	14 00	14 05	14 09							14 15	14 20	14 24			14 30	14 35						
Shadwell	d	14 02	14 07	14 11							14 17	14 22	14 26			14 32	14 37						
Whitechapel	d	14 04	14 09	14 14							14 19	14 24	14 29			14 34	14 39						
Shoreditch High Street	d	14 06	14 11	14 16							14 21	14 26	14 31			14 36	14 41						
Hoxton	d	14 08	14 13	14 18							14 23	14 28	14 33			14 38	14 43						
Haggerston	d	14 10	14 15	14 20							14 25	14 30	14 35			14 40	14 45						
Dalston Junction Stn ELL	a	14 14	14 19	14 25							14 29	14 34	14 40			14 44	14 49						
London Bridge	a						14 06		13 56	14 44				14 29	14 41					14 36		14 26	15 11

Station		LO	LO	LO	LO	LO	SN	SN	LO	LO	LO	SE	SN	SN	SE	SN	SN	LO	LO	LO	SN	SN	SE
East Croydon	d						14 30														15 00		
West Croydon	d	14 09			14 22			14 31		14 39									14 52			15 01	
Norwood Junction	d	14 13			14 28		14 35			14 43									14 58		15 05		
Anerley	d	14 16			14 31		14 38			14 46									15 01		15 08		
Penge West	d	14 18			14 33		14 40			14 48									15 03		15 10		
London Victoria	d											14 39		14 41	14 43.		14 49						15 09.
Battersea Park	d													14 45			14 53						
Wandsworth Road	d													14 47									
Clapham High Street	d													14 49									
London Blackfriars	d																						
Denmark Hill	d											14 48		14 54	14 52								15 18
Peckham Rye	d							15 01				14 51	14 42	14 56	14 55	14 46						15 31	15 21
Queens Rd Peckham	d							15 04						14 59		14 49						15 34	
South Bermondsey	d							15 06						15 01		14 51						15 36	
Clapham Junction	d																14 57						
Wandsworth Common	d																15 00						
Balham	d																15 02						
Streatham Hill	d																15 05						
West Norwood	d												14 53				15 10						
Gipsy Hill	d												14 56				15 13						
Crystal Palace	d			14 28					14 43				14 59				15 21	14 58					
Sydenham	d	14 21		14 31	14 36		14 42		14 46	14 51							15 24	15 01	15 06		15 12		
Forest Hill	d	14 23		14 34	14 38		14 45		14 49	14 53							15 27	15 04	15 08		15 15		
Honor Oak Park	d	14 26		14 36	14 41		14 47		14 51	14 56							15 29	15 06	15 11		15 17		
Brockley	d	14 28		14 39	14 43		14 50		14 54	14 58							15 32	15 09	15 13		15 20		
New Cross Gate Station ELL	a																						
	d																						
New Cross Gate	d	14 31		14 41	14 46		14 52		14 56	15 01							15 34	15 11	15 16		15 22		
New Cross ELL	d		14 36			14 51					15 06									15 21			
Surrey Quays	d	14 34	14 40	14 45	14 49	14 55			15 00	15 04	15 10							15 15	15 19	15 25			
Canada Water	d	14 36	14 42	14 47	14 51	14 57			15 02	15 06	15 12							15 17	15 21	15 27			
Rotherhithe	d	14 38	14 43	14 48	14 53	14 58			15 03	15 08	15 13							15 18	15 23	15 28			
Wapping	d	14 39	14 45	14 50	14 54	15 00			15 05	15 09	15 15							15 20	15 24	15 30			
Shadwell	d	14 41	14 47	14 52	14 56	15 02			15 07	15 11	15 17							15 22	15 26	15 32			
Whitechapel	d	14 44	14 49	14 54	14 59	15 04			15 09	15 14	15 19							15 24	15 29	15 34			
Shoreditch High Street	d	14 46	14 51	14 56	15 01	15 06			15 11	15 16	15 21							15 26	15 31	15 36			
Hoxton	d	14 48	14 53	14 58	15 03	15 08			15 13	15 18	15 23							15 28	15 33	15 38			
Haggerston	d	14 50	14 55	15 00	15 05	15 10			15 15	15 20	15 25							15 30	15 35	15 40			
Dalston Junction Stn ELL	a	14 55	14 59	15 04	15 10	15 14			15 19	15 25	15 29							15 34	15 40	15 44			
London Bridge	a						14 59	15 11						15 06		14 56	15 44				15 29	15 41	

Table 178

East London Line and Croydon-London Victoria to London Bridge

Station		SN	LO	LO	SN	SE	SN	SN	LO	LO	LO	SN	SN	LO	LO	LO	SE	SN	SN	SE	SN	SN
East Croydon	d											15 30										
West Croydon	d			15 09							15 22		15 31			15 39						
Norwood Junction	d			15 13							15 28	15 35				15 43						
Anerley	d			15 16							15 31	15 38				15 46						
Penge West	d			15 18							15 33	15 40				15 48						
London Victoria	d				15 11	15 13		15 19									15 39.		15 41	15 43.		15 49
Battersea Park	d				15 15			15 23											15 45			15 53
Wandsworth Road	d				15 17														15 47			
Clapham High Street	d				15 19														15 49			
London Blackfriars	d																					
Denmark Hill	d				15 24	15 22											15 48		15 54	15 52		
Peckham Rye	d	15 12			15 26	15 25	15 16						16 01				15 51	15 42	15 56	15 55	15 46	
Queens Rd Peckham	d				15 29		15 19						16 04						15 59		15 49	
South Bermondsey	d				15 31		15 21						16 06						16 01		15 51	
Clapham Junction	d							15 27														15 57
Wandsworth Common	d							15 30														16 00
Balham	d							15 32														16 02
Streatham Hill	d							15 35														16 05
West Norwood	d	15 23						15 40										15 53				16 10
Gipsy Hill	d	15 26						15 43										15 56				16 13
Crystal Palace	d	15 29	15 13					15 51		15 28					15 43			15 59				16 21
Sydenham	d		15 16	15 21				15 54		15 31	15 36	15 42			15 46	15 51						16 24
Forest Hill	d		15 19	15 23				15 57		15 34	15 38	15 45			15 49	15 53						16 27
Honor Oak Park	d		15 21	15 26				15 59		15 36	15 41	15 47			15 51	15 56						16 29
Brockley	d		15 24	15 28				16 02		15 39	15 43	15 50			15 54	15 58						16 32
New Cross Gate Station ELL	a																					
	d																					
New Cross Gate	d		15 26	15 31				16 04		15 41	15 46	15 52			15 56	16 01						16 34
New Cross ELL	d								15 36					15 51								
Surrey Quays	d		15 30	15 34					15 40	15 45	15 49			15 55	16 00	16 04						
Canada Water	d		15 32	15 36					15 42	15 47	15 51			15 57	16 02	16 06						
Rotherhithe	d		15 33	15 38					15 43	15 48	15 53			15 58	16 03	16 08						
Wapping	d		15 35	15 39					15 45	15 50	15 54			16 00	16 05	16 09						
Shadwell	d		15 37	15 41					15 47	15 52	15 56			16 02	16 07	16 11						
Whitechapel	d		15 39	15 44					15 49	15 54	15 59			16 04	16 09	16 14						
Shoreditch High Street	d		15 41	15 46					15 51	15 56	16 01			16 06	16 11	16 16						
Hoxton	d		15 43	15 48					15 53	15 58	16 03			16 08	16 13	16 18						
Haggerston	d		15 45	15 50					15 55	16 00	16 05			16 10	16 15	16 20						
Dalston Junction Stn ELL	a		15 49	15 55					15 59	16 04	16 10			16 14	16 19	16 25						
London Bridge	a				15 36		15 26	16 11				15 59	16 11						16 06		15 56	16 41

Station		LO	LO	LO	SN	SN	SE	SN	SN	LO	LO	LO	SE	SN	SN	LO	LO	LO	LO	SN	SN	LO	SE	SN
East Croydon	d				16 00															16 30				
West Croydon	d			15 52		16 01						16 09						16 22			16 31			
Norwood Junction	d			15 58	16 05							16 13						16 28		16 35				
Anerley	d			16 01	16 08							16 16						16 31		16 38				
Penge West	d			16 03	16 10							16 18						16 33		16 40				
London Victoria	d						16 09.		16 11				16 13.		16 19								16 39.	
Battersea Park	d								16 15						16 23									
Wandsworth Road	d								16 17															
Clapham High Street	d								16 19															
London Blackfriars	d																							
Denmark Hill	d						16 18		16 24				16 22										16 48	
Peckham Rye	d					16 31	16 21	16 12	16 26				16 25	16 16							17 01		16 51	16 42
Queens Rd Peckham	d					16 34			16 29					16 19							17 04			
South Bermondsey	d					16 36			16 31					16 21							17 06			
Clapham Junction	d														16 27									
Wandsworth Common	d														16 30									
Balham	d														16 32									
Streatham Hill	d														16 35									
West Norwood	d							16 23							16 40									16 53
Gipsy Hill	d							16 26							16 43									16 56
Crystal Palace	d		15 58					16 29			16 13				16 51		16 28					16 43		16 59
Sydenham	d		16 01	16 06	16 12						16 16	16 21			16 54		16 31	16 36		16 42		16 46		
Forest Hill	d		16 04	16 08	16 15						16 19	16 23			16 57		16 34	16 38		16 45		16 49		
Honor Oak Park	d		16 06	16 11	16 17						16 21	16 26			16 59		16 36	16 41		16 47		16 51		
Brockley	d		16 09	16 13	16 20						16 24	16 28			17 02		16 39	16 43		16 50		16 54		
New Cross Gate Station ELL	a																							
	d																							
New Cross Gate	d		16 11	16 16	16 22						16 26	16 31			17 04		16 41	16 46		16 52		16 56		
New Cross ELL	d	16 06								16 21						16 36			16 51					
Surrey Quays	d	16 10	16 15	16 19						16 25	16 30	16 34				16 40	16 45	16 49	16 55			17 00		
Canada Water	d	16 12	16 17	16 21						16 27	16 32	16 36				16 42	16 47	16 51	16 57			17 02		
Rotherhithe	d	16 13	16 18	16 23						16 28	16 33	16 38				16 43	16 48	16 53	16 58			17 03		
Wapping	d	16 15	16 20	16 24						16 30	16 35	16 39				16 45	16 50	16 54	17 00			17 05		
Shadwell	d	16 17	16 22	16 26						16 32	16 37	16 41				16 47	16 52	16 56	17 02			17 07		
Whitechapel	d	16 19	16 24	16 29						16 34	16 39	16 44				16 49	16 54	16 59	17 04			17 09		
Shoreditch High Street	d	16 21	16 26	16 31						16 36	16 41	16 46				16 51	16 56	17 01	17 06			17 11		
Hoxton	d	16 23	16 28	16 33						16 38	16 43	16 48				16 53	16 58	17 03	17 08			17 13		
Haggerston	d	16 25	16 30	16 35						16 40	16 45	16 50				16 55	17 00	17 05	17 10			17 15		
Dalston Junction Stn ELL	a	16 29	16 34	16 40						16 44	16 49	16 55				16 59	17 04	17 10	17 14			17 19		
London Bridge	a				16 29	16 41			16 36					16 26	17 11					16 59	17 11			

East London Line and Croydon-London Victoria to London Bridge

		SN		SE	LO	LO	LO	SN	SN		LO	SN	SN	LO	LO	LO	LO	SE	SN	SN	SE	SN	SN	LO	LO
East Croydon	d											17 00													
West Croydon 4	d				16 39						16 52		17 01			17 09									17 22
Norwood Junction 2	d				16 43						16 58	17 05				17 13									17 28
Anerley	d				16 46						17 01	17 08				17 16									17 31
Penge West	d				16 48						17 03	17 10				17 18									17 33
London Victoria 15	⊖ d	16 41		16 43.					16 49									17 09.		17 11	17 13		17 19		
Battersea Park 4	d	16 45							16 53											17 15			17 23		
Wandsworth Road	d	16 47																		17 17					
Clapham High Street	⊖ d	16 49																		17 19					
London Blackfriars 3	⊖ d																								
Denmark Hill 4	d	16 54		16 52														17 18		17 24	17 22				
Peckham Rye 4	d	16 56		16 55				16 46					17 31					17 21	17 12	17 26	17 25	17 16			
Queens Rd Peckham	d	16 59						16 49					17 34							17 29		17 19			
South Bermondsey	d	17 01						16 51					17 36							17 31		17 21			
Clapham Junction 10	d								16 57														17 27		
Wandsworth Common	d								17 00														17 30		
Balham 4	⊖ d								17 02														17 32		
Streatham Hill	d								17 05														17 35		
West Norwood 4	d								17 10										17 23				17 40		
Gipsy Hill	d								17 13										17 26				17 43		
Crystal Palace 4	d						16 58		17 21						17 13				17 29				17 51	17 28	
Sydenham	d				16 51		17 01		17 24		17 06	17 12			17 16	17 21							17 54	17 31	17 36
Forest Hill 4	d				16 53		17 04		17 27		17 08	17 15			17 19	17 23							17 57	17 34	17 38
Honor Oak Park	d				16 56		17 06		17 29		17 11	17 17			17 21	17 26							17 59	17 36	17 41
Brockley	d				16 58		17 09		17 32		17 13	17 20			17 24	17 28							18 02	17 39	17 43
New Cross Gate Station Ell	a																								
	d																								
New Cross Gate 4	d				17 01		17 11		17 34		17 16	17 22			17 26	17 31							18 04	17 41	17 46
New Cross Ell	d					17 06								17 21			17 36								
Surrey Quays	d				17 04	17 10	17 15				17 19			17 25	17 30	17 34	17 40							17 45	17 49
Canada Water	d				17 06	17 12	17 17				17 21			17 27	17 32	17 36	17 42							17 47	17 51
Rotherhithe	d				17 08	17 13	17 18				17 23			17 28	17 33	17 38	17 43							17 48	17 53
Wapping	d				17 09	17 15	17 20				17 24			17 30	17 35	17 39	17 45							17 50	17 54
Shadwell	d				17 11	17 17	17 22				17 26			17 32	17 37	17 41	17 47							17 52	17 56
Whitechapel	d				17 14	17 19	17 24				17 29			17 34	17 39	17 44	17 49							17 54	17 59
Shoreditch High Street	d				17 16	17 21	17 26				17 31			17 36	17 41	17 46	17 51							17 56	18 01
Hoxton	d				17 18	17 23	17 28				17 33			17 38	17 43	17 48	17 53							17 58	18 03
Haggerston	d				17 20	17 25	17 30				17 35			17 40	17 45	17 50	17 55							18 00	18 05
Dalston Junction Stn Ell	a				17 25	17 29	17 34				17 40			17 44	17 49	17 55	17 59							18 04	18 10
London Bridge 4	⊖ a	17 06						16 56	17 41			17 30	17 41							17 36		17 26	18 11		

		LO	LO		SN	SN		LO	SE	SN	SN		SE	SN	SN	LO	LO	LO	SN	SN	LO		SE	SN	SN
East Croydon	d				17 30														18 00						
West Croydon 4	d					17 31		17 39										17 52		18 01					
Norwood Junction 2	d				17 35			17 43										17 58	18 05						
Anerley	d				17 38			17 46										18 01	18 08						
Penge West	d				17 40			17 48										18 03	18 10						
London Victoria 15	⊖ d								17 39		17 41		17 43.		17 49								18 09.		18 11
Battersea Park 4	d										17 45				17 53										18 15
Wandsworth Road	d										17 47														18 17
Clapham High Street	⊖ d										17 49														18 19
London Blackfriars 3	⊖ d																								
Denmark Hill 4	d								17 48		17 54		17 52										18 18		18 24
Peckham Rye 4	d					18 01			17 51	17 42	17 56		17 55	17 46						18 31			18 21	18 12	18 26
Queens Rd Peckham	d					18 04					17 59			17 49						18 34					18 29
South Bermondsey	d					18 06					18 01			17 51						18 36					18 31
Clapham Junction 10	d														17 57										
Wandsworth Common	d														18 00										
Balham 4	⊖ d														18 02										
Streatham Hill	d														18 05										
West Norwood 4	d									17 53					18 10									18 23	
Gipsy Hill	d									17 56					18 13									18 26	
Crystal Palace 4	d		17 43							17 59					18 21		17 58							18 29	
Sydenham	d		17 46		17 42			17 51							18 24		18 01	18 06	18 12						
Forest Hill 4	d		17 49		17 45			17 53							18 27		18 04	18 08	18 15						
Honor Oak Park	d		17 51		17 47			17 56							18 29		18 06	18 11	18 17						
Brockley	d		17 54		17 50			17 58							18 32		18 09	18 13	18 20						
New Cross Gate Station Ell	a																								
	d																								
New Cross Gate 4	d		17 56		17 52			18 01							18 34		18 11	18 16	18 22						
New Cross Ell	d	17 51														18 06					18 21				
Surrey Quays	d	17 55	18 00					18 04								18 10	18 15	18 19			18 25				
Canada Water	d	17 57	18 02					18 06								18 12	18 17	18 21			18 27				
Rotherhithe	d	17 58	18 03					18 08								18 13	18 18	18 23			18 28				
Wapping	d	18 00	18 05					18 09								18 15	18 20	18 24			18 30				
Shadwell	d	18 02	18 07					18 11								18 17	18 22	18 26			18 32				
Whitechapel	d	18 04	18 09					18 14								18 19	18 24	18 29			18 34				
Shoreditch High Street	d	18 06	18 11					18 16								18 21	18 26	18 31			18 36				
Hoxton	d	18 08	18 13					18 18								18 23	18 28	18 33			18 38				
Haggerston	d	18 10	18 15					18 20								18 25	18 30	18 35			18 40				
Dalston Junction Stn Ell	a	18 14	18 19					18 25								18 29	18 34	18 40			18 44				
London Bridge 4	⊖ a				17 59	18 11					18 06			17 56	18 41				18 29	18 41					18 36

Table 178

Saturdays

East London Line and Croydon-London Victoria to London Bridge

		LO	SE	SN	SN	LO	LO		LO	LO	LO	LO	SN	SN	LO	SE	SN	SN		SE	SN	LO	LO	SN	SN
East Croydon	d												18 30												19 00
West Croydon 4	d					18 09				18 22				18 31	18 39										
Norwood Junction 2	d					18 13				18 28			18 35		18 43										19 05
Anerley	d					18 16				18 31			18 38		18 46										19 08
Penge West	d					18 18				18 33			18 40		18 48										19 10
London Victoria 15	⊖ d		18 13.		18 19											18 39.		18 41		18 43.				18 53	
Battersea Park 4	d				18 23													18 45						18 57	
Wandsworth Road	d																	18 47							
Clapham High Street	⊖ d																	18 49							
London Blackfriars 3	⊖ d																								
Denmark Hill 4	d		18 22													18 48		18 54		18 52					
Peckham Rye 4	d		18 25	18 16										19 01		18 51	18 42	18 56		18 55	18 46				
Queens Rd Peckham	d			18 19										19 04				18 59			18 49				
South Bermondsey	d			18 21										19 06				19 01			18 51				
Clapham Junction 10	d				18 27																			19 01	
Wandsworth Common	d				18 30																			19 04	
Balham 4	⊖ d				18 32																			19 06	
Streatham Hill	d				18 35																			19 09	
West Norwood 4	d				18 40												18 53							19 13	
Gipsy Hill	d				18 43												18 56							19 16	
Crystal Palace 4	d	18 13			18 51				18 28			18 43					18 59						18 58	19 21	
Sydenham	d	18 16			18 54	18 21			18 31	18 36		18 46	18 42		18 51								19 01	19 24	19 12
Forest Hill 4	d	18 19			18 57	18 23			18 34	18 38		18 49	18 45		18 53								19 04	19 27	19 15
Honor Oak Park	d	18 21			18 59	18 26			18 36	18 41		18 51	18 47		18 56								19 06	19 29	19 17
Brockley	d	18 24			19 02	18 28			18 39	18 43		18 54	18 50		18 58								19 09	19 32	19 20
New Cross Gate Station Ell	a																								
	d																								
New Cross Gate 4	d	18 26			19 04	18 31			18 41	18 46		18 56	18 52		19 01								19 11	19 34	19 22
New Cross Ell	d						18 36				18 51											19 06			
Surrey Quays	d	18 30				18 34	18 40		18 45	18 49	18 55	19 00			19 04							19 10	19 15		
Canada Water	d	18 32				18 36	18 42		18 47	18 51	18 57	19 02			19 06							19 12	19 17		
Rotherhithe	d	18 33				18 38	18 43		18 48	18 53	18 58	19 03			19 08							19 13	19 18		
Wapping	d	18 35				18 39	18 45		18 50	18 54	19 00	19 05			19 09							19 15	19 20		
Shadwell	d	18 37				18 41	18 47		18 52	18 56	19 02	19 07			19 11							19 17	19 22		
Whitechapel	d	18 39				18 44	18 49		18 54	18 59	19 04	19 09			19 14							19 19	19 24		
Shoreditch High Street	d	18 41				18 46	18 51		18 56	19 01	19 06	19 11			19 16							19 21	19 26		
Hoxton	d	18 43				18 48	18 53		18 58	19 03	19 08	19 13			19 18							19 23	19 28		
Haggerston	d	18 45				18 50	18 55		19 00	19 05	19 10	19 15			19 20							19 25	19 30		
Dalston Junction Stn Ell	a	18 49				18 55	18 59		19 04	19 10	19 14	19 19			19 25							19 29	19 34		
London Bridge 4	⊖ a			18 26	19 11								18 59	19 11				19 06			18 56			19 41	19 29

		SN	LO	LO	LO		LO	LO	SE	SN	SN	SE	SN		SN	LO	LO	SN	SN	LO	LO	SE	SN		SN
East Croydon	d																	19 30							
West Croydon 4	d	19 01	18 52				19 09										19 22		19 31						
Norwood Junction 2	d		18 58				19 13										19 28	19 35							
Anerley	d		19 01				19 16										19 31	19 38							
Penge West	d		19 03				19 18										19 33	19 40							
London Victoria 15	⊖ d								19 09		19 11	19 13.			19 23							19 39.			19 41
Battersea Park 4	d										19 15				19 27										19 45
Wandsworth Road	d										19 17														19 47
Clapham High Street	⊖ d										19 19														19 49
London Blackfriars 3	⊖ d																								
Denmark Hill 4	d								19 18		19 24	19 22										19 48			19 54
Peckham Rye 4	d	19 31							19 21	19 12	19 26	19 25	19 16						20 01			19 51	19 42		19 56
Queens Rd Peckham	d	19 34									19 29		19 19						20 04						19 59
South Bermondsey	d	19 36									19 31		19 21						20 06						20 01
Clapham Junction 10	d														19 31										
Wandsworth Common	d														19 34										
Balham 4	⊖ d														19 36										
Streatham Hill	d														19 39										
West Norwood 4	d									19 23					19 43								19 53		
Gipsy Hill	d									19 26					19 46								19 56		
Crystal Palace 4	d				19 13					19 29					19 51	19 28					19 43		19 59		
Sydenham	d		19 06		19 16		19 21								19 54	19 31	19 36	19 42			19 46				
Forest Hill 4	d		19 08		19 19		19 23								19 57	19 34	19 38	19 45			19 49				
Honor Oak Park	d		19 11		19 21		19 26								19 59	19 36	19 41	19 47			19 51				
Brockley	d		19 13		19 24		19 28								20 02	19 39	19 43	19 50			19 54				
New Cross Gate Station Ell	a																								
	d																								
New Cross Gate 4	d		19 16		19 26		19 31								20 04	19 41	19 46	19 52			19 56				
New Cross Ell	d			19 21				19 36												19 51					
Surrey Quays	d		19 19	19 25	19 30		19 34	19 40								19 45	19 49			19 55	20 00				
Canada Water	d		19 21	19 27	19 32		19 36	19 42								19 47	19 51			19 57	20 02				
Rotherhithe	d		19 23	19 28	19 33		19 38	19 43								19 48	19 53			19 58	20 03				
Wapping	d		19 24	19 30	19 35		19 39	19 45								19 50	19 54			20 00	20 05				
Shadwell	d		19 26	19 32	19 37		19 41	19 47								19 52	19 56			20 02	20 07				
Whitechapel	d		19 29	19 34	19 39		19 44	19 49								19 54	19 59			20 04	20 09				
Shoreditch High Street	d		19 31	19 36	19 41		19 46	19 51								19 56	20 01			20 06	20 11				
Hoxton	d		19 33	19 38	19 43		19 48	19 53								19 58	20 03			20 08	20 13				
Haggerston	d		19 35	19 40	19 45		19 50	19 55								20 00	20 05			20 10	20 15				
Dalston Junction Stn Ell	a		19 40	19 44	19 49		19 55	19 59								20 04	20 10			20 14	20 19				
London Bridge 4	⊖ a	19 41									19 36		19 26		20 11			19 59	20 11						20 06

Table 178

Saturdays

East London Line and Croydon-London Victoria to London Bridge

		LO	LO	SE	SN	LO	LO	SN	SN	SN	LO	LO	LO	SN	SE	SN	LO	LO	LO	LO	SN	SN	SN	LO
East Croydon	d								20 00													20 30		
West Croydon	d	19 39					19 52			20 01			20 09						20 22				20 31	
Norwood Junction	d	19 43					19 58		20 05				20 13						20 28			20 35		
Anerley	d	19 46					20 01		20 08				20 16						20 31			20 38		
Penge West	d	19 48					20 03		20 10				20 18						20 33			20 40		
London Victoria	d			19 43.				19 53						20 11	20 13.						20 23			
Battersea Park	d							19 57						20 15							20 27			
Wandsworth Road	d													20 17										
Clapham High Street	d													20 19										
London Blackfriars	d																							
Denmark Hill	d			19 52										20 24	20 22									
Peckham Rye	d			19 55	19 46					20 31				20 26	20 25	20 17							21 01	
Queens Rd Peckham	d				19 49					20 34				20 29		20 20							21 04	
South Bermondsey	d				19 51					20 36				20 31		20 22							21 06	
Clapham Junction	d							20 01													20 31			
Wandsworth Common	d							20 04													20 34			
Balham	d							20 06													20 36			
Streatham Hill	d							20 09													20 39			
West Norwood	d							20 13													20 43			
Gipsy Hill	d							20 16													20 46			
Crystal Palace	d					19 58		20 21				20 13						20 28			20 51			20 43
Sydenham	d	19 51				20 01	20 06	20 24	20 12			20 16	20 21					20 31	20 36		20 54	20 42		20 46
Forest Hill	d	19 53				20 04	20 08	20 27	20 15			20 19	20 23					20 34	20 38		20 57	20 45		20 49
Honor Oak Park	d	19 56				20 06	20 11	20 29	20 17			20 21	20 26					20 36	20 41		20 59	20 47		20 51
Brockley	d	19 58				20 09	20 13	20 32	20 20			20 24	20 28					20 39	20 43		21 02	20 50		20 54
New Cross Gate Station Ell	a																							
	d																							
New Cross Gate	d	20 01				20 11	20 16	20 34	20 22			20 26	20 31					20 41	20 46		21 04	20 52		20 56
New Cross Ell	d		20 06								20 21						20 36			20 51				
Surrey Quays	d	20 04	20 10			20 15	20 19				20 25	20 30	20 34				20 40	20 45	20 49	20 55				21 00
Canada Water	d	20 06	20 12			20 17	20 21				20 27	20 32	20 36				20 42	20 47	20 51	20 57				21 02
Rotherhithe	d	20 08	20 13			20 18	20 23				20 28	20 33	20 38				20 43	20 48	20 53	20 58				21 03
Wapping	d	20 09	20 15			20 20	20 24				20 30	20 35	20 39				20 45	20 50	20 54	21 00				21 05
Shadwell	d	20 11	20 17			20 22	20 26				20 32	20 37	20 41				20 47	20 52	20 56	21 02				21 07
Whitechapel	d	20 14	20 19			20 24	20 29				20 34	20 39	20 44				20 49	20 54	20 59	21 04				21 09
Shoreditch High Street	d	20 16	20 21			20 26	20 31				20 36	20 41	20 46				20 51	20 56	21 01	21 06				21 11
Hoxton	d	20 18	20 23			20 28	20 33				20 38	20 43	20 48				20 53	20 58	21 03	21 08				21 13
Haggerston	d	20 20	20 25			20 30	20 35				20 40	20 45	20 50				20 55	21 00	21 05	21 10				21 15
Dalston Junction Stn Ell	a	20 25	20 29			20 34	20 40				20 44	20 49	20 55				20 59	21 04	21 10	21 14				21 19
London Bridge	a				19 56			20 41	20 29	20 41				20 36		20 27					21 13	20 59	21 11	

		LO	SN	LO	LO	SE	SN	LO	LO	LO	SN	SN	SN	LO	SN	LO	LO	LO	SN	SN	SN
East Croydon	d											21 00								21 30	
West Croydon	d	20 39						20 52					21 01	21 09				21 22			21 31
Norwood Junction	d	20 43						20 58				21 05		21 13				21 28		21 35	
Anerley	d	20 46						21 01				21 08		21 16				21 31		21 38	
Penge West	d	20 48						21 03				21 10		21 18				21 33		21 40	
London Victoria	d		20 41			20 43.					20 53				21 11				21 23		
Battersea Park	d		20 45								20 57				21 15				21 27		
Wandsworth Road	d		20 47												21 17						
Clapham High Street	d		20 49												21 19						
London Blackfriars	d																				
Denmark Hill	d		20 54			20 52									21 24						
Peckham Rye	d		20 56			20 55	20 46						21 31		21 26						22 01
Queens Rd Peckham	d		20 59				20 49						21 34		21 29						22 04
South Bermondsey	d		21 01				20 51						21 36		21 31						22 06
Clapham Junction	d										21 01								21 31		
Wandsworth Common	d										21 04								21 34		
Balham	d										21 06								21 36		
Streatham Hill	d										21 09								21 39		
West Norwood	d										21 13								21 43		
Gipsy Hill	d										21 16								21 46		
Crystal Palace	d				20 58					21 13	21 21						21 28		21 51		
Sydenham	d	20 51			21 01			21 06		21 16	21 24	21 12		21 21			21 31	21 36	21 54	21 42	
Forest Hill	d	20 53			21 04			21 08		21 19	21 27	21 15		21 23			21 34	21 38	21 57	21 45	
Honor Oak Park	d	20 56			21 06			21 11		21 21	21 29	21 17		21 26			21 36	21 41	21 59	21 47	
Brockley	d	20 58			21 09			21 13		21 24	21 32	21 20		21 28			21 39	21 43	22 02	21 50	
New Cross Gate Station Ell	a																				
	d																				
New Cross Gate	d	21 01			21 11			21 16		21 26	21 34	21 22		21 31			21 41	21 46	22 04	21 52	
New Cross Ell	d			21 06					21 21							21 36					
Surrey Quays	d	21 04		21 10	21 15			21 19	21 25	21 30				21 34		21 40	21 45	21 49			
Canada Water	d	21 06		21 12	21 17			21 21	21 27	21 32				21 36		21 42	21 47	21 51			
Rotherhithe	d	21 08		21 13	21 18			21 23	21 28	21 33				21 38		21 43	21 48	21 53			
Wapping	d	21 09		21 15	21 20			21 24	21 30	21 35				21 39		21 45	21 50	21 54			
Shadwell	d	21 11		21 17	21 22			21 26	21 32	21 37				21 41		21 47	21 52	21 56			
Whitechapel	d	21 14		21 19	21 24			21 29	21 34	21 39				21 44		21 49	21 54	21 59			
Shoreditch High Street	d	21 16		21 21	21 26			21 31	21 36	21 41				21 46		21 51	21 56	22 01			
Hoxton	d	21 18		21 23	21 28			21 33	21 38	21 43				21 48		21 53	21 58	22 03			
Haggerston	d	21 20		21 25	21 30			21 35	21 40	21 45				21 50		21 55	22 00	22 05			
Dalston Junction Stn Ell	a	21 25		21 29	21 34			21 40	21 44	21 49				21 55		21 59	22 04	22 10			
London Bridge	a		21 06				20 56				21 43	21 29	21 41		21 36				22 13	21 59	22 11

Table 178

Saturdays

East London Line and Croydon-London Victoria to London Bridge

		LO	LO	LO	LO	SN	SE	LO	LO	SN	SN	SN	LO	LO	LO	SN	SE	LO	LO	SN	SN	SN
East Croydon	d										22 00										22 30	
West Croydon	d			21 39					21 52			22 01		22 09					22 22			22 31
Norwood Junction	d			21 43					21 58		22 05			22 13					22 28		22 35	
Anerley	d			21 46					22 01		22 08			22 16					22 31		22 38	
Penge West	d			21 48					22 03		22 10			22 18					22 33		22 40	
London Victoria	d					21 41	21 43.			21 53						22 11	22 13			22 23		
Battersea Park	d					21 45				21 57						22 15				22 27		
Wandsworth Road	d					21 47										22 17						
Clapham High Street	d					21 49										22 19						
London Blackfriars	d																					
Denmark Hill	d					21 54	21 52									22 24	22 22					
Peckham Rye	d					21 56	21 55					22 31				22 26	22 25					23 01
Queens Rd Peckham	d					21 59						22 34				22 29						23 04
South Bermondsey	d					22 01						22 36				22 31						23 06
Clapham Junction	d									22 01										22 31		
Wandsworth Common	d									22 04										22 34		
Balham	d									22 06										22 36		
Streatham Hill	d									22 09										22 39		
West Norwood	d									22 13										22 43		
Gipsy Hill	d									22 16										22 46		
Crystal Palace	d		21 43					21 58		22 21			22 13					22 28		22 51		
Sydenham	d		21 46	21 51				22 01	22 06	22 24	22 12		22 16	22 21				22 31	22 36	22 54	22 42	
Forest Hill	d		21 49	21 53				22 04	22 08	22 27	22 15		22 19	22 23				22 34	22 38	22 57	22 45	
Honor Oak Park	d		21 51	21 56				22 06	22 11	22 29	22 17		22 21	22 26				22 36	22 41	22 59	22 47	
Brockley	d		21 54	21 58				22 09	22 13	22 32	22 20		22 24	22 28				22 39	22 43	23 02	22 50	
New Cross Gate Station Ell	a																					
	d																					
New Cross Gate	d		21 56	22 01				22 11	22 16	22 34	22 22		22 26	22 31				22 41	22 46	23 04	22 52	
New Cross Ell	d	21 51			22 06										22 36							
Surrey Quays	d	21 55	22 00	22 04	22 10			22 15	22 19				22 30	22 34	22 40			22 45	22 49			
Canada Water	d	21 57	22 02	22 06	22 12			22 17	22 21				22 32	22 36	22 42			22 47	22 51			
Rotherhithe	d	21 58	22 03	22 08	22 13			22 18	22 23				22 33	22 38	22 43			22 48	22 53			
Wapping	d	22 00	22 05	22 09	22 15			22 20	22 24				22 35	22 39	22 45			22 50	22 54			
Shadwell	d	22 02	22 07	22 11	22 17			22 22	22 26				22 37	22 41	22 47			22 52	22 56			
Whitechapel	d	22 04	22 09	22 14	22 19			22 24	22 29				22 39	22 44	22 49			22 54	22 59			
Shoreditch High Street	d	22 06	22 11	22 16	22 21			22 26	22 31				22 41	22 46	22 51			22 56	23 01			
Hoxton	d	22 08	22 13	22 18	22 23			22 28	22 33				22 43	22 48	22 53			22 58	23 03			
Haggerston	d	22 10	22 15	22 20	22 25			22 30	22 35				22 45	22 50	22 55			23 00	23 05			
Dalston Junction Stn Ell	a	22 14	22 19	22 25	22 29			22 34	22 40				22 49	22 55	22 59			23 05	23 10			
London Bridge	a					22 06				22 43	22 29	22 41				22 36				23 13	22 59	23 11

		LO	LO	SN	SE	LO	LO	SN	SN	SN	SN	LO	SE	LO	LO	SN	LO	SE	SN
East Croydon	d								23 01										
West Croydon	d		22 39				22 52			23 01					23 22				
Norwood Junction	d		22 43				22 58		23 06						23 28				
Anerley	d		22 46				23 01		23 09						23 31				
Penge West	d		22 48				23 03		23 11						23 33				
London Victoria	d			22 41	22 43.			22 53			23 11		23 13.			23 22		23 43.	
Battersea Park	d			22 45				22 57			23 15					23 26			
Wandsworth Road	d			22 47							23 17								
Clapham High Street	d			22 49							23 19								
London Blackfriars	d																		
Denmark Hill	d			22 54	22 52						23 24		23 22					23 52	
Peckham Rye	d			22 56	22 55					23 31	23 26		23 25					23 55	23 57
Queens Rd Peckham	d			22 59						23 34	23 29								
South Bermondsey	d			23 01						23 36	23 31								
Clapham Junction	d							23 01								23 30			
Wandsworth Common	d							23 04								23 33			
Balham	d							23 06								23 35			
Streatham Hill	d							23 09								23 38			
West Norwood	d							23 13								23 42			00 10
Gipsy Hill	d							23 16								23 45			00 13
Crystal Palace	d	22 43						23 21				23 13				23 51	23 43		00 15
Sydenham	d	22 46	22 51				23 06	23 24	23 13			23 16			23 36	23 54	23 46		
Forest Hill	d	22 49	22 53				23 08	23 27	23 16			23 19			23 38	23 57	23 49		
Honor Oak Park	d	22 51	22 56				23 11	23 29	23 18			23 21			23 41	23 59	23 51		
Brockley	d	22 54	22 58				23 13	23 32	23 21			23 24			23 43	00 02	23 54		
New Cross Gate Station Ell	a																		
	d																		
New Cross Gate	d	22 56	23 01				23 16	23 34	23 23			23 26			23 46	00 04	23 56		
New Cross Ell	d					23 06								23 36					
Surrey Quays	d	23 00	23 04			23 10	23 19					23 30		23 40	23 49		23 59		
Canada Water	d	23 02	23 06			23 12	23 21					23 32		23 42	23 51		00 02		
Rotherhithe	d	23 03	23 08			23 13	23 23					23 33		23 43	23 53		00 03		
Wapping	d	23 05	23 09			23 15	23 24					23 35		23 45	23 54		00 05		
Shadwell	d	23 07	23 11			23 17	23 26					23 37		23 47	23 56		00 07		
Whitechapel	d	23 09	23 14			23 19	23 29					23 39		23 49	23 59		00 09		
Shoreditch High Street	d	23 11	23 16			23 21	23 31					23 41		23 51	00 01		00 11		
Hoxton	d	23 13	23 18			23 23	23 33					23 43		23 53	00 03		00 13		
Haggerston	d	23 15	23 20			23 25	23 35					23 45		23 55	00 05		00 15		
Dalston Junction Stn Ell	a	23 19	23 25			23 29	23 40					23 49		23 59	00 10		00 19		
London Bridge	a			23 06				23 43	23 30	23 41	23 36					00 11			

Table 178

Sundays

East London Line and Croydon-London Victoria to London Bridge

		LO	SN	LO	SN	LO	SN	LO	SN	LO		SN	SN	SN	SN	LO	SE	SN	LO	SN		SN	SN	SN	LO
East Croydon ⇌	d						06 47					07 14	07 17							07 44		07 47			
West Croydon 4 ⇌	d	23p22				06 42				07 12				07 22	07 35				07 42				07 52	08 05	
Norwood Junction 2	d	23p28				06 47	06 52			07 17			07 22	07 29	07 40				07 47			07 52	07 59	08 10	
Anerley	d	23p31				06 50	06 55			07 20			07 25						07 50			07 55			
Penge West	d	23p33				06 52	06 57			07 22			07 27						07 52			07 57			
London Victoria 15 ⊖	d		23p22															07 41							
London Victoria-I 15 ⊖	d																07 39								
Battersea Park 4	d		23p26															07 45							
Wandsworth Road	d																	07 47							
Clapham High Street ⊖	d																	07 49							
London Blackfriars 3 ⊖	d																								
Denmark Hill 4	d																07 48	07 54							
Peckham Rye 4	d				23p57				07 09			07 39					07 51	07 56		08 09					
Queens Rd Peckham	d								07 12			07 42						07 59		08 12					
South Bermondsey	d								07 14			07 44						08 01		08 14					
Clapham Junction 10	d		23p30																						
Wandsworth Common	d		23p33																						
Balham 4 ⊖	d		23p35																						
Streatham Hill	d		23p38																						
West Norwood 4	d		23p42		00 10																				
Gipsy Hill	d		23p45		00 13																				
Crystal Palace 4	d		23p51	23p43	00 15			07 07						07 35		07 37							08 05		08 07
Sydenham	d	23p36	23p54	23p46		06 55	06 59	07 10		07 25			07 29		07 44	07 40			07 55			07 59		08 14	08 10
Forest Hill 4	d	23p38	23p57	23p49		06 57	07 02	07 13		07 27			07 32		07 47	07 43			07 57			08 02		08 17	08 13
Honor Oak Park	d	23p41	23p59	23p51		07 00	07 04	07 15		07 30			07 34		07 49	07 45			08 00			08 04		08 19	08 15
Brockley	d	23p43	00 02	23p54		07 02	07 07	07 18		07 32			07 37		07 52	07 48			08 02			08 07		08 22	08 18
New Cross Gate Station Ell	a																								
	d																								
New Cross Gate 4	d	23p46	00 04	23p56		07 05	07 09	07 20		07 35			07 39		07 54	07 50			08 05			08 09		08 24	08 20
New Cross Ell	d																								
Surrey Quays	d	23p49		23p59		07 09		07 24		07 39						07 54			08 09						08 24
Canada Water	d	23p51		00 02		07 11		07 26		07 41						07 56			08 11						08 26
Rotherhithe	d	23p53		00 03		07 12		07 27		07 42						07 57			08 12						08 27
Wapping	d	23p54		00 05		07 14		07 29		07 44						07 59			08 14						08 29
Shadwell	d	23p56		00 07		07 16		07 31		07 46						08 01			08 16						08 31
Whitechapel	d	23p59		00 09		07 18		07 33		07 48						08 03			08 18						08 33
Shoreditch High Street	d	00 01		00 11		07 20		07 35		07 50						08 05			08 20						08 35
Hoxton	d	00 03		00 13		07 22		07 37		07 52						08 07			08 22						08 37
Haggerston	d	00 05		00 15		07 24		07 39		07 54						08 09			08 24						08 39
Dalston Junction Stn Ell	a	00 10		00 19		07 29		07 42		07 59						08 12			08 29						08 42
London Bridge 4 ⊖	a		00 11				07 18		07 19			07 49	07 48		08 01			08 06		08 19		08 18		08 31	

		SE	SN	LO	SN	SN		SN	LO	SE	SN	LO	LO	SN	SN	SN		LO	LO	SE	SN	LO	LO	SN	SN
East Croydon ⇌	d				08 14	08 17								08 44	08 47									09 14	09 17
West Croydon 4 ⇌	d			08 12				08 35					08 42			09 05							09 12		
Norwood Junction 2	d			08 17		08 22		08 40					08 47		08 52	09 10							09 17		09 22
Anerley	d			08 20		08 25							08 50		08 55								09 20		09 25
Penge West	d			08 22		08 27							08 52		08 57								09 22		09 27
London Victoria 15 ⊖	d		08 11								08 41										09 11				
London Victoria-I 15 ⊖	d	08 09								08 39										09 09					
Battersea Park 4	d		08 15								08 45										09 15				
Wandsworth Road	d		08 17								08 47										09 17				
Clapham High Street ⊖	d		08 19								08 49										09 19				
London Blackfriars 3 ⊖	d																								
Denmark Hill 4	d	08 18	08 24							08 48	08 54									09 18	09 24				
Peckham Rye 4	d	08 21	08 26		08 39					08 51	08 56			09 09						09 21	09 26			09 39	
Queens Rd Peckham	d		08 29		08 42						08 59			09 12							09 29			09 42	
South Bermondsey	d		08 31		08 44						09 01			09 14							09 31			09 44	
Clapham Junction 10	d																								
Wandsworth Common	d																								
Balham 4 ⊖	d																								
Streatham Hill	d																								
West Norwood 4	d																								
Gipsy Hill	d																								
Crystal Palace 4	d								08 37										09 07						
Sydenham	d			08 25		08 29		08 44	08 40				08 55		08 59	09 14			09 10				09 25		09 29
Forest Hill 4	d			08 27		08 32		08 47	08 43				08 57		09 02	09 17			09 13				09 27		09 32
Honor Oak Park	d			08 30		08 34		08 49	08 45				09 00		09 04	09 19			09 15				09 30		09 34
Brockley	d			08 32		08 37		08 52	08 48				09 02		09 07	09 22			09 18				09 32		09 37
New Cross Gate Station Ell	a																								
	d																								
New Cross Gate 4	d			08 35		08 39		08 54	08 50				09 05		09 09	09 24			09 20				09 35		09 39
New Cross Ell	d											08 54						09 09				09 24			
Surrey Quays	d			08 39					08 54			08 58	09 09					09 13	09 24			09 28	09 39		
Canada Water	d			08 41					08 56			09 00	09 11					09 15	09 26			09 30	09 41		
Rotherhithe	d			08 42					08 57			09 01	09 12					09 16	09 27			09 31	09 42		
Wapping	d			08 44					08 59			09 03	09 14					09 18	09 29			09 33	09 44		
Shadwell	d			08 46					09 01			09 05	09 16					09 20	09 31			09 35	09 46		
Whitechapel	d			08 48					09 03			09 07	09 18					09 22	09 33			09 37	09 48		
Shoreditch High Street	d			08 50					09 05			09 09	09 20					09 24	09 35			09 39	09 50		
Hoxton	d			08 52					09 07			09 11	09 22					09 26	09 37			09 41	09 52		
Haggerston	d			08 54					09 09			09 13	09 24					09 28	09 39			09 43	09 54		
Dalston Junction Stn Ell	a			08 59					09 12			09 17	09 29					09 32	09 42			09 47	09 59		
London Bridge 4 ⊖	a		08 36		08 49	08 48		09 01			09 06			09 19	09 18	09 31					09 36			09 49	09 48

Table 178

Sundays

East London Line and Croydon-London Victoria to London Bridge

		SN		LO	LO	SE	SN	LO	LO	SN	SN	SN		LO	LO	SE	SN	SN	SN	LO	LO	SN		LO	LO
East Croydon ⇌	d									09 44	09 47							10 14	10 17						
West Croydon 4 ⇌	d	09 35							09 42			10 05									10 12	10 35			
Norwood Junction 2	d	09 40							09 47		09 52	10 10							10 22		10 17	10 40			
Anerley	d								09 50		09 55								10 25		10 20				
Penge West	d								09 52		09 57								10 27		10 22				
London Victoria 15 ⊖	d					09 39	09 41									10 09	10 11								
Battersea Park 4	d						09 45										10 15								
Wandsworth Road	d						09 47										10 17								
Clapham High Street ⊖	d						09 49										10 19								
London Blackfriars 3 ⊖	d																								
Denmark Hill 4	d					09 48	09 54									10 18	10 24								
Peckham Rye 4	d					09 51	09 56			10 09						10 21	10 26	10 39							
Queens Rd Peckham	d						09 59			10 12							10 29	10 42							
South Bermondsey	d						10 01			10 14							10 31	10 44							
Clapham Junction 10	d																								
Wandsworth Common	d																								
Balham 4 ⊖	d																								
Streatham Hill	d																								
West Norwood 4	d																								
Gipsy Hill	d																								
Crystal Palace 4	d				09 37										10 07										10 37
Sydenham	d	09 44			09 40				09 55		09 59	10 14			10 10				10 29		10 25	10 44			10 40
Forest Hill 4	d	09 47			09 43				09 57		10 02	10 17			10 13				10 32		10 27	10 47			10 43
Honor Oak Park	d	09 49			09 45				10 00		10 04	10 19			10 15				10 34		10 30	10 49			10 45
Brockley	d	09 52			09 48				10 02		10 07	10 22			10 18				10 37		10 32	10 52			10 48
New Cross Gate Station Ell	a																								
	d																								
New Cross Gate 4	d	09 54			09 50				10 05		10 09	10 24			10 20				10 39		10 35	10 54			10 50
New Cross Ell	d			09 39				09 54						10 09						10 24				10 39	
Surrey Quays	d			09 43	09 54			09 58	10 09					10 13	10 24					10 28	10 39			10 43	10 54
Canada Water	d			09 45	09 56			10 00	10 11					10 15	10 26					10 30	10 41			10 45	10 56
Rotherhithe	d			09 46	09 57			10 01	10 12					10 16	10 27					10 31	10 42			10 46	10 57
Wapping	d			09 48	09 59			10 03	10 14					10 18	10 29					10 33	10 44			10 48	10 59
Shadwell	d			09 50	10 01			10 05	10 16					10 20	10 31					10 35	10 46			10 50	11 01
Whitechapel	d			09 52	10 03			10 07	10 18					10 22	10 33					10 37	10 48			10 52	11 03
Shoreditch High Street	d			09 54	10 05			10 09	10 20					10 24	10 35					10 39	10 50			10 54	11 05
Hoxton	d			09 56	10 07			10 11	10 22					10 26	10 37					10 41	10 52			10 56	11 07
Haggerston	d			09 58	10 09			10 13	10 24					10 28	10 39					10 43	10 54			10 58	11 09
Dalston Junction Stn Ell	a			10 02	10 12			10 17	10 29					10 32	10 42					10 47	10 59			11 02	11 12
London Bridge 4 ⊖	a	10 01					10 06			10 19	10 18	10 31					10 36	10 49	10 48			11 01			

		LO	SE	SN	LO	SN	SN	SN		LO	LO	SE	SN	LO	LO	SN	SN	SN	LO	LO	SE	LO	SN	LO	SN
East Croydon ⇌	d					10 44	10 47									11 14	11 17								11 44
West Croydon 4 ⇌	d				10 42			11 05							11 12			11 35						11 42	
Norwood Junction 2	d				10 47		10 52	11 10							11 17		11 22	11 40						11 47	
Anerley	d				10 50		10 55								11 20		11 25							11 50	
Penge West	d				10 52		10 57								11 22		11 27							11 52	
London Victoria 15 ⊖	d		10 39	10 41								11 09	11 11								11 39		11 41		
Battersea Park 4	d			10 45									11 15										11 45		
Wandsworth Road	d			10 47									11 17										11 47		
Clapham High Street ⊖	d			10 49									11 19										11 49		
London Blackfriars 3 ⊖	d																								
Denmark Hill 4	d		10 48	10 54								11 18	11 24								11 48		11 54		
Peckham Rye 4	d		10 51	10 56		11 09						11 21	11 26			11 39					11 51		11 56		12 09
Queens Rd Peckham	d			10 59		11 12							11 29			11 42							11 59		12 12
South Bermondsey	d			11 01		11 14							11 31			11 44							12 01		12 14
Clapham Junction 10	d																								
Wandsworth Common	d																								
Balham 4 ⊖	d																								
Streatham Hill	d																								
West Norwood 4	d																								
Gipsy Hill	d																								
Crystal Palace 4	d										11 07									11 37					
Sydenham	d				10 55		10 59	11 14			11 10				11 25		11 29	11 44		11 40				11 55	
Forest Hill 4	d				10 57		11 02	11 17			11 13				11 27		11 32	11 47		11 43				11 57	
Honor Oak Park	d				11 00		11 04	11 19			11 15				11 30		11 34	11 49		11 45				12 00	
Brockley	d				11 02		11 07	11 22			11 18				11 32		11 37	11 52		11 48				12 02	
New Cross Gate Station Ell	a																								
	d																								
New Cross Gate 4	d				11 05		11 09	11 24			11 20				11 35		11 39	11 54		11 50				12 05	
New Cross Ell	d	10 54								11 09				11 24					11 39			11 54			
Surrey Quays	d	10 58			11 09					11 13	11 24			11 28	11 39				11 43	11 54		11 58		12 09	
Canada Water	d	11 00			11 11					11 15	11 26			11 30	11 41				11 45	11 56		12 00		12 11	
Rotherhithe	d	11 01			11 12					11 16	11 27			11 31	11 42				11 46	11 57		12 01		12 12	
Wapping	d	11 03			11 14					11 18	11 29			11 33	11 44				11 48	11 59		12 03		12 14	
Shadwell	d	11 05			11 16					11 20	11 31			11 35	11 46				11 50	12 01		12 05		12 16	
Whitechapel	d	11 07			11 18					11 22	11 33			11 37	11 48				11 52	12 03		12 07		12 18	
Shoreditch High Street	d	11 09			11 20					11 24	11 35			11 39	11 50				11 54	12 05		12 09		12 20	
Hoxton	d	11 11			11 22					11 26	11 37			11 41	11 52				11 56	12 07		12 11		12 22	
Haggerston	d	11 13			11 24					11 28	11 39			11 43	11 54				11 58	12 09		12 13		12 24	
Dalston Junction Stn Ell	a	11 17			11 29					11 32	11 42			11 47	11 59				12 02	12 12		12 18		12 29	
London Bridge 4 ⊖	a			11 06		11 19	11 18	11 31					11 36			11 49	11 48	12 01					12 06		12 19

Table 178

Sundays

East London Line and Croydon-London Victoria to London Bridge

		SN	SN	LO	LO	SE	SN	LO	LO	SN	SN	LO	LO	SN	SE	SN	SN	SN	LO	LO	LO	LO
East Croydon	d	11 47								12 14	12 17						12 44	12 47				
West Croydon 4	d		12 05						12 12					12 35								12 42
Norwood Junction 2	d	11 52	12 10						12 16		12 22			12 40				12 52				12 46
Anerley	d	11 55							12 19		12 25							12 55				12 49
Penge West	d	11 57							12 21		12 27							12 57				12 51
London Victoria 15 ⊖	d					12 09.	12 11								12 39.	12 41						
Battersea Park 4	d						12 15									12 45						
Wandsworth Road	d						12 17									12 47						
Clapham High Street ⊖	d						12 19									12 49						
London Blackfriars 3 ⊖	d																					
Denmark Hill 4	d					12 18	12 24								12 48	12 54						
Peckham Rye 4	d					12 21	12 26			12 39					12 51	12 56	13 09					
Queens Rd Peckham	d						12 29			12 42						12 59	13 12					
South Bermondsey	d						12 31			12 44						13 01	13 14					
Clapham Junction 10	d																					
Wandsworth Common	d																					
Balham 4 ⊖	d																					
Streatham Hill	d																					
West Norwood 4	d																					
Gipsy Hill	d																					
Crystal Palace 4	d				12 07								12 31						12 46			
Sydenham	d	11 59	12 14		12 10				12 24		12 29		12 34	12 44				12 59	12 49			12 54
Forest Hill 4	d	12 02	12 17		12 13				12 26		12 32		12 37	12 47				13 02	12 52			12 56
Honor Oak Park	d	12 04	12 19		12 15				12 29		12 34		12 39	12 49				13 04	12 54			12 59
Brockley	d	12 07	12 22		12 18				12 31		12 37		12 42	12 52				13 07	12 57			13 01
New Cross Gate Station Ell	a																					
	d																					
New Cross Gate 4	d	12 09	12 24		12 20				12 34		12 39		12 44	12 54				13 09	12 59			13 04
New Cross Ell	d			12 09				12 24				12 39									12 54	
Surrey Quays	d			12 13	12 24			12 28	12 38			12 43	12 48						13 03	12 53	12 58	13 08
Canada Water	d			12 15	12 26			12 30	12 40			12 45	12 50						13 05	12 55	13 00	13 10
Rotherhithe	d			12 16	12 27			12 31	12 41			12 46	12 51						13 06	12 56	13 01	13 11
Wapping	d			12 18	12 29			12 33	12 43			12 48	12 53						13 08	12 58	13 03	13 13
Shadwell	d			12 20	12 31			12 35	12 45			12 50	12 55						13 10	13 00	13 05	13 15
Whitechapel	d			12 22	12 33			12 37	12 47			12 52	12 57						13 12	13 02	13 07	13 17
Shoreditch High Street	d			12 24	12 35			12 39	12 49			12 54	12 59						13 14	13 04	13 09	13 19
Hoxton	d			12 26	12 37			12 41	12 51			12 56	13 02						13 17	13 06	13 11	13 21
Haggerston	d			12 28	12 39			12 43	12 53			12 58	13 04						13 19	13 08	13 13	13 23
Dalston Junction Stn Ell	a			12 32	12 42			12 48	12 58			13 02	13 06						13 21	13 13	13 17	13 28
London Bridge 4 ⊖	a	12 18	12 31				12 36			12 49	12 48			13 01		13 06	13 19	13 18				

		LO	LO	LO	LO	SN	SE	SN	LO	LO	SN	SN	LO	LO	LO	SN	SE	SN	LO	LO	LO	SN	SN
East Croydon	d										13 14	13 17										13 44	13 47
West Croydon 4	d			12 57		13 05				13 12					13 27	13 35					13 42		
Norwood Junction 2	d			13 01		13 10				13 16		13 22			13 31	13 40					13 46		13 52
Anerley	d			13 04						13 19		13 25			13 34						13 49		13 55
Penge West	d			13 06						13 21		13 27			13 36						13 51		13 57
London Victoria 15 ⊖	d						13 09	13 11									13 39	13 41					
Battersea Park 4	d							13 15										13 45					
Wandsworth Road	d							13 17										13 47					
Clapham High Street ⊖	d							13 19										13 49					
London Blackfriars 3 ⊖	d																						
Denmark Hill 4	d						13 18	13 24									13 48	13 54					
Peckham Rye 4	d						13 21	13 26			13 39						13 51	13 56				14 09	
Queens Rd Peckham	d							13 29			13 42							13 59				14 12	
South Bermondsey	d							13 31			13 44							14 01				14 14	
Clapham Junction 10	d																						
Wandsworth Common	d																						
Balham 4 ⊖	d																						
Streatham Hill	d																						
West Norwood 4	d																						
Gipsy Hill	d																						
Crystal Palace 4	d		13 01						13 16					13 31						13 46			
Sydenham	d		13 04	13 09		13 14			13 19	13 24		13 29		13 34	13 39	13 44				13 49	13 54		13 59
Forest Hill 4	d		13 07	13 11		13 17			13 22	13 26		13 32		13 37	13 41	13 47				13 52	13 56		14 02
Honor Oak Park	d		13 09	13 14		13 19			13 24	13 29		13 34		13 39	13 44	13 49				13 54	13 59		14 04
Brockley	d		13 12	13 16		13 22			13 27	13 31		13 37		13 42	13 46	13 52				13 57	14 01		14 07
New Cross Gate Station Ell	a																						
	d																						
New Cross Gate 4	d		13 14	13 19		13 24			13 29	13 34		13 39		13 44	13 49	13 54				13 59	14 04		14 09
New Cross Ell	d	13 09			13 24								13 39						13 54				
Surrey Quays	d	13 13	13 18	13 23	13 28				13 33	13 38			13 43	13 48	13 53				13 58	14 03	14 08		
Canada Water	d	13 15	13 20	13 25	13 30				13 35	13 40			13 45	13 50	13 55				14 00	14 05	14 10		
Rotherhithe	d	13 16	13 21	13 26	13 31				13 36	13 41			13 46	13 51	13 56				14 01	14 06	14 11		
Wapping	d	13 18	13 23	13 28	13 33				13 38	13 43			13 48	13 53	13 58				14 03	14 08	14 13		
Shadwell	d	13 20	13 25	13 30	13 35				13 40	13 45			13 50	13 55	14 00				14 05	14 10	14 15		
Whitechapel	d	13 22	13 27	13 32	13 37				13 42	13 47			13 52	13 57	14 02				14 07	14 12	14 17		
Shoreditch High Street	d	13 24	13 29	13 34	13 39				13 44	13 49			13 54	13 59	14 04				14 09	14 14	14 19		
Hoxton	d	13 26	13 32	13 36	13 41				13 47	13 51			13 56	14 02	14 06				14 11	14 17	14 21		
Haggerston	d	13 28	13 34	13 38	13 43				13 49	13 53			13 58	14 04	14 08				14 13	14 19	14 23		
Dalston Junction Stn Ell	a	13 32	13 36	13 43	13 47				13 51	13 58			14 02	14 06	14 13				14 17	14 21	14 28		
London Bridge 4 ⊖	a					13 31		13 36			13 49	13 48				14 01		14 06				14 19	14 18

Table 178

Sundays

East London Line and Croydon-London Victoria to London Bridge

		LO	LO	LO	SN	LO	SE	SN	SN	SN	LO	LO	LO	LO	LO	LO	SN	SE	SN	LO	SN	SN
East Croydon	d								14 14	14 17											14 44	14 47
West Croydon 4	d			13 57	14 05							14 12			14 27		14 35					
Norwood Junction 2	d			14 01	14 10					14 22		14 16			14 31		14 40					14 52
Anerley	d			14 04						14 25		14 19			14 34							14 55
Penge West	d			14 06						14 27		14 21			14 36							14 57
London Victoria 15 ⊖	d						14 09.	14 11										14 39.	14 41			
Battersea Park 4	d							14 15											14 45			
Wandsworth Road	d							14 17											14 47			
Clapham High Street ⊖	d							14 19											14 49			
London Blackfriars 3 ⊖	d																					
Denmark Hill 4	d						14 18	14 24										14 48	14 54			
Peckham Rye 4	d						14 21	14 26	14 39									14 51	14 56		15 09	
Queens Rd Peckham	d							14 29	14 42										14 59		15 12	
South Bermondsey	d							14 31	14 44										15 01		15 14	
Clapham Junction 10	d																					
Wandsworth Common	d																					
Balham 4 ⊖	d																					
Streatham Hill	d																					
West Norwood 4	d																					
Gipsy Hill	d																					
Crystal Palace 4	d		14 01								14 16			14 31						14 46		
Sydenham	d		14 04	14 09	14 14					14 29	14 19	14 24		14 34	14 39		14 44			14 49		14 59
Forest Hill 4	d		14 07	14 11	14 17					14 32	14 22	14 26		14 37	14 41		14 47			14 52		15 02
Honor Oak Park	d		14 09	14 14	14 19					14 34	14 24	14 29		14 39	14 44		14 49			14 54		15 04
Brockley	d		14 12	14 16	14 22					14 37	14 27	14 31		14 42	14 46		14 52			14 57		15 07
New Cross Gate Station Ell	a																					
	d																					
New Cross Gate 4	d		14 14	14 19	14 24					14 39	14 29	14 34		14 44	14 49		14 54			14 59		15 09
New Cross Ell	d	14 09				14 24							14 39			14 54						
Surrey Quays	d	14 13	14 18	14 23		14 28					14 33	14 38	14 43	14 48	14 53	14 58				15 03		
Canada Water	d	14 15	14 20	14 25		14 30					14 35	14 40	14 45	14 50	14 55	15 00				15 05		
Rotherhithe	d	14 16	14 21	14 26		14 31					14 36	14 41	14 46	14 51	14 56	15 01				15 06		
Wapping	d	14 18	14 23	14 28		14 33					14 38	14 43	14 48	14 53	14 58	15 03				15 08		
Shadwell	d	14 20	14 25	14 30		14 35					14 40	14 45	14 50	14 55	15 00	15 05				15 10		
Whitechapel	d	14 22	14 27	14 32		14 37					14 42	14 47	14 52	14 57	15 02	15 07				15 12		
Shoreditch High Street	d	14 24	14 29	14 34		14 39					14 44	14 49	14 54	14 59	15 04	15 09				15 14		
Hoxton	d	14 26	14 32	14 36		14 41					14 47	14 51	14 56	15 02	15 06	15 11				15 17		
Haggerston	d	14 28	14 34	14 38		14 43					14 49	14 53	14 58	15 04	15 08	15 13				15 19		
Dalston Junction Stn Ell	a	14 32	14 36	14 43		14 47					14 51	14 58	15 02	15 06	15 13	15 17				15 21		
London Bridge 4 ⊖	a				14 31			14 36	14 49	14 48							15 01		15 06		15 19	15 18

		LO	LO	LO	LO	SN	LO	LO	SE	SN	LO	SN	SN	LO	LO	LO	SN	LO	SE	SN	LO	SN	SN
East Croydon	d											15 14	15 17									15 44	15 47
West Croydon 4	d	14 42			14 57	15 05					15 12					15 27	15 35						
Norwood Junction 2	d	14 46			15 01	15 10					15 16		15 22			15 31	15 40						15 52
Anerley	d	14 49			15 04						15 19		15 25			15 34							15 55
Penge West	d	14 51			15 06						15 21		15 27			15 36							15 57
London Victoria 15 ⊖	d								15 09.	15 11									15 39.	15 41			
Battersea Park 4	d									15 15										15 45			
Wandsworth Road	d									15 17										15 47			
Clapham High Street ⊖	d									15 19										15 49			
London Blackfriars 3 ⊖	d																						
Denmark Hill 4	d								15 18	15 24									15 48	15 54			
Peckham Rye 4	d								15 21	15 26		15 39							15 51	15 56		16 09	
Queens Rd Peckham	d									15 29		15 42								15 59		16 12	
South Bermondsey	d									15 31		15 44								16 01		16 14	
Clapham Junction 10	d																						
Wandsworth Common	d																						
Balham 4 ⊖	d																						
Streatham Hill	d																						
West Norwood 4	d																						
Gipsy Hill	d																						
Crystal Palace 4	d			15 01				15 16							15 31						15 46		
Sydenham	d	14 54		15 04	15 09	15 14		15 19			15 24		15 29		15 34	15 39	15 44				15 49		15 59
Forest Hill 4	d	14 56		15 07	15 11	15 17		15 22			15 26		15 32		15 37	15 41	15 47				15 52		16 02
Honor Oak Park	d	14 59		15 09	15 14	15 19		15 24			15 29		15 34		15 39	15 44	15 49				15 54		16 04
Brockley	d	15 01		15 12	15 16	15 22		15 27			15 31		15 37		15 42	15 46	15 52				15 57		16 07
New Cross Gate Station Ell	a																						
	d																						
New Cross Gate 4	d	15 04		15 14	15 19	15 24		15 29			15 34		15 39		15 44	15 49	15 54				15 59		16 09
New Cross Ell	d		15 09				15 24							15 39				15 54					
Surrey Quays	d	15 08	15 13	15 18	15 23		15 28	15 33			15 38			15 43	15 48	15 53		15 58			16 03		
Canada Water	d	15 10	15 15	15 20	15 25		15 30	15 35			15 40			15 45	15 50	15 55		16 00			16 05		
Rotherhithe	d	15 11	15 16	15 21	15 26		15 31	15 36			15 41			15 46	15 51	15 56		16 01			16 06		
Wapping	d	15 13	15 18	15 23	15 28		15 33	15 38			15 43			15 48	15 53	15 58		16 03			16 08		
Shadwell	d	15 15	15 20	15 25	15 30		15 35	15 40			15 45			15 50	15 55	16 00		16 05			16 10		
Whitechapel	d	15 17	15 22	15 27	15 32		15 37	15 42			15 47			15 52	15 57	16 02		16 07			16 12		
Shoreditch High Street	d	15 19	15 24	15 29	15 34		15 39	15 44			15 49			15 54	15 59	16 04		16 09			16 14		
Hoxton	d	15 21	15 26	15 32	15 36		15 41	15 47			15 51			15 56	16 02	16 06		16 11			16 17		
Haggerston	d	15 23	15 28	15 34	15 38		15 43	15 49			15 53			15 58	16 04	16 08		16 13			16 19		
Dalston Junction Stn Ell	a	15 28	15 32	15 36	15 43		15 47	15 51			15 58			16 02	16 06	16 13		16 17			16 21		
London Bridge 4 ⊖	a					15 31				15 36		15 49	15 48				16 01			16 06		16 19	16 18

Table 178

Sundays

East London Line and Croydon-London Victoria to London Bridge

		LO		LO	LO	LO	SN	SE	LO		LO	SN	LO	LO	SN	SN	LO	LO	SN	LO	SE	SN	LO	SN	SN
East Croydon	d														16 14	16 17								16 44	16 47
West Croydon	d	15 42				15 57	16 05						16 12					16 27	16 35						
Norwood Junction	d	15 46				16 01	16 10						16 16			16 22		16 31	16 40						16 52
Anerley	d	15 49				16 04							16 19			16 25		16 34							16 55
Penge West	d	15 51				16 06							16 21			16 27		16 36							16 57
London Victoria	d							16 09				16 11									16 39.	16 41			
Battersea Park	d											16 15										16 45			
Wandsworth Road	d											16 17										16 47			
Clapham High Street	d											16 19										16 49			
London Blackfriars	d																								
Denmark Hill	d							16 18				16 24									16 48	16 54			
Peckham Rye	d							16 21				16 26			16 39						16 51	16 56		17 09	
Queens Rd Peckham	d											16 29			16 42							16 59		17 12	
South Bermondsey	d											16 31			16 44							17 01		17 14	
Clapham Junction	d																								
Wandsworth Common	d																								
Balham	d																								
Streatham Hill	d																								
West Norwood	d																								
Gipsy Hill	d																								
Crystal Palace	d				16 01						16 16						16 31						16 46		
Sydenham	d	15 54			16 04	16 09	16 14				16 19		16 24			16 29	16 34	16 39	16 44				16 49		16 59
Forest Hill	d	15 56			16 07	16 11	16 17				16 22		16 26			16 32	16 37	16 41	16 47				16 52		17 02
Honor Oak Park	d	15 59			16 09	16 14	16 19				16 24		16 29			16 34	16 39	16 44	16 49				16 54		17 04
Brockley	d	16 01			16 12	16 16	16 22				16 27		16 31			16 37	16 42	16 46	16 52				16 57		17 07
New Cross Gate Station Ell	a																								
	d																								
New Cross Gate	d	16 04			16 14	16 19	16 24				16 29		16 34			16 39	16 44	16 49	16 54				16 59		17 09
New Cross Ell	d			16 09					16 24					16 39						16 54					
Surrey Quays	d	16 08		16 13	16 18	16 23			16 28		16 33		16 38	16 43			16 48	16 53		16 58			17 03		
Canada Water	d	16 10		16 15	16 20	16 25			16 30		16 35		16 40	16 45			16 50	16 55		17 00			17 05		
Rotherhithe	d	16 11		16 16	16 21	16 26			16 31		16 36		16 41	16 46			16 51	16 56		17 01			17 06		
Wapping	d	16 13		16 18	16 23	16 28			16 33		16 38		16 43	16 48			16 53	16 58		17 03			17 08		
Shadwell	d	16 15		16 20	16 25	16 30			16 35		16 40		16 45	16 50			16 55	17 00		17 05			17 10		
Whitechapel	d	16 17		16 22	16 27	16 32			16 37		16 42		16 47	16 52			16 57	17 02		17 07			17 12		
Shoreditch High Street	d	16 19		16 24	16 29	16 34			16 39		16 44		16 49	16 54			16 59	17 04		17 09			17 14		
Hoxton	d	16 21		16 26	16 32	16 36			16 41		16 47		16 51	16 56			17 02	17 06		17 11			17 17		
Haggerston	d	16 23		16 28	16 34	16 38			16 43		16 49		16 53	16 58			17 04	17 08		17 13			17 19		
Dalston Junction Stn Ell	a	16 28		16 32	16 36	16 43			16 47		16 51		16 58	17 02			17 06	17 13		17 17			17 21		
London Bridge	a						16 31					16 36			16 49	16 48			17 01			17 06		17 19	17 18

		LO	LO		LO	LO		SN	SE	SN	LO	LO	LO	SN	SN		LO	LO	LO	SN	SE	LO	SN		SN
East Croydon	d													17 14	17 17										17 44
West Croydon	d	16 42				16 57		17 05					17 12						17 27	17 35					
Norwood Junction	d	16 46				17 01		17 10					17 16		17 22				17 31	17 40					
Anerley	d	16 49				17 04							17 19		17 25				17 34						
Penge West	d	16 51				17 06							17 21		17 27				17 36						
London Victoria	d								17 09.	17 11											17 39.		17 41		
Battersea Park	d									17 15													17 45		
Wandsworth Road	d									17 17													17 47		
Clapham High Street	d									17 19													17 49		
London Blackfriars	d																								
Denmark Hill	d								17 18	17 24											17 48		17 54		
Peckham Rye	d								17 21	17 26				17 39							17 51		17 56		18 09
Queens Rd Peckham	d									17 29				17 42									17 59		18 12
South Bermondsey	d									17 31				17 44									18 01		18 14
Clapham Junction	d																								
Wandsworth Common	d																								
Balham	d																								
Streatham Hill	d																								
West Norwood	d																								
Gipsy Hill	d																								
Crystal Palace	d				17 01							17 16						17 31							
Sydenham	d	16 54			17 04	17 09		17 14				17 19	17 24		17 29			17 34	17 39	17 44					
Forest Hill	d	16 56			17 07	17 11		17 17				17 22	17 26		17 32			17 37	17 41	17 47					
Honor Oak Park	d	16 59			17 09	17 14		17 19				17 24	17 29		17 34			17 39	17 44	17 49					
Brockley	d	17 01			17 12	17 16		17 22				17 27	17 31		17 37			17 42	17 46	17 52					
New Cross Gate Station Ell	a																								
	d																								
New Cross Gate	d	17 04			17 14	17 19		17 24				17 29	17 34		17 39			17 44	17 49	17 54					
New Cross Ell	d		17 09								17 24						17 39					17 54			
Surrey Quays	d	17 08	17 13		17 18	17 23					17 28	17 33	17 38				17 43	17 48	17 53			17 58			
Canada Water	d	17 10	17 15		17 20	17 25					17 30	17 35	17 40				17 45	17 50	17 55			18 00			
Rotherhithe	d	17 11	17 16		17 21	17 26					17 31	17 36	17 41				17 46	17 51	17 56			18 01			
Wapping	d	17 13	17 18		17 23	17 28					17 33	17 38	17 43				17 48	17 53	17 58			18 03			
Shadwell	d	17 15	17 20		17 25	17 30					17 35	17 40	17 45				17 50	17 55	18 00			18 05			
Whitechapel	d	17 17	17 22		17 27	17 32					17 37	17 42	17 47				17 52	17 57	18 02			18 07			
Shoreditch High Street	d	17 19	17 24		17 29	17 34					17 39	17 44	17 49				17 54	17 59	18 04			18 09			
Hoxton	d	17 21	17 26		17 32	17 36					17 41	17 47	17 51				17 56	18 02	18 06			18 11			
Haggerston	d	17 23	17 28		17 34	17 38					17 43	17 49	17 53				17 58	18 04	18 08			18 13			
Dalston Junction Stn Ell	a	17 28	17 32		17 36	17 43					17 47	17 51	17 58				18 02	18 06	18 13			18 17			
London Bridge	a							17 31		17 36				17 49	17 48					18 01			18 06		18 19

Table 178

Sundays

East London Line and Croydon-London Victoria to London Bridge

		SN	LO	LO	LO	LO	LO	SN	SE	SN		LO	LO	SN	SN	LO	LO	LO	LO	SN		SE	SN	LO	SN
East Croydon	d	17 47												18 14	18 17										18 44
West Croydon	d			17 42			17 57	18 05					18 12						18 27	18 35					
Norwood Junction	d	17 52		17 46			18 01	18 10					18 16		18 22				18 31	18 40					
Anerley	d	17 55		17 49			18 04						18 19		18 25				18 34						
Penge West	d	17 57		17 51			18 06						18 21		18 27				18 36						
London Victoria	d								18 09.	18 11												18 39.	18 41		
Battersea Park	d									18 15													18 45		
Wandsworth Road	d									18 17													18 47		
Clapham High Street	d									18 19													18 49		
London Blackfriars	d																								
Denmark Hill	d								18 18	18 24												18 48	18 54		
Peckham Rye	d								18 21	18 26				18 39								18 51	18 56		19 09
Queens Rd Peckham	d									18 29				18 42									18 59		19 12
South Bermondsey	d									18 31				18 44									19 01		19 14
Clapham Junction	d																								
Wandsworth Common	d																								
Balham	d																								
Streatham Hill	d																								
West Norwood	d																								
Gipsy Hill	d																								
Crystal Palace	d		17 46			18 01										18 16		18 31							
Sydenham	d	17 59	17 49	17 54		18 04	18 09	18 14					18 24		18 29	18 19		18 34	18 39	18 44					
Forest Hill	d	18 02	17 52	17 56		18 07	18 11	18 17					18 26		18 32	18 22		18 37	18 41	18 47					
Honor Oak Park	d	18 04	17 54	17 59		18 09	18 14	18 19					18 29		18 34	18 24		18 39	18 44	18 49					
Brockley	d	18 07	17 57	18 01		18 12	18 16	18 22					18 31		18 37	18 27		18 42	18 46	18 52					
New Cross Gate Station Ell	a																								
	d																								
New Cross Gate	d	18 09	17 59	18 04		18 14	18 19	18 24					18 34		18 39	18 29		18 44	18 49	18 54					
New Cross Ell	d				18 09							18 24					18 39							18 54	
Surrey Quays	d		18 03	18 08	18 13	18 18	18 23					18 28	18 38			18 33	18 43	18 48	18 53					18 58	
Canada Water	d		18 05	18 10	18 15	18 20	18 25					18 30	18 40			18 35	18 45	18 50	18 55					19 00	
Rotherhithe	d		18 06	18 11	18 16	18 21	18 26					18 31	18 41			18 36	18 46	18 51	18 56					19 01	
Wapping	d		18 08	18 13	18 18	18 23	18 28					18 33	18 43			18 38	18 48	18 53	18 58					19 03	
Shadwell	d		18 10	18 15	18 20	18 25	18 30					18 35	18 45			18 40	18 50	18 55	19 00					19 05	
Whitechapel	d		18 12	18 17	18 22	18 27	18 32					18 37	18 47			18 42	18 52	18 57	19 02					19 07	
Shoreditch High Street	d		18 14	18 19	18 24	18 29	18 34					18 39	18 49			18 44	18 54	18 59	19 04					19 09	
Hoxton	d		18 17	18 21	18 26	18 32	18 36					18 41	18 51			18 47	18 56	19 02	19 06					19 11	
Haggerston	d		18 19	18 23	18 28	18 34	18 38					18 43	18 53			18 49	18 58	19 04	19 08					19 13	
Dalston Junction Stn Ell	a		18 21	18 28	18 32	18 36	18 43					18 47	18 58			18 51	19 02	19 06	19 13					19 17	
London Bridge	a	18 18						18 31		18 36				18 49	18 48					19 01			19 06		19 19

		SN	LO	LO	LO		LO	LO	LO	SN	SE	SN	LO	LO	SN	SN		LO	LO	LO	SN	SE	SN		SN
East Croydon	d	18 47													19 14	19 17									19 44
West Croydon	d			18 42				18 57		19 05				19 12						19 27	19 35				
Norwood Junction	d	18 52		18 46				19 01		19 10				19 16		19 22				19 31	19 40				
Anerley	d	18 55		18 49				19 04						19 19		19 25				19 34					
Penge West	d	18 57		18 51				19 06						19 21		19 27				19 36					
London Victoria	d										19 09.	19 11										19 39.	19 41		
Battersea Park	d											19 15											19 45		
Wandsworth Road	d											19 17											19 47		
Clapham High Street	d											19 19											19 49		
London Blackfriars	d																								
Denmark Hill	d										19 18	19 24										19 48	19 54		
Peckham Rye	d										19 21	19 26			19 39							19 51	19 56		20 09
Queens Rd Peckham	d											19 29			19 42								19 59		20 12
South Bermondsey	d											19 31			19 44								20 01		20 14
Clapham Junction	d																								
Wandsworth Common	d																								
Balham	d																								
Streatham Hill	d																								
West Norwood	d																								
Gipsy Hill	d																								
Crystal Palace	d		18 46				19 01						19 16						19 31						
Sydenham	d	18 59	18 49	18 54			19 04	19 09		19 14			19 19	19 24		19 29			19 34	19 39	19 44				
Forest Hill	d	19 02	18 52	18 56			19 07	19 11		19 17			19 22	19 26		19 32			19 37	19 41	19 47				
Honor Oak Park	d	19 04	18 54	18 59			19 09	19 14		19 19			19 24	19 29		19 34			19 39	19 44	19 49				
Brockley	d	19 07	18 57	19 01			19 12	19 16		19 22			19 27	19 31		19 37			19 42	19 46	19 52				
New Cross Gate Station Ell	a																								
	d																								
New Cross Gate	d	19 09	18 59	19 04			19 14	19 19		19 24			19 29	19 34		19 39			19 44	19 49	19 54				
New Cross Ell	d				19 09				19 24									19 39							
Surrey Quays	d		19 03	19 08	19 13		19 18	19 23	19 28				19 33	19 38				19 43	19 48	19 53					
Canada Water	d		19 05	19 10	19 15		19 20	19 25	19 30				19 35	19 40				19 45	19 50	19 55					
Rotherhithe	d		19 06	19 11	19 16		19 21	19 26	19 31				19 36	19 41				19 46	19 51	19 56					
Wapping	d		19 08	19 13	19 18		19 23	19 28	19 33				19 38	19 43				19 48	19 53	19 58					
Shadwell	d		19 10	19 15	19 20		19 25	19 30	19 35				19 40	19 45				19 50	19 55	20 00					
Whitechapel	d		19 12	19 17	19 22		19 27	19 32	19 37				19 42	19 47				19 52	19 57	20 02					
Shoreditch High Street	d		19 14	19 19	19 24		19 29	19 34	19 39				19 44	19 49				19 54	19 59	20 04					
Hoxton	d		19 17	19 21	19 26		19 32	19 36	19 41				19 47	19 51				19 56	20 02	20 06					
Haggerston	d		19 19	19 23	19 28		19 34	19 38	19 43				19 49	19 53				19 58	20 04	20 08					
Dalston Junction Stn Ell	a		19 21	19 28	19 32		19 36	19 43	19 47				19 51	19 58				20 02	20 06	20 13					
London Bridge	a	19 18								19 31		19 36			19 49	19 48					20 01		20 06		20 19

Table 178

East London Line and Croydon-London Victoria to London Bridge

		SN	LO	LO	LO	LO	LO	LO	SN	SE	SN	LO	LO	LO		SN	SN	LO	LO	LO		SN	SE	LO	SN
East Croydon	d	19 47														20 14	20 17								
West Croydon	d				19 42			19 57	20 05					20 12						20 27		20 35			
Norwood Junction	d	19 52			19 46			20 01	20 10					20 16			20 22			20 31		20 40			
Anerley	d	19 55			19 49			20 04						20 19			20 25			20 34					
Penge West	d	19 57			19 51			20 06						20 21			20 27			20 36					
London Victoria ⊖	d									20 09	20 11												20 39		20 41
Battersea Park	d										20 15														20 45
Wandsworth Road	d										20 17														20 47
Clapham High Street ⊖	d										20 19														20 49
London Blackfriars ⊖	d																								
Denmark Hill	d									20 18	20 24												20 48		20 54
Peckham Rye	d									20 21	20 26					20 39							20 51		20 56
Queens Rd Peckham	d										20 29					20 42									20 59
South Bermondsey	d										20 31					20 44									21 01
Clapham Junction	d																								
Wandsworth Common	d																								
Balham ⊖	d																								
Streatham Hill	d																								
West Norwood	d																								
Gipsy Hill	d																								
Crystal Palace	d			19 46			20 01						20 16						20 31						
Sydenham	d	19 59		19 49	19 54		20 04	20 09	20 14				20 19	20 24			20 29		20 34	20 39		20 44			
Forest Hill	d	20 02		19 52	19 56		20 07	20 11	20 17				20 22	20 26			20 32		20 37	20 41		20 47			
Honor Oak Park	d	20 04		19 54	19 59		20 09	20 14	20 19				20 24	20 29			20 34		20 39	20 44		20 49			
Brockley	d	20 07		19 57	20 01		20 12	20 16	20 22				20 27	20 31			20 37		20 42	20 46		20 52			
New Cross Gate Station Ell	a																								
	d																								
New Cross Gate	d	20 09		19 59	20 04		20 14	20 19	20 24				20 29	20 34			20 39		20 44	20 49		20 54			
New Cross Ell	d		19 54			20 09						20 24						20 39						20 54	
Surrey Quays	d		19 58	20 03	20 08	20 13	20 18	20 23				20 28	20 33	20 38				20 43	20 48	20 53				20 58	
Canada Water	d		20 00	20 05	20 10	20 15	20 20	20 25				20 30	20 35	20 40				20 45	20 50	20 55				21 00	
Rotherhithe	d		20 01	20 06	20 11	20 16	20 21	20 26				20 31	20 36	20 41				20 46	20 51	20 56				21 01	
Wapping	d		20 03	20 08	20 13	20 18	20 23	20 28				20 33	20 38	20 43				20 48	20 53	20 58				21 03	
Shadwell	d		20 05	20 10	20 15	20 20	20 25	20 30				20 35	20 40	20 45				20 50	20 55	21 00				21 05	
Whitechapel	d		20 07	20 12	20 17	20 22	20 27	20 32				20 37	20 42	20 47				20 52	20 57	21 02				21 07	
Shoreditch High Street	d		20 09	20 14	20 19	20 24	20 29	20 34				20 39	20 44	20 49				20 54	20 59	21 04				21 09	
Hoxton	d		20 11	20 17	20 21	20 26	20 32	20 36				20 41	20 47	20 51				20 56	21 02	21 06				21 11	
Haggerston	d		20 13	20 19	20 23	20 28	20 34	20 38				20 43	20 49	20 53				20 58	21 04	21 08				21 13	
Dalston Junction Stn Ell	a		20 17	20 21	20 28	20 32	20 36	20 43				20 47	20 51	20 58				21 02	21 06	21 13				21 17	
London Bridge ⊖	a	20 18							20 31		20 36					20 49	20 48					21 01			21 06

		SN	SN	LO	LO	LO	LO	LO	SN		SE	SN	LO	LO	LO	SN	SN	LO	LO	LO		SN	SE	SN	LO
East Croydon	d	20 44	20 47													21 14	21 17								
West Croydon	d				20 42			20 57	21 05						21 12					21 27		21 35			
Norwood Junction	d		20 52		20 46			21 01	21 10						21 16		21 22			21 31		21 40			
Anerley	d		20 55		20 49			21 04							21 19		21 25			21 34					
Penge West	d		20 57		20 51			21 06							21 21		21 27			21 36					
London Victoria ⊖	d										21 09	21 11											21 39	21 41	
Battersea Park	d											21 15												21 45	
Wandsworth Road	d											21 17												21 47	
Clapham High Street ⊖	d											21 19												21 49	
London Blackfriars ⊖	d																								
Denmark Hill	d										21 18	21 24											21 48	21 54	
Peckham Rye	d	21 09									21 21	21 26				21 39							21 51	21 56	
Queens Rd Peckham	d	21 12										21 29				21 42								21 59	
South Bermondsey	d	21 14										21 31				21 44								22 01	
Clapham Junction	d																								
Wandsworth Common	d																								
Balham ⊖	d																								
Streatham Hill	d																								
West Norwood	d																								
Gipsy Hill	d																								
Crystal Palace	d			20 46			21 01							21 16					21 31						21 46
Sydenham	d		20 59	20 49	20 54		21 04	21 09	21 14					21 19	21 24		21 29		21 34	21 39		21 44			21 49
Forest Hill	d		21 02	20 52	20 56		21 07	21 11	21 17					21 22	21 26		21 32		21 37	21 41		21 47			21 52
Honor Oak Park	d		21 04	20 54	20 59		21 09	21 14	21 19					21 24	21 29		21 34		21 39	21 44		21 49			21 54
Brockley	d		21 07	20 57	21 01		21 12	21 16	21 22					21 27	21 31		21 37		21 42	21 46		21 52			21 57
New Cross Gate Station Ell	a																								
	d																								
New Cross Gate	d		21 09	20 59	21 04		21 14	21 19	21 24					21 29	21 34		21 39		21 44	21 49		21 54			21 59
New Cross Ell	d					21 09							21 24					21 39							
Surrey Quays	d			21 03	21 08	21 13	21 18	21 23					21 28	21 33	21 38			21 43	21 48	21 53					22 03
Canada Water	d			21 05	21 10	21 15	21 20	21 25					21 30	21 35	21 40			21 45	21 50	21 55					22 05
Rotherhithe	d			21 06	21 11	21 16	21 21	21 26					21 31	21 36	21 41			21 46	21 51	21 56					22 06
Wapping	d			21 08	21 13	21 18	21 23	21 28					21 33	21 38	21 43			21 48	21 53	21 58					22 08
Shadwell	d			21 10	21 15	21 20	21 25	21 30					21 35	21 40	21 45			21 50	21 55	22 00					22 10
Whitechapel	d			21 12	21 17	21 22	21 27	21 32					21 37	21 42	21 47			21 52	21 57	22 02					22 12
Shoreditch High Street	d			21 14	21 19	21 24	21 29	21 34					21 39	21 44	21 49			21 54	21 59	22 04					22 14
Hoxton	d			21 17	21 21	21 26	21 32	21 36					21 41	21 47	21 51			21 56	22 02	22 06					22 17
Haggerston	d			21 19	21 23	21 28	21 34	21 38					21 43	21 49	21 53			21 58	22 04	22 08					22 19
Dalston Junction Stn Ell	a			21 21	21 28	21 32	21 36	21 43					21 47	21 51	21 58			22 02	22 06	22 13					22 21
London Bridge ⊖	a	21 19	21 18						21 31			21 36				21 49	21 48					22 02		22 06	

Table 178

Sundays

East London Line and Croydon-London Victoria to London Bridge

		SN	SN		LO	LO	LO	LO	LO	SN	SE	SN	LO	LO	SN		SN	LO	LO	SN	SE	SN	LO	SN	LO
East Croydon	d	21 44	21 47												22 14		22 17							22 44	
West Croydon	d					21 42			21 57	22 05				22 12					22 27	22 35					22 42
Norwood Junction	d		21 52			21 46			22 01	22 10				22 16			22 22		22 31	22 40					22 46
Anerley	d		21 55			21 49			22 04					22 19			22 25		22 34						22 49
Penge West	d		21 57			21 51			22 06					22 21			22 27		22 36						22 51
London Victoria ⊖	d										22 09	22 11									22 39	22 41			
Battersea Park	d											22 15										22 45			
Wandsworth Road	d											22 17										22 47			
Clapham High Street ⊖	d											22 19										22 49			
London Blackfriars ⊖	d																								
Denmark Hill	d										22 18	22 24									22 48	22 54			
Peckham Rye	d	22 09									22 21	22 26			22 39						22 51	22 56		23 09	
Queens Rd Peckham	d	22 12										22 29			22 42							22 59		23 12	
South Bermondsey	d	22 14										22 31			22 44							23 01		23 14	
Clapham Junction	d																								
Wandsworth Common	d																								
Balham ⊖	d																								
Streatham Hill	d																								
West Norwood	d																								
Gipsy Hill	d																								
Crystal Palace	d							22 01					22 16										22 46		
Sydenham	d		21 59			21 54		22 04	22 09	22 14			22 19	22 24			22 29		22 39	22 44			22 49		22 54
Forest Hill	d		22 02			21 56		22 07	22 11	22 17			22 22	22 26			22 32		22 41	22 47			22 52		22 56
Honor Oak Park	d		22 04			21 59		22 09	22 14	22 19			22 24	22 29			22 34		22 44	22 49			22 54		22 59
Brockley	d		22 07			22 01		22 12	22 16	22 22			22 27	22 31			22 37		22 46	22 52			22 57		23 01
New Cross Gate Station Ell	a																								
	d																								
New Cross Gate	d		22 09			22 04		22 14	22 19	22 24			22 29	22 34			22 39		22 49	22 54			22 59		23 04
New Cross Ell	d				21 54		22 09											22 39							
Surrey Quays	d				21 58	22 08	22 13	22 18	22 23				22 33	22 38				22 43	22 53				23 03		23 08
Canada Water	d				22 00	22 10	22 15	22 20	22 25				22 35	22 40				22 45	22 55				23 05		23 10
Rotherhithe	d				22 01	22 11	22 16	22 21	22 26				22 36	22 41				22 46	22 56				23 06		23 11
Wapping	d				22 03	22 13	22 18	22 23	22 28				22 38	22 43				22 48	22 58				23 08		23 13
Shadwell	d				22 05	22 15	22 20	22 25	22 30				22 40	22 45				22 50	23 00				23 10		23 15
Whitechapel	d				22 07	22 17	22 22	22 27	22 32				22 42	22 47				22 52	23 02				23 12		23 17
Shoreditch High Street	d				22 09	22 19	22 24	22 29	22 34				22 44	22 49				22 54	23 04				23 14		23 19
Hoxton	d				22 11	22 21	22 26	22 31	22 36				22 47	22 51				22 56	23 06				23 17		23 21
Haggerston	d				22 13	22 23	22 28	22 33	22 38				22 49	22 53				22 58	23 08				23 19		23 23
Dalston Junction Stn Ell	a				22 17	22 28	22 32	22 38	22 43				22 51	22 58				23 02	23 13				23 21		23 28
London Bridge ⊖	a	22 19	22 18							22 32		22 36			22 49		22 48			23 02		23 06		23 20	

		SN		LO	LO	SE	SN	LO
East Croydon	d	22 47						
West Croydon	d				22 57			
Norwood Junction	d	22 52			23 01			
Anerley	d	22 55			23 04			
Penge West	d	22 57			23 06			
London Victoria ⊖	d					23 09	23 11	
Battersea Park	d						23 15	
Wandsworth Road	d						23 17	
Clapham High Street ⊖	d						23 19	
London Blackfriars ⊖	d							
Denmark Hill	d					23 18	23 24	
Peckham Rye	d					23 21	23 26	
Queens Rd Peckham	d						23 29	
South Bermondsey	d						23 31	
Clapham Junction	d							
Wandsworth Common	d							
Balham ⊖	d							
Streatham Hill	d							
West Norwood	d							
Gipsy Hill	d							
Crystal Palace	d							23 16
Sydenham	d	22 59			23 09			23 19
Forest Hill	d	23 02			23 11			23 22
Honor Oak Park	d	23 04			23 14			23 24
Brockley	d	23 07			23 16			23 27
New Cross Gate Station Ell	a							
	d							
New Cross Gate	d	23 09			23 19			23 29
New Cross Ell	d			23 09				
Surrey Quays	d			23 13	23 23			23 33
Canada Water	d			23 15	23 25			23 35
Rotherhithe	d			23 16	23 26			23 36
Wapping	d			23 18	23 28			23 38
Shadwell	d			23 20	23 30			23 40
Whitechapel	d			23 22	23 32			23 42
Shoreditch High Street	d			23 24	23 34			23 44
Hoxton	d			23 26	23 36			23 47
Haggerston	d			23 28	23 38			23 49
Dalston Junction Stn Ell	a			23 32	23 43			23 51
London Bridge ⊖	a	23 18					23 36	

Luton and London - Wimbledon and Sutton via Streatham

		FC MX	FC MX	SN	SN	FC	FC	SN	FC	SN	FC	FC	FC	SN	FC	FC	SN	FC	SN	FC	FC	FC	FC
												1	1							1 A	1		
Luton 10	d					05 08			05 48		06 06	06 34	06 40		06 50	07 10		07 30			07 56	08 02	
Luton Airport Parkway 7	d					05 10			05 50		06 08		06 42		06 52	07 12		07 32			07 58	08 04	
St Pancras International 15	d					05 54	06 12		06 34		06 52	07 06	07 16		07 32	07 52		08 12		08 24	08 32	08 44	08 56
Farringdon 3	d					05 58	06 17		06 39		06 57	07 11	07 21		07 37	07 57		08 17		08 29	08 37	08 49	09 01
City Thameslink 3	d					06 01	06 21		06 43		07 01	07 15	07 25		07 41	08 01		08 21		08 33	08 41	08 53	09 05
London Blackfriars 3	d					06 06	06 24		06 46		07 04	07 18	07 28		07 44	08 04		08 24		08 36	08 44	08 56	09 08
Elephant & Castle	d					06 09	06 27		06 49		07 07	07 21	07 33		07 47	08 07		08 27			08 47	09 00	09 12
Loughborough Jn	d					06 13	06 31		06 53		07 11	07 25	07 37		07 51	08 11		08 31			08 51	09 04	09 16
Herne Hill 4	d					06 16	06 34		06 57		07 16	07 31	07 41		07 56	08 15		08 36		08 46	08 57	09 11	09 25
London Bridge 4	d	23p28	23p58		06 00			06 30		06 58				07 29			08 06		08 24				
South Bermondsey	d				06 04			06 34		07 02				07 33			08 11		08 28				
Queens Rd Peckham	d				06 06			06 36		07 04				07 35			08 13		08 30				
Peckham Rye 4	d				06 09			06 39		07 07				07 38			08 16		08 33				
East Dulwich	d				06 12			06 42		07 10				07 41			08 19		08 36				
North Dulwich	d				06 14			06 44		07 12				07 43			08 21		08 38				
Tulse Hill 3	d	23p40	00 10		06 18	06 22	06 42	06 48	07 02	07 16	07 20	07 37	07 45	07 47	08 05	08 20	08 25	08 40	08 47	08 50	09 01	09 16	09 31
Streatham 4	d	23p44	00 14		06 21	06 25	06 46	06 51	07 05	07 19	07 23	07 40	07 48	07 51	08 09	08 24	08 28	08 44	08 50	08 54	09 05	09 20	09 35
Mitcham Eastfields	d					06 29	06 50				07 27		07 52			08 28				08 58		09 24	
Mitcham Junction	d					06 32	06 53				07 30		07 55			08 31				09 01		09 27	
Hackbridge	d					06 35	06 56				07 33		07 58			08 34				09 04		09 30	
Carshalton	d					06 38	06 59				07 36		08 01			08 37				09 07		09 33	
Tooting	d	23p48	00 18		06 25			06 55	07 10	07 23		07 44		07 55	08 12		08 33	08 48			09 10		09 40
Haydons Road	d	23p51	00 21		06 28			06 58	07 13	07 26		07 47		07 58	08 15		08 36	08 51			09 13		09 43
Wimbledon 6	a	23p54	00 24		06 31			07 01	07 16	07 30		07 50		08 01	08 18		08 38	08 54			09 16		09 46
	d	23p55	00 25	05 56	06 32			07 02	07 17	07 31		07 51		08 02	08 19		08 39	08 55			09 17		09 47
Wimbledon Chase	d	23p58	00 28	05 59	06 35			07 10	07 20	07 34		07 54		08 05	08 22		08 42	08 58			09 20		09 50
South Merton	d	00 01	00 30	06 01	06 37			07 12	07 22	07 36		07 56		08 07	08 24		08 44	09 00			09 22		09 52
Morden South	d	00 03	00 32	06 03	06 39			07 14	07 24	07 38		07 58		08 09	08 26		08 46	09 02			09 24		09 54
St Helier	d	00 05	00 34	06 05	06 41			07 16	07 26	07 40		08 00		08 11	08 28		08 48	09 04			09 26		09 56
Sutton Common	d	00 07	00 36	06 07	06 43			07 18	07 28	07 42		08 02		08 13	08 30		08 50	09 06			09 28		09 58
West Sutton	d	00 10	00 39	06 10	06 46			07 21	07 31	07 45		08 05		08 16	08 33		08 53	09 09			09 31		10 01
Sutton (Surrey) 4	a	00 13	00 43	06 13	06 49	06 43	07 04	07 25	07 35	07 48	07 39	08 08	08 04	08 19	08 37	08 40	08 56	09 12	09 02	09 10	09 37	09 36	10 05

		FC	FC	FC	FC	FC	FC	FC	FC	FC	FC	FC	FC	FC	FC	FC	FC	FC	FC	FC	FC	FC	FC
Luton 10	d		08 54		09 14		09 44		10 14		10 44		11 14		11 44		12 14		12 44		13 14		13 44
Luton Airport Parkway 7	d		08 56		09 16		09 46		10 16		10 46		11 16		11 46		12 16		12 46		13 16		13 46
St Pancras International 15	d	09 16	09 34	09 48	10 04	10 18	10 34	10 48	11 04	11 18	11 34	11 48	12 04	12 18	12 34	12 48	13 04	13 18	13 34	13 48	14 04	14 18	14 34
Farringdon 3	d	09 21	09 39	09 53	10 09	10 23	10 39	10 53	11 09	11 23	11 39	11 53	12 09	12 23	12 39	12 53	13 09	13 23	13 39	13 53	14 09	14 23	14 39
City Thameslink 3	d	09 25	09 43	09 57	10 13	10 27	10 43	10 57	11 13	11 27	11 43	11 57	12 13	12 27	12 43	12 57	13 13	13 27	13 43	13 57	14 13	14 27	14 43
London Blackfriars 3	d	09 28	09 46	10 00	10 16	10 30	10 46	11 00	11 16	11 30	11 46	12 00	12 16	12 30	12 46	13 00	13 16	13 30	13 46	14 00	14 16	14 30	14 46
Elephant & Castle	d	09 31	09 49	10 03	10 19	10 33	10 49	11 03	11 19	11 33	11 49	12 03	12 19	12 33	12 49	13 03	13 19	13 33	13 49	14 03	14 19	14 33	14 49
Loughborough Jn	d	09 35	09 53	10 07	10 23	10 37	10 53	11 07	11 23	11 37	11 53	12 07	12 23	12 37	12 53	13 07	13 23	13 37	13 53	14 07	14 23	14 37	14 53
Herne Hill 4	d	09 41	09 57	10 11	10 27	10 41	10 57	11 11	11 27	11 41	11 57	12 11	12 27	12 41	12 57	13 11	13 27	13 41	13 57	14 11	14 27	14 41	14 57
London Bridge 4	d																						
South Bermondsey	d																						
Queens Rd Peckham	d																						
Peckham Rye 4	d																						
East Dulwich	d																						
North Dulwich	d																						
Tulse Hill 3	d	09 46	10 01	10 16	10 31	10 46	11 01	11 16	11 31	11 46	12 01	12 16	12 31	12 46	13 01	13 16	13 31	13 46	14 01	14 16	14 31	14 46	15 01
Streatham 4	d	09 50	10 05	10 20	10 35	10 50	11 05	11 20	11 35	11 50	12 05	12 20	12 35	12 50	13 05	13 20	13 35	13 50	14 05	14 20	14 35	14 50	15 05
Mitcham Eastfields	d	09 54		10 24		10 54		11 24		11 54		12 24		12 54		13 24		13 54		14 24		14 54	
Mitcham Junction	d	09 57		10 27		10 57		11 27		11 57		12 27		12 57		13 27		13 57		14 27		14 57	
Hackbridge	d	10 00		10 30		11 00		11 30		12 00		12 30		13 00		13 30		14 00		14 30		15 00	
Carshalton	d	10 03		10 33		11 03		11 33		12 03		12 33		13 03		13 33		14 03		14 33		15 03	
Tooting	d		10 10		10 40		11 10		11 40		12 10		12 40		13 10		13 40		14 10		14 40		15 10
Haydons Road	d		10 13		10 43		11 13		11 43		12 13		12 43		13 13		13 43		14 13		14 43		15 13
Wimbledon 6	a		10 16		10 46		11 16		11 46		12 16		12 46		13 16		13 46		14 16		14 46		15 16
	d		10 17		10 47		11 17		11 47		12 17		12 47		13 17		13 47		14 17		14 47		15 17
Wimbledon Chase	d		10 20		10 50		11 20		11 50		12 20		12 50		13 20		13 50		14 20		14 50		15 20
South Merton	d		10 22		10 52		11 22		11 52		12 22		12 52		13 22		13 52		14 22		14 52		15 22
Morden South	d		10 24		10 54		11 24		11 54		12 24		12 54		13 24		13 54		14 24		14 54		15 24
St Helier	d		10 26		10 56		11 26		11 56		12 26		12 56		13 26		13 56		14 26		14 56		15 26
Sutton Common	d		10 28		10 58		11 28		11 58		12 28		12 58		13 28		13 58		14 28		14 58		15 28
West Sutton	d		10 31		11 01		11 31		12 01		12 31		13 01		13 31		14 01		14 31		15 01		15 31
Sutton (Surrey) 4	a	10 06	10 35	10 36	11 05	11 06	11 35	11 36	12 05	12 06	12 35	12 36	13 05	13 06	13 35	13 36	14 05	14 06	14 35	14 36	15 05	15 06	15 35

A 1 from London Blackfriars

Luton and London - Wimbledon and Sutton via Streatham

		FC	FC	FC	FC	FC	FC	FC	FC	FC	SN	FC	FC	SN	FC	FC	SN	FC
Luton 10	d		14 14		14 44		15 14		15 44			16 16			16 46			17 18
Luton Airport Parkway 7	d		14 16		14 46		15 16		15 46			16 18			16 48			17 20
St Pancras International 15	d	14 48	15 04	15 18	15 34	15 48	16 04	16 18	16 34	16 52		17 02	17 18		17 32	17 52		18 04
Farringdon 3	d	14 53	15 09	15 23	15 39	15 53	16 09	16 23	16 39	16 57		17 07	17 23		17 37	17 57		18 09
City Thameslink 3	d	14 57	15 13	15 27	15 43	15 57	16 13	16 27	16 43	17 01		17 11	17 27		17 41	18 01		18 13
London Blackfriars 3	d	15 00	15 16	15 30	15 46	16 00	16 16	16 30	16 46	17 04		17 14	17 30		17 44	18 04		18 16
Elephant & Castle	d	15 03	15 19	15 33	15 49	16 03	16 19	16 33	16 49	17 08		17 18	17 34		17 48	18 08		18 20
Loughborough Jn	d	15 07	15 23	15 37	15 53	16 07	16 23	16 37	16 53	17 12		17 22	17 38		17 52	18 12		18 24
Herne Hill 4	d	15 11	15 27	15 41	15 57	16 11	16 27	16 41	16 57	17 16		17 26	17 44		17 57	18 18		18 28
London Bridge 4	d										17 06			17 37			18 08	
South Bermondsey	d										17 10			17 41			18 12	
Queens Rd Peckham	d										17 12			17 43			18 14	
Peckham Rye 4	d										17 15			17 46			18 17	
East Dulwich	d										17 18			17 49			18 20	
North Dulwich	d										17 20			17 51			18 22	
Tulse Hill 3	d	15 16	15 31	15 46	16 01	16 16	16 32	16 46	17 02	17 20	17 24	17 31	17 48	17 55	18 02	18 22	18 27	18 32
Streatham 4	d	15 20	15 35	15 50	16 05	16 20	16 36	16 50	17 06	17 24	17 28	17 36	17 52	17 58	18 06	18 26	18 30	18 36
Mitcham Eastfields	d	15 24		15 54		16 24		16 56		17 28	17 32		17 56	18 02		18 30	18 34	
Mitcham Junction	d	15 27		15 57		16 27		16 59		17 31	17 35		17 59	18 05		18 33	18 37	
Hackbridge	d	15 30		16 00		16 30		17 02		17 34	17 38		18 02	18 09		18 36	18 41	
Carshalton	d	15 33		16 03		16 33		17 05		17 37	17 41		18 05	18 11		18 39	18 43	
Tooting	d		15 40		16 10		16 40		17 10			17 40			18 10			18 40
Haydons Road	d		15 43		16 13		16 43		17 13			17 43			18 13			18 43
Wimbledon 6	a		15 46		16 16		16 46		17 16			17 46			18 16			18 46
	d		15 47		16 17		16 47		17 19			17 47			18 19			18 47
Wimbledon Chase	d		15 50		16 20		16 50		17 22			17 50			18 22			18 50
South Merton	d		15 52		16 22		16 52		17 24			17 52			18 24			18 52
Morden South	d		15 54		16 24		16 54		17 26			17 54			18 26			18 54
St Helier	d		15 56		16 26		16 56		17 28			17 56			18 28			18 56
Sutton Common	d		15 58		16 28		16 58		17 30			17 58			18 30			18 58
West Sutton	d		16 01		16 31		17 01		17 33			18 01			18 33			19 01
Sutton (Surrey) 4	a	15 36	16 05	16 06	16 35	16 36	17 05	17 08	17 39	17 40	17 44	18 05	18 08	18 15	18 37	18 42	18 47	19 07

		FC	SN	FC	FC	FC	FC	FC	FC	FC	FC	FC	FC	FC	FC	FC	FC	FC
Luton 10	d	17 38			18 08	18 22		18 54		19 24		19 50	20 20	20 50	21 20			
Luton Airport Parkway 7	d	17 40			18 10	18 25		18 57		19 27		19 52	20 22	20 52	21 22			
St Pancras International 15	d	18 24		18 38	18 48	19 04	19 18	19 34	19 48	20 04	20 18	20 36	21 06	21 36	22 06			
Farringdon 3	d	18 29		18 43	18 53	19 09	19 23	19 39	19 53	20 09	20 23	20 40	21 10	21 40	22 10			
City Thameslink 3	d	18 33		18 47	18 57	19 13	19 27	19 43	19 57	20 13	20 27	20 43	21 13	21 43	22 13			
London Blackfriars 3	d	18 36		18 50	19 00	19 16	19 30	19 46	20 00	20 16	20 30	20 46	21 16	21 46	22 16			
Elephant & Castle	d	18 40		18 54	19 04	19 19	19 33	19 49	20 03	20 19	20 33	20 49	21 19	21 49	22 19			
Loughborough Jn	d	18 44		18 58	19 08	19 23	19 37	19 53	20 07	20 23	20 37	20 53	21 23	21 53	22 23			
Herne Hill 4	d	18 48		19 02	19 12	19 27	19 41	19 57	20 11	20 27	20 41	20 57	21 27	21 57	22 27			
London Bridge 4	d		18 38													23 02	23 28	23 58
South Bermondsey	d		18 42															
Queens Rd Peckham	d		18 44															
Peckham Rye 4	d		18 47															
East Dulwich	d		18 50															
North Dulwich	d		18 52															
Tulse Hill 3	d	18 52	18 56	19 07	19 16	19 31	19 46	20 01	20 16	20 31	20 46	21 01	21 31	22 01	22 31	23 12	23 40	00 10
Streatham 4	d	18 56	18 59	19 11	19 20	19 35	19 50	20 05	20 20	20 35	20 50	21 05	21 35	22 05	22 35	23 16	23 44	00 14
Mitcham Eastfields	d	19 00	19 03		19 24		19 54		20 24		20 54							
Mitcham Junction	d	19 03	19 06		19 27		19 57		20 27		20 57							
Hackbridge	d	19 06	19 10		19 30		20 00		20 30		21 00							
Carshalton	d	19 09	19 12		19 33		20 03		20 33		21 03							
Tooting	d			19 16		19 40		20 10		20 40		21 10	21 40	22 10	22 40	23 20	23 48	00 18
Haydons Road	d			19 19		19 43		20 13		20 43		21 13	21 43	22 13	22 43	23 23	23 51	00 21
Wimbledon 6	a			19 22		19 46		20 16		20 46		21 16	21 46	22 16	22 46	23 26	23 54	00 24
	d			19 23		19 49		20 19		20 47		21 19	21 47	22 19	22 47	23 27	23 55	00 25
Wimbledon Chase	d			19 26		19 52		20 22		20 50		21 22	21 50	22 22	22 50	23 30	23 58	00 28
South Merton	d			19 28		19 54		20 24		20 52		21 24	21 52	22 24	22 52	23 32	00 01	00 30
Morden South	d			19 30		19 56		20 26		20 54		21 26	21 54	22 26	22 54	23 34	00 03	00 32
St Helier	d			19 32		19 58		20 28		20 56		21 28	21 56	22 28	22 56	23 36	00 05	00 34
Sutton Common	d			19 34		20 00		20 30		20 58		21 30	21 58	22 30	22 58	23 38	00 07	00 36
West Sutton	d			19 37		20 03		20 33		21 01		21 33	22 01	22 33	23 01	23 41	00 10	00 39
Sutton (Surrey) 4	a	19 12	19 16	19 40	19 36	20 07	20 06	20 37	20 36	21 05	21 06	21 39	22 05	22 39	23 05	23 45	00 13	00 43

Table 179

Luton and London - Wimbledon and Sutton via Streatham

Station		FC	FC	FC ▬	FC	FC	FC ▬	FC	FC	FC ▬		FC	FC	FC ▬	FC	FC	FC ▬	FC	FC	FC ▬		FC	FC	FC ▬	FC
Luton	d																								
Luton Airport Parkway	d																								
St Pancras International ⊖	d																								
Farringdon ⊖	d																								
City Thameslink	d																								
London Blackfriars ⊖	d			06 00			06 16			06 46				07 16			07 46			08 16				08 46	
Elephant & Castle ⊖	d			06 08			06 24			06 54				07 24			07 54			08 24				08 54	
Loughborough Jn	d						06 36			07 06				07 36			08 06			08 36				09 06	
Herne Hill	d			06 16		06 42	06 44		07 12	07 14			07 42	07 44		08 12	08 14		08 42	08 44			09 12	09 14	
London Bridge ⊖	d	23p28	23p58		06 21			06 45				07 15			07 45			08 15				08 45			09 15
South Bermondsey	d																								
Queens Rd Peckham	d																								
Peckham Rye	d																								
East Dulwich	d																								
North Dulwich	d																								
Tulse Hill	d	23p40	00 10	06a24	06 31	06 46	06a52	07 01	07 16	07a22		07 31	07 46	07a52	08 01	08 16	08a22	08 31	08 46	08a52		09 01	09 16	09a22	09 31
Streatham	d	23p44	00 14		06 35	06 50		07 05	07 20			07 35	07 50		08 05	08 20		08 35	08 50			09 05	09 20		09 35
Mitcham Eastfields	d					06 54			07 24				07 54			08 24			08 54				09 24		
Mitcham Junction	d					06 57			07 27				07 57			08 27			08 57				09 27		
Hackbridge	d					07 00			07 30				08 00			08 30			09 00				09 30		
Carshalton	d					07 03			07 33				08 03			08 33			09 03				09 33		
Tooting	d	23p48	00 18		06 40			07 10				07 40			08 10			08 40				09 10			09 40
Haydons Road	d	23p51	00 21		06 43			07 13				07 43			08 13			08 43				09 13			09 43
Wimbledon ⊖	a	23p54	00 24		06 46			07 16				07 46			08 16			08 46				09 16			09 46
	d	23p55	00 25		06 47			07 17				07 47			08 17			08 47				09 17			09 47
Wimbledon Chase	d	23p58	00 28		06 50			07 20				07 50			08 20			08 50				09 20			09 50
South Merton	d	00 01	00 30		06 52			07 22				07 52			08 22			08 52				09 22			09 52
Morden South	d	00 03	00 32		06 54			07 24				07 54			08 24			08 54				09 24			09 54
St Helier	d	00 05	00 34		06 56			07 26				07 56			08 26			08 56				09 26			09 56
Sutton Common	d	00 07	00 36		06 58			07 28				07 58			08 28			08 58				09 28			09 58
West Sutton	d	00 10	00 39		07 01			07 31				08 01			08 31			09 01				09 31			10 01
Sutton (Surrey)	a	00 13	00 43		07 05	07 06		07 35	07 36			08 05	08 06		08 35	08 36		09 05	09 06			09 35	09 36		10 05

Station		FC	FC ▬	FC	FC	FC ▬		FC	FC	FC ▬	FC	FC	FC ▬	FC	FC	FC ▬		FC	FC	FC ▬	FC	FC	FC ▬	FC	FC
Luton	d																								
Luton Airport Parkway	d																								
St Pancras International ⊖	d																								
Farringdon ⊖	d																								
City Thameslink	d																								
London Blackfriars ⊖	d		09 16			09 46				10 16			10 46			11 16				11 46			12 16		
Elephant & Castle ⊖	d		09 24			09 54				10 24			10 54			11 24				11 54			12 24		
Loughborough Jn	d		09 36			10 06				10 36			11 06			11 36				12 06			12 36		
Herne Hill	d	09 42	09 44		10 12	10 14			10 42	10 44		11 12	11 14		11 42	11 44			12 12	12 14		12 42	12 44		13 12
London Bridge ⊖	d			09 45				10 15			10 45			11 15				11 45			12 15			12 45	
South Bermondsey	d																								
Queens Rd Peckham	d																								
Peckham Rye	d																								
East Dulwich	d																								
North Dulwich	d																								
Tulse Hill	d	09 46	09a52	10 01	10 16	10a22		10 31	10 46	10a52	11 01	11 16	11a22	11 31	11 46	11a52		12 01	12 16	12a22	12 31	12 46	12a52	13 01	13 16
Streatham	d	09 50		10 05	10 20			10 35	10 50		11 05	11 20		11 35	11 50			12 05	12 20		12 35	12 50		13 05	13 20
Mitcham Eastfields	d	09 54			10 24				10 54			11 24			11 54				12 24			12 54			13 24
Mitcham Junction	d	09 57			10 27				10 57			11 27			11 57				12 27			12 57			13 27
Hackbridge	d	10 00			10 30				11 00			11 30			12 00				12 30			13 00			13 30
Carshalton	d	10 03			10 33				11 03			11 33			12 03				12 33			13 03			13 33
Tooting	d			10 10				10 40			11 10			11 40				12 10			12 40			13 10	
Haydons Road	d			10 13				10 43			11 13			11 43				12 13			12 43			13 13	
Wimbledon ⊖	a			10 16				10 46			11 16			11 46				12 16			12 46			13 16	
	d			10 17				10 47			11 17			11 47				12 17			12 47			13 17	
Wimbledon Chase	d			10 20				10 50			11 20			11 50				12 20			12 50			13 20	
South Merton	d			10 22				10 52			11 22			11 52				12 22			12 52			13 22	
Morden South	d			10 24				10 54			11 24			11 54				12 24			12 54			13 24	
St Helier	d			10 26				10 56			11 26			11 56				12 26			12 56			13 26	
Sutton Common	d			10 28				10 58			11 28			11 58				12 28			12 58			13 28	
West Sutton	d			10 31				11 01			11 31			12 01				12 31			13 01			13 31	
Sutton (Surrey)	a	10 06		10 35	10 36			11 05	11 06		11 35	11 36		12 05	12 06			12 35	12 36		13 05	13 06		13 35	13 36

Table 179

Saturdays

Luton and London - Wimbledon and Sutton via Streatham

Station		FC ▬		FC	FC	FC ▬	FC	FC	FC ▬	FC	FC	FC ▬		FC	FC	FC ▬	FC	FC	FC ▬	FC	FC	FC ▬		FC	FC
Luton	d																								
Luton Airport Parkway	d																								
St Pancras International ⊖	d																								
Farringdon ⊖	d																								
City Thameslink	d																								
London Blackfriars ⊖	d	12 46				13 16			13 46			14 16				14 46			15 16			15 46			
Elephant & Castle ⊖	d	12 54				13 24			13 54			14 24				14 54			15 24			15 54			
Loughborough Jn	d	13 06				13 36			14 06			14 36				15 06			15 36			16 06			
Herne Hill	d	13 14			13 42	13 44		14 12	14 14		14 42	14 44			15 12	15 14		15 42	15 44		16 12	16 14			16 42
London Bridge ⊖	d			13 15			13 45			14 15				14 45			15 15			15 45				16 15	
South Bermondsey	d																								
Queens Rd Peckham	d																								
Peckham Rye	d																								
East Dulwich	d																								
North Dulwich	d																								
Tulse Hill	d	13a22		13 31	13 46	13a52	14 01	14 16	14a22	14 31	14 46	14a52		15 01	15 16	15a22	15 31	15 46	15a52	16 01	16 16	16a22		16 31	16 46
Streatham	d			13 35	13 50		14 05	14 20		14 35	14 50			15 05	15 20		15 35	15 50		16 05	16 20			16 35	16 50
Mitcham Eastfields	d				13 54			14 24			14 54				15 24			15 54			16 24				16 54
Mitcham Junction	d				13 57			14 27			14 57				15 27			15 57			16 27				16 57
Hackbridge	d				14 00			14 30			15 00				15 30			16 00			16 30				17 00
Carshalton	d				14 03			14 33			15 03				15 33			16 03			16 33				17 03
Tooting	d			13 40			14 10			14 40				15 10			15 40			16 10				16 40	
Haydons Road	d			13 43			14 13			14 43				15 13			15 43			16 13				16 43	
Wimbledon ⊖	a			13 46			14 16			14 46				15 16			15 46			16 16				16 46	
	d			13 47			14 17			14 47				15 17			15 47			16 17				16 47	
Wimbledon Chase	d			13 50			14 20			14 50				15 20			15 50			16 20				16 50	
South Merton	d			13 52			14 22			14 52				15 22			15 52			16 22				16 52	
Morden South	d			13 54			14 24			14 54				15 24			15 54			16 24				16 54	
St Helier	d			13 56			14 26			14 56				15 26			15 56			16 26				16 56	
Sutton Common	d			13 58			14 28			14 58				15 28			15 58			16 28				16 58	
West Sutton	d			14 01			14 31			15 01				15 31			16 01			16 31				17 01	
Sutton (Surrey)	a			14 05	14 06		14 35	14 36		15 05	15 06			15 35	15 36		16 05	16 06		16 35	16 36			17 05	17 06

Station		FC ▬	FC	FC	FC ▬	FC	FC	FC ▬		FC	FC	FC ▬	FC	FC	FC ▬	FC	FC	FC ▬		FC	FC	FC ▬	FC	FC ▬	FC
Luton	d																								
Luton Airport Parkway	d																								
St Pancras International ⊖	d																								
Farringdon ⊖	d																								
City Thameslink	d																								
London Blackfriars ⊖	d	16 16			16 46			17 16				17 46			18 16			18 46				19 16		19 46	
Elephant & Castle ⊖	d	16 24			16 54			17 24				17 54			18 24			18 54				19 24		19 54	
Loughborough Jn	d	16 36			17 06			17 36				18 06			18 36			19 06				19 36		20 06	
Herne Hill	d	16 44		17 12	17 14		17 42	17 44			18 12	18 14		18 42	18 44		19 12	19 14			19 42	19 44		20 14	
London Bridge ⊖	d		16 45			17 15				17 45			18 15			18 45				19 15			19 45		20 15
South Bermondsey	d																								
Queens Rd Peckham	d																								
Peckham Rye	d																								
East Dulwich	d																								
North Dulwich	d																								
Tulse Hill	d	16a52	17 01	17 16	17a22	17 31	17 46	17a52		18 01	18 16	18a22	18 31	18 46	18a52	19 01	19 16	19a22		19 31	19 46	19a53	20 01	20a22	20 31
Streatham	d		17 05	17 20		17 35	17 50			18 05	18 20		18 35	18 50		19 05	19 20			19 35	19 51		20 05		20 35
Mitcham Eastfields	d			17 24			17 54				18 24			18 54			19 24				19 55				
Mitcham Junction	d			17 27			17 57				18 27			18 57			19 27				19 58				
Hackbridge	d			17 30			18 00				18 30			19 00			19 30				20 01				
Carshalton	d			17 33			18 03				18 33			19 03			19 33				20 04				
Tooting	d		17 10			17 40				18 10			18 40			19 10				19 40			20 10		20 40
Haydons Road	d		17 13			17 43				18 13			18 43			19 13				19 43			20 13		20 43
Wimbledon ⊖	a		17 16			17 46				18 16			18 46			19 16				19 46			20 16		20 46
	d		17 17			17 47				18 17			18 47			19 17				19 47			20 17		20 47
Wimbledon Chase	d		17 20			17 50				18 20			18 50			19 20				19 50			20 20		20 50
South Merton	d		17 22			17 52				18 22			18 52			19 22				19 52			20 22		20 52
Morden South	d		17 24			17 54				18 24			18 54			19 24				19 54			20 24		20 54
St Helier	d		17 26			17 56				18 26			18 56			19 26				19 56			20 26		20 56
Sutton Common	d		17 28			17 58				18 28			18 58			19 28				19 58			20 28		20 58
West Sutton	d		17 31			18 01				18 31			19 01			19 31				20 01			20 31		21 01
Sutton (Surrey)	a		17 35	17 36		18 05	18 06			18 35	18 36		19 05	19 06		19 39	19 36			20 05	20 07		20 39		21 05

Table 179

Saturdays

Luton and London - Wimbledon and Sutton via Streatham

		FC 🚌	FC	FC 🚌	FC	FC 🚌	FC	FC 🚌	FC	FC 🚌	FC	FC 🚌	FC	FC 🚌	FC
Luton 10	d														
Luton Airport Parkway 7	d														
St Pancras International 15 ⊖	d														
Farringdon 3 ⊖	d														
City Thameslink 3	d														
London Blackfriars 3 ⊖	d	20 16		20 46		21 16		21 46		22 16		22 46		23 16	
Elephant & Castle ⊖	d	20 24		20 54		21 24		21 54		22 24		22 54		23 24	
Loughborough Jn	d	20 36		21 06		21 36		22 06		22 36		23 06		23 36	
Herne Hill 4	d	20 44		21 14		21 44		22 14		22 44		23 14		23 44	
London Bridge 4 ⊖	d		20 45		21 15		21 45		22 15		22 45		23 15		23 45
South Bermondsey	d														
Queens Rd Peckham	d														
Peckham Rye 4	d														
East Dulwich	d														
North Dulwich	d														
Tulse Hill 3	d	20a52	21 01	21a22	21 31	21a52	22 01	22a22	22 31	22a52	23 01	23a22	23 31	23a52	00 01
Streatham 4	d		21 05		21 35		22 05		22 35		23 05		23 35		00 05
Mitcham Eastfields	d														
Mitcham Junction ⇌	d														
Hackbridge	d														
Carshalton	d														
Tooting	d		21 10		21 40		22 10		22 40		23 10		23 40		00 10
Haydons Road	d		21 13		21 43		22 13		22 43		23 13		23 43		00 13
Wimbledon 6 ⊖ ⇌	a		21 16		21 46		22 16		22 46		23 16		23 46		00 16
	d		21 17		21 47		22 17		22 47		23 17		23 47		00 17
Wimbledon Chase	d		21 20		21 50		22 20		22 50		23 20		23 50		00 20
South Merton	d		21 22		21 52		22 22		22 52		23 22		23 52		00 22
Morden South	d		21 24		21 54		22 24		22 54		23 24		23 54		00 24
St Helier	d		21 26		21 56		22 26		22 56		23 26		23 56		00 26
Sutton Common	d		21 28		21 58		22 28		22 58		23 28		23 58		00 28
West Sutton	d		21 31		22 01		22 31		23 01		23 31		00 01		00 31
Sutton (Surrey) 4	a		21 39		22 05		22 39		23 05		23 35		00 05		00 35

Sundays

		FC	FC	FC 🚌	FC	FC 🚌	FC	FC 🚌	FC	FC 🚌	FC	FC 🚌	FC	FC 🚌	FC	FC 🚌	FC	FC 🚌	FC	FC 🚌	FC	FC 🚌	FC
Luton 10	d																						
Luton Airport Parkway 7	d																						
St Pancras International 15 ⊖	d																						
Farringdon 3 ⊖	d																						
City Thameslink 3	d																						
London Blackfriars 3 ⊖	d			08 49		09 19		09 49		10 19		10 49		11 19		11 49		12 19		12 49		13 19	
Elephant & Castle ⊖	d			08 57		09 27		09 57		10 27		10 57		11 27		11 57		12 27		12 57		13 27	
Loughborough Jn	d			09 09		09 39		10 09		10 39		11 09		11 39		12 09		12 39		13 09		13 39	
Herne Hill 4	d			09 17		09 47		10 17		10 47		11 17		11 47		12 17		12 47		13 17		13 47	
London Bridge 4 ⊖	d	23p15	23p45		09 21		09 51		10 21		10 51		11 21		11 51		12 21		12 51		13 21		13 51
South Bermondsey	d																						
Queens Rd Peckham	d																						
Peckham Rye 4	d																						
East Dulwich	d																						
North Dulwich	d																						
Tulse Hill 3	d	23p31	00 01	09a25	09 31	09a55	10 01	10a25	10 31	10a55	11 01	11a25	11 31	11a55	12 01	12a25	12 31	12a55	13 01	13a25	13 31	13a55	14 01
Streatham 4	d	23p35	00 05		09 35		10 05		10 35		11 05		11 35		12 05		12 35		13 05		13 35		14 05
Mitcham Eastfields	d																						
Mitcham Junction ⇌	d																						
Hackbridge	d																						
Carshalton	d																						
Tooting	d	23p40	00 10		09 40		10 10		10 40		11 10		11 40		12 10		12 40		13 10		13 40		14 10
Haydons Road	d	23p43	00 13		09 43		10 13		10 43		11 13		11 43		12 13		12 43		13 13		13 43		14 13
Wimbledon 6 ⊖ ⇌	a	23p46	00 16		09 46		10 16		10 46		11 16		11 46		12 16		12 46		13 16		13 46		14 16
	d	23p47	00 17		09 47		10 17		10 47		11 17		11 47		12 17		12 47		13 17		13 47		14 17
Wimbledon Chase	d	23p50	00 20		09 50		10 20		10 50		11 20		11 50		12 20		12 50		13 20		13 50		14 20
South Merton	d	23p52	00 22		09 52		10 22		10 52		11 22		11 52		12 22		12 52		13 22		13 52		14 22
Morden South	d	23p54	00 24		09 54		10 24		10 54		11 24		11 54		12 24		12 54		13 24		13 54		14 24
St Helier	d	23p56	00 26		09 56		10 26		10 56		11 26		11 56		12 26		12 56		13 26		13 56		14 26
Sutton Common	d	23p58	00 28		09 58		10 28		10 58		11 28		11 58		12 28		12 58		13 28		13 58		14 28
West Sutton	d	00 01	00 31		10 01		10 31		11 01		11 31		12 01		12 31		13 01		13 31		14 01		14 31
Sutton (Surrey) 4	a	00 05	00 35		10 05		10 35		11 05		11 35		12 05		12 35		13 05		13 35		14 05		14 35

Table 179

Sundays

Luton and London - Wimbledon and Sutton via Streatham

		FC 🚌	FC	FC 🚌	FC	FC 🚌	FC	FC 🚌	FC	FC 🚌	FC	FC 🚌	FC	FC 🚌	FC	FC 🚌	FC	FC 🚌	FC	FC 🚌	FC	FC 🚌	FC
Luton 10	d																						
Luton Airport Parkway 7	d																						
St Pancras International-2 15 ⊖	d																						
Farringdon 3 ⊖	d																						
City Thameslink 3	d																						
London Blackfriars 3 ⊖	d	13 49		14 19		14 49		15 19		15 49		16 19		16 49		17 19		17 49		18 19		18 49	
Elephant & Castle ⊖	d	13 57		14 27		14 57		15 27		15 57		16 27		16 57		17 27		17 57		18 27		18 57	
Loughborough Jn	d	14 09		14 39		15 09		15 39		16 09		16 39		17 09		17 39		18 09		18 39		19 09	
Herne Hill 4	d	14 17		14 47		15 17		15 47		16 17		16 47		17 17		17 47		18 17		18 47		19 17	
London Bridge 4 ⊖	d		14 21		14 51		15 21		15 51		16 21		16 51		17 21		17 51		18 21		18 51		19 21
South Bermondsey	d																						
Queens Rd Peckham	d																						
Peckham Rye 4	d																						
East Dulwich	d																						
North Dulwich	d																						
Tulse Hill 3	d	14a25	14 31	14a55	15 01	15a25	15 31	15a55	16 01	16a25	16 31	16a55	17 01	17a25	17 31	17a55	18 01	18a25	18 31	18a55	19 01	19a25	19 31
Streatham 4	d		14 35		15 05		15 35		16 05		16 35		17 05		17 35		18 05		18 35		19 05		19 35
Mitcham Eastfields	d																						
Mitcham Junction ⇌	d																						
Hackbridge	d																						
Carshalton	d																						
Tooting	d		14 40		15 10		15 40		16 10		16 40		17 10		17 40		18 10		18 40		19 10		19 40
Haydons Road	d		14 43		15 13		15 43		16 13		16 43		17 13		17 43		18 13		18 43		19 13		19 43
Wimbledon 6 ⊖ ⇌	a		14 46		15 16		15 46		16 16		16 46		17 16		17 46		18 16		18 46		19 16		19 46
	d		14 47		15 17		15 47		16 17		16 47		17 17		17 47		18 17		18 47		19 17		19 47
Wimbledon Chase	d		14 50		15 20		15 50		16 20		16 50		17 20		17 50		18 20		18 50		19 20		19 50
South Merton	d		14 52		15 22		15 52		16 22		16 52		17 22		17 52		18 22		18 52		19 22		19 52
Morden South	d		14 54		15 24		15 54		16 24		16 54		17 24		17 54		18 24		18 54		19 24		19 54
St Helier	d		14 56		15 26		15 56		16 26		16 56		17 26		17 56		18 26		18 56		19 26		19 56
Sutton Common	d		14 58		15 28		15 58		16 28		16 58		17 28		17 58		18 28		18 58		19 28		19 58
West Sutton	d		15 01		15 31		16 01		16 31		17 01		17 31		18 01		18 31		19 01		19 31		20 01
Sutton (Surrey) 4	a		15 05		15 35		16 05		16 35		17 05		17 35		18 05		18 35		19 05		19 35		20 05

		FC 🚌	FC	FC 🚌	FC	FC 🚌	FC
Luton 10	d						
Luton Airport Parkway 7	d						
St Pancras International-2 15 ⊖	d						
Farringdon 3 ⊖	d						
City Thameslink 3	d						
London Blackfriars 3 ⊖	d	19 19		19 49		20 19	
Elephant & Castle ⊖	d	19 27		19 57		20 27	
Loughborough Jn	d	19 39		20 09		20 39	
Herne Hill 4	d	19 47		20 17		20 47	
London Bridge 4 ⊖	d		19 51		20 21		20 51
South Bermondsey	d						
Queens Rd Peckham	d						
Peckham Rye 4	d						
East Dulwich	d						
North Dulwich	d						
Tulse Hill 3	d	19a55	20 01	20a25	20 31	20a55	21 01
Streatham 4	d		20 05		20 35		21 05
Mitcham Eastfields	d						
Mitcham Junction ⇌	d						
Hackbridge	d						
Carshalton	d						
Tooting	d		20 10		20 40		21 10
Haydons Road	d		20 13		20 43		21 13
Wimbledon 6 ⊖ ⇌	a		20 16		20 46		21 16
	d		20 17		20 47		21 17
Wimbledon Chase	d		20 20		20 50		21 20
South Merton	d		20 22		20 52		21 22
Morden South	d		20 24		20 54		21 24
St Helier	d		20 26		20 56		21 26
Sutton Common	d		20 28		20 58		21 28
West Sutton	d		20 31		21 01		21 31
Sutton (Surrey) 4	a		20 35		21 05		21 35

Sutton and Wimbledon - London and Luton via Streatham

		SN	SN	FC	FC	SN	FC	SN	FC	FC	SN	FC	FC	SN	FC	FC	FC	SN
Sutton (Surrey) 4	d	05 37	06 14		06 20	06 50	06 48	07 20	07 06	07 37	07 49	07 40	08 09	08 20	08 08	08 39	08 41	08 57
West Sutton	d				06 23		06 51		07 09			07 43			08 11		08 44	
Sutton Common	d				06 25		06 53		07 11			07 45			08 13		08 46	
St Helier	d				06 28		06 56		07 14			07 48			08 16		08 49	
Morden South	d				06 30		06 58		07 16			07 50			08 18		08 51	
South Merton	d				06 32		07 00		07 18			07 52			08 20		08 53	
Wimbledon Chase	d				06 34		07 02		07 20			07 54			08 22		08 55	
Wimbledon 6 ⊖	a				06 37		07 05		07 23			07 57			08 25		08 58	
	d			06 26	06 38		07 06		07 26			07 58			08 28		08 58	
Haydons Road	d			06 28	06 40		07 08		07 28			08 00			08 30		09 00	
Tooting	d			06 31	06 43		07 11		07 31			08 03			08 33		09 03	
Carshalton	d	05 40	06 17			06 53		07 23		07 40	07 52		08 12	08 23		08 42		09 00
Hackbridge	d	05 42	06 19			06 55		07 25		07 42	07 54		08 14	08 25		08 44		09 02
Mitcham Junction	d	05 46	06 23			06 59		07 29		07 45	07 58		08 17	08 29		08 47		09 06
Mitcham Eastfields	d	05 49	06 26			07 02		07 32		07 48	08 01		08 20	08 32		08 50		09 09
Streatham 4	d	05 53	06 30	06 36	06 49	07 05	07 16	07 35	07 38	07 52	08 05	08 09	08 24	08 36	08 39	08 54	09 08	09 12
Tulse Hill 3	d	05 57	06 34	06 40	06 52	07 10	07 20	07 41	07 42	07 57	08 09	08 13	08 28	08 40	08 43	08 58	09 16	09 16
North Dulwich	d		06 37			07 13		07 44			08 12			08 43				09 19
East Dulwich	d		06 39			07 15		07 46			08 14			08 45				09 21
Peckham Rye 4	d	06 02	06 42			07 17		07 48			08 16			08 48				09 23
Queens Rd Peckham	d		06 44			07 20		07 51			08 19			08 50				09 26
South Bermondsey	d		06 47			07 22		07 53			08 21			08 53				09 28
London Bridge 4 ⊖	a	06 08	06 51			07 29		08 00			08 29			08 59				09 35
Herne Hill 4	d			06 46	06 56		07 24		07 46	08 01		08 20	08 31		08 47	09 02	09 20	
Loughborough Jn	d			06 49	07 00		07 27		07 50	08 04		08 23	08 35		08 50	09 05	09 23	
Elephant & Castle ⊖	d			06 54	07 06		07 32		07 54	08 09		08 28	08 40		08 58	09 10	09 30	
London Blackfriars 3 ⊖	a			06 57	07 09		07 35		07 58	08 12		08 32	08 45		09 01	09 13	09 33	
City Thameslink 3	a			07 02	07 14		07 38		08 00	08 15		08 35	08 48		09 04	09 16	09 36	
Farringdon 3 ⊖	a			07 06	07 18		07 42		08 03	08 19		08 39	08 52		09 08	09 20	09 40	
St Pancras International-2 15 ⊖	a			07 09	07 21		07 45		08 07	08 23		08 43	08 55		09 11	09 23	09 43	
Luton Airport Parkway 7	a			07 49			08 21					09 27			09 59	10 03	10 30	
Luton 10	a			07 54			08 24					09 32			10 04	10 06	10 34	

		FC	FC	FC	FC	FC	FC	FC	FC	FC	FC	FC	FC	FC	FC	FC	FC	FC	FC	FC	FC	FC	FC
Sutton (Surrey) 4	d	09 13	09 11	09 38	09 37	10 08	10 07	10 38	10 37	11 08	11 07	11 38	11 37	12 08	12 07	12 38	12 37	13 08	13 07	13 38	13 37	14 08	14 07
West Sutton	d		09 14		09 40		10 10		10 40		11 10		11 40		12 10		12 40		13 10		13 40		14 10
Sutton Common	d		09 16		09 42		10 12		10 42		11 12		11 42		12 12		12 42		13 12		13 42		14 12
St Helier	d		09 19		09 45		10 15		10 45		11 15		11 45		12 15		12 45		13 15		13 45		14 15
Morden South	d		09 21		09 47		10 17		10 47		11 17		11 47		12 17		12 47		13 17		13 47		14 17
South Merton	d		09 23		09 49		10 19		10 49		11 19		11 49		12 19		12 49		13 19		13 49		14 19
Wimbledon Chase	d		09 25		09 51		10 21		10 51		11 21		11 51		12 21		12 51		13 21		13 51		14 21
Wimbledon 6 ⊖	a		09 28		09 54		10 24		10 54		11 24		11 54		12 24		12 54		13 24		13 54		14 24
	d		09 28		09 58		10 28		10 58		11 28		11 58		12 28		12 58		13 28		13 58		14 28
Haydons Road	d		09 30		10 00		10 30		11 00		11 30		12 00		12 30		13 00		13 30		14 00		14 30
Tooting	d		09 33		10 03		10 33		11 03		11 33		12 03		12 33		13 03		13 33		14 03		14 33
Carshalton	d	09 16		09 41		10 11		10 41		11 11		11 41		12 11		12 41		13 11		13 41		14 11	
Hackbridge	d	09 18		09 43		10 13		10 43		11 13		11 43		12 13		12 43		13 13		13 43		14 13	
Mitcham Junction	d	09 21		09 46		10 16		10 46		11 16		11 46		12 16		12 46		13 16		13 46		14 16	
Mitcham Eastfields	d	09 24		09 49		10 19		10 49		11 19		11 49		12 19		12 49		13 19		13 49		14 19	
Streatham 4	d	09 28	09 38	09 53	10 08	10 23	10 38	10 53	11 08	11 23	11 38	11 53	12 08	12 23	12 38	12 53	13 08	13 23	13 38	13 53	14 08	14 23	14 38
Tulse Hill 3	d	09 32	09 42	09 57	10 12	10 27	10 42	10 57	11 12	11 27	11 42	11 57	12 12	12 27	12 42	12 57	13 12	13 27	13 42	13 57	14 12	14 27	14 42
North Dulwich	d																						
East Dulwich	d																						
Peckham Rye 4	d																						
Queens Rd Peckham	d																						
South Bermondsey	d																						
London Bridge 4 ⊖	a																						
Herne Hill 4	d	09 35	09 47	10 01	10 16	10 31	10 46	11 01	11 16	11 31	11 46	12 01	12 16	12 31	12 46	13 01	13 16	13 31	13 46	14 01	14 16	14 31	14 46
Loughborough Jn	d	09 39	09 50	10 04	10 19	10 34	10 49	11 04	11 19	11 34	11 49	12 04	12 19	12 34	12 49	13 04	13 19	13 34	13 49	14 04	14 19	14 34	14 49
Elephant & Castle ⊖	d	09 46	09 55	10 09	10 24	10 39	10 54	11 09	11 24	11 39	11 54	12 09	12 24	12 39	12 54	13 09	13 24	13 39	13 54	14 09	14 24	14 39	14 54
London Blackfriars 3 ⊖	a	09 49	09 59	10 12	10 27	10 42	10 57	11 12	11 27	11 42	11 57	12 12	12 27	12 42	12 57	13 12	13 27	13 42	13 57	14 12	14 27	14 42	14 57
City Thameslink 3	a	09 52	10 02	10 15	10 30	10 45	11 00	11 15	11 30	11 45	12 00	12 15	12 30	12 45	13 00	13 15	13 30	13 45	14 00	14 15	14 30	14 45	15 00
Farringdon 3 ⊖	a	09 56	10 06	10 19	10 34	10 49	11 04	11 19	11 34	11 49	12 04	12 19	12 34	12 49	13 04	13 19	13 34	13 49	14 04	14 19	14 34	14 49	15 04
St Pancras International-2 15 ⊖	a	09 59	10 09	10 22	10 37	10 52	11 07	11 22	11 37	11 52	12 07	12 22	12 37	12 52	13 07	13 22	13 37	13 52	14 07	14 22	14 37	14 52	15 07
Luton Airport Parkway 7	a		10 59		11 26		11 56		12 26		12 56		13 26		13 56		14 26		14 56		15 26		15 56
Luton 10	a		11 04		11 30		12 00		12 30		13 00		13 30		14 00		14 30		15 00		15 30		16 00

Sutton and Wimbledon - London and Luton via Streatham

		FC	FC	FC	FC	FC	FC	FC	FC	FC 1 A	FC	FC	FC	FC	FC	SN	FC	FC	FC	SN	FC	FC
Sutton (Surrey) 4	d	14 38	14 37	15 08	15 07	15 38	15 37	16 08	16 07	16 38	16 37	17 08	17 11	17 42	17 41	17 48.	18 08	18 09	18 38	18 16.	18 43	19 08
West Sutton	d		14 40		15 10		15 40		16 10		16 40		17 14		17 44	17 51.		18 12		18 20	18 46	
Sutton Common	d		14 42		15 12		15 42		16 12		16 42		17 16		17 46	17 54		18 14		18 22	18 48	
St Helier	d		14 45		15 15		15 45		16 15		16 45		17 19		17 49	17 56		18 17		18 25	18 51	
Morden South	d		14 47		15 17		15 47		16 17		16 47		17 21		17 51	17 58		18 19		18 27	18 53	
South Merton	d		14 49		15 19		15 49		16 19		16 49		17 23		17 53	18 00		18 21		18 29	18 55	
Wimbledon Chase	d		14 51		15 21		15 51		16 21		16 51		17 25		17 55	18 02		18 23		18 31	18 57	
Wimbledon 6 ⊖	a		14 54		15 24		15 54		16 24		16 54		17 28		17 58	18 08		18 26		18 36	19 00	
	d		14 58		15 28		15 58		16 30		17 00		17 30		18 00	18 10		18 28		18 43	19 00	
Haydons Road	d		15 00		15 30		16 00		16 32		17 02		17 32		18 02	18 12		18 30		18 45	19 02	
Tooting	d		15 03		15 33		16 03		16 35		17 05		17 35		18 05	18 15		18 33		18 48	19 05	
Carshalton	d	14 41		15 11		15 41		16 11		16 41		17 11		17 45			18 11		18 41			19 11
Hackbridge	d	14 43		15 13		15 43		16 13		16 43		17 13		17 47			18 13		18 43			19 13
Mitcham Junction	d	14 46		15 16		15 46		16 16		16 46		17 16		17 50			18 16		18 46			19 16
Mitcham Eastfields	d	14 49		15 19		15 49		16 19		16 49		17 19		17 53			18 19		18 49			19 19
Streatham 4	d	14 53	15 08	15 23	15 38	15 53	16 08	16 23	16 40	16 53	17 10	17 23	17 40	17 57	18 10	18 19	18 23	18 40	18 53	18 56	19 10	19 23
Tulse Hill 3	d	14 57	15 12	15 27	15 42	15 57	16 12	16 27	16 46	16 57	17 16	17 27	17 44	18 01	18 16	18 24	18 27	18 44	18 57	19 00	19 14	19 27
North Dulwich	d															18 27				19 03		
East Dulwich	d															18 29				19 05		
Peckham Rye 4	d															18 32				19 07		
Queens Rd Peckham	d															18 35				19 10		
South Bermondsey	d															18 37				19 12		
London Bridge 4 ⊖	a															18 42				19 17		
Herne Hill 4	d	15 01	15 16	15 31	15 46	16 01	16 16	16 31	16 50	17 01	17 20	17 31	17 48	18 06	18 20		18 31	18 48	19 01		19 17	19 31
Loughborough Jn	d	15 04	15 19	15 34	15 49	16 04	16 19	16 34	16 53		17 23	17 34	17 51	18 09	18 23		18 34	18 51	19 04		19 20	19 34
Elephant & Castle ⊖	d	15 09	15 24	15 39	15 54	16 09	16 24	16 39	17 00	17 08	17 28	17 39	17 56	18 14	18 28		18 40	18 56	19 09		19 25	19 39
London Blackfriars 3 ⊖	a	15 12	15 27	15 42	15 57	16 13	16 29	16 43	17 03	17 11	17 31	17 43	17 59	18 17	18 31		18 43	18 59	19 14		19 28	19 43
City Thameslink 3	a	15 15	15 30	15 45	16 00	16 16	16 32	16 46	17 06	17 14	17 34	17 48	18 02	18 20	18 34		18 46	19 02	19 20		19 32	19 48
Farringdon 3 ⊖	a	15 19	15 34	15 49	16 04	16 19	16 35	16 49	17 09	17 17	17 37	17 51	18 05	18 23	18 37		18 49	19 05	19 23		19 36	19 52
St Pancras International-2 15 ⊖	a	15 22	15 37	15 52	16 07	16 23	16 39	16 53	17 13	17 21	17 41	17 55	18 09	18 27	18 41		18 53	19 09	19 27		19 39	19 55
Luton Airport Parkway 7	a		16 30		17 00		17 26			17 56	18 27		18 57		19 29		19 35	19 53			20 26	
Luton 10	a		16 32		17 02		17 30			17 59	18 32		19 02		19 34		19 40	19 58			20 30	

		SN	FC	FC	FC	FC	FC	FC	FC	FC	FC	FC
Sutton (Surrey) 4	d	18 48	19 13	19 42	19 38	20 10	20 07	20 40	20 37	21 10	21 12	22 12
West Sutton	d	18 54	19 16		19 41		20 10		20 40		21 15	22 15
Sutton Common	d	18 56	19 18		19 43		20 12		20 42		21 17	22 17
St Helier	d	18 59	19 21		19 46		20 15		20 45		21 20	22 20
Morden South	d	19 01	19 23		19 48		20 17		20 47		21 22	22 22
South Merton	d	19 03	19 25		19 50		20 19		20 49		21 24	22 24
Wimbledon Chase	d	19 05	19 27		19 52		20 21		20 51		21 26	22 26
Wimbledon 6 ⊖	a	19 10	19 30		19 55		20 24		20 54		21 29	22 29
	d	19 17	19 30		19 56		20 26		20 56		21 36	22 30
Haydons Road	d	19 19	19 32		19 58		20 28		20 58		21 38	22 32
Tooting	d	19 22	19 35		20 01		20 31		21 01		21 41	22 35
Carshalton	d			19 45		20 13		20 43		21 13		
Hackbridge	d			19 47		20 15		20 45		21 15		
Mitcham Junction	d			19 50		20 18		20 48		21 18		
Mitcham Eastfields	d			19 53		20 21		20 51		21 21		
Streatham 4	d	19 26	19 40	19 57	20 06	20 25	20 36	20 55	21 06	21 25	21 46	22 40
Tulse Hill 3	d	19 31	19 44	20 01	20 12	20 29	20 42	20 59	21 12	21 29	21 50	22 43
North Dulwich	d	19 34										
East Dulwich	d	19 36										
Peckham Rye 4	d	19 38										
Queens Rd Peckham	d	19 41										
South Bermondsey	d	19 43										
London Bridge 4 ⊖	a	19 51										22 55
Herne Hill 4	d		19 47	20 05	20 16	20 35	20 46	21 05	21 16	21 35	21 54	
Loughborough Jn	d		19 50	20 08	20 19	20 38	20 49	21 08	21 19	21 38	21 57	
Elephant & Castle ⊖	d		19 55	20 13	20 24	20 43	20 54	21 13	21 24	21 43	22 02	
London Blackfriars 3 ⊖	a		19 58	20 16	20 27	20 46	20 57	21 16	21 27	21 46	22 05	
City Thameslink 3	a		20 02	20 20	20 32	20 50	21 02	21 20	21 32	21 50	22 10	
Farringdon 3 ⊖	a		20 06	20 24	20 36	20 54	21 06	21 24	21 36	21 54	22 14	
St Pancras International-2 15 ⊖	a		20 09	20 27	20 39	20 57	21 09	21 27	21 39	21 57	22 17	
Luton Airport Parkway 7	a		20 56		21 26		21 56		22 26		23 01	
Luton 10	a		21 00		21 30		22 00		22 30		23 04	

A 1 to City Thameslink

Table 179

Sutton and Wimbledon - London and Luton via Streatham

		FC 🚌	FC 🚌	FC	FC 🚌	FC 🚌	FC	FC	FC 🚌	FC 🚌		FC	FC	FC 🚌	FC 🚌	FC	FC	FC 🚌	FC 🚌	FC		FC	FC 🚌	FC 🚌	FC
Sutton (Surrey) [4]	d						07 08	07 07				07 38	07 37			08 08	08 07			08 38		08 37			09 08
West Sutton	d							07 10					07 40				08 10					08 40			
Sutton Common	d							07 12					07 42				08 12					08 42			
St Helier	d							07 15					07 45				08 15					08 45			
Morden South	d							07 17					07 47				08 17					08 47			
South Merton	d							07 19					07 49				08 19					08 49			
Wimbledon Chase	d							07 21					07 51				08 21					08 51			
Wimbledon [6] ⊖ 🚊	a							07 25					07 55				08 25					08 55			
	d			07 00				07 30					08 00				08 30					09 00			
Haydons Road	d			07 02				07 32					08 02				08 32					09 02			
Tooting	d			07 05				07 35					08 05				08 35					09 05			
Carshalton	d						07 11					07 41				08 11				08 41					09 11
Hackbridge	d						07 13					07 43				08 13				08 43					09 13
Mitcham Junction 🚊	d						07 16					07 46				08 16				08 46					09 16
Mitcham Eastfields	d						07 19					07 49				08 19				08 49					09 19
Streatham [4]	d			07 10			07 23	07 40				07 53	08 10			08 23	08 40			08 53		09 10			09 23
Tulse Hill [3]	d	06 00	06 30	07 17		07 20	07 27	07 47		07 50		07 57	08 17		08 20	08 27	08 47		08 50	08 57		09 17		09 20	09 27
North Dulwich	d																								
East Dulwich	d																								
Peckham Rye [4]	d																								
Queens Rd Peckham	d																								
South Bermondsey	d																								
London Bridge [4] ⊖	a			07 30				08 00					08 30				09 00					09 30			
Herne Hill [4]	d	06 08	06 38		07 08	07 28	07a31		07 38	07 58		08a01		08 08	08 28	08a31		08 38	08 58	09a01			09 08	09 28	09a31
Loughborough Jn	d	06 16	06 46		07 16	07 36			07 46	08 06				08 16	08 36			08 46	09 06				09 16	09 36	
Elephant & Castle ⊖	d	06 28	06 58		07 28	07 48			07 58	08 18				08 28	08 48			08 58	09 18				09 28	09 48	
London Blackfriars [3] ⊖	a	06 36	07 06		07 36	07 56			08 06	08 26				08 36	08 56			09 06	09 26				09 36	09 56	
City Thameslink [3]	a																								
Farringdon [3] ⊖	a																								
St Pancras International-2 [15] ⊖	a																								
Luton Airport Parkway [7]	a																								
Luton [10]	a																								

		FC	FC 🚌	FC 🚌	FC	FC		FC 🚌	FC 🚌	FC	FC	FC 🚌	FC 🚌	FC	FC	FC 🚌		FC 🚌	FC	FC	FC 🚌	FC 🚌	FC	FC	FC 🚌
Sutton (Surrey) [4]	d	09 07			09 38	09 37				10 08	10 07			10 38	10 37				11 08	11 07			11 38	11 37	
West Sutton	d	09 10				09 40					10 10				10 40					11 10				11 40	
Sutton Common	d	09 12				09 42					10 12				10 42					11 12				11 42	
St Helier	d	09 15				09 45					10 15				10 45					11 15				11 45	
Morden South	d	09 17				09 47					10 17				10 47					11 17				11 47	
South Merton	d	09 19				09 49					10 19				10 49					11 19				11 49	
Wimbledon Chase	d	09 21				09 51					10 21				10 51					11 21				11 51	
Wimbledon [6] ⊖ 🚊	a	09 25				09 55					10 25				10 55					11 25				11 55	
	d	09 30				10 00					10 30				11 00					11 30				12 00	
Haydons Road	d	09 32				10 02					10 32				11 02					11 32				12 02	
Tooting	d	09 35				10 05					10 35				11 05					11 35				12 05	
Carshalton	d				09 41					10 11				10 41					11 11				11 41		
Hackbridge	d				09 43					10 13				10 43					11 13				11 43		
Mitcham Junction 🚊	d				09 46					10 16				10 46					11 16				11 46		
Mitcham Eastfields	d				09 49					10 19				10 49					11 19				11 49		
Streatham [4]	d	09 40			09 53	10 10				10 23	10 40			10 53	11 10				11 23	11 40			11 53	12 10	
Tulse Hill [3]	d	09 47		09 50	09 57	10 17			10 20	10 27	10 47		10 50	10 57	11 17			11 20	11 27	11 47		11 50	11 57	12 17	
North Dulwich	d																								
East Dulwich	d																								
Peckham Rye [4]	d																								
Queens Rd Peckham	d																								
South Bermondsey	d																								
London Bridge [4] ⊖	a	10 00				10 30					11 00				11 30					12 00				12 30	
Herne Hill [4]	d		09 38	09 58	10a01			10 08	10 28	10a31		10 38	10 58	11a01		11 08		11 28	11a31		11 38	11 58	12a01		12 08
Loughborough Jn	d		09 46	10 06				10 16	10 36			10 46	11 06			11 16		11 36			11 46	12 06			12 16
Elephant & Castle ⊖	d		09 58	10 18				10 28	10 48			10 58	11 18			11 28		11 48			11 58	12 18			12 28
London Blackfriars [3] ⊖	a		10 06	10 26				10 36	10 56			11 06	11 26			11 36		11 56			12 06	12 26			12 36
City Thameslink [3]	a																								
Farringdon [3] ⊖	a																								
St Pancras International-2 [15] ⊖	a																								
Luton Airport Parkway [7]	a																								
Luton [10]	a																								

Table 179

Sutton and Wimbledon - London and Luton via Streatham

		FC 🚌		FC	FC	FC 🚌	FC 🚌	FC	FC	FC 🚌	FC 🚌	FC		FC	FC 🚌	FC 🚌	FC	FC	FC 🚌	FC 🚌	FC	FC		FC 🚌	FC 🚌
Sutton (Surrey) [4]	d			12 08	12 07			12 38	12 37			13 08		13 07			13 38	13 37			14 08	14 07			
West Sutton	d				12 10				12 40					13 10				13 40				14 10			
Sutton Common	d				12 12				12 42					13 12				13 42				14 12			
St Helier	d				12 15				12 45					13 15				13 45				14 15			
Morden South	d				12 17				12 47					13 17				13 47				14 17			
South Merton	d				12 19				12 49					13 19				13 49				14 19			
Wimbledon Chase	d				12 21				12 51					13 21				13 51				14 21			
Wimbledon [6] ⊖ 🚊	a				12 25				12 55					13 25				13 55				14 25			
	d				12 30				13 00					13 30				14 00				14 30			
Haydons Road	d				12 32				13 02					13 32				14 02				14 32			
Tooting	d				12 35				13 05					13 35				14 05				14 35			
Carshalton	d			12 11				12 41				13 11					13 41				14 11				
Hackbridge	d			12 13				12 43				13 13					13 43				14 13				
Mitcham Junction 🚊	d			12 16				12 46				13 16					13 46				14 16				
Mitcham Eastfields	d			12 19				12 49				13 19					13 49				14 19				
Streatham [4]	d			12 23	12 40			12 53	13 10			13 23		13 40			13 53	14 10			14 23	14 40			
Tulse Hill [3]	d	12 20		12 27	12 47		12 50	12 57	13 17		13 20	13 27		13 47		13 50	13 57	14 17		14 20	14 27	14 47			14 50
North Dulwich	d																								
East Dulwich	d																								
Peckham Rye [4]	d																								
Queens Rd Peckham	d																								
South Bermondsey	d																								
London Bridge [4] ⊖	a				13 00				13 30					14 00				14 30				15 00			
Herne Hill [4]	d	12 28		12a31		12 38	12 58	13a01		13 08	13 28	13a31			13 38	13 58	14a01		14 08	14 28	14a31			14 38	14 58
Loughborough Jn	d	12 36				12 46	13 06			13 16	13 36				13 46	14 06			14 16	14 36				14 46	15 06
Elephant & Castle ⊖	d	12 48				12 58	13 18			13 28	13 48				13 58	14 18			14 28	14 48				14 58	15 18
London Blackfriars [3] ⊖	a	12 56				13 06	13 26			13 36	13 56				14 06	14 26			14 36	14 56				15 06	15 26
City Thameslink [3]	a																								
Farringdon [3] ⊖	a																								
St Pancras International-2 [15] ⊖	a																								
Luton Airport Parkway [7]	a																								
Luton [10]	a																								

		FC	FC	FC 🚌	FC 🚌	FC	FC	FC 🚌		FC 🚌	FC	FC	FC 🚌	FC 🚌	FC	FC	FC 🚌	FC 🚌		FC	FC	FC 🚌	FC 🚌	FC	FC
Sutton (Surrey) [4]	d	14 38	14 37			15 08	15 07				15 38	15 37			16 08	16 07				16 38	16 37			17 08	17 07
West Sutton	d		14 40				15 10					15 40				16 10					16 40				17 10
Sutton Common	d		14 42				15 12					15 42				16 12					16 42				17 12
St Helier	d		14 45				15 15					15 45				16 15					16 45				17 15
Morden South	d		14 47				15 17					15 47				16 17					16 47				17 17
South Merton	d		14 49				15 19					15 49				16 19					16 49				17 19
Wimbledon Chase	d		14 51				15 21					15 51				16 21					16 51				17 21
Wimbledon [6] ⊖ 🚊	a		14 55				15 25					15 55				16 25					16 55				17 25
	d		15 00				15 30					16 00				16 30					17 00				17 30
Haydons Road	d		15 02				15 32					16 02				16 32					17 02				17 32
Tooting	d		15 05				15 35					16 05				16 35					17 05				17 35
Carshalton	d	14 41				15 11					15 41				16 11					16 41				17 11	
Hackbridge	d	14 43				15 13					15 43				16 13					16 43				17 13	
Mitcham Junction 🚊	d	14 46				15 16					15 46				16 16					16 46				17 16	
Mitcham Eastfields	d	14 49				15 19					15 49				16 19					16 49				17 19	
Streatham [4]	d	14 53	15 10			15 23	15 40				15 53	16 10			16 23	16 40				16 53	17 10			17 23	17 40
Tulse Hill [3]	d	14 57	15 17		15 20	15 27	15 47			15 50	15 57	16 17		16 20	16 27	16 47		16 50		16 57	17 17		17 20	17 27	17 47
North Dulwich	d																								
East Dulwich	d																								
Peckham Rye [4]	d																								
Queens Rd Peckham	d																								
South Bermondsey	d																								
London Bridge [4] ⊖	a		15 30				16 00					16 30				17 00					17 30				18 00
Herne Hill [4]	d	15a01		15 08	15 28	15a31		15 38		15 58	16a01		16 08	16 28	16a31		16 38	16 58		17a01		17 08	17 28	17a31	
Loughborough Jn	d			15 16	15 36			15 46		16 06			16 16	16 36			16 46	17 06				17 16	17 36		
Elephant & Castle ⊖	d			15 28	15 48			15 58		16 18			16 28	16 48			16 58	17 18				17 28	17 48		
London Blackfriars [3] ⊖	a			15 36	15 56			16 06		16 26			16 36	16 57			17 06	17 26				17 36	17 56		
City Thameslink [3]	a																								
Farringdon [3] ⊖	a																								
St Pancras International-2 [15] ⊖	a																								
Luton Airport Parkway [7]	a																								
Luton [10]	a																								

Table 179

Saturdays

Sutton and Wimbledon - London and Luton via Streatham

		FC	FC	FC	FC	FC	FC	FC	FC	FC	FC	FC	FC	FC	FC	FC	FC	FC	FC	FC	FC	FC
Sutton (Surrey) 4	d		17 38	17 37			18 08	18 07			18 38	18 37			19 08	19 07			19 37		20 08	
West Sutton	d			17 40				18 10				18 40				19 10			19 40		20 11	
Sutton Common	d			17 42				18 12				18 42				19 12			19 42		20 13	
St Helier	d			17 45				18 15				18 45				19 15			19 45		20 16	
Morden South	d			17 47				18 17				18 47				19 17			19 47		20 18	
South Merton	d			17 49				18 19				18 49				19 19			19 49		20 20	
Wimbledon Chase	d			17 51				18 21				18 51				19 21			19 51		20 22	
Wimbledon 6 ⊖	a			17 55				18 25				18 55				19 25			19 55		20 25	
	d			18 00				18 30				19 00				19 30			20 00		20 30	
Haydons Road	d			18 02				18 32				19 02				19 32			20 02		20 32	
Tooting	d			18 05				18 35				19 05				19 35			20 05		20 35	
Carshalton	d		17 41				18 11				18 41				19 11							
Hackbridge	d		17 43				18 13				18 43				19 13							
Mitcham Junction	d		17 46				18 16				18 46				19 16							
Mitcham Eastfields	d		17 49				18 19				18 49				19 19							
Streatham 4	d		17 53	18 10			18 23	18 40			18 53	19 10			19 23	19 40			20 10		20 40	
Tulse Hill 3	d	17 50	17 57	18 17		18 20	18 27	18 47		18 50	18 57	19 17		19 20	19 27	19 47		19 50	20 17	20 20	20 47	20 50
North Dulwich	d																					
East Dulwich	d																					
Peckham Rye 4	d																					
Queens Rd Peckham	d																					
South Bermondsey	d																					
London Bridge 4 ⊖	a			18 30				19 00				19 30				20 00			20 30		21 00	
Herne Hill 4	d	17 58	18a01		18 08	18 28	18a31		18 38	18 58	19a01		19 08	19 28	19a31		19 38	19 58		20 28		20 58
Loughborough Jn	d	18 06			18 16	18 36			18 46	19 06			19 16	19 36			19 46	20 06		20 36		21 06
Elephant & Castle ⊖	d	18 18			18 28	18 48			18 58	19 18			19 28	19 48			19 58	20 18		20 48		21 18
London Blackfriars 3 ⊖	a	18 26			18 36	18 56			19 06	19 26			19 36	19 56			20 06	20 26		20 56		21 26
City Thameslink 3	a																					
Farringdon 3 ⊖	a																					
St Pancras International-2 15 ⊖	a																					
Luton Airport Parkway 7	a																					
Luton 10	a																					

		FC	FC	FC	FC	FC	FC	FC	FC
Sutton (Surrey) 4	d	20 37		21 07		21 37		22 07	
West Sutton	d	20 40		21 10		21 40		22 10	
Sutton Common	d	20 42		21 12		21 42		22 12	
St Helier	d	20 45		21 15		21 45		22 15	
Morden South	d	20 47		21 17		21 47		22 17	
South Merton	d	20 49		21 19		21 49		22 19	
Wimbledon Chase	d	20 51		21 21		21 51		22 21	
Wimbledon 6 ⊖	a	20 55		21 25		21 55		22 25	
	d	21 00		21 30		22 00		22 30	
Haydons Road	d	21 02		21 32		22 02		22 32	
Tooting	d	21 05		21 35		22 05		22 35	
Carshalton	d								
Hackbridge	d								
Mitcham Junction	d								
Mitcham Eastfields	d								
Streatham 4	d	21 10		21 40		22 10		22 40	
Tulse Hill 3	d	21 17	21 20	21 47	21 50	22 17	22 20	22 47	22 50
North Dulwich	d								
East Dulwich	d								
Peckham Rye 4	d								
Queens Rd Peckham	d								
South Bermondsey	d								
London Bridge 4 ⊖	a	21 30		22 00		22 30		23 00	
Herne Hill 4	d		21 28		21 58		22 28		22 58
Loughborough Jn	d		21 36		22 06		22 36		23 06
Elephant & Castle ⊖	d		21 48		22 18		22 48		23 18
London Blackfriars 3 ⊖	a		21 56		22 26		22 56		23 26
City Thameslink 3	a								
Farringdon 3 ⊖	a								
St Pancras International-2 15 ⊖	a								
Luton Airport Parkway 7	a								
Luton 10	a								

Table 179

Sundays

Sutton and Wimbledon - London and Luton via Streatham

		FC	FC	FC	FC	FC	FC	FC	FC	FC	FC	FC	FC	FC	FC	FC	FC	FC	FC	FC	FC	FC	FC
Sutton (Surrey) 4	d	10 16		10 46		11 16		11 46		12 16		12 46		13 16		13 46		14 16		14 46		15 16	
West Sutton	d	10 19		10 49		11 19		11 49		12 19		12 49		13 19		13 49		14 19		14 49		15 19	
Sutton Common	d	10 21		10 51		11 21		11 51		12 21		12 51		13 21		13 51		14 21		14 51		15 21	
St Helier	d	10 24		10 54		11 24		11 54		12 24		12 54		13 24		13 54		14 24		14 54		15 24	
Morden South	d	10 26		10 56		11 26		11 56		12 26		12 56		13 26		13 56		14 26		14 56		15 26	
South Merton	d	10 28		10 58		11 28		11 58		12 28		12 58		13 28		13 58		14 28		14 58		15 28	
Wimbledon Chase	d	10 30		11 00		11 30		12 00		12 30		13 00		13 30		14 00		14 30		15 00		15 30	
Wimbledon 6 ⊖	a	10 33		11 03		11 33		12 03		12 33		13 03		13 33		14 03		14 33		15 03		15 33	
	d	10 33		11 03		11 33		12 03		12 33		13 03		13 33		14 03		14 33		15 03		15 33	
Haydons Road	d	10 35		11 05		11 35		12 05		12 35		13 05		13 35		14 05		14 35		15 05		15 35	
Tooting	d	10 38		11 08		11 38		12 08		12 38		13 08		13 38		14 08		14 38		15 08		15 38	
Carshalton	d																						
Hackbridge	d																						
Mitcham Junction	d																						
Mitcham Eastfields	d																						
Streatham 4	d	10 43		11 13		11 43		12 13		12 43		13 13		13 43		14 13		14 43		15 13		15 43	
Tulse Hill 3	d	10 47	10 55	11 17	11 25	11 47	11 55	12 17	12 25	12 47	12 55	13 17	13 25	13 47	13 55	14 17	14 25	14 47	14 55	15 17	15 25	15 47	15 55
North Dulwich	d																						
East Dulwich	d																						
Peckham Rye 4	d																						
Queens Rd Peckham	d																						
South Bermondsey	d																						
London Bridge 4 ⊖	a	10 59		11 29		11 59		12 29		12 59		13 29		13 59		14 29		14 59		15 29		15 59	
Herne Hill 4	d		11 03		11 33		12 03		12 33		13 03		13 33		14 03		14 33		15 03		15 33		16 03
Loughborough Jn	d		11 11		11 41		12 11		12 41		13 11		13 41		14 11		14 41		15 11		15 41		16 11
Elephant & Castle ⊖	d		11 23		11 53		12 23		12 53		13 23		13 53		14 23		14 53		15 23		15 53		16 23
London Blackfriars 3 ⊖	a		11 31		12 01		12 31		13 01		13 31		14 01		14 31		15 01		15 31		16 01		16 31
City Thameslink 3	a																						
Farringdon 3 ⊖	a																						
St Pancras International-2 15 ⊖	a																						
Luton Airport Parkway 7	a																						
Luton 10	a																						

		FC	FC	FC	FC	FC	FC	FC	FC	FC	FC	FC	FC	FC	FC	FC	FC	FC	FC	FC	FC	FC	FC
Sutton (Surrey) 4	d	15 46		16 16		16 46		17 16		17 46		18 16		18 46		19 16		19 46		20 16		20 46	
West Sutton	d	15 49		16 19		16 49		17 19		17 49		18 19		18 49		19 19		19 49		20 19		20 49	
Sutton Common	d	15 51		16 21		16 51		17 21		17 51		18 21		18 51		19 21		19 51		20 21		20 51	
St Helier	d	15 54		16 24		16 54		17 24		17 54		18 24		18 54		19 24		19 54		20 24		20 54	
Morden South	d	15 56		16 26		16 56		17 26		17 56		18 26		18 56		19 26		19 56		20 26		20 56	
South Merton	d	15 58		16 28		16 58		17 28		17 58		18 28		18 58		19 28		19 58		20 28		20 58	
Wimbledon Chase	d	16 00		16 30		17 00		17 30		18 00		18 30		19 00		19 30		20 00		20 30		21 00	
Wimbledon 6 ⊖	a	16 03		16 33		17 03		17 33		18 03		18 33		19 03		19 33		20 03		20 33		21 03	
	d	16 03		16 33		17 03		17 33		18 03		18 33		19 03		19 33		20 03		20 33		21 03	
Haydons Road	d	16 05		16 35		17 05		17 35		18 05		18 35		19 05		19 35		20 05		20 35		21 05	
Tooting	d	16 08		16 38		17 08		17 38		18 08		18 38		19 08		19 38		20 08		20 38		21 08	
Carshalton	d																						
Hackbridge	d																						
Mitcham Junction	d																						
Mitcham Eastfields	d																						
Streatham 4	d	16 13		16 43		17 13		17 43		18 13		18 43		19 13		19 43		20 13		20 43		21 13	
Tulse Hill 3	d	16 17	16 25	16 47	16 55	17 17	17 25	17 47	17 55	18 17	18 25	18 47	18 55	19 17	19 25	19 47	19 55	20 17	20 25	20 47	20 55	21 17	21 25
North Dulwich	d																						
East Dulwich	d																						
Peckham Rye 4	d																						
Queens Rd Peckham	d																						
South Bermondsey	d																						
London Bridge 4 ⊖	a	16 29		16 59		17 29		17 59		18 29		18 59		19 29		19 59		20 29		20 59		21 29	
Herne Hill 4	d		16 33		17 03		17 33		18 03		18 33		19 03		19 33		20 03		20 33		21 03		21 33
Loughborough Jn	d		16 41		17 11		17 41		18 11		18 41		19 11		19 41		20 11		20 41		21 11		21 41
Elephant & Castle ⊖	d		16 53		17 23		17 53		18 23		18 53		19 23		19 53		20 23		20 53		21 23		21 53
London Blackfriars 3 ⊖	a		17 01		17 31		18 01		18 31		19 01		19 31		20 01		20 31		21 01		21 31		22 01
City Thameslink 3	a																						
Farringdon 3 ⊖	a																						
St Pancras International-2 15 ⊖	a																						
Luton Airport Parkway 7	a																						
Luton 10	a																						

Table 179

Sundays

Sutton and Wimbledon - London and Luton via Streatham

		FC		FC
Sutton (Surrey) 4	d	21 16		
West Sutton	d	21 19		
Sutton Common	d	21 21		
St Helier	d	21 24		
Morden South	d	21 26		
South Merton	d	21 28		
Wimbledon Chase	d	21 30		
Wimbledon 6 ⊖ ⇌	a	21 33		
	d	21 33		
Haydons Road	d	21 35		
Tooting	d	21 38		
Carshalton	d			
Hackbridge	d			
Mitcham Junction ⇌	d			
Mitcham Eastfields	d			
Streatham 4	d	21 43		
Tulse Hill 3	d	21 47		21 55
North Dulwich	d			
East Dulwich	d			
Peckham Rye 4	d			
Queens Rd Peckham	d			
South Bermondsey	d			
London Bridge 4 ⊖	a	21 59		
Herne Hill 4	d			22 03
Loughborough Jn	d			22 11
Elephant & Castle ⊖	d			22 23
London Blackfriars 3 ⊖	a			22 31
City Thameslink 3	a			
Farringdon 3 ⊖	a			
St Pancras International-2 15 ⊖	a			
Luton Airport Parkway 7	a			
Luton 10	a			

Table 181

Mondays to Fridays

London and Croydon-Caterham and Tattenham Corner

		SN MX	SN MX	SN MO	SN MX	SN	SN	SN	SN	SN		SN	SN	SN	SN	SN	SN	SN	SN	SN		SN	SN	SN	SN
London Victoria 15 ⊖	d	23p15					06 15						07 20			07 45			08 15				08 43		
Clapham Junction 10	d	23p23					06 23						07 28			07 51			08 23				08 51		
London Bridge 4 ⊖	d		23p36	23p39	00 06	06 06		06 36	06 54			07 06		07 36			08 14	08 06		08 47		08 36		09 06	09 20
New Cross Gate 4 ⊖	d		23p41	23p44	00 11	06 11		06 41	06 59			07 11		07 41				08 11				08 41		09 12	
Norwood Junction 2	d		23p59	00 05	00 30	06 30		07 00	07 18			07 31		08 00			08 27	08 30				09 00		09 30	09 33
East Croydon ⇌	d	23p45	00 03	00 09	00 35	06 34	06 49	07 04	07 22			07 38	07 49	08 04		08 13	08 31	08 34	08 45	09 03		09 07	09 13	09 34	09 37
South Croydon 4	d	23p47	00 06	00 11	00 37	06 36		07 06	07 25			07 40		08 06		08 15		08 36	08 47			09 09	09 15	09 36	
Purley Oaks	d	23p50	00 09	00 14	00 40	06 39		07 09	07 28			07 43		08 09		08 18		08 39	08 50			09 12	09 18	09 39	
Purley 4	a	23p53	00 12	00 17	00 43	06 42	06 56	07 12	07 31	>		07 46	07 55	08 12	>	08 21	08 38	08 42	08 53	09 09		09 15	09 21	09 42	09 45
	d	23p54	00 15	00 18	00 46	06 45	07 00	07 13	07 34	07 36		07 49	07 58	08 16	08 18	08 24	08 39	08 43	08 54	09 11		09 18	09 26	09 43	09 46
Kenley	d		00 18	00 21	00 49	06 48		07 16	07 37			07 52		08 19		08 27		08 46	08 57			09 21	09 29	09 46	
Whyteleafe	d		00 21	00 24	00 52	06 51		07 19	07 40			07 55		08 22		08 30		08 49	09 00			09 24	09 32	09 49	
Whyteleafe South	d		00 23	00 26	00 54	06 53		07 21	07 42			07 57		08 24		08 32		08 51	09 02			09 26	09 34	09 51	
Caterham	a		00 28	00 31	00 59	06 58		07 26	07 48			08 02		08 29		08 37		08 56	09 07			09 31	09 40	09 56	
Reedham	d	23p56					07 02			07 38			08 00		08 20		08 42			09 14					09 48
Smitham	d	23p59					07 05			07 41			08 03		08 23		08 44			09 16					09 51
Woodmansterne	d	00 02					07 08			07 44			08 06		08 26		08 47			09 19					09 54
Chipstead	d	00 05					07 11			07 47			08 09		08 29		08 50			09 22					09 57
Kingswood	d	00 10					07 16			07 52			08 14		08 34		08 56			09 28					10 02
Tadworth	d	00 14					07 20			07 56			08 18		08 38		08 59			09 31					10 06
Tattenham Corner	a	00 17					07 23			07 59			08 21		08 41		09 03			09 36					10 09

		SN	SN	SN	SN	SN		SN	SN	SN	SN	SN	SN	SN	SN	SN	SN	SN	SN	SN	SN	SN	SN	SN	SN
London Victoria 15 ⊖	d	09 13				09 43				10 13				10 43			11 13				11 43			12 13	
Clapham Junction 10	d	09 21				09 51				10 21				10 51			11 21				11 51			12 21	
London Bridge 4 ⊖	d			09 36	09 50			10 06	10 20			10 36	10 50		11 06	11 20			11 36	11 50		12 06	12 20		
New Cross Gate 4 ⊖	d			09 41				10 11				10 41			11 11				11 41			12 11			
Norwood Junction 2	d			10 00	10 03			10 30	10 33			11 00	11 03		11 30	11 33			12 00	12 03		12 30	12 33		
East Croydon ⇌	d	09 43		10 04	10 07	10 13		10 34	10 37	10 43		11 04	11 07	11 13	11 34	11 37	11 43		12 04	12 07	12 13	12 34	12 37	12 43	
South Croydon 4	d	09 45		10 06		10 15		10 36		10 45		11 06		11 15	11 36		11 45		12 06		12 15	12 36		12 45	
Purley Oaks	d	09 48		10 09		10 18		10 39		10 48		11 09		11 18	11 39		11 48		12 09		12 18	12 39		12 48	
Purley 4	a	09 51		10 12	10 15	10 21		10 42	10 45	10 51		11 12	11 15	11 21	11 42	11 45	11 51		12 12	12 15	12 21	12 42	12 45	12 51	
	d	09 52	10 02	10 13	10 16	10 22		10 43	10 46	10 52	11 02	11 13	11 16	11 22	11 43	11 46	11 52	12 02	12 13	12 16	12 22	12 43	12 46	12 52	13 02
Kenley	d	09 55		10 16		10 25		10 46		10 55		11 16		11 25	11 46		11 55		12 16		12 25	12 46		12 55	
Whyteleafe	d	09 58		10 19		10 28		10 49		10 58		11 19		11 28	11 49		11 58		12 19		12 28	12 49		12 58	
Whyteleafe South	d	10 00		10 21		10 30		10 51		11 00		11 21		11 30	11 51		12 00		12 21		12 30	12 51		13 00	
Caterham	a	10 05		10 26		10 35		10 56		11 05		11 26		11 35	11 56		12 05		12 26		12 35	12 56		13 05	
Reedham	d		10 04		10 18				10 48		11 04		11 18			11 48		12 04		12 18			12 48		13 04
Smitham	d		10 07		10 21				10 51		11 07		11 21			11 51		12 07		12 21			12 51		13 07
Woodmansterne	d		10 10		10 24				10 54		11 10		11 24			11 54		12 10		12 24			12 54		13 10
Chipstead	d		10 13		10 27				10 57		11 13		11 27			11 57		12 13		12 27			12 57		13 13
Kingswood	d		10 18		10 32				11 02		11 18		11 32			12 02		12 18		12 32			13 02		13 18
Tadworth	d		10 22		10 36				11 06		11 22		11 36			12 06		12 22		12 36			13 06		13 22
Tattenham Corner	a		10 25		10 39				11 09		11 25		11 39			12 09		12 25		12 39			13 09		13 25

			SN	SN	SN	SN	SN	SN	SN	SN	SN		SN	SN	SN	SN	SN	SN	SN	SN	SN		SN	SN	SN
London Victoria 15 ⊖	d				12 43			13 13					13 43			14 13				14 43				15 13	
Clapham Junction 10	d				12 51			13 21					13 51			14 21				14 51				15 21	
London Bridge 4 ⊖	d		12 36	12 50		13 06	13 20			13 36	13 50			14 06	14 20			14 36	14 50		15 06		15 20		
New Cross Gate 4 ⊖	d		12 41			13 11				13 41				14 11				14 41			15 11				
Norwood Junction 2	d		13 00	13 03		13 30	13 33			14 00	14 03			14 30	14 33			15 00	15 03		15 30		15 33		
East Croydon ⇌	d		13 04	13 07	13 13	13 34	13 37	13 43		14 04	14 07		14 13	14 34	14 37	14 43		15 04	15 07	15 13	15 34		15 37	15 43	
South Croydon 4	d		13 06		13 15	13 36		13 45		14 06			14 15	14 36		14 46		15 06		15 15	15 36			15 46	
Purley Oaks	d		13 09		13 18	13 39		13 48		14 09			14 18	14 39		14 49		15 09		15 18	15 39			15 49	
Purley 4	a		13 12	13 15	13 21	13 42	13 45	13 51		14 12	14 15		14 21	14 42	14 45	14 52		15 12	15 18	15 21	15 42		15 45	15 52	
	d		13 13	13 16	13 22	13 43	13 46	13 52	14 02	14 13	14 16		14 22	14 43	14 46	14 54	15 02	15 13	15 18	15 22	15 43		15 46	15 52	16 02
Kenley	d		13 16		13 25	13 46		13 55		14 16			14 25	14 46		14 57		15 16		15 25	15 46			15 55	
Whyteleafe	d		13 19		13 28	13 49		13 58		14 19			14 28	14 49		15 01		15 19		15 28	15 49			15 59	
Whyteleafe South	d		13 21		13 30	13 51		14 00		14 21			14 30	14 51		15 03		15 21		15 30	15 51			16 01	
Caterham	a		13 26		13 35	13 56		14 05		14 26			14 35	14 56		15 07		15 26		15 35	15 56			16 05	
Reedham	d			13 18			13 48		14 04		14 18				14 48		15 04		15 21				15 48		16 04
Smitham	d			13 21			13 51		14 07		14 21				14 51		15 07		15 23				15 51		16 07
Woodmansterne	d			13 24			13 54		14 10		14 24				14 54		15 10		15 26				15 54		16 10
Chipstead	d			13 27			13 57		14 13		14 27				14 57		15 13		15 29				15 57		16 13
Kingswood	d			13 32			14 02		14 18		14 32				15 02		15 18		15 35				16 02		16 18
Tadworth	d			13 36			14 06		14 22		14 36				15 06		15 22		15 38				16 06		16 22
Tattenham Corner	a			13 39			14 09		14 25		14 39				15 09		15 25		15 42				16 09		16 25

London and Croydon-Caterham and Tattenham Corner

		SN	SN	SN	SN	SN	SN			SN	SN	SN	SN	SN	SN	SN	SN	SN	SN			SN	SN	SN	SN
London Victoria 15 ⊖	d			15 43			16 13			16 39			16 43	17 09				17 39						18 09	
Clapham Junction 10	d			15 51			16 21			16 45			16 51	17 15				17 45						18 15	
London Bridge 4 ⊖	d	15 36	15 50		16 06	16 20					16 48					17 17						17 49			
New Cross Gate 4 ⊖	d	15 41			16 11																				
Norwood Junction 2	d	16 00	16 03		16 30	16 33					17 02					17 31						18 02			
East Croydon	d	16 04	16 07	16 13	16 34	16 37	16 43			16 56	17 06		17 17	17 27		17 35		17 56				18 06		18 28	
South Croydon 4	d	16 06		16 15	16 36		16 45			16 58	17 08		17 19	17 30		17 37		17 58				18 08		18 30	
Purley Oaks	d	16 09		16 18	16 39		16 48			17 01	17 11		17 22	17 33		17 40		18 01				18 11		18 33	
Purley 4	a	16 12	16 15	16 21	16 42	16 45	16 51			17 04	17 14	>	17 25	17 36	>	17 44	>	18 04	>			18 14	>	18 36	>
	d	16 13	16 16	16 24	16 43	16 48	16 52			17 05	17 18	17 22	17 28	17 40	17 42	17 48	17 50	18 08	18 10			18 18	18 21	18 40	18 42
Kenley	d	16 16		16 27	16 46		16 55			17 08	17 21		17 31	17 43		17 51		18 11				18 21		18 43	
Whyteleafe	d	16 19		16 30	16 49		16 58			17 11	17 24		17 34	17 46		17 54		18 14				18 24		18 46	
Whyteleafe South	d	16 21		16 32	16 51		17 00			17 13	17 26		17 36	17 48		17 56		18 16				18 26		18 48	
Caterham	a	16 26		16 37	16 58		17 07			17 20	17 33		17 43	17 55		18 03		18 23				18 33		18 55	
Reedham	d		16 18			16 50						17 24			17 44		17 52		18 12				18 23		18 44
Smitham	d		16 21			16 53						17 27			17 47		17 55		18 15				18 26		18 47
Woodmansterne	d		16 24			16 56						17 30			17 50		17 58		18 18				18 29		18 50
Chipstead	d		16 27			16 59						17 33			17 53		18 01		18 21				18 32		18 53
Kingswood	d		16 32			17 04						17 38			17 58		18 06		18 26				18 37		18 58
Tadworth	d		16 36			17 08						17 42			18 02		18 10		18 30				18 41		19 02
Tattenham Corner	a		16 39			17 11						17 47			18 07		18 15		18 35				18 45		19 07

		SN	SN	SN	SN		SN	SN	SN	SN	SN	SN	SN	SN	SN		SN	SN	SN	SN	SN	SN	SN	SN	SN
London Victoria 15 ⊖	d			18 39					18 45			19 15		19 45			20 15		20 45		21 15		21 45		22 15
Clapham Junction 10	d			18 45					18 53			19 23		19 53			20 23		20 53		21 23		21 53		22 23
London Bridge 4 ⊖	d	18 18					18 49				19 06		19 36		20 06			20 36		21 06		21 36		22 08	
New Cross Gate 4 ⊖	d										19 11		19 41		20 11			20 41		21 11		21 41		22 13	
Norwood Junction 2	d	18 31					19 02				19 30		20 00		20 30			21 00		21 30		22 00		22 32	
East Croydon	d	18 37		18 57			19 06		19 14		19 34	19 44	20 04	20 15	20 34		20 44	21 04	21 14	21 34	21 45	22 04	22 14	22 36	22 45
South Croydon 4	d	18 42		19 00			19 08		19 16		19 36	19 47	20 06	20 17	20 36		20 47	21 06	21 17	21 36	21 47	22 06	22 17	22 38	22 47
Purley Oaks	d	18 45		19 03			19 11		19 19		19 39	19 50	20 09	20 21	20 39		20 50	21 09	21 20	21 39	21 50	22 09	22 20	22 41	22 50
Purley 4	a	18 48	>	19 06	>		19 14	>	19 22	>	19 42	19 53	20 12	20 24	20 42		20 53	21 12	21 23	21 42	21 53	22 12	22 23	22 44	22 53
	d	18 51	18 54	19 10	19 12		19 18	19 21	19 26	19 28	19 45	19 53	20 15	20 24	20 45		20 53	21 15	21 23	21 45	21 54	22 15	22 23	22 47	22 54
Kenley	d	18 54		19 13			19 21		19 29		19 48		20 18		20 48			21 18		21 48		22 18		22 50	
Whyteleafe	d	18 57		19 16			19 24		19 32		19 51		20 21		20 51			21 21		21 51		22 21		22 53	
Whyteleafe South	d	18 59		19 18			19 26		19 34		19 53		20 23		20 53			21 23		21 53		22 23		22 55	
Caterham	a	19 06		19 25			19 33		19 41		19 58		20 28		20 58			21 28		21 58		22 28		23 00	
Reedham	d		18 56		19 14			19 23		19 31		19 56		20 27			20 56		21 26		21 56		22 26		22 56
Smitham	d		18 59		19 17			19 26		19 34		19 58		20 29			20 58		21 28		21 59		22 28		22 59
Woodmansterne	d		19 02		19 20			19 29		19 37		20 01		20 32			21 01		21 31		22 02		22 31		23 02
Chipstead	d		19 05		19 23			19 32		19 40		20 04		20 35			21 04		21 34		22 05		22 34		23 05
Kingswood	d		19 10		19 28			19 37		19 45		20 10		20 41			21 10		21 40		22 10		22 40		23 10
Tadworth	d		19 14		19 32			19 41		19 49		20 13		20 44			21 13		21 43		22 14		22 43		23 14
Tattenham Corner	a		19 19		19 37			19 45		19 52		20 17		20 48			21 17		21 47		22 17		22 47		23 17

		SN	SN	SN	SN	SN
London Victoria 15 ⊖	d		22 45		23 15	
Clapham Junction 10	d		22 53		23 23	
London Bridge 4 ⊖	d	22 38		23 06		23 36
New Cross Gate 4 ⊖	d	22 43		23 11		23 41
Norwood Junction 2	d	23 02		23 30		23 59
East Croydon	d	23 06	23 14	23 34	23 45	00 03
South Croydon 4	d	23 08	23 17	23 36	23 47	00 06
Purley Oaks	d	23 11	23 20	23 39	23 50	00 09
Purley 4	a	23 14	23 23	23 42	23 53	00 12
	d	23 15	23 24	23 45	23 54	00 15
Kenley	d	23 18		23 48		00 18
Whyteleafe	d	23 21		23 51		00 21
Whyteleafe South	d	23 23		23 53		00 23
Caterham	a	23 28		23 58		00 28
Reedham	d		23 26		23 56	
Smitham	d		23 29		23 59	
Woodmansterne	d		23 32		00 02	
Chipstead	d		23 35		00 05	
Kingswood	d		23 40		00 10	
Tadworth	d		23 44		00 14	
Tattenham Corner	a		23 47		00 17	

London and Croydon-Caterham and Tattenham Corner

		SN	SN	SN	SN	SN	SN	SN	SN	SN		SN	SN	SN	SN	SN	SN	SN	SN	SN		SN	SN	SN	SN
London Victoria 15 ⊖	d	23p15						06 43				07 13				07 43			08 13					08 43	
Clapham Junction 10	d	23p23						06 51				07 21				07 51			08 21					08 51	
London Bridge 4 ⊖	d		23p36	00 06		06 36	06 50		07 06	07 20				07 36	07 50		08 06	08 20				08 36	08 50		09 06
New Cross Gate 4 ⊖	d		23p41	00 11		06 41			07 11					07 41			08 11					08 41			09 11
Norwood Junction 2	d		23p59	00 30	06 33	07 00	07 03		07 30	07 33				08 00	08 03		08 30	08 33				09 00	09 03		09 30
East Croydon	d	23p45	00 03	00 34	06 37	07 04	07 07	07 13	07 34	07 37		07 43		08 04	08 07	08 13	08 34	08 37	08 43			09 04	09 07	09 13	09 34
South Croydon 4	d	23p47	00 06	00 36		07 06		07 15	07 36			07 45		08 06		08 15	08 36		08 45			09 06		09 15	09 36
Purley Oaks	d	23p50	00 09	00 39		07 09		07 18	07 39			07 48		08 09		08 18	08 39		08 48			09 09		09 18	09 39
Purley 4	a	23p53	00 12	00 42	06 45	07 12	07 15	07 21	07 42	07 45		07 51		08 12	08 15	08 21	08 42	08 45	08 51			09 12	09 15	09 21	09 42
	d	23p54	00 15	00 45	06 46	07 13	07 16	07 22	07 43	07 46		07 52	08 02	08 13	08 16	08 22	08 43	08 46	08 52	09 02		09 13	09 16	09 22	09 43
Kenley	d		00 18	00 48		07 16		07 25	07 46			07 55		08 16		08 25	08 46		08 55			09 16		09 25	09 46
Whyteleafe	d		00 21	00 51		07 19		07 28	07 49			07 58		08 19		08 28	08 49		08 58			09 19		09 28	09 49
Whyteleafe South	d		00 23	00 53		07 21		07 30	07 51			08 00		08 21		08 30	08 51		09 00			09 21		09 30	09 51
Caterham	a		00 28	00 58		07 26		07 35	07 56			08 05		08 26		08 35	08 56		09 05			09 26		09 35	09 56
Reedham	d	23p56			06 48		07 18			07 48			08 04		08 18			08 48		09 04			09 18		
Smitham	d	23p59			06 51		07 21			07 51			08 07		08 21			08 51		09 07			09 21		
Woodmansterne	d	00 02			06 54		07 24			07 54			08 10		08 24			08 54		09 10			09 24		
Chipstead	d	00 05			06 57		07 27			07 57			08 13		08 27			08 57		09 13			09 27		
Kingswood	d	00 10			07 02		07 32			08 02			08 18		08 32			09 02		09 18			09 32		
Tadworth	d	00 14			07 06		07 36			08 06			08 22		08 36			09 06		09 22			09 36		
Tattenham Corner	a	00 17			07 09		07 39			08 09			08 25		08 39			09 09		09 25			09 39		

		SN	SN	SN	SN	SN		SN	SN	SN	SN	SN	SN	SN	SN	SN		SN	SN	SN	SN	SN	SN	SN	SN
London Victoria 15 ⊖	d		09 13					09 43			10 13				10 43				11 13				11 43		
Clapham Junction 10	d		09 21					09 51			10 21				10 51				11 21				11 51		
London Bridge 4 ⊖	d	09 20			09 36	09 50			10 06	10 20			10 36	10 50		11 06		11 20			11 36	11 50		12 06	12 20
New Cross Gate 4 ⊖	d				09 41				10 11				10 41			11 11					11 41			12 11	
Norwood Junction 2	d	09 33			10 00	10 03			10 30	10 33			11 00	11 03		11 30		11 33			12 00	12 03		12 30	12 33
East Croydon	d	09 37	09 43		10 04	10 07		10 13	10 34	10 37	10 43		11 04	11 07	11 13	11 34		11 37	11 43		12 04	12 07	12 13	12 34	12 37
South Croydon 4	d		09 45		10 06			10 15	10 36		10 45		11 06		11 15	11 36			11 45		12 06		12 15	12 36	
Purley Oaks	d		09 48		10 09			10 18	10 39		10 48		11 09		11 18	11 39			11 48		12 09		12 18	12 39	
Purley 4	a	09 45	09 51		10 12	10 15		10 21	10 42	10 45	10 51		11 12	11 15	11 21	11 42		11 45	11 51		12 12	12 15	12 21	12 42	12 45
	d	09 46	09 52	10 02	10 13	10 16		10 22	10 43	10 46	10 52	11 02	11 13	11 16	11 22	11 43		11 46	11 52	12 02	12 13	12 16	12 22	12 43	12 46
Kenley	d		09 55		10 16			10 25	10 46		10 55		11 16		11 25	11 46			11 55		12 16		12 25	12 46	
Whyteleafe	d		09 58		10 19			10 28	10 49		10 58		11 19		11 28	11 49			11 58		12 19		12 28	12 49	
Whyteleafe South	d		10 00		10 21			10 30	10 51		11 00		11 21		11 30	11 51			12 00		12 21		12 30	12 51	
Caterham	a		10 05		10 26			10 35	10 56		11 05		11 26		11 35	11 56			12 05		12 26		12 35	12 56	
Reedham	d	09 48		10 04		10 18				10 48		11 04		11 18				11 48		12 04		12 18			12 48
Smitham	d	09 51		10 07		10 21				10 51		11 07		11 21				11 51		12 07		12 21			12 51
Woodmansterne	d	09 54		10 10		10 24				10 54		11 10		11 24				11 54		12 10		12 24			12 54
Chipstead	d	09 57		10 13		10 27				10 57		11 13		11 27				11 57		12 13		12 27			12 57
Kingswood	d	10 02		10 18		10 32				11 02		11 18		11 32				12 02		12 18		12 32			13 02
Tadworth	d	10 06		10 22		10 36				11 06		11 22		11 36				12 06		12 22		12 36			13 06
Tattenham Corner	a	10 09		10 25		10 39				11 09		11 25		11 39				12 09		12 25		12 39			13 09

		SN		SN	SN	SN	SN	SN	SN	SN	SN	SN		SN	SN	SN	SN	SN	SN	SN	SN	SN		SN	SN
London Victoria 15 ⊖	d	12 13					12 43			13 13					13 43			14 13				14 43			
Clapham Junction 10	d	12 21					12 51			13 21					13 51			14 21				14 51			
London Bridge 4 ⊖	d				12 36	12 50		13 06	13 20			13 36		13 50		14 06	14 20			14 36	14 50			15 06	15 20
New Cross Gate 4 ⊖	d				12 41			13 11				13 41				14 11				14 41				15 11	
Norwood Junction 2	d				13 00	13 03		13 30	13 33			14 00		14 03		14 30	14 33			15 00	15 03			15 30	15 33
East Croydon	d	12 43			13 04	13 07	13 13	13 34	13 37	13 43		14 04		14 07	14 13	14 34	14 37	14 43		15 04	15 07	15 13		15 34	15 37
South Croydon 4	d	12 45			13 06		13 15	13 36		13 45		14 06			14 15	14 36		14 45		15 06		15 15		15 36	
Purley Oaks	d	12 48			13 09		13 18	13 39		13 48		14 09			14 18	14 39		14 48		15 09		15 18		15 39	
Purley 4	a	12 51			13 12	13 15	13 21	13 42	13 45	13 51		14 12		14 15	14 21	14 42	14 45	14 51		15 12	15 15	15 21		15 42	15 45
	d	12 52		13 02	13 13	13 16	13 22	13 43	13 46	13 52	14 02	14 13		14 16	14 22	14 43	14 46	14 52	15 02	15 13	15 16	15 22		15 43	15 46
Kenley	d	12 55			13 16		13 25	13 46		13 55		14 16			14 25	14 46		14 55		15 16		15 25		15 46	
Whyteleafe	d	12 58			13 19		13 28	13 49		13 58		14 19			14 28	14 49		14 58		15 19		15 28		15 49	
Whyteleafe South	d	13 00			13 21		13 30	13 51		14 00		14 21			14 30	14 51		15 00		15 21		15 30		15 51	
Caterham	a	13 05			13 26		13 35	13 56		14 05		14 26			14 35	14 56		15 05		15 26		15 35		15 56	
Reedham	d			13 04		13 18			13 48		14 04			14 18			14 48		15 04		15 18				15 48
Smitham	d			13 07		13 21			13 51		14 07			14 21			14 51		15 07		15 21				15 51
Woodmansterne	d			13 10		13 24			13 54		14 10			14 24			14 54		15 10		15 24				15 54
Chipstead	d			13 13		13 27			13 57		14 13			14 27			14 57		15 13		15 27				15 57
Kingswood	d			13 18		13 32			14 02		14 18			14 32			15 02		15 18		15 32				16 02
Tadworth	d			13 22		13 36			14 06		14 22			14 36			15 06		15 22		15 36				16 06
Tattenham Corner	a			13 25		13 39			14 09		14 25			14 39			15 09		15 25		15 39				16 09

Table 181

Saturdays

London and Croydon-Caterham and Tattenham Corner

		SN	SN	SN	SN	SN	SN	SN	SN	SN	SN	SN	SN	SN	SN	SN	SN	SN	SN	SN	SN	SN	SN
London Victoria 15 ⊖	d	15 13				15 43			16 13				16 43			17 13				17 43			18 13
Clapham Junction 10	d	15 21				15 51			16 21				16 51			17 21				17 51			18 21
London Bridge 4 ⊖	d			15 36	15 50		16 06	16 20			16 36	16 50		17 06	17 20			17 36	17 50		18 06	18 20	
New Cross Gate 4 ⊖	d			15 41			16 11				16 41			17 11				17 41			18 11		
Norwood Junction 2	d			16 00	16 03		16 30	16 33			17 00	17 03		17 30	17 33			18 00	18 03		18 30	18 33	
East Croydon	d	15 43		16 04	16 07	16 13	16 34	16 37	16 43		17 04	17 07	17 13	17 34	17 37	17 43		18 04	18 07	18 13	18 34	18 37	18 43
South Croydon 4	d	15 45		16 06		16 15	16 36		16 45		17 06		17 15	17 36		17 45		18 06		18 15	18 36		18 45
Purley Oaks	d	15 48		16 09		16 18	16 39		16 48		17 09		17 18	17 39		17 48		18 09		18 18	18 39		18 48
Purley 4	a	15 51		16 12	16 15	16 21	16 42	16 45	16 51		17 12	17 15	17 21	17 42	17 45	17 51		18 12	18 15	18 21	18 42	18 45	18 51
	d	15 52	16 02	16 13	16 16	16 22	16 43	16 46	16 52	17 02	17 13	17 16	17 22	17 43	17 46	17 52	18 02	18 13	18 16	18 22	18 43	18 46	18 52
Kenley	d	15 55		16 16		16 25	16 46		16 55		17 16		17 25	17 46		17 55		18 16		18 25	18 46		18 55
Whyteleafe	d	15 58		16 19		16 28	16 49		16 58		17 19		17 28	17 49		17 58		18 19		18 28	18 49		18 58
Whyteleafe South	d	16 00		16 21		16 30	16 51		17 00		17 21		17 30	17 51		18 00		18 21		18 30	18 51		19 00
Caterham	a	16 05		16 26		16 35	16 56		17 05		17 26		17 35	17 56		18 05		18 26		18 35	18 56		19 05
Reedham	d		16 04		16 18			16 48		17 04		17 18			17 48		18 04		18 18			18 48	
Smitham	d		16 07		16 21			16 51		17 07		17 21			17 51		18 07		18 21			18 51	
Woodmansterne	d		16 10		16 24			16 54		17 10		17 24			17 54		18 10		18 24			18 54	
Chipstead	d		16 13		16 27			16 57		17 13		17 27			17 57		18 13		18 27			18 57	
Kingswood	d		16 18		16 32			17 02		17 18		17 32			18 02		18 18		18 32			19 02	
Tadworth	d		16 22		16 36			17 06		17 22		17 36			18 06		18 22		18 36			19 06	
Tattenham Corner	a		16 25		16 39			17 09		17 25		17 39			18 09		18 25		18 39			19 09	

		SN	SN	SN	SN	SN	SN	SN	SN	SN	SN	SN	SN	SN	SN	SN	SN	SN	SN	SN	SN	SN	SN
London Victoria 15 ⊖	d			18 43		19 15		19 45		20 15		20 45		21 15		21 45		22 15		22 45		23 15	
Clapham Junction 10	d			18 51		19 23		19 53		20 23		20 53		21 23		21 53		22 23		22 53		23 23	
London Bridge 4 ⊖	d	18 36	18 50		19 06		19 36		20 06		20 36		21 06		21 36		22 06		22 36		23 06		23 36
New Cross Gate 4 ⊖	d	18 41			19 11		19 41		20 11		20 41		21 11		21 41		22 11		22 41		23 11		23 41
Norwood Junction 2	d	19 00	19 03		19 30		20 00		20 30		21 00		21 30		22 00		22 30		23 00		23 30		23 59
East Croydon	d	19 04	19 07	19 13	19 34	19 44	20 04	20 14	20 34	20 44	21 04	21 14	21 34	21 44	22 05	22 14	22 36	22 44	23 04	23 14	23 34	23 45	00 03
South Croydon 4	d	19 06		19 15	19 36	19 47	20 06	20 17	20 36	20 47	21 06	21 17	21 36	21 47	22 07	22 17	22 38	22 47	23 06	23 17	23 36	23 47	00 06
Purley Oaks	d	19 09		19 18	19 39	19 50	20 09	20 20	20 39	20 50	21 09	21 20	21 39	21 50	22 10	22 20	22 41	22 50	23 09	23 20	23 39	23 50	00 09
Purley 4	a	19 12	19 15	19 21	19 42	19 53	20 12	20 23	20 42	20 53	21 12	21 23	21 42	21 53	22 13	22 23	22 44	22 53	23 12	23 23	23 42	23 53	00 12
	d	19 13	19 16	19 22	19 45	19 53	20 15	20 23	20 45	20 53	21 15	21 23	21 45	21 53	22 16	22 23	22 47	22 53	23 15	23 24	23 45	23 54	00 15
Kenley	d	19 16		19 25	19 48		20 18		20 48		21 18		21 48		22 19		22 50		23 18		23 48		00 18
Whyteleafe	d	19 19		19 28	19 51		20 21		20 51		21 21		21 51		22 22		22 53		23 21		23 51		00 21
Whyteleafe South	d	19 21		19 30	19 53		20 23		20 53		21 23		21 53		22 24		22 55		23 23		23 53		00 23
Caterham	a	19 26		19 35	19 58		20 28		20 58		21 28		21 58		22 29		23 00		23 28		23 58		00 28
Reedham	d		19 18			19 56		20 26		20 56		21 26		21 56		22 26		22 56		23 26		23 56	
Smitham	d		19 21			19 58		20 28		20 58		21 28		21 58		22 28		22 58		23 29		23 59	
Woodmansterne	d		19 24			20 01		20 31		21 01		21 31		22 01		22 31		23 01		23 32		00 02	
Chipstead	d		19 27			20 04		20 34		21 04		21 34		22 04		22 34		23 04		23 35		00 05	
Kingswood	d		19 32			20 10		20 40		21 10		21 40		22 10		22 40		23 10		23 40		00 10	
Tadworth	d		19 36			20 13		20 43		21 13		21 43		22 13		22 43		23 13		23 44		00 14	
Tattenham Corner	a		19 39			20 17		20 47		21 17		21 47		22 17		22 47		23 17		23 47		00 17	

Table 181

Sundays

London and Croydon-Caterham and Tattenham Corner

		SN	SN	SN	SN	SN	SN	SN	SN	SN	SN	SN	SN	SN	SN	SN	SN	SN	SN	SN	SN	SN	SN
London Victoria 15 ⊖	d	23p15																					
Clapham Junction 10	d	23p23																					
London Bridge 4 ⊖	d		23p36	00 06	07 39	08 09	08 39	09 09	09 39	10 09	10 39	11 09	11 39	12 09	12 39	13 09	13 39	14 09	14 39	15 09	15 39	16 09	16 39
New Cross Gate 4 ⊖	d		23p41	00 11	07 44	08 14	08 44	09 14	09 44	10 14	10 44	11 14	11 44	12 14	12 44	13 14	13 44	14 14	14 44	15 14	15 44	16 14	16 44
Norwood Junction 2	d		23p59	00 30	08 03	08 33	09 03	09 33	10 03	10 33	11 03	11 33	12 03	12 33	13 03	13 33	14 03	14 33	15 03	15 33	16 03	16 33	17 03
East Croydon	d	23p45	00 03	00 34	08 07	08 37	09 07	09 37	10 07	10 37	11 07	11 37	12 07	12 37	13 07	13 37	14 07	14 37	15 07	15 37	16 07	16 37	17 07
South Croydon 4	d	23p47	00 06	00 36	08 09	08 39	09 09	09 39	10 09	10 39	11 09	11 39	12 09	12 39	13 09	13 39	14 09	14 39	15 09	15 39	16 09	16 39	17 09
Purley Oaks	d	23p50	00 09	00 39	08 12	08 42	09 12	09 42	10 12	10 42	11 12	11 42	12 12	12 42	13 12	13 42	14 12	14 42	15 12	15 42	16 12	16 42	17 12
Purley 4	a	23p53	00 12	00 42	08 15	08 45	09 15	09 45	10 15	10 45	11 15	11 45	12 15	12 45	13 15	13 45	14 15	14 45	15 15	15 45	16 15	16 45	17 15
	d	23p54	00 15	00 45	08 16	08 46	09 16	09 46	10 16	10 46	11 16	11 46	12 16	12 46	13 16	13 46	14 16	14 46	15 16	15 46	16 16	16 46	17 16
Kenley	d		00 18	00 48		08 49		09 49		10 49		11 49		12 49		13 49		14 49		15 49		16 49	
Whyteleafe	d		00 21	00 51		08 52		09 52		10 52		11 52		12 52		13 52		14 52		15 52		16 52	
Whyteleafe South	d		00 23	00 53		08 54		09 54		10 54		11 54		12 54		13 54		14 54		15 54		16 54	
Caterham	a		00 28	00 58		08 59		09 59		10 59		11 59		12 59		13 59		14 59		15 59		16 59	
Reedham	d	23p56			08 18		09 18		10 18		11 18		12 18		13 18		14 18		15 18		16 18		17 18
Smitham	d	23p59			08 21		09 21		10 21		11 21		12 21		13 21		14 21		15 21		16 21		17 21
Woodmansterne	d	00 02			08 24		09 24		10 24		11 24		12 24		13 24		14 24		15 24		16 24		17 24
Chipstead	d	00 05			08 27		09 27		10 27		11 27		12 27		13 27		14 27		15 27		16 27		17 27
Kingswood	d	00 10			08 32		09 32		10 32		11 32		12 32		13 32		14 32		15 32		16 32		17 32
Tadworth	d	00 14			08 36		09 36		10 36		11 36		12 36		13 36		14 36		15 36		16 36		17 36
Tattenham Corner	a	00 17			08 39		09 39		10 39		11 39		12 39		13 39		14 39		15 39		16 39		17 39

		SN	SN	SN	SN	SN	SN	SN	SN	SN	SN	SN	SN	SN	SN
London Victoria 15 ⊖	d														
Clapham Junction 10	d														
London Bridge 4 ⊖	d	17 09	17 39	18 09	18 39	19 09	19 39	20 09	20 39	21 09	21 39	22 09	22 39	23 09	23 39
New Cross Gate 4 ⊖	d	17 14	17 44	18 14	18 44	19 14	19 44	20 14	20 44	21 14	21 44	22 14	22 44	23 14	23 44
Norwood Junction 2	d	17 33	18 03	18 33	19 03	19 33	20 03	20 33	21 03	21 33	22 03	22 33	23 03	23 33	00 05
East Croydon	d	17 37	18 07	18 37	19 07	19 37	20 07	20 37	21 07	21 37	22 07	22 37	23 07	23 37	00 09
South Croydon 4	d	17 39	18 09	18 39	19 09	19 39	20 09	20 39	21 09	21 39	22 09	22 39	23 09	23 39	00 11
Purley Oaks	d	17 42	18 12	18 42	19 12	19 42	20 12	20 42	21 12	21 42	22 12	22 42	23 12	23 42	00 14
Purley 4	a	17 45	18 15	18 45	19 15	19 45	20 15	20 45	21 15	21 45	22 15	22 45	23 15	23 45	00 17
	d	17 46	18 16	18 46	19 16	19 46	20 16	20 46	21 16	21 46	22 16	22 46	23 32	23 46	00 18
Kenley	d	17 49		18 49		19 49		20 49		21 49		22 49		23 49	00 21
Whyteleafe	d	17 52		18 52		19 52		20 52		21 52		22 52		23 52	00 24
Whyteleafe South	d	17 54		18 54		19 54		20 54		21 54		22 54		23 54	00 26
Caterham	a	17 59		18 59		19 59		20 59		21 59		22 59		23 59	00 31
Reedham	d		18 18		19 18		20 18		21 18		22 18		23 34		
Smitham	d		18 21		19 21		20 21		21 21		22 21		23 37		
Woodmansterne	d		18 24		19 24		20 24		21 24		22 24		23 40		
Chipstead	d		18 27		19 27		20 27		21 27		22 27		23 43		
Kingswood	d		18 32		19 32		20 32		21 32		22 32		23 48		
Tadworth	d		18 36		19 36		20 36		21 36		22 36		23 52		
Tattenham Corner	a		18 39		19 39		20 39		21 39		22 39		23 55		

Table 181

Mondays to Fridays

Tattenham Corner and Caterham-Croydon and London

		SN	SN	SN	SN	SN	SN	SN	SN	SN		SN	SN	SN	SN	SN	SN	SN	SN	SN	SN	SN	SN	SN	
Tattenham Corner	d		05 56		06 32		06 48		07 02			07 18		07 32		07 48		08 04		08 16		08 27			
Tadworth	d		05 59		06 35		06 51		07 05			07 21		07 35		07 51		08 07		08 19		08 30			
Kingswood	d		06 02		06 38		06 54		07 08			07 24		07 38		07 54		08 10		08 22		08 33			
Chipstead	d		06 08		06 44		07 00		07 14			07 30		07 44		08 00		08 16		08 28		08 39			
Woodmansterne	d		06 11		06 47		07 03		07 17			07 33		07 47		08 03		08 19		08 31		08 42			
Smitham	d		06 14		06 50		07 06		07 20			07 36		07 50		08 06		08 22		08 34		08 45			
Reedham	d		06 16		06 52		07 08		07 22			07 38		07 52		08 08		08 24		08 36		08 47			
Caterham	d	05 52		06 18		06 45		07 01		07 15			07 31		07 45		08 01		08 17		08 29		08 40	08 56	
Whyteleafe South	d	05 55		06 21		06 48		07 04		07 18			07 34		07 48		08 04		08 20		08 32		08 43	08 59	
Whyteleafe	d	05 57		06 23		06 50		07 06		07 20			07 36		07 50		08 06		08 22		08 34		08 45	09 01	
Kenley	d	06 00		06 26		06 53		07 09		07 23			07 39		07 53		08 09		08 25		08 37		08 48	09 04	
Purley 4	a	06 03	06 19	06 29	06 55	06 57	07 11	07 13	07 25	07 27		07 41	07 43	07 55	07 57	08 11	08 13	08 27	08 29	08 39	08 41	08 50	08 52	09 07	
	d	06 04	06 22	06 30	07 01	<	07 17	<	07 31	<		07 47	<	08 01	<	08 17	<	08 33	<	08 45	<	08 56	<	09 08	
Purley Oaks	d	06 07	06 25	06 33	07 04		07 20		07 34			07 50		08 04		08 20		08 36		08 48		08 59		09 11	
South Croydon 4	d	06 10	06 28	06 36	07 07		07 23		07 37			07 53		08 07		08 23		08 39		08 51		09 02		09 14	
East Croydon	⇌ d	06 13	06 31	06 39	07 10		07 26		07 40			07 56		08 10		08 26		08 42		08 54		09 05		09 17	
Norwood Junction 2	d	06 18	06 37	06 43	07 14				07 44					08 14				08 47				09 09			
New Cross Gate 4	⊖ a	06 35																							
London Bridge 4	⊖ a	06 42	06 49	06 55	07 28				07 58					08 28				09 01				09 23			
Clapham Junction 10	a						07 36					08 06				08 36				09 04				09 38	
London Victoria 15	⊖ a						07 46					08 15				08 45				09 13				09 48	

		SN	SN	SN	SN	SN		SN	SN	SN	SN	SN	SN	SN	SN	SN		SN	SN	SN	SN	SN	SN	SN	SN
Tattenham Corner	d	08 51			09 21			09 33		09 49			10 21		10 33			10 51			11 21		11 33		11 51
Tadworth	d	08 54			09 24			09 36		09 52			10 24		10 36			10 54			11 24		11 36		11 54
Kingswood	d	08 57			09 27			09 39		09 55			10 27		10 39			10 57			11 27		11 39		11 57
Chipstead	d	09 03			09 33			09 45		10 01			10 33		10 45			11 03			11 33		11 45		12 03
Woodmansterne	d	09 06			09 36			09 48		10 04			10 36		10 48			11 06			11 36		11 48		12 06
Smitham	d	09 09			09 39			09 51		10 07			10 39		10 51			11 09			11 39		11 51		12 09
Reedham	d	09 11			09 41			09 53		10 09			10 41		10 53			11 11			11 41		11 53		12 11
Caterham	d		09 09	09 26		09 37			09 56		10 09	10 26		10 39		10 56			11 09	11 26		11 39		11 56	
Whyteleafe South	d		09 12	09 29		09 40			09 59		10 12	10 29		10 42		10 59			11 12	11 29		11 42		11 59	
Whyteleafe	d		09 14	09 31		09 42			10 01		10 14	10 31		10 44		11 01			11 14	11 31		11 44		12 01	
Kenley	d		09 17	09 34		09 45			10 04		10 17	10 34		10 47		11 04			11 17	11 34		11 47		12 04	
Purley 4	a	09 14	09 20	09 37	09 44	09 48		09 56	10 07	10 12	10 20	10 37	10 44	10 50	10 56	11 07		11 14	11 20	11 37	11 44	11 50	11 56	12 07	12 14
	d	09 14	09 21	09 38	09 45	09 51			10 08	10 15	10 21	10 38	10 45	10 51		11 08		11 15	11 21	11 38	11 45	11 51		12 08	12 15
Purley Oaks	d		09 24	09 41		09 54			10 11		10 24	10 41		10 54		11 11			11 24	11 41		11 54		12 11	
South Croydon 4	d		09 27	09 44		09 57			10 14		10 27	10 44		10 57		11 14			11 27	11 44		11 57		12 14	
East Croydon	⇌ d	09 20	09 30	09 47	09 51	10 00			10 17	10 21	10 30	10 47	10 51	11 00		11 17		11 21	11 30	11 47	11 51	12 00		12 17	12 21
Norwood Junction 2	d	09 25	09 35		09 55	10 05				10 25	10 35		10 55	11 05				11 26	11 35		11 55	12 05			12 25
New Cross Gate 4	⊖ a	09 32	09 52			10 22					10 52			11 22					11 52			12 22			
London Bridge 4	⊖ a	09 42	10 01		10 09	10 29				10 39	10 59		11 09	11 29				11 39	11 59		12 09	12 29			12 39
Clapham Junction 10	a			10 07					10 37			11 07				11 37				12 07				12 37	
London Victoria 15	⊖ a			10 16					10 46			11 16				11 46				12 16				12 46	

		SN		SN	SN	SN	SN	SN	SN	SN	SN	SN		SN	SN	SN	SN	SN	SN	SN	SN	SN		SN	SN
Tattenham Corner	d				12 21		12 33		12 51			13 21			13 33		13 51			14 21		14 33			14 51
Tadworth	d				12 24		12 36		12 54			13 24			13 36		13 54			14 24		14 36			14 54
Kingswood	d				12 27		12 39		12 57			13 27			13 39		13 57			14 27		14 39			14 57
Chipstead	d				12 33		12 45		13 03			13 33			13 45		14 03			14 33		14 45			15 03
Woodmansterne	d				12 36		12 48		13 06			13 36			13 48		14 06			14 36		14 48			15 06
Smitham	d				12 39		12 51		13 09			13 39			13 51		14 09			14 39		14 51			15 09
Reedham	d				12 41		12 53		13 11			13 41			13 53		14 11			14 41		14 53			15 11
Caterham	d	12 09		12 26		12 39		12 56		13 09	13 26			13 39		13 56		14 09	14 26		14 39			14 56	
Whyteleafe South	d	12 12		12 29		12 42		12 59		13 12	13 29			13 42		13 59		14 12	14 29		14 42			14 59	
Whyteleafe	d	12 14		12 31		12 44		13 01		13 14	13 31			13 44		14 01		14 14	14 31		14 44			15 01	
Kenley	d	12 17		12 34		12 47		13 04		13 17	13 34			13 47		14 04		14 17	14 34		14 47			15 04	
Purley 4	a	12 20		12 37	12 44	12 50	12 56	13 07	13 14	13 20	13 37	13 44		13 50	13 56	14 07	14 14	14 20	14 37	14 44	14 50	14 56		15 07	15 14
	d	12 21		12 38	12 45	12 51		13 08	13 15	13 21	13 38	13 45		13 51		14 08	14 15	14 21	14 38	14 45	14 51			15 08	15 15
Purley Oaks	d	12 24		12 41		12 54		13 11		13 24	13 41			13 54		14 11		14 24	14 41		14 54			15 11	
South Croydon 4	d	12 27		12 44		12 57		13 14		13 27	13 44			13 57		14 14		14 27	14 44		14 57			15 14	
East Croydon	⇌ d	12 30		12 47	12 51	13 00		13 17	13 21	13 30	13 47	13 51		14 00		14 17	14 21	14 30	14 47	14 51	15 00			15 17	15 21
Norwood Junction 2	d	12 35			12 55	13 05			13 25	13 35		13 55		14 05			14 25	14 35		14 55	15 05				15 25
New Cross Gate 4	⊖ a	12 52				13 22				13 52				14 22				14 52			15 22				
London Bridge 4	⊖ a																								
London Bridge 4	⊖ a	12 59			13 09	13 29			13 39	13 59		14 09		14 29			14 39	14 59		15 09	15 29				15 39
Clapham Junction 10	a			13 07				13 37			14 07					14 37			15 07					15 37	
London Victoria 15	⊖ a			13 16				13 46			14 16					14 46			15 16					15 46	

Table 181

Mondays to Fridays

Tattenham Corner and Caterham-Croydon and London

		SN	SN	SN	SN	SN	SN	SN		SN	SN	SN	SN	SN	SN	SN	SN	SN		SN	SN	SN	SN	SN	SN
Tattenham Corner	d			15 21		15 33		15 51				16 21		16 33		16 51				17 19			17 51		18 12
Tadworth	d			15 24		15 36		15 54				16 24		16 36		16 54				17 22			17 54		18 15
Kingswood	d			15 27		15 39		15 57				16 27		16 39		16 57				17 25			17 57		18 18
Chipstead	d			15 33		15 45		16 03				16 33		16 45		17 03				17 31			18 03		18 24
Woodmansterne	d			15 36		15 48		16 06				16 36		16 48		17 06				17 34			18 06		18 27
Smitham	d			15 39		15 51		16 09				16 39		16 51		17 09				17 37			18 09		18 30
Reedham	d			15 41		15 53		16 11				16 41		16 53		17 11				17 39			18 11		18 32
Caterham	d	15 09	15 26		15 39		15 56			16 09	16 26		16 39		16 52		17 09	17 26			17 45	17 56		18 09	
Whyteleafe South	d	15 12	15 29		15 42		15 59			16 12	16 29		16 42		16 55		17 12	17 29			17 48	17 59		18 12	
Whyteleafe	d	15 14	15 31		15 44		16 01			16 14	16 31		16 44		16 57		17 14	17 31			17 50	18 01		18 14	
Kenley	d	15 17	15 34		15 47		16 04			16 17	16 34		16 47		17 00		17 17	17 34			17 53	18 04		18 17	
Purley 4	a	15 20	15 37	15 44	15 50	15 56	16 07	16 14		16 20	16 37	16 44	16 50	16 56	17 04	17 14	17 20	17 37		17 42	17 56	18 07	18 14	18 20	18 35
	d	15 21	15 38	15 45	15 51		16 08	16 15		16 21	16 38	16 45	16 51	17 08	<	17 15	17 21	17 38		17 45	17 59	18 08	18 15	18 21	18 37
Purley Oaks	d	15 24	15 41		15 54		16 11			16 24	16 41		16 54	17 11			17 24	17 41			18 02	18 11		18 24	18 40
South Croydon 4	d	15 27	15 44		15 57		16 14			16 27	16 44		16 57	17 14			17 27	17 44			18 05	18 14		18 27	18 44
East Croydon	⇌ d	15 30	15 47	15 51	16 00		16 17	16 21		16 30	16 47	16 51	17 00	17 17		17 21	17 30	17 47		17 51	18 08	18 17	18 21	18 30	18 47
Norwood Junction 2	d	15 35		15 55	16 05			16 25		16 35		16 55	17 05			17 25	17 35			17 55	18 12		18 29	18 35	
New Cross Gate 4	⊖ a	15 52			16 22					16 52			17 22				17 52							18 52	
London Bridge 4	⊖ a	15 59		16 09	16 29			16 39		17 00		17 08	17 30			17 37	17 59			18 09	18 26		18 41	18 59	
Clapham Junction 10	a		16 07				16 37				17 07			17 37				18 07				18 39			19 08
London Victoria 15	⊖ a		16 16				16 46				17 16			17 48				18 16				18 46			19 15

		SN	SN	SN		SN	SN	SN	SN	SN	SN	SN	SN	SN		SN	SN	SN	SN	SN	SN	SN	SN		
Tattenham Corner	d		18 42			19 14		19 42	19 53		20 12		20 42			21 12		21 42		22 12		22 42			
Tadworth	d		18 45			19 17		19 45	19 56		20 15		20 45			21 15		21 45		22 15		22 45			
Kingswood	d		18 48			19 20		19 48	19 59		20 18		20 48			21 18		21 48		22 18		22 48			
Chipstead	d		18 54			19 26		19 54	20 05		20 24		20 54			21 24		21 54		22 24		22 54			
Woodmansterne	d		18 57			19 29		19 57	20 08		20 27		20 57			21 27		21 57		22 27		22 57			
Smitham	d		19 00			19 32		20 00	20 11		20 30		21 00			21 30		22 00		22 30		23 00			
Reedham	d		19 02			19 34		20 02	20 13		20 32		21 02			21 32		22 02		22 32		23 02			
Caterham	d	18 39		19 09			19 39			20 08		20 37		21 07			21 39		22 09		22 38		23 20		
Whyteleafe South	d	18 42		19 12			19 42			20 11		20 40		21 10			21 42		22 12		22 41		23 23		
Whyteleafe	d	18 44		19 14			19 44			20 13		20 42		21 12			21 44		22 14		22 43		23 25		
Kenley	d	18 47		19 17			19 47			20 16		20 45		21 15			21 47		22 17		22 46		23 28		
Purley 4	a	18 50	19 05	19 20		19 37	19 50	20 05	20 16	20 19	20 35	20 48	21 05	21 18		21 35	21 50	22 05	22 20	22 35	22 49	23 05	23 31		
	d	18 51	19 08	19 21		19 38	19 51	20 08		20 22	20 38	20 51	21 08	21 21		21 38	21 51	22 08	22 21	22 38	22 52	23 08	23 34		
Purley Oaks	d	18 54	19 11	19 24		19 41	19 54	20 11		20 25	20 41	20 54	21 11	21 24		21 41	21 54	22 11	22 24	22 41	22 55	23 11	23 37		
South Croydon 4	d	18 57	19 14	19 27		19 44	19 57	20 14		20 28	20 44	20 57	21 14	21 27		21 44	21 57	22 14	22 27	22 44	22 58	23 14	23 40		
East Croydon	⇌ d	19 00	19 17	19 30		19 47	20 00	20 17		20 31	20 47	21 00	21 17	21 30		21 47	22 00	22 17	22 30	22 47	23 01	23 17	23 43		
Norwood Junction 2	d	19 05		19 35			20 05			20 35		21 05		21 35			22 05		22 35		23 06		23a47		
New Cross Gate 4	⊖ a	19 22		19 52			20 22			20 52		21 22		21 52			22 22		22 52		23 23				
London Bridge 4	⊖ a	19 29		19 59			20 29			20 59		21 29		21 59			22 29		22 59		23 30				
Clapham Junction 10	a		19 37			20 07		20 37			21 07		21 37			22 07		22 37		23 07		23 37			
London Victoria 15	⊖ a		19 48			20 18		20 46			21 18		21 46			22 16		22 48		23 18		23 46			

Saturdays

		SN	SN	SN	SN	SN	SN	SN	SN	SN		SN	SN	SN	SN	SN	SN	SN	SN	SN		SN	SN	SN	SN
Tattenham Corner	d		06 12		06 42			07 21				07 51			08 21		08 35		08 51				09 21		09 33
Tadworth	d		06 15		06 45			07 24				07 54			08 24		08 38		08 54				09 24		09 36
Kingswood	d		06 18		06 48			07 27				07 57			08 27		08 41		08 57				09 27		09 39
Chipstead	d		06 24		06 54			07 33				08 03			08 33		08 47		09 03				09 33		09 45
Woodmansterne	d		06 27		06 57			07 36				08 06			08 36		08 50		09 06				09 36		09 48
Smitham	d		06 30		07 00			07 39				08 09			08 39		08 53		09 09				09 39		09 51
Reedham	d		06 32		07 02			07 41				08 11			08 41		08 55		09 11				09 41		09 53
Caterham	d	06 07		06 39		07 09	07 26		07 39	07 56			08 09	08 26		08 39		08 56		09 09		09 26		09 39	
Whyteleafe South	d	06 10		06 42		07 12	07 29		07 42	07 59			08 12	08 29		08 42		08 59		09 12		09 29		09 42	
Whyteleafe	d	06 12		06 44		07 14	07 31		07 44	08 01			08 14	08 31		08 44		09 01		09 14		09 31		09 44	
Kenley	d	06 15		06 47		07 17	07 34		07 47	08 04			08 17	08 34		08 47		09 04		09 17		09 34		09 47	
Purley 4	a	06 18	06 35	06 50	07 05	07 20	07 37	07 44	07 50	08 07		08 14	08 20	08 37	08 44	08 50	08 58	09 07	09 14	09 20		09 37	09 44	09 50	09 56
	d	06 21	06 38	06 51	07 08	07 21	07 38	07 45	07 51	08 08		08 15	08 21	08 38	08 45	08 51		09 08	09 15	09 21		09 38	09 45	09 51	
Purley Oaks	d	06 24	06 41	06 54	07 11	07 24	07 41		07 54	08 11			08 24	08 41		08 54		09 11		09 24		09 41		09 54	
South Croydon 4	d	06 27	06 44	06 57	07 14	07 27	07 44		07 57	08 14			08 27	08 44		08 57		09 14		09 27		09 44		09 57	
East Croydon	⇌ d	06 30	06 47	07 00	07 17	07 30	07 47	07 51	08 00	08 17		08 21	08 30	08 47	08 51	09 00		09 17	09 21	09 30		09 47	09 51	10 00	
Norwood Junction 2	d	06 35		07 05		07 35		07 55	08 05			08 25	08 35		08 55	09 05			09 25	09 35			09 55	10 05	
New Cross Gate 4	⊖ a	06 52		07 22		07 52			08 22				08 52			09 22				09 52				10 22	
London Bridge 4	⊖ a	06 59		07 29		07 59		08 09	08 29			08 39	08 59		09 09	09 29			09 39	09 59			10 09	10 29	
Clapham Junction 10	a		07 07		07 37		08 07			08 37				09 07				09 37				10 07			
London Victoria 15	⊖ a		07 16		07 46		08 16			08 46				09 16				09 46				10 16			

Table 181

Saturdays

Tattenham Corner and Caterham-Croydon and London

		SN	SN	SN	SN	SN	SN	SN	SN	SN	SN	SN	SN	SN	SN	SN	SN	SN	SN	SN	SN	SN	SN
Tattenham Corner	d		09 51			10 21		10 33		10 51			11 21		11 33		11 51			12 21		12 33	
Tadworth	d		09 54			10 24		10 36		10 54			11 24		11 36		11 54			12 24		12 36	
Kingswood	d		09 57			10 27		10 39		10 57			11 27		11 39		11 57			12 27		12 39	
Chipstead	d		10 03			10 33		10 45		11 03			11 33		11 45		12 03			12 33		12 45	
Woodmansterne	d		10 06			10 36		10 48		11 06			11 36		11 48		12 06			12 36		12 48	
Smitham	d		10 09			10 39		10 51		11 09			11 39		11 51		12 09			12 39		12 51	
Reedham	d		10 11			10 41		10 53		11 11			11 41		11 53		12 11			12 41		12 53	
Caterham	d	09 56		10 09	10 26		10 39		10 56		11 09	11 26		11 39		11 56		12 09	12 26		12 39		12 56
Whyteleafe South	d	09 59		10 12	10 29		10 42		10 59		11 12	11 29		11 42		11 59		12 12	12 29		12 42		12 59
Whyteleafe	d	10 01		10 14	10 31		10 44		11 01		11 14	11 31		11 44		12 01		12 14	12 31		12 44		13 01
Kenley	d	10 04		10 17	10 34		10 47		11 04		11 17	11 34		11 47		12 04		12 17	12 34		12 47		13 04
Purley 4	a	10 07	10 14	10 20	10 37	10 44	10 50	10 56	11 07	11 14	11 20	11 37	11 44	11 50	11 56	12 07	12 14	12 20	12 37	12 44	12 50	12 56	13 07
	d	10 08	10 15	10 21	10 38	10 45	10 51		11 08	11 15	11 21	11 38	11 45	11 51		12 08	12 15	12 21	12 38	12 45	12 51		13 08
Purley Oaks	d	10 11		10 24	10 41		10 54		11 11		11 24	11 41		11 54		12 11		12 24	12 41		12 54		13 11
South Croydon 4	d	10 14		10 27	10 44		10 57		11 14		11 27	11 44		11 57		12 14		12 27	12 44		12 57		13 14
East Croydon	d	10 17	10 21	10 30	10 47	10 51	11 00		11 17	11 21	11 30	11 47	11 51	12 00		12 17	12 21	12 30	12 47	12 51	13 00		13 17
Norwood Junction 2	d		10 25	10 35		10 55	11 05			11 25	11 35		11 55	12 05			12 25	12 35		12 55	13 05		
New Cross Gate 4 ⊖	a			10 52			11 22				11 52			12 22				12 52			13 22		
London Bridge 4 ⊖	a		10 39	10 59		11 09	11 29			11 39	11 59		12 09	12 29			12 39	12 59		13 09	13 29		
Clapham Junction 10	a	10 37			11 07				11 37			12 07				12 37			13 07				13 37
London Victoria 15 ⊖	a	10 46			11 16				11 46			12 16				12 46			13 16				13 46

		SN	SN	SN	SN	SN	SN	SN	SN	SN	SN	SN	SN	SN	SN	SN	SN	SN	SN	SN	SN	SN
Tattenham Corner	d	12 51			13 21		13 33		13 51			14 21		14 33		14 51			15 21		15 33	
Tadworth	d	12 54			13 24		13 36		13 54			14 24		14 36		14 54			15 24		15 36	
Kingswood	d	12 57			13 27		13 39		13 57			14 27		14 39		14 57			15 27		15 39	
Chipstead	d	13 03			13 33		13 45		14 03			14 33		14 45		15 03			15 33		15 45	
Woodmansterne	d	13 06			13 36		13 48		14 06			14 36		14 48		15 06			15 36		15 48	
Smitham	d	13 09			13 39		13 51		14 09			14 39		14 51		15 09			15 39		15 51	
Reedham	d	13 11			13 41		13 53		14 11			14 41		14 53		15 11			15 41		15 53	
Caterham	d		13 09	13 26		13 39		13 56		14 09	14 26		14 39		14 56		15 09	15 26		15 39		15 56
Whyteleafe South	d		13 12	13 29		13 42		13 59		14 12	14 29		14 42		14 59		15 12	15 29		15 42		15 59
Whyteleafe	d		13 14	13 31		13 44		14 01		14 14	14 31		14 44		15 01		15 14	15 31		15 44		16 01
Kenley	d		13 17	13 34		13 47		14 04		14 17	14 34		14 47		15 04		15 17	15 34		15 47		16 04
Purley 4	a	13 14	13 20	13 37	13 44	13 50	13 56	14 07	14 14	14 20	14 37	14 44	14 50	14 56	15 07	15 14	15 20	15 37	15 44	15 50	15 56	16 07
	d	13 15	13 21	13 38	13 45	13 51		14 08	14 15	14 21	14 38	14 45	14 51		15 08	15 15	15 21	15 38	15 45	15 51		16 08
Purley Oaks	d		13 24	13 41		13 54		14 11		14 24	14 41		14 54		15 11		15 24	15 41		15 54		16 11
South Croydon 4	d		13 27	13 44		13 57		14 14		14 27	14 44		14 57		15 14		15 27	15 44		15 57		16 14
East Croydon	d	13 21	13 30	13 47	13 51	14 00		14 17	14 21	14 30	14 47	14 51	15 00		15 17	15 21	15 30	15 47	15 51	16 00		16 17
Norwood Junction 2	d	13 25	13 35		13 55	14 05			14 25	14 35		14 55	15 05			15 25	15 35		15 55	16 05		
New Cross Gate 4 ⊖	a		13 52			14 22				14 52			15 22				15 52			16 22		
London Bridge 4 ⊖	a	13 39	13 59		14 09	14 29			14 39	14 59		15 09	15 29			15 39	15 59		16 09	16 29		
Clapham Junction 10	a			14 07				14 37			15 07				15 37			16 07				16 37
London Victoria 15 ⊖	a			14 16				14 46			15 16				15 46			16 16				16 46

		SN	SN	SN	SN	SN	SN	SN	SN	SN	SN	SN	SN	SN	SN	SN	SN	SN	SN	SN	SN	SN	SN
Tattenham Corner	d	15 51			16 21		16 33		16 51			17 21		17 33		17 51			18 21		18 31	18 42	
Tadworth	d	15 54			16 24		16 36		16 54			17 24		17 36		17 54			18 24		18 34	18 45	
Kingswood	d	15 57			16 27		16 39		16 57			17 27		17 39		17 57			18 27		18 37	18 48	
Chipstead	d	16 03			16 33		16 45		17 03			17 33		17 45		18 03			18 33		18 43	18 54	
Woodmansterne	d	16 06			16 36		16 48		17 06			17 36		17 48		18 06			18 36		18 46	18 57	
Smitham	d	16 09			16 39		16 51		17 09			17 39		17 51		18 09			18 39		18 49	19 00	
Reedham	d	16 11			16 41		16 53		17 11			17 41		17 53		18 11			18 41		18 51	19 02	
Caterham	d		16 09	16 26		16 39		16 56		17 09	17 26		17 39		17 56		18 09	18 26		18 39			19 09
Whyteleafe South	d		16 12	16 29		16 42		16 59		17 12	17 29		17 42		17 59		18 12	18 29		18 42			19 12
Whyteleafe	d		16 14	16 31		16 44		17 01		17 14	17 31		17 44		18 01		18 14	18 31		18 44			19 14
Kenley	d		16 17	16 34		16 47		17 04		17 17	17 34		17 47		18 04		18 17	18 34		18 47			19 17
Purley 4	a	16 14	16 20	16 37	16 44	16 50	16 56	17 07	17 14	17 20	17 37	17 44	17 50	17 56	18 07	18 14	18 20	18 37	18 44	18 50	18 54	19 05	19 20
	d	16 15	16 21	16 38	16 45	16 51		17 08	17 15	17 21	17 38	17 45	17 51		18 08	18 15	18 21	18 38	18 45	18 51		19 08	19 21
Purley Oaks	d		16 24	16 41		16 54		17 11		17 24	17 41		17 54		18 11		18 24	18 41		18 54		19 11	19 24
South Croydon 4	d		16 27	16 44		16 57		17 14		17 27	17 44		17 57		18 14		18 27	18 44		18 57		19 14	19 27
East Croydon	d	16 21	16 30	16 47	16 51	17 00		17 17	17 21	17 30	17 47	17 51	18 00		18 17	18 21	18 30	18 47	18 51	19 00		19 17	19 30
Norwood Junction 2	d	16 25	16 35		16 55	17 05			17 25	17 35		17 55	18 05			18 25	18 35		18 55	19 05			19 35
New Cross Gate 4 ⊖	a		16 52			17 22				17 52			18 22				18 52			19 22			19 52
London Bridge 4 ⊖	a	16 39	16 59		17 09	17 30			17 39	17 59		18 09	18 29			18 39	18 59		19 09	19 29			19 59
Clapham Junction 10	a			17 07				17 38			18 07				18 37			19 07				19 37	
London Victoria 15 ⊖	a			17 16				17 47			18 16				18 46			19 16				19 46	

Table 181

Saturdays

Tattenham Corner and Caterham-Croydon and London

		SN	SN	SN	SN	SN	SN	SN	SN	SN	SN	SN	SN	SN	SN	SN	SN
Tattenham Corner	d	19 12		19 42		20 12		20 42		21 12		21 42		22 12		22 42	
Tadworth	d	19 15		19 45		20 15		20 45		21 15		21 45		22 15		22 45	
Kingswood	d	19 18		19 48		20 18		20 48		21 18		21 48		22 18		22 48	
Chipstead	d	19 24		19 54		20 24		20 54		21 24		21 54		22 24		22 54	
Woodmansterne	d	19 27		19 57		20 27		20 57		21 27		21 57		22 27		22 57	
Smitham	d	19 30		20 00		20 30		21 00		21 30		22 00		22 30		23 00	
Reedham	d	19 32		20 02		20 32		21 02		21 32		22 02		22 32		23 02	
Caterham	d		19 39		20 09		20 37		21 07		21 37		22 07		22 38		23 20
Whyteleafe South	d		19 42		20 12		20 40		21 10		21 40		22 10		22 41		23 23
Whyteleafe	d		19 44		20 14		20 42		21 12		21 42		22 12		22 43		23 25
Kenley	d		19 47		20 17		20 45		21 15		21 45		22 15		22 46		23 28
Purley 4	a	19 35	19 50	20 05	20 20	20 35	20 48	21 05	21 18	21 35	21 48	22 05	22 18	22 35	22 49	23 05	23 31
	d	19 38	19 51	20 08	20 21	20 38	20 51	21 08	21 21	21 38	21 51	22 08	22 21	22 38	22 52	23 08	23 34
Purley Oaks	d	19 41	19 54	20 11	20 24	20 41	20 54	21 11	21 24	21 41	21 54	22 11	22 24	22 41	22 55	23 11	23 37
South Croydon 4	d	19 44	19 57	20 14	20 27	20 44	20 57	21 14	21 27	21 44	21 57	22 14	22 27	22 44	22 58	23 14	23 40
East Croydon	d	19 47	20 00	20 17	20 30	20 47	21 00	21 17	21 30	21 47	22 00	22 17	22 30	22 47	23 01	23 17	23 43
Norwood Junction 2	d		20 05		20 35		21 05		21 35		22 05		22 35		23 06		23a47
New Cross Gate 4 ⊖	a		20 22		20 52		21 22		21 52		22 22		22 52		23 23		
London Bridge 4 ⊖	a		20 29		20 59		21 29		21 59		22 29		22 59		23 30		
Clapham Junction 10	a	20 07		20 37		21 07		21 37		22 07		22 37		23 07		23 37	
London Victoria 15 ⊖	a	20 16		20 46		21 16		21 46		22 16		22 46		23 18		23 46	

Sundays

		SN	SN	SN	SN	SN	SN	SN	SN	SN	SN	SN	SN	SN	SN	SN	SN	SN	SN	SN	SN	SN	SN
Tattenham Corner	d		07 45		08 45		09 45		10 45		11 45		12 45		13 45		14 45		15 45		16 45		17 45
Tadworth	d		07 48		08 48		09 48		10 48		11 48		12 48		13 48		14 48		15 48		16 48		17 48
Kingswood	d		07 51		08 51		09 51		10 51		11 51		12 51		13 51		14 51		15 51		16 51		17 51
Chipstead	d		07 57		08 57		09 57		10 57		11 57		12 57		13 57		14 57		15 57		16 57		17 57
Woodmansterne	d		08 00		09 00		10 00		11 00		12 00		13 00		14 00		15 00		16 00		17 00		18 00
Smitham	d		08 03		09 03		10 03		11 03		12 03		13 03		14 03		15 03		16 03		17 03		18 03
Reedham	d		08 05		09 05		10 05		11 05		12 05		13 05		14 05		15 05		16 05		17 05		18 05
Caterham	d	07 24		08 26		09 26		10 26		11 26		12 26		13 26		14 26		15 26		16 26		17 26	
Whyteleafe South	d	07 27		08 29		09 29		10 29		11 29		12 29		13 29		14 29		15 29		16 29		17 29	
Whyteleafe	d	07 29		08 31		09 31		10 31		11 31		12 31		13 31		14 31		15 31		16 31		17 31	
Kenley	d	07 32		08 34		09 34		10 34		11 34		12 34		13 34		14 34		15 34		16 34		17 34	
Purley 4	a	07 35	08 08	08 37	09 08	09 37	10 08	10 37	11 08	11 37	12 08	12 37	13 08	13 37	14 08	14 37	15 08	15 37	16 08	16 37	17 08	17 37	18 08
	d	07 38	08 08	08 38	09 08	09 38	10 08	10 38	11 08	11 38	12 08	12 38	13 08	13 38	14 08	14 38	15 08	15 38	16 08	16 38	17 08	17 38	18 08
Purley Oaks	d	07 41	08 11	08 41	09 11	09 41	10 11	10 41	11 11	11 41	12 11	12 41	13 11	13 41	14 11	14 41	15 11	15 41	16 11	16 41	17 11	17 41	18 11
South Croydon 4	d	07 44	08 14	08 44	09 14	09 44	10 14	10 44	11 14	11 44	12 14	12 44	13 14	13 44	14 14	14 44	15 14	15 44	16 14	16 44	17 14	17 44	18 14
East Croydon	d	07 47	08 17	08 47	09 17	09 47	10 17	10 47	11 17	11 47	12 17	12 47	13 17	13 47	14 17	14 47	15 17	15 47	16 17	16 47	17 17	17 47	18 17
Norwood Junction 2	d	07 52	08 22	08 52	09 22	09 52	10 22	10 52	11 22	11 52	12 22	12 52	13 22	13 52	14 22	14 52	15 22	15 52	16 22	16 52	17 22	17 52	18 22
New Cross Gate 4 ⊖	a	08 09	08 39	09 09	09 39	10 09	10 39	11 09	11 39	12 09	12 39	13 09	13 39	14 09	14 39	15 09	15 39	16 09	16 39	17 09	17 39	18 09	18 39
London Bridge-I 4 ⊖	a																						
London Bridge 4 ⊖	a	08 18	08 48	09 18	09 48	10 18	10 48	11 18	11 48	12 18	12 48	13 18	13 48	14 18	14 48	15 18	15 48	16 18	16 48	17 18	17 48	18 18	18 48
Clapham Junction 10	a																						
London Victoria 15 ⊖	a																						

		SN	SN	SN	SN	SN	SN	SN	SN	SN	SN	SN
Tattenham Corner	d		18 45		19 45		20 45		21 45		22 44	
Tadworth	d		18 48		19 48		20 48		21 48		22 47	
Kingswood	d		18 51		19 51		20 51		21 51		22 50	
Chipstead	d		18 57		19 57		20 57		21 57		22 56	
Woodmansterne	d		19 00		20 00		21 00		22 00		22 59	
Smitham	d		19 03		20 03		21 03		22 03		23 02	
Reedham	d		19 05		20 05		21 05		22 05		23 04	
Caterham	d	18 26		19 26		20 26		21 26		22 26		23 10
Whyteleafe South	d	18 29		19 29		20 29		21 29		22 29		23 13
Whyteleafe	d	18 31		19 31		20 31		21 31		22 31		23 15
Kenley	d	18 34		19 34		20 34		21 34		22 34		23 18
Purley 4	a	18 37	19 08	19 37	20 08	20 37	21 08	21 37	22 08	22 37	23 07	23 21
	d	18 38	19 08	19 38	20 08	20 38	21 08	21 38	22 08	22 38	23 07	23 23
Purley Oaks	d	18 41	19 11	19 41	20 11	20 41	21 11	21 41	22 11	22 41	23 10	23 26
South Croydon 4	d	18 44	19 14	19 44	20 14	20 44	21 14	21 44	22 14	22 44	23 13	23 29
East Croydon	d	18 47	19 17	19 47	20 17	20 47	21 17	21 47	22 17	22 47	23 16	23a31
Norwood Junction 2	d	18 52	19 22	19 52	20 22	20 52	21 22	21 52	22 22	22 52	23a20	
New Cross Gate 4 ⊖	a	19 09	19 39	20 09	20 39	21 09	21 39	22 09	22 39	23 09		
London Bridge 4 ⊖	a	19 18	19 48	20 18	20 48	21 18	21 48	22 18	22 48	23 18		
Clapham Junction 10	a											
London Victoria 15 ⊖	a											

Table 182

London - Sutton, Epsom, Guildford, Dorking and Horsham

		SW MX	SN MO	SN MO	SW MO	SN MX	FC MX	SN MX	SW MX	SN MX		FC MX	SW MX	SN	SW	SN	SN	SN	SN	SN		SN	FC	SW	SN
London Victoria 15 ⊖	d		23p08	23p19		23p26		23p34		23p51								05 57		06 00		06 07			06 25
London Waterloo 15 ⊖	d	23p09			23p32				23p42				00 15		05 47									06 24	
Clapham Junction 10	d	23p18	23p16	23p27	23p41	23p34		23p42	23p51	23p59			00 24		05 56			06 03		06 08		06 15		06 33	06 31
Balham 4 ⊖	d		23p21	23p32		23p40		23p47		00 04								06 08		06 13		06 20			06 36
London Bridge 4 ⊖	d						23p28					23p58					05 36								
Tulse Hill 3	d						23p40					00 10											06 22		
Norwood Junction 2	d															05 53	06 00					06 39			
West Croydon 4	d			23p50				00 04		00 21				05 46		05 58	06 05			06 32		06 46			
Waddon	d			23p52				00 06		00 24				05 48		06 00	06 08			06 34		06 48			
Wallington	d			23p56				00 10		00 27				05 52		06 04	06 11			06 38		06 52			
Carshalton Beeches	d			23p58				00 12		00 30				05 54		06 06	06 14			06 40		06 54			
Mitcham Eastfields	d		23p28			23p46												06 14					06 29		06 42
Mitcham Junction	d		23p31			23p49												06 17					06 32		06 45
Hackbridge	d		23p34			23p53												06 21					06 35		06 49
Carshalton	d		23p37			23p55												06 23					06 38		06 51
Sutton (Surrey) 4	a		23p40	00 02		00 01	00 13	00 16		00 33		00 43		05 58		06 10	06 17	06 29		06 44		06 58	06 43		06 55
	d		23p41	00 04		00 02										06 11		06 30	06 39	06 48		07 00			06 55
Belmont	d															06 14				06 51					
Banstead	d															06 18				06 55					
Epsom Downs	a															06 21				06 58					
Cheam	d		23p43	00 06		00 04												06 32	06 41			07 02			06 58
Ewell East	d		23p47	00 10		00 08												06 36	06 45			07 06			07 01
Epsom 3	a	23p42	23p51	00 14	00 06	00 12			00 15				00 48		06 20			06 40	06 49			07 10		06 57	07 05
	d	23p47	23p51			00 12			00 19						06 21			06 40	06 50					06 58	07 06
Ashtead	d	23p51	23p55			00 16			00 23						06 25			06 44						07 02	07 10
Leatherhead	d	23p54	23p58			00 19			00 26						06 28			06 47	06 56					07 05	07 13
Bookham	d								00 31						06 33				07 01						
Effingham Junction 6	d								00 37						06 37				07 05						
Guildford	a								00 54						06 50				07 17						
Boxhill & Westhumble	d	23p59	00 03			00 24												06 52							
Dorking 4	a	00 01	00 06			00 27												06 55						07 11	07 19
	d					00 27												06 56							07 20
Holmwood	d					00s34												07 03							07 27
Ockley	d					00s38												07 07							07 31
Warnham	d					00s44												07 13							07 37
Horsham 4	a					00 48												07 17							07 43

		FC	SN	SW	SW	SN		SN	FC	SN	SW	FC	SN	SW	SW	FC 1		FC 1	SN	SN	SN	SW	SN	FC	SW
London Victoria 15 ⊖	d		06 32			06 36		07 00		07 06			07 15						07 30	07 36	07 47		07 55		
London Waterloo 15 ⊖	d			06 39	06 54						07 09			07 24	07 39							07 54			08 09
Clapham Junction 10	d		06 40	06 48	07 03	06 44		07 08		07 14	07 18		07 21	07 33	07 48				07 38	07 44	07 55	08 03	08 02		08 18
Balham 4 ⊖	d		06 45			06 49		07 13		07 20			07 26						07 44	07 50	08 00				
London Bridge 4 ⊖	d																								
Tulse Hill 3	d	06 42							07 02			07 20				07 45		07 37						08 05	
Norwood Junction 2	d					07 09				07 39										08 09					
West Croydon 4	d		07 03			07 14		07 32		07 46									08 04	08 15					
Waddon	d		07 05			07 16		07 35		07 48									08 06	08 17					
Wallington	d		07 09			07 20		07 38		07 52									08 10	08 21					
Carshalton Beeches	d		07 11			07 22		07 41		07 54									08 12	08 23					
Mitcham Eastfields	d	06 50										07 27				07 52					08 07				
Mitcham Junction	d	06 53										07 30	07 34			07 55					08 10				
Hackbridge	d	06 56										07 33	07 37			07 58					08 13				
Carshalton	d	06 59										07 36	07 40			08 01					08 16				
Sutton (Surrey) 4	a	07 04	07 15			07 26		07 44	07 35	07 58		07 39	07 43			08 04		08 08	08 16	08 27	08 19		08 22	08 37	
	d		07 18			07 26		07 45		07 59			07 44						08 16	08 27			08 23		
Belmont	d		07 21					07 48											08 20						
Banstead	d		07 25					07 52											08 23						
Epsom Downs	a		07 28					07 55											08 27						
Cheam	d					07 29				08 01			07 46							08 30			08 25		
Ewell East	d					07 32				08 05			07 50							08 33			08 29		
Epsom 3	a			07 11	07 27	07 36				08 09	07 42		07 54	07 58	08 13					08 37		08 27	08 33		08 42
	d			07 12	07 28	07 37							07 54	07 58	08 17					08 38		08 28	08 33		08 47
Ashtead	d			07 16	07 32	07 41							07 58	08 02	08 21					08 42		08 32	08 37		08 51
Leatherhead	d			07 19	07 35	07 44							08 01	08 05	08 24					08 45		08 35	08 40		08 54
Bookham	d			07 24		07 49									08 29										08 59
Effingham Junction 6	d			07a28		07 53									08 33										09 03
Guildford	a					08 06									08 50										09 20
Boxhill & Westhumble	d												08 06							08 50					
Dorking 4	a				07 41								08 09	08 12						08 52		08 41	08 46		
	d												08 09										08 47		
Holmwood	d												08 17												
Ockley	d												08 21												
Warnham	d												08 26												
Horsham 4	a												08 30										09 03		

Table 182

London - Sutton, Epsom, Guildford, Dorking and Horsham

		FC		SN	SN	SW	SN	SN	SN	SW	FC 1	FC		SN	SN	SW	SN	SN	SN	SW	FC	FC 1		SN	SN
London Victoria 15 ⊖	d			08 03	08 07		08 19		08 26					08 31	08 36		08 47	08 52	09 01					09 03	09 05
London Waterloo 15 ⊖	d					08 24				08 39						08 54				09 09					
Clapham Junction 10	d			08 11	08 15	08 33	08 26		08 33	08 48				08 40	08 44	09 03	08 54	09 00	09 08	09 18				09 11	09 14
Balham 4 ⊖	d			08 16	08 20		08 30		08 38					08 46	08 50		09 00	09 05						09 16	09 20
London Bridge 4 ⊖	d							08 24																	
Tulse Hill 3	d	08 20						08 47			08 50	08 40									09 16	09 01			
Norwood Junction 2	d				08 39										09 09										09 39
West Croydon 4	d			08 36	08 45				08 56					09 06	09 14			09 24						09 34	09 44
Waddon	d			08 39	08 47				08 58					09 08	09 16			09 26						09 36	09 46
Wallington	d			08 42	08 51				09 02					09 12	09 20			09 30						09 40	09 50
Carshalton Beeches	d			08 45	08 53				09 04					09 14	09 22			09 32						09 42	09 52
Mitcham Eastfields	d	08 28					08 37				08 58						09 06				09 24				
Mitcham Junction	d	08 31					08 40				09 01						09 09				09 27				
Hackbridge	d	08 34					08 44				09 04						09 13				09 30				
Carshalton	d	08 37					08 46				09 07						09 15				09 33				
Sutton (Surrey) 4	a	08 40		08 48	08 57		08 50	09 02	09 08		09 10	09 12		09 18	09 26		09 19	09 39	09 28		09 36	09 37		09 46	09 56
	d			08 53			08 50	09 02						09 19			09 19	09 40	09 29						
Belmont	d			08 56										09 22											
Banstead	d			09 00										09 26											
Epsom Downs	a			09 03										09 29											
Cheam	d						08 53	09 05									09 22	09 42	09 31						
Ewell East	d						08 56	09 08									09 25	09 46							
Epsom 3	a					08 57	09 00	09 12		09 16						09 27	09 29	09 50	09 37	09 42					
	d					08 58	09 01			09 17						09 28			09 37	09 47					
Ashtead	d					09 02	09 05			09 21						09 32			09 41	09 51					
Leatherhead	d					09 05	09 08			09 24						09 35			09 44	09 54					
Bookham	d									09 29										09 59					
Effingham Junction 6	d									09 33										10 03					
Guildford	a									09 50										10 20					
Boxhill & Westhumble	d						09 13												09 49						
Dorking 4	a					09 11	09 15									09 41			09 52						
	d						09 16																		
Holmwood	d						09 23																		
Ockley	d						09 27																		
Warnham	d						09 33																		
Horsham 4	a						09 37																		

		SW	SN	SN	SN	FC	SW	FC		SN	SN	SW	SN	SN	SN	FC	SW	FC		SN	SN	SW	SN	SN	SN
London Victoria 15 ⊖	d		09 17	09 22	09 31					09 33	09 35		09 47	09 53	10 01					10 03	10 06		10 17	10 23	10 31
London Waterloo 15 ⊖	d	09 24					09 39					09 54					10 09					10 24			
Clapham Junction 10	d	09 33	09 24	09 30	09 38		09 48			09 41	09 44	10 03	09 54	10 00	10 08		10 18			10 11	10 14	10 33	10 24	10 30	10 38
Balham 4 ⊖	d		09 30	09 35						09 46	09 50		10 00	10 05						10 16	10 20		10 30	10 35	
London Bridge 4 ⊖	d																								
						09 31		09 46								10 01		10 16							
Norwood Junction 2	d										10 09										10 39				
West Croydon 4	d			09 54						10 04	10 14			10 24						10 34	10 44			10 54	
Waddon	d			09 56						10 06	10 16			10 26						10 36	10 46			10 56	
Wallington	d			10 00						10 10	10 20			10 30						10 40	10 50			11 00	
Carshalton Beeches	d			10 02						10 12	10 22			10 32						10 42	10 52			11 02	
Mitcham Eastfields	d		09 36					09 54					10 06					10 24					10 36		
Mitcham Junction	d		09 39					09 57					10 09					10 27					10 39		
Hackbridge	d		09 43					10 00					10 13					10 30					10 43		
Carshalton	d		09 45					10 03					10 15					10 33					10 45		
Sutton (Surrey) 4	a		09 49	10 06	09 58	10 05		10 06		10 16	10 26		10 19	10 39	10 28	10 35		10 36		10 46	10 56		10 49	11 06	10 58
	d		09 49	10 07	09 59								10 19	10 40	10 29								10 49	11 07	10 59
Belmont	d			10 10																				11 10	
Banstead	d			10 14																				11 14	
Epsom Downs	a			10 17																				11 17	
Cheam	d		09 52		10 01								10 22	10 42	10 31								10 52		11 01
Ewell East	d		09 55		10 05								10 25	10 46									10 55		11 05
Epsom 3	a	09 57	09 59		10 09		10 16					10 27	10 29	10 52	10 37		10 46					10 57	10 59		11 09
	d	09 58			10 09		10 17					10 28			10 37		10 47					10 58			11 09
Ashtead	d	10 02			10 13		10 21					10 32			10 41		10 51					11 02			11 13
Leatherhead	d	10 05			10 16		10 24					10 35			10 44		10 54					11 05			11 16
Bookham	d						10 29										10 59								
Effingham Junction 6	d						10 33										11 03								
Guildford	a						10 50										11 20								
Boxhill & Westhumble	d				10 21																				11 21
Dorking 4	a	10 11			10 24							10 41			10 50							11 11			11 24
	d				10 24																				11 24
Holmwood	d				10 32																				11 32
Ockley	d				10 36																				11 36
Warnham	d				10 41																				11 41
Horsham 4	a				10 45																				11 45

Table 182

Mondays to Fridays
24 May to 24 September

London - Sutton, Epsom, Guildford, Dorking and Horsham

		FC	SW	FC	SN	SN	SW	SN	SN	SN	FC	SW	FC	SN	SN	SW	SN	SN	SN	FC	SW	FC
London Victoria 15 ⊖	d				10 33	10 36		10 47	10 53	11 01				11 03	11 06		11 17	11 23	11 31			
London Waterloo 15 ⊖	d		10 39				10 54					11 09				11 24					11 39	
Clapham Junction 10	d		10 48		10 41	10 44	11 03	10 54	11 00	11 08		11 18		11 11	11 14	11 33	11 24	11 30	11 38		11 48	
Balham 4 ⊖	d				10 46	10 50		11 00	11 05					11 16	11 20		11 30	11 35				
London Bridge 4 ⊖	d																					
Tulse Hill 3	d	10 31		10 46							11 01		11 16							11 31		11 46
Norwood Junction 2	d					11 09									11 39							
West Croydon 4	d				11 04	11 14			11 24					11 34	11 44			11 54				
Waddon	d				11 06	11 16			11 26					11 36	11 46			11 56				
Wallington	d				11 10	11 20			11 30					11 40	11 50			12 00				
Carshalton Beeches	d				11 12	11 22			11 32					11 42	11 52			12 02				
Mitcham Eastfields	d			10 54				11 06					11 24				11 36					11 54
Mitcham Junction	d			10 57				11 09					11 27				11 39					11 57
Hackbridge	d			11 00				11 13					11 30				11 43					12 00
Carshalton	d			11 03				11 15					11 33				11 45					12 03
Sutton (Surrey) 4	a	11 05		11 06	11 16	11 26		11 19	11 39	11 28	11 35		11 36	11 46	11 56		11 49	12 06	11 58	12 05		12 06
	d							11 19	11 40	11 29							11 49	12 07	11 59			
Belmont	d																	12 10				
Banstead	d																	12 14				
Epsom Downs	a																	12 17				
Cheam	d							11 22	11 42	11 31							11 52		12 01			
Ewell East	d							11 25	11 46								11 55		12 05			
Epsom 3	a		11 16				11 27	11 29	11 52	11 37		11 46				11 57	11 59		12 09		12 16	
	d		11 17				11 28			11 37		11 47				11 58			12 09		12 17	
Ashtead	d		11 21				11 32			11 41		11 51				12 02			12 13		12 21	
Leatherhead	d		11 24				11 35			11 44		11 54				12 05			12 16		12 24	
Bookham	d		11 29									11 59									12 29	
Effingham Junction 6	d		11 33									12 03									12 33	
Guildford	a		11 50									12 20									12 50	
Boxhill & Westhumble	d																		12 21			
Dorking 4	a						11 41			11 50						12 11			12 24			
	d																		12 24			
Holmwood	d																		12 32			
Ockley	d																		12 36			
Warnham	d																		12 41			
Horsham 4	a																		12 45			

		SN	SN	SW	SN	SN	FC	SW	FC	SN	SN	SN	SW	SN	SN	FC	SN	SW	FC	SN	SN	SW	SN
London Victoria 15 ⊖	d	11 33	11 36		11 47	12 01				11 53	12 03	12 06		12 17	12 31		12 23			12 33	12 36		12 47
London Waterloo 15 ⊖	d			11 54				12 09					12 24					12 39				12 54	
Clapham Junction 10	d	11 41	11 44	12 03	11 54	12 08		12 18		12 00	12 11	12 14	12 33	12 24	12 38		12 30	12 48		12 41	12 44	13 03	12 54
Balham 4 ⊖	d	11 46	11 50		12 00					12 05	12 16	12 20		12 30			12 35			12 46	12 50		13 00
London Bridge 4 ⊖	d																						
Tulse Hill 3	d						12 01		12 16							12 31			12 46				
Norwood Junction 2	d		12 09									12 39									13 09		
West Croydon 4	d	12 04	12 14							12 24	12 34	12 44					12 54			13 04	13 14		
Waddon	d	12 06	12 16							12 26	12 36	12 46					12 56			13 06	13 16		
Wallington	d	12 10	12 20							12 30	12 40	12 50					13 00			13 10	13 20		
Carshalton Beeches	d	12 12	12 22							12 32	12 42	12 52					13 02			13 12	13 22		
Mitcham Eastfields	d				12 06				12 24					12 36					12 54				13 06
Mitcham Junction	d				12 09				12 27					12 39					12 57				13 09
Hackbridge	d				12 13				12 30					12 43					13 00				13 13
Carshalton	d				12 15				12 33					12 45					13 03				13 15
Sutton (Surrey) 4	a	12 16	12 26		12 19	12 28	12 35		12 36	12 39	12 46	12 56		12 49	12 58	13 05	13 06		13 06	13 16	13 26		13 19
	d				12 19	12 29				12 40				12 49	12 59		13 07						13 19
Belmont	d																13 10						
Banstead	d																13 14						
Epsom Downs	a																13 17						
Cheam	d				12 22	12 31				12 42				12 52	13 01								13 22
Ewell East	d				12 25					12 46				12 55	13 05								13 25
Epsom 3	a			12 27	12 29	12 37		12 46		12 52			12 57	12 59	13 09			13 16				13 27	13 29
	d			12 28		12 37		12 47					12 58		13 09			13 17				13 28	
Ashtead	d			12 32		12 41		12 51					13 02		13 13			13 21				13 32	
Leatherhead	d			12 35		12 44		12 54					13 05		13 16			13 24				13 35	
Bookham	d							12 59										13 29					
Effingham Junction 6	d							13 03										13 33					
Guildford	a							13 20										13 50					
Boxhill & Westhumble	d														13 21								
Dorking 4	a			12 41		12 50							13 11		13 24							13 41	
	d														13 24								
Holmwood	d														13 32								
Ockley	d														13 36								
Warnham	d														13 41								
Horsham 4	a														13 45								

Table 182

Mondays to Fridays
24 May to 24 September

London - Sutton, Epsom, Guildford, Dorking and Horsham

		SN	FC	SW	FC	SN	SN	SN	SW	SN	SN	SN	FC	SW	FC	SN	SN	SW	SN	SN	FC	SW	FC
London Victoria 15 ⊖	d	13 01				12 53	13 03	13 06		13 17	13 23	13 31				13 33	13 36		13 47	14 01			
London Waterloo 15 ⊖	d			13 09					13 24					13 39				13 54				14 09	
Clapham Junction 10	d	13 08		13 18		13 00	13 11	13 14	13 33	13 24	13 30	13 38		13 48		13 41	13 44	14 03	13 54	14 08		14 18	
Balham 4 ⊖	d					13 05	13 16	13 20		13 30	13 35					13 46	13 50		14 00				
London Bridge 4 ⊖	d																						
Tulse Hill 3	d		13 01		13 16								13 31		13 46						14 01		14 16
Norwood Junction 2	d							13 39									14 09						
West Croydon 4	d					13 24	13 34	13 44			13 54					14 04	14 14						
Waddon	d					13 26	13 36	13 46			13 56					14 06	14 16						
Wallington	d					13 30	13 40	13 50			14 00					14 10	14 20						
Carshalton Beeches	d					13 32	13 42	13 52			14 02					14 12	14 22						
Mitcham Eastfields	d				13 24					13 36					13 54				14 06				14 24
Mitcham Junction	d				13 27					13 39					13 57				14 09				14 27
Hackbridge	d				13 30					13 43					14 00				14 13				14 30
Carshalton	d				13 33					13 45					14 03				14 15				14 33
Sutton (Surrey) 4	a	13 28	13 35		13 36	13 39	13 46	13 56		13 49	14 06	13 58	14 05		14 06	14 16	14 26		14 19	14 28	14 35		14 36
	d	13 29				13 40				13 49	14 07	13 59							14 19	14 29			
Belmont	d										14 10												
Banstead	d										14 14												
Epsom Downs	a										14 17												
Cheam	d	13 31				13 42				13 52		14 01							14 22	14 31			
Ewell East	d					13 46				13 55		14 05							14 25				
Epsom 3	a	13 37		13 46		13 52			13 57	13 59		14 09		14 16				14 27	14 29	14 37		14 46	
	d	13 37		13 47					13 58			14 09		14 17				14 28		14 37		14 47	
Ashtead	d	13 41		13 51					14 02			14 13		14 21				14 32		14 41		14 51	
Leatherhead	d	13 44		13 54					14 05			14 16		14 24				14 35		14 44		14 54	
Bookham	d			13 59										14 29								14 59	
Effingham Junction 6	d			14 03										14 33								15 03	
Guildford	a			14 20										14 50								15 20	
Boxhill & Westhumble	d											14 21											
Dorking 4	a	13 50							14 11			14 24						14 41		14 50			
	d											14 24											
Holmwood	d											14 32											
Ockley	d											14 36											
Warnham	d											14 41											
Horsham 4	a											14 45											

		SN	SN	SN	SW	SN	SN	FC	SN	SW	FC	SN	SN	SW	SN	SN	FC	SW	FC	SN	SN	SN
London Victoria 15 ⊖	d	13 53	14 03	14 06		14 17	14 31		14 23			14 33	14 36		14 47	15 01				14 53	15 03	15 06
London Waterloo 15 ⊖	d				14 24					14 39				14 54				15 09				
Clapham Junction 10	d	14 00	14 11	14 14	14 33	14 24	14 38		14 30	14 48		14 41	14 44	15 03	14 54	15 08		15 18		15 00	15 11	15 14
Balham 4 ⊖	d	14 05	14 16	14 20		14 30			14 35			14 46	14 50		15 00					15 05	15 16	15 20
London Bridge 4 ⊖	d																					
Tulse Hill 3	d							14 31			14 46						15 01		15 16			
Norwood Junction 2	d			14 39									15 09									15 39
West Croydon 4	d	14 24	14 34	14 44					14 54			15 04	15 14							15 24	15 34	15 44
Waddon	d	14 26	14 36	14 46					14 56			15 06	15 16							15 26	15 36	15 46
Wallington	d	14 30	14 40	14 50					15 00			15 10	15 20							15 30	15 40	15 50
Carshalton Beeches	d	14 32	14 42	14 52					15 02			15 12	15 22							15 32	15 42	15 52
Mitcham Eastfields	d					14 36					14 54				15 06				15 24			
Mitcham Junction	d					14 39					14 57				15 09				15 27			
Hackbridge	d					14 43					15 00				15 13				15 30			
Carshalton	d					14 45					15 03				15 15				15 33			
Sutton (Surrey) 4	a	14 39	14 46	14 56		14 50	14 58	15 05	15 06		15 06	15 16	15 26		15 19	15 28	15 35		15 36	15 39	15 47	15 56
	d	14 40				14 50	14 59		15 07						15 19	15 29				15 40		
Belmont	d								15 10													
Banstead	d								15 14													
Epsom Downs	a								15 17													
Cheam	d	14 42				14 53	15 01								15 22	15 31				15 42		
Ewell East	d	14 46				14 56	15 05								15 25					15 46		
Epsom 3	a	14 52			14 57	15 00	15 09			15 16				15 27	15 29	15 37		15 46		15 52		
	d				14 58		15 09			15 17				15 28		15 37		15 47				
Ashtead	d				15 02		15 13			15 21				15 32		15 41		15 51				
Leatherhead	d				15 05		15 16			15 24				15 35		15 44		15 54				
Bookham	d									15 29								15 59				
Effingham Junction 6	d									15 33								16 03				
Guildford	a									15 50								16 20				
Boxhill & Westhumble	d						15 21															
Dorking 4	a				15 11		15 24							15 41		15 50						
	d						15 24															
Holmwood	d						15 32															
Ockley	d						15 36															
Warnham	d						15 41															
Horsham 4	a						15 45															

London - Sutton, Epsom, Guildford, Dorking and Horsham

		SW	SN	SN	SN	FC	SW	FC		SN	SN	SW	SN	SN	SN	FC	SW	FC		SN	SN	SW	SN	SN	FC
London Victoria 15 ⊖	d		15 17	15 23	15 31					15 33	15 36		15 47	15 53	16 01					16 03	16 07		16 17	16 31	
London Waterloo 15 ⊖	d	15 24					15 39					15 54					16 09					16 24			
Clapham Junction 10	d	15 33	15 24	15 30	15 38		15 48			15 41	15 44	16 03	15 54	16 00	16 08		16 18			16 11	16 15	16 33	16 24	16 38	
Balham 4 ⊖	d		15 30	15 35						15 46	15 50		16 00	16 05						16 16	16 20		16 30		
London Bridge 4 ⊖	d																								
Tulse Hill 3	d					15 31		15 46								16 01		16 16							16 32
Norwood Junction 2	d										16 09										16 39				
West Croydon 4	d			15 54						16 04	16 14			16 24						16 34	16 44				
Waddon	d			15 56						16 06	16 16			16 26						16 36	16 46				
Wallington	d			16 00						16 10	16 20			16 30						16 40	16 50				
Carshalton Beeches	d			16 02						16 12	16 22			16 32						16 42	16 52				
Mitcham Eastfields	d		15 36					15 54					16 06					16 24					16 36	16 51	
Mitcham Junction	d		15 39					15 57					16 09		16 22			16 27					16 39	16 54	
Hackbridge	d		15 43					16 00					16 13					16 30					16 43	16 57	
Carshalton	d		15 45					16 03					16 15					16 33					16 45	17 00	
Sutton (Surrey) 4	a		15 49	16 06	15 58	16 05		16 06		16 16	16 26		16 19	16 36	16 29	16 35		16 36		16 48	16 58		16 49	17 03	17 05
	d		15 49	16 07	15 59								16 19	16 37	16 30								16 49	17 04	
Belmont	d			16 10										16 40											
Banstead	d			16 14										16 44											
Epsom Downs	a			16 17										16 47											
Cheam	d		15 52		16 01								16 22		16 32								16 52	17 06	
Ewell East	d		15 55		16 05								16 25		16 36								16 55	17 10	
Epsom 3	a	15 57	15 59		16 09		16 15					16 27	16 29		16 40		16 46					16 57	17 01	17 16	
	d	15 58			16 09		16 17					16 28			16 40		16 47					16 58	17 02		
Ashtead	d	16 02			16 13		16 21					16 32			16 44		16 51					17 02	17 06		
Leatherhead	d	16 05			16 16		16 24					16 35			16 47		16 54					17 05	17 09		
Bookham	d						16 29										16 59								
Effingham Junction 6	d						16 33										17 03								
Guildford	a						16 50										17 22								
Boxhill & Westhumble	d				16 21										16 52							17 10	17 14		
Dorking 4	a	16 11			16 24							16 41			16 57							17 14	17 16		
	d				16 24																		17 17		
Holmwood	d				16 32																		17 24		
Ockley	d				16 36																		17 28		
Warnham	d				16 41																		17 34		
Horsham 4	a				16 45																		17 40		

		SW	FC	SN		SN	SW	SN	SW	SN	FC	FC	SN	SN		SN	SW	SN	SW	SN	SN	FC	SW	FC	
London Victoria 15 ⊖	d			16 33		16 37		16 50					17 01	17 06				17 20		17 31					
London Waterloo 15 ⊖	d	16 39					16 54		17 09								17 24		17 30				17 39		
Clapham Junction 10	d	16 48		16 41		16 45	17 03	16 56	17 18				17 09	17 14			17 33	17 26	17 39	17 37			17 48		
Balham 4 ⊖	d			16 46		16 50		17 01					17 14	17 19				17 32		17 42					
London Bridge 4 ⊖	d									17 03						17 06					17 32				
Tulse Hill 3	d		16 46								17 02	17 20				17 24						17 31		17 48	
Norwood Junction 2	d					17 09				17 16				17 39							17 46				
West Croydon 4	d			17 04		17 14				17 22			17 33	17 44							17 51				
Waddon	d			17 06		17 16				17 24			17 35	17 46							17 53				
Wallington	d			17 10		17 20				17 28			17 39	17 50							17 57				
Carshalton Beeches	d			17 12		17 22				17 30			17 41	17 52							17 59				
Mitcham Eastfields	d		16 56					17 08				17 28				17 32		17 38		17 48				17 56	
Mitcham Junction	d		16 59					17 11				17 31				17 35		17 41		17 51				17 59	
Hackbridge	d		17 02					17 15				17 34				17 38		17 45		17 55				18 02	
Carshalton	d		17 05					17 17				17 37				17 41		17 47		17 57				18 05	
Sutton (Surrey) 4	a		17 08	17 16		17 26		17 21		17 34	17 39	17 40	17 45	17 58		17 44		17 51		18 01	18 04	18 05		18 08	
	d			17 16		17 27		17 21		17 36			17 45			17 48		17 51		18 01	18 05				
Belmont	d			17 20									17 49												
Banstead	d			17 23									17 52												
Epsom Downs	a			17 29									17 58												
Cheam	d					17 29		17 24		17 38								17 54		18 04	18 07				
Ewell East	d					17 33		17 27		17 42								17 57		18 07	18 11				
Epsom 3	a	17 12				17 37	17 27	17 31	17 42	17 48							17 54	18 01	18 07	18 13	18 15		18 20		
	d	17 17				17 37	17 28	17 32	17 47								17 54	18 02			18 16		18 21		
Ashtead	d	17 21				17 41	17 32	17 36	17 51								17 58	18 06			18 20		18 25		
Leatherhead	d	17 24				17 44	17 35	17 39	17 54								18 01	18 09			18 23		18 28		
Bookham	d	17 29				17 50			17 59												18 28		18 34		
Effingham Junction 6	d	17 33				17 53			18a05												18 32		18a44		
Guildford	a	17 52				18 13															18 50				
Boxhill & Westhumble	d						17 40	17 44									18 06	18 14							
Dorking 4	a						17 44	17 46									18 11	18 16							
	d							17 47										18 19							
Holmwood	d							17 54										18 26							
Ockley	d							17 58										18 30							
Warnham	d							18 04										18 36							
Horsham 4	a							18 10										18 42							

London - Sutton, Epsom, Guildford, Dorking and Horsham

		SN	SN	SN	SW	SN	SW	SN	SW	SN		FC	FC	SN	SN	SN	SW	SN	SW	SN		FC	SW	FC	SW
London Victoria 15 ⊖	d		17 33	17 37		17 50				18 01				18 03	18 07			18 20							
London Waterloo 15 ⊖	d				17 54		18 00		18 09								18 24		18 30				18 39		18 54
Clapham Junction 10	d		17 41	17 45	18 03	17 56	18 09		18 18	18 08				18 11	18 15		18 33	18 26	18 39				18 48		19 03
Balham 4 ⊖	d		17 46	17 50		18 02				18 12				18 16	18 20			18 32							
London Bridge 4 ⊖	d	17 37						18 02								18 08				18 32					
Tulse Hill 3	d	17 55										18 02	18 22			18 27						18 32		18 52	
Norwood Junction 2	d			18 09				18 16							18 39					18 46					
West Croydon 4	d		18 04	18 15				18 21						18 35	18 45					18 51					
Waddon	d		18 06	18 17				18 23						18 37	18 47					18 53					
Wallington	d		18 10	18 21				18 27						18 41	18 51					18 57					
Carshalton Beeches	d		18 12	18 23				18 29						18 43	18 53					18 59					
Mitcham Eastfields	d	18 02				18 08				18 19			18 30			18 34		18 38						19 00	
Mitcham Junction	d	18 05				18 11				18 22			18 33			18 37		18 41						19 03	
Hackbridge	d	18 09				18 15				18 25			18 36			18 41		18 45						19 06	
Carshalton	d	18 11				18 17				18 28			18 39			18 43		18 47						19 09	
Sutton (Surrey) 4	a	18 15	18 18	18 29		18 21		18 33		18 36		18 37	18 42	18 47	18 58	18 47		18 51		19 03		19 07		19 12	
	d	18 16	18 19			18 21		18 33		18 36				18 48		18 48		18 51		19 03					
Belmont	d		18 22											18 51											
Banstead	d		18 26											18 55											
Epsom Downs	a		18 31											19 00											
Cheam	d					18 24		18 36		18 39								18 54		19 06					
Ewell East	d					18 27		18 39		18 42								18 57		19 09					
Epsom 3	a				18 24	18 31	18 35	18 43	18 46	18 48							18 54	19 01	19 07	19 13			19 12		19 24
	d				18 24	18 34		18 44	18 47								18 54	19 02		19 14			19 17		19 24
Ashtead	d				18 28	18 38		18 48	18 51								18 58	19 06		19 18			19 21		19 28
Leatherhead	d				18 31	18 41		18 51	18 54								19 01	19 09		19 21			19 24		19 31
Bookham	d								18 59														19 29		
Effingham Junction 6	d								19 03														19 33		
Guildford	a								19 22														19 52		
Boxhill & Westhumble	d				18 36	18 46		18 56									19 06	19 14		19 26					19 36
Dorking 4	a				18 41	18 48		19 00									19 11	19 16		19 30					19 41
	d					18 49												19 19							
Holmwood	d					18 56												19 26							
Ockley	d					19 00												19 30							
Warnham	d					19 06												19 36							
Horsham 4	a					19 12												19 42							

		SN	SN	SN	SN	SW		SW	FC	FC	SN	SN	SW	SN	SN	SW		FC	FC	SN	SN	SW	SN	SW	FC
London Victoria 15 ⊖	d		18 32	18 36	18 50						19 00	19 06		19 20						19 31	19 36		19 50		
London Waterloo 15 ⊖	d					19 00		19 09					19 24			19 39						19 54		20 09	
Clapham Junction 10	d		18 40	18 44	18 56	19 09		19 18			19 08	19 14	19 33	19 26		19 48				19 39	19 44	20 03	19 56	20 18	
Balham 4 ⊖	d		18 45	18 49	19 02						19 14	19 20		19 32						19 44	19 50		20 02		
London Bridge 4 ⊖	d	18 38													19 31										
Tulse Hill 3	d	18 56							19 16	19 07								19 46	19 31						20 16
Norwood Junction 2	d			19 09								19 39			19 44						20 09				
West Croydon 4	d		19 04	19 15							19 32	19 45			19 49					20 02	20 14				
Waddon	d		19 07	19 17							19 35	19 47			19 52					20 05	20 16				
Wallington	d		19 10	19 21							19 38	19 51			19 55					20 08	20 20				
Carshalton Beeches	d		19 13	19 23							19 41	19 53			19 58					20 11	20 22				
Mitcham Eastfields	d	19 03			19 08				19 24					19 38				19 54					20 08		20 24
Mitcham Junction	d	19 06			19 11				19 27					19 41				19 57					20 11		20 27
Hackbridge	d	19 10			19 15				19 30					19 45				20 00					20 15		20 30
Carshalton	d	19 12			19 17				19 33					19 47				20 03					20 17		20 33
Sutton (Surrey) 4	a	19 16	19 16	19 28	19 21				19 36	19 40	19 44	19 57		19 51	20 01			20 06	20 07	20 14	20 26		20 21		20 36
	d	19 16	19 17		19 21						19 45	19 58		19 51	20 02						20 27		20 21		
Belmont	d		19 20									20 01									20 30				
Banstead	d		19 24									20 05									20 34				
Epsom Downs	a		19 29									20 08									20 37				
Cheam	d	19 19			19 24						19 47			19 54	20 04								20 24		
Ewell East	d	19 22			19 27						19 51			19 57	20 08								20 27		
Epsom 3	a	19 28			19 31	19 35		19 43			19 55		19 57	20 01	20 12	20 16						20 27	20 31	20 42	
	d				19 34			19 47					19 58	20 02	20 13	20 17							20 32	20 47	
Ashtead	d				19 38			19 51					20 02	20 06		20 21							20 36	20 51	
Leatherhead	d				19 41			19 54					20 05	20 09	20 19	20 24							20 39	20 54	
Bookham	d							19 59								20 29									
Effingham Junction 6	d							20 03								20 33									
Guildford	a							20 20								20 50									
Boxhill & Westhumble	d				19 46								20 10	20 14									20 44	20 59	
Dorking 4	a				19 50								20 12	20 16	20 25								20 46	21 01	
	d													20 17											
Holmwood	d													20 24											
Ockley	d													20 28											
Warnham	d													20 34											
Horsham 4	a													20 38											

Table 182

London - Sutton, Epsom, Guildford, Dorking and Horsham

Mondays to Fridays

24 May to 24 September

		FC		SN	SN	SW	SN	FC	SW	FC	SN	SN		SW	SN	FC	SN	SN	SW	SW	SN	FC		SN	SN
London Victoria 15	⊖ d			20 00	20 06		20 20				20 30	20 36			20 50		21 00	21 06			21 20			21 30	21 36
London Waterloo 15	⊖ d					20 24			20 39					20 54					21 09	21 24					
Clapham Junction 10	d			20 08	20 14	20 33	20 26		20 48		20 38	20 44		21 03	20 56		21 08	21 14	21 18	21 33	21 26			21 38	21 44
Balham 4	⊖ d			20 14	20 20		20 31				20 44	20 50			21 02		21 14	21 20			21 31			21 44	21 50
London Bridge 4	⊖ d																								
Tulse Hill 3	d	20 01						20 31		20 46						21 01						21 31			
Norwood Junction 2	d				20 39							21 09						21 39							22 09
West Croydon 4	d			20 32	20 44						21 02	21 14					21 32	21 44						22 02	22 14
Waddon	d			20 35	20 46						21 05	21 16					21 35	21 46						22 05	22 16
Wallington	d			20 38	20 50						21 08	21 20					21 38	21 50						22 08	22 20
Carshalton Beeches	d			20 41	20 52						21 11	21 22					21 41	21 52						22 11	22 22
Mitcham Eastfields	d						20 38			20 54					21 08						21 38				
Mitcham Junction	d						20 41			20 57					21 11						21 41				
Hackbridge	d						20 45			21 00					21 15						21 45				
Carshalton	d						20 47			21 03					21 17						21 47				
Sutton (Surrey) 4	a	20 37		20 44	20 56		20 51	21 05		21 06	21 14	21 26			21 21	21 39	21 44	21 56			21 51	22 05		22 14	22 26
	d				20 57		20 51					21 27			21 21			21 57			21 51				22 27
Belmont	d											21 30													22 30
Banstead	d											21 34													22 34
Epsom Downs	a											21 37													22 37
Cheam	d				20 59		20 54								21 24			21 59			21 54				
Ewell East	d				21 03		20 57								21 27			22 03			21 57				
Epsom 3	a				21 07	20 57	21 01		21 12					21 27	21 31			22 07	21 42	21 57	22 01				
	d						21 02		21 17						21 32				21 47		22 02				
Ashtead	d						21 06		21 21						21 36				21 51		22 06				
Leatherhead	d						21 09		21 24						21 39				21 54		22 09				
Bookham	d								21 29																
Effingham Junction 6	d								21 33																
Guildford	a								21 50																
Boxhill & Westhumble	d						21 14								21 44				21 59						
Dorking 4	a						21 16								21 46				22 01		22 15				
	d																								
Holmwood	d																								
Ockley	d																								
Warnham	d																								
Horsham 4	a																								

		SW	SW	SN	FC	SN	SN	SW		SN	FC	SN	SN	SW	SN	SW	SN	FC		SN	SN	FC	SN	SW	SN
London Victoria 15	⊖ d			21 50		22 00	22 06			22 20		22 30	22 36		22 50		23 00			23 06	23 26		23 34		23 51
London Waterloo 15	⊖ d	21 39	21 54					22 09						22 39		23 09								23 42	
Clapham Junction 10	d	21 48	22 03	21 56		22 08	22 14	22 18		22 26		22 38	22 44	22 48	22 56	23 18	23 08			23 14	23 34		23 42	23 51	23 59
Balham 4	⊖ d			22 02		22 14	22 20			22 32		22 44	22 50		23 01		23 14			23 20	23 40		23 47		00 04
London Bridge 4	⊖ d																	23 02				23 28			
Tulse Hill 3	d				22 01						22 31							23 12				23 40			
Norwood Junction 2	d						22 39						23 09							23 39					
West Croydon 4	d					22 32	22 44					23 02	23 14				23 32			23 44			00 04		00 21
Waddon	d					22 35	22 46					23 05	23 16				23 35			23 46			00 06		00 24
Wallington	d					22 38	22 50					23 08	23 20				23 38			23 50			00 10		00 27
Carshalton Beeches	d					22 41	22 52					23 11	23 22				23 41			23 52			00 12		00 30
Mitcham Eastfields	d			22 08						22 38					23 07						23 46				
Mitcham Junction	d			22 11						22 41					23 10						23 49				
Hackbridge	d			22 15						22 45					23 14						23 53				
Carshalton	d			22 17						22 47					23 16						23 55				
Sutton (Surrey) 4	a			22 21	22 39	22 44	22 56			22 51	23 05	23 14	23 26		23 20		23 44	23 45		23 56	00 01	00 13	00 16		00 33
	d			22 21			22 57			22 51			23 27		23 20		23 45				00 02				
Belmont	d												23 30												
Banstead	d												23 34												
Epsom Downs	a												23 37												
Cheam	d			22 24			22 59			22 54					23 23		23 47				00 04				
Ewell East	d			22 27			23 03			22 57					23 26		23 51				00 08				
Epsom 3	a	22 12	22 27	22 31			23 07	22 42		23 01				23 12	23 30	23 42	23 55				00 12			00 15	
	d	22 17		22 32				22 47		23 02				23 17	23 31	23 47					00 12			00 19	
Ashtead	d	22 21		22 36				22 51		23 06				23 21	23 35	23 51					00 16			00 23	
Leatherhead	d	22 24		22 39				22 54		23 09				23 24	23 38	23 54					00 19			00 26	
Bookham	d	22 29												23 29										00 31	
Effingham Junction 6	d	22 33												23 33										00 37	
Guildford	a	22 50												23 54										00 54	
Boxhill & Westhumble	d			22 44				22 59							23 43	23 59					00 24				
Dorking 4	a			22 46				23 01		23 15					23 45	00 01					00 27				
	d																				00 27				
Holmwood	d																				00s34				
Ockley	d																				00s38				
Warnham	d																				00s44				
Horsham 4	a																				00 48				

Table 182

London - Sutton, Epsom, Guildford, Dorking and Horsham

Mondays to Fridays

24 May to 24 September

		FC
London Victoria 15	⊖ d	
London Waterloo 15	⊖ d	
Clapham Junction 10	d	
Balham 4	⊖ d	
London Bridge 4	⊖ d	23 58
Tulse Hill 3	d	00 10
Norwood Junction 2	d	
West Croydon 4	d	
Waddon	d	
Wallington	d	
Carshalton Beeches	d	
Mitcham Eastfields	d	
Mitcham Junction	d	
Hackbridge	d	
Carshalton	d	
Sutton (Surrey) 4	a	00 43
	d	
Belmont	d	
Banstead	d	
Epsom Downs	a	
Cheam	d	
Ewell East	d	
Epsom 3	a	
	d	
Ashtead	d	
Leatherhead	d	
Bookham	d	
Effingham Junction 6	d	
Guildford	a	
Boxhill & Westhumble	d	
Dorking 4	a	
	d	
Holmwood	d	
Ockley	d	
Warnham	d	
Horsham 4	a	

Mondays to Fridays

from 27 September

		SW MX	SN MO	SN MO	SW MO	SN MX	FC MX	SN MX	SW MX	SN MX		FC MX	SW MX	SN	SW	SN	SN	SN	SN	SN		SN	FC	SW	SN
London Victoria 15	⊖ d		23p08	23p19		23p26		23p34		23p51								05 57		06 00		06 07			06 25
London Waterloo 15	⊖ d	23p09			23p32				23p42				00 15		05 47									06 24	
Clapham Junction 10	d	23p18	23p16	23p27	23p41	23p34		23p42	23p51	23p59			00 24		05 56			06 03		06 08		06 15		06 33	06 31
Balham 4	⊖ d		23p21	23p32		23p40		23p47		00 04								06 08		06 13		06 20			06 36
London Bridge 4	⊖ d						23p28					23p58					05 36								
Tulse Hill 3	d						23p40					00 10											06 22		
Norwood Junction 2	d															05 53	06 00					06 39			
West Croydon 4	d			23p50				00 04		00 21				05 46		05 58	06 05			06 32		06 46			
Waddon	d			23p52				00 06		00 24				05 48		06 00	06 08			06 34		06 48			
Wallington	d			23p56				00 10		00 27				05 52		06 04	06 11			06 38		06 52			
Carshalton Beeches	d			23p58				00 12		00 30				05 54		06 06	06 14			06 40		06 54			
Mitcham Eastfields	d		23p28			23p46												06 14					06 29		06 42
Mitcham Junction	d		23p31			23p49												06 17					06 32		06 45
Hackbridge	d		23p34			23p53												06 21					06 35		06 49
Carshalton	d		23p37			23p55												06 23					06 38		06 51
Sutton (Surrey) 4	a		23p40	00 02		00 01	00 13	00 16		00 33		00 43		05 58		06 10	06 17	06 29		06 44		06 58	06 43		06 55
	d		23p41	00 04		00 02										06 11		06 30	06 39	06 48		07 00			06 55
Belmont	d															06 14				06 51					
Banstead	d															06 18				06 55					
Epsom Downs	a															06 21				06 58					
Cheam	d		23p43	00 06		00 04												06 32	06 41			07 02			06 58
Ewell East	d		23p47	00 10		00 08												06 36	06 45			07 06			07 01
Epsom 3	a	23p42	23p51	00 14	00 06	00 12			00 15				00 48		06 20			06 40	06 49			07 10		06 57	07 05
	d	23p47	23p51			00 12			00 19						06 21			06 40	06 50					06 58	07 06
Ashtead	d	23p51	23p55			00 16			00 23						06 25			06 44						07 02	07 10
Leatherhead	d	23p54	23p58			00 19			00 26						06 28			06 47	06 56					07 05	07 13
Bookham	d								00 31						06 33				07 01						
Effingham Junction 6	d								00 37						06 37				07 05						
Guildford	a								00 57						06 53				07 17						
Boxhill & Westhumble	d	23p59	00 03			00 24												06 52							
Dorking 4	a	00 03	00 06			00 27												06 55						07 13	07 19
	d					00 27												06 56							07 20
Holmwood	d					00s34												07 03							07 27
Ockley	d					00s38												07 07							07 31
Warnham	d					00s44												07 13							07 37
Horsham 4	a					00 48												07 17							07 43

Table 182

London - Sutton, Epsom, Guildford, Dorking and Horsham

		FC	SN	SW	SW	SN		SN	FC	SN	SW	FC	SN	SW	SW	FC 1		FC 1	SN	SN	SN	SW	SN	FC	SW
London Victoria	⊖ d		06 32			06 36		07 00		07 06			07 15						07 30	07 36	07 47		07 55		
London Waterloo	⊖ d			06 39	06 54						07 09			07 24	07 39							07 54			08 09
Clapham Junction	d		06 40	06 48	07 03	06 44		07 08		07 14	07 18		07 21	07 33	07 48				07 38	07 44	07 55	08 03	08 02		08 18
Balham	⊖ d		06 45			06 49		07 13		07 20			07 26						07 44	07 50	08 00				
London Bridge	⊖ d																								
Tulse Hill	d	06 42							07 02			07 20				07 45		07 37						08 05	
Norwood Junction	d					07 09				07 39										08 09					
West Croydon	d		07 03			07 14		07 32		07 46									08 04	08 15					
Waddon	d		07 05			07 16		07 35		07 48									08 06	08 17					
Wallington	d		07 09			07 20		07 38		07 52									08 10	08 21					
Carshalton Beeches	d		07 11			07 22		07 41		07 54									08 12	08 23					
Mitcham Eastfields	d	06 50										07 27				07 52					08 07				
Mitcham Junction	d	06 53										07 30	07 34			07 55					08 10				
Hackbridge	d	06 56										07 33	07 37			07 58					08 13				
Carshalton	d	06 59										07 36	07 40			08 01					08 16				
Sutton (Surrey)	a	07 04	07 15			07 26		07 44	07 35	07 58		07 39	07 43			08 04		08 08	08 16	08 27	08 19		08 22	08 37	
	d		07 18			07 26		07 45		07 59			07 44						08 16	08 27			08 23		
Belmont	d		07 21					07 48											08 20						
Banstead	d		07 25					07 52											08 23						
Epsom Downs	a		07 28					07 55											08 27						
Cheam	d					07 29				08 01			07 46							08 30			08 25		
Ewell East	d					07 32				08 05			07 50							08 33			08 29		
Epsom	a			07 11	07 27	07 36				08 09	07 42		07 54	07 58	08 13					08 37		08 27	08 33		08 42
	d			07 12	07 28	07 37							07 54	07 58	08 17					08 38		08 28	08 33		08 47
Ashtead	d			07 16	07 32	07 41							07 58	08 02	08 21					08 42		08 32	08 37		08 51
Leatherhead	d			07 19	07 35	07 44							08 01	08 05	08 24					08 45		08 35	08 40		08 54
Bookham	d			07 24		07 49									08 29										08 59
Effingham Junction	d			07a28		07 53									08 33										09 03
Guildford	a					08 06									08 53										09 23
Boxhill & Westhumble	d												08 06							08 50					
Dorking	a				07 43								08 09	08 14						08 52		08 43	08 46		
	d												08 09										08 47		
Holmwood	d												08 17												
Ockley	d												08 21												
Warnham	d												08 26												
Horsham	a												08 30										09 03		

		FC		SN	SN	SW	SN	SN	SN	SW	FC 1	FC		SN	SN	SW	SN	SN	SN	SW	FC	FC 1		SN	SN
London Victoria	⊖ d			08 03	08 07		08 19		08 26					08 31	08 36		08 47	08 52	09 01					09 03	09 05
London Waterloo	⊖ d					08 24				08 39						08 54				09 09					
Clapham Junction	d			08 11	08 15	08 33	08 26		08 33	08 48				08 40	08 44	09 03	08 54	09 00	09 08	09 18				09 11	09 14
Balham	⊖ d			08 16	08 20		08 30		08 38					08 46	08 50		09 00	09 05						09 16	09 20
London Bridge	⊖ d							08 24																	
Tulse Hill	d	08 20						08 47			08 50	08 40									09 16	09 01			
Norwood Junction	d				08 39										09 09										09 39
West Croydon	d			08 36	08 45				08 56					09 06	09 14			09 24						09 34	09 44
Waddon	d			08 39	08 47				08 58					09 08	09 16			09 26						09 36	09 46
Wallington	d			08 42	08 51				09 02					09 12	09 20			09 30						09 40	09 50
Carshalton Beeches	d			08 45	08 53				09 04					09 14	09 22			09 32						09 42	09 52
Mitcham Eastfields	d	08 28					08 37				08 58						09 06				09 24				
Mitcham Junction	d	08 31					08 40				09 01						09 09				09 27				
Hackbridge	d	08 34					08 44				09 04						09 13				09 30				
Carshalton	d	08 37					08 46				09 07						09 15				09 33				
Sutton (Surrey)	a	08 40		08 48	08 57		08 50	09 02	09 08		09 10	09 12		09 18	09 26		09 19	09 39	09 28		09 36	09 37		09 46	09 56
	d			08 53			08 50	09 02						09 19			09 19	09 40	09 29						
Belmont	d			08 56										09 22											
Banstead	d			09 00										09 26											
Epsom Downs	a			09 03										09 29											
Cheam	d						08 53	09 05									09 22	09 42	09 31						
Ewell East	d						08 56	09 08									09 25	09 46							
Epsom	a					08 57	09 00	09 12		09 16						09 27	09 29	09 50	09 37	09 42					
	d					08 58	09 01			09 17						09 28			09 37	09 47					
Ashtead	d					09 02	09 05			09 21						09 32			09 41	09 51					
Leatherhead	d					09 05	09 08			09 24						09 35			09 44	09 54					
Bookham	d									09 29										09 59					
Effingham Junction	d									09 33										10 03					
Guildford	a									09 53										10 23					
Boxhill & Westhumble	d						09 13												09 49						
Dorking	a					09 13	09 15									09 43			09 52						
	d						09 16																		
Holmwood	d						09 23																		
Ockley	d						09 27																		
Warnham	d						09 33																		
Horsham	a						09 37																		

Table 182

London - Sutton, Epsom, Guildford, Dorking and Horsham

		SW	SN	SN	SN	FC	SW	FC		SN	SN	SW	SN	SN	SN	FC	SW	FC		SN	SN	SW	SN	SN	SN
London Victoria	⊖ d		09 17	09 22	09 31					09 33	09 35		09 47	09 53	10 01					10 03	10 06		10 17	10 23	10 31
London Waterloo	⊖ d	09 24					09 39					09 54					10 09					10 24			
Clapham Junction	d	09 33	09 24	09 30	09 38		09 48			09 41	09 44	10 03	09 54	10 00	10 08		10 18			10 11	10 14	10 33	10 24	10 30	10 38
Balham	⊖ d		09 30	09 35						09 46	09 50		10 00	10 05						10 16	10 20		10 30	10 35	
London Bridge	⊖ d																								
Tulse Hill	d					09 31		09 46								10 01		10 16							
Norwood Junction	d										10 09										10 39				
West Croydon	d			09 54						10 04	10 14			10 24						10 34	10 44			10 54	
Waddon	d			09 56						10 06	10 16			10 26						10 36	10 46			10 56	
Wallington	d			10 00						10 10	10 20			10 30						10 40	10 50			11 00	
Carshalton Beeches	d			10 02						10 12	10 22			10 32						10 42	10 52			11 02	
Mitcham Eastfields	d		09 36					09 54					10 06					10 24					10 36		
Mitcham Junction	d		09 39					09 57					10 09					10 27					10 39		
Hackbridge	d		09 43					10 00					10 13					10 30					10 43		
Carshalton	d		09 45					10 03					10 15					10 33					10 45		
Sutton (Surrey)	a		09 49	10 06	09 58	10 05		10 06		10 16	10 26		10 19	10 39	10 28	10 35		10 36		10 46	10 56		10 49	11 06	10 58
	d		09 49	10 07	09 59								10 19	10 40	10 29								10 49	11 07	10 59
Belmont	d			10 10																				11 10	
Banstead	d			10 14																				11 14	
Epsom Downs	a			10 17																				11 17	
Cheam	d		09 52		10 01								10 22	10 42	10 31								10 52		11 01
Ewell East	d		09 55		10 05								10 25	10 46									10 55		11 05
Epsom	a	09 57	09 59		10 09		10 16					10 27	10 29	10 52	10 37		10 46					10 57	10 59		11 09
	d	09 58			10 09		10 17					10 28			10 37		10 47					10 58			11 09
Ashtead	d	10 02			10 13		10 21					10 32			10 41		10 51					11 02			11 13
Leatherhead	d	10 05			10 16		10 24					10 35			10 44		10 54					11 05			11 16
Bookham	d						10 29										10 59								
Effingham Junction	d						10 33										11 03								
Guildford	a						10 53										11 23								
Boxhill & Westhumble	d				10 21																				11 21
Dorking	a	10 13			10 24							10 43			10 50							11 13			11 24
	d				10 24																				11 24
Holmwood	d				10 32																				11 32
Ockley	d				10 36																				11 36
Warnham	d				10 41																				11 41
Horsham	a				10 45																				11 45

		FC	SW	FC		SN	SN	SW	SN	SN	SN	FC	SW	FC		SN	SN	SW	SN	SN	SN	FC	SW	FC	
London Victoria	⊖ d					10 33	10 36		10 47	10 53	11 01					11 03	11 06		11 17	11 23	11 31				
London Waterloo	⊖ d		10 39					10 54					11 09					11 24					11 39		
Clapham Junction	d		10 48			10 41	10 44	11 03	10 54	11 00	11 08		11 18			11 11	11 14	11 33	11 24	11 30	11 38		11 48		
Balham	⊖ d					10 46	10 50		11 00	11 05						11 16	11 20		11 30	11 35					
London Bridge	⊖ d																								
Tulse Hill	d	10 31		10 46								11 01		11 16								11 31		11 46	
Norwood Junction	d						11 09										11 39								
West Croydon	d					11 04	11 14			11 24						11 34	11 44			11 54					
Waddon	d					11 06	11 16			11 26						11 36	11 46			11 56					
Wallington	d					11 10	11 20			11 30						11 40	11 50			12 00					
Carshalton Beeches	d					11 12	11 22			11 32						11 42	11 52			12 02					
Mitcham Eastfields	d			10 54					11 06					11 24					11 36					11 54	
Mitcham Junction	d			10 57					11 09					11 27					11 39					11 57	
Hackbridge	d			11 00					11 13					11 30					11 43					12 00	
Carshalton	d			11 03					11 15					11 33					11 45					12 03	
Sutton (Surrey)	a	11 05		11 06		11 16	11 26		11 19	11 39	11 28	11 35		11 36		11 46	11 56		11 49	12 06	11 58	12 05		12 06	
	d								11 19	11 40	11 29								11 49	12 07	11 59				
Belmont	d																			12 10					
Banstead	d																			12 14					
Epsom Downs	a																			12 17					
Cheam	d								11 22	11 42	11 31								11 52		12 01				
Ewell East	d								11 25	11 46									11 55		12 05				
Epsom	a		11 16					11 27	11 29	11 52	11 37		11 46					11 57	11 59		12 09		12 16		
	d		11 17					11 28			11 37		11 47					11 58			12 09		12 17		
Ashtead	d		11 21					11 32			11 41		11 51					12 02			12 13		12 21		
Leatherhead	d		11 24					11 35			11 44		11 54					12 05			12 16		12 24		
Bookham	d		11 29										11 59										12 29		
Effingham Junction	d		11 33										12 03										12 33		
Guildford	a		11 53										12 23										12 53		
Boxhill & Westhumble	d																				12 21				
Dorking	a							11 43			11 50							12 13			12 24				
	d																				12 24				
Holmwood	d																				12 32				
Ockley	d																				12 36				
Warnham	d																				12 41				
Horsham	a																				12 45				

Table 182

Mondays to Fridays
from 27 September

London - Sutton, Epsom, Guildford, Dorking and Horsham

Station		SN	SN	SW	SN	SN	FC	SW	FC	SN	SN	SN	SW	SN	SN	FC	SN	SW	FC	SN	SN	SW	SN
London Victoria 15 ⊖	d	11 33	11 36		11 47	12 01				11 53	12 03	12 06		12 17	12 31		12 23			12 33	12 36		12 47
London Waterloo 15 ⊖	d			11 54				12 09					12 24					12 39				12 54	
Clapham Junction 10	d	11 41	11 44	12 03	11 54	12 08		12 18		12 00	12 11	12 14	12 33	12 24	12 38		12 30	12 48		12 41	12 44	13 03	12 54
Balham 4 ⊖	d	11 46	11 50		12 00					12 05	12 16	12 20		12 30			12 35			12 46	12 50		13 00
London Bridge 4 ⊖	d																						
Tulse Hill 3	d						12 01		12 16							12 31			12 46				
Norwood Junction 2	d		12 09									12 39									13 09		
West Croydon 4	d	12 04	12 14							12 24	12 34	12 44					12 54			13 04	13 14		
Waddon	d	12 06	12 16							12 26	12 36	12 46					12 56			13 06	13 16		
Wallington	d	12 10	12 20							12 30	12 40	12 50					13 00			13 10	13 20		
Carshalton Beeches	d	12 12	12 22							12 32	12 42	12 52					13 02			13 12	13 22		
Mitcham Eastfields	d				12 06				12 24					12 36					12 54				13 06
Mitcham Junction	d				12 09				12 27					12 39					12 57				13 09
Hackbridge	d				12 13				12 30					12 43					13 00				13 13
Carshalton	d				12 15				12 33					12 45					13 03				13 15
Sutton (Surrey) 4	a	12 16	12 26		12 19	12 28	12 35		12 36	12 39	12 46	12 56		12 49	12 58	13 05	13 06		13 06	13 16	13 26		13 19
	d				12 19	12 29				12 40				12 49	12 59		13 07						13 19
Belmont	d																13 10						
Banstead	d																13 14						
Epsom Downs	a																13 17						
Cheam	d				12 22	12 31				12 42				12 52	13 01								13 22
Ewell East	d				12 25					12 46				12 55	13 05								13 25
Epsom 3	a			12 27	12 29	12 37		12 46		12 52			12 57	12 59	13 09			13 16				13 27	13 29
	d			12 28		12 37		12 47					12 58		13 09			13 17				13 28	
Ashtead	d			12 32		12 41		12 51					13 02		13 13			13 21				13 32	
Leatherhead	d			12 35		12 44		12 54					13 05		13 16			13 24				13 35	
Bookham	d							12 59										13 29					
Effingham Junction 6	d							13 03										13 33					
Guildford	a							13 23										13 53					
Boxhill & Westhumble	d														13 21								
Dorking 4	a			12 43		12 50							13 13		13 24							13 43	
	d														13 24								
Holmwood	d														13 32								
Ockley	d														13 36								
Warnham	d														13 41								
Horsham 4	a														13 45								

Station		SN	FC	SW	FC	SN	SN	SN	SW	SN	SN	SN	FC	SW	FC	SN	SN	SW	SN	SN	FC	SW	FC
London Victoria 15 ⊖	d	13 01				12 53	13 03	13 06		13 17	13 23	13 31				13 33	13 36		13 47	14 01			
London Waterloo 15 ⊖	d			13 09					13 24					13 39				13 54				14 09	
Clapham Junction 10	d	13 08		13 18		13 00	13 11	13 14	13 33	13 24	13 30	13 38		13 48		13 41	13 44	14 03	13 54	14 08		14 18	
Balham 4 ⊖	d					13 05	13 16	13 20		13 30	13 35					13 46	13 50		14 00				
London Bridge 4 ⊖	d																						
Tulse Hill 3	d		13 01		13 16								13 31		13 46						14 01		14 16
Norwood Junction 2	d							13 39									14 09						
West Croydon 4	d					13 24	13 34	13 44			13 54					14 04	14 14						
Waddon	d					13 26	13 36	13 46			13 56					14 06	14 16						
Wallington	d					13 30	13 40	13 50			14 00					14 10	14 20						
Carshalton Beeches	d					13 32	13 42	13 52			14 02					14 12	14 22						
Mitcham Eastfields	d				13 24					13 36					13 54				14 06				14 24
Mitcham Junction	d				13 27					13 39					13 57				14 09				14 27
Hackbridge	d				13 30					13 43					14 00				14 13				14 30
Carshalton	d				13 33					13 45					14 03				14 15				14 33
Sutton (Surrey) 4	a	13 28	13 35		13 36	13 39	13 46	13 56		13 49	14 06	13 58	14 05		14 06	14 16	14 26		14 19	14 28	14 35		14 36
	d	13 29				13 40				13 49	14 07	13 59							14 19	14 29			
Belmont	d										14 10												
Banstead	d										14 14												
Epsom Downs	a										14 17												
Cheam	d	13 31				13 42				13 52		14 01							14 22	14 31			
Ewell East	d					13 46				13 55		14 05							14 25				
Epsom 3	a	13 37		13 46		13 52			13 57	13 59		14 09		14 16				14 27	14 29	14 37		14 46	
	d	13 37		13 47					13 58			14 09		14 17				14 28		14 37		14 47	
Ashtead	d	13 41		13 51					14 02			14 13		14 21				14 32		14 41		14 51	
Leatherhead	d	13 44		13 54					14 05			14 16		14 24				14 35		14 44		14 54	
Bookham	d			13 59										14 29								14 59	
Effingham Junction 6	d			14 03										14 33								15 03	
Guildford	a			14 23										14 53								15 23	
Boxhill & Westhumble	d											14 21											
Dorking 4	a	13 50							14 13			14 24						14 43		14 50			
	d											14 24											
Holmwood	d											14 32											
Ockley	d											14 36											
Warnham	d											14 41											
Horsham 4	a											14 45											

Table 182

Mondays to Fridays
from 27 September

London - Sutton, Epsom, Guildford, Dorking and Horsham

Station		SN	SN	SN	SW	SN	SN	FC	SN	SW	FC	SN	SN	SW	SN	SN	FC	SW	FC	SN	SN	SN
London Victoria 15 ⊖	d	13 53	14 03	14 06		14 17	14 31		14 23			14 33	14 36		14 47	15 01				14 53	15 03	15 06
London Waterloo 15 ⊖	d				14 24					14 39				14 54				15 09				
Clapham Junction 10	d	14 00	14 11	14 14	14 33	14 24	14 38		14 30	14 48		14 41	14 44	15 03	14 54	15 08		15 18		15 00	15 11	15 14
Balham 4 ⊖	d	14 05	14 16	14 20		14 30			14 35			14 46	14 50		15 00					15 05	15 16	15 20
London Bridge 4 ⊖	d																					
Tulse Hill 3	d							14 31			14 46						15 01		15 16			
Norwood Junction 2	d			14 39									15 09									15 39
West Croydon 4	d	14 24	14 34	14 44					14 54			15 04	15 14							15 24	15 34	15 44
Waddon	d	14 26	14 36	14 46					14 56			15 06	15 16							15 26	15 36	15 46
Wallington	d	14 30	14 40	14 50					15 00			15 10	15 20							15 30	15 40	15 50
Carshalton Beeches	d	14 32	14 42	14 52					15 02			15 12	15 22							15 32	15 42	15 52
Mitcham Eastfields	d					14 36					14 54				15 06				15 24			
Mitcham Junction	d					14 39					14 57				15 09				15 27			
Hackbridge	d					14 43					15 00				15 13				15 30			
Carshalton	d					14 45					15 03				15 15				15 33			
Sutton (Surrey) 4	a	14 39	14 46	14 56		14 50	14 58	15 05	15 06		15 06	15 16	15 26		15 19	15 28	15 35		15 36	15 39	15 47	15 56
	d	14 40				14 50	14 59		15 07						15 19	15 29				15 40		
Belmont	d								15 10													
Banstead	d								15 14													
Epsom Downs	a								15 17													
Cheam	d	14 42				14 53	15 01								15 22	15 31				15 42		
Ewell East	d	14 46				14 56	15 05								15 25					15 46		
Epsom 3	a	14 52			14 57	15 00	15 09			15 16				15 27	15 29	15 37		15 46		15 52		
	d				14 58		15 09			15 17				15 28		15 37		15 47				
Ashtead	d				15 02		15 13			15 21				15 32		15 41		15 51				
Leatherhead	d				15 05		15 16			15 24				15 35		15 44		15 54				
Bookham	d									15 29								15 59				
Effingham Junction 6	d									15 33								16 03				
Guildford	a									15 53								16 23				
Boxhill & Westhumble	d						15 21															
Dorking 4	a				15 13		15 24							15 43		15 50						
	d						15 24															
Holmwood	d						15 32															
Ockley	d						15 36															
Warnham	d						15 41															
Horsham 4	a						15 45															

Station		SW	SN	SN	SN	FC	SW	FC	SN	SN	SW	SN	SN	SN	FC	SW	FC	SN	SN	SW	SN	SN	FC
London Victoria 15 ⊖	d		15 17	15 23	15 31				15 33	15 36		15 47	15 53	16 01				16 03	16 07		16 17	16 31	
London Waterloo 15 ⊖	d	15 24					15 39				15 54					16 09				16 24			
Clapham Junction 10	d	15 33	15 24	15 30	15 38		15 48		15 41	15 44	16 03	15 54	16 00	16 08		16 18		16 11	16 15	16 33	16 24	16 38	
Balham 4 ⊖	d		15 30	15 35					15 46	15 50		16 00	16 05					16 16	16 20		16 30		
London Bridge 4 ⊖	d																						
Tulse Hill 3	d					15 31		15 46							16 01		16 16						16 32
Norwood Junction 2	d									16 09									16 39				
West Croydon 4	d			15 54					16 04	16 14			16 24					16 34	16 44				
Waddon	d			15 56					16 06	16 16			16 26					16 36	16 46				
Wallington	d			16 00					16 10	16 20			16 30					16 40	16 50				
Carshalton Beeches	d			16 02					16 12	16 22			16 32					16 42	16 52				
Mitcham Eastfields	d		15 36					15 54				16 06					16 24				16 36	16 51	
Mitcham Junction	d		15 39					15 57				16 09		16 22			16 27				16 39	16 54	
Hackbridge	d		15 43					16 00				16 13					16 30				16 43	16 57	
Carshalton	d		15 45					16 03				16 15					16 33				16 45	17 00	
Sutton (Surrey) 4	a		15 49	16 06	15 58	16 05		16 06	16 16	16 26		16 19	16 36	16 29	16 35		16 36	16 48	16 58		16 49	17 03	17 05
	d		15 49	16 07	15 59							16 19	16 37	16 30							16 49	17 04	
Belmont	d			16 10									16 40										
Banstead	d			16 14									16 44										
Epsom Downs	a			16 17									16 47										
Cheam	d		15 52		16 01							16 22		16 32							16 52	17 06	
Ewell East	d		15 55		16 05							16 25		16 36							16 55	17 10	
Epsom 3	a	15 57	15 59		16 09		16 15				16 27	16 29		16 40		16 46				16 57	17 01	17 16	
	d	15 58			16 09		16 17				16 28			16 40		16 47				16 58	17 02		
Ashtead	d	16 02			16 13		16 21				16 32			16 44		16 51				17 02	17 06		
Leatherhead	d	16 05			16 16		16 24				16 35			16 47		16 54				17 05	17 09		
Bookham	d						16 29									16 59							
Effingham Junction 6	d						16 33									17 03							
Guildford	a						16 53									17 25							
Boxhill & Westhumble	d				16 21									16 52						17 10	17 14		
Dorking 4	a	16 13			16 24						16 43			16 57						17 16	17 16		
	d				16 24																17 17		
Holmwood	d				16 32																17 24		
Ockley	d				16 36																17 28		
Warnham	d				16 41																17 34		
Horsham 4	a				16 45																17 40		

London - Sutton, Epsom, Guildford, Dorking and Horsham

		SW	FC	SN	SN	SW	SN	SW	SN	FC	FC	SN	SN	SN	SW	SN	SW	SN	SN	FC	SW	FC
London Victoria ⊖	d			16 33	16 37		16 50					17 01	17 06			17 20		17 31				
London Waterloo ⊖	d	16 39				16 54		17 09							17 24		17 30				17 39	
Clapham Junction	d	16 48		16 41	16 45	17 03	16 56	17 18				17 09	17 14		17 33	17 26	17 39	17 37			17 48	
Balham ⊖	d			16 46	16 50		17 01					17 14	17 19			17 32		17 42				
London Bridge ⊖	d								17 03					17 06					17 32			
Tulse Hill	d		16 46							17 02	17 20			17 24						17 31		17 48
Norwood Junction	d				17 09				17 16				17 39						17 46			
West Croydon	d			17 04	17 14				17 22			17 33	17 44						17 51			
Waddon	d			17 06	17 16				17 24			17 35	17 46						17 53			
Wallington	d			17 10	17 20				17 28			17 39	17 50						17 57			
Carshalton Beeches	d			17 12	17 22				17 30			17 41	17 52						17 59			
Mitcham Eastfields	d		16 56				17 08				17 28			17 32		17 38		17 48				17 56
Mitcham Junction	d		16 59				17 11				17 31			17 35		17 41		17 51				17 59
Hackbridge	d		17 02				17 15				17 34			17 38		17 45		17 55				18 02
Carshalton	d		17 05				17 17				17 37			17 41		17 47		17 57				18 05
Sutton (Surrey)	a		17 08	17 16	17 26		17 21		17 34	17 39	17 40	17 45	17 58	17 44		17 51		18 01	18 04	18 05		18 08
	d			17 16	17 27		17 21		17 36			17 45		17 48		17 51		18 01	18 05			
Belmont	d			17 20								17 49										
Banstead	d			17 23								17 52										
Epsom Downs	a			17 29								17 58										
Cheam	d				17 29		17 24		17 38							17 54		18 04	18 07			
Ewell East	d				17 33		17 27		17 42							17 57		18 07	18 11			
Epsom	a	17 12			17 37	17 27	17 31	17 42	17 48						17 54	18 01	18 07	18 13	18 15		18 20	
	d	17 17			17 37	17 28	17 32	17 47							17 54	18 02			18 16		18 21	
Ashtead	d	17 21			17 41	17 32	17 36	17 51							17 58	18 06			18 20		18 25	
Leatherhead	d	17 24			17 44	17 35	17 39	17 54							18 01	18 09			18 23		18 28	
Bookham	d	17 29			17 50			17 59											18 28		18 34	
Effingham Junction	d	17 33			17 53			18a05											18 32		18a44	
Guildford	a	17 55			18 13														18 50			
Boxhill & Westhumble	d					17 40	17 44								18 06	18 14						
Dorking	a					17 46	17 46								18 13	18 16						
	d						17 47									18 19						
Holmwood	d						17 54									18 26						
Ockley	d						17 58									18 30						
Warnham	d						18 04									18 36						
Horsham	a						18 10									18 42						

		SN	SN	SN	SW	SN	SW	SN	SW	SN	FC	FC	SN	SN	SN	SW	SN	SW	SN	FC	SW	FC	SW
London Victoria ⊖	d		17 33	17 37		17 50				18 01			18 03	18 07			18 20						
London Waterloo ⊖	d				17 54		18 00		18 09							18 24		18 30			18 39		18 54
Clapham Junction	d		17 41	17 45	18 03	17 56	18 09		18 18	18 08			18 11	18 15		18 33	18 26	18 39			18 48		19 03
Balham ⊖	d		17 46	17 50		18 02				18 12			18 16	18 20			18 32						
London Bridge ⊖	d	17 37						18 02							18 08				18 32				
Tulse Hill	d	17 55									18 02	18 22			18 27					18 32		18 52	
Norwood Junction	d			18 09				18 16						18 39					18 46				
West Croydon	d		18 04	18 15				18 21					18 35	18 45					18 51				
Waddon	d		18 06	18 17				18 23					18 37	18 47					18 53				
Wallington	d		18 10	18 21				18 27					18 41	18 51					18 57				
Carshalton Beeches	d		18 12	18 23				18 29					18 43	18 53					18 59				
Mitcham Eastfields	d	18 02				18 08				18 19		18 30			18 34		18 38					19 00	
Mitcham Junction	d	18 05				18 11				18 22		18 33			18 37		18 41					19 03	
Hackbridge	d	18 09				18 15				18 25		18 36			18 41		18 45					19 06	
Carshalton	d	18 11				18 17				18 28		18 39			18 43		18 47					19 09	
Sutton (Surrey)	a	18 15	18 18	18 29		18 21		18 33		18 36	18 37	18 42	18 47	18 58	18 47		18 51		19 03	19 07		19 12	
	d	18 16	18 19			18 21		18 33		18 36			18 48		18 48		18 51		19 03				
Belmont	d		18 22										18 51										
Banstead	d		18 26										18 55										
Epsom Downs	a		18 31										19 00										
Cheam	d					18 24		18 36		18 39							18 54		19 06				
Ewell East	d					18 27		18 39		18 42							18 57		19 09				
Epsom	a				18 24	18 31	18 35	18 43	18 46	18 48						18 54	19 01	19 07	19 13		19 12		19 24
	d				18 24	18 34		18 44	18 47							18 54	19 02		19 14		19 17		19 24
Ashtead	d				18 28	18 38		18 48	18 51							18 58	19 06		19 18		19 21		19 28
Leatherhead	d				18 31	18 41		18 51	18 54							19 01	19 09		19 21		19 24		19 31
Bookham	d								18 59												19 29		
Effingham Junction	d								19 03												19 33		
Guildford	a								19 25												19 55		
Boxhill & Westhumble	d				18 36	18 46		18 56								19 06	19 14		19 26				19 36
Dorking	a				18 43	18 48		19 00								19 13	19 16		19 30				19 43
	d					18 49											19 19						
Holmwood	d					18 56											19 26						
Ockley	d					19 00											19 30						
Warnham	d					19 06											19 36						
Horsham	a					19 12											19 42						

Table 182

Mondays to Fridays
from 27 September

London - Sutton, Epsom, Guildford, Dorking and Horsham

		SN	SN	SN	SN	SW	SW	FC	FC	SN	SN	SW	SN	SN	SW	FC	FC	SN	SN	SW	SN	SW	FC
London Victoria ⊖	d		18 32	18 36	18 50					19 00	19 06		19 20					19 31	19 36		19 50		
London Waterloo ⊖	d					19 00	19 09					19 24			19 39					19 54		20 09	
Clapham Junction	d		18 40	18 44	18 56	19 09	19 18		19 09	19 08	19 14	19 33	19 26		19 48			19 39	19 44	20 03	19 56	20 18	
Balham ⊖	d		18 45	18 49	19 02					19 14	19 20		19 32					19 44	19 50		20 02		
London Bridge ⊖	d	18 38												19 31									
Tulse Hill	d	18 56						19 16	19 07							19 46	19 31						20 16
Norwood Junction	d			19 09							19 39			19 44					20 09				
West Croydon	d		19 04	19 15						19 32	19 45			19 49				20 02	20 14				
Waddon	d		19 07	19 17						19 35	19 47			19 52				20 05	20 16				
Wallington	d		19 10	19 21						19 38	19 51			19 55				20 08	20 20				
Carshalton Beeches	d		19 13	19 23						19 41	19 53			19 58				20 11	20 22				
Mitcham Eastfields	d	19 03			19 08			19 24					19 38			19 54					20 08		20 24
Mitcham Junction	d	19 06			19 11			19 27					19 41			19 57					20 11		20 27
Hackbridge	d	19 10			19 15			19 30					19 45			20 00					20 15		20 30
Carshalton	d	19 12			19 17			19 33					19 47			20 03					20 17		20 33
Sutton (Surrey)	a	19 16	19 16	19 28	19 21			19 36	19 40	19 44	19 57		19 51	20 01		20 06	20 07	20 14	20 26		20 21		20 36
	d	19 16	19 17		19 21					19 45	19 58		19 51	20 02					20 27		20 21		
Belmont	d		19 20								20 01								20 30				
Banstead	d		19 24								20 05								20 34				
Epsom Downs	a		19 29								20 08								20 37				
Cheam	d	19 19			19 24					19 47			19 54	20 04							20 24		
Ewell East	d	19 22			19 27					19 51			19 57	20 08							20 27		
Epsom	a	19 28			19 31	19 35	19 43			19 55		19 57	20 01	20 12	20 16					20 27	20 31	20 42	
	d				19 34		19 47					19 58	20 02	20 13	20 17						20 32	20 47	
Ashtead	d				19 38		19 51					20 02	20 06		20 21						20 36	20 51	
Leatherhead	d				19 41		19 54					20 05	20 09	20 19	20 24						20 39	20 54	
Bookham	d						19 59								20 29								
Effingham Junction	d						20 03								20 33								
Guildford	a						20 23								20 53								
Boxhill & Westhumble	d				19 46							20 10	20 14								20 44	20 59	
Dorking	a				19 50							20 14	20 16	20 25							20 46	21 03	
	d												20 17										
Holmwood	d												20 24										
Ockley	d												20 28										
Warnham	d												20 34										
Horsham	a												20 38										

		FC	SN	SN	SW	SN	FC	SW	FC	SN	SN	SW	SN	FC	SN	SN	SW	SW	SN	FC	SN	SN
London Victoria ⊖	d		20 00	20 06		20 20				20 30	20 36		20 50		21 00	21 06			21 20		21 30	21 36
London Waterloo ⊖	d				20 24			20 39				20 54					21 09	21 24				
Clapham Junction	d		20 08	20 14	20 33	20 26		20 48		20 38	20 44	21 03	20 56		21 08	21 14	21 18	21 33	21 26		21 38	21 44
Balham ⊖	d		20 14	20 20		20 31				20 44	20 50		21 02		21 14	21 20			21 31		21 44	21 50
London Bridge ⊖	d																					
Tulse Hill	d	20 01					20 31		20 46					21 01						21 31		
Norwood Junction	d			20 39							21 09					21 39						22 09
West Croydon	d		20 32	20 44						21 02	21 14				21 32	21 44					22 02	22 14
Waddon	d		20 35	20 46						21 05	21 16				21 35	21 46					22 05	22 16
Wallington	d		20 38	20 50						21 08	21 20				21 38	21 50					22 08	22 20
Carshalton Beeches	d		20 41	20 52						21 11	21 22				21 41	21 52					22 11	22 22
Mitcham Eastfields	d					20 38			20 54				21 08						21 38			
Mitcham Junction	d					20 41			20 57				21 11						21 41			
Hackbridge	d					20 45			21 00				21 15						21 45			
Carshalton	d					20 47			21 03				21 17						21 47			
Sutton (Surrey)	a	20 37	20 44	20 56		20 51	21 05		21 06	21 14	21 26		21 21	21 39	21 44	21 56			21 51	22 05	22 14	22 26
	d			20 57		20 51					21 27		21 21			21 57			21 51			22 27
Belmont	d										21 30											22 30
Banstead	d										21 34											22 34
Epsom Downs	a										21 37											22 37
Cheam	d			20 59		20 54							21 24			21 59			21 54			
Ewell East	d			21 03		20 57							21 27			22 03			21 57			
Epsom	a			21 07	20 57	21 01		21 12				21 27	21 31			22 07	21 42	21 57	22 01			
	d					21 02		21 17					21 32				21 47		22 02			
Ashtead	d					21 06		21 21					21 36				21 51		22 06			
Leatherhead	d					21 09		21 24					21 39				21 54		22 09			
Bookham	d							21 29														
Effingham Junction	d							21 33														
Guildford	a							21 53														
Boxhill & Westhumble	d					21 14							21 44				21 59					
Dorking	a					21 16							21 46				22 03		22 15			
	d																					
Holmwood	d																					
Ockley	d																					
Warnham	d																					
Horsham	a																					

London - Sutton, Epsom, Guildford, Dorking and Horsham

Mondays to Fridays
from 27 September

		SW	SW	SN	FC	SN	SN	SW	SN	FC	SN	SN	SW	SN	SW	SN	FC	SN	SN	FC	SN	SW	SN
London Victoria ⊖	d			21 50		22 00	22 06		22 20		22 30	22 36		22 50		23 00		23 06	23 26		23 34		23 51
London Waterloo ⊖	d	21 39	21 54					22 09					22 39		23 09							23 42	
Clapham Junction	d	21 48	22 03	21 56		22 08	22 14	22 18	22 26		22 38	22 44	22 48	22 56	23 18	23 08		23 14	23 34		23 42	23 51	23 59
Balham ⊖	d			22 02		22 14	22 20		22 32		22 44	22 50		23 01		23 14		23 20	23 40		23 47		00 04
London Bridge ⊖	d																23 02			23 28			
Tulse Hill	d				22 01					22 31							23 12			23 40			
Norwood Junction	d						22 39					23 09						23 39					
West Croydon	d					22 32	22 44				23 02	23 14				23 32		23 44			00 04		00 21
Waddon	d					22 35	22 46				23 05	23 16				23 35		23 46			00 06		00 24
Wallington	d					22 38	22 50				23 08	23 20				23 38		23 50			00 10		00 27
Carshalton Beeches	d					22 41	22 52				23 11	23 22				23 41		23 52			00 12		00 30
Mitcham Eastfields	d			22 08					22 38					23 07					23 46				
Mitcham Junction	d			22 11					22 41					23 10					23 49				
Hackbridge	d			22 15					22 45					23 14					23 53				
Carshalton	d			22 17					22 47					23 16					23 55				
Sutton (Surrey)	a			22 21	22 39	22 44	22 56		22 51	23 05	23 14	23 26		23 20		23 44	23 45	23 56	00 01	00 13	00 16		00 33
	d			22 21			22 57		22 51			23 27		23 20		23 45			00 02				
Belmont	d											23 30											
Banstead	d											23 34											
Epsom Downs	a											23 37											
Cheam	d			22 24			22 59		22 54					23 23		23 47			00 04				
Ewell East	d			22 27			23 03		22 57					23 26		23 51			00 08				
Epsom	a	22 12	22 27	22 31			23 07	22 42	23 01				23 12	23 30	23 42	23 55			00 12			00 15	
	d	22 17		22 32				22 47	23 02				23 17	23 31	23 47				00 12			00 19	
Ashtead	d	22 21		22 36				22 51	23 06				23 21	23 35	23 51				00 16			00 23	
Leatherhead	d	22 24		22 39				22 54	23 09				23 24	23 38	23 54				00 19			00 26	
Bookham	d	22 29											23 29									00 31	
Effingham Junction	d	22 33											23 33									00 37	
Guildford	a	22 53											23 54									00 57	
Boxhill & Westhumble	d			22 44				22 59						23 43	23 59				00 24				
Dorking	a			22 46				23 03	23 15					23 45	00 03				00 27				
	d																		00 27				
Holmwood	d																		00s34				
Ockley	d																		00s38				
Warnham	d																		00s44				
Horsham	a																		00 48				

		FC
London Victoria ⊖	d	
London Waterloo ⊖	d	
Clapham Junction	d	
Balham ⊖	d	
London Bridge ⊖	d	23 58
Tulse Hill	d	00 10
Norwood Junction	d	
West Croydon	d	
Waddon	d	
Wallington	d	
Carshalton Beeches	d	
Mitcham Eastfields	d	
Mitcham Junction	d	
Hackbridge	d	
Carshalton	d	
Sutton (Surrey)	a	00 43
	d	
Belmont	d	
Banstead	d	
Epsom Downs	a	
Cheam	d	
Ewell East	d	
Epsom	a	
	d	
Ashtead	d	
Leatherhead	d	
Bookham	d	
Effingham Junction	d	
Guildford	a	
Boxhill & Westhumble	d	
Dorking	a	
	d	
Holmwood	d	
Ockley	d	
Warnham	d	
Horsham	a	

London - Sutton, Epsom, Guildford, Dorking and Horsham

Saturdays
29 May to 25 September

		SW	SN	FC	SN	SW	SN	FC	SW	SN	FC	SN	SW	FC	SN	SN	FC	SW	FC	SN	SN	SW	SN
London Victoria ⊖	d		23p26		23p34		23p51					06 23			06 47					06 53	07 06		07 17
London Waterloo ⊖	d	23p09				23p42			00 15				06 39					07 09				07 24	
Clapham Junction	d	23p18	23p34		23p42	23p51	23p59		00 24			06 30	06 48		06 54			07 18		07 00	07 14	07 33	07 24
Balham ⊖	d		23p40		23p47		00 04					06 35			07 00					07 05	07 20		07 30
London Bridge ⊖	d			23p28				23p58			06 21						06 45						
Tulse Hill	d			23p40				00 10			06 31			06 46			07 01		07 16				
Norwood Junction	d															07 09					07 39		
West Croydon	d				00 04		00 21			06 45		06 54				07 15				07 24	07 44		
Waddon	d				00 06		00 24			06 47		06 56				07 17				07 26	07 46		
Wallington	d				00 10		00 27			06 51		07 00				07 21				07 30	07 50		
Carshalton Beeches	d				00 12		00 30			06 53		07 02				07 23				07 32	07 52		
Mitcham Eastfields	d		23p46											06 54	07 06				07 24				07 36
Mitcham Junction	d		23p49											06 57	07 09				07 27				07 39
Hackbridge	d		23p53											07 00	07 13				07 30				07 43
Carshalton	d		23p55											07 03	07 15				07 33				07 45
Sutton (Surrey)	a		00 01	00 13	00 16		00 33	00 43		06 57	07 05	07 06		07 06	07 19	07 27	07 35		07 36	07 39	07 56		07 49
	d		00 02							06 57		07 07			07 19					07 40			07 49
Belmont	d											07 10											
Banstead	d											07 14											
Epsom Downs	a											07 17											
Cheam	d		00 04							07 00					07 22					07 42			07 52
Ewell East	d		00 08							07 03					07 25					07 46			07 55
Epsom	a	23p42	00 12			00 15			00 48	07 07			07 16		07 29			07 46		07 52		07 57	07 59
	d	23p47	00 12			00 19				07 08			07 17		07 30			07 47				07 58	
Ashtead	d	23p51	00 16			00 23				07 12			07 21		07 34			07 51				08 02	
Leatherhead	d	23p54	00 19			00 26				07 15			07 24		07 37			07 54				08 05	
Bookham	d					00 31							07 29					07 59					
Effingham Junction	d					00 37							07 33					08 03					
Guildford	a					00 54							07 50					08 20					
Boxhill & Westhumble	d	23p59	00 24												07 42								
Dorking	a	00 01	00 27							07 21					07 44							08 11	
	d		00 27																				
Holmwood	d		00s34																				
Ockley	d		00s38																				
Warnham	d		00s44																				
Horsham	a		00 48																				

		SN	SN	FC	SW	FC	SN	SN	SW	SN	SN	SN	FC	SW	FC	SN	SN	SW	SN	SN	SN	FC	SW
London Victoria ⊖	d	07 23	07 31				07 33	07 36		07 47	07 53	08 01				08 03	08 06		08 17	08 23	08 31		
London Waterloo ⊖	d				07 39				07 54					08 09				08 24					08 39
Clapham Junction	d	07 30	07 38		07 48		07 41	07 44	08 03	07 54	08 00	08 08		08 18		08 11	08 14	08 33	08 24	08 30	08 38		08 48
Balham ⊖	d	07 35					07 46	07 50		08 00	08 05					08 16	08 20		08 30	08 35			
London Bridge ⊖	d			07 15									07 45									08 15	
Tulse Hill	d			07 31		07 46							08 01		08 16							08 31	
Norwood Junction	d							08 09									08 39						
West Croydon	d	07 54					08 04	08 14			08 24					08 34	08 44			08 54			
Waddon	d	07 56					08 06	08 16			08 26					08 36	08 46			08 56			
Wallington	d	08 00					08 10	08 20			08 30					08 40	08 50			09 00			
Carshalton Beeches	d	08 02					08 12	08 22			08 32					08 42	08 52			09 02			
Mitcham Eastfields	d					07 54				08 06					08 24				08 36				
Mitcham Junction	d					07 57				08 09					08 27				08 39				
Hackbridge	d					08 00				08 13					08 30				08 43				
Carshalton	d					08 03				08 15					08 33				08 45				
Sutton (Surrey)	a	08 06	07 58	08 05		08 06	08 16	08 26		08 19	08 39	08 28	08 35		08 36	08 46	08 56		08 49	09 06	08 58	09 05	
	d	08 07	07 59							08 19	08 40	08 29							08 49	09 07	08 59		
Belmont	d	08 10																		09 10			
Banstead	d	08 14																		09 14			
Epsom Downs	a	08 17																		09 17			
Cheam	d		08 01							08 22	08 42	08 31							08 52		09 01		
Ewell East	d		08 05							08 25	08 46								08 55		09 05		
Epsom	a		08 09		08 16				08 27	08 29	08 52	08 37		08 46				08 57	08 59		09 09		09 16
	d		08 09		08 17				08 28			08 37		08 47				08 58			09 09		09 17
Ashtead	d		08 13		08 21				08 32			08 41		08 51				09 02			09 13		09 21
Leatherhead	d		08 16		08 24				08 35			08 44		08 54				09 05			09 16		09 24
Bookham	d				08 29									08 59									09 29
Effingham Junction	d				08 33									09 03									09 33
Guildford	a				08 50									09 20									09 50
Boxhill & Westhumble	d		08 21																		09 21		
Dorking	a		08 24						08 41			08 50						09 11			09 24		
	d		08 24																		09 24		
Holmwood	d		08 32																		09 32		
Ockley	d		08 36																		09 36		
Warnham	d		08 41																		09 41		
Horsham	a		08 45																		09 45		

London - Sutton, Epsom, Guildford, Dorking and Horsham

		FC	SN	SN	SW	SN	SN	SN	FC	SW	FC	SN	SN	SW	SN	SN	SN	FC	SW	FC	SN	SN
London Victoria 15 ⊖	d		08 33	08 36		08 47	08 53	09 01				09 03	09 06		09 17	09 23	09 31				09 33	09 36
London Waterloo 15 ⊖	d				08 54					09 09				09 24					09 39			
Clapham Junction 10	d		08 41	08 44	09 03	08 54	09 00	09 08		09 18		09 11	09 14	09 33	09 24	09 30	09 38		09 48		09 41	09 44
Balham 4 ⊖	d		08 46	08 50		09 00	09 05					09 16	09 20		09 30	09 35					09 46	09 50
London Bridge 4 ⊖	d								08 45									09 15				
Tulse Hill 3	d	08 46							09 01		09 16							09 31		09 46		
Norwood Junction 2	d			09 09									09 39									10 09
West Croydon 4	d		09 04	09 14			09 24					09 34	09 44			09 54					10 04	10 14
Waddon	d		09 06	09 16			09 26					09 36	09 46			09 56					10 06	10 16
Wallington	d		09 10	09 20			09 30					09 40	09 50			10 00					10 10	10 20
Carshalton Beeches	d		09 12	09 22			09 32					09 42	09 52			10 02					10 12	10 22
Mitcham Eastfields	d	08 54				09 06					09 24				09 36					09 54		
Mitcham Junction	d	08 57				09 09					09 27				09 39					09 57		
Hackbridge	d	09 00				09 13					09 30				09 43					10 00		
Carshalton	d	09 03				09 15					09 33				09 45					10 03		
Sutton (Surrey) 4	a	09 06	09 16	09 26		09 19	09 39	09 28	09 35		09 36	09 46	09 56		09 49	10 06	09 58	10 05		10 06	10 16	10 26
	d					09 19	09 40	09 29							09 49	10 07	09 59					
Belmont	d															10 10						
Banstead	d															10 14						
Epsom Downs	a															10 17						
Cheam	d					09 22	09 42	09 31							09 52		10 01					
Ewell East	d					09 25	09 46								09 55		10 05					
Epsom 3	a				09 27	09 29	09 52	09 37		09 46				09 57	09 59		10 09		10 16			
	d				09 28			09 37		09 47				09 58			10 09		10 17			
Ashtead	d				09 32			09 41		09 51				10 02			10 13		10 21			
Leatherhead	d				09 35			09 44		09 54				10 05			10 16		10 24			
Bookham	d									09 59									10 29			
Effingham Junction 6	d									10 03									10 33			
Guildford	a									10 20									10 50			
Boxhill & Westhumble	d																10 21					
Dorking 4	a				09 41			09 50						10 11			10 24					
	d																10 24					
Holmwood	d																10 32					
Ockley	d																10 36					
Warnham	d																10 41					
Horsham 4	a																10 45					

		SW	SN	SN	SN	FC	SW	FC	SN	SN	SW	SN	SN	SN	FC	SW	FC	SN	SN	SW	SN	SN	SN
London Victoria 15 ⊖	d		09 47	09 53	10 01				10 03	10 06		10 17	10 23	10 31				10 33	10 36		10 47	10 53	11 01
London Waterloo 15 ⊖	d	09 54					10 09				10 24					10 39				10 54			
Clapham Junction 10	d	10 03	09 54	10 00	10 08		10 18		10 11	10 14	10 33	10 24	10 30	10 38		10 48		10 41	10 44	11 03	10 54	11 00	11 08
Balham 4 ⊖	d		10 00	10 05					10 16	10 20		10 30	10 35					10 46	10 50		11 00	11 05	
London Bridge 4 ⊖	d					09 45									10 15								
Tulse Hill 3	d					10 01		10 16							10 31		10 46						
Norwood Junction 2	d									10 39									11 09				
West Croydon 4	d			10 24					10 34	10 44			10 54					11 04	11 14			11 24	
Waddon	d			10 26					10 36	10 46			10 56					11 06	11 16			11 26	
Wallington	d			10 30					10 40	10 50			11 00					11 10	11 20			11 30	
Carshalton Beeches	d			10 32					10 42	10 52			11 02					11 12	11 22			11 32	
Mitcham Eastfields	d		10 06					10 24				10 36					10 54				11 08		
Mitcham Junction	d		10 09					10 27				10 39					10 57				11 11		
Hackbridge	d		10 13					10 30				10 43					11 00				11 15		
Carshalton	d		10 15					10 33				10 45					11 03				11 17		
Sutton (Surrey) 4	a		10 19	10 39	10 28	10 35		10 36	10 46	10 56		10 49	11 06	10 58	11 05		11 06	11 16	11 26		11 21	11 39	11 28
	d		10 19	10 40	10 29							10 49	11 07	10 59							11 21	11 40	11 29
Belmont	d												11 10										
Banstead	d												11 14										
Epsom Downs	a												11 17										
Cheam	d		10 22	10 42	10 31							10 52		11 01							11 24	11 42	11 31
Ewell East	d		10 25	10 46								10 55		11 05							11 27	11 46	
Epsom 3	a	10 27	10 29	10 52	10 37		10 46				10 57	10 59		11 09		11 16				11 27	11 31	11 52	11 37
	d	10 28			10 37		10 47				10 58			11 09		11 17				11 28			11 37
Ashtead	d	10 32			10 41		10 51				11 02			11 13		11 21				11 32			11 41
Leatherhead	d	10 35			10 44		10 54				11 05			11 16		11 24				11 35			11 44
Bookham	d						10 59									11 29							
Effingham Junction 6	d						11 03									11 33							
Guildford	a						11 20									11 50							
Boxhill & Westhumble	d													11 21									
Dorking 4	a	10 41			10 50						11 11			11 24						11 41			11 50
	d													11 24									
Holmwood	d													11 32									
Ockley	d													11 36									
Warnham	d													11 41									
Horsham 4	a													11 45									

London - Sutton, Epsom, Guildford, Dorking and Horsham

		FC	SW	FC	SN	SN	SW	SN	SN	SN	FC	SW	FC	SN	SN	SW	SN	SN	SN	FC	SW	FC
London Victoria 15 ⊖	d				11 03	11 06		11 17	11 23	11 31				11 33	11 36		11 47	11 53	12 01			
London Waterloo 15 ⊖	d		11 09				11 24					11 39				11 54					12 09	
Clapham Junction 10	d		11 18		11 11	11 14	11 33	11 24	11 30	11 38		11 48		11 41	11 44	12 03	11 54	12 00	12 08		12 18	
Balham 4 ⊖	d				11 16	11 20		11 30	11 35					11 46	11 50		12 00	12 05				
London Bridge 4 ⊖	d	10 45									11 15									11 45		
Tulse Hill 3	d	11 01		11 16							11 31		11 46							12 01		12 16
Norwood Junction 2	d					11 39									12 09							
West Croydon 4	d				11 34	11 44			11 54					12 04	12 14			12 24				
Waddon	d				11 36	11 46			11 56					12 06	12 16			12 26				
Wallington	d				11 40	11 50			12 00					12 10	12 20			12 30				
Carshalton Beeches	d				11 42	11 52			12 02					12 12	12 22			12 32				
Mitcham Eastfields	d			11 24				11 36					11 54				12 06					12 24
Mitcham Junction	d			11 27				11 39					11 57				12 09					12 27
Hackbridge	d			11 30				11 43					12 00				12 13					12 30
Carshalton	d			11 33				11 45					12 03				12 15					12 33
Sutton (Surrey) 4	a	11 35		11 36	11 46	11 56		11 49	12 06	11 58	12 05		12 06	12 16	12 26		12 19	12 39	12 28	12 35		12 36
	d							11 49	12 07	11 59							12 19	12 40	12 29			
Belmont	d								12 10													
Banstead	d								12 14													
Epsom Downs	a								12 17													
Cheam	d							11 52		12 01							12 22	12 42	12 31			
Ewell East	d							11 55		12 05							12 25	12 46				
Epsom 3	a		11 46				11 57	11 59		12 09		12 16				12 27	12 29	12 52	12 37		12 46	
	d		11 47				11 58			12 09		12 17				12 28			12 37		12 47	
Ashtead	d		11 51				12 02			12 13		12 21				12 32			12 41		12 51	
Leatherhead	d		11 54				12 05			12 16		12 24				12 35			12 44		12 54	
Bookham	d		11 59									12 29									12 59	
Effingham Junction 6	d		12 03									12 33									13 03	
Guildford	a		12 20									12 50									13 20	
Boxhill & Westhumble	d									12 21												
Dorking 4	a						12 11			12 24						12 41			12 50			
	d									12 24												
Holmwood	d									12 32												
Ockley	d									12 36												
Warnham	d									12 41												
Horsham 4	a									12 45												

		SN	SN	SW	SN	SN	SN	FC	SW	FC	SN	SN	SW	SN	SN	SN	FC	SW	FC	SN	SN	SW	SN
London Victoria 15 ⊖	d	12 03	12 06		12 17	12 23	12 31				12 33	12 36		12 47	12 53	13 01				13 03	13 06		13 17
London Waterloo 15 ⊖	d			12 24					12 39				12 54					13 09				13 24	
Clapham Junction 10	d	12 11	12 14	12 33	12 24	12 30	12 38		12 48		12 41	12 44	13 03	12 54	13 00	13 08		13 18		13 11	13 14	13 33	13 24
Balham 4 ⊖	d	12 16	12 20		12 30	12 35					12 46	12 50		13 00	13 05					13 16	13 20		13 30
London Bridge 4 ⊖	d							12 15									12 45						
Tulse Hill 3	d							12 31		12 46							13 01		13 16				
Norwood Junction 2	d		12 39									13 09									13 39		
West Croydon 4	d	12 34	12 44			12 54					13 04	13 14			13 24					13 34	13 44		
Waddon	d	12 36	12 46			12 56					13 06	13 16			13 26					13 36	13 46		
Wallington	d	12 40	12 50			13 00					13 10	13 20			13 30					13 40	13 50		
Carshalton Beeches	d	12 42	12 52			13 02					13 12	13 22			13 32					13 42	13 52		
Mitcham Eastfields	d				12 36					12 54				13 06					13 24				13 36
Mitcham Junction	d				12 39					12 57				13 09					13 27				13 39
Hackbridge	d				12 43					13 00				13 13					13 30				13 43
Carshalton	d				12 45					13 03				13 15					13 33				13 45
Sutton (Surrey) 4	a	12 46	12 56		12 49	13 06	12 58	13 05		13 06	13 16	13 26		13 19	13 39	13 28	13 35		13 36	13 46	13 56		13 49
	d				12 49	13 07	12 59							13 19	13 40	13 29							13 49
Belmont	d					13 10																	
Banstead	d					13 14																	
Epsom Downs	a					13 17																	
Cheam	d				12 52		13 01							13 22	13 42	13 31							13 52
Ewell East	d				12 55		13 05							13 25	13 46								13 55
Epsom 3	a			12 57	12 59		13 09		13 16				13 27	13 29	13 52	13 37		13 46				13 57	13 59
	d			12 58			13 09		13 17				13 28			13 37		13 47				13 58	
Ashtead	d			13 02			13 13		13 21				13 32			13 41		13 51				14 02	
Leatherhead	d			13 05			13 16		13 24				13 35			13 44		13 54				14 05	
Bookham	d								13 29									13 59					
Effingham Junction 6	d								13 33									14 03					
Guildford	a								13 50									14 20					
Boxhill & Westhumble	d						13 21																
Dorking 4	a			13 11			13 24						13 41			13 50						14 11	
	d						13 24																
Holmwood	d						13 32																
Ockley	d						13 36																
Warnham	d						13 41																
Horsham 4	a						13 45																

London - Sutton, Epsom, Guildford, Dorking and Horsham

		SN	SN	FC	SW	FC		SN	SN	SW	SN	SN	SN	FC	SW	FC		SN	SN	SW	SN	SN	SN	FC	SW
London Victoria 15	⊖ d	13 23	13 31					13 33	13 36		13 47	13 53	14 01					14 03	14 06		14 17	14 23	14 31		
London Waterloo 15	⊖ d				13 39					13 54					14 09					14 24					14 39
Clapham Junction 10	d	13 30	13 38		13 48			13 41	13 44	14 03	13 54	14 00	14 08		14 18			14 11	14 14	14 33	14 24	14 30	14 38		14 48
Balham 4	⊖ d	13 35						13 46	13 50		14 00	14 05						14 16	14 20		14 30	14 35			
London Bridge 4	⊖ d			13 15										13 45										14 15	
Tulse Hill 3	d			13 31		13 46								14 01		14 16								14 31	
Norwood Junction 2	d								14 09										14 39						
West Croydon 4	d	13 54						14 04	14 14			14 24						14 34	14 44			14 54			
Waddon	d	13 56						14 06	14 16			14 26						14 36	14 46			14 56			
Wallington	d	14 00						14 10	14 20			14 30						14 40	14 50			15 00			
Carshalton Beeches	d	14 02						14 12	14 22			14 32						14 42	14 52			15 02			
Mitcham Eastfields	d					13 54					14 06					14 24					14 36				
Mitcham Junction	d					13 57					14 09					14 27					14 39				
Hackbridge	d					14 00					14 13					14 30					14 43				
Carshalton	d					14 03					14 15					14 33					14 45				
Sutton (Surrey) 4	a	14 06	13 58	14 05		14 06		14 16	14 26		14 19	14 39	14 28	14 35		14 36		14 46	14 56		14 49	15 06	14 58	15 05	
	d	14 07	13 59								14 19	14 40	14 29								14 49	15 07	14 59		
Belmont	d	14 10																				15 10			
Banstead	d	14 14																				15 14			
Epsom Downs	a	14 17																				15 17			
Cheam	d		14 01								14 22	14 42	14 31								14 52		15 01		
Ewell East	d		14 05								14 25	14 46									14 55		15 05		
Epsom 3	a		14 09		14 16					14 27	14 29	14 52	14 37		14 46					14 57	14 59		15 09		15 16
	d		14 09		14 17					14 28			14 37		14 47					14 58			15 09		15 17
Ashtead	d		14 13		14 21					14 32			14 41		14 51					15 02			15 13		15 21
Leatherhead	d		14 16		14 24					14 35			14 44		14 54					15 05			15 16		15 24
Bookham	d				14 29										14 59										15 29
Effingham Junction 6	d				14 33										15 03										15 33
Guildford	a				14 50										15 20										15 50
Boxhill & Westhumble	d		14 21																				15 21		
Dorking 4	a		14 24							14 41			14 50							15 11			15 24		
	d		14 24																				15 24		
Holmwood	d		14 32																				15 32		
Ockley	d		14 36																				15 36		
Warnham	d		14 41																				15 41		
Horsham 4	a		14 45																				15 45		

		FC		SN	SN	SW	SN	SN	SN	FC	SW	FC		SN	SN	SW	SN	SN	SN	FC	SW	FC		SN	SN
London Victoria 15	⊖ d			14 33	14 36		14 47	14 53	15 01					15 03	15 06		15 17	15 23	15 31					15 33	15 36
London Waterloo 15	⊖ d					14 54					15 09					15 24					15 39				
Clapham Junction 10	d			14 41	14 44	15 03	14 54	15 00	15 08		15 18			15 11	15 14	15 33	15 24	15 30	15 38		15 48			15 41	15 44
Balham 4	⊖ d			14 46	14 50		15 00	15 05						15 16	15 20		15 30	15 35						15 46	15 50
London Bridge 4	⊖ d									14 45										15 15					
Tulse Hill 3	d	14 46								15 01		15 16								15 31		15 46			
Norwood Junction 2	d				15 09										15 39										16 09
West Croydon 4	d			15 04	15 14			15 24						15 34	15 44			15 54						16 04	16 14
Waddon	d			15 06	15 16			15 26						15 36	15 46			15 56						16 06	16 16
Wallington	d			15 10	15 20			15 30						15 40	15 50			16 00						16 10	16 20
Carshalton Beeches	d			15 12	15 22			15 32						15 42	15 52			16 02						16 12	16 22
Mitcham Eastfields	d	14 54					15 06					15 24					15 36					15 54			
Mitcham Junction	d	14 57					15 09					15 27					15 39					15 57			
Hackbridge	d	15 00					15 13					15 30					15 43					16 00			
Carshalton	d	15 03					15 15					15 33					15 45					16 03			
Sutton (Surrey) 4	a	15 06		15 16	15 26		15 19	15 39	15 28	15 35		15 36		15 46	15 56		15 49	16 06	15 58	16 05		16 06		16 16	16 26
	d						15 19	15 40	15 29								15 49	16 07	15 59						
Belmont	d																	16 10							
Banstead	d																	16 14							
Epsom Downs	a																	16 17							
Cheam	d						15 22	15 42	15 31								15 52		16 01						
Ewell East	d						15 25	15 46									15 55		16 05						
Epsom 3	a					15 27	15 29	15 52	15 37		15 46					15 57	15 59		16 09		16 16				
	d					15 28			15 37		15 47					15 58			16 09		16 17				
Ashtead	d					15 32			15 41		15 51					16 02			16 13		16 21				
Leatherhead	d					15 35			15 44		15 54					16 05			16 16		16 24				
Bookham	d										15 59										16 29				
Effingham Junction 6	d										16 03										16 33				
Guildford	a										16 20										16 50				
Boxhill & Westhumble	d																		16 21						
Dorking 4	a					15 41			15 50							16 11			16 24						
	d																		16 24						
Holmwood	d																		16 32						
Ockley	d																		16 36						
Warnham	d																		16 41						
Horsham 4	a																		16 45						

London - Sutton, Epsom, Guildford, Dorking and Horsham

		SW	SN	SN	SN	FC	SW	FC		SN	SN	SW	SN	SN	SN	FC	SW	FC		SN	SN	SW	SN	SN	SN
London Victoria 15	⊖ d		15 47	15 53	16 01					16 03	16 06		16 17	16 23	16 31					16 33	16 36		16 47	16 53	17 01
London Waterloo 15	⊖ d	15 54					16 09					16 24					16 39					16 54			
Clapham Junction 10	d	16 03	15 54	16 00	16 08		16 18			16 11	16 14	16 33	16 24	16 30	16 38		16 48			16 41	16 44	17 03	16 54	17 00	17 08
Balham 4	⊖ d		16 00	16 05						16 16	16 20		16 30	16 35						16 46	16 50		17 00	17 05	
London Bridge 4	⊖ d					15 45										16 15									
Tulse Hill 3	d					16 01		16 16								16 31		16 46							
Norwood Junction 2	d										16 39										17 09				
West Croydon 4	d			16 24						16 34	16 44			16 54						17 04	17 14			17 24	
Waddon	d			16 26						16 36	16 46			16 56						17 06	17 16			17 26	
Wallington	d			16 30						16 40	16 50			17 00						17 10	17 20			17 30	
Carshalton Beeches	d			16 32						16 42	16 52			17 02						17 12	17 22			17 32	
Mitcham Eastfields	d		16 06					16 24					16 36					16 54					17 06		
Mitcham Junction	d		16 09					16 27					16 39					16 57					17 09		
Hackbridge	d		16 13					16 30					16 43					17 00					17 13		
Carshalton	d		16 15					16 33					16 45					17 03					17 15		
Sutton (Surrey) 4	a		16 19	16 39	16 28	16 35		16 36		16 46	16 56		16 49	17 06	16 58	17 05		17 06		17 16	17 26		17 19	17 39	17 28
	d		16 19	16 40	16 29								16 49	17 07	16 59								17 19	17 40	17 29
Belmont	d													17 10											
Banstead	d													17 14											
Epsom Downs	a													17 17											
Cheam	d		16 22	16 42	16 31								16 52		17 01								17 22	17 42	17 31
Ewell East	d		16 25	16 46									16 55		17 05								17 25	17 46	
Epsom 3	a	16 27	16 29	16 52	16 37		16 46					16 57	16 59		17 09		17 16					17 27	17 29	17 52	17 37
	d	16 28			16 37		16 47					16 58			17 09		17 17					17 28			17 37
Ashtead	d	16 32			16 41		16 51					17 02			17 13		17 21					17 32			17 41
Leatherhead	d	16 35			16 44		16 54					17 05			17 16		17 24					17 35			17 44
Bookham	d						16 59										17 29								
Effingham Junction 6	d						17 03										17 33								
Guildford	a						17 20										17 50								
Boxhill & Westhumble	d														17 21										
Dorking 4	a	16 41			16 50							17 11			17 24							17 41			17 50
	d														17 24										
Holmwood	d														17 32										
Ockley	d														17 36										
Warnham	d														17 41										
Horsham 4	a														17 45										

		FC	SW	FC		SN	SN	SW	SN	SN	SN	FC	SW	FC		SN	SN	SW	SN	SN	SN	FC	SN	SW	
London Victoria 15	⊖ d					17 03	17 06		17 17	17 23	17 31					17 33	17 36		17 47	17 53	18 01		18 06		
London Waterloo 15	⊖ d		17 09					17 24					17 39					17 54						18 09	
Clapham Junction 10	d		17 18			17 11	17 14	17 33	17 24	17 30	17 38		17 48			17 41	17 44	18 03	17 54	18 00	18 08		18 14	18 18	
Balham 4	⊖ d					17 16	17 20		17 30	17 35						17 46	17 50		18 00	18 05			18 20		
London Bridge 4	⊖ d	16 45										17 15										17 45			
Tulse Hill 3	d	17 01		17 16								17 31		17 46								18 01			
Norwood Junction 2	d						17 39										18 09						18 39		
West Croydon 4	d					17 34	17 44			17 54						18 04	18 14			18 24			18 44		
Waddon	d					17 36	17 46			17 56						18 06	18 16			18 26			18 46		
Wallington	d					17 40	17 50			18 00						18 10	18 20			18 30			18 50		
Carshalton Beeches	d					17 42	17 52			18 02						18 12	18 22			18 32			18 52		
Mitcham Eastfields	d			17 24					17 36					17 54					18 06						
Mitcham Junction	d			17 27					17 39					17 57					18 09						
Hackbridge	d			17 30					17 43					18 00					18 13						
Carshalton	d			17 33					17 45					18 03					18 15						
Sutton (Surrey) 4	a	17 35		17 36		17 46	17 56		17 49	18 06	17 58	18 05		18 06		18 16	18 26		18 19	18 39	18 28	18 35	18 56		
	d								17 49	18 07	17 59								18 19	18 40	18 29		18 57		
Belmont	d									18 10													19 00		
Banstead	d									18 14													19 04		
Epsom Downs	a									18 17													19 07		
Cheam	d								17 52		18 01								18 22	18 42	18 31				
Ewell East	d								17 55		18 05								18 25	18 46					
Epsom 3	a		17 46					17 57	17 59		18 09		18 16					18 27	18 29	18 50	18 37			18 46	
	d		17 47					17 58			18 09		18 17					18 28			18 37			18 47	
Ashtead	d		17 51					18 02			18 13		18 21					18 32			18 41			18 51	
Leatherhead	d		17 54					18 05			18 16		18 24					18 35			18 44			18 54	
Bookham	d		17 59										18 29											18 59	
Effingham Junction 6	d		18 03										18 33											19 03	
Guildford	a		18 20										18 50											19 20	
Boxhill & Westhumble	d										18 21														
Dorking 4	a							18 11			18 24							18 41			18 50				
	d										18 24														
Holmwood	d										18 32														
Ockley	d										18 36														
Warnham	d										18 41														
Horsham 4	a										18 45														

Table 182

Saturdays

29 May to 25 September

London - Sutton, Epsom, Guildford, Dorking and Horsham

		FC	SW	SN	FC	SN	SN	SW	FC	SW		SN	SW	FC	FC	SN	SN	SW	SN	FC		SW	FC	SN	SN
London Victoria ⊖	d			18 17		18 23	18 36					18 50				19 01	19 06		19 20					19 31	19 36
London Waterloo ⊖	d		18 24					18 39		18 54			19 09					19 24				19 39			
Clapham Junction	d		18 33	18 24		18 30	18 44	18 48		19 03		18 57	19 18			19 09	19 14	19 33	19 26			19 48		19 39	19 44
Balham ⊖	d			18 30		18 35	18 50					19 01				19 14	19 20		19 32					19 44	19 50
London Bridge ⊖	d				18 15										18 45					19 15					
Tulse Hill	d	18 16			18 31				18 46					19 16	19 01					19 31			19 46		
Norwood Junction	d						19 09										19 39								20 09
West Croydon	d					18 54	19 14									19 32	19 44							20 03	20 15
Waddon	d					18 56	19 16									19 35	19 46							20 05	20 18
Wallington	d					19 00	19 20									19 38	19 50							20 09	20 21
Carshalton Beeches	d					19 02	19 22									19 41	19 52							20 11	20 24
Mitcham Eastfields	d	18 24		18 36					18 54			19 08		19 24					19 38				19 55		
Mitcham Junction	d	18 27		18 39					18 57			19 11		19 27					19 41				19 58		
Hackbridge	d	18 30		18 43					19 00			19 15		19 30					19 45				20 01		
Carshalton	d	18 33		18 45					19 03			19 17		19 33					19 47				20 04		
Sutton (Surrey)	a	18 36		18 49	19 05	19 06	19 26		19 06			19 21		19 36	19 39	19 44	19 56		19 51	20 05			20 07	20 15	20 27
	d			18 49			19 27					19 21					19 57		19 51						20 28
Belmont	d						19 30																		20 31
Banstead	d						19 34																		20 35
Epsom Downs	a						19 37																		20 38
Cheam	d			18 52								19 24					19 59		19 54						
Ewell East	d			18 55								19 27					20 03		19 57						
Epsom	a		18 57	18 59				19 12		19 27		19 31	19 42				20 07	19 57	20 01			20 12			
	d		18 58	19 02				19 17		19 28		19 32	19 47					19 58	20 02			20 17			
Ashtead	d		19 02	19 06				19 21		19 32		19 36	19 51					20 02	20 06			20 21			
Leatherhead	d		19 05	19 09				19 24		19 35		19 39	19 54					20 05	20 09			20 24			
Bookham	d							19 29					19 59									20 29			
Effingham Junction	d							19 33					20 03									20 33			
Guildford	a							19 50					20 20									20 50			
Boxhill & Westhumble	d			19 14								19 44													
Dorking	a		19 11	19 16						19 41		19 46						20 11	20 15						
	d																								
Holmwood	d																								
Ockley	d																								
Warnham	d																								
Horsham	a																								

		SW	SN	FC	SN	SN		SW	SW	SN	FC	SN	SN	SW	SW	SN		FC	SN	SN	SW	SW	SN	FC	SN
London Victoria ⊖	d		19 50		20 01	20 06				20 20		20 30	20 36			20 50			21 00	21 06			21 20		21 30
London Waterloo ⊖	d	19 54						20 09	20 24					20 39	20 54						21 09	21 24			
Clapham Junction	d	20 03	19 56		20 09	20 14		20 18	20 33	20 26		20 38	20 44	20 48	21 03	20 56			21 08	21 14	21 18	21 33	21 26		21 38
Balham ⊖	d		20 02		20 14	20 20				20 32		20 44	20 50			21 02			21 14	21 20			21 32		21 44
London Bridge ⊖	d			19 45							20 15							20 45						21 15	
Tulse Hill	d			20 01							20 31							21 01						21 31	
Norwood Junction	d					20 39							21 09							21 39					
West Croydon	d				20 32	20 45						21 03	21 15						21 32	21 45					22 02
Waddon	d				20 35	20 48						21 05	21 18						21 35	21 48					22 05
Wallington	d				20 38	20 51						21 09	21 21						21 38	21 51					22 08
Carshalton Beeches	d				20 41	20 54						21 11	21 24						21 41	21 54					22 11
Mitcham Eastfields	d		20 08							20 38						21 08							21 38		
Mitcham Junction	d		20 11							20 41						21 11							21 41		
Hackbridge	d		20 15							20 45						21 15							21 45		
Carshalton	d		20 17							20 47						21 17							21 47		
Sutton (Surrey)	a		20 21	20 39	20 44	20 57				20 51	21 05	21 15	21 27			21 21		21 39	21 44	21 57			21 51	22 05	22 14
	d		20 21			20 58				20 51			21 28			21 21				21 58			21 51		
Belmont	d												21 31												
Banstead	d												21 35												
Epsom Downs	a												21 38												
Cheam	d		20 24			21 00				20 54						21 24				22 00			21 54		
Ewell East	d		20 27			21 04				20 57						21 27				22 04			21 57		
Epsom	a	20 27	20 31			21 08		20 42	20 57	21 01				21 12	21 27	21 31				22 08	21 42	21 57	22 01		
	d		20 32					20 47		21 02				21 17		21 32					21 47		22 02		
Ashtead	d		20 36					20 51		21 06				21 21		21 36					21 51		22 06		
Leatherhead	d		20 39					20 54		21 09				21 24		21 39					21 54		22 09		
Bookham	d													21 29											
Effingham Junction	d													21 33											
Guildford	a													21 50											
Boxhill & Westhumble	d		20 44													21 44									
Dorking	a		20 46					21 00		21 15						21 46					22 00		22 15		
	d																								
Holmwood	d																								
Ockley	d																								
Warnham	d																								
Horsham	a																								

Table 182

Saturdays

29 May to 25 September

London - Sutton, Epsom, Guildford, Dorking and Horsham

		SN		SW	SW	SN	FC	SN	SN	SW	SN	FC		SN	SN	SW	SN	FC	SW	SN	SN	SN		FC	SN
London Victoria ⊖	d	21 36				21 50		22 00	22 06		22 20			22 30	22 36		22 50			23 00	23 06	23 26			23 34
London Waterloo ⊖	d			21 39	21 54					22 09						22 39			23 09						
Clapham Junction	d	21 44		21 48	22 03	21 56		22 08	22 14	22 18	22 26			22 38	22 44	22 48	22 56		23 18	23 08	23 14	23 34			23 42
Balham ⊖	d	21 50				22 02		22 14	22 20		22 32			22 44	22 50		23 01			23 14	23 20	23 40			23 47
London Bridge ⊖	d						21 45					22 15						22 45						23 15	
Tulse Hill	d						22 01					22 31						23 01						23 31	
Norwood Junction	d	22 09							22 39						23 09						23 39				
West Croydon	d	22 14						22 33	22 44					23 03	23 14					23 32	23 44				00 04
Waddon	d	22 16						22 35	22 46					23 05	23 16					23 35	23 46				00 06
Wallington	d	22 20						22 39	22 50					23 09	23 20					23 38	23 50				00 10
Carshalton Beeches	d	22 22						22 41	22 52					23 11	23 22					23 41	23 52				00 12
Mitcham Eastfields	d					22 08					22 38						23 07					23 46			
Mitcham Junction	d					22 11					22 41						23 10					23 49			
Hackbridge	d					22 15					22 45						23 14					23 53			
Carshalton	d					22 17					22 47						23 16					23 55			
Sutton (Surrey)	a	22 26				22 21	22 39	22 45	22 56		22 51	23 05		23 15	23 26		23 20	23 35		23 44	23 56	00 01		00 05	00 16
	d	22 27				22 21			22 57		22 51				23 27		23 20			23 45		00 02			
Belmont	d	22 30													23 30										
Banstead	d	22 34													23 34										
Epsom Downs	a	22 37													23 37										
Cheam	d					22 24			22 59		22 54						23 23			23 47		00 04			
Ewell East	d					22 27			23 03		22 57						23 26			23 51		00 08			
Epsom	a			22 12	22 27	22 31			23 07	22 42	23 01					23 12	23 30		23 42	23 55		00 12			
	d			22 17		22 32				22 47	23 02					23 17	23 31		23 47			00 12			
Ashtead	d			22 21		22 36				22 51	23 06					23 21	23 35		23 51			00 16			
Leatherhead	d			22 24		22 39				22 54	23 09					23 24	23 38		23 54			00 19			
Bookham	d			22 29												23 29									
Effingham Junction	d			22 33												23 33									
Guildford	a			22 50												23 54									
Boxhill & Westhumble	d					22 44											23 43					00 24			
Dorking	a					22 46				23 00	23 15						23 45		00 01			00 27			
	d																								
Holmwood	d																								
Ockley	d																								
Warnham	d																								
Horsham	a																								

		SW	SN	FC
London Victoria ⊖	d		23 51	
London Waterloo ⊖	d	23 42		
Clapham Junction	d	23 51	23 59	
Balham ⊖	d		00 04	
London Bridge ⊖	d			23 45
Tulse Hill	d			00 01
Norwood Junction	d			
West Croydon	d		00 21	
Waddon	d		00 24	
Wallington	d		00 27	
Carshalton Beeches	d		00 30	
Mitcham Eastfields	d			
Mitcham Junction	d			
Hackbridge	d			
Carshalton	d			
Sutton (Surrey)	a		00 33	00 35
	d			
Belmont	d			
Banstead	d			
Epsom Downs	a			
Cheam	d			
Ewell East	d			
Epsom	a	00 15		
	d	00 19		
Ashtead	d	00 23		
Leatherhead	d	00 26		
Bookham	d	00 31		
Effingham Junction	d	00 37		
Guildford	a	00 54		
Boxhill & Westhumble	d			
Dorking	a			
	d			
Holmwood	d			
Ockley	d			
Warnham	d			
Horsham	a			

Table 182

London - Sutton, Epsom, Guildford, Dorking and Horsham

Saturdays
from 02 October

		SW	SN	FC	SN	SW	SN	FC	SW	SN	FC	SN	SW	FC	SN	SN	FC	SW	FC	SN	SN	SW	SN
London Victoria 15	⊖ d		23p26		23p34		23p51					06 23			06 47					06 53	07 06		07 17
London Waterloo 15	⊖ d	23p09				23p42			00 15				06 39					07 09				07 24	
Clapham Junction 10	d	23p18	23p34		23p42	23p51	23p59		00 24			06 30	06 48		06 54			07 18		07 00	07 14	07 33	07 24
Balham 4	⊖ d		23p40		23p47		00 04					06 35			07 00					07 05	07 20		07 30
London Bridge 4	⊖ d			23p28				23p58			06 21						06 45						
Tulse Hill 3	d			23p40				00 10			06 31			06 46			07 01		07 16				
Norwood Junction 2	d															07 09					07 39		
West Croydon 4	d				00 04		00 21			06 45		06 54				07 15				07 24	07 44		
Waddon	d				00 06		00 24			06 47		06 56				07 17				07 26	07 46		
Wallington	d				00 10		00 27			06 51		07 00				07 21				07 30	07 50		
Carshalton Beeches	d				00 12		00 30			06 53		07 02				07 23				07 32	07 52		
Mitcham Eastfields	d		23p46											06 54	07 06				07 24				07 36
Mitcham Junction	d		23p49											06 57	07 09				07 27				07 39
Hackbridge	d		23p53											07 00	07 13				07 30				07 43
Carshalton	d		23p55											07 03	07 15				07 33				07 45
Sutton (Surrey) 4	a		00 01	00 13	00 16		00 33	00 43		06 57	07 05	07 06		07 06	07 19	07 27	07 35		07 36	07 39	07 56		07 49
	d		00 02							06 57		07 07			07 19					07 40			07 49
Belmont	d											07 10											
Banstead	d											07 14											
Epsom Downs	a											07 17											
Cheam	d		00 04							07 00					07 22					07 42			07 52
Ewell East	d		00 08							07 03					07 25					07 46			07 55
Epsom 3	a	23p42	00 12			00 15			00 48	07 07			07 16		07 29			07 46		07 52		07 57	07 59
	d	23p47	00 12			00 19				07 08			07 17		07 30			07 47				07 58	
Ashtead	d	23p51	00 16			00 23				07 12			07 21		07 34			07 51				08 02	
Leatherhead	d	23p54	00 19			00 26				07 15			07 24		07 37			07 54				08 05	
Bookham	d					00 31							07 29					07 59					
Effingham Junction 6	d					00 37							07 33					08 03					
Guildford	a					00 57							07 53					08 23					
Boxhill & Westhumble	d	23p59	00 24												07 42								
Dorking 4	a	00 03	00 27							07 21					07 44							08 13	
	d		00 27																				
Holmwood	d		00s34																				
Ockley	d		00s38																				
Warnham	d		00s44																				
Horsham 4	a		00 48																				

		SN	SN	FC	SW	FC	SN	SN	SW	SN	SN	SN	FC	SW	FC	SN	SN	SW	SN	SN	SN	FC	SW
London Victoria 15	⊖ d	07 23	07 31				07 33	07 36		07 47	07 53	08 01				08 03	08 06		08 17	08 23	08 31		
London Waterloo 15	⊖ d				07 39				07 54					08 09				08 24					08 39
Clapham Junction 10	d	07 30	07 38		07 48		07 41	07 44	08 03	07 54	08 00	08 08		08 18		08 11	08 14	08 33	08 24	08 30	08 38		08 48
Balham 4	⊖ d	07 35					07 46	07 50		08 00	08 05					08 16	08 20		08 30	08 35			
London Bridge 4	⊖ d			07 15									07 45									08 15	
Tulse Hill 3	d			07 31		07 46							08 01		08 16							08 31	
Norwood Junction 2	d							08 09									08 39						
West Croydon 4	d	07 54					08 04	08 14			08 24					08 34	08 44			08 54			
Waddon	d	07 56					08 06	08 16			08 26					08 36	08 46			08 56			
Wallington	d	08 00					08 10	08 20			08 30					08 40	08 50			09 00			
Carshalton Beeches	d	08 02					08 12	08 22			08 32					08 42	08 52			09 02			
Mitcham Eastfields	d					07 54				08 06					08 24				08 36				
Mitcham Junction	d					07 57				08 09					08 27				08 39				
Hackbridge	d					08 00				08 13					08 30				08 43				
Carshalton	d					08 03				08 15					08 33				08 45				
Sutton (Surrey) 4	a	08 06	07 58	08 05		08 06	08 16	08 26		08 19	08 39	08 28	08 35		08 36	08 46	08 56		08 49	09 06	08 58	09 05	
	d	08 07	07 59							08 19	08 40	08 29							08 49	09 07	08 59		
Belmont	d	08 10																		09 10			
Banstead	d	08 14																		09 14			
Epsom Downs	a	08 17																		09 17			
Cheam	d		08 01							08 22	08 42	08 31							08 52		09 01		
Ewell East	d		08 05							08 25	08 46								08 55		09 05		
Epsom 3	a		08 09		08 16				08 27	08 29	08 52	08 37		08 46				08 57	08 59		09 09		09 16
	d		08 09		08 17				08 28			08 37		08 47				08 58			09 09		09 17
Ashtead	d		08 13		08 21				08 32			08 41		08 51				09 02			09 13		09 21
Leatherhead	d		08 16		08 24				08 35			08 44		08 54				09 05			09 16		09 24
Bookham	d				08 29									08 59									09 29
Effingham Junction 6	d				08 33									09 03									09 33
Guildford	a				08 53									09 23									09 53
Boxhill & Westhumble	d		08 21																		09 21		
Dorking 4	a		08 24						08 43			08 50						09 13			09 24		
	d		08 24																		09 24		
Holmwood	d		08 32																		09 32		
Ockley	d		08 36																		09 36		
Warnham	d		08 41																		09 41		
Horsham 4	a		08 45																		09 45		

Table 182

London - Sutton, Epsom, Guildford, Dorking and Horsham

Saturdays
from 02 October

		FC	SN	SN	SW	SN	SN	SN	FC	SW	FC	SN	SN	SW	SN	SN	SN	FC	SW	FC	SN	SN
London Victoria 15	⊖ d		08 33	08 36		08 47	08 53	09 01				09 03	09 06		09 17	09 23	09 31				09 33	09 36
London Waterloo 15	⊖ d				08 54					09 09				09 24					09 39			
Clapham Junction 10	d		08 41	08 44	09 03	08 54	09 00	09 08		09 18		09 11	09 14	09 33	09 24	09 30	09 38		09 48		09 41	09 44
Balham 4	⊖ d		08 46	08 50		09 00	09 05					09 16	09 20		09 30	09 35					09 46	09 50
London Bridge 4	⊖ d								08 45									09 15				
Tulse Hill 3	d	08 46							09 01		09 16							09 31		09 46		
Norwood Junction 2	d			09 09									09 39									10 09
West Croydon 4	d		09 04	09 14			09 24					09 34	09 44			09 54					10 04	10 14
Waddon	d		09 06	09 16			09 26					09 36	09 46			09 56					10 06	10 16
Wallington	d		09 10	09 20			09 30					09 40	09 50			10 00					10 10	10 20
Carshalton Beeches	d		09 12	09 22			09 32					09 42	09 52			10 02					10 12	10 22
Mitcham Eastfields	d	08 54				09 06					09 24				09 36					09 54		
Mitcham Junction	d	08 57				09 09					09 27				09 39					09 57		
Hackbridge	d	09 00				09 13					09 30				09 43					10 00		
Carshalton	d	09 03				09 15					09 33				09 45					10 03		
Sutton (Surrey) 4	a	09 06	09 16	09 26		09 19	09 39	09 28	09 35		09 36	09 46	09 56		09 49	10 06	09 58	10 05		10 06	10 16	10 26
	d					09 19	09 40	09 29							09 49	10 07	09 59					
Belmont	d															10 10						
Banstead	d															10 14						
Epsom Downs	a															10 17						
Cheam	d					09 22	09 42	09 31							09 52		10 01					
Ewell East	d					09 25	09 46								09 55		10 05					
Epsom 3	a				09 27	09 29	09 52	09 37		09 46				09 57	09 59		10 09		10 16			
	d				09 28			09 37		09 47				09 58			10 09		10 17			
Ashtead	d				09 32			09 41		09 51				10 02			10 13		10 21			
Leatherhead	d				09 35			09 44		09 54				10 05			10 16		10 24			
Bookham	d									09 59									10 29			
Effingham Junction 6	d									10 03									10 33			
Guildford	a									10 23									10 53			
Boxhill & Westhumble	d																10 21					
Dorking 4	a				09 43			09 50						10 13			10 24					
	d																10 24					
Holmwood	d																10 32					
Ockley	d																10 36					
Warnham	d																10 41					
Horsham 4	a																10 45					

		SW	SN	SN	SN	FC	SW	FC	SN	SN	SW	SN	SN	SN	FC	SW	FC	SN	SN	SW	SN	SN	SN
London Victoria 15	⊖ d		09 47	09 53	10 01				10 03	10 06		10 17	10 23	10 31				10 33	10 36		10 47	10 53	11 01
London Waterloo 15	⊖ d	09 54					10 09				10 24					10 39				10 54			
Clapham Junction 10	d	10 03	09 54	10 00	10 08		10 18		10 11	10 14	10 33	10 24	10 30	10 38		10 48		10 41	10 44	11 03	10 54	11 00	11 08
Balham 4	⊖ d		10 00	10 05					10 16	10 20		10 30	10 35					10 46	10 50		11 00	11 05	
London Bridge 4	⊖ d					09 45									10 15								
Tulse Hill 3	d					10 01		10 16							10 31		10 46						
Norwood Junction 2	d									10 39									11 09				
West Croydon 4	d			10 24					10 34	10 44			10 54					11 04	11 14			11 24	
Waddon	d			10 26					10 36	10 46			10 56					11 06	11 16			11 26	
Wallington	d			10 30					10 40	10 50			11 00					11 10	11 20			11 30	
Carshalton Beeches	d			10 32					10 42	10 52			11 02					11 12	11 22			11 32	
Mitcham Eastfields	d		10 06					10 24				10 36					10 54				11 08		
Mitcham Junction	d		10 09					10 27				10 39					10 57				11 11		
Hackbridge	d		10 13					10 30				10 43					11 00				11 15		
Carshalton	d		10 15					10 33				10 45					11 03				11 17		
Sutton (Surrey) 4	a		10 19	10 39	10 28	10 35		10 36	10 46	10 56		10 49	11 06	10 58	11 05		11 06	11 16	11 26		11 21	11 39	11 28
	d		10 19	10 40	10 29							10 49	11 07	10 59							11 21	11 40	11 29
Belmont	d												11 10										
Banstead	d												11 14										
Epsom Downs	a												11 17										
Cheam	d		10 22	10 42	10 31							10 52		11 01							11 24	11 42	11 31
Ewell East	d		10 25	10 46								10 55		11 05							11 27	11 46	
Epsom 3	a	10 27	10 29	10 52	10 37		10 46				10 57	10 59		11 09		11 16				11 27	11 31	11 52	11 37
	d	10 28			10 37		10 47				10 58			11 09		11 17				11 28			11 37
Ashtead	d	10 32			10 41		10 51				11 02			11 13		11 21				11 32			11 41
Leatherhead	d	10 35			10 44		10 54				11 05			11 16		11 24				11 35			11 44
Bookham	d						10 59									11 29							
Effingham Junction 6	d						11 03									11 33							
Guildford	a						11 23									11 53							
Boxhill & Westhumble	d													11 21									
Dorking 4	a	10 43			10 50						11 13			11 24						11 43			11 50
	d													11 24									
Holmwood	d													11 32									
Ockley	d													11 36									
Warnham	d													11 41									
Horsham 4	a													11 45									

Table 182

London - Sutton, Epsom, Guildford, Dorking and Horsham

Saturdays
from 02 October

Station		FC	SW	FC		SN	SN	SW	SN	SN	SN	FC	SW	FC		SN	SN	SW	SN	SN	SN	FC	SW	FC	
London Victoria 15 ⊖	d					11 03	11 06		11 17	11 23	11 31					11 33	11 36		11 47	11 53	12 01				
London Waterloo 15 ⊖	d		11 09					11 24					11 39					11 54					12 09		
Clapham Junction 10	d		11 18			11 11	11 14	11 33	11 24	11 30	11 38		11 48			11 41	11 44	12 03	11 54	12 00	12 08		12 18		
Balham 4 ⊖	d					11 16	11 20		11 30	11 35						11 46	11 50		12 00	12 05					
London Bridge 4 ⊖	d	10 45										11 15										11 45			
Tulse Hill 3	d	11 01		11 16								11 31		11 46								12 01		12 16	
Norwood Junction 2	d						11 39										12 09								
West Croydon 4	d					11 34	11 44			11 54						12 04	12 14			12 24					
Waddon	d					11 36	11 46			11 56						12 06	12 16			12 26					
Wallington	d					11 40	11 50			12 00						12 10	12 20			12 30					
Carshalton Beeches	d					11 42	11 52			12 02						12 12	12 22			12 32					
Mitcham Eastfields	d			11 24					11 36					11 54					12 06					12 24	
Mitcham Junction	d			11 27					11 39					11 57					12 09					12 27	
Hackbridge	d			11 30					11 43					12 00					12 13					12 30	
Carshalton	d			11 33					11 45					12 03					12 15					12 33	
Sutton (Surrey) 4	a	11 35		11 36		11 46	11 56		11 49	12 06	11 58	12 05		12 06		12 16	12 26		12 19	12 39	12 28	12 35		12 36	
	d								11 49	12 07	11 59								12 19	12 40	12 29				
Belmont	d									12 10															
Banstead	d									12 14															
Epsom Downs	a									12 17															
Cheam	d								11 52		12 01								12 22	12 42	12 31				
Ewell East	d								11 55		12 05								12 25	12 46					
Epsom 3	a		11 46					11 57	11 59		12 09		12 16					12 27	12 29	12 52	12 37		12 46		
	d		11 47					11 58			12 09		12 17					12 28			12 37		12 47		
Ashtead	d		11 51					12 02			12 13		12 21					12 32			12 41		12 51		
Leatherhead	d		11 54					12 05			12 16		12 24					12 35			12 44		12 54		
Bookham	d		11 59										12 29										12 59		
Effingham Junction 6	d		12 03										12 33										13 03		
Guildford	a		12 23										12 53										13 23		
Boxhill & Westhumble	d										12 21														
Dorking 4	a							12 13			12 24							12 43			12 50				
	d										12 24														
Holmwood	d										12 32														
Ockley	d										12 36														
Warnham	d										12 41														
Horsham 4	a										12 45														

Station		SN	SN	SW	SN	SN	SN	FC	SW	FC		SN	SN	SW	SN	SN	SN	FC	SW	FC		SN	SN	SW	SN
London Victoria 15 ⊖	d	12 03	12 06		12 17	12 23	12 31					12 33	12 36		12 47	12 53	13 01					13 03	13 06		13 17
London Waterloo 15 ⊖	d			12 24					12 39					12 54					13 09					13 24	
Clapham Junction 10	d	12 11	12 14	12 33	12 24	12 30	12 38		12 48			12 41	12 44	13 03	12 54	13 00	13 08		13 18			13 11	13 14	13 33	13 24
Balham 4 ⊖	d	12 16	12 20		12 30	12 35						12 46	12 50		13 00	13 05						13 16	13 20		13 30
London Bridge 4 ⊖	d							12 15										12 45							
Tulse Hill 3	d							12 31		12 46								13 01		13 16					
Norwood Junction 2	d		12 39										13 09										13 39		
West Croydon 4	d	12 34	12 44			12 54						13 04	13 14			13 24						13 34	13 44		
Waddon	d	12 36	12 46			12 56						13 06	13 16			13 26						13 36	13 46		
Wallington	d	12 40	12 50			13 00						13 10	13 20			13 30						13 40	13 50		
Carshalton Beeches	d	12 42	12 52			13 02						13 12	13 22			13 32						13 42	13 52		
Mitcham Eastfields	d				12 36					12 54					13 06					13 24					13 36
Mitcham Junction	d				12 39					12 57					13 09					13 27					13 39
Hackbridge	d				12 43					13 00					13 13					13 30					13 43
Carshalton	d				12 45					13 03					13 15					13 33					13 45
Sutton (Surrey) 4	a	12 46	12 56		12 49	13 06	12 58	13 05		13 06		13 16	13 26		13 19	13 39	13 28	13 35		13 36		13 46	13 56		13 49
	d				12 49	13 07	12 59								13 19	13 40	13 29								13 49
Belmont	d					13 10																			
Banstead	d					13 14																			
Epsom Downs	a					13 17																			
Cheam	d				12 52		13 01								13 22	13 42	13 31								13 52
Ewell East	d				12 55		13 05								13 25	13 46									13 55
Epsom 3	a			12 57	12 59		13 09		13 16					13 27	13 29	13 52	13 37		13 46					13 57	13 59
	d			12 58			13 09		13 17					13 28			13 37		13 47					13 58	
Ashtead	d			13 02			13 13		13 21					13 32			13 41		13 51					14 02	
Leatherhead	d			13 05			13 16		13 24					13 35			13 44		13 54					14 05	
Bookham	d								13 29										13 59						
Effingham Junction 6	d								13 33										14 03						
Guildford	a								13 53										14 23						
Boxhill & Westhumble	d						13 21																		
Dorking 4	a			13 13			13 24							13 43			13 50							14 13	
	d						13 24																		
Holmwood	d						13 32																		
Ockley	d						13 36																		
Warnham	d						13 41																		
Horsham 4	a						13 45																		

Table 182

London - Sutton, Epsom, Guildford, Dorking and Horsham

Saturdays
from 02 October

Station		SN	SN	FC	SW	FC		SN	SN	SW	SN	SN	SN	FC	SW	FC		SN	SN	SW	SN	SN	SN	FC	SW
London Victoria 15 ⊖	d	13 23	13 31					13 33	13 36		13 47	13 53	14 01					14 03	14 06		14 17	14 23	14 31		
London Waterloo 15 ⊖	d				13 39					13 54					14 09					14 24					14 39
Clapham Junction 10	d	13 30	13 38		13 48			13 41	13 44	14 03	13 54	14 00	14 08		14 18			14 11	14 14	14 33	14 24	14 30	14 38		14 48
Balham 4 ⊖	d	13 35						13 46	13 50		14 00	14 05						14 16	14 20		14 30	14 35			
London Bridge 4 ⊖	d			13 15										13 45										14 15	
Tulse Hill 3	d			13 31		13 46								14 01		14 16								14 31	
Norwood Junction 2	d								14 09										14 39						
West Croydon 4	d	13 54						14 04	14 14			14 24						14 34	14 44			14 54			
Waddon	d	13 56						14 06	14 16			14 26						14 36	14 46			14 56			
Wallington	d	14 00						14 10	14 20			14 30						14 40	14 50			15 00			
Carshalton Beeches	d	14 02						14 12	14 22			14 32						14 42	14 52			15 02			
Mitcham Eastfields	d					13 54					14 06					14 24					14 36				
Mitcham Junction	d					13 57					14 09					14 27					14 39				
Hackbridge	d					14 00					14 13					14 30					14 43				
Carshalton	d					14 03					14 15					14 33					14 45				
Sutton (Surrey) 4	a	14 06	13 58	14 05		14 06		14 16	14 26		14 19	14 39	14 28	14 35		14 36		14 46	14 56		14 49	15 06	14 58	15 05	
	d	14 07	13 59								14 19	14 40	14 29								14 49	15 07	14 59		
Belmont	d	14 10																				15 10			
Banstead	d	14 14																				15 14			
Epsom Downs	a	14 17																				15 17			
Cheam	d		14 01								14 22	14 42	14 31								14 52		15 01		
Ewell East	d		14 05								14 25	14 46									14 55		15 05		
Epsom 3	a		14 09		14 16					14 27	14 29	14 52	14 37		14 46					14 57	14 59		15 09		15 16
	d		14 09		14 17					14 28			14 37		14 47					14 58			15 09		15 17
Ashtead	d		14 13		14 21					14 32			14 41		14 51					15 02			15 13		15 21
Leatherhead	d		14 16		14 24					14 35			14 44		14 54					15 05			15 16		15 24
Bookham	d				14 29										14 59										15 29
Effingham Junction 6	d				14 33										15 03										15 33
Guildford	a				14 53										15 23										15 53
Boxhill & Westhumble	d		14 21																				15 21		
Dorking 4	a		14 24							14 43			14 50							15 13			15 24		
	d		14 24																				15 24		
Holmwood	d		14 32																				15 32		
Ockley	d		14 36																				15 36		
Warnham	d		14 41																				15 41		
Horsham 4	a		14 45																				15 45		

Station		FC		SN	SN	SW	SN	SN	SN	FC	SW	FC		SN	SN	SW	SN	SN	SN	FC	SW	FC		SN	SN
London Victoria 15 ⊖	d			14 33	14 36		14 47	14 53	15 01					15 03	15 06		15 17	15 23	15 31					15 33	15 36
London Waterloo 15 ⊖	d					14 54					15 09					15 24					15 39				
Clapham Junction 10	d			14 41	14 44	15 03	14 54	15 00	15 08		15 18			15 11	15 14	15 33	15 24	15 30	15 38		15 48			15 41	15 44
Balham 4 ⊖	d			14 46	14 50		15 00	15 05						15 16	15 20		15 30	15 35						15 46	15 50
London Bridge 4 ⊖	d									14 45										15 15					
Tulse Hill 3	d	14 46								15 01		15 16								15 31		15 46			
Norwood Junction 2	d				15 09										15 39										16 09
West Croydon 4	d			15 04	15 14			15 24						15 34	15 44			15 54						16 04	16 14
Waddon	d			15 06	15 16			15 26						15 36	15 46			15 56						16 06	16 16
Wallington	d			15 10	15 20			15 30						15 40	15 50			16 00						16 10	16 20
Carshalton Beeches	d			15 12	15 22			15 32						15 42	15 52			16 02						16 12	16 22
Mitcham Eastfields	d	14 54					15 06					15 24					15 36					15 54			
Mitcham Junction	d	14 57					15 09					15 27					15 39					15 57			
Hackbridge	d	15 00					15 13					15 30					15 43					16 00			
Carshalton	d	15 03					15 15					15 33					15 45					16 03			
Sutton (Surrey) 4	a	15 06		15 16	15 26		15 19	15 39	15 28	15 35		15 36		15 46	15 56		15 49	16 06	15 58	16 05		16 06		16 16	16 26
	d						15 19	15 40	15 29								15 49	16 07	15 59						
Belmont	d																	16 10							
Banstead	d																	16 14							
Epsom Downs	a																	16 17							
Cheam	d						15 22	15 42	15 31								15 52		16 01						
Ewell East	d						15 25	15 46									15 55		16 05						
Epsom 3	a					15 27	15 29	15 52	15 37		15 46					15 57	15 59		16 09		16 16				
	d					15 28			15 37		15 47					15 58			16 09		16 17				
Ashtead	d					15 32			15 41		15 51					16 02			16 13		16 21				
Leatherhead	d					15 35			15 44		15 54					16 05			16 16		16 24				
Bookham	d										15 59										16 29				
Effingham Junction 6	d										16 03										16 33				
Guildford	a										16 23										16 53				
Boxhill & Westhumble	d																		16 21						
Dorking 4	a					15 43			15 50							16 13			16 24						
	d																		16 24						
Holmwood	d																		16 32						
Ockley	d																		16 36						
Warnham	d																		16 41						
Horsham 4	a																		16 45						

Table 182

Saturdays
from 02 October

London - Sutton, Epsom, Guildford, Dorking and Horsham

		SW	SN	SN	SN	FC	SW	FC		SN	SN	SW	SN	SN	SN	FC	SW	FC		SN	SN	SW	SN	SN	SN
London Victoria 15	⊖ d		15 47	15 53	16 01					16 03	16 06		16 17	16 23	16 31					16 33	16 36		16 47	16 53	17 01
London Waterloo 15	⊖ d	15 54					16 09					16 24					16 39					16 54			
Clapham Junction 10	d	16 03	15 54	16 00	16 08		16 18			16 11	16 14	16 33	16 24	16 30	16 38		16 48			16 41	16 44	17 03	16 54	17 00	17 08
Balham 4	⊖ d		16 00	16 05						16 16	16 20		16 30	16 35						16 46	16 50		17 00	17 05	
London Bridge 4	⊖ d					15 45										16 15									
Tulse Hill 3	d					16 01		16 16								16 31		16 46							
Norwood Junction 2	d										16 39										17 09				
West Croydon 4	d			16 24						16 34	16 44			16 54						17 04	17 14			17 24	
Waddon	d			16 26						16 36	16 46			16 56						17 06	17 16			17 26	
Wallington	d			16 30						16 40	16 50			17 00						17 10	17 20			17 30	
Carshalton Beeches	d			16 32						16 42	16 52			17 02						17 12	17 22			17 32	
Mitcham Eastfields	d		16 06					16 24					16 36					16 54					17 06		
Mitcham Junction	d		16 09					16 27					16 39					16 57					17 09		
Hackbridge	d		16 13					16 30					16 43					17 00					17 13		
Carshalton	d		16 15					16 33					16 45					17 03					17 15		
Sutton (Surrey) 4	a		16 19	16 39	16 28	16 35		16 36		16 46	16 56		16 49	17 06	16 58	17 05		17 06		17 16	17 26		17 19	17 39	17 28
	d		16 19	16 40	16 29								16 49	17 07	16 59								17 19	17 40	17 29
Belmont	d													17 10											
Banstead	d													17 14											
Epsom Downs	a													17 17											
Cheam	d		16 22	16 42	16 31								16 52		17 01								17 22	17 42	17 31
Ewell East	d		16 25	16 46									16 55		17 05								17 25	17 46	
Epsom 3	a	16 27	16 29	16 52	16 37		16 46					16 57	16 59		17 09		17 16					17 27	17 29	17 52	17 37
	d	16 28			16 37		16 47					16 58			17 09		17 17					17 28			17 37
Ashtead	d	16 32			16 41		16 51					17 02			17 13		17 21					17 32			17 41
Leatherhead	d	16 35			16 44		16 54					17 05			17 16		17 24					17 35			17 44
Bookham	d						16 59										17 29								
Effingham Junction 6	d						17 03										17 33								
Guildford	a						17 23										17 53								
Boxhill & Westhumble	d														17 21										
Dorking 4	a	16 43			16 50							17 13			17 24							17 43			17 50
	d														17 24										
Holmwood	d														17 32										
Ockley	d														17 36										
Warnham	d														17 41										
Horsham 4	a														17 45										

		FC	SW	FC		SN	SN	SW	SN	SN	SN	FC	SW	FC		SN	SN	SW	SN	SN	SN	FC	SN	SW	
London Victoria 15	⊖ d					17 03	17 06		17 17	17 23	17 31					17 33	17 36		17 47	17 53	18 01		18 06		
London Waterloo 15	⊖ d		17 09					17 24					17 39					17 54						18 09	
Clapham Junction 10	d		17 18			17 11	17 14	17 33	17 24	17 30	17 38		17 48			17 41	17 44	18 03	17 54	18 00	18 08		18 14	18 18	
Balham 4	⊖ d					17 16	17 20		17 30	17 35						17 46	17 50		18 00	18 05			18 20		
London Bridge 4	⊖ d	16 45										17 15										17 45			
Tulse Hill 3	d	17 01		17 16								17 31		17 46								18 01			
Norwood Junction 2	d						17 39										18 09						18 39		
West Croydon 4	d					17 34	17 44			17 54						18 04	18 14			18 24			18 44		
Waddon	d					17 36	17 46			17 56						18 06	18 16			18 26			18 46		
Wallington	d					17 40	17 50			18 00						18 10	18 20			18 30			18 50		
Carshalton Beeches	d					17 42	17 52			18 02						18 12	18 22			18 32			18 52		
Mitcham Eastfields	d			17 24					17 36					17 54					18 06						
Mitcham Junction	d			17 27					17 39					17 57					18 09						
Hackbridge	d			17 30					17 43					18 00					18 13						
Carshalton	d			17 33					17 45					18 03					18 15						
Sutton (Surrey) 4	a	17 35		17 36		17 46	17 56		17 49	18 06	17 58	18 05		18 06		18 16	18 26		18 19	18 39	18 28	18 35	18 56		
	d								17 49	18 07	17 59								18 19	18 40	18 29		18 57		
Belmont	d									18 10													19 00		
Banstead	d									18 14													19 04		
Epsom Downs	a									18 17													19 07		
Cheam	d								17 52		18 01								18 22	18 42	18 31				
Ewell East	d								17 55		18 05								18 25	18 46					
Epsom 3	a		17 46					17 57	17 59		18 09		18 16					18 27	18 29	18 50	18 37			18 46	
	d		17 47					17 58			18 09		18 17					18 28			18 37			18 47	
Ashtead	d		17 51					18 02			18 13		18 21					18 32			18 41			18 51	
Leatherhead	d		17 54					18 05			18 16		18 24					18 35			18 44			18 54	
Bookham	d		17 59										18 29											18 59	
Effingham Junction 6	d		18 03										18 33											19 03	
Guildford	a		18 23										18 53											19 23	
Boxhill & Westhumble	d										18 21														
Dorking 4	a							18 13			18 24							18 43			18 50				
	d										18 24														
Holmwood	d										18 32														
Ockley	d										18 36														
Warnham	d										18 41														
Horsham 4	a										18 45														

Table 182

Saturdays
from 02 October

London - Sutton, Epsom, Guildford, Dorking and Horsham

		FC	SW	SN	FC	SN	SN	SW	FC	SW		SN	SW	FC	FC	SN	SN	SW	SN	FC		SW	FC	SN	SN
London Victoria 15	⊖ d			18 17		18 23	18 36					18 50				19 01	19 06		19 20					19 31	19 36
London Waterloo 15	⊖ d		18 24					18 39		18 54			19 09					19 24				19 39			
Clapham Junction 10	d		18 33	18 24		18 30	18 44	18 48		19 03		18 57	19 18			19 09	19 14	19 33	19 26			19 48		19 39	19 44
Balham 4	⊖ d			18 30		18 35	18 50					19 01				19 14	19 20		19 32					19 44	19 50
London Bridge 4	⊖ d				18 15										18 45					19 15					
Tulse Hill 3	d	18 16			18 31				18 46					19 16	19 01					19 31			19 46		
Norwood Junction 2	d						19 09										19 39								20 09
West Croydon 4	d					18 54	19 14									19 32	19 44							20 03	20 15
Waddon	d					18 56	19 16									19 35	19 46							20 05	20 18
Wallington	d					19 00	19 20									19 38	19 50							20 09	20 21
Carshalton Beeches	d					19 02	19 22									19 41	19 52							20 11	20 24
Mitcham Eastfields	d	18 24		18 36					18 54			19 08		19 24					19 38				19 55		
Mitcham Junction	d	18 27		18 39					18 57			19 11		19 27					19 41				19 58		
Hackbridge	d	18 30		18 43					19 00			19 15		19 30					19 45				20 01		
Carshalton	d	18 33		18 45					19 03			19 17		19 33					19 47				20 04		
Sutton (Surrey) 4	a	18 36		18 49	19 05	19 06	19 26		19 06			19 21		19 36	19 39	19 44	19 56		19 51	20 05			20 07	20 15	20 27
	d			18 49			19 27					19 21					19 57		19 51						20 28
Belmont	d						19 30																		20 31
Banstead	d						19 34																		20 35
Epsom Downs	a						19 37																		20 38
Cheam	d			18 52								19 24					19 59		19 54						
Ewell East	d			18 55								19 27					20 03		19 57						
Epsom 3	a		18 57	18 59				19 12		19 27		19 31	19 42				20 07	19 57	20 01			20 12			
	d		18 58	19 02				19 17		19 28		19 32	19 47					19 58	20 02			20 17			
Ashtead	d		19 02	19 06				19 21		19 32		19 36	19 51					20 02	20 06			20 21			
Leatherhead	d		19 05	19 09				19 24		19 35		19 39	19 54					20 05	20 09			20 24			
Bookham	d							19 29					19 59									20 29			
Effingham Junction 6	d							19 33					20 03									20 33			
Guildford	a							19 53					20 23									20 53			
Boxhill & Westhumble	d			19 14								19 44													
Dorking 4	a		19 13	19 16						19 43		19 46						20 13	20 15						
	d																								
Holmwood	d																								
Ockley	d																								
Warnham	d																								
Horsham 4	a																								

		SW	SN	FC	SN	SN		SW	SW	SN	FC	SN	SN	SW	SW	SN		FC	SN	SN	SW	SW	SN	FC	SN
London Victoria 15	⊖ d		19 50		20 01	20 06				20 20		20 30	20 36			20 50			21 00	21 06			21 20		21 30
London Waterloo 15	⊖ d	19 54						20 09	20 24					20 39	20 54						21 09	21 24			
Clapham Junction 10	d	20 03	19 56		20 09	20 14		20 18	20 33	20 26		20 38	20 44	20 48	21 03	20 56			21 08	21 14	21 18	21 33	21 26		21 38
Balham 4	⊖ d		20 02		20 14	20 20				20 32		20 44	20 50			21 02			21 14	21 20			21 32		21 44
London Bridge 4	⊖ d			19 45							20 15							20 45						21 15	
Tulse Hill 3	d			20 01							20 31							21 01						21 31	
Norwood Junction 2	d					20 39							21 09							21 39					
West Croydon 4	d				20 32	20 45						21 03	21 15						21 32	21 45					22 02
Waddon	d				20 35	20 48						21 05	21 18						21 35	21 48					22 05
Wallington	d				20 38	20 51						21 09	21 21						21 38	21 51					22 08
Carshalton Beeches	d				20 41	20 54						21 11	21 24						21 41	21 54					22 11
Mitcham Eastfields	d		20 08							20 38						21 08							21 38		
Mitcham Junction	d		20 11							20 41						21 11							21 41		
Hackbridge	d		20 15							20 45						21 15							21 45		
Carshalton	d		20 17							20 47						21 17							21 47		
Sutton (Surrey) 4	a		20 21	20 39	20 44	20 57				20 51	21 05	21 15	21 27			21 21		21 39	21 44	21 57			21 51	22 05	22 14
	d		20 21			20 58				20 51			21 28			21 21				21 58			21 51		
Belmont	d												21 31												
Banstead	d												21 35												
Epsom Downs	a												21 38												
Cheam	d		20 24			21 00				20 54						21 24				22 00			21 54		
Ewell East	d		20 27			21 04				20 57						21 27				22 04			21 57		
Epsom 3	a	20 27	20 31			21 08		20 42	20 57	21 01				21 12	21 27	21 31				22 08	21 42	21 57	22 01		
	d		20 32					20 47		21 02				21 17		21 32					21 47		22 02		
Ashtead	d		20 36					20 51		21 06				21 21		21 36					21 51		22 06		
Leatherhead	d		20 39					20 54		21 09				21 24		21 39					21 54		22 09		
Bookham	d													21 29											
Effingham Junction 6	d													21 33											
Guildford	a													21 53											
Boxhill & Westhumble	d		20 44													21 44									
Dorking 4	a		20 46					21 02		21 15						21 46					22 02		22 15		
	d																								
Holmwood	d																								
Ockley	d																								
Warnham	d																								
Horsham 4	a																								

Table 182

London - Sutton, Epsom, Guildford, Dorking and Horsham

Saturdays
from 02 October

		SN	SW	SW	SN	FC	SN	SN	SW	SN	FC	SN	SN	SW	SN	FC	SW	SN	SN	SN	FC	SN
London Victoria 15 ⊖	d	21 36			21 50		22 00	22 06		22 20		22 30	22 36		22 50			23 00	23 06	23 26		23 34
London Waterloo 15 ⊖	d		21 39	21 54					22 09					22 39			23 09					
Clapham Junction 10	d	21 44	21 48	22 03	21 56		22 08	22 14	22 18	22 26		22 38	22 44	22 48	22 56		23 18	23 08	23 14	23 34		23 42
Balham 4 ⊖	d	21 50			22 02		22 14	22 20		22 32		22 44	22 50		23 01			23 14	23 20	23 40		23 47
London Bridge 4 ⊖	d					21 45					22 15					22 45					23 15	
Tulse Hill 3	d					22 01					22 31					23 01					23 31	
Norwood Junction 2	d	22 09						22 39					23 09						23 39			
West Croydon 4	d	22 14					22 33	22 44				23 03	23 14					23 32	23 44			00 04
Waddon	d	22 16					22 35	22 46				23 05	23 16					23 35	23 46			00 06
Wallington	d	22 20					22 39	22 50				23 09	23 20					23 38	23 50			00 10
Carshalton Beeches	d	22 22					22 41	22 52				23 11	23 22					23 41	23 52			00 12
Mitcham Eastfields	d				22 08					22 38					23 07					23 46		
Mitcham Junction	d				22 11					22 41					23 10					23 49		
Hackbridge	d				22 15					22 45					23 14					23 53		
Carshalton	d				22 17					22 47					23 16					23 55		
Sutton (Surrey) 4	a	22 26			22 21	22 39	22 45	22 56		22 51	23 05	23 15	23 26		23 20	23 35		23 44	23 56	00 01	00 05	00 16
	d	22 27			22 21			22 57		22 51			23 27		23 20			23 45		00 02		
Belmont	d	22 30											23 30									
Banstead	d	22 34											23 34									
Epsom Downs	a	22 37											23 37									
Cheam	d				22 24			22 59		22 54					23 23			23 47		00 04		
Ewell East	d				22 27			23 03		22 57					23 26			23 51		00 08		
Epsom 3	a		22 12	22 27	22 31			23 07	22 42	23 01				23 12	23 30		23 42	23 55		00 12		
	d		22 17		22 32				22 47	23 02				23 17	23 31		23 47			00 12		
Ashtead	d		22 21		22 36				22 51	23 06				23 21	23 35		23 51			00 16		
Leatherhead	d		22 24		22 39				22 54	23 09				23 24	23 38		23 54			00 19		
Bookham	d		22 29											23 29								
Effingham Junction 6	d		22 33											23 33								
Guildford	a		22 53											23 54								
Boxhill & Westhumble	d				22 44										23 43					00 24		
Dorking 4	a				22 46				23 02	23 15					23 45		00 03			00 27		
	d																					
Holmwood	d																					
Ockley	d																					
Warnham	d																					
Horsham 4	a																					

		SW	SN	FC
London Victoria 15 ⊖	d		23 51	
London Waterloo 15 ⊖	d	23 42		
Clapham Junction 10	d	23 51	23 59	
Balham 4 ⊖	d		00 04	
London Bridge 4 ⊖	d			23 45
Tulse Hill 3	d			00 01
Norwood Junction 2	d			
West Croydon 4	d		00 21	
Waddon	d		00 24	
Wallington	d		00 27	
Carshalton Beeches	d		00 30	
Mitcham Eastfields	d			
Mitcham Junction	d			
Hackbridge	d			
Carshalton	d			
Sutton (Surrey) 4	a		00 33	00 35
	d			
Belmont	d			
Banstead	d			
Epsom Downs	a			
Cheam	d			
Ewell East	d			
Epsom 3	a	00 15		
	d	00 19		
Ashtead	d	00 23		
Leatherhead	d	00 26		
Bookham	d	00 31		
Effingham Junction 6	d	00 37		
Guildford	a	00 57		
Boxhill & Westhumble	d			
Dorking 4	a			
	d			
Holmwood	d			
Ockley	d			
Warnham	d			
Horsham 4	a			

Table 182

London - Sutton, Epsom, Guildford, Dorking and Horsham

Sundays
until 19 September

		SW	SN	FC	SN	SW	SN	FC	SW	SN	SW	SN	SN	SN	SW	SN	SN	SN	SW	SN	SN	SN	SW
London Victoria 15 ⊖	d		23p26		23p34		23p51			06 49		07 19	07 36	07 49		08 06	08 08	08 19		08 36	08 38	08 49	
London Waterloo 15 ⊖	d	23p09				23p42			00 15						08 02				08 32				09 02
Clapham Junction 10	d	23p18	23p34		23p42	23p51	23p59		00 24	06 57		07 27	07 42	07 57	08 11	08 12	08 16	08 27	08 41	08 42	08 46	08 57	09 11
Balham 4 ⊖	d		23p40		23p47		00 04			07 02		07 32	07 47	08 02		08 17	08 21	08 32		08 47	08 51	09 02	
London Bridge 4 ⊖	d			23p15				23p45															
Tulse Hill 3	d			23p31				00 01															
Norwood Junction 2	d												08 03			08 33				09 03			
West Croydon 4	d				00 04		00 21			07 20		07 50	08 08	08 20		08 38		08 50		09 08		09 20	
Waddon	d				00 06		00 24			07 22		07 52	08 11	08 22		08 41		08 52		09 11		09 22	
Wallington	d				00 10		00 27			07 26		07 56	08 14	08 26		08 44		08 56		09 14		09 26	
Carshalton Beeches	d				00 12		00 30			07 28		07 58	08 17	08 28		08 47		08 58		09 17		09 28	
Mitcham Eastfields	d		23p46														08 28				08 58		
Mitcham Junction	d		23p49														08 31				09 01		
Hackbridge	d		23p53														08 34				09 04		
Carshalton	d		23p55														08 37				09 07		
Sutton (Surrey) 4	a		00 01	00 05	00 16		00 33	00 35		07 32		08 02	08 20	08 32		08 50	08 40	09 02		09 20	09 10	09 32	
	d		00 02							07 41		08 11					08 41				09 11		
Belmont	d																						
Banstead	d																						
Epsom Downs	a																						
Cheam	d		00 04							07 43		08 13					08 43				09 13		
Ewell East	d		00 08							07 47		08 17					08 47				09 17		
Epsom 3	a	23p42	00 12			00 15			00 48	07 51	08 06	08 21			08 36		08 51		09 06		09 21		09 36
	d	23p47	00 12			00 19				07 51	08 08	08 21			08 38		08 51		09 08		09 21		09 38
Ashtead	d	23p51	00 16			00 23				07 55	08 12	08 25			08 42		08 55		09 12		09 25		09 42
Leatherhead	d	23p54	00 19			00 26				07 58	08 15	08 28			08 45		08 58		09 15		09 28		09 45
Bookham	d					00 31					08 21								09 21				
Effingham Junction 6	d					00 37					08 25								09 25				
Guildford	a					00 54					08 41								09 41				
Boxhill & Westhumble	d		00 24							08 03		08 33					09 03				09 33		
Dorking 4	a	00 01	00 27							08 06		08 36			08 51		09 06				09 36		09 51
	d																						
Holmwood	d																						
Ockley	d																						
Warnham	d																						
Horsham 4	a																						

		SN	SN	SN	FC	SW	SN	SN	SN	FC	SW	SN	SN	SN	FC	SW	SN	SN	SN	FC	SW	SN	SN
London Victoria 15 ⊖	d	09 06	09 08	09 19			09 36	09 38	09 49			10 06	10 08	10 19			10 36	10 38	10 49			11 06	11 08
London Waterloo 15 ⊖	d					09 32					10 02					10 32					11 02		
Clapham Junction 10	d	09 12	09 16	09 27		09 41	09 42	09 46	09 57		10 11	10 12	10 16	10 27		10 41	10 42	10 46	10 57		11 11	11 12	11 16
Balham 4 ⊖	d	09 17	09 21	09 32			09 47	09 51	10 02			10 17	10 21	10 32			10 47	10 51	11 02			11 17	11 21
London Bridge 4 ⊖	d				09 21					09 51					10 21					10 51			
Tulse Hill 3	d				09 31					10 01					10 31					11 01			
Norwood Junction 2	d	09 33					10 03					10 33					11 03					11 33	
West Croydon 4	d	09 38		09 50			10 08		10 20			10 38		10 50			11 08		11 20			11 38	
Waddon	d	09 41		09 52			10 11		10 22			10 41		10 52			11 11		11 22			11 41	
Wallington	d	09 44		09 56			10 14		10 26			10 44		10 56			11 14		11 26			11 44	
Carshalton Beeches	d	09 47		09 58			10 17		10 28			10 47		10 58			11 17		11 28			11 47	
Mitcham Eastfields	d		09 28					09 58					10 28					10 58					11 28
Mitcham Junction	d		09 31					10 01					10 31					11 01					11 31
Hackbridge	d		09 34					10 04					10 34					11 04					11 34
Carshalton	d		09 37					10 07					10 37					11 07					11 37
Sutton (Surrey) 4	a	09 50	09 40	10 02	10 05		10 20	10 10	10 32	10 35		10 50	10 40	11 02	11 05		11 20	11 10	11 32	11 35		11 50	11 40
	d		09 41					10 11					10 41					11 11					11 41
Belmont	d																						
Banstead	d																						
Epsom Downs	a																						
Cheam	d		09 43					10 13					10 43					11 13					11 43
Ewell East	d		09 47					10 17					10 47					11 17					11 47
Epsom 3	a		09 51			10 06		10 21			10 36		10 51			11 06		11 21			11 36		11 51
	d		09 51			10 08		10 21			10 38		10 51			11 08		11 21			11 38		11 51
Ashtead	d		09 55			10 12		10 25			10 42		10 55			11 12		11 25			11 42		11 55
Leatherhead	d		09 58			10 15		10 28			10 45		10 58			11 15		11 28			11 45		11 58
Bookham	d					10 21										11 21							
Effingham Junction 6	d					10 25										11 25							
Guildford	a					10 41										11 41							
Boxhill & Westhumble	d		10 03					10 33					11 03					11 33					12 03
Dorking 4	a		10 06					10 36			10 51		11 06					11 36			11 51		12 06
	d																						
Holmwood	d																						
Ockley	d																						
Warnham	d																						
Horsham 4	a																						

Table 182

Sundays until 19 September

London - Sutton, Epsom, Guildford, Dorking and Horsham

		SN		FC	SW	SN	SN	SN	FC	SW	SN	SN		SN	FC	SW	SN	SN	SN	FC	SW	SN		SN	SN
London Victoria 15 ⊖	d	11 19				11 36	11 38	11 49			12 06	12 08		12 19			12 36	12 38	12 49			13 06		13 08	13 19
London Waterloo 15 ⊖	d				11 32					12 02						12 32					13 02				
Clapham Junction 10	d	11 27			11 41	11 42	11 46	11 57		12 11	12 12	12 16		12 27		12 41	12 42	12 46	12 57		13 11	13 12		13 16	13 27
Balham 4 ⊖	d	11 32				11 47	11 51	12 02			12 17	12 21		12 32			12 47	12 51	13 02			13 17		13 21	13 32
London Bridge 4 ⊖	d			11 21					11 51						12 21					12 51					
Tulse Hill 3	d			11 31					12 01						12 31					13 01					
Norwood Junction 2	d					12 03					12 33						13 03					13 33			
West Croydon 4	d	11 50				12 08		12 20			12 38			12 50			13 08		13 20			13 38			13 50
Waddon	d	11 52				12 11		12 22			12 41			12 52			13 11		13 22			13 41			13 52
Wallington	d	11 56				12 14		12 26			12 44			12 56			13 14		13 26			13 44			13 56
Carshalton Beeches	d	11 58				12 17		12 28			12 47			12 58			13 17		13 28			13 47			13 58
Mitcham Eastfields	d						11 58					12 28						12 58						13 28	
Mitcham Junction	d						12 01					12 31						13 01						13 31	
Hackbridge	d						12 04					12 34						13 04						13 34	
Carshalton	d						12 07					12 37						13 07						13 37	
Sutton (Surrey) 4	a	12 02		12 05		12 20	12 10	12 32	12 35		12 50	12 40		13 02	13 05		13 20	13 10	13 32	13 35		13 50		13 40	14 02
	d						12 11					12 41						13 11						13 41	
Belmont	d																								
Banstead	d																								
Epsom Downs	a																								
Cheam	d						12 13					12 43						13 13						13 43	
Ewell East	d						12 17					12 47						13 17						13 47	
Epsom 3	a				12 06		12 21			12 36		12 51				13 06		13 21			13 36			13 51	
	d				12 08		12 21			12 38		12 51				13 08		13 21			13 38			13 51	
Ashtead	d				12 12		12 25			12 42		12 55				13 12		13 25			13 42			13 55	
Leatherhead	d				12 15		12 28			12 45		12 58				13 15		13 28			13 45			13 58	
Bookham	d				12 21											13 21									
Effingham Junction 6	d				12 25											13 25									
Guildford	a				12 41											13 41									
Boxhill & Westhumble	d						12 33					13 03						13 33						14 03	
Dorking 4	a						12 36			12 51		13 06						13 36			13 51			14 06	
	d																								
Holmwood	d																								
Ockley	d																								
Warnham	d																								
Horsham 4	a																								

		FC	SW	SN	SN	SN	FC	SW		SN	SN	SN	FC	SW	SN	SN	SN	FC		SW	SN	SN	SN	FC	SW
London Victoria 15 ⊖	d			13 36	13 38	13 49				14 06	14 08	14 19			14 36	14 38	14 49				15 06	15 08	15 19		
London Waterloo 15 ⊖	d		13 32					14 02						14 32						15 02					15 32
Clapham Junction 10	d		13 41	13 42	13 46	13 57		14 11		14 12	14 16	14 27		14 41	14 42	14 46	14 57			15 11	15 12	15 16	15 27		15 41
Balham 4 ⊖	d			13 47	13 51	14 02				14 17	14 21	14 32			14 47	14 51	15 02				15 17	15 21	15 32		
London Bridge 4 ⊖	d	13 21					13 51						14 21					14 51						15 21	
Tulse Hill 3	d	13 31					14 01						14 31					15 01						15 31	
Norwood Junction 2	d			14 03						14 33					15 03						15 33				
West Croydon 4	d			14 08		14 20				14 38		14 50			15 08		15 20				15 38		15 50		
Waddon	d			14 11		14 22				14 41		14 52			15 11		15 22				15 41		15 52		
Wallington	d			14 14		14 26				14 44		14 56			15 14		15 26				15 44		15 56		
Carshalton Beeches	d			14 17		14 28				14 47		14 58			15 17		15 28				15 47		15 58		
Mitcham Eastfields	d				13 58						14 28					14 58						15 28			
Mitcham Junction	d				14 01						14 31					15 01						15 31			
Hackbridge	d				14 04						14 34					15 04						15 34			
Carshalton	d				14 07						14 37					15 07						15 37			
Sutton (Surrey) 4	a	14 05		14 20	14 10	14 32	14 35			14 50	14 40	15 02	15 05		15 20	15 10	15 32	15 35			15 50	15 40	16 02	16 05	
	d				14 11						14 41					15 11						15 41			
Belmont	d																								
Banstead	d																								
Epsom Downs	a																								
Cheam	d				14 13						14 43					15 13						15 43			
Ewell East	d				14 17						14 47					15 17						15 47			
Epsom 3	a		14 06		14 21			14 36			14 51			15 06		15 21				15 36		15 51			16 06
	d		14 08		14 21			14 38			14 51			15 08		15 21				15 38		15 51			16 08
Ashtead	d		14 12		14 25			14 42			14 55			15 12		15 25				15 42		15 55			16 12
Leatherhead	d		14 15		14 28			14 45			14 58			15 15		15 28				15 45		15 58			16 15
Bookham	d		14 21											15 21											16 21
Effingham Junction 6	d		14 25											15 25											16 25
Guildford	a		14 41											15 41											16 41
Boxhill & Westhumble	d				14 33						15 03					15 33						16 03			
Dorking 4	a				14 36			14 51			15 06					15 36				15 51		16 06			
	d																								
Holmwood	d																								
Ockley	d																								
Warnham	d																								
Horsham 4	a																								

Table 182

Sundays until 19 September

London - Sutton, Epsom, Guildford, Dorking and Horsham

		SN	SN	SN		FC	SW	SN	SN	SN	FC	SW	SN	SN		SN	FC	SW	SN	SN	SN	FC	SW	SN	
London Victoria 15 ⊖	d	15 36	15 38	15 49				16 06	16 08	16 19			16 36	16 38		16 49			17 06	17 08	17 19			17 36	
London Waterloo 15 ⊖	d						16 02					16 32						17 02					17 32		
Clapham Junction 10	d	15 42	15 46	15 57			16 11	16 12	16 16	16 27		16 41	16 42	16 46		16 57		17 11	17 12	17 16	17 27		17 41	17 42	
Balham 4 ⊖	d	15 47	15 51	16 02				16 17	16 21	16 32			16 47	16 51		17 02			17 17	17 21	17 32			17 47	
London Bridge 4 ⊖	d					15 51					16 21						16 51					17 21			
Tulse Hill 3	d					16 01					16 31						17 01					17 31			
Norwood Junction 2	d	16 03						16 33					17 03						17 33					18 03	
West Croydon 4	d	16 08		16 20				16 38		16 50			17 08			17 20			17 38		17 50			18 08	
Waddon	d	16 11		16 22				16 41		16 52			17 11			17 22			17 41		17 52			18 11	
Wallington	d	16 14		16 26				16 44		16 56			17 14			17 26			17 44		17 56			18 14	
Carshalton Beeches	d	16 17		16 28				16 47		16 58			17 17			17 28			17 47		17 58			18 17	
Mitcham Eastfields	d		15 58						16 28					16 58						17 28					
Mitcham Junction	d		16 01						16 31					17 01						17 31					
Hackbridge	d		16 04						16 34					17 04						17 34					
Carshalton	d		16 07						16 37					17 07						17 37					
Sutton (Surrey) 4	a	16 20	16 10	16 32		16 35		16 50	16 40	17 02	17 05		17 20	17 10		17 32	17 35		17 50	17 40	18 02	18 05		18 20	
	d		16 11						16 41					17 11						17 41					
Belmont	d																								
Banstead	d																								
Epsom Downs	a																								
Cheam	d		16 13						16 43					17 13						17 43					
Ewell East	d		16 17						16 47					17 17						17 47					
Epsom 3	a		16 21				16 36		16 51			17 06		17 21				17 36		17 51			18 06		
	d		16 21				16 38		16 51			17 08		17 21				17 38		17 51			18 08		
Ashtead	d		16 25				16 42		16 55			17 12		17 25				17 42		17 55			18 12		
Leatherhead	d		16 28				16 45		16 58			17 15		17 28				17 45		17 58			18 15		
Bookham	d											17 21											18 21		
Effingham Junction 6	d											17 25											18 25		
Guildford	a											17 41											18 41		
Boxhill & Westhumble	d		16 33						17 03					17 33						18 03					
Dorking 4	a		16 36				16 51		17 06					17 36				17 51		18 06					
	d																								
Holmwood	d																								
Ockley	d																								
Warnham	d																								
Horsham 4	a																								

		SN	SN	FC	SW	SN	SN	SN	FC	SW		SN	SN	SN	FC	SW	SN	SN	SN	FC		SW	SN	SN	SN
London Victoria 15 ⊖	d	17 38	17 49			18 06	18 08	18 19				18 36	18 38	18 49			19 06	19 08	19 19				19 36	19 38	19 49
London Waterloo 15 ⊖	d				18 02					18 32						19 02						19 32			
Clapham Junction 10	d	17 46	17 57		18 11	18 12	18 16	18 27		18 41		18 42	18 46	18 57		19 11	19 12	19 16	19 27			19 41	19 42	19 46	19 57
Balham 4 ⊖	d	17 51	18 02			18 17	18 21	18 32				18 47	18 51	19 02			19 17	19 21	19 32				19 47	19 51	20 02
London Bridge 4 ⊖	d			17 51					18 21						18 51					19 21					
Tulse Hill 3	d			18 01					18 31						19 01					19 31					
Norwood Junction 2	d					18 33						19 03					19 33						20 03		
West Croydon 4	d		18 20			18 38		18 50				19 08		19 20			19 38		19 50				20 08		20 20
Waddon	d		18 22			18 41		18 52				19 11		19 22			19 41		19 52				20 11		20 22
Wallington	d		18 26			18 44		18 56				19 14		19 26			19 44		19 56				20 14		20 26
Carshalton Beeches	d		18 28			18 47		18 58				19 17		19 28			19 47		19 58				20 17		20 28
Mitcham Eastfields	d	17 58					18 28						18 58					19 28						19 58	
Mitcham Junction	d	18 01					18 31						19 01					19 31						20 01	
Hackbridge	d	18 04					18 34						19 04					19 34						20 04	
Carshalton	d	18 07					18 37						19 07					19 37						20 07	
Sutton (Surrey) 4	a	18 10	18 32	18 35		18 50	18 40	19 02	19 05			19 20	19 10	19 32	19 35		19 50	19 40	20 02	20 05			20 20	20 10	20 32
	d	18 11					18 41						19 11					19 41						20 11	
Belmont	d																								
Banstead	d																								
Epsom Downs	a																								
Cheam	d	18 13					18 43						19 13					19 43						20 13	
Ewell East	d	18 17					18 47						19 17					19 47						20 17	
Epsom 3	a	18 21			18 36		18 51			19 06			19 21			19 36		19 51				20 06		20 21	
	d	18 21			18 38		18 51			19 08			19 21			19 38		19 51				20 08		20 21	
Ashtead	d	18 25			18 42		18 55			19 12			19 25			19 42		19 55				20 12		20 25	
Leatherhead	d	18 28			18 45		18 58			19 15			19 28			19 45		19 58				20 15		20 28	
Bookham	d									19 21												20 21			
Effingham Junction 6	d									19 25												20 25			
Guildford	a									19 41												20 41			
Boxhill & Westhumble	d	18 33					19 03						19 33					20 03						20 33	
Dorking 4	a	18 36			18 51		19 06						19 36			19 51		20 06						20 36	
	d																								
Holmwood	d																								
Ockley	d																								
Warnham	d																								
Horsham 4	a																								

Table 182

Sundays until 19 September

London - Sutton, Epsom, Guildford, Dorking and Horsham

		FC	SW	SN	SN	SN	FC	SW	SN	SN	SN	FC	SW	SN	SN	SN	SW	SN	SN	SN	SW	SN	SN
London Victoria ⊖	d			20 06	20 08	20 19			20 36	20 38	20 49			21 06	21 08	21 19		21 36	21 38	21 49		22 06	22 08
London Waterloo ⊖	d		20 02					20 32					21 02				21 32				22 02		
Clapham Junction	d		20 11	20 12	20 16	20 27		20 41	20 42	20 46	20 57		21 11	21 12	21 16	21 27	21 41	21 42	21 46	21 57	22 11	22 12	22 16
Balham ⊖	d			20 17	20 21	20 32			20 47	20 51	21 02			21 17	21 21	21 32		21 47	21 51	22 02		22 17	22 21
London Bridge ⊖	d	19 51					20 21					20 51											
Tulse Hill	d	20 01					20 31					21 01											
Norwood Junction	d			20 33					21 03					21 33				22 03				22 33	
West Croydon	d			20 38		20 50			21 08		21 20			21 38		21 50		22 08		22 20		22 38	
Waddon	d			20 41		20 52			21 11		21 22			21 41		21 52		22 11		22 22		22 41	
Wallington	d			20 44		20 56			21 14		21 26			21 44		21 56		22 14		22 26		22 44	
Carshalton Beeches	d			20 47		20 58			21 17		21 28			21 47		21 58		22 17		22 28		22 47	
Mitcham Eastfields	d				20 28					20 58					21 28				21 58				22 28
Mitcham Junction	d				20 31					21 01					21 31				22 01				22 31
Hackbridge	d				20 34					21 04					21 34				22 04				22 34
Carshalton	d				20 37					21 07					21 37				22 07				22 37
Sutton (Surrey)	a	20 35		20 50	20 40	21 02	21 05		21 20	21 10	21 32	21 35		21 50	21 40	22 02		22 20	22 10	22 32		22 50	22 40
	d				20 41					21 11					21 41				22 11				22 41
Belmont	d																						
Banstead	d																						
Epsom Downs	a																						
Cheam	d				20 43					21 13					21 43				22 13				22 43
Ewell East	d				20 47					21 17					21 47				22 17				22 47
Epsom	a		20 36		20 51			21 06		21 21			21 36		21 51		22 06		22 21		22 36		22 51
	d		20 38		20 51			21 08		21 21			21 38		21 51		22 08		22 21		22 38		22 51
Ashtead	d		20 42		20 55			21 12		21 25			21 42		21 55		22 12		22 25		22 42		22 55
Leatherhead	d		20 45		20 58			21 15		21 28			21 45		21 58		22 15		22 28		22 45		22 58
Bookham	d							21 21									22 21						
Effingham Junction	d							21 25									22 25						
Guildford	a							21 41									22 41						
Boxhill & Westhumble	d				21 03					21 33					22 03				22 33				23 03
Dorking	a		20 51		21 06					21 36			21 51		22 06				22 36		22 51		23 06
	d																						
Holmwood	d																						
Ockley	d																						
Warnham	d																						
Horsham	a																						

		SN	SW	SN	SN	SN	SW	SN	SW	SN
London Victoria ⊖	d	22 19		22 36	22 38	22 49		23 08		23 19
London Waterloo ⊖	d		22 32				23 02		23 32	
Clapham Junction	d	22 26	22 41	22 42	22 46	22 57	23 11	23 16	23 41	23 27
Balham ⊖	d	22 32		22 47	22 51	23 02		23 21		23 32
London Bridge ⊖	d									
Tulse Hill	d									
Norwood Junction	d			23 03						
West Croydon	d	22 50		23 08		23 20				23 50
Waddon	d	22 52		23 11		23 22				23 52
Wallington	d	22 56		23 14		23 26				23 56
Carshalton Beeches	d	22 58		23 17		23 28				23 58
Mitcham Eastfields	d				22 58			23 28		
Mitcham Junction	d				23 01			23 31		
Hackbridge	d				23 04			23 34		
Carshalton	d				23 07			23 37		
Sutton (Surrey)	a	23 02		23 20	23 10	23 32		23 40		00 02
	d				23 11			23 41		00 04
Belmont	d									
Banstead	d									
Epsom Downs	a									
Cheam	d				23 13			23 43		00 06
Ewell East	d				23 17			23 47		00 10
Epsom	a		23 06		23 21		23 36	23 51	00 06	00 14
	d		23 08		23 21			23 51		
Ashtead	d		23 12		23 25			23 55		
Leatherhead	d		23 15		23 28			23 58		
Bookham	d		23 21							
Effingham Junction	d		23 25							
Guildford	a		23 41							
Boxhill & Westhumble	d				23 33			00 03		
Dorking	a				23 36			00 06		
	d									
Holmwood	d									
Ockley	d									
Warnham	d									
Horsham	a									

Table 182

Sundays from 26 September

London - Sutton, Epsom, Guildford, Dorking and Horsham

		SW A	SW B	SN	FC	SN	SW A	SW B	SN	FC	SW	SN	SW	SN	SN	SN	SW	SN	SN	SN	SW	SN	SN
London Victoria ⊖	d			23p26		23p34			23p51			06 49		07 19	07 36	07 49		08 06	08 08	08 19		08 36	08 38
London Waterloo ⊖	d	23p09	23p09				23p42	23p42			00 15						08 02				08 32		
Clapham Junction	d	23p18	23p18	23p34		23p42	23p51	23p51	23p59		00 24	06 57		07 27	07 42	07 57	08 11	08 12	08 16	08 27	08 41	08 42	08 46
Balham ⊖	d			23p40		23p47			00 04			07 02		07 32	07 47	08 02		08 17	08 21	08 32		08 47	08 51
London Bridge ⊖	d				23p15					23p45													
Tulse Hill	d				23p31					00 01													
Norwood Junction	d														08 03			08 33				09 03	
West Croydon	d					00 04			00 21			07 20		07 50	08 08	08 20		08 38		08 50		09 08	
Waddon	d					00 06			00 24			07 22		07 52	08 11	08 22		08 41		08 52		09 11	
Wallington	d					00 10			00 27			07 26		07 56	08 14	08 26		08 44		08 56		09 14	
Carshalton Beeches	d					00 12			00 30			07 28		07 58	08 17	08 28		08 47		08 58		09 17	
Mitcham Eastfields	d			23p46															08 28				08 58
Mitcham Junction	d			23p49															08 31				09 01
Hackbridge	d			23p53															08 34				09 04
Carshalton	d			23p55															08 37				09 07
Sutton (Surrey)	a			00 01	00 05	00 16			00 33	00 35		07 32		08 02	08 20	08 32		08 50	08 40	09 02		09 20	09 10
	d			00 02								07 41		08 11					08 41				09 11
Belmont	d																						
Banstead	d																						
Epsom Downs	a																						
Cheam	d			00 04								07 43		08 13					08 43				09 13
Ewell East	d			00 08								07 47		08 17					08 47				09 17
Epsom	a	23p42	23p42	00 12			00 15	00 15			00 48	07 51	08 06	08 21			08 36		08 51		09 06		09 21
	d	23p47	23p47	00 12			00 19	00 19				07 51	08 08	08 21			08 38		08 51		09 08		09 21
Ashtead	d	23p51	23p51	00 16			00 23	00 23				07 55	08 12	08 25			08 42		08 55		09 12		09 25
Leatherhead	d	23p54	23p54	00 19			00 26	00 26				07 58	08 15	08 28			08 45		08 58		09 15		09 28
Bookham	d						00 31	00 31					08 21								09 21		
Effingham Junction	d						00 37	00 37					08 25								09 25		
Guildford	a						00 54	00 57					08 44								09 44		
Boxhill & Westhumble	d			00 24								08 03		08 33					09 03				09 33
Dorking	a	00 01	00 03	00 27								08 06		08 36			08 53		09 06				09 36
	d																						
Holmwood	d																						
Ockley	d																						
Warnham	d																						
Horsham	a																						

		SN	SW	SN	SN	SN	FC	SW	SN	SN	SN	FC	SW	SN	SN	SN	FC	SW	SN	SN	SN	FC	SW
London Victoria ⊖	d	08 49		09 06	09 08	09 19			09 36	09 38	09 49			10 06	10 08	10 19			10 36	10 38	10 49		
London Waterloo ⊖	d		09 02					09 32					10 02					10 32					11 02
Clapham Junction	d	08 57	09 11	09 12	09 16	09 27		09 41	09 42	09 46	09 57		10 11	10 12	10 16	10 27		10 41	10 42	10 46	10 57		11 11
Balham ⊖	d	09 02		09 17	09 21	09 32			09 47	09 51	10 02			10 17	10 21	10 32			10 47	10 51	11 02		
London Bridge ⊖	d						09 21					09 51					10 21					10 51	
Tulse Hill	d						09 31					10 01					10 31					11 01	
Norwood Junction	d			09 33					10 03					10 33					11 03				
West Croydon	d	09 20		09 38		09 50			10 08		10 20			10 38		10 50			11 08		11 20		
Waddon	d	09 22		09 41		09 52			10 11		10 22			10 41		10 52			11 11		11 22		
Wallington	d	09 26		09 44		09 56			10 14		10 26			10 44		10 56			11 14		11 26		
Carshalton Beeches	d	09 28		09 47		09 58			10 17		10 28			10 47		10 58			11 17		11 28		
Mitcham Eastfields	d				09 28					09 58					10 28					10 58			
Mitcham Junction	d				09 31					10 01					10 31					11 01			
Hackbridge	d				09 34					10 04					10 34					11 04			
Carshalton	d				09 37					10 07					10 37					11 07			
Sutton (Surrey)	a	09 32		09 50	09 40	10 02	10 05		10 20	10 10	10 32	10 35		10 50	10 40	11 02	11 05		11 20	11 10	11 32	11 35	
	d				09 41					10 11					10 41					11 11			
Belmont	d																						
Banstead	d																						
Epsom Downs	a																						
Cheam	d				09 43					10 13					10 43					11 13			
Ewell East	d				09 47					10 17					10 47					11 17			
Epsom	a		09 36		09 51			10 06		10 21			10 36		10 51			11 06		11 21			11 36
	d		09 38		09 51			10 08		10 21			10 38		10 51			11 08		11 21			11 38
Ashtead	d		09 42		09 55			10 12		10 25			10 42		10 55			11 12		11 25			11 42
Leatherhead	d		09 45		09 58			10 15		10 28			10 45		10 58			11 15		11 28			11 45
Bookham	d							10 21										11 21					
Effingham Junction	d							10 25										11 25					
Guildford	a							10 44										11 44					
Boxhill & Westhumble	d				10 03					10 33					11 03					11 33			
Dorking	a		09 53		10 06					10 36			10 53		11 06					11 36			11 53
	d																						
Holmwood	d																						
Ockley	d																						
Warnham	d																						
Horsham	a																						

A 26 September

B not 26 September

London - Sutton, Epsom, Guildford, Dorking and Horsham

Sundays
from 26 September

		SN		SN	SN	FC	SW	SN	SN	SN	FC	SW		SN	SN	SN	FC	SW	SN	SN	SN	FC		SW	SN
London Victoria 15 ⊖	d	11 06		11 08	11 19			11 36	11 38	11 49				12 06	12 08	12 19			12 36	12 38	12 49				13 06
London Waterloo 15 ⊖	d						11 32					12 02						12 32						13 02	
Clapham Junction 10	d	11 12		11 16	11 27		11 41	11 42	11 46	11 57		12 11		12 12	12 16	12 27		12 41	12 42	12 46	12 57			13 11	13 12
Balham 4 ⊖	d	11 17		11 21	11 32			11 47	11 51	12 02				12 17	12 21	12 32			12 47	12 51	13 02				13 17
London Bridge 4 ⊖	d					11 21					11 51						12 21					12 51			
Tulse Hill 3	d					11 31					12 01						12 31					13 01			
Norwood Junction 2	d	11 33						12 03						12 33					13 03						13 33
West Croydon 4	d	11 38			11 50			12 08		12 20				12 38		12 50			13 08		13 20				13 38
Waddon	d	11 41			11 52			12 11		12 22				12 41		12 52			13 11		13 22				13 41
Wallington	d	11 44			11 56			12 14		12 26				12 44		12 56			13 14		13 26				13 44
Carshalton Beeches	d	11 47			11 58			12 17		12 28				12 47		12 58			13 17		13 28				13 47
Mitcham Eastfields	d			11 28					11 58						12 28					12 58					
Mitcham Junction	d			11 31					12 01						12 31					13 01					
Hackbridge	d			11 34					12 04						12 34					13 04					
Carshalton	d			11 37					12 07						12 37					13 07					
Sutton (Surrey) 4	a	11 50		11 40	12 02	12 05		12 20	12 10	12 32	12 35			12 50	12 40	13 02	13 05		13 20	13 10	13 32	13 35			13 50
	d			11 41					12 11						12 41					13 11					
Belmont	d																								
Banstead	d																								
Epsom Downs	a																								
Cheam	d			11 43					12 13						12 43					13 13					
Ewell East	d			11 47					12 17						12 47					13 17					
Epsom 3	a			11 51			12 06		12 21			12 36			12 51			13 06		13 21				13 36	
	d			11 51			12 08		12 21			12 38			12 51			13 08		13 21				13 38	
Ashtead	d			11 55			12 12		12 25			12 42			12 55			13 12		13 25				13 42	
Leatherhead	d			11 58			12 15		12 28			12 45			12 58			13 15		13 28				13 45	
Bookham	d						12 21											13 21							
Effingham Junction 6	d						12 25											13 25							
Guildford	a						12 44											13 44							
Boxhill & Westhumble	d			12 03					12 33						13 03					13 33					
Dorking 4	a			12 06					12 36			12 53			13 06					13 36				13 53	
	d																								
Holmwood	d																								
Ockley	d																								
Warnham	d																								
Horsham 4	a																								

		SN	SN	FC	SW	SN	SN	SN		FC	SW	SN	SN	SN	FC	SW	SN	SN		SN	FC	SW	SN	SN	SN
London Victoria 15 ⊖	d	13 08	13 19			13 36	13 38	13 49				14 06	14 08	14 19			14 36	14 38		14 49			15 06	15 08	15 19
London Waterloo 15 ⊖	d				13 32						14 02					14 32						15 02			
Clapham Junction 10	d	13 16	13 27		13 41	13 42	13 46	13 57			14 11	14 12	14 16	14 27		14 41	14 42	14 46		14 57		15 11	15 12	15 16	15 27
Balham 4 ⊖	d	13 21	13 32			13 47	13 51	14 02				14 17	14 21	14 32			14 47	14 51		15 02			15 17	15 21	15 32
London Bridge 4 ⊖	d			13 21						13 51					14 21						14 51				
Tulse Hill 3	d			13 31						14 01					14 31						15 01				
Norwood Junction 2	d					14 03						14 33					15 03						15 33		
West Croydon 4	d		13 50			14 08		14 20				14 38		14 50			15 08			15 20			15 38		15 50
Waddon	d		13 52			14 11		14 22				14 41		14 52			15 11			15 22			15 41		15 52
Wallington	d		13 56			14 14		14 26				14 44		14 56			15 14			15 26			15 44		15 56
Carshalton Beeches	d		13 58			14 17		14 28				14 47		14 58			15 17			15 28			15 47		15 58
Mitcham Eastfields	d	13 28					13 58						14 28					14 58						15 28	
Mitcham Junction	d	13 31					14 01						14 31					15 01						15 31	
Hackbridge	d	13 34					14 04						14 34					15 04						15 34	
Carshalton	d	13 37					14 07						14 37					15 07						15 37	
Sutton (Surrey) 4	a	13 40	14 02	14 05		14 20	14 10	14 32		14 35		14 50	14 40	15 02	15 05		15 20	15 10		15 32	15 35		15 50	15 40	16 02
	d	13 41					14 11						14 41					15 11						15 41	
Belmont	d																								
Banstead	d																								
Epsom Downs	a																								
Cheam	d	13 43					14 13						14 43					15 13						15 43	
Ewell East	d	13 47					14 17						14 47					15 17						15 47	
Epsom 3	a	13 51			14 06		14 21				14 36		14 51			15 06		15 21				15 36		15 51	
	d	13 51			14 08		14 21				14 38		14 51			15 08		15 21				15 38		15 51	
Ashtead	d	13 55			14 12		14 25				14 42		14 55			15 12		15 25				15 42		15 55	
Leatherhead	d	13 58			14 15		14 28				14 45		14 58			15 15		15 28				15 45		15 58	
Bookham	d				14 21											15 21									
Effingham Junction 6	d				14 25											15 25									
Guildford	a				14 44											15 44									
Boxhill & Westhumble	d	14 03					14 33						15 03					15 33						16 03	
Dorking 4	a	14 06					14 36				14 53		15 06					15 36				15 53		16 06	
	d																								
Holmwood	d																								
Ockley	d																								
Warnham	d																								
Horsham 4	a																								

Table 182

London - Sutton, Epsom, Guildford, Dorking and Horsham

Sundays
from 26 September

		FC	SW	SN		SN	SN	FC	SW	SN	SN	SN	FC	SW		SN	SN	SN	FC	SW	SN	SN	SN	FC	
London Victoria 15 ⊖	d			15 36		15 38	15 49			16 06	16 08	16 19				16 36	16 38	16 49			17 06	17 08	17 19		
London Waterloo 15 ⊖	d		15 32						16 02					16 32						17 02					
Clapham Junction 10	d		15 41	15 42		15 46	15 57		16 11	16 12	16 16	16 27		16 41		16 42	16 46	16 57		17 11	17 12	17 16	17 27		
Balham 4 ⊖	d			15 47		15 51	16 02			16 17	16 21	16 32				16 47	16 51	17 02			17 17	17 21	17 32		
London Bridge 4 ⊖	d	15 21						15 51					16 21						16 51					17 21	
Tulse Hill 3	d	15 31						16 01					16 31						17 01					17 31	
Norwood Junction 2	d			16 03						16 33						17 03					17 33				
West Croydon 4	d			16 08			16 20			16 38		16 50				17 08		17 20			17 38		17 50		
Waddon	d			16 11			16 22			16 41		16 52				17 11		17 22			17 41		17 52		
Wallington	d			16 14			16 26			16 44		16 56				17 14		17 26			17 44		17 56		
Carshalton Beeches	d			16 17			16 28			16 47		16 58				17 17		17 28			17 47		17 58		
Mitcham Eastfields	d					15 58					16 28						16 58					17 28			
Mitcham Junction	d					16 01					16 31						17 01					17 31			
Hackbridge	d					16 04					16 34						17 04					17 34			
Carshalton	d					16 07					16 37						17 07					17 37			
Sutton (Surrey) 4	a	16 05		16 20		16 10	16 32	16 35		16 50	16 40	17 02	17 05			17 20	17 10	17 32	17 35		17 50	17 40	18 02	18 05	
	d					16 11					16 41						17 11					17 41			
Belmont	d																								
Banstead	d																								
Epsom Downs	a																								
Cheam	d					16 13					16 43						17 13					17 43			
Ewell East	d					16 17					16 47						17 17					17 47			
Epsom 3	a		16 06			16 21			16 36		16 51			17 06			17 21			17 36		17 51			
	d		16 08			16 21			16 38		16 51			17 08			17 21			17 38		17 51			
Ashtead	d		16 12			16 25			16 42		16 55			17 12			17 25			17 42		17 55			
Leatherhead	d		16 15			16 28			16 45		16 58			17 15			17 28			17 45		17 58			
Bookham	d		16 21											17 21											
Effingham Junction 6	d		16 25											17 25											
Guildford	a		16 44											17 44											
Boxhill & Westhumble	d					16 33					17 03						17 33					18 03			
Dorking 4	a					16 36			16 53		17 06						17 36			17 53		18 06			
	d																								
Holmwood	d																								
Ockley	d																								
Warnham	d																								
Horsham 4	a																								

		SW	SN	SN	SN	FC	SW	SN	SN	SN		FC	SW	SN	SN	SN	FC	SW	SN	SN		SN	FC	SW	SN
London Victoria 15 ⊖	d		17 36	17 38	17 49			18 06	18 08	18 19				18 36	18 38	18 49			19 06	19 08		19 19			19 36
London Waterloo 15 ⊖	d	17 32					18 02						18 32					19 02						19 32	
Clapham Junction 10	d	17 41	17 42	17 46	17 57		18 11	18 12	18 16	18 27			18 41	18 42	18 46	18 57		19 11	19 12	19 16		19 27		19 41	19 42
Balham 4 ⊖	d		17 47	17 51	18 02			18 17	18 21	18 32				18 47	18 51	19 02			19 17	19 21		19 32			19 47
London Bridge 4 ⊖	d					17 51						18 21					18 51						19 21		
Tulse Hill 3	d					18 01						18 31					19 01						19 31		
Norwood Junction 2	d		18 03					18 33						19 03					19 33						20 03
West Croydon 4	d		18 08		18 20			18 38		18 50				19 08		19 20			19 38			19 50			20 08
Waddon	d		18 11		18 22			18 41		18 52				19 11		19 22			19 41			19 52			20 11
Wallington	d		18 14		18 26			18 44		18 56				19 14		19 26			19 44			19 56			20 14
Carshalton Beeches	d		18 17		18 28			18 47		18 58				19 17		19 28			19 47			19 58			20 17
Mitcham Eastfields	d			17 58					18 28						18 58					19 28					
Mitcham Junction	d			18 01					18 31						19 01					19 31					
Hackbridge	d			18 04					18 34						19 04					19 34					
Carshalton	d			18 07					18 37						19 07					19 37					
Sutton (Surrey) 4	a		18 20	18 10	18 32	18 35		18 50	18 40	19 02		19 05		19 20	19 10	19 32	19 35		19 50	19 40		20 02	20 05		20 20
	d			18 11					18 41						19 11					19 41					
Belmont	d																								
Banstead	d																								
Epsom Downs	a																								
Cheam	d			18 13					18 43						19 13					19 43					
Ewell East	d			18 17					18 47						19 17					19 47					
Epsom 3	a	18 06		18 21			18 36		18 51				19 06		19 21			19 36		19 51				20 06	
	d	18 08		18 21			18 38		18 51				19 08		19 21			19 38		19 51				20 08	
Ashtead	d	18 12		18 25			18 42		18 55				19 12		19 25			19 42		19 55				20 12	
Leatherhead	d	18 15		18 28			18 45		18 58				19 15		19 28			19 45		19 58				20 15	
Bookham	d	18 21											19 21											20 21	
Effingham Junction 6	d	18 25											19 25											20 25	
Guildford	a	18 44											19 44											20 44	
Boxhill & Westhumble	d			18 33					19 03						19 33					20 03					
Dorking 4	a			18 36			18 53		19 06						19 36			19 53		20 06					
	d																								
Holmwood	d																								
Ockley	d																								
Warnham	d																								
Horsham 4	a																								

Table 182

Sundays from 26 September

London - Sutton, Epsom, Guildford, Dorking and Horsham

		SN	SN	FC	SW	SN		SN	SN	FC	SW	SN	SN	SN	FC	SW		SN	SN	SN	SW	SN	SN	SN	SW
London Victoria 15 ⊖	d	19 38	19 49			20 06		20 08	20 19			20 36	20 38	20 49				21 06	21 08	21 19		21 36	21 38	21 49	
London Waterloo 15 ⊖	d				20 02						20 32					21 02					21 32				22 02
Clapham Junction 10	d	19 46	19 57		20 11	20 12		20 16	20 27		20 41	20 42	20 46	20 57		21 11		21 12	21 16	21 27	21 41	21 42	21 46	21 57	22 11
Balham 4 ⊖	d	19 51	20 02			20 17		20 21	20 32			20 47	20 51	21 02				21 17	21 21	21 32		21 47	21 51	22 02	
London Bridge 4 ⊖	d			19 51						20 21					20 51										
Tulse Hill 3	d			20 01						20 31					21 01										
Norwood Junction 2	d					20 33						21 03						21 33				22 03			
West Croydon 4	d		20 20			20 38			20 50			21 08		21 20				21 38		21 50		22 08		22 20	
Waddon	d		20 22			20 41			20 52			21 11		21 22				21 41		21 52		22 11		22 22	
Wallington	d		20 26			20 44			20 56			21 14		21 26				21 44		21 56		22 14		22 26	
Carshalton Beeches	d		20 28			20 47			20 58			21 17		21 28				21 47		21 58		22 17		22 28	
Mitcham Eastfields	d	19 58						20 28					20 58						21 28				21 58		
Mitcham Junction	d	20 01						20 31					21 01						21 31				22 01		
Hackbridge	d	20 04						20 34					21 04						21 34				22 04		
Carshalton	d	20 07						20 37					21 07						21 37				22 07		
Sutton (Surrey) 4	a	20 10	20 32	20 35		20 50		20 40	21 02	21 05		21 20	21 10	21 32	21 35			21 50	21 40	22 02		22 20	22 10	22 32	
	d	20 11						20 41					21 11						21 41				22 11		
Belmont	d																								
Banstead	d																								
Epsom Downs	a																								
Cheam	d	20 13						20 43					21 13						21 43				22 13		
Ewell East	d	20 17						20 47					21 17						21 47				22 17		
Epsom 3	a	20 21			20 36			20 51			21 06		21 21			21 36			21 51		22 06		22 21		22 36
	d	20 21			20 38			20 51			21 08		21 21			21 38			21 51		22 08		22 21		22 38
Ashtead	d	20 25			20 42			20 55			21 12		21 25			21 42			21 55		22 12		22 25		22 42
Leatherhead	d	20 28			20 45			20 58			21 15		21 28			21 45			21 58		22 15		22 28		22 45
Bookham	d										21 21										22 21				
Effingham Junction 6	d										21 25										22 25				
Guildford	a										21 44										22 44				
Boxhill & Westhumble	d	20 33						21 03					21 33						22 03				22 33		
Dorking 4	a	20 36			20 53			21 06					21 36			21 53			22 06				22 36		22 53
	d																								
Holmwood	d																								
Ockley	d																								
Warnham	d																								
Horsham 4	a																								

		SN		SN	SN	SW	SN	SN	SN	SW	SN	SW		SN
London Victoria 15 ⊖	d	22 06		22 08	22 19		22 36	22 38	22 49		23 08			23 19
London Waterloo 15 ⊖	d					22 32				23 02		23 32		
Clapham Junction 10	d	22 12		22 16	22 26	22 41	22 42	22 46	22 57	23 11	23 16	23 41		23 27
Balham 4 ⊖	d	22 17		22 21	22 32		22 47	22 51	23 02		23 21			23 32
London Bridge 4 ⊖	d													
Tulse Hill 3	d													
Norwood Junction 2	d	22 33					23 03							
West Croydon 4	d	22 38			22 50		23 08		23 20					23 50
Waddon	d	22 41			22 52		23 11		23 22					23 52
Wallington	d	22 44			22 56		23 14		23 26					23 56
Carshalton Beeches	d	22 47			22 58		23 17		23 28					23 58
Mitcham Eastfields	d			22 28				22 58			23 28			
Mitcham Junction	d			22 31				23 01			23 31			
Hackbridge	d			22 34				23 04			23 34			
Carshalton	d			22 37				23 07			23 37			
Sutton (Surrey) 4	a	22 50		22 40	23 02		23 20	23 10	23 32		23 40			00 02
	d			22 41				23 11			23 41			00 04
Belmont	d													
Banstead	d													
Epsom Downs	a													
Cheam	d			22 43				23 13			23 43			00 06
Ewell East	d			22 47				23 17			23 47			00 10
Epsom 3	a			22 51		23 06		23 21		23 36	23 51	00 06		00 14
	d			22 51		23 08		23 21			23 51			
Ashtead	d			22 55		23 12		23 25			23 55			
Leatherhead	d			22 58		23 15		23 28			23 58			
Bookham	d					23 21								
Effingham Junction 6	d					23 25								
Guildford	a					23 44								
Boxhill & Westhumble	d			23 03				23 33			00 03			
Dorking 4	a			23 06				23 36			00 06			
	d													
Holmwood	d													
Ockley	d													
Warnham	d													
Horsham 4	a													

Table 182

Mondays to Fridays until 24 September

Horsham, Dorking, Guildford, Epsom and Sutton - London

		SN MX	SN	SW	SN	SN	SN	SN	SW	SN		SN	SW	FC	SN	SN	SW	SW	SN	FC		SN	SN	FC	SN
Horsham 4	d															05 49									06 20
Warnham	d															05 53									06 24
Ockley	d															06 00									06 31
Holmwood	d															06 04									06 35
Dorking 4	a															06 10									06 41
	d								05 48							06 11		06 32							06 44
Boxhill & Westhumble	d								05 50							06 13		06 34							06 46
Guildford	d			04 58													05 58								
Effingham Junction 6	d			05 16													06 16								
Bookham	d			05 19													06 19								
Leatherhead	d			05 24					05 56							06 18	06 24	06 39							06 51
Ashtead	d			05 28					05 59							06 22	06 28	06 43							06 55
Epsom 3	a			05 32					06 04							06 26	06 32	06 47							06 59
	d		05 23	05 34		05 39		05 57	06 04				06 18			06 27	06 34	06 48					06 49		07 00
Ewell East	d		05 27			05 43		06 01								06 31							06 53		07 04
Cheam	d		05 30			05 46		06 04								06 34							06 56		07 07
Epsom Downs	d	23p43																	06 34						
Banstead	d	23p46																	06 37						
Belmont	d	23p49																	06 40						
Sutton (Surrey) 4	a	23p52	05 33			05 49		06 07		06 13						06 37			06 43			06 49	06 59		07 10
	d	23p53	05 33		05 37	05 49	06 03	06 07		06 14		06 14		06 20	06 33	06 37			06 44	06 48		06 50	07 00	07 06	07 10
Carshalton	d				05 40			06 10		06 17						06 40						06 53			07 13
Hackbridge	d				05 42			06 13		06 19						06 43						06 55			07 16
Mitcham Junction	d				05 46			06 16		06 23						06 46						06 59			07 19
Mitcham Eastfields	d				05 49			06 19		06 26						06 49						07 02			07 22
Carshalton Beeches	d	23p56	05 36			05 52	06 06					06 17			06 36				06 47				07 03		
Wallington	d	23p58	05 39			05 55	06 08					06 20			06 38				06 50				07 05		
Waddon	d	00 01	05 42			05 58	06 11					06 23			06 41				06 53				07 08		
West Croydon 4	d	00a04	05 45			06 01	06 15					06 26			06 45				06 58				07 13		
Norwood Junction 2	d		05 50				06 20								06 50								07 18		
New Cross Gate 4 ⊖	d		06 08																						
Tulse Hill 3	d				05 57					06 34				06 52						07 20		07 10		07 42	
London Bridge 4 ⊖	a		06 14		06 08		06 33			06 51					07 04							07 29	07 32		
Balham 4 ⊖	d					06 17		06 27				06 42				06 57			07 14						07 29
Clapham Junction 10	a			06 00		06 23		06 31	06 30			06 48	06 45			07 01	07 00	07 15	07 19						07 34
London Waterloo 15 ⊖	a			06 11					06 40				06 55				07 12	07 27							
London Victoria 15 ⊖	a					06 31		06 38				06 58				07 10			07 30						07 43

		SW	SN	SN	SW	SN		SN	SW	SN	FC	SN	SW	SW	FC	SN		SN	SW	SN	SN	SN	FC	FC	SN
Horsham 4	d											06 55													07 22
Warnham	d											06 59													07 26
Ockley	d											07 06													07 33
Holmwood	d											07 10													07 37
Dorking 4	a											07 16													07 43
	d							06 52	07 02			07 17		07 32											07 46
Boxhill & Westhumble	d							06 59	07 04					07 34											
Guildford	d	06 28											06 58									07 26			
Effingham Junction 6	d	06 48											07 16									07 38			
Bookham	d	06 51											07 19									07 41			
Leatherhead	d	06 56						07 04	07 09			07 23	07 26	07 39								07 46			07 52
Ashtead	d	06 59						07 08	07 13			07 26	07 29	07 43								07 50			07 55
Epsom 3	a	07 04						07 12	07 17			07 31	07 34	07 47								07 54			08 00
	d	07 04			07 22			07 15	07 18	07 21		07 31	07 34	07 48					07 52		07 49	07 55			08 02
Ewell East	d							07 19		07 25											07 53	07 59			08 06
Cheam	d							07 22		07 28		07 37									07 56	08 02			08 09
Epsom Downs	d		07 04													07 34									
Banstead	d		07 07													07 37									
Belmont	d		07 10													07 40									
Sutton (Surrey) 4	a		07 13	07 19				07 25		07 31		07 40				07 43		07 48			07 59	08 05			08 12
	d		07 14	07 20		07 22		07 26		07 32	07 37	07 42			07 40	07 44		07 49		07 53	08 00	08 05	08 08	08 09	08 13
Carshalton	d			07 23				07 29			07 40	07 45						07 52			08 03			08 12	08 16
Hackbridge	d			07 25				07 31			07 42							07 54			08 05			08 14	08 18
Mitcham Junction	d			07 29				07 35			07 45	07 49						07 58			08 09			08 17	08 22
Mitcham Eastfields	d			07 32				07 38			07 48	07 52						08 01			08 12			08 20	08 25
Carshalton Beeches	d		07 17			07 25				07 35						07 47				07 56		08 08			
Wallington	d		07 20			07 27				07 37						07 50				07 58		08 11			
Waddon	d		07 23			07 30				07 40						07 53				08 01					
West Croydon 4	d		07 28			07 34				07 44						07 58				08 05		08 16			
Norwood Junction 2	d									07 49												08 21			
New Cross Gate 4 ⊖	d																								
Tulse Hill 3	d			07 41							07 57				08 13			08 09					08 43	08 28	
London Bridge 4 ⊖	a			08 00						08 05								08 29				08 35			
Balham 4 ⊖	d		07 44			07 50		07 47				07 59				08 14				08 21	08 18				
Clapham Junction 10	a	07 30	07 49		07 48	07 55		07 51	07 42			08 04	08 01	08 12		08 19			08 18	08 25	08 22				08 32
London Waterloo 15 ⊖	a	07 42			08 00				07 54				08 13	08 24					08 30						
London Victoria 15 ⊖	a		08 00			08 06		08 02				08 13				08 30				08 36	08 32				08 41

Table 182

Mondays to Fridays

until 24 September

Horsham, Dorking, Guildford, Epsom and Sutton - London

		SW		SW	SN	SN	SW	SN	SN	SW	FC	FC		SN	SN	SW	SN	SN	SW	SN	FC	FC		SN	SN
Horsham [4]	d														08 00										
Warnham	d														08 04										
Ockley	d														08 11										
Holmwood	d														08 15										
Dorking [4]	a														08 21										
	d			08 02											08 22	08 31									08 57
Boxhill & Westhumble	d			08 04											08 24	08 33									08 59
Guildford	d									07 58								08 16							
Effingham Junction [6]	d	07 46								08 16								08 32	08 48						
Bookham	d	07 49								08 19								08 35	08 51						
Leatherhead	d	07 56		08 09						08 25					08 29	08 38		08 41	08 56						09 04
Ashtead	d	07 59		08 13						08 28					08 33	08 42		08 45	08 59						09 08
Epsom [3]	a	08 04		08 17						08 33					08 37	08 46		08 49	09 04						09 12
	d	08 04		08 18			08 22		08 22	08 34					08 38	08 48		08 50	09 04						09 13
Ewell East	d								08 26						08 42			08 54							09 17
Cheam	d								08 29						08 45			08 57							09 20
Epsom Downs	d				08 04									08 34											
Banstead	d				08 07									08 37											
Belmont	d				08 10									08 40											
Sutton (Surrey) [4]	a				08 13	08 19			08 32					08 43	08 48		08 56	09 00							09 23
	d				08 14	08 20		08 29	08 32		08 39	08 41		08 44	08 48		08 57	09 00		09 03	09 11	09 13		09 15	09 23
Carshalton	d					08 23		08 32			08 42				08 51		09 00	09 03				09 16			
Hackbridge	d					08 25		08 34			08 44				08 54		09 02	09 06				09 18			
Mitcham Junction	d					08 29		08 38			08 47				08 57		09 06	09 09				09 21			
Mitcham Eastfields	d					08 32		08 41			08 50				09 00		09 09	09 12				09 24			09 32
Carshalton Beeches	d				08 17				08 35					08 47						09 06				09 18	
Wallington	d				08 19				08 38					08 50						09 08				09 20	
Waddon	d				08 22				08 41					08 53						09 11				09 23	
West Croydon [4]	d				08 26				08 44					08 56						09 15				09 28	
Norwood Junction [2]	d								08 49											09 22					
New Cross Gate [4] ⊖	d																								
Tulse Hill [3]	d					08 40					08 58	09 16					09 16				09 42	09 32			
London Bridge [4] ⊖	a					08 59			09 04								09 35								
Balham [4] ⊖	d				08 43			08 47						09 13	09 07			09 18		09 41				09 44	
Clapham Junction [10]	a	08 31		08 42	08 49		08 48	08 52		09 00				09 18	09 11	09 15		09 22	09 30	09 46				09 49	09 42
London Waterloo [15] ⊖	a	08 43		08 54			09 00			09 12						09 27			09 42						
London Victoria [15] ⊖	a				09 00			09 02						09 31	09 22			09 33		09 58				10 00	09 54

		SW	SN	SN	SW	SN	SN	FC	FC		SN	SN	SN	SW	SW	SN	FC	FC	SN	SN	SN	SW	SN	SW	SN
Horsham [4]	d												09 09												
Warnham	d												09 13												
Ockley	d												09 20												
Holmwood	d												09 24												
Dorking [4]	a												09 30												
	d	09 02											09 31	09 35							09 57	10 05			
Boxhill & Westhumble	d	09 04											09 33								09 59				
Guildford	d				08 58										09 28									09 58	
Effingham Junction [6]	d				09 16										09 46									10 16	
Bookham	d				09 19										09 49									10 19	
Leatherhead	d	09 09			09 24								09 38	09 41	09 54						10 04	10 11		10 24	
Ashtead	d	09 13			09 28								09 42	09 45	09 58						10 08	10 14		10 28	
Epsom [3]	a	09 17			09 32								09 46	09 49	10 02						10 12	10 19		10 32	
	d	09 18		09 19	09 35	09 42							09 49	09 50	10 05				10 04		10 13	10 20	10 19	10 35	
Ewell East	d			09 23		09 46							09 53						10 08		10 17		10 23		
Cheam	d			09 26		09 49							09 56						10 11		10 20		10 26		
Epsom Downs	d		09 09								09 34														
Banstead	d		09 12								09 37														
Belmont	d		09 15								09 40														
Sutton (Surrey) [4]	a		09 18	09 29		09 53					09 43		09 59						10 14		10 23		10 29		
	d		09 23	09 30		09 53	09 33	09 37	09 38		09 44	09 52	10 00			10 03	10 07	10 08	10 14	10 22	10 23		10 30		10 33
Carshalton	d			09 33					09 41				10 03					10 11					10 33		
Hackbridge	d			09 35					09 43				10 05					10 13					10 35		
Mitcham Junction	d			09 39					09 46				10 09					10 16					10 39		
Mitcham Eastfields	d			09 42					09 49				10 12					10 19					10 42		
Carshalton Beeches	d		09 26				09 36				09 47	09 55				10 06			10 17	10 25					10 36
Wallington	d		09 28				09 38				09 50	09 57				10 08			10 20	10 27					10 38
Waddon	d		09 31				09 41				09 53	10 00				10 11			10 23	10 30					10 41
West Croydon [4]	d		09 35				09 45				09 58	10 04				10 15			10 28	10 34					10 45
Norwood Junction [2]	d						09 52									10 22									10 52
New Cross Gate [4] ⊖	d																								
Tulse Hill [3]	d							10 12	09 57								10 42	10 27							
London Bridge [4] ⊖	a																								
Balham [4] ⊖	d		09 52	09 48			10 09				10 14	10 21	10 18			10 39			10 44	10 51			10 48		11 09
Clapham Junction [10]	a	09 45	09 57	09 52	10 00	10 11	10 15				10 19	10 26	10 22	10 15	10 30	10 45			10 49	10 56	10 40	10 45	10 52	11 00	11 14
London Waterloo [15] ⊖	a	09 57			10 10									10 25	10 40							10 55		11 10	
London Victoria [15] ⊖	a		10 05	10 00		10 20	10 24				10 28	10 34	10 31			10 53			10 58	11 04	10 48		11 00		11 23

Table 182

Mondays to Fridays

until 24 September

Horsham, Dorking, Guildford, Epsom and Sutton - London

		FC	FC	SN		SN	SW	SN	SN	SW	SN	FC	FC	SN		SN	SW	SN	SN	SW	SN	FC	FC	SN	
Horsham [4]	d					10 04																			
Warnham	d					10 08																			
Ockley	d					10 15																			
Holmwood	d					10 19																			
Dorking [4]	a					10 25																			
	d					10 26	10 35									10 58	11 05								
Boxhill & Westhumble	d					10 28																			
Guildford	d									10 28										10 58					
Effingham Junction [6]	d									10 46										11 16					
Bookham	d									10 49										11 19					
Leatherhead	d					10 33	10 41			10 54						11 04	11 11			11 24					
Ashtead	d					10 37	10 44			10 58						11 07	11 14			11 28					
Epsom [3]	a					10 41	10 49			11 02						11 12	11 19			11 32					
	d					10 42	10 50		10 49	11 05				11 04		11 13	11 20		11 19	11 35					
Ewell East	d					10 46			10 53					11 08					11 23						
Cheam	d					10 49			10 56					11 11		11 18			11 26						
Epsom Downs	d			10 34																				11 34	
Banstead	d			10 37																				11 37	
Belmont	d			10 40																				11 40	
Sutton (Surrey) [4]	a			10 43		10 52			10 59					11 14		11 21			11 29					11 43	
	d	10 37	10 38	10 44		10 53		10 52	11 00		11 04	11 07	11 08	11 14		11 23		11 22	11 30		11 33	11 37	11 38	11 44	
Carshalton	d		10 41						11 03				11 11						11 33				11 41		
Hackbridge	d		10 43						11 05				11 13						11 35				11 43		
Mitcham Junction	d		10 46						11 09				11 16						11 39				11 46		
Mitcham Eastfields	d		10 49						11 12				11 19						11 42				11 49		
Carshalton Beeches	d			10 47				10 55			11 07			11 17				11 25			11 36			11 47	
Wallington	d			10 50				10 57			11 09			11 20				11 27			11 38			11 50	
Waddon	d			10 53				11 00			11 12			11 23				11 30			11 41			11 53	
West Croydon [4]	d			10 58				11 04			11 16			11 28				11 34			11 45			11 58	
Norwood Junction [2]	d										11 22										11 52				
New Cross Gate [4] ⊖	d																								
Tulse Hill [3]	d	11 12	10 57									11 42	11 27									12 12	11 57		
London Bridge [4] ⊖	a																								
Balham [4] ⊖	d			11 14				11 21	11 18		11 40			11 44				11 51	11 48		12 09			12 14	
Clapham Junction [10]	a			11 19		11 10	11 15	11 26	11 22	11 30	11 45			11 49		11 40	11 45	11 56	11 52	12 00	12 14			12 19	
London Waterloo [15] ⊖	a						11 25			11 40							11 55			12 10					
London Victoria [15] ⊖	a			11 28		11 20		11 34	11 30		11 54			11 58		11 50		12 04	12 00		12 23			12 28	

		SN	SW	SN	SN	SW	SN	FC	FC	SN		SN	SW	SN	SN	SW	SN	FC	FC	SN		SN	SW	SN	SN
Horsham [4]	d	11 04																				12 04			
Warnham	d	11 08																				12 08			
Ockley	d	11 15																				12 15			
Holmwood	d	11 19																				12 19			
Dorking [4]	a	11 25																				12 25			
	d	11 26	11 35									11 58	12 05									12 26	12 35		
Boxhill & Westhumble	d	11 28																				12 28			
Guildford	d					11 28										11 58									
Effingham Junction [6]	d					11 46										12 16									
Bookham	d					11 49										12 19									
Leatherhead	d	11 33	11 41			11 54						12 04	12 11			12 24						12 33	12 41		
Ashtead	d	11 37	11 44			11 58						12 07	12 14			12 28						12 37	12 44		
Epsom [3]	a	11 41	11 49			12 02						12 12	12 19			12 32						12 41	12 49		
	d	11 42	11 50		11 49	12 05				12 04		12 13	12 20		12 19	12 35						12 42	12 50		12 49
Ewell East	d	11 46			11 53					12 08					12 23							12 46			12 53
Cheam	d	11 49			11 56					12 11		12 18			12 26							12 49			12 56
Epsom Downs	d																			12 34					
Banstead	d																			12 37					
Belmont	d																			12 40					
Sutton (Surrey) [4]	a	11 52			11 59					12 14		12 21			12 29					12 43		12 52			12 59
	d	11 53		11 52	12 00		12 03	12 07	12 08	12 14		12 23		12 22	12 30		12 33	12 37	12 38	12 44		12 53		12 52	13 00
Carshalton	d				12 03				12 11						12 33				12 41						13 03
Hackbridge	d				12 05				12 13						12 35				12 43						13 05
Mitcham Junction	d				12 09				12 16						12 39				12 46						13 09
Mitcham Eastfields	d				12 12				12 19						12 42				12 49						13 12
Carshalton Beeches	d			11 55			12 06			12 17				12 25			12 36			12 47				12 55	
Wallington	d			11 57			12 08			12 20				12 27			12 38			12 50				12 57	
Waddon	d			12 00			12 11			12 23				12 30			12 41			12 53				13 00	
West Croydon [4]	d			12 04			12 15			12 28				12 34			12 45			12 58				13 04	
Norwood Junction [2]	d						12 22										12 52								
New Cross Gate [4] ⊖	d																								
Tulse Hill [3]	d							12 42	12 27									13 12	12 57						
London Bridge [4] ⊖	a																								
Balham [4] ⊖	d			12 21	12 18		12 39			12 44				12 51	12 48		13 09			13 13				13 21	13 18
Clapham Junction [10]	a	12 10	12 15	12 26	12 22	12 30	12 44			12 49		12 40	12 45	12 56	12 52	13 00	13 14			13 20		13 10	13 15	13 26	13 22
London Waterloo [15] ⊖	a		12 25			12 40							12 55			13 10							13 25		
London Victoria [15] ⊖	a	12 18		12 34	12 30		12 53			12 58		12 48		13 04	13 00		13 23			13 28		13 18		13 34	13 30

Table 182

Mondays to Fridays
until 24 September

Horsham, Dorking, Guildford, Epsom and Sutton - London

		SW	SN	FC	FC	SN		SN	SW	SN	SN	SW	SN	FC	FC	SN		SN	SW	SN	SN	SW	SN	FC	FC
Horsham 4	d																	13 04							
Warnham	d																	13 08							
Ockley	d																	13 15							
Holmwood	d																	13 19							
Dorking 4	a																	13 25							
	d							12 59	13 05									13 26	13 35						
Boxhill & Westhumble	d																	13 28							
Guildford	d	12 28										12 58										13 28			
Effingham Junction 6	d	12 46										13 16										13 46			
Bookham	d	12 49										13 19										13 49			
Leatherhead	d	12 54						13 05	13 11			13 24						13 33	13 41			13 54			
Ashtead	d	12 58						13 08	13 14			13 28						13 37	13 44			13 58			
Epsom 3	a	13 02						13 13	13 19			13 32						13 41	13 49			14 02			
	d	13 05				13 04		13 13	13 20		13 19	13 35						13 42	13 50		13 49	14 05			
Ewell East	d					13 08					13 23							13 46			13 53				
Cheam	d					13 11		13 19			13 26							13 49			13 56				
Epsom Downs	d															13 34									
Banstead	d															13 37									
Belmont	d															13 40									
Sutton (Surrey) 4	a					13 14		13 22			13 29					13 43		13 52			13 59				
	d		13 03	13 07	13 08	13 14		13 23		13 22	13 30		13 33	13 37	13 38	13 44		13 53		13 52	14 00		14 03	14 07	14 08
Carshalton	d				13 11						13 33				13 41						14 03				14 11
Hackbridge	d				13 13						13 35				13 43						14 05				14 13
Mitcham Junction	d				13 16						13 39				13 46						14 09				14 16
Mitcham Eastfields	d				13 19						13 42				13 49						14 12				14 19
Carshalton Beeches	d		13 06			13 17				13 25			13 36			13 47				13 55			14 06		
Wallington	d		13 08			13 20				13 27			13 38			13 50				13 57			14 08		
Waddon	d		13 11			13 23				13 30			13 41			13 53				14 00			14 11		
West Croydon 4	d		13 15			13 28				13 34			13 45			13 58				14 04			14 15		
Norwood Junction 2	d		13 22										13 52										14 22		
New Cross Gate 4 ⊖	d																								
Tulse Hill 3	d			13 42	13 27									14 12	13 57									14 42	14 27
London Bridge 4 ⊖	a																								
Balham 4 ⊖	d		13 39			13 44				13 51	13 48		14 09			14 14				14 21	14 18		14 39		
Clapham Junction 10	a	13 30	13 44			13 49		13 40	13 45	13 56	13 52	14 00	14 14			14 19		14 10	14 15	14 26	14 22	14 30	14 44		
London Waterloo 15 ⊖	a	13 40							13 55			14 10							14 25			14 40			
London Victoria 15 ⊖	a		13 53			13 58		13 48		14 04	14 00		14 23			14 28		14 18		14 34	14 30		14 53		

		SN		SN	SW	SN	SN	SW	SN	FC	FC	SN		SN	SW	SN	SN	SW	SN	FC	FC	SN		SN	SW
Horsham 4	d													14 04											
Warnham	d													14 08											
Ockley	d													14 15											
Holmwood	d													14 19											
Dorking 4	a													14 25											
	d			13 58	14 05									14 26	14 35									14 58	15 05
Boxhill & Westhumble	d													14 28											
Guildford	d							13 58										14 28							
Effingham Junction 6	d							14 16										14 46							
Bookham	d							14 19										14 49							
Leatherhead	d			14 04	14 11			14 24						14 33	14 41			14 54						15 04	15 11
Ashtead	d			14 07	14 14			14 28						14 37	14 44			14 58						15 07	15 14
Epsom 3	a			14 12	14 19			14 32						14 41	14 49			15 02						15 12	15 19
	d	14 04		14 13	14 20		14 19	14 35						14 42	14 50		14 49	15 05				15 04		15 13	15 20
Ewell East	d	14 08					14 23							14 46			14 53					15 08			
Cheam	d	14 11		14 18			14 26							14 49			14 56					15 11		15 18	
Epsom Downs	d											14 34													
Banstead	d											14 37													
Belmont	d											14 40													
Sutton (Surrey) 4	a	14 14		14 21			14 29					14 43		14 52			14 59					15 14		15 21	
	d	14 14		14 23		14 22	14 30		14 33	14 37	14 38	14 44		14 53		14 52	15 00		15 03	15 07	15 08	15 14		15 23	
Carshalton	d						14 33				14 41						15 03				15 11				
Hackbridge	d						14 35				14 43						15 05				15 13				
Mitcham Junction	d						14 39				14 46						15 09				15 16				
Mitcham Eastfields	d						14 42				14 49						15 12				15 19				
Carshalton Beeches	d	14 17				14 25			14 36			14 47				14 55			15 06			15 17			
Wallington	d	14 20				14 27			14 38			14 50				14 57			15 08			15 20			
Waddon	d	14 23				14 30			14 41			14 53				15 00			15 11			15 23			
West Croydon 4	d	14 28				14 34			14 45			14 58				15 04			15 15			15 28			
Norwood Junction 2	d								14 52										15 22						
New Cross Gate 4 ⊖	d																								
Tulse Hill 3	d									15 12	14 57									15 42	15 27				
London Bridge 4 ⊖	a																								
Balham 4 ⊖	d	14 44				14 51	14 48		15 09			15 14				15 21	15 18		15 39			15 44			
Clapham Junction 10	a	14 49		14 40	14 45	14 56	14 52	15 00	15 14			15 19		15 10	15 15	15 26	15 22	15 30	15 44			15 49		15 40	15 45
London Waterloo 15 ⊖	a				14 55			15 10							15 25			15 40							15 55
London Victoria 15 ⊖	a	14 58		14 48		15 04	15 00		15 24			15 28		15 22		15 34	15 30		15 54			15 58		15 52	

Table 182

Mondays to Fridays
until 24 September

Horsham, Dorking, Guildford, Epsom and Sutton - London

		SN	SN	SW	SN	FC	FC	SN		SN	SW	SN	SN	SW	SN	FC	FC	SN		SN	SW	SN	SN	SW	SN
Horsham 4	d									15 04															
Warnham	d									15 08															
Ockley	d									15 15															
Holmwood	d									15 19															
Dorking 4	a									15 25															
	d									15 26	15 35									15 56	16 05				
Boxhill & Westhumble	d									15 28										15 58					
Guildford	d			14 58										15 28										15 58	
Effingham Junction 6	d			15 16										15 46										16 16	
Bookham	d			15 19										15 49										16 19	
Leatherhead	d			15 24						15 33	15 41			15 54						16 03	16 11			16 24	
Ashtead	d			15 28						15 37	15 44			15 58						16 07	16 14			16 28	
Epsom 3	a			15 32						15 41	15 49			16 02						16 11	16 19			16 32	
	d		15 19	15 35						15 42	15 50		15 49	16 05				16 04		16 12	16 20		16 19	16 35	
Ewell East	d		15 23							15 46			15 53					16 08		16 16			16 23		
Cheam	d		15 26							15 49			15 56					16 11		16 19			16 26		
Epsom Downs	d							15 34																	
Banstead	d							15 37																	
Belmont	d							15 40																	
Sutton (Surrey) 4	a		15 29					15 43		15 52			15 59					16 14		16 22			16 29		
	d	15 22	15 30		15 33	15 37	15 38	15 44		15 53		15 52	16 00		16 03	16 07	16 08	16 14		16 23		16 22	16 30		16 33
Carshalton	d		15 33				15 41						16 03				16 11						16 33		
Hackbridge	d		15 35				15 43						16 05				16 13						16 35		
Mitcham Junction	d		15 39				15 46						16 09				16 16						16 39		
Mitcham Eastfields	d		15 42				15 49						16 12				16 19						16 42		
Carshalton Beeches	d	15 25			15 36			15 47				15 55			16 06			16 17				16 25			16 36
Wallington	d	15 27			15 38			15 50				15 57			16 08			16 20				16 27			16 38
Waddon	d	15 30			15 41			15 53				16 00			16 11			16 23				16 30			16 41
West Croydon 4	d	15 34			15 45			15 58				16 04			16 15			16 28				16 34			16 45
Norwood Junction 2	d				15 52										16 22										16 52
New Cross Gate 4 ⊖	d																								
Tulse Hill 3	d					16 12	15 57									16 46	16 27								
London Bridge 4 ⊖	a																								
Balham 4 ⊖	d	15 51	15 48		16 09			16 14				16 21	16 18		16 39			16 44				16 51	16 48		17 09
Clapham Junction 10	a	15 56	15 52	16 00	16 14			16 19		16 10	16 15	16 26	16 23	16 30	16 45			16 49		16 40	16 45	16 56	16 53	17 00	17 14
London Waterloo 15 ⊖	a			16 10							16 25			16 40							16 55			17 10	
London Victoria 15 ⊖	a	16 04	16 00		16 23			16 28		16 18		16 34	16 30		16 55			16 58		16 48		17 04	17 00		17 23

		SN	FC	FC 1		SN	SW	SN	SN	SW	SN	FC	FC	SN		SN	SW	SN	SW	FC	FC	SN	SN	SW	
Horsham 4	d					16 04																	17 07		
Warnham	d					16 08																	17 11		
Ockley	d					16 15																	17 18		
Holmwood	d					16 19																	17 22		
Dorking 4	a					16 25																	17 28		
	d					16 26	16 35									17 00	17 05						17 31	17 35	
Boxhill & Westhumble	d					16 28										17 02							17 33		
Guildford	d									16 28									16 58						
Effingham Junction 6	d									16 46									17 16						
Bookham	d									16 49									17 19						
Leatherhead	d					16 33	16 41			16 54						17 07	17 11		17 24				17 38	17 41	
Ashtead	d					16 37	16 44			16 58						17 11	17 14		17 28				17 42	17 44	
Epsom 3	a					16 41	16 49			17 02						17 15	17 19		17 32				17 46	17 49	
	d					16 42	16 50		16 49	17 05						17 19	17 20	17 23	17 35				17 49	17 50	
Ewell East	d					16 46			16 53							17 23		17 27					17 53		
Cheam	d					16 49			16 56							17 26		17 30					17 56		
Epsom Downs	d	16 26												17 02								17 34			
Banstead	d	16 29												17 05								17 37			
Belmont	d	16 32												17 08								17 40			
Sutton (Surrey) 4	a	16 35				16 52			16 59					17 11		17 29		17 33				17 43	17 59		
	d	16 44	16 37	16 38		16 53		16 52	17 00		17 03	17 08	17 11	17 14		17 30		17 33		17 41	17 42	17 44	18 00		
Carshalton	d			16 41					17 03			17 11				17 33					17 45		18 03		
Hackbridge	d			16 43					17 05			17 13				17 35					17 47		18 05		
Mitcham Junction	d			16 46					17 09			17 16				17 39					17 50		18 09		
Mitcham Eastfields	d			16 49					17 12			17 19				17 42					17 53		18 12		
Carshalton Beeches	d	16 47						16 55			17 06			17 17				17 36				17 47			
Wallington	d	16 50						16 57			17 08			17 20				17 39				17 50			
Waddon	d	16 53						17 00			17 11			17 23				17 42				17 53			
West Croydon 4	d	16 56						17 04			17 18			17 28				17 48				17 58			
Norwood Junction 2	d										17 23							17 55							
New Cross Gate 4 ⊖	d																								
Tulse Hill 3	d		17 16	16 57								17 27	17 44							18 16	18 01				
London Bridge 4 ⊖	a																								
Balham 4 ⊖	d	17 12						17 21	17 18		17 39			17 44		17 48		18 11				18 14	18 18		
Clapham Junction 10	a	17 18				17 10	17 15	17 26	17 23	17 30	17 44			17 49		17 52	17 45	18 16	18 00			18 19	18 22	18 15	
London Waterloo 15 ⊖	a						17 25			17 40							17 55		18 10					18 25	
London Victoria 15 ⊖	a	17 26				17 18		17 34	17 30		17 55			17 58		18 00		18 25				18 28	18 33		

Table 182

Mondays to Fridays
until 24 September

Horsham, Dorking, Guildford, Epsom and Sutton - London

		SN	SW	FC	FC	SN	SN	SW	SN	SW		FC	FC	SN	SN	SW	SN	SW	FC	FC		SN	SN	SW	SN
Horsham 4	d						17 34								18 04								18 34		
Warnham	d						17 38								18 08								18 38		
Ockley	d						17 45								18 15								18 45		
Holmwood	d						17 49								18 19								18 49		
Dorking 4	a						17 55								18 25								18 55		
	d						18 01	18 05							18 31	18 35		18 50					18 56		19 05
Boxhill & Westhumble	d						18 03								18 33								18 58		
Guildford	d		17 28							17 58							18 22								
Effingham Junction 6	d		17 46							18 16							18 39							18 59	
Bookham	d		17 49							18 19							18 42							19 02	
Leatherhead	d		17 54				18 08	18 11		18 24					18 38	18 41	18 47	18 56					19 03	19 08	19 11
Ashtead	d		17 58				18 12	18 14		18 28					18 42	18 44	18 51	18 59					19 07	19 12	19 15
Epsom 3	a		18 02				18 16	18 19		18 32					18 46	18 49	18 57	19 04					19 11	19 16	19 19
	d	17 52	18 05				18 17	18 20	18 22	18 35					18 49	18 50	18 57	19 05					19 12	19 20	19 20
Ewell East	d	17 56					18 23		18 26						18 53								19 16		19 24
Cheam	d	17 59					18 26		18 29						18 56								19 19		19 27
Epsom Downs	d					18 02								18 35								19 06			
Banstead	d					18 05								18 38								19 09			
Belmont	d					18 08								18 41								19 12			
Sutton (Surrey) 4	a	18 02				18 11	18 29		18 32					18 44	18 59		19 04					19 15	19 22		19 30
	d	18 03		18 08	18 09	18 12	18 30		18 33			18 38	18 43	18 45	19 00		19 05		19 08	19 13		19 16	19 22		19 33
Carshalton	d			18 11			18 33					18 41			19 03				19 11				19 25		
Hackbridge	d			18 13			18 35					18 43			19 05				19 13				19 28		
Mitcham Junction	d			18 16			18 39					18 46			19 09				19 16				19 31		
Mitcham Eastfields	d			18 19			18 42					18 49			19 12				19 19				19 34		
Carshalton Beeches	d	18 06				18 15			18 36					18 48			19 08					19 19			19 36
Wallington	d	18 08				18 17			18 38					18 50			19 10					19 21			19 38
Waddon	d	18 11				18 20			18 41					18 53			19 13					19 24			19 41
West Croydon 4	d	18 18				18 28			18 47					18 58			19 17					19 28			19 47
Norwood Junction 2	d	18 24							18 52								19 22								19 52
New Cross Gate 4 ⊖	d																								
Tulse Hill 3	d			18 27	18 44							18 57	19 14						19 27	19 44					
London Bridge 4 ⊖	a																								
Balham 4 ⊖	d	18 40				18 44	18 48		19 09					19 14	19 18		19 39					19 45	19 42		20 08
Clapham Junction 10	a	18 45	18 30			18 49	18 52	18 45	19 14	19 00				19 19	19 22	19 16	19 44	19 30				19 50	19 47	19 45	20 14
London Waterloo 15 ⊖	a		18 40					18 55		19 10						19 27		19 41						19 55	
London Victoria 15 ⊖	a	18 54				18 57	19 01		19 25					19 28	19 30		19 53					19 59	19 55		20 25

		SW	FC	FC	SN	SN		SN	SW	SN	SW	FC	FC	SN	SW	SN		SN	SW	FC	FC	SN	SN	SW	SN
Horsham 4	d							19 04															20 06		
Warnham	d							19 08															20 10		
Ockley	d							19 15															20 17		
Holmwood	d							19 19															20 21		
Dorking 4	a							19 25															20 27		
	d							19 28	19 33	19 37				19 57	20 05								20 30	20 35	
Boxhill & Westhumble	d							19 30						19 59											
Guildford	d				18 58						19 28								19 58						
Effingham Junction 6	d				19 15						19 46								20 16						
Bookham	d				19 18						19 49								20 19						
Leatherhead	d				19 23			19 35	19 39	19 43	19 54			20 04	20 11				20 24				20 36	20 41	
Ashtead	d				19 27			19 39	19 42	19 46	19 58			20 08	20 14				20 28				20 39	20 44	
Epsom 3	a				19 32			19 45	19 47	19 51	20 02			20 12	20 19				20 32				20 44	20 49	
	d	19 35			19 35			19 46	19 50	19 52	20 05			20 13	20 20			20 22	20 35				20 45	20 50	
Ewell East	d				19 39			19 50		19 56				20 17				20 26					20 49		
Cheam	d				19 42			19 53		19 59				20 20				20 29					20 52		
Epsom Downs	d					19 36										20 13									20 54
Banstead	d					19 39										20 16									20 57
Belmont	d					19 42										20 19									21 00
Sutton (Surrey) 4	a				19 45	19 45		19 56		20 02				20 23		20 22		20 32					20 55		21 03
	d		19 38	19 42		19 46		19 56		20 03		20 07	20 10	20 25		20 23		20 33		20 37	20 40	20 52	20 55		21 06
Carshalton	d			19 45				19 59					20 13	20 28							20 43		20 58		
Hackbridge	d			19 47				20 02					20 15	20 31							20 45		21 01		
Mitcham Junction	d			19 50				20 05					20 18	20 34							20 48		21 04		
Mitcham Eastfields	d			19 53				20 08					20 21	20 37							20 51		21 07		
Carshalton Beeches	d					19 49				20 06						20 26		20 36				20 55			21 09
Wallington	d					19 51				20 08						20 28		20 38				20 57			21 11
Waddon	d					19 54				20 11						20 31		20 41				21 00			21 14
West Croydon 4	d					19 58				20 18						20 35		20 45				21 04			21 18
Norwood Junction 2	d									20 23								20 52							21 23
New Cross Gate 4 ⊖	d																								
Tulse Hill 3	d		20 12	20 01								20 42	20 29							21 12	20 59				
London Bridge 4 ⊖	a																								
Balham 4 ⊖	d					20 14		20 17		20 39				20 44		20 51		21 09				21 21	21 14		21 39
Clapham Junction 10	a	20 00				20 19		20 22	20 15	20 44	20 30			20 48	20 45	20 56		21 14	21 00			21 26	21 18	21 15	21 44
London Waterloo 15 ⊖	a	20 10							20 25		20 41				20 55				21 10					21 25	
London Victoria 15 ⊖	a					20 28		20 30		20 53				20 56		21 04		21 23				21 34	21 26		21 53

Table 182

Mondays to Fridays
until 24 September

Horsham, Dorking, Guildford, Epsom and Sutton - London

		SW		FC	FC	SN	SN	SW	SN	SW	SN	SN		SW	SN	FC	SN	SN	SW	SN	SN	SN		SW	SN
Horsham 4	d																								
Warnham	d																								
Ockley	d																								
Holmwood	d																								
Dorking 4	a																								
	d						20 59					21 30		21 35				21 59				22 30		22 35	
Boxhill & Westhumble	d						21 01											22 01							
Guildford	d							20 46											21 46						
Effingham Junction 6	d							21 03											22 03						
Bookham	d							21 06											22 06						
Leatherhead	d						21 06	21 11				21 36		21 41				22 06	22 11			22 36		22 41	
Ashtead	d						21 10	21 14				21 40		21 44				22 10	22 14			22 40		22 44	
Epsom 3	a						21 14	21 19				21 44		21 49				22 14	22 19			22 44		22 49	
	d	21 05					21 15	21 20	21 25	21 35		21 45		21 50				22 15	22 20	22 25		22 45		22 50	
Ewell East	d						21 19		21 29			21 49						22 19		22 29		22 49			
Cheam	d						21 22		21 32			21 52						22 22		22 32		22 52			
Epsom Downs	d														21 54										22 54
Banstead	d														21 57										22 57
Belmont	d														22 00										23 00
Sutton (Surrey) 4	a						21 25		21 35			21 55			22 03			22 25		22 35		22 55			23 03
	d			21 10	21 12	21 22	21 25		21 36		21 52	21 55			22 06	22 12	22 22	22 25		22 36	22 52	22 55			23 06
Carshalton	d			21 13			21 28					21 58						22 28				22 58			
Hackbridge	d			21 15			21 31					22 01						22 31				23 01			
Mitcham Junction	d			21 18			21 34					22 04						22 34				23 04			
Mitcham Eastfields	d			21 21			21 37					22 07						22 37				23 07			
Carshalton Beeches	d					21 25			21 39		21 55				22 09		22 25			22 39	22 55				23 09
Wallington	d					21 27			21 41		21 57				22 11		22 27			22 41	22 57				23 11
Waddon	d					21 30			21 44		22 00				22 14		22 30			22 44	23 00				23 14
West Croydon 4	d					21 34			21 48		22 04				22 18		22 34			22 48	23 04				23 18
Norwood Junction 2	d								21 53						22 23					22 53					23 23
New Cross Gate 4 ⊖	d																								
Tulse Hill 3	d			21 29	21 50											22 43									
London Bridge 4 ⊖	a															22 55									
Balham 4 ⊖	d					21 51	21 44		22 09		22 21	22 14			22 39		22 51	22 44		23 09	23 21	23 14			23 40
Clapham Junction 10	a	21 30				21 56	21 48	21 45	22 14	22 00	22 26	22 19		22 15	22 44		22 56	22 48	22 45	23 15	23 26	23 18		23 15	23 45
London Waterloo 15 ⊖	a	21 40						21 55		22 10				22 25					22 55					23 27	
London Victoria 15 ⊖	a					22 04	21 56		22 25		22 34	22 27			22 53		23 04	22 56		23 23	23 34	23 26			23 54

		SN	SN	SW	SN	SN	SN
Horsham 4	d						
Warnham	d						
Ockley	d						
Holmwood	d						
Dorking 4	a						
	d		23 00			23 30	
Boxhill & Westhumble	d		23 02				
Guildford	d			22 46			
Effingham Junction 6	d			23 03			
Bookham	d			23 06			
Leatherhead	d		23 07	23 11		23 36	
Ashtead	d		23 11	23 14		23 39	
Epsom 3	a		23 15	23 19		23 45	
	d		23 16	23 20	23 25		
Ewell East	d		23 20		23 29		
Cheam	d		23 23		23 32		
Epsom Downs	d						23 43
Banstead	d						23 46
Belmont	d						23 49
Sutton (Surrey) 4	a		23 26		23 35		23 52
	d	23 20	23 30		23 40		23 53
Carshalton	d						
Hackbridge	d						
Mitcham Junction	d						
Mitcham Eastfields	d						
Carshalton Beeches	d	23 23	23 33		23 43		23 56
Wallington	d	23 25	23 35		23 45		23 58
Waddon	d	23 28	23 38		23 48		00 01
West Croydon 4	d	23a31	23a41		23a57		00a04
Norwood Junction 2	d						
New Cross Gate 4 ⊖	d						
Tulse Hill 3	d						
London Bridge 4 ⊖	a						
Balham 4 ⊖	d						
Clapham Junction 10	a			23 48			
London Waterloo 15 ⊖	a			23 58			
London Victoria 15 ⊖	a						

Horsham, Dorking, Guildford, Epsom and Sutton - London

		SN MX	SN	SW	SN	SN	SN	SN	SW	SN		SN	SW	FC	SN	SN	SW	SW	SN	FC		SN	SN	FC	SN
Horsham 4	d															05 49									06 20
Warnham	d															05 53									06 24
Ockley	d															06 00									06 31
Holmwood	d															06 04									06 35
Dorking 4	a															06 10									06 41
	d								05 48							06 11		06 32							06 44
Boxhill & Westhumble	d								05 50							06 13		06 34							06 46
Guildford	d			04 58													05 58								
Effingham Junction 6	d			05 16													06 16								
Bookham	d			05 19													06 19								
Leatherhead	d			05 24					05 56							06 18	06 24	06 39							06 51
Ashtead	d			05 28					05 59							06 22	06 28	06 43							06 55
Epsom 3	a			05 32					06 04							06 26	06 32	06 47							06 59
	d		05 23	05 34		05 39		05 57	06 04				06 18			06 27	06 34	06 48					06 49		07 00
Ewell East	d		05 27			05 43		06 01								06 31							06 53		07 04
Cheam	d		05 30			05 46		06 04								06 34							06 56		07 07
Epsom Downs	d	23p43																	06 34						
Banstead	d	23p46																	06 37						
Belmont	d	23p49																	06 40						
Sutton (Surrey) 4	a	23p52	05 33			05 49		06 07		06 13						06 37			06 43			06 49	06 59		07 10
	d	23p53	05 33		05 37	05 49	06 03	06 07		06 14		06 14		06 20	06 33	06 37			06 44	06 48		06 50	07 00	07 06	07 10
Carshalton	d				05 40			06 10		06 17						06 40						06 53			07 13
Hackbridge	d				05 42			06 13		06 19						06 43						06 55			07 16
Mitcham Junction	d				05 46			06 16		06 23						06 46						06 59			07 19
Mitcham Eastfields	d				05 49			06 19		06 26						06 49						07 02			07 22
Carshalton Beeches	d	23p56	05 36			05 52	06 06					06 17			06 36				06 47				07 03		
Wallington	d	23p58	05 39			05 55	06 08					06 20			06 38				06 50				07 05		
Waddon	d	00 01	05 42			05 58	06 11					06 23			06 41				06 53				07 08		
West Croydon 4	d	00a04	05 45			06 01	06 15					06 26			06 45				06 58				07 13		
Norwood Junction 2	d		05 50				06 20								06 50								07 18		
New Cross Gate 4	⊖ d		06 08																						
Tulse Hill 3	d				05 57					06 34				06 52						07 20		07 10		07 42	
London Bridge 4	⊖ a		06 14		06 08		06 33			06 51					07 04							07 29	07 32		
Balham 4	⊖ d					06 17		06 27				06 42				06 57			07 14						07 29
Clapham Junction 10	a			06 00		06 23		06 31	06 30			06 48	06 45			07 01	07 00	07 15	07 19						07 34
London Waterloo 15	⊖ a			06 11					06 40				06 55				07 12	07 27							
London Victoria 15	⊖ a					06 31		06 38				06 58				07 10			07 30						07 43

		SW	SN	SN	SW	SN		SN	SW	SN	FC	SN	SW	SW	FC	SN		SN	SW	SN	SN	SN	FC	FC	SN
Horsham 4	d											06 55													07 22
Warnham	d											06 59													07 26
Ockley	d											07 06													07 33
Holmwood	d											07 10													07 37
Dorking 4	a											07 16													07 43
	d							06 52	07 02			07 17		07 32											07 46
Boxhill & Westhumble	d							06 59	07 04					07 34											
Guildford	d	06 28											06 58									07 26			
Effingham Junction 6	d	06 48											07 16									07 38			
Bookham	d	06 51											07 19									07 41			
Leatherhead	d	06 56						07 04	07 09			07 23	07 26	07 39								07 46			07 52
Ashtead	d	06 59						07 08	07 13			07 26	07 29	07 43								07 50			07 55
Epsom 3	a	07 04						07 12	07 17			07 31	07 34	07 47								07 54			08 00
	d	07 04			07 22			07 15	07 18	07 21		07 31	07 34	07 48					07 52		07 49	07 55			08 02
Ewell East	d							07 19		07 25											07 53	07 59			08 06
Cheam	d							07 22		07 28		07 37									07 56	08 02			08 09
Epsom Downs	d		07 04													07 34									
Banstead	d		07 07													07 37									
Belmont	d		07 10													07 40									
Sutton (Surrey) 4	a		07 13	07 19				07 25		07 31		07 40				07 43		07 48			07 59	08 05			08 12
	d		07 14	07 20		07 22		07 26		07 32	07 37	07 42			07 40	07 44		07 49		07 53	08 00	08 05	08 08	08 09	08 13
Carshalton	d			07 23				07 29			07 40	07 45						07 52			08 03			08 12	08 16
Hackbridge	d			07 25				07 31			07 42							07 54			08 05			08 14	08 18
Mitcham Junction	d			07 29				07 35			07 45	07 49						07 58			08 09			08 17	08 22
Mitcham Eastfields	d			07 32				07 38			07 48	07 52						08 01			08 12			08 20	08 25
Carshalton Beeches	d		07 17			07 25				07 35						07 47				07 56		08 08			
Wallington	d		07 20			07 27				07 37						07 50				07 58		08 11			
Waddon	d		07 23			07 30				07 40						07 53				08 01					
West Croydon 4	d		07 28			07 34				07 44						07 58				08 05		08 16			
Norwood Junction 2	d									07 49												08 21			
New Cross Gate 4	⊖ d																								
Tulse Hill 3	d			07 41							07 57				08 13			08 09					08 43	08 28	
London Bridge 4	⊖ a			08 00						08 05								08 29				08 35			
Balham 4	⊖ d		07 44			07 50		07 47				07 59				08 14				08 21	08 18				
Clapham Junction 10	a	07 30	07 49		07 48	07 55		07 51	07 42			08 04	08 01	08 12		08 19			08 18	08 25	08 22				08 32
London Waterloo 15	⊖ a	07 42			08 00				07 54				08 13	08 24					08 30						
London Victoria 15	⊖ a		08 00			08 06		08 02				08 13				08 30				08 36	08 32				08 41

		SW		SW	SN	SN	SW	SN	SN	SW	FC	FC		SN	SN	SW	SN	SN	SW	SN	FC	FC		SN	SN
Horsham 4	d														08 00										
Warnham	d														08 04										
Ockley	d														08 11										
Holmwood	d														08 15										
Dorking 4	a														08 21										
	d			08 02											08 22	08 31									08 57
Boxhill & Westhumble	d			08 04											08 24	08 33									08 59
Guildford	d									07 58								08 16							
Effingham Junction 6	d	07 46								08 16								08 32	08 48						
Bookham	d	07 49								08 19								08 35	08 51						
Leatherhead	d	07 56		08 09						08 25					08 29	08 38		08 41	08 56						09 04
Ashtead	d	07 59		08 13						08 28					08 33	08 42		08 45	08 59						09 08
Epsom 3	a	08 04		08 17						08 33					08 37	08 46		08 49	09 04						09 12
	d	08 04		08 18			08 22		08 22	08 34					08 38	08 48		08 50	09 04						09 13
Ewell East	d								08 26						08 42			08 54							09 17
Cheam	d								08 29						08 45			08 57							09 20
Epsom Downs	d				08 04									08 34											
Banstead	d				08 07									08 37											
Belmont	d				08 10									08 40											
Sutton (Surrey) 4	a				08 13	08 19			08 32					08 43	08 48		08 56	09 00							09 23
	d				08 14	08 20		08 29	08 32		08 39	08 41		08 44	08 48		08 57	09 00		09 03	09 11	09 13		09 15	09 23
Carshalton	d					08 23		08 32			08 42				08 51		09 00	09 03				09 16			
Hackbridge	d					08 25		08 34			08 44				08 54		09 02	09 06				09 18			
Mitcham Junction	d					08 29		08 38			08 47				08 57		09 06	09 09				09 21			
Mitcham Eastfields	d					08 32		08 41			08 50				09 00		09 09	09 12				09 24			09 32
Carshalton Beeches	d				08 17				08 35					08 47						09 06				09 18	
Wallington	d				08 19				08 38					08 50						09 08				09 20	
Waddon	d				08 22				08 41					08 53						09 11				09 23	
West Croydon 4	d				08 26				08 44					08 56						09 15				09 28	
Norwood Junction 2	d								08 49											09 22					
New Cross Gate 4	⊖ d																								
Tulse Hill 3	d					08 40					08 58	09 16					09 16				09 42	09 32			
London Bridge 4	⊖ a					08 59			09 04								09 35								
Balham 4	⊖ d				08 43			08 47						09 13	09 07			09 18		09 41				09 44	
Clapham Junction 10	a	08 31		08 42	08 49		08 48	08 52		09 00				09 18	09 11	09 15		09 22	09 30	09 46				09 49	09 42
London Waterloo 15	⊖ a	08 43		08 54			09 00			09 12						09 27			09 42						
London Victoria 15	⊖ a				09 00			09 02						09 31	09 22			09 33		09 58				10 00	09 54

		SW	SN	SN	SW	SN	FC	FC		SN	SN	SN	SW	SW	SN	FC	FC	SN		SN	SN	SW	SN	SW	SN
Horsham 4	d											09 09													
Warnham	d											09 13													
Ockley	d											09 20													
Holmwood	d											09 24													
Dorking 4	a											09 30													
	d	09 02										09 31	09 35								09 57	10 05			
Boxhill & Westhumble	d	09 04										09 33									09 59				
Guildford	d				08 58									09 28										09 58	
Effingham Junction 6	d				09 16									09 46										10 16	
Bookham	d				09 19									09 49										10 19	
Leatherhead	d	09 09			09 24							09 38	09 41	09 54							10 04	10 11		10 24	
Ashtead	d	09 13			09 28							09 42	09 45	09 58							10 08	10 14		10 28	
Epsom 3	a	09 17			09 32							09 46	09 49	10 02							10 12	10 19		10 32	
	d	09 18		09 19	09 35							09 49	09 50	10 05				10 04			10 13	10 20	10 19	10 35	
Ewell East	d			09 23								09 53						10 08			10 17		10 23		
Cheam	d			09 26								09 56						10 11			10 20		10 26		
Epsom Downs	d		09 09							09 34															
Banstead	d		09 12							09 37															
Belmont	d		09 15							09 40															
Sutton (Surrey) 4	a		09 18	09 29						09 43		09 59						10 14			10 23		10 29		
	d		09 23	09 30		09 33	09 37	09 38		09 44	09 52	10 00			10 03	10 07	10 08	10 14		10 22	10 23		10 30		10 33
Carshalton	d			09 33				09 41				10 03					10 11						10 33		
Hackbridge	d			09 35				09 43				10 05					10 13						10 35		
Mitcham Junction	d			09 39				09 46				10 09					10 16						10 39		
Mitcham Eastfields	d			09 42				09 49				10 12					10 19						10 42		
Carshalton Beeches	d		09 26			09 36				09 47	09 55				10 06			10 17		10 25					10 36
Wallington	d		09 28			09 38				09 50	09 57				10 08			10 20		10 27					10 38
Waddon	d		09 31			09 41				09 53	10 00				10 11			10 23		10 30					10 41
West Croydon 4	d		09 35			09 45				09 58	10 04				10 15			10 28		10 34					10 45
Norwood Junction 2	d					09 52									10 22										10 52
New Cross Gate 4	⊖ d																								
Tulse Hill 3	d						10 12	09 57								10 42	10 27								
London Bridge 4	⊖ a																								
Balham 4	⊖ d		09 52	09 48		10 09				10 14	10 21	10 18			10 39			10 44		10 51			10 48		11 09
Clapham Junction 10	a	09 45	09 57	09 52	10 00	10 15				10 19	10 26	10 22	10 15	10 30	10 45			10 49		10 56	10 40	10 45	10 52	11 00	11 14
London Waterloo 15	⊖ a	09 57			10 10								10 25	10 40								10 55		11 10	
London Victoria 15	⊖ a		10 05	10 00		10 24				10 28	10 34	10 31			10 53			10 58		11 04	10 48		11 00		11 23

Table 182

Mondays to Fridays
from 27 September

Horsham, Dorking, Guildford, Epsom and Sutton - London

		FC	FC	SN	SN	SW	SN	SN	SW	SN	FC	FC	SN	SN	SW	SN	SN	SW	SN	FC	FC	SN
Horsham	d				10 04																	
Warnham	d				10 08																	
Ockley	d				10 15																	
Holmwood	d				10 19																	
Dorking	a				10 25																	
	d				10 26	10 35								10 58	11 05							
Boxhill & Westhumble	d				10 28																	
Guildford	d								10 28									10 58				
Effingham Junction	d								10 46									11 16				
Bookham	d								10 49									11 19				
Leatherhead	d				10 33	10 41			10 54					11 04	11 11			11 24				
Ashtead	d				10 37	10 44			10 58					11 07	11 14			11 28				
Epsom	a				10 41	10 49			11 02					11 12	11 19			11 32				
	d				10 42	10 50		10 49	11 05				11 04	11 13	11 20		11 19	11 35				
Ewell East	d				10 46			10 53					11 08				11 23					
Cheam	d				10 49			10 56					11 11	11 18			11 26					
Epsom Downs	d			10 34																		11 34
Banstead	d			10 37																		11 37
Belmont	d			10 40																		11 40
Sutton (Surrey)	a			10 43	10 52			10 59					11 14	11 21			11 29					11 43
	d	10 37	10 38	10 44	10 53		10 52	11 00		11 04	11 07	11 08	11 14	11 23		11 22	11 30		11 33	11 37	11 38	11 44
Carshalton	d		10 41					11 03				11 11					11 33				11 41	
Hackbridge	d		10 43					11 05				11 13					11 35				11 43	
Mitcham Junction	d		10 46					11 09				11 16					11 39				11 46	
Mitcham Eastfields	d		10 49					11 12				11 19					11 42				11 49	
Carshalton Beeches	d			10 47			10 55			11 07			11 17			11 25			11 36			11 47
Wallington	d			10 50			10 57			11 09			11 20			11 27			11 38			11 50
Waddon	d			10 53			11 00			11 12			11 23			11 30			11 41			11 53
West Croydon	d			10 58			11 04			11 16			11 28			11 34			11 45			11 58
Norwood Junction	d									11 22									11 52			
New Cross Gate ⊖	d																					
Tulse Hill	d	11 12	10 57								11 42	11 27								12 12	11 57	
London Bridge ⊖	a																					
Balham ⊖	d			11 14			11 21	11 18		11 40			11 44			11 51	11 48		12 09			12 14
Clapham Junction	a			11 19	11 10	11 15	11 26	11 22	11 30	11 45			11 49	11 40	11 45	11 56	11 52	12 00	12 14			12 19
London Waterloo ⊖	a					11 25			11 40						11 55			12 10				
London Victoria ⊖	a			11 28	11 20		11 34	11 30		11 54			11 58	11 50		12 04	12 00		12 23			12 28

		SN	SW	SN	SN	SW	SN	FC	FC	SN	SN	SW	SN	SN	SW	SN	FC	FC	SN	SN	SW	SN	SN
Horsham	d	11 04																		12 04			
Warnham	d	11 08																		12 08			
Ockley	d	11 15																		12 15			
Holmwood	d	11 19																		12 19			
Dorking	a	11 25																		12 25			
	d	11 26	11 35								11 58	12 05								12 26	12 35		
Boxhill & Westhumble	d	11 28																		12 28			
Guildford	d					11 28									11 58								
Effingham Junction	d					11 46									12 16								
Bookham	d					11 49									12 19								
Leatherhead	d	11 33	11 41			11 54					12 04	12 11			12 24					12 33	12 41		
Ashtead	d	11 37	11 44			11 58					12 07	12 14			12 28					12 37	12 44		
Epsom	a	11 41	11 49			12 02					12 12	12 19			12 32					12 41	12 49		
	d	11 42	11 50		11 49	12 05				12 04	12 13	12 20		12 19	12 35					12 42	12 50		12 49
Ewell East	d	11 46			11 53					12 08				12 23						12 46			12 53
Cheam	d	11 49			11 56					12 11	12 18			12 26						12 49			12 56
Epsom Downs	d																		12 34				
Banstead	d																		12 37				
Belmont	d																		12 40				
Sutton (Surrey)	a	11 52			11 59					12 14	12 21			12 29					12 43	12 52			12 59
	d	11 53		11 52	12 00		12 03	12 07	12 08	12 14	12 23		12 22	12 30		12 33	12 37	12 38	12 44	12 53		12 52	13 00
Carshalton	d				12 03				12 11					12 33				12 41					13 03
Hackbridge	d				12 05				12 13					12 35				12 43					13 05
Mitcham Junction	d				12 09				12 16					12 39				12 46					13 09
Mitcham Eastfields	d				12 12				12 19					12 42				12 49					13 12
Carshalton Beeches	d			11 55			12 06			12 17			12 25			12 36			12 47			12 55	
Wallington	d			11 57			12 08			12 20			12 27			12 38			12 50			12 57	
Waddon	d			12 00			12 11			12 23			12 30			12 41			12 53			13 00	
West Croydon	d			12 04			12 15			12 28			12 34			12 45			12 58			13 04	
Norwood Junction	d						12 22									12 52							
New Cross Gate ⊖	d																						
Tulse Hill	d							12 42	12 27								13 12	12 57					
London Bridge ⊖	a																						
Balham ⊖	d			12 21	12 18		12 39			12 44			12 51	12 48		13 09			13 13			13 21	13 18
Clapham Junction	a	12 10	12 15	12 26	12 22	12 30	12 44			12 49	12 40	12 45	12 56	12 52	13 00	13 14			13 20	13 10	13 15	13 26	13 22
London Waterloo ⊖	a		12 25			12 40						12 55			13 10						13 25		
London Victoria ⊖	a	12 18		12 34	12 30		12 53			12 58	12 48		13 04	13 00		13 23			13 28	13 18		13 34	13 30

Table 182

Mondays to Fridays
from 27 September

Horsham, Dorking, Guildford, Epsom and Sutton - London

		SW	SN	FC	FC	SN	SN	SW	SN	SN	SW	SN	FC	FC	SN	SN	SW	SN	SN	SW	SN	FC	FC
Horsham	d															13 04							
Warnham	d															13 08							
Ockley	d															13 15							
Holmwood	d															13 19							
Dorking	a															13 25							
	d						12 59	13 05								13 26	13 35						
Boxhill & Westhumble	d															13 28							
Guildford	d	12 28									12 58									13 28			
Effingham Junction	d	12 46									13 16									13 46			
Bookham	d	12 49									13 19									13 49			
Leatherhead	d	12 54					13 05	13 11			13 24					13 33	13 41			13 54			
Ashtead	d	12 58					13 08	13 14			13 28					13 37	13 44			13 58			
Epsom	a	13 02					13 13	13 19			13 32					13 41	13 49			14 02			
	d	13 05				13 04	13 13	13 20		13 19	13 35					13 42	13 50		13 49	14 05			
Ewell East	d					13 08				13 23						13 46			13 53				
Cheam	d					13 11	13 19			13 26						13 49			13 56				
Epsom Downs	d														13 34								
Banstead	d														13 37								
Belmont	d														13 40								
Sutton (Surrey)	a					13 14	13 22			13 29					13 43	13 52			13 59				
	d		13 03	13 07	13 08	13 14	13 23		13 22	13 30		13 33	13 37	13 38	13 44	13 53		13 52	14 00		14 03	14 07	14 08
Carshalton	d				13 11					13 33				13 41					14 03				14 11
Hackbridge	d				13 13					13 35				13 43					14 05				14 13
Mitcham Junction	d				13 16					13 39				13 46					14 09				14 16
Mitcham Eastfields	d				13 19					13 42				13 49					14 12				14 19
Carshalton Beeches	d		13 06			13 17			13 25			13 36			13 47			13 55			14 06		
Wallington	d		13 08			13 20			13 27			13 38			13 50			13 57			14 08		
Waddon	d		13 11			13 23			13 30			13 41			13 53			14 00			14 11		
West Croydon	d		13 15			13 28			13 34			13 45			13 58			14 04			14 15		
Norwood Junction	d		13 22									13 52									14 22		
New Cross Gate ⊖	d																						
Tulse Hill	d			13 42	13 27								14 12	13 57								14 42	14 27
Balham ⊖	d		13 39			13 44			13 51	13 48		14 09			14 14			14 21	14 18		14 39		
Clapham Junction	a	13 30	13 44			13 49	13 40	13 45	13 56	13 52	4 00	14 14			14 19	14 10	14 15	14 26	14 22	14 30	14 44		
London Waterloo ⊖	a	13 40						13 55			14 10						14 25			14 40			
London Victoria ⊖	a		13 53			13 58	13 48		14 04	14 00		14 23			14 28	14 18		14 34	14 30		14 53		

		SN	SN	SW	SN	SN	SW	SN	FC	FC	SN	SN	SW	SN	SN	SW	SN	FC	FC	SN	SN	SW
Horsham	d											14 04										
Warnham	d											14 08										
Ockley	d											14 15										
Holmwood	d											14 19										
Dorking	a											14 25										
	d		13 58	14 05								14 26	14 35								14 58	15 05
Boxhill & Westhumble	d											14 28										
Guildford	d						13 58									14 28						
Effingham Junction	d						14 16									14 46						
Bookham	d						14 19									14 49						
Leatherhead	d		14 04	14 11			14 24					14 33	14 41			14 54					15 04	15 11
Ashtead	d		14 07	14 14			14 28					14 37	14 44			14 58					15 07	15 14
Epsom	a		14 12	14 19			14 32					14 41	14 49			15 02					15 12	15 19
	d	14 04	14 13	14 20		14 19	14 35					14 42	14 50		14 49	15 05				15 04	15 13	15 20
Ewell East	d	14 08				14 23						14 46			14 53					15 08		
Cheam	d	14 11	14 18			14 26						14 49			14 56					15 11	15 18	
Epsom Downs	d										14 34											
Banstead	d										14 37											
Belmont	d										14 40											
Sutton (Surrey)	a	14 14	14 21			14 29					14 43	14 52			14 59					15 14	15 21	
	d	14 14	14 23		14 22	14 30		14 33	14 37	14 38	14 44	14 53		14 52	15 00		15 03	15 07	15 08	15 14	15 23	
Carshalton	d					14 33				14 41					15 03				15 11			
Hackbridge	d					14 35				14 43					15 05				15 13			
Mitcham Junction	d					14 39				14 46					15 09				15 16			
Mitcham Eastfields	d					14 42				14 49					15 12				15 19			
Carshalton Beeches	d	14 17			14 25			14 36			14 47			14 55			15 06			15 17		
Wallington	d	14 20			14 27			14 38			14 50			14 57			15 08			15 20		
Waddon	d	14 23			14 30			14 41			14 53			15 00			15 11			15 23		
West Croydon	d	14 28			14 34			14 45			14 58			15 04			15 15			15 28		
Norwood Junction	d							14 52									15 22					
New Cross Gate ⊖	d																					
Tulse Hill	d								15 12	14 57								15 42	15 27			
London Bridge ⊖	a																					
Balham ⊖	d	14 44			14 51	14 48		15 09			15 14			15 21	15 18		15 39			15 44		
Clapham Junction	a	14 49	14 40	14 45	14 56	14 52	15 00	15 14			15 19	15 10	15 15	15 26	15 22	15 30	15 44			15 49	15 40	15 45
London Waterloo ⊖	a			14 55			15 10						15 25			15 40						15 55
London Victoria ⊖	a	14 58	14 48		15 04	15 00		15 24			15 28	15 22		15 34	15 30		15 54			15 58	15 52	

Table 182

Mondays to Fridays
from 27 September

Horsham, Dorking, Guildford, Epsom and Sutton - London

		SN	SN	SW	SN	FC	FC	SN	SN	SW	SN	SN	SW	SN	FC	FC	SN	SN	SW	SN	SN	SW	SN
Horsham 4	d								15 04														
Warnham	d								15 08														
Ockley	d								15 15														
Holmwood	d								15 19														
Dorking 4	a								15 25														
	d								15 26	15 35								15 56	16 05				
Boxhill & Westhumble	d								15 28									15 58					
Guildford	d			14 58									15 28									15 58	
Effingham Junction 6	d			15 16									15 46									16 16	
Bookham	d			15 19									15 49									16 19	
Leatherhead	d			15 24					15 33	15 41			15 54					16 03	16 11			16 24	
Ashtead	d			15 28					15 37	15 44			15 58					16 07	16 14			16 28	
Epsom 3	a			15 32					15 41	15 49			16 02					16 11	16 19			16 32	
	d		15 19	15 35					15 42	15 50		15 49	16 05				16 04	16 12	16 20		16 19	16 35	
Ewell East	d		15 23						15 46			15 53					16 08	16 16			16 23		
Cheam	d		15 26						15 49			15 56					16 11	16 19			16 26		
Epsom Downs	d							15 34															
Banstead	d							15 37															
Belmont	d							15 40															
Sutton (Surrey) 4	a		15 29					15 43	15 52			15 59					16 14	16 22			16 29		
	d	15 22	15 30		15 33	15 37	15 38	15 44	15 53		15 52	16 00		16 03	16 07	16 08	16 14	16 23		16 22	16 30		16 33
Carshalton	d		15 33				15 41					16 03				16 11					16 33		
Hackbridge	d		15 35				15 43					16 05				16 13					16 35		
Mitcham Junction	d		15 39				15 46					16 09				16 16					16 39		
Mitcham Eastfields	d		15 42				15 49					16 12				16 19					16 42		
Carshalton Beeches	d	15 25			15 36			15 47			15 55			16 06			16 17			16 25			16 36
Wallington	d	15 27			15 38			15 50			15 57			16 08			16 20			16 27			16 38
Waddon	d	15 30			15 41			15 53			16 00			16 11			16 23			16 30			16 41
West Croydon 4	d	15 34			15 45			15 58			16 04			16 15			16 28			16 34			16 45
Norwood Junction 2	d				15 52									16 22									16 52
New Cross Gate 4 ⊖	d																						
Tulse Hill 3	d					16 12	15 57								16 46	16 27							
London Bridge 4 ⊖	a																						
Balham 4 ⊖	d	15 51	15 48		16 09			16 14			16 21	16 18		16 39			16 44			16 51	16 48		17 09
Clapham Junction 10	a	15 56	15 52	16 00	16 14			16 19	16 10	16 15	16 26	16 23	16 30	16 45			16 49	16 40	16 45	16 56	16 53	17 00	17 14
London Waterloo 15 ⊖	a			16 10						16 25			16 40						16 55			17 10	
London Victoria 15 ⊖	a	16 04	16 00		16 23			16 28	16 18		16 34	16 30		16 55			16 58	16 48		17 04	17 00		17 23

		SN	FC	FC 1	SN	SW	SN	SN	SW	SN	FC	FC	SN	SN	SW	SN	SW	FC	FC	SN	SN	SW
Horsham 4	d				16 04																17 07	
Warnham	d				16 08																17 11	
Ockley	d				16 15																17 18	
Holmwood	d				16 19																17 22	
Dorking 4	a				16 25																17 28	
	d				16 26	16 35								17 00	17 05						17 31	17 35
Boxhill & Westhumble	d				16 28									17 02							17 33	
Guildford	d								16 28								16 58					
Effingham Junction 6	d								16 46								17 16					
Bookham	d								16 49								17 19					
Leatherhead	d				16 33	16 41			16 54					17 07	17 11		17 24				17 38	17 41
Ashtead	d				16 37	16 44			16 58					17 11	17 14		17 28				17 42	17 44
Epsom 3	a				16 41	16 49			17 02					17 15	17 19		17 32				17 46	17 49
	d				16 42	16 50		16 49	17 05					17 19	17 20	17 23	17 35				17 49	17 50
Ewell East	d				16 46			16 53						17 23		17 27					17 53	
Cheam	d				16 49			16 56						17 26		17 30					17 56	
Epsom Downs	d	16 26											17 02							17 34		
Banstead	d	16 29											17 05							17 37		
Belmont	d	16 32											17 08							17 40		
Sutton (Surrey) 4	a	16 35			16 52			16 59					17 11	17 29		17 33				17 43	17 59	
	d	16 44	16 37	16 38	16 53		16 52	17 00		17 03	17 08	17 11	17 14	17 30		17 33		17 41	17 42	17 44	18 00	
Carshalton	d			16 41				17 03			17 11			17 33					17 45		18 03	
Hackbridge	d			16 43				17 05			17 13			17 35					17 47		18 05	
Mitcham Junction	d			16 46				17 09			17 16			17 39					17 50		18 09	
Mitcham Eastfields	d			16 49				17 12			17 19			17 42					17 53		18 12	
Carshalton Beeches	d	16 47					16 55			17 06			17 17			17 36				17 47		
Wallington	d	16 50					16 57			17 08			17 20			17 39				17 50		
Waddon	d	16 53					17 00			17 11			17 23			17 42				17 53		
West Croydon 4	d	16 56					17 04			17 18			17 28			17 48				17 58		
Norwood Junction 2	d									17 23						17 55						
New Cross Gate 4 ⊖	d																					
Tulse Hill 3	d		17 16	16 57							17 27	17 44						18 16	18 01			
London Bridge 4 ⊖	a																					
Balham 4 ⊖	d	17 12					17 21	17 18		17 39			17 44	17 48		18 11				18 14	18 18	
Clapham Junction 10	a	17 18			17 10	17 15	17 26	17 23	17 30	17 44			17 49	17 52	17 45	18 16	18 00			18 19	18 22	18 15
London Waterloo 15 ⊖	a					17 25			17 40						17 55		18 10					18 25
London Victoria 15 ⊖	a	17 26			17 18		17 34	17 30		17 55			17 58	18 00		18 25				18 28	18 33	

Table 182

Mondays to Fridays
from 27 September

Horsham, Dorking, Guildford, Epsom and Sutton - London

		SN	SW	FC	FC	SN	SN	SW	SN	SW	FC	FC	SN	SN	SW	SN	SW	FC	FC	SN	SN	SW	SN
Horsham 4	d						17 34							18 04							18 34		
Warnham	d						17 38							18 08							18 38		
Ockley	d						17 45							18 15							18 45		
Holmwood	d						17 49							18 19							18 49		
Dorking 4	a						17 55							18 25							18 55		
	d						18 01	18 05						18 31	18 35		18 50				18 56		19 05
Boxhill & Westhumble	d						18 03							18 33							18 58		
Guildford	d		17 28							17 58						18 22							
Effingham Junction 6	d		17 46							18 16						18 39						18 59	
Bookham	d		17 49							18 19						18 42						19 02	
Leatherhead	d		17 54				18 08	18 11		18 24				18 38	18 41	18 47	18 56				19 03	19 08	19 11
Ashtead	d		17 58				18 12	18 14		18 28				18 42	18 44	18 51	18 59				19 07	19 12	19 15
Epsom 3	a		18 02				18 16	18 19		18 32				18 46	18 49	18 57	19 04				19 11	19 16	19 19
	d	17 52	18 05				18 17	18 20	18 22	18 35				18 49	18 50	18 57	19 05				19 12	19 20	19 20
Ewell East	d	17 56					18 23		18 26					18 53							19 16		19 24
Cheam	d	17 59					18 26		18 29					18 56							19 19		19 27
Epsom Downs	d					18 02							18 35							19 06			
Banstead	d					18 05							18 38							19 09			
Belmont	d					18 08							18 41							19 12			
Sutton (Surrey) 4	a	18 02				18 11	18 29		18 32				18 44	18 59		19 04				19 15	19 22		19 30
	d	18 03		18 08	18 09	18 12	18 30		18 33		18 38	18 43	18 45	19 00		19 05		19 08	19 13	19 16	19 22		19 33
Carshalton	d			18 11			18 33				18 41			19 03				19 11			19 25		
Hackbridge	d			18 13			18 35				18 43			19 05				19 13			19 28		
Mitcham Junction	d			18 16			18 39				18 46			19 09				19 16			19 31		
Mitcham Eastfields	d			18 19			18 42				18 49			19 12				19 19			19 34		
Carshalton Beeches	d	18 06				18 15			18 36				18 48			19 08				19 19			19 36
Wallington	d	18 08				18 17			18 38				18 50			19 10				19 21			19 38
Waddon	d	18 11				18 20			18 41				18 53			19 13				19 24			19 41
West Croydon 4	d	18 18				18 28			18 47				18 58			19 17				19 28			19 47
Norwood Junction 2	d	18 24							18 52							19 22							19 52
New Cross Gate 4 ⊖	d																						
Tulse Hill 3	d			18 27	18 44						18 57	19 14						19 27	19 44				
London Bridge 4 ⊖	a																						
Balham 4 ⊖	d	18 40				18 44	18 48		19 09				19 14	19 18		19 39				19 45	19 42		20 08
Clapham Junction 10	a	18 45	18 30			18 49	18 52	18 45	19 14	19 00			19 19	19 22	19 16	19 44	19 30			19 50	19 47	19 45	20 14
London Waterloo 15 ⊖	a		18 40					18 55		19 10					19 27		19 41					19 55	
London Victoria 15 ⊖	a	18 54				18 57	19 01		19 25				19 28	19 30		19 53				19 59	19 55		20 25

		SW	FC	FC	SN	SN	SN	SW	SN	SW	FC	FC	SN	SW	SN	SN	SW	FC	FC	SN	SN	SW	SN
Horsham 4	d						19 04														20 06		
Warnham	d						19 08														20 10		
Ockley	d						19 15														20 17		
Holmwood	d						19 19														20 21		
Dorking 4	a						19 25														20 27		
	d						19 28	19 33	19 37				19 57	20 05							20 30	20 35	
Boxhill & Westhumble	d						19 30						19 59										
Guildford	d				18 58					19 28							19 58						
Effingham Junction 6	d				19 15					19 46							20 16						
Bookham	d				19 18					19 49							20 19						
Leatherhead	d				19 23		19 35	19 39	19 43	19 54			20 04	20 11			20 24				20 36	20 41	
Ashtead	d				19 27		19 39	19 42	19 46	19 58			20 08	20 14			20 28				20 39	20 44	
Epsom 3	a				19 32		19 45	19 47	19 51	20 02			20 12	20 19			20 32				20 44	20 49	
	d	19 35			19 35		19 46	19 50	19 52	20 05			20 13	20 20		20 22	20 35				20 45	20 50	
Ewell East	d				19 39		19 50		19 56				20 17			20 26					20 49		
Cheam	d				19 42		19 53		19 59				20 20			20 29					20 52		
Epsom Downs	d					19 36									20 13								20 54
Banstead	d					19 39									20 16								20 57
Belmont	d					19 42									20 19								21 00
Sutton (Surrey) 4	a				19 45	19 45	19 56		20 02				20 23		20 22	20 32					20 55		21 03
	d		19 38	19 42		19 46	19 56		20 03		20 07	20 10	20 25		20 23	20 33		20 37	20 40	20 52	20 55		21 06
Carshalton	d			19 45			19 59					20 13	20 28						20 43		20 58		
Hackbridge	d			19 47			20 02					20 15	20 31						20 45		21 01		
Mitcham Junction	d			19 50			20 05					20 18	20 34						20 48		21 04		
Mitcham Eastfields	d			19 53			20 08					20 21	20 37						20 51		21 07		
Carshalton Beeches	d					19 49			20 06						20 26	20 36				20 55			21 09
Wallington	d					19 51			20 08						20 28	20 38				20 57			21 11
Waddon	d					19 54			20 11						20 31	20 41				21 00			21 14
West Croydon 4	d					19 58			20 18						20 35	20 45				21 04			21 18
Norwood Junction 2	d								20 23							20 52							21 23
New Cross Gate 4 ⊖	d																						
Tulse Hill 3	d		20 12	20 01							20 42	20 29						21 12	20 59				
London Bridge 4 ⊖	a																						
Balham 4 ⊖	d					20 14	20 17		20 39				20 44		20 51	21 09				21 21	21 14		21 39
Clapham Junction 10	a	20 00				20 19	20 22	20 15	20 44	20 30			20 48	20 45	20 56	21 14	21 00			21 26	21 18	21 15	21 44
London Waterloo 15 ⊖	a	20 10						20 25		20 41				20 55			21 10					21 25	
London Victoria 15 ⊖	a					20 28	20 30		20 53				20 56		21 04	21 23				21 34	21 26		21 53

Table 182

Horsham, Dorking, Guildford, Epsom and Sutton - London

Mondays to Fridays
from 27 September

		SW		FC	FC	SN	SN	SW	SN	SW	SN	SN		SW	SN	FC	SN	SN	SW	SN	SN	SN		SW	SN
Horsham 4	d																								
Warnham	d																								
Ockley	d																								
Holmwood	d																								
Dorking 4	a																								
	d						20 59					21 30		21 35				21 59				22 30		22 35	
Boxhill & Westhumble	d						21 01											22 01							
Guildford	d							20 46											21 46						
Effingham Junction 6	d							21 03											22 03						
Bookham	d							21 06											22 06						
Leatherhead	d						21 06	21 11				21 36		21 41				22 06	22 11			22 36		22 41	
Ashtead	d						21 10	21 14				21 40		21 44				22 10	22 14			22 40		22 44	
Epsom 3	a						21 14	21 19				21 44		21 49				22 14	22 19			22 44		22 49	
	d	21 05					21 15	21 20	21 25	21 35		21 45		21 50				22 15	22 20	22 25		22 45		22 50	
Ewell East	d						21 19		21 29			21 49						22 19		22 29		22 49			
Cheam	d						21 22		21 32			21 52						22 22		22 32		22 52			
Epsom Downs	d														21 54										22 54
Banstead	d														21 57										22 57
Belmont	d														22 00										23 00
Sutton (Surrey) 4	a						21 25		21 35			21 55			22 03			22 25		22 35		22 55			23 03
	d			21 10	21 12	21 22	21 25		21 36		21 52	21 55			22 06	22 12	22 22	22 25		22 36	22 52	22 55			23 06
Carshalton	d			21 13			21 28					21 58						22 28				22 58			
Hackbridge	d			21 15			21 31					22 01						22 31				23 01			
Mitcham Junction	d			21 18			21 34					22 04						22 34				23 04			
Mitcham Eastfields	d			21 21			21 37					22 07						22 37				23 07			
Carshalton Beeches	d					21 25			21 39		21 55				22 09		22 25			22 39	22 55				23 09
Wallington	d					21 27			21 41		21 57				22 11		22 27			22 41	22 57				23 11
Waddon	d					21 30			21 44		22 00				22 14		22 30			22 44	23 00				23 14
West Croydon 4	d					21 34			21 48		22 04				22 18		22 34			22 48	23 04				23 18
Norwood Junction 2	d								21 53						22 23					22 53					23 23
New Cross Gate 4	⊖ d																								
Tulse Hill 3	d			21 29	21 50											22 43									
London Bridge 4	⊖ a															22 55									
Balham 4	⊖ d					21 51	21 44		22 09		22 21	22 14			22 39		22 51	22 44		23 09	23 21	23 14			23 40
Clapham Junction 10	a	21 30				21 56	21 48	21 45	22 14	22 00	22 26	22 19		22 15	22 44		22 56	22 48	22 45	23 15	23 26	23 18		23 15	23 45
London Waterloo 15	⊖ a	21 40						21 55		22 10				22 25					22 55					23 27	
London Victoria 15	⊖ a					22 04	21 56		22 25		22 34	22 27			22 53		23 04	22 56		23 23	23 34	23 26			23 54

		SN	SN	SW	SN	SN	SN
Horsham 4	d						
Warnham	d						
Ockley	d						
Holmwood	d						
Dorking 4	a						
	d		23 00			23 30	
Boxhill & Westhumble	d		23 02				
Guildford	d			22 46			
Effingham Junction 6	d			23 03			
Bookham	d			23 06			
Leatherhead	d		23 07	23 11		23 36	
Ashtead	d		23 11	23 14		23 39	
Epsom 3	a		23 15	23 19		23 45	
	d		23 16	23 20	23 25		
Ewell East	d		23 20		23 29		
Cheam	d		23 23		23 32		
Epsom Downs	d						23 43
Banstead	d						23 46
Belmont	d						23 49
Sutton (Surrey) 4	a		23 26		23 35		23 52
	d	23 20	23 30		23 40		23 53
Carshalton	d						
Hackbridge	d						
Mitcham Junction	d						
Mitcham Eastfields	d						
Carshalton Beeches	d	23 23	23 33		23 43		23 56
Wallington	d	23 25	23 35		23 45		23 58
Waddon	d	23 28	23 38		23 48		00 01
West Croydon 4	d	23a31	23a41		23a57		00a04
Norwood Junction 2	d						
New Cross Gate 4	⊖ d						
Tulse Hill 3	d						
London Bridge 4	⊖ a						
Balham 4	⊖ d						
Clapham Junction 10	a			23 48			
London Waterloo 15	⊖ a			23 58			
London Victoria 15	⊖ a						

Table 182

Horsham, Dorking, Guildford, Epsom and Sutton - London

Saturdays
29 May to 25 September

		SN	SW	SW	SW	SN	SN	SN	SW	SN		FC	FC	SN	SN	SN	SW	SN	FC	FC		SN	SN	SN	SW
Horsham 4	d																								
Warnham	d																								
Ockley	d																								
Holmwood	d																								
Dorking 4	a																								
	d						06 27								06 57								07 26		
Boxhill & Westhumble	d														06 59								07 28		
Guildford	d								06 28								06 58								07 28
Effingham Junction 6	d								06 46								07 16								07 46
Bookham	d								06 49								07 19								07 49
Leatherhead	d						06 33		06 54						07 04		07 24						07 33		07 54
Ashtead	d						06 37		06 58						07 08		07 28						07 37		07 58
Epsom 3	a						06 41		07 02						07 12		07 32						07 41		08 02
	d		05 35	06 05	06 35		06 42	06 49	07 05					07 04	07 13	07 19	07 35						07 42	07 49	08 05
Ewell East	d						06 46	06 53						07 08		07 23							07 46	07 53	
Cheam	d						06 49	06 56						07 11	07 18	07 26							07 49	07 56	
Epsom Downs	d	23p43																				07 34			
Banstead	d	23p46																				07 37			
Belmont	d	23p49																				07 40			
Sutton (Surrey) 4	a	23p52					06 52	06 59						07 14	07 22	07 29						07 43	07 52	07 59	
	d	23p53				06 44	06 53	07 00		07 03		07 07	07 08	07 14	07 23	07 30		07 33	07 37	07 38		07 44	07 53	08 00	
Carshalton	d							07 03					07 11			07 33				07 41				08 03	
Hackbridge	d							07 05					07 13			07 35				07 43				08 05	
Mitcham Junction	d							07 09					07 16			07 39				07 46				08 09	
Mitcham Eastfields	d							07 12					07 19			07 42				07 49				08 12	
Carshalton Beeches	d	23p56				06 47				07 06				07 17				07 36				07 47			
Wallington	d	23p58				06 50				07 08				07 20				07 38				07 50			
Waddon	d	00 01				06 53				07 11				07 23				07 41				07 53			
West Croydon 4	d	00a04				06 58				07 15				07 28				07 45				07 58			
Norwood Junction 2	d									07 20								07 50							
New Cross Gate 4	⊖ d									07 34								08 04							
Tulse Hill 3	d											07 47	07 27						08 17	07 57					
London Bridge 4	⊖ a									07 41		08 00						08 11	08 30						
Balham 4	⊖ d					07 14		07 18						07 44		07 48						08 14		08 18	
Clapham Junction 10	a		06 01	06 30	07 00	07 19	07 10	07 22	07 30					07 49	07 40	07 52	08 00					08 19	08 10	08 22	08 30
London Waterloo 15	⊖ a		06 11	06 40	07 10				07 40								08 10								08 40
London Victoria 15	⊖ a					07 28	07 18	07 30						07 58	07 50	08 00						08 28	08 18	08 30	

		SN	FC	FC	SN	SN		SW	SN	SN	SW	SN	FC	FC	SN	SN		SW	SN	SN	SW	SN	FC	FC	SN
Horsham 4	d															08 04									
Warnham	d															08 08									
Ockley	d															08 15									
Holmwood	d															08 19									
Dorking 4	a															08 25									
	d					07 58		08 05								08 26		08 35							
Boxhill & Westhumble	d															08 28									
Guildford	d										07 58										08 28				
Effingham Junction 6	d										08 16										08 46				
Bookham	d										08 19										08 49				
Leatherhead	d					08 04		08 11			08 24					08 33		08 41			08 54				
Ashtead	d					08 07		08 14			08 28					08 37		08 44			08 58				
Epsom 3	a					08 12		08 19			08 32					08 41		08 49			09 02				
	d				08 04	08 13		08 20		08 19	08 35					08 42		08 50		08 49	09 05				09 04
Ewell East	d				08 08					08 23						08 46				08 53					09 08
Cheam	d				08 11	08 18				08 26						08 49				08 56					09 11
Epsom Downs	d														08 34										
Banstead	d														08 37										
Belmont	d														08 40										
Sutton (Surrey) 4	a				08 14	08 21				08 29					08 43	08 52				08 59					09 14
	d	08 03	08 07	08 08	08 14	08 23			08 22	08 30		08 33	08 37	08 38	08 44	08 53			08 52	09 00		09 03	09 07	09 08	09 14
Carshalton	d			08 11						08 33				08 41						09 03				09 11	
Hackbridge	d			08 13						08 35				08 43						09 05				09 13	
Mitcham Junction	d			08 16						08 39				08 46						09 09				09 16	
Mitcham Eastfields	d			08 19						08 42				08 49						09 12				09 19	
Carshalton Beeches	d	08 06			08 17				08 25			08 36			08 47				08 55			09 06			09 17
Wallington	d	08 08			08 20				08 27			08 38			08 50				08 57			09 08			09 20
Waddon	d	08 11			08 23				08 30			08 41			08 53				09 00			09 11			09 23
West Croydon 4	d	08 15			08 28				08 34			08 45			08 58				09 04			09 15			09 28
Norwood Junction 2	d	08 22										08 52										09 22			
New Cross Gate 4	⊖ d																								
Tulse Hill 3	d		08 47	08 27									09 17	08 57									09 47	09 27	
London Bridge 4	⊖ a		09 00										09 30										10 00		
Balham 4	⊖ d	08 39			08 44				08 51	08 48		09 09			09 14				09 21	09 18		09 39			09 44
Clapham Junction 10	a	08 44			08 49	08 40		08 45	08 56	08 52	09 00	09 14			09 19	09 10		09 15	09 26	09 22	09 30	09 44			09 49
London Waterloo 15	⊖ a							08 55			09 10							09 25			09 40				
London Victoria 15	⊖ a	08 53			08 58	08 48			09 04	09 00		09 23			09 28	09 18			09 34	09 30		09 53			09 58

Table 182

Saturdays

29 May to 25 September

Horsham, Dorking, Guildford, Epsom and Sutton - London

		SN		SW	SN	SN	SW	SN	FC	FC	SN	SN		SW	SN	SN	SW	SN	FC	FC	SN	SN		SW	SN
Horsham [4]	d										09 04													
Warnham	d										09 08													
Ockley	d										09 15													
Holmwood	d										09 19													
Dorking [4]	a										09 25													
	d	08 58		09 05								09 26		09 35								09 58		10 05	
Boxhill & Westhumble	d										09 28													
Guildford	d						08 58										09 28								
Effingham Junction [6]	d						09 16										09 46								
Bookham	d						09 19										09 49								
Leatherhead	d	09 04		09 11			09 24					09 33		09 41			09 54					10 04		10 11	
Ashtead	d	09 07		09 14			09 28					09 37		09 44			09 58					10 07		10 14	
Epsom [3]	a	09 12		09 19			09 32					09 41		09 49			10 02					10 12		10 19	
	d	09 13		09 20		09 19	09 35					09 42		09 50		09 49	10 05				10 04	10 12		10 20	
Ewell East	d					09 23						09 46				09 53					10 08				
Cheam	d	09 18				09 26						09 49				09 56					10 11	10 18			
Epsom Downs	d										09 34														
Banstead	d										09 37														
Belmont	d										09 40														
Sutton (Surrey) [4]	a	09 21				09 29					09 43	09 52				09 59					10 14	10 22			
	d	09 23			09 22	09 30		09 33	09 37	09 38	09 44	09 53			09 52	10 00		10 03	10 07	10 08	10 14	10 23			10 22
Carshalton	d					09 33				09 41						10 03				10 11					
Hackbridge	d					09 35				09 43						10 05				10 13					
Mitcham Junction	d					09 39				09 46						10 09				10 16					
Mitcham Eastfields	d					09 42				09 49						10 12				10 19					
Carshalton Beeches	d				09 25			09 36			09 47				09 55			10 06			10 17				10 25
Wallington	d				09 27			09 38			09 50				09 57			10 08			10 20				10 27
Waddon	d				09 30			09 41			09 53				10 00			10 11			10 23				10 30
West Croydon [4]	d				09 34			09 45			09 58				10 04			10 15			10 28				10 34
Norwood Junction [2]	d							09 52										10 22							
New Cross Gate [4] ⊖	d																								
Tulse Hill [3]	d								10 17	09 57									10 47	10 27					
London Bridge [4] ⊖	a								10 30										11 00						
Balham [4] ⊖	d				09 51	09 48		10 09			10 14				10 21	10 18		10 39			10 44				10 51
Clapham Junction [10]	a	09 40		09 45	09 56	09 52	10 00	10 14			10 19	10 10		10 15	10 26	10 22	10 30	10 44			10 49	10 40		10 45	10 56
London Waterloo [15] ⊖	a			09 55			10 10							10 25			10 40							10 55	
London Victoria [15] ⊖	a	09 48			10 04	10 00		10 23			10 28	10 18			10 34	10 30		10 53			10 58	10 48			11 04

		SN	SW	SN	FC	FC	SN	SN		SW	SN	SN	SW	SN	FC	FC	SN	SN		SW	SN	SN	SW	SN	FC
Horsham [4]	d							10 04																	
Warnham	d							10 08																	
Ockley	d							10 15																	
Holmwood	d							10 19																	
Dorking [4]	a							10 25																	
	d							10 26		10 35								10 58		11 05					
Boxhill & Westhumble	d							10 28																	
Guildford	d		09 58										10 28										10 58		
Effingham Junction [6]	d		10 16										10 46										11 16		
Bookham	d		10 19										10 49										11 19		
Leatherhead	d		10 24					10 33		10 41			10 54					11 04		11 11			11 24		
Ashtead	d		10 28					10 37		10 44			10 58					11 07		11 14			11 28		
Epsom [3]	a		10 32					10 41		10 49			11 02					11 12		11 19			11 32		
	d	10 19	10 35					10 42		10 50		10 49	11 05				11 04	11 13		11 20		11 19	11 35		
Ewell East	d	10 23						10 46				10 53					11 08					11 23			
Cheam	d	10 26						10 49				10 56					11 11	11 18				11 26			
Epsom Downs	d						10 34																		
Banstead	d						10 37																		
Belmont	d						10 40																		
Sutton (Surrey) [4]	a	10 29					10 43	10 52				10 59					11 14	11 21				11 29			
	d	10 30		10 33	10 37	10 38	10 44	10 53			10 52	11 00		11 03	11 07	11 08	11 14	11 23			11 22	11 30		11 33	11 37
Carshalton	d	10 33				10 41						11 03				11 11						11 33			
Hackbridge	d	10 35				10 43						11 05				11 13						11 35			
Mitcham Junction	d	10 39				10 46						11 09				11 16						11 39			
Mitcham Eastfields	d	10 42				10 49						11 12				11 19						11 42			
Carshalton Beeches	d			10 36			10 47				10 55			11 06			11 17				11 25			11 36	
Wallington	d			10 38			10 50				10 57			11 08			11 20				11 27			11 38	
Waddon	d			10 41			10 53				11 00			11 11			11 23				11 30			11 41	
West Croydon [4]	d			10 45			10 58				11 04			11 15			11 28				11 34			11 45	
Norwood Junction [2]	d			10 52										11 22										11 52	
New Cross Gate [4] ⊖	d																								
Tulse Hill [3]	d				11 17	10 57									11 47	11 27									12 17
London Bridge [4] ⊖	a				11 30										12 00										12 30
Balham [4] ⊖	d	10 48		11 09			11 14				11 21	11 18		11 39			11 44				11 51	11 48		12 09	
Clapham Junction [10]	a	10 52	11 00	11 14			11 19	11 10		11 15	11 26	11 22	11 30	11 44			11 49	11 40		11 45	11 56	11 52	12 00	12 14	
London Waterloo [15] ⊖	a		11 10							11 25			11 40							11 55			12 10		
London Victoria [15] ⊖	a	11 00		11 23			11 28	11 18			11 34	11 30		11 53			11 58	11 48			12 04	12 00		12 23	

Table 182

Saturdays

29 May to 25 September

Horsham, Dorking, Guildford, Epsom and Sutton - London

		FC	SN	SN		SW	SN	SN	SW	SN	FC	FC	SN	SN		SW	SN	SN	SW	SN	FC	FC	SN	SN	
Horsham [4]	d			11 04																				12 04	
Warnham	d			11 08																				12 08	
Ockley	d			11 15																				12 15	
Holmwood	d			11 19																				12 19	
Dorking [4]	a			11 25																				12 25	
	d			11 26		11 35								11 58		12 05								12 26	
Boxhill & Westhumble	d			11 28																				12 28	
Guildford	d								11 28										11 58						
Effingham Junction [6]	d								11 46										12 16						
Bookham	d								11 49										12 19						
Leatherhead	d			11 33		11 41			11 54					12 04		12 11			12 24					12 33	
Ashtead	d			11 37		11 44			11 58					12 07		12 14			12 28					12 37	
Epsom [3]	a			11 41		11 49			12 02					12 12		12 19			12 32					12 41	
	d			11 42		11 50		11 49	12 05				12 04	12 13		12 20		12 19	12 35					12 42	
Ewell East	d			11 46				11 53					12 08					12 23						12 46	
Cheam	d			11 49				11 56					12 11	12 18				12 26						12 49	
Epsom Downs	d		11 34																				12 34		
Banstead	d		11 37																				12 37		
Belmont	d		11 40																				12 40		
Sutton (Surrey) [4]	a		11 43	11 52				11 59					12 14	12 21				12 29					12 43	12 52	
	d	11 38	11 44	11 53			11 52	12 00		12 03	12 07	12 08	12 14	12 23			12 22	12 30		12 33	12 37	12 38	12 44	12 53	
Carshalton	d	11 41						12 03				12 11						12 33				12 41			
Hackbridge	d	11 43						12 05				12 13						12 35				12 43			
Mitcham Junction	d	11 46						12 09				12 16						12 39				12 46			
Mitcham Eastfields	d	11 49						12 12				12 19						12 42				12 49			
Carshalton Beeches	d		11 47				11 55			12 06			12 17				12 25			12 36			12 47		
Wallington	d		11 50				11 57			12 08			12 20				12 27			12 38			12 50		
Waddon	d		11 53				12 00			12 11			12 23				12 30			12 41			12 53		
West Croydon [4]	d		11 58				12 04			12 15			12 28				12 34			12 45			12 58		
Norwood Junction [2]	d									12 22										12 52					
New Cross Gate [4] ⊖	d																								
Tulse Hill [3]	d	11 57									12 47	12 27									13 17	12 57			
London Bridge [4] ⊖	a										13 00										13 30				
Balham [4] ⊖	d		12 14				12 21	12 18		12 39			12 44				12 51	12 48		13 09			13 14		
Clapham Junction [10]	a		12 19	12 10		12 15	12 26	12 22	12 30	12 44			12 49	12 40		12 45	12 56	12 52	13 00	13 14			13 19	13 10	
London Waterloo [15] ⊖	a					12 25			12 40							12 55			13 10						
London Victoria [15] ⊖	a		12 28	12 18			12 34	12 30		12 53			12 58	12 48			13 04	13 00		13 23			13 28	13 18	

		SW	SN	SN	SW	SN	FC	FC	SN	SN		SW	SN	SN	SW	SN	FC	FC	SN	SN		SW	SN	SN	SW
Horsham [4]	d																			13 04					
Warnham	d																			13 08					
Ockley	d																			13 15					
Holmwood	d																			13 19					
Dorking [4]	a																			13 25					
	d	12 35								12 58		13 05								13 26		13 35			
Boxhill & Westhumble	d																			13 28					
Guildford	d				12 28										12 58										13 28
Effingham Junction [6]	d				12 46										13 16										13 46
Bookham	d				12 49										13 19										13 49
Leatherhead	d	12 41			12 54					13 04		13 11			13 24					13 33		13 41			13 54
Ashtead	d	12 44			12 58					13 07		13 14			13 28					13 37		13 44			13 58
Epsom [3]	a	12 49			13 02					13 12		13 19			13 32					13 41		13 49			14 02
	d	12 50		12 49	13 05				13 04	13 13		13 20		13 19	13 35					13 42		13 50		13 49	14 05
Ewell East	d			12 53					13 08					13 23						13 46				13 53	
Cheam	d			12 56					13 11	13 18				13 26						13 49				13 56	
Epsom Downs	d																		13 34						
Banstead	d																		13 37						
Belmont	d																		13 40						
Sutton (Surrey) [4]	a			12 59					13 14	13 21				13 29					13 43	13 52				13 59	
	d		12 52	13 00		13 03	13 07	13 08	13 14	13 23			13 22	13 30		13 33	13 37	13 38	13 44	13 53			13 52	14 00	
Carshalton	d			13 03				13 11						13 33				13 41						14 03	
Hackbridge	d			13 05				13 13						13 35				13 43						14 05	
Mitcham Junction	d			13 09				13 16						13 39				13 46						14 09	
Mitcham Eastfields	d			13 12				13 19						13 42				13 49						14 12	
Carshalton Beeches	d		12 55			13 06			13 17				13 25			13 36			13 47				13 55		
Wallington	d		12 57			13 08			13 20				13 27			13 38			13 50				13 57		
Waddon	d		13 00			13 11			13 23				13 30			13 41			13 53				14 00		
West Croydon [4]	d		13 04			13 15			13 28				13 34			13 45			13 58				14 04		
Norwood Junction [2]	d					13 22										13 52									
New Cross Gate [4] ⊖	d																								
Tulse Hill [3]	d						13 47	13 27									14 17	13 57							
London Bridge [4] ⊖	a						14 00										14 30								
Balham [4] ⊖	d		13 21	13 18		13 39			13 44				13 51	13 48		14 09			14 14				14 21	14 18	
Clapham Junction [10]	a	13 15	13 26	13 22	13 30	13 44			13 49	13 40		13 45	13 56	13 52	14 00	14 14			14 19	14 10		14 15	14 26	14 22	14 30
London Waterloo [15] ⊖	a	13 25			13 40							13 55			14 10							14 25			14 40
London Victoria [15] ⊖	a		13 34	13 30		13 53			13 58	13 48			14 04	14 00		14 23			14 28	14 18			14 34	14 30	

Table 182

Saturdays

29 May to 25 September

Horsham, Dorking, Guildford, Epsom and Sutton - London

		SN	FC	FC	SN	SN	SW	SN	SN	SW	SN	FC	FC	SN	SN	SW	SN	SN	SW	SN	FC	FC	SN
Horsham	d														14 04								
Warnham	d														14 08								
Ockley	d														14 15								
Holmwood	d														14 19								
Dorking	a														14 25								
	d					13 58	14 05								14 26	14 35							
Boxhill & Westhumble	d														14 28								
Guildford	d									13 58									14 28				
Effingham Junction	d									14 16									14 46				
Bookham	d									14 19									14 49				
Leatherhead	d					14 04	14 11			14 24					14 33	14 41			14 54				
Ashtead	d					14 07	14 14			14 28					14 37	14 44			14 58				
Epsom	a					14 12	14 19			14 32					14 41	14 49			15 02				
	d				14 04	14 13	14 20		14 19	14 35					14 42	14 50		14 49	15 05				15 04
Ewell East	d				14 08				14 23						14 46			14 53					15 08
Cheam	d				14 11	14 18			14 26						14 49			14 56					15 11
Epsom Downs	d													14 34									
Banstead	d													14 37									
Belmont	d													14 40									
Sutton (Surrey)	a				14 14	14 21			14 29					14 43	14 52			14 59					15 14
	d	14 03	14 07	14 08	14 14	14 23		14 22	14 30		14 33	14 37	14 38	14 44	14 53		14 52	15 00		15 03	15 07	15 08	15 14
Carshalton	d			14 11					14 33				14 41					15 03				15 11	
Hackbridge	d			14 13					14 35				14 43					15 05				15 13	
Mitcham Junction	d			14 16					14 39				14 46					15 09				15 16	
Mitcham Eastfields	d			14 19					14 42				14 49					15 12				15 19	
Carshalton Beeches	d	14 06			14 17			14 25			14 36			14 47			14 55			15 06			15 17
Wallington	d	14 08			14 20			14 27			14 38			14 50			14 57			15 08			15 20
Waddon	d	14 11			14 23			14 30			14 41			14 53			15 00			15 11			15 23
West Croydon	d	14 15			14 28			14 34			14 45			14 58			15 04			15 15			15 28
Norwood Junction	d	14 22									14 52									15 22			
New Cross Gate ⊖	d																						
Tulse Hill	d		14 47	14 27								15 17	14 57								15 47	15 27	
London Bridge ⊖	a		15 00									15 30									16 00		
Balham ⊖	d	14 39			14 44			14 51	14 48		15 09			15 14			15 21	15 18		15 39			15 44
Clapham Junction	a	14 44			14 49	14 40	14 45	14 56	14 52	15 00	15 14			15 19	15 10	15 15	15 26	15 22	15 30	15 44			15 49
London Waterloo ⊖	a						14 55			15 10						15 25			15 40				
London Victoria ⊖	a	14 53			14 58	14 48		15 04	15 00		15 23			15 28	15 18		15 34	15 30		15 53			15 58

		SN	SW	SN	SN	SW	SN	FC	FC	SN	SN	SW	SN	SN	SW	SN	FC	FC	SN	SN	SW	SN
Horsham	d										15 04											
Warnham	d										15 08											
Ockley	d										15 15											
Holmwood	d										15 19											
Dorking	a										15 25											
	d	14 58	15 05								15 26	15 35								15 58	16 05	
Boxhill & Westhumble	d										15 28											
Guildford	d					14 58									15 28							
Effingham Junction	d					15 16									15 46							
Bookham	d					15 19									15 49							
Leatherhead	d	15 04	15 11			15 24					15 33	15 41			15 54					16 04	16 11	
Ashtead	d	15 07	15 14			15 28					15 37	15 44			15 58					16 07	16 14	
Epsom	a	15 12	15 19			15 32					15 41	15 49			16 02					16 12	16 19	
	d	15 13	15 20		15 19	15 35					15 42	15 50		15 49	16 05				16 04	16 13	16 20	
Ewell East	d				15 23						15 46			15 53					16 08			
Cheam	d	15 18			15 26						15 49			15 56					16 11	16 18		
Epsom Downs	d									15 34												
Banstead	d									15 37												
Belmont	d									15 40												
Sutton (Surrey)	a	15 21			15 29					15 43	15 52			15 59					16 14	16 21		
	d	15 23		15 22	15 30		15 33	15 37	15 38	15 44	15 53		15 52	16 00		16 03	16 07	16 08	16 14	16 23		16 22
Carshalton	d				15 33				15 41					16 03				16 11				
Hackbridge	d				15 35				15 43					16 05				16 13				
Mitcham Junction	d				15 39				15 46					16 09				16 16				
Mitcham Eastfields	d				15 42				15 49					16 12				16 19				
Carshalton Beeches	d			15 25			15 36			15 47			15 55			16 06			16 17			16 25
Wallington	d			15 27			15 38			15 50			15 57			16 08			16 20			16 27
Waddon	d			15 30			15 41			15 53			16 00			16 11			16 23			16 30
West Croydon	d			15 34			15 45			15 58			16 04			16 15			16 28			16 34
Norwood Junction	d						15 52									16 22						
New Cross Gate ⊖	d																					
Tulse Hill	d							16 17	15 57								16 47	16 27				
London Bridge ⊖	a							16 30									17 00					
Balham ⊖	d			15 51	15 48		16 09			16 14			16 21	16 18		16 39			16 44			16 51
Clapham Junction	a	15 40	15 45	15 56	15 52	16 00	16 14			16 19	16 10	16 15	16 26	16 22	16 30	16 44			16 49	16 40	16 45	16 56
London Waterloo ⊖	a		15 55			16 10						16 25			16 40						16 55	
London Victoria ⊖	a	15 48		16 04	16 00		16 23			16 28	16 18		16 34	16 30		16 53			16 58	16 48		17 04

Table 182

Saturdays

29 May to 25 September

Horsham, Dorking, Guildford, Epsom and Sutton - London

		SN	SW	SN	FC	FC	SN	SN	SW	SN	SN	SW	SN	FC	FC	SN	SN	SW	SN	SN	SW	SN	FC
Horsham	d							16 04															
Warnham	d							16 08															
Ockley	d							16 15															
Holmwood	d							16 19															
Dorking	a							16 25															
	d							16 26	16 35								16 58	17 05					
Boxhill & Westhumble	d							16 28															
Guildford	d		15 58									16 28									16 58		
Effingham Junction	d		16 16									16 46									17 16		
Bookham	d		16 19									16 49									17 19		
Leatherhead	d		16 24					16 33	16 41			16 54					17 04	17 11			17 24		
Ashtead	d		16 28					16 37	16 44			16 58					17 07	17 14			17 28		
Epsom	a		16 32					16 41	16 49			17 02					17 12	17 19			17 32		
	d	16 19	16 35					16 42	16 50		16 49	17 05				17 04	17 13	17 20		17 19	17 35		
Ewell East	d	16 23						16 46			16 53					17 08				17 23			
Cheam	d	16 26						16 49			16 56					17 11	17 18			17 26			
Epsom Downs	d						16 34																
Banstead	d						16 37																
Belmont	d						16 40																
Sutton (Surrey)	a	16 29					16 43	16 52			16 59					17 14	17 21			17 29			
	d	16 30		16 33	16 37	16 38	16 44	16 53		16 52	17 00		17 03	17 07	17 08	17 14	17 23		17 22	17 30		17 33	17 37
Carshalton	d	16 33				16 41					17 03				17 11					17 33			
Hackbridge	d	16 35				16 43					17 05				17 13					17 35			
Mitcham Junction	d	16 39				16 46					17 09				17 16					17 39			
Mitcham Eastfields	d	16 42				16 49					17 12				17 19					17 42			
Carshalton Beeches	d			16 36			16 47			16 55			17 06			17 17			17 25			17 36	
Wallington	d			16 38			16 50			16 57			17 08			17 20			17 27			17 38	
Waddon	d			16 41			16 53			17 00			17 11			17 23			17 30			17 41	
West Croydon	d			16 45			16 58			17 04			17 15			17 28			17 34			17 45	
Norwood Junction	d			16 52									17 22									17 52	
New Cross Gate ⊖	d																						
Tulse Hill	d				17 17	16 57								17 47	17 27								18 17
London Bridge ⊖	a				17 30									18 00									18 30
Balham ⊖	d	16 48		17 09			17 14			17 21	17 18		17 39			17 44			17 51	17 48		18 09	
Clapham Junction	a	16 52	17 00	17 14			17 19	17 10	17 15	17 26	17 22	17 30	17 44			17 49	17 41	17 45	17 56	17 52	18 00	18 14	
London Waterloo ⊖	a		17 10						17 25			17 40						17 55			18 10		
London Victoria ⊖	a	17 00		17 23			17 28	17 18		17 34	17 30		17 53			17 58	17 49		18 04	18 00		18 23	

		FC	SN	SN	SW	SN	SN	SW	SN	FC	FC	SN	SN	SW	SN	SN	SW	SN	FC	FC	SN	SN
Horsham	d			17 04																		18 04
Warnham	d			17 08																		18 08
Ockley	d			17 15																		18 15
Holmwood	d			17 19																		18 19
Dorking	a			17 25																		18 25
	d			17 26	17 35								17 58	18 05								18 26
Boxhill & Westhumble	d			17 28																		18 28
Guildford	d							17 28									17 58					
Effingham Junction	d							17 46									18 16					
Bookham	d							17 49									18 19					
Leatherhead	d			17 33	17 41			17 54					18 04	18 11			18 24					18 33
Ashtead	d			17 37	17 44			17 58					18 07	18 14			18 28					18 37
Epsom	a			17 41	17 49			18 02					18 12	18 19			18 32					18 41
	d			17 42	17 50		17 49	18 05				18 04	18 13	18 20		18 19	18 35					18 42
Ewell East	d			17 46			17 53					18 08				18 23						18 46
Cheam	d			17 49			17 56					18 11	18 18			18 26						18 49
Epsom Downs	d		17 34																		18 34	
Banstead	d		17 37																		18 37	
Belmont	d		17 40																		18 40	
Sutton (Surrey)	a		17 43	17 52			17 59					18 14	18 21			18 29					18 43	18 52
	d	17 38	17 44	17 53		17 52	18 00		18 03	18 07	18 08	18 14	18 23		18 22	18 30		18 33	18 37	18 38	18 44	18 53
Carshalton	d	17 41					18 03				18 11					18 33				18 41		
Hackbridge	d	17 43					18 05				18 13					18 35				18 43		
Mitcham Junction	d	17 46					18 09				18 16					18 39				18 46		
Mitcham Eastfields	d	17 49					18 12				18 19					18 42				18 49		
Carshalton Beeches	d		17 47			17 55			18 06			18 17			18 25			18 36			18 47	
Wallington	d		17 50			17 57			18 08			18 20			18 27			18 38			18 50	
Waddon	d		17 53			18 00			18 11			18 23			18 30			18 41			18 53	
West Croydon	d		17 58			18 04			18 15			18 28			18 34			18 45			18 58	
Norwood Junction	d								18 22									18 52				
New Cross Gate ⊖	d																					
Tulse Hill	d	17 57								18 47	18 27								19 17	18 57		
London Bridge ⊖	a									19 00									19 30			
Balham ⊖	d		18 14			18 21	18 18		18 39			18 44			18 51	18 48		19 09			19 14	
Clapham Junction	a		18 19	18 10	18 15	18 26	18 22	18 30	18 44			18 49	18 40	18 45	18 56	18 52	19 00	19 14			19 19	19 10
London Waterloo ⊖	a				18 25			18 40						18 55			19 10					
London Victoria ⊖	a		18 28	18 18		18 34	18 30		18 53			18 58	18 48		19 04	19 00		19 23			19 28	19 18

Horsham, Dorking, Guildford, Epsom and Sutton - London

		SW	SN	SN	SW	FC	FC	SN	SN	SN	SW	SN	SW	FC	SN	SN	SW	SW	SN	FC	SN	SN	SW
Horsham	d																						
Warnham	d																						
Ockley	d																						
Holmwood	d																						
Dorking	a																						
	d	18 35								19 00	19 05					19 28	19 35					19 59	20 05
Boxhill & Westhumble	d									19 02												20 01	
Guildford	d				18 28								18 58					19 28					
Effingham Junction	d				18 46								19 16					19 46					
Bookham	d				18 49								19 19					19 49					
Leatherhead	d	18 41			18 54					19 07	19 11		19 24			19 34	19 41	19 54				20 06	20 11
Ashtead	d	18 44			18 58					19 11	19 14		19 28			19 37	19 44	19 58				20 10	20 14
Epsom	a	18 49			19 02					19 15	19 19		19 32			19 42	19 49	20 02				20 14	20 19
	d	18 50	18 49	18 55	19 05					19 19	19 20	19 25	19 35			19 42	19 50	20 05				20 15	20 20
Ewell East	d		18 53							19 23		19 29				19 46						20 19	
Cheam	d		18 56							19 26		19 32				19 49						20 22	
Epsom Downs	d								19 15										19 54				
Banstead	d								19 18										19 57				
Belmont	d								19 21										20 00				
Sutton (Surrey)	a		18 59	19 02					19 24	19 29		19 35				19 52			20 03			20 25	
	d		19 00	19 03		19 07	19 08	19 14	19 25	19 30		19 36		19 37	19 52	19 53			20 06	20 08	20 22	20 25	
Carshalton	d		19 03				19 11			19 33						19 56						20 28	
Hackbridge	d		19 05				19 13			19 35						19 58						20 31	
Mitcham Junction	d		19 09				19 16			19 39						20 02						20 34	
Mitcham Eastfields	d		19 12				19 19			19 42						20 05						20 37	
Carshalton Beeches	d			19 06				19 17	19 28			19 39			19 55				20 09		20 25		
Wallington	d			19 08				19 20	19 30			19 41			19 57				20 11		20 27		
Waddon	d			19 11				19 23	19 33			19 44			20 00				20 14		20 30		
West Croydon	d			19 15				19 28	19a41			19 48			20 04				20 18		20 34		
Norwood Junction	d			19 22								19 53							20 23				
New Cross Gate ⊖	d																						
Tulse Hill	d					19 47	19 27							20 17						20 47			
London Bridge ⊖	a					20 00								20 30						21 00			
Balham ⊖	d		19 18	19 39				19 44		19 48		20 09			20 21	20 12			20 39		20 51	20 44	
Clapham Junction	a	19 15	19 22	19 44	19 30			19 49		19 52	19 45	20 14	20 00		20 26	20 17	20 15	20 30	20 44		20 56	20 48	20 45
London Waterloo ⊖	a	19 25			19 40						19 55		20 10				20 25	20 40					20 55
London Victoria ⊖	a		19 30	19 53				19 58		20 00		20 23			20 34	20 25			20 53		21 04	20 56	

		SN	SW	FC	SN	SN	SW	SN	SW	FC	SN	SN	SW	SN	SW	FC	SN	SN	SW	SN	FC	SN	SN
Horsham	d																						
Warnham	d																						
Ockley	d																						
Holmwood	d																						
Dorking	a																						
	d					20 30	20 35					20 59						21 30	21 35				21 59
Boxhill & Westhumble	d											21 01											22 01
Guildford	d		19 58										20 46										
Effingham Junction	d		20 16										21 03										
Bookham	d		20 19										21 06										
Leatherhead	d		20 24			20 36	20 41					21 06	21 11					21 36	21 41				22 06
Ashtead	d		20 28			20 40	20 44					21 10	21 14					21 40	21 44				22 10
Epsom	a		20 32			20 44	20 49					21 14	21 19					21 44	21 49				22 14
	d	20 25	20 35			20 45	20 50		21 05			21 15	21 20	21 25	21 35			21 45	21 50				22 15
Ewell East	d	20 29				20 49						21 19		21 29				21 49					22 19
Cheam	d	20 32				20 52						21 22		21 32				21 52					22 22
Epsom Downs	d							20 54												21 54			
Banstead	d							20 57												21 57			
Belmont	d							21 00												22 00			
Sutton (Surrey)	a	20 35				20 55		21 03				21 25		21 35				21 55		22 03			22 25
	d	20 36		20 37	20 52	20 55		21 06		21 07	21 22	21 25		21 36		21 37	21 52	21 55		22 06	22 07	22 22	22 25
Carshalton	d					20 58						21 28						21 58					22 28
Hackbridge	d					21 01						21 31						22 01					22 31
Mitcham Junction	d					21 04						21 34						22 04					22 34
Mitcham Eastfields	d					21 07						21 37						22 07					22 37
Carshalton Beeches	d	20 39			20 55			21 09			21 25			21 39			21 55			22 09		22 25	
Wallington	d	20 41			20 57			21 11			21 27			21 41			21 57			22 11		22 27	
Waddon	d	20 44			21 00			21 14			21 30			21 44			22 00			22 14		22 30	
West Croydon	d	20 48			21 04			21 18			21 34			21 48			22 04			22 18		22 34	
Norwood Junction	d	20 53						21 23						21 53						22 23			
New Cross Gate ⊖	d																						
Tulse Hill	d			21 17						21 47						22 17					22 47		
London Bridge ⊖	a			21 30						22 00						22 30					23 00		
Balham ⊖	d	21 09			21 21	21 14		21 39			21 51	21 44		22 09			22 21	22 14		22 39		22 51	22 44
Clapham Junction	a	21 14	21 00		21 26	21 18	21 15	21 44	21 30		21 56	21 48	21 45	22 14	22 00		22 26	22 18	22 15	22 44		22 56	22 48
London Waterloo ⊖	a		21 10				21 25		21 40				21 55		22 10				22 25				
London Victoria ⊖	a	21 23			21 34	21 26		21 53			22 04	21 56		22 23			22 34	22 26		22 53		23 04	22 56

Horsham, Dorking, Guildford, Epsom and Sutton - London

		SW	SN	SN	SN	SW	SN	SN	SN	SW	SN	SN	SN
Horsham	d												
Warnham	d												
Ockley	d												
Holmwood	d												
Dorking	a												
	d				22 30	22 35			23 00			23 30	
Boxhill & Westhumble	d								23 02				
Guildford	d	21 46								22 46			
Effingham Junction	d	22 03								23 03			
Bookham	d	22 06								23 06			
Leatherhead	d	22 11			22 36	22 41			23 07	23 11		23 36	
Ashtead	d	22 14			22 40	22 44			23 11	23 14		23 39	
Epsom	a	22 19			22 44	22 49			23 15	23 19		23 45	
	d	22 20	22 25		22 45	22 50			23 16	23 20	23 25		
Ewell East	d		22 29		22 49				23 20		23 29		
Cheam	d		22 32		22 52				23 23		23 32		
Epsom Downs	d						22 54						23 43
Banstead	d						22 57						23 46
Belmont	d						23 00						23 49
Sutton (Surrey)	a		22 35		22 55		23 03		23 26		23 39		23 52
	d		22 36	22 52	22 55		23 06	23 20	23 27		23 40		23 53
Carshalton	d				22 58								
Hackbridge	d				23 01								
Mitcham Junction	d				23 04								
Mitcham Eastfields	d				23 07								
Carshalton Beeches	d		22 39	22 55			23 09	23 23	23 30		23 43		23 56
Wallington	d		22 41	22 57			23 11	23 25	23 32		23 45		23 58
Waddon	d		22 44	23 00			23 14	23 28	23 35		23 48		00 01
West Croydon	d		22 48	23 04			23 18	23a31	23a41		23a57		00a04
Norwood Junction	d		22 53				23 23						
New Cross Gate ⊖	d												
Tulse Hill	d												
London Bridge ⊖	a												
Balham ⊖	d		23 09	23 21	23 14		23 40						
Clapham Junction	a	22 45	23 14	23 26	23 18	23 15	23 45			23 48			
London Waterloo ⊖	a	22 55				23 25				23 58			
London Victoria ⊖	a		23 23	23 34	23 26		23 54						

Saturdays
from 02 October

		SN	SW	SW	SW	SN	SN	SN	SW	SN	FC	FC	SN	SN	SN	SW	SN	FC	FC	SN	SN	SN	SW
Horsham	d																						
Warnham	d																						
Ockley	d																						
Holmwood	d																						
Dorking	a																						
	d						06 27							06 57							07 26		
Boxhill & Westhumble	d													06 59							07 28		
Guildford	d								06 28							06 58							07 28
Effingham Junction	d								06 46							07 16							07 46
Bookham	d								06 49							07 19							07 49
Leatherhead	d						06 33		06 54					07 04		07 24					07 33		07 54
Ashtead	d						06 37		06 58					07 08		07 28					07 37		07 58
Epsom	a						06 41		07 02					07 12		07 32					07 41		08 02
	d		05 35	06 05	06 35		06 42	06 49	07 05				07 04	07 13	07 19	07 35					07 42	07 49	08 05
Ewell East	d						06 46	06 53					07 08		07 23						07 46	07 53	
Cheam	d						06 49	06 56					07 11	07 18	07 26						07 49	07 56	
Epsom Downs	d	23p43																		07 34			
Banstead	d	23p46																		07 37			
Belmont	d	23p49																		07 40			
Sutton (Surrey)	a	23p52					06 52	06 59					07 14	07 22	07 29					07 43	07 52	07 59	
	d	23p53				06 44	06 53	07 00		07 03	07 07	07 08	07 14	07 23	07 30		07 33	07 37	07 38	07 44	07 53	08 00	
Carshalton	d							07 03				07 11			07 33				07 41			08 03	
Hackbridge	d							07 05				07 13			07 35				07 43			08 05	
Mitcham Junction	d							07 09				07 16			07 39				07 46			08 09	
Mitcham Eastfields	d							07 12				07 19			07 42				07 49			08 12	
Carshalton Beeches	d	23p56				06 47				07 06			07 17				07 36			07 47			
Wallington	d	23p58				06 50				07 08			07 20				07 38			07 50			
Waddon	d	00 01				06 53				07 11			07 23				07 41			07 53			
West Croydon	d	00a04				06 58				07 15			07 28				07 45			07 58			
Norwood Junction	d									07 20							07 50						
New Cross Gate ⊖	d									07 34							08 04						
Tulse Hill	d										07 47	07 27						08 17	07 57				
London Bridge ⊖	a									07 41	08 00						08 11	08 30					
Balham ⊖	d					07 14		07 18					07 44		07 48					08 14		08 18	
Clapham Junction	a		06 01	06 30	07 00	07 19	07 10	07 22	07 30				07 49	07 40	07 52	08 00				08 19	08 10	08 22	08 30
London Waterloo ⊖	a		06 11	06 40	07 10				07 40							08 10							08 40
London Victoria ⊖	a					07 28	07 18	07 30					07 58	07 50	08 00					08 28	08 18	08 30	

Table 182

Saturdays from 02 October

Horsham, Dorking, Guildford, Epsom and Sutton - London

		SN	FC	FC	SN	SN		SW	SN	SN	SW	SN	FC	FC	SN	SN		SW	SN	SN	SW	SN	FC	FC	SN
Horsham 4	d															08 04									
Warnham	d															08 08									
Ockley	d															08 15									
Holmwood	d															08 19									
Dorking 4	a															08 25									
	d					07 58		08 05								08 26		08 35							
Boxhill & Westhumble	d															08 28									
Guildford	d										07 58										08 28				
Effingham Junction 6	d										08 16										08 46				
Bookham	d										08 19										08 49				
Leatherhead	d					08 04		08 11			08 24					08 33		08 41			08 54				
Ashtead	d					08 07		08 14			08 28					08 37		08 44			08 58				
Epsom 3	a					08 12		08 19			08 32					08 41		08 49			09 02				
	d				08 04	08 13		08 20		08 19	08 35					08 42		08 50		08 49	09 05				09 04
Ewell East	d				08 08					08 23						08 46				08 53					09 08
Cheam	d				08 11	08 18				08 26						08 49				08 56					09 11
Epsom Downs	d														08 34										
Banstead	d														08 37										
Belmont	d														08 40										
Sutton (Surrey) 4	a				08 14	08 21				08 29					08 43	08 52				08 59					09 14
	d	08 03	08 07	08 08	08 14	08 23			08 22	08 30		08 33	08 37	08 38	08 44	08 53			08 52	09 00		09 03	09 07	09 08	09 14
Carshalton	d			08 11						08 33				08 41						09 03				09 11	
Hackbridge	d			08 13						08 35				08 43						09 05				09 13	
Mitcham Junction	d			08 16						08 39				08 46						09 09				09 16	
Mitcham Eastfields	d			08 19						08 42				08 49						09 12				09 19	
Carshalton Beeches	d	08 06			08 17				08 25			08 36			08 47				08 55			09 06			09 17
Wallington	d	08 08			08 20				08 27			08 38			08 50				08 57			09 08			09 20
Waddon	d	08 11			08 23				08 30			08 41			08 53				09 00			09 11			09 23
West Croydon 4	d	08 15			08 28				08 34			08 45			08 58				09 04			09 15			09 28
Norwood Junction 2	d	08 22										08 52										09 22			
New Cross Gate 4 ⊖	d																								
Tulse Hill 3	d		08 47	08 27									09 17	08 57									09 47	09 27	
London Bridge 4 ⊖	a		09 00										09 30										10 00		
Balham 4 ⊖	d	08 39			08 44				08 51	08 48		09 09			09 14				09 21	09 18		09 39			09 44
Clapham Junction 10	a	08 44			08 49	08 40		08 45	08 56	08 52	09 00	09 14			09 19	09 10		09 15	09 26	09 22	09 30	09 44			09 49
London Waterloo 15 ⊖	a							08 55			09 10							09 25			09 40				
London Victoria 15 ⊖	a	08 53			08 58	08 48			09 04	09 00		09 23			09 28	09 18			09 34	09 30		09 53			09 58

		SN		SW	SN	SN	SW	SN	FC	FC	SN	SN		SW	SN	SN	SW	SN	FC	FC	SN	SN		SW	SN
Horsham 4	d											09 04													
Warnham	d											09 08													
Ockley	d											09 15													
Holmwood	d											09 19													
Dorking 4	a											09 25													
	d	08 58		09 05								09 26		09 35								09 58		10 05	
Boxhill & Westhumble	d											09 28													
Guildford	d						08 58										09 28								
Effingham Junction 6	d						09 16										09 46								
Bookham	d						09 19										09 49								
Leatherhead	d	09 04		09 11			09 24					09 33		09 41			09 54					10 04		10 11	
Ashtead	d	09 07		09 14			09 28					09 37		09 44			09 58					10 07		10 14	
Epsom 3	a	09 12		09 19			09 32					09 41		09 49			10 02					10 12		10 19	
	d	09 13		09 20		09 19	09 35					09 42		09 50		09 49	10 05				10 04	10 12		10 20	
Ewell East	d					09 23						09 46				09 53					10 08				
Cheam	d	09 18				09 26						09 49				09 56					10 11	10 18			
Epsom Downs	d										09 34														
Banstead	d										09 37														
Belmont	d										09 40														
Sutton (Surrey) 4	a	09 21				09 29					09 43	09 52				09 59					10 14	10 22			
	d	09 23			09 22	09 30		09 33	09 37	09 38	09 44	09 53			09 52	10 00		10 03	10 07	10 08	10 14	10 23			10 22
Carshalton	d					09 33				09 41						10 03				10 11					
Hackbridge	d					09 35				09 43						10 05				10 13					
Mitcham Junction	d					09 39				09 46						10 09				10 16					
Mitcham Eastfields	d					09 42				09 49						10 12				10 19					
Carshalton Beeches	d				09 25			09 36			09 47				09 55			10 06			10 17				10 25
Wallington	d				09 27			09 38			09 50				09 57			10 08			10 20				10 27
Waddon	d				09 30			09 41			09 53				10 00			10 11			10 23				10 30
West Croydon 4	d				09 34			09 45			09 58				10 04			10 15			10 28				10 34
Norwood Junction 2	d							09 52										10 22							
New Cross Gate 4 ⊖	d																								
Tulse Hill 3	d								10 17	09 57									10 47	10 27					
London Bridge 4 ⊖	a								10 30										11 00						
Balham 4 ⊖	d				09 51	09 48		10 09			10 14				10 21	10 18		10 39			10 44				10 51
Clapham Junction 10	a	09 40		09 45	09 56	09 52	10 00	10 14			10 19	10 10		10 15	10 26	10 22	10 30	10 44			10 49	10 40		10 45	10 56
London Waterloo 15 ⊖	a			09 55			10 10							10 25			10 40							10 55	
London Victoria 15 ⊖	a	09 48			10 04	10 00		10 23			10 28	10 18			10 34	10 30		10 53			10 58	10 48			11 04

Table 182

Saturdays from 02 October

Horsham, Dorking, Guildford, Epsom and Sutton - London

		SN	SW	SN	FC	FC	SN	SN		SW	SN	SN	SW	SN	FC	FC	SN	SN		SW	SN	SN	SW	SN	FC
Horsham 4	d							10 04																	
Warnham	d							10 08																	
Ockley	d							10 15																	
Holmwood	d							10 19																	
Dorking 4	a							10 25																	
	d							10 26		10 35								10 58		11 05					
Boxhill & Westhumble	d							10 28																	
Guildford	d		09 58										10 28										10 58		
Effingham Junction 6	d		10 16										10 46										11 16		
Bookham	d		10 19										10 49										11 19		
Leatherhead	d		10 24					10 33		10 41			10 54					11 04		11 11			11 24		
Ashtead	d		10 28					10 37		10 44			10 58					11 07		11 14			11 28		
Epsom 3	a		10 32					10 41		10 49			11 02					11 12		11 19			11 32		
	d	10 19	10 35					10 42		10 50		10 49	11 05				11 04	11 13		11 20		11 19	11 35		
Ewell East	d	10 23						10 46				10 53					11 08					11 23			
Cheam	d	10 26						10 49				10 56					11 11	11 18				11 26			
Epsom Downs	d						10 34																		
Banstead	d						10 37																		
Belmont	d						10 40																		
Sutton (Surrey) 4	a	10 29					10 43	10 52				10 59					11 14	11 21				11 29			
	d	10 30		10 33	10 37	10 38	10 44	10 53			10 52	11 00		11 03	11 07	11 08	11 14	11 23			11 22	11 30		11 33	11 37
Carshalton	d	10 33				10 41						11 03				11 11						11 33			
Hackbridge	d	10 35				10 43						11 05				11 13						11 35			
Mitcham Junction	d	10 39				10 46						11 09				11 16						11 39			
Mitcham Eastfields	d	10 42				10 49						11 12				11 19						11 42			
Carshalton Beeches	d			10 36			10 47				10 55			11 06			11 17				11 25			11 36	
Wallington	d			10 38			10 50				10 57			11 08			11 20				11 27			11 38	
Waddon	d			10 41			10 53				11 00			11 11			11 23				11 30			11 41	
West Croydon 4	d			10 45			10 58				11 04			11 15			11 28				11 34			11 45	
Norwood Junction 2	d			10 52										11 22										11 52	
New Cross Gate 4 ⊖	d																								
Tulse Hill 3	d				11 17	10 57									11 47	11 27									12 17
London Bridge 4 ⊖	a				11 30										12 00										12 30
Balham 4 ⊖	d	10 48		11 09			11 14				11 21	11 18		11 39			11 44				11 51	11 48		12 09	
Clapham Junction 10	a	10 52	11 00	11 14			11 19	11 10		11 15	11 26	11 22	11 30	11 44			11 49	11 40		11 45	11 56	11 52	12 00	12 14	
London Waterloo 15 ⊖	a		11 10							11 25			11 40							11 55			12 10		
London Victoria 15 ⊖	a	11 00		11 23			11 28	11 18			11 34	11 30		11 53			11 58	11 48			12 04	12 00		12 23	

		FC	SN	SN		SW	SN	SN	SW	SN	FC	FC	SN	SN		SW	SN	SN	SW	SN	FC	FC	SN	SN	
Horsham 4	d			11 04																				12 04	
Warnham	d			11 08																				12 08	
Ockley	d			11 15																				12 15	
Holmwood	d			11 19																				12 19	
Dorking 4	a			11 25																				12 25	
	d			11 26		11 35								11 58		12 05								12 26	
Boxhill & Westhumble	d			11 28																				12 28	
Guildford	d								11 28										11 58						
Effingham Junction 6	d								11 46										12 16						
Bookham	d								11 49										12 19						
Leatherhead	d			11 33		11 41			11 54					12 04		12 11			12 24					12 33	
Ashtead	d			11 37		11 44			11 58					12 07		12 14			12 28					12 37	
Epsom 3	a			11 41		11 49			12 02					12 12		12 19			12 32					12 41	
	d			11 42		11 50		11 49	12 05				12 04	12 13		12 20		12 19	12 35					12 42	
Ewell East	d			11 46				11 53					12 08					12 23						12 46	
Cheam	d			11 49				11 56					12 11	12 18				12 26						12 49	
Epsom Downs	d		11 34																				12 34		
Banstead	d		11 37																				12 37		
Belmont	d		11 40																				12 40		
Sutton (Surrey) 4	a		11 43	11 52				11 59					12 14	12 21				12 29					12 43	12 52	
	d	11 38	11 44	11 53			11 52	12 00		12 03	12 07	12 08	12 14	12 23			12 22	12 30		12 33	12 37	12 38	12 44	12 53	
Carshalton	d	11 41						12 03				12 11						12 33				12 41			
Hackbridge	d	11 43						12 05				12 13						12 35				12 43			
Mitcham Junction	d	11 46						12 09				12 16						12 39				12 46			
Mitcham Eastfields	d	11 49						12 12				12 19						12 42				12 49			
Carshalton Beeches	d		11 47				11 55			12 06			12 17				12 25			12 36			12 47		
Wallington	d		11 50				11 57			12 08			12 20				12 27			12 38			12 50		
Waddon	d		11 53				12 00			12 11			12 23				12 30			12 41			12 53		
West Croydon 4	d		11 58				12 04			12 15			12 28				12 34			12 45			12 58		
Norwood Junction 2	d									12 22										12 52					
New Cross Gate 4 ⊖	d																								
Tulse Hill 3	d	11 57									12 47	12 27									13 17	12 57			
London Bridge 4 ⊖	a										13 00										13 30				
Balham 4 ⊖	d		12 14				12 21	12 18		12 39			12 44				12 51	12 48		13 09			13 14		
Clapham Junction 10	a		12 19	12 10		12 15	12 26	12 22	12 30	12 44			12 49	12 40		12 45	12 56	12 52	13 00	13 14			13 19	13 10	
London Waterloo 15 ⊖	a					12 25			12 40							12 55			13 10						
London Victoria 15 ⊖	a		12 28	12 18			12 34	12 30		12 53			12 58	12 48			13 04	13 00		13 23			13 28	13 18	

Horsham, Dorking, Guildford, Epsom and Sutton - London

		SW	SN	SN	SW	SN	FC	FC	SN	SN		SW	SN	SN	SW	SN	FC	FC	SN	SN		SW	SN	SN	SW
Horsham	d																			13 04					
Warnham	d																			13 08					
Ockley	d																			13 15					
Holmwood	d																			13 19					
Dorking	a																			13 25					
	d	12 35								12 58		13 05								13 26		13 35			
Boxhill & Westhumble	d																			13 28					
Guildford	d				12 28										12 58										13 28
Effingham Junction	d				12 46										13 16										13 46
Bookham	d				12 49										13 19										13 49
Leatherhead	d	12 41			12 54					13 04		13 11			13 24					13 33		13 41			13 54
Ashtead	d	12 44			12 58					13 07		13 14			13 28					13 37		13 44			13 58
Epsom	a	12 49			13 02					13 12		13 19			13 32					13 41		13 49			14 02
	d	12 50		12 49	13 05				13 04	13 13		13 20		13 19	13 35					13 42		13 50		13 49	14 05
Ewell East	d			12 53					13 08					13 23						13 46				13 53	
Cheam	d			12 56					13 11	13 18				13 26						13 49				13 56	
Epsom Downs	d																		13 34						
Banstead	d																		13 37						
Belmont	d																		13 40						
Sutton (Surrey)	a			12 59					13 14	13 21				13 29					13 43	13 52				13 59	
	d		12 52	13 00		13 03	13 07	13 08	13 14	13 23			13 22	13 30		13 33	13 37	13 38	13 44	13 53			13 52	14 00	
Carshalton	d			13 03				13 11						13 33				13 41						14 03	
Hackbridge	d			13 05				13 13						13 35				13 43						14 05	
Mitcham Junction	d			13 09				13 16						13 39				13 46						14 09	
Mitcham Eastfields	d			13 12				13 19						13 42				13 49						14 12	
Carshalton Beeches	d		12 55			13 06			13 17				13 25			13 36			13 47				13 55		
Wallington	d		12 57			13 08			13 20				13 27			13 38			13 50				13 57		
Waddon	d		13 00			13 11			13 23				13 30			13 41			13 53				14 00		
West Croydon	d		13 04			13 15			13 28				13 34			13 45			13 58				14 04		
Norwood Junction	d					13 22										13 52									
New Cross Gate ⊖	d																								
Tulse Hill	d						13 47	13 27									14 17	13 57							
London Bridge ⊖	a						14 00										14 30								
Balham ⊖	d		13 21	13 18		13 39			13 44				13 51	13 48		14 09			14 14				14 21	14 18	
Clapham Junction	a	13 15	13 26	13 22	13 30	13 44			13 49	13 40		13 45	13 56	13 52	14 00	14 14			14 19	14 10		14 15	14 26	14 22	14 30
London Waterloo ⊖	a	13 25			13 40							13 55			14 10							14 25			14 40
London Victoria ⊖	a		13 34	13 30		13 53			13 58	13 48			14 04	14 00		14 23			14 28	14 18			14 34	14 30	

		SN	FC	FC	SN	SN		SW	SN	SN	SW	SN	FC	FC	SN	SN		SW	SN	SN	SW	SN	FC	FC	SN
Horsham	d															14 04									
Warnham	d															14 08									
Ockley	d															14 15									
Holmwood	d															14 19									
Dorking	a															14 25									
	d					13 58		14 05								14 26		14 35							
Boxhill & Westhumble	d															14 28									
Guildford	d										13 58										14 28				
Effingham Junction	d										14 16										14 46				
Bookham	d										14 19										14 49				
Leatherhead	d					14 04		14 11			14 24					14 33		14 41			14 54				
Ashtead	d					14 07		14 14			14 28					14 37		14 44			14 58				
Epsom	a					14 12		14 19			14 32					14 41		14 49			15 02				
	d				14 04	14 13		14 20		14 19	14 35					14 42		14 50		14 49	15 05				15 04
Ewell East	d				14 08					14 23						14 46				14 53					15 08
Cheam	d				14 11	14 18				14 26						14 49				14 56					15 11
Epsom Downs	d														14 34										
Banstead	d														14 37										
Belmont	d														14 40										
Sutton (Surrey)	a				14 14	14 21				14 29					14 43	14 52				14 59					15 14
	d	14 03	14 07	14 08	14 14	14 23			14 22	14 30		14 33	14 37	14 38	14 44	14 53			14 52	15 00		15 03	15 07	15 08	15 14
Carshalton	d			14 11						14 33				14 41						15 03				15 11	
Hackbridge	d			14 13						14 35				14 43						15 05				15 13	
Mitcham Junction	d			14 16						14 39				14 46						15 09				15 16	
Mitcham Eastfields	d			14 19						14 42				14 49						15 12				15 19	
Carshalton Beeches	d	14 06			14 17				14 25			14 36			14 47				14 55			15 06			15 17
Wallington	d	14 08			14 20				14 27			14 38			14 50				14 57			15 08			15 20
Waddon	d	14 11			14 23				14 30			14 41			14 53				15 00			15 11			15 23
West Croydon	d	14 15			14 28				14 34			14 45			14 58				15 04			15 15			15 28
Norwood Junction	d	14 22										14 52										15 22			
New Cross Gate ⊖	d																								
Tulse Hill	d		14 47	14 27									15 17	14 57									15 47	15 27	
London Bridge ⊖	a		15 00										15 30										16 00		
Balham ⊖	d	14 39			14 44				14 51	14 48		15 09			15 14				15 21	15 18		15 39			15 44
Clapham Junction	a	14 44			14 49	14 40		14 45	14 56	14 52	15 00	15 14			15 19	15 10		15 15	15 26	15 22	15 30	15 44			15 49
London Waterloo ⊖	a							14 55			15 10							15 25			15 40				
London Victoria ⊖	a	14 53			14 58	14 48			15 04	15 00		15 23			15 28	15 18			15 34	15 30		15 53			15 58

Table 182

Saturdays
from 02 October

Horsham, Dorking, Guildford, Epsom and Sutton - London

		SN		SW	SN	SN	SW	SN	FC	FC	SN	SN		SW	SN	SN	SW	SN	FC	FC	SN	SN		SW	SN
Horsham	d											15 04													
Warnham	d											15 08													
Ockley	d											15 15													
Holmwood	d											15 19													
Dorking	a											15 25													
	d	14 58		15 05								15 26		15 35								15 58		16 05	
Boxhill & Westhumble	d											15 28													
Guildford	d						14 58										15 28								
Effingham Junction	d						15 16										15 46								
Bookham	d						15 19										15 49								
Leatherhead	d	15 04		15 11			15 24					15 33		15 41			15 54					16 04		16 11	
Ashtead	d	15 07		15 14			15 28					15 37		15 44			15 58					16 07		16 14	
Epsom	a	15 12		15 19			15 32					15 41		15 49			16 02					16 12		16 19	
	d	15 13		15 20		15 19	15 35					15 42		15 50		15 49	16 05				16 04	16 13		16 20	
Ewell East	d					15 23						15 46				15 53					16 08				
Cheam	d	15 18				15 26						15 49				15 56					16 11	16 18			
Epsom Downs	d										15 34														
Banstead	d										15 37														
Belmont	d										15 40														
Sutton (Surrey)	a	15 21				15 29					15 43	15 52				15 59					16 14	16 21			
	d	15 23			15 22	15 30		15 33	15 37	15 38	15 44	15 53			15 52	16 00		16 03	16 07	16 08	16 14	16 23			16 22
Carshalton	d					15 33				15 41						16 03				16 11					
Hackbridge	d					15 35				15 43						16 05				16 13					
Mitcham Junction	d					15 39				15 46						16 09				16 16					
Mitcham Eastfields	d					15 42				15 49						16 12				16 19					
Carshalton Beeches	d				15 25			15 36			15 47				15 55			16 06			16 17				16 25
Wallington	d				15 27			15 38			15 50				15 57			16 08			16 20				16 27
Waddon	d				15 30			15 41			15 53				16 00			16 11			16 23				16 30
West Croydon	d				15 34			15 45			15 58				16 04			16 15			16 28				16 34
Norwood Junction	d							15 52										16 22							
New Cross Gate ⊖	d																								
Tulse Hill	d								16 17	15 57									16 47	16 27					
London Bridge ⊖	a								16 30										17 00						
Balham ⊖	d				15 51	15 48		16 09			16 14				16 21	16 18		16 39			16 44				16 51
Clapham Junction	a	15 40		15 45	15 56	15 52	16 00	16 14			16 19	16 10		16 15	16 26	16 22	16 30	16 44			16 49	16 40		16 45	16 56
London Waterloo ⊖	a			15 55			16 10							16 25			16 40							16 55	
London Victoria ⊖	a	15 48			16 04	16 00		16 23			16 28	16 18			16 34	16 30		16 53			16 58	16 48			17 04

		SN	SW	SN	FC	FC	SN	SN		SW	SN	SN	SW	SN	FC	FC	SN	SN		SW	SN	SN	SW	SN	FC
Horsham	d							16 04																	
Warnham	d							16 08																	
Ockley	d							16 15																	
Holmwood	d							16 19																	
Dorking	a							16 25																	
	d							16 26		16 35								16 58		17 05					
Boxhill & Westhumble	d							16 28																	
Guildford	d		15 58										16 28										16 58		
Effingham Junction	d		16 16										16 46										17 16		
Bookham	d		16 19										16 49										17 19		
Leatherhead	d		16 24					16 33		16 41			16 54					17 04		17 11			17 24		
Ashtead	d		16 28					16 37		16 44			16 58					17 07		17 14			17 28		
Epsom	a		16 32					16 41		16 49			17 02					17 12		17 19			17 32		
	d	16 19	16 35					16 42		16 50		16 49	17 05				17 04	17 13		17 20		17 19	17 35		
Ewell East	d	16 23						16 46				16 53					17 08					17 23			
Cheam	d	16 26						16 49				16 56					17 11	17 18				17 26			
Epsom Downs	d						16 34																		
Banstead	d						16 37																		
Belmont	d						16 40																		
Sutton (Surrey)	a	16 29					16 43	16 52				16 59					17 14	17 21				17 29			
	d	16 30		16 33	16 37	16 38	16 44	16 53			16 52	17 00		17 03	17 07	17 08	17 14	17 23			17 22	17 30		17 33	17 37
Carshalton	d	16 33				16 41						17 03				17 11						17 33			
Hackbridge	d	16 35				16 43						17 05				17 13						17 35			
Mitcham Junction	d	16 39				16 46						17 09				17 16						17 39			
Mitcham Eastfields	d	16 42				16 49						17 12				17 19						17 42			
Carshalton Beeches	d			16 36			16 47				16 55			17 06			17 17				17 25			17 36	
Wallington	d			16 38			16 50				16 57			17 08			17 20				17 27			17 38	
Waddon	d			16 41			16 53				17 00			17 11			17 23				17 30			17 41	
West Croydon	d			16 45			16 58				17 04			17 15			17 28				17 34			17 45	
Norwood Junction	d			16 52										17 22										17 52	
New Cross Gate ⊖	d																								
Tulse Hill	d				17 17	16 57									17 47	17 27									18 17
London Bridge ⊖	a				17 30										18 00										18 30
Balham ⊖	d	16 48		17 09			17 14				17 21	17 18		17 39			17 44				17 51	17 48		18 09	
Clapham Junction	a	16 52	17 00	17 14			17 19	17 10		17 15	17 26	17 22	17 30	17 44			17 49	17 41		17 45	17 56	17 52	18 00	18 14	
London Waterloo ⊖	a		17 10							17 25			17 40							17 55			18 10		
London Victoria ⊖	a	17 00		17 23			17 28	17 18			17 34	17 30		17 53			17 58	17 49			18 04	18 00		18 23	

Table 182

Horsham, Dorking, Guildford, Epsom and Sutton - London

		FC	SN	SN		SW	SN	SN	SW	SN	FC	FC	SN	SN		SW	SN	SN	SW	SN	FC	FC	SN	SN
Horsham 4	d			17 04																				18 04
Warnham	d			17 08																				18 08
Ockley	d			17 15																				18 15
Holmwood	d			17 19																				18 19
Dorking 4	a			17 25																				18 25
	d			17 26		17 35								17 58		18 05								18 26
Boxhill & Westhumble	d			17 28																				18 28
Guildford	d								17 28										17 58					
Effingham Junction 6	d								17 46										18 16					
Bookham	d								17 49										18 19					
Leatherhead	d			17 33		17 41			17 54					18 04		18 11			18 24					18 33
Ashtead	d			17 37		17 44			17 58					18 07		18 14			18 28					18 37
Epsom 3	a			17 41		17 49			18 02					18 12		18 19			18 32					18 41
	d			17 42		17 50		17 49	18 05				18 04	18 13		18 20		18 19	18 35					18 42
Ewell East	d			17 46				17 53					18 08					18 23						18 46
Cheam	d			17 49				17 56					18 11	18 18				18 26						18 49
Epsom Downs	d		17 34																				18 34	
Banstead	d		17 37																				18 37	
Belmont	d		17 40																				18 40	
Sutton (Surrey) 4	a		17 43	17 52				17 59					18 14	18 21				18 29					18 43	18 52
	d	17 38	17 44	17 53			17 52	18 00		18 03	18 07	18 08	18 14	18 23			18 22	18 30		18 33	18 37	18 38	18 44	18 53
Carshalton	d	17 41						18 03				18 11						18 33				18 41		
Hackbridge	d	17 43						18 05				18 13						18 35				18 43		
Mitcham Junction	d	17 46						18 09				18 16						18 39				18 46		
Mitcham Eastfields	d	17 49						18 12				18 19						18 42				18 49		
Carshalton Beeches	d		17 47				17 55			18 06			18 17				18 25			18 36			18 47	
Wallington	d		17 50				17 57			18 08			18 20				18 27			18 38			18 50	
Waddon	d		17 53				18 00			18 11			18 23				18 30			18 41			18 53	
West Croydon 4	d		17 58				18 04			18 15			18 28				18 34			18 45			18 58	
Norwood Junction 2	d									18 22										18 52				
New Cross Gate 4 ⊖	d																							
Tulse Hill 3	d	17 57									18 47	18 27									19 17	18 57		
London Bridge 4 ⊖	a										19 00										19 30			
Balham 4 ⊖	d		18 14				18 21	18 18		18 39			18 44				18 51	18 48		19 09			19 14	
Clapham Junction 10	a		18 19	18 10		18 15	18 26	18 22	18 30	18 44			18 49	18 40		18 45	18 56	18 52	19 00	19 14			19 19	19 10
London Waterloo 15 ⊖	a					18 25			18 40							18 55			19 10					
London Victoria 15 ⊖	a		18 28	18 18			18 34	18 30		18 53			18 58	18 48			19 04	19 00		19 23			19 28	19 18

		SW	SN	SN	SW	FC	FC	SN	SN	SN		SW	SN	SW	FC	SN	SN	SW	SW	SN		FC	SN	SN	SW
Horsham 4	d																								
Warnham	d																								
Ockley	d																								
Holmwood	d																								
Dorking 4	a																								
	d	18 35								19 00		19 05					19 28	19 35						19 59	20 05
Boxhill & Westhumble	d									19 02														20 01	
Guildford	d				18 28									18 58					19 28						
Effingham Junction 6	d				18 46									19 16					19 46						
Bookham	d				18 49									19 19					19 49						
Leatherhead	d	18 41			18 54					19 07		19 11		19 24			19 34	19 41	19 54					20 06	20 11
Ashtead	d	18 44			18 58					19 11		19 14		19 28			19 37	19 44	19 58					20 10	20 14
Epsom 3	a	18 49			19 02					19 15		19 19		19 32			19 42	19 49	20 02					20 14	20 19
	d	18 50	18 49	18 55	19 05					19 19		19 20	19 25	19 35			19 42	19 50	20 05					20 15	20 20
Ewell East	d		18 53							19 23			19 29				19 46							20 19	
Cheam	d		18 56							19 26			19 32				19 49							20 22	
Epsom Downs	d								19 15											19 54					
Banstead	d								19 18											19 57					
Belmont	d								19 21											20 00					
Sutton (Surrey) 4	a		18 59	19 02					19 24	19 29			19 35				19 52			20 03				20 25	
	d		19 00	19 03		19 07	19 08	19 14	19 25	19 30			19 36		19 37	19 52	19 53			20 06		20 08	20 22	20 25	
Carshalton	d		19 03				19 11			19 33							19 56							20 28	
Hackbridge	d		19 05				19 13			19 35							19 58							20 31	
Mitcham Junction	d		19 09				19 16			19 39							20 02							20 34	
Mitcham Eastfields	d		19 12				19 19			19 42							20 05							20 37	
Carshalton Beeches	d			19 06				19 17	19 28				19 39			19 55				20 09			20 25		
Wallington	d			19 08				19 20	19 30				19 41			19 57				20 11			20 27		
Waddon	d			19 11				19 23	19 33				19 44			20 00				20 14			20 30		
West Croydon 4	d			19 15				19 28	19a41				19 48			20 04				20 18			20 34		
Norwood Junction 2	d			19 22									19 53							20 23					
New Cross Gate 4 ⊖	d																								
Tulse Hill 3	d					19 47	19 27								20 17							20 47			
London Bridge 4 ⊖	a					20 00									20 30							21 00			
Balham 4 ⊖	d		19 18	19 39				19 44		19 48			20 09			20 21	20 12			20 39			20 51	20 44	
Clapham Junction 10	a	19 15	19 22	19 44	19 30			19 49		19 52		19 45	20 14	20 00		20 26	20 17	20 15	20 30	20 44			20 56	20 48	v
London Waterloo 15 ⊖	a	19 25			19 40							19 55		20 10				20 25	20 40						20 55
London Victoria 15 ⊖	a		19 30	19 53				19 58		20 00			20 23			20 34	20 25			20 53			21 04	20 56	

Table 182

Horsham, Dorking, Guildford, Epsom and Sutton - London

		SN	SW	FC	SN	SN		SW	SN	SW	FC	SN	SN	SW	SN	SW		FC	SN	SN	SW	SN	FC	SN	SN
Horsham 4	d																								
Warnham	d																								
Ockley	d																								
Holmwood	d																								
Dorking 4	a																								
	d					20 30		20 35					20 59							21 30	21 35				21 59
Boxhill & Westhumble	d												21 01												22 01
Guildford	d		19 58											20 46											
Effingham Junction 6	d		20 16											21 03											
Bookham	d		20 19											21 06											
Leatherhead	d		20 24			20 36		20 41					21 06	21 11						21 36	21 41				22 06
Ashtead	d		20 28			20 40		20 44					21 10	21 14						21 40	21 44				22 10
Epsom 3	a		20 32			20 44		20 49					21 14	21 19						21 44	21 49				22 14
	d	20 25	20 35			20 45		20 50		21 05			21 15	21 20	21 25	21 35				21 45	21 50				22 15
Ewell East	d	20 29				20 49							21 19		21 29					21 49					22 19
Cheam	d	20 32				20 52							21 22		21 32					21 52					22 22
Epsom Downs	d								20 54													21 54			
Banstead	d								20 57													21 57			
Belmont	d								21 00													22 00			
Sutton (Surrey) 4	a	20 35				20 55			21 03				21 25		21 35					21 55		22 03			22 25
	d	20 36		20 37	20 52	20 55			21 06		21 07	21 22	21 25		21 36			21 37	21 52	21 55		22 06	22 07	22 22	22 25
Carshalton	d					20 58							21 28							21 58					22 28
Hackbridge	d					21 01							21 31							22 01					22 31
Mitcham Junction	d					21 04							21 34							22 04					22 34
Mitcham Eastfields	d					21 07							21 37							22 07					22 37
Carshalton Beeches	d	20 39			20 55				21 09			21 25			21 39				21 55			22 09		22 25	
Wallington	d	20 41			20 57				21 11			21 27			21 41				21 57			22 11		22 27	
Waddon	d	20 44			21 00				21 14			21 30			21 44				22 00			22 14		22 30	
West Croydon 4	d	20 48			21 04				21 18			21 34			21 48				22 04			22 18		22 34	
Norwood Junction 2	d	20 53							21 23						21 53							22 23			
New Cross Gate 4 ⊖	d																								
Tulse Hill 3	d			21 17							21 47							22 17					22 47		
London Bridge 4 ⊖	a			21 30							22 00							22 30					23 00		
Balham 4 ⊖	d	21 09			21 21	21 14			21 39			21 51	21 44		22 09				22 21	22 14		22 39		22 51	22 44
Clapham Junction 10	a	21 14	21 00		21 26	21 18		21 15	21 44	21 30		21 56	21 48	21 45	22 14	22 00			22 26	22 18	22 15	22 44		22 56	22 48
London Waterloo 15 ⊖	a		21 10					21 25		21 40				21 55		22 10					22 25				
London Victoria 15 ⊖	a	21 23			21 34	21 26			21 53			22 04	21 56		22 23				22 34	22 26		22 53		23 04	22 56

		SW		SN	SN	SN	SW	SN	SN	SN	SW	SN		SN	SN
Horsham 4	d														
Warnham	d														
Ockley	d														
Holmwood	d														
Dorking 4	a														
	d					22 30	22 35			23 00				23 30	
Boxhill & Westhumble	d									23 02					
Guildford	d	21 46									22 46				
Effingham Junction 6	d	22 03									23 03				
Bookham	d	22 06									23 06				
Leatherhead	d	22 11				22 36	22 41			23 07	23 11			23 36	
Ashtead	d	22 14				22 40	22 44			23 11	23 14			23 39	
Epsom 3	a	22 19				22 44	22 49			23 15	23 19			23 45	
	d	22 20		22 25		22 45	22 50			23 16	23 20	23 25			
Ewell East	d			22 29		22 49				23 20		23 29			
Cheam	d			22 32		22 52				23 23		23 32			
Epsom Downs	d							22 54							23 43
Banstead	d							22 57							23 46
Belmont	d							23 00							23 49
Sutton (Surrey) 4	a			22 35		22 55		23 03		23 26		23 39			23 52
	d			22 36	22 52	22 55		23 06	23 20	23 27		23 40			23 53
Carshalton	d					22 58									
Hackbridge	d					23 01									
Mitcham Junction	d					23 04									
Mitcham Eastfields	d					23 07									
Carshalton Beeches	d			22 39	22 55			23 09	23 23	23 30		23 43			23 56
Wallington	d			22 41	22 57			23 11	23 25	23 32		23 45			23 58
Waddon	d			22 44	23 00			23 14	23 28	23 35		23 48			00 01
West Croydon 4	d			22 48	23 04			23 18	23a31	23a41		23a57			00a04
Norwood Junction 2	d			22 53				23 23							
New Cross Gate 4 ⊖	d														
Tulse Hill 3	d														
London Bridge 4 ⊖	a														
Balham 4 ⊖	d			23 09	23 21	23 14		23 40							
Clapham Junction 10	a	22 45		23 14	23 26	23 18	23 15	23 45			23 48				
London Waterloo 15 ⊖	a	22 55					23 25				23 58				
London Victoria 15 ⊖	a			23 23	23 34	23 26		23 54							

Table 182

Sundays until 19 September

Horsham, Dorking, Guildford, Epsom and Sutton - London

		SN	SN	SN	SW	SN	SN	SW	SN	SN		SN	SW	SN	SN	SN	SW	SN	SN	SN		SW	SN	SN	SN
Horsham 4	d																								
Warnham	d																								
Ockley	d																								
Holmwood	d																								
Dorking 4	a																								
	d			06 54			07 24					07 54				08 24				08 54		09 08			09 24
Boxhill & Westhumble	d			06 56			07 26					07 56				08 26				08 56					09 26
Guildford	d																08 20								
Effingham Junction 6	d																08 36								
Bookham	d																08 39								
Leatherhead	d			07 01			07 31					08 01				08 31	08 45			09 01		09 15			09 31
Ashtead	d			07 05			07 35					08 05				08 35	08 48			09 05		09 18			09 35
Epsom 3	a			07 09			07 39					08 09				08 39	08 53			09 09		09 23			09 39
	d		06 45	07 10	07 24		07 40	07 54				08 10	08 24			08 40	08 54			09 10		09 24			09 40
Ewell East	d		06 49	07 14			07 44					08 14				08 44				09 14					09 44
Cheam	d		06 52	07 17			07 47					08 17				08 47				09 17					09 47
Epsom Downs	d	23p43																							
Banstead	d	23p46																							
Belmont	d	23p49																							
Sutton (Surrey) 4	a	23p52	06 55	07 20			07 50					08 20				08 50				09 20					09 50
	d	23p53	06 56	07 21		07 26	07 51		07 56	08 10		08 21		08 26	08 40	08 51		08 56	09 10	09 21			09 26	09 40	09 51
Carshalton	d			07 24			07 54					08 24				08 54				09 24					09 54
Hackbridge	d			07 26			07 56					08 26				08 56				09 26					09 56
Mitcham Junction	d			07 30			08 00					08 30				09 00				09 30					10 00
Mitcham Eastfields	d			07 33			08 03					08 33				09 03				09 33					10 03
Carshalton Beeches	d	23p56	06 59			07 29			07 59	08 13				08 29	08 43			08 59	09 13				09 29	09 43	
Wallington	d	23p58	07 01			07 31			08 01	08 15				08 31	08 45			09 01	09 15				09 31	09 45	
Waddon	d	00 01	07 04			07 34			08 04	08 18				08 34	08 48			09 04	09 18				09 34	09 48	
West Croydon 4	d	00a04	07 08			07 38			08 08	08 22				08 38	08 52			09 08	09 22				09 38	09 52	
Norwood Junction 2	d									08 29					08 59				09 29					09 59	
New Cross Gate 4 ⊖	d																								
Tulse Hill 3	d																								
London Bridge 4 ⊖	a																								
Balham 4 ⊖	d		07 25	07 39		07 55	08 09		08 25	08 47		08 39		08 55	09 17	09 09		09 25	09 47	09 39			09 55	10 17	10 09
Clapham Junction 10	a		07 30	07 44	07 49	08 00	08 14	08 19	08 30	08 51		08 44	08 49	09 00	09 21	09 14	09 19	09 30	09 51	09 44		09 49	10 00	10 21	10 14
London Waterloo 15 ⊖	a				08 04			08 34					09 04				09 34					10 04			
London Victoria 15 ⊖	a		07 39	07 53		08 09	08 23		08 39	08 59		08 53		09 09	09 29	09 23		09 39	09 59	09 53			10 09	10 29	10 23

		SW	SN	SN	FC	SN		SW	SN	SN	FC	SN	SW	SN	SN	FC		SN	SW	SN	SN	FC	SN	SW	SN
Horsham 4	d																								
Warnham	d																								
Ockley	d																								
Holmwood	d																								
Dorking 4	a																								
	d					09 54		10 08				10 24						10 54	11 08				11 24		
Boxhill & Westhumble	d					09 56						10 26						10 56					11 26		
Guildford	d	09 20											10 20											11 20	
Effingham Junction 6	d	09 36											10 36											11 36	
Bookham	d	09 39											10 39											11 39	
Leatherhead	d	09 45				10 01		10 15				10 31	10 45					11 01	11 15				11 31	11 45	
Ashtead	d	09 48				10 05		10 18				10 35	10 48					11 05	11 18				11 35	11 48	
Epsom 3	a	09 53				10 09		10 23				10 39	10 53					11 09	11 23				11 39	11 53	
	d	09 54				10 10		10 24				10 40	10 54					11 10	11 24				11 40	11 54	
Ewell East	d					10 14						10 44						11 14					11 44		
Cheam	d					10 17						10 47						11 17					11 47		
Epsom Downs	d																								
Banstead	d																								
Belmont	d																								
Sutton (Surrey) 4	a					10 20						10 50						11 20					11 50		
	d		09 56	10 10	10 16	10 21			10 26	10 40	10 46	10 51		10 56	11 10	11 16		11 21		11 26	11 40	11 46	11 51		11 56
Carshalton	d					10 24						10 54						11 24					11 54		
Hackbridge	d					10 26						10 56						11 26					11 56		
Mitcham Junction	d					10 30						11 00						11 30					12 00		
Mitcham Eastfields	d					10 33						11 03						11 33					12 03		
Carshalton Beeches	d		09 59	10 13					10 29	10 43				10 59	11 13					11 29	11 43				11 59
Wallington	d		10 01	10 15					10 31	10 45				11 01	11 15					11 31	11 45				12 01
Waddon	d		10 04	10 18					10 34	10 48				11 04	11 18					11 34	11 48				12 04
West Croydon 4	d		10 08	10 22					10 38	10 52				11 08	11 22					11 38	11 52				12 08
Norwood Junction 2	d			10 29						10 59					11 29						11 59				
New Cross Gate 4 ⊖	d																								
Tulse Hill 3	d				10 47						11 17					11 47						12 17			
London Bridge 4 ⊖	a				10 59						11 29					11 59						12 29			
Balham 4 ⊖	d		10 25	10 47		10 39			10 55	11 17		11 09		11 25	11 47			11 39		11 55	12 17		12 09		12 25
Clapham Junction 10	a	10 19	10 30	10 51		10 44		10 49	11 00	11 21		11 14	11 19	11 30	11 51			11 44	11 49	12 00	12 21		12 14	12 19	12 30
London Waterloo 15 ⊖	a	10 34						11 03					11 34						12 04					12 34	
London Victoria 15 ⊖	a		10 39	10 59		10 53			11 09	11 29		11 23		11 39	11 59			11 53		12 09	12 29		12 23		12 39

A not 23 May

Table 182

Sundays until 19 September

Horsham, Dorking, Guildford, Epsom and Sutton - London

		SN		FC	SN	SW	SN	SN	FC	SN	SW	SN		SN	FC	SN	SW	SN	SN	FC	SN	SW		SN	SN
Horsham 4	d																								
Warnham	d																								
Ockley	d																								
Holmwood	d																								
Dorking 4	a																								
	d				11 54	12 08				12 24						12 54	13 08				13 24				
Boxhill & Westhumble	d				11 56					12 26						12 56					13 26				
Guildford	d										12 20											13 20			
Effingham Junction 6	d										12 36											13 36			
Bookham	d										12 39											13 39			
Leatherhead	d				12 01	12 15				12 31	12 45					13 01	13 15				13 31	13 45			
Ashtead	d				12 05	12 18				12 35	12 48					13 05	13 18				13 35	13 48			
Epsom 3	a				12 09	12 23				12 39	12 53					13 09	13 23				13 39	13 53			
	d				12 10	12 24				12 40	12 54					13 10	13 24				13 40	13 54			
Ewell East	d				12 14					12 44						13 14					13 44				
Cheam	d				12 17					12 47						13 17					13 47				
Epsom Downs	d																								
Banstead	d																								
Belmont	d																								
Sutton (Surrey) 4	a				12 20					12 50						13 20					13 50				
	d	12 10		12 16	12 21		12 26	12 40	12 46	12 51		12 56		13 10	13 16	13 21		13 26	13 40	13 46	13 51			13 56	14 10
Carshalton	d				12 24					12 54						13 24					13 54				
Hackbridge	d				12 26					12 56						13 26					13 56				
Mitcham Junction	d				12 30					13 00						13 30					14 00				
Mitcham Eastfields	d				12 33					13 03						13 33					14 03				
Carshalton Beeches	d	12 13					12 29	12 43				12 59		13 13				13 29	13 43					13 59	14 13
Wallington	d	12 15					12 31	12 45				13 01		13 15				13 31	13 45					14 01	14 15
Waddon	d	12 18					12 34	12 48				13 04		13 18				13 34	13 48					14 04	14 18
West Croydon 4	d	12 22					12 38	12 52				13 08		13 22				13 38	13 52					14 08	14 22
Norwood Junction 2	d	12 29						12 59						13 29					13 59						14 29
New Cross Gate 4 ⊖	d																								
Tulse Hill 3	d			12 47					13 17						13 47					14 17					
London Bridge 4 ⊖	a			12 59					13 29						13 59					14 29					
Balham 4 ⊖	d	12 47			12 39		12 55	13 17		13 09		13 25		13 47		13 39		13 55	14 17		14 09			14 25	14 47
Clapham Junction 10	a	12 51			12 44	12 49	13 00	13 21		13 14	13 19	13 30		13 51		13 44	13 49	14 00	14 21		14 14	14 19		14 30	14 51
London Waterloo 15 ⊖	a					13 04					13 34						14 04					14 34			
London Victoria 15 ⊖	a	12 59			12 53		13 09	13 29		13 23		13 39		13 59		13 53		14 09	14 29		14 23			14 39	14 59

		FC	SN	SW	SN	SN	FC	SN		SW	SN	SN	FC	SN	SW	SN	SN	FC		SN	SW	SN	SN	FC	SN
Horsham 4	d																								
Warnham	d																								
Ockley	d																								
Holmwood	d																								
Dorking 4	a																								
	d		13 54	14 08				14 24						14 54	15 08					15 24					15 54
Boxhill & Westhumble	d		13 56					14 26						14 56						15 26					15 56
Guildford	d									14 20											15 20				
Effingham Junction 6	d									14 36											15 36				
Bookham	d									14 39											15 39				
Leatherhead	d		14 01	14 15				14 31		14 45				15 01	15 15					15 31	15 45				16 01
Ashtead	d		14 05	14 18				14 35		14 48				15 05	15 18					15 35	15 48				16 05
Epsom 3	a		14 09	14 23				14 39		14 53				15 09	15 23					15 39	15 53				16 09
	d		14 10	14 24				14 40		14 54				15 10	15 24					15 40	15 54				16 10
Ewell East	d		14 14					14 44						15 14						15 44					16 14
Cheam	d		14 17					14 47						15 17						15 47					16 17
Epsom Downs	d																								
Banstead	d																								
Belmont	d																								
Sutton (Surrey) 4	a		14 20					14 50						15 20						15 50					16 20
	d	14 16	14 21		14 26	14 40	14 46	14 51			14 56	15 10	15 16	15 21		15 26	15 40	15 46		15 51		15 56	16 10	16 16	16 21
Carshalton	d		14 24					14 54						15 24						15 54					16 24
Hackbridge	d		14 26					14 56						15 26						15 56					16 26
Mitcham Junction	d		14 30					15 00						15 30						16 00					16 30
Mitcham Eastfields	d		14 33					15 03						15 33						16 03					16 33
Carshalton Beeches	d				14 29	14 43					14 59	15 13				15 29	15 43					15 59	16 13		
Wallington	d				14 31	14 45					15 01	15 15				15 31	15 45					16 01	16 15		
Waddon	d				14 34	14 48					15 04	15 18				15 34	15 48					16 04	16 18		
West Croydon 4	d				14 38	14 52					15 08	15 22				15 38	15 52					16 08	16 22		
Norwood Junction 2	d					14 59						15 29					15 59						16 29		
New Cross Gate 4 ⊖	d																								
Tulse Hill 3	d	14 47					15 17						15 47					16 17						16 47	
London Bridge 4 ⊖	a	14 59					15 29						15 59					16 29						16 59	
Balham 4 ⊖	d		14 39		14 55	15 17		15 09			15 25	15 47		15 39		15 55	16 17			16 09		16 25	16 47		16 39
Clapham Junction 10	a		14 44	14 49	15 00	15 21		15 14		15 19	15 30	15 51		15 44	15 49	16 00	16 21			16 14	16 19	16 30	16 51		16 44
London Waterloo 15 ⊖	a			14 59						15 29					15 59						16 29				
London Victoria 15 ⊖	a		14 53		15 09	15 29		15 23			15 39	15 59		15 53		16 09	16 29			16 23		16 39	16 59		16 53

Table 182

Sundays

until 19 September

Horsham, Dorking, Guildford, Epsom and Sutton - London

Station		SW	SN	SN	FC	SN	SW	SN	SN	FC	SN	SW	SN	SN	FC	SN	SW	SN	SN	FC	SN	SW
Horsham 4	d																					
Warnham	d																					
Ockley	d																					
Holmwood	d																					
Dorking 4	a																					
	d	16 08				16 24					16 54	17 08				17 24					17 54	18 08
Boxhill & Westhumble	d					16 26					16 56					17 26					17 56	
Guildford	d						16 20										17 20					
Effingham Junction 6	d						16 36										17 36					
Bookham	d						16 39										17 39					
Leatherhead	d	16 15				16 31	16 45				17 01	17 15				17 31	17 45				18 01	18 15
Ashtead	d	16 18				16 35	16 48				17 05	17 18				17 35	17 48				18 05	18 18
Epsom 3	a	16 23				16 39	16 53				17 09	17 23				17 39	17 53				18 09	18 23
	d	16 24				16 40	16 54				17 10	17 24				17 40	17 54				18 10	18 24
Ewell East	d					16 44					17 14					17 44					18 14	
Cheam	d					16 47					17 17					17 47					18 17	
Epsom Downs	d																					
Banstead	d																					
Belmont	d																					
Sutton (Surrey) 4	a					16 50					17 20					17 50					18 20	
	d		16 26	16 40	16 46	16 51		16 56	17 10	17 16	17 21		17 26	17 40	17 46	17 51		17 56	18 10	18 16	18 21	
Carshalton	d					16 54					17 24					17 54					18 24	
Hackbridge	d					16 56					17 26					17 56					18 26	
Mitcham Junction	d					17 00					17 30					18 00					18 30	
Mitcham Eastfields	d					17 03					17 33					18 03					18 33	
Carshalton Beeches	d		16 29	16 43				16 59	17 13				17 29	17 43				17 59	18 13			
Wallington	d		16 31	16 45				17 01	17 15				17 31	17 45				18 01	18 15			
Waddon	d		16 34	16 48				17 04	17 18				17 34	17 48				18 04	18 18			
West Croydon 4	d		16 38	16 52				17 08	17 22				17 38	17 52				18 08	18 22			
Norwood Junction 2	d			16 59					17 29					17 59					18 29			
New Cross Gate 4 ⊖	d																					
Tulse Hill 3	d				17 17					17 47					18 17					18 47		
London Bridge 4 ⊖	a				17 29					17 59					18 29					18 59		
Balham 4 ⊖	d		16 55	17 17		17 09		17 25	17 47		17 39		17 55	18 17		18 09		18 25	18 47		18 39	
Clapham Junction 10	a	16 49	17 00	17 21		17 14	17 19	17 30	17 51		17 44	17 49	18 00	18 21		18 14	18 19	18 30	18 51		18 45	18 49
London Waterloo 15 ⊖	a	16 59					17 29					17 59					18 29					18 59
London Victoria 15 ⊖	a		17 09	17 29		17 23		17 39	17 59		17 53		18 09	18 29		18 23		18 39	18 59		18 53	

Station		SN	SN	FC	SN	SW	SN	SN	FC	SN	SW	SN	SN	FC	SN	SW	SN	SN	FC	SN	SW	SN	SN
Horsham 4	d																						
Warnham	d																						
Ockley	d																						
Holmwood	d																						
Dorking 4	a																						
	d				18 24					18 54	19 08				19 24					19 54	20 08		
Boxhill & Westhumble	d				18 26					18 56					19 26					19 56			
Guildford	d					18 20										19 20							
Effingham Junction 6	d					18 36										19 36							
Bookham	d					18 39										19 39							
Leatherhead	d				18 31	18 45				19 01	19 15				19 31	19 45				20 01	20 15		
Ashtead	d				18 35	18 48				19 05	19 18				19 35	19 48				20 05	20 18		
Epsom 3	a				18 39	18 53				19 09	19 23				19 39	19 53				20 09	20 23		
	d				18 40	18 54				19 10	19 24				19 40	19 54				20 10	20 24		
Ewell East	d				18 44					19 14					19 44					20 14			
Cheam	d				18 47					19 17					19 47					20 17			
Epsom Downs	d																						
Banstead	d																						
Belmont	d																						
Sutton (Surrey) 4	a				18 50					19 20					19 50					20 20			
	d	18 26	18 40	18 46	18 51		18 56	19 10	19 16	19 21		19 26	19 40	19 46	19 51		19 56	20 10	20 16	20 21		20 26	20 40
Carshalton	d				18 54					19 24					19 54					20 24			
Hackbridge	d				18 56					19 26					19 56					20 26			
Mitcham Junction	d				19 00					19 30					20 00					20 30			
Mitcham Eastfields	d				19 03					19 33					20 03					20 33			
Carshalton Beeches	d	18 29	18 43				18 59	19 13				19 29	19 43				19 59	20 13				20 29	20 43
Wallington	d	18 31	18 45				19 01	19 15				19 31	19 45				20 01	20 15				20 31	20 45
Waddon	d	18 34	18 48				19 04	19 18				19 34	19 48				20 04	20 18				20 34	20 48
West Croydon 4	d	18 38	18 52				19 08	19 22				19 38	19 52				20 08	20 22				20 38	20 52
Norwood Junction 2	d		18 59					19 29					19 59					20 29					20 59
New Cross Gate 4 ⊖	d																						
Tulse Hill 3	d			19 17					19 47					20 17					20 47				
London Bridge 4 ⊖	a			19 29					19 59					20 29					20 59				
Balham 4 ⊖	d	18 55	19 17		19 09		19 25	19 47		19 39		19 55	20 17		20 09		20 25	20 47		20 39		20 55	21 17
Clapham Junction 10	a	19 00	19 21		19 14	19 19	19 30	19 51		19 44	19 49	20 00	20 21		20 14	20 19	20 30	20 51		20 44	20 49	21 00	21 21
London Waterloo 15 ⊖	a					19 29					19 59					20 29					21 00		
London Victoria 15 ⊖	a	19 09	19 29		19 23		19 39	19 59		19 53		20 09	20 29		20 23		20 39	20 59		20 53		21 09	21 29

Table 182

Sundays

until 19 September

Horsham, Dorking, Guildford, Epsom and Sutton - London

Station		FC	SN	SW	SN	SN	FC	SN	SW	SN	SN	SN	SW	SN	SN	SN	SW	SN	SN	SN	SW	SN	SN
Horsham 4	d																						
Warnham	d																						
Ockley	d																						
Holmwood	d																						
Dorking 4	a																						
	d		20 24					20 54	21 08			21 24				21 54	22 08			22 24			
Boxhill & Westhumble	d		20 26					20 56				21 26				21 56				22 26			
Guildford	d			20 20									21 20								22 20		
Effingham Junction 6	d			20 36									21 36								22 36		
Bookham	d			20 39									21 39								22 39		
Leatherhead	d		20 31	20 45				21 01	21 15			21 31	21 45			22 01	22 15			22 31	22 45		
Ashtead	d		20 35	20 48				21 05	21 18			21 35	21 48			22 05	22 18			22 35	22 48		
Epsom 3	a		20 39	20 53				21 09	21 23			21 39	21 53			22 09	22 23			22 39	22 53		
	d		20 40	20 54				21 10	21 24			21 40	21 54			22 10	22 24			22 40	22 54		
Ewell East	d		20 44					21 14				21 44				22 14				22 44			
Cheam	d		20 47					21 17				21 47				22 17				22 47			
Epsom Downs	d																						
Banstead	d																						
Belmont	d																						
Sutton (Surrey) 4	a		20 50					21 20				21 50				22 20				22 50			
	d	20 46	20 51		20 56	21 10	21 16	21 21		21 26	21 40	21 51		21 56	22 10	22 21		22 26	22 40	22 51		22 56	23 10
Carshalton	d		20 54					21 24				21 54				22 24				22 54			
Hackbridge	d		20 56					21 26				21 56				22 26				22 56			
Mitcham Junction	d		21 00					21 30				22 00				22 30				23 00			
Mitcham Eastfields	d		21 03					21 33				22 03				22 33				23 03			
Carshalton Beeches	d				20 59	21 13				21 29	21 43			21 59	22 13			22 29	22 43			22 59	23 13
Wallington	d				21 01	21 15				21 31	21 45			22 01	22 15			22 31	22 45			23 01	23 15
Waddon	d				21 04	21 18				21 34	21 48			22 04	22 18			22 34	22 48			23 04	23 18
West Croydon 4	d				21 08	21 22				21 38	21 52			22 08	22 22			22 38	22 52			23 08	23 22
Norwood Junction 2	d					21 29					21 59				22 29				22 59				23 29
New Cross Gate 4 ⊖	d																						
Tulse Hill 3	d	21 17					21 47																
London Bridge 4 ⊖	a	21 29					21 59																
Balham 4 ⊖	d		21 09		21 25	21 47		21 39		21 55	22 17	22 09		22 25	22 47	22 39		22 55	23 17	23 09		23 25	23 47
Clapham Junction 10	a		21 14	21 19	21 30	21 51		21 44	21 49	22 00	22 21	22 14	22 19	22 30	22 51	22 44	22 49	23 00	23 21	23 14	23 19	23 30	23 51
London Waterloo 15 ⊖	a			21 29					22 00				22 29				23 00				23 29		
London Victoria 15 ⊖	a		21 23		21 39	21 59		21 53		22 09	22 29	22 23		22 39	22 59	22 53		23 09	23 29	23 23		23 39	23 59

Station		SN	SW	SN	SN
Horsham 4	d				
Warnham	d				
Ockley	d				
Holmwood	d				
Dorking 4	a				
	d	22 54	23 08		
Boxhill & Westhumble	d	22 56			
Guildford	d				
Effingham Junction 6	d				
Bookham	d				
Leatherhead	d	23 01	23 15		
Ashtead	d	23 05	23 18		
Epsom 3	a	23 09	23 23		
	d	23 10	23 24		
Ewell East	d	23 14			
Cheam	d	23 17			
Epsom Downs	d				
Banstead	d				
Belmont	d				
Sutton (Surrey) 4	a	23 20			
	d	23 21		23 26	23 40
Carshalton	d	23 24			
Hackbridge	d	23 26			
Mitcham Junction	d	23 30			
Mitcham Eastfields	d	23 33			
Carshalton Beeches	d			23 29	23 43
Wallington	d			23 31	23 45
Waddon	d			23 34	23 48
West Croydon 4	d			23 38	23a51
Norwood Junction 2	d				
New Cross Gate 4 ⊖	d				
Tulse Hill 3	d				
London Bridge 4 ⊖	a				
Balham 4 ⊖	d	23 39			
Clapham Junction 10	a	23 44	23 49		
London Waterloo 15 ⊖	a		23 59		
London Victoria 15 ⊖	a	23 53			

Table 182

Sundays
from 26 September

Horsham, Dorking, Guildford, Epsom and Sutton - London

		SN	SN	SN	SW	SN	SN	SW	SN	SN		SN	SW	SN	SN	SN	SW	SN	SN	SN		SW	SN	SN	SN
Horsham 4	d																								
Warnham	d																								
Ockley	d																								
Holmwood	d																								
Dorking 4	a																								
	d			06 54			07 24					07 54				08 24				08 54		09 08			09 24
Boxhill & Westhumble	d			06 56			07 26					07 56				08 26				08 56					09 26
Guildford	d																08 18								
Effingham Junction 6	d																08 34								
Bookham	d																08 37								
Leatherhead	d			07 01			07 31					08 01				08 31	08 45			09 01		09 15			09 31
Ashtead	d			07 05			07 35					08 05				08 35	08 48			09 05		09 18			09 35
Epsom 3	a			07 09			07 39					08 09				08 39	08 53			09 09		09 23			09 39
	d		06 45	07 10	07 24		07 40	07 54				08 10	08 24			08 40	08 54			09 10		09 24			09 40
Ewell East	d		06 49	07 14			07 44					08 14				08 44				09 14					09 44
Cheam	d		06 52	07 17			07 47					08 17				08 47				09 17					09 47
Epsom Downs	d	23p43																							
Banstead	d	23p46																							
Belmont	d	23p49																							
Sutton (Surrey) 4	a	23p52	06 55	07 20			07 50					08 20				08 50				09 20					09 50
	d	23p53	06 56	07 21		07 26	07 51		07 56	08 10		08 21		08 26	08 40	08 51		08 56	09 10	09 21			09 26	09 40	09 51
Carshalton	d			07 24			07 54					08 24				08 54				09 24					09 54
Hackbridge	d			07 26			07 56					08 26				08 56				09 26					09 56
Mitcham Junction	d			07 30			08 00					08 30				09 00				09 30					10 00
Mitcham Eastfields	d			07 33			08 03					08 33				09 03				09 33					10 03
Carshalton Beeches	d	23p56	06 59			07 29			07 59	08 13				08 29	08 43			08 59	09 13				09 29	09 43	
Wallington	d	23p58	07 01			07 31			08 01	08 15				08 31	08 45			09 01	09 15				09 31	09 45	
Waddon	d	00 01	07 04			07 34			08 04	08 18				08 34	08 48			09 04	09 18				09 34	09 48	
West Croydon 4	d	00a04	07 08			07 38			08 08	08 22				08 38	08 52			09 08	09 22				09 38	09 52	
Norwood Junction 2	d									08 29					08 59				09 29					09 59	
New Cross Gate 4 ⊖	d																								
Tulse Hill 3	d																								
London Bridge 4 ⊖	a																								
Balham 4 ⊖	d		07 25	07 39		07 55	08 09		08 25	08 47		08 39		08 55	09 17	09 09		09 25	09 47	09 39			09 55	10 17	10 09
Clapham Junction 10	a		07 30	07 44	07 49	08 00	08 14	08 19	08 30	08 51		08 44	08 49	09 00	09 21	09 14	09 19	09 30	09 51	09 44		09 49	10 00	10 21	10 14
London Waterloo 15 ⊖	a				08 04			08 34					09 04				09 34					10 04			
London Victoria 15 ⊖	a		07 39	07 53		08 09	08 23		08 39	08 59		08 53		09 09	09 29	09 23		09 39	09 59	09 53			10 09	10 29	10 23

		SW	SN	SN	FC	SN		SW	SN	SN	FC	SN	SW	SN	SN	FC		SN	SW	SN	SN	FC	SN	SW	SN
Horsham 4	d																								
Warnham	d																								
Ockley	d																								
Holmwood	d																								
Dorking 4	a																								
	d					09 54		10 08				10 24						10 54	11 08				11 24		
Boxhill & Westhumble	d					09 56						10 26						10 56					11 26		
Guildford	d	09 18											10 18											11 18	
Effingham Junction 6	d	09 34											10 34											11 34	
Bookham	d	09 37											10 37											11 37	
Leatherhead	d	09 45				10 01		10 15				10 31	10 45					11 01	11 15				11 31	11 45	
Ashtead	d	09 48				10 05		10 18				10 35	10 48					11 05	11 18				11 35	11 48	
Epsom 3	a	09 53				10 09		10 23				10 39	10 53					11 09	11 23				11 39	11 53	
	d	09 54				10 10		10 24				10 40	10 54					11 10	11 24				11 40	11 54	
Ewell East	d					10 14						10 44						11 14					11 44		
Cheam	d					10 17						10 47						11 17					11 47		
Epsom Downs	d																								
Banstead	d																								
Belmont	d																								
Sutton (Surrey) 4	a					10 20						10 50						11 20					11 50		
	d		09 56	10 10	10 16	10 21			10 26	10 40	10 46	10 51		10 56	11 10	11 16		11 21		11 26	11 40	11 46	11 51		11 56
Carshalton	d					10 24						10 54						11 24					11 54		
Hackbridge	d					10 26						10 56						11 26					11 56		
Mitcham Junction	d					10 30						11 00						11 30					12 00		
Mitcham Eastfields	d					10 33						11 03						11 33					12 03		
Carshalton Beeches	d		09 59	10 13					10 29	10 43				10 59	11 13					11 29	11 43				11 59
Wallington	d		10 01	10 15					10 31	10 45				11 01	11 15					11 31	11 45				12 01
Waddon	d		10 04	10 18					10 34	10 48				11 04	11 18					11 34	11 48				12 04
West Croydon 4	d		10 08	10 22					10 38	10 52				11 08	11 22					11 38	11 52				12 08
Norwood Junction 2	d			10 29						10 59					11 29						11 59				
New Cross Gate 4 ⊖	d																								
Tulse Hill 3	d				10 47						11 17					11 47						12 17			
London Bridge 4 ⊖	a				10 59						11 29					11 59						12 29			
Balham 4 ⊖	d		10 25	10 47		10 39			10 55	11 17		11 09		11 25	11 47			11 39		11 55	12 17		12 09		12 25
Clapham Junction 10	a	10 19	10 30	10 51		10 44		10 49	11 00	11 21		11 14	11 19	11 30	11 51			11 44	11 49	12 00	12 21		12 14	12 19	12 30
London Waterloo 15 ⊖	a	10 34						11 03					11 34						12 04					12 34	
London Victoria 15 ⊖	a		10 39	10 59		10 53			11 09	11 29		11 23		11 39	11 59			11 53		12 09	12 29		12 23		12 39

Table 182

Sundays
from 26 September

Horsham, Dorking, Guildford, Epsom and Sutton - London

		SN		FC	SN	SW	SN	SN	FC	SN	SW	SN		SN	FC	SN	SW	SN	SN	FC	SN	SW		SN	SN
Horsham 4	d																								
Warnham	d																								
Ockley	d																								
Holmwood	d																								
Dorking 4	a																								
	d				11 54	12 08				12 24						12 54	13 08				13 24				
Boxhill & Westhumble	d				11 56					12 26						12 56					13 26				
Guildford	d										12 18											13 18			
Effingham Junction 6	d										12 34											13 34			
Bookham	d										12 37											13 37			
Leatherhead	d				12 01	12 15				12 31	12 45					13 01	13 15				13 31	13 45			
Ashtead	d				12 05	12 18				12 35	12 48					13 05	13 18				13 35	13 48			
Epsom 3	a				12 09	12 23				12 39	12 53					13 09	13 23				13 39	13 53			
	d				12 10	12 24				12 40	12 54					13 10	13 24				13 40	13 54			
Ewell East	d				12 14					12 44						13 14					13 44				
Cheam	d				12 17					12 47						13 17					13 47				
Epsom Downs	d																								
Banstead	d																								
Belmont	d																								
Sutton (Surrey) 4	a				12 20					12 50						13 20					13 50				
	d	12 10		12 16	12 21		12 26	12 40	12 46	12 51		12 56		13 10	13 16	13 21		13 26	13 40	13 46	13 51			13 56	14 10
Carshalton	d				12 24					12 54						13 24					13 54				
Hackbridge	d				12 26					12 56						13 26					13 56				
Mitcham Junction	d				12 30					13 00						13 30					14 00				
Mitcham Eastfields	d				12 33					13 03						13 33					14 03				
Carshalton Beeches	d	12 13					12 29	12 43				12 59		13 13				13 29	13 43					13 59	14 13
Wallington	d	12 15					12 31	12 45				13 01		13 15				13 31	13 45					14 01	14 15
Waddon	d	12 18					12 34	12 48				13 04		13 18				13 34	13 48					14 04	14 18
West Croydon 4	d	12 22					12 38	12 52				13 08		13 22				13 38	13 52					14 08	14 22
Norwood Junction 2	d	12 29						12 59						13 29					13 59						14 29
New Cross Gate 4 ⊖	d																								
Tulse Hill 3	d			12 47					13 17						13 47					14 17					
London Bridge 4 ⊖	a			12 59					13 29						13 59					14 29					
Balham 4 ⊖	d	12 47			12 39		12 55	13 17		13 09		13 25		13 47		13 39		13 55	14 17		14 09			14 25	14 47
Clapham Junction 10	a	12 51			12 44	12 49	13 00	13 21		13 14	13 19	13 30		13 51		13 44	13 49	14 00	14 21		14 14	14 19		14 30	14 51
London Waterloo 15 ⊖	a					13 04					13 34						14 04					14 34			
London Victoria 15 ⊖	a	12 59			12 53		13 09	13 29		13 23		13 39		13 59		13 53		14 09	14 29		14 23			14 39	14 59

		FC	SN	SW	SN	SN	FC	SN		SW	SN	SN	FC	SN	SW	SN	SN	FC		SN	SW	SN	SN	FC	SN
Horsham 4	d																								
Warnham	d																								
Ockley	d																								
Holmwood	d																								
Dorking 4	a																								
	d		13 54	14 08				14 24						14 54	15 08					15 24					15 54
Boxhill & Westhumble	d		13 56					14 26						14 56						15 26					15 56
Guildford	d									14 18											15 18				
Effingham Junction 6	d									14 34											15 34				
Bookham	d									14 37											15 37				
Leatherhead	d		14 01	14 15				14 31		14 45				15 01	15 15					15 31	15 45				16 01
Ashtead	d		14 05	14 18				14 35		14 48				15 05	15 18					15 35	15 48				16 05
Epsom 3	a		14 09	14 23				14 39		14 53				15 09	15 23					15 39	15 53				16 09
	d		14 10	14 24				14 40		14 54				15 10	15 24					15 40	15 54				16 10
Ewell East	d		14 14					14 44						15 14						15 44					16 14
Cheam	d		14 17					14 47						15 17						15 47					16 17
Epsom Downs	d																								
Banstead	d																								
Belmont	d																								
Sutton (Surrey) 4	a		14 20					14 50						15 20						15 50					16 20
	d	14 16	14 21		14 26	14 40	14 46	14 51			14 56	15 10	15 16	15 21		15 26	15 40	15 46		15 51		15 56	16 10	16 16	16 21
Carshalton	d		14 24					14 54						15 24						15 54					16 24
Hackbridge	d		14 26					14 56						15 26						15 56					16 26
Mitcham Junction	d		14 30					15 00						15 30						16 00					16 30
Mitcham Eastfields	d		14 33					15 03						15 33						16 03					16 33
Carshalton Beeches	d				14 29	14 43					14 59	15 13				15 29	15 43					15 59	16 13		
Wallington	d				14 31	14 45					15 01	15 15				15 31	15 45					16 01	16 15		
Waddon	d				14 34	14 48					15 04	15 18				15 34	15 48					16 04	16 18		
West Croydon 4	d				14 38	14 52					15 08	15 22				15 38	15 52					16 08	16 22		
Norwood Junction 2	d					14 59						15 29					15 59						16 29		
New Cross Gate 4 ⊖	d																								
Tulse Hill 3	d	14 47					15 17						15 47					16 17						16 47	
London Bridge 4 ⊖	a	14 59					15 29						15 59					16 29						16 59	
Balham 4 ⊖	d		14 39		14 55	15 17		15 09			15 25	15 47		15 39		15 55	16 17			16 09		16 25	16 47		16 39
Clapham Junction 10	a		14 44	14 49	15 00	15 21		15 14		15 19	15 30	15 51		15 44	15 49	16 00	16 21			16 14	16 19	16 30	16 51		16 44
London Waterloo 15 ⊖	a			14 59						15 29					15 59						16 29				
London Victoria 15 ⊖	a		14 53		15 09	15 29		15 23			15 39	15 59		15 53		16 09	16 29			16 23		16 39	16 59		16 53

Table 182

Horsham, Dorking, Guildford, Epsom and Sutton - London

Sundays

from 26 September

Station		SW	SN	SN		FC	SN	SW	SN	SN	FC	SN	SW	SN		SN	FC	SN	SW	SN	SN	FC	SN	SW
Horsham 4	d																							
Warnham	d																							
Ockley	d																							
Holmwood	d																							
Dorking 4	a																							
	d	16 08					16 24					16 54	17 08					17 24					17 54	18 08
Boxhill & Westhumble	d						16 26					16 56						17 26					17 56	
Guildford	d							16 18											17 18					
Effingham Junction 6	d							16 34											17 34					
Bookham	d							16 37											17 37					
Leatherhead	d	16 15					16 31	16 45				17 01	17 15					17 31	17 45				18 01	18 15
Ashtead	d	16 18					16 35	16 48				17 05	17 18					17 35	17 48				18 05	18 18
Epsom 3	a	16 23					16 39	16 53				17 09	17 23					17 39	17 53				18 09	18 23
	d	16 24					16 40	16 54				17 10	17 24					17 40	17 54				18 10	18 24
Ewell East	d						16 44					17 14						17 44					18 14	
Cheam	d						16 47					17 17						17 47					18 17	
Epsom Downs	d																							
Banstead	d																							
Belmont	d																							
Sutton (Surrey) 4	a						16 50					17 20						17 50					18 20	
	d		16 26	16 40		16 46	16 51		16 56	17 10	17 16	17 21		17 26		17 40	17 46	17 51		17 56	18 10	18 16	18 21	
Carshalton	d						16 54					17 24						17 54					18 24	
Hackbridge	d						16 56					17 26						17 56					18 26	
Mitcham Junction	d						17 00					17 30						18 00					18 30	
Mitcham Eastfields	d						17 03					17 33						18 03					18 33	
Carshalton Beeches	d		16 29	16 43					16 59	17 13				17 29		17 43				17 59	18 13			
Wallington	d		16 31	16 45					17 01	17 15				17 31		17 45				18 01	18 15			
Waddon	d		16 34	16 48					17 04	17 18				17 34		17 48				18 04	18 18			
West Croydon 4	d		16 38	16 52					17 08	17 22				17 38		17 52				18 08	18 22			
Norwood Junction 2	d			16 59						17 29						17 59					18 29			
New Cross Gate 4 ⊖	d																							
Tulse Hill 3	d					17 17					17 47						18 17					18 47		
London Bridge 4 ⊖	a					17 29					17 59						18 29					18 59		
Balham 4 ⊖	d		16 55	17 17			17 09		17 25	17 47		17 39		17 55		18 17		18 09		18 25	18 47		18 39	
Clapham Junction 10	a	16 49	17 00	17 21			17 14	17 19	17 30	17 51		17 44	17 49	18 00		18 21		18 14	18 19	18 30	18 51		18 45	18 49
London Waterloo 15 ⊖	a	16 59						17 29					17 59						18 29					18 59
London Victoria 15 ⊖	a		17 09	17 29			17 23		17 39	17 59		17 53		18 09		18 29		18 23		18 39	18 59		18 53	

Station		SN	SN	FC	SN	SW	SN	SN	FC	SN		SW	SN	SN	FC	SN	SW	SN	SN	FC		SN	SW	SN	SN
Horsham 4	d																								
Warnham	d																								
Ockley	d																								
Holmwood	d																								
Dorking 4	a																								
	d				18 24					18 54		19 08				19 24						19 54	20 08		
Boxhill & Westhumble	d				18 26					18 56						19 26						19 56			
Guildford	d					18 18											19 18								
Effingham Junction 6	d					18 34											19 34								
Bookham	d					18 37											19 37								
Leatherhead	d				18 31	18 45				19 01		19 15				19 31	19 45					20 01	20 15		
Ashtead	d				18 35	18 48				19 05		19 18				19 35	19 48					20 05	20 18		
Epsom 3	a				18 39	18 53				19 09		19 23				19 39	19 53					20 09	20 23		
	d				18 40	18 54				19 10		19 24				19 40	19 54					20 10	20 24		
Ewell East	d				18 44					19 14						19 44						20 14			
Cheam	d				18 47					19 17						19 47						20 17			
Epsom Downs	d																								
Banstead	d																								
Belmont	d																								
Sutton (Surrey) 4	a				18 50					19 20						19 50						20 20			
	d	18 26	18 40	18 46	18 51		18 56	19 10	19 16	19 21			19 26	19 40	19 46	19 51		19 56	20 10	20 16		20 21		20 26	20 40
Carshalton	d				18 54					19 24						19 54						20 24			
Hackbridge	d				18 56					19 26						19 56						20 26			
Mitcham Junction	d				19 00					19 30						20 00						20 30			
Mitcham Eastfields	d				19 03					19 33						20 03						20 33			
Carshalton Beeches	d	18 29	18 43				18 59	19 13					19 29	19 43				19 59	20 13					20 29	20 43
Wallington	d	18 31	18 45				19 01	19 15					19 31	19 45				20 01	20 15					20 31	20 45
Waddon	d	18 34	18 48				19 04	19 18					19 34	19 48				20 04	20 18					20 34	20 48
West Croydon 4	d	18 38	18 52				19 08	19 22					19 38	19 52				20 08	20 22					20 38	20 52
Norwood Junction 2	d		18 59					19 29						19 59					20 29						20 59
New Cross Gate 4 ⊖	d																								
Tulse Hill 3	d			19 17					19 47						20 17					20 47					
London Bridge 4 ⊖	a			19 29					19 59						20 29					20 59					
Balham 4 ⊖	d	18 55	19 17		19 09		19 25	19 47		19 39			19 55	20 17		20 09		20 25	20 47			20 39		20 55	21 17
Clapham Junction 10	a	19 00	19 21		19 14	19 19	19 30	19 51		19 44		19 49	20 00	20 21		20 14	20 19	20 30	20 51			20 44	20 49	21 00	21 21
London Waterloo 15 ⊖	a					19 29						19 59					20 29						21 00		
London Victoria 15 ⊖	a	19 09	19 29		19 23		19 39	19 59		19 53			20 09	20 29		20 23		20 39	20 59			20 53		21 09	21 29

Table 182

Horsham, Dorking, Guildford, Epsom and Sutton - London

Sundays

from 26 September

Station		FC	SN	SW	SN	SN		FC	SN	SW	SN	SN	SN	SW	SN	SN		SN	SW	SN	SN	SN	SW	SN	SN
Horsham 4	d																								
Warnham	d																								
Ockley	d																								
Holmwood	d																								
Dorking 4	a																								
	d		20 24						20 54	21 08			21 24					21 54	22 08			22 24			
Boxhill & Westhumble	d		20 26						20 56				21 26					21 56				22 26			
Guildford	d			20 18										21 18									22 20		
Effingham Junction 6	d			20 34										21 34									22 36		
Bookham	d			20 37										21 37									22 39		
Leatherhead	d		20 31	20 45					21 01	21 15			21 31	21 45				22 01	22 15			22 31	22 45		
Ashtead	d		20 35	20 48					21 05	21 18			21 35	21 48				22 05	22 18			22 35	22 48		
Epsom 3	a		20 39	20 53					21 09	21 23			21 39	21 53				22 09	22 23			22 39	22 53		
	d		20 40	20 54					21 10	21 24			21 40	21 54				22 10	22 24			22 40	22 54		
Ewell East	d		20 44						21 14				21 44					22 14				22 44			
Cheam	d		20 47						21 17				21 47					22 17				22 47			
Epsom Downs	d																								
Banstead	d																								
Belmont	d																								
Sutton (Surrey) 4	a		20 50						21 20				21 50					22 20				22 50			
	d	20 46	20 51		20 56	21 10		21 16	21 21		21 26	21 40	21 51		21 56	22 10		22 21		22 26	22 40	22 51		22 56	23 10
Carshalton	d		20 54						21 24				21 54					22 24				22 54			
Hackbridge	d		20 56						21 26				21 56					22 26				22 56			
Mitcham Junction	d		21 00						21 30				22 00					22 30				23 00			
Mitcham Eastfields	d		21 03						21 33				22 03					22 33				23 03			
Carshalton Beeches	d				20 59	21 13					21 29	21 43			21 59	22 13				22 29	22 43			22 59	23 13
Wallington	d				21 01	21 15					21 31	21 45			22 01	22 15				22 31	22 45			23 01	23 15
Waddon	d				21 04	21 18					21 34	21 48			22 04	22 18				22 34	22 48			23 04	23 18
West Croydon 4	d				21 08	21 22					21 38	21 52			22 08	22 22				22 38	22 52			23 08	23 22
Norwood Junction 2	d					21 29						21 59				22 29					22 59				23 29
New Cross Gate 4 ⊖	d																								
Tulse Hill 3	d	21 17						21 47																	
London Bridge 4 ⊖	a	21 29						21 59																	
Balham 4 ⊖	d		21 09		21 25	21 47			21 39		21 55	22 17	22 09		22 25	22 47		22 39		22 55	23 17	23 09		23 25	23 47
Clapham Junction 10	a		21 14	21 19	21 30	21 51			21 44	21 49	22 00	22 21	22 14	22 19	22 30	22 51		22 44	22 49	23 00	23 21	23 14	23 19	23 30	23 51
London Waterloo 15 ⊖	a			21 29						22 00				22 29					23 00				23 29		
London Victoria 15 ⊖	a		21 23		21 39	21 59			21 53		22 09	22 29	22 23		22 39	22 59		22 53		23 09	23 29	23 23		23 39	23 59

Station		SN		SW	SN	SN
Horsham 4	d					
Warnham	d					
Ockley	d					
Holmwood	d					
Dorking 4	a					
	d	22 54		23 08		
Boxhill & Westhumble	d	22 56				
Guildford	d					
Effingham Junction 6	d					
Bookham	d					
Leatherhead	d	23 01		23 15		
Ashtead	d	23 05		23 18		
Epsom 3	a	23 09		23 23		
	d	23 10		23 24		
Ewell East	d	23 14				
Cheam	d	23 17				
Epsom Downs	d					
Banstead	d					
Belmont	d					
Sutton (Surrey) 4	a	23 20				
	d	23 21			23 26	23 40
Carshalton	d	23 24				
Hackbridge	d	23 26				
Mitcham Junction	d	23 30				
Mitcham Eastfields	d	23 33				
Carshalton Beeches	d				23 29	23 43
Wallington	d				23 31	23 45
Waddon	d				23 34	23 48
West Croydon 4	d				23 38	23a51
Norwood Junction 2	d					
New Cross Gate 4 ⊖	d					
Tulse Hill 3	d					
London Bridge 4 ⊖	a					
Balham 4 ⊖	d	23 39				
Clapham Junction 10	a	23 44		23 49		
London Waterloo 15 ⊖	a			23 59		
London Victoria 15 ⊖	a	23 53				

Network Diagram for Tables 184, 189

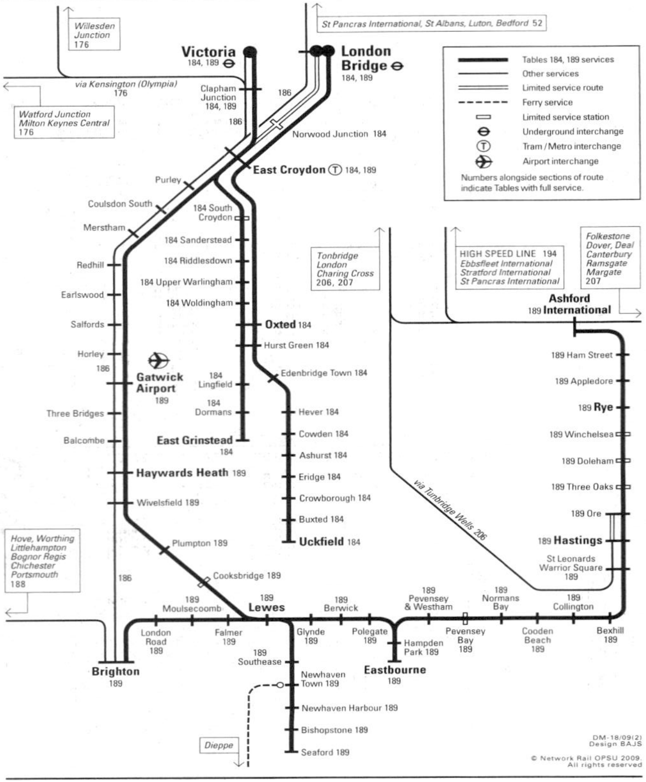

London - Oxted, East Grinstead and Uckfield

	SN MX	SN MX	SN	SN	SN	SN	SN	SN	SN	SN	SN	SN	SN	SN	SN	SN	SN	SN	SN	SN	SN	SN
London Victoria ⊖ 175,177 d	23p24	23p49		05 23	05 53		06 24		06 54		07 10		07 40		08 10		08 53		09 23	09 53		10 23
Clapham Junction 175,177 d	23p30	23p56		05 33	05 59		06 30		07 00		07 16		07 46		08 16		08 59		09 29	09 59		10 29
London Bridge ⊖ 175,177 d						06 08				07 03		07 19		08 00		08 25		09 08			10 08	
Norwood Junction 175,177 d				05 50								07 30				08 36						
East Croydon 175,177 d	23p43	00 10	05 26	05 54	06 10	06 22	06 41		07 11	07 17	07 27	07 35	07 57	08 16	08 27	08 41	09 10	09 23	09 40	10 10	10 23	10 40
South Croydon 175 d				05 56																		
Sanderstead d	23p47	00s14			06 14		06 45		07 15	07 21	07 31	07 39	08 01	08 20	08 31	08 45	09 14		09 44	10 14		10 44
Riddlesdown d	23p50	00s17			06 17		06 48			07 24		07 42		08 23		08 48	09 17		09 47	10 17		10 47
Upper Warlingham d	23p54	00s21			06 21		06 52			07 28		07 46		08 27		08 52	09 21		09 51	10 21		10 51
Woldingham d	23p58	00s25			06 25		06 56			07 32		07 50		08 31		08 56	09 25		09 55	10 25		10 55
Oxted a	00 03	00 30	05 41	06 08	06 30	06 36	07 01		07 26	07 37	07 43	07 55	08 12	08 36	08 42	09 01	09 30	09 36	10 00	10 30	10 36	11 00
Oxted d	00 03		05 41	06 08	06 31	06 36	07 02	07 08	07 26	07 38	07 43	07 56	08 12	08 37	08 42	09 02	09 31	09 37	10 00	10 30	10 37	11 00
Hurst Green d	00 06		05 44	06 10	06 33	06 39	07 04	07 11	07 29	07 40	07 46	07 58	08 16	08 39	08 46	09 04	09 33	09 39	10 03	10 33	10 39	11 03
Lingfield d	00 12			06 16	06 39		07 10		07 35		07 52	08 04	08 22		08 52	09 10	09 39		10 09	10 39		11 09
Dormans d	00 15			06 20	06 43		07 14		07 38		07 55	08 08	08 25		08 55	09 14	09 43		10 12	10 42		11 12
East Grinstead a	00 20			06 24	06 47		07 18		07 43		08 00	08 12	08 30		09 00	09 18	09 47		10 17	10 47		11 17
Edenbridge Town d			05 50			06 45		07 17		07 46				08 45				09 45			10 45	
Hever d						06 48		07 20		07 50				08 49				09 49			10 49	
Cowden d						06 52		07 24		07 54				08 53				09 53			10 53	
Ashurst d						06 57		07 29		07 58				08 57				09 57			10 57	
Eridge d			06 02			07 02		07 34		08 04				09 03				10 03			11 03	
Crowborough d			06 12			07b13		07 40		08 10				09 09				10 09			11 09	
Buxted d			06 18			07 19		07 46		08 16				09 15				10 15			11 15	
Uckfield a			06 24			07 25		07 52		08 22				09 21				10 21			11 21	

	SN	SN	SN	SN	SN	SN	SN	SN	SN	SN	SN	SN	SN	SN	SN	SN	SN	SN	SN	SN	SN	SN
London Victoria ⊖ 175,177 d	10 53		11 23	11 53		12 23	12 53		13 23	13 53		14 23	14 53		15 23		15 53		16 23		16 53	
Clapham Junction 175,177 d	10 59		11 29	11 59		12 29	12 59		13 29	13 59		14 29	14 59		15 29		15 59		16 29		16 59	
London Bridge ⊖ 175,177 d		11 08			12 08			13 08			14 08			15 08		15 38		16 08		16 38		17 09
Norwood Junction 175,177 d								13 19			14 19			15 19				16 19				
East Croydon 175,177 d	11 10	11 24	11 40	12 11	12 23	12 40	13 10	13 23	13 40	14 10	14 23	14 40	15 10	15 23	15 40	15 53	16 10	16 23	16 40	16 53	17 10	17 23
South Croydon 175 d															15 43		16 12		16 42		17 12	
Sanderstead d	11 14		11 44	12 15		12 44	13 14		13 44	14 14		14 45	15 14		15 46		16 15		16 45		17 15	
Riddlesdown d	11 17		11 47	12 18		12 47	13 17		13 47	14 17		14 48	15 17		15 49		16 18		16 48		17 18	
Upper Warlingham d	11 21		11 51	12 22		12 51	13 21		13 51	14 21		14 52	15 21		15 53		16 22		16 52		17 22	
Woldingham d	11 25		11 55	12 26		12 55	13 25		13 55	14 25		14 56	15 25		15 57		16 26		16 56		17 26	
Oxted a	11 30	11 36	12 00	12 31	12 36	13 00	13 30	13 36	14 00	14 30	14 36	15 01	15 30	15 36	16 02	16 06	16 31	16 36	17 01	17 06	17 31	17 36
Oxted d	11 30	11 37	12 00	12 31	12 37	13 00	13 30	13 37	14 00	14 30	14 37	15 01	15 30	15 37	16 02	16 07	16 31	16 37	17 02	17 07	17 32	17 37
Hurst Green d	11 33	11 39	12 03	12 34	12 39	13 03	13 33	13 39	14 03	14 33	14 39	15 03	15 33	15 39	16 04	16 09	16 34	16 39	17 04	17 09	17 34	17 40
Lingfield d	11 39		12 09	12 40		13 09	13 39		14 09	14 39		15 09	15 39		16 10		16 40		17 10		17 40	
Dormans d	11 42		12 12	12 43		13 12	13 42		14 12	14 42		15 13	15 42		16 14		16 43		17 14		17 44	
East Grinstead a	11 47		12 17	12 48		13 17	13 47		14 17	14 47		15 17	15 47		16 18		16 48		17 20		17 50	
Edenbridge Town d		11 45			12 45			13 45			14 45			15 45		16 15		16 45		17 15		17 46
Hever d		11 49			12 49			13 49			14 49			15 49		16 19		16 49		17 19		
Cowden d		11 53			12 53			13 53			14 53			15 53		16 23		16 53		17 23		
Ashurst d		11 57			12 57			13 57			14 57			15 57		16 27		16 57		17 27		
Eridge d		12 03			13 03			14 03			15 03			16 03		16 33		17 03		17 33		17 58
Crowborough d		12 09			13 09			14 09			15 09			16 09		16 39		17 09		17 39		18 04
Buxted d		12 15			13 15			14 15			15 15			16 15		16 45		17 15		17 45		18 10
Uckfield a		12 21			13 21			14 21			15 21			16 21		16 51		17 21		17 51		18 18

	SN	SN	SN	SN	SN	SN	SN	SN	SN	SN	SN	SN	SN	SN	SN	SN	SN	SN	SN	SN	SN
London Victoria ⊖ 175,177 d		17 23			17 53			18 23			18 53		19 23	19 53		20 23	20 53		21 23	21 53	
Clapham Junction 175,177 d		17 30			18 00			18 30			19 00		19 29	19 59		20 29	20 59		21 29	21 59	
London Bridge ⊖ 175,177 d	17 15			17 44		18 08	18 16			18 47		19 08			20 04			21 04			22 04
Norwood Junction 175,177 d															20 16			21 15			22 15
East Croydon 175,177 d	17 30	17 41		17 58	18 11	18 22	18 31	18 42		19 00	19 11	19 23	19 40	20 10	20 20	20 40	21 10	21 19	21 40	22 10	22 19
South Croydon 175 d	17 32			18 01			18 33			19 03											
Sanderstead d	17 35	17 45		18 04	18 15		18 36	18 47		19 06	19 15		19 44	20 14	20 24	20 44	21 14	21 24	21 44	22 14	22 24
Riddlesdown d	17 38	17 48		18 07	18 18		18 39	18 50		19 09	19 18		19 47	20 17		20 47	21 17		21 47	22 17	
Upper Warlingham d	17 42	17 52		18 11	18 22		18 43	18 54		19 13	19 22		19 51	20 21	20 30	20 51	21 21	21 29	21 51	22 21	22 29
Woldingham d	17 46	17 56		18 15	18 26		18 47	18 58		19 17	19 26		19 55	20 25		20 55	21 25		21 55	22 25	
Oxted a	17 51	18 01		18 20	18 31	18 36	18 52	19 03		19 22	19 31	19 36	20 00	20 30	20 37	21 00	21 30	21 36	22 00	22 30	22 36
Oxted d	17 52	18 02	18 07	18 20	18 32	18 37	18 53	19 03	19 07	19 22	19 32	19 37	20 00	20 30	20 37	21 00	21 30	21 37	22 00	22 30	22 37
Hurst Green d	17 54	18 04	18 09	18 23	18 34	18 39	18 55	19 06	19 09	19 25	19 34	19 39	20 03	20 33	20 40	21 03	21 33	21 39	22 03	22 33	22 39
Lingfield d	18 00	18 10		18 29	18 40		19 01	19 12		19 31	19 40		20 09	20 39		21 09	21 39		22 09	22 39	
Dormans d	18 04	18 14		18 32	18 44		19 05	19 15		19 34	19 44		20 12	20 42		21 12	21 42		22 12	22 42	
East Grinstead a	18 12	18 22		18 40	18 52		19 12	19 22		19 42	19 52		20 17	20 47		21 17	21 47		22 17	22 47	
Edenbridge Town d			18 15			18 45			19 15			19 45			20 46			21 45			22 45
Hever d			18 19						19 19			19 49			20 49			21 49			
Cowden d			18 23						19 23			19 53			20 53			21 53			
Ashurst d			18 27						19 27			19 57			20 58			21 57			
Eridge d			18 33			18 57			19 33			20 03			21 03			22 03			22 58
Crowborough d			18 39			19 03			19 39			20 09			21 09			22 09			23 04
Buxted d			18 45			19 09			19 45			20 15			21 15			22 15			23 10
Uckfield a			18 51			19 17			19 51			20 21			21 21			22 21			23 16

b arr. 0708

Table 184

Mondays to Fridays

London - Oxted, East Grinstead and Uckfield

	SN	SN	SN	SN
London Victoria ⊖175,177 d	22 23	22 53	23 24	23 49
Clapham Junction-I 175,177 d	22 29	22 59	23 30	23 56
London Bridge ⊖175,177 d				
Norwood Junction 175,177 d				
East Croydon 175,177 d	22 40	23 10	23 43	00 10
South Croydon 175 d				
Sanderstead d	22 44	23 14	23 47	00s14
Riddlesdown d	22 47	23 17	23 50	00s17
Upper Warlingham d	22 51	23 21	23 54	00s21
Woldingham d	22 55	23 25	23 58	00s25
Oxted a	23 00	23 30	00 03	00 30
d	23 00	23 30	00 03	
Hurst Green d	23 03	23 33	00 06	
Lingfield d	23 09	23 39	00 12	
Dormans d	23 12	23 42	00 15	
East Grinstead a	23 17	23 47	00 20	
Edenbridge Town d				
Hever d				
Cowden d				
Ashurst d				
Eridge d				
Crowborough d				
Buxted d				
Uckfield a				

Saturdays

	SN	SN	SN	SN	SN	SN	SN	SN	SN	SN	SN	SN	SN	SN	SN	SN	SN	SN	SN	SN	SN	SN
London Victoria ⊖175,177 d	23p24	23p49	05 25		06 23	06 53		07 23	07 53		08 23	08 53		09 23	09 53		10 23	10 53		11 23	11 53	
Clapham Junction-I 175,177 d	23p30	23p56	05 31		06 29	06 59		07 29	07 59		08 29	08 59		09 29	09 59		10 29	10 59		11 29	11 59	
London Bridge ⊖175,177 d				06 08			07 08			08 08			09 08			10 08			11 08			12 08
Norwood Junction 175,177 d			05 48																			
East Croydon 175,177 d	23p43	00 10	05 52	06 23	06 40	07 10	07 23	07 40	08 10	08 23	08 40	09 10	09 23	09 40	10 10	10 23	10 40	11 10	11 23	11 40	12 10	12 23
South Croydon 175 d			05 54																			
Sanderstead d	23p47	00s14			06 44	07 14		07 44	08 14		08 44	09 14		09 44	10 14		10 44	11 14		11 44	12 14	
Riddlesdown d	23p50	00s17			06 47	07 17		07 47	08 17		08 47	09 17		09 47	10 17		10 47	11 17		11 47	12 17	
Upper Warlingham d	23p54	00s21			06 51	07 21		07 51	08 21		08 51	09 21		09 51	10 21		10 51	11 21		11 51	12 21	
Woldingham d	23p58	00s25			06 55	07 25		07 55	08 25		08 55	09 25		09 55	10 25		10 55	11 25		11 55	12 25	
Oxted a	00 03	00 30	06 06	06 36	07 00	07 30	07 36	08 00	08 30	08 36	09 00	09 30	09 36	10 00	10 30	10 36	11 00	11 30	11 36	12 00	12 30	12 36
d	00 03		06 06	06 37	07 00	07 30	07 37	08 00	08 30	08 37	09 00	09 30	09 37	10 00	10 30	10 37	11 00	11 30	11 37	12 00	12 30	12 37
Hurst Green d	00 06		06 09	06 39	07 03	07 33	07 39	08 03	08 33	08 39	09 03	09 33	09 39	10 03	10 33	10 39	11 03	11 33	11 39	12 03	12 33	12 39
Lingfield d	00 12		06 15		07 09	07 39		08 09	08 39		09 09	09 39		10 09	10 39		11 09	11 39		12 09	12 39	
Dormans d	00 15		06 18		07 12	07 42		08 12	08 42		09 12	09 42		10 12	10 42		11 12	11 42		12 12	12 42	
East Grinstead a	00 20		06 23		07 17	07 47		08 17	08 47		09 17	09 47		10 17	10 47		11 17	11 47		12 17	12 47	
Edenbridge Town d				06 45			07 45			08 45			09 45			10 45			11 45			12 45
Hever d				06 49			07 49			08 49			09 49			10 49			11 49			12 49
Cowden d				06 53			07 53			08 53			09 53			10 53			11 53			12 53
Ashurst d				06 57			07 57			08 57			09 57			10 57			11 57			12 57
Eridge d				07 03			08 03			09 03			10 03			11 03			12 03			13 03
Crowborough d				07 09			08 09			09 09			10 09			11 09			12 09			13 09
Buxted d				07 15			08 15			09 15			10 15			11 15			12 15			13 15
Uckfield a				07 21			08 21			09 21			10 21			11 21			12 21			13 21

	SN	SN	SN	SN	SN	SN	SN	SN	SN	SN	SN	SN	SN	SN	SN	SN	SN	SN	SN	SN	SN	SN
London Victoria ⊖175,177 d	12 23	12 53		13 23	13 53		14 23	14 53		15 23	15 53		16 23	16 53		17 23	17 53		18 23	18 53		19 23
Clapham Junction-I 175,177 d	12 29	12 59		13 29	13 59		14 29	14 59		15 29	15 59		16 29	16 59		17 29	17 59		18 29	18 59		19 29
London Bridge ⊖175,177 d			13 08			14 08			15 08			16 08			17 08			18 08			19 08	
Norwood Junction 175,177 d																						
East Croydon 175,177 d	12 40	13 10	13 23	13 40	14 10	14 23	14 40	15 10	15 23	15 40	16 10	16 23	16 40	17 10	17 23	17 40	18 10	18 23	18 40	19 10	19 23	19 40
South Croydon 175 d																						
Sanderstead d	12 44	13 14		13 44	14 14		14 44	15 14		15 44	16 14		16 44	17 14		17 44	18 14		18 44	19 14		19 44
Riddlesdown d	12 47	13 17		13 47	14 17		14 47	15 17		15 47	16 17		16 47	17 17		17 47	18 17		18 47	19 17		19 47
Upper Warlingham d	12 51	13 21		13 51	14 21		14 51	15 21		15 51	16 21		16 51	17 21		17 51	18 21		18 51	19 21		19 51
Woldingham d	12 55	13 25		13 55	14 25		14 55	15 25		15 55	16 25		16 55	17 25		17 55	18 25		18 55	19 25		19 55
Oxted a	13 00	13 30	13 36	14 00	14 30	14 36	15 00	15 30	15 36	16 00	16 30	16 36	17 00	17 30	17 36	18 00	18 30	18 36	19 00	19 30	19 36	20 00
d	13 00	13 30	13 37	14 00	14 30	14 37	15 00	15 30	15 37	16 00	16 30	16 37	17 00	17 30	17 37	18 00	18 30	18 37	19 00	19 30	19 37	20 00
Hurst Green d	13 03	13 33	13 39	14 03	14 33	14 39	15 03	15 33	15 39	16 03	16 33	16 39	17 03	17 33	17 39	18 03	18 33	18 39	19 03	19 33	19 39	20 03
Lingfield d	13 09	13 39		14 09	14 39		15 09	15 39		16 09	16 39		17 09	17 39		18 09	18 39		19 09	19 39		20 09
Dormans d	13 12	13 42		14 12	14 42		15 12	15 42		16 12	16 42		17 12	17 42		18 12	18 42		19 12	19 42		20 12
East Grinstead a	13 17	13 47		14 17	14 47		15 17	15 47		16 17	16 47		17 17	17 47		18 17	18 47		19 17	19 47		20 17
Edenbridge Town d			13 45			14 45			15 45			16 45			17 45			18 45			19 45	
Hever d			13 49			14 49			15 49			16 49			17 49			18 49			19 49	
Cowden d			13 53			14 53			15 53			16 53			17 53			18 53			19 53	
Ashurst d			13 57			14 57			15 57			16 57			17 57			18 57			19 57	
Eridge d			14 03			15 03			16 03			17 03			18 03			19 03			20 03	
Crowborough d			14 09			15 09			16 09			17 09			18 09			19 09			20 09	
Buxted d			14 15			15 15			16 15			17 15			18 15			19 15			20 15	
Uckfield a			14 21			15 21			16 21			17 21			18 21			19 21			20 21	

Table 184

Saturdays

London - Oxted, East Grinstead and Uckfield

	SN	SN	SN	SN	SN	SN	SN	SN	SN	SN	SN	SN
London Victoria ⊖175,177 d	19 53		20 23	20 53		21 23	21 53		22 23	22 53	23 24	23 49
Clapham Junction-I 175,177 d	19 59		20 29	20 59		21 29	21 59		22 29	22 59	23 30	23 56
London Bridge ⊖175,177 d		20 08			21 08			22 08				
Norwood Junction 175,177 d		20 19			21 19			22 19				
East Croydon 175,177 d	20 10	20 23	20 40	21 10	21 23	21 40	22 10	22 23	22 40	23 10	23 43	00 10
South Croydon 175 d												
Sanderstead d	20 14		20 44	21 14		21 44	22 14		22 44	23 14	23 47	00s14
Riddlesdown d	20 17		20 47	21 17		21 47	22 17		22 47	23 17	23 50	00s17
Upper Warlingham d	20 21		20 51	21 21		21 51	22 21		22 51	23 21	23 54	00s21
Woldingham d	20 25		20 55	21 25		21 55	22 25		22 55	23 25	23 58	00s25
Oxted a	20 30	20 36	21 00	21 30	21 36	22 00	22 30	22 36	23 00	23 30	00 03	00 30
d	20 30	20 37	21 00	21 30	21 37	22 00	22 30	22 37	23 00	23 30	00 03	
Hurst Green d	20 33	20 39	21 03	21 33	21 39	22 03	22 33	22 39	23 03	23 33	00 06	
Lingfield d	20 39		21 09	21 39		22 09	22 39		23 09	23 39	00 12	
Dormans d	20 42		21 12	21 42		22 12	22 42		23 12	23 42	00 15	
East Grinstead a	20 47		21 17	21 47		22 17	22 47		23 17	23 47	00 20	
Edenbridge Town d		20 45			21 45			22 45				
Hever d		20 49			21 49							
Cowden d		20 53			21 53							
Ashurst d		20 57			21 57							
Eridge d		21 03			22 03			22 57				
Crowborough d		21 09			22 09			23 03				
Buxted d		21 15			22 15			23 09				
Uckfield a		21 21			22 21			23 15				

Sundays

	SN	SN	SN B	SN C	SN B	SN C	SN	SN B	SN C	SN	SN B	SN C	SN	SN B	SN C	SN	SN B	SN C	SN	SN B	SN C	SN
London Victoria ⊖175,177 d	23p24	23p49	07 22	07 25	08 22	08 25		09 22	09 25		10 22	10 25		11 22	11 25		12 22	12 25		13 22	13 25	
Clapham Junction-I 175,177 d	23p30	23p56	07 28	07 31	08 28	08 31		09 28	09 31		10 28	10 31		11 28	11 31		12 28	12 31		13 28	13 31	
London Bridge ⊖175,177 d																						
Norwood Junction 175,177 d																						
East Croydon 175,177 d	23p43	00 10	07 43	07 43	08 43	08 43	09 05	09 43	09 43	10 05	10 43	10 43		11 43	11 43		12 43	12 43		13 43	13 43	
South Croydon 175 d																						
Sanderstead d	23p47	00s14	07 47	07 47	08 47	08 47		09 47	09 47		10 47	10 47		11 47	11 47		12 47	12 47		13 47	13 47	
Riddlesdown d	23p50	00s17	07 50	07 50	08 50	08 50		09 50	09 50		10 50	10 50		11 50	11 50		12 50	12 50		13 50	13 50	
Upper Warlingham d	23p54	00s21	07 54	07 54	08 54	08 54		09 54	09 54		10 54	10 54		11 54	11 54		12 54	12 54		13 54	13 54	
Woldingham d	23p58	00s25	07 58	07 58	08 58	08 58		09 58	09 58		10 58	10 58		11 58	11 58		12 58	12 58		13 58	13 58	
Oxted a	00 03	00 30	08 03	08 03	09 03	09 03	09 17	10 03	10 03	10 17	11 03	11 03		12 03	12 03		13 03	13 03		14 03	14 03	
d	00 03		08 03	08 03	09 03	09 03	09 18	10 03	10 03	10 18	11 03	11 03	11 18	12 03	12 03	12 18	13 03	13 03	13 18	14 03	14 03	14 18
Hurst Green d	00 06		08 06	08 06	09 06	09 06	09 21	10 06	10 06	10 21	11 06	11 06	11 21	12 06	12 06	12 21	13 06	13 06	13 21	14 06	14 06	14 21
Lingfield d	00 12		08 12	08 12	09 12	09 12		10 12	10 12		11 12	11 12		12 12	12 12		13 12	13 12		14 12	14 12	
Dormans d	00 15		08 15	08 15	09 15	09 15		10 15	10 15		11 15	11 15		12 15	12 15		13 15	13 15		14 15	14 15	
East Grinstead a	00 20		08 20	08 20	09 20	09 20		10 20	10 20		11 20	11 20		12 20	12 20		13 20	13 20		14 20	14 20	
Edenbridge Town d							09 27			10 27			11 27			12 27			13 27			14 27
Hever d							09 31			10 31			11 31			12 31			13 31			14 31
Cowden d							09 35			10 35			11 35			12 35			13 35			14 35
Ashurst d							09 39			10 39			11 39			12 39			13 39			14 39
Eridge d							09 45			10 45			11 45			12 45			13 45			14 45
Crowborough d							09 51			10 51			11 51			12 51			13 51			14 51
Buxted d							09 57			10 57			11 57			12 57			13 57			14 57
Uckfield a							10 03			11 03			12 03			13 03			14 03			15 03

	SN B	SN C	SN	SN B	SN C	SN	SN B	SN C	SN	SN B	SN C	SN	SN B	SN C	SN	SN B	SN C	SN	SN B	SN C	SN	SN B
London Victoria ⊖175,177 d	14 22	14 25		15 22	15 25		16 22	16 25		17 22	17 25		18 22	18 25		19 22	19 25		20 22	20 25		21 22
Clapham Junction-I 175,177 d	14 28	14 31		15 28	15 31		16 28	16 31		17 28	17 31		18 28	18 31		19 28	19 31		20 28	20 31		21 28
London Bridge ⊖175,177 d																						
Norwood Junction 175,177 d																						
East Croydon 175,177 d	14 43	14 43		15 43	15 43		16 43	16 43		17 43	17 43		18 43	18 43		19 43	19 43		20 43	20 43		21 43
South Croydon 175 d																						
Sanderstead d	14 47	14 47		15 47	15 47		16 47	16 47		17 47	17 47		18 47	18 47		19 47	19 47		20 47	20 47		21 47
Riddlesdown d	14 50	14 50		15 50	15 50		16 50	16 50		17 50	17 50		18 50	18 50		19 50	19 50		20 50	20 50		21 50
Upper Warlingham d	14 54	14 54		15 54	15 54		16 54	16 54		17 54	17 54		18 54	18 54		19 54	19 54		20 54	20 54		21 54
Woldingham d	14 58	14 58		15 58	15 58		16 58	16 58		17 58	17 58		18 58	18 58		19 58	19 58		20 58	20 58		21 58
Oxted a	15 03	15 03		16 03	16 03		17 03	17 03		18 03	18 03		19 03	19 03		20 03	20 03		21 03	21 03		22 03
d	15 03	15 03	15 18	16 03	16 03	16 18	17 03	17 03	17 18	18 03	18 03	18 18	19 03	19 03	19 18	20 03	20 03	20 18	21 03	21 03	21 18	22 03
Hurst Green d	15 06	15 06	15 21	16 06	16 06	16 21	17 06	17 06	17 21	18 06	18 06	18 21	19 06	19 06	19 21	20 06	20 06	20 21	21 06	21 06	21 21	22 06
Lingfield d	15 12	15 12		16 12	16 12		17 12	17 12		18 12	18 12		19 12	19 12		20 12	20 12		21 12	21 12		22 12
Dormans d	15 15	15 15		16 15	16 15		17 15	17 15		18 15	18 15		19 15	19 15		20 15	20 15		21 15	21 15		22 15
East Grinstead a	15 20	15 20		16 20	16 20		17 20	17 20		18 20	18 20		19 20	19 20		20 20	20 20		21 20	21 20		22 20
Edenbridge Town d			15 27			16 27			17 27			18 27			19 27			20 27			21 27	
Hever d			15 31			16 31			17 31			18 31			19 31			20 31			21 31	
Cowden d			15 35			16 35			17 35			18 35			19 35			20 35			21 35	
Ashurst d			15 39			16 39			17 39			18 39			19 39			20 39			21 39	
Eridge d			15 45			16 45			17 45			18 45			19 45			20 45			21 45	
Crowborough d			15 51			16 51			17 51			18 51			19 51			20 51			21 51	
Buxted d			15 57			16 57			17 57			18 57			19 57			20 57			21 57	
Uckfield a			16 03			17 03			18 03			19 03			20 03			21 03			22 03	

A not 23 May

B from 12 September

C until 5 September

London - Oxted, East Grinstead and Uckfield

		SN 1 A		SN 1	SN 1 A	SN 1 B
London Victoria 15 ⊖175,177	d	21 25			22 25	22 22
Clapham Junction-I 10 175,177	d	21 31			22 31	22 28
London Bridge 4 ⊖175,177	d					
Norwood Junction 2 175,177	d					
East Croydon 175,177 ⇌	d	21 43			22 43	22 44
South Croydon 4 175	d					
Sanderstead	d	21 47			22 47	22 48
Riddlesdown	d	21 50			22 50	22 51
Upper Warlingham	d	21 54			22 54	22 55
Woldingham	d	21 58			22 58	22 59
Oxted 3	a	22 03			23 03	23 04
	d	22 03		22 18	23 03	23 04
Hurst Green	d	22 06		22 21	23 06	23 07
Lingfield	d	22 12			23 12	23 13
Dormans	d	22 15			23 15	23 16
East Grinstead	a	22 20			23 20	23 21
Edenbridge Town	d			22 27		
Hever	d			22 31		
Cowden	d			22 35		
Ashurst	d			22 39		
Eridge	d			22 45		
Crowborough	d			22 51		
Buxted	d			22 57		
Uckfield	a			23 03		

A until 5 September

B from 12 September

Uckfield, East Grinstead and Oxted - London

		SN 1	SN 1	SN 1	SN 1	SN 1	SN 1	SN 1	SN 1	SN 1		SN 1	SN 1
Uckfield	d				06 00			06 34				07 08	
Buxted	d				06 05			06 39				07 14	
Crowborough	d				06 12			06 46				07 21	
Eridge	d				06 17			06 51				07 27	
Ashurst	d				06 22			06 56					
Cowden	d				06 27			07 01					
Hever	d				06 31			07 05					
Edenbridge Town	d				06 34			07 09				07 39	
East Grinstead	d		05 58	06 16		06 37	06 49		07 07	07 19			07 37
Dormans	d		06 02	06 20		06 41	06 53		07 11	07 23			07 41
Lingfield	d		06 05	06 23		06 44	06 56		07 14	07 26			07 44
Hurst Green	d	06 00	06 12	06 30	06 41	06 51	07 03	07 17	07 21	07 33		07 47	07 51
Oxted 3	a	06 02	06 14	06 32	06 44	06 53	07 05	07 19	07 23	07 35		07 49	07 53
	d	06 03	06 15	06 33		06 54	07 06	07 20	07 24	07 36		07 50	07 54
Woldingham	d	06 08		06 38		06 59	07 11		07 29	07 41			07 59
Upper Warlingham	d	06 12		06 42		07 03	07 15		07 33	07 45			08 03
Riddlesdown	d	06 15		06 45		07 06	07 18		07 36	07 48			08 06
Sanderstead	d	06 18		06 48		07 10	07 22		07 40	07 51			08 10
South Croydon 4 175	d			06 51			07 25			07 54			
East Croydon 175,177 ⇌	a	06 23	06 27	06 54		07 14	07 27	07 31	07 44	07 58		08 04	08 14
Norwood Junction 2 175,177	a												
London Bridge 4 ⊖175,177	a	06 39		07 11			07 47	07 50		08 17		08 23	
Clapham Junction-I 10 175,177	a		06 38			07 27			07 55				08 26
London Victoria 15 ⊖175,177	a		06 45			07 36			08 04				08 35

		SN 1	SN 1	SN 1	SN 1	SN 1	SN 1	SN 1		SN 1	SN 1	SN 1	SN 1
Uckfield	d		07 34			08 04		08 34				09 34	
Buxted	d		07 39			08 09		08 39				09 39	
Crowborough	d		07 46			08 16		08 46				09 46	
Eridge	d		07 51			08 21		08 51				09 51	
Ashurst	d		07 56			08 26		08 56				09 56	
Cowden	d		08 01			08 31		09 01				10 01	
Hever	d		08 05			08 35		09 05				10 05	
Edenbridge Town	d		08 09			08 39		09 08				10 08	
East Grinstead	d	07 49		08 07	08 19		08 37			09 07	09 37		10 07
Dormans	d	07 53		08 11	08 23		08 41			09 11	09 41		10 11
Lingfield	d	07 56		08 14	08 26		08 44			09 14	09 44		10 14
Hurst Green	d	08 03	08 16	08 21	08 33	08 46	08 51	09 15		09 21	09 51	10 15	10 21
Oxted 3	a	08 05	08 19	08 23	08 35	08 48	08 53	09 18		09 23	09 53	10 17	10 23
	d	08 06	08 20	08 24	08 36	08 50	08 53	09 19		09 23	09 53	10 18	10 23
Woldingham	d	08 11		08 29	08 41		08 59			09 29	09 59		10 29
Upper Warlingham	d	08 15		08 33	08 45		09 02			09 32	10 02		10 32
Riddlesdown	d	08 18		08 36	08 48		09 06			09 36	10 06		10 36
Sanderstead	d	08 22		08 39	08 51		09 09			09 39	10 09		10 39
South Croydon 4 175	d	08 26		08 42	08 54								
East Croydon 175,177 ⇌	a	08 29	08 32	08 45	08 57	09 01	09 13	09 32		09 43	10 13	10 32	10 43
Norwood Junction 2 175,177	a												
London Bridge 4 ⊖175,177	a	08 47	08 54		09 16	09 20		09 51				10 49	
Clapham Junction-I 10 175,177	a			08 55			09 26			09 55	10 25		10 55
London Victoria 15 ⊖175,177	a			09 04			09 35			10 02	10 35		11 05

		SN 1	SN 1	SN 1	SN 1	SN 1		SN 1	SN 1	SN 1	SN 1	SN 1	SN 1
Uckfield	d		10 34			11 34				12 34			13 34
Buxted	d		10 39			11 39				12 39			13 39
Crowborough	d		10 46			11 46				12 46			13 46
Eridge	d		10 51			11 51				12 51			13 51
Ashurst	d		10 56			11 56				12 56			13 56
Cowden	d		11 01			12 01				13 01			14 01
Hever	d		11 05			12 05				13 05			14 05
Edenbridge Town	d		11 08			12 08				13 08			14 08
East Grinstead	d	10 37		11 07	11 37			12 07	12 37		13 07	13 37	
Dormans	d	10 41		11 11	11 41			12 11	12 41		13 11	13 41	
Lingfield	d	10 44		11 14	11 44			12 14	12 44		13 14	13 44	
Hurst Green	d	10 51	11 15	11 21	11 51	12 15		12 21	12 51	13 15	13 21	13 51	14 15
Oxted 3	a	10 53	11 17	11 23	11 53	12 17		12 23	12 53	13 17	13 23	13 53	14 17
	d	10 53	11 18	11 23	11 53	12 18		12 23	12 53	13 18	13 23	13 53	14 18
Woldingham	d	10 59		11 29	11 59			12 29	12 59		13 29	13 59	
Upper Warlingham	d	11 02		11 32	12 02			12 32	13 02		13 32	14 02	
Riddlesdown	d	11 06		11 36	12 06			12 36	13 06		13 36	14 06	
Sanderstead	d	11 09		11 39	12 09			12 39	13 09		13 39	14 09	
South Croydon 4 175	d												
East Croydon 175,177 ⇌	a	11 13	11 32	11 43	12 13	12 32		12 43	13 13	13 32	13 43	14 13	14 32
Norwood Junction 2 175,177	a												
London Bridge 4 ⊖175,177	a		11 49			12 49				13 49			14 49
Clapham Junction-I 10 175,177	a	11 25		11 55	12 25			12 55	13 25		13 55	14 25	
London Victoria 15 ⊖175,177	a	11 32		12 02	12 32			13 02	13 32		14 02	14 32	

		SN 1	SN 1	SN 1		SN 1	SN 1	SN 1	SN 1	SN 1	SN 1	SN 1	SN 1
Uckfield	d			14 34				15 34			16 33		17 03
Buxted	d			14 39				15 39			16 38		17 08
Crowborough	d			14 46				15 46			16 46		17 16
Eridge	d			14 51				15 51			16 51		17 21
Ashurst	d			14 56				15 56			16 56		
Cowden	d			15 01				16 01			17 01		
Hever	d			15 05				16 05			17 05		
Edenbridge Town	d			15 08				16 08			17 08		17 34
East Grinstead	d	14 07	14 37			15 07	15 37		16 07	16 37		17 07	
Dormans	d	14 11	14 41			15 11	15 41		16 11	16 41		17 11	
Lingfield	d	14 14	14 44			15 14	15 44		16 14	16 44		17 14	
Hurst Green	d	14 21	14 51	15 15		15 21	15 51	16 15	16 21	16 51	17 15	17 21	17 40
Oxted 3	a	14 23	14 53	15 17		15 23	15 53	16 17	16 23	16 53	17 17	17 23	17 43
	d	14 23	14 53	15 18		15 23	15 53	16 18	16 23	16 53	17 18	17 23	
Woldingham	d	14 29	14 59			15 29	15 59		16 29	16 59		17 29	
Upper Warlingham	d	14 32	15 02			15 32	16 02		16 32	17 02		17 32	
Riddlesdown	d	14 36	15 06			15 36	16 06		16 36	17 06		17 36	
Sanderstead	d	14 39	15 09			15 39	16 09		16 39	17 09		17 39	
South Croydon 4 175	d												
East Croydon 175,177 ⇌	a	14 43	15 13	15 32		15 43	16 13	16 32	16 43	17 13	17 35	17 43	
Norwood Junction 2 175,177	a												
London Bridge 4 ⊖175,177	a			15 49				16 47			17 52		
Clapham Junction-I 10 175,177	a	14 55	15 25			15 55	16 25		16 55	17 25		17 55	
London Victoria 15 ⊖175,177	a	15 02	15 32			16 05	16 35		17 05	17 32		18 02	

		SN 1		SN 1	SN 1	SN 1	SN 1	SN 1	SN 1	SN 1	SN 1	SN 1	
Uckfield	d			17 32			17 58			18 30			
Buxted	d			17 37			18 03			18 35			
Crowborough	d			17 44			18b16			18 43			
Eridge	d			17 49			18 21			18 48			
Ashurst	d			17 54						18 53			
Cowden	d			17 59						18 57			
Hever	d			18 03						19 01			
Edenbridge Town	d			18 06			18 34			19 05			
East Grinstead	d	17 37			18 07	18 17		18 37	18 47		19 07	19 17	
Dormans	d	17 41			18 11	18 21		18 41	18 51		19 11	19 21	
Lingfield	d	17 44			18 14	18 24		18 44	18 54		19 14	19 24	
Hurst Green	d	17 51		18 13	18 21	18 31	18 40	18 51	19 01	19 11	19 21	19 31	
Oxted 3	a	17 53		18 15	18 23	18 33	18 43	18 53	19 03	19 14	19 23	19 33	
	d	17 53		18 20	18 23	18 34		18 53	19 04	19 18	19 23	19 34	
Woldingham	d	17 59			18 29	18 39		18 59	19 09		19 29	19 39	
Upper Warlingham	d	18 02			18 32	18 43		19 02	19 13		19 32	19 43	
Riddlesdown	d	18 06			18 36	18 46		19 06	19 16		19 36	19 46	
Sanderstead	d	18 09			18 39	18 49		19 09	19 19		19 39	19 49	
South Croydon 4 175	d												
East Croydon 175,177 ⇌	a	18 13		18 35	18 43	18 56		19 13	19 25	19 31	19 43	19 55	
Norwood Junction 2 175,177	a					19 01							
London Bridge 4 ⊖175,177	a			18 50		19 15				19 49			
Clapham Junction-I 10 175,177	a	18 25			18 55			19 25			19 55		
London Victoria 15 ⊖175,177	a	18 32			19 05			19 32			20 02		

		SN 1	SN 1	SN 1	SN 1	SN 1	SN 1	SN 1	SN 1	SN 1		SN 1	SN 1
Uckfield	d	18 57			19 33		20 04		20 34				21 34
Buxted	d	19 02			19 38		20 09		20 39				21 39
Crowborough	d	19c16			19 46		20 16		20 46				21 46
Eridge	d	19 21			19 51		20 21		20 51				21 51
Ashurst	d	19 26			19 56				20 56				21 56
Cowden	d	19 31			20 01				21 01				22 01
Hever	d	19 35			20 05				21 05				22 05
Edenbridge Town	d	19 38			20 08		20 33		21 08				22 08
East Grinstead	d		19 37	19 47		20 07		20 37		21 07		21 37	
Dormans	d		19 41	19 51		20 11		20 41		21 11		21 41	
Lingfield	d		19 44	19 54		20 14		20 44		21 14		21 44	
Hurst Green	d	19 45	19 51	20 01	20 15	20 21	20 39	20 51	21 15	21 21		21 51	22 15
Oxted 3	a	19 47	19 53	20 03	20 17	20 23	20 42	20 53	21 17	21 23		21 53	22 17
	d	19 48	19 53	20 04	20 18	20 23	20 42	20 53	21 18	21 23		21 53	22 18
Woldingham	d		19 59	20 09		20 29		20 59		21 29		21 59	
Upper Warlingham	d		20 02	20 13		20 32		21 02		21 32		22 02	
Riddlesdown	d		20 06	20 16		20 36		21 06		21 36		22 06	
Sanderstead	d		20 09	20 19		20 39		21 09		21 39		22 09	
South Croydon 4 175	d												
East Croydon 175,177 ⇌	a	20 06	20 13	20 25	20 30	20 43	20 54	21 13	21 30	21 43		22 13	22 33
Norwood Junction 2 175,177	a												
London Bridge 4 ⊖175,177	a	20 21			20 48		21 09		21 49				22 49
Clapham Junction-I 10 175,177	a		20 25			20 55		21 25		21 55		22 25	
London Victoria 15 ⊖175,177	a		20 32			21 05		21 35		22 05		22 35	

b arr. 1810

c arr. 1909

Table 184

Mondays to Fridays

Uckfield, East Grinstead and Oxted - London

		SN 1	SN 1	SN 1	SN 1
Uckfield	d				22 32
Buxted	d				22 37
Crowborough	d				22 44
Eridge	d				22 49
Ashurst	d				
Cowden	d				
Hever	d				
Edenbridge Town	d				23 01
East Grinstead	d	22 07	22 37	22 54	
Dormans	d	22 11	22 41		
Lingfield	d	22 14	22 44		
Hurst Green	d	22 21	22 51		23 08
Oxted 3	a	22 23	22 53	23 06	23 10
	d	22 23	22 53	23 07	23 11
Woldingham	d	22 29	22 59		
Upper Warlingham	d	22 32	23 02		
Riddlesdown	d	22 36	23 06		
Sanderstead	d	22 39	23 09		
South Croydon 4 175	d				
East Croydon 175,177 ⇌	a	22 43	23 13	23 19	23 28
Norwood Junction 2 175,177	a				
London Bridge 4 ⊖175,177	a				
Clapham Junction-1 10 175,177	a	22 55	23 25	23 32	
London Victoria 15 ⊖175,177	a	23 05	23 35	23 40	

Saturdays

		SN 1	SN 1	SN 1	SN 1	SN 1	SN 1	SN 1	SN 1	SN 1	SN 1	SN 1	SN 1	SN 1	SN 1	SN 1	SN 1	SN 1	SN 1	SN 1	SN 1	SN 1	SN 1
Uckfield	d		06 34			07 34			08 34			09 34			10 34			11 34			12 34		
Buxted	d		06 39			07 39			08 39			09 39			10 39			11 39			12 39		
Crowborough	d		06 46			07 46			08 46			09 46			10 46			11 46			12 46		
Eridge	d		06 51			07 51			08 51			09 51			10 51			11 51			12 51		
Ashurst	d		06 56			07 56			08 56			09 56			10 56			11 56			12 56		
Cowden	d		07 01			08 01			09 01			10 01			11 01			12 01			13 01		
Hever	d		07 05			08 05			09 05			10 05			11 05			12 05			13 05		
Edenbridge Town	d		07 08			08 08			09 08			10 08			11 08			12 08			13 08		
East Grinstead	d	06 37		07 07	07 37		08 07	08 37		09 07	09 37		10 07	10 37		11 07	11 37		12 07	12 37		13 07	13 37
Dormans	d	06 41		07 11	07 41		08 11	08 41		09 11	09 41		10 11	10 41		11 11	11 41		12 11	12 41		13 11	13 41
Lingfield	d	06 44		07 14	07 44		08 14	08 44		09 14	09 44		10 14	10 44		11 14	11 44		12 14	12 44		13 14	13 44
Hurst Green	d	06 51	07 15	07 21	07 51	08 15	08 21	08 51	09 15	09 21	09 51	10 15	10 21	10 51	11 15	11 21	11 51	12 15	12 21	12 51	13 15	13 21	13 51
Oxted 3	a	06 53	07 18	07 23	07 53	08 18	08 23	08 53	09 17	09 23	09 53	10 17	10 23	10 53	11 17	11 23	11 53	12 17	12 23	12 53	13 17	13 23	13 53
	d	06 53	07 19	07 23	07 53	08 19	08 23	08 53	09 18	09 23	09 53	10 18	10 23	10 53	11 18	11 23	11 53	12 18	12 23	12 53	13 18	13 23	13 53
Woldingham	d	06 59		07 29	07 59		08 29	08 59		09 29	09 59		10 29	10 59		11 29	11 59		12 29	12 59		13 29	13 59
Upper Warlingham	d	07 02		07 32	08 02		08 32	09 02		09 32	10 02		10 32	11 02		11 32	12 02		12 32	13 02		13 32	14 02
Riddlesdown	d	07 06		07 36	08 06		08 36	09 06		09 36	10 06		10 36	11 06		11 36	12 06		12 36	13 06		13 36	14 06
Sanderstead	d	07 09		07 39	08 09		08 39	09 09		09 39	10 09		10 39	11 09		11 39	12 09		12 39	13 09		13 39	14 09
South Croydon 4 175	d																						
East Croydon 175,177 ⇌	a	07 13	07 33	07 43	08 13	08 32	08 43	09 13	09 32	09 43	10 13	10 32	10 43	11 13	11 32	11 43	12 13	12 32	12 43	13 13	13 32	13 43	14 13
Norwood Junction 2 175,177	a																						
London Bridge 4 ⊖175,177	a		07 49			08 49			09 49			10 49			11 49			12 49			13 49		
Clapham Junction-1 10 175,177	a	07 25		07 55	08 25		08 55	09 25		09 55	10 25		10 55	11 25		11 55	12 25		12 55	13 25		13 55	14 25
London Victoria 15 ⊖175,177	a	07 32		08 02	08 32		09 02	09 32		10 02	10 32		11 02	11 32		12 02	12 32		13 02	13 32		14 02	14 32

		SN 1	SN 1	SN 1	SN 1	SN 1	SN 1	SN 1	SN 1	SN 1	SN 1	SN 1	SN 1	SN 1	SN 1	SN 1	SN 1	SN 1	SN 1	SN 1	SN 1	SN 1	SN 1
Uckfield	d	13 34			14 34			15 34			16 34			17 34			18 34			19 34			20 34
Buxted	d	13 39			14 39			15 39			16 39			17 39			18 39			19 39			20 39
Crowborough	d	13 46			14 46			15 46			16 46			17 46			18 46			19 46			20 46
Eridge	d	13 51			14 51			15 51			16 51			17 51			18 51			19 51			20 51
Ashurst	d	13 56			14 56			15 56			16 56			17 56			18 56			19 56			20 56
Cowden	d	14 01			15 01			16 01			17 01			18 01			19 01			20 01			21 01
Hever	d	14 05			15 05			16 05			17 05			18 05			19 05			20 05			21 05
Edenbridge Town	d	14 08			15 08			16 08			17 08			18 08			19 08			20 08			21 08
East Grinstead	d		14 07	14 37		15 07	15 37		16 07	16 37		17 07	17 37		18 07	18 37		19 07	19 37		20 07	20 37	
Dormans	d		14 11	14 41		15 11	15 41		16 11	16 41		17 11	17 41		18 11	18 41		19 11	19 41		20 11	20 41	
Lingfield	d		14 14	14 44		15 14	15 44		16 14	16 44		17 14	17 44		18 14	18 44		19 14	19 44		20 14	20 44	
Hurst Green	d	14 15	14 21	14 51	15 15	15 21	15 51	16 15	16 21	16 51	17 15	17 21	17 51	18 15	18 21	18 51	19 15	19 21	19 51	20 15	20 21	20 51	21 15
Oxted 3	a	14 17	14 23	14 53	15 17	15 23	15 53	16 17	16 23	16 53	17 17	17 23	17 53	18 17	18 23	18 53	19 17	19 23	19 53	20 17	20 23	20 53	21 17
	d	14 18	14 23	14 53	15 18	15 23	15 53	16 18	16 23	16 53	17 18	17 23	17 53	18 18	18 23	18 53	19 18	19 23	19 53	20 18	20 23	20 53	21 18
Woldingham	d		14 29	14 59		15 29	15 59		16 29	16 59		17 29	17 59		18 29	18 59		19 29	19 59		20 29	20 59	
Upper Warlingham	d		14 32	15 02		15 32	16 02		16 32	17 02		17 32	18 02		18 32	19 02		19 32	20 02		20 32	21 02	
Riddlesdown	d		14 36	15 06		15 36	16 06		16 36	17 06		17 36	18 06		18 36	19 06		19 36	20 06		20 36	21 06	
Sanderstead	d		14 39	15 09		15 39	16 09		16 39	17 09		17 39	18 09		18 39	19 09		19 39	20 09		20 39	21 09	
South Croydon 4 175	d																						
East Croydon 175,177 ⇌	a	14 32	14 43	15 13	15 32	15 43	16 13	16 32	16 43	17 13	17 32	17 43	18 13	18 32	18 43	19 13	19 32	19 43	20 13	20 32	20 43	21 13	21 32
Norwood Junction 2 175,177	a																						
London Bridge 4 ⊖175,177	a	14 49			15 49			16 49			17 49			18 49			19 49			20 49			21 49
Clapham Junction-1 10 175,177	a		14 55	15 25		15 55	16 25		16 55	17 25		17 55	18 25		18 55	19 25		19 55	20 25		20 55	21 25	
London Victoria 15 ⊖175,177	a		15 02	15 32		16 02	16 32		17 02	17 32		18 02	18 32		19 02	19 32		20 02	20 32		21 02	21 32	

Table 184

Saturdays

Uckfield, East Grinstead and Oxted - London

		SN 1	SN 1	SN 1	SN 1	SN 1	SN 1
Uckfield	d			21 34			22 32
Buxted	d			21 39			22 37
Crowborough	d			21 46			22 44
Eridge	d			21 51			22 49
Ashurst	d			21 56			
Cowden	d			22 01			
Hever	d			22 05			
Edenbridge Town	d			22 08			23 01
East Grinstead	d	21 07	21 37		22 07	22 37	
Dormans	d	21 11	21 41		22 11	22 41	
Lingfield	d	21 14	21 44		22 14	22 44	
Hurst Green	d	21 21	21 51	22 15	22 21	22 51	23 08
Oxted 3	a	21 23	21 53	22 17	22 23	22 53	23 10
	d	21 23	21 53	22 18	22 23	22 53	23 11
Woldingham	d	21 29	21 59		22 29	22 59	
Upper Warlingham	d	21 32	22 02		22 32	23 02	
Riddlesdown	d	21 36	22 06		22 36	23 06	
Sanderstead	d	21 39	22 09		22 39	23 09	
South Croydon 4 175	d						
East Croydon 175,177 ⇌	a	21 43	22 13	22 32	22 43	23 13	23 26
Norwood Junction 2 175,177	a						
London Bridge 4 ⊖175,177	a			22 49			
Clapham Junction-1 10 175,177	a	21 55	22 25		22 55	23 25	
London Victoria 15 ⊖175,177	a	22 02	22 32		23 02	23 32	

Sundays

		SN 1	SN 1	SN 1	SN 1	SN 1	SN 1	SN 1	SN 1	SN 1	SN 1	SN 1	SN 1	SN 1	SN 1	SN 1	SN 1	SN 1	SN 1	SN 1	SN 1	SN 1	SN 1
Uckfield	d				10 17		11 17		12 17		13 17		14 17		15 17		16 17		17 17		18 17		19 17
Buxted	d				10 22		11 22		12 22		13 22		14 22		15 22		16 22		17 22		18 22		19 22
Crowborough	d				10 29		11 29		12 29		13 29		14 29		15 29		16 29		17 29		18 29		19 29
Eridge	d				10 34		11 34		12 34		13 34		14 34		15 34		16 34		17 34		18 34		19 34
Ashurst	d				10 39		11 39		12 39		13 39		14 39		15 39		16 39		17 39		18 39		19 39
Cowden	d				10 44		11 44		12 44		13 44		14 44		15 44		16 44		17 44		18 44		19 44
Hever	d				10 48		11 48		12 48		13 48		14 48		15 48		16 48		17 48		18 48		19 48
Edenbridge Town	d				10 51		11 51		12 51		13 51		14 51		15 51		16 51		17 51		18 51		19 51
East Grinstead	d	07 52	08 52	09 52		10 52		11 52		12 52		13 52		14 52		15 52		16 52		17 52		18 52	
Dormans	d	07 56	08 56	09 56		10 56		11 56		12 56		13 56		14 56		15 56		16 56		17 56		18 56	
Lingfield	d	07 59	08 59	09 59		10 59		11 59		12 59		13 59		14 59		15 59		16 59		17 59		18 59	
Hurst Green	d	08 06	09 06	10 06	10 58	11 06	11 58	12 06	12 58	13 06	13 58	14 06	14 58	15 06	15 58	16 06	16 58	17 06	17 58	18 06	18 58	19 06	19 58
Oxted 3	a	08 08	09 08	10 08	11 01	11 08	12 01	12 08	13 01	13 08	14 01	14 08	15 01	15 08	16 01	16 08	17 01	17 08	18 01	18 08	19 01	19 08	20 01
	d	08 08	09 08	10 08		11 08		12 08		13 08		14 08		15 08		16 08		17 08		18 08		19 08	
Woldingham	d	08 14	09 14	10 14		11 14		12 14		13 14		14 14		15 14		16 14		17 14		18 14		19 14	
Upper Warlingham	d	08 17	09 17	10 17		11 17		12 17		13 17		14 17		15 17		16 17		17 17		18 17		19 17	
Riddlesdown	d	08 21	09 21	10 21		11 21		12 21		13 21		14 21		15 21		16 21		17 21		18 21		19 21	
Sanderstead	d	08 24	09 24	10 24		11 24		12 24		13 24		14 24		15 24		16 24		17 24		18 24		19 24	
South Croydon 4 175	d																						
East Croydon 175,177 ⇌	a	08 28	09 28	10 28		11 28		12 28		13 28		14 28		15 28		16 28		17 28		18 28		19 28	
Norwood Junction 2 175,177	a																						
London Bridge 4 ⊖175,177	a																						
Clapham Junction-1 10 175,177	a	08 41	09 41	10 41		11 41		12 41		13 41		14 41		15 41		16 41		17 41		18 41		19 41	
London Victoria 15 ⊖175,177	a	08 48	09 48	10 48		11 48		12 48		13 48		14 48		15 48		16 48		17 48		18 48		19 48	

		SN 1	SN 1	SN 1	SN 1	SN 1	SN 1	SN 1
Uckfield	d		20 17		21 17		22 17	
Buxted	d		20 22		21 22		22 22	
Crowborough	d		20 29		21 29		22 29	
Eridge	d		20 34		21 34		22 34	
Ashurst	d		20 39		21 39		22 39	
Cowden	d		20 44		21 44		22 44	
Hever	d		20 48		21 48		22 48	
Edenbridge Town	d		20 51		21 51		22 51	
East Grinstead	d	19 52		20 52		21 52		22 52
Dormans	d	19 56		20 56		21 56		22 56
Lingfield	d	19 59		20 59		21 59		22 59
Hurst Green	d	20 06	20 58	21 06	21 58	22 06	22 58	23 06
Oxted 3	a	20 08	21 01	21 08	22 01	22 08	23 01	23 08
	d	20 08		21 08		22 08	23 02	23 08
Woldingham	d	20 14		21 14		22 14		23 14
Upper Warlingham	d	20 17		21 17		22 17		23 17
Riddlesdown	d	20 21		21 21		22 21		23 21
Sanderstead	d	20 24		21 24		22 24		23 24
South Croydon 4 175	d							
East Croydon 175,177 ⇌	a	20 28		21 28		22 28	23 14	23 28
Norwood Junction 2 175,177	a							
London Bridge 4 ⊖175,177	a							
Clapham Junction-1 10 175,177	a	20 41		21 41		22 41		23 41
London Victoria 15 ⊖175,177	a	20 48		21 48		22 50		23 50

Network Diagram for Tables 186, 188

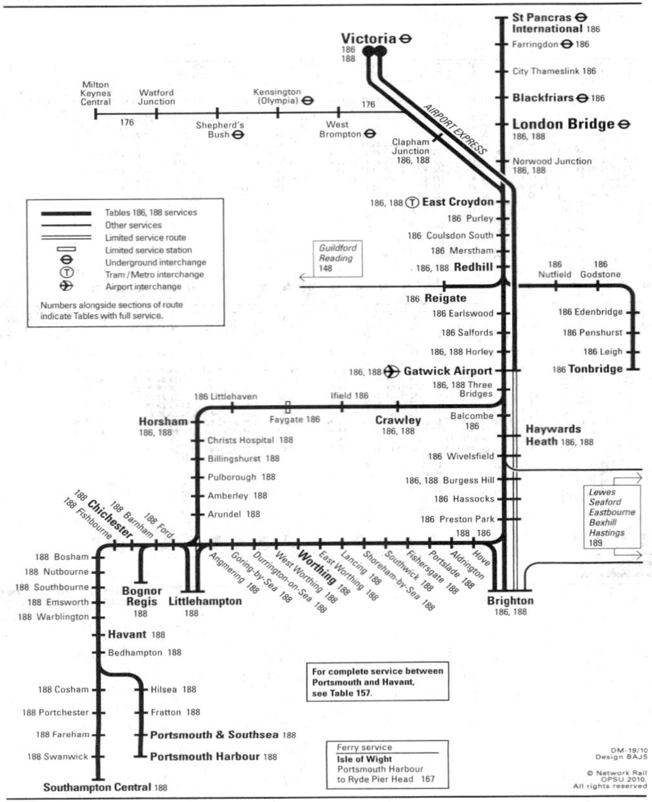

Bedford and London - Brighton

		SN MX ◇1	SN MO 1	FC 1 A	FC MX 1	SN MX 1	FC 1 B	SN MX ◇1	SN MO ◇1	GX 1	SN MX 1	GW MX 1	SN MX ◇1	SN MO ◇1	FC MX 1	FC MO 1	GX 1	SN MX 1	GX 1	GW MO 1	SN MX ◇1	SN MX ◇1	FC
London Victoria [15] ⊖	d	23p02	23p04			23p10		23p17	23p17	23p30			23p32	23p32			23p45	23p47	00 02		00 05		
Clapham Junction [10]	d	23p08	23p10			23p16		23p23	23p23				23p38	23p38				23p53			00 11		
Bedford	d																						
Luton [10]	d																						
Luton Airport Parkway [7]	d																						
St Albans City	d																						
St Pancras International [15] ⊖	d																						
Farringdon [3] ⊖	d																						
City Thameslink [3]	d																						
London Blackfriars [3] ⊖	d																						
London Bridge [4] ⊖	d			23p12	23p12		23p12								23p42	23p42							00 12
London Bridge [4] ⊖	d																						
Norwood Junction [2]	d																						
East Croydon	a	23p19	23p22	23p24	23p24	23p27	23p27	23p33	23p37				23p51	23p52	23p56	23p56		00 05			00 24		00 26
	d	23p20	23p22	23p24	23p24	23p28	23p27	23p33	23p38				23p52	23p53	23p56	23p57		00 06			00 25		00 26
Purley [4]	d		23p29			23p33												00 12					
Coulsdon South	d		23p33			23p37												00 15					
Merstham	d		23p38			23p42												00 21					
Redhill	a	23p31	23p42			23p46						23p58	00 03	00 05				00 24		00 30			
	d	23p31	23p42			23p46					23p55	00 03	00 05	00 05				00 25		00 34			
Reigate	a																						
Nutfield	d																						
Godstone	d																						
Edenbridge	d										00 06												
Penshurst	d																						
Leigh (Kent)	d																						
Tonbridge [4]	a										00 15												
Earlswood (Surrey)	d					23p49																	
Salfords	d					23p52																	
Horley [4]	d		23p50			23p56												00 31					
Gatwick Airport [10]	a	23p38	23p54	23p41	23p40	23p58	23p48	23p50	23p59	00 05		00 11	00 14	00 14	00 18	00 18	00 20	00 33	00 37	00 41	00 42		00 48
	d	23p39	23p55	23p41	23p41	23p59	23p50	23p51	00 01				00 15	00 15	00 18	00 19		00 34			00 43		00 48
Three Bridges [15]	a	23p44	00 01	23p47	23p47	00 04	23p54	23p55	00 05				00 20	00 19	00 24	00 24		00 39			00 48		00 54
	d	23p44	00 01	23p47	23p47	00 04	23p54	23p56	00 06				00 20	00 20				00 39			00 48		
Crawley	d		00 05			00 07												00 43					
Ifield	d		00 07			00 10												00 46					
Faygate	d																						
Littlehaven	d		00 14			00 16												00 52					
Horsham [4]	a		00 17			00 19												00 55					
Balcombe	d				23p53								00 26	00 26								>	
Haywards Heath	d	23p53		23p56	23p58		00 03	00 05	00 15				00 31	00 31							01 03	01 06	
Wivelsfield	d	23p57			00 02								00 35	00 35									
Lewes [4]	a																					01 20	
Burgess Hill [4]	d	23p59		00 01	00 04		00 08	00 10					00 37	00 37									
Hassocks [4]	d	00 02			00 08								00 41	00 41									
Preston Park	d	00 09			00 15								00 48	00 48									
Hove [2]	a							00 21	00 28												01s25		
Brighton [10]	a	00 15		00 13	00 19		00 22						00 52	00 52							01s17		

A MO until 6 September

B MO from 13 September

Table 186

Mondays to Fridays

Bedford and London - Brighton

		SN 1	GW MX 1	FC	GX 1	SN ◇1	FC 1	FC 1	SN 1	FC 1	SN 1	FC	GX 1	FC 1	SN ◇1	FC 1	GX 1	FC 1	GX 1	SN ◇1	GX 1	SN 1
		00 14																				
London Victoria 15 ⊖	d	00 20			00 30	01 00			02 00		03 00		03 30		04 00		04 30		05 00	05 02	05 15	
Clapham Junction 10	d					01 08			02 08		03 08				04 08					05 08		
Bedford	d																					
Luton 10	d																					
Luton Airport Parkway 7	d																					
St Albans City	d																					
St Pancras International 15 ⊖	d																					
Farringdon 3 ⊖	d																					
City Thameslink 3	d																					
London Blackfriars 3 ⊖	d																					
London Bridge 4 ⊖	d			00 42			01 05	01 35		02 05		03 05		03 35		04 05		04 35				
Norwood Junction 2	d																					
East Croydon	a	00 31		00 56		01 21	01 32	02 02	02 21	02 30	03 21	03 30		04 00	04 21	04 30		05 00		05 20		
	d	00 32		00 56		01 22	01 32	02 02	02 22	02 32	03 22	03 32		04 02	04 22	04 32		05 02		05 20		
Purley 4	d	00 37				01 27			02 27		03 27				04 27					05 25		
Coulsdon South	d	00 41																		05 28		
Merstham	d	00 47																		05 34		
Redhill	a	00 50	00 49																	05 37		
	d	00 51	00 54																	05 38		
Reigate	a																					05 35
Nutfield	d																					05 39
Godstone	d																					05 45
Edenbridge	d																					05 50
Penshurst	d																					05 57
Leigh (Kent)	d																					06 00
Tonbridge 4	a																					06 05
Earlswood (Surrey)	d																					
Salfords	d																					
Horley 4	d	00 57				01 42			02 42		03 42				04 43					05 44		
Gatwick Airport 10	a	00 59	01 03	01 18	01 20	01 44	01 51	02 21	02 44	02 51	03 44	03 51	04 05	04 24	04 46	04 51	05 05	05 21	05 35	05 46	05 50	
	d			01 18		01 46	01 52	02 22	02 46	02 52	03 46	03 52		04 24	04 47	04 52		05 22		05 47		
Three Bridges 15	a			01 24		01 50	01 58	02 28	02 50	02 58	03 50	03 58		04 30	04 52	04 58		05 26		05 52		
	d					01 52									04 52	05 00		05 26		05 52		
Crawley	d																					
Ifield	d																					
Faygate	d																					
Littlehaven	d																					
Horsham 4	a																					
Balcombe	d																			05 58		
Haywards Heath	d					02 06									05 01	05 10		05 36		06 04		
Wivelsfield	d																	05 40		06 08		
Lewes 4	a																					
Burgess Hill 4	d															05 15		05 42		06 10		
Hassocks 4	d															05 18		05 46		06 13		
Preston Park	d																	05 53		06 20		
Hove 2	a																					
Brighton 10	a					02 23									05 16	05 29		05 57		06 26		

Table 186

Mondays to Fridays

Bedford and London - Brighton

		GW 1	SN 1	SN 1	SN	FC 1	GX 1	SN ◇1	FC 1	GX 1	FC 1	GX 1	SN ◇1	SN ◇1	GX ◇1	FC 1	GW 1	SN 1	GW 1	GX 1	SN 1
London Victoria 15 ⊖	d						05 30	05 32		05 45		06 00	06 02		06 15					06 30	
Clapham Junction 10	d							05 38					06 08								
Bedford	d					03 42			04 10		04 20					05 00					
Luton 10	d					04 06			04 34		04 44					05 24					
Luton Airport Parkway 7	d					04 08			04 36		04 46					05 26					
St Albans City	d					04 20			04 48		04 58					05 38					
St Pancras International 15 ⊖	d					04 54			05 12		05 32					06 02					
Farringdon 3 ⊖	d					04 59			05 17		05 37					06 07					
City Thameslink 3	d								05 21		05 41					06 11					
London Blackfriars 3 ⊖	d					05 04			05 24		05 44					06 14					
London Bridge 4 ⊖	d								05 30		05 50					06 20					
Norwood Junction 2	d																				
East Croydon	a					05 30		05 48	05 51		06 04		06 17			06 35					
	d					05 32		05 49	05 52		06 06		06 18			06 36					
Purley 4	d							05 54					06 23								
Coulsdon South	d							05 58					06 26								
Merstham	d							06 03					06 32								
Redhill	a	05 40						06 07					06 35	>					06 39		
	d	05 44	05 56					06 07					06 40	06 42			06 24	06 39	06 46		07 00
Reigate	a																06 28	06 43			07 04
Nutfield	d		06 00										06 44								
Godstone	d		06 06										06 50								
Edenbridge	d		06 11										06 55								
Penshurst	d		06 18										07 02								
Leigh (Kent)	d		06 21										07 05								
Tonbridge 4	a		06 26										07 10								
Earlswood (Surrey)	d							06 10						06 44							
Salfords	d							06 13						06 48							
Horley 4	d							06 17						06 51							
Gatwick Airport 10	a	05 54				05 53	06 00	06 19	06 08	06 15	06 21	06 30		06 54	06 44	06 51			06 56	07 00	
	d			05 59		05 56		06 20	06 10		06 22			06 55	06 48	06 52					
Three Bridges 15	a			06 03		06 00		06 25	06 14		06 27			06 59		06 57					
	d			06 04		06 00		06 25	06 14		06 27			07 00		06 57					
Crawley	d			06 07										07 03							
Ifield	d			06 10																	
Faygate	d																				
Littlehaven	d			06 16																	
Horsham 4	a			06 19										07 11							
Balcombe	d								06 20		06 34										
Haywards Heath	d				06 07	06 10		06 34	06 26		06 39				07 00	07 06					
Wivelsfield	d				06 11	06 14		06 38	06 30		06 43					07 10					
Lewes 4	a				06 22			06 49													
Burgess Hill 4	d					06 16			06 32		06 45					07 12					
Hassocks 4	d					06 20			06 36		06 49					07 16					
Preston Park	d					06 27			06 43		06 56					07 23					
Hove 2	a																				
Brighton 10	a					06 31			06 47		07 00				07 13	07 27					

Bedford and London - Brighton

		SN ■	SN ◇■	SN ■	SN ◇■	SN ◇■	FC ■	GX ■	SN ◇■	SN ■	SN ■	GX ■	FC ■	SN ■	GX ■	FC ■	GW ■	GW ■	SN ◇■	GX ■	SN ■	SN ■	SN ■	FC ■	GX ■
London Victoria 15 ⊖	d		06 21		06 32			06 45	06 47	06 51		07 00		07 02	07 15				07 17	07 30			07 36		07 45
Clapham Junction 10	d		06 27		06 38				06 53	06 57				07 08					07 23				07 42		
Bedford	d						05 20						05 40			05 58								06 22	
Luton 10	d						05 44						06 04			06 22								06 46	
Luton Airport Parkway 7	d						05 46						06 06			06 24								06 48	
St Albans City	d						05 58						06 18			06 36								07 00	
St Pancras International 15 ⊖	d						06 22						06 38			06 58								07 20	
Farringdon 3 ⊖	d						06 27						06 43			07 03								07 25	
City Thameslink 3	d						06 31						06 47			07 07								07 29	
London Blackfriars 3 ⊖	d						06 34						06 50			07 09								07 32	
London Bridge 4 ⊖	d						06 42						07 00			07 16					07 30	07 33		07 42	
Norwood Junction 2	d																				07 42				
East Croydon	a		06 38		06 48		06 55		07 03	07 06			07 14	07 17		07 30			07 33		07 45	07 48	07 52	07 55	
	d		06 39		06 49		06 56		07 03	07 07			07 15	07 18		07 31			07 34		07 46	07 49	07 52	07 56	
Purley 4	d		06 44		06 54									07 23									07 57		
Coulsdon South	d				06 57					07 13				07 26							07 52		08 01		
Merstham	d				07 03					07 19				07 32							07 58		08 07		
Redhill	a		06 52	>	07 06					07 22	>			07 35				07 38	07 45		08 01		08 10		
	d		06 56	07 03	07 07					07 27	07 29			07 40			07 28	07 41	07 45		08 02		08 11		
Reigate	a													07 44			07 32								
Nutfield	d			07 07							07 33										08 06				
Godstone	d			07 13							07 39										08 12				
Edenbridge	d			07 18							07 44										08 17				
Penshurst	d			07 25							07 51										08 24				
Leigh (Kent)	d			07 28							07 54										08 27				
Tonbridge 4	a			07 33							08 02										08 32				
Earlswood (Surrey)	d				07 09					07 29									07 48				08 13		
Salfords	d				07 13					07 33									07 51				08 17		
Horley 4	d		07 02		07 16					07 36									07 55				08 21		
Gatwick Airport 10	a		07 04		07 19		07 11	07 15	07 18	07 39		07 30	07 31		07 45	07 46		07 50	07 57	08 02		08 04	08 24	08 11	08 15
	d		07 05		07 20		07 12		07 19	07 40			07 32			07 47			07 58			08 05	08 25	08 12	
Three Bridges 15	a		07 10		07 24	>	07 17		07 24	07 44			07 37			07 52			08 04			08 09	08 30	08 16	
	d		07 10		07 28	07 30	07 17		07 24	07 45			07 37			07 52			08 05			08 10	08 31	08 16	
Crawley	d					07 34				07 49									08 09				08 35		
Ifield	d					07 36				07 52									08 11				08 37		
Faygate	d																		08 15				08 41		
Littlehaven	d					07 43				07 58									08 19				08 45		
Horsham 4	a					07 46				08 01									08 22				08 49		
Balcombe	d		07 16		07 35											07 58								08 22	
Haywards Heath	d	07 10	07 22		07 40		07 26		07 33				07 46			08 04						08 19		08 28	
Wivelsfield	d	07 14	07 26		07 44		07 30		07 37				07 50			08 08								08 32	
Lewes 4	a	07 29							07 52																
Burgess Hill 4	d		07 28		07 46		07 32						07 52			08 10						08 25		08 34	
Hassocks 4	d		07 31		07 50		07 36						07 56			08 14								08 38	
Preston Park	d		07 38		07 57		07 43									08 21								08 45	
Hove 2	a																								
Brighton 10	a		07 43		08 02		07 47						08 05			08 25						08 36		08 49	

Table 186

Mondays to Fridays

Bedford and London - Brighton

		SN ◇■	SN ■	SN ■	SN ◇■	SN ■	GX ■	SN ■	SN ◇■	GW ■	SN ■	SN ◇■	FC ■	GX ■	SN ◇■	SN ◇■	FC ■	SN ■	SN ■	SN ◇■	GX ■	GW ■
London Victoria 15 ⊖	d	07 47			07 52		08 00		08 02			08 07		08 15	08 17					08 21	08 30	
Clapham Junction 10	d	07 53			07 58				08 08			08 13			08 23					08 27		
Bedford	d												06 56				07 00					
Luton 10	d												07 16				07 24					
Luton Airport Parkway 7	d																07 26					
St Albans City	d												07 28				07 38					
St Pancras International 15 ⊖	d												07 48				07 59					
Farringdon 3 ⊖	d												07 53				08 03					
City Thameslink 3	d												07 57				08 07					
London Blackfriars 3 ⊖	d												08 00				08 10					
London Bridge 4 ⊖	d		07 53								08 02						08 18	08 23				
Norwood Junction 2	d										08 14											
East Croydon	a	08 03	08 06		08 09				08 18		08 18	08 22	08 25		08 33		08 36	08 37		08 39		
	d	08 03	08 06		08 09				08 18		08 19	08 23	08 26		08 33		08 37	08 38		08 40		
Purley 4	d										08 25											
Coulsdon South	d										08 28							08 47				
Merstham	d										08 34											
Redhill	a		08 17	>					08 31		08 37							08 54	>			08 46
	d		08 21	08 23		08 00		08 17	08 32	08 33	08 41							08 58	09 00			08 52
Reigate	a					08 04		08 21		08 37									09 04			
Nutfield	d			08 27														09 02				
Godstone	d			08 33														09 08				
Edenbridge	d			08 38														09 13				
Penshurst	d			08 45														09 20				
Leigh (Kent)	d			08 48														09 23				
Tonbridge 4	a			08 53														09 28				
Earlswood (Surrey)	d										08 43											
Salfords	d										08 47											
Horley 4	d										08 50											
Gatwick Airport 10	a	08 18	08 28		08 24		08 30		08 39		08 53		08 41	08 45	08 48		08 51			08 55	09 00	09 01
	d	08 19	08 29		08 25				08 40		08 54		08 42		08 49		08 52			08 56		
Three Bridges 15	a		08 33						08 44		08 59	08 41	08 46				08 57			09 00		
	d		08 34						08 45		08 59	08 42	08 46				08 57			09 01		
Crawley	d								08 48		09 03											
Ifield	d										09 06											
Faygate	d										09 10											
Littlehaven	d										09 14											
Horsham 4	a								08 56		09 17											
Balcombe	d												08 52									
Haywards Heath	d	08 31	08 43		08 37							08 51	08 58		09 04	> 09 10	09 08			09b17		
Wivelsfield	d	08 35	08 47										09 02			09 14				09 21		
Lewes 4	a	08 50														09 25						
Burgess Hill 4	d		08 49										09 04		09 09		09 13			09 23		
Hassocks 4	d		08 52										09 08							09 27		
Preston Park	d		08 59										09 15							09 34		
Hove 2	a				08 53										09 21							
Brighton 10	a		09 04									09 07	09 19				09 24			09 40		

b arr. 0912

Table 186

Mondays to Fridays

Bedford and London - Brighton

		SN ◇1 ⊼	SN 1	SN ◇1 ⊼	FC 1	GX 1 ⊼	SN 1	SN ◇1 ⊼	SN ◇1 ⊼	GX 1 ⊼	SN ◇1 ⊼	SN 1	SN ◇1 ⊼	GW 1	FC 1	GX 1 ⊼	SN 1	SN ◇1 ⊼	SN ◇1 ⊼	SN ◇1	FC 1	GW 1	GX 1 ⊼
London Victoria 15 ⊖	d	08 32		08 36		08 45		08 47		09 00	09 02		09 06			09 15		09 17		09 21			09 30
Clapham Junction 10	d	08 38		08 43				08 53			09 08		09 12					09 23					
Bedford	d				07 28										07 48						08 04		
Luton 10	d				07 48										08 12						08 28		
Luton Airport Parkway 7	d														08 14						08 30		
St Albans City	d				08 00										08 27						08 43		
St Pancras International 15 ⊖	d				08 20										08 48						09 04		
Farringdon 3 ⊖	d				08 25										08 53						09 09		
City Thameslink 3	d				08 29										08 57						09 13		
London Blackfriars 3 ⊖	d				08 32										09 00						09 16		
London Bridge 4 ⊖	d		08 32				08 45					09 03			09 12		09 15						
Norwood Junction 2	d		08 45				08 56					09 15					09 26						
East Croydon	a	08 48	08 48	08 52	08 56		08 59	09 03			09 18	09 18	09 22		09 24		09 30	09 33		09 37	09 39		
	d	08 48	08 49	08 53	08 56		09 00	09 03			09 18	09 21	09 22		09 24		09 30	09 33		09 37	09 39		
Purley 4	d		08 56				09 06					09 27					09 36						
Coulsdon South	d		08 59				09 09					09 30					09 39						
Merstham	d		09 05									09 36					09 45						
Redhill	a	09 02	09 08				09 16				09 30	09 39					09 48					09 42	
	d	09 03	09 12				09 17				09 30	09 40		09 34			09 53					09 51	
Reigate	a													09 38			09 57						
Nutfield	d						09 21																
Godstone	d						09 27																
Edenbridge	d						09 32																
Penshurst	d						09 39																
Leigh (Kent)	d						09 42																
Tonbridge 4	a						09 47																
Earlswood (Surrey)	d		09 14									09 42											
Salfords	d		09 18									09 46											
Horley 4	d		09 21								09 36	09 50											
Gatwick Airport 10	a	09 10	09 24		09 11	09 15		09 18		09 30	09 39	09 53			09 40	09 45		09 48		09 52	09 56	09 59	10 00
	d	09 11	09 25		09 12			09 19			09 40	09 54			09 41			09 49		09 53	09 57		
Three Bridges 15	a	09 16	09 29		09 17						09 44	09 59			09 45					09 58	10 01		
	d	09 16	09 30		09 17						09 45	10 00			09 45					09 58	10 02		
Crawley	d	09 19	09 34								09 48	10 03											
Ifield	d		09 36									10 06											
Faygate	d																						
Littlehaven	d		09 43									10 12											
Horsham 4	a	09 27	09 46								09 56	10 15											
Balcombe	d								>						09 51				>				
Haywards Heath	d				09 26			09 34	09 37						09 57			10 04	10 07	10b17	10 10		
Wivelsfield	d				09 30										10 01				10 11	10 21			
Lewes 4	a							09 52											10 22				
Burgess Hill 4	d				09 33										10 03			10 09		10 23			
Hassocks 4	d				09 36										10 06					10 26			
Preston Park	d				09 43										10 13					10 33			
Hove 2	a								09 51									10 21					
Brighton 10	a			09 29	09 49								09 58		10 19					10 40	10 24		

b arr. 1008

Table 186

Mondays to Fridays

Bedford and London - Brighton

		SN ◇1 ⊼	SN 1	SN ◇1	FC 1	GX 1 ⊼	SN 1	SN ◇1 ⊼	SN ◇1	GW 1	FC 1	GX 1 ⊼	SN ◇1 ⊼	SN 1	SN ◇1 ⊼	FC 1	GX 1 ⊼	SN 1	SN ◇1 ⊼	SN ◇1 ⊼	GW 1	SN ◇1	FC 1
London Victoria 15 ⊖	d	09 32		09 36		09 45		09 47				10 00	10 02		10 06		10 15		10 17			10 21	
Clapham Junction 10	d	09 38		09 42				09 53					10 08		10 12				10 23				
Bedford	d				08 24						08 40					08 54							09 10
Luton 10	d				08 48						09 04					09 18							09 34
Luton Airport Parkway 7	d				08 50						09 06					09 20							09 36
St Albans City	d				09 03						09 18					09 34							09 48
St Pancras International 15 ⊖	d				09 24						09 40					09 54							10 10
Farringdon 3 ⊖	d				09 29						09 44					09 59							10 14
City Thameslink 3	d				09 32						09 47					10 02							10 17
London Blackfriars 3 ⊖	d				09 34						09 50					10 05							10 20
London Bridge 4 ⊖	d		09 32		09 42		09 45				09 57			10 03		10 12		10 15					10 27
Norwood Junction 2	d		09 45				09 56							10 15				10 26					
East Croydon	a	09 48	09 48	09 52	09 54		10 00	10 03			10 09		10 18	10 18	10 22	10 24		10 30	10 33			10 37	10 39
	d	09 48	09 51	09 52	09 54		10 00	10 03			10 09		10 18	10 21	10 22	10 24		10 30	10 33			10 37	10 39
Purley 4	d		09 57				10 06							10 27				10 36					
Coulsdon South	d		10 00				10 09							10 30				10 39					
Merstham	d		10 06											10 36				10 45					
Redhill	a	10 00	10 09				10 16						10 30	10 39				10 48			10 38		
	d	10 00	10 10				10 17			10 34			10 30	10 44				10 52			10 41		
Reigate	a									10 38								10 56					
Nutfield	d						10 21																
Godstone	d						10 27																
Edenbridge	d						10 32																
Penshurst	d						10 39																
Leigh (Kent)	d						10 42																
Tonbridge 4	a						10 47																
Earlswood (Surrey)	d		10 12																				
Salfords	d		10 16																				
Horley 4	d		10 19										10 36	10 51									
Gatwick Airport 10	a	10 08	10 23		10 10	10 15		10 18			10 25	10 30	10 39	10 55		10 40	10 45		10 48		10 50	10 52	10 55
	d	10 09	10 24		10 11			10 19			10 26		10 40	10 56		10 41			10 49			10 58	10 56
Three Bridges 15	a	10 14	10 29		10 15								10 44	11 01		10 45						11 03	
	d	10 14	10 30		10 15								10 45	11 01		10 45						11 03	
Crawley	d	10 18	10 33										10 48	11 05									
Ifield	d		10 36											11 07									
Faygate	d																						
Littlehaven	d		10 42											11 14									
Horsham 4	a	10 26	10 47										10 56	11 17									
Balcombe	d				10 21				>											>			
Haywards Heath	d				10 27			10 34	10 37		10 38					10 55			11 04	11 07		11 17	11 08
Wivelsfield	d				10 31											10 59				11 11		11 21	
Lewes 4	a							10 51												11 22			
Burgess Hill 4	d				10 33											11 01			11 09			11 23	
Hassocks 4	d				10 36											11 04						11 26	
Preston Park	d				10 43											11 11						11 33	
Hove 2	a								10 51										11 21				
Brighton 10	a			10 27	10 49						10 54				10 58	11 17						11 40	11 24

Table 186

Bedford and London - Brighton

Station		GX		SN	SN	SN	FC	GX	SN	SN	SN	GW	FC	GX	SN	SN	SN	FC	GX	SN	SN	SN		GW	SN
		1		◇1	1	◇1	1	1	1	◇1	◇1	1	1	1	◇1	1	◇1	1	1	1	◇1	◇1		1	◇1
		✠		✠		✠		✠		✠				✠			✠		✠						
London Victoria 15 ⊖	d	10 30		10 32		10 36		10 45		10 47				11 00	11 02		11 06		11 15		11 17				11 21
Clapham Junction 10	d			10 38		10 42				10 53					11 08		11 12				11 23				
Bedford	d						09 24						09 40					09 54							
Luton 10	d						09 48						10 04					10 18							
Luton Airport Parkway 7	d						09 50						10 06					10 20							
St Albans City	d						10 03						10 18					10 34							
St Pancras International 15 ⊖	d						10 24						10 40					10 54							
Farringdon 3 ⊖	d						10 29						10 44					10 59							
City Thameslink 3	d						10 32						10 47					11 02							
London Blackfriars 3 ⊖	d						10 35						10 50					11 05							
London Bridge 4 ⊖	d				10 33		10 42		10 45				10 57			11 03		11 12		11 15					
Norwood Junction 2	d				10 45				10 56							11 15				11 26					
East Croydon	a			10 48	10 48	10 52	10 54		11 00	11 03			11 09		11 18	11 18	11 22	11 24		11 30	11 33				11 37
	d			10 48	10 51	10 52	10 54		11 00	11 03			11 09		11 18	11 21	11 22	11 24		11 30	11 33				11 37
Purley 4	d				10 57				11 06							11 27				11 36					
Coulsdon South	d				11 00				11 09							11 30				11 39					
Merstham	d				11 06											11 36				11 45					
Redhill	a			11 00	11 10				11 16						11 30	11 39				11 48				11 38	
	d			11 00	11 11				11 17			11 34			11 30	11 44				11 52				11 41	
Reigate	a											11 38								11 56					
Nutfield	d								11 21																
Godstone	d								11 27																
Edenbridge	d								11 32																
Penshurst	d								11 39																
Leigh (Kent)	d								11 42																
Tonbridge 4	a								11 47																
Earlswood (Surrey)	d				11 13																				
Salfords	d				11 17																				
Horley 4	d				11 20										11 36	11 51									
Gatwick Airport 10	a	11 00		11 08	11 23		11 10	11 15		11 18			11 25	11 30	11 39	11 55		11 40	11 45		11 48			11 50	11 52
	d			11 09	11 24		11 11			11 19			11 26		11 40	11 56		11 41			11 49				11 58
Three Bridges 15	a			11 14	11 29		11 15								11 44	12 01		11 45							12 03
	d			11 14	11 30		11 15								11 45	12 01		11 45							12 03
Crawley	d			11 18	11 33										11 48	12 05									
Ifield	d				11 36											12 07									
Faygate	d															12 11									
Littlehaven	d				11 42											12 15									
Horsham 4	a			11 26	11 45										11 56	12 18									
Balcombe	d						11 21				>											>			
Haywards Heath	d						11 27			11 34	11 37		11 38					11 55			12 04	12 07			12 17
Wivelsfield	d						11 31											11 59				12 11			12 21
Lewes 4	a									11 48												12 22			
Burgess Hill 4	d						11 33											12 01			12 09				12 23
Hassocks 4	d						11 36											12 04							12 26
Preston Park	d						11 43											12 11							12 33
Hove 2	a										11 51										12 21				
Brighton 10	a					11 27	11 49						11 54				11 58	12 17							12 40

Table 186

Bedford and London - Brighton

Station		FC	GX	SN	SN	SN	FC		GX	SN	SN	SN	GW	FC	GX	SN	SN		SN	FC	GX	SN	SN	SN	GW
		1	1	◇1	1	◇1	1		1	1	◇1	◇1	1	1	1	◇1	1		◇1	1	1	1	◇1	◇1	1
			✠			✠			✠						✠				✠		✠				
London Victoria 15 ⊖	d		11 30	11 32		11 36			11 45		11 47				12 00	12 02			12 06		12 15		12 17		
Clapham Junction 10	d			11 38		11 42					11 53					12 08			12 12				12 23		
Bedford	d	10 10					10 24							10 40						10 54					
Luton 10	d	10 34					10 48							11 04						11 18					
Luton Airport Parkway 7	d	10 36					10 50							11 06						11 20					
St Albans City	d	10 48					11 04							11 18						11 34					
St Pancras International 15 ⊖	d	11 10					11 24							11 40						11 54					
Farringdon 3 ⊖	d	11 14					11 29							11 44						11 59					
City Thameslink 3	d	11 17					11 32							11 47						12 02					
London Blackfriars 3 ⊖	d	11 20					11 35							11 50						12 05					
London Bridge 4 ⊖	d	11 27.			11 33		11 42			11 45				11 57			12 03			12 12		12 15			
Norwood Junction 2	d				11 45					11 56							12 15					12 26			
East Croydon	a	11 39		11 48	11 48	11 52	11 54			12 00	12 03			12 09		12 18	12 18		12 22	12 24		12 30	12 33		
	d	11 39		11 48	11 51	11 52	11 54			12 00	12 03			12 09		12 18	12 21		12 22	12 24		12 30	12 33		
Purley 4	d				11 57					12 06							12 27					12 36			
Coulsdon South	d				12 00					12 09							12 30					12 39			
Merstham	d				12 06												12 36					12 45			
Redhill	a			12 00	12 09					12 16						12 30	12 39					12 48			12 38
	d			12 00	12 10					12 17			12 34			12 30	12 44					12 52			12 41
Reigate	a												12 38									12 56			
Nutfield	d									12 21															
Godstone	d									12 27															
Edenbridge	d									12 32															
Penshurst	d									12 39															
Leigh (Kent)	d									12 42															
Tonbridge 4	a									12 47															
Earlswood (Surrey)	d				12 12																				
Salfords	d				12 16																				
Horley 4	d				12 19											12 36	12 51								
Gatwick Airport 10	a	11 55	12 00	12 08	12 23		12 10		12 15		12 18			12 25	12 30	12 39	12 55			12 40	12 45		12 48		12 50
	d	11 56		12 09	12 24		12 11				12 19			12 26		12 40	12 56			12 41			12 49		
Three Bridges 15	a			12 14	12 29		12 15									12 44	13 01			12 45					
	d			12 14	12 30		12 15									12 45	13 01			12 45					
Crawley	d			12 18	12 33											12 48	13 05								
Ifield	d				12 36												13 07								
Faygate	d																								
Littlehaven	d				12 42												13 14								
Horsham 4	a			12 26	12 45											12 56	13 17								
Balcombe	d						12 21					>												>	
Haywards Heath	d	12 08					12 27				12 34	12 37		12 38						12 55			13 04	13 07	
Wivelsfield	d						12 31													12 59				13 11	
Lewes 4	a										12 51													13 22	
Burgess Hill 4	d						12 33													13 01			13 09		
Hassocks 4	d						12 36													13 04					
Preston Park	d						12 43													13 11					
Hove 2	a											12 51											13 21		
Brighton 10	a	12 24				12 27	12 49							12 54					12 58	13 17					

Table 186

Mondays to Fridays

Bedford and London - Brighton

		SN ◇1	FC 1	GX 1 ⊼	SN ◇1	SN 1	SN ◇1 ⊼	FC 1	GX 1 ⊼	SN 1	SN ◇1	SN ◇1	GW 1	FC 1	GX 1 ⊼	SN ◇1	SN 1	SN ◇1 ⊼	FC 1	GX 1 ⊼	SN 1
London Victoria 15 ⊖	d	12 21		12 30	12 32		12 36		12 45		12 47				13 00	13 02		13 06		13 15	
Clapham Junction 10	d				12 38		12 42				12 53					13 08		13 12			
Bedford	d		11 10					11 24						11 40					11 54		
Luton 10	d		11 34					11 48						12 04					12 18		
Luton Airport Parkway 7	d		11 36					11 50						12 06					12 20		
St Albans City	d		11 48					12 04						12 18					12 34		
St Pancras International 15 ⊖	d		12 10					12 24						12 40					12 54		
Farringdon 3 ⊖	d		12 14					12 29						12 44					12 59		
City Thameslink 3	d		12 17					12 32						12 47					13 02		
London Blackfriars 3 ⊖	d		12 20					12 35						12 50					13 05		
London Bridge 4 ⊖	d		12 27			12 33		12 42		12 45				12 57			13 03		13 12		13 15
Norwood Junction 2	d					12 47				12 56							13 15				13 26
East Croydon	a	12 37	12 39		12 48	12 51	12 52	12 54		13 00	13 03			13 09		13 18	13 18	13 22	13 24		13 30
	d	12 37	12 39		12 48	12 51	12 52	12 54		13 00	13 03			13 09		13 18	13 21	13 22	13 24		13 30
Purley 4	d					12 57				13 06							13 27				13 36
Coulsdon South	d					13 00				13 09							13 30				13 39
Merstham	d					13 06											13 36				13 45
Redhill	a				13 00	13 09				13 16						13 30	13 39				13 48
	d				13 00	13 10				13 17			13 34			13 30	13 44				13 52
Reigate	a												13 38								13 56
Nutfield	d									13 21											
Godstone	d									13 27											
Edenbridge	d									13 32											
Penshurst	d									13 39											
Leigh (Kent)	d									13 42											
Tonbridge 4	a									13 47											
Earlswood (Surrey)	d					13 12															
Salfords	d					13 16															
Horley 4	d					13 19										13 36	13 51				
Gatwick Airport 10	a	12 52	12 55	13 00	13 08	13 23		13 10	13 15		13 18			13 25	13 30	13 39	13 55		13 40	13 45	
	d	12 58	12 56		13 09	13 24		13 11			13 19			13 26		13 40	13 56		13 41		
Three Bridges 15	a	13 03			13 14	13 29		13 15								13 44	14 01		13 45		
	d	13 03			13 14	13 30		13 15								13 45	14 01		13 45		
Crawley	d				13 18	13 33										13 48	14 05				
Ifield	d					13 36											14 07				
Faygate	d																				
Littlehaven	d					13 42											14 14				
Horsham 4	a				13 26	13 45										13 56	14 17				
Balcombe	d							13 21				>									
Haywards Heath	d	13 17	13 08					13 27			13 34	13 37		13 38					13 55		
Wivelsfield	d	13 21						13 31											13 59		
Lewes 4	a										13 48										
Burgess Hill 4	d	13 23						13 33											14 01		
Hassocks 4	d	13 26						13 36											14 04		
Preston Park	d	13 33						13 43											14 11		
Hove 2	a											13 51									
Brighton 10	a	13 40	13 24				13 27	13 49						13 54				13 58	14 17		

Table 186

Mondays to Fridays

Bedford and London - Brighton

		SN ◇1	SN ◇1	GW 1	SN ◇1	FC 1	GX 1 ⊼	SN ◇1 ⊼	SN 1	SN ◇1 ⊼	FC 1	GX 1 ⊼	SN 1	SN ◇1	SN ◇1	GW 1	FC 1	GX 1 ⊼	SN ◇1	SN 1	SN ◇1 ⊼	FC 1	GX 1 ⊼
London Victoria 15 ⊖	d	13 17			13 21		13 30	13 32		13 36		13 45		13 47				14 00	14 02		14 06		14 15
Clapham Junction 10	d	13 23						13 38		13 42				13 53					14 08		14 12		
Bedford	d					12 10					12 24						12 40					12 54	
Luton 10	d					12 34					12 48						13 04					13 18	
Luton Airport Parkway 7	d					12 36					12 50						13 06					13 20	
St Albans City	d					12 48					13 04						13 18					13 34	
St Pancras International 15 ⊖	d					13 10					13 24						13 40					13 54	
Farringdon 3 ⊖	d					13 14					13 29						13 44					13 59	
City Thameslink 3	d					13 17					13 32						13 47					14 02	
London Blackfriars 3 ⊖	d					13 20					13 35						13 50					14 05	
London Bridge 4 ⊖	d					13 27			13 33		13 42		13 45				13 57			14 03		14 12	
Norwood Junction 2	d								13 45				13 56							14 15			
East Croydon	a	13 33			13 37	13 39		13 48	13 48	13 52	13 54		14 00	14 03			14 09		14 18	14 18	14 22	14 24	
	d	13 33			13 37	13 39		13 48	13 51	13 52	13 54		14 00	14 03			14 09		14 18	14 21	14 22	14 24	
Purley 4	d								13 57				14 06							14 27			
Coulsdon South	d								14 00				14 09							14 30			
Merstham	d								14 06											14 36			
Redhill	a			13 38				14 00	14 09				14 16						14 30	14 39			
	d			13 41				14 00	14 10				14 17			14 34			14 30	14 44			
Reigate	a															14 38							
Nutfield	d												14 21										
Godstone	d												14 27										
Edenbridge	d												14 32										
Penshurst	d												14 39										
Leigh (Kent)	d												14 42										
Tonbridge 4	a												14 47										
Earlswood (Surrey)	d								14 12														
Salfords	d								14 16														
Horley 4	d								14 19										14 36	14 51			
Gatwick Airport 10	a	13 48		13 50	13 52	13 55	14 00	14 08	14 23		14 10	14 15		14 18			14 25	14 30	14 39	14 55		14 40	14 45
	d	13 49			13 58	13 56		14 09	14 24		14 11			14 19			14 26		14 40	14 56		14 41	
Three Bridges 15	a				14 03			14 14	14 29		14 15								14 44	15 01		14 45	
	d				14 03			14 14	14 30		14 15								14 45	15 01		14 45	
Crawley	d							14 18	14 33										14 48	15 05			
Ifield	d								14 36											15 07			
Faygate	d																						
Littlehaven	d								14 42											15 14			
Horsham 4	a							14 26	14 45										14 56	15 17			
Balcombe	d		>								14 21				>								
Haywards Heath	d	14 04	14 07		14 17	14 08					14 27			14 34	14 37		14 38					14 55	
Wivelsfield	d		14 11		14 21						14 31											14 59	
Lewes 4	a		14 22											14 48									
Burgess Hill 4	d	14 09			14 23						14 33											15 01	
Hassocks 4	d				14 26						14 36											15 04	
Preston Park	d				14 33						14 43											15 11	
Hove 2	a	14 21													14 51								
Brighton 10	a				14 40	14 24				14 27	14 49						14 54				14 58	15 17	

Table 186

Bedford and London - Brighton

		SN 1	SN ◇1	SN ◇1	GW 1	SN ◇1	FC 1	GX 1	SN ◇1	SN 1	SN ◇1	FC 1	GX 1	SN 1	SN ◇1	SN ◇1	GW 1	FC 1	GX 1	SN ◇1	SN 1	SN ◇1	FC 1
London Victoria [15] ⊖	d		14 17			14 21		14 30	14 32		14 36		14 45		14 47				15 00	15 02		15 06	
Clapham Junction [10]	d		14 23						14 38		14 42				14 53					15 08		15 12	
Bedford	d						13 10					13 24						13 40					13 54
Luton [10]	d						13 34					13 48						14 04					14 18
Luton Airport Parkway [7]	d						13 36					13 50						14 06					14 20
St Albans City	d						13 48					14 04						14 18					14 34
St Pancras International [15] ⊖	d						14 10					14 24						14 40					14 54
Farringdon [3] ⊖	d						14 14					14 29						14 44					14 59
City Thameslink [3]	d						14 17					14 32						14 47					15 02
London Blackfriars [3] ⊖	d						14 20					14 35						14 50					15 05
London Bridge [4] ⊖	d	14 15					14 27			14 33		14 42		14 45				14 57			15 03		15 12
Norwood Junction [2]	d	14 26								14 45				14 56							15 15		
East Croydon	a	14 30	14 33			14 37	14 39		14 48	14 48	14 52	14 54		15 00	15 03			15 09		15 18	15 18	15 22	15 24
	d	14 30	14 33			14 37	14 39		14 48	14 51	14 52	14 54		15 00	15 03			15 09		15 18	15 21	15 22	15 24
Purley [4]	d	14 36								14 57				15 06							15 27		
Coulsdon South	d	14 39								15 00				15 09							15 30		
Merstham	d	14 45								15 06											15 36		
Redhill	a	14 48			14 38				15 00	15 09				15 16						15 30	15 39		
	d	14 52			14 41				15 00	15 10				15 17			15 29			15 30	15 44		
Reigate	a	14 56															15 33						
Nutfield	d													15 21									
Godstone	d													15 27									
Edenbridge	d													15 32									
Penshurst	d													15 39									
Leigh (Kent)	d													15 42									
Tonbridge [4]	a													15 47									
Earlswood (Surrey)	d									15 12											15 46		
Salfords	d									15 16											15 50		
Horley [4]	d									15 19										15 36	15 53		
Gatwick Airport [10]	a		14 48		14 50	14 52	14 55	15 00	15 08	15 23		15 10	15 15		15 18			15 25	15 30	15 39	15 56		15 40
	d		14 49			14 58	14 56		15 09	15 24		15 11			15 19			15 26		15 40	15 57		15 41
Three Bridges [15]	a					15 03			15 14	15 29		15 15								15 44	16 01		15 45
	d					15 03			15 14	15 30		15 15								15 45	16 02		15 45
Crawley	d								15 18	15 33										15 48	16 06		
Ifield	d									15 36											16 08		
Faygate	d																				16 12		
Littlehaven	d									15 42											16 16		
Horsham [4]	a								15 26	15 48										15 56	16 19		
Balcombe	d			>								15 21				>							
Haywards Heath	d		15 04	15 07		15 17	15 08					15 27			15 34	15 37		15 38					15 55
Wivelsfield	d			15 11		15 21						15 31			15 38								15 59
Lewes [4]	a			15 22											15 51								
Burgess Hill [4]	d		15 09			15 23						15 33											16 01
Hassocks [4]	d					15 26						15 36											16 04
Preston Park	d					15 33						15 43											16 11
Hove [2]	a		15 21													15 51							
Brighton [10]	a					15 40	15 24				15 28	15 49						15 54				15 58	16 17

Table 186

Bedford and London - Brighton

		GX 1	SN 1	SN ◇1	SN ◇1	GW 1	SN ◇1	FC 1	GX 1	SN ◇1	SN 1	SN ◇1	FC 1	GX 1	SN 1	SN ◇1	SN ◇1	GW 1	FC 1	GX 1	SN ◇1	SN 1	SN 1
London Victoria [15] ⊖	d	15 15		15 17			15 21		15 30	15 32		15 36		15 45		15 47				16 00	16 02		
Clapham Junction [10]	d			15 23						15 38		15 42				15 53					16 08		
Bedford	d							14 10					14 24						14 40				
Luton [10]	d							14 34					14 48						15 04				
Luton Airport Parkway [7]	d							14 36					14 50						15 06				
St Albans City	d							14 48					15 04						15 18				
St Pancras International [15] ⊖	d							15 10					15 24						15 40				
Farringdon [3] ⊖	d							15 14					15 29						15 44				
City Thameslink [3]	d							15 17					15 32						15 47				
London Blackfriars [3] ⊖	d							15 20					15 35						15 50				
London Bridge [4] ⊖	d		15 15					15 27			15 33		15 42		15 45				15 57			16 03	
Norwood Junction [2]	d		15 26								15 45				15 56							16 15	
East Croydon	a		15 30	15 33			15 37	15 39		15 48	15 48	15 52	15 54		16 00	16 03			16 09		16 18	16 18	
	d		15 30	15 33			15 37	15 39		15 48	15 51	15 52	15 54		16 00	16 03			16 09		16 18	16 21	
Purley [4]	d		15 36								15 57				16 06							16 27	
Coulsdon South	d		15 39								16 00				16 09							16 30	
Merstham	d		15 45								16 06				16 15							16 36	
Redhill	a		15 48			15 38				16 00	16 09				16 18						16 30	16 39	>
	d		15 52			15 41				16 00	16 10				16 20			16 32			16 30	16 43	16 45
Reigate	a		15 56															16 36					
Nutfield	d														16 24								16 49
Godstone	d														16 30								16 55
Edenbridge	d														16 35								17 00
Penshurst	d														16 42								17 07
Leigh (Kent)	d														16 45								17 10
Tonbridge [4]	a														16 52								17 17
Earlswood (Surrey)	d										16 12											16 45	
Salfords	d										16 16											16 49	
Horley [4]	d										16 19										16 36	16 52	
Gatwick Airport [10]	a	15 45		15 48		15 50	15 52	15 56	16 00	16 08	16 23		16 10	16 15		16 18			16 25	16 30	16 39	16 55	
	d			15 49			15 53	15 56		16 09	16 24		16 11			16 19			16 26		16 40	16 56	
Three Bridges [15]	a						15 57	16 01		16 14	16 29		16 15						16 31		16 44	17 00	
	d						15 57	16 01		16 14	16 30		16 15						16 31		16 45	17 02	
Crawley	d									16 18	16 34										16 48	17 06	
Ifield	d										16 36											17 08	
Faygate	d										16 40											17 12	
Littlehaven	d										16 44											17 16	
Horsham [4]	a									16 26	16 47										16 56	17 21	
Balcombe	d				>								16 21				>						
Haywards Heath	d			16 04	16 07		16b17	16 10					16 27			16 33	16 37		16 40				
Wivelsfield	d				16 11		16 21						16 31			16 37							
Lewes [4]	a				16 22											16 52							
Burgess Hill [4]	d			16 09			16 23						16 33										
Hassocks [4]	d						16 26						16 36										
Preston Park	d						16 33						16 43										
Hove [2]	a			16 21													16 51						
Brighton [10]	a						16 40	16 24				16 27	16 49						16 54				

b arr. 1609

Table 186

Mondays to Fridays

Bedford and London - Brighton

		SN 1	FC 1	SN 1	GX 1	SN ◇1	SN ◇1	SN 1		FC 1	GW 1	GX 1	SN ◇1	SN 1	SN 1	SN 1	SN 1	GX 1	SN 1	FC 1	SN ◇1	GX 1	SN 1	SN 1	SN 1
		✠				✠	✠					✠	✠			✠		✠			✠	✠			
London Victoria 15 ⊖	d	16 06			16 15	16 17		16 19				16 30	16 32			16 36		16 45			16 47	17 00	16 49		
Clapham Junction 10	d	16 12				16 23		16 26					16 38			16 42					16 53		16 56		
Bedford	d		14 54							15 10										15 24					
Luton 10	d		15 18							15 34										15 48					
Luton Airport Parkway 7	d		15 20							15 36										15 50					
St Albans City	d		15 34							15 48										16 04					
St Pancras International 15 ⊖	d		15 54							16 10										16 24					
Farringdon 3 ⊖	d		15 59							16 14										16 29					
City Thameslink 3	d		16 02							16 17										16 33					
London Blackfriars 3 ⊖	d		16 05							16 20										16 36					
London Bridge 4 ⊖	d		16 12	16 15						16 27					16 33					16 43					16 57
Norwood Junction 2	d			16 26											16 45										
East Croydon	a	16 22	16 24	16 30		16 33		16 36		16 39			16 47		16 48	16 52				16 59	17 03		17 06		17 09
	d	16 22	16 24	16 30		16 33		16 36		16 40			16 48		16 49	16 52				17 00	17 03		17 07		17 10
Purley 4	d			16 36											16 55										
Coulsdon South	d			16 39											16 59								17 13		
Merstham	d			16 45											17 04								17 19		
Redhill	a			16 48							16 42		16 59		17 08								17 22	>	
	d			16 53							16 51		17 00		17 08				17 12				17 27	17 29	
Reigate	a			16 59																				17 35	
Nutfield	d																		17 16						
Godstone	d																		17 22						
Edenbridge	d																		17 27						
Penshurst	d																		17 34						
Leigh (Kent)	d																		17 37						
Tonbridge 4	a																		17 42						
Earlswood (Surrey)	d														17 11								17 29		
Salfords	d														17 14								17 33		
Horley 4	d												17 06		17 18								17 36		
Gatwick Airport 10	a		16 40		16 43	16 48		16 52		16 55	16 59	17 00	17 08		17 20			17 15		17 15	17 19	17 30	17 39		
	d		16 41		16 46	16 49		16 53		16 56			17 09		17 21					17 16	17 20		17 40		
Three Bridges 15	a		16 45					16 57		17 01			17 14	>	17 26	17 10				17 21	17 25		17 46		17 29
	d		16 46					16 58		17 01			17 18	17 20	17 26	17 10				17 21	17 25				17 29
Crawley	d							17 02					17 22	17 26	17 30										
Ifield	d													17 28	17 33										
Faygate	d														17 37										
Littlehaven	d													17 35	17 41										
Horsham 4	a							17 12					17 30	17 38	17 46										
Balcombe	d						>										>			17 27					
Haywards Heath	d		16 55		16a57	17 04	17 06			17 10						17 23	17 26			17 33	17 36				17 39
Wivelsfield	d		16 59				17 10										17 30			17 37	17 41				
Lewes 4	a						17 21														17 56				
Burgess Hill 4	d		17 01			17 09				17 16							17 32			17 40					17 46
Hassocks 4	d		17 04														17 35			17 44					17 49
Preston Park	d		17 11														17 42			17 51					17 56
Hove 2	a					17 20																			18 00
Brighton 10	a	17 00	17 17							17 27						17 39	17 49			17 56					

Table 186

Mondays to Fridays

Bedford and London - Brighton

		SN 1	SN 1	SN 1	SN 1	FC 1	GX 1	SN ◇1	SN 1	SN 1	SN 1	SN 1	FC 1	GW 1	GX 1	SN 1	SN ◇1	SN 1	SN 1	GW 1	GX 1	SN ◇1	SN 1	SN 1	FC 1
					✠		✠								✠		A ✠				✠				
London Victoria 15 ⊖	d			17 02	17 06		17 15	17 17		17 21					17 30	17 32	17 36				17 45	17 47	17 49		
Clapham Junction 10	d			17 08	17 12			17 23		17 27						17 38	17 42					17 53	17 56		
Bedford	d					15 52							16 10												16 26
Luton 10	d					16 14							16 34												16 50
Luton Airport Parkway 7	d					16 17							16 36												16 52
St Albans City	d					16 24							16 48												17 04
St Pancras International 15 ⊖	d					16 46							17 10												17 28
Farringdon 3 ⊖	d					16 51							17 15												17 33
City Thameslink 3	d					16 55							17 19												17 37
London Blackfriars 3 ⊖	d					17 00							17 22												17 40
London Bridge 4 ⊖	d	16 59							17 23		17 29							17 42	17 47						
Norwood Junction 2	d	17 11									17 41														
East Croydon	a	17 14		17 17	17 21	17 25		17 32	17 35	17 36	17 44		17 45			17 48	17 51	17 54	17 59			18 02	18 05		18 08
	d	17 15		17 18	17 22	17 26		17 33	17 36	17 38	17 45		17 46			17 49	17 52	17 55	18 00			18 03	18 06		18 09
Purley 4	d	17 21									17 51														
Coulsdon South	d	17 24								17 44	17 54												18 12		
Merstham	d	17 30								17 50	18 00												18 18		
Redhill	a	17 33	>							17 53	18 03	>	17 59	17 38									18 21	>	
	d	17 37	17 39							17 55	18 07	18 09	18 00	17 41						17 43			18 25	18 27	
Reigate	a										18 13									17 48				18 33	
Nutfield	d		17 43																						
Godstone	d		17 49																						
Edenbridge	d		17 54																						
Penshurst	d		18 01																						
Leigh (Kent)	d		18 04																						
Tonbridge 4	a		18 11																						
Earlswood (Surrey)	d	17 39								17 57		18 11											18 27		
Salfords	d	17 43								18 01		18 15											18 31		
Horley 4	d	17 46							17 50	18 04		18 18										18 18	18 34		
Gatwick Airport 10	a	17 49				17 40	17 45	17 47		18 08		18 21	18 13	17 54	17 57		18 06				18 12	18 20	18 37		18 24
	d	17 50				17 41		17 48		18 10		18 22	18 14		18 00		18 07				18 15	18 21	18 38		18 25
Three Bridges 15	a	17 54		17 36		17 46			17 55	18 16		18 26	18 18			18 06			18 21				18 44		18 30
	d	17 55		17 37		17 46			17 56			18 27	18 19			18 07			18 22						18 30
Crawley	d	17 59		17 41								18 31				18 11			18 26						
Ifield	d	18 01										18 33							18 28						
Faygate	d											18 37													
Littlehaven	d	18 08										18 41				18 19			18 35						
Horsham 4	a	18 13		17 49								18 47				18 22			18 38						
Balcombe	d					17 52							18 25												
Haywards Heath	d				17 47	17 58		18 01	18 05				18 31		18 12		18 18	18 22			18 26	18 33			18 39
Wivelsfield	d				17 52				18 09								18 23								18 43
Lewes 4	a								18 20								18 38								
Burgess Hill 4	d				17 54	18 03		18 07					18 36		18 18			18 27				18 41			18 46
Hassocks 4	d				17 58	18 07		18 11					18 40		18 22			18 31				18 45			18 50
Preston Park	d				18 06	18 15							18 48					18 39			18 43	18 53			18 57
Hove 2	a							18 21										18 43				18 57			
Brighton 10	a				18 12	18 20							18 52		18 34						18 50				19 02

Table 186

Bedford and London - Brighton

Mondays to Fridays

		SN	SN	GX	SN	SN ◇	SN	SN	GX	FC	SN ◇	SN	SN	SN	FC	GX	SN	SN	SN	SN	SN	GW	GW	FC	GX
London Victoria	d			18 00	18 02	18 06			18 15		18 17		18 19			18 30			18 32		18 36				18 45
Clapham Junction	d				18 08	18 12					18 23		18 26						18 38		18 42				
Bedford	d														17 08									17 22	
Luton	d														17 32									17 46	
Luton Airport Parkway	d														17 34									17 48	
St Albans City	d														17 46									18 00	
St Pancras International	d									17 40					18 08									18 20	
Farringdon	d									17 45					18 13									18 25	
City Thameslink	d									17 49					18 17									18 29	
London Blackfriars	d									17 52					18 20									18 32	
London Bridge	d	17 57	17 59					18 12				18 23			18 27		18 30								
Norwood Junction	d		18 11														18 42								
East Croydon	a	18 11	18 15		18 17	18 22		18 24		18 24	18 33	18 36	18 37		18 41		18 45		18 48		18 52			18 55	
	d	18 15	18 15		18 18	18 22		18 25		18 26	18 33	18 37	18 38		18 41		18 46		18 48		18 52			18 56	
Purley	d		18 21										18 43				18 51								
Coulsdon South	d		18 24										18 46				18 54								
Merstham	d		18 30										18 52				19 00								
Redhill	a		18 33							18 37			18 55	>			19 03	>					18 47		
	d		18 34				18 12			18 39			18 59	19 01			19 07	19 09		18 32		18 43	18 51		
Reigate	a																	19 15				18 47			
Nutfield	d						18 16							19 05						18 36					
Godstone	d						18 22							19 11						18 42					
Edenbridge	d						18 27							19 16						18 47					
Penshurst	d						18 34							19 23						18 54					
Leigh (Kent)	d						18 37							19 26						18 57					
Tonbridge	a						18 42							19 34						19 02					
Earlswood (Surrey)	d		18 36										19 01				19 09								
Salfords	d		18 40										19 05				19 13								
Horley	d		18 43								18 48		19 08				19 16								
Gatwick Airport	a		18 46	18 28		18 37			18 43	18 49			19 13		18 56	19 00	19 19						19 00	19 10	19 14
	d		18 47	18 35		18 38			18 46	18 50			19 14		18 57	19 05	19 20							19 11	19 16
Three Bridges	a	18 34	18 51		18 36			18 44		18 56		18 55	19 19		19 02		19 24		19 06						
	d	18 34	18 52		18 37			18 45				18 56	19 19		19 02		19 25		19 07						
Crawley	d		18 56		18 41								19 23				19 29		19 11						
Ifield	d		18 58										19 26				19 31								
Faygate	d																19 35								
Littlehaven	d		19 05										19 32				19 39		19 19						
Horsham	a		19 10		18 49								19 37				19 45		19 22						
Balcombe	d										18 57				19 08									19 19	
Haywards Heath	d	18 44		18 47		18 50		18 54	18 58		19 03	19 06			19 14	19 17					19 20			19b31	19 28
Wivelsfield	d					18 54						19 11									19 24				
Lewes	a					19 09						19 27													
Burgess Hill	d	18 49		18 53				19 00			19 08				19 19	19 23								19 36	
Hassocks	d	18 53		18 57				19 04			19 12				19 23	19 27								19 40	
Preston Park	d	19 01						19 11	19 15															19 48	19 40
Hove	a							19 17			19 22														
Brighton	a	19 07		19 10					19 22						19 34	19 39					19 42			19 52	19 47

b arr. 1924

Table 186

Bedford and London - Brighton

Mondays to Fridays

		SN ◇	SN ◇	SN	SN	SN	FC	GX	SN ◇	SN	SN	FC	SN	GX	SN ◇	SN ◇	GW	SN	SN	FC	GX	SN ◇
London Victoria	d	18 47		18 51				19 00	19 02		19 06		19 10	19 15	19 17						19 30	19 32
Clapham Junction	d	18 53		18 57					19 08		19 12		19 16		19 23							19 38
Bedford	d						17 36					17 54								18 10		
Luton	d						18 00					18 18								18 34		
Luton Airport Parkway	d						18 02					18 20								18 36		
St Albans City	d						18 14					18 34								18 48		
St Pancras International	d						18 34					18 54								19 10		
Farringdon	d						18 39					18 59								19 14		
City Thameslink	d						18 43					19 03								19 17		
London Blackfriars	d						18 46					19 05								19 20		
London Bridge	d						18 57			19 03		19 12								19 27		
Norwood Junction	d									19 15												
East Croydon	a	19 02		19 07			19 10		19 18	19 18	19 22	19 24	19 27		19 33					19 39		19 48
	d	19 03		19 08			19 11		19 18	19 19	19 22	19 24	19 28		19 33					19 39		19 48
Purley	d									19 24			19 33									
Coulsdon South	d			19 14						19 28			19 36									
Merstham	d			19 20						19 33			19 42									
Redhill	a			19 23					19 30	19 37			19 45				19 39					20 00
	d			19 24	18 54	19 36			19 31	19 37			19 46				19 43	19 51	20 05			20 00
Reigate	a				18 58	19 40													20 10			
Nutfield	d																	19 55				
Godstone	d																	20 01				
Edenbridge	d																	20 06				
Penshurst	d																	20 13				
Leigh (Kent)	d																	20 16				
Tonbridge	a																	20 21				
Earlswood (Surrey)	d			19 26						19 40			19 48									
Salfords	d			19 30						19 43			19 52									
Horley	d			19 33						19 47			19 55									
Gatwick Airport	a	19 19		19 36			19 25	19 30	19 39	19 49		19 40	19 58	19 45	19 48		19 55			19 55	20 00	20 08
	d	19 20		19 37			19 26		19 40	19 50		19 41	19 59		19 49					19 56		20 09
Three Bridges	a			19 43			19 31		19 45	19 55		19 45	20 03							20 00		20 14
	d						19 31		19 45	19 55		19 45	20 04							20 01		20 14
Crawley	d								19 49	19 59			20 08									20 18
Ifield	d									20 02			20 10									
Faygate	d												20 14									
Littlehaven	d									20 08			20 18									
Horsham	a								19 57	20 11			20 21									20 26
Balcombe	d		>									19 51				>						
Haywards Heath	d	19 34	19 37				19 40				19 45	19 57			20 04	20 07				20 10		
Wivelsfield	d	19 38										20 01				20 11						
Lewes	a	19 53														20 22						
Burgess Hill	d		19 42				19 45					20 03			20 09					20 15		
Hassocks	d		19 46				19 49					20 06								20 19		
Preston Park	d											20 13										
Hove	a		19 56												20 21							
Brighton	a						19 58				20 02	20 19								20 28		

Bedford and London - Brighton

		SN 1	FC 1	SN 1	GX 1	SN ◇1	SN ◇1	SN 1	GW 1	FC 1	GX 1	SN ◇1	SN ◇1	FC 1	SN 1	GX 1	SN ◇1	SN ◇1	GW 1	SN 1	SN 1	SN 1
					⌶	⌶	⌶				⌶	⌶										
London Victoria 15 ⊖	d	19 36		19 40	19 45	19 47					20 00	20 02	20 06		20 10	20 15	20 17					
Clapham Junction 10	d	19 42		19 46		19 53						20 08	20 12		20 16		20 23					
Bedford	d		18 24							18 40				18 54								
Luton 10	d		18 48							19 04				19 18								
Luton Airport Parkway 7	d		18 50							19 06				19 20								
St Albans City	d		19 02							19 18				19 33								
St Pancras International 15 ⊖	d		19 24							19 40				19 54								
Farringdon 3 ⊖	d		19 29							19 44				19 59								
City Thameslink 3	d		19 32							19 47				20 02								
London Blackfriars 3 ⊖	d		19 35							19 50				20 05								
London Bridge 4 ⊖	d		19 42					19 52		19 57				20 12								20 28
Norwood Junction 2	d							20 03														
East Croydon	a	19 52	19 54	19 57		20 03		20 06		20 09		20 19	20 22	20 24	20 27		20 33					20 40
	d	19 53	19 54	19 58		20 03		20 07		20 09		20 19	20 23	20 24	20 28		20 33					20 41
Purley 4	d			20 03				20 12							20 33							
Coulsdon South	d			20 06				20 15							20 36							
Merstham	d			20 12				20 21							20 42							
Redhill	a			20 15				20 24				20 30			20 45				20 38			
	d			20 16				20 25	20 34			20 31			20 46				20 41	20 51	21 05	
Reigate	a							20 30	20 38												21 09	
Nutfield	d																			20 55		
Godstone	d																			21 01		
Edenbridge	d																			21 06		
Penshurst	d																			21 13		
Leigh (Kent)	d																			21 16		
Tonbridge 4	a																			21 21		
Earlswood (Surrey)	d			20 18											20 48							
Salfords	d			20 22																		
Horley 4	d			20 25											20 54							
Gatwick Airport 10	a		20 10	20 28	20 15	20 18				20 25	20 30	20 38		20 40	20 56	20 45	20 48		20 50			20 55
	d		20 11	20 29		20 19				20 26		20 39		20 41	20 57		20 49					20 56
Three Bridges 10	a		20 16	20 33						20 30		20 44		20 45	21 02							21 01
	d		20 16	20 34						20 31		20 44		20 45	21 03							21 01
Crawley	d			20 37								20 48			21 06							
Ifield	d			20 40											21 09							
Faygate	d																					
Littlehaven	d			20 46											21 15							
Horsham 4	a			20 49								20 56			21 18							
Balcombe	d						>							20 51				>				
Haywards Heath	d	20 18	20 26			20 34	20 36			20 40			20 47	20 57			21 04	21 07				21 11
Wivelsfield	d		20 30				20 40							21 01				21 11				
Lewes 4	a						20 55											21 22				
Burgess Hill 4	d		20 32			20 39				20 45				21 03			21 09					
Hassocks 4	d		20 36			20 42								21 06								
Preston Park	d		20 43			20 49								21 13								
Hove 2	a					20 53											21 21					
Brighton 10	a	20 33	20 47							20 56			21 01	21 19								21 26

Bedford and London - Brighton

		GX 1	SN ◇1	SN ◇1	FC 1	SN 1	GX 1	SN ◇1	SN ◇1	SN 1	GW 1	SN 1	GX 1	SN 1	SN ◇1	FC 1	SN 1	GX 1	SN ◇1	SN ◇1	GX 1	GW 1	SN 1	SN 1
London Victoria 15 ⊖	d	20 30	20 32	20 36		20 40	20 45	20 47					21 00	21 02	21 06		21 10	21 15	21 17		21 30		21 32	
Clapham Junction 10	d		20 38	20 42		20 46		20 53						21 08	21 12		21 16		21 23				21 38	
Bedford	d				19 22											19 52								
Luton 10	d				19 46											20 16								
Luton Airport Parkway 7	d				19 48											20 18								
St Albans City	d				20 00											20 30								
St Pancras International 15 ⊖	d				20 24											20 54								
Farringdon 3 ⊖	d				20 29											20 59								
City Thameslink 3	d				20 32											21 02								
London Blackfriars 3 ⊖	d				20 35											21 05								
London Bridge 4 ⊖	d				20 42							20 58				21 12								
Norwood Junction 2	d																							
East Croydon	a		20 48	20 52	20 54	20 57		21 03				21 10		21 18	21 22	21 24	21 27		21 33				21 48	
	d		20 48	20 52	20 54	20 58		21 04				21 11		21 18	21 23	21 24	21 28		21 33				21 48	
Purley 4	d					21 03											21 33							
Coulsdon South	d					21 06											21 36							
Merstham	d					21 12											21 42							
Redhill	a		21 00			21 15								21 30			21 45					21 49	21 59	
	d		21 00			21 16				21 22	21 35			21 31			21 46					21 53	22 00	21 55
Reigate	a									21 26	21 39													
Nutfield	d																							21 59
Godstone	d																							22 05
Edenbridge	d																							22 10
Penshurst	d																							22 17
Leigh (Kent)	d																							22 20
Tonbridge 4	a																							22 28
Earlswood (Surrey)	d					21 18											21 48							
Salfords	d					21 22																		
Horley 4	d					21 25											21 54							
Gatwick Airport 10	a	21 00	21 08		21 10	21 28	21 15	21 18				21 26	21 30	21 38		21 40	21 56	21 45	21 48		22 00	22 06	22 08	
	d		21 09		21 11	21 29		21 19				21 27		21 39		21 41	21 57		21 49				22 09	
Three Bridges 10	a		21 14		21 15	21 33						21 31		21 44		21 45	22 02		21 53				22 14	
	d		21 14		21 15	21 34						21 32		21 44		21 45	22 03		21 53				22 14	
Crawley	d		21 18			21 37											22 06						22 18	
Ifield	d					21 40											22 09							
Faygate	d																							
Littlehaven	d					21 46											22 15							
Horsham 4	a		21 26			21 49											22 18						22 26	
Balcombe	d								>							21 53				>				
Haywards Heath	d			21 15	21 26			21 34	21 37			21 41		21 53	21 47	21 58			22 06	22 08				
Wivelsfield	d				21 30				21 41					21 57		22 02				22 12				
Lewes 4	a								21 54											22 23				
Burgess Hill 4	d				21 32			21 39						21 59		22 04			22 11					
Hassocks 4	d				21 36			21 42						22 02		22 08								
Preston Park	d				21 43			21 49						22 09		22 15								
Hove 2	a							21 53											22 22					
Brighton 10	a			21 30	21 47							21 55		22 15	22 01	22 19								

Table 186

Bedford and London - Brighton

		SN 1	SN ◇1	FC 1	SN 1	GX 1	SN ◇1	SN ◇1	GX 1	SN ◇1	SN 1	SN ◇1	FC 1	SN 1	GX 1	SN ◇1	GX 1	GW 1	SN 1	SN 1	FC 1
London Victoria 15 ⊖	d		21 36		21 40	21 45	21 47		22 00	22 02		22 06		22 10	22 15	22 17	22 30		22 32	22 36	
Clapham Junction 10	d		21 42		21 46		21 53			22 08		22 12		22 16		22 23			22 38	22 42	
Bedford	d			20 22									20 52								
Luton 10	d			20 46									21 16								
Luton Airport Parkway 7	d			20 48									21 18								
St Albans City	d			21 00									21 30								
St Pancras International 15 ⊖	d			21 24									21 54								
Farringdon 3 ⊖	d			21 29									21 59								
City Thameslink 3	d			21 32									22 02								
London Blackfriars 3 ⊖	d			21 35									22 05								
London Bridge 4 ⊖	d			21 42									22 12								22 42
Norwood Junction 2	d																				
East Croydon ⇌	a		21 52	21 54	21 57		22 03			22 18		22 22	22 24	22 27		22 33			22 48	22 52	22 54
	d		21 52	21 54	21 58		22 03			22 18		22 23	22 24	22 28		22 34			22 48	22 53	22 56
Purley 4	d				22 03									22 33							
Coulsdon South	d				22 06									22 36							
Merstham	d				22 12									22 42							
Redhill	a				22 15					22 30				22 45				22 48	23 00		
	d	22 05			22 16					22 31	22 22			22 46				22 52	23 01		
Reigate	a	22 09									22 26										
Nutfield	d																				
Godstone	d																				
Edenbridge	d																				
Penshurst	d																				
Leigh (Kent)	d																				
Tonbridge 4	a																				
Earlswood (Surrey)	d				22 18									22 48							
Salfords	d				22 22																
Horley 4	d				22 25									22 54							
Gatwick Airport 10	a			22 10	22 28	22 15	22 18		22 30	22 38			22 40	22 56	22 45	22 48	23 00	23 06	23 08		23 10
	d			22 11	22 29		22 19			22 39			22 41	22 57		22 49			23 09		23 11
Three Bridges 15	a			22 15	22 33					22 44			22 45	23 02		22 54			23 15		23 15
	d			22 15	22 36					22 44			22 45	23 03		22 54			23 16		23 15
Crawley	d				22 39									23 06					23 19		
Ifield	d				22 42									23 09							
Faygate	d																				
Littlehaven	d				22 48									23 15							
Horsham 4	a				22 51									23 18					23 27		
Balcombe	d							>					22 53								
Haywards Heath	d		22 15	22 26			22 34	22 37		22 53		22 47	22 58			23 03				23 17	23 26
Wivelsfield	d			22 30			22 38			22 57			23 02								23 30
Lewes 4	a						22 51														
Burgess Hill 4	d			22 32						22 59			23 04			23 08					23 32
Hassocks 4	d			22 36						23 02			23 08								23 36
Preston Park	d			22 43						23 09			23 15								23 43
Hove 2	a							22 51								23 21					
Brighton 10	a		22 30	22 47						23 15		23 00	23 19							23 30	23 47

Table 186

Bedford and London - Brighton

		SN 1	GX 1	SN ◇1	SN ◇1	SN 1	GX 1	SN ◇1	SN 1	SN ◇1	FC 1	SN 1	GX 1	SN ◇1	GX 1	SN 1	GW 1	SN ◇1	FC 1	GX 1	SN 1
London Victoria 15 ⊖	d	22 40	22 45	22 47			23 00	23 02		23 06		23 10	23 15	23 17	23 30			23 32		23 45	23 47
Clapham Junction 10	d	22 46		22 53				23 08		23 12		23 16		23 23				23 38			23 53
Bedford	d																				
Luton 10	d																				
Luton Airport Parkway 7	d																				
St Albans City	d																				
St Pancras International 15 ⊖	d																				
Farringdon 3 ⊖	d																				
City Thameslink 3	d																				
London Blackfriars 3 ⊖	d																				
London Bridge 4 ⊖	d										23 12								23 42		
Norwood Junction 2	d																				
East Croydon ⇌	a	22 57		23 03				23 19		23 22	23 24	23 27		23 33				23 51	23 56		00 05
	d	22 58		23 03				23 20		23 22	23 24	23 28		23 33				23 52	23 56		00 06
Purley 4	d	23 03										23 33									00 12
Coulsdon South	d	23 06										23 37									00 15
Merstham	d	23 12										23 42									00 21
Redhill	a	23 15						23 31				23 46					23 58	00 03			00 24
	d	23 16				22 55		23 31	23 05			23 46				23 55	00 03	00 05			00 25
Reigate	a								23 09												
Nutfield	d					22 59															
Godstone	d					23 05															
Edenbridge	d					23 10										00 06					
Penshurst	d					23 17															
Leigh (Kent)	d					23 20															
Tonbridge 4	a					23 25										00 15					
Earlswood (Surrey)	d	23 18										23 49									
Salfords	d	23 22										23 52									
Horley 4	d	23 25										23 56									00 31
Gatwick Airport 10	a	23 28	23 15	23 18			23 30	23 38			23 40	23 58	23 45	23 50	00 05		00 11	00 14	00 18	00 20	00 33
	d	23 29		23 19				23 39			23 41	23 59		23 51				00 15	00 18		00 34
Three Bridges 15	a	23 33						23 44			23 47	00 04		23 55				00 20	00 24		00 39
	d	23 38						23 44			23 47	00 04		23 56				00 20			00 39
Crawley	d	23 41										00 07									00 43
Ifield	d	23 44										00 10									00 46
Faygate	d																				
Littlehaven	d	23 50										00 16									00 52
Horsham 4	a	23 53										00 19									00 55
Balcombe	d				>						23 53							00 26			
Haywards Heath	d			23 34	23 37			23 53		23 45	23 58			00 05				00 31			
Wivelsfield	d			23 38				23 57			00 02							00 35			
Lewes 4	a			23 51																	
Burgess Hill 4	d							23 59			00 04			00 10				00 37			
Hassocks 4	d							00 02			00 08							00 41			
Preston Park	d							00 09			00 15							00 48			
Hove 2	a				23 51									00 21							
Brighton 10	a							00 15		23 59	00 19							00 52			

Bedford and London - Brighton

		SN	FC	SN	SN	GX	SN	GW	SN	FC		GX	SN	GX	SN	SN	FC	SN	GW	FC	GX		SN	FC	FC
		◇1	1	1	◇1	1	1	1	◇1	1		1	1	1	◇1	◇1		1	1		1		◇1	1	1
London Victoria 15 ⊖	d	23p02		23p10	23p17	23p30			23p32			23p45	23p47	00 02	00 05			00 14			00 30		01 00		
Clapham Junction 10	d	23p08		23p16	23p23				23p38				23p53		00 11			00 20					01 08		
Bedford	d																								
Luton 10	d																								
Luton Airport Parkway 7	d																								
St Albans City	d																								
St Pancras International 15 ⊖	d																								
Farringdon 3 ⊖	d																								
City Thameslink 3	d																								
London Blackfriars 3 ⊖	d																								
London Bridge 4 ⊖	d		23p12							23p42							00 12			00 42				01 05	01 35
Norwood Junction 2	d																								
East Croydon	a	23p19	23p24	23p27	23p33				23p51	23p56			00 05		00 24		00 26	00 31		00 56			01 21	01 32	02 02
	d	23p20	23p24	23p28	23p33				23p52	23p56			00 06		00 25		00 26	00 32		00 56			01 22	01 32	02 02
Purley 4	d			23p33									00 12					00 37					01 27		
Coulsdon South	d			23p37									00 15					00 41							
Merstham	d			23p42									00 21					00 47							
Redhill	a	23p31		23p46				23p58	00 03				00 24					00 50	00 49						
	d	23p31		23p46			23p55	00 03	00 05				00 25					00 51	00 54						
Reigate	a																								
Nutfield	d																								
Godstone	d																								
Edenbridge	d						00 06																		
Penshurst	d																								
Leigh (Kent)	d																								
Tonbridge 4	a						00 15																		
Earlswood (Surrey)	d			23p49																					
Salfords	d			23p52																					
Horley 4	d			23p56									00 31					00 57					01 43		
Gatwick Airport 10	a	23p38	23p40	23p58	23p50	00 05		00 11	00 14	00 18		00 20	00 33	00 37	00 43		00 48	00 59	01 03	01 18	01 20		01 45	01 51	02 21
	d	23p39	23p41	23p59	23p51				00 15	00 18			00 34		00 44		00 48			01 18			01 47	01 52	02 22
Three Bridges 15	a	23p44	23p47	00 04	23p55				00 20	00 24			00 39		00 48		00 54			01 24			01 51	01 58	02 28
	d	23p44	23p47	00 04	23p56				00 20				00 39		00 48								01 52		
Crawley	d			00 07									00 43												
Ifield	d			00 10									00 46												
Faygate	d																								
Littlehaven	d			00 16									00 52												
Horsham 4	a			00 19									00 55												
Balcombe	d		23p53						00 26							>									
Haywards Heath	d	23p53	23p58		00 05				00 31						01 03	01 06							02 06		
Wivelsfield	d	23p57	00 02						00 35																
Lewes 4	a															01 20									
Burgess Hill 4	d	23p59	00 04		00 10				00 37																
Hassocks 4	d	00 02	00 08						00 41																
Preston Park	d	00 09	00 15						00 48																
Hove 2	a				00 21										01s25										
Brighton 10	a	00 15	00 19						00 52						01s17								02 23		

Bedford and London - Brighton

		SN	FC	SN	FC	GX		FC	SN	FC	GX	FC	GX	SN	GX	FC		SN	GW	SN	GX	SN	GX	FC	GX
		1	1	1	1	1		1	◇1	1	1	1	1	◇1	1	1		◇1	1	1	1	1	1	1	1 🚌
London Victoria 15 ⊖	d	02 00		03 00		03 30			04 00		04 30		05 00	05 02	05 15			05 32			05 30		05 45		06 00
Clapham Junction 10	d	02 08		03 08					04 08					05 08				05 38							
Bedford	d																								
Luton 10	d																								
Luton Airport Parkway 7	d																								
St Albans City	d																								
St Pancras International 15 ⊖	d																								
Farringdon 3 ⊖	d																								
City Thameslink 3	d																								
London Blackfriars 3 ⊖	d																								
London Bridge 4 ⊖	d		02 05		03 05			03 35		04 05		04 35				05 05								05 52	
Norwood Junction 2	d																								
East Croydon	a	02 21	02 30	03 21	03 30			04 00	04 21	04 30		05 00		05 21		05 32		05 48						06 04	
	d	02 22	02 32	03 22	03 32			04 02	04 22	04 32		05 02		05 22		05 32		05 48						06 05	
Purley 4	d	02 27		03 27					04 27					05 26				05 53							
Coulsdon South	d													05 30				05 57							
Merstham	d													05 35				06 03							
Redhill	a													05 39				06 06	05 39						
	d													05 39				06 07	05 49						
Reigate	a																								
Nutfield	d																								
Godstone	d																								
Edenbridge	d																								
Penshurst	d																								
Leigh (Kent)	d																								
Tonbridge 4	a																								
Earlswood (Surrey)	d																	06 11							
Salfords	d																	06 15							
Horley 4	d	02 42		03 42					04 43					05 45				06 18							
Gatwick Airport 10	a	02 44	02 51	03 44	03 51	04 05		04 24	04 45	04 51	05 05	05 21	05 35	05 48	05 52	05 55		06 21	05 58		06 00		06 15	06 20	06 30
	d	02 46	02 52	03 46	03 52			04 24	04 47	04 52		05 22		05 49		05 56		06 22		05 58		06 11		06 21	
Three Bridges 15	a	02 50	02 58	03 50	03 58			04 30	04 51	04 58		05 27		05 53		06 00		06 26		06 02		06 15		06 25	
	d								04 52			05 28		05 54		06 00		06 30		06 03		06 16		06 25	
Crawley	d																			06 06					
Ifield	d																			06 09					
Faygate	d																								
Littlehaven	d																			06 15					
Horsham 4	a																			06 18					
Balcombe	d											05 35				06 06		06 36						06 31	
Haywards Heath	d								05 01			05 42		06 03		06 12		06 41				06 25		06 38	
Wivelsfield	d											05 46		06 07		06 16		06 45				06 29			
Lewes 4	a																					06 40			
Burgess Hill 4	d											05 48		06 09		06 18		06 47							
Hassocks 4	d											05 52		06 12		06 22		06 51							
Preston Park	d											05 59		06 19		06 29		06 58							
Hove 2	a																								
Brighton 10	a								05 16			06 07		06 24		06 34		07 02						06 52	

Table 186

Saturdays

Bedford and London - Brighton

		SN 1	SN 1		GX 1	SN 1	GW 1	GW 1	FC 1	GX 1	SN 1	SN 1	FC 1	GX 1	SN 1	GW 1	SN ◇1	FC 1	GX 1	SN 1	SN 1	SN ◇1		FC 1	GX 1
London Victoria 15 ⊖	d	06 02			06 15					06 30	06 32			06 45					07 00			07 06			07 15
Clapham Junction 10	d	06 08									06 38											07 12			
Bedford	d																								
Luton 10	d																								
Luton Airport Parkway 7	d																								
St Albans City	d																								
St Pancras International 15 ⊖	d																								
Farringdon 3 ⊖	d																								
City Thameslink 3	d																								
London Blackfriars 3 ⊖	d																								
London Bridge 4 ⊖	d								06 27				06 42					06 57		07 03				07 12	
Norwood Junction 2	d																			07 15					
East Croydon	a	06 18							06 39		06 48		06 54					07 09		07 18		07 22		07 24	
	d	06 18							06 39		06 48		06 54					07 09		07 21		07 22		07 24	
Purley 4	d	06 23									06 53									07 27					
Coulsdon South	d	06 27									06 57									07 30					
Merstham	d	06 32									07 02									07 36					
Redhill	a	06 36	>					06 39			07 06	>								07 39	>				
	d	06 46	06 52			06 22	06 34	06 41			07 10	07 22				07 34				07 44	07 52				
Reigate	a		06 56				06 38									07 38					07 56				
Nutfield	d					06 26						07 26													
Godstone	d					06 32						07 32													
Edenbridge	d					06 37						07 37													
Penshurst	d					06 44						07 44													
Leigh (Kent)	d					06 47						07 47													
Tonbridge 4	a					06 52						07 52													
Earlswood (Surrey)	d	06 48									07 12														
Salfords	d	06 52									07 16														
Horley 4	d	06 55									07 19									07 51					
Gatwick Airport 10	a	06 58			06 45			06 50	06 55	07 00	07 23		07 10	07 15				07 25	07 30	07 55				07 40	07 45
	d	06 59							06 56		07 24		07 11					07 26		07 56				07 41	
Three Bridges 15	a	07 03							07 00		07 29		07 15							08 01				07 45	
	d	07 04							07 00		07 30		07 15							08 01				07 45	
Crawley	d	07 07									07 33									08 05					
Ifield	d	07 10									07 36									08 07					
Faygate	d																								
Littlehaven	d	07 16									07 42									08 14					
Horsham 4	a	07 19									07 45									08 17					
Balcombe	d												07 21												
Haywards Heath	d								07 10				07 27		07 33		07 37	07 38						07 55	
Wivelsfield	d												07 31		07 37									07 59	
Lewes 4	a														07 48										
Burgess Hill 4	d												07 33											08 01	
Hassocks 4	d												07 36											08 04	
Preston Park	d												07 43											08 11	
Hove 2	a																07 51								
Brighton 10	a								07 24				07 49					07 54				07 58		08 17	

Table 186

Saturdays

Bedford and London - Brighton

		GW 1	SN ◇1	FC 1	GX 1	SN ◇1	SN 1	SN ◇1	FC 1	GX 1	SN 1	SN ◇1	SN ◇1	GW 1	FC 1	GX 1			SN ◇1	SN 1	SN ◇1	FC 1	GX 1		SN 1
London Victoria 15 ⊖	d		07 21		07 30	07 32		07 36		07 45		07 47				08 00			08 02		08 06		08 15		
Clapham Junction 10	d					07 38		07 42				07 53							08 08		08 12				
Bedford	d																								
Luton 10	d																								
Luton Airport Parkway 7	d																								
St Albans City	d																								
St Pancras International 15 ⊖	d																								
Farringdon 3 ⊖	d																								
City Thameslink 3	d																								
London Blackfriars 3 ⊖	d																								
London Bridge 4 ⊖	d			07 27			07 33		07 42		07 45				07 57					08 03		08 12			08 15
Norwood Junction 2	d						07 45				07 56									08 15					08 26
East Croydon	a		07 37	07 39		07 48	07 48	07 52	07 54		08 00	08 03			08 09				08 18	08 18	08 22	08 24			08 30
	d		07 37	07 39		07 48	07 51	07 52	07 54		08 00	08 03			08 09				08 18	08 21	08 22	08 24			08 30
Purley 4	d						07 57				08 06									08 27					08 36
Coulsdon South	d						08 00				08 09									08 30					08 39
Merstham	d						08 06													08 36					08 45
Redhill	a	07 39				08 00	08 09				08 16								08 30	08 39					08 48
	d	07 41				08 00	08 10				08 17			08 34					08 30	08 44					08 56
Reigate	a													08 38											09 00
Nutfield	d										08 21														
Godstone	d										08 27														
Edenbridge	d										08 32														
Penshurst	d										08 39														
Leigh (Kent)	d										08 42														
Tonbridge 4	a										08 47														
Earlswood (Surrey)	d						08 12																		
Salfords	d						08 16																		
Horley 4	d						08 19												08 36	08 51					
Gatwick Airport 10	a	07 50	07 53	07 55	08 00	08 08	08 23		08 10	08 15		08 18			08 25	08 30			08 39	08 55		08 40	08 45		
	d		07 58	07 56		08 09	08 24		08 11			08 19			08 26				08 40	08 56		08 41			
Three Bridges 15	a		08 03			08 14	08 29		08 15										08 44	09 01		08 45			
	d		08 03			08 14	08 30		08 15										08 45	09 01		08 45			
Crawley	d					08 18	08 33												08 48	09 05					
Ifield	d						08 36													09 07					
Faygate	d																								
Littlehaven	d						08 42													09 14					
Horsham 4	a					08 26	08 45												08 56	09 17					
Balcombe	d								08 21				>												
Haywards Heath	d		08 17	08 08					08 27			08 34	08 37		08 38							08 55			
Wivelsfield	d		08 21						08 31													08 59			
Lewes 4	a											08 48													
Burgess Hill 4	d		08 23						08 33													09 01			
Hassocks 4	d		08 26						08 36													09 04			
Preston Park	d		08 33						08 43													09 11			
Hove 2	a												08 51												
Brighton 10	a		08 40	08 24				08 27	08 49						08 54						08 58	09 17			

Bedford and London - Brighton

		SN	SN	GW	SN	FC	GX	SN	SN	SN	FC	GX	SN	SN	SN	GW	FC	GX	SN	SN	SN	FC
		◇1	◇1	1	◇1	1	1	◇1	1	◇1	1	1	1	◇1	◇1	1	1	1	◇1	1	◇1	1
							T					T						T			T	
London Victoria 15 ⊖	d	08 17			08 21		08 30	08 32		08 36		08 45		08 47				09 00	09 02		09 06	
Clapham Junction 10	d	08 23						08 38		08 42				08 53					09 08		09 12	
Bedford	d																					
Luton 10	d																					
Luton Airport Parkway 7	d																					
St Albans City	d																					
St Pancras International 15 ⊖	d																					
Farringdon 3 ⊖	d																					
City Thameslink 3	d																					
London Blackfriars 3 ⊖	d																					
London Bridge 4 ⊖	d					08 27			08 33		08 42		08 45				08 57			09 03		09 12
Norwood Junction 2	d								08 45				08 56							09 15		
East Croydon	a	08 33			08 37	08 39		08 48	08 48	08 52	08 54		09 00	09 03			09 09		09 18	09 18	09 22	09 24
	d	08 33			08 37	08 39		08 48	08 51	08 52	08 54		09 00	09 03			09 09		09 18	09 21	09 22	09 24
Purley 4	d								08 57				09 06							09 27		
Coulsdon South	d								09 00				09 09							09 30		
Merstham	d								09 06											09 36		
Redhill	a			08 38				09 00	09 09				09 16						09 30	09 39		
	d			08 41				09 00	09 10				09 17			09 34			09 30	09 44		
Reigate	a															09 38						
Nutfield	d												09 21									
Godstone	d												09 27									
Edenbridge	d												09 32									
Penshurst	d												09 39									
Leigh (Kent)	d												09 42									
Tonbridge 4	a												09 47									
Earlswood (Surrey)	d								09 12													
Salfords	d								09 16													
Horley 4	d								09 19										09 36	09 51		
Gatwick Airport 10	a	08 48		08 50	08 53	08 55	09 00	09 08	09 23		09 10	09 15		09 18			09 25	09 30	09 39	09 55		09 40
	d	08 49			08 58	08 56		09 09	09 24		09 11			09 19			09 26		09 40	09 56		09 41
Three Bridges 15	a				09 03			09 14	09 29		09 15								09 44	10 01		09 45
	d				09 03			09 14	09 30		09 15								09 45	10 01		09 45
Crawley	d							09 18	09 33										09 48	10 05		
Ifield	d								09 36											10 07		
Faygate	d																					
Littlehaven	d								09 42											10 14		
Horsham 4	a							09 26	09 45										09 56	10 17		
Balcombe	d		>								09 21				>							
Haywards Heath	d	09 04	09 07		09 17	09 08					09 27			09 34	09 37		09 38					09 55
Wivelsfield	d		09 11		09 21						09 31											09 59
Lewes 4	a		09 22											09 51								
Burgess Hill 4	d	09 09			09 23						09 33											10 01
Hassocks 4	d				09 26						09 36											10 04
Preston Park	d				09 33						09 43											10 11
Hove 2	a	09 21													09 51							
Brighton 10	a				09 40	09 24				09 27	09 49						09 54				09 58	10 17

Bedford and London - Brighton

		GX	SN	SN	SN	GW	SN	FC	GX	SN	SN	SN	FC	GX	SN	SN	SN	GW	FC	GX	SN	SN	SN
		1	1	◇1	◇1	1	◇1	1	1	◇1	1	◇1	1	1	1	◇1	◇1	1	1	1	◇1	1	◇1
		T							T			T		T						T	T		T
London Victoria 15 ⊖	d	09 15		09 17			09 21		09 30	09 32		09 36		09 45		09 47				10 00	10 02		10 06
Clapham Junction 10	d			09 23						09 38		09 42				09 53					10 08		10 12
Bedford	d																						
Luton 10	d																						
Luton Airport Parkway 7	d																						
St Albans City	d																						
St Pancras International 15 ⊖	d																						
Farringdon 3 ⊖	d																						
City Thameslink 3	d																						
London Blackfriars 3 ⊖	d																						
London Bridge 4 ⊖	d		09 15					09 27			09 33		09 42		09 45				09 57			10 03	
Norwood Junction 2	d		09 26								09 45				09 56							10 15	
East Croydon	a		09 30	09 33			09 37	09 39		09 48	09 48	09 52	09 54		10 00	10 03			10 09		10 18	10 18	10 22
	d		09 30	09 33			09 37	09 39		09 48	09 51	09 52	09 54		10 00	10 03			10 09		10 18	10 21	10 22
Purley 4	d		09 36								09 57				10 06							10 27	
Coulsdon South	d		09 39								10 00				10 09							10 30	
Merstham	d		09 45								10 06											10 36	
Redhill	a		09 48			09 38				10 00	10 09				10 16						10 30	10 39	
	d		09 52			09 41				10 00	10 10				10 17			10 34			10 30	10 44	
Reigate	a		09 56															10 38					
Nutfield	d														10 21								
Godstone	d														10 27								
Edenbridge	d														10 32								
Penshurst	d														10 39								
Leigh (Kent)	d														10 42								
Tonbridge 4	a														10 47								
Earlswood (Surrey)	d										10 12												
Salfords	d										10 16												
Horley 4	d										10 19										10 36	10 51	
Gatwick Airport 10	a	09 45		09 48		09 50	09 53	09 55	10 00	10 08	10 23		10 10	10 15		10 18			10 25	10 30	10 39	10 55	
	d			09 49			09 58	09 56		10 09	10 24		10 11			10 19			10 26		10 40	10 56	
Three Bridges 15	a						10 03			10 14	10 29		10 15								10 44	11 01	
	d						10 03			10 14	10 30		10 15								10 45	11 01	
Crawley	d									10 18	10 33										10 48	11 05	
Ifield	d										10 36											11 07	
Faygate	d																						
Littlehaven	d										10 42											11 14	
Horsham 4	a									10 26	10 45										10 56	11 17	
Balcombe	d				>								10 21				>						
Haywards Heath	d			10 04	10 07		10 17	10 08					10 27			10 34	10 37		10 38				
Wivelsfield	d				10 11		10 21						10 31										
Lewes 4	a				10 22											10 51							
Burgess Hill 4	d			10 09			10 23						10 33										
Hassocks 4	d						10 26						10 36										
Preston Park	d						10 33						10 43										
Hove 2	a			10 21													10 51						
Brighton 10	a						10 40	10 24				10 27	10 49						10 54				10 58

Bedford and London - Brighton

		FC ■	GX ■ ⊥	SN ■	SN ◇■	SN ◇■	GW ■	SN ◇■	FC ■	GX ■ ⊥	SN ◇■	SN ■	SN ◇■ ⊥	FC ■	GX ■ ⊥	SN ■	SN ◇■	SN ◇■	GW ■	FC ■	GX ■ ⊥	SN ◇■ ⊥	SN ■
London Victoria ■ ⊖	d		10 15		10 17			10 21		10 30	10 32		10 36		10 45		10 47				11 00	11 02	
Clapham Junction ■	d				10 23						10 38		10 42				10 53					11 08	
Bedford	d																						
Luton ■	d																						
Luton Airport Parkway ■	d																						
St Albans City	d																						
St Pancras International ■ ⊖	d																						
Farringdon ■ ⊖	d																						
City Thameslink ■	d																						
London Blackfriars ■ ⊖	d																						
London Bridge ■ ⊖	d	10 12		10 15					10 27			10 33		10 42		10 45				10 57			11 03
Norwood Junction ■	d			10 26								10 45				10 56							11 15
East Croydon	a	10 24		10 30	10 33			10 37	10 39		10 48	10 48	10 52	10 54		11 00	11 03			11 09		11 18	11 18
	d	10 24		10 30	10 33			10 37	10 39		10 48	10 51	10 52	10 54		11 00	11 03			11 09		11 18	11 21
Purley ■	d			10 36								10 57				11 06							11 27
Coulsdon South	d			10 39								11 00				11 09							11 30
Merstham	d			10 45								11 06											11 36
Redhill	a			10 48			10 38				11 00	11 09				11 16						11 30	11 39
	d			10 52			10 41				11 00	11 10				11 17			11 34			11 30	11 44
Reigate	a			10 56															11 38				
Nutfield	d															11 21							
Godstone	d															11 27							
Edenbridge	d															11 32							
Penshurst	d															11 39							
Leigh (Kent)	d															11 42							
Tonbridge ■	a															11 47							
Earlswood (Surrey)	d											11 12											
Salfords	d											11 16											
Horley ■	d											11 19										11 36	11 51
Gatwick Airport ■	a	10 40	10 45		10 48		10 50	10 53	10 55	11 00	11 08	11 23		11 10	11 15		11 18			11 25	11 30	11 39	11 55
	d	10 41			10 49			10 58	10 56		11 09	11 24		11 11			11 19			11 26		11 40	11 56
Three Bridges ■	a	10 45						11 03			11 14	11 29		11 15								11 44	12 01
	d	10 45						11 03			11 14	11 30		11 15								11 45	12 01
Crawley	d										11 18	11 33										11 48	12 05
Ifield	d											11 36											12 07
Faygate	d																						
Littlehaven	d											11 42											12 14
Horsham ■	a										11 26	11 45										11 56	12 17
Balcombe	d					>								11 21				>					
Haywards Heath	d	10 55			11 04	11 07		11 17	11 08					11 27			11 34	11 37		11 38			
Wivelsfield	d	10 59				11 11		11 21						11 31									
Lewes ■	a					11 22											11 51						
Burgess Hill ■	d	11 01			11 09			11 23						11 33									
Hassocks ■	d	11 04						11 26						11 36									
Preston Park	d	11 11						11 33						11 43									
Hove ■	a				11 21													11 51					
Brighton ■	a	11 17						11 40	11 24				11 27	11 49						11 54			

Bedford and London - Brighton

		SN ◇■ ⊥	FC ■	GX ■ ⊥	SN ■	SN ◇■	SN ◇■	GW ■	SN ◇■	FC ■	GX ■ ⊥	SN ◇■	SN ■	SN ◇■ ⊥	FC ■	GX ■ ⊥	SN ■	SN ◇■	SN ◇■	GW ■	FC ■	GX ■ ⊥
London Victoria ■ ⊖	d	11 06		11 15		11 17			11 21		11 30	11 32		11 36		11 45		11 47				12 00
Clapham Junction ■	d	11 12				11 23						11 38		11 42				11 53				
Bedford	d																					
Luton ■	d																					
Luton Airport Parkway ■	d																					
St Albans City	d																					
St Pancras International ■ ⊖	d																					
Farringdon ■ ⊖	d																					
City Thameslink ■	d																					
London Blackfriars ■ ⊖	d																					
London Bridge ■ ⊖	d		11 12		11 15					11 27			11 33		11 42		11 45				11 57	
Norwood Junction ■	d				11 26								11 45				11 56					
East Croydon	a	11 22	11 24		11 30	11 33			11 37	11 39		11 48	11 48	11 52	11 54		12 00	12 03			12 09	
	d	11 22	11 24		11 30	11 33			11 37	11 39		11 48	11 51	11 52	11 54		12 00	12 03			12 09	
Purley ■	d				11 36								11 57				12 06					
Coulsdon South	d				11 39								12 00				12 09					
Merstham	d				11 45								12 06									
Redhill	a				11 48			11 38				12 00	12 09				12 16					
	d				11 52			11 41				12 00	12 10				12 17			12 34		
Reigate	a				11 56															12 38		
Nutfield	d																12 21					
Godstone	d																12 27					
Edenbridge	d																12 32					
Penshurst	d																12 39					
Leigh (Kent)	d																12 42					
Tonbridge ■	a																12 47					
Earlswood (Surrey)	d												12 12									
Salfords	d												12 16									
Horley ■	d												12 19									
Gatwick Airport ■	a		11 40	11 45		11 48		11 50	11 53	11 55	12 00	12 08	12 23		12 10	12 15		12 18			12 25	12 30
	d		11 41			11 49			11 58	11 56		12 09	12 24		12 11			12 19			12 26	
Three Bridges ■	a		11 45						12 03			12 14	12 29		12 15							
	d		11 45						12 03			12 14	12 30		12 15							
Crawley	d											12 18	12 33									
Ifield	d												12 36									
Faygate	d																					
Littlehaven	d												12 42									
Horsham ■	a											12 26	12 45									
Balcombe	d						>								12 21				>			
Haywards Heath	d		11 55			12 04	12 07		12 17	12 08					12 27			12 34	12 37		12 38	
Wivelsfield	d		11 59				12 11		12 21						12 31							
Lewes ■	a						12 22											12 51				
Burgess Hill ■	d		12 01			12 09			12 23						12 33							
Hassocks ■	d		12 04						12 26						12 36							
Preston Park	d		12 11						12 33						12 43							
Hove ■	a					12 21													12 51			
Brighton ■	a	11 58	12 17						12 40	12 24				12 27	12 49						12 54	

Table 186

Saturdays

Bedford and London - Brighton

		SN ◇1 (trolley)	SN 1	SN ◇1 (trolley)	FC 1	GX 1 (trolley)	SN 1	SN ◇1	SN ◇1		GW 1	SN ◇1	FC 1	GX 1 (trolley)	SN ◇1	SN 1	SN ◇1 (trolley)	FC 1		GX 1 (trolley)	SN 1	SN ◇1	SN ◇1	GW 1	FC 1
London Victoria 15 ⊖	d	12 02		12 06		12 15		12 17				12 21		12 30	12 32		12 36			12 45		12 47			
Clapham Junction 10	d	12 08		12 12				12 23							12 38		12 42					12 53			
Bedford	d																								
Luton 10	d																								
Luton Airport Parkway 7	d																								
St Albans City	d																								
St Pancras International 15 ⊖	d																								
Farringdon 3 ⊖	d																								
City Thameslink 3	d																								
London Blackfriars 3 ⊖	d																								
London Bridge 4 ⊖	d		12 03		12 12		12 15						12 27			12 33		12 42			12 45				12 57
Norwood Junction 2	d		12 15				12 26									12 45					12 56				
East Croydon	a	12 18	12 18	12 22	12 24		12 30	12 33				12 37	12 39		12 48	12 48	12 52	12 54			13 00	13 03			13 09
	d	12 18	12 21	12 22	12 24		12 30	12 33				12 37	12 39		12 48	12 51	12 52	12 54			13 00	13 03			13 09
Purley 4	d		12 27				12 36									12 57					13 06				
Coulsdon South	d		12 30				12 39									13 00					13 09				
Merstham	d		12 36				12 45									13 06									
Redhill	a	12 30	12 39				12 48				12 38				13 00	13 09					13 16				
	d	12 30	12 44				12 52				12 41				13 00	13 10					13 17			13 34	
Reigate	a						12 56																	13 38	
Nutfield	d																				13 21				
Godstone	d																				13 27				
Edenbridge	d																				13 32				
Penshurst	d																				13 39				
Leigh (Kent)	d																				13 42				
Tonbridge 4	a																				13 47				
Earlswood (Surrey)	d															13 12									
Salfords	d															13 16									
Horley 4	d	12 36	12 51													13 19									
Gatwick Airport 10	a	12 39	12 55		12 40	12 45		12 48			12 50	12 53	12 55	13 00	13 08	13 23		13 10		13 15		13 18			13 25
	d	12 40	12 56		12 41			12 49				12 58	12 56		13 09	13 24		13 11				13 19			13 26
Three Bridges 5	a	12 44	13 01		12 45							13 03			13 14	13 29		13 15							
	d	12 45	13 01		12 45							13 03			13 14	13 30		13 15							
Crawley	d	12 48	13 05												13 18	13 33									
Ifield	d		13 07													13 36									
Faygate	d																								
Littlehaven	d		13 14													13 42									
Horsham 4	a	12 56	13 17												13 26	13 45									
Balcombe	d								>									13 21					>		
Haywards Heath	d				12 55			13 04	13 07			13 17	13 08					13 27				13 34	13 37		13 38
Wivelsfield	d				12 59				13 11			13 21						13 31							
Lewes 4	a								13 22													13 48			
Burgess Hill 4	d				13 01			13 09				13 23						13 33							
Hassocks 4	d				13 04							13 26						13 36							
Preston Park	d				13 11							13 33						13 43							
Hove 2	a							13 21															13 51		
Brighton 10	a			12 58	13 17							13 40	13 24				13 27	13 49							13 54

Table 186

Saturdays

Bedford and London - Brighton

		GX 1 (trolley)	SN ◇1 (trolley)	SN 1		SN ◇1 (trolley)	FC 1	GX 1 (trolley)	SN 1	SN ◇1	SN ◇1	GW 1	SN ◇1	FC 1		GX 1 (trolley)	SN ◇1	SN 1	SN ◇1 (trolley)	FC 1	GX 1 (trolley)	SN 1	SN ◇1	SN ◇1	GW 1	
London Victoria 15 ⊖	d	13 00	13 02			13 06		13 15		13 17			13 21			13 30	13 32		13 36		13 45		13 47			
Clapham Junction 10	d		13 08			13 12				13 23							13 38		13 42				13 53			
Bedford	d																									
Luton 10	d																									
Luton Airport Parkway 7	d																									
St Albans City	d																									
St Pancras International 15 ⊖	d																									
Farringdon 3 ⊖	d																									
City Thameslink 3	d																									
London Blackfriars 3 ⊖	d																									
London Bridge 4 ⊖	d			13 03			13 12		13 15					13 27				13 33		13 42		13 45				
Norwood Junction 2	d			13 15					13 26									13 45				13 56				
East Croydon	a		13 18	13 18		13 22	13 24		13 30	13 33			13 37	13 39			13 48	13 48	13 52	13 54		14 00	14 03			
	d		13 18	13 21		13 22	13 24		13 30	13 33			13 37	13 39			13 48	13 51	13 52	13 54		14 00	14 03			
Purley 4	d			13 27					13 36									13 57				14 06				
Coulsdon South	d			13 30					13 39									14 00				14 09				
Merstham	d			13 36					13 45									14 06								
Redhill	a		13 30	13 39					13 48			13 38					14 00	14 09				14 16				
	d		13 30	13 44					13 52			13 41					14 00	14 10				14 17			14 34	
Reigate	a								13 56																14 38	
Nutfield	d																					14 21				
Godstone	d																					14 27				
Edenbridge	d																					14 32				
Penshurst	d																					14 39				
Leigh (Kent)	d																					14 42				
Tonbridge 4	a																					14 47				
Earlswood (Surrey)	d																	14 12								
Salfords	d																	14 16								
Horley 4	d		13 36	13 51														14 19								
Gatwick Airport 10	a	13 30	13 39	13 55			13 40	13 45		13 48		13 50	13 53	13 55		14 00	14 08	14 23		14 10	14 15		14 18			
	d		13 40	13 56			13 41			13 49			13 58	13 56			14 09	14 24		14 11			14 19			
Three Bridges 5	a		13 44	14 01			13 45						14 03				14 14	14 29		14 15						
	d		13 45	14 01			13 45						14 03				14 14	14 30		14 15						
Crawley	d		13 48	14 05													14 18	14 33								
Ifield	d			14 07														14 36								
Faygate	d																									
Littlehaven	d			14 14														14 42								
Horsham 4	a		13 56	14 17													14 26	14 45								
Balcombe	d										>									14 21				>		
Haywards Heath	d						13 55			14 04	14 07		14 17	14 08						14 27			14 34	14 37		
Wivelsfield	d						13 59				14 11		14 21							14 31						
Lewes 4	a										14 22												14 48			
Burgess Hill 4	d						14 01			14 09			14 23							14 33						
Hassocks 4	d						14 04						14 26							14 36						
Preston Park	d						14 11						14 33							14 43						
Hove 2	a									14 21														14 51		
Brighton 10	a					13 58	14 17						14 40	14 24					14 27	14 49						

Bedford and London - Brighton

		FC 1	GX 1 ⌶	SN ◇1 ⌶	SN 1	SN ◇1 ⌶	FC 1	GX 1 ⌶	SN 1	SN ◇1	SN ◇1	GW 1	SN ◇1	FC 1	GX 1 ⌶	SN ◇1	SN 1	SN ◇1 ⌶	FC 1	GX 1 ⌶	SN 1	SN ◇1	SN ◇1
London Victoria 15 ⊖	d		14 00	14 02		14 06		14 15		14 17			14 21		14 30	14 32		14 36		14 45		14 47	
Clapham Junction 10	d			14 08		14 12				14 23						14 38		14 42				14 53	
Bedford	d																						
Luton 10	d																						
Luton Airport Parkway 7	d																						
St Albans City	d																						
St Pancras International 15 ⊖	d																						
Farringdon 3 ⊖	d																						
City Thameslink 3	d																						
London Blackfriars 3 ⊖	d																						
London Bridge 4 ⊖	d	13 57			14 03		14 12		14 15					14 27			14 33		14 42		14 45		
Norwood Junction 2	d				14 15				14 26								14 45				14 56		
East Croydon	a	14 09		14 18	14 18	14 22	14 24		14 30	14 33			14 37	14 39		14 48	14 48	14 52	14 54		15 00	15 03	
	d	14 09		14 18	14 21	14 22	14 24		14 30	14 33			14 37	14 39		14 48	14 51	14 52	14 54		15 00	15 03	
Purley 4	d				14 27				14 36								14 57				15 06		
Coulsdon South	d				14 30				14 39								15 00				15 09		
Merstham	d				14 36				14 45								15 06						
Redhill	a			14 30	14 39				14 48			14 38				15 00	15 09				15 16		
	d			14 30	14 44				14 52			14 41				15 00	15 10				15 17		
Reigate	a								14 56														
Nutfield	d																				15 21		
Godstone	d																				15 27		
Edenbridge	d																				15 32		
Penshurst	d																				15 39		
Leigh (Kent)	d																				15 42		
Tonbridge 4	a																				15 47		
Earlswood (Surrey)	d																15 12						
Salfords	d																15 16						
Horley 4	d			14 36	14 51												15 19						
Gatwick Airport 10	a	14 25	14 30	14 39	14 55		14 40	14 45		14 48		14 50	14 53	14 55	15 00	15 08	15 23		15 10	15 15		15 18	
	d	14 26		14 40	14 56		14 41			14 49			14 58	14 56		15 09	15 24		15 11			15 19	
Three Bridges 15	a			14 44	15 01		14 45						15 03			15 14	15 29		15 15				
	d			14 45	15 01		14 45						15 03			15 14	15 30		15 15				
Crawley	d			14 48	15 05											15 18	15 33						
Ifield	d				15 07												15 36						
Faygate	d																						
Littlehaven	d				15 14												15 42						
Horsham 4	a			14 56	15 17											15 26	15 45						
Balcombe	d										>								15 21				>
Haywards Heath	d	14 38					14 55			15 04	15 07		15 17	15 08					15 27			15 34	15 37
Wivelsfield	d						14 59				15 11		15 21						15 31				
Lewes 4	a										15 22											15 48	
Burgess Hill 4	d						15 01			15 09			15 23						15 33				
Hassocks 4	d						15 04						15 26						15 36				
Preston Park	d						15 11						15 33						15 43				
Hove 2	a									15 21													15 51
Brighton 10	a	14 54				14 58	15 17						15 40	15 24				15 27	15 49				

Bedford and London - Brighton

		GW 1	FC 1	GX 1 ⌶	SN ◇1 ⌶	SN 1	SN ◇1 ⌶	FC 1	GX 1 ⌶	SN 1	SN ◇1	SN ◇1	GW 1	SN ◇1	FC 1	GX 1 ⌶	SN ◇1	SN 1	SN ◇1 ⌶	FC 1	GX 1 ⌶	SN 1
London Victoria 15 ⊖	d			15 00	15 02		15 06		15 15		15 17			15 21		15 30	15 32		15 36		15 45	
Clapham Junction 10	d				15 08		15 12				15 23						15 38		15 42			
Bedford	d																					
Luton 10	d																					
Luton Airport Parkway 7	d																					
St Albans City	d																					
St Pancras International 15 ⊖	d																					
Farringdon 3 ⊖	d																					
City Thameslink 3	d																					
London Blackfriars 3 ⊖	d																					
London Bridge 4 ⊖	d		14 57			15 03		15 12		15 15					15 27			15 33		15 42		15 45
Norwood Junction 2	d					15 15				15 26								15 45				15 56
East Croydon	a		15 09		15 18	15 18	15 22	15 24		15 30	15 33			15 37	15 39		15 48	15 48	15 52	15 54		16 00
	d		15 09		15 18	15 21	15 22	15 24		15 30	15 33			15 37	15 39		15 48	15 51	15 52	15 54		16 00
Purley 4	d					15 27				15 36								15 57				16 06
Coulsdon South	d					15 30				15 39								16 00				16 09
Merstham	d					15 36				15 45								16 06				
Redhill	a				15 30	15 39				15 48			15 38				16 00	16 09				16 16
	d	15 34			15 30	15 44				15 52			15 41				16 00	16 10				16 17
Reigate	a	15 38								15 56												
Nutfield	d																					16 21
Godstone	d																					16 27
Edenbridge	d																					16 32
Penshurst	d																					16 39
Leigh (Kent)	d																					16 42
Tonbridge 4	a																					16 47
Earlswood (Surrey)	d																	16 12				
Salfords	d																	16 16				
Horley 4	d				15 36	15 51												16 19				
Gatwick Airport 10	a		15 25	15 30	15 39	15 55		15 40	15 45		15 48		15 50	15 53	15 55	16 00	16 08	16 23		16 10	16 15	
	d		15 26		15 40	15 56		15 41			15 49			15 58	15 56		16 09	16 24		16 11		
Three Bridges 15	a				15 44	16 01		15 45						16 03			16 14	16 29		16 15		
	d				15 45	16 01		15 45						16 03			16 14	16 30		16 15		
Crawley	d				15 48	16 05											16 18	16 33				
Ifield	d					16 07												16 36				
Faygate	d																					
Littlehaven	d					16 14												16 42				
Horsham 4	a				15 56	16 17											16 26	16 45				
Balcombe	d											>								16 21		
Haywards Heath	d		15 38					15 55			16 04	16 07		16 17	16 08					16 27		
Wivelsfield	d							15 59				16 11		16 21						16 31		
Lewes 4	a											16 22										
Burgess Hill 4	d							16 01			16 09			16 23						16 33		
Hassocks 4	d							16 04						16 26						16 36		
Preston Park	d							16 11						16 33						16 43		
Hove 2	a										16 21											
Brighton 10	a		15 54				15 58	16 17						16 40	16 24				16 27	16 49		

Table 186

Saturdays

Bedford and London - Brighton

		SN ◇1	SN ◇1	GW 1	FC 1	GX 1	SN ◇1	SN 1	SN ◇1	FC 1	GX 1	SN 1	SN ◇1	SN ◇1	GW 1	SN ◇1	FC 1	GX 1	SN ◇1	SN 1	SN ◇1	FC 1
London Victoria 15 ⊖	d	15 47				16 00	16 02		16 06		16 15		16 17			16 21		16 30	16 32		16 36	
Clapham Junction 10	d	15 53					16 08		16 12				16 23						16 38		16 42	
Bedford	d																					
Luton 10	d																					
Luton Airport Parkway 7	d																					
St Albans City	d																					
St Pancras International 15 ⊖	d																					
Farringdon 3 ⊖	d																					
City Thameslink 3	d																					
London Blackfriars 3 ⊖	d																					
London Bridge 4 ⊖	d				15 57			16 03		16 12		16 15					16 27			16 33		16 42
Norwood Junction 2	d							16 15				16 26								16 45		
East Croydon	a	16 03			16 09		16 18	16 18	16 22	16 24		16 30	16 33			16 37	16 39		16 48	16 48	16 52	16 54
	d	16 03			16 09		16 18	16 21	16 22	16 24		16 30	16 33			16 37	16 39		16 48	16 51	16 52	16 54
Purley 4	d							16 27				16 36								16 57		
Coulsdon South	d							16 30				16 39								17 00		
Merstham	d							16 36				16 45								17 06		
Redhill	a						16 30	16 39				16 48			16 38				17 00	17 09		
	d			16 34			16 30	16 44				16 52			16 41				17 00	17 10		
Reigate	a			16 38								16 56										
Nutfield	d																					
Godstone	d																					
Edenbridge	d																					
Penshurst	d																					
Leigh (Kent)	d																					
Tonbridge 4	a																					
Earlswood (Surrey)	d																			17 12		
Salfords	d																			17 16		
Horley 4	d						16 36	16 51												17 19		
Gatwick Airport 10	a	16 18			16 25	16 30	16 39	16 55		16 40	16 45		16 48		16 50	16 53	16 55	17 00	17 08	17 23		17 10
	d	16 19			16 26		16 40	16 56		16 41			16 49			16 58	16 56		17 09	17 24		17 11
Three Bridges 15	a						16 44	17 01		16 45						17 03			17 14	17 29		17 15
	d						16 45	17 01		16 45						17 03			17 14	17 30		17 15
Crawley	d						16 48	17 05											17 18	17 33		
Ifield	d							17 07												17 36		
Faygate	d																					
Littlehaven	d							17 14												17 42		
Horsham 4	a						16 56	17 17											17 26	17 45		
Balcombe	d		>											>								17 21
Haywards Heath	d	16 34	16 37		16 38					16 55			17 04	17 07		17 17	17 08					17 27
Wivelsfield	d									16 59				17 11		17 21						17 31
Lewes 4	a	16 51												17 22								
Burgess Hill 4	d									17 01			17 09			17 23						17 33
Hassocks 4	d									17 04						17 26						17 36
Preston Park	d									17 11						17 33						17 43
Hove 2	a		16 51										17 21									
Brighton 10	a				16 54				16 58	17 17						17 40	17 24				17 27	17 49

Table 186

Saturdays

Bedford and London - Brighton

		GX 1	SN 1	SN ◇1	SN ◇1	GW 1	FC 1	GX 1	SN ◇1	SN 1	SN ◇1	FC 1	GX 1	SN 1	SN ◇1	SN ◇1	GW 1	SN ◇1	FC 1	GX 1	SN ◇1	SN 1	SN ◇1
London Victoria 15 ⊖	d	16 45		16 47				17 00	17 02		17 06		17 15		17 17			17 21		17 30	17 32		17 36
Clapham Junction 10	d			16 53					17 08		17 12				17 23						17 38		17 42
Bedford	d																						
Luton 10	d																						
Luton Airport Parkway 7	d																						
St Albans City	d																						
St Pancras International 15 ⊖	d																						
Farringdon 3 ⊖	d																						
City Thameslink 3	d																						
London Blackfriars 3 ⊖	d																						
London Bridge 4 ⊖	d		16 45				16 57			17 03		17 12		17 15					17 27			17 33	
Norwood Junction 2	d		16 56							17 15				17 26								17 45	
East Croydon	a		17 00	17 03			17 09		17 18	17 18	17 22	17 24		17 30	17 33			17 37	17 39		17 48	17 48	17 52
	d		17 00	17 03			17 09		17 18	17 21	17 22	17 24		17 30	17 33			17 37	17 39		17 48	17 51	17 52
Purley 4	d		17 06							17 27				17 36								17 57	
Coulsdon South	d		17 09							17 30				17 39								18 00	
Merstham	d									17 36				17 45								18 06	
Redhill	a		17 16						17 30	17 39				17 48			17 38				18 00	18 09	
	d		17 17			17 34			17 30	17 44				17 52			17 41				18 00	18 10	
Reigate	a					17 38								17 56									
Nutfield	d		17 21																				
Godstone	d		17 27																				
Edenbridge	d		17 32																				
Penshurst	d		17 39																				
Leigh (Kent)	d		17 42																				
Tonbridge 4	a		17 47																				
Earlswood (Surrey)	d																					18 12	
Salfords	d																					18 16	
Horley 4	d								17 36	17 51												18 19	
Gatwick Airport 10	a	17 15		17 18			17 25	17 30	17 39	17 55		17 40	17 45		17 48		17 50	17 53	17 55	18 00	18 08	18 23	
	d			17 19			17 26		17 40	17 56		17 41			17 49			17 58	17 56		18 09	18 24	
Three Bridges 15	a								17 44	18 01		17 45						18 03			18 14	18 29	
	d								17 45	18 01		17 45						18 03			18 14	18 30	
Crawley	d								17 48	18 05											18 18	18 33	
Ifield	d									18 07												18 36	
Faygate	d																						
Littlehaven	d									18 14												18 42	
Horsham 4	a								17 56	18 17											18 26	18 47	
Balcombe	d				>											>							
Haywards Heath	d			17 34	17 37		17 38					17 55			18 04	18 07		18 17	18 08				
Wivelsfield	d											17 59				18 11		18 21					
Lewes 4	a			17 51												18 22							
Burgess Hill 4	d											18 01			18 09			18 23					
Hassocks 4	d											18 04						18 26					
Preston Park	d											18 11						18 33					
Hove 2	a				17 51										18 21								
Brighton 10	a						17 54				17 58	18 17						18 40	18 24				18 27

Table 186

Bedford and London - Brighton

		FC 1	GX 1	SN 1	SN ◇1	SN ◇1	GW 1	FC 1	GX 1	SN ◇1	SN 1	SN ◇1	FC 1	GX 1	SN 1	SN ◇1	SN ◇1	GW 1	SN ◇1	FC 1	GX 1	SN ◇1
London Victoria 15 ⊖	d		17 45		17 47				18 00	18 02		18 06		18 15		18 17			18 21		18 30	18 32
Clapham Junction 10	d				17 53					18 08		18 12				18 23						18 38
Bedford	d																					
Luton 10	d																					
Luton Airport Parkway 7	d																					
St Albans City	d																					
St Pancras International 15 ⊖	d																					
Farringdon 3 ⊖	d																					
City Thameslink 3	d																					
London Blackfriars 3 ⊖	d																					
London Bridge 4 ⊖	d	17 42		17 45				17 57			18 03		18 12		18 15					18 27		
Norwood Junction 2	d			17 56							18 15				18 26							
East Croydon ⇌	a	17 54		18 00	18 03			18 09		18 18	18 18	18 22	18 24		18 30	18 33			18 38	18 39		18 48
	d	17 54		18 00	18 03			18 09		18 18	18 21	18 22	18 24		18 30	18 33			18 38	18 39		18 48
Purley 4	d			18 06							18 27				18 36							
Coulsdon South	d			18 09							18 30				18 39							
Merstham	d										18 36				18 45							
Redhill	a			18 16						18 30	18 39				18 48			18 38				19 00
	d			18 17			18 34			18 30	18 44				18 52			18 41				19 00
Reigate	a						18 38								18 56							
Nutfield	d			18 21																		
Godstone	d			18 27																		
Edenbridge	d			18 32																		
Penshurst	d			18 39																		
Leigh (Kent)	d			18 42																		
Tonbridge 4	a			18 47																		
Earlswood (Surrey)	d																					
Salfords	d																					
Horley 4	d									18 36	18 51											
Gatwick Airport 10	a	18 10	18 15		18 18			18 25	18 30	18 39	18 55		18 40	18 45		18 48		18 50	18 53	18 55	19 00	19 08
	d	18 11			18 19			18 26		18 40	18 56		18 41			18 49			18 58	18 56		19 09
Three Bridges 15	a	18 15								18 44	19 01		18 45						19 03			19 14
	d	18 15								18 45	19 01		18 45						19 03			19 14
Crawley	d									18 48	19 05											19 18
Ifield	d										19 07											
Faygate	d																					
Littlehaven	d										19 14											
Horsham 4	a									18 56	19 17											19 26
Balcombe	d	18 21				>											>					
Haywards Heath	d	18 27			18 34	18 37		18 38					18 55			19 04	19 07		19 17	19 08		
Wivelsfield	d	18 31											18 59				19 11		19 21			
Lewes 4	a				18 51												19 22					
Burgess Hill 4	d	18 33											19 01			19 09			19 23			
Hassocks 4	d	18 36											19 04						19 26			
Preston Park	d	18 43											19 11						19 33			
Hove 2	a					18 51										19 21						
Brighton 10	a	18 49						18 54				18 58	19 17						19 40	19 24		

Table 186

Bedford and London - Brighton

		SN 1	SN ◇1	FC 1	GX 1	SN 1	SN ◇1	SN ◇1	GW 1	FC 1	GX 1	SN ◇1	SN 1	SN ◇1	FC 1	GX 1	SN ◇1	SN 1	GW 1	SN ◇1	SN 1	FC 1	GX 1
London Victoria 15 ⊖	d		18 36		18 45		18 47				19 00	19 02		19 06		19 15	19 17			19 21			19 30
Clapham Junction 10	d		18 42				18 53					19 08		19 12			19 23						
Bedford	d																						
Luton 10	d																						
Luton Airport Parkway 7	d																						
St Albans City	d																						
St Pancras International 15 ⊖	d																						
Farringdon 3 ⊖	d																						
City Thameslink 3	d																						
London Blackfriars 3 ⊖	d																						
London Bridge 4 ⊖	d	18 33		18 42		18 45				18 57			19 03		19 12							19 27	
Norwood Junction 2	d	18 45				18 56							19 15										
East Croydon ⇌	a	18 48	18 52	18 54		19 00	19 03			19 09		19 18	19 18	19 22	19 24		19 33			19 37		19 39	
	d	18 51	18 52	18 54		19 00	19 03			19 09		19 18	19 21	19 22	19 24		19 33			19 37		19 39	
Purley 4	d	18 57				19 06							19 27										
Coulsdon South	d	19 00				19 09							19 30										
Merstham	d	19 06											19 36										
Redhill	a	19 09				19 16						19 30	19 39						19 38				
	d	19 10				19 17			19 34			19 30	19 46						19 41		19 51		
Reigate	a								19 38														
Nutfield	d					19 21															19 55		
Godstone	d					19 27															20 01		
Edenbridge	d					19 32															20 06		
Penshurst	d					19 39															20 13		
Leigh (Kent)	d					19 42															20 16		
Tonbridge 4	a					19 47															20 21		
Earlswood (Surrey)	d	19 12																					
Salfords	d	19 16																					
Horley 4	d	19 19										19 36	19 52										
Gatwick Airport 10	a	19 23		19 10	19 15		19 18			19 25	19 30	19 39	19 55		19 40	19 45	19 48		19 50	19 53		19 55	20 00
	d	19 24		19 11			19 19			19 26		19 40	19 56		19 41		19 49			19 58		19 56	
Three Bridges 15	a	19 28		19 15								19 44	20 01		19 45					20 03			
	d	19 30		19 15								19 45	20 01		19 45					20 03			
Crawley	d	19 33										19 48	20 05										
Ifield	d	19 36											20 07										
Faygate	d																						
Littlehaven	d	19 42											20 14										
Horsham 4	a	19 45										19 56	20 17										
Balcombe	d			19 21				>										>					
Haywards Heath	d			19 27			19 34	19 37		19 38					19 55		20 04	20 07		20 17		20 08	
Wivelsfield	d			19 31											19 59			20 11		20 21			
Lewes 4	a						19 51											20 22					
Burgess Hill 4	d			19 33											20 01		20 09			20 23			
Hassocks 4	d			19 36											20 04					20 26			
Preston Park	d			19 43											20 11					20 33			
Hove 2	a							19 51									20 21						
Brighton 10	a		19 27	19 49						19 54				19 58	20 17					20 40		20 24	

Table 186

Bedford and London - Brighton

		SN ◇1	SN 1	SN ◇1	FC 1	GX 1	SN ◇1	SN ◇1	GW 1	FC 1	GX 1	SN ◇1	SN ◇1	FC 1	SN 1	GX 1	SN ◇1	SN ◇1	GW 1	SN 1	SN ◇1	GX 1	SN ◇1
London Victoria 15 ⊖	d	19 32		19 36		19 45	19 47				20 00	20 02	20 06		20 10	20 15	20 17				20 21	20 30	20 32
Clapham Junction 10	d	19 38		19 42			19 53					20 08	20 12		20 16		20 23						20 38
Bedford	d																						
Luton 10	d																						
Luton Airport Parkway 7	d																						
St Albans City	d																						
St Pancras International 15 ⊖	d																						
Farringdon 3 ⊖	d																						
City Thameslink 3	d																						
London Blackfriars 3 ⊖	d																						
London Bridge 4 ⊖	d		19 33		19 42					19 57				20 12									
Norwood Junction 2	d		19 45																				
East Croydon	a	19 48	19 49	19 52	19 54		20 03			20 09		20 19	20 22	20 24	20 27		20 33				20 37		20 48
	d	19 48	19 51	19 52	19 54		20 03			20 09		20 19	20 22	20 24	20 28		20 33				20 37		20 48
Purley 4	d		19 57												20 33								
Coulsdon South	d		20 00												20 37								
Merstham	d		20 06												20 42								
Redhill	a	20 00	20 09									20 30			20 46				20 38				21 00
	d	20 00	20 10						20 34			20 31			20 46				20 41	20 51			21 00
Reigate	a								20 38														
Nutfield	d																			20 55			
Godstone	d																			21 01			
Edenbridge	d																			21 06			
Penshurst	d																			21 13			
Leigh (Kent)	d																			21 16			
Tonbridge 4	a																			21 21			
Earlswood (Surrey)	d		20 12																				
Salfords	d		20 16																				
Horley 4	d		20 19												20 52								
Gatwick Airport 10	a	20 08	20 23		20 10	20 15	20 18			20 25	20 30	20 38		20 40	20 56	20 45	20 48		20 50		20 52	21 00	21 08
	d	20 09	20 24		20 11		20 19			20 26		20 39		20 41	20 57		20 49				20 55		21 09
Three Bridges 15	a	20 14	20 29		20 15							20 44		20 45	21 02						20 59		21 14
	d	20 14	20 33		20 15							20 44		20 45	21 02						21 00		21 14
Crawley	d	20 18	20 36									20 48			21 06								21 18
Ifield	d		20 39												21 08								
Faygate	d																						
Littlehaven	d		20 45												21 15								
Horsham 4	a	20 26	20 48									20 56			21 18								21 26
Balcombe	d				20 21			>						20 53				>					
Haywards Heath	d				20 27		20 34	20 37		20 38				20 58			21 04	21 07			21b17		
Wivelsfield	d				20 31		20 38							21 02				21 11			21 21		
Lewes 4	a						20 51											21 22					
Burgess Hill 4	d				20 33									21 04			21 09				21 23		
Hassocks 4	d				20 36									21 08							21 26		
Preston Park	d				20 43									21 15							21 33		
Hove 2	a							20 51									21 21						
Brighton 10	a			20 27	20 49					20 54			20 58	21 19							21 40		

b arr. 2110

Table 186

Bedford and London - Brighton

		SN ◇1	FC 1	SN 1	GX 1	SN ◇1	SN ◇1	GX 1	SN ◇1	GW 1	SN ◇1	FC 1	SN 1	GX 1	SN ◇1	SN ◇1	GW 1	GX 1	SN 1	SN 1	SN ◇1	FC 1
London Victoria 15 ⊖	d	20 36		20 40	20 45	20 47		21 00	21 02		21 06		21 10	21 15	21 17			21 30	21 32		21 36	
Clapham Junction 10	d	20 42		20 46		20 53			21 08		21 12		21 16		21 23				21 38		21 42	
Bedford	d																					
Luton 10	d																					
Luton Airport Parkway 7	d																					
St Albans City	d																					
St Pancras International 15 ⊖	d																					
Farringdon 3 ⊖	d																					
City Thameslink 3	d																					
London Blackfriars 3 ⊖	d																					
London Bridge 4 ⊖	d		20 42									21 12										21 42
Norwood Junction 2	d																					
East Croydon	a	20 52	20 53	20 57		21 03			21 18		21 22	21 24	21 27		21 33				21 48		21 52	21 54
	d	20 52	20 54	20 58		21 03			21 18		21 22	21 24	21 28		21 33				21 48		21 52	21 54
Purley 4	d			21 03									21 33									
Coulsdon South	d			21 06									21 37									
Merstham	d			21 12									21 42									
Redhill	a			21 15					21 30				21 46				21 44		21 59			
	d			21 16					21 31	21 36			21 46				21 49		22 00	21 51		
Reigate	a									21 40												
Nutfield	d																			21 55		
Godstone	d																			22 01		
Edenbridge	d																			22 06		
Penshurst	d																			22 13		
Leigh (Kent)	d																			22 16		
Tonbridge 4	a																			22 21		
Earlswood (Surrey)	d			21 18																		
Salfords	d			21 22																		
Horley 4	d			21 25									21 52									
Gatwick Airport 10	a		21 10	21 28	21 15	21 18		21 30	21 38			21 40	21 55	21 45	21 48		21 59	22 00	22 08			22 10
	d		21 11	21 29		21 19			21 39			21 41	21 56		21 49				22 09			22 11
Three Bridges 15	a		21 15	21 33					21 44			21 45	22 00		21 53				22 14			22 15
	d		21 15	21 36					21 44			21 45	22 01		21 53				22 14			22 15
Crawley	d			21 39									22 04						22 18			
Ifield	d			21 42									22 07									
Faygate	d																					
Littlehaven	d			21 48									22 13									
Horsham 4	a			21 52									22 16						22 26			
Balcombe	d						>					21 53				>						
Haywards Heath	d		21 26			21 34	21 37		21 53		21 45	21 58			22 06	22 08					22 15	22 26
Wivelsfield	d		21 30			21 38			21 57			22 02				22 12						22 30
Lewes 4	a					21 51										22 23						
Burgess Hill 4	d		21 32						21 59			22 04			22 11							22 32
Hassocks 4	d		21 36						22 02			22 08										22 36
Preston Park	d		21 43						22 09			22 15										22 43
Hove 2	a						21 51								22 22							
Brighton 10	a	21 27	21 47						22 15		22 00	22 19									22 30	22 47

Table 186

Saturdays

Bedford and London - Brighton

		SN 1	GX 1	SN ◇1	SN ◇1	GX 1	SN ◇1	SN ◇1		FC 1	SN 1	GX 1	SN ◇1	GX 1	GW 1	SN 1	SN ◇1	FC 1	SN 1	GX 1	SN ◇1	SN ◇1	SN 1	GX 1	SN ◇1
London Victoria 15 ⊖	d	21 40	21 45	21 47		22 00	22 02	22 06			22 10	22 15	22 17	22 30		22 32	22 36		22 40	22 45	22 47			23 00	23 02
Clapham Junction 10	d	21 46		21 53			22 08	22 12			22 16		22 23			22 38	22 42		22 46		22 53				23 08
Bedford	d																								
Luton 10	d																								
Luton Airport Parkway 7	d																								
St Albans City	d																								
St Pancras International 15 ⊖	d																								
Farringdon 3 ⊖	d																								
City Thameslink 3	d																								
London Blackfriars 3 ⊖	d																								
London Bridge 4 ⊖	d									22 12								22 42							
Norwood Junction 2	d																								
East Croydon	a	21 57		22 03			22 18	22 22		22 24	22 27		22 33			22 48	22 52	22 54	22 57		23 03				23 18
	d	21 58		22 03			22 18	22 22		22 24	22 28		22 33			22 48	22 52	22 54	22 58		23 03				23 18
Purley 4	d	22 03									22 33								23 03						
Coulsdon South	d	22 06									22 37								23 07						
Merstham	d	22 12									22 42								23 12						
Redhill	a	22 15					22 30				22 46				22 52	23 00			23 16						23 30
	d	22 16					22 31				22 46				22 56	23 01			23 16				22 55		23 31
Reigate	a																								
Nutfield	d																						22 59		
Godstone	d																						23 05		
Edenbridge	d																						23 10		
Penshurst	d																						23 17		
Leigh (Kent)	d																						23 20		
Tonbridge 4	a																						23 25		
Earlswood (Surrey)	d	22 18																	23 19						
Salfords	d	22 22																	23 22						
Horley 4	d	22 25									22 52								23 26						
Gatwick Airport 10	a	22 28	22 15	22 18		22 30	22 38			22 40	22 55	22 45	22 48	23 00	23 05	23 08		23 10	23 28	23 15	23 18			23 30	23 38
	d	22 29		22 19			22 39			22 41	22 56		22 49			23 09		23 11	23 29		23 19				23 39
Three Bridges 15	a	22 33					22 44			22 45	23 00		22 54			23 14		23 15	23 34						23 44
	d	22 36					22 44			22 45	23 01		22 54			23 15		23 15	23 38						23 44
Crawley	d	22 39									23 04					23 18			23 41						
Ifield	d	22 42									23 07								23 44						
Faygate	d																								
Littlehaven	d	22 48									23 13								23 50						
Horsham 4	a	22 52									23 16					23 26			23 53						
Balcombe	d				>					22 53												>			
Haywards Heath	d			22 34	22 37		22 53	22 45		22 58			23 03				23 15	23 26			23 34	23 37			23 53
Wivelsfield	d			22 38			22 57			23 02								23 30			23 38				23 57
Lewes 4	a			22 51																	23 51				
Burgess Hill 4	d						22 59			23 04			23 08					23 32							23 59
Hassocks 4	d						23 02			23 08								23 36							00 02
Preston Park	d						23 09			23 15								23 43							00 09
Hove 2	a				22 51								23 21									23 51			
Brighton 10	a						23 15	23 00		23 19							23 30	23 47							00 15

Table 186

Saturdays

Bedford and London - Brighton

		SN ◇1	FC 1		SN 1	GX 1	SN ◇1	GX 1	SN 1	GW 1	SN 1	FC 1	GX
London Victoria 15 ⊖	d	23 06			23 10	23 15	23 17	23 30			23 32		23 45
Clapham Junction 10	d	23 12			23 16		23 23				23 38		
Bedford	d												
Luton 10	d												
Luton Airport Parkway 7	d												
St Albans City	d												
St Pancras International 15 ⊖	d												
Farringdon 3 ⊖	d												
City Thameslink 3	d												
London Blackfriars 3 ⊖	d												
London Bridge 4 ⊖	d		23 12									23 42	
Norwood Junction 2	d												
East Croydon	a	23 22	23 24		23 27		23 33				23 52	23 56	
	d	23 22	23 24		23 28		23 33				23 52	23 56	
Purley 4	d				23 33								
Coulsdon South	d				23 37								
Merstham	d				23 42								
Redhill	a				23 46					23 58	00 03		
	d				23 46				23 55	00 03	00 05		
Reigate	a												
Nutfield	d												
Godstone	d												
Edenbridge	d								00 06				
Penshurst	d												
Leigh (Kent)	d												
Tonbridge 4	a								00 15				
Earlswood (Surrey)	d				23 49								
Salfords	d				23 52								
Horley 4	d				23 56								
Gatwick Airport 10	a		23 40		23 58	23 45	23 50	00 05		00 10	00 14	00 18	00 20
	d		23 41		23 59		23 51				00 15	00 18	
Three Bridges 15	a		23 47		00 04		23 55				00 20	00 24	
	d		23 47		00 04		23 56				00 20		
Crawley	d				00 07								
Ifield	d				00 10								
Faygate	d												
Littlehaven	d				00 16								
Horsham 4	a				00 19								
Balcombe	d		23 53								00 27		
Haywards Heath	d	23 45	23 58				00 05				00 34		
Wivelsfield	d		00 02								00 38		
Lewes 4	a												
Burgess Hill 4	d		00 04				00 10				00 40		
Hassocks 4	d		00 08								00 44		
Preston Park	d		00 15								00 51		
Hove 2	a						00 21						
Brighton 10	a	23 59	00 19								00 55		

Table 186

Bedford and London - Brighton

Sundays
until 05 September

		SN ◇1	FC 1	SN 1	SN ◇1	GX 1	SN 1	GW 1	SN 1	FC 1		GX	GX 1	SN ◇1	SN ◇1	FC 1	SN 1	GW 1	FC 1	GX 1		SN 1	FC 1	SN 1	SN 1
London Victoria ⊖	d	23p02		23p10	23p17	23p30			23p32			23p45	00 02	00 05			00 14			00 30		01 00		02 00	03 00
Clapham Junction	d	23p08		23p16	23p23				23p38					00 11			00 20					01 08		02 08	03 08
Bedford	d																								
Luton	d																								
Luton Airport Parkway	d																								
St Albans City	d																								
St Pancras International ⊖	d																								
Farringdon ⊖	d																								
City Thameslink	d																								
London Blackfriars ⊖	d																								
London Bridge ⊖	d		23p12							23p42						00 12			00 42				01 05		
Norwood Junction	d																								
East Croydon	a	23p18	23p24	23p27	23p33				23p52	23p56				00 24		00 27	00 31		00 56			01 21	01 32	02 21	03 21
	d	23p18	23p24	23p28	23p33				23p52	23p56				00 25		00 28	00 32		00 57			01 22	01 32	02 22	03 22
Purley	d			23p33													00 37					01 27		02 27	03 27
Coulsdon South	d			23p37													00 41								
Merstham	d			23p42													00 47								
Redhill	a	23p30		23p46				23p58	00 03								00 50	00 49							
	d	23p31		23p46			23p55	00 03	00 05								00 51	00 54							
Reigate	a																								
Nutfield	d																								
Godstone	d																								
Edenbridge	d						00 06																		
Penshurst	d																								
Leigh (Kent)	d																								
Tonbridge	a						00 15																		
Earlswood (Surrey)	d			23p49																					
Salfords	d			23p52																					
Horley	d			23p56													00 57					01 43		02 42	03 42
Gatwick Airport	a	23p38	23p40	23p58	23p50	00 05		00 10	00 14	00 18		00 20	00 37	00 43		00 49	00 59	01 02	01 16	01 20		01 45	01 51	02 44	03 44
	d	23p39	23p41	23p59	23p51				00 15	00 18				00 44		00 50	01 00		01 17			01 47	01 52	02 46	03 46
Three Bridges	a	23p44	23p47	00 04	23p55				00 20	00 24				00 48		00 54	01 05		01 24			01 51	01 58	03 00	04 00
	d	23p44	23p47	00 04	23p56									00 48								01 52			
Crawley	d			00 07																					
Ifield	d			00 10																					
Faygate	d																								
Littlehaven	d			00 16																					
Horsham	a			00 19																					
Balcombe	d		23p53						00 27						>										
Haywards Heath	d	23p53	23p58		00 05				00 34					01 03	01 06							02 06			
Wivelsfield	d	23p57	00 02						00 38																
Lewes	a														01 20										
Burgess Hill	d	23p59	00 04		00 10				00 40																
Hassocks	d	00 02	00 08						00 44																
Preston Park	d	00 09	00 15						00 51																
Hove	a				00 21									01s25											
Brighton	a	00 15	00 19						00 55					01s17								02 23			

Table 186

Bedford and London - Brighton

Sundays
until 05 September

		GX 1	SN 1	GX 1	GX 1	SN A 🚌		SN 1	GX 1	GX 1	GX 1	SN 1	SN ◇1	GX 1 ⌶	GX 1 ⌶	SN 1		GX 1 ⌶	GX 1 ⌶	SN ◇1	SN ◇1	SN 1	GW 1	GX 1 ⌶	FC 1
London Victoria ⊖	d	03 30	04 00	04 30	05 00			05 02	05 15	05 30	05 45		05 47	06 00	06 15			06 30	06 45	06 32	07 02			07 00	
Clapham Junction	d		04 08					05 08					05 53							06 38	07 08				
Bedford	d																								
Luton	d																								
Luton Airport Parkway	d																								
St Albans City	d																								
St Pancras International ⊖	d																								
Farringdon ⊖	d																								
City Thameslink	d																								
London Blackfriars ⊖	d																								
London Bridge ⊖	d																					07 05			07 12
Norwood Junction	d																					07 17			
East Croydon	a		04 21					05 22					06 05							06 51	07 19	07 21			07 24
	d		04 22					05 23					06 06							06 52	07 20	07 22			07 24
Purley	d		04 27					05 29												06 56	07 25	07 28			
Coulsdon South	d																			07 00		07 31			
Merstham	d																			07 05		07 37			
Redhill	a							05 37					06 18							07 09	07 33	07 40	07 09		
	d							05 38					06 19							07 09	07 34	07 41	07 15		
Reigate	a																								
Nutfield	d																					07 45			
Godstone	d																					07 51			
Edenbridge	d																					07 56			
Penshurst	d																					08 03			
Leigh (Kent)	d																					08 06			
Tonbridge	a																					08 11			
Earlswood (Surrey)	d																								
Salfords	d																								
Horley	d		04 43										06 25							07 15	07 40				
Gatwick Airport	a	04 05	04 45	05 05	05 35			05 45	05 50	06 05	06 20		06 31	06 35	06 47			07 05	07 15	07 18	07 42		07 27	07 30	07 41
	d		04 47					05 46				06 29	06 32			06 58				07 19	07 43				07 41
Three Bridges	a		04 54					05 50				06 33	06 36			07 02				07 23	07 48				07 47
	d		04 55			05 00		05 51				06 40	06 36			07 03				07 24	07 48				07 47
Crawley	d											06 43									07 52				
Ifield	d											06 46									07 54				
Faygate	d																								
Littlehaven	d											06 52									08 01				
Horsham	a											06 56									08 04				
Balcombe	d																			07 30					
Haywards Heath	d		05 07			05 20		06 00					06 47			07 12				07 36					07 56
Wivelsfield	d												06 51							07 40					
Lewes	a															07 27									
Burgess Hill	d												06 53							07 42					08 01
Hassocks	d												06 56							07 45					
Preston Park	d												07 03							07 52					
Hove	a																								
Brighton	a		05 21			05 55		06 18					07 08							07 58					08 13

A 23 May

Table 186

Bedford and London - Brighton

Sundays until 05 September

		GX 1	SN ◇1	GX 1	SN 1	FC 1	GX 1	GX 1	GW 1	SN ◇1	SN 1	FC 1	GX 1	SN ◇1	SN ◇1	GX 1	SN 1	FC 1	GX 1	SN ◇1	GX 1	SN ◇1
London Victoria 15 ⊖	d	07 15	07 17	07 30	07 32		07 45	08 00		08 02			08 15	08 17	08 21	08 30	08 32		08 45	08 47	09 00	09 02
Clapham Junction 10	d		07 23		07 38					08 08				08 23	08 27		08 38			08 53		09 08
Bedford	d																					
Luton 10	d																					
Luton Airport Parkway 7	d																					
St Albans City	d																					
St Pancras International 15 ⊖	d																					
Farringdon 3 ⊖	d																					
City Thameslink 3	d																					
London Blackfriars 3 ⊖	d																					
London Bridge 4 ⊖	d					07 42					08 05	08 12						08 42				
Norwood Junction 2	d										08 16											
East Croydon	a		07 35		07 49	07 54				08 17	08 20	08 24		08 32	08 38		08 47	08 54		09 02		09 17
	d		07 36		07 50	07 54				08 18	08 21	08 24		08 33	08 38		08 48	08 54		09 03		09 18
Purley 4	d				07 55					08 23	08 27						08 53					09 23
Coulsdon South	d				07 59						08 30						08 57					
Merstham	d				08 04						08 36						09 02					
Redhill	a		07 49		08 08				08 18	08 31	08 39				08 49		09 06					09 31
	d		07 50		08 08				08 20	08 32	08 40				08 50		09 06					09 32
Reigate	a																					
Nutfield	d										08 44											
Godstone	d										08 50											
Edenbridge	d										08 55											
Penshurst	d										09 02											
Leigh (Kent)	d										09 05											
Tonbridge 4	a										09 10											
Earlswood (Surrey)	d				08 11												09 09					
Salfords	d				08 14												09 12					
Horley 4	d				08 18					08 38							09 16					09 38
Gatwick Airport 10	a	07 45	07 57	08 00	08 20	08 11	08 15	08 30	08 31	08 40		08 41	08 45	08 48	08 57	09 00	09 18	09 11	09 15	09 18	09 30	09 40
	d		07 58		08 21	08 11				08 41		08 41		08 49	08 58		09 19	09 11		09 19		09 41
Three Bridges 15	a		08 02		08 26	08 17				08 46		08 47			09 02		09 24	09 17				09 46
	d		08 09		08 26	08 17				08 46		08 47			09 09		09 24	09 17				09 46
Crawley	d				08 30					08 50							09 28					09 50
Ifield	d				08 33												09 31					
Faygate	d																					
Littlehaven	d				08 39												09 37					
Horsham 4	a				08 42					08 58							09 40					09 58
Balcombe	d		08 15												09 15							
Haywards Heath	d		08 21			08 26						08 56		09 00	09 21			09 26		09 30		
Wivelsfield	d		08 25												09 25					09 34		
Lewes 4	a																			09 48		
Burgess Hill 4	d		08 27			08 31						09 01		09 06	09 27			09 31				
Hassocks 4	d		08 30			08 35									09 30			09 35				
Preston Park	d		08 37												09 37							
Hove 2	a													09 18								
Brighton 10	a		08 41			08 44						09 13			09 41			09 44				

Table 186

Bedford and London - Brighton

Sundays until 05 September

		SN 1	GW 1	SN ◇1	FC 1	GX 1	SN ◇1	SN ◇1	GX 1	SN 1	SN ◇1	FC 1	GX 1	SN ◇1	GX 1	SN ◇1	SN 1	GW 1	SN ◇1	FC 1	GX 1	SN ◇1	SN ◇1
London Victoria 15 ⊖	d			09 06		09 15	09 17	09 21	09 30	09 32	09 36		09 45	09 47	10 00	10 02			10 06		10 15	10 17	10 21
Clapham Junction 10	d			09 12			09 23	09 27		09 38	09 42			09 53		10 08			10 12			10 23	10 27
Bedford	d																						
Luton 10	d																						
Luton Airport Parkway 7	d																						
St Albans City	d																						
St Pancras International 15 ⊖	d																						
Farringdon 3 ⊖	d																						
City Thameslink 3	d																						
London Blackfriars 3 ⊖	d																						
London Bridge 4 ⊖	d	09 05			09 12							09 42					10 05			10 12			
Norwood Junction 2	d	09 16															10 16						
East Croydon	a	09 20		09 22	09 24		09 32	09 38		09 47	09 52	09 54		10 02		10 17	10 20		10 22	10 24		10 32	10 38
	d	09 21		09 22	09 24		09 33	09 38		09 48	09 52	09 54		10 03		10 18	10 21		10 22	10 24		10 33	10 38
Purley 4	d	09 27								09 53						10 23	10 27						
Coulsdon South	d	09 30								09 57							10 30						
Merstham	d	09 36								10 02							10 36						
Redhill	a	09 39	09 18					09 49		10 06						10 31	10 39	10 17					10 49
	d	09 40	09 20					09 50		10 06						10 32	10 40	10 20					10 50
Reigate	a																						
Nutfield	d	09 44															10 44						
Godstone	d	09 50															10 50						
Edenbridge	d	09 55															10 55						
Penshurst	d	10 02															11 02						
Leigh (Kent)	d	10 05															11 05						
Tonbridge 4	a	10 10															11 10						
Earlswood (Surrey)	d									10 09													
Salfords	d									10 12													
Horley 4	d									10 16						10 38							
Gatwick Airport 10	a		09 31	09 37	09 41	09 45	09 48	09 57	10 00	10 18		10 11	10 15	10 18	10 30	10 40		10 31	10 37	10 41	10 45	10 48	10 57
	d			09 38	09 41		09 49	09 58		10 19		10 11		10 19		10 41			10 38	10 41		10 49	10 58
Three Bridges 15	a				09 47			10 02		10 24		10 17				10 46				10 47			11 02
	d				09 47			10 09		10 24		10 17				10 46				10 47			11 09
Crawley	d									10 28						10 50							
Ifield	d									10 31													
Faygate	d																						
Littlehaven	d									10 37													
Horsham 4	a									10 40						10 58							
Balcombe	d							10 15															11 15
Haywards Heath	d				09 56		10 00	10 21				10 26		10 30						10 56		11 00	11 21
Wivelsfield	d							10 25						10 34									11 25
Lewes 4	a													10 48									
Burgess Hill 4	d				10 01		10 06	10 27				10 31								11 01		11 06	11 27
Hassocks 4	d							10 30				10 35											11 30
Preston Park	d							10 37															11 37
Hove 2	a						10 18															11 18	
Brighton 10	a			10 00	10 13			10 41			10 27	10 44							11 00	11 13			11 41

Table 186

Bedford and London - Brighton

Sundays
until 05 September

		GX	SN	SN	FC	GX	SN	GX	SN	SN	GW	SN	FC	GX	SN	SN	GX	SN	SN	FC	GX	SN
		1 🛒	1	◇1 🛒	1	1 🛒	◇1 🛒	1 🛒	◇1 🛒	1	1	◇1 🛒	1	1 🛒	◇1	◇1	1 🛒	1	◇1 🛒	1	1 🛒	◇1 🛒
London Victoria 15 ⊖	d	10 30	10 32	10 36		10 45	10 47	11 00	11 02			11 06		11 15	11 17	11 21	11 30	11 32	11 36		11 45	11 47
Clapham Junction 10	d		10 38	10 42			10 53		11 08			11 12			11 23	11 27		11 38	11 42			11 53
Bedford	d																					
Luton 10	d																					
Luton Airport Parkway 7	d																					
St Albans City	d																					
St Pancras International 15 ⊖	d																					
Farringdon 3 ⊖	d																					
City Thameslink 3	d																					
London Blackfriars 3 ⊖	d																					
London Bridge 4 ⊖	d				10 42					11 05			11 12							11 42		
Norwood Junction 2	d									11 16												
East Croydon	a		10 47	10 52	10 54		11 02		11 17	11 20		11 22	11 24		11 32	11 38		11 47	11 52	11 54		12 02
	d		10 48	10 52	10 54		11 03		11 18	11 21		11 22	11 24		11 33	11 38		11 48	11 52	11 54		12 03
Purley 4	d		10 53						11 23	11 27								11 53				
Coulsdon South	d		10 57							11 30								11 57				
Merstham	d		11 02							11 36								12 02				
Redhill	a		11 06						11 31	11 39	11 18					11 49		12 06				
	d		11 06						11 32	11 40	11 20					11 50		12 06				
Reigate	a																					
Nutfield	d									11 44												
Godstone	d									11 50												
Edenbridge	d									11 55												
Penshurst	d									12 02												
Leigh (Kent)	d									12 05												
Tonbridge 4	a									12 10												
Earlswood (Surrey)	d		11 09															12 09				
Salfords	d		11 12															12 12				
Horley 4	d		11 16						11 38									12 16				
Gatwick Airport 10	a	11 00	11 18		11 11	11 15	11 18	11 30	11 40		11 31	11 37	11 41	11 45	11 48	11 57	12 00	12 18		12 11	12 15	12 18
	d		11 19		11 11		11 19		11 41			11 38	11 41		11 49	11 58		12 19		12 11		12 19
Three Bridges 15	a		11 24		11 17				11 46				11 47			12 02		12 24		12 17		
	d		11 24		11 17				11 46				11 47			12 09		12 24		12 17		
Crawley	d		11 28						11 50									12 28				
Ifield	d		11 31															12 31				
Faygate	d																					
Littlehaven	d		11 37															12 37				
Horsham 4	a		11 40						11 58									12 40				
Balcombe	d															12 15						
Haywards Heath	d				11 26		11 30						11 56		12 00	12 21				12 26		12 30
Wivelsfield	d						11 34									12 25						12 34
Lewes 4	a						11 48															12 48
Burgess Hill 4	d				11 31								12 01		12 06	12 27				12 31		
Hassocks 4	d				11 35											12 30				12 35		
Preston Park	d															12 37						
Hove 2	a														12 18							
Brighton 10	a			11 27	11 44							12 00	12 13			12 41			12 27	12 44		

Table 186

Bedford and London - Brighton

Sundays
until 05 September

		GX	SN	SN	GW	SN	FC	GX	SN	SN	GX	SN	SN	FC	GX	SN	GX	SN	SN	GW	SN	FC	GX
		1 🛒	◇1	1	1	◇1 🛒	1	1 🛒	◇1	◇1	1 🛒	1	◇1 🛒	1	1 🛒	◇1 🛒	1 🛒	◇1	1	1	◇1 🛒	1	1 🛒
London Victoria 15 ⊖	d	12 00	12 02			12 06		12 15	12 17	12 21	12 30	12 32	12 36		12 45	12 47	13 00	13 02			13 06		13 15
Clapham Junction 10	d		12 08			12 12			12 23	12 27		12 38	12 42			12 53		13 08			13 12		
Bedford	d																						
Luton 10	d																						
Luton Airport Parkway 7	d																						
St Albans City	d																						
St Pancras International 15 ⊖	d																						
Farringdon 3 ⊖	d																						
City Thameslink 3	d																						
London Blackfriars 3 ⊖	d																						
London Bridge 4 ⊖	d			12 05			12 12							12 42					13 05			13 12	
Norwood Junction 2	d			12 16															13 16				
East Croydon	a		12 17	12 20		12 22	12 24		12 32	12 38		12 47	12 52	12 54		13 02		13 17	13 20		13 22	13 24	
	d		12 18	12 21		12 22	12 24		12 33	12 38		12 48	12 52	12 54		13 03		13 18	13 21		13 22	13 24	
Purley 4	d		12 23	12 27								12 53						13 23	13 27				
Coulsdon South	d			12 30								12 57							13 30				
Merstham	d			12 36								13 02							13 36				
Redhill	a		12 31	12 39	12 17					12 49		13 06						13 31	13 39	13 18			
	d		12 32	12 40	12 20					12 50		13 06						13 32	13 40	13 20			
Reigate	a																						
Nutfield	d			12 44															13 44				
Godstone	d			12 50															13 50				
Edenbridge	d			12 55															13 55				
Penshurst	d			13 02															14 02				
Leigh (Kent)	d			13 05															14 05				
Tonbridge 4	a			13 10															14 10				
Earlswood (Surrey)	d											13 09											
Salfords	d											13 12											
Horley 4	d		12 38									13 16						13 38					
Gatwick Airport 10	a	12 30	12 40		12 31	12 37	12 41	12 45	12 48	12 57	13 00	13 18		13 11	13 15	13 18	13 31	13 40		13 31	13 37	13 41	13 45
	d		12 41			12 38	12 41		12 49	12 58		13 19		13 11		13 19		13 41			13 38	13 41	
Three Bridges 15	a		12 46				12 47			13 02		13 24		13 17				13 46				13 47	
	d		12 46				12 47			13 09		13 24		13 17				13 46				13 47	
Crawley	d		12 50									13 28						13 50					
Ifield	d											13 31											
Faygate	d																						
Littlehaven	d											13 37											
Horsham 4	a		12 58									13 40						13 58					
Balcombe	d									13 15													
Haywards Heath	d						12 56		13 00	13 21				13 26		13 30						13 56	
Wivelsfield	d									13 25						13 34							
Lewes 4	a															13 48							
Burgess Hill 4	d						13 01		13 06	13 27				13 31								14 01	
Hassocks 4	d									13 30				13 35									
Preston Park	d									13 37													
Hove 2	a								13 18														
Brighton 10	a					13 00	13 13			13 41			13 27	13 44							14 00	14 13	

Table 186

Bedford and London - Brighton

		SN	SN	GX	SN	SN	FC	GX	SN	GX	SN	SN	GW	SN	FC	GX	SN	SN	GX	SN	SN	FC	GX
		◇1	◇1	1	1	◇1	1	1	◇1	1	◇1	1	1	◇1	1	1	◇1	◇1	1	1	◇1	1	1
				⊼		⊼		⊼	⊼	⊼				⊼		⊼			⊼		⊼		⊼
London Victoria 15 ⊖	d	13 17	13 21	13 30	13 32	13 36		13 45	13 47	14 00	14 02			14 06		14 15	14 17	14 21	14 30	14 32	14 36		14 45
Clapham Junction 10	d	13 23	13 27		13 38	13 42			13 53		14 08			14 12			14 23	14 27		14 38	14 42		
Bedford	d																						
Luton 10	d																						
Luton Airport Parkway 7	d																						
St Albans City	d																						
St Pancras International 15 ⊖	d																						
Farringdon 3 ⊖	d																						
City Thameslink 3	d																						
London Blackfriars 3 ⊖	d																						
London Bridge 4 ⊖	d						13 42					14 05			14 12							14 42	
Norwood Junction 2	d											14 16											
East Croydon	a	13 32	13 38		13 47	13 52	13 54		14 02		14 17	14 20		14 22	14 24		14 32	14 38		14 47	14 52	14 54	
	d	13 33	13 38		13 48	13 52	13 54		14 03		14 18	14 21		14 22	14 24		14 33	14 38		14 48	14 52	14 54	
Purley 4	d				13 53						14 23	14 27								14 53			
Coulsdon South	d				13 57							14 30								14 57			
Merstham	d				14 02							14 36								15 02			
Redhill	a		13 49		14 06						14 31	14 39	14 17					14 49		15 06			
	d		13 50		14 06						14 32	14 40	14 20					14 50		15 06			
Reigate	a																						
Nutfield	d											14 44											
Godstone	d											14 50											
Edenbridge	d											14 55											
Penshurst	d											15 02											
Leigh (Kent)	d											15 05											
Tonbridge 4	a											15 10											
Earlswood (Surrey)	d				14 09															15 09			
Salfords	d				14 12															15 12			
Horley 4	d				14 16						14 38									15 16			
Gatwick Airport 10	a	13 48	13 57	14 00	14 18		14 11	14 15	14 18	14 30	14 40		14 31	14 37	14 41	14 45	14 48	14 57	15 00	15 18		15 11	15 15
	d	13 49	13 58		14 19		14 11		14 19		14 41			14 38	14 41		14 49	14 58		15 19		15 11	
Three Bridges 5	a		14 02		14 24		14 17				14 46				14 47			15 02		15 24		15 17	
	d		14 09		14 24		14 17				14 46				14 47			15 09		15 24		15 17	
Crawley	d				14 28						14 50									15 28			
Ifield	d				14 31															15 31			
Faygate	d																						
Littlehaven	d				14 37															15 37			
Horsham 4	a				14 40						14 58									15 40			
Balcombe	d		14 15															15 15					
Haywards Heath	d	14 00	14 21				14 26		14 30						14 56		15 00	15 21				15 26	
Wivelsfield	d		14 25						14 34									15 25					
Lewes 4	a								14 48														
Burgess Hill 4	d	14 06	14 27				14 31								15 01		15 06	15 27				15 31	
Hassocks 4	d		14 30				14 35											15 30				15 35	
Preston Park	d		14 37															15 37					
Hove 2	a	14 18															15 18						
Brighton 10	a		14 41			14 27	14 44							15 00	15 13			15 41			15 27	15 44	

Table 186

Bedford and London - Brighton

		SN	GX	SN	SN	GW	SN	FC	GX	SN	SN	GX	SN	SN	FC	GX	SN	GX	SN	SN	GW	SN
		◇1	1	◇1	1	1	◇1	1	1	◇1	◇1	1	1	◇1	1	1	◇1	1	◇1	1	1	◇1
		A ⊼	⊼				⊼		⊼			⊼		⊼		⊼	A ⊼	⊼				⊼
London Victoria 15 ⊖	d	14 47	15 00	15 02			15 06		15 15	15 17	15 21	15 30	15 32	15 36		15 45	15 47	16 00	16 02			16 06
Clapham Junction 10	d	14 53		15 08			15 12			15 23	15 27		15 38	15 42			15 53		16 08			16 12
Bedford	d																					
Luton 10	d																					
Luton Airport Parkway 7	d																					
St Albans City	d																					
St Pancras International 15 ⊖	d																					
Farringdon 3 ⊖	d																					
City Thameslink 3	d																					
London Blackfriars 3 ⊖	d																					
London Bridge 4 ⊖	d				15 05			15 12							15 42					16 05		
Norwood Junction 2	d				15 16															16 16		
East Croydon	a	15 02		15 17	15 20		15 22	15 24		15 32	15 38		15 47	15 52	15 54		16 02		16 17	16 20		16 22
	d	15 03		15 18	15 21		15 22	15 24		15 33	15 38		15 48	15 52	15 54		16 03		16 18	16 21		16 22
Purley 4	d			15 23	15 27								15 53						16 23	16 27		
Coulsdon South	d				15 30								15 57							16 30		
Merstham	d				15 36								16 02							16 36		
Redhill	a			15 31	15 39	15 18					15 49		16 06						16 31	16 39	16 17	
	d			15 32	15 40	15 20					15 50		16 06						16 32	16 40	16 20	
Reigate	a																					
Nutfield	d				15 44															16 44		
Godstone	d				15 50															16 50		
Edenbridge	d				15 55															16 55		
Penshurst	d				16 02															17 02		
Leigh (Kent)	d				16 05															17 05		
Tonbridge 4	a				16 10															17 10		
Earlswood (Surrey)	d												16 09									
Salfords	d												16 12									
Horley 4	d			15 38									16 16						16 38			
Gatwick Airport 10	a	15 18	15 30	15 40		15 31	15 37	15 41	15 45	15 48	15 57	16 00	16 18		16 11	16 15	16 18	16 30	16 40		16 31	16 37
	d	15 19		15 41			15 38	15 41		15 49	15 58		16 19		16 11		16 19		16 41			16 38
Three Bridges 5	a			15 46				15 47			16 02		16 24		16 17				16 46			
	d			15 46				15 47			16 09		16 24		16 17				16 46			
Crawley	d			15 50									16 28						16 50			
Ifield	d												16 31									
Faygate	d																					
Littlehaven	d												16 37									
Horsham 4	a			15 58									16 40						16 58			
Balcombe	d										16 15											
Haywards Heath	d	15 30						15 56		16 00	16 21				16 26		16 30					
Wivelsfield	d	15 34									16 25						16 34					
Lewes 4	a	15 48															16 48					
Burgess Hill 4	d							16 01		16 06	16 27				16 31							
Hassocks 4	d										16 30				16 35							
Preston Park	d										16 37											
Hove 2	a									16 18												
Brighton 10	a						16 00	16 13			16 41			16 27	16 44							17 00

Table 186

Bedford and London - Brighton

Sundays
until 05 September

		FC	GX	SN	SN	GX	SN	SN	FC	GX	SN	GX	SN	SN	GW	SN	FC	GX	SN	SN	GX	SN	SN
		1	1	◇1	◇1	1	1	◇1	1	1	◇1	1	◇1	1	1	◇1	1	1	◇1	◇1	1	1	◇1
			⊤			⊤		⊤		⊤	⊤	⊤				⊤		⊤			⊤		⊤
London Victoria 15 ⊖	d		16 15	16 17	16 21	16 30	16 32	16 36		16 45	16 47	17 00	17 02			17 06		17 15	17 17	17 21	17 30	17 32	17 36
Clapham Junction 10	d			16 23	16 27		16 38	16 42			16 53		17 08			17 12			17 23	17 27		17 38	17 42
Bedford	d																						
Luton 10	d																						
Luton Airport Parkway 7	d																						
St Albans City	d																						
St Pancras International 15 ⊖	d																						
Farringdon 3 ⊖	d																						
City Thameslink 3	d																						
London Blackfriars 3 ⊖	d																						
London Bridge 4 ⊖	d	16 12							16 42					17 05			17 12						
Norwood Junction 2	d													17 16									
East Croydon	a	16 24		16 32	16 38		16 47	16 52	16 54		17 02		17 17	17 20		17 22	17 24		17 32	17 38		17 47	17 52
	d	16 24		16 33	16 38		16 48	16 52	16 54		17 03		17 18	17 21		17 22	17 24		17 33	17 38		17 48	17 52
Purley 4	d						16 53						17 23	17 27								17 53	
Coulsdon South	d						16 57							17 30								17 57	
Merstham	d						17 02							17 36								18 02	
Redhill	a				16 49		17 06						17 31	17 39	17 18					17 49		18 06	
	d				16 50		17 06						17 32	17 40	17 20					17 50		18 06	
Reigate	a																						
Nutfield	d													17 44									
Godstone	d													17 50									
Edenbridge	d													17 55									
Penshurst	d													18 02									
Leigh (Kent)	d													18 05									
Tonbridge 4	a													18 10									
Earlswood (Surrey)	d						17 09															18 09	
Salfords	d						17 12															18 12	
Horley 4	d						17 16						17 38									18 16	
Gatwick Airport 10	a	16 41	16 45	16 48	16 57	17 00	17 18		17 11	17 15	17 18	17 30	17 40		17 31	17 37	17 41	17 45	17 48	17 57	18 00	18 18	
	d	16 41		16 49	16 58		17 19		17 11		17 19		17 41			17 38	17 41		17 49	17 58		18 19	
Three Bridges 15	a	16 47			17 02		17 24		17 17				17 46				17 47			18 02		18 24	
	d	16 47			17 09		17 24		17 17				17 46				17 47			18 09		18 24	
Crawley	d						17 28						17 50									18 28	
Ifield	d						17 31															18 31	
Faygate	d																						
Littlehaven	d						17 37															18 37	
Horsham 4	a						17 40						17 58									18 40	
Balcombe	d				17 15															18 15			
Haywards Heath	d	16 56		17 00	17 21				17 26		17 30						17 56		18 00	18 21			
Wivelsfield	d				17 25						17 34									18 25			
Lewes 4	a										17 48												
Burgess Hill 4	d	17 01		17 06	17 27				17 31								18 01		18 06	18 27			
Hassocks 4	d				17 30				17 35											18 30			
Preston Park	d				17 37															18 37			
Hove 2	a			17 18															18 18				
Brighton 10	a	17 13			17 41			17 27	17 44							18 00	18 13			18 41			18 27

Table 186

Bedford and London - Brighton

Sundays
until 05 September

		FC	GX	SN	GX	SN	SN	GW	SN	FC	GX	SN	SN	GX	SN	SN	FC	GX	SN	SN	SN	GW
		1	1	◇1	1	◇1	1	1	◇1	1	1	◇1	◇1	1	1	◇1	1	1	◇1	◇1	1	1
			⊤	⊤	⊤				⊤		⊤			⊤		⊤		⊤	⊤			
London Victoria 15 ⊖	d		17 45	17 47	18 00	18 02			18 06		18 15	18 17	18 21	18 30	18 32	18 36		18 45	18 47	19 02		
Clapham Junction 10	d			17 53		18 08			18 12			18 23	18 27		18 38	18 42			18 53	19 08		
Bedford	d																					
Luton 10	d																					
Luton Airport Parkway 7	d																					
St Albans City	d																					
St Pancras International 15 ⊖	d																					
Farringdon 3 ⊖	d																					
City Thameslink 3	d																					
London Blackfriars 3 ⊖	d																					
London Bridge 4 ⊖	d	17 42					18 05			18 12							18 42				19 05	
Norwood Junction 2	d						18 16														19 16	
East Croydon	a	17 54		18 02		18 17	18 20		18 22	18 24		18 32	18 38		18 47	18 52	18 54		19 02	19 17	19 20	
	d	17 54		18 03		18 18	18 21		18 22	18 24		18 33	18 38		18 48	18 52	18 54		19 03	19 18	19 21	
Purley 4	d					18 23	18 27								18 53					19 23	19 27	
Coulsdon South	d						18 30								18 57						19 30	
Merstham	d						18 36								19 02						19 36	
Redhill	a					18 31	18 39	18 17					18 49		19 06					19 31	19 39	19 18
	d					18 32	18 40	18 20					18 50		19 06					19 32	19 40	19 20
Reigate	a																					
Nutfield	d						18 44														19 44	
Godstone	d						18 50														19 50	
Edenbridge	d						18 55														19 55	
Penshurst	d						19 02														20 02	
Leigh (Kent)	d						19 05														20 05	
Tonbridge 4	a						19 10														20 10	
Earlswood (Surrey)	d														19 09							
Salfords	d														19 12							
Horley 4	d					18 38									19 16					19 38		
Gatwick Airport 10	a	18 11	18 15	18 18	18 31	18 40		18 31	18 37	18 41	18 45	18 48	18 57	19 00	19 18		19 11	19 15	19 18	19 40		19 30
	d	18 11		18 19		18 41			18 38	18 41		18 49	18 58		19 19		19 11		19 19	19 41		
Three Bridges 15	a	18 17				18 46				18 47			19 02		19 24		19 17			19 46		
	d	18 17				18 46				18 47			19 09		19 24		19 17			19 46		
Crawley	d					18 50									19 28					19 50		
Ifield	d														19 31							
Faygate	d																					
Littlehaven	d														19 37							
Horsham 4	a					18 58									19 40					19 58		
Balcombe	d												19 15									
Haywards Heath	d	18 26		18 30						18 56		19 00	19 21				19 26		19 30			
Wivelsfield	d			18 34									19 25						19 34			
Lewes 4	a			18 48															19 48			
Burgess Hill 4	d	18 31								19 01		19 06	19 27				19 31					
Hassocks 4	d	18 35											19 30				19 35					
Preston Park	d												19 37									
Hove 2	a											19 18										
Brighton 10	a	18 44							19 00	19 13			19 41			19 27	19 44					

Table 186

Sundays until 05 September

Bedford and London - Brighton

		GX 1 ⊼	SN ◇1 ⊼	FC 1	GX 1	SN ◇1	SN ◇1	GX 1	SN 1	SN ◇1	FC 1	GX 1	SN ◇1 ⊼	SN ◇1	SN 1	GW 1	GX 1	SN ◇1	FC 1	GX 1	SN ◇1	SN ◇1	GX 1
London Victoria 15 ⊖	d	19 00	19 06		19 15	19 17	19 21	19 30	19 32	19 36		19 45	19 47	20 02			20 00	20 06		20 15	20 17	20 21	20 30
Clapham Junction 10	d		19 12			19 23	19 27		19 38	19 42			19 53	20 08				20 12			20 23	20 27	
Bedford	d																						
Luton 10	d																						
Luton Airport Parkway 7	d																						
St Albans City	d																						
St Pancras International 15 ⊖	d																						
Farringdon 3 ⊖	d																						
City Thameslink 3	d																						
London Blackfriars 3 ⊖	d																						
London Bridge 4 ⊖	d			19 12							19 42				20 05				20 12				
Norwood Junction 2	d														20 16								
East Croydon ⇌	a		19 22	19 24		19 32	19 38		19 47	19 52	19 54		20 02	20 17	20 20			20 22	20 24		20 32	20 38	
	d		19 22	19 24		19 33	19 38		19 48	19 52	19 54		20 03	20 18	20 21			20 22	20 24		20 33	20 38	
Purley 4	d								19 53					20 23	20 27								
Coulsdon South	d								19 57						20 30								
Merstham	d								20 02						20 36								
Redhill	a						19 49		20 06					20 31	20 39	20 17						20 49	
	d						19 50		20 06					20 32	20 40	20 20						20 50	
Reigate	a																						
Nutfield	d														20 44								
Godstone	d														20 50								
Edenbridge	d														20 55								
Penshurst	d														21 02								
Leigh (Kent)	d														21 05								
Tonbridge 4	a														21 10								
Earlswood (Surrey)	d								20 09														
Salfords	d								20 12														
Horley 4	d								20 16					20 38									
Gatwick Airport 10	a	19 32	19 37	19 41	19 45	19 48	19 57	20 00	20 18		20 11	20 15	20 18	20 40		20 30	20 31	20 37	20 41	20 45	20 48	20 57	21 00
	d		19 38	19 41		19 49	19 58		20 19		20 11		20 19	20 41				20 38	20 41		20 49	20 58	
Three Bridges 15	a			19 47			20 02		20 24		20 17			20 46					20 47			21 02	
	d			19 47			20 09		20 24		20 17			20 46					20 47			21 09	
Crawley	d								20 28					20 50									
Ifield	d								20 31														
Faygate	d																						
Littlehaven	d								20 37														
Horsham 4	a								20 40					20 58									
Balcombe	d						20 15															21 15	
Haywards Heath	d			19 56		20 00	20 21				20 26		20 30						20 56		21 00	21 21	
Wivelsfield	d						20 25						20 34									21 25	
Lewes 4	a												20 48										
Burgess Hill 4	d			20 01		20 06	20 27				20 31								21 01		21 06	21 27	
Hassocks 4	d						20 30				20 35											21 30	
Preston Park	d						20 37															21 37	
Hove 2	a					20 18															21 18		
Brighton 10	a		20 00	20 13			20 41			20 27	20 44							21 00	21 13			21 41	

Table 186

Sundays until 05 September

Bedford and London - Brighton

		SN 1	SN ◇1	FC 1	GX 1	SN ◇1	SN ◇1	SN 1	GW 1	GX 1	SN ◇1	FC 1	GX 1	SN ◇1	SN ◇1	GX 1	SN 1	FC 1	GX 1	SN ◇1	GX 1	GW 1	SN ◇1
London Victoria 15 ⊖	d	20 32	20 36		20 45	20 47	21 02			21 00	21 06		21 15	21 17	21 21	21 30	21 32		21 45	21 47	22 00		22 02
Clapham Junction 10	d	20 38	20 42			20 53	21 08				21 12			21 23	21 27		21 38			21 53			22 08
Bedford	d																						
Luton 10	d																						
Luton Airport Parkway 7	d																						
St Albans City	d																						
St Pancras International 15 ⊖	d																						
Farringdon 3 ⊖	d																						
City Thameslink 3	d																						
London Blackfriars 3 ⊖	d																						
London Bridge 4 ⊖	d			20 42				21 05				21 12						21 42					
Norwood Junction 2	d							21 16															
East Croydon ⇌	a	20 47	20 52	20 54		21 02	21 17	21 20			21 22	21 24		21 32	21 38		21 47	21 54		22 02			22 17
	d	20 48	20 52	20 54		21 03	21 18	21 21			21 22	21 24		21 33	21 38		21 48	21 54		22 03			22 18
Purley 4	d	20 53					21 23	21 27									21 53						22 23
Coulsdon South	d	20 57						21 30									21 57						
Merstham	d	21 02						21 36									22 02						
Redhill	a	21 06					21 31	21 39	21 18						21 49		22 06					22 18	22 31
	d	21 06					21 32	21 40	21 20						21 50		22 06					22 20	22 32
Reigate	a																						
Nutfield	d							21 44															
Godstone	d							21 50															
Edenbridge	d							21 55															
Penshurst	d							22 02															
Leigh (Kent)	d							22 05															
Tonbridge 4	a							22 10															
Earlswood (Surrey)	d	21 09															22 09						
Salfords	d	21 12															22 12						
Horley 4	d	21 16					21 38										22 16						22 38
Gatwick Airport 10	a	21 18		21 11	21 15	21 18	21 40		21 30	21 32	21 37	21 41	21 45	21 48	21 57	22 00	22 18	22 11	22 15	22 18	22 30	22 31	22 40
	d	21 19		21 11		21 19	21 41				21 38	21 41		21 49	21 58		22 19	22 11		22 19			22 41
Three Bridges 15	a	21 24		21 17			21 46					21 47			22 02		22 24	22 17					22 46
	d	21 24		21 17			21 46					21 47			22 03		22 24	22 17					22 46
Crawley	d	21 28					21 50										22 28						22 50
Ifield	d	21 31															22 31						
Faygate	d																						
Littlehaven	d	21 37															22 37						
Horsham 4	a	21 40					21 58										22 40						22 58
Balcombe	d														22 09								
Haywards Heath	d			21 26		21 30						21 56		22 00	22 15			22 26		22 30			
Wivelsfield	d					21 34									22 19					22 34			
Lewes 4	a					21 48														22 48			
Burgess Hill 4	d			21 31								22 01		22 06	22 21			22 31					
Hassocks 4	d			21 35											22 24			22 35					
Preston Park	d														22 31								
Hove 2	a													22 18									
Brighton 10	a		21 27	21 44							22 00	22 13			22 35			22 44					

Table 186

Bedford and London - Brighton

Sundays until 05 September

		SN 1		FC 1	GX 1	SN ◇1	SN ◇1	GX 1	SN 1	FC 1	GX 1	SN ◇1		GX 1	SN 1	SN 1	GW 1	FC 1	GX 1	SN ◇1	GX 1	SN ◇1		FC 1	GX 1
London Victoria 15 ⊖	d				22 15	22 17	22 21	22 30	22 32		22 45	22 47		23 00	23 04				23 15	23 17	23 30	23 32			23 45
Clapham Junction 10	d					22 23	22 27		22 38			22 53			23 10					23 23		23 38			
Bedford	d																								
Luton 10	d																								
Luton Airport Parkway 7	d																								
St Albans City	d																								
St Pancras International 15 ⊖	d																								
Farringdon 3 ⊖	d																								
City Thameslink 3	d																								
London Blackfriars 3 ⊖	d																								
London Bridge 4 ⊖	d	22 05		22 12						22 42								23 12						23 42	
Norwood Junction 2	d	22 16																							
East Croydon	a	22 20		22 24		22 32	22 38		22 47	22 54		23 02			23 22			23 24		23 37		23 52		23 56	
	d	22 21		22 24		22 33	22 38		22 48	22 54		23 03			23 22			23 24		23 38		23 53		23 57	
Purley 4	d	22 27							22 53						23 29										
Coulsdon South	d	22 30							22 57						23 33										
Merstham	d	22 36							23 02						23 38										
Redhill	a	22 39					22 49		23 06						23 42		23 18					00 05			
	d	22 40					22 50		23 06						23 42	23 10	23 20					00 05			
Reigate	a																								
Nutfield	d	22 44														23 14									
Godstone	d	22 50														23 20									
Edenbridge	d	22 55														23 25									
Penshurst	d	23 02														23 32									
Leigh (Kent)	d	23 05														23 35									
Tonbridge 4	a	23 10														23 40									
Earlswood (Surrey)	d								23 09																
Salfords	d								23 12																
Horley 4	d								23 16						23 50										
Gatwick Airport 10	a			22 41	22 45	22 48	22 57	23 00	23 18	23 11	23 15	23 18		23 30	23 54		23 31	23 41	23 50	23 59	00 05	00 14		00 18	00 20
	d			22 41		22 49	22 58		23 19	23 11		23 19			23 55			23 41		00 01		00 15		00 19	
Three Bridges 15	a			22 47			23 02		23 24	23 17					00 01			23 47		00 05		00 19		00 24	
	d			22 47			23 03		23 24	23 17					00 01			23 47		00 06		00 20			
Crawley	d								23 28						00 05										
Ifield	d								23 31						00 07										
Faygate	d																								
Littlehaven	d								23 37						00 14										
Horsham 4	a								23 40						00 17										
Balcombe	d						23 09															00 26			
Haywards Heath	d			22 56		23 00	23 15			23 26		23 30						23 56		00 15		00 31			
Wivelsfield	d						23 19					23 34										00 35			
Lewes 4	a											23 48													
Burgess Hill 4	d			23 01		23 06	23 21			23 31								00 01				00 37			
Hassocks 4	d						23 24			23 35												00 41			
Preston Park	d						23 31															00 48			
Hove 2	a					23 19														00 28					
Brighton 10	a			23 13			23 35			23 44								00 13				00 52			

Table 186

Bedford and London - Brighton

Sundays from 12 September

		SN ◇1	FC 1	SN 1	SN ◇1	GX 1	SN 1	GW 1	SN 1	FC 1		GX	GX 1	SN ◇1	SN ◇1	FC 1	SN 1	GW 1	FC 1	GX 1		SN 1	FC 1	SN 1	SN 1
London Victoria 15 ⊖	d	23p02		23p10	23p17	23p30			23p32			23p45	00 02	00 05			00 14			00 30		01 00		02 00	03 00
Clapham Junction 10	d	23p08		23p16	23p23				23p38					00 11			00 20					01 08		02 08	03 08
Bedford	d																								
Luton 10	d																								
Luton Airport Parkway 7	d																								
St Albans City	d																								
St Pancras International 15 ⊖	d																								
Farringdon 3 ⊖	d																								
City Thameslink 3	d																								
London Blackfriars 3 ⊖	d																								
London Bridge 4 ⊖	d		23p12							23p42						00 12			00 42				01 05		
Norwood Junction 2	d																								
East Croydon	a	23p18	23p24	23p27	23p33				23p52	23p56				00 24		00 27	00 31		00 56			01 21	01 32	02 21	03 21
	d	23p18	23p24	23p28	23p33				23p52	23p56				00 25		00 28	00 32		00 57			01 22	01 32	02 22	03 22
Purley 4	d			23p33													00 37					01 27		02 27	03 27
Coulsdon South	d			23p37													00 41								
Merstham	d			23p42													00 47								
Redhill	a	23p30		23p46				23p58	00 03								00 50	00 49							
	d	23p31		23p46			23p55	00 03	00 05								00 51	00 54							
Reigate	a																								
Nutfield	d																								
Godstone	d																								
Edenbridge	d						00 06																		
Penshurst	d																								
Leigh (Kent)	d																								
Tonbridge 4	a						00 15																		
Earlswood (Surrey)	d			23p49																					
Salfords	d			23p52																					
Horley 4	d			23p56													00 57					01 43		02 42	03 42
Gatwick Airport 10	a	23p38	23p40	23p58	23p50	00 05		00 10	00 14	00 18		00 20	00 37	00 43		00 49	00 59	01 02	01 16	01 20		01 45	01 51	02 44	03 44
	d	23p39	23p41	23p59	23p51				00 15	00 18				00 44		00 50	01 00		01 17			01 47	01 52	02 46	03 46
Three Bridges 15	a	23p44	23p47	00 04	23p55				00 20	00 24				00 48		00 54	01 05		01 24			01 51	01 58	03 00	04 00
	d	23p44	23p47	00 04	23p56				00 20					00 48								01 52			
Crawley	d			00 07																					
Ifield	d			00 10																					
Faygate	d																								
Littlehaven	d			00 16																					
Horsham 4	a			00 19																					
Balcombe	d		23p53						00 27						>										
Haywards Heath	d	23p53	23p58		00 05				00 34					01 03	01 06							02 06			
Wivelsfield	d	23p57	00 02						00 38																
Lewes 4	a														01 20										
Burgess Hill 4	d	23p59	00 04		00 10				00 40																
Hassocks 4	d	00 02	00 08						00 44																
Preston Park	d	00 09	00 15						00 51																
Hove 2	a				00 21									01s25											
Brighton 10	a	00 15	00 19						00 55					01s17								02 23			

Table 186

Sundays
from 12 September

Bedford and London - Brighton

		GX 1	SN 1	GX 1	GX 1	SN 1	GX 1	GX 1	GX 1	SN 1	SN ◇1	GX 1	GX 1	GX 1	SN ◇1	GX 1	GW 1	GX 1	SN ◇1	FC 1	GX 1	GX 1	SN ◇1
London Victoria 15 ⊖	d	03 30	04 00	04 30	05 00	05 02	05 15	05 30	05 45		05 47	06 00	06 15	06 30	06 32	06 45		07 00	07 02		07 15	07 30	07 32
Clapham Junction 10	d		04 08			05 08					05 53				06 38				07 08				07 38
Bedford	d																						
Luton 10	d																						
Luton Airport Parkway 7	d																						
St Albans City	d																						
St Pancras International 15 ⊖	d																						
Farringdon 3 ⊖	d																						
City Thameslink 3	d																						
London Blackfriars 3 ⊖	d																						
London Bridge 4 ⊖	d																			07 12			
Norwood Junction 2	d																						
East Croydon	a		04 21			05 22					06 05				06 51				07 23	07 26			07 50
	d		04 22			05 23					06 06				06 52				07 23	07 27			07 51
Purley 4	d		04 27			05 29									06 56				07 29				
Coulsdon South	d														07 00								
Merstham	d														07 05								
Redhill	a					05 37					06 18				07 09		07 09		07 37				08 03
	d					05 38					06 19				07 09		07 15		07 37				08 04
Reigate	a																						
Nutfield	d																						
Godstone	d																						
Edenbridge	d																						
Penshurst	d																						
Leigh (Kent)	d																						
Tonbridge 4	a																						
Earlswood (Surrey)	d																						
Salfords	d																						
Horley 4	d		04 43								06 25				07 15				07 43				
Gatwick Airport 10	a	04 05	04 45	05 05	05 35	05 45	05 50	06 05	06 20		06 31	06 35	06 47	07 05	07 18	07 20	07 27	07 35	07 46	07 48	07 50	08 05	08 11
	d		04 47			05 46				06 29	06 32				07 19				07 47	07 50			08 12
Three Bridges 15	a		04 54			05 50				06 33	06 36				07 23				07 51	07 54			08 16
	d		04 55			05 51				06 40	06 36				07 24				07 52	07 54			08 17
Crawley	d									06 43									07 55				
Ifield	d									06 46									07 58				
Faygate	d																						
Littlehaven	d									06 52									08 04				
Horsham 4	a									06 56									08 07				
Balcombe	d														07 30								08 23
Haywards Heath	d		05 07			06 00					06 47				07 36					08 03			08 28
Wivelsfield	d										06 51				07 40								08 32
Lewes 4	a																						
Burgess Hill 4	d										06 53				07 42					08 08			08 34
Hassocks 4	d										06 56				07 45								08 38
Preston Park	d										07 03				07 52								08 45
Hove 2	a																						
Brighton 10	a		05 21			06 18					07 08				07 58					08 22			08 50

Table 186

Sundays
from 12 September

Bedford and London - Brighton

		SN 1	FC 1	GX 1	SN 1	GW 1	GX 1	SN ◇1	FC 1	GX 1	SN ◇1	GX 1	SN ◇1	SN 1	FC 1	GX 1	SN ◇1	SN 1	GW 1	GX 1	SN ◇1	SN ◇1
London Victoria 15 ⊖	d	07 34		07 45			08 00	08 04		08 15	08 17	08 30	08 32	08 34		08 45	08 47			09 00	09 02	09 04
Clapham Junction 10	d	07 41						08 10			08 23		08 38	08 41			08 53				09 08	09 10
Bedford	d																					
Luton 10	d																					
Luton Airport Parkway 7	d																					
St Albans City	d																					
St Pancras International 15 ⊖	d																					
Farringdon 3 ⊖	d																					
City Thameslink 3	d																					
London Blackfriars 3 ⊖	d																					
London Bridge 4 ⊖	d		07 42						08 12						08 42							
Norwood Junction 2	d																					
East Croydon	a	07 53	07 56					08 24	08 27		08 36		08 50	08 53	08 56		09 06				09 21	09 24
	d	07 54	07 57					08 24	08 27		08 37		08 51	08 54	08 57		09 07				09 22	09 24
Purley 4	d	07 59						08 30						08 59								09 30
Coulsdon South	d	08 03												09 03								
Merstham	d	08 08												09 08								
Redhill	a	08 12				08 18		08 38					09 03	09 12					09 18			09 38
	d	08 12			08 10	08 20		08 39					09 04	09 12				09 10	09 20			09 39
Reigate	a																					
Nutfield	d				08 14													09 14				
Godstone	d				08 20													09 20				
Edenbridge	d				08 25													09 25				
Penshurst	d				08 32													09 32				
Leigh (Kent)	d				08 35													09 35				
Tonbridge 4	a				08 40													09 40				
Earlswood (Surrey)	d																					
Salfords	d																					
Horley 4	d	08 22						08 45						09 22								09 45
Gatwick Airport 10	a	08 24	08 18	08 20		08 31	08 35	08 47	08 48	08 50	08 54	09 05	09 11	09 24	09 18	09 20	09 27		09 31	09 35	09 39	09 47
	d	08 25	08 20					08 48	08 50		08 56		09 12	09 25	09 20		09 29				09 40	09 48
Three Bridges 15	a	08 30	08 24					08 53	08 54				09 16	09 30	09 24							09 53
	d	08 33	08 24					08 53	08 54				09 17	09 33	09 24							09 53
Crawley	d	08 36						08 56						09 37								09 56
Ifield	d	08 39												09 39								
Faygate	d																					
Littlehaven	d	08 45												09 46								
Horsham 4	a	08 49						09 04						09 49								10 04
Balcombe	d												09 23									
Haywards Heath	d		08 33						09 03		09 07		09 28		09 33		09 41					
Wivelsfield	d												09 32				09 45					
Lewes 4	a																09 58					
Burgess Hill 4	d		08 38						09 08		09 12		09 34		09 38							
Hassocks 4	d		08 42										09 38		09 42							
Preston Park	d												09 45									
Hove 2	a										09 24											
Brighton 10	a		08 52						09 22				09 50		09 52						10 03	

Table 186

Bedford and London - Brighton

Sundays from 12 September

		FC 1	GX 1	SN ◇1	GX 1	SN ◇1	SN 1	FC 1	GX 1	SN ◇1	SN 1	GW 1	GX 1	SN ◇1	SN ◇1	FC 1	GX 1	SN ◇1	GX 1	SN ◇1	SN 1	FC 1	GX 1
			╤		╤				╤	╤			╤	╤	╤		╤		╤				╤
London Victoria 15 ⊖	d		09 15	09 17	09 30	09 32	09 34		09 45	09 47			10 00	10 02	10 04		10 15	10 17	10 30	10 32	10 34		10 45
Clapham Junction 10	d			09 23		09 38	09 41			09 53				10 08	10 10			10 23		10 38	10 41		
Bedford	d																						
Luton 10	d																						
Luton Airport Parkway 7	d																						
St Albans City	d																						
St Pancras International 15 ⊖	d																						
Farringdon 3 ⊖	d																						
City Thameslink 3	d																						
London Blackfriars 3 ⊖	d																						
London Bridge 4 ⊖	d	09 12						09 42								10 12						10 42	
Norwood Junction 2	d																						
East Croydon	a	09 27		09 36		09 50	09 53	09 56		10 06				10 21	10 24	10 27		10 36		10 50	10 53	10 56	
	d	09 27		09 37		09 51	09 54	09 57		10 07				10 22	10 24	10 27		10 37		10 51	10 54	10 57	
Purley 4	d						09 59								10 30						10 59		
Coulsdon South	d						10 03														11 03		
Merstham	d						10 08														11 08		
Redhill	a					10 03	10 12					10 17			10 38					11 03	11 12		
	d					10 04	10 12				10 10	10 20			10 39					11 04	11 12		
Reigate	a																						
Nutfield	d										10 14												
Godstone	d										10 20												
Edenbridge	d										10 25												
Penshurst	d										10 32												
Leigh (Kent)	d										10 35												
Tonbridge 4	a										10 40												
Earlswood (Surrey)	d																						
Salfords	d																						
Horley 4	d						10 22								10 45						11 22		
Gatwick Airport 10	a	09 48	09 50	09 54	10 05	10 11	10 24	10 18	10 20	10 27		10 31	10 35	10 39	10 47	10 48	10 50	10 54	11 05	11 11	11 24	11 18	11 20
	d	09 50		09 56		10 12	10 25	10 20		10 29				10 40	10 48	10 50		10 56		11 12	11 25	11 20	
Three Bridges 15	a	09 54				10 16	10 30	10 24							10 53	10 54				11 16	11 30	11 24	
	d	09 54				10 17	10 33	10 24							10 53	10 54				11 17	11 33	11 24	
Crawley	d						10 37								10 56						11 37		
Ifield	d						10 39														11 39		
Faygate	d																						
Littlehaven	d						10 46														11 46		
Horsham 4	a						10 49								11 04						11 49		
Balcombe	d					10 23														11 23			
Haywards Heath	d	10 03		10 07		10 28		10 33		10 41						11 03		11 07		11 28		11 33	
Wivelsfield	d					10 32				10 45										11 32			
Lewes 4	a									10 58													
Burgess Hill 4	d	10 08		10 12		10 34		10 38								11 08		11 12		11 34		11 38	
Hassocks 4	d					10 38		10 42												11 38		11 42	
Preston Park	d					10 45														11 45			
Hove 2	a			10 24														11 24					
Brighton 10	a	10 22				10 50		10 52						11 03		11 22				11 50		11 52	

Table 186

Bedford and London - Brighton

Sundays from 12 September

		SN ◇1	SN 1	GW 1	GX 1	SN ◇1	SN ◇1	FC 1	GX 1	SN ◇1	GX 1	SN ◇1	SN 1	FC 1	GX 1	SN ◇1	SN 1	GW 1	GX 1	SN ◇1	SN ◇1	FC 1
		╤			╤	╤	╤		╤		╤				╤	╤			╤	╤	╤	
London Victoria 15 ⊖	d	10 47			11 00	11 02	11 04		11 15	11 17	11 30	11 32	11 34		11 45	11 47			12 00	12 02	12 04	
Clapham Junction 10	d	10 53				11 08	11 10			11 23		11 38	11 41			11 53				12 08	12 10	
Bedford	d																					
Luton 10	d																					
Luton Airport Parkway 7	d																					
St Albans City	d																					
St Pancras International 15 ⊖	d																					
Farringdon 3 ⊖	d																					
City Thameslink 3	d																					
London Blackfriars 3 ⊖	d																					
London Bridge 4 ⊖	d							11 12						11 42								12 12
Norwood Junction 2	d																					
East Croydon	a	11 06				11 21	11 24	11 27		11 36		11 50	11 53	11 56		12 06				12 21	12 24	12 27
	d	11 07				11 22	11 24	11 27		11 37		11 51	11 54	11 57		12 07				12 22	12 24	12 27
Purley 4	d						11 30						11 59								12 30	
Coulsdon South	d												12 03									
Merstham	d												12 08									
Redhill	a			11 18			11 38					12 03	12 12					12 17			12 38	
	d		11 10	11 20			11 39					12 04	12 12				12 10	12 20			12 39	
Reigate	a																					
Nutfield	d		11 14														12 14					
Godstone	d		11 20														12 20					
Edenbridge	d		11 25														12 25					
Penshurst	d		11 32														12 32					
Leigh (Kent)	d		11 35														12 35					
Tonbridge 4	a		11 40														12 40					
Earlswood (Surrey)	d																					
Salfords	d																					
Horley 4	d						11 45						12 22								12 45	
Gatwick Airport 10	a	11 27		11 31	11 35	11 39	11 47	11 48	11 50	11 54	12 05	12 11	12 24	12 18	12 20	12 27		12 31	12 35	12 39	12 47	12 48
	d	11 29				11 40	11 48	11 50		11 56		12 12	12 25	12 20		12 29				12 40	12 48	12 50
Three Bridges 15	a						11 53	11 54				12 16	12 30	12 24							12 53	12 54
	d						11 53	11 54				12 17	12 33	12 24							12 53	12 54
Crawley	d						11 56						12 37								12 56	
Ifield	d												12 39									
Faygate	d																					
Littlehaven	d												12 46									
Horsham 4	a						12 04						12 49								13 04	
Balcombe	d											12 23										
Haywards Heath	d	11 41						12 03		12 07		12 28		12 33		12 41						13 03
Wivelsfield	d	11 45										12 32				12 45						
Lewes 4	a	11 58														12 58						
Burgess Hill 4	d							12 08		12 12		12 34		12 38								13 08
Hassocks 4	d											12 38		12 42								
Preston Park	d											12 45										
Hove 2	a									12 24												
Brighton 10	a					12 03		12 22				12 49		12 52						13 03		13 22

Table 186

Sundays
from 12 September

Bedford and London - Brighton

		GX	SN	GX	SN	SN	FC	GX	SN	SN	GW	GX	SN	SN	FC	GX	SN	GX	SN	SN	FC	GX	SN
		1	◇1	1	◇1	1	1	1	◇1	1	1	1	◇1	◇1	1	1	◇1	1	◇1	1	1	1	◇1
		H		H				H	H			H	H	H		H		H				H	H
London Victoria 15 ⊖	d	12 15	12 17	12 30	12 32	12 34		12 45	12 47			13 00	13 02	13 04		13 15	13 17	13 30	13 32	13 34		13 45	13 47
Clapham Junction 10	d		12 23		12 38	12 41			12 53				13 08	13 10			13 23		13 38	13 41			13 53
Bedford	d																						
Luton 10	d																						
Luton Airport Parkway 7	d																						
St Albans City	d																						
St Pancras International 15 ⊖	d																						
Farringdon 3 ⊖	d																						
City Thameslink 3	d																						
London Blackfriars 3 ⊖	d																						
London Bridge 4 ⊖	d						12 42								13 12						13 42		
Norwood Junction 2	d																						
East Croydon	a		12 36		12 50	12 53	12 56		13 06				13 21	13 24	13 27		13 36		13 50	13 53	13 56		14 06
	d		12 37		12 51	12 54	12 57		13 07				13 22	13 24	13 27		13 37		13 51	13 54	13 57		14 07
Purley 4	d					12 59								13 30						13 59			
Coulsdon South	d					13 03														14 03			
Merstham	d					13 08														14 08			
Redhill	a				13 03	13 12					13 18			13 38					14 03	14 12			
	d				13 04	13 12				13 10	13 20			13 39					14 04	14 12			
Reigate	a																						
Nutfield	d									13 14													
Godstone	d									13 20													
Edenbridge	d									13 25													
Penshurst	d									13 32													
Leigh (Kent)	d									13 35													
Tonbridge 4	a									13 40													
Earlswood (Surrey)	d																						
Salfords	d																						
Horley 4	d					13 22								13 45						14 22			
Gatwick Airport 10	a	12 50	12 54	13 05	13 11	13 24	13 18	13 20	13 27		13 31	13 35	13 39	13 47	13 48	13 50	13 54	14 05	14 11	14 24	14 18	14 20	14 27
	d		12 56		13 12	13 25	13 20		13 29				13 40	13 48	13 50		13 56		14 12	14 25	14 20		14 29
Three Bridges 15	a				13 16	13 30	13 24							13 53	13 54				14 16	14 30	14 24		
	d				13 17	13 33	13 24							13 53	13 54				14 17	14 33	14 24		
Crawley	d					13 37								13 56						14 37			
Ifield	d					13 39														14 39			
Faygate	d																						
Littlehaven	d					13 46														14 46			
Horsham 4	a					13 49								14 04						14 49			
Balcombe	d				13 23														14 23				
Haywards Heath	d		13 07		13 28		13 33		13 41						14 03		14 07		14 28		14 33		14 41
Wivelsfield	d				13 32				13 45										14 32				14 45
Lewes 4	a								13 56														14 56
Burgess Hill 4	d		13 12		13 34		13 38								14 08		14 12		14 34		14 38		
Hassocks 4	d				13 38		13 42												14 38		14 42		
Preston Park	d				13 45														14 45				
Hove 2	a		13 24														14 24						
Brighton 10	a				13 50		13 52						14 03		14 22				14 50		14 52		

Table 186

Sundays
from 12 September

Bedford and London - Brighton

		SN	GW	GX	SN	SN	FC	GX	SN	GX	SN	SN	FC	GX	SN	SN	GW	GX	SN	SN	FC	GX	SN
		1	1	1	◇1	◇1	1	1	◇1	1	◇1	1	1	1	◇1	1	1	1	◇1	◇1	1	1	◇1
				H	H	H		H		H				H	H			H	H	H		H	
London Victoria 15 ⊖	d			14 00	14 02	14 04		14 15	14 17	14 30	14 32	14 34		14 45	14 47			15 00	15 02	15 04		15 15	15 17
Clapham Junction 10	d				14 08	14 10			14 23		14 38	14 41			14 53				15 08	15 10			15 23
Bedford	d																						
Luton 10	d																						
Luton Airport Parkway 7	d																						
St Albans City	d																						
St Pancras International 15 ⊖	d																						
Farringdon 3 ⊖	d																						
City Thameslink 3	d																						
London Blackfriars 3 ⊖	d																						
London Bridge 4 ⊖	d						14 12						14 42								15 12		
Norwood Junction 2	d																						
East Croydon	a				14 21	14 24	14 27		14 36		14 50	14 53	14 56		15 06				15 21	15 24	15 27		15 36
	d				14 22	14 24	14 27		14 37		14 51	14 54	14 57		15 07				15 22	15 24	15 27		15 37
Purley 4	d					14 30						14 59								15 30			
Coulsdon South	d											15 03											
Merstham	d											15 08											
Redhill	a		14 17			14 38					15 03	15 12					15 18			15 38			
	d	14 10	14 20			14 39					15 04	15 12				15 10	15 20			15 39			
Reigate	a																						
Nutfield	d	14 14														15 14							
Godstone	d	14 20														15 20							
Edenbridge	d	14 25														15 25							
Penshurst	d	14 32														15 32							
Leigh (Kent)	d	14 35														15 35							
Tonbridge 4	a	14 40														15 40							
Earlswood (Surrey)	d																						
Salfords	d																						
Horley 4	d					14 45						15 22								15 45			
Gatwick Airport 10	a		14 31	14 35	14 39	14 47	14 48	14 50	14 54	15 05	15 11	15 24	15 18	15 20	15 27		15 31	15 35	15 39	15 47	15 48	15 50	15 54
	d				14 40	14 48	14 50		14 56		15 12	15 25	15 20		15 29				15 40	15 48	15 50		15 56
Three Bridges 15	a					14 53	14 54				15 16	15 30	15 24							15 53	15 54		
	d					14 53	14 54				15 17	15 33	15 24							15 53	15 54		
Crawley	d					14 56						15 37								15 56			
Ifield	d											15 39											
Faygate	d																						
Littlehaven	d											15 46											
Horsham 4	a					15 04						15 49								16 04			
Balcombe	d										15 23												
Haywards Heath	d						15 03		15 07		15 28		15 33		15 41						16 03		16 07
Wivelsfield	d										15 32				15 45								
Lewes 4	a														15 56								
Burgess Hill 4	d						15 08		15 12		15 34		15 38								16 08		16 12
Hassocks 4	d										15 38		15 42										
Preston Park	d										15 45												
Hove 2	a								15 24														16 24
Brighton 10	a				15 03		15 22				15 50		15 52						16 03		16 22		

Table 186

Bedford and London - Brighton

Sundays from 12 September

		GX 1 ✕		SN ◇1	SN 1	FC 1	GX 1 ✕	SN ◇1 ✕	SN 1	GW 1	GX 1 ✕	SN ◇1 ✕		SN ◇1 ✕	FC 1	GX 1 ✕	SN ◇1	SN 1 ✕	SN ◇1	SN 1	FC 1	GX 1 ✕		SN ◇1 ✕	SN 1
London Victoria 15 ⊖	d	15 30		15 32	15 34		15 45	15 47			16 00	16 02		16 04		16 15	16 17	16 30	16 32	16 34		16 45		16 47	
Clapham Junction 10	d			15 38	15 41			15 53				16 08		16 10			16 23		16 38	16 41				16 53	
Bedford	d																								
Luton 10	d																								
Luton Airport Parkway 7	d																								
St Albans City	d																								
St Pancras International 15 ⊖	d																								
Farringdon 3 ⊖	d																								
City Thameslink 3	d																								
London Blackfriars 3 ⊖	d																								
London Bridge 4 ⊖	d					15 42									16 12						16 42				
Norwood Junction 2	d																								
East Croydon	a			15 50	15 53	15 56		16 06				16 21		16 24	16 27		16 36		16 50	16 53	16 56			17 06	
	d			15 51	15 54	15 57		16 07				16 22		16 24	16 27		16 37		16 51	16 54	16 57			17 07	
Purley 4	d				15 59									16 30						16 59					
Coulsdon South	d				16 03															17 03					
Merstham	d				16 08															17 08					
Redhill	a			16 03	16 12					16 17				16 38					17 03	17 12					
	d			16 04	16 12				16 10	16 20				16 39					17 04	17 12					17 10
Reigate	a																								
Nutfield	d								16 14																17 14
Godstone	d								16 20																17 20
Edenbridge	d								16 25																17 25
Penshurst	d								16 32																17 32
Leigh (Kent)	d								16 35																17 35
Tonbridge 4	a								16 40																17 40
Earlswood (Surrey)	d																								
Salfords	d																								
Horley 4	d				16 22									16 45						17 22					
Gatwick Airport 10	a	16 05		16 11	16 24	16 18	16 20	16 27		16 31	16 35	16 39		16 47	16 48	16 50	16 54	17 05	17 11	17 24	17 18	17 20		17 27	
	d			16 12	16 25	16 20		16 29				16 40		16 48	16 50		16 56		17 12	17 25	17 20			17 29	
Three Bridges 15	a			16 16	16 30	16 24								16 53	16 54				17 16	17 30	17 24				
	d			16 17	16 33	16 24								16 53	16 54				17 17	17 33	17 24				
Crawley	d				16 37									16 56						17 37					
Ifield	d				16 39															17 39					
Faygate	d																								
Littlehaven	d				16 46															17 46					
Horsham 4	a				16 49									17 04						17 49					
Balcombe	d			16 23															17 23						
Haywards Heath	d			16 28		16 33		16 41							17 03		17 07		17 28		17 33			17 41	
Wivelsfield	d			16 32				16 45											17 32					17 45	
Lewes 4	a							16 58																17 58	
Burgess Hill 4	d			16 34		16 38									17 08		17 12		17 34		17 38				
Hassocks 4	d			16 38		16 42													17 38		17 42				
Preston Park	d			16 45															17 45						
Hove 2	a																17 24								
Brighton 10	a			16 50		16 52						17 03			17 22				17 50		17 52				

Table 186

Bedford and London - Brighton

Sundays from 12 September

		GW 1	GX 1 ✕	SN ◇1 ✕	SN ◇1 ✕	FC 1	GX 1 ✕	SN ◇1		GX 1 ✕	SN ◇1	SN 1	FC 1	GX 1 ✕	SN ◇1 ✕	SN 1	GW 1	GX 1 ✕		SN ◇1 ✕	SN ◇1 ✕	FC 1	GX 1 ✕	SN ◇1	GX 1 ✕
London Victoria 15 ⊖	d		17 00	17 02	17 04		17 15	17 17		17 30	17 32	17 34		17 45	17 47			18 00		18 02	18 04		18 15	18 17	18 30
Clapham Junction 10	d			17 08	17 10			17 23			17 38	17 41			17 53					18 08	18 10			18 23	
Bedford	d																								
Luton 10	d																								
Luton Airport Parkway 7	d																								
St Albans City	d																								
St Pancras International 15 ⊖	d																								
Farringdon 3 ⊖	d																								
City Thameslink 3	d																								
London Blackfriars 3 ⊖	d																								
London Bridge 4 ⊖	d					17 12							17 42									18 12			
Norwood Junction 2	d																								
East Croydon	a			17 21	17 24	17 27		17 36			17 50	17 53	17 56		18 06					18 21	18 24	18 27		18 36	
	d			17 22	17 24	17 27		17 37			17 51	17 54	17 57		18 07					18 22	18 24	18 27		18 37	
Purley 4	d				17 30							17 59									18 30				
Coulsdon South	d											18 03													
Merstham	d											18 08													
Redhill	a	17 18			17 38						18 03	18 12					18 17				18 38				
	d	17 20			17 39						18 04	18 12				18 10	18 20				18 39				
Reigate	a																								
Nutfield	d															18 14									
Godstone	d															18 20									
Edenbridge	d															18 25									
Penshurst	d															18 32									
Leigh (Kent)	d															18 35									
Tonbridge 4	a															18 40									
Earlswood (Surrey)	d																								
Salfords	d																								
Horley 4	d				17 45							18 22									18 45				
Gatwick Airport 10	a	17 31	17 35	17 39	17 47	17 48	17 50	17 54		18 05	18 11	18 24	18 18	18 20	18 27		18 31	18 35		18 39	18 47	18 48	18 50	18 54	19 05
	d			17 40	17 48	17 50		17 56			18 12	18 25	18 20		18 29					18 40	18 48	18 50		18 56	
Three Bridges 15	a				17 53	17 54					18 16	18 30	18 24								18 53	18 54			
	d				17 53	17 54					18 17	18 33	18 24								18 53	18 54			
Crawley	d				17 56							18 37									18 56				
Ifield	d											18 39													
Faygate	d																								
Littlehaven	d											18 46													
Horsham 4	a				18 04							18 49									19 04				
Balcombe	d										18 23														
Haywards Heath	d					18 03		18 07			18 28		18 33		18 41							19 03		19 07	
Wivelsfield	d										18 32				18 45										
Lewes 4	a														18 58										
Burgess Hill 4	d					18 08		18 12			18 34		18 38									19 08		19 12	
Hassocks 4	d										18 38		18 42												
Preston Park	d										18 45														
Hove 2	a							18 24																19 24	
Brighton 10	a			18 03		18 22					18 50		18 52							19 03		19 22			

Table 186

Sundays from 12 September

Bedford and London - Brighton

		SN ◇1	SN 1	FC 1	GX 1	SN ◇1	SN 1	GW 1	GX 1	SN ◇1	SN ◇1	FC 1	GX 1	SN ◇1	GX 1	SN ◇1	SN 1	FC 1	GX 1	SN ◇1	SN 1	GW 1
					⌶	⌶			⌶	⌶	⌶									⌶		
London Victoria 15 ⊖	d	18 32	18 34		18 45	18 47			19 00	19 02	19 04		19 15	19 17	19 30	19 32	19 34		19 45	19 47		
Clapham Junction 10	d	18 38	18 41			18 53				19 08	19 10			19 23		19 38	19 41			19 53		
Bedford	d																					
Luton 10	d																					
Luton Airport Parkway 7	d																					
St Albans City	d																					
St Pancras International 15 ⊖	d																					
Farringdon 3 ⊖	d																					
City Thameslink 3	d																					
London Blackfriars 3 ⊖	d																					
London Bridge 4 ⊖	d			18 42								19 12						19 42				
Norwood Junction 2	d																					
East Croydon	a	18 50	18 53	18 56		19 06				19 21	19 24	19 27		19 36		19 50	19 53	19 56		20 06		
	d	18 51	18 54	18 57		19 07				19 22	19 24	19 27		19 37		19 51	19 54	19 57		20 07		
Purley 4	d		18 59								19 30						19 59					
Coulsdon South	d		19 03														20 03					
Merstham	d		19 08														20 08					
Redhill	a	19 03	19 12					19 18			19 38					20 03	20 12					20 17
	d	19 04	19 12				19 10	19 20			19 39					20 04	20 12				20 10	20 20
Reigate	a																					
Nutfield	d						19 14														20 14	
Godstone	d						19 20														20 20	
Edenbridge	d						19 25														20 25	
Penshurst	d						19 32														20 32	
Leigh (Kent)	d						19 35														20 35	
Tonbridge 4	a						19 40														20 40	
Earlswood (Surrey)	d																					
Salfords	d																					
Horley 4	d		19 22								19 45						20 22					
Gatwick Airport 10	a	19 11	19 24	19 18	19 20	19 27		19 30	19 35	19 39	19 47	19 48	19 50	19 54	20 05	20 11	20 24	20 18	20 20	20 27		20 30
	d	19 12	19 25	19 20		19 29				19 40	19 48	19 50		19 56		20 12	20 25	20 20		20 29		
Three Bridges 15	a	19 16	19 30	19 24							19 53	19 54				20 16	20 30	20 24				
	d	19 17	19 33	19 24							19 53	19 54				20 17	20 33	20 24				
Crawley	d		19 37								19 56						20 37					
Ifield	d		19 39														20 39					
Faygate	d																					
Littlehaven	d		19 46														20 46					
Horsham 4	a		19 49								20 04						20 49					
Balcombe	d	19 23														20 23						
Haywards Heath	d	19 28		19 33		19 41						20 03		20 07		20 28		20 33		20 41		
Wivelsfield	d	19 32				19 45										20 32				20 45		
Lewes 4	a					19 58														20 58		
Burgess Hill 4	d	19 34		19 38								20 08		20 12		20 34		20 38				
Hassocks 4	d	19 38		19 42												20 38		20 42				
Preston Park	d	19 45														20 45						
Hove 2	a													20 24								
Brighton 10	a	19 50		19 52						20 03		20 22				20 50		20 52				

Table 186

Sundays from 12 September

Bedford and London - Brighton

		GX 1	SN ◇1	SN ◇1	FC 1	GX 1	SN ◇1	GX 1	SN ◇1	SN 1	FC 1	GX 1	SN ◇1	SN 1	GW 1	GX 1	SN ◇1	SN ◇1	FC 1	GX 1	SN ◇1	GX 1	SN ◇1
London Victoria 15 ⊖	d	20 00	20 02	20 04		20 15	20 17	20 30	20 32	20 34		20 45	20 47			21 00	21 02	21 04		21 15	21 17	21 30	21 32
Clapham Junction 10	d		20 08	20 10			20 23		20 38	20 41			20 53				21 08	21 10			21 23		21 38
Bedford	d																						
Luton 10	d																						
Luton Airport Parkway 7	d																						
St Albans City	d																						
St Pancras International 15 ⊖	d																						
Farringdon 3 ⊖	d																						
City Thameslink 3	d																						
London Blackfriars 3 ⊖	d																						
London Bridge 4 ⊖	d				20 12						20 42								21 12				
Norwood Junction 2	d																						
East Croydon	a		20 21	20 24	20 27		20 36		20 50	20 53	20 56		21 06				21 21	21 24	21 27		21 36		21 50
	d		20 22	20 24	20 27		20 37		20 51	20 54	20 57		21 07				21 22	21 24	21 27		21 37		21 51
Purley 4	d			20 30						20 59								21 30					
Coulsdon South	d									21 03													
Merstham	d									21 08													
Redhill	a			20 38					21 03	21 12					21 18			21 38					22 03
	d			20 39					21 04	21 12				21 10	21 20			21 39					22 04
Reigate	a																						
Nutfield	d													21 14									
Godstone	d													21 20									
Edenbridge	d													21 25									
Penshurst	d													21 32									
Leigh (Kent)	d													21 35									
Tonbridge 4	a													21 40									
Earlswood (Surrey)	d																						
Salfords	d																						
Horley 4	d			20 45						21 22								21 45					
Gatwick Airport 10	a	20 35	20 39	20 47	20 48	20 50	20 54	21 05	21 11	21 24	21 18	21 20	21 27		21 30	21 35	21 39	21 47	21 48	21 50	21 55	22 05	22 11
	d		20 40	20 48	20 50		20 56		21 12	21 25	21 20		21 29				21 40	21 48	21 50		21 56		22 12
Three Bridges 15	a			20 53	20 54				21 16	21 30	21 24							21 53	21 54				22 16
	d			20 53	20 54				21 17	21 33	21 24							21 53	21 54				22 17
Crawley	d			20 56						21 37								21 56					
Ifield	d									21 39													
Faygate	d																						
Littlehaven	d									21 46													
Horsham 4	a			21 04						21 49								22 04					
Balcombe	d								21 23														22 23
Haywards Heath	d				21 03		21 07		21 28		21 33		21 41						22 03		22 07		22 28
Wivelsfield	d								21 32				21 45										22 32
Lewes 4	a												21 58										
Burgess Hill 4	d				21 08		21 12		21 34		21 38								22 08		22 12		22 34
Hassocks 4	d								21 38		21 42												22 38
Preston Park	d								21 45														22 45
Hove 2	a						21 24														22 24		
Brighton 10	a		21 03		21 22				21 50		21 52						22 03		22 22				22 50

Table 186

Bedford and London - Brighton

Sundays from 12 September

Station		SN 1	FC 1	GX 1	SN ◇1	SN 1	GW 1	GX 1	SN ◇1	FC 1	GX 1	SN ◇1	GX 1	SN ◇1	SN 1	FC 1	GX 1	SN ◇1	SN 1	SN 1	GW 1	GX 1	FC 1
London Victoria 15 ⊖	d	21 34		21 45	21 47			22 00	22 04		22 15	22 17	22 30	22 32	22 34		22 45	22 47	23 04			23 00	
Clapham Junction 10	d	21 41			21 53				22 10			22 23		22 38	22 41			22 53	23 10				
Bedford	d																						
Luton 10	d																						
Luton Airport Parkway 7	d																						
St Albans City	d																						
St Pancras International 15 ⊖	d																						
Farringdon 3 ⊖	d																						
City Thameslink 3	d																						
London Blackfriars 3 ⊖	d																						
London Bridge 4 ⊖	d		21 42							22 12						22 42							23 12
Norwood Junction 2	d																						
East Croydon	a	21 53	21 56		22 06				22 24	22 27		22 36		22 50	22 53	22 56		23 06	23 22				23 27
	d	21 54	21 57		22 07				22 24	22 27		22 37		22 51	22 54	22 57		23 07	23 22				23 27
Purley 4	d	21 59							22 30						22 59				23 29				
Coulsdon South	d	22 03													23 03				23 33				
Merstham	d	22 08													23 08				23 38				
Redhill	a	22 12					22 18		22 38					23 03	23 12				23 42		23 18		
	d	22 12				22 10	22 20		22 39					23 04	23 12				23 42	23 10	23 20		
Reigate	a																						
Nutfield	d					22 14														23 14			
Godstone	d					22 20														23 20			
Edenbridge	d					22 25														23 25			
Penshurst	d					22 32														23 32			
Leigh (Kent)	d					22 35														23 35			
Tonbridge 4	a					22 40														23 40			
Earlswood (Surrey)	d																						
Salfords	d																						
Horley 4	d	22 22							22 45						23 22				23 50				
Gatwick Airport 10	a	22 24	22 18	22 20	22 27		22 31	22 35	22 47	22 48	22 50	22 54	23 05	23 11	23 24	23 18	23 20	23 27	23 54		23 31	23 35	23 48
	d	22 25	22 20		22 29				22 48	22 50		22 56		23 12	23 25	23 20		23 29	23 55				23 50
Three Bridges 15	a	22 30	22 24						22 53	22 54				23 16	23 30	23 24			00 01				23 54
	d	22 33	22 24						22 53	22 54				23 17	23 33	23 24			00 01				23 54
Crawley	d	22 37							22 56						23 37				00 05				
Ifield	d	22 39													23 39				00 07				
Faygate	d																						
Littlehaven	d	22 46													23 46				00 14				
Horsham 4	a	22 49							23 04						23 49				00 17				
Balcombe	d													23 23									
Haywards Heath	d		22 33		22 41					23 03		23 07		23 28		23 33		23 41					00 03
Wivelsfield	d				22 45									23 32				23 45					
Lewes 4	a				22 58													23 58					
Burgess Hill 4	d		22 38							23 08		23 12		23 34		23 38							00 08
Hassocks 4	d		22 42											23 38		23 42							
Preston Park	d													23 45									
Hove 2	a											23 24											
Brighton 10	a		22 52							23 22				23 50		23 52							00 22

Table 186

Bedford and London - Brighton

Sundays from 12 September

Station		GX 1	SN ◇1	GX 1	SN ◇1	FC 1	GX 1
London Victoria 15 ⊖	d	23 15	23 17	23 30	23 32		23 45
Clapham Junction 10	d		23 23		23 38		
Bedford	d						
Luton 10	d						
Luton Airport Parkway 7	d						
St Albans City	d						
St Pancras International 15 ⊖	d						
Farringdon 3 ⊖	d						
City Thameslink 3	d						
London Blackfriars 3 ⊖	d						
London Bridge 4 ⊖	d					23 42	
Norwood Junction 2	d						
East Croydon	a		23 37		23 52	23 56	
	d		23 38		23 53	23 57	
Purley 4	d						
Coulsdon South	d						
Merstham	d						
Redhill	a				00 05		
	d				00 05		
Reigate	a						
Nutfield	d						
Godstone	d						
Edenbridge	d						
Penshurst	d						
Leigh (Kent)	d						
Tonbridge 4	a						
Earlswood (Surrey)	d						
Salfords	d						
Horley 4	d						
Gatwick Airport 10	a	23 50	23 59	00 05	00 14	00 18	00 20
	d		00 01		00 15	00 19	
Three Bridges 15	a		00 05		00 19	00 24	
	d		00 06		00 20		
Crawley	d						
Ifield	d						
Faygate	d						
Littlehaven	d						
Horsham 4	a						
Balcombe	d				00 26		
Haywards Heath	d		00 15		00 31		
Wivelsfield	d				00 35		
Lewes 4	a						
Burgess Hill 4	d				00 37		
Hassocks 4	d				00 41		
Preston Park	d				00 48		
Hove 2	a		00 28				
Brighton 10	a				00 52		

Table 186

Brighton - London, Bedford

		SN MX 1	SN MX ◇1	SN MO ◇1	SN MO 1	GX 1	FC 1	GX 1	GX 1	FC MX 1	FC MO 1	GX 1	GX 1	SN	GX 1	SN 1	GX 1	SN 1	FC 1	SN 1	FC 1
Brighton 10	d		23p02	23p02			23p11			23p37	23p44										
Hove 2	d																				
Preston Park	d		23p06	23p06						23p41											
Hassocks 4	d		23p12	23p12			23p19			23p47	23p52										
Burgess Hill 4	d		23p16	23p16			23p23			23p51	23p56										
Lewes 4	d																				
Wivelsfield 4	d		23p19	23p19						23p53											
Haywards Heath 3	a		23p23	23p23			23p27			23p58	00 01										
	d		23p24	23p24			23p28			23p59	00 01										
Balcombe	d			23p29						00 04											
Horsham 4	d	23p02			23p04																
Littlehaven	d	23p05			23p07																
Faygate	d																				
Ifield	d	23p11			23p13																
Crawley	d	23p14			23p17																
Three Bridges 4	a	23p18	23p33	23p35	23p20		23p38			00 10	00 10										
	d	23p18	23p47	23p42	23p22		23p38			00 10	00 10							01 59	02 25	02 55	03 25
Gatwick Airport 10	a	23p22	23p52	23p46	23p26		23p42			00 14	00 14							02 03	02 29	02 59	03 29
	d	23p23	23p53	23p47	23p27	23p35	23p43	23p50	00 05	00 15	00 15	00 20	00 35		00 50	01 05	01 35	02 05	02 30	03 05	03 30
Horley 4	d	23p26	23p56	23p49	23p30											01 07		02 07		03 07	
Salfords	d	23p29																			
Earlswood (Surrey)	d	23p33																			
Tonbridge 4	d																				
Leigh (Kent)	d																				
Penshurst	d																				
Edenbridge	d																				
Godstone	d																				
Nutfield	d																				
Reigate	d																				
Redhill 5	a	23p36	00 03	23p57	23p36					00 22	00 22										
	d	23p37	00 03	00 02	23p37					00 22	00 22										
Merstham	d	23p41			23p41																
Coulsdon South	d	23p46			23p46																
Purley 4	d	23p49	00 11	00 11	23p50											01 22		02 22		03 22	
East Croydon ⇌	a	23p55	00 16	00 16	23p55		00 02			00 35	00 35					01 27		02 27	02 47	03 27	03 47
	d	23p58	00 17	00 17	23p56		00 04			00 36	00 36			00 49		01 28		02 28	02 47	03 28	03 47
Norwood Junction 2	a																				
London Bridge 4 ⊖	a						00 19			00 52	00 52								03 12		04 12
London Blackfriars 3 ⊖	a																				
City Thameslink 3	a																				
Farringdon 3 ⊖	a																				
St Pancras International 15 ⊖	a																				
St Albans City	a																				
Luton Airport Parkway 4	a																				
Luton 7	a																				
Bedford 10	a																				
Clapham Junction 10	d	00 11	00 30	00 30	00 11									01 01		01 41		02 41		03 41	
London Victoria 15 ⊖	a	00 18	00 37	00 37	00 18	00 10		00 25	00 40			00 55	01 11	01 09	01 25	01 49	02 20	02 49		03 49	

Table 186

Brighton - London, Bedford

		FC	GX 1	FC 1	SN 1	SN 1	SN 1	GX 1	GW 1	SN 1	FC 1	GX 1	SN 1	GW 1	SN ◇1
Brighton 10	d				03 50						05 09		05 23		
Hove 2	d														
Preston Park	d										05 13				
Hassocks 4	d										05 19				
Burgess Hill 4	d										05 23		05 33		
Lewes 4	d														05 29
Wivelsfield 4	d										05 25				
Haywards Heath 3	a				04 25						05 30		05 38		05 46
	d				04 25						05 30		05 38		05 47
Balcombe	d										05 36		05 44		
Horsham 4	d									05 17					
Littlehaven	d									05 20					
Faygate	d														
Ifield	d									05 26					
Crawley	d									05 29					
Three Bridges 4	a				04 45					05 33	05 41		05 49		
	d	04 25		04 55	04 54					05 33	05 41		05 50		
Gatwick Airport 10	a	04 29		04 59	05 02					05 37	05 45		05 54		05 58
	d	04 30	04 35	05 00	05 03			05 20	05 31	05 38	05 46	05 50	05 55	05 56	06 00
Horley 4	d				05 05					05 40					
Salfords	d														
Earlswood (Surrey)	d														
Tonbridge 4	d					04 59	05 20								
Leigh (Kent)	d					05 03	05 24								
Penshurst	d					05 07	05 28								
Edenbridge	d					05 13	05 34								
Godstone	d					05 20	05 41								
Nutfield	d					05 25	05 46								
Reigate	d														
Redhill 5	a					05 30	05 51		05 41	05 47				06 07	
	d								05 43	05 48				06 13	
Merstham	d									05 52					
Coulsdon South	d									05 57					
Purley 4	d				05 23					06 00					
East Croydon ⇌	a	04 47		05 17	05 28					06 06	06 01		06 10		06 15
	d	04 47		05 17	05 29					06 07	06 02		06 11		06 15
Norwood Junction 2	a														
London Bridge 4 ⊖	a			05 34							06 15				
London Blackfriars 3 ⊖	a	05 13		05 43							06 24				
City Thameslink 3	a	05 16		05 46							06 26				
Farringdon 3 ⊖	a	05 20		05 50							06 30				
St Pancras International 15 ⊖	a	05 23		05 53							06 33				
St Albans City	a	05 57		06 25							06 56				
Luton Airport Parkway 4	a	06 10		06 37							07 08				
Luton 7	a	06 12		06 40							07 11				
Bedford 10	a	06 40		07 08							07 36				
Clapham Junction 10	d				05 49					06 18			06 21		06 25
London Victoria 15 ⊖	a		05 12		05 58			05 55		06 25		06 20	06 28		06 32

Brighton - London, Bedford

Station		GX 1	GX 1	SN 1	SN 1	FC 1	FC 1	SN 1	SN 1	GX 1	SN 1	SN 1	SN 1	FC 1	SN 1	SN ◇1	SN 1	SN 1
Brighton 10	d					05 39	05 49				06 01			06 07	06 17			
Hove 2	d							05 57										
Preston Park	d					05 43	05 53							06 11				
Hassocks 4	d					05 49	05 59				06 09			06 18	06 25			
Burgess Hill 4	d					05 53	06 03				06 12			06 22	06 29			
Lewes 4	d											06 05						
Wivelsfield 4	d					05 55	06 05				06 15			06 25				
Haywards Heath 3	a					06 00	06 10	06 12			06 19	06 22		06 29	06 34			
	d					06 00	06 10	06 12			06 27	<		06 30	06 34			
Balcombe	d					06 06								06 35				
Horsham 4	d				05 38				06 10							06 24		
Littlehaven	d				05 41				06 13							06 27		
Faygate	d																	
Ifield	d				05 47				06 19							06 33		
Crawley	d				05 50				06 23							06 37		
Three Bridges 4	a				05 54	06 11	06 19	06 21	06 26		06 36			06 41	06 44	06 40		
	d				05 54	06 11	06 20	06 21	06 27		06 36			06 41	>	06 48		
Gatwick Airport 10	a				05 58	06 15	06 24	06 25	06 31		06 40			06 45		06 52		
	d	06 05	06 20		06 00	06 16	06 24	06 26	06 32	06 35	06 41			06 46		06 53		
Horley 4	d				06 02				06 35							06 56		
Salfords	d				06 06				06 39									
Earlswood (Surrey)	d				06 10				06 42									
Tonbridge 4	d												06 10				06 47	
Leigh (Kent)	d												06 14				06 51	
Penshurst	d												06 18				06 55	
Edenbridge	d												06 24				07 01	
Godstone	d												06 31				07 08	
Nutfield	d												06 36				07 13	
Reigate	d																	06 49
Redhill 5	a				06 13		06 32		06 45				06 41	06 54		07 02	07 18	06 53
	d				06 13		06 33		06 46				06 43	06 56		07 03		
Merstham	d				06 17				06 50									
Coulsdon South	d				06 22				06 55				06 50					
Purley 4	d				06 26				06 59				06 54					
East Croydon	a			06 27	06 30	06 32	06 43	06 41	07 04		06 56		06 59	07 08		07 14		
	d			06 27	06 31	06 32	06 44	06 42	07 05		06 57		07 00	07 09		07 15		
Norwood Junction 2	a																	
London Bridge 4 ⊖	a					06 46	06 58				07 13		07 16	07 23				
London Blackfriars 3 ⊖	a					06 52	07 04							07 30				
City Thameslink 3	a					06 54	07 08							07 32				
Farringdon 3 ⊖	a					06 58	07 12							07 36				
St Pancras International 15 ⊖	a					07 01	07 15							07 39				
St Albans City	a					07 25	07 41											
Luton Airport Parkway 4	a					07 37	07 53							08 09				
Luton 7	a					07 40	07 56							08 12				
Bedford 10	a					08 06	08 22											
Clapham Junction 10	d			06 38	06 41			06 51	07 17							07 24		
London Victoria 15 ⊖	a	06 35	06 50	06 45	06 48			07 00	07 25	07 05						07 33		

Brighton - London, Bedford

Station		GX 1	GW 1	SN 1	FC 1	SN 1	GX 1	SN 1	SN 1	SN 1	GX 1	SN ◇1	SN ◇1	SN 1	SN 1	GX 1
Brighton 10	d				06 24		06 30		06 37		06 40		06 51			06 56
Hove 2	d							06 31								
Preston Park	d				06 28			06 35			06 44					07 00
Hassocks 4	d				06 35			06 42			06 52					
Burgess Hill 4	d				06 39		06 42	06 46			06 56		07 01			07 10
Lewes 4	d														06 51	
Wivelsfield 4	d						06 45	06 49							07 08	07 14
Haywards Heath 3	a				06 43		06 49	06 54	06 56		07 01		07 05		07 12	07 18
	d				06 44		06 51	07 00	<		07 03		07 06		07 13	07 20
Balcombe	d				06 50										07 19	
Horsham 4	d					06 38						06 51		07 04		
Littlehaven	d					06 41						06 54				
Faygate	d					06 45										
Ifield	d					06 49						07 01				
Crawley	d					06 52						07 05		07 13		
Three Bridges 4	a				06 55	06 56						07 08	07 16	07 18	07 24	
	d				06 56	06 56				07 04		07 09	07 22	<	07 25	
Gatwick Airport 10	a				07 00	07 01	07 03	07 11		07 08	07 15				07 29	07 32
	d	06 50	07 00		07 01	07 02	07 05	07 12		07 09	07 20				07 30	07 35
Horley 4	d					07 04				07 12		07 16				
Salfords	d					07 08				07 16						
Earlswood (Surrey)	d					07 12				07 19						
Tonbridge 4	d															
Leigh (Kent)	d															
Penshurst	d															
Edenbridge	d															
Godstone	d															
Nutfield	d															
Reigate	d															
Redhill 5	a		07 07		07 10	07 15				07 22						
	d		07 10		07 11	07 15				07 23						
Merstham	d					07 19				07 27						
Coulsdon South	d					07 25				07 33						
Purley 4	d					07 29										
East Croydon	a			07 14	07 23	07 34		07 27		07 39		07 31	07 42		07 45	
	d			07 15	07 24	07 35		07 27		07 39		07 31	07 43		07 46	
Norwood Junction 2	a															
London Bridge 4 ⊖	a					07 51		07 43							08 01	
London Blackfriars 3 ⊖	a				07 51											
City Thameslink 3	a				07 56											
Farringdon 3 ⊖	a				08 00											
St Pancras International 15 ⊖	a				08 03											
St Albans City	a				08 23											
Luton Airport Parkway 4	a				08 37											
Luton 7	a				08 40											
Bedford 10	a				09 06											
Clapham Junction 10	d			07 27						07 49		07 41	07 52			
London Victoria 15 ⊖	a	07 20		07 36			07 36			07 57	07 50	07 49	08 01			08 05

b arr. 0726

Table 186

Mondays to Fridays

Brighton - London, Bedford

		GW	SN	FC	SN	SN	SN ◇	SN	SN	SN	SN	SN	SN	GX	SN ◇	SN ◇
Brighton	d			07 00										07 15		
Hove	d				07 11										07 20	
Preston Park	d			07 04										07 19		
Hassocks	d			07 10	07 21										07 30	
Burgess Hill	d			07 14										07 29		
Lewes	d															07b22
Wivelsfield	d			07 18	07 26										07 35	07 39
Haywards Heath	a			07 23	07 30									07 34	07 40	07 43
	d			07 23	07 31									07 35	07 40	07 44
Balcombe	d															
Horsham	d					07 19	07 25				07 09					
Littlehaven	d					07 22	07 29				07 12					
Faygate	d										07 16					
Ifield	d					07 28					07 20					
Crawley	d					07 32	07 37				07 23					
Three Bridges	a			07 32		07 35	07 40				07 27					
	d			07 32		07 36	07 41		07 14		07 28					
Gatwick Airport	a			07 37		07 40			07 21		07 32			07 47		
	d			07 38		07 41			07 22		07 33		07 45	07 50		
Horley	d					07 43			07 25		07 36		07 48			07 58
Salfords	d					07 47			07 29		07 40		07 52			
Earlswood (Surrey)	d					07 51			07 32		07 43		07 55			
Tonbridge	d											07 25				
Leigh (Kent)	d											07 29				
Penshurst	d											07 33				
Edenbridge	d											07 39				
Godstone	d											07 46				
Nutfield	d											07 51				
Reigate	d	07 18						07 27		07 40						
Redhill	a	07 24				07 54		07 31	07 36	07 45	07 47	07 56	07 58			
	d					07 54		07 40	<	07 51	<	08 02	<			
Merstham	d					07 59		07 44				08 06				
Coulsdon South	d					08 04		07 50				08 11				
Purley	d							07 55				08 15				
East Croydon	a		07 44	07 53	07 57	08 11	08 00	08 01		08 02		08 20			08 08	08 14
	d		07 45	07 54	07 57	08 11	08 01	08 02		08 03		08 21			08 08	08 14
Norwood Junction	a															
London Bridge ⊖	a				08 13			08 19		08 21		08 39				
London Blackfriars ⊖	a			08 20												
City Thameslink	a			08 23												
Farringdon ⊖	a			08 27												
St Pancras International ⊖	a			08 31												
St Albans City	a			08 51												
Luton Airport Parkway	a			09 00												
Luton	a			09 04												
Bedford	a			09 26												
Clapham Junction	d		07 56			08 21	08 11								08 18	08 24
London Victoria ⊖	a		08 04			08 29	08 19							08 20	08 26	08 32

b arr. 0714

Table 186

Mondays to Fridays

Brighton - London, Bedford

		GW	SN	SN	FC	GX	SN	SN	SN ◇	SN	SN	SN	GX	FC	SN ◇	SN ◇
Brighton	d				07 24	07 30	07 33						07 44	07 50		
Hove	d								07 41							
Preston Park	d				07 28		07 37						07 48	07 54		
Hassocks	d				07 35	07 39							07 56	08 00		
Burgess Hill	d				07 39		07 46		07 52				08 00			
Lewes	d									07 42						07 55
Wivelsfield	d					07 45	07 49									08 11
Haywards Heath	a				07 45	07 50	07 53		07 57	08 02			08 05	08 09		08 16
	d				07 46	07 51	07 54		07 59	08 03			08 06	08 09		08 16
Balcombe	d						07 59							08 15		08 22
Horsham	d							07 40			07 51				08b09	
Littlehaven	d							07 43			07 54					
Faygate	d										07 58					
Ifield	d							07 50			08 02					
Crawley	d							07 53			08 06				08 18	
Three Bridges	a				07 55		08 05	07 57			08 09				08 22	08 28
	d				07 56		08 05	07 58			08 10				08 22	08 28
Gatwick Airport	a				08 00	08 02		08 04	08 12		08 14		08 17	08 22		
	d	07 58			08 01	08 05		08 05	08 13		08 15	08 17	08 20	08 23		
Horley	d							08 07			08 17				08 28	
Salfords	d							08 11			08 21					
Earlswood (Surrey)	d							08 15			08 25					
Tonbridge	d															
Leigh (Kent)	d															
Penshurst	d															
Edenbridge	d															
Godstone	d															
Nutfield	d															
Reigate	d		08 09													
Redhill	a	08 05	08 13		08 08			08 18			08 28					
	d	08 08			08 09			08 18			08 28					
Merstham	d							08 22								
Coulsdon South	d							08 27			08 36					
Purley	d							08 31								
East Croydon	a			08 14	08 20		08 24	08 36	08 29	08 31	08 50			08 38	08 43	08 46
	d			08 15	08 21		08 25	08 37	08 30	08 33	08 51			08 39	08 43	08 50
Norwood Junction	a															
London Bridge ⊖	a						08 41			08 52	09 08					
London Blackfriars ⊖	a				08 53									09 09		
City Thameslink	a				08 56									09 12		
Farringdon ⊖	a				09 00									09 16		
St Pancras International ⊖	a				09 03									09 19		
St Albans City	a				09 25									09 40		
Luton Airport Parkway	a				09 37									09 52		
Luton	a				09 40									09 56		
Bedford	a				10 08									10 22		
Clapham Junction	d			08 27				08 48	08 40						08 53	09 01
London Victoria ⊖	a			08 35		08 35		08 58	08 48			08 50	08 52		09 01	09 09
London Victoria ⊖	a															

b arr. 0758

Table 186

Mondays to Fridays

Brighton - London, Bedford

		SN 1	SN 1	GW 1	GX 1 (trolley)	FC 1	SN 1	SN 1	SN ◇1	GX 1 (trolley)	FC 1	SN ◇1 (trolley)
Brighton 10	d					08 02					08 16	
Hove 2	d								08 11			
Preston Park	d					08 06			08 15		08 20	
Hassocks 4	d					08 12			08 22		08 26	
Burgess Hill 4	d					08 16			08 26		08 30	
Lewes 4	d											08 23
Wivelsfield 4	d					08 18					08 33	08 39
Haywards Heath 3	a					08 23			08 31		08 37	08 44
	d					08 23			08 31		08 38	08 44
Balcombe	d											
Horsham 4	d		08 12									
Littlehaven	d		08 15									
Faygate	d		08 19									
Ifield	d		08 23									
Crawley	d		08 26									
Three Bridges 4	a		08 29			08 33			08 41		08 47	
	d		08 30			08 34			08 42		08 47	
Gatwick Airport 10	a		08 34			08 38					08 51	08 55
	d		08 35		08 35	08 38				08 50	08 53	08 56
Horley 4	d		08 38									08 59
Salfords	d		08 42									
Earlswood (Surrey)	d		08 45									
Tonbridge 4	d	08 16					07 59					
Leigh (Kent)	d	08 20					08 03					
Penshurst	d	08 24					08 07					
Edenbridge	d	08 30					08 13					
Godstone	d	08 37					08 20					
Nutfield	d	08 42					08 25					
Reigate	d			08 24				08 27				
Redhill 5	a	08 47	08 49	08 30			08 31	08 33				
	d	08 53	<				08 36	<				
Merstham	d	08 57					08 41					
Coulsdon South	d	09 02					08 46					
Purley 4	d	09 05					08 50					
East Croydon	a	09 10				08 54	08 56		09 01		09 08	09 14
	d	09 11				08 54	08 57		09 01		09 09	09 14
Norwood Junction 2	a											
London Bridge 4 ⊖	a					09 08	09 13					
London Blackfriars 3 ⊖	a					09 21					09 37	
City Thameslink 3	a					09 25					09 40	
Farringdon 3 ⊖	a					09 28					09 44	
St Pancras International 15 ⊖	a					09 32					09 47	
St Albans City	a					09 52					10 10	
Luton Airport Parkway 4	a					10 01					10 21	
Luton 7	a					10 04					10 24	
Bedford 10	a					10 28					10 50	
Clapham Junction 10	d	09 21							09 11			09 24
London Victoria 15 ⊖	a	09 29			09 05				09 22	09 20		09 32

Table 186

Mondays to Fridays

Brighton - London, Bedford

		GX 1 (trolley)	GW 1	SN 1	SN ◇1 (trolley)	SN 1 (trolley)	SN 1	SN 1	FC 1	SN 1	GX 1 (trolley)	SN ◇1 (trolley)	SN 1	SN ◇1	GW 1
Brighton 10	d					08 45			08 36						
Hove 2	d													08 52	
Preston Park	d								08 40					08 57	
Hassocks 4	d								08 46					09 04	
Burgess Hill 4	d								08 50					09 08	
Lewes 4	d											08b48			
Wivelsfield 4	d											09 00			
Haywards Heath 3	a					08 58			08 55			09 05		09 12	
	d					08 58			09 00			09 08		09 14	
Balcombe	d								09 06						
Horsham 4	d				08b49			08 35					09 00		
Littlehaven	d							08 38					09 03		
Faygate	d														
Ifield	d							08 44					09 09		
Crawley	d				08 58			08 47					09 13		
Three Bridges 4	a				09 01			08 51	09 11			09 17	09 16		
	d				09 02			08 51	09 12			09 17	09 18		
Gatwick Airport 10	a				09 06	09 10		08 55	09 16			09 21	09 22	09 26	
	d	09 05	09 07		09 07	09 11		08 56	09 16		09 20	09 23	09 23	09 27	
Horley 4	d							08 59					09 26		
Salfords	d							09 03					09 30		
Earlswood (Surrey)	d							09 06					09 33		
Tonbridge 4	d						08 37								
Leigh (Kent)	d						08 41								
Penshurst	d						08 45								
Edenbridge	d						08 51								
Godstone	d						08 58								
Nutfield	d						09 03								
Reigate	d									09 14					09 24
Redhill 5	a		09 15				09 08	09 10		09 18			09 36		09 30
	d		09 23				09 14	<		09 19			09 37		
Merstham	d						09 18			09 23			09 41		
Coulsdon South	d						09 23			09 28			09 46		
Purley 4	d									09 32			09 49		
East Croydon	a			09 13	09 22	09 26	09 29		09 32	09 37		09 38	09 54	09 42	
	d			09 14	09 22	09 26	09 29		09 32	09 37		09 39	09 55	09 43	
Norwood Junction 2	a									09 41			10 00		
London Bridge 4 ⊖	a								09 46	09 56			10 13		
London Blackfriars 3 ⊖	a								09 53						
City Thameslink 3	a								09 56						
Farringdon 3 ⊖	a								10 00						
St Pancras International 15 ⊖	a								10 03						
St Albans City	a								10 24						
Luton Airport Parkway 4	a								10 37						
Luton 7	a								10 40						
Bedford 10	a								11 06						
Clapham Junction 10	d			09 27	09 33	09 36	09 39					09 48		09 53	
London Victoria 15 ⊖	a	09 35		09 35	09 41	09 44	09 48				09 50	09 58		10 00	

b arr. 0839

Table 186

Brighton - London, Bedford

Station		GX 1 🛒	SN 1	FC 1	SN ◇1 🛒	SN ◇1 🛒	FC 1	SN 1	GX 1 🛒	SN 1	SN ◇1 🛒	SN ◇1	GW 1	GX 1 🛒	SN 1	FC 1
Brighton 10	d			09 00	09 19		09 07									09 34
Hove 2	d											09 22				
Preston Park	d						09 11									
Hassocks 4	d			09 08			09 17									
Burgess Hill 4	d			09 12			09 21					09 33				
Lewes 4	d										09 17					
Wivelsfield 4	d						09 23				09 33					
Haywards Heath 3	a			09 16			09 28				09 38	09 40				09 47
	d			09 16			09 32				09 43	<				09 48
Balcombe	d						09 37									
Horsham 4	d					09b20				09 30						
Littlehaven	d									09 33						
Faygate	d									09 37						
Ifield	d									09 41						
Crawley	d					09 29				09 44						
Three Bridges 4	a			09 26		09 32	09 42			09 48						
	d			09 27		09 33	09 42			09 48						
Gatwick Airport 10	a			09 31		09 37	09 46			09 53	09 54					10 00
	d	09 35		09 31		09 38	09 46		09 50	09 54	09 55		10 03	10 05		10 01
Horley 4	d					09 41				09 56						
Salfords	d															
Earlswood (Surrey)	d															
Tonbridge 4	d							09 19								
Leigh (Kent)	d							09 23								
Penshurst	d							09 27								
Edenbridge	d							09 33								
Godstone	d							09 40								
Nutfield	d							09 45								
Reigate	d															
Redhill 5	a					09 47		09 50		10 03			10 10			
	d					09 48		09 51		10 07			10 13			
Merstham	d									10 11						
Coulsdon South	d							09 58		10 16						
Purley 4	d							10 02		10 19						
East Croydon ⇌	a		09 43	09 47	09 54	09 59	10 02	10 07		10 24	10 11				10 13	10 16
	d		09 44	09 47	09 55	10 00	10 02	10 07		10 25	10 11				10 14	10 17
Norwood Junction 2	a							10 12		10 29						
London Bridge 4 ⊖	a			10 00			10 15	10 25		10 43						10 30
London Blackfriars 3 ⊖	a			10 08			10 23									10 37
City Thameslink 3	a			10 10			10 26									10 40
Farringdon 3 ⊖	a			10 14			10 30									10 44
St Pancras International 15 ⊖	a			10 17			10 33									10 47
St Albans City	a			10 39			10 54									11 10
Luton Airport Parkway 4	a			10 51			11 06									11 21
Luton 7	a			10 54			11 09									11 24
Bedford 10	a			11 20			11 36									11 50
Clapham Junction 10	d		09 56		10 04	10 09					10 21				10 26	
London Victoria 15 ⊖	a	10 05	10 02		10 11	10 16			10 20		10 28			10 35	10 35	

b arr. 0911

Table 186

Brighton - London, Bedford

Station		SN ◇1 🛒	SN ◇1	FC 1	SN 1	GW 1	GX 1 🛒	SN 1	SN ◇1	SN 1	SN ◇1	GX 1 🛒	SN 1	FC 1	SN ◇1 🛒	SN ◇1	FC 1
Brighton 10	d	09 49		09 37							09 55			10 04	10 19		10 07
Hove 2	d								09 51								
Preston Park	d			09 41							09 58						10 11
Hassocks 4	d			09 47							10 05						10 17
Burgess Hill 4	d			09 51					10 02		10 08						10 21
Lewes 4	d									09 50							
Wivelsfield 4	d			09 53							10 11						10 23
Haywards Heath 3	a			09 58					10 06	10 09	10 15			10 18			10 28
	d			09 58					10 13	<	10 16			10 18			10 32
Balcombe	d																10 37
Horsham 4	d		09b51					10 00								10c20	
Littlehaven	d							10 03									
Faygate	d																
Ifield	d							10 09									
Crawley	d		10 00					10 13								10 29	
Three Bridges 4	a		10 03	10 07				10 16			10 25					10 32	10 42
	d		10 04	10 10				10 18			10 31					10 33	10 42
Gatwick Airport 10	a		10 08	10 15				10 22	10 24		10 35			10 30		10 37	10 46
	d		10 09	10 16			10 20	10 23	10 25		10 38	10 35		10 31		10 38	10 46
Horley 4	d							10 26								10 41	
Salfords	d							10 30									
Earlswood (Surrey)	d							10 33									
Tonbridge 4	d																
Leigh (Kent)	d																
Penshurst	d																
Edenbridge	d																
Godstone	d																
Nutfield	d																
Reigate	d				10 14	10 19											
Redhill 5	a		10 16		10 18	10 25		10 36								10 47	
	d		10 17		10 20			10 37								10 48	
Merstham	d				10 24			10 41									
Coulsdon South	d				10 29			10 46									
Purley 4	d				10 33			10 49									
East Croydon ⇌	a	10 24	10 28	10 32	10 38			10 54	10 40		10 53		10 43	10 46	10 56	10 59	11 02
	d	10 24	10 28	10 32	10 38			10 55	10 41		10 53		10 44	10 47	10 56	11 00	11 02
Norwood Junction 2	a				10 42			11 00									
London Bridge 4 ⊖	a			10 45	10 55			11 13						11 00			11 15
London Blackfriars 3 ⊖	a			10 52										11 07			11 22
City Thameslink 3	a			10 56										11 10			11 26
Farringdon 3 ⊖	a			11 00										11 14			11 30
St Pancras International 15 ⊖	a			11 03										11 17			11 33
St Albans City	a			11 24										11 39			11 54
Luton Airport Parkway 4	a			11 37										11 51			12 07
Luton 7	a			11 40										11 54			12 10
Bedford 10	a			12 06										12 20			12 36
Clapham Junction 10	d	10 34	10 38						10 50		11 03		10 56		11 06	11 10	
London Victoria 15 ⊖	a	10 40	10 44				10 50		10 57		11 09	11 05	11 05		11 12	11 16	

b arr. 0940

c arr. 1010

Table 186

Mondays to Fridays

Brighton - London, Bedford

Station		SN 1	GX 1	SN 1	SN ◇1	SN 1	GW 1	GX 1	SN 1	FC 1	SN ◇1	SN ◇1	FC 1	SN 1	GW 1	GX 1
Brighton 10	d									10 34	10 49		10 37			
Hove 2	d				10 21											
Preston Park	d												10 41			
Hassocks 4	d												10 47			
Burgess Hill 4	d												10 51			
Lewes 4	d					10 19										
Wivelsfield 4	d					10 35							10 53			
Haywards Heath 3	a				10 35	10 40				10 47			10 58			
	d				10 43	<				10 48			11 02			
Balcombe	d															
Horsham 4	d			10 30								10b50				
Littlehaven	d			10 33												
Faygate	d															
Ifield	d			10 39												
Crawley	d			10 43								10 59				
Three Bridges 4	a			10 46								11 02	11 11			
	d			10 48								11 03	11 12			
Gatwick Airport 10	a			10 52	10 54					11 00		11 07	11 16			
	d		10 50	10 53	10 55		11 03	11 05		11 01		11 08	11 16			11 20
Horley 4	d			10 56												
Salfords	d															
Earlswood (Surrey)	d															
Tonbridge 4	d	10 19														
Leigh (Kent)	d	10 23														
Penshurst	d	10 27														
Edenbridge	d	10 33														
Godstone	d	10 40														
Nutfield	d	10 45														
Reigate	d													11 14	11 19	
Redhill 5	a	10 50		11 02			11 10					11 15		11 18	11 25	
	d	10 51		11 07			11 13					11 16		11 19		
Merstham	d			11 11										11 23		
Coulsdon South	d	10 58		11 16										11 28		
Purley 4	d	11 01		11 19										11 32		
East Croydon ⇌	a	11 06		11 24	11 10				11 13	11 16	11 23	11 27	11 32	11 37		
	d	11 07		11 25	11 11				11 14	11 17	11 24	11 28	11 32	11 37		
Norwood Junction 2	a	11 12		11 29										11 42		
London Bridge 4 ⊖	a	11 25		11 43						11 30			11 45	11 55		
London Blackfriars 3 ⊖	a									11 37			11 52			
City Thameslink 3	a									11 40			11 56			
Farringdon 3 ⊖	a									11 44			12 00			
St Pancras International 15 ⊖	a									11 47			12 03			
St Albans City	a									12 09			12 24			
Luton Airport Parkway 4	a									12 21			12 37			
Luton 7	a									12 24			12 40			
Bedford 10	a									12 50			13 06			
Clapham Junction 10	d				11 20				11 26		11 33	11 37				
London Victoria 15 ⊖	a		11 20		11 27			11 35	11 32		11 40	11 44				11 50

b arr. 1040

Table 186

Mondays to Fridays

Brighton - London, Bedford

Station		SN 1	SN ◇1	SN ◇1	SN ◇1	GX 1	SN 1	FC 1	SN ◇1	SN ◇1	FC 1	SN 1	GX 1	SN 1	SN ◇1	SN 1
Brighton 10	d				10 55			11 04	11 19		11 07					
Hove 2	d			10 51											11 21	
Preston Park	d				10 58						11 11					
Hassocks 4	d				11 05						11 17					
Burgess Hill 4	d			11 02	11 08						11 21					
Lewes 4	d		10 50													11 20
Wivelsfield 4	d				11 11						11 23					11 34
Haywards Heath 3	a		11 05	11 08	11 15			11 18			11 28				11 35	11 40
	d		11 13	<	11 16			11 18			11 32				11 43	<
Balcombe	d										11 37					
Horsham 4	d	11 00								11b20				11 30		
Littlehaven	d	11 03												11 33		
Faygate	d															
Ifield	d	11 09												11 39		
Crawley	d	11 13								11 29				11 43		
Three Bridges 4	a	11 16			11 25					11 32	11 42			11 46		
	d	11 18			11 31					11 33	11 42			11 48		
Gatwick Airport 10	a	11 22	11 24		11 35			11 30		11 37	11 46			11 52	11 54	
	d	11 23	11 25		11 38	11 35		11 31		11 38	11 46		11 50	11 53	11 55	
Horley 4	d	11 26								11 41				11 56		
Salfords	d	11 30														
Earlswood (Surrey)	d	11 33														
Tonbridge 4	d											11 19				
Leigh (Kent)	d											11 23				
Penshurst	d											11 27				
Edenbridge	d											11 33				
Godstone	d											11 40				
Nutfield	d											11 45				
Reigate	d															
Redhill 5	a	11 36								11 47		11 50		12 02		
	d	11 37								11 48		11 51		12 07		
Merstham	d	11 41												12 11		
Coulsdon South	d	11 46										11 58		12 16		
Purley 4	d	11 49										12 02		12 19		
East Croydon ⇌	a	11 54	11 40		11 53		11 43	11 46	11 56	11 59	12 02	12 07		12 24	12 10	
	d	11 55	11 41		11 53		11 44	11 47	11 56	12 00	12 02	12 07		12 25	12 11	
Norwood Junction 2	a	12 00										12 12		12 29		
London Bridge 4 ⊖	a	12 13						12 00			12 15	12 15		12 43		
London Bridge 4 ⊖	a	12 13										12 25		12 43		
London Blackfriars 3 ⊖	a							12 07			12 22					
City Thameslink 3	a							12 10			12 26					
Farringdon 3 ⊖	a							12 14			12 30					
St Pancras International 15 ⊖	a							12 17			12 33					
St Albans City	a							12 39			12 54					
Luton Airport Parkway 4	a							12 51			13 07					
Luton 7	a							12 54			13 10					
Bedford 10	a							13 20			13 36					
Clapham Junction 10	d		11 50		12 03		11 56		12 06	12 12					12 20	
London Victoria 15 ⊖	a		11 57		12 09	12 05	12 02		12 12	12 18			12 20		12 28	

b arr. 1110

Table 186

Mondays to Fridays

Brighton - London, Bedford

Station		GW		GX	SN	FC	SN ◇	SN ◇	FC		SN	GW	GX	SN	SN ◇	SN ◇	SN ◇
Brighton	d					11 34	11 49		11 37								11 55
Hove	d															11 51	
Preston Park	d								11 41								11 58
Hassocks	d								11 47								12 05
Burgess Hill	d								11 51							12 02	12 08
Lewes	d														11 50		
Wivelsfield	d								11 53								12 11
Haywards Heath	a					11 47			11 58						12 05	12 09	12 15
	d					11 48			12 02						12 13	<	12 16
Balcombe	d																
Horsham	d							11b50						12 00			
Littlehaven	d													12 03			
Faygate	d																
Ifield	d													12 09			
Crawley	d							11 59						12 13			
Three Bridges	a							12 02	12 11					12 16			12 25
	d							12 03	12 12					12 18			12 31
Gatwick Airport	a					12 00		12 07	12 16					12 22	12 24		12 35
	d	12 03		12 05		12 01		12 08	12 16				12 20	12 23	12 25		12 38
Horley	d													12 26			
Salfords	d													12 30			
Earlswood (Surrey)	d													12 33			
Tonbridge	d																
Leigh (Kent)	d																
Penshurst	d																
Edenbridge	d																
Godstone	d																
Nutfield	d																
Reigate	d										12 14	12 19					
Redhill	a	12 10						12 15			12 18	12 25		12 36			
	d	12 13						12 16			12 19			12 37			
Merstham	d										12 23			12 41			
Coulsdon South	d										12 28			12 46			
Purley	d										12 32			12 49			
East Croydon	a				12 13	12 16	12 23	12 27	12 32		12 37			12 54	12 40		12 53
	d				12 14	12 17	12 24	12 28	12 32		12 37			12 55	12 41		12 53
Norwood Junction	a										12 42			13 00			
London Bridge ⊖	a					12 30			12 45		12 55			13 13			
London Blackfriars ⊖	a					12 37			12 52								
City Thameslink	a					12 40			12 56								
Farringdon ⊖	a					12 44			13 00								
St Pancras International ⊖	a					12 47			13 03								
St Albans City	a					13 09			13 24								
Luton Airport Parkway	a					13 21			13 37								
Luton	a					13 24			13 40								
Bedford	a					13 50			14 06								
Clapham Junction	d				12 26		12 33	12 37							12 50		13 03
London Victoria ⊖	a			12 35	12 32		12 40	12 44					12 50		12 57		13 09

b arr. 1140

Table 186

Mondays to Fridays

Brighton - London, Bedford

Station		GX	SN	FC	SN ◇	SN ◇	FC		SN	GX	SN	SN ◇	SN	GW		GX	SN	FC	SN ◇
Brighton	d			12 04	12 19		12 07											12 34	12 49
Hove	d											12 21							
Preston Park	d						12 11												
Hassocks	d						12 17												
Burgess Hill	d						12 21												
Lewes	d												12 20						
Wivelsfield	d						12 23						12 34						
Haywards Heath	a			12 18			12 28					12 35	12 40					12 47	
	d			12 18			12 32					12 43	<					12 48	
Balcombe	d						12 37												
Horsham	d					12b20					12 30								
Littlehaven	d										12 33								
Faygate	d										12 37								
Ifield	d										12 41								
Crawley	d					12 29					12 44								
Three Bridges	a					12 32	12 42				12 47								
	d					12 33	12 42				12 48								
Gatwick Airport	a			12 30		12 37	12 46				12 52	12 54						13 00	
	d	12 35		12 31		12 38	12 46			12 50	12 53	12 55		13 03		13 05		13 01	
Horley	d					12 41					12 56								
Salfords	d																		
Earlswood (Surrey)	d																		
Tonbridge	d								12 19										
Leigh (Kent)	d								12 23										
Penshurst	d								12 27										
Edenbridge	d								12 33										
Godstone	d								12 40										
Nutfield	d								12 45										
Reigate	d																		
Redhill	a					12 47			12 50		13 02			13 10					
	d					12 48			12 51		13 07			13 13					
Merstham	d										13 11								
Coulsdon South	d								12 58		13 16								
Purley	d								13 02		13 19								
East Croydon	a		12 43	12 46	12 56	12 59	13 02		13 07		13 24	13 10					13 13	13 16	13 23
	d		12 44	12 47	12 56	13 00	13 02		13 07		13 25	13 11					13 14	13 17	13 24
Norwood Junction	a								13 12		13 29								
London Bridge ⊖	a			13 00			13 15		13 25		13 43							13 30	
London Blackfriars ⊖	a			13 07			13 22											13 37	
City Thameslink	a			13 10			13 26											13 40	
Farringdon ⊖	a			13 14			13 30											13 44	
St Pancras International ⊖	a			13 17			13 33											13 47	
St Albans City	a			13 40			13 54											14 09	
Luton Airport Parkway	a			13 52			14 07											14 21	
Luton	a			13 55			14 10											14 24	
Bedford	a			14 20			14 36											14 50	
Clapham Junction	d		12 56		13 06	13 10						13 20					13 26		13 33
London Victoria ⊖	a	13 05	13 02		13 12	13 16				13 20		13 28				13 35	13 32		13 40

b arr. 1210

Brighton - London, Bedford

		SN ◇1	FC 1	SN 1	GW 1	GX 1 🛒	SN 1	SN ◇1	SN ◇1	SN ◇1	GX 1 🛒	SN 1	FC 1	SN ◇1 🛒	SN ◇1	FC 1
Brighton 10	d		12 37							12 55			13 04	13 19		13 07
Hove 2	d								12 51							
Preston Park	d		12 41							12 58						13 11
Hassocks 4	d		12 47							13 05						13 17
Burgess Hill 4	d		12 51						13 02	13 08						13 21
Lewes 4	d							12 50								
Wivelsfield 4	d		12 53							13 11						13 23
Haywards Heath 3	a		12 58					13 05	13 09	13 15			13 18			13 28
	d		13 02					13 13	<	13 16			13 18			13 32
Balcombe	d															13 37
Horsham 4	d	12b50					13 00								13c20	
Littlehaven	d						13 03									
Faygate	d															
Ifield	d						13 09									
Crawley	d	12 59					13 13								13 29	
Three Bridges 4	a	13 02	13 11				13 16			13 25					13 32	13 42
	d	13 03	13 12				13 18			13 31					13 33	13 42
Gatwick Airport 10	a	13 07	13 16				13 22	13 24		13 35			13 30		13 37	13 46
	d	13 08	13 16			13 20	13 23	13 25		13 38	13 35		13 31		13 38	13 46
Horley 4	d						13 26								13 41	
Salfords	d						13 30									
Earlswood (Surrey)	d						13 33									
Tonbridge 4	d															
Leigh (Kent)	d															
Penshurst	d															
Edenbridge	d															
Godstone	d															
Nutfield	d															
Reigate	d			13 14	13 19											
Redhill 5	a	13 15		13 18	13 25		13 36								13 47	
	d	13 16		13 19			13 37								13 48	
Merstham	d			13 23			13 41									
Coulsdon South	d			13 28			13 46									
Purley 4	d			13 32			13 49									
East Croydon	a	13 27	13 32	13 37			13 54	13 40		13 53		13 43	13 46	13 56	13 59	14 02
	d	13 28	13 32	13 37			13 55	13 41		13 53		13 44	13 47	13 56	14 00	14 02
Norwood Junction 2	a			13 42			14 00									
London Bridge 4 ⊖	a		13 45	13 55			14 13						14 00			14 15
London Blackfriars 3 ⊖	a		13 52										14 07			14 22
City Thameslink 3	a		13 56										14 10			14 26
Farringdon 3 ⊖	a		14 00										14 14			14 30
St Pancras International 15 ⊖	a		14 03										14 17			14 33
St Albans City	a		14 24										14 39			14 54
Luton Airport Parkway 4	a		14 37										14 51			15 07
Luton 7	a		14 40										14 54			15 10
Bedford 10	a		15 06										15 20			15 36
Clapham Junction 10	d	13 37						13 50		14 03		13 56		14 06	14 10	
London Victoria 15 ⊖	a	13 44				13 50		13 57		14 09	14 05	14 02		14 12	14 16	

b arr. 1240 c arr. 1310

Brighton - London, Bedford

		SN 1	GX 1 🛒	SN 1	SN ◇1	SN 1	GW 1	GX 1 🛒	SN 1	FC 1	SN ◇1 🛒	SN ◇1	FC 1	SN 1	GW 1	GX 1 🛒
Brighton 10	d									13 34	13 49		13 37			
Hove 2	d				13 21											
Preston Park	d												13 41			
Hassocks 4	d												13 47			
Burgess Hill 4	d												13 51			
Lewes 4	d					13 20										
Wivelsfield 4	d					13 34							13 53			
Haywards Heath 3	a				13 35	13 40				13 47			13 58			
	d				13 43	<				13 48			14 02			
Balcombe	d															
Horsham 4	d			13 30								13b50				
Littlehaven	d			13 33												
Faygate	d															
Ifield	d			13 39												
Crawley	d			13 43								13 59				
Three Bridges 4	a			13 46								14 02	14 11			
	d			13 48								14 03	14 12			
Gatwick Airport 10	a			13 52	13 54					14 00		14 07	14 16			
	d		13 50	13 53	13 55		14 03	14 05		14 01		14 08	14 16			14 20
Horley 4	d			13 56												
Salfords	d															
Earlswood (Surrey)	d															
Tonbridge 4	d	13 19														
Leigh (Kent)	d	13 23														
Penshurst	d	13 27														
Edenbridge	d	13 33														
Godstone	d	13 40														
Nutfield	d	13 45														
Reigate	d													14 14	14 19	
Redhill 5	a	13 50		14 02			14 10					14 15		14 18	14 25	
	d	13 51		14 07			14 13					14 16		14 19		
Merstham	d			14 11										14 23		
Coulsdon South	d	13 58		14 16										14 28		
Purley 4	d	14 02		14 19										14 32		
East Croydon	a	14 07		14 24	14 10				14 13	14 16	14 23	14 27	14 32	14 37		
	d	14 08		14 25	14 11				14 14	14 17	14 24	14 28	14 32	14 37		
Norwood Junction 2	a	14 12		14 29										14 42		
London Bridge 4 ⊖	a	14 25		14 43						14 30			14 45	14 55		
London Blackfriars 3 ⊖	a									14 37			14 52			
City Thameslink 3	a									14 40			14 56			
Farringdon 3 ⊖	a									14 44			15 00			
St Pancras International 15 ⊖	a									14 47			15 03			
St Albans City	a									15 09			15 24			
Luton Airport Parkway 4	a									15 21			15 37			
Luton 7	a									15 24			15 40			
Bedford 10	a									15 50			16 06			
Clapham Junction 10	d				14 20				14 26		14 33	14 37				
London Victoria 15 ⊖	a		14 20		14 27			14 35	14 32		14 40	14 44				14 50

b arr. 1340

Brighton - London, Bedford

		SN 1	SN ◇1	SN ◇1	SN ◇1	GX 1	SN 1	FC 1	SN ◇1	SN ◇1	FC 1	SN 1	GX 1	SN 1	SN ◇1	SN 1
Brighton 10	d				13 55			14 04	14 19		14 07					
Hove 2	d			13 51											14 21	
Preston Park	d				13 58						14 11					
Hassocks 4	d				14 05						14 17					
Burgess Hill 4	d			14 02	14 08						14 21					
Lewes 4	d		13 50													14 20
Wivelsfield 4	d				14 11						14 23					14 34
Haywards Heath 3	a		14 05	14 09	14 15			14 18			14 28				14 35	14 40
	d		14 13	<	14 16			14 18			14 32				14 43	<
Balcombe	d										14 37					
Horsham 4	d	14 00								14b20				14 30		
Littlehaven	d	14 03												14 33		
Faygate	d															
Ifield	d	14 09												14 39		
Crawley	d	14 13								14 29				14 43		
Three Bridges 4	a	14 16			14 25					14 32	14 42			14 46		
	d	14 18			14 31					14 33	14 42			14 48		
Gatwick Airport 10	a	14 22	14 24		14 35			14 30		14 37	14 46			14 52	14 54	
	d	14 23	14 25		14 38	14 35		14 31		14 38	14 46		14 50	14 53	14 55	
Horley 4	d	14 26								14 41				14 56		
Salfords	d	14 30														
Earlswood (Surrey)	d	14 33														
Tonbridge 4	d											14 19				
Leigh (Kent)	d											14 23				
Penshurst	d											14 27				
Edenbridge	d											14 33				
Godstone	d											14 40				
Nutfield	d											14 45				
Reigate	d															
Redhill 5	a	14 36								14 47		14 50		15 02		
	d	14 37								14 48		14 51		15 07		
Merstham	d	14 41												15 11		
Coulsdon South	d	14 46										14 58		15 16		
Purley 4	d	14 49										15 02		15 19		
East Croydon	a	14 54	14 40		14 53		14 43	14 46	14 56	14 59	15 02	15 07		15 24	15 10	
	d	14 55	14 41		14 53		14 44	14 47	14 56	15 00	15 02	15 07		15 25	15 11	
Norwood Junction 2	a	15 00										15 12		15 29		
London Bridge 4 ⊖	a	15 13						15 00			15 15	15 25		15 43		
London Blackfriars 3 ⊖	a							15 07			15 22					
City Thameslink 3	a							15 10			15 26					
Farringdon 3 ⊖	a							15 14			15 30					
St Pancras International 15 ⊖	a							15 17			15 33					
St Albans City	a							15 39			15 54					
Luton Airport Parkway 4	a							15 51			16 06					
Luton 7	a							15 54			16 09					
Bedford 10	a							16 20			16 36					
Clapham Junction 10	d		14 50		15 03		14 56		15 06	15 10					15 20	
London Victoria 15 ⊖	a		14 57		15 09	15 05	15 02		15 12	15 20			15 20		15 27	

b arr. 1410

Table 186

Mondays to Fridays

Brighton - London, Bedford

		GW 1	GX 1	SN 1	FC 1	SN ◇1	SN ◇1	FC 1	SN 1	GW 1	GX 1	SN 1	SN ◇1	SN ◇1	SN ◇1
Brighton 10	d				14 34	14 49		14 37							14 55
Hove 2	d													14 51	
Preston Park	d							14 41							14 58
Hassocks 4	d							14 47							15 05
Burgess Hill 4	d							14 51						15 02	15 08
Lewes 4	d												14 50		
Wivelsfield 4	d							14 53							15 11
Haywards Heath 3	a				14 47			14 58					15 05	15 09	15 15
	d				14 48			15 02					15 13	<	15 16
Balcombe	d														
Horsham 4	d						14b50					15 00			
Littlehaven	d											15 03			
Faygate	d														
Ifield	d											15 09			
Crawley	d						14 59					15 13			
Three Bridges 4	a						15 02	15 11				15 16			15 25
	d						15 03	15 12				15 18			15 31
Gatwick Airport 10	a				15 00		15 07	15 16				15 22	15 24		15 35
	d	15 03	15 05		15 01		15 08	15 16			15 20	15 23	15 25		15 38
Horley 4	d											15 26			
Salfords	d											15 30			
Earlswood (Surrey)	d											15 33			
Tonbridge 4	d														
Leigh (Kent)	d														
Penshurst	d														
Edenbridge	d														
Godstone	d														
Nutfield	d														
Reigate	d								15 14	15 19					
Redhill 5	a	15 10					15 16		15 18	15 25		15 36			
	d	15 13					15 17		15 19			15 37			
Merstham	d								15 23			15 41			
Coulsdon South	d								15 28			15 46			
Purley 4	d								15 32			15 49			
East Croydon	a			15 13	15 16	15 23	15 28	15 32	15 37			15 54	15 40		15 53
	d			15 14	15 17	15 24	15 28	15 32	15 37			15 55	15 41		15 53
Norwood Junction 2	a								15 42			16 00			
London Bridge 4 ⊖	a				15 30			15 45	15 55			16 13			
London Blackfriars 3 ⊖	a				15 37			15 52							
City Thameslink 3	a				15 40			15 56							
Farringdon 3 ⊖	a				15 44			16 00							
St Pancras International 15 ⊖	a				15 47			16 03							
St Albans City	a				16 09			16 24							
Luton Airport Parkway 4	a				16 21			16 37							
Luton 7	a				16 24			16 40							
Bedford 10	a				16 50			17 06							
Clapham Junction 10	d			15 26		15 33	15 38						15 50		16 03
London Victoria 15 ⊖	a		15 35	15 32		15 40	15 44				15 50		15 57		16 09

b arr. 1440

Table 186

Mondays to Fridays

Brighton - London, Bedford

		GX 1	SN 1	FC 1	SN ◇1	SN ◇1	FC 1	SN 1	GX 1	SN 1	SN ◇1	SN 1	GW 1	GX 1	SN 1	FC 1	SN ◇1
		🍴			🍴	🍴			🍴		🍴			🍴			🍴
Brighton 10	d			15 04	15 19		15 07									15 34	
Hove 2	d										15 21						
Preston Park	d						15 11										
Hassocks 4	d						15 17										
Burgess Hill 4	d						15 21										
Lewes 4	d											15 19					
Wivelsfield 4	d						15 23					15 35					
Haywards Heath 3	a			15 18			15 28				15 35	15 39				15 48	
	d			15 18			15 32				15 43	<				15 48	
Balcombe	d						15 37										
Horsham 4	d					15b20				15 30							15c50
Littlehaven	d									15 33							
Faygate	d																
Ifield	d									15 39							
Crawley	d					15 29				15 43							15 59
Three Bridges 4	a					15 32	15 42			15 46							16 02
	d					15 33	15 42			15 48							16 03
Gatwick Airport 10	a			15 30		15 37	15 46			15 52	15 54					16 00	16 07
	d	15 35		15 31		15 38	15 46		15 50	15 53	15 55		16 03	16 05		16 01	16 08
Horley 4	d					15 41				15 56							
Salfords	d																
Earlswood (Surrey)	d																
Tonbridge 4	d							15 19									
Leigh (Kent)	d							15 23									
Penshurst	d							15 27									
Edenbridge	d							15 33									
Godstone	d							15 40									
Nutfield	d							15 45									
Reigate	d																
Redhill 5	a					15 47		15 50		16 02			16 10				16 17
	d					15 48		15 51		16 06			16 13				16 18
Merstham	d									16 10							
Coulsdon South	d							15 58		16 15							
Purley 4	d							16 02		16 18							
East Croydon	a		15 43	15 46	15 56	15 59	16 02	16 07		16 23	16 10				16 13	16 16	16 30
	d		15 44	15 47	15 56	16 00	16 02	16 07		16 24	16 11				16 14	16 17	16 30
Norwood Junction 2	a							16 12		16 28							
London Bridge 4 ⊖	a			16 00			16 15	16 25		16 43							
London Blackfriars 3 ⊖	a			16 07			16 25									16 47	
City Thameslink 3	a			16 10			16 28									16 54	
Farringdon 3 ⊖	a			16 13			16 31									16 57	
St Pancras International 15 ⊖	a			16 17			16 35									17 01	
St Albans City	a			16 39			16 56									17 21	
Luton Airport Parkway 4	a			16 51			17 09										
Luton 7	a			16 54			17 12									17 34	
Bedford 10	a			17 20			17 38									17 58	
Clapham Junction 10	d		15 56		16 06	16 09					16 20				16 26		16 40
London Victoria 15 ⊖	a	16 05	16 05		16 12	16 20			16 22		16 27			16 35	16 35		16 46

b arr. 1510 c arr. 1540

Table 186

Mondays to Fridays

Brighton - London, Bedford

		SN ◇1	FC 1	SN 1	GW 1	GX 1	SN 1	SN ◇1	SN ◇1	SN ◇1	GX 1	SN 1	FC 1	SN ◇1	SN 1	FC 1
		🍴				🍴		🍴			🍴				🍴	
Brighton 10	d	15 49	15 37							15 55			16 04		16 19	16 07
Hove 2	d								15 51							
Preston Park	d		15 41							15 58						16 11
Hassocks 4	d		15 47							16 05						16 17
Burgess Hill 4	d		15 51						16 02	16 08						16 21
Lewes 4	d							15 50								
Wivelsfield 4	d		15 53							16 11						
Haywards Heath 3	a		15 58					16 05	16 09	16 15			16 18			16 25
	d		15 58					16 13	<	16 16			16 18			16 26
Balcombe	d															16 31
Horsham 4	d						16 00							16b20		
Littlehaven	d						16 03									
Faygate	d															
Ifield	d						16 09									
Crawley	d						16 13							16 29		
Three Bridges 4	a		16 07				16 16			16 25				16 32		16 37
	d		16 07				16 18			16 31				16 33		16 37
Gatwick Airport 10	a		16 11				16 22	16 24		16 35			16 30	16 37		16 41
	d		16 11			16 20	16 23	16 25		16 38	16 35		16 31	16 38		16 41
Horley 4	d						16 26									
Salfords	d						16 30									
Earlswood (Surrey)	d						16 33									
Tonbridge 4	d															
Leigh (Kent)	d															
Penshurst	d															
Edenbridge	d															
Godstone	d															
Nutfield	d															
Reigate	d			16 14	16 21											
Redhill 5	a			16 18	16 27		16 36							16 46		
	d			16 21			16 37							16 47		
Merstham	d			16 25			16 41									
Coulsdon South	d			16 30			16 46									
Purley 4	d			16 34			16 49									
East Croydon	a	16 24	16 28	16 39			16 54	16 40		16 53		16 43	16 46	17 01	16 56	16 57
	d	16 26	16 28	16 40			16 55	16 41		16 53		16 44	16 47	17 01	16 56	16 57
Norwood Junction 2	a			16 44			16 59									
London Bridge 4 ⊖	a			16 57			17 14									
London Blackfriars 3 ⊖	a		16 55										17 19			17 25
City Thameslink 3	a		16 58										17 24			17 28
Farringdon 3 ⊖	a		17 01										17 27			17 31
St Pancras International 15 ⊖	a		17 05										17 31			17 35
St Albans City	a		17 26										17 51			17 56
Luton Airport Parkway 4	a		17 39													18 09
Luton 7	a		17 42										18 04			18 12
Bedford 10	a		18 08										18 28			18 38
Clapham Junction 10	d	16 36						16 50		17 03		16 56		17 11	17 06	
London Victoria 15 ⊖	a	16 42				16 52		16 58		17 09	17 05	17 05		17 17	17 12	

b arr. 1610

Table 186 — Mondays to Fridays

Brighton - London, Bedford

		SN 1	GX 1	FC 1	SN 1	SN ◇1	SN 1	SN 1	GW 1	GX 1	SN 1	FC 1	SN 1	SN ◇1	SN 1	SN 1
Brighton 10	d			16 24								16 30	16 49			
Hove 2	d					16 21										
Preston Park	d											16 34				
Hassocks 4	d											16 40				
Burgess Hill 4	d											16 44				
Lewes 4	d						16 19									
Wivelsfield 4	d						16 37					16 46				
Haywards Heath 3	a			16 37		16 34	16 41					16 50				
	d			16 38		16 45	<					16 50				
Balcombe	d											16 57				
Horsham 4	d				16 30									16b52		
Littlehaven	d				16 33											
Faygate	d				16 37											
Ifield	d				16 41											
Crawley	d				16 44									17 01		
Three Bridges 4	a			16 47	16 47							17 02		17 04		
	d			16 47	16 48							17 03		17 05		
Gatwick Airport 10	a			16 52	16 52	16 56						17 07		17 09		
	d		16 50	16 53	16 53	16 57			17 03	17 05		17 08		17 10		
Horley 4	d				16 56											
Salfords	d				17 00											
Earlswood (Surrey)	d				17 03											
Tonbridge 4	d	16 19													16 49	17 03
Leigh (Kent)	d	16 23													16 53	
Penshurst	d	16 27													16 57	
Edenbridge	d	16 33													17 03	17 13
Godstone	d	16 40													17 10	
Nutfield	d	16 45													17 15	
Reigate	d							17 03								
Redhill 5	a	16 50			17 06			17 07	17 10					17 17	17 20	17 25
	d	16 51			17 07				17 13					17 18	17 21	17 28
Merstham	d				17 11										17 25	
Coulsdon South	d	16 58			17 16										17 30	
Purley 4	d	17 02			17 19											
East Croydon ⇌	a	17 07		17 08	17 24	17 12					17 13	17 23	17 26	17 30	17 37	17 40
	d	17 07		17 09	17 25	17 12					17 14	17 23	17 26	17 30	17 38	17 41
Norwood Junction 2	a	17 11			17 30											17 45
London Bridge 4 ⊖	a	17 26		17 27	17 45											17 58
London Blackfriars 3 ⊖	a			17 35								17 49				
City Thameslink 3	a			17 38								17 54				
Farringdon 3 ⊖	a			17 41								17 57				
St Pancras International 15 ⊖	a			17 45								18 01				
St Albans City	a			18 06								18 21				
Luton Airport Parkway 4	a			18 20												
Luton 7	a			18 23								18 34				
Bedford 10	a			18 48								18 58				
Clapham Junction 10	d					17 22					17 25		17 36	17 40	17 47	
London Victoria 15 ⊖	a		17 20			17 28				17 35	17 32		17 42	17 46	17 54	

b arr. 1640

Table 186 — Mondays to Fridays

Brighton - London, Bedford

		GX 1	SN	SN ◇1	SN ◇1	SN 1	GW 1	GX 1	SN 1	FC 1	SN 1	SN 1	FC 1	SN ◇1	SN 1	SN 1	GX 1	SN 1
Brighton 10	d									17 03	16 55	17 19	17 07					
Hove 2	d				16 51													
Preston Park	d										16 58		17 11					
Hassocks 4	d										17 05		17 17					
Burgess Hill 4	d				17 02					17 13	17 08		17 21					
Lewes 4	d			16 51														
Wivelsfield 4	d										17 11							
Haywards Heath 3	a			17 05	17 09					17 17	17 15		17 25					
	d			17 13	<					17 18	17 21		17 26					
Balcombe	d										17 26							
Horsham 4	d		17 00											17c22				17 30
Littlehaven	d		17 03															17 33
Faygate	d		17 07															17 37
Ifield	d		17 11															17 41
Crawley	d		17 14											17 31				17 44
Three Bridges 4	a		17 17							17 27	17 32			17 34				17 47
	d		17 18							17 27	17 32			17 36				17 48
Gatwick Airport 10	a		17 22	17 24						17 31	17 36		17 38	17 40				17 52
	d	17 20	17 23	17 25				17 35		17 31	17 38		17 39	17 41			17 50	17 53
Horley 4	d		17 26															17 56
Salfords	d		17 30															18 00
Earlswood (Surrey)	d		17 33															18 03
Tonbridge 4	d					17 23										17 49		
Leigh (Kent)	d					17 27										17 53		
Penshurst	d					17 31										17 57		
Edenbridge	d					17 37										18 03		
Godstone	d					17 44										18 10		
Nutfield	d					17 49										18 15		
Reigate	d						17 26								17 44			
Redhill 5	a		17 36			17 54	17 32							17 48	17 48	18 21		18 06
	d		17 37											17 49	17 52			18 07
Merstham	d		17 41												17 56			18 11
Coulsdon South	d		17 46												18 01			18 16
Purley 4	d		17 49															18 19
East Croydon ⇌	a		17 54	17 40					17 43	17 46	17 53	17 56	17 57	18 01	18 08			18 24
	d		17 55	17 41					17 44	17 47	17 53	17 56	17 58	18 02	18 08			18 26
Norwood Junction 2	a		17 59															
London Bridge 4 ⊖	a		18 13							18 13								
London Blackfriars 3 ⊖	a									18 21			18 25					
City Thameslink 3	a									18 24			18 28					
Farringdon 3 ⊖	a									18 27			18 31					
St Pancras International 15 ⊖	a									18 31			18 35					
St Albans City	a									18 51			18 56					
Luton Airport Parkway 4	a												19 09					
Luton 7	a									19 04			19 12					
Bedford 10	a									19 26			19 38					
Clapham Junction 10	d			17 51					17 56		18 03	18 06		18 13	18 19			18 37
London Victoria 15 ⊖	a	17 52		17 58				18 05	18 02		18 09	18 12		18 20	18 26		18 22	18 44

b arr. 1755

c arr. 1712

Table 186

Mondays to Fridays

Brighton - London, Bedford

Station		SN ◇[1] ✠	SN [1]	GW [1]	GX [1] ✠	SN [1]	FC [1]	SN [1] ✠	SN ◇[1] ✠	FC [1]	SN [1]	GX [1] ✠	SN [1]	SN ◇[1] ✠	SN ◇[1]	GW [1]
Brighton [10]	d						17 24	17 49		17 37						
Hove [2]	d	17 21													17 51	
Preston Park	d						17 28			17 41						
Hassocks [4]	d						17 34			17 47						
Burgess Hill [4]	d						17 38			17 51					18 02	
Lewes [4]	d		17 19											17 50		
Wivelsfield [4]	d		17 35				17 40			17 53						
Haywards Heath [3]	a	17 35	17 39				17 45			17 58				18 06	18 09	
	d	17 43	<				17 46			18 02				18 13	<	
Balcombe	d									18 07						
Horsham [4]	d								17b52				18 00			
Littlehaven	d												18 03			
Faygate	d												18 07			
Ifield	d												18 11			
Crawley	d								18 01				18 14			
Three Bridges [4]	a						17 55		18 04	18 13			18 17			
	d						17 55		18 05	18 13			18 18			
Gatwick Airport [10]	a	17 54					17 59		18 09	18 17			18 22	18 26		
	d	17 55		18 03	18 05		18 00		18 10	18 17		18 20	18 23	18 27		
Horley [4]	d												18 26			
Salfords	d												18 30			
Earlswood (Surrey)	d												18 33			
Tonbridge [4]	d															
Leigh (Kent)	d															
Penshurst	d															
Edenbridge	d															
Godstone	d															
Nutfield	d															
Reigate	d										18 15					18 26
Redhill [5]	a			18 10					18 17		18 19		18 36			18 32
	d			18 13					18 18		18 24		18 37			
Merstham	d										18 28		18 41			
Coulsdon South	d										18 33		18 46			
Purley [4]	d												18 49			
East Croydon ⇌	a	18 11				18 13	18 15	18 24	18 29	18 32	18 39		18 54	18 42		
	d	18 12				18 14	18 17	18 25	18 30	18 33	18 40		18 55	18 43		
Norwood Junction [2]	a															
London Bridge [4] ⊖	a									18 46						
London Blackfriars [3] ⊖	a						18 51			18 55						
City Thameslink [3]	a						18 54			18 58						
Farringdon [3] ⊖	a						18 57			19 01						
St Pancras International [15] ⊖	a						19 01			19 05						
St Albans City	a						19 21			19 26						
Luton Airport Parkway [4]	a									19 39						
Luton [7]	a						19 34			19 43						
Bedford [10]	a						19 58			20 08						
Clapham Junction [10]	d	18 22				18 26		18 34	18 40		18 49		19 06	18 52		
London Victoria [15] ⊖	a	18 29			18 35	18 32		18 41	18 47		18 56	18 50	19 13	18 59		

b arr. 1740 c arr. 1832

Table 186

Mondays to Fridays

Brighton - London, Bedford

Station		GX [1] ✠	SN [1]	SN [1]	FC [1]	SN [1]	SN [1]	SN ◇[1]	FC [1]	SN [1]	GX [1] ✠	SN [1]	SN ◇[1] ✠	SN ◇[1]	SN [1]	GX [1] ✠	SN [1]
Brighton [10]	d				18 04	17 55	18 19		18 07								
Hove [2]	d													18 21			
Preston Park	d					17 59			18 11								
Hassocks [4]	d					18 05			18 17								
Burgess Hill [4]	d				18 14	18 09			18 21					18 33			
Lewes [4]	d												18 18				
Wivelsfield [4]	d					18 11			18 23				18 34				
Haywards Heath [3]	a				18 18	18 16			18 28				18 38	18 41			
	d				18 18	18 22			18 32				18 45	<			
Balcombe	d								18 37								
Horsham [4]	d							18b22				18 30					
Littlehaven	d											18 33					
Faygate	d											18 37					
Ifield	d											18 41					
Crawley	d							18 31				18 44					
Three Bridges [4]	a					18 31		18 34	18 42			18 47					
	d					18 31		18 35	18 42			18 48					
Gatwick Airport [10]	a				18 30	18 36		18 39	18 46			18 52	18 56				
	d	18 35			18 31	18 38		18 40	18 46		18 50	18 53	18 57			19 05	
Horley [4]	d											18 56					
Salfords	d											19 00					
Earlswood (Surrey)	d											19 03					
Tonbridge [4]	d									18 23							19 10
Leigh (Kent)	d									18 27							19 14
Penshurst	d									18 31							19 18
Edenbridge	d									18 37							19 24
Godstone	d									18 44							19 31
Nutfield	d									18 49							19 36
Reigate	d		18 38												19 02		
Redhill [5]	a		18 42					18 47		18 54		19 06			19 06		19 41
	d							18 48		18 57		19 07					
Merstham	d											19 11					
Coulsdon South	d											19 16					
Purley [4]	d											19 19					
East Croydon ⇌	a			18 43	18 46	18 53	18 56	18 59	19 02	19 09		19 24	19 12				
	d			18 44	18 47	18 53	18 57	19 00	19 02	19 09		19 25	19 12				
Norwood Junction [2]	a									19 12							
London Bridge [4] ⊖	a				19 00				19 15	19 25							
London Blackfriars [3] ⊖	a				19 09				19 22								
City Thameslink [3]	a				19 12				19 26								
Farringdon [3] ⊖	a				19 15				19 30								
St Pancras International [15] ⊖	a				19 19				19 33								
St Albans City	a				19 45				19 55								
Luton Airport Parkway [4]	a				19 57				20 07								
Luton [7]	a				20 00				20 10								
Bedford [10]	a				20 26				20 36								
Clapham Junction [10]	d			18 56		19 03	19 09	19 12				19 37	19 22				
London Victoria [15] ⊖	a	19 05		19 05		19 09	19 15	19 18			19 20	19 43	19 29			19 35	

b arr. 1812 c arr. 1923

Table 186

Mondays to Fridays

Brighton - London, Bedford

Station		SN	FC	SN ◇	SN ◇	FC	SN	GW	GX	SN	SN ◇	SN	SN	GW	GX	SN	FC
Brighton	d		18 34	18 49		18 37											
Hove	d										18 52						
Preston Park	d					18 41											
Hassocks	d					18 47											
Burgess Hill	d					18 51											
Lewes	d											18 50					
Wivelsfield	d					18 53						19 05					
Haywards Heath	a		18 47			18 58					19 05	19 10					
	d		18 48			19 02					19 14	<					
Balcombe	d																
Horsham	d				18b52					19 02							
Littlehaven	d									19 05							
Faygate	d																
Ifield	d									19 11							
Crawley	d				19 01					19 14							
Three Bridges	a				19 04	19 12				19 18							
	d				19 05	19 12				19 18							19 27
Gatwick Airport	a		19 00		19 09	19 16				19 22	19 25						19 31
	d		19 01		19 10	19 16		19 16	19 20	19 23	19 26				19 35		19 31
Horley	d									19 26							
Salfords	d									19 30							
Earlswood (Surrey)	d									19 33							
Tonbridge	d						18 50										
Leigh (Kent)	d						18 54										
Penshurst	d						18 58										
Edenbridge	d						19 04										
Godstone	d						19 11										
Nutfield	d						19 16										
Reigate	d												19 21	19 26			
Redhill	a				19 17		19 21	19 23		19 38			19 25	19 32			
	d				19 18		19 23	19 26		19 39							
Merstham	d						19 27			19 43							
Coulsdon South	d						19 32			19 48							
Purley	d									19 53							
East Croydon	a	19 13	19 16	19 23	19 28	19 32	19 39			19 58	19 42					19 43	19 47
	d	19 14	19 17	19 24	19 29	19 32	19 40			19 59	19 43					19 44	19 47
Norwood Junction	a																
London Bridge ⊖	a		19 30			19 45											20 00
London Blackfriars ⊖	a		19 37			19 52											20 07
City Thameslink	a		19 40			19 56											20 10
Farringdon ⊖	a		19 44			20 00											20 14
St Pancras International ⊖	a		19 47			20 03											20 17
St Albans City	a		20 09			20 25											20 39
Luton Airport Parkway	a		20 21			20 37											20 51
Luton	a		20 24			20 40											20 54
Bedford	a		20 50			21 06											21 20
Clapham Junction	d	19 26		19 34	19 40		19 49			20 08	19 52					19 56	
London Victoria ⊖	a	19 32		19 40	19 47		19 56		19 50	20 15	19 59				20 05	20 02	

b arr. 1842

Table 186

Mondays to Fridays

Brighton - London, Bedford

Station		SN ◇	SN	SN ◇	FC	GX	SN ◇	SN	SN	SN	GW	GX	SN	SN	FC	SN ◇	SN ◇	FC	SN	GX
Brighton	d	19 19		18 59	19 07										19 34	19 49		19 37		
Hove	d						19 22													
Preston Park	d			19 03	19 11													19 41		
Hassocks	d			19 09	19 17													19 47		
Burgess Hill	d			19 13	19 21		19 32											19 51		
Lewes	d							19 21												
Wivelsfield	d			19 15	19 23													19 53		
Haywards Heath	a			19 20	19 28		19 36	19 40							19 47			19 58		
	d			19 21	19 32		19 44	<							19 48			20 02		
Balcombe	d				19 37															
Horsham	d		19 17						19 32								19 52			
Littlehaven	d								19 35											
Faygate	d																			
Ifield	d								19 41											
Crawley	d		19 26						19 45								20 01			
Three Bridges	a		19 29	19 31	19 42				19 49								20 04	20 11		
	d		19 35	<	19 42				19 51								20 05	20 12		
Gatwick Airport	a		19 39		19 46		19 55		19 55						20 00		20 10	20 16		
	d		19 40		19 46	19 50	19 56		19 56		20 03	20 05			20 01		20 11	20 16		20 20
Horley	d								19 59											
Salfords	d																			
Earlswood (Surrey)	d																			
Tonbridge	d												20 10							
Leigh (Kent)	d												20 14							
Penshurst	d												20 18							
Edenbridge	d												20 24							
Godstone	d												20 31							
Nutfield	d												20 36							
Reigate	d									19 51									20 14	
Redhill	a		19 47						20 05	19 55	20 10		20 45				20 18		20 18	
	d		19 48						20 06		20 13						20 18			
Merstham	d								20 10											
Coulsdon South	d								20 15											
Purley	d								20 18											
East Croydon	a	19 54	20 00		20 02		20 11		20 23					20 13	20 16	20 22	20 30	20 32		
	d	19 54	20 01		20 02		20 11		20 26					20 14	20 17	20 24	20 30	20 32		
Norwood Junction	a																			
London Bridge ⊖	a				20 15										20 30			20 45		
London Blackfriars ⊖	a				20 22										20 37			20 52		
City Thameslink	a				20 26										20 40			20 56		
Farringdon ⊖	a				20 30										20 44			21 00		
St Pancras International ⊖	a				20 33										20 47			21 03		
St Albans City	a				20 55										21 09			21 25		
Luton Airport Parkway	a				21 07										21 21			21 37		
Luton	a				21 10										21 24			21 40		
Bedford	a				21 36										21 50			22 06		
Clapham Junction	d	20 04	20 11				20 21		20 37					20 26		20 34	20 41			
London Victoria ⊖	a	20 10	20 20			20 20	20 28		20 44			20 35		20 32		20 40	20 50			20 50

Table 186

Mondays to Fridays

Brighton - London, Bedford

Station		SN 1	SN ◇1	SN 1	GX 1		SN 1	FC 1	SN ◇1	SN ◇1	FC 1	SN 1	GX 1		SN ◇1	SN 1	GW 1	GX 1	SN 1	SN 1
Brighton 10	d							20 04	20 19	19 55	20 07									
Hove 2	d		19 52												20 22					
Preston Park	d									19 59	20 11									
Hassocks 4	d									20 05	20 17									
Burgess Hill 4	d									20 09	20 21				20 33					
Lewes 4	d			19 50																
Wivelsfield 4	d			20 05						20 11	20 23									
Haywards Heath 3	a		20 04	20 10				20 18		20 16	20 28				20 37					
	d		20 14	<				20 18		20 22	20 32				20 38					
Balcombe	d										20 37									
Horsham 4	d	20 02														20 32				
Littlehaven	d	20 05														20 35				
Faygate	d																			
Ifield	d	20 11														20 41				
Crawley	d	20 14														20 45				
Three Bridges 4	a	20 18								20 32	20 42				20 47	20 48				
	d	20 18								20 32	20 42				20 47	20 51				
Gatwick Airport 10	a	20 22	20 25					20 31		20 37	20 46				20 51	20 56				
	d	20 23	20 26		20 35			20 31		20 38	20 46		20 50		20 53	20 57	21 03	21 05		
Horley 4	d	20 26														20 59				
Salfords	d	20 30																		
Earlswood (Surrey)	d	20 33																		
Tonbridge 4	d																		21 10	
Leigh (Kent)	d																		21 14	
Penshurst	d																		21 18	
Edenbridge	d																		21 24	
Godstone	d																		21 31	
Nutfield	d																		21 36	
Reigate	d											20 50								
Redhill 5	a	20 36								20 47		20 54				21 06	21 10		21 42	
	d	20 37								20 48						21 07	21 13			
Merstham	d	20 41														21 11				
Coulsdon South	d	20 46														21 16				
Purley 4	d	20 49														21 19				
East Croydon ⇌	a	20 57	20 41				20 43	20 47	20 54	20 59	21 02				21 09	21 25				21 13
	d	20 57	20 41				20 44	20 47	20 54	21 00	21 02				21 10	21 26				21 14
Norwood Junction 2	a																			
London Bridge 4 ⊖	a							21 00			21 15									
London Blackfriars 3 ⊖	a							21 07			21 22									
City Thameslink 3	a							21 10			21 26									
Farringdon 3 ⊖	a							21 14			21 30									
St Pancras International 15 ⊖	a							21 17			21 33									
St Albans City	a							21 39			21 55									
Luton Airport Parkway 4	a							21 51			22 07									
Luton 7	a							21 54			22 10									
Bedford 10	a							22 20			22 36									
Clapham Junction 10	d	21 08	20 51				20 57		21 04	21 11					21 20	21 38				21 26
London Victoria 15 ⊖	a	21 15	20 58		21 05		21 05		21 10	21 20			21 20		21 27	21 45		21 35		21 35

b arr. 2119

Table 186

Mondays to Fridays

Brighton - London, Bedford

Station		FC 1		SN ◇1	SN ◇1	FC 1	SN 1	GX 1	SN 1	SN ◇1	SN 1	GW 1		GX 1	SN 1	SN ◇1	SN ◇1	FC 1		GX 1	SN ◇1
Brighton 10	d	20 34		20 49		20 37										21 19	21 02	21 11			
Hove 2	d									20 52											21 22
Preston Park	d					20 41											21 06				
Hassocks 4	d					20 47											21 12	21 19			
Burgess Hill 4	d					20 51											21 16	21 23			21 32
Lewes 4	d										20 50										
Wivelsfield 4	d					20 53					21 05						21 18				
Haywards Heath 3	a	20 47				20 58				21 05	21 09						21 23	21 27			21 37
	d	20 48				21 02				21 13	<						21 23	21 32			21 38
Balcombe	d																	21 37			
Horsham 4	d				20 52				21 02												
Littlehaven	d								21 05												
Faygate	d																				
Ifield	d								21 11												
Crawley	d				21 01				21 14												
Three Bridges 4	a				21 05	21 11			21 18								21 32	21 42			21 47
	d				21 05	21 12			21 18								21 33	21 42			21 47
Gatwick Airport 10	a	21 00			21 10	21 16			21 22	21 25							21 37	21 46			21 51
	d	21 01			21 11	21 16		21 20	21 23	21 26				21 35			21 38	21 46		21 50	21 53
Horley 4	d								21 26												
Salfords	d								21 30												
Earlswood (Surrey)	d								21 33												
Tonbridge 4	d																				
Leigh (Kent)	d																				
Penshurst	d																				
Edenbridge	d																				
Godstone	d																				
Nutfield	d																				
Reigate	d						21 13					21 24									
Redhill 5	a				21 18		21 17		21 36			21 30					21 45				
	d				21 18				21 37								21 46				
Merstham	d								21 41												
Coulsdon South	d								21 46												
Purley 4	d								21 49												
East Croydon ⇌	a	21 16		21 22	21 30	21 32			21 54	21 41					21 43	21 53	21 59	22 02			22 09
	d	21 17		21 24	21 30	21 32			21 57	21 42					21 44	21 54	22 00	22 02			22 10
Norwood Junction 2	a																				
London Bridge 4 ⊖	a	21 30				21 45												22 17			
London Blackfriars 3 ⊖	a	21 37				21 52															
City Thameslink 3	a	21 40				21 56															
Farringdon 3 ⊖	a	21 44				22 00															
St Pancras International 15 ⊖	a	21 47				22 03															
St Albans City	a	22 09				22 25															
Luton Airport Parkway 4	a	22 21				22 37															
Luton 7	a	22 24				22 40															
Bedford 10	a	22 50				23 06															
Clapham Junction 10	d			21 34	21 41				22 08	21 51					21 56	22 04	22 11				22 20
London Victoria 15 ⊖	a			21 43	21 48			21 50	22 14	21 58				22 05	22 05	22 11	22 20			22 20	22 27

Brighton - London, Bedford

		SN 1	SN 1	GX 1	SN 1	SN 1	SN 1	SN ◇1	SN ◇1	FC 1	SN 1	SN 1	GX 1	GW 1	SN ◇1	SN ◇1	SN 1	GX 1
Brighton 10	d						21 34	21 49		21 37								
Hove 2	d															21 52		
Preston Park	d									21 41								
Hassocks 4	d									21 47								
Burgess Hill 4	d									21 51						22 02		
Lewes 4	d										21 50				21 50			
Wivelsfield 4	d									21 53	22 02				22 02			
Haywards Heath 3	a						21 46			21 58	22 06				22 06	22 09		
	d						21 46			22 02					22 13	<		
Balcombe	d																	
Horsham 4	d	21 32							21 52									
Littlehaven	d	21 35																
Faygate	d																	
Ifield	d	21 41																
Crawley	d	21 45							22 01									
Three Bridges 4	a	21 48					21 55		22 05	22 11								
	d	21 51					21 56		22 05	22 12								
Gatwick Airport 10	a	21 55					22 00		22 10	22 16					22 24			
	d	21 56		22 05			22 02		22 11	22 16			22 20	22 22	22 25			22 35
Horley 4	d	21 59																
Salfords	d																	
Earlswood (Surrey)	d																	
Tonbridge 4	d				22 10													
Leigh (Kent)	d				22 14													
Penshurst	d				22 18													
Edenbridge	d				22 24													
Godstone	d				22 31													
Nutfield	d				22 36													
Reigate	d		21 52									22 13					22 33	
Redhill 5	a	22 05	21 57		22 42				22 18			22 17		22 30			22 37	
	d	22 06							22 18					22 33				
Merstham	d	22 10																
Coulsdon South	d	22 15																
Purley 4	d	22 19																
East Croydon ⇌	a	22 24				22 13	22 17	22 23	22 30	22 32					22 40			
	d	22 25				22 14	22 17	22 24	22 30	22 32					22 40			
Norwood Junction 2	a																	
London Bridge 4 ⊖	a						22 33			22 47								
London Blackfriars 3 ⊖	a																	
City Thameslink 3	a																	
Farringdon 3 ⊖	a																	
St Pancras International 15 ⊖	a																	
St Albans City	a																	
Luton Airport Parkway 4	a																	
Luton 7	a																	
Bedford 10	a																	
Clapham Junction 10	d	22 38				22 26		22 33	22 41						22 50			
London Victoria 15 ⊖	a	22 44		22 35		22 35		22 41	22 50				22 50		22 57			23 05

b arr. 2219 c arr. 2249

Table 186 Mondays to Fridays

Brighton - London, Bedford

		SN 1	SN ◇1	SN 1	SN ◇1	FC 1	FC 1	GX 1	GX 1	SN 1	SN 1	GW 1	SN 1	SN ◇1	SN ◇1	GX 1	SN 1
Brighton 10	d		22 19		22 00	22 07	22 33								23 02		
Hove 2	d																
Preston Park	d				22 04	22 11	22 37								23 06		
Hassocks 4	d				22 10	22 17	22 43								23 12		
Burgess Hill 4	d				22 14	22 21	22 47								23 16		
Lewes 4	d													22 40			
Wivelsfield 4	d				22 16	22 23	22 49							22 54	23 19		
Haywards Heath 3	a				22 21	22 28	22 54							22 58	23 23		
	d				22 22	22 32	22 54							22 59	23 24		
Balcombe	d					22 37	23 00										
Horsham 4	d			22 02													23 02
Littlehaven	d			22 05													23 05
Faygate	d																
Ifield	d			22 11													23 11
Crawley	d			22 14													23 14
Three Bridges 4	a			22 18	22 32	22 42	23 05							23 08	23 33		23 18
	d			22 19	22 32	22 42	23 12							23 08	23 47		23 18
Gatwick Airport 10	a			22 23	22 37	22 46	23 16							23 12	23 52		23 22
	d			22 24	22 38	22 46	23 16	22 50	23 05			23 18		23 13	23 53	23 20	23 23
Horley 4	d			22 27											23 56		23 26
Salfords	d			22 31													23 29
Earlswood (Surrey)	d			22 34													23 33
Tonbridge 4	d										23 17						
Leigh (Kent)	d										23 21						
Penshurst	d										23 25						
Edenbridge	d										23 31						
Godstone	d										23 38						
Nutfield	d										23 43						
Reigate	d																
Redhill 5	a			22 37	22 45						23 49	23 25			00 03		23 36
	d			22 38	22 46							23 28			00 03		23 37
Merstham	d			22 42													23 41
Coulsdon South	d			22 47													23 46
Purley 4	d			22 50											00 11		23 49
East Croydon ⇌	a	22 43	22 52	22 55	22 59	23 02	23 32			23 13			23 19	23 30	00 16		23 55
	d	22 44	22 54	22 56	23 00	23 02	23 32			23 14			23 20	23 30	00 17		23 58
Norwood Junction 2	a																
London Bridge 4 ⊖	a					23 17	23 47										
London Blackfriars 3 ⊖	a																
City Thameslink 3	a																
Farringdon 3 ⊖	a																
St Pancras International 15 ⊖	a																
St Albans City	a																
Luton Airport Parkway 4	a																
Luton 7	a																
Bedford 10	a																
Clapham Junction 10	d	22 56	23 04	23 07	23 11					23 26			23 33	23 42	00 30		00 11
London Victoria 15 ⊖	a	23 05	23 13	23 15	23 20			23 20	23 35	23 35			23 40	23 52	00 37	23 55	00 18

b arr. 2349

Table 186

Mondays to Fridays

Brighton - London, Bedford

		GX 1	FC 1	GX 1	FC 1
Brighton 10	d		23 11		23 37
Hove 2	d				
Preston Park	d				23 41
Hassocks 3	d		23 19		23 47
Burgess Hill 4	d		23 23		23 51
Lewes 4	d				
Wivelsfield 4	d				23 53
Haywards Heath 3	a		23 27		23 58
	d		23 28		23 59
Balcombe	d				00 04
Horsham 4	d				
Littlehaven	d				
Faygate	d				
Ifield	d				
Crawley	d				
Three Bridges 4	a		23 38		00 10
	d		23 38		00 10
Gatwick Airport 10	a		23 42		00 14
	d	23 35	23 43	23 50	00 15
Horley 4	d				
Salfords	d				
Earlswood (Surrey)	d				
Tonbridge 4	d				
Leigh (Kent)	d				
Penshurst	d				
Edenbridge	d				
Godstone	d				
Nutfield	d				
Reigate	d				
Redhill 5	a				00 22
	d				00 22
Merstham	d				
Coulsdon South	d				
Purley 4	d				
East Croydon ⇌	a		00 02		00 35
	d		00 04		00 36
Norwood Junction 2	a				
London Bridge 4 ⊖	a		00 19		00 52
London Blackfriars 3 ⊖	a				
City Thameslink 3	a				
Farringdon 3 ⊖	a				
St Pancras International 15 ⊖	a				
St Albans City	a				
Luton Airport Parkway 4	a				
Luton 7	a				
Bedford 10	a				
Clapham Junction 10	d				
London Victoria 15 ⊖	a	00 10		00 25	

Table 186

Saturdays

Brighton - London, Bedford

		SN 1	SN ◇1	GX 1	FC 1	GX 1	GX 1	FC 1	GX 1	GX 1	SN	GX 1	SN 1	GX 1	SN 1	FC 1	SN 1	FC 1	SN 1	FC 1	GX 1	FC 1
Brighton 10	d		23p02		23p11			23p37														
Hove 2	d																					
Preston Park	d		23p06					23p41														
Hassocks 3	d		23p12		23p19			23p47														
Burgess Hill 4	d		23p16		23p23			23p51														
Lewes 4	d																					
Wivelsfield 4	d		23p19					23p53														
Haywards Heath 3	a		23p23		23p27			23p58														
	d		23p24		23p28			23p59														
Balcombe	d							00 04														
Horsham 4	d	23p02																				
Littlehaven	d	23p05																				
Faygate	d																					
Ifield	d	23p11																				
Crawley	d	23p14																				
Three Bridges 4	a	23p18	23p33		23p38			00 10														
	d	23p18	23p47		23p38			00 10							01 59	02 25	02 55	03 25	03 55	04 25		04 55
Gatwick Airport 10	a	23p22	23p52		23p42			00 14							02 03	02 29	02 59	03 29	03 59	04 29		04 59
	d	23p23	23p53	23p35	23p43	23p50	00 05	00 15	00 20	00 35		00 50	01 05	01 35	02 05	02 30	03 05	03 30	04 05	04 30	04 35	05 00
Horley 4	d	23p26	23p56										01 07		02 07		03 07		04 07			
Salfords	d	23p29																				
Earlswood (Surrey)	d	23p33																				
Tonbridge 4	d																					
Leigh (Kent)	d																					
Penshurst	d																					
Edenbridge	d																					
Godstone	d																					
Nutfield	d																					
Reigate	d																					
Redhill 5	a	23p36	00 03					00 22											04 14			
	d	23p37	00 03					00 22											04 14			
Merstham	d	23p41																				
Coulsdon South	d	23p46																				
Purley 4	d	23p49	00 11										01 22		02 22		03 22		04 22			
East Croydon ⇌	a	23p55	00 16		00 02			00 35					01 27		02 27	02 47	03 27	03 47	04 27	04 47		05 17
	d	23p58	00 17		00 04			00 36			00 49		01 28		02 28	02 47	03 28	03 47	04 28	04 47		05 17
Norwood Junction 2	a																					
London Bridge 4 ⊖	a				00 19			00 52								03 12		04 12		05 12		05 42
London Blackfriars 3 ⊖	a																					
City Thameslink 3	a																					
Farringdon 3 ⊖	a																					
St Pancras International 15 ⊖	a																					
St Albans City	a																					
Luton Airport Parkway 4	a																					
Luton 7	a																					
Bedford 10	a																					
Clapham Junction 10	d	00 11	00 30								01 01		01 41		02 41		03 41		04 41			
London Victoria 15 ⊖	a	00 18	00 37	00 10		00 25	00 40		00 55	01 10	01 08	01 25	01 49	02 20	02 49		03 49		04 49		05 10	

Table 186

Saturdays

Brighton - London, Bedford

Station		SN 1	GX 1	FC 1	SN 1	GW 1	SN ◇1	GX 1	SN ◇1	SN 1	FC 1	SN 1	GW 1	GX 1
Brighton 10	d	03 50							05 21		05 24			
Hove 2	d													
Preston Park	d										05 28			
Hassocks 4	d										05 34			
Burgess Hill 4	d								05 31		05 38			
Lewes 4	d											05 25		
Wivelsfield 4	d										05 40			
Haywards Heath 3	a	04 24							05 36		05 45	05 40		
	d	04 25							05 37		05 45	05 49		
Balcombe	d										05 51			
Horsham 4	d									05 30				
Littlehaven	d									05 33				
Faygate	d													
Ifield	d									05 39				
Crawley	d									05 43				
Three Bridges 4	a	04 45							05 46	05 46	05 56	05 59		
	d	04 58		05 20			05 33		05 46	05 48	05 56	05 59		
Gatwick Airport 10	a	05 02		05 24			05 37		05 50	05 52	06 00	06 03		
	d	05 03	05 20	05 26		05 31	05 38	05 50	05 53	05 53	06 01		06 03	06 05
Horley 4	d	05 05					05 40			05 56				
Salfords	d									06 00				
Earlswood (Surrey)	d									06 03				
Tonbridge 4	d				05 24									
Leigh (Kent)	d				05 28									
Penshurst	d				05 32									
Edenbridge	d				05 38									
Godstone	d				05 45									
Nutfield	d				05 50									
Reigate	d													
Redhill 5	a				05 55	05 38	05 47			06 06			06 12	
	d					05 41	05 48			06 07			06 13	
Merstham	d									06 11				
Coulsdon South	d									06 16				
Purley 4	d	05 24					05 58			06 19				
East Croydon ⇌	a	05 29		05 42			06 02		06 10	06 24	06 16			
	d	05 29		05 42			06 07		06 11	06 25	06 17			
Norwood Junction 2	a									06 29				
London Bridge 4 ⊖	a			05 57						06 43	06 32			
London Blackfriars 3 ⊖	a													
City Thameslink 3	a													
Farringdon 3 ⊖	a													
St Pancras International 15 ⊖	a													
St Albans City	a													
Luton Airport Parkway 4	a													
Luton 7	a													
Bedford 10	a													
Clapham Junction 10	d	05 49					06 18		06 22					
London Victoria 15 ⊖	a	05 58	05 55				06 26	06 20	06 30					06 35

Table 186

Saturdays

Brighton - London, Bedford

Station		GX 1	SN 1	SN ◇1	SN ◇1	SN ◇1	FC 1	SN 1	SN	GX 1	GX 1	SN 1	SN ◇1	SN ◇1
Brighton 10	d			05 50		05 56	06 04						06 10	
Hove 2	d				05 54									06 21
Preston Park	d					06 00							06 14	
Hassocks 4	d					06 06							06 20	
Burgess Hill 4	d						06 14						06 24	
Lewes 4	d													
Wivelsfield 4	d					06 11							06 26	
Haywards Heath 3	a			06 02	06 07	06 15	06 18						06 31	06 35
	d			06 11	<	06 16	06 18						06 40	<
Balcombe	d													
Horsham 4	d		06 00									06 30		
Littlehaven	d		06 03									06 33		
Faygate	d													
Ifield	d		06 09									06 39		
Crawley	d		06 13									06 43		
Three Bridges 4	a		06 16	06 20		06 25						06 46	06 49	
	d		06 18	06 20		06 31						06 48	06 49	
Gatwick Airport 10	a		06 22	06 24		06 35	06 30					06 52	06 53	
	d	06 20	06 23	06 25		06 38	06 31			06 35	06 50	06 53	06 55	
Horley 4	d		06 26									06 56		
Salfords	d		06 30											
Earlswood (Surrey)	d		06 33											
Tonbridge 4	d							06 19						
Leigh (Kent)	d							06 23						
Penshurst	d							06 27						
Edenbridge	d							06 33						
Godstone	d							06 40						
Nutfield	d							06 45						
Reigate	d													
Redhill 5	a		06 36					06 50				07 02		
	d		06 37					06 51				07 07		
Merstham	d		06 41									07 11		
Coulsdon South	d		06 46					06 58				07 16		
Purley 4	d		06 49					07 02				07 19		
East Croydon ⇌	a		06 54	06 40		06 53	06 46	07 07				07 24	07 10	
	d		06 55	06 41		06 53	06 47	07 07				07 25	07 11	
Norwood Junction 2	a		07 00					07 12				07 29		
London Bridge 4 ⊖	a		07 13				07 02	07 25				07 43		
London Blackfriars 3 ⊖	a													
City Thameslink 3	a													
Farringdon 3 ⊖	a													
St Pancras International 15 ⊖	a													
St Albans City	a													
Luton Airport Parkway 4	a													
Luton 7	a													
Bedford 10	a													
Clapham Junction 10	d			06 50		07 03			07 11				07 20	
London Victoria 15 ⊖	a	06 50		06 57		07 09			07 18	07 05	07 20		07 27	

Table 186

Brighton - London, Bedford

		GW	GX	SN	FC	SN ◇	SN ◇	FC	SN	GW	GX	SN	SN ◇	SN ◇	SN ◇
Brighton	d				06 24	06 49		06 37							06 55
Hove	d													06 51	
Preston Park	d				06 28			06 41							06 58
Hassocks	d				06 34			06 47							07 05
Burgess Hill	d				06 38			06 51						07 02	07 08
Lewes	d												06 50		
Wivelsfield	d				06 40			06 53							07 11
Haywards Heath	a				06 45			06 58					07 05	07 08	07 15
	d				06 45			07 02					07 13	<	07 16
Balcombe	d				06 51										
Horsham	d						06 52					07 00			
Littlehaven	d											07 03			
Faygate	d														
Ifield	d											07 09			
Crawley	d						07 01					07 13			
Three Bridges	a				06 56		07 04	07 11				07 16			07 25
	d				06 56		07 05	07 12				07 18			07 31
Gatwick Airport	a				07 00		07 09	07 16				07 22	07 24		07 35
	d	07 03	07 05		07 01		07 10	07 16			07 20	07 23	07 25		07 38
Horley	d											07 26			
Salfords	d											07 30			
Earlswood (Surrey)	d											07 33			
Tonbridge	d														
Leigh (Kent)	d														
Penshurst	d														
Edenbridge	d														
Godstone	d														
Nutfield	d														
Reigate	d								07 14	07 18					
Redhill	a	07 10					07 17		07 18	07 25		07 36			
	d	07 13					07 18		07 21			07 37			
Merstham	d								07 25			07 41			
Coulsdon South	d								07 30			07 46			
Purley	d								07 34			07 49			
East Croydon	a			07 13	07 16	07 23	07 29	07 32	07 39			07 54	07 40		07 53
	d			07 14	07 17	07 24	07 30	07 32	07 39			07 55	07 41		07 53
Norwood Junction	a								07 44			08 00			
London Bridge ⊖	a				07 32			07 47	07 57			08 13			
London Blackfriars ⊖	a														
City Thameslink	a														
Farringdon ⊖	a														
St Pancras International ⊖	a														
St Albans City	a														
Luton Airport Parkway	a														
Luton	a														
Bedford	a														
Clapham Junction	d			07 26		07 33	07 39						07 50		08 03
London Victoria ⊖	a		07 35	07 32		07 40	07 46				07 50		07 57		08 09

Table 186

Brighton - London, Bedford

		GX	SN	FC	SN ◇	SN ◇	FC	SN	GX	SN	SN ◇	SN	GW	GX	SN	FC
Brighton	d			07 04	07 19		07 07									07 34
Hove	d										07 22					
Preston Park	d						07 11									
Hassocks	d						07 17									
Burgess Hill	d						07 21									
Lewes	d											07 20				
Wivelsfield	d						07 23					07 34				
Haywards Heath	a			07 18			07 28				07 35	07 40				07 48
	d			07 18			07 32				07 43	<				07 48
Balcombe	d						07 37									
Horsham	d					07b20				07 30						
Littlehaven	d									07 33						
Faygate	d															
Ifield	d									07 39						
Crawley	d					07 29				07 43						
Three Bridges	a					07 32	07 42			07 46						
	d					07 33	07 42			07 48						
Gatwick Airport	a			07 30		07 37	07 46			07 52	07 54					08 00
	d	07 35		07 31		07 38	07 46		07 50	07 53	07 55		08 03	08 05		08 01
Horley	d					07 41				07 56						
Salfords	d															
Earlswood (Surrey)	d															
Tonbridge	d							07 19								
Leigh (Kent)	d							07 23								
Penshurst	d							07 27								
Edenbridge	d							07 33								
Godstone	d							07 40								
Nutfield	d							07 45								
Reigate	d															
Redhill	a					07 47		07 50		08 02			08 10			
	d					07 48		07 51		08 07			08 13			
Merstham	d									08 11						
Coulsdon South	d							07 58		08 16						
Purley	d							08 02		08 19						
East Croydon	a		07 43	07 46	07 56	07 59	08 02	08 07		08 24	08 10				08 13	08 16
	d		07 44	07 47	07 56	08 00	08 02	08 07		08 25	08 11				08 14	08 17
Norwood Junction	a							08 12		08 29						
London Bridge ⊖	a			08 02			08 17	08 25		08 43						08 32
London Blackfriars ⊖	a															
City Thameslink	a															
Farringdon ⊖	a															
St Pancras International ⊖	a															
St Albans City	a															
Luton Airport Parkway	a															
Luton	a															
Bedford	a															
Clapham Junction	d		07 56		08 06	08 10					08 20				08 26	
London Victoria ⊖	a	08 05	08 02		08 12	08 16			08 20		08 27			08 35	08 32	

b arr. 0710

Table 186

Saturdays

Brighton - London, Bedford

		SN ◇1 🛒	SN ◇1	FC 1	SN 1	GW 1	GX 1 🛒	SN 1	SN ◇1	SN ◇1	SN ◇1	GX 1 🛒	SN 1	FC 1	SN ◇1 🛒	SN ◇1	FC 1
Brighton 10	d	07 49		07 37							07 55			08 04	08 19		08 07
Hove 2	d									07 51							
Preston Park	d			07 41							07 58						08 11
Hassocks 4	d			07 47							08 05						08 17
Burgess Hill 4	d			07 51						08 02	08 08						08 21
Lewes 4	d								07 50								
Wivelsfield 4	d			07 53							08 11						08 23
Haywards Heath 3	a			07 58					08 05	08 09	08 15			08 18			08 28
	d			08 02					08 13	<	08 16			08 18			08 32
Balcombe	d																08 37
Horsham 4	d		07b50					08 00								08c20	
Littlehaven	d							08 03									
Faygate	d																
Ifield	d							08 09									
Crawley	d		07 59					08 13								08 29	
Three Bridges 4	a		08 02	08 11				08 16			08 25					08 32	08 42
	d		08 03	08 12				08 18			08 31					08 33	08 42
Gatwick Airport 10	a		08 07	08 16				08 22	08 24		08 35			08 30		08 37	08 46
	d		08 08	08 16			08 20	08 23	08 25		08 38	08 35		08 31		08 38	08 46
Horley 4	d							08 26								08 41	
Salfords	d							08 30									
Earlswood (Surrey)	d							08 33									
Tonbridge 4	d																
Leigh (Kent)	d																
Penshurst	d																
Edenbridge	d																
Godstone	d																
Nutfield	d																
Reigate	d				08 14	08 19											
Redhill 5	a		08 15		08 18	08 25		08 36								08 47	
	d		08 16		08 19			08 37								08 48	
Merstham	d				08 23			08 41									
Coulsdon South	d				08 28			08 46									
Purley 4	d				08 32			08 49									
East Croydon ⇌	a	08 23	08 27	08 32	08 37			08 54	08 40		08 53		08 43	08 46	08 56	08 59	09 02
	d	08 24	08 28	08 32	08 37			08 55	08 41		08 53		08 44	08 47	08 56	09 00	09 02
Norwood Junction 2	a				08 42			09 00									
London Bridge 4 ⊖	a			08 47	08 55			09 13						09 02			09 17
London Blackfriars 3 ⊖	a																
City Thameslink 3	a																
Farringdon 3 ⊖	a																
St Pancras International 15 ⊖	a																
St Albans City	a																
Luton Airport Parkway 4	a																
Luton 7	a																
Bedford 10	a																
Clapham Junction 10	d	08 33	08 37						08 50		09 03		08 56		09 06	09 10	
London Victoria 15 ⊖	a	08 40	08 44				08 50		08 57		09 09	09 05	09 02		09 12	09 16	

b arr. 0740

c arr. 0810

Table 186

Saturdays

Brighton - London, Bedford

		SN 1	GX 1 🛒	SN 1	SN ◇1	SN 1	GW 1	GX 1 🛒	SN 1	FC 1	SN ◇1 🛒	SN ◇1 🛒	FC 1	SN 1	GW 1
Brighton 10	d									08 34	08 49		08 37		
Hove 2	d				08 21										
Preston Park	d												08 41		
Hassocks 4	d												08 47		
Burgess Hill 4	d												08 51		
Lewes 4	d					08 20									
Wivelsfield 4	d					08 34							08 53		
Haywards Heath 3	a				08 35	08 40				08 48			08 58		
	d				08 43	<				08 48			09 02		
Balcombe	d														
Horsham 4	d			08 30								08b50			
Littlehaven	d			08 33											
Faygate	d														
Ifield	d			08 39											
Crawley	d			08 43								08 59			
Three Bridges 4	a			08 46								09 02	09 11		
	d			08 48								09 03	09 12		
Gatwick Airport 10	a			08 52	08 54					09 00		09 07	09 16		
	d		08 50	08 53	08 55		09 03	09 05		09 01		09 08	09 16		
Horley 4	d			08 56											
Salfords	d														
Earlswood (Surrey)	d														
Tonbridge 4	d	08 19													
Leigh (Kent)	d	08 23													
Penshurst	d	08 27													
Edenbridge	d	08 33													
Godstone	d	08 40													
Nutfield	d	08 45													
Reigate	d													09 14	09 18
Redhill 5	a	08 50		09 02			09 10					09 15		09 18	09 25
	d	08 51		09 07			09 13					09 16		09 19	
Merstham	d			09 11										09 23	
Coulsdon South	d	08 58		09 16										09 28	
Purley 4	d	09 02		09 19										09 32	
East Croydon ⇌	a	09 07		09 24	09 10				09 13	09 16	09 23	09 27	09 32	09 37	
	d	09 07		09 25	09 11				09 14	09 17	09 24	09 28	09 32	09 37	
Norwood Junction 2	a	09 12		09 29										09 42	
London Bridge 4 ⊖	a	09 25		09 43						09 32			09 47	09 55	
London Blackfriars 3 ⊖	a														
City Thameslink 3	a														
Farringdon 3 ⊖	a														
St Pancras International 15 ⊖	a														
St Albans City	a														
Luton Airport Parkway 4	a														
Luton 7	a														
Bedford 10	a														
Clapham Junction 10	d				09 20				09 26		09 33	09 37			
London Victoria 15 ⊖	a		09 20		09 27			09 35	09 32		09 40	09 44			

b arr. 0840

Table 186

Saturdays

Brighton - London, Bedford

		GX 1 ✕	SN 1	SN ◇1	SN ◇1	SN ◇1	GX 1 ✕	SN 1	FC 1	SN ◇1 ✕	SN ◇1	FC 1	SN 1	GX 1 ✕	SN 1	SN ◇1	SN 1
Brighton 10	d					08 55			09 04	09 19		09 07					
Hove 2	d				08 51											09 21	
Preston Park	d					08 58						09 11					
Hassocks 4	d					09 05						09 17					
Burgess Hill 4	d				09 02	09 08						09 21					
Lewes 4	d			08 50													09 20
Wivelsfield 4	d					09 11						09 23					09 34
Haywards Heath 3	a			09 05	09 09	09 15			09 18			09 28				09 35	09 40
	d			09 13	<	09 16			09 18			09 32				09 43	<
Balcombe	d											09 37					
Horsham 4	d		09 00								09b20				09 30		
Littlehaven	d		09 03												09 33		
Faygate	d																
Ifield	d		09 09												09 39		
Crawley	d		09 13								09 29				09 43		
Three Bridges 4	a		09 16			09 25					09 32	09 42			09 46		
	d		09 18			09 31					09 33	09 42			09 48		
Gatwick Airport 10	a		09 22	09 24		09 35			09 30		09 37	09 46			09 52	09 54	
	d	09 20	09 23	09 25		09 38	09 35		09 31		09 38	09 46		09 50	09 53	09 55	
Horley 4	d		09 26								09 41				09 56		
Salfords	d		09 30														
Earlswood (Surrey)	d		09 33														
Tonbridge 4	d												09 19				
Leigh (Kent)	d												09 23				
Penshurst	d												09 27				
Edenbridge	d												09 33				
Godstone	d												09 40				
Nutfield	d												09 45				
Reigate	d																
Redhill 5	a		09 36								09 47		09 50		10 02		
	d		09 37								09 48		09 51		10 07		
Merstham	d		09 41												10 11		
Coulsdon South	d		09 46										09 58		10 16		
Purley 4	d		09 49										10 02		10 19		
East Croydon	a		09 54	09 41		09 53		09 43	09 46	09 56	09 59	10 02	10 07		10 24	10 10	
	d		09 55	09 42		09 53		09 44	09 47	09 56	10 00	10 02	10 07		10 25	10 11	
Norwood Junction 2	a		10 00										10 12		10 29		
London Bridge 4 ⊖	a		10 13						10 02			10 17	10 25		10 43		
London Blackfriars 3 ⊖	a																
City Thameslink 3	a																
Farringdon 3 ⊖	a																
St Pancras International 15 ⊖	a																
St Albans City	a																
Luton Airport Parkway 4	a																
Luton 7	a																
Bedford 10	a																
Clapham Junction 10	d			09 51		10 03		09 56		10 06	10 10					10 20	
London Victoria 15 ⊖	a	09 50		09 58		10 09	10 05	10 02		10 12	10 16			10 20		10 27	

b arr. 0910

Table 186

Saturdays

Brighton - London, Bedford

		GW 1	GX 1 ✕	SN 1	FC 1	SN ◇1 ✕	SN ◇1 ✕	FC 1	SN 1	GW 1	GX 1 ✕	SN ◇1	SN 1	SN ◇1	SN ◇1
Brighton 10	d				09 34	09 49		09 37							09 55
Hove 2	d													09 51	
Preston Park	d							09 41							09 58
Hassocks 4	d							09 47							10 05
Burgess Hill 4	d							09 51						10 02	10 08
Lewes 4	d											09 50			
Wivelsfield 4	d							09 53							10 11
Haywards Heath 3	a				09 48			09 58				10 05		10 08	10 15
	d				09 48			10 02				10 09		10 12	10 16
Balcombe	d														
Horsham 4	d						09b50						10 00		
Littlehaven	d												10 03		
Faygate	d														
Ifield	d												10 09		
Crawley	d						09 59						10 13		
Three Bridges 4	a						10 02	10 11					10 16		10 25
	d						10 03	10 12					10 18		10 31
Gatwick Airport 10	a				10 00		10 07	10 16				10 21	10 22	10 25	10 35
	d	10 03	10 05		10 01		10 08	10 16			10 20	10 22	10 23	10 26	10 38
Horley 4	d												10 26		
Salfords	d												10 30		
Earlswood (Surrey)	d												10 33		
Tonbridge 4	d														
Leigh (Kent)	d														
Penshurst	d														
Edenbridge	d														
Godstone	d														
Nutfield	d														
Reigate	d								10 14	10 19					
Redhill 5	a	10 10					10 15		10 18	10 25			10 36		
	d	10 13					10 16		10 19				10 37		
Merstham	d								10 23				10 41		
Coulsdon South	d								10 28				10 46		
Purley 4	d								10 32				10 49		
East Croydon	a			10 13	10 16	10 23	10 27	10 32	10 37			10 38	10 54	10 42	10 53
	d			10 14	10 17	10 24	10 28	10 32	10 37			10 38	10 55	10 42	10 53
Norwood Junction 2	a								10 42				11 00		
London Bridge 4 ⊖	a				10 32			10 47	10 55				11 13		
London Blackfriars 3 ⊖	a														
City Thameslink 3	a														
Farringdon 3 ⊖	a														
St Pancras International 15 ⊖	a														
St Albans City	a														
Luton Airport Parkway 4	a														
Luton 7	a														
Bedford 10	a														
Clapham Junction 10	d			10 26		10 33	10 37					10 48		10 52	11 03
London Victoria 15 ⊖	a		10 35	10 32		10 40	10 44				10 50	10 56		10 59	11 09

b arr. 0940

Table 186

Saturdays

Brighton - London, Bedford

		GX ■ ⌶	SN ■	FC ■	SN ◇■ ⌶	SN ◇■	FC ■	SN ■	GX ■ ⌶	SN ■	SN ◇■	SN ■	SN	GW ■	GX ■ ⌶	SN ■
Brighton	d			10 04	10 19		10 07									
Hove	d										10 21					
Preston Park	d						10 11									
Hassocks	d						10 17									
Burgess Hill	d						10 21									
Lewes	d											10 20				
Wivelsfield	d						10 23					10 34				
Haywards Heath	a			10 18			10 28				10 35	10 40				
	d			10 18			10 32				10 43	<				
Balcombe	d						10 37									
Horsham	d					10b20				10 30						
Littlehaven	d									10 33						
Faygate	d															
Ifield	d									10 39						
Crawley	d					10 29				10 43						
Three Bridges	a					10 32	10 42			10 46						
	d					10 33	10 42			10 48						
Gatwick Airport	a			10 30		10 37	10 46			10 52	10 54					
	d	10 35		10 31		10 38	10 46		10 50	10 53	10 55			11 03	11 05	
Horley	d					10 41				10 56						
Salfords	d															
Earlswood (Surrey)	d															
Tonbridge	d							10 19								
Leigh (Kent)	d							10 23								
Penshurst	d							10 27								
Edenbridge	d							10 33								
Godstone	d							10 40								
Nutfield	d							10 45								
Reigate	d															
Redhill	a					10 47		10 50		11 02				11 10		
	d					10 48		10 51		11 07				11 13		
Merstham	d									11 11						
Coulsdon South	d							10 58		11 16						
Purley	d							11 02		11 19						
East Croydon	a		10 43	10 46	10 56	10 59	11 02	11 07		11 24	11 10					11 13
	d		10 44	10 47	10 56	11 00	11 02	11 07		11 25	11 11					11 14
Norwood Junction	a							11 12		11 29						
London Bridge	a			11 02			11 17	11 25		11 43						
London Blackfriars	a															
City Thameslink	a															
Farringdon	a															
St Pancras International	a															
St Albans City	a															
Luton Airport Parkway	a															
Luton	a															
Bedford	a															
Clapham Junction	d		10 56		11 06	11 10					11 20		11 41			11 26
London Victoria	a	11 05	11 02		11 12	11 16			11 20		11 27		11 48		11 35	11 32

b arr. 1010

Table 186

Saturdays

Brighton - London, Bedford

		FC ■	SN ◇■ ⌶	SN ◇■ ⌶	FC ■	SN ■	GW ■	GX ■ ⌶	SN ■	SN ◇■	SN ◇■	SN ◇■	GX ■ ⌶	SN ■	FC ■	SN ◇■ ⌶	SN ◇■
Brighton	d	10 34	10 49		10 37							10 55			11 04	11 19	
Hove	d										10 51						
Preston Park	d				10 41							10 58					
Hassocks	d				10 47							11 05					
Burgess Hill	d				10 51						11 02	11 08					
Lewes	d									10 50							
Wivelsfield	d				10 53							11 11					
Haywards Heath	a	10 48			10 58					11 05	11 09	11 15			11 18		
	d	10 48			11 02					11 13	<	11 16			11 18		
Balcombe	d																
Horsham	d			10b50					11 00								11c20
Littlehaven	d								11 03								
Faygate	d																
Ifield	d								11 09								
Crawley	d			10 59					11 13								11 29
Three Bridges	a			11 02	11 11				11 16			11 25					11 32
	d			11 03	11 12				11 18			11 31					11 33
Gatwick Airport	a	11 00		11 07	11 16				11 22	11 24		11 35			11 30		11 37
	d	11 01		11 08	11 16			11 20	11 23	11 25		11 38	11 35		11 31		11 38
Horley	d								11 26								11 41
Salfords	d								11 30								
Earlswood (Surrey)	d								11 33								
Tonbridge	d																
Leigh (Kent)	d																
Penshurst	d																
Edenbridge	d																
Godstone	d																
Nutfield	d																
Reigate	d					11 14	11 18										
Redhill	a			11 15		11 18	11 25		11 36								11 47
	d			11 16		11 19			11 37								11 48
Merstham	d					11 23			11 41								
Coulsdon South	d					11 28			11 46								
Purley	d					11 32			11 49								
East Croydon	a	11 16	11 23	11 27	11 32	11 37			11 54	11 40		11 53		11 43	11 46	11 56	11 59
	d	11 17	11 24	11 28	11 32	11 37			11 55	11 41		11 53		11 44	11 47	11 56	12 00
Norwood Junction	a					11 42			12 00								
London Bridge	a	11 32			11 47	11 55			12 13						12 02		
London Blackfriars	a																
City Thameslink	a																
Farringdon	a																
St Pancras International	a																
St Albans City	a																
Luton Airport Parkway	a																
Luton	a																
Bedford	a																
Clapham Junction	d		11 33	11 37						11 50		12 03		11 56		12 06	12 10
London Victoria	a		11 40	11 44				11 50		11 57		12 09	12 05	12 02		12 12	12 16

b arr. 1040

c arr. 1110

Table 186

Saturdays

Brighton - London, Bedford

		FC 1	SN 1	GX 1 ✠	SN 1	SN ◇1	SN 1	GW 1	GX 1 ✠	SN 1	FC 1	SN ◇1 ✠	SN ◇1 ✠	FC 1	SN 1	GW 1
Brighton 10	d	11 07									11 34	11 49		11 37		
Hove 2	d					11 21										
Preston Park	d	11 11												11 41		
Hassocks 4	d	11 17												11 47		
Burgess Hill 4	d	11 21												11 51		
Lewes 4	d						11 20									
Wivelsfield 4	d	11 23					11 34							11 53		
Haywards Heath 3	a	11 28				11 35	11 40				11 48			11 58		
	d	11 32				11 43	<				11 48			12 02		
Balcombe	d	11 37														
Horsham 4	d				11 30								11b50			
Littlehaven	d				11 33											
Faygate	d															
Ifield	d				11 39											
Crawley	d				11 43								11 59			
Three Bridges 4	a	11 42			11 46								12 02	12 11		
	d	11 42			11 48								12 03	12 12		
Gatwick Airport 10	a	11 46			11 52	11 54					12 00		12 07	12 16		
	d	11 46		11 50	11 53	11 55		12 03	12 05		12 01		12 08	12 16		
Horley 4	d				11 56											
Salfords	d															
Earlswood (Surrey)	d															
Tonbridge 4	d		11 19													
Leigh (Kent)	d		11 23													
Penshurst	d		11 27													
Edenbridge	d		11 33													
Godstone	d		11 40													
Nutfield	d		11 45													
Reigate	d														12 14	12 19
Redhill 5	a		11 50		12 02			12 10					12 15		12 18	12 25
	d		11 51		12 07			12 13					12 16		12 19	
Merstham	d				12 11										12 23	
Coulsdon South	d		11 58		12 16										12 28	
Purley 4	d		12 02		12 19										12 32	
East Croydon	a	12 02	12 07		12 24	12 10				12 13	12 16	12 23	12 27	12 32	12 37	
	d	12 02	12 07		12 25	12 11				12 14	12 17	12 24	12 28	12 32	12 37	
Norwood Junction 2	a		12 12		12 29										12 42	
London Bridge 4 ⊖	a	12 17	12 25		12 43						12 32			12 47	12 55	
London Blackfriars 3 ⊖	a															
City Thameslink 3	a															
Farringdon 3 ⊖	a															
St Pancras International 15 ⊖	a															
St Albans City	a															
Luton Airport Parkway 4	a															
Luton 7	a															
Bedford 10	a															
Clapham Junction 10	d					12 20				12 26		12 33	12 37			
London Victoria 15 ⊖	a			12 20		12 27			12 35	12 32		12 40	12 44			

b arr. 1140

Table 186

Saturdays

Brighton - London, Bedford

		GX 1 ✠	SN 1	SN ◇1	SN ◇1	SN ◇1	GX 1 ✠	SN 1	FC 1	SN ◇1 ✠	SN ◇1	FC 1	SN 1	GX 1 ✠	SN 1	SN ◇1	SN 1
Brighton 10	d					11 55			12 04	12 19		12 07					
Hove 2	d				11 51											12 21	
Preston Park	d					11 58						12 11					
Hassocks 4	d					12 05						12 17					
Burgess Hill 4	d				12 02	12 08						12 21					
Lewes 4	d			11 50													12 20
Wivelsfield 4	d					12 11						12 23					12 34
Haywards Heath 3	a			12 05	12 09	12 15			12 18			12 28				12 35	12 40
	d			12 13	<	12 16			12 18			12 32				12 43	<
Balcombe	d											12 37					
Horsham 4	d		12 00								12b20				12 30		
Littlehaven	d		12 03												12 33		
Faygate	d																
Ifield	d		12 09												12 39		
Crawley	d		12 13								12 29				12 43		
Three Bridges 4	a		12 16			12 25					12 32	12 42			12 46		
	d		12 18			12 31					12 33	12 42			12 48		
Gatwick Airport 10	a		12 22	12 24		12 35			12 30		12 37	12 46			12 52	12 54	
	d	12 20	12 23	12 25		12 38	12 35		12 31		12 38	12 46		12 50	12 53	12 55	
Horley 4	d		12 26								12 41				12 56		
Salfords	d		12 30														
Earlswood (Surrey)	d		12 33														
Tonbridge 4	d												12 19				
Leigh (Kent)	d												12 23				
Penshurst	d												12 27				
Edenbridge	d												12 33				
Godstone	d												12 40				
Nutfield	d												12 45				
Reigate	d																
Redhill 5	a		12 36								12 47		12 50		13 02		
	d		12 37								12 48		12 51		13 07		
Merstham	d		12 41												13 11		
Coulsdon South	d		12 46										12 58		13 16		
Purley 4	d		12 49										13 02		13 19		
East Croydon	a		12 54	12 40		12 53		12 43	12 46	12 56	12 59	13 02	13 07		13 24	13 10	
	d		12 55	12 41		12 53		12 44	12 47	12 56	13 00	13 02	13 07		13 25	13 11	
Norwood Junction 2	a		13 00										13 12		13 29		
London Bridge 4 ⊖	a		13 13						13 02			13 17	13 25		13 43		
London Blackfriars 3 ⊖	a																
City Thameslink 3	a																
Farringdon 3 ⊖	a																
St Pancras International 15 ⊖	a																
St Albans City	a																
Luton Airport Parkway 4	a																
Luton 7	a																
Bedford 10	a																
Clapham Junction 10	d			12 50		13 03		12 56		13 06	13 10					13 20	
London Victoria 15 ⊖	a	12 50		12 57		13 09	13 05	13 02		13 12	13 16			13 20		13 27	

b arr. 1210

Brighton - London, Bedford

		GW 1	GX 1 ⌶	SN 1	FC 1	SN ◇1 ⌶	SN ◇1 ⌶	FC 1	SN 1	GW 1	GX 1 ⌶	SN 1	SN ◇1	SN ◇1	SN ◇1
Brighton 10	d				12 34	12 49		12 37							12 55
Hove 2	d													12 51	
Preston Park	d							12 41							12 58
Hassocks 4	d							12 47							13 05
Burgess Hill 4	d							12 51						13 02	13 08
Lewes 4	d												12 50		
Wivelsfield 4	d							12 53							13 11
Haywards Heath 3	a				12 48			12 58					13 05	13 09	13 15
	d				12 48			13 02					13 13	<	13 16
Balcombe	d														
Horsham 4	d						12b50					13 00			
Littlehaven	d											13 03			
Faygate	d														
Ifield	d											13 09			
Crawley	d						12 59					13 13			
Three Bridges 4	a						13 02	13 11				13 16			13 25
	d						13 03	13 12				13 18			13 31
Gatwick Airport 10	a				13 00		13 07	13 16				13 22	13 24		13 35
	d	13 03	13 05		13 01		13 08	13 16			13 20	13 23	13 25		13 38
Horley 4	d											13 26			
Salfords	d											13 30			
Earlswood (Surrey)	d											13 33			
Tonbridge 4	d														
Leigh (Kent)	d														
Penshurst	d														
Edenbridge	d														
Godstone	d														
Nutfield	d														
Reigate	d								13 14	13 18					
Redhill 5	a	13 10					13 15		13 18	13 25		13 36			
	d	13 13					13 16		13 19			13 37			
Merstham	d								13 23			13 41			
Coulsdon South	d								13 28			13 46			
Purley 4	d								13 32			13 49			
East Croydon taxi	a			13 13	13 16	13 23	13 27	13 32	13 37			13 54	13 40		13 53
	d			13 14	13 17	13 24	13 28	13 32	13 37			13 55	13 41		13 53
Norwood Junction 2	a								13 42			14 00			
London Bridge 4 ⊖	a				13 32			13 47	13 55			14 13			
London Blackfriars 3 ⊖	a														
City Thameslink 3	a														
Farringdon 3 ⊖	a														
St Pancras International 15 ⊖	a														
St Albans City	a														
Luton Airport Parkway 4	a														
Luton 7	a														
Bedford 10	a														
Clapham Junction 10	d			13 26		13 33	13 37						13 50		14 03
London Victoria 15 ⊖	a		13 35	13 32		13 40	13 44				13 50		13 57		14 09

b arr. 1240

Table 186

Saturdays

Brighton - London, Bedford

		GX 1 ⌶	SN 1	FC 1	SN ◇1 ⌶	SN ◇1	FC 1	SN 1	GX 1 ⌶	SN 1	SN ◇1	SN 1	GW 1	GX 1 ⌶	SN 1
Brighton 10	d			13 04	13 19		13 07								
Hove 2	d										13 21				
Preston Park	d						13 11								
Hassocks 4	d						13 17								
Burgess Hill 4	d						13 21								
Lewes 4	d											13 20			
Wivelsfield 4	d						13 23					13 34			
Haywards Heath 3	a			13 18			13 28				13 35	13 40			
	d			13 18			13 32				13 43	<			
Balcombe	d						13 37								
Horsham 4	d					13b20				13 30					
Littlehaven	d									13 33					
Faygate	d														
Ifield	d									13 39					
Crawley	d					13 29				13 43					
Three Bridges 4	a					13 32	13 42			13 46					
	d					13 33	13 42			13 48					
Gatwick Airport 10	a			13 30		13 37	13 46			13 52	13 54				
	d	13 35		13 31		13 38	13 46		13 50	13 53	13 55		14 03	14 05	
Horley 4	d					13 41				13 56					
Salfords	d														
Earlswood (Surrey)	d														
Tonbridge 4	d							13 19							
Leigh (Kent)	d							13 23							
Penshurst	d							13 27							
Edenbridge	d							13 33							
Godstone	d							13 40							
Nutfield	d							13 45							
Reigate	d														
Redhill 5	a					13 47		13 50		14 02			14 10		
	d					13 48		13 51		14 07			14 13		
Merstham	d									14 11					
Coulsdon South	d							13 58		14 16					
Purley 4	d							14 02		14 19					
East Croydon taxi	a		13 43	13 46	13 56	13 59	14 02	14 07		14 24	14 10				14 13
	d		13 44	13 47	13 56	14 00	14 02	14 07		14 25	14 11				14 14
Norwood Junction 2	a							14 12		14 29					
London Bridge 4 ⊖	a			14 02			14 17	14 25		14 43					
London Blackfriars 3 ⊖	a														
City Thameslink 3	a														
Farringdon 3 ⊖	a														
St Pancras International 15 ⊖	a														
St Albans City	a														
Luton Airport Parkway 4	a														
Luton 7	a														
Bedford 10	a														
Clapham Junction 10	d		13 56		14 06	14 10					14 20				14 26
London Victoria 15 ⊖	a	14 05	14 02		14 12	14 16			14 20		14 27			14 35	14 32

b arr. 1310

Table 186

Saturdays

Brighton - London, Bedford

		FC	SN	SN	FC	SN	GW	GX	SN	SN	SN	SN	GX	SN	FC	SN	SN
		■	◇■	◇■	■	■	■	■	■	◇■	◇■	◇■	■	■	■	◇■	◇■
Brighton	d	13 34	13 49		13 37							13 55			14 04	14 19	
Hove	d										13 51						
Preston Park	d				13 41							13 58					
Hassocks	d				13 47							14 05					
Burgess Hill	d				13 51						14 02	14 08					
Lewes	d									13 50							
Wivelsfield	d				13 53							14 11					
Haywards Heath	a	13 48			13 58					14 05	14 09	14 15			14 18		
	d	13 48			14 02					14 13	<	14 16			14 18		
Balcombe	d																
Horsham	d			13b50					14 00								14c20
Littlehaven	d								14 03								
Faygate	d																
Ifield	d								14 09								
Crawley	d			13 59					14 13								14 29
Three Bridges	a			14 02	14 11				14 16			14 25					14 32
	d			14 03	14 12				14 18			14 31					14 33
Gatwick Airport	a	14 00		14 07	14 16				14 22	14 24		14 35			14 30		14 37
	d	14 01		14 08	14 16			14 20	14 23	14 25		14 38	14 35		14 31		14 38
Horley	d								14 26								14 41
Salfords	d								14 30								
Earlswood (Surrey)	d								14 33								
Tonbridge	d																
Leigh (Kent)	d																
Penshurst	d																
Edenbridge	d																
Godstone	d																
Nutfield	d																
Reigate	d					14 14	14 19										
Redhill	a			14 15		14 18	14 25		14 36								14 47
	d			14 16		14 19			14 37								14 48
Merstham	d					14 23			14 41								
Coulsdon South	d					14 28			14 46								
Purley	d					14 32			14 49								
East Croydon	a	14 16	14 23	14 27	14 32	14 37			14 54	14 40		14 53		14 43	14 46	14 56	14 59
	d	14 17	14 24	14 28	14 32	14 37			14 55	14 41		14 53		14 44	14 47	14 56	15 00
Norwood Junction	a					14 42			15 00								
London Bridge ⊖	a	14 32			14 47	14 55			15 13						15 02		
London Blackfriars ⊖	a																
City Thameslink	a																
Farringdon ⊖	a																
St Pancras International ⊖	a																
St Albans City	a																
Luton Airport Parkway	a																
Luton	a																
Bedford	a																
Clapham Junction	d		14 33	14 37						14 50		15 03		14 56		15 06	15 10
London Victoria ⊖	a		14 40	14 44				14 50		14 57		15 09	15 05	15 02		15 12	15 16

b arr. 1340

c arr. 1410

Table 186

Saturdays

Brighton - London, Bedford

		FC	SN	GX	SN	SN	SN	GW	GX	SN	FC	SN	SN	FC	SN	GW
		■	■	■	■	◇■	■	■	■	■	■	◇■	◇■	■	■	■
Brighton	d	14 07									14 34	14 49		14 37		
Hove	d					14 21										
Preston Park	d	14 11												14 41		
Hassocks	d	14 17												14 47		
Burgess Hill	d	14 21												14 51		
Lewes	d						14 20									
Wivelsfield	d	14 23					14 34							14 53		
Haywards Heath	a	14 28				14 35	14 39				14 48			14 58		
	d	14 32				14 43	<				14 48			15 02		
Balcombe	d	14 37														
Horsham	d				14 30								14b50			
Littlehaven	d				14 33											
Faygate	d															
Ifield	d				14 39											
Crawley	d				14 43								14 59			
Three Bridges	a	14 42			14 46								15 02	15 11		
	d	14 42			14 48								15 03	15 12		
Gatwick Airport	a	14 46			14 52	14 54					15 00		15 07	15 16		
	d	14 46		14 50	14 53	14 55		15 03	15 05		15 01		15 08	15 16		
Horley	d				14 56											
Salfords	d															
Earlswood (Surrey)	d															
Tonbridge	d		14 19													
Leigh (Kent)	d		14 23													
Penshurst	d		14 27													
Edenbridge	d		14 33													
Godstone	d		14 40													
Nutfield	d		14 45													
Reigate	d														15 14	15 18
Redhill	a		14 50		15 02			15 10					15 15		15 18	15 25
	d		14 51		15 07			15 13					15 16		15 19	
Merstham	d				15 11										15 23	
Coulsdon South	d		14 58		15 16										15 28	
Purley	d		15 02		15 19										15 32	
East Croydon	a	15 02	15 07		15 24	15 10				15 13	15 16	15 23	15 27	15 32	15 37	
	d	15 02	15 07		15 25	15 11				15 14	15 17	15 24	15 28	15 32	15 37	
Norwood Junction	a		15 12		15 29										15 42	
London Bridge ⊖	a	15 17	15 25		15 43						15 32			15 47	15 55	
London Blackfriars ⊖	a															
City Thameslink	a															
Farringdon ⊖	a															
St Pancras International ⊖	a															
St Albans City	a															
Luton Airport Parkway	a															
Luton	a															
Bedford	a															
Clapham Junction	d					15 20				15 26		15 33	15 37			
London Victoria ⊖	a			15 20		15 27			15 35	15 32		15 40	15 44			

b arr. 1440

Table 186

Brighton - London, Bedford

Saturdays

		GX 1	SN 1	SN ◇1	SN ◇1	SN ◇1	GX 1	SN 1	FC 1	SN ◇1	SN ◇1	FC 1	SN 1	GX 1	SN 1	SN ◇1	SN 1
Brighton 10	d					14 55			15 04	15 19		15 07					
Hove 2	d				14 51											15 21	
Preston Park	d					14 58						15 11					
Hassocks 4	d					15 05						15 17					
Burgess Hill 4	d				15 02	15 08						15 21					
Lewes 4	d			14 50													15 20
Wivelsfield 4	d					15 11						15 23					15 34
Haywards Heath 3	a			15 05	15 09	15 15			15 18			15 28				15 35	15 40
	d			15 13	<	15 16			15 18			15 32				15 43	<
Balcombe	d											15 37					
Horsham 4	d		15 00								15b20				15 30		
Littlehaven	d		15 03												15 33		
Faygate	d																
Ifield	d		15 09												15 39		
Crawley	d		15 13								15 29				15 43		
Three Bridges 4	a		15 16			15 25					15 32	15 42			15 46		
	d		15 18			15 31					15 33	15 42			15 48		
Gatwick Airport 10	a		15 22	15 24		15 35			15 30		15 37	15 46			15 52	15 54	
	d	15 20	15 23	15 25		15 38	15 35		15 31		15 38	15 46		15 50	15 53	15 55	
Horley 4	d		15 26								15 41				15 56		
Salfords	d		15 30														
Earlswood (Surrey)	d		15 33														
Tonbridge 4	d												15 19				
Leigh (Kent)	d												15 23				
Penshurst	d												15 27				
Edenbridge	d												15 33				
Godstone	d												15 40				
Nutfield	d												15 45				
Reigate	d																
Redhill 5	a		15 36								15 47		15 50		16 02		
	d		15 37								15 48		15 51		16 07		
Merstham	d		15 41												16 11		
Coulsdon South	d		15 46										15 58		16 16		
Purley 4	d		15 49										16 02		16 19		
East Croydon	a		15 54	15 40		15 53		15 43	15 46	15 56	15 59	16 02	16 07		16 24	16 10	
	d		15 55	15 41		15 53		15 44	15 47	15 56	16 00	16 02	16 07		16 25	16 11	
Norwood Junction 2	a		16 00										16 12		16 29		
London Bridge 4 ⊖	a		16 13						16 02			16 17	16 25		16 43		
London Blackfriars 3 ⊖	a																
City Thameslink 3	a																
Farringdon 3 ⊖	a																
St Pancras International 15 ⊖	a																
St Albans City	a																
Luton Airport Parkway 4	a																
Luton 7	a																
Bedford 10	a																
Clapham Junction 10	d			15 50		16 03		15 56		16 06	16 10					16 20	
London Victoria 15 ⊖	a	15 50		15 57		16 09	16 05	16 02		16 12	16 16			16 20		16 27	

b arr. 1510

Table 186

Brighton - London, Bedford

Saturdays

		GW 1	GX 1	SN 1	FC 1	SN ◇1	SN ◇1	FC 1	SN 1	GW 1	GX 1	SN 1	SN ◇1	SN ◇1	SN ◇1
Brighton 10	d				15 34	15 49		15 37							15 55
Hove 2	d													15 51	
Preston Park	d							15 41							15 58
Hassocks 4	d							15 47							16 05
Burgess Hill 4	d							15 51						16 02	16 08
Lewes 4	d												15 50		
Wivelsfield 4	d							15 53							16 11
Haywards Heath 3	a				15 48			15 58					16 05	16 09	16 15
	d				15 48			16 02					16 13	<	16 16
Balcombe	d														
Horsham 4	d						15b50					16 00			
Littlehaven	d											16 03			
Faygate	d														
Ifield	d											16 09			
Crawley	d						15 59					16 13			
Three Bridges 4	a						16 02	16 11				16 16			16 25
	d						16 03	16 12				16 18			16 31
Gatwick Airport 10	a				16 00		16 07	16 16				16 22	16 24		16 35
	d	16 03	16 05		16 01		16 08	16 16			16 20	16 23	16 25		16 38
Horley 4	d											16 26			
Salfords	d											16 30			
Earlswood (Surrey)	d											16 33			
Tonbridge 4	d														
Leigh (Kent)	d														
Penshurst	d														
Edenbridge	d														
Godstone	d														
Nutfield	d														
Reigate	d								16 14	16 19					
Redhill 5	a	16 10					16 15		16 18	16 25		16 36			
	d	16 13					16 16		16 19			16 37			
Merstham	d								16 23			16 41			
Coulsdon South	d								16 28			16 46			
Purley 4	d								16 32			16 49			
East Croydon	a			16 13	16 16	16 23	16 27	16 32	16 37			16 54	16 40		16 53
	d			16 14	16 17	16 24	16 28	16 32	16 37			16 55	16 41		16 53
Norwood Junction 2	a								16 42			17 00			
London Bridge 4 ⊖	a				16 32			16 47	16 55			17 13			
London Blackfriars 3 ⊖	a														
City Thameslink 3	a														
Farringdon 3 ⊖	a														
St Pancras International 15 ⊖	a														
St Albans City	a														
Luton Airport Parkway 4	a														
Luton 7	a														
Bedford 10	a														
Clapham Junction 10	d			16 26		16 33	16 37						16 50		17 03
London Victoria 15 ⊖	a		16 35	16 32		16 40	16 44				16 50		16 57		17 09

b arr. 1540

Table 186

Saturdays

Brighton - London, Bedford

		GX 1 (trolley)		SN 1	FC 1	SN ◇1 (trolley)	SN ◇1	FC 1	SN 1	GX 1 (trolley)	SN 1		SN ◇1	SN 1	GW 1	GX 1 (trolley)
Brighton 10	d				16 04	16 19		16 07								
Hove 2	d												16 21			
Preston Park	d							16 11								
Hassocks 4	d							16 17								
Burgess Hill 4	d							16 21								
Lewes 4	d													16 20		
Wivelsfield 4	d							16 23						16 34		
Haywards Heath 3	a				16 18			16 28					16 35	16 40		
	d				16 18			16 32					16 43	<		
Balcombe	d							16 37								
Horsham 4	d						16b20				16 30					
Littlehaven	d										16 33					
Faygate	d															
Ifield	d										16 39					
Crawley	d						16 29				16 43					
Three Bridges 4	a						16 32	16 42			16 46					
	d						16 33	16 42			16 48					
Gatwick Airport 10	a				16 30		16 37	16 46			16 52		16 54			
	d	16 35			16 31		16 38	16 46		16 50	16 53		16 55		17 03	17 05
Horley 4	d						16 41				16 56					
Salfords	d															
Earlswood (Surrey)	d															
Tonbridge 4	d								16 19							
Leigh (Kent)	d								16 23							
Penshurst	d								16 27							
Edenbridge	d								16 33							
Godstone	d								16 40							
Nutfield	d								16 45							
Reigate	d															
Redhill 5	a						16 47		16 50		17 02				17 10	
	d						16 48		16 51		17 07				17 13	
Merstham	d										17 11					
Coulsdon South	d								16 58		17 16					
Purley 4	d								17 02		17 19					
East Croydon	a			16 43	16 46	16 56	16 59	17 02	17 07		17 24		17 10			
	d			16 44	16 47	16 56	17 00	17 02	17 07		17 25		17 11			
Norwood Junction 2	a								17 12		17 29					
London Bridge 4 ⊖	a				17 02			17 17	17 25		17 43					
London Blackfriars 3 ⊖	a															
City Thameslink 3	a															
Farringdon 3 ⊖	a															
St Pancras International 15 ⊖	a															
St Albans City	a															
Luton Airport Parkway 4	a															
Luton 7	a															
Bedford 10	a															
Clapham Junction 10	d			16 56		17 06	17 10						17 20			
London Victoria 15 ⊖	a	17 05		17 02		17 12	17 16			17 20			17 28			17 35

b arr. 1610

Table 186

Saturdays

Brighton - London, Bedford

		SN 1	FC 1	SN ◇1 (trolley)	SN ◇1 (trolley)	FC 1	SN 1	GW 1		GX 1 (trolley)	SN 1	SN ◇1	SN ◇1	SN ◇1	GX 1 (trolley)			SN 1	FC 1	SN ◇1 (trolley)
Brighton 10	d		16 34	16 49		16 37								16 55					17 04	17 19
Hove 2	d												16 51							
Preston Park	d					16 41								16 58						
Hassocks 4	d					16 47								17 05						
Burgess Hill 4	d					16 51							17 02	17 08						
Lewes 4	d											16 50								
Wivelsfield 4	d					16 53								17 11						
Haywards Heath 3	a		16 48			16 58						17 05	17 09	17 15					17 18	
	d		16 48			17 02						17 13	<	17 16					17 18	
Balcombe	d																			
Horsham 4	d				16b50						17 00									
Littlehaven	d										17 03									
Faygate	d																			
Ifield	d										17 09									
Crawley	d				16 59						17 13									
Three Bridges 4	a				17 02	17 11					17 16			17 25						
	d				17 03	17 12					17 18			17 31						
Gatwick Airport 10	a		17 00		17 07	17 16					17 22	17 24		17 35					17 30	
	d		17 01		17 08	17 16				17 20	17 23	17 25		17 38	17 35				17 31	
Horley 4	d										17 26									
Salfords	d										17 30									
Earlswood (Surrey)	d										17 33									
Tonbridge 4	d																			
Leigh (Kent)	d																			
Penshurst	d																			
Edenbridge	d																			
Godstone	d																			
Nutfield	d																			
Reigate	d						17 14	17 18												
Redhill 5	a				17 15		17 18	17 25			17 36									
	d				17 16		17 19				17 37									
Merstham	d						17 23				17 41									
Coulsdon South	d						17 28				17 46									
Purley 4	d						17 32				17 49									
East Croydon	a	17 13	17 16	17 23	17 27	17 32	17 37				17 54	17 40		17 53				17 43	17 46	17 56
	d	17 14	17 17	17 24	17 28	17 32	17 37				17 55	17 41		17 53				17 44	17 47	17 56
Norwood Junction 2	a						17 42				18 00									
London Bridge 4 ⊖	a		17 32			17 47	17 55				18 13								18 02	
London Blackfriars 3 ⊖	a																			
City Thameslink 3	a																			
Farringdon 3 ⊖	a																			
St Pancras International 15 ⊖	a																			
St Albans City	a																			
Luton Airport Parkway 4	a																			
Luton 7	a																			
Bedford 10	a																			
Clapham Junction 10	d	17 26		17 33	17 37							17 50		18 03				17 56		18 06
London Victoria 15 ⊖	a	17 32		17 40	17 44					17 50		17 57		18 09	18 05			18 02		18 12

b arr. 1640

Brighton - London, Bedford

Station		SN ◇1	FC 1	SN 1	GX 1 H		SN 1	SN ◇1	SN 1	GW 1	GX 1 H		SN 1	FC 1	SN ◇1 H	SN ◇1 H	FC 1	SN 1
Brighton 10	d		17 07											17 34	17 49		17 37	
Hove 2	d							17 21										
Preston Park	d		17 11														17 41	
Hassocks 4	d		17 17														17 47	
Burgess Hill 4	d		17 21														17 51	
Lewes 4	d								17 20									
Wivelsfield 4	d		17 23						17 34								17 53	
Haywards Heath 3	a		17 28					17 35	17 40					17 48			17 58	
	d		17 32					17 43	<					17 48			18 02	
Balcombe	d		17 37															
Horsham 4	d	17b20					17 30									17c50		
Littlehaven	d						17 33											
Faygate	d																	
Ifield	d						17 39											
Crawley	d	17 29					17 43									17 59		
Three Bridges 4	a	17 32	17 42				17 46									18 02	18 11	
	d	17 33	17 42				17 48									18 03	18 12	
Gatwick Airport 10	a	17 37	17 46				17 52	17 54						18 00		18 07	18 16	
	d	17 38	17 46		17 50		17 53	17 55		18 03	18 05			18 01		18 08	18 16	
Horley 4	d	17 41					17 56											
Salfords	d																	
Earlswood (Surrey)	d																	
Tonbridge 4	d			17 19														
Leigh (Kent)	d			17 23														
Penshurst	d			17 27														
Edenbridge	d			17 33														
Godstone	d			17 40														
Nutfield	d			17 45														
Reigate	d																	18 14
Redhill 5	a	17 47		17 50			18 02			18 10						18 15		18 18
	d	17 48		17 51			18 07			18 13						18 16		18 19
Merstham	d						18 11											18 23
Coulsdon South	d			17 58			18 16											18 28
Purley 4	d			18 02			18 19											18 32
East Croydon ⇌	a	17 59	18 02	18 07			18 24	18 10					18 13	18 16	18 23	18 27	18 32	18 37
	d	18 00	18 02	18 07			18 25	18 11					18 14	18 17	18 24	18 28	18 32	18 37
Norwood Junction 2	a			18 12			18 29											18 42
London Bridge 4 ⊖	a		18 17	18 25			18 43							18 32			18 47	18 55
London Blackfriars 3 ⊖	a																	
City Thameslink 3	a																	
Farringdon 3 ⊖	a																	
St Pancras International 15 ⊖	a																	
St Albans City	a																	
Luton Airport Parkway 4	a																	
Luton 7	a																	
Bedford 10	a																	
Clapham Junction 10	d	18 10						18 20					18 26		18 33	18 37		
London Victoria 15 ⊖	a	18 16			18 20			18 27			18 35		18 32		18 40	18 44		

b arr. 1710   c arr. 1740

Table 186

Saturdays

Brighton - London, Bedford

Station		GW 1		GX 1 H	SN 1	SN ◇1	SN ◇1	SN ◇1	GX 1 H		SN 1	FC 1	SN ◇1	SN ◇1	FC 1	SN 1	GX 1 H		SN ◇1	SN 1	SN 1
Brighton 10	d							17 55				18 04	18 19		18 07						
Hove 2	d						17 51												18 21		
Preston Park	d							17 58							18 11						
Hassocks 4	d							18 05							18 17						
Burgess Hill 4	d						18 02	18 08							18 21						
Lewes 4	d					17 50														18 20	
Wivelsfield 4	d							18 11							18 23					18 34	
Haywards Heath 3	a					18 05	18 09	18 15				18 18			18 28				18 35	18 40	
	d					18 13	<	18 16				18 18			18 32				18 43	<	
Balcombe	d														18 37						
Horsham 4	d				18 00									18b20							18 32
Littlehaven	d				18 03																18 35
Faygate	d																				
Ifield	d				18 09																18 41
Crawley	d				18 13									18 29							18 45
Three Bridges 4	a				18 16			18 25						18 32	18 42						18 48
	d				18 18			18 31						18 33	18 42						18 50
Gatwick Airport 10	a				18 22	18 24		18 35				18 30		18 37	18 46				18 54		18 54
	d			18 20	18 23	18 25		18 38	18 35			18 31		18 38	18 46		18 50		18 55		18 55
Horley 4	d				18 26									18 41							18 58
Salfords	d				18 30																
Earlswood (Surrey)	d				18 33																
Tonbridge 4	d															18 19					
Leigh (Kent)	d															18 23					
Penshurst	d															18 27					
Edenbridge	d															18 33					
Godstone	d															18 40					
Nutfield	d															18 45					
Reigate	d	18 19																			
Redhill 5	a	18 25			18 36									18 47		18 50					19 04
	d				18 37									18 48		18 51					19 07
Merstham	d				18 41																19 11
Coulsdon South	d				18 46											18 58					19 16
Purley 4	d				18 49											19 02					19 19
East Croydon ⇌	a				18 54	18 40		18 53			18 43	18 46	18 56	18 59	19 02	19 07			19 10		19 24
	d				18 55	18 41		18 53			18 44	18 47	18 56	19 00	19 02	19 07			19 11		19 25
Norwood Junction 2	a				19 00											19 12					
London Bridge 4 ⊖	a				19 13							19 02			19 17	19 25					
London Blackfriars 3 ⊖	a																				
City Thameslink 3	a																				
Farringdon 3 ⊖	a																				
St Pancras International 15 ⊖	a																				
St Albans City	a																				
Luton Airport Parkway 4	a																				
Luton 7	a																				
Bedford 10	a																				
Clapham Junction 10	d					18 50		19 03			18 56		19 06	19 10					19 20		19 37
London Victoria 15 ⊖	a			18 50		18 57		19 09	19 05		19 02		19 12	19 16			19 20		19 27		19 44

b arr. 1810

Table 186

Saturdays

Brighton - London, Bedford

		GW 1	GX 1	SN 1	SN 1	FC 1	SN ◇1	SN ◇1	FC 1	SN	GW 1	GX 1	SN 1	SN ◇1	SN ◇1	SN ◇1
Brighton 10	d					18 34	18 49		18 37							18 55
Hove 2	d														18 51	
Preston Park	d								18 41							18 58
Hassocks 4	d								18 47							19 05
Burgess Hill 4	d								18 51						19 02	19 08
Lewes 4	d													18 50		
Wivelsfield 4	d								18 53							19 11
Haywards Heath 3	a					18 48			18 58					19 05	19 09	19 15
	d					18 48			19 02					19 13	<	19 16
Balcombe	d															
Horsham 4	d							18b50					19 02			
Littlehaven	d												19 05			
Faygate	d															
Ifield	d												19 11			
Crawley	d							18 59					19 14			
Three Bridges 4	a							19 02	19 11				19 18			19 25
	d							19 03	19 12				19 18			19 31
Gatwick Airport 10	a					19 00		19 07	19 16				19 22	19 24		19 35
	d	19 03	19 05			19 01		19 08	19 16			19 20	19 23	19 25		19 38
Horley 4	d							19 11					19 26			
Salfords	d												19 30			
Earlswood (Surrey)	d												19 33			
Tonbridge 4	d			19 10												
Leigh (Kent)	d			19 14												
Penshurst	d			19 18												
Edenbridge	d			19 24												
Godstone	d			19 31												
Nutfield	d			19 36												
Reigate	d									19 14	19 18					
Redhill 5	a	19 10		19 45				19 17		19 18	19 25		19 36			
	d	19 13						19 18					19 37			
Merstham	d												19 41			
Coulsdon South	d												19 46			
Purley 4	d												19 49			
East Croydon	a				19 13	19 16	19 23	19 28	19 32				19 54	19 40		19 53
	d				19 14	19 17	19 24	19 29	19 32				19 57	19 41		19 53
Norwood Junction 2	a															
London Bridge 4 ⊖	a					19 32			19 47							
London Blackfriars 3 ⊖	a															
City Thameslink 3	a															
Farringdon 3 ⊖	a															
St Pancras International 15 ⊖	a															
St Albans City	a															
Luton Airport Parkway 4	a															
Luton 7	a															
Bedford 10	a															
Clapham Junction 10	d				19 26		19 33	19 40					20 09	19 50		20 03
London Victoria 15 ⊖	a		19 35		19 32		19 40	19 47				19 50	20 15	19 57		20 09

b arr. 1840

Table 186

Saturdays

Brighton - London, Bedford

		GX 1	SN 1	FC 1	SN ◇1	SN 1	FC 1	GX 1	SN ◇1	SN 1	SN 1	GW 1	GX 1	SN 1	SN 1	FC 1	SN ◇1	SN ◇1
Brighton 10	d			19 04	19 19		19 07									19 34	19 49	
Hove 2	d								19 21									
Preston Park	d						19 11											
Hassocks 4	d						19 17											
Burgess Hill 4	d						19 21											
Lewes 4	d									19 20								
Wivelsfield 4	d						19 23			19 34								
Haywards Heath 3	a			19 18			19 28		19 35	19 40						19 48		
	d			19 18			19 32		19 43	<						19 48		
Balcombe	d						19 37											
Horsham 4	d					19 21					19 32							19 52
Littlehaven	d										19 35							
Faygate	d																	
Ifield	d										19 41							
Crawley	d					19 30					19 45							20 01
Three Bridges 4	a					19 33	19 42				19 48							20 05
	d					19 34	19 42				19 50							20 05
Gatwick Airport 10	a			19 30		19 38	19 46		19 54		19 54					20 00		20 10
	d	19 35		19 31		19 39	19 46	19 50	19 55		19 55	20 03	20 05			20 01		20 11
Horley 4	d										19 58							
Salfords	d																	
Earlswood (Surrey)	d																	
Tonbridge 4	d													20 10				
Leigh (Kent)	d													20 14				
Penshurst	d													20 18				
Edenbridge	d													20 24				
Godstone	d													20 31				
Nutfield	d													20 36				
Reigate	d																	
Redhill 5	a					19 47					20 04	20 10		20 45				20 18
	d					19 48					20 07	20 13						20 18
Merstham	d										20 11							
Coulsdon South	d										20 16							
Purley 4	d										20 19							
East Croydon	a		19 43	19 46	19 56	19 59	20 02		20 10		20 24				20 13	20 16	20 23	20 30
	d		19 44	19 47	19 56	20 00	20 02		20 11		20 26				20 14	20 17	20 24	20 30
Norwood Junction 2	a																	
London Bridge 4 ⊖	a			20 02			20 17									20 32		
London Blackfriars 3 ⊖	a																	
City Thameslink 3	a																	
Farringdon 3 ⊖	a																	
St Pancras International 15 ⊖	a																	
St Albans City	a																	
Luton Airport Parkway 4	a																	
Luton 7	a																	
Bedford 10	a																	
Clapham Junction 10	d		19 56		20 06	20 12			20 20		20 37				20 26		20 33	20 41
London Victoria 15 ⊖	a	20 05	20 02		20 12	20 20		20 20	20 27		20 44		20 35		20 32		20 40	20 50

Brighton - London, Bedford

		FC 1	GW 1	GX 1	SN 1	SN ◇1	SN ◇1	GX 1	SN 1	FC 1	SN ◇1	SN ◇1	FC 1	GX 1	SN ◇1	SN 1	GW 1
Brighton 10	d	19 37								20 04	20 19	19 55	20 07				
Hove 2	d						19 52								20 22		
Preston Park	d	19 41										19 59	20 11				
Hassocks 4	d	19 47										20 05	20 17				
Burgess Hill 4	d	19 51					20 02					20 09	20 21				
Lewes 4	d					19 51											
Wivelsfield 4	d	19 53				20 03						20 11	20 23				
Haywards Heath 3	a	19 58				20 07	20 09			20 18		20 16	20 28		20 36		
	d	20 02				20 13	<			20 18		20 22	20 32		20 38		
Balcombe	d												20 37				
Horsham 4	d				20 02											20 32	
Littlehaven	d				20 05											20 35	
Faygate	d																
Ifield	d				20 11											20 41	
Crawley	d				20 14											20 45	
Three Bridges 4	a	20 11			20 18							20 32	20 42		20 47	20 48	
	d	20 12			20 18							20 32	20 42		20 48	20 51	
Gatwick Airport 10	a	20 16			20 22	20 24				20 30		20 37	20 46		20 52	20 56	
	d	20 16		20 20	20 23	20 25		20 35		20 31		20 38	20 46	20 50	20 53	20 57	21 03
Horley 4	d				20 26											20 59	
Salfords	d				20 30												
Earlswood (Surrey)	d				20 33												
Tonbridge 4	d																
Leigh (Kent)	d																
Penshurst	d																
Edenbridge	d																
Godstone	d																
Nutfield	d																
Reigate	d		20 19														
Redhill 5	a		20 25		20 36							20 47				21 06	21 10
	d				20 37							20 48				21 07	21 13
Merstham	d				20 41											21 11	
Coulsdon South	d				20 46											21 16	
Purley 4	d				20 49											21 19	
East Croydon ⇌	a	20 32			20 54	20 40			20 43	20 46	20 53	20 59	21 02		21 09	21 24	
	d	20 32			20 56	20 41			20 44	20 47	20 54	21 00	21 02		21 11	21 26	
Norwood Junction 2	a																
London Bridge 4 ⊖	a	20 47								21 02			21 17				
London Blackfriars 3 ⊖	a																
City Thameslink 3	a																
Farringdon 3 ⊖	a																
St Pancras International 15 ⊖	a																
St Albans City	a																
Luton Airport Parkway 4	a																
Luton 7	a																
Bedford 10	a																
Clapham Junction 10	d				21 07	20 50			20 56		21 03	21 11			21 20	21 37	
London Victoria 15 ⊖	a			20 50	21 14	20 57		21 05	21 02		21 10	21 17		21 20	21 27	21 44	

Brighton - London, Bedford

		GX 1	SN 1	SN 1	FC 1	SN ◇1	SN ◇1	FC 1	GW 1	GX 1	SN 1	SN ◇1	SN ◇1	GX 1	SN 1	SN ◇1	SN ◇1	FC 1
Brighton 10	d				20 34	20 49		20 37								21 19	21 00	21 07
Hove 2	d												20 52					
Preston Park	d							20 41									21 04	21 11
Hassocks 4	d							20 47									21 10	21 17
Burgess Hill 4	d							20 51					21 02				21 14	21 21
Lewes 4	d											20 50						
Wivelsfield 4	d							20 53				21 02					21 16	21 23
Haywards Heath 3	a				20 48			20 58				21 06	21 09				21 21	21 28
	d				20 48			21 02				21 13	<				21 22	21 32
Balcombe	d																	21 37
Horsham 4	d						20 52				21 02							
Littlehaven	d										21 05							
Faygate	d																	
Ifield	d										21 11							
Crawley	d						21 01				21 14							
Three Bridges 4	a						21 05	21 11			21 18						21 32	21 42
	d						21 05	21 12			21 18						21 32	21 42
Gatwick Airport 10	a				21 00		21 10	21 16			21 22	21 24					21 37	21 46
	d	21 05			21 01		21 11	21 16		21 20	21 23	21 25		21 35			21 38	21 46
Horley 4	d										21 26							
Salfords	d										21 30							
Earlswood (Surrey)	d										21 33							
Tonbridge 4	d		21 10															
Leigh (Kent)	d		21 14															
Penshurst	d		21 18															
Edenbridge	d		21 24															
Godstone	d		21 31															
Nutfield	d		21 36															
Reigate	d								21 18									
Redhill 5	a		21 41				21 18		21 25		21 36						21 47	
	d						21 18				21 37						21 48	
Merstham	d										21 41							
Coulsdon South	d										21 46							
Purley 4	d										21 49							
East Croydon ⇌	a			21 13	21 16	21 23	21 30	21 32			21 54	21 40			21 43	21 53	21 59	22 02
	d			21 14	21 17	21 24	21 30	21 32			21 56	21 41			21 44	21 54	22 00	22 02
Norwood Junction 2	a																	
London Bridge 4 ⊖	a				21 32			21 47										22 17
London Blackfriars 3 ⊖	a																	
City Thameslink 3	a																	
Farringdon 3 ⊖	a																	
St Pancras International 15 ⊖	a																	
St Albans City	a																	
Luton Airport Parkway 4	a																	
Luton 7	a																	
Bedford 10	a																	
Clapham Junction 10	d			21 26		21 33	21 41				22 07	21 50			21 56	22 03	22 11	
London Victoria 15 ⊖	a	21 35		21 32		21 40	21 47			21 50	22 14	21 57		22 05	22 02	22 10	22 20	

b arr. 2119

Table 186

Saturdays

Brighton - London, Bedford

		GX	SN ◇	GX	SN	SN	SN ◇	SN	SN ◇	FC	GX	GW	SN ◇	SN ◇	GX
Brighton	d						21 49			21 37					
Hove	d		21 22											21 52	
Preston Park	d									21 41					
Hassocks	d									21 47					
Burgess Hill	d									21 51				22 02	
Lewes	d												21 50		
Wivelsfield	d									21 53			22 02		
Haywards Heath	a		21 36							21 58			22 06	22 08	
	d		21 38							22 02			22 12	<	
Balcombe	d														
Horsham	d							21 32	21 52						
Littlehaven	d							21 35							
Faygate	d														
Ifield	d							21 41							
Crawley	d							21 45	22 01						
Three Bridges	a		21 47					21 48	22 05	22 11					
	d		21 48					21 52	22 05	22 12					
Gatwick Airport	a		21 52					21 56	22 10	22 16			22 23		
	d	21 50	21 53	22 05				21 57	22 11	22 16	22 20	22 22	22 25		22 35
Horley	d							22 00							
Salfords	d														
Earlswood (Surrey)	d														
Tonbridge	d				22 10										
Leigh (Kent)	d				22 14										
Penshurst	d				22 18										
Edenbridge	d				22 24										
Godstone	d				22 31										
Nutfield	d				22 36										
Reigate	d														
Redhill	a				22 42			22 06	22 18			22 30			
	d							22 07	22 18			22 33			
Merstham	d							22 11							
Coulsdon South	d							22 16							
Purley	d							22 19							
East Croydon	a		22 09			22 13	22 23	22 24	22 30	22 32			22 40		
	d		22 11			22 14	22 24	22 26	22 30	22 32			22 40		
Norwood Junction	a														
London Bridge ⊖	a									22 47					
London Blackfriars ⊖	a														
City Thameslink	a														
Farringdon ⊖	a														
St Pancras International ⊖	a														
St Albans City	a														
Luton Airport Parkway	a														
Luton	a														
Bedford	a														
Clapham Junction	d		22 20			22 26	22 33	22 37	22 41				22 50		
London Victoria ⊖	a	22 20	22 28	22 35		22 32	22 40	22 44	22 50		22 50		22 58		23 05

b arr. 2219

c arr. 2249

Table 186

Saturdays

Brighton - London, Bedford

		SN	SN	SN ◇	FC	FC	GX	GX	SN	SN ◇	SN ◇	SN	GW	GX	SN	GX	FC
Brighton	d			22 00	22 07	22 33					23 02						23 11
Hove	d																
Preston Park	d			22 04	22 11	22 37					23 06						
Hassocks	d			22 10	22 17	22 43					23 12						23 19
Burgess Hill	d			22 14	22 21	22 47					23 16						23 23
Lewes	d									22 40							
Wivelsfield	d			22 16	22 23	22 49				22 54	23 19						
Haywards Heath	a			22 21	22 28	22 54				22 58	23 23						23 27
	d			22 22	22 32	22 54				22 59	23 24						23 28
Balcombe	d				22 37	23 00											
Horsham	d		22 02												23 02		
Littlehaven	d		22 05												23 05		
Faygate	d																
Ifield	d		22 11												23 11		
Crawley	d		22 14												23 14		
Three Bridges	a		22 18	22 32	22 42	23 05				23 08	23 33				23 18		23 38
	d		22 19	22 32	22 42	23 12				23 08	23 47				23 18		23 38
Gatwick Airport	a		22 23	22 37	22 46	23 16				23 12	23 52				23 22		23 42
	d		22 24	22 38	22 46	23 16	22 50	23 05		23 13	23 53		23 18	23 20	23 23	23 35	23 43
Horley	d		22 27								23 56				23 26		
Salfords	d		22 31												23 30		
Earlswood (Surrey)	d		22 34												23 33		
Tonbridge	d											23 17					
Leigh (Kent)	d											23 21					
Penshurst	d											23 25					
Edenbridge	d											23 31					
Godstone	d											23 38					
Nutfield	d											23 43					
Reigate	d																
Redhill	a		22 37	22 46							00 03	23 49	23 25		23 36		
	d		22 38	22 47							00 03		23 28		23 37		
Merstham	d		22 42												23 41		
Coulsdon South	d		22 47												23 46		
Purley	d		22 50								00 11				23 49		
East Croydon	a	22 43	22 55	22 59	23 02	23 32			23 13	23 30	00 16				23 55		00 02
	d	22 44	22 56	23 00	23 02	23 32			23 14	23 30	00 17				23 56		00 04
Norwood Junction	a																
London Bridge ⊖	a				23 17	23 47											00 19
London Blackfriars ⊖	a																
City Thameslink	a																
Farringdon ⊖	a																
St Pancras International ⊖	a																
St Albans City	a																
Luton Airport Parkway	a																
Luton	a																
Bedford	a																
Clapham Junction	d	22 56	23 07	23 11					23 26	23 42	00 29				00 11		
London Victoria ⊖	a	23 02	23 14	23 17			23 20	23 35	23 32	23 52	00 36			23 55	00 18	00 10	

b arr. 2349

Table 186

Saturdays

Brighton - London, Bedford

		GX 1	FC 1
Brighton 10	d		23 37
Hove 2	d		
Preston Park	d		23 41
Hassocks 4	d		23 47
Burgess Hill 4	d		23 51
Lewes 4	d		
Wivelsfield 4	d		23 53
Haywards Heath 3	a		23 58
	d		23 59
Balcombe	d		00 04
Horsham 4	d		
Littlehaven	d		
Faygate	d		
Ifield	d		
Crawley	d		
Three Bridges 4	a		00 10
	d		00 10
Gatwick Airport 10	a		00 14
	d	23 50	00 15
Horley 4	d		
Salfords	d		
Earlswood (Surrey)	d		
Tonbridge 4	d		
Leigh (Kent)	d		
Penshurst	d		
Edenbridge	d		
Godstone	d		
Nutfield	d		
Reigate	d		
Redhill 5	a		00 22
	d		00 22
Merstham	d		
Coulsdon South	d		
Purley 4	d		
East Croydon	a		00 35
	d		00 36
Norwood Junction 2	a		
London Bridge 4 ⊖	a		00 52
London Blackfriars 3 ⊖	a		
City Thameslink 3	a		
Farringdon 3 ⊖	a		
St Pancras International 15 ⊖	a		
St Albans City	a		
Luton Airport Parkway 4	a		
Luton 7	a		
Bedford 10	a		
Clapham Junction 10	d		
London Victoria 15 ⊖	a	00 25	

Table 186

Sundays

until 05 September

Brighton - London, Bedford

		SN 1	SN ◇1	GX 1	FC 1	GX 1	GX 1	FC 1	GX 1	GX 1	SN	GX 1	SN 1	GX 1	SN 1	SN 1	SN 1	GX 1	SN 1	FC 1	GX 1	SN 1
Brighton 10	d		23p02		23p11			23p37											03 50			
Hove 2	d																					
Preston Park	d		23p06					23p41														
Hassocks 4	d		23p12		23p19			23p47														
Burgess Hill 4	d		23p16		23p23			23p51														
Lewes 4	d																					
Wivelsfield 4	d		23p19					23p53														
Haywards Heath 3	a		23p23		23p27			23p58														
	d		23p24		23p28			23p59														
Balcombe	d							00 04														
Horsham 4	d	23p02																				
Littlehaven	d	23p05																				
Faygate	d																					
Ifield	d	23p11																				
Crawley	d	23p14																				
Three Bridges 4	a	23p18	23p33		23p38			00 10											04 45			
	d	23p18	23p47		23p38			00 10					01 10		02 10	03 10	04 10		04 58	05 10		05 30
Gatwick Airport 10	a	23p22	23p52		23p42			00 14					01 19		02 14	03 14	04 14		05 02	05 14		05 34
	d	23p23	23p53	23p35	23p43	23p50	00 05	00 15	00 20	00 35		00 50	01 20	01 35	02 15	03 15	04 15	04 35	05 03	05 15	05 20	05 36
Horley 4	d	23p26	23p56										01 22		02 18	03 18	04 18		05 05			05 38
Salfords	d	23p30																				
Earlswood (Surrey)	d	23p33																				
Tonbridge 4	d																					
Leigh (Kent)	d																					
Penshurst	d																					
Edenbridge	d																					
Godstone	d																					
Nutfield	d																					
Reigate	d																					
Redhill 5	a	23p36	00 03					00 22														05 46
	d	23p37	00 03					00 22														05 46
Merstham	d	23p41																				
Coulsdon South	d	23p46																				
Purley 4	d	23p49	00 11										01 37		02 33	03 33	04 33		05 22			05 56
East Croydon	a	23p55	00 16		00 02			00 35					01 42		02 39	03 39	04 39		05 27	05 31		06 01
	d	23p56	00 17		00 04			00 36			00 49		01 43		02 40	03 40	04 40		05 28	05 32		06 02
Norwood Junction 2	a																			05 36		
London Bridge 4 ⊖	a				00 19			00 52												05 59		
London Blackfriars 3 ⊖	a																					
City Thameslink 3	a																					
Farringdon 3 ⊖	a																					
St Pancras International 15 ⊖	a																					
St Albans City	a																					
Luton Airport Parkway 4	a																					
Luton 7	a																					
Bedford 10	a																					
Clapham Junction 10	d	00 11	00 29								01 02		01 54		02 53	03 53	04 53		05 49			06 14
London Victoria 15 ⊖	a	00 18	00 36	00 10		00 25	00 42		00 55	01 11	01 09	01 25	02 05	02 20	03 05	04 05	05 05	05 10	05 58		05 55	06 22

Table 186

Sundays until 05 September

Brighton - London, Bedford

		GX 1	GX 1	GW 1	FC 1	GX 1	SN 1	GX 1	FC 1	GX 1	SN 1	SN ◇1	SN 1	GX 1	GW 1	FC 1	GX 1	SN 1	GX 1	SN ◇1
Brighton 10	d				05 44				06 13		06b16					06 45				07 04
Hove 2	d											06 27								
Preston Park	d										06 19									07 07
Hassocks 4	d				05 52						06 26					06 53				07 14
Burgess Hill 4	d				05 56				06 26		06 29					06 57				07 17
Lewes 4	d										05 57									
Wivelsfield 4	d										06 32									07 20
Haywards Heath 3	a				06 00				06 30		06 36	06 39				07 02				07 24
	d				06 01				06 31		06 37	06 40				07 02				07 25
Balcombe	d																			07 30
Horsham 4	d						06 04						06 34					07 00		
Littlehaven	d						06 07						06 37					07 03		
Faygate	d																			
Ifield	d						06 13						06 43					07 09		
Crawley	d						06 17						06 47					07 13		
Three Bridges 4	a				06 10		06 20		06 40		06 46		06 51			07 11		07 16		07 36
	d				06 10		06 21		06 40		06 46		06 53			07 12		07 18		07 36
Gatwick Airport 10	a				06 14		06 25		06 44		06 51	06 52	06 56			07 16		07 22		07 41
	d	05 50	06 05	06 08	06 15	06 20		06 35	06 45	06 50		06 53	06 58	07 05	07 08	07 17	07 20	07 23	07 35	07 42
Horley 4	d												07 00					07 26		
Salfords	d																	07 30		
Earlswood (Surrey)	d																	07 33		
Tonbridge 4	d																			
Leigh (Kent)	d																			
Penshurst	d																			
Edenbridge	d																			
Godstone	d																			
Nutfield	d																			
Reigate	d																			
Redhill 5	a			06 17									07 06		07 18			07 36		07 49
	d			06 21									07 07		07 21			07 37		07 49
Merstham	d												07 11					07 41		
Coulsdon South	d												07 16					07 46		
Purley 4	d												07 20					07 50		
East Croydon	a				06 31				07 01			07 09	07 26			07 33		07 55		08 00
	d				06 32				07 02			07 09	07 27			07 33		07 56		08 00
Norwood Junction 2	a				06 36															
London Bridge 4 ⊖	a				06 59				07 16							07 46				
London Blackfriars 3 ⊖	a																			
City Thameslink 3	a																			
Farringdon 3 ⊖	a																			
St Pancras International 15 ⊖	a																			
St Albans City	a																			
Luton Airport Parkway 4	a																			
Luton 7	a																			
Bedford 10	a																			
Clapham Junction 10	d											07 19	07 41					08 07		08 11
London Victoria 15 ⊖	a	06 25	06 40			06 55		07 10		07 20		07 25	07 48	07 35			07 50	08 13	08 05	08 17

b arr. 0609

Table 186

Sundays until 05 September

Brighton - London, Bedford

		FC 1	GX 1	SN ◇1	SN ◇1	GX 1	GW 1	GX 1	SN 1	SN 1	FC 1	SN ◇1	SN ◇1	SN 1	GX 1
Brighton 10	d	07 17									07 45		08 10		
Hove 2	d											07 54			
Preston Park	d														
Hassocks 4	d										07 53				
Burgess Hill 4	d	07 27									07 57	08 04			
Lewes 4	d			07 22											
Wivelsfield 4	d			07 36											
Haywards Heath 3	a	07 32		07 40							08 02	08 09			
	d	07 32		07 41							08 02	08 11			
Balcombe	d														
Horsham 4	d				07 37									08 00	
Littlehaven	d													08 03	
Faygate	d														
Ifield	d													08 09	
Crawley	d				07 46									08 13	
Three Bridges 4	a	07 41			07 50						08 11			08 16	
	d	07 42			07 50						08 12			08 18	
Gatwick Airport 10	a	07 46		07 52	07 55						08 16	08 22		08 22	
	d	07 47	07 50	07 53	07 56	08 05	08 08	08 20			08 17	08 23		08 23	08 35
Horley 4	d				07 58									08 26	
Salfords	d													08 30	
Earlswood (Surrey)	d													08 33	
Tonbridge 4	d									07 41					
Leigh (Kent)	d									07 45					
Penshurst	d									07 49					
Edenbridge	d									07 55					
Godstone	d									08 02					
Nutfield	d									08 07					
Reigate	d														
Redhill 5	a				08 05		08 15			08 12				08 36	
	d				08 05		08 19			08 13				08 37	
Merstham	d									08 17				08 41	
Coulsdon South	d									08 22				08 46	
Purley 4	d				08 14					08 27				08 50	
East Croydon	a	08 03		08 09	08 20				08 28	08 32	08 33	08 39	08 45	08 55	
	d	08 03		08 09	08 21				08 29	08 34	08 33	08 39	08 46	08 56	
Norwood Junction 2	a									08 38					
London Bridge 4 ⊖	a	08 16								08 51	08 46				
London Blackfriars 3 ⊖	a														
City Thameslink 3	a														
Farringdon 3 ⊖	a														
St Pancras International 15 ⊖	a														
St Albans City	a														
Luton Airport Parkway 4	a														
Luton 7	a														
Bedford 10	a														
Clapham Junction 10	d			08 19	08 32				08 41			08 49	08 55	09 07	
London Victoria 15 ⊖	a		08 20	08 25	08 39	08 35		08 50	08 48			08 55	09 02	09 13	09 05

Table 186

Sundays
until 05 September

Brighton - London, Bedford

		SN ◇1	FC 1	GX 1 H	SN ◇1 H	SN ◇1	SN ◇1 H	GX 1 H	GW 1	GX 1 H	SN 1	SN 1	FC 1	SN ◇1	SN ◇1 H	SN 1
Brighton 10	d	08 00	08 17				08 40						08 45		09 10	
Hove 2	d													08 54		
Preston Park	d	08 03														
Hassocks 4	d	08 10											08 53			
Burgess Hill 4	d	08 13	08 27										08 57	09 04		
Lewes 4	d				08 22											
Wivelsfield 4	d	08 16			08 36											
Haywards Heath 3	a	08 20	08 32		08 40								09 02	09 09		
	d	08 25	08 32		08 41								09 02	09 11		
Balcombe	d	08 30														
Horsham 4	d					08 37										09 00
Littlehaven	d															09 03
Faygate	d															
Ifield	d															09 09
Crawley	d					08 46										09 13
Three Bridges 4	a	08 36	08 41			08 50							09 11			09 16
	d	08 36	08 42			08 50							09 12			09 18
Gatwick Airport 10	a	08 41	08 46		08 52	08 55	09 01						09 16	09 22		09 22
	d	08 42	08 47	08 50	08 53	08 56	09 02	09 05	09 08	09 20			09 17	09 23		09 23
Horley 4	d					08 58										09 26
Salfords	d															09 30
Earlswood (Surrey)	d															09 33
Tonbridge 4	d											08 41				
Leigh (Kent)	d											08 45				
Penshurst	d											08 49				
Edenbridge	d											08 55				
Godstone	d											09 02				
Nutfield	d											09 07				
Reigate	d															
Redhill 5	a	08 49				09 05			09 16			09 12				09 36
	d	08 49				09 05			09 20			09 13				09 37
Merstham	d											09 17				09 41
Coulsdon South	d											09 22				09 46
Purley 4	d					09 14						09 27				09 50
East Croydon ⇌	a	09 00	09 03		09 09	09 20	09 17				09 28	09 32	09 33	09 39	09 45	09 55
	d	09 00	09 03		09 09	09 21	09 17				09 29	09 34	09 33	09 39	09 46	09 56
Norwood Junction 2	a											09 38				
London Bridge 4 ⊖	a		09 16									09 51	09 46			
London Blackfriars 3 ⊖	a															
City Thameslink 3	a															
Farringdon 3 ⊖	a															
St Pancras International 15 ⊖	a															
St Albans City	a															
Luton Airport Parkway 4	a															
Luton 7	a															
Bedford 10	a															
Clapham Junction 10	d	09 11			09 19	09 32	09 27				09 41			09 49	09 55	10 07
London Victoria 15 ⊖	a	09 17		09 20	09 25	09 39	09 33	09 35		09 50	09 48			09 55	10 02	10 13

b arr. 0915
c arr. 0944

Table 186

Sundays
until 05 September

Brighton - London, Bedford

		GX 1 H	SN ◇1	FC 1	GX 1 H	SN ◇1 H	SN ◇1	SN ◇1 H	GX 1 H	GW 1	GX 1 H	SN 1	SN 1	FC 1	SN ◇1	SN ◇1 H	SN 1
Brighton 10	d		09 00	09 17				09 40						09 45		10 10	
Hove 2	d														09 54		
Preston Park	d		09 03														
Hassocks 4	d		09 10											09 53			
Burgess Hill 4	d		09 13	09 27										09 57	10 04		
Lewes 4	d					09 22											
Wivelsfield 4	d		09 16			09 36											
Haywards Heath 3	a		09 20	09 32		09 40								10 02	10 09		
	d		09 25	09 32		09 41								10 02	10 11		
Balcombe	d		09 30														
Horsham 4	d						09 37										10 00
Littlehaven	d																10 03
Faygate	d																
Ifield	d																10 09
Crawley	d						09 46										10 13
Three Bridges 4	a		09 36	09 41			09 50							10 11			10 16
	d		09 36	09 42			09 50							10 12			10 18
Gatwick Airport 10	a		09 41	09 46		09 52	09 55	10 01						10 16	10 22		10 22
	d	09 35	09 42	09 47	09 50	09 53	09 56	10 02	10 05	10 08	10 20			10 17	10 23		10 23
Horley 4	d						09 58										10 26
Salfords	d																10 30
Earlswood (Surrey)	d																10 33
Tonbridge 4	d												09 41				
Leigh (Kent)	d												09 45				
Penshurst	d												09 49				
Edenbridge	d												09 55				
Godstone	d												10 02				
Nutfield	d												10 07				
Reigate	d																
Redhill 5	a		09 49				10 05			10 15			10 12				10 36
	d		09 49				10 05			10 19			10 13				10 37
Merstham	d												10 17				10 41
Coulsdon South	d												10 22				10 46
Purley 4	d						10 14						10 27				10 50
East Croydon ⇌	a		10 00	10 03		10 09	10 20	10 17				10 28	10 32	10 33	10 39	10 45	10 55
	d		10 00	10 03		10 09	10 21	10 17				10 29	10 34	10 33	10 39	10 46	10 56
Norwood Junction 2	a												10 38				
London Bridge 4 ⊖	a			10 16									10 51	10 46			
London Blackfriars 3 ⊖	a																
City Thameslink 3	a																
Farringdon 3 ⊖	a																
St Pancras International 15 ⊖	a																
St Albans City	a																
Luton Airport Parkway 4	a																
Luton 7	a																
Bedford 10	a																
Clapham Junction 10	d		10 11			10 19	10 32	10 27				10 41			10 49	10 55	11 07
London Victoria 15 ⊖	a	10 05	10 17		10 20	10 25	10 39	10 33	10 35		10 50	10 48			10 55	11 02	11 13

b arr. 1015
c arr. 1044

Table 186

Sundays
until 05 September

Brighton - London, Bedford

		GX 1 ⌶	SN ◇1	FC 1	GX 1 ⌶	SN ◇1 ⌶	SN ◇1 ⌶	SN ◇1 ⌶	GX 1 ⌶	GW 1	GX 1 ⌶	SN 1	SN 1	FC 1	SN ◇1	SN ◇1 ⌶	SN 1
Brighton 10	d		10 00	10 17				10 40						10 45		11 10	
Hove 2	d														10 54		
Preston Park	d		10 03														
Hassocks 4	d		10 10											10 53			
Burgess Hill 4	d		10 13	10 27										10 57	11 04		
Lewes 4	d					10 22											
Wivelsfield 4	d		10 16			10 36											
Haywards Heath 3	a		10 20	10 32		10 40								11 02	11 09		
	d		10 25	10 32		10 41								11 02	11 11		
Balcombe	d		10 30														
Horsham 4	d						10 37										11 00
Littlehaven	d																11 03
Faygate	d																
Ifield	d																11 09
Crawley	d						10 46										11 13
Three Bridges 4	a		10 36	10 41			10 50							11 11			11 16
	d		10 36	10 42			10 50							11 12			11 18
Gatwick Airport 10	a		10 41	10 46		10 52	10 55	11 01						11 16	11 22		11 22
	d	10 35	10 42	10 47	10 50	10 53	10 56	11 02	11 05	11 08	11 20			11 17	11 23		11 23
Horley 4	d						10 58										11 26
Salfords	d																11 30
Earlswood (Surrey)	d																11 33
Tonbridge 4	d												10 41				
Leigh (Kent)	d												10 45				
Penshurst	d												10 49				
Edenbridge	d												10 55				
Godstone	d												11 02				
Nutfield	d												11 07				
Reigate	d																
Redhill 5	a		10 49				11 05			11 16			11 12				11 36
	d		10 49				11 05			11 20			11 13				11 37
Merstham	d												11 17				11 41
Coulsdon South	d												11 22				11 46
Purley 4	d						11 14						11 27				11 50
East Croydon	a		11 00	11 03		11 09	11 20	11 17				11 28	11 32	11 33	11 39	11 45	11 55
	d		11 00	11 03		11 09	11 21	11 17				11 29	11 34	11 33	11 39	11 46	11 56
Norwood Junction 2	a												11 38				
London Bridge 4 ⊖	a			11 16									11 51	11 46			
London Blackfriars 3 ⊖	a																
City Thameslink 3	a																
Farringdon 3 ⊖	a																
St Pancras International 15 ⊖	a																
St Albans City	a																
Luton Airport Parkway 4	a																
Luton 7	a																
Bedford 10	a																
Clapham Junction 10	d		11 11			11 19	11 32	11 27				11 41			11 49	11 55	12 07
London Victoria 15 ⊖	a	11 05	11 17		11 20	11 25	11 39	11 33	11 35		11 50	11 48			11 55	12 02	12 13

b arr. 1115 c arr. 1144

Table 186

Sundays
until 05 September

Brighton - London, Bedford

		GX 1 ⌶	SN ◇1	FC 1	GX 1 ⌶	SN ◇1 ⌶	SN ◇1 ⌶	SN ◇1 ⌶	GX 1 ⌶	GW 1	GX 1 ⌶	SN 1	SN 1	FC 1	SN ◇1	SN ◇1 ⌶	SN 1	GX 1 ⌶
Brighton 10	d		11 00	11 17				11 40						11 45		12 10		
Hove 2	d														11 54			
Preston Park	d		11 03															
Hassocks 4	d		11 10											11 53				
Burgess Hill 4	d		11 13	11 27										11 57	12 04			
Lewes 4	d					11 22												
Wivelsfield 4	d		11 16			11 36												
Haywards Heath 3	a		11 20	11 32		11 40								12 02	12 09			
	d		11 25	11 32		11 41								12 02	12 11			
Balcombe	d		11 30															
Horsham 4	d						11 37										12 00	
Littlehaven	d																12 03	
Faygate	d																	
Ifield	d																12 09	
Crawley	d						11 46										12 13	
Three Bridges 4	a		11 36	11 41			11 50							12 11			12 16	
	d		11 36	11 42			11 50							12 12			12 18	
Gatwick Airport 10	a		11 41	11 46		11 52	11 55	12 01						12 16	12 22		12 22	
	d	11 35	11 42	11 47	11 50	11 53	11 56	12 02	12 05	12 08	12 20			12 17	12 23		12 23	12 35
Horley 4	d						11 58										12 26	
Salfords	d																12 30	
Earlswood (Surrey)	d																12 33	
Tonbridge 4	d												11 41					
Leigh (Kent)	d												11 45					
Penshurst	d												11 49					
Edenbridge	d												11 55					
Godstone	d												12 02					
Nutfield	d												12 07					
Reigate	d																	
Redhill 5	a		11 49				12 05			12 15			12 12				12 36	
	d		11 49				12 05			12 19			12 13				12 37	
Merstham	d												12 17				12 41	
Coulsdon South	d												12 22				12 46	
Purley 4	d						12 14						12 27				12 50	
East Croydon	a		12 00	12 03		12 09	12 20	12 17				12 28	12 32	12 33	12 39	12 45	12 55	
	d		12 00	12 03		12 09	12 21	12 17				12 29	12 34	12 33	12 39	12 46	12 56	
Norwood Junction 2	a												12 38					
London Bridge 4 ⊖	a			12 16									12 51	12 46				
London Blackfriars 3 ⊖	a																	
City Thameslink 3	a																	
Farringdon 3 ⊖	a																	
St Pancras International 15 ⊖	a																	
St Albans City	a																	
Luton Airport Parkway 4	a																	
Luton 7	a																	
Bedford 10	a																	
Clapham Junction 10	d		12 11			12 19	12 32	12 27				12 41			12 49	12 55	13 07	
London Victoria 15 ⊖	a	12 05	12 17		12 20	12 25	12 39	12 33	12 35		12 50	12 48			12 55	13 02	13 13	13 05

b arr. 1215 c arr. 1244

Table 186

Sundays
until 05 September

Brighton - London, Bedford

		SN		FC	GX	SN	SN	SN	GX	GW	GX	SN	SN	SN	FC	SN	SN	SN		GX
		◇1		1	1	◇1	◇1	◇1	1	1	1	1	1	1	1	◇1	◇1	1		1
					H	H	H	H	H		H						H			H
Brighton 10	d	12 00		12 17				12 40				13 20			12 45		13 10			
Hove 2	d															12 54				
Preston Park	d	12 03																		
Hassocks 4	d	12 10													12 53					
Burgess Hill 4	d	12 13		12 27											12 57	13 04				
Lewes 4	d					12 22						13 32								
Wivelsfield 4	d	12 16				12 36														
Haywards Heath 3	a	12 20		12 32		12 40									13 02	13 09				
	d	12 25		12 32		12 41									13 02	13 11				
Balcombe	d	12 30																		
Horsham 4	d						12 37											13 00		
Littlehaven	d																	13 03		
Faygate	d																			
Ifield	d																	13 09		
Crawley	d						12 46											13 13		
Three Bridges 4	a	12 36		12 41			12 50								13 11			13 16		
	d	12 36		12 42			12 50								13 12			13 18		
Gatwick Airport 10	a	12 41		12 46		12 52	12 55	13 01							13 16	13 22		13 22		
	d	12 42		12 47	12 50	12 53	12 56	13 02	13 05	13 08	13 20				13 17	13 23		13 23		13 35
Horley 4	d						12 58											13 26		
Salfords	d																	13 30		
Earlswood (Surrey)	d																	13 33		
Tonbridge 4	d													12 41						
Leigh (Kent)	d													12 45						
Penshurst	d													12 49						
Edenbridge	d													12 55						
Godstone	d													13 02						
Nutfield	d													13 07						
Reigate	d																			
Redhill 5	a	12 49					13 05			13 16				13 12				13 36		
	d	12 49					13 05			13 20				13 13				13 37		
Merstham	d													13 17				13 41		
Coulsdon South	d													13 22				13 46		
Purley 4	d						13 14							13 27				13 50		
East Croydon	a	13 00		13 03		13 09	13 20	13 17					13 28	13 32	13 33	13 39	13 45	13 55		
	d	13 00		13 03		13 09	13 21	13 17					13 29	13 34	13 33	13 39	13 46	13 56		
Norwood Junction 2	a													13 38						
London Bridge 4 ⊖	a			13 16										13 51	13 46					
London Blackfriars 3 ⊖	a																			
City Thameslink 3	a																			
Farringdon 3 ⊖	a																			
St Pancras International 15 ⊖	a																			
St Albans City	a																			
Luton Airport Parkway 4	a																			
Luton 7	a																			
Bedford 10	a																			
Clapham Junction 10	d	13 11				13 19	13 32	13 27					13 41			13 49	13 55	14 07		
London Victoria 15 ⊖	a	13 17			13 20	13 25	13 39	13 33	13 35		13 50		13 48			13 55	14 02	14 13		14 05

b arr. 1315 c arr. 1344

Table 186

Sundays
until 05 September

Brighton - London, Bedford

		SN	FC		GX	SN	SN	SN		GX	GW	GX	SN	SN	FC		SN	SN	SN	GX	SN
		◇1	1		1	◇1	◇1	◇1		1	1	1	1	1	1		◇1	◇1	1	1	◇1
					H	H	H	H		H		H						H		H	
Brighton 10	d	13 00	13 17					13 40							13 45			14 10			14 00
Hove 2	d																13 54				
Preston Park	d	13 03																			14 03
Hassocks 4	d	13 10													13 53						14 10
Burgess Hill 4	d	13 13	13 27												13 57		14 04				14 13
Lewes 4	d					13 22															
Wivelsfield 4	d	13 16				13 36															14 16
Haywards Heath 3	a	13 20	13 32			13 40									14 02		14 09				14 20
	d	13 25	13 32			13 41									14 02		14 11				14 25
Balcombe	d	13 30																			14 30
Horsham 4	d						13 37												14 00		
Littlehaven	d																		14 03		
Faygate	d																				
Ifield	d																		14 09		
Crawley	d						13 46												14 13		
Three Bridges 4	a	13 36	13 41				13 50								14 11				14 16		14 36
	d	13 36	13 42				13 50								14 12				14 18		14 36
Gatwick Airport 10	a	13 41	13 46			13 52	13 55	14 01							14 16		14 22		14 22		14 41
	d	13 42	13 47		13 50	13 53	13 56	14 02		14 05	14 08	14 20			14 17		14 23		14 23	14 35	14 42
Horley 4	d						13 58												14 26		
Salfords	d																		14 30		
Earlswood (Surrey)	d																		14 33		
Tonbridge 4	d													13 41							
Leigh (Kent)	d													13 45							
Penshurst	d													13 49							
Edenbridge	d													13 55							
Godstone	d													14 02							
Nutfield	d													14 07							
Reigate	d																				
Redhill 5	a	13 49					14 05				14 15			14 12					14 36		14 49
	d	13 49					14 05				14 19			14 13					14 37		14 49
Merstham	d													14 17					14 41		
Coulsdon South	d													14 22					14 46		
Purley 4	d						14 14							14 27					14 50		
East Croydon	a	14 00	14 03			14 09	14 20	14 17					14 28	14 32	14 33		14 39	14 45	14 55		15 00
	d	14 00	14 03			14 09	14 21	14 17					14 29	14 34	14 33		14 39	14 46	14 56		15 00
Norwood Junction 2	a													14 38							
London Bridge 4 ⊖	a		14 16											14 51	14 46						
London Blackfriars 3 ⊖	a																				
City Thameslink 3	a																				
Farringdon 3 ⊖	a																				
St Pancras International 15 ⊖	a																				
St Albans City	a																				
Luton Airport Parkway 4	a																				
Luton 7	a																				
Bedford 10	a																				
Clapham Junction 10	d	14 11				14 19	14 32	14 27					14 41				14 49	14 55	15 07		15 11
London Victoria 15 ⊖	a	14 17			14 20	14 25	14 39	14 33		14 35		14 50	14 48				14 55	15 02	15 13	15 05	15 17

b arr. 1415 c arr. 1444

Table 186

Brighton - London, Bedford

Sundays until 05 September

		FC 1	GX 1	SN ◇1	SN ◇1	SN ◇1	GX 1	GW 1	GX 1	SN 1	SN 1	FC 1	SN ◇1	SN ◇1	SN 1	GX 1	SN ◇1
Brighton 10	d	14 17				14 40						14 45		15 10			15 00
Hove 2	d												14 54				
Preston Park	d																15 03
Hassocks 4	d											14 53					15 10
Burgess Hill 4	d	14 27										14 57	15 04				15 13
Lewes 4	d			14 22													
Wivelsfield 4	d			14 36													15 16
Haywards Heath 3	a	14 32		14 40								15 02	15 09				15 20
	d	14 32		14 41								15 02	15 11				15 25
Balcombe	d																15 30
Horsham 4	d				14 37										15 00		
Littlehaven	d														15 03		
Faygate	d																
Ifield	d														15 09		
Crawley	d				14 46										15 13		
Three Bridges 4	a	14 41			14 50							15 11			15 16		15 36
	d	14 42			14 50							15 12			15 18		15 36
Gatwick Airport 10	a	14 46		14 52	14 55	15 01						15 16	15 22		15 22		15 41
	d	14 47	14 50	14 53	14 56	15 02	15 05	15 08	15 20			15 17	15 23		15 23	15 35	15 42
Horley 4	d				14 58										15 26		
Salfords	d														15 30		
Earlswood (Surrey)	d														15 33		
Tonbridge 4	d										14 41						
Leigh (Kent)	d										14 45						
Penshurst	d										14 49						
Edenbridge	d										14 55						
Godstone	d										15 02						
Nutfield	d										15 07						
Reigate	d																
Redhill 5	a				15 05			15 16			15 12				15 36		15 49
	d				15 05			15 20			15 13				15 37		15 49
Merstham	d										15 17				15 41		
Coulsdon South	d										15 22				15 46		
Purley 4	d				15 14						15 27				15 50		
East Croydon	a	15 03		15 09	15 20	15 17				15 28	15 32	15 33	15 39	15 45	15 55		16 00
	d	15 03		15 09	15 21	15 17				15 29	15 34	15 33	15 39	15 46	15 56		16 00
Norwood Junction 2	a										15 38						
London Bridge 4 ⊖	a	15 16									15 51	15 46					
London Blackfriars 3 ⊖	a																
City Thameslink 3	a																
Farringdon 3 ⊖	a																
St Pancras International 15 ⊖	a																
St Albans City	a																
Luton Airport Parkway 4	a																
Luton 7	a																
Bedford 10	a																
Clapham Junction 10	d			15 19	15 32	15 27				15 41			15 49	15 55	16 07		16 11
London Victoria 15 ⊖	a		15 20	15 25	15 39	15 33	15 35		15 50	15 48			15 55	16 02	16 13	16 05	16 17

b arr. 1515

c arr. 1544

Table 186

Brighton - London, Bedford

Sundays until 05 September

		FC 1	GX 1	SN ◇1	SN ◇1	SN ◇1	GX 1	GW 1	GX 1	SN 1	SN 1	FC 1	SN ◇1	SN ◇1	SN 1	GX 1	SN ◇1
Brighton 10	d	15 17				15 40						15 45		16 10			16 00
Hove 2	d												15 54				
Preston Park	d																16 03
Hassocks 4	d											15 53					16 10
Burgess Hill 4	d	15 27										15 57	16 04				16 13
Lewes 4	d			15 22													
Wivelsfield 4	d			15 36													16 16
Haywards Heath 3	a	15 32		15 40								16 02	16 09				16 20
	d	15 32		15 41								16 02	16 11				16 25
Balcombe	d																16 30
Horsham 4	d				15 37										16 00		
Littlehaven	d														16 03		
Faygate	d																
Ifield	d														16 09		
Crawley	d				15 46										16 13		
Three Bridges 4	a	15 41			15 50							16 11			16 16		16 36
	d	15 42			15 50							16 12			16 18		16 36
Gatwick Airport 10	a	15 46		15 52	15 55	16 01						16 16	16 22		16 22		16 41
	d	15 47	15 50	15 53	15 56	16 02	16 05	16 08	16 20			16 17	16 23		16 23	16 35	16 42
Horley 4	d				15 58										16 26		
Salfords	d														16 30		
Earlswood (Surrey)	d														16 33		
Tonbridge 4	d										15 41						
Leigh (Kent)	d										15 45						
Penshurst	d										15 49						
Edenbridge	d										15 55						
Godstone	d										16 02						
Nutfield	d										16 07						
Reigate	d																
Redhill 5	a				16 05			16 15			16 12				16 36		16 49
	d				16 05			16 19			16 13				16 37		16 49
Merstham	d										16 17				16 41		
Coulsdon South	d										16 22				16 46		
Purley 4	d				16 14						16 27				16 50		
East Croydon	a	16 03		16 09	16 20	16 17				16 28	16 32	16 33	16 39	16 45	16 55		17 00
	d	16 03		16 09	16 21	16 17				16 29	16 34	16 33	16 39	16 46	16 56		17 00
Norwood Junction 2	a										16 38						
London Bridge 4 ⊖	a	16 16									16 51	16 46					
London Blackfriars 3 ⊖	a																
City Thameslink 3	a																
Farringdon 3 ⊖	a																
St Pancras International 15 ⊖	a																
St Albans City	a																
Luton Airport Parkway 4	a																
Luton 7	a																
Bedford 10	a																
Clapham Junction 10	d			16 19	16 32	16 27				16 41			16 49	16 55	17 07		17 11
London Victoria 15 ⊖	a		16 20	16 25	16 39	16 33	16 35		16 50	16 48			16 55	17 02	17 13	17 05	17 17

b arr. 1615

c arr. 1644

Table 186

Sundays
until 05 September

Brighton - London, Bedford

		FC	GX	SN	SN	SN	GX	GW	GX	SN	SN	FC	SN	SN	SN	GX	SN	FC
		1	1 ⌶	◇1 ⌶	◇1 ⌶	◇1 ⌶	1 ⌶	1	1 ⌶	1	1	1	◇1	◇1 ⌶	1	1 ⌶	◇1	1
Brighton 10	d	16 17				16 40						16 45		17 10			17 00	17 17
Hove 2	d												16 54					
Preston Park	d																17 03	
Hassocks 4	d											16 53					17 10	
Burgess Hill 4	d	16 27										16 57	17 04				17 13	17 27
Lewes 4	d			16 22														
Wivelsfield 4	d			16 36													17 16	
Haywards Heath 3	a	16 32		16 40								17 02	17 09				17 20	17 32
	d	16 32		16 41								17 02	17 11				17 25	17 32
Balcombe	d																17 30	
Horsham 4	d				16 37										17 00			
Littlehaven	d														17 03			
Faygate	d																	
Ifield	d														17 09			
Crawley	d				16 46										17 13			
Three Bridges 4	a	16 41			16 50							17 11			17 16		17 36	17 41
	d	16 42			16 50							17 12			17 18		17 36	17 42
Gatwick Airport 10	a	16 46		16 52	16 55	17 01						17 16	17 22		17 22		17 41	17 46
	d	16 47	16 50	16 53	16 56	17 02	17 05	17 08	17 20			17 17	17 23		17 23	17 35	17 42	17 47
Horley 4	d				16 58										17 26			
Salfords	d														17 30			
Earlswood (Surrey)	d														17 33			
Tonbridge 4	d										16 41							
Leigh (Kent)	d										16 45							
Penshurst	d										16 49							
Edenbridge	d										16 55							
Godstone	d										17 02							
Nutfield	d										17 07							
Reigate	d																	
Redhill 5	a				17 05			17 16			17 12				17 36		17 49	
	d				17 05			17 20			17 13				17 37		17 49	
Merstham	d										17 17				17 41			
Coulsdon South	d										17 22				17 46			
Purley 4	d				17 14						17 27				17 50			
East Croydon ⇌	a	17 03		17 09	17 20	17 17				17 28	17 32	17 33	17 39	17 45	17 55		18 00	18 03
	d	17 03		17 09	17 21	17 17				17 29	17 34	17 33	17 39	17 46	17 56		18 00	18 03
Norwood Junction 2	a										17 38							
London Bridge 4 ⊖	a	17 16									17 51	17 46						18 16
London Blackfriars 3 ⊖	a																	
City Thameslink 3	a																	
Farringdon 3 ⊖	a																	
St Pancras International 15 ⊖	a																	
St Albans City	a																	
Luton Airport Parkway 4	a																	
Luton 7	a																	
Bedford 10	a																	
Clapham Junction 10	d			17 19	17 32	17 27				17 41			17 49	17 55	18 07		18 11	
London Victoria 15 ⊖	a		17 20	17 25	17 39	17 33	17 35		17 50	17 48			17 55	18 02	18 13	18 05	18 17	

b arr. 1715 c arr. 1744

Table 186

Sundays
until 05 September

Brighton - London, Bedford

		GX	SN	SN	SN	GX	GW	GX	SN	SN	FC	SN	SN	SN	GX	SN
		1 ⌶	◇1 ⌶	◇1 ⌶	◇1 ⌶	1 ⌶	1	1 ⌶	1	1	1	◇1	◇1	1	1 ⌶	◇1
Brighton 10	d				17 40						17 45		18 10			18 00
Hove 2	d											17 54				
Preston Park	d															18 03
Hassocks 4	d										17 53					18 10
Burgess Hill 4	d										17 57	18 04				18 13
Lewes 4	d		17 22													
Wivelsfield 4	d		17 36													18 16
Haywards Heath 3	a		17 40								18 02	18 09				18 20
	d		17 41								18 02	18 11				18 25
Balcombe	d															18 30
Horsham 4	d			17 37										18 00		
Littlehaven	d													18 03		
Faygate	d															
Ifield	d													18 09		
Crawley	d			17 46										18 13		
Three Bridges 4	a			17 50							18 11			18 16		18 36
	d			17 50							18 12			18 18		18 36
Gatwick Airport 10	a		17 52	17 55	18 01						18 16	18 22		18 22		18 41
	d	17 50	17 53	17 56	18 02	18 05	18 08	18 20			18 17	18 23		18 23	18 35	18 42
Horley 4	d			17 58										18 26		
Salfords	d													18 30		
Earlswood (Surrey)	d													18 33		
Tonbridge 4	d									17 41						
Leigh (Kent)	d									17 45						
Penshurst	d									17 49						
Edenbridge	d									17 55						
Godstone	d									18 02						
Nutfield	d									18 07						
Reigate	d															
Redhill 5	a			18 05			18 15			18 12				18 36		18 49
	d			18 05			18 19			18 13				18 37		18 49
Merstham	d									18 17				18 41		
Coulsdon South	d									18 22				18 46		
Purley 4	d			18 14						18 27				18 50		
East Croydon ⇌	a		18 09	18 20	18 17				18 28	18 32	18 33	18 39	18 45	18 55		19 00
	d		18 09	18 21	18 17				18 29	18 34	18 33	18 39	18 46	18 56		19 00
Norwood Junction 2	a									18 38						
London Bridge 4 ⊖	a									18 51	18 46					
London Blackfriars 3 ⊖	a															
City Thameslink 3	a															
Farringdon 3 ⊖	a															
St Pancras International 15 ⊖	a															
St Albans City	a															
Luton Airport Parkway 4	a															
Luton 7	a															
Bedford 10	a															
Clapham Junction 10	d		18 19	18 32	18 27				18 41			18 49	18 55	19 07		19 11
London Victoria 15 ⊖	a	18 20	18 25	18 39	18 33	18 35		18 50	18 48			18 55	19 02	19 13	19 05	19 17

b arr. 1815 c arr. 1844

Table 186

Sundays until 05 September

Brighton - London, Bedford

Station		FC	GX	SN ◇	SN ◇	SN ◇	GX	GW	GX	SN	SN	FC	SN ◇	SN ◇	SN	GX	SN ◇	FC
Brighton	d	18 17				18 40						18 45		19 10			19 00	19 17
Hove	d												18 54					
Preston Park	d																19 03	
Hassocks	d											18 53					19 10	
Burgess Hill	d	18 27										18 57	19 04				19 13	19 27
Lewes	d			18 22														
Wivelsfield	d			18 36													19 16	
Haywards Heath	a	18 32		18 40								19 02	19 09				19 20	19 32
	d	18 32		18 41								19 02	19 11				19 25	19 32
Balcombe	d																19 30	
Horsham	d				18 37										19 00			
Littlehaven	d														19 03			
Faygate	d																	
Ifield	d														19 09			
Crawley	d				18 46										19 13			
Three Bridges	a	18 41			18 50							19 11			19 16		19 36	19 41
	d	18 42			18 50							19 12			19 18		19 36	19 42
Gatwick Airport	a	18 46		18 52	18 55	19 01						19 16	19 22		19 22		19 41	19 46
	d	18 47	18 50	18 53	18 56	19 02	19 05	19 08	19 20			19 17	19 23		19 23	19 35	19 42	19 47
Horley	d				18 58										19 26			
Salfords	d														19 30			
Earlswood (Surrey)	d														19 33			
Tonbridge	d										18 41							
Leigh (Kent)	d										18 45							
Penshurst	d										18 49							
Edenbridge	d										18 55							
Godstone	d										19 02							
Nutfield	d										19 07							
Reigate	d																	
Redhill	a				19 05			19 16			19 12				19 36		19 49	
	d				19 05			19 20			19 13				19 37		19 49	
Merstham	d										19 17				19 41			
Coulsdon South	d										19 22				19 46			
Purley	d				19 14						19 27				19 50			
East Croydon	a	19 03		19 09	19 20	19 17				19 28	19 32	19 33	19 39	19 45	19 55		20 00	20 03
	d	19 03		19 09	19 21	19 17				19 29	19 34	19 33	19 39	19 46	19 56		20 00	20 03
Norwood Junction	a										19 38							
London Bridge ⊖	a	19 16									19 51	19 46						20 16
London Blackfriars ⊖	a																	
City Thameslink	a																	
Farringdon ⊖	a																	
St Pancras International ⊖	a																	
St Albans City	a																	
Luton Airport Parkway	a																	
Luton	a																	
Bedford	a																	
Clapham Junction	d			19 19	19 32	19 27				19 41			19 49	19 55	20 07		20 11	
London Victoria ⊖	a		19 20	19 25	19 39	19 33	19 35		19 50	19 48			19 55	20 02	20 13	20 05	20 17	

b arr. 1915 c arr. 1944

Table 186

Sundays until 05 September

Brighton - London, Bedford

Station		GX	SN ◇	SN ◇	SN ◇	GX	GW	GX	SN	SN	FC	SN ◇	SN ◇	SN	GX	SN ◇	FC
Brighton	d				19 40						19 45		20 10			20 00	20 17
Hove	d											19 54					
Preston Park	d															20 03	
Hassocks	d										19 53					20 10	
Burgess Hill	d										19 57	20 04				20 13	20 27
Lewes	d		19 22														
Wivelsfield	d		19 36													20 16	
Haywards Heath	a		19 40								20 02	20 09				20 20	20 32
	d		19 41								20 02	20 11				20 25	20 32
Balcombe	d															20 30	
Horsham	d			19 37										20 00			
Littlehaven	d													20 03			
Faygate	d																
Ifield	d													20 09			
Crawley	d			19 46										20 13			
Three Bridges	a			19 50							20 11			20 16		20 36	20 41
	d			19 50							20 12			20 18		20 36	20 42
Gatwick Airport	a		19 52	19 55	20 01						20 16	20 22		20 22		20 41	20 46
	d	19 50	19 53	19 56	20 02	20 05	20 08	20 20			20 17	20 23		20 23	20 35	20 42	20 47
Horley	d			19 58										20 26			
Salfords	d													20 30			
Earlswood (Surrey)	d													20 33			
Tonbridge	d									19 41							
Leigh (Kent)	d									19 45							
Penshurst	d									19 49							
Edenbridge	d									19 55							
Godstone	d									20 02							
Nutfield	d									20 07							
Reigate	d																
Redhill	a			20 05			20 15			20 12				20 36		20 49	
	d			20 05			20 19			20 13				20 37		20 49	
Merstham	d									20 17				20 41			
Coulsdon South	d									20 22				20 46			
Purley	d			20 14						20 27				20 50			
East Croydon	a		20 09	20 20	20 17				20 28	20 32	20 33	20 39	20 45	20 55		21 00	21 03
	d		20 09	20 21	20 17				20 29	20 34	20 33	20 39	20 46	20 56		21 00	21 03
Norwood Junction	a									20 38							
London Bridge ⊖	a									20 51	20 46						21 16
London Blackfriars ⊖	a																
City Thameslink	a																
Farringdon ⊖	a																
St Pancras International ⊖	a																
St Albans City	a																
Luton Airport Parkway	a																
Luton	a																
Bedford	a																
Clapham Junction	d		20 19	20 32	20 27				20 41			20 49	20 55	21 07		21 11	
London Victoria ⊖	a	20 20	20 25	20 39	20 33	20 35		20 50	20 48			20 55	21 02	21 13	21 05	21 17	

b arr. 2015 c arr. 2044

Table 186

Sundays
until 05 September

Brighton - London, Bedford

		GX	SN	SN	SN	GX	GW	GX	SN	SN	FC	SN	SN	GX	SN	FC
		1	◇1	◇1	◇1	1	1	1	1	1	1	◇1	1	1	◇1	1
Brighton 10	d				20 40						20 45				21 04	21 17
Hove 2	d											20 54				
Preston Park	d														21 07	
Hassocks 4	d										20 53				21 14	
Burgess Hill 4	d										20 57	21 04			21 17	21 27
Lewes 4	d		20 22													
Wivelsfield 4	d		20 36												21 20	
Haywards Heath 3	a		20 40								21 02	21 09			21 24	21 32
	d		20 41								21 02	21 11			21 25	21 32
Balcombe	d														21 30	
Horsham 4	d			20 37									21 00			
Littlehaven	d												21 03			
Faygate	d															
Ifield	d												21 09			
Crawley	d			20 46									21 13			
Three Bridges 4	a			20 50							21 11		21 16		21 36	21 41
	d			20 50							21 12		21 18		21 36	21 42
Gatwick Airport 10	a		20 52	20 55	21 01						21 16	21 22	21 22		21 41	21 46
	d	20 50	20 53	20 56	21 02	21 05	21 08	21 20			21 17	21 23	21 23	21 35	21 42	21 47
Horley 4	d			20 58									21 26			
Salfords	d												21 30			
Earlswood (Surrey)	d												21 33			
Tonbridge 4	d									20 41						
Leigh (Kent)	d									20 45						
Penshurst	d									20 49						
Edenbridge	d									20 55						
Godstone	d									21 02						
Nutfield	d									21 07						
Reigate	d															
Redhill 5	a			21 05			21 16			21 12			21 36		21 49	
	d			21 05			21 19			21 13			21 37		21 49	
Merstham	d									21 17			21 41			
Coulsdon South	d									21 22			21 46			
Purley 4	d			21 14						21 27			21 50			
East Croydon	a		21 09	21 20	21 17				21 28	21 32	21 33	21 39	21 55		22 00	22 03
	d		21 09	21 21	21 17				21 29	21 34	21 33	21 39	21 56		22 00	22 03
Norwood Junction 2	a									21 38						
London Bridge 4 ⊖	a									21 51	21 46					22 16
London Blackfriars 3 ⊖	a															
City Thameslink 3	a															
Farringdon 3 ⊖	a															
St Pancras International 15 ⊖	a															
St Albans City	a															
Luton Airport Parkway 4	a															
Luton 7	a															
Bedford 10	a															
Clapham Junction 10	d		21 19	21 32	21 27				21 41			21 49	22 07		22 11	
London Victoria 15 ⊖	a	21 20	21 25	21 39	21 33	21 35		21 50	21 48			21 55	22 13	22 05	22 17	

b arr. 2115
c arr. 2144

Table 186

Sundays
until 05 September

Brighton - London, Bedford

		GX	SN	SN	GX	GW	GX	SN	SN	FC	SN	SN	GX	SN	FC	GX	SN	GX
		1	◇1	◇1	1	1	1	1	1	1	1	1	1	◇1	1	1	◇1	1
Brighton 10	d									21 45				22 04	22 17			
Hove 2	d																	
Preston Park	d													22 07				
Hassocks 4	d									21 53				22 14				
Burgess Hill 4	d									21 57				22 17	22 27			
Lewes 4	d		21 22															
Wivelsfield 4	d		21 36											22 20				
Haywards Heath 3	a		21 40							22 02				22 24	22 32			
	d		21 41							22 02				22 25	22 32			
Balcombe	d													22 30				
Horsham 4	d			21 37							22 00						22 37	
Littlehaven	d										22 03							
Faygate	d																	
Ifield	d										22 09							
Crawley	d			21 46							22 13						22 46	
Three Bridges 4	a			21 50						22 11	22 16			22 36	22 41		22 50	
	d			21 50						22 12	22 18			22 36	22 42		22 50	
Gatwick Airport 10	a		21 52	21 55						22 16	22 22			22 41	22 46		22 55	
	d	21 50	21 53	21 56	22 05	22 07	22 20			22 17	22 23		22 35	22 42	22 47	22 50	22 56	23 05
Horley 4	d			21 58							22 26						22 58	
Salfords	d										22 30							
Earlswood (Surrey)	d										22 33							
Tonbridge 4	d								21 41			22 29						
Leigh (Kent)	d								21 45			22 33						
Penshurst	d								21 49			22 37						
Edenbridge	d								21 55			22 43						
Godstone	d								22 02			22 50						
Nutfield	d								22 07			22 55						
Reigate	d																	
Redhill 5	a			22 05		22 15			22 12		22 36	23 00		22 49			23 05	
	d			22 05		22 20			22 13		22 37			22 49			23 05	
Merstham	d								22 17		22 41							
Coulsdon South	d								22 22		22 46							
Purley 4	d			22 14					22 27		22 50						23 14	
East Croydon	a		22 09	22 20				22 28	22 32	22 33	22 55			23 00	23 03		23 20	
	d		22 09	22 21				22 29	22 34	22 33	22 56			23 00	23 03		23 21	
Norwood Junction 2	a								22 38									
London Bridge 4 ⊖	a								22 51	22 46					23 16			
London Blackfriars 3 ⊖	a																	
City Thameslink 3	a																	
Farringdon 3 ⊖	a																	
St Pancras International 15 ⊖	a																	
St Albans City	a																	
Luton Airport Parkway 4	a																	
Luton 7	a																	
Bedford 10	a																	
Clapham Junction 10	d		22 19	22 32				22 41			23 07			23 11			23 32	
London Victoria 15 ⊖	a	22 20	22 25	22 39	22 35		22 50	22 50			23 14		23 07	23 17		23 20	23 38	23 35

b arr. 2254

Table 186

Brighton - London, Bedford

Sundays
until 05 September

		GW ■		GX ■	SN ■	FC ■	SN ◇■	SN ■	GX ■		FC ■	GX ■	FC ■
Brighton ■	d					22 45	23 02				23 11		23 44
Hove ■	d												
Preston Park	d						23 06						
Hassocks ■	d					22 53	23 12				23 19		23 52
Burgess Hill ■	d					22 57	23 16				23 23		23 56
Lewes ■	d												
Wivelsfield ■	d						23 19						
Haywards Heath ■	a					23 02	23 23				23 27		00 01
	d					23 02	23 24				23 28		00 01
Balcombe	d						23 29						
Horsham ■	d							23 04					
Littlehaven	d							23 07					
Faygate	d												
Ifield	d							23 13					
Crawley	d							23 17					
Three Bridges ■	a					23 11	23 35	23 20			23 38		00 10
	d					23 12	23 42	23 22			23 38		00 10
Gatwick Airport ■	a					23 16	23 46	23 26			23 42		00 14
	d	23 08		23 20		23 17	23 47	23 27	23 35		23 43	23 50	00 15
Horley ■	d						23 49	23 30					
Salfords	d												
Earlswood (Surrey)	d												
Tonbridge ■	d												
Leigh (Kent)	d												
Penshurst	d												
Edenbridge	d												
Godstone	d												
Nutfield	d												
Reigate	d												
Redhill ■	a	23 16					23 57	23 36					00 22
	d	23 20					00 02	23 37					00 22
Merstham	d							23 41					
Coulsdon South	d							23 46					
Purley ■	d						00 11	23 50					
East Croydon ⇌	a				23 28	23 33	00 16	23 55			00 02		00 35
	d				23 29	23 33	00 17	23 56			00 04		00 36
Norwood Junction ■	a												
London Bridge ■ ⊖	a					23 46					00 19		00 52
London Blackfriars ■ ⊖	a												
City Thameslink ■	a												
Farringdon ■ ⊖	a												
St Pancras International ■ ⊖	a												
St Albans City	a												
Luton Airport Parkway ■	a												
Luton ■	a												
Bedford ■	a												
Clapham Junction ■	d				23 41		00 30	00 11					
London Victoria ■ ⊖	a			23 55	23 50		00 37	00 18	00 10			00 25	

Table 186

Brighton - London, Bedford

Sundays
from 12 September

		SN ■	SN ◇■	GX ■	FC ■	GX ■	GX ■	FC ■	GX ■		GX ■	SN	GX ■	SN ■	GX ■	SN ■	SN ■	SN ■	GX ■		SN ■	FC ■	GX ■	SN ■	GX ■
Brighton ■	d		23p02		23p11			23p37													03 50				
Hove ■	d																								
Preston Park	d		23p06					23p41																	
Hassocks ■	d		23p12		23p19			23p47																	
Burgess Hill ■	d		23p16		23p23			23p51																	
Lewes ■	d																								
Wivelsfield ■	d		23p19					23p53																	
Haywards Heath ■	a		23p23		23p27			23p58																	
	d		23p24		23p28			23p59																	
Balcombe	d							00 04																	
Horsham ■	d	23p02																							
Littlehaven	d	23p05																							
Faygate	d																								
Ifield	d	23p11																							
Crawley	d	23p14																							
Three Bridges ■	a	23p18	23p33		23p38			00 10													04 45				
	d	23p18	23p47		23p38			00 10						01 10		02 10	03 10	04 10			04 58	05 10		05 30	
Gatwick Airport ■	a	23p22	23p52		23p42			00 14						01 19		02 14	03 14	04 14			05 02	05 14		05 34	
	d	23p23	23p53	23p35	23p43	23p50	00 05	00 15	00 20		00 35		00 50	01 20	01 35	02 15	03 15	04 15	04 35		05 03	05 15	05 20	05 36	05 50
Horley ■	d	23p26	23p56											01 22		02 18	03 18	04 18			05 05			05 38	
Salfords	d	23p30																							
Earlswood (Surrey)	d	23p33																							
Tonbridge ■	d																								
Leigh (Kent)	d																								
Penshurst	d																								
Edenbridge	d																								
Godstone	d																								
Nutfield	d																								
Reigate	d																								
Redhill ■	a	23p36	00 03					00 22																05 46	
	d	23p37	00 03					00 22																05 46	
Merstham	d	23p41																							
Coulsdon South	d	23p46																							
Purley ■	d	23p49	00 11											01 37		02 33	03 33	04 33			05 22			05 56	
East Croydon ⇌	a	23p55	00 16		00 02			00 35						01 42		02 39	03 39	04 39			05 27	05 31		06 01	
	d	23p56	00 17		00 04			00 36				00 49		01 43		02 40	03 40	04 40			05 28	05 32		06 02	
Norwood Junction ■	a																					05 36			
London Bridge ■ ⊖	a				00 19			00 52														05 59			
London Blackfriars ■ ⊖	a																								
City Thameslink ■	a																								
Farringdon ■ ⊖	a																								
St Pancras International ■ ⊖	a																								
St Albans City	a																								
Luton Airport Parkway ■	a																								
Luton ■	a																								
Bedford ■	a																								
Clapham Junction ■	d	00 11	00 29									01 02		01 54		02 53	03 53	04 53			05 48			06 14	
London Victoria ■ ⊖	a	00 18	00 36	00 10		00 25	00 42		00 55		01 11	01 09	01 25	02 05	02 20	03 05	04 05	05 05	05 10		05 56		05 58	06 22	06 25

Table 186

Sundays from 12 September

Brighton - London, Bedford

		GX [1] 🛒	GW [1]	FC [1]	GX [1] 🛒	SN [1]	GX [1] 🛒	FC [1]	GX [1] 🛒	SN ◇[1]	SN [1]	GX [1] 🛒	GW [1]	GX [1] 🛒	SN [1]	SN [1]	GX [1] 🛒	SN ◇[1]	FC [1]
Brighton [10]	d			05 44				06 13		06 16								07 00	07 16
Hove [2]	d																		
Preston Park	d									06 19								07 03	
Hassocks [4]	d			05 52						06 26								07 10	
Burgess Hill [4]	d			05 56				06 26		06 29								07 13	07 26
Lewes [4]	d																		
Wivelsfield [4]	d									06 32								07 16	
Haywards Heath [3]	a			06 00				06 30		06 36								07 20	07 30
	d			06 01				06 31		06 40								07 21	07 31
Balcombe	d																	07 26	
Horsham [4]	d					06 04					06 34				07 04				
Littlehaven	d					06 07					06 37				07 07				
Faygate	d																		
Ifield	d					06 13					06 43				07 13				
Crawley	d					06 17					06 47				07 17				
Three Bridges [4]	a			06 10		06 20		06 40		06 49	06 51				07 20			07 32	07 40
	d			06 10		06 21		06 40		06 49	06 53				07 22			07 32	07 40
Gatwick Airport [10]	a			06 14		06 25		06 44		06 53	06 56				07 26			07 37	07 44
	d	06 05	06 08	06 15	06 20		06 35	06 45	06 50	06 54	06 58	07 05	07 08	07 20	07 27		07 35	07 38	07 45
Horley [4]	d										07 00				07 30				
Salfords	d																		
Earlswood (Surrey)	d																		
Tonbridge [4]	d															07 29			
Leigh (Kent)	d															07 33			
Penshurst	d															07 37			
Edenbridge	d															07 43			
Godstone	d															07 50			
Nutfield	d															07 55			
Reigate	d																		
Redhill [5]	a		06 17								07 06		07 18		07 36	08 00		07 45	
	d		06 21								07 07		07 21		07 37			07 46	
Merstham	d										07 11				07 41				
Coulsdon South	d										07 16				07 46				
Purley [4]	d										07 20				07 49				
East Croydon	a			06 31				07 01		07 10	07 26				07 54			07 58	08 01
	d			06 32				07 02		07 10	07 27				07 58			08 00	08 02
Norwood Junction [2]	a			06 36															
London Bridge [4] ⊖	a			06 59				07 16											08 16
London Blackfriars [3] ⊖	a																		
City Thameslink [3]	a																		
Farringdon [3] ⊖	a																		
St Pancras International [15] ⊖	a																		
St Albans City	a																		
Luton Airport Parkway [4]	a																		
Luton [7]	a																		
Bedford [10]	a																		
Clapham Junction [10]	d									07 24	07 41				08 09			08 12	
London Victoria [15] ⊖	a	06 40			06 55		07 10		07 25	07 31	07 48	07 40		07 55	08 16		08 10	08 18	

Table 186

Sundays from 12 September

Brighton - London, Bedford

		GX [1] 🛒	SN ◇[1] 🛒	SN ◇[1]	GX [1] 🛒	GW [1]	GX [1] 🛒	SN [1]	FC [1]	SN ◇[1]	SN [1]	SN [1]	GX [1] 🛒	SN ◇[1]	FC [1]	GX [1] 🛒
Brighton [10]	d								07 44					08 00	08 16	
Hove [2]	d									07 54						
Preston Park	d													08 03		
Hassocks [4]	d								07 52					08 10		
Burgess Hill [4]	d								07 56	08 04				08 13	08 26	
Lewes [4]	d		07b20													
Wivelsfield [4]	d		07 32											08 16		
Haywards Heath [3]	a		07 36						08 00	08 09				08 20	08 30	
	d		07 39						08 01	08 10				08 21	08 31	
Balcombe	d													08 26		
Horsham [4]	d			07 42							08 04					
Littlehaven	d										08 07					
Faygate	d															
Ifield	d										08 13					
Crawley	d			07 51							08 17					
Three Bridges [4]	a			07 54					08 10		08 20			08 32	08 40	
	d			07 55					08 10		08 22			08 32	08 40	
Gatwick Airport [10]	a		07 51	07 59					08 14	08 22	08 26			08 37	08 44	
	d	07 50	07 53	08 00	08 05	08 08	08 20		08 15	08 23	08 27		08 35	08 38	08 45	08 50
Horley [4]	d			08 02							08 30					
Salfords	d															
Earlswood (Surrey)	d															
Tonbridge [4]	d											08 29				
Leigh (Kent)	d											08 33				
Penshurst	d											08 37				
Edenbridge	d											08 43				
Godstone	d											08 50				
Nutfield	d											08 55				
Reigate	d															
Redhill [5]	a			08 09		08 15					08 36	09 00		08 45		
	d			08 09		08 19					08 37			08 46		
Merstham	d										08 41					
Coulsdon South	d										08 46					
Purley [4]	d			08 19							08 49					
East Croydon	a		08 09	08 24				08 28	08 31	08 39	08 54			08 58	09 01	
	d		08 10	08 26				08 29	08 32	08 40	08 58			09 00	09 02	
Norwood Junction [2]	a															
London Bridge [4] ⊖	a								08 46						09 16	
London Blackfriars [3] ⊖	a															
City Thameslink [3]	a															
Farringdon [3] ⊖	a															
St Pancras International [15] ⊖	a															
St Albans City	a															
Luton Airport Parkway [4]	a															
Luton [7]	a															
Bedford [10]	a															
Clapham Junction [10]	d		08 25	08 38				08 41		08 55	09 09			09 12		
London Victoria [15] ⊖	a	08 25	08 31	08 46	08 40		08 55	08 48		09 01	09 16		09 10	09 18		09 25

b arr. 0714

Table 186

Sundays from 12 September

Brighton - London, Bedford

		SN ◇1 ⟂	SN ◇1 ⟂	SN ◇1 ⟂	GX 1 ⟂	GW 1	GX 1 ⟂	SN 1	FC 1	SN ◇1	SN 1	SN 1	GX 1 ⟂	SN ◇1	FC 1	GX 1 ⟂	SN ◇1 ⟂	SN ◇1 ⟂
Brighton 10	d		08 34						08 44					09 00	09 16			09 34
Hove 2	d									08 54								
Preston Park	d													09 03				
Hassocks 4	d								08 52					09 10				
Burgess Hill 4	d								08 56	09 04				09 13	09 26			
Lewes 4	d	08 16															09 16	
Wivelsfield 4	d	08 31												09 16			09 31	
Haywards Heath 3	a	08 36							09 00	09 09				09 20	09 30		09 35	
	d	08 39							09 01	09 10				09 21	09 31		09 39	
Balcombe	d													09 26				
Horsham 4	d			08 42							09 04							
Littlehaven	d										09 07							
Faygate	d																	
Ifield	d										09 13							
Crawley	d			08 51							09 17							
Three Bridges 4	a			08 54					09 10		09 20			09 32	09 40			
	d			08 55					09 10		09 22			09 32	09 40			
Gatwick Airport 10	a	08 51	08 55	08 59					09 14	09 21	09 26			09 37	09 44		09 51	09 55
	d	08 53	08 56	09 00	09 05	09 08	09 20		09 15	09 23	09 27		09 35	09 38	09 45	09 50	09 53	09 56
Horley 4	d			09 02							09 30							
Salfords	d																	
Earlswood (Surrey)	d																	
Tonbridge 4	d											09 29						
Leigh (Kent)	d											09 33						
Penshurst	d											09 37						
Edenbridge	d											09 43						
Godstone	d											09 50						
Nutfield	d											09 55						
Reigate	d																	
Redhill 5	a			09 09		09 16					09 36	10 00		09 45				
	d			09 09		09 20					09 37			09 46				
Merstham	d										09 41							
Coulsdon South	d										09 46							
Purley 4	d			09 19							09 49							
East Croydon	a	09 09	09 12	09 24				09 28	09 31	09 39	09 54			09 58	10 01		10 09	10 12
	d	09 10	09 13	09 25				09 29	09 32	09 40	09 58			10 00	10 02		10 10	10 13
Norwood Junction 2	a																	
London Bridge 4 ⊖	a								09 46						10 16			
London Blackfriars 3 ⊖	a																	
City Thameslink 3	a																	
Farringdon 3 ⊖	a																	
St Pancras International 15 ⊖	a																	
St Albans City	a																	
Luton Airport Parkway 4	a																	
Luton 7	a																	
Bedford 10	a																	
Clapham Junction 10	d	09 25	09 28	09 38				09 41		09 55	10 09			10 12			10 25	10 28
London Victoria 15 ⊖	a	09 31	09 35	09 46	09 40		09 55	09 48		10 01	10 16		10 10	10 18		10 25	10 31	10 35

b arr. 0920 c arr. 0954

Table 186

Sundays from 12 September

Brighton - London, Bedford

		SN ◇1 ⟂	GX 1 ⟂	GW 1	GX 1 ⟂	SN 1	FC 1	SN ◇1	SN 1	SN 1	GX 1 ⟂	SN ◇1	FC 1	GX 1 ⟂	SN ◇1 ⟂	SN ◇1 ⟂	SN ◇1 ⟂
Brighton 10	d						09 44					10 00	10 16			10 34	
Hove 2	d							09 54									
Preston Park	d											10 03					
Hassocks 4	d						09 52					10 10					
Burgess Hill 4	d						09 56	10 04				10 13	10 26				
Lewes 4	d														10 16		
Wivelsfield 4	d											10 16			10 31		
Haywards Heath 3	a						10 00	10 09				10 20	10 30		10 35		
	d						10 01	10 10				10 21	10 31		10 39		
Balcombe	d											10 26					
Horsham 4	d	09 42							10 04								10 42
Littlehaven	d								10 07								
Faygate	d																
Ifield	d								10 13								
Crawley	d	09 51							10 17								10 51
Three Bridges 4	a	09 54					10 10		10 20			10 32	10 40				10 54
	d	09 55					10 10		10 22			10 32	10 40				10 55
Gatwick Airport 10	a	09 59					10 14	10 21	10 26			10 37	10 44		10 51	10 55	10 59
	d	10 00	10 05	10 08	10 20		10 15	10 23	10 27		10 35	10 38	10 45	10 50	10 53	10 56	11 00
Horley 4	d	10 02							10 30								11 02
Salfords	d																
Earlswood (Surrey)	d																
Tonbridge 4	d									10 29							
Leigh (Kent)	d									10 33							
Penshurst	d									10 37							
Edenbridge	d									10 43							
Godstone	d									10 50							
Nutfield	d									10 55							
Reigate	d																
Redhill 5	a	10 09		10 15					10 36	11 00		10 45					11 09
	d	10 09		10 19					10 37			10 46					11 09
Merstham	d								10 41								
Coulsdon South	d								10 46								
Purley 4	d	10 19							10 49								11 19
East Croydon	a	10 24				10 28	10 31	10 39	10 54			10 58	11 01		11 09	11 12	11 24
	d	10 25				10 29	10 32	10 40	10 58			11 00	11 02		11 10	11 13	11 25
Norwood Junction 2	a																
London Bridge 4 ⊖	a						10 46						11 16				
London Blackfriars 3 ⊖	a																
City Thameslink 3	a																
Farringdon 3 ⊖	a																
St Pancras International 15 ⊖	a																
St Albans City	a																
Luton Airport Parkway 4	a																
Luton 7	a																
Bedford 10	a																
Clapham Junction 10	d	10 38				10 41		10 55	11 09			11 12			11 25	11 28	11 38
London Victoria 15 ⊖	a	10 46	10 40		10 55	10 48		11 01	11 16		11 10	11 18		11 25	11 31	11 35	11 46

b arr. 1020 c arr. 1054

Table 186

Sundays from 12 September

Brighton - London, Bedford

		GX	GW	GX	SN	FC	SN ◇	SN	SN	GX	SN ◇	FC	GX	SN ◇	SN ◇	SN ◇
Brighton	d					10 44					11 00	11 16			11 34	
Hove	d						10 54									
Preston Park	d										11 03					
Hassocks	d					10 52					11 10					
Burgess Hill	d					10 56	11 04				11 13	11 26				
Lewes	d													11 16		
Wivelsfield	d										11 16			11 31		
Haywards Heath	a					11 00	11 09				11 20	11 30		11 35		
	d					11 01	11 10				11 21	11 31		11 39		
Balcombe	d										11 26					
Horsham	d							11 04								11 42
Littlehaven	d							11 07								
Faygate	d															
Ifield	d							11 13								
Crawley	d							11 17								11 51
Three Bridges	a					11 10		11 20			11 32	11 40				11 54
	d					11 10		11 22			11 32	11 40				11 55
Gatwick Airport	a					11 14	11 21	11 26			11 37	11 44		11 51	11 55	11 59
	d	11 05	11 08	11 20		11 15	11 23	11 27		11 35	11 38	11 45	11 50	11 53	11 56	12 00
Horley	d							11 30								12 02
Salfords	d															
Earlswood (Surrey)	d															
Tonbridge	d								11 29							
Leigh (Kent)	d								11 33							
Penshurst	d								11 37							
Edenbridge	d								11 43							
Godstone	d								11 50							
Nutfield	d								11 55							
Reigate	d															
Redhill	a		11 16					11 36	12 00		11 45					12 09
	d		11 20					11 37			11 46					12 09
Merstham	d							11 41								
Coulsdon South	d							11 46								
Purley	d							11 49								12 19
East Croydon	a				11 28	11 31	11 39	11 54			11 58	12 01		12 09	12 12	12 24
	d				11 29	11 32	11 40	11 58			12 00	12 02		12 10	12 13	12 25
Norwood Junction	a															
London Bridge ⊖	a					11 46						12 16				
London Blackfriars ⊖	a															
City Thameslink	a															
Farringdon ⊖	a															
St Pancras International ⊖	a															
St Albans City	a															
Luton Airport Parkway	a															
Luton	a															
Bedford	a															
Clapham Junction	d				11 41		11 55	12 09			12 12			12 25	12 28	12 38
London Victoria ⊖	a	11 40		11 55	11 48		12 01	12 16		12 10	12 18		12 25	12 31	12 35	12 46

b arr. 1120 c arr. 1154

Table 186

Sundays from 12 September

Brighton - London, Bedford

		GX	GW	GX	SN	FC	SN ◇	SN	SN	GX	SN ◇	FC	GX	SN ◇	SN ◇	SN ◇	GX	GW
Brighton	d					11 44					12 00	12 16			12 34			
Hove	d						11 54											
Preston Park	d										12 03							
Hassocks	d					11 52					12 10							
Burgess Hill	d					11 56	12 04				12 13	12 26						
Lewes	d													12 16				
Wivelsfield	d										12 16			12 31				
Haywards Heath	a					12 00	12 09				12 20	12 30		12 35				
	d					12 01	12 10				12 21	12 31		12 39				
Balcombe	d										12 26							
Horsham	d							12 04								12 42		
Littlehaven	d							12 07										
Faygate	d																	
Ifield	d							12 13										
Crawley	d							12 17								12 51		
Three Bridges	a					12 10		12 20			12 32	12 40				12 54		
	d					12 10		12 22			12 32	12 40				12 55		
Gatwick Airport	a					12 14	12 22	12 26			12 37	12 44		12 52	12 55	12 59		
	d	12 05	12 08	12 20		12 15	12 23	12 27		12 35	12 38	12 45	12 50	12 53	12 56	13 00	13 05	13 08
Horley	d							12 30								13 02		
Salfords	d																	
Earlswood (Surrey)	d																	
Tonbridge	d								12 29									
Leigh (Kent)	d								12 33									
Penshurst	d								12 37									
Edenbridge	d								12 43									
Godstone	d								12 50									
Nutfield	d								12 55									
Reigate	d																	
Redhill	a		12 15					12 36	13 00		12 45					13 09		13 16
	d		12 19					12 37			12 46					13 09		13 20
Merstham	d							12 41										
Coulsdon South	d							12 46										
Purley	d							12 49								13 19		
East Croydon	a				12 28	12 31	12 39	12 54			12 58	13 01		13 09	13 12	13 24		
	d				12 29	12 32	12 40	12 58			13 00	13 02		13 10	13 13	13 25		
Norwood Junction	a																	
London Bridge ⊖	a					12 46						13 16						
London Blackfriars ⊖	a																	
City Thameslink	a																	
Farringdon ⊖	a																	
St Pancras International ⊖	a																	
St Albans City	a																	
Luton Airport Parkway	a																	
Luton	a																	
Bedford	a																	
Clapham Junction	d				12 41		12 55	13 09			13 12			13 25	13 28	13 38		
London Victoria ⊖	a	12 40		12 55	12 48		13 01	13 16		13 10	13 18		13 25	13 31	13 35	13 46	13 40	

b arr. 1220 c arr. 1254

Table 186

Brighton - London, Bedford

Sundays
from 12 September

Station		GX 1	SN 1	FC 1	SN ◇1	SN 1	SN 1	GX 1	SN ◇1	FC 1	GX 1	SN ◇1	SN ◇1	SN ◇1	GX 1	GW 1
Brighton 10	d			12 44					13 00	13 16			13 34			
Hove 2	d				12 54											
Preston Park	d								13 03							
Hassocks 4	d			12 52					13 10							
Burgess Hill 4	d			12 56	13 04				13 13	13 26						
Lewes 4	d											13 16				
Wivelsfield 4	d								13 16			13 31				
Haywards Heath 3	a			13 00	13 09				13 20	13 30		13 35				
	d			13 01	13 10				13 21	13 31		13 39				
Balcombe	d								13 26							
Horsham 4	d					13 04								13 42		
Littlehaven	d					13 07										
Faygate	d															
Ifield	d					13 13										
Crawley	d					13 17								13 51		
Three Bridges 4	a			13 10		13 20			13 32	13 40				13 54		
	d			13 10		13 22			13 32	13 40				13 55		
Gatwick Airport 10	a			13 14	13 22	13 26			13 37	13 44		13 52	13 55	13 59		
	d	13 20		13 15	13 23	13 27		13 35	13 38	13 45	13 50	13 53	13 56	14 00	14 05	14 08
Horley 4	d					13 30								14 02		
Salfords	d															
Earlswood (Surrey)	d															
Tonbridge 4	d						13 29									
Leigh (Kent)	d						13 33									
Penshurst	d						13 37									
Edenbridge	d						13 43									
Godstone	d						13 50									
Nutfield	d						13 55									
Reigate	d															
Redhill 5	a					13 36	14 00		13 45					14 09		14 15
	d					13 37			13 46					14 09		14 19
Merstham	d					13 41										
Coulsdon South	d					13 46										
Purley 4	d					13 49								14 19		
East Croydon	a		13 28	13 31	13 39	13 54			13 58	14 01		14 09	14 12	14 24		
	d		13 29	13 32	13 40	13 58			14 00	14 02		14 10	14 13	14 25		
Norwood Junction 2	a															
London Bridge 4 ⊖	a			13 46						14 16						
London Blackfriars 3 ⊖	a															
City Thameslink 3	a															
Farringdon 3 ⊖	a															
St Pancras International 15 ⊖	a															
St Albans City	a															
Luton Airport Parkway 4	a															
Luton 7	a															
Bedford 10	a															
Clapham Junction 10	d		13 41		13 55	14 09			14 12			14 25	14 28	14 38		
London Victoria 15 ⊖	a	13 55	13 48		14 01	14 16		14 10	14 18		14 25	14 31	14 35	14 46	14 40	

b arr. 1320

c arr. 1354

Table 186

Brighton - London, Bedford

Sundays
from 12 September

Station		GX 1	SN 1	FC 1	SN ◇1	SN 1	SN 1	GX 1	SN ◇1	FC 1	GX 1	SN ◇1	SN ◇1	SN ◇1	GX 1	GW 1	GX 1
Brighton 10	d			13 44					14 00	14 16			14 34				
Hove 2	d				13 54												
Preston Park	d								14 03								
Hassocks 4	d			13 52					14 10								
Burgess Hill 4	d			13 56	14 04				14 13	14 26							
Lewes 4	d											14 16					
Wivelsfield 4	d								14 16			14 31					
Haywards Heath 3	a			14 00	14 09				14 20	14 30		14 35					
	d			14 01	14 10				14 21	14 31		14 39					
Balcombe	d								14 26								
Horsham 4	d					14 04								14 42			
Littlehaven	d					14 07											
Faygate	d																
Ifield	d					14 13											
Crawley	d					14 17								14 51			
Three Bridges 4	a			14 10		14 20			14 32	14 40				14 54			
	d			14 10		14 22			14 32	14 40				14 55			
Gatwick Airport 10	a			14 14	14 22	14 26			14 37	14 44		14 52	14 55	14 59			
	d	14 20		14 15	14 23	14 27		14 35	14 38	14 45	14 50	14 53	14 56	15 00	15 05	15 08	15 20
Horley 4	d					14 30								15 02			
Salfords	d																
Earlswood (Surrey)	d																
Tonbridge 4	d						14 29										
Leigh (Kent)	d						14 33										
Penshurst	d						14 37										
Edenbridge	d						14 43										
Godstone	d						14 50										
Nutfield	d						14 55										
Reigate	d																
Redhill 5	a					14 36	15 00		14 45					15 09		15 16	
	d					14 37			14 46					15 09		15 20	
Merstham	d					14 41											
Coulsdon South	d					14 46											
Purley 4	d					14 49								15 19			
East Croydon	a		14 28	14 31	14 39	14 54			14 58	15 01		15 09	15 12	15 24			
	d		14 29	14 32	14 40	14 58			15 00	15 02		15 10	15 13	15 25			
Norwood Junction 2	a																
London Bridge 4 ⊖	a			14 46						15 16							
London Blackfriars 3 ⊖	a																
City Thameslink 3	a																
Farringdon 3 ⊖	a																
St Pancras International 15 ⊖	a																
St Albans City	a																
Luton Airport Parkway 4	a																
Luton 7	a																
Bedford 10	a																
Clapham Junction 10	d		14 41		14 55	15 09			15 12			15 25	15 28	15 38			
London Victoria 15 ⊖	a	14 55	14 48		15 01	15 16		15 10	15 18		15 25	15 31	15 35	15 46	15 40		15 55

b arr. 1420

c arr. 1454

e arr. 1520

Table 186

Sundays
from 12 September

Brighton - London, Bedford

		SN 1	FC 1	SN ◇1	SN 1	SN 1	GX 1 H	SN ◇1	FC 1	GX 1 H	SN ◇1 H	SN ◇1 H	SN ◇1 H	GX 1 H	GW 1	GX 1 H
Brighton 10	d		14 44					15 00	15 16			15 34				
Hove 2	d			14 54												
Preston Park	d							15 03								
Hassocks 4	d		14 52					15 10								
Burgess Hill 4	d		14 56	15 04				15 13	15 26							
Lewes 4	d										15 16					
Wivelsfield 4	d							15 16			15 31					
Haywards Heath 3	a		15 00	15 09				15 20	15 30		15 35					
	d		15 01	15 10				15 21	15 31		15 39					
Balcombe	d							15 26								
Horsham 4	d				15 04								15 42			
Littlehaven	d				15 07											
Faygate	d															
Ifield	d				15 13											
Crawley	d				15 17								15 51			
Three Bridges 4	a		15 10		15 20			15 32	15 40				15 54			
	d		15 10		15 22			15 32	15 40				15 55			
Gatwick Airport 10	a		15 14	15 22	15 26			15 37	15 44		15 52	15 55	15 59			
	d		15 15	15 23	15 27		15 35	15 38	15 45	15 50	15 53	15 56	16 00	16 05	16 08	16 20
Horley 4	d				15 30								16 02			
Salfords	d															
Earlswood (Surrey)	d															
Tonbridge 4	d					15 29										
Leigh (Kent)	d					15 33										
Penshurst	d					15 37										
Edenbridge	d					15 43										
Godstone	d					15 50										
Nutfield	d					15 55										
Reigate	d															
Redhill 5	a				15 36	16 00		15 45					16 09		16 15	
	d				15 37			15 46					16 09		16 19	
Merstham	d				15 41											
Coulsdon South	d				15 46											
Purley 4	d				15 49								16 19			
East Croydon ⇌	a	15 28	15 31	15 39	15 54			15 58	16 01		16 09	16 12	16 24			
	d	15 29	15 32	15 40	15 58			16 00	16 02		16 10	16 13	16 25			
Norwood Junction 2	a															
London Bridge 4 ⊖	a		15 46						16 16							
London Blackfriars 3 ⊖	a															
City Thameslink 3	a															
Farringdon 3 ⊖	a															
St Pancras International 15 ⊖	a															
St Albans City	a															
Luton Airport Parkway 4	a															
Luton 7	a															
Bedford 10	a															
Clapham Junction 10	d	15 41		15 55	16 09			16 12			16 25	16 28	16 38			
London Victoria 15 ⊖	a	15 48		16 01	16 16		16 10	16 18		16 25	16 31	16 35	16 46	16 40		16 55

b arr. 1554 c arr. 1620

Table 186

Sundays
from 12 September

Brighton - London, Bedford

		SN 1	FC 1	SN ◇1	SN 1	SN 1	GX 1 H	SN ◇1	FC 1	GX 1 H	SN ◇1 H	SN ◇1 H	SN ◇1 H	GX 1 H	GW 1	GX 1 H	SN 1
Brighton 10	d		15 44					16 00	16 16			16 34					
Hove 2	d			15 54													
Preston Park	d							16 03									
Hassocks 4	d		15 52					16 10									
Burgess Hill 4	d		15 56	16 04				16 13	16 26								
Lewes 4	d										16 16						
Wivelsfield 4	d							16 16			16 31						
Haywards Heath 3	a		16 00	16 09				16 20	16 30		16 35						
	d		16 01	16 10				16 21	16 31		16 39						
Balcombe	d							16 26									
Horsham 4	d				16 04								16 42				
Littlehaven	d				16 07												
Faygate	d																
Ifield	d				16 13												
Crawley	d				16 17								16 51				
Three Bridges 4	a		16 10		16 20			16 32	16 40				16 54				
	d		16 10		16 22			16 32	16 40				16 55				
Gatwick Airport 10	a		16 14	16 22	16 26			16 37	16 44		16 52	16 55	16 59				
	d		16 15	16 23	16 27		16 35	16 38	16 45	16 50	16 53	16 56	17 00	17 05	17 08	17 20	
Horley 4	d				16 30								17 02				
Salfords	d																
Earlswood (Surrey)	d																
Tonbridge 4	d					16 29											
Leigh (Kent)	d					16 33											
Penshurst	d					16 37											
Edenbridge	d					16 43											
Godstone	d					16 50											
Nutfield	d					16 55											
Reigate	d																
Redhill 5	a				16 36	17 00		16 45					17 09		17 16		
	d				16 37			16 46					17 09		17 20		
Merstham	d				16 41												
Coulsdon South	d				16 46												
Purley 4	d				16 49								17 19				
East Croydon ⇌	a	16 28	16 31	16 39	16 54			16 58	17 01		17 09	17 12	17 24				17 28
	d	16 29	16 32	16 40	16 58			17 00	17 02		17 10	17 13	17 25				17 29
Norwood Junction 2	a																
London Bridge 4 ⊖	a		16 46						17 16								
London Blackfriars 3 ⊖	a																
City Thameslink 3	a																
Farringdon 3 ⊖	a																
St Pancras International 15 ⊖	a																
St Albans City	a																
Luton Airport Parkway 4	a																
Luton 7	a																
Bedford 10	a																
Clapham Junction 10	d	16 41		16 55	17 09			17 12			17 25	17 28	17 38				17 41
London Victoria 15 ⊖	a	16 48		17 01	17 16		17 10	17 18		17 25	17 31	17 35	17 46	17 40		17 55	17 48

b arr. 1654 c arr. 1720

Table 186

Sundays
from 12 September

Brighton - London, Bedford

		FC ■	SN ◇■	SN ■	SN ■	GX ■ H	SN ◇■	FC ■	GX ■ H	SN ◇■ H	SN ◇■ H	SN ◇■ H	GX ■ H	GW ■	GX ■ H	SN ■	FC ■
Brighton	d	16 44					17 00	17 16			17 34						17 44
Hove	d		16 54														
Preston Park	d						17 03										
Hassocks	d	16 52					17 10										17 52
Burgess Hill	d	16 56	17 04				17 13	17 26									17 56
Lewes	d									17 16							
Wivelsfield	d						17 16			17 31							
Haywards Heath	a	17 00	17 09				17 20	17 30		17 35							18 00
	d	17 01	17 10				17 21	17 31		17 39							18 01
Balcombe	d						17 26										
Horsham	d			17 04								17 42					
Littlehaven	d			17 07													
Faygate	d																
Ifield	d			17 13													
Crawley	d			17 17								17 51					
Three Bridges	a	17 10		17 20			17 32	17 40				17 54					18 10
	d	17 10		17 22			17 32	17 40				17 55					18 10
Gatwick Airport	a	17 14	17 22	17 26			17 37	17 44		17 52	17 55	17 59					18 14
	d	17 15	17 23	17 27		17 35	17 38	17 45	17 50	17 53	17 56	18 00	18 05	18 08	18 20		18 15
Horley	d			17 30								18 02					
Salfords	d																
Earlswood (Surrey)	d																
Tonbridge	d				17 29												
Leigh (Kent)	d				17 33												
Penshurst	d				17 37												
Edenbridge	d				17 43												
Godstone	d				17 50												
Nutfield	d				17 55												
Reigate	d																
Redhill	a			17 36	18 00		17 45					18 09		18 15			
	d			17 37			17 46					18 09		18 19			
Merstham	d			17 41													
Coulsdon South	d			17 46													
Purley	d			17 49								18 19					
East Croydon	a	17 31	17 39	17 54			17 58	18 01		18 09	18 12	18 24				18 28	18 31
	d	17 32	17 40	17 58			18 00	18 02		18 10	18 13	18 25				18 29	18 32
Norwood Junction	a																
London Bridge ⊖	a	17 46						18 16									18 46
London Blackfriars ⊖	a																
City Thameslink	a																
Farringdon ⊖	a																
St Pancras International ⊖	a																
St Albans City	a																
Luton Airport Parkway	a																
Luton	a																
Bedford	a																
Clapham Junction	d		17 55	18 09			18 12			18 25	18 28	18 38				18 41	
London Victoria ⊖	a		18 01	18 16		18 10	18 18		18 25	18 31	18 35	18 46	18 40		18 55	18 48	

b arr. 1754 c arr. 1820

Table 186

Sundays
from 12 September

Brighton - London, Bedford

		SN ◇■	SN ■	SN ■	GX ■ H	SN ◇■	FC ■	GX ■ H	SN ◇■ H	SN ◇■	SN ◇■	GX ■	GW ■	GX ■	SN ■	FC ■	SN ◇■
Brighton	d					18 00	18 16			18 34						18 44	
Hove	d	17 54															18 54
Preston Park	d					18 03											
Hassocks	d					18 10										18 52	
Burgess Hill	d	18 04				18 13	18 26									18 56	19 04
Lewes	d								18 16								
Wivelsfield	d					18 16			18 31								
Haywards Heath	a	18 09				18 20	18 30		18 35							19 00	19 09
	d	18 10				18 21	18 31		18 39							19 01	19 10
Balcombe	d					18 26											
Horsham	d		18 04								18 42						
Littlehaven	d		18 07														
Faygate	d																
Ifield	d		18 13														
Crawley	d		18 17								18 51						
Three Bridges	a		18 20			18 32	18 40				18 54					19 10	
	d		18 22			18 32	18 40				18 55					19 10	
Gatwick Airport	a	18 22	18 26			18 37	18 44		18 52	18 55	18 59					19 14	19 22
	d	18 23	18 27		18 35	18 38	18 45	18 50	18 53	18 56	19 00	19 05	19 08	19 20		19 15	19 23
Horley	d		18 30								19 02						
Salfords	d																
Earlswood (Surrey)	d																
Tonbridge	d			18 29													
Leigh (Kent)	d			18 33													
Penshurst	d			18 37													
Edenbridge	d			18 43													
Godstone	d			18 50													
Nutfield	d			18 55													
Reigate	d																
Redhill	a		18 36	19 00		18 45					19 09		19 16				
	d		18 37			18 46					19 09		19 20				
Merstham	d		18 41														
Coulsdon South	d		18 46														
Purley	d		18 49								19 19						
East Croydon	a	18 39	18 54			18 58	19 01		19 09	19 12	19 24				19 28	19 31	19 39
	d	18 40	18 58			19 00	19 02		19 10	19 13	19 25				19 29	19 32	19 40
Norwood Junction	a																
London Bridge ⊖	a						19 16									19 46	
London Blackfriars ⊖	a																
City Thameslink	a																
Farringdon ⊖	a																
St Pancras International ⊖	a																
St Albans City	a																
Luton Airport Parkway	a																
Luton	a																
Bedford	a																
Clapham Junction	d	18 55	19 09			19 12			19 25	19 28	19 38				19 41		19 55
London Victoria ⊖	a	19 01	19 16		19 10	19 18		19 25	19 31	19 35	19 46	19 40		19 55	19 48		20 01

b arr. 1854 c arr. 1920

Table 186

Sundays from 12 September

Brighton - London, Bedford

		SN 1	SN 1	GX 1	SN ◇1	FC 1	GX 1	SN ◇1	SN ◇1	SN ◇1	GX 1	GW 1	GX 1	SN 1	FC 1	SN ◇1	SN 1	SN 1
Brighton 10	d				19 00	19 16			19 34						19 44			
Hove 2	d															19 54		
Preston Park	d				19 03													
Hassocks 4	d				19 10										19 52			
Burgess Hill 4	d				19 13	19 26									19 56	20 04		
Lewes 4	d							19 16										
Wivelsfield 4	d				19 16			19 31										
Haywards Heath 3	a				19 20	19 30		19 35							20 00	20 09		
	d				19 21	19 31		19 39							20 01	20 10		
Balcombe	d				19 26													
Horsham 4	d	19 04								19 42							20 04	
Littlehaven	d	19 07															20 07	
Faygate	d																	
Ifield	d	19 13															20 13	
Crawley	d	19 17								19 51							20 17	
Three Bridges 4	a	19 20			19 32	19 40				19 54					20 10		20 20	
	d	19 22			19 32	19 40				19 55					20 10		20 22	
Gatwick Airport 10	a	19 26			19 37	19 44		19 52	19 55	19 59					20 14	20 22	20 26	
	d	19 27		19 35	19 38	19 45	19 50	19 53	19 56	20 00	20 05	20 08	20 20		20 15	20 23	20 27	
Horley 4	d	19 30								20 02							20 30	
Salfords	d																	
Earlswood (Surrey)	d																	
Tonbridge 4	d		19 29															20 29
Leigh (Kent)	d		19 33															20 33
Penshurst	d		19 37															20 37
Edenbridge	d		19 43															20 43
Godstone	d		19 50															20 50
Nutfield	d		19 55															20 55
Reigate	d																	
Redhill 5	a	19 36	20 00		19 45					20 09		20 15					20 36	21 00
	d	19 37			19 46					20 09		20 19					20 37	
Merstham	d	19 41															20 41	
Coulsdon South	d	19 46															20 46	
Purley 4	d	19 49								20 19							20 49	
East Croydon	a	19 54			19 58	20 01		20 09	20 12	20 24				20 28	20 31	20 39	20 54	
	d	19 58			20 00	20 02		20 10	20 13	20 25				20 29	20 32	20 40	20 58	
Norwood Junction 2	a																	
London Bridge 4 ⊖	a					20 16									20 46			
London Blackfriars 3 ⊖	a																	
City Thameslink 3	a																	
Farringdon 3 ⊖	a																	
St Pancras International 15 ⊖	a																	
St Albans City	a																	
Luton Airport Parkway 4	a																	
Luton 7	a																	
Bedford 10	a																	
Clapham Junction 10	d	20 09			20 12			20 25	20 28	20 38				20 41		20 55	21 09	
London Victoria 15 ⊖	a	20 16		20 10	20 18		20 25	20 31	20 35	20 46	20 40		20 55	20 48		21 01	21 16	

b arr. 1954 c arr. 2020

Table 186

Sundays from 12 September

Brighton - London, Bedford

		GX 1	SN ◇1	FC 1	GX 1	SN ◇1	SN ◇1	SN ◇1	GX 1	GW 1	GX 1	SN 1	FC 1	SN ◇1	SN 1	SN 1	GX 1
Brighton 10	d		20 00	20 16			20 34						20 44				
Hove 2	d													20 54			
Preston Park	d		20 03														
Hassocks 4	d		20 10										20 52				
Burgess Hill 4	d		20 13	20 26									20 56	21 04			
Lewes 4	d					20 16											
Wivelsfield 4	d		20 16			20 31											
Haywards Heath 3	a		20 20	20 30		20 35							21 00	21 09			
	d		20 21	20 31		20 39							21 01	21 10			
Balcombe	d		20 26														
Horsham 4	d							20 42							21 04		
Littlehaven	d														21 07		
Faygate	d																
Ifield	d														21 13		
Crawley	d							20 51							21 17		
Three Bridges 4	a		20 32	20 40				20 54					21 10		21 20		
	d		20 32	20 40				20 55					21 10		21 22		
Gatwick Airport 10	a		20 37	20 44		20 52	20 55	20 59					21 14	21 22	21 26		
	d	20 35	20 38	20 45	20 50	20 53	20 56	21 00	21 05	21 08	21 20		21 15	21 23	21 27		21 35
Horley 4	d							21 02							21 30		
Salfords	d																
Earlswood (Surrey)	d																
Tonbridge 4	d															21 29	
Leigh (Kent)	d															21 33	
Penshurst	d															21 37	
Edenbridge	d															21 43	
Godstone	d															21 50	
Nutfield	d															21 55	
Reigate	d																
Redhill 5	a		20 45					21 09		21 16					21 36	22 00	
	d		20 46					21 09		21 19					21 37		
Merstham	d														21 41		
Coulsdon South	d														21 46		
Purley 4	d							21 19							21 49		
East Croydon	a		20 58	21 01		21 09	21 12	21 24				21 28	21 31	21 39	21 54		
	d		21 00	21 02		21 10	21 13	21 25				21 29	21 32	21 40	21 58		
Norwood Junction 2	a																
London Bridge 4 ⊖	a			21 16									21 46				
London Blackfriars 3 ⊖	a																
City Thameslink 3	a																
Farringdon 3 ⊖	a																
St Pancras International 15 ⊖	a																
St Albans City	a																
Luton Airport Parkway 4	a																
Luton 7	a																
Bedford 10	a																
Clapham Junction 10	d		21 12			21 25	21 28	21 38				21 41		21 55	22 09		
London Victoria 15 ⊖	a	21 10	21 18		21 25	21 31	21 35	21 46	21 40		21 55	21 48		22 01	22 16		22 10

b arr. 2054 c arr. 2120

Table 186

Sundays
from 12 September

Brighton - London, Bedford

		SN	FC	GX	SN	SN	GX	GW	GX	SN	FC	SN	SN	GX	SN	FC
		◇1	1	1	◇1	◇1	1	1	1	1	1	1	1	1	◇1	1
Brighton 10	d	21 00	21 16								21 44				22 00	22 16
Hove 2	d															
Preston Park	d	21 03													22 03	
Hassocks 4	d	21 10									21 52				22 10	
Burgess Hill 4	d	21 13	21 26								21 56				22 13	22 26
Lewes 4	d				21 16											
Wivelsfield 4	d	21 16			21 31										22 16	
Haywards Heath 3	a	21 20	21 30		21 35						22 00				22 20	22 30
	d	21 21	21 31		21 39						22 01				22 21	22 31
Balcombe	d	21 26													22 26	
Horsham 4	d					21 42						22 04				
Littlehaven	d											22 07				
Faygate	d															
Ifield	d											22 13				
Crawley	d					21 51						22 17				
Three Bridges 4	a	21 32	21 40			21 54					22 10	22 20			22 32	22 40
	d	21 32	21 40			21 55					22 10	22 22			22 32	22 40
Gatwick Airport 10	a	21 37	21 44		21 52	21 59					22 14	22 26			22 37	22 44
	d	21 38	21 45	21 50	21 53	22 00	22 05	22 07	22 20		22 15	22 27		22 35	22 38	22 45
Horley 4	d					22 02						22 30				
Salfords	d															
Earlswood (Surrey)	d															
Tonbridge 4	d												22 29			
Leigh (Kent)	d												22 33			
Penshurst	d												22 37			
Edenbridge	d												22 43			
Godstone	d												22 50			
Nutfield	d												22 55			
Reigate	d															
Redhill 5	a	21 45				22 09		22 15				22 36	23 00		22 45	
	d	21 46				22 09		22 20				22 37			22 46	
Merstham	d											22 41				
Coulsdon South	d											22 46				
Purley 4	d					22 18						22 49				
East Croydon ⇌	a	21 58	22 01		22 09	22 24				22 28	22 31	22 54			22 58	23 01
	d	22 00	22 02		22 10	22 25				22 29	22 32	22 58			23 00	23 02
Norwood Junction 2	a															
London Bridge 4 ⊖	a		22 16								22 46					23 16
London Blackfriars 3 ⊖	a															
City Thameslink 3	a															
Farringdon 3 ⊖	a															
St Pancras International 15 ⊖	a															
St Albans City	a															
Luton Airport Parkway 4	a															
Luton 7	a															
Bedford 10	a															
Clapham Junction 10	d	22 12			22 25	22 38				22 41		23 10			23 13	
London Victoria 15 ⊖	a	22 18		22 25	22 31	22 46	22 40		22 55	22 50		23 16		23 10	23 20	

b arr. 2154

c arr. 2254

Table 186

Sundays
from 12 September

Brighton - London, Bedford

		GX	SN	GX	GW	GX	SN	FC	SN	SN	GX	FC	GX	FC
		1	◇1	1	1	1	1	1	◇1	1	1	1	1	1
Brighton 10	d							22 44	23 02			23 11		23 44
Hove 2	d													
Preston Park	d								23 06					
Hassocks 4	d							22 52	23 12			23 19		23 52
Burgess Hill 4	d							22 56	23 16			23 23		23 56
Lewes 4	d													
Wivelsfield 4	d								23 19					
Haywards Heath 3	a							23 00	23 23			23 27		00 01
	d							23 01	23 24			23 28		00 01
Balcombe	d								23 29					
Horsham 4	d		22 42							23 04				
Littlehaven	d									23 07				
Faygate	d													
Ifield	d									23 13				
Crawley	d		22 51							23 17				
Three Bridges 4	a		22 54					23 10	23 35	23 20		23 38		00 10
	d		22 55					23 10	23 42	23 22		23 38		00 10
Gatwick Airport 10	a		22 59					23 14	23 46	23 26		23 42		00 14
	d	22 50	23 00	23 05	23 08	23 20		23 15	23 47	23 27	23 35	23 43	23 50	00 15
Horley 4	d		23 02						23 49	23 30				
Salfords	d													
Earlswood (Surrey)	d													
Tonbridge 4	d													
Leigh (Kent)	d													
Penshurst	d													
Edenbridge	d													
Godstone	d													
Nutfield	d													
Reigate	d													
Redhill 5	a		23 09		23 16				23 57	23 36				00 22
	d		23 09		23 20				00 02	23 37				00 22
Merstham	d									23 41				
Coulsdon South	d									23 46				
Purley 4	d		23 18						00 11	23 50				
East Croydon ⇌	a		23 24				23 28	23 31	00 16	23 55		00 02		00 35
	d		23 25				23 29	23 32	00 17	23 56		00 04		00 36
Norwood Junction 2	a													
London Bridge 4 ⊖	a							23 46				00 19		00 52
London Blackfriars 3 ⊖	a													
City Thameslink 3	a													
Farringdon 3 ⊖	a													
St Pancras International 15 ⊖	a													
St Albans City	a													
Luton Airport Parkway 4	a													
Luton 7	a													
Bedford 10	a													
Clapham Junction 10	d		23 38				23 41		00 30	00 11				
London Victoria 15 ⊖	a	23 25	23 46	23 40		23 55	23 50		00 37	00 18	00 10		00 25	

London, Gatwick Airport, Brighton - Sussex Coast, Portsmouth and Southampton

		SN MX ◇■	SN MX ■	SN MX ◇■	SN	SN MX ◇■	SN MO ■	SN MX ■	SN MO ◇■	SN MX ■		SN MX ◇■	SN ■	SN ■	SN ■	SN ■	SN ■	SN ■	SN ■	SN ■	SN ■	SN	SN ■	SN ■	SN ■
London Victoria ■ ⊖	d	22p17	22p32	22p47		23p17	23p04	23p10	23p17	23p47		00 05													
Clapham Junction ■	d	22p23	22p38	22p53		23p23	23p10	23p16	23p23	23p53		00 11													
London Bridge ■ ⊖	d																								
East Croydon	d	22p34	22p48	23p03		23p33	23p22	23p28	23p38	00 06		00 25													
Redhill ■	d		23p01				23p42	23p46		00 25															
Horley	d						23p50	23p56		00 31															
Gatwick Airport ■	d	22p49	23p09	23p19		23p51	23p55	23p59	00 01	00 34		00 43													
Three Bridges ■	a	22p54	23p15			23p55	00 01	00 04	00 05	00 39		00 48													
	d	22p54	23p16			23p56	00 01	00 04	00 06	00 39		00 48													
Crawley	d		23p19				00 05	00 07		00 43															
Horsham ■	a		23p27				00 17	00 19		00 55															
	d		23p28																						
Christs Hospital	d		23p31																						
Billingshurst	d		23p37																						
Pulborough	d		23p44																						
Amberley	d		23p50																						
Arundel	d		23p55																						
Haywards Heath ■	d	23p03		23p37		00 05			00 15			01 03													
Burgess Hill	d	23p08				00 10																			
Brighton ■	d				00 10							01s22					05 14			05 30	05 44		05 53	05 57
Hove ■	d	23p22		23p52	00a13	00 22			00 29			01s25					05 18			05 34	05a47		05 57	06 01
Aldrington	d																05 20			05 36				06 03
Portslade	d	23p25		23p55		00s25			00s32			01s28					05 22			05 38				06 05
Fishersgate	d																05 24			05 40				06 07
Southwick	d	23p28		23p58		00s28			00s35			01s31					05 26			05 42				06 09
Shoreham-by-Sea	d	23p31		00 01		00s31			00s38			01s34					05 29			05 45			06 03	06 12
Lancing	d	23p35		00 05		00s35			00s42			01s38					05 33			05 49				06 16
East Worthing	d																05 36			05 52				06 19
Worthing ■	a	23p39		00 09		00 39			00 46			01 42					05 39			05 55			06 09	06 22
	d	23p39															05 39			05 55			06 09	06 22
West Worthing	d	23p41															05 41			05 57				06 24
Durrington-on-Sea	d	23p44															05 44			06 00				06 27
Goring-by-Sea	d	23p46															05 46			06 02				06 29
Angmering ■	d	23p50															05 50			06 06				06 33
Littlehampton ■	a																							06 42
	d															05 35			06 04					
Ford ■	d	23p56	00 01													05 39	05 56		06 08	06 13				
Bognor Regis ■	d																					06 13		
Barnham	a	00 01	00 06													05 43	06 01		06 12	06 17		06 19	06 24	
	d	00 09	00 06										04 58	05 02	05 21	05 36	05 44	06 01	06 06	06 13	06 18			06 24	
Bognor Regis	a	00 15														05 42			06 12	06 19					
Chichester ■	a		00 14										05 05	05 09	05 28		05 51	06 09			06 25			06 32	
	d												05 06	05 10	05 29		05 52	06 09			06 26			06 32	
Fishbourne (Sussex)	d																05 55							06 35	
Bosham	d																05 58							06 38	
Nutbourne	d																06 01							06 42	
Southbourne	d																06 04				06 33			06 44	
Emsworth	d																06 07				06 36			06 47	
Warblington	d																06 10							06 50	
Havant	d												05 17	05 21	05 40		06 13	06 20			06 40			06 53	
Bedhampton	a																06 15							06 56	
Hilsea	a																06 20							07 01	
Fratton	a													05 29	05 48		06 24							07 05	
Portsmouth & Southsea	a													05 33	05 52		06 28							07 08	
Portsmouth Harbour	a													05 37	05 56		06 32							07 12	
Cosham	a												05 23					06 27			06 49				
Portchester	a												05 28								06 54				
Fareham	a												05 33					06 36			06 59				
Swanwick	a												05 40					06 43			07 06				
Southampton Central	a												05 59					07 02			07 25				

London, Gatwick Airport, Brighton - Sussex Coast, Portsmouth and Southampton

		SN ■	SN ■	SN ■	SN ■	SN ■		SN ■	SN ■	SN ■	SN ■	SN ■	SN ■	SN ■	SN ■	SN ◇■		SN ■	SN ■	SN ■	SN ■	SN ■	SN ■	SN ■	SN ■
London Victoria ■ ⊖	d															06 02									
Clapham Junction ■	d															06 08									
London Bridge ■ ⊖	d																								
East Croydon	d															06 18									
Redhill ■	d															06 42									
Horley	d															06 51									
Gatwick Airport ■	d				05 59											06 55									
Three Bridges ■	a				06 03											06 59									
	d				06 04											07 00		07 05							
Crawley	d				06 07											07 03		07 08							
Horsham ■	a				06 19											07 11		07 22							
	d				06 20											07 12									
Christs Hospital	d				06 23											07 15									
Billingshurst	d				06 29											07 21									
Pulborough	d				06 36											07 28									
Amberley	d				06 42											07 34									
Arundel	d				06 47											07 39									
Haywards Heath ■	d																								
Burgess Hill	d																								
Brighton ■	d	06 15				06 27				06 35	06 53				07 06				07 15		07 20		07 30	07 37	07 47
Hove ■	d	06 19				06 31				06 39	06 57				07 10				07 19		07 24		07 34	07 41	07 51
Aldrington	d	06 21									06 59										07 26				
Portslade	d	06 23								06 42	07 01								07 22		07 28		07 37	07 44	07 54
Fishersgate	d	06 25									07 03										07 30				
Southwick	d	06 27								06 45	07 05								07 25		07 32		07 40	07 47	07 57
Shoreham-by-Sea	d	06 30				06 37				06 48	07 09				07 16				07 28		07 35		07 43	07 50	08 00
Lancing	d	06 34								06 52	07 13								07 32		07 39		07 47	07 54	08 04
East Worthing	d	06 37									07 16										07 42				
Worthing ■	a	06 40				06 43				06 56	07 18				07 22				07 36		07 45		07 51	07 58	08 08
	d	06 40				06 43				06 56	07 19				07 23				07 36		07 45		07 52	07 59	08 08
West Worthing	d	06a42				06 45				06 58	07 21				07 25						07 47		07 54	08 01	
Durrington-on-Sea	d					06 48				07 01	07 23				07 27						07 50		07 56	08 03	08 12
Goring-by-Sea	d					06 50				07 03	07 26				07 30						07 52		07 59	08 06	
Angmering ■	d					06 54				07 07	07 30				07 34						07 56		08 03	08 10	08 17
Littlehampton ■	a										07 38										08 05				
	d			06 39				07 00			07 48	07 18										07 58			
Ford ■	d			06 43	06 52			07 04		07 13	07 52	07 22				07 44			07 48			08 02	08 09	08 17	
Bognor Regis ■	d												07 27							←					
Barnham	a			06 47	06 56	07 04		07 08		07 18	07 56	07 26	07 33		07 43	07 49			07 53	07 56		08 06	08 13	08 21	08 27
	d		06 27	06 48	07 00	07 05		07 09	07 13	07 18	07 57	07 27		07 39	07 44	07 50			07 53	07 57		08 07	08 14	08 22	08 28
Bognor Regis	a		06 33	06 54					07 20		→			07 45		07 58						08 13			08 35
Chichester ■	a				07 07	07 12		07 16		07 26		07 34			07 51				08 01	08 05			08 21	08 29	
	d				07 08	07 13		07 17		07 28		07 35			07 52				08 01				08 22	08 30	
Fishbourne (Sussex)	d							07 20				07 38							08 04						
Bosham	d					07 17						07 41							08 07						
Nutbourne	d							07 25				07 44							08 11						
Southbourne	d					07 22		07 27				07 47							08 13				08 29	08 37	
Emsworth	d					07 25		07 30				07 50							08 16				08 32	08 40	
Warblington	d					07 28						07 53							08 19						
Havant	d				07 19	07 31		07 35		07 41		07 58			08 03				08 22				08 37	08 44	
Bedhampton	a							07 37				08 00							08 25						
Hilsea	a							07 42				08 05							08 30						
Fratton	a							07 46		07 49		08 09							08 34					08 53	
Portsmouth & Southsea	a							07 50		07 53		08 15							08 37					08 56	
Portsmouth Harbour	a									07 58		08 19							08 41					09 00	
Cosham	a				07 25	07 38									08 09								08 45		
Portchester	a				07 30										08 13								08 49		
Fareham	a				07 35	07 46									08 18								08 54		
Swanwick	a				07 42	07 53									08 26								09 01		
Southampton Central	a				08 01	08 13									08 52								09 19		

Table 188

Mondays to Fridays

London, Gatwick Airport, Brighton - Sussex Coast, Portsmouth and Southampton

		SN ■		SN ■	SN ■	SN ■	SN ■	SN ■	SN ■	SN ■	SN ◇■		SN ◇■	SN ■	SN ■	SN ■	SN	SN ■		SN ■	SN ■		SN ◇■	SN ◇■	SN ◇■
London Victoria [15] ⊖	d	06 32									07 17		07 52										08 02		08 17
Clapham Junction [10]	d	06 38									07 23		07 58										08 08		08 23
London Bridge [4] ⊖	d																								
East Croydon	d	06 49									07 34		08 09										08 18		08 33
Redhill [5]	d	07 07									07 45												08 32		
Horley	d	07 16									07 55														
Gatwick Airport [10]	d	07 20									07 58		08 25										08 40		08 49
Three Bridges [4]	a	07 24									08 04												08 44		
	d	07 30									08 05												08 45		
Crawley	d	07 34									08 09												08 48		
Horsham [4]	a	07 46									08 22												08 56	>	
	d	07 46									08 23												09 00	09 05	
Christs Hospital	d	07 50									08 26													09 08	
Billingshurst	d	07 56									08 32													09 14	
Pulborough	d	08 03									08 39													09 21	
Amberley	d	08 09									08 45													09 27	
Arundel	d	08 14									08 50													09 32	
Haywards Heath [3]	d												08 37												09 04
Burgess Hill	d																								09 09
Brighton [10]	d			07 50		08 03		08 07	08 23							08 39	08 44	08 53							
Hove [2]	d			07 54		08 07		08 11	08 27				08 54			08 43	08a47	08 57							09 22
Aldrington	d			07 56					08 29									08 59							
Portslade	d			07 58				08 14	08 31									09 01							09 25
Fishersgate	d			08 00					08 33									09 03							
Southwick	d			08 02				08 17	08 35									09 05							
Shoreham-by-Sea	d			08 06		08 13		08 20	08 39				09 00			08 49		09 08							09 30
Lancing	d			08 10				08 24	08 43				09 04					09 12							
East Worthing	d			08 13					08 46									09 15							
Worthing [4]	a			08 15		08 19		08 28	08 48				09 08			08 55		09 18							09 36
	d			08 16		08 20		08 28	08 49				09 08			08 56		09 18							09 37
West Worthing	d			08 18		08 22		08 30	08a51				09 10					09a20							09 39
Durrington-on-Sea	d			08 20		08 24		08 33					09 13			08 59									09 41
Goring-by-Sea	d			08 23		08 27		08 35					09 15			09 02									09 44
Angmering [3]	d			08 27		08 31		08 39					09 19			09 06									09 48
Littlehampton [4]	a	08 21		08 35									09 28												09 58
	d	08 26												08 54											
Ford [4]	d	08 30				08 37		08 45			08 55			08 59										09 37	
Bognor Regis [4]	d				08 32					08 48										09 09					
Barnham	a	08 34			08 38	08 41		08 50		08 55	08 59			09 03		09 15				09 15			09 26	09 41	
	d	08 35				08 42	08 45	08 52			09 00			09 04	09 12	09 16					09 25		09 27	09 42	
Bognor Regis	a						08 51	08 58							09 18						09 31			09 48	
Chichester [4]	a	08 42				08 49					09 07			09 11		09 23							09 34		
	d					08 50					09 08			09 12		09 24							09 35		
Fishbourne (Sussex)	d													09 15											
Bosham	d													09 18											
Nutbourne	d													09 21											
Southbourne	d										09 15			09 24		09 31									
Emsworth	d										09 18			09 27		09 34									
Warblington	d													09 30											
Havant	d					09 01					09 23			09 33		09 38							09 46		
Bedhampton	a													09 36											
Hilsea	a													09 42											
Fratton	a					09 11								09 46									09 54		
Portsmouth & Southsea	a					09 17								09 50									09 58		
Portsmouth Harbour	a					09 21																	10 02		
Cosham	a										09 29					09 45									
Portchester	a																								
Fareham	a										09 37					09 53									
Swanwick	a										09 44					10 00									
Southampton Central	a										10 01					10 20									

Table 188

Mondays to Fridays

London, Gatwick Airport, Brighton - Sussex Coast, Portsmouth and Southampton

		GW ◇	SN ■	SN	SN ■		SN ■	SN ■	SN ◇■ 🛒	SN ◇■ 🛒	SN ■	SN ■	SN	SN ◇■	SN ■		SN ■	SN ◇■ 🛒	SN ◇■ 🛒	SN ◇■ 🛒	SN ■				
London Victoria [15] ⊖	d								08 32					08 47				09 02		09 17					
Clapham Junction [10]	d								08 38					08 53				09 08		09 23					
London Bridge [4] ⊖	d																								
East Croydon	d								08 48					09 03				09 18		09 33					
Redhill [5]	d								09 03									09 30							
Horley	d																	09 36							
Gatwick Airport [10]	d								09 11					09 19				09 40		09 49					
Three Bridges [4]	a								09 16									09 44							
	d								09 16									09 45							
Crawley	d								09 19									09 48							
Horsham [4]	a								09 27	>								09 56	>						
	d								09 31	09 36								10 00	10 05						
Christs Hospital	d									09 39															
Billingshurst	d									09 45									10 14						
Pulborough	d									09 52									10 20						
Amberley	d									09 58															
Arundel	d									10 03									10 29						
Haywards Heath [3]	d													09 37						10 04					
Burgess Hill	d																			10 09					
Brighton [10]	d	09 00	09 03	09 14	09 23							09 33	09 44		09 53						10 03				
Hove [2]	d	09 04	09 07	09a18	09 27							09 37	09a47	09 52	09 57					10 22	10 07				
Aldrington	d				09 29										09 59										
Portslade	d		09 10		09 31							09 40			10 01					10 25	10 10				
Fishersgate	d				09 33										10 03										
Southwick	d		09 13		09 35							09 43			10 05						10 13				
Shoreham-by-Sea	d	09 13	09 17		09 39							09 46		09 58	10 09					10 30	10 16				
Lancing	d		09 21		09 43							09 50		10 02	10 13						10 20				
East Worthing	d				09 46										10 16										
Worthing [4]	a	09 21	09 25		09 48							09 54		10 06	10 18					10 36	10 24				
	d	09 22	09 25		09 49							09 55		10 07	10 19					10 37	10 25				
West Worthing	d				09a51							09 57		10 09	10a21					10 39					
Durrington-on-Sea	d											09 59		10 11						10 41					
Goring-by-Sea	d											10 02		10 14						10 44					
Angmering [3]	d		09 34									10 06		10 18						10 48	10 31				
Littlehampton [4]	a													10 27						10 57					
	d										09 54						10 11								
Ford [4]	d									10 08	09 58	10 12					10 16		10 34						
Bognor Regis [4]	d						09 39																		
Barnham	a	09 37	09 44				09 45		09 57	10 12	10 02	10 16					10 20	10 26	10 39		10 42				
	d	09 38	09 45					09 52	09 58	10 13	10 03	10 17					10 22	10 27	10 39		10 42				
Bognor Regis	a							09 58		10 19							10 28		10 46						
Chichester [4]	a	09 45	09 52						10 05		10 10	10 24						10 34			10 50				
	d	09 47	09 53						10 06		10 11	10 25						10 35			10 50				
Fishbourne (Sussex)	d										10 14														
Bosham	d										10 17														
Nutbourne	d										10 20														
Southbourne	d		10 00						10 13		10 23										10 57				
Emsworth	d		10 03						10 16		10 26	10 33									11 00				
Warblington	d										10 29														
Havant	d	09 59	10 07						10 20		10 32	10 37						10 46			11 05				
Bedhampton	a										10 34														
Hilsea	a										10 42														
Fratton	a		10 16								10 46							10 54			11 13				
Portsmouth & Southsea	a		10 19								10 50							10 58			11 17				
Portsmouth Harbour	a		10 23															11 02			11 21				
Cosham	a	10 05							10 28			10 45													
Portchester	a								10 32																
Fareham	a	10 14							10 37			10 53													
Swanwick	a								10 44			11 00													
Southampton Central	a	10 41							11 01			11 19													

London, Gatwick Airport, Brighton - Sussex Coast, Portsmouth and Southampton

		SN	SN 1	SN 1	SN 1	SN ◇1 ✕	SN ◇1 ✕	SN 1	SN 1	SN	SN ◇1	SN 1	SN 1	SN ◇1 ✕	SN ◇1 ✕	SN 1	SN	SN ◇1 ✕	SN 1
London Victoria 15 ⊖	d					09 32					09 47			10 02				10 17	
Clapham Junction 10	d					09 38					09 53			10 08				10 23	
London Bridge 4 ⊖	d																		
East Croydon	d					09 48					10 03			10 18				10 33	
Redhill 5	d					10 00								10 30					
Horley	d													10 36					
Gatwick Airport 10	d					10 09					10 19			10 40				10 49	
Three Bridges 4	a					10 14								10 44					
	d					10 14								10 45					
Crawley	d					10 18								10 48					
Horsham 4	a					10 26	>							10 56	>				
	d					10 30	10 35							11 00	11 05				
Christs Hospital	d						10 38												
Billingshurst	d						10 44								11 14				
Pulborough	d						10 51								11 20				
Amberley	d						10 57												
Arundel	d						11 02								11 29				
Haywards Heath 3	d										10 37							11 04	
Burgess Hill	d																	11 09	
Brighton 10	d	10 14	10 23						10 33	10 44		10 53				11 03	11 14		11 23
Hove 2	d	10a17	10 27						10 37	10a47	10 52	10 57				11 07	11a17	11 22	11 27
Aldrington	d		10 29									10 59							11 29
Portslade	d		10 31						10 40			11 01				11 10		11 25	11 31
Fishersgate	d		10 33									11 03							11 33
Southwick	d		10 35						10 43			11 05				11 13			11 35
Shoreham-by-Sea	d		10 39						10 46		10 58	11 09				11 16		11 30	11 39
Lancing	d		10 43						10 50		11 02	11 13				11 20			11 43
East Worthing	d		10 46									11 16							11 46
Worthing 4	a		10 48						10 54		11 06	11 18				11 24		11 36	11 48
	d		10 49						10 55		11 07	11 19				11 25		11 37	11 49
West Worthing	d		10a51						10 57		11 09	11a21						11 39	11a51
Durrington-on-Sea	d								10 59		11 11							11 41	
Goring-by-Sea	d								11 02		11 14							11 44	
Angmering 3	d								11 06		11 18					11 31		11 48	
Littlehampton 4	a										11 27							11 57	
	d							10 54					11 11						
Ford 4	d						11 07	10 58	11 12				11 16		11 34				
Bognor Regis 4	d			10 39															
Barnham	a			10 45		10 56	11 11	11 02	11 16				11 20	11 26	11 39	11 42			
	d				10 52	10 57	11 12	11 03	11 17				11 22	11 27	11 39	11 42			
Bognor Regis	a				10 58		11 18						11 28		11 46				
Chichester 4	a					11 04		11 10	11 24					11 34		11 50			
	d					11 05		11 11	11 25					11 35		11 50			
Fishbourne (Sussex)	d							11 14											
Bosham	d							11 17											
Nutbourne	d							11 20											
Southbourne	d					11 12		11 23								11 57			
Emsworth	d					11 15		11 26	11 33							12 00			
Warblington	d							11 29											
Havant	d					11 19		11 32	11 37					11 46		12 05			
Bedhampton	a							11 34											
Hilsea	a							11 42											
Fratton	a							11 46						11 54		12 13			
Portsmouth & Southsea	a							11 50						11 58		12 17			
Portsmouth Harbour	a													12 02		12 21			
Cosham	a					11 26			11 45										
Portchester	a					11 30													
Fareham	a					11 35			11 53										
Swanwick	a					11 42			12 00										
Southampton Central	a					12 01			12 19										

London, Gatwick Airport, Brighton - Sussex Coast, Portsmouth and Southampton

		SN 1	SN 1	SN ◇1 ✕	SN ◇1 ✕	SN 1	SN 1	SN	SN ◇1	SN 1	SN 1	SN ◇1	SN ◇1	SN ◇1	SN 1	SN	SN 1	SN 1	SN 1
London Victoria 15 ⊖	d			10 32					10 47			11 02		11 17					
Clapham Junction 10	d			10 38					10 53			11 08		11 23					
London Bridge 4 ⊖	d																		
East Croydon	d			10 48					11 03			11 18		11 33					
Redhill 5	d			11 00								11 30							
Horley	d											11 36							
Gatwick Airport 10	d			11 09					11 19			11 40		11 49					
Three Bridges 4	a			11 14								11 44							
	d			11 14								11 45							
Crawley	d			11 18								11 48							
Horsham 4	a			11 26	>							11 56	>						
	d			11 30	11 35							12 00	12 05						
Christs Hospital	d				11 38														
Billingshurst	d				11 44								12 14						
Pulborough	d				11 51								12 20						
Amberley	d				11 57														
Arundel	d				12 02								12 29						
Haywards Heath 3	d								11 37					12 04					
Burgess Hill	d													12 09					
Brighton 10	d						11 33	11 44		11 53					12 03	12 14	12 23		
Hove 2	d						11 37	11a47	11 52	11 57				12 22	12 07	12a17	12 27		
Aldrington	d									11 59							12 29		
Portslade	d						11 40			12 01				12 25	12 10		12 31		
Fishersgate	d									12 03							12 33		
Southwick	d						11 43			12 05					12 13		12 35		
Shoreham-by-Sea	d						11 46		11 58	12 09				12 30	12 16		12 39		
Lancing	d						11 50		12 02	12 13					12 20		12 43		
East Worthing	d									12 16							12 46		
Worthing 4	a						11 54		12 06	12 18				12 36	12 24		12 48		
	d						11 55		12 07	12 19				12 37	12 25		12 49		
West Worthing	d						11 57		12 09	12a21				12 39			12a51		
Durrington-on-Sea	d						11 59		12 11					12 41					
Goring-by-Sea	d						12 02		12 14					12 44					
Angmering 3	d						12 06		12 18					12 48	12 31				
Littlehampton 4	a								12 27					12 57					
	d					11 54					12 11								
Ford 4	d				12 07	11 58	12 12				12 16		12 34						
Bognor Regis 4	d	11 39																12 39	
Barnham	a	11 45		11 56	12 11	12 02	12 16				12 20	12 26	12 39		12 42			12 45	
	d		11 52	11 57	12 12	12 03	12 17				12 22	12 27	12 39		12 42				12 52
Bognor Regis	a		11 58		12 18						12 28		12 46						12 58
Chichester 4	a			12 04		12 10	12 24					12 34			12 50				
	d			12 05		12 11	12 25					12 35			12 50				
Fishbourne (Sussex)	d					12 14													
Bosham	d					12 17													
Nutbourne	d					12 20													
Southbourne	d			12 12		12 23									12 57				
Emsworth	d			12 15		12 26	12 33								13 00				
Warblington	d					12 29													
Havant	d			12 19		12 32	12 37					12 46			13 05				
Bedhampton	a					12 34													
Hilsea	a					12 42													
Fratton	a					12 46						12 54			13 13				
Portsmouth & Southsea	a					12 50						12 58			13 17				
Portsmouth Harbour	a											13 02			13 21				
Cosham	a			12 26			12 45												
Portchester	a			12 30															
Fareham	a			12 35			12 53												
Swanwick	a			12 42			13 00												
Southampton Central	a			12 59			13 19												

Table 188

Mondays to Fridays

London, Gatwick Airport, Brighton - Sussex Coast, Portsmouth and Southampton

		SN ◇1	SN ◇1	SN 1	SN 1	SN	SN ◇1	SN 1	SN 1	SN ◇1	SN ◇1	SN ◇1	SN 1	SN	SN 1	SN 1	SN 1	SN ◇1	SN ◇1	SN 1	SN 1	SN	SN ◇1
London Victoria ⊖	d	11 32					11 47			12 02		12 17						12 32					12 47
Clapham Junction	d	11 38					11 53			12 08		12 23						12 38					12 53
London Bridge ⊖	d																						
East Croydon	d	11 48					12 03			12 18		12 33						12 48					13 03
Redhill	d	12 00								12 30								13 00					
Horley	d									12 36													
Gatwick Airport	d	12 09					12 19			12 40		12 49						13 09					13 19
Three Bridges	a	12 14								12 44								13 14					
	d	12 14								12 45								13 14					
Crawley	d	12 18								12 48								13 18					
Horsham	a	12 26	>							12 56	>							13 26	>				
	d	12 30	12 35							13 00	13 05							13 30	13 35				
Christs Hospital	d		12 38																13 38				
Billingshurst	d		12 44								13 14								13 44				
Pulborough	d		12 51								13 20								13 51				
Amberley	d		12 57																13 57				
Arundel	d		13 02								13 29								14 02				
Haywards Heath	d						12 37					13 04											13 37
Burgess Hill	d											13 09											
Brighton	d				12 33	12 44		12 53					13 03	13 14	13 23						13 33	13 44	
Hove	d				12 37	12a47	12 52	12 57				13 22	13 07	13a19	13 27						13 37	13a47	13 52
Aldrington	d							12 59							13 29								
Portslade	d				12 40			13 01				13 25	13 10		13 31						13 40		
Fishersgate	d							13 03							13 33								
Southwick	d				12 43			13 05					13 13		13 35						13 43		
Shoreham-by-Sea	d				12 46		12 58	13 09				13 30	13 16		13 39						13 46		13 58
Lancing	d				12 50		13 02	13 13					13 20		13 43						13 50		14 02
East Worthing	d							13 16							13 46								
Worthing	a				12 54		13 06	13 18				13 36	13 24		13 48						13 54		14 06
	d				12 55		13 07	13 19				13 37	13 25		13 49						13 55		14 07
West Worthing	d				12 57		13 09	13a21				13 39			13a51						13 57		14 09
Durrington-on-Sea	d				12 59		13 11					13 41									13 59		14 11
Goring-by-Sea	d				13 02		13 14					13 44									14 02		14 14
Angmering	d				13 06		13 18					13 48	13 31								14 06		14 18
Littlehampton	a						13 27					13 57											14 27
	d			12 54					13 11											13 54			
Ford	d		13 07	12 58	13 12				13 16		13 34								14 07	13 58	14 12		
Bognor Regis	d															13 39							
Barnham	a	12 56	13 11	13 02	13 16				13 20	13 26	13 39		13 42			13 45		13 56	14 11	14 02	14 16		
	d	12 57	13 12	13 03	13 17				13 22	13 27	13 39		13 42				13 52	13 57	14 12	14 03	14 17		
Bognor Regis	a		13 18						13 28		13 46						13 58		14 18				
Chichester	a	13 04		13 10	13 24					13 34			13 50					14 04		14 10	14 24		
	d	13 05		13 11	13 25					13 35			13 50					14 05		14 11	14 25		
Fishbourne (Sussex)	d			13 14																14 14			
Bosham	d			13 17																14 17			
Nutbourne	d			13 20																14 20			
Southbourne	d	13 12		13 23									13 57					14 12		14 23			
Emsworth	d	13 15		13 26	13 33								14 00					14 15		14 26	14 33		
Warblington	d			13 29																14 29			
Havant	d	13 19		13 32	13 37					13 46			14 05					14 19		14 32	14 37		
Bedhampton	a			13 34																14 34			
Hilsea	a			13 42																14 42			
Fratton	a			13 46						13 54			14 13							14 46			
Portsmouth & Southsea	a			13 50						13 58			14 17							14 50			
Portsmouth Harbour	a									14 02			14 21										
Cosham	a	13 26			13 45													14 26			14 45		
Portchester	a	13 30																14 30					
Fareham	a	13 35			13 53													14 35			14 53		
Swanwick	a	13 42			14 00													14 42			15 00		
Southampton Central	a	13 59			14 19													14 59			15 19		

Table 188

Mondays to Fridays

London, Gatwick Airport, Brighton - Sussex Coast, Portsmouth and Southampton

		SN 1	SN 1	SN ◇1	SN ◇1	SN ◇1	SN 1	SN	SN 1	SN 1	SN 1	SN ◇1	SN ◇1	SN 1	SN 1	SN	SN ◇1	SN 1	SN 1	SN ◇1	SN ◇1	SN 1
London Victoria ⊖	d			13 02		13 17						13 32					13 47			14 02		
Clapham Junction	d			13 08		13 23						13 38					13 53			14 08		
London Bridge ⊖	d																					
East Croydon	d			13 18		13 33						13 48					14 03			14 18		
Redhill	d			13 30								14 00								14 30		
Horley	d			13 36																14 36		
Gatwick Airport	d			13 40		13 49						14 09					14 19			14 40		
Three Bridges	a			13 44								14 14								14 44		
	d			13 45								14 14								14 45		
Crawley	d			13 48								14 18								14 48		
Horsham	a			13 56	>							14 26	>							14 56	>	
	d			14 00	14 05							14 30	14 35							15 00	15 05	
Christs Hospital	d												14 38								15 08	
Billingshurst	d				14 14								14 44								15 14	
Pulborough	d				14 20								14 51								15 21	
Amberley	d												14 57									
Arundel	d				14 29								15 02								15 30	
Haywards Heath	d					14 04											14 37					
Burgess Hill	d					14 09																
Brighton	d	13 53					14 03	14 14	14 23						14 33	14 44		14 53				
Hove	d	13 57				14 22	14 07	14a17	14 27						14 37	14a47	14 52	14 57				
Aldrington	d	13 59							14 29									14 59				
Portslade	d	14 01				14 25	14 10		14 31						14 40			15 01				
Fishersgate	d	14 03							14 33									15 03				
Southwick	d	14 05					14 13		14 35						14 43			15 05				
Shoreham-by-Sea	d	14 09				14 30	14 16		14 39						14 46		14 58	15 09				
Lancing	d	14 13					14 20		14 43						14 50		15 02	15 13				
East Worthing	d	14 16							14 46									15 16				
Worthing	a	14 18				14 36	14 24		14 48						14 54		15 06	15 18				
	d	14 19				14 37	14 25		14 49						14 55		15 07	15 19				
West Worthing	d	14a21				14 39			14a51						14 57		15 09	15a21				
Durrington-on-Sea	d					14 41									14 59		15 11					
Goring-by-Sea	d					14 44									15 02		15 14					
Angmering	d					14 48	14 31								15 06		15 18					
Littlehampton	a					14 57											15 27					
	d		14 11											14 54					15 11			15 23
Ford	d		14 16		14 34								15 07	14 58	15 12				15 16		15 35	15 27
Bognor Regis	d									14 40												
Barnham	a		14 20	14 27	14 39		14 42			14 46		14 56	15 11	15 02	15 16				15 20	15 26	15 39	15 31
	d		14 22	14 28	14 39		14 42				14 52	14 57	15 12	15 03	15 17				15 22	15 27	15 39	15 33
Bognor Regis	a		14 28		14 46						14 58		15 18						15 28		15 46	
Chichester	a			14 35			14 50					15 04		15 10	15 24					15 34		15 40
	d			14 36			14 50					15 05		15 11	15 25					15 35		15 41
Fishbourne (Sussex)	d													15 14								15 44
Bosham	d													15 17								15 47
Nutbourne	d													15 20								15 50
Southbourne	d						14 57					15 12		15 23								15 53
Emsworth	d						15 00					15 15		15 26	15 33							15 56
Warblington	d													15 29								15 59
Havant	d			14 47			15 05					15 19		15 32	15 37					15 46		16 02
Bedhampton	a													15 34								16 04
Hilsea	a													15 42								
Fratton	a			14 55			15 13							15 46						15 54		16 12
Portsmouth & Southsea	a			14 59			15 17							15 50						15 58		16 15
Portsmouth Harbour	a			15 03			15 21													16 02		16 21
Cosham	a											15 26			15 45							
Portchester	a											15 30										
Fareham	a											15 35			15 53							
Swanwick	a											15 42			16 00							
Southampton Central	a											15 59			16 19							

Table 188

London, Gatwick Airport, Brighton - Sussex Coast, Portsmouth and Southampton

		SN	SN	SN	SN	SN	SN	SN	SN	SN	SN	SN	SN	SN	SN	SN	SN	SN	SN	SN
		1	1	◇1		1	1	◇1	◇1	1	1	1		◇1	1	1	◇1	◇1	◇1	1
London Victoria ⊖	d			14 17				14 32						14 47			15 02		15 17	
Clapham Junction	d			14 23				14 38						14 53			15 08		15 23	
London Bridge ⊖	d																			
East Croydon	d			14 33				14 48						15 03			15 18		15 33	
Redhill	d							15 00									15 30			
Horley	d																15 36			
Gatwick Airport	d			14 49				15 09						15 19			15 40		15 49	
Three Bridges	a							15 14									15 44			
	d							15 14									15 45			
Crawley	d							15 18									15 48			
Horsham	a							15 26	>								15 56	>		
	d							15 30	15 35								16 00	16 05		
Christs Hospital	d								15 38									16 08		
Billingshurst	d								15 44									16 14		
Pulborough	d								15 51									16 21		
Amberley	d								15 57											
Arundel	d								16 02									16 30		
Haywards Heath	d			15 04										15 37					16 04	
Burgess Hill	d			15 09															16 09	
Brighton	d		15 03		15 14	15 23						15 33	15 44		15 53					
Hove	d		15 07	15 22	15a17	15 27						15 37	15a47	15 52	15 57				16 22	
Aldrington	d					15 29									15 59					
Portslade	d		15 10	15 25		15 31						15 40			16 01				16 25	
Fishersgate	d					15 33									16 03					
Southwick	d		15 13			15 35						15 43			16 05					
Shoreham-by-Sea	d		15 16	15 30		15 39						15 46		15 58	16 09				16 30	
Lancing	d		15 20			15 43						15 50		16 02	16 13					
East Worthing	d					15 46									16 16					
Worthing	a		15 24	15 36		15 48						15 54		16 06	16 18				16 36	
	d		15 25	15 37		15 49						15 55		16 07	16 19				16 37	
West Worthing	d		15 27	15 39		15 51						15 57		16 09	16a21				16 39	
Durrington-on-Sea	d		15 29	15 41		15 53						15 59		16 11					16 41	
Goring-by-Sea	d		15 32	15 44		15 56						16 02		16 14					16 44	
Angmering	d		15 36	15 48		16 00						16 06		16 18					16 48	
Littlehampton	a			15 58		16 11								16 27					16 57	
	d									15 54										16 22
Ford	d		15 42						16 07	15 58		16 12						16 35		16 26
Bognor Regis	d	15 39									16 09									
Barnham	a	15 45	15 46					15 56	16 11	16 02	16 15	16 16					16 26	16 39		16 30
	d		15 47				15 53	15 57	16 12	16 03		16 17				16 24	16 27	16 40		16 31
Bognor Regis	a						15 59		16 18							16 30		16 46		
Chichester	a		15 54					16 04		16 10		16 24					16 34			16 38
	d		15 55					16 05		16 11		16 25					16 35			16 39
Fishbourne (Sussex)	d									16 14										16 42
Bosham	d									16 17										16 45
Nutbourne	d									16 20										16 48
Southbourne	d		16 02					16 12		16 23										16 51
Emsworth	d		16 05					16 15		16 26		16 33								16 54
Warblington	d									16 29										16 57
Havant	d		16 09					16 19		16 32		16 37					16 46			17 00
Bedhampton	a									16 34										17 02
Hilsea	a									16 42										17 07
Fratton	a		16 18							16 46							16 54			17 11
Portsmouth & Southsea	a		16 21							16 50							16 58			17 16
Portsmouth Harbour	a		16 26														17 02			17 20
Cosham	a							16 26				16 45								
Portchester	a							16 30												
Fareham	a							16 35				16 53								
Swanwick	a							16 42												
Southampton Central	a							17 01				17 28								

Table 188

London, Gatwick Airport, Brighton - Sussex Coast, Portsmouth and Southampton

		SN	SN	SN	SN	SN	SN	SN	SN	SN	SN	SN	SN	SN	SN	SN	GW	SN
		1	1		1	1	◇1	◇1	1	1		◇1	1	1	◇1	◇1	◇	◇1
London Victoria ⊖	d						15 32					15 47			16 02			16 17
Clapham Junction	d						15 38					15 53			16 08			16 23
London Bridge ⊖	d																	
East Croydon	d						15 48					16 03			16 18			16 33
Redhill	d						16 00								16 30			
Horley	d														16 36			
Gatwick Airport	d						16 09					16 19			16 40			16 49
Three Bridges	a						16 14								16 44			
	d						16 14								16 45			
Crawley	d						16 18								16 48			
Horsham	a						16 26	>							16 56	>		
	d						16 30	16 35							17 00	17 05		
Christs Hospital	d							16 38								17 08		
Billingshurst	d							16 44								17 15		
Pulborough	d							16 51								17 21		
Amberley	d							16 57								17 27		
Arundel	d							17 02								17 32		
Haywards Heath	d											16 37						17 04
Burgess Hill	d																	17 09
Brighton	d		16 03	16 14	16 24					16 33	16 44		16 53				17 00	
Hove	d		16 07	16a17	16 28					16 37	16a47	16 52	16 57				17 04	17 21
Aldrington	d				16 30								16 59					
Portslade	d		16 10		16 32					16 40		16 55	17 01					17 24
Fishersgate	d				16 34								17 03					
Southwick	d		16 13		16 36					16 43			17 05					
Shoreham-by-Sea	d		16 16		16 40					16 46		17 00	17 08				17 13	17 29
Lancing	d		16 20		16 44					16 50		17 04	17 12					17 33
East Worthing	d				16 47								17 15					
Worthing	a		16 24		16 49					16 54		17 08	17 18				17 21	17 37
	d		16 25		16 50					16 55		17 08	17 18				17 22	17 38
West Worthing	d		16 27		16a52					16 57		17 10	17 20					17 40
Durrington-on-Sea	d		16 29							16 59		17 13						17 42
Goring-by-Sea	d		16 32							17 02		17 15						17 45
Angmering	d		16 36							17 06		17 19						17 49
Littlehampton	a											17 28	17 33					18 00
	d								16 54				17 41	17 11				
Ford	d		16 42					17 07	16 58	17 12			17 46	17 16		17 37		
Bognor Regis	d	16 39																
Barnham	a	16 45	16 46				16 56	17 11	17 02	17 16			17 50	17 20	17 26	17 42	17 38	
	d		16 47			16 54	16 57	17 12	17 03	17 17			17 54	17 24	17 27	17 42	17 39	
Bognor Regis	a					17 00		17 18					→	17 30		17 49		
Chichester	a		16 54				17 04		17 10	17 24					17 34		17 46	
	d		16 55				17 05		17 11	17 25					17 35		17 47	
Fishbourne (Sussex)	d								17 14						17 38			
Bosham	d								17 17						17 41			
Nutbourne	d								17 20									
Southbourne	d		17 02				17 12		17 23						17 45			
Emsworth	d		17 05				17 15		17 26	17 33					17 48			
Warblington	d								17 29									
Havant	d		17 09				17 19		17 32	17 37					17 54		17 58	
Bedhampton	a								17 34						17 56			
Hilsea	a								17 42						18 01			
Fratton	a		17 18						17 46						18 05			
Portsmouth & Southsea	a		17 22						17 50						18 09			
Portsmouth Harbour	a														18 15			
Cosham	a						17 26			17 45							18 04	
Portchester	a						17 31											
Fareham	a						17 36			17 53							18 12	
Swanwick	a						17 43			18 00								
Southampton Central	a						18 03			18 20							18 41	

London, Gatwick Airport, Brighton - Sussex Coast, Portsmouth and Southampton

Station		SN ■1	SN ■1	SN ◇■1 ⌶	SN ◇■1 ⌶	SN	SN ■1	SN ■1	SN ■1	SN ■1	SN ■1	SN ■1	SN ■1	SN	SN ■1	SN ◇■1 ⌶	SN ◇■1	SN ■1
London Victoria ■15 ⊖	d			16 32												17 02		
Clapham Junction ■10	d			16 38												17 08		
London Bridge ■4 ⊖	d														16 57			
East Croydon	d			16 48											17 10	17 18		
Redhill ■5	d			17 00														
Horley	d			17 06														
Gatwick Airport ■10	d			17 09														
Three Bridges ■4	a			17 14	>										17 29	17 36		
	d			17 18	17 20										17 29	17 37		
Crawley	d			17 22	17 26											17 41		
Horsham ■4	a			17 30	17 38											17 49	>	
	d			17 30	17 38											17 53	17 58	
Christs Hospital	d				17 42												18 01	
Billingshurst	d				17 48												18 07	
Pulborough	d				17 54												18 14	
Amberley	d																18 20	
Arundel	d				18 03												18 25	
Haywards Heath ■3	d														17 39			
Burgess Hill	d														17 46			
Brighton ■10	d	17 03				17 14	17 23				17 33		17 45	17 53				
Hove ■2	d	17 07				17a17	17 27				17 37		17 49	17a56	18 01			
Aldrington	d						17 29						17 51					
Portslade	d	17 10					17 31				17 40		17 53		18 04			
Fishersgate	d						17 33						17 55					
Southwick	d	17 13					17 35				17 43		17 57					
Shoreham-by-Sea	d	17 16					17 39				17 46		18 01		18 09			
Lancing	d	17 20					17 43				17 50		18 05		18 13			
East Worthing	d						17 46						18 08					
Worthing ■4	a	17 24					17 48				17 54		18 10		18 17			
	d	17 25					17 49				17 55		18 11		18 17			
West Worthing	d	17 27					17 51				17 57		18 13		18 19			
Durrington-on-Sea	d	17 29					17 53				17 59		18 15		18 22			
Goring-by-Sea	d	17 32					17 56				18 02		18 18		18 24			
Angmering ■3	d	17 36					18 00				18 06		18 22		18 28			
Littlehampton ■4	a						18 08						18 30		18 39			
	d								17 54									18 18
Ford ■4	d	17 42			18 08				17 58		18 12						18 30	18 22
Bognor Regis ■4	d		⟵					17 51				18 19						
Barnham	a	17 46	17 50	17 57	18 13			17 57	18 02		18 16	18 25				18 20	18 34	18 26
	d	17 47	17 54	17 57	18 14				18 04	18 08	18 17					18 21	18 35	18 27
Bognor Regis	a		18 00		18 22					18 14							18 43	18 33
Chichester ■4	a	17 54		18 05					18 11		18 24					18 28		
	d	17 55		18 05					18 12		18 25					18 29		
Fishbourne (Sussex)	d								18 15							18 32		
Bosham	d			18 10					18 18							18 35		
Nutbourne	d								18 21							18 38		
Southbourne	d	18 04		18 14					18 24							18 41		
Emsworth	d	18 07		18 17					18 27		18 33					18 44		
Warblington	d	18 10							18 30							18 47		
Havant	d	18 13		18 23					18 34		18 37					18 54		
Bedhampton	a								18 36							18 57		
Hilsea	a								18 42							19 02		
Fratton	a	18 22							18 46							19 06		
Portsmouth & Southsea	a	18 25							18 49							19 09		
Portsmouth Harbour	a	18 31																
Cosham	a			18 29							18 44							
Portchester	a			18 33														
Fareham	a			18 38							18 52							
Swanwick	a			18 45							18 59							
Southampton Central	a			19 04							19 20							

London, Gatwick Airport, Brighton - Sussex Coast, Portsmouth and Southampton

Station		SN ■1	SN	SN ◇■1	SN ◇■1	SN ■1	SN ◇■1	SN ■1	SN ■1	SN ◇■1	SN ■1	SN ■1	SN ◇■1	SN ◇■1	SN	SN ■1	SN ■1	SN ◇■1	SN ◇■1	SN ◇■1	SN	SN ■1
London Victoria ■15 ⊖	d			17 32			17 17			17 47			18 02					18 17	18 32			
Clapham Junction ■10	d			17 38			17 23			17 53			18 08					18 23	18 38			
London Bridge ■4 ⊖	d								17 42			17 47					18 12					
East Croydon	d			17 49			17 33		17 55	18 03		18 00	18 18				18 25	18 33	18 48			
Redhill ■5	d																					
Horley	d									18 18												
Gatwick Airport ■10	d						17 48			18 21								18 48				
Three Bridges ■4	a			18 06								18 21	18 36				18 44		19 06			
	d			18 07								18 22	18 37				18 45		19 07			
Crawley	d			18 11								18 26	18 41						19 11			
Horsham ■4	a			18 22	>							18 38	18 49	>					19 22	>		
	d			18 26	18 31							18 39	18 53	18 58					19 26	19 31		
Christs Hospital	d				18 35							18 42		19 01						19 34		
Billingshurst	d				18 41							18 49		19 07						19 41		
Pulborough	d				18 48							18 56		19 14						19 48		
Amberley	d											19 02								19 54		
Arundel	d				18 57							19 07		19 23						19 59		
Haywards Heath ■3	d						18 01			18 33							18 54	19 03				
Burgess Hill	d						18 07			18 41							19 00	19 08				
Brighton ■10	d	18 00	18 14					18 28							18 48	19 00					19 15	
Hove ■2	d	18 04	18a17				18 21	18 32	18 44	18 58					18a53	19 04	19 18	19 23			19a19	
Aldrington	d	18 06						18 34								19 06						
Portslade	d	18 08					18 24	18 36	18 47	19 01						19 08	19 21	19 26				
Fishersgate	d	18 10						18 38								19 10						
Southwick	d	18 12						18 40								19 12						
Shoreham-by-Sea	d	18 16					18 29	18 44	18 52	19 06						19 16	19 26	19 31				
Lancing	d	18 20					18 33	18 48	18 56	19 10						19 20	19 30	19 36				
East Worthing	d	18 23						18 51								19 23						
Worthing ■4	a	18 25					18 38	18 53	18 59	19 14						19 25	19 34	19 39				
	d	18 27					18 38	18 54	19 00	19 14						19 26	19 35	19 40				
West Worthing	d	18 29					18 40		19 02	19 16						19 28	19 37	19 42				
Durrington-on-Sea	d	18 31					18 42		19 05	19 19						19 30	19 39	19 45				
Goring-by-Sea	d	18 34					18 45		19 07	19 21						19 33	19 42	19 47				
Angmering ■3	d	18 38					18 49	19 00	19 11	19 25						19 37	19 46	19 51				
Littlehampton ■4	a						18 58		19 22	19 36							19 55	20 01				
	d					18 48																19 35
Ford ■4	d	18 44			19 02	18 53		19 07						19 28		19 43						19 39
Bognor Regis ■4	d																					
Barnham	a	18 48		18 53	19 06	18 57		19 11				19 15	19 19	19 32		19 47			19 52	20 08		19 43
	d	18 49		18 54	19 07	19 00		19 12			18 55	19 16	19 20	19 33		19 48			19 53	20 08		19 55
Bognor Regis	a				19 15						19 01	19 24		19 41						20 14		20 01
Chichester ■4	a	18 56		19 01		19 07		19 19					19 27			19 55			20 00			
	d	18 57		19 02		19 11		19 20					19 28			19 56			20 01			
Fishbourne (Sussex)	d			19 05		19 14													20 04			
Bosham	d			19 08		19 17													20 07			
Nutbourne	d					19 20													20 10			
Southbourne	d			19 12		19 23							19 35						20 13			
Emsworth	d			19 15		19 26		19 30					19 38						20 16			
Warblington	d					19 29													20 19			
Havant	d	19 08		19 20		19 33		19 37					19 46			20 07			20 22			
Bedhampton	a					19 35																
Hilsea	a					19 43																
Fratton	a	19 17				19 47							19 56			20 15						
Portsmouth & Southsea	a	19 21				19 50							20 01			20 19						
Portsmouth Harbour	a	19 26											20 07									
Cosham	a			19 29				19 46											20 28			
Portchester	a			19 33																		
Fareham	a			19 38				19 54											20 36			
Swanwick	a			19 45				20 01											20 43			
Southampton Central	a			20 03				20 18											21 01			

London, Gatwick Airport, Brighton - Sussex Coast, Portsmouth and Southampton

		SN ■	SN ◇■	SN	SN ■	SN ◇■ ⊼	SN ◇■ ⊼	SN ■	SN	SN ◇■ ⊼	SN ■	SN ◇■ ⊼	SN ◇■ ⊼	SN ■	SN	SN ◇■ ⊼	SN ■
London Victoria ■ ⊖	d					19 02				19 17		19 32				19 47	
Clapham Junction ■	d					19 08				19 23		19 38				19 53	
London Bridge ■ ⊖	d																
East Croydon	d					19 18				19 33		19 48				20 03	
Redhill ■	d					19 31						20 00					
Horley	d																
Gatwick Airport ■	d					19 40				19 49		20 09				20 19	
Three Bridges ■	a					19 45						20 14					
	d					19 45						20 14					
Crawley	d					19 49						20 18					
Horsham ■	a					19 57	>					20 26	>				
	d					20 01	20 06					20 30	20 35				
Christs Hospital	d						20 09						20 38				
Billingshurst	d						20 15						20 44				
Pulborough	d						20 22						20 51				
Amberley	d						20 28						20 57				
Arundel	d						20 33						21 02				
Haywards Heath ■	d		19 37							20 04						20 34	
Burgess Hill	d		19 42							20 09						20 39	
Brighton ■	d	19 30		19 44				20 03	20 14					20 30	20 44		
Hove ■	d	19 34	19 57	19a48				20 07	20a17	20 22				20 34	20a48	20 54	
Aldrington	d	19 36						20 09						20 36			
Portslade	d	19 38	20 00					20 11		20 25				20 38		20 57	
Fishersgate	d	19 40						20 13						20 40			
Southwick	d	19 42						20 15						20 42			
Shoreham-by-Sea	d	19 46	20 04					20 19		20 30				20 46		21 01	
Lancing	d	19 50	20 08					20 23		20 34				20 50		21 05	
East Worthing	d	19 53						20 26						20 53			
Worthing ■	a	19 55	20 12					20 28		20 38				20 55		21 09	
	d	19 56	20 13					20 29		20 38				20 56		21 10	
West Worthing	d	19 58	20 15					20 31		20 40				20 58		21 12	
Durrington-on-Sea	d	20 00	20 17					20 33		20 43				21 00		21 14	
Goring-by-Sea	d	20 03	20 20					20 36		20 45				21 03		21 17	
Angmering ■	d	20 07	20 24					20 40		20 49				21 07		21 21	
Littlehampton ■	a		20 35							20 58						21 29	
	d				20 06						20 37						21 06
Ford ■	d	20 13			20 10		20 38	20 46			20 42		21 07	21 13			21 10
Bognor Regis ■	d																
Barnham	a	20 18			20 14	20 27	20 42	20 50			20 46	20 56	21 11	21 17			21 14
	d	20 18			20 22	20 28	20 43	20 51			20 52	20 57	21 12	21 18			21 22
Bognor Regis	a				20 28		20 49				20 58		21 18				21 28
Chichester ■	a	20 26				20 35		20 58				21 04		21 25			
	d	20 26				20 36		20 59				21 05		21 26			
Fishbourne (Sussex)	d											21 08					
Bosham	d											21 11					
Nutbourne	d											21 14					
Southbourne	d					20 43						21 17					
Emsworth	d					20 46						21 20					
Warblington	d											21 23					
Havant	d	20 37				20 52		21 10				21 26		21 37			
Bedhampton	a																
Hilsea	a																
Fratton	a					21 01		21 18									
Portsmouth & Southsea	a					21 06		21 23									
Portsmouth Harbour	a							21 27									
Cosham	a	20 44										21 32		21 43			
Portchester	a	20 48										21 37					
Fareham	a	20 53										21 42		21 51			
Swanwick	a	21 00										21 48		21 58			
Southampton Central	a	21 19										22 06		22 16			

Table 188

Mondays to Fridays

London, Gatwick Airport, Brighton - Sussex Coast, Portsmouth and Southampton

		SN ◇■ ⊼	SN ◇■ ⊼	SN ■	SN ■	SN	SN ◇■	SN ■	SN ◇■	SN ◇■	SN ■	SN ■	SN ■	SN	SN ◇■	SN ■	SN ■	SN	SN ■	SN ◇■
London Victoria ■ ⊖	d	20 02					20 17		20 32						20 47					21 17
Clapham Junction ■	d	20 08					20 23		20 38						20 53					21 23
London Bridge ■ ⊖	d																			
East Croydon	d	20 19					20 33		20 48						21 04					21 33
Redhill ■	d	20 31							21 00											
Horley	d																			
Gatwick Airport ■	d	20 39					20 49		21 09						21 19					21 49
Three Bridges ■	a	20 44							21 14											21 53
	d	20 44							21 14											21 53
Crawley	d	20 48							21 18											
Horsham ■	a	20 56	>						21 26	>										
	d	21 00	21 05						21 30	21 35										
Christs Hospital	d		21 08							21 38										
Billingshurst	d		21 14							21 44										
Pulborough	d		21 21							21 51										
Amberley	d		21 27							21 57										
Arundel	d		21 32							22 02										
Haywards Heath ■	d						21 04								21 34					22 06
Burgess Hill	d						21 09								21 39					22 11
Brighton ■	d				21 03	21 14							21 33	21 44			22 03	22 14		
Hove ■	d				21 07	21a17	21 22						21 37	21a48	21 54		22 07	22a17		22 23
Aldrington	d				21 09								21 39				22 09			
Portslade	d				21 11		21 25						21 41		21 57		22 11			22 26
Fishersgate	d				21 13								21 43				22 13			
Southwick	d				21 15								21 45				22 15			
Shoreham-by-Sea	d				21 19		21 30						21 49		22 01		22 19			22 31
Lancing	d				21 23		21 34						21 53		22 05		22 23			22 35
East Worthing	d				21 26								21 56				22 26			
Worthing ■	a				21 28		21 38						21 58		22 09		22 28			22 39
	d				21 29		21 38						21 59		22 10		22 29			22 39
West Worthing	d				21 31		21 40						22 01		22 12		22 31			22 41
Durrington-on-Sea	d				21 33		21 43						22 03		22 14		22 33			22 44
Goring-by-Sea	d				21 36		21 45						22 06		22 17		22 36			22 46
Angmering ■	d				21 40		21 49						22 10		22 21		22 40			22 50
Littlehampton ■	a						21 58								22 30					
	d											22 08							22 38	
Ford ■	d		21 37		21 46					22 07		22 12	22 16				22 46		22 42	22 56
Bognor Regis ■	d			21 39							22 00									
Barnham	a	21 26	21 41	21 45	21 50				21 56	22 11	22 06	22 16	22 20				22 50		22 46	23 01
	d	21 27	21 42		21 51			21 52	21 57	22 12		22 17	22 21			22 22	22 51		22 52	23 06
Bognor Regis	a		21 48					21 58		22 18						22 28			22 58	23 12
Chichester ■	a	21 34			21 58				22 04			22 24	22 28				22 58			
	d	21 35			21 59				22 05				22 29				22 59			
Fishbourne (Sussex)	d								22 08											
Bosham	d								22 11											
Nutbourne	d								22 14											
Southbourne	d	21 42							22 17				22 36							
Emsworth	d	21 45							22 20				22 39							
Warblington	d								22 23											
Havant	d	21 49			22 10				22 26				22 43				23 11			
Bedhampton	a																			
Hilsea	a																			
Fratton	a	21 58			22 18								22 52				23 20			
Portsmouth & Southsea	a	22 01			22 22								22 55				23 23			
Portsmouth Harbour	a	22 05			22 26								22 59				23 27			
Cosham	a								22 33											
Portchester	a																			
Fareham	a								22 42											
Swanwick	a								22 49											
Southampton Central	a								23 07											

Table 188

Mondays to Fridays

London, Gatwick Airport, Brighton - Sussex Coast, Portsmouth and Southampton

		SN 1	SN 1	SN 1	SN	SN ◇1	SN	SN 1	SN ◇1	SN 1	SN	SN ◇1	SN ◇1
London Victoria 15 ⊖	d	21 32				21 47			22 17	22 32		22 47	23 17
Clapham Junction 10	d	21 38				21 53			22 23	22 38		22 53	23 23
London Bridge 4 ⊖	d												
East Croydon	d	21 48				22 03			22 34	22 48		23 03	23 33
Redhill 5	d	22 00								23 01			
Horley	d												
Gatwick Airport 10	d	22 09				22 19			22 49	23 09		23 19	23 51
Three Bridges 4	a	22 14							22 54	23 15			23 55
	d	22 14							22 54	23 16			23 56
Crawley	d	22 18								23 19			
Horsham 4	a	22 26								23 27			
	d	22 27								23 28			
Christs Hospital	d	22 30								23 31			
Billingshurst	d	22 36								23 37			
Pulborough	d	22 43								23 44			
Amberley	d	22 49								23 50			
Arundel	d	22 54								23 55			
Haywards Heath 3	d					22 37			23 03			23 37	00 05
Burgess Hill	d								23 08				00 10
Brighton 10	d			22 33	22 44		23 14				23 44		
Hove 2	d			22 37	22a47	22 52	23a17		23 22		23a47	23 52	00 22
Aldrington	d			22 39									
Portslade	d			22 41		22 55			23 25			23 55	00s25
Fishersgate	d			22 43									
Southwick	d			22 45					23 28			23 58	00s28
Shoreham-by-Sea	d			22 49		23 00			23 31			00 01	00s31
Lancing	d			22 53		23 04			23 35			00 05	00s35
East Worthing	d			22 56									
Worthing 4	a			22 58		23 08			23 39			00 09	00 39
	d			22 59		23 08			23 39				
West Worthing	d			23 01		23 10			23 41				
Durrington-on-Sea	d			23 03		23 13			23 44				
Goring-by-Sea	d			23 06		23 15			23 46				
Angmering 3	d			23 10		23 19			23 50				
Littlehampton 4	a			23 18		23 28							
	d			23 23									
Ford 4	d	23 00		23 27					23 56	00 01			
Bognor Regis 4	d		23 15										
Barnham	a	23 04	23 21	23 31					00 01	00 06			
	d	23 05		23 32				23 36	00 09	00 06			
Bognor Regis	a							23 42	00 15				
Chichester 4	a	23 12		23 39						00 14			
	d	23 13											
Fishbourne (Sussex)	d	23 16											
Bosham	d	23 19											
Nutbourne	d	23 22											
Southbourne	d	23 25											
Emsworth	d	23 28											
Warblington	d	23 31											
Havant	d	23 34											
Bedhampton	a												
Hilsea	a												
Fratton	a	23 47											
Portsmouth & Southsea	a	23 51											
Portsmouth Harbour	a												
Cosham	a												
Portchester	a												
Fareham	a												
Swanwick	a												
Southampton Central	a												

Table 188

Saturdays

London, Gatwick Airport, Brighton - Sussex Coast, Portsmouth and Southampton

		SN ◇1	SN 1	SN ◇1	SN	SN ◇1	SN 1	SN 1	SN ◇1	SN 1
London Victoria 15 ⊖	d	22p17	22p32	22p47		23p17	23p10	23p47	00 05	
Clapham Junction 10	d	22p23	22p38	22p53		23p23	23p16	23p53	00 11	
London Bridge 4 ⊖	d									
East Croydon	d	22p34	22p48	23p03		23p33	23p28	00 06	00 25	
Redhill 5	d		23p01				23p46	00 25		
Horley	d						23p56	00 31		
Gatwick Airport 10	d	22p49	23p09	23p19		23p51	23p59	00 34	00 44	
Three Bridges 4	a	22p54	23p15			23p55	00 04	00 39	00 48	
	d	22p54	23p16			23p56	00 04	00 39	00 48	
Crawley	d		23p19				00 07	00 43		
Horsham 4	a		23p27				00 19	00 55		
	d		23p28							
Christs Hospital	d		23p31							
Billingshurst	d		23p37							
Pulborough	d		23p44							
Amberley	d		23p50							
Arundel	d		23p55							
Haywards Heath 3	d	23p03		23p37		00 05			01 03	
Burgess Hill	d	23p08				00 10				
Brighton 10	d				00 10				01s22	
Hove 2	d	23p22		23p52	00a13	00 22			01s25	
Aldrington	d									
Portslade	d	23p25		23p55		00s25			01s28	
Fishersgate	d									
Southwick	d	23p28		23p58		00s28			01s31	
Shoreham-by-Sea	d	23p31		00 01		00s31			01s34	
Lancing	d	23p35		00 05		00s35			01s38	
East Worthing	d									
Worthing 4	a	23p39		00 09		00 39			01 42	
	d	23p39								
West Worthing	d	23p41								
Durrington-on-Sea	d	23p44								
Goring-by-Sea	d	23p46								
Angmering 3	d	23p50								
Littlehampton 4	a									
	d									
Ford 4	d	23p56	00 01							
Bognor Regis 4	d									
Barnham	a	00 01	00 06							
	d	00 09	00 06							04 57
Bognor Regis	a	00 15								
Chichester 4	a		00 14							05 04
	d									05 05
Fishbourne (Sussex)	d									
Bosham	d									
Nutbourne	d									
Southbourne	d									
Emsworth	d									
Warblington	d									
Havant	d									05 16
Bedhampton	a									
Hilsea	a									
Fratton	a									
Portsmouth & Southsea	a									
Portsmouth Harbour	a									
Cosham	a									05 22
Portchester	a									05 27
Fareham	a									05 32
Swanwick	a									05 39
Southampton Central	a									05 58

		SN 1	SN 1	SN 1	SN 1	SN 1	SN 1	SN 1	SN 1	SN	SN 1	SN 1	SN 1	SN 1
London Victoria 15 ⊖	d													
Clapham Junction 10	d													
London Bridge 4 ⊖	d													
East Croydon	d													
Redhill 5	d													
Horley	d													
Gatwick Airport 10	d													
Three Bridges 4	a													
	d													
Crawley	d													
Horsham 4	a													
	d													
Christs Hospital	d													
Billingshurst	d													
Pulborough	d													
Amberley	d													
Arundel	d													
Haywards Heath 3	d													
Burgess Hill	d													
Brighton 10	d					05 15			05 27	05 44	05 53			06 01
Hove 2	d					05 20			05 31	05a47	05 57			06 05
Aldrington	d								05 33		05 59			
Portslade	d					05 23			05 35		06 01			06 08
Fishersgate	d								05 37		06 03			
Southwick	d								05 39		06 05			06 11
Shoreham-by-Sea	d					05 27			05 43		06 09			06 14
Lancing	d					05 31			05 47		06 13			06 18
East Worthing	d								05 50		06 16			
Worthing 4	a					05 35			05 52		06 18			06 22
	d					05 36			05 53		06 19			06 23
West Worthing	d					05 38			05 55		06a21			06 25
Durrington-on-Sea	d					05 40			05 57					06 27
Goring-by-Sea	d					05 43			06 00					06 30
Angmering 3	d					05 47			06 04					06 34
Littlehampton 4	a													
	d						05 54						06 19	
Ford 4	d					05 53	05 58		06 10					06 40
Bognor Regis 4	d							06 04						
Barnham	a					05 57	06 02	06 10	06 14				06 26	06 44
	d	05 15	05 20	05 30	05 38	05 58	06 03		06 15			06 22	06 27	06 45
Bognor Regis	a											06 28		
Chichester 4	a	05 22	05 27	05 37	05 45	06 05	06 10		06 22				06 34	06 52
	d	05 23	05 28	05 38	05 46	06 06	06 11		06 23				06 35	06 53
Fishbourne (Sussex)	d						06 14							
Bosham	d					06 10	06 17							
Nutbourne	d						06 20							
Southbourne	d					06 15	06 23		06 30					
Emsworth	d					06 18	06 26		06 33					
Warblington	d					06 21	06 29							
Havant	d	05 34	05 39	05 49	05 57	06 24	06 32		06 37				06 46	07 04
Bedhampton	a						06 34							
Hilsea	a						06 42							
Fratton	a	05 42		05 57	06 05		06 46						06 54	07 12
Portsmouth & Southsea	a	05 46		06 01	06 09		06 50						06 58	07 16
Portsmouth Harbour	a			06 05	06 16								07 02	07 20
Cosham	a		05 49			06 30			06 45					
Portchester	a					06 34								
Fareham	a		05 57			06 39			06 53					
Swanwick	a		06 04			06 46			07 00					
Southampton Central	a		06 24			07 05			07 18					

Table 188

London, Gatwick Airport, Brighton - Sussex Coast, Portsmouth and Southampton

		SN	SN 1	SN 1	SN 1	SN 1	SN 1	SN 1	SN 1	SN	SN 1	SN 1	SN 1	SN 1	SN 1	SN	SN 1	SN ◇1	SN 1	SN 1	SN 1	SN 1	SN 1
London Victoria 15 ⊖	d													05 32							06 02		
Clapham Junction 10	d													05 38							06 08		
London Bridge 4 ⊖	d																						
East Croydon	d													05 48							06 18		
Redhill 5	d													06 07							06b46		
Horley	d													06 18							06 55		
Gatwick Airport 10	d					05 58								06 22							06 59		
Three Bridges 4	a					06 02								06 26							07 03		
	d					06 03								06 34							07 04		
Crawley	d					06 06								06 37							07 07		
Horsham 4	a					06 18								06 49							07 19		
	d					06 19								06 50							07 20		
Christs Hospital	d					06 22								06 53							07 23		
Billingshurst	d					06 28								06 59							07 29		
Pulborough	d					06 35								07 06							07 36		
Amberley	d					06 41								07 12							07 42		
Arundel	d					06 46								07 17							07 47		
Haywards Heath 3	d																	07 37					
Burgess Hill	d																						
Brighton 10	d	06 14	06 23						06 33	06 44	06 48	06 53			07 03	07 14	07 23						07 33
Hove 2	d	06a17	06 27						06 37	06a47	06 52	06 57			07 07	07a17	07 27	07 52					07 37
Aldrington	d		06 29									06 59					07 29						
Portslade	d		06 31						06 40		06 55	07 01			07 10		07 31						07 40
Fishersgate	d		06 33									07 03					07 33						
Southwick	d		06 35						06 43			07 05			07 13		07 35						07 43
Shoreham-by-Sea	d		06 39						06 46		06 59	07 09			07 16		07 39	07 58					07 46
Lancing	d		06 43						06 50		07 03	07 13			07 20		07 43	08 02					07 50
East Worthing	d		06 46									07 16					07 46						
Worthing 4	a		06 48						06 54		07 07	07 18			07 24		07 48	08 06					07 54
	d		06 49						06 55		07 08	07 19			07 25		07 49	08 07					07 55
West Worthing	d		06a51						06 57		07 10	07a21					07a51	08 09					07 57
Durrington-on-Sea	d								06 59		07 12							08 11					07 59
Goring-by-Sea	d								07 02		07 15							08 14					08 02
Angmering 3	d								07 06		07 19				07 31			08 18					08 06
Littlehampton 4	a										07 27							08 27					
	d							06 54					07 11									07 54	
Ford 4	d					06 51		06 58	07 12				07 16	07 22							07 52	07 58	08 12
Bognor Regis 4	d			06 39															07 39				
Barnham	a			06 45		06 55	>	07 02	07 16				07 20	07 27	07 41				07 45		07 57	08 02	08 16
	d				06 52	06 59	07 05	07 03	07 17				07 22	07 27	07 41					07 52	07 57	08 03	08 17
Bognor Regis	a				06 58		07 11						07 28							07 58			
Chichester 4	a					07 06		07 10	07 24					07 35	07 49						08 05	08 10	08 24
	d					07 07		07 11	07 25					07 35	07 49						08 05	08 11	08 25
Fishbourne (Sussex)	d							07 14														08 14	
Bosham	d							07 17														08 17	
Nutbourne	d							07 20														08 20	
Southbourne	d					07 14		07 23							07 56						08 12	08 23	
Emsworth	d					07 17		07 26	07 33						07 59						08 15	08 26	08 33
Warblington	d							07 29														08 29	
Havant	d					07 23		07 32	07 37					07 46	08 04						08 20	08 32	08 37
Bedhampton	a							07 34														08 34	
Hilsea	a							07 42														08 42	
Fratton	a							07 46						07 55	08 12							08 46	
Portsmouth & Southsea	a							07 50						07 58	08 16							08 50	
Portsmouth Harbour	a													08 02	08 20								
Cosham	a					07 29			07 45												08 28		08 45
Portchester	a					07 34															08 32		
Fareham	a					07 39			07 53												08 37		08 53
Swanwick	a					07 45			08 00												08 44		09 00
Southampton Central	a					08 03			08 17												09 01		09 19

b arr. 0636

Table 188

London, Gatwick Airport, Brighton - Sussex Coast, Portsmouth and Southampton

		SN	SN 1	SN 1	SN 1	SN 1	SN	SN 1	SN 1	SN 1	SN ◇1	SN ◇1	SN 1	SN 1	SN	SN ◇1	SN 1	SN 1	SN ◇1	SN ◇1	SN ◇1
London Victoria 15 ⊖	d				06 32						07 32					07 47			08 02		08 17
Clapham Junction 10	d				06 38						07 38					07 53			08 08		08 23
London Bridge 4 ⊖	d																				
East Croydon	d				06 48						07 48					08 03			08 18		08 33
Redhill 5	d				07 10						08 00								08 30		
Horley	d				07 19														08 36		
Gatwick Airport 10	d				07 24						08 09					08 19			08 40		08 49
Three Bridges 4	a				07 29						08 14								08 44		
	d				07 30						08 14								08 45		
Crawley	d				07 33						08 18								08 48		
Horsham 4	a				07 45						08 26	>							08 56	>	
	d				07 50						08 30	08 35							09 00	09 05	
Christs Hospital	d				07 53							08 38									
Billingshurst	d				07 59							08 44								09 13	
Pulborough	d				08 06							08 51								09 19	
Amberley	d				08 12							08 57									
Arundel	d				08 17							09 02								09 28	
Haywards Heath 3	d															08 37					09 04
Burgess Hill	d																				09 09
Brighton 10	d	07 44	07 53			08 03	08 14	08 23						08 33	08 44		08 53				
Hove 2	d	07a47	07 57			08 07	08a17	08 27						08 37	08a47	08 52	08 57				09 22
Aldrington	d		07 59					08 29									08 59				
Portslade	d		08 01			08 10		08 31						08 40			09 01				09 25
Fishersgate	d		08 03					08 33									09 03				
Southwick	d		08 05			08 13		08 35						08 43			09 05				
Shoreham-by-Sea	d		08 09			08 16		08 39						08 46		08 58	09 09				09 30
Lancing	d		08 13			08 20		08 43						08 50		09 02	09 13				
East Worthing	d		08 16					08 46									09 16				
Worthing 4	a		08 18			08 24		08 48						08 54		09 06	09 18				09 36
	d		08 19			08 25		08 49						08 55		09 07	09 19				09 37
West Worthing	d		08a21					08a51						08 57		09 09	09a21				09 39
Durrington-on-Sea	d													08 59		09 11					09 41
Goring-by-Sea	d													09 02		09 14					09 44
Angmering 3	d					08 31								09 06		09 18					09 48
Littlehampton 4	a															09 27					09 57
	d			08 11									08 54					09 11			
Ford 4	d			08 16	08 22							09 07	08 58	09 12				09 16		09 33	
Bognor Regis 4	d								08 39												
Barnham	a			08 20	08 27	08 41			08 45		08 56	09 11	09 02	09 16				09 20	09 26	09 38	
	d			08 22	08 27	08 41				08 52	08 57	09 12	09 03	09 17				09 22	09 27	09 38	
Bognor Regis	a			08 28						08 58		09 18						09 28		09 45	
Chichester 4	a				08 35	08 49					09 04		09 10	09 24					09 34		
	d				08 35	08 49					09 05		09 11	09 25					09 35		
Fishbourne (Sussex)	d												09 14								
Bosham	d												09 17								
Nutbourne	d												09 20								
Southbourne	d					08 56					09 12		09 23								
Emsworth	d					08 59					09 15		09 26	09 33							
Warblington	d												09 29								
Havant	d				08 46	09 04					09 19		09 32	09 37					09 46		
Bedhampton	a												09 34								
Hilsea	a												09 42								
Fratton	a				08 55	09 12							09 46						09 54		
Portsmouth & Southsea	a				08 58	09 16							09 50						09 58		
Portsmouth Harbour	a				09 02	09 20													10 02		
Cosham	a										09 26			09 45							
Portchester	a										09 30										
Fareham	a										09 35			09 53							
Swanwick	a										09 42			10 00							
Southampton Central	a										09 59			10 17							

Table 188

London, Gatwick Airport, Brighton - Sussex Coast, Portsmouth and Southampton

		GW	SN	SN	SN		SN	SN	SN	SN	SN	SN	SN	SN	SN		SN	SN	SN	SN	SN
		◇	■		■		■	■	◇■	◇■	■	■		◇■	■		■	◇■	◇■	■	◇■
London Victoria ■ ⊖	d								08 32									09 02			09 17
Clapham Junction ■	d								08 38									09 08			09 23
London Bridge ■ ⊖	d																				
East Croydon	d								08 48									09 18			09 33
Redhill ■	d								09 00									09 30			
Horley	d																	09 36			
Gatwick Airport ■	d								09 09									09 40			09 49
Three Bridges ■	a								09 14									09 44			
	d								09 14									09 45			
Crawley	d								09 18									09 48			
Horsham ■	a								09 26	>								09 56	>		
	d								09 30	09 35								10 00	10 05		
Christs Hospital	d									09 38											
Billingshurst	d									09 44									10 14		
Pulborough	d									09 51									10 20		
Amberley	d									09 57											
Arundel	d									10 02									10 29		
Haywards Heath ■	d													09 37							10 04
Burgess Hill	d																				10 09
Brighton ■	d	09 00	09 03	09 14	09 23							09 33	09 44		09 53					10 03	
Hove ■	d	09 04	09 07	09a17	09 27							09 37	09a47	09 52	09 57					10 07	10 22
Aldrington	d				09 29										09 59						
Portslade	d		09 10		09 31							09 40			10 01					10 10	10 25
Fishersgate	d				09 33										10 03						
Southwick	d		09 13		09 35							09 43			10 05					10 13	
Shoreham-by-Sea	d	09 13	09 17		09 39							09 46		09 58	10 09					10 16	10 30
Lancing	d		09 21		09 43							09 50		10 02	10 13					10 20	
East Worthing	d				09 46										10 16						
Worthing ■	a	09 22	09 25		09 48							09 54		10 06	10 18					10 24	10 36
	d	09 22	09 25		09 49							09 55		10 07	10 19					10 25	10 37
West Worthing	d				09a51							09 57		10 09	10a21						10 39
Durrington-on-Sea	d											09 59		10 11							10 41
Goring-by-Sea	d											10 02		10 14							10 44
Angmering ■	d		09 34									10 06		10 18						10 31	10 48
Littlehampton ■	a													10 27							10 57
	d										09 54						10 11				
Ford ■	d									10 07	09 58	10 12					10 16		10 34		
Bognor Regis ■	d						09 39														
Barnham	a	09 40	09 44				09 45		09 56	10 11	10 02	10 16					10 20	10 26	10 39	10 42	
	d	09 41	09 45					09 52	09 57	10 12	10 03	10 17					10 22	10 27	10 39	10 42	
Bognor Regis	a							09 58		10 18							10 28		10 46		
Chichester ■	a	09 48	09 52						10 04		10 10	10 24						10 34		10 50	
	d	09 49	09 53						10 05		10 11	10 25						10 35		10 50	
Fishbourne (Sussex)	d										10 14										
Bosham	d										10 17										
Nutbourne	d										10 20										
Southbourne	d		10 00						10 12		10 23									10 57	
Emsworth	d		10 03						10 15		10 26	10 33								11 00	
Warblington	d										10 29										
Havant	d	10 00	10 07						10 19		10 32	10 37						10 46		11 05	
Bedhampton	a										10 34										
Hilsea	a										10 43										
Fratton	a		10 16								10 47							10 54		11 13	
Portsmouth & Southsea	a		10 19								10 50							10 58		11 17	
Portsmouth Harbour	a		10 23															11 02		11 21	
Cosham	a	10 06							10 26			10 45									
Portchester	a								10 30												
Fareham	a	10 15							10 35			10 53									
Swanwick	a								10 42			11 00									
Southampton Central	a	10 40							10 59			11 19									

Table 188

London, Gatwick Airport, Brighton - Sussex Coast, Portsmouth and Southampton

		SN	SN		SN	SN	SN	SN	SN	SN	SN		SN	SN	SN	SN	SN	SN	SN	SN	SN
			■		■	■	◇■	◇■	■	■			■	◇■	■	◇■	◇■	■		◇■	■
																🍴	🍴				
London Victoria ■ ⊖	d						09 32							09 47		10 02				10 17	
Clapham Junction ■	d						09 38							09 53		10 08				10 23	
London Bridge ■ ⊖	d																				
East Croydon	d						09 48							10 03		10 18				10 33	
Redhill ■	d						10 00									10 30					
Horley	d															10 36					
Gatwick Airport ■	d						10 09							10 19		10 40				10 49	
Three Bridges ■	a						10 14									10 44					
	d						10 14									10 45					
Crawley	d						10 18									10 48					
Horsham ■	a						10 26	>								10 56	>				
	d						10 30	10 35								11 00	11 05				
Christs Hospital	d							10 38													
Billingshurst	d							10 44									11 14				
Pulborough	d							10 51									11 20				
Amberley	d							10 57													
Arundel	d							11 02									11 29				
Haywards Heath ■	d													10 37						11 04	
Burgess Hill	d																			11 09	
Brighton ■	d	10 14	10 23							10 33	10 44				10 53			11 03	11 14		11 23
Hove ■	d	10a17	10 27							10 37	10a47			10 52	10 57			11 07	11a17	11 22	11 27
Aldrington	d		10 29												10 59						11 29
Portslade	d		10 31							10 40					11 01			11 10		11 25	11 31
Fishersgate	d		10 33												11 03						11 33
Southwick	d		10 35							10 43					11 05			11 13			11 35
Shoreham-by-Sea	d		10 39							10 46				10 58	11 09			11 16		11 30	11 39
Lancing	d		10 43							10 50				11 02	11 13			11 20			11 43
East Worthing	d		10 46												11 16						11 46
Worthing ■	a		10 48							10 54				11 06	11 18			11 24		11 36	11 48
	d		10 49							10 55				11 07	11 19			11 25		11 37	11 49
West Worthing	d		10a51							10 57				11 09	11a21					11 39	11a51
Durrington-on-Sea	d									10 59				11 11						11 41	
Goring-by-Sea	d									11 02				11 14						11 44	
Angmering ■	d									11 06				11 18				11 31		11 48	
Littlehampton ■	a													11 27						11 57	
	d								10 54				11 11								
Ford ■	d							11 07	10 58	11 12			11 16				11 34				
Bognor Regis ■	d				10 39																
Barnham	a				10 45		10 56	11 11	11 02	11 16			11 20			11 26	11 39	11 42			
	d					10 52	10 57	11 12	11 03	11 17			11 22			11 27	11 39	11 42			
Bognor Regis	a					10 58		11 18					11 28				11 46				
Chichester ■	a						11 04		11 10	11 24						11 34		11 50			
	d						11 05		11 11	11 25						11 35		11 50			
Fishbourne (Sussex)	d								11 14												
Bosham	d								11 17												
Nutbourne	d								11 20												
Southbourne	d						11 12		11 23									11 57			
Emsworth	d						11 15		11 26	11 33								12 00			
Warblington	d								11 29												
Havant	d						11 19		11 32	11 37						11 46		12 05			
Bedhampton	a								11 34												
Hilsea	a								11 42												
Fratton	a								11 46							11 54		12 13			
Portsmouth & Southsea	a								11 50							11 58		12 17			
Portsmouth Harbour	a															12 02		12 21			
Cosham	a						11 26			11 45											
Portchester	a						11 30														
Fareham	a						11 35			11 53											
Swanwick	a						11 42			12 00											
Southampton Central	a						11 59			12 19											

Table 188 — Saturdays

London, Gatwick Airport, Brighton - Sussex Coast, Portsmouth and Southampton

Station		SN 1	SN 1	SN ◇1	SN ◇1	SN 1	SN 1	SN	SN ◇1	SN 1	SN 1	SN ◇1 🚌	SN ◇1 🚌	SN ◇1	SN 1	SN	SN 1	SN 1	SN 1	SN ◇1	SN ◇1	SN 1
London Victoria 15 ⊖	d			10 32					10 47			11 02		11 17						11 32		
Clapham Junction 10	d			10 38					10 53			11 08		11 23						11 38		
London Bridge 4 ⊖	d																					
East Croydon 🚊	d			10 48					11 03			11 18		11 33						11 48		
Redhill 5	d			11 00								11 30								12 00		
Horley	d											11 36										
Gatwick Airport 10	d			11 09					11 19			11 40		11 49						12 09		
Three Bridges 4	a			11 14								11 44								12 14		
	d			11 14								11 45								12 14		
Crawley	d			11 18								11 48								12 18		
Horsham 4	a			11 26	>							11 56	>							12 26	>	
	d			11 30	11 35							12 00	12 05							12 30	12 35	
Christs Hospital	d				11 38																12 38	
Billingshurst	d				11 44								12 14								12 44	
Pulborough	d				11 51								12 20								12 51	
Amberley	d				11 57																12 57	
Arundel	d				12 02								12 29								13 02	
Haywards Heath 3	d								11 37					12 04								
Burgess Hill	d													12 09								
Brighton 10	d						11 33	11 44		11 53					12 03	12 14	12 23					
Hove 2	d						11 37	11a47	11 52	11 57				12 22	12 07	12a17	12 27					
Aldrington	d									11 59							12 29					
Portslade	d						11 40			12 01				12 25	12 10		12 31					
Fishersgate	d									12 03							12 33					
Southwick	d						11 43			12 05					12 13		12 35					
Shoreham-by-Sea	d						11 46		11 58	12 09				12 30	12 16		12 39					
Lancing	d						11 50		12 02	12 13					12 20		12 43					
East Worthing	d									12 16							12 46					
Worthing 4	a						11 54		12 06	12 18				12 36	12 24		12 48					
	d						11 55		12 07	12 19				12 37	12 25		12 49					
West Worthing	d						11 57		12 09	12a21				12 39			12a51					
Durrington-on-Sea	d						11 59		12 11					12 41								
Goring-by-Sea	d						12 02		12 14					12 44								
Angmering 3	d						12 06		12 18					12 48	12 31							
Littlehampton 4	a								12 27					12 57								
	d					11 54					12 11											12 54
Ford 4	d				12 07	11 58	12 12				12 16		12 34								13 07	12 58
Bognor Regis 4	d	11 39																12 39				
Barnham	a	11 45		11 56	12 11	12 02	12 16				12 20	12 26	12 39		12 42			12 45		12 56	13 11	13 02
	d		11 52	11 57	12 12	12 03	12 17				12 22	12 27	12 39		12 42				12 52	12 57	13 12	13 03
Bognor Regis	a		11 58		12 18						12 28		12 46						12 58		13 18	
Chichester 4	a			12 04		12 10	12 24					12 34			12 50					13 04		13 10
	d			12 05		12 11	12 25					12 35			12 50					13 05		13 11
Fishbourne (Sussex)	d					12 14																13 14
Bosham	d					12 17																13 17
Nutbourne	d					12 20																13 20
Southbourne	d			12 12		12 23									12 57					13 12		13 23
Emsworth	d			12 15		12 26	12 33								13 00					13 15		13 26
Warblington	d					12 29																13 29
Havant	d			12 19		12 32	12 37					12 46			13 05					13 19		13 32
Bedhampton	a					12 34																13 34
Hilsea	a					12 42																13 42
Fratton	a					12 46						12 54			13 13							13 46
Portsmouth & Southsea	a					12 50						12 58			13 17							13 50
Portsmouth Harbour	a											13 02			13 21							
Cosham	a			12 26			12 45													13 26		
Portchester	a			12 30																13 30		
Fareham	a			12 35			12 53													13 35		
Swanwick	a			12 42			13 00													13 42		
Southampton Central	a			12 59			13 19													13 59		

Table 188 — Saturdays

London, Gatwick Airport, Brighton - Sussex Coast, Portsmouth and Southampton

Station		SN 1	SN	SN 1	SN ◇1	SN 1	SN ◇1 🚌	SN ◇1 🚌	SN 1	SN	SN ◇1	SN 1	SN 1	SN 1	SN ◇1	SN ◇1	SN 1	SN 1	SN
London Victoria 15 ⊖	d				11 47		12 02				12 17				12 32				
Clapham Junction 10	d				11 53		12 08				12 23				12 38				
London Bridge 4 ⊖	d																		
East Croydon 🚊	d				12 03		12 18				12 33				12 48				
Redhill 5	d						12 30								13 00				
Horley	d						12 36												
Gatwick Airport 10	d				12 19		12 40				12 49				13 09				
Three Bridges 4	a						12 44								13 14				
	d						12 45								13 14				
Crawley	d						12 48								13 18				
Horsham 4	a						12 56	>							13 26	>			
	d						13 00	13 05							13 30	13 35			
Christs Hospital	d															13 38			
Billingshurst	d							13 14								13 44			
Pulborough	d							13 20								13 51			
Amberley	d															13 57			
Arundel	d							13 29								14 02			
Haywards Heath 3	d				12 37						13 04								
Burgess Hill	d										13 09								
Brighton 10	d	12 33	12 44			12 53			13 03	13 14		13 23						13 33	13 44
Hove 2	d	12 37	12a47		12 52	12 57			13 07	13a17	13 22	13 27						13 37	13a47
Aldrington	d					12 59						13 29							
Portslade	d	12 40				13 01			13 10		13 25	13 31						13 40	
Fishersgate	d					13 03						13 33							
Southwick	d	12 43				13 05			13 13			13 35						13 43	
Shoreham-by-Sea	d	12 46			12 58	13 09			13 16		13 30	13 39						13 46	
Lancing	d	12 50			13 02	13 13			13 20			13 43						13 50	
East Worthing	d					13 16						13 46							
Worthing 4	a	12 54			13 06	13 18			13 24		13 36	13 48						13 54	
	d	12 55			13 07	13 19			13 25		13 37	13 49						13 55	
West Worthing	d	12 57			13 09	13a21					13 39	13a51						13 57	
Durrington-on-Sea	d	12 59			13 11						13 41							13 59	
Goring-by-Sea	d	13 02			13 14						13 44							14 02	
Angmering 3	d	13 06			13 18				13 31		13 48							14 06	
Littlehampton 4	a				13 27						13 57								
	d			13 11													13 54		
Ford 4	d	13 12		13 16				13 34								14 07	13 58	14 12	
Bognor Regis 4	d												13 39						
Barnham	a	13 16		13 20			13 26	13 39	13 42				13 45		13 56	14 11	14 02	14 16	
	d	13 17		13 22			13 27	13 39	13 42					13 52	13 57	14 12	14 03	14 17	
Bognor Regis	a			13 28				13 46						13 58		14 18			
Chichester 4	a	13 24					13 34		13 50						14 04		14 10	14 24	
	d	13 25					13 35		13 50						14 05		14 11	14 25	
Fishbourne (Sussex)	d																14 14		
Bosham	d																14 17		
Nutbourne	d																14 20		
Southbourne	d								13 57						14 12		14 23		
Emsworth	d	13 33							14 00						14 15		14 26	14 33	
Warblington	d																14 29		
Havant	d	13 37					13 46		14 05						14 19		14 32	14 37	
Bedhampton	a																14 34		
Hilsea	a																14 42		
Fratton	a						13 54		14 13								14 46		
Portsmouth & Southsea	a						13 58		14 17								14 50		
Portsmouth Harbour	a						14 02		14 21										
Cosham	a	13 45													14 26			14 45	
Portchester	a														14 30				
Fareham	a	13 53													14 35			14 53	
Swanwick	a	14 00													14 42			15 00	
Southampton Central	a	14 19													14 59			15 19	

Table 188

Saturdays

London, Gatwick Airport, Brighton - Sussex Coast, Portsmouth and Southampton

		SN ◇1	SN 1	SN 1	SN ◇1 🚌	SN ◇1 🚌	SN 1	SN	SN ◇1	SN 1	SN 1	SN 1	SN ◇1	SN ◇1	SN 1	SN 1	SN	SN 1	SN ◇1	SN 1
London Victoria [15] ⊖	d	12 47			13 02				13 17				13 32						13 47	
Clapham Junction [10]	d	12 53			13 08				13 23				13 38						13 53	
London Bridge [4] ⊖	d																			
East Croydon	d	13 03			13 18				13 33				13 48						14 03	
Redhill [5]	d				13 30								14 00							
Horley	d				13 36															
Gatwick Airport [10]	d	13 19			13 40				13 49				14 09						14 19	
Three Bridges [4]	a				13 44								14 14							
	d				13 45								14 14							
Crawley	d				13 48								14 18							
Horsham [4]	a				13 56	>							14 26	>						
	d				14 00	14 05							14 30	14 35						
Christs Hospital	d													14 38						
Billingshurst	d					14 14								14 44						
Pulborough	d					14 20								14 51						
Amberley	d													14 57						
Arundel	d					14 29								15 02						
Haywards Heath [3]	d	13 37							14 04										14 37	
Burgess Hill	d								14 09											
Brighton [10]	d		13 53				14 03	14 14		14 23						14 33	14 44			14 53
Hove [2]	d	13 52	13 57				14 07	14a17	14 22	14 27						14 37	14a47		14 52	14 57
Aldrington	d		13 59							14 29										14 59
Portslade	d		14 01				14 10		14 25	14 31						14 40				15 01
Fishersgate	d		14 03							14 33										15 03
Southwick	d		14 05				14 13			14 35						14 43				15 05
Shoreham-by-Sea	d	13 58	14 09				14 16		14 30	14 39						14 46			14 58	15 09
Lancing	d	14 02	14 13				14 20			14 43						14 50			15 02	15 13
East Worthing	d		14 16							14 46										15 16
Worthing [4]	a	14 06	14 18				14 24		14 36	14 48						14 54			15 06	15 18
	d	14 07	14 19				14 25		14 37	14 49						14 55			15 07	15 19
West Worthing	d	14 09	14a21						14 39	14a51						14 57			15 09	15a21
Durrington-on-Sea	d	14 11							14 41							14 59			15 11	
Goring-by-Sea	d	14 14							14 44							15 02			15 14	
Angmering [3]	d	14 18					14 31		14 48							15 06			15 18	
Littlehampton [4]	a	14 27							14 57										15 27	
	d			14 11											14 54			15 11		
Ford [4]	d			14 16		14 34								15 07	14 58	15 12		15 16		
Bognor Regis [4]	d										14 39									
Barnham	a			14 20	14 26	14 39	14 42				14 45		14 56	15 11	15 02	15 16		15 20		
	d			14 22	14 27	14 39	14 42					14 52	14 57	15 12	15 03	15 17		15 22		
Bognor Regis	a			14 28		14 46						14 58		15 18				15 28		
Chichester [4]	a				14 34		14 50						15 04		15 10	15 24				
	d				14 35		14 50						15 05		15 11	15 25				
Fishbourne (Sussex)	d														15 14					
Bosham	d														15 17					
Nutbourne	d														15 20					
Southbourne	d						14 57						15 12		15 23					
Emsworth	d						15 00						15 15		15 26	15 33				
Warblington	d														15 29					
Havant	d				14 46		15 05						15 19		15 32	15 37				
Bedhampton	a														15 34					
Hilsea	a														15 42					
Fratton	a				14 54		15 13								15 46					
Portsmouth & Southsea	a				14 58		15 17								15 50					
Portsmouth Harbour	a				15 02		15 21													
Cosham	a												15 26			15 45				
Portchester	a												15 30							
Fareham	a												15 35			15 53				
Swanwick	a												15 42			16 00				
Southampton Central	a												15 59			16 19				

Table 188

Saturdays

London, Gatwick Airport, Brighton - Sussex Coast, Portsmouth and Southampton

		SN ◇1 🚌	SN ◇1 🚌	SN 1	SN	SN ◇1	SN 1	SN 1	SN 1	SN ◇1	SN ◇1	SN 1	SN 1	SN	SN ◇1	SN 1	SN 1	SN ◇1 🚌	SN ◇1 🚌	SN 1	SN 1	SN 1	SN ◇1
London Victoria [15] ⊖	d	14 02				14 17				14 32					14 47			15 02					15 17
Clapham Junction [10]	d	14 08				14 23				14 38					14 53			15 08					15 23
London Bridge [4] ⊖	d																						
East Croydon	d	14 18				14 33				14 48					15 03			15 18					15 33
Redhill [5]	d	14 30								15 00								15 30					
Horley	d	14 36																15 36					
Gatwick Airport [10]	d	14 40				14 49				15 09					15 19			15 40					15 49
Three Bridges [4]	a	14 44								15 14								15 44					
	d	14 45								15 14								15 45					
Crawley	d	14 48								15 18								15 48					
Horsham [4]	a	14 56	>							15 26	>							15 56	>				
	d	15 00	15 05							15 30	15 35							16 00	16 05				
Christs Hospital	d										15 38												
Billingshurst	d		15 14								15 44								16 14				
Pulborough	d		15 20								15 51								16 20				
Amberley	d										15 57												
Arundel	d		15 29								16 02								16 29				
Haywards Heath [3]	d					15 04									15 37								16 04
Burgess Hill	d					15 09																	16 09
Brighton [10]	d			15 03	15 14		15 23						15 33	15 44		15 53				16 03	16 14		
Hove [2]	d			15 07	15a17	15 22	15 27						15 37	15a47	15 52	15 57				16 07	16 17		16 22
Aldrington	d						15 29									15 59							
Portslade	d			15 10		15 25	15 31						15 40			16 01				16 10			16 25
Fishersgate	d						15 33									16 03							
Southwick	d			15 13			15 35						15 43			16 05				16 13			
Shoreham-by-Sea	d			15 16		15 30	15 39						15 46		15 58	16 09				16 16			16 30
Lancing	d			15 20			15 43						15 50		16 02	16 13				16 20			
East Worthing	d						15 46									16 16							
Worthing [4]	a			15 24		15 36	15 48						15 54		16 06	16 18				16 24			16 36
	d			15 25		15 37	15 49						15 55		16 07	16 19				16 25			16 37
West Worthing	d					15 39	15a51						15 57		16 09	16a21							16 39
Durrington-on-Sea	d					15 41							15 59		16 11								16 41
Goring-by-Sea	d					15 44							16 02		16 14								16 44
Angmering [3]	d			15 31		15 48							16 06		16 18					16 31			16 48
Littlehampton [4]	a					15 58									16 27								16 57
	d											15 54					16 11						
Ford [4]	d		15 34								16 07	15 58	16 12				16 16		16 34				
Bognor Regis [4]	d							15 39															
Barnham	a	15 26	15 39	15 42				15 45		15 56	16 11	16 02	16 16				16 20	16 26	16 39	16 42			
	d	15 27	15 39	15 42					15 52	15 57	16 12	16 03	16 17				16 22	16 27	16 39	16 42		16 52	
Bognor Regis	a		15 46						15 58		16 18						16 28		16 46			16 58	
Chichester [4]	a	15 34		15 50						16 04		16 10	16 24					16 34		16 50			
	d	15 35		15 50						16 05		16 11	16 25					16 35		16 50			
Fishbourne (Sussex)	d											16 14											
Bosham	d											16 17											
Nutbourne	d											16 20											
Southbourne	d			15 57						16 12		16 23								16 57			
Emsworth	d			16 00						16 15		16 26	16 33							17 00			
Warblington	d											16 29											
Havant	d	15 46		16 05						16 19		16 32	16 37					16 46		17 05			
Bedhampton	a											16 34											
Hilsea	a											16 42											
Fratton	a	15 54		16 13								16 46						16 54		17 13			
Portsmouth & Southsea	a	15 58		16 17								16 50						16 58		17 17			
Portsmouth Harbour	a	16 02		16 21														17 02		17 21			
Cosham	a									16 26			16 45										
Portchester	a									16 30													
Fareham	a									16 35			16 53										
Swanwick	a									16 42			17 00										
Southampton Central	a									16 59			17 19										

Table 188

Saturdays

London, Gatwick Airport, Brighton - Sussex Coast, Portsmouth and Southampton

		SN		SN	SN	SN	SN	SN	SN		SN	SN	SN	SN	SN	GW	SN	SN	SN	SN
		■		■	◇■	◇■	■	■			■	◇■	■	◇■	◇■	◇	■		◇■	■
														⌶	⌶					
London Victoria ■ ⊖	d				15 32							15 47		16 02					16 17	
Clapham Junction ■	d				15 38							15 53		16 08					16 23	
London Bridge ■ ⊖	d																			
East Croydon	d				15 48							16 03		16 18					16 33	
Redhill ■	d				16 00									16 30						
Horley	d													16 36						
Gatwick Airport ■	d				16 09							16 19		16 40					16 49	
Three Bridges ■	a				16 14									16 44						
	d				16 14									16 45						
Crawley	d				16 18									16 48						
Horsham ■	a				16 26	>								16 56	>					
	d				16 30	16 35								17 00	17 05					
Christs Hospital	d					16 38														
Billingshurst	d					16 44									17 14					
Pulborough	d					16 51									17 20					
Amberley	d					16 57														
Arundel	d					17 02									17 29					
Haywards Heath ■	d											16 37							17 04	
Burgess Hill	d																		17 09	
Brighton ■	d	16 23						16 33	16 44				16 53			17 00	17 03	17 14		17 23
Hove ■	d	16 27						16 37	16a47			16 52	16 57			17 04	17 07	17a17	17 22	17 27
Aldrington	d	16 29											16 59							17 29
Portslade	d	16 31						16 40					17 01				17 10		17 25	17 31
Fishersgate	d	16 33											17 03							17 33
Southwick	d	16 35						16 43					17 05				17 13			17 35
Shoreham-by-Sea	d	16 39						16 46				16 58	17 09			17 13	17 17		17 30	17 39
Lancing	d	16 43						16 50				17 02	17 13				17 21			17 43
East Worthing	d	16 46											17 16							17 46
Worthing ■	a	16 48						16 54				17 06	17 18			17 22	17 25		17 36	17 48
	d	16 49						16 55				17 07	17 19			17 22	17 25		17 37	17 49
West Worthing	d	16a51						16 57				17 09	17a21						17 39	17a51
Durrington-on-Sea	d							16 59				17 11							17 41	
Goring-by-Sea	d							17 02				17 14							17 44	
Angmering ■	d							17 06				17 18					17 34		17 48	
Littlehampton ■	a											17 27							17 57	
	d						16 54				17 11									
Ford ■	d					17 07	16 58	17 12			17 16				17 36					
Bognor Regis ■	d			16 39																
Barnham	a			16 45	16 56	17 11	17 02	17 16			17 20			17 26	17 40	17 37	17 43			
	d				16 57	17 12	17 03	17 17			17 22			17 27	17 41	17 38	17 44			
Bognor Regis	a					17 18					17 28				17 47					
Chichester ■	a				17 04		17 10	17 24						17 34		17 45	17 51			
	d				17 05		17 11	17 25						17 35		17 46	17 52			
Fishbourne (Sussex)	d						17 14													
Bosham	d						17 17													
Nutbourne	d						17 20													
Southbourne	d				17 12		17 23										17 59			
Emsworth	d				17 15		17 26	17 33									18 02			
Warblington	d						17 29													
Havant	d				17 19		17 32	17 37						17 46		18 00	18 06			
Bedhampton	a						17 34													
Hilsea	a						17 42													
Fratton	a						17 46							17 54			18 15			
Portsmouth & Southsea	a						17 50							17 58			18 18			
Portsmouth Harbour	a													18 02			18 22			
Cosham	a				17 26			17 45								18 06				
Portchester	a				17 30															
Fareham	a				17 35			17 53								18 14				
Swanwick	a				17 42			18 00												
Southampton Central	a				17 59			18 19								18 43				

Table 188

Saturdays

London, Gatwick Airport, Brighton - Sussex Coast, Portsmouth and Southampton

		SN	SN	SN	SN	SN	SN	SN		SN	SN	SN	SN	SN	SN	SN	SN		SN	SN	SN	SN
		■	■	◇■	◇■	■	■			■	◇■	■	◇■	◇■	■		■		■	◇■	◇■	◇■
													⌶	⌶								
London Victoria ■ ⊖	d			16 32							16 47		17 02							17 17	17 32	
Clapham Junction ■	d			16 38							16 53		17 08							17 23	17 38	
London Bridge ■ ⊖	d																					
East Croydon	d			16 48							17 03		17 18							17 33	17 48	
Redhill ■	d			17 00									17 30								18 00	
Horley	d												17 36									
Gatwick Airport ■	d			17 09							17 19		17 40							17 49	18 09	
Three Bridges ■	a			17 14									17 44								18 14	
	d			17 14									17 45								18 14	
Crawley	d			17 18									17 48								18 18	
Horsham ■	a			17 26	>								17 56	>							18 26	>
	d			17 30	17 35								18 00	18 05							18 30	18 35
Christs Hospital	d				17 38																	18 38
Billingshurst	d				17 44									18 14								18 44
Pulborough	d				17 51									18 20								18 51
Amberley	d				17 57																	18 57
Arundel	d				18 02									18 29								19 02
Haywards Heath ■	d										17 37									18 04		
Burgess Hill	d																			18 09		
Brighton ■	d						17 33	17 44				17 53			18 03	18 14						
Hove ■	d						17 37	17a47			17 52	17 57			18 07	18a17				18 22		
Aldrington	d											17 59										
Portslade	d						17 40					18 01			18 10					18 25		
Fishersgate	d											18 03										
Southwick	d						17 43					18 05			18 13							
Shoreham-by-Sea	d						17 46				17 58	18 09			18 16					18 30		
Lancing	d						17 50				18 02	18 13			18 20							
East Worthing	d											18 16										
Worthing ■	a						17 54				18 06	18 18			18 24					18 36		
	d						17 55				18 07	18 19			18 25					18 37		
West Worthing	d						17 57				18 09	18a21								18 39		
Durrington-on-Sea	d						17 59				18 11									18 41		
Goring-by-Sea	d						18 02				18 14									18 44		
Angmering ■	d						18 06				18 18				18 31					18 48		
Littlehampton ■	a										18 27									18 57		
	d					17 54				18 11												
Ford ■	d				18 07	17 58	18 12			18 16				18 34								19 07
Bognor Regis ■	d	17 39																	18 39			
Barnham	a	17 45		17 56	18 11	18 02	18 16			18 20			18 26	18 39	18 42				18 46		18 56	19 11
	d		17 52	17 57	18 12	18 03	18 17			18 22			18 27	18 39	18 42		18 52				18 57	19 12
Bognor Regis	a		17 58		18 18					18 28				18 46			18 58					19 18
Chichester ■	a			18 04		18 10	18 24						18 34		18 50						19 04	
	d			18 05		18 11	18 25						18 35		18 50						19 05	
Fishbourne (Sussex)	d					18 14																
Bosham	d					18 17																
Nutbourne	d					18 20																
Southbourne	d			18 12		18 23									18 57						19 12	
Emsworth	d			18 15		18 26	18 33								19 00						19 15	
Warblington	d					18 29																
Havant	d			18 19		18 32	18 37						18 46		19 05						19 19	
Bedhampton	a					18 34																
Hilsea	a					18 42																
Fratton	a					18 46							18 54		19 13							
Portsmouth & Southsea	a					18 50							18 58		19 17							
Portsmouth Harbour	a												19 02		19 21							
Cosham	a			18 26			18 45														19 26	
Portchester	a			18 30																	19 30	
Fareham	a			18 35			18 53														19 35	
Swanwick	a			18 42			19 00														19 42	
Southampton Central	a			18 59			19 19														19 59	

London, Gatwick Airport, Brighton - Sussex Coast, Portsmouth and Southampton

		SN ■	SN ■	SN ■	SN	SN ■	SN ◇■	SN ◇■	SN ◇■	SN ■	SN	SN ◇■	SN ■	SN ■	SN ◇■	SN ◇■	SN ■	SN	SN ■	SN ◇■	SN ◇■	SN ◇■
								🚲	🚲												🚲	🚲
London Victoria 15 ⊖	d						17 47	18 02				18 17			18 32					18 47	19 02	
Clapham Junction 10	d						17 53	18 08				18 23			18 38					18 53	19 08	
London Bridge 4 ⊖	d																					
East Croydon	d						18 03	18 18				18 33			18 48					19 03	19 18	
Redhill 5	d							18 30							19 00						19 30	
Horley	d							18 36													19 36	
Gatwick Airport 10	d						18 19	18 40				18 49			19 09					19 19	19 40	
Three Bridges 4	a							18 44							19 14						19 44	
	d							18 45							19 14						19 45	
Crawley	d							18 48							19 18						19 48	
Horsham 4	a							18 56	>						19 26	>					19 56	>
	d							19 00	19 05						19 30	19 35					20 00	20 05
Christs Hospital	d															19 38						
Billingshurst	d								19 14							19 44						20 14
Pulborough	d								19 20							19 51						20 20
Amberley	d															19 57						
Arundel	d								19 29							20 02						20 29
Haywards Heath 3	d						18 37					19 04								19 37		
Burgess Hill	d											19 09										
Brighton 10	d		18 23	18 33	18 44					19 03	19 14						19 29	19 44				
Hove 2	d		18 27	18 37	18a47		18 52			19 07	19a17	19 22					19 33	19a47		19 52		
Aldrington	d		18 29							19 09							19 35					
Portslade	d		18 31	18 40			18 55			19 11		19 25					19 37			19 55		
Fishersgate	d		18 33							19 13							19 39					
Southwick	d		18 35	18 43						19 15							19 41					
Shoreham-by-Sea	d		18 39	18 46			19 00			19 19		19 30					19 45			20 00		
Lancing	d		18 43	18 50			19 04			19 23		19 34					19 49			20 04		
East Worthing	d		18 46							19 26							19 52					
Worthing 4	a		19 28	18 54			19 08			19 28		19 38					19 54			20 08		
	d		19 29	18 55			19 08			19 29		19 38					19 55			20 08		
West Worthing	d		19 31	18 57			19 10			19 31		19 40					19 57			20 10		
Durrington-on-Sea	d		19 33	18 59			19 13			19 33		19 43					19 59			20 13		
Goring-by-Sea	d		19 36	19 02			19 15			19 36		19 45					20 02			20 15		
Angmering 3	d		19 40	19 06			19 19			19 40		19 49					20 06			20 19		
Littlehampton 4	a		19 11				19 28					19 58								20 28		
	d	18 54				19 11													20 11			
Ford 4	d	18 58		19 12		19 16			19 34	19 46						20 07	20 12		20 16			20 34
Bognor Regis 4	d												19 39									
Barnham	a	19 02		19 16		19 20		19 26	19 39	19 50			19 46		19 56	20 11	20 16		20 20		20 26	20 39
	d	19 03		19 17		19 22		19 27	19 39	19 51				19 52	19 57	20 12	20 17		20 22		20 27	20 39
Bognor Regis	a					19 28			19 46					19 58		20 18			20 28			20 46
Chichester 4	a	19 10		19 24				19 34		19 58					20 04		20 24				20 34	
	d	19 11		19 25				19 35		19 59					20 05		20 25				20 35	
Fishbourne (Sussex)	d	19 14													20 08							
Bosham	d	19 17													20 11							
Nutbourne	d	19 20													20 14							
Southbourne	d	19 23													20 17							
Emsworth	d	19 26		19 33											20 20		20 33					
Warblington	d	19 29													20 23							
Havant	d	19 32		19 37				19 46		20 10					20 26		20 37				20 46	
Bedhampton	a	19 34																				
Hilsea	a	19 42																				
Fratton	a	19 46						19 54		20 18											20 54	
Portsmouth & Southsea	a	19 50						19 58		20 22											20 58	
Portsmouth Harbour	a							20 02		20 26											21 02	
Cosham	a			19 45											20 32		20 45					
Portchester	a														20 36							
Fareham	a			19 53											20 41		20 53					
Swanwick	a			20 00											20 48		21 00					
Southampton Central	a			20 19											21 05		21 19					

Table 188

Saturdays

London, Gatwick Airport, Brighton - Sussex Coast, Portsmouth and Southampton

		SN ■	SN	SN ◇■	SN ■	SN ■	SN ◇■	SN ◇■	SN ■	SN	SN ■	SN ◇■	SN ◇■	SN ◇■	SN ■	SN	SN ◇■	SN ■
London Victoria 15 ⊖	d			19 17			19 32					19 47	20 02				20 17	
Clapham Junction 10	d			19 23			19 38					19 53	20 08				20 23	
London Bridge 4 ⊖	d																	
East Croydon	d			19 33			19 48					20 03	20 19				20 33	
Redhill 5	d						20 00						20 31					
Horley	d																	
Gatwick Airport 10	d			19 49			20 09					20 19	20 39				20 49	
Three Bridges 4	a						20 14						20 44					
	d						20 14						20 44					
Crawley	d						20 18						20 48					
Horsham 4	a						20 26	>					20 56	>				
	d						20 30	20 35					21 00	21 05				
Christs Hospital	d							20 38						21 08				
Billingshurst	d							20 44						21 14				
Pulborough	d							20 51						21 21				
Amberley	d							20 57						21 27				
Arundel	d							21 02						21 32				
Haywards Heath 3	d			20 04								20 37					21 04	
Burgess Hill	d			20 09													21 09	
Brighton 10	d	19 56	20 14						20 30	20 44					21 03	21 14		
Hove 2	d	20 00	20a18	20 22					20 34	20a48		20 52			21 07	21a17	21 22	
Aldrington	d	20 02							20 36						21 09			
Portslade	d	20 04		20 25					20 38			20 55			21 11		21 25	
Fishersgate	d	20 06							20 40						21 13			
Southwick	d	20 08							20 42						21 15			
Shoreham-by-Sea	d	20 12		20 30					20 46			21 00			21 19		21 30	
Lancing	d	20 16		20 34					20 50			21 04			21 23		21 34	
East Worthing	d	20 19							20 53						21 26			
Worthing 4	a	20 21		20 38					20 55			21 08			21 28		21 38	
	d	20 22		20 38					20 56			21 08			21 29		21 38	
West Worthing	d	20 24		20 40					20 58			21 10			21 31		21 40	
Durrington-on-Sea	d	20 26		20 43					21 00			21 13			21 33		21 43	
Goring-by-Sea	d	20 29		20 45					21 03			21 15			21 36		21 45	
Angmering 3	d	20 33		20 49					21 07			21 19			21 40		21 49	
Littlehampton 4	a			20 58								21 28					21 58	
	d										21 07							
Ford 4	d	20 39						21 07	21 15		21 11			21 37	21 46			
Bognor Regis 4	d				20 39													21 39
Barnham	a	20 43			20 45		20 56	21 11	21 19		21 15		21 26	21 41	21 50			21 45
	d	20 44				20 52	20 57	21 12	21 20		21 22		21 27	21 42	21 51			
Bognor Regis	a					20 58		21 18			21 28			21 48				
Chichester 4	a	20 51					21 04		21 27				21 34		21 58			
	d	20 52					21 05		21 28				21 35		21 59			
Fishbourne (Sussex)	d	20 55																
Bosham	d						21 09											
Nutbourne	d	21 00																
Southbourne	d	21 02					21 14						21 42					
Emsworth	d	21 05					21 17		21 36				21 45					
Warblington	d						21 20											
Havant	d	21 10					21 23		21 40				21 49		22 10			
Bedhampton	a																	
Hilsea	a																	
Fratton	a	21 18											21 59		22 18			
Portsmouth & Southsea	a	21 22											22 02		22 22			
Portsmouth Harbour	a	21 26											22 06		22 26			
Cosham	a						21 29		21 46									
Portchester	a						21 33											
Fareham	a						21 38		21 54									
Swanwick	a						21 45		22 01									
Southampton Central	a						22 02		22 20									

b arr. 1939

Table 188

London, Gatwick Airport, Brighton - Sussex Coast, Portsmouth and Southampton

		SN ■	SN ◇■	SN ◇■	SN ■	SN ■	SN ■	SN	SN ◇■	SN ■	SN ■	SN	SN ■	SN ◇■	SN ■	SN ■	SN ■	SN	SN ◇■	SN
London Victoria ■ ⊖	d		20 32						20 47					21 17	21 32				21 47	
Clapham Junction ■	d		20 38						20 53					21 23	21 38				21 53	
London Bridge ■ ⊖	d																			
East Croydon	d		20 48						21 03					21 33	21 48				22 03	
Redhill ■	d		21 00												22 00					
Horley	d																			
Gatwick Airport ■	d		21 09						21 19					21 49	22 09				22 19/	
Three Bridges ■	a		21 14											21 53	22 14					
	d		21 14											21 53	22 14					
Crawley	d		21 18												22 18					
Horsham ■	a		21 26	>											22 26					
	d		21 30	21 35											22 27					
Christs Hospital	d			21 38											22 30					
Billingshurst	d			21 44											22 36					
Pulborough	d			21 51											22 43					
Amberley	d			21 57											22 49					
Arundel	d			22 02											22 54					
Haywards Heath ■	d								21 37					22 06					22 37	
Burgess Hill	d													22 11						
Brighton ■	d						21 33	21 44			22 03	22 14					22 33	22 44		23 14
Hove ■	d						21 37	21a48	21 52		22 07	22a17		22 23			22 37	22a47	22 52	23a17
Aldrington	d						21 39				22 09						22 39			
Portslade	d						21 41		21 55		22 11			22 26			22 41		22 55	
Fishersgate	d						21 43				22 13						22 43			
Southwick	d						21 45				22 15						22 45			
Shoreham-by-Sea	d						21 49		22 00		22 19			22 31			22 49		23 00	
Lancing	d						21 53		22 04		22 23			22 35			22 53		23 04	
East Worthing	d						21 56				22 26						22 56			
Worthing ■	a						21 58		22 08		22 28			22 39			22 58		23 08	
	d						21 59		22 08		22 29			22 39			22 59		23 08	
West Worthing	d						22 01		22 10		22 31			22 41			23 01		23 10	
Durrington-on-Sea	d						22 03		22 13		22 33			22 44			23 03		23 13	
Goring-by-Sea	d						22 06		22 15		22 36			22 46			23 06		23 15	
Angmering ■	d						22 10		22 19		22 40			22 50			23 10		23 19	
Littlehampton ■	a								22 28								23 18		23 28	
	d					22 08							22 38				23 23			
Ford ■	d			22 07		22 12	22 16				22 46		22 42	22 56	23 00		23 27			
Bognor Regis ■	d				22 00											23 15				
Barnham	a		21 56	22 11	22 06	22 16	22 20				22 50		22 46	23 01	23 04	23 21	23 31			
	d	21 52	21 57	22 12		22 17	22 21			22 22	22 51		22 52	23 06	23 05		23 32			
Bognor Regis	a	21 58		22 18						22 28			22 58	23 12						
Chichester ■	a		22 04			22 24	22 28				22 58				23 12		23 39			
	d		22 05				22 29				22 59				23 13					
Fishbourne (Sussex)	d		22 08												23 16					
Bosham	d		22 11												23 19					
Nutbourne	d		22 14												23 22					
Southbourne	d		22 17				22 36								23 25					
Emsworth	d		22 20				22 39								23 28					
Warblington	d		22 23												23 31					
Havant	d		22 26				22 43				23 10				23 36					
Bedhampton	a																			
Hilsea	a																			
Fratton	a						22 52				23 18				23 48					
Portsmouth & Southsea	a						22 55				23 22				23 51					
Portsmouth Harbour	a						22 59				23 26									
Cosham	a		22 33																	
Portchester	a																			
Fareham	a		22 41																	
Swanwick	a		22 48																	
Southampton Central	a		23 05																	

Table 188

London, Gatwick Airport, Brighton - Sussex Coast, Portsmouth and Southampton

		SN ■	SN ◇■	SN	SN ■	SN ◇■	SN ◇■
London Victoria ■ ⊖	d		22 17		22 32	22 47	23 17
Clapham Junction ■	d		22 23		22 38	22 53	23 23
London Bridge ■ ⊖	d						
East Croydon	d		22 33		22 48	23 03	23 33
Redhill ■	d				23 01		
Horley	d						
Gatwick Airport ■	d		22 49		23 09	23 19	23 51
Three Bridges ■	a		22 54		23 14		23 55
	d		22 54		23 15		23 56
Crawley	d				23 18		
Horsham ■	a				23 26		
	d				23 27		
Christs Hospital	d				23 30		
Billingshurst	d				23 36		
Pulborough	d				23 43		
Amberley	d				23 49		
Arundel	d				23 54		
Haywards Heath ■	d		23 03			23 37	00 05
Burgess Hill	d		23 08				00 10
Brighton ■	d			23 44			
Hove ■	d		23 22	23a47		23 52	00 22
Aldrington	d						
Portslade	d		23 25			23 55	00s25
Fishersgate	d						
Southwick	d		23 28			23 58	00s28
Shoreham-by-Sea	d		23 31			00 01	00s31
Lancing	d		23 35			00 05	00s35
East Worthing	d						
Worthing ■	a		23 39			00 09	00s39
	d		23 39				00s39
West Worthing	d		23 41				00s41
Durrington-on-Sea	d		23 44				00s44
Goring-by-Sea	d		23 46				00s46
Angmering ■	d		23 50				00s50
Littlehampton ■	a						
	d						
Ford ■	d		23 56		23 59		00s56
Bognor Regis ■	d						
Barnham	a		00 01		00 04		01s01
	d	23 36	00 09		00 05		01s01
Bognor Regis	a	23 42	00 15				
Chichester ■	a				00 12		01 09
	d						
Fishbourne (Sussex)	d						
Bosham	d						
Nutbourne	d						
Southbourne	d						
Emsworth	d						
Warblington	d						
Havant	d						
Bedhampton	a						
Hilsea	a						
Fratton	a						
Portsmouth & Southsea	a						
Portsmouth Harbour	a						
Cosham	a						
Portchester	a						
Fareham	a						
Swanwick	a						
Southampton Central	a						

London, Gatwick Airport, Brighton - Sussex Coast, Portsmouth and Southampton

		SN	SN	SN	SN	SN	SN	SN	SN	SN	SN	SN	SN	SN	SN	SN	SN	SN	SN	SN	SN
		◇1	1	◇1	1	◇1	◇1	1	1	1	1	1	1	1	1	◇1	1	1	1	1	◇1
London Victoria 15 ⊖	d	22p17	22p32	22p47		23p17	00 05									07 02					08 02
Clapham Junction 10	d	22p23	22p38	22p53		23p23	00 11									07 08					08 08
London Bridge 4 ⊖	d																				
East Croydon	d	22p33	22p48	23p03		23p33	00 25									07 20					08 18
Redhill 5	d		23p01													07 34					08 32
Horley	d															07 40					08 38
Gatwick Airport 10	d	22p49	23p09	23p19		23p51	00 44	06 29								07 43					08 41
Three Bridges 4	a	22p54	23p14			23p55	00 48	06 33								07 48					08 46
	d	22p54	23p15			23p56	00 48	06 40								07 48					08 46
Crawley	d		23p18					06 43								07 52					08 50
Horsham 4	a		23p26					06 56								08 04					08 58
	d		23p27													08 04					08 59
Christs Hospital	d		23p30																		09 02
Billingshurst	d		23p36													08 13					09 09
Pulborough	d		23p43													08 19					09 15
Amberley	d		23p49																		09 21
Arundel	d		23p54													08 29					09 27
Haywards Heath 3	d	23p03		23p37		00 05	01 03														
Burgess Hill	d	23p08				00 10															
Brighton 10	d				00 10		01s22					07 12	07 18	07 45			08 12		08 18	08 48	
Hove 2	d	23p22		23p52	00a13	00 22	01s25					07 16	07 22	07 49			08 16		08 22	08 52	
Aldrington	d												07 24	07 51					08 24	08 54	
Portslade	d	23p25		23p55		00s25	01s28						07 26	07 53					08 26	08 56	
Fishersgate	d												07 28	07 55					08 28	08 58	
Southwick	d	23p28		23p58		00s28	01s31						07 30	07 57					08 30	09 00	
Shoreham-by-Sea	d	23p31		00 01		00s31	01s34					07 22	07 33	08 00			08 22		08 33	09 03	
Lancing	d	23p35		00 05		00s35	01s38						07 37	08 04					08 37	09 07	
East Worthing	d												07 40	08 07					08 40	09 10	
Worthing 4	a	23p39		00 09		00s39	01 42					07 28	07 43	08 10			08 28		08 43	09 13	
	d	23p39				00s39						07 28	07 43	08 10			08 28		08 43	09 13	
West Worthing	d	23p41				00s41							07 45	08 12					08 45	09 15	
Durrington-on-Sea	d	23p44				00s44							07 48	08 15					08 48	09 18	
Goring-by-Sea	d	23p46				00s46							07 50	08 17					08 50	09 20	
Angmering 3	d	23p50				00s50						07 35	07 54	08 21			08 35		08 54	09 24	
Littlehampton 4	a													08 30						09 33	
	d									06 42	07 19				07 54			08 54			
Ford 4	d	23p56	23p59			00s56				06 46	07 23	07 41	08 01		07 58	08 34	08 41	08 58	09 01		09 32
Bognor Regis 4	d																				
Barnham	a	00 01	00 04			01s01				06 50	07 27	07 46	08 05		08 02	08 38	08 46	09 02	09 05		09 37
	d	00 09	00 05			01s01			06 45	06 51	07 28	07 46	08 06		08 09	08 39	08 46	09 09	09 06		09 37
Bognor Regis	a	00 15							06 51		07 34				08 15	08 45		09 15			09 44
Chichester 4	a		00 12			01 09				06 58		07 54	08 13				08 54		09 13		
	d									06 59		07 54	08 14				08 54		09 14		
Fishbourne (Sussex)	d												08 17						09 17		
Bosham	d												08 20						09 20		
Nutbourne	d												08 23						09 23		
Southbourne	d											08 01	08 26				09 01		09 26		
Emsworth	d											08 04	08 29				09 04		09 29		
Warblington	d												08 32						09 32		
Havant	d									07 10		08 09	08 35				09 09		09 35		
Bedhampton	a												08 37						09 37		
Hilsea	a																				
Fratton	a									07 18		08 17	08 45				09 17		09 45		
Portsmouth & Southsea	a									07 22		08 21	08 48				09 21		09 48		
Portsmouth Harbour	a									07 26		08 25	08 52				09 25		09 52		
Cosham	a																				
Portchester	a																				
Fareham	a																				
Swanwick	a																				
Southampton Central	a																				

London, Gatwick Airport, Brighton - Sussex Coast, Portsmouth and Southampton

		SN	SN	SN	SN	SN	SN	SN	SN	SN	SN	SN	SN	GW	SN	SN	SN	SN	SN	SN
		◇1	◇1	1	1	1	◇1	◇1	◇1	1	1	1	◇1	◇	◇1	◇1	1	1	1	◇1
London Victoria 15 ⊖	d	08 17					09 02	09 17					10 02		10 17					11 02
Clapham Junction 10	d	08 23					09 08	09 23					10 08		10 23					11 08
London Bridge 4 ⊖	d																			
East Croydon	d	08 33					09 18	09 33					10 18		10 33					11 18
Redhill 5	d						09 32						10 32							11 32
Horley	d						09 38						10 38							11 38
Gatwick Airport 10	d	08 49					09 41	09 49					10 41		10 49					11 41
Three Bridges 4	a						09 46						10 46							11 46
	d						09 46						10 46							11 46
Crawley	d						09 50						10 50							11 50
Horsham 4	a						09 58						10 58							11 58
	d						09 59						10 59							11 59
Christs Hospital	d						10 02						11 02							12 02
Billingshurst	d						10 09						11 09							12 09
Pulborough	d						10 15						11 15							12 15
Amberley	d						10 21						11 21							12 21
Arundel	d						10 27						11 27							12 27
Haywards Heath 3	d	09 00						10 00							11 00					
Burgess Hill	d	09 06						10 06							11 06					
Brighton 10	d				09 12	09 48					10 12	10 48		11 08				11 12	11 48	
Hove 2	d	09 19			09b22	09 52		10 19			10c22	10 52		11 12	11 19			11f22	11 52	
Aldrington	d				09 24	09 54					10 24	10 54						11 24	11 54	
Portslade	d				09 26	09 56					10 26	10 56						11 26	11 56	
Fishersgate	d				09 28	09 58					10 28	10 58						11 28	11 58	
Southwick	d				09 30	10 00					10 30	11 00						11 30	12 00	
Shoreham-by-Sea	d	09 25			09 33	10 03		10 25			10 33	11 03		11 18	11 25			11 33	12 03	
Lancing	d				09 37	10 07					10 37	11 07						11 37	12 07	
East Worthing	d				09 40	10 10					10 40	11 10						11 40	12 10	
Worthing 4	a	09 31	>		09 43	10 13		10 31	>		10 43	11 13		11 24	11 31	>		11 43	12 13	
	d	09 35	09 37		09 43	10 13		10 35	10 37		10 43	11 13		11 27	11 35	11 37		11 43	12 13	
West Worthing	d		09 39		09 45	10 15			10 39		10 45	11 15				11 39		11 45	12 15	
Durrington-on-Sea	d		09 41		09 48	10 18			10 41		10 48	11 18				11 41		11 48	12 18	
Goring-by-Sea	d		09 44		09 50	10 20			10 44		10 50	11 20				11 44		11 50	12 20	
Angmering 3	d		09 48		09 54	10 24			10 48		10 54	11 24				11 48		11 54	12 24	
Littlehampton 4	a		09 57			10 33			10 57			11 33				11 57			12 33	
	d			09 54						10 54							11 54			
Ford 4	d			09 58	10 01		10 32			10 58	11 01		11 32				11 58	12 01		12 32
Bognor Regis 4	d																			
Barnham	a	09 49		10 02	10 05		10 37	10 49		11 02	11 05		11 37	11 45	11 49		12 02	12 05		12 37
	d	09 50		10 09	10 06		10 37	10 50		11 09	11 06		11 37	11 46	11 50		12 09	12 06		12 37
Bognor Regis	a			10 15			10 44			11 15			11 44				12 15			12 44
Chichester 4	a	09 57			10 13			10 57			11 13			11 53	11 57			12 13		
	d	09 58			10 14			10 58			11 14			11 54	11 58			12 14		
Fishbourne (Sussex)	d				10 17						11 17							12 17		
Bosham	d				10 20						11 20							12 20		
Nutbourne	d				10 23						11 23							12 23		
Southbourne	d	10 05			10 26			11 05			11 26				12 05			12 26		
Emsworth	d	10 08			10 29			11 08			11 29				12 08			12 29		
Warblington	d				10 32						11 32							12 32		
Havant	d	10 12			10 35			11 12			11 35			12e10	12 13			12 35		
Bedhampton	a				10 37						11 37							12 37		
Hilsea	a																			
Fratton	a	10 21			10 45			11 21			11 45				12 22			12 46		
Portsmouth & Southsea	a	10 24			10 50			11 24			11 49				12 25			12 57		
Portsmouth Harbour	a	10 28			10 54			11 28			11 53				12 29			13 01		
Cosham	a													12 16						
Portchester	a																			
Fareham	a													12 31						
Swanwick	a																			
Southampton Central	a													12 53						

b arr. 0915
c arr. 1015
e arr. 1204
f arr. 1115

Table 188

Sundays
until 05 September

London, Gatwick Airport, Brighton - Sussex Coast, Portsmouth and Southampton

		SN ◇1	SN ◇1	SN 1	SN 1	SN 1	SN ◇1	SN ◇1	SN ◇1	SN 1	SN 1	SN 1	SN ◇1	SN ◇1	SN ◇1	SN 1	SN 1	SN 1	SN ◇1
London Victoria 15 ⊖	d	11 17					12 02	12 17					13 02	13 17					14 02
Clapham Junction 10	d	11 23					12 08	12 23					13 08	13 23					14 08
London Bridge 4 ⊖	d																		
East Croydon	d	11 33					12 18	12 33					13 18	13 33					14 18
Redhill 5	d						12 32						13 32						14 32
Horley	d						12 38						13 38						14 38
Gatwick Airport 10	d	11 49					12 41	12 49					13 41	13 49					14 41
Three Bridges 4	a						12 46						13 46						14 46
	d						12 46						13 46						14 46
Crawley	d						12 50						13 50						14 50
Horsham 4	a						12 58						13 58						14 58
	d						12 59						13 59						14 59
Christs Hospital	d						13 02						14 02						15 02
Billingshurst	d						13 09						14 09						15 09
Pulborough	d						13 15						14 15						15 15
Amberley	d						13 21						14 21						15 21
Arundel	d						13 27						14 27						15 27
Haywards Heath 3	d	12 00						13 00						14 00					
Burgess Hill	d	12 06						13 06						14 06					
Brighton 10	d				12 12	12 48				13 12	13 48						14 12	14 48	
Hove 2	d	12 19			12b22	12 52		13 19		13c22	13 52			14 19			14e22	14 52	
Aldrington	d				12 24	12 54				13 24	13 54						14 24	14 54	
Portslade	d				12 26	12 56				13 26	13 56						14 26	14 56	
Fishersgate	d				12 28	12 58				13 28	13 58						14 28	14 58	
Southwick	d				12 30	13 00				13 30	14 00						14 30	15 00	
Shoreham-by-Sea	d	12 25			12 33	13 03		13 25		13 33	14 03			14 25			14 33	15 03	
Lancing	d				12 37	13 07				13 37	14 07						14 37	15 07	
East Worthing	d				12 40	13 10				13 40	14 10						14 40	15 10	
Worthing 4	a	12 31	>		12 43	13 13		13 31	>	13 43	14 13			14 31	>		14 43	15 13	
	d	12 35	12 37		12 43	13 13		13 35	13 37	13 43	14 13			14 35	14 37		14 43	15 13	
West Worthing	d		12 39		12 45	13 15			13 39	13 45	14 15				14 39		14 45	15 15	
Durrington-on-Sea	d		12 41		12 48	13 18			13 41	13 48	14 18				14 41		14 48	15 18	
Goring-by-Sea	d		12 44		12 50	13 20			13 44	13 50	14 20				14 44		14 50	15 20	
Angmering 3	d		12 48		12 54	13 24			13 48	13 54	14 24				14 48		14 54	15 24	
Littlehampton 4	a		12 57			13 33			13 57		14 33				14 57			15 33	
	d			12 54								13 54				14 54			
Ford 4	d			12 58	13 01		13 32			14 01		13 58	14 32			14 58	15 01		15 32
Bognor Regis 4	d																		
Barnham	a	12 49		13 02	13 05		13 37	13 49		14 05		14 02	14 37	14 49		15 02	15 05		15 37
	d	12 50		13 09	13 06		13 37	13 50		14 06		14 09	14 37	14 50		15 09	15 06		15 37
Bognor Regis	a			13 15			13 44					14 15	14 44			15 15			15 44
Chichester 4	a	12 57			13 13			13 57		14 13				14 57			15 13		
	d	12 58			13 14			13 58		14 14				14 58			15 14		
Fishbourne (Sussex)	d				13 17					14 17							15 17		
Bosham	d				13 20					14 20							15 20		
Nutbourne	d				13 23					14 23							15 23		
Southbourne	d	13 05			13 26			14 05		14 26				15 05			15 26		
Emsworth	d	13 08			13 29			14 08		14 29				15 08			15 29		
Warblington	d				13 32					14 32							15 32		
Havant	d	13 12			13 35			14 12		14 35				15 12			15 35		
Bedhampton	a				13 37					14 37							15 37		
Hilsea	a																		
Fratton	a	13 21			13 45			14 21		14 45				15 21			15 45		
Portsmouth & Southsea	a	13 24			13 48			14 24		14 48				15 24			15 48		
Portsmouth Harbour	a	13 28			13 52			14 28		14 52				15 28			15 52		
Cosham	a																		
Portchester	a																		
Fareham	a																		
Swanwick	a																		
Southampton Central	a																		

b arr. 1215 c arr. 1315 e arr. 1415

Table 188

Sundays
until 05 September

London, Gatwick Airport, Brighton - Sussex Coast, Portsmouth and Southampton

		SN ◇1	SN ◇1	SN 1	SN 1	GW ◇	SN 1	SN ◇1	SN ◇1	SN ◇1	SN 1	SN 1	SN 1	SN ◇1	SN ◇1	SN ◇1	SN 1	SN 1	GW ◇	SN 1	SN ◇1
London Victoria 15 ⊖	d	14 17						15 02	15 17					16 02	16 17						17 02
Clapham Junction 10	d	14 23						15 08	15 23					16 08	16 23						17 08
London Bridge 4 ⊖	d																				
East Croydon	d	14 33						15 18	15 33					16 18	16 33						17 18
Redhill 5	d							15 32						16 32							17 32
Horley	d							15 38						16 38							17 38
Gatwick Airport 10	d	14 49						15 41	15 49					16 41	16 49						17 41
Three Bridges 4	a							15 46						16 46							17 46
	d							15 46						16 46							17 46
Crawley	d							15 50						16 50							17 50
Horsham 4	a							15 58						16 58							17 58
	d							15 59						16 59							17 59
Christs Hospital	d							16 02						17 02							18 02
Billingshurst	d							16 09						17 09							18 09
Pulborough	d							16 15						17 15							18 15
Amberley	d							16 21						17 21							18 21
Arundel	d							16 27						17 27							18 27
Haywards Heath 3	d	15 00							16 00						17 00						
Burgess Hill	d	15 06							16 06						17 06						
Brighton 10	d				15 12	15 45	15 48					16 12	16 48					17 12	17 45	17 48	
Hove 2	d	15 19			15b22	15 49	15 52		16 19			16c22	16 52		17 19			17e22	17 49	17 52	
Aldrington	d				15 24		15 54					16 24	16 54					17 24		17 54	
Portslade	d				15 26		15 56					16 26	16 56					17 26		17 56	
Fishersgate	d				15 28		15 58					16 28	16 58					17 28		17 58	
Southwick	d				15 30		16 00					16 30	17 00					17 30		18 00	
Shoreham-by-Sea	d	15 25			15 33	15 55	16 03		16 25			16 33	17 03		17 25			17 33	17 55	18 03	
Lancing	d				15 37		16 07					16 37	17 07					17 37		18 07	
East Worthing	d				15 40		16 10					16 40	17 10					17 40		18 10	
Worthing 4	a	15 31	>		15 43	16 01	16 13		16 31	>		16 43	17 13		17 31			17 43	18 01	18 13	
	d	15 35	15 37		15 43	16 06	16 13		16 35	16 37		16 43	17 13		17 35	17 37		17 43	18 06	18 13	
West Worthing	d		15 39		15 45		16 15			16 39		16 45	17 15			17 39		17 45		18 15	
Durrington-on-Sea	d		15 41		15 48		16 18			16 41		16 48	17 18			17 41		17 48		18 18	
Goring-by-Sea	d		15 44		15 50		16 20			16 44		16 50	17 20			17 44		17 50		18 20	
Angmering 3	d		15 48		15 54		16 24			16 48		16 54	17 24			17 48		17 54		18 24	
Littlehampton 4	a		15 57				16 33			16 57			17 33			17 57				18 33	
	d			15 54							16 54						17 54				
Ford 4	d			15 58	16 01			16 32			16 58	17 01		17 32			17 58	18 01			18 32
Bognor Regis 4	d																				
Barnham	a	15 49		16 02	16 05	16 23		16 37	16 49		17 02	17 05		17 37	17 49		18 02	18 05	18 23		18 37
	d	15 50		16 09	16 06	16 23		16 37	16 50		17 09	17 06		17 37	17 50		18 09	18 06	18 23		18 37
Bognor Regis	a			16 15				16 44			17 15			17 44			18 15				18 44
Chichester 4	a	15 57			16 13	16 31			16 57			17 13			17 57			18 13	18 31		
	d	15 58			16 14	16 34			16 58			17 14			17 58			18 14	18 34		
Fishbourne (Sussex)	d				16 17							17 17						18 17			
Bosham	d				16 20							17 20						18 20			
Nutbourne	d				16 23							17 23						18 23			
Southbourne	d	16 05			16 26				17 05			17 26			18 05			18 26			
Emsworth	d	16 08			16 29				17 08			17 29			18 08			18 29			
Warblington	d				16 32							17 32						18 32			
Havant	d	16 12			16 35	16 48			17 12			17 35			18 12			18 35	18 48		
Bedhampton	a				16 37							17 37						18 37			
Hilsea	a																				
Fratton	a	16 23			16 46				17 21			17 46			18 21			18 46			
Portsmouth & Southsea	a	16 26			16 57				17 24			17 57			18 24			18 57			
Portsmouth Harbour	a	16 30			17 01				17 28			18 01			18 28			19 01			
Cosham	a					16 54													18 54		
Portchester	a																				
Fareham	a					17 02													19 02		
Swanwick	a																				
Southampton Central	a					17 24													19 25		

b arr. 1515 c arr. 1615 e arr. 1715

Table 188

Sundays
until 05 September

London, Gatwick Airport, Brighton - Sussex Coast, Portsmouth and Southampton

		SN ◇■	SN ◇■	SN ■	SN ■	SN ■	SN ◇■	SN ◇■	SN ◇■	SN ■	SN ■	SN ■	SN ◇■	SN ◇■	SN ◇■	SN ■	SN ■	SN ■
London Victoria ■ ⊖	d	17 17					18 02	18 17					19 02	19 17				
Clapham Junction ■	d	17 23					18 08	18 23					19 08	19 23				
London Bridge ■ ⊖	d																	
East Croydon ⇌	d	17 33					18 18	18 33					19 18	19 33				
Redhill ■	d						18 32						19 32					
Horley	d						18 38						19 38					
Gatwick Airport ■	d	17 49					18 41	18 49					19 41	19 49				
Three Bridges ■	a						18 46						19 46					
	d						18 46						19 46					
Crawley	d						18 50						19 50					
Horsham ■	a						18 58						19 58					
	d						18 59						19 59					
Christs Hospital	d						19 02						20 02					
Billingshurst	d						19 09						20 09					
Pulborough	d						19 15						20 15					
Amberley	d						19 21						20 21					
Arundel	d						19 27						20 27					
Haywards Heath ■	d	18 00						19 00						20 00				
Burgess Hill	d	18 06						19 06						20 06				
Brighton ■	d				18 12	18 48					19 12	19 48					20 12	20 48
Hove ■	d	18 19			18b22	18 52		19 19			19c22	19 52		20 19			20e22	20 52
Aldrington	d				18 24	18 54					19 24	19 54					20 24	20 54
Portslade	d				18 26	18 56					19 26	19 56					20 26	20 56
Fishersgate	d				18 28	18 58					19 28	19 58					20 28	20 58
Southwick	d				18 30	19 00					19 30	20 00					20 30	21 00
Shoreham-by-Sea	d	18 25			18 33	19 03		19 25			19 33	20 03		20 25			20 33	21 03
Lancing	d				18 37	19 07					19 37	20 07					20 37	21 07
East Worthing	d				18 40	19 10					19 40	20 10					20 40	21 10
Worthing ■	a	18 31	>		18 43	19 13		19 31	>		19 43	20 13		20 31	>		20 43	21 13
	d	18 35	18 37		18 43	19 13		19 35	19 37		19 43	20 13		20 35	20 37		20 43	21 13
West Worthing	d		18 39		18 45	19 15			19 39		19 45	20 15			20 39		20 45	21 15
Durrington-on-Sea	d		18 41		18 48	19 18			19 41		19 48	20 18			20 41		20 48	21 18
Goring-by-Sea	d		18 44		18 50	19 20			19 44		19 50	20 20			20 44		20 50	21 20
Angmering ■	d		18 48		18 54	19 24			19 48		19 54	20 24			20 48		20 54	21 24
Littlehampton ■	a		18 57			19 33			19 57			20 33			20 57			21 34
	d			18 54						19 54						20 54		
Ford ■	d			18 58	19 01		19 32			19 58	20 01		20 32			20 58	21 01	
Bognor Regis ■	d																	
Barnham	a	18 49		19 02	19 05		19 37	19 49		20 02	20 05		20 37	20 49		21 02	21 05	
	d	18 50		19 09	19 06		19 37	19 50		20 09	20 06		20 37	20 50		21 09	21 06	
Bognor Regis	a			19 15			19 44			20 15			20 44			21 15		
Chichester ■	a	18 57			19 13			19 57			20 13			20 57			21 13	
	d	18 58			19 14			19 58			20 14			20 58			21 14	
Fishbourne (Sussex)	d				19 17						20 17						21 17	
Bosham	d				19 20						20 20						21 20	
Nutbourne	d				19 23						20 23						21 23	
Southbourne	d	19 05			19 26			20 05			20 26			21 05			21 26	
Emsworth	d	19 08			19 29			20 08			20 29			21 08			21 29	
Warblington	d				19 32						20 32						21 32	
Havant	d	19 12			19 35			20 12			20 35			21 12			21 35	
Bedhampton	a				19 37						20 37						21 37	
Hilsea	a																	
Fratton	a	19 21			19 46			20 21			20 45			21 21			21 45	
Portsmouth & Southsea	a	19 24			19 57			20 24			20 48			21 24			21 48	
Portsmouth Harbour	a	19 28			20 01			20 28			20 52			21 28			21 52	
Cosham	a																	
Portchester	a																	
Fareham	a																	
Swanwick	a																	
Southampton Central	a																	

b arr. 1815 c arr. 1915 e arr. 2015

Table 188

Sundays
until 05 September

London, Gatwick Airport, Brighton - Sussex Coast, Portsmouth and Southampton

		SN ◇■	SN ◇■	SN ◇■	SN ■	SN ■	GW	SN ■	SN ■	SN ■	SN ◇■	SN ◇■	SN ◇■	SN ■	SN ■	SN ■	SN ■	SN ◇■	SN ◇■
London Victoria ■ ⊖	d	20 02	20 17								21 02	21 17						22 02	22 17
Clapham Junction ■	d	20 08	20 23								21 08	21 23						22 08	22 23
London Bridge ■ ⊖	d																		
East Croydon ⇌	d	20 18	20 33								21 18	21 33						22 18	22 33
Redhill ■	d	20 32									21 32							22 32	
Horley	d	20 38									21 38							22 38	
Gatwick Airport ■	d	20 41	20 49								21 41	21 49						22 41	22 49
Three Bridges ■	a	20 46									21 46							22 46	
	d	20 46									21 46							22 46	
Crawley	d	20 50									21 50							22 50	
Horsham ■	a	20 58									21 58							22 58	
	d	20 59									21 59							22 59	
Christs Hospital	d	21 02									22 02							23 02	
Billingshurst	d	21 09									22 09							23 09	
Pulborough	d	21 15									22 15							23 15	
Amberley	d	21 21									22 21							23 21	
Arundel	d	21 27									22 27							23 27	
Haywards Heath ■	d		21 00									22 00							23 00
Burgess Hill	d		21 06									22 06							23 06
Brighton ■	d					21 12	21 43	21 48	22 10							22 40	23 15		
Hove ■	d		21 19			21b22	21 47	21 52	22a13			22 19				22 44	23a18		23c25
Aldrington	d					21 24		21 54								22 46			
Portslade	d					21 26		21 56								22 48			23 28
Fishersgate	d					21 28		21 58								22 50			
Southwick	d					21 30		22 00								22 52			23 31
Shoreham-by-Sea	d		21 25			21 33	21 53	22 03				22 25				22 55			23 34
Lancing	d					21 37		22 07								22 59			23 38
East Worthing	d					21 40		22 10								23 02			
Worthing ■	a		21 31	>		21 43	21 59	22 13				22 31	>			23 05			23 42
	d		21 35	21 37		21 43	22 00	22 13				22 35	22 37			23 05			
West Worthing	d			21 39		21 45		22 15					22 39			23 07			
Durrington-on-Sea	d			21 41		21 48		22 18					22 41			23 09			
Goring-by-Sea	d			21 44		21 50		22 20					22 44			23 12			
Angmering ■	d			21 48		21 54		22 24					22 48			23 16			
Littlehampton ■	a			21 57				22 34					22 57			23 24			
	d				21 54										23 06	23 29			
Ford ■	d	21 32			21 58	22 01					22 32				23 10	23 36		23 32	
Bognor Regis ■	d									22 11									
Barnham	a	21 37	21 49		22 02	22 05	22 14			22 18	22 37	22 49			23 14	23 40		23 36	
	d	21 37	21 50		22 09	22 06	22 15				22 37	22 56		22 52	23 15	23 45		23 42	
Bognor Regis	a	21 44			22 15						22 44			22 58	23 21			23 48	
Chichester ■	a		21 57			22 13	22 22					23 03				23 52			
	d		21 58			22 14	22 23					23 04							
Fishbourne (Sussex)	d					22 17													
Bosham	d					22 20						23 08							
Nutbourne	d					22 23						23 12							
Southbourne	d		22 05			22 26						23 14							
Emsworth	d		22 08			22 29						23 17							
Warblington	d					22 32													
Havant	d		22 12			22 35	22 44					23 22							
Bedhampton	a					22 37													
Hilsea	a																		
Fratton	a		22 21			22 45	22 54					23 32							
Portsmouth & Southsea	a		22 24			22 48	22 57					23 35							
Portsmouth Harbour	a		22 28			22 52	23 01					23 39							
Cosham	a																		
Portchester	a																		
Fareham	a																		
Swanwick	a																		
Southampton Central	a																		

b arr. 2115 c arr. 2319

Table 188

Sundays until 05 September

London, Gatwick Airport, Brighton - Sussex Coast, Portsmouth and Southampton

		SN ◇1
London Victoria 15 ⊖	d	23 17
Clapham Junction 10	d	23 23
London Bridge 4 ⊖	d	
East Croydon ⇌	d	23 38
Redhill 5	d	
Horley	d	
Gatwick Airport 10	d	00 01
Three Bridges 4	a	00 05
	d	00 06
Crawley	d	
Horsham 4	a	
	d	
Christs Hospital	d	
Billingshurst	d	
Pulborough	d	
Amberley	d	
Arundel	d	
Haywards Heath 3	d	00 15
Burgess Hill	d	
Brighton 10	d	
Hove 2	d	00 29
Aldrington	d	
Portslade	d	00s32
Fishersgate	d	
Southwick	d	00s35
Shoreham-by-Sea	d	00s38
Lancing	d	00s42
East Worthing	d	
Worthing 4	a	00 46
	d	
West Worthing	d	
Durrington-on-Sea	d	
Goring-by-Sea	d	
Angmering 3	d	
Littlehampton 4	a	
	d	
Ford 4	d	
Bognor Regis 4	d	
Barnham	a	
	d	
Bognor Regis	a	
Chichester 4	a	
	d	
Fishbourne (Sussex)	d	
Bosham	d	
Nutbourne	d	
Southbourne	d	
Emsworth	d	
Warblington	d	
Havant	d	
Bedhampton	a	
Hilsea	a	
Fratton	a	
Portsmouth & Southsea	a	
Portsmouth Harbour	a	
Cosham	a	
Portchester	a	
Fareham	a	
Swanwick	a	
Southampton Central	a	

Table 188

Sundays from 12 September

London, Gatwick Airport, Brighton - Sussex Coast, Portsmouth and Southampton

		SN ◇1	SN 1	SN ◇1	SN 1	SN ◇1	SN 1	SN ◇1	SN 1	SN 1	SN 1	SN 1	SN 1	SN 1	SN ◇1	SN 1	SN 1	SN 1	SN 1	SN ◇1	SN ◇1	SN ◇1
London Victoria 15 ⊖	d	22p17	22p32	22p47		23p17	23p10	00 05							07 02					08 04	08 17	
Clapham Junction 10	d	22p23	22p38	22p53		23p23	23p16	00 11							07 08					08 10	08 23	
London Bridge 4 ⊖	d																					
East Croydon ⇌	d	22p33	22p48	23p03		23p33	23p28	00 25							07 23					08 24	08 37	
Redhill 5	d		23p01				23p46								07 37					08 39		
Horley	d						23p56								07 43					08 45		
Gatwick Airport 10	d	22p49	23p09	23p19		23p51	23p59	00 44							07 47					08 48	08 56	
Three Bridges 4	a	22p54	23p14			23p55	00 04	00 48							07 51					08 53		
	d	22p54	23p15			23p56	00 04	00 48							07 52					08 53		
Crawley	d		23p18				00 07								07 55					08 56		
Horsham 4	a		23p26				00 19								08 07					09 04		
	d		23p27												08 08					09 05		
Christs Hospital	d		23p30																	09 08		
Billingshurst	d		23p36												08 16					09 15		
Pulborough	d		23p43												08 23					09 21		
Amberley	d		23p49																	09 27		
Arundel	d		23p54												08 33					09 33		
Haywards Heath 3	d	23p03		23p37		00 05		01 03													09 07	
Burgess Hill	d	23p08				00 10															09 12	
Brighton 10	d				00 10			01s22				07 14	07 22			08 14	08 22	08 50				
Hove 2	d	23p22		23p52	00a13	00 22		01s25				07 18	07 26			08 18	08 26	08 54			09 24	
Aldrington	d												07 28				08 28	08 56				
Portslade	d	23p25		23p55		00s25		01s28					07 30				08 30	08 58				
Fishersgate	d												07 32				08 32	09 00				
Southwick	d	23p28		23p58		00s28		01s31					07 34				08 34	09 02				
Shoreham-by-Sea	d	23p31		00 01		00s31		01s34				07 24	07 37			08 24	08 37	09 05			09 30	
Lancing	d	23p35		00 05		00s35		01s38					07 41				08 41	09 09				
East Worthing	d												07 44				08 44	09 12				
Worthing 4	a	23p39		00 09		00s39		01 42				07 30	07 47			08 30	08 47	09 15			09 36	>
	d	23p39				00s39						07 30	07 47			08 30	08 47	09 15			09 40	09 42
West Worthing	d	23p41				00s41							07 49				08 49	09 17				09 44
Durrington-on-Sea	d	23p44				00s44							07 51				08 51	09 20				09 46
Goring-by-Sea	d	23p46				00s46							07 54				08 54	09 22				09 49
Angmering 3	d	23p50				00s50						07 37	07 58			08 37	08 58	09 26				09 53
Littlehampton 4	a												08 06				09 06	09 35				10 02
	d									06 42	07 19		08 11	07 57			09 11		08 57			
Ford 4	d	23p56	23p59			00s56				06 46	07 23	07 43	08 15	08 01	08 38	08 43	09 15		09 01	09 39		
Bognor Regis 4	d																					
Barnham	a	00 01	00 04			01s01				06 50	07 27	07 48	08 19	08 08	08 42	08 48	09 19		09 08	09 43	09 54	
	d	00 09	00 05			01s01			06 45	06 51	07 28	07 48	08 20	08 26	08 43	08 48	09 20		09 26	09 44	09 55	
Bognor Regis	a	00 15							06 51		07 34			08 32	08 49				09 32	09 50		
Chichester 4	a		00 12			01 09				06 58		07 56	08 27			08 56	09 27				10 02	
	d									06 59		07 56	08 28			08 56	09 28				10 03	
Fishbourne (Sussex)	d												08 31				09 31					
Bosham	d												08 34				09 34					
Nutbourne	d												08 37				09 37					
Southbourne	d											08 03	08 40			09 03	09 40				10 10	
Emsworth	d											08 06	08 43			09 06	09 43				10 13	
Warblington	d												08 46				09 46					
Havant	d									07 10		08 11	08 49			09 11	09 49				10 17	
Bedhampton	a												08 51				09 51					
Hilsea	a																					
Fratton	a									07 18		08 19	08 59			09 19	09 59				10 26	
Portsmouth & Southsea	a									07 22		08 23	09 03			09 23	10 03				10 29	
Portsmouth Harbour	a									07 26		08 27	09 07			09 27	10 07				10 35	
Cosham	a																					
Portchester	a																					
Fareham	a																					
Swanwick	a																					
Southampton Central	a																					

Table 188

Sundays from 12 September

London, Gatwick Airport, Brighton - Sussex Coast, Portsmouth and Southampton

		SN 1	SN 1	SN 1	SN ◇1	SN ◇1	SN ◇1	SN 1	SN 1	SN 1	SN ◇1 (trolley)	GW ◇	SN ◇1	SN ◇1	SN 1	SN 1	SN 1	SN ◇1 (trolley)	SN ◇1	SN ◇1
London Victoria 15 ⊖	d				09 04	09 17					10 04		10 17					11 04	11 17	
Clapham Junction 10	d				09 10	09 23					10 10		10 23					11 10	11 23	
London Bridge 4 ⊖	d																			
East Croydon (tram)	d				09 24	09 37					10 24		10 37					11 24	11 37	
Redhill 5	d				09 39						10 39							11 39		
Horley	d				09 45						10 45							11 45		
Gatwick Airport 10	d				09 48	09 56					10 48		10 56					11 48	11 56	
Three Bridges 4	a				09 53						10 53							11 53		
	d				09 53						10 53							11 53		
Crawley	d				09 56						10 56							11 56		
Horsham 4	a				10 04						11 04							12 04		
	d				10 05						11 05							12 05		
Christs Hospital	d				10 08						11 08							12 08		
Billingshurst	d				10 15						11 15							12 15		
Pulborough	d				10 21						11 21							12 21		
Amberley	d				10 27						11 27							12 27		
Arundel	d				10 33						11 33							12 33		
Haywards Heath 3	d					10 07							11 07						12 07	
Burgess Hill	d					10 12							11 12						12 12	
Brighton 10	d		09 17	09 50				10 17	10 50			11 10				11 17	11 50			
Hove 2	d		09b26	09 54		10 24		10c26	10 54			11 14	11 24			11f26	11 54		12 24	
Aldrington	d		09 28	09 56				10 28	10 56							11 28	11 56			
Portslade	d		09 31	09 58				10 31	10 58							11 31	11 58			
Fishersgate	d		09 33	10 00				10 33	11 00							11 33	12 00			
Southwick	d		09 35	10 02				10 35	11 02							11 35	12 02			
Shoreham-by-Sea	d		09 38	10 05		10 30		10 38	11 05			11 20	11 30			11 38	12 05		12 30	
Lancing	d		09 42	10 09				10 42	11 09							11 42	12 09			
East Worthing	d		09 45	10 12				10 45	11 12							11 45	12 12			
Worthing 4	a		09 47	10 15		10 36	>	10 47	11 15			11 26	11 36	>		11 47	12 15		12 36	>
	d		09 48	10 15		10 40	10 42	10 48	11 15			11 29	11 40	11 42		11 48	12 15		12 40	12 42
West Worthing	d		09 50	10 17			10 44	10 50	11 17					11 44		11 50	12 17			12 44
Durrington-on-Sea	d		09 52	10 20			10 46	10 52	11 20					11 46		11 52	12 20			12 46
Goring-by-Sea	d		09 55	10 22			10 49	10 55	11 22					11 49		11 55	12 22			12 49
Angmering 3	d		09 59	10 26			10 53	10 59	11 26					11 53		11 59	12 26			12 53
Littlehampton 4	a			10 35			11 02		11 35					12 02			12 35			13 02
	d	09 57								10 57					11 57					
Ford 4	d	10 01	10 05		10 38			11 05		11 01	11 38				12 01	12 05		12 38		
Bognor Regis 4	d																			
Barnham	a	10 08	10 11		10 42	10 54		11 11		11 08	11 42	11 45	11 54		12 08	12 11		12 42	12 54	
	d	10 15	10 12		10 43	10 55		11 12		11 15	11 43	11 46	11 55		12 15	12 12		12 43	12 55	
Bognor Regis	a	10 21			10 49					11 21	11 49				12 21			12 49		
Chichester 4	a		10 19			11 02		11 19				11 53	12 02			12 19			13 02	
	d		10 20			11 03		11 20				11 54	12 03			12 20			13 03	
Fishbourne (Sussex)	d		10 23					11 23								12 23				
Bosham	d		10 26					11 26								12 26				
Nutbourne	d		10 29					11 29								12 29				
Southbourne	d		10 32			11 10		11 32					12 10			12 32			13 10	
Emsworth	d		10 35			11 13		11 35					12 13			12 35			13 13	
Warblington	d		10 38					11 38								12 38				
Havant	d		10 41			11 17		11 44				12e10	12 17			12 44			13 17	
Bedhampton	a		10 43					11 46								12 46				
Hilsea	a																			
Fratton	a		10 51			11 26		11 54					12 26			12 54			13 26	
Portsmouth & Southsea	a		10 54			11 29		11 57					12 29			12 57			13 29	
Portsmouth Harbour	a		10 58			11 35		12 01					12 35			13 01			13 35	
Cosham	a											12 16								
Portchester	a																			
Fareham	a											12 31								
Swanwick	a																			
Southampton Central	a											12 53								

b arr. 0920
c arr. 1020
e arr. 1204
f arr. 1120

Table 188

Sundays from 12 September

London, Gatwick Airport, Brighton - Sussex Coast, Portsmouth and Southampton

		SN 1	SN 1	SN 1	SN ◇1 (trolley)	SN ◇1	SN ◇1	SN 1	SN 1	SN 1	SN ◇1 (trolley)	SN ◇1	SN ◇1	SN 1	SN 1	SN 1	SN ◇1 (trolley)	SN ◇1	SN ◇1
London Victoria 15 ⊖	d				12 04	12 17					13 04	13 17					14 04	14 17	
Clapham Junction 10	d				12 10	12 23					13 10	13 23					14 10	14 23	
London Bridge 4 ⊖	d																		
East Croydon (tram)	d				12 24	12 37					13 24	13 37					14 24	14 37	
Redhill 5	d				12 39						13 39						14 39		
Horley	d				12 45						13 45						14 45		
Gatwick Airport 10	d				12 48	12 56					13 48	13 56					14 48	14 56	
Three Bridges 4	a				12 53						13 53						14 53		
	d				12 53						13 53						14 53		
Crawley	d				12 56						13 56						14 56		
Horsham 4	a				13 04						14 04						15 04		
	d				13 05						14 05						15 05		
Christs Hospital	d				13 08						14 08						15 08		
Billingshurst	d				13 15						14 15						15 15		
Pulborough	d				13 21						14 21						15 21		
Amberley	d				13 27						14 27						15 27		
Arundel	d				13 33						14 33						15 33		
Haywards Heath 3	d					13 07						14 07						15 07	
Burgess Hill	d					13 12						14 12						15 12	
Brighton 10	d		12 17	12 50					13 17	13 50					14 17	14 50			
Hove 2	d		12b26	12 54		13 24			13c26	13 54		14 24			14e26	14 54		15 24	
Aldrington	d		12 28	12 56					13 28	13 56					14 28	14 56			
Portslade	d		12 31	12 58					13 31	13 58					14 31	14 58			
Fishersgate	d		12 33	13 00					13 33	14 00					14 33	15 00			
Southwick	d		12 35	13 02					13 35	14 02					14 35	15 02			
Shoreham-by-Sea	d		12 38	13 05		13 30			13 38	14 05		14 30			14 38	15 05		15 30	
Lancing	d		12 42	13 09					13 42	14 09					14 42	15 09			
East Worthing	d		12 45	13 12					13 45	14 12					14 45	15 12			
Worthing 4	a		12 47	13 15		13 36	>		13 47	14 15		14 36	>		14 47	15 15		15 36	>
	d		12 48	13 15		13 40	13 42		13 48	14 15		14 40	14 42		14 48	15 15		15 40	15 42
West Worthing	d		12 50	13 17			13 44		13 50	14 17			14 44		14 50	15 17			15 44
Durrington-on-Sea	d		12 52	13 20			13 46		13 52	14 20			14 46		14 52	15 20			15 46
Goring-by-Sea	d		12 55	13 22			13 49		13 55	14 22			14 49		14 55	15 22			15 49
Angmering 3	d		12 59	13 26			13 53		13 59	14 26			14 53		14 59	15 26			15 53
Littlehampton 4	a			13 35			14 02			14 35			15 02			15 35			16 02
	d	12 57						13 57						14 57					
Ford 4	d	13 01	13 05		13 38			14 01	14 05		14 38			15 01	15 05		15 38		
Bognor Regis 4	d																		
Barnham	a	13 08	13 11		13 42	13 54		14 08	14 11		14 42	14 54		15 08	15 11		15 42	15 54	
	d	13 15	13 12		13 43	13 55		14 15	14 12		14 43	14 55		15 15	15 12		15 43	15 55	
Bognor Regis	a	13 21			13 49			14 21			14 49			15 21			15 49		
Chichester 4	a		13 19			14 02			14 19			15 02			15 19			16 02	
	d		13 20			14 03			14 20			15 03			15 20			16 03	
Fishbourne (Sussex)	d		13 23						14 23						15 23				
Bosham	d		13 26						14 26						15 26				
Nutbourne	d		13 29						14 29						15 29				
Southbourne	d		13 32			14 10			14 32			15 10			15 32			16 10	
Emsworth	d		13 35			14 13			14 35			15 13			15 35			16 13	
Warblington	d		13 38						14 38						15 38				
Havant	d		13 44			14 17			14 44			15 17			15 44			16 17	
Bedhampton	a		13 46						14 46						15 46				
Hilsea	a																		
Fratton	a		13 54			14 26			14 54			15 26			15 54			16 26	
Portsmouth & Southsea	a		13 57			14 29			14 57			15 29			15 57			16 29	
Portsmouth Harbour	a		14 01			14 35			15 01			15 35			16 01			16 35	
Cosham	a																		
Portchester	a																		
Fareham	a																		
Swanwick	a																		
Southampton Central	a																		

b arr. 1220
c arr. 1320
e arr. 1420

Table 188

Sundays from 12 September

London, Gatwick Airport, Brighton - Sussex Coast, Portsmouth and Southampton

		SN ■	SN ■	GW ◇	SN ■	SN ◇■ bus	SN ◇■	SN ◇■	SN ■	SN ■	SN ■	SN ◇■ bus	SN ◇■	SN ◇■	SN ■	SN ■	GW ◇	SN ■	SN ◇■ bus	SN ◇■	SN ◇■
London Victoria ■ ⊖	d					15 04	15 17					16 04	16 17						17 04	17 17	
Clapham Junction ■	d					15 10	15 23					16 10	16 23						17 10	17 23	
London Bridge ■ ⊖	d																				
East Croydon	d					15 24	15 37					16 24	16 37						17 24	17 37	
Redhill ■	d					15 39						16 39							17 39		
Horley	d					15 45						16 45							17 45		
Gatwick Airport ■	d					15 48	15 56					16 48	16 56						17 48	17 56	
Three Bridges ■	a					15 53						16 53							17 53		
	d					15 53						16 53							17 53		
Crawley	d					15 56						16 56							17 56		
Horsham ■	a					16 04						17 04							18 04		
	d					16 05						17 05							18 05		
Christs Hospital	d					16 08						17 08							18 08		
Billingshurst	d					16 15						17 15							18 15		
Pulborough	d					16 21						17 21							18 21		
Amberley	d					16 27						17 27							18 27		
Arundel	d					16 33						17 33							18 33		
Haywards Heath ■	d						16 07						17 07							18 07	
Burgess Hill	d						16 12						17 12							18 12	
Brighton ■	d		15 17	15 46	15 50					16 17	16 50					17 17	17 46	17 50			
Hove ■	d		15b26	15 50	15 54		16 24			16c26	16 54		17 24			17e26	17 50	17 54		18 24	
Aldrington	d		15 28		15 56					16 28	16 56					17 28		17 56			
Portslade	d		15 31		15 58					16 31	16 58					17 31		17 58			
Fishersgate	d		15 33		16 00					16 33	17 00					17 33		18 00			
Southwick	d		15 35		16 02					16 35	17 02					17 35		18 02			
Shoreham-by-Sea	d		15 38	15 56	16 05		16 30			16 38	17 05		17 30			17 38	17 56	18 05		18 30	
Lancing	d		15 42		16 09					16 42	17 09					17 42		17 09			
East Worthing	d		15 45		16 12					16 45	17 12					17 45		17 12			
Worthing ■	a		15 47	16 03	16 15		16 36	>		16 47	17 15		17 36	>		17 47	18 03	17 15		18 36	>
	d		15 48	16 08	16 15		16 40	16 42		16 48	17 15		17 40	17 42		17 48	18 08	17 15		18 40	18 42
West Worthing	d		15 50		16 17			16 44		16 50	17 17			17 44		17 50		17 17			18 44
Durrington-on-Sea	d		15 52		16 20			16 46		16 52	17 20			17 46		17 52		17 20			18 46
Goring-by-Sea	d		15 55		16 22			16 49		16 55	17 22			17 49		17 55		17 22			18 49
Angmering ■	d		15 59		16 26			16 53		16 59	17 26			17 53		17 59		17 26			18 53
Littlehampton ■	a				16 35			17 02			17 35			18 02				17 35			19 02
	d	15 57							16 57						17 57						
Ford ■	d	16 01	16 05			16 38			17 01	17 05		17 38			18 01	18 05			18 38		
Bognor Regis ■	d																				
Barnham	a	16 08	16 11	16 25		16 42	16 54		17 08	17 11		17 42	17 54		18 08	18 11	18 25		18 42	18 54	
	d	16 15	16 12	16 25		16 43	16 55		17 15	17 12		17 43	17 55		18 15	18 12	18 25		18 43	18 55	
Bognor Regis	a	16 21				16 49			17 21			17 49			18 21				18 49		
Chichester ■	a		16 19	16 33			17 02			17 19			18 02			18 19	18 33			19 02	
	d		16 20	16 34			17 03			17 20			18 03			18 20	18 34			19 03	
Fishbourne (Sussex)	d		16 23							17 23						18 23					
Bosham	d		16 26							17 26						18 26					
Nutbourne	d		16 29							17 29						18 29					
Southbourne	d		16 32				17 10			17 32			18 10			18 32				19 10	
Emsworth	d		16 35				17 13			17 35			18 13			18 35				19 13	
Warblington	d		16 38							17 38						18 38					
Havant	d		16 44	16 48			17 17			17 44			18 17			18 44	18 48			19 17	
Bedhampton	a		16 46							17 46						18 46					
Hilsea	a																				
Fratton	a		16 54				17 26			17 54			18 26			18 54				19 26	
Portsmouth & Southsea	a		16 57				17 29			17 57			18 29			18 57				19 29	
Portsmouth Harbour	a		17 01				17 35			18 01			18 35			19 01				19 35	
Cosham	a			16 54													18 54				
Portchester	a																				
Fareham	a			17 02													19 02				
Swanwick	a																				
Southampton Central	a			17 24													19 24				

b arr. 1520 c arr. 1620 e arr. 1720

Table 188

Sundays from 12 September

London, Gatwick Airport, Brighton - Sussex Coast, Portsmouth and Southampton

		SN ■	SN ■	SN ■	SN ◇■ bus	SN ◇■	SN ◇■	SN ■	SN ■	SN ■	SN ◇■ bus	SN ◇■	SN ◇■	SN ■	SN ■	SN ■	SN ◇■
London Victoria ■ ⊖	d				18 04	18 17					19 04	19 17					20 04
Clapham Junction ■	d				18 10	18 23					19 10	19 23					20 10
London Bridge ■ ⊖	d																
East Croydon	d				18 24	18 37					19 24	19 37					20 24
Redhill ■	d				18 39						19 39						20 39
Horley	d				18 45						19 45						20 45
Gatwick Airport ■	d				18 48	18 56					19 48	19 56					20 48
Three Bridges ■	a				18 53						19 53						20 53
	d				18 53						19 53						20 53
Crawley	d				18 56						19 56						20 56
Horsham ■	a				19 04						20 04						21 04
	d				19 05						20 05						21 05
Christs Hospital	d				19 08						20 08						21 08
Billingshurst	d				19 15						20 15						21 15
Pulborough	d				19 21						20 21						21 21
Amberley	d				19 27						20 27						21 27
Arundel	d				19 33						20 33						21 33
Haywards Heath ■	d					19 07						20 07					
Burgess Hill	d					19 12						20 12					
Brighton ■	d		18 17	18 50					19 17	19 50					20 17	20 50	
Hove ■	d		18b26	18 54		19 24			19c26	19 54		20 24			20e26	20 54	
Aldrington	d		18 28	18 56					19 28	19 56					20 28	20 56	
Portslade	d		18 31	18 58					19 31	19 58					20 31	20 58	
Fishersgate	d		18 33	19 00					19 33	20 00					20 33	21 00	
Southwick	d		18 35	19 02					19 35	20 02					20 35	21 02	
Shoreham-by-Sea	d		18 38	19 05		19 30			19 38	20 05		20 30			20 38	21 05	
Lancing	d		18 42	19 09					19 42	20 09					20 42	21 09	
East Worthing	d		18 45	19 12					19 45	20 12					20 45	21 12	
Worthing ■	a		18 47	19 15		19 36	>		19 47	20 15		20 36	>		20 47	21 15	
	d		18 48	19 15		19 40	19 42		19 48	20 15		20 40	20 42		20 48	21 15	
West Worthing	d		18 50	19 17			19 44		19 50	20 17			20 44		20 50	21 17	
Durrington-on-Sea	d		18 52	19 20			19 46		19 52	20 20			20 46		20 52	21 20	
Goring-by-Sea	d		18 55	19 22			19 49		19 55	20 22			20 49		20 55	21 22	
Angmering ■	d		18 59	19 26			19 53		19 59	20 26			20 53		20 59	21 26	
Littlehampton ■	a			19 35			20 02			20 35			21 02			21 35	
	d	18 57						19 57						20 57			
Ford ■	d	19 01	19 05		19 38			20 01	20 05		20 38			21 01	21 05		21 38
Bognor Regis ■	d																
Barnham	a	19 08	19 11		19 42	19 54		20 08	20 11		20 42	20 54		21 08	21 11		21 42
	d	19 15	19 12		19 43	19 55		20 15	20 12		20 43	20 55		21 15	21 12		21 43
Bognor Regis	a	19 21			19 49			20 21			20 49			21 21			21 49
Chichester ■	a		19 19			20 02			20 19			21 02			21 19		
	d		19 20			20 03			20 20			21 03			21 20		
Fishbourne (Sussex)	d		19 23						20 23						21 23		
Bosham	d		19 26						20 26						21 26		
Nutbourne	d		19 29						20 29						21 29		
Southbourne	d		19 32			20 10			20 32			21 10			21 32		
Emsworth	d		19 35			20 13			20 35			21 13			21 35		
Warblington	d		19 38						20 38						21 38		
Havant	d		19 44			20 17			20 44			21 17			21 44		
Bedhampton	a		19 46						20 46						21 46		
Hilsea	a																
Fratton	a		19 54			20 26			20 54			21 26			21 54		
Portsmouth & Southsea	a		19 57			20 29			20 57			21 29			21 57		
Portsmouth Harbour	a		20 01			20 35			21 01			21 35			22 01		
Cosham	a																
Portchester	a																
Fareham	a																
Swanwick	a																
Southampton Central	a																

b arr. 1820 c arr. 1920 e arr. 2020

Table 188

Sundays from 12 September

London, Gatwick Airport, Brighton - Sussex Coast, Portsmouth and Southampton

		SN	SN	SN	SN	GW	SN	SN	SN	SN	SN	SN	SN	SN	SN	SN	SN	SN	SN
		◇■	◇■	■	■		■	■	■	◇■	◇■	◇■	■	■	◇■	◇■	■	■	◇■
London Victoria [15] ⊖	d	20 17								21 04	21 17				22 04	22 17			23 17
Clapham Junction [10]	d	20 23								21 10	21 23				22 10	22 23			23 23
London Bridge [4] ⊖	d																		
East Croydon	d	20 37								21 24	21 37				22 24	22 37			23 38
Redhill [5]	d									21 39					22 39				
Horley	d									21 45					22 45				
Gatwick Airport [10]	d	20 56								21 48	21 56				22 48	22 56			00 01
Three Bridges [4]	a									21 53					22 53				00 05
	d									21 53					22 53				00 06
Crawley	d									21 56					22 56				
Horsham [4]	a									22 04					23 04				
	d									22 05					23 05				
Christs Hospital	d									22 08					23 08				
Billingshurst	d									22 15					23 15				
Pulborough	d									22 21					23 21				
Amberley	d									22 27					23 27				
Arundel	d									22 33					23 33				
Haywards Heath [3]	d	21 07									22 07					23 07			00 15
Burgess Hill	d	21 12									22 12					23 12			
Brighton [10]	d				21 17	21 46	21 50	22 10									22 40	23 15	
Hove [2]	d	21 24			21b26	21 50	21 54	22a13			22 25					23 25	22 44	23a18	00 29
Aldrington	d				21 28		21 56										22 46		
Portslade	d				21 31		21 58									23 28	22 48		00s32
Fishersgate	d				21 33		22 00										22 50		
Southwick	d				21 35		22 02									23 31	22 52		00s35
Shoreham-by-Sea	d	21 30			21 38	21 56	22 05				22 31					23 34	22 55		00s38
Lancing	d				21 42		22 09									23 38	22 59		00s42
East Worthing	d				21 45		22 12										23 02		
Worthing [4]	a	21 36	>		21 47	22 02	22 15				22 37	>				23 42	23 05		00 46
	d	21 40	21 42		21 48	22 03	22 15				22 41	22 43					23 05		
West Worthing	d		21 44		21 50		22 17					22 45					23 07		
Durrington-on-Sea	d		21 46		21 52		22 20					22 47					23 09		
Goring-by-Sea	d		21 49		21 55		22 22					22 50					23 12		
Angmering [3]	d		21 53		21 59		22 26					22 54					23 16		
Littlehampton [4]	a		22 02				22 35					23 02					23 24		
	d			21 57										23 06			23 29		
Ford [4]	d			22 01	22 05					22 38				23 10	23 38		23 33		
Bognor Regis [4]	d								22 11										
Barnham	a	21 54		22 08	22 11	22 17			22 18	22 42	22 55			23 14	23 42		23 37		
	d	21 55		22 15	22 12	22 18				22 43	22 56		22 57	23 15	23 43		23 45		
Bognor Regis	a			22 21						22 49			23 03	23 21	23 49				
Chichester [4]	a	22 02			22 19	22 25					23 03						23 52		
	d	22 03			22 20	22 26					23 04								
Fishbourne (Sussex)	d				22 23														
Bosham	d				22 26						23 08								
Nutbourne	d				22 29						23 12								
Southbourne	d	22 10			22 32						23 14								
Emsworth	d	22 13			22 35						23 17								
Warblington	d				22 38														
Havant	d	22 17			22 44	22 47					23 22								
Bedhampton	a				22 46														
Hilsea	a																		
Fratton	a	22 26			22 54	22 57					23 32								
Portsmouth & Southsea	a	22 29			22 57	23 00					23 35								
Portsmouth Harbour	a	22 35			23 01	23 04					23 39								
Cosham	a																		
Portchester	a																		
Fareham	a																		
Swanwick	a																		
Southampton Central	a																		

b arr. 2120

Table 188

Mondays to Fridays

Southampton, Portsmouth and Sussex Coast - Brighton, Gatwick Airport & London

		SN	SN	SN	SN	SN	SN	SN	SN	SN	SN	SN	SN	SN	SN	SN
		MX	MX	MX												
		■	■	■	■	■	■	■		■	■	◇■	■		■	◇■ 🍴
Southampton Central	d															
Swanwick	d															
Fareham	d															
Portchester	d															
Cosham	d															
Portsmouth Harbour	d	22p44		23p15												
Portsmouth & Southsea	d	22p48		23p19												
Fratton	d	22p52		23p23												
Hilsea	d	22p56		23p27												
Bedhampton	d	23p01		23p33												
Havant	d	23p05		23p36		05 01						05 30				
Warblington	d			23p38												
Emsworth	d			23p41												
Southbourne	d			23p44												
Nutbourne	d			23p47												
Bosham	d			23p50												
Fishbourne (Sussex)	d			23p53												
Chichester [4]	a	23p16		23p57		05 15						05 40				
	d	23p17	23p52	23p57		05 16						05 41				
Bognor Regis [4]	d						05 13			05 35			05 49		05 55	06 07
Barnham	a	23p24	23p59	00 05		05 23	05 19			05 41		05 48	05 55		06 01	06 13
	d	23p25	00 01	00 06	04 48	05 24	05 27	05 36		05 42		05 49	05 56		06 02	06 14
Bognor Regis	a							05 42								
Ford [4]	d	23p29	00 05	00 10	04 52		05 31			05 46			06 00		06 06	
Littlehampton [4]	a	23p34	00 10	00 15	04 57		05 36						06 05			
	d	23p39			05 02						05 54					
Angmering [3]	d	23p47			05 10	05 33				05 53	06 02				06 13	
Goring-by-Sea	d	23p51			05 14					05 57	06 06				06 17	
Durrington-on-Sea	d	23p53			05 17					05 59	06 09				06 19	
West Worthing	d	23p55			05 19					06 01	06 11				06 21	
Worthing [4]	a	23p58			05 21	05 40				06 04	06 13				06 24	
	d	23p59			05 22	05 41				06 04	06 14				06 24	
East Worthing	d	00 01			05 24					06 07					06 27	
Lancing	d	00 04			05 27	05 45				06 10	06 18				06 30	
Shoreham-by-Sea	d	00 08			05 32	05 49				06 14	06 22				06 34	
Southwick	d	00 11			05 35					06 17					06 37	
Fishersgate	d	00 13			05 37					06 19					06 39	
Portslade	d	00 15			05 39	05 53				06 21	06 27				06 41	
Aldrington	d	00 18			05 41					06 23					06 43	
Hove [2]	d	00 20			05 44	05 57			05 59	06 26	06 31			06 36	06 46	
Brighton [10]	a	00 25			05 48				06 03	06 30				06 40	06 50	
Burgess Hill	a										06 46					
Haywards Heath [3]	a					06 12					06 54					
Arundel	d											05 57				06 22
Amberley	d															06 27
Pulborough	d											06 06				06 33
Billingshurst	d											06 13				06 40
Christs Hospital	d											06 19				06 46
Horsham [4]	a											06 23				06 50
	d											06 24				06 51
Crawley	d											06 37				07 05
Three Bridges [4]	a					06 21						06 40				07 08
Gatwick Airport [10]	a					06 25					07 11	06 52				
	d					06 26					07 12	06 53				
Horley	a											06 56				07 16
Redhill [5]	a											07 02				
East Croydon	a					06 41					07 27	07 14				07 31
London Bridge [4] ⊖	a										07 43					
Clapham Junction [10]	a					06 51						07 24				07 40
London Victoria [15] ⊖	a					07 00						07 33				07 49

Southampton, Portsmouth and Sussex Coast - Brighton, Gatwick Airport & London

		SN 1	SN 1	SN 1	SN 1	SN 1	SN 1	SN	SN ◇1 ✠	SN ◇1	SN 1	SN 1	SN 1	SN ◇1	SN 1	SN ◇1	SN 1	SN 1	SN 1
Southampton Central	d													05 48				06 10	
Swanwick	d													06 06				06 27	
Fareham	d													06 13				06 34	
Portchester	d													06 18				06 40	
Cosham	d													06 23				06 44	
Portsmouth Harbour	d		05 33			05 47					06 04								
Portsmouth & Southsea	d		05 37			05 51					06 08								
Fratton	d		05 41			05 55					06 12								
Hilsea	d		05 45			05 59													
Bedhampton	d		05 50			06 04								06 34					
Havant	d		05 53			06 07					06 20			06 37				06 53	
Warblington	d		05 55											06 39					
Emsworth	d		05 58			06 11					06 24			06 42				06 57	
Southbourne	d		06 01			06 14					06 27			06 45				07 00	
Nutbourne	d		06 03			06 18								06 48					
Bosham	d		06 07			06 21								06 51					
Fishbourne (Sussex)	d		06 10			06 25								06 54					
Chichester 4	a		06 13			06 29					06 34			06 58				07 07	
	d		06 14								06 35			06 59				07 08	
Bognor Regis 4	d	06 13			06 22				06 41				06 50		06 57				
Barnham	a	06 19	06 21		06 28	06 36			06 47		06 42		06 56	07 07	07 03			07 15	
	d		06 22	06 27	06 29	06 37			06 48		06 43		06 57	>	07 11		07 13	07 16	
Bognor Regis	a			06 33													07 20		
Ford 4	d		06 26		06 33				06 52		06 47		07 01					07 20	
Littlehampton 4	a				06 38								07 06						
	d						06 32			06 42						07 03			07 22
Angmering 3	d		06 32				06 40			06 50	06 56					07 11		07 26	07 33
Goring-by-Sea	d		06 36				06 44			06 54	07 00					07 15		07 30	07 37
Durrington-on-Sea	d		06 39				06 47			06 57	07 03					07 17		07 33	07 39
West Worthing	d		06 41				06 49			06 59	07 05	07 12				07 20		07 35	07 42
Worthing 4	a		06 43				06 52			07 02	07 07	07 14				07 22		07 37	07 44
	d		06 44				06 52			07 02	07 08	07 15				07 23		07 38	07 45
East Worthing	d		06 46									07 17							07 47
Lancing	d		06 49				06 57			07 07	07 12	07 20				07 27		07 42	07 50
Shoreham-by-Sea	d		06 53				07 01			07 11	07 16	07 25				07 31		07 46	07 55
Southwick	d		06 56								07 19	07 28						07 49	07 58
Fishersgate	d		06 58									07 30							08 00
Portslade	d		07 00				07 06			07 16	07 22	07 32				07 36		07 52	08 02
Aldrington	d		07 03									07 34							08 04
Hove 2	d		07 05				07 11	07 17		07 20	07 26	07 37				07 41		07 56	08 07
Brighton 10	a		07 09					07 21			07 30	07 41						08 00	08 11
Burgess Hill	a															07 51			
Haywards Heath 3	a						07 29			07 40						07 57			
Arundel	d								06 58						07 18				
Amberley	d																		
Pulborough	d								07 07						07 28				
Billingshurst	d								07 14						07 35				
Christs Hospital	d								07 20						07 41				
Horsham 4	a					07 03			07 24						07 45				
	d					07 04			07 25						07 46				
Crawley	d					07 13			07 37						08 00				
Three Bridges 4	a					07 18			07 40						08 05				
Gatwick Airport 10	a															08 12			
	d															08 13			
Horley	a																		
Redhill 5	a																		
East Croydon ⇌	a					07 42	07 57		08 00	08 08					08 26	08 29			
London Bridge 4 ⊖	a						08 11								08 45				
Clapham Junction 10	a					07 51			08 10	08 17						08 39			
London Victoria 15 ⊖	a					07 59			08 19	08 26						08 48			

Southampton, Portsmouth and Sussex Coast - Brighton, Gatwick Airport & London

		SN	SN ◇1 ✠	SN ◇1	SN 1	SN ◇1	SN 1	GW	SN 1	SN 1	SN 1	SN 1	SN ◇1 ✠	SN ◇1	SN ◇1	SN	SN	SN 1
Southampton Central	d													07 06				
Swanwick	d													07 24				
Fareham	d													07 31				
Portchester	d													07 36				
Cosham	d													07 40				
Portsmouth Harbour	d			06 46				07 01			07 20							
Portsmouth & Southsea	d			06 50				07 05			07 24							
Fratton	d			06 54				07 10			07 28							
Hilsea	d			06 58														
Bedhampton	d			07 03														
Havant	d			07 06				07 20			07 36			07 47				
Warblington	d			07 08										07 49				
Emsworth	d			07 11										07 52				
Southbourne	d			07 14										07 55				
Nutbourne	d			07 16										07 58				
Bosham	d			07 20										08 01				
Fishbourne (Sussex)	d			07 23										08 04				
Chichester 4	a			07 26				07 31			07 47			08 08				
	d			07 28				07 32			07 47			08 08				08 21
Bognor Regis 4	d		07 16		07 27					07 36			07 55				08 13	
Barnham	a		07 22	07 35	07 33			07 39		07 42	07 55		08 01	08 16			08 19	08 28
	d		07 23	07 36			07 39	07 40		07 45	07 55		08 02	08 16			08 20	08 29
Bognor Regis	a						07 45											
Ford 4	d									07 50	08 00		08 06				08 24	08 33
Littlehampton 4	a									07 54								08 38
	d					07 32			07 45			08 01			08 15			
Angmering 3	d					07 41			07 53		08 06	08 10			08 23		08 30	
Goring-by-Sea	d					07 45			07 57			08 14			08 27		08 34	
Durrington-on-Sea	d					07 47			08 00		08 12	08 17			08 30		08 37	
West Worthing	d					07 50			08 02			08 19			08 32		08 39	
Worthing 4	a					07 52		07 56	08 04		08 16	08 21			08 34		08 41	
	d					07 53		08 00	08 05		08 16	08 22			08 35		08 42	
East Worthing	d								08 07			08 24					08 44	
Lancing	d					07 57			08 10		08 20	08 27			08 39		08 47	
Shoreham-by-Sea	d					08 01		08 06	08 15		08 24	08 32			08 43		08 52	
Southwick	d								08 18		08 27	08 35					08 55	
Fishersgate	d								08 20			08 37					08 57	
Portslade	d					08 06			08 22		08 31	08 39			08 48		08 59	
Aldrington	d								08 24			08 41					09 01	
Hove 2	d	07 49				08 11		08 14	08 27		08 34	08 44			08 52	08 54	09 04	
Brighton 10	a	07 54						08 20	08 31		08 38	08 48				08 58	09 08	
Burgess Hill	a					08 26									09 07			
Haywards Heath 3	a					08 31									09 12			
Arundel	d		07 30										08 11					
Amberley	d		07 35										08 16					
Pulborough	d		07 41										08 22					
Billingshurst	d		07 48										08 29					
Christs Hospital	d		07 54										08 35					
Horsham 4	a		07 58	08 05									08 39	08 45				
	d		08 09	<									08 49	<				
Crawley	d		08 18										08 58					
Three Bridges 4	a		08 22			08 41							09 01					
Gatwick Airport 10	a												09 06		09 26			
	d												09 07		09 27			
Horley	a		08 28															
Redhill 5	a																	
East Croydon ⇌	a		08 43			09 01							09 22		09 42			
London Bridge 4 ⊖	a																	
Clapham Junction 10	a		08 52			09 10							09 32		09 52			
London Victoria 15 ⊖	a		09 01			09 22							09 41		10 00			

Table 188

Mondays to Fridays

Southampton, Portsmouth and Sussex Coast - Brighton, Gatwick Airport & London

		SN ◇■1	SN ◇■1	SN ■1	SN ◇■1	SN ■1	SN ■1	SN ■1	SN ■1	SN	SN ■1	SN ■1	SN ■1	SN ◇■1	SN ◇■1	SN ◇■1	SN ■1	SN ■1	SN ■1	SN ■1	SN ■1
Southampton Central	d			07 33											08 10						08 33
Swanwick	d			07 51											08 28						08 50
Fareham	d			07 58											08 35						08 57
Portchester	d														08 40						
Cosham	d			08 07											08 44						09 05
Portsmouth Harbour	d		08 10										08 29								
Portsmouth & Southsea	d		08 14				08 03						08 33								
Fratton	d		08 18				08 07						08 37								
Hilsea	d						08 11														
Bedhampton	d						08 16														
Havant	d		08 27	08 13			08 19						08 46		08 51						09 12
Warblington	d						08 21								08 53						
Emsworth	d		08 31				08 24						08 50		08 56						09 16
Southbourne	d						08 27						08 53		08 59						
Nutbourne	d						08 29								09 01						
Bosham	d			08 21											09 05						
Fishbourne (Sussex)	d			08 24											09 08						
Chichester ■4	a		08 40	08 27			08 35						09 00		09 11						09 24
	d		08 41	08 28			08 36						09 00		09 12		09 07				09 25
Bognor Regis ■4	d	08 26				08 32			08 48					08 56				09 09			
Barnham	a	08 32	08 48	08 35		08 38	08 43		08 55				09 08	09 02	09 19		09 14	09 15			09 32
	d	08 33	08 49	08 36			08 44	08 45				09 12	09 08	09 03	09 20		09 15		09 25		09 33
Bognor Regis	a							08 51				09 18							09 31		
Ford ■4	d	08 37		08 40			08 48							09 07			09 19				09 37
Littlehampton ■4	a						08 53										09 24				
	d				08 45											09 15					
Angmering ■3	d			08 46	08 53								09 17			09 23					09 43
Goring-by-Sea	d				08 57											09 27					09 47
Durrington-on-Sea	d			08 52	09 00											09 30					09 50
West Worthing	d				09 02						09 09					09 32				09 39	09 52
Worthing ■4	a			08 56	09 04						09 11		09 24			09 34				09 41	09 54
	d			08 56	09 05						09 12		09 26			09 36				09 42	09 56
East Worthing	d										09 14									09 44	
Lancing	d			09 00	09 09						09 17		09 30							09 47	10 00
Shoreham-by-Sea	d			09 04	09 13						09 22		09 34			09 42				09 52	10 04
Southwick	d			09 07							09 25		09 37							09 55	10 07
Fishersgate	d										09 27									09 57	
Portslade	d			09 11	09 18						09 29		09 40			09 47				09 59	10 10
Aldrington	d										09 31									10 01	
Hove ■2	d			09 14	09 22					09 24	09 34		09 44			09 51				10 04	10 14
Brighton ■10	a			09 18						09 28	09 38		09 48							10 08	10 18
Burgess Hill	a				09 33											10 01					
Haywards Heath ■3	a				09 40											10 06					
Arundel	d	08 42												09 12							
Amberley	d	08 47												09 17							
Pulborough	d	08 53												09 23							
Billingshurst	d	09 00												09 29							
Christs Hospital	d	09 06												09 36							
Horsham ■4	a	09 11	09 16											09 40	09 47						
	d	09 20	<											09 51	<						
Crawley	d	09 29												10 00							
Three Bridges ■4	a	09 32												10 03							
Gatwick Airport ■10	a	09 37			09 55									10 08		10 24					
	d	09 38			09 55									10 09		10 25					
Horley	a	09 41																			
Redhill ■5	a	09 47												10 16							
East Croydon	a	09 59			10 11									10 28		10 40					
London Bridge ■4	a																				
Clapham Junction ■10	a	10 09			10 21									10 37		10 50					
London Victoria ■15	a	10 16			10 28									10 44		10 57					

Table 188

Mondays to Fridays

Southampton, Portsmouth and Sussex Coast - Brighton, Gatwick Airport & London

		SN	SN ◇■1	SN ◇■1	SN ■1	SN ◇■1	SN	SN ■1	SN ■1	SN ■1	SN ■1	SN ■1	SN ◇■1	SN ◇■1	SN ◇■1	SN	SN ■1	SN ■1
Southampton Central	d													09 10				09 33
Swanwick	d													09 28				09 50
Fareham	d													09 37				09 56
Portchester	d													09 42				
Cosham	d													09 46				10 05
Portsmouth Harbour	d			09 12	08 51						09 29							
Portsmouth & Southsea	d			09 16	08 55						09 33							
Fratton	d			09 20	08 59						09 37							
Hilsea	d				09 04													
Bedhampton	d				09 13													
Havant	d			09 30	09 16						09 46			09 54				10 11
Warblington	d				09 18													
Emsworth	d				09 21						09 50			10 00				10 15
Southbourne	d				09 24						09 53			10 03				
Nutbourne	d				09 26													
Bosham	d				09 30													
Fishbourne (Sussex)	d				09 33													
Chichester ■4	a			09 40	09 36						10 00			10 10				10 23
	d			09 41	09 37						10 00			10 11				10 25
Bognor Regis ■4	d		09 30					09 39				10 07	09 56					
Barnham	a		09 36	09 48	09 44			09 45			10 08	10 13	10 02	10 18				10 32
	d		09 37	09 49	09 45				09 52		10 08	10 15	10 03	10 19				10 33
Bognor Regis	a								09 58									
Ford ■4	d		09 41		09 49							10 19	10 07					10 37
Littlehampton ■4	a				09 54							10 24						
	d					09 45									10 15			
Angmering ■3	d					09 54					10 17				10 23			10 43
Goring-by-Sea	d					09 58									10 27			10 47
Durrington-on-Sea	d					10 00									10 30			10 50
West Worthing	d					10 02				10 09					10 32		10 39	10 52
Worthing ■4	a					10 05				10 11	10 24				10 34		10 41	10 54
	d					10 06				10 12	10 26				10 36		10 42	10 56
East Worthing	d									10 14							10 44	
Lancing	d					10 10				10 17	10 30						10 47	11 00
Shoreham-by-Sea	d					10 14				10 22	10 34				10 42		10 52	11 04
Southwick	d									10 25	10 37						10 55	11 07
Fishersgate	d									10 27							10 57	
Portslade	d									10 29	10 40				10 47		10 59	11 10
Aldrington	d									10 31							11 01	
Hove ■2	d	09 54				10 21	10 24			10 34	10 44				10 51	10 54	11 04	11 14
Brighton ■10	a	09 58					10 28			10 38	10 48					10 58	11 08	11 18
Burgess Hill	a														11 01			
Haywards Heath ■3	a					10 35									11 08			
Arundel	d		09 46										10 12					
Amberley	d												10 17					
Pulborough	d		09 55										10 23					
Billingshurst	d		10 01										10 29					
Christs Hospital	d												10 36					
Horsham ■4	a		10 10	10 16									10 40	10 46				
	d		10 20	<									10 50	<				
Crawley	d		10 29										10 59					
Three Bridges ■4	a		10 32										11 02					
Gatwick Airport ■10	a		10 37			10 54							11 07		11 24			
	d		10 38			10 55							11 08		11 24			
Horley	a		10 41															
Redhill ■5	a		10 47										11 15					
East Croydon	a		10 59			11 10							11 27		11 40			
London Bridge ■4	a																	
Clapham Junction ■10	a		11 09			11 20							11 37		11 50			
London Victoria ■15	a		11 16			11 27							11 44		11 57			

Southampton, Portsmouth and Sussex Coast - Brighton, Gatwick Airport & London

Station		SN 1	SN 1	SN ◇1	SN ◇1	SN ◇1	SN	SN 1	SN 1	SN ◇1	SN ◇1	SN ◇1	SN 1	SN	SN 1	SN 1	SN 1	SN 1
Southampton Central	d										10 13						10 33	
Swanwick	d										10 32						10 50	
Fareham	d										10 39						10 57	
Portchester	d										10 44							
Cosham	d										10 48						11 05	
Portsmouth Harbour	d				10 12								10 29					
Portsmouth & Southsea	d	09 56			10 16								10 33					10 56
Fratton	d	10 01			10 20								10 37					11 01
Hilsea	d	10 05																11 05
Bedhampton	d	10 13																11 13
Havant	d	10 16			10 30						10 56		10 46				11 12	11 16
Warblington	d	10 18																11 18
Emsworth	d	10 21									11 00		10 50				11 16	11 21
Southbourne	d	10 24									11 03		10 53					11 24
Nutbourne	d	10 26																11 26
Bosham	d	10 30																11 30
Fishbourne (Sussex)	d	10 33																11 33
Chichester 4	a	10 36			10 40						11 10		11 00				11 24	11 36
	d	10 37			10 41						11 11		11 00				11 25	11 37
Bognor Regis 4	d		10 39	10 30						10 56					11 07			
Barnham	a	10 44	10 45	10 36	10 48					11 02	11 18		11 08		11 13		11 32	11 44
	d	10 45		10 37	10 49			10 52		11 03	11 19		11 08		11 15		11 33	11 45
Bognor Regis	a							10 58										
Ford 4	d	10 49		10 41						11 07					11 19		11 37	11 49
Littlehampton 4	a	10 54													11 24			11 54
	d					10 45						11 15						
Angmering 3	d					10 53						11 23	11 17				11 43	
Goring-by-Sea	d					10 57						11 27					11 47	
Durrington-on-Sea	d					11 00						11 30					11 50	
West Worthing	d					11 02			11 09			11 32				11 39	11 52	
Worthing 4	a					11 04			11 11			11 34	11 24			11 41	11 54	
	d					11 06			11 12			11 36	11 26			11 42	11 56	
East Worthing	d								11 14							11 44		
Lancing	d					11 10			11 17				11 30			11 47	12 00	
Shoreham-by-Sea	d					11 14			11 22			11 42	11 34			11 52	12 04	
Southwick	d								11 25				11 37			11 55	12 07	
Fishersgate	d								11 27							11 57		
Portslade	d								11 29			11 47	11 40			11 59	12 10	
Aldrington	d								11 31							12 01		
Hove 2	d					11 21	11 24		11 34			11 51	11 44	11 54		12 04	12 14	
Brighton 10	a						11 28		11 38				11 48	11 58		12 08	12 18	
Burgess Hill	a											12 01						
Haywards Heath 3	a					11 35						12 09						
Arundel	d			10 46						11 12								
Amberley	d									11 17								
Pulborough	d			10 55						11 23								
Billingshurst	d			11 01						11 29								
Christs Hospital	d									11 36								
Horsham 4	a			11 10	11 16					11 40	11 46							
	d			11 20	<					11 50	<							
Crawley	d			11 29						11 59								
Three Bridges 4	a			11 32						12 02								
Gatwick Airport 10	a			11 37		11 54				12 07		12 24						
	d			11 38		11 55				12 08		12 24						
Horley	a			11 41														
Redhill 5	a			11 47						12 15								
East Croydon	a			11 59		12 10				12 27		12 40						
London Bridge 4 ⊖	a																	
Clapham Junction 10	a			12 09		12 19				12 37		12 50						
London Victoria 15 ⊖	a			12 18		12 28				12 44		12 57						

Table 188 — Mondays to Fridays

Southampton, Portsmouth and Sussex Coast - Brighton, Gatwick Airport & London

Station		SN ◇1	SN ◇1	SN ◇1	SN 1	SN 1	SN	SN 1	SN 1	SN ◇1	SN ◇1	SN ◇1	SN	SN 1	SN 1	SN 1	SN 1	SW 1	SN 1	SN ◇1	SN ◇1	SN ◇1
Southampton Central	d										11 13					11 33		11 44				
Swanwick	d										11 33					11 50		12 11				
Fareham	d										11 40					11 57		12 18				
Portchester	d										11 45							12 23				
Cosham	d										11 49					12 05		12 28				
Portsmouth Harbour	d		11 12						11 29												12 12	
Portsmouth & Southsea	d		11 16						11 33								11 56				12 16	
Fratton	d		11 20						11 37								12 01				12 20	
Hilsea	d																12 05	12 33				
Bedhampton	d																12 13					
Havant	d		11 30						11 46		11 56					12 12	12 16				12 30	
Warblington	d																12 18					
Emsworth	d								11 50		12 00					12 16	12 21					
Southbourne	d								11 53		12 03						12 24					
Nutbourne	d																12 26					
Bosham	d																12 30					
Fishbourne (Sussex)	d																12 33					
Chichester 4	a		11 40						12 00		12 10					12 24	12 36				12 40	
	d		11 41						12 00		12 11					12 25	12 37				12 41	
Bognor Regis 4	d	11 30			11 39					11 56				12 07					12 39	12 30		
Barnham	a	11 36	11 48		11 45				12 08	12 02	12 18			12 13		12 32	12 44		12 45	12 36	12 48	
	d	11 37	11 49			11 52			12 08	12 03	12 19			12 15		12 33	12 45			12 37	12 49	
Bognor Regis	a					11 58																
Ford 4	d	11 41								12 07				12 19		12 37	12 49			12 41		
Littlehampton 4	a													12 24			12 54					
	d			11 45								12 15										12 45
Angmering 3	d			11 53					12 17			12 23				12 43						12 53
Goring-by-Sea	d			11 57								12 27				12 47						12 57
Durrington-on-Sea	d			12 00								12 30				12 50						13 00
West Worthing	d			12 02				12 09				12 32			12 39	12 52						13 02
Worthing 4	a			12 04				12 11	12 24			12 34			12 41	12 54						13 04
	d			12 06				12 12	12 26			12 36			12 42	12 56						13 06
East Worthing	d							12 14							12 44							
Lancing	d			12 10				12 17	12 30						12 47	13 00						13 10
Shoreham-by-Sea	d			12 14				12 22	12 34			12 42			12 52	13 04						13 14
Southwick	d							12 25	12 37						12 55	13 07						
Fishersgate	d							12 27							12 57							
Portslade	d							12 29	12 40			12 47			12 59	13 10						
Aldrington	d							12 31							13 01							
Hove 2	d			12 21			12 24	12 34	12 44			12 51	12 54		13 04	13 14						13 21
Brighton 10	a						12 28	12 38	12 48				12 58		13 08	13 18						
Burgess Hill	a											13 01										
Haywards Heath 3	a			12 35								13 09										13 35
Arundel	d	11 46								12 12										12 46		
Amberley	d									12 17												
Pulborough	d	11 55								12 23										12 55		
Billingshurst	d	12 01								12 29										13 01		
Christs Hospital	d									12 36												
Horsham 4	a	12 10	12 16							12 40	12 46									13 10	13 16	
	d	12 20	<							12 50	<									13 20	<	
Crawley	d	12 29								12 59										13 29		
Three Bridges 4	a	12 32								13 02										13 32		
Gatwick Airport 10	a	12 37		12 54						13 07		13 24								13 37		13 54
	d	12 38		12 55						13 08		13 24								13 38		13 55
Horley	a	12 41																		13 41		
Redhill 5	a	12 47								13 15										13 47		
East Croydon	a	12 59		13 10						13 27		13 40								13 59		14 10
London Bridge 4 ⊖	a																					
Clapham Junction 10	a	13 09		13 20						13 37		13 50								14 09		14 20
London Victoria 15 ⊖	a	13 16		13 28						13 44		13 57								14 16		14 27

Table 188

Mondays to Fridays

Southampton, Portsmouth and Sussex Coast - Brighton, Gatwick Airport & London

Station		SN 1		SN	SN 1	SN 1	SN 1	SN ◇1	SN ◇1	SN ◇1		SN	SN 1	SN 1	SN 1	SN 1	SN ◇1	SN ◇1	SN ◇1		SN 1	SN 1
Southampton Central	d								12 13					12 33								
Swanwick	d								12 33					12 50								
Fareham	d								12 40					12 56								
Portchester	d								12 45													
Cosham	d								12 49					13 05								
Portsmouth Harbour	d					12 29												13 12				
Portsmouth & Southsea	d					12 33									12 56			13 16				
Fratton	d					12 37									13 01			13 20				
Hilsea	d														13 05							
Bedhampton	d														13 13							
Havant	d					12 46			12 56					13 11	13 16			13 30				
Warblington	d														13 18							
Emsworth	d					12 50			13 00					13 15	13 21							
Southbourne	d					12 53			13 03						13 24							
Nutbourne	d														13 26							
Bosham	d														13 30							
Fishbourne (Sussex)	d														13 33							
Chichester 4	a					13 00			13 10					13 23	13 36			13 40				
	d					13 00			13 11					13 25	13 37			13 41				
Bognor Regis 4	d						13 07	12 56								13 39	13 30					
Barnham	a					13 08	13 13	13 02	13 18					13 32	13 44	13 45	13 36	13 48				
	d	12 52				13 08	13 15	13 03	13 19					13 33	13 45		13 37	13 49			13 52	
Bognor Regis	a	12 58																			13 58	
Ford 4	d						13 19	13 07						13 37	13 49		13 41					
Littlehampton 4	a						13 24								13 54							
	d									13 15									13 45			
Angmering 3	d					13 17				13 23				13 43					13 53			
Goring-by-Sea	d									13 27				13 47					13 57			
Durrington-on-Sea	d									13 30				13 50					14 00			
West Worthing	d				13 09					13 32			13 39	13 52					14 02			14 09
Worthing 4	a				13 11	13 24				13 34			13 41	13 54					14 04			14 11
	d				13 12	13 26				13 36			13 42	13 56					14 06			14 12
East Worthing	d				13 14								13 44									14 14
Lancing	d				13 17	13 30							13 47	14 00					14 10			14 17
Shoreham-by-Sea	d				13 22	13 34				13 42			13 52	14 04					14 14			14 22
Southwick	d				13 25	13 37							13 55	14 07								14 25
Fishersgate	d				13 27								13 57									14 27
Portslade	d				13 29	13 40				13 47			13 59	14 10								14 29
Aldrington	d				13 31								14 01									14 31
Hove 2	d			13 24	13 34	13 44				13 51		13 54	14 04	14 14					14 21			14 34
Brighton 10	a			13 28	13 38	13 48						13 58	14 08	14 18								14 38
Burgess Hill	a									14 01												
Haywards Heath 3	a									14 09									14 35			
Arundel	d							13 12									13 46					
Amberley	d							13 17														
Pulborough	d							13 23									13 55					
Billingshurst	d							13 29									14 01					
Christs Hospital	d							13 36														
Horsham 4	a							13 40	13 46								14 10	14 16				
	d							13 50	<								14 20	<				
Crawley	d							13 59									14 29					
Three Bridges 4	a							14 02									14 32					
Gatwick Airport 10	a							14 07		14 24							14 37		14 54			
	d							14 08		14 24							14 38		14 55			
Horley	a																14 41					
Redhill 5	a							14 15									14 47					
East Croydon	a							14 27		14 40							14 59		15 10			
London Bridge 4 ⊖	a																					
Clapham Junction 10	a							14 37		14 50							15 09		15 20			
London Victoria 15 ⊖	a							14 44		14 57							15 20		15 27			

Table 188

Mondays to Fridays

Southampton, Portsmouth and Sussex Coast - Brighton, Gatwick Airport & London

Station		SN	SN 1	SN 1	SN ◇1	SN ◇1	SN ◇1	SN		SN 1	SN 1	SN 1	SN 1		SN ◇1 [trolley symbol]	SN ◇1	SN ◇1 [trolley symbol]	SN 1	SN	SN 1
Southampton Central	d					13 13					13 33									
Swanwick	d					13 33					13 50									
Fareham	d					13 40					13 56									
Portchester	d					13 45														
Cosham	d					13 49					14 05									
Portsmouth Harbour	d		13 29													14 12				
Portsmouth & Southsea	d		13 33									13 56				14 16				
Fratton	d		13 37									14 01				14 20				
Hilsea	d											14 05								
Bedhampton	d											14 13								
Havant	d		13 46			13 56					14 11	14 16				14 30				
Warblington	d											14 18								
Emsworth	d		13 50			14 00					14 15	14 21								
Southbourne	d		13 53			14 03						14 24								
Nutbourne	d											14 26								
Bosham	d											14 30								
Fishbourne (Sussex)	d											14 33								
Chichester 4	a		14 00			14 10					14 23	14 36				14 40				
	d		14 00			14 11					14 25	14 37				14 41				
Bognor Regis 4	d			14 07	13 56								14 40		14 30					
Barnham	a		14 08	14 13	14 02	14 18					14 32	14 44	14 46		14 36	14 48				
	d		14 08	14 15	14 03	14 19					14 33	14 45			14 37	14 49		14 52		
Bognor Regis	a																	14 58		
Ford 4	d			14 19	14 07						14 37	14 49			14 41					
Littlehampton 4	a			14 24								14 54								
	d						14 15										14 45			
Angmering 3	d		14 17				14 23				14 43						14 53			
Goring-by-Sea	d						14 27				14 47						14 57			
Durrington-on-Sea	d						14 30				14 50						15 00			
West Worthing	d						14 32			14 39	14 52						15 02			15 09
Worthing 4	a		14 24				14 34			14 41	14 54						15 04			15 11
	d		14 26				14 36			14 42	14 56						15 06			15 12
East Worthing	d									14 44										15 14
Lancing	d		14 30							14 47	15 00						15 10			15 17
Shoreham-by-Sea	d		14 34				14 42			14 52	15 04						15 14			15 22
Southwick	d		14 37							14 55	15 07									15 25
Fishersgate	d									14 57										15 27
Portslade	d		14 40				14 47			14 59	15 10									15 29
Aldrington	d									15 01										15 31
Hove 2	d	14 24	14 44				14 51	14 54		15 04	15 14						15 21		15 24	15 34
Brighton 10	a	14 28	14 48					14 58		15 08	15 18								15 28	15 38
Burgess Hill	a						15 01													
Haywards Heath 3	a						15 09										15 35			
Arundel	d				14 12										14 46					
Amberley	d				14 17															
Pulborough	d				14 23										14 55					
Billingshurst	d				14 29										15 01					
Christs Hospital	d				14 36															
Horsham 4	a				14 40	14 46									15 10	15 16				
	d				14 50	<									15 20	<				
Crawley	d				14 59										15 29					
Three Bridges 4	a				15 02										15 32					
Gatwick Airport 10	a				15 07		15 24								15 37		15 54			
	d				15 08		15 24								15 38		15 55			
Horley	a														15 41					
Redhill 5	a				15 16										15 47					
East Croydon	a				15 28		15 40								15 59		16 10			
London Bridge 4 ⊖	a																			
Clapham Junction 10	a				15 37		15 50								16 09		16 20			
London Victoria 15 ⊖	a				15 44		15 57								16 20		16 27			

Southampton, Portsmouth and Sussex Coast - Brighton, Gatwick Airport & London

		SN ■	SN ■	SN ◇■ H	SN ◇■	SN ◇■	SN	SN ■	GW ◇	SN ■	SN ■	SN ■	SN ◇■	SN ◇■	SN ◇■ H	SN	SN ■	SN ■
Southampton Central	d				14 13				14 34	14 27								
Swanwick	d				14 33													
Fareham	d				14 40				14 56	15 00								
Portchester	d				14 45													
Cosham	d				14 49				15 04									
Portsmouth Harbour	d	14 29												15 12				
Portsmouth & Southsea	d	14 33										14 56		15 16				
Fratton	d	14 37										15 01		15 20				
Hilsea	d											15 05						
Bedhampton	d											15 14						
Havant	d	14 46			14 56				15 11	15 15		15 17		15 30				
Warblington	d											15 19						
Emsworth	d	14 50			15 00							15 22						
Southbourne	d	14 53			15 03							15 25						
Nutbourne	d											15 28						
Bosham	d											15 31						
Fishbourne (Sussex)	d											15 34						
Chichester [4]	a	15 00			15 10				15 21	15 25		15 37		15 41				
	d	15 00			15 11				15 22	15 29		15 38		15 42				
Bognor Regis [4]	d		15 07	14 56							15 39		15 27					
Barnham	a	15 08	15 13	15 02	15 18				15 29	15 36	15 45	15 45	15 33	15 49				
	d	15 08	15 15	15 03	15 19				15 30	15 37		15 46	15 34	15 50			15 53	
Bognor Regis	a																15 59	
Ford [4]	d		15 19	15 07						15 41		15 50	15 38					
Littlehampton [4]	a		15 24									15 55						
	d					15 15									15 45			15 50
Angmering [3]	d	15 17				15 23				15 47					15 53			16 00
Goring-by-Sea	d					15 27				15 51					15 57			16 04
Durrington-on-Sea	d					15 30				15 54					16 00			16 07
West Worthing	d					15 32		15 39		15 56					16 02			16 09
Worthing [4]	a	15 24				15 34		15 41	15 45	15 58					16 04			16 11
	d	15 26				15 36		15 42	15 50	15 59					16 06			16 12
East Worthing	d							15 44										16 14
Lancing	d	15 30						15 47		16 03					16 10			16 17
Shoreham-by-Sea	d	15 34				15 42		15 52	15 57	16 07					16 14			16 22
Southwick	d	15 37						15 55		16 10								16 25
Fishersgate	d							15 57										16 27
Portslade	d	15 40				15 47		15 59		16 13								16 29
Aldrington	d							16 01										16 31
Hove [2]	d	15 44				15 51	15 54	16 04	16 08	16 17					16 21	16 24		16 34
Brighton [10]	a	15 48					15 58	16 08	16 14	16 21						16 28		16 38
Burgess Hill	a					16 01												
Haywards Heath [3]	a					16 09									16 34			
Arundel	d			15 12									15 43					
Amberley	d			15 17														
Pulborough	d			15 23									15 52					
Billingshurst	d			15 29									15 58					
Christs Hospital	d			15 36									16 05					
Horsham [4]	a			15 40	15 46								16 10	16 16				
	d			15 50	<								16 20	<				
Crawley	d			15 59									16 29					
Three Bridges [4]	a			16 02									16 32					
Gatwick Airport [10]	a			16 07		16 24							16 37		16 56			
	d			16 08		16 24							16 38		16 57			
Horley	a																	
Redhill [5]	a			16 17									16 46					
East Croydon	a			16 30		16 40							17 01		17 12			
London Bridge [4] ⊖	a																	
Clapham Junction [10]	a			16 39		16 50							17 10		17 21			
London Victoria [15] ⊖	a			16 46		16 58							17 17		17 28			

Southampton, Portsmouth and Sussex Coast - Brighton, Gatwick Airport & London

		SN ■	SN ■	SN ◇■ H	SN ◇■	SN ◇■	SN	SN ■	SN ■	SN ■	SN ■	SN ■	SN ◇■ H	SN ◇■	SN ■	SN ◇■ H	SN	SN ■	SN ■	SN ◇■ H	SN ◇■	SN ◇■
Southampton Central	d				15 13					15 33											16 12	
Swanwick	d				15 33					15 50											16 29	
Fareham	d				15 40					15 57											16 36	
Portchester	d				15 45																16 41	
Cosham	d				15 49					16 05											16 45	
Portsmouth Harbour	d	15 29												16 12					16 29			
Portsmouth & Southsea	d	15 33									15 56			16 16					16 33			
Fratton	d	15 37									16 01			16 20					16 37			
Hilsea	d										16 05											
Bedhampton	d										16 13											
Havant	d	15 46			15 58					16 12	16 16			16 30					16 46		16 52	
Warblington	d										16 18											
Emsworth	d	15 50			16 02					16 16	16 21			16 34					16 50		16 56	
Southbourne	d	15 53			16 05						16 24								16 53		16 59	
Nutbourne	d										16 26											
Bosham	d										16 30										17 03	
Fishbourne (Sussex)	d										16 33											
Chichester [4]	a	16 00			16 12					16 24	16 36			16 42					17 00		17 08	
	d	16 00			16 13					16 25	16 37			16 43					17 00		17 13	
Bognor Regis [4]	d		16 09	15 56								16 39	16 30							16 56		
Barnham	a	16 08	16 15	16 02	16 20					16 32	16 44	16 45	16 36	16 50					17 08	17 02	17 20	
	d	16 08		16 03	16 21				16 24	16 33	16 45		16 37	16 51	16 54				17 08	17 03	17 21	
Bognor Regis	a								16 30						17 00							
Ford [4]	d			16 07						16 37	16 49		16 41							17 07		
Littlehampton [4]	a										16 54											
	d					16 15										16 45						17 15
Angmering [3]	d	16 17				16 23				16 43						16 53			17 17			17 23
Goring-by-Sea	d					16 27				16 47						16 57						17 27
Durrington-on-Sea	d					16 30				16 50						17 00						17 30
West Worthing	d					16 32		16 39		16 52						17 02		17 09				17 32
Worthing [4]	a	16 24				16 34		16 41		16 54						17 04		17 11	17 24			17 34
	d	16 26				16 36		16 42		16 56						17 06		17 12	17 26			17 36
East Worthing	d							16 44										17 14				
Lancing	d	16 30						16 47		17 00						17 10		17 17	17 30			
Shoreham-by-Sea	d	16 34				16 42		16 52		17 04						17 14		17 22	17 34			17 42
Southwick	d	16 37						16 55		17 07								17 25	17 37			
Fishersgate	d							16 57										17 27				
Portslade	d	16 40				16 47		16 59		17 10								17 29	17 40			17 47
Aldrington	d							17 01										17 31				
Hove [2]	d	16 44				16 51	16 54	17 04		17 14						17 21	17 24	17 34	17 44			17 51
Brighton [10]	a	16 48					16 58	17 08		17 18							17 28	17 38	17 48			
Burgess Hill	a					17 01																18 01
Haywards Heath [3]	a					17 09										17 35						18 09
Arundel	d			16 12									16 46							17 12		
Amberley	d			16 17																17 17		
Pulborough	d			16 23									16 55							17 23		
Billingshurst	d			16 29									17 01							17 29		
Christs Hospital	d			16 36									17 08							17 36		
Horsham [4]	a			16 40	16 48								17 12	17 18						17 40	17 48	
	d			16 52	<								17 22	<						17 52	<	
Crawley	d			17 01									17 31							18 01		
Three Bridges [4]	a			17 04									17 34							18 04		
Gatwick Airport [10]	a			17 09		17 24							17 40			17 54				18 09		18 26
	d			17 10		17 24							17 41			17 55				18 10		18 26
Horley	a																					
Redhill [5]	a			17 17									17 48							18 17		
East Croydon	a			17 30		17 40							18 01			18 11				18 29		18 42
London Bridge [4] ⊖	a																					
Clapham Junction [10]	a			17 39		17 50							18 13			18 21				18 40		18 52
London Victoria [15] ⊖	a			17 46		17 58							18 20			18 29				18 47		18 59

Table 188

Mondays to Fridays

Southampton, Portsmouth and Sussex Coast - Brighton, Gatwick Airport & London

		SN ■	SN	SN ■	SN ■	SN ■	SN ◇■	SN ◇■	SN ◇■	SN	SN ■	SN ■	SN ■	SN ◇■	SN ◇■	SN ◇■	SN ■	SN ■	SN	SN ■
Southampton Central	d				16 33										17 13					17 33
Swanwick	d				16 50										17 33					17 50
Fareham	d				16 57										17 40					17 56
Portchester	d														17 45					
Cosham	d				17 05										17 49					18 05
Portsmouth Harbour	d			16 40				17 12					17 29							
Portsmouth & Southsea	d			16 46		16 56		17 16					17 33					17 46		
Fratton	d			16 50		17 01		17 20					17 37					17 50		
Hilsea	d			16 54		17 05												17 54		
Bedhampton	d					17 14														
Havant	d			17 00	17 12	17 17		17 30					17 46		17 56			18 00		18 11
Warblington	d			17 02		17 19												18 02		
Emsworth	d			17 05	17 17	17 22							17 50		18 00			18 05		18 15
Southbourne	d			17 08		17 25							17 53		18 03			18 08		
Nutbourne	d			17 10		17 28												18 10		
Bosham	d			17 14		17 31												18 14		
Fishbourne (Sussex)	d			17 17		17 34												18 17		
Chichester 4	a			17 20	17 25	17 37		17 42					18 00		18 10			18 20		18 24
	d			17 21	17 25	17 38		17 43					18 00		18 13			18 21		18 25
Bognor Regis 4	d	17 18					17 30				17 51			17 57			18 19			
Barnham	a	17 24		17 28	17 33	17 45	17 36	17 50			17 57		18 08	18 03	18 20		18 25	18 28		18 32
	d	17 25		17 29	17 33	17 46	17 37	17 51				18 08	18 08	18 04	18 21			18 29		18 33
Bognor Regis	a											18 14								
Ford 4	d	17 29			17 38	17 50	17 41							18 08				18 33		
Littlehampton 4	a	17 37				17 55												18 40		
	d								17 45							18 15				
Angmering 3	d				17 44				17 53				18 18			18 23				18 42
Goring-by-Sea	d				17 48				17 57							18 27				
Durrington-on-Sea	d				17 50				18 00							18 30				18 48
West Worthing	d				17 52				18 02							18 32				
Worthing 4	a			17 43	17 55				18 04				18 25			18 34				18 52
	d			17 43	17 56				18 06				18 25			18 35				18 52
East Worthing	d			17 46									18 28							18 55
Lancing	d			17 49	18 00				18 10				18 31			18 39				18 58
Shoreham-by-Sea	d			17 53	18 04				18 14				18 35			18 43				19 02
Southwick	d			17 56	18 07								18 38							19 05
Fishersgate	d			17 58									18 40							19 07
Portslade	d			18 00	18 10								18 42			18 48				19 09
Aldrington	d			18 02									18 44							19 11
Hove 2	d		18 01	18 05	18 14				18 21	18 24			18 47			18 52			19 00	19 14
Brighton 10	a		18 05	18 09	18 18					18 28			18 51						19 04	19 18
Burgess Hill	a								18 32											
Haywards Heath 3	a								18 41							19 05				
Arundel	d						17 46							18 13						
Amberley	d													18 18						
Pulborough	d						17 55							18 24						
Billingshurst	d						18 01							18 30						
Christs Hospital	d						18 08							18 37						
Horsham 4	a						18 12	18 18						18 42	18 48					
	d						18 22	<						18 52	<					
Crawley	d						18 31							19 01						
Three Bridges 4	a						18 34							19 04						
Gatwick Airport 10	a						18 39		18 56					19 09		19 25				
	d						18 40		18 56					19 10		19 26				
Horley	a																			
Redhill 5	a						18 47							19 17						
East Croydon	a						18 59		19 12					19 28		19 42				
London Bridge 4 ⊖	a																			
Clapham Junction 10	a						19 11		19 21					19 40		19 52				
London Victoria 15 ⊖	a						19 18		19 29					19 47		19 59				

Table 188

Mondays to Fridays

Southampton, Portsmouth and Sussex Coast - Brighton, Gatwick Airport & London

		SN ■	SN ◇■	SN	SN ■	SN ■	SN ■	SN ■	SN ■	SN ◇■	SN ◇■	SN	SN ■	SN ■	SN ◇■	SN	SN ■	SN ■	SN ■
Southampton Central	d									18 11				18 33					
Swanwick	d									18 28				18 50					
Fareham	d									18 35				18 56					
Portchester	d									18 40									
Cosham	d									18 44				19 05					
Portsmouth Harbour	d							18 28					18 37						
Portsmouth & Southsea	d	17 56						18 32					18 42				18 56	19 32	
Fratton	d	18 01						18 36					18 46				19 01	19 36	
Hilsea	d	18 05											18 50				19 05		
Bedhampton	d	18 13															19 13		
Havant	d	18 16						18 44		18 51			18 56	19 11			19 16	19 46	
Warblington	d	18 18											18 58				19 18		
Emsworth	d	18 21						18 48		18 55			19 01				19 21	19 50	
Southbourne	d	18 24						18 51		18 58			19 04				19 24	19 53	
Nutbourne	d	18 26											19 07				19 26		
Bosham	d	18 30											19 10				19 30		
Fishbourne (Sussex)	d	18 33											19 13				19 33		
Chichester 4	a	18 36						18 58		19 05			19 17	19 22			19 36	20 00	
	d	18 37						18 59		19 06			19 17	19 22			19 40	20 01	
Bognor Regis 4	d		18 33				18 46		19 03						19 36				
Barnham	a	18 44	18 39				18 52	19 06	19 09	19 13			19 25	19 30	19 42		19 47	20 08	
	d	18 45	18 40			18 55	18 53	19 07	19 10	19 14			19 25	19 30	19 43		19 48	20 09	
Bognor Regis	a					19 01													
Ford 4	d		18 44				18 57		19 14	19 18			19 30		19 47		19 52		
Littlehampton 4	a						19 02		19 19				19 38				19 58		
	d				18 52						19 15								19 52
Angmering 3	d		18 53		19 00			19 16			19 23			19 40	19 53			20 18	20 00
Goring-by-Sea	d		18 57		19 04						19 27			19 44	19 57				20 04
Durrington-on-Sea	d		19 00		19 07						19 30			19 46	20 00				20 07
West Worthing	d		19 02		19 09						19 32			19 48	20 02				20 09
Worthing 4	a		19 04		19 11			19 23			19 34			19 51	20 04			20 25	20 11
	d		19 05		19 12			19 24			19 35			19 52	20 05			20 25	20 12
East Worthing	d				19 14			19 26						19 55				20 28	20 14
Lancing	d		19 09		19 17			19 29			19 39			19 58	20 09			20 31	20 17
Shoreham-by-Sea	d		19 13		19 22			19 33			19 43			20 02	20 13			20 35	20 22
Southwick	d				19 25			19 36						20 05				20 38	20 25
Fishersgate	d				19 27			19 38						20 07				20 40	20 27
Portslade	d		19 18		19 29			19 40			19 48			20 09	20 18			20 42	20 29
Aldrington	d				19 31			19 43						20 11				20 44	20 31
Hove 2	d		19 22	19 24	19 34			19 45			19 52	19 54		20 14	20 22	20 24		20 47	20 34
Brighton 10	a			19 28	19 38			19 49				19 58		20 18		20 28		20 51	20 38
Burgess Hill	a		19 32												20 32				
Haywards Heath 3	a		19 36								20 04				20 37				
Arundel	d	18 52								19 23									
Amberley	d									19 28									
Pulborough	d	19 01								19 34									
Billingshurst	d	19 08								19 41									
Christs Hospital	d									19 47									
Horsham 4	a	19 16								19 51									
	d	19 17								19 52									
Crawley	d	19 26								20 01									
Three Bridges 4	a	19 29								20 04					20 47				
Gatwick Airport 10	a	19 39	19 55							20 10	20 25				20 51				
	d	19 40	19 56							20 11	20 26				20 53				
Horley	a																		
Redhill 5	a	19 47								20 18									
East Croydon	a	20 00	20 11							20 30	20 41				21 09				
London Bridge 4 ⊖	a																		
Clapham Junction 10	a	20 11	20 20							20 40	20 50				21 19				
London Victoria 15 ⊖	a	20 20	20 28							20 50	20 58				21 27				

Southampton, Portsmouth and Sussex Coast - Brighton, Gatwick Airport & London

		SN 1	SN ◇1	SN ◇1	SN	SN 1	SN 1	SN ◇1	SN	SN 1	SN 1	SN 1	SN 1	SN ◇1	SN	SN ◇1	SN 1	SN 1	SN
Southampton Central	d		19 12				19 33									20 11		20 33	
Swanwick	d		19 29				19 51									20 28		20 50	
Fareham	d		19 36				19 57									20 35		20 57	
Portchester	d		19 41													20 40			
Cosham	d		19 46				20 06									20 44		21 06	
Portsmouth Harbour	d					19 40											20 40		
Portsmouth & Southsea	d					19 44					19 56	20 32					20 44		
Fratton	d					19 48					20 01	20 36					20 48		
Hilsea	d										20 05								
Bedhampton	d										20 14								
Havant	d		19 52			19 57	20 12				20 17	20 44				20 51	20 57	21 12	
Warblington	d					19 59					20 19						20 59		
Emsworth	d		19 56			20 02	20 16				20 22	20 48				20 55	21 02	21 16	
Southbourne	d		19 59			20 05					20 25	20 51				20 58	21 05		
Nutbourne	d					20 07					20 27						21 07		
Bosham	d					20 11					20 31						21 11		
Fishbourne (Sussex)	d					20 14					20 34						21 14		
Chichester 4	a		20 06			20 17	20 24				20 37	20 58				21 05	21 17	21 24	
	d		20 07			20 18	20 25				20 38	20 59				21 07	21 18	21 25	
Bognor Regis 4	d	20 04						20 33					21 04						
Barnham	a	20 10	20 14			20 25	20 32	20 39			20 45	21 06	21 10			21 14	21 25	21 32	
	d	20 11	20 15			20 27	20 33	20 40			20 46	21 07	21 11			21 15	21 26	21 33	
Bognor Regis	a																		
Ford 4	d	20 15	20 19			20 31		20 44			20 50		21 15			21 19	21 30	21 37	
Littlehampton 4	a	20 20				20 36					20 55		21 20				21 35		
	d			20 15						20 52				21 15					
Angmering 3	d			20 23			20 42	20 53		21 00		21 16		21 23				21 43	
Goring-by-Sea	d			20 27				20 57		21 04				21 27				21 47	
Durrington-on-Sea	d			20 30			20 48	21 00		21 07				21 30				21 50	
West Worthing	d			20 32				21 02		21 09				21 32				21 52	
Worthing 4	a			20 34			20 52	21 04		21 11		21 23		21 34				21 54	
	d			20 35			20 52	21 05		21 12		21 23		21 35				21 55	
East Worthing	d						20 55			21 14		21 26						21 57	
Lancing	d			20 39			20 58	21 09		21 17		21 29		21 39				22 00	
Shoreham-by-Sea	d			20 43			21 02	21 13		21 22		21 33		21 43				22 04	
Southwick	d						21 05			21 25		21 36						22 07	
Fishersgate	d						21 07			21 27		21 38						22 09	
Portslade	d			20 48			21 09	21 18		21 29		21 40		21 48				22 11	
Aldrington	d						21 11			21 31		21 42						22 14	
Hove 2	d			20 52	20 54		21 14	21 22	21 24	21 34		21 45		21 52	21 54			22 16	22 24
Brighton 10	a				20 58		21 18		21 28	21 38		21 49			21 58			22 21	22 28
Burgess Hill	a							21 32						22 02					
Haywards Heath 3	a			21 05				21 37						22 09					
Arundel	d		20 24													21 24			
Amberley	d		20 29													21 29			
Pulborough	d		20 35													21 35			
Billingshurst	d		20 41													21 41			
Christs Hospital	d		20 48													21 48			
Horsham 4	a		20 52													21 52			
	d		20 52													21 52			
Crawley	d		21 01													22 01			
Three Bridges 4	a		21 05					21 47								22 05			
Gatwick Airport 10	a		21 10	21 25				21 51								22 10			
	d		21 11	21 26				21 53								22 11			
Horley	a																		
Redhill 5	a		21 18													22 18			
East Croydon	a		21 30	21 41				22 09								22 30			
London Bridge 4 ⊖	a																		
Clapham Junction 10	a		21 40	21 51				22 19								22 40			
London Victoria 15 ⊖	a		21 48	21 58				22 27								22 50			

Southampton, Portsmouth and Sussex Coast - Brighton, Gatwick Airport & London

		SN 1	SN 1	SN 1	SN 1	SN	SN 1	SN 1	SN 1	SN 1	SN 1	SN ◇1	SN 1	SN	SN 1	SN ◇1	SN 1
Southampton Central	d							21 13				21 32				22 13	
Swanwick	d							21 33				21 51				22 30	
Fareham	d							21 40				21 58				22 37	
Portchester	d							21 45				22 03				22 42	
Cosham	d							21 49				22 07				22 47	
Portsmouth Harbour	d								21 40						22 15		
Portsmouth & Southsea	d				21 15				21 44						22 19		
Fratton	d				21 19				21 48						22 23		
Hilsea	d				21 23				21 52						22 27		
Bedhampton	d				21 28				21 57						22 32		
Havant	d				21 31			21 56	22 00			22 14			22 35	22 57	
Warblington	d				21 33							22 16					
Emsworth	d				21 36							22 19			22 39	23 01	
Southbourne	d				21 39							22 22			22 42	23 04	
Nutbourne	d				21 41							22 24					
Bosham	d				21 45							22 28					
Fishbourne (Sussex)	d				21 48							22 31					
Chichester 4	a				21 51			22 06	22 10			22 34			22 49	23 11	
	d				21 52			22 07	22 11			22 34	22 40		22 52	23 11	
Bognor Regis 4	d	21 39					22 00				22 30						23 15
Barnham	a	21 45			21 59		22 06	22 14	22 18		22 36	22 42	22 47		22 59	23 19	23 21
	d		21 52		22 00			22 15	22 19	22 22	22 37		22 48		23 00	23 19	
Bognor Regis	a		21 58							22 28							
Ford 4	d				22 04			22 19	22 23		22 41		22 52		23 04		
Littlehampton 4	a							22 24			22 46					23 31	
	d			21 52				22 33									
Angmering 3	d			22 00	22 11			22 41							23 11		
Goring-by-Sea	d			22 04	22 15			22 45							23 15		
Durrington-on-Sea	d			22 07	22 18			22 47							23 17		
West Worthing	d			22 09	22 20			22 49							23 19		
Worthing 4	a			22 11	22 22			22 52							23 22		
	d			22 12	22 23			22 52							23 22		
East Worthing	d			22 14	22 25			22 55							23 25		
Lancing	d			22 17	22 28			22 58							23 28		
Shoreham-by-Sea	d			22 22	22 32			23 02							23 32		
Southwick	d			22 25	22 35			23 05							23 35		
Fishersgate	d			22 27	22 37			23 07							23 37		
Portslade	d			22 29	22 39			23 09							23 39		
Aldrington	d			22 31	22 42			23 11							23 41		
Hove 2	d			22 34	22 44	22 54		23 14						23 24	23 44		
Brighton 10	a			22 38	22 48	22 58		23 18						23 28	23 48		
Burgess Hill	a																
Haywards Heath 3	a																
Arundel	d								22 28				22 57				
Amberley	d												23 02				
Pulborough	d								22 37				23 08				
Billingshurst	d								22 43				23 14				
Christs Hospital	d								22 50				23 21				
Horsham 4	a								22 54				23 25				
	d								22 55				23 25				
Crawley	d								23 03				23 38				
Three Bridges 4	a								23 07				23 42				
Gatwick Airport 10	a																
	d																
Horley	a																
Redhill 5	a																
East Croydon	a																
London Bridge 4 ⊖	a																
Clapham Junction 10	a																
London Victoria 15 ⊖	a																

Table 188

Mondays to Fridays

Southampton, Portsmouth and Sussex Coast - Brighton, Gatwick Airport & London

		SN ■	SN ■	SN ■	SN ■	SN ■	SN
Southampton Central	d		22 22				
Swanwick	d						
Fareham	d		23 00				
Portchester	d						
Cosham	d		23 08				
Portsmouth Harbour	d	22 44				23 15	
Portsmouth & Southsea	d	22 48				23 19	
Fratton	d	22 52				23 23	
Hilsea	d	22 56				23 27	
Bedhampton	d	23 01				23 33	
Havant	d	23 05	23 15			23 36	
Warblington	d					23 38	
Emsworth	d					23 41	
Southbourne	d					23 44	
Nutbourne	d					23 47	
Bosham	d					23 50	
Fishbourne (Sussex)	d					23 53	
Chichester	a	23 16	23 25			23 57	
	d	23 17	23 26		23 52	23 57	
Bognor Regis	d						
Barnham	a	23 24	23 33		23 59	00 05	
	d	23 25	23 34	23 36	00 01	00 06	
Bognor Regis	a			23 42			
Ford	d	23 29			00 05	00 10	
Littlehampton	a	23 34	23 42		00 10	00 15	
	d	23 39					
Angmering	d	23 47					
Goring-by-Sea	d	23 51					
Durrington-on-Sea	d	23 53					
West Worthing	d	23 55					
Worthing	a	23 58					
	d	23 59					
East Worthing	d	00 01					
Lancing	d	00 04					
Shoreham-by-Sea	d	00 08					
Southwick	d	00 11					
Fishersgate	d	00 13					
Portslade	d	00 15					
Aldrington	d	00 18					
Hove	d	00 20					23 54
Brighton	a	00 25					23 58
Burgess Hill	a						
Haywards Heath	a						
Arundel	d						
Amberley	d						
Pulborough	d						
Billingshurst	d						
Christs Hospital	d						
Horsham	a						
	d						
Crawley	d						
Three Bridges	a						
Gatwick Airport	a						
	d						
Horley	a						
Redhill	a						
East Croydon	a						
London Bridge ⊖	a						
Clapham Junction	a						
London Victoria ⊖	a						

Table 188

Saturdays

Southampton, Portsmouth and Sussex Coast - Brighton, Gatwick Airport & London

		SN ■	SN ■	SN ■	SN ■	SN ◇■	SN	SN ■	SN ■	SN ◇■	SN	SN ■	SN ◇■	SN ◇■	SN ■	SN ■	SN	SN ■	SN ■
Southampton Central	d																		
Swanwick	d																		
Fareham	d																		
Portchester	d																		
Cosham	d																		
Portsmouth Harbour	d	22p44		23p15															
Portsmouth & Southsea	d	22p48		23p19		04 56													
Fratton	d	22p52		23p23		05 00													
Hilsea	d	22p56		23p27															
Bedhampton	d	23p01		23p33															
Havant	d	23p05		23p36		05 08							05 52						
Warblington	d			23p38															
Emsworth	d			23p41									05 56						
Southbourne	d			23p44									05 59						
Nutbourne	d			23p47															
Bosham	d			23p50															
Fishbourne (Sussex)	d			23p53															
Chichester	a	23p16		23p57		05 19							06 06						
	d	23p17	23p52	23p57		05 19							06 06						06 25
Bognor Regis	d							05 13	06 04			05 43				06 13			
Barnham	a	23p24	23p59	00 05		05 27		05 19	06 10			05 49	06 14			06 19			06 32
	d	23p25	00 01	00 06	04 48	05 27		05 31				05 50	06 14		06 22	06 20			06 33
Bognor Regis	a														06 28				
Ford	d	23p29	00 05	00 10	04 52			05 35				05 54	06 19			06 24			06 37
Littlehampton	a	23p34	00 10	00 15	04 57			05 40								06 29			
	d	23p39			05 02					05 45				06 15					
Angmering	d	23p47			05 10					05 53		06 00		06 23					06 43
Goring-by-Sea	d	23p51			05 14					05 57		06 04		06 27					06 47
Durrington-on-Sea	d	23p53			05 17					06 00		06 07		06 30					06 50
West Worthing	d	23p55			05 19					06 02		06 09		06 32				06 39	06 52
Worthing	a	23p58			05 21	05 41				06 04		06 11		06 34				06 41	06 54
	d	23p59			05 22	05 42				06 05		06 12		06 35				06 42	06 56
East Worthing	d	00 01			05 24							06 14						06 44	
Lancing	d	00 04			05 27					06 09		06 17		06 39				06 47	07 00
Shoreham-by-Sea	d	00 08			05 32	05 48				06 13		06 22		06 43				06 52	07 04
Southwick	d	00 11			05 35							06 25						06 55	07 07
Fishersgate	d	00 13			05 37							06 27						06 57	
Portslade	d	00 15			05 39					06 17		06 29		06 47				06 59	07 10
Aldrington	d	00 18			05 41							06 31						07 01	
Hove	d	00 20			05 44	05 54	05 56			06 21	06 24	06 34		06 51			06 54	07 04	07 14
Brighton	a	00 25			05 48		06 00				06 28	06 38					06 58	07 08	07 18
Burgess Hill	a													07 01					
Haywards Heath	a					06 07				06 35				07 08					
Arundel	d												06 23						
Amberley	d												06 28						
Pulborough	d												06 34						
Billingshurst	d												06 41						
Christs Hospital	d												06 47						
Horsham	a												06 51						
	d												06 52						
Crawley	d												07 01						
Three Bridges	a					06 20							07 04						
Gatwick Airport	a					06 24							07 09	07 24					
	d					06 24							07 10	07 24					
Horley	a																		
Redhill	a												07 17						
East Croydon	a					06 40							07 29	07 40					
London Bridge ⊖	a																		
Clapham Junction	a					06 50							07 39	07 50					
London Victoria ⊖	a					06 57							07 46	07 57					

Table 188

Southampton, Portsmouth and Sussex Coast - Brighton, Gatwick Airport & London

		SN 1	SN ◇1	SN 1	SN 1	SN ◇1	SN ◇1	SN	SN 1	SN 1	SN 1	SN 1	SN ◇1	SN ◇1	SN ◇1	SN	SN 1	GW	SN 1
Southampton Central	d													06 13					06 33
Swanwick	d													06 33					06 50
Fareham	d													06 40					06 56
Portchester	d													06 45					
Cosham	d													06 49					07 05
Portsmouth Harbour	d					06 12					06 29							06 48	
Portsmouth & Southsea	d	05 59				06 16					06 33							06 54	
Fratton	d	06 04				06 20					06 37							06 58	
Hilsea	d	06 08																	
Bedhampton	d	06 13																	
Havant	d	06 16				06 30					06 46			06 56				07 08	07 11
Warblington	d	06 18																	
Emsworth	d	06 21									06 50			07 00					07 15
Southbourne	d	06 24									06 53			07 03					
Nutbourne	d	06 26																	
Bosham	d	06 30																	
Fishbourne (Sussex)	d	06 33																	
Chichester 4	a	06 36				06 40					07 00			07 10				07 19	07 23
	d	06 37				06 41					07 00			07 11				07 20	07 25
Bognor Regis 4	d		06 30	06 39								07 07	06 56						
Barnham	a	06 44	06 36	06 45		06 48					07 08	07 13	07 02	07 18				07 27	07 32
	d	06 45	06 37		06 52	06 49				07 05	07 08	07 15	07 03	07 19				07 28	07 33
Bognor Regis	a				06 58					07 11									
Ford 4	d	06 49	06 41									07 19	07 07						07 37
Littlehampton 4	a	06 54										07 24							
	d						06 45								07 15				
Angmering 3	d						06 55				07 17				07 23				07 43
Goring-by-Sea	d						06 59								07 27				07 47
Durrington-on-Sea	d						07 02								07 30				07 50
West Worthing	d						07 04		07 09						07 32		07 39		07 52
Worthing 4	a						07 06		07 11		07 24				07 34		07 41	07 45	07 54
	d						07 07		07 12		07 26				07 36		07 42	07 50	07 56
East Worthing	d								07 14								07 44		
Lancing	d						07 11		07 17		07 30						07 47		08 00
Shoreham-by-Sea	d						07 15		07 22		07 34				07 42		07 52	07 57	08 04
Southwick	d								07 25		07 37						07 55		08 07
Fishersgate	d								07 27								07 57		
Portslade	d								07 29		07 40				07 47		07 59		08 10
Aldrington	d								07 31								08 01		
Hove 2	d						07 22	07 24	07 34		07 44				07 51	07 54	08 04	08 08	08 14
Brighton 10	a							07 28	07 38		07 48					07 58	08 08	08 15	08 18
Burgess Hill	a														08 01				
Haywards Heath 3	a						07 35								08 09				
Arundel	d		06 46										07 12						
Amberley	d												07 17						
Pulborough	d		06 55										07 23						
Billingshurst	d		07 01										07 29						
Christs Hospital	d												07 36						
Horsham 4	a		07 10			07 16							07 40	07 46					
	d		07 20			<							07 50	<					
Crawley	d		07 29										07 59						
Three Bridges 4	a		07 32										08 02						
Gatwick Airport 10	a		07 37				07 54						08 07		08 24				
	d		07 38				07 55						08 08		08 24				
Horley	a		07 41																
Redhill 5	a		07 47										08 15						
East Croydon ⇌	a		07 59				08 10						08 27		08 40				
London Bridge 4 ⊖	a																		
Clapham Junction 10	a		08 09				08 20						08 37		08 50				
London Victoria 15 ⊖	a		08 16				08 27						08 44		08 57				

Table 188

Southampton, Portsmouth and Sussex Coast - Brighton, Gatwick Airport & London

		SN 1	SN 1	SN ◇1	SN ◇1	SN ◇1	SN 1	SN	SN 1	SN 1	SN 1	SN ◇1 🍴	SN ◇1	SN ◇1	SN	SN 1	SN 1	SN 1	SN 1	SN ◇1	SN ◇1	SN ◇1
Southampton Central	d												07 13				07 33					
Swanwick	d												07 33				07 50					
Fareham	d												07 40				07 56					
Portchester	d												07 45									
Cosham	d												07 49				08 05					
Portsmouth Harbour	d				07 12					07 29											08 12	
Portsmouth & Southsea	d	06 56			07 16					07 33								07 56			08 16	
Fratton	d	07 01			07 20					07 37								08 01			08 20	
Hilsea	d	07 05																08 05				
Bedhampton	d	07 13																08 13				
Havant	d	07 16			07 30					07 46			07 56				08 11	08 16			08 30	
Warblington	d	07 18																08 18				
Emsworth	d	07 21								07 50			08 00				08 15	08 21				
Southbourne	d	07 24								07 53			08 03					08 24				
Nutbourne	d	07 26																08 27				
Bosham	d	07 30																08 30				
Fishbourne (Sussex)	d	07 33																08 33				
Chichester 4	a	07 36			07 40					08 00			08 10				08 23	08 36			08 40	
	d	07 37			07 41					08 00			08 11				08 25	08 37			08 41	
Bognor Regis 4	d		07 39	07 30							08 07	07 56							08 39	08 30		
Barnham	a	07 44	07 45	07 36	07 48					08 08	08 13	08 02	08 18				08 32	08 44	08 45	08 36	08 48	
	d	07 45		07 37	07 49		07 52			08 08	08 15	08 03	08 19				08 33	08 45		08 37	08 49	
Bognor Regis	a						07 58															
Ford 4	d	07 49		07 41							08 19	08 07					08 37	08 49		08 41		
Littlehampton 4	a	07 54									08 24							08 54				
	d					07 45								08 15								08 45
Angmering 3	d					07 53				08 17				08 23			08 43					08 53
Goring-by-Sea	d					07 57								08 27			08 47					08 57
Durrington-on-Sea	d					08 00								08 30			08 50					09 00
West Worthing	d					08 02			08 09					08 32		08 39	08 52					09 02
Worthing 4	a					08 04			08 11	08 24				08 34		08 41	08 54					09 04
	d					08 06			08 12	08 26				08 36		08 42	08 56					09 06
East Worthing	d								08 14							08 44						
Lancing	d					08 10			08 17	08 30						08 47	09 00					09 10
Shoreham-by-Sea	d					08 14			08 22	08 34				08 42		08 52	09 04					09 14
Southwick	d								08 25	08 37						08 55	09 07					
Fishersgate	d								08 27							08 57						
Portslade	d								08 29	08 40				08 47		08 59	09 10					
Aldrington	d								08 31							09 01						
Hove 2	d					08 21		08 24	08 34	08 44				08 51	08 54	09 04	09 14					09 21
Brighton 10	a							08 28	08 38	08 48					08 58	09 08	09 18					
Burgess Hill	a													09 01								
Haywards Heath 3	a					08 35								09 09								09 35
Arundel	d			07 46								08 12								08 46		
Amberley	d											08 17										
Pulborough	d			07 55								08 23								08 55		
Billingshurst	d			08 01								08 29								09 01		
Christs Hospital	d											08 36										
Horsham 4	a			08 10	08 16							08 40	08 46							09 10	09 16	
	d			08 20	<							08 50	<							09 20	<	
Crawley	d			08 29								08 59								09 29		
Three Bridges 4	a			08 32								09 02								09 32		
Gatwick Airport 10	a			08 37		08 54						09 07		09 24						09 37		09 54
	d			08 38		08 55						09 08		09 24						09 38		09 55
Horley	a			08 41																09 41		
Redhill 5	a			08 47								09 15								09 47		
East Croydon ⇌	a			08 59		09 10						09 27		09 40						09 59		10 10
London Bridge 4 ⊖	a																					
Clapham Junction 10	a			09 09		09 20						09 37		09 50						10 09		10 20
London Victoria 15 ⊖	a			09 16		09 27						09 44		09 57						10 16		10 27

Southampton, Portsmouth and Sussex Coast - Brighton, Gatwick Airport & London

		SN 1	SN	SN 1	SN 1	SN 1	SN ◇1 (bus)	SN ◇1	SN ◇1	SN	SN 1	SN 1	SN 1	SN 1	SN ◇1	SN ◇1	SN ◇1
Southampton Central	d							08 13				08 33					
Swanwick	d							08 33				08 50					
Fareham	d							08 40				08 56					
Portchester	d							08 45									
Cosham	d							08 49				09 05					
Portsmouth Harbour	d				08 29											09 12	
Portsmouth & Southsea	d				08 33								08 56			09 16	
Fratton	d				08 37								09 01			09 20	
Hilsea	d												09 05				
Bedhampton	d												09 13				
Havant	d				08 46			08 56				09 11	09 16			09 30	
Warblington	d												09 18				
Emsworth	d				08 50			09 00				09 15	09 21				
Southbourne	d				08 53			09 03					09 24				
Nutbourne	d												09 26				
Bosham	d												09 30				
Fishbourne (Sussex)	d												09 33				
Chichester 4	a				09 00			09 10				09 23	09 36			09 40	
	d				09 00			09 11				09 25	09 37			09 41	
Bognor Regis 4	d					09 07	08 56							09 39	09 30		
Barnham	a				09 08	09 13	09 02	09 18				09 32	09 44	09 45	09 36	09 48	
	d	08 52			09 08	09 15	09 03	09 19				09 33	09 45		09 37	09 49	
Bognor Regis	a	08 58															
Ford 4	d					09 19	09 07					09 37	09 49		09 41		
Littlehampton 4	a					09 24							09 54				
	d								09 15								09 45
Angmering 3	d				09 17				09 23			09 43					09 53
Goring-by-Sea	d								09 27			09 47					09 57
Durrington-on-Sea	d								09 30			09 50					10 00
West Worthing	d			09 09					09 32		09 39	09 52					10 02
Worthing 4	a			09 11	09 24				09 34		09 41	09 54					10 04
	d			09 12	09 26				09 36		09 42	09 56					10 06
East Worthing	d			09 14							09 44						
Lancing	d			09 17	09 30						09 47	10 00					10 10
Shoreham-by-Sea	d			09 22	09 34				09 42		09 52	10 04					10 14
Southwick	d			09 25	09 37						09 55	10 07					
Fishersgate	d			09 27							09 57						
Portslade	d			09 29	09 40				09 47		09 59	10 10					
Aldrington	d			09 31							10 01						
Hove 2	d		09 24	09 34	09 44				09 51	09 54	10 04	10 14					10 21
Brighton 10	a		09 28	09 38	09 48					09 58	10 08	10 18					
Burgess Hill	a								10 01								
Haywards Heath 3	a								10 08								10 35
Arundel	d						09 12								09 46		
Amberley	d						09 17										
Pulborough	d						09 23								09 55		
Billingshurst	d						09 29								10 01		
Christs Hospital	d						09 36										
Horsham 4	a						09 40	09 46							10 10	10 16	
	d						09 50	<							10 20	<	
Crawley	d						09 59								10 29		
Three Bridges 4	a						10 02								10 32		
Gatwick Airport 10	a						10 07		10 25						10 37		10 54
	d						10 08		10 26						10 38		10 55
Horley	a														10 41		
Redhill 5	a						10 15								10 47		
East Croydon	a						10 27		10 42						10 59		11 10
London Bridge 4 ⊖	a																
Clapham Junction 10	a						10 37		10 51						11 09		11 20
London Victoria 15 ⊖	a						10 44		10 59						11 16		11 27

Southampton, Portsmouth and Sussex Coast - Brighton, Gatwick Airport & London

		SN 1	SN	SN 1	SN 1	SN 1	SN ◇1 (bus)	SN ◇1	SN ◇1	SN	SN 1	SN 1	SN 1	SN 1	SN ◇1	SN ◇1	SN ◇1	SN 1
Southampton Central	d							09 13			09 33							
Swanwick	d							09 33			09 50							
Fareham	d							09 40			09 56							
Portchester	d							09 45										
Cosham	d							09 49			10 05							
Portsmouth Harbour	d				09 29											10 12		
Portsmouth & Southsea	d				09 33								09 56			10 16		
Fratton	d				09 37								10 01			10 20		
Hilsea	d												10 05					
Bedhampton	d												10 13					
Havant	d				09 46			09 56			10 11		10 16			10 30		
Warblington	d												10 18					
Emsworth	d				09 50			10 00			10 15		10 21					
Southbourne	d				09 53			10 03					10 24					
Nutbourne	d												10 26					
Bosham	d												10 30					
Fishbourne (Sussex)	d												10 33					
Chichester 4	a				10 00			10 10			10 23		10 36			10 40		
	d				10 00			10 11			10 25		10 37			10 41		
Bognor Regis 4	d					10 07	09 56							10 39	10 30			
Barnham	a				10 08	10 13	10 02	10 18			10 32		10 44	10 45	10 36	10 48		
	d	09 52			10 08	10 15	10 03	10 19			10 33		10 45		10 37	10 49		10 52
Bognor Regis	a	09 58																10 58
Ford 4	d					10 19	10 07				10 37		10 49		10 41			
Littlehampton 4	a					10 24							10 54					
	d								10 15								10 45	
Angmering 3	d				10 17				10 23		10 43						10 53	
Goring-by-Sea	d								10 27		10 47						10 57	
Durrington-on-Sea	d								10 30		10 50						11 00	
West Worthing	d			10 09					10 32		10 52	10 39					11 02	
Worthing 4	a			10 11	10 24				10 34		10 54	10 41					11 04	
	d			10 12	10 26				10 36		10 56	10 42					11 06	
East Worthing	d			10 14								10 44						
Lancing	d			10 17	10 30						11 00	10 47					11 10	
Shoreham-by-Sea	d			10 22	10 34				10 42		11 04	10 52					11 14	
Southwick	d			10 25	10 37						11 07	10 55						
Fishersgate	d			10 27								10 57						
Portslade	d			10 29	10 40				10 47		11 10	10 59						
Aldrington	d			10 31								11 01						
Hove 2	d		10 24	10 34	10 44				10 51	10 54	11 14	11 04					11 21	
Brighton 10	a		10 28	10 38	10 48					10 58	11 18	11 08						
Burgess Hill	a								11 01									
Haywards Heath 3	a								11 09								11 35	
Arundel	d						10 12								10 46			
Amberley	d						10 17											
Pulborough	d						10 23								10 55			
Billingshurst	d						10 29								11 01			
Christs Hospital	d						10 36											
Horsham 4	a						10 40	10 46							11 10	11 16		
	d						10 50	<							11 20	<		
Crawley	d						10 59								11 29			
Three Bridges 4	a						11 02								11 32			
Gatwick Airport 10	a						11 07		11 24						11 37		11 54	
	d						11 08		11 24						11 38		11 55	
Horley	a														11 41			
Redhill 5	a						11 15								11 47			
East Croydon	a						11 27		11 40						11 59		12 10	
London Bridge 4 ⊖	a																	
Clapham Junction 10	a						11 37		11 50						12 09		12 20	
London Victoria 15 ⊖	a						11 44		11 57						12 16		12 27	

Table 188

Saturdays

Southampton, Portsmouth and Sussex Coast - Brighton, Gatwick Airport & London

Station		SN	SN ■	SN ■	SN ■	SN ◇■ ⌶	SN ◇■	SN ◇■	SN	SN ■	SN ■	SN ■	SN ◇■	SN ◇■	SN ◇■	SN ■	SN	SN ■	SN ■
Southampton Central	d						10 13				10 33								
Swanwick	d						10 33				10 50								
Fareham	d						10 40				10 56								
Portchester	d						10 45												
Cosham	d						10 49				11 05								
Portsmouth Harbour	d			10 29										11 12					
Portsmouth & Southsea	d			10 33								10 56		11 16					
Fratton	d			10 37								11 01		11 20					
Hilsea	d											11 05							
Bedhampton	d											11 13							
Havant	d			10 46			10 56				11 11	11 16		11 30					
Warblington	d											11 18							
Emsworth	d			10 50			11 00				11 15	11 21							
Southbourne	d			10 53			11 03					11 24							
Nutbourne	d											11 26							
Bosham	d											11 30							
Fishbourne (Sussex)	d											11 33							
Chichester ■	a			11 00			11 10				11 23	11 36		11 40					
	d			11 00			11 11				11 25	11 37		11 41					
Bognor Regis ■	d				11 07	10 56							11 30			11 39			
Barnham	a			11 08	11 13	11 02	11 18				11 32	11 44	11 36	11 48		11 45			
	d			11 08	11 15	11 03	11 19				11 33	11 45	11 37	11 49				11 52	
Bognor Regis	a																	11 58	
Ford ■	d				11 19	11 07					11 37	11 49	11 41						
Littlehampton ■	a				11 24							11 54							
	d							11 15							11 45				
Angmering ■	d			11 17				11 23			11 43				11 53				
Goring-by-Sea	d							11 27			11 47				11 57				
Durrington-on-Sea	d							11 30			11 50				12 00				
West Worthing	d		11 09					11 32		11 39	11 52				12 02				12 09
Worthing ■	a		11 11	11 24				11 34		11 41	11 54				12 04				12 11
	d		11 12	11 26				11 36		11 42	11 56				12 06				12 12
East Worthing	d		11 14							11 44									12 14
Lancing	d		11 17	11 30						11 47	12 00				12 10				12 17
Shoreham-by-Sea	d		11 22	11 34				11 42		11 52	12 04				12 14				12 22
Southwick	d		11 25	11 37						11 55	12 07								12 25
Fishersgate	d		11 27							11 57									12 27
Portslade	d		11 29	11 40				11 47		11 59	12 10								12 29
Aldrington	d		11 31							12 01									12 31
Hove ■	d	11 24	11 34	11 44				11 51	11 54	12 04	12 14				12 21		12 24		12 34
Brighton ■	a	11 28	11 38	11 48					11 58	12 08	12 18						12 28		12 38
Burgess Hill	a							12 01											
Haywards Heath ■	a							12 09							12 35				
Arundel	d					11 12							11 46						
Amberley	d					11 17													
Pulborough	d					11 23							11 55						
Billingshurst	d					11 29							12 01						
Christs Hospital	d					11 36													
Horsham ■	a					11 40	11 46						12 10	12 16					
	d					11 50	<						12 20	<					
Crawley	d					11 59							12 29						
Three Bridges ■	a					12 02							12 32						
Gatwick Airport ■	a					12 07		12 24					12 37		12 54				
	d					12 08		12 24					12 38		12 55				
Horley	a												12 41						
Redhill ■	a					12 15							12 47						
East Croydon	a					12 27		12 40					12 59		13 10				
London Bridge ■ ⊖	a																		
Clapham Junction ■	a					12 37		12 50					13 09		13 20				
London Victoria ■ ⊖	a					12 44		12 57					13 16		13 27				

Table 188

Saturdays

Southampton, Portsmouth and Sussex Coast - Brighton, Gatwick Airport & London

Station		SN ■	SN ■	SN ◇■ ⌶	SN ◇■	SN ◇■	SN	SN ■	SN ■	SN ■	SN ■	SN ◇■	SN ◇■	SN ◇■	SN	SN ■	SN ■	SN ■	SN ■	SN ◇■ ⌶	SN ◇■	SN ◇■
Southampton Central	d				11 13				11 33												12 13	
Swanwick	d				11 33				11 50												12 33	
Fareham	d				11 40				11 56												12 40	
Portchester	d				11 45																12 45	
Cosham	d				11 49				12 05												12 49	
Portsmouth Harbour	d	11 29											12 12					12 29				
Portsmouth & Southsea	d	11 33								11 56			12 16					12 33				
Fratton	d	11 37								12 01			12 20					12 37				
Hilsea	d									12 05												
Bedhampton	d									12 13												
Havant	d	11 46			11 56				12 11	12 16			12 30					12 46			12 56	
Warblington	d									12 18												
Emsworth	d	11 50			12 00				12 15	12 21								12 50			13 00	
Southbourne	d	11 53			12 03					12 24								12 53			13 03	
Nutbourne	d									12 26												
Bosham	d									12 30												
Fishbourne (Sussex)	d									12 33												
Chichester ■	a	12 00			12 10				12 23	12 36			12 40					13 00			13 10	
	d	12 00			12 11				12 25	12 37			12 41					13 00			13 11	
Bognor Regis ■	d		12 07	11 56							12 39	12 30							13 07	12 56		
Barnham	a	12 08	12 13	12 02	12 18				12 32	12 44	12 45	12 36	12 48					13 08	13 13	13 02	13 18	
	d	12 08	12 15	12 03	12 19				12 33	12 45		12 37	12 49			12 52		13 08	13 15	13 03	13 19	
Bognor Regis	a															12 58						
Ford ■	d		12 19	12 07					12 37	12 49		12 41							13 19	13 07		
Littlehampton ■	a		12 24							12 54									13 24			
	d					12 15								12 45								13 15
Angmering ■	d	12 17				12 23			12 43					12 53				13 17				13 23
Goring-by-Sea	d					12 27			12 47					12 57								13 27
Durrington-on-Sea	d					12 30			12 50					13 00								13 30
West Worthing	d					12 32		12 39	12 52					13 02			13 09					13 32
Worthing ■	a	12 24				12 34		12 41	12 54					13 04			13 11	13 24				13 34
	d	12 26				12 36		12 42	12 56					13 06			13 12	13 26				13 36
East Worthing	d							12 44									13 14					
Lancing	d	12 30						12 47	13 00					13 10			13 17	13 30				
Shoreham-by-Sea	d	12 34				12 42		12 52	13 04					13 14			13 22	13 34				13 42
Southwick	d	12 37						12 55	13 07								13 25	13 37				
Fishersgate	d							12 57									13 27					
Portslade	d	12 40				12 47		12 59	13 10								13 29	13 40				13 47
Aldrington	d							13 01									13 31					
Hove ■	d	12 44				12 51	12 54	13 04	13 14					13 21	13 24		13 34	13 44				13 51
Brighton ■	a	12 48					12 58	13 08	13 18						13 28		13 38	13 48				
Burgess Hill	a					13 01																14 01
Haywards Heath ■	a					13 09								13 35								14 09
Arundel	d			12 12								12 46								13 12		
Amberley	d			12 17																13 17		
Pulborough	d			12 23								12 55								13 23		
Billingshurst	d			12 29								13 01								13 29		
Christs Hospital	d			12 36																13 36		
Horsham ■	a			12 40	12 46							13 10	13 16							13 40	13 46	
	d			12 50	<							13 20	<							13 50	<	
Crawley	d			12 59								13 29								13 59		
Three Bridges ■	a			13 02								13 32								14 02		
Gatwick Airport ■	a			13 07		13 24						13 37		13 54						14 07		14 24
	d			13 08		13 24						13 38		13 55						14 08		14 24
Horley	a											13 41										
Redhill ■	a			13 15								13 47								14 15		
East Croydon	a			13 27		13 40						13 59		14 10						14 27		14 40
London Bridge ■ ⊖	a																					
Clapham Junction ■	a			13 37		13 50						14 09		14 20						14 37		14 50
London Victoria ■ ⊖	a			13 44		13 57						14 16		14 27						14 44		14 57

Table 188

Southampton, Portsmouth and Sussex Coast - Brighton, Gatwick Airport & London

		SN	SN 1	SN 1	SN 1	SN 1	SN ◇1	SN ◇1	SN ◇1	SN	SN 1	SN 1	SN 1	SN 1	SN 1	SN ◇1	SN ◇1	SN ◇1
Southampton Central	d			12 33													13 13	
Swanwick	d			12 50													13 33	
Fareham	d			12 56													13 40	
Portchester	d																13 45	
Cosham	d			13 05													13 49	
Portsmouth Harbour	d							13 12						13 29				
Portsmouth & Southsea	d				12 56			13 16						13 33				
Fratton	d				13 01			13 20						13 37				
Hilsea	d				13 05													
Bedhampton	d				13 13													
Havant	d			13 11	13 16			13 30						13 46			13 56	
Warblington	d				13 18													
Emsworth	d			13 15	13 21									13 50			14 00	
Southbourne	d				13 24									13 53			14 03	
Nutbourne	d				13 26													
Bosham	d				13 30													
Fishbourne (Sussex)	d				13 33													
Chichester 4	a			13 23	13 36			13 40						14 00			14 10	
	d			13 25	13 37			13 41						14 00			14 11	
Bognor Regis 4	d					13 39	13 30								14 07	13 56		
Barnham	a			13 32	13 44	13 45	13 36	13 48						14 08	14 13	14 02	14 18	
	d			13 33	13 45		13 37	13 49			13 52			14 08	14 15	14 03	14 19	
Bognor Regis	a										13 58							
Ford 4	d			13 37	13 49		13 41								14 19	14 07		
Littlehampton 4	a				13 54										14 24			
	d								13 45									14 15
Angmering 3	d			13 43					13 53					14 17				14 23
Goring-by-Sea	d			13 47					13 57									14 27
Durrington-on-Sea	d			13 50					14 00									14 30
West Worthing	d		13 39	13 52					14 02			14 09						14 32
Worthing 4	a		13 41	13 54					14 04			14 11		14 24				14 34
	d		13 42	13 56					14 06			14 12		14 26				14 36
East Worthing	d		13 44									14 14						
Lancing	d		13 47	14 00					14 10			14 17		14 30				
Shoreham-by-Sea	d		13 52	14 04					14 14			14 22		14 34				14 42
Southwick	d		13 55	14 07								14 25		14 37				
Fishersgate	d		13 57									14 27						
Portslade	d		13 59	14 10								14 29		14 40				14 47
Aldrington	d		14 01									14 31						
Hove 2	d	13 54	14 04	14 14					14 21	14 24		14 34		14 44				14 51
Brighton 10	a	13 58	14 08	14 18						14 28		14 38		14 48				
Burgess Hill	a																	15 01
Haywards Heath 5	a								14 35									15 09
Arundel	d						13 46									14 12		
Amberley	d															14 17		
Pulborough	d						13 55									14 23		
Billingshurst	d						14 01									14 29		
Christs Hospital	d															14 36		
Horsham 4	a						14 10	14 16								14 40	14 46	
	d						14 20	<					14 30			14 50	<	
Crawley	d						14 29						14 43			14 59		
Three Bridges 4	a						14 32						14 46			15 02		
Gatwick Airport 10	a						14 37		14 54				14 52			15 07		15 24
	d						14 38		14 55				14 53			15 08		15 24
Horley	a						14 41						14 56					
Redhill 5	a						14 47						15 02			15 15		
East Croydon	a						14 59		15 10				15 24			15 27		15 40
London Bridge 4 ⊖	a												15 43					
Clapham Junction 10	a						15 09		15 20							15 37		15 50
London Victoria 15 ⊖	a						15 16		15 27							15 44		15 57

Table 188

Southampton, Portsmouth and Sussex Coast - Brighton, Gatwick Airport & London

		SN	SN 1	SN 1	SN 1	SN 1	SN ◇1	SN ◇1	SN ◇1	SN 1	SN	SN 1	SN 1	SN 1	SN 1	SN ◇1	SN ◇1	SN ◇1	SN	SN 1	GW ◇	SN 1
Southampton Central	d			13 33													14 13				14 34	14 27
Swanwick	d			13 50													14 33					
Fareham	d			13 56													14 40				14 55	15 00
Portchester	d																14 45					
Cosham	d			14 05													14 49				15 03	
Portsmouth Harbour	d							14 12						14 29								
Portsmouth & Southsea	d				13 56			14 16						14 33								
Fratton	d				14 01			14 20						14 37								
Hilsea	d				14 05																	
Bedhampton	d				14 13																	
Havant	d			14 11	14 16			14 30						14 46			14 56				15 10	15 14
Warblington	d				14 18																	
Emsworth	d			14 15	14 21									14 50			15 00					
Southbourne	d				14 24									14 53			15 03					
Nutbourne	d				14 26																	
Bosham	d				14 30																	
Fishbourne (Sussex)	d				14 33																	
Chichester 4	a			14 23	14 36			14 40						15 00			15 10				15 21	15 25
	d			14 25	14 37			14 41						15 00			15 11				15 21	15 25
Bognor Regis 4	d					14 39	14 30								15 07	14 56						
Barnham	a			14 32	14 44	14 45	14 36	14 48						15 08	15 13	15 02	15 18				15 29	15 33
	d			14 33	14 45		14 37	14 49		14 52				15 08	15 15	15 03	15 19				15 29	15 33
Bognor Regis	a									14 58												
Ford 4	d			14 37	14 49		14 41								15 19	15 07						15 38
Littlehampton 4	a				14 54										15 24							
	d								14 45									15 15				
Angmering 3	d			14 43					14 53					15 17				15 23				15 44
Goring-by-Sea	d			14 47					14 57									15 27				15 48
Durrington-on-Sea	d			14 50					15 00									15 30				15 50
West Worthing	d		14 39	14 52					15 02			15 09						15 32		15 39		15 52
Worthing 4	a		14 41	14 54					15 04			15 11		15 24				15 34		15 41	15 44	15 55
	d		14 42	14 56					15 06			15 12		15 26				15 36		15 42	15 48	15 56
East Worthing	d		14 44									15 14								15 44		
Lancing	d		14 47	15 00					15 10			15 17		15 30						15 47		16 00
Shoreham-by-Sea	d		14 52	15 04					15 14			15 22		15 34				15 42		15 52	15 56	16 04
Southwick	d		14 55	15 07								15 25		15 37						15 55		16 07
Fishersgate	d		14 57									15 27								15 57		
Portslade	d		14 59	15 10								15 29		15 40				15 47		15 59		16 10
Aldrington	d		15 01									15 31								16 01		
Hove 2	d	14 54	15 04	15 14					15 21		15 24	15 34		15 44				15 51	15 54	16 04	16 08	16 14
Brighton 10	a	14 58	15 08	15 18							15 28	15 38		15 48					15 58	16 08	16 14	16 18
Burgess Hill	a																	16 01				
Haywards Heath 5	a								15 35									16 09				
Arundel	d						14 46									15 12						
Amberley	d															15 17						
Pulborough	d						14 55									15 23						
Billingshurst	d						15 01									15 29						
Christs Hospital	d															15 36						
Horsham 4	a						15 10	15 16								15 40	15 46					
	d						15 20	<					15 30			15 50	<					
Crawley	d						15 29						15 43			15 59						
Three Bridges 4	a						15 32						15 46			16 02						
Gatwick Airport 10	a						15 37		15 54				15 52			16 07		16 24				
	d						15 38		15 55				15 53			16 08		16 24				
Horley	a						15 41						15 56									
Redhill 5	a						15 47						16 02			16 15						
East Croydon	a						15 59		16 10				16 24			16 27		16 40				
London Bridge 4 ⊖	a												16 43									
Clapham Junction 10	a						16 09		16 20							16 37		16 50				
London Victoria 15 ⊖	a						16 16		16 27							16 44		16 57				

Table 188

Southampton, Portsmouth and Sussex Coast - Brighton, Gatwick Airport & London

		SN 1	SN 1	SN ◇1	SN ◇1	SN ◇1	SN 1	SN	SN 1	SN 1	SN 1	SN ◇1 ⊥	SN ◇1	SN ◇1	SN	SN 1	SN 1
Southampton Central	d												15 13				15 33
Swanwick	d												15 33				15 50
Fareham	d												15 40				15 56
Portchester	d												15 45				
Cosham	d												15 49				16 05
Portsmouth Harbour	d				15 12					15 29							
Portsmouth & Southsea	d		14 56		15 16					15 33							
Fratton	d		15 01		15 20					15 37							
Hilsea	d		15 05														
Bedhampton	d		15 14														
Havant	d		15 17		15 30					15 46			15 56				16 11
Warblington	d		15 19														
Emsworth	d		15 22							15 50			16 00				16 15
Southbourne	d		15 25							15 53			16 03				
Nutbourne	d		15 28														
Bosham	d		15 31														
Fishbourne (Sussex)	d		15 34														
Chichester 4	a		15 37		15 41					16 00			16 10				16 23
	d		15 38		15 42					16 00			16 11				16 25
Bognor Regis 4	d	15 39		15 30							16 07	15 56					
Barnham	a	15 45	15 45	15 36	15 49					16 08	16 13	16 02	16 18				16 32
	d		15 46	15 37	15 50		15 52			16 08	16 15	16 03	16 19				16 33
Bognor Regis	a				<		15 58										
Ford 4	d		15 50	15 41							16 19	16 07					16 37
Littlehampton 4	a		15 55								16 24						
	d					15 45								16 15			
Angmering 3	d					15 53				16 17				16 23			16 43
Goring-by-Sea	d					15 57								16 27			16 47
Durrington-on-Sea	d					16 00								16 30			16 50
West Worthing	d					16 02			16 09					16 32		16 39	16 52
Worthing 4	a					16 04			16 11	16 24				16 34		16 41	16 54
	d					16 06			16 12	16 26				16 36		16 42	16 56
East Worthing	d								16 14							16 44	
Lancing	d					16 10			16 17	16 30						16 47	17 00
Shoreham-by-Sea	d					16 14			16 22	16 34				16 42		16 52	17 04
Southwick	d								16 25	16 37						16 55	17 07
Fishersgate	d								16 27							16 57	
Portslade	d								16 29	16 40				16 47		16 59	17 10
Aldrington	d								16 31							17 01	
Hove 2	d					16 21		16 24	16 34	16 44				16 51	16 54	17 04	17 14
Brighton 10	a							16 28	16 38	16 48					16 58	17 08	17 18
Burgess Hill	a													17 01			
Haywards Heath 3	a					16 35								17 09			
Arundel	d			15 46								16 12					
Amberley	d											16 17					
Pulborough	d			15 55								16 23					
Billingshurst	d			16 01								16 29					
Christs Hospital	d											16 36					
Horsham 4	a			16 10	16 16							16 40	16 46				
	d			16 20	<							16 50	<				
Crawley	d			16 29								16 59					
Three Bridges 4	a			16 32								17 02					
Gatwick Airport 10	a			16 37		16 54						17 07		17 24			
	d			16 38		16 55						17 08		17 24			
Horley	a			16 41													
Redhill 5	a			16 47								17 15					
East Croydon	a			16 59		17 10						17 27		17 40			
London Bridge 4 ⊖	a																
Clapham Junction 10	a			17 09		17 20						17 37		17 50			
London Victoria 15 ⊖	a			17 16		17 28						17 44		17 57			

Table 188

Southampton, Portsmouth and Sussex Coast - Brighton, Gatwick Airport & London

		SN 1	SN 1	SN ◇1	SN ◇1	SN ◇1	SN 1	SN	SN 1	SN 1	SN 1	SN ◇1 ⊥	SN ◇1	SN ◇1	SN	SN 1	SN 1	SN 1
Southampton Central	d												16 13				16 33	
Swanwick	d												16 33				16 50	
Fareham	d												16 40				16 56	
Portchester	d												16 45					
Cosham	d												16 49				17 05	
Portsmouth Harbour	d				16 12					16 29								
Portsmouth & Southsea	d	15 56			16 16					16 33								16 56
Fratton	d	16 01			16 20					16 37								17 01
Hilsea	d	16 05																17 05
Bedhampton	d	16 13																17 13
Havant	d	16 16			16 30					16 46			16 56				17 11	17 16
Warblington	d	16 18																17 18
Emsworth	d	16 21								16 50			17 00				17 15	17 21
Southbourne	d	16 24								16 53			17 03					17 24
Nutbourne	d	16 26																17 26
Bosham	d	16 30																17 30
Fishbourne (Sussex)	d	16 33																17 33
Chichester 4	a	16 36			16 40					17 00			17 10				17 23	17 36
	d	16 37			16 41					17 00			17 11				17 25	17 37
Bognor Regis 4	d		16 39	16 30							17 07	16 56						
Barnham	a	16 44	16 45	16 36	16 48					17 08	17 13	17 02	17 18				17 32	17 44
	d	16 45		16 37	16 49		16 52			17 08	17 15	17 03	17 19				17 33	17 45
Bognor Regis	a						16 58											
Ford 4	d	16 49		16 41							17 19	17 07					17 37	17 49
Littlehampton 4	a	16 54									17 24							17 54
	d					16 45								17 15				
Angmering 3	d					16 53				17 17				17 23			17 43	
Goring-by-Sea	d					16 57								17 27			17 47	
Durrington-on-Sea	d					17 00								17 30			17 50	
West Worthing	d					17 02			17 09					17 32		17 39	17 52	
Worthing 4	a					17 04			17 11	17 24				17 34		17 41	17 54	
	d					17 06			17 12	17 26				17 36		17 42	17 56	
East Worthing	d								17 14							17 44		
Lancing	d					17 10			17 17	17 30						17 47	18 00	
Shoreham-by-Sea	d					17 14			17 22	17 34				17 42		17 52	18 04	
Southwick	d								17 25	17 37						17 55	18 07	
Fishersgate	d								17 27							17 57		
Portslade	d								17 29	17 40				17 47		17 59	18 10	
Aldrington	d								17 31							18 01		
Hove 2	d					17 21		17 24	17 34	17 44				17 51	17 54	18 04	18 14	
Brighton 10	a							17 28	17 38	17 48					17 58	18 08	18 18	
Burgess Hill	a													18 01				
Haywards Heath 3	a					17 35								18 09				
Arundel	d			16 46								17 12						
Amberley	d											17 17						
Pulborough	d			16 55								17 23						
Billingshurst	d			17 01								17 29						
Christs Hospital	d											17 36						
Horsham 4	a			17 10	17 16							17 40	17 46					
	d			17 20	<							17 50	<					
Crawley	d			17 29								17 59						
Three Bridges 4	a			17 32								18 02						
Gatwick Airport 10	a			17 37		17 54						18 07		18 24				
	d			17 38		17 55						18 08		18 24				
Horley	a			17 41														
Redhill 5	a			17 47								18 15						
East Croydon	a			17 59		18 10						18 27		18 40				
London Bridge 4 ⊖	a																	
Clapham Junction 10	a			18 09		18 20						18 37		18 50				
London Victoria 15 ⊖	a			18 16		18 27						18 44		18 57				

Table 188

Saturdays

Southampton, Portsmouth and Sussex Coast - Brighton, Gatwick Airport & London

Station		SN ■	SN ◇■	SN ◇■	SN ◇■	SN	SN ■	SN ■	SN ■	SN ■	SN ◇■	SN ◇■	SN ◇■	SN	SN ■	SN ■	SN ■	SN ■	SN ◇■	SN	SN ■	SN ■	SN ■
Southampton Central	d											17 13						17 33					
Swanwick	d											17 33						17 50					
Fareham	d											17 40						17 56					
Portchester	d											17 45											
Cosham	d											17 49						18 05					
Portsmouth Harbour	d			17 12					17 29														18 12
Portsmouth & Southsea	d			17 16					17 33							17 56							18 16
Fratton	d			17 20					17 37							18 01							18 20
Hilsea	d															18 05							
Bedhampton	d															18 13							
Havant	d			17 30					17 46			17 56				18 16		18 11					18 30
Warblington	d															18 18							
Emsworth	d								17 50			18 00				18 21		18 15					18 34
Southbourne	d								17 53			18 03				18 24							18 37
Nutbourne	d															18 26							
Bosham	d															18 30							
Fishbourne (Sussex)	d															18 33							
Chichester ■	a			17 40					18 00			18 10				18 36		18 23					18 44
	d			17 41					18 00			18 11				18 37		18 25					18 45
Bognor Regis ■	d		17 30							18 07	17 56						18 39		18 33				
Barnham	a		17 36	17 48					18 08	18 13	18 02	18 18				18 44	18 46	18 32	18 40				18 52
	d	17 39	17 37	17 49			17 52		18 08	18 15	18 03	18 19				18 45		18 33	18 41			18 52	18 53
Bognor Regis	a	17 45					17 58															18 58	
Ford ■	d		17 41							18 19	18 07					18 49		18 37	18 45				18 57
Littlehampton ■	a									18 24													19 02
	d				17 45								18 15								18 51		
Angmering ■	d				17 53				18 17				18 23					18 43	18 53		19 00		
Goring-by-Sea	d				17 57								18 27					18 47	18 57		19 04		
Durrington-on-Sea	d				18 00								18 30					18 50	19 00		19 07		
West Worthing	d				18 02			18 09					18 32		18 39			18 52	19 02		19 09		
Worthing ■	a				18 04			18 11	18 24				18 34		18 41			18 54	19 04		19 11		
	d				18 06			18 12	18 26				18 36		18 42			18 56	19 06		19 12		
East Worthing	d							18 14							18 44						19 14		
Lancing	d				18 10			18 17	18 30						18 47			19 00	19 10		19 17		
Shoreham-by-Sea	d				18 14			18 22	18 34				18 42		18 52			19 04	19 14		19 22		
Southwick	d							18 25	18 37						18 55			19 07			19 25		
Fishersgate	d							18 27							18 57						19 27		
Portslade	d							18 29	18 40				18 47		18 59			19 10			19 29		
Aldrington	d							18 31							19 01						19 31		
Hove ■	d				18 21	18 24		18 34	18 44				18 51	18 54	19 04			19 14	19 21	19 24	19 34		
Brighton ■	a					18 28		18 38	18 48					18 58	19 08			19 18		19 28	19 38		
Burgess Hill	a												19 01										
Haywards Heath ■	a				18 35								19 09						19 35				
Arundel	d		17 46								18 12					18 54							
Amberley	d										18 17					18 59							
Pulborough	d		17 55								18 23					19 05							
Billingshurst	d		18 01								18 29					19 11							
Christs Hospital	d										18 36												
Horsham ■	a		18 10	18 16							18 40	18 46				19 20							
	d		18 20	<							18 50	<				19 21							
Crawley	d		18 29								18 59					19 30							
Three Bridges ■	a		18 32								19 02					19 33							
Gatwick Airport ■	a		18 37		18 54						19 07		19 24			19 38			19 54				
	d		18 37		18 54						19 08		19 24			19 39			19 55				
Horley	a		18 41								19 11												
Redhill ■	a		18 47								19 17					19 47							
East Croydon ■	a		18 59		19 10						19 28		19 40			19 59			20 10				
London Bridge ■ ⊖	a																						
Clapham Junction ■	a		19 09		19 20						19 40		19 50			20 11			20 20				
London Victoria ■ ⊖	a		19 16		19 27						19 47		19 57			20 20			20 27				

Table 188

Saturdays

Southampton, Portsmouth and Sussex Coast - Brighton, Gatwick Airport & London

Station		SN ■		SN ■	SN ◇■	SN ◇■	SN	SN ■	SN ◇■	SN	SN ■	SN ■	SN ■		SN ■	SN ■	SN ■	SN ■	SN ◇■	SN ◇■
Southampton Central	d				18 11			18 33											19 11	
Swanwick	d				18 28			18 50											19 28	
Fareham	d				18 35			18 56											19 35	
Portchester	d				18 40														19 40	
Cosham	d				18 44			19 05											19 44	
Portsmouth Harbour	d	18 29														19 12	19 29			
Portsmouth & Southsea	d	18 33										18 56				19 16	19 33			
Fratton	d	18 37										19 01				19 20	19 37			
Hilsea	d											19 05								
Bedhampton	d											19 13								
Havant	d	18 46			18 51			19 11				19 16				19 30	19 46		19 52	
Warblington	d											19 18								
Emsworth	d	18 50			18 55			19 15				19 21				19 34			19 56	
Southbourne	d	18 53			18 58							19 24				19 37			19 59	
Nutbourne	d											19 26								
Bosham	d											19 30								
Fishbourne (Sussex)	d											19 33								
Chichester ■	a	19 00			19 05			19 23				19 36				19 44	19 57		20 06	
	d	19 00			19 07			19 25				19 37				19 45	19 59		20 07	
Bognor Regis ■	d			19 03					19 33				19 39					20 04		
Barnham	a	19 08		19 09	19 14			19 32	19 40			19 44	19 46			19 52	20 06	20 10	20 14	
	d	19 08		19 22	19 15			19 33	19 41			19 45			19 52	19 53	20 07	20 11	20 15	
Bognor Regis	a														19 58					
Ford ■	d			19 26	19 19			19 37	19 45			19 49				19 57		20 15	20 19	
Littlehampton ■	a			19 32								19 55				20 02		20 20		
	d					19 15					19 52									20 15
Angmering ■	d	19 17				19 23		19 43	19 53		20 00						20 16			20 23
Goring-by-Sea	d					19 27			19 57		20 04									20 27
Durrington-on-Sea	d					19 30		19 49	20 00		20 07									20 30
West Worthing	d					19 32			20 02		20 09									20 32
Worthing ■	a	19 24				19 34		19 53	20 04		20 11						20 23			20 34
	d	19 26				19 35		19 53	20 05		20 12						20 23			20 35
East Worthing	d							19 56			20 14						20 26			
Lancing	d	19 30				19 39		19 59	20 09		20 17						20 29			20 39
Shoreham-by-Sea	d	19 34				19 43		20 03	20 13		20 22						20 33			20 43
Southwick	d	19 37						20 06			20 25						20 36			
Fishersgate	d							20 08			20 27						20 38			
Portslade	d	19 40				19 48		20 10	20 17		20 29						20 40			20 48
Aldrington	d							20 12			20 31						20 42			
Hove ■	d	19 44				19 52	19 54	20 15	20 22	20 24	20 34						20 45			20 52
Brighton ■	a	19 48					19 58	20 19		20 28	20 38						20 49			
Burgess Hill	a					20 02														21 02
Haywards Heath ■	a					20 09			20 36											21 09
Arundel	d				19 24														20 24	
Amberley	d				19 29														20 29	
Pulborough	d				19 35														20 35	
Billingshurst	d				19 41														20 41	
Christs Hospital	d				19 48														20 48	
Horsham ■	a				19 52														20 52	
	d				19 52														20 52	
Crawley	d				20 01														21 01	
Three Bridges ■	a				20 05				20 47										21 05	
Gatwick Airport ■	a				20 10	20 24			20 52										21 10	21 24
	d				20 11	20 24			20 53										21 11	21 24
Horley	a																			
Redhill ■	a				20 18														21 18	
East Croydon ■	a				20 30	20 40			21 09										21 30	21 40
London Bridge ■ ⊖	a																			
Clapham Junction ■	a				20 40	20 50			21 20										21 40	21 50
London Victoria ■ ⊖	a				20 50	20 57			21 27										21 47	21 57

Southampton, Portsmouth and Sussex Coast - Brighton, Gatwick Airport & London

		SN	SN 1	SN ◇1	SN	SN 1	SN 1	SN 1	SN 1	SN 1	SN 1	SN ◇1	SN ◇1	SN 1	SN	SN 1	SN 1	SN 1	SN 1	SN	SN 1	SN 1
Southampton Central	d		19 33									20 11				20 33						
Swanwick	d		19 50									20 28				20 50						
Fareham	d		19 56									20 35				20 56						
Portchester	d											20 40										
Cosham	d		20 05									20 44				21 05						
Portsmouth Harbour	d									20 28				20 40								21 11
Portsmouth & Southsea	d						19 56			20 32				20 44								21 15
Fratton	d						20 01			20 36				20 48								21 19
Hilsea	d						20 05															21 23
Bedhampton	d						20 13															21 28
Havant	d		20 11				20 16			20 44		20 51		20 57		21 11						21 31
Warblington	d						20 18							20 59								21 33
Emsworth	d		20 15				20 21			20 48		20 55		21 02		21 15						21 36
Southbourne	d						20 24			20 51		20 58		21 05								21 39
Nutbourne	d						20 26							21 07								21 41
Bosham	d						20 30							21 11								21 45
Fishbourne (Sussex)	d						20 33							21 14								21 48
Chichester 4	a		20 23				20 36			20 58		21 05		21 17		21 23						21 51
	d		20 25				20 37			20 59		21 07		21 18		21 25						21 52
Bognor Regis 4	d			20 33				20 39			21 04						21 39		22 00			
Barnham	a		20 32	20 39			20 44	20 45		21 06	21 10	21 14		21 25		21 32	21 45		22 06			21 59
	d		20 33	20 40			20 45		20 52	21 07	21 11	21 15		21 26		21 33		21 52				22 00
Bognor Regis	a								20 58									21 58				
Ford 4	d			20 44			20 49				21 15	21 19		21 30		21 37						22 04
Littlehampton 4	a						20 55				21 20			21 35								
	d					20 52							21 15								21 52	
Angmering 3	d		20 42	20 53		21 00				21 16			21 23			21 43					22 00	22 11
Goring-by-Sea	d			20 57		21 04							21 27			21 47					22 04	22 15
Durrington-on-Sea	d		20 48	21 00		21 07							21 30			21 50					22 07	22 18
West Worthing	d			21 02		21 09							21 32			21 52					22 09	22 20
Worthing 4	a		20 52	21 04		21 11				21 23			21 34			21 54					22 11	22 22
	d		20 52	21 05		21 12				21 23			21 35			21 55					22 12	22 23
East Worthing	d		20 55			21 14				21 26						21 57					22 14	22 25
Lancing	d		20 58	21 09		21 17				21 29			21 39			22 00					22 17	22 28
Shoreham-by-Sea	d		21 02	21 13		21 22				21 33			21 43			22 04					22 22	22 32
Southwick	d		21 05			21 25				21 36						22 07					22 25	22 35
Fishersgate	d		21 07			21 27				21 38						22 09					22 27	22 37
Portslade	d		21 09	21 18		21 29				21 40			21 48			22 11					22 29	22 39
Aldrington	d		21 11			21 31				21 42						22 14					22 31	22 42
Hove 2	d	20 54	21 14	21 22	21 24	21 34				21 45			21 52		21 54	22 16				22 24	22 34	22 44
Brighton 10	a	20 58	21 18		21 28	21 38				21 49					21 58	22 21				22 28	22 38	22 48
Burgess Hill	a												22 02									
Haywards Heath 3	a			21 36									22 08									
Arundel	d											21 24										
Amberley	d											21 29										
Pulborough	d											21 35										
Billingshurst	d											21 41										
Christs Hospital	d											21 48										
Horsham 4	a											21 52										
	d											21 52										
Crawley	d											22 01										
Three Bridges 4	a			21 47								22 05										
Gatwick Airport 10	a			21 52								22 10	22 23									
	d			21 53								22 11	22 23									
Horley	a																					
Redhill 5	a											22 18										
East Croydon ⇌	a			22 09								22 30	22 40									
London Bridge 4 ⊖	a																					
Clapham Junction 10	a			22 20								22 40	22 49									
London Victoria 15 ⊖	a			22 28								22 50	22 58									

Southampton, Portsmouth and Sussex Coast - Brighton, Gatwick Airport & London

		SN 1	SN 1	SN 1	SN 1	SN 1	SN	SN 1	SN	SN 1	SN ◇1	SN 1	SN	SN 1	SN ◇1	SN 1
Southampton Central	d	21 13				21 23					22 13				22 33	
Swanwick	d	21 33				21 45					22 31				22 50	
Fareham	d	21 40				21 56					22 39				23 00	
Portchester	d	21 45				22 01					22 44					
Cosham	d	21 49				22 06					22 48				23 08	
Portsmouth Harbour	d		21 40							22 15				22 44		
Portsmouth & Southsea	d		21 44							22 19				22 48		
Fratton	d		21 48							22 23				22 52		
Hilsea	d		21 52							22 27				22 56		
Bedhampton	d		21 57							22 32				23 01		
Havant	d	21 56	22 00			22 12				22 35	22 55			23 05	23 15	
Warblington	d					22 14										
Emsworth	d					22 17				22 39	22 59					
Southbourne	d					22 20				22 42	23 02					
Nutbourne	d					22 23										
Bosham	d					22 26										
Fishbourne (Sussex)	d					22 29										
Chichester 4	a	22 06	22 10			22 33				22 49	23 09			23 16	23 25	
	d	22 07	22 11			22 33		22 40		22 52	23 09			23 18	23 26	
Bognor Regis 4	d				22 30							23 15				
Barnham	a	22 14	22 18		22 36	22 41		22 47		22 59	23 17	23 21		23 26	23 33	
	d	22 15	22 19	22 22	22 37			22 48		23 00	23 17			23 26	23 34	23 36
Bognor Regis	a			22 28												23 42
Ford 4	d	22 19	22 23		22 41			22 52		23 04				23 31		
Littlehampton 4	a	22 24			22 46						23 25			23 35	23 42	
	d	22 33												23 40		
Angmering 3	d	22 41								23 11				23 48		
Goring-by-Sea	d	22 45								23 15				23 52		
Durrington-on-Sea	d	22 47								23 17				23 54		
West Worthing	d	22 49								23 19				23 56		
Worthing 4	a	22 52								23 22				23 59		
	d	22 52								23 22				23 59		
East Worthing	d	22 55								23 25				00 02		
Lancing	d	22 58								23 28				00 05		
Shoreham-by-Sea	d	23 02								23 32				00 09		
Southwick	d	23 05								23 35				00 12		
Fishersgate	d	23 07								23 37				00 14		
Portslade	d	23 09								23 39				00 16		
Aldrington	d	23 11								23 41				00 18		
Hove 2	d	23 14					22 54		23 24	23 44			23 54	00 21		
Brighton 10	a	23 18					22 58		23 28	23 48			23 58	00 25		
Burgess Hill	a															
Haywards Heath 3	a															
Arundel	d		22 28					22 57								
Amberley	d							23 02								
Pulborough	d		22 37					23 08								
Billingshurst	d		22 43					23 14								
Christs Hospital	d		22 50					23 21								
Horsham 4	a		22 54					23 25								
	d		22 55					23 25								
Crawley	d		23 03					23 38								
Three Bridges 4	a		23 07					23 42								
Gatwick Airport 10	a															
	d															
Horley	a															
Redhill 5	a															
East Croydon ⇌	a															
London Bridge 4 ⊖	a															
Clapham Junction 10	a															
London Victoria 15 ⊖	a															

Table 188

Saturdays

Southampton, Portsmouth and Sussex Coast - Brighton, Gatwick Airport & London

Station		SN [1]	SN [1]
Southampton Central	d		
Swanwick	d		
Fareham	d		
Portchester	d		
Cosham	d		
Portsmouth Harbour	d		23 15
Portsmouth & Southsea	d		23 19
Fratton	d		23 23
Hilsea	d		23 27
Bedhampton	d		23 33
Havant	d		23 36
Warblington	d		23 38
Emsworth	d		23 41
Southbourne	d		23 44
Nutbourne	d		23 47
Bosham	d		23 50
Fishbourne (Sussex)	d		23 53
Chichester [4]	a		23 57
	d	23 52	23 57
Bognor Regis [4]	d		
Barnham	a	23 59	00 05
	d	00 01	00 06
Bognor Regis	a		
Ford [4]	d	00 05	00 10
Littlehampton [4]	a	00 10	00 15
	d		
Angmering [3]	d		
Goring-by-Sea	d		
Durrington-on-Sea	d		
West Worthing	d		
Worthing [4]	a		
	d		
East Worthing	d		
Lancing	d		
Shoreham-by-Sea	d		
Southwick	d		
Fishersgate	d		
Portslade	d		
Aldrington	d		
Hove [2]	d		
Brighton [10]	a		
Burgess Hill	a		
Haywards Heath [3]	a		
Arundel	d		
Amberley	d		
Pulborough	d		
Billingshurst	d		
Christs Hospital	d		
Horsham [4]	a		
	d		
Crawley	d		
Three Bridges [4]	a		
Gatwick Airport [10]	a		
	d		
Horley	a		
Redhill [5]	a		
East Croydon ⇌	a		
London Bridge [4] ⊖	a		
Clapham Junction [10]	a		
London Victoria [15] ⊖	a		

Table 188

Sundays
until 05 September

Southampton, Portsmouth and Sussex Coast - Brighton, Gatwick Airport & London

Station		SN [1]	SN [1]	SN [1]	SN [1]	SN ◇[1]	SN [1]	SN [1]	SN ◇[1]	SN ◇[1]	SN [1]	SN [1]	SN [1]	SN [1]	SN ◇[1]	SN ◇[1]	SN ◇[1]	SN [1]
Southampton Central	d																	
Swanwick	d																	
Fareham	d																	
Portchester	d																	
Cosham	d																	
Portsmouth Harbour	d	22p44			23p15									07 05			07 43	
Portsmouth & Southsea	d	22p48			23p19									07 09			07 47	
Fratton	d	22p52			23p23									07 13			07 51	
Hilsea	d	22p56			23p27													
Bedhampton	d	23p01			23p33									07 21				
Havant	d	23p05			23p36									07 27			08 00	
Warblington	d				23p38									07 29				
Emsworth	d				23p41									07 32			08 04	
Southbourne	d				23p44									07 35			08 07	
Nutbourne	d				23p47									07 38				
Bosham	d				23p50									07 41				
Fishbourne (Sussex)	d				23p53									07 44				
Chichester [4]	a	23p16			23p57									07 47			08 14	
	d	23p18		23p52	23p57	05 45								07 48			08 14	
Bognor Regis [4]	d								06 52			07 30			07 52			08 30
Barnham	a	23p26		23p59	00 05	05 52			06 58			07 36		07 55	07 58		08 22	08 36
	d	23p26		00 01	00 06	05 53	06 06	06 45	06 59			07 37		08 02	07 59		08 22	08 37
Bognor Regis	a							06 51										
Ford [4]	d	23p31		00 05	00 10				07 03			07 41		08 06	08 03			08 41
Littlehampton [4]	a	23p35		00 10	00 15		06 13					07 46						08 46
	d	23p40					06 20			07 14			07 38			08 14		
Angmering [3]	d	23p48								07 22			07 46	08 12		08 22		
Goring-by-Sea	d	23p52								07 26			07 50	08 16		08 26		
Durrington-on-Sea	d	23p54								07 29			07 52	08 19		08 29		
West Worthing	d	23p56								07 31			07 54	08 21		08 31		
Worthing [4]	a	23p59				06 07	06 33			07 33			07 57	08 23		08 33	08 37	
	d	23p59				06 08	06 33			07 35			07 57	08 24		08 41	<	
East Worthing	d	00 02											08 00	08 26				
Lancing	d	00 05				06 12	06 37			07 39			08 03	08 29				
Shoreham-by-Sea	d	00 09				06 16	06 41			07 43			08 07	08 33		08 47		
Southwick	d	00 12				06 19	06 44			07 46			08 10	08 36				
Fishersgate	d	00 14											08 12	08 38				
Portslade	d	00 16				06 23	06 48			07 49			08 14	08 40				
Aldrington	d	00 18											08 16	08 43				
Hove [2]	d	00 21				06 27	06 51			07 54	07 56		08 19	08 45		08 54		
Brighton [10]	a	00 25					06 55				08 00		08 23	08 49				
Burgess Hill	a									08 04						09 04		
Haywards Heath [3]	a					06 39				08 09						09 09		
Arundel	d								07 08						08 08			
Amberley	d								07 13						08 13			
Pulborough	d								07 19						08 19			
Billingshurst	d								07 26						08 26			
Christs Hospital	d								07 32						08 32			
Horsham [4]	a								07 37						08 37			
	d		23p02						07 37						08 37			
Crawley	d		23p14						07 46						08 46			
Three Bridges [4]	a		23p18						07 50						08 50			
Gatwick Airport [10]	a		23p22			06 52			07 55	08 22					08 55	09 22		
	d		23p23			06 53			07 56	08 23					08 56	09 23		
Horley	a		23p26						07 58						08 58			
Redhill [5]	a		23p36						08 05						09 05			
East Croydon ⇌	a		23p55			07 09			08 20	08 39					09 20	09 39		
London Bridge [4] ⊖	a																	
Clapham Junction [10]	a		00 11			07 18			08 31	08 48					09 31	09 48		
London Victoria [15] ⊖	a		00 18			07 25			08 39	08 55					09 39	09 55		

Table 188

Sundays
until 05 September

Southampton, Portsmouth and Sussex Coast - Brighton, Gatwick Airport & London

		SN ■	SN ■	SN ◇■	SN ■	SN ◇■	SN ◇■	GW	SN ■	SN ■	SN ■	SN ■	SN ■	SN ◇■ H	SN ◇■	SN ◇■	SN ■	SN ■	SN ■
Southampton Central	d							08 31											
Swanwick	d																		
Fareham	d							08 52											
Portchester	d																		
Cosham	d							09 00											
Portsmouth Harbour	d				08 05		08 43				09 05					09 43			10 05
Portsmouth & Southsea	d				08 09		08 47				09 09					09 47			10 09
Fratton	d				08 13		08 51				09 13					09 51			10 13
Hilsea	d																		
Bedhampton	d				08 20						09 20								10 20
Havant	d				08 27		09 00	09 11			09 27					10 00			10 27
Warblington	d				08 29						09 29								10 29
Emsworth	d				08 32		09 04				09 32					10 04			10 32
Southbourne	d				08 35		09 07				09 35					10 07			10 35
Nutbourne	d				08 38						09 38								10 38
Bosham	d				08 41						09 41								10 41
Fishbourne (Sussex)	d				08 44						09 44								10 44
Chichester ■	a				08 47		09 14	09 22			09 47					10 14			10 47
	d				08 48		09 14	09 22			09 48					10 14			10 48
Bognor Regis ■	d			08 52						09 30				09 52			10 30		
Barnham	a			08 58	08 55		09 22	09 30		09 36	09 55			09 58		10 22	10 36		10 55
	d			08 59	09 02		09 22	09 30		09 37	10 02			09 59		10 22	10 37		11 02
Bognor Regis	a																		
Ford ■	d			09 03	09 06					09 41	10 06			10 03			10 41		11 06
Littlehampton ■	a									09 46							10 46		
	d		08 38			09 14						09 38			10 14			10 38	
Angmering ■	d		08 46		09 12	09 22					10 12	09 46			10 22			10 46	11 12
Goring-by-Sea	d		08 50		09 16	09 26					10 16	09 50			10 26			10 50	11 16
Durrington-on-Sea	d		08 52		09 19	09 29					10 19	09 52			10 29			10 52	11 19
West Worthing	d		08 54		09 21	09 31					10 21	09 54			10 31			10 54	11 21
Worthing ■	a		08 57		09 23	09 33	09 37	09 45			10 23	09 57			10 33	10 37		10 57	11 23
	d		08 57		09 24	09 41	<	09 45			10 24	09 57			10 41	<		10 57	11 24
East Worthing	d		09 00		09 26						10 26	10 00						11 00	11 26
Lancing	d		09 03		09 29						10 29	10 03						11 03	11 29
Shoreham-by-Sea	d		09 07		09 33	09 47		09 52			10 33	10 07			10 47			11 07	11 33
Southwick	d		09 10		09 36						10 36	10 10						11 10	11 36
Fishersgate	d		09 12		09 38						10 38	10 12						11 12	11 38
Portslade	d		09 14		09 40						10 40	10 14						11 14	11 40
Aldrington	d		09 16		09 43						10 43	10 16						11 16	11 43
Hove ■	d	09 01	09 19		09 45	09 54		09 59	10 02		10 45	10 19			10 54			11 19	11 45
Brighton ■	a	09 05	09 23		09 49			10 05	10 06		10 49	10 23						11 23	11 49
Burgess Hill	a					10 04									11 04				
Haywards Heath ■	a					10 09									11 09				
Arundel	d			09 08										10 08					
Amberley	d			09 13										10 13					
Pulborough	d			09 19										10 19					
Billingshurst	d			09 26										10 26					
Christs Hospital	d			09 32										10 32					
Horsham ■	a			09 37										10 37					
	d			09 37									10 00	10 37					
Crawley	d			09 46									10 13	10 46					
Three Bridges ■	a			09 50									10 16	10 50					
Gatwick Airport ■	a			09 55		10 22							10 22	10 55	11 22				
	d			09 56		10 23							10 23	10 56	11 23				
Horley	a			09 58									10 26	10 58					
Redhill ■	a			10 05									10 36	11 05					
East Croydon	a			10 20		10 39							10 55	11 20	11 39				
London Bridge ■ ⊖	a																		
Clapham Junction ■	a			10 31		10 48							11 06	11 31	11 48				
London Victoria ■ ⊖	a			10 39		10 55							11 13	11 39	11 55				

Table 188

Sundays
until 05 September

Southampton, Portsmouth and Sussex Coast - Brighton, Gatwick Airport & London

		SN ■	SN ◇■ H	SN ◇■	SN ◇■	SN ■	SN ■	SN ■	SN ■	SN ◇■ H	SN ◇■	SN ◇■	SN ■	SN ■	SN ■	SN ■	SN ◇■ H
Southampton Central	d																
Swanwick	d																
Fareham	d																
Portchester	d																
Cosham	d																
Portsmouth Harbour	d				10 43				11 05			11 43				12 05	
Portsmouth & Southsea	d				10 47				11 09			11 47				12 09	
Fratton	d				10 51				11 13			11 51				12 13	
Hilsea	d																
Bedhampton	d								11 20							12 20	
Havant	d				11 00				11 27			12 00				12 27	
Warblington	d								11 29							12 29	
Emsworth	d				11 04				11 32			12 04				12 32	
Southbourne	d				11 07				11 35			12 07				12 35	
Nutbourne	d								11 38							12 38	
Bosham	d								11 41							12 41	
Fishbourne (Sussex)	d								11 44							12 44	
Chichester ■	a				11 14				11 47			12 14				12 47	
	d				11 14				11 48			12 14				12 48	
Bognor Regis ■	d		10 52					11 30		11 52			12 30				12 52
Barnham	a		10 58		11 22			11 36	11 55	11 58		12 22	12 36			12 55	12 58
	d		10 59		11 22			11 37	12 02	11 59		12 22	12 37			13 02	12 59
Bognor Regis	a																
Ford ■	d		11 03					11 41	12 06	12 03			12 41			13 06	13 03
Littlehampton ■	a							11 46					12 46				
	d			11 14			11 38				12 14				12 38		
Angmering ■	d			11 22			11 46		12 12		12 22				12 46	13 12	
Goring-by-Sea	d			11 26			11 50		12 16		12 26				12 50	13 16	
Durrington-on-Sea	d			11 29			11 52		12 19		12 29				12 52	13 19	
West Worthing	d			11 31			11 54		12 21		12 31				12 54	13 21	
Worthing ■	a			11 33	11 37		11 57		12 23		12 33	12 37			12 57	13 23	
	d			11 41	<		11 57		12 24		12 41	<			12 57	13 24	
East Worthing	d						12 00		12 26						13 00	13 26	
Lancing	d						12 03		12 29						13 03	13 29	
Shoreham-by-Sea	d			11 47			12 07		12 33		12 47				13 07	13 33	
Southwick	d						12 10		12 36						13 10	13 36	
Fishersgate	d						12 12		12 38						13 12	13 38	
Portslade	d						12 14		12 40						13 14	13 40	
Aldrington	d						12 16		12 43						13 16	13 43	
Hove ■	d	11 01		11 54		12 01	12 19		12 45		12 54			13 01	13 19	13 45	
Brighton ■	a	11 05				12 05	12 23		12 49					13 05	13 23	13 49	
Burgess Hill	a			12 04							13 04						
Haywards Heath ■	a			12 09							13 09						
Arundel	d		11 08							12 08							13 08
Amberley	d		11 13							12 13							13 13
Pulborough	d		11 19							12 19							13 19
Billingshurst	d		11 26							12 26							13 26
Christs Hospital	d		11 32							12 32							13 32
Horsham ■	a		11 37							12 37							13 37
	d		11 37							12 37							13 37
Crawley	d		11 46							12 46							13 46
Three Bridges ■	a		11 50							12 50							13 50
Gatwick Airport ■	a		11 55	12 22						12 55	13 22						13 55
	d		11 56	12 23						12 56	13 23						13 56
Horley	a		11 58							12 58							13 58
Redhill ■	a		12 05							13 05							14 05
East Croydon	a		12 20	12 39						13 20	13 39						14 20
London Bridge ■ ⊖	a																
Clapham Junction ■	a		12 31	12 48						13 31	13 48						14 31
London Victoria ■ ⊖	a		12 39	12 55						13 39	13 55						14 39

Table 188

Sundays
until 05 September

Southampton, Portsmouth and Sussex Coast - Brighton, Gatwick Airport & London

		SN ◇1	SN ◇1	SN 1	SN 1	SN 1	SN 1	SN ◇1 ⊼	SN ◇1	SN ◇1	GW ◇	SN 1	SN 1	SN 1	SN 1	SN ◇1 ⊼	SN ◇1	SN ◇1	SN 1
Southampton Central	d										13 08								
Swanwick	d																		
Fareham	d										13 34								
Portchester	d																		
Cosham	d										13 42								
Portsmouth Harbour	d		12 43				13 05			13 43					14 05			14 43	
Portsmouth & Southsea	d		12 47				13 09			13 47					14 09			14 47	
Fratton	d		12 51				13 13			13 51					14 13			14 51	
Hilsea	d																		
Bedhampton	d						13 20								14 20				
Havant	d		13 00				13 27			14 00	14 04				14 27			15 00	
Warblington	d						13 29								14 29				
Emsworth	d		13 04				13 32			14 04					14 32			15 04	
Southbourne	d		13 07				13 35			14 07					14 35			15 07	
Nutbourne	d						13 38								14 38				
Bosham	d						13 41								14 41				
Fishbourne (Sussex)	d						13 44								14 44				
Chichester 4	a		13 14				13 47			14 14	14 19				14 47			15 14	
	d		13 14				13 48			14 14	14 19				14 48			15 14	
Bognor Regis 4	d				13 30			13 52					14 30			14 52			15 30
Barnham	a		13 22		13 36		13 55	13 58		14 22	14 27		14 36		14 55	14 58		15 22	15 36
	d		13 22		13 37		14 02	13 59		14 22	14 27		14 37		15 02	14 59		15 22	15 37
Bognor Regis	a																		
Ford 4	d				13 41		14 06	14 03					14 41		15 06	15 03			15 41
Littlehampton 4	a				13 46								14 46						15 46
	d	13 14				13 38			14 14					14 38			15 14		
Angmering 3	d	13 22				13 46	14 12		14 22					14 46	15 12		15 22		
Goring-by-Sea	d	13 26				13 50	14 16		14 26					14 50	15 16		15 26		
Durrington-on-Sea	d	13 29				13 52	14 19		14 29					14 52	15 19		15 29		
West Worthing	d	13 31				13 54	14 21		14 31					14 54	15 21		15 31		
Worthing 4	a	13 33	13 37			13 57	14 23		14 33	14 37	14 44			14 57	15 23		15 33	15 37	
	d	13 41	<			13 57	14 24		14 41	<	14 45			14 57	15 24		15 41	<	
East Worthing	d					14 00	14 26							15 00	15 26				
Lancing	d					14 03	14 29							15 03	15 29				
Shoreham-by-Sea	d	13 47				14 07	14 33		14 47		14 51			15 07	15 33		15 47		
Southwick	d					14 10	14 36							15 10	15 36				
Fishersgate	d					14 12	14 38							15 12	15 38				
Portslade	d					14 14	14 40							15 14	15 40				
Aldrington	d					14 16	14 43							15 16	15 43				
Hove 2	d	13 54		14 01		14 19	14 45		14 54		15 00	15 01		15 19	15 45		15 54		
Brighton 10	a			14 05		14 23	14 49				15 06	15 05		15 23	15 49				
Burgess Hill	a	14 04							15 04								16 04		
Haywards Heath 3	a	14 09							15 09								16 09		
Arundel	d							14 08								15 08			
Amberley	d							14 13								15 13			
Pulborough	d							14 19								15 19			
Billingshurst	d							14 26								15 26			
Christs Hospital	d							14 32								15 32			
Horsham 4	a							14 37								15 37			
	d							14 37								15 37			
Crawley	d							14 46								15 46			
Three Bridges 4	a							14 50								15 50			
Gatwick Airport 10	a	14 22						14 55	15 22							15 55	16 22		
	d	14 23						14 56	15 23							15 56	16 23		
Horley	a							14 58								15 58			
Redhill 5	a							15 05								16 05			
East Croydon	a	14 39						15 20	15 39							16 20	16 39		
London Bridge 4 ⊖	a																		
Clapham Junction 10	a	14 48						15 31	15 48							16 31	16 48		
London Victoria 15 ⊖	a	14 55						15 39	15 55							16 39	16 55		

Table 188

Sundays
until 05 September

Southampton, Portsmouth and Sussex Coast - Brighton, Gatwick Airport & London

		SN 1	SN 1	SN 1	SN ◇1 ⊼	GW ◇	SN ◇1	SN ◇1	SN 1	SN 1	SN 1	SN 1	SN ◇1 ⊼	SN ◇1	SN ◇1	SN 1	SN 1
Southampton Central	d					15 22											
Swanwick	d																
Fareham	d					15 51											
Portchester	d																
Cosham	d					16 01											
Portsmouth Harbour	d			15 05				15 43				16 05			16 43		17 05
Portsmouth & Southsea	d			15 09				15 47				16 09			16 47		17 09
Fratton	d			15 13				15 51				16 13			16 51		17 13
Hilsea	d																
Bedhampton	d			15 20								16 20					17 20
Havant	d			15 27		16 11		16 00				16 27			17 00		17 27
Warblington	d			15 29								16 29					17 29
Emsworth	d			15 32				16 04				16 32			17 04		17 32
Southbourne	d			15 35				16 07				16 35			17 07		17 35
Nutbourne	d			15 38								16 38					17 38
Bosham	d			15 41								16 41					17 41
Fishbourne (Sussex)	d			15 44								16 44					17 44
Chichester 4	a			15 47		16 22		16 14				16 47			17 14		17 47
	d			15 48		16 22		16 14				16 48			17 14		17 48
Bognor Regis 4	d				15 52					16 30			16 52			17 30	
Barnham	a			15 55	15 58	16 30		16 22		16 40		16 55	16 58		17 22	17 36	17 55
	d			16 02	15 59	16 30		16 22		16 41		17 02	16 59		17 22	17 37	18 02
Bognor Regis	a																
Ford 4	d			16 06	16 03					16 46		17 06	17 03			17 41	18 06
Littlehampton 4	a									16 50						17 46	
	d		15 38				16 14				16 38			17 14			
Angmering 3	d		15 46	16 12			16 22				16 46	17 12		17 22			18 12
Goring-by-Sea	d		15 50	16 16			16 26				16 50	17 16		17 26			18 16
Durrington-on-Sea	d		15 52	16 19			16 29				16 52	17 19		17 29			18 19
West Worthing	d		15 54	16 21			16 31				16 54	17 21		17 31			18 21
Worthing 4	a		15 57	16 23		16 45	16 33	16 37			16 57	17 23		17 33	17 37		18 23
	d		15 57	16 24		16 45	16 41	<			16 57	17 24		17 41	<		18 24
East Worthing	d		16 00	16 26							17 00	17 26					18 26
Lancing	d		16 03	16 29							17 03	17 29					18 29
Shoreham-by-Sea	d		16 07	16 33		16 52	16 47				17 07	17 33		17 47			18 33
Southwick	d		16 10	16 36							17 10	17 36					18 36
Fishersgate	d		16 12	16 38							17 12	17 38					18 38
Portslade	d		16 14	16 40							17 14	17 40					18 40
Aldrington	d		16 16	16 43							17 16	17 43					18 43
Hove 2	d	16 01	16 19	16 45		16 59	16 54		17 02		17 19	17 45		17 54			18 45
Brighton 10	a	16 05	16 23	16 49		17 05			17 06		17 23	17 49					18 49
Burgess Hill	a						17 04							18 04			
Haywards Heath 3	a						17 09							18 09			
Arundel	d				16 08								17 08				
Amberley	d				16 13								17 13				
Pulborough	d				16 19								17 19				
Billingshurst	d				16 26								17 26				
Christs Hospital	d				16 32								17 32				
Horsham 4	a				16 37								17 37				
	d				16 37								17 37				
Crawley	d				16 46								17 46				
Three Bridges 4	a				16 50								17 50				
Gatwick Airport 10	a				16 55		17 22						17 55	18 22			
	d				16 56		17 23						17 56	18 23			
Horley	a				16 58								17 58				
Redhill 5	a				17 05								18 05				
East Croydon	a				17 20		17 39						18 20	18 39			
London Bridge 4 ⊖	a																
Clapham Junction 10	a				17 31		17 48						18 31	18 48			
London Victoria 15 ⊖	a				17 39		17 55						18 39	18 55			

Sundays
until 05 September

Southampton, Portsmouth and Sussex Coast - Brighton, Gatwick Airport & London

		SN	SN	SN	SN	SN	SN	SN	SN	SN	SN	SN	SN	SN	SN	SN	SN	SN
		1	1	◇1	◇1	◇1	1	1	1	1	◇1	◇1	◇1	1	1	1	1	◇1
Southampton Central	d																	
Swanwick	d																	
Fareham	d																	
Portchester	d																	
Cosham	d																	
Portsmouth Harbour	d					17 43				18 05			18 43				19 05	
Portsmouth & Southsea	d					17 47				18 09			18 47				19 09	
Fratton	d					17 51				18 13			18 51				19 13	
Hilsea	d																	
Bedhampton	d									18 20							19 20	
Havant	d					18 00				18 27			19 00				19 27	
Warblington	d									18 29							19 29	
Emsworth	d					18 04				18 32			19 04				19 32	
Southbourne	d					18 07				18 35			19 07				19 35	
Nutbourne	d									18 38							19 38	
Bosham	d									18 41							19 41	
Fishbourne (Sussex)	d									18 44							19 44	
Chichester 4	a					18 14				18 47			19 14				19 47	
	d					18 14				18 48			19 14				19 48	
Bognor Regis 4	d			17 52			18 30				18 52			19 30				19 52
Barnham	a			17 58		18 22	18 36			18 55	18 58		19 22	19 36			19 55	19 58
	d			17 59		18 22	18 37			19 02	18 59		19 22	19 37			20 02	19 59
Bognor Regis	a																	
Ford 4	d			18 03			18 41			19 06	19 03			19 41			20 06	20 03
Littlehampton 4	a						18 46							19 46				
	d		17 38		18 14				18 38			19 14				19 38		
Angmering 3	d		17 46		18 22				18 46	19 12		19 22				19 46	20 12	
Goring-by-Sea	d		17 50		18 26				18 50	19 16		19 26				19 50	20 16	
Durrington-on-Sea	d		17 52		18 29				18 52	19 19		19 29				19 52	20 19	
West Worthing	d		17 54		18 31				18 54	19 21		19 31				19 54	20 21	
Worthing 4	a		17 57		18 33	18 37			18 57	19 23		19 33	19 37			19 57	20 23	
	d		17 57		18 41	<			18 57	19 24		19 41	<			19 57	20 24	
East Worthing	d		18 00						19 00	19 26						20 00	20 26	
Lancing	d		18 03						19 03	19 29						20 03	20 29	
Shoreham-by-Sea	d		18 07		18 47				19 07	19 33		19 47				20 07	20 33	
Southwick	d		18 10						19 10	19 36						20 10	20 36	
Fishersgate	d		18 12						19 12	19 38						20 12	20 38	
Portslade	d		18 14						19 14	19 40						20 14	20 40	
Aldrington	d		18 16						19 16	19 43						20 16	20 43	
Hove 2	d	18 01	18 19		18 54			19 01	19 19	19 45		19 54			20 01	20 19	20 45	
Brighton 10	a	18 05	18 23					19 05	19 23	19 49					20 05	20 23	20 49	
Burgess Hill	a				19 04							20 04						
Haywards Heath 3	a				19 09							20 09						
Arundel	d			18 08							19 08							20 08
Amberley	d			18 13							19 13							20 13
Pulborough	d			18 19							19 19							20 19
Billingshurst	d			18 26							19 26							20 26
Christs Hospital	d			18 32							19 32							20 32
Horsham 4	a			18 37							19 37							20 37
	d			18 37							19 37							20 37
Crawley	d			18 46							19 46							20 46
Three Bridges 4	a			18 50							19 50							20 50
Gatwick Airport 10	a			18 55	19 22						19 55	20 22						20 55
	d			18 56	19 23						19 56	20 23						20 56
Horley	a			18 58							19 58							20 58
Redhill 5	a			19 05							20 05							21 05
East Croydon ⇌	a			19 20	19 39						20 20	20 39						21 20
London Bridge 4 ⊖	a																	
Clapham Junction 10	a			19 31	19 48						20 31	20 48						21 31
London Victoria 15 ⊖	a			19 39	19 55						20 39	20 55						21 39

Sundays
until 05 September

Southampton, Portsmouth and Sussex Coast - Brighton, Gatwick Airport & London

		SN	SN	SN	GW	SN	SN	SN	SN	SN	SN	SN	SN	SN	SN	SN	SN	SN
		◇1	◇1	1	◇	1	1	1	◇1	1	1	1	◇1	1	1	1	1	1
Southampton Central	d				19 27													
Swanwick	d																	
Fareham	d				19 49													
Portchester	d																	
Cosham	d				19 59													
Portsmouth Harbour	d		19 43					20 05		20 43		21 05			21 43		22 14	22 43
Portsmouth & Southsea	d		19 47					20 09		20 47		21 09			21 47		22 18	22 47
Fratton	d		19 51					20 13		20 51		21 13			21 51		22 22	22 51
Hilsea	d																	
Bedhampton	d							20 20				21 20					22 30	
Havant	d		20 00		20 11			20 27		21 00		21 27			22 00		22 33	23 00
Warblington	d							20 29				21 29					22 35	
Emsworth	d		20 04					20 32		21 04		21 32			22 04		22 38	23 04
Southbourne	d		20 07					20 35		21 07		21 35			22 07		22 41	23 07
Nutbourne	d							20 38				21 38					22 43	
Bosham	d							20 41				21 41					22 47	
Fishbourne (Sussex)	d							20 44				21 44					22 50	
Chichester 4	a		20 14		20 21			20 47		21 14		21 47			22 14		22 53	23 14
	d		20 14		20 22			20 48		21 14		21 48			22 14		22 53	23 14
Bognor Regis 4	d					20 30			20 52		21 30		21 52	22 11				
Barnham	a		20 22		20 29	20 36		20 55	20 58	21 22	21 36	21 55	21 58	22 18	22 22		23 01	23 22
	d		20 22		20 30	20 37		21 02	20 59	21 22	21 37	22 02	21 59		22 22	22 52	23 01	23 22
Bognor Regis	a															22 58		
Ford 4	d					20 41		21 06	21 03	21 27	21 41	22 06	22 03		22 27		23 06	23 27
Littlehampton 4	a					20 46				21 31	21 46				22 31		23 10	23 32
	d	20 14					20 38			21 42					22 42			
Angmering 3	d	20 22					20 46	21 12		21 50		22 12			22 50			
Goring-by-Sea	d	20 26					20 50	21 16		21 54		22 16			22 54			
Durrington-on-Sea	d	20 29					20 52	21 19		21 57		22 19			22 57			
West Worthing	d	20 31					20 54	21 21		21 59		22 21			22 59			
Worthing 4	a	20 33	20 37		20 51		20 57	21 23		22 01		22 23			23 01			
	d	20 41	<		20 51		20 57	21 24		22 02		22 24			23 02			
East Worthing	d						21 00	21 26		22 04		22 26			23 04			
Lancing	d						21 03	21 29		22 07		22 29			23 07			
Shoreham-by-Sea	d	20 47			20 58		21 07	21 33		22 11		22 33			23 11			
Southwick	d						21 10	21 36		22 14		22 36			23 14			
Fishersgate	d						21 12	21 38		22 16		22 38			23 16			
Portslade	d						21 14	21 40		22 18		22 40			23 18			
Aldrington	d						21 16	21 43		22 21		22 43			23 21			
Hove 2	d	20 54		21 01	21 05		21 19	21 45		22 23		22 45			23 25			
Brighton 10	a			21 05	21 10		21 23	21 49		22 27		22 49			23 29			
Burgess Hill	a	21 04																
Haywards Heath 3	a	21 09																
Arundel	d								21 08				22 08					
Amberley	d								21 13				22 13					
Pulborough	d								21 19				22 19					
Billingshurst	d								21 26				22 26					
Christs Hospital	d								21 32				22 32					
Horsham 4	a								21 37				22 37					
	d								21 37				22 37					
Crawley	d								21 46				22 46					
Three Bridges 4	a								21 50				22 50					
Gatwick Airport 10	a	21 22							21 55				22 55					
	d	21 23							21 56				22 56					
Horley	a								21 58				22 58					
Redhill 5	a								22 05				23 05					
East Croydon ⇌	a	21 39							22 20				23 20					
London Bridge 4 ⊖	a																	
Clapham Junction 10	a	21 48							22 31				23 31					
London Victoria 15 ⊖	a	21 55							22 39				23 38					

Table 188

Sundays
from 12 September

Southampton, Portsmouth and Sussex Coast - Brighton, Gatwick Airport & London

		SN 1	SN 1	SN 1	SN 1	SN 1	SN ◇1	SN ◇1	SN 1	SN 1	SN 1	SN 1	SN ◇1 [trolley]	SN ◇1	SN ◇1	SN 1
Southampton Central	d															
Swanwick	d															
Fareham	d															
Portchester	d															
Cosham	d															
Portsmouth Harbour	d	22p44		23p15								07 14			07 43	
Portsmouth & Southsea	d	22p48		23p19								07 18			07 47	
Fratton	d	22p52		23p23								07 22			07 51	
Hilsea	d	22p56		23p27												
Bedhampton	d	23p01		23p33								07 30				
Havant	d	23p05		23p36								07 33			08 00	
Warblington	d			23p38								07 35				
Emsworth	d			23p41								07 38			08 04	
Southbourne	d			23p44								07 41			08 07	
Nutbourne	d			23p47								07 43				
Bosham	d			23p50								07 47				
Fishbourne (Sussex)	d			23p53								07 50				
Chichester 4	a	23p16		23p57								07 53			08 14	
	d	23p18	23p52	23p57								07 53			08 14	
Bognor Regis 4	d						06 57			07 36			07 57			08 36
Barnham	a	23p26	23p59	00 05			07 03			07 42		08 01	08 03		08 22	08 42
	d	23p26	00 01	00 06	06 06	06 45	07 05			07 43		08 08	08 05		08 22	08 43
Bognor Regis	a					06 51										
Ford 4	d	23p31	00 05	00 10			07 09			07 47		08 12	08 09			08 47
Littlehampton 4	a	23p35	00 10	00 15	06 13					07 52						08 52
	d	23p40			06 20			07 14			07 40			08 14		
Angmering 3	d	23p48						07 22			07 48	08 18		08 22		
Goring-by-Sea	d	23p52						07 26			07 52	08 22		08 26		
Durrington-on-Sea	d	23p54						07 29			07 55	08 25		08 29		
West Worthing	d	23p56						07 31			07 57	08 27		08 31		
Worthing 4	a	23p59			06 33			07 33			07 59	08 29		08 33	08 37	
	d	23p59			06 33			07 35			08 00	08 30		08 41	<	
East Worthing	d	00 02									08 02	08 32				
Lancing	d	00 05			06 37			07 39			08 05	08 35				
Shoreham-by-Sea	d	00 09			06 41			07 43			08 09	08 39		08 47		
Southwick	d	00 12			06 44			07 46			08 12	08 42				
Fishersgate	d	00 14									08 14	08 44				
Portslade	d	00 16			06 48			07 49			08 16	08 46				
Aldrington	d	00 18									08 19	08 49				
Hove 2	d	00 21			06 51			07 54	07 56		08 21	08 56		08 54		
Brighton 10	a	00 25			06 55				08 00		08 25	09 00				
Burgess Hill	a							08 04						09 04		
Haywards Heath 3	a							08 09						09 09		
Arundel	d						07 14						08 14			
Amberley	d						07 19						08 19			
Pulborough	d						07 25						08 25			
Billingshurst	d						07 31						08 31			
Christs Hospital	d						07 38						08 38			
Horsham 4	a						07 42						08 42			
	d						07 42						08 42			
Crawley	d						07 51						08 51			
Three Bridges 4	a						07 54						08 54			
Gatwick Airport 10	a						07 59	08 22					08 59	09 21		
	d						08 00	08 23					09 00	09 23		
Horley	a						08 02						09 02			
Redhill 5	a						08 09						09 09			
East Croydon	a						08 24	08 39					09 24	09 39		
London Bridge 4 ⊖	a															
Clapham Junction 10	a						08 37	08 54					09 37	09 54		
London Victoria 15 ⊖	a						08 46	09 01					09 46	10 01		

Table 188

Sundays
from 12 September

Southampton, Portsmouth and Sussex Coast - Brighton, Gatwick Airport & London

		SN 1	SN 1	SN ◇1 [trolley]	SN ◇1	GW	SN ◇1	SN 1	SN 1	SN 1	SN ◇1 [trolley]	SN ◇1	SN ◇1	SN 1	SN 1	SN 1	SN ◇1 [trolley]
Southampton Central	d					08 31											
Swanwick	d																
Fareham	d					08 52											
Portchester	d																
Cosham	d					09 00											
Portsmouth Harbour	d		08 14				08 43			09 14			09 43			10 14	
Portsmouth & Southsea	d		08 18				08 47			09 18			09 47			10 18	
Fratton	d		08 22				08 51			09 22			09 51			10 22	
Hilsea	d																
Bedhampton	d		08 30							09 30						10 30	
Havant	d		08 33			09 11	09 00			09 33			10 00			10 33	
Warblington	d		08 35							09 35						10 35	
Emsworth	d		08 38				09 04			09 38			10 04			10 38	
Southbourne	d		08 41				09 07			09 41			10 07			10 41	
Nutbourne	d		08 43							09 43						10 43	
Bosham	d		08 47							09 47						10 47	
Fishbourne (Sussex)	d		08 50							09 50						10 50	
Chichester 4	a		08 53			09 22	09 14			09 53			10 14			10 53	
	d		08 53			09 22	09 14			09 53			10 14			10 53	
Bognor Regis 4	d			08 57				09 36			09 57			10 36			10 57
Barnham	a		09 01	09 03		09 30	09 22	09 42		10 01	10 03		10 22	10 42		11 01	11 03
	d		09 08	09 05		09 30	09 22	09 43		10 08	10 05		10 22	10 43		11 08	11 05
Bognor Regis	a																
Ford 4	d		09 12	09 09				09 47		10 12	10 09			10 47		11 12	11 09
Littlehampton 4	a							09 52						10 52			
	d	08 40			09 14				09 40			10 14			10 40		
Angmering 3	d	08 48	09 18		09 22				09 48	10 18		10 22			10 48	11 18	
Goring-by-Sea	d	08 52	09 22		09 26				09 52	10 22		10 26			10 52	11 22	
Durrington-on-Sea	d	08 55	09 25		09 29				09 55	10 25		10 29			10 55	11 25	
West Worthing	d	08 57	09 27		09 31				09 57	10 27		10 31			10 57	11 27	
Worthing 4	a	08 59	09 29		09 33	09 45	09 37		09 59	10 29		10 33	10 37		10 59	11 29	
	d	09 00	09 30		09 41	09 45	<		10 00	10 30		10 41	<		11 00	11 30	
East Worthing	d	09 02	09 32						10 02	10 32					11 02	11 32	
Lancing	d	09 05	09 35						10 05	10 35					11 05	11 35	
Shoreham-by-Sea	d	09 09	09 39		09 47	09 52			10 09	10 39		10 47			11 09	11 39	
Southwick	d	09 12	09 42						10 12	10 42					11 12	11 42	
Fishersgate	d	09 14	09 44						10 14	10 44					11 14	11 44	
Portslade	d	09 16	09 46						10 16	10 46					11 16	11 46	
Aldrington	d	09 19	09 49						10 19	10 49					11 19	11 49	
Hove 2	d	09 21	09 56		09 54	09 59			10 21	10 56		10 54			11 21	11 56	
Brighton 10	a	09 25	10 00			10 05			10 25	11 00					11 25	12 00	
Burgess Hill	a				10 04							11 04					
Haywards Heath 3	a				10 09							11 09					
Arundel	d			09 14							10 14						11 14
Amberley	d			09 19							10 19						11 19
Pulborough	d			09 25							10 25						11 25
Billingshurst	d			09 31							10 31						11 31
Christs Hospital	d			09 38							10 38						11 38
Horsham 4	a			09 42							10 42						11 42
	d			09 42							10 42						11 42
Crawley	d			09 51							10 51						11 51
Three Bridges 4	a			09 54							10 54						11 54
Gatwick Airport 10	a			09 59	10 21						10 59	11 21					11 59
	d			10 00	10 23						11 00	11 23					12 00
Horley	a			10 02							11 02						12 02
Redhill 5	a			10 09							11 09						12 09
East Croydon	a			10 24	10 39						11 24	11 39					12 24
London Bridge 4 ⊖	a																
Clapham Junction 10	a			10 37	10 54						11 37	11 54					12 37
London Victoria 15 ⊖	a			10 46	11 01						11 46	12 01					12 46

Table 188

Sundays

from 12 September

Southampton, Portsmouth and Sussex Coast - Brighton, Gatwick Airport & London

		SN ◇1	SN ◇1	SN 1	SN 1	SN 1	SN ◇1 🚲	SN ◇1	SN ◇1	SN 1	SN 1	SN 1	SN ◇1 🚲	SN ◇1	SN ◇1	SN 1	SN 1	SN 1
Southampton Central	d																	
Swanwick	d																	
Fareham	d																	
Portchester	d																	
Cosham	d																	
Portsmouth Harbour	d		10 43			11 14			11 43			12 14			12 43			13 14
Portsmouth & Southsea	d		10 47			11 18			11 47			12 18			12 47			13 18
Fratton	d		10 51			11 22			11 51			12 22			12 51			13 22
Hilsea	d																	
Bedhampton	d					11 30						12 30						13 30
Havant	d		11 00			11 33			12 00			12 33			13 00			13 33
Warblington	d					11 35						12 35						13 35
Emsworth	d		11 04			11 38			12 04			12 38			13 04			13 38
Southbourne	d		11 07			11 41			12 07			12 41			13 07			13 41
Nutbourne	d					11 43						12 43						13 43
Bosham	d					11 47						12 47						13 47
Fishbourne (Sussex)	d					11 50						12 50						13 50
Chichester 4	a		11 14			11 53			12 14			12 53			13 14			13 53
	d		11 14			11 53			12 14			12 53			13 14			13 53
Bognor Regis 4	d			11 36			11 57			12 36			12 57			13 36		
Barnham	a		11 22	11 42		12 01	12 03		12 22	12 42		13 01	13 03		13 22	13 42		14 01
	d		11 22	11 43		12 08	12 05		12 22	12 43		13 08	13 05		13 22	13 43		14 08
Bognor Regis	a																	
Ford 4	d			11 47		12 12	12 09			12 47		13 12	13 09			13 47		14 12
Littlehampton 4	a			11 52						12 52						13 52		
	d	11 14			11 40			12 14			12 40			13 14			13 40	
Angmering 3	d	11 22			11 48	12 18		12 22			12 48	13 18		13 22			13 48	14 18
Goring-by-Sea	d	11 26			11 52	12 22		12 26			12 52	13 22		13 26			13 52	14 22
Durrington-on-Sea	d	11 29			11 55	12 25		12 29			12 55	13 25		13 29			13 55	14 25
West Worthing	d	11 31			11 57	12 27		12 31			12 57	13 27		13 31			13 57	14 27
Worthing 4	a	11 33	11 37		11 59	12 29		12 33	12 37		12 59	13 29		13 33	13 37		13 59	14 29
	d	11 41	<		12 00	12 30		12 41	<		13 00	13 30		13 41	<		14 00	14 30
East Worthing	d				12 02	12 32					13 02	13 32					14 02	14 32
Lancing	d				12 05	12 35					13 05	13 35					14 05	14 35
Shoreham-by-Sea	d	11 47			12 09	12 39		12 47			13 09	13 39		13 47			14 09	14 39
Southwick	d				12 12	12 42					13 12	13 42					14 12	14 42
Fishersgate	d				12 14	12 44					13 14	13 44					14 14	14 44
Portslade	d				12 16	12 46					13 16	13 46					14 16	14 46
Aldrington	d				12 19	12 49					13 19	13 49					14 19	14 49
Hove 2	d	11 54			12 21	12 56		12 54			13 21	13 56		13 54			14 21	14 55
Brighton 10	a				12 25	13 00					13 25	14 00					14 25	14 59
Burgess Hill	a	12 04						13 04						14 04				
Haywards Heath 3	a	12 09						13 09						14 09				
Arundel	d						12 14						13 14					
Amberley	d						12 19						13 19					
Pulborough	d						12 25						13 25					
Billingshurst	d						12 31						13 31					
Christs Hospital	d						12 38						13 38					
Horsham 4	a						12 42						13 42					
	d						12 42						13 42					
Crawley	d						12 51						13 51					
Three Bridges 4	a						12 54						13 54					
Gatwick Airport 10	a	12 22					12 59	13 22					13 59	14 22				
	d	12 23					13 00	13 23					14 00	14 23				
Horley	a						13 02						14 02					
Redhill 5	a						13 09						14 09					
East Croydon ⇌	a	12 39					13 24	13 39					14 24	14 39				
London Bridge 4 ⊖	a																	
Clapham Junction 10	a	12 54					13 37	13 54					14 37	14 54				
London Victoria 15 ⊖	a	13 01					13 46	14 01					14 46	15 01				

Table 188

Sundays

from 12 September

Southampton, Portsmouth and Sussex Coast - Brighton, Gatwick Airport & London

		SN ◇1 🚲	SN ◇1	SN ◇1	GW ◇	SN 1	SN 1	SN 1	SN ◇1 🚲	SN ◇1	SN ◇1	SN 1	SN 1	SN 1	SN ◇1 🚲	SN ◇1	SN ◇1	GW ◇
Southampton Central	d				13 08													15 22
Swanwick	d																	
Fareham	d				13 34													15 51
Portchester	d																	
Cosham	d				13 42													16 01
Portsmouth Harbour	d			13 43				14 14			14 43			15 14			15 43	
Portsmouth & Southsea	d			13 47				14 18			14 47			15 18			15 47	
Fratton	d			13 51				14 22			14 51			15 22			15 51	
Hilsea	d																	
Bedhampton	d							14 30						15 30				
Havant	d			14 00	14 04			14 33			15 00			15 33			16 00	16 11
Warblington	d							14 35						15 35				
Emsworth	d			14 04				14 38			15 04			15 38			16 04	
Southbourne	d			14 07				14 41			15 07			15 41			16 07	
Nutbourne	d							14 43						15 43				
Bosham	d							14 47						15 47				
Fishbourne (Sussex)	d							14 50						15 50				
Chichester 4	a			14 14	14 19			14 53			15 14			15 53			16 14	16 22
	d			14 14	14 19			14 53			15 14			15 53			16 14	16 22
Bognor Regis 4	d	13 57				14 36			14 57			15 36			15 57			
Barnham	a	14 03		14 22	14 27	14 42		15 01	15 03		15 22	15 42		16 01	16 03		16 22	16 30
	d	14 05		14 22	14 27	14 43		15 08	15 05		15 22	15 43		16 08	16 05		16 22	16 30
Bognor Regis	a																	
Ford 4	d	14 09				14 47		15 12	15 09			15 47		16 12	16 09			
Littlehampton 4	a					14 52						15 52						
	d		14 14				14 40			15 14			15 40			16 14		
Angmering 3	d		14 22				14 48	15 18		15 22			15 48	16 18		16 22		
Goring-by-Sea	d		14 26				14 52	15 22		15 26			15 52	16 22		16 26		
Durrington-on-Sea	d		14 29				14 55	15 25		15 29			15 55	16 25		16 29		
West Worthing	d		14 31				14 57	15 27		15 31			15 57	16 27		16 31		
Worthing 4	a		14 33	14 37	14 44		14 59	15 29		15 33	15 37		15 59	16 29		16 33	16 37	16 45
	d		14 41	<	14 45		15 00	15 30		15 41	<		16 00	16 30		16 41	<	16 45
East Worthing	d						15 02	15 32					16 02	16 32				
Lancing	d						15 05	15 35					16 05	16 35				
Shoreham-by-Sea	d		14 47		14 51		15 09	15 39		15 47			16 09	16 39		16 47		16 52
Southwick	d						15 12	15 42					16 12	16 42				
Fishersgate	d						15 14	15 44					16 14	16 44				
Portslade	d						15 16	15 46					16 16	16 46				
Aldrington	d						15 19	15 49					16 19	16 49				
Hove 2	d		14 54		15 00		15 21	15 56		15 54			16 21	16 56		16 54		16 59
Brighton 10	a				15 06		15 25	16 00					16 25	17 00				17 05
Burgess Hill	a		15 04							16 04						17 04		
Haywards Heath 3	a		15 09							16 09						17 09		
Arundel	d	14 14							15 14						16 14			
Amberley	d	14 19							15 19						16 19			
Pulborough	d	14 25							15 25						16 25			
Billingshurst	d	14 31							15 31						16 31			
Christs Hospital	d	14 38							15 38						16 38			
Horsham 4	a	14 42							15 42						16 42			
	d	14 42							15 42						16 42			
Crawley	d	14 51							15 51						16 51			
Three Bridges 4	a	14 54							15 54						16 54			
Gatwick Airport 10	a	14 59	15 22						15 59	16 22					16 59	17 22		
	d	15 00	15 23						16 00	16 23					17 00	17 23		
Horley	a	15 02							16 02						17 02			
Redhill 5	a	15 09							16 09						17 09			
East Croydon ⇌	a	15 24	15 39						16 24	16 39					17 24	17 39		
London Bridge 4 ⊖	a																	
Clapham Junction 10	a	15 37	15 54						16 37	16 54					17 37	17 54		
London Victoria 15 ⊖	a	15 46	16 01						16 46	17 01					17 46	18 01		

Table 188

Sundays from 12 September

Southampton, Portsmouth and Sussex Coast - Brighton, Gatwick Airport & London

		SN 1	SN 1	SN 1	SN ◇1	SN ◇1	SN ◇1	SN 1	SN 1	SN 1	SN ◇1	SN ◇1	SN ◇1	SN 1	SN 1	SN 1
Southampton Central	d															
Swanwick	d															
Fareham	d															
Portchester	d															
Cosham	d															
Portsmouth Harbour	d			16 14			16 43			17 14			17 43			18 14
Portsmouth & Southsea	d			16 18			16 47			17 18			17 47			18 18
Fratton	d			16 22			16 51			17 22			17 51			18 22
Hilsea	d															
Bedhampton	d			16 30						17 30						18 30
Havant	d			16 33			17 00			17 33			18 00			18 33
Warblington	d			16 35						17 35						18 35
Emsworth	d			16 38			17 04			17 38			18 04			18 38
Southbourne	d			16 41			17 07			17 41			18 07			18 41
Nutbourne	d			16 43						17 43						18 43
Bosham	d			16 47						17 47						18 47
Fishbourne (Sussex)	d			16 50						17 50						18 50
Chichester 4	a			16 53			17 14			17 53			18 14			18 53
	d			16 53			17 14			17 53			18 14			18 53
Bognor Regis 4	d	16 36			16 57			17 36			17 57			18 36		
Barnham	a	16 42		17 01	17 03		17 22	17 42		18 01	18 03		18 22	18 42		19 01
	d	16 43		17 08	17 05		17 22	17 43		18 08	18 05		18 22	18 43		19 08
Bognor Regis	a															
Ford 4	d	16 47		17 12	17 09			17 47		18 12	18 09			18 47		19 12
Littlehampton 4	a	16 52						17 52						18 52		
	d		16 40			17 14			17 40			18 14			18 40	
Angmering 3	d		16 48	17 18		17 22			17 48	18 18		18 22			18 48	19 18
Goring-by-Sea	d		16 52	17 22		17 26			17 52	18 22		18 26			18 52	19 22
Durrington-on-Sea	d		16 55	17 25		17 29			17 55	18 25		18 29			18 55	19 25
West Worthing	d		16 57	17 27		17 31			17 57	18 27		18 31			18 57	19 27
Worthing 4	a		16 59	17 29		17 33	17 37		17 59	18 29		18 33	18 37		18 59	19 29
	d		17 00	17 30		17 41	<		18 00	18 30		18 41	<		19 00	19 30
East Worthing	d		17 02	17 32					18 02	18 32					19 02	19 32
Lancing	d		17 05	17 35					18 05	18 35					19 05	19 35
Shoreham-by-Sea	d		17 09	17 39		17 47			18 09	18 39		18 47			19 09	19 39
Southwick	d		17 12	17 42					18 12	18 42					19 12	19 42
Fishersgate	d		17 14	17 44					18 14	18 44					19 14	19 44
Portslade	d		17 16	17 46					18 16	18 46					19 16	19 46
Aldrington	d		17 19	17 49					18 19	18 49					19 19	19 49
Hove 2	d		17 21	17 56		17 54			18 21	18 56		18 54			19 21	19 56
Brighton 10	a		17 25	18 00					18 25	19 00					19 25	20 00
Burgess Hill	a					18 04						19 04				
Haywards Heath 3	a					18 09						19 09				
Arundel	d				17 14						18 14					
Amberley	d				17 19						18 19					
Pulborough	d				17 25						18 25					
Billingshurst	d				17 31						18 31					
Christs Hospital	d				17 38						18 38					
Horsham 4	a				17 42						18 42					
	d				17 42						18 42					
Crawley	d				17 51						18 51					
Three Bridges 4	a				17 54						18 54					
Gatwick Airport 10	a				17 59	18 22					18 59	19 22				
	d				18 00	18 23					19 00	19 23				
Horley	a				18 02						19 02					
Redhill 5	a				18 09						19 09					
East Croydon	a				18 24	18 39					19 24	19 39				
London Bridge 4 ⊖	a															
Clapham Junction 10	a				18 37	18 54					19 37	19 54				
London Victoria 15 ⊖	a				18 46	19 01					19 46	20 01				

Table 188

Sundays from 12 September

Southampton, Portsmouth and Sussex Coast - Brighton, Gatwick Airport & London

		SN ◇1	SN ◇1	SN ◇1	SN 1	SN 1	SN 1	SN ◇1	GW ◇	SN ◇1	SN ◇1	SN 1	SN 1	SN 1	SN ◇1	SN 1	SN 1	SN 1
Southampton Central	d								19 27									
Swanwick	d																	
Fareham	d								19 49									
Portchester	d																	
Cosham	d								19 59									
Portsmouth Harbour	d			18 43			19 14				19 43			20 14		20 43		21 14
Portsmouth & Southsea	d			18 47			19 18				19 47			20 18		20 47		21 18
Fratton	d			18 51			19 22				19 51			20 22		20 51		21 22
Hilsea	d																	
Bedhampton	d						19 30							20 30				21 30
Havant	d			19 00			19 33		20 11		20 00			20 33		21 00		21 33
Warblington	d						19 35							20 35				21 35
Emsworth	d			19 04			19 38				20 04			20 38		21 04		21 38
Southbourne	d			19 07			19 41				20 07			20 41		21 07		21 41
Nutbourne	d						19 43							20 43				21 43
Bosham	d						19 47							20 47				21 47
Fishbourne (Sussex)	d						19 50							20 50				21 50
Chichester 4	a			19 14			19 53		20 21		20 14			20 53		21 14		21 53
	d			19 14			19 53		20 22		20 14			20 53		21 14		21 53
Bognor Regis 4	d	18 57			19 36			19 57				20 36			20 57		21 36	
Barnham	a	19 03		19 22	19 42		20 01	20 03	20 29		20 22	20 42		21 01	21 03	21 22	21 42	22 01
	d	19 05		19 22	19 43		20 08	20 05	20 30		20 22	20 43		21 08	21 05	21 22	21 43	22 08
Bognor Regis	a																	
Ford 4	d	19 09			19 47		20 12	20 09				20 47		21 12	21 09	21 27	21 47	22 12
Littlehampton 4	a				19 52							20 52				21 31	21 52	
	d		19 14			19 40				20 14			20 40			21 42		
Angmering 3	d		19 22			19 48	20 18			20 22			20 48	21 18		21 50		22 18
Goring-by-Sea	d		19 26			19 52	20 22			20 26			20 52	21 22		21 54		22 22
Durrington-on-Sea	d		19 29			19 55	20 25			20 29			20 55	21 25		21 57		22 25
West Worthing	d		19 31			19 57	20 27			20 31			20 57	21 27		21 59		22 27
Worthing 4	a		19 33	19 37		19 59	20 29		20 51	20 33	20 37		20 59	21 29		22 01		22 29
	d		19 41	<		20 00	20 30		20 51	20 41	<		21 00	21 30		22 02		22 30
East Worthing	d					20 02	20 32						21 02	21 32		22 04		22 32
Lancing	d					20 05	20 35						21 05	21 35		22 07		22 35
Shoreham-by-Sea	d		19 47			20 09	20 39		20 58	20 47			21 09	21 39		22 11		22 39
Southwick	d					20 12	20 42						21 12	21 42		22 14		22 42
Fishersgate	d					20 14	20 44						21 14	21 44		22 16		22 44
Portslade	d					20 16	20 46						21 16	21 46		22 18		22 46
Aldrington	d					20 19	20 49						21 19	21 49		22 21		22 49
Hove 2	d		19 54			20 21	20 56		21 05	20 54			21 21	21 51		22 23		22 51
Brighton 10	a					20 25	21 00		21 10				21 25	21 55		22 27		22 56
Burgess Hill	a		20 04							21 04								
Haywards Heath 3	a		20 09							21 09								
Arundel	d	19 14						20 14							21 14			
Amberley	d	19 19						20 19							21 19			
Pulborough	d	19 25						20 25							21 25			
Billingshurst	d	19 31						20 31							21 31			
Christs Hospital	d	19 38						20 38							21 38			
Horsham 4	a	19 42						20 42							21 42			
	d	19 42						20 42							21 42			
Crawley	d	19 51						20 51							21 51			
Three Bridges 4	a	19 54						20 54							21 54			
Gatwick Airport 10	a	19 59	20 22					20 59		21 22					21 59			
	d	20 00	20 23					21 00		21 23					22 00			
Horley	a	20 02						21 02							22 02			
Redhill 5	a	20 09						21 09							22 09			
East Croydon	a	20 24	20 39					21 24		21 39					22 24			
London Bridge 4 ⊖	a																	
Clapham Junction 10	a	20 37	20 54					21 37		21 54					22 37			
London Victoria 15 ⊖	a	20 46	21 01					21 46		22 01					22 46			

Table 188

Sundays
from 12 September

Southampton, Portsmouth and Sussex Coast - Brighton, Gatwick Airport & London

		SN	SN	SN	SN	SN	SN
		◇[1]	[1]	[1]	[1]	[1]	[1]
Southampton Central	d						
Swanwick	d						
Fareham	d						
Portchester	d						
Cosham	d						
Portsmouth Harbour	d			21 43		22 14	22 43
Portsmouth & Southsea	d			21 47		22 18	22 47
Fratton	d			21 51		22 22	22 51
Hilsea	d						
Bedhampton	d					22 30	
Havant	d			22 00		22 33	23 00
Warblington	d					22 35	
Emsworth	d			22 04		22 38	23 04
Southbourne	d			22 07		22 41	23 07
Nutbourne	d					22 43	
Bosham	d					22 47	
Fishbourne (Sussex)	d					22 50	
Chichester [4]	a			22 14		22 53	23 14
	d			22 14		22 53	23 14
Bognor Regis [4]	d	21 57	22 11				
Barnham	a	22 03	22 18	22 22		23 01	23 22
	d	22 05		22 22	22 57	23 01	23 22
Bognor Regis	a				23 03		
Ford [4]	d	22 09		22 27		23 06	23 27
Littlehampton [4]	a			22 31		23 10	23 32
	d			22 42			
Angmering [3]	d			22 50			
Goring-by-Sea	d			22 54			
Durrington-on-Sea	d			22 57			
West Worthing	d			22 59			
Worthing [4]	a			23 01			
	c			23 02			
East Worthing	d			23 04			
Lancing	d			23 07			
Shoreham-by-Sea	d			23 11			
Southwick	d			23 14			
Fishersgate	d			23 16			
Portslade	d			23 18			
Aldrington	d			23 21			
Hove [2]	d			23 25			
Brighton [10]	a			23 29			
Burgess Hill	a						
Haywards Heath [3]	a						
Arundel	d	22 14					
Amberley	d	22 19					
Pulborough	d	22 25					
Billingshurst	d	22 31					
Christs Hospital	d	22 38					
Horsham [4]	a	22 42					
	d	22 42					
Crawley	d	22 51					
Three Bridges [4]	a	22 54					
Gatwick Airport [10]	a	22 59					
	d	23 00					
Horley	a	23 02					
Redhill [6]	a	23 09					
East Croydon ⇌	a	23 24					
London Bridge [4] ⊖	a						
Clapham Junction [10]	a	23 37					
London Victoria [15] ⊖	a	23 46					

Table 189

Mondays to Fridays

London, Haywards Heath and Brighton-Lewes, Seaford, Eastbourne, Hastings and Ashford

		SN	SN MX	SN MX	SN	SN MX	SN	SN	SN	SN	SN	SN	SN	SN	SN	SN	SN	SN	SN	SN	SN	SN	SN
		◇[1]	◇[1]		◇[1]	◇[1]	[1]	[1]	[1]		[1]	[1]	[1]		[1]	[1]	[1]	[1]	[1]	◇[1]			[1]
		A			B																		
London Victoria [15] ⊖	d	22p47	22p47		22p47	00 05														05 32			
Clapham Junction [10]	d	22p53	22p53		22p53	00 11														05 38			
London Bridge [4] ⊖	d																						
East Croydon ⇌	d	23p03	23p03		23p07	00 25														05 49			
Gatwick Airport [10]	d	23p19	23p19		23p29	00 43														06 20			
Haywards Heath [3]	d	23p30	23p34		23p41	01 06								06 07						06 34			
Wivelsfield [4]	d	23p34	23p38		23p45									06 11						06 38			
Plumpton	d	23p40	23p44		23p51																		
Cooksbridge	d																						
Brighton [10]	d			23p34				05 12		05 45			06 00				06 18	06 26			06 39	06 52	07 00
London Road (Brighton)	d			23p37						05 48			06 03					06 29			06 42	06 55	07 03
Moulsecoomb	d			23p39						05 50			06 05					06 31			06 44	06 57	07 05
Falmer	d			23p43						05 54			06 09					06 35			06 48	07 01	07 09
Lewes [4]	a	23p48	23p51	23p49	23p58	01 20		05 23		06 00			06 15	06 22			06 29	06 41		06 49	06 54	07 08	07 17
	d	23p59	23p53	23p56	23p59	01 20		05 23		06 05				06 27			06 30	06 42		06 51	06 55	07 10	
Southease	d																						
Newhaven Town	d			00 04						06 13				06 35							07 03	07 18	
Newhaven Harbour	d			00 06						06 15				06 37							07 05	07 23	
Bishopstone	d			00 09						06 18				06 40							07 08	07 26	
Seaford	a			00 12						06 21				06 43							07 11	07 29	
Glynde	d																	06 47		06 56			
Berwick	d		00 02															06 53		07 02			
Polegate	d	00 11	00 07		00 11	01s32		05 35									06 43	06 58		07 07			
Hampden Park [4]	d	00 15	00 11		00 15	01s36												07 02		07 11			
Eastbourne [4]	a	00 20	00 16		00 20	01 41		05 42									06 50	07 07		07 16			
	d		00 22				04 50		05 15			05 53			06 14	06 33	06 54		07 02	07 21			
Hampden Park [4]	d														06 18				07 06	07 25			
Pevensey & Westham	d		00 29						05 22						06 23	06 40			07 11	07 30			
Pevensey Bay	d																						
Normans Bay	d															06 45							
Cooden Beach	d		00 35												06 29				07 17	07 36			
Collington	d		00 38												06 32				07 20	07 39			
Bexhill [4]	d		00 41				05 05		05 31			06 07			06 34	06 51	07 09		07 22	07 41			
St Leonards Warrior Sq [4]	d		00 47				05 12		05 37			06 14			06 41	06 58	07 16		07 29	07 49			
Hastings [4]	a		00 50				05 15		05 41			06 18			06 44	07 01	07 19		07 32	07 52			
Ore	d						05 23				05 49									07a56			
Three Oaks	d										05 55												
Doleham	d										05 58												
Winchelsea	d										06 04												
Rye	a						05 44				06 08	06 36					07 38						
	d						05 44				06 08	06 38					07 41						
Appledore (Kent)	d						05 53				06 17	06 47					07 50						
Ham Street	d						05 58				06 22	06 52					07 55						
Ashford International	a						06 06				06 30	07 00					08 03						

A MO until 6 September

B MO from 13 September

Table 189 | Mondays to Fridays

London, Haywards Heath and Brighton-Lewes, Seaford, Eastbourne, Hastings and Ashford

		SN	SN	SN	SN	SN	SN	SN	SN	SN	SN	SN	SN	SN	SN	SN	SN	SN	SN	SN	SN	SN	SN
			1	1	1	1	1	◇1		1	1	1		1	1	◇1	1		1		◇1	1	1
London Victoria 15 ⊖	d							06 47								07 47					08 17		
Clapham Junction 10	d							06 53								07 53					08 23		
London Bridge 4 ⊖	d																						
East Croydon	d							07 03								08 03					08 33		
Gatwick Airport 10	d							07 19								08 19					08 49		
Haywards Heath 3	d		07 10					07 33								08 31					09 10		
Wivelsfield 4	d		07 14					07 37								08 35					09 14		
Plumpton	d		07 20					07 43								08 41							
Cooksbridge	d		07 24					07 47								08 45							
Brighton 10	d	07 10			07 22		07 32		07 40	07 52	08 03		08 13	08 22	08 32		08 38	08 45	08 52	09 10		09 22	09 32
London Road (Brighton)	d	07 13			07 25				07 43	07 55	08 06		08 16	08 25			08 41	08 48	08 55	09 13		09 25	
Moulsecoomb	d	07 15			07 27				07 45	07 57	08 08		08 18	08 27			08 43	08 50	08 57	09 15		09 27	
Falmer	d	07 19			07 31				07 49	08 01	08 12		08 22	08 31			08 47	08 54	09 01	09 19		09 31	
Lewes 4	a	07 26	07 29		07 37		07 43	07 52	07 56	08 08	08 19		08 29	08 37	08 43	08 50	08 53	09 00	09 07	09 25	09 25	09 37	09 43
	d	07 34	07 31				07 44	07 53	07 58	08 09	08 23		08 30		08 44	08 51		09 02	09 09	09 29	09 26		09 44
Southease	d																			09 35			
Newhaven Town	d	07 42							08 06				08 38					09 10		09 39			
Newhaven Harbour	d	07 44							08 08				08 40					09 12		09 41			
Bishopstone	d	07 47							08 11				08 43					09 15		09 44			
Seaford	a	07 50							08 14				08 46					09 18		09 47			
Glynde	d		07 36							08 14	08 28								09 14				
Berwick	d		07 42							08 20	08 34								09 20				
Polegate	d		07 47				07 57	08 05		08 25	08 39				08 57	09 03			09 25		09 38		09 57
Hampden Park 4	d		07 51					08 09		08 29	08 43					09 07			09 29		09 42		
Eastbourne 4	a		07 56				08 04	08 14		08 34	08 48				09 04	09 12			09 34		09 50		10 04
	d					07 38	08 09	08 21		08 40					09 09	09 19			09 40				10 09
Hampden Park 4	d					07 42		08 25		08 44						09 23			09 44				
Pevensey & Westham	d					07 47	08 17	08 30		08 49						09 28			09 49				
Pevensey Bay	d					07 49		08 32															
Normans Bay	d					07 53		08 36		08 53									09 53				
Cooden Beach	d					07 56		08 39		08 57						09 34			09 57				
Collington	d					07 59		08 42		09 00						09 37			10 00				
Bexhill 4	d					08 02	08 25	08 45		09 02					09 24	09 39			10 02				10 24
St Leonards Warrior Sq 4	d					08 08	08 32	08 51		09 09					09 32	09 46			10 09				10 31
Hastings 4	a					08 11	08 35	08 55		09 12					09 35	09 49			10 12				10 35
Ore	d					08a15		08a59		09a16						09a53			10a16				
Three Oaks	d																						
Doleham	d																						
Winchelsea	d																						
Rye	a						08 53								09 53								10 53
	d			07 11			08 56					08 13			09 56								10 56
Appledore (Kent)	d			07 20			09 05					08 22			10 05								11 05
Ham Street	d			07 25			09 10					08 27			10 10								11 10
Ashford International	a			07 33			09 18					08 35			10 18								11 18

Table 189 | Mondays to Fridays

London, Haywards Heath and Brighton-Lewes, Seaford, Eastbourne, Hastings and Ashford

		SN	SN	SN	SN	SN	SN	SN	SN	SN	SN	SN	SN	SN	SN	SN	SN	SN	SN	SN	SN	SN
		◇1		1	◇1		1	1	◇1		1	◇1		1	1	◇1		1	◇1		1	1
		A ⌶			A ⌶				A ⌶			A ⌶				A ⌶						
London Victoria 15 ⊖	d	08 47			09 17				09 47			10 17				10 47			11 17			
Clapham Junction 10	d	08 53			09 23				09 53			10 23				10 53			11 23			
London Bridge 4 ⊖	d																					
East Croydon	d	09 03			09 33				10 03			10 33				11 03			11 33			
Gatwick Airport 10	d	09 19			09 49				10 19			10 49				11 19			11 49			
Haywards Heath 3	d	09 34			10 07				10 34			11 07				11 34			12 07			
Wivelsfield 4	d				10 11							11 11							12 11			
Plumpton	d	09 43							10 43													
Cooksbridge	d	09 48																				
Brighton 10	d		09 40	09 52		10 10	10 22	10 32		10 40	10 52		11 10	11 22	11 32		11 40	11 52		12 10	12 22	12 32
London Road (Brighton)	d		09 43	09 55		10 13	10 25			10 43	10 55		11 13	11 25			11 43	11 55		12 13	12 25	
Moulsecoomb	d		09 45	09 57		10 15	10 27			10 45	10 57		11 15	11 27			11 45	11 57		12 15	12 27	
Falmer	d		09 49	10 01		10 19	10 31			10 49	11 01		11 19	11 31			11 49	12 01		12 19	12 31	
Lewes 4	a	09 52	09 56	10 07	10 22	10 25	10 37	10 43	10 51	10 55	11 07	11 22	11 25	11 37	11 43	11 48	11 55	12 07	12 22	12 25	12 37	12 43
	d	09 53	09 58	10 09	10 23	10 28		10 44	10 53	10 58	11 09	11 23	11 28		11 44	11 53	11 58	12 09	12 23	12 28		12 44
Southease	d					10 34							11 34							12 34		
Newhaven Town	d		10 06			10 38				11 06			11 38				12 06			12 38		
Newhaven Harbour	d		10 08			10 40				11 08			11 40				12 08			12 40		
Bishopstone	d		10 11			10 43				11 11			11 43				12 11			12 43		
Seaford	a		10 14			10 46				11 14			11 46				12 14			12 46		
Glynde	d			10 14							11 14							12 14				
Berwick	d			10 20							11 20							12 20				
Polegate	d	10 05		10 25	10 35			10 57	11 05		11 25	11 35			11 57	12 05		12 25	12 35			12 57
Hampden Park 4	d			10 29	10 39						11 29	11 39						12 29	12 39			
Eastbourne 4	a	10 13		10 34	10 44			11 04	11 13		11 34	11 44			12 04	12 13		12 34	12 44			13 04
	d	10 19		10 40				11 09	11 19		11 40				12 09	12 19		12 40				13 09
Hampden Park 4	d	10 23		10 44					11 23		11 44					12 23		12 44				
Pevensey & Westham	d	10 28		10 49					11 28		11 49					12 28		12 49				
Pevensey Bay	d																					
Normans Bay	d			10 53							11 53							12 53				
Cooden Beach	d	10 34		10 57					11 34		11 57					12 34		12 57				
Collington	d	10 37		11 00					11 37		12 00					12 37		13 00				
Bexhill 4	d	10 39		11 02				11 24	11 39		12 02				12 24	12 39		13 02				13 24
St Leonards Warrior Sq 4	d	10 46		11 09				11 31	11 46		12 09				12 31	12 46		13 09				13 31
Hastings 4	a	10 49		11 12				11 35	11 49		12 12				12 35	12 49		13 12				13 35
Ore	d	10a53		11a16					11a53		12a16					12a53		13a16				
Three Oaks	d																					
Doleham	d																					
Winchelsea	d																					
Rye	a							11 53							12 53							13 53
	d							11 56							12 56							13 56
Appledore (Kent)	d							12 05							13 05							14 05
Ham Street	d							12 10							13 10							14 10
Ashford International	a							12 18							13 18							14 18

A ⌶ to Lewes

Table 189 | Mondays to Fridays

London, Haywards Heath and Brighton-Lewes, Seaford, Eastbourne, Hastings and Ashford

		SN	SN	SN	SN	SN	SN	SN	SN	SN	SN	SN	SN	SN	SN	SN	SN	SN	SN	SN	SN	SN	SN
		◇1		1	◇1		1	1	◇1		1	◇1		1	1	◇1		1	◇1		1	1	◇1
London Victoria 15 ⊖	d	11 47			12 17				12 47			13 17				13 47			14 17				14 47
Clapham Junction 10	d	11 53			12 23				12 53			13 23				13 53			14 23				14 53
London Bridge 4 ⊖	d																						
East Croydon ⇌	d	12 03			12 34				13 03			13 33				14 03			14 33				15 03
Gatwick Airport 10	d	12 19			12 50				13 19			13 49				14 19			14 49				15 19
Haywards Heath 3	d	12 34			13 07				13 34			14 07				14 34			15 07				15 34
Wivelsfield 4	d				13 11							14 11							15 11				15 38
Plumpton	d	12 43																					15 44
Cooksbridge	d																						
Brighton 10	d		12 40	12 52		13 10	13 22	13 32		13 40	13 52		14 10	14 22	14 32		14 40	14 52		15 10	15 22	15 32	
London Road (Brighton)	d		12 43	12 55		13 13	13 25			13 43	13 55		14 13	14 25			14 43	14 55		15 13	15 25		
Moulsecoomb	d		12 45	12 57		13 15	13 27			13 45	13 57		14 15	14 27			14 45	14 57		15 15	15 27		
Falmer	d		12 49	13 01		13 19	13 31			13 49	14 01		14 19	14 31			14 49	15 01		15 19	15 31		
Lewes 4	a	12 51	12 55	13 07	13 22	13 25	13 37	13 43	13 48	13 55	14 07	14 22	14 25	14 37	14 43	14 48	14 55	15 07	15 22	15 25	15 37	15 43	15 51
	d	12 53	12 58	13 09	13 23	13 28		13 44	13 53	13 58	14 09	14 23	14 28		14 44	14 53	14 58	15 09	15 23	15 28		15 44	15 53
Southease	d					13 34							14 34							15 34			
Newhaven Town	d		13 06			13 38				14 06			14 38				15 06			15 38			
Newhaven Harbour	d		13 08			13 40				14 08			14 40				15 08			15 40			
Bishopstone	d		13 11			13 43				14 11			14 43				15 11			15 43			
Seaford	a		13 14			13 46				14 14			14 46				15 14			15 46			
Glynde	d			13 14							14 14							15 14					
Berwick	d			13 20							14 20							15 20					
Polegate	d	13 05		13 25	13 35			13 57	14 05		14 25	14 35			14 57	15 05		15 25	15 35			15 57	16 05
Hampden Park 4	d			13 29	13 39						14 29	14 39						15 29	15 39				
Eastbourne 4	a	13 13		13 34	13 44			14 04	14 13		14 34	14 44			15 04	15 13		15 34	15 44			16 04	16 13
	d	13 19		13 40				14 09	14 19		14 40				15 09	15 19		15 40				16 09	16 19
Hampden Park 4	d	13 23		13 44					14 23		14 44					15 23		15 44					16 23
Pevensey & Westham	d	13 28		13 49					14 28		14 49					15 28		15 49					16 28
Pevensey Bay	d															15 30							
Normans Bay	d			13 53							14 53					15 34		15 53					
Cooden Beach	d	13 34		13 57					14 34		14 57					15 37		15 57					16 34
Collington	d	13 37		14 00					14 37		15 00					15 40		16 00					16 37
Bexhill 4	d	13 39		14 02				14 24	14 39		15 02				15 24	15 43		16 02				16 24	16 39
St Leonards Warrior Sq 4	d	13 46		14 09				14 31	14 46		15 09				15 31	15 49		16 09				16 31	16 46
Hastings 4	a	13 49		14 12				14 35	14 49		15 12				15 35	15 52		16 12				16 35	16 49
Ore	d	13a53		14a16					14a53		15a16					15a57		16a16					16a53
Three Oaks	d																						
Doleham	d																						
Winchelsea	d																						
Rye	a							14 53							15 53							16 53	
	d							14 56							15 56							16 56	
Appledore (Kent)	d							15 05							16 05							17 05	
Ham Street	d							15 10							16 10							17 10	
Ashford International	a							15 18							16 18							17 18	

Table 189 | Mondays to Fridays

London, Haywards Heath and Brighton-Lewes, Seaford, Eastbourne, Hastings and Ashford

		SN	SN	SN	SN	SN	SN	SN	SN	SN	SN	SN	SN	SN	SN	SN	SN	SN	SN	SN	SN	SN
			1	◇1		1	1	◇1		1	◇1		1	1	1	◇1		1	1		◇1	
											A ⌶					A ⌶					A ⌶	
London Victoria 15 ⊖	d			15 17				15 47			16 17					16 47					17 36	
Clapham Junction 10	d			15 23				15 53			16 23					16 53					17 42	
London Bridge 4 ⊖	d																		17 23			
East Croydon ⇌	d			15 33				16 03			16 33					17 03			17 36		17 52	
Gatwick Airport 10	d			15 49				16 19			16 49					17 20					18 07	
Haywards Heath 3	d			16 07				16 33			17 06					17 36			18 05		18 18	
Wivelsfield 4	d			16 11				16 37			17 10					17 41			18 09		18 23	
Plumpton	d							16 43								17 47					18 29	
Cooksbridge	d							16 48								17 52					18 33	
Brighton 10	d	15 40	15 52		16 10	16 22	16 32		16 40	16 52		17 10		17 20	17 32		17 40	17 52		18 08		18 17
London Road (Brighton)	d	15 43	15 55		16 13	16 25			16 43	16 55		17 13		17 23			17 43	17 55		18 11		18 20
Moulsecoomb	d	15 45	15 57		16 15	16 27			16 45	16 57		17 15		17 25			17 45	17 57		18 13		18 22
Falmer	d	15 49	16 01		16 19	16 31			16 49	17 01		17 19		17 29			17 49	18 01		18 17		18 26
Lewes 4	a	15 55	16 07	16 22	16 25	16 37	16 43	16 52	16 55	17 07	17 21	17 25		17 35	17 43	17 56	17 55	18 07	18 20	18 23	18 38	18 32
	d	15 58	16 09	16 23	16 28		16 44	16 53	16 58	17 09	17 22	17 28		17 36	17 44	17 57	18 01	18 08	18 21	18 24	18 38	18 42
Southease	d	16 04			16 34							17 34					18 07					
Newhaven Town	d	16 08			16 38				17 06			17 38					18 11			18 33		18 50
Newhaven Harbour	d	16 10			16 40				17 08			17 40					18 13					
Bishopstone	d	16 13			16 43				17 11			17 43					18 16			18 37		18 54
Seaford	a	16 16			16 46				17 14			17 46					18 19			18 40		18 58
Glynde	d		16 14							17 14								18 13	18 26			
Berwick	d		16 20					17 02		17 20	17 31			17 45				18 19	18 32			
Polegate	d		16 25	16 35			16 57	17 07		17 25	17 36			17 50	17 57	18 09		18 24	18 37		18 51	
Hampden Park 4	d		16 29	16 39						17 29	17 40			17 55		18 13		18 28	18 41		18 55	
Eastbourne 4	a		16 34	16 44			17 04	17 14		17 34	17 48			18 00	18 04	18 18		18 34	18 48		19 01	
	d		16 40				17 09	17 21		17 40					18 09	18 25		18 43			19 19	
Hampden Park 4	d		16 44					17 25		17 44						18 29		18 47			19 23	
Pevensey & Westham	d		16 49					17 30		17 49						18 34		18 52			19 28	
Pevensey Bay	d							17 32		17 51												
Normans Bay	d		16 53					17 36		17 55								18 56				
Cooden Beach	d		16 57					17 39		17 58						18 40		19 00			19 34	
Collington	d		17 00					17 42		18 01						18 43		19 03			19 37	
Bexhill 4	d		17 02				17 24	17 45		18 04					18 24	18 45		19 05			19 39	
St Leonards Warrior Sq 4	d		17 09				17 31	17 53		18 10					18 31	18 56		19 11			19 46	
Hastings 4	a		17 12				17 35	17 57		18 13			17 09		18 34	19 00		19 14			19 49	
Ore	d		17a16					18a01		18a17			17 11					19a18			19a55	
Three Oaks	d												17 17									
Doleham	d												17 20									
Winchelsea	d												17 26									
Rye	a						17 53						17 30		18 53							
	d						17 56						17 30		18 56							
Appledore (Kent)	d						18 05						17 39		19 05							
Ham Street	d						18 10						17 44		19 10							
Ashford International	a						18 18						17 52		19 18							

A ⌶ to Lewes

Table 189

Mondays to Fridays

London, Haywards Heath and Brighton-Lewes, Seaford, Eastbourne, Hastings and Ashford

		SN	SN	SN	SN	SN	SN	SN	SN	SN	SN	SN	SN	SN	SN	SN	SN	SN	SN	SN	SN	SN	SN
		■	■		■	◇■	◇■	■		■	■	■	◇■		■	◇■		■	◇■			◇■	■
						A ⌶							A ⌶			A ⌶			A ⌶				
London Victoria 15 ⊖	d					18 06							18 47			19 17			19 47			20 17	
Clapham Junction 10	d					18 12							18 53			19 23			19 53			20 23	
London Bridge 4 ⊖	d							18 23															
East Croydon	d					18 22		18 37					19 03			19 33			20 03			20 33	
Gatwick Airport 10	d					18 38							19 20			19 49			20 19			20 49	
Haywards Heath 3	d					18 50		19 06					19 34			20 07			20 36			21 07	
Wivelsfield 4	d					18 54		19 11					19 38			20 11			20 40			21 11	
Plumpton	d					19 00		19 17					19 44						20 46				
Cooksbridge	d					19 05		19 22					19 49						20 50				
Brighton 10	d		18 32	18 38	18 51				19 08	19 22		19 32		19 40	19 52		20 10	20 30		20 40	21 04		21 32
London Road (Brighton)	d			18 41	18 54				19 11	19 25				19 43	19 55		20 13			20 43	21 07		
Moulsecoomb	d			18 43	18 56				19 13	19 27				19 45	19 57		20 15			20 45	21 09		
Falmer	d			18 47	19 00				19 17	19 31				19 49	20 01		20 19			20 49	21 13		
Lewes 4	a		18 44	18 53	19 06	19 09	>	19 27	19 23	19 37		19 43	19 53	19 55	20 07	20 22	20 25	20 43	20 55	20 55	21 19	21 22	21 43
	d		18 45	18 54	19 07	19 13	19 16	19 27	19 31			19 44	19 54	19 58	20 09	20 23	20 28	20 44	20 55	21 00	21 28	21 23	21 44
Southease	d			19 00					19 37					20 04									
Newhaven Town	d			19 04		19 21			19 41					20 08			20 36			21 08	21 36		
Newhaven Harbour	d			19 09					19 44					20 10			20 38			21 10	21 38		
Bishopstone	d			19 12		19 29			19 47					20 13			20 41			21 13	21 41		
Seaford	a			19 15		19 34			19 50					20 16			20 44			21 16	21 44		
Glynde	d						19 21	19 33							20 14	20 28						21 28	
Berwick	d						19 27	19 39							20 20	20 34						21 34	
Polegate	d		18 58		19 19		19 32	19 45				19 57	20 06		20 25	20 39		20 57	21 08			21 39	21 57
Hampden Park 4	d						19 36	19 49							20 29	20 43						21 43	
Eastbourne 4	a		19 05		19 28		19 41	19 56				20 04	20 14		20 34	20 48		21 04	21 15			21 48	22 04
	d		19 09				19 51					20 09	20 19					21 09	21 21				22 09
Hampden Park 4	d						19 55						20 23						21 25				
Pevensey & Westham	d		19 17				20 00						20 28						21 30				
Pevensey Bay	d																						
Normans Bay	d																						
Cooden Beach	d						20 06						20 34						21 36				
Collington	d						20 09						20 37						21 39				
Bexhill 4	d		19 25				20 11					20 24	20 39					21 24	21 41				22 23
St Leonards Warrior Sq 4	d		19 32				20 18					20 31	20 46					21 31	21 48				22 30
Hastings 4	a		19 35				20 21					20 34	20 49					21 34	21 53				22 33
Ore	d						20a27						20a55					21 37	21a57				
Three Oaks	d																	21 43					
Doleham	d																	21 46					
Winchelsea	d																	21 52					
Rye	a		19 53									20 53						21 56					
	d	18 31	19 56								19 31	20 56						21 56					
Appledore (Kent)	d	18 40	20 05								19 40	21 05						22 05					
Ham Street	d	18 45	20 10								19 45	21 10						22 10					
Ashford International	a	18 53	20 18								19 53	21 18						22 18					

A ⌶ to Lewes

Table 189

Mondays to Fridays

London, Haywards Heath and Brighton-Lewes, Seaford, Eastbourne, Hastings and Ashford

		SN	SN	SN	SN	SN	SN	SN	SN	SN	SN	SN
		◇■			◇■	■	◇■		■	■	◇■	
London Victoria 15 ⊖	d	20 47			21 17		21 47				22 47	
Clapham Junction 10	d	20 53			21 23		21 53				22 53	
London Bridge 4 ⊖	d											
East Croydon	d	21 04			21 33		22 03				23 03	
Gatwick Airport 10	d	21 19			21 49		22 19				23 19	
Haywards Heath 3	d	21 37			22 08		22 34				23 34	
Wivelsfield 4	d	21 41			22 12		22 38				23 38	
Plumpton	d	21 47					22 44				23 44	
Cooksbridge	d											
Brighton 10	d		21 40	22 04		22 28		22 34	23 06	23 28		23 34
London Road (Brighton)	d		21 43	22 07				22 37	23 09			23 37
Moulsecoomb	d		21 45	22 09				22 39	23 11			23 39
Falmer	d		21 49	22 13				22 43	23 15			23 43
Lewes 4	a	21 54	21 55	22 19	22 23	22 39	22 51	22 49	23 21	23 39	23 51	23 49
	d	21 55	21 58	22 28	22 23	22 39	22 53	22 56	23 22	23 39	23 53	23 56
Southease	d		22 04					23 02				
Newhaven Town	d		22 08	22 36				23 06				00 04
Newhaven Harbour	d		22 10	22 38				23 08				00 06
Bishopstone	d		22 13	22 41				23 11				00 09
Seaford	a		22 16	22 44				23 14				00 12
Glynde	d				22 29				23 27			
Berwick	d				22 34				23 33		00 02	
Polegate	d	22 07			22 39	22 52	23 05		23 38	23 52	00 07	
Hampden Park 4	d				22 43		23 09		23 42		00 11	
Eastbourne 4	a	22 15			22 48	23 03	23 14		23 47	23 59	00 16	
	d	22 21					23 20				00 22	
Hampden Park 4	d	22 25					23 24					
Pevensey & Westham	d	22 30					23 29				00 29	
Pevensey Bay	d											
Normans Bay	d											
Cooden Beach	d	22 36					23 35				00 35	
Collington	d	22 39					23 38				00 38	
Bexhill 4	d	22 41					23 40				00 41	
St Leonards Warrior Sq 4	d	22 48					23 47				00 47	
Hastings 4	a	22 51					23 50				00 50	
Ore	d											
Three Oaks	d											
Doleham	d											
Winchelsea	d											
Rye	a											
	d											
Appledore (Kent)	d											
Ham Street	d											
Ashford International	a											

London, Haywards Heath and Brighton-Lewes, Seaford, Eastbourne, Hastings and Ashford

		SN ◇1	SN	SN ◇1	SN 1	SN 1	SN 1	SN	SN 1	SN 1	SN	SN 1	SN 1	SN 1	SN 1	SN	SN 1	SN	SN 1	SN 1	SN 1	SN	SN 1
London Victoria 15 ⊖	d	22p47		00 05																			
Clapham Junction 10	d	22p53		00 11																			
London Bridge 4 ⊖	d																						
East Croydon	d	23p03		00 25																			
Gatwick Airport 10	d	23p19		00 44											06 11								
Haywards Heath 3	d	23p34		01 06											06 25						07 33		
Wivelsfield 4	d	23p38													06 29						07 37		
Plumpton	d	23p44																					
Cooksbridge	d																						
Brighton 10	d		23p34		05 12			05 52			06 10			06 32		06 40	06 52	07 10	07 22	07 32		07 40	07 52
London Road (Brighton)	d		23p37					05 55			06 13					06 43	06 55	07 13	07 25			07 43	07 55
Moulsecoomb	d		23p39					05 57			06 15					06 45	06 57	07 15	07 27			07 45	07 57
Falmer	d		23p43					06 01			06 19					06 49	07 01	07 19	07 31			07 49	08 01
Lewes 4	a	23p51	23p49	01 20	05 23			06 07			06 25			06 43	06 40	06 55	07 07	07 25	07 37	07 43	07 48	07 55	08 07
	d	23p53	23p56	01 20	05 23			06 08			06 28			06 44	06 53	06 58	07 09	07 28		07 44	07 53	07 58	08 09
Southease	d																						
Newhaven Town	d		00 04					06 16			06 36					07 06		07 36				08 06	
Newhaven Harbour	d		00 06					06 18			06 38					07 08		07 38				08 08	
Bishopstone	d		00 09								06 41					07 11		07 41				08 11	
Seaford	a		00 12					06 23			06 44					07 14		07 44				08 14	
Glynde	d																07 14						08 14
Berwick	d	00 02													07 02		07 20						08 20
Polegate	d	00 07		01s32	05 35									06 57	07 07		07 25			07 57	08 05		08 25
Hampden Park 4	d	00 11		01s36											07 11		07 29						08 29
Eastbourne 4	a	00 16		01 41	05 42									07 04	07 16		07 34			08 05	08 13		08 34
	d	00 22					05 38		05 53	06 04		06 18	06 45	07 09	07 21		07 40			08 09	08 19		08 40
Hampden Park 4	d											06 22			07 25		07 44				08 23		08 44
Pevensey & Westham	d	00 29										06 27			07 30		07 49				08 28		08 49
Pevensey Bay	d																						
Normans Bay	d											06 31					07 53						08 53
Cooden Beach	d	00 35										06 35			07 36		07 57				08 34		08 57
Collington	d	00 38										06 38			07 39		08 00				08 37		09 00
Bexhill 4	d	00 41					05 52		06 07	06 18		06 40	07 00	07 24	07 41		08 02			08 24	08 39		09 02
St Leonards Warrior Sq 4	d	00 47					06 00		06 14	06 24		06 49	07 06	07 31	07 48		08 09			08 31	08 46		09 09
Hastings 4	a	00 50					06 04		06 17	06 28		06 53	07 10	07 35	07 51		08 12			08 35	08 50		09 12
Ore	d					05 23	06a08			06a32		06a57	07a14		07a55		08a16				08a54		09a16
Three Oaks	d					05 29																	
Doleham	d					05 32																	
Winchelsea	d					05 38																	
Rye	a					05 41			06 35					07 53						08 53			
	d					05 43			06 38					07 56						08 56			
Appledore (Kent)	d					05 52			06 47					08 05						09 05			
Ham Street	d					05 57			06 52					08 10						09 10			
Ashford International	a					06 05			07 00					08 18						09 18			

		SN	SN 1	SN 1	SN ◇1	SN	SN 1	SN ◇1	SN	SN 1	SN 1	SN ◇1	SN	SN 1	SN ◇1	SN	SN 1	SN 1	SN ◇1	SN	SN 1	SN ◇1	SN
London Victoria 15 ⊖	d				07 47				08 17			08 47			09 17				09 47				
Clapham Junction 10	d				07 53				08 23			08 53			09 23				09 53				
London Bridge 4 ⊖	d																						
East Croydon	d				08 03				08 33			09 03			09 33				10 03				
Gatwick Airport 10	d				08 19				08 49			09 19			09 49				10 19				
Haywards Heath 3	d				08 34			09 07				09 34			10 07				10 34			11 07	
Wivelsfield 4	d							09 11							10 11							11 11	
Plumpton	d											09 43							10 43				
Cooksbridge	d																						
Brighton 10	d	08 10	08 22	08 32		08 40	08 52		09 10	09 22	09 32		09 40	09 52		10 10	10 22	10 32		10 40	10 52		11 10
London Road (Brighton)	d	08 13	08 25			08 43	08 55		09 13	09 25			09 43	09 55		10 13	10 25			10 43	10 55		11 13
Moulsecoomb	d	08 15	08 27			08 45	08 57		09 15	09 27			09 45	09 57		10 15	10 27			10 45	10 57		11 15
Falmer	d	08 19	08 31			08 49	09 01		09 19	09 31			09 49	10 01		10 19	10 31			10 49	11 01		11 19
Lewes 4	a	08 25	08 37	08 43	08 48	08 55	09 07	09 22	09 25	09 37	09 43	09 51	09 55	10 07	10 22	10 25	10 37	10 43	10 51	10 55	11 07	11 22	11 25
	d	08 28		08 44	08 53	08 58	09 09	09 23	09 28		09 44	09 53	09 58	10 09	10 23	10 28		10 44	10 53	10 58	11 09	11 23	11 28
Southease	d								09 34							10 34							11 34
Newhaven Town	d	08 36				09 06			09 38				10 06			10 38				11 06			11 38
Newhaven Harbour	d	08 38				09 08			09 40				10 08			10 40				11 08			11 40
Bishopstone	d	08 41				09 11			09 43				10 11			10 43				11 11			11 43
Seaford	a	08 44				09 14			09 46				10 14			10 46				11 14			11 46
Glynde	d						09 14							10 14							11 14		
Berwick	d						09 20							10 20							11 20		
Polegate	d			08 57	09 05		09 25	09 35			09 57	10 05		10 25	10 35			10 57	11 05		11 25	11 35	
Hampden Park 4	d						09 29	09 39						10 29	10 39						11 29	11 39	
Eastbourne 4	a			09 04	09 13		09 34	09 44			10 04	10 13		10 34	10 44			11 04	11 13		11 34	11 44	
	d			09 09	09 19		09 40				10 09	10 19		10 40				11 09	11 19		11 40		
Hampden Park 4	d				09 23		09 44					10 23		10 44					11 23		11 44		
Pevensey & Westham	d				09 28		09 49					10 28		10 49					11 28		11 49		
Pevensey Bay	d																						
Normans Bay	d						09 53							10 53							11 53		
Cooden Beach	d				09 34		09 57					10 34		10 57					11 34		11 57		
Collington	d				09 37		10 00					10 37		11 00					11 37		12 00		
Bexhill 4	d			09 24	09 39		10 02				10 24	10 39		11 02				11 24	11 39		12 02		
St Leonards Warrior Sq 4	d			09 31	09 46		10 09				10 31	10 46		11 09				11 31	11 46		12 09		
Hastings 4	a			09 35	09 49		10 12				10 35	10 49		11 12				11 35	11 49		12 12		
Ore	d				09a53		10a16					10a53		11a16					11a53		12a16		
Three Oaks	d																						
Doleham	d																						
Winchelsea	d																						
Rye	a			09 53							10 53							11 53					
	d			09 56							10 56							11 56					
Appledore (Kent)	d			10 05							11 05							12 05					
Ham Street	d			10 10							11 10							12 10					
Ashford International	a			10 18							11 18							12 18					

		SN 1	SN 1	SN ◇1	SN	SN 1	SN ◇1	SN	SN 1	SN 1	SN ◇1	SN	SN 1	SN ◇1	SN	SN 1	SN 1	SN ◇1	SN	SN 1	SN ◇1	SN
London Victoria 15 ⊖	d	10 17		10 47			11 17				11 47			12 17				12 47			13 17	
Clapham Junction 10	d	10 23		10 53			11 23				11 53			12 23				12 53			13 23	
London Bridge 4 ⊖	d																					
East Croydon	d	10 33		11 03			11 33				12 03			12 33				13 03			13 33	
Gatwick Airport 10	d	10 49		11 19			11 49				12 19			12 49				13 19			13 49	
Haywards Heath 3	d			11 34			12 07				12 34			13 07				13 34			14 07	
Wivelsfield 4	d						12 11							13 11							14 11	
Plumpton	d			11 43							12 43											
Cooksbridge	d																					
Brighton 10	d	11 22	11 32		11 40	11 52		12 10	12 22	12 32		12 40	12 52		13 10	13 22	13 32		13 40	13 52		14 10
London Road (Brighton)	d	11 25			11 43	11 55		12 13	12 25			12 43	12 55		13 13	13 25			13 43	13 55		14 13
Moulsecoomb	d	11 27			11 45	11 57		12 15	12 27			12 45	12 57		13 15	13 27			13 45	13 57		14 15
Falmer	d	11 31			11 49	12 01		12 19	12 31			12 49	13 01		13 19	13 31			13 49	14 01		14 19
Lewes 4	a	11 37	11 43	11 51	11 55	12 07	12 22	12 25	12 37	12 43	12 51	12 55	13 07	13 22	13 25	13 37	13 43	13 48	13 55	14 07	14 22	14 25
	d		11 44	11 53	11 58	12 09	12 23	12 28		12 44	12 53	12 58	13 09	13 23	13 28		13 44	13 53	13 58	14 09	14 23	14 28
Southease	d							12 34							13 34							14 34
Newhaven Town	d				12 06			12 38				13 06			13 38				14 06			14 38
Newhaven Harbour	d				12 08			12 40				13 08			13 40				14 08			14 40
Bishopstone	d				12 11			12 43				13 11			13 43				14 11			14 43
Seaford	a				12 14			12 46				13 14			13 46				14 14			14 46
Glynde	d					12 14							13 14							14 14		
Berwick	d					12 20							13 20							14 20		
Polegate	d		11 57	12 05		12 25	12 35			12 57	13 05		13 25	13 35			13 57	14 05		14 25	14 35	
Hampden Park 4	d					12 29	12 39						13 29	13 39						14 29	14 39	
Eastbourne 4	a		12 04	12 13		12 34	12 44			13 04	13 13		13 34	13 44			14 04	14 13		14 34	14 44	
	d		12 09	12 19		12 40				13 09	13 19		13 40				14 09	14 19		14 40		
Hampden Park 4	d			12 23		12 44					13 23		13 44					14 23		14 44		
Pevensey & Westham	d			12 28		12 49					13 28		13 49					14 28		14 49		
Pevensey Bay	d																					
Normans Bay	d					12 53							13 53							14 53		
Cooden Beach	d			12 34		12 57					13 34		13 57					14 34		14 57		
Collington	d			12 37		13 00					13 37		14 00					14 37		15 00		
Bexhill 4	d		12 24	12 39		13 02				13 24	13 39		14 02				14 24	14 39		15 02		
St Leonards Warrior Sq 4	d		12 31	12 46		13 09				13 31	13 46		14 09				14 31	14 46		15 09		
Hastings 4	a		12 35	12 49		13 12				13 35	13 49		14 12				14 35	14 49		15 12		
Ore	d			12a53		13a16					13a53		14a16					14a53		15a16		
Three Oaks	d																					
Doleham	d																					
Winchelsea	d																					
Rye	a		12 53							13 53							14 53					
	d		12 56							13 56							14 56					
Appledore (Kent)	d		13 05							14 05							15 05					
Ham Street	d		13 10							14 10							15 10					
Ashford International	a		13 18							14 18							15 18					

		SN 1	SN 1	SN ◇1	SN	SN 1	SN ◇1	SN	SN 1	SN 1	SN ◇1	SN	SN 1	SN ◇1	SN	SN 1	SN 1	SN ◇1	SN	SN 1	SN ◇1	SN	SN 1
London Victoria 15 ⊖	d			13 47			14 17				14 47			15 17				15 47			16 17		
Clapham Junction 10	d			13 53			14 23				14 53			15 23				15 53			16 23		
London Bridge 4 ⊖	d																						
East Croydon	d			14 03			14 33				15 03			15 33				16 03			16 33		
Gatwick Airport 10	d			14 19			14 49				15 19			15 49				16 19			16 49		
Haywards Heath 3	d			14 34			15 07				15 34			16 07				16 34			17 07		
Wivelsfield 4	d						15 11							16 11							17 11		
Plumpton	d																	16 43					
Cooksbridge	d																						
Brighton 10	d	14 22	14 32		14 40	14 52		15 10	15 22	15 32		15 40	15 52		16 10	16 22	16 32		16 40	16 52		17 10	17 22
London Road (Brighton)	d	14 25			14 43	14 55		15 13	15 25			15 43	15 55		16 13	16 25			16 43	16 55		17 13	17 25
Moulsecoomb	d	14 27			14 45	14 57		15 15	15 27			15 45	15 57		16 15	16 27			16 45	16 57		17 15	17 27
Falmer	d	14 31			14 49	15 01		15 19	15 31			15 49	16 01		16 19	16 31			16 49	17 01		17 19	17 31
Lewes 4	a	14 37	14 43	14 48	14 55	15 07	15 22	15 25	15 37	15 43	15 48	15 55	16 07	16 22	16 25	16 37	16 43	16 51	16 55	17 07	17 22	17 25	17 37
	d		14 44	14 53	14 58	15 09	15 23	15 28		15 44	15 53	15 58	16 09	16 23	16 28		16 44	16 53	16 58	17 09	17 23	17 28	
Southease	d							15 34							16 34							17 34	
Newhaven Town	d				15 06			15 38				16 06			16 38				17 06			17 38	
Newhaven Harbour	d				15 08			15 40				16 08			16 40				17 08			17 40	
Bishopstone	d				15 11			15 43				16 11			16 43				17 11			17 43	
Seaford	a				15 14			15 50				16 14			16 46				17 14			17 46	
Glynde	d					15 14							16 14							17 14			
Berwick	d					15 20							16 20							17 20			
Polegate	d		14 57	15 05		15 25	15 35			15 57	16 05		16 25	16 35			16 57	17 05		17 25	17 35		
Hampden Park 4	d					15 29	15 39						16 29	16 39						17 29	17 39		
Eastbourne 4	a		15 04	15 13		15 34	15 44			16 04	16 13		16 34	16 44			17 04	17 13		17 34	17 44		
	d		15 09	15 19		15 40				16 09	16 19		16 40				17 09	17 19		17 40			
Hampden Park 4	d			15 23		15 44					16 23		16 44					17 23		17 44			
Pevensey & Westham	d			15 28		15 49					16 28		16 49					17 28		17 49			
Pevensey Bay	d																						
Normans Bay	d					15 53							16 53							17 53			
Cooden Beach	d			15 34		15 57					16 34		16 57					17 34		17 57			
Collington	d			15 37		16 00					16 37		17 00					17 37		18 00			
Bexhill 4	d		15 24	15 39		16 02				16 24	16 39		17 02				17 24	17 39		18 02			
St Leonards Warrior Sq 4	d		15 31	15 46		16 09				16 31	16 46		17 09				17 31	17 46		18 09			
Hastings 4	a		15 35	15 49		16 12				16 35	16 49		17 12				17 35	17 49		18 12			
Ore	d			15a53		16a16					16a53		17a16					17a53		18a16			
Three Oaks	d																						
Doleham	d																						
Winchelsea	d																						
Rye	a		15 53							16 53							17 53						
	d		15 56							16 56							17 56						
Appledore (Kent)	d		16 05							17 05							18 05						
Ham Street	d		16 10							17 10							18 10						
Ashford International	a		16 18							17 18							18 18						

Table 189

Saturdays

London, Haywards Heath and Brighton-Lewes, Seaford, Eastbourne, Hastings and Ashford

		SN ■	SN ◇■	SN	SN ■	SN ◇■	SN	SN ■	SN ■	SN ◇■	SN	SN ■	SN ◇■	SN	SN ■	SN ■	SN ◇■	SN	SN ■	SN ■	SN	SN ■
London Victoria 15 ⊖	d		16 47			17 17				17 47			18 17				18 47			19 17		
Clapham Junction 10	d		16 53			17 23				17 53			18 23				18 53			19 23		
London Bridge 4 ⊖	d																					
East Croydon ⇌	d		17 03			17 33				18 03			18 33				19 03			19 33		
Gatwick Airport 10	d		17 19			17 49				18 19			18 49				19 19			19 49		
Haywards Heath 3	d		17 34			18 07				18 34			19 07				19 34			20 07		
Wivelsfield 4	d					18 11							19 11							20 11		
Plumpton	d		17 43							18 43							19 43					
Cooksbridge	d																					
Brighton 10	d	17 32		17 40	17 52		18 10	18 22	18 32		18 40	18 52		19 10	19 22	19 32		19 40	19 53		20 10	20 32
London Road (Brighton)	d			17 43	17 55		18 13	18 25			18 43	18 55		19 13	19 25			19 43	19 56		20 13	
Moulsecoomb	d			17 45	17 57		18 15	18 27			18 45	18 57		19 15	19 27			19 45	19 58		20 15	
Falmer	d			17 49	18 01		18 19	18 31			18 49	19 01		19 19	19 31			19 49	20 02		20 19	
Lewes 4	a	17 43	17 51	17 55	18 07	18 22	18 25	18 37	18 43	18 51	18 55	19 07	19 22	19 25	19 37	19 43	19 51	19 55	20 08	20 22	20 25	20 43
	d	17 44	17 53	17 58	18 09	18 23	18 28		18 44	18 53	18 58	19 09	19 23	19 28		19 44	19 53	19 58	20 09	20 23	20 28	20 44
Southease	d						18 34							19 34								
Newhaven Town	d			18 06			18 38				19 06			19 38				20 06			20 36	
Newhaven Harbour	d			18 08			18 40				19 08			19 40				20 08			20 38	
Bishopstone	d			18 11			18 43				19 11			19 43				20 11			20 41	
Seaford	a			18 14			18 46				19 14			19 46				20 14			20 44	
Glynde	d				18 14							19 14							20 14	20 28		
Berwick	d				18 20							19 20							20 20	20 34		
Polegate	d	17 57	18 05		18 25	18 35			18 57	19 05		19 25	19 35			19 57	20 05		20 25	20 39		20 57
Hampden Park 4	d				18 29	18 39						19 29	19 39						20 29	20 43		
Eastbourne 4	a	18 04	18 13		18 34	18 44			19 04	19 13		19 34	19 44			20 04	20 13		20 34	20 48		21 04
	d	18 09	18 19		18 40				19 09	19 19		19 40				20 09	20 19			20 54		21 09
Hampden Park 4	d		18 23		18 44					19 23		19 44					20 23					
Pevensey & Westham	d		18 28		18 49					19 28		19 49					20 28			21 01		
Pevensey Bay	d																					
Normans Bay	d				18 53							19 53										
Cooden Beach	d		18 34		18 57					19 34		19 57					20 34			21 07		
Collington	d		18 37		19 00					19 37		20 00					20 37					
Bexhill 4	d	18 24	18 39		19 02				19 24	19 39		20 02				20 24	20 39			21 12		21 23
St Leonards Warrior Sq 4	d	18 31	18 46		19 09				19 31	19 46		20 09				20 31	20 46			21 18		21 30
Hastings 4	a	18 35	18 49		19 12				19 35	19 49		20 12				20 35	20 49			21 21		21 33
Ore	d		18a53		19a16					19a53		20a16					20a53					21 36
Three Oaks	d																					21 42
Doleham	d																					21 45
Winchelsea	d																					21 51
Rye	a	18 53							19 53							20 53						21 55
	d	18 56							19 56							20 56						21 56
Appledore (Kent)	d	19 05							20 05							21 05						22 05
Ham Street	d	19 10							20 10							21 10						22 10
Ashford International	a	19 18							20 18							21 18						22 18

		SN ◇■	SN	SN	SN ◇■	SN ■	SN ◇■	SN	SN	SN ◇■	SN ■	SN ◇■	SN	SN ■	SN ■	SN ◇■	SN
London Victoria 15 ⊖	d	19 47			20 17		20 47			21 17		21 47				22 47	
Clapham Junction 10	d	19 53			20 23		20 53			21 23		21 53				22 53	
London Bridge 4 ⊖	d																
East Croydon ⇌	d	20 03			20 33		21 03			21 33		22 03				23 03	
Gatwick Airport 10	d	20 19			20 49		21 19			21 49		22 19				23 19	
Haywards Heath 3	d	20 34			21 07		21 34			22 08		22 34				23 34	
Wivelsfield 4	d	20 38			21 11		21 38			22 12		22 38				23 38	
Plumpton	d	20 44					21 44					22 44				23 44	
Cooksbridge	d																
Brighton 10	d		20 40	21 04		21 32		21 40	22 04		22 28		22 34	23 06	23 28		23 34
London Road (Brighton)	d		20 43	21 07				21 43	22 07				22 37	23 09			23 37
Moulsecoomb	d		20 45	21 09				21 45	22 09				22 39	23 11			23 39
Falmer	d		20 49	21 13				21 49	22 13				22 43	23 15			23 43
Lewes 4	a	20 51	20 55	21 19	21 22	21 43	21 51	21 55	22 19	22 23	22 39	22 51	22 49	23 21	23 39	23 51	23 49
	d	20 53	20 58	21 28	21 23	21 44	21 53	21 58	22 28	22 23	22 39	22 53	22 56	23 22	23 39	23 53	23 56
Southease	d																
Newhaven Town	d		21 06	21 36				22 06	22 36				23 04				00 04
Newhaven Harbour	d		21 08	21 38				22 08	22 38				23 06				00 06
Bishopstone	d		21 11	21 41				22 11	22 41				23 09				00 09
Seaford	a		21 14	21 44				22 14	22 44				23 12				00 12
Glynde	d				21 28					22 29				23 27			
Berwick	d				21 34					22 34				23 33		00 02	
Polegate	d	21 05			21 39	21 57	22 05			22 39	22 52	23 05		23 38	23 52	00 07	
Hampden Park 4	d				21 43					22 43		23 09		23 42		00 11	
Eastbourne 4	a	21 13			21 48	22 04	22 15			22 48	23 03	23 14		23 47	23 59	00 16	
	d	21 19				22 09	22 21				23 10	23 20				00 22	
Hampden Park 4	d	21 23					22 25					23 24					
Pevensey & Westham	d	21 28					22 30					23 29				00 29	
Pevensey Bay	d																
Normans Bay	d																
Cooden Beach	d	21 34					22 36					23 35				00 35	
Collington	d	21 37					22 39					23 38				00 38	
Bexhill 4	d	21 39				22 23	22 41				23 24	23 40				00 41	
St Leonards Warrior Sq 4	d	21 46				22 30	22 48				23 31	23 47				00 47	
Hastings 4	a	21 49				22 33	22 51				23 34	23 50				00 50	
Ore	d	21a53															
Three Oaks	d																
Doleham	d																
Winchelsea	d																
Rye	a																
	d																
Appledore (Kent)	d																
Ham Street	d																
Ashford International	a																

Table 189

Sundays
until 05 September

London, Haywards Heath and Brighton-Lewes, Seaford, Eastbourne, Hastings and Ashford

		SN ◇■	SN	SN ◇■	SN	SN ■	SN ■	SN	SN ■	SN ■	SN ■	SN ■	SN	SN	SN ■	SN ■	SN	SN	SN ■	SN ◇■ B 🚌	SN	SN	SN ■
London Victoria 15 ⊖	d	22p47		00 05																08 47			
Clapham Junction 10	d	22p53		00 11																08 53			
London Bridge 4 ⊖	d																						
East Croydon ⇌	d	23p03		00 25																09 03			
Gatwick Airport 10	d	23p19		00 43			06 58													09 19			
Haywards Heath 3	d	23p34		01 06			07 12													09 30			
Wivelsfield 4	d	23p38																		09 34			
Plumpton	d	23p44																		09 40			
Cooksbridge	d																						
Brighton 10	d		23p34		06 20	07 09		07 15				07 43	07 49	08 09	08 20	08 43	08 49	09 09	09 20		09 29	10 09	10 20
London Road (Brighton)	d		23p37			07 12		07 18				07 46	07 52	08 12		08 46	08 52	09 12			09 32	10 12	
Moulsecoomb	d		23p39			07 14		07 20				07 48	07 54	08 14		08 48	08 54	09 14			09 34	10 14	
Falmer	d		23p43			07 18		07 24				07 52	07 58	08 18		08 52	08 58	09 18			09 38	10 18	
Lewes 4	a	23p51	23p49	01 20	06 31	07 24	07 27	07 31				07 58	08 04	08 24	08 31	08 58	09 04	09 24	09 31	09 48	09 44	10 24	10 31
	d	23p53	23p56	01 20	06 31	07 25	07 37	07 32				07 59	08 05	08 25	08 32	08 59	09 05	09 25	09 32	09 48	09 52	10 25	10 32
Southease	d												08 11				09 11				09 58		
Newhaven Town	d		00 04		06 40			07 40					08 15	08 33			09 15	09 33			10 02	10 33	
Newhaven Harbour	d		00 06		06 41			07 42					08 17	08 35			09 17	09 35			10 04	10 35	
Bishopstone	d		00 09					07 45					08 20	08 38			09 20	09 38			10 07	10 38	
Seaford	a		00 12		06 46			07 48					08 23	08 41			09 23	09 41			10 10	10 41	
Glynde	d					07 30									08 37				09 37				10 37
Berwick	d	00 02				07 36									08 43				09 43				10 43
Polegate	d	00 07		01s32		07 41	07 49					08 11			08 49	09 11			09 49	10 01			10 49
Hampden Park 4	d	00 11		01s36		07 45	07 53								08 53				09 53				10 53
Eastbourne 4	a	00 16		01 41		07 50	08 01					08 19			08 58	09 19			09 58	10 08			10 58
	d	00 22								07 26	07 58	08 26			09 02	09 26			10 02	10 15			11 02
Hampden Park 4	d									07 30		08 30				09 30				10 19			
Pevensey & Westham	d	00 29								07 35		08 35				09 35				10 24			
Pevensey Bay	d																						
Normans Bay	d																						
Cooden Beach	d	00 35								07 41		08 41				09 41				10 30			
Collington	d	00 38								07 44		08 44				09 44				10 33			
Bexhill 4	d	00 41								07 46	08 11	08 46			09 16	09 46			10 16	10 35			11 16
St Leonards Warrior Sq 4	d	00 47								07 53	08 18	08 53			09 23	09 53			10 23	10 42			11 23
Hastings 4	a	00 50								07 56	08 22	08 56			09 26	09 56			10 26	10 45			11 26
Ore	d								07 24	08a00		09a00				10a00				10a49			
Three Oaks	d								07 30														
Doleham	d								07 33														
Winchelsea	d								07 39														
Rye	a								07 43		08 39				09 44				10 44				11 44
	d								07 43		08 41				09 46				10 46				11 46
Appledore (Kent)	d								07 52		08 50				09 55				10 55				11 55
Ham Street	d								07 57		08 55				10 00				11 00				12 00
Ashford International	a								08 06		09 03				10 08				11 08				12 08

B 🚌 to Lewes

Table 189

Sundays
until 05 September

London, Haywards Heath and Brighton-Lewes, Seaford, Eastbourne, Hastings and Ashford

		SN ◇1 A ⌶	SN	SN	SN 1	SN ◇1 A ⌶	SN	SN	SN 1	SN ◇1 A ⌶	SN	SN	SN 1	SN ◇1 A ⌶	SN	SN	SN 1	SN ◇1 A ⌶	SN	SN	SN 1	SN ◇1 A ⌶	SN
London Victoria 15 ⊖	d	09 47				10 47				11 47				12 47				13 47				14 47	
Clapham Junction 10	d	09 53				10 53				11 53				12 53				13 53				14 53	
London Bridge 4 ⊖	d																						
East Croydon ⇌	d	10 03				11 03				12 03				13 03				14 03				15 03	
Gatwick Airport 10	d	10 19				11 19				12 19				13 19				14 19				15 19	
Haywards Heath 3	d	10 30				11 30				12 30				13 30				14 30				15 30	
Wivelsfield 4	d	10 34				11 34				12 34				13 34				14 34				15 34	
Plumpton	d	10 40				11 40				12 40													
Cooksbridge	d																						
Brighton 10	d		10 29	11 09	11 20		11 29	12 09	12 20		12 29	13 09	13 20		13 29	14 09	14 20		14 29	15 09	15 20		15 29
London Road (Brighton)	d		10 32	11 12			11 32	12 12			12 32	13 12			13 32	14 12			14 32	15 12			15 32
Moulsecoomb	d		10 34	11 14			11 34	12 14			12 34	13 14			13 34	14 14			14 34	15 14			15 34
Falmer	d		10 38	11 18			11 38	12 18			12 38	13 18			13 38	14 18			14 38	15 18			15 38
Lewes 4	a	10 48	10 44	11 24	11 31	11 48	11 44	12 24	12 31	12 48	12 44	13 24	13 31	13 48	13 44	14 24	14 31	14 48	14 44	15 24	15 31	15 48	15 44
	d	10 48	10 52	11 25	11 32	11 48	11 52	12 25	12 32	12 48	12 52	13 25	13 32	13 48	13 52	14 25	14 32	14 48	14 52	15 25	15 32	15 48	15 52
Southease	d		10 58				11 58				12 58				13 58				14 58				15 58
Newhaven Town	d		11 02	11 33			12 02	12 33			13 02	13 33			14 02	14 33			15 02	15 33			16 02
Newhaven Harbour	d		11 04	11 35			12 04	12 35			13 04	13 35			14 04	14 35			15 04	15 35			16 04
Bishopstone	d		11 07	11 38			12 07	12 38			13 07	13 38			14 07	14 38			15 07	15 38			16 07
Seaford	a		11 10	11 41			12 10	12 41			13 10	13 41			14 10	14 41			15 10	15 41			16 10
Glynde	d				11 37				12 37				13 37				14 37				15 37		
Berwick	d				11 43				12 43				13 43				14 43				15 43		
Polegate	d	11 01			11 49	12 01			12 49	13 01			13 49	14 01			14 49	15 01			15 49	16 01	
Hampden Park 4	d				11 53				12 53				13 53				14 53				15 53		
Eastbourne 4	a	11 08			11 58	12 08			12 58	13 08			13 58	14 08			14 58	15 08			15 58	16 08	
	d	11 15			12 02	12 15			13 02	13 15			14 02	14 15			15 02	15 15			16 02	16 15	
Hampden Park 4	d	11 19				12 19				13 19				14 19				15 19				16 19	
Pevensey & Westham	d	11 24				12 24				13 24				14 24				15 24				16 24	
Pevensey Bay	d																						
Normans Bay	d																						
Cooden Beach	d	11 30				12 30				13 30				14 30				15 30				16 30	
Collington	d	11 33				12 33				13 33				14 33				15 33				16 33	
Bexhill 4	d	11 35			12 16	12 35			13 16	13 35			14 16	14 35			15 16	15 35			16 16	16 35	
St Leonards Warrior Sq 4	d	11 42			12 23	12 42			13 23	13 42			14 23	14 42			15 23	15 42			16 23	16 42	
Hastings 4	a	11 45			12 26	12 45			13 26	13 45			14 26	14 45			15 26	15 45			16 26	16 45	
Ore	d	11a49				12a49				13a49				14a49				15a49				16a49	
Three Oaks	d																						
Doleham	d																						
Winchelsea	d																						
Rye	a				12 44				13 44				14 44				15 44				16 44		
	d				12 46				13 46				14 46				15 46				16 46		
Appledore (Kent)	d				12 55				13 55				14 55				15 55				16 55		
Ham Street	d				13 00				14 00				15 00				16 00				17 00		
Ashford International	a				13 08				14 08				15 08				16 08				17 08		

A ⌶ to Lewes

Table 189

Sundays
until 05 September

London, Haywards Heath and Brighton-Lewes, Seaford, Eastbourne, Hastings and Ashford

		SN	SN 1	SN ◇1 A ⌶	SN	SN	SN 1	SN ◇1 A ⌶	SN	SN	SN 1	SN ◇1 A ⌶	SN	SN	SN 1	SN ◇1 A ⌶	SN	SN	SN 1	SN ◇1 A ⌶	SN	SN
London Victoria 15 ⊖	d			15 47				16 47				17 47				18 47				19 47		
Clapham Junction 10	d			15 53				16 53				17 53				18 53				19 53		
London Bridge 4 ⊖	d																					
East Croydon ⇌	d			16 03				17 03				18 03				19 03				20 03		
Gatwick Airport 10	d			16 19				17 19				18 19				19 19				20 19		
Haywards Heath 3	d			16 30				17 30				18 30				19 30				20 30		
Wivelsfield 4	d			16 34				17 34				18 34				19 34				20 34		
Plumpton	d			16 40				17 40				18 40				19 40				20 40		
Cooksbridge	d																					
Brighton 10	d	16 09	16 20		16 29	17 09	17 20		17 29	18 09	18 20		18 29	19 09	19 20		19 29	20 09	20 20		20 29	21 09
London Road (Brighton)	d	16 12			16 32	17 12			17 32	18 12			18 32	19 12			19 32	20 12			20 32	21 12
Moulsecoomb	d	16 14			16 34	17 14			17 34	18 14			18 34	19 14			19 34	20 14			20 34	21 14
Falmer	d	16 18			16 38	17 18			17 38	18 18			18 38	19 18			19 38	20 18			20 38	21 18
Lewes 4	a	16 24	16 31	16 48	16 44	17 24	17 31	17 48	17 44	18 24	18 31	18 48	18 44	19 24	19 31	19 48	19 44	20 24	20 31	20 48	20 44	21 24
	d	16 25	16 32	16 48	16 52	17 25	17 32	17 48	17 52	18 25	18 32	18 48	18 52	19 25	19 32	19 48	19 52	20 25	20 32	20 48	20 52	21 25
Southease	d				16 58				17 58				18 58				19 58					
Newhaven Town	d	16 33			17 02	17 33			18 02	18 33			19 02	19 33			20 02	20 33			21 00	21 33
Newhaven Harbour	d	16 35			17 04	17 35			18 04	18 35			19 04	19 35			20 04	20 35			21 04	21 35
Bishopstone	d	16 38			17 07	17 38			18 07	18 38			19 07	19 38			20 07	20 38			21 07	21 38
Seaford	a	16 41			17 10	17 41			18 10	18 41			19 10	19 41			20 10	20 41			21 10	21 41
Glynde	d		16 37				17 37				18 37				19 37				20 37			
Berwick	d		16 43				17 43				18 43				19 43				20 43			
Polegate	d		16 49	17 01			17 49	18 01			18 49	19 01			19 49	20 01			20 49	21 01		
Hampden Park 4	d		16 53				17 53				18 53				19 53				20 53			
Eastbourne 4	a		16 58	17 08			17 58	18 08			18 58	19 08			19 58	20 08			20 58	21 08		
	d		17 02	17 15			18 02	18 15			19 02	19 15			20 02	20 15			21 02	21 15		
Hampden Park 4	d			17 19				18 19				19 19				20 19				21 19		
Pevensey & Westham	d			17 24				18 24				19 24				20 24				21 24		
Pevensey Bay	d																					
Normans Bay	d																					
Cooden Beach	d			17 30				18 30				19 30				20 30				21 30		
Collington	d			17 33				18 33				19 33				20 33				21 33		
Bexhill 4	d		17 16	17 35			18 16	18 35			19 16	19 35			20 16	20 35			21 16	21 35		
St Leonards Warrior Sq 4	d		17 23	17 42			18 23	18 42			19 23	19 42			20 23	20 42			21 23	21 42		
Hastings 4	a		17 26	17 45			18 26	18 45			19 26	19 45			20 26	20 45			21 26	21 45		
Ore	d			17a49				18a49				19a49				20a49				21a49		
Three Oaks	d																					
Doleham	d																					
Winchelsea	d																					
Rye	a		17 44				18 44				19 44				20 44				21 44			
	d		17 46				18 46				19 46				20 46				21 46			
Appledore (Kent)	d		17 55				18 55				19 55				20 55				21 55			
Ham Street	d		18 00				19 00				20 00				21 00				22 00			
Ashford International	a		18 08				19 08				20 08				21 08				22 08			

A ⌶ to Lewes

Table 189

Sundays until 05 September

London, Haywards Heath and Brighton-Lewes, Seaford, Eastbourne, Hastings and Ashford

		SN 1	SN ◇1	SN	SN	SN 1	SN ◇1	SN	SN 1	SN 1	SN ◇1	SN 1
London Victoria 15 ⊖	d		20 47				21 47				22 47	
Clapham Junction 10	d		20 53				21 53				22 53	
London Bridge 4 ⊖	d											
East Croydon	d		21 03				22 03				23 03	
Gatwick Airport 10	d		21 19				22 19				23 19	
Haywards Heath 3	d		21 30				22 30				23 30	
Wivelsfield 4	d		21 34				22 34				23 34	
Plumpton	d		21 40				22 40				23 40	
Cooksbridge	d											
Brighton 10	d	21 20		21 29	22 09	22 20		22 39	23 09	23 20		23 39
London Road (Brighton)	d			21 32	22 12			22 42	23 12			23 42
Moulsecoomb	d			21 34	22 14			22 44	23 14			23 44
Falmer	d			21 38	22 18			22 48	23 18			23 48
Lewes 4	a	21 31	21 48	21 44	22 24	22 31	22 48	22 54	23 24	23 31	23 48	23 54
	d	21 32	21 48	21 52	22 25	22 32	22 59	23 03		23 32	23 59	
Southease	d											
Newhaven Town	d			22 00	22 33			23 11				
Newhaven Harbour	d			22 02	22 35			23 13				
Bishopstone	d			22 05	22 38			23 16				
Seaford	a			22 08	22 41			23 19				
Glynde	d	21 37				22 37				23 37		
Berwick	d	21 43				22 43				23 43		
Polegate	d	21 49	22 01			22 49	23 11			23 49	00 11	
Hampden Park 4	d	21 53				22 53				23 53	00 15	
Eastbourne 4	a	21 58	22 08			22 58	23 19			23 58	00 20	
	d	22 02	22 15				23 26					
Hampden Park 4	d		22 19				23 30					
Pevensey & Westham	d		22 24				23 35					
Pevensey Bay	d											
Normans Bay	d											
Cooden Beach	d		22 30				23 41					
Collington	d		22 33				23 44					
Bexhill 4	d	22 16	22 35				23 46					
St Leonards Warrior Sq 4	d	22 23	22 42				23 53					
Hastings 4	a	22 26	22 45				23 56					
Ore	d											
Three Oaks	d											
Doleham	d											
Winchelsea	d											
Rye	a											
	d											
Appledore (Kent)	d											
Ham Street	d											
Ashford International	a											

Table 189

Sundays from 12 September

London, Haywards Heath and Brighton-Lewes, Seaford, Eastbourne, Hastings and Ashford

		SN ◇1	SN	SN ◇1	SN 1	SN	SN 1	SN 1	SN 1	SN 1	SN	SN
London Victoria 15 ⊖	d	22p47										
Clapham Junction 10	d	22p53										
London Bridge 4 ⊖	d											
East Croydon	d	23p03										
Gatwick Airport 10	d	23p19										
Haywards Heath 3	d	23p34		01 06								
Wivelsfield 4	d	23p38										
Plumpton	d	23p44										
Cooksbridge	d											
Brighton 10	d		23p34		07 09	07 15				07 43	07 49	08 09
London Road (Brighton)	d		23p37		07 12	07 18				07 46	07 52	08 12
Moulsecoomb	d		23p39		07 14	07 20				07 48	07 54	08 14
Falmer	d		23p43		07 18	07 24				07 52	07 58	08 18
Lewes 4	a	23p51	23p49	01 20	07 24	07 31				07 58	08 04	08 24
	d	23p53	23p56	01 20	07 25	07 32				07 59	08 05	08 25
Southease	d										08 11	
Newhaven Town	d		00 04			07 40					08 15	08 33
Newhaven Harbour	d		00 06			07 42					08 17	08 35
Bishopstone	d		00 09			07 45					08 20	08 38
Seaford	a		00 12			07 48					08 23	08 41
Glynde	d				07 30							
Berwick	d	00 02			07 36							
Polegate	d	00 07		01s32	07 41					08 11		
Hampden Park 4	d	00 11		01s36	07 45							
Eastbourne 4	a	00 16		01 41	07 50					08 19		
	d	00 22						07 26	07 58	08 26		
Hampden Park 4	d							07 30		08 30		
Pevensey & Westham	d	00 29						07 35		08 35		
Pevensey Bay	d											
Normans Bay	d											
Cooden Beach	d	00 35						07 41		08 41		
Collington	d	00 38						07 44		08 44		
Bexhill 4	d	00 41						07 46	08 11	08 46		
St Leonards Warrior Sq 4	d	00 47						07 53	08 18	08 53		
Hastings 4	a	00 50						07 56	08 22	08 56		
Ore	d						07 24	08a00		09a00		
Three Oaks	d						07 30					
Doleham	d						07 33					
Winchelsea	d						07 39					
Rye	a						07 43		08 39			
	d						07 43		08 41			
Appledore (Kent)	d						07 52		08 50			
Ham Street	d						07 57		08 55			
Ashford International	a						08 06		09 03			

		SN 1	SN 1	SN	SN	SN 1	SN ◇1 A	SN	SN	SN 1	SN ◇1 A	SN
London Victoria 15 ⊖	d						08 47				09 47	
Clapham Junction 10	d						08 53				09 53	
London Bridge 4 ⊖	d											
East Croydon	d						09 07				10 07	
Gatwick Airport 10	d						09 29				10 29	
Haywards Heath 3	d						09 41				10 41	
Wivelsfield 4	d						09 45				10 45	
Plumpton	d						09 51				10 51	
Cooksbridge	d											
Brighton 10	d	08 20	08 43	08 49	09 09	09 20		09 39	10 09	10 20		10 39
London Road (Brighton)	d		08 46	08 52	09 12			09 42	10 12			10 42
Moulsecoomb	d		08 48	08 54	09 14			09 44	10 14			10 44
Falmer	d		08 52	08 58	09 18			09 48	10 18			10 48
Lewes 4	a	08 31	08 58	09 04	09 24	09 31	09 58	09 54	10 24	10 31	10 58	10 54
	d	08 32	08 59	09 05	09 25	09 32	09 59	10 03	10 25	10 32	10 59	11 03
Southease	d			09 11				10 09				11 09
Newhaven Town	d			09 15	09 33			10 13	10 33			11 13
Newhaven Harbour	d			09 17	09 35			10 15	10 35			11 15
Bishopstone	d			09 20	09 38			10 18	10 38			11 18
Seaford	a			09 23	09 41			10 21	10 41			11 21
Glynde	d	08 37				09 37				10 37		
Berwick	d	08 43				09 43				10 43		
Polegate	d	08 49	09 11			09 49	10 11			10 49	11 11	
Hampden Park 4	d	08 53				09 53				10 53		
Eastbourne 4	a	08 58	09 19			09 58	10 19			10 58	11 19	
	d	09 02	09 26			10 02	10 26			11 02	11 26	
Hampden Park 4	d		09 30				10 30				11 30	
Pevensey & Westham	d		09 35				10 35				11 35	
Pevensey Bay	d											
Normans Bay	d											
Cooden Beach	d		09 41				10 41				11 41	
Collington	d		09 44				10 44				11 44	
Bexhill 4	d	09 16	09 46			10 16	10 46			11 16	11 46	
St Leonards Warrior Sq 4	d	09 23	09 53			10 23	10 53			11 23	11 53	
Hastings 4	a	09 26	09 56			10 26	10 56			11 26	11 56	
Ore	d		10a00				11a00				12a00	
Three Oaks	d											
Doleham	d											
Winchelsea	d											
Rye	a	09 44				10 44				11 44		
	d	09 46				10 46				11 46		
Appledore (Kent)	d	09 55				10 55				11 55		
Ham Street	d	10 00				11 00				12 00		
Ashford International	a	10 08				11 08				12 08		

A to Lewes

Table 189

Sundays from 12 September

London, Haywards Heath and Brighton-Lewes, Seaford, Eastbourne, Hastings and Ashford

		SN	SN 1	SN ◇1 A 🚌	SN	SN	SN 1	SN ◇1 A 🚌	SN	SN	SN 1	SN ◇1 A 🚌	SN	SN	SN 1	SN ◇1 A 🚌	SN	SN	SN 1	SN ◇1 A 🚌	SN	SN	SN 1
London Victoria 15 ⊖	d			10 47				11 47				12 47				13 47				14 47			
Clapham Junction 10	d			10 53				11 53				12 53				13 53				14 53			
London Bridge 4 ⊖	d																						
East Croydon	d			11 07				12 07				13 07				14 07				15 07			
Gatwick Airport 10	d			11 29				12 29				13 29				14 29				15 29			
Haywards Heath 3	d			11 41				12 41				13 41				14 41				15 41			
Wivelsfield 4	d			11 45				12 45				13 45				14 45				15 45			
Plumpton	d			11 51				12 51															
Cooksbridge	d																						
Brighton 10	d	11 09	11 20		11 39	12 09	12 20		12 39	13 09	13 20		13 39	14 09	14 20		14 39	15 09	15 20		15 39	16 09	16 20
London Road (Brighton)	d	11 12			11 42	12 12			12 42	13 12			13 42	14 12			14 42	15 12			15 42	16 12	
Moulsecoomb	d	11 14			11 44	12 14			12 44	13 14			13 44	14 14			14 44	15 14			15 44	16 14	
Falmer	d	11 18			11 48	12 18			12 48	13 18			13 48	14 18			14 48	15 18			15 48	16 18	
Lewes 4	a	11 24	11 31	11 58	11 54	12 24	12 31	12 58	12 54	13 24	13 31	13 56	13 54	14 24	14 31	14 56	14 54	15 24	15 31	15 56	15 54	16 24	16 31
	d	11 25	11 32	11 59	12 03	12 25	12 32	12 59	13 03	13 25	13 32	13 59	14 03	14 25	14 32	14 59	15 03	15 25	15 32	15 59	16 03	16 25	16 32
Southease	d				12 09				13 09				14 09				15 09				16 09		
Newhaven Town	d	11 33			12 13	12 33			13 13	13 33			14 13	14 33			15 13	15 33			16 13	16 33	
Newhaven Harbour	d	11 35			12 15	12 35			13 15	13 35			14 15	14 35			15 15	15 35			16 15	16 35	
Bishopstone	d	11 38			12 18	12 38			13 18	13 38			14 18	14 38			15 18	15 38			16 18	16 38	
Seaford	a	11 41			12 21	12 41			13 21	13 41			14 21	14 41			15 21	15 41			16 21	16 41	
Glynde	d		11 37				12 37				13 37				14 37				15 37				16 37
Berwick	d		11 43				12 43				13 43				14 43				15 43				16 43
Polegate	d		11 49	12 11			12 49	13 11			13 49	14 11			14 49	15 11			15 49	16 11			16 49
Hampden Park 4	d		11 53				12 53				13 53				14 53				15 53				16 53
Eastbourne 4	a		11 58	12 19			12 58	13 19			13 58	14 19			14 58	15 19			15 58	16 19			16 58
	d		12 02	12 26			13 02	13 26			14 02	14 26			15 02	15 26			16 02	16 26			17 02
Hampden Park 4	d			12 30				13 30				14 30				15 30				16 30			
Pevensey & Westham	d			12 35				13 35				14 35				15 35				16 35			
Pevensey Bay	d																						
Normans Bay	d																						
Cooden Beach	d			12 41				13 41				14 41				15 41				16 41			
Collington	d			12 44				13 44				14 44				15 44				16 44			
Bexhill 4	d		12 16	12 46			13 16	13 46			14 16	14 46			15 16	15 46			16 16	16 46			17 16
St Leonards Warrior Sq 4	d		12 23	12 53			13 23	13 53			14 23	14 53			15 23	15 53			16 23	16 53			17 23
Hastings 4	a		12 26	12 56			13 26	13 56			14 26	14 56			15 26	15 56			16 26	16 56			17 26
Ore	d			13a00				14a00				15a00				16a00				17a00			
Three Oaks	d																						
Doleham	d																						
Winchelsea	d																						
Rye	a		12 44				13 44				14 44				15 44				16 44				17 44
	d		12 46				13 46				14 46				15 46				16 46				17 46
Appledore (Kent)	d		12 55				13 55				14 55				15 55				16 55				17 55
Ham Street	d		13 00				14 00				15 00				16 00				17 00				18 00
Ashford International	a		13 08				14 08				15 08				16 08				17 08				18 08

A 🚌 to Lewes

Table 189

Sundays from 12 September

London, Haywards Heath and Brighton-Lewes, Seaford, Eastbourne, Hastings and Ashford

		SN ◇1 A 🚌	SN	SN	SN 1	SN ◇1 A 🚌	SN	SN	SN 1	SN ◇1 A 🚌	SN	SN	SN 1	SN ◇1 A 🚌	SN	SN	SN 1	SN ◇1 A 🚌	SN	SN	SN 1	SN ◇1
London Victoria 15 ⊖	d	15 47				16 47				17 47				18 47				19 47				20 47
Clapham Junction 10	d	15 53				16 53				17 53				18 53				19 53				20 53
London Bridge 4 ⊖	d																					
East Croydon	d	16 07				17 07				18 07				19 07				20 07				21 07
Gatwick Airport 10	d	16 29				17 29				18 29				19 29				20 29				21 29
Haywards Heath 3	d	16 41				17 41				18 41				19 41				20 41				21 41
Wivelsfield 4	d	16 45				17 45				18 45				19 45				20 45				21 45
Plumpton	d	16 51				17 51				18 51				19 51				20 51				21 51
Cooksbridge	d																					
Brighton 10	d		16 39	17 09	17 20		17 39	18 09	18 20		18 39	19 09	19 20		19 39	20 09	20 20		20 39	21 09	21 20	
London Road (Brighton)	d		16 42	17 12			17 42	18 12			18 42	19 12			19 42	20 12			20 42	21 12		
Moulsecoomb	d		16 44	17 14			17 44	18 14			18 44	19 14			19 44	20 14			20 44	21 14		
Falmer	d		16 48	17 18			17 48	18 18			18 48	19 18			19 48	20 18			20 48	21 18		
Lewes 4	a	16 58	16 54	17 24	17 31	17 58	17 54	18 24	18 31	18 58	18 54	19 24	19 31	19 58	19 54	20 24	20 31	20 58	20 54	21 24	21 31	21 58
	d	16 59	17 03	17 25	17 32	17 59	18 03	18 25	18 32	18 59	19 03	19 25	19 32	19 59	20 03	20 25	20 32	20 59	21 03	21 25	21 32	21 59
Southease	d		17 09				18 09				19 09				20 09							
Newhaven Town	d		17 13	17 33			18 13	18 33			19 13	19 33			20 13	20 33			21 11	21 33		
Newhaven Harbour	d		17 15	17 35			18 15	18 35			19 15	19 35			20 15	20 35			21 13	21 35		
Bishopstone	d		17 18	17 38			18 18	18 38			19 18	19 38			20 18	20 38			21 16	21 38		
Seaford	a		17 21	17 41			18 21	18 41			19 21	19 41			20 21	20 41			21 19	21 41		
Glynde	d				17 37				18 37				19 37				20 37				21 37	
Berwick	d				17 43				18 43				19 43				20 43				21 43	
Polegate	d	17 11			17 49	18 11			18 49	19 11			19 49	20 11			20 49	21 11			21 49	22 11
Hampden Park 4	d				17 53				18 53				19 53				20 53				21 53	
Eastbourne 4	a	17 19			17 58	18 19			18 58	19 19			19 58	20 19			20 58	21 19			21 58	22 19
	d	17 26			18 02	18 26			19 02	19 26			20 02	20 26			21 02	21 26			22 02	22 26
Hampden Park 4	d	17 30				18 30				19 30				20 30				21 30				22 30
Pevensey & Westham	d	17 35				18 35				19 35				20 35				21 35				22 35
Pevensey Bay	d																					
Normans Bay	d																					
Cooden Beach	d	17 41				18 41				19 41				20 41				21 41				22 41
Collington	d	17 44				18 44				19 44				20 44				21 44				22 44
Bexhill 4	d	17 46			18 16	18 46			19 16	19 46			20 16	20 46			21 16	21 46			22 16	22 46
St Leonards Warrior Sq 4	d	17 53			18 23	18 53			19 23	19 53			20 23	20 53			21 23	21 53			22 23	22 53
Hastings 4	a	17 56			18 26	18 56			19 26	19 56			20 26	20 56			21 26	21 56			22 26	22 56
Ore	d	18a00				19a00				20a00				21a00				22a00				
Three Oaks	d																					
Doleham	d																					
Winchelsea	d																					
Rye	a				18 44				19 44				20 44				21 44					
	d				18 46				19 46				20 46				21 46					
Appledore (Kent)	d				18 55				19 55				20 55				21 55					
Ham Street	d				19 00				20 00				21 00				22 00					
Ashford International	a				19 08				20 08				21 08				22 08					

A 🚌 to Lewes

Table 189

Sundays from 12 September

London, Haywards Heath and Brighton-Lewes, Seaford, Eastbourne, Hastings and Ashford

		SN	SN	SN 1	SN ◇1	SN	SN 1	SN 1		SN 1	SN ◇1
London Victoria 15 ⊖	d				21 47						22 47
Clapham Junction 10	d				21 53						22 53
London Bridge 4 ⊖	d										
East Croydon	d				22 07						23 07
Gatwick Airport 10	d				22 29						23 29
Haywards Heath 3	d				22 41						23 41
Wivelsfield 4	d				22 45						23 45
Plumpton	d				22 51						23 51
Cooksbridge	d										
Brighton 10	d	21 39	22 09	22 20		22 39	23 09	23 20		23 39	
London Road (Brighton)	d	21 42	22 12			22 42	23 12			23 42	
Moulsecoomb	d	21 44	22 14			22 44	23 14			23 44	
Falmer	d	21 48	22 18			22 48	23 18			23 48	
Lewes 4	a	21 54	22 24	22 31	22 58	22 54	23 24	23 31		23 54	23 58
	d	22 03	22 25	22 32	22 59	23 03		23 32			23 59
Southease	d										
Newhaven Town	d	22 11	22 33			23 11					
Newhaven Harbour	d	22 13	22 35			23 13					
Bishopstone	d	22 16	22 38			23 16					
Seaford	a	22 19	22 41			23 19					
Glynde	d			22 37				23 37			
Berwick	d			22 43				23 43			
Polegate	d			22 49	23 11			23 49			00 11
Hampden Park 4	d			22 53				23 53			00 15
Eastbourne 4	a			22 58	23 19			23 58			00 20
	d				23 26						
Hampden Park 4	d				23 30						
Pevensey & Westham	d				23 35						
Pevensey Bay	d										
Normans Bay	d										
Cooden Beach	d				23 41						
Collington	d				23 44						
Bexhill 4	d				23 46						
St Leonards Warrior Sq 4	d				23 53						
Hastings 4	a				23 56						
Ore	d										
Three Oaks	d										
Doleham	d										
Winchelsea	d										
Rye	a										
	d										
Appledore (Kent)	d										
Ham Street	d										
Ashford International	a										

Table 189

Mondays to Fridays

Ashford, Hastings, Eastbourne, Seaford and Lewes - Brighton, Haywards Heath and London

		SN MX 1	SN ◇1	SN	SN 1	SN 1	SN 1	SN	SN 1	SN		SN 1	SN 1	SN 1	SN 1	SN ◇1	SN ◇1 A ✠	SN 1	SN	SN 1		SN	SN ◇1 A ✠	SN 1	SN 1
Ashford International	d													06 39										07 39	
Ham Street	d													06 48										07 48	
Appledore (Kent)	d													06 53										07 53	
Rye	a													07 02										08 02	
	d																								
Winchelsea	d																								
Doleham	d																								
Three Oaks	d																								
Ore	d																								
Hastings 4	a																								
	d	23p22				05 07	05 42						05 58			06 15							06 49		
St Leonards Warrior Sq 4	d	23p24				05 09	05 45						06 01			06 18							06 52		
Bexhill 4	d	23p31				05 16	05 52						06 12			06 26							06 59		
Collington	d	23p33				05 18	05 54									06 28							07 01		
Cooden Beach	d	23p36				05 21	05 57									06 31							07 04		
Normans Bay	d																								
Pevensey Bay	d																								
Pevensey & Westham	d	23p42				05 27	06 03									06 37							07 10		
Hampden Park 4	d	23p47				05 32	06 08						06 24			06 42							07 15		
Eastbourne 4	a	23p52				05 37	06 13						06 29			06 47							07 20		
	d	23p56	05 08		05 32	05 42						06 24	06 37		06 47	06 57				07 14			07 32		
Hampden Park 4	d	00 01	05 12		05 36	05 46						06 28			06 51	07 01				07 19					
Polegate	d	00 05	05 16		05 41	05 50						06 33	06 44		06 55	07 05				07 23			07 39		
Berwick	d					05 55						06 39			07 00					07 29			07 44		
Glynde	d											06 45			07 06					07 35					
Seaford	d			05 09				05 45		06 30							06 56		07 16			07 33			
Bishopstone	d			05 11				05 47		06 32							06 58		07 18			07 35			
Newhaven Harbour	d			05 14				05 50		06 35							07 01		07 21			07 38			
Newhaven Town	d			05 16				05 52		06 37							07 03		07 23			07 40			
Southease	d																07 07		07 27			07 44			
Lewes 4	a	00 17	05 28	05 25	05 53	06 04		06 01		06 46		06 50	06 57		07 11	07 18	07 14		07 33	07 41		07 50	07 53		
	d	00 18	05 29	05 32	05 54	06 05		06 09	06 26	06 47		06 51	06 59		07 12	>	07 22	07 23	07 34	07 42		07 51	07 55		07 58
Falmer	d	00 25		05 39	06 01			06 16	06 33	06 54			07 06		07 19			07 30	07 41			07 58			08 05
Moulsecoomb	d	00 28		05 42	06 05			06 19	06 36	06 57			07 10		07 22			07 33	07 44			08 01			08 08
London Road (Brighton)	d	00 30		05 44	06 07			06 21	06 38	06 59			07 12		07 24			07 35	07 46			08 03			08 10
Brighton 10	a	00 34		05 48	06 11			06 25	06 42	07 03			07 16		07 28			07 39	07 50			08 07			08 14
Cooksbridge	d											06 56					07 27			07 48			08 00		
Plumpton	d		05 37			06 13						07 01					07 32			07 53			08 05		
Wivelsfield 4	a											07 07					07 39						08 11		
Haywards Heath 3	a		05 46			06 22						07 12					07 43			08 02			08 16		
Gatwick Airport 10	a		05 58			06 40						07 29													
East Croydon	a		06 15			06 56						07 45					08 14			08 31			08 46		
London Bridge 4 ⊖	a					07 13						08 01								08 52					
Clapham Junction 10	a		06 25														08 23						09 00		
London Victoria 15 ⊖	a		06 32														08 32						09 09		

A ✠ from Lewes

Table 189

Ashford, Hastings, Eastbourne, Seaford and Lewes - Brighton, Haywards Heath and London

Station		SN ■	SN	SN ◇■ A ⌶	SN ■	SN ◇■	SN ◇■ A ⌶	SN ■	SN ■	SN ■	SN	SN ◇■ A ⌶	SN ■	SN	SN ◇■ A ⌶	SN ■	SN ■	SN	SN ◇■	SN ■	SN ■	SN	SN ◇■
Ashford International	d	06 13								07 17							08 32				08 52		
Ham Street	d	06 22								07 26							08 41				09 01		
Appledore (Kent)	d	06 27								07 31							08 46				09 06		
Rye	a	06 36								07 40							08 55				09 15		
	d	06 36								07 45							08 56				09 16		
Winchelsea	d	06 40								07 48											09 19		
Doleham	d	06 46								07 55											09 26		
Three Oaks	d	06 50								07 58											09 29		
Ore	d	06 55								08 04			08 22		08 47					09 20	09 35		09 50
Hastings 4	a	06 58								08 07			08 25		08 50		09 13			09 23	09 38		09 53
	d	07 12		07 20		07 38				08 10			08 26		08 52		09 14			09 24			09 55
St Leonards Warrior Sq 4	d	07 15		07 23		07 40				08 13			08 28		08 55		09 17			09 26			09 58
Bexhill 4	d	07 22		07 31		07 47				08 22			08 35		09 02		09 24			09 35			10 05
Collington	d			07 33		07 49							08 37		09 04					09 37			10 07
Cooden Beach	d			07 36		07 52							08 40		09 07					09 40			10 10
Normans Bay	d					07 55							08 43							09 43			
Pevensey Bay	d					07 59																	
Pevensey & Westham	d			07 42		08 01							08 48		09 13					09 48			10 16
Hampden Park 4	d			07 46		08 06							08 52		09 17					09 52			10 20
Eastbourne 4	a	07 37		07 51		08 11				08 37			08 57		09 23		09 39			09 57			10 25
	d	07 47		07 57	08 04	08 18				08 45		08 56	09 03		09 30		09 47		09 56	10 03			10 31
Hampden Park 4	d			08 01	08 08							09 00	09 07						10 00	10 07			
Polegate	d	07 54		08 05	08 12	08 25				08 52		09 04	09 11		09 37		09 54		10 04	10 11			10 37
Berwick	d			08 11	08 18	08 30							09 17						10 09	10 17			
Glynde	d			08 16	08 23	08 36							09 22							10 22			
Seaford	d		07 58				08 21				08 57			09 25				09 58				10 25	
Bishopstone	d		08 00				08 23				08 59			09 27				10 00				10 27	
Newhaven Harbour	d		08 03				08 26				09 02			09 30				10 03				10 30	
Newhaven Town	d		08 05				08 28				09 04			09 32				10 05				10 32	
Southease	d		08 09				08 32							09 36								10 36	
Lewes 4	a	08 07	08 16	08 22	08 29	08 42	08 39			09 07	09 13	09 16	09 28	09 44	09 49		10 07	10 14	10 18	10 28		10 44	10 49
	d	08 07	08 17	08 23	08 30	>	08 48	08 46	08 58	09 07	09 14	09 17	09 28	09 44	09 50	09 58	10 07	10 14	10 19	10 28		10 44	10 50
Falmer	d		08 25		08 37			08 53	09 05		09 21		09 35	09 51		10 05		10 21		10 35		10 51	
Moulsecoomb	d		08 28		08 40			08 56	09 08		09 24		09 38	09 54		10 08		10 24		10 38		10 54	
London Road (Brighton)	d		08 30		08 42			08 58	09 10		09 27		09 41	09 57		10 10		10 27		10 41		10 57	
Brighton 10	a	08 20	08 35		08 46			09 02	09 14	09 20	09 30		09 44	10 00		10 14	10 20	10 30		10 44		11 00	
Cooksbridge	d			08 28								09 22			09 55				10 24				
Plumpton	d			08 33								09 27			10 00				10 29				
Wivelsfield 4	a			08 39			09 00					09 33							10 35				
Haywards Heath 3	a			08 44			09 05					09 38			10 09				10 40				11 05
Gatwick Airport 10	a			08 55			09 21					09 54			10 24				10 54				11 24
East Croydon	a			09 14			09 38					10 11			10 40				11 10				11 40
London Bridge 4 ⊖	a																						
Clapham Junction 10	a			09 23			09 48					10 20			10 50				11 20				11 50
London Victoria 15 ⊖	a			09 32			09 58					10 28			10 57				11 27				11 57

A ⌶ from Lewes

Table 189

Mondays to Fridays

Ashford, Hastings, Eastbourne, Seaford and Lewes - Brighton, Haywards Heath and London

Station		SN ■	SN ■	SN	SN ◇■	SN ■	SN	SN ◇■	SN ■	SN ■	SN	SN ◇■	SN ■	SN	SN ◇■	SN ■	SN ■	SN	SN ◇■	SN ■	SN	SN ◇■
Ashford International	d		09 32							10 32							11 32					
Ham Street	d		09 41							10 41							11 41					
Appledore (Kent)	d		09 46							10 46							11 46					
Rye	a		09 55							10 55							11 55					
	d		09 56							10 56							11 56					
Winchelsea	d																					
Doleham	d																					
Three Oaks	d																					
Ore	d					10 22		10 50					11 22		11 50					12 22		12 50
Hastings 4	a		10 13			10 25		10 53		11 13			11 25		11 53		12 13			12 25		12 53
	d		10 14			10 26		10 55		11 14			11 26		11 55		12 14			12 26		12 55
St Leonards Warrior Sq 4	d		10 17			10 28		10 58		11 17			11 28		11 58		12 17			12 28		12 58
Bexhill 4	d		10 24			10 35		11 05		11 24			11 35		12 05		12 24			12 35		13 05
Collington	d					10 37		11 07					11 37		12 07					12 37		13 07
Cooden Beach	d					10 40		11 10					11 40		12 10					12 40		13 10
Normans Bay	d					10 43							11 43							12 43		
Pevensey Bay	d																					
Pevensey & Westham	d					10 48		11 16					11 48		12 16					12 48		13 16
Hampden Park 4	d					10 52		11 20					11 52		12 20					12 52		13 20
Eastbourne 4	a		10 39			10 57		11 25		11 39			11 57		12 25		12 39			12 57		13 25
	d		10 47		10 58	11 03		11 31		11 47		11 58	12 03		12 31		12 47		12 58	13 03		13 31
Hampden Park 4	d				11 02	11 07						12 02	12 07						13 02	13 07		
Polegate	d		10 54		11 06	11 11		11 37		11 54		12 06	12 11		12 37		12 54		13 06	13 11		13 37
Berwick	d					11 17							12 17							13 17		
Glynde	d					11 22							12 22							13 22		
Seaford	d			10 58			11 25				11 58			12 25				12 58			13 25	
Bishopstone	d			11 00			11 27				12 00			12 27				13 00			13 27	
Newhaven Harbour	d			11 03			11 30				12 03			12 30				13 03			13 30	
Newhaven Town	d			11 05			11 32				12 05			12 32				13 05			13 32	
Southease	d						11 36							12 36							13 36	
Lewes 4	a		11 07	11 14	11 18	11 28	11 44	11 49		12 07	12 14	12 18	12 28	12 44	12 49		13 07	13 14	13 18	13 28	13 44	13 49
	d	10 58	11 07	11 14	11 20	11 28	11 44	11 50	11 58	12 07	12 14	12 20	12 28	12 44	12 50	12 58	13 07	13 14	13 20	13 28	13 44	13 50
Falmer	d	11 05		11 21		11 35	11 51		12 05		12 21		12 35	12 51		13 05		13 21		13 35	13 51	
Moulsecoomb	d	11 08		11 24		11 38	11 54		12 08		12 24		12 38	12 54		13 08		13 24		13 38	13 54	
London Road (Brighton)	d	11 10		11 27		11 41	11 57		12 10		12 27		12 41	12 57		13 10		13 27		13 41	13 57	
Brighton 10	a	11 14	11 20	11 30		11 44	12 00		12 14	12 20	12 30		12 44	13 00		13 14	13 20	13 30		13 44	14 00	
Cooksbridge	d																					
Plumpton	d				11 28							12 28										
Wivelsfield 4	a				11 34							12 34							13 34			
Haywards Heath 3	a				11 40			12 05				12 40			13 05				13 40			14 05
Gatwick Airport 10	a				11 54			12 24				12 54			13 24				13 54			14 24
East Croydon	a				12 10			12 40				13 10			13 40				14 10			14 40
London Bridge 4 ⊖	a																					
Clapham Junction 10	a				12 19			12 50				13 20			13 50				14 20			14 50
London Victoria 15 ⊖	a				12 28			12 57				13 28			13 57				14 27			14 57

Table 189

Mondays to Fridays

Ashford, Hastings, Eastbourne, Seaford and Lewes - Brighton, Haywards Heath and London

		SN 1	SN 1	SN	SN ◇1	SN 1	SN	SN ◇1 A 🛒	SN 1	SN 1	SN	SN ◇1 A 🛒	SN 1	SN	SN ◇1 A 🛒	SN 1	SN 1	SN	SN ◇1 A 🛒	SN 1	SN	SN ◇1 A 🛒	SN 1
Ashford International	d		12 32							13 32							14 32						
Ham Street	d		12 41							13 41							14 41						
Appledore (Kent)	d		12 46							13 46							14 46						
Rye	a		12 55							13 55							14 55						
	d		12 56							13 56							14 56						
Winchelsea	d																						
Doleham	d																						
Three Oaks	d																						
Ore	d					13 22		13 50					14 22		14 50					15 20		15 48	
Hastings 4	a		13 13			13 25		13 53		14 13			14 25		14 53		15 13			15 23		15 51	
	d		13 14			13 26		13 55		14 14			14 26		14 55		15 14			15 24		15 53	
St Leonards Warrior Sq 4	d		13 17			13 28		13 58		14 17			14 28		14 58		15 17			15 26		15 56	
Bexhill 4	d		13 24			13 35		14 05		14 24			14 35		15 05		15 24			15 33		16 03	
Collington	d					13 37		14 07					14 37		15 07					15 35		16 05	
Cooden Beach	d					13 40		14 10					14 40		15 10					15 38		16 08	
Normans Bay	d					13 43							14 43							15 41		16 11	
Pevensey Bay	d																			15 45		16 14	
Pevensey & Westham	d					13 48		14 16					14 48		15 16					15 47		16 17	
Hampden Park 4	d					13 52		14 20					14 52		15 20					15 52		16 21	
Eastbourne 4	a		13 39			13 57		14 25		14 39			14 57		15 25		15 39			15 57		16 26	
	d		13 47		13 58	14 03		14 31		14 47		14 58	15 03		15 31		15 47		15 58	16 03		16 32	
Hampden Park 4	d				14 02	14 07						15 02	15 07						16 02	16 07			
Polegate	d		13 54		14 06	14 11		14 37		14 54		15 06	15 11		15 37		15 54		16 06	16 11		16 38	
Berwick	d					14 17							15 17							16 17			
Glynde	d					14 22							15 22							16 22			
Seaford	d			13 58			14 25				14 58			15 25				15 58			16 26		
Bishopstone	d			14 00			14 27				15 00			15 27				16 00			16 28		
Newhaven Harbour	d			14 03			14 30				15 03			15 30				16 03			16 31		
Newhaven Town	d			14 05			14 32				15 05			15 32				16 05			16 33		
Southease	d						14 36							15 36							16 37		
Lewes 4	a		14 07	14 14	14 18	14 28	14 44	14 49		15 07	15 14	15 18	15 28	15 44	15 49		16 07	16 14	16 18	16 28	16 44	16 50	
	d	13 58	14 07	14 14	14 20	14 28	14 44	14 50	14 58	15 07	15 14	15 19	15 28	15 44	15 50	15 58	16 07	16 14	16 19	16 28	16 44	16 51	16 58
Falmer	d	14 05		14 21		14 35	14 51		15 05		15 21		15 35	15 51		16 05		16 21		16 35	16 51		17 05
Moulsecoomb	d	14 08		14 24		14 38	14 54		15 08		15 24		15 38	15 54		16 08		16 24		16 38	16 54		17 08
London Road (Brighton)	d	14 10		14 27		14 41	14 57		15 10		15 27		15 41	15 57		16 10		16 27		16 41	16 57		17 10
Brighton 10	a	14 14	14 20	14 30		14 44	15 00		15 14	15 20	15 30		15 44	16 00		16 14	16 20	16 30		16 44	17 00		17 14
Cooksbridge	d											15 24							16 24				
Plumpton	d											15 29							16 29				
Wivelsfield 4	a				14 34							15 35							16 37				
Haywards Heath 3	a				14 40			15 05				15 39			16 05				16 41			17 05	
Gatwick Airport 10	a				14 54			15 24				15 55			16 24				16 56			17 24	
East Croydon	a				15 10			15 40				16 11			16 40				17 12			17 40	
London Bridge 4 ⊖	a																						
Clapham Junction 10	a				15 20			15 50				16 20			16 50				17 21			17 50	
London Victoria 15 ⊖	a				15 27			15 57				16 28			16 58				17 28			17 58	

A 🛒 from Lewes

Table 189

Mondays to Fridays

Ashford, Hastings, Eastbourne, Seaford and Lewes - Brighton, Haywards Heath and London

		SN 1	SN	SN ◇1 A 🛒	SN 1	SN	SN ◇1 A 🛒	SN 1	SN 1	SN	SN ◇1 A 🛒	SN 1	SN	SN ◇1	SN	SN 1	SN 1	SN	SN ◇1	SN 1	SN	SN ◇1
Ashford International	d	15 32						16 32	17 58							17 32	18 58					
Ham Street	d	15 41						16 41	18 07							17 41	19 07					
Appledore (Kent)	d	15 46						16 46	18 12							17 46	19 12					
Rye	a	15 55						16 55	18 21							17 55	19 21					
	d	15 56						16 56								17 56						
Winchelsea	d																					
Doleham	d																					
Three Oaks	d																					
Ore	d				16 22		16 50					17 22		17 50						18 22		18 50
Hastings 4	a	16 13			16 25		16 53	17 13				17 25		17 53		18 13				18 25		18 53
	d	16 14			16 26		16 55	17 14				17 26		17 55		18 14				18 26		18 55
St Leonards Warrior Sq 4	d	16 17			16 28		16 58	17 17				17 28		17 58		18 17				18 28		18 58
Bexhill 4	d	16 24			16 35		17 05	17 24				17 35		18 05		18 24				18 35		19 05
Collington	d				16 37		17 07					17 37		18 07						18 37		19 07
Cooden Beach	d				16 40		17 10					17 40		18 10						18 40		19 10
Normans Bay	d				16 43							17 43								18 43		
Pevensey Bay	d																					
Pevensey & Westham	d				16 48		17 16					17 48		18 16						18 48		19 16
Hampden Park 4	d				16 52		17 20					17 52		18 20						18 52		19 20
Eastbourne 4	a	16 39			16 57		17 25	17 39				17 57		18 25		18 39				18 57		19 25
	d	16 45		16 58	17 03		17 31	17 45			17 57	18 01		18 31		18 47			18 58	19 04		19 31
Hampden Park 4	d	16 49		17 02	17 07						18 01	18 05							19 02	19 08		
Polegate	d	16 54		17 06	17 11		17 37	17 52			18 05	18 11		18 37		18 54			19 06	19 12		19 37
Berwick	d				17 17							18 17								19 17		
Glynde	d				17 22							18 22								19 23		
Seaford	d		16 58			17 25				17 58			18 26		18 44			19 02			19 19	
Bishopstone	d		17 00			17 27				18 00			18 28		18 46			19 04			19 21	
Newhaven Harbour	d		17 03			17 30				18 03			18 31								19 24	
Newhaven Town	d		17 05			17 32				18 05			18 33		18 50			19 08			19 26	
Southease	d					17 36							18 37									
Lewes 4	a	17 07	17 14	17 18	17 28	17 44	17 49	18 04		18 14	18 17	18 28	18 44	18 49	18 59	19 07		19 17	19 20	19 28	19 35	19 49
	d	17 07	17 14	17 19	17 28	17 44	17 50	18 05		18 14	18 18	18 28	18 44	18 50	18 59	19 07		19 18	19 21	19 29	19 38	19 50
Falmer	d		17 21		17 35	17 51		18 12		18 21		18 36	18 51		19 06			19 25		19 36	19 45	
Moulsecoomb	d		17 24		17 38	17 54		18 16		18 24		18 39	18 54		19 09			19 28		19 39	19 48	
London Road (Brighton)	d		17 27		17 41	17 57		18 18		18 27		18 42	18 57		19 12			19 30		19 41	19 50	
Brighton 10	a	17 20	17 30		17 44	18 00		18 22		18 30		18 45	19 00		19 15	19 21		19 34		19 45	19 55	
Cooksbridge	d			17 24							18 23								19 26			
Plumpton	d			17 29							18 28			18 58					19 31			
Wivelsfield 4	a			17 35							18 34			19 05								20 05
Haywards Heath 3	a			17 39			18 06				18 38			19 10					19 40			20 10
Gatwick Airport 10	a			17 54			18 26				18 56			19 25					19 55			20 25
East Croydon	a			18 11			18 42				19 12			19 42					20 11			20 41
London Bridge 4 ⊖	a																					
Clapham Junction 10	a			18 21			18 52				19 21			19 52					20 20			20 50
London Victoria 15 ⊖	a			18 29			18 59				19 29			19 59					20 28			20 58

A 🛒 from Lewes

Table 189

Mondays to Fridays

Ashford, Hastings, Eastbourne, Seaford and Lewes - Brighton, Haywards Heath and London

Station		SN	SN 1	SN	SN 1	SN ◇1	SN	SN 1	SN	SN 1	SN 1	SN ◇1
Ashford International	d		18 32					19 32			19 58	
Ham Street	d		18 41					19 41			20 07	
Appledore (Kent)	d		18 46					19 46			20 12	
Rye	a		18 55					19 55			20 21	
	d		18 56					19 56			20 22	
Winchelsea	d											
Doleham	d											
Three Oaks	d											
Ore	d				19 22	19 50				20 22		20 50
Hastings 4	a		19 13			19 53		20 13		20 25	20 39	20 53
	d		19 14		19 27	19 55		20 14		20 26		20 55
St Leonards Warrior Sq 4	d		19 17		19 30	19 58		20 17		20 28		20 58
Bexhill 4	d		19 24		19 37	20 05		20 24		20 35		21 05
Collington	d				19 39	20 07				20 37		21 07
Cooden Beach	d				19 42	20 10				20 40		21 10
Normans Bay	d				19 43							
Pevensey Bay	d											
Pevensey & Westham	d				19 48	20 16				20 46		21 16
Hampden Park 4	d				19 52	20 20				20 52		21 20
Eastbourne 4	a		19 44		19 57	20 25		20 39		20 57		21 25
	d		19 48		20 03	20 31		20 45		21 03		21 31
Hampden Park 4	d				20 07					21 07		
Polegate	d		19 55		20 11	20 37		20 52		21 11		21 37
Berwick	d				20 17					21 17		
Glynde	d				20 22					21 22		
Seaford	d	19 37		19 58			20 28		20 58			
Bishopstone	d	19 39		20 00			20 30		21 00			
Newhaven Harbour	d	19 42		20 03			20 33		21 03			
Newhaven Town	d	19 44		20 05			20 35		21 05			
Southease	d	19 48					20 39					
Lewes 4	a	19 55	20 07	20 14	20 28	20 49	20 46	21 07	21 14	21 28		21 49
	d	19 58	20 08	20 14	20 28	20 50	20 53	21 07	21 14	21 28		21 50
Falmer	d	20 05		20 21	20 35		21 00		21 21	21 35		
Moulsecoomb	d	20 08		20 24	20 38		21 03		21 24	21 38		
London Road (Brighton)	d	20 10		20 27	20 41		21 05		21 27	21 41		
Brighton 10	a	20 14	20 20	20 33	20 44		21 09	21 20	21 30	21 45		
Cooksbridge	d											
Plumpton	d					20 58						
Wivelsfield 4	a					21 05						22 02
Haywards Heath 3	a					21 09						22 06
Gatwick Airport 10	a					21 24						22 24
East Croydon	a					21 40						22 40
London Bridge 4	a											
Clapham Junction 10	a					21 50						22 49
London Victoria 15	a					21 57						22 57

Station		SN	SN 1	SN	SN 1	SN ◇1	SN	SN 1	SN	SN 1	SN 1	SN
Ashford International	d		20 32					21 32			22 32	
Ham Street	d		20 41					21 41			22 41	
Appledore (Kent)	d		20 46					21 46			22 46	
Rye	a		20 55					21 55			22 55	
	d		20 56					21 57			22 55	
Winchelsea	d										22 58	
Doleham	d										23 05	
Three Oaks	d										23 08	
Ore	d					21 22				22 22	23 14	
Hastings 4	a		21 13			21 25		22 14		22 25	23 17	
	d		21 14			21 30		22 15		22 26		
St Leonards Warrior Sq 4	d		21 17			21 32		22 18		22 29		
Bexhill 4	d		21 24			21 39		22 25		22 38		
Collington	d					21 41				22 40		
Cooden Beach	d					21 44				22 43		
Normans Bay	d									22 46		
Pevensey Bay	d											
Pevensey & Westham	d					21 50				22 51		
Hampden Park 4	d					21 55				22 55		
Eastbourne 4	a		21 39			22 00		22 40		23 00		
	d		21 45		22 03	22 15		22 45		23 05		
Hampden Park 4	d				22 07	22 19				23 09		
Polegate	d		21 52		22 11	22 23		22 52		23 13		
Berwick	d				22 17	22 29				23 18		
Glynde	d				22 22					23 24		
Seaford	d	21 28		21 58			22 20		22 58			23 25
Bishopstone	d	21 30		22 00			22 22		23 00			23 27
Newhaven Harbour	d	21 33		22 03			22 25		23 03			23 30
Newhaven Town	d	21 35		22 05			22 27		23 05			23 32
Southease	d											
Lewes 4	a	21 44	22 07	22 14	22 28	22 38	22 35	23 07	23 14	23 29		23 40
	d	21 53	22 07	22 14	22 28	22 40	22 42	23 07	23 14	23 30		23 40
Falmer	d	22 00		22 21	22 37		22 49		23 21	23 37		23 47
Moulsecoomb	d	22 03		22 24	22 40		22 52		23 24	23 40		23 50
London Road (Brighton)	d	22 05		22 27	22 42		22 54		23 27	23 42		23 53
Brighton 10	a	22 09	22 20	22 31	22 46		22 58	23 20	23 31	23 46		23 56
Cooksbridge	d											
Plumpton	d					22 48						
Wivelsfield 4	a					22 54						
Haywards Heath 3	a					22 58						
Gatwick Airport 10	a					23 12						
East Croydon	a					23 30						
London Bridge 4	a											
Clapham Junction 10	a					23 42						
London Victoria 15	a					23 52						

Station		SN 1
Ashford International	d	
Ham Street	d	
Appledore (Kent)	d	
Rye	a	
	d	
Winchelsea	d	
Doleham	d	
Three Oaks	d	
Ore	d	
Hastings 4	a	
	d	23 22
St Leonards Warrior Sq 4	d	23 24
Bexhill 4	d	23 31
Collington	d	23 33
Cooden Beach	d	23 36
Normans Bay	d	
Pevensey Bay	d	
Pevensey & Westham	d	23 42
Hampden Park 4	d	23 47
Eastbourne 4	a	23 52
	d	23 56
Hampden Park 4	d	00 01
Polegate	d	00 05
Berwick	d	
Glynde	d	
Seaford	d	
Bishopstone	d	
Newhaven Harbour	d	
Newhaven Town	d	
Southease	d	
Lewes 4	a	00 17
	d	00 18
Falmer	d	00 25
Moulsecoomb	d	00 28
London Road (Brighton)	d	00 30
Brighton 10	a	00 34
Cooksbridge	d	
Plumpton	d	
Wivelsfield 4	a	
Haywards Heath 3	a	
Gatwick Airport 10	a	
East Croydon	a	
London Bridge 4	a	
Clapham Junction 10	a	
London Victoria 15	a	

Table 189

Saturdays

Ashford, Hastings, Eastbourne, Seaford and Lewes - Brighton, Haywards Heath and London

Station		SN 1	SN 1	SN	SN 1	SN	SN ◇1	SN 1	SN	SN ◇1	SN 1	SN
Ashford International	d											
Ham Street	d											
Appledore (Kent)	d											
Rye	a											
	d											
Winchelsea	d											
Doleham	d											
Three Oaks	d											
Ore	d										06 22	
Hastings 4	a										06 25	
	d	23p22									06 26	
St Leonards Warrior Sq 4	d	23p24									06 28	
Bexhill 4	d	23p31									06 35	
Collington	d	23p33									06 37	
Cooden Beach	d	23p36									06 40	
Normans Bay	d										06 43	
Pevensey Bay	d											
Pevensey & Westham	d	23p42									06 48	
Hampden Park 4	d	23p47									06 52	
Eastbourne 4	a	23p52									06 57	
	d	23p56	05 03		05 50		06 24	06 38		06 58	07 03	
Hampden Park 4	d	00 01	05 07				06 28			07 02	07 07	
Polegate	d	00 05	05 11		05 57		06 32	06 45		07 06	07 11	
Berwick	d						06 38				07 17	
Glynde	d						06 43				07 22	
Seaford	d			05 05		06 28			06 58			07 28
Bishopstone	d			05 07		06 30			07 00			07 30
Newhaven Harbour	d			05 10		06 33			07 03			07 33
Newhaven Town	d			05 12		06 35			07 05			07 35
Southease	d											
Lewes 4	a	00 17	05 24	05 21	06 10	06 44	06 49	06 57	07 14	07 18	07 28	07 44
	d	00 18	05 25	05 28	06 10	06 44	06 50	06 58	07 14	07 20	07 28	07 44
Falmer	d	00 25		05 35	06 18	06 51		07 05	07 21		07 35	07 51
Moulsecoomb	d	00 28		05 38	06 21	06 54		07 09	07 24		07 38	07 54
London Road (Brighton)	d	00 30		05 40	06 24	06 57		07 11	07 27		07 40	07 57
Brighton 10	a	00 34		05 44	06 27	07 00		07 15	07 30		07 44	08 00
Cooksbridge	d											
Plumpton	d									07 28		
Wivelsfield 4	a									07 34		
Haywards Heath 3	a		05 40				07 05			07 40		
Gatwick Airport 10	a		06 03				07 24			07 54		
East Croydon	a						07 40			08 10		
London Bridge 4	a											
Clapham Junction 10	a						07 50			08 20		
London Victoria 15	a						07 57			08 27		

Station		SN ◇1	SN 1	SN 1	SN	SN ◇1	SN 1	SN	SN ◇1	SN 1	SN 1	SN
Ashford International	d			06 13							07 32	
Ham Street	d			06 22							07 41	
Appledore (Kent)	d			06 27							07 46	
Rye	a			06 36							07 55	
	d			06 51							07 56	
Winchelsea	d			06 54								
Doleham	d			07 01								
Three Oaks	d			07 04								
Ore	d	06 50		07 10			07 22		07 50			
Hastings 4	a	06 53		07 13			07 25		07 53		08 13	
	d	06 55		07 14			07 26		07 55		08 14	
St Leonards Warrior Sq 4	d	06 58		07 17			07 28		07 58		08 17	
Bexhill 4	d	07 05		07 24			07 35		08 05		08 24	
Collington	d	07 07					07 37		08 07			
Cooden Beach	d	07 10					07 40		08 10			
Normans Bay	d						07 43					
Pevensey Bay	d											
Pevensey & Westham	d	07 16					07 48		08 16			
Hampden Park 4	d	07 20					07 52		08 20			
Eastbourne 4	a	07 25		07 39			07 57		08 25		08 39	
	d	07 31		07 47		07 58	08 03		08 31		08 47	
Hampden Park 4	d					08 02	08 07					
Polegate	d	07 37		07 54		08 06	08 11		08 37		08 54	
Berwick	d						08 17					
Glynde	d						08 22					
Seaford	d				07 58			08 25				08 58
Bishopstone	d				08 00			08 27				09 00
Newhaven Harbour	d				08 03			08 30				09 03
Newhaven Town	d				08 05			08 32				09 05
Southease	d							08 36				
Lewes 4	a	07 49		08 07	08 14	08 18	08 28	08 44	08 49		09 07	09 14
	d	07 50	07 58	08 07	08 14	08 20	08 28	08 44	08 50	08 58	09 07	09 14
Falmer	d		08 05		08 21		08 35	08 51		09 05		09 21
Moulsecoomb	d		08 08		08 24		08 38	08 54		09 08		09 24
London Road (Brighton)	d		08 10		08 27		08 40	08 57		09 10		09 27
Brighton 10	a		08 14	08 20	08 30		08 44	09 00		09 14	09 20	09 30
Cooksbridge	d											
Plumpton	d					08 28						
Wivelsfield 4	a					08 34						
Haywards Heath 3	a	08 05				08 40			09 05			
Gatwick Airport 10	a	08 24				08 54			09 24			
East Croydon	a	08 40				09 10			09 41			
London Bridge 4	a											
Clapham Junction 10	a	08 50				09 20			09 51			
London Victoria 15	a	08 57				09 27			09 58			

Station		SN ◇1	SN 1	SN	SN ◇1	SN 1	SN 1	SN	SN ◇1	SN 1	SN	SN ◇1
Ashford International	d						08 32					
Ham Street	d						08 41					
Appledore (Kent)	d						08 46					
Rye	a						08 55					
	d						08 56					
Winchelsea	d											
Doleham	d											
Three Oaks	d											
Ore	d		08 22		08 50					09 22		09 50
Hastings 4	a		08 25		08 53		09 13			09 25		09 53
	d		08 26		08 55		09 14			09 26		09 55
St Leonards Warrior Sq 4	d		08 28		08 58		09 17			09 28		09 58
Bexhill 4	d		08 35		09 05		09 24			09 35		10 05
Collington	d		08 37		09 07					09 37		10 07
Cooden Beach	d		08 40		09 10					09 40		10 10
Normans Bay	d		08 43							09 43		
Pevensey Bay	d											
Pevensey & Westham	d		08 48		09 16					09 48		10 16
Hampden Park 4	d		08 52		09 20					09 52		10 20
Eastbourne 4	a		08 57		09 25		09 39			09 57		10 25
	d	08 58	09 03		09 31		09 47		09 58	10 03		10 31
Hampden Park 4	d	09 02	09 07						10 02	10 07		
Polegate	d	09 06	09 11		09 37		09 54		10 06	10 11		10 37
Berwick	d		09 17							10 17		
Glynde	d		09 22							10 22		
Seaford	d			09 25				09 58			10 25	
Bishopstone	d			09 27				10 00			10 27	
Newhaven Harbour	d			09 30				10 03			10 30	
Newhaven Town	d			09 32				10 05			10 32	
Southease	d			09 36							10 36	
Lewes 4	a	09 18	09 28	09 44	09 49		10 07	10 14	10 18	10 28	10 44	10 49
	d	09 20	09 28	09 44	09 50	09 58	10 07	10 14	10 20	10 28	10 44	10 50
Falmer	d		09 35	09 51		10 05		10 21		10 35	10 51	
Moulsecoomb	d		09 38	09 54		10 08		10 24		10 38	10 54	
London Road (Brighton)	d		09 41	09 57		10 10		10 27		10 41	10 57	
Brighton 10	a		09 44	10 00		10 14	10 20	10 30		10 44	11 00	
Cooksbridge	d											
Plumpton	d	09 28							10 28			
Wivelsfield 4	a	09 34							10 34			
Haywards Heath 3	a	09 40			10 05				10 40			11 05
Gatwick Airport 10	a	09 54			10 21				10 54			11 24
East Croydon	a	10 10			10 38				11 10			11 40
London Bridge 4	a											
Clapham Junction 10	a	10 20			10 47				11 20			11 50
London Victoria 15	a	10 27			10 56				11 27			11 57

Station		SN 1	SN 1	SN	SN ◇1	SN 1	SN	SN ◇1	SN 1	SN 1	SN	SN ◇1
Ashford International	d		09 32							10 32		
Ham Street	d		09 41							10 41		
Appledore (Kent)	d		09 46							10 46		
Rye	a		09 55							10 55		
	d		09 56							10 56		
Winchelsea	d											
Doleham	d											
Three Oaks	d											
Ore	d					10 22		10 50				
Hastings 4	a		10 13			10 25		10 53		11 13		
	d		10 14			10 26		10 55		11 14		
St Leonards Warrior Sq 4	d		10 17			10 28		10 58		11 17		
Bexhill 4	d		10 24			10 35		11 05		11 24		
Collington	d					10 37		11 07				
Cooden Beach	d					10 40		11 10				
Normans Bay	d					10 43						
Pevensey Bay	d											
Pevensey & Westham	d					10 48		11 16				
Hampden Park 4	d					10 52		11 20				
Eastbourne 4	a		10 39			10 57		11 25		11 39		
	d		10 47		10 58	11 03		11 31		11 47		11 58
Hampden Park 4	d				11 02	11 07						12 02
Polegate	d		10 54		11 06	11 11		11 37		11 54		12 06
Berwick	d					11 17						
Glynde	d					11 22						
Seaford	d			10 58			11 25				11 58	
Bishopstone	d			11 00			11 27				12 00	
Newhaven Harbour	d			11 03			11 30				12 03	
Newhaven Town	d			11 05			11 32				12 05	
Southease	d						11 36					
Lewes 4	a		11 07	11 14	11 18	11 28	11 44	11 49		12 07	12 14	12 18
	d	10 58	11 07	11 14	11 20	11 28	11 44	11 50	11 58	12 07	12 14	12 20
Falmer	d	11 05		11 21		11 35	11 51		12 05		12 21	
Moulsecoomb	d	11 08		11 24		11 38	11 54		12 08		12 24	
London Road (Brighton)	d	11 10		11 27		11 41	11 57		12 10		12 27	
Brighton 10	a	11 14	11 20	11 30		11 44	12 00		12 14	12 20	12 30	
Cooksbridge	d											
Plumpton	d											12 28
Wivelsfield 4	a				11 34							12 34
Haywards Heath 3	a				11 40			12 05				12 40
Gatwick Airport 10	a				11 54			12 24				12 54
East Croydon	a				12 10			12 40				13 10
London Bridge 4	a											
Clapham Junction 10	a				12 20			12 50				13 20
London Victoria 15	a				12 27			12 57				13 27

Ashford, Hastings, Eastbourne, Seaford and Lewes - Brighton, Haywards Heath and London

		SN 1	SN	SN ◇1	SN 1	SN 1	SN	SN ◇1	SN 1	SN	SN ◇1	SN 1	SN 1	SN	SN ◇1	SN 1	SN	SN ◇1	SN 1	SN 1	SN	SN ◇1
Ashford International	d					11 32							12 32							13 32		
Ham Street	d					11 41							12 41							13 41		
Appledore (Kent)	d					11 46							12 46							13 46		
Rye	a					11 55							12 55							13 55		
	d					11 56							12 56							13 56		
Winchelsea	d																					
Doleham	d																					
Three Oaks	d																					
Ore	d	11 22		11 50					12 22		12 50					13 22		13 50				
Hastings 4	a	11 25		11 53		12 13			12 25		12 53		13 13			13 25		13 53		14 13		
	d	11 26		11 55		12 14			12 26		12 55		13 14			13 26		13 55		14 14		
St Leonards Warrior Sq 4	d	11 28		11 58		12 17			12 28		12 58		13 17			13 28		13 58		14 17		
Bexhill 4	d	11 35		12 05		12 24			12 35		13 05		13 24			13 35		14 05		14 24		
Collington	d	11 37		12 07					12 37		13 07					13 37		14 07				
Cooden Beach	d	11 40		12 10					12 40		13 10					13 40		14 10				
Normans Bay	d	11 43							12 43							13 43						
Pevensey Bay	d																					
Pevensey & Westham	d	11 48		12 16					12 48		13 16					13 48		14 16				
Hampden Park 4	d	11 52		12 20					12 52		13 20					13 52		14 20				
Eastbourne 4	a	11 57		12 25		12 39			12 57		13 25		13 39			13 57		14 25		14 39		
	d	12 03		12 31		12 47		12 58	13 03		13 31		13 47		13 58	14 03		14 31		14 47		14 58
Hampden Park 4	d	12 07						13 02	13 07						14 02	14 07						15 02
Polegate	d	12 11		12 37		12 54		13 06	13 11		13 37		13 54		14 06	14 11		14 37		14 54		15 06
Berwick	d	12 17							13 17							14 17						
Glynde	d	12 22							13 22							14 22						
Seaford	d		12 25				12 58			13 25				13 58			14 25				14 58	
Bishopstone	d		12 27				13 00			13 27				14 00			14 27				15 00	
Newhaven Harbour	d		12 30				13 03			13 30				14 03			14 30				15 03	
Newhaven Town	d		12 32				13 05			13 32				14 05			14 32				15 05	
Southease	d		12 36							13 36							14 36					
Lewes 4	a	12 28	12 44	12 49		13 07	13 14	13 18	13 28	13 44	13 49		14 07	14 14	14 18	14 28	14 44	14 49		15 07	15 14	15 18
	d	12 28	12 44	12 50	12 58	13 07	13 14	13 20	13 28	13 44	13 50	13 58	14 07	14 14	14 20	14 28	14 44	14 50	14 58	15 07	15 14	15 20
Falmer	d	12 35	12 51		13 05		13 21		13 35	13 51		14 05		14 21		14 35	14 51		15 05		15 21	
Moulsecoomb	d	12 38	12 54		13 08		13 24		13 38	13 54		14 08		14 24		14 38	14 54		15 08		15 24	
London Road (Brighton)	d	12 41	12 57		13 10		13 27		13 41	13 57		14 10		14 27		14 41	14 57		15 10		15 27	
Brighton 10	a	12 44	13 00		13 14	13 20	13 30		13 44	14 00		14 14	14 20	14 30		14 44	15 00		15 14	15 20	15 30	
Cooksbridge	d																					
Plumpton	d																					
Wivelsfield 4	a							13 34							14 34							15 34
Haywards Heath 5	a			13 05				13 40			14 05				14 39			15 05				15 40
Gatwick Airport 10	a			13 24				13 54			14 24				14 54			15 24				15 54
East Croydon	a			13 40				14 10			14 40				15 10			15 40				16 10
London Bridge 4	a																					
Clapham Junction 10	a			13 50				14 20			14 50				15 20			15 50				16 20
London Victoria 15	a			13 57				14 27			14 57				15 27			15 57				16 27

		SN 1	SN	SN ◇1	SN 1	SN 1	SN	SN ◇1	SN 1	SN	SN ◇1	SN 1	SN 1	SN	SN ◇1	SN 1	SN	SN ◇1	SN 1	SN 1	SN	SN ◇1	SN 1
Ashford International	d					14 32							15 32							16 32			
Ham Street	d					14 41							15 41							16 41			
Appledore (Kent)	d					14 46							15 46							16 46			
Rye	a					14 55							15 55							16 55			
	d					14 56							15 56							16 56			
Winchelsea	d																						
Doleham	d																						
Three Oaks	d																						
Ore	d	14 22		14 50					15 22		15 50					16 22		16 50					17 22
Hastings 4	a	14 25		14 53		15 13			15 25		15 53		16 13			16 25		16 53		17 13			17 25
	d	14 26		14 55		15 14			15 26		15 55		16 14			16 26		16 55		17 14			17 26
St Leonards Warrior Sq 4	d	14 28		14 58		15 17			15 28		15 58		16 17			16 28		16 58		17 17			17 28
Bexhill 4	d	14 35		15 05		15 24			15 35		16 05		16 24			16 35		17 05		17 24			17 35
Collington	d	14 37		15 07					15 37		16 07					16 37		17 07					17 37
Cooden Beach	d	14 40		15 10					15 40		16 10					16 40		17 10					17 40
Normans Bay	d	14 43							15 43							16 43							17 43
Pevensey Bay	d																						
Pevensey & Westham	d	14 48		15 16					15 48		16 16					16 48		17 16					17 48
Hampden Park 4	d	14 52		15 20					15 52		16 20					16 52		17 20					17 52
Eastbourne 4	a	14 57		15 25		15 39			15 57		16 25		16 39			16 57		17 25		17 39			17 57
	d	15 03		15 31		15 47		15 58	16 03		16 31		16 47		16 58	17 03		17 31		17 47		17 58	18 03
Hampden Park 4	d	15 07						16 02	16 07						17 02	17 07						18 02	18 07
Polegate	d	15 11		15 37		15 54		16 06	16 11		16 37		16 54		17 06	17 11		17 37		17 54		18 06	18 11
Berwick	d	15 17							16 17							17 17							18 17
Glynde	d	15 22							16 22							17 22							18 22
Seaford	d		15 25				15 58			16 25				16 58			17 25				17 58		
Bishopstone	d		15 27				16 00			16 27				17 00			17 27				18 00		
Newhaven Harbour	d		15 30				16 03			16 30				17 03			17 30				18 03		
Newhaven Town	d		15 32				16 05			16 32				17 05			17 32				18 05		
Southease	d		15 36							16 36							17 36						
Lewes 4	a	15 28	15 44	15 49		16 07	16 14	16 18	16 28	16 44	16 49		17 07	17 14	17 18	17 28	17 44	17 49		18 07	18 14	18 18	18 28
	d	15 28	15 44	15 50	15 58	16 07	16 14	16 20	16 28	16 44	16 50	16 58	17 07	17 14	17 20	17 28	17 44	17 50	17 58	18 07	18 14	18 20	18 28
Falmer	d	15 35	15 51		16 05		16 21		16 35	16 51		17 05		17 21		17 35	17 51		18 05		18 21		18 35
Moulsecoomb	d	15 38	15 54		16 08		16 24		16 38	16 54		17 08		17 24		17 38	17 54		18 08		18 24		18 38
London Road (Brighton)	d	15 41	15 57		16 10		16 27		16 41	16 57		17 10		17 27		17 41	17 57		18 10		18 27		18 41
Brighton 10	a	15 44	16 00		16 14	16 20	16 30		16 44	17 00		17 14	17 20	17 30		17 44	18 00		18 14	18 20	18 30		18 44
Cooksbridge	d																						
Plumpton	d							16 28							17 28							18 28	
Wivelsfield 4	a							16 34							17 34							18 34	
Haywards Heath 5	a			16 05				16 40			17 05				17 40			18 05				18 40	
Gatwick Airport 10	a			16 24				16 54			17 24				17 54			18 24				18 54	
East Croydon	a			16 40				17 10			17 40				18 10			18 40				19 10	
London Bridge 4	a																						
Clapham Junction 10	a			16 50				17 20			17 50				18 20			18 50				19 20	
London Victoria 15	a			16 57				17 27			17 57				18 27			18 57				19 27	

Table 189

Saturdays

Ashford, Hastings, Eastbourne, Seaford and Lewes - Brighton, Haywards Heath and London

		SN	SN ◇1	SN 1	SN 1	SN	SN ◇1	SN 1	SN	SN ◇1	SN 1	SN 1	SN	SN 1	SN ◇1	SN	SN 1	SN	SN 1	SN ◇1	SN	SN 1
Ashford International	d				17 32							18 32					19 32					20 32
Ham Street	d				17 41							18 41					19 41					20 41
Appledore (Kent)	d				17 46							18 46					19 46					20 46
Rye	a				17 55							18 55					19 55					20 55
	d				17 56							18 56					19 56					20 56
Winchelsea	d																					
Doleham	d																					
Three Oaks	d																					
Ore	d		17 50					18 22		18 50				19 22	19 50				20 22	20 50		
Hastings 4	a		17 53		18 13			18 25		18 53		19 13		19 25	19 53		20 13		20 25	20 53		21 13
	d		17 55		18 14			18 26		18 55		19 14		19 26	19 55		20 14		20 26	20 55		21 14
St Leonards Warrior Sq 4	d		17 58		18 17			18 28		18 58		19 17		19 28	19 58		20 17		20 28	20 58		21 17
Bexhill 4	d		18 05		18 24			18 35		19 05		19 24		19 35	20 05		20 24		20 35	21 05		21 24
Collington	d		18 07					18 37		19 07				19 37	20 07				20 37	21 07		
Cooden Beach	d		18 10					18 40		19 10				19 40	20 10				20 40	21 10		
Normans Bay	d							18 43						19 43					20 43			
Pevensey Bay	d																					
Pevensey & Westham	d		18 16					18 48		19 16				19 48	20 16				20 48	21 16		
Hampden Park 4	d		18 20					18 52		19 21				19 52	20 20				20 52	21 20		
Eastbourne 4	a		18 25		18 39			18 57		19 26		19 39		19 57	20 25		20 39		20 57	21 25		21 39
	d		18 31		18 47		18 58	19 03		19 32		19 47		20 03	20 31		20 45		21 03	21 31		21 45
Hampden Park 4	d						19 02	19 07						20 07					21 07			
Polegate	d		18 37		18 54		19 06	19 11		19 38		19 54		20 11	20 37		20 52		21 11	21 37		21 52
Berwick	d							19 17						20 17					21 17			
Glynde	d							19 22						20 22					21 22			
Seaford	d	18 25				18 58			19 25				19 58			20 28		20 58			21 28	
Bishopstone	d	18 27				19 00			19 27				20 00			20 30		21 00			21 30	
Newhaven Harbour	d	18 30				19 03			19 30				20 03			20 33		21 03			21 33	
Newhaven Town	d	18 32				19 05			19 32				20 05			20 35		21 05			21 35	
Southease	d	18 36							19 36													
Lewes 4	a	18 44	18 49		19 07	19 14	19 18	19 28	19 44	19 50		20 07	20 14	20 28	20 49	20 44	21 07	21 14	21 28	21 49	21 44	22 07
	d	18 44	18 50	18 58	19 07	19 14	19 20	19 28	19 44	19 51	19 58	20 07	20 14	20 30	20 50	20 53	21 07	21 14	21 28	21 50	21 53	22 07
Falmer	d	18 51		19 05		19 21		19 35	19 51		20 05		20 21	20 37		21 00		21 21	21 36		22 00	
Moulsecoomb	d	18 54		19 08		19 24		19 38	19 54		20 08		20 24	20 40		21 03		21 24	21 39		22 03	
London Road (Brighton)	d	18 57		19 10		19 27		19 41	19 57		20 10		20 27	20 42		21 05		21 27	21 41		22 05	
Brighton 10	a	19 00		19 14	19 20	19 30		19 44	20 00		20 14	20 20	20 30	20 46		21 10	21 20	21 30	21 45		22 09	22 20
Cooksbridge	d																					
Plumpton	d						19 28															
Wivelsfield 4	a						19 34			20 03					21 02					22 02		
Haywards Heath 5	a		19 05				19 40			20 07					21 06					22 06		
Gatwick Airport 10	a		19 24				19 34			20 24					21 24					22 23		
East Croydon	a		19 40				20 10			20 40					21 40					22 40		
London Bridge 4	a																					
Clapham Junction 10	a		19 50				20 20			20 50					21 50					22 49		
London Victoria 15	a		19 57				20 27			20 57					21 57					22 58		

		SN	SN 1	SN ◇1	SN	SN 1	SN	SN 1	SN 1	SN	SN 1
Ashford International	d					21 32			22 32		
Ham Street	d					21 41			22 41		
Appledore (Kent)	d					21 46			22 46		
Rye	a					21 55			22 55		
	d					21 56			22 55		
Winchelsea	d								22 59		
Doleham	d								23 05		
Three Oaks	d								23 09		
Ore	d		21 22					22 22	23 14		
Hastings 4	a		21 25			22 13		22 25	23 17		
	d		21 26	21 42		22 15		22 26			23 22
St Leonards Warrior Sq 4	d		21 28	21 44		22 18		22 29			23 24
Bexhill 4	d		21 35	21 51		22 25		22 38			23 31
Collington	d		21 37	21 53				22 40			23 33
Cooden Beach	d		21 40	21 56				22 43			23 36
Normans Bay	d							22 46			
Pevensey Bay	d										
Pevensey & Westham	d		21 46	22 02				22 51			23 42
Hampden Park 4	d		21 51	22 07				22 55			23 47
Eastbourne 4	a		21 56	22 12		22 40		23 00			23 52
	d		22 03	22 18		22 45		23 05			23 56
Hampden Park 4	d		22 07					23 09			00 01
Polegate	d		22 11	22 25		22 52		23 13			00 05
Berwick	d		22 17					23 18			
Glynde	d		22 22					23 24			
Seaford	d	21 58			22 20		22 58			23 25	
Bishopstone	d	22 00			22 22		23 30			23 27	
Newhaven Harbour	d	22 03			22 25		23 03			23 30	
Newhaven Town	d	22 05			22 27		23 05			23 32	
Southease	d										
Lewes 4	a	22 14	22 28	22 38	22 35	23 07	23 14	23 29		23 40	00 17
	d	22 14	22 28	22 40	22 42	23 07	23 14	23 30		23 40	00 18
Falmer	d	22 21	22 35		22 49		23 21	23 37		23 47	00 25
Moulsecoomb	d	22 24	22 38		22 52		23 24	23 40		23 50	00 28
London Road (Brighton)	d	22 27	22 41		22 54		23 27	23 42		23 53	00 30
Brighton 10	a	22 31	22 44		22 58	23 20	23 31	23 46		23 56	00 34
Cooksbridge	d										
Plumpton	d			22 48							
Wivelsfield 4	a			22 54							
Haywards Heath 5	a			22 58							
Gatwick Airport 10	a			23 12							
East Croydon	a			23 30							
London Bridge 4	a										
Clapham Junction 10	a			23 42							
London Victoria 15	a			23 52							

Table 189

Sundays
until 05 September

Ashford, Hastings, Eastbourne, Seaford and Lewes - Brighton, Haywards Heath and London

		SN 1	SN 1	SN	SN ◇1 B ✠	SN 1	SN ◇1 B ✠	SN	SN	SN 1	SN ◇1 B ✠	SN	SN	SN 1	SN ◇1 B ✠	SN	SN	SN 1	SN ◇1 B ✠	SN	SN	SN 1	SN ◇1 B ✠
Ashford International	d													08 15				09 21				10 21	
Ham Street	d													08 24				09 30				10 30	
Appledore (Kent)	d													08 29				09 35				10 35	
Rye	a													08 38				09 44				10 44	
	d													08 40				09 45				10 45	
Winchelsea	d													08 43									
Doleham	d													08 50									
Three Oaks	d													08 53									
Ore	d										08 14			08 59	09 14				10 14				11 14
Hastings 4	a										08 17			09 02	09 17			10 02	10 17			11 02	11 17
	d	23p22									08 18			09 03	09 18			10 03	10 18			11 03	11 18
St Leonards Warrior Sq 4	d	23p24									08 21			09 06	09 21			10 06	10 21			11 06	11 21
Bexhill 4	d	23p31									08 28			09 13	09 28			10 13	10 28			11 13	11 28
Collington	d	23p33									08 30				09 30				10 30				11 30
Cooden Beach	d	23p36									08 33				09 33				10 33				11 33
Normans Bay	d																						
Pevensey Bay	d																						
Pevensey & Westham	d	23p42									08 39				09 39				10 39				11 39
Hampden Park 4	d	23p47									08 43				09 43				10 43				11 43
Eastbourne 4	a	23p52									08 49			09 29	09 49			10 29	10 49			11 29	11 49
	d	23p56	05 37		06 58	07 30	07 55			08 34	08 59			09 34	09 59			10 34	10 59			11 34	11 59
Hampden Park 4	d	00 01			07 02	07 34				08 38				09 38				10 38				11 38	
Polegate	d	00 05	05 44		07 06	07 38	08 02			08 42	09 06			09 42	10 06			10 42	11 06			11 42	12 06
Berwick	d					07 44				08 48				09 48				10 48				11 48	
Glynde	d					07 49				08 53				09 53				10 53				11 53	
Seaford	d							07 57	08 27			08 57	09 27			09 57	10 27			10 57	11 27		
Bishopstone	d							07 59	08 29			08 59	09 29			09 59	10 29			10 59	11 29		
Newhaven Harbour	d							08 02	08 32			09 02	09 32			10 02	10 32			11 02	11 32		
Newhaven Town	d							08 04	08 34			09 04	09 34			10 04	10 34			11 04	11 34		
Southease	d							08 08				09 08				10 08				11 08			
Lewes 4	a	00 17	05 56	07 15	07 18	07 55	08 18	08 15	08 43	08 59	09 18	09 15	09 43	09 59	10 18	10 15	10 43	10 59	11 18	11 15	11 43	11 59	12 18
	d	00 18	05 57	07 22	07 22	07 56	08 22	08 22	08 44	09 00	09 22	09 22	09 44	10 00	10 22	10 22	10 44	11 00	11 22	11 22	11 44	12 00	12 22
Falmer	d	00 25		07 29		08 03		08 29	08 51			09 29	09 51			10 29	10 51			11 29	11 51		
Moulsecoomb	d	00 28		07 32		08 07		08 32	08 54			09 32	09 54			10 32	10 54			11 32	11 54		
London Road (Brighton)	d	00 30		07 34		08 09		08 34	08 56			09 34	09 56			10 34	10 56			11 34	11 56		
Brighton 10	a	00 34	06 09	07 38		08 13		08 38	09 00	09 12		09 38	10 00	10 12		10 38	11 00	11 12		11 38	12 00	12 12	
Cooksbridge	d																						
Plumpton	d						08 30				09 30				10 30				11 30				12 30
Wivelsfield 4	a		06 32		07 36		08 36				09 36				10 36				11 36				12 36
Haywards Heath 3	a		06 36		07 40		08 40				09 40				10 40				11 40				12 40
Gatwick Airport 10	a		06 51		07 52		08 52				09 52				10 52				11 52				12 52
East Croydon	a				08 09		09 09				10 09				11 09				12 09				13 09
London Bridge 4 ⊖	a																						
Clapham Junction 10	a				08 18		09 18				10 18				11 18				12 18				13 18
London Victoria 15 ⊖	a				08 25		09 25				10 25				11 25				12 25				13 25

B ✠ from Lewes

Table 189

Sundays
until 05 September

Ashford, Hastings, Eastbourne, Seaford and Lewes - Brighton, Haywards Heath and London

		SN	SN	SN 1	SN ◇1 A ✠	SN	SN	SN 1	SN ◇1 A ✠	SN	SN	SN 1	SN ◇1 A ✠	SN	SN	SN 1	SN ◇1 A ✠	SN	SN	SN 1	SN ◇1 A ✠	SN	SN
Ashford International	d			11 21				12 21				13 21				14 21				15 21			
Ham Street	d			11 30				12 30				13 30				14 30				15 30			
Appledore (Kent)	d			11 35				12 35				13 35				14 35				15 35			
Rye	a			11 44				12 44				13 44				14 44				15 44			
	d			11 45				12 45				13 45				14 45				15 45			
Winchelsea	d																						
Doleham	d																						
Three Oaks	d																						
Ore	d				12 14				13 14				14 14				15 14				16 14		
Hastings 4	a			12 02	12 17			13 02	13 17			14 02	14 17			15 02	15 17			16 02	16 17		
	d			12 03	12 18			13 03	13 18			14 03	14 18			15 03	15 18			16 03	16 18		
St Leonards Warrior Sq 4	d			12 06	12 21			13 06	13 21			14 06	14 21			15 06	15 21			16 06	16 21		
Bexhill 4	d			12 13	12 28			13 13	13 28			14 13	14 28			15 13	15 28			16 13	16 28		
Collington	d				12 30				13 30				14 30				15 30				16 30		
Cooden Beach	d				12 33				13 33				14 33				15 33				16 33		
Normans Bay	d																						
Pevensey Bay	d																						
Pevensey & Westham	d				12 39				13 39				14 39				15 39				16 39		
Hampden Park 4	d				12 43				13 43				14 43				15 43				16 43		
Eastbourne 4	a			12 29	12 49			13 29	13 49			14 29	14 49			15 29	15 49			16 29	16 49		
	d			12 34	12 59			13 34	13 59			14 34	14 59			15 34	15 59			16 34	16 59		
Hampden Park 4	d			12 38				13 38				14 38				15 38				16 38			
Polegate	d			12 42	13 06			13 42	14 06			14 42	15 06			15 42	16 06			16 42	17 06		
Berwick	d			12 48				13 48				14 48				15 48				16 48			
Glynde	d			12 53				13 53				14 53				15 53				16 53			
Seaford	d	11 57	12 27			12 57	13 27			13 57	14 27			14 57	15 27			15 57	16 27			16 57	17 27
Bishopstone	d	11 59	12 29			12 59	13 29			13 59	14 29			14 59	15 29			15 59	16 29			16 59	17 29
Newhaven Harbour	d	12 02	12 32			13 02	13 32			14 02	14 32			15 02	15 32			16 02	16 32			17 02	17 32
Newhaven Town	d	12 04	12 34			13 04	13 34			14 04	14 34			15 04	15 34			16 04	16 34			17 04	17 34
Southease	d	12 08				13 08				14 08				15 08				16 08				17 08	
Lewes 4	a	12 15	12 43	12 59	13 18	13 15	13 43	13 59	14 18	14 15	14 43	14 59	15 18	15 15	15 43	15 59	16 18	16 15	16 43	16 59	17 18	17 15	17 43
	d	12 22	12 44	13 00	13 22	13 22	13 44	14 00	14 22	14 22	14 44	15 00	15 22	15 22	15 44	16 00	16 22	16 22	16 44	17 00	17 22	17 22	17 44
Falmer	d	12 29	12 51			13 29	13 51			14 29	14 51			15 29	15 51			16 29	16 51			17 29	17 51
Moulsecoomb	d	12 32	12 54			13 32	13 54			14 32	14 54			15 32	15 54			16 32	16 54			17 32	17 54
London Road (Brighton)	d	12 34	12 56			13 34	13 56			14 34	14 56			15 34	15 56			16 34	16 56			17 34	17 56
Brighton 10	a	12 38	13 00	13 12		13 38	14 00	14 12		14 38	15 00	15 12		15 38	16 00	16 12		16 38	17 00	17 12		17 38	18 00
Cooksbridge	d																						
Plumpton	d																16 30				17 30		
Wivelsfield 4	a				13 36				14 36				15 36				16 36				17 36		
Haywards Heath 3	a				13 40				14 40				15 40				16 40				17 40		
Gatwick Airport 10	a				13 52				14 52				15 52				16 52				17 52		
East Croydon	a				14 09				15 09				16 09				17 09				18 09		
London Bridge 4 ⊖	a																						
Clapham Junction 10	a				14 18				15 18				16 18				17 18				18 18		
London Victoria 15 ⊖	a				14 25				15 25				16 25				17 25				18 25		

A ✠ from Lewes

Ashford, Hastings, Eastbourne, Seaford and Lewes - Brighton, Haywards Heath and London

		SN 1	SN ◇1 A ⌶	SN	SN	SN 1	SN ◇1	SN	SN	SN 1	SN ◇1	SN	SN	SN 1	SN ◇1	SN	SN	SN 1	SN	SN 1	SN	SN 1
Ashford International	d	16 21				17 21				18 21				19 21				20 21				21 21
Ham Street	d	16 30				17 30				18 30				19 30				20 30				21 30
Appledore (Kent)	d	16 35				17 35				18 35				19 35				20 35				21 35
Rye	a	16 44				17 44				18 44				19 44				20 44				21 44
	d	16 45				17 45				18 45				19 45				20 45				21 45
Winchelsea	d																					
Doleham	d																					
Three Oaks	d																					
Ore	d		17 14				18 14				19 14				20 14					21 14		
Hastings 4	a	17 02	17 17			18 02	18 17			19 02	19 17			20 02	20 17			21 02		21 17		22 02
	d	17 03	17 18			18 03	18 18			19 03	19 18			20 03	20 18			21 03		21 18		22 03
St Leonards Warrior Sq 4	d	17 06	17 21			18 06	18 21			19 06	19 21			20 06	20 21			21 06		21 21		22 06
Bexhill 4	d	17 13	17 28			18 13	18 28			19 13	19 28			20 13	20 28			21 13		21 28		22 13
Collington	d		17 30				18 30				19 30				20 30					21 30		
Cooden Beach	d		17 33				18 33				19 33				20 33					21 33		
Normans Bay	d																					
Pevensey Bay	d																					
Pevensey & Westham	d		17 39				18 39				19 39				20 39					21 39		
Hampden Park 4	d		17 43				18 43				19 43				20 43					21 43		
Eastbourne 4	a	17 29	17 49			18 29	18 49			19 29	19 49			20 29	20 49			21 29		21 49		22 29
	d	17 34	17 59			18 34	18 59			19 34	19 59			20 34	20 59			21 34		21 59		22 34
Hampden Park 4	d	17 38				18 38				19 38				20 38				21 38				22 38
Polegate	d	17 42	18 06			18 42	19 06			19 42	20 06			20 42	21 06			21 42		22 06		22 42
Berwick	d	17 48				18 48				19 48				20 48				21 48				22 48
Glynde	d	17 53				18 53				19 53				20 53				21 53				22 53
Seaford	d			17 57	18 27			18 57	19 27			19 57	20 27			20 57	21 27		21 53		22 27	
Bishopstone	d			17 59	18 29			18 59	19 29			19 59	20 29			20 59	21 29		21 55		22 29	
Newhaven Harbour	d			18 02	18 32			19 02	19 32			20 02	20 32			21 02	21 32		21 58		22 32	
Newhaven Town	d			18 04	18 34			19 04	19 34			20 04	20 34			21 04	21 34		22 00		22 34	
Southease	d			18 08				19 08				20 08										
Lewes 4	a	17 59	18 18	18 15	18 43	18 59	19 18	19 15	19 43	19 59	20 18	20 15	20 43	20 59	21 18	21 13	21 43	21 59	22 09	22 18	22 43	22 59
	d	18 00	18 22	18 22	18 44	19 00	19 22	19 22	19 44	20 00	20 22	20 22	20 44	21 00	21 22	21 22	21 44	22 00	22 10	22 19	22 44	23 00
Falmer	d			18 29	18 51			19 29	19 51			20 29	20 51			21 29	21 51		22 17	22 26	22 51	
Moulsecoomb	d			18 32	18 54			19 32	19 54			20 32	20 54			21 32	21 54		22 20	22 29	22 54	
London Road (Brighton)	d			18 34	18 56			19 34	19 56			20 34	20 56			21 34	21 56		22 22	22 31	22 56	
Brighton 10	a	18 12		18 38	19 00	19 12		19 38	20 00	20 12		20 38	21 00	21 12		21 38	22 00	22 12	22 26	22 35	23 00	23 12
Cooksbridge	d																					
Plumpton	d		18 30				19 30				20 30				21 30							
Wivelsfield 4	a		18 36				19 36				20 36				21 36							
Haywards Heath 3	a		18 40				19 40				20 40				21 40							
Gatwick Airport 10	a		18 52				19 52				20 52				21 52							
East Croydon ⇌	a		19 09				20 09				21 09				22 09							
London Bridge 4 ⊖	a																					
Clapham Junction 10	a		19 18				20 18				21 18				22 18							
London Victoria 15 ⊖	a		19 25				20 25				21 25				22 25							

A ⌶ from Lewes

Ashford, Hastings, Eastbourne, Seaford and Lewes - Brighton, Haywards Heath and London

		SN	SN 1	SN 1	SN 1
Ashford International	d			22 32	
Ham Street	d			22 41	
Appledore (Kent)	d			22 46	
Rye	a			22 55	
	d			22 55	
Winchelsea	d			22 58	
Doleham	d			23 05	
Three Oaks	d			23 08	
Ore	d		22 14	23 14	
Hastings 4	a		22 17	23 17	
	d		22 18		23 22
St Leonards Warrior Sq 4	d		22 21		23 24
Bexhill 4	d		22 28		23 31
Collington	d		22 30		23 33
Cooden Beach	d		22 33		23 36
Normans Bay	d				
Pevensey Bay	d				
Pevensey & Westham	d		22 39		23 42
Hampden Park 4	d		22 43		23 47
Eastbourne 4	a		22 49		23 52
	d		22 59		
Hampden Park 4	d				
Polegate	d		23 06		
Berwick	d				
Glynde	d				
Seaford	d	22 53			
Bishopstone	d	22 55			
Newhaven Harbour	d	22 58			
Newhaven Town	d	23 00			
Southease	d				
Lewes 4	a	23 09	23 18		
	d	23 10	23 19		
Falmer	d	23 17	23 26		
Moulsecoomb	d	23 20	23 29		
London Road (Brighton)	d	23 22	23 31		
Brighton 10	a	23 26	23 35		
Cooksbridge	d				
Plumpton	d				
Wivelsfield 4	a				
Haywards Heath 3	a				
Gatwick Airport 10	a				
East Croydon ⇌	a				
London Bridge 4 ⊖	a				
Clapham Junction 10	a				
London Victoria 15 ⊖	a				

Table 189

Sundays
from 12 September

Ashford, Hastings, Eastbourne, Seaford and Lewes - Brighton, Haywards Heath and London

		SN [1]	SN ◇[1] A 🛒	SN [1]	SN [1]	SN	SN ◇[1] A 🛒	SN	SN [1]	SN ◇[1] A 🛒	SN	SN	SN [1]	SN ◇[1] A 🛒	SN	SN	SN [1]	SN ◇[1] A 🛒	SN	SN	SN [1]	SN ◇[1] A 🛒	SN
Ashford International	d												08 15				09 21				10 21		
Ham Street	d												08 24				09 30				10 30		
Appledore (Kent)	d												08 29				09 35				10 35		
Rye	a												08 38				09 44				10 44		
	d												08 40				09 45				10 45		
Winchelsea	d												08 43										
Doleham	d												08 50										
Three Oaks	d												08 53										
Ore	d									08 14			08 59	09 14				10 14				11 14	
Hastings [4]	a									08 17			09 02	09 17			10 02	10 17			11 02	11 17	
	d	23p22								08 18			09 03	09 18			10 03	10 18			11 03	11 18	
St Leonards Warrior Sq [4]	d	23p24								08 21			09 06	09 21			10 06	10 21			11 06	11 21	
Bexhill [4]	d	23p31								08 28			09 13	09 28			10 13	10 28			11 13	11 28	
Collington	d	23p33								08 30				09 30				10 30				11 30	
Cooden Beach	d	23p36								08 33				09 33				10 33				11 33	
Normans Bay	d																						
Pevensey Bay	d																						
Pevensey & Westham	d	23p42								08 39				09 39				10 39				11 39	
Hampden Park [4]	d	23p47								08 43				09 43				10 43				11 43	
Eastbourne [4]	a	23p52								08 49			09 29	09 49			10 29	10 49			11 29	11 49	
	d	23p56	06 54		07 30		07 55		08 34	08 55			09 34	09 55			10 34	10 55			11 34	11 55	
Hampden Park [4]	d	00 01	06 58		07 34				08 38				09 38				10 38				11 38		
Polegate	d	00 05	07 02		07 38		08 02		08 42	09 02			09 42	10 02			10 42	11 02			11 42	12 02	
Berwick	d				07 44				08 48				09 48				10 48				11 48		
Glynde	d				07 49				08 53				09 53				10 53				11 53		
Seaford	d					07 53		08 27			08 53	09 27			09 53	10 27			10 53	11 27			11 53
Bishopstone	d					07 55		08 29			08 55	09 29			09 55	10 29			10 55	11 29			11 55
Newhaven Harbour	d					07 58		08 32			08 58	09 32			09 58	10 32			10 58	11 32			11 58
Newhaven Town	d					08 00		08 34			09 00	09 34			10 00	10 34			11 00	11 34			12 00
Southease	d					08 04					09 04				10 04				11 04				12 04
Lewes [4]	a	00 17	07 14		07 55	08 11	08 14	08 43	08 59	09 14	09 11	09 43	09 59	10 14	10 11	10 43	10 59	11 14	11 11	11 43	11 59	12 14	12 11
	d	00 18	07 20	07 18	07 56	08 18	08 16	08 44	09 00	09 16	09 18	09 44	10 00	10 16	10 18	10 44	11 00	11 16	11 18	11 44	12 00	12 16	12 18
Falmer	d	00 25		07 25	08 03	08 25		08 51			09 25	09 51			10 25	10 51			11 25	11 51			12 25
Moulsecoomb	d	00 28		07 28	08 07	08 28		08 54			09 28	09 54			10 28	10 54			11 28	11 54			12 28
London Road (Brighton)	d	00 30		07 30	08 09	08 30		08 56			09 30	09 56			10 30	10 56			11 30	11 56			12 30
Brighton [10]	a	00 34		07 34	08 13	08 34		09 00	09 12		09 34	10 00	10 12		10 34	11 00	11 12		11 34	12 00	12 12		12 34
Cooksbridge	d																						
Plumpton	d						08 24			09 24				10 24				11 24				12 24	
Wivelsfield [4]	a		07 32				08 31			09 31				10 31				11 31				12 31	
Haywards Heath [3]	a		07 36				08 36			09 35				10 35				11 35				12 35	
Gatwick Airport [10]	a		07 51				08 51			09 51				10 51				11 51				12 52	
East Croydon	a		08 09				09 09			10 09				11 09				12 09				13 09	
London Bridge [4] ⊖	a																						
Clapham Junction [10]	a		08 24				09 24			10 24				11 24				12 24				13 24	
London Victoria [15] ⊖	a		08 31				09 31			10 31				11 31				12 31				13 31	

A 🛒 from Lewes

Table 189

Sundays
from 12 September

Ashford, Hastings, Eastbourne, Seaford and Lewes - Brighton, Haywards Heath and London

		SN	SN [1]	SN ◇[1] A 🛒	SN	SN	SN [1]	SN ◇[1] A 🛒	SN	SN	SN [1]	SN ◇[1] A 🛒	SN	SN	SN [1]	SN ◇[1] A 🛒	SN	SN	SN [1]	SN ◇[1] A 🛒	SN	SN	SN [1]
Ashford International	d		11 21				12 21				13 21				14 21				15 21				16 21
Ham Street	d		11 30				12 30				13 30				14 30				15 30				16 30
Appledore (Kent)	d		11 35				12 35				13 35				14 35				15 35				16 35
Rye	a		11 44				12 44				13 44				14 44				15 44				16 44
	d		11 45				12 45				13 45				14 45				15 45				16 45
Winchelsea	d																						
Doleham	d																						
Three Oaks	d																						
Ore	d			12 14				13 14				14 14				15 14				16 14			
Hastings [4]	a		12 02	12 17			13 02	13 17			14 02	14 17			15 02	15 17			16 02	16 17			17 02
	d		12 03	12 18			13 03	13 18			14 03	14 18			15 03	15 18			16 03	16 18			17 03
St Leonards Warrior Sq [4]	d		12 06	12 21			13 06	13 21			14 06	14 21			15 06	15 21			16 06	16 21			17 06
Bexhill [4]	d		12 13	12 28			13 13	13 28			14 13	14 28			15 13	15 28			16 13	16 28			17 13
Collington	d			12 30				13 30				14 30				15 30				16 30			
Cooden Beach	d			12 33				13 33				14 33				15 33				16 33			
Normans Bay	d																						
Pevensey Bay	d																						
Pevensey & Westham	d			12 39				13 39				14 39				15 39				16 39			
Hampden Park [4]	d			12 43				13 43				14 43				15 43				16 43			
Eastbourne [4]	a		12 29	12 49			13 29	13 49			14 29	14 49			15 29	15 49			16 29	16 49			17 29
	d		12 34	12 55			13 34	13 55			14 34	14 55			15 34	15 55			16 34	16 55			17 34
Hampden Park [4]	d		12 38				13 38				14 38				15 38				16 38				17 38
Polegate	d		12 42	13 02			13 42	14 02			14 42	15 02			15 42	16 02			16 42	17 02			17 42
Berwick	d		12 48				13 48				14 48				15 48				16 48				17 48
Glynde	d		12 53				13 53				14 53				15 53				16 53				17 53
Seaford	d	12 27			12 53	13 27			13 53	14 27			14 53	15 27			15 53	16 27			16 53	17 27	
Bishopstone	d	12 29			12 55	13 29			13 55	14 29			14 55	15 29			15 55	16 29			16 55	17 29	
Newhaven Harbour	d	12 32			12 58	13 32			13 58	14 32			14 58	15 32			15 58	16 32			16 58	17 32	
Newhaven Town	d	12 34			13 00	13 34			14 00	14 34			15 00	15 34			16 00	16 34			17 00	17 34	
Southease	d				13 04				14 04				15 04				16 04				17 04		
Lewes [4]	a	12 43	12 59	13 14	13 11	13 43	13 59	14 14	14 11	14 43	14 59	15 14	15 11	15 43	15 59	16 14	16 11	16 43	16 59	17 14	17 11	17 43	17 59
	d	12 44	13 00	13 16	13 18	13 44	14 00	14 16	14 18	14 44	15 00	15 16	15 18	15 44	16 00	16 16	16 18	16 44	17 00	17 16	17 18	17 44	18 00
Falmer	d	12 51			13 25	13 51			14 25	14 51			15 25	15 51			16 25	16 51			17 25	17 51	
Moulsecoomb	d	12 54			13 28	13 54			14 28	14 54			15 28	15 54			16 28	16 54			17 28	17 54	
London Road (Brighton)	d	12 56			13 30	13 56			14 30	14 56			15 30	15 56			16 30	16 56			17 30	17 56	
Brighton [10]	a	13 00	13 12		13 34	14 00	14 12		14 34	15 00	15 12		15 34	16 00	16 12		16 34	17 00	17 12		17 34	18 00	18 12
Cooksbridge	d																						
Plumpton	d															16 24				17 24			
Wivelsfield [4]	a			13 31				14 31				15 31				16 31				17 31			
Haywards Heath [3]	a			13 35				14 35				15 35				16 35				17 35			
Gatwick Airport [10]	a			13 52				14 52				15 52				16 52				17 52			
East Croydon	a			14 09				15 09				16 09				17 09				18 09			
London Bridge [4] ⊖	a																						
Clapham Junction [10]	a			14 24				15 24				16 24				17 24				18 24			
London Victoria [15] ⊖	a			14 31				15 31				16 31				17 31				18 31			

A 🛒 from Lewes

Table 189

Sundays
from 12 September

Ashford, Hastings, Eastbourne, Seaford and Lewes - Brighton, Haywards Heath and London

		SN ◇1 A ✠	SN	SN	SN 1	SN ◇1	SN	SN	SN 1	SN ◇1	SN	SN	SN 1	SN ◇1	SN	SN	SN 1	SN	SN 1	SN	SN 1	SN
Ashford International	d				17 21				18 21				19 21				20 21				21 21	
Ham Street	d				17 30				18 30				19 30				20 30				21 30	
Appledore (Kent)	d				17 35				18 35				19 35				20 35				21 35	
Rye	a				17 44				18 44				19 44				20 44				21 44	
	d				17 45				18 45				19 45				20 45				21 45	
Winchelsea	d																					
Doleham	d																					
Three Oaks	d																					
Ore	d	17 14				18 14				19 14				20 14					21 14			
Hastings 4	a	17 17			18 02	18 17			19 02	19 17			20 02	20 17			21 02		21 17		22 02	
	d	17 18			18 03	18 18			19 03	19 18			20 03	20 18			21 03		21 18		22 03	
St Leonards Warrior Sq 4	d	17 21			18 06	18 21			19 06	19 21			20 06	20 21			21 06		21 21		22 06	
Bexhill 4	d	17 28			18 13	18 28			19 13	19 28			20 13	20 28			21 13		21 28		22 13	
Collington	d	17 30				18 30				19 30				20 30					21 30			
Cooden Beach	d	17 33				18 33				19 33				20 33					21 33			
Normans Bay	d																					
Pevensey Bay	d																					
Pevensey & Westham	d	17 39				18 39				19 39				20 39					21 39			
Hampden Park 4	d	17 43				18 43				19 43				20 43					21 43			
Eastbourne 4	a	17 49			18 29	18 49			19 29	19 49			20 29	20 49			21 29		21 49		22 29	
	d	17 55			18 34	18 55			19 34	19 55			20 34	20 55			21 34		21 59		22 34	
Hampden Park 4	d				18 38				19 38				20 38				21 38				22 38	
Polegate	d	18 02			18 42	19 02			19 42	20 02			20 42	21 02			21 42		22 06		22 42	
Berwick	d				18 48				19 48				20 48				21 48				22 48	
Glynde	d				18 53				19 53				20 53				21 53				22 53	
Seaford	d		17 53	18 27			18 53	19 27			19 53	20 27			20 53	21 27		21 53		22 27		22 53
Bishopstone	d		17 55	18 29			18 55	19 29			19 55	20 29			20 55	21 29		21 55		22 29		22 55
Newhaven Harbour	d		17 58	18 32			18 58	19 32			19 58	20 32			20 58	21 32		21 58		22 32		22 58
Newhaven Town	d		18 00	18 34			19 00	19 34			20 00	20 34			21 00	21 34		22 00		22 34		23 00
Southease	d		18 04				19 04				20 04											
Lewes 4	a	18 14	18 11	18 43	18 59	19 14	19 11	19 43	19 59	20 14	20 11	20 43	20 59	21 14	21 09	21 43	21 59	22 09	22 18	22 43	22 59	23 09
	d	18 16	18 18	18 44	19 00	19 16	19 18	19 44	20 00	20 16	20 18	20 44	21 00	21 16	21 18	21 44	22 00	22 10	22 19	22 44	23 00	23 10
Falmer	d		18 25	18 51			19 25	19 51			20 25	20 51			21 25	21 51		22 17	22 26	22 51		23 17
Moulsecoomb	d		18 28	18 54			19 28	19 54			20 28	20 54			21 28	21 54		22 20	22 29	22 54		23 20
London Road (Brighton)	d		18 30	18 56			19 30	19 56			20 30	20 56			21 30	21 56		22 22	22 31	22 56		23 22
Brighton 10	a		18 34	19 00	19 12		19 34	20 00	20 12		20 34	21 00	21 12		21 34	22 00	22 12	22 26	22 35	23 00	23 12	23 26
Cooksbridge	d																					
Plumpton	d	18 24				19 24				20 24				21 24								
Wivelsfield 4	a	18 31				19 31				20 31				21 31								
Haywards Heath 3	a	18 35				19 35				20 35				21 35								
Gatwick Airport 10	a	18 52				19 52				20 52				21 52								
East Croydon	a	19 09				20 09				21 09				22 09								
London Bridge 4 ⊖	a																					
Clapham Junction 10	a	19 24				20 24				21 24				22 24								
London Victoria 15 ⊖	a	19 31				20 31				21 31				22 31								

A ✠ from Lewes

Table 189

Sundays
from 12 September

Ashford, Hastings, Eastbourne, Seaford and Lewes - Brighton, Haywards Heath and London

		SN 1	SN 1	SN 1
Ashford International	d		22 32	
Ham Street	d		22 41	
Appledore (Kent)	d		22 46	
Rye	a		22 55	
	d		22 55	
Winchelsea	d		22 58	
Doleham	d		23 05	
Three Oaks	d		23 08	
Ore	d	22 14	23 14	
Hastings 4	a	22 17	23 17	
	d	22 18		23 22
St Leonards Warrior Sq 4	d	22 21		23 24
Bexhill 4	d	22 28		23 31
Collington	d	22 30		23 33
Cooden Beach	d	22 33		23 36
Normans Bay	d			
Pevensey Bay	d			
Pevensey & Westham	d	22 39		23 42
Hampden Park 4	d	22 43		23 47
Eastbourne 4	a	22 49		23 52
	d	22 59		
Hampden Park 4	d			
Polegate	d	23 06		
Berwick	d			
Glynde	d			
Seaford	d			
Bishopstone	d			
Newhaven Harbour	d			
Newhaven Town	d			
Southease	d			
Lewes 4	a	23 18		
	d	23 19		
Falmer	d	23 26		
Moulsecoomb	d	23 29		
London Road (Brighton)	d	23 31		
Brighton 10	a	23 35		
Cooksbridge	d			
Plumpton	d			
Wivelsfield 4	a			
Haywards Heath 3	a			
Gatwick Airport 10	a			
East Croydon	a			
London Bridge 4 ⊖	a			
Clapham Junction 10	a			
London Victoria 15 ⊖	a			

Route Diagram for Table 194 — SUMMARY OF HIGH SPEED SERVICES

DM-28/09
Design BAJS

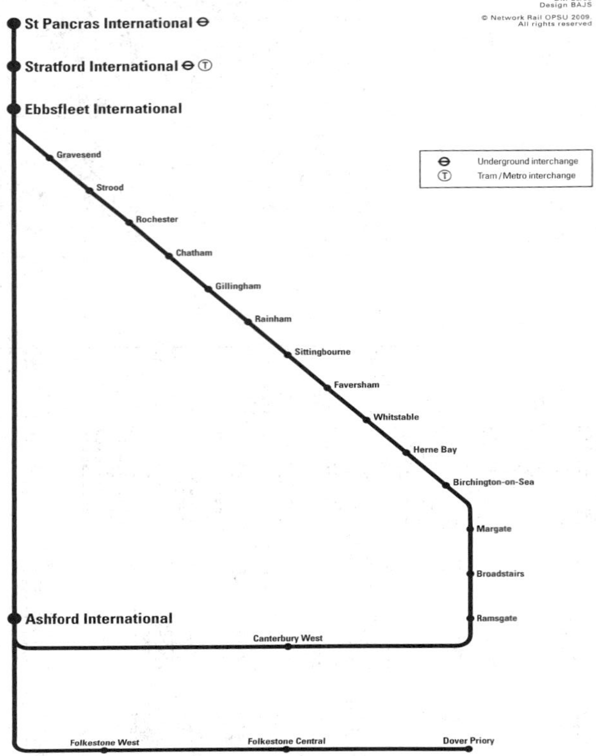

St Pancras International -Kent, High Speed Domestic Services

		SE	SE	SE MO	SE MX	SE MO	SE MX	SE MX	SE	SE	SE	SE
St Pancras International ⊖	d	22p55	23p12	23p25	23p25	23p42	23p55	00 12	06 25	06 40	06 58	07 10
Stratford International ⊖	d	23p02	23p19	23p32	23p32	23p49	00 02	00 19	06 32	06 47	07 05	07 17
Ebbsfleet International	a	23p12	23p30	23p42	23p42	23p59	00 12	00 30	06 42	06 58	07 15	07 29
	d	23p13	23p31	23p43	23p43	00 01	00 13	00 31	06 42	06 59	07 16	07 30
Gravesend	d	23p18		23p48	23p48		00 18		06 46		07 21	
Strood	d	23p28		23p58	23p58		00 28		06 56		07 31	
Rochester	d	23p33		00 03	00 03		00 33		07a00		07 36	
Chatham	d	23p35		00 05	00 06		00 35				07 38	
Gillingham (Kent)	d	23p40		00 10	00 10		00 40				07 43	
Rainham (Kent)	d	23p45		00 15	00 15		00 45				07 48	
Sittingbourne	d	23p53		00 23	00 23		00 53				07 55	
Faversham	a	00 03		00 33	00 33		01 03				08 03	
Whitstable	d											
Herne Bay	d											
Birchington-on-Sea	d											
Margate	d											
Broadstairs	a											
Ashford International	a		23p50			00 19		00 50		07 19		07 50
	d		23p52							07 22		07 52
Folkestone West	d		00 07									08 07
Folkestone Central	d		00 10									08 10
Dover Priory	a		00 21									08 21
Canterbury West	a									07 39		
	d									07 40		
Ramsgate	d									08 02		
Broadstairs	d									08 07		
Margate	a									08 12		

		SE	SE	SE	SE	SE	SE	SE	SE	SE	SE	SE
St Pancras International ⊖	d	07 22	07 40	07 55	08 10	08 22	08 40	08 58	09 12	09 25	09 40	09 55
Stratford International ⊖	d	07 28	07 47	08 02	08 17	08 29	08 47	09 05	09 19	09 32	09 47	10 02
Ebbsfleet International	a	07 38	07 59	08 12	08 29	08 39	08 59	09 15	09 30	09 42	09 58	10 12
	d	07 43	08 00	08 13	08 30	08 43	09 00	09 16	09 31	09 43	09 59	10 13
Gravesend	d	07 48		08 18		08 48		09 21		09 48		10 18
Strood	d	07 58		08 28		08 58		09 31		09 58		10 28
Rochester	d	08 03		08 33		09 03		09 36		10 03		10 33
Chatham	d	08 05		08 35		09 05		09 38		10 05		10 35
Gillingham (Kent)	d	08 10		08 40		09 10		09 43		10 10		10 40
Rainham (Kent)	d	08 15		08 45		09 15		09 48		10 15		10 45
Sittingbourne	d	08 23		08 53		09 23		09 55		10 23		10 53
Faversham	a	08 31		09 01		09 31		10 03		10 31		11 01
Whitstable	d											
Herne Bay	d											
Birchington-on-Sea	d											
Margate	d											
Broadstairs	a											
Ashford International	a		08 20		08 50		09 20		09 50		10 18	
	d		08 22		08 52		09 22		09 52		10 22	
Folkestone West	d				09 07				10 07			
Folkestone Central	d				09 10				10 10			
Dover Priory	a				09 21				10 21			
Canterbury West	a		08 39				09 39				10 39	
	d		08 40				09 40				10 40	
Ramsgate	d		08 59				09 59				10 59	
Broadstairs	d		09 05				10 05				11 05	
Margate	a		09 10				10 10				11 10	

		SE	SE	SE	SE	SE	SE	SE	SE	SE	SE	SE
St Pancras International ⊖	d	10 12	10 28	10 42	10 55	11 12	11 25	11 42	11 55	12 12	12 25	12 42
Stratford International ⊖	d	10 19	10 35	10 49	11 02	11 19	11 32	11 49	12 02	12 19	12 36	12 49
Ebbsfleet International	a	10 30	10 45	11 00	11 12	11 30	11 42	12 00	12 12	12 30	12 46	13 00
	d	10 31	10 46	11 01	11 13	11 31	11 43	12 01	12 13	12 31	12 47	13 01
Gravesend	d		10 51		11 18		11 48		12 18		12 51	
Strood	d		11 01		11 28		11 58		12 28		13 01	
Rochester	d		11 06		11 33		12 03		12 33		13 06	
Chatham	d		11 08		11 35		12 05		12 35		13 08	
Gillingham (Kent)	d		11 13		11 40		12 10		12 40		13 13	
Rainham (Kent)	d		11 18		11 45		12 15		12 45		13 18	
Sittingbourne	d		11 25		11 53		12 23		12 53		13 25	
Faversham	a		11 33		12 01		12 31		13 01		13 33	
Whitstable	d											
Herne Bay	d											
Birchington-on-Sea	d											
Margate	d											
Broadstairs	a											
Ashford International	a	10 50		11 20		11 50		12 20		12 50		13 20
	d	10 52		11 22		11 52		12 22		12 52		13 22
Folkestone West	d	11 07				12 07				13 07		
Folkestone Central	d	11 10				12 10				13 10		
Dover Priory	a	11 21				12 21				13 21		
Canterbury West	a			11 39				12 39				13 39
	d			11 40				12 40				13 40
Ramsgate	d			11 59				12 59				13 59
Broadstairs	d			12 05				13 05				14 05
Margate	a			12 10				13 10				14 10

		SE	SE	SE	SE	SE	SE	SE	SE	SE	SE	SE
St Pancras International ⊖	d	12 52	13 12	13 25	13 42	13 55	14 12	14 28	14 42	14 55	15 12	15 28
Stratford International ⊖	d	12 58	13 19	13 32	13 49	14 02	14 19	14 35	14 49	15 02	15 19	15 35
Ebbsfleet International	a	13 08	13 30	13 42	14 00	14 12	14 30	14 45	15 00	15 12	15 30	15 45
	d	13 13	13 31	13 43	14 01	14 13	14 31	14 46	15 01	15 13	15 31	15 46
Gravesend	d	13 18		13 48		14 18		14 51		15 18		15 51
Strood	d	13 28		13 58		14 28		15 01		15 28		16 01
Rochester	d	13 33		14 03		14 33		15 06		15 33		16 06
Chatham	d	13 35		14 05		14 35		15 08		15 35		16 08
Gillingham (Kent)	d	13 40		14 10		14 40		15 13		15 40		16 13
Rainham (Kent)	d	13 45		14 15		14 45		15 18		15 45		16 18
Sittingbourne	d	13 53		14 23		14 53		15 25		15 53		16 25
Faversham	a	14 01		14 31		15 01		15 33		16 01		16 33
Whitstable	d											
Herne Bay	d											
Birchington-on-Sea	d											
Margate	d											
Broadstairs	a											
Ashford International	a		13 50		14 20		14 50		15 20		15 50	
	d		13 52		14 22		14 52		15 22		15 52	
Folkestone West	d		14 07				15 07				16 07	
Folkestone Central	d		14 10				15 10				16 10	
Dover Priory	a		14 21				15 21				16 21	
Canterbury West	a				14 39				15 39			
	d				14 40				15 40			
Ramsgate	d				14 59				15 59			
Broadstairs	d				15 05				16 05			
Margate	a				15 10				16 10			

		SE	SE	SE	SE	SE	SE	SE	SE	SE	SE	SE	SE
St Pancras International ⊖	d	15 42	15 55	16 12	16 25	16 42	16 58	17 10		17 14	17 18	17 25	17 40
Stratford International ⊖	d	15 49	16 02	16 19	16 32	16 49	17 05	17 17		17 21	17 25	17b38	17 47
Ebbsfleet International	a	16 00	16 12	16 30	16 42	17 00	17 15				17 35	17 48	
	d	16 01	16 13	16 31	16 43	17 01	17 16					17 49	
Gravesend	d		16 18		16 48		17 21			17 36			
Strood	d		16 28		16 58		17 31			17 46			
Rochester	d		16 33		17 03		17 36			17a52			
Chatham	d		16 35		17 05		17 38					18 06	
Gillingham (Kent)	d		16 40		17 10		17 43					18 10	
Rainham (Kent)	d		16 45		17 15		17 48					18 15	
Sittingbourne	d		16 53		17 23		17 55					18 23	
Faversham	a		17 01		17 31		18 03					18 31	
Whitstable	d											18 40	
Herne Bay	d											18 45	
Birchington-on-Sea	d											18 54	
Margate	d											19 00	
Broadstairs	a											19 08	
Ashford International	a	16 20		16 50		17 20		17 46	>				18 16
	d	16 22		16 52		17 22		17 50	17 52				18 20
Folkestone West	d			17 07				18 03					18 33
Folkestone Central	d			17 10				18 06					18 36
Dover Priory	a			17 21				18 18					18 48
Canterbury West	a	16 39				17 39			18 09				
	d	16 40				17 40			18 10				
Ramsgate	d	16 59				17 59			18 29				
Broadstairs	d	17 05				18 05			18 35				
Margate	a	17 10				18 10			18 40				

		SE	SE	SE	SE	SE	SE	SE	SE	SE	SE	SE	SE
St Pancras International ⊖	d		17 44	17 48	17 58	18 10		18 14	18 18	18 25	18 40		18 48
Stratford International ⊖	d		17 51	17 55	18 05	18 17		18 21	18 25	18 32	18 47		18 55
Ebbsfleet International	a			18 05	18 15				18 35	18 42			19 05
	d				18 16					18 43			
Gravesend	d		18 06					18 36					
Strood	d		18 16					18 46					
Rochester	d		18 24					18 51					
Chatham	d		18 26		18 36			18 53		19 02			
Gillingham (Kent)	d		18 31		18 40			18 58		19 07			
Rainham (Kent)	d		18 36		18 45			19 03		19 12			
Sittingbourne	d		18 44		18 53			19 10		19 22			
Faversham	a		18 54		19 01			19 18		19 30			
Whitstable	d				19 10					19 39			
Herne Bay	d				19 15					19 45			
Birchington-on-Sea	d				19 24					19 54			
Margate	d				19 30					20 01			
Broadstairs	a				19 35					20 07			
Ashford International	a	>				18 46	>				19 16	>	
	d	18 22				18 50	18 52				19 20	19 22	
Folkestone West	d					19 03					19 33		
Folkestone Central	d					19 06					19 36		
Dover Priory	a					19 18					19 47		
Canterbury West	a	18 39					19 09					19 39	
	d	18 40					19 10					19 40	
Ramsgate	d	18 59					19 29					19 59	
Broadstairs	d	19 05					19 35					20 05	
Margate	a	19 10					19 40					20 10	

b arr. 1731

Table 194

Mondays to Fridays

St Pancras International -Kent, High Speed Domestic Services

		SE	SE	SE	SE	SE	SE	SE	SE	SE	SE	SE	SE	SE	SE	SE	SE	SE	SE	SE	SE
St Pancras International ⊖	d	18 55	19 12	19 25	19 42	19 55	20 12	20 25	20 42	20 55	21 12	21 25	21 42	21 55	22 12	22 25	22 42	22 55	23 12	23 25	23 55
Stratford International ⊖	d	19 02	19 19	19 32	19 49	20 02	20 19	20 32	20 49	21 02	21 19	21 32	21 49	22 02	22 19	22 32	22 49	23 02	23 19	23 32	00 02
Ebbsfleet International	a	19 12	19 30	19 42	20 00	20 12	20 30	20 42	21 00	21 12	21 30	21 42	22 00	22 12	22 30	22 42	23 00	23 12	23 30	23 42	00 12
	d	19 13	19 31	19 44	20 01	20 13	20 31	20 43	21 01	21 13	21 31	21 43	22 01	22 13	22 31	22 43	23 01	23 13	23 31	23 43	00 13
Gravesend	d	19 18		19 50		20 18		20 48		21 18		21 48		22 18		22 48		23 18		23 48	00 18
Strood	d	19 28		20 01		20 28		20 58		21 28		21 58		22 28		22 58		23 28		23 58	00 28
Rochester	d	19 33		20 06		20 33		21 03		21 33		22 03		22 33		23 03		23 33		00 03	00 33
Chatham	d	19 35		20 09		20 35		21 05		21 35		22 05		22 35		23 05		23 35		00 06	00 35
Gillingham (Kent)	d	19 40		20 13		20 40		21 10		21 40		22 10		22 40		23 10		23 40		00 10	00 40
Rainham (Kent)	d	19 45		20 18		20 45		21 15		21 45		22 15		22 45		23 15		23 45		00 15	00 45
Sittingbourne	d	19 52		20 26		20 53		21 23		21 53		22 23		22 53		23 23		23 53		00 23	00 53
Faversham	a	20 02		20 34		21 03		21 33		22 03		22 33		23 03		23 33		00 03		00 33	01 03
Whitstable	d																				
Herne Bay	d																				
Birchington-on-Sea	d																				
Margate	d																				
Broadstairs	a																				
Ashford International	a		19 50		20 20		20 50		21 20		21 50		22 20		22 50		23 20		23 50		
	d		19 52		20 22		20 52		21 22		21 52		22 22		22 52		23 22		23 52		
Folkestone West	d		20 07				21 07				22 07				23 07				00 07		
Folkestone Central	d		20 10				21 10				22 10				23 10				00 10		
Dover Priory	a		20 21				21 21				22 21				23 21				00 21		
Canterbury West	a				20 39				21 39				22 39				23 39				
	d				20 40				21 40				22 40				23 40				
Ramsgate	d				20 59				21 59				22 59				23a58				
Broadstairs	d				21 05				22 05				23 05								
Margate	a				21 10				22 10				23 10								

Saturdays

		SE	SE	SE	SE	SE	SE	SE	SE	SE	SE	SE	SE	SE	SE	SE	SE	SE	SE	SE	SE	SE
St Pancras International ⊖	d	22p55	23p12	23p25	23p55	00 12	06 40	07 12	07 22	08 42	08 52	09 12	09 28	09 40	09 55	10 12	10 28	10 42	10 52	11 12	11 25	11 42
Stratford International ⊖	d	23p02	23p19	23p32	00 02	00 19	06 47	07 19	07 28	08 49	08 58	09 19	09 35	09 47	10 02	10 19	10 35	10 49	10 58	11 19	11 32	11 49
Ebbsfleet International	a	23p12	23p30	23p42	00 12	00 30	06 58	07 30	07 38	09 00	09 08	09 30	09 45	09 58	10 12	10 30	10 45	11 00	11 08	11 30	11 42	12 00
	d	23p13	23p31	23p43	00 13	00 31	06 59	07 31	07 43	09 01	09 13	09 31	09 46	09 59	10 13	10 31	10 46	11 01	11 13	11 31	11 43	12 01
Gravesend	d	23p18		23p48	00 18				07 48		09 18		09 51		10 18		10 51		11 18		11 48	
Strood	d	23p28		23p58	00 28				07 58		09 28		10 01		10 28		11 01		11 28		11 58	
Rochester	d	23p33		00 03	00 33				08 03		09 33		10 06		10 33		11 06		11 33		12 03	
Chatham	d	23p35		00 06	00 35				08 05		09 35		10 08		10 35		11 08		11 35		12 05	
Gillingham (Kent)	d	23p40		00 10	00 40				08 10		09 40		10 13		10 40		11 13		11 40		12 10	
Rainham (Kent)	d	23p45		00 15	00 45				08 15		09 45		10 18		10 45		11 18		11 45		12 15	
Sittingbourne	d	23p53		00 23	00 53				08 23		09 53		10 25		10 53		11 25		11 53		12 23	
Faversham	a	00 03		00 33	01 03				08 31		10 01		10 34		11 01		11 34		12 01		12 31	
Whitstable	d																					
Herne Bay	d																					
Birchington-on-Sea	d																					
Margate	d																					
Broadstairs	a																					
Ashford International	a		23p50			00 50	07 19	07 50		09 20		09 50		10 18		10 50		11 20		11 50		12 20
	d		23p52				07 22	07 52		09 22		09 52		10 22		10 52		11 22		11 52		12 22
Folkestone West	d		00 07					08 07				10 07				11 07				12 07		
Folkestone Central	d		00 10					08 10				10 10				11 10				12 10		
Dover Priory	a		00 21					08 21				10 21				11 21				12 21		
Canterbury West	a						07 39			09 39				10 39				11 39				12 39
	d						07 40			09 40				10 40				11 40				12 40
Ramsgate	d						07 59			09 59				10 59				11 59				12 59
Broadstairs	d						08 05			10 05				11 05				12 05				13 05
Margate	a						08 10			10 10				11 10				12 10				13 10

		SE	SE	SE	SE	SE	SE	SE	SE	SE	SE	SE	SE	SE	SE	SE	SE	SE	SE	SE	SE	SE	SE
St Pancras International ⊖	d	11 55	12 12	12 25	12 42	12 52	13 12	13 25	13 42	13 55	14 12	14 28	14 42	14 58	15 12	15 25	15 42	15 55	16 12	16 28	16 42	16 55	17 12
Stratford International ⊖	d	12 02	12 19	12 36	12 49	12 58	13 19	13 32	13 49	14 02	14 19	14 35	14 49	15 05	15 19	15 32	15 49	16 02	16 19	16 35	16 49	17 02	17 19
Ebbsfleet International	a	12 12	12 30	12 46	13 00	13 08	13 30	13 42	14 00	14 12	14 30	14 45	15 00	15 15	15 30	15 42	16 00	16 12	16 30	16 45	17 00	17 12	17 30
	d	12 13	12 31	12 47	13 01	13 13	13 31	13 43	14 01	14 13	14 31	14 46	15 01	15 16	15 31	15 43	16 01	16 13	16 31	16 46	17 01	17 13	17 31
Gravesend	d	12 18		12 51		13 18		13 48		14 18		14 51		15 21		15 48		16 18		16 51		17 18	
Strood	d	12 28		13 01		13 28		13 58		14 28		15 01		15 31		15 58		16 28		17 01		17 28	
Rochester	d	12 33		13 06		13 33		14 03		14 33		15 06		15 36		16 03		16 33		17 06		17 33	
Chatham	d	12 35		13 08		13 35		14 05		14 35		15 08		15 38		16 05		16 35		17 08		17 35	
Gillingham (Kent)	d	12 40		13 13		13 40		14 10		14 40		15 13		15 43		16 10		16 40		17 13		17 40	
Rainham (Kent)	d	12 45		13 18		13 45		14 15		14 45		15 18		15 48		16 15		16 45		17 18		17 45	
Sittingbourne	d	12 53		13 25		13 53		14 23		14 53		15 25		15 55		16 23		16 53		17 25		17 53	
Faversham	a	13 01		13 34		14 01		14 31		15 01		15 34		16 04		16 31		17 01		17 34		18 01	
Whitstable	d																						
Herne Bay	d																						
Birchington-on-Sea	d																						
Margate	d																						
Broadstairs	a																						
Ashford International	a		12 50		13 20		13 50		14 20		14 50		15 20		15 50		16 20		16 50		17 20		17 50
	d		12 52		13 22		13 52		14 22		14 52		15 22		15 52		16 22		16 52		17 22		17 52
Folkestone West	d		13 07				14 07				15 07				16 07				17 07				18 07
Folkestone Central	d		13 10				14 10				15 10				16 10				17 10				18 10
Dover Priory	a		13 21				14 21				15 21				16 21				17 21				18 21
Canterbury West	a				13 39				14 39				15 39				16 39				17 39		
	d				13 40				14 40				15 40				16 40				17 40		
Ramsgate	d				13 59				14 59				15 59				16 59				17 59		
Broadstairs	d				14 05				15 05				16 05				17 05				18 05		
Margate	a				14 10				15 10				16 10				17 10				18 10		

b arr. 0656

Table 194

Saturdays

St Pancras International -Kent, High Speed Domestic Services

		SE	SE	SE	SE	SE	SE	SE	SE	SE	SE	SE	SE	SE	SE	SE	SE	SE	SE	SE	SE	SE
St Pancras International ⊖	d	17 28	17 42	17 58	18 12	18 25	18 42	18 55	19 12	19 25	19 42	19 55	20 12	20 25	20 42	20 55	21 12	21 25	21 42	21 55	22 12	22 25
Stratford International ⊖	d	17 35	17 49	18 05	18 19	18 32	18 49	19 02	19 19	19 32	19 49	20 02	20 19	20 32	20 49	21 02	21 19	21 32	21 49	22 02	22 19	22 32
Ebbsfleet International	a	17 45	18 00	18 15	18 30	18 42	19 00	19 12	19 30	19 42	20 00	20 12	20 30	20 42	21 00	21 12	21 30	21 42	22 00	22 12	22 30	22 42
	d	17 46	18 01	18 16	18 31	18 43	19 01	19 13	19 31	19 43	20 01	20 13	20 31	20 43	21 01	21 13	21 31	21 43	22 01	22 13	22 31	22 43
Gravesend	d	17 51		18 21		18 48		19 18		19 48		20 18		20 48		21 18		21 48		22 18		22 48
Strood	d	18 01		18 31		18 58		19 28		19 58		20 28		20 58		21 28		21 58		22 28		22 58
Rochester	d	18 06		18 36		19 03		19 33		20 03		20 33		21 03		21 33		22 03		22 33		23 03
Chatham	d	18 08		18 38		19 05		19 35		20 05		20 35		21 05		21 35		22 05		22 35		23 05
Gillingham (Kent)	d	18 13		18 43		19 10		19 40		20 10		20 40		21 10		21 40		22 10		22 40		23 10
Rainham (Kent)	d	18 18		18 48		19 15		19 45		20 15		20 45		21 15		21 45		22 15		22 45		23 15
Sittingbourne	d	18 25		18 55		19 23		19 53		20 23		20 53		21 23		21 53		22 23		22 53		23 23
Faversham	a	18 34		19 04		19 31		20 01		20 31		21 01		21 31		22 01		22 31		23 01		23 31
Whitstable	d																					
Herne Bay	d																					
Birchington-on-Sea	d																					
Margate	d																					
Broadstairs	a																					
Ashford International	a		18 20		18 50		19 20		19 50		20 20		20 50		21 20		21 50		22 20		22 50	
	d		18 22		18 52		19 22		19 52		20 22		20 52		21 22		21 52		22 22		22 52	
Folkestone West	d				19 07				20 07				21 07				22 07				23 07	
Folkestone Central	d				19 10				20 10				21 10				22 10				23 10	
Dover Priory	a				19 21				20 21				21 21				22 21				23 21	
Canterbury West	a		18 39				19 39				20 39				21 39				22 39			
	d		18 40				19 40				20 40				21 40				22 40			
Ramsgate	d		18 59				20 00				21 00				22 00				23 00			
Broadstairs	d		19 05				20 06				21 06				22 06				23 06			
Margate	a		19 10				20 10				21 10				22 10				23 10			

		SE	SE	SE	SE	SE
St Pancras International ⊖	d	22 42	22 55	23 12	23 25	23 55
Stratford International ⊖	d	22 49	23 02	23 19	23 32	00 02
Ebbsfleet International	a	23 00	23 12	23 30	23 42	00 12
	d	23 01	23 13	23 31	23 43	00 13
Gravesend	d		23 18		23 48	00 18
Strood	d		23 28		23 58	00 28
Rochester	d		23 33		00 03	00 33
Chatham	d		23 35		00 05	00 35
Gillingham (Kent)	d		23 40		00 09	00 40
Rainham (Kent)	d		23 45		00 14	00 45
Sittingbourne	d		23 53		00 22	00 53
Faversham	a		00 01		00 31	01 01
Whitstable	d					
Herne Bay	d					
Birchington-on-Sea	d					
Margate	d					
Broadstairs	a					
Ashford International	a	23 20		23 50		
	d	23 22		23 52		
Folkestone West	d			00 07		
Folkestone Central	d			00 10		
Dover Priory	a			00 21		
Canterbury West	a	23 39				
	d	23 40				
Ramsgate	d	00a01				
Broadstairs	d					
Margate	a					

Sundays

		SE	SE	SE	SE	SE	SE	SE	SE	SE	SE	SE	SE	SE	SE	SE	SE	SE	SE	SE
St Pancras International ⊖	d	22p55	23p12	23p25	23p55	00 12	08 42	09 12	09 25	09 40	10 12	10 28	10 42	11 12	11 25	11 42	12 12	12 25	12 42	12 52
Stratford International ⊖	d	23p02	23p19	23p32	00 02	00 19	08 49	09 19	09 32	09 47	10 19	10 35	10 49	11 19	11 32	11 49	12 19	12 36	12 49	12 58
Ebbsfleet International	a	23p12	23p30	23p42	00 12	00 30	09 00	09 30	09 42	09 58	10 30	10 45	11 00	11 30	11 42	12 00	12 30	12 46	13 00	13 08
	d	23p13	23p31	23p43	00 13	00 31	09 01	09 31	09 43	09 59	10 31	10 46	11 01	11 31	11 43	12 01	12 31	12 47	13 01	13 13
Gravesend	d	23p18		23p48	00 18				09 48			10 51			11 48			12 51		13 18
Strood	d	23p28		23p58	00 28				09 58			11 01			11 58			13 01		13 28
Rochester	d	23p33		00 03	00 33				10 03			11 06			12 03			13 06		13 33
Chatham	d	23p35		00 05	00 35				10 05			11 08			12 05			13 08		13 35
Gillingham (Kent)	d	23p40		00 09	00 40				10 10			11 13			12 10			13 13		13 40
Rainham (Kent)	d	23p45		00 14	00 45				10 15			11 18			12 15			13 18		13 45
Sittingbourne	d	23p53		00 22	00 53				10 23			11 25			12 23			13 25		13 53
Faversham	a	00 01		00 31	01 01				10 31			11 33			12 31			13 33		14 01
Whitstable	d																			
Herne Bay	d																			
Birchington-on-Sea	d																			
Margate	d																			
Broadstairs	a																			
Ashford International	a		23p50			00 50	09 20	09 50		10 18	10 50		11 20	11 50		12 20	12 50		13 20	
	d		23p52				09 22	09 52		10 22	10 52		11 22	11 52		12 22	12 52		13 22	
Folkestone West	d		00 07					10 07			11 07			12 07			13 07			
Folkestone Central	d		00 10					10 10			11 10			12 10			13 10			
Dover Priory	a		00 21					10 21			11 21			12 21			13 21			
Canterbury West	a						09 39			10 39			11 39			12 39			13 39	
	d						09 40			10 40			11 40			12 40			13 40	
Ramsgate	d						09 59			10 59			11 59			12 59			13 59	
Broadstairs	d						10 05			11 05			12 05			13 05			14 05	
Margate	a						10 10			11 10			12 10			13 10			14 10	

Table 194 — Sundays

St Pancras International -Kent, High Speed Domestic Services

Station		SE	SE	SE	SE	SE		SE	SE	SE	SE	SE	SE	SE	SE	SE		SE	SE	SE	SE	SE	SE	SE	SE
St Pancras International 15 ⊖	d	13 12	13 25	13 42	13 55	14 12		14 28	14 42	14 55	15 12	15 25	15 42	15 55	16 12	16 28		16 42	16 55	17 04	17 12	17 25	17 42	17 58	18 12
Stratford International ⊖	d	13 19	13 32	13 49	14 02	14 19		14 35	14 49	15 02	15 19	15 32	15 49	16 02	16 19	16 35		16 49	17 05	17 11	17 19	17 32	17 49	18 05	18 19
Ebbsfleet International	a	13 30	13 42	14 00	14 12	14 30		14 45	15 00	15 12	15 30	15 42	16 00	16 12	16 30	16 45		17 00	17 15	17 21	17 30	17 42	18 00	18 15	18 30
	d	13 31	13 43	14 01	14 13	14 31		14 46	15 01	15 13	15 31	15 43	16 01	16 13	16 31	16 46		17 01	17 16	17 23	17 31	17 43	18 01	18 16	18 31
Gravesend 4	d		13 48		14 18			14 51		15 18		15 48		16 18		16 51			17 21	17 28		17 48		18 21	
Strood 4	d		13 58		14 28			15 01		15 28		15 58		16 28		17 01			17 31	17 38		17 58		18 31	
Rochester 4	d		14 03		14 33			15 06		15 33		16 03		16 33		17 06			17 35	17 42		18 03		18 35	
Chatham 4	d		14 05		14 35			15 08		15 35		16 05		16 35		17 08			17 38	17 45		18 05		18 38	
Gillingham (Kent) 4	d		14 10		14 40			15 13		15 40		16 10		16 40		17 13			17 42	17 49		18 10		18 42	
Rainham (Kent)	d		14 15		14 45			15 18		15 45		16 15		16 45		17 18			17 47	17 54		18 15		18 47	
Sittingbourne 4	d		14 23		14 53			15 25		15 53		16 23		16 53		17 25			17 55	18 02		18 23		18 55	
Faversham 2	a		14 31		15 01			15 33		16 01		16 31		17 01		17 33			18 03	18 10		18 31		19 03	
Whitstable	d																								
Herne Bay	d																								
Birchington-on-Sea	d																								
Margate 4	d																								
Broadstairs	a																								
Ashford International	a	13 50		14 20		14 50			15 20		15 50		16 20		16 50			17 20			17 50		18 20		18 50
	d	13 52		14 22		14 52			15 22		15 52		16 22		16 52			17 22			17 52		18 22		18 52
Folkestone West	d	14 07				15 07					16 07				17 07						18 07				19 07
Folkestone Central	d	14 10				15 10					16 10				17 10						18 10				19 10
Dover Priory 4	a	14 21				15 21					16 21				17 21						18 21				19 21
Canterbury West 4	a			14 39					15 39				16 39					17 39					18 39		
	d			14 40					15 40				16 40					17 40					18 40		
Ramsgate 4	d			14 59					15 59				16 59					17 59					18 59		
Broadstairs	d			15 05					16 05				17 05					18 05					19 05		
Margate 4	a			15 10					16 10				17 10					18 10					19 10		

Station		SE		SE	SE	SE	SE	SE	SE	SE	SE	SE		SE	SE	SE	SE	SE	SE	SE	SE	SE		SE	SE
St Pancras International 15 ⊖	d	18 28		18 42	18 55	19 12	19 25	19 42	19 55	20 12	20 25	20 42		20 55	21 12	21 25	21 42	21 55	22 12	22 25	22 42	22 55		23 12	23 25
Stratford International ⊖	d	18 35		18 49	19 02	19 19	19 32	19 49	20 02	20 19	20 32	20 49		21 02	21 19	21 32	21 49	22 02	22 19	22 32	22 49	23 02		23 19	23 32
Ebbsfleet International	a	18 45		19 00	19 12	19 30	19 42	20 00	20 12	20 30	20 42	21 00		21 12	21 30	21 42	22 00	22 12	22 30	22 42	23 00	23 12		23 30	23 42
	d	18 46		19 01	19 13	19 31	19 43	20 01	20 13	20 31	20 43	21 01		21 13	21 31	21 43	22 01	22 13	22 31	22 43	23 01	23 13		23 31	23 43
Gravesend 4	d	18 51			19 18		19 48		20 18		20 48			21 18		21 48		22 18		22 48		23 18			23 48
Strood 4	d	19 01			19 28		19 58		20 28		20 58			21 28		21 58		22 28		22 58		23 28			23 58
Rochester 4	d	19 06			19 33		20 03		20 33		21 03			21 33		22 03		22 33		23 03		23 33			00 03
Chatham 4	d	19 08			19 35		20 05		20 35		21 05			21 35		22 05		22 35		23 05		23 35			00 05
Gillingham (Kent) 4	d	19 13			19 40		20 10		20 40		21 10			21 40		22 10		22 40		23 10		23 40			00 10
Rainham (Kent)	d	19 18			19 45		20 15		20 45		21 15			21 45		22 15		22 45		23 15		23 45			00 15
Sittingbourne 4	d	19 25			19 53		20 23		20 53		21 23			21 53		22 23		22 53		23 23		23 53			00 23
Faversham 2	a	19 33			20 01		20 31		21 03		21 33			22 03		22 33		23 03		23 31		00 03			00 33
Whitstable	d																								
Herne Bay	d																								
Birchington-on-Sea	d																								
Margate 4	d																								
Broadstairs	a																								
Ashford International	a			19 20		19 50		20 20		20 50		21 20			21 50		22 20		22 50		23 20			23 50	
	d			19 22		19 52		20 22		20 52		21 22			21 52		22 22		22 52		23 22			23 52	
Folkestone West	d					20 07				21 07					22 07				23 07					00 07	
Folkestone Central	d					20 10				21 10					22 10				23 10					00 10	
Dover Priory 4	a					20 21				21 21					22 21				23 21					00 21	
Canterbury West 4	a			19 39				20 39				21 39					22 39				23 39				
	d			19 40				20 40				21 40					22 40				23 40				
Ramsgate 4	d			19 59				20 59				21 59					22 59				23a58				
Broadstairs	d			20 05				21 05				22 05					23 05								
Margate 4	a			20 10				21 10				22 10					23 10								

Station		SE
St Pancras International 15 ⊖	d	23 42
Stratford International ⊖	d	23 49
Ebbsfleet International	a	23 59
	d	00 01
Gravesend 4	d	
Strood 4	d	
Rochester 4	d	
Chatham 4	d	
Gillingham (Kent) 4	d	
Rainham (Kent)	d	
Sittingbourne 4	d	
Faversham 2	a	
Whitstable	d	
Herne Bay	d	
Birchington-on-Sea	d	
Margate 4	d	
Broadstairs	a	
Ashford International	a	00 19
	d	
Folkestone West	d	
Folkestone Central	d	
Dover Priory 4	a	
Canterbury West 4	a	
	d	
Ramsgate 4	d	
Broadstairs	d	
Margate 4	a	

Table 194 — Mondays to Fridays

Kent, High Speed Domestic Services - St Pancras International

Station		SE	SE	SE	SE	SE	SE	SE	SE	SE	SE	SE	SE	SE	SE	SE	SE	SE	SE	SE	SE	SE	SE	SE	SE
Margate 4	d							05 47										06 44							
Broadstairs	d							05 54										06 50							
Ramsgate 4	d			05 00				06 00					06 26					06 56					07 26		
Canterbury West 4	a			05 23				06 19					06 45					07 15					07 45		
	d			05 25				06 20					06 46					07 16					07 46		
Dover Priory	d					05 44			06 12					06 38					07 08					07 38	
Folkestone Central	d					05 56			06 24					06 50					07 20					07 50	
Folkestone West	d					05 58			06 26					06 52					07 22					07 52	
Ashford International	a			05 41		06 11		06 36	06 39				07 03	07 06				07 32	07 35				08 03	08 06	
	d	05 13		05 43		06 13		>	06 43				>	07 13				>	07 43				>	08 13	
Broadstairs	d										06 00					06 30					07 00				
Margate 4	d										06 05					06 35					07 05				
Birchington-on-Sea	d										06 10					06 40					07 10				
Herne Bay	d										06 19					06 49					07 19				
Whitstable	d										06 25					06 55					07 25				
Faversham 2	a										06 33					07 03					07 33				
	d		04 56		05 28		05 58				06 34					07 04					07 34				
Sittingbourne 4	d		05 07		05 37		06 06				06 43					07 12					07 42				
Rainham (Kent)	d		05 15		05 45		06 14				06 51					07 20					07 50				
Gillingham (Kent) 4	d		05 20		05 50		06 19				06 56					07 25					07 55				
Chatham 4	d		05 24		05 54		06 24				07 01					07 30					08 00				
Rochester 4	d		05 27		05 57		06 26					07 07					07 37					08 07			
Strood 4	d		05 32		06 02		06 32					07 12					07 42					08 12			
Gravesend	d		05 43		06 13		06 43					07 22					07 52					08 22			
Ebbsfleet International	a	05 32	05 47	06 02	06 17	06 32	06 47				07 17					07 47					08 17				
	d	05 33	05 48	06 03	06 18	06 33	06 48			07 06	07 18				07 34	07 48				08 04	08 18				08 34
Stratford International ⊖	a	05 44	05 59	06 15	06 29	06 44	06 59		07 11	07 18	07 29	07 36		07 40	07 45	07 59	08 06		08 11	08 15	08 29	08 36		08 40	08 45
St Pancras International 4 ⊖	a	05 51	06 06	06 23	06 36	06 53	07 07		07 18	07 25	07 36	07 43		07 48	07 52	08 06	08 13		08 19	08 22	08 36	08 43		08 48	08 52

Station		SE	SE	SE	SE	SE	SE	SE	SE	SE	SE	SE	SE	SE	SE	SE	SE	SE	SE	SE	SE	SE	SE	SE	SE
Margate 4	d		07 49				08 53				09 53				10 53				11 53				12 53		
Broadstairs	d		07 55				08 59				09 59				10 59				11 59				12 59		
Ramsgate 4	d		08 01				09 05				10 05				11 05				12 05				13 05		
Canterbury West 4	a		08 24				09 24				10 24				11 24				12 24				13 24		
	d		08 25				09 25				10 25				11 25				12 25				13 25		
Dover Priory	d				08 44				09 44				10 44				11 44				12 44				13 44
Folkestone Central	d				08 56				09 56				10 56				11 56				12 56				13 56
Folkestone West	d				08 58				09 58				10 58				11 58				12 58				13 58
Ashford International	a		08 41		09 11		09 41		10 11		10 41		11 11		11 41		12 11		12 41		13 11		13 41		14 11
	d		08 43		09 13		09 43		10 13		10 43		11 13		11 43		12 13		12 43		13 13		13 43		14 13
Broadstairs	d																								
Margate 4	d																								
Birchington-on-Sea	d																								
Herne Bay	d																								
Whitstable	d																								
Faversham 2	a																								
	d	07 58		08 28		08 58		09 28		09 58		10 28		10 58		11 28		11 58		12 28		12 58		13 28	
Sittingbourne 4	d	08 06		08 37		09 07		09 37		10 07		10 37		11 07		11 37		12 07		12 37		13 07		13 37	
Rainham (Kent)	d	08 14		08 45		09 15		09 45		10 15		10 45		11 15		11 45		12 15		12 45		13 15		13 45	
Gillingham (Kent) 4	d	08 19		08 50		09 20		09 50		10 20		10 50		11 20		11 50		12 20		12 50		13 20		13 50	
Chatham 4	d	08 24		08 54		09 24		09 54		10 24		10 54		11 24		11 54		12 24		12 54		13 24		13 54	
Rochester 4	d	08 26		08 57		09 27		09 57		10 27		10 57		11 27		11 57		12 27		12 57		13 27		13 57	
Strood 4	d	08 32		09 02		09 32		10 02		10 32		11 02		11 32		12 02		12 32		13 02		13 32		14 02	
Gravesend	d	08 43		09 13		09 43		10 12		10 43		11 13		11 43		12 13		12 43		13 13		13 43		14 13	
Ebbsfleet International	a	08 47	09 02	09 17	09 32	09 47	10 02	10 16	10 32	10 47	11 02	11 17	11 32	11 47	12 02	12 17	12 32	12 47	13 02	13 17	13 32	13 47	14 02	14 17	14 32
	d	08 48	09 03	09 18	09 33	09 48	10 03	10 17	10 33	10 48	11 03	11 18	11 33	11 48	12 03	12 21	12 33	12 48	13 03	13 18	13 33	13 48	14 03	14 21	14 33
Stratford International ⊖	a	08 59	09 14	09 29	09 44	09 59	10 14	10 27	10 44	10 59	11 14	11 29	11 44	11 59	12 14	12 32	12 45	12 59	13 14	13 29	13 44	13 59	14 14	14 32	14 44
St Pancras International 4 ⊖	a	09 07	09 21	09 39	09 51	10 06	10 21	10 38	10 51	11 06	11 21	11 36	11 51	12 06	12 21	12 39	12 54	13 06	13 21	13 36	13 51	14 06	14 21	14 39	14 51

Station		SE	SE	SE	SE	SE	SE	SE	SE	SE	SE	SE		SE	SE	SE	SE	SE	SE	SE	SE	SE		SE	SE
Margate 4	d		13 53				14 53				15 53						16 53				17 53				
Broadstairs	d		13 59				14 59				15 59						16 59				17 59				
Ramsgate 4	d		14 05				15 05				16 05						17 05				18 05				
Canterbury West 4	a		14 24				15 24				16 24						17 24				18 24				
	d		14 25				15 25				16 25						17 25				18 25				
Dover Priory	d				14 44				15 44					16 44					17 44					18 44	
Folkestone Central	d				14 56				15 56					16 56					17 56					18 56	
Folkestone West	d				14 58				15 58					16 58					17 58					18 58	
Ashford International	a		14 41		15 11		15 41		16 11		16 41			17 11			17 41		18 11		18 41			19 11	
	d		14 43		15 13		15 43		16 13		16 43			17 13			17 43		18 13		18 43			19 13	
Broadstairs	d																								
Margate 4	d																								
Birchington-on-Sea	d																								
Herne Bay	d																								
Whitstable	d																								
Faversham 2	a																								
	d	13 58		14 28		14 58		15 28		15 58		16 28			16 58	16 58		17 28		17 58		18 28			18 58
Sittingbourne 4	d	14 07		14 37		15 07		15 37		16 07		16 37			17 07	17 07		17 37		18 07		18 37			19 07
Rainham (Kent)	d	14 15		14 45		15 15		15 45		16 15		16 45			17 15	17 15		17 45		18 15		18 45			19 15
Gillingham (Kent) 4	d	14 20		14 50		15 20		15 50		16 20		16 50			17 20	17 20		17 50		18 20		18 50			19 20
Chatham 4	d	14 24		14 54		15 24		15 54		16 24		16 54			17 24	17 24		17 54		18 24		18 54			19 24
Rochester 4	d	14 27		14 57		15 27		15 57		16 27		16 57			17 27	17 27		17 57		18 27		18 57			19 27
Strood 4	d	14 32		15 02		15 32		16 02		16 32		17 02			17 32	17 32		18 02		18 32		19 02			19 32
Gravesend	d	14 43		15 13		15 43		16 13		16 43		17 12			17 42	17 42		18 13		18 43		19 12			19 43
Ebbsfleet International	a	14 47	15 02	15 17	15 32	15 47	16 02	16 17	16 32	16 47	17 02	17 16		17 32	17 46	17 46	18 02	18 17	18 32	18 47	19 02	19 16		19 32	19 47
	d	14 48	15 03	15 18	15 33	15 48	16 03	16 18	16 33	16 51	17 03	17 17		17 33	17 47	17 51	18 03	18 18	18 33	18 51	19 03	19 17		19 33	19 48
Stratford International ⊖	a	14 59	15 14	15 29	15 44	15 59	16 14	16 29	16 44	17 02	17 14	17 27		17 44	17 57	18 02	18 14	18 28	18 44	19 02	19 14	19 27		19 44	19 59
St Pancras International 4 ⊖	a	15 06	15 21	15 36	15 51	16 06	16 21	16 40	16 51	17 09	17 21	17 38		17 51	18 08	18 09	18 21	18 35	18 51	19 09	19 21	19 38		19 51	20 06

Kent, High Speed Domestic Services - St Pancras International

		SE	SE	SE	SE	SE	SE	SE	SE	SE	SE	SE	SE	SE	SE
Margate 4	d	18 53				19 53				20 53				21 53	
Broadstairs	d	18 59				19 59				20 59				21 59	
Ramsgate 4	d	19 05				20 05				21 05				22 05	
Canterbury West 4	a	19 24				20 24				21 24				22 24	
	d	19 25				20 25				21 25				22 25	
Dover Priory	d			19 44				20 44				21 44			22 44
Folkestone Central	d			19 56				20 56				21 56			22 56
Folkestone West	d			19 58				20 58				21 58			22 58
Ashford International	a	19 41		20 12		20 41		21 11		21 41		22 11		22 41	23 11
	d	19 43		20 13		20 47		21 13		21 43		22 13		22 43	23 13
Broadstairs	d														
Margate 4	d														
Birchington-on-Sea	d														
Herne Bay	d														
Whitstable	d														
Faversham 2	a														
	d		19 28		19 58		20 28		20 58		21 28		21 58		
Sittingbourne 4	d		19 37		20 07		20 37		21 07		21 37		22 07		
Rainham (Kent)	d		19 45		20 15		20 45		21 15		21 45		22 15		
Gillingham (Kent) 4	d		19 50		20 20		20 50		21 20		21 50		22 20		
Chatham 4	d		19 54		20 24		20 54		21 24		21 54		22 24		
Rochester 4	d		19 57		20 27		20 57		21 27		21 57		22 27		
Strood 4	d		20 02		20 32		21 02		21 32		22 02		22 32		
Gravesend	d		20 12		20 43		21 13		21 43		22 12		22 43		
Ebbsfleet International	a	20 02	20 16	20 32	20 47	21 06	21 17	21 32	21 47	22 02	22 16	22 32	22 47	23 02	23 32
	d	20 03	20 17	20 33	20 48	21 07	21 21	21 33	21 48	22 03	22 17	22 33	22 48	23 03	23 33
Stratford International ⊖	a	20 14	20 27	20 44	20 59	21 18	21 32	21 44	21 59	22 14	22 27	22 44	22 59	23 14	23 44
St Pancras International 4 ⊖	a	20 21	20 38	20 51	21 06	21 25	21 39	21 51	22 06	22 21	22 38	22 51	23 06	23 21	23 51

Saturdays

		SE	SE	SE	SE	SE	SE	SE	SE	SE	SE	SE	SE	SE	SE	SE	SE	SE	SE	SE
Margate 4	d				05 43						07 53				08 53				09 53	
Broadstairs	d				05 49						07 59				08 59				09 59	
Ramsgate 4	d	05 05			05 55	06 26					08 05				09 05				10 05	
Canterbury West 4	a	05 24			06 14	06 45					08 24				09 24				10 24	
	d	05 25			06 15	06 46					08 25				09 25				10 25	
Dover Priory	d			05 44				06 44					08 44				09 44			
Folkestone Central	d			05 56				06 56					08 56				09 56			
Folkestone West	d			05 58				06 58					08 58				09 58			
Ashford International	a	05 41		06 11	06 31	07 03		07 11			08 41		09 11		09 41		10 11		10 41	
	d	05 43		06 13	06 33	07 13		07 13			08 43		09 13		09 43		10 13		10 43	
Broadstairs	d																			
Margate 4	d																			
Birchington-on-Sea	d																			
Herne Bay	d																			
Whitstable	d																			
Faversham 2	a																			
	d		05 28				06 28		07 28	07 58		08 28		08 58		09 28		09 58		10 28
Sittingbourne 4	d		05 37				06 37		07 37	08 07		08 37		09 07		09 37		10 07		10 37
Rainham (Kent)	d		05 45				06 45		07 45	08 15		08 45		09 15		09 45		10 15		10 45
Gillingham (Kent) 4	d		05 50				06 50		07 50	08 20		08 50		09 20		09 50		10 20		10 50
Chatham 4	d		05 54				06 54		07 54	08 24		08 54		09 24		09 54		10 24		10 54
Rochester 4	d		05 57				06 57		07 57	08 27		08 57		09 27		09 57		10 27		10 57
Strood 4	d		06 02				07 02		08 02	08 32		09 02		09 32		10 02		10 32		11 02
Gravesend	d		06 13				07 13		08 13	08 43		09 13		09 43		10 12		10 43		11 13
Ebbsfleet International	a	06 02	06 17	06 32	06 52		07 17	07 32	08 17	08 47	09 02	09 17	09 32	09 47	10 02	10 16	10 32	10 47	11 02	11 17
	d	06 03	06 18	06 33	06 53		07 18	07 33	08 18	08 48	09 03	09 18	09 33	09 48	10 03	10 17	10 33	10 48	11 03	11 18
Stratford International ⊖	a	06 15	06 29	06 44	07 04	07 42	07 29	07 44	08 29	08 59	09 14	09 29	09 44	09 59	10 14	10 27	10 44	10 59	11 14	11 29
St Pancras International 4 ⊖	a	06 23	06 36	06 53	07 10	07 48	07 36	07 50	08 36	09 07	09 21	09 39	09 51	10 06	10 21	10 38	10 51	11 06	11 21	11 36

		SE	SE	SE	SE	SE	SE	SE	SE	SE	SE	SE	SE	SE	SE	SE	SE	SE	SE	SE	SE	SE	SE
Margate 4	d			10 53				11 53				12 53				13 53				14 53			
Broadstairs	d			10 59				11 59				12 59				13 59				14 59			
Ramsgate 4	d			11 05				12 05				13 05				14 05				15 05			
Canterbury West 4	a			11 24				12 24				13 24				14 24				15 24			
	d			11 25				12 25				13 25				14 25				15 25			
Dover Priory	d	10 44				11 44				12 44				13 44				14 44				15 44	
Folkestone Central	d	10 56				11 56				12 56				13 56				14 56				15 56	
Folkestone West	d	10 58				11 58				12 58				13 58				14 58				15 58	
Ashford International	a	11 11		11 41		12 11		12 41		13 11		13 41		14 11		14 41		15 11		15 41		16 11	
	d	11 13		11 43		12 13		12 43		13 13		13 43		14 13		14 43		15 13		15 43		16 13	
Broadstairs	d																						
Margate 4	d																						
Birchington-on-Sea	d																						
Herne Bay	d																						
Whitstable	d																						
Faversham 2	a																						
	d		10 58		11 28		11 58		12 28		12 58		13 28		13 58		14 28		14 58		15 28		15 58
Sittingbourne 4	d		11 07		11 37		12 07		12 37		13 07		13 37		14 07		14 37		15 07		15 37		16 07
Rainham (Kent)	d		11 15		11 45		12 15		12 45		13 15		13 45		14 15		14 45		15 15		15 45		16 15
Gillingham (Kent) 4	d		11 20		11 50		12 20		12 50		13 20		13 50		14 20		14 50		15 20		15 50		16 20
Chatham 4	d		11 24		11 54		12 24		12 54		13 24		13 54		14 24		14 54		15 24		15 54		16 24
Rochester 4	d		11 27		11 57		12 27		12 57		13 27		13 57		14 27		14 57		15 27		15 57		16 27
Strood 4	d		11 32		12 02		12 32		13 02		13 32		14 02		14 32		15 02		15 32		16 02		16 32
Gravesend	d		11 43		12 13		12 43		13 13		13 43		14 13		14 43		15 13		15 43		16 13		16 43
Ebbsfleet International	a	11 32	11 47	12 02	12 17	12 32	12 47	13 02	13 17	13 32	13 47	14 02	14 17	14 32	14 47	15 02	15 17	15 32	15 47	16 02	16 17	16 32	16 47
	d	11 33	11 48	12 03	12 21	12 33	12 48	13 03	13 18	13 33	13 48	14 03	14 21	14 33	14 51	15 03	15 18	15 33	15 48	16 03	16 18	16 33	16 48
Stratford International ⊖	a	11 44	11 59	12 14	12 32	12 45	12 59	13 14	13 29	13 44	13 59	14 14	14 32	14 44	15 02	15 14	15 29	15 44	15 59	16 14	16 29	16 44	16 59
St Pancras International 4 ⊖	a	11 51	12 06	12 21	12 39	12 54	13 06	13 21	13 36	13 51	14 06	14 21	14 39	14 51	15 09	15 21	15 36	15 51	16 06	16 21	16 40	16 51	17 06

Kent, High Speed Domestic Services - St Pancras International

		SE	SE	SE	SE	SE	SE	SE	SE	SE	SE	SE	SE	SE	SE	SE	SE	SE	SE	SE	SE	SE
Margate 4	d	15 53	15 53				16 53				17 53				18 53				19 53			
Broadstairs	d	15 59	15 59				16 59				17 59				18 59				19 59			
Ramsgate 4	d	16 05	16 05				17 05				18 05				19 05				20 05			
Canterbury West 4	a	16 24	16 24				17 24				18 24				19 24				20 24			
	d	16 25	16 25				17 25				18 25				19 25				20 25			
Dover Priory	d				16 44				17 44				18 44				19 44				20 44	
Folkestone Central	d				16 56				17 56				18 56				19 56				20 56	
Folkestone West	d				16 58				17 58				18 58				19 58				20 58	
Ashford International	a	16 41	16 41		17 11		17 41		18 11		18 41		19 11		19 41		20 11		20 41		21 11	
	d	16 43	16 47		17 13		17 43		18 13		18 43		19 13		19 43		20 13		20 47		21 13	
Broadstairs	d																					
Margate 4	d																					
Birchington-on-Sea	d																					
Herne Bay	d																					
Whitstable	d																					
Faversham 2	a																					
	d			16 28		16 58		17 28		17 58		18 28		18 58		19 28		19 58		20 28		20 58
Sittingbourne 4	d			16 37		17 07		17 37		18 07		18 37		19 07		19 37		20 07		20 37		21 07
Rainham (Kent)	d			16 45		17 15		17 45		18 15		18 45		19 15		19 45		20 15		20 45		21 15
Gillingham (Kent) 4	d			16 50		17 20		17 50		18 20		18 50		19 20		19 50		20 20		20 50		21 20
Chatham 4	d			16 54		17 24		17 54		18 24		18 54		19 24		19 54		20 24		20 54		21 24
Rochester 4	d			16 57		17 27		17 57		18 27		18 57		19 27		19 57		20 27		20 57		21 27
Strood 4	d			17 02		17 32		18 02		18 32		19 02		19 32		20 02		20 32		21 02		21 32
Gravesend	d			17 12		17 43		18 13		18 43		19 12		19 43		20 12		20 43		21 13		21 43
Ebbsfleet International	a	17 02	17 06	17 16	17 32	17 47	18 02	18 17	18 32	18 47	19 02	19 16	19 32	19 47	20 02	20 16	20 32	20 47	21 06	21 17	21 32	21 47
	d	17 03	17 07	17 17	17 33	17 51	18 03	18 18	18 33	18 51	19 03	19 17	19 33	19 48	20 03	20 17	20 33	20 51	21 07	21 21	21 33	21 48
Stratford International ⊖	a	17 14	17 18	17 27	17 44	18 02	18 14	18 29	18 44	19 02	19 14	19 27	19 44	19 59	20 14	20 27	20 44	21 02	21 18	21 31	21 44	21 59
St Pancras International 4 ⊖	a	17 21	17 25	17 38	17 51	18 09	18 21	18 36	18 51	19 09	19 21	19 38	19 51	20 06	20 21	20 38	20 51	21 09	21 25	21 42	21 51	22 06

		SE	SE	SE	SE	SE	SE
Margate 4	d	20 53				21 53	
Broadstairs	d	20 59				21 59	
Ramsgate 4	d	21 05				22 05	
Canterbury West 4	a	21 24				22 24	
	d	21 25				22 25	
Dover Priory	d			21 44			22 44
Folkestone Central	d			21 56			22 56
Folkestone West	d			21 58			22 58
Ashford International	a	21 41		22 11		22 41	23 11
	d	21 43		22 13		22 43	23 13
Broadstairs	d						
Margate 4	d						
Birchington-on-Sea	d						
Herne Bay	d						
Whitstable	d						
Faversham 2	a						
	d		21 28		21 58		
Sittingbourne 4	d		21 37		22 07		
Rainham (Kent)	d		21 45		22 15		
Gillingham (Kent) 4	d		21 50		22 20		
Chatham 4	d		21 54		22 24		
Rochester 4	d		21 57		22 27		
Strood 4	d		22 02		22 32		
Gravesend	d		22 13		22 43		
Ebbsfleet International	a	22 02	22 17	22 32	22 47	23 02	23 32
	d	22 03	22 18	22 33	22 48	23 03	23 33
Stratford International ⊖	a	22 14	22 29	22 44	22 59	23 14	23 44
St Pancras International 4 ⊖	a	22 21	22 36	22 51	23 06	23 21	23 51

Sundays

		SE	SE	SE	SE	SE	SE	SE	SE	SE	SE	SE	SE	SE	SE	SE	SE	SE	SE	SE
Margate 4	d			07 53			08 53			09 53			10 53				11 53			
Broadstairs	d			07 59			08 59			09 59			10 59				11 59			
Ramsgate 4	d			08 05			09 05			10 05			11 05				12 05			
Canterbury West 4	a			08 24			09 24			10 24			11 24				12 24			
	d			08 25			09 25			10 25			11 25				12 25			
Dover Priory	d	07 44			08 44			09 44			10 44				11 44				12 44	
Folkestone Central	d	07 56			08 56			09 56			10 56				11 56				12 56	
Folkestone West	d	07 58			08 58			09 58			10 58				11 58				12 58	
Ashford International	a	08 11		08 41	09 11		09 41	10 11		10 41	11 11		11 41		12 11		12 41		13 11	
	d	08 13		08 43	09 13		09 43	10 13		10 43	11 13		11 43		12 13		12 43		13 13	
Broadstairs	d																			
Margate 4	d																			
Birchington-on-Sea	d																			
Herne Bay	d																			
Whitstable	d																			
Faversham 2	a																			
	d		07 58			08 58			09 58			10 58		11 28		11 58		12 28		12 58
Sittingbourne 4	d		08 07			09 07			10 07			11 07		11 37		12 07		12 37		13 07
Rainham (Kent)	d		08 15			09 15			10 15			11 15		11 45		12 15		12 45		13 15
Gillingham (Kent) 4	d		08 20			09 20			10 20			11 20		11 50		12 20		12 50		13 20
Chatham 4	d		08 24			09 24			10 24			11 24		11 54		12 24		12 54		13 24
Rochester 4	d		08 27			09 27			10 27			11 27		11 57		12 27		12 57		13 27
Strood 4	d		08 32			09 32			10 32			11 32		12 02		12 32		13 02		13 32
Gravesend	d		08 43			09 43			10 43			11 43		12 13		12 43		13 13		13 43
Ebbsfleet International	a	08 32	08 47	09 02	09 32	09 47	10 02	10 32	10 47	11 02	11 32	11 47	12 02	12 17	12 32	12 47	13 02	13 17	13 32	13 47
	d	08 33	08 48	09 03	09 33	09 48	10 03	10 33	10 48	11 03	11 33	11 48	12 03	12 21	12 33	12 48	13 03	13 18	13 33	13 48
Stratford International ⊖	a	08 44	08 59	09 14	09 44	09 59	10 14	10 44	10 59	11 14	11 44	11 59	12 14	12 32	12 45	12 59	13 14	13 29	13 44	13 59
St Pancras International 4 ⊖	a	08 51	09 07	09 21	09 51	10 06	10 21	10 51	11 06	11 21	11 51	12 06	12 21	12 39	12 54	13 06	13 21	13 36	13 51	14 06

Kent, High Speed Domestic Services - St Pancras International

		SE	SE	SE	SE	SE		SE	SE	SE	SE	SE	SE	SE	SE	SE		SE	SE	SE	SE	SE	SE	SE	SE
Margate [4]	d	12 53				13 53					14 53				15 53	15 53						16 53			
Broadstairs	d	12 59				13 59					14 59				15 59	15 59						16 59			
Ramsgate [4]	d	13 05				14 05					15 05				16 05	16 05						17 05			
Canterbury West [4]	a	13 24				14 24					15 24				16 24	16 24						17 24			
	d	13 25				14 25					15 25				16 25	16 25						17 25			
Dover Priory	d			13 44					14 44				15 44							16 44				17 44	
Folkestone Central	d			13 56					14 56				15 56							16 56				17 56	
Folkestone West	d			13 58					14 58				15 58							16 58				17 58	
Ashford International	a	13 41		14 11		14 41			15 11		15 41		16 11		16 41	16 41				17 11		17 41		18 11	
	d	13 43		14 13		14 43			15 13		15 43		16 13		16 43	16 47				17 13		17 43		18 13	
Broadstairs	d																								
Margate [4]	d																								
Birchington-on-Sea	d																								
Herne Bay	d																								
Whitstable	d																								
Faversham [2]	a																								
	d		13 28		13 58			14 28		14 58		15 28		15 58				16 28	16 28		16 58		17 28		17 58
Sittingbourne [4]	d		13 37		14 07			14 37		15 07		15 37		16 07				16 37	16 37		17 07		17 37		18 07
Rainham (Kent)	d		13 45		14 15			14 45		15 15		15 45		16 15				16 45	16 45		17 15		17 45		18 15
Gillingham (Kent) [4]	d		13 50		14 20			14 50		15 20		15 50		16 20				16 50	16 50		17 20		17 50		18 20
Chatham [4]	d		13 54		14 24			14 54		15 24		15 54		16 24				16 54	16 54		17 24		17 54		18 24
Rochester [4]	d		13 57		14 27			14 57		15 27		15 57		16 27				16 57	16 57		17 27		17 57		18 27
Strood [4]	d		14 02		14 32			15 02		15 32		16 02		16 32				17 02	17 02		17 32		18 02		18 32
Gravesend	d		14 13		14 43			15 13		15 43		16 13		16 43				17 12	17 12		17 43		18 12		18 43
Ebbsfleet International	a	14 02	14 17	14 32	14 47	15 02		15 17	15 32	15 47	16 02	16 17	16 32	16 47	17 02	17 06		17 16	17 16	17 32	17 47	18 02	18 16	18 32	18 47
	d	14 03	14 21	14 33	14 51	15 03		15 18	15 33	15 48	16 03	16 18	16 33	16 48	17 03	17 07		17 17	17 17	17 33	17 48	18 03	18 17	18 33	18 51
Stratford International ⊖	a	14 14	14 32	14 44	15 02	15 14		15 29	15 44	15 59	16 14	16 29	16 44	16 59	17 14	17 18		17 27	17 27	17 44	17 59	18 14	18 27	18 44	19 02
St Pancras International [4] ⊖	a	14 21	14 39	14 51	15 09	15 21		15 36	15 51	16 06	16 21	16 40	16 51	17 06	17 21	17 28		17 34	17 38	17 51	18 09	18 21	18 38	18 51	19 09

		SE		SE	SE	SE	SE	SE	SE	SE	SE	SE		SE	SE	SE	SE	SE	SE	SE	SE				
Margate [4]	d	17 53					18 53				19 53					20 53					21 53				
Broadstairs	d	17 59					18 59				19 59					20 59					21 59				
Ramsgate [4]	d	18 05					19 05				20 05					21 05					22 05				
Canterbury West [4]	a	18 24					19 24				20 24					21 24					22 24				
	d	18 25					19 25				20 25					21 25					22 25				
Dover Priory	d				18 44				19 44					20 44				21 44							
Folkestone Central	d				18 56				19 56					20 56				21 56							
Folkestone West	d				18 58				19 58					20 58				21 58							
Ashford International	a	18 41			19 11		19 41		20 11		20 41			21 11		21 41		22 11			22 41				
	d	18 43			19 13		19 43		20 13		20 47			21 13		21 43		22 13			22 43				
Broadstairs	d																								
Margate [4]	d																								
Birchington-on-Sea	d																								
Herne Bay	d																								
Whitstable	d																								
Faversham [2]	a																								
	d			18 28		18 58		19 28		19 58		20 28			20 58		21 28		21 58	21 58					
Sittingbourne [4]	d			18 37		19 07		19 37		20 07		20 37			21 07		21 37		22 07	22 07					
Rainham (Kent)	d			18 45		19 15		19 45		20 15		20 45			21 15		21 45		22 15	22 15					
Gillingham (Kent) [4]	d			18 50		19 20		19 50		20 20		20 50			21 20		21 50		22 20	22 20					
Chatham [4]	d			18 54		19 24		19 54		20 24		20 54			21 24		21 54		22 24	22 24					
Rochester [4]	d			18 57		19 27		19 57		20 27		20 57			21 27		21 57		22 27	22 27					
Strood [4]	d			19 02		19 32		20 02		20 32		21 02			21 32		22 02		22 32	22 32					
Gravesend	d			19 13		19 43		20 12		20 43		21 13			21 43		22 13		22 43	22 43					
Ebbsfleet International	a	19 02		19 17	19 32	19 47	20 02	20 16	20 32	20 47	21 06	21 17		21 32	21 47	22 02	22 17	22 32	22 47	22 47	23 02				
	d	19 03		19 18	19 33	19 48	20 03	20 17	20 33	20 48	21 07	21 21		21 33	21 48	22 03	22 18	22 33	22 48	22 51	23 03				
Stratford International ⊖	a	19 14		19 29	19 44	19 59	20 14	20 27	20 44	20 59	21 18	21 31		21 44	21 59	22 14	22 29	22 44	22 59	23 02	23 14				
St Pancras International [4] ⊖	a	19 21		19 36	19 51	20 06	20 21	20 38	20 51	21 06	21 25	21 42		21 51	22 06	22 21	22 36	22 51	23 06	23 09	23 21				

Network Diagram for Tables 195, 196 | also 199★

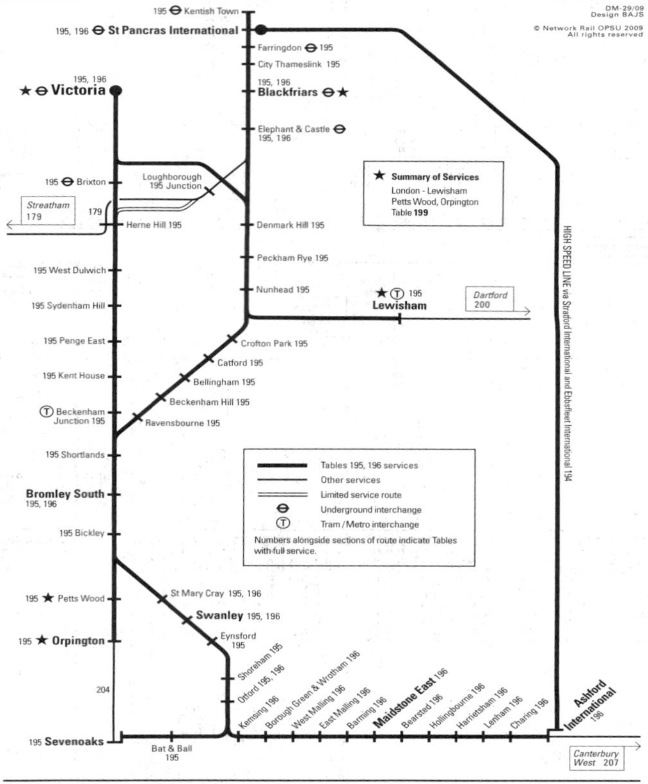

London - Catford, Beckenham Junction, Bromley South, Orpington, Otford and Sevenoaks

		SE MO ■1	SE MX ■1	SE MX	SE MX	SE MX ■1	SE	SE ■1	SE	SE		FC	SE ■1	SE	SE ■1	SE	FC	SE ■1	SE ■1	SE		SE	FC	SE ■1	SE ■1
London Victoria ■15	⊖ d	23p45	23p52	23p43	23p55	00 07	00 35	05 22		05 40			05 52		06 07	06 10		06 22	06 22			06 30		06 37	06 45
Brixton	⊖ d				00 02					05 47						06 17						06 37			
Kentish Town	⊖ d											05 50					06 08						06 30		
St Pancras International ■15	⊖ d											05 54					06 12						06 34		
Farringdon	⊖ d											05 58					06 17						06 39		
City Thameslink ■3	d								05 26			06 01					06 21			06 07			06 43		
London Blackfriars ■3	⊖ d								05 28			06 06					06 24			06 10			06 46		
Elephant & Castle	⊖ d								05 32			06 09					06 27			06 16			06 49		
Loughborough Jn	d											06 13					06 31						06 53		
Herne Hill ■4	d				00 04		00 43			05 49		06 16				06 19	06 34					06 39	06 57		
West Dulwich	d				00 06					05 51						06 21						06 41			
Sydenham Hill	d				00 08					05 53						06 23						06 43			
Penge East	d				00 11		00 48			05 56						06 26						06 46			
Kent House ■4	d				00 13					05 58						06 28						06 48			
Beckenham Junction ■4	d				00 15		00 50			06 00						06 30						06 50			
Denmark Hill ■4	d			23p52					05 39											06 22					
Peckham Rye ■4	d			23p55					05 41											06 25					
Nunhead ■4	d			23p57					05 44											06 27					
Lewisham ■4	a																								
Crofton Park	d			23p59					05 47											06 30					
Catford	d			00 03					05 49											06 33					
Bellingham	d			00 05					05 52											06 35					
Beckenham Hill	d			00 07					05 54											06 37					
Ravensbourne	d			00 09					05 56											06 39					
Shortlands ■4	d			00 11	00 18				05 58	06 03						06 33				06 41		06 54			
Bromley South ■4	d	00 02	00 09	00 14	00 21	00 25	00 55	05 39	06 01	06 06			06 09	06 16	06 23	06 37		06 39	06 39	06 44		06 57		06 58	07 02
Bickley ■4	d			00 17	00 24				06 03	06 09				06 18		06 39				06 47		07 00			
Petts Wood ■4	d			00 21	00 29					06 14						06 44						07 04			
Orpington ■4	d			00a25	00a32					06a18						06a49						07a08			
St Mary Cray	d	00 08	00 15			00 31	01 01	05 45	06 08					06 23	06 30			06 45	06 45	06 51				07 04	07 08
Swanley ■4	d	00 12	00 19			00 36	01 05	05 49	06 12				06 19	06 27	06 34			06 49	06 49	06 56				07 08	07 13
Eynsford	d					00 40			06 17					06 31						07 00					
Shoreham (Kent)	d					00 44			06 20					06 35						07 04					
Otford ■4	d					00 47			06 23					06 38	06 42					07 07				07 16	
Bat & Ball	d								06 26					06 41						07 10					
Sevenoaks ■4	a								06 29					06 44						07 14					

		SE ■1	SE	SE	FC	SE ■1		FC ■1	SE ■1	FC ■1	SE ■1	SE ■1	SE	FC ■1	FC	FC ■1		SE ■1	FC	SE	FC	SE	SE	FC	SE ■1
London Victoria ■15	⊖ d	06 45		06 50		06 58			07 07		07 22	07 22	07 25					07 36		07 40		07 43	07 55		08 07
Brixton	⊖ d			06 57									07 32							07 47			08 02		
Kentish Town	⊖ d				06 48										07 20				07 08						
St Pancras International ■15	⊖ d				06 52			07 06		06 45				07 16	07 24	07 28			07 12		07 32			07 52	
Farringdon	⊖ d				06 57			07 11		06 50				07 21	07 29	07 33			07 17		07 37			07 57	
City Thameslink ■3	d		06 39		07 01			07 15		06 54				07 25	07 33	07 37			07 21		07 41			08 01	
London Blackfriars ■3	⊖ d		06 42		07 04			07 18		06 58				07 28	07 36	07 40			07 24		07 44			08 04	
Elephant & Castle	⊖ d		06 46		07 07			07 21		07 02				07 33	07 40	07 44			07 28		07 47			08 07	
Loughborough Jn	d				07 11			07 25						07 37							07 51			08 11	
Herne Hill ■4	d			06 59	07 16			07 31					07 34	07 41	07 46					07 49	07 56		08 04	08 15	
West Dulwich	d			07 02									07 36							07 51			08 06		
Sydenham Hill	d			07 04									07 38							07 53			08 08		
Penge East	d			07 07									07 41							07 56			08 11		
Kent House ■4	d			07 09									07 43							07 58			08 13		
Beckenham Junction ■4	d			07 11									07 45		07a53					08 00			08 15		
Denmark Hill ■4	d		06 52							07 09						07 50			07 34			07 53			
Peckham Rye ■4	d		06 55							07 12						07 53			07 36			07 56			
Nunhead ■4	d		06 57							07 14						07 56			07 39			07 59			
Lewisham ■4	a																					08 07			
Crofton Park	d		07 00							07 17									07 42						
Catford	d		07 03							07 20						08 00			07 44						
Bellingham	d		07 05							07 22						08 02			07 47						
Beckenham Hill	d		07 07							07 24									07 49						
Ravensbourne	d		07 09							07 26									07 51						
Shortlands ■4	d		07 11	07 14						07 28			07 48						07 54	08 03					
Bromley South ■4	d	07 02	07 14	07 17		07 19			07 23	07 31	07 40	07 40	07 51			08a10		07 53	07 57	08 06			08 22		08 23
Bickley ■4	d		07 17	07 20						07 34			07 54						08 00	08 09			08 24		
Petts Wood ■4	d			07 24									07 59							08 14			08 29		
Orpington ■4	d			07a28									08a02							08a19			08a32		
St Mary Cray	d	07 08	07 21			07 25			07 30	07 38								08 00	08 04						08 30
Swanley ■4	d	07 13	07 26			07 29			07 34	07 44	07 49	07 49						08 04	08 10						08 34
Eynsford	d		07 30							07 48									08 15						
Shoreham (Kent)	d		07 34							07 52									08 18						
Otford ■4	d		07 37						07 42	07 55								08 12	08 21						08 42
Bat & Ball	d		07 40							07 58									08 24						
Sevenoaks ■4	a		07 43							08 01									08 27						

London - Catford, Beckenham Junction, Bromley South, Orpington, Otford and Sevenoaks

		FC		SE ■1	FC	SE	SE	SE ■1	SE	FC	FC ■1 A	SE ■1		FC ■1	SE	SE	FC ■1	FC	SE ■1 (trolley)	FC	FC	SE	SE ■1	SE ■1	SE
London Victoria ■15	⊖ d			07 58		08 09	08 10	08 22	08 25			08 37			08 39	08 40			08 52			08 55	08 58	09 07	09 09
Brixton	⊖ d						08 17		08 32							08 47						09 02			
Kentish Town	⊖ d				07 40						08 19										08 35				
St Pancras International ■15	⊖ d	07 38			07 44					08 12	08 24			08 16			08 32	08 44		08 28	08 40				
Farringdon	⊖ d	07 43			07 49					08 17	08 29			08 21			08 37	08 49		08 33	08 45				
City Thameslink ■3	d	07 47			07 53					08 21	08 33			08 25			08 41	08 53		08 37	08 49				
London Blackfriars ■3	⊖ d	07 50			07 56					08 24	08 36			08 28			08 44	08 56		08 40	08 52				
Elephant & Castle	⊖ d	07 54			08 00					08 27				08 32			08 47	09 00		08 44	08 56				
Loughborough Jn	d									08 31							08 51	09 04							
Herne Hill ■4	d						08 19		08 34	08 36	08 46					08 48	08 57	09 11				09 04			
West Dulwich	d						08 21		08 36							08 51						09 06			
Sydenham Hill	d						08 23		08 38							08 53						09 08			
Penge East	d						08 26		08 41							08 56						09 11			
Kent House ■4	d						08 28		08 43							08 58						09 13			
Beckenham Junction ■4	d						08 30		08 45							09 00						09 15			
Denmark Hill ■4	d	08 00			08 09	08 19								08 38	08 48					08 52	09 02				09 18
Peckham Rye ■4	d	08 03			08 12	08 23								08 41	08 51					08 55					09 21
Nunhead ■4	d	08 06			08 14	08 25								08 43	08 53					08 57					09 23
Lewisham ■4	a					08 30									09 01										09 31
Crofton Park	d	08 09			08 17									08 46						09 00					
Catford	d	08 12			08 20									08 49						09 03	09 09				
Bellingham	d	08 15			08 22									08 51						09 05					
Beckenham Hill	d	08 17			08 24									08 53						09 07					
Ravensbourne	d	08 19			08 26									08 55						09 09					
Shortlands ■4	d	08 22			08 30		08 33		08 48					08 57		09 03				09 11		09 18			
Bromley South ■4	d	08 25		08 27	08 33		08 36	08 39	08 51			08 53		09 00		09 07			09 09	09 14	09 18	09 21	09 19	09 23	
Bickley ■4	d	08 28			08 35		08 39		08 54					09 03		09 09				09 17	09 20	09 24			
Petts Wood ■4	d	08 32					08 44		08 59							09 14						09 29			
Orpington ■4	d	08a35					08a47		09a02							09a17						09a33			
St Mary Cray	d			08 33	08 40							09 00		09 07						09 21	09 25		09 25		
Swanley ■4	d			08 38	08 44							09 04		09 12						09 26	09b36		09 29	09 33	
Eynsford	d				08 49									09 16						09 30	09 40				
Shoreham (Kent)	d				08 52									09 20						09 34	09 44				
Otford ■4	d				08 55							09 12		09 23						09 37	09 47			09 41	
Bat & Ball	d				08 58									09 26						09 40	09 50				
Sevenoaks ■4	a				09 01									09 29						09 45	09 53				

		SE	FC	SE ■1 (trolley)	FC	SE	FC	SE ■1		SE	SE	FC	SE ■1	FC	SE ■1	SE	FC	SE ■1		SE	SE	FC	SE ■1 (trolley)	FC	SE
London Victoria ■15	⊖ d	09 10		09 22		09 25		09 37		09 39	09 40		09 52		09 58	09 55		10 07		10 09	10 10		10 22		10 25
Brixton	⊖ d	09 17				09 32					09 47					10 02					10 17				10 32
Kentish Town	⊖ d		08 51				09 11							09 26			09 43					10 00		09 54	
St Pancras International ■15	⊖ d		08 56		09 00		09 16					09 34		09 30			09 48					10 04		10 00	
Farringdon	⊖ d		09 01		09 05		09 21					09 39		09 35			09 53					10 09		10 05	
City Thameslink ■3	d		09 05		09 09		09 25					09 43		09 39			09 57					10 13		10 09	
London Blackfriars ■3	⊖ d		09 08		09 12		09 28					09 46		09 42			10 00					10 16		10 12	
Elephant & Castle	⊖ d		09 12		09 16		09 31					09 49		09 46			10 03					10 19		10 16	
Loughborough Jn	d		09 16				09 35					09 53					10 07					10 23			
Herne Hill ■4	d	09 19	09 25			09 34	09 41				09 49	09 57				10 04	10 11				10 19	10 27			10 34
West Dulwich	d	09 21				09 36					09 51					10 06					10 21				10 36
Sydenham Hill	d	09 23				09 38					09 53					10 08					10 23				10 38
Penge East	d	09 26				09 41					09 56					10 11					10 26				10 41
Kent House ■4	d	09 28				09 43					09 58					10 13					10 28				10 43
Beckenham Junction ■4	d	09 30				09 45					10 00					10 15					10 30				10 45
Denmark Hill ■4	d				09 22					09 48				09 52						10 18				10 22	
Peckham Rye ■4	d				09 25					09 51				09 55						10 21				10 25	
Nunhead ■4	d				09 27					09 53				09 57						10 23				10 27	
Lewisham ■4	a									10 01										10 31					
Crofton Park	d				09 30									10 00										10 30	
Catford	d				09 33									10 03										10 33	
Bellingham	d				09 35									10 05										10 35	
Beckenham Hill	d				09 37									10 07										10 37	
Ravensbourne	d				09 39									10 09										10 39	
Shortlands ■4	d	09 33			09 41	09 48					10 03			10 11		10 18					10 33			10 41	10 48
Bromley South ■4	d	09 36		09 39	09 44	09 52		09 53			10 07		10 09	10 14	10 19	10 21		10 23			10 36		10 39	10 44	10 51
Bickley ■4	d	09 39			09 47	09 54					10 09			10 17		10 24					10 39			10 47	10 54
Petts Wood ■4	d	09 44				09 59					10 14					10 29					10 44				10 59
Orpington ■4	d	09a47				10a02					10a17					10a32					10a47				11a02
St Mary Cray	d				09 51			10 00						10 21	10 25									10 51	
Swanley ■4	d				09 56			10 04						10 26	10 29			10 33						10 56	
Eynsford	d				10 00									10 30										11 00	
Shoreham (Kent)	d				10 04									10 34										11 04	
Otford ■4	d				10 07			10 12						10 37				10 41						11 07	
Bat & Ball	d				10 10									10 40										11 10	
Sevenoaks ■4	a				10 13									10 43										11 13	

A ■1 from London Blackfriars

b arr. 0929

London - Catford, Beckenham Junction, Bromley South, Orpington, Otford and Sevenoaks

		FC	SE 1	SE	SE	FC	SE 1 ⌶	FC	SE 1	SE	FC	SE 1	SE	SE	FC	SE 1 ⌶	FC	SE	FC	SE 1	SE	SE
London Victoria 15 ⊖	d		10 37	10 39	10 40		10 52		10 58	10 55		11 07	11 09	11 10		11 22		11 25		11 37	11 39	11 40
Brixton ⊖	d				10 47					11 02				11 17				11 32				11 47
Kentish Town ⊖	d	10 13				10 30		10 26			10 44				11 00		10 56		11 14			
St Pancras International 15 ⊖	d	10 18				10 34		10 30			10 48				11 04		11 00		11 18			
Farringdon ⊖	d	10 23				10 39		10 35			10 53				11 09		11 05		11 23			
City Thameslink 3	d	10 27				10 43		10 39			10 57				11 13		11 09		11 27			
London Blackfriars 3 ⊖	d	10 30				10 46		10 42			11 00				11 16		11 12		11 30			
Elephant & Castle ⊖	d	10 33				10 49		10 46			11 03				11 19		11 16		11 33			
Loughborough Jn	d	10 37				10 53					11 07				11 23				11 37			
Herne Hill 4	d	10 41			10 49	10 57				11 04	11 11			11 19	11 27			11 34	11 41			11 49
West Dulwich	d				10 51					11 06				11 21				11 36				11 51
Sydenham Hill	d				10 53					11 08				11 23				11 38				11 53
Penge East	d				10 56					11 11				11 26				11 41				11 56
Kent House 4	d				10 58					11 13				11 28				11 43				11 58
Beckenham Junction 4	d				11 00					11 15				11 30				11 45				12 00
Denmark Hill 4	d			10 48				10 52					11 18				11 22				11 48	
Peckham Rye 4	d			10 51				10 55					11 21				11 25				11 51	
Nunhead 4	d			10 53				10 57					11 23				11 27				11 53	
Lewisham 4	a			11 01									11 31								12 02	
Crofton Park	d							11 00									11 30					
Catford	d							11 03									11 33					
Bellingham	d							11 05									11 35					
Beckenham Hill	d							11 07									11 37					
Ravensbourne	d							11 09									11 39					
Shortlands 4	d				11 03			11 11		11 18				11 33			11 41	11 48				12 03
Bromley South 4	d		10 53		11 06		11 09	11 14	11 19	11 21		11 23		11 36		11 39	11 44	11 51		11 53		12 06
Bickley 4	d				11 09			11 17		11 24				11 39			11 47	11 54				12 09
Petts Wood 4	d				11 14					11 29				11 44				11 59				12 14
Orpington 4	d				11a17					11a32				11a47				12a02				12a17
St Mary Cray	d		11 00					11 21	11 25								11 51			12 00		
Swanley 4	d		11 04					11 26	11 29			11 33					11 56			12 04		
Eynsford	d							11 30									12 00					
Shoreham (Kent)	d							11 34									12 04					
Otford 4	d		11 12					11 37				11 41					12 07			12 12		
Bat & Ball	d							11 40									12 10					
Sevenoaks 4	a							11 43									12 13					

		FC	SE 1 ⌶	FC	SE 1	SE	FC	SE 1	SE	SE	FC	SE 1 ⌶	FC	SE	FC	SE 1	SE	SE	FC	SE 1 ⌶	FC	SE 1	SE
London Victoria 15 ⊖	d		11 52		11 58	11 55		12 07	12 09	12 10		12 22		12 25		12 37	12 39	12 40		12 52		12 58	12 55
Brixton ⊖	d					12 02				12 17				12 32				12 47					13 02
Kentish Town ⊖	d	11 30		11 26			11 43				12 00		11 56		12 13				12 30		12 26		
St Pancras International 15 ⊖	d	11 34		11 30			11 48				12 04		12 00		12 18				12 34		12 30		
Farringdon ⊖	d	11 39		11 35			11 53				12 09		12 05		12 23				12 39		12 35		
City Thameslink 3	d	11 43		11 39			11 57				12 13		12 09		12 27				12 43		12 39		
London Blackfriars 3 ⊖	d	11 46		11 42			12 00				12 16		12 12		12 30				12 46		12 42		
Elephant & Castle ⊖	d	11 49		11 46			12 03				12 19		12 16		12 33				12 49		12 46		
Loughborough Jn	d	11 53					12 07				12 23				12 37				12 53				
Herne Hill 4	d	11 57				12 04	12 11			12 19	12 27			12 34	12 41			12 49	12 57				13 04
West Dulwich	d					12 06				12 21				12 36				12 51					13 06
Sydenham Hill	d					12 08				12 23				12 38				12 53					13 08
Penge East	d					12 11				12 26				12 41				12 56					13 11
Kent House 4	d					12 13				12 28				12 43				12 58					13 13
Beckenham Junction 4	d					12 15				12 30				12 45				13 00					13 15
Denmark Hill 4	d			11 52					12 18				12 22				12 48				12 52		
Peckham Rye 4	d			11 55					12 21				12 25				12 51				12 55		
Nunhead 4	d			11 57					12 23				12 27				12 53				12 57		
Lewisham 4	a								12 31								13 02						
Crofton Park	d			12 00									12 30								13 00		
Catford	d			12 03									12 33								13 03		
Bellingham	d			12 05									12 35								13 05		
Beckenham Hill	d			12 07									12 37								13 07		
Ravensbourne	d			12 09									12 39								13 09		
Shortlands 4	d			12 11		12 18				12 33			12 41	12 48				13 03			13 11		13 18
Bromley South 4	d		12 09	12 14	12 19	12 21		12 23		12 36		12 39	12 44	12 51		12 53		13 06		13 09	13 14	13 19	13 21
Bickley 4	d			12 17		12 24				12 39			12 47	12 54				13 09			13 17		13 24
Petts Wood 4	d					12 29				12 44				12 59				13 14					13 29
Orpington 4	d					12a32				12a47				13a02				13a17					13a32
St Mary Cray	d			12 21	12 25								12 51			13 00					13 21	13 25	
Swanley 4	d			12 26	12 29			12 33					12 56			13 04					13 26	13 29	
Eynsford	d			12 30									13 00								13 30		
Shoreham (Kent)	d			12 34									13 04								13 34		
Otford 4	d			12 37				12 41					13 07			13 12					13 37		
Bat & Ball	d			12 40									13 10								13 40		
Sevenoaks 4	a			12 43									13 13								13 43		

Table 195 — Mondays to Fridays

London - Catford, Beckenham Junction, Bromley South, Orpington, Otford and Sevenoaks

		FC	SE 1	SE	SE	FC	SE 1 ⌶	FC	SE	FC	SE 1	SE	SE	FC	SE 1 ⌶	FC	SE 1	SE	FC	SE 1	SE	SE	FC
London Victoria 15 ⊖	d		13 07	13 09	13 10		13 22		13 25		13 37	13 39	13 40		13 52		13 58	13 55		14 07	14 09	14 10	
Brixton ⊖	d				13 17				13 32				13 47					14 02				14 17	
Kentish Town ⊖	d	12 43				13 00		12 56		13 13				13 30		13 26			13 43				14 00
St Pancras International 15 ⊖	d	12 48				13 04		13 00		13 18				13 34		13 30			13 48				14 04
Farringdon ⊖	d	12 53				13 09		13 05		13 23				13 39		13 35			13 53				14 09
City Thameslink 3	d	12 57				13 13		13 09		13 27				13 43		13 39			13 57				14 13
London Blackfriars 3 ⊖	d	13 00				13 16		13 12		13 30				13 46		13 42			14 00				14 16
Elephant & Castle ⊖	d	13 03				13 19		13 16		13 33				13 49		13 46			14 03				14 19
Loughborough Jn	d	13 07				13 23				13 37				13 53					14 07				14 23
Herne Hill 4	d	13 11			13 19	13 27			13 34	13 41			13 49	13 57				14 04	14 11			14 19	14 27
West Dulwich	d				13 21				13 36				13 51					14 06				14 21	
Sydenham Hill	d				13 23				13 38				13 53					14 08				14 23	
Penge East	d				13 26				13 41				13 56					14 11				14 26	
Kent House 4	d				13 28				13 43				13 58					14 13				14 28	
Beckenham Junction 4	d				13 30				13 45				14 00					14 15				14 30	
Denmark Hill 4	d			13 18				13 22				13 48				13 52					14 18		
Peckham Rye 4	d			13 21				13 25				13 51				13 55					14 21		
Nunhead 4	d			13 23				13 27				13 53				13 57					14 23		
Lewisham 4	a			13 31								14 01									14 31		
Crofton Park	d							13 30								14 00							
Catford	d							13 33								14 03							
Bellingham	d							13 35								14 05							
Beckenham Hill	d							13 37								14 07							
Ravensbourne	d							13 39								14 09							
Shortlands 4	d				13 33			13 41	13 48				14 03			14 11		14 18				14 33	
Bromley South 4	d		13 23		13 36		13 39	13 44	13 51		13 53		14 06		14 09	14 14	14 19	14 21		14 23		14 36	
Bickley 4	d				13 39			13 47	13 54				14 09			14 17		14 24				14 39	
Petts Wood 4	d				13 44				13 59				14 14					14 29				14 44	
Orpington 4	d				13a47				14a02				14a17					14a32				14a47	
St Mary Cray	d							13 51			14 00					14 21	14 25						
Swanley 4	d		13 33					13 56			14 04					14 26	14 29			14 33			
Eynsford	d							14 00								14 30							
Shoreham (Kent)	d							14 04								14 34							
Otford 4	d		13 41					14 07			14 12					14 37				14 41			
Bat & Ball	d							14 10								14 40							
Sevenoaks 4	a							14 13								14 43							

		SE 1 ⌶	FC	SE	FC	SE 1	SE	SE	FC	SE 1 ⌶	FC	SE 1	SE	FC	SE 1	SE	SE	FC	SE 1 ⌶	FC	SE	FC
London Victoria 15 ⊖	d	14 22		14 25		14 37	14 39	14 40		14 52		14 58	14 55		15 07	15 09	15 10		15 22		15 25	
Brixton ⊖	d			14 32				14 47					15 02				15 17				15 32	
Kentish Town ⊖	d		13 56		14 13				14 30		14 26			14 43				15 00		14 56		15 13
St Pancras International 15 ⊖	d		14 00		14 18				14 34		14 30			14 48				15 04		15 00		15 18
Farringdon ⊖	d		14 05		14 23				14 39		14 35			14 53				15 09		15 05		15 23
City Thameslink 3	d		14 09		14 27				14 43		14 39			14 57				15 13		15 09		15 27
London Blackfriars 3 ⊖	d		14 12		14 30				14 46		14 42			15 00				15 16		15 12		15 30
Elephant & Castle ⊖	d		14 16		14 33				14 49		14 46			15 03				15 19		15 16		15 33
Loughborough Jn	d				14 37				14 53					15 07				15 23				15 37
Herne Hill 4	d			14 34	14 41			14 49	14 57				15 04	15 11			15 19	15 27			15 34	15 41
West Dulwich	d			14 36				14 51					15 06				15 21				15 36	
Sydenham Hill	d			14 38				14 53					15 08				15 23				15 38	
Penge East	d			14 41				14 56					15 11				15 26				15 41	
Kent House 4	d			14 43				14 58					15 13				15 28				15 43	
Beckenham Junction 4	d			14 45				15 00					15 15				15 30				15 45	
Denmark Hill 4	d		14 22				14 48				14 52					15 18				15 22		
Peckham Rye 4	d		14 25				14 51				14 55					15 21				15 25		
Nunhead 4	d		14 27				14 53				14 57					15 23				15 27		
Lewisham 4	a						15 01									15 31						
Crofton Park	d		14 30								15 00									15 30		
Catford	d		14 33								15 03									15 33		
Bellingham	d		14 35								15 05									15 35		
Beckenham Hill	d		14 37								15 07									15 37		
Ravensbourne	d		14 39								15 09									15 39		
Shortlands 4	d		14 41	14 48				15 03			15 11		15 18				15 33			15 41	15 48	
Bromley South 4	d	14 39	14 44	14 51		14 53		15 06		15 09	15 14	15 19	15 21		15 23		15 36		15 39	15 44	15 51	
Bickley 4	d		14 47	14 54				15 09			15 17		15 24				15 39			15 47	15 54	
Petts Wood 4	d			14 59				15 14					15 29				15 44				15 59	
Orpington 4	d			15a02				15a17					15a32				15a47				16a02	
St Mary Cray	d		14 51			15 00					15 21	15 25								15 51		
Swanley 4	d		14 56			15 04					15 26	15 29			15 33					15 56		
Eynsford	d		15 00								15 30									16 00		
Shoreham (Kent)	d		15 04								15 34									16 04		
Otford 4	d		15 07			15 12					15 37				15 41					16 07		
Bat & Ball	d		15 10								15 40									16 10		
Sevenoaks 4	a		15 13								15 43									16 13		

Table 195

Mondays to Fridays

London - Catford, Beckenham Junction, Bromley South, Orpington, Otford and Sevenoaks

		SE 1	SE	SE	FC	SE 1 🍴	FC	SE 1	SE	FC	SE 1	SE	SE	FC	SE	SE 1	FC	SE 1	SE	FC	SE 1	FC	SE
London Victoria 15 ⊖	d	15 37	15 39	15 40		15 52		15 58	15 55		16 07	16 09	16 10			16 22		16 28	16 25		16 37		16 39
Brixton ⊖	d			15 47					16 02				16 17						16 32				
Kentish Town ⊖	d				15 30		15 26			15 43				16 00			15 56			16 13		16 09	
St Pancras International 15 ⊖	d				15 34		15 30			15 48				16 04			16 00			16 18		16 14	
Farringdon ⊖	d				15 39		15 35			15 53				16 09			16 05			16 23		16 19	
City Thameslink 3	d				15 43		15 39			15 57				16 13			16 09			16 27		16 23	
London Blackfriars 3 ⊖	d				15 46		15 42			16 00				16 16			16 12			16 30		16 26	
Elephant & Castle ⊖	d				15 49		15 46			16 03				16 19			16 16			16 33		16 30	
Loughborough Jn	d				15 53					16 07				16 23						16 37			
Herne Hill 4	d			15 49	15 57				16 04	16 11			16 19	16 27					16 34	16 41			
West Dulwich	d			15 51					16 06				16 21						16 36				
Sydenham Hill	d			15 53					16 08				16 23						16 38				
Penge East	d			15 56					16 11				16 26						16 41				
Kent House 4	d			15 58					16 13				16 28						16 43				
Beckenham Junction 4 🚊	d			16 00					16 15				16 30		16 12				16 45				
Denmark Hill 4	d		15 48				15 52					16 18					16 22					16 39	16 48
Peckham Rye 4	d		15 51				15 55					16 21					16 25					16 42	16 51
Nunhead 4	d		15 53				15 57					16 23					16 27					16 44	16 53
Lewisham 4 🚊	a		16 01									16 31											16 58
Crofton Park	d						16 00										16 30					16 47	
Catford	d						16 03										16 33					16 50	
Bellingham	d						16 05										16 35					16 52	
Beckenham Hill	d						16 07										16 37					16 54	
Ravensbourne	d						16 09										16 39					16 56	
Shortlands 4	d			16 03			16 11		16 18				16 33				16 41		16 48			16 58	
Bromley South 4	d	15 53		16 06		16 09	16 14	16 19	16 21		16 23		16 36			16 39	16 44	16 49	16 51		16 53	17 01	
Bickley 4	d			16 09			16 17		16 24				16 39				16 47		16 54			17 04	
Petts Wood 4	d			16 14					16 29				16 44						16 59			17 08	
Orpington 4	d			16a17					16a32				16a48						17a03			17a14	
St Mary Cray	d	16 00					16 21	16 25									16 51	16 55			17 00		
Swanley 4	d	16 04					16 26	16 29			16 33						16 56	16 59			17 04		
Eynsford	d						16 30										17 00						
Shoreham (Kent)	d						16 34										17 04						
Otford 4	d	16 12					16 37				16 41						17 07				17 12		
Bat & Ball	d						16 40										17 10						
Sevenoaks 4	a						16 43										17 14						

		SE	FC	FC 1	SE 1 🍴	FC	SE 1	SE	SE 1	SE	FC	SE 1	SE	FC	SE 1 🍴	FC	FC 1	SE 1	SE	FC	SE	SE 1
London Victoria 15 ⊖	d	16 40			16 57		16 58	17 04	17 04	17 00		17 12	17 15		17 27			17 28	17 30		17 34	17 42
Brixton ⊖	d	16 47								17 07			17 22						17 37			
Kentish Town ⊖	d		16 30			16 24					16 44			16 58						17 14		
St Pancras International 15 ⊖	d		16 34	16 40		16 28					16 52			17 02		16 58	17 14			17 18		
Farringdon ⊖	d		16 39	16 45		16 33					16 57			17 07		17 03	17 19			17 23		
City Thameslink 3	d		16 43	16 49		16 37					17 01			17 11		17 07	17 23			17 27		
London Blackfriars 3 ⊖	d		16 46	16 52		16 42					17 04			17 14		17 10	17 26			17 30		
Elephant & Castle ⊖	d		16 49	16 56		16 46					17 08			17 18		17 14	17 30			17 34		
Loughborough Jn	d		16 53	17 00							17 12			17 22						17 38		
Herne Hill 4	d	16 49	16 57	17 06						17 09	17 16		17 24	17 26			17 36		17 39	17 44		
West Dulwich	d	16 51		17 09						17 12			17 27						17 42			
Sydenham Hill	d	16 53		17 11						17 14			17 29						17 44			
Penge East	d	16 56		17 14						17 17			17 32						17 47			
Kent House 4	d	16 58		17 16						17 19			17 34						17 49			
Beckenham Junction 4 🚊	d	17 00		17a19						17 21			17 37						17 51			
Denmark Hill 4	d					16 52		17 13								17 20					17 43	
Peckham Rye 4	d					16 55		17 16								17 23					17 46	
Nunhead 4	d					16 57		17 18								17 26					17 49	
Lewisham 4 🚊	a							17 23													17 55	
Crofton Park	d					17 00										17 29						
Catford	d					17 03										17 32						
Bellingham	d					17 05										17 35						
Beckenham Hill	d					17 07										17 37						
Ravensbourne	d					17 09										17 39						
Shortlands 4	d	17 03				17 11				17 25			17 40			17 43			17 55			
Bromley South 4	d	17 06			17 13	17 14	17 19		17 24	17 28		17 28	17 43		17 44	17 46	17 48	17 50	17 58			17 59
Bickley 4	d	17 09				17 17				17 30			17 45				17 50		18 00			
Petts Wood 4	d	17 14								17 35			17 50						18 05			
Orpington 4	d	17a18								17a39			17a54						18a09			
St Mary Cray	d					17 21			17 30			17 35					17 55	17 57				18 06
Swanley 4	d					17 30			17 34			17 39				17 55	18 00	18 01				18 11
Eynsford	d					17 34										18 00						
Shoreham (Kent)	d					17 38										18 03						
Otford 4	d					17 41	17 35					17 48				18 06		18 10				18 19
Bat & Ball	d					17 44										18 14						
Sevenoaks 4	a					17 48										18 22						

Table 195

Mondays to Fridays

London - Catford, Beckenham Junction, Bromley South, Orpington, Otford and Sevenoaks

		FC	FC 1	SE	FC	FC	SE	SE 1 🍴	SE 1	SE 1	SE	FC	FC 1	FC	SE	SE 1	SE	FC	SE 1 🍴	SE 1	SE	FC	SE
London Victoria 15 ⊖	d			17 45			17 56	17 57	17 54	18 03	18 00				18 18	18 18	18 15		18 27	18 24	18 30		18 39
Brixton ⊖	d			17 52							18 07						18 22				18 37		
Kentish Town ⊖	d	17 18			17 28							17 48		17 44				18 00				18 20	
St Pancras International 15 ⊖	d	17 22	17 37		17 32	17 44						17 52	17 58	17 48				18 04				18 24	
Farringdon ⊖	d	17 27	17 42		17 37	17 49						17 57	18 03	17 53				18 09				18 29	
City Thameslink 3	d	17 31	17 45		17 41	17 53						18 01	18 07	17 57				18 13				18 33	
London Blackfriars 3 ⊖	d	17 36	17 48		17 44	17 56						18 04	18 10	18 00				18 16				18 36	
Elephant & Castle ⊖	d	17 40	17 52		17 48	18 00						18 08	18 14	18 05				18 20				18 40	
Loughborough Jn	d				17 52							18 12						18 24				18 44	
Herne Hill 4	d			17 54	17 57	18 06					18 09	18 18	18 21				18 24	18 28			18 39	18 48	
West Dulwich	d			17 57		18 09					18 12						18 27				18 42		
Sydenham Hill	d			17 59		18 11					18 14						18 29				18 44		
Penge East	d			18 02		18 14					18 17						18 32				18 47		
Kent House 4	d			18 04		18a16					18 19						18 34				18 49		
Beckenham Junction 4 🚊	d			18 06							18 21						18 36				18 51		
Denmark Hill 4	d	17 47					18 06							18 15	18 28								18 48
Peckham Rye 4	d	17 50					18 09							18 18	18 32								18 51
Nunhead 4	d	17 52					18 11							18 20	18 34								18 54
Lewisham 4 🚊	a						18 17								18 42								19 01
Crofton Park	d	17 55												18 23									
Catford	d	17 58												18 26									
Bellingham	d	18 01												18 29									
Beckenham Hill	d	18 03												18 31									
Ravensbourne	d	18 05												18 33									
Shortlands 4	d	18 07		18 10							18 25			18 35			18 39				18 55		
Bromley South 4	d	18 10	18 11	18 13				18 15	18 17	18 24	18 28		18 31	18 38		18 39	18 42		18 44	18 46	18 58		
Bickley 4	d	18 12		18 16							18 31			18 40			18 45				19 00		
Petts Wood 4	d			18 21							18 36						18 52				19 07		
Orpington 4	d			18a24							18a40						18a56				19a11		
St Mary Cray	d	18 21	18 17						18 24				18 38	18 45		18 45				18 52			
Swanley 4	d	18 26	18 22						18 29				18 43	18 53		18 50				18 57			
Eynsford	d	18 30												18 57									
Shoreham (Kent)	d	18 34												19 01									
Otford 4	d	18 37	18 30							18 41				19 04		18 58							
Bat & Ball	d	18 40												19 07									
Sevenoaks 4	a	18 44												19 11									

		SE 1	FC	SE	FC	SE 1 🍴	FC 1	SE 1	SE 1	SE	FC	SE	SE	FC	SE 1 🍴	FC	SE	SE	FC	SE 1	SE	SE	FC
London Victoria 15 ⊖	d	18 42		18 45		18 57		18 58	19 07	19 00		19 09	19 10		19 22		19 28	19 25		19 37	19 39	19 40	
Brixton ⊖	d			18 52						19 07			19 17					19 32				19 47	
Kentish Town ⊖	d				18 34											18 54							
St Pancras International 15 ⊖	d		18 12		18 38		18 30				18 48			19 04		19 00			19 18				19 34
Farringdon ⊖	d		18 17		18 43		18 35				18 53			19 09		19 05			19 23				19 39
City Thameslink 3	d		18 21		18 47		18 39				18 57			19 13		19 09			19 27				19 43
London Blackfriars 3 ⊖	d		18 24		18 50		18 42				19 00			19 16		19 12			19 30				19 46
Elephant & Castle ⊖	d		18 28		18 54		18 46				19 04			19 19		19 16			19 33				19 49
Loughborough Jn	d				18 58						19 08			19 23					19 37				19 53
Herne Hill 4	d			18 54	19 02					19 09	19 12		19 19	19 27				19 34	19 41			19 49	19 57
West Dulwich	d			18 56						19 12			19 21					19 36				19 51	
Sydenham Hill	d			18 58						19 14			19 23					19 38				19 53	
Penge East	d			19 01						19 17			19 26					19 41				19 56	
Kent House 4	d			19 03						19 19			19 28					19 43				19 58	
Beckenham Junction 4 🚊	d			19 06						19 21			19 30					19 45				20 00	
Denmark Hill 4	d		18 34				18 52					19 18				19 22					19 48		
Peckham Rye 4	d		18 38				18 55					19 22				19 25					19 51		
Nunhead 4	d		18 40				18 57					19 24				19 27					19 53		
Lewisham 4 🚊	a											19 32									20 01		
Crofton Park	d		18 43				19 00									19 30							
Catford	d		18 46				19 03									19 33							
Bellingham	d		18 49				19 05									19 35							
Beckenham Hill	d		18 51				19 07									19 37							
Ravensbourne	d		18 53				19 09									19 39							
Shortlands 4	d		18 57	19 09			19 13			19 25			19 33			19 41		19 48				20 03	
Bromley South 4	d	18 59	19 00	19 12		19 13	19 16	19 19	19 27	19 28			19 36		19 39	19 44	19 49	19 51		19 53		20 06	
Bickley 4	d		19 03	19 15			19 19			19 30			19 39			19 47		19 54				20 09	
Petts Wood 4	d			19 19						19 35			19 44					19 59				20 14	
Orpington 4	d			19a23						19a38			19a48					20a02				20a18	
St Mary Cray	d	19 06	19 10				19 23	19 25								19 51	19 55			20 00			
Swanley 4	d	19 11	19 15				19 28	19 29	19 36							19 56	19 59			20 04			
Eynsford	d		19 19				19 32									20 00							
Shoreham (Kent)	d		19 23				19 36									20 04							
Otford 4	d	19 19	19 26				19 39		19 44							20 07				20 12			
Bat & Ball	d		19 29				19 42									20 10							
Sevenoaks 4	a		19 36				19 49									20 13							

Table 195

Mondays to Fridays

London - Catford, Beckenham Junction, Bromley South, Orpington, Otford and Sevenoaks

		SE ■		FC	SE ■	SE	FC	SE ■	SE	FC	SE ■	FC		SE	FC	FC	SE ■	SE ■	FC	SE ■	SE	FC		SE ■	SE ■
London Victoria 15	d	19 52			19 58	19 55		20 07	20 10		20 22			20 25			20 37	20 52		20 58	20 55			21 07	21 22
Brixton	d					20 02			20 17					20 32							21 02				
Kentish Town	d			19 26								19 56				20 30			20 26			21 00			
St Pancras International 15	d			19 30			19 48			20 04		20 00			20 18	20 36			20 30			21 06			
Farringdon	d			19 35			19 53			20 09		20 05			20 23	20 40			20 35			21 10			
City Thameslink 3	d			19 39			19 57			20 13		20 09			20 27	20 43			20 39			21 13			
London Blackfriars 3	d			19 42			20 00			20 16		20 12			20 30	20 46			20 42			21 16			
Elephant & Castle	d			19 46			20 03			20 19		20 16			20 33	20 49			20 46			21 19			
Loughborough Jn	d						20 07			20 23					20 37	20 53						21 23			
Herne Hill 4	d					20 04	20 11		20 19	20 27				20 34	20 41	20 57					21 04	21 27			
West Dulwich	d					20 06			20 21					20 36							21 06				
Sydenham Hill	d					20 08			20 23					20 38							21 08				
Penge East	d					20 11			20 26					20 41							21 11				
Kent House 4	d					20 13			20 28					20 43							21 13				
Beckenham Junction 4	d					20 15			20 30					20 45							21 15				
Denmark Hill 4	d			19 52								20 22							20 52						
Peckham Rye 4	d			19 55								20 25							20 55						
Nunhead 4	d			19 57								20 27							20 57						
Lewisham 4	a																								
Crofton Park	d			20 00								20 30							21 00						
Catford	d			20 03								20 33							21 03						
Bellingham	d			20 05								20 35							21 05						
Beckenham Hill	d			20 07								20 37							21 07						
Ravensbourne	d			20 09								20 39							21 09						
Shortlands 4	d			20 11		20 18			20 33			20 41		20 48					21 11		21 18				
Bromley South 4	d	20 09		20 14	20 19	20 21		20 23	20 36		20 39	20 44		20 51			20 53	21 09	21 14	21 19	21 21			21 23	21 39
Bickley 4	d			20 17		20 24			20 39			20 47		20 54					21 17		21 24				
Petts Wood 4	d					20 29			20 44					20 59							21 29				
Orpington 4	d					20a32			20a47					21a02							21a32				
St Mary Cray	d			20 21	20 25							20 51					21 00		21 21	21 25				21 30	
Swanley 4	d			20 26	20 29			20 33				20 56					21 04		21 26	21 29				21 34	
Eynsford	d			20 30								21 00							21 30						
Shoreham (Kent)	d			20 34								21 04							21 34						
Otford 4	d			20 37				20 41				21 07					21 12		21 37					21 42	
Bat & Ball	d			20 40								21 10							21 40						
Sevenoaks 4	a			20 43								21 13							21 43						

		FC	SE	FC	SE ■	SE	SE	FC		SE ■	SE ■	SE	SE	SE ■	SE	SE	SE ■	SE ■		SE	SE	SE ■	SE	SE	
London Victoria 15	d		21 25		21 52	21 43	21 55			22 07	22 22	22 13	22 25	22 52	22 43	22 55	23 07	23 22		23 13	23 25	23 52	23 43	23 55	
Brixton	d		21 32				22 02						22 32			23 02					23 32			00 02	
Kentish Town	d	20 56		21 30				22 00																	
St Pancras International 15	d	21 00		21 36				22 06																	
Farringdon	d	21 05		21 40				22 10																	
City Thameslink 3	d	21 09		21 43				22 13																	
London Blackfriars 3	d	21 12		21 46				22 16																	
Elephant & Castle	d	21 16		21 49				22 19																	
Loughborough Jn	d			21 53				22 23																	
Herne Hill 4	d		21 34	21 57			22 04	22 27					22 34			23 04					23 34			00 04	
West Dulwich	d		21 36				22 06						22 36			23 06					23 36			00 06	
Sydenham Hill	d		21 38				22 08						22 38			23 08					23 38			00 08	
Penge East	d		21 41				22 11						22 41			23 11					23 41			00 11	
Kent House 4	d		21 43				22 13						22 43			23 13					23 43			00 13	
Beckenham Junction 4	d		21 45				22 15						22 45			23 15					23 45			00 15	
Denmark Hill 4	d	21 22				21 52						22 22			22 52					23 22			23 52		
Peckham Rye 4	d	21 25				21 55						22 25			22 55					23 25			23 55		
Nunhead 4	d	21 27				21 57						22 27			22 57					23 27			23 57		
Lewisham 4	a																								
Crofton Park	d	21 30				22 00						22 30			23 00					23 30			23 59		
Catford	d	21 33				22 03						22 33			23 03					23 33			00 03		
Bellingham	d	21 35				22 05						22 35			23 05					23 35			00 05		
Beckenham Hill	d	21 37				22 07						22 37			23 07					23 37			00 07		
Ravensbourne	d	21 39				22 09						22 39			23 09					23 39			00 09		
Shortlands 4	d	21 41	21 48			22 11	22 18					22 41	22 48		23 11	23 18				23 41	23 48		00 11	00 18	
Bromley South 4	d	21 44	21 51		22 09	22 14	22 21			22 23	22 39	22 44	22 51	23 09	23 14	23 21	23 23	23 39		23 44	23 51	00 09	00 14	00 21	
Bickley 4	d	21 47	21 54			22 17	22 24					22 47	22 54		23 17	23 24				23 47	23 54		00 17	00 24	
Petts Wood 4	d		21 59				22 29						22 59		23 21	23 29				23 54	23 59		00 21	00 29	
Orpington 4	d		22a02				22a32						23a02		23a25	23a32				23a57	00a02		00a25	00a32	
St Mary Cray	d	21 51			22 15	22 21				22 30		22 51		23 15			23 30					00 15			
Swanley 4	d	21 56			22 19	22 26				22 34		22 56		23 19			23 34					00 19			
Eynsford	d	22 00				22 30						23 00													
Shoreham (Kent)	d	22 04				22 34						23 04													
Otford 4	d	22 07				22 37				22 42		23 07					23 42								
Bat & Ball	d	22 10				22 40						23 10													
Sevenoaks 4	a	22 13				22 43						23 13													

Table 195

Saturdays

London - Catford, Beckenham Junction, Bromley South, Orpington, Otford and Sevenoaks

		SE ■	SE	SE	SE ■	SE	SE ■	SE	FC (bus)	SE ■	SE ■	SE	SE	FC (bus)	SE	SE ■	SE	FC (bus)	SE ■	SE		SE ■	SE	SE	FC (bus)
London Victoria 15	d	23p52	23p43	23p55	00 07	00 35	05 22	05 55		06 07	06 22	06 13	06 25		06 43	06 58	06 55		07 07	07 10		07 22	07 13	07 25	
Brixton	d			00 02				06 02					06 32				07 02			07 17				07 32	
Kentish Town	d																								
St Pancras International 15	d																								
Farringdon	d																								
City Thameslink 3	d																								
London Blackfriars 3	d								06 00					06 16				06 46							07 16
Elephant & Castle	d								06 08					06 24				06 54							07 24
Loughborough Jn	d													06 36				07 06							07 36
Herne Hill 4	d			00 04		00 43		06 04	06 16				06 34	06 44			07 04	07 14		07 19				07 34	07 44
West Dulwich	d			00 06				06 06					06 36				07 06			07 21				07 36	
Sydenham Hill	d			00 08				06 08					06 38				07 08			07 23				07 38	
Penge East	d			00 11		00 48		06 11					06 41				07 11			07 26				07 41	
Kent House 4	d			00 13				06 13					06 43				07 13			07 28				07 43	
Beckenham Junction 4	d			00 15		00 50		06 15					06 45				07 15			07 30				07 45	
Denmark Hill 4	d		23p52									06 22			06 52								07 22		
Peckham Rye 4	d		23p55									06 25			06 55								07 25		
Nunhead 4	d		23p57									06 27			06 57								07 27		
Lewisham 4	a																								
Crofton Park	d		23p59									06 30			07 00								07 30		
Catford	d		00 03									06 33			07 03								07 33		
Bellingham	d		00 05									06 35			07 05								07 35		
Beckenham Hill	d		00 07									06 37			07 07								07 37		
Ravensbourne	d		00 09									06 39			07 09								07 39		
Shortlands 4	d		00 11	00 18				06 18				06 41	06 48		07 11		07 18			07 33			07 41	07 48	
Bromley South 4	d	00 09	00 14	00 21	00 25	00 55	05 39	06 21		06 23	06 39	06 44	06 51		07 14	07 19	07 21		07 23	07 36		07 39	07 44	07 51	
Bickley 4	d		00 17	00 24				06 24				06 47	06 54		07 17		07 24			07 39			07 47	07 54	
Petts Wood 4	d		00 21	00 29				06 29					06 59				07 29			07 44				07 59	
Orpington 4	d		00a25	00a32				06a32					07a02				07a32			07a47				08a02	
St Mary Cray	d	00 15			00 31	01 01	05 45			06 30	06 45	06 51			07 21	07 25			07 30				07 51		
Swanley 4	d	00 19			00 36	01 05	05 49			06 34	06 49	06 56			07 26	07 29			07 34				07 56		
Eynsford	d				00 40							07 00			07 30								08 00		
Shoreham (Kent)	d				00 44							07 04			07 34								08 04		
Otford 4	d				00 47					06 42		07 07			07 37				07 42				08 07		
Bat & Ball	d											07 10			07 40								08 10		
Sevenoaks 4	a											07 13			07 43								08 13		

		SE ■	SE	SE	SE ■	SE		SE ■	SE	FC (bus)	SE ■	SE	SE	SE ■	SE	SE		FC (bus)	SE ■	SE	SE	SE ■	SE	SE ■	SE
London Victoria 15	d	07 37	07 39	07 40	07 52	07 43		07 58	07 55		08 07	08 09	08 10	08 22	08 13	08 25			08 37	08 39	08 40	08 52	08 43	08 58	08 55
Brixton	d			07 47					08 02				08 17			08 32					08 47				09 02
Kentish Town	d																								
St Pancras International 15	d																								
Farringdon	d																								
City Thameslink 3	d																								
London Blackfriars 3	d									07 46								08 16							
Elephant & Castle	d									07 54								08 24							
Loughborough Jn	d									08 06								08 36							
Herne Hill 4	d			07 49					08 04	08 14			08 19			08 34		08 44			08 49				09 04
West Dulwich	d			07 51					08 06				08 21			08 36					08 51				09 06
Sydenham Hill	d			07 53					08 08				08 23			08 38					08 53				09 08
Penge East	d			07 56					08 11				08 26			08 41					08 56				09 11
Kent House 4	d			07 58					08 13				08 28			08 43					08 58				09 13
Beckenham Junction 4	d			08 00					08 15				08 30			08 45					09 00				09 15
Denmark Hill 4	d		07 48			07 52						08 18			08 22					08 48			08 52		
Peckham Rye 4	d		07 51			07 55						08 21			08 25					08 51			08 55		
Nunhead 4	d		07 53			07 57						08 23			08 27					08 53			08 57		
Lewisham 4	a		08 02									08 31								09 01					
Crofton Park	d					08 00									08 30								09 00		
Catford	d					08 03									08 33								09 03		
Bellingham	d					08 05									08 35								09 05		
Beckenham Hill	d					08 07									08 37								09 07		
Ravensbourne	d					08 09									08 39								09 09		
Shortlands 4	d			08 03		08 11			08 18				08 33		08 41	08 48					09 03		09 11		09 18
Bromley South 4	d	07 53		08 06	08 09	08 14		08 19	08 21		08 23		08 36	08 39	08 44	08 51			08 53		09 06	09 09	09 14	09 19	09 21
Bickley 4	d			08 09		08 17			08 24				08 39		08 47	08 54					09 09		09 17		09 24
Petts Wood 4	d			08 14					08 29				08 44			08 59					09 14				09 29
Orpington 4	d			08a17					08a32				08a47			09a02					09a17				09a32
St Mary Cray	d	08 00				08 21		08 25							08 51				09 00				09 21	09 25	
Swanley 4	d	08 04				08 26		08 29			08 33				08 56				09 04				09 26	09 29	
Eynsford	d					08 30									09 00								09 30		
Shoreham (Kent)	d					08 34									09 04								09 34		
Otford 4	d	08 12				08 37					08 41				09 07				09 12				09 37		
Bat & Ball	d					08 40									09 10								09 40		
Sevenoaks 4	a					08 43									09 13								09 43		

Table 195

London - Catford, Beckenham Junction, Bromley South, Orpington, Otford and Sevenoaks

	FC		SE ■	SE	SE	SE ■	SE	SE	FC	SE ■	SE		SE	SE ■	SE	SE ■	SE	FC	SE ■	SE	SE		SE ■	SE
London Victoria d			09 07	09 09	09 10	09 22	09 13	09 25		09 37	09 39		09 40	09 52	09 43	09 58	09 55		10 07	10 09	10 10		10 22	10 13
Brixton d					09 17			09 32					09 47				10 02				10 17			
Kentish Town d																								
St Pancras International d																								
Farringdon d																								
City Thameslink d																								
London Blackfriars d	08 46								09 16									09 46						
Elephant & Castle d	08 54								09 24									09 54						
Loughborough Jn d	09 06								09 36									10 06						
Herne Hill d	09 14				09 19			09 34	09 44				09 49				10 04	10 14			10 19			
West Dulwich d					09 21			09 36					09 51				10 06				10 21			
Sydenham Hill d					09 23			09 38					09 53				10 08				10 23			
Penge East d					09 26			09 41					09 56				10 11				10 26			
Kent House d					09 28			09 43					09 58				10 13				10 28			
Beckenham Junction d					09 30			09 45					10 00				10 15				10 30			
Denmark Hill d				09 18			09 22				09 48				09 52					10 18				10 22
Peckham Rye d				09 21			09 25				09 51				09 55					10 21				10 25
Nunhead d				09 23			09 27				09 53				09 57					10 23				10 27
Lewisham a				09 31							10 01									10 32				
Crofton Park d							09 30								10 00									10 30
Catford d							09 33								10 03									10 33
Bellingham d							09 35								10 05									10 35
Beckenham Hill d							09 37								10 07									10 37
Ravensbourne d							09 39								10 09									10 39
Shortlands d					09 33		09 41	09 48					10 03		10 11		10 18				10 33			10 41
Bromley South d			09 23		09 36	09 39	09 44	09 51		09 53			10 06	10 09	10 14	10 19	10 21		10 23		10 36		10 39	10 44
Bickley d					09 39		09 47	09 54					10 09		10 17		10 24				10 39			10 47
Petts Wood d					09 44			09 59					10 14				10 29				10 44			
Orpington d					09a47			10a02					10a17				10a32				10a47			
St Mary Cray d							09 51			10 00					10 21	10 25								10 51
Swanley d			09 33				09 56			10 04					10 26	10 29			10 33					10 56
Eynsford d							10 00								10 30									11 00
Shoreham (Kent) d							10 04								10 34									11 04
Otford d			09 41				10 07			10 12					10 37				10 41					11 07
Bat & Ball d							10 10								10 40									11 10
Sevenoaks a							10 13								10 43									11 13

	SE	FC	SE ■	SE	SE	SE ■	SE		SE ■	SE	FC	SE ■	SE	SE	SE ■	SE	SE		FC	SE ■	SE	SE	SE ■	SE
London Victoria d	10 25		10 37	10 39	10 40	10 52	10 43		10 58	10 55		11 07	11 09	11 10	11 22	11 13	11 25			11 37	11 39	11 40	11 52	11 43
Brixton d	10 32				10 47					11 02				11 17			11 32					11 47		
Kentish Town d																								
St Pancras International d																								
Farringdon d																								
City Thameslink d																								
London Blackfriars d		10 16									10 46								11 16					
Elephant & Castle d		10 24									10 54								11 24					
Loughborough Jn d		10 36									11 06								11 36					
Herne Hill d	10 34	10 44			10 49					11 04	11 14			11 19			11 34		11 44			11 49		
West Dulwich d	10 36				10 51					11 06				11 21			11 36					11 51		
Sydenham Hill d	10 38				10 53					11 08				11 23			11 38					11 53		
Penge East d	10 41				10 56					11 11				11 26			11 41					11 56		
Kent House d	10 43				10 58					11 13				11 28			11 43					11 58		
Beckenham Junction d	10 45				11 00					11 15				11 30			11 45					12 00		
Denmark Hill d				10 48			10 52						11 18			11 22					11 48			11 52
Peckham Rye d				10 51			10 55						11 21			11 25					11 51			11 55
Nunhead d				10 53			10 57						11 23			11 27					11 53			11 57
Lewisham a				11 01									11 31								12 01			
Crofton Park d							11 00									11 30								12 00
Catford d							11 03									11 33								12 03
Bellingham d							11 05									11 35								12 05
Beckenham Hill d							11 07									11 37								12 07
Ravensbourne d							11 09									11 39								12 09
Shortlands d	10 48				11 03		11 11			11 18				11 33		11 41	11 48					12 03		12 11
Bromley South d	10 51		10 53		11 06	11 09	11 14		11 19	11 21		11 23		11 36	11 39	11 44	11 51			11 53		12 06	12 09	12 14
Bickley d	10 54				11 09		11 17			11 24				11 39		11 47	11 54					12 09		12 17
Petts Wood d	10 59				11 14					11 29				11 44			11 59					12 14		
Orpington d	11a02				11a17					11a32				11a47			12a02					12a17		
St Mary Cray d			11 00				11 21		11 25							11 51				12 00				12 21
Swanley d			11 04				11 26		11 29			11 33				11 56				12 04				12 26
Eynsford d							11 30									12 00								12 30
Shoreham (Kent) d							11 34									12 04								12 34
Otford d			11 12				11 37					11 41				12 07				12 12				12 37
Bat & Ball d							11 40									12 10								12 40
Sevenoaks a							11 43									12 13								12 43

Table 195

London - Catford, Beckenham Junction, Bromley South, Orpington, Otford and Sevenoaks

	SE ■	SE	FC		SE ■	SE	SE	SE ■	SE	SE	FC	SE ■	SE		SE	SE ■	SE	SE ■	SE	FC	SE ■	SE	SE	
London Victoria d	11 58	11 55			12 07	12 09	12 10	12 22	12 13	12 25		12 37	12 39		12 40	12 52	12 43	12 58	12 55		13 07	13 09	13 10	
Brixton d		12 02					12 17			12 32					12 47				13 02				13 17	
Kentish Town d																								
St Pancras International d																								
Farringdon d																								
City Thameslink d																								
London Blackfriars d			11 46								12 16									12 46				
Elephant & Castle d			11 54								12 24									12 54				
Loughborough Jn d			12 06								12 36									13 06				
Herne Hill d		12 04	12 14				12 19			12 34	12 44				12 49				13 04	13 14			13 19	
West Dulwich d		12 06					12 21			12 36					12 51				13 06				13 21	
Sydenham Hill d		12 08					12 23			12 38					12 53				13 08				13 23	
Penge East d		12 11					12 26			12 41					12 56				13 11				13 26	
Kent House d		12 13					12 28			12 43					12 58				13 13				13 28	
Beckenham Junction d		12 15					12 30			12 45					13 00				13 15				13 30	
Denmark Hill d						12 18			12 22				12 48				12 52					13 18		
Peckham Rye d						12 21			12 25				12 51				12 55					13 21		
Nunhead d						12 23			12 27				12 53				12 57					13 23		
Lewisham a						12 31							13 01									13 31		
Crofton Park d									12 30								13 00							
Catford d									12 33								13 03							
Bellingham d									12 35								13 05							
Beckenham Hill d									12 37								13 07							
Ravensbourne d									12 39								13 09							
Shortlands d		12 18					12 33		12 41	12 48					13 03		13 11		13 18				13 33	
Bromley South d	12 19	12 21			12 23		12 36	12 39	12 44	12 51		12 53			13 06	13 09	13 14	13 19	13 21		13 23		13 36	
Bickley d		12 24					12 39		12 47	12 54					13 09		13 17		13 24				13 39	
Petts Wood d		12 29					12 44			12 59					13 14				13 29				13 44	
Orpington d		12a32					12a47			13a02					13a17				13a32				13a47	
St Mary Cray d	12 25								12 51			13 00					13 21	13 25						
Swanley d	12 29				12 33				12 56			13 04					13 26	13 29			13 33			
Eynsford d									13 00								13 30							
Shoreham (Kent) d									13 04								13 34							
Otford d					12 41				13 07			13 12					13 37				13 41			
Bat & Ball d									13 10								13 40							
Sevenoaks a									13 13								13 43							

	SE ■	SE	SE	FC	SE ■	SE	SE	SE ■	SE		SE ■	SE	FC	SE ■	SE	SE	SE ■	SE	SE		FC	SE ■	SE	SE
London Victoria d	13 22	13 13	13 25		13 37	13 39	13 40	13 52	13 43		13 58	13 55		14 07	14 09	14 10	14 22	14 13	14 25			14 37	14 39	14 40
Brixton d			13 32				13 47					14 02				14 17			14 32					14 47
Kentish Town d																								
St Pancras International d																								
Farringdon d																								
City Thameslink d																								
London Blackfriars d				13 16									13 46								14 16			
Elephant & Castle d				13 24									13 54								14 24			
Loughborough Jn d				13 36									14 06								14 36			
Herne Hill d			13 34	13 44			13 49					14 04	14 14			14 19			14 34		14 44			14 49
West Dulwich d			13 36				13 51					14 06				14 21			14 36					14 51
Sydenham Hill d			13 38				13 53					14 08				14 23			14 38					14 53
Penge East d			13 41				13 56					14 11				14 26			14 41					14 56
Kent House d			13 43				13 58					14 13				14 28			14 43					14 58
Beckenham Junction d			13 45				14 00					14 15				14 30			14 45					15 00
Denmark Hill d		13 22				13 48			13 52						14 18			14 22					14 48	
Peckham Rye d		13 25				13 51			13 55						14 21			14 25					14 51	
Nunhead d		13 27				13 53			13 57						14 23			14 27					14 53	
Lewisham a						14 01									14 31								15 01	
Crofton Park d		13 30							14 00									14 30						
Catford d		13 33							14 03									14 33						
Bellingham d		13 35							14 05									14 35						
Beckenham Hill d		13 37							14 07									14 37						
Ravensbourne d		13 39							14 09									14 39						
Shortlands d		13 41	13 48				14 03		14 11			14 18				14 33		14 41	14 48					15 03
Bromley South d	13 39	13 44	13 51		13 53		14 06	14 09	14 14		14 19	14 21		14 23		14 36	14 39	14 44	14 51			14 53		15 06
Bickley d		13 47	13 54				14 09		14 17			14 24				14 39		14 47	14 54					15 09
Petts Wood d			13 59				14 14					14 29				14 44			14 59					15 14
Orpington d			14a02				14a17					14a32				14a47			15a02					15a17
St Mary Cray d		13 51			14 00				14 21		14 25							14 51				15 00		
Swanley d		13 56			14 04				14 26		14 29			14 33				14 56				15 04		
Eynsford d		14 00							14 30									15 00						
Shoreham (Kent) d		14 04							14 34									15 04						
Otford d		14 07			14 12				14 37					14 41				15 07				15 12		
Bat & Ball d		14 10							14 40									15 10						
Sevenoaks a		14 13							14 43									15 13						

Table 195

Saturdays

London - Catford, Beckenham Junction, Bromley South, Orpington, Otford and Sevenoaks

		SE 1	SE	SE 1	SE	FC		SE 1	SE	SE	SE 1	SE	SE	FC	SE 1	SE		SE	SE 1	SE	SE 1	SE	FC	SE 1	SE
London Victoria 15 ⊖	d	14 52	14 43	14 58	14 55			15 07	15 09	15 10	15 22	15 13	15 25		15 37	15 39		15 40	15 52	15 43	15 58	15 55		16 07	16 09
Brixton ⊖	d				15 02					15 17			15 32					15 47				16 02			
Kentish Town ⊖	d																								
St Pancras International 15 ⊖	d																								
Farringdon ⊖	d																								
City Thameslink 3	d																								
London Blackfriars 3 ⊖	d					14 46								15 16									15 46		
Elephant & Castle ⊖	d					14 54								15 24									15 54		
Loughborough Jn	d					15 06								15 36									16 06		
Herne Hill 4	d				15 04	15 14				15 19			15 34	15 44				15 49				16 04	16 14		
West Dulwich	d				15 06					15 21			15 36					15 51				16 06			
Sydenham Hill	d				15 08					15 23			15 38					15 53				16 08			
Penge East	d				15 11					15 26			15 41					15 56				16 11			
Kent House 4	d				15 13					15 28			15 43					15 58				16 13			
Beckenham Junction 4	d				15 15					15 30			15 45					16 00				16 15			
Denmark Hill 4	d		14 52						15 18			15 22				15 48				15 52					16 18
Peckham Rye 4	d		14 55						15 21			15 25				15 51				15 55					16 21
Nunhead 4	d		14 57						15 23			15 27				15 53				15 57					16 23
Lewisham 4	a								15 31							16 01									16 31
Crofton Park	d		15 00									15 30								16 00					
Catford	d		15 03									15 33								16 03					
Bellingham	d		15 05									15 35								16 05					
Beckenham Hill	d		15 07									15 37								16 07					
Ravensbourne	d		15 09									15 39								16 09					
Shortlands 4	d		15 11		15 18					15 33		15 41	15 48					16 03		16 11		16 18			
Bromley South 4	d	15 09	15 14	15 19	15 21			15 23		15 36	15 39	15 44	15 51		15 53			16 06	16 09	16 14	16 19	16 21		16 23	
Bickley 4	d		15 17		15 24					15 39		15 47	15 54					16 09		16 17		16 24			
Petts Wood 4	d				15 29					15 44			15 59					16 14				16 29			
Orpington 4	d				15a32					15a47			16a02					16a17				16a32			
St Mary Cray	d		15 21	15 25								15 51			16 00					16 21	16 25				
Swanley 4	d		15 26	15 29				15 33				15 56			16 04					16 26	16 29			16 33	
Eynsford	d		15 30									16 00								16 30					
Shoreham (Kent)	d		15 34									16 04								16 34					
Otford 4	d		15 37					15 41				16 07			16 12					16 37				16 41	
Bat & Ball	d		15 40									16 10								16 40					
Sevenoaks 4	a		15 43									16 13								16 43					

		SE		SE 1	SE	SE	FC	SE 1	SE	SE	SE 1	SE		SE 1	SE	FC	SE 1	SE	SE	SE 1	SE	SE		FC	SE 1
London Victoria 15 ⊖	d	16 10		16 22	16 13	16 25		16 37	16 39	16 40	16 52	16 43		16 58	16 55		17 07	17 09	17 10	17 22	17 13	17 25			17 37
Brixton ⊖	d	16 17				16 32				16 47					17 02				17 17			17 32			
Kentish Town ⊖	d																								
St Pancras International 15 ⊖	d																								
Farringdon ⊖	d																								
City Thameslink 3	d																								
London Blackfriars 3 ⊖	d						16 16									16 46								17 16	
Elephant & Castle ⊖	d						16 24									16 54								17 24	
Loughborough Jn	d						16 36									17 06								17 36	
Herne Hill 4	d	16 19				16 34	16 44			16 49					17 04	17 14			17 19			17 34		17 44	
West Dulwich	d	16 21				16 36				16 51					17 06				17 21			17 36			
Sydenham Hill	d	16 23				16 38				16 53					17 08				17 23			17 38			
Penge East	d	16 26				16 41				16 56					17 11				17 26			17 41			
Kent House 4	d	16 28				16 43				16 58					17 13				17 28			17 43			
Beckenham Junction 4	d	16 30				16 45				17 00					17 15				17 30			17 45			
Denmark Hill 4	d				16 22				16 48			16 52						17 18			17 22				
Peckham Rye 4	d				16 25				16 51			16 55						17 21			17 25				
Nunhead 4	d				16 27				16 53			16 57						17 23			17 27				
Lewisham 4	a								17 01									17 31							
Crofton Park	d				16 30							17 00									17 30				
Catford	d				16 33							17 03									17 33				
Bellingham	d				16 35							17 05									17 35				
Beckenham Hill	d				16 37							17 07									17 37				
Ravensbourne	d				16 39							17 09									17 39				
Shortlands 4	d	16 33			16 41	16 48				17 03		17 11			17 18				17 33		17 41	17 48			
Bromley South 4	d	16 36		16 39	16 44	16 51		16 53		17 06	17 09	17 14		17 19	17 21		17 23		17 36	17 39	17 44	17 51			17 53
Bickley 4	d	16 39			16 47	16 54				17 09		17 17			17 24				17 39		17 47	17 54			
Petts Wood 4	d	16 44				16 59				17 14					17 29				17 44			17 59			
Orpington 4	d	16a47				17a02				17a17					17a32				17a47			18a02			
St Mary Cray	d				16 51			17 00				17 21		17 25							17 51				18 00
Swanley 4	d				16 56			17 04				17 26		17 29			17 33				17 56				18 04
Eynsford	d				17 00							17 30									18 00				
Shoreham (Kent)	d				17 04							17 34									18 04				
Otford 4	d				17 07			17 12				17 37					17 41				18 07				18 12
Bat & Ball	d				17 10							17 40									18 10				
Sevenoaks 4	a				17 13							17 43									18 13				

Table 195

Saturdays

London - Catford, Beckenham Junction, Bromley South, Orpington, Otford and Sevenoaks

		SE	SE	SE 1	SE	SE 1	SE	FC		SE 1	SE	SE	SE 1	SE	SE	FC	SE 1	SE		SE	SE 1	SE	SE 1	SE	FC
London Victoria 15 ⊖	d	17 39	17 40	17 52	17 43	17 58	17 55			18 07	18 09	18 10	18 22	18 13	18 25		18 37	18 39		18 40	18 52	18 43	18 58	18 55	
Brixton ⊖	d		17 47				18 02					18 17			18 32					18 47				19 02	
Kentish Town ⊖	d																								
St Pancras International 15 ⊖	d																								
Farringdon ⊖	d																								
City Thameslink 3	d																								
London Blackfriars 3 ⊖	d							17 46								18 16									18 46
Elephant & Castle ⊖	d							17 54								18 24									18 54
Loughborough Jn	d							18 06								18 36									19 06
Herne Hill 4	d		17 49				18 04	18 14				18 19			18 34	18 44				18 49				19 04	19 14
West Dulwich	d		17 51				18 06					18 21			18 36					18 51				19 06	
Sydenham Hill	d		17 53				18 08					18 23			18 38					18 53				19 08	
Penge East	d		17 56				18 11					18 26			18 41					18 56				19 11	
Kent House 4	d		17 58				18 13					18 28			18 43					18 58				19 13	
Beckenham Junction 4	d		18 00				18 15					18 30			18 45					19 00				19 15	
Denmark Hill 4	d	17 48			17 52						18 18			18 22				18 48				18 52			
Peckham Rye 4	d	17 51			17 55						18 21			18 25				18 51				18 55			
Nunhead 4	d	17 53			17 57						18 23			18 27				18 53				18 57			
Lewisham 4	a	18 01									18 31							19 02							
Crofton Park	d				18 00									18 30								19 00			
Catford	d				18 03									18 33								19 03			
Bellingham	d				18 05									18 35								19 05			
Beckenham Hill	d				18 07									18 37								19 07			
Ravensbourne	d				18 09									18 39								19 09			
Shortlands 4	d		18 03		18 11		18 18					18 33		18 41	18 48					19 03		19 11		19 18	
Bromley South 4	d		18 06	18 09	18 14	18 19	18 21			18 23		18 36	18 39	18 44	18 51		18 53			19 06	19 09	19 14	19 19	19 21	
Bickley 4	d		18 09		18 17		18 24					18 39		18 47	18 54					19 09		19 17		19 24	
Petts Wood 4	d		18 14				18 29					18 44			18 59					19 14				19 29	
Orpington 4	d		18a17				18a32					18a47			19a02					19a17				19a32	
St Mary Cray	d				18 21	18 25								18 51			19 00					19 21	19 25		
Swanley 4	d				18 26	18 29				18 33				18 56			19 04					19 26	19 29		
Eynsford	d				18 30									19 00								19 30			
Shoreham (Kent)	d				18 34									19 04								19 34			
Otford 4	d				18 37					18 41				19 07			19 12					19 37			
Bat & Ball	d				18 40									19 10								19 40			
Sevenoaks 4	a				18 43									19 13								19 43			

		SE 1	SE	SE		SE 1	SE	SE	FC	SE 1	SE	SE	SE 1	SE		SE 1	SE	FC	SE 1	SE	SE 1	SE	SE	FC	
London Victoria 15 ⊖	d	19 07	19 09	19 10		19 22	19 13	19 25		19 37	19 39	19 40	19 52	19 43		19 58	19 55		20 07	20 10	20 22	20 13	20 25		
Brixton ⊖	d			19 17				19 32				19 47					20 02			20 17			20 32		
Kentish Town ⊖	d																								
St Pancras International 15 ⊖	d																								
Farringdon ⊖	d																								
City Thameslink 3	d																								
London Blackfriars 3 ⊖	d								19 16									19 46						20 16	
Elephant & Castle ⊖	d								19 24									19 54						20 24	
Loughborough Jn	d								19 36									20 06						20 36	
Herne Hill 4	d			19 19				19 34	19 44			19 49					20 04	20 14		20 19			20 34	20 44	
West Dulwich	d			19 21				19 36				19 51					20 06			20 21			20 36		
Sydenham Hill	d			19 23				19 38				19 53					20 08			20 23			20 38		
Penge East	d			19 26				19 41				19 56					20 11			20 26			20 41		
Kent House 4	d			19 28				19 43				19 58					20 13			20 28			20 43		
Beckenham Junction 4	d			19 30				19 45				20 00					20 15			20 30			20 45		
Denmark Hill 4	d		19 18				19 22				19 48			19 52								20 22			
Peckham Rye 4	d		19 21				19 25				19 51			19 55								20 25			
Nunhead 4	d		19 23				19 27				19 53			19 57								20 27			
Lewisham 4	a		19 31								20 01														
Crofton Park	d						19 30							20 00								20 30			
Catford	d						19 33							20 03								20 33			
Bellingham	d						19 35							20 05								20 35			
Beckenham Hill	d						19 37							20 07								20 37			
Ravensbourne	d						19 39							20 09								20 39			
Shortlands 4	d			19 33			19 41	19 48				20 03		20 11			20 18			20 33		20 41	20 48		
Bromley South 4	d	19 23		19 36		19 39	19 44	19 51		19 53		20 06	20 09	20 14		20 19	20 21		20 23	20 36	20 39	20 44	20 51		
Bickley 4	d			19 39			19 47	19 54				20 09		20 17			20 24			20 39		20 47	20 54		
Petts Wood 4	d			19 44				19 59				20 14					20 29			20 44			20 59		
Orpington 4	d			19a48				20a02				20a18					20a32			20a47			21a02		
St Mary Cray	d						19 51			20 00				20 21		20 25			20 30			20 51			
Swanley 4	d	19 33					19 56			20 04				20 26		20 29			20 34			20 56			
Eynsford	d						20 00							20 30								21 00			
Shoreham (Kent)	d						20 04							20 34								21 04			
Otford 4	d	19 41					20 07			20 12				20 37					20 42			21 07			
Bat & Ball	d						20 10							20 40								21 10			
Sevenoaks 4	a						20 13							20 43								21 13			

Table 195

Saturdays

London - Catford, Beckenham Junction, Bromley South, Orpington, Otford and Sevenoaks

		SE 1	SE	SE	FC	SE 1	SE 1	SE	SE	FC	SE 1	SE	SE	FC	SE 1	SE 1	SE	SE	FC	SE 1	SE	SE	FC
London Victoria 15 ⊖	d	20 52	20 43	20 55		21 07	21 22	21 13	21 25		21 52	21 43	21 55		22 07	22 22	22 13	22 25		22 52	22 43	22 55	
Brixton ⊖	d			21 02					21 32				22 02					22 32				23 02	
Kentish Town ⊖	d																						
St Pancras International 15 ⊖	d																						
Farringdon ⊖	d																						
City Thameslink 3	d																						
London Blackfriars 3 ⊖	d				20 46					21 16				21 46					22 16				22 46
Elephant & Castle ⊖	d				20 54					21 24				21 54					22 24				22 54
Loughborough Jn	d				21 06					21 36				22 06					22 36				23 06
Herne Hill 4	d			21 04	21 14				21 34	21 44			22 04	22 14				22 34	22 44			23 04	23 14
West Dulwich	d			21 06					21 36				22 06					22 36				23 06	
Sydenham Hill	d			21 08					21 38				22 08					22 38				23 08	
Penge East	d			21 11					21 41				22 11					22 41				23 11	
Kent House 4	d			21 13					21 43				22 13					22 43				23 13	
Beckenham Junction 4	d			21 15					21 45				22 15					22 45				23 15	
Denmark Hill 4	d		20 52					21 22				21 52					22 22				22 52		
Peckham Rye 4	d		20 55					21 25				21 55					22 25				22 55		
Nunhead 4	d		20 57					21 27				21 57					22 27				22 57		
Lewisham 4	a																						
Crofton Park	d		21 00					21 30				22 00					22 30				23 00		
Catford	d		21 03					21 33				22 03					22 33				23 03		
Bellingham	d		21 05					21 35				22 05					22 35				23 05		
Beckenham Hill	d		21 07					21 37				22 07					22 37				23 07		
Ravensbourne	d		21 09					21 39				22 09					22 39				23 09		
Shortlands 4	d		21 11	21 18				21 41	21 48			22 11	22 18				22 41	22 48			23 11	23 18	
Bromley South 4	d	21 09	21 14	21 21		21 23	21 39	21 44	21 51		22 09	22 14	22 21		22 23	22 39	22 44	22 51		23 09	23 14	23 21	
Bickley 4	d		21 17	21 24				21 47	21 54			22 17	22 24				22 47	22 54			23 17	23 24	
Petts Wood 4	d			21 29					21 59				22 29					22 59			23 22	23 29	
Orpington 4	d			21a32					22a02				22a32					23a02			23a25	23a32	
St Mary Cray	d	21 15	21 21			21 30		21 51			22 15	22 21			22 30		22 51			23 15			
Swanley 4	d	21 19	21 26			21 34		21 56			22 19	22 26			22 34		22 56			23 19			
Eynsford	d		21 30					22 00				22 30					23 00						
Shoreham (Kent)	d		21 34					22 04				22 34					23 04						
Otford 4	d		21 37			21 42		22 07				22 37			22 42		23 07						
Bat & Ball	d		21 40					22 10				22 40					23 10						
Sevenoaks 4	a		21 43					22 13				22 43					23 13						

		SE 1	SE 1	SE	SE	FC	SE 1	SE	SE
London Victoria 15 ⊖	d	23 07	23 22	23 13	23 25		23 52	23 43	23 55
Brixton ⊖	d				23 32				00 02
Kentish Town ⊖	d								
St Pancras International 15 ⊖	d								
Farringdon ⊖	d								
City Thameslink 3	d								
London Blackfriars 3 ⊖	d					23 16			
Elephant & Castle ⊖	d					23 24			
Loughborough Jn	d					23 36			
Herne Hill 4	d				23 34	23 44			00 04
West Dulwich	d				23 36				00 06
Sydenham Hill	d				23 38				00 08
Penge East	d				23 41				00 11
Kent House 4	d				23 43				00 13
Beckenham Junction 4	d				23 45				00 15
Denmark Hill 4	d			23 22				23 52	
Peckham Rye 4	d			23 25				23 55	
Nunhead 4	d			23 27				23 57	
Lewisham 4	a								
Crofton Park	d			23 30				23 59	
Catford	d			23 33				00 03	
Bellingham	d			23 35				00 05	
Beckenham Hill	d			23 37				00 07	
Ravensbourne	d			23 39				00 09	
Shortlands 4	d			23 41	23 48			00 11	00 18
Bromley South 4	d	23 23	23 39	23 44	23 51		00 09	00 14	00 21
Bickley 4	d			23 47	23 54			00 17	00 24
Petts Wood 4	d			23 52	23 59			00 22	00 29
Orpington 4	d			23a55	00a02			00a25	00a32
St Mary Cray	d	23 30					00 15		
Swanley 4	d	23 34					00 19		
Eynsford	d								
Shoreham (Kent)	d								
Otford 4	d	23 42							
Bat & Ball	d								
Sevenoaks 4	a								

Table 195

Sundays

London - Catford, Beckenham Junction, Bromley South, Orpington, Otford and Sevenoaks

		SE 1	SE	SE	SE 1	SE	SE 1	SE 1	SE	SE	SE 1	SE	SE 1	SE	SE 1	SE	SE	FC	SE 1	SE	SE 1	SE	FC
London Victoria 15 ⊖	d	23p52	23p43	23p55	00 07	00 35	07 38	07 45	07 39	07 51	08 05	08 09	08 24	08 21	08 45	08 39	08 51		09 05	09 09	09 24	09 21	
Brixton ⊖	d			00 02						07 58				08 28			08 58					09 28	
Kentish Town ⊖	d																						
St Pancras International 15 ⊖	d																						
Farringdon ⊖	d																						
City Thameslink 3	d																						
London Blackfriars 3 ⊖	d																	08 49					09 19
Elephant & Castle ⊖	d																	08 57					09 27
Loughborough Jn	d																	09 09					09 39
Herne Hill 4	d			00 04		00 43				08 00				08 30			09 00	09 17				09 30	09 47
West Dulwich	d			00 06						08 02				08 32			09 02					09 32	
Sydenham Hill	d			00 08						08 04				08 34			09 04					09 34	
Penge East	d			00 11		00 48				08 07				08 37			09 07					09 37	
Kent House 4	d			00 13						08 09				08 39			09 09					09 39	
Beckenham Junction 4	d			00 15		00 50				08 11				08 41			09 11					09 41	
Denmark Hill 4	d		23p52						07 48			08 18				08 48				09 18			
Peckham Rye 4	d		23p55						07 51			08 21				08 51				09 21			
Nunhead 4	d		23p57						07 53			08 23				08 53				09 23			
Lewisham 4	a																						
Crofton Park	d		23p59						07 56			08 26				08 56				09 26			
Catford	d		00 03						07 59			08 29				08 59				09 29			
Bellingham	d		00 05						08 01			08 31				09 01				09 31			
Beckenham Hill	d		00 07						08 03			08 33				09 03				09 33			
Ravensbourne	d		00 09						08 05			08 35				09 05				09 35			
Shortlands 4	d		00 11	00 18					08 07	08 14		08 37		08 44		09 07	09 14			09 37		09 44	
Bromley South 4	d	00 09	00 14	00 21	00 25	00 55	07 55	08 01	08 10	08 18	08 22	08 40	08 44	08 48	09 01	09 10	09 18		09 22	09 40	09 44	09 48	
Bickley 4	d		00 17	00 24					08 13	08 20		08 43		08 50		09 13	09 20			09 43		09 50	
Petts Wood 4	d		00 22	00 29						08 25				08 55			09 25					09 55	
Orpington 4	d		00a25	00a32						08a28				08a58			09a28					09a58	
St Mary Cray	d	00 15			00 31	01 01	08 01	08 08	08 17			08 47	08 50		09 08	09 17				09 47	09 50		
Swanley 4	d	00 19			00 36	01 05	08 05	08 12	08 22			08 52	08 54		09 12	09 22				09 52	09 54		
Eynsford	d				00 40				08 26			08 56				09 26				09 56			
Shoreham (Kent)	d				00 44				08 30			09 00				09 30				10 00			
Otford 4	d				00 47			08 20	08 33			09 03			09 20	09 33				10 03			
Bat & Ball	d								08 36			09 06				09 36				10 06			
Sevenoaks 4	a								08 39			09 09				09 39				10 09			

		SE 1	SE	SE	FC	SE 1	SE	SE 1	SE	FC	SE 1	SE	SE	FC	SE 1	SE	SE 1	SE	FC	SE 1	SE	SE	FC
London Victoria 15 ⊖	d	09 45	09 39	09 51		10 05	10 09	10 24	10 21		10 45	10 39	10 51		11 05	11 09	11 24	11 21		11 45	11 39	11 51	
Brixton ⊖	d			09 58					10 28				10 58					11 28				11 58	
Kentish Town ⊖	d																						
St Pancras International 15 ⊖	d																						
Farringdon ⊖	d																						
City Thameslink 3	d																						
London Blackfriars 3 ⊖	d				09 49					10 19				10 49					11 19				11 49
Elephant & Castle ⊖	d				09 57					10 27				10 57					11 27				11 57
Loughborough Jn	d				10 09					10 39				11 09					11 39				12 09
Herne Hill 4	d			10 00	10 17				10 30	10 47			11 00	11 17				11 30	11 47			12 00	12 17
West Dulwich	d			10 02					10 32				11 02					11 32				12 02	
Sydenham Hill	d			10 04					10 34				11 04					11 34				12 04	
Penge East	d			10 07					10 37				11 07					11 37				12 07	
Kent House 4	d			10 09					10 39				11 09					11 39				12 09	
Beckenham Junction 4	d			10 11					10 41				11 11					11 41				12 11	
Denmark Hill 4	d		09 48				10 18					10 48				11 18					11 48		
Peckham Rye 4	d		09 51				10 21					10 51				11 21					11 51		
Nunhead 4	d		09 53				10 23					10 53				11 23					11 53		
Lewisham 4	a																						
Crofton Park	d		09 56				10 26					10 56				11 26					11 56		
Catford	d		09 59				10 29					10 59				11 29					11 59		
Bellingham	d		10 01				10 31					11 01				11 31					12 01		
Beckenham Hill	d		10 03				10 33					11 03				11 33					12 03		
Ravensbourne	d		10 05				10 35					11 05				11 35					12 05		
Shortlands 4	d		10 07	10 14			10 37		10 44			11 07	11 14			11 37		11 44			12 07	12 14	
Bromley South 4	d	10 01	10 10	10 18		10 22	10 40	10 44	10 48		11 01	11 10	11 18		11 22	11 40	11 44	11 48		12 01	12 10	12 18	
Bickley 4	d		10 13	10 20			10 43		10 50			11 13	11 20			11 43		11 50			12 13	12 20	
Petts Wood 4	d			10 25					10 55				11 25					11 55				12 25	
Orpington 4	d			10a28					10a58				11a28					11a58				12a28	
St Mary Cray	d	10 08	10 17				10 47	10 50			11 08	11 17				11 47	11 50			12 08	12 17		
Swanley 4	d	10 12	10 22				10 52	10 54			11 12	11 22				11 52	11 54			12 12	12 22		
Eynsford	d		10 26				10 56					11 26				11 56					12 26		
Shoreham (Kent)	d		10 30				11 00					11 30				12 00					12 30		
Otford 4	d	10 20	10 33				11 03				11 20	11 33				12 03				12 20	12 33		
Bat & Ball	d		10 36				11 06					11 36				12 06					12 36		
Sevenoaks 4	a		10 39				11 09					11 39				12 09					12 39		

Table 195

Sundays

London - Catford, Beckenham Junction, Bromley South, Orpington, Otford and Sevenoaks

		SE ■		SE	SE ■	SE	FC	SE ■	SE	SE	FC	SE ■		SE	SE ■	SE	FC	SE ■	SE	SE	FC	SE ■		SE	SE ■
London Victoria	⊖ d	12 05		12 09	12 24	12 21		12 45	12 39	12 51		13 05		13 09	13 24	13 21		13 45	13 39	13 51		14 05		14 09	14 24
Brixton	⊖ d					12 28				12 58						13 28				13 58					
Kentish Town	⊖ d																								
St Pancras International	⊖ d																								
Farringdon	⊖ d																								
City Thameslink	d																								
London Blackfriars	⊖ d						12 19				12 49						13 19				13 49				
Elephant & Castle	⊖ d						12 27				12 57						13 27				13 57				
Loughborough Jn	d						12 39				13 09						13 39				14 09				
Herne Hill	d					12 30	12 47			13 00	13 17					13 30	13 47			14 00	14 17				
West Dulwich	d					12 32				13 02						13 32				14 02					
Sydenham Hill	d					12 34				13 04						13 34				14 04					
Penge East	d					12 37				13 07						13 37				14 07					
Kent House	d					12 39				13 09						13 39				14 09					
Beckenham Junction	d					12 41				13 11						13 41				14 11					
Denmark Hill	d			12 18					12 48					13 18					13 48					14 18	
Peckham Rye	d			12 21					12 51					13 21					13 51					14 21	
Nunhead	d			12 23					12 53					13 23					13 53					14 23	
Lewisham	a																								
Crofton Park	d			12 26					12 56					13 26					13 56					14 26	
Catford	d			12 29					12 59					13 29					13 59					14 29	
Bellingham	d			12 31					13 01					13 31					14 01					14 31	
Beckenham Hill	d			12 33					13 03					13 33					14 03					14 33	
Ravensbourne	d			12 35					13 05					13 35					14 05					14 35	
Shortlands	d			12 37		12 44			13 07	13 14				13 37		13 44			14 07	14 14				14 37	
Bromley South	d	12 22		12 40	12 44	12 48		13 01	13 10	13 18		13 22		13 40	13 44	13 48		14 01	14 10	14 18		14 22		14 40	14 44
Bickley	d			12 43		12 50			13 13	13 20				13 43		13 50			14 13	14 20				14 43	
Petts Wood	d					12 55				13 25						13 55				14 25					
Orpington	d					12a58				13a28						13a58				14a28					
St Mary Cray	d			12 47	12 50			13 08	13 17					13 47	13 50			14 08	14 17					14 47	14 50
Swanley	d			12 52	12 54			13 12	13 22					13 52	13 54			14 12	14 22					14 52	14 54
Eynsford	d			12 56					13 26					13 56					14 26					14 56	
Shoreham (Kent)	d			13 00					13 30					14 00					14 30					15 00	
Otford	d			13 03				13 20	13 33					14 03				14 20	14 33					15 03	
Bat & Ball	d			13 06					13 36					14 06					14 36					15 06	
Sevenoaks	a			13 09					13 39					14 09					14 39					15 09	

		SE	FC	SE ■	SE	SE	FC	SE ■		SE	SE ■	SE	FC	SE ■	SE	SE	FC	SE ■		SE	SE ■	SE	FC	SE ■	SE
London Victoria	⊖ d	14 21		14 45	14 39	14 51		15 05		15 09	15 24	15 21		15 45	15 39	15 51		16 05		16 09	16 24	16 21		16 45	16 39
Brixton	⊖ d	14 28				14 58						15 28				15 58						16 28			
Kentish Town	⊖ d																								
St Pancras International	⊖ d																								
Farringdon	⊖ d																								
City Thameslink	d																								
London Blackfriars	⊖ d		14 19				14 49						15 19				15 49						16 19		
Elephant & Castle	⊖ d		14 27				14 57						15 27				15 57						16 27		
Loughborough Jn	d		14 39				15 09						15 39				16 09						16 39		
Herne Hill	d	14 30	14 47			15 00	15 17					15 30	15 47			16 00	16 17					16 30	16 47		
West Dulwich	d	14 32				15 02						15 32				16 02						16 32			
Sydenham Hill	d	14 34				15 04						15 34				16 04						16 34			
Penge East	d	14 37				15 07						15 37				16 07						16 37			
Kent House	d	14 39				15 09						15 39				16 09						16 39			
Beckenham Junction	d	14 41				15 11						15 41				16 11						16 41			
Denmark Hill	d				14 48					15 18					15 48					16 18					16 48
Peckham Rye	d				14 51					15 21					15 51					16 21					16 51
Nunhead	d				14 53					15 23					15 53					16 23					16 53
Lewisham	a																								
Crofton Park	d				14 56					15 26					15 56					16 26					16 56
Catford	d				14 59					15 29					15 59					16 29					16 59
Bellingham	d				15 01					15 31					16 01					16 31					17 01
Beckenham Hill	d				15 03					15 33					16 03					16 33					17 03
Ravensbourne	d				15 05					15 35					16 05					16 35					17 05
Shortlands	d	14 44			15 07	15 14				15 37		15 44			16 07	16 14				16 37		16 44			17 07
Bromley South	d	14 48		15 01	15 10	15 18		15 22		15 40	15 44	15 48		16 01	16 10	16 18		16 22		16 40	16 44	16 48		17 01	17 10
Bickley	d	14 50			15 13	15 20				15 43		15 50			16 13	16 20				16 43		16 50			17 13
Petts Wood	d	14 55				15 25						15 55				16 25						16 55			
Orpington	d	14a58				15a28						15a58				16a28						16a58			
St Mary Cray	d			15 08	15 17					15 47	15 50			16 08	16 17					16 47	16 50			17 08	17 17
Swanley	d			15 12	15 22					15 52	15 54			16 12	16 22					16 52	16 54			17 12	17 22
Eynsford	d				15 26					15 56					16 26					16 56					17 26
Shoreham (Kent)	d				15 30					16 00					16 30					17 00					17 30
Otford	d			15 20	15 33					16 03				16 20	16 33					17 03				17 20	17 33
Bat & Ball	d				15 36					16 06					16 36					17 06					17 36
Sevenoaks	a				15 39					16 09					16 39					17 09					17 39

Table 195

Sundays

London - Catford, Beckenham Junction, Bromley South, Orpington, Otford and Sevenoaks

		SE	FC	SE ■		SE	SE ■	SE	FC	SE ■	SE	SE	FC	SE ■		SE	SE ■	SE	FC	SE ■	SE	SE	FC	SE ■	
London Victoria	⊖ d	16 51		17 05		17 09	17 24	17 21		17 45	17 39	17 51		18 05		18 09	18 24	18 21		18 45	18 39	18 51		19 05	
Brixton	⊖ d	16 58						17 28				17 58						18 28				18 58			
Kentish Town	⊖ d																								
St Pancras International	⊖ d																								
Farringdon	⊖ d																								
City Thameslink	d																								
London Blackfriars	⊖ d		16 49						17 19				17 49						18 19				18 49		
Elephant & Castle	⊖ d		16 57						17 27				17 57						18 27				18 57		
Loughborough Jn	d		17 09						17 39				18 09						18 39				19 09		
Herne Hill	d	17 00	17 17					17 30	17 47			18 00	18 17					18 30	18 47			19 00	19 17		
West Dulwich	d	17 02						17 32				18 02						18 32				19 02			
Sydenham Hill	d	17 04						17 34				18 04						18 34				19 04			
Penge East	d	17 07						17 37				18 07						18 37				19 07			
Kent House	d	17 09						17 39				18 09						18 39				19 09			
Beckenham Junction	d	17 11						17 41				18 11						18 41				19 11			
Denmark Hill	d					17 18					17 48					18 18					18 48				
Peckham Rye	d					17 21					17 51					18 21					18 51				
Nunhead	d					17 23					17 53					18 23					18 53				
Lewisham	a																								
Crofton Park	d					17 26					17 56					18 26					18 56				
Catford	d					17 29					17 59					18 29					18 59				
Bellingham	d					17 31					18 01					18 31					19 01				
Beckenham Hill	d					17 33					18 03					18 33					19 03				
Ravensbourne	d					17 35					18 05					18 35					19 05				
Shortlands	d	17 14				17 37		17 44			18 07	18 14				18 37		18 44			19 07	19 14			
Bromley South	d	17 18		17 22		17 40	17 44	17 48		18 01	18 10	18 18		18 22		18 40	18 44	18 48		19 01	19 10	19 18		19 22	
Bickley	d	17 20				17 43		17 50			18 13	18 20				18 43		18 50			19 13	19 20			
Petts Wood	d	17 25						17 55				18 25						18 55				19 25			
Orpington	d	17a28						17a58				18a28						18a58				19a28			
St Mary Cray	d					17 47	17 50			18 08	18 17					18 47	18 50			19 08	19 17				
Swanley	d					17 52	17 54			18 12	18 22					18 52	18 54			19 12	19 22				
Eynsford	d					17 56					18 26					18 56					19 26				
Shoreham (Kent)	d					18 00					18 30					19 00					19 30				
Otford	d					18 03				18 20	18 33					19 03				19 20	19 33				
Bat & Ball	d					18 06					18 36					19 06					19 36				
Sevenoaks	a					18 09					18 39					19 09					19 39				

		SE	SE ■	SE	FC	SE ■	SE	SE	FC	SE ■		SE	SE ■	SE	FC	SE ■	SE	SE	SE ■	SE		SE ■	SE	SE ■	SE
London Victoria	⊖ d	19 09	19 24	19 21		19 45	19 39	19 51		20 05		20 09	20 24	20 21		20 45	20 39	20 51	21 05	21 09		21 24	21 21	21 45	21 39
Brixton	⊖ d			19 28				19 58						20 28				20 58					21 28		
Kentish Town	⊖ d																								
St Pancras International	⊖ d																								
Farringdon	⊖ d																								
City Thameslink	d																								
London Blackfriars	⊖ d				19 19				19 49						20 19										
Elephant & Castle	⊖ d				19 27				19 57						20 27										
Loughborough Jn	d				19 39				20 09						20 39										
Herne Hill	d			19 30	19 47			20 00	20 17					20 30	20 47			21 00					21 30		
West Dulwich	d			19 32				20 02						20 32				21 02					21 32		
Sydenham Hill	d			19 34				20 04						20 34				21 04					21 34		
Penge East	d			19 37				20 07						20 37				21 07					21 37		
Kent House	d			19 39				20 09						20 39				21 09					21 39		
Beckenham Junction	d			19 41				20 11						20 41				21 11					21 41		
Denmark Hill	d	19 18					19 48					20 18					20 48			21 18					21 48
Peckham Rye	d	19 21					19 51					20 21					20 51			21 21					21 51
Nunhead	d	19 23					19 53					20 23					20 53			21 23					21 53
Lewisham	a																								
Crofton Park	d	19 26					19 56					20 26					20 56			21 26					21 56
Catford	d	19 29					19 59					20 29					20 59			21 29					21 59
Bellingham	d	19 31					20 01					20 31					21 01			21 31					22 01
Beckenham Hill	d	19 33					20 03					20 33					21 03			21 33					22 03
Ravensbourne	d	19 35					20 05					20 35					21 05			21 35					22 05
Shortlands	d	19 37		19 44			20 07	20 14				20 37		20 44			21 07	21 14		21 37			21 44		22 07
Bromley South	d	19 40	19 44	19 48		20 01	20 10	20 18		20 22		20 40	20 44	20 48		21 01	21 10	21 18	21 22	21 40		21 44	21 48	22 01	22 10
Bickley	d	19 43		19 50			20 13	20 20				20 43		20 50			21 13	21 20		21 43			21 50		22 13
Petts Wood	d			19 55				20 25						20 55				21 25					21 55		
Orpington	d			19a58				20a28						20a58				21a28					21a58		
St Mary Cray	d	19 47	19 50			20 08	20 17					20 47	20 50			21 08	21 17			21 47		21 50		22 08	22 17
Swanley	d	19 52	19 54			20 12	20 22					20 52	20 54			21 12	21 22			21 52		21 54		22 12	22 22
Eynsford	d	19 56					20 26					20 56					21 26			21 56					22 26
Shoreham (Kent)	d	20 00					20 30					21 00					21 30			22 00					22 30
Otford	d	20 03				20 20	20 33					21 03				21 20	21 33			22 03				22 20	22 33
Bat & Ball	d	20 06					20 36					21 06					21 36			22 06					22 36
Sevenoaks	a	20 09					20 39					21 09					21 39			22 09					22 39

Table 195

Sundays

London - Catford, Beckenham Junction, Bromley South, Orpington, Otford and Sevenoaks

		SE	SE [1]	SE	SE [1]	SE		SE [1]	SE	SE	SE [1]	SE	SE	SE [1]
London Victoria [15]	⊖ d	21 51	22 05	22 09	22 24	22 21		22 45	22 39	22 51	23 05	23 09	23 21	23 45
Brixton	⊖ d	21 58				22 28				22 58			23 28	
Kentish Town	⊖ d													
St Pancras International [15]	⊖ d													
Farringdon	⊖ d													
City Thameslink [3]	d													
London Blackfriars [3]	⊖ d													
Elephant & Castle	⊖ d													
Loughborough Jn	d													
Herne Hill [4]	d	22 00				22 30				23 00			23 30	
West Dulwich	d	22 02				22 32				23 02			23 32	
Sydenham Hill	d	22 04				22 34				23 04			23 34	
Penge East	d	22 07				22 37				23 07			23 37	
Kent House [4]	d	22 09				22 39				23 09			23 39	
Beckenham Junction [4]	d	22 11				22 41				23 11			23 41	
Denmark Hill [4]	d			22 18					22 48			23 18		
Peckham Rye [4]	d			22 21					22 51			23 21		
Nunhead [4]	d			22 23					22 53			23 23		
Lewisham [4]	a													
Crofton Park	d			22 26					22 56			23 26		
Catford	d			22 29					22 59			23 29		
Bellingham	d			22 31					23 01			23 31		
Beckenham Hill	d			22 33					23 03			23 33		
Ravensbourne	d			22 35					23 05			23 35		
Shortlands [4]	d	22 14		22 37		22 44			23 07	23 14		23 37	23 44	
Bromley South [4]	d	22 18	22 22	22 40	22 44	22 48		23 01	23 10	23 18	23 22	23 40	23 48	00 02
Bickley [4]	d	22 20		22 43		22 50			23 13	23 20		23 43	23 50	
Petts Wood [4]	d	22 25				22 55			23 22	23 25		23 52	23 55	
Orpington [4]	d	22a28				22a58			23a26	23a29		23a56	23a59	
St Mary Cray	d			22 47	22 50			23 08						00 08
Swanley [4]	d			22 52	22 54			23 12						00 12
Eynsford	d			22 56										
Shoreham (Kent)	d			23 00										
Otford [4]	d			23 03				23 20						
Bat & Ball	d			23 06										
Sevenoaks [4]	a			23 09										

Table 195

Mondays to Fridays

Sevenoaks, Otford, Orpington, Bromley South, Beckenham Junction and Catford - London

		SE MO [1]	SE MX [1]	SE MX [1]	SE MO [1]	SE	SE	SE	SE	SE		SE	FC	SE	SE [1]	SE [1]	FC	SE	SE [1]	SE		SE [1]	SE [1]	SE	FC
Sevenoaks [4]	d											05 40								06 13					
Bat & Ball	d											05 43								06 16					
Otford [4]	d											05 46							06 15	06 19			06 38		
Shoreham (Kent)	d											05 49								06 22					
Eynsford	d											05 53								06 26					
Swanley [4]	d	23p32		00 10		04 33						05 58			06 02				06 25	06 31		06 35	06 48		
St Mary Cray	d	23p36		00 14		04 37						06 02			06 06					06 35		06 39			
Orpington [4]	d						04 34	04 55	05 10	05 34				05 40				06 10							
Petts Wood [4]	d						04 37	04 58	05 13	05 37				05 43				06 13							
Bickley [4]	d					04 41	04 41	05 02	05 17	05 41		06 06		05 47				06 17		06 39					
Bromley South [4]	d	23p43	23p50	00 20	00 13	04b50	04 44	05 05	05 20	05 44		06 10		05 50	06 15	06 13		06 20	06 33	06 42		06 46	06 57		
Shortlands [4]	d					04 53	04 47	05 08	05 23	05 47		06 13		05 53				06 23		06 45					
Ravensbourne	d						04 49			05 49		06 15								06 47					
Beckenham Hill	d						04 51			05 51		06 17								06 49					
Bellingham	d						04 53			05 53		06 19								06 51					
Catford	d						04 56			05 56		06 22								06 54					
Crofton Park	d						04 58			05 58		06 25								06 57					
Lewisham [4]	d																							06 41	
Nunhead [4]	d						05 01			06 01		06 27								06 59					
Peckham Rye [4]	d						05 04			06 04		06 30								07 02				06 47	
Denmark Hill [4]	d						05 07			06 07		06 33								07 05				06 50	
Beckenham Junction [4]	d					04 56		05 11	05 26					05 56				06 26							
Kent House [4]	d					04 58		05 13	05 28					05 58				06 28							
Penge East	d					05 00		05 15	05 30					06 00				06 30							
Sydenham Hill	d					05 03		05 18	05 33					06 03				06 33							
West Dulwich	d					05 05		05 20	05 35					06 05				06 35							
Herne Hill [4]	d					05 08		05 23	05 38				05 54	06 08			06 16	06 38	06 43						06 46
Loughborough Jn	d																06 19								06 49
Elephant & Castle	⊖ d						05 13	05 29		06 13		06 40	06 00				06 24			07 12			07 16		06 54
London Blackfriars [3]	⊖ d						05 17	05 33		06 17		06 48	06 04				06 30			07 18			07 24		07 00
City Thameslink [3]	a						05 19	05 35		06 19		06 50	06 06				06 32			07 20			07 26		07 02
Farringdon	⊖ a											06 54	06 10				06 36			07 24			07 30		07 06
St Pancras International [15]	⊖ a											06 57	06 13				06 39			07 27			07 33		07 09
Kentish Town	⊖ a											07 02	06 18				06 44			07 32					
Brixton	⊖ d					05 10			05 40					06 10				06 40							
London Victoria [15]	⊖ a	00 02	00 07	00 38	00 29	05 17			05 47					06 18	06 31	06 29		06 47	06 51			07 07		07 04	

		SE	SE [1]	SE [1]	FC	SE		SE [1]	SE	SE [1]	SE	SE [1]	SE [1]	SE	SE [1]	SE		SE [1]	FC	SE	SE	SE [1]	SE [1]	SE	FC [1]
Sevenoaks [4]	d								06 42							07 11								07 36	
Bat & Ball	d								06 48							07 14								07 39	
Otford [4]	d		06 46						06 51	07 01		07 14				07 18		07 23					07 38	07 43	
Shoreham (Kent)	d								06 54							07 21								07 46	
Eynsford	d								06 58							07 24								07 49	
Swanley [4]	d		06 54					06 57	07 03	07 10		07 22			07 23	07 30		07 32				07 40	07 47	07 54	
St Mary Cray	d							07 01	07 07						07 27	07 34						07 45		07 59	
Orpington [4]	d					06 40														06 58	07 10				
Petts Wood [4]	d					06 43														07 01	07 13				
Bickley [4]	d					06 47			07 11							07 39				07 05	07 17			08 03	
Bromley South [4]	d		07 02	06 50		06 50		07 08	07 14	07 20		07 31	07 16		07 34	07 42		07 40		07 08	07 20	07 53	07 57	08 08	
Shortlands [4]	d					06 53			07 17							07 44				07 11	07 23			08 10	
Ravensbourne	d								07 19							07 47								08 13	
Beckenham Hill	d								07 21							07 49								08 15	
Bellingham	d								07 23							07 51								08 17	
Catford	d								07 26							07 53								08 20	
Crofton Park	d								07 29							07 56									
Lewisham [4]	d													07 15											
Nunhead [4]	d								07 31					07 20		07 58									
Peckham Rye [4]	d								07 34					07 23		08 01									
Denmark Hill [4]	d								07 37					07 29		08 04								08 26	
Beckenham Junction [4]	d	06 40				06 56					07 08									07 14	07 26				
Kent House [4]	d	06 42				06 58					07 11									07 17	07 28				
Penge East	d	06 44				07 00					07 14									07 19	07 30				
Sydenham Hill	d	06 47				07 03					07 17									07 22	07 33				
West Dulwich	d	06 49				07 05					07 19									07 24	07 35				
Herne Hill [4]	d	06 52			06 56	07 08					07 22								07 24	07 31	07 38				07 41
Loughborough Jn	d				07 00														07 27	07 34					
Elephant & Castle	⊖ d				07 06				07 44							08 13		08 00	07 32	07 38				08 35	
London Blackfriars [3]	⊖ d				07 12				07 48							08 17		08 04	07 36	07 42				08 42	07 54
City Thameslink [3]	a				07 14				07 50							08 19		08 06	07 38	07 44				08 44	07 56
Farringdon	⊖ a				07 18				07 54							08 23		08 10	07 42	07 48				08 48	08 00
St Pancras International [15]	⊖ a				07 21				07 57							08 27		08 13	07 45	07 51				08 51	08 03
Kentish Town	⊖ a								08 02															08 58	
Brixton	⊖ d	06 54				07 10					07 24										07 40				
London Victoria [15]	⊖ a	07 03	07 22	07 09		07 19		07 30		07 43	07 33	07 53	07 38	07 42	07 57						07 49	08 17	08 23		

b arr. 0444

Sevenoaks, Otford, Orpington, Bromley South, Beckenham Junction and Catford - London

		SE	FC	SE	SE	SE	SE 1	SE 1	FC	SE	SE 1	SE 1	SE 1	SE	SE	SE 1	SE 1 🍴	FC	SE	SE 1	SE 1	SE
Sevenoaks 4	d													07 53								
Bat & Ball	d													07 56								
Otford 4	d												07 56	08 00		08 09						
Shoreham (Kent)	d													08 03								
Eynsford	d													08 06								
Swanley 4	d							07 55				08 02	08 05	08 11							08 22	
St Mary Cray	d							08 00				08 06		08 16							08 27	
Orpington 4	d				07 28	07 47				07 38												
Petts Wood 4	d				07 31	07 50				07 41												
Bickley 4	d				07 35	07 55				07 45				08 20								
Bromley South 4	d			07 34	07 38	07 58	07 49	08 06		07 50		08 12	08 13	08 26		08 25	08 16		08 04	08 18	08 33	
Shortlands 4	d			07 36	07 41	08 00				07 53				08 29					08 06	08 20		
Ravensbourne	d																			08 23		
Beckenham Hill	d																			08 25		
Bellingham	d					08 05								08 33						08 27		
Catford	d					08 08								08 36						08 30		
Crofton Park	d					08 10								08 39								
Lewisham 4	d	07 46													08 05							08 26
Nunhead 4	d	07 51				08 14								08 41	08 11							08 31
Peckham Rye 4	d	07 54				08 16								08 44	08 13					08 36		08 33
Denmark Hill 4	d	07 59				08 19						08 30		08 47	08 17					08 39		08 36
Beckenham Junction 4	d			07 39	07 44					07 56	07 59								08 10			
Kent House 4	d			07 42	07 47					07 58	08 02								08 12			
Penge East	d			07 44	07 49					08 00	08 04								08 14			
Sydenham Hill	d			07 47	07 52					08 03	08 07								08 17			
West Dulwich	d			07 49	07 54					08 05	08 09								08 19			
Herne Hill 4	d		07 46	07 52	07 57				08 01	08 08	08 12							08 20	08 23			
Loughborough Jn	d		07 50		08 00				08 04		08 16							08 23				
Elephant & Castle ⊖	d		07 54		08 05	08 25		08 31	08 09		08 21			08 54				08 28		08 46		
London Blackfriars 3 ⊖	d		07 58		08 09	08 29		08 37	08 13		08 25			08 58				08 33		08 50		
City Thameslink 3	a		08 00		08 11	08 31		08 39	08 15		08 27			09 00				08 35		08 52		
Farringdon ⊖	a		08 03		08 15	08 35		08 43	08 19		08 30			09 04				08 39		08 56		
St Pancras International 15 ⊖	a		08 07		08 19	08 39		08 47	08 23		08 35			09 07				08 43		08 59		
Kentish Town ⊖	a		08 14						08 28					09 14				08 48				
Brixton ⊖	d			07 54						08 10									08 25			
London Victoria 15 ⊖	a	08 11		08 03			08 09			08 20		08 42	08 36		08 29	08 53	08 39		08 35		08 53	08 49

		SE 1	FC	SE	SE	SE	SE 1	SE	SE	FC	SE 1	SE	SE	SE 1 🍴	FC 1	FC	SE	SE 1	SE	SE 1	SE	SE 1	FC
Sevenoaks 4	d	08 24						08 43													09 13		
Bat & Ball	d	08 27						08 46													09 16		
Otford 4	d	08 31					08 45	08 49												09 17	09 21		
Shoreham (Kent)	d	08 34						08 52													09 24		
Eynsford	d	08 37						08 56													09 28		
Swanley 4	d	08 42					08 54	09 01										09 05		09 26	09 33		
St Mary Cray	d	08 46					08 58	09 05										09 09			09 37		
Orpington 4	d				08 10							08 26	08 47				08 40						
Petts Wood 4	d				08 13							08 29	08 50				08 43						
Bickley 4	d	08 51			08 17			09 09				08 33	08 55				08 47				09 42		
Bromley South 4	d	08 54			08 22	08 44	09 05	09 12				08 36	08 58	08 50			08 50	09 15		09 34	09 45	09 20	
Shortlands 4	d	08 56			08 24	08 46		09 15				08 39	09 00				08 53				09 48		
Ravensbourne	d					08 49		09 17					09 03								09 50		
Beckenham Hill	d					08 51		09 19					09 05								09 52		
Bellingham	d	09 01				08 53		09 21					09 07								09 54		
Catford	d	09 04				08 56		09 24					09 09								09 57		
Crofton Park	d					08 58		09 26					09 12								09 59		
Lewisham 4	d								08 46										09 06				
Nunhead 4	d					09 01		09 29	08 52				09 14						09 11		10 02		
Peckham Rye 4	d	09 09				09 04		09 31	08 55				09 17						09 14		10 04		
Denmark Hill 4	d	09 12				09 07		09 34	09 02				09 19						09 17		10 07		
Beckenham Junction 4	d			08 22	08 28							08 42					08 56						
Kent House 4	d			08 24	08 30						08 42	08 45					08 58						
Penge East	d			08 26							08 44	08 47					09 00						
Sydenham Hill	d			08 29							08 47	08 50					09 03						
West Dulwich	d			08 31	08 35						08 49	08 52					09 05						
Herne Hill 4	d		08 31	08 34	08 39					08 47	08 52	08 54			08 57	09 02	09 08						09 20
Loughborough Jn	d		08 35							08 50	08 55					09 05							09 23
Elephant & Castle ⊖	d	09 20	08 40			09 14		09 42		08 58	09 02		09 26		09 06	09 10					10 14		09 30
London Blackfriars 3 ⊖	d	09 26	08 46			09 18		09 46		09 02	09 06		09 30		09 10	09 14					10 18		09 34
City Thameslink 3	a	09 27	08 48			09 20		09 48		09 04	09 08		09 32		09 12	09 16					10 20		09 36
Farringdon ⊖	a	09 32	08 52			09 24		09 52		09 08	09 12		09 36		09 16	09 20					10 24		09 40
St Pancras International 15 ⊖	a	09 35	08 55			09 27		09 55		09 11	09 15		09 39		09 19	09 23					10 27		09 43
Kentish Town ⊖	a		09 00			09 34		10 00		09 16			09 46								10 34		09 48
Brixton ⊖	d			08 36	08 41							08 57					09 10						
London Victoria 15 ⊖	a			08 45	08 50		09 23		09 11			09 06		09 09			09 19	09 38	09 29	09 51		09 43	

Table 195 — Mondays to Fridays

Sevenoaks, Otford, Orpington, Bromley South, Beckenham Junction and Catford - London

		SE	FC	SE	SE	SE 1	SE	FC	SE	SE 1 🍴	FC	SE	SE 1	SE	SE	FC	SE	SE 1	SE 1 🍴	FC	SE	SE
Sevenoaks 4	d						09 42							10 02								10 32
Bat & Ball	d						09 46							10 05								10 35
Otford 4	d					09 45	09 50							10 08				10 17				10 38
Shoreham (Kent)	d						09 53							10 11								10 41
Eynsford	d						09 56							10 15								10 45
Swanley 4	d					09 54	10 01						10 05	10 20				10 26				10 50
St Mary Cray	d					09 58	10 05						10 09	10 24								10 54
Orpington 4	d	08 55		09 10					09 25			09 40					09 55				10 10	
Petts Wood 4	d	08 58		09 13					09 28			09 43					09 58				10 13	
Bickley 4	d	09 02		09 17			10 10		09 32			09 47		10 28			10 02				10 17	10 58
Bromley South 4	d	09 05		09 20		10 05	10 15		09 35	09 50		09 50	10 15	10 31			10 05	10 35	10 20		10 20	11 01
Shortlands 4	d	09 08		09 23			10 18		09 38			09 53		10 34			10 08				10 23	11 04
Ravensbourne	d						10 20							10 36								11 06
Beckenham Hill	d						10 22							10 38								11 08
Bellingham	d						10 24							10 40								11 10
Catford	d						10 27							10 43								11 13
Crofton Park	d						10 29							10 45								11 15
Lewisham 4	d				09 38										10 08							
Nunhead 4	d				09 43		10 32							10 48	10 13							11 18
Peckham Rye 4	d				09 45		10 34							10 50	10 15							11 20
Denmark Hill 4	d				09 49		10 37							10 54	10 19							11 24
Beckenham Junction 4	d	09 11		09 26					09 41			09 56					10 11				10 26	
Kent House 4	d	09 13		09 28					09 43			09 58					10 13				10 28	
Penge East	d	09 15		09 30					09 45			10 00					10 15				10 30	
Sydenham Hill	d	09 18		09 33					09 48			10 03					10 18				10 33	
West Dulwich	d	09 20		09 35					09 50			10 05					10 20				10 35	
Herne Hill 4	d	09 23	09 35	09 38				09 47	09 53		10 01	10 08				10 16	10 23			10 31	10 38	
Loughborough Jn	d		09 39					09 50			10 04					10 19				10 34		
Elephant & Castle ⊖	d		09 46				10 44	09 55			10 09			11 00		10 24				10 39		11 30
London Blackfriars 3 ⊖	d		09 50				10 48	10 00			10 13			11 04		10 28				10 43		11 34
City Thameslink 3	a		09 52				10 50	10 02			10 15			11 06		10 30				10 45		11 36
Farringdon ⊖	a		09 56				10 54	10 06			10 19			11 10		10 34				10 49		11 40
St Pancras International 15 ⊖	a		09 59				10 57	10 09			10 22			11 13		10 37				10 52		11 43
Kentish Town ⊖	a		10 06				11 03	10 14			10 27			11 20		10 42				10 57		11 50
Brixton ⊖	d	09 25		09 40					09 55			10 10					10 25				10 40	
London Victoria 15 ⊖	a	09 34		09 49	10 00	10 21			10 02	10 07		10 17	10 41		10 28		10 32	10 51	10 37		10 47	

		SE	SE 1	FC	SE	SE 1 🍴	FC	SE	SE 1	SE	SE	FC	SE	SE 1	SE 1 🍴	FC	SE	SE	SE	SE 1	FC	SE	SE 1 🍴
Sevenoaks 4	d									11 02								11 32					
Bat & Ball	d									11 05								11 35					
Otford 4	d		10 46							11 08				11 17				11 38		11 46			
Shoreham (Kent)	d									11 11								11 41					
Eynsford	d									11 15								11 45					
Swanley 4	d		10 54						11 05	11 20				11 26				11 50		11 54			
St Mary Cray	d		10 58						11 09	11 24								11 54		11 58			
Orpington 4	d				10 25			10 40					10 55				11 10					11 25	
Petts Wood 4	d				10 28			10 43					10 58				11 13					11 28	
Bickley 4	d				10 32			10 47		11 28			11 02				11 17	11 58				11 32	
Bromley South 4	d		11 05		10 35	10 50		10 50	11 15	11 31			11 05	11 35	11 20		11 20	12 01		12 05		11 35	11 50
Shortlands 4	d				10 38			10 53		11 34			11 08				11 23	12 04				11 38	
Ravensbourne	d									11 36								12 06					
Beckenham Hill	d									11 38								12 08					
Bellingham	d									11 40								12 10					
Catford	d									11 43								12 13					
Crofton Park	d									11 45								12 15					
Lewisham 4	d	10 38									11 08								11 38				
Nunhead 4	d	10 43								11 48	11 13							12 18	11 43				
Peckham Rye 4	d	10 45								11 50	11 15							12 20	11 45				
Denmark Hill 4	d	10 49								11 54	11 19							12 24	11 49				
Beckenham Junction 4	d				10 41			10 56					11 11				11 26					11 41	
Kent House 4	d				10 43			10 58					11 13				11 28					11 43	
Penge East	d				10 45			11 00					11 15				11 30					11 45	
Sydenham Hill	d				10 48			11 03					11 18				11 33					11 48	
West Dulwich	d				10 50			11 05					11 20				11 35					11 50	
Herne Hill 4	d			10 46	10 53		11 01	11 08				11 16	11 23			11 31	11 38				11 46	11 53	
Loughborough Jn	d			10 49			11 04					11 19				11 34					11 49		
Elephant & Castle ⊖	d			10 54			11 09			12 00		11 24				11 39		12 30			11 54		
London Blackfriars 3 ⊖	d			10 58			11 13			12 04		11 28				11 43		12 34			11 58		
City Thameslink 3	a			11 00			11 15			12 06		11 30				11 45		12 36			12 00		
Farringdon ⊖	a			11 04			11 19			12 10		11 34				11 49		12 40			12 04		
St Pancras International 15 ⊖	a			11 07			11 22			12 13		11 37				11 52		12 43			12 07		
Kentish Town ⊖	a			11 12			11 27			12 20		11 42				11 57		12 50			12 12		
Brixton ⊖	d				10 55			11 10					11 25				11 40					11 55	
London Victoria 15 ⊖	a	10 58	11 21		11 02	11 07		11 17	11 37		11 28		11 32	11 51	11 37		11 47		11 58	12 21		12 02	12 07

Sevenoaks, Otford, Orpington, Bromley South, Beckenham Junction and Catford - London

		FC	SE	SE 1	SE	SE		FC	SE	SE 1	SE 1 ⊼	FC	SE	SE	SE	SE 1		FC	SE	SE 1 ⊼	FC	SE	SE 1	SE	SE
Sevenoaks 4	d				12 02										12 32									13 02	
Bat & Ball	d				12 05										12 35									13 05	
Otford 4	d				12 08					12 17					12 38	12 46								13 08	
Shoreham (Kent)	d				12 11										12 41									13 11	
Eynsford	d				12 15										12 45									13 15	
Swanley 4	d			12 05	12 20					12 26					12 50	12 54							13 05	13 20	
St Mary Cray	d			12 09	12 24										12 54	12 58							13 09	13 24	
Orpington 4	d		11 40						11 55				12 10						12 25			12 40			
Petts Wood 4	d		11 43						11 58				12 13						12 28			12 43			
Bickley 4	d		11 47		12 28				12 02				12 17	12 58					12 32			12 47		13 28	
Bromley South 4	d		11 50	12 15	12 31				12 05	12 35	12 20		12 20	13 01		13 05			12 35	12 50		12 50	13 15	13 31	
Shortlands 4	d		11 53		12 34				12 08				12 23	13 04					12 38			12 53		13 34	
Ravensbourne	d				12 36									13 06										13 36	
Beckenham Hill	d				12 38									13 08										13 38	
Bellingham	d				12 40									13 10										13 40	
Catford	d				12 43									13 13										13 43	
Crofton Park	d				12 45									13 15										13 45	
Lewisham 4	d					12 08									12 38										13 08
Nunhead 4	d				12 48	12 13								13 18	12 43									13 48	13 13
Peckham Rye 4	d				12 50	12 15								13 20	12 45									13 50	13 15
Denmark Hill 4	d				12 54	12 19								13 24	12 49									13 54	13 19
Beckenham Junction 4	d		11 56						12 11				12 26						12 41			12 56			
Kent House 4	d		11 58						12 13				12 28						12 43			12 58			
Penge East	d		12 00						12 15				12 30						12 45			13 00			
Sydenham Hill	d		12 03						12 18				12 33						12 48			13 03			
West Dulwich	d		12 05						12 20				12 35						12 50			13 05			
Herne Hill 4	d	12 01	12 08					12 16	12 23			12 31	12 38					12 46	12 53		13 01	13 08			
Loughborough Jn	d	12 04						12 19				12 34						12 49			13 04				
Elephant & Castle ⊖	d	12 09			13 00			12 24				12 39			13 30			12 54			13 09			14 00	
London Blackfriars 3 ⊖	d	12 13			13 04			12 28				12 43			13 34			12 58			13 13			14 04	
City Thameslink 3	a	12 15			13 06			12 30				12 45			13 36			13 00			13 15			14 06	
Farringdon ⊖	a	12 19			13 10			12 34				12 49			13 40			13 04			13 19			14 10	
St Pancras International 15 ⊖	a	12 22			13 13			12 37				12 52			13 43			13 07			13 22			14 13	
Kentish Town ⊖	a	12 27			13 20			12 42				12 57			13 50			13 12			13 27			14 20	
Brixton ⊖	d		12 10						12 25				12 40						12 55			13 10			
London Victoria 15 ⊖	a		12 17	12 37		12 28			12 32	12 51	12 37		12 47		12 58	13 21			13 02	13 07		13 17	13 37		13 28

		FC		SE	SE 1	SE 1 ⊼	FC	SE	SE	SE	SE 1	FC		SE	SE 1 ⊼	FC	SE	SE 1	SE	SE	FC	SE		SE 1	SE 1 ⊼
Sevenoaks 4	d								13 32										14 02						
Bat & Ball	d								13 35										14 05						
Otford 4	d				13 17				13 38		13 46								14 08					14 17	
Shoreham (Kent)	d								13 41										14 11						
Eynsford	d								13 45										14 15						
Swanley 4	d				13 26				13 50		13 54							14 05	14 20					14 26	
St Mary Cray	d								13 54		13 58							14 09	14 24						
Orpington 4	d			12 55				13 10						13 25			13 40					13 55			
Petts Wood 4	d			12 58				13 13						13 28			13 43					13 58			
Bickley 4	d			13 02				13 17	13 58					13 32			13 47		14 28			14 02			
Bromley South 4	d			13 05	13 35	13 20		13 20	14 01		14 05			13 35	13 50		13 50	14 15	14 31			14 05		14 35	14 20
Shortlands 4	d			13 08				13 23	14 04					13 38			13 53		14 34			14 08			
Ravensbourne	d								14 06										14 36						
Beckenham Hill	d								14 08										14 38						
Bellingham	d								14 10										14 40						
Catford	d								14 13										14 43						
Crofton Park	d								14 15										14 45						
Lewisham 4	d									13 38										14 08					
Nunhead 4	d								14 18	13 43									14 48	14 13					
Peckham Rye 4	d								14 20	13 45									14 50	14 15					
Denmark Hill 4	d								14 24	13 49									14 54	14 19					
Beckenham Junction 4	d			13 11				13 26						13 41			13 56					14 11			
Kent House 4	d			13 13				13 28						13 43			13 58					14 13			
Penge East	d			13 15				13 30						13 45			14 00					14 15			
Sydenham Hill	d			13 18				13 33						13 48			14 03					14 18			
West Dulwich	d			13 20				13 35						13 50			14 05					14 20			
Herne Hill 4	d	13 16		13 23			13 31	13 38				13 46		13 53		14 01	14 08				14 16	14 23			
Loughborough Jn	d	13 19					13 34					13 49				14 04					14 19				
Elephant & Castle ⊖	d	13 24					13 39		14 30			13 54				14 09			15 00		14 24				
London Blackfriars 3 ⊖	d	13 28					13 43		14 34			13 58				14 13			15 04		14 28				
City Thameslink 3	a	13 30					13 45		14 36			14 00				14 15			15 06		14 30				
Farringdon ⊖	a	13 34					13 49		14 40			14 04				14 19			15 10		14 34				
St Pancras International 15 ⊖	a	13 37					13 52		14 43			14 07				14 22			15 13		14 37				
Kentish Town ⊖	a	13 42					13 57		14 50			14 12				14 27			15 20		14 42				
Brixton ⊖	d			13 25				13 40						13 55			14 10					14 25			
London Victoria 15 ⊖	a			13 32	13 51	13 37		13 47		13 58	14 21			14 02	14 07		14 17	14 37		14 28		14 32		14 51	14 37

Sevenoaks, Otford, Orpington, Bromley South, Beckenham Junction and Catford - London

		FC	SE	SE	SE	SE 1	FC	SE		SE 1 ⊼	FC	SE	SE 1	SE	SE	FC	SE	SE 1		SE 1 ⊼	FC	SE	SE 1	SE	SE 1
Sevenoaks 4	d			14 32										15 02									15 32		
Bat & Ball	d			14 35										15 05									15 35		
Otford 4	d			14 38		14 46								15 08				15 17					15 38		15 46
Shoreham (Kent)	d			14 41										15 11									15 41		
Eynsford	d			14 45										15 15									15 45		
Swanley 4	d			14 50		14 54							15 05	15 20				15 26					15 50		15 54
St Mary Cray	d			14 54		14 58							15 09	15 24									15 54		15 58
Orpington 4	d		14 10					14 25				14 40					14 55					15 10			
Petts Wood 4	d		14 13					14 28				14 43					14 58					15 13			
Bickley 4	d		14 17	14 58				14 32				14 47		15 28			15 02					15 17	15 58		
Bromley South 4	d		14 20	15 01		15 05		14 35		14 50		14 50	15 15	15 31			15 05	15 35		15 20		15 20	16 01		16 05
Shortlands 4	d		14 23	15 04				14 38				14 53		15 34			15 08					15 23	16 04		
Ravensbourne	d			15 06										15 36									16 06		
Beckenham Hill	d			15 08										15 38									16 08		
Bellingham	d			15 10										15 40									16 10		
Catford	d			15 13										15 43									16 13		
Crofton Park	d			15 15										15 45									16 15		
Lewisham 4	d				14 38										15 08									15 38	
Nunhead 4	d			15 18	14 43									15 48	15 13								16 18	15 43	
Peckham Rye 4	d			15 20	14 45									15 50	15 15								16 20	15 45	
Denmark Hill 4	d			15 24	14 49									15 54	15 19								16 24	15 49	
Beckenham Junction 4	d		14 26					14 41				14 56					15 11					15 26			
Kent House 4	d		14 28					14 43				14 58					15 13					15 28			
Penge East	d		14 30					14 45				15 00					15 15					15 30			
Sydenham Hill	d		14 33					14 48				15 03					15 18					15 33			
West Dulwich	d		14 35					14 50				15 05					15 20					15 35			
Herne Hill 4	d	14 31	14 38				14 46	14 53			15 01	15 08				15 16	15 23				15 31	15 38			
Loughborough Jn	d	14 34					14 49				15 04					15 19					15 34				
Elephant & Castle ⊖	d	14 39		15 30			14 54				15 09			16 00		15 24					15 39		16 30		
London Blackfriars 3 ⊖	d	14 43		15 34			14 58				15 13			16 04		15 28					15 43		16 36		
City Thameslink 3	a	14 45		15 36			15 00				15 15			16 06		15 30					15 45		16 38		
Farringdon ⊖	a	14 49		15 40			15 04				15 19			16 10		15 34					15 49		16 41		
St Pancras International 15 ⊖	a	14 52		15 43			15 07				15 22			16 13		15 37					15 52		16 45		
Kentish Town ⊖	a	14 57		15 50			15 12				15 27			16 20		15 42					15 57				
Brixton ⊖	d		14 40					14 55				15 10					15 25					15 40			
London Victoria 15 ⊖	a		14 47		14 58	15 21		15 02		15 07		15 17	15 37		15 28		15 32	15 51		15 37		15 47		15 58	16 21

		FC	SE	SE 1 ⊼		FC	SE	SE	SE 1	SE	FC	SE	SE 1	SE 1 ⊼		SE	FC	SE	SE	SE	SE 1	SE 1 ⊼	FC	SE	
Sevenoaks 4	d								16 02							16 22			16 32						
Bat & Ball	d								16 05							16 25			16 35						
Otford 4	d								16 08				16 17			16 28			16 38		16 46				
Shoreham (Kent)	d								16 11										16 41						
Eynsford	d								16 15										16 45						
Swanley 4	d							16 05	16 20				16 26			16 37			16 50		16 54				
St Mary Cray	d							16 09	16 24							16 41			16 54		16 58				
Orpington 4	d		15 25				15 40					15 55						16 10						16 25	
Petts Wood 4	d		15 28				15 43					15 58						16 13						16 28	
Bickley 4	d		15 32				15 47		16 28			16 02						16 17	16 58					16 32	
Bromley South 4	d		15 35	15 50			15 50	16 15	16 31			16 05	16 35	16 20		16 47		16 20	17 01		17 05	16 50		16 35	
Shortlands 4	d		15 38				15 53		16 34			16 08						16 23	17 04					16 38	
Ravensbourne	d								16 36										17 06						
Beckenham Hill	d								16 38										17 08						
Bellingham	d								16 40							16 52			17 10						
Catford	d								16 43							16 55			17 13						
Crofton Park	d								16 45										17 15						
Lewisham 4	d									16 08										16 38					
Nunhead 4	d								16 48	16 13						16 59			17 18	16 43					
Peckham Rye 4	d								16 50	16 15						17 02			17 20	16 45					
Denmark Hill 4	d								16 54	16 19						17 05			17 24	16 49					
Beckenham Junction 4	d		15 41				15 56					16 11						16 26						16 41	
Kent House 4	d		15 43				15 58					16 13						16 28						16 43	
Penge East	d		15 45				16 00					16 15						16 30						16 45	
Sydenham Hill	d		15 48				16 03					16 18						16 33						16 48	
West Dulwich	d		15 50				16 05					16 20						16 35						16 50	
Herne Hill 4	d	15 46	15 53			16 01	16 08				16 16	16 23					16 31	16 38					16 50	16 53	
Loughborough Jn	d	15 49				16 04					16 19						16 34						16 53		
Elephant & Castle ⊖	d	15 54				16 09			17 04		16 24					17 12	16 39		17 34				17 00		
London Blackfriars 3 ⊖	d	15 58				16 14			17 08		16 30					17 16	16 44		17 40				17 04		
City Thameslink 3	a	16 00				16 16			17 10		16 32					17 18	16 46		17 42				17 06		
Farringdon ⊖	a	16 04				16 19			17 13		16 35					17 23	16 49		17 45				17 09		
St Pancras International 15 ⊖	a	16 07				16 23			17 17		16 39					17 27	16 53		17 49				17 13		
Kentish Town ⊖	a	16 12				16 28					16 44					17 32	16 58						17 18		
Brixton ⊖	d		15 55				16 10					16 25						16 40						16 55	
London Victoria 15 ⊖	a		16 02	16 07			16 17	16 37		16 28		16 32	16 51	16 38				16 47		16 58	17 21	17 07		17 03	

Sevenoaks, Otford, Orpington, Bromley South, Beckenham Junction and Catford - London

		FC [1] A	SE	SE [1]	SE [1]	SE	SE [1]	SE [1] ⌶	FC	SE		FC	SE	SE [1]	SE [1]	SE	SE [1]	FC	SE	SE [1]		SE [1]	SE [1] B	FC	SE
Sevenoaks [4]	d				17 02										17 32								18 02		
Bat & Ball	d				17 05										17 35								18 05		
Otford [4]	d				17 08		17 17								17 38		17 46						18 08		
Shoreham (Kent)	d				17 11										17 41								18 11		
Eynsford	d				17 15										17 45								18 15		
Swanley [4]	d			17 05	17 20		17 26							17 35	17 50		17 54					18 05	18 20		
St Mary Cray	d			17 09	17 24									17 39	17 54		17 58					18 09	18 24		
Orpington [4]	d		16 40							16 55			17 10						17 24						17 40
Petts Wood [4]	d		16 43							16 58			17 13						17 28						17 43
Bickley [4]	d		16 47		17 28					17 02			17 17		17 58				17 32				18 28		17 47
Bromley South [4]	d		16 50	17 15	17 31		17 35	17 20		17 05			17 20	17 46	18 01		18 05		17 35	17 50		18 15	18 31		17 50
Shortlands [4]	d		16 53		17 34					17 08			17 23		18 04				17 38				18 34		17 53
Ravensbourne	d				17 36										18 06								18 36		
Beckenham Hill	d				17 38										18 08								18 38		
Bellingham	d				17 40										18 10								18 40		
Catford	d				17 43										18 13								18 43		
Crofton Park	d				17 45										18 15								18 45		
Lewisham [4]	d					17 08										17 38									
Nunhead [4]	d				17 48	17 13									18 18	17 43							18 48		
Peckham Rye [4]	d				17 50	17 15									18 20	17 45							18 50		
Denmark Hill [4]	d				17 54	17 19									18 23	17 49							18 54		
Beckenham Junction [4]	d		16 56							17 11			17 26						17 41						17 56
Kent House [4]	d		16 58							17 13			17 28						17 43						17 58
Penge East	d		17 00							17 15			17 30						17 45						18 00
Sydenham Hill	d		17 03							17 18			17 33						17 48						18 03
West Dulwich	d		17 05							17 20			17 35						17 50						18 05
Herne Hill [4]	d	17 01	17 08						17 20	17 23		17 31	17 38					17 48	17 53					18 06	18 09
Loughborough Jn	d								17 23			17 34						17 51						18 09	
Elephant & Castle	⊖ d	17 08			18 00				17 28			17 39			18 32			17 56					19 00	18 14	
London Blackfriars [3]	⊖ d	17 12			18 06				17 32			17 46			18 36			18 00					19 06	18 18	
City Thameslink [3]	a	17 14			18 08				17 34			17 48			18 38			18 02					19 08	18 20	
Farringdon	⊖ a	17 17			18 11				17 37			17 51			18 41			18 05					19 11	18 23	
St Pancras International [15]	⊖ a	17 21			18 15				17 41			17 55			18 45			18 09					19 15	18 27	
Kentish Town	⊖ a								17 46			18 00						18 14						18 32	
Brixton	⊖ d		17 10							17 25			17 40						17 55						18 11
London Victoria [15]	⊖ a		17 18	17 38		17 28	17 53	17 37		17 33			17 48	18 08		17 59	18 21		18 03	18 07		18 37			18 18

		SE	SE [1]	SE	FC	SE		SE [1] ⌶	FC	SE	SE	SE	SE [1]	SE	FC	SE		SE [1] ⌶	FC	SE	SE [1]	SE	SE	SE [1]	SE [1]
Sevenoaks [4]	d			18 18							18 32			18 45								19 02			
Bat & Ball	d			18 21							18 35			18 48								19 05			
Otford [4]	d		18 17	18 24							18 38		18 46	18 51								19 08			19 17
Shoreham (Kent)	d			18 27							18 41			18 54								19 11			
Eynsford	d			18 31							18 45			18 58								19 15			
Swanley [4]	d		18 26	18 36							18 50		18 54	19 03							19 05	19 20			19 26
St Mary Cray	d			18 40							18 54		18 58								19 09	19 24			
Orpington [4]	d					17 53				18 09						18 25				18 40					
Petts Wood [4]	d					17 56				18 12						18 28				18 43					
Bickley [4]	d					18 02				18 17	18 58					18 32				18 47		19 28			
Bromley South [4]	d		18 35	18 46		18 05		18 20		18 20	19 01		19 05	19 11		18 35		18 50		18 50	19 15	19 31		19 17	19 35
Shortlands [4]	d					18 08				18 23	19 04					18 38				18 53		19 34			
Ravensbourne	d										19 06											19 36			
Beckenham Hill	d										19 08											19 38			
Bellingham	d										19 10											19 40			
Catford	d										19 13											19 43			
Crofton Park	d										19 15											19 45			
Lewisham [4]	d	18 08										18 38											19 08		
Nunhead [4]	d	18 13									19 18	18 43										19 48	19 13		
Peckham Rye [4]	d	18 15									19 20	18 45										19 50	19 15		
Denmark Hill [4]	d	18 19		18 59							19 24	18 49		19 28								19 54	19 19		
Beckenham Junction [4]	d					18 11				18 26						18 41				18 56					
Kent House [4]	d					18 13				18 28						18 43				18 58					
Penge East	d					18 15				18 30						18 45				19 00					
Sydenham Hill	d					18 18				18 33						18 48				19 03					
West Dulwich	d					18 20				18 35						18 50				19 05					
Herne Hill [4]	d				18 20	18 24			18 31	18 38					18 48	18 53			19 01	19 08					
Loughborough Jn	d				18 23				18 34						18 51				19 04						
Elephant & Castle	⊖ d				18 28				18 40		19 30				18 56				19 09			20 00			
London Blackfriars [3]	⊖ d				18 32				18 44		19 34				19 00				19 18			20 04			
City Thameslink [3]	a				18 34				18 46		19 36				19 02				19 20			20 06			
Farringdon	⊖ a				18 37				18 49		19 40				19 05				19 23			20 10			
St Pancras International [15]	⊖ a				18 41				18 53		19 43				19 09				19 27			20 13			
Kentish Town	⊖ a				18 46						19 50				19 14				19 32			20 20			
Brixton	⊖ d					18 26				18 40						18 55				19 10					
London Victoria [15]	⊖ a	18 29	18 53	19 13		18 33		18 37		18 47		18 58	19 21	19 42		19 03		19 07		19 17	19 37		19 28	19 35	19 51

A [1] to City Thameslink

B [1] from London Blackfriars

Table 195

Mondays to Fridays

Sevenoaks, Otford, Orpington, Bromley South, Beckenham Junction and Catford - London

		FC		SE	SE [1]	SE	FC	SE	SE	SE [1]	SE	FC		SE	SE [1]	SE	SE	FC	SE	SE [1]	FC	SE		SE [1]	FC
Sevenoaks [4]	d					19 22			19 32		19 45						20 02								
Bat & Ball	d					19 25			19 35		19 48						20 05								
Otford [4]	d					19 28			19 38	19 46	19 51						20 08			20 16					
Shoreham (Kent)	d					19 31			19 41		19 54						20 11								
Eynsford	d					19 35			19 45		19 58						20 15								
Swanley [4]	d					19a39			19 50	19 54	20 03					20 05	20 20			20 24					
St Mary Cray	d								19 54	19 58						20 09	20 24			20 28					
Orpington [4]	d			18 55				19 10						19 25					19 40			19 55			
Petts Wood [4]	d			18 58				19 13						19 28					19 43			19 58			
Bickley [4]	d			19 02				19 17	19 58					19 32			20 28		19 47			20 02			
Bromley South [4]	d			19 05	19 20			19 20	20 01	20 05	20a11			19 35	19 50	20 15	20 31		19 50	20 35		20 05		20 20	
Shortlands [4]	d			19 08				19 23	20 04					19 38			20 34		19 53			20 08			
Ravensbourne	d								20 06								20 36								
Beckenham Hill	d								20 08								20 38								
Bellingham	d								20 10								20 40								
Catford	d								20 13								20 43								
Crofton Park	d								20 15								20 45								
Lewisham [4]	d																								
Nunhead [4]	d								20 18								20 48								
Peckham Rye [4]	d								20 20								20 50								
Denmark Hill [4]	d								20 24								20 54								
Beckenham Junction [4]	d			19 11				19 26						19 41					19 56			20 11			
Kent House [4]	d			19 13				19 28						19 43					19 58			20 13			
Penge East	d			19 15				19 30						19 45					20 00			20 15			
Sydenham Hill	d			19 18				19 33						19 48					20 03			20 18			
West Dulwich	d			19 20				19 35						19 50					20 05			20 20			
Herne Hill [4]	d	19 17		19 23			19 31	19 38				19 47		19 53				20 05	20 08		20 16	20 23			20 35
Loughborough Jn	d	19 20					19 34					19 50						20 08			20 19				20 38
Elephant & Castle	⊖ d	19 25					19 39		20 30			19 55					21 00	20 13			20 24				20 43
London Blackfriars [3]	⊖ d	19 30					19 46		20 34			20 00					21 04	20 18			20 30				20 48
City Thameslink [3]	a	19 32					19 48		20 36			20 02					21 06	20 20			20 32				20 50
Farringdon	⊖ a	19 36					19 52		20 40			20 06					21 10	20 24			20 36				20 54
St Pancras International [15]	⊖ a	19 39					19 55		20 43			20 09					21 13	20 27			20 39				20 57
Kentish Town	⊖ a	19 44					20 00		20 50			20 14					21 20	20 32			20 44				21 02
Brixton	⊖ d			19 25				19 40						19 55					20 10			20 25			
London Victoria [15]	⊖ a			19 32	19 37			19 47		20 21				20 02	20 07	20 37			20 17	20 51		20 32		20 38	

		SE	SE	FC	SE [1]	FC	SE	SE [1]		SE	SE [1]	FC	FC	SE	SE	SE [1]	FC	SE		SE [1]	SE	SE	SE [1]	SE	SE
Sevenoaks [4]	d		20 32							21 02					21 32						22 02			22 32	
Bat & Ball	d		20 35							21 05					21 35						22 05			22 35	
Otford [4]	d		20 38							21 08	21 16				21 38						22 08		22 16	22 38	
Shoreham (Kent)	d		20 41							21 11					21 41						22 11			22 41	
Eynsford	d		20 45							21 15					21 45						22 15			22 45	
Swanley [4]	d		20 50					21 10		21 20	21 24				21 50					22 10	22 20		22 24	22 50	
St Mary Cray	d		20 54					21 14		21 24	21 28				21 54					22 14	22 24		22 28	22 54	
Orpington [4]	d	20 10					20 40							21 10				21 40				22 10			22 40
Petts Wood [4]	d	20 13					20 43							21 13				21 43				22 13			22 43
Bickley [4]	d	20 17	20 58				20 47			21 28				21 17	21 58			21 47			22 28	22 17		22 58	22 47
Bromley South [4]	d	20 20	21 01		20 50		20 50	21 20		21 31	21 35			21 20	22 01	21 50		21 50		22 20	22 31	22 20	22 35	23 01	22 50
Shortlands [4]	d	20 23	21 04				20 53			21 34				21 23	22 04			21 53			22 34	22 23		23 04	22 53
Ravensbourne	d		21 06							21 36					22 06						22 36			23 06	
Beckenham Hill	d		21 08							21 38					22 08						22 38			23 08	
Bellingham	d		21 10							21 40					22 10						22 40			23 10	
Catford	d		21 13							21 43					22 13						22 43			23 13	
Crofton Park	d		21 15							21 45					22 15						22 45			23 15	
Lewisham [4]	d																								
Nunhead [4]	d		21 18							21 48					22 18						22 48			23 18	
Peckham Rye [4]	d		21 20							21 50					22 20						22 50			23 20	
Denmark Hill [4]	d		21 23							21 53					22 23						22 53			23 23	
Beckenham Junction [4]	d	20 26					20 56							21 26				21 56				22 26			22 56
Kent House [4]	d	20 28					20 58							21 28				21 58				22 28			22 58
Penge East	d	20 30					21 00							21 30				22 00				22 30			23 00
Sydenham Hill	d	20 33					21 03							21 33				22 03				22 33			23 03
West Dulwich	d	20 35					21 05							21 35				22 05				22 35			23 05
Herne Hill [4]	d	20 38		20 46		21 05	21 08					21 16	21 35	21 38			21 54	22 08				22 38			23 08
Loughborough Jn	d			20 49		21 08						21 19	21 38				21 57								
Elephant & Castle	⊖ d			20 54		21 13						21 24	21 43				22 02								
London Blackfriars [3]	⊖ d			21 00		21 18						21 30	21 48				22 08								
City Thameslink [3]	a			21 02		21 20						21 32	21 50				22 10								
Farringdon	⊖ a			21 06		21 24						21 36	21 54				22 14								
St Pancras International [15]	⊖ a			21 09		21 27						21 39	21 57				22 17								
Kentish Town	⊖ a			21 14		21 32						21 44	22 02				22 22								
Brixton	⊖ d	20 40					21 10							21 40				22 10				22 40			23 10
London Victoria [15]	⊖ a	20 47	21 33		21 07		21 17	21 37		22 03	21 51			21 47	22 33	22 07		22 17		22 37	23 03	22 47	22 51	23 33	23 17

Table 195

Mondays to Fridays

Sevenoaks, Otford, Orpington, Bromley South, Beckenham Junction and Catford - London

Station		SE 1	SE 1	SE	SE 1	SE 1
Sevenoaks	d					
Bat & Ball	d					
Otford	d				23 16	
Shoreham (Kent)	d					
Eynsford	d					
Swanley	d		23 10		23 24	
St Mary Cray	d		23 14		23 28	
Orpington	d			23 10		
Petts Wood	d			23 13		
Bickley	d			23 17		
Bromley South	d	22 50	23 20	23 20	23 35	23 50
Shortlands	d			23 23		
Ravensbourne	d					
Beckenham Hill	d					
Bellingham	d					
Catford	d					
Crofton Park	d					
Lewisham	d					
Nunhead	d					
Peckham Rye	d					
Denmark Hill	d					
Beckenham Junction	d			23 26		
Kent House	d			23 28		
Penge East	d			23 30		
Sydenham Hill	d			23 33		
West Dulwich	d			23 35		
Herne Hill	d			23 38		
Loughborough Jn	d					
Elephant & Castle	d					
London Blackfriars	d					
City Thameslink	a					
Farringdon	a					
St Pancras International	a					
Kentish Town	a					
Brixton	d			23 40		
London Victoria	a	23 07	23 37	23 47	23 51	00 07

Saturdays

Station		SE 1	SE 1	SE	SE 1	SE	FC	SE	SE 1	SE	FC	SE	SE	SE 1	SE 1	SE 1	SE	SE	FC	SE	SE 1	SE 1	SE
Sevenoaks	d					05 55				06 25							06 55						07 25
Bat & Ball	d					05 58				06 28							06 58						07 28
Otford	d					06 01			06 16	06 31				06 46			07 01				07 17		07 31
Shoreham (Kent)	d					06 04				06 34							07 04						07 34
Eynsford	d					06 08				06 38							07 08						07 38
Swanley	d		00 10		06 05	06 13			06 24	06 43				06 54		07 05	07 13				07 26		07 43
St Mary Cray	d		00 14		06 09	06 17			06 28	06 47				06 58		07 09	07 17						07 47
Orpington	d			05 44				06 10				06 25	06 40							06 55			
Petts Wood	d			05 47				06 13				06 28	06 43							06 58			
Bickley	d			05 51		06 21		06 17		06 51		06 32	06 47				07 21			07 02			07 51
Bromley South	d	23p50	00 20	05 54	06 16	06 24		06 20	06 35	06 54		06 35	06 50	07 05	06 50	07 15	07 24			07 05	07 35	07 20	07 54
Shortlands	d			05 57		06 27		06 23		06 57		06 38	06 53				07 27			07 08			07 57
Ravensbourne	d			05 59		06 29				06 59							07 29						07 59
Beckenham Hill	d			06 01		06 31				07 01							07 31						08 01
Bellingham	d			06 03		06 33				07 03							07 33						08 03
Catford	d			06 06		06 36				07 06							07 36						08 06
Crofton Park	d			06 08		06 38				07 08							07 38						08 08
Lewisham	d																	07 08					
Nunhead	d			06 11		06 41				07 11							07 41	07 15					08 11
Peckham Rye	d			06 13		06 43				07 13							07 43	07 17					08 13
Denmark Hill	d			06 17		06 47				07 17							07 47	07 21					08 17
Beckenham Junction	d							06 26				06 41	06 56							07 11			
Kent House	d							06 28				06 43	06 58							07 13			
Penge East	d							06 30				06 45	07 00							07 15			
Sydenham Hill	d							06 33				06 48	07 03							07 18			
West Dulwich	d							06 35				06 50	07 05							07 20			
Herne Hill	d						06 08	06 38			06 38	06 53	07 08						07 08	07 23			
Loughborough Jn	d						06 16				06 46								07 16				
Elephant & Castle	d						06 28				06 58								07 28				
London Blackfriars	d						06a36				07a06								07a36				
City Thameslink	a																						
Farringdon	a																						
St Pancras International	a																						
Kentish Town	a																						
Brixton	d							06 40				06 55	07 10							07 25			
London Victoria	a	00 07	00 38	06 26	06 37	06 56		06 47	06 51	07 26		07 02	07 17	07 21	07 07	07 37	07 56	07 30		07 32	07 51	07 37	08 26

Table 195

Saturdays

Sevenoaks, Otford, Orpington, Bromley South, Beckenham Junction and Catford - London

Station		FC	SE	SE	FC	SE	SE 1	SE 1	FC	SE	SE 1	SE	SE	FC	SE	SE 1	SE 1	SE	FC	SE	SE	FC	SE
Sevenoaks	d											07 55						08 25					
Bat & Ball	d											07 58						08 28					
Otford	d						07 46					08 01				08 17		08 31					
Shoreham (Kent)	d											08 04						08 34					
Eynsford	d											08 08						08 38					
Swanley	d						07 54				08 05	08 13				08 26		08 43					
St Mary Cray	d						07 58				08 09	08 17						08 47					
Orpington	d		07 10			07 25				07 40					07 55					08 10			08 25
Petts Wood	d		07 13			07 28				07 43					07 58					08 13			08 28
Bickley	d		07 17			07 32				07 47		08 21			08 02			08 51		08 17			08 32
Bromley South	d		07 20			07 35	08 05	07 50		07 50	08 15	08 24			08 05	08 35	08 20	08 54		08 20			08 35
Shortlands	d		07 23			07 38				07 53		08 27			08 08			08 57		08 23			08 38
Ravensbourne	d											08 29						08 59					
Beckenham Hill	d											08 31						09 01					
Bellingham	d											08 33						09 03					
Catford	d											08 36						09 06					
Crofton Park	d											08 38						09 08					
Lewisham	d			07 38									08 08								08 38		
Nunhead	d			07 45								08 41	08 15					09 11			08 45		
Peckham Rye	d			07 47								08 43	08 17					09 13			08 47		
Denmark Hill	d			07 51								08 47	08 21					09 17			08 51		
Beckenham Junction	d		07 26			07 41				07 56					08 11					08 26			08 41
Kent House	d		07 28			07 43				07 58					08 13					08 28			08 43
Penge East	d		07 30			07 45				08 00					08 15					08 30			08 45
Sydenham Hill	d		07 33			07 48				08 03					08 18					08 33			08 48
West Dulwich	d		07 35			07 50				08 05					08 20					08 35			08 50
Herne Hill	d	07 28	07 38		07 38	07 53			07 58	08 08				08 08	08 23				08 28	08 38		08 38	08 53
Loughborough Jn	d	07 36			07 46				08 06					08 16					08 36			08 46	
Elephant & Castle	d	07 48			07 58				08 18					08 28					08 48			08 58	
London Blackfriars	d	07a56			08a06				08a26					08a36					08a56			09a06	
City Thameslink	a																						
Farringdon	a																						
St Pancras International	a																						
Kentish Town	a																						
Brixton	d		07 40			07 55				08 10					08 25					08 40			08 55
London Victoria	a		07 47	08 00		08 02	08 21	08 07		08 17	08 37	08 56	08 30		08 32	08 51	08 37	09 26		08 47	09 00		09 02

Station		SE 1	SE 1	FC	SE	SE 1	SE	SE	FC	SE	SE 1	SE 1	SE	FC	SE	SE	FC	SE	SE 1	SE 1	FC	SE
Sevenoaks	d						08 55						09 25									
Bat & Ball	d						08 58						09 28									
Otford	d	08 46					09 01				09 17		09 31						09 46			
Shoreham (Kent)	d						09 04						09 34									
Eynsford	d						09 08						09 38									
Swanley	d	08 54				09 05	09 13				09 26		09 43						09 54			
St Mary Cray	d	08 58				09 09	09 17						09 47						09 58			
Orpington	d				08 40					08 55					09 10			09 25				09 40
Petts Wood	d				08 43					08 58					09 13			09 28				09 43
Bickley	d				08 47		09 21			09 02			09 51		09 17			09 32				09 47
Bromley South	d	09 05	08 50		08 50	09 15	09 24			09 05	09 35	09 20	09 54		09 20			09 35	10 05	09 50		09 50
Shortlands	d				08 53		09 27			09 08			09 57		09 23			09 38				09 53
Ravensbourne	d						09 29						09 59									
Beckenham Hill	d						09 31						10 01									
Bellingham	d						09 33						10 03									
Catford	d						09 36						10 06									
Crofton Park	d						09 38						10 08									
Lewisham	d							09 08								09 38						
Nunhead	d						09 41	09 15					10 11			09 45						
Peckham Rye	d						09 43	09 17					10 13			09 47						
Denmark Hill	d						09 47	09 21					10 17			09 51						
Beckenham Junction	d				08 56					09 11					09 26			09 41				09 56
Kent House	d				08 58					09 13					09 28			09 43				09 58
Penge East	d				09 00					09 15					09 30			09 45				10 00
Sydenham Hill	d				09 03					09 18					09 33			09 48				10 03
West Dulwich	d				09 05					09 20					09 35			09 50				10 05
Herne Hill	d			08 58	09 08				09 08	09 23				09 28	09 38		09 38	09 53			09 58	10 08
Loughborough Jn	d			09 06					09 16					09 36			09 46				10 06	
Elephant & Castle	d			09 18					09 28					09 48			09 58				10 18	
London Blackfriars	d			09a26					09a36					09a56			10a06				10a26	
City Thameslink	a																					
Farringdon	a																					
St Pancras International	a																					
Kentish Town	a																					
Brixton	d				09 10					09 25					09 40			09 55				10 10
London Victoria	a	09 21	09 07		09 17	09 37	09 56	09 30		09 32	09 51	09 37	10 26		09 47	10 00		10 02	10 21	10 07		10 17

Table 195

Saturdays

Sevenoaks, Otford, Orpington, Bromley South, Beckenham Junction and Catford - London

		SE [1]	SE	SE	FC	SE	SE [1]	SE [1]	SE	FC	SE	SE	FC	SE	SE [1]	SE [1]	FC	SE	SE [1]	SE	SE	FC	SE
Sevenoaks [4]	d		09 55						10 25											10 55			
Bat & Ball	d		09 58						10 28											10 58			
Otford [4]	d		10 01				10 17		10 31						10 46					11 01			
Shoreham (Kent)	d		10 04						10 34											11 04			
Eynsford	d		10 08						10 38											11 08			
Swanley [4]	d	10 05	10 13				10 26		10 43						10 54				11 05	11 13			
St Mary Cray	d	10 09	10 17						10 47						10 58				11 09	11 17			
Orpington [4]	d					09 55					10 10			10 25				10 40					10 55
Petts Wood [4]	d					09 58					10 13			10 28				10 43					10 58
Bickley [4]	d		10 21			10 02			10 51		10 17			10 32				10 47		11 21			11 02
Bromley South [4]	d	10 15	10 24			10 05	10 35	10 20	10 54		10 20			10 35	11 05	10 50		10 50	11 15	11 24			11 05
Shortlands [4]	d		10 27			10 08			10 57		10 23			10 38				10 53		11 27			11 08
Ravensbourne	d		10 29						10 59											11 29			
Beckenham Hill	d		10 31						11 01											11 31			
Bellingham	d		10 33						11 03											11 33			
Catford	d		10 36						11 06											11 36			
Crofton Park	d		10 38						11 08											11 38			
Lewisham [4]	d			10 08								10 38									11 08		
Nunhead [4]	d		10 41	10 15					11 11			10 45								11 41	11 15		
Peckham Rye [4]	d		10 43	10 17					11 13			10 47								11 43	11 17		
Denmark Hill [4]	d		10 47	10 21					11 17			10 51								11 47	11 21		
Beckenham Junction [4]	d					10 11					10 26			10 41				10 56					11 11
Kent House [4]	d					10 13					10 28			10 43				10 58					11 13
Penge East	d					10 15					10 30			10 45				11 00					11 15
Sydenham Hill	d					10 18					10 33			10 48				11 03					11 18
West Dulwich	d					10 20					10 35			10 50				11 05					11 20
Herne Hill [4]	d				10 08	10 23				10 28	10 38		10 38	10 53			10 58	11 08				11 08	11 23
Loughborough Jn	d				10 16					10 36			10 46				11 06					11 16	
Elephant & Castle ⊖	d				10 28					10 48			10 58				11 18					11 28	
London Blackfriars [3] ⊖	d				10a36					10a56			11a06				11a26					11a36	
City Thameslink [3]	a																						
Farringdon ⊖	a																						
St Pancras International [15] ⊖	a																						
Kentish Town ⊖	a																						
Brixton ⊖	d					10 25					10 40			10 55				11 10					11 25
London Victoria [15] ⊖	a	10 37	10 56	10 30		10 32	10 51	10 37	11 26		10 47	11 00		11 02	11 21	11 07		11 17	11 37	11 56	11 30		11 32

		SE [1]	SE [1]	SE	FC	SE	SE	FC	SE	SE [1]	SE [1]	FC	SE	SE [1]	SE	SE	FC	SE	SE [1]	SE [1]	SE	FC
Sevenoaks [4]	d			11 25											11 55						12 25	
Bat & Ball	d			11 28											11 58						12 28	
Otford [4]	d	11 17		11 31						11 46					12 01				12 17		12 31	
Shoreham (Kent)	d			11 34											12 04						12 34	
Eynsford	d			11 38											12 08						12 38	
Swanley [4]	d	11 26		11 43						11 54				12 05	12 13				12 26		12 43	
St Mary Cray	d			11 47						11 58				12 09	12 17						12 47	
Orpington [4]	d					11 10			11 25				11 40					11 55				
Petts Wood [4]	d					11 13			11 28				11 43					11 58				
Bickley [4]	d			11 51		11 17			11 32				11 47		12 21			12 02			12 51	
Bromley South [4]	d	11 35	11 20	11 54		11 20			11 35	12 05	11 50		11 50	12 15	12 24			12 05	12 35	12 20	12 54	
Shortlands [4]	d			11 57		11 23			11 38				11 53		12 27			12 08			12 57	
Ravensbourne	d			11 59											12 29						12 59	
Beckenham Hill	d			12 01											12 31						13 01	
Bellingham	d			12 03											12 33						13 03	
Catford	d			12 06											12 36						13 06	
Crofton Park	d			12 08											12 38						13 08	
Lewisham [4]	d						11 38									12 08						
Nunhead [4]	d			12 11			11 45								12 41	12 15					13 11	
Peckham Rye [4]	d			12 13			11 47								12 43	12 17					13 13	
Denmark Hill [4]	d			12 17			11 51								12 47	12 21					13 17	
Beckenham Junction [4]	d					11 26			11 41				11 56					12 11				
Kent House [4]	d					11 28			11 43				11 58					12 13				
Penge East	d					11 30			11 45				12 00					12 15				
Sydenham Hill	d					11 33			11 48				12 03					12 18				
West Dulwich	d					11 35			11 50				12 05					12 20				
Herne Hill [4]	d				11 28	11 38		11 38	11 53			11 58	12 08				12 08	12 23				12 28
Loughborough Jn	d				11 36			11 46				12 06					12 16					12 36
Elephant & Castle ⊖	d				11 48			11 58				12 18					12 28					12 48
London Blackfriars [3] ⊖	d				11a56			12a06				12a26					12a36					12a56
City Thameslink [3]	a																					
Farringdon ⊖	a																					
St Pancras International [15] ⊖	a																					
Kentish Town ⊖	a																					
Brixton ⊖	d					11 40			11 55				12 10					12 25				
London Victoria [15] ⊖	a	11 51	11 37	12 26		11 47	12 00		12 02	12 21	12 07		12 17	12 37	12 56	12 30		12 32	12 51	12 37	13 26	

Table 195

Saturdays

Sevenoaks, Otford, Orpington, Bromley South, Beckenham Junction and Catford - London

		SE	SE	FC	SE	SE [1]	SE [1]	FC	SE	SE [1]	SE	SE	FC	SE	SE [1]	SE [1]	SE	FC	SE	SE	FC	SE	SE [1]
Sevenoaks [4]	d										12 55						13 25						
Bat & Ball	d										12 58						13 28						
Otford [4]	d					12 46					13 01				13 17		13 31						13 46
Shoreham (Kent)	d										13 04						13 34						
Eynsford	d										13 08						13 38						
Swanley [4]	d					12 54				13 05	13 13				13 26		13 43						13 54
St Mary Cray	d					12 58				13 09	13 17						13 47						13 58
Orpington [4]	d	12 10			12 25				12 40					12 55					13 10			13 25	
Petts Wood [4]	d	12 13			12 28				12 43					12 58					13 13			13 28	
Bickley [4]	d	12 17			12 32				12 47		13 21			13 02			13 51		13 17			13 32	
Bromley South [4]	d	12 20			12 35	13 05	12 50		12 50	13 15	13 24			13 05	13 35	13 20	13 54		13 20			13 35	14 05
Shortlands [4]	d	12 23			12 38				12 53		13 27			13 08			13 57		13 23			13 38	
Ravensbourne	d										13 29						13 59						
Beckenham Hill	d										13 31						14 01						
Bellingham	d										13 33						14 03						
Catford	d										13 36						14 06						
Crofton Park	d										13 38						14 08						
Lewisham [4]	d		12 38									13 08								13 38			
Nunhead [4]	d		12 45								13 41	13 15					14 11			13 45			
Peckham Rye [4]	d		12 47								13 43	13 17					14 13			13 47			
Denmark Hill [4]	d		12 51								13 47	13 21					14 17			13 51			
Beckenham Junction [4]	d	12 26			12 41				12 56					13 11					13 26			13 41	
Kent House [4]	d	12 28			12 43				12 58					13 13					13 28			13 43	
Penge East	d	12 30			12 45				13 00					13 15					13 30			13 45	
Sydenham Hill	d	12 33			12 48				13 03					13 18					13 33			13 48	
West Dulwich	d	12 35			12 50				13 05					13 20					13 35			13 50	
Herne Hill [4]	d	12 38		12 38	12 53			12 58	13 08				13 08	13 23				13 28	13 38		13 38	13 53	
Loughborough Jn	d			12 46				13 06					13 16					13 36			13 46		
Elephant & Castle ⊖	d			12 58				13 18					13 28					13 48			13 58		
London Blackfriars [3] ⊖	d			13a06				13a26					13a36					13a56			14a06		
City Thameslink [3]	a																						
Farringdon ⊖	a																						
St Pancras International [15] ⊖	a																						
Kentish Town ⊖	a																						
Brixton ⊖	d	12 40			12 55				13 10					13 25					13 40			13 55	
London Victoria [15] ⊖	a	12 47	13 00		13 02	13 21	13 07		13 17	13 37	13 56	13 30		13 32	13 51	13 37	14 26		13 47	14 00		14 02	14 21

		SE [1]	FC	SE	SE [1]	SE	SE	FC	SE	SE [1]	SE [1]	SE	FC	SE	SE	FC	SE	SE [1]	SE [1]	FC	SE	SE [1]	SE
Sevenoaks [4]	d					13 55						14 25											14 55
Bat & Ball	d					13 58						14 28											14 58
Otford [4]	d					14 01				14 17		14 31						14 46					15 01
Shoreham (Kent)	d					14 04						14 34											15 04
Eynsford	d					14 08						14 38											15 08
Swanley [4]	d				14 05	14 13				14 26		14 43						14 54				15 05	15 13
St Mary Cray	d				14 09	14 17						14 47						14 58				15 09	15 17
Orpington [4]	d			13 40					13 55					14 10			14 25				14 40		
Petts Wood [4]	d			13 43					13 58					14 13			14 28				14 43		
Bickley [4]	d			13 47		14 21			14 02			14 51		14 17			14 32				14 47		15 21
Bromley South [4]	d	13 50		13 50	14 15	14 24			14 05	14 35	14 20	14 54		14 20			14 35	15 05	14 50		14 50	15 15	15 24
Shortlands [4]	d			13 53		14 27			14 08			14 57		14 23			14 38				14 53		15 27
Ravensbourne	d					14 29						14 59											15 29
Beckenham Hill	d					14 31						15 01											15 31
Bellingham	d					14 33						15 03											15 33
Catford	d					14 36						15 06											15 36
Crofton Park	d					14 38						15 08											15 38
Lewisham [4]	d						14 08								14 38								
Nunhead [4]	d					14 41	14 15					15 11			14 45								15 41
Peckham Rye [4]	d					14 43	14 17					15 13			14 47								15 43
Denmark Hill [4]	d					14 47	14 21					15 17			14 51								15 47
Beckenham Junction [4]	d			13 56					14 11					14 26			14 41				14 56		
Kent House [4]	d			13 58					14 13					14 28			14 43				14 58		
Penge East	d			14 00					14 15					14 30			14 45				15 00		
Sydenham Hill	d			14 03					14 18					14 33			14 48				15 03		
West Dulwich	d			14 05					14 20					14 35			14 50				15 05		
Herne Hill [4]	d		13 58	14 08				14 08	14 23				14 28	14 38		14 38	14 53			14 58	15 08		
Loughborough Jn	d		14 06					14 16					14 36			14 46				15 06			
Elephant & Castle ⊖	d		14 18					14 28					14 48			14 58				15 18			
London Blackfriars [3] ⊖	d		14a26					14a36					14a56			15a06				15a26			
City Thameslink [3]	a																						
Farringdon ⊖	a																						
St Pancras International [15] ⊖	a																						
Kentish Town ⊖	a																						
Brixton ⊖	d			14 10					14 25					14 40			14 55				15 10		
London Victoria [15] ⊖	a	14 07		14 17	14 37	14 56	14 30		14 32	14 51	14 37	15 26		14 47	15 00		15 02	15 21	15 07		15 17	15 37	15 56

Sevenoaks, Otford, Orpington, Bromley South, Beckenham Junction and Catford - London

		SE	FC	SE	SE	SE	SE	FC	SE	SE	FC	SE	SE	SE	FC	SE	SE	SE	SE	FC	SE	SE
					1	1							1	1			1					1
Sevenoaks 4	d						15 25											15 55				
Bat & Ball	d						15 28											15 58				
Otford 4	d				15 17		15 31						15 46					16 01				16 17
Shoreham (Kent)	d						15 34											16 04				
Eynsford	d						15 38											16 08				
Swanley 4	d				15 26		15 43						15 54				16 05	16 13				16 26
St Mary Cray	d						15 47						15 58				16 09	16 17				
Orpington 4	d			14 55					15 10			15 25				15 40					15 55	
Petts Wood 4	d			14 58					15 13			15 28				15 43					15 58	
Bickley 4	d			15 02			15 51		15 17			15 32				15 47		16 21			16 02	
Bromley South 4	d			15 05	15 35	15 20	15 54		15 20			15 35	16 05	15 50		15 50	16 15	16 24			16 05	16 35
Shortlands 4	d			15 08			15 57		15 23			15 38				15 53		16 27			16 08	
Ravensbourne	d						15 59											16 29				
Beckenham Hill	d						16 01											16 31				
Bellingham	d						16 03											16 33				
Catford	d						16 06											16 36				
Crofton Park	d						16 08											16 38				
Lewisham 4	d	15 08								15 38									16 08			
Nunhead 4	d	15 15					16 11			15 45								16 41	16 15			
Peckham Rye 4	d	15 17					16 13			15 47								16 43	16 17			
Denmark Hill 4	d	15 21					16 17			15 51								16 47	16 21			
Beckenham Junction 4	d			15 11					15 26			15 41				15 56					16 11	
Kent House 4	d			15 13					15 28			15 43				15 58					16 13	
Penge East	d			15 15					15 30			15 45				16 00					16 15	
Sydenham Hill	d			15 18					15 33			15 48				16 03					16 18	
West Dulwich	d			15 20					15 35			15 50				16 05					16 20	
Herne Hill 4	d		15 08	15 23				15 28	15 38		15 38	15 53			15 58	16 08				16 08	16 23	
Loughborough Jn	d		15 16					15 36			15 46				16 06					16 16		
Elephant & Castle ⊖	d		15 28					15 48			15 58				16 18					16 28		
London Blackfriars 3 ⊖	d		15a36					15a56			16a06				16a26					16a36		
City Thameslink 3	a																					
Farringdon ⊖	a																					
St Pancras International 15 ⊖	a																					
Kentish Town ⊖	a																					
Brixton ⊖	d			15 25					15 40			15 55				16 10					16 25	
London Victoria 15 ⊖	a	15 30		15 32	15 51	15 37	16 26		15 47	16 00		16 02	16 21	16 07		16 17	16 37	16 56	16 30		16 32	16 51

		SE	SE	FC	SE	SE	FC	SE	SE	SE	FC	SE	SE	SE	SE	FC	SE	SE	SE	SE	FC	SE	SE
		1							1	1			1					1	1				
Sevenoaks 4	d		16 25											16 55						17 25			
Bat & Ball	d		16 28											16 58						17 28			
Otford 4	d		16 31						16 46					17 01				17 17		17 31			
Shoreham (Kent)	d		16 34											17 04						17 34			
Eynsford	d		16 38											17 08						17 38			
Swanley 4	d		16 43						16 54				17 05	17 13				17 26		17 43			
St Mary Cray	d		16 47						16 58				17 09	17 17						17 47			
Orpington 4	d				16 10			16 25				16 40					16 55					17 10	17 25
Petts Wood 4	d				16 13			16 28				16 43					16 58					17 13	17 28
Bickley 4	d		16 51		16 17			16 32				16 47		17 21			17 02			17 51		17 17	17 32
Bromley South 4	d	16 20	16 54		16 20			16 35	17 05	16 50		16 50	17 15	17 24			17 05	17 35	17 20	17 54		17 20	17 35
Shortlands 4	d		16 57		16 23			16 38				16 53		17 27			17 08			17 57		17 23	17 38
Ravensbourne	d		16 59											17 29						17 59			
Beckenham Hill	d		17 01											17 31						18 01			
Bellingham	d		17 03											17 33						18 03			
Catford	d		17 06											17 36						18 06			
Crofton Park	d		17 08											17 38						18 08			
Lewisham 4	d					16 38									17 08								
Nunhead 4	d		17 11			16 45								17 41	17 15					18 11			
Peckham Rye 4	d		17 13			16 47								17 43	17 17					18 13			
Denmark Hill 4	d		17 17			16 51								17 47	17 21					18 17			
Beckenham Junction 4	d				16 26			16 41				16 56					17 11					17 26	17 41
Kent House 4	d				16 28			16 43				16 58					17 13					17 28	17 43
Penge East	d				16 30			16 45				17 00					17 15					17 30	17 45
Sydenham Hill	d				16 33			16 48				17 03					17 18					17 33	17 48
West Dulwich	d				16 35			16 50				17 05					17 20					17 35	17 50
Herne Hill 4	d			16 28	16 38		16 38	16 53			16 58	17 08				17 08	17 23				17 28	17 38	17 53
Loughborough Jn	d			16 36			16 46				17 06					17 16					17 36		
Elephant & Castle ⊖	d			16 48			16 58				17 18					17 28					17 48		
London Blackfriars 3 ⊖	d			16a57			17a06				17a26					17a36					17a56		
City Thameslink 3	a																						
Farringdon ⊖	a																						
St Pancras International 15 ⊖	a																						
Kentish Town ⊖	a																						
Brixton ⊖	d				16 40			16 55				17 10					17 25					17 40	17 55
London Victoria 15 ⊖	a	16 37	17 26		16 47	17 00		17 02	17 21	17 07		17 17	17 37	17 56	17 30		17 32	17 51	17 37	18 26		17 47	18 02

Sevenoaks, Otford, Orpington, Bromley South, Beckenham Junction and Catford - London

		SE	SE	SE	FC	SE	SE	SE	SE	FC	SE	SE	SE	SE	FC	SE	SE	FC	SE	SE	SE	FC
			1	1			1					1	1							1	1	
Sevenoaks 4	d							17 55						18 25								
Bat & Ball	d							17 58						18 28								
Otford 4	d		17 46					18 01				18 17		18 31						18 46		
Shoreham (Kent)	d							18 04						18 34								
Eynsford	d							18 08						18 38								
Swanley 4	d		17 54				18 05	18 13				18 26		18 43						18 54		
St Mary Cray	d		17 58				18 09	18 17						18 47						18 58		
Orpington 4	d					17 40					17 55					18 10			18 25			
Petts Wood 4	d					17 43					17 58					18 13			18 28			
Bickley 4	d					17 47		18 21			18 02			18 51		18 17			18 32			
Bromley South 4	d		18 05	17 50		17 50	18 15	18 24			18 05	18 35	18 20	18 54		18 20			18 35	19 05	18 50	
Shortlands 4	d					17 53		18 27			18 08			18 57		18 23			18 38			
Ravensbourne	d							18 29						18 59								
Beckenham Hill	d							18 31						19 01								
Bellingham	d							18 33						19 03								
Catford	d							18 36						19 06								
Crofton Park	d							18 38						19 08								
Lewisham 4	d	17 38							18 08								18 38					
Nunhead 4	d	17 45						18 41	18 15					19 11			18 45					
Peckham Rye 4	d	17 47						18 43	18 17					19 13			18 47					
Denmark Hill 4	d	17 51						18 47	18 21					19 17			18 51					
Beckenham Junction 4	d					17 56					18 11					18 26			18 41			
Kent House 4	d					17 58					18 13					18 28			18 43			
Penge East	d					18 00					18 15					18 30			18 45			
Sydenham Hill	d					18 03					18 18					18 33			18 48			
West Dulwich	d					18 05					18 20					18 35			18 50			
Herne Hill 4	d				17 58	18 08				18 08	18 23				18 28	18 38		18 38	18 53			18 58
Loughborough Jn	d				18 06					18 16					18 36			18 46				19 06
Elephant & Castle ⊖	d				18 18					18 28					18 48			18 58				19 18
London Blackfriars 3 ⊖	d				18a26					18a36					18a56			19a06				19a26
City Thameslink 3	a																					
Farringdon ⊖	a																					
St Pancras International 15 ⊖	a																					
Kentish Town ⊖	a																					
Brixton ⊖	d					18 10					18 25					18 40			18 55			
London Victoria 15 ⊖	a	18 00	18 21	18 07		18 17	18 37	18 56	18 30		18 32	18 51	18 37	19 26		18 47	19 00		19 02	19 21	19 07	

		SE	SE	SE	SE	FC	SE	SE	SE	SE	FC	SE	FC	SE	SE	SE	FC	SE	SE	SE	SE	SE	SE
			1					1	1						1	1				1		1	
Sevenoaks 4	d			18 55						19 25											19 55		20 25
Bat & Ball	d			18 58						19 28											19 58		20 28
Otford 4	d			19 01				19 17		19 31					19 46						20 01		20 31
Shoreham (Kent)	d			19 04						19 34											20 04		20 34
Eynsford	d			19 08						19 38											20 08		20 38
Swanley 4	d		19 05	19 13				19 26		19 43					19 54					20 05	20 13		20 43
St Mary Cray	d		19 09	19 17						19 47					19 58					20 09	20 17		20 47
Orpington 4	d	18 40					18 55					19 10		19 25				19 40	19 55				
Petts Wood 4	d	18 43					18 58					19 13		19 28				19 43	19 58				
Bickley 4	d	18 47		19 21			19 02			19 51		19 17		19 32				19 47	20 02		20 21		20 51
Bromley South 4	d	18 50	19 15	19 24			19 05	19 35	19 20	19 54		19 20		19 35	20 05	19 50		19 50	20 05	20 15	20 24	20 20	20 54
Shortlands 4	d	18 53		19 27			19 08			19 57		19 23		19 38				19 53	20 08		20 27		20 57
Ravensbourne	d			19 29						19 59											20 29		20 59
Beckenham Hill	d			19 31						20 01											20 31		21 01
Bellingham	d			19 33						20 03											20 33		21 03
Catford	d			19 36						20 06											20 36		21 06
Crofton Park	d			19 38						20 08											20 38		21 08
Lewisham 4	d				19 08																		
Nunhead 4	d			19 41	19 15					20 11											20 41		21 11
Peckham Rye 4	d			19 43	19 17					20 13											20 43		21 13
Denmark Hill 4	d			19 47	19 21					20 17											20 47		21 17
Beckenham Junction 4	d	18 56					19 11					19 26		19 41				19 56	20 11				
Kent House 4	d	18 58					19 13					19 28		19 43				19 58	20 13				
Penge East	d	19 00					19 15					19 30		19 45				20 00	20 15				
Sydenham Hill	d	19 03					19 18					19 33		19 48				20 03	20 18				
West Dulwich	d	19 05					19 20					19 35		19 50				20 05	20 20				
Herne Hill 4	d	19 08				19 08	19 23				19 28	19 38	19 38	19 53			19 58	20 08	20 23				
Loughborough Jn	d					19 16					19 36		19 46				20 06						
Elephant & Castle ⊖	d					19 28					19 48		19 58				20 18						
London Blackfriars 3 ⊖	d					19a36					19a56		20a06				20a26						
City Thameslink 3	a																						
Farringdon ⊖	a																						
St Pancras International 15 ⊖	a																						
Kentish Town ⊖	a																						
Brixton ⊖	d	19 10					19 25					19 40		19 55				20 10	20 25				
London Victoria 15 ⊖	a	19 17	19 37	19 56	19 30		19 32	19 51	19 37	20 26		19 47		20 02	20 21	20 07		20 17	20 32	20 37	20 56	20 37	21 26

Table 195 — Saturdays

Sevenoaks, Otford, Orpington, Bromley South, Beckenham Junction and Catford - London

		FC	SE	SE [1]	SE [1]	FC	SE	SE [1]	SE	SE	FC	SE	SE [1]	SE [1]	FC	SE	SE [1]	SE	SE	FC	SE	SE [1]	FC
Sevenoaks [4]	d								20 55	21 25								21 55	22 25				
Bat & Ball	d								20 58	21 28								21 58	22 28				
Otford [4]	d			20 46					21 01	21 31			21 46					22 01	22 31				
Shoreham (Kent)	d								21 04	21 34								22 04	22 34				
Eynsford	d								21 08	21 38								22 08	22 38				
Swanley [4]	d			20 54				21 10	21 13	21 43			21 54				22 10	22 13	22 43				
St Mary Cray	d			20 58				21 14	21 17	21 47			21 58				22 14	22 17	22 47				
Orpington [4]	d		20 10				20 40					21 10				21 40					22 10		
Petts Wood [4]	d		20 13				20 43					21 13				21 43					22 13		
Bickley [4]	d		20 17				20 47		21 21	21 51		21 17				21 47		22 21	22 51		22 17		
Bromley South [4]	d		20 20	21 05	20 50		20 50	21 20	21 24	21 54		21 20	22 05	21 50		21 50	22 20	22 24	22 54		22 20	22 50	
Shortlands [4]	d		20 23				20 53		21 27	21 57		21 23				21 53		22 27	22 57		22 23		
Ravensbourne	d								21 29	21 59								22 29	22 59				
Beckenham Hill	d								21 31	22 01								22 31	23 01				
Bellingham	d								21 33	22 03								22 33	23 03				
Catford	d								21 36	22 06								22 36	23 06				
Crofton Park	d								21 38	22 08								22 38	23 08				
Lewisham [4]	d																						
Nunhead [4]	d								21 41	22 11								22 41	23 11				
Peckham Rye [4]	d								21 43	22 13								22 43	23 13				
Denmark Hill [4]	d								21 47	22 17								22 47	23 17				
Beckenham Junction [4]	d		20 26				20 56					21 26				21 56					22 26		
Kent House [4]	d		20 28				20 58					21 28				21 58					22 28		
Penge East	d		20 30				21 00					21 30				22 00					22 30		
Sydenham Hill	d		20 33				21 03					21 33				22 03					22 33		
West Dulwich	d		20 35				21 05					21 35				22 05					22 35		
Herne Hill [4]	d	20 28	20 38			20 58	21 08				21 28	21 38			21 58	22 08				22 28	22 38		22 58
Loughborough Jn	d	20 36				21 06					21 36				22 06					22 36			23 06
Elephant & Castle	⊖ d	20 48				21 18					21 48				22 18					22 48			23 18
London Blackfriars [3]	⊖ d	20a56				21a26					21a56				22a26					22a56			23a26
City Thameslink [3]	a																						
Farringdon	⊖ a																						
St Pancras International [15]	⊖ a																						
Kentish Town	⊖ a																						
Brixton	⊖ d		20 40				21 10					21 40				22 10					22 40		
London Victoria [15]	⊖ a		20 47	21 21	21 07		21 17	21 37	21 56	22 26		21 47	22 21	22 07		22 17	22 37	22 56	23 26		22 47	23 07	

		SE	SE [1]	SE	SE [1]	SE [1]
Sevenoaks [4]	d					
Bat & Ball	d					
Otford [4]	d				23 16	
Shoreham (Kent)	d					
Eynsford	d					
Swanley [4]	d		23 10		23 24	
St Mary Cray	d		23 14		23 28	
Orpington [4]	d	22 40		23 10		
Petts Wood [4]	d	22 43		23 13		
Bickley [4]	d	22 47		23 17		
Bromley South [4]	d	22 50	23 20	23 20	23 35	23 50
Shortlands [4]	d	22 53		23 23		
Ravensbourne	d					
Beckenham Hill	d					
Bellingham	d					
Catford	d					
Crofton Park	d					
Lewisham [4]	d					
Nunhead [4]	d					
Peckham Rye [4]	d					
Denmark Hill [4]	d					
Beckenham Junction [4]	d	22 56		23 26		
Kent House [4]	d	22 58		23 28		
Penge East	d	23 00		23 30		
Sydenham Hill	d	23 03		23 33		
West Dulwich	d	23 05		23 35		
Herne Hill [4]	d	23 08		23 38		
Loughborough Jn	d					
Elephant & Castle	⊖ d					
London Blackfriars [3]	⊖ d					
City Thameslink [3]	a					
Farringdon	⊖ a					
St Pancras International [15]	⊖ a					
Kentish Town	⊖ a					
Brixton	⊖ d	23 10		23 40		
London Victoria [15]	⊖ a	23 17	23 37	23 47	23 51	00 10

Table 195 — Sundays

Sevenoaks, Otford, Orpington, Bromley South, Beckenham Junction and Catford - London

		SE [1]	SE	SE	SE	SE [1]	SE	SE [1]	SE	SE	SE	SE [1]	SE [1]	SE	SE	SE [1]	SE	SE	SE [1]	SE [1]	SE	SE	SE [1]
Sevenoaks [4]	d									07 54				08 24			08 54				09 24		
Bat & Ball	d									07 57				08 27			08 57				09 27		
Otford [4]	d							07 43		08 00				08 30		08 43	09 00				09 30		09 43
Shoreham (Kent)	d									08 03				08 33			09 03				09 33		
Eynsford	d									08 07				08 37			09 07				09 37		
Swanley [4]	d					07 32		07 51		08 12			08 32	08 42		08 51	09 12			09 32	09 42		09 51
St Mary Cray	d					07 36		07 55		08 16			08 36	08 46		08 55	09 16			09 36	09 46		09 55
Orpington [4]	d		06 43	07 06	07 13		07 36		07 43		08 06				08 36			09 06				09 36	
Petts Wood [4]	d		06 46	07 09	07 16		07 39		07 46		08 09				08 39			09 09				09 39	
Bickley [4]	d		06 50	07 13	07 20		07 43		07 50	08 20	08 13			08 50	08 43		09 20	09 13			09 50	09 43	
Bromley South [4]	d	23p50	06 53	07 16	07 23	07 43	07 46	08 02	07 53	08 23	08 16	08 13	08 43	08 53	08 46	09 02	09 23	09 16	09 13	09 43	09 53	09 46	10 02
Shortlands [4]	d		06 56	07 19	07 26		07 49		07 55	08 26	08 19			08 56	08 49		09 26	09 19			09 56	09 49	
Ravensbourne	d		06 58		07 28				07 58	08 28				08 58			09 28				09 58		
Beckenham Hill	d		07 00		07 30				08 00	08 30				09 00			09 30				10 00		
Bellingham	d		07 02		07 32				08 02	08 32				09 02			09 32				10 02		
Catford	d		07 05		07 35				08 05	08 35				09 05			09 35				10 05		
Crofton Park	d		07 07		07 37				08 07	08 37				09 07			09 37				10 07		
Lewisham [4]	d																						
Nunhead [4]	d		07 10		07 40				08 10	08 40				09 10			09 40				10 10		
Peckham Rye [4]	d		07 12		07 42				08 12	08 42				09 12			09 42				10 12		
Denmark Hill [4]	d		07 16		07 46				08 16	08 46				09 16			09 46				10 16		
Beckenham Junction [4]	d			07 22			07 52				08 22				08 52			09 22				09 52	
Kent House [4]	d			07 24			07 54				08 24				08 54			09 24				09 54	
Penge East	d			07 26			07 56				08 26				08 56			09 26				09 56	
Sydenham Hill	d			07 29			07 59				08 29				08 59			09 29				09 59	
West Dulwich	d			07 31			08 01				08 31				09 01			09 31				10 01	
Herne Hill [4]	d			07 34			08 04				08 34				09 04			09 34				10 04	
Loughborough Jn	d																						
Elephant & Castle	⊖ d																						
London Blackfriars [3]	⊖ d																						
City Thameslink [3]	a																						
Farringdon	⊖ a																						
St Pancras International [15]	⊖ a																						
Kentish Town	⊖ a																						
Brixton	⊖ d			07 36			08 06				08 36				09 06			09 36				10 06	
London Victoria [15]	⊖ a	00 10	07 25	07 43	07 56	08 03	08 13	08 18	08 26	08 55	08 43	08 30	09 02	09 25	09 13	09 18	09 55	09 43	09 29	10 02	10 25	10 13	10 18

		SE	SE	SE [1]	SE [1]	SE	SE [1]	SE	FC	SE	SE [1]	SE [1]	SE	FC	SE	SE [1]	SE	FC	SE	SE [1]	SE [1]	SE	FC
Sevenoaks [4]	d	09 54				10 24		10 54					11 24				11 54					12 24	
Bat & Ball	d	09 57				10 27		10 57					11 27				11 57					12 27	
Otford [4]	d	10 00				10 30	10 43	11 00					11 30			11 43	12 00					12 30	
Shoreham (Kent)	d	10 03				10 33		11 03					11 33				12 03					12 33	
Eynsford	d	10 07				10 37		11 07					11 37				12 07					12 37	
Swanley [4]	d	10 12			10 32	10 42	10 51	11 12				11 32	11 42			11 51	12 12				12 32	12 42	
St Mary Cray	d	10 16			10 36	10 46	10 55	11 16				11 36	11 46			11 55	12 16				12 36	12 46	
Orpington [4]	d		10 06							10 36					11 06				11 36				
Petts Wood [4]	d		10 09							10 39					11 09				11 39				
Bickley [4]	d	10 20	10 13			10 50		11 20		10 43			11 50		11 13		12 20		11 43			12 50	
Bromley South [4]	d	10 23	10 16	10 13	10 43	10 53	11 02	11 23		10 46	11 13	11 43	11 53		11 16	12 02	12 23		11 46	12 13	12 43	12 53	
Shortlands [4]	d	10 26	10 19			10 56		11 26		10 49			11 56		11 19		12 26		11 49			12 56	
Ravensbourne	d	10 28				10 58		11 28					11 58				12 28					12 58	
Beckenham Hill	d	10 30				11 00		11 30					12 00				12 30					13 00	
Bellingham	d	10 32				11 02		11 32					12 02				12 32					13 02	
Catford	d	10 35				11 05		11 35					12 05				12 35					13 05	
Crofton Park	d	10 37				11 07		11 37					12 07				12 37					13 07	
Lewisham [4]	d																						
Nunhead [4]	d	10 40				11 10		11 40					12 10				12 40					13 10	
Peckham Rye [4]	d	10 42				11 12		11 42					12 12				12 42					13 12	
Denmark Hill [4]	d	10 46				11 16		11 46					12 16				12 46					13 16	
Beckenham Junction [4]	d		10 22							10 52					11 22				11 52				
Kent House [4]	d		10 24							10 54					11 24				11 54				
Penge East	d		10 26							10 56					11 26				11 56				
Sydenham Hill	d		10 29							10 59					11 29				11 59				
West Dulwich	d		10 31							11 01					11 31				12 01				
Herne Hill [4]	d		10 34						11 03	11 04				11 33	11 34			12 03	12 04				12 33
Loughborough Jn	d								11 11					11 41				12 11					12 41
Elephant & Castle	⊖ d								11 23					11 53				12 23					12 53
London Blackfriars [3]	⊖ d								11a31					12a01				12a31					13a01
City Thameslink [3]	a																						
Farringdon	⊖ a																						
St Pancras International [15]	⊖ a																						
Kentish Town	⊖ a																						
Brixton	⊖ d		10 36							11 06					11 36				12 06				
London Victoria [15]	⊖ a	10 55	10 43	10 29	11 02	11 25	11 18	11 55		11 13	11 29	12 02	12 25		11 43	12 18	12 55		12 13	12 29	13 02	13 25	

Table 195

Sundays

Sevenoaks, Otford, Orpington, Bromley South, Beckenham Junction and Catford - London

		SE		SE ■1	SE	FC	SE	SE ■1	SE ■1	SE	FC	SE		SE ■1	SE	FC	SE	SE ■1	SE ■1	SE	FC	SE		SE ■1	SE
Sevenoaks ■4	d				12 54					13 24					13 54					14 24					14 54
Bat & Ball	d				12 57					13 27					13 57					14 27					14 57
Otford ■4	d			12 43	13 00					13 30				13 43	14 00					14 30				14 43	15 00
Shoreham (Kent)	d				13 03					13 33					14 03					14 33					15 03
Eynsford	d				13 07					13 37					14 07					14 37					15 07
Swanley ■4	d			12 51	13 12				13 32	13 42				13 51	14 12				14 32	14 42				14 51	15 12
St Mary Cray	d			12 55	13 16				13 36	13 46				13 55	14 16				14 36	14 46				14 55	15 16
Orpington ■4	d	12 06					12 36					13 06					13 36					14 06			
Petts Wood ■4	d	12 09					12 39					13 09					13 39					14 09			
Bickley ■4	d	12 13			13 20		12 43			13 50		13 13			14 20		13 43			14 50		14 13			15 20
Bromley South ■4	d	12 16		13 02	13 23		12 46	13 13	13 43	13 53		13 16		14 02	14 23		13 46	14 13	14 43	14 53		14 16		15 02	15 23
Shortlands ■4	d	12 19			13 26		12 49			13 56		13 19			14 26		13 49			14 56		14 19			15 26
Ravensbourne	d				13 28					13 58					14 28					14 58					15 28
Beckenham Hill	d				13 30					14 00					14 30					15 00					15 30
Bellingham	d				13 32					14 02					14 32					15 02					15 32
Catford	d				13 35					14 05					14 35					15 05					15 35
Crofton Park	d				13 37					14 07					14 37					15 07					15 37
Lewisham ■4	d																								
Nunhead ■4	d				13 40					14 10					14 40					15 10					15 40
Peckham Rye ■4	d				13 42					14 12					14 42					15 12					15 42
Denmark Hill ■4	d				13 46					14 16					14 46					15 16					15 46
Beckenham Junction ■4	d	12 22					12 52					13 22					13 52					14 22			
Kent House ■4	d	12 24					12 54					13 24					13 54					14 24			
Penge East	d	12 26					12 56					13 26					13 56					14 26			
Sydenham Hill	d	12 29					12 59					13 29					13 59					14 29			
West Dulwich	d	12 31					13 01					13 31					14 01					14 31			
Herne Hill ■4	d	12 34				13 03	13 04				13 33	13 34				14 03	14 04				14 33	14 34			
Loughborough Jn	d					13 11					13 41					14 11					14 41				
Elephant & Castle ⊖	d					13 23					13 53					14 23					14 53				
London Blackfriars ■3 ⊖	d					13a31					14a01					14a31					15a01				
City Thameslink ■3	a																								
Farringdon ⊖	a																								
St Pancras International ■15 ⊖	a																								
Kentish Town ⊖	a																								
Brixton ⊖	d	12 36					13 06					13 36					14 06					14 36			
London Victoria ■15 ⊖	a	12 43		13 18	13 55		13 13	13 29	14 02	14 25		13 43		14 18	14 55		14 13	14 29	15 02	15 25		14 43		15 18	15 55

		FC	SE	SE ■1	SE ■1	SE	FC	SE		SE ■1	SE	FC	SE	SE ■1	SE ■1	SE	FC	SE		SE ■1	SE	FC	SE	SE ■1	SE ■1
Sevenoaks ■4	d					15 24					15 54					16 24					16 54				
Bat & Ball	d					15 27					15 57					16 27					16 57				
Otford ■4	d					15 30				15 43	16 00					16 30				16 43	17 00				
Shoreham (Kent)	d					15 33					16 03					16 33					17 03				
Eynsford	d					15 37					16 07					16 37					17 07				
Swanley ■4	d				15 32	15 42				15 51	16 12				16 32	16 42				16 51	17 12				17 32
St Mary Cray	d				15 36	15 46				15 55	16 16				16 36	16 46				16 55	17 16				17 36
Orpington ■4	d		14 36					15 06					15 36					16 06					16 36		
Petts Wood ■4	d		14 39					15 09					15 39					16 09					16 39		
Bickley ■4	d		14 43			15 50		15 13			16 20		15 43			16 50		16 13			17 20		16 43		
Bromley South ■4	d		14 46	15 13	15 43	15 53		15 16		16 02	16 23		15 46	16 13	16 43	16 53		16 16		17 02	17 23		16 46	17 13	17 43
Shortlands ■4	d		14 49			15 56		15 19			16 26		15 49			16 56		16 19			17 26		16 49		
Ravensbourne	d					15 58					16 28					16 58					17 28				
Beckenham Hill	d					16 00					16 30					17 00					17 30				
Bellingham	d					16 02					16 32					17 02					17 32				
Catford	d					16 05					16 35					17 05					17 35				
Crofton Park	d					16 07					16 37					17 07					17 37				
Lewisham ■4	d																								
Nunhead ■4	d					16 10					16 40					17 10					17 40				
Peckham Rye ■4	d					16 12					16 42					17 12					17 42				
Denmark Hill ■4	d					16 16					16 46					17 16					17 46				
Beckenham Junction ■4	d		14 52					15 22					15 52					16 22					16 52		
Kent House ■4	d		14 54					15 24					15 54					16 24					16 54		
Penge East	d		14 56					15 26					15 56					16 26					16 56		
Sydenham Hill	d		14 59					15 29					15 59					16 29					16 59		
West Dulwich	d		15 01					15 31					16 01					16 31					17 01		
Herne Hill ■4	d	15 03	15 04				15 33	15 34				16 03	16 04				16 33	16 34				17 03	17 04		
Loughborough Jn	d	15 11					15 41					16 11					16 41					17 11			
Elephant & Castle ⊖	d	15 23					15 53					16 23					16 53					17 23			
London Blackfriars ■3 ⊖	d	15a31					16a01					16a31					17a01					17a31			
City Thameslink ■3	a																								
Farringdon ⊖	a																								
St Pancras International ■ ⊖	a																								
Kentish Town ⊖	a																								
Brixton ⊖	d		15 06					15 36					16 06					16 36					17 06		
London Victoria ■15 ⊖	a		15 13	15 29	16 02	16 25		15 43		16 18	16 55		16 13	16 29	17 02	17 25		16 43		17 18	17 55		17 13	17 29	18 02

Table 195

Sundays

Sevenoaks, Otford, Orpington, Bromley South, Beckenham Junction and Catford - London

		SE	FC	SE		SE ■1	SE	FC	SE	SE ■1	SE ■1	SE	FC	SE		SE ■1	SE	FC	SE	SE ■1	SE ■1	SE	FC	SE	
Sevenoaks ■4	d	17 24					17 54					18 24					18 54					19 24			
Bat & Ball	d	17 27					17 57					18 27					18 57					19 27			
Otford ■4	d	17 30				17 43	18 00					18 30				18 43	19 00					19 30			
Shoreham (Kent)	d	17 33					18 03					18 33					19 03					19 33			
Eynsford	d	17 37					18 07					18 37					19 07					19 37			
Swanley ■4	d	17 42				17 51	18 12				18 32	18 42				18 51	19 12				19 32	19 42			
St Mary Cray	d	17 46				17 55	18 16				18 36	18 46				18 55	19 16				19 36	19 46			
Orpington ■4	d			17 06					17 36					18 06					18 36					19 06	
Petts Wood ■4	d			17 09					17 39					18 09					18 39					19 09	
Bickley ■4	d	17 50		17 13			18 20		17 43			18 50		18 13			19 20		18 43			19 50		19 13	
Bromley South ■4	d	17 53		17 16		18 02	18 23		17 46	18 13	18 43	18 53		18 16		19 02	19 23		18 46	19 13	19 43	19 53		19 16	
Shortlands ■4	d	17 56		17 19			18 26		17 49			18 56		18 19			19 26		18 49			19 56		19 19	
Ravensbourne	d	17 58					18 28					18 58					19 28					19 58			
Beckenham Hill	d	18 00					18 30					19 00					19 30					20 00			
Bellingham	d	18 02					18 32					19 02					19 32					20 02			
Catford	d	18 05					18 35					19 05					19 35					20 05			
Crofton Park	d	18 07					18 37					19 07					19 37					20 07			
Lewisham ■4	d																								
Nunhead ■4	d	18 10					18 40					19 10					19 40					20 10			
Peckham Rye ■4	d	18 12					18 42					19 12					19 42					20 12			
Denmark Hill ■4	d	18 16					18 46					19 16					19 46					20 16			
Beckenham Junction ■4	d			17 22					17 52					18 22					18 52					19 22	
Kent House ■4	d			17 24					17 54					18 24					18 54					19 24	
Penge East	d			17 26					17 56					18 26					18 56					19 26	
Sydenham Hill	d			17 29					17 59					18 29					18 59					19 29	
West Dulwich	d			17 31					18 01					18 31					19 01					19 31	
Herne Hill ■4	d		17 33	17 34				18 03	18 04				18 33	18 34				19 03	19 04				19 33	19 34	
Loughborough Jn	d		17 41					18 11					18 41					19 11					19 41		
Elephant & Castle ⊖	d		17 53					18 23					18 53					19 23					19 53		
London Blackfriars ■3 ⊖	d		18a01					18a31					19a01					19a31					20a01		
City Thameslink ■3	a																								
Farringdon ⊖	a																								
St Pancras International ■15 ⊖	a																								
Kentish Town ⊖	a																								
Brixton ⊖	d			17 36					18 06					18 36					19 06					19 36	
London Victoria ■15 ⊖	a	18 25		17 43		18 18	18 55		18 13	18 29	19 02	19 25		18 43		19 18	19 55		19 13	19 29	20 02	20 25		19 43	

		SE ■1	SE	FC	SE	SE ■1	SE ■1	SE	FC	SE		SE ■1	SE	FC	SE	SE ■1	SE ■1	SE	FC	SE		SE ■1	SE	FC	SE
Sevenoaks ■4	d		19 54					20 24					20 54					21 24					21 54		
Bat & Ball	d		19 57					20 27					20 57					21 27					21 57		
Otford ■4	d	19 43	20 00					20 30				20 43	21 00					21 30				21 43	22 00		
Shoreham (Kent)	d		20 03					20 33					21 03					21 33					22 03		
Eynsford	d		20 07					20 37					21 07					21 37					22 07		
Swanley ■4	d	19 51	20 12				20 32	20 42				20 51	21 12				21 32	21 42				21 51	22 12		
St Mary Cray	d	19 55	20 16				20 36	20 46				20 55	21 16				21 36	21 46				21 55	22 16		
Orpington ■4	d				19 36					20 06					20 36					21 06					21 36
Petts Wood ■4	d				19 39					20 09					20 39					21 09					21 39
Bickley ■4	d		20 20		19 43			20 50		20 13			21 20		20 43			21 50		21 13			22 20		21 43
Bromley South ■4	d	20 02	20 23		19 46	20 13	20 43	20 53		20 16		21 02	21 23		20 46	21 13	21 43	21 53		21 16		22 02	22 23		21 46
Shortlands ■4	d		20 26		19 49			20 56		20 19			21 26		20 49			21 56		21 19			22 26		21 49
Ravensbourne	d		20 28					20 58					21 28					21 58					22 28		
Beckenham Hill	d		20 30					21 00					21 30					22 00					22 30		
Bellingham	d		20 32					21 02					21 32					22 02					22 32		
Catford	d		20 35					21 05					21 35					22 05					22 35		
Crofton Park	d		20 37					21 07					21 37					22 07					22 37		
Lewisham ■4	d																								
Nunhead ■4	d		20 40					21 10					21 40					22 10					22 40		
Peckham Rye ■4	d		20 42					21 12					21 42					22 12					22 42		
Denmark Hill ■4	d		20 46					21 16					21 46					22 16					22 46		
Beckenham Junction ■4	d				19 52					20 22					20 52					21 22					21 52
Kent House ■4	d				19 54					20 24					20 54					21 24					21 54
Penge East	d				19 56					20 26					20 56					21 26					21 56
Sydenham Hill	d				19 59					20 29					20 59					21 29					21 59
West Dulwich	d				20 01					20 31					21 01					21 31					22 01
Herne Hill ■4	d			20 03	20 04				20 33	20 34				21 03	21 04				21 33	21 34				22 03	22 04
Loughborough Jn	d			20 11					20 41					21 11					21 41					22 11	
Elephant & Castle ⊖	d			20 23					20 53					21 23					21 53					22 23	
London Blackfriars ■3 ⊖	d			20a31					21a01					21a31					22a01					22a31	
City Thameslink ■3	a																								
Farringdon ⊖	a																								
St Pancras International ■15 ⊖	a																								
Kentish Town ⊖	a																								
Brixton ⊖	d				20 06					20 36					21 06					21 36					22 06
London Victoria ■15 ⊖	a	20 18	20 55		20 13	20 29	21 02	21 25		20 43		21 18	21 55		21 13	21 29	22 02	22 25		21 43		22 18	22 55		22 13

Table 195

Sundays

Sevenoaks, Otford, Orpington, Bromley South, Beckenham Junction and Catford - London

	SE	SE ■	SE ■	SE	SE	SE ■	SE	SE ■	SE ■
Sevenoaks d				22 24			22 54		
Bat & Ball d				22 27			22 57		
Otford d				22 30		22 43	23 00		
Shoreham (Kent) d				22 33			23 03		
Eynsford d				22 37			23 07		
Swanley d			22 32	22 42		22 51	23 12		23 32
St Mary Cray d			22 36	22 46		22 55	23 16		23 36
Orpington d	22 06				22 36				
Petts Wood d	22 09				22 39				
Bickley d	22 13			22 50	22 43		23 20		
Bromley South d	22 16	22 13	22 43	22 53	22 46	23 02	23 23	23 13	23 43
Shortlands d	22 19			22 56	22 49		23 26		
Ravensbourne d				22 58			23 28		
Beckenham Hill d				23 00			23 30		
Bellingham d				23 02			23 32		
Catford d				23 05			23 35		
Crofton Park d				23 07			23 37		
Lewisham d									
Nunhead d				23 10			23 40		
Peckham Rye d				23 12			23 42		
Denmark Hill d				23 16			23 46		
Beckenham Junction d	22 22				22 52				
Kent House d	22 24				22 54				
Penge East d	22 26				22 56				
Sydenham Hill d	22 29				22 59				
West Dulwich d	22 31				23 01				
Herne Hill d	22 34				23 04				
Loughborough Jn d									
Elephant & Castle ⊖ d									
London Blackfriars ⊖ d									
City Thameslink a									
Farringdon ⊖ a									
St Pancras International ⊖ a									
Kentish Town ⊖ a									
Brixton ⊖ d	22 36				23 06				
London Victoria ⊖ a	22 43	22 29	23 02	23 25	23 13	23 18	23 55	23 29	00 02

Table 196

Mondays to Fridays

London - Maidstone East and Ashford International

	SE MO ■	SE MX ■	SE MO	SE MX ■	SE MX ■	SE MX	SE MX ■	SE ■	SE ■	SE ■	SE ■	SE	SE ■	SE	SE ■	SE	SE ■	SE ■	SE	SE ■	SE ■	SE
St Pancras International 195 d			23p42			00 12						06 40		07 10		07 40			08 10			08 40
Stratford International ⊖ d			23p49			00 19						06 47		07 17		07 47			08 17			08 47
Ebbsfleet International d			00 01			00 31						06 59		07 30		08 00			08 30			09 00
London Victoria ⊖ d	22p45	23p07			00 07			06 07			06 37		07 07		07 36			08 07			08 37	
London Blackfriars ⊖ 195 d																						
Elephant & Castle ⊖ 195 d																						
Bromley South 195 d	23p01	23p23			00 25			06 23			06 58		07 23		07 53			08 23			08 53	
St Mary Cray 195 d	23p08	23p30			00 31			06 30			07 04		07 30		08 00			08 30			09 00	
Swanley 195 d	23p12	23p34			00 36			06 34			07 08		07 34		08 04			08 34			09 04	
Otford 195 d	23p20	23p42			00 47			06 42			07 16		07 42		08 12			08 42			09 12	
Kemsing d		23p47			00 52			06 47			07 21		07 47		08 17			08 47			09 17	
Borough Green & Wrotham d	23p28	23p52			00 56			06 52			07 26		07 52		08 22			08 52			09 22	
West Malling d	23p34	23p58			01 02			06 58			07 32		07 58		08 28			08 58			09 28	
East Malling d	23p37	00 02			01 05			07 01			07 35		08 01		08 31			09 01			09 31	
Barming d	23p40	00 05			01 09			07 04			07 38		08 04		08 34			09 04			09 34	
Maidstone East a	23p44	00 09			01 13			07 08			07 42		08 08		08 38			09 08			09 38	
d	23p45	00 09			01 13			07 09		06 35	07 43		08 09		08 39			09 09			09 39	
Bearsted d	23p50	00 14			01 18			07 14		06 40	07 48		08 14		08 44			09 14			09 44	
Hollingbourne d	23p54	00 18			01 22			07 18		06 43	07 52		08 18		08 48			09 18			09 48	
Harrietsham d	23p57	00 21			01 25			07 21		06 47	07 55		08 21		08 51			09 21			09 51	
Lenham d	00 01	00 24			01 28			07 24		06 50	07 58		08 24		08 54			09 24			09 54	
Charing d	00 06	00 29			01 33			07 29		06 55	08 03		08 29		08 59			09 29			09 59	
Ashford International a	00 14	00 38	00 19		01 41	00 50		07 38		07 02	08 11	07 19	08 38	07 50	09 08	08 20	07 50	09 38	08 50		10 08	09 20
d				00 03			01 03		06 33	07 03		07 22		07 52		08 22	07 55		08 52	08 33		09 22
Canterbury West 207 a				00 25			01 24		06 55	07 24		07 39				08 39	08 16			08 54		09 39

	SE ■	SE ■	SE	SE ■	SE ■	SE	SE ■	SE ■	SE	SE ■	SE ■	SE	SE ■	SE ■	SE	SE ■	SE ■	SE	SE ■	SE ■	SE	SE ■
St Pancras International ⊖ 195 d			09 12			09 40			10 12			10 42			11 12			11 42			12 12	
Stratford International ⊖ d			09 19			09 47			10 19			10 49			11 19			11 49			12 19	
Ebbsfleet International d			09 31			09 59			10 31			11 01			11 31			12 01			12 31	
London Victoria ⊖ d		09 07			09 37			10 07			10 37			11 07			11 37			12 07		
London Blackfriars ⊖ 195 d																						
Elephant & Castle ⊖ 195 d																						
Bromley South 195 d		09 23			09 53			10 23			10 53			11 23			11 53			12 23		
St Mary Cray 195 d					10 00						11 00						12 00					
Swanley 195 d		09 33			10 04			10 33			11 04			11 33			12 04			12 33		
Otford 195 d		09 41			10 12			10 41			11 12			11 41			12 12			12 41		
Kemsing d					10 17						11 17						12 17					
Borough Green & Wrotham d		09 48			10 22			10 48			11 22			11 48			12 22			12 48		
West Malling d		09 54			10 28			10 54			11 28			11 54			12 28			12 54		
East Malling d					10 31						11 31						12 31					
Barming d					10 34						11 34						12 34					
Maidstone East a		10 01			10 38			11 01			11 38			12 01			12 38			13 01		
d		10 02			10 39			11 02			11 39			12 02			12 39			13 02		
Bearsted d		10 07			10 44			11 07			11 44			12 07			12 44			13 07		
Hollingbourne d					10 48						11 48						12 48					
Harrietsham d					10 51						11 51						12 51					
Lenham d					10 54						11 54						12 54					
Charing d					10 59						11 59						12 59					
Ashford International a		10 27	09 50		11 08	10 18		11 27	10 50		12 08	11 20		12 27	11 50		13 08	12 20		13 27	12 50	
d	09 03		09 52	09 33		10 22	10 03		10 52	10 33		11 22	11 03		11 52	11 33		12 22	12 03		12 52	12 33
Canterbury West 207 a	09 21			09 54		10 39	10 21			10 54		11 39	11 21			11 54		12 39	12 21			12 54

	SE ■	SE	SE ■	SE ■	SE	SE ■	SE ■	SE	SE ■	SE ■	SE	SE ■	SE ■	SE	SE ■	SE ■	SE	SE ■	SE ■	SE	SE ■
St Pancras International ⊖ 195 d		12 42			13 12			13 42			14 12			14 42			15 12			15 42	
Stratford International ⊖ d		12 49			13 19			13 49			14 19			14 49			15 19			15 49	
Ebbsfleet International d		13 01			13 31			14 01			14 31			15 01			15 31			16 01	
London Victoria ⊖ d	12 37			13 07			13 37			14 07			14 37			15 07			15 37		
London Blackfriars ⊖ 195 d																					
Elephant & Castle ⊖ 195 d																					
Bromley South 195 d	12 53			13 23			13 53			14 23			14 53			15 23			15 53		
St Mary Cray 195 d	13 00						14 00						15 00						16 00		
Swanley 195 d	13 04			13 33			14 04			14 33			15 04			15 33			16 04		
Otford 195 d	13 12			13 41			14 12			14 41			15 12			15 41			16 12		
Kemsing d	13 17						14 17						15 17						16 17		
Borough Green & Wrotham d	13 22			13 48			14 22			14 48			15 22			15 48			16 22		
West Malling d	13 28			13 54			14 28			14 54			15 28			15 54			16 28		
East Malling d	13 31						14 31						15 31						16 31		
Barming d	13 34						14 34						15 34						16 34		
Maidstone East a	13 38			14 01			14 38			15 01			15 38			16 01			16 38		
d	13 39			14 02			14 39			15 02			15 39			16 02			16 39		
Bearsted d	13 44			14 07			14 44			15 07			15 44			16 07			16 44		
Hollingbourne d	13 48						14 48						15 48			16 11			16 48		
Harrietsham d	13 51						14 51						15 51			16 14			16 51		
Lenham d	13 54						14 54						15 54			16 17			16 54		
Charing d	13 59						14 59						15 59			16 22			16 59		
Ashford International a	14 08	13 20		14 27	13 50		15 08	14 20		15 27	14 50		16 08	15 20		16 30	15 50		17 08	16 20	
d		13 22	13 03		13 52	13 33		14 22	14 03		14 52	14 33		15 22	15 03		15 52	15 33		16 22	16 03
Canterbury West 207 a		13 39	13 21			13 54		14 39	14 21			14 54		15 39	15 21			15 54		16 39	16 21

Table 196

London - Maidstone East and Ashford International

Mondays to Fridays

	SE ■	SE	SE ■	SE ■	SE	SE ■	SE ■		SE	SE ■	SE ■	SE ■	SE	SE ■	FC ■	SE	SE ■		SE ■	SE	SE ■	SE	SE ■	SE
St Pancras International ⊖195 d		16 12			16 42				17 10				17 40							18 10				18 40
Stratford International ⊖ d		16 19			16 49				17 17				17 47							18 17				18 47
Ebbsfleet International d		16 31			17 01																			
London Victoria ⊖ d	16 07			16 37		16 58				17 12	17 28			17 42					18 03		18 18			
London Blackfriars ⊖195 d															17 48									
Elephant & Castle ⊖195 d															17 52									
Bromley South 195 d	16 23			16 53		17 19				17 28	17 50			17 59	18 11				18 24		18 39			
St Mary Cray 195 d				17 00						17 35	17 57			18 06	18 17						18 45			
Swanley 195 d	16 33			17 04						17 39	18 01			18 11	18 22						18 50			
Otford 195 d	16 41			17 12		17 35				17 48	18 10			18 19	18 30				18 41		18 58			
Kemsing d				17 17						17 53				18 24	18 35						19 03			
Borough Green & Wrotham d	16 48			17 22		17 43				17 57	18 17			18 29	18 40				18 49		19 08			
West Malling d	16 54			17 28		17 49				18 03	18 23			18 35	18 46				18 55		19 14			
East Malling d				17 31						18 06				18 38	18 49						19 17			
Barming d				17 34						18 10				18 41	18 52						19 20			
Maidstone East a	17 01			17 38		17 56				18 14	18 33			18 45	18 56				19 02		19 24			
d	17 02			17 39		17 57				18 15				18 46	18 57				19 03		19 25			
Bearsted d	17 07			17 44		18 02				18 20				18 51	19 02				19 08		19 30			
Hollingbourne d	17 11			17 48		18 05				18 23				18 55	19 06				19 11		19 34			
Harrietsham d	17 14			17 51		18 09				18 27				18 58	19 09				19 15		19 37			
Lenham d	17 17			17 54		18 12				18 30				19 01	19 12				19 18		19 40			
Charing d	17 22			17 59		18 17				18 35				19 06	19 17				19 23		19 45			
Ashford International a	17 32	16 50		18 10	17 20	18 27			17 46	18 45			18 16	19 16	19 27				19 32	18 46	19 55			19 16
d		16 52	16 35		17 22		17 03		17 50			17 35	18 20			17 52	18 03			18 50		18 22	18 34	19 20
Canterbury West 207 a			16 56		17 39		17 25					17 58				18 09	18 25					18 39	18 56	

	SE ■	SE	SE ■		SE ■	SE	SE	SE ■	SE ■	SE	SE ■	SE ■	SE		SE ■	SE ■	SE	SE ■	SE ■	SE	SE	SE ■	SE ■	
St Pancras International ⊖195 d						19 12				19 42			20 12				20 42			21 12	21 42			
Stratford International ⊖ d						19 19				19 49			20 19				20 49			21 19	21 49			
Ebbsfleet International d						19 31				20 01			20 31				21 01			21 31	22 01			
London Victoria ⊖ d	18 42				19 07				19 37			20 07				20 37			21 07				22 07	
London Blackfriars ⊖195 d																								
Elephant & Castle ⊖195 d																								
Bromley South 195 d	18 59				19 27				19 53			20 23				20 53			21 23				22 23	
St Mary Cray 195 d	19 06								20 00							21 00			21 30				22 30	
Swanley 195 d	19 11				19 36				20 04			20 33				21 04			21 34				22 34	
Otford 195 d	19 19				19 44				20 12			20 41				21 12			21 42				22 42	
Kemsing d	19 24								20 17							21 17			21 47				22 47	
Borough Green & Wrotham d	19 29				19 51				20 22			20 48				21 22			21 52				22 52	
West Malling d	19 35				19 57				20 28			20 54				21 28			21 58				22 58	
East Malling d	19 38								20 31							21 31			22 01				23 01	
Barming d	19 41								20 34							21 34			22 04				23 04	
Maidstone East a	19 45				20 04				20 38			21 01				21 38			22 08				23 08	
d	19 46				20 05				20 39			21 02				21 39			22 09				23 09	
Bearsted d	19 51				20 10				20 44			21 07				21 44			22 14				23 14	
Hollingbourne d	19 55				20 14				20 48			21 11				21 48			22 18				23 18	
Harrietsham d	19 58				20 17				20 51			21 14				21 51			22 21				23 21	
Lenham d	20 01				20 20				20 54			21 17				21 54			22 24				23 24	
Charing d	20 06				20 25				20 59			21 22				21 59			22 29				23 29	
Ashford International a	20 16		19 00		20 33	19 50			21 08	20 20		21 30	20 50			22 09	21 20		22 38	21 50	22 20		23 38	
d		18 52	19 04			19 52	19 22	19 29		20 22	20 06		20 52		20 35		21 22	21 03		21 52	22 22	22 03		
Canterbury West 207 a		19 09	19 25				19 39	19 52		20 39	20 24				20 56		21 39	21 25			22 39	22 25		

	SE	SE	SE ■	SE ■	SE
St Pancras International ⊖195 d	22 12	22 42			23 12
Stratford International ⊖ d	22 19	22 49			23 19
Ebbsfleet International d	22 31	23 01			23 31
London Victoria ⊖ d				23 07	
London Blackfriars ⊖195 d					
Elephant & Castle ⊖195 d					
Bromley South 195 d				23 23	
St Mary Cray 195 d				23 30	
Swanley 195 d				23 34	
Otford 195 d				23 42	
Kemsing d				23 47	
Borough Green & Wrotham d				23 52	
West Malling d				23 58	
East Malling d				00 02	
Barming d				00 05	
Maidstone East a				00 09	
d				00 09	
Bearsted d				00 14	
Hollingbourne d				00 18	
Harrietsham d				00 21	
Lenham d				00 24	
Charing d				00 29	
Ashford International a	22 50	23 20		00 38	23 50
d	22 52	23 22	23 03		23 52
Canterbury West 207 a		23 39	23 25		

Table 196

London - Maidstone East and Ashford International

Saturdays

	SE ■	SE ■	SE	SE ■	SE ■	SE ■	SE ■	SE ■	SE	SE ■		SE ■	SE	SE ■	SE ■	SE ■	SE ■	SE ■	SE ■	SE	SE ■	SE ■	SE	SE ■
St Pancras International ⊖195 d			00 12						06 40				07 12							08 42			09 12	
Stratford International ⊖ d			00 19						06 47				07 19							08 49			09 19	
Ebbsfleet International d			00 31						06 59				07 31							09 01			09 31	
London Victoria ⊖ d	23p07				00 07	06 07						07 07			07 37		08 07		08 37			09 07		
London Blackfriars ⊖195 d																								
Elephant & Castle ⊖195 d																								
Bromley South 195 d	23p23				00 25	06 23						07 23			07 53		08 23		08 53			09 23		
St Mary Cray 195 d	23p30				00 31	06 30						07 30			08 00				09 00					
Swanley 195 d	23p34				00 36	06 34						07 34			08 04		08 33		09 04			09 33		
Otford 195 d	23p42				00 47	06 42						07 42			08 12		08 41		09 12			09 41		
Kemsing d	23p47				00 52	06 47						07 47			08 17				09 17					
Borough Green & Wrotham d	23p52				00 56	06 52						07 52			08 22		08 48		09 22			09 48		
West Malling d	23p58				01 02	06 58						07 58			08 28		08 54		09 28			09 54		
East Malling d	00 02				01 05	07 01						08 01			08 31				09 31					
Barming d	00 05				01 09	07 04						08 04			08 34				09 34					
Maidstone East a	00 09				01 13	07 08						08 08			08 38		09 01		09 38			10 01		
d	00 09				01 13	07 09	06 30					08 09			08 39		09 02		09 39			10 02		
Bearsted d	00 14				01 18	07 14	06 35					08 14			08 44		09 07		09 44			10 07		
Hollingbourne d	00 18				01 22	07 18	06 38					08 18			08 48				09 48					
Harrietsham d	00 21				01 25	07 21	06 42					08 21			08 51				09 51					
Lenham d	00 24				01 28	07 24	06 45					08 24			08 54				09 54					
Charing d	00 29				01 33	07 29	06 50					08 29			08 59				09 59					
Ashford International a	00 38		00 50		01 41	07 38	06 58		07 19	06 56		08 38	07 50		09 08		09 27		10 08	09 20	08 56	10 27	09 50	
d		00 03		01 03				06 33	07 22	07 03			07 52	07 33		08 03		08 33		09 22	09 03		09 52	09 33
Canterbury West 207 a		00 25		01 24				06 54	07 39	07 21				07 54		08 21		08 54		09 39	09 21			09 54

	SE ■	SE	SE ■	SE ■	SE		SE ■	SE ■	SE	SE ■	SE ■	SE	SE ■	SE ■	SE		SE ■	SE ■	SE	SE ■	SE ■	SE	SE ■	SE ■
St Pancras International ⊖195 d		09 40			10 12				10 42			11 12			11 42				12 12			12 42		
Stratford International ⊖ d		09 47			10 19				10 49			11 19			11 49				12 19			12 49		
Ebbsfleet International d		09 59			10 31				11 01			11 31			12 01				12 31			13 01		
London Victoria ⊖ d	09 37			10 07				10 37			11 07			11 37				12 07			12 37			13 07
London Blackfriars ⊖195 d																								
Elephant & Castle ⊖195 d																								
Bromley South 195 d	09 53			10 23				10 53			11 23			11 53				12 23			12 53			13 23
St Mary Cray 195 d	10 00							11 00						12 00							13 00			
Swanley 195 d	10 04			10 33				11 04			11 33			12 04				12 33			13 04			13 33
Otford 195 d	10 12			10 41				11 12			11 41			12 12				12 41			13 12			13 41
Kemsing d	10 17							11 17						12 17							13 17			
Borough Green & Wrotham d	10 22			10 48				11 22			11 48			12 22				12 48			13 22			13 48
West Malling d	10 28			10 54				11 28			11 54			12 28				12 54			13 28			13 54
East Malling d	10 31							11 31						12 31							13 31			
Barming d	10 34							11 34						12 34							13 34			
Maidstone East a	10 38			11 01				11 38			12 01			12 38				13 01			13 38			14 01
d	10 39			11 02				11 39			12 02			12 39				13 02			13 39			14 02
Bearsted d	10 44			11 07				11 44			12 07			12 44				13 07			13 44			14 07
Hollingbourne d	10 48							11 48						12 48							13 48			
Harrietsham d	10 51							11 51						12 51							13 51			
Lenham d	10 54							11 54						12 54							13 54			
Charing d	10 59							11 59						12 59							13 59			
Ashford International a	11 08	10 18	09 56	11 27	10 50			12 08	11 20	10 56	12 27	11 50		13 08	12 20		11 56	13 27	12 50		14 08	13 20	12 56	14 27
d		10 22	10 03		10 52		10 33		11 22	11 03		11 52	11 33		12 22		12 03		12 52	12 33		13 22	13 03	
Canterbury West 207 a		10 39	10 21				10 54		11 39	11 21			11 54		12 39		12 21			12 54		13 39	13 21	

	SE		SE ■	SE ■	SE	SE ■	SE ■	SE	SE ■	SE ■	SE		SE ■	SE ■	SE	SE ■	SE ■	SE	SE ■	SE ■	SE		SE ■	SE ■
St Pancras International ⊖195 d	13 12				13 42			14 12			14 42				15 12			15 42			16 12			
Stratford International ⊖ d	13 19				13 49			14 19			14 49				15 19			15 49			16 19			
Ebbsfleet International d	13 31				14 01			14 31			15 01				15 31			16 01			16 31			
London Victoria ⊖ d				13 37			14 07			14 37				15 07			15 37			16 07				16 37
London Blackfriars ⊖195 d																								
Elephant & Castle ⊖195 d																								
Bromley South 195 d				13 53			14 23			14 53				15 23			15 53			16 23				16 53
St Mary Cray 195 d				14 00						15 00							16 00							17 00
Swanley 195 d				14 04			14 33			15 04				15 33			16 04			16 33				17 04
Otford 195 d				14 12			14 41			15 12				15 41			16 12			16 41				17 12
Kemsing d				14 17						15 17							16 17							17 17
Borough Green & Wrotham d				14 22			14 48			15 22				15 48			16 22			16 48				17 22
West Malling d				14 28			14 54			15 28				15 54			16 28			16 54				17 28
East Malling d				14 31						15 31							16 31							17 31
Barming d				14 34						15 34							16 34							17 34
Maidstone East a				14 38			15 01			15 38				16 01			16 38			17 01				17 38
d				14 39			15 02			15 39				16 02			16 39			17 02				17 39
Bearsted d				14 44			15 07			15 44				16 07			16 44			17 07				17 44
Hollingbourne d				14 48						15 48							16 48							17 48
Harrietsham d				14 51						15 51							16 51							17 51
Lenham d				14 54						15 54							16 54							17 54
Charing d				14 59						15 59							16 59							17 59
Ashford International a	13 50			15 08	14 20	13 56	15 27	14 50		16 08	15 20		14 56	16 27	15 50		17 08	16 20	15 56	17 27	16 50			18 08
d	13 52		13 33		14 22	14 03		14 52	14 33		15 22		15 03		15 52	15 33		16 22	16 03		16 52		16 33	
Canterbury West 207 a			13 54		14 39	14 21			14 54		15 39		15 21			15 54		16 39	16 21				16 54	

Table 196

London - Maidstone East and Ashford International

Saturdays

	SE	SE 1	SE 1	SE	SE 1	SE 1	SE	SE 1	SE 1	SE	SE 1	SE 1	SE	SE 1	SE 1	SE	SE 1	SE	SE 1	SE 1	SE	SE
St Pancras International ⊖195 d	16 42			17 12			17 42			18 12			18 42			19 12		19 42			20 12	20 42
Stratford International ⊖ d	16 49			17 19			17 49			18 19			18 49			19 19		19 49			20 19	20 49
Ebbsfleet International d	17 01			17 31			18 01			18 31			19 01			19 31		20 01			20 31	21 01
London Victoria ⊖ d			17 07			17 37			18 07			18 37			19 07		19 37			20 07		
London Blackfriars ⊖195 d																						
Elephant & Castle ⊖195 d																						
Bromley South 195 d			17 23			17 53			18 23			18 53			19 23		19 53			20 23		
St Mary Cray 195 d						18 00						19 00					20 00			20 30		
Swanley 195 d			17 33			18 04			18 33			19 04			19 33		20 04			20 34		
Otford 195 d			17 41			18 12			18 41			19 12			19 41		20 12			20 42		
Kemsing d						18 17						19 17					20 17			20 47		
Borough Green & Wrotham d			17 48			18 22			18 48			19 22			19 48		20 22			20 52		
West Malling d			17 54			18 28			18 54			19 28			19 54		20 28			20 58		
East Malling d						18 31						19 31					20 31			21 01		
Barming d						18 34						19 34					20 34			21 04		
Maidstone East a			18 01			18 38			19 01			19 38			20 01		20 38			21 08		
d			18 02			18 39			19 02			19 39			20 02		20 39			21 09		
Bearsted d			18 07			18 44			19 07			19 44			20 07		20 44			21 14		
Hollingbourne d						18 48						19 48					20 48			21 18		
Harrietsham d						18 51						19 51					20 51			21 21		
Lenham d						18 54						19 54					20 54			21 24		
Charing d						18 59						19 59					20 59			21 29		
Ashford International a	17 20	16 56	18 27	17 50		19 08	18 20	17 56	19 27	18 50		20 08	19 20	18 56	20 27	19 50	21 08	20 20	19 56	21 38	20 50	21 20
d	17 22	17 03		17 52	17 33		18 22	18 03		18 52	18 33		19 22	19 03		19 52		20 22	20 03		20 52	21 22
Canterbury West 207 a	17 39	17 21			17 54		18 39	18 21			18 54		19 39	19 25				20 39	20 25			21 39

	SE 1	SE 1	SE	SE	SE 1	SE 1	SE	SE	SE 1	SE 1	SE	SE 1
St Pancras International ⊖195 d			21 12	21 42			22 12	22 42			23 12	
Stratford International ⊖ d			21 19	21 49			22 19	22 49			23 19	
Ebbsfleet International d			21 31	22 01			22 31	23 01			23 31	
London Victoria ⊖ d		21 07				22 07				23 07		
London Blackfriars ⊖195 d												
Elephant & Castle ⊖195 d												
Bromley South 195 d		21 23				22 23				23 23		
St Mary Cray 195 d		21 30				22 30				23 30		
Swanley 195 d		21 34				22 34				23 34		
Otford 195 d		21 42				22 42				23 42		
Kemsing d		21 47				22 47				23 47		
Borough Green & Wrotham d		21 52				22 52				23 52		
West Malling d		21 58				22 58				23 58		
East Malling d		22 01				23 01				00 01		
Barming d		22 04				23 04				00 04		
Maidstone East a		22 08				23 08				00 08		
d		22 09				23 09				00 09		
Bearsted d		22 14				23 14				00 14		
Hollingbourne d		22 18				23 18				00 18		
Harrietsham d		22 21				23 21				00 21		
Lenham d		22 24				23 24				00 24		
Charing d		22 29				23 29				00 29		
Ashford International a	20 56	22 38	21 50	22 20	21 57	23 38	22 50	23 20	22 57	00 38	23 50	23 57
d	21 03		21 52	22 22	22 03		22 52	23 22	23 03		23 52	00 03
Canterbury West 207 a	21 25			22 39	22 25			23 39	23 25			00 25

Sundays

	SE 1	SE 1	SE 1	SE 1	SE	SE 1	SE 1	SE 1	SE	SE 1	SE 1	SE 1	SE	SE 1	SE 1	SE	SE 1	SE	SE 1	SE 1	SE	SE 1
St Pancras International ⊖195 d					00 12				08 42				09 40			10 12		10 42			11 12	
Stratford International ⊖ d					00 19				08 49				09 47			10 19		10 49			11 19	
Ebbsfleet International d					00 31				09 01				09 59			10 31		11 01			11 31	
London Victoria ⊖ d	23p07			00 07			07 45			08 45				09 45					10 45			
London Blackfriars ⊖195 d																						
Elephant & Castle ⊖195 d																						
Bromley South 195 d	23p23			00 25			08 01			09 01				10 01					11 01			
St Mary Cray 195 d	23p30			00 31			08 08			09 08				10 08					11 08			
Swanley 195 d	23p34			00 36			08 12			09 12				10 12					11 12			
Otford 195 d	23p42			00 47			08 20			09 20				10 20					11 20			
Kemsing d	23p47			00 52																		
Borough Green & Wrotham d	23p52			00 56			08 28			09 28				10 28					11 28			
West Malling d	23p58			01 02			08 34			09 34				10 34					11 34			
East Malling d	00 01			01 05			08 37			09 37				10 37					11 37			
Barming d	00 04			01 09			08 40			09 40				10 40					11 40			
Maidstone East a	00 08			01 13			08 44			09 44				10 44					11 44			
d	00 09			01 13			08 45			09 45				10 45					11 45			
Bearsted d	00 14			01 18			08 50			09 50				10 50					11 50			
Hollingbourne d	00 18			01 22			08 54			09 54				10 54					11 54			
Harrietsham d	00 21			01 25			08 57			09 57				10 57					11 57			
Lenham d	00 24			01 28			09 00			10 00				11 00					12 00			
Charing d	00 29			01 33			09 05			10 05				11 05					12 05			
Ashford International a	00 38	23p57		01 41	00 50		09 13		09 20	10 13	08 56		10 18	11 13	09 56	10 50		11 20	12 13	10 56	11 50	
d		00 03	00 03			01 03		08 33	09 22		09 03	09 33	10 22		10 03	10 52	10 33	11 22		11 03	11 52	11 33
Canterbury West 207 a		00 25	00 25			01 24		08 54	09 39		09 21	09 54	10 39		10 21		10 54	11 39		11 21		11 54

Table 196

London - Maidstone East and Ashford International

Sundays

	SE	SE 1	SE 1	SE	SE 1	SE	SE 1	SE 1	SE	SE 1	SE	SE 1	SE 1	SE	SE 1	SE	SE 1	SE 1	SE	SE 1	SE	SE 1
St Pancras International ⊖195 d	11 42			12 12		12 42			13 12		13 42			14 12		14 42			15 12		15 42	
Stratford International ⊖ d	11 49			12 19		12 49			13 19		13 49			14 19		14 49			15 19		15 49	
Ebbsfleet International d	12 01			12 31		13 01			13 31		14 01			14 31		15 01			15 31		16 01	
London Victoria ⊖ d		11 45					12 45					13 45					14 45					15 45
London Blackfriars ⊖195 d																						
Elephant & Castle ⊖195 d																						
Bromley South 195 d		12 01					13 01					14 01					15 01					16 01
St Mary Cray 195 d		12 08					13 08					14 08					15 08					16 08
Swanley 195 d		12 12					13 12					14 12					15 12					16 12
Otford 195 d		12 20					13 20					14 20					15 20					16 20
Kemsing d																						
Borough Green & Wrotham d		12 28					13 28					14 28					15 28					16 28
West Malling d		12 34					13 34					14 34					15 34					16 34
East Malling d		12 37					13 37					14 37					15 37					16 37
Barming d		12 40					13 40					14 40					15 40					16 40
Maidstone East a		12 44					13 44					14 44					15 44					16 44
d		12 45					13 45					14 45					15 45					16 45
Bearsted d		12 50					13 50					14 50					15 50					16 50
Hollingbourne d		12 54					13 54					14 54					15 54					16 54
Harrietsham d		12 57					13 57					14 57					15 57					16 57
Lenham d		13 00					14 00					15 00					16 00					17 00
Charing d		13 05					14 05					15 05					16 05					17 05
Ashford International a	12 20	13 13	11 56	12 50		13 20	14 13	12 56	13 50		14 20	15 13	13 56	14 50		15 20	16 13	14 56	15 50		16 20	17 13
d	12 22		12 03	12 52	12 33	13 22		13 03	13 52	13 33	14 22		14 03	14 52	14 33	15 22		15 03	15 52	15 33	16 22	
Canterbury West 207 a	12 39		12 21		12 54	13 39		13 21		13 54	14 39		14 21		14 54	15 39		15 21		15 54	16 39	

	SE 1	SE	SE 1	SE	SE 1	SE 1	SE	SE 1	SE	SE 1	SE 1	SE	SE	SE 1	SE 1	SE	SE	SE 1	SE 1	SE	SE
St Pancras International ⊖195 d		16 12		16 42			17 12		17 42			18 12	18 42			19 12	19 42			20 12	20 42
Stratford International ⊖ d		16 19		16 49			17 19		17 49			18 19	18 49			19 19	19 49			20 19	20 49
Ebbsfleet International d		16 31		17 01			17 31		18 01			18 31	19 01			19 31	20 01			20 31	21 01
London Victoria ⊖ d					16 45					17 45				18 45				19 45			
London Blackfriars ⊖195 d																					
Elephant & Castle ⊖195 d																					
Bromley South 195 d					17 01					18 01				19 01				20 01			
St Mary Cray 195 d					17 08					18 08				19 08				20 08			
Swanley 195 d					17 12					18 12				19 12				20 12			
Otford 195 d					17 20					18 20				19 20				20 20			
Kemsing d																					
Borough Green & Wrotham d					17 28					18 28				19 28				20 28			
West Malling d					17 34					18 34				19 34				20 34			
East Malling d					17 37					18 37				19 37				20 37			
Barming d					17 40					18 40				19 40				20 40			
Maidstone East a					17 44					18 44				19 44				20 44			
d					17 45					18 45				19 45				20 45			
Bearsted d					17 50					18 50				19 50				20 50			
Hollingbourne d					17 54					18 54				19 54				20 54			
Harrietsham d					17 57					18 57				19 57				20 57			
Lenham d					18 00					19 00				20 00				21 00			
Charing d					18 05					19 05				20 05				21 05			
Ashford International a	15 56	16 50		17 20	18 13	16 56	17 50		18 20	19 13	17 56	18 50	19 20	20 13	18 56	19 50	20 20	21 13	19 56	20 50	21 20
d	16 03	16 52	16 33	17 22		17 03	17 52	17 33	18 22		18 03	18 52	19 22		19 03	19 52	20 22		20 03	20 52	21 22
Canterbury West 207 a	16 21		16 54	17 39		17 21		17 54	18 39		18 24		19 39		19 24		20 39		20 24		21 39

	SE 1	SE 1	SE	SE	SE 1	SE 1	SE	SE	SE 1	SE 1	SE	SE
St Pancras International ⊖195 d			21 12	21 42			22 12	22 42			23 12	23 42
Stratford International ⊖ d			21 19	21 49			22 19	22 49			23 19	23 49
Ebbsfleet International d			21 31	22 01			22 31	23 01			23 31	00 01
London Victoria ⊖ d	20 45				21 45				22 45			
London Blackfriars ⊖195 d												
Elephant & Castle ⊖195 d												
Bromley South 195 d	21 01				22 01				23 01			
St Mary Cray 195 d	21 08				22 08				23 08			
Swanley 195 d	21 12				22 12				23 12			
Otford 195 d	21 20				22 20				23 20			
Kemsing d												
Borough Green & Wrotham d	21 28				22 28				23 28			
West Malling d	21 34				22 34				23 34			
East Malling d	21 37				22 37				23 37			
Barming d	21 40				22 40				23 40			
Maidstone East a	21 44				22 44				23 44			
d	21 45				22 45				23 45			
Bearsted d	21 50				22 50				23 50			
Hollingbourne d	21 54				22 54				23 54			
Harrietsham d	21 57				22 57				23 57			
Lenham d	22 00				23 00				00 01			
Charing d	22 05				23 05				00 06			
Ashford International a	22 13	20 56	21 50	22 20	23 13	21 56	22 50	23 20	00 14	22 56	23 50	00 19
d		21 03	21 52	22 22		22 03	22 52	23 22		23 03	23 52	
Canterbury West 207 a		21 24		22 39		22 24		23 39		23 24		

Table 196

Ashford International and Maidstone East to London

Mondays to Fridays

Station		SE	SE ■	SE	SE ■	SE ■	SE ■	SE	SE ■	SE	SE ■	SE ■	SE ■	SE	SE ■	SE ■	SE	SE ■	SE	SE ■	SE ■	SE ■	SE
Canterbury West [4]	207 d			05 25	05 35					06 20				07 16		07 35	07 46		08 25		08 37		
Ashford International	a			05 41	05 57			06 11		06 36				07 32		07 58	08 03		08 41		08 58		09 11
	d	05 13	05 20	05 43	06 03	05 50		06 13	06 16	06 43	06 25	06 40	06 58	07 43	07 15		08 13	07 47	08 43	08 26		08 47	09 13
Charing	d		05 28		06 11	05 58			06 24		06 33	06 48	07 06		07 23			07 55		08 34		08 55	
Lenham	d		05 33		06 16	06 03			06 29		06 38	06 53	07 11		07 28			08 00		08 39		09 00	
Harrietsham	d		05 36		06 19	06 06			06 32		06 41	06 56	07 14		07 31			08 03		08 42		09 03	
Hollingbourne	d		05 40		06 23	06 10			06 36		06 45	07 00	07 18		07 35			08 07		08 46		09 07	
Bearsted	d		05 43		06 26	06 13	06 09		06 39		06 48	07 03	07 21		07 38			08 10		08 49		09 10	
Maidstone East [4]	a		05 48		06 31	06 20	06 14		06 44		06 53	07 08	07 26		07 43			08 15		08 54		09 15	
	d		05 49		06 32	06 20	06 15		06 45		06 54	07 09	07 27		07 44			08 18		08 55		09 18	
Barming	d		05 54		06 37	06 25			06 50		06 59	07 14	07 32		07 49			08 23				09 23	
East Malling	d		05 58		06 41	06 29			06 54		07 03	07 18	07 36					08 26				09 26	
West Malling	d		06 00		06 43	06 31	06 22		06 56		07 05	07 20	07 38		07 53			08 29		09 02		09 29	
Borough Green & Wrotham	d		06 07		06 51	06 38	06 30		07 04		07 13	07 28	07 46		08 01			08 36		09 09		09 36	
Kemsing	d				06 55				07 08		07 17	07 32	07 50					08 40				09 40	
Otford [4]	195 a		06 15		07 00	06 46	06 38		07 13		07 22	07 37	07 55		08 09			08 45		09 17		09 45	
Swanley [4]	195 a		06 24		07 09	06 54	06 47		07 22		07 31	07 46	08 04					08 54		09 25		09 54	
St Mary Cray	195 a																	08 58				09 58	
Bromley South [4]	195 a		06 33		07 19	07 02	06 56		07 30		07 40	07 57	08 13		08 25			09 04		09 34		10 04	
Elephant & Castle	⊖195 a						07 15				07 59												
London Blackfriars [3]	⊖195 a						07 22				08 04												
London Victoria [15]	⊖ a		06 51		07 43	07 22			07 53			08 23	08 36		08 53			09 23		09 51		10 21	
Ebbsfleet International	a	05 32		06 02				06 32											09 02				09 32
Stratford International	⊖ a	05 44		06 15				06 44		07 11				08 11			08 41		09 14				09 44
St Pancras International [15]	⊖195 a	05 51		06 23				06 53		07 18				08 19			08 48		09 21				09 51

Station		SE	SE ■	SE ■	SE ■	SE	SE	SE ■	SE ■	SE ■	SE	SE	SE ■	SE ■	SE ■	SE	SE	SE ■	SE ■	SE ■	SE	SE	SE ■
Canterbury West [4]	207 d	09 25		09 35			10 25		10 35			11 25		11 35			12 25		12 35			13 25	
Ashford International	a	09 41		09 58		10 11	10 41		10 58		11 11	11 41		11 58		12 11	12 41		12 58		13 11	13 41	
	d	09 43	09 28		09 47	10 13	10 43	10 28		10 47	11 13	11 43	11 28		11 47	12 13	12 43	12 28		12 47	13 13	13 43	13 28
Charing	d				09 55					10 55					11 55					12 55			
Lenham	d				10 00					11 00					12 00					13 00			
Harrietsham	d				10 03					11 03					12 03					13 03			
Hollingbourne	d				10 07					11 07					12 07					13 07			
Bearsted	d		09 46		10 10			10 46		11 10			11 46		12 10			12 46		13 10			13 46
Maidstone East [4]	a		09 51		10 15			10 51		11 15			11 51		12 15			12 51		13 15			13 51
	d		09 55		10 18			10 55		11 18			11 55		12 18			12 55		13 18			13 55
Barming	d				10 23					11 23					12 23					13 23			
East Malling	d				10 26					11 26					12 26					13 26			
West Malling	d		10 02		10 29			11 02		11 29			12 02		12 29			13 02		13 29			14 02
Borough Green & Wrotham	d		10 09		10 36			11 09		11 36			12 09		12 36			13 09		13 36			14 09
Kemsing	d				10 40					11 40					12 40					13 40			
Otford [4]	195 a		10 17		10 46			11 17		11 46			12 17		12 46			13 17		13 46			14 17
Swanley [4]	195 a		10 25		10 54			11 25		11 54			12 25		12 54			13 25		13 54			14 25
St Mary Cray	195 a				10 58					11 58					12 58					13 58			
Bromley South [4]	195 a		10 34		11 04			11 34		12 04			12 34		13 04			13 34		14 04			14 34
Elephant & Castle	⊖195 a																						
London Blackfriars [3]	⊖195 a																						
London Victoria [15]	⊖ a		10 51		11 21			11 51		12 21			12 51		13 21			13 51		14 21			14 51
Ebbsfleet International	a	10 02				10 32	11 02				11 32	12 02				12 32	13 02				13 32	14 02	
Stratford International	⊖ a	10 14				10 44	11 14				11 44	12 14				12 45	13 14				13 44	14 14	
St Pancras International [15]	⊖195 a	10 21				10 51	11 21				11 51	12 21				12 54	13 21				13 51	14 21	

Station		SE ■	SE ■	SE	SE	SE ■	SE ■	SE ■	SE	SE	SE ■	SE ■	SE ■	SE	SE	SE ■	SE ■	SE ■	SE	SE	SE ■	SE ■
Canterbury West [4]	207 d	13 35			14 25		14 35			15 25		15 35			16 25		16 35			17 25		17 35
Ashford International	a	13 58		14 11	14 41		14 58		15 11	15 41		15 58		16 11	16 41		16 58		17 11	17 41		17 58
	d		13 47	14 13	14 43	14 28		14 47	15 13	15 43	15 26		15 47	16 13	16 43	16 26		16 47	17 13	17 43	17 26	
Charing	d		13 55					14 55			15 34		15 55			16 34		16 55			17 34	
Lenham	d		14 00					15 00			15 39		16 00			16 39		17 00			17 39	
Harrietsham	d		14 03					15 03			15 42		16 03			16 42		17 03			17 42	
Hollingbourne	d		14 07					15 07			15 46		16 07			16 46		17 07			17 46	
Bearsted	d		14 10			14 46		15 10			15 49		16 10			16 49		17 10			17 49	
Maidstone East [4]	a		14 15			14 51		15 15			15 54		16 15			16 54		17 15			17 54	
	d		14 18			14 55		15 18			15 55		16 18			16 55		17 18			17 55	
Barming	d		14 23					15 23					16 23					17 23				
East Malling	d		14 26					15 26					16 26					17 26				
West Malling	d		14 29			15 02		15 29			16 02		16 29			17 02		17 29			18 02	
Borough Green & Wrotham	d		14 36			15 09		15 36			16 09		16 36			17 09		17 36			18 09	
Kemsing	d		14 40					15 40					16 40					17 40				
Otford [4]	195 a		14 46			15 17		15 46			16 17		16 46			17 17		17 46			18 17	
Swanley [4]	195 a		14 54			15 25		15 54			16 25		16 54			17 25		17 54			18 25	
St Mary Cray	195 a		14 58					15 58					16 58					17 58				
Bromley South [4]	195 a		15 04			15 34		16 04			16 34		17 04			17 34		18 05			18 [illegible]	
Elephant & Castle	⊖195 a																					
London Blackfriars [3]	⊖195 a																					
London Victoria [15]	⊖ a		15 21			15 51		16 21			16 51		17 21			17 53		18 21			18 53	
Ebbsfleet International	a			14 32	15 02				15 32	16 02				16 32	17 02				17 32	18 02		
Stratford International	⊖ a			14 44	15 14				15 44	16 14				16 44	17 14				17 44	18 14		
St Pancras International [15]	⊖195 a			14 51	15 21				15 51	16 21				16 51	17 21				17 51	18 21		

Table 196

Ashford International and Maidstone East to London

Mondays to Fridays

Station		SE ■	SE	SE	SE ■	SE ■	SE ■	SE ■	SE	SE ■	SE	SE ■	SE	SE ■	SE	SE ■	SE	SE ■	SE	SE ■	SE	SE ■	SE
Canterbury West [4]	207 d			18 25		18 35					19 25	19 35			20 25	20 35			21 25	21 35			22 25
Ashford International	a		18 11	18 41		18 58			19 11		19 41	19 58	20 12		20 41	20 58	21 11		21 41	21 58	22 11		22 41
	d	17 49	18 13	18 43	18 26			18 49	19 13	19 19	19 43		20 13	20 17	20 47		21 13	21 17	21 43		22 13	22 17	22 43
Charing	d	17 57			18 34			18 57		19 27				20 25				21 25				22 25	
Lenham	d	18 02			18 39			19 02		19 32				20 30				21 30				22 30	
Harrietsham	d	18 05			18 42			19 05		19 35				20 33				21 33				22 33	
Hollingbourne	d	18 09			18 46			19 09		19 39				20 37				21 37				22 37	
Bearsted	d	18 12			18 49			19 12		19 42				20 40				21 40				22 40	
Maidstone East [4]	a	18 17			18 54			19 17		19 47				20 45				21 45				22 45	
	d	18 18			18 55		18 40	19 18		19 48				20 48				21 48				22 48	
Barming	d	18 23						19 23		19 53				20 53				21 53				22 53	
East Malling	d	18 26						19 26		19 56				20 56				21 56				22 56	
West Malling	d	18 29			19 02		18 47	19 29		19 59				20 59				21 59				22 59	
Borough Green & Wrotham	d	18 36			19 09		18 54	19 36		20 06				21 06				22 06				23 06	
Kemsing	d	18 40						19 40		20 10				21 10				22 10				23 10	
Otford [4]	195 a	18 46			19 17			19 46		20 16				21 16				22 16				23 16	
Swanley [4]	195 a	18 54			19 25			19 54		20 24				21 24				22 24				23 24	
St Mary Cray	195 a	18 58						19 58		20 28				21 28				22 28				23 28	
Bromley South [4]	195 a	19 04			19 34		19 16	20 04		20 34				21 34				22 34				23 34	
Elephant & Castle	⊖195 a																						
London Blackfriars [3]	⊖195 a																						
London Victoria [15]	⊖ a	19 21			19 51		19 35	20 21		20 51				21 51				22 51				23 51	
Ebbsfleet International	a		18 32	19 02					19 32		20 02		20 32		21 06		21 32		22 02		22 32		23 02
Stratford International	⊖ a		18 44	19 14					19 44		20 14		20 44		21 18		21 44		22 14		22 44		23 14
St Pancras International [15]	⊖195 a		18 51	19 21					19 51		20 21		20 51		21 25		21 51		22 21		22 51		23 21

Station		SE ■	SE
Canterbury West [4]	207 d	22 46	
Ashford International	a	23 08	23 11
	d		23 13
Charing	d		
Lenham	d		
Harrietsham	d		
Hollingbourne	d		
Bearsted	d		
Maidstone East [4]	a		
	d		
Barming	d		
East Malling	d		
West Malling	d		
Borough Green & Wrotham	d		
Kemsing	d		
Otford [4]	195 a		
Swanley [4]	195 a		
St Mary Cray	195 a		
Bromley South [4]	195 a		
Elephant & Castle	⊖195 a		
London Blackfriars [3]	⊖195 a		
London Victoria [15]	⊖ a		
Ebbsfleet International	a		23 32
Stratford International	⊖ a		23 44
St Pancras International [15]	⊖195 a		23 51

Saturdays

Station		SE	SE ■	SE	SE ■	SE	SE	SE ■	SE	SE ■	SE	SE ■	SE ■	SE ■	SE	SE ■	SE ■	SE ■	SE	SE	SE ■	SE ■	SE ■
Canterbury West [4]	207 d			05 25			06 15		06 46				07 35		08 25		08 35			09 25		09 35	
Ashford International	a			05 41		06 11	06 31		07 03		07 11		07 58		08 41		08 58		09 11	09 41		09 58	
	d	05 13	05 20	05 43	05 47	06 13	06 33	06 28	07 13	06 47	07 13	07 28		07 47	08 43	08 28		08 47	09 13	09 43	09 28		09 47
Charing	d		05 28		05 55					06 55				07 55				08 55					09 55
Lenham	d		05 33		06 00					07 00				08 00				09 00					10 00
Harrietsham	d		05 36		06 03					07 03				08 03				09 03					10 03
Hollingbourne	d		05 40		06 07					07 07				08 07				09 07					10 07
Bearsted	d		05 43		06 10			06 46		07 10		07 46		08 10		08 46		09 10			09 46		10 10
Maidstone East [4]	a		05 48		06 15			06 51		07 15		07 51		08 15		08 51		09 15			09 51		10 15
	d		05 49		06 18			06 55		07 18		07 55		08 18		08 55		09 18			09 55		10 18
Barming	d		05 54		06 23					07 23				08 23				09 23					10 23
East Malling	d		05 58		06 26					07 26				08 26				09 26					10 26
West Malling	d		06 00		06 29			07 02		07 29		08 02		08 29		09 02		09 29			10 02		10 29
Borough Green & Wrotham	d		06 08		06 36			07 09		07 36		08 09		08 36		09 09		09 36			10 09		10 36
Kemsing	d				06 40					07 40				08 40				09 40					10 40
Otford [4]	195 a		06 16		06 46			07 17		07 46		08 17		08 46		09 17		09 46			10 17		10 46
Swanley [4]	195 a		06 24		06 54			07 25		07 54		08 25		08 54		09 25		09 54			10 25		10 54
St Mary Cray	195 a		06 28		06 58					07 58				08 58				09 58					10 58
Bromley South [4]	195 a		06 34		07 04			07 34		08 04		08 34		09 04		09 34		10 04			10 34		11 04
Elephant & Castle	⊖195 a																						
London Blackfriars [3]	⊖195 a																						
London Victoria [15]	⊖ a		06 51		07 21			07 51		08 21		08 51		09 21		09 51		10 21			10 51		11 21
Ebbsfleet International	a	05 32		06 02		06 32	06 52				07 32				09 02				09 32	10 02			
Stratford International	⊖ a	05 44		06 15		06 44	07 04		07 42		07 44				09 14				09 44	10 14			
St Pancras International [15]	⊖195 a	05 51		06 23		06 53	07 10		07 48		07 50				09 21				09 51	10 21			

Table 196

Saturdays

Ashford International and Maidstone East to London

	SE	SE	SE ■1	SE ■1	SE ■1	SE	SE	SE ■1	SE ■1	SE ■1	SE	SE	SE ■1	SE ■1	SE ■1	SE	SE	SE ■1	SE ■1	SE ■1	SE	SE
Canterbury West ■4 207 d		10 25		10 35			11 25		11 35			12 25		12 35			13 25		13 35			14 25
Ashford International a	10 11	10 41		10 58		11 11	11 41		11 58		12 11	12 41		12 58		13 11	13 41		13 58		14 11	14 41
d	10 13	10 43	10 28		10 47	11 13	11 43	11 28		11 47	12 13	12 43	12 28		12 47	13 13	13 43	13 28		13 47	14 13	14 43
Charing d					10 55					11 55					12 55					13 55		
Lenham d					11 00					12 00					13 00					14 00		
Harrietsham d					11 03					12 03					13 03					14 03		
Hollingbourne d					11 07					12 07					13 07					14 07		
Bearsted d			10 46		11 10			11 46		12 10			12 46		13 10			13 46		14 10		
Maidstone East ■4 a			10 51		11 15			11 51		12 15			12 51		13 15			13 51		14 15		
d			10 55		11 18			11 55		12 18			12 55		13 18			13 55		14 18		
Barming d					11 23					12 23					13 23					14 23		
East Malling d					11 26					12 26					13 26					14 26		
West Malling d			11 02		11 29			12 02		12 29			13 02		13 29			14 02		14 29		
Borough Green & Wrotham d			11 09		11 36			12 09		12 36			13 09		13 36			14 09		14 36		
Kemsing d					11 40					12 40					13 40					14 40		
Otford ■4 195 a			11 17		11 46			12 17		12 46			13 17		13 46			14 17		14 46		
Swanley ■4 195 a			11 25		11 54			12 25		12 54			13 25		13 54			14 25		14 54		
St Mary Cray 195 a					11 58					12 58					13 58					14 58		
Bromley South ■4 195 a			11 34		12 04			12 34		13 04			13 34		14 04			14 34		15 04		
Elephant & Castle ⊖195 a																						
London Blackfriars ■3 ⊖195 a																						
London Victoria ■15 ⊖ a			11 51		12 21			12 51		13 21			13 51		14 21			14 51		15 21		
Ebbsfleet International a	10 32	11 02				11 32	12 02				12 32	13 02				13 32	14 02				14 32	15 02
Stratford International ⊖ a	10 44	11 14				11 44	12 14				12 45	13 14				13 44	14 14				14 44	15 14
St Pancras International ■15 ⊖195 a	10 51	11 21				11 51	12 21				12 54	13 21				13 51	14 21				14 51	15 21

	SE ■1	SE ■1	SE ■1	SE	SE	SE ■1	SE ■1	SE ■1	SE	SE	SE	SE ■1	SE ■1	SE ■1	SE	SE	SE ■1	SE ■1	SE ■1	SE	SE
Canterbury West ■4 207 d		14 35			15 25		15 35			16 25	16 25		16 35			17 25		17 35			18 25
Ashford International a		14 58		15 11	15 41		15 58		16 11	16 41	16 41		16 58		17 11	17 41		17 58		18 11	18 41
d	14 28		14 47	15 13	15 43	15 28		15 47	16 13	16 43	16 47	16 28		16 47	17 13	17 43	17 28		17 47	18 13	18 43
Charing d			14 55					15 55						16 55					17 55		
Lenham d			15 00					16 00						17 00					18 00		
Harrietsham d			15 03					16 03						17 03					18 03		
Hollingbourne d			15 07					16 07						17 07					18 07		
Bearsted d	14 46		15 10			15 46		16 10				16 46		17 10			17 46		18 10		
Maidstone East ■4 a	14 51		15 15			15 51		16 15				16 51		17 15			17 51		18 15		
d	14 55		15 18			15 55		16 18				16 55		17 18			17 55		18 18		
Barming d			15 23					16 23						17 23					18 23		
East Malling d			15 26					16 26						17 26					18 26		
West Malling d	15 02		15 29			16 02		16 29				17 02		17 29			18 02		18 29		
Borough Green & Wrotham d	15 09		15 36			16 09		16 36				17 09		17 36			18 09		18 36		
Kemsing d			15 40					16 40						17 40					18 40		
Otford ■4 195 a	15 17		15 46			16 17		16 46				17 17		17 46			18 17		18 46		
Swanley ■4 195 a	15 25		15 54			16 25		16 54				17 25		17 54			18 25		18 54		
St Mary Cray 195 a			15 58					16 58						17 58					18 58		
Bromley South ■4 195 a	15 34		16 04			16 34		17 04				17 34		18 04			18 34		19 04		
Elephant & Castle ⊖195 a																					
London Blackfriars ■3 ⊖195 a																					
London Victoria ■15 ⊖ a	15 51		16 21			16 51		17 21				17 51		18 21			18 51		19 21		
Ebbsfleet International a				15 32	16 02				16 32	17 02	17 06				17 32	18 02				18 32	19 02
Stratford International ⊖ a				15 44	16 14				16 44	17 14	17 18				17 44	18 14				18 44	19 14
St Pancras International ■15 ⊖195 a				15 51	16 21				16 51	17 21	17 25				17 51	18 21				18 51	19 21

	SE ■1	SE ■1	SE ■1	SE	SE	SE ■1	SE ■1	SE	SE	SE ■1	SE	SE	SE	SE ■1	SE	SE ■1	SE
Canterbury West ■4 207 d		18 35			19 25	19 35			20 25			21 25			22 25	22 46	
Ashford International a		18 58		19 11	19 41	19 58		20 11	20 41		21 11	21 41	22 11		22 41	23 08	23 11
d	18 28		18 47	19 13	19 43		19 47	20 13	20 47	20 47	21 13	21 43	22 13	22 17	22 43		23 13
Charing d			18 55				19 55			20 55				22 25			
Lenham d			19 00				20 00			21 00				22 30			
Harrietsham d			19 03				20 03			21 03				22 33			
Hollingbourne d			19 07				20 07			21 07				22 37			
Bearsted d	18 46		19 10				20 10			21 10				22 40			
Maidstone East ■4 a	18 51		19 15				20 15			21 15				22 45			
d	18 55		19 18				20 18			21 18				22 48			
Barming d			19 23				20 23			21 23				22 53			
East Malling d			19 26				20 26			21 26				22 56			
West Malling d	19 02		19 29				20 29			21 29				22 59			
Borough Green & Wrotham d	19 09		19 36				20 36			21 36				23 06			
Kemsing d			19 40				20 40			21 40				23 10			
Otford ■4 195 a	19 17		19 46				20 46			21 46				23 16			
Swanley ■4 195 a	19 25		19 54				20 54			21 54				23 24			
St Mary Cray 195 a			19 58				20 58			21 58				23 28			
Bromley South ■4 195 a	19 34		20 04				21 04			22 04				23 34			
Elephant & Castle ⊖195 a																	
London Blackfriars ■3 ⊖195 a																	
London Victoria ■15 ⊖ a	19 51		20 21				21 21			22 21				23 51			
Ebbsfleet International a				19 32	20 02			20 32	21 06		21 32	22 02	22 32		23 02		23 32
Stratford International ⊖ a				19 44	20 14			20 44	21 18		21 44	22 14	22 44		23 14		23 44
St Pancras International ■15 ⊖195 a				19 51	20 21			20 51	21 25		21 51	22 21	22 51		23 21		23 51

Table 196

Sundays

Ashford International and Maidstone East to London

	SE ■1	SE ■1	SE	SE	SE ■1	SE	SE	SE ■1	SE ■1	SE	SE	SE ■1	SE ■1	SE	SE	SE ■1	SE ■1	SE	SE	SE ■1	SE ■1	SE
Canterbury West ■4 207 d				08 25			09 25	09 35			10 25	10 35			11 25	11 35			12 25	12 35		
Ashford International a			08 11	08 41		09 11	09 41	09 58		10 11	10 41	10 58		11 11	11 41	11 58		12 11	12 41	12 58		13 11
d	06 47	07 47	08 13	08 43	08 47	09 13	09 43		09 47	10 13	10 43		10 47	11 13	11 43		11 47	12 13	12 43		12 47	13 13
Charing d	06 55	07 55			08 55				09 55				10 55				11 55				12 55	
Lenham d	07 00	08 00			09 00				10 00				11 00				12 00				13 00	
Harrietsham d	07 03	08 03			09 03				10 03				11 03				12 03				13 03	
Hollingbourne d	07 07	08 07			09 07				10 07				11 07				12 07				13 07	
Bearsted d	07 10	08 10			09 10				10 10				11 10				12 10				13 10	
Maidstone East ■4 a	07 15	08 15			09 15				10 15				11 15				12 15				13 15	
d	07 16	08 16			09 16				10 16				11 16				12 16				13 16	
Barming d	07 21	08 21			09 21				10 21				11 21				12 21				13 21	
East Malling d	07 25	08 25			09 25				10 25				11 25				12 25				13 25	
West Malling d	07 27	08 27			09 27				10 27				11 27				12 27				13 27	
Borough Green & Wrotham d	07 35	08 35			09 35				10 35				11 35				12 35				13 35	
Kemsing d																						
Otford ■4 195 a	07 43	08 43			09 43				10 43				11 43				12 43				13 43	
Swanley ■4 195 a	07 51	08 51			09 51				10 51				11 51				12 51				13 51	
St Mary Cray 195 a	07 55	08 55			09 55				10 55				11 55				12 55				13 55	
Bromley South ■4 195 a	08 02	09 02			10 02				11 02				12 02				13 02				14 02	
Elephant & Castle ⊖195 a																						
London Blackfriars ■3 ⊖195 a																						
London Victoria ■15 ⊖ a	08 18	09 18			10 18				11 18				12 18				13 18				14 18	
Ebbsfleet International a			08 32	09 02		09 32	10 02			10 32	11 02			11 32	12 02			12 32	13 02			13 32
Stratford International ⊖ a			08 44	09 14		09 44	10 14			10 44	11 14			11 44	12 14			12 45	13 14			13 44
St Pancras International ■15 ⊖195 a			08 51	09 21		09 51	10 21			10 51	11 21			11 51	12 21			12 54	13 21			13 51

	SE	SE ■1	SE ■1	SE	SE	SE ■1	SE ■1	SE	SE	SE ■1	SE ■1	SE	SE	SE	SE ■1	SE ■1	SE	SE	SE ■1	SE ■1	SE	SE
Canterbury West ■4 207 d	13 25	13 35			14 25	14 35			15 25	15 35			16 25	16 25	16 35			17 25	17 35			18 25
Ashford International a	13 41	13 58		14 11	14 41	14 58		15 11	15 41	15 58		16 11	16 41	16 41	16 58		17 11	17 41	17 58		18 11	18 41
d	13 43		13 47	14 13	14 43		14 47	15 13	15 43		15 47	16 13	16 43	16 47		16 47	17 13	17 43		17 47	18 13	18 43
Charing d			13 55				14 55				15 55					16 55				17 55		
Lenham d			14 00				15 00				16 00					17 00				18 00		
Harrietsham d			14 03				15 03				16 03					17 03				18 03		
Hollingbourne d			14 07				15 07				16 07					17 07				18 07		
Bearsted d			14 10				15 10				16 10					17 10				18 10		
Maidstone East ■4 a			14 15				15 15				16 15					17 15				18 15		
d			14 16				15 16				16 16					17 16				18 16		
Barming d			14 21				15 21				16 21					17 21				18 21		
East Malling d			14 25				15 25				16 25					17 25				18 25		
West Malling d			14 27				15 27				16 27					17 27				18 27		
Borough Green & Wrotham d			14 35				15 35				16 35					17 35				18 35		
Kemsing d																						
Otford ■4 195 a			14 43				15 43				16 43					17 43				18 43		
Swanley ■4 195 a			14 51				15 51				16 51					17 51				18 51		
St Mary Cray 195 a			14 55				15 55				16 55					17 55				18 55		
Bromley South ■4 195 a			15 02				16 02				17 02					18 02				19 02		
Elephant & Castle ⊖195 a																						
London Blackfriars ■3 ⊖195 a																						
London Victoria ■15 ⊖ a			15 18				16 18				17 18					18 18				19 18		
Ebbsfleet International a	14 02			14 32	15 02			15 32	16 02			16 32	17 02	17 06			17 32	18 02			18 32	19 02
Stratford International ⊖ a	14 14			14 44	15 14			15 44	16 14			16 44	17 14	17 18			17 44	18 14			18 44	19 14
St Pancras International ■15 ⊖195 a	14 21			14 51	15 21			15 51	16 21			16 51	17 21	17 28			17 51	18 21			18 51	19 21

	SE ■1	SE ■1	SE	SE	SE ■1	SE	SE	SE ■1	SE	SE	SE ■1	SE ■1	SE	SE
Canterbury West ■4 207 d	18 35			19 25			20 25			21 25		22 00		22 25
Ashford International a	18 58		19 11	19 41		20 11	20 41		21 11	21 41		22 22	22 11	22 41
d		18 47	19 13	19 43	19 47	20 13	20 47	20 47	21 13	21 43	21 47		22 13	22 43
Charing d		18 55			19 55			20 55			21 55			
Lenham d		19 00			20 00			21 00			22 00			
Harrietsham d		19 03			20 03			21 03			22 03			
Hollingbourne d		19 07			20 07			21 07			22 07			
Bearsted d		19 10			20 10			21 10			22 10			
Maidstone East ■4 a		19 15			20 15			21 15			22 15			
d		19 16			20 16			21 16			22 16			
Barming d		19 21			20 21			21 21			22 21			
East Malling d		19 25			20 25			21 25			22 25			
West Malling d		19 27			20 27			21 27			22 27			
Borough Green & Wrotham d		19 35			20 35			21 35			22 35			
Kemsing d														
Otford ■4 195 a		19 43			20 43			21 43			22 43			
Swanley ■4 195 a		19 51			20 51			21 51			22 51			
St Mary Cray 195 a		19 55			20 55			21 55			22 55			
Bromley South ■4 195 a		20 02			21 02			22 02			23 02			
Elephant & Castle ⊖195 a														
London Blackfriars ■3 ⊖195 a														
London Victoria ■15 ⊖ a		20 18			21 18			22 18			23 18			
Ebbsfleet International a			19 32	20 02		20 32	21 06		21 32	22 02			22 32	23 02
Stratford International ⊖ a			19 44	20 14		20 44	21 18		21 44	22 14			22 44	23 14
St Pancras International ■15 ⊖195 a			19 51	20 21		20 51	21 25		21 51	22 21			22 51	23 21

Table 199

Mondays to Fridays

London - Lewisham, Hither Green, Petts Wood and Orpington (Summary of Services)

		SE MX	SE MX	SE MO [1]	SE MX	SE MX [1]	SE MO	SE MO	SE MX	SE MX		SE MO	SE MX	SE MX	SE MX	SE MX	SE	SE	SE	SE		SE	SE	FC [1]	SE
London Charing Cross 4	⊖ d		23p36	23p38		23p45	23p46	23p50	23p52			23p56	23p56	00 02	00 05	00 10	00 15	00 48	04 50	04 56		05 02	05 20		05 26
London Waterloo (East) 4	⊖ d		23p39	23p41		23p48	23p49	23p53	23p55			23p59	23p59	00 05	00 08	00 13	00 18	00 51	04 53	04 59		05 05	05 23		05 29
London Cannon Street 4	⊖ d																								
London Blackfriars 3	⊖ d																							05 24	
London Bridge 4	⊖ d		23p44	23p46		23p53	23p54	23p58	23p59			00 04	00 04	00 10	00 13	00 18	00 23	00 56	04 58	05 04		05 10	05 28	05 30	05 34
London Victoria 15	⊖ d	23p25			23p43					23p55															
New Cross 4	⊖ d							00 04	00 05					00 15	00 18		00 28	01 01		05 09		05 15			05 39
St Johns	d								00 07																
Lewisham 4	a		23p51				00 02	00 07	00 10			00 11		00 19	00 22		00 32	01 05		05 13		05 19			05 43
Hither Green 4	a		23p56				00 06					00 16			00 26			01 09		05 17					05 47
Petts Wood 4	a	23p59	00 08		00 21		00 19			00 29						00 40		01 22							
Orpington 4	a	00 02	00 12	00 01	00 25	00 08	00 22			00 32						00 43		01 25							

		SE [1]	SE	SE	SE	SE		SE	FC [1]	SE	SE	SE	SE	SE	SE	SE		SE	SE	FC [1]	SE [1]	SE	SE	SE	SE
London Charing Cross 4	⊖ d	05 30		05 32	05 36	05 39				05 47		05 52	05 56	06 02	06 06	06 09					06 15	06 17	06 26		
London Waterloo (East) 4	⊖ d	05 33		05 35	05 39	05 42				05 50		05 55	05 59	06 05	06 09	06 12					06 18	06 20	06 29		
London Cannon Street 4	⊖ d										05 52								06 12					06 27	
London Blackfriars 3	⊖ d								05 44											06 14					
London Bridge 4	⊖ d	05 39		05 42	05 44	05 47			05 50	05 55	05a55	06 01	06 04	06 10	06 14	06 17			06a15	06 20	06 24	06 26	06 34	06 31	
London Victoria 15	⊖ d							05 40										06 10							06 30
New Cross 4	⊖ d		05 31	05 48		05 52				06 01			06 09	06 15								06 32	06 40		
St Johns	d		05 33							06 03												06 34			
Lewisham 4	a		05 35	05 51	05 53	05 56				06 05			06 13	06 19	06 22	06 26						06 37	06 43		
Hither Green 4	a				05 57								06 17		06 27								06 48		
Petts Wood 4	a				06 09			06 14							06 39			06 44							07 04
Orpington 4	a	05 54			06 12			06 18							06 42			06 49			06 40				07 08

		SE [1]		SE	FC [1]	SE	SE	SE [1]	SE	FC [1]	SE	SE		SE	SE	SE	SE [1]	SE	SE	FC [1]	SE	SE		SE [1]	SE
London Charing Cross 4	⊖ d	06 30		06 32		06 36	06 39	06 45	06 47					06 52	06 56		07 00	07 02	07 06					07 10	07 12
London Waterloo (East) 4	⊖ d	06 33		06 35		06 39	06 42	06 48	06 50					06 55	06 59		07 03	07 05	07 09					07 13	07 15
London Cannon Street 4	⊖ d										06 50					07 00						07 10			
London Blackfriars 3	⊖ d				06 34					06 50										07 09					
London Bridge 4	⊖ d	06 38		06 40	06 42	06 44	06 47	06 53	06 55	07 00	06 54			07 00	07 05	07 04	07 08	07 10	07 14	07 16		07 14		07 20	07 21
London Victoria 15	⊖ d											06 50									07 09				
New Cross 4	⊖ d			06 46					07 02		06 59					07 09						07 20			
St Johns	d								07 04		07 01					07 11						07 22			
Lewisham 4	a			06 49		06 52	06 56		07 07		07 04					07 14		07 18			07 24	07 26			07 29
Hither Green 4	a					06 58					07 08				07 18				07 23			07 31			
Petts Wood 4	a					07 10					07 21	07 24							07 36						
Orpington 4	a	06 53				07 13		07 09			07 25	07 28					07 25		07 40						

		SE	SE [1]	SE	SE	SE	SE	SE		SE	SE [1]	SE	FC [1]	SE	SE	SE	SE	SE		SE [1]	SE	SE	SE	SE	SE [1]
London Charing Cross 4	⊖ d		07 15	07 17				07 26			07 29					07 36	07 39			07 40			07 44		
London Waterloo (East) 4	⊖ d		07 18	07 20				07 29			07 32					07 39	07 42			07 43			07 47		
London Cannon Street 4	⊖ d	07 13			07 20	07 24				07 27		07 30		07 32	07 36						07 41			07 44	07 47
London Blackfriars 3	⊖ d												07 32												
London Bridge 4	⊖ d	07 17	07 23	07 25	07 24	07 28		07 34		07 31	07 38	07 34	07 42	07 37	07 40	07 44	07 47			07 49	07 44		07 53	07 48	07 51
London Victoria 15	⊖ d						07 25											07 40				07 43			
New Cross 4	⊖ d					07 33						07 39									07 49				
St Johns	d											07 41													
Lewisham 4	a					07 37						07 44			07 48		07 56				07 54	08 07			
Hither Green 4	a				07 34			07 45								07 53					07 58				
Petts Wood 4	a						07 59									08 06		08 14							
Orpington 4	a		07 38		07 48		08 02				07 53					08 09		08 19							08 08

		SE	FC	SE		SE [1]	SE	SE	SE	SE	SE	SE [1]	SE	SE		SE	FC [1]	SE	SE	SE	SE	SE [1]	SE	SE [1] (trolley)	
London Charing Cross 4	⊖ d	07 48				07 52				07 59		08 00	08 03			08 05					08 11	08 13		08 17	
London Waterloo (East) 4	⊖ d	07 51				07 55				08 02		08 03	08 06			08 08					08 14	08 16		08 20	
London Cannon Street 4	⊖ d			07 51			07 54		07 56		08 00			08 05						08 10			08 16		
London Blackfriars 3	⊖ d		07 50														08 10								
London Bridge 4	⊖ d	07 56		07 55		08 01	07 58		08 01	08 07	08 04	08 09	08 11	08 09		08 13	08 18			08 14	08 19	08 21	08 20	08 25	
London Victoria 15	⊖ d							07 55										08 09	08 10						
New Cross 4	⊖ d			08 00			08 05				08 09									08 20			09 38		
St Johns	d						08 07				08 11									08 22					
Lewisham 4	a			08 04			08 10				08 14		08 18					08 30		08 25	08 28				
Hither Green 4	a			08 10												08 23				08 29					
Petts Wood 4	a		08 32	08 22				08 29								08 36			08 44						
Orpington 4	a	08 12	08 35	08 25				08 32				08 25				08 39			08 47					08 41	

Table 199

Mondays to Fridays

London - Lewisham, Hither Green, Petts Wood and Orpington (Summary of Services)

		SE	SE	SE	SE	SE	SE [1]	SE	SE	SE [1]		SE	SE	SE	SE	SE	SE	SE [1] (trolley)	SE	SE		SE	SE	SE [1]	SE
London Charing Cross 4	⊖ d		08 20	08 23			08 27		08 31	08 33			08 37				08 41		08 44			08 49		08 53	
London Waterloo (East) 4	⊖ d		08 23	08 26			08 30		08 34	08 36			08 40				08 44		08 47			08 52		08 56	
London Cannon Street 4	⊖ d	08 19				08 25		08 30				08 36			08 39			08 42		08 47			08 51		08 54
London Blackfriars 3	⊖ d																								
London Bridge 4	⊖ d	08 23	08 29	08 31		08 29	08 35	08 34	08 39	08 41		08 40	08 45		08 43		08 49	08 46	08 53	08 51		08 57	08 55	09 01	08 58
London Victoria 15	⊖ d				08 25									08 39		08 40									
New Cross 4	⊖ d	08 29		08 38				08 41							08 49								09 00		09 05
St Johns	d	08 31						08 43							08 51								09 02		
Lewisham 4	a	08 33		08 42				08 45	08 48					09 01	08 54		08 56						09 05		09 08
Hither Green 4	a	08 38	08 41										08 54		08 59							09 08	09 10		
Petts Wood 4	a	08 51			08 59								09 08			09 14							09 23		
Orpington 4	a	08 54			09 02		08 53			08 57			09 11			09 17		09 07					09 26	09 20	

		SE	SE	FC [1]	SE	SE [1]		SE	SE	SE	SE	SE	SE	SE	SE	SE [1]		SE	FC [1]	SE	SE	SE [1] (trolley)	SE	SE	SE
London Charing Cross 4	⊖ d	08 55				09 00		09 02		09 06					09 11	09 13				09 17			09 21		
London Waterloo (East) 4	⊖ d	08 58				09 03		09 05		09 09					09 14	09 16				09 20			09 24		
London Cannon Street 4	⊖ d		08 56		09 00				09 03		09 07		09 09					09 15			09 18	09 20		09 24	
London Blackfriars 3	⊖ d			09 00															09 16						
London Bridge 4	⊖ d	09 03	09 01	09 12	09 04	09 08		09 10	09 07	09 14	09 11		09 14		09 19	09 21		09 19	09 27	09 25	09 22	09 25	09 31	09 28	
London Victoria 15	⊖ d											09 09		09 10											09 25
New Cross 4	⊖ d				09 09								09 19								09 27			09 34	
St Johns	d				09 11								09 21								09 29				
Lewisham 4	a				09 14			09 20				09 31	09 24		09 28						09 33			09 37	
Hither Green 4	a	09 14								09 23			09 28								09 38				
Petts Wood 4	a									09 36				09 44							09 51				09 59
Orpington 4	a					09 26				09 39				09 47							09 54	09 41			10 02

		SE		SE	SE	SE [1]	SE	FC [1]	SE	SE	SE	SE		SE	SE	SE [1] (trolley)	SE [1] (trolley)	SE	SE	FC [1]	SE	SE		SE	SE
London Charing Cross 4	⊖ d	09 26				09 30	09 32		09 36			09 39				09 40	09 45	09 47							09 56
London Waterloo (East) 4	⊖ d	09 29				09 33	09 35		09 39			09 42				09 43	09 48	09 50							09 59
London Cannon Street 4	⊖ d			09 27	09 30					09 37					09 40				09 47		09 50	09 54			
London Blackfriars 3	⊖ d							09 34												09 50					
London Bridge 4	⊖ d	09 34		09 31	09 34	09 39	09 40	09 42	09 44	09 41		09 47			09 44	09 49	09 53	09 55	09 51	09 57	09 54	09 58			10 04
London Victoria 15	⊖ d										09 39			09 40										09 55	
New Cross 4	⊖ d				09 39										09 49						09 59	10 04			
St Johns	d				09 41										09 51						10 01				
Lewisham 4	a				09 44		09 49				10 01	09 56			09 54						10 04	10 07			
Hither Green 4	a	09 43							09 53						09 58						10 08				10 13
Petts Wood 4	a								10 06					10 14							10 21			10 29	
Orpington 4	a					09 55			10 09					10 17			10 08				10 24			10 32	

		SE	SE	SE [1]	SE	FC [1]	SE	SE		SE	SE	SE	SE	SE [1] (trolley)	SE [1] (trolley)	SE	SE	FC [1]		SE	SE	SE	SE	SE	SE [1]
London Charing Cross 4	⊖ d			10 00	10 02		10 06				10 09			10 10	10 15	10 17						10 26			10 30
London Waterloo (East) 4	⊖ d			10 03	10 05		10 09				10 12			10 13	10 18	10 20						10 29			10 33
London Cannon Street 4	⊖ d	09 57	10 00					10 07					10 10				10 17			10 20			10 27	10 30	
London Blackfriars 3	⊖ d					10 05												10 20							
London Bridge 4	⊖ d	10 01	10 04	10 09	10 10	10 12	10 14	10 11			10 17		10 14	10 19	10 23	10 25	10 21	10 27		10 24		10 34	10 31	10 34	10 39
London Victoria 15	⊖ d									10 09		10 10									10 25				
New Cross 4	⊖ d		10 09										10 19							10 29				10 39	
St Johns	d		10 11										10 21							10 31				10 41	
Lewisham 4	a		10 14		10 19					10 31	10 26		10 24							10 34				10 44	
Hither Green 4	a						10 23						10 28							10 38		10 43			
Petts Wood 4	a						10 36					10 44								10 51	10 59				
Orpington 4	a			10 25			10 39					10 47			10 38					10 54	11 02				10 55

		SE	FC [1]	SE		SE	SE	SE	SE	SE	SE [1]	SE [1] (trolley)	SE	SE		FC [1]	SE	SE	SE	SE	SE	SE	SE [1]	SE	
London Charing Cross 4	⊖ d	10 32		10 36				10 39			10 40	10 45	10 47							10 56			11 00	11 02	
London Waterloo (East) 4	⊖ d	10 35		10 39				10 42			10 43	10 48	10 50							10 59			11 03	11 05	
London Cannon Street 4	⊖ d					10 37				10 40				10 47			10 50	10 54			10 57	11 00			
London Blackfriars 3	⊖ d		10 35													10 50									
London Bridge 4	⊖ d	10 40	10 42	10 44		10 41		10 47		10 44	10 49	10 53	10 55	10 51		10 57	10 54	10 58		11 04	11 01	11 04	11 09	11 10	
London Victoria 15	⊖ d						10 39		10 40										10 55						
New Cross 4	⊖ d									10 49							10 59	11 04				11 09			
St Johns	d									10 51							11 01					11 11			
Lewisham 4	a	10 49					11 01	10 56		10 54							11 04	11 10				11 14		11 19	
Hither Green 4	a			10 53						10 58							11 08			11 13					
Petts Wood 4	a			11 06					11 14								11 21		11 29						
Orpington 4	a			11 09					11 17			11 08					11 24		11 32				11 25		

London - Lewisham, Hither Green, Petts Wood and Orpington (Summary of Services)

	FC ■	SE	SE	SE	SE	SE	SE	SE ■ 🍴	SE ■ 🍴		SE	SE	FC ■	SE	SE	SE	SE	SE	SE		SE ■	SE	FC ■	SE
London Charing Cross ■ ⊖ d		11 06			11 09			11 10	11 15		11 17						11 26				11 30	11 32		11 36
London Waterloo (East) ■ ⊖ d		11 09			11 12			11 13	11 18		11 20						11 29				11 33	11 35		11 39
London Cannon Street ■ ⊖ d			11 07				11 10					11 17		11 20	11 24			11 27	11 30					
London Blackfriars ■ ⊖ d	11 05												11 20										11 35	
London Bridge ■ ⊖ d	11 12	11 14	11 11		11 17		11 14	11 19	11 23		11 25	11 21	11 27	11 24	11 28		11 34	11 31	11 34		11 39	11 40	11 42	11 44
London Victoria ■ ⊖ d				11 09		11 10										11 25								
New Cross ■ ⊖ d							11 19							11 29	11 34				11 39					
St Johns d							11 21							11 31					11 41					
Lewisham ■ a				11 31	11 26		11 24							11 34	11 37				11 44			11 49		
Hither Green ■ a		11 23					11 28							11 38			11 43							11 53
Petts Wood ■ a		11 36				11 44								11 51		11 59								12 06
Orpington ■ a		11 39				11 47			11 38					11 54		12 02					11 55			12 09

	SE	SE	SE	SE	SE		SE ■ 🍴	SE ■ 🍴	SE	SE	FC ■	SE	SE	SE	SE		SE	SE	SE ■	SE	FC ■	SE	SE	SE
London Charing Cross ■ ⊖ d			11 39				11 40	11 45	11 47						11 56				12 00	12 02		12 06		
London Waterloo (East) ■ ⊖ d			11 42				11 43	11 48	11 50						11 59				12 03	12 05		12 09		
London Cannon Street ■ ⊖ d	11 37				11 40					11 47		11 50	11 54				11 57	12 00					12 07	
London Blackfriars ■ ⊖ d											11 50										12 05			
London Bridge ■ ⊖ d	11 41		11 47		11 44		11 49	11 53	11 55	11 51	11 57	11 54	11 58		12 04		12 01	12 04	12 09	12 10	12 12	12 14	12 11	
London Victoria ■ ⊖ d		11 39		11 40										11 55										12 09
New Cross ■ ⊖ d					11 49							11 59	12 04					12 09						
St Johns d					11 51							12 01						12 11						
Lewisham ■ a		12 02	11 56		11 54							12 04	12 07					12 14		12 19				12 31
Hither Green ■ a					11 58							12 08			12 13							12 23		
Petts Wood ■ a				12 14								12 21		12 29								12 36		
Orpington ■ a				12 17				12 08				12 24		12 32					12 25			12 39		

	SE		SE	SE	SE ■ 🍴	SE ■ 🍴	SE	SE	FC ■	SE	SE		SE	SE	SE	SE	SE ■	SE	FC ■	SE	SE		SE	SE
London Charing Cross ■ ⊖ d	12 09				12 10	12 15	12 17							12 26			12 30	12 32		12 36				12 39
London Waterloo (East) ■ ⊖ d	12 12				12 13	12 18	12 20							12 29			12 33	12 35		12 39				12 42
London Cannon Street ■ ⊖ d				12 10				12 17		12 20	12 24				12 27	12 30					12 37			
London Blackfriars ■ ⊖ d									12 20										12 35					
London Bridge ■ ⊖ d	12 17			12 14	12 19	12 23	12 25	12 21	12 27	12 24	12 28			12 34	12 31	12 34	12 39	12 40	12 42	12 44	12 41			12 47
London Victoria ■ ⊖ d			12 10										12 25										12 39	
New Cross ■ ⊖ d				12 19						12 29	12 34					12 39								
St Johns d				12 21						12 31						12 41								
Lewisham ■ a	12 26			12 24						12 34	12 37					12 44		12 49					13 02	12 56
Hither Green ■ a				12 28						12 38				12 43						12 53				
Petts Wood ■ a			12 44							12 51			12 59							13 06				
Orpington ■ a			12 47			12 38				12 54			13 02				12 55			13 09				

	SE	SE	SE ■ 🍴	SE ■ 🍴	SE	SE	FC ■		SE	SE	SE	SE	SE	SE	SE ■	SE	FC ■		SE	SE	SE	SE	SE	SE
London Charing Cross ■ ⊖ d			12 40	12 45	12 47							12 56			13 00	13 02			13 06			13 09		
London Waterloo (East) ■ ⊖ d			12 43	12 48	12 50							12 59			13 03	13 05			13 09			13 12		
London Cannon Street ■ ⊖ d		12 40				12 47			12 50	12 54			12 57	13 00						13 07				13 10
London Blackfriars ■ ⊖ d							12 50										13 05							
London Bridge ■ ⊖ d		12 44	12 49	12 53	12 55	12 51	12 57		12 54	12 58		13 04	13 01	13 04	13 09	13 10	13 12		13 14	13 11		13 17		13 14
London Victoria ■ ⊖ d	12 40										12 55										13 09		13 10	
New Cross ■ ⊖ d		12 49							12 59	13 04				13 09										13 19
St Johns d		12 51							13 01					13 11										13 21
Lewisham ■ a		12 54							13 04	13 07				13 14		13 19					13 31	13 26		13 24
Hither Green ■ a		12 58							13 08			13 13							13 23					13 28
Petts Wood ■ a	13 14								13 21		13 29								13 36				13 44	
Orpington ■ a	13 17			13 08					13 24		13 32				13 25				13 39				13 47	

	SE ■ 🍴	SE ■ 🍴	SE		SE	FC ■	SE	SE	SE	SE	SE	SE	SE ■		SE	FC ■	SE	SE	SE	SE	SE	SE	SE ■ 🍴	
London Charing Cross ■ ⊖ d	13 10	13 15	13 17							13 26			13 30		13 32		13 36			13 39			13 40	
London Waterloo (East) ■ ⊖ d	13 13	13 18	13 20							13 29			13 33		13 35		13 39			13 42			13 43	
London Cannon Street ■ ⊖ d					13 17		13 20	13 24			13 27	13 30						13 37				13 40		
London Blackfriars ■ ⊖ d						13 20										13 35								
London Bridge ■ ⊖ d	13 19	13 23	13 25		13 21	13 27	13 24	13 28		13 34	13 31	13 34	13 39		13 40	13 42	13 44	13 41		13 47		13 44	13 49	
London Victoria ■ ⊖ d									13 25										13 39		13 40			
New Cross ■ ⊖ d							13 29	13 34				13 39										13 49		
St Johns d							13 31					13 41										13 51		
Lewisham ■ a							13 34	13 37				13 44			13 49				14 01	13 56		13 54		
Hither Green ■ a							13 39			13 43							13 53					13 58		
Petts Wood ■ a							13 51		13 59								14 06				14 14			
Orpington ■ a		13 38					13 54		14 02				13 55				14 09				14 17			

Table 199

Mondays to Fridays

London - Lewisham, Hither Green, Petts Wood and Orpington (Summary of Services)

	SE ■ 🍴	SE	SE	FC ■	SE	SE	SE	SE	SE		SE	SE ■	SE	FC ■	SE	SE	SE	SE	SE		SE	SE ■ 🍴	SE ■ 🍴	SE
London Charing Cross ■ ⊖ d	13 45	13 47						13 56				14 00	14 02		14 06			14 09				14 10	14 15	14 17
London Waterloo (East) ■ ⊖ d	13 48	13 50						13 59				14 03	14 05		14 09			14 12				14 13	14 18	14 20
London Cannon Street ■ ⊖ d			13 47		13 50	13 54			13 57		14 00					14 07					14 10			
London Blackfriars ■ ⊖ d				13 50										14 05										
London Bridge ■ ⊖ d	13 53	13 55	13 51	13 57	13 54	13 58		14 04	14 01		14 04	14 09	14 10	14 12	14 14	14 11		14 17			14 14	14 19	14 23	14 25
London Victoria ■ ⊖ d							13 55										14 09		14 10					
New Cross ■ ⊖ d					13 59	14 04					14 09										14 19			
St Johns d					14 01						14 11										14 21			
Lewisham ■ a					14 04	14 07					14 14		14 19				14 31	14 26			14 24			
Hither Green ■ a					14 08			14 13							14 23						14 28			
Petts Wood ■ a					14 21		14 29								14 36				14 44					
Orpington ■ a	14 08				14 24		14 32					14 25			14 39				14 47				14 38	

	SE	FC ■	SE	SE	SE		SE	SE	SE	SE ■	SE	FC ■	SE	SE	SE		SE	SE	SE	SE ■ 🍴	SE ■ 🍴	SE	SE	FC ■
London Charing Cross ■ ⊖ d							14 26			14 30	14 32		14 36				14 39			14 40	14 45	14 47		
London Waterloo (East) ■ ⊖ d							14 29			14 33	14 35		14 39				14 42			14 43	14 48	14 50		
London Cannon Street ■ ⊖ d	14 17		14 20	14 24				14 27	14 30					14 37					14 40				14 47	
London Blackfriars ■ ⊖ d		14 20										14 35												14 50
London Bridge ■ ⊖ d	14 21	14 27	14 24	14 28			14 34	14 31	14 34	14 39	14 40	14 42	14 44	14 41			14 47		14 44	14 49	14 53	14 55	14 51	14 57
London Victoria ■ ⊖ d					14 25										14 39			14 40						
New Cross ■ ⊖ d			14 29	14 34					14 39										14 49					
St Johns d			14 31						14 41										14 51					
Lewisham ■ a			14 34	14 37					14 44		14 49				15 01		14 56		14 54					
Hither Green ■ a			14 38				14 43						14 53						14 58					
Petts Wood ■ a			14 51		14 59								15 06					15 14						
Orpington ■ a			14 54		15 02					14 55			15 09					15 17			15 08			

	SE		SE	SE	SE	SE	SE	SE ■	SE	FC ■	SE		SE	SE	SE	SE	SE	SE ■ 🍴	SE ■ 🍴	SE	SE		FC ■	SE
London Charing Cross ■ ⊖ d					14 56			15 00	15 02		15 06				15 09			15 10	15 15	15 17				
London Waterloo (East) ■ ⊖ d					14 59			15 03	15 05		15 09				15 12			15 13	15 18	15 20				
London Cannon Street ■ ⊖ d	14 50		14 54			14 57	15 00						15 07				15 10				15 17			15 20
London Blackfriars ■ ⊖ d										15 05													15 20	
London Bridge ■ ⊖ d	14 54		14 58		15 04	15 01	15 04	15 09	15 10	15 12	15 14		15 11		15 17		15 14	15 19	15 23	15 25	15 21		15 27	15 24
London Victoria ■ ⊖ d				14 55										15 09		15 10								
New Cross ■ ⊖ d	14 59		15 04				15 09										15 19							15 29
St Johns d	15 01						15 11										15 21							15 31
Lewisham ■ a	15 04		15 07				15 14		15 19					15 31	15 26		15 24							15 34
Hither Green ■ a	15 08				15 13						15 23						15 28							15 38
Petts Wood ■ a	15 21			15 29							15 36					15 44								15 51
Orpington ■ a	15 24			15 32				15 25			15 39					15 47			15 38					15 54

	SE	SE	SE	SE	SE	SE ■	SE		FC ■	SE	SE	SE	SE	SE	SE	SE ■ 🍴	SE ■ 🍴		SE	SE	FC ■	SE	SE	SE
London Charing Cross ■ ⊖ d			15 26			15 30	15 32			15 36			15 39			15 40	15 45		15 47					
London Waterloo (East) ■ ⊖ d			15 29			15 33	15 35			15 39			15 42			15 43	15 48		15 50					
London Cannon Street ■ ⊖ d	15 24			15 27	15 30						15 37				15 40					15 47		15 50	15 54	
London Blackfriars ■ ⊖ d									15 35												15 50			
London Bridge ■ ⊖ d	15 28		15 34	15 31	15 34	15 39	15 40		15 42	15 44	15 41		15 47		15 44	15 49	15 53		15 55	15 51	15 57	15 54	15 58	
London Victoria ■ ⊖ d		15 25										15 39		15 40										15 55
New Cross ■ ⊖ d	15 34				15 39										15 49							15 59	16 04	
St Johns d					15 41										15 51							16 01		
Lewisham ■ a	15 37				15 44		15 49					16 01	15 56		15 54							16 04	16 07	
Hither Green ■ a			15 43							15 53					15 58							16 08		
Petts Wood ■ a		15 59								16 06				16 14								16 21		16 29
Orpington ■ a		16 02				15 55				16 09				16 17			16 08					16 24		16 32

	SE	SE	SE		SE ■	SE	FC ■	SE	SE	SE	SE	SE	SE		SE ■ 🍴	SE ■	SE	FC ■	SE	SE	SE	SE	FC	
London Charing Cross ■ ⊖ d	15 56				16 00	16 02		16 06			16 09				16 10	16 15				16 20				
London Waterloo (East) ■ ⊖ d	15 59				16 03	16 05		16 09			16 12				16 13	16 18				16 23				
London Cannon Street ■ ⊖ d		15 57	16 00						16 07				16 10				16 17		16 20		16 24			
London Blackfriars ■ ⊖ d							16 05											16 20					16 26	
London Bridge ■ ⊖ d	16 04	16 01	16 04		16 09	16 10	16 12	16 14	16 11		16 17		16 14		16 19	16 23	16 21	16 27	16 24	16 29	16 28			
London Victoria ■ ⊖ d										16 09		16 10										16 25		
New Cross ■ ⊖ d			16 10										16 20						16 30		16 34			
St Johns d			16 12										16 22						16 32					
Lewisham ■ a			16 14			16 19				16 31	16 26		16 24						16 34		16 37			
Hither Green ■ a	16 13							16 23					16 29						16 39					
Petts Wood ■ a								16 36				16 44							16 51			16 59	17 08	
Orpington ■ a					16 25			16 39				16 48							16 56			17 03	17 14	

Table 199

Mondays to Fridays

London - Lewisham, Hither Green, Petts Wood and Orpington (Summary of Services)

		SE	SE	SE 1	SE	SE	SE	SE	FC 1	SE 1 🛒		SE	SE	SE	SE	SE 1 🛒	SE	SE	SE	SE		SE 1	SE	SE	SE
London Charing Cross 4 ⊖	d	16 26		16 28		16 30	16 32			16 37		16 39				16 41	16 42			16 45			16 49		16 51
London Waterloo (East) 4 ⊖	d	16 29		16 31		16 33	16 35			16 40		16 42				16 44	16 45			16 48			16 52		16 54
London Cannon Street 4 ⊖	d		16 27		16 30			16 35						16 39				16 42	16 44			16 46		16 51	
London Blackfriars 3 ⊖	d								16 36																
London Bridge 4 ⊖	d	16 34	16 31	16 36	16 34	16 38	16 40	16 39	16 43	16 45		16 47		16 43		16 49	16 51	16 46	16 48	16 53		16 50	16 57	16 55	16 59
London Victoria 15 ⊖	d												16 39		16 40										
New Cross 4 ⊖	d				16 40									16 49				16 52						17 01	
St Johns	d				16 42									16 51										17 03	
Lewisham 4	a				16 44	16 47							16 58	16 53			17 00	16 55						17 05	17 07
Hither Green 4	a	16 43					16 49							16 58			17 05						17 07		
Petts Wood 4	a						17 03								17 14		17 18								
Orpington 4	a			16 52			17 06								17 18		17 23								

		SE	SE	SE	SE 1	SE		SE	SE	SE 1	SE 1	SE	SE	SE	SE	SE		SE 1	SE	SE	SE	SE 1 🛒	SE	SE	SE
London Charing Cross 4 ⊖	d		16 55		16 57			16 59		17 01		17 03			17 06				17 10		17 12	17 14			17 17
London Waterloo (East) 4 ⊖	d		16 58		17 00			17 02		17 04		17 06			17 09				17 13		17 15	17 18			17 20
London Cannon Street 4 ⊖	d	16 54		16 56		16 58					17 02		17 04			17 06		17 08		17 12				17 16	
London Blackfriars 3 ⊖	d																								
London Bridge 4 ⊖	d	16 58	17 04	17 00		17 02		17 07		17 09	17 06	17 11	17 08		17 14	17 10		17 12	17 19	17 16	17 21			17 20	17 26
London Victoria 15 ⊖	d								17 00					17 04									17 15		
New Cross 4 ⊖	d					17 08							17 14							17 22					
St Johns	d					17 10														17 24					
Lewisham 4	a					17 12						17 20	17 17	17 23						17 26	17 30				
Hither Green 4	a					17 19						17 25							17 28						
Petts Wood 4	a			17 23					17 35			17 39											17 50		
Orpington 4	a			17 27					17 39			17 43											17 54		

		SE		SE 1 🛒	SE	SE	SE 1	SE 1	SE	SE	SE	SE		SE	SE	SE 1	SE	SE	SE	SE	SE 1	SE		SE	SE
London Charing Cross 4 ⊖	d			17 19		17 21	17 23			17 26		17 29			17 30		17 32		17 34					17 39	
London Waterloo (East) 4 ⊖	d			17 22		17 24	17 26			17 29		17 32			17 33		17 35		17 37					17 42	
London Cannon Street 4 ⊖	d	17 19			17 21			17 24	17 26		17 28					17 30		17 34			17 37	17 39			17 41
London Blackfriars 3 ⊖	d																								
London Bridge 4 ⊖	d	17 23			17 25	17 29	17 31	17 28	17 30	17 35	17 32	17 37				17 34	17 41	17 39	17 43		17 42	17 43		17 48	17 45
London Victoria 15 ⊖	d													17 30						17 34					
New Cross 4 ⊖	d				17 31				17 36									17 45							
St Johns	d				17 33													17 47							
Lewisham 4	a				17 35				17 39	17 43								17 49	17 52	17 55					
Hither Green 4	a				17 40					17 48							17 51								
Petts Wood 4	a	17 43								18 01				18 05											18 08
Orpington 4	a	17 47								18 06				18 09											18 11

		SE 1 🛒	SE	SE	SE	SE 1	SE 1	SE		SE	SE	SE	SE	SE 1	SE	SE	SE	SE		SE 1 🛒	SE	SE	SE	SE	SE 1
London Charing Cross 4 ⊖	d	17 41	17 43			17 45		17 47			17 50		17 52		17 54	17 56				17 59			18 01		18 03
London Waterloo (East) 4 ⊖	d	17 44	17 46			17 48		17 50			17 53		17 55		17 57	17 59				18 02			18 04		18 06
London Cannon Street 4 ⊖	d			17 43			17 45			17 47		17 50		17 52			17 56					18 00		18 03	
London Blackfriars 3 ⊖	d																								
London Bridge 4 ⊖	d		17 52	17 47		17 53	17 49	17 55		17 51	17 58	17 54		17 56	18 02	18 04	18 00					18 05	18 10	18 07	
London Victoria 15 ⊖	d				17 45													17 56			18 00				
New Cross 4 ⊖	d			17 53						17 58							18 06								
St Johns	d			17 55													18 08								
Lewisham 4	a			17 58				18 04		18 01						18 13	18 10	18 17							
Hither Green 4	a			18 03				18 09							18 12										
Petts Wood 4	a				18 20			18 24													18 35			18 27	
Orpington 4	a				18 24			18 28													18 40			18 31	

		SE	SE	SE 1		SE 1	SE	SE	SE	SE	SE	SE 1	SE	SE		SE	SE	FC 1	SE	SE 1	SE	SE	SE	SE	
London Charing Cross 4 ⊖	d	18 05		18 07			18 09		18 12		18 14					18 18				18 21		18 23	18 27		
London Waterloo (East) 4 ⊖	d	18 08		18 10			18 12		18 15		18 17					18 21				18 24		18 26	18 30		
London Cannon Street 4 ⊖	d		18 05			18 08		18 10		18 12		18 14		18 18					18 21		18 23				
London Blackfriars 3 ⊖	d																	18 20							
London Bridge 4 ⊖	d	18 13	18 09	18 15		18 12	18 17	18 14	18 21	18 16	18 23	18 18		18 23		18 26		18 27	18 25		18 27	18 32	18 35		
London Victoria 15 ⊖	d												18 15				18 18								
New Cross 4 ⊖	d		18 15					18 20						18 28										18 30	
St Johns	d		18 17											18 30											
Lewisham 4	a		18 19				18 26	18 23						18 33		18 35	18 42								
Hither Green 4	a		18 24				18 31				18 35														
Petts Wood 4	a						18 44						18 52								18 49			19 06	
Orpington 4	a						18 48						18 56								18 52			19 11	

Table 199

Mondays to Fridays

London - Lewisham, Hither Green, Petts Wood and Orpington (Summary of Services)

		SE	SE	SE 1	SE 1	SE	SE	SE	SE	SE		SE	SE 1 🛒	SE 1	SE	SE 1 🛒	FC 1	SE	SE	SE		SE	SE	SE	SE
London Charing Cross 4 ⊖	d	18 30		18 32			18 34	18 37	18 39				18 41			18 45				18 48			18 52		18 56
London Waterloo (East) 4 ⊖	d	18 33		18 35			18 37	18 40	18 42				18 44			18 48				18 51			18 55		18 59
London Cannon Street 4 ⊖	d		18 30		18 32	18 34						18 40		18 44				18 46	18 48			18 50		18 54	
London Blackfriars 3 ⊖	d																18 46								
London Bridge 4 ⊖	d	18 38	18 34	18 40	18 36	18 38	18 42	18 46	18 48			18 44	18 50	18 48		18 53	18 57	18 50	18 52	18 57		18 54	19 00	18 58	19 04
London Victoria 15 ⊖	d									18 39					18 45										
New Cross 4 ⊖	d					18 44			18 55			18 50										19 00		19 05	
St Johns	d											18 52										19 02			
Lewisham 4	a					18 47			18 58	19 01		18 54								19 06		19 04		19 08	
Hither Green 4	a	18 48						18 55														19 09			19 14
Petts Wood 4	a	19 03													19 19				19 13						
Orpington 4	a	19 06											19 06		19 23				19 18						

		SE	SE	SE	SE 1	SE		FC 1	SE 1	SE	SE	SE	SE	SE	SE	SE 1 🛒		SE 1 🛒	SE	SE	FC 1	SE	SE	SE	SE
London Charing Cross 4 ⊖	d				19 00	19 02				19 06			19 09			19 10		19 15	19 17						19 26
London Waterloo (East) 4 ⊖	d				19 03	19 05				19 09			19 12			19 13		19 18	19 20						19 29
London Cannon Street 4 ⊖	d	18 57		19 00					19 04		19 07				19 10					19 17		19 20	19 24		
London Blackfriars 3 ⊖	d							19 05													19 20				
London Bridge 4 ⊖	d	19 01		19 04	19 09	19 10		19 12	19 08	19 14	19 11		19 17		19 14	19 19		19 23	19 25	19 21	19 27	19 24	19 28		19 34
London Victoria 15 ⊖	d		19 00									19 09		19 10										19 25	
New Cross 4 ⊖	d			19 09											19 19							19 29	19 34		
St Johns	d			19 11											19 21							19 31			
Lewisham 4	a			19 14		19 19						19 32	19 25		19 24							19 34	19 37		
Hither Green 4	a									19 23					19 28							19 39			19 43
Petts Wood 4	a		19 35							19 37				19 44								19 51		19 59	
Orpington 4	a		19 38		19 25					19 43				19 48				19 38				19 54		20 02	

		SE		SE	SE 1	SE	FC 1	SE	SE	SE	SE	SE		SE	SE 1 🛒	SE 1	SE	SE	FC 1	SE	SE	SE		SE	SE
London Charing Cross 4 ⊖	d				19 30	19 32		19 36			19 39				19 40	19 45		19 47						19 56	
London Waterloo (East) 4 ⊖	d				19 33	19 35		19 39			19 42				19 43	19 48		19 50						19 59	
London Cannon Street 4 ⊖	d	19 27		19 30					19 37					19 40			19 47			19 50	19 54				19 57
London Blackfriars 3 ⊖	d						19 35												19 50						
London Bridge 4 ⊖	d	19 31		19 34	19 39	19 40	19 42	19 44	19 41		19 47			19 44	19 49	19 53	19 51	19 55	19 57	19 54	19 58			20 04	20 01
London Victoria 15 ⊖	d									19 39		19 40										19 55			
New Cross 4 ⊖	d			19 39										19 49						19 59	20 04				
St Johns	d			19 41										19 51						20 01					
Lewisham 4	a			19 44		19 49				20 01	19 56			19 54						20 04	20 07				
Hither Green 4	a							19 53						19 58						20 08				20 13	
Petts Wood 4	a							20 06				20 14								20 21		20 29			
Orpington 4	a				19 55			20 09				20 18				20 08				20 24		20 32			

		SE	SE 1	SE	FC 1	SE	SE	SE		SE	SE 1 🛒	SE 1	SE	SE	SE	SE	SE	SE		SE 1	SE	FC 1	SE	SE	SE 1 🛒
London Charing Cross 4 ⊖	d		20 00	20 02		20 06	20 09				20 10	20 15	20 17			20 22				20 30	20 32		20 36	20 39	20 40
London Waterloo (East) 4 ⊖	d		20 03	20 05		20 09	20 12				20 13	20 18	20 20			20 25				20 33	20 35		20 39	20 42	20 43
London Cannon Street 4 ⊖	d	20 00								20 10				20 17	20 20			20 27							
London Blackfriars 3 ⊖	d				20 05																	20 35			
London Bridge 4 ⊖	d	20 04	20 09	20 10	20 12	20 14	20 17			20 14	20 19	20 23	20 25	20 21	20 24	20 30		20 31		20 39	20 40	20 42	20 44	20 47	20 49
London Victoria 15 ⊖	d							20 10									20 25								
New Cross 4 ⊖	d	20 09								20 19			20 32		20 29	20 35					20 45				
St Johns	d	20 11								20 21			20 34		20 31										
Lewisham 4	a	20 14		20 19			20 26			20 24			20 36		20 34	20 39					20 49			20 56	
Hither Green 4	a					20 23				20 28					20 38	20 44							20 53		
Petts Wood 4	a					20 36		20 44							20 51		20 59						21 06		
Orpington 4	a		20 25			20 39		20 47				20 38			20 54		21 02			20 55			21 09		

		SE 1	SE	SE		SE	SE	SE	SE 1	SE	FC 1	SE	SE	SE 1 🛒		SE	SE	SE	SE	SE 1	SE	FC 1	SE	SE	
London Charing Cross 4 ⊖	d	20 45	20 47			20 52			21 00	21 02		21 06	21 09	21 10		21 17	21 22		21 26	21 30	21 32		21 36	21 39	
London Waterloo (East) 4 ⊖	d	20 48	20 50			20 55			21 03	21 05		21 09	21 12	21 13		21 20	21 25		21 29	21 33	21 35		21 39	21 42	
London Cannon Street 4 ⊖	d			20 47				20 57																	
London Blackfriars 3 ⊖	d										21 05											21 35			
London Bridge 4 ⊖	d	20 53	20 55	20 51		21 00		21 01	21 09	21 10	21 12	21 14	21 17	21 19		21 25	21 30		21 34	21 39	21 40	21 42	21 44	21 47	
London Victoria 15 ⊖	d						20 55											21 25							
New Cross 4 ⊖	d		21 00			21 05				21 15						21 30	21 35				21 45				
St Johns	d		21 02													21 32									
Lewisham 4	a		21 05			21 09				21 19		21 21	21 26			21 35	21 39				21 49		21 51	21 56	
Hither Green 4	a					21 13						21 26					21 43						21 56		
Petts Wood 4	a						21 29					21 38						21 59					22 08		
Orpington 4	a	21 08					21 32		21 25			21 42		21 34				22 02		21 55			22 12		

London - Lewisham, Hither Green, Petts Wood and Orpington (Summary of Services)

		SE ■	SE ■	SE	SE	SE	SE	SE ■	SE	FC ■		SE	SE	SE ■	SE	SE	SE	SE	SE ■	SE		SE	SE	SE ■	SE
London Charing Cross 4	⊖ d	21 40	21 45	21 47	21 52		21 56	22 00	22 02			22 06	22 09	22 10	22 17	22 22		22 26	22 30	22 32		22 36	22 39	22 40	
London Waterloo (East) 4	⊖ d	21 43	21 48	21 50	21 55		21 59	22 03	22 05			22 09	22 12	22 13	22 20	22 25		22 29	22 33	22 35		22 39	22 42	22 43	
London Cannon Street 4	⊖ d																								
London Blackfriars 3	⊖ d									22 05															
London Bridge 4	⊖ d	21 49	21 53	21 55	22 00		22 04	22 09	22 10	22 12		22 14	22 17	22 19	22 25	22 30		22 34	22 39	22 40		22 44	22 47	22 49	
London Victoria 15	⊖ d					21 55											22 25								22 43
New Cross 4	⊖ d			22 00	22 05				22 15						22 30	22 35				22 45					
St Johns	d			22 02											22 32										
Lewisham 4	a			22 05	22 09				22 19			22 21	22 26		22 35	22 39				22 49		22 51	22 56		
Hither Green 4	a				22 13							22 26				22 43						22 56			
Petts Wood 4	a					22 29						22 38					22 59					23 08			23 21
Orpington 4	a		22 08			22 32		22 25				22 42		22 34			23 02		22 54			23 12			23 25

		SE ■	SE	SE	SE	SE		SE ■	SE	SE	SE	SE ■	SE	SE	SE	SE		SE	SE ■	SE	SE	SE	SE ■	SE	SE ■
London Charing Cross 4	⊖ d	22 45	22 47	22 52		22 56		23 00	23 02	23 06	23 09	23 10		23 17	23 22			23 26	23 30	23 32	23 36	23 39	23 40		23 45
London Waterloo (East) 4	⊖ d	22 48	22 50	22 55		22 59		23 03	23 05	23 09	23 12	23 13		23 20	23 25			23 29	23 33	23 35	23 39	23 42	23 43		23 48
London Cannon Street 4	⊖ d																								
London Blackfriars 3	⊖ d																								
London Bridge 4	⊖ d	22 53	22 55	23 00		23 04		23 09	23 10	23 14	23 17	23 19		23 25	23 30			23 34	23 39	23 40	23 44	23 47	23 49		23 53
London Victoria 15	⊖ d				22 55								23 13			23 25								23 43	
New Cross 4	⊖ d		23 00	23 05					23 15					23 30	23 35					23 45					
St Johns	d		23 02											23 32											
Lewisham 4	a		23 05	23 09					23 19	23 21	23 25			23 35	23 39					23 49	23 51	23 56			
Hither Green 4	a			23 13						23 26					23 43						23 56				
Petts Wood 4	a				23 29					23 38			23 51			23 59					00 08			00 21	
Orpington 4	a	23 08			23 32			23 24		23 42		23 34	23 57			00 02			23 54		00 12			00 25	00 08

		SE		SE	SE
London Charing Cross 4	⊖ d	23 52			23 56
London Waterloo (East) 4	⊖ d	23 55			23 59
London Cannon Street 4	⊖ d				
London Blackfriars 3	⊖ d				
London Bridge 4	⊖ d	23 59			00 04
London Victoria 15	⊖ d			23 55	
New Cross 4	⊖ d	00 05			
St Johns	d	00 07			
Lewisham 4	a	00 10			
Hither Green 4	a				
Petts Wood 4	a			00 29	
Orpington 4	a			00 32	

Saturdays

		SE	SE	SE	SE ■	SE	SE	SE	SE	SE		SE	SE	SE	SE	SE	SE	SE	SE	SE		SE	SE	SE	SE
London Charing Cross 4	⊖ d		23p36		23p45	23p52		23p56	00 02	00 05		00 10	00 15	00 48	04 52	05 22	05 26	05 32	05 36	05 39		05 47	05 52		05 56
London Waterloo (East) 4	⊖ d		23p39		23p48	23p55		23p59	00 05	00 08		00 13	00 18	00 51	04 55	05 25	05 29	05 35	05 39	05 42		05 50	05 55		05 59
London Cannon Street 4	⊖ d																								
London Blackfriars 3	⊖ d																								
London Bridge 4	⊖ d		23p44		23p53	23p59		00 04	00 10	00 13		00 18	00 23	00 56	05 00	05 30	05 34	05 40	05 44	05 47		05 55	06 00		06 04
London Victoria 15	⊖ d	23p25		23p43			23p55																	05 55	
New Cross 4	⊖ d					00 05			00 15	00 18			00 28	01 01	05 05	05 35		05 45				06 00	06 05		
St Johns	d					00 07																06 02			
Lewisham 4	a		23p51			00 10			00 19	00 22			00 32	01 05	05 09	05 39		05 49	05 52	05 56		06 05	06 09		
Hither Green 4	a		23p56							00 26				01 09	05 13	05 43			05 57				06 13		
Petts Wood 4	a	23p59	00 08	00 21			00 29					00 40		01 22					06 09					06 29	
Orpington 4	a	00 02	00 12	00 25	00 08		00 32					00 43		01 25					06 12					06 32	

		SE ■	SE	SE	SE	SE		SE	SE	SE	SE	SE	SE	SE	SE	SE		SE	SE ■	SE	SE	SE	SE	SE	SE
London Charing Cross 4	⊖ d	06 00	06 02	06 06	06 09	06 17		06 22		06 26	06 32	06 36	06 39	06 47	06 52			06 56	07 00	07 02	07 06	07 09		07 17	07 22
London Waterloo (East) 4	⊖ d	06 03	06 05	06 09	06 12	06 20		06 25		06 29	06 35	06 39	06 42	06 50	06 55			06 59	07 03	07 05	07 09	07 12		07 20	07 25
London Cannon Street 4	⊖ d																								
London Blackfriars 3	⊖ d																								
London Bridge 4	⊖ d	06 08	06 10	06 14	06 17	06 25		06 30		06 34	06 40	06 44	06 47	06 55	07 00			07 04	07 08	07 10	07 14	07 17		07 25	07 30
London Victoria 15	⊖ d								06 25							06 55							07 10		
New Cross 4	⊖ d		06 15			06 30		06 35			06 45			07 00	07 05					07 15				07 30	07 35
St Johns	d					06 32								07 02										07 32	
Lewisham 4	a		06 19	06 22	06 26	06 35		06 39			06 49	06 52	06 56	07 05	07 08					07 19	07 22	07 26		07 35	07 39
Hither Green 4	a			06 27				06 43				06 57			07 14						07 27				07 44
Petts Wood 4	a			06 39					06 59			07 09				07 29					07 39		07 44		
Orpington 4	a	06 23		06 42					07 02			07 12				07 32			07 23		07 42		07 47		

London - Lewisham, Hither Green, Petts Wood and Orpington (Summary of Services)

		SE		SE	SE ■	SE	SE	SE	SE	SE	SE ■	SE		SE	SE	SE	SE ■	SE	SE	SE	SE	SE		SE	SE
London Charing Cross 4	⊖ d			07 26	07 30	07 32	07 36		07 39		07 45	07 47		07 52		07 56	08 00	08 02		08 06		08 09			
London Waterloo (East) 4	⊖ d			07 29	07 33	07 35	07 39		07 42		07 48	07 50		07 55		07 59	08 03	08 05		08 09		08 12			
London Cannon Street 4	⊖ d																		08 05						08 10
London Blackfriars 3	⊖ d																								
London Bridge 4	⊖ d			07 34	07 38	07 40	07 44		07 47		07 53	07 55		08 00		08 04	08 08	08 10	08 11	08 14		08 17			08 14
London Victoria 15	⊖ d	07 25						07 39		07 40					07 55						08 09			08 10	
New Cross 4	⊖ d					07 45								08 05				08 15							08 19
St Johns	d																								08 21
Lewisham 4	a					07 49	07 52	08 02	07 56					08 08				08 18			08 31	08 26			08 24
Hither Green 4	a						07 57							08 14						08 23					08 28
Petts Wood 4	a	07 59					08 09			08 14					08 29					08 36				08 44	
Orpington 4	a	08 02			07 54		08 12			08 17	08 08				08 32		08 23			08 39				08 47	

		SE	SE ■	SE	SE	SE	SE	SE		SE	SE	SE ■	SE	SE	SE	SE	SE	SE		SE	SE ■	SE ■	SE	SE	SE
London Charing Cross 4	⊖ d		08 15	08 17				08 26				08 30	08 32		08 36		08 39				08 40	08 45		08 47	
London Waterloo (East) 4	⊖ d		08 18	08 20				08 29				08 33	08 35		08 39		08 42				08 43	08 48		08 50	
London Cannon Street 4	⊖ d	08 15			08 20		08 25				08 30			08 35						08 40			08 45		08 50
London Blackfriars 3	⊖ d																								
London Bridge 4	⊖ d	08 21	08 23	08 25	08 24		08 31	08 34		08 28	08 34	08 39	08 40	08 41	08 44		08 47			08 44	08 49	08 53	08 51	08 55	08 54
London Victoria 15	⊖ d					08 25										08 39		08 40							
New Cross 4	⊖ d	09 38			08 29					08 34	08 39									08 49					08 59
St Johns	d				08 31						08 41									08 51					09 01
Lewisham 4	a				08 34					08 37	08 44		08 49			09 01	08 56			08 54					09 04
Hither Green 4	a				08 38			08 43							08 53					08 58					09 08
Petts Wood 4	a				08 51	08 59									09 06			09 14							09 21
Orpington 4	a		08 38		08 54	09 02						08 55			09 09			09 17				09 08			09 24

		SE	SE	SE		SE	SE	SE ■	SE	SE	SE	SE	SE	SE		SE	SE ■	SE	SE ■	SE	SE	SE	SE	SE	
London Charing Cross 4	⊖ d			08 56				09 00	09 02		09 06		09 09				09 10		09 15	09 17				09 26	
London Waterloo (East) 4	⊖ d			08 59				09 03	09 05		09 09		09 12				09 13		09 18	09 20				09 29	
London Cannon Street 4	⊖ d		08 55				09 00			09 05						09 10		09 15			09 20		09 25		
London Blackfriars 3	⊖ d																								
London Bridge 4	⊖ d		09 01	09 04		08 58	09 04	09 09	09 10	09 11	09 14		09 17			09 14	09 19	09 21	09 23	09 25	09 24		09 31	09 34	
London Victoria 15	⊖ d	08 55										09 09		09 10								09 25			
New Cross 4	⊖ d					09 04	09 09									09 19					09 29				
St Johns	d						09 11									09 21					09 31				
Lewisham 4	a					09 07	09 14		09 19			09 31	09 26			09 24					09 34				
Hither Green 4	a			09 13							09 23					09 28					09 38			09 43	
Petts Wood 4	a	09 29									09 36			09 44							09 51	09 59			
Orpington 4	a	09 32						09 25			09 39			09 47					09 38		09 54	10 02			

		SE	SE	SE ■	SE	SE	SE	SE	SE	SE		SE	SE ■	SE ■	SE	SE	SE	SE	SE	SE		SE	SE	SE ■	SE
London Charing Cross 4	⊖ d			09 30	09 32		09 36		09 39				09 40	09 45		09 47				09 56				10 00	10 02
London Waterloo (East) 4	⊖ d			09 33	09 35		09 39		09 42				09 43	09 48		09 50				09 59				10 03	10 05
London Cannon Street 4	⊖ d		09 30			09 35						09 40			09 45		09 50		09 55				10 00		
London Blackfriars 3	⊖ d																								
London Bridge 4	⊖ d	09 28	09 34	09 39	09 40	09 41	09 44		09 47			09 44	09 49	09 53	09 51	09 55	09 54		10 01	10 04		09 58	10 04	10 09	10 10
London Victoria 15	⊖ d							09 39		09 40								09 55							
New Cross 4	⊖ d	09 34	09 39									09 49					09 59					10 04	10 09		
St Johns	d		09 41									09 51					10 01						10 11		
Lewisham 4	a	09 37	09 44		09 49			10 01	09 56			09 54					10 04					10 07	10 14		10 19
Hither Green 4	a						09 53					09 58					10 08			10 13					
Petts Wood 4	a						10 06			10 14							10 21	10 29							
Orpington 4	a			09 55			10 09			10 17				10 08			10 24	10 32						10 25	

		SE	SE	SE	SE	SE		SE	SE ■	SE	SE ■ ⚲	SE	SE	SE	SE	SE		SE	SE	SE ■	SE	SE	SE	SE	SE
London Charing Cross 4	⊖ d		10 06		10 09				10 10		10 15	10 17				10 26				10 30	10 32		10 36		10 39
London Waterloo (East) 4	⊖ d		10 09		10 12				10 13		10 18	10 20				10 29				10 33	10 35		10 39		10 42
London Cannon Street 4	⊖ d	10 05						10 10		10 15			10 20		10 25				10 30			10 35			
London Blackfriars 3	⊖ d																								
London Bridge 4	⊖ d	10 11	10 14		10 17			10 14	10 19	10 21	10 23	10 25	10 24		10 31	10 34		10 28	10 34	10 39	10 40	10 41	10 44		10 47
London Victoria 15	⊖ d			10 09		10 10								10 25										10 39	
New Cross 4	⊖ d							10 19					10 29					10 34	10 39						
St Johns	d							10 21					10 31						10 41						
Lewisham 4	a			10 32	10 26			10 24					10 34					10 37	10 44		10 49			11 01	10 56
Hither Green 4	a		10 23					10 28					10 39			10 43							10 53		
Petts Wood 4	a		10 36			10 44							10 51	10 59									11 06		
Orpington 4	a		10 39			10 47					10 38		10 54	11 02						10 55			11 09		

Table 199

London - Lewisham, Hither Green, Petts Wood and Orpington (Summary of Services)

	SE		SE	SE ■ ✕	SE ■ ✕	SE	SE	SE	SE	SE	SE		SE	SE	SE ■	SE	SE	SE	SE	SE	SE		SE	SE ■ ✕
London Charing Cross 4 ⊖ d				10 40	10 45		10 47				10 56				11 00	11 02		11 06		11 09				11 10
London Waterloo (East) 4 ⊖ d				10 43	10 48		10 50				10 59				11 03	11 05		11 09		11 12				11 13
London Cannon Street 4 ⊖ d			10 40			10 45		10 50		10 55				11 00			11 05						11 10	
London Blackfriars 3 ⊖ d																								
London Bridge 4 ⊖ d			10 44	10 49	10 53	10 51	10 55	10 54		11 01	11 04		10 58	11 04	11 09	11 10	11 11	11 14		11 17			11 14	11 19
London Victoria 15 ⊖ d	10 40								10 55										11 09		11 10			
New Cross 4 ⊖ d			10 49					10 59					11 04	11 09									11 19	
St Johns d			10 51					11 01						11 11									11 21	
Lewisham 4 a			10 54					11 04					11 07	11 14		11 19			11 31	11 26			11 24	
Hither Green 4 a			10 58					11 08			11 13							11 23					11 28	
Petts Wood 4 a	11 14							11 21	11 29									11 36			11 44			
Orpington 4 a	11 17				11 08			11 24	11 32						11 25			11 39			11 47			

	SE	SE ■ ✕	SE	SE	SE	SE	SE		SE	SE	SE ■	SE	SE	SE	SE	SE	SE		SE	SE ■ ✕	SE ■ ✕	SE	SE	SE
London Charing Cross 4 ⊖ d		11 15	11 17				11 26				11 30	11 32		11 36		11 39				11 40	11 45		11 47	
London Waterloo (East) 4 ⊖ d		11 18	11 20				11 29				11 33	11 35		11 39		11 42				11 43	11 48		11 50	
London Cannon Street 4 ⊖ d	11 15			11 20		11 25				11 30			11 35						11 40			11 45		11 50
London Blackfriars 3 ⊖ d																								
London Bridge 4 ⊖ d	11 21	11 23	11 25	11 24		11 31	11 34		11 28	11 34	11 39	11 40	11 41	11 44		11 47			11 44	11 49	11 53	11 51	11 55	11 54
London Victoria 15 ⊖ d					11 25										11 39		11 40							
New Cross 4 ⊖ d				11 29					11 34	11 39									11 49					11 59
St Johns d				11 31						11 41									11 51					12 01
Lewisham 4 a				11 34					11 37	11 44		11 49			12 01	11 56			11 54					12 04
Hither Green 4 a				11 38			11 43							11 53					11 58					12 08
Petts Wood 4 a				11 51	11 59									12 06			12 14							12 21
Orpington 4 a		11 38		11 54	12 02						11 55			12 09			12 17				12 08			12 24

	SE	SE	SE		SE	SE	SE ■	SE	SE	SE	SE	SE	SE		SE	SE ■ ✕	SE	SE ■ ✕	SE	SE	SE	SE	SE	
London Charing Cross 4 ⊖ d			11 56				12 00	12 02		12 06		12 09				12 10		12 15	12 17				12 26	
London Waterloo (East) 4 ⊖ d			11 59				12 03	12 05		12 09		12 12				12 13		12 18	12 20				12 29	
London Cannon Street 4 ⊖ d		11 55				12 00			12 05						12 10		12 15			12 20		12 25		
London Blackfriars 3 ⊖ d																								
London Bridge 4 ⊖ d		12 01	12 04		11 58	12 04	12 09	12 10	12 11	12 14		12 17			12 14	12 19	12 21	12 23	12 25	12 24		12 31	12 34	
London Victoria 15 ⊖ d	11 55										12 09		12 10								12 25			
New Cross 4 ⊖ d					12 04	12 09									12 19					12 29				
St Johns d						12 11									12 21					12 31				
Lewisham 4 a					12 07	12 14		12 19			12 31	12 26			12 24					12 34				
Hither Green 4 a			12 13							12 23					12 28					12 38			12 43	
Petts Wood 4 a	12 29									12 36			12 44							12 51	12 59			
Orpington 4 a	12 32						12 25			12 39			12 47					12 38		12 54	13 02			

	SE	SE	SE ■	SE	SE	SE	SE	SE	SE		SE	SE ■ ✕	SE ■ ✕	SE	SE	SE	SE	SE	SE		SE	SE	SE ■	SE
London Charing Cross 4 ⊖ d			12 30	12 32		12 36		12 39				12 40	12 45		12 47				12 56				13 00	13 02
London Waterloo (East) 4 ⊖ d			12 33	12 35		12 39		12 42				12 43	12 48		12 50				12 59				13 03	13 05
London Cannon Street 4 ⊖ d		12 30			12 35						12 40			12 45		12 50		12 55				13 00		
London Blackfriars 3 ⊖ d																								
London Bridge 4 ⊖ d	12 28	12 34	12 39	12 40	12 41	12 44		12 47			12 44	12 49	12 53	12 51	12 55	12 54		13 01	13 04		12 58	13 04	13 09	13 10
London Victoria 15 ⊖ d							12 39		12 40								12 55							
New Cross 4 ⊖ d	12 34	12 39									12 49					12 59					13 04	13 09		
St Johns d		12 41									12 51					13 01						13 11		
Lewisham 4 a	12 37	12 44		12 49			13 01	12 56			12 54					13 04					13 07	13 14		13 19
Hither Green 4 a						12 53					12 58					13 08			13 13					
Petts Wood 4 a						13 06			13 14							13 21	13 29							
Orpington 4 a			12 55			13 09			13 17				13 08			13 24	13 32						13 25	

	SE	SE	SE	SE	SE		SE	SE ■ ✕	SE	SE ■ ✕	SE	SE	SE	SE	SE		SE	SE	SE ■	SE	SE	SE	SE	SE
London Charing Cross 4 ⊖ d		13 06		13 09				13 10		13 15	13 17				13 26				13 30	13 32		13 36		13 39
London Waterloo (East) 4 ⊖ d		13 09		13 12				13 13		13 18	13 20				13 29				13 33	13 35		13 39		13 42
London Cannon Street 4 ⊖ d	13 05						13 10		13 15			13 20		13 25				13 30			13 35			
London Blackfriars 3 ⊖ d																								
London Bridge 4 ⊖ d	13 11	13 14		13 17			13 14	13 19	13 21	13 23	13 25	13 24		13 31	13 34		13 28	13 34	13 39	13 40	13 41	13 44		13 47
London Victoria 15 ⊖ d			13 09		13 10								13 25										13 39	
New Cross 4 ⊖ d							13 19					13 29					13 34	13 39						
St Johns d							13 21					13 31						13 41						
Lewisham 4 a			13 31	13 26			13 24					13 34					13 37	13 44		13 49			14 01	13 56
Hither Green 4 a		13 23					13 28					13 38			13 43							13 53		
Petts Wood 4 a		13 36			13 44							13 51	13 59									14 06		
Orpington 4 a		13 39			13 47					13 38		13 54	14 02						13 55			14 09		

Table 199

London - Lewisham, Hither Green, Petts Wood and Orpington (Summary of Services)

	SE		SE	SE ■ ✕	SE ■ ✕	SE	SE	SE	SE	SE	SE		SE	SE	SE ■	SE	SE	SE	SE	SE	SE		SE	SE ■ ✕
London Charing Cross 4 ⊖ d				13 40	13 45		13 47				13 56				14 00	14 02		14 06		14 09				14 10
London Waterloo (East) 4 ⊖ d				13 43	13 48		13 50				13 59				14 03	14 05		14 09		14 12				14 13
London Cannon Street 4 ⊖ d			13 40			13 45		13 50		13 55				14 00			14 05						14 10	
London Blackfriars 3 ⊖ d																								
London Bridge 4 ⊖ d			13 44	13 49	13 53	13 51	13 55	13 54		14 01	14 04		13 58	14 04	14 09	14 10	14 11	14 14		14 17			14 14	14 19
London Victoria 15 ⊖ d	13 40								13 55										14 09		14 10			
New Cross 4 ⊖ d			13 49					13 59					14 04	14 09									14 19	
St Johns d			13 51					14 01						14 11									14 21	
Lewisham 4 a			13 54					14 04					14 07	14 14		14 19			14 31	14 26			14 24	
Hither Green 4 a			13 58					14 08			14 13							14 23					14 28	
Petts Wood 4 a	14 14							14 21	14 29									14 36			14 44			
Orpington 4 a	14 17				14 08			14 24	14 32						14 25			14 39			14 47			

	SE	SE ■ ✕	SE	SE	SE	SE	SE		SE	SE	SE ■	SE	SE	SE	SE	SE	SE		SE	SE ■ ✕	SE ■ ✕	SE	SE	SE
London Charing Cross 4 ⊖ d		14 15	14 17				14 26				14 30	14 32		14 36		14 39				14 40	14 45		14 47	
London Waterloo (East) 4 ⊖ d		14 18	14 20				14 29				14 33	14 35		14 39		14 42				14 43	14 48		14 50	
London Cannon Street 4 ⊖ d	14 15			14 20		14 25				14 30			14 35						14 40			14 45		14 50
London Blackfriars 3 ⊖ d																								
London Bridge 4 ⊖ d	14 21	14 23	14 25	14 24		14 31	14 34		14 28	14 34	14 39	14 40	14 41	14 44		14 47			14 44	14 49	14 53	14 51	14 55	14 54
London Victoria 15 ⊖ d					14 25										14 39		14 40							
New Cross 4 ⊖ d				14 29					14 34	14 39									14 49					14 59
St Johns d				14 31						14 41									14 51					15 01
Lewisham 4 a				14 34					14 37	14 44		14 49			15 01	14 56			14 54					15 04
Hither Green 4 a				14 38			14 43							14 53					14 58					15 08
Petts Wood 4 a				14 51	14 59									15 06			15 14							15 21
Orpington 4 a		14 38		14 54	15 02						14 55			15 09			15 17				15 08			15 24

	SE	SE	SE		SE	SE	SE ■	SE	SE	SE	SE	SE	SE		SE	SE ■ ✕	SE	SE ■ ✕	SE	SE	SE	SE	SE	
London Charing Cross 4 ⊖ d			14 56				15 00	15 02		15 06		15 09				15 10		15 15	15 17				15 26	
London Waterloo (East) 4 ⊖ d			14 59				15 03	15 05		15 09		15 12				15 13		15 18	15 20				15 29	
London Cannon Street 4 ⊖ d		14 55				15 00			15 05						15 10		15 15			15 20		15 25		
London Blackfriars 3 ⊖ d																								
London Bridge 4 ⊖ d		15 01	15 04		14 58	15 04	15 09	15 10	15 11	15 14		15 17			15 14	15 19	15 21	15 23	15 25	15 24		15 31	15 34	
London Victoria 15 ⊖ d	14 55										15 09		15 10								15 25			
New Cross 4 ⊖ d					15 04	15 09									15 19					15 29				
St Johns d						15 11									15 21					15 31				
Lewisham 4 a					15 07	15 14		15 19			15 31	15 26			15 24					15 34				
Hither Green 4 a			15 13							15 23					15 28					15 38			15 43	
Petts Wood 4 a	15 29									15 36			15 44							15 51	15 59			
Orpington 4 a	15 32						15 25			15 39			15 47					15 38		15 54	16 02			

	SE	SE	SE ■	SE	SE	SE	SE	SE	SE		SE	SE ■ ✕	SE ■ ✕	SE	SE	SE	SE	SE	SE		SE	SE	SE ■	SE
London Charing Cross 4 ⊖ d			15 30	15 32		15 36		15 39				15 40	15 45		15 47				15 56				16 00	16 02
London Waterloo (East) 4 ⊖ d			15 33	15 35		15 39		15 42				15 43	15 48		15 50				15 59				16 03	16 05
London Cannon Street 4 ⊖ d		15 30			15 35						15 40			15 45		15 50		15 55				16 00		
London Blackfriars 3 ⊖ d																								
London Bridge 4 ⊖ d	15 28	15 34	15 39	15 40	15 41	15 44		15 47			15 44	15 49	15 53	15 51	15 55	15 54		16 01	16 04		15 58	16 04	16 09	16 10
London Victoria 15 ⊖ d							15 39		15 40								15 55							
New Cross 4 ⊖ d	15 34	15 39									15 49					15 59					16 04	16 09		
St Johns d		15 41									15 51					16 01						16 11		
Lewisham 4 a	15 37	15 44		15 49			16 01	15 56			15 54					16 04					16 07	16 14		16 19
Hither Green 4 a						15 53					15 58					16 08			16 13					
Petts Wood 4 a						16 06			16 14							16 21	16 29							
Orpington 4 a			15 55			16 09			16 17				16 08			16 24	16 32						16 25	

	SE	SE	SE	SE	SE		SE	SE ■ ✕	SE	SE ■ ✕	SE	SE	SE	SE	SE		SE	SE	SE ■	SE	SE	SE	SE	SE
London Charing Cross 4 ⊖ d		16 06		16 09				16 10		16 15	16 17				16 26				16 30	16 32		16 36		16 39
London Waterloo (East) 4 ⊖ d		16 09		16 12				16 13		16 18	16 20				16 29				16 33	16 35		16 39		16 42
London Cannon Street 4 ⊖ d	16 05						16 10		16 15			16 20		16 25				16 30			16 35			
London Blackfriars 3 ⊖ d																								
London Bridge 4 ⊖ d	16 11	16 14		16 17			16 14	16 19	16 21	16 23	16 25	16 24		16 31	16 34		16 28	16 34	16 39	16 40	16 41	16 44		16 47
London Victoria 15 ⊖ d			16 09		16 10								16 25										16 39	
New Cross 4 ⊖ d							16 19					16 29					16 34	16 39						
St Johns d							16 21					16 31						16 41						
Lewisham 4 a			16 31	16 26			16 24					16 34					16 37	16 44		16 49			17 01	16 56
Hither Green 4 a		16 23					16 28					16 38			16 43							16 53		
Petts Wood 4 a		16 36			16 44							16 51	16 59									17 06		
Orpington 4 a		16 39			16 47					16 38		16 54	17 02						16 55			17 09		

London - Lewisham, Hither Green, Petts Wood and Orpington (Summary of Services)

	SE		SE	SE 1 ⌶	SE 1 ⌶	SE	SE	SE	SE	SE	SE		SE	SE	SE 1	SE	SE	SE	SE	SE	SE		SE	SE 1 ⌶
London Charing Cross 4 ⊖ d				16 40	16 45		16 47				16 56				17 00	17 02		17 06		17 09				17 10
London Waterloo (East) 4 ⊖ d				16 43	16 48		16 50				16 59				17 03	17 05		17 09		17 12				17 13
London Cannon Street 4 ⊖ d			16 40			16 45		16 50		16 55				17 00			17 05						17 10	
London Blackfriars 3 ⊖ d																								
London Bridge 4 ⊖ d			16 44	16 49	16 53	16 51	16 55	16 54		17 01	17 04		16 58	17 04	17 09	17 10	17 11	17 14		17 17			17 14	17 19
London Victoria 15 ⊖ d	16 40								16 55										17 09		17 10			
New Cross 4 ⊖ d			16 49					16 59					17 04	17 09									17 19	
St Johns d			16 51					17 01						17 11									17 21	
Lewisham 4 ⇌ a			16 54					17 04					17 07	17 14		17 19			17 31	17 26			17 24	
Hither Green 4 a			16 58					17 08			17 13							17 23					17 28	
Petts Wood 4 a	17 14							17 21	17 29									17 36			17 44			
Orpington 4 a	17 17				17 08			17 24	17 32						17 25			17 39			17 47			

	SE	SE 1 ⌶	SE	SE	SE	SE	SE		SE	SE	SE 1	SE	SE	SE	SE	SE	SE		SE	SE 1 ⌶	SE 1 ⌶	SE	SE	SE
London Charing Cross 4 ⊖ d		17 15	17 17				17 26				17 30	17 32		17 36		17 39				17 40	17 45		17 47	
London Waterloo (East) 4 ⊖ d		17 18	17 20				17 29				17 33	17 35		17 39		17 42				17 43	17 48		17 50	
London Cannon Street 4 ⊖ d	17 15			17 20		17 25				17 30			17 35						17 40			17 45		17 50
London Blackfriars 3 ⊖ d																								
London Bridge 4 ⊖ d	17 21	17 23	17 25	17 24		17 31	17 34		17 28	17 34	17 39	17 40	17 41	17 44		17 47			17 44	17 49	17 53	17 51	17 55	17 54
London Victoria 15 ⊖ d					17 25										17 39		17 40							
New Cross 4 ⊖ d				17 29					17 34	17 39									17 49					17 59
St Johns d				17 31						17 41									17 51					18 01
Lewisham 4 ⇌ a				17 34					17 37	17 44		17 49			18 01	17 56			17 54					18 04
Hither Green 4 a				17 38			17 43							17 53					17 58					18 08
Petts Wood 4 a				17 51	17 59									18 06			18 14							18 21
Orpington 4 a		17 38		17 54	18 02						17 55			18 09			18 17				18 08			18 24

	SE	SE	SE		SE	SE	SE 1	SE	SE	SE	SE	SE	SE		SE	SE 1 ⌶	SE	SE 1 ⌶	SE	SE	SE	SE	SE	
London Charing Cross 4 ⊖ d			17 56				18 00	18 02		18 06		18 09				18 10		18 15	18 17				18 26	
London Waterloo (East) 4 ⊖ d			17 59				18 03	18 05		18 09		18 12				18 13		18 18	18 20				18 29	
London Cannon Street 4 ⊖ d		17 55				18 00			18 05						18 10		18 15			18 20		18 25		
London Blackfriars 3 ⊖ d																								
London Bridge 4 ⊖ d		18 01	18 04		17 58	18 04	18 09	18 10	18 11	18 14		18 17			18 14	18 19	18 21	18 23	18 25	18 24		18 31	18 34	
London Victoria 15 ⊖ d	17 55										18 09		18 10								18 25			
New Cross 4 ⊖ d					18 04	18 09									18 19					18 29				
St Johns d						18 11									18 21					18 31				
Lewisham 4 ⇌ a					18 07	18 14		18 19			18 31	18 26			18 24					18 34				
Hither Green 4 a			18 13							18 23					18 28					18 38			18 43	
Petts Wood 4 a	18 29									18 36			18 44							18 51	18 59			
Orpington 4 a	18 32						18 25			18 39			18 47					18 38		18 54	19 02			

	SE	SE	SE 1	SE	SE	SE	SE	SE	SE		SE	SE 1 ⌶	SE	SE 1 ⌶	SE	SE	SE	SE	SE		SE	SE	SE 1	SE
London Charing Cross 4 ⊖ d			18 30	18 32		18 36		18 39				18 40		18 45	18 47				18 56				19 00	19 02
London Waterloo (East) 4 ⊖ d			18 33	18 35		18 39		18 42				18 43		18 48	18 50				18 59				19 03	19 05
London Cannon Street 4 ⊖ d		18 30			18 35						18 40		18 45			18 50		18 55				19 00		
London Blackfriars 3 ⊖ d																								
London Bridge 4 ⊖ d	18 28	18 34	18 39	18 40	18 41	18 44		18 47			18 44	18 49	18 51	18 53	18 55	18 54		19 01	19 04		18 58	19 04	19 09	19 10
London Victoria 15 ⊖ d							18 39		18 40								18 55							
New Cross 4 ⊖ d	18 34	18 39									18 49					18 59					19 04	19 09		
St Johns d		18 41									18 51					19 01						19 11		
Lewisham 4 ⇌ a	18 37	18 44		18 49			19 02	18 56			18 54					19 04					19 07	19 14		19 19
Hither Green 4 a						18 53					18 58					19 09			19 13					
Petts Wood 4 a						19 06			19 14							19 21	19 29							
Orpington 4 a			18 55			19 09			19 17					19 08		19 24	19 32						19 25	

	SE	SE	SE	SE	SE		SE	SE 1 ⌶	SE 1	SE	SE	SE	SE	SE	SE 1		SE	SE	SE	SE	SE	SE 1 ⌶	SE	SE
London Charing Cross 4 ⊖ d		19 06		19 09				19 10	19 15	19 17			19 26		19 30		19 32	19 36		19 39		19 40	19 47	19 52
London Waterloo (East) 4 ⊖ d		19 09		19 12				19 13	19 18	19 20			19 29		19 33		19 35	19 39		19 42		19 43	19 50	19 55
London Cannon Street 4 ⊖ d	19 05						19 10					19 25												
London Blackfriars 3 ⊖ d																								
London Bridge 4 ⊖ d	19 11	19 14		19 17			19 14	19 19	19 23	19 25		19 31	19 34	19 28	19 39		19 40	19 44		19 47		19 49	19 55	20 00
London Victoria 15 ⊖ d			19 09		19 10						19 25								19 39		19 40			
New Cross 4 ⊖ d							19 19			19 30				19 34			19 45						20 00	20 05
St Johns d							19 21			19 32													20 02	
Lewisham 4 ⇌ a			19 31	19 26			19 24			19 35				19 37			19 49	19 51	20 01	19 56			20 05	20 09
Hither Green 4 a		19 23					19 28						19 43					19 56						20 13
Petts Wood 4 a		19 36			19 44						19 59							20 08			20 14			
Orpington 4 a		19 39			19 48				19 38		20 02				19 55			20 12			20 18			

London - Lewisham, Hither Green, Petts Wood and Orpington (Summary of Services)

	SE		SE 1	SE	SE	SE	SE	SE	SE 1 ⌶	SE	SE		SE	SE 1	SE	SE	SE	SE	SE 1 ⌶	SE	SE		SE	SE 1
London Charing Cross 4 ⊖ d			19 55	19 56	20 02	20 06	20 09		20 10	20 17	20 22			20 25	20 26	20 32	20 36	20 39	20 40	20 47	20 52			20 55
London Waterloo (East) 4 ⊖ d			19 58	19 59	20 05	20 09	20 12		20 13	20 20	20 25			20 28	20 29	20 35	20 39	20 42	20 43	20 50	20 55			20 58
London Cannon Street 4 ⊖ d																								
London Blackfriars 3 ⊖ d																								
London Bridge 4 ⊖ d			20 03	20 05	20 10	20 14	20 17		20 19	20 25	20 30			20 33	20 35	20 40	20 44	20 47	20 49	20 55	21 00			21 03
London Victoria 15 ⊖ d	19 55							20 10					20 25										20 55	
New Cross 4 ⊖ d					20 15					20 30	20 35					20 45				21 00	21 05			
St Johns d										20 32										21 02				
Lewisham 4 ⇌ a					20 19	20 21	20 26			20 35	20 39					20 49	20 51	20 56		21 05	21 09			
Hither Green 4 a						20 26					20 43						20 56				21 13			
Petts Wood 4 a	20 29					20 38		20 44					20 59				21 08						21 29	
Orpington 4 a	20 32		20 18			20 42		20 47	20 34				21 02	20 48			21 12		21 04				21 32	21 18

	SE	SE	SE	SE	SE 1	SE	SE		SE	SE 1	SE	SE	SE	SE	SE 1	SE	SE		SE	SE 1	SE	SE	SE	SE
London Charing Cross 4 ⊖ d	20 56	21 02	21 06	21 09	21 10	21 17	21 22			21 25	21 26	21 32	21 36	21 39	21 40	21 47	21 52			21 55	21 56	22 02	22 06	22 09
London Waterloo (East) 4 ⊖ d	20 59	21 05	21 09	21 12	21 13	21 20	21 25			21 28	21 29	21 35	21 39	21 42	21 43	21 50	21 55			21 58	21 59	22 05	22 09	22 12
London Cannon Street 4 ⊖ d																								
London Blackfriars 3 ⊖ d																								
London Bridge 4 ⊖ d	21 05	21 10	21 14	21 17	21 19	21 25	21 30			21 33	21 35	21 40	21 44	21 47	21 49	21 55	22 00			22 03	22 05	22 10	22 14	22 17
London Victoria 15 ⊖ d									21 25										21 55					
New Cross 4 ⊖ d		21 15				21 30	21 35					21 45				22 00	22 05					22 15		
St Johns d						21 32										22 02								
Lewisham 4 ⇌ a		21 19	21 21	21 26		21 35	21 39					21 49	21 51	21 56		22 05	22 09					22 19	22 21	22 26
Hither Green 4 a			21 26				21 43						21 56				22 13						22 26	
Petts Wood 4 a			21 38						21 59				22 08						22 29				22 38	
Orpington 4 a			21 42		21 34				22 02	21 48			22 12		22 04				22 32	22 18			22 42	

	SE 1	SE	SE		SE	SE 1	SE	SE	SE	SE	SE 1	SE	SE		SE	SE 1	SE	SE	SE	SE	SE	SE 1	SE	
London Charing Cross 4 ⊖ d	22 10	22 17	22 22			22 25	22 26	22 32	22 36	22 39	22 40		22 47		22 52	22 55		22 56	23 02	23 06	23 09	23 10		
London Waterloo (East) 4 ⊖ d	22 13	22 20	22 25			22 28	22 29	22 35	22 39	22 42	22 43		22 50		22 55	22 58		22 59	23 05	23 09	23 12	23 13		
London Cannon Street 4 ⊖ d																								
London Blackfriars 3 ⊖ d																								
London Bridge 4 ⊖ d	22 19	22 25	22 30			22 33	22 35	22 40	22 44	22 47	22 49		22 55		23 00	23 03		23 05	23 10	23 14	23 17	23 19		
London Victoria 15 ⊖ d					22 25							22 43					22 55						23 13	
New Cross 4 ⊖ d		22 30	22 35					22 45					23 00		23 05				23 15					
St Johns d		22 32											23 02											
Lewisham 4 ⇌ a		22 35	22 39					22 49	22 51	22 56			23 05		23 09				23 19	23 21	23 25			
Hither Green 4 a			22 43						22 56						23 13					23 26				
Petts Wood 4 a					22 59				23 08			23 22					23 29			23 38			23 52	
Orpington 4 a	22 34				23 02	22 48			23 12		23 04	23 25				23 18	23 32			23 42		23 34	23 55	

	SE	SE	SE	SE 1	SE	SE	SE	SE	SE 1		SE	SE 1	SE	SE	SE
London Charing Cross 4 ⊖ d	23 17	23 22		23 25	23 26	23 32	23 36	23 39	23 40			23 45	23 52		23 56
London Waterloo (East) 4 ⊖ d	23 20	23 25		23 28	23 29	23 35	23 39	23 42	23 43			23 48	23 55		23 59
London Cannon Street 4 ⊖ d															
London Blackfriars 3 ⊖ d															
London Bridge 4 ⊖ d	23 25	23 30		23 33	23 35	23 40	23 44	23 47	23 49			23 53	23 59		00 05
London Victoria 15 ⊖ d			23 25								23 43			23 55	
New Cross 4 ⊖ d	23 30	23 35				23 45							00 05		
St Johns d	23 32												00 07		
Lewisham 4 ⇌ a	23 35	23 39				23 49	23 51	23 55					00 10		
Hither Green 4 a		23 43					23 56								
Petts Wood 4 a			23 59				00 08				00 22			00 29	
Orpington 4 a			00 02	23 48			00 12		00 04		00 25	00 08		00 32	

Sundays

	SE	SE	SE 1	SE	SE 1	SE	SE	SE	SE		SE	SE	SE	SE	SE	SE	SE	SE	SE		SE	SE	SE	SE 1
London Charing Cross 4 ⊖ d		23p36	23p40		23p45	23p52		23p56	00 02		00 05	00 10	00 15	00 48	07 30	07 35	07 46	07 50			07 56	08 00	08 05	08 08
London Waterloo (East) 4 ⊖ d		23p39	23p43		23p48	23p55		23p59	00 05		00 08	00 13	00 18	00 51	07 33	07 38	07 49	07 53			07 59	08 03	08 08	08 11
London Cannon Street 4 ⊖ d																								
London Blackfriars 3 ⊖ d																								
London Bridge 4 ⊖ d		23p44	23p49		23p53	23p59		00 05	00 10		00 13	00 18	00 23	00 56	07 38	07 43	07 54	07 58			08 04	08 08	08 13	08 16
London Victoria 15 ⊖ d	23p25			23p43			23p55												07 51					
New Cross 4 ⊖ d						00 05			00 15		00 18		00 28	01 01		07 49		08 04					08 19	
St Johns d						00 07										07 51							08 21	
Lewisham 4 ⇌ a		23p51				00 10			00 19		00 22		00 32	01 05		07 53	08 02	08 07			08 11		08 23	
Hither Green 4 a		23p56									00 26			01 09			08 07				08 16			
Petts Wood 4 a	23p59	00 08		00 22			00 29					00 40		01 22			08 19		08 25					
Orpington 4 a	00 02	00 12	00 04	00 25	00 08		00 32					00 43		01 25			08 22		08 28					08 31

Table 199

Sundays

London - Lewisham, Hither Green, Petts Wood and Orpington (Summary of Services)

		SE	SE	SE	SE	SE [1]		SE	SE	SE	SE [1]	SE	SE	SE	SE	SE		SE	SE	SE [1]	SE	SE	SE	SE	SE [1]
London Charing Cross [4]	⊖ d	08 10	08 16	08 20		08 23		08 26	08 30	08 35	08 38	08 40	08 46	08 50		08 56		09 00	09 05	09 08	09 10	09 16	09 20		09 23
London Waterloo (East) [4]	⊖ d	08 13	08 19	08 23		08 26		08 29	08 33	08 38	08 41	08 43	08 49	08 53		08 59		09 03	09 08	09 11	09 13	09 19	09 23		09 26
London Cannon Street [4]	⊖ d																								
London Blackfriars [3]	⊖ d																								
London Bridge [4]	⊖ d	08 18	08 24	08 28		08 31		08 34	08 38	08 43	08 46	08 48	08 54	08 58		09 04		09 08	09 13	09 16	09 18	09 24	09 28		09 31
London Victoria [15]	⊖ d				08 21										08 51									09 21	
New Cross [4]	⊖ d			08 34						08 49				09 04					09 19				09 34		
St Johns	d									08 51									09 21						
Lewisham [4]	a	08 27	08 32	08 37				08 41		08 53		08 57	09 02	09 07		09 11			09 23		09 27	09 32	09 37		
Hither Green [4]	a		08 37					08 46					09 07			09 16						09 37			
Petts Wood [4]	a		08 49		08 55								09 19		09 25							09 49		09 55	
Orpington [4]	a		08 52		08 58	08 46					09 01		09 22		09 28					09 31		09 52		09 58	09 46

		SE		SE	SE	SE [1] ⊤	SE	SE	SE	SE	SE [1]	SE		SE	SE	SE [1] ⊤	SE	SE	SE	SE	SE [1]	SE		SE	SE
London Charing Cross [4]	⊖ d	09 26		09 30	09 35	09 38	09 40	09 46	09 50		09 53	09 56		10 00	10 05	10 08	10 10	10 16	10 20		10 23	10 26		10 30	10 35
London Waterloo (East) [4]	⊖ d	09 29		09 33	09 38	09 41	09 43	09 49	09 53		09 56	09 59		10 03	10 08	10 11	10 13	10 19	10 23		10 26	10 29		10 33	10 38
London Cannon Street [4]	⊖ d																								
London Blackfriars [3]	⊖ d																								
London Bridge [4]	⊖ d	09 34		09 38	09 43	09 46	09 48	09 54	09 58		10 01	10 04		10 08	10 13	10 16	10 18	10 24	10 28		10 31	10 34		10 38	10 43
London Victoria [15]	⊖ d									09 51										10 21					
New Cross [4]	⊖ d				09 49				10 04						10 19				10 34						10 49
St Johns	d				09 51										10 21										10 51
Lewisham [4]	a	09 41			09 53		09 57	10 02	10 07			10 11			10 23		10 27	10 32	10 37			10 41			10 53
Hither Green [4]	a	09 46						10 07				10 16						10 37				10 46			
Petts Wood [4]	a							10 19		10 25								10 49		10 55					
Orpington [4]	a					10 01		10 22		10 28	10 16					10 31		10 52		10 58	10 46				

		SE [1] ⊤	SE	SE	SE	SE	SE [1]	SE		SE	SE	SE [1] ⊤	SE	SE	SE	SE	SE [1]	SE		SE	SE	SE [1] ⊤	SE	SE	SE
London Charing Cross [4]	⊖ d	10 38	10 40	10 46	10 50		10 53	10 56		11 00	11 05	11 08	11 10	11 16	11 20		11 23	11 26		11 30	11 35	11 38	11 40	11 46	11 50
London Waterloo (East) [4]	⊖ d	10 41	10 43	10 49	10 53		10 56	10 59		11 03	11 08	11 11	11 13	11 19	11 23		11 26	11 29		11 33	11 38	11 41	11 43	11 49	11 53
London Cannon Street [4]	⊖ d																								
London Blackfriars [3]	⊖ d																								
London Bridge [4]	⊖ d	10 46	10 48	10 54	10 58		11 01	11 04		11 08	11 13	11 16	11 18	11 24	11 28		11 31	11 34		11 38	11 43	11 46	11 48	11 54	11 58
London Victoria [15]	⊖ d					10 51										11 21									
New Cross [4]	⊖ d				11 04						11 19				11 34						11 49				12 04
St Johns	d										11 21										11 51				
Lewisham [4]	a		10 57	11 02	11 07			11 11			11 23		11 27	11 32	11 37			11 41			11 53		11 57	12 02	12 07
Hither Green [4]	a			11 07				11 16						11 37				11 46						12 07	
Petts Wood [4]	a			11 19		11 25								11 49		11 55								12 19	
Orpington [4]	a	11 01		11 22		11 28	11 16					11 31		11 52		11 58	11 46					12 01		12 22	

		SE	SE [1]	SE		SE	SE	SE [1] ⊤	SE	SE	SE	SE	SE [1]	SE		SE	SE	SE [1] ⊤	SE	SE	SE	SE	SE [1]	SE	
London Charing Cross [4]	⊖ d		11 53	11 56		12 00	12 05	12 08	12 10	12 16	12 20		12 23	12 26		12 30	12 35	12 38	12 40	12 46	12 50		12 53	12 56	
London Waterloo (East) [4]	⊖ d		11 56	11 59		12 03	12 08	12 11	12 13	12 19	12 23		12 26	12 29		12 33	12 38	12 41	12 43	12 49	12 53		12 56	12 59	
London Cannon Street [4]	⊖ d																								
London Blackfriars [3]	⊖ d																								
London Bridge [4]	⊖ d		12 01	12 04		12 08	12 13	12 16	12 18	12 24	12 28		12 31	12 34		12 38	12 43	12 46	12 48	12 54	12 58		13 01	13 04	
London Victoria [15]	⊖ d	11 51										12 21										12 51			
New Cross [4]	⊖ d						12 19				12 34						12 49				13 04				
St Johns	d						12 21										12 51								
Lewisham [4]	a			12 11			12 23		12 27	12 32	12 37			12 41			12 53		12 57	13 02	13 07			13 11	
Hither Green [4]	a			12 16						12 37				12 46						13 07				13 16	
Petts Wood [4]	a	12 25								12 49		12 55								13 19		13 25			
Orpington [4]	a	12 28	12 16					12 31		12 52		12 58	12 46					13 01		13 22		13 28	13 16		

		SE	SE	SE [1] ⊤	SE	SE	SE	SE	SE [1]	SE		SE	SE	SE [1] ⊤	SE	SE	SE	SE	SE [1]	SE		SE	SE	SE [1] ⊤	SE
London Charing Cross [4]	⊖ d	13 00	13 05	13 08	13 10	13 16	13 20		13 23	13 26		13 30	13 35	13 38	13 40	13 46	13 50		13 53	13 56		14 00	14 05	14 08	14 10
London Waterloo (East) [4]	⊖ d	13 03	13 08	13 11	13 13	13 19	13 23		13 26	13 29		13 33	13 38	13 41	13 43	13 49	13 53		13 56	13 59		14 03	14 08	14 11	14 13
London Cannon Street [4]	⊖ d																								
London Blackfriars [3]	⊖ d																								
London Bridge [4]	⊖ d	13 08	13 13	13 16	13 18	13 24	13 28		13 31	13 34		13 38	13 43	13 46	13 48	13 54	13 58		14 01	14 04		14 08	14 13	14 16	14 18
London Victoria [15]	⊖ d							13 21										13 51							
New Cross [4]	⊖ d		13 19				13 34						13 49				14 04						14 19		
St Johns	d		13 21										13 51										14 21		
Lewisham [4]	a		13 23		13 27	13 32	13 37			13 41			13 53		13 57	14 02	14 07			14 11			14 23		14 27
Hither Green [4]	a					13 37				13 46						14 07				14 16					
Petts Wood [4]	a					13 49		13 55								14 19		14 25							
Orpington [4]	a			13 31		13 52		13 58	13 46					14 01		14 22		14 28	14 16					14 31	

Table 199

Sundays

London - Lewisham, Hither Green, Petts Wood and Orpington (Summary of Services)

		SE	SE	SE	SE [1]	SE		SE	SE	SE [1] ⊤	SE	SE	SE	SE	SE [1]	SE		SE	SE	SE [1] ⊤	SE	SE	SE	SE	SE [1]
London Charing Cross [4]	⊖ d	14 16	14 20		14 23	14 26		14 30	14 35	14 38	14 40	14 46	14 50		14 53	14 56		15 00	15 05	15 08	15 10	15 16	15 20		15 23
London Waterloo (East) [4]	⊖ d	14 19	14 23		14 26	14 29		14 33	14 38	14 41	14 43	14 49	14 53		14 56	14 59		15 03	15 08	15 11	15 13	15 19	15 23		15 26
London Cannon Street [4]	⊖ d																								
London Blackfriars [3]	⊖ d																								
London Bridge [4]	⊖ d	14 24	14 28		14 31	14 34		14 38	14 43	14 46	14 48	14 54	14 58		15 01	15 04		15 08	15 13	15 16	15 18	15 24	15 28		15 31
London Victoria [15]	⊖ d			14 21										14 51										15 21	
New Cross [4]	⊖ d		14 34						14 49				15 04						15 19				15 34		
St Johns	d								14 51										15 21						
Lewisham [4]	a	14 32	14 37			14 41			14 53		14 57	15 02	15 07			15 11			15 23		15 27	15 32	15 37		
Hither Green [4]	a	14 37				14 46						15 07				15 16						15 37			
Petts Wood [4]	a	14 49		14 55								15 19		15 25								15 49		15 55	
Orpington [4]	a	14 52		14 58	14 46					15 01		15 22		15 28	15 16					15 31		15 52		15 58	15 46

		SE		SE	SE	SE [1] ⊤	SE	SE	SE	SE	SE [1]	SE		SE	SE	SE [1] ⊤	SE	SE	SE	SE	SE [1]	SE		SE	SE
London Charing Cross [4]	⊖ d	15 26		15 30	15 35	15 38	15 40	15 46	15 50		15 53	15 56		16 00	16 05	16 08	16 10	16 16	16 20		16 23	16 26		16 30	16 35
London Waterloo (East) [4]	⊖ d	15 29		15 33	15 38	15 41	15 43	15 49	15 53		15 56	15 59		16 03	16 08	16 11	16 13	16 19	16 23		16 26	16 29		16 33	16 38
London Cannon Street [4]	⊖ d																								
London Blackfriars [3]	⊖ d																								
London Bridge [4]	⊖ d	15 34		15 38	15 43	15 46	15 48	15 54	15 58		16 01	16 04		16 08	16 13	16 16	16 18	16 24	16 28		16 31	16 34		16 38	16 43
London Victoria [15]	⊖ d									15 51										16 21					
New Cross [4]	⊖ d				15 49				16 04						16 19				16 34						16 49
St Johns	d				15 51										16 21										16 51
Lewisham [4]	a	15 41			15 53		15 57	16 02	16 07			16 11			16 23		16 27	16 32	16 37			16 41			16 53
Hither Green [4]	a	15 46						16 07				16 16						16 37				16 46			
Petts Wood [4]	a							16 19		16 25								16 49		16 55					
Orpington [4]	a					16 01		16 22		16 28	16 16					16 31		16 52		16 58	16 46				

		SE [1] ⊤	SE	SE	SE	SE	SE [1]	SE		SE	SE	SE [1] ⊤	SE	SE	SE	SE	SE [1]	SE		SE	SE	SE [1] ⊤	SE	SE	SE
London Charing Cross [4]	⊖ d	16 38	16 40	16 46	16 50		16 53	16 56		17 00	17 05	17 08	17 10	17 16	17 20		17 23	17 26		17 30	17 35	17 38	17 40	17 46	17 50
London Waterloo (East) [4]	⊖ d	16 41	16 43	16 49	16 53		16 56	16 59		17 03	17 08	17 11	17 13	17 19	17 23		17 26	17 29		17 33	17 38	17 41	17 43	17 49	17 53
London Cannon Street [4]	⊖ d																								
London Blackfriars [3]	⊖ d																								
London Bridge [4]	⊖ d	16 46	16 48	16 54	16 58		17 01	17 04		17 08	17 13	17 16	17 18	17 24	17 28		17 31	17 34		17 38	17 43	17 46	17 48	17 54	17 58
London Victoria [15]	⊖ d					16 51										17 21									
New Cross [4]	⊖ d				17 04						17 19				17 34						17 49				18 04
St Johns	d										17 21										17 51				
Lewisham [4]	a		16 57	17 02	17 07			17 11			17 23		17 27	17 32	17 37			17 41			17 53		17 57	18 02	18 07
Hither Green [4]	a			17 07				17 16						17 37				17 46						18 07	
Petts Wood [4]	a			17 19		17 25								17 49		17 55								18 19	
Orpington [4]	a	17 01		17 22		17 28	17 16					17 31		17 52		17 58	17 46					18 01		18 22	

		SE	SE [1]	SE		SE	SE	SE [1] ⊤	SE	SE	SE	SE	SE [1]	SE		SE	SE	SE [1] ⊤	SE	SE	SE	SE	SE [1]	SE	
London Charing Cross [4]	⊖ d		17 53	17 56		18 00	18 05	18 08	18 10	18 16	18 20		18 23	18 26		18 30	18 35	18 38	18 40	18 46	18 50		18 53	18 56	
London Waterloo (East) [4]	⊖ d		17 56	17 59		18 03	18 08	18 11	18 13	18 19	18 23		18 26	18 29		18 33	18 38	18 41	18 43	18 49	18 53		18 56	18 59	
London Cannon Street [4]	⊖ d																								
London Blackfriars [3]	⊖ d																								
London Bridge [4]	⊖ d		18 01	18 04		18 08	18 13	18 16	18 18	18 24	18 28		18 31	18 34		18 38	18 43	18 46	18 48	18 54	18 58		19 01	19 04	
London Victoria [15]	⊖ d	17 51										18 21										18 51			
New Cross [4]	⊖ d						18 19				18 34						18 49				19 04				
St Johns	d						18 21										18 51								
Lewisham [4]	a			18 11			18 23		18 27	18 32	18 37			18 41			18 53		18 57	19 02	19 07			19 11	
Hither Green [4]	a			18 16						18 37				18 46						19 07				19 16	
Petts Wood [4]	a	18 25								18 49		18 55								19 19		19 25			
Orpington [4]	a	18 28	18 16					18 31		18 52		18 58	18 46					19 01		19 22		19 28	19 16		

		SE	SE	SE [1] ⊤	SE	SE	SE	SE	SE [1]	SE		SE	SE	SE [1] ⊤	SE	SE	SE	SE	SE [1]	SE		SE	SE	SE [1] ⊤	SE
London Charing Cross [4]	⊖ d	19 00	19 05	19 08	19 10	19 16	19 20		19 23	19 26		19 30	19 35	19 38	19 40	19 46	19 50		19 53	19 56		20 00	20 05	20 08	20 10
London Waterloo (East) [4]	⊖ d	19 03	19 08	19 11	19 13	19 19	19 23		19 26	19 29		19 33	19 38	19 41	19 43	19 49	19 53		19 56	19 59		20 03	20 08	20 11	20 13
London Cannon Street [4]	⊖ d																								
London Blackfriars [3]	⊖ d																								
London Bridge [4]	⊖ d	19 08	19 13	19 16	19 18	19 24	19 28		19 31	19 34		19 38	19 43	19 46	19 48	19 54	19 58		20 01	20 04		20 08	20 13	20 16	20 18
London Victoria [15]	⊖ d							19 21										19 51							
New Cross [4]	⊖ d		19 19				19 34						19 49				20 04						20 19		
St Johns	d		19 21										19 51										20 21		
Lewisham [4]	a		19 23		19 27	19 32	19 37			19 41			19 53		19 57	20 02	20 07			20 11			20 23		20 27
Hither Green [4]	a					19 37				19 46						20 07				20 16					
Petts Wood [4]	a					19 49		19 55								20 19		20 25							
Orpington [4]	a			19 31		19 52		19 58	19 46					20 01		20 22		20 28	20 16					20 31	

Table 199

Sundays

London - Lewisham, Hither Green, Petts Wood and Orpington (Summary of Services)

	SE	SE	SE	SE ■	SE		SE	SE	SE ■	SE	SE	SE	SE	SE	SE		SE	SE ■	SE	SE	SE	SE	SE ■	SE
London Charing Cross ■ ⊖ d	20 16	20 20		20 23	20 26		20 30	20 35	20 38	20 40	20 46	20 50		20 56	21 00		21 05	21 08	21 10	21 16	21 20		21 23	21 26
London Waterloo (East) ■ ⊖ d	20 19	20 23		20 26	20 29		20 33	20 38	20 41	20 43	20 49	20 53		20 59	21 03		21 08	21 11	21 13	21 19	21 23		21 26	21 29
London Cannon Street ■ ⊖ d																								
London Blackfriars ■ ⊖ d																								
London Bridge ■ ⊖ d	20 24	20 28		20 31	20 34		20 38	20 43	20 46	20 48	20 54	20 58		21 04	21 08		21 13	21 16	21 18	21 24	21 28		21 31	21 34
London Victoria ■ ⊖ d			20 21										20 51									21 21		
New Cross ■ ⊖ d		20 34						20 49				21 04					21 19				21 34			
St Johns d								20 51									21 21							
Lewisham ■ a	20 32	20 37			20 41			20 53		20 57	21 02	21 07		21 11			21 23		21 27	21 32	21 37			21 41
Hither Green ■ a	20 37				20 46						21 07			21 16						21 37				21 46
Petts Wood ■ a	20 49		20 55								21 19		21 25							21 49		21 55		
Orpington ■ a	20 52		20 58	20 46					21 01		21 22		21 28					21 31		21 52		21 58	21 46	

	SE		SE	SE ■	SE	SE	SE	SE	SE	SE	SE		SE ■	SE	SE	SE	SE	SE ■	SE	SE	SE		SE ■	SE
London Charing Cross ■ ⊖ d	21 30		21 35	21 38	21 40	21 46	21 50		21 56	22 00	22 05		22 08	22 10	22 16	22 20		22 23	22 26	22 30	22 35		22 38	
London Waterloo (East) ■ ⊖ d	21 33		21 38	21 41	21 43	21 49	21 53		21 59	22 03	22 08		22 11	22 13	22 19	22 23		22 26	22 29	22 33	22 38		22 41	
London Cannon Street ■ ⊖ d																								
London Blackfriars ■ ⊖ d																								
London Bridge ■ ⊖ d	21 38		21 43	21 46	21 48	21 54	21 58		22 04	22 08	22 13		22 16	22 18	22 24	22 28		22 31	22 34	22 38	22 43		22 46	
London Victoria ■ ⊖ d								21 51									22 21							22 39
New Cross ■ ⊖ d			21 49				22 04				22 19					22 34					22 49			
St Johns d			21 51								22 21										22 51			
Lewisham ■ a			21 53		21 57	22 02	22 07		22 11		22 23			22 27	22 32	22 37			22 41		22 53			
Hither Green ■ a						22 07			22 16						22 37				22 46					
Petts Wood ■ a						22 19		22 25							22 49		22 55							23 22
Orpington ■ a				22 01		22 22		22 28					22 31		22 52		22 58	22 46					23 01	23 26

	SE	SE	SE	SE	SE	SE	SE		SE ■	SE	SE	SE	SE	SE	SE ■	SE	SE		SE	SE ■	SE	SE	SE	
London Charing Cross ■ ⊖ d	22 40	22 46	22 50		22 56	23 00	23 05		23 08		23 10	23 16	23 20		23 23	23 26	23 30		23 35	23 38	23 46	23 50	23 56	
London Waterloo (East) ■ ⊖ d	22 43	22 49	22 53		22 59	23 03	23 08		23 11		23 13	23 19	23 23		23 26	23 29	23 33		23 38	23 41	23 49	23 53	23 59	
London Cannon Street ■ ⊖ d																								
London Blackfriars ■ ⊖ d																								
London Bridge ■ ⊖ d	22 48	22 54	22 58		23 04	23 08	23 13		23 16		23 18	23 24	23 28		23 31	23 34	23 38		23 43	23 46	23 54	23 58	00 04	
London Victoria ■ ⊖ d				22 51						23 09				23 21										
New Cross ■ ⊖ d			23 04				23 19						23 34						23 49			00 04		
St Johns d							23 21												23 51					
Lewisham ■ a	22 57	23 02	23 07		23 11		23 23				23 26	23 32	23 37			23 41			23 53		00 02	00 07	00 11	
Hither Green ■ a		23 07			23 16							23 37				23 46					00 06		00 16	
Petts Wood ■ a		23 19		23 25						23 52		23 49		23 55							00 19			
Orpington ■ a		23 22		23 29					23 31	23 56		23 52		23 59	23 46					00 01	00 22			

Table 199

Mondays to Fridays

Orpington, Petts Wood, Hither Green and Lewisham - London (Summary of Services)

	SE MX ■	SE	SE	SE	SE	FC ■	SE	SE	SE		SE	SE	SE	SE	SE	SE	SE	SE ■	SE		SE	FC ■	SE	SE
Orpington ■ d	23p37	04 34	04 55		05 10			05 34	05 40			05 20						05 54	06 10					
Petts Wood ■ d		04 37	04 58		05 13			05 37	05 43			05 23							06 13					
Hither Green ■ d				05 08			05 23					05 35		05 38										
Lewisham ■ d				05 13			05 28						05 39	05 43	05 50		05 56						06 09	
St Johns d													05 41										06 11	
New Cross ■ ⊖ d				05 16			05 31					05 40	05 43	05 46	05 53								06 13	
London Victoria ■ ⊖ a					05 47				06 18										06 47					
London Bridge ■ ⊖ d	23p53			05 22		05 34	05 37				05 42	05 46	05 49	05 53	05 59	06 02	06 04	06 10			06 13	06 16	06 19	06 20
London Blackfriars ■ ⊖ a		05 17	05 33			05 43		06 17														06 24		
London Cannon Street ■ ⊖ a							05 41									06 06								06 24
London Waterloo (East) ■ ⊖ d	23p58			05 27							05 47	05 50	05 53	05 57	06 04		06 09	06 15			06 18		06 24	
London Charing Cross ■ ⊖ a	00 01			05 30							05 50	05 53	05 56	06 01	06 07		06 12	06 18			06 21		06 27	

	SE	SE ■	SE	SE	SE		SE	SE	SE ■	SE ■	SE	SE	SE	SE	SE		FC ■	SE	SE	SE ■	SE	FC ■	SE	SE
Orpington ■ d		06 09			06 01				06 20	06 24		06 40			06 43				06b22					
Petts Wood ■ d					06 04							06 43			06 46				06 25					
Hither Green ■ d	06 08				06 16			06 22							06 58				06 38					
Lewisham ■ d	06 13			06 20	06 22		06 25	06 27			06 41			06 35	07 04			06 39	06 43				06 48	06 50
St Johns d								06 29										06 41					06 50	
New Cross ■ ⊖ d	06 16				06 25			06 31						06 38				06 43					06 52	
London Victoria ■ ⊖ a											07 04	07 19												
London Bridge ■ ⊖ d	06 22	06 25	06 28	06 29	06 32		06 34	06 37	06 38	06 40			06 43	06 44			06 46	06 49	06 52	06 55	06 57	06 58	07 00	07 01
London Blackfriars ■ ⊖ a																	06 52					07 04		
London Cannon Street ■ ⊖ a			06 32						06 42					06 48							07 03		07 05	
London Waterloo (East) ■ ⊖ d	06 27	06 30		06 33	06 36		06 40	06 42		06 45			06 49		07 17			06 54	06 57	07 00				07 06
London Charing Cross ■ ⊖ a	06 30	06 33		06 36	06 39		06 43	06 45		06 49			06 52		07 22			06 57	07 02	07 05				07 11

	SE		SE	SE	SE ■	SE	SE	SE	SE	SE ■	SE		SE	SE	SE	SE	SE	SE ■	SE ■	FC ■	SE		SE	SE
Orpington ■ d					06 54	06 58		07 03	07 10							06 53			07 04					
Petts Wood ■ d						07 01		07 06	07 13							06 56								
Hither Green ■ d			06 56	06 51				07 18								07 08					07 11		07 16	
Lewisham ■ d	06 55			06 57			07 00	07 25					07 08	07 15			07 11				07 17			07 20
St Johns d				06 59																	07 19			
New Cross ■ ⊖ d				07 01			07 04						07 11								07 21			07 23
London Victoria ■ ⊖ a									07 49					07 42										
London Bridge ■ ⊖ d	07 04		07 07	07 08	07 10		07 10			07 15	07 15		07 18		07 18	07 19	07 21	07 21	07 23	07 24	07 27		07 27	07 29
London Blackfriars ■ ⊖ a						07 42														07 30				
London Cannon Street ■ ⊖ a				07 14			07 16				07 21		07 23			07 25		07 27	07 29		07 33			07 35
London Waterloo (East) ■ ⊖ d	07 10		07 12		07 15			07 37		07 20					07 23		07 26						07 32	
London Charing Cross ■ ⊖ a	07 14		07 17		07 20			07 42		07 25					07 28		07 31						07 37	

	SE ■	SE	SE	SE	SE	SE ■	SE		SE	SE	SE	SE	SE	SE ■	SE	SE	SE		SE	SE	SE ■	SE ■	SE	SE ■
Orpington ■ d	07 14		07 28				07 13				07 38	07 42								07 47			07 22	
Petts Wood ■ d			07 31				07 16				07 41	07 45								07 50			07 25	
Hither Green ■ d							07 28					07 57					07 32		07 36				07 39	
Lewisham ■ d		07 22							07 30	07 35		08 03			07 46		07 38						07 44	
St Johns d		07 24															07 40							
New Cross ■ ⊖ d		07 26								07 38							07 42							
London Victoria ■ ⊖ a											08 20				08 11									
London Bridge ■ ⊖ d	07 30	07 34		07 34	07 36	07 37	07 38		07 42	07 44			07 45			07 46	07 48		07 48		07 51	07 52	07 54	07 54
London Blackfriars ■ ⊖ a			08 08																	08 29				
London Cannon Street ■ ⊖ a		07 39			07 42		07 44			07 50						07 52	07 54					07 57		07 59
London Waterloo (East) ■ ⊖ d	07 35			07 39		07 42			07 47			08 17	07 51	07 45					07 53		07 56		07 59	
London Charing Cross ■ ⊖ a	07 40			07 44		07 47			07 52			08 22	07 56	07 50					07 58		08 01		08 04	

	SE	SE	SE		SE	SE	SE	SE	SE ■	SE	SE ■ (trolley)	SE	SE		SE	SE	SE ■	SE ■	SE	SE	SE	SE	SE ■	
Orpington ■ d			07 33					07 57		08 02											08 10			
Petts Wood ■ d			07 36					08 00		08 05											08 13			
Hither Green ■ d			07 48							08 17						07 52			08 02					
Lewisham ■ d					07 48	07 50	07 55			08 23			08 05			07 57								
St Johns d					07 50											08 00								
New Cross ■ ⊖ d					07 53		07 58									08 02								
London Victoria ■ ⊖ a													08 29								08 50			
London Bridge ■ ⊖ d	07 58	07 58	08 00		08 02	08 02	08 04					08 06			08 06	08 09	08 10	08 11	08 14				08 14	
London Blackfriars ■ ⊖ a																								
London Cannon Street ■ ⊖ a		08 04	08 06		08 08		08 10								08 12	08 15		08 17					08 20	
London Waterloo (East) ■ ⊖ d	08 03					08 07		08 25	08 01	08 37	08 05	08 11					08 15		08 19	08 09		08 13		
London Charing Cross ■ ⊖ a	08 08					08 12		08 30	08 06	08 42	08 08	08 16					08 20		08 24	08 14		08 18		

b arr. 0616

Table 199

Mondays to Fridays

Orpington, Petts Wood, Hither Green and Lewisham - London (Summary of Services)

		SE	SE	SE	SE	SE 1	SE	SE 1 ⌶	SE	SE		SE	SE	SE	SE	SE 1	SE	SE 1	SE	SE		SE 1	SE	SE	SE
Orpington 4	d		07 53				08 22								08 26										08 13
Petts Wood 4	d		07 56				08 25								08 29										08 16
Hither Green 4	d						08 37							08 12					08 22						
Lewisham 4 ⇌	d			08 08	08 10				08 15			08 26		08 17											
St Johns	d			08 12										08 21											
New Cross 4 ⊖	d			08 14					08 18					08 23											
London Victoria 15 ⊖	a											08 49			09 06										
London Bridge 4 ⊖	d	08 18	08 20	08 22	08 22			08 24	08 26	08 26			08 28	08 30		08 30		08 32	08 34			08 36	08 38	08 39	08 40
London Blackfriars 3 ⊖	a																								
London Cannon Street 4 ⊖	a	08 24	08 26	08 28				08 30	08 32				08 34	08 36				08 38				08 41		08 44	08 46
London Waterloo (East) 4 ⊖	d				08 27	08 21	08 53			08 31						08 35	08 29		08 39	08 33			08 43		
London Charing Cross 4 ⊖	a				08 32	08 26	08 58			08 36						08 40	08 34		08 44	08 39			08 48		

		SE	SE	SE	SE 1 ⌶	SE		SE 1 ⌶	SE	SE	SE	SE	SE	SE 1	SE 1	SE		SE	SE 1	SE	SE	SE	SE	SE	SE 1
Orpington 4	d					08 40							08 47								08 55		08 32		
Petts Wood 4	d					08 43							08 50								08 58		08 35		
Hither Green 4	d										08 32					08 42									
Lewisham 4 ⇌	d	08 28	08 31	08 35							08 37	08 46								08 48				08 51	
St Johns	d	08 30									08 40									08 50					
New Cross 4 ⊖	d	08 32		08 38							08 42									08 52					
London Victoria 15 ⊖	a					09 19						09 11									09 34				
London Bridge 4 ⊖	d	08 42	08 42	08 44					08 46	08 46	08 50			08 50	08 51	08 54			08 56	08 58		08 58	09 00	09 01	
London Blackfriars 3 ⊖	a												09 30												
London Cannon Street 4 ⊖	a	08 48		08 50						08 52	08 55				08 57				09 02	09 04			09 06		
London Waterloo (East) 4 ⊖	d		08 47		08 41			08 45	08 51					08 55		08 59		08 49				09 03		09 06	09 01
London Charing Cross 4 ⊖	a		08 52		08 46			08 50	08 56					09 00		09 04		08 54				09 08		09 12	09 04

		SE		SE 1 ⌶	SE	SE	SE	SE	SE	FC 1	SE	SE 1		SE 1	SE	SE 1	SE	SE	SE	SE 1	SE	SE		SE 1	SE
Orpington 4	d														09 10		08 43		08 52	09 04				09 09	
Petts Wood 4	d														09 13		08 46		08 55						
Hither Green 4	d				08 49	08 55											08 58		09 08		09 14				
Lewisham 4 ⇌	d				08 54			09 06			08 59						09 04					09 14			
St Johns	d				08 57												09 06					09 17			
New Cross 4 ⊖	d				08 59						09 02						09 08					09 19			
London Victoria 15 ⊖	a							09 29							09 49										
London Bridge 4 ⊖	d	09 02		09 04	09 06	09 06	09 08			09 09	09 10	09 12		09 12		09 15	09 18	09 18	09 21	09 23	09 24	09 26		09 27	09 30
London Blackfriars 3 ⊖	a									09 21															
London Cannon Street 4 ⊖	a	09 08		09 10	09 12		09 14				09 18	09 18					09 23			09 28		09 32			09 36
London Waterloo (East) 4 ⊖	d					09 11			09 08					09 17		09 20		09 23	09 26		09 29			09 32	
London Charing Cross 4 ⊖	a					09 16			09 13					09 22		09 25		09 28	09 31		09 34			09 37	

		SE	SE	SE	SE	SE	SE	SE		SE 1	SE	SE	SE 1 ⌶	SE	FC 1	SE	SE	SE		SE 1 ⌶	SE	SE	SE	SE	FC 1
Orpington 4	d		09 03		09 25					09 24		09 40				09 21				09 39				09 55	
Petts Wood 4	d		09 06		09 28							09 43				09 24								09 58	
Hither Green 4	d		09 18											09 28		09 36		09 42							
Lewisham 4 ⇌	d	09 20	09 24	09 26		09 29	09 38							09 34							09 45	09 50			
St Johns	d		09 26											09 36							09 47				
New Cross 4 ⊖	d		09 28			09 32								09 38							09 49				
London Victoria 15 ⊖	a				10 02		10 00					10 17												10 32	
London Bridge 4 ⊖	d	09 30	09 34	09 35		09 38		09 38		09 41	09 42		09 44	09 45	09 46	09 50	09 51	09 52		09 55	09 55	09 58	10 00		10 00
London Blackfriars 3 ⊖	a														09 53										10 08
London Cannon Street 4 ⊖	a		09 40			09 45					09 48			09 51			09 57				10 00		10 04		
London Waterloo (East) 4 ⊖	d	09 35		09 40				09 43		09 46			09 49			09 55		09 57		10 00		10 03			
London Charing Cross 4 ⊖	a	09 40		09 45				09 48		09 51			09 54			10 00		10 00		10 03		10 06			

		SE	SE	SE		SE	SE	SE 1	SE	SE	SE	SE 1	FC 1	SE		SE	SE	SE	SE 1 ⌶	SE	SE	SE	FC 1	SE	
Orpington 4	d	09 33						09 54			10 10			09 51					10 09			10 25		10 03	
Petts Wood 4	d	09 36									10 13			09 54								10 28		10 06	
Hither Green 4	d	09 49								09 58				10 07			10 12							10 19	
Lewisham 4 ⇌	d	09 54	09 56	09 59		10 08				10 04								10 14		10 20				10 24	
St Johns	d	09 56								10 06								10 16						10 26	
New Cross 4 ⊖	d	09 58		10 02						10 08								10 18						10 28	
London Victoria 15 ⊖	a					10 28					10 47											11 02			
London Bridge 4 ⊖	d	10 04	10 05	10 08			10 08	10 11	10 11	10 14		10 14	10 16	10 19		10 20	10 22	10 24	10 25	10 28	10 30		10 30	10 34	
London Blackfriars 3 ⊖	a												10 23										10 37		
London Cannon Street 4 ⊖	a	10 08		10 13					10 15	10 19						10 24		10 28			10 36			10 38	
London Waterloo (East) 4 ⊖	d		10 10				10 13	10 15				10 19		10 24			10 27		10 30	10 33					
London Charing Cross 4 ⊖	a		10 13				10 16	10 19				10 22		10 27			10 30		10 33	10 36					

Table 199

Mondays to Fridays

Orpington, Petts Wood, Hither Green and Lewisham - London (Summary of Services)

		SE	SE	SE	SE	SE 1	SE	SE	SE 1 ⌶	SE		FC 1	SE	SE	SE	SE	SE 1 ⌶	SE	SE	SE		FC 1	SE	SE	SE
Orpington 4	d					10 24		10 40					10 21				10 39			10 55			10 33		
Petts Wood 4	d							10 43					10 24							10 58			10 36		
Hither Green 4	d									10 28			10 37		10 42								10 49		
Lewisham 4 ⇌	d	10 26	10 29	10 38						10 34						10 44		10 50					10 54	10 56	10 59
St Johns	d									10 36						10 46							10 56		
New Cross 4 ⊖	d		10 32							10 38						10 48							10 58		11 02
London Victoria 15 ⊖	a			10 58				11 17												11 32					
London Bridge 4 ⊖	d	10 35	10 38		10 38	10 41	10 41		10 44	10 45		10 45	10 49	10 50	10 52	10 54	10 55	10 58	11 00			11 00	11 04	11 05	11 08
London Blackfriars 3 ⊖	a											10 52										11 07			
London Cannon Street 4 ⊖	a		10 43				10 45			10 49				10 54		10 58			11 06				11 08		11 13
London Waterloo (East) 4 ⊖	d	10 40			10 43	10 45			10 49				10 54		10 57		11 00	11 03						11 10	
London Charing Cross 4 ⊖	a	10 43			10 46	10 49			10 52				10 57		11 00		11 03	11 06						11 13	

		SE	SE	SE 1	SE	SE		SE 1 ⌶	SE	FC 1	SE	SE	SE	SE	SE 1 ⌶	SE		SE	SE	FC 1	SE	SE	SE	SE	SE
Orpington 4	d			10 54		11 10					10 51				11 09				11 25		11 03				
Petts Wood 4	d					11 13					10 54								11 28		11 06				
Hither Green 4	d								10 58		11 07		11 12								11 19				
Lewisham 4 ⇌	d	11 08							11 04					11 14		11 20					11 24	11 26	11 29	11 38	
St Johns	d								11 06					11 16							11 26				
New Cross 4 ⊖	d								11 08					11 18							11 28		11 32		
London Victoria 15 ⊖	a	11 28				11 47													12 02					11 58	
London Bridge 4 ⊖	d		11 08	11 11	11 11			11 14	11 15	11 15	11 19	11 20	11 22	11 24	11 25	11 28		11 30		11 30	11 34	11 35	11 38		11 38
London Blackfriars 3 ⊖	a									11 22										11 37					
London Cannon Street 4 ⊖	a				11 15				11 19			11 24		11 28				11 36			11 38		11 43		
London Waterloo (East) 4 ⊖	d		11 13	11 15				11 19			11 24		11 27		11 30	11 33						11 40			11 43
London Charing Cross 4 ⊖	a		11 16	11 19				11 22			11 27		11 30		11 33	11 36						11 43			11 46

		SE 1		SE	SE	SE 1 ⌶	SE	FC 1	SE	SE	SE	SE		SE 1 ⌶	SE	SE	SE	FC 1	SE	SE	SE	SE		SE	SE 1
Orpington 4	d	11 24				11 40				11 21					11 39			11 55		11 33						11 54
Petts Wood 4	d				11 43				11 24								11 58		11 36						
Hither Green 4	d						11 28		11 37		11 42								11 49						
Lewisham 4 ⇌	d						11 34					11 44			11 50				11 54	11 56	11 59	12 08			
St Johns	d						11 36					11 46							11 56						
New Cross 4 ⊖	d						11 38					11 48							11 58		12 02				
London Victoria 15 ⊖	a				12 17												12 32					12 28			
London Bridge 4 ⊖	d	11 41		11 41		11 44	11 45	11 45	11 49	11 50	11 52	11 54		11 55	11 58	12 00		12 00	12 04	12 05	12 08			12 08	12 11
London Blackfriars 3 ⊖	a							11 52										12 07							
London Cannon Street 4 ⊖	a			11 45			11 49			11 54		11 58				12 04			12 08		12 13				
London Waterloo (East) 4 ⊖	d	11 45				11 49			11 54		11 57			12 00	12 03					12 10				12 13	12 15
London Charing Cross 4 ⊖	a	11 49				11 52			11 57		12 00			12 03	12 06					12 13				12 16	12 19

		SE	SE	SE 1 ⌶	SE	FC 1	SE	SE		SE	SE	SE 1 ⌶	SE	SE	SE	FC 1	SE	SE		SE	SE	SE	SE 1	SE	SE
Orpington 4	d		12 10				11 51					12 09			12 25		12 03						12 24		12 40
Petts Wood 4	d		12 13				11 54								12 28		12 06								12 43
Hither Green 4	d				11 58		12 07			12 12							12 19								
Lewisham 4 ⇌	d				12 04						12 14		12 20				12 24	12 26		12 29	12 38				
St Johns	d				12 06						12 16						12 26								
New Cross 4 ⊖	d				12 08						12 18						12 28			12 32					
London Victoria 15 ⊖	a		12 47												13 02						12 58				13 17
London Bridge 4 ⊖	d	12 11		12 14	12 15	12 15	12 19	12 20		12 22	12 24	12 25	12 28	12 30		12 30	12 34	12 35		12 38		12 38	12 41	12 41	
London Blackfriars 3 ⊖	a					12 22										12 37									
London Cannon Street 4 ⊖	a	12 15			12 19			12 24			12 28			12 36			12 38			12 43				12 45	
London Waterloo (East) 4 ⊖	d			12 19			12 24			12 27		12 30	12 33					12 40				12 43	12 45		
London Charing Cross 4 ⊖	a			12 22			12 27			12 30		12 33	12 36					12 43				12 46	12 49		

		SE 1 ⌶	SE	FC 1		SE	SE	SE	SE	SE 1 ⌶	SE	SE	SE	FC 1		SE	SE	SE	SE	SE	SE 1	SE	SE	SE 1 ⌶	
Orpington 4	d					12 21				12 39			12 55			12 33					12 54		13 10		
Petts Wood 4	d					12 24							12 58			12 36							13 13		
Hither Green 4	d		12 28			12 37		12 42								12 49									
Lewisham 4 ⇌	d		12 34						12 44		12 50					12 54	12 56	12 59	13 08						
St Johns	d		12 36						12 46							12 56									
New Cross 4 ⊖	d		12 38						12 48							12 58		13 02							
London Victoria 15 ⊖	a												13 32						13 28				13 47		
London Bridge 4 ⊖	d	12 44	12 45	12 45		12 49	12 50	12 52	12 54	12 55	12 58	13 00		13 00		13 04	13 05	13 08		13 08	13 11	13 11		13 14	
London Blackfriars 3 ⊖	a			12 52										13 07											
London Cannon Street 4 ⊖	a		12 49				12 54		12 58			13 06				13 08		13 13				13 15			
London Waterloo (East) 4 ⊖	d	12 49				12 54		12 57		13 00	13 03						13 10			13 13	13 15			13 19	
London Charing Cross 4 ⊖	a	12 52				12 57		13 00		13 03	13 06						13 13			13 16	13 19			13 22	

Orpington, Petts Wood, Hither Green and Lewisham - London (Summary of Services)

		SE	FC ■	SE	SE	SE	SE	SE ■ ⚭	SE	SE		SE	FC ■	SE	SE	SE	SE	SE	SE ■	SE		SE	SE ■ ⚭	SE	FC ■
Orpington 4	d			12 51				13 09				13 25		13 03					13 24			13 40			
Petts Wood 4	d			12 54								13 28		13 06								13 43			
Hither Green 4	d	12 58		13 07		13 12								13 19										13 28	
Lewisham 4	⇌ d	13 04					13 14		13 20					13 24	13 26	13 29	13 38							13 34	
St Johns	d	13 06					13 16							13 26										13 36	
New Cross 4	⊖ d	13 08					13 18							13 28		13 32								13 38	
London Victoria 15	⊖ a											14 02					13 58					14 17			
London Bridge 4	⊖ d	13 15	13 15	13 19	13 20	13 22	13 24	13 25	13 28	13 30			13 30	13 34	13 35	13 38		13 38	13 41	13 41			13 44	13 45	13 45
London Blackfriars 3	⊖ a		13 22										13 37												13 52
London Cannon Street 4	⊖ a	13 19			13 24		13 28			13 36				13 38		13 43				13 45				13 49	
London Waterloo (East) 4	⊖ d			13 24		13 27		13 30	13 33						13 40			13 43	13 45				13 49		
London Charing Cross 4	⊖ a			13 27		13 30		13 33	13 36						13 43			13 46	13 49				13 52		

		SE	SE	SE	SE	SE ■ ⚭		SE	SE	SE	FC ■	SE	SE	SE	SE	SE		SE ■	SE	SE	SE ■ ⚭	SE	FC ■	SE	SE
Orpington 4	d	13 21				13 39				13 55		13 33						13 54		14 10				13 51	
Petts Wood 4	d	13 24								13 58		13 36								14 13				13 54	
Hither Green 4	d	13 37		13 42								13 49										13 58		14 07	
Lewisham 4	⇌ d				13 44			13 50				13 54	13 56	13 59	14 08							14 04			
St Johns	d				13 46							13 56										14 06			
New Cross 4	⊖ d				13 48							13 58		14 02								14 08			
London Victoria 15	⊖ a									14 32					14 28					14 47					
London Bridge 4	⊖ d	13 49	13 50	13 52	13 54	13 55		13 58	14 00		14 00	14 04	14 05	14 08		14 08		14 11	14 11		14 14	14 15	14 15	14 19	14 20
London Blackfriars 3	⊖ a										14 07												14 22		
London Cannon Street 4	⊖ a		13 54		13 58				14 06			14 08		14 13					14 15			14 19			14 24
London Waterloo (East) 4	⊖ d	13 54		13 57		14 00		14 03					14 10			14 13		14 15			14 19			14 24	
London Charing Cross 4	⊖ a	13 57		14 00		14 03		14 06					14 13			14 16		14 19			14 22			14 27	

		SE		SE	SE ■ ⚭	SE	SE	SE	FC ■	SE	SE	SE		SE	SE	SE ■	SE	SE	SE ■ ⚭	SE	FC ■	SE		SE	SE
Orpington 4	d				14 09			14 25		14 03						14 24		14 40				14 21			
Petts Wood 4	d							14 28		14 06								14 43				14 24			
Hither Green 4	d	14 12								14 19										14 28		14 37			14 42
Lewisham 4	⇌ d			14 14		14 20				14 24	14 26	14 29		14 38						14 34					
St Johns	d			14 16						14 26										14 36					
New Cross 4	⊖ d			14 18						14 28		14 32								14 38					
London Victoria 15	⊖ a							15 02						14 58				15 17							
London Bridge 4	⊖ d	14 22		14 24	14 25	14 28	14 30		14 30	14 34	14 35	14 38			14 38	14 41	14 41		14 44	14 45	14 45	14 49		14 50	14 52
London Blackfriars 3	⊖ a								14 37												14 52				
London Cannon Street 4	⊖ a			14 28			14 36			14 38		14 43					14 45			14 49				14 54	
London Waterloo (East) 4	⊖ d	14 27			14 30	14 33					14 40				14 43	14 45			14 49			14 54			14 57
London Charing Cross 4	⊖ a	14 30			14 33	14 36					14 43				14 46	14 49			14 52			14 57			15 00

		SE	SE ■ ⚭	SE	SE	SE	FC ■	SE		SE	SE	SE	SE	SE ■	SE	SE	SE ■ ⚭	SE		FC ■	SE	SE	SE	SE	SE ■ ⚭
Orpington 4	d		14 39			14 55		14 33						14 54		15 10					14 51				15 09
Petts Wood 4	d					14 58		14 36								15 13					14 54				
Hither Green 4	d							14 49										14 58			15 07		15 12		
Lewisham 4	⇌ d	14 44		14 50				14 54		14 56	14 59	15 08						15 04						15 14	
St Johns	d	14 46						14 56										15 06						15 16	
New Cross 4	⊖ d	14 48						14 58			15 02							15 08						15 18	
London Victoria 15	⊖ a					15 32						15 28				15 47									
London Bridge 4	⊖ d	14 54	14 55	14 58	15 00		15 00	15 04		15 05	15 08		15 08	15 11	15 11		15 14	15 15		15 15	15 19	15 20	15 22	15 24	15 25
London Blackfriars 3	⊖ a						15 07													15 22					
London Cannon Street 4	⊖ a	14 58			15 06			15 08			15 13				15 15			15 19				15 24		15 28	
London Waterloo (East) 4	⊖ d		15 00	15 03						15 10			15 13	15 15			15 19				15 24		15 27		15 30
London Charing Cross 4	⊖ a		15 03	15 06						15 13			15 16	15 19			15 22				15 27		15 30		15 33

		SE	SE	SE		FC ■	SE	SE	SE	SE	SE	SE ■	SE	SE		SE ■ ⚭	SE	FC ■	SE	SE	SE	SE	SE ■	SE	
Orpington 4	d			15 25			15 03					15 24		15 40					15 21				15 39		
Petts Wood 4	d			15 28			15 06							15 43					15 24						
Hither Green 4	d						15 19										15 28		15 37		15 42				
Lewisham 4	⇌ d	15 20					15 24	15 26	15 29	15 38							15 34					15 44		15 50	
St Johns	d						15 26										15 36					15 46			
New Cross 4	⊖ d						15 28		15 32								15 38					15 48			
London Victoria 15	⊖ a			16 02						15 58				16 17											
London Bridge 4	⊖ d	15 28	15 30			15 30	15 34	15 35	15 38		15 38	15 41	15 41			15 43	15 45	15 45	15 50	15 50	15 53	15 54	15 55	15 58	
London Blackfriars 3	⊖ a					15 37												15 52							
London Cannon Street 4	⊖ a		15 36				15 38		15 43				15 45				15 49			15 54		15 58			
London Waterloo (East) 4	⊖ d	15 33						15 40			15 43	15 46				15 49			15 55		15 58		16 00	16 03	
London Charing Cross 4	⊖ a	15 36						15 43			15 46	15 49				15 52			15 58		16 01		16 03	16 06	

Orpington, Petts Wood, Hither Green and Lewisham - London (Summary of Services)

		SE	SE	FC ■	SE	SE	SE	SE	SE	SE ■		SE	SE	SE ■ ⚭	SE	FC ■	SE	SE	SE	SE		SE ■ ⚭	SE	SE	SE
Orpington 4	d		15 55		15 33					15 54		16 10					15 51					16 08			16 25
Petts Wood 4	d		15 58		15 36							16 13					15 54								16 28
Hither Green 4	d				15 49										15 58		16 07		16 12						
Lewisham 4	⇌ d				15 54	15 56	15 59	16 08							16 04					16 14			16 20		
St Johns	d				15 56										16 06					16 16					
New Cross 4	⊖ d				15 58		16 02								16 08					16 18					
London Victoria 15	⊖ a		16 32					16 28				16 47													17 03
London Bridge 4	⊖ d	16 00		16 00	16 04	16 05	16 09		16 09	16 12			16 12	16 14	16 15	16 16	16 19	16 20	16 22	16 24		16 25	16 29	16 30	
London Blackfriars 3	⊖ a			16 07												16 25									
London Cannon Street 4	⊖ a	16 06			16 08		16 13						16 16		16 19			16 24		16 28				16 36	
London Waterloo (East) 4	⊖ d					16 10			16 14	16 17				16 20			16 25		16 28			16 30	16 34		
London Charing Cross 4	⊖ a					16 13			16 18	16 20				16 24			16 28		16 31			16 33	16 37		

		SE	SE	SE	SE	SE		SE	SE ■	SE	SE	SE	SE ■ ⚭	SE	SE	SE		SE	SE ■ ⚭	SE	SE	SE	SE	SE	SE A
Orpington 4	d		16 03						16 25	16 40				16 21					16 39			16 33	16 51		
Petts Wood 4	d		16 06							16 43				16 24								16 36	16 54		
Hither Green 4	d		16 19									16 28		16 37		16 42						16 49	17 09	16 49	16 55
Lewisham 4	⇌ d		16 24	16 26	16 38			16 29				16 34						16 44		16 50					
St Johns	d		16 26									16 36						16 46						16 54	
New Cross 4	⊖ d		16 28					16 32				16 38						16 48						16 56	
London Victoria 15	⊖ a				16 58					17 18															
London Bridge 4	⊖ d	16 32	16 34	16 35		16 38		16 39	16 42		16 42	16 45	16 46	16 49	16 50	16 52		16 54	16 56	16 59	17 01	17 02		17 04	17 06
London Blackfriars 3	⊖ a																								
London Cannon Street 4	⊖ a		16 38					16 43			16 46	16 49			16 54			16 58			17 05			17 09	
London Waterloo (East) 4	⊖ d	16 38		16 40		16 43			16 49				16 53	16 55		16 57			17 01	17 04		17 07	17 25		17 11
London Charing Cross 4	⊖ a	16 42		16 44		16 46			16 52				16 56	16 58		17 00			17 04	17 07		17 10	17 29		17 15

		SE		SE	SE	SE	SE	SE ■	SE	SE	SE	SE ■ ⚭		SE	SE	SE	SE	SE	FC ■	SE ■ ⚭	SE	SE		SE	SE
Orpington 4	d			16 55				16 54	17 10		17 13							17 24		17 09				17 03	
Petts Wood 4	d			16 58					17 13									17 28						17 06	
Hither Green 4	d										17 21			17 00	17 08									17 19	
Lewisham 4	⇌ d	16 56			17 08		16 59							17 05			17 14				17 20			17 24	17 27
St Johns	d													17 09			17 16							17 26	
New Cross 4	⊖ d						17 03							17 11			17 18							17 28	
London Victoria 15	⊖ a			17 33	17 28				17 48									18 03							
London Bridge 4	⊖ d	17 07				17 09	17 10	17 12		17 13		17 18		17 19	17 22	17 22	17 25		17 27	17 28	17 30	17 31		17 34	17 36
London Blackfriars 3	⊖ a																		17 35						
London Cannon Street 4	⊖ a	17 11					17 15			17 17				17 24		17 26	17 29			17 32		17 36		17 38	
London Waterloo (East) 4	⊖ d					17 14		17 16			17 37	17 23			17 29						17 35				17 41
London Charing Cross 4	⊖ a					17 18		17 20			17 40	17 26			17 33						17 38				17 44

		SE	SE	SE	SE ■	SE	SE	SE		SE ■ ⚭	SE	SE	SE	SE	SE ■	SE	SE	SE		SE	SE	SE	SE	SE ■	SE
Orpington 4	d				17 24	17 40					17 20				17 39			17 53			17 37			17 54	
Petts Wood 4	d					17 43					17 23							17 56			17 40				
Hither Green 4	d							17 28			17 37		17 42								17 53				
Lewisham 4	⇌ d	17 38		17 30				17 35						17 44		17 50				17 56			17 59		18 08
St Johns	d							17 37						17 46							17 57				
New Cross 4	⊖ d			17 33				17 39						17 48							17 59		18 02		
London Victoria 15	⊖ a	17 59				18 18												18 33							18 29
London Bridge 4	⊖ d		17 38	17 39	17 42		17 42	17 45		17 45	17 49	17 52	17 54	17 55	17 58	18 00	18 03			18 04	18 06	18 07	18 09	18 10	
London Blackfriars 3	⊖ a																								
London Cannon Street 4	⊖ a			17 44			17 46	17 49				17 56		17 59		18 04	18 07				18 11		18 13		
London Waterloo (East) 4	⊖ d		17 43		17 47					17 50	17 54		17 59		18 03					18 09		18 13		18 15	
London Charing Cross 4	⊖ a		17 46		17 50					17 53	17 57		18 03		18 06					18 12		18 16		18 18	

		SE	FC ■	SE		SE	SE ■ ⚭	SE	SE	SE	SE	SE ■ ⚭	SE	SE		SE	SE	SE	SE	SE	SE	SE	SE ■	SE	
Orpington 4	d	18 09						17 50				18 09		18 25				18 03					18 24	18 40	
Petts Wood 4	d	18 12						17 53						18 28				18 06						18 43	
Hither Green 4	d					17 58		18 07		18 12							18 21	18 19							
Lewisham 4	⇌ d					18 05					18 14		18 20					18 24	18 26	18 29	18 38				
St Johns	d					18 07					18 16							18 26							
New Cross 4	⊖ d					18 09					18 18							18 28		18 32					
London Victoria 15	⊖ a	18 47												19 03							18 58			19 17	
London Bridge 4	⊖ d		18 13	18 13		18 16	18 16	18 19	18 20	18 23	18 24	18 25	18 28			18 31	18 33	18 34	18 36	18 38		18 38	18 41		
London Blackfriars 3	⊖ a		18 21																						
London Cannon Street 4	⊖ a			18 17		18 20			18 24		18 29					18 35		18 38		18 42					
London Waterloo (East) 4	⊖ d						18 21	18 24		18 28		18 30	18 33				18 38		18 42			18 45	18 46		
London Charing Cross 4	⊖ a						18 25	18 27		18 31		18 35	18 37				18 41		18 45			18 48	18 49		

A not 31 May

Orpington, Petts Wood, Hither Green and Lewisham - London (Summary of Services)

		SE ■ 🍴	SE	SE	FC ■	SE	SE	SE	SE	SE ■ 🍴		SE	SE	FC ■	SE	SE	SE	SE	SE	SE		SE ■	SE	SE	SE ■ 🍴
Orpington 4	d					18 21							18 55			18 33						18 54	19 10		
Petts Wood 4	d					18 24							18 58			18 36							19 13		
Hither Green 4	d			18 28		18 37		18 42								18 49									
Lewisham 4	d			18 35					18 45			18 50				18 54	18 56	19 08		18 59					
St Johns	d			18 37					18 47							18 56									
New Cross 4	⊖ d			18 39					18 49							18 58				19 03					
London Victoria 15	⊖ a												19 32					19 28					19 47		
London Bridge 4	⊖ d	18 43	18 43	18 46	18 46	18 49	18 50	18 53	18 55	18 55		18 58		19 00	19 00	19 05	19 05		19 08	19 09		19 10		19 12	19 13
London Blackfriars 3	⊖ a				18 55									19 09											
London Cannon Street 4	⊖ a		18 47	18 51			18 54		18 59						19 06	19 10				19 13				19 16	
London Waterloo (East) 4	⊖ d	18 49				18 54		18 58		19 00		19 03					19 10		19 13			19 15			19 18
London Charing Cross 4	⊖ a	18 52				18 57		19 01		19 04		19 06					19 13		19 16			19 18			19 21

		SE	FC ■	SE	SE	SE		SE ■	SE	SE	SE	FC ■	SE	SE	SE	SE		SE ■	SE	SE	SE ■ 🍴	SE	FC ■	SE	SE
Orpington 4	d			18 50				19 08			19 25		19 03					19 24		19 40					19 21
Petts Wood 4	d			18 54							19 28		19 06							19 43					19 24
Hither Green 4	d	18 59		19 07	19 12								19 19									19 28			19 37
Lewisham 4	d	19 05				19 14				19 20			19 24	19 26	19 29							19 34		19 38	19 43
St Johns	d	19 07				19 16							19 26									19 36		19 40	
New Cross 4	⊖ d	19 09				19 18							19 28		19 32							19 38		19 42	
London Victoria 15	⊖ a										20 02									20 17					
London Bridge 4	⊖ d	19 15	19 17	19 19	19 22	19 24		19 25	19 28	19 28		19 30	19 34	19 35	19 38	19 38		19 41	19 41		19 43	19 45	19 45	19 49	19 52
London Blackfriars 3	⊖ a		19 22									19 37											19 52		
London Cannon Street 4	⊖ a	19 19				19 28			19 33				19 38		19 43				19 45			19 49			
London Waterloo (East) 4	⊖ d			19 24	19 27			19 30		19 33				19 40		19 43		19 46			19 49			19 54	19 57
London Charing Cross 4	⊖ a			19 27	19 30			19 33		19 36				19 43		19 46		19 49			19 52			19 57	20 00

		SE ■		SE	SE	SE	FC ■	SE	SE	SE ■	SE	SE		SE ■ 🍴	FC ■	SE	SE	SE ■	SE	SE	FC ■	SE		SE	SE ■
Orpington 4	d	19 39			19 55					19 54		20 10					19 51	20 09							20 24
Petts Wood 4	d				19 58							20 13					19 54								
Hither Green 4	d			19 43													20 07		20 13						
Lewisham 4	d			19 48				19 52	19 55							20 08	20 13		20 18			20 22		20 26	
St Johns	d															20 10									
New Cross 4	⊖ d			19 51				19 56								20 12			20 21			20 26			
London Victoria 15	⊖ a				20 32							20 47													
London Bridge 4	⊖ d	19 55		19 58		19 59	20 00	20 04	20 06	20 11	20 11			20 13	20 15	20 19	20 22	20 25	20 28	20 28	20 30	20 34		20 36	20 40
London Blackfriars 3	⊖ a						20 07								20 22						20 37				
London Cannon Street 4	⊖ a					20 03					20 15									20 31					
London Waterloo (East) 4	⊖ d	20 00		20 03				20 09	20 11	20 16				20 19		20 24	20 27	20 30	20 33			20 39		20 41	20 45
London Charing Cross 4	⊖ a	20 03		20 06				20 12	20 14	20 19				20 22		20 27	20 30	20 33	20 36			20 42		20 44	20 48

		SE	SE	SE ■ 🍴	FC ■	SE	SE	SE		FC ■	SE	SE	SE ■	SE	SE	SE ■	FC ■	SE		SE	SE ■	SE	FC ■	SE	SE
Orpington 4	d		20 40				20 21						20 53		21 10					20 51	21 09				
Petts Wood 4	d		20 43				20 24								21 13					20 54					
Hither Green 4	d						20 37	20 43												21 07		21 13			
Lewisham 4	d					20 38	20 43	20 48			20 53	20 56						21 08		21 13		21 18		21 23	21 25
St Johns	d					20 40												21 10							
New Cross 4	⊖ d					20 42		20 51			20 56							21 12				21 21		21 26	
London Victoria 15	⊖ a		21 17												21 47										
London Bridge 4	⊖ d	20 41		20 43	20 45	20 49	20 52	20 58		21 00	21 04	21 06	21 09	21 11		21 14	21 15	21 19		21 22	21 25	21 28	21 30	21 34	21 36
London Blackfriars 3	⊖ a				20 52					21 07							21 22						21 37		
London Cannon Street 4	⊖ a	20 45																							
London Waterloo (East) 4	⊖ d			20 48		20 54	20 57	21 03			21 09	21 11	21 14	21 16		21 19		21 24		21 27	21 30	21 33		21 39	21 41
London Charing Cross 4	⊖ a			20 51		20 57	21 00	21 06			21 12	21 14	21 18	21 19		21 22		21 27		21 30	21 33	21 36		21 42	21 44

		SE ■	SE	SE		SE ■	FC ■	SE	SE	SE	SE	SE	SE ■	SE		SE	SE ■	SE	SE	SE ■	SE	SE	SE	SE ■	
Orpington 4	d	21 23		21 40					21 21				21 53			22 10			21 51	22 09				22 23	
Petts Wood 4	d			21 43					21 24							22 13			21 54						
Hither Green 4	d								21 37	21 43									22 07		22 13				
Lewisham 4	d							21 38	21 43	21 48	21 53	21 56						22 08	22 13		22 18	22 23	22 26		
St Johns	d							21 40										22 10							
New Cross 4	⊖ d							21 42		21 51	21 56							22 12			22 21	22 26			
London Victoria 15	⊖ a			22 17												22 47									
London Bridge 4	⊖ d	21 39	21 41			21 44	21 45	21 49	21 52	21 58	22 02	22 05	22 09	22 11			22 14	22 19	22 22	22 25	22 28	22 32	22 35	22 39	
London Blackfriars 3	⊖ a						21 52																		
London Cannon Street 4	⊖ a																								
London Waterloo (East) 4	⊖ d	21 44	21 46			21 49		21 54	21 57	22 03	22 07	22 10	22 14	22 16			22 19	22 24	22 27	22 30	22 33	22 37	22 40	22 44	
London Charing Cross 4	⊖ a	21 48	21 49			21 52		21 57	22 00	22 06	22 10	22 13	22 18	22 19			22 22	22 27	22 30	22 33	22 36	22 40	22 43	22 48	

Orpington, Petts Wood, Hither Green and Lewisham - London (Summary of Services)

		SE	SE	SE ■	SE	SE	SE	SE	SE	SE ■		SE	SE	SE ■	SE	SE	SE ■	SE	SE	SE		SE	SE	SE ■	
Orpington 4	d		22 40			22 21				22 53			23 10			22 51	23 09						23 21	23 37	
Petts Wood 4	d		22 43			22 24							23 13			22 54							23 24		
Hither Green 4	d					22 37	22 43									23 07		23 13					23 37		
Lewisham 4	d				22 38	22 43	22 48	22 53	22 56						23 08	23 13		23 18	23 23	23 26			23 43		
St Johns	d				22 40										23 10										
New Cross 4	⊖ d				22 42		22 51	22 56							23 12			23 21	23 26						
London Victoria 15	⊖ a		23 17										23 47												
London Bridge 4	⊖ d	22 41		22 44	22 49	22 52	22 58	23 02	23 05	23 09		23 11		23 14	23 19	23 22	23 25	23 28	23 32	23 35		23 41	23 50	23 53	
London Blackfriars 3	⊖ a																								
London Cannon Street 4	⊖ a																								
London Waterloo (East) 4	⊖ d	22 46		22 49	22 54	22 57	23 03	23 07	23 10	23 14		23 16		23 19	23 24	23 27	23 30	23 33	23 37	23 40		23 46	23 55	23 58	
London Charing Cross 4	⊖ a	22 49		22 52	22 57	23 00	23 06	23 10	23 13	23 18		23 19		23 22	23 27	23 30	23 33	23 36	23 40	23 43		23 49	23 59	00 01	

Saturdays

		SE ■	SE	SE	SE	SE	SE	SE	SE	SE		SE	SE	SE	SE	SE	SE ■	SE	SE	SE		SE	SE	SE	SE
Orpington 4	d	23p37				05 44				06 10			05 51				06 24	06 25		06 40			06 21		
Petts Wood 4	d					05 47				06 13			05 54					06 28		06 43			06 24		
Hither Green 4	d				05 42								06 07	06 12									06 37	06 42	
Lewisham 4	d			05 39	05 48		05 50	05 56	06 02				06 12	06 18	06 20	06 26			06 32				06 42	06 48	06 50
St Johns	d			05 41					06 04										06 34						
New Cross 4	⊖ d			05 43	05 51				06 06					06 21					06 36					06 51	
London Victoria 15	⊖ a					06 26				06 47								07 02		07 17					
London Bridge 4	⊖ d	23p53	05 45	05 49	05 57		05 59	06 05	06 12			06 15	06 21	06 27	06 29	06 35	06 39		06 42			06 45	06 51	06 57	06 59
London Blackfriars 3	⊖ a																								
London Cannon Street 4	⊖ a																								
London Waterloo (East) 4	⊖ d	23p58	05 50	05 53	06 02		06 04	06 10	06 17			06 20	06 26	06 32	06 34	06 40	06 44		06 47			06 50	06 56	07 02	07 04
London Charing Cross 4	⊖ a	00 01	05 53	05 56	06 05		06 07	06 13	06 20			06 25	06 29	06 35	06 37	06 43	06 47		06 50			06 55	06 59	07 05	07 07

		SE	SE ■	SE	SE	SE		SE	SE	SE	SE ■	SE	SE	SE	SE ■	SE		SE	SE	SE	SE	SE	SE	SE ■	SE
Orpington 4	d		06 54	06 55				07 10		06 51	07 09				07 24	07 25					07 21	07 40		07 39	
Petts Wood 4	d			06 58				07 13		06 54						07 28					07 24	07 43			
Hither Green 4	d									07 07		07 12									07 37		07 42		
Lewisham 4	d	06 56			07 02	07 08				07 12		07 18	07 20	07 26				07 38		07 32					07 50
St Johns	d				07 04															07 34					
New Cross 4	⊖ d				07 06							07 21								07 36					
London Victoria 15	⊖ a			07 32		07 30		07 47								08 02		08 00				08 17			
London Bridge 4	⊖ d	07 05	07 09		07 12				07 15	07 21	07 24	07 27	07 29	07 35	07 39				07 41	07 42	07 49		07 52	07 55	07 58
London Blackfriars 3	⊖ a																								
London Cannon Street 4	⊖ a																		07 45						
London Waterloo (East) 4	⊖ d	07 10	07 14		07 17				07 20	07 26	07 29	07 32	07 34	07 40	07 44					07 47	07 54		07 57	08 00	08 03
London Charing Cross 4	⊖ a	07 13	07 17		07 20				07 25	07 29	07 33	07 35	07 40	07 43	07 48					07 50	07 57		08 00	08 03	08 06

		SE		SE	SE	SE	SE	SE	SE ■	SE	SE	SE		SE ■	SE	SE	SE	SE	SE	SE ■	SE	SE		SE	SE
Orpington 4	d	07 55				07 33			07 54			08 10				07 51				08 09		08 25			
Petts Wood 4	d	07 58				07 36						08 13				07 54						08 28			
Hither Green 4	d					07 49									07 58	08 07		08 12							
Lewisham 4	d			07 59		07 54	07 56	07 59		08 08					08 04				08 14		08 20			08 29	
St Johns	d					07 56									08 06				08 16						
New Cross 4	⊖ d			08 02		07 58									08 08				08 18					08 32	
London Victoria 15	⊖ a	08 32								08 30		08 47										09 02			
London Bridge 4	⊖ d			08a08	08 00	08 04	08 05	08 08	08 11		08 11			08 14	08 15	08 19	08 20	08 22	08 24	08 25	08 28			08a38	08 30
London Blackfriars 3	⊖ a																								
London Cannon Street 4	⊖ a				08 04	08 08					08 18				08 20		08 24		08 28						08 34
London Waterloo (East) 4	⊖ d						08 10	08 13	08 15					08 19		08 24		08 27		08 30	08 33				
London Charing Cross 4	⊖ a						08 13	08 16	08 19					08 22		08 27		08 30		08 33	08 36				

		SE	SE	SE	SE	SE ■	SE	SE		SE ■	SE	SE	SE	SE	SE	SE ■	SE	SE		SE	SE	SE	SE	SE	SE
Orpington 4	d	08 03				08 24		08 40				08 21				08 39		08 55				08 33			
Petts Wood 4	d	08 06						08 43				08 24						08 58				08 36			
Hither Green 4	d	08 19									08 28	08 37		08 42								08 49			
Lewisham 4	d	08 24	08 26	08 38							08 34				08 44		08 50			08 59		08 54	08 56	09 08	
St Johns	d	08 26									08 36				08 46							08 56			
New Cross 4	⊖ d	08 28									08 38				08 48					09 02		08 58			
London Victoria 15	⊖ a			09 00				09 17										09 32						09 30	
London Bridge 4	⊖ d	08 34	08 35		08 38	08 41	08 41			08 44	08 45	08 49	08 50	08 52	08 54	08 55	08 58			09a08	09 00	09 04	09 05		09 08
London Blackfriars 3	⊖ a																								
London Cannon Street 4	⊖ a	08 38					08 45				08 49		08 54		08 58						09 04	09 08			
London Waterloo (East) 4	⊖ d		08 40		08 43	08 45				08 49		08 54		08 57		09 00	09 03						09 10		09 13
London Charing Cross 4	⊖ a		08 43		08 46	08 49				08 52		08 57		09 00		09 03	09 06						09 13		09 16

Orpington, Petts Wood, Hither Green and Lewisham - London (Summary of Services)

		SE 1	SE	SE	SE 1	SE	SE	SE	SE	SE	SE 1	SE	SE	SE	SE	SE	SE	SE	SE	SE 1	SE	SE
Orpington 4	d	08 54		09 10			08 51				09 09			09 03		09 25				09 24		09 40
Petts Wood 4	d			09 13			08 54							09 06		09 28						09 43
Hither Green 4	d					08 58	09 07		09 12					09 19								
Lewisham 4	d					09 04				09 14		09 20		09 24	09 26		09 29	09 38				
St Johns	d					09 06				09 16				09 26								
New Cross 4	d					09 08				09 18				09 28			09 32					
London Victoria 15	a			09 47												10 02		10 00				10 17
London Bridge 4	d	09 11	09 11		09 14	09 15	09 19	09 20	09 22	09 24	09 25	09 28	09 30	09 34	09 35		09a38		09 38	09 41	09 41	
London Blackfriars 3	a																					
London Cannon Street 4	a		09 15			09 19		09 24		09 28			09 34	09 38							09 45	
London Waterloo (East) 4	d	09 15			09 19		09 24		09 27		09 30	09 33			09 40				09 43	09 45		
London Charing Cross 4	a	09 19			09 22		09 27		09 30		09 33	09 36			09 43				09 46	09 49		

		SE 1	SE	SE	SE	SE	SE	SE 1 ⌶	SE	SE	SE	SE	SE	SE	SE	SE	SE 1	SE	SE	SE 1 ⌶	SE	SE	SE
Orpington 4	d			09 21				09 39			09 33		09 55				09 54		10 10			09 51	
Petts Wood 4	d			09 24							09 36		09 58						10 13			09 54	
Hither Green 4	d		09 28	09 37		09 42					09 49										09 58	10 07	
Lewisham 4	d		09 34				09 44		09 50		09 54	09 56		09 59	10 08						10 04		
St Johns	d		09 36				09 46				09 56										10 06		
New Cross 4	d		09 38				09 48				09 58			10 02							10 08		
London Victoria 15	a												10 32		10 30				10 47				
London Bridge 4	d	09 44	09 45	09 49	09 50	09 52	09 54	09 55	09 58	10 00	10 04	10 05		10a08		10 08	10 11	10 11		10 14	10 15	10 19	10 20
London Blackfriars 3	a																						
London Cannon Street 4	a		09 49		09 54		09 58			10 04	10 08							10 15			10 19		10 24
London Waterloo (East) 4	d	09 49		09 54		09 57		10 00	10 03			10 10				10 13	10 15			10 19		10 24	
London Charing Cross 4	a	09 52		09 57		10 00		10 03	10 06			10 13				10 16	10 19			10 22		10 27	

		SE	SE	SE 1 ⌶	SE	SE	SE	SE	SE	SE	SE	SE	SE 1	SE	SE	SE 1 ⌶	SE	SE	SE	SE	SE	SE 1 ⌶	SE
Orpington 4	d			10 09			10 03		10 25				10 24		10 40			10 21				10 39	
Petts Wood 4	d						10 06		10 28						10 43			10 24					
Hither Green 4	d	10 12					10 19										10 28	10 37		10 42			
Lewisham 4	d		10 14		10 20		10 24	10 26		10 29	10 38						10 34				10 44		10 50
St Johns	d		10 16				10 26										10 36				10 46		
New Cross 4	d		10 18				10 28			10 32							10 38				10 48		
London Victoria 15	a								11 02		11 00				11 17								
London Bridge 4	d	10 22	10 24	10 25	10 28	10 30	10 34	10 35		10a38		10 38	10 41	10 41		10 44	10 45	10 49	10 50	10 52	10 54	10 55	10 58
London Blackfriars 3	a																						
London Cannon Street 4	a		10 28			10 34	10 38							10 45			10 49		10 54		10 58		
London Waterloo (East) 4	d	10 27		10 30	10 33			10 40				10 43	10 45			10 49		10 54		10 57		11 00	11 03
London Charing Cross 4	a	10 30		10 33	10 36			10 43				10 46	10 49			10 52		10 57		11 00		11 03	11 06

		SE	SE	SE	SE	SE	SE	SE	SE 1	SE	SE	SE 1 ⌶	SE	SE	SE	SE	SE	SE 1 ⌶	SE	SE	SE	SE
Orpington 4	d		10 33		10 55				10 54		11 10			10 51				11 09			11 03	
Petts Wood 4	d		10 36		10 58						11 13			10 54							11 06	
Hither Green 4	d		10 49										10 58	11 07		11 12					11 19	
Lewisham 4	d		10 54	10 56		10 59	11 08						11 04				11 14		11 20		11 24	11 26
St Johns	d		10 56										11 06				11 16				11 26	
New Cross 4	d		10 58			11 02							11 08				11 18				11 28	
London Victoria 15	a				11 32		11 30				11 47											
London Bridge 4	d	11 00	11 04	11 05		11a08		11 08	11 11	11 11		11 14	11 15	11 19	11 20	11 22	11 24	11 25	11 28	11 30	11 34	11 35
London Blackfriars 3	a																					
London Cannon Street 4	a	11 04	11 08							11 15			11 19		11 24		11 28			11 34	11 38	
London Waterloo (East) 4	d			11 10				11 13	11 15			11 19		11 24		11 27		11 30	11 33			11 40
London Charing Cross 4	a			11 13				11 16	11 19			11 22		11 27		11 30		11 33	11 36			11 43

		SE	SE	SE	SE	SE 1	SE	SE	SE 1 ⌶	SE	SE	SE	SE	SE	SE 1 ⌶	SE	SE	SE	SE	SE	SE	SE	SE
Orpington 4	d	11 25				11 24		11 40			11 21				11 39			11 33		11 55			
Petts Wood 4	d	11 28						11 43			11 24							11 36		11 58			
Hither Green 4	d									11 28	11 37		11 42					11 49					
Lewisham 4	d		11 29	11 38						11 34				11 44		11 50		11 54	11 56		11 59	12 08	
St Johns	d									11 36				11 46				11 56					
New Cross 4	d		11 32							11 38				11 48				11 58			12 02		
London Victoria 15	a	12 02		12 00				12 17												12 32		12 30	
London Bridge 4	d		11a38		11 38	11 41	11 41		11 44	11 45	11 49	11 50	11 52	11 54	11 55	11 58	12 00	12 04	12 05		12a08		12 08
London Blackfriars 3	a																						
London Cannon Street 4	a						11 45			11 49		11 54		11 58			12 04	12 08					
London Waterloo (East) 4	d				11 43	11 45			11 49		11 54		11 57		12 00	12 03			12 10				12 13
London Charing Cross 4	a				11 46	11 49			11 52		11 57		12 00		12 03	12 06			12 13				12 16

Orpington, Petts Wood, Hither Green and Lewisham - London (Summary of Services)

		SE 1	SE	SE	SE 1 ⌶	SE	SE	SE	SE	SE	SE 1 ⌶	SE	SE	SE	SE	SE	SE	SE	SE	SE 1	SE	SE
Orpington 4	d	11 54		12 10			11 51				12 09			12 03		12 25				12 24		12 40
Petts Wood 4	d			12 13			11 54							12 06		12 28						12 43
Hither Green 4	d					11 58	12 07		12 12					12 19								
Lewisham 4	d					12 04				12 14		12 20		12 24	12 26		12 29	12 38				
St Johns	d					12 06				12 16				12 26								
New Cross 4	d					12 08				12 18				12 28			12 32					
London Victoria 15	a			12 47												13 02		13 00				13 17
London Bridge 4	d	12 11	12 11		12 14	12 15	12 19	12 20	12 22	12 24	12 25	12 28	12 30	12 34	12 35		12a38		12 38	12 41	12 41	
London Blackfriars 3	a																					
London Cannon Street 4	a		12 15			12 19		12 24		12 28			12 34	12 38							12 45	
London Waterloo (East) 4	d	12 15			12 19		12 24		12 27		12 30	12 33			12 40				12 43	12 45		
London Charing Cross 4	a	12 19			12 22		12 27		12 30		12 33	12 36			12 43				12 46	12 49		

		SE 1 ⌶	SE	SE	SE	SE	SE	SE 1 ⌶	SE	SE	SE	SE	SE	SE	SE	SE	SE 1	SE	SE	SE 1 ⌶	SE	SE	SE
Orpington 4	d			12 21				12 39			12 33		12 55				12 54		13 10			12 51	
Petts Wood 4	d			12 24							12 36		12 58						13 13			12 54	
Hither Green 4	d		12 28	12 37		12 42					12 49										12 58	13 07	
Lewisham 4	d		12 34				12 44		12 50		12 54	12 56		12 59	13 08						13 04		
St Johns	d		12 36				12 46				12 56										13 06		
New Cross 4	d		12 38				12 48				12 58			13 02							13 08		
London Victoria 15	a												13 32		13 30				13 47				
London Bridge 4	d	12 44	12 45	12 49	12 50	12 52	12 54	12 55	12 58	13 00	13 04	13 05		13a08		13 08	13 11	13 11		13 14	13 15	13 19	13 20
London Blackfriars 3	a																						
London Cannon Street 4	a		12 49		12 54		12 58			13 04	13 08							13 15			13 19		13 24
London Waterloo (East) 4	d	12 49		12 54		12 57		13 00	13 03			13 10				13 13	13 15			13 19		13 24	
London Charing Cross 4	a	12 52		12 57		13 00		13 03	13 06			13 13				13 16	13 19			13 22		13 27	

		SE	SE	SE 1 ⌶	SE	SE	SE	SE	SE	SE	SE	SE	SE 1	SE	SE	SE 1 ⌶	SE	SE	SE	SE	SE	SE 1 ⌶	SE
Orpington 4	d			13 09			13 03		13 25				13 24		13 40			13 21				13 39	
Petts Wood 4	d						13 06		13 28						13 43			13 24					
Hither Green 4	d	13 12					13 19										13 28	13 37		13 42			
Lewisham 4	d		13 14		13 20		13 24	13 26		13 29	13 38						13 34				13 44		13 50
St Johns	d		13 16				13 26										13 36				13 46		
New Cross 4	d		13 18				13 28			13 32							13 38				13 48		
London Victoria 15	a								14 02		14 00				14 17								
London Bridge 4	d	13 22	13 24	13 25	13 28	13 30	13 34	13 35		13a38		13 38	13 41	13 41		13 44	13 45	13 49	13 50	13 52	13 54	13 55	13 58
London Blackfriars 3	a																						
London Cannon Street 4	a		13 28			13 34	13 38							13 45			13 49		13 54		13 58		
London Waterloo (East) 4	d	13 27		13 30	13 33			13 40				13 43	13 45			13 49		13 54		13 57		14 00	14 03
London Charing Cross 4	a	13 30		13 33	13 37			13 43				13 46	13 49			13 52		13 57		14 00		14 03	14 06

		SE	SE	SE	SE	SE	SE	SE	SE 1	SE	SE	SE 1 ⌶	SE	SE	SE	SE	SE	SE 1 ⌶	SE	SE	SE	SE
Orpington 4	d		13 33		13 55				13 54		14 10			13 51				14 09			14 03	
Petts Wood 4	d		13 36		13 58						14 13			13 54							14 06	
Hither Green 4	d		13 49										13 58	14 07		14 12					14 19	
Lewisham 4	d		13 54	13 56		13 59	14 08						14 04				14 14		14 20		14 24	14 26
St Johns	d		13 56										14 06				14 16				14 26	
New Cross 4	d		13 58			14 02							14 08				14 18				14 28	
London Victoria 15	a				14 32		14 30				14 47											
London Bridge 4	d	14 00	14 04	14 05		14a08		14 08	14 11	14 11		14 14	14 15	14 19	14 20	14 22	14 24	14 25	14 28	14 30	14 34	14 35
London Blackfriars 3	a																					
London Cannon Street 4	a	14 04	14 08							14 15			14 19		14 24		14 28			14 34	14 38	
London Waterloo (East) 4	d			14 10				14 13	14 15			14 19		14 24		14 27		14 30	14 33			14 40
London Charing Cross 4	a			14 13				14 16	14 19			14 22		14 27		14 30		14 33	14 36			14 43

		SE	SE	SE	SE	SE 1	SE	SE	SE 1 ⌶	SE	SE	SE	SE	SE	SE 1 ⌶	SE	SE	SE	SE	SE	SE	SE	SE
Orpington 4	d	14 25				14 24		14 40			14 21				14 39			14 33		14 55			
Petts Wood 4	d	14 28						14 43			14 24							14 36		14 58			
Hither Green 4	d									14 28	14 37		14 42					14 49					
Lewisham 4	d		14 29	14 38						14 34				14 44		14 50		14 54	14 56		14 59	15 08	
St Johns	d									14 36				14 46				14 56					
New Cross 4	d		14 32							14 38				14 48				14 58			15 02		
London Victoria 15	a	15 02		15 00				15 17												15 32		15 30	
London Bridge 4	d		14a38		14 38	14 41	14 41		14 44	14 45	14 49	14 50	14 52	14 54	14 55	14 58	15 00	15 04	15 05		15a08		15 08
London Blackfriars 3	a																						
London Cannon Street 4	a						14 45			14 49		14 54		14 58			15 04	15 08					
London Waterloo (East) 4	d				14 43	14 45			14 49		14 54		14 57		15 00	15 03			15 10				15 13
London Charing Cross 4	a				14 46	14 49			14 52		14 57		15 00		15 03	15 06			15 13				15 16

Table 199

Saturdays

Orpington, Petts Wood, Hither Green and Lewisham - London (Summary of Services)

		SE 1	SE	SE		SE 1 🛒	SE	SE	SE	SE	SE	SE 1 🛒	SE	SE		SE	SE	SE	SE	SE	SE	SE 1	SE	SE
Orpington 4	d	14 54		15 10				14 51				15 09				15 03		15 25				15 24		15 40
Petts Wood 4	d			15 13				14 54								15 06		15 28						15 43
Hither Green 4	d						14 58	15 07		15 12						15 19								
Lewisham 4	d						15 04				15 14		15 20			15 24	15 26		15 29	15 38				
St Johns	d						15 06				15 16					15 26								
New Cross 4	⊖ d						15 08				15 18					15 28			15 32					
London Victoria 15	⊖ a			15 47														16 02		16 00				16 17
London Bridge 4	⊖ d	15 11	15 11			15 14	15 15	15 19	15 20	15 22	15 24	15 25	15 28	15 30		15 34	15 35		15a38		15 38	15 41	15 41	
London Blackfriars 3	⊖ a																							
London Cannon Street 4	⊖ a		15 15				15 19		15 24		15 28			15 34		15 38							15 45	
London Waterloo (East) 4	⊖ d	15 15				15 19		15 24		15 27		15 30	15 33				15 40				15 43	15 45		
London Charing Cross 4	⊖ a	15 19				15 22		15 27		15 30		15 33	15 36				15 43				15 46	15 49		

		SE 1 🛒	SE	SE	SE	SE	SE	SE 1 🛒	SE	SE		SE	SE	SE	SE	SE	SE	SE 1	SE	SE		SE 1 🛒	SE	SE	SE
Orpington 4	d			15 21				15 39				15 33		15 55				15 54		16 10				15 51	
Petts Wood 4	d			15 24								15 36		15 58						16 13				15 54	
Hither Green 4	d		15 28	15 37		15 42						15 49											15 58	16 07	
Lewisham 4	d		15 34				15 44		15 50			15 54	15 56		15 59	16 08							16 04		
St Johns	d		15 36				15 46					15 56											16 06		
New Cross 4	⊖ d		15 38				15 48					15 58			16 02								16 08		
London Victoria 15	⊖ a													16 32		16 30				16 47					
London Bridge 4	⊖ d	15 44	15 45	15 49	15 50	15 52	15 54	15 55	15 58	16 00		16 04	16 05		16a08		16 08	16 11	16 11			16 14	16 15	16 19	16 20
London Blackfriars 3	⊖ a																								
London Cannon Street 4	⊖ a		15 49		15 54		15 58			16 04		16 08							16 15				16 19		16 24
London Waterloo (East) 4	⊖ d	15 49		15 54		15 57		16 00	16 03				16 10				16 13	16 15				16 19		16 24	
London Charing Cross 4	⊖ a	15 52		15 57		16 00		16 03	16 06				16 13				16 16	16 19				16 22		16 27	

		SE	SE	SE 1 🛒	SE	SE		SE	SE	SE	SE	SE	SE	SE 1	SE	SE		SE 1 🛒	SE	SE	SE	SE	SE	SE 1 🛒	SE
Orpington 4	d			16 09				16 03		16 25				16 24		16 40				16 21				16 39	
Petts Wood 4	d							16 06		16 28						16 43				16 24					
Hither Green 4	d	16 12						16 19											16 28	16 37		16 42			
Lewisham 4	d		16 14		16 20			16 24	16 26		16 29	16 38							16 34				16 44		16 50
St Johns	d		16 16					16 26											16 36				16 46		
New Cross 4	⊖ d		16 18					16 28			16 32								16 38				16 48		
London Victoria 15	⊖ a									17 02		17 00				17 17									
London Bridge 4	⊖ d	16 22	16 24	16 25	16 28	16 30		16 34	16 35		16a38		16 38	16 41	16 41			16 44	16 45	16 49	16 50	16 52	16 54	16 55	16 58
London Blackfriars 3	⊖ a																								
London Cannon Street 4	⊖ a		16 28			16 34		16 38							16 45				16 49		16 54		16 58		
London Waterloo (East) 4	⊖ d	16 27		16 30	16 33				16 40				16 43	16 45				16 49		16 54		16 57		17 00	17 03
London Charing Cross 4	⊖ a	16 30		16 33	16 36				16 43				16 46	16 49				16 52		16 57		17 00		17 03	17 06

		SE		SE	SE	SE	SE	SE	SE	SE 1	SE	SE		SE 1 🛒	SE	SE	SE	SE	SE	SE 1 🛒	SE	SE		SE	SE
Orpington 4	d			16 33		16 55				16 54		17 10				16 51				17 09				17 03	
Petts Wood 4	d			16 36		16 58						17 13				16 54								17 06	
Hither Green 4	d			16 49											16 58	17 07		17 12						17 19	
Lewisham 4	d			16 54	16 56		16 59	17 08							17 04				17 14		17 20			17 24	17 26
St Johns	d			16 56											17 06				17 16					17 26	
New Cross 4	⊖ d			16 58			17 02								17 08				17 18					17 28	
London Victoria 15	⊖ a					17 32		17 30				17 47													
London Bridge 4	⊖ d	17 00		17 04	17 05		17a08		17 08	17 11	17 11			17 14	17 15	17 19	17 20	17 22	17 24	17 25	17 28	17 30		17 34	17 35
London Blackfriars 3	⊖ a																								
London Cannon Street 4	⊖ a	17 04		17 08							17 15				17 19		17 24		17 28			17 34		17 38	
London Waterloo (East) 4	⊖ d				17 10				17 13	17 15				17 19		17 24		17 27		17 30	17 33				17 40
London Charing Cross 4	⊖ a				17 13				17 16	17 19				17 22		17 27		17 30		17 33	17 36				17 43

		SE	SE	SE	SE	SE 1	SE	SE		SE 1 🛒	SE	SE	SE	SE	SE	SE 1 🛒	SE	SE		SE	SE	SE	SE	SE	SE
Orpington 4	d	17 25				17 24		17 40				17 21				17 39				17 33		17 55			
Petts Wood 4	d	17 28						17 43				17 24								17 36		17 58			
Hither Green 4	d										17 28	17 37		17 42						17 49					
Lewisham 4	d		17 29	17 38							17 34				17 44		17 50			17 54	17 56		17 59	18 08	
St Johns	d										17 36				17 46					17 56					
New Cross 4	⊖ d		17 32								17 38				17 48					17 58			18 02		
London Victoria 15	⊖ a	18 02		18 00				18 17														18 32		18 30	
London Bridge 4	⊖ d		17a38		17 38	17 41	17 41			17 44	17 45	17 49	17 50	17 52	17 54	17 55	17 58	18 00		18 04	18 05		18a08		18 08
London Blackfriars 3	⊖ a																								
London Cannon Street 4	⊖ a						17 45				17 49		17 54		17 58			18 04		18 08					
London Waterloo (East) 4	⊖ d				17 43	17 45				17 49		17 54		17 57		18 00	18 03				18 10				18 13
London Charing Cross 4	⊖ a				17 46	17 49				17 52		17 57		18 00		18 03	18 06				18 13				18 16

Table 199

Saturdays

Orpington, Petts Wood, Hither Green and Lewisham - London (Summary of Services)

		SE 1	SE	SE		SE 1 🛒	SE	SE	SE	SE	SE	SE 1 🛒	SE	SE		SE	SE	SE	SE	SE	SE	SE	SE 1	SE
Orpington 4	d	17 54		18 10				17 51				18 09				18 03			18 25				18 24	
Petts Wood 4	d			18 13				17 54								18 06			18 28					
Hither Green 4	d						17 58	18 07		18 12						18 19								
Lewisham 4	d						18 04				18 14		18 20			18 24		18 26		18 29	18 38			
St Johns	d						18 06				18 16					18 26								
New Cross 4	⊖ d						18 08				18 18					18 28				18 32				
London Victoria 15	⊖ a			18 47															19 02		19 00			
London Bridge 4	⊖ d	18 11	18 11			18 14	18 15	18 19	18 20	18 22	18 24	18 25	18 28	18 30		18 34		18 35		18a38		18 38	18 41	18 41
London Blackfriars 3	⊖ a																							
London Cannon Street 4	⊖ a		18 15				18 19		18 24		18 28			18 34		18 38								18 45
London Waterloo (East) 4	⊖ d	18 15				18 19		18 24		18 27		18 30	18 33					18 40				18 43	18 45	
London Charing Cross 4	⊖ a	18 19				18 22		18 27		18 30		18 33	18 36					18 43				18 46	18 49	

		SE	SE 1 🛒	SE	SE	SE	SE	SE	SE 1	SE		SE	SE	SE	SE	SE	SE	SE	SE 1	SE		SE	SE 1 🛒	SE	SE
Orpington 4	d	18 40			18 21				18 39						18 55				18 54			19 10			18 51
Petts Wood 4	d	18 43			18 24										18 58							19 13			18 54
Hither Green 4	d			18 28	18 37		18 42																	18 58	19 07
Lewisham 4	d			18 34				18 44		18 50				18 56		18 59	19 08							19 04	19 12
St Johns	d			18 36				18 46																19 06	
New Cross 4	⊖ d			18 38				18 48								19 02								19 08	
London Victoria 15	⊖ a	19 17													19 32		19 30					19 47			
London Bridge 4	⊖ d		18 44	18 45	18 49	18 50	18 52	18 54	18 55	18 58		19 00		19 05		19a08		19 08	19 11	19 11			19 14	19 15	19 21
London Blackfriars 3	⊖ a																								
London Cannon Street 4	⊖ a			18 49		18 54		18 58				19 04								19 15				19 19	
London Waterloo (East) 4	⊖ d		18 49		18 54		18 57		19 00	19 03				19 10				19 13	19 15				19 19		19 26
London Charing Cross 4	⊖ a		18 52		18 57		19 00		19 03	19 06				19 13				19 16	19 19				19 22		19 29

		SE 1	SE	SE	SE	SE		SE	SE	SE	SE 1 🛒	SE	SE	SE 1	SE	SE		SE	SE	SE	SE	SE 1 🛒	SE	SE	SE 1
Orpington 4	d	19 09							19 25		19 28		19 21	19 39	19 40					19 55		19 58		19 51	20 09
Petts Wood 4	d								19 28				19 24		19 43					19 58				19 54	
Hither Green 4	d		19 13										19 37			19 43								20 07	
Lewisham 4	d		19 18	19 14	19 20			19 26				19 38	19 43			19 48		19 53	19 56				20 08	20 13	
St Johns	d			19 16								19 40											20 10		
New Cross 4	⊖ d			19 18	19 23							19 42				19 51		19 56					20 12		
London Victoria 15	⊖ a								20 02						20 17					20 32					
London Bridge 4	⊖ d	19 25	19 28	19a24	19 34			19 37		19 41	19 44	19 49	19 52	19 55		19 58		20 04	20 06		20 11	20 14	20 19	20 22	20 25
London Blackfriars 3	⊖ a																								
London Cannon Street 4	⊖ a																								
London Waterloo (East) 4	⊖ d	19 30	19 32		19 39			19 42		19 46	19 48	19 54	19 57	20 00		20 04		20 09	20 11		20 16	20 18	20 24	20 27	20 30
London Charing Cross 4	⊖ a	19 33	19 35		19 42			19 45		19 49	19 51	19 58	20 00	20 03		20 07		20 12	20 14		20 19	20 21	20 28	20 30	20 33

		SE		SE	SE	SE	SE	SE 1	SE	SE	SE 1	SE		SE	SE	SE	SE	SE 1	SE	SE	SE 1	SE		SE	SE
Orpington 4	d	20 10						20 28		20 21	20 39	20 40						20 58		20 51	21 09	21 10			
Petts Wood 4	d	20 13								20 24		20 43								20 54		21 13			
Hither Green 4	d			20 13						20 37				20 43						21 07				21 13	
Lewisham 4	d			20 18	20 23	20 26			20 38	20 43				20 48	20 53	20 56			21 08	21 13				21 18	21 23
St Johns	d								20 40										21 10						
New Cross 4	⊖ d			20 21	20 26				20 42					20 51	20 56				21 12					21 21	21 26
London Victoria 15	⊖ a	20 47										21 17										21 47			
London Bridge 4	⊖ d			20 28	20 34	20 36	20 41	20 44	20 49	20 52	20 55			20 58	21 04	21 06	21 11	21 14	21 19	21 22	21 25			21 28	21 34
London Blackfriars 3	⊖ a																								
London Cannon Street 4	⊖ a																								
London Waterloo (East) 4	⊖ d			20 34	20 39	20 41	20 46	20 48	20 54	20 57	21 00			21 04	21 09	21 11	21 16	21 18	21 24	21 27	21 30			21 34	21 39
London Charing Cross 4	⊖ a			20 37	20 42	20 44	20 49	20 51	20 58	21 00	21 03			21 07	21 12	21 14	21 19	21 21	21 28	21 30	21 33			21 37	21 42

		SE	SE	SE 1	SE	SE	SE 1	SE		SE	SE	SE	SE	SE 1	SE	SE	SE 1	SE		SE	SE	SE	SE	SE 1	SE
Orpington 4	d			21 28		21 21	21 39	21 40						21 58		21 51	22 09	22 10						22 28	
Petts Wood 4	d					21 24		21 43								21 54		22 13							
Hither Green 4	d					21 37				21 43						22 07				22 13					
Lewisham 4	d	21 26			21 38	21 43				21 48	21 53	21 56			22 08	22 13				22 18	22 23	22 26			22 38
St Johns	d				21 40										22 10										22 40
New Cross 4	⊖ d				21 42					21 51	21 56				22 12					22 21	22 26				22 42
London Victoria 15	⊖ a							22 17										22 47							
London Bridge 4	⊖ d	21 36	21 41	21 44	21 49	21 52	21 55			21 58	22 02	22 05	22 11	22 14	22 19	22 22	22 25			22 28	22 32	22 35	22 41	22 44	22 49
London Blackfriars 3	⊖ a																								
London Cannon Street 4	⊖ a																								
London Waterloo (East) 4	⊖ d	21 41	21 46	21 48	21 54	21 57	22 00			22 04	22 07	22 10	22 16	22 18	22 24	22 27	22 30			22 34	22 37	22 40	22 46	22 48	22 54
London Charing Cross 4	⊖ a	21 44	21 49	21 51	21 58	22 00	22 03			22 07	22 10	22 13	22 19	22 21	22 28	22 30	22 33			22 37	22 40	22 43	22 49	22 51	22 58

Table 199

Saturdays

Orpington, Petts Wood, Hither Green and Lewisham - London (Summary of Services)

		SE	SE ■	SE	SE	SE	SE	SE	SE ■	SE	SE	SE ■	SE	SE	SE	SE	SE	SE	SE ■
Orpington ■	d	22 21	22 39	22 40					22 58		22 51	23 09	23 10					23 21	23 37
Petts Wood ■	d	22 24		22 43							22 54		23 13					23 24	
Hither Green ■	d	22 37			22 43						23 07			23 13				23 37	
Lewisham ■	d	22 43			22 48	22 53	22 56			23 08	23 13			23 18	23 23	23 26		23 43	
St Johns	d									23 10									
New Cross ■ ⊖	d				22 51	22 56				23 12				23 21	23 26				
London Victoria ■ ⊖	a			23 17									23 47						
London Bridge ■ ⊖	d	22 52	22 55		22 58	23 02	23 05	23 11	23 14	23 19	23 22	23 25		23 28	23 32	23 35	23 41	23 50	23 53
London Blackfriars ■ ⊖	a																		
London Cannon Street ■ ⊖	a																		
London Waterloo (East) ■ ⊖	d	22 57	23 00		23 04	23 07	23 10	23 16	23 18	23 24	23 27	23 30		23 34	23 37	23 40	23 46	23 55	23 58
London Charing Cross ■ ⊖	a	23 00	23 03		23 07	23 10	23 13	23 20	23 21	23 27	23 30	23 33		23 37	23 40	23 43	23 49	23 58	00 01

Sundays

		SE ■	SE	SE	SE	SE	SE	SE	SE	SE ■	SE	SE	SE	SE	SE	SE ■	SE	SE	SE	SE ■	SE	SE	SE
Orpington ■	d	23p37	06 43	07 06		07 13			07 10	07 29	07 36		07 43			07 43			07 40	07 59	08 06		
Petts Wood ■	d		06 46	07 09		07 16			07 13		07 39		07 46						07 43		08 09		
Hither Green ■	d							07 13	07 26						07 43				07 56				
Lewisham ■	d				07 08			07 18	07 31			07 38			07 48		07 52	07 56	08 01			08 08	
St Johns	d																07 54						
New Cross ■ ⊖	d				07 11							07 41					07 56					08 11	
London Victoria ■ ⊖	a		07 25	07 43		07 56					08 13		08 26								08 43		
London Bridge ■ ⊖	d	23p53			07 20		07 23	07 26	07 40	07 45		07 50		07 53	07 56	07 59	08 04	08 07	08 10	08 15		08 20	08 23
London Blackfriars ■ ⊖	a																						
London Cannon Street ■ ⊖	a																						
London Waterloo (East) ■ ⊖	d	23p58			07 25		07 28	07 31	07 45	07 50		07 55		07 58	08 01	08 04	08 08	08 11	08 15	08 20		08 25	08 28
London Charing Cross ■ ⊖	a	00 01			07 28		07 31	07 34	07 48	07 53		07 58		08 01	08 04	08 07	08 11	08 14	08 18	08 23		08 28	08 31

		SE	SE	SE	SE	SE ■	SE	SE	SE	SE	SE ■	SE	SE	SE	SE ■	SE	SE	SE	SE	SE ■	SE	SE	SE
Orpington ■	d				08 10	08 29	08 36				08 43			08 40	08 59	09 06				09 13			09 10
Petts Wood ■	d				08 13		08 39							08 43		09 09							09 13
Hither Green ■	d	08 13			08 26					08 43				08 56					09 13				09 26
Lewisham ■	d	08 18	08 22	08 26	08 31			08 38		08 48		08 52	08 56	09 01			09 08		09 18		09 22	09 26	09 31
St Johns	d		08 24									08 54									09 24		
New Cross ■ ⊖	d		08 26					08 41				08 56					09 11				09 26		
London Victoria ■ ⊖	a						09 13									09 43							
London Bridge ■ ⊖	d	08 26	08 34	08 37	08 40	08 45		08 50	08 53	08 56	08 59	09 04	09 07	09 10	09 15		09 20	09 23	09 26	09 29	09 34	09 37	09 40
London Blackfriars ■ ⊖	a																						
London Cannon Street ■ ⊖	a																						
London Waterloo (East) ■ ⊖	d	08 31	08 38	08 41	08 45	08 50		08 55	08 58	09 01	09 04	09 08	09 11	09 15	09 20		09 25	09 28	09 31	09 34	09 38	09 41	09 45
London Charing Cross ■ ⊖	a	08 34	08 41	08 44	08 49	08 53		08 58	09 01	09 04	09 07	09 11	09 14	09 18	09 23		09 28	09 31	09 34	09 37	09 41	09 44	09 49

		SE ■ 🛒	SE	SE	SE	SE	SE ■	SE	SE	SE	SE ■ 🛒	SE	SE	SE	SE	SE ■	SE	SE	SE	SE ■ 🛒	SE	SE
Orpington ■	d	09 29	09 36				09 43			09 41	09 59	10 06				10 13			10 10	10 29	10 36	
Petts Wood ■	d		09 39							09 44		10 09							10 13		10 39	
Hither Green ■	d					09 43				09 57					10 13				10 26			
Lewisham ■	d			09 38		09 48		09 52	09 56	10 02			10 08		10 18		10 22	10 26	10 31			10 38
St Johns	d							09 54									10 24					
New Cross ■ ⊖	d			09 41				09 56					10 11				10 26					10 41
London Victoria ■ ⊖	a		10 13									10 43									11 13	
London Bridge ■ ⊖	d	09 45		09 50	09 53	09 56	09 59	10 04	10 07	10 11	10 15		10 20	10 23	10 26	10 29	10 34	10 37	10 40	10 45		10 50
London Blackfriars ■ ⊖	a																					
London Cannon Street ■ ⊖	a																					
London Waterloo (East) ■ ⊖	d	09 50		09 55	09 58	10 01	10 04	10 08	10 11	10 16	10 20		10 25	10 28	10 31	10 34	10 38	10 41	10 45	10 50		10 55
London Charing Cross ■ ⊖	a	09 53		09 58	10 01	10 04	10 07	10 11	10 14	10 19	10 23		10 28	10 31	10 34	10 37	10 41	10 44	10 49	10 53		10 58

		SE	SE	SE ■	SE	SE	SE	SE ■ 🛒	SE	SE	SE	SE	SE ■	SE	SE	SE	SE ■ 🛒	SE	SE	SE	SE	SE ■	SE
Orpington ■	d			10 43			10 40	10 59	11 06				11 13			11 10	11 29	11 36				11 43	
Petts Wood ■	d						10 43		11 09							11 13		11 39					
Hither Green ■	d		10 43				10 56					11 13				11 26					11 43		
Lewisham ■	d		10 48		10 52	10 56	11 01			11 08		11 18		11 22	11 26	11 31			11 38		11 48		11 52
St Johns	d				10 54									11 24									11 54
New Cross ■ ⊖	d				10 56					11 11				11 26					11 41				11 56
London Victoria ■ ⊖	a								11 43									12 13					
London Bridge ■ ⊖	d	10 53	10 56	10 59	11 04	11 07	11 10	11 15		11 20	11 23	11 26	11 29	11 34	11 37	11 40	11 45		11 50	11 53	11 56	11 59	12 04
London Blackfriars ■ ⊖	a																						
London Cannon Street ■ ⊖	a																						
London Waterloo (East) ■ ⊖	d	10 58	11 01	11 04	11 08	11 11	11 15	11 20		11 25	11 28	11 31	11 34	11 38	11 41	11 45	11 50		11 55	11 58	12 01	12 04	12 08
London Charing Cross ■ ⊖	a	11 01	11 04	11 07	11 11	11 14	11 18	11 23		11 28	11 31	11 34	11 37	11 41	11 44	11 49	11 53		11 58	12 01	12 04	12 07	12 11

Table 199

Sundays

Orpington, Petts Wood, Hither Green and Lewisham - London (Summary of Services)

		SE	SE	SE ■ 🛒	SE	SE	SE	SE	SE ■	SE	SE	SE	SE ■ 🛒	SE	SE	SE	SE	SE ■	SE	SE	SE	SE ■ 🛒
Orpington ■	d		11 40	11 59	12 06				12 13			12 10	12 29	12 36				12 43			12 40	12 59
Petts Wood ■	d		11 43		12 09							12 13		12 39							12 43	
Hither Green ■	d		11 56					12 13				12 26					12 43				12 56	
Lewisham ■	d	11 56	12 01			12 08		12 18		12 22	12 26	12 31			12 38		12 48		12 52	12 56	13 01	
St Johns	d									12 24									12 54			
New Cross ■ ⊖	d					12 11				12 26					12 41				12 56			
London Victoria ■ ⊖	a				12 43									13 13								
London Bridge ■ ⊖	d	12 07	12 10	12 15		12 20	12 23	12 26	12 29	12 34	12 37	12 40	12 45		12 50	12 53	12 56	12 59	13 04	13 07	13 10	13 15
London Blackfriars ■ ⊖	a																					
London Cannon Street ■ ⊖	a																					
London Waterloo (East) ■ ⊖	d	12 11	12 15	12 20		12 25	12 28	12 31	12 34	12 38	12 41	12 45	12 50		12 55	12 58	13 01	13 04	13 08	13 11	13 15	13 20
London Charing Cross ■ ⊖	a	12 14	12 18	12 23		12 28	12 31	12 34	12 37	12 41	12 44	12 49	12 53		12 58	13 01	13 04	13 07	13 11	13 14	13 18	13 23

		SE	SE	SE	SE	SE ■	SE	SE	SE	SE ■ 🛒	SE	SE	SE	SE	SE ■	SE	SE	SE	SE ■ 🛒	SE	SE	SE	SE
Orpington ■	d	13 06				13 13			13 10	13 29	13 36				13 43			13 40	13 59	14 06			
Petts Wood ■	d	13 09							13 13		13 39							13 43		14 09			
Hither Green ■	d				13 13				13 26					13 43				13 56					14 13
Lewisham ■	d		13 08		13 18		13 22	13 26	13 31			13 38		13 48		13 52	13 56	14 01			14 08		14 18
St Johns	d						13 24									13 54							
New Cross ■ ⊖	d		13 11				13 26					13 41				13 56					14 11		
London Victoria ■ ⊖	a	13 43									14 13									14 43			
London Bridge ■ ⊖	d		13 20	13 23	13 26	13 29	13 34	13 37	13 40	13 45		13 50	13 53	13 56	13 59	14 04	14 07	14 10	14 15		14 20	14 23	14 26
London Blackfriars ■ ⊖	a																						
London Cannon Street ■ ⊖	a																						
London Waterloo (East) ■ ⊖	d		13 25	13 28	13 31	13 34	13 38	13 41	13 45	13 50		13 55	13 58	14 01	14 04	14 08	14 11	14 15	14 20		14 25	14 28	14 31
London Charing Cross ■ ⊖	a		13 28	13 31	13 34	13 37	13 41	13 44	13 49	13 53		13 58	14 01	14 04	14 07	14 11	14 14	14 18	14 23		14 28	14 31	14 34

		SE ■	SE	SE	SE	SE ■ 🛒	SE	SE	SE	SE	SE ■	SE	SE	SE	SE ■ 🛒	SE	SE	SE	SE	SE ■	SE	SE	SE
Orpington ■	d	14 13			14 10	14 29	14 36				14 43			14 40	14 59	15 06				15 13			15 10
Petts Wood ■	d				14 13		14 39							14 43		15 09							15 13
Hither Green ■	d				14 26					14 43				14 56					15 13				15 26
Lewisham ■	d		14 22	14 26	14 31			14 38		14 48		14 52	14 56	15 01			15 08		15 18		15 22	15 26	15 31
St Johns	d		14 24									14 54									15 24		
New Cross ■ ⊖	d		14 26					14 41				14 56					15 11				15 26		
London Victoria ■ ⊖	a						15 13									15 43							
London Bridge ■ ⊖	d	14 29	14 34	14 37	14 40	14 45		14 50	14 53	14 56	14 59	15 04	15 07	15 10	15 15		15 20	15 23	15 26	15 29	15 34	15 37	15 40
London Blackfriars ■ ⊖	a																						
London Cannon Street ■ ⊖	a																						
London Waterloo (East) ■ ⊖	d	14 34	14 38	14 41	14 45	14 50		14 55	14 58	15 01	15 04	15 08	15 11	15 15	15 20		15 25	15 28	15 31	15 34	15 38	15 41	15 45
London Charing Cross ■ ⊖	a	14 37	14 41	14 44	14 49	14 53		14 58	15 01	15 04	15 07	15 11	15 14	15 18	15 23		15 28	15 31	15 34	15 37	15 41	15 44	15 49

		SE ■ 🛒	SE	SE	SE	SE	SE ■	SE	SE	SE	SE ■ 🛒	SE	SE	SE	SE	SE ■	SE	SE	SE	SE ■ 🛒	SE	SE
Orpington ■	d	15 29	15 36				15 43			15 40	15 59	16 06				16 13			16 10	16 29	16 36	
Petts Wood ■	d		15 39							15 43		16 09							16 13		16 39	
Hither Green ■	d					15 43				15 56					16 13				16 26			
Lewisham ■	d			15 38		15 48		15 52	15 56	16 01			16 08		16 18		16 22	16 26	16 31			16 38
St Johns	d							15 54									16 24					
New Cross ■ ⊖	d			15 41				15 56					16 11				16 26					16 41
London Victoria ■ ⊖	a		16 13									16 43									17 13	
London Bridge ■ ⊖	d	15 45		15 50	15 53	15 56	15 59	16 04	16 07	16 10	16 15		16 20	16 23	16 26	16 29	16 34	16 37	16 40	16 45		16 50
London Blackfriars ■ ⊖	a																					
London Cannon Street ■ ⊖	a																					
London Waterloo (East) ■ ⊖	d	15 50		15 55	15 58	16 01	16 04	16 08	16 11	16 15	16 20		16 25	16 28	16 31	16 34	16 38	16 41	16 45	16 50		16 55
London Charing Cross ■ ⊖	a	15 53		15 58	16 01	16 04	16 07	16 11	16 14	16 18	16 23		16 28	16 31	16 34	16 37	16 41	16 44	16 49	16 53		16 58

		SE	SE	SE ■	SE	SE	SE	SE ■ 🛒	SE	SE	SE	SE	SE ■	SE	SE	SE	SE ■ 🛒	SE	SE	SE	SE	SE ■	SE
Orpington ■	d			16 43			16 40	16 59	17 06				17 13			17 10	17 29	17 36				17 43	
Petts Wood ■	d						16 43		17 09							17 13		17 39					
Hither Green ■	d		16 43				16 56					17 13				17 26					17 43		
Lewisham ■	d		16 48		16 52	16 56	17 01			17 08		17 18		17 22	17 26	17 31			17 38		17 48		17 52
St Johns	d				16 54									17 24									17 54
New Cross ■ ⊖	d				16 56					17 11				17 26					17 41				17 56
London Victoria ■ ⊖	a								17 43									18 13					
London Bridge ■ ⊖	d	16 53	16 56	16 59	17 04	17 07	17 10	17 15		17 20	17 23	17 26	17 29	17 34	17 37	17 40	17 45		17 50	17 53	17 56	17 59	18 04
London Blackfriars ■ ⊖	a																						
London Cannon Street ■ ⊖	a																						
London Waterloo (East) ■ ⊖	d	16 58	17 01	17 04	17 08	17 11	17 15	17 20		17 25	17 28	17 31	17 34	17 38	17 41	17 45	17 50		17 55	17 58	18 01	18 04	18 08
London Charing Cross ■ ⊖	a	17 01	17 04	17 07	17 11	17 14	17 18	17 23		17 28	17 31	17 34	17 37	17 41	17 44	17 49	17 53		17 58	18 01	18 04	18 07	18 11

Table 199 | **Sundays**

Orpington, Petts Wood, Hither Green and Lewisham - London (Summary of Services)

		SE	SE	SE 1 ⊥		SE	SE	SE	SE	SE 1	SE	SE	SE	SE 1 ⊥		SE	SE	SE	SE	SE 1	SE	SE	SE	SE 1 ⊥	
Orpington 4	d		17 40	17 59		18 06				18 13			18 10	18 29		18 36				18 43			18 40	18 59	
Petts Wood 4	d		17 43			18 09							18 13			18 39							18 43		
Hither Green 4	d		17 56						18 13				18 26						18 43				18 56		
Lewisham 4	d	17 56	18 01				18 08		18 18		18 22	18 26	18 31				18 38		18 48		18 52	18 56	19 01		
St Johns	d										18 24										18 54				
New Cross 4 ⊖	d						18 11				18 26						18 41				18 56				
London Victoria 15 ⊖	a					18 43										19 13									
London Bridge 4 ⊖	d	18 07	18 10	18 15			18 20	18 23	18 26	18 29	18 34	18 37	18 40	18 45			18 50	18 53	18 56	18 59	19 04	19 07	19 10	19 15	
London Blackfriars 3 ⊖	a																								
London Cannon Street 4 ⊖	a																								
London Waterloo (East) 4 ⊖	d	18 11	18 15	18 20			18 25	18 28	18 31	18 34	18 38	18 41	18 45	18 50			18 55	18 58	19 01	19 04	19 08	19 11	19 15	19 20	
London Charing Cross 4 ⊖	a	18 14	18 18	18 23			18 28	18 31	18 34	18 37	18 41	18 44	18 49	18 53			18 58	19 01	19 04	19 07	19 11	19 14	19 18	19 23	

		SE	SE	SE	SE	SE 1	SE	SE	SE	SE 1 ⊥		SE	SE	SE	SE	SE 1	SE	SE	SE	SE 1		SE	SE	SE	SE
Orpington 4	d	19 06				19 13			19 10	19 29		19 36				19 43			19 40	19 59		20 06			
Petts Wood 4	d	19 09							19 13			19 39							19 43			20 09			
Hither Green 4	d				19 13				19 26						19 43				19 56						20 13
Lewisham 4	d		19 08		19 18		19 22	19 26	19 31				19 38		19 48		19 52	19 56	20 01				20 08		20 18
St Johns	d						19 24										19 54								
New Cross 4 ⊖	d		19 11				19 26						19 41				19 56						20 11		
London Victoria 15 ⊖	a	19 43										20 13										20 43			
London Bridge 4 ⊖	d		19 20	19 23	19 26	19 29	19 34	19 37	19 40	19 45			19 50	19 53	19 56	19 59	20 04	20 07	20 10	20 15			20 20	20 23	20 26
London Blackfriars 3 ⊖	a																								
London Cannon Street 4 ⊖	a																								
London Waterloo (East) 4 ⊖	d		19 25	19 28	19 31	19 34	19 38	19 41	19 45	19 50			19 55	19 58	20 01	20 04	20 08	20 11	20 15	20 20			20 25	20 28	20 31
London Charing Cross 4 ⊖	a		19 28	19 31	19 34	19 37	19 41	19 44	19 49	19 53			19 58	20 01	20 04	20 07	20 11	20 14	20 18	20 23			20 28	20 31	20 34

		SE	SE	SE	SE 1	SE		SE	SE	SE	SE 1	SE	SE	SE	SE 1	SE		SE	SE	SE	SE	SE	SE	SE 1	SE
Orpington 4	d			20 10	20 29	20 36					20 43			20 40	20 59	21 06							21 10	21 29	21 36
Petts Wood 4	d			20 13		20 39								20 43		21 09							21 13		21 39
Hither Green 4	d			20 26						20 43				20 56						21 13			21 26		
Lewisham 4	d	20 22	20 26	20 31				20 38		20 48		20 52	20 56	21 01				21 08		21 18	21 22	21 26	21 31		
St Johns	d	20 24										20 54									21 24				
New Cross 4 ⊖	d	20 26						20 41				20 56						21 11			21 26				
London Victoria 15 ⊖	a					21 13										21 43									22 13
London Bridge 4 ⊖	d	20 34	20 37	20 40	20 45			20 50	20 53	20 56	20 59	21 04	21 07	21 10	21 15			21 20	21 23	21 26	21 34	21 37	21 40	21 45	
London Blackfriars 3 ⊖	a																								
London Cannon Street 4 ⊖	a																								
London Waterloo (East) 4 ⊖	d	20 38	20 41	20 45	20 50			20 55	20 58	21 01	21 04	21 08	21 11	21 15	21 20			21 25	21 28	21 31	21 38	21 41	21 45	21 50	
London Charing Cross 4 ⊖	a	20 41	20 44	20 49	20 53			20 58	21 01	21 04	21 07	21 11	21 14	21 18	21 23			21 28	21 31	21 34	21 41	21 44	21 49	21 53	

		SE		SE	SE	SE 1	SE	SE	SE	SE 1	SE	SE		SE	SE	SE	SE	SE	SE 1	SE	SE	SE		SE	SE 1
Orpington 4	d					21 43			21 40	21 59	22 06							22 10	22 29	22 36					22 43
Petts Wood 4	d								21 43		22 09							22 13		22 39					
Hither Green 4	d				21 43				21 56						22 13			22 26						22 43	
Lewisham 4	d	21 38			21 48		21 52	21 56	22 01			22 08			22 18	22 22	22 26	22 31			22 38			22 48	
St Johns	d						21 54									22 24									
New Cross 4 ⊖	d	21 41					21 56					22 11				22 26					22 41				
London Victoria 15 ⊖	a										22 43									23 13					
London Bridge 4 ⊖	d	21 50		21 53	21 56	21 59	22 04	22 07	22 10	22 15		22 20		22 23	22 26	22 34	22 37	22 40	22 45		22 50	22 53		22 56	22 59
London Blackfriars 3 ⊖	a																								
London Cannon Street 4 ⊖	a																								
London Waterloo (East) 4 ⊖	d	21 55		21 58	22 01	22 04	22 08	22 11	22 15	22 20		22 25		22 28	22 31	22 38	22 41	22 45	22 50		22 55	22 58		23 01	23 04
London Charing Cross 4 ⊖	a	21 58		22 01	22 04	22 07	22 11	22 14	22 18	22 23		22 28		22 31	22 34	22 41	22 44	22 49	22 53		22 58	23 01		23 04	23 07

		SE	SE	SE	SE 1	SE	SE	SE		SE	SE	SE
Orpington 4	d			22 40	22 59							23 10
Petts Wood 4	d			22 43								23 13
Hither Green 4	d			22 56				23 13				23 26
Lewisham 4	d	22 52	22 56	23 01		23 08		23 18		23 22	23 26	23 31
St Johns	d	22 54								23 24		
New Cross 4 ⊖	d	22 56				23 11				23 26		
London Victoria 15 ⊖	a											
London Bridge 4 ⊖	d	23 04	23 07	23 10	23 15	23 20	23 23	23 26		23 34	23 37	23 40
London Blackfriars 3 ⊖	a											
London Cannon Street 4 ⊖	a											
London Waterloo (East) 4 ⊖	d	23 08	23 11	23 15	23 20	23 25	23 28	23 31		23 38	23 41	23 45
London Charing Cross 4 ⊖	a	23 11	23 14	23 18	23 23	23 28	23 31	23 34		23 41	23 44	23 49

Network Diagram for Tables 200, 203, 204 | also 199★

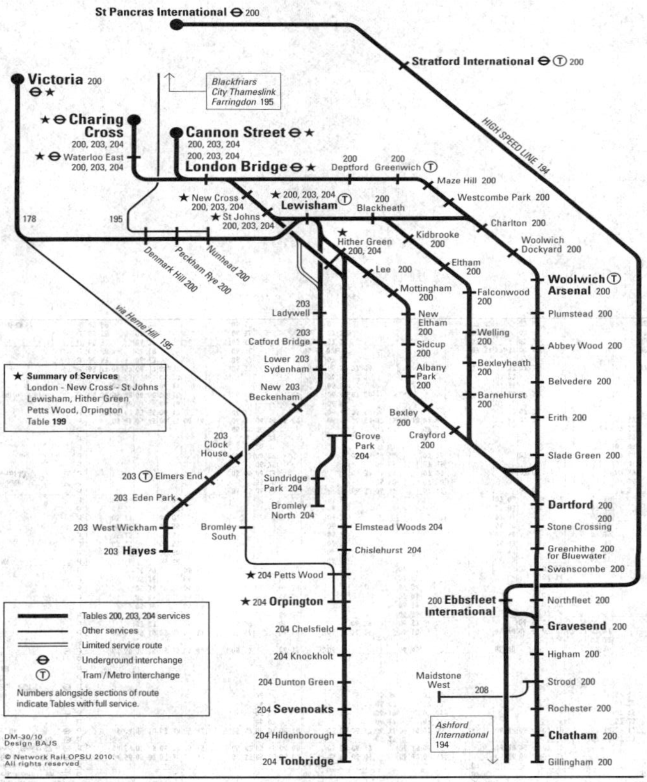

DM-30/10
Design BAJS

London - Dartford and Gillingham

		SE MX	SE MO	SE MO	SE MX	SE MO	SE MX	SE MX	SE MO	SE MO	SE MX	SE MO	SE MX	SE MO	SE MX	SE MX	SE MO	SE MX	SE MX	SE MX	SE	SE	SE
St Pancras International	d					23p25	23p25								23p55								
Stratford International	d					23p32	23p32								00 02								
Ebbsfleet International	d					23p43	23p43								00 13								
London Charing Cross	d	22p39	22p40	23p20	23p22			23p09	23p10	23p26	23p26	23p30	23p32	23p50		23p39	23p56	23p56	00 02	00 05	00 15	04 50	05 20
London Waterloo (East)	d	22p42	22p43	23p23	23p25			23p12	23p13	23p29	23p29	23p33	23p35	23p53		23p42	23p59	23p59	00 05	00 08	00 18	04 53	05 23
London Cannon Street	d																						
London Bridge	d	22p47	22p48	23p28	23p30			23p17	23p18	23p34	23p34	23p38	23p40	23p58		23p47	00 04	00 04	00 10	00 13	00 23	04 58	05 28
Deptford	d										23p40	23p44						00 10				05 04	05 34
Greenwich	d										23p42	23p46						00 12				05 06	05 36
Maze Hill	d										23p45	23p49						00 15				05 09	05 39
Westcombe Park	d										23p47	23p51						00 17				05 11	05 41
London Victoria	d																						
Denmark Hill	d																						
Peckham Rye	d																						
Nunhead	d																						
New Cross	d			23p34	23p35								23p45	00 04					00 15	00 18	00 28		
St Johns	d																						
Lewisham	d	22p56	22p57	23p38	23p39			23p26	23p27	23p42			23p49	00 08		23p56	00 12		00 19	00 22	00 33		
Blackheath	d	22p59	23p00	23p40				23p29	23p30				23p53	00 10		23p59			00 23		00 35		
Kidbrooke	d			23p43									23p56	00 13					00 26				
Eltham	d			23p47									23p59	00 17					00 29				
Falconwood	d			23p49									00 01	00 19					00 31				
Welling	d			23p52									00 04	00 22					00 34				
Bexleyheath	d			23p54									00 06	00 24					00 36				
Barnehurst	d			23p57									00 09	00 27					00 39				
Hither Green	d				23p44					23p46							00 16			00 27			
Lee	d				23p46					23p48							00 18			00 29			
Mottingham	d				23p49					23p51							00 21			00 32			
New Eltham	d				23p51					23p53							00 23			00 34			
Sidcup	d				23p55					23p57							00 27			00 38			
Albany Park	d				23p57					23p59							00 29			00 40			
Bexley	d				23p59					00 01							00 31			00 42			
Crayford	d				00 03					00 04							00 34			00 46			
Charlton	d	23p03	23p04					23p33	23p34		23p50	23p54				00 03		00 20			00 40	05 14	05 44
Woolwich Dockyard	d										23p53	23p57						00 23				05 17	05 47
Woolwich Arsenal	d	23p09	23p10					23p39	23p40		23p56	23p59				00 09		00 26			00 45	05 20	05 50
Plumstead	d										23p58	00 02						00 28			00 47	05 22	05 52
Abbey Wood	d	23p13	23p14					23p43	23p44		00 01	00 05				00 13		00 31			00 50	05 25	05 55
Belvedere	d										00 04	00 08						00 34			00 53	05 28	05 58
Erith	d										00 06	00 10						00 36			00 55	05 30	06 00
Slade Green	d										00 09	00 14						00 39			00 58	05 34	06 04
Dartford	a	23p24	23p24	00 03	00 08			23p54	23p54	00 09	00 14	00 19	00 16	00 33		00 24	00 39	00 44	00 46	00 51	01 03	05 38	06 08
	d	23p25	23p25					23p55	23p55							00 25					01 03		
Stone Crossing	d	23p29	23p29					23p59	23p59							00 29							
Greenhithe for Bluewater	d	23p31	23p31					00 02	00 01							00 31					01 08		
Swanscombe	d	23p34	23p34					00 05	00 04							00 34							
Northfleet	d	23p36	23p36					00 07	00 06							00 36							
Gravesend	d	23p40	23p40			23p48	23p48	00 10	00 10						00 18	00 40					01 15		
Higham	d	23p46	23p46					00 16	00 16							00 46					01 21		
Strood	d	23p52	23p52			23p58	23p58	00 22	00 22						00 28	00 52					01 26		
Rochester	d	23p56	23p56			00 03	00 03	00 26	00 26						00 33	00 56					01 32		
Chatham	d	23p58	23p58			00 05	00 06	00 28	00 28						00 35	00 58					01 35		
Gillingham (Kent)	a	00 03	00 03			00 09	00 10	00 33	00 33						00 39	01 03					01 41		

Table 200 Mondays to Fridays

London - Dartford and Gillingham

		SE	SE	SE	SE	SE	SE	SE	SE	SE	SE	SE	SE	SE	SE	SE	SE	SE	SE	SE	SE	SE	SE
St Pancras International	d									06 25						06 58							07 22
Stratford International	d									06 32						07 05							07 28
Ebbsfleet International	d									06 42						07 16							07 43
London Charing Cross	d		04 56	05 02	05 26	05 32	05 39	05 52	06 02		05 56	06 09		06 32	06 52		06 26	06 39	07 02				
London Waterloo (East)	d		04 59	05 05	05 29	05 35	05 42	05 55	06 05		05 59	06 12		06 35	06 55		06 29	06 42	07 05				
London Cannon Street	d												06 27								07 10	07 13	
London Bridge	d		05 04	05 10	05 34	05 42	05 47	06 01	06 10		06 04	06 17	06 31	06 40	07 00		06 34	06 47	07 10		07 14	07 17	
Deptford	d							06 07					06 37		07 07							07 23	
Greenwich	d							06 09					06 39		07 09							07 25	
Maze Hill	d							06 12					06 42		07 12							07 28	
Westcombe Park	d							06 14					06 44		07 14							07 30	
London Victoria	d																			07 09			
Denmark Hill	d																						
Peckham Rye	d																						
Nunhead	d																						
New Cross	d		05 09	05 15	05 39	05 48	05 52		06 15		06 09			06 46			06 40				07 20		
St Johns	d																				07 22		
Lewisham	d		05 13	05 19	05 43	05 52	05 56		06 19		06 13	06 26		06 50			06 44	06 56	07 18	07 27	07 27		
Blackheath	d			05 23		05 54	05 59		06 23			06 29		06 53				06 59	07 21	07 29			
Kidbrooke	d			05 26		05 57			06 26					06 56					07 24				
Eltham	d			05 29		06 00			06 29					06 59					07 27				
Falconwood	d			05 31		06 03			06 31					07 01					07 29				
Welling	d			05 34		06 05			06 34					07 04					07 32				
Bexleyheath	d			05 36		06 08			06 36					07 06					07 34				
Barnehurst	d			05 39		06 10			06 39					07 12					07 37	07 40			
Hither Green	d		05 18		05 48						06 18						06 48				07 31		
Lee	d		05 20		05 50						06 20						06 50				07 33		
Mottingham	d		05 23		05 53						06 23						06 53				07 36		
New Eltham	d		05 25		05 55						06 25						06 55				07 39		
Sidcup	d		05 29		05 59						06 29						06 59				07 42		
Albany Park	d		05 31		06 01						06 31						07 01				07 44		
Bexley	d		05 33		06 03						06 33						07 03				07 47		
Crayford	d		05 36		06 06						06 36						07 06		07a46		07 50		
Charlton	d						06 03	06 17				06 33	06 47		07 17			07 04				07 33	
Woolwich Dockyard	d							06 20					06 50		07 20							07 36	
Woolwich Arsenal	d						06 09	06 23				06 39	06 53		07 23			07 09				07 39	
Plumstead	d							06 25					06 55		07 25							07 41	
Abbey Wood	d						06 13	06 28				06 43	06 58		07 28			07 13				07 44	
Belvedere	d							06 31					07 01		07 31							07 47	
Erith	d							06 33					07 03		07 33							07 49	
Slade Green	d						06 19	06 37					07 07		07 37						07a57	07 52	
Dartford	a		05 41	05 45	06 11	06 16	06 24	06 44	06 49		06 41	06 54	07 12	07 18	07 46		07 11	07 23		07 48		07 57	
	d	05 25	05 42	05 55	06 12		06 25				06 42	06 55					07 12	07 25					
Stone Crossing	d		05 46		06 16						06 46						07 16						
Greenhithe for Bluewater	d	05 30	05 48	06 00	06 18		06 30				06 48	07 00					07 18	07 30					
Swanscombe	d		05 51		06 21						06 51						07 21						
Northfleet	d		05 53		06 23						06 53						07 23						
Gravesend	d	05 37	05a57	06 07	06a27		06 37			06 46	06 59	07a06				07 21	07 27	07 37					07 48
Higham	d	05 43		06 13			06 43				07 05							07 43					
Strood	d	05 48		06 18			06 48			06 56	07b17					07 31	07a37	07 48					07 58
Rochester	d	05 52		06 22			06 52			07a00	07 21					07 36		07 52					08 03
Chatham	d	05 55		06 25			06 55				07 24					07 38		07 55					08 05
Gillingham (Kent)	a	05 59		06 29			06 59				07 28					07 42		07 59					08 09

b arr. 0710

Table 200

Mondays to Fridays

London - Dartford and Gillingham

		SE		SE	SE	SE	SE	SE	SE	SE	SE	SE		SE	SE	SE	SE	SE	SE	SE	SE	SE		SE	SE
St Pancras International ⊖	d													07 55										08 22	
Stratford International ⊖	d													08 02										08 29	
Ebbsfleet International	d													08 13										08 43	
London Charing Cross ⊖	d	06 56		07 12											07 26	07 39		08 03							07 59
London Waterloo (East) ⊖	d	06 59		07 15											07 29	07 42		08 06							08 02
London Cannon Street ⊖	d				07 24	07 27	07 32	07 36	07 41		07 44	07 54					07 56		08 05		08 10	08 16			
London Bridge ⊖	d	07 05		07 21	07 28	07 31	07 37	07 40	07 44		07 48	07 58			07 34	07 47	08 01	08 11	08 09		08 14	08 20			08 07
Deptford	d						07 43				07 54						08 07		08 15			08 27			
Greenwich	d					07 38	07 45				07 59						08 09		08 19			08 29			
Maze Hill	d						07 48				08 02						08 12		08 22			08 32			
Westcombe Park	d						07 50				08 04						08 14		08 24			08 34			
London Victoria ⊖	d									07 43										08 09					
Denmark Hill	d									07 53										08 19					
Peckham Rye	d									07 56										08 23					
Nunhead	d									07 59										08 25					
New Cross ⊖	d				07 33				07 49			08 05									08 20				
St Johns	d											08 07									08 22				
Lewisham	d			07 30	07 39			07 49	07 54	08 08		08 11				07 56		08 19		08 32	08 25				
Blackheath	d			07 32	07 42			07 53		08 10		08 13				07 59		08 23		08 35					
Kidbrooke	d				07 45			07 56				08 16						08 26		08 38					
Eltham	d				07 48			07 59				08 19						08 29		08 41					
Falconwood	d				07 51			08 01				08 22						08 31		08 44					
Welling	d				07 53			08 04				08 24						08 34		08 46					
Bexleyheath	d				07 56			08 06				08 27						08 36		08 49					
Barnehurst	d				07 59			08 09				08 30						08 39		08 51					
Hither Green	d	07 18							07 59						07 45						08 29				
Lee	d	07 20							08 01						07 47						08 31				
Mottingham	d	07 23							08 04						07 50						08 34				
New Eltham	d	07 26							08 06						07 53						08 37				08 21
Sidcup	d	07 29							08 11						07 56						08 40				08 25
Albany Park	d	07 31							08 13						07 58						08 42				08 27
Bexley	d	07 34							08 15						08 01						08 45				08 29
Crayford	d	07 37			08a08				08 20						08 05						08 48				08 33
Charlton	d			07 37		07 44	07 53		08 50		08 07					08 04	08 17		08 26		09 13	08 37			
Woolwich Dockyard	d						07 56				08 10						08 20		08 29			08 40			
Woolwich Arsenal	d			07 43		07 49	07 59				08 13					08 09	08 23		08 32			08 43			
Plumstead	d						08 01				08 15						08 25		08 34			08 45			
Abbey Wood	d			07 48		07 53	08 04				08 19					08 13	08 28		08 37			08 48			
Belvedere	d						08 07				08 21						08 31		08 40			08 51			
Erith	d						08 09				08 24						08 33		08 42			08 53			
Slade Green	d					08 00	08a12				08 32	08a35				08 20	08 37		08a45			08 57			
Dartford	a	07 42		07 59				08 15		08 27					08 11	08 25	08 42	08 45		08 58					08 38
	d	07 43		08 00											08 12	08 25									08 38
Stone Crossing	d	07 47													08 16										08 42
Greenhithe for Bluewater	d	07 49		08 05											08 18	08 30									08 45
Swanscombe	d	07 52													08 21										08 48
Northfleet	d	07 54													08 23										08 50
Gravesend	d	07a58		08 12										08 18	08a27	08 37								08 48	08a55
Higham	d			08 18												08 43									
Strood	d			08 23										08 28		08 48								08 58	
Rochester	d			08 27										08 33		08 52								09 03	
Chatham	d			08 30										08 35		08 55								09 05	
Gillingham (Kent)	a			08 35										08 39		08 59								09 09	

Table 200

Mondays to Fridays

London - Dartford and Gillingham

		SE	SE	SE	SE	SE	SE	SE		SE	SE	SE	SE	SE	SE	SE	SE	SE		SE	SE	SE	SE	SE	SE
St Pancras International ⊖	d													08 58											09 25
Stratford International ⊖	d													09 05											09 32
Ebbsfleet International	d													09 16											09 43
London Charing Cross ⊖	d	08 11	08 23		08 31						08 49				08 20	08 41	09 02						09 21		
London Waterloo (East) ⊖	d	08 14	08 26		08 34						08 52				08 23	08 44	09 05						09 24		
London Cannon Street ⊖	d			08 25		08 36		08 39		08 47		08 54	08 56					09 07			09 09	09 15		09 24	
London Bridge ⊖	d	08 19	08 31	08 29	08 39	08 40		08 43		08 51	08 57	08 58	09 01		08 29	08 49	09 10	09 11			09 14	09 19	09 31	09 28	
Deptford	d			08 35		08 46				08 57			09 07					09 17				09 25			
Greenwich	d			08 39		08 49				08 59			09 09					09 19				09 29			
Maze Hill	d			08 42		08 52				09 02			09 12					09 22				09 32			
Westcombe Park	d			08 44		08 54				09 04			09 14					09 24				09 34			
London Victoria ⊖	d						08 39													09 09					
Denmark Hill	d						08 48													09 18					
Peckham Rye	d						08 51													09 21					
Nunhead	d						08 53													09 23					
New Cross ⊖	d		08 38					08 49				09 05									09 19			09 34	
St Johns	d							08 51													09 21				
Lewisham	d	08 28	08 42		08 49		09 02	08 54				09 09				08 56	09 20			09 32	09 24			09 38	
Blackheath	d	08 31	08 45		08 53		09 05					09 12				08 59	09 23			09 35				09 41	
Kidbrooke	d		08 48		08 56		09 08					09 15					09 26			09 38				09 44	
Eltham	d		08 51		08 59		09 11					09 18					09 29			09 41				09 47	
Falconwood	d		08 53		09 01		09 14					09 21					09 32			09 44				09 50	
Welling	d		08 56		09 04		09 16					09 23					09 34			09 46				09 52	
Bexleyheath	d		08 58		09 06		09 19					09 26					09 37			09 49				09 55	
Barnehurst	d		09a01		09 09		09 21					09a28					09 39			09 51				09a57	
Hither Green	d							08 59			09 09				08 44						09 29				
Lee	d							09 01			09 11				08 46						09 31				
Mottingham	d							09 04			09 14				08 49						09 34				
New Eltham	d							09 06			09 16				08 51						09 36				
Sidcup	d							09 10			09a19				08 55						09 40		09a48		
Albany Park	d							09 12							08 57						09 42				
Bexley	d							09 14							08 59						09 44				
Crayford	d							09 18							09 03						09 48				
Charlton	d	08 35		08 47		08 56		09 44		09 07			09 17			09 03		09 26			10 14	09 38			
Woolwich Dockyard	d			08 50		08 59				09 10			09 20					09 29				09 41			
Woolwich Arsenal	d	08 40		08 53		09 02				09 13			09 23			09 09		09 32				09 44			
Plumstead	d			08 55		09 04				09 15			09 25					09 34				09 46			
Abbey Wood	d	08 45		08 58		09 07				09 18			09 28			09 13		09 37				09 49			
Belvedere	d			09 01		09 10				09 21			09 31					09 40				09 52			
Erith	d			09 03		09 12				09 23			09 33					09 42				09 54			
Slade Green	d			09 07		09a15				09 27			09 37					09a45				09 58			
Dartford	a	08 54		09 12	09 15		09 28						09 42		09 08	09 24	09 45			09 58					
	d	08 55													09 08	09 25									
Stone Crossing	d														09 12										
Greenhithe for Bluewater	d	09 00													09 15	09 30									
Swanscombe	d														09 18										
Northfleet	d														09 20										
Gravesend	d	09 07												09 21	09a25	09 37									09 48
Higham	d	09 13														09 43									
Strood	d	09 18												09 31		09 48									09 58
Rochester	d	09 22												09 36		09 52									10 03
Chatham	d	09 25												09 38		09 55									10 05
Gillingham (Kent)	a	09 29												09 42		09 59									10 09

Table 200

Mondays to Fridays

London - Dartford and Gillingham

Station		SE	SE	SE	SE	SE	SE	SE	SE	SE	SE	SE	SE	SE	SE	SE	SE	SE	SE	SE	SE	SE
St Pancras International [15] ⊖	d										09 55										10 28	
Stratford International ⊖ ⛴	d										10 02										10 35	
Ebbsfleet International	d										10 13										10 46	
London Charing Cross [4] ⊖	d	08 55	09 11		09 32							09 26	09 39		10 02							09 56
London Waterloo (East) [4] ⊖	d	08 58	09 14		09 35							09 29	09 42		10 05							09 59
London Cannon Street [4] ⊖	d			09 27		09 37		09 40	09 47	09 54				09 57		10 07		10 10	10 17	10 27		
London Bridge [4] ⊖	d	09 03	09 19	09 31	09 40	09 41		09 44	09 51	09 58		09 34	09 47	10 01	10 10	10 11		10 14	10 21	10 31		10 04
Deptford	d			09 37		09 47			09 57					10 07		10 17			10 27	10 37		
Greenwich [4] ⛴	d			09 39		09 49			09 59					10 09		10 19			10 29	10 39		
Maze Hill	d			09 42		09 52			10 02					10 12		10 22			10 32	10 42		
Westcombe Park	d			09 44		09 54			10 04					10 14		10 24			10 34	10 44		
London Victoria [15] ⊖	d						09 39										10 09					
Denmark Hill [4]	d						09 48										10 18					
Peckham Rye [4]	d						09 51										10 21					
Nunhead [4]	d						09 53										10 23					
New Cross [4] ⊖	d							09 49		10 04								10 19				
St Johns	d							09 51										10 21				
Lewisham [4] ⛴	d		09 29		09 49		10 02	09 54		10 08			09 56		10 19		10 32	10 24				
Blackheath [4]	d		09 31		09 53		10 05			10 11			09 59		10 23		10 35					
Kidbrooke	d				09 56		10 08			10 14					10 26		10 38					
Eltham	d				09 59		10 11			10 17					10 29		10 41					
Falconwood	d				10 01		10 14			10 20					10 31		10 44					
Welling	d				10 04		10 16			10 22					10 34		10 46					
Bexleyheath	d				10 06		10 19			10 25					10 36		10 49					
Barnehurst [4]	d				10 09		10 21			10a27					10 39		10 51					
Hither Green [4]	d	09 15						09 59				09 44						10 29				10 14
Lee	d	09 17						10 01				09 46						10 31				10 16
Mottingham	d	09 20						10 04				09 49						10 34				10 19
New Eltham	d	09 22						10 06				09 51						10 36				10 21
Sidcup [4]	d	09 26						10 10				09 55						10 40				10 25
Albany Park	d	09 28						10 12				09 57						10 42				10 27
Bexley	d	09 30						10 14				09 59						10 44				10 29
Crayford	d	09 33						10 18				10 03						10 48				10 33
Charlton [4]	d		09 37	09 47		09 56		10 44	10 07				10 03	10 17		10 26		11 14	10 37	10 47		
Woolwich Dockyard	d			09 50		09 59			10 10					10 20		10 29			10 40	10 50		
Woolwich Arsenal [4] ⛴	d		09 42	09 53		10 02			10 13				10 09	10 23		10 32			10 43	10 53		
Plumstead	d			09 55		10 04			10 15					10 25		10 34			10 45	10 55		
Abbey Wood	d		09 46	09 58		10 07			10 18				10 13	10 28		10 37			10 48	10 58		
Belvedere	d			10 01		10 10			10 21					10 31		10 40			10 51	11 01		
Erith	d			10 03		10 12			10 23					10 33		10 42			10 53	11 03		
Slade Green [4]	d			10 07		10a15			10 27					10 37		10a45			10 57	11 07		
Dartford [4]	a	09 38	09 54	10 12	10 15		10 28					10 08	10 24	10 42	10 45		10 58			11 12		10 38
	d	09 38	09 55									10 08	10 25									10 38
Stone Crossing	d	09 42										10 12										10 42
Greenhithe for Bluewater	d	09 45	10 00									10 15	10 30									10 45
Swanscombe	d	09 48										10 18										10 48
Northfleet	d	09 50										10 20										10 50
Gravesend [4]	d	09a55	10 07								10 18	10a25	10 37								10 51	10a55
Higham	d		10 13										10 43									
Strood [4]	d		10 18								10 28		10 48								11 01	
Rochester [4]	d		10 22								10 33		10 52								11 06	
Chatham [4]	d		10 25								10 35		10 55								11 08	
Gillingham (Kent) [4]	a		10 29								10 39		10 59								11 12	

Table 200

Mondays to Fridays

London - Dartford and Gillingham

Station		SE	SE	SE	SE	SE	SE	SE	SE	SE	SE	SE	SE	SE	SE	SE	SE	SE	SE	SE	SE	SE	SE
St Pancras International [15] ⊖	d								10 55										11 25				
Stratford International ⊖ ⛴	d								11 02										11 32				
Ebbsfleet International	d								11 13										11 43				
London Charing Cross [4] ⊖	d	10 09	10 32							10 26	10 39		11 02							10 56	11 09		11 32
London Waterloo (East) [4] ⊖	d	10 12	10 35							10 29	10 42		11 05							10 59	11 12		11 35
London Cannon Street [4] ⊖	d			10 37		10 40	10 47	10 54				10 57		11 07		11 10	11 17	11 24				11 27	
London Bridge [4] ⊖	d	10 17	10 40	10 41		10 44	10 51	10 58		10 34	10 47	11 01	11 10	11 11		11 14	11 21	11 28		11 04	11 17	11 31	11 40
Deptford	d			10 47			10 57					11 07		11 17			11 27					11 37	
Greenwich [4] ⛴	d			10 49			10 59					11 09		11 19			11 29					11 39	
Maze Hill	d			10 52			11 02					11 12		11 22			11 32					11 42	
Westcombe Park	d			10 54			11 04					11 14		11 24			11 34					11 44	
London Victoria [15] ⊖	d				10 39										11 09								
Denmark Hill [4]	d				10 48										11 18								
Peckham Rye [4]	d				10 51										11 21								
Nunhead [4]	d				10 53										11 23								
New Cross [4] ⊖	d					10 49		11 04								11 19		11 34					
St Johns	d					10 51										11 21							
Lewisham [4] ⛴	d	10 26	10 49		11 02	10 54		11 11			10 56		11 19		11 32	11 24		11 38			11 26		11 49
Blackheath [4]	d	10 29	10 53		11 05			11 14			10 59		11 23		11 35			11 41			11 29		11 53
Kidbrooke	d		10 56		11 08			11 17					11 26		11 38			11 44					11 56
Eltham	d		10 59		11 11			11 20					11 29		11 41			11 47					11 59
Falconwood	d		11 01		11 14			11 23					11 31		11 44			11 50					12 01
Welling	d		11 04		11 16			11 25					11 34		11 46			11 52					12 04
Bexleyheath	d		11 06		11 19			11 28					11 36		11 49			11 55					12 06
Barnehurst [4]	d		11 09		11 21			11a30					11 39		11 51			11a57					12 09
Hither Green [4]	d					10 59				10 44						11 29				11 14			
Lee	d					11 01				10 46						11 31				11 16			
Mottingham	d					11 04				10 49						11 34				11 19			
New Eltham	d					11 06				10 51						11 36				11 21			
Sidcup [4]	d					11 10				10 55						11 40				11 25			
Albany Park	d					11 12				10 57						11 42				11 27			
Bexley	d					11 14				10 59						11 44				11 29			
Crayford	d					11 18				11 03						11 48				11 33			
Charlton [4]	d	10 33		10 56		11 44	11 07				11 03	11 17		11 26		12 14	11 37				11 33	11 47	
Woolwich Dockyard	d			10 59			11 10					11 20		11 29			11 40					11 50	
Woolwich Arsenal [4] ⛴	d	10 39		11 02			11 13				11 09	11 23		11 32			11 43				11 39	11 53	
Plumstead	d			11 04			11 15					11 25		11 34			11 45					11 55	
Abbey Wood	d	10 43		11 07			11 18				11 13	11 28		11 37			11 48				11 43	11 58	
Belvedere	d			11 10			11 21					11 31		11 40			11 51					12 01	
Erith	d			11 12			11 23					11 33		11 42			11 53					12 03	
Slade Green [4]	d			11a15			11 27					11 37		11a45			11 57					12 07	
Dartford [4]	a	10 54	11 15		11 28					11 08	11 24	11 42	11 45		11 58					11 38	11 54	12 12	12 15
	d	10 55								11 08	11 25									11 38	11 55		
Stone Crossing	d									11 12										11 42			
Greenhithe for Bluewater	d	11 00								11 15	11 30									11 45	12 00		
Swanscombe	d									11 18										11 48			
Northfleet	d									11 20										11 50			
Gravesend [4]	d	11 07							11 18	11a25	11 37								11 48	11a55	12 07		
Higham	d	11 13									11 43										12 13		
Strood [4]	d	11 18							11 28		11 48								11 58		12 18		
Rochester [4]	d	11 22							11 33		11 52								12 03		12 22		
Chatham [4]	d	11 25							11 35		11 55								12 05		12 25		
Gillingham (Kent) [4]	a	11 29							11 39		11 59								12 09		12 29		

London - Dartford and Gillingham

Station		SE	SE	SE	SE	SE		SE	SE	SE	SE	SE	SE	SE	SE	SE		SE	SE	SE	SE	SE	SE	SE	SE
St Pancras International ⊖	d							11 55											12 25						
Stratford International ⊖	d							12 02											12 36						
Ebbsfleet International	d							12 13											12 47						
London Charing Cross ⊖	d								11 26	11 39		12 02								11 56	12 09		12 32		
London Waterloo (East) ⊖	d								11 29	11 42		12 05								11 59	12 12		12 35		
London Cannon Street ⊖	d	11 37		11 40	11 47	11 54					11 57		12 07		12 10	12 17		12 24				12 27		12 37	
London Bridge ⊖	d	11 41		11 44	11 51	11 58			11 34	11 47	12 01	12 10	12 11		12 14	12 21		12 28		12 04	12 17	12 31	12 40	12 41	
Deptford	d	11 47			11 57						12 07		12 17			12 27						12 37		12 47	
Greenwich	d	11 49			11 59						12 09		12 19			12 29						12 39		12 49	
Maze Hill	d	11 52			12 02						12 12		12 22			12 32						12 42		12 52	
Westcombe Park	d	11 54			12 04						12 14		12 24			12 34						12 44		12 54	
London Victoria ⊖	d		11 39											12 09											12 39
Denmark Hill	d		11 48											12 18											12 48
Peckham Rye	d		11 51											12 21											12 51
Nunhead	d		11 53											12 23											12 53
New Cross ⊖	d			11 49		12 04									12 19			12 34							
St Johns	d			11 51											12 21										
Lewisham	d		12 02	11 54		12 08				11 56		12 19		12 32	12 24			12 38			12 26		12 49		13 02
Blackheath	d		12 05			12 11				11 59		12 23		12 35				12 41			12 29		12 53		13 05
Kidbrooke	d		12 08			12 14						12 26		12 38				12 44					12 56		13 08
Eltham	d		12 11			12 17						12 29		12 41				12 47					12 59		13 11
Falconwood	d		12 14			12 20						12 31		12 44				12 50					13 01		13 14
Welling	d		12 16			12 22						12 34		12 46				12 52					13 04		13 16
Bexleyheath	d		12 19			12 22						12 36		12 49				12 55					13 06		13 19
Barnehurst	d		12 21			12a27						12 39		12 51				12a57					13 09		13 21
Hither Green	d			11 59					11 44						12 29					12 14					
Lee	d			12 01					11 46						12 31					12 16					
Mottingham	d			12 04					11 49						12 34					12 19					
New Eltham	d			12 06					11 51						12 36					12 21					
Sidcup	d			12 10					11 55						12 40					12 25					
Albany Park	d			12 12					11 57						12 42					12 27					
Bexley	d			12 14					11 59						12 44					12 29					
Crayford	d			12 18					12 03						12 48					12 33					
Charlton	d	11 56		12 44	12 07					12 03	12 17		12 26		13 14	12 37					12 33	12 47		12 56	
Woolwich Dockyard	d	11 59			12 10						12 20		12 29			12 40						12 50		12 59	
Woolwich Arsenal	d	12 02			12 13					12 09	12 23		12 32			12 43					12 39	12 53		13 02	
Plumstead	d	12 04			12 15						12 25		12 34			12 45						12 55		13 04	
Abbey Wood	d	12 07			12 18					12 13	12 28		12 37			12 48					12 43	12 58		13 07	
Belvedere	d	12 10			12 21						12 31		12 40			12 51						13 01		13 10	
Erith	d	12 12			12 23						12 33		12 42			12 53						13 03		13 12	
Slade Green	d	12a15			12 27						12 37		12a45			12 57						13 07		13a15	
Dartford	a		12 28						12 08	12 24	12 42	12 45		12 58						12 38	12 54	13 12	13 15		13 28
	d								12 08	12 25										12 38	12 55				
Stone Crossing	d								12 12											12 42					
Greenhithe for Bluewater	d								12 15	12 30										12 45	13 00				
Swanscombe	d								12 18											12 48					
Northfleet	d								12 20											12 50					
Gravesend	d							12 18	12a25	12 37									12 51	12a55	13 07				
Higham	d									12 43											13 13				
Strood	d							12 28		12 48									13 01		13 18				
Rochester	d							12 33		12 52									13 06		13 22				
Chatham	d							12 35		12 55									13 08		13 25				
Gillingham (Kent)	a							12 39		12 59									13 12		13 29				

London - Dartford and Gillingham

Station		SE		SE	SE	SE	SE	SE	SE	SE	SE	SE		SE	SE	SE	SE	SE	SE	SE	SE	SE		SE	SE
St Pancras International ⊖	d				12 52												13 25								
Stratford International ⊖	d				12 58												13 32								
Ebbsfleet International	d				13 13												13 43								
London Charing Cross ⊖	d					12 26	12 39			13 02								12 56	13 09		13 32				
London Waterloo (East) ⊖	d					12 29	12 42			13 05								12 59	13 12		13 35				
London Cannon Street ⊖	d	12 40		12 47				12 54	12 57		13 07			13 10	13 17	13 24				13 27		13 37			13 40
London Bridge ⊖	d	12 44		12 51		12 34	12 47	12 58	13 01	13 10	13 11			13 14	13 21	13 28		13 04	13 17	13 31	13 40	13 41			13 44
Deptford	d			12 57					13 07		13 17				13 27					13 37		13 47			
Greenwich	d			12 59					13 09		13 19				13 29					13 39		13 49			
Maze Hill	d			13 02					13 12		13 22				13 32					13 42		13 52			
Westcombe Park	d			13 04					13 14		13 24				13 34					13 44		13 54			
London Victoria ⊖	d											13 09												13 39	
Denmark Hill	d											13 18												13 48	
Peckham Rye	d											13 21												13 51	
Nunhead	d											13 23												13 53	
New Cross ⊖	d	12 49						13 04						13 19		13 34									13 49
St Johns	d	12 51												13 21											13 51
Lewisham	d	12 54					12 56	13 08		13 19		13 32		13 24		13 38			13 26		13 49			14 02	13 54
Blackheath	d						12 59	13 11		13 23		13 35				13 41			13 29		13 53			14 05	
Kidbrooke	d							13 14		13 26		13 38				13 44					13 56			14 08	
Eltham	d							13 17		13 29		13 41				13 47					13 59			14 11	
Falconwood	d							13 20		13 31		13 44				13 50					14 01			14 14	
Welling	d							13 22		13 34		13 46				13 52					14 04			14 16	
Bexleyheath	d							13 25		13 36		13 49				13 55					14 06			14 19	
Barnehurst	d							13a27		13 39		13 51				13a57					14 09			14 21	
Hither Green	d	12 59				12 44								13 29				13 14							13 59
Lee	d	13 01				12 46								13 31				13 16							14 01
Mottingham	d	13 04				12 49								13 34				13 19							14 04
New Eltham	d	13 06				12 51								13 36				13 21							14 06
Sidcup	d	13 10				12 55								13 40				13 25							14 10
Albany Park	d	13 12				12 57								13 42				13 27							14 12
Bexley	d	13 14				12 59								13 44				13 29							14 14
Crayford	d	13 18				13 03								13 48				13 33							14 18
Charlton	d	13 44		13 07			13 03		13 17		13 26			14 14	13 37				13 33	13 47		13 56			14 44
Woolwich Dockyard	d			13 10					13 20		13 29				13 40					13 50		13 59			
Woolwich Arsenal	d			13 13			13 09		13 23		13 32				13 43				13 39	13 53		14 02			
Plumstead	d			13 15					13 25		13 34				13 45					13 55		14 04			
Abbey Wood	d			13 18			13 13		13 28		13 37				13 48				13 43	13 58		14 07			
Belvedere	d			13 21					13 31		13 40				13 51					14 01		14 10			
Erith	d			13 23					13 33		13 42				13 53					14 03		14 12			
Slade Green	d			13 27					13 37		13a45				13 57					14 07		14a15			
Dartford	a					13 08	13 24		13 42	13 45		13 58						13 38	13 54	14 12	14 15			14 28	
	d					13 08	13 25											13 38	13 55						
Stone Crossing	d					13 12												13 42							
Greenhithe for Bluewater	d					13 15	13 30											13 45	14 00						
Swanscombe	d					13 18												13 48							
Northfleet	d					13 20												13 50							
Gravesend	d				13 18	13a25	13 37										13 48	13a55	14 07						
Higham	d						13 43												14 13						
Strood	d				13 28		13 48										13 58		14 18						
Rochester	d				13 33		13 52										14 03		14 22						
Chatham	d				13 35		13 55										14 05		14 25						
Gillingham (Kent)	a				13 39		13 59										14 09		14 29						

Table 200

Mondays to Fridays

London - Dartford and Gillingham

		SE	SE	SE	SE	SE	SE	SE	SE	SE	SE	SE	SE	SE	SE	SE	SE	SE	SE	SE	SE	SE	SE
St Pancras International	d			13 55											14 28								
Stratford International	d			14 02											14 35								
Ebbsfleet International	d			14 13											14 46								
London Charing Cross	d				13 26	13 39		14 02								13 56	14 09	14 32					
London Waterloo (East)	d				13 29	13 42		14 05								13 59	14 12	14 35					
London Cannon Street	d	13 47	13 54				13 57		14 07		14 10	14 17	14 24	14 27					14 37		14 40	14 47	14 54
London Bridge	d	13 51	13 58		13 34	13 47	14 01	14 10	14 11		14 14	14 21	14 28	14 31		14 04	14 17	14 40	14 41		14 44	14 51	14 58
Deptford	d	13 57					14 07		14 17			14 27		14 37					14 47			14 57	
Greenwich	d	13 59					14 09		14 19			14 29		14 39					14 49			14 59	
Maze Hill	d	14 02					14 12		14 22			14 32		14 42					14 52			15 02	
Westcombe Park	d	14 04					14 14		14 24			14 34		14 44					14 54			15 04	
London Victoria	d									14 09										14 39			
Denmark Hill	d									14 18										14 48			
Peckham Rye	d									14 21										14 51			
Nunhead	d									14 23										14 53			
New Cross	d		14 04								14 19		14 34								14 49		15 04
St Johns	d										14 21										14 51		
Lewisham	d		14 08			13 56		14 19		14 32	14 24		14 38				14 26	14 49		15 02	14 54		15 08
Blackheath	d		14 11			13 59		14 23		14 35			14 41				14 29	14 53		15 05			15 11
Kidbrooke	d		14 14					14 26		14 38			14 44					14 56		15 08			15 14
Eltham	d		14 17					14 29		14 41			14 47					14 59		15 11			15 17
Falconwood	d		14 20					14 31		14 44			14 50					15 01		15 14			15 20
Welling	d		14 22					14 34		14 46			14 52					15 04		15 16			15 22
Bexleyheath	d		14 25					14 36		14 49			14 55					15 06		15 19			15 25
Barnehurst	d		14a27					14 39		14 51			14a57					15 09		15 21			15a27
Hither Green	d				13 44						14 29					14 14					14 59		
Lee	d				13 46						14 31					14 16					15 01		
Mottingham	d				13 49						14 34					14 19					15 04		
New Eltham	d				13 51						14 36					14 21					15 06		
Sidcup	d				13 55						14 40					14 25					15 10		
Albany Park	d				13 57						14 42					14 27					15 12		
Bexley	d				13 59						14 44					14 29					15 14		
Crayford	d				14 03						14 48					14 33					15 18		
Charlton	d	14 07				14 03	14 17		14 26		15 14	14 37		14 47			14 33		14 56		15 44	15 07	
Woolwich Dockyard	d	14 10					14 20		14 29			14 40		14 50					14 59			15 10	
Woolwich Arsenal	d	14 13				14 09	14 23		14 32			14 43		14 53			14 39		15 02			15 13	
Plumstead	d	14 15					14 25		14 34			14 45		14 55					15 04			15 15	
Abbey Wood	d	14 18				14 13	14 28		14 37			14 48		14 58			14 43		15 07			15 18	
Belvedere	d	14 21					14 31		14 40			14 51		15 01					15 10			15 21	
Erith	d	14 23					14 33		14 42			14 53		15 03					15 12			15 23	
Slade Green	d	14 27					14 37		14a45			14 57		15 07					15a15			15 27	
Dartford	a				14 08	14 24	14 42	14 45		14 58				15 12		14 38	14 54	15 15		15 28			
	d				14 08	14 25										14 38	14 55						
Stone Crossing	d				14 12											14 42							
Greenhithe for Bluewater	d				14 15	14 30										14 45	15 00						
Swanscombe	d				14 18											14 48							
Northfleet	d				14 20											14 50							
Gravesend	d			14 18	14a25	14 37									14 51	14a55	15 07						
Higham	d					14 43											15 13						
Strood	d			14 28		14 48									15 01		15 18						
Rochester	d			14 33		14 52									15 06		15 22						
Chatham	d			14 35		14 55									15 08		15 25						
Gillingham (Kent)	a			14 39		14 59									15 12		15 29						

Table 200

Mondays to Fridays

London - Dartford and Gillingham

		SE	SE	SE	SE	SE	SE	SE	SE	SE	SE	SE	SE	SE	SE	SE	SE	SE	SE	SE	SE	SE
St Pancras International	d	14 55											15 28									15 55
Stratford International	d	15 02											15 35									16 02
Ebbsfleet International	d	15 13											15 46									16 13
London Charing Cross	d		14 26	14 39		15 02								14 56	15 09	15 32						
London Waterloo (East)	d		14 29	14 42		15 05								14 59	15 12	15 35						
London Cannon Street	d				14 57		15 07		15 10	15 17	15 24	15 27					15 37		15 40	15 47	15 54	
London Bridge	d		14 34	14 47	15 01	15 10	15 11		15 14	15 21	15 28	15 31		15 04	15 17	15 40	15 41		15 44	15 51	15 58	
Deptford	d				15 07		15 17			15 27		15 37					15 47			15 57		
Greenwich	d				15 09		15 19			15 29		15 39					15 49			15 59		
Maze Hill	d				15 12		15 22			15 32		15 42					15 52			16 02		
Westcombe Park	d				15 14		15 24			15 34		15 44					15 54			16 04		
London Victoria	d							15 09										15 39				
Denmark Hill	d							15 18										15 48				
Peckham Rye	d							15 21										15 51				
Nunhead	d							15 23										15 53				
New Cross	d								15 19		15 34								15 49		16 04	
St Johns	d								15 21										15 51			
Lewisham	d			14 56		15 19		15 32	15 24		15 38				15 26	15 49		16 02	15 54		16 08	
Blackheath	d			14 59		15 23		15 35			15 41				15 29	15 53		16 05			16 11	
Kidbrooke	d					15 26		15 38			15 44					15 56		16 08			16 14	
Eltham	d					15 29		15 41			15 47					15 59		16 11			16 17	
Falconwood	d					15 31		15 44			15 50					16 01		16 14			16 20	
Welling	d					15 34		15 46			15 52					16 04		16 16			16 22	
Bexleyheath	d					15 36		15 49			15 55					16 06		16 19			16 25	
Barnehurst	d					15 39		15 51			15a57					16 09		16 21			16 30	
Hither Green	d		14 44						15 29					15 14					15 59			
Lee	d		14 46						15 31					15 16					16 01			
Mottingham	d		14 49						15 34					15 19					16 04			
New Eltham	d		14 51						15 36					15 21					16 06			
Sidcup	d		14 55						15 40					15 25					16 10			
Albany Park	d		14 57						15 42					15 27					16 12			
Bexley	d		14 59						15 44					15 29					16 14			
Crayford	d		15 03						15 48					15 33					16 18			
Charlton	d			15 03	15 17		15 26		16 14	15 37		15 47			15 33		15 56		16 44	16 07		
Woolwich Dockyard	d				15 20		15 29			15 40		15 50					15 59			16 10		
Woolwich Arsenal	d			15 09	15 23		15 32			15 43		15 53			15 39		16 02			16 13		
Plumstead	d				15 25		15 34			15 45		15 55					16 04			16 15		
Abbey Wood	d			15 13	15 28		15 37			15 48		15 58			15 43		16 07			16 18		
Belvedere	d				15 31		15 40			15 51		16 01					16 10			16 21		
Erith	d				15 33		15 42			15 53		16 03					16 12			16 23		
Slade Green	d				15 37		15a45			15 57		16 07					16a15			16 27		
Dartford	a		15 08	15 24	15 42	15 45		15 58				16 12		15 38	15 54	16 15		16 28			16 42	
	d		15 08	15 25										15 38	15 55							
Stone Crossing	d		15 12											15 42								
Greenhithe for Bluewater	d		15 15	15 30										15 45	16 00							
Swanscombe	d		15 18											15 48								
Northfleet	d		15 20											15 50								
Gravesend	d	15 18	15a25	15 37									15 51	15a55	16 07							16 18
Higham	d			15 43											16 13							
Strood	d	15 28		15 48									16 01		16 18							16 28
Rochester	d	15 33		15 52									16 06		16 22							16 33
Chatham	d	15 35		15 55									16 08		16 25							16 35
Gillingham (Kent)	a	15 39		15 59									16 12		16 29							16 39

Table 200

Mondays to Fridays

London - Dartford and Gillingham

		SE	SE	SE	SE	SE	SE	SE	SE	SE	SE	SE	SE	SE	SE	SE	SE	SE	SE	SE	SE	SE	SE
St Pancras International ⊖	d										16 25												
Stratford International ⊖	d										16 32												
Ebbsfleet International	d										16 43												
London Charing Cross ⊖	d	15 26	15 39		16 02							15 56	16 09		16 30					16 45	16 49	16 51	
London Waterloo (East) ⊖	d	15 29	15 42		16 05							15 59	16 12		16 33					16 48	16 52	16 54	
London Cannon Street ⊖	d			15 57		16 07		16 10	16 17	16 24				16 27		16 35		16 39	16 42				16 54
London Bridge ⊖	d	15 34	15 47	16 01	16 10	16 11		16 14	16 21	16 28		16 04	16 17	16 31	16 38	16 39		16 43	16 46	16 53	16 57	16 59	16 58
Deptford	d			16 07		16 17			16 27					16 37		16 45				16 59			17 04
Greenwich	d			16 09		16 20			16 30					16 40		16 48				17 02			17 07
Maze Hill	d			16 12		16 23			16 33					16 43		16 51				17 05			17 10
Westcombe Park	d			16 14		16 25			16 35					16 45		16 53				17 07			17 12
London Victoria ⊖	d						16 09										16 39						
Denmark Hill	d						16 18										16 48						
Peckham Rye	d						16 21										16 51						
Nunhead	d						16 23										16 53						
New Cross ⊖	d							16 20		16 34								16 49	16 52				
St Johns	d							16 22										16 51					
Lewisham	d		15 56		16 19		16 32	16 25		16 38			16 27		16 49		17 00	16 54	16 56			17 08	
Blackheath	d		15 59		16 23		16 35			16 41			16 29		16 53		17 03		16 59			17 11	
Kidbrooke	d				16 26		16 38			16 44					16 56		17 06		17 02			17 14	
Eltham	d				16 29		16 41			16 47					16 59		17 10		17 06			17 17	
Falconwood	d				16 32		16 44			16 50					17 02		17 12		17 08			17 20	
Welling	d				16 34		16 46			16 52					17 04		17 15		17 11			17 22	
Bexleyheath	d				16 37		16 49			16 55					17 07		17 17		17 13			17 25	
Barnehurst	d				16 39		16 51			16a57					17 09		17 22		17 17			17 27	
Hither Green	d	15 44						16 29				16 14						16 58			17 07		
Lee	d	15 46						16 31				16 16						17 00			17 09		
Mottingham	d	15 49						16 34				16 19						17 03			17 12		
New Eltham	d	15 51						16 37				16 21						17 06			17 15		
Sidcup	d	15 55						16 40				16 25						17 09			17a19		
Albany Park	d	15 57						16 42				16 27						17 11					
Bexley	d	15 59						16 45				16 29						17 14					
Crayford	d	16 03						16 48				16 33						17 17	17a28				
Charlton	d		16 03	16 17		16 27		17 14	16 37				16 34	16 47		16 55		17 44		17 09			17 14
Woolwich Dockyard	d			16 20		16 30			16 40					16 50		16 58				17 12			17 17
Woolwich Arsenal	d		16 09	16 23		16 33			16 43				16 39	16 53		17 01				17 15			17 20
Plumstead	d			16 25		16 35			16 45					16 55		17 03				17 17			17 22
Abbey Wood	d		16 13	16 28		16 38			16 48				16 43	16 58		17 06				17 20			17 25
Belvedere	d			16 31		16 41			16 51					17 01		17 09				17 23			17 28
Erith	d			16 33		16 43			16 53					17 03		17 11				17 25			17 30
Slade Green	d			16 37		16a47			16 57					17 07		17 15				17 28			17 34
Dartford	a	16 08	16 24	16 45	16 47		16 59					16 38	16 54	17 13	17 17	17 21	17 30					17 35	17 42
	d	16 08	16 25									16 38	16 55										
Stone Crossing	d	16 12										16 42											
Greenhithe for Bluewater	d	16 15	16 30									16 45	17 00										
Swanscombe	d	16 18										16 48											
Northfleet	d	16 20										16 50											
Gravesend	d	16a25	16 37								16 48	16a55	17 07										
Higham	d		16 43										17 13										
Strood	d		16 48								16 58		17 18										
Rochester	d		16 52								17 03		17 22										
Chatham	d		16 55								17 05		17 25										
Gillingham (Kent)	a		16 59								17 09		17 30										

Table 200

Mondays to Fridays

London - Dartford and Gillingham

		SE	SE	SE	SE	SE	SE	SE	SE	SE	SE	SE	SE	SE	SE	SE	SE	SE	SE	SE	SE	SE	SE
St Pancras International ⊖	d	16 58								17 14													
Stratford International ⊖	d	17 05								17 21													
Ebbsfleet International	d	17 16																					
London Charing Cross ⊖	d		16 26				17 06	17 10	17 12			16 55					17 29	17 30	17 32	17 34			
London Waterloo (East) ⊖	d		16 29				17 09	17 13	17 15			16 58					17 32	17 33	17 35	17 37			
London Cannon Street ⊖	d			16 58	17 04						16 44		17 06	17 16	17 21	17 26						17 39	17 43
London Bridge ⊖	d		16 34	17 02	17 08		17 14	17 19	17 21		16 48	17 04	17 10	17 20	17 25	17 30	17 37		17 41	17 43		17 43	17 47
Deptford	d						17 20							17 26			17 43					17 49	
Greenwich	d						17 23				16 56		17 18	17 29			17 46					17 52	
Maze Hill	d						17 26							17 32			17 49					17 55	
Westcombe Park	d						17 28							17 34			17 51					17 57	
London Victoria ⊖	d					17 04															17 34		
Denmark Hill	d					17 13															17 43		
Peckham Rye	d					17 16															17 46		
Nunhead	d					17 18															17 49		
New Cross ⊖	d			17 08	17 14										17 31	17 36							17 53
St Johns	d			17 10											17 33								17 55
Lewisham	d			17 13	17 19	17 25			17 30						17 36	17 40				17 53	17 56		17 59
Blackheath	d				17 23	17 28			17 33							17 43		17 49		17 56	18 00		
Kidbrooke	d				17 26	17 31			17 36							17 46		17 52		17 59	18 03		
Eltham	d				17 29	17 35			17 40							17 50		17 56		18 02	18 06		
Falconwood	d				17 32	17 37			17 42							17 52		17 58		18 05	18 09		
Welling	d				17 34	17 40			17 45							17 55		18 01		18 07	18 11		
Bexleyheath	d				17 37	17 42			17 47							17 57		18 03		18 10	18 14		
Barnehurst	d				17a40	17 45			17 50							18a01		18 06		18 13	18 16		
Hither Green	d		16 44	17 19				17 29							17 41				17 51				18 03
Lee	d		16 46	17 21				17 31							17 43				17 53				18 05
Mottingham	d		16 49	17 24				17 34							17 46				17 56				18 08
New Eltham	d		16 51	17 27				17 36				17 19			17 48				17 59				18 11
Sidcup	d		16 55	17 30				17a40				17 24			17 52				18a03				18 14
Albany Park	d		16 57	17 32								17 26			17 54								18 16
Bexley	d		16 59	17 35								17 28			17 56								18 19
Crayford	d		17 03	17 38								17 31			18a00								18 24
Charlton	d			18 04			17 30				17 02		17 24	17 36			17 53					17 59	
Woolwich Dockyard	d						17 33							17 39			17 56					18 02	
Woolwich Arsenal	d						17 36				17 07		17 29	17 42			17 59					18 05	
Plumstead	d						17 38							17 44			18 01					18 07	
Abbey Wood	d						17 41				17 11		17 33	17 47			18 04					18 10	
Belvedere	d						17 44							17 50			18 07					18 13	
Erith	d						17 46							17 52			18 09					18 15	
Slade Green	d						17a50							17 55			18a13			18a21		18 18	
Dartford	a		17 08			17 53			17 58		17 26	17 37	17 44	18 05				18 14			18 24	18 26	
	d		17 08								17 27	17 37	17 47										
Stone Crossing	d		17 12									17 41											
Greenhithe for Bluewater	d		17 15								17 32	17 43	17 52										
Swanscombe	d		17 18									17 46											
Northfleet	d		17 20									17 48											
Gravesend	d	17 21	17a26							17 36	17 40	17a56	18 00										
Higham	d										17 46		18 06										
Strood	d	17 31								17 46	17 51		18 12										
Rochester	d	17 36								17a52	17 55		18 17										
Chatham	d	17 38									17 58		18 19										
Gillingham (Kent)	a	17 42									18 03		18 24										

Table 200

Mondays to Fridays

London - Dartford and Gillingham

		SE		SE	SE	SE	SE	SE	SE	SE	SE	SE		SE	SE	SE	SE	SE	SE	SE	SE	SE		SE	SE
St Pancras International ⊖	d	17 44																	18 14						
Stratford International ⊖	d	17 51																	18 21						
Ebbsfleet International	d																								
London Charing Cross ⊖	d			17 17		17 39		17 50	17 52	17 54	17 56						18 12	18 14			18 01			18 18	
London Waterloo (East) ⊖	d			17 20		17 42		17 53	17 55	17 57	17 59						18 15	18 17			18 04			18 21	
London Cannon Street ⊖	d				17 28		17 47							18 00	18 05	18 10				17 50		18 12			
London Bridge ⊖	d			17 26	17 32	17 48	17 51	17 58		18 02	18 04			18 05	18 09	18 14	18 21	18 23		17 54	18 10	18 16		18 26	
Deptford	d							18 04						18 11			18 27								
Greenwich	d				17 40			18 07						18 14			18 29			18 02		18 24			
Maze Hill	d							18 10						18 17			18 32								
Westcombe Park	d							18 12						18 19			18 34								
London Victoria ⊖	d											17 56													18 18
Denmark Hill	d											18 06													18 28
Peckham Rye	d											18 09													18 32
Nunhead	d											18 11													18 34
New Cross ⊖	d						17 58								18 15	18 20									
St Johns	d														18 17										
Lewisham	d						18 02				18 13	18 19			18 20	18 24								18 35	18 43
Blackheath	d						18 05		18 10		18 16	18 23				18 27								18 38	18 46
Kidbrooke	d						18 08		18 13		18 19	18 26				18 30								18 41	18 49
Eltham	d						18 12		18 17		18 23	18 30				18 34								18 45	18 52
Falconwood	d						18 14		18 19		18 25	18 32				18 36								18 47	18 55
Welling	d						18 17		18 22		18 28	18 35				18 39								18 50	18 57
Bexleyheath	d						18 19		18 24		18 30	18 37				18 41								18 52	19 00
Barnehurst	d						18 24		18 27		18a34	18 41				18a45								18 55	19 02
Hither Green	d									18 12					18 25			18 35							
Lee	d									18 14					18 27			18 37							
Mottingham	d									18 17					18 30			18 40							
New Eltham	d			17 41		18 03				18 20					18 32			18 43			18 25				
Sidcup	d			17 46		18 07				18a24					18 36			18 46			18 29				
Albany Park	d			17 48		18 09									18 38			18 48			18 31				
Bexley	d			17 50		18 11									18 40			18 51			18 33				
Crayford	d			17 53		18 14	18a33								18 44			18 54			18 36				
Charlton	d				17 46			18 14						18 21	19 10		18 36			18 08		18 30			
Woolwich Dockyard	d							18 17						18 24			18 39								
Woolwich Arsenal	d				17 51			18 20						18 27			18 42			18 13		18 35			
Plumstead	d							18 22						18 29			18 44								
Abbey Wood	d				17 55			18 25						18 32			18 47			18 17		18 39			
Belvedere	d							18 28						18 35			18 50								
Erith	d							18 30						18 37			18 52								
Slade Green	d							18a34						18 40			18a56								
Dartford	a			17 58	18 06	18 19			18 35			18 52		18 47						18 28	18 41	18 52		19 03	19 12
	d			17 59	18 08	18 20														18 29	18 42	18 53			
Stone Crossing	d				18 12																18 46				
Greenhithe for Bluewater	d			18 04	18 14	18 25														18 34	18 48				
Swanscombe	d				18 17																18 51				
Northfleet	d				18 19																18 53				
Gravesend	d	18 06		18 11	18 24	18 32													18 36	18a41	18a58	19 03			
Higham	d			18 17	18 30																	19 09			
Strood	d	18 16		18 22	18a36	18 42													18 46			19 14			
Rochester	d	18 24		18 29		18 46													18 51			19 18			
Chatham	d	18 26		18 32		18 48													18 53			19 21			
Gillingham (Kent)	a	18 30		18 37		18 54													18 57			19 26			

Table 200

Mondays to Fridays

London - Dartford and Gillingham

		SE	SE	SE	SE	SE	SE	SE		SE	SE	SE	SE	SE	SE	SE	SE	SE		SE	SE	SE	SE	SE	SE
St Pancras International ⊖	d										18 55													19 25	
Stratford International ⊖	d										19 02													19 32	
Ebbsfleet International	d										19 13													19 44	
London Charing Cross ⊖	d			18 34	18 39							18 23		18 37	18 48		19 02								18 56
London Waterloo (East) ⊖	d			18 37	18 42							18 26		18 40	18 51		19 05								18 59
London Cannon Street ⊖	d	18 21	18 34				18 46	18 50		18 54			18 30			18 57		19 07			19 10	19 17	19 24		
London Bridge ⊖	d	18 25	18 38	18 42	18 48		18 50	18 54		18 58		18 32	18 34	18 46	18 57	19 01	19 10	19 11			19 14	19 21	19 28		19 04
Deptford	d	18 31		18 48			18 56									19 07		19 17				19 27			
Greenwich	d	18 34		18 51			18 59						18 42			19 10		19 19				19 29			
Maze Hill	d	18 37		18 54			19 02									19 13		19 22				19 32			
Westcombe Park	d	18 39		18 56			19 04									19 15		19 24				19 34			
London Victoria ⊖	d					18 39														19 09					
Denmark Hill	d					18 48														19 18					
Peckham Rye	d					18 51														19 22					
Nunhead	d					18 54														19 24					
New Cross ⊖	d		18 44		18 55			19 00		19 05											19 19		19 34		
St Johns	d							19 02													19 21				
Lewisham	d		18 49		18 59	19 03		19 05		19 09					19 07		19 19			19 33	19 24		19 38		
Blackheath	d		18 53		19 02	19 06				19 12					19 09		19 23			19 35			19 41		
Kidbrooke	d		18 56		19 05	19 09				19 15							19 26			19 38			19 44		
Eltham	d		19 00		19 08	19 12				19 18							19 29			19 41			19 47		
Falconwood	d		19 02		19 11	19 15				19 21							19 31			19 44			19 50		
Welling	d		19 05		19 13	19 17				19 23							19 34			19 46			19 52		
Bexleyheath	d		19 07		19 16	19 20				19 26							19 36			19 49			19 55		
Barnehurst	d		19a11		19a19	19 24				19a29							19 39			19 51			19a57		
Hither Green	d							19 09						18 56							19 29				19 14
Lee	d							19 11						18 58							19 31				19 16
Mottingham	d							19 14						19 01							19 34				19 19
New Eltham	d							19 17				18 48		19 03							19 36				19 22
Sidcup	d							19 20				18 51		19 07							19 40				19 25
Albany Park	d							19 22				18 53		19 09							19 42				19 27
Bexley	d							19 25				18 56		19 11							19 44				19 30
Crayford	d							19 28				18 59		19 14							19 48				19 33
Charlton	d	18 41		18 58			19 06						18 48		19 14	19 17		19 26				19 36			
Woolwich Dockyard	d	18 44		19 01			19 09									19 20		19 29				19 39			
Woolwich Arsenal	d	18 47		19 04			19 12						18 53		19 19	19 23		19 32				19 42			
Plumstead	d	18 49		19 06			19 14									19 25		19 34				19 44			
Abbey Wood	d	18 52		19 09			19 17						18 57		19 23	19 28		19 37				19 47			
Belvedere	d	18 55		19 12			19 19									19 31		19 40				19 50			
Erith	d	18 57		19 14			19 22									19 33		19 42				19 52			
Slade Green	d	19 01		19 17			19a25	19a40								19 37		19a45				19a55			
Dartford	a	19 08		19 23		19 32						19 04	19 09	19 21	19 34	19 43	19 45			19 59	19 53				19 38
	d											19 05	19 10	19 22	19 34										19 38
Stone Crossing	d											19 09	19 14	19 26											19 42
Greenhithe for Bluewater	d											19 11	19 16	19 28	19 39										19 45
Swanscombe	d											19 14	19 19	19 31											19 48
Northfleet	d											19 16	19 21	19 33											19 50
Gravesend	d										19 18	19a22	19 26	19 37	19 46									19 50	19a56
Higham	d												19 32	19 43	19 52										
Strood	d										19 28		19 37	19a49	19 57									20 01	
Rochester	d										19 33		19 43		20 02									20 06	
Chatham	d										19 35		19 46		20 05									20 09	
Gillingham (Kent)	a										19 39		19 50		20 10									20 13	

Table 200

Mondays to Fridays

London - Dartford and Gillingham

		SE	SE	SE		SE	SE	SE	SE	SE	SE	SE	SE	SE		SE	SE	SE	SE	SE	SE	SE	SE	SE
St Pancras International	d										19 55								20 25					
Stratford International	d										20 02								20 32					
Ebbsfleet International	d										20 13								20 43					
London Charing Cross	d	19 09		19 32								19 26	19 39			20 02				19 56	20 09		20 32	
London Waterloo (East)	d	19 12		19 35								19 29	19 42			20 05				19 59	20 12		20 35	
London Cannon Street	d		19 27			19 37		19 40	19 47	19 54				19 57			20 10	20 17				20 27		20 47
London Bridge	d	19 17	19 31	19 40		19 41		19 44	19 51	19 58		19 34	19 47	20 01		20 10	20 14	20 21		20 04	20 17	20 31	20 40	20 51
Deptford	d		19 37			19 47			19 57					20 07				20 27				20 39		20 57
Greenwich	d		19 39			19 49			19 59					20 09				20 29				20 41		20 59
Maze Hill	d		19 42			19 52			20 02					20 12				20 32				20 44		21 02
Westcombe Park	d		19 44			19 54			20 04					20 14				20 34				20 46		21 04
London Victoria	d						19 39																	
Denmark Hill	d						19 48																	
Peckham Rye	d						19 51																	
Nunhead	d						19 53																	
New Cross	d							19 49		20 04							20 19						20 45	
St Johns	d							19 51									20 21							
Lewisham	d	19 26		19 49			20 02	19 54		20 08			19 56			20 19	20 24				20 26		20 49	
Blackheath	d	19 29		19 53			20 05			20 11			19 59			20 23					20 29		20 53	
Kidbrooke	d			19 56			20 08			20 14						20 26							20 56	
Eltham	d			19 59			20 11			20 17						20 29							20 59	
Falconwood	d			20 01			20 14			20 20						20 31							21 01	
Welling	d			20 04			20 16			20 22						20 34							21 04	
Bexleyheath	d			20 06			20 19			20 25						20 36							21 06	
Barnehurst	d			20 09			20 21			20a27						20 39							21 09	
Hither Green	d							19 59				19 44					20 29			20 14				
Lee	d							20 01				19 46					20 31			20 16				
Mottingham	d							20 04				19 49					20 34			20 19				
New Eltham	d							20 06				19 51					20 36			20 21				
Sidcup	d							20 10				19 55					20 40			20 25				
Albany Park	d							20 12				19 57					20 42			20 27				
Bexley	d							20 14				19 59					20 44			20 29				
Crayford	d							20 18				20 03					20 48			20 33				
Charlton	d	19 33	19 47			19 56			20 06				20 03	20 17				20 37			20 33	20 48		21 07
Woolwich Dockyard	d		19 50			19 59			20 09					20 20				20 40				20 51		21 10
Woolwich Arsenal	d	19 38	19 53			20 02			20 12				20 09	20 23				20 43			20 39	20 54		21 13
Plumstead	d		19 55			20 04			20 14					20 25				20 45				20 56		21 15
Abbey Wood	d	19 43	19 58			20 07			20 17				20 13	20 28				20 48			20 43	21 00		21 18
Belvedere	d		20 01			20 10			20 20					20 31				20 51				21 02		21 21
Erith	d		20 03			20 12			20 22					20 33				20 53				21 05		21 23
Slade Green	d		20 07			20a15			20a25					20 37				20 57				21 08		21 27
Dartford	a	19 54	20 13	20 15			20 28	20 23				20 08	20 24	20 43		20 45	20 53	21 02		20 38	20 54	21 12	21 15	21 32
	d	19 55										20 08	20 25							20 38	20 55			
Stone Crossing	d											20 12								20 42				
Greenhithe for Bluewater	d	20 00										20 15	20 30							20 45	21 00			
Swanscombe	d											20 18								20 48				
Northfleet	d											20 20								20 50				
Gravesend	d	20 07									20 18	20a25	20 37						20 48	20a55	21 07			
Higham	d	20 13											20 43								21 13			
Strood	d	20 18									20 28		20 48						20 58		21 18			
Rochester	d	20 22									20 33		20 52						21 03		21 22			
Chatham	d	20 25									20 35		20 55						21 05		21 25			
Gillingham (Kent)	a	20 29									20 39		20 59						21 09		21 29			

Table 200

Mondays to Fridays

London - Dartford and Gillingham

		SE	SE	SE	SE	SE	SE	SE	SE	SE		SE	SE	SE	SE	SE	SE	SE	SE	SE		SE	SE	SE	SE
St Pancras International	d	20 55						21 25							21 55							22 25			
Stratford International	d	21 02						21 32							22 02							22 32			
Ebbsfleet International	d	21 13						21 43							22 13							22 43			
London Charing Cross	d		20 22	20 39		21 02			20 52	21 09		21 26	21 32			21 22	21 39	21 56	22 02				21 52	22 09	22 26
London Waterloo (East)	d		20 25	20 42		21 05			20 55	21 12		21 29	21 35			21 25	21 42	21 59	22 05				21 55	22 12	22 29
London Cannon Street	d				20 57																				
London Bridge	d		20 30	20 47	21 01	21 10	21 20		21 00	21 17		21 34	21 40	21 50		21 30	21 47	22 04	22 10	22 20			22 00	22 17	22 34
Deptford	d				21 08		21 26					21 40		21 56				22 10		22 26					22 40
Greenwich	d				21 10		21 28					21 42		21 58				22 12		22 28					22 42
Maze Hill	d				21 13		21 31					21 45		22 01				22 15		22 31					22 45
Westcombe Park	d				21 15		21 33					21 47		22 03				22 17		22 33					22 47
London Victoria	d																								
Denmark Hill	d																								
Peckham Rye	d																								
Nunhead	d																								
New Cross	d		20 35			21 15			21 05				21 45			21 35			22 15				22 05		
St Johns	d																								
Lewisham	d		20 39	20 56		21 19			21 09	21 26			21 49			21 39	21 56		22 19				22 09	22 26	
Blackheath	d			20 59		21 23				21 29			21 53				21 59		22 23					22 29	
Kidbrooke	d					21 26							21 56						22 26						
Eltham	d					21 29							21 59						22 29						
Falconwood	d					21 31							22 01						22 31						
Welling	d					21 34							22 04						22 34						
Bexleyheath	d					21 36							22 06						22 36						
Barnehurst	d					21 39							22 09						22 39						
Hither Green	d		20 44						21 14							21 44							22 14		
Lee	d		20 46						21 16							21 46							22 16		
Mottingham	d		20 49						21 19							21 49							22 19		
New Eltham	d		20 51						21 21							21 51							22 21		
Sidcup	d		20 55						21 25							21 55							22 25		
Albany Park	d		20 57						21 27							21 57							22 27		
Bexley	d		20 59						21 29							21 59							22 29		
Crayford	d		21 03						21 33							22 03							22 33		
Charlton	d			21 03	21 17		21 36			21 33		21 50		22 06			22 03	22 20		22 36				22 33	22 50
Woolwich Dockyard	d				21 20		21 39					21 53		22 09				22 23		22 39					22 53
Woolwich Arsenal	d			21 09	21 23		21 42			21 39		21 56		22 12			22 09	22 26		22 42				22 39	22 56
Plumstead	d				21 25		21 44					21 58		22 14				22 28		22 44					22 58
Abbey Wood	d			21 13	21 29		21 48			21 43		22 01		22 18			22 13	22 31		22 48				22 43	23 01
Belvedere	d				21 31		21 50					22 04		22 20				22 34		22 50					23 04
Erith	d				21 34		21 53					22 06		22 23				22 36		22 53					23 06
Slade Green	d				21 37		21 56					22 09		22 26				22 39		22 56					23 09
Dartford	a		21 08	21 24	21 42	21 45	22 00		21 38	21 54		22 14	22 16	22 30		22 08	22 24	22 44	22 46	23 00			22 38	22 54	23 14
	d		21 08	21 25					21 38	21 55						22 08	22 25						22 38	22 55	
Stone Crossing	d		21 12						21 42							22 12							22 42		
Greenhithe for Bluewater	d		21 15	21 30					21 45	22 00						22 15	22 30						22 45	23 00	
Swanscombe	d		21 18						21 48							22 18							22 48		
Northfleet	d		21 20						21 50							22 20							22 50		
Gravesend	d	21 18	21a25	21 37				21 48	21a55	22 07					22 18	22a25	22 37					22 48	22a55	23 07	
Higham	d			21 43						22 13							22 43							23 13	
Strood	d	21 28		21 48				21 58		22 18					22 28		22 48					22 58		23 18	
Rochester	d	21 33		21 52				22 03		22 22					22 33		22 52					23 03		23 22	
Chatham	d	21 35		21 55				22 05		22 25					22 35		22 55					23 05		23 25	
Gillingham (Kent)	a	21 39		21 59				22 09		22 29					22 39		22 59					23 09		23 29	

Table 200

Mondays to Fridays

London - Dartford and Gillingham

		SE	SE	SE	SE	SE	SE	SE	SE	SE	SE	SE	SE	SE	SE	SE	SE
St Pancras International	d				22 55						23 25				23 55		
Stratford International	d				23 02						23 32				00 02		
Ebbsfleet International	d				23 13						23 43				00 13		
London Charing Cross	d	22 32		22 52		22 22	22 39	22 56	23 02	23 22		23 09	23 26	23 32		23 39	23 56
London Waterloo (East)	d	22 35		22 55		22 25	22 42	22 59	23 05	23 25		23 12	23 29	23 35		23 42	23 59
London Cannon Street	d																
London Bridge	d	22 40	22 50	23 00		22 30	22 47	23 04	23 10	23 30		23 17	23 34	23 40		23 47	00 04
Deptford	d		22 56					23 10					23 40				00 10
Greenwich	d		22 58					23 12					23 42				00 12
Maze Hill	d		23 01					23 15					23 45				00 15
Westcombe Park	d		23 03					23 17					23 47				00 17
London Victoria	d																
Denmark Hill	d																
Peckham Rye	d																
Nunhead	d																
New Cross	d	22 45		23 05		22 35			23 15	23 35				23 45			
St Johns	d																
Lewisham	d	22 49		23 09		22 39	22 56		23 19	23 39		23 26		23 49		23 56	
Blackheath	d	22 53					22 59		23 23			23 29		23 53		23 59	
Kidbrooke	d	22 56							23 26					23 56			
Eltham	d	22 59							23 29					23 59			
Falconwood	d	23 01							23 31					00 01			
Welling	d	23 04							23 34					00 04			
Bexleyheath	d	23 06							23 36					00 06			
Barnehurst	d	23 09							23 39					00 09			
Hither Green	d			23 14		22 44				23 44							
Lee	d			23 16		22 46				23 46							
Mottingham	d			23 19		22 49				23 49							
New Eltham	d			23 21		22 51				23 51							
Sidcup	d			23 25		22 55				23 55							
Albany Park	d			23 27		22 57				23 57							
Bexley	d			23 29		22 59				23 59							
Crayford	d			23 33		23 03				00 03							
Charlton	d		23 06				23 03	23 20				23 33	23 50			00 03	00 20
Woolwich Dockyard	d		23 09					23 23					23 53				00 23
Woolwich Arsenal	d		23 12				23 09	23 26				23 39	23 56			00 09	00 26
Plumstead	d		23 14					23 28					23 58				00 28
Abbey Wood	d		23 18				23 13	23 31				23 43	00 01			00 13	00 31
Belvedere	d		23 20					23 34					00 04				00 34
Erith	d		23 23					23 36					00 06				00 36
Slade Green	d		23 26					23 39					00 09				00 39
Dartford	a	23 16	23 30	23 38		23 08	23 24	23 44	23 46	00 08		23 54	00 14	00 16		00 24	00 44
	d					23 08	23 25					23 55				00 25	
Stone Crossing	d					23 12	23 29					23 59				00 29	
Greenhithe for Bluewater	d					23 15	23 31					00 02				00 31	
Swanscombe	d					23 18	23 34					00 05				00 34	
Northfleet	d					23 20	23 36					00 07				00 36	
Gravesend	d				23 18	23a25	23 40				23 48	00 10			00 18	00 40	
Higham	d						23 46					00 16				00 46	
Strood	d				23 28		23 52				23 58	00 22			00 28	00 52	
Rochester	d				23 33		23 56				00 03	00 26			00 33	00 56	
Chatham	d				23 35		23 58				00 06	00 28			00 35	00 58	
Gillingham (Kent)	a				23 39		00 03				00 10	00 33			00 39	01 03	

Table 200

Saturdays

London - Dartford and Gillingham

		SE	SE	SE	SE	SE	SE	SE	SE	SE	SE	SE	SE	SE	SE	SE	SE	SE	SE	SE	SE	SE	SE
St Pancras International	d			23p25				23p55															
Stratford International	d			23p32				00 02															
Ebbsfleet International	d			23p43				00 13															
London Charing Cross	d	22p39	23p22		23p09	23p26	23p32		23p39	23p56	00 02	00 05	00 15	04 52	05 26	05 32		05 22	05 39	05 52	05 56	06 02	06 09
London Waterloo (East)	d	22p42	23p25		23p12	23p29	23p35		23p42	23p59	00 05	00 08	00 18	04 55	05 29	05 35		05 25	05 42	05 55	05 59	06 05	06 12
London Cannon Street	d																						
London Bridge	d	22p47	23p30		23p17	23p34	23p40		23p47	00 04	00 10	00 13	00 23	05 00	05 34	05 40		05 30	05 47	06 00	06 04	06 10	06 17
Deptford	d					23p40				00 10					05 40						06 10		
Greenwich	d					23p42				00 12					05 42						06 12		
Maze Hill	d					23p45				00 15					05 45						06 15		
Westcombe Park	d					23p47				00 17					05 47						06 17		
London Victoria	d																						
Denmark Hill	d																						
Peckham Rye	d																						
Nunhead	d																						
New Cross	d		23p35				23p45				00 15	00 18	00 28	05 05		05 45		05 35		06 05		06 15	
St Johns	d																						
Lewisham	d	22p56	23p39		23p26		23p49		23p56		00 19	00 22	00 33	05 09		05 49		05 39	05 56	06 09		06 19	06 26
Blackheath	d	22p59			23p29		23p53		23p59		00 23		00 35			05 53			05 59			06 23	06 29
Kidbrooke	d						23p56				00 26					05 56						06 26	
Eltham	d						23p59				00 29					05 59						06 29	
Falconwood	d						00 01				00 31					06 01						06 31	
Welling	d						00 04				00 34					06 04						06 34	
Bexleyheath	d						00 06				00 36					06 06						06 36	
Barnehurst	d						00 09				00 39					06 09						06 39	
Hither Green	d		23p44									00 27		05 14				05 44		06 14			
Lee	d		23p46									00 29		05 16				05 46		06 16			
Mottingham	d		23p49									00 32		05 19				05 49		06 19			
New Eltham	d		23p51									00 34		05 21				05 51		06 21			
Sidcup	d		23p55									00 38		05 25				05 55		06 25			
Albany Park	d		23p57									00 40		05 27				05 57		06 27			
Bexley	d		23p59									00 42		05 29				05 59		06 29			
Crayford	d		00 03									00 46		05 33				06 03		06 33			
Charlton	d	23p03			23p33	23p50			00 03	00 20			00 40		05 50				06 03		06 20		06 33
Woolwich Dockyard	d					23p53				00 23					05 53						06 23		
Woolwich Arsenal	d	23p09			23p39	23p56			00 09	00 26			00 45		05 56				06 09		06 26		06 39
Plumstead	d					23p58				00 28			00 47		05 58						06 28		
Abbey Wood	d	23p13			23p43	00 01			00 13	00 31			00 50		06 01				06 13		06 31		06 43
Belvedere	d					00 04				00 34			00 53		06 04						06 34		
Erith	d					00 06				00 36			00 55		06 06						06 36		
Slade Green	d					00 09				00 39			00 58		06 09						06 39		
Dartford	a	23p24	00 08		23p54	00 14	00 16		00 24	00 44	00 46	00 51	01 03	05 38	06 14	06 16		06 08	06 24	06 38	06 44	06 46	06 54
	d	23p25			23p55				00 25				01 03	05 38			05 55	06 08	06 25	06 38			06 55
Stone Crossing	d	23p29			23p59				00 29					05 42				06 12		06 42			
Greenhithe for Bluewater	d	23p31			00 02				00 31				01 08	05 45			06 00	06 15	06 30	06 45			07 00
Swanscombe	d	23p34			00 05				00 34					05 48				06 18		06 48			
Northfleet	d	23p36			00 07				00 36					05 50				06 20		06 50			
Gravesend	d	23p40		23p48	00 10			00 18	00 40				01 15	05a55			06 07	06a25	06 37	06a55			07 07
Higham	d	23p46			00 16				00 46				01 21				06 13		06 43				07 13
Strood	d	23p52		23p58	00 22			00 28	00 52				01 26				06 18		06 48				07 18
Rochester	d	23p56		00 03	00 26			00 33	00 56				01 32				06 22		06 52				07 22
Chatham	d	23p58		00 06	00 28			00 35	00 58				01 35				06 25		06 55				07 25
Gillingham (Kent)	a	00 03		00 10	00 33			00 39	01 03				01 41				06 29		06 59				07 29

Table 200

Saturdays

London - Dartford and Gillingham

	SE	SE		SE	SE		SE	SE	SE	SE	SE	SE	SE	SE	SE		SE	SE	SE	SE	SE	SE	SE	SE
St Pancras International d									07 22															
Stratford International d									07 28															
Ebbsfleet International d									07 43															
London Charing Cross d	06 26	06 32		06 22	06 39		06 56	07 02		06 52	07 09	07 22	07 26	07 32			07 39	07 52	07 56	08 02			08 09	
London Waterloo (East) d	06 29	06 35		06 25	06 42		06 59	07 05		06 55	07 12	07 25	07 29	07 35			07 42	07 55	07 59	08 05			08 12	
London Cannon Street d																					08 05			08 10
London Bridge d	06 34	06 40		06 30	06 47		07 04	07 10		07 00	07 17	07 30	07 34	07 40			07 47	08 00	08 04	08 10	08 11		08 17	08 14
Deptford d	06 40						07 10						07 40						08 10		08 17			
Greenwich d	06 42						07 12						07 42						08 13		08 19			
Maze Hill d	06 45						07 15						07 45						08 16		08 22			
Westcombe Park d	06 47						07 17						07 47						08 18		08 24			
London Victoria d															07 39							08 09		
Denmark Hill d															07 48							08 18		
Peckham Rye d															07 51							08 21		
Nunhead d															07 53							08 23		
New Cross d		06 45		06 35				07 15		07 05		07 35		07 45				08 05		08 15				08 19
St Johns d																								08 21
Lewisham d		06 49		06 39	06 56			07 19		07 09	07 26	07 39		07 49	08 02		07 56	08 09		08 19		08 32	08 26	08 24
Blackheath d		06 53			06 59			07 23			07 29			07 53	08 05		07 59			08 23		08 35	08 29	
Kidbrooke d		06 56						07 26						07 56	08 08					08 26		08 38		
Eltham d		06 59						07 29						07 59	08 11					08 29		08 41		
Falconwood d		07 01						07 31						08 01	08 14					08 31		08 44		
Welling d		07 04						07 34						08 04	08 16					08 34		08 46		
Bexleyheath d		07 06						07 36						08 06	08 19					08 36		08 49		
Barnehurst d		07 09						07 39						08 09	08 21					08 39		08 51		
Hither Green d				06 44						07 14		07 44						08 14						08 29
Lee d				06 46						07 16		07 46						08 16						08 31
Mottingham d				06 49						07 19		07 49						08 19						08 34
New Eltham d				06 51						07 21		07 51						08 21						08 36
Sidcup d				06 55						07 25		07 55						08 25						08 40
Albany Park d				06 57						07 27		07 57						08 27						08 42
Bexley d				06 59						07 29		07 59						08 29						08 44
Crayford d				07 03						07 33		08 03						08 33						08 48
Charlton d	06 50				07 03		07 20				07 33		07 50				08 03		08 20		08 26		08 33	09 14
Woolwich Dockyard d	06 53						07 23						07 53						08 23		08 29			
Woolwich Arsenal d	06 56				07 09		07 26				07 39		07 56				08 09		08 26		08 32		08 39	
Plumstead d	06 58						07 28						07 58						08 28		08 34			
Abbey Wood d	07 01				07 13		07 31				07 43		08 01				08 13		08 31		08 37		08 43	
Belvedere d	07 04						07 34						08 04						08 34		08 40			
Erith d	07 06						07 36						08 06						08 36		08 42			
Slade Green d	07 09						07 39						08 09						08 39		08a45			
Dartford a	07 14	07 16		07 08	07 24		07 44	07 46		07 38	07 54	08 08	08 14	08 16	08 29		08 24	08 38	08 44	08 46		08 58	08 54	
d				07 08	07 25					07 38	07 55	08 08					08 25	08 38					08 55	
Stone Crossing d				07 12						07 42		08 12						08 42						
Greenhithe for Bluewater d				07 15	07 30					07 45	08 00	08 15					08 30	08 45					09 00	
Swanscombe d				07 18						07 48		08 18						08 48						
Northfleet d				07 20						07 50		08 20						08 50						
Gravesend d				07a25	07 37				07 48	07a55	08 07	08a25					08 37	08a55					09 07	
Higham d					07 43						08 13						08 43						09 13	
Strood d					07 48				07 58		08 18						08 48						09 18	
Rochester d					07 52				08 03		08 22						08 52						09 22	
Chatham d					07 55				08 05		08 25						08 55						09 25	
Gillingham (Kent) a					07 59				08 09		08 29						08 59						09 29	

b arr. 0656

Table 200

Saturdays

London - Dartford and Gillingham

	SE		SE	SE	SE	SE	SE	SE	SE	SE	SE		SE	SE	SE	SE	SE	SE	SE	SE	SE		SE	SE
St Pancras International d										08 52														09 28
Stratford International d										08 58														09 35
Ebbsfleet International d										09 13														09 46
London Charing Cross d					08 32						08 26		08 39			09 02								
London Waterloo (East) d					08 35						08 29		08 42			09 05								
London Cannon Street d	08 15		08 25			08 35		08 40	08 45					08 55			09 05		09 10	09 15	09 25			
London Bridge d	08 21		08 31	08 28	08 40	08 41		08 44	08 51		08 34		08 47	09 01	08 58	09 10	09 11		09 14	09 21	09 31		09 28	
Deptford d	08 27		08 37			08 47			08 57					09 07			09 17			09 27	09 37			
Greenwich d	08 29		08 39			08 49			08 59					09 09			09 19			09 29	09 39			
Maze Hill d	08 32		08 42			08 52			09 02					09 12			09 22			09 32	09 42			
Westcombe Park d	08 34		08 44			08 54			09 04					09 14			09 24			09 34	09 44			
London Victoria d							08 39											09 09						
Denmark Hill d							08 48											09 18						
Peckham Rye d							08 51											09 21						
Nunhead d							08 53											09 23						
New Cross d				08 34				08 49							09 04				09 19				09 34	
St Johns d								08 51											09 21					
Lewisham d				08 38	08 49		09 02	08 54					08 56		09 08	09 19		09 32	09 24				09 38	
Blackheath d				08 41	08 53		09 05						08 59		09 11	09 23		09 35					09 41	
Kidbrooke d				08 44	08 56		09 08								09 14	09 26		09 38					09 44	
Eltham d				08 47	08 59		09 11								09 17	09 29		09 41					09 47	
Falconwood d				08 50	09 01		09 14								09 20	09 31		09 44					09 50	
Welling d				08 52	09 04		09 16								09 22	09 34		09 46					09 52	
Bexleyheath d				08 55	09 06		09 19								09 25	09 36		09 49					09 55	
Barnehurst d				08a57	09 09		09 21								09a27	09 39		09 51					09a57	
Hither Green d								08 59			08 44								09 29					
Lee d								09 01			08 46								09 31					
Mottingham d								09 04			08 49								09 34					
New Eltham d								09 06			08 51								09 36					
Sidcup d								09 10			08 55								09 40					
Albany Park d								09 12			08 57								09 42					
Bexley d								09 14			08 59								09 44					
Crayford d								09 18			09 03								09 48					
Charlton d	08 37		08 47			08 56		09 44	09 07				09 03	09 17			09 26		10 14	09 37	09 47			
Woolwich Dockyard d	08 40		08 50			08 59			09 10					09 20			09 29			09 40	09 50			
Woolwich Arsenal d	08 43		08 53			09 02			09 13				09 09	09 23			09 32			09 43	09 53			
Plumstead d	08 45		08 55			09 04			09 15					09 25			09 34			09 45	09 55			
Abbey Wood d	08 48		08 58			09 07			09 18				09 13	09 28			09 37			09 48	09 58			
Belvedere d	08 51		09 01			09 10			09 21					09 31			09 40			09 51	10 01			
Erith d	08 53		09 03			09 12			09 23					09 33			09 42			09 53	10 03			
Slade Green d	08 57		09 07			09a15			09 27					09 37			09a45			09 57	10 07			
Dartford a			09 12		09 15		09 28				09 08		09 24	09 42		09 45		09 58			10 12			
d											09 08		09 25											
Stone Crossing d											09 12													
Greenhithe for Bluewater d											09 15		09 30											
Swanscombe d											09 18													
Northfleet d											09 20													
Gravesend d										09 18	09a25		09 37											09 51
Higham d													09 43											
Strood d										09 28			09 48											10 01
Rochester d										09 33			09 52											10 06
Chatham d										09 35			09 55											10 08
Gillingham (Kent) a										09 39			09 59											10 12

Table 200

Saturdays

London - Dartford and Gillingham

Station		SE	SE	SE	SE	SE	SE	SE	SE	SE	SE	SE	SE	SE	SE	SE	SE	SE	SE	SE	SE	SE	SE
St Pancras International	d									09 55											10 28		
Stratford International	d									10 02											10 35		
Ebbsfleet International	d									10 13											10 46		
London Charing Cross	d	08 56	09 09	09 32							09 26	09 39		10 02								09 56	10 09
London Waterloo (East)	d	08 59	09 12	09 35							09 29	09 42		10 05								09 59	10 12
London Cannon Street	d				09 35		09 40	09 45	09 55						10 05		10 10	10 15	10 25				
London Bridge	d	09 04	09 17	09 40	09 41		09 44	09 51	10 01		09 34	09 47	09 58	10 10	10 11		10 14	10 21	10 31	10 28		10 04	10 17
Deptford	d				09 47			09 57	10 07						10 17			10 27	10 37				
Greenwich	d				09 49			09 59	10 09						10 19			10 29	10 39				
Maze Hill	d				09 52			10 02	10 12						10 22			10 32	10 42				
Westcombe Park	d				09 54			10 04	10 14						10 24			10 34	10 44				
London Victoria	d					09 39										10 09							
Denmark Hill	d					09 48										10 18							
Peckham Rye	d					09 51										10 21							
Nunhead	d					09 53										10 23							
New Cross	d						09 49						10 04				10 19			10 34			
St Johns	d						09 51										10 21						
Lewisham	d		09 26	09 49		10 02	09 54					09 56	10 08	10 19		10 33	10 24			10 38			10 26
Blackheath	d		09 29	09 53		10 05						09 59	10 11	10 23		10 35				10 41			10 29
Kidbrooke	d			09 56		10 08							10 14	10 26		10 38				10 44			
Eltham	d			09 59		10 11							10 17	10 29		10 41				10 47			
Falconwood	d			10 01		10 14							10 20	10 31		10 44				10 50			
Welling	d			10 04		10 16							10 22	10 34		10 46				10 52			
Bexleyheath	d			10 06		10 19							10 25	10 36		10 49				10 55			
Barnehurst	d			10 09		10 21							10a27	10 39		10 51				10a57			
Hither Green	d	09 14					09 59				09 44						10 29					10 14	
Lee	d	09 16					10 01				09 46						10 31					10 16	
Mottingham	d	09 19					10 04				09 49						10 34					10 19	
New Eltham	d	09 21					10 06				09 51						10 36					10 21	
Sidcup	d	09 25					10 10				09 55						10 40					10 25	
Albany Park	d	09 27					10 12				09 57						10 42					10 27	
Bexley	d	09 29					10 14				09 59						10 44					10 29	
Crayford	d	09 33					10 18				10 03						10 48					10 33	
Charlton	d		09 33		09 56		10 44	10 07	10 17			10 03			10 26		11 14	10 37	10 47				10 33
Woolwich Dockyard	d				09 59			10 10	10 20						10 29			10 40	10 50				
Woolwich Arsenal	d		09 39		10 02			10 13	10 23			10 09			10 32			10 43	10 53				10 39
Plumstead	d				10 04			10 15	10 25						10 34			10 45	10 55				
Abbey Wood	d		09 43		10 07			10 18	10 28			10 13			10 37			10 48	10 58				10 43
Belvedere	d				10 10			10 21	10 31						10 40			10 51	11 01				
Erith	d				10 12			10 23	10 33						10 42			10 53	11 03				
Slade Green	d				10a15			10 27	10 37						10a45			10 57	11 07				
Dartford	a	09 38	09 54	10 15		10 28			10 42		10 08	10 24		10 45		10 58			11 12			10 38	10 54
	d	09 38	09 55								10 08	10 25										10 38	10 55
Stone Crossing	d	09 42									10 12											10 42	
Greenhithe for Bluewater	d	09 45	10 00								10 15	10 30										10 45	11 00
Swanscombe	d	09 48									10 18											10 48	
Northfleet	d	09 50									10 20											10 50	
Gravesend	d	09a55	10 07							10 18	10a25	10 37									10 51	10a55	11 07
Higham	d		10 13									10 43											11 13
Strood	d		10 18							10 28		10 48									11 01		11 18
Rochester	d		10 22							10 33		10 52									11 06		11 22
Chatham	d		10 25							10 35		10 55									11 08		11 25
Gillingham (Kent)	a		10 29							10 39		10 59									11 12		11 29

Table 200

Saturdays

London - Dartford and Gillingham

Station		SE	SE	SE	SE	SE	SE	SE	SE	SE	SE	SE	SE	SE	SE	SE	SE	SE	SE	SE	SE	SE
St Pancras International	d						10 52											11 25				
Stratford International	d						10 58											11 32				
Ebbsfleet International	d						11 13											11 43				
London Charing Cross	d	10 32						10 26	10 39			11 02							10 56	11 09		11 32
London Waterloo (East)	d	10 35						10 29	10 42			11 05							10 59	11 12		11 35
London Cannon Street	d		10 35		10 40	10 45				10 55			11 05		11 10	11 15	11 25					
London Bridge	d	10 40	10 41		10 44	10 51		10 34	10 47	11 01	10 58	11 10	11 11		11 14	11 21	11 31		11 04	11 17	11 28	11 40
Deptford	d		10 47			10 57				11 07			11 17			11 27	11 37					
Greenwich	d		10 49			10 59				11 09			11 19			11 29	11 39					
Maze Hill	d		10 52			11 02				11 12			11 22			11 32	11 42					
Westcombe Park	d		10 54			11 04				11 14			11 24			11 34	11 44					
London Victoria	d			10 39										11 09								
Denmark Hill	d			10 48										11 18								
Peckham Rye	d			10 51										11 21								
Nunhead	d			10 53										11 23								
New Cross	d				10 49						11 04				11 19						11 34	
St Johns	d				10 51										11 21							
Lewisham	d	10 49		11 02	10 54				10 56		11 08	11 19		11 32	11 24					11 26	11 38	11 49
Blackheath	d	10 53		11 05					10 59		11 11	11 23		11 35						11 29	11 41	11 53
Kidbrooke	d	10 56		11 08							11 14	11 26		11 38							11 44	11 56
Eltham	d	10 59		11 11							11 17	11 29		11 41							11 47	11 59
Falconwood	d	11 01		11 14							11 20	11 31		11 44							11 50	12 01
Welling	d	11 04		11 16							11 22	11 34		11 46							11 52	12 04
Bexleyheath	d	11 06		11 19							11 25	11 36		11 49							11 55	12 06
Barnehurst	d	11 09		11 21							11a27	11 39		11 51							11a57	12 09
Hither Green	d				10 59			10 44							11 29				11 14			
Lee	d				11 01			10 46							11 31				11 16			
Mottingham	d				11 04			10 49							11 34				11 19			
New Eltham	d				11 06			10 51							11 36				11 21			
Sidcup	d				11 10			10 55							11 40				11 25			
Albany Park	d				11 12			10 57							11 42				11 27			
Bexley	d				11 14			10 59							11 44				11 29			
Crayford	d				11 18			11 03							11 48				11 33			
Charlton	d		10 56		11 44	11 07			11 03	11 17			11 26		12 14	11 37	11 47			11 33		
Woolwich Dockyard	d		10 59			11 10				11 20			11 29			11 40	11 50					
Woolwich Arsenal	d		11 02			11 13			11 09	11 23			11 32			11 43	11 53			11 39		
Plumstead	d		11 04			11 15				11 25			11 34			11 45	11 55					
Abbey Wood	d		11 07			11 18			11 13	11 28			11 37			11 48	11 58			11 43		
Belvedere	d		11 10			11 21				11 31			11 40			11 51	12 01					
Erith	d		11 12			11 23				11 33			11 42			11 53	12 03					
Slade Green	d		11a15			11 27				11 37			11a45			11 57	12 07					
Dartford	a	11 15		11 28				11 08	11 24	11 42		11 45		11 58			12 12		11 38	11 54		12 15
	d							11 08	11 25										11 38	11 55		
Stone Crossing	d							11 12											11 42			
Greenhithe for Bluewater	d							11 15	11 30										11 45	12 00		
Swanscombe	d							11 18											11 48			
Northfleet	d							11 20											11 50			
Gravesend	d						11 18	11a25	11 37									11 48	11a55	12 07		
Higham	d								11 43											12 13		
Strood	d						11 28		11 48									11 58		12 18		
Rochester	d						11 33		11 52									12 03		12 22		
Chatham	d						11 35		11 55									12 05		12 25		
Gillingham (Kent)	a						11 39		11 59									12 09		12 29		

Table 200

Saturdays

London - Dartford and Gillingham

		SE	SE	SE	SE	SE	SE	SE	SE	SE	SE	SE	SE	SE	SE	SE	SE	SE	SE	SE	SE	SE	SE
St Pancras International	d						11 55										12 25						
Stratford International	d						12 02										12 36						
Ebbsfleet International	d						12 13										12 47						
London Charing Cross	d							11 26	11 39		12 02							11 56	12 09		12 32		
London Waterloo (East)	d							11 29	11 42		12 05							11 59	12 12		12 35		
London Cannon Street	d	11 35		11 40	11 45	11 55						12 05		12 10	12 15	12 25						12 35	
London Bridge	d	11 41		11 44	11 51	12 01		11 34	11 47	11 58	12 10	12 11		12 14	12 21	12 31		12 04	12 17	12 28	12 40	12 41	
Deptford	d	11 47			11 57	12 07						12 17			12 27	12 37						12 47	
Greenwich	d	11 49			11 59	12 09						12 19			12 29	12 39						12 49	
Maze Hill	d	11 52			12 02	12 12						12 22			12 32	12 42						12 52	
Westcombe Park	d	11 54			12 04	12 14						12 24			12 34	12 44						12 54	
London Victoria	d		11 39										12 09										12 39
Denmark Hill	d		11 48										12 18										12 48
Peckham Rye	d		11 51										12 21										12 51
Nunhead	d		11 53										12 23										12 53
New Cross	d			11 49						12 04				12 19						12 34			
St Johns	d			11 51										12 21									
Lewisham	d		12 02	11 54					11 56	12 08	12 19		12 32	12 24					12 26	12 38	12 49		13 02
Blackheath	d		12 05						11 59	12 11	12 23		12 35						12 29	12 41	12 53		13 05
Kidbrooke	d		12 08							12 14	12 26		12 38							12 44	12 56		13 08
Eltham	d		12 11							12 17	12 29		12 41							12 47	12 59		13 11
Falconwood	d		12 14							12 20	12 31		12 44							12 50	13 01		13 14
Welling	d		12 16							12 22	12 34		12 46							12 52	13 04		13 16
Bexleyheath	d		12 19							12 25	12 36		12 49							12 55	13 06		13 19
Barnehurst	d		12 21							12a27	12 39		12 51							12a57	13 09		13 21
Hither Green	d			11 59				11 44						12 29				12 14					
Lee	d			12 01				11 46						12 31				12 16					
Mottingham	d			12 04				11 49						12 34				12 19					
New Eltham	d			12 06				11 51						12 36				12 21					
Sidcup	d			12 10				11 55						12 40				12 25					
Albany Park	d			12 12				11 57						12 42				12 27					
Bexley	d			12 14				11 59						12 44				12 29					
Crayford	d			12 18				12 03						12 48				12 33					
Charlton	d	11 56		12 44	12 07	12 17			12 03			12 26		13 14	12 37	12 47			12 33			12 56	
Woolwich Dockyard	d	11 59			12 10	12 20						12 29			12 40	12 50						12 59	
Woolwich Arsenal	d	12 02			12 13	12 23			12 09			12 32			12 43	12 53			12 39			13 02	
Plumstead	d	12 04			12 15	12 25						12 34			12 45	12 55						13 04	
Abbey Wood	d	12 07			12 18	12 28			12 13			12 37			12 48	12 58			12 43			13 07	
Belvedere	d	12 10			12 21	12 31						12 40			12 51	13 01						13 10	
Erith	d	12 12			12 23	12 33						12 42			12 53	13 03						13 12	
Slade Green	d	12a15			12 27	12 37						12a45			12 57	13 07						13a15	
Dartford	a		12 28			12 42		12 08	12 24		12 45		12 58			13 12		12 38	12 54		13 15		13 28
	d							12 08	12 25									12 38	12 55				
Stone Crossing	d							12 12										12 42					
Greenhithe for Bluewater	d							12 15	12 30									12 45	13 00				
Swanscombe	d							12 18										12 48					
Northfleet	d							12 20										12 50					
Gravesend	d						12 18	12a25	12 37								12 51	12a55	13 07				
Higham	d								12 43										13 13				
Strood	d						12 28		12 48								13 01		13 18				
Rochester	d						12 33		12 52								13 06		13 22				
Chatham	d						12 35		12 55								13 08		13 25				
Gillingham (Kent)	a						12 39		12 59								13 12		13 29				

Table 200

Saturdays

London - Dartford and Gillingham

		SE	SE	SE	SE	SE	SE	SE	SE	SE	SE	SE	SE	SE	SE	SE	SE	SE	SE	SE	SE	SE	SE
St Pancras International	d			12 52											13 25								
Stratford International	d			12 58											13 32								
Ebbsfleet International	d			13 13											13 43								
London Charing Cross	d				12 26	12 39			13 02							12 56	13 09		13 32				
London Waterloo (East)	d				12 29	12 42			13 05							12 59	13 12		13 35				
London Cannon Street	d	12 40	12 45				12 55			13 05		13 10	13 15	13 25						13 35		13 40	13 45
London Bridge	d	12 44	12 51		12 34	12 47	13 01	12 58	13 10	13 11		13 14	13 21	13 31		13 04	13 17	13 28	13 40	13 41		13 44	13 51
Deptford	d		12 57				13 07			13 17			13 27	13 37						13 47			13 57
Greenwich	d		12 59				13 09			13 19			13 29	13 39						13 49			13 59
Maze Hill	d		13 02				13 12			13 22			13 32	13 42						13 52			14 02
Westcombe Park	d		13 04				13 14			13 24			13 34	13 44						13 54			14 04
London Victoria	d										13 09										13 39		
Denmark Hill	d										13 18										13 48		
Peckham Rye	d										13 21										13 51		
Nunhead	d										13 23										13 53		
New Cross	d	12 49						13 04				13 19						13 34				13 49	
St Johns	d	12 51										13 21										13 51	
Lewisham	d	12 54				12 56		13 08	13 19		13 32	13 24					13 26	13 38	13 49		14 02	13 54	
Blackheath	d					12 59		13 11	13 23		13 35						13 29	13 41	13 53		14 05		
Kidbrooke	d							13 14	13 26		13 38							13 44	13 56		14 08		
Eltham	d							13 17	13 29		13 41							13 47	13 59		14 11		
Falconwood	d							13 20	13 31		13 44							13 50	14 01		14 14		
Welling	d							13 22	13 34		13 46							13 52	14 04		14 16		
Bexleyheath	d							13 25	13 36		13 49							13 55	14 06		14 19		
Barnehurst	d							13a27	13 39		13 51							13a57	14 09		14 21		
Hither Green	d	12 59			12 44							13 29				13 14						13 59	
Lee	d	13 01			12 46							13 31				13 16						14 01	
Mottingham	d	13 04			12 49							13 34				13 19						14 04	
New Eltham	d	13 06			12 51							13 36				13 21						14 06	
Sidcup	d	13 10			12 55							13 40				13 25						14 10	
Albany Park	d	13 12			12 57							13 42				13 27						14 12	
Bexley	d	13 14			12 59							13 44				13 29						14 14	
Crayford	d	13 18			13 03							13 48				13 33						14 18	
Charlton	d	13 44	13 07			13 03	13 17			13 26		14 14	13 37	13 47			13 33			13 56		14 44	14 07
Woolwich Dockyard	d		13 10				13 20			13 29			13 40	13 50						13 59			14 10
Woolwich Arsenal	d		13 13			13 09	13 23			13 32			13 43	13 53			13 39			14 02			14 13
Plumstead	d		13 15				13 25			13 34			13 45	13 55						14 04			14 15
Abbey Wood	d		13 18			13 13	13 28			13 37			13 48	13 58			13 43			14 07			14 18
Belvedere	d		13 21				13 31			13 40			13 51	14 01						14 10			14 21
Erith	d		13 23				13 33			13 42			13 53	14 03						14 12			14 23
Slade Green	d		13 27				13 37			13a45			13 57	14 07						14a15			14 27
Dartford	a				13 08	13 24	13 42		13 45		13 58			14 12		13 38	13 54		14 15		14 28		
	d				13 08	13 25										13 38	13 55						
Stone Crossing	d				13 12											13 42							
Greenhithe for Bluewater	d				13 15	13 30										13 45	14 00						
Swanscombe	d				13 18											13 48							
Northfleet	d				13 20											13 50							
Gravesend	d			13 18	13a25	13 37									13 48	13a55	14 07						
Higham	d					13 43											14 13						
Strood	d			13 28		13 48									13 58		14 18						
Rochester	d			13 33		13 52									14 03		14 22						
Chatham	d			13 35		13 55									14 05		14 25						
Gillingham (Kent)	a			13 39		13 59									14 09		14 29						

Table 200

Saturdays

London - Dartford and Gillingham

		SE	SE	SE	SE	SE	SE	SE	SE	SE	SE	SE	SE	SE	SE	SE	SE	SE	SE	SE	SE	SE
St Pancras International ⊖	d		13 55											14 28								
Stratford International ⊖	d		14 02											14 35								
Ebbsfleet International	d		14 13											14 46								
London Charing Cross ⊖	d			13 26	13 39		14 02								13 56	14 09	14 32					
London Waterloo (East) ⊖	d			13 29	13 42		14 05								13 59	14 12	14 35					
London Cannon Street ⊖	d	13 55						14 05		14 10	14 15	14 25						14 35		14 40	14 45	14 55
London Bridge ⊖	d	14 01		13 34	13 47	13 58	14 10	14 11		14 14	14 21	14 31	14 28		14 04	14 17	14 40	14 41		14 44	14 51	15 01
Deptford	d	14 07						14 17			14 27	14 37						14 47			14 57	15 07
Greenwich	d	14 09						14 19			14 29	14 39						14 49			14 59	15 09
Maze Hill	d	14 12						14 22			14 32	14 42						14 52			15 02	15 12
Westcombe Park	d	14 14						14 24			14 34	14 44						14 54			15 04	15 14
London Victoria ⊖	d								14 09										14 39			
Denmark Hill	d								14 18										14 48			
Peckham Rye	d								14 21										14 51			
Nunhead	d								14 23										14 53			
New Cross ⊖	d					14 04				14 19			14 34							14 49		
St Johns	d									14 21										14 51		
Lewisham	d				13 56	14 08	14 19		14 32	14 24			14 38			14 26	14 49		15 02	14 54		
Blackheath	d				13 59	14 11	14 23		14 35				14 41			14 29	14 53		15 05			
Kidbrooke	d					14 14	14 26		14 38				14 44				14 56		15 08			
Eltham	d					14 17	14 29		14 41				14 47				14 59		15 11			
Falconwood	d					14 20	14 31		14 44				14 50				15 01		15 14			
Welling	d					14 22	14 34		14 46				14 52				15 04		15 16			
Bexleyheath	d					14 25	14 36		14 49				14 55				15 06		15 19			
Barnehurst	d					14a27	14 39		14 51				14a57				15 09		15 21			
Hither Green	d			13 44						14 29					14 14					14 59		
Lee	d			13 46						14 31					14 16					15 01		
Mottingham	d			13 49						14 34					14 19					15 04		
New Eltham	d			13 51						14 36					14 21					15 06		
Sidcup	d			13 55						14 40					14 25					15 10		
Albany Park	d			13 57						14 42					14 27					15 12		
Bexley	d			13 59						14 44					14 29					15 14		
Crayford	d			14 03						14 48					14 33					15 18		
Charlton	d	14 17			14 03			14 26		15 14	14 37	14 47				14 33		14 56		15 44	15 07	15 17
Woolwich Dockyard	d	14 20						14 29			14 40	14 50						14 59			15 10	15 20
Woolwich Arsenal	d	14 23			14 09			14 32			14 43	14 53				14 39		15 02			15 13	15 23
Plumstead	d	14 25						14 34			14 45	14 55						15 04			15 15	15 25
Abbey Wood	d	14 28			14 13			14 37			14 48	14 58				14 43		15 07			15 18	15 28
Belvedere	d	14 31						14 40			14 51	15 01						15 10			15 21	15 31
Erith	d	14 33						14 42			14 53	15 03						15 12			15 23	15 33
Slade Green	d	14 37						14a45			14 57	15 07						15a15			15 27	15 37
Dartford	a	14 42		14 08	14 24		14 45		14 58			15 12			14 38	14 54	15 15		15 28			15 42
	d			14 08	14 25										14 38	14 55						
Stone Crossing	d			14 12											14 42							
Greenhithe for Bluewater	d			14 15	14 30										14 45	15 00						
Swanscombe	d			14 18											14 48							
Northfleet	d			14 20											14 50							
Gravesend	d		14 18	14a25	14 37									14 51	14a55	15 07						
Higham	d				14 43											15 13						
Strood	d		14 28		14 48									15 01		15 18						
Rochester	d		14 33		14 52									15 06		15 22						
Chatham	d		14 35		14 55									15 08		15 25						
Gillingham (Kent)	a		14 39		14 59									15 12		15 29						

Table 200

Saturdays

London - Dartford and Gillingham

		SE	SE	SE	SE	SE	SE	SE	SE	SE	SE	SE	SE	SE	SE	SE	SE	SE	SE	SE	SE	SE	SE
St Pancras International ⊖	d		14 58									15 25										15 55	
Stratford International ⊖	d		15 05									15 32										16 02	
Ebbsfleet International	d		15 16									15 43										16 13	
London Charing Cross ⊖	d			14 26	14 39	15 02							14 56	15 09		15 32							15 26
London Waterloo (East) ⊖	d			14 29	14 42	15 05							14 59	15 12		15 35							15 29
London Cannon Street ⊖	d						15 05		15 10	15 15	15 25						15 35		15 40	15 45	15 55		
London Bridge ⊖	d	14 58		14 34	14 47	15 10	15 11		15 14	15 21	15 31		15 04	15 17	15 28	15 40	15 41		15 44	15 51	16 01		15 34
Deptford	d						15 17			15 27	15 37						15 47			15 57	16 07		
Greenwich	d						15 19			15 29	15 39						15 49			15 59	16 09		
Maze Hill	d						15 22			15 32	15 42						15 52			16 02	16 12		
Westcombe Park	d						15 24			15 34	15 44						15 54			16 04	16 14		
London Victoria ⊖	d							15 09										15 39					
Denmark Hill	d							15 18										15 48					
Peckham Rye	d							15 21										15 51					
Nunhead	d							15 23										15 53					
New Cross ⊖	d	15 04							15 19						15 34				15 49				
St Johns	d								15 21										15 51				
Lewisham	d	15 08			14 56	15 19		15 32	15 24					15 26	15 38	15 49		16 02	15 54				
Blackheath	d	15 11			14 59	15 23		15 35						15 29	15 41	15 53		16 05					
Kidbrooke	d	15 14				15 26		15 38							15 44	15 56		16 08					
Eltham	d	15 17				15 29		15 41							15 47	15 59		16 11					
Falconwood	d	15 20				15 31		15 44							15 50	16 01		16 14					
Welling	d	15 22				15 34		15 46							15 52	16 04		16 16					
Bexleyheath	d	15 25				15 36		15 49							15 55	16 06		16 19					
Barnehurst	d	15a27				15 39		15 51							15a57	16 09		16 21					
Hither Green	d			14 44					15 29				15 14						15 59				15 44
Lee	d			14 46					15 31				15 16						16 01				15 46
Mottingham	d			14 49					15 34				15 19						16 04				15 49
New Eltham	d			14 51					15 36				15 21						16 06				15 51
Sidcup	d			14 55					15 40				15 25						16 10				15 55
Albany Park	d			14 57					15 42				15 27						16 12				15 57
Bexley	d			14 59					15 44				15 29						16 14				15 59
Crayford	d			15 03					15 48				15 33						16 18				16 03
Charlton	d				15 03		15 26		16 14	15 37	15 47			15 33			15 56		16 44	16 07	16 17		
Woolwich Dockyard	d						15 29			15 40	15 50						15 59			16 10	16 20		
Woolwich Arsenal	d				15 09		15 32			15 43	15 53			15 39			16 02			16 13	16 23		
Plumstead	d						15 34			15 45	15 55						16 04			16 15	16 25		
Abbey Wood	d				15 13		15 37			15 48	15 58			15 43			16 07			16 18	16 28		
Belvedere	d						15 40			15 51	16 01						16 10			16 21	16 31		
Erith	d						15 42			15 53	16 03						16 12			16 23	16 33		
Slade Green	d						15a45			15 57	16 07						16a15			16 27	16 37		
Dartford	a			15 08	15 24	15 45		15 58			16 12		15 38	15 54		16 15		16 28			16 42		16 08
	d			15 08	15 25								15 38	15 55									16 08
Stone Crossing	d			15 12									15 42										16 12
Greenhithe for Bluewater	d			15 15	15 30								15 45	16 00									16 15
Swanscombe	d			15 18									15 48										16 18
Northfleet	d			15 20									15 50										16 20
Gravesend	d		15 21	15a25	15 37							15 48	15a55	16 07								16 18	16a25
Higham	d				15 43									16 13									
Strood	d		15 31		15 48							15 58		16 18								16 28	
Rochester	d		15 36		15 52							16 03		16 22								16 33	
Chatham	d		15 38		15 55							16 05		16 25								16 35	
Gillingham (Kent)	a		15 42		15 59							16 09		16 29								16 39	

Table 200

Saturdays

London - Dartford and Gillingham

Station		SE	SE	SE	SE	SE	SE	SE	SE	SE	SE	SE	SE	SE	SE	SE	SE	SE	SE	SE	SE	SE
St Pancras International 15 ⊖	d										16 28									16 55		
Stratford International ⊖ ⛴	d										16 35									17 02		
Ebbsfleet International	d										16 46									17 13		
London Charing Cross 4 ⊖	d	15 39		16 02								15 56	16 09	16 32							16 26	16 39
London Waterloo (East) 4 ⊖	d	15 42		16 05								15 59	16 12	16 35							16 29	16 42
London Cannon Street 4 ⊖	d				16 05		16 10	16 15	16 25						16 35		16 40	16 45	16 55			
London Bridge 4 ⊖	d	15 47	15 58	16 10	16 11		16 14	16 21	16 31	16 28		16 04	16 17	16 40	16 41		16 44	16 51	17 01		16 34	16 47
Deptford	d				16 17			16 27	16 37						16 47			16 57	17 07			
Greenwich 4 ⛴	d				16 19			16 29	16 39						16 49			16 59	17 09			
Maze Hill	d				16 22			16 32	16 42						16 52			17 02	17 12			
Westcombe Park	d				16 24			16 34	16 44						16 54			17 04	17 14			
London Victoria 15 ⊖	d					16 09										16 39						
Denmark Hill 4	d					16 18										16 48						
Peckham Rye 4	d					16 21										16 51						
Nunhead 4	d					16 23										16 53						
New Cross 4 ⊖	d		16 04				16 19			16 34							16 49					
St Johns	d						16 21										16 51					
Lewisham 4 ⛴	d	15 56	16 08	16 19		16 32	16 24			16 38			16 26	16 49		17 02	16 54					16 56
Blackheath 4	d	15 59	16 11	16 23		16 35				16 41			16 29	16 53		17 05						16 59
Kidbrooke	d		16 14	16 26		16 38				16 44				16 56		17 08						
Eltham	d		16 17	16 29		16 41				16 47				16 59		17 11						
Falconwood	d		16 20	16 31		16 44				16 50				17 01		17 14						
Welling	d		16 22	16 34		16 46				16 52				17 04		17 16						
Bexleyheath	d		16 25	16 36		16 49				16 55				17 06		17 19						
Barnehurst 4	d		16a27	16 39		16 51				16a57				17 09		17 21						
Hither Green 4	d						16 29					16 14					16 59				16 44	
Lee	d						16 31					16 16					17 01				16 46	
Mottingham	d						16 34					16 19					17 04				16 49	
New Eltham	d						16 36					16 21					17 06				16 51	
Sidcup 4	d						16 40					16 25					17 10				16 55	
Albany Park	d						16 42					16 27					17 12				16 57	
Bexley	d						16 44					16 29					17 14				16 59	
Crayford	d						16 48					16 33					17 18				17 03	
Charlton 4	d	16 03			16 26		17 14	16 37	16 47				16 33		16 56		17 44	17 07	17 17			17 03
Woolwich Dockyard	d				16 29			16 40	16 50						16 59			17 10	17 20			
Woolwich Arsenal 4 ⛴	d	16 09			16 32			16 43	16 53				16 39		17 02			17 13	17 23			17 09
Plumstead	d				16 34			16 45	16 55						17 04			17 15	17 25			
Abbey Wood	d	16 13			16 37			16 48	16 58				16 43		17 07			17 18	17 28			17 13
Belvedere	d				16 40			16 51	17 01						17 10			17 21	17 31			
Erith	d				16 42			16 53	17 03						17 12			17 23	17 33			
Slade Green 4	d				16a45			16 57	17 07						17a15			17 27	17 37			
Dartford 4	a	16 24		16 45		16 58			17 12			16 38	16 54	17 15		17 28			17 42		17 08	17 24
	d	16 25										16 38	16 55								17 08	17 25
Stone Crossing	d											16 42									17 12	
Greenhithe for Bluewater	d	16 30										16 45	17 00								17 15	17 30
Swanscombe	d											16 48									17 18	
Northfleet	d											16 50									17 20	
Gravesend 4	d	16 37									16 51	16a55	17 07							17 18	17a25	17 37
Higham	d	16 43											17 13									17 43
Strood 4	d	16 48									17 01		17 18							17 28		17 48
Rochester 4	d	16 52									17 06		17 22							17 33		17 52
Chatham 4	d	16 55									17 08		17 25							17 35		17 55
Gillingham (Kent) 4	a	16 59									17 12		17 29							17 39		17 59

Table 200

Saturdays

London - Dartford and Gillingham

Station		SE	SE	SE	SE	SE	SE	SE	SE	SE	SE	SE	SE	SE	SE	SE	SE	SE	SE	SE	SE	SE	SE
St Pancras International 15 ⊖	d									17 28										17 58			
Stratford International ⊖ ⛴	d									17 35										18 05			
Ebbsfleet International	d									17 46										18 16			
London Charing Cross 4 ⊖	d		17 02								16 56	17 09	17 32								17 26	17 39	18 02
London Waterloo (East) 4 ⊖	d		17 05								16 59	17 12	17 35								17 29	17 42	18 05
London Cannon Street 4 ⊖	d			17 05		17 10	17 15	17 25						17 35		17 40	17 45	17 55					
London Bridge 4 ⊖	d	16 58	17 10	17 11		17 14	17 21	17 31	17 28		17 04	17 17	17 40	17 41		17 44	17 51	18 01	17 58		17 34	17 47	18 10
Deptford	d			17 17			17 27	17 37						17 47			17 57	18 07					
Greenwich 4 ⛴	d			17 19			17 29	17 39						17 49			17 59	18 09					
Maze Hill	d			17 22			17 32	17 42						17 52			18 02	18 12					
Westcombe Park	d			17 24			17 34	17 44						17 54			18 04	18 14					
London Victoria 15 ⊖	d				17 09										17 39								
Denmark Hill 4	d				17 18										17 48								
Peckham Rye 4	d				17 21										17 51								
Nunhead 4	d				17 23										17 53								
New Cross 4 ⊖	d	17 04				17 19			17 34							17 49			18 04				
St Johns	d					17 21										17 51							
Lewisham 4 ⛴	d	17 08	17 19		17 32	17 24			17 38			17 26	17 49		18 02	17 54			18 08			17 56	18 19
Blackheath 4	d	17 11	17 23		17 35				17 41			17 29	17 53		18 05				18 11			17 59	18 23
Kidbrooke	d	17 14	17 26		17 38				17 44				17 56		18 08				18 14				18 26
Eltham	d	17 17	17 29		17 41				17 47				17 59		18 11				18 17				18 29
Falconwood	d	17 20	17 31		17 44				17 50				18 01		18 14				18 20				18 31
Welling	d	17 22	17 34		17 46				17 52				18 04		18 16				18 22				18 34
Bexleyheath	d	17 25	17 36		17 49				17 55				18 06		18 19				18 25				18 36
Barnehurst 4	d	17a27	17 39		17 51				17a57				18 09		18 21				18a27				18 39
Hither Green 4	d					17 29					17 14					17 59					17 44		
Lee	d					17 31					17 16					18 01					17 46		
Mottingham	d					17 34					17 19					18 04					17 49		
New Eltham	d					17 36					17 21					18 06					17 51		
Sidcup 4	d					17 40					17 25					18 10					17 55		
Albany Park	d					17 42					17 27					18 12					17 57		
Bexley	d					17 44					17 29					18 14					17 59		
Crayford	d					17 48					17 33					18 18					18 03		
Charlton 4	d			17 26		18 14	17 37	17 47				17 33		17 56		18 44	18 07	18 17				18 03	
Woolwich Dockyard	d			17 29			17 40	17 50						17 59			18 10	18 20					
Woolwich Arsenal 4 ⛴	d			17 32			17 43	17 53				17 39		18 02			18 13	18 23				18 09	
Plumstead	d			17 34			17 45	17 55						18 04			18 15	18 25					
Abbey Wood	d			17 37			17 48	17 58				17 43		18 07			18 18	18 28				18 13	
Belvedere	d			17 40			17 51	18 01						18 10			18 21	18 31					
Erith	d			17 42			17 53	18 03						18 12			18 23	18 33					
Slade Green 4	d			17a45			17 57	18 07						18a15			18 27	18 37					
Dartford 4	a		17 45		17 58			18 12			17 38	17 54	18 15		18 28			18 42			18 08	18 24	18 45
	d										17 38	17 55									18 08	18 25	
Stone Crossing	d										17 42										18 12		
Greenhithe for Bluewater	d										17 45	18 00									18 15	18 30	
Swanscombe	d										17 48										18 18		
Northfleet	d										17 50										18 20		
Gravesend 4	d									17 51	17a55	18 07								18 21	18a25	18 37	
Higham	d											18 13										18 43	
Strood 4	d									18 01		18 18								18 31		18 48	
Rochester 4	d									18 06		18 22								18 36		18 52	
Chatham 4	d									18 08		18 25								18 38		18 55	
Gillingham (Kent) 4	a									18 12		18 29								18 42		18 59	

Table 200

Saturdays

London - Dartford and Gillingham

		SE	SE	SE	SE	SE		SE	SE	SE	SE	SE	SE	SE	SE	SE		SE	SE	SE	SE	SE	SE	SE	SE
St Pancras International	d							18 25											18 55						
Stratford International	d							18 32											19 02						
Ebbsfleet International	d							18 43											19 13						
London Charing Cross	d								17 56	18 09		18 32								18 26	18 39		19 02		
London Waterloo (East)	d								17 59	18 12		18 35								18 29	18 42		19 05		
London Cannon Street	d	18 05		18 10	18 15	18 25							18 35		18 40	18 45		18 55						19 05	
London Bridge	d	18 11		18 14	18 21	18 31			18 04	18 17	18 28	18 40	18 41		18 44	18 51		19 01		18 34	18 47	18 58	19 10	19 11	
Deptford	d	18 17			18 27	18 37							18 47			18 57		19 07						19 17	
Greenwich	d	18 19			18 29	18 39							18 49			18 59		19 09						19 19	
Maze Hill	d	18 22			18 32	18 42							18 52			19 02		19 12						19 22	
Westcombe Park	d	18 24			18 34	18 44							18 54			19 04		19 14						19 24	
London Victoria	d		18 09											18 39											19 09
Denmark Hill	d		18 18											18 48											19 18
Peckham Rye	d		18 21											18 51											19 21
Nunhead	d		18 23											18 53											19 23
New Cross	d			18 19							18 34				18 49							19 04			
St Johns	d			18 21											18 51										
Lewisham	d		18 32	18 24						18 26	18 38	18 49		19 03	18 54						18 56	19 08	19 19		19 32
Blackheath	d		18 35							18 29	18 41	18 53		19 05							18 59	19 11	19 23		19 35
Kidbrooke	d		18 38								18 44	18 56		19 08								19 14	19 26		19 38
Eltham	d		18 41								18 47	18 59		19 11								19 17	19 29		19 41
Falconwood	d		18 44								18 50	19 01		19 14								19 20	19 31		19 44
Welling	d		18 46								18 52	19 04		19 16								19 22	19 34		19 46
Bexleyheath	d		18 49								18 55	19 06		19 19								19 25	19 36		19 49
Barnehurst	d		18 51								18a57	19 09		19 21								19a27	19 39		19 51
Hither Green	d			18 29					18 14						18 59					18 44					
Lee	d			18 31					18 16						19 01					18 46					
Mottingham	d			18 34					18 19						19 04					18 49					
New Eltham	d			18 36					18 21						19 06					18 51					
Sidcup	d			18 40					18 25						19 10					18 55					
Albany Park	d			18 42					18 27						19 12					18 57					
Bexley	d			18 44					18 29						19 14					18 59					
Crayford	d			18 48					18 33						19 18					19 03					
Charlton	d	18 26		19 14	18 37	18 47				18 33			18 56		19 44	19 07		19 17			19 03			19 26	
Woolwich Dockyard	d	18 29			18 40	18 50							18 59			19 10		19 20						19 29	
Woolwich Arsenal	d	18 32			18 43	18 53				18 39			19 02			19 13		19 23			19 09			19 32	
Plumstead	d	18 34			18 45	18 55							19 04			19 15		19 25						19 34	
Abbey Wood	d	18 37			18 48	18 58				18 43			19 07			19 18		19 28			19 13			19 37	
Belvedere	d	18 40			18 51	19 01							19 10			19 21		19 31						19 40	
Erith	d	18 42			18 53	19 03							19 12			19 23		19 33						19 42	
Slade Green	d	18a45			18a56	19 07							19a15			19a26		19 37						19 46	
Dartford	a		18 58			19 12			18 38	18 54		19 15		19 28				19 42		19 08	19 24		19 45	19 52	19 58
	d								18 38	18 55										19 08	19 25				
Stone Crossing	d								18 42											19 12					
Greenhithe for Bluewater	d								18 45	19 00										19 15	19 30				
Swanscombe	d								18 48											19 18					
Northfleet	d								18 50											19 20					
Gravesend	d							18 48	18a55	19 07									19 18	19a25	19 37				
Higham	d									19 13											19 43				
Strood	d							18 58		19 18									19 28		19 48				
Rochester	d							19 03		19 22									19 33		19 52				
Chatham	d							19 05		19 25									19 35		19 55				
Gillingham (Kent)	a							19 09		19 29									19 39		19 59				

Table 200

Saturdays

London - Dartford and Gillingham

		SE		SE	SE	SE	SE	SE	SE	SE	SE	SE		SE	SE	SE	SE	SE	SE	SE	SE	SE		SE	SE
St Pancras International	d				19 25							19 55							20 25						
Stratford International	d				19 32							20 02							20 32						
Ebbsfleet International	d				19 43							20 13							20 43						
London Charing Cross	d					18 56	19 09		19 32					19 26	19 39	19 56	20 02			19 52	20 09	20 26		20 32	
London Waterloo (East)	d					18 59	19 12		19 35					19 29	19 42	19 59	20 05			19 55	20 12	20 29		20 35	
London Cannon Street	d	19 10		19 25																					
London Bridge	d	19 14		19 31		19 04	19 17	19 28	19 40		19 51			19 34	19 47	20 05	20 10	20 21		20 00	20 17	20 35		20 40	20 51
Deptford	d			19 37							19 57					20 11		20 27				20 41			20 57
Greenwich	d			19 39							19 59					20 13		20 29				20 43			20 59
Maze Hill	d			19 42							20 02					20 16		20 32				20 46			21 02
Westcombe Park	d			19 44							20 04					20 18		20 34				20 48			21 04
London Victoria	d									19 39															
Denmark Hill	d									19 48															
Peckham Rye	d									19 51															
Nunhead	d									19 53															
New Cross	d	19 19						19 34	19 45								20 15			20 05				20 45	
St Johns	d	19 21																							
Lewisham	d	19 24					19 26	19 38	19 49	20 02					19 56		20 19			20 09	20 26			20 49	
Blackheath	d						19 29	19 41	19 53	20 05					19 59		20 23				20 29			20 53	
Kidbrooke	d							19 44	19 56	20 08							20 26							20 56	
Eltham	d							19 47	19 59	20 11							20 29							20 59	
Falconwood	d							19 50	20 01	20 14							20 31							21 01	
Welling	d							19 52	20 04	20 16							20 34							21 04	
Bexleyheath	d							19 55	20 06	20 19							20 36							21 06	
Barnehurst	d							19a57	20 09	20 21							20 39							21 09	
Hither Green	d	19 29				19 14								19 44						20 14					
Lee	d	19 31				19 16								19 46						20 16					
Mottingham	d	19 34				19 19								19 49						20 19					
New Eltham	d	19 36				19 21								19 51						20 21					
Sidcup	d	19 40				19 25								19 55						20 25					
Albany Park	d	19 42				19 27								19 57						20 27					
Bexley	d	19 44				19 29								19 59						20 29					
Crayford	d	19 48				19 33								20 03						20 33					
Charlton	d	20 14		19 47			19 33				20 07				20 03	20 20		20 37			20 33	20 50			21 07
Woolwich Dockyard	d			19 50							20 10					20 23		20 40				20 53			21 10
Woolwich Arsenal	d			19 53			19 39				20 13				20 09	20 26		20 43			20 39	20 56			21 13
Plumstead	d			19 55							20 15					20 28		20 45				20 58			21 15
Abbey Wood	d			19 58			19 43				20 18				20 13	20 32		20 48			20 43	21 02			21 18
Belvedere	d			20 01							20 21					20 34		20 51				21 04			21 21
Erith	d			20 03							20 23					20 37		20 53				21 07			21 23
Slade Green	d			20 07							20 27					20 39		20 57				21 09			21 27
Dartford	a			20 12		19 38	19 54		20 15	20 28	20 32			20 08	20 24	20 44	20 46	21 02		20 38	20 54	21 14		21 16	21 32
	d					19 38	19 55							20 08	20 25					20 38	20 55				
Stone Crossing	d					19 42								20 12						20 42					
Greenhithe for Bluewater	d					19 45	20 00							20 15	20 30					20 45	21 00				
Swanscombe	d					19 48								20 18						20 48					
Northfleet	d					19 50								20 20						20 50					
Gravesend	d				19 48	19a55	20 07					20 18		20a25	20 37				20 48	20a55	21 07				
Higham	d						20 13								20 43						21 13				
Strood	d				19 58		20 18					20 28			20 48				20 58		21 18				
Rochester	d				20 03		20 22					20 33			20 52				21 03		21 22				
Chatham	d				20 05		20 25					20 35			20 55				21 05		21 25				
Gillingham (Kent)	a				20 09		20 29					20 39			20 59				21 09		21 29				

Table 200

Saturdays

London - Dartford and Gillingham

		SE	SE	SE	SE	SE	SE	SE		SE	SE	SE	SE	SE	SE	SE	SE	SE		SE	SE	SE	SE	SE	SE
St Pancras International 15 ⊖	d	20 55					21 25							21 55							22 25				
Stratford International ⊖ ⛴	d	21 02					21 32							22 02							22 32				
Ebbsfleet International	d	21 13					21 43							22 13							22 43				
London Charing Cross 4 ⊖	d		20 22	20 39	20 56	21 02		20 52		21 09	21 26	21 32	21 52		21 22	21 39	21 56	22 02		22 22		22 09	22 26	22 32	22 52
London Waterloo (East) 4 ⊖	d		20 25	20 42	20 59	21 05		20 55		21 12	21 29	21 35	21 55		21 25	21 42	21 59	22 05		22 25		22 12	22 29	22 35	22 55
London Cannon Street 4 ⊖	d																								
London Bridge 4 ⊖	d		20 30	20 47	21 05	21 10		21 00		21 17	21 35	21 40	22 00		21 30	21 47	22 05	22 10		22 30		22 17	22 35	22 40	23 00
Deptford	d				21 11						21 41						22 11						22 41		
Greenwich 4 ⛴	d				21 13						21 43						22 13						22 43		
Maze Hill	d				21 16						21 46						22 16						22 46		
Westcombe Park	d				21 18						21 48						22 18						22 48		
London Victoria 15 ⊖	d																								
Denmark Hill 4	d																								
Peckham Rye 4	d																								
Nunhead 4	d																								
New Cross 4 ⊖	d		20 35			21 15		21 05				21 45	22 05		21 35			22 15		22 35				22 45	23 05
St Johns	d																								
Lewisham 4 ⛴	d		20 39	20 56		21 19		21 09		21 26		21 49	22 09		21 39	21 56		22 19		22 39		22 26		22 49	23 09
Blackheath 4	d			20 59		21 23				21 29		21 53				21 59		22 23				22 29		22 53	
Kidbrooke	d					21 26						21 56						22 26						22 56	
Eltham	d					21 29						21 59						22 29						22 59	
Falconwood	d					21 31						22 01						22 31						23 01	
Welling	d					21 34						22 04						22 34						23 04	
Bexleyheath	d					21 36						22 06						22 36						23 06	
Barnehurst 4	d					21 39						22 09						22 39						23 09	
Hither Green 4	d		20 44					21 14					22 14		21 44					22 44					23 14
Lee	d		20 46					21 16					22 16		21 46					22 46					23 16
Mottingham	d		20 49					21 19					22 19		21 49					22 49					23 19
New Eltham	d		20 51					21 21					22 21		21 51					22 51					23 21
Sidcup 4	d		20 55					21 25					22 25		21 55					22 55					23 25
Albany Park	d		20 57					21 27					22 27		21 57					22 57					23 27
Bexley	d		20 59					21 29					22 29		21 59					22 59					23 29
Crayford	d		21 03					21 33					22 33		22 03					23 03					23 33
Charlton 4	d			21 03	21 20					21 33	21 50					22 03	22 20					22 33	22 50		
Woolwich Dockyard	d				21 23						21 53						22 23						22 53		
Woolwich Arsenal 4 ⛴	d			21 09	21 26					21 39	21 56					22 09	22 26					22 39	22 56		
Plumstead	d				21 28						21 58						22 28						22 58		
Abbey Wood	d			21 13	21 32					21 43	22 02					22 13	22 32					22 43	23 02		
Belvedere	d				21 34						22 04						22 34						23 04		
Erith	d				21 37						22 07						22 37						23 07		
Slade Green 4	d				21 39						22 09						22 39						23 09		
Dartford 4	a		21 08	21 24	21 44	21 46		21 38		21 54	22 14	22 16	22 38		22 08	22 24	22 44	22 46		23 08		22 54	23 14	23 16	23 38
	d		21 08	21 25				21 38		21 55					22 08	22 25						22 55			
Stone Crossing	d		21 12					21 42							22 12	22 29						22 59			
Greenhithe for Bluewater	d		21 15	21 30				21 45		22 00					22 15	22 31						23 01			
Swanscombe	d		21 18					21 48							22 18	22 34						23 04			
Northfleet	d		21 20					21 50							22 20	22 36						23 06			
Gravesend 4	d	21 18	21a25	21 37			21 48	21a55		22 07				22 18	22a25	22 40					22 48	23 10			
Higham	d			21 43						22 13						22 46						23 16			
Strood 4	d	21 28		21 48			21 58			22 18				22 28		22 51					22 58	23 21			
Rochester 4	d	21 33		21 52			22 03			22 22				22 33		22 55					23 03	23 25			
Chatham 4	d	21 35		21 55			22 05			22 25				22 35		22 58					23 05	23 28			
Gillingham (Kent) 4	a	21 39		21 59			22 09			22 29				22 39		23 02					23 09	23 32			

Table 200

Saturdays

London - Dartford and Gillingham

		SE	SE	SE		SE	SE	SE	SE	SE	SE	SE	SE	SE
St Pancras International 15 ⊖	d	22 55						23 25				23 55		
Stratford International ⊖ ⛴	d	23 02						23 32				00 02		
Ebbsfleet International	d	23 13						23 43				00 13		
London Charing Cross 4 ⊖	d		22 39	22 56		23 02	23 22		23 09	23 26	23 32		23 39	23 56
London Waterloo (East) 4 ⊖	d		22 42	22 59		23 05	23 25		23 12	23 29	23 35		23 42	23 59
London Cannon Street 4 ⊖	d													
London Bridge 4 ⊖	d		22 47	23 05		23 10	23 30		23 17	23 35	23 40		23 47	00 05
Deptford	d			23 11						23 41				00 11
Greenwich 4 ⛴	d			23 13						23 43				00 13
Maze Hill	d			23 16						23 46				00 16
Westcombe Park	d			23 18						23 48				00 18
London Victoria 15 ⊖	d													
Denmark Hill 4	d													
Peckham Rye 4	d													
Nunhead 4	d													
New Cross 4 ⊖	d					23 15	23 35				23 45			
St Johns	d													
Lewisham 4 ⛴	d		22 56			23 19	23 39		23 26		23 49		23 56	
Blackheath 4	d		22 59			23 23			23 29		23 53		23 58	
Kidbrooke	d					23 26					23 56			
Eltham	d					23 29					23 59			
Falconwood	d					23 31					00 01			
Welling	d					23 34					00 04			
Bexleyheath	d					23 36					00 06			
Barnehurst 4	d					23 39					00 09			
Hither Green 4	d						23 44							
Lee	d						23 46							
Mottingham	d						23 49							
New Eltham	d						23 51							
Sidcup 4	d						23 55							
Albany Park	d						23 57							
Bexley	d						23 59							
Crayford	d						00 03							
Charlton 4	d		23 03	23 20					23 33	23 50			00 03	00 20
Woolwich Dockyard	d			23 23						23 53				00 23
Woolwich Arsenal 4 ⛴	d		23 09	23 26					23 39	23 56			00 09	00 26
Plumstead	d			23 28						23 58				00 28
Abbey Wood	d		23 13	23 32					23 43	00 02			00 13	00 32
Belvedere	d			23 34						00 04				00 34
Erith	d			23 37						00 07				00 37
Slade Green 4	d			23 39						00 09				00 39
Dartford 4	a		23 24	23 44		23 46	00 08		23 54	00 14	00 16		00 24	00 44
	d		23 25						23 55				00 25	
Stone Crossing	d		23 29						23 58				00 29	
Greenhithe for Bluewater	d		23 31						23 59				00 31	
Swanscombe	d		23 34						00 04				00 34	
Northfleet	d		23 36						00 06				00 36	
Gravesend 4	d	23 18	23 40					23 48	00 09			00 18	00 40	
Higham	d		23 46						00 15				00 46	
Strood 4	d	23 28	23 51					23 58	00 21			00 28	00 51	
Rochester 4	d	23 33	23 55					00 03	00 25			00 33	00 55	
Chatham 4	d	23 35	23 58					00 05	00 27			00 35	00 58	
Gillingham (Kent) 4	a	23 39	00 02					00 09	00 32			00 39	01 02	

Table 200

Sundays

London - Dartford and Gillingham

		SE	SE	SE	SE	SE	SE	SE	SE	SE	SE	SE	SE	SE	SE	SE	SE	SE	SE	SE	SE	SE	SE
St Pancras International 15 ⊖	d			23p25				23p55															
Stratford International ⊖ ⛴	d			23p32				00 02															
Ebbsfleet International	d			23p43				00 13															
London Charing Cross 4 ⊖	d	22p39	23p22		23p09	23p26	23p32		23p39	23p56	00 02	00 05	00 15	07 30	07 50		08 00	08 20		07 56	08 10	08 30	08 50
London Waterloo (East) 4 ⊖	d	22p42	23p25		23p12	23p29	23p35		23p42	23p59	00 05	00 08	00 18	07 33	07 53		08 03	08 23		07 59	08 13	08 33	08 53
London Cannon Street 4 ⊖	d																						
London Bridge 4 ⊖	d	22p47	23p30		23p17	23p35	23p40		23p47	00 05	00 10	00 13	00 23	07 38	07 58		08 08	08 28		08 04	08 18	08 38	08 58
Deptford	d					23p41				00 11				07 44			08 14					08 44	
Greenwich 4 ⛴	d					23p43				00 13				07 46			08 16					08 46	
Maze Hill	d					23p46				00 16				07 49			08 19					08 49	
Westcombe Park	d					23p48				00 18				07 51			08 21					08 51	
London Victoria 15 ⊖	d																						
Denmark Hill 4	d																						
Peckham Rye 4	d																						
Nunhead 4	d																						
New Cross 4 ⊖	d		23p35				23p45				00 15	00 18	00 28		08 04			08 34					09 04
St Johns	d																						
Lewisham 4 ⛴	d	22p56	23p39		23p26		23p49		23p56		00 19	00 22	00 33		08 08			08 38		08 12	08 27		09 08
Blackheath 4	d	22p59			23p29		23p53		23p58		00 23		00 35		08 10			08 40			08 30		09 10
Kidbrooke	d						23p56				00 26				08 13			08 43					09 13
Eltham	d						23p59				00 29				08 17			08 47					09 17
Falconwood	d						00 01				00 31				08 19			08 49					09 19
Welling	d						00 04				00 34				08 22			08 52					09 22
Bexleyheath	d						00 06				00 36				08 24			08 54					09 24
Barnehurst 4	d						00 09				00 39				08 27			08 57					09 27
Hither Green 4	d		23p44									00 27								08 16			
Lee	d		23p46									00 29								08 18			
Mottingham	d		23p49									00 32								08 21			
New Eltham	d		23p51									00 34								08 23			
Sidcup 4	d		23p55									00 38								08 27			
Albany Park	d		23p57									00 40								08 29			
Bexley	d		23p59									00 42								08 31			
Crayford	d		00 03									00 46								08 34			
Charlton 4	d	23p03			23p33	23p50			00 03	00 20			00 40	07 54			08 24				08 34	08 54	
Woolwich Dockyard	d					23p53				00 23				07 57			08 27					08 57	
Woolwich Arsenal 4 ⛴	d	23p09			23p39	23p56			00 09	00 26			00 45	08 00			08 30				08 40	09 00	
Plumstead	d					23p58				00 28			00 47	08 02			08 32					09 02	
Abbey Wood	d	23p13			23p43	00 02			00 13	00 32			00 50	08 05			08 35				08 44	09 05	
Belvedere	d					00 04				00 34			00 53	08 08			08 38					09 08	
Erith	d					00 07				00 37			00 55	08 10			08 40					09 10	
Slade Green 4	d					00 09				00 39			00 58	08 14			08 44					09 14	
Dartford 4	a	23p24	00 08		23p54	00 14	00 16		00 24	00 44	00 46	00 51	01 03	08 19	08 33		08 49	09 03		08 39	08 54	09 19	09 33
	d	23p25			23p55				00 25				01 03			07 55			08 25	08 40	08 55		
Stone Crossing	d	23p29			23p58				00 29							07 59			08 29	08 44			
Greenhithe for Bluewater	d	23p31			23p59				00 31				01 08			08 01			08 31	08 46	09 00		
Swanscombe	d	23p34			00 04				00 34							08 04			08 34	08 49			
Northfleet	d	23p36			00 06				00 36							08 06			08 36	08 51			
Gravesend 4	d	23p40		23p48	00 09			00 18	00 40				01 15			08 10			08 40	08a55	09 07		
Higham	d	23p46			00 15				00 46				01 21			08 16			08 46		09 13		
Strood 4	d	23p51		23p58	00 21			00 28	00 51				01 26			08 22			08 52		09 18		
Rochester 4	d	23p55		00 03	00 25			00 33	00 55				01 32			08 26			08 56		09 23		
Chatham 4	d	23p58		00 05	00 27			00 35	00 58				01 35			08 28			08 58		09 26		
Gillingham (Kent) 4	a	00 02		00 09	00 32			00 39	01 02				01 41			08 33			09 03		09 30		

Table 200

Sundays

London - Dartford and Gillingham

		SE	SE	SE	SE	SE	SE	SE	SE	SE	SE	SE	SE	SE	SE	SE	SE	SE	SE	SE	SE
St Pancras International 15 ⊖	d						09 25											10 28			
Stratford International ⊖ ⛴	d						09 32											10 35			
Ebbsfleet International	d						09 43											10 46			
London Charing Cross 4 ⊖	d	08 26	08 40	09 00	09 20			08 56	09 10	09 30	09 50		09 26	09 40	10 00	10 20			09 56	10 10	10 30
London Waterloo (East) 4 ⊖	d	08 29	08 43	09 03	09 23			08 59	09 13	09 33	09 53		09 29	09 43	10 03	10 23			09 59	10 13	10 33
London Cannon Street 4 ⊖	d																				
London Bridge 4 ⊖	d	08 34	08 48	09 08	09 28	09 23		09 04	09 18	09 38	09 58	09 53	09 34	09 48	10 08	10 28	10 23		10 04	10 18	10 38
Deptford	d			09 14		09 29				09 44		09 59			10 14		10 29				10 44
Greenwich 4 ⛴	d			09 16		09 31				09 46		10 01			10 16		10 31				10 46
Maze Hill	d			09 19		09 34				09 49		10 04			10 19		10 34				10 49
Westcombe Park	d			09 21		09 36				09 51		10 06			10 21		10 36				10 51
London Victoria 15 ⊖	d																				
Denmark Hill 4	d																				
Peckham Rye 4	d																				
Nunhead 4	d																				
New Cross 4 ⊖	d				09 34						10 04					10 34					
St Johns	d																				
Lewisham 4 ⛴	d	08 42	08 57		09 38			09 12	09 27		10 08		09 42	09 57		10 38			10 12	10 27	
Blackheath 4	d		09 00		09 40				09 30		10 10			10 00		10 40				10 30	
Kidbrooke	d				09 43						10 13					10 43					
Eltham	d				09 47						10 17					10 47					
Falconwood	d				09 49						10 19					10 49					
Welling	d				09 52						10 22					10 52					
Bexleyheath	d				09 54						10 24					10 54					
Barnehurst 4	d				09 57						10 27					10 57					
Hither Green 4	d	08 46						09 16					09 46						10 16		
Lee	d	08 48						09 18					09 48						10 18		
Mottingham	d	08 51						09 21					09 51						10 21		
New Eltham	d	08 53						09 23					09 53						10 23		
Sidcup 4	d	08 57						09 27					09 57						10 27		
Albany Park	d	08 59						09 29					09 59						10 29		
Bexley	d	09 01						09 31					10 01						10 31		
Crayford	d	09 04						09 34					10 04						10 34		
Charlton 4	d		09 04	09 24		09 39			09 34	09 54		10 09		10 04	10 24		10 39			10 34	10 54
Woolwich Dockyard	d			09 27		09 42				09 57		10 12			10 27		10 42				10 57
Woolwich Arsenal 4 ⛴	d		09 10	09 30		09 45			09 40	10 00		10 15		10 10	10 30		10 45			10 40	11 00
Plumstead	d			09 32		09a47				10 02		10a17			10 32		10a47				11 02
Abbey Wood	d		09 14	09 35					09 44	10 05				10 14	10 35					10 44	11 05
Belvedere	d			09 38						10 08					10 38						11 08
Erith	d			09 40						10 10					10 40						11 10
Slade Green 4	d			09 44						10 14					10 44						11 14
Dartford 4	a	09 09	09 24	09 49	10 03			09 39	09 54	10 19	10 33		10 09	10 24	10 49	11 03			10 39	10 54	11 19
	d	09 10	09 25					09 40	09 55				10 10	10 25					10 40	10 55	
Stone Crossing	d	09 14						09 44					10 14						10 44		
Greenhithe for Bluewater	d	09 16	09 30					09 46	10 00				10 16	10 30					10 46	11 00	
Swanscombe	d	09 19						09 49					10 19						10 49		
Northfleet	d	09 21						09 51					10 21						10 51		
Gravesend 4	d	09a25	09 37				09 48	09a55	10 07				10a25	10 37				10 51	10a55	11 07	
Higham	d		09 43						10 13					10 43						11 13	
Strood 4	d		09 48				09 58		10 18					10 48				11 01		11 18	
Rochester 4	d		09 52				10 03		10 23					10 52				11 06		11 23	
Chatham 4	d		09 55				10 05		10 26					10 55				11 08		11 26	
Gillingham (Kent) 4	a		10 02				10 09		10 30					11 02				11 12		11 30	

Table 200

Sundays

London - Dartford and Gillingham

		SE			SE	SE	SE	SE	SE	SE	SE	SE		SE	SE	SE		SE	SE	SE	SE	SE		SE	SE
St Pancras International	d										11 25														12 25
Stratford International	d										11 32														12 36
Ebbsfleet International	d										11 43														12 47
London Charing Cross	d	10 50			10 26	10 40		11 00	11 20			10 56		11 10	11 30	11 50		11 26	11 40		12 00	12 20			
London Waterloo (East)	d	10 53			10 29	10 43		11 03	11 23			10 59		11 13	11 33	11 53		11 29	11 43		12 03	12 23			
London Cannon Street	d																								
London Bridge	d	10 58			10 34	10 48	10 53	11 08	11 28	11 23		11 04		11 18	11 38	11 58		11 34	11 48	11 53	12 08	12 28		12 23	
Deptford	d						10 59	11 14		11 29					11 44					11 59	12 14			12 29	
Greenwich	d						11 01	11 16		11 31					11 46					12 01	12 16			12 31	
Maze Hill	d						11 04	11 19		11 34					11 49					12 04	12 19			12 34	
Westcombe Park	d						11 06	11 21		11 36					11 51					12 06	12 21			12 36	
London Victoria	d																								
Denmark Hill	d																								
Peckham Rye	d																								
Nunhead	d																								
New Cross	d	11 04							11 34							12 04						12 34			
St Johns	d																								
Lewisham	d	11 08			10 42	10 57			11 38			11 12		11 27		12 08		11 42	11 57			12 38			
Blackheath	d	11 10				11 00			11 40					11 30		12 10			12 00			12 40			
Kidbrooke	d	11 13							11 43							12 13						12 43			
Eltham	d	11 17							11 47							12 17						12 47			
Falconwood	d	11 19							11 49							12 19						12 49			
Welling	d	11 22							11 52							12 22						12 52			
Bexleyheath	d	11 24							11 54							12 24						12 54			
Barnehurst	d	11 27							11 57							12 27						12 57			
Hither Green	d				10 46							11 16						11 46							
Lee	d				10 48							11 18						11 48							
Mottingham	d				10 51							11 21						11 51							
New Eltham	d				10 53							11 23						11 53							
Sidcup	d				10 57							11 27						11 57							
Albany Park	d				10 59							11 29						11 59							
Bexley	d				11 01							11 31						12 01							
Crayford	d				11 04							11 34						12 04							
Charlton	d					11 04	11 09	11 24		11 39				11 34	11 54				12 04	12 09	12 24			12 39	
Woolwich Dockyard	d						11 12	11 27		11 42					11 57					12 12	12 27			12 42	
Woolwich Arsenal	d					11 10	11 15	11 30		11 45				11 40	12 00				12 10	12 15	12 30			12 45	
Plumstead	d						11a17	11 32		11a47					12 02					12a17	12 32			12a47	
Abbey Wood	d					11 14		11 35						11 44	12 05				12 14		12 35				
Belvedere	d							11 38							12 08						12 38				
Erith	d							11 40							12 10						12 40				
Slade Green	d							11 44							12 14						12 44				
Dartford	a	11 33			11 09	11 24		11 49	12 03			11 39		11 54	12 19	12 33		12 09	12 24		12 49	13 03			
	d				11 10	11 25						11 40		11 55				12 10	12 25						
Stone Crossing	d				11 14							11 44						12 14							
Greenhithe for Bluewater	d				11 16	11 30						11 46		12 00				12 16	12 30						
Swanscombe	d				11 19							11 49						12 19							
Northfleet	d				11 21							11 51						12 21							
Gravesend	d				11a25	11 37					11 48	11a55		12 07				12a25	12 37						12 51
Higham	d					11 43								12 13					12 43						
Strood	d					11 48					11 58			12 18					12 48						13 01
Rochester	d					11 52					12 03			12 23					12 52						13 06
Chatham	d					11 55					12 05			12 26					12 55						13 08
Gillingham (Kent)	a					12 02					12 09			12 30					13 02						13 12

Table 200

Sundays

London - Dartford and Gillingham

		SE	SE	SE	SE	SE	SE	SE		SE	SE	SE	SE	SE	SE	SE	SE	SE		SE	SE	SE	SE	SE	SE
St Pancras International	d					12 52								13 25							13 55				
Stratford International	d					12 58								13 32							14 02				
Ebbsfleet International	d					13 13								13 43							14 13				
London Charing Cross	d	11 56	12 10	12 30	12 50		12 26	12 40			13 00	13 20			12 56	13 10	13 30	13 50				13 26	13 40	14 00	14 20
London Waterloo (East)	d	11 59	12 13	12 33	12 53		12 29	12 43			13 03	13 23			12 59	13 13	13 33	13 53				13 29	13 43	14 03	14 23
London Cannon Street	d																								
London Bridge	d	12 04	12 18	12 38	12 58		12 34	12 48		12 53	13 08	13 28	13 23		13 04	13 18	13 38	13 58		13 53		13 34	13 48	14 08	14 28
Deptford	d			12 44						12 59	13 14		13 29				13 44			13 59				14 14	
Greenwich	d			12 46						13 01	13 16		13 31				13 46			14 01				14 16	
Maze Hill	d			12 49						13 04	13 19		13 34				13 49			14 04				14 19	
Westcombe Park	d			12 51						13 06	13 21		13 36				13 51			14 06				14 21	
London Victoria	d																								
Denmark Hill	d																								
Peckham Rye	d																								
Nunhead	d																								
New Cross	d				13 04							13 34						14 04							14 34
St Johns	d																								
Lewisham	d	12 12	12 27		13 08		12 42	12 57				13 38			13 12	13 27		14 08				13 42	13 57		14 38
Blackheath	d		12 30		13 10			13 00				13 40				13 30		14 10					14 00		14 40
Kidbrooke	d				13 13							13 43						14 13							14 43
Eltham	d				13 17							13 47						14 17							14 47
Falconwood	d				13 19							13 49						14 19							14 49
Welling	d				13 22							13 52						14 22							14 52
Bexleyheath	d				13 24							13 54						14 24							14 54
Barnehurst	d				13 27							13 57						14 27							14 57
Hither Green	d	12 16					12 46								13 16							13 46			
Lee	d	12 18					12 48								13 18							13 48			
Mottingham	d	12 21					12 51								13 21							13 51			
New Eltham	d	12 23					12 53								13 23							13 53			
Sidcup	d	12 27					12 57								13 27							13 57			
Albany Park	d	12 29					12 59								13 29							13 59			
Bexley	d	12 31					13 01								13 31							14 01			
Crayford	d	12 34					13 04								13 34							14 04			
Charlton	d		12 34	12 54				13 04		13 09	13 24		13 39			13 34	13 54			14 09			14 04	14 24	
Woolwich Dockyard	d			12 57						13 12	13 27		13 42				13 57			14 12				14 27	
Woolwich Arsenal	d		12 40	13 00				13 10		13 15	13 30		13 45			13 40	14 00			14 15			14 10	14 30	
Plumstead	d			13 02						13a17	13 32		13a47				14 02			14a17				14 32	
Abbey Wood	d		12 44	13 05				13 14			13 35					13 44	14 05						14 14	14 35	
Belvedere	d			13 08							13 38						14 08							14 38	
Erith	d			13 10							13 40						14 10							14 40	
Slade Green	d			13 14							13 44						14 14							14 44	
Dartford	a	12 39	12 54	13 19	13 33		13 09	13 24			13 49	14 03			13 39	13 54	14 19	14 33				14 09	14 24	14 49	15 03
	d	12 40	12 55				13 10	13 25							13 40	13 55						14 10	14 25		
Stone Crossing	d	12 44					13 14								13 44							14 14			
Greenhithe for Bluewater	d	12 46	13 00				13 16	13 30							13 46	14 00						14 16	14 30		
Swanscombe	d	12 49					13 19								13 49							14 19			
Northfleet	d	12 51					13 21								13 51							14 21			
Gravesend	d	12a55	13 07			13 18	13a25	13 37						13 48	13a55	14 07					14 18	14a25	14 37		
Higham	d		13 13					13 43								14 13							14 43		
Strood	d		13 18			13 28		13 48						13 58		14 18					14 28		14 48		
Rochester	d		13 23			13 33		13 52						14 03		14 23					14 33		14 52		
Chatham	d		13 26			13 35		13 55						14 05		14 26					14 35		14 55		
Gillingham (Kent)	a		13 30			13 39		14 02						14 09		14 30					14 39		15 02		

Table 200

Sundays

London - Dartford and Gillingham

		SE	SE	SE	SE	SE	SE	SE	SE	SE	SE	SE	SE	SE	SE	SE	SE	SE	SE	SE	SE	SE
St Pancras International ⊖	d		14 28						14 55						15 25						15 55	
Stratford International ⊖	d		14 35						15 02						15 32						16 02	
Ebbsfleet International	d		14 46						15 13						15 43						16 13	
London Charing Cross ⊖	d			13 56	14 10	14 30	14 50			14 26	14 40	15 00	15 20			14 56	15 10	15 30	15 50			15 26
London Waterloo (East) ⊖	d			13 59	14 13	14 33	14 53			14 29	14 43	15 03	15 23			14 59	15 13	15 33	15 53			15 29
London Cannon Street ⊖	d																					
London Bridge ⊖	d	14 23		14 04	14 18	14 38	14 58	14 53		14 34	14 48	15 08	15 28	15 23		15 04	15 18	15 38	15 58	15 53		15 34
Deptford	d	14 29				14 44		14 59				15 14		15 29				15 44		15 59		
Greenwich	d	14 31				14 46		15 01				15 16		15 31				15 46		16 01		
Maze Hill	d	14 34				14 49		15 04				15 19		15 34				15 49		16 04		
Westcombe Park	d	14 36				14 51		15 06				15 21		15 36				15 51		16 06		
London Victoria ⊖	d																					
Denmark Hill	d																					
Peckham Rye	d																					
Nunhead	d																					
New Cross ⊖	d						15 04						15 34						16 04			
St Johns	d																					
Lewisham	d			14 12	14 27		15 08			14 42	14 57		15 38			15 12	15 27		16 08			15 42
Blackheath	d				14 30		15 10				15 00		15 40				15 30		16 10			
Kidbrooke	d						15 13						15 43						16 13			
Eltham	d						15 17						15 47						16 17			
Falconwood	d						15 19						15 49						16 19			
Welling	d						15 22						15 52						16 22			
Bexleyheath	d						15 24						15 54						16 24			
Barnehurst	d						15 27						15 57						16 27			
Hither Green	d			14 16						14 46						15 16						15 46
Lee	d			14 18						14 48						15 18						15 48
Mottingham	d			14 21						14 51						15 21						15 51
New Eltham	d			14 23						14 53						15 23						15 53
Sidcup	d			14 27						14 57						15 27						15 57
Albany Park	d			14 29						14 59						15 29						15 59
Bexley	d			14 31						15 01						15 31						16 01
Crayford	d			14 34						15 04						15 34						16 04
Charlton	d	14 39			14 34	14 54		15 09			15 04	15 24		15 39			15 34	15 54		16 09		
Woolwich Dockyard	d	14 42				14 57		15 12				15 27		15 42				15 57		16 12		
Woolwich Arsenal	d	14 45			14 40	15 00		15 15			15 10	15 30		15 45			15 40	16 00		16 15		
Plumstead	d	14a47				15 02		15a17				15 32		15a47				16 02		16a17		
Abbey Wood	d				14 44	15 05					15 14	15 35					15 44	16 05				
Belvedere	d					15 08						15 38						16 08				
Erith	d					15 10						15 40						16 10				
Slade Green	d					15 14						15 44						16 14				
Dartford	a			14 39	14 54	15 19	15 33			15 09	15 24	15 49	16 03			15 39	15 54	16 19	16 33			16 09
	d			14 40	14 55					15 10	15 25					15 40	15 55					16 10
Stone Crossing	d			14 44						15 14						15 44						16 14
Greenhithe for Bluewater	d			14 46	15 00					15 16	15 30					15 46	16 00					16 16
Swanscombe	d			14 49						15 19						15 49						16 19
Northfleet	d			14 51						15 21						15 51						16 21
Gravesend	d		14 51	14a55	15 07				15 18	15a25	15 37				15 48	15a55	16 07				16 18	16a25
Higham	d				15 13						15 43						16 13					
Strood	d		15 01		15 18				15 28		15 48				15 58		16 18				16 28	
Rochester	d		15 06		15 23				15 33		15 52				16 03		16 23				16 33	
Chatham	d		15 08		15 26				15 35		15 55				16 05		16 26				16 35	
Gillingham (Kent)	a		15 12		15 30				15 39		16 02				16 09		16 30				16 39	

Table 200

Sundays

London - Dartford and Gillingham

		SE	SE	SE	SE	SE	SE	SE	SE	SE	SE	SE	SE	SE	SE	SE	SE	SE	SE	SE	SE	SE	SE
St Pancras International ⊖	d					16 28						16 55			17 04				17 25				
Stratford International ⊖	d					16 35						17 05			17 11				17 32				
Ebbsfleet International	d					16 46						17 16			17 23				17 43				
London Charing Cross ⊖	d	15 40	16 00	16 20			15 56	16 10	16 30	16 50			16 26	17 00		16 40	17 20			16 56	17 10	17 30	17 50
London Waterloo (East) ⊖	d	15 43	16 03	16 23			15 59	16 13	16 33	16 53			16 29	17 03		16 43	17 23			16 59	17 13	17 33	17 53
London Cannon Street ⊖	d																						
London Bridge ⊖	d	15 48	16 08	16 28	16 23		16 04	16 18	16 38	16 58	16 53		16 34	17 08		16 48	17 28	17 23		17 04	17 18	17 38	17 58
Deptford	d		16 14		16 29				16 44		16 59			17 14				17 29				17 44	
Greenwich	d		16 16		16 31				16 46		17 01			17 16				17 31				17 46	
Maze Hill	d		16 19		16 34				16 49		17 04			17 19				17 34				17 49	
Westcombe Park	d		16 21		16 36				16 51		17 06			17 21				17 36				17 51	
London Victoria ⊖	d																						
Denmark Hill	d																						
Peckham Rye	d																						
Nunhead	d																						
New Cross ⊖	d			16 34						17 04							17 34						18 04
St Johns	d																						
Lewisham	d	15 57		16 38			16 12	16 27		17 08			16 42			16 57	17 38			17 12	17 27		18 08
Blackheath	d	16 00		16 40				16 30		17 10						17 00	17 40				17 30		18 10
Kidbrooke	d			16 43						17 13							17 43						18 13
Eltham	d			16 47						17 17							17 47						18 17
Falconwood	d			16 49						17 19							17 49						18 19
Welling	d			16 52						17 22							17 52						18 22
Bexleyheath	d			16 54						17 24							17 54						18 24
Barnehurst	d			16 57						17 27							17 57						18 27
Hither Green	d						16 16						16 46							17 16			
Lee	d						16 18						16 48							17 18			
Mottingham	d						16 21						16 51							17 21			
New Eltham	d						16 23						16 53							17 23			
Sidcup	d						16 27						16 57							17 27			
Albany Park	d						16 29						16 59							17 29			
Bexley	d						16 31						17 01							17 31			
Crayford	d						16 34						17 04							17 34			
Charlton	d	16 04	16 24		16 39			16 34	16 54		17 09			17 24		17 04		17 39			17 34	17 54	
Woolwich Dockyard	d		16 27		16 42				16 57		17 12			17 27				17 42				17 57	
Woolwich Arsenal	d	16 10	16 30		16 45			16 40	17 00		17 15			17 30		17 10		17 45			17 40	18 00	
Plumstead	d		16 32		16a47				17 02		17a17			17 32				17a47				18 02	
Abbey Wood	d	16 14	16 35					16 44	17 05					17 35		17 14					17 44	18 05	
Belvedere	d		16 38						17 08					17 38								18 08	
Erith	d		16 40						17 10					17 40								18 10	
Slade Green	d		16 44						17 14					17 44								18 14	
Dartford	a	16 24	16 49	17 03			16 39	16 54	17 19	17 33			17 09	17 49		17 24	18 03			17 39	17 54	18 19	18 33
	d	16 25					16 40	16 55					17 10			17 25				17 40	17 55		
Stone Crossing	d						16 44						17 14							17 44			
Greenhithe for Bluewater	d	16 30					16 46	17 00					17 16			17 30				17 46	18 00		
Swanscombe	d						16 49						17 19							17 49			
Northfleet	d						16 51						17 21							17 51			
Gravesend	d	16 37				16 51	16a55	17 07				17 21	17a25		17 28	17 37			17 48	17a55	18 07		
Higham	d	16 43						17 13								17 43					18 13		
Strood	d	16 48				17 01		17 18				17 31			17 38	17 48			17 58		18 18		
Rochester	d	16 52				17 06		17 23				17 35			17 42	17 52			18 03		18 23		
Chatham	d	16 55				17 08		17 26				17 38			17 45	17 55			18 05		18 26		
Gillingham (Kent)	a	17 02				17 12		17 30				17 42			17 49	18 02			18 09		18 30		

Table 200

Sundays

London - Dartford and Gillingham

		SE	SE	SE	SE	SE		SE	SE	SE	SE	SE	SE	SE	SE	SE		SE	SE	SE	SE	SE	SE	SE	SE
St Pancras International [15] ⊖	d		17 58							18 28						18 55							19 25		
Stratford International ⊖ ⛴	d		18 05							18 35						19 02							19 32		
Ebbsfleet International	d		18 16							18 46						19 13							19 43		
London Charing Cross [4] ⊖	d			17 26	17 40	18 00		18 20			17 56	18 10	18 30	18 50				18 26	18 40	18 56	19 00	19 20		19 10	19 26
London Waterloo (East) [4] ⊖	d			17 29	17 43	18 03		18 23			17 59	18 13	18 33	18 53				18 29	18 43	18 59	19 03	19 23		19 13	19 29
London Cannon Street [4] ⊖	d																								
London Bridge [4] ⊖	d	17 53		17 34	17 48	18 08		18 28	18 23		18 04	18 18	18 38	18 58	18 53			18 34	18 48	19 04	19 08	19 28		19 18	19 34
Deptford	d	17 59				18 14			18 29				18 44		18 59						19 14				
Greenwich [4] ⛴	d	18 01				18 16			18 31				18 46		19 01						19 16				
Maze Hill	d	18 04				18 19			18 34				18 49		19 04						19 19				
Westcombe Park	d	18 06				18 21			18 36				18 51		19 06						19 21				
London Victoria [15] ⊖	d																								
Denmark Hill [4]	d																								
Peckham Rye [4]	d																								
Nunhead [4]	d																								
New Cross [4] ⊖	d							18 34						19 04								19 34			
St Johns	d																								
Lewisham [4] ⛴	d			17 42	17 57			18 38			18 12	18 27		19 08				18 42	18 57	19 12		19 38		19 27	19 42
Blackheath [4]	d				18 00			18 40				18 30		19 10					19 00			19 40		19 30	
Kidbrooke	d							18 43						19 13								19 43			
Eltham	d							18 47						19 17								19 47			
Falconwood	d							18 49						19 19								19 49			
Welling	d							18 52						19 22								19 52			
Bexleyheath	d							18 54						19 24								19 54			
Barnehurst [4]	d							18 57						19 27								19 57			
Hither Green [4]	d			17 46							18 16							18 46		19 16					19 46
Lee	d			17 48							18 18							18 48		19 18					19 48
Mottingham	d			17 51							18 21							18 51		19 21					19 51
New Eltham	d			17 53							18 23							18 53		19 23					19 53
Sidcup [4]	d			17 57							18 27							18 57		19 27					19 57
Albany Park	d			17 59							18 29							18 59		19 29					19 59
Bexley	d			18 01							18 31							19 01		19 31					20 01
Crayford	d			18 04							18 34							19 04		19 34					20 04
Charlton [4]	d	18 09			18 04	18 24			18 39			18 34	18 54		19 09				19 04		19 24			19 34	
Woolwich Dockyard	d	18 12				18 27			18 42				18 57		19 12						19 27				
Woolwich Arsenal [4] ⛴	d	18 15			18 10	18 30			18 45			18 40	19 00		19 15				19 10		19 30			19 40	
Plumstead	d	18a17				18 32			18a47				19 02		19a17						19 32				
Abbey Wood	d				18 14	18 35						18 44	19 05						19 14		19 35			19 44	
Belvedere	d					18 38							19 08								19 38				
Erith	d					18 40							19 10								19 40				
Slade Green [4]	d					18 44							19 14								19 44				
Dartford [4]	a			18 09	18 24	18 49		19 03			18 39	18 54	19 19	19 33				19 09	19 24	19 39	19 49	20 03		19 54	20 09
	d			18 10	18 25						18 40	18 55						19 10	19 25					19 55	
Stone Crossing	d			18 14							18 44							19 14	19 29					19 59	
Greenhithe for Bluewater	d			18 16	18 30						18 46	19 00						19 16	19 31					20 01	
Swanscombe	d			18 19							18 49							19 19	19 34					20 04	
Northfleet	d			18 21							18 51							19 21	19 36					20 06	
Gravesend [4]	d		18 21	18a25	18 37					18 51	18a55	19 07				19 18		19a25	19 40				19 48	20 10	
Higham	d				18 43							19 13							19 46					20 16	
Strood [4]	d		18 31		18 48					19 01		19 18				19 28			19 52				19 58	20 22	
Rochester [4]	d		18 35		18 52					19 06		19 23				19 33			19 56				20 03	20 26	
Chatham [4]	d		18 38		18 55					19 08		19 26				19 35			19 58				20 05	20 28	
Gillingham (Kent) [4]	a		18 42		19 02					19 12		19 30				19 39			20 03				20 09	20 33	

Table 200

Sundays

London - Dartford and Gillingham

		SE		SE	SE	SE	SE	SE	SE	SE	SE	SE		SE	SE	SE	SE	SE	SE	SE	SE	SE		SE	SE
St Pancras International [15] ⊖	d				19 55					20 25						20 55					21 25				
Stratford International ⊖ ⛴	d				20 02					20 32						21 02					21 32				
Ebbsfleet International	d				20 13					20 43						21 13					21 43				
London Charing Cross [4] ⊖	d	19 30		19 50		19 40	19 56	20 00	20 20		20 10	20 26		20 30	20 50		20 40	20 56	21 00	21 20		21 10		21 26	21 30
London Waterloo (East) [4] ⊖	d	19 33		19 53		19 43	19 59	20 03	20 23		20 13	20 29		20 33	20 53		20 43	20 59	21 03	21 23		21 13		21 29	21 33
London Cannon Street [4] ⊖	d																								
London Bridge [4] ⊖	d	19 38		19 58		19 48	20 04	20 08	20 28		20 18	20 34		20 38	20 58		20 48	21 04	21 08	21 28		21 18		21 34	21 38
Deptford	d	19 44						20 14						20 44					21 14						21 44
Greenwich [4] ⛴	d	19 46						20 16						20 46					21 16						21 46
Maze Hill	d	19 49						20 19						20 49					21 19						21 49
Westcombe Park	d	19 51						20 21						20 51					21 21						21 51
London Victoria [15] ⊖	d																								
Denmark Hill [4]	d																								
Peckham Rye [4]	d																								
Nunhead [4]	d																								
New Cross [4] ⊖	d			20 04					20 34						21 04					21 34					
St Johns	d																								
Lewisham [4] ⛴	d			20 08		19 57	20 12		20 38		20 27	20 42			21 08		20 57	21 12		21 38		21 27		21 42	
Blackheath [4]	d			20 10		20 00			20 40		20 30				21 10		21 00			21 40		21 30			
Kidbrooke	d			20 13					20 43						21 13					21 43					
Eltham	d			20 17					20 47						21 17					21 47					
Falconwood	d			20 19					20 49						21 19					21 49					
Welling	d			20 22					20 52						21 22					21 52					
Bexleyheath	d			20 24					20 54						21 24					21 54					
Barnehurst [4]	d			20 27					20 57						21 27					21 57					
Hither Green [4]	d						20 16					20 46						21 16						21 46	
Lee	d						20 18					20 48						21 18						21 48	
Mottingham	d						20 21					20 51						21 21						21 51	
New Eltham	d						20 23					20 53						21 23						21 53	
Sidcup [4]	d						20 27					20 57						21 27						21 57	
Albany Park	d						20 29					20 59						21 29						21 59	
Bexley	d						20 31					21 01						21 31						22 01	
Crayford	d						20 34					21 04						21 34						22 04	
Charlton [4]	d	19 54				20 04		20 24			20 34			20 54			21 04		21 24			21 34			21 54
Woolwich Dockyard	d	19 57						20 27						20 57					21 27						21 57
Woolwich Arsenal [4] ⛴	d	20 00				20 10		20 30			20 40			21 00			21 10		21 30			21 40			22 00
Plumstead	d	20 02						20 32						21 02					21 32						22 02
Abbey Wood	d	20 05				20 14		20 35			20 44			21 05			21 14		21 35			21 44			22 05
Belvedere	d	20 08						20 38						21 08					21 38						22 08
Erith	d	20 10						20 40						21 10					21 40						22 10
Slade Green [4]	d	20 14						20 44						21 14					21 44						22 14
Dartford [4]	a	20 19		20 33		20 24	20 39	20 49	21 03		20 54	21 09		21 19	21 33		21 24	21 39	21 49	22 03		21 54		22 09	22 19
	d					20 25					20 55						21 25					21 55			
Stone Crossing	d					20 29					20 59						21 29					21 59			
Greenhithe for Bluewater	d					20 31					21 01						21 31					22 01			
Swanscombe	d					20 34					21 04						21 34					22 04			
Northfleet	d					20 36					21 06						21 36					22 06			
Gravesend [4]	d				20 18	20 40				20 48	21 10					21 18	21 40				21 48	22 10			
Higham	d					20 46					21 16						21 46					22 16			
Strood [4]	d				20 28	20 52				20 58	21 22					21 28	21 52				21 58	22 22			
Rochester [4]	d				20 33	20 56				21 03	21 26					21 33	21 56				22 03	22 26			
Chatham [4]	d				20 35	20 58				21 05	21 28					21 35	21 58				22 05	22 28			
Gillingham (Kent) [4]	a				20 39	21 03				21 09	21 33					21 39	22 03				22 09	22 33			

Table 200

Sundays

London - Dartford and Gillingham

		SE	SE	SE	SE	SE	SE	SE	SE	SE	SE	SE	SE	SE	SE	SE	SE	SE	SE	SE	SE	SE	SE
St Pancras International	d		21 55					22 25					22 55					23 25					
Stratford International	d		22 02					22 32					23 02					23 32					
Ebbsfleet International	d		22 13					22 43					23 13					23 43					
London Charing Cross	d	21 50		21 40	21 56	22 00	22 20		22 10	22 26	22 30	22 50		22 40	22 56	23 00	23 20		23 10	23 26	23 30	23 50	23 56
London Waterloo (East)	d	21 53		21 43	21 59	22 03	22 23		22 13	22 29	22 33	22 53		22 43	22 59	23 03	23 23		23 13	23 29	23 33	23 53	23 59
London Cannon Street	d																						
London Bridge	d	21 58		21 48	22 04	22 08	22 28		22 18	22 34	22 38	22 58		22 48	23 04	23 08	23 28		23 18	23 34	23 38	23 58	00 04
Deptford	d					22 14					22 44					23 14					23 44		
Greenwich	d					22 16					22 46					23 16					23 46		
Maze Hill	d					22 19					22 49					23 19					23 49		
Westcombe Park	d					22 21					22 51					23 21					23 51		
London Victoria	d																						
Denmark Hill	d																						
Peckham Rye	d																						
Nunhead	d																						
New Cross	d	22 04					22 34					23 04					23 34					00 04	
St Johns	d																						
Lewisham	d	22 08		21 57	22 12		22 38		22 27	22 42		23 08		22 57	23 12		23 38		23 27	23 42		00 08	00 12
Blackheath	d	22 10		22 00			22 40		22 30			23 10		23 00			23 40		23 30			00 10	
Kidbrooke	d	22 13					22 43					23 13					23 43					00 13	
Eltham	d	22 17					22 47					23 17					23 47					00 17	
Falconwood	d	22 19					22 49					23 19					23 49					00 19	
Welling	d	22 22					22 52					23 22					23 52					00 22	
Bexleyheath	d	22 24					22 54					23 24					23 54					00 24	
Barnehurst	d	22 27					22 57					23 27					23 57					00 27	
Hither Green	d				22 16					22 46					23 16					23 46			00 16
Lee	d				22 18					22 48					23 18					23 48			00 18
Mottingham	d				22 21					22 51					23 21					23 51			00 21
New Eltham	d				22 23					22 53					23 23					23 53			00 23
Sidcup	d				22 27					22 57					23 27					23 57			00 27
Albany Park	d				22 29					22 59					23 29					23 59			00 29
Bexley	d				22 31					23 01					23 31					00 01			00 31
Crayford	d				22 34					23 04					23 34					00 04			00 34
Charlton	d			22 04		22 24			22 34		22 54			23 04		23 24			23 34		23 54		
Woolwich Dockyard	d					22 27					22 57					23 27					23 57		
Woolwich Arsenal	d			22 10		22 30			22 40		23 00			23 10		23 30			23 40		23 59		
Plumstead	d					22 32					23 02					23 32					00 02		
Abbey Wood	d			22 14		22 35			22 44		23 05			23 14		23 35			23 44		00 05		
Belvedere	d					22 38					23 08					23 38					00 08		
Erith	d					22 40					23 10					23 40					00 10		
Slade Green	d					22 44					23 14					23 44					00 14		
Dartford	a	22 33		22 24	22 39	22 49	23 03		22 54	23 09	23 19	23 33		23 24	23 39	23 49	00 03		23 54	00 09	00 19	00 33	00 39
	d			22 25					22 55					23 25					23 55				
Stone Crossing	d			22 29					22 59					23 29					23 59				
Greenhithe for Bluewater	d			22 31					23 01					23 31					00 01				
Swanscombe	d			22 34					23 04					23 34					00 04				
Northfleet	d			22 36					23 06					23 36					00 06				
Gravesend	d		22 18	22 40				22 48	23 10				23 18	23 40				23 48	00 10				
Higham	d			22 46					23 16					23 46					00 16				
Strood	d		22 28	22 52				22 58	23 22				23 28	23 52				23 58	00 22				
Rochester	d		22 33	22 56				23 03	23 26				23 33	23 56				00 03	00 26				
Chatham	d		22 35	22 58				23 05	23 28				23 35	23 58				00 05	00 28				
Gillingham (Kent)	a		22 39	23 03				23 09	23 33				23 39	00 03				00 09	00 33				

Table 200

Mondays to Fridays

Gillingham and Dartford - London

		SE	SE	SE	SE	SE	SE	SE	SE	SE	SE	SE	SE	SE	SE	SE	SE	SE	SE	SE	SE	SE	SE
Gillingham (Kent)	d	04 10		04 35	05 20		04 54			05 50			05 24						05 54	06 19			
Chatham	d	04 14		04 39	05 24		04 58			05 54			05 28						05 58	06 24			
Rochester	d	04 16		04 41	05 27		05 00			05 57			05 30						06 00	06 26			
Strood	d	04 21		04 46	05 32		05 05			06 02			05 35						06 05	06 32			
Higham	d	04 26		04 51			05 10						05 40						06 10				
Gravesend	d	04 34		04 59	05 43		05 18		05 28	06 13			05 48					06 06	06 18	06 43			
Northfleet	d			05 02					05 32									06 10					
Swanscombe	d			05 04					05 34									06 12					
Greenhithe for Bluewater	d	04 39		05 07			05 23		05 37				05 53					06 15	06 23				
Stone Crossing	d			05 09					05 39									06 17					
Dartford	a	04 44		05 13			05 28		05 43				05 58					06 21	06 28				
	d	04 44	05 01	05 14		05 22	05 28	05 31	05 44		05 52	05 56	05 58	06 01	06 13		06 16	06 22	06 28		06 31		06 32
Slade Green	d		05 06					05 36						06 06			06 21				06 36		
Erith	d		05 08					05 38						06 08			06 23				06 39		
Belvedere	d		05 11					05 41						06 11			06 26				06 41		
Abbey Wood	d		05 14				05 37	05 44					06 07	06 14			06 29		06 37		06 44		
Plumstead	d		05 17					05 47						06 17			06 32				06 47		
Woolwich Arsenal	d		05 20				05 42	05 50					06 12	06 20			06 35		06 42		06 50		
Woolwich Dockyard	d		05 22					05 52						06 22			06 37				06 53		
Charlton	d		05 25				05 47	05 55					06 17	06 25			06 40		06 47		06 56		
Crayford	d	04 49		05 19					05 49			06 03										06 32	06 36
Bexley	d	04 52		05 22					05 52			06 06										06 35	06 39
Albany Park	d	04 54		05 24					05 54			06 08										06 37	06 42
Sidcup	d	04 57		05 27					05 57			06 11										06 40	06 45
New Eltham	d	05 00		05 30					06 00			06 14										06 43	06 48
Mottingham	d	05 03		05 33					06 03			06 17										06 46	06 50
Lee	d	05 06		05 36					06 06			06 20										06 49	06 53
Hither Green	d	05 08		05 38					06 08			06 22										06 51	06 56
Barnehurst	d					05 29					05 59				06 20	06 14		06 29					
Bexleyheath	d					05 31					06 01				06 22	06 16		06 31					
Welling	d					05 34					06 04				06 25	06 19		06 34					
Falconwood	d					05 37					06 07				06 28	06 22		06 37					
Eltham	d					05 40					06 10				06 31	06 25		06 40					
Kidbrooke	d					05 43					06 13				06 34	06 28		06 43					
Blackheath	d					05 46	05 51				06 16		06 21		06 37	06 31		06 46	06 51				
Lewisham	d	05 13		05 43		05 50	05 56		06 13		06 20	06 27	06 25		06 41	06 35		06 50	06 55			06 57	
St Johns	d											06 29										06 59	
New Cross	d	05 16		05 46		05 53			06 16			06 31				06 38						07 01	
Nunhead	d																						
Peckham Rye	d														06 47								
Denmark Hill	d														06 50								
London Victoria	a														07 04								
Westcombe Park	d		05 27					05 57						06 27			06 42				06 58		
Maze Hill	d		05 27					05 57						06 27			06 42				06 58		
Greenwich	d		05 29					05 59						06 29			06 44				07 00		
Deptford	d		05 33					06 03						06 33			06 48				07 03		
London Bridge	a		05 35					06 05						06 35			06 50				07 05		
London Cannon Street	a															06 48	07 03				07 21	07 14	
London Waterloo (East)	a	05 26	05 46	05 57		06 03	06 08	06 17	06 26		06 33	06 41	06 39	06 48				07 05	07 09				07 11
London Charing Cross	a	05 30	05 50	06 01		06 07	06 12	06 21	06 30		06 36	06 45	06 43	06 52				07 11	07 14				07 17
Ebbsfleet International	a				05 47					06 17										06 47			
Stratford International	a				05 59					06 29										06 59			
St Pancras International	a				06 06					06 36										07 07			

Table 200

Gillingham and Dartford - London

Mondays to Fridays

		SE	SE	SE	SE	SE	SE	SE	SE	SE	SE	SE	SE	SE	SE	SE	SE	SE	SE	SE	SE	SE	SE
Gillingham (Kent)	d			06 08									06 38										
Chatham	d			06 12									06 42										
Rochester	d			06 14									06 44	07 07									
Strood	d			06 19									06 49	07 12				06 57					
Higham	d			06 24									06 54					07 02					
Gravesend	d			06 32	06 37						06 48		07 02	07 22				07 09				07 17	
Northfleet	d				06 40						06 52											07 21	
Swanscombe	d				06 42						06 54											07 23	
Greenhithe for Bluewater	d			06 37	06 45						06 57		07 07					07 15				07 26	
Stone Crossing	d				06 47						06 59											07 28	
Dartford	a			06 42	06 51						07 03		07 12					07 20				07 33	
	d		06 40	06 42	06 52					07 02	07 04	07 06	07 12				07 17	07 24		07 22	07 26	07 34	
Slade Green	d							06 56				07 10							07 20		07 30		
Erith	d							06 58				07 13							07 22		07 33		
Belvedere	d							07 01				07 15							07 25		07 35		
Abbey Wood	d			06 51				07 04			07 13	07 18						07 33	07 28		07 38		
Plumstead	d							07 07				07 21							07 31		07 41		
Woolwich Arsenal	d			06 56				07 10			07 18	07 24						07 38	07 34		07 44		
Woolwich Dockyard	d							07 12				07 27							07 36		07 47		
Charlton	d							07 15			07 22	07 30						07 42	07 39		07 50		
Crayford	d				06 56	06 52							07 17		07 12							07 38	07 32
Bexley	d				06 59	06 55							07 20		07 15							07 41	07 35
Albany Park	d				07 02	06 57							07 22		07 17							07 44	07 37
Sidcup	d				07 05	07 00							07 25		07 20							07 47	07 40
New Eltham	d				07 08	07 03							07 28		07 23							07 50	07 43
Mottingham	d				07 10	07 06							07 31		07 26								07 46
Lee	d				07 13	07 09							07 34		07 29								07 49
Hither Green	d				07 16	07 11							07 36		07 32								07 52
Barnehurst	d	06 39	06 49				06 54		07 01	07 09						07 14	07 24			07 29			
Bexleyheath	d	06 41	06 51				06 56		07 03	07 11						07 16	07 26			07 31			
Welling	d	06 44	06 54				06 59		07 06	07 14						07 19	07 29			07 34			
Falconwood	d	06 47	06 57				07 02		07 09	07 17						07 22	07 32			07 37			
Eltham	d	06 50	07 00				07 05		07 12	07 20						07 25	07 35			07 40			
Kidbrooke	d	06 53	07 03				07 08		07 15	07 23						07 28	07 38			07 43			
Blackheath	d	06 56	07 07	07 04			07 11		07 18	07 26						07 31	07 41			07 46			
Lewisham	d	07 00	07 11	07 08		07 17	07 15		07 22	07 30					07 38	07 35	07 46			07 50			07 57
St Johns	d					07 19			07 24						07 40								08 00
New Cross	d	07 04		07 11		07 21			07 26						07 42	07 38							08 02
Nunhead	d						07 20										07 51						
Peckham Rye	d						07 23										07 54						
Denmark Hill	d						07 29										07 59						
London Victoria	a						07 42										08 11						
Westcombe Park	d							07 17				07 32							07 41		07 52		
Maze Hill	d							07 17				07 32							07 41		07 52		
Greenwich	d							07 19				07 34							07 43		07 54		
Deptford	d							07 23			07 28	07 37						07 50	07 47		07 57		
London Bridge	a							07 25				07 39							07 49		07 59		
London Cannon Street	a	07 16		07 23		07 33			07 39		07 42	07 52			07 54	07 50		08 04			08 12		08 15
London Waterloo (East)	a		07 25		07 31			07 38		07 46			07 52						08 02	08 06		08 10	
London Charing Cross	a		07 31		07 37			07 44		07 52			07 58						08 08	08 12		08 16	
Ebbsfleet International	a																						
Stratford International	a													07 36									
St Pancras International	a													07 43									

Table 200

Gillingham and Dartford - London

Mondays to Fridays

		SE	SE	SE	SE	SE	SE	SE	SE	SE	SE	SE	SE	SE	SE	SE	SE	SE	SE	SE	SE	SE
Gillingham (Kent)	d								07 12										07 38			
Chatham	d								07 16										07 42			
Rochester	d			07 37					07 18										07 44		08 07	
Strood	d			07 42			07 19		07 25										07 49		08 12	
Higham	d						07 24		07 30										07 54			
Gravesend	d			07 52			07 32		07 37								07 48		08 02	08 06	08 22	
Northfleet	d								07 41								07 52			08 09		
Swanscombe	d								07 43								07 54			08 11		
Greenhithe for Bluewater	d						07 38		07 46								07 57		08 08	08 15		
Stone Crossing	d								07 48								07 59			08 17		
Dartford	a						07 43		07 52								08 03		08 12	08 21		
	d		07 36			07 42	07 44	07 46	07 54				07 56			08 02	08 04	08 06	08 13	08 22		
Slade Green	d							07 50							08 00			08 10		08 27		
Erith	d							07 53							08 02			08 13				
Belvedere	d							07 55							08 05			08 15				
Abbey Wood	d						07 53	07 58							08 08		08 13	08 18		08 33		
Plumstead	d							08 01							08 11			08 21				
Woolwich Arsenal	d						07 58	08 04							08 14		08 18	08 24		08 38		
Woolwich Dockyard	d							08 07							08 16			08 27				
Charlton	d						08 02	08 10							08 19		08 22	08 30		08 43		
Crayford	d								07 58		07 52								08 17			
Bexley	d								08 01		07 55								08 20			
Albany Park	d								08 04		07 57								08 23			
Sidcup	d								08 07	07 51	08 00								08 26			08 11
New Eltham	d								08 10	07 54	08 03								08 29			08 14
Mottingham	d									07 56	08 06											08 16
Lee	d									07 59	08 09											08 19
Hither Green	d									08 02	08 12											08 22
Barnehurst	d	07 34	07 44		07 40	07 49						07 54	08 04	08 00		08 09						
Bexleyheath	d	07 36	07 46		07 42	07 51						07 56	08 06	08 02		08 11						
Welling	d	07 39	07 49		07 45	07 54						07 59	08 09	08 05		08 14						
Falconwood	d	07 42	07 52		07 48	07 57						08 02	08 12	08 08		08 17						
Eltham	d	07 45	07 55		07 51	08 00						08 05	08 15	08 11		08 20						
Kidbrooke	d	07 48	07 58		07 54	08 03						08 08	08 18	08 14		08 23						
Blackheath	d	07 51	08 01		07 57	08 06						08 11	08 21	08 17		08 26						
Lewisham	d	07 55	08 05			08 10					08 17	08 15	08 26			08 31						
St Johns	d										08 21											
New Cross	d	07 58									08 23	08 18										
Nunhead	d		08 11										08 31									
Peckham Rye	d		08 13										08 33									
Denmark Hill	d		08 17										08 36									
London Victoria	a		08 29										08 49									
Westcombe Park	d							08 12							08 21			08 32				
Maze Hill	d							08 12							08 21			08 32				
Greenwich	d							08 14							08 23			08 34				
Deptford	d						08 10	08 17							08 27		08 30	08 37		08 50		
London Bridge	a							08 19							08 29			08 39				
London Cannon Street	a	08 10					08 24	08 34			08 36	08 32					08 44	08 52		09 08		
London Waterloo (East)	a				08 12	08 26			08 30	08 18				08 32	08 42	08 46			08 50			08 38
London Charing Cross	a				08 18	08 32			08 36	08 24				08 39	08 48	08 52			08 56			08 44
Ebbsfleet International	a																					
Stratford International	a			08 06																	08 36	
St Pancras International	a			08 13																	08 43	

Gillingham and Dartford - London

		SE	SE	SE	SE	SE	SE	SE		SE	SE	SE	SE	SE	SE	SE	SE	SE		SE	SE	SE	SE	SE	SE
Gillingham (Kent) [4]	d			08 19												08 08		08 50							
Chatham [4]	d			08 24												08 12		08 54							
Rochester [4]	d			08 26												08 14		08 57							
Strood [4]	d			08 32				07 58								08 19		09 02							
Higham	d							08 03								08 24									
Gravesend [4]	d			08 43				08b18								08 33		09 13			08 48				
Northfleet	d															08 37									
Swanscombe	d															08 39									
Greenhithe for Bluewater	d							08 24								08 42					08 53				
Stone Crossing	d															08 44									
Dartford [4]	a							08 29								08 49					08 58				
	d						08 24	08 31							08 38	08 49				08 52	08 58		09 01		
Slade Green [4]	d				08 18	08 18					08 31						08 40					08 54	09 05		
Erith	d				08 20						08 34						08 42					08 56	09 08		
Belvedere	d				08 23						08 36						08 45					08 59	09 10		
Abbey Wood	d				08 26						08 39						08 48				09 07	09 02	09 13		
Plumstead	d				08 29						08 42						08 51					09 05	09 16		
Woolwich Arsenal [4] ⛴	d				08 32						08 45						08 54				09 12	09 08	09 19		
Woolwich Dockyard	d				08 34						08 47						08 56					09 10	09 22		
Charlton [4]	d				08 37						08 50		08 37				08 59				09 17	09 13	09 25	09 07	
Crayford	d	08 12						08 36		08 29			09c08			08 54								09 38	
Bexley	d	08 15						08 39		08 32			09 11			08 57								09 41	
Albany Park	d	08 17						08 41		08 34			09 14			09 00								09 44	
Sidcup [4]	d	08 20						08 44		08 37		08 31	09 17			09 03								09 47	
New Eltham	d	08 23						08 47		08 40		08 34	09 20			09 06								09 50	
Mottingham	d	08 26						08 50		08 43		08 36	09 22			09 08								09 52	
Lee	d	08 29						08 53		08 46		08 39	09 25			09 11								09 55	
Hither Green [4]	d	08 32						08 55		08 49		08 42	09 28			09 14								09 58	
Barnehurst [4]	d		08 14			08 25	08 30							08 38	08 45					08 59					09 08
Bexleyheath	d		08 16			08 27	08 33							08 40	08 47					09 01					09 10
Welling	d		08 19			08 30	08 36							08 43	08 50					09 04					09 13
Falconwood	d		08 22			08 33	08 38							08 46	08 53					09 07					09 16
Eltham	d		08 25			08 36	08 41							08 49	08 56					09 10					09 19
Kidbrooke	d		08 28			08 39	08 44							08 52	08 59					09 13					09 22
Blackheath [4]	d		08 31			08 42	08 48							08 55	09 02					09 16	09 21				09 25
Lewisham [4] ⛴	d	08 37	08 35			08 46	08 51			08 54			09 34	08 59	09 06					09 20	09 26			10 04	09 29
St Johns	d	08 40								08 57			09 36											10 06	
New Cross [4] ⊖	d	08 42	08 38							08 59			09 38	09 02										10 08	09 32
Nunhead [4]	d					08 52									09 11										
Peckham Rye [4]	d					08 55									09 14										
Denmark Hill [4]	d					09 02									09 17										
London Victoria [15] ⊖	a					09 11									09 29										
Westcombe Park	d				08 39						08 52						09 01					09 15	09 27		
Maze Hill	d				08 39						08 52						09 01					09 15	09 27		
Greenwich [4] ⛴	d				08 41						08 54						09 03					09 17	09 29		
Deptford	d				08 45						08 57						09 07					09 21	09 32		
London Bridge [4] ⊖	a				08 47						08 59						09 09					09 23	09 34		
London Cannon Street [4] ⊖	a	08 55	08 50							09 12	09 14		09 51	09 18								09 36	09 48	10 19	09 45
London Waterloo (East) [4] ⊖	a				09 02		09 05	09 10				08 58				09 28	09 22			09 34	09 39				
London Charing Cross [4] ⊖	a				09 08		09 12	09 16				09 04				09 34	09 28			09 40	09 45				
Ebbsfleet International	a			08 47														09 17							
Stratford International ⊖ ⛴	a			08 59														09 29							
St Pancras International [15] ⊖	a			09 07														09 39							

b arr. 0810

c arr. 0903

Gillingham and Dartford - London

		SE	SE	SE		SE	SE	SE	SE	SE	SE	SE	SE	SE		SE	SE	SE	SE	SE	SE	SE	SE	SE	
Gillingham (Kent) [4]	d					09 20		08 54									09 50		09 24						
Chatham [4]	d					09 24		08 58									09 54		09 28						
Rochester [4]	d					09 27		09 00									09 57		09 30						
Strood [4]	d					09 32		09 06									10 02		09 35						
Higham	d							09 11											09 40						
Gravesend [4]	d		09 03			09 43		09 18						09 33			10 12		09 48						
Northfleet	d		09 07											09 37											
Swanscombe	d		09 09											09 39											
Greenhithe for Bluewater	d		09 12					09 23						09 42					09 53						
Stone Crossing	d		09 14											09 44											
Dartford [4]	a		09 18					09 27						09 48					09 58						
	d	09 08	09 18				09 22	09 28		09 31			09 38	09 48				09 52	09 58		10 01			10 08	
Slade Green [4]	d			09 15					09 25	09 35						09 45				09 55	10 05				
Erith	d			09 17					09 27	09 38						09 47				09 57	10 08				
Belvedere	d			09 20					09 30	09 40						09 50				10 00	10 10				
Abbey Wood	d			09 23				09 37	09 33	09 43						09 53			10 07	10 03	10 13				
Plumstead	d			09 26					09 36	09 46						09 56				10 06	10 16				
Woolwich Arsenal [4] ⛴	d			09 29				09 43	09 39	09 49						09 59			10 12	10 09	10 19				
Woolwich Dockyard	d			09 31					09 41	09 52						10 01				10 11	10 22				
Charlton [4]	d			09 34				09 47	09 44	09 55	09 38					10 04			10 17	10 14	10 25	10 07			
Crayford	d		09 23								10 08			09 53								10 38			
Bexley	d		09 26								10 11			09 56								10 41			
Albany Park	d		09 29								10 14			09 59								10 44			
Sidcup [4]	d		09 32								10 17			10 02								10 47			
New Eltham	d		09 35								10 20			10 05								10 50			
Mottingham	d		09 37								10 22			10 07								10 52			
Lee	d		09 40								10 25			10 10								10 55			
Hither Green [4]	d		09 42								10 28			10 12								10 58			
Barnehurst [4]	d	09 16					09 29					09 38	09 46					09 59					10 08	10 16	
Bexleyheath	d	09 19					09 31					09 40	09 49					10 01					10 10	10 19	
Welling	d	09 22					09 34					09 43	09 52					10 04					10 13	10 22	
Falconwood	d	09 24					09 37					09 46	09 54					10 07					10 16	10 24	
Eltham	d	09 27					09 40					09 49	09 57					10 10					10 19	10 27	
Kidbrooke	d	09 30					09 43					09 52	10 00					10 13					10 22	10 30	
Blackheath [4]	d	09 34					09 46	09 52				09 55	10 04					10 16	10 21				10 25	10 34	
Lewisham [4] ⛴	d	09 38					09 50	09 56			10 34	09 59	10 08					10 20	10 26			11 04	10 29	10 38	
St Johns	d										10 36											11 06			
New Cross [4] ⊖	d										10 38	10 02										11 08	10 32		
Nunhead [4]	d	09 43											10 13											10 43	
Peckham Rye [4]	d	09 45											10 15											10 45	
Denmark Hill [4]	d	09 49											10 19											10 49	
London Victoria [15] ⊖	a	10 00											10 28											10 58	
Westcombe Park	d			09 36					09 46	09 57						10 06				10 16	10 27				
Maze Hill	d			09 36					09 46	09 57						10 06				10 16	10 27				
Greenwich [4] ⛴	d			09 38					09 48	09 59						10 08				10 18	10 29				
Deptford	d			09 42					09 52	10 02						10 12				10 22	10 32				
London Bridge [4] ⊖	a			09 44					09 54	10 04						10 14				10 24	10 34				
London Cannon Street [4] ⊖	a			09 57					10 04	10 15	10 49	10 13				10 24				10 36	10 45	11 19	10 43		
London Waterloo (East) [4] ⊖	a		09 56				10 02	10 09						10 26				10 32	10 39						
London Charing Cross [4] ⊖	a		10 00				10 06	10 13						10 30				10 36	10 43						
Ebbsfleet International	a					09 47											10 16								
Stratford International ⊖ ⛴	a					09 59											10 27								
St Pancras International [15] ⊖	a					10 06											10 38								

Table 200

Mondays to Fridays

Gillingham and Dartford - London

		SE	SE	SE	SE	SE	SE	SE	SE	SE		SE	SE	SE	SE	SE	SE	SE	SE	SE		SE	SE	SE	SE
Gillingham (Kent) [4]	d			10 20		09 54									10 50		10 24								
Chatham [4]	d			10 24		09 58									10 54		10 28								
Rochester [4]	d			10 27		10 00									10 57		10 30								
Strood [4]	d			10 32		10 05									11 02		10 35								
Higham	d					10 10											10 40								
Gravesend [4]	d	10 03		10 43		10 18							10 33		11 13		10 48							11 03	
Northfleet	d	10 07											10 37											11 07	
Swanscombe	d	10 09											10 39											11 09	
Greenhithe for Bluewater	d	10 12				10 23							10 42				10 53							11 12	
Stone Crossing	d	10 14											10 44											11 14	
Dartford [4]	a	10 18				10 28							10 48				10 58							11 18	
	d	10 18			10 22	10 28		10 31				10 38	10 48			10 52	10 58		11 01				11 08	11 18	
Slade Green [4]	d		10 15				10 25	10 35						10 45				10 55	11 05						11 15
Erith	d		10 17				10 27	10 38						10 47				10 57	11 08						11 17
Belvedere	d		10 20				10 30	10 40						10 50				11 00	11 10						11 20
Abbey Wood	d		10 23			10 37	10 33	10 43						10 53			11 07	11 03	11 13						11 23
Plumstead	d		10 26				10 36	10 46						10 56				11 06	11 16						11 26
Woolwich Arsenal [4] ⛴	d		10 29			10 42	10 39	10 49						10 59			11 12	11 09	11 19						11 29
Woolwich Dockyard	d		10 31				10 41	10 52						11 01				11 11	11 22						11 31
Charlton [4]	d		10 34			10 47	10 44	10 55	10 37					11 04			11 17	11 14	11 25	11 07					11 34
Crayford	d	10 23							11 08				10 53							11 38				11 23	
Bexley	d	10 26							11 11				10 56							11 41				11 26	
Albany Park	d	10 29							11 14				10 59							11 44				11 29	
Sidcup [4]	d	10 32							11 17				11 02							11 47				11 32	
New Eltham	d	10 35							11 20				11 05							11 50				11 35	
Mottingham	d	10 37							11 22				11 07							11 52				11 37	
Lee	d	10 40							11 25				11 10							11 55				11 40	
Hither Green [4]	d	10 42							11 28				11 12							11 58				11 42	
Barnehurst [4]	d				10 29					10 38		10 46				10 59						11 08	11 16		
Bexleyheath	d				10 31					10 40		10 49				11 01						11 10	11 19		
Welling	d				10 34					10 43		10 52				11 04						11 13	11 22		
Falconwood	d				10 37					10 46		10 54				11 07						11 16	11 24		
Eltham	d				10 40					10 49		10 57				11 10						11 19	11 27		
Kidbrooke	d				10 43					10 52		11 00				11 13						11 22	11 30		
Blackheath [4]	d				10 46	10 51				10 55		11 04				11 16	11 21					11 25	11 34		
Lewisham [4] ⛴	d				10 50	10 56			11 34	10 59		11 08				11 20	11 26			12 04		11 29	11 38		
St Johns	d								11 36											12 06					
New Cross [4] ⊖	d								11 38	11 02										12 08		11 32			
Nunhead [4]	d											11 13											11 43		
Peckham Rye [4]	d											11 15											11 45		
Denmark Hill [4]	d											11 19											11 49		
London Victoria [15] ⊖	a											11 28											11 58		
Westcombe Park	d		10 36				10 46	10 57						11 06				11 16	11 27						11 36
Maze Hill	d		10 36				10 46	10 57						11 06				11 16	11 27						11 36
Greenwich [4] ⛴	d		10 38				10 48	10 59						11 08				11 18	11 29						11 38
Deptford	d		10 42				10 52	11 02						11 12				11 22	11 32						11 42
London Bridge [4] ⊖	a		10 44				10 54	11 04						11 14				11 24	11 34						11 44
London Cannon Street [4] ⊖	a		10 54				11 06	11 15	11 49	11 13				11 24				11 36	11 45	12 19		11 43			11 54
London Waterloo (East) [4] ⊖	a	10 56			11 02	11 09							11 26			11 32	11 39							11 56	
London Charing Cross [4] ⊖	a	11 00			11 06	11 13							11 30			11 36	11 43							12 00	
Ebbsfleet International	a			10 47											11 17										
Stratford International ⊖ ⛴	a			10 59											11 29										
St Pancras International [15] ⊖	a			11 06											11 36										

Table 200

Mondays to Fridays

Gillingham and Dartford - London

		SE	SE	SE	SE	SE		SE	SE	SE	SE	SE	SE	SE	SE	SE		SE	SE	SE	SE	SE	SE	SE	SE
Gillingham (Kent) [4]	d	11 20		10 54								11 50		11 24										12 20	
Chatham [4]	d	11 24		10 58								11 54		11 28										12 24	
Rochester [4]	d	11 27		11 00								11 57		11 30										12 27	
Strood [4]	d	11 32		11 05								12 02		11 35										12 32	
Higham	d			11 10										11 40											
Gravesend [4]	d	11 43		11 18							11 33		12 13		11 48							12 03		12 43	
Northfleet	d										11 37											12 07			
Swanscombe	d										11 39											12 09			
Greenhithe for Bluewater	d			11 23							11 42				11 53							12 12			
Stone Crossing	d										11 44											12 14			
Dartford [4]	a			11 28							11 48				11 58							12 18			
	d		11 22	11 28		11 31				11 38	11 48			11 52	11 58			12 01			12 08	12 18			12 22
Slade Green [4]	d				11 25	11 35						11 45				11 55		12 05					12 15		
Erith	d				11 27	11 38						11 47				11 57		12 08					12 17		
Belvedere	d				11 30	11 40						11 50				12 00		12 10					12 20		
Abbey Wood	d			11 37	11 33	11 43						11 53			12 07	12 03		12 13					12 23		
Plumstead	d				11 36	11 46						11 56				12 06		12 16					12 26		
Woolwich Arsenal [4] ⛴	d			11 42	11 39	11 49						11 59			12 12	12 09		12 19					12 29		
Woolwich Dockyard	d				11 41	11 52						12 01				12 11		12 22					12 31		
Charlton [4]	d			11 47	11 44	11 55		11 37				12 04			12 17	12 14		12 25	12 07				12 34		
Crayford	d							12 08			11 53								12 38			12 23			
Bexley	d							12 11			11 56								12 41			12 26			
Albany Park	d							12 14			11 59								12 44			12 29			
Sidcup [4]	d							12 17			12 02								12 47			12 32			
New Eltham	d							12 20			12 05								12 50			12 35			
Mottingham	d							12 22			12 07								12 52			12 37			
Lee	d							12 25			12 10								12 55			12 40			
Hither Green [4]	d							12 28			12 12								12 58			12 42			
Barnehurst [4]	d		11 29						11 38	11 46				11 59						12 08	12 16				12 29
Bexleyheath	d		11 31						11 40	11 49				12 01						12 10	12 19				12 31
Welling	d		11 34						11 43	11 52				12 04						12 13	12 22				12 34
Falconwood	d		11 37						11 46	11 54				12 07						12 16	12 24				12 37
Eltham	d		11 40						11 49	11 57				12 10						12 19	12 27				12 40
Kidbrooke	d		11 43						11 52	12 00				12 13						12 22	12 30				12 43
Blackheath [4]	d		11 46	11 51					11 55	12 04				12 16	12 21					12 25	12 34				12 46
Lewisham [4] ⛴	d		11 50	11 56				12 34	11 59	12 08				12 20	12 26				13 04	12 29	12 38				12 50
St Johns	d							12 36											13 06						
New Cross [4] ⊖	d							12 38	12 02										13 08	12 32					
Nunhead [4]	d									12 13											12 43				
Peckham Rye [4]	d									12 15											12 45				
Denmark Hill [4]	d									12 19											12 49				
London Victoria [15] ⊖	a									12 28											12 58				
Westcombe Park	d				11 46	11 57						12 06				12 16		12 27					12 36		
Maze Hill	d				11 46	11 57						12 06				12 16		12 27					12 36		
Greenwich [4] ⛴	d				11 48	11 59						12 08				12 18		12 29					12 38		
Deptford	d				11 52	12 02						12 12				12 22		12 32					12 42		
London Bridge [4] ⊖	a				11 54	12 04						12 14				12 24		12 34					12 44		
London Cannon Street [4] ⊖	a				12 04	12 15		12 49	12 13			12 24				12 36		12 45	13 19	12 43			12 54		
London Waterloo (East) [4] ⊖	a		12 02	12 09							12 26			12 32	12 39							12 56			13 02
London Charing Cross [4] ⊖	a		12 06	12 13							12 30			12 36	12 43							13 00			13 06
Ebbsfleet International	a	11 47											12 17											12 47	
Stratford International ⊖ ⛴	a	11 59											12 32											12 59	
St Pancras International [15] ⊖	a	12 06											12 39											13 06	

Table 200

Mondays to Fridays

Gillingham and Dartford - London

		SE	SE	SE	SE	SE	SE	SE	SE	SE	SE	SE	SE	SE	SE	SE	SE	SE	SE	SE	SE	SE
Gillingham (Kent)	d	11 54								12 50		12 24								13 20		12 54
Chatham	d	11 58								12 54		12 28								13 24		12 58
Rochester	d	12 00								12 57		12 30								13 27		13 00
Strood	d	12 05								13 02		12 35								13 32		13 05
Higham	d	12 10										12 40										13 10
Gravesend	d	12 18						12 33		13 13		12 48						13 03		13 43		13 18
Northfleet	d							12 37										13 07				
Swanscombe	d							12 39										13 09				
Greenhithe for Bluewater	d	12 23						12 42				12 53						13 12				13 23
Stone Crossing	d							12 44										13 14				
Dartford	a	12 28						12 48				12 58						13 18				13 28
	d	12 28		12 31			12 38	12 48			12 52	12 58		13 01			13 08	13 18			13 22	13 28
Slade Green	d		12 25	12 35					12 45				12 55	13 05					13 15			
Erith	d		12 27	12 38					12 47				12 57	13 08					13 17			
Belvedere	d		12 30	12 40					12 50				13 00	13 10					13 20			
Abbey Wood	d	12 37	12 33	12 43					12 53			13 07	13 03	13 13					13 23			13 37
Plumstead	d		12 36	12 46					12 56				13 06	13 16					13 26			
Woolwich Arsenal	d	12 42	12 39	12 49					12 59			13 12	13 09	13 19					13 29			13 42
Woolwich Dockyard	d		12 41	12 52					13 01				13 11	13 22					13 31			
Charlton	d	12 47	12 44	12 55	12 37				13 04			13 17	13 14	13 25	13 07				13 34			13 47
Crayford	d				13 08			12 53							13 38			13 23				
Bexley	d				13 11			12 56							13 41			13 26				
Albany Park	d				13 14			12 59							13 44			13 29				
Sidcup	d				13 17			13 02							13 47			13 32				
New Eltham	d				13 20			13 05							13 50			13 35				
Mottingham	d				13 22			13 07							13 52			13 37				
Lee	d				13 25			13 10							13 55			13 40				
Hither Green	d				13 28			13 12							13 58			13 42				
Barnehurst	d					12 38	12 46				12 59					13 08	13 16				13 29	
Bexleyheath	d					12 40	12 49				13 01					13 10	13 19				13 31	
Welling	d					12 43	12 52				13 04					13 13	13 22				13 34	
Falconwood	d					12 46	12 54				13 07					13 16	13 24				13 37	
Eltham	d					12 49	12 57				13 10					13 19	13 27				13 40	
Kidbrooke	d					12 52	13 00				13 13					13 22	13 30				13 43	
Blackheath	d	12 51				12 55	13 04				13 16	13 21				13 25	13 34				13 46	13 51
Lewisham	d	12 56			13 34	12 59	13 08				13 20	13 26			14 04	13 29	13 38				13 50	13 56
St Johns	d				13 36										14 06							
New Cross	d				13 38	13 02									14 08	13 32						
Nunhead	d						13 13										13 43					
Peckham Rye	d						13 15										13 45					
Denmark Hill	d						13 19										13 49					
London Victoria	a						13 28										13 58					
Westcombe Park	d		12 46	12 57					13 06				13 16	13 27					13 36			
Maze Hill	d		12 46	12 57					13 06				13 16	13 27					13 36			
Greenwich	d		12 48	12 59					13 08				13 18	13 29					13 38			
Deptford	d		12 52	13 02					13 12				13 22	13 32					13 42			
London Bridge	a		12 54	13 04					13 14				13 24	13 34					13 44			
London Cannon Street	a		13 06	13 15	13 49	13 13			13 24				13 36	13 45	14 19	13 43			13 54			
London Waterloo (East)	a	13 09						13 26			13 32	13 39						13 56			14 02	14 09
London Charing Cross	a	13 13						13 30			13 36	13 43						14 00			14 06	14 13
Ebbsfleet International	a									13 17										13 47		
Stratford International	a									13 29										13 59		
St Pancras International	a									13 36										14 06		

Table 200

Mondays to Fridays

Gillingham and Dartford - London

		SE	SE	SE	SE	SE	SE	SE	SE	SE	SE	SE	SE	SE	SE	SE	SE	SE	SE	SE	SE	SE	SE
Gillingham (Kent)	d								13 50		13 24								14 20		13 54		
Chatham	d								13 54		13 28								14 24		13 58		
Rochester	d								13 57		13 30								14 27		14 00		
Strood	d								14 02		13 35								14 32		14 05		
Higham	d										13 40										14 10		
Gravesend	d						13 33		14 13		13 48						14 03		14 43		14 18		
Northfleet	d						13 37										14 07						
Swanscombe	d						13 39										14 09						
Greenhithe for Bluewater	d						13 42				13 53						14 12				14 23		
Stone Crossing	d						13 44										14 14						
Dartford	a						13 48				13 58						14 18				14 28		
	d		13 31			13 38	13 48			13 52	13 58		14 01			14 08	14 18			14 22	14 28		14 31
Slade Green	d	13 25	13 35					13 45				13 55	14 05					14 15				14 25	14 35
Erith	d	13 27	13 38					13 47				13 57	14 08					14 17				14 27	14 38
Belvedere	d	13 30	13 40					13 50				14 00	14 10					14 20				14 30	14 40
Abbey Wood	d	13 33	13 43					13 53			14 07	14 03	14 13					14 23			14 37	14 33	14 43
Plumstead	d	13 36	13 46					13 56				14 06	14 16					14 26				14 36	14 46
Woolwich Arsenal	d	13 39	13 49					13 59			14 12	14 09	14 19					14 29			14 42	14 39	14 49
Woolwich Dockyard	d	13 41	13 52					14 01				14 11	14 22					14 31				14 41	14 52
Charlton	d	13 44	13 55	13 37				14 04			14 17	14 14	14 25	14 07				14 34			14 47	14 44	14 55
Crayford	d			14 08			13 53							14 38			14 23						
Bexley	d			14 11			13 56							14 41			14 26						
Albany Park	d			14 14			13 59							14 44			14 29						
Sidcup	d			14 17			14 02							14 47			14 32						
New Eltham	d			14 20			14 05							14 50			14 35						
Mottingham	d			14 22			14 07							14 52			14 37						
Lee	d			14 25			14 10							14 55			14 40						
Hither Green	d			14 28			14 12							14 58			14 42						
Barnehurst	d				13 38	13 46				13 59					14 08	14 16				14 29			
Bexleyheath	d				13 40	13 49				14 01					14 10	14 19				14 31			
Welling	d				13 43	13 52				14 04					14 13	14 22				14 34			
Falconwood	d				13 46	13 54				14 07					14 16	14 24				14 37			
Eltham	d				13 49	13 57				14 10					14 19	14 27				14 40			
Kidbrooke	d				13 52	14 00				14 13					14 22	14 30				14 43			
Blackheath	d				13 55	14 04				14 16	14 21				14 25	14 34				14 46	14 51		
Lewisham	d			14 34	13 59	14 08				14 20	14 26			15 04	14 29	14 38				14 50	14 56		
St Johns	d			14 36										15 06									
New Cross	d			14 38	14 02									15 08	14 32								
Nunhead	d					14 13										14 43							
Peckham Rye	d					14 15										14 45							
Denmark Hill	d					14 19										14 49							
London Victoria	a					14 28										14 58							
Westcombe Park	d	13 46	13 57					14 06				14 16	14 27					14 36				14 46	14 57
Maze Hill	d	13 46	13 57					14 06				14 16	14 27					14 36				14 46	14 57
Greenwich	d	13 48	13 59					14 08				14 18	14 29					14 38				14 48	14 59
Deptford	d	13 52	14 02					14 12				14 22	14 32					14 42				14 52	15 02
London Bridge	a	13 54	14 04					14 14				14 24	14 34					14 44				14 54	15 04
London Cannon Street	a	14 06	14 15	14 49	14 13			14 24				14 36	14 45	15 19	14 43			14 54				15 06	15 15
London Waterloo (East)	a						14 26			14 32	14 39						14 56			15 02	15 09		
London Charing Cross	a						14 30			14 36	14 43						15 00			15 06	15 13		
Ebbsfleet International	a								14 17										14 47				
Stratford International	a								14 32										14 59				
St Pancras International	a								14 39										15 06				

Table 200

Mondays to Fridays

Gillingham and Dartford - London

		SE	SE	SE		SE	SE	SE	SE	SE	SE	SE	SE	SE		SE	SE	SE	SE	SE	SE	SE	SE	SE	
Gillingham (Kent)	d							14 50		14 24									15 20		14 54				
Chatham	d							14 54		14 28									15 24		14 58				
Rochester	d							14 57		14 30									15 27		15 00				
Strood	d							15 02		14 35									15 32		15 05				
Higham	d									14 40											15 10				
Gravesend	d					14 33		15 13		14 48							15 03		15 43		15 18				
Northfleet	d					14 37											15 07								
Swanscombe	d					14 39											15 09								
Greenhithe for Bluewater	d					14 42				14 53							15 12				15 23				
Stone Crossing	d					14 44											15 14								
Dartford	a					14 48				14 58							15 18				15 28				
	d			14 38		14 48			14 52	14 58		15 01				15 08	15 18			15 22	15 28		15 31		
Slade Green	d						14 45				14 55	15 05						15 15				15 25	15 35		
Erith	d						14 47				14 57	15 08						15 17				15 27	15 38		
Belvedere	d						14 50				15 00	15 10						15 20				15 30	15 40		
Abbey Wood	d						14 53			15 07	15 03	15 13						15 23			15 37	15 33	15 43		
Plumstead	d						14 56				15 06	15 16						15 26				15 36	15 46		
Woolwich Arsenal	d						14 59			15 12	15 09	15 19						15 29			15 42	15 39	15 49		
Woolwich Dockyard	d						15 01				15 11	15 22						15 31				15 41	15 52		
Charlton	d	14 37					15 04			15 17	15 14	15 25	15 07					15 34			15 47	15 44	15 55	15 37	
Crayford	d	15 08				14 53							15 38				15 23							16 08	
Bexley	d	15 11				14 56							15 41				15 26							16 11	
Albany Park	d	15 14				14 59							15 44				15 29							16 14	
Sidcup	d	15 17				15 02							15 47				15 32							16 17	
New Eltham	d	15 20				15 05							15 50				15 35							16 20	
Mottingham	d	15 22				15 07							15 52				15 37							16 22	
Lee	d	15 25				15 10							15 55				15 40							16 25	
Hither Green	d	15 28				15 12							15 58				15 42							16 28	
Barnehurst	d		14 38	14 46					14 59					15 08		15 16				15 29					
Bexleyheath	d		14 40	14 49					15 01					15 10		15 19				15 31					
Welling	d		14 43	14 52					15 04					15 13		15 22				15 34					
Falconwood	d		14 46	14 54					15 07					15 16		15 24				15 37					
Eltham	d		14 49	14 57					15 10					15 19		15 27				15 40					
Kidbrooke	d		14 52	15 00					15 13					15 22		15 30				15 43					
Blackheath	d		14 55	15 04					15 16	15 21				15 25		15 34				15 46	15 51				
Lewisham	d	15 34	14 59	15 08					15 20	15 26			16 04	15 29		15 38				15 50	15 56			16 34	
St Johns	d	15 36											16 06											16 36	
New Cross ⊖	d	15 38	15 02										16 08	15 32										16 38	
Nunhead	d			15 13												15 43									
Peckham Rye	d			15 15												15 45									
Denmark Hill	d			15 19												15 49									
London Victoria ⊖	a			15 28												15 58									
Westcombe Park	d						15 06				15 16	15 27						15 36				15 46	15 57		
Maze Hill	d						15 06				15 16	15 27						15 36				15 46	15 57		
Greenwich	d						15 08				15 18	15 29						15 38				15 48	15 59		
Deptford	d						15 12				15 22	15 32						15 42				15 52	16 02		
London Bridge ⊖	a						15 14				15 24	15 34						15 44				15 54	16 04		
London Cannon Street ⊖	a	15 49	15 13				15 24				15 36	15 45	16 19	15 43				15 54				16 06	16 16	16 49	
London Waterloo (East) ⊖	a					15 26			15 32	15 39							15 57			16 02	16 09				
London Charing Cross ⊖	a					15 30			15 36	15 43							16 01			16 06	16 13				
Ebbsfleet International	a							15 17											15 47						
Stratford International ⊖	a							15 29											15 59						
St Pancras International ⊖	a							15 36											16 06						

Table 200

Mondays to Fridays

Gillingham and Dartford - London

		SE	SE	SE	SE	SE	SE	SE	SE	SE		SE	SE	SE	SE	SE	SE	SE	SE	SE		SE	SE	SE	SE
Gillingham (Kent)	d					15 50		15 24									16 20		15 54						
Chatham	d					15 54		15 28									16 24		15 58						
Rochester	d					15 57		15 30									16 27		16 00						
Strood	d					16 02		15 35									16 32		16 05						
Higham	d							15 40											16 10						
Gravesend	d			15 33		16 13		15 48							16 03		16 43		16 18						
Northfleet	d			15 37											16 07										
Swanscombe	d			15 39											16 09										
Greenhithe for Bluewater	d			15 42				15 53							16 12				16 23						
Stone Crossing	d			15 44											16 14										
Dartford	a			15 48				15 58							16 18				16 28						
	d		15 38	15 48			15 52	15 58		16 01				16 08	16 18			16 22	16 28			16 31			16 38
Slade Green	d				15 45				15 55	16 05						16 15				16 25		16 35			
Erith	d				15 47				15 57	16 08						16 17				16 27		16 38			
Belvedere	d				15 50				16 00	16 10						16 20				16 30		16 40			
Abbey Wood	d				15 53			16 07	16 03	16 13						16 23			16 37	16 33		16 43			
Plumstead	d				15 56				16 06	16 16						16 26				16 36		16 46			
Woolwich Arsenal	d				15 59			16 12	16 09	16 19						16 29			16 42	16 39		16 49			
Woolwich Dockyard	d				16 01				16 11	16 22						16 31				16 41		16 52			
Charlton	d				16 04			16 17	16 14	16 25		16 07				16 34			16 47	16 44		16 55	16 37		
Crayford	d			15 53								16 38			16 23								17 08		
Bexley	d			15 56								16 41			16 26								17 11		
Albany Park	d			15 59								16 44			16 29								17 14		
Sidcup	d			16 02								16 47			16 32								17 17		
New Eltham	d			16 05								16 50			16 35								17 20		
Mottingham	d			16 07								16 52			16 37								17 22		
Lee	d			16 10								16 55			16 40								17 25		
Hither Green	d			16 12								17 00			16 42								17 28		
Barnehurst	d	15 38	15 46				15 59						16 08	16 16				16 29						16 38	16 46
Bexleyheath	d	15 40	15 49				16 01						16 10	16 19				16 31						16 40	16 49
Welling	d	15 43	15 52				16 04						16 13	16 22				16 34						16 43	16 52
Falconwood	d	15 46	15 54				16 07						16 16	16 24				16 37						16 46	16 54
Eltham	d	15 49	15 57				16 10						16 19	16 27				16 40						16 49	16 57
Kidbrooke	d	15 52	16 00				16 13						16 22	16 30				16 43						16 52	17 00
Blackheath	d	15 55	16 04				16 16	16 21					16 25	16 34				16 46	16 51					16 55	17 04
Lewisham	d	15 59	16 08				16 20	16 26				17 05	16 29	16 38				16 50	16 56				17 35	16 59	17 08
St Johns	d											17 09											17 37		
New Cross ⊖	d	16 02										17 11	16 32										17 39	17 03	
Nunhead	d		16 13											16 43											17 13
Peckham Rye	d		16 15											16 45											17 15
Denmark Hill	d		16 19											16 49											17 19
London Victoria ⊖	a		16 28											16 58											17 28
Westcombe Park	d				16 06				16 16	16 27						16 36				16 46		16 57			
Maze Hill	d				16 06				16 16	16 27						16 36				16 46		16 57			
Greenwich	d				16 08				16 18	16 29						16 38				16 48		16 59			
Deptford	d				16 12				16 22	16 32						16 42				16 52		17 02			
London Bridge ⊖	a				16 14				16 24	16 34						16 44				16 54		17 04			
London Cannon Street ⊖	a	16 13			16 24				16 36	16 46		17 24	16 43			16 54			17 11	17 05		17 17	17 49	17 15	
London Waterloo (East) ⊖	a			16 27			16 33	16 39							16 56			17 03							
London Charing Cross ⊖	a			16 31			16 37	16 44							17 00			17 07							
Ebbsfleet International	a					16 17											16 47								
Stratford International ⊖	a					16 29											17 02								
St Pancras International ⊖	a					16 40											17 09								

Table 200

Mondays to Fridays

Gillingham and Dartford - London

		SE	SE	SE	SE	SE		SE	SE	SE	SE	SE	SE	SE	SE	SE		SE	SE	SE	SE	SE	SE	SE	SE
Gillingham (Kent) [4]	d				16 24			16 50							17 20	17 20			16 54						
Chatham [4]	d				16 28			16 54							17 24	17 24			16 58						
Rochester [4]	d				16 30			16 57							17 27	17 27			17 00						
Strood [4]	d				16 35			17 02							17 32	17 32			17 05						
Higham	d				16 40														17 10						
Gravesend [4]	d			16 33	16 48			17 12					17 03		17 42	17 42			17 18						17 33
Northfleet	d			16 37									17 07												17 37
Swanscombe	d			16 39									17 09												17 39
Greenhithe for Bluewater	d			16 42	16 53								17 12						17 23						17 42
Stone Crossing	d			16 44									17 14												17 44
Dartford [4]	a			16 48	16 58								17 18						17 28						17 48
	d		16 43	16 52	16 58					17 01		17 08	17 18					17 22	17 28		17 31			17 38	17 48
Slade Green [4]	d					16 44			16 55	17 05				17 15						17 25	17 35				
Erith	d					16 46			16 57	17 08				17 17						17 27	17 38				
Belvedere	d					16 49			17 00	17 10				17 20						17 30	17 40				
Abbey Wood	d				17 07	16 52			17 03	17 13				17 23					17 37	17 33	17 43				
Plumstead	d					16 55			17 06	17 16				17 26						17 36	17 46				
Woolwich Arsenal [4] ⛴	d				17 12	16 58			17 09	17 19				17 29					17 42	17 39	17 49				
Woolwich Dockyard	d					17 00			17 11	17 22				17 31						17 41	17 52				
Charlton [4]	d				17 17	17 03			17 14	17 25				17 34					17 47	17 44	17 55				
Crayford	d		16 48										17 23										17 38		17 53
Bexley	d		16 51										17 26										17 41		17 56
Albany Park	d		16 54										17 29										17 44		17 59
Sidcup [4]	d	16 39	16 57										17 32										17 47		18 02
New Eltham	d	16 42	17 00										17 35										17 50		18 05
Mottingham	d	16 44	17 02										17 37										17 52		18 07
Lee	d	16 47	17 05										17 40										17 55		18 10
Hither Green [4]	d	16 49	17 08										17 42										17 58		18 12
Barnehurst [4]	d			16 59							17 08	17 16						17 29				17 38		17 46	
Bexleyheath	d			17 01							17 10	17 19						17 31				17 40		17 49	
Welling	d			17 04							17 13	17 22						17 34				17 43		17 52	
Falconwood	d			17 07							17 16	17 24						17 37				17 46		17 54	
Eltham	d			17 10							17 19	17 27						17 40				17 49		17 57	
Kidbrooke	d			17 13							17 22	17 30						17 43				17 52		18 00	
Blackheath [4]	d			17 16	17 21						17 25	17 34						17 46	17 51			17 55		18 04	
Lewisham [4] ⛴	d			17 20	17 27						17 30	17 38						17 50	17 56			17 59	18 05	18 08	
St Johns	d	16 54																					18 07		
New Cross [4] ⊖	d	16 56									17 33											18 02	18 09		
Nunhead [4]	d											17 43												18 13	
Peckham Rye [4]	d											17 45												18 15	
Denmark Hill [4]	d											17 49												18 19	
London Victoria [15] ⊖	a											17 59												18 29	
Westcombe Park	d					17 05			17 16	17 27				17 36						17 46	17 57				
Maze Hill	d					17 05			17 16	17 27				17 36						17 46	17 57				
Greenwich [4] ⛴	d					17 07			17 18	17 29				17 38						17 48	17 59				
Deptford	d					17 11			17 22	17 32				17 42						17 52	18 02				
London Bridge [4] ⊖	a					17 13			17 24	17 34				17 44						17 54	18 04				
London Cannon Street [4] ⊖	a	17 09				17 26			17 36	17 46	17 44			17 56				18 04		18 07	18 17	18 13	18 20		
London Waterloo (East) [4] ⊖	a		17 28	17 34	17 40								17 58						18 08						18 27
London Charing Cross [4] ⊖	a		17 33	17 38	17 44								18 03						18 12						18 31
Ebbsfleet International	a							17 16							17 46	17 46									
Stratford International ⊖ ⛴	a							17 27							17 57	18 02									
St Pancras International [15] ⊖	a							17 38							18 08	18 09									

Table 200

Mondays to Fridays

Gillingham and Dartford - London

		SE		SE	SE	SE	SE	SE	SE	SE	SE	SE		SE	SE	SE	SE	SE	SE	SE	SE	SE		SE	SE
Gillingham (Kent) [4]	d			17 50			17 24								18 20			17 54							18 09
Chatham [4]	d			17 54			17 28								18 24			17 58							18 13
Rochester [4]	d			17 57			17 30								18 27			18 00							18 15
Strood [4]	d			18 02			17 35								18 32			18 05							18 20
Higham	d						17 40											18 10							18 25
Gravesend [4]	d			18 13			17 48					18 03			18 43			18 18							18 33
Northfleet	d											18 07													18 37
Swanscombe	d											18 09													18 39
Greenhithe for Bluewater	d						17 53					18 12						18 24							18 42
Stone Crossing	d											18 14													18 44
Dartford [4]	a						17 58					18 18						18 28							18 48
	d					17 52	17 58			18 01	18 08	18 18					18 22	18 29		18 31				18 38	18 48
Slade Green [4]	d	17 45			17 50			17 55		18 05				18 15					18 25	18 36					
Erith	d	17 47						17 57		18 08				18 17					18 27	18 38					
Belvedere	d	17 50						18 00		18 10				18 20					18 30	18 41					
Abbey Wood	d	17 53					18 07	18 03		18 13				18 23				18 37	18 33	18 44					
Plumstead	d	17 56						18 06		18 16				18 26					18 36	18 47					
Woolwich Arsenal [4] ⛴	d	17 59					18 12	18 09		18 19				18 29				18 42	18 39	18 50					
Woolwich Dockyard	d	18 01						18 11		18 22				18 31					18 41	18 52					
Charlton [4]	d	18 04					18 17	18 14		18 25				18 34				18 47	18 44	18 55					
Crayford	d				18 01				18 01			18 23										18 38			18 53
Bexley	d				18 04							18 26										18 41			18 56
Albany Park	d				18 07							18 29										18 44			18 59
Sidcup [4]	d				18 10							18 32				18 20						18 47			19 02
New Eltham	d				18 13							18 35				18 23						18 50			19 05
Mottingham	d				18 15							18 37										18 52			19 07
Lee	d				18 18							18 40										18 55			19 10
Hither Green [4]	d				18 21							18 42				18 28						18 59			19 12
Barnehurst [4]	d					17 59			18 09		18 16						18 29				18 38			18 46	
Bexleyheath	d					18 01			18 12		18 19						18 31				18 40			18 49	
Welling	d					18 04			18 15		18 22						18 34				18 43			18 52	
Falconwood	d					18 07			18 17		18 24						18 37				18 46			18 54	
Eltham	d					18 10			18 20		18 27						18 40				18 49			18 57	
Kidbrooke	d					18 13			18 23		18 30						18 43				18 52			19 00	
Blackheath [4]	d					18 16	18 21				18 34						18 46	18 51			18 55			19 04	
Lewisham [4] ⛴	d					18 20	18 26		18 29		18 38					18 35	18 50	18 56			18 59	19 05		19 08	
St Johns	d															18 37						19 07			
New Cross [4] ⊖	d								18 32							18 39					19 03	19 09			
Nunhead [4]	d										18 43													19 13	
Peckham Rye [4]	d										18 45													19 15	
Denmark Hill [4]	d										18 49													19 19	
London Victoria [15] ⊖	a										18 58													19 28	
Westcombe Park	d	18 06						18 16		18 27				18 36					18 46	18 57					
Maze Hill	d	18 06						18 16		18 27				18 36					18 46	18 57					
Greenwich [4] ⛴	d	18 08						18 18		18 29				18 38					18 48	18 59					
Deptford	d	18 12						18 22		18 32				18 42					18 52	19 03					
London Bridge [4] ⊖	a	18 14						18 24		18 34				18 44					18 54	19 05					
London Cannon Street [4] ⊖	a	18 24						18 35	18 42	18 47				18 54		18 51			19 06	19 16	19 13	19 19			
London Waterloo (East) [4] ⊖	a				18 37	18 32	18 41					18 57					19 02	19 09							19 26
London Charing Cross [4] ⊖	a				18 41	18 37	18 45					19 01					19 06	19 13							19 30
Ebbsfleet International	a			18 17											18 47										
Stratford International ⊖ ⛴	a			18 28											19 02										
St Pancras International [15] ⊖	a			18 35											19 09										

Table 200

Mondays to Fridays

Gillingham and Dartford - London

		SE	SE	SE	SE	SE	SE	SE		SE	SE	SE	SE	SE	SE	SE	SE	SE		SE	SE	SE	SE	SE	SE
Gillingham (Kent)	d		18 50									19 20		18 54				19 50			19 24				20 20
Chatham	d		18 54									19 24		18 58				19 54			19 28				20 24
Rochester	d		18 57									19 27		19 00				19 57			19 30				20 27
Strood	d		19 02									19 32		19 05				20 02			19 35				20 32
Higham	d													19 10							19 40				
Gravesend	d		19 12		18 48						19 03	19 43		19 18			19 33	20 12			19 48			20 03	20 43
Northfleet	d										19 07						19 37							20 07	
Swanscombe	d										19 09						19 39							20 09	
Greenhithe for Bluewater	d				18 53						19 12			19 23			19 42				19 53			20 12	
Stone Crossing	d										19 14						19 44							20 14	
Dartford	a				18 58						19 18			19 27			19 48				19 58			20 18	
	d			18 52	18 58		19 01			19 15	19 18		19 25	19 27	19 31	19 46	19 48			19 55	19 58	20 01	20 16	20 18	
Slade Green	d	18 51				18 56	19 06			19 21					19 36	19 51						20 06	20 21		
Erith	d	18 53					19 08			19 23					19 38	19 53						20 08	20 23		
Belvedere	d	18 56					19 11			19 26					19 41	19 56						20 11	20 26		
Abbey Wood	d	18 59			19 07		19 14			19 29				19 37	19 44	19 59					20 07	20 14	20 29		
Plumstead	d	19 02					19 17			19 32					19 47	20 02						20 17	20 32		
Woolwich Arsenal	d	19 05			19 12		19 20			19 35				19 42	19 50	20 05					20 12	20 20	20 35		
Woolwich Dockyard	d	19 07					19 22			19 37					19 52	20 07						20 22	20 37		
Charlton	d	19 10			19 17		19 25			19 40				19 47	19 55	20 10					20 17	20 25	20 40		
Crayford	d					19 08					19 23						19 53							20 23	
Bexley	d					19 11					19 26						19 56							20 26	
Albany Park	d					19 14					19 29						19 59							20 29	
Sidcup	d					19 17					19 32						20 02							20 32	
New Eltham	d					19 20					19 35						20 05							20 35	
Mottingham	d					19 22					19 37						20 07							20 37	
Lee	d					19 25					19 40						20 10							20 40	
Hither Green	d					19 28					19 43						20 13							20 43	
Barnehurst	d			18 59				19 08					19 32							20 02					
Bexleyheath	d			19 01				19 10					19 34							20 04					
Welling	d			19 04				19 13					19 37							20 07					
Falconwood	d			19 07				19 16					19 40							20 10					
Eltham	d			19 10				19 19					19 42							20 12					
Kidbrooke	d			19 13				19 22					19 45							20 15					
Blackheath	d			19 16	19 21			19 25					19 49	19 51						20 19	20 21				
Lewisham	d			19 20	19 26	19 34		19 29			19 48		19 52	19 55			20 18			20 22	20 26			20 48	
St Johns	d					19 36																			
New Cross	d					19 38		19 32			19 51		19 56				20 21			20 26				20 51	
Nunhead	d																								
Peckham Rye	d																								
Denmark Hill	d																								
London Victoria	a																								
Westcombe Park	d	19 12					19 27			19 42					19 57	20 12						20 27	20 42		
Maze Hill	d	19 12					19 27			19 42					19 57	20 12						20 27	20 42		
Greenwich	d	19 14					19 29			19 44					19 59	20 14						20 29	20 44		
Deptford	d	19 18					19 33			19 48					20 03	20 18						20 33	20 48		
London Bridge	a	19 20					19 35			19 50					20 05	20 20						20 35	20 50		
London Cannon Street	a	19 33				19 49	19 45	19 43		20 03					20 15	20 31						20 45			
London Waterloo (East)	a			19 32	19 39						20 02		20 08	20 11			20 32			20 38	20 40			21 02	
London Charing Cross	a			19 36	19 43						20 06		20 12	20 14			20 36			20 42	20 44			21 06	
Ebbsfleet International	a		19 16									19 47						20 16							20 47
Stratford International	a		19 27									19 59						20 27							20 59
St Pancras International	a		19 38									20 06						20 38							21 06

Table 200

Mondays to Fridays

Gillingham and Dartford - London

		SE	SE	SE		SE	SE	SE	SE	SE	SE	SE	SE	SE		SE	SE	SE	SE	SE	SE	SE	SE	SE	
Gillingham (Kent)	d		19 54					20 50		20 24				21 20			20 54				21 50		21 24		
Chatham	d		19 58					20 54		20 28				21 24			20 58				21 54		21 28		
Rochester	d		20 00					20 57		20 30				21 27			21 00				21 57		21 30		
Strood	d		20 05					21 02		20 35				21 32			21 05				22 02		21 35		
Higham	d		20 10							20 40							21 10						21 40		
Gravesend	d		20 18				20 33	21 13		20 48			21 03	21 43			21 18			21 33	22 12		21 48		
Northfleet	d						20 37						21 07							21 37					
Swanscombe	d						20 39						21 09							21 39					
Greenhithe for Bluewater	d		20 23				20 42			20 53			21 12				21 23			21 42			21 53		
Stone Crossing	d						20 44						21 14							21 44					
Dartford	a		20 28				20 48			20 58			21 18				21 28			21 48			21 58		
	d	20 25	20 28	20 31		20 46	20 48		20 55	20 58	21 01	21 16	21 18			21 25	21 28	21 31	21 46	21 48		21 55	21 58	22 01	
Slade Green	d			20 36		20 51					21 06	21 21						21 36	21 51					22 06	
Erith	d			20 38		20 53					21 08	21 23						21 38	21 53					22 08	
Belvedere	d			20 41		20 56					21 11	21 26						21 41	21 56					22 11	
Abbey Wood	d		20 37	20 44		20 59				21 07	21 14	21 29					21 37	21 44	21 59				22 07	22 14	
Plumstead	d			20 47		21 02					21 17	21 32						21 47	22 02					22 17	
Woolwich Arsenal	d		20 42	20 50		21 05				21 12	21 20	21 35					21 42	21 50	22 05				22 12	22 20	
Woolwich Dockyard	d			20 52		21 07					21 22	21 37						21 52	22 07					22 22	
Charlton	d		20 47	20 55		21 10				21 17	21 25	21 40					21 47	21 55	22 10				22 17	22 25	
Crayford	d						20 53						21 23							21 53					
Bexley	d						20 56						21 26							21 56					
Albany Park	d						20 59						21 29							21 59					
Sidcup	d						21 02						21 32							22 02					
New Eltham	d						21 05						21 35							22 05					
Mottingham	d						21 07						21 37							22 07					
Lee	d						21 10						21 40							22 10					
Hither Green	d						21 13						21 43							22 13					
Barnehurst	d	20 32							21 02							21 32						22 02			
Bexleyheath	d	20 34							21 04							21 34						22 04			
Welling	d	20 37							21 07							21 37						22 07			
Falconwood	d	20 40							21 10							21 40						22 10			
Eltham	d	20 42							21 12							21 42						22 12			
Kidbrooke	d	20 45							21 15							21 45						22 15			
Blackheath	d	20 49	20 51						21 19	21 21						21 49	21 51					22 19	22 21		
Lewisham	d	20 53	20 56				21 18		21 23	21 25			21 48			21 53	21 56			22 18		22 23	22 26		
St Johns	d																								
New Cross	d	20 56					21 21		21 26				21 51			21 56				22 21		22 26			
Nunhead	d																								
Peckham Rye	d																								
Denmark Hill	d																								
London Victoria	a																								
Westcombe Park	d			20 57		21 12					21 27	21 42						21 57	22 12					22 27	
Maze Hill	d			20 57		21 12					21 27	21 42						21 57	22 12					22 27	
Greenwich	d			20 59		21 14					21 29	21 44						21 59	22 14					22 29	
Deptford	d			21 03		21 18					21 33	21 48						22 03	22 18					22 33	
London Bridge	a			21 05		21 20					21 35	21 50						22 05	22 20					22 35	
London Cannon Street	a																								
London Waterloo (East)	a	21 08	21 10	21 15			21 32		21 38	21 40	21 45		22 02			22 06	22 09	22 15		22 32		22 36	22 39	22 45	
London Charing Cross	a	21 12	21 14	21 19			21 36		21 42	21 44	21 49		22 06			22 10	22 13	22 19		22 36		22 40	22 43	22 49	
Ebbsfleet International	a							21 17						21 47							22 16				
Stratford International	a							21 32						21 59							22 27				
St Pancras International	a							21 39						22 06							22 38				

Table 200

Mondays to Fridays

Gillingham and Dartford - London

		SE	SE	SE	SE	SE	SE	SE	SE	SE	SE	SE
Gillingham (Kent)	d		22 20	22 20		21 54				22 24		22 54
Chatham	d		22 24	22 24		21 58				22 28		22 58
Rochester	d		22 27	22 27		22 00				22 30		23 00
Strood	d		22 32	22 32		22 05				22 35		23 05
Higham	d					22 10				22 40		23 10
Gravesend	d	22 03	22 43	22 43		22 18		22 33		22 48		23 18
Northfleet	d	22 07						22 37				
Swanscombe	d	22 09						22 39				
Greenhithe for Bluewater	d	22 12				22 23		22 42		22 53		23 23
Stone Crossing	d	22 14						22 44				
Dartford	a	22 18				22 28		22 48		22 58		23 28
	d	22 18			22 25	22 28	22 31	22 48	22 55	22 58	23 01	
Slade Green	d						22 36				23 06	
Erith	d						22 38				23 08	
Belvedere	d						22 41				23 11	
Abbey Wood	d					22 37	22 44			23 07	23 14	
Plumstead	d						22 47				23 17	
Woolwich Arsenal	d					22 42	22 50			23 12	23 20	
Woolwich Dockyard	d						22 52				23 22	
Charlton	d					22 47	22 55			23 17	23 25	
Crayford	d	22 23						22 53				
Bexley	d	22 26						22 56				
Albany Park	d	22 29						22 59				
Sidcup	d	22 32						23 02				
New Eltham	d	22 35						23 05				
Mottingham	d	22 37						23 07				
Lee	d	22 40						23 10				
Hither Green	d	22 43						23 13				
Barnehurst	d				22 32				23 02			
Bexleyheath	d				22 34				23 04			
Welling	d				22 37				23 07			
Falconwood	d				22 40				23 10			
Eltham	d				22 42				23 12			
Kidbrooke	d				22 45				23 15			
Blackheath	d				22 49	22 51			23 19	23 21		
Lewisham	d	22 48			22 53	22 56		23 18	23 23	23 26		
St Johns	d											
New Cross	d	22 51			22 56			23 21	23 26			
Nunhead	d											
Peckham Rye	d											
Denmark Hill	d											
London Victoria	a											
Westcombe Park	d						22 57				23 27	
Maze Hill	d						22 57				23 27	
Greenwich	d						22 59				23 29	
Deptford	d						23 03				23 33	
London Bridge	a						23 05				23 35	
London Cannon Street	a											
London Waterloo (East)	a	23 02			23 06	23 09	23 15	23 32	23 36	23 39	23 45	
London Charing Cross	a	23 06			23 10	23 13	23 19	23 36	23 40	23 43	23 49	
Ebbsfleet International	a		22 47	22 47								
Stratford International	a		22 59	23 02								
St Pancras International	a		23 06	23 09								

Table 200

Saturdays

Gillingham and Dartford - London

		SE	SE	SE	SE	SE	SE	SE	SE	SE	SE	SE
Gillingham (Kent)	d				04 48			05 50		05 18		
Chatham	d				04 52			05 54		05 22		
Rochester	d				04 54			05 57		05 24		
Strood	d				04 59			06 02		05 29		
Higham	d				05 04					05 34		
Gravesend	d				05 12			06 13		05 42		06 03
Northfleet	d				05 15					05 45		06 07
Swanscombe	d				05 17					05 47		06 09
Greenhithe for Bluewater	d				05 21					05 51		06 12
Stone Crossing	d				05 23					05 53		06 14
Dartford	a				05 27					05 57		06 18
	d	05 05	05 18	05 22	05 28	05 35	05 48		05 52	05 58	06 05	06 18
Slade Green	d	05 10				05 40					06 10	
Erith	d	05 12				05 42					06 12	
Belvedere	d	05 15				05 45					06 15	
Abbey Wood	d	05 18			05 37	05 48				06 07	06 18	
Plumstead	d	05 21				05 51					06 21	
Woolwich Arsenal	d	05 24			05 42	05 54				06 12	06 24	
Woolwich Dockyard	d	05 26				05 56					06 26	
Charlton	d	05 29			05 47	05 59				06 17	06 29	
Crayford	d		05 23				05 53					06 23
Bexley	d		05 26				05 56					06 26
Albany Park	d		05 29				05 59					06 29
Sidcup	d		05 32				06 02					06 32
New Eltham	d		05 35				06 05					06 35
Mottingham	d		05 37				06 07					06 37
Lee	d		05 40				06 10					06 40
Hither Green	d		05 42				06 12					06 42
Barnehurst	d			05 29					05 59			
Bexleyheath	d			05 31					06 01			
Welling	d			05 34					06 04			
Falconwood	d			05 37					06 07			
Eltham	d			05 40					06 10			
Kidbrooke	d			05 43					06 13			
Blackheath	d			05 46	05 51				06 16	06 21		
Lewisham	d		05 48	05 50	05 56		06 18		06 20	06 26		06 48
St Johns	d											
New Cross	d		05 51				06 21					06 51
Nunhead	d											
Peckham Rye	d											
Denmark Hill	d											
London Victoria	a											
Westcombe Park	d	05 31				06 01					06 31	
Maze Hill	d	05 31				06 01					06 31	
Greenwich	d	05 33				06 03					06 33	
Deptford	d	05 37				06 07					06 37	
London Bridge	a	05 39				06 09					06 39	
London Cannon Street	a											
London Waterloo (East)	a	05 49	06 01	06 03	06 09	06 19	06 31		06 33	06 39	06 49	07 01
London Charing Cross	a	05 53	06 05	06 07	06 13	06 25	06 35		06 37	06 43	06 55	07 05
Ebbsfleet International	a							06 17				
Stratford International	a							06 29				
St Pancras International	a							06 36				

		SE	SE	SE	SE	SE	SE	SE	SE	SE	SE
Gillingham (Kent)	d		05 54				06 50		06 24		
Chatham	d		05 58				06 54		06 28		
Rochester	d		06 00				06 57		06 30		
Strood	d		06 05				07 02		06 35		
Higham	d		06 10						06 40		
Gravesend	d		06 18			06 33	07 13		06 48		
Northfleet	d					06 37					
Swanscombe	d					06 39					
Greenhithe for Bluewater	d		06 23			06 42			06 53		
Stone Crossing	d					06 44					
Dartford	a		06 28			06 48			06 58		
	d	06 22	06 28	06 35	06 38	06 48		06 52	06 58	07 01	07 08
Slade Green	d			06 40						07 06	
Erith	d			06 42						07 08	
Belvedere	d			06 45						07 11	
Abbey Wood	d		06 37	06 48					07 07	07 14	
Plumstead	d			06 51						07 17	
Woolwich Arsenal	d		06 42	06 54					07 12	07 20	
Woolwich Dockyard	d			06 56						07 22	
Charlton	d		06 47	06 59					07 17	07 25	
Crayford	d					06 53					
Bexley	d					06 56					
Albany Park	d					06 59					
Sidcup	d					07 02					
New Eltham	d					07 05					
Mottingham	d					07 07					
Lee	d					07 10					
Hither Green	d					07 12					
Barnehurst	d	06 29			06 46			06 59			07 16
Bexleyheath	d	06 31			06 49			07 01			07 19
Welling	d	06 34			06 52			07 04			07 22
Falconwood	d	06 37			06 54			07 07			07 24
Eltham	d	06 40			06 57			07 10			07 27
Kidbrooke	d	06 43			07 00			07 13			07 30
Blackheath	d	06 46	06 51		07 04			07 16	07 21		07 34
Lewisham	d	06 50	06 56		07 08	07 18		07 20	07 26		07 38
St Johns	d										
New Cross	d					07 21					
Nunhead	d				07 15						07 45
Peckham Rye	d				07 17						07 47
Denmark Hill	d				07 21						07 51
London Victoria	a				07 30						08 00
Westcombe Park	d			07 01						07 27	
Maze Hill	d			07 01						07 27	
Greenwich	d			07 03						07 29	
Deptford	d			07 07						07 33	
London Bridge	a			07 09						07 35	
London Cannon Street	a									07 45	
London Waterloo (East)	a	07 03	07 09	07 19		07 31		07 33	07 39		
London Charing Cross	a	07 07	07 13	07 25		07 35		07 40	07 43		
Ebbsfleet International	a						07 17				
Stratford International	a						07 29				
St Pancras International	a						07 36				

Table 200

Gillingham and Dartford - London

Station		SE	SE	SE	SE	SE	SE	SE	SE	SE	SE	SE	SE	SE	SE	SE	SE	SE	SE	SE	SE	SE
Gillingham (Kent) 4	d			06 54								07 50		07 24								08 20
Chatham 4	d			06 58								07 54		07 28								08 24
Rochester 4	d			07 00								07 57		07 30								08 27
Strood 4	d			07 05								08 02		07 35								08 32
Higham	d			07 10										07 40								
Gravesend 4	d	07 03		07 18						07 33		08 13		07 48						08 03		08 43
Northfleet	d	07 07								07 37										08 07		
Swanscombe	d	07 09								07 39										08 09		
Greenhithe for Bluewater	d	07 12		07 23						07 42				07 53						08 12		
Stone Crossing	d	07 14								07 44										08 14		
Dartford 4	a	07 18		07 28						07 48				07 58						08 18		
	d	07 18	07 22	07 28		07 31			07 38	07 48			07 52	07 58		08 01			08 08	08 18		
Slade Green 4	d				07 25	07 36					07 45				07 55	08 06					08 15	
Erith	d				07 27	07 38					07 47				07 57	08 08					08 17	
Belvedere	d				07 30	07 41					07 50				08 00	08 11					08 20	
Abbey Wood	d			07 37	07 33	07 44					07 53			08 07	08 03	08 14					08 23	
Plumstead	d				07 36	07 47					07 56				08 06	08 17					08 26	
Woolwich Arsenal 4	d			07 42	07 39	07 50					07 59			08 12	08 09	08 20					08 29	
Woolwich Dockyard	d				07 41	07 52					08 01				08 11	08 22					08 31	
Charlton 4	d			07 47	07 44	07 55					08 04			08 17	08 14	08 25					08 34	
Crayford	d	07 23						07 38		07 53								08 08		08 23		
Bexley	d	07 26						07 41		07 56								08 11		08 26		
Albany Park	d	07 29						07 44		07 59								08 14		08 29		
Sidcup 4	d	07 32						07 47		08 02								08 17		08 32		
New Eltham	d	07 35						07 50		08 05								08 20		08 35		
Mottingham	d	07 37						07 52		08 07								08 22		08 37		
Lee	d	07 40						07 55		08 10								08 25		08 40		
Hither Green 4	d	07 42						07 58		08 12								08 28		08 42		
Barnehurst 4	d		07 29				07 38		07 46				07 59				08 08		08 16			
Bexleyheath	d		07 31				07 40		07 49				08 01				08 10		08 19			
Welling	d		07 34				07 43		07 52				08 04				08 13		08 22			
Falconwood	d		07 37				07 46		07 54				08 07				08 16		08 24			
Eltham	d		07 40				07 49		07 57				08 10				08 19		08 27			
Kidbrooke	d		07 43				07 52		08 00				08 13				08 22		08 30			
Blackheath 4	d		07 46	07 51			07 55		08 04				08 16	08 21			08 25		08 34			
Lewisham 4 ⛴	d		07 50	07 56			07 59	08 04	08 08				08 20	08 26			08 29	08 34	08 38			
St Johns	d							08 06										08 36				
New Cross 4 ⊖	d						08 02	08 08									08 32	08 38				
Nunhead 4	d								08 15										08 45			
Peckham Rye 4	d								08 17										08 47			
Denmark Hill 4	d								08 21										08 51			
London Victoria 15 ⊖	a								08 30										09 00			
Westcombe Park	d				07 46	07 57					08 06				08 16	08 27					08 36	
Maze Hill	d				07 46	07 57					08 06				08 16	08 27					08 36	
Greenwich 4 ⛴	d				07 48	07 59					08 08				08 18	08 29					08 38	
Deptford	d				07 52	08 03					08 12				08 22	08 33					08 42	
London Bridge 4 ⊖	a				07 54	08 05					08 14				08 24	08 35					08 44	
London Cannon Street 4 ⊖	a				08 04	08 18		08 20			08 24				08 34	08 45		08 49			08 54	
London Waterloo (East) 4 ⊖	a	07 56	08 02	08 09						08 26			08 32	08 39						08 56		
London Charing Cross 4 ⊖	a	08 00	08 06	08 13						08 30			08 36	08 43						09 00		
Ebbsfleet International	a											08 17										08 47
Stratford International ⊖ ⛴	a											08 29										08 59
St Pancras International 15 ⊖	a											08 36										09 07

Table 200

Gillingham and Dartford - London

Station		SE	SE	SE	SE	SE	SE	SE	SE	SE	SE	SE	SE	SE	SE	SE	SE	SE	SE	SE	SE	SE
Gillingham (Kent) 4	d		07 54									08 50		08 24								09 20
Chatham 4	d		07 58									08 54		08 28								09 24
Rochester 4	d		08 00									08 57		08 30								09 27
Strood 4	d		08 05									09 02		08 35								09 32
Higham	d		08 10											08 40								
Gravesend 4	d		08 18							08 33		09 13		08 48						09 03		09 43
Northfleet	d									08 37										09 07		
Swanscombe	d									08 39										09 09		
Greenhithe for Bluewater	d		08 23							08 42				08 53						09 12		
Stone Crossing	d									08 44										09 14		
Dartford 4	a		08 28							08 48				08 58						09 18		
	d	08 22	08 28		08 31				08 38	08 48			08 52	08 58		09 01			09 08	09 18		
Slade Green 4	d			08 25	08 36						08 45				08 55	09 06					09 15	
Erith	d			08 27	08 38						08 47				08 57	09 08					09 17	
Belvedere	d			08 30	08 41						08 50				09 00	09 11					09 20	
Abbey Wood	d		08 37	08 33	08 44						08 53			09 07	09 03	09 14					09 23	
Plumstead	d			08 36	08 47						08 56				09 06	09 17					09 26	
Woolwich Arsenal 4	d		08 42	08 39	08 50						08 59			09 12	09 09	09 20					09 29	
Woolwich Dockyard	d			08 41	08 52						09 01				09 11	09 22					09 31	
Charlton 4	d		08 47	08 44	08 55	08 37					09 04			09 17	09 14	09 25	09 07				09 34	
Crayford	d					09 08		08 38		08 53							09 38			09 23		
Bexley	d					09 11		08 41		08 56							09 41			09 26		
Albany Park	d					09 14		08 44		08 59							09 44			09 29		
Sidcup 4	d					09 17		08 47		09 02							09 47			09 32		
New Eltham	d					09 20		08 50		09 05							09 50			09 35		
Mottingham	d					09 22		08 52		09 07							09 52			09 37		
Lee	d					09 25		08 55		09 10							09 55			09 40		
Hither Green 4	d					09 28		08 58		09 12							09 58			09 42		
Barnehurst 4	d	08 29					08 38		08 46				08 59					09 08	09 16			
Bexleyheath	d	08 31					08 40		08 49				09 01					09 10	09 19			
Welling	d	08 34					08 43		08 52				09 04					09 13	09 22			
Falconwood	d	08 37					08 46		08 54				09 07					09 16	09 24			
Eltham	d	08 40					08 49		08 57				09 10					09 19	09 27			
Kidbrooke	d	08 43					08 52		09 00				09 13					09 22	09 30			
Blackheath 4	d	08 46	08 51				08 55		09 04				09 16	09 21				09 25	09 34			
Lewisham 4 ⛴	d	08 50	08 56			09 34	08 59	09 04	09 08				09 20	09 26			10 04	09 29	09 38			
St Johns	d					09 36		09 06									10 06					
New Cross 4 ⊖	d					09 38	09 02	09 08									10 08	09 32				
Nunhead 4	d								09 15										09 45			
Peckham Rye 4	d								09 17										09 47			
Denmark Hill 4	d								09 21										09 51			
London Victoria 15 ⊖	a								09 30										10 00			
Westcombe Park	d			08 46	08 57						09 06				09 16	09 27					09 36	
Maze Hill	d			08 46	08 57						09 06				09 16	09 27					09 36	
Greenwich 4 ⛴	d			08 48	08 59						09 08				09 18	09 29					09 38	
Deptford	d			08 52	09 03						09 12				09 22	09 33					09 42	
London Bridge 4 ⊖	a			08 54	09 05						09 14				09 24	09 35					09 44	
London Cannon Street 4 ⊖	a			09 04	09 15	09 49		09 19			09 24				09 34	09 45	10 19				09 54	
London Waterloo (East) 4 ⊖	a	09 02	09 09							09 26			09 32	09 39						09 56		
London Charing Cross 4 ⊖	a	09 06	09 13							09 30			09 36	09 43						10 00		
Ebbsfleet International	a											09 17										09 47
Stratford International ⊖ ⛴	a											09 29										09 59
St Pancras International 15 ⊖	a											09 39										10 06

Gillingham and Dartford - London

		SE	SE	SE	SE	SE	SE	SE		SE	SE	SE	SE	SE	SE	SE	SE	SE		SE	SE	SE	SE	SE	SE
Gillingham (Kent) 4	d		08 54									09 50		09 24									10 20		09 54
Chatham 4	d		08 58									09 54		09 28									10 24		09 58
Rochester 4	d		09 00									09 57		09 30									10 27		10 00
Strood 4	d		09 05									10 02		09 35									10 32		10 05
Higham	d		09 10											09 40											10 10
Gravesend 4	d		09 18							09 33		10 12		09 48							10 03		10 43		10 18
Northfleet	d									09 37											10 07				
Swanscombe	d									09 39											10 09				
Greenhithe for Bluewater	d		09 23							09 42				09 53							10 12				10 23
Stone Crossing	d									09 44											10 14				
Dartford 4	a		09 28							09 48				09 58							10 18				10 28
	d	09 22	09 28		09 31			09 38		09 48			09 52	09 58		10 01				10 08	10 18			10 22	10 28
Slade Green 4	d			09 25	09 36						09 45				09 55	10 06						10 15			
Erith	d			09 27	09 38						09 47				09 57	10 08						10 17			
Belvedere	d			09 30	09 41						09 50				10 00	10 11						10 20			
Abbey Wood	d		09 37	09 33	09 44						09 53			10 07	10 03	10 14						10 23			10 37
Plumstead	d			09 36	09 47						09 56				10 06	10 17						10 26			
Woolwich Arsenal 4 ⛴	d		09 42	09 39	09 50						09 59			10 12	10 09	10 20						10 29			10 42
Woolwich Dockyard	d			09 41	09 52						10 01				10 11	10 22						10 31			
Charlton 4	d		09 47	09 44	09 55	09 37					10 04			10 17	10 14	10 25	10 07					10 34			10 47
Crayford	d					10 08				09 53							10 38				10 23				
Bexley	d					10 11				09 56							10 41				10 26				
Albany Park	d					10 14				09 59							10 44				10 29				
Sidcup 4	d					10 17				10 02							10 47				10 32				
New Eltham	d					10 20				10 05							10 50				10 35				
Mottingham	d					10 22				10 07							10 52				10 37				
Lee	d					10 25				10 10							10 55				10 40				
Hither Green 4	d					10 28				10 12							10 58				10 42				
Barnehurst 4	d	09 29					09 38	09 46					09 59					10 08		10 16				10 29	
Bexleyheath	d	09 31					09 40	09 49					10 01					10 10		10 19				10 31	
Welling	d	09 34					09 43	09 52					10 04					10 13		10 22				10 34	
Falconwood	d	09 37					09 46	09 54					10 07					10 16		10 24				10 37	
Eltham	d	09 40					09 49	09 57					10 10					10 19		10 27				10 40	
Kidbrooke	d	09 43					09 52	10 00					10 13					10 22		10 30				10 43	
Blackheath 4	d	09 46	09 51				09 55	10 04					10 16	10 21				10 25		10 34				10 46	10 51
Lewisham 4 ⛴	d	09 50	09 56			10 34	09 59	10 08					10 20	10 26			11 04	10 29		10 38				10 50	10 56
St Johns	d					10 36											11 06								
New Cross 4 ⊖	d					10 38	10 02										11 08	10 32							
Nunhead 4	d							10 15												10 45					
Peckham Rye 4	d							10 17												10 47					
Denmark Hill 4	d							10 21												10 51					
London Victoria 15 ⊖	a							10 30												11 00					
Westcombe Park	d			09 46	09 57						10 06				10 16	10 27						10 36			
Maze Hill	d			09 46	09 57						10 06				10 16	10 27						10 36			
Greenwich 4 ⛴	d			09 48	09 59						10 08				10 18	10 29						10 38			
Deptford	d			09 52	10 03						10 12				10 22	10 33						10 42			
London Bridge 4 ⊖	a			09 54	10 05						10 14				10 24	10 35						10 44			
London Cannon Street 4 ⊖	a			10 04	10 15	10 49					10 24				10 34	10 45	11 19					10 54			
London Waterloo (East) 4 ⊖	a	10 02	10 09							10 26			10 32	10 39							10 56			11 02	11 09
London Charing Cross 4 ⊖	a	10 06	10 13							10 30			10 36	10 43							11 00			11 06	11 13
Ebbsfleet International	a											10 16											10 47		
Stratford International ⊖ ⛴	a											10 27											10 59		
St Pancras International 15 ⊖	a											10 38											11 06		

Table 200

Saturdays

Gillingham and Dartford - London

		SE	SE	SE		SE	SE	SE	SE	SE	SE	SE	SE	SE		SE	SE	SE	SE	SE	SE	SE	SE	SE
Gillingham (Kent) 4	d									10 50		10 24									11 20		10 54	
Chatham 4	d									10 54		10 28									11 24		10 58	
Rochester 4	d									10 57		10 30									11 27		11 00	
Strood 4	d									11 02		10 35									11 32		11 05	
Higham	d											10 40											11 10	
Gravesend 4	d							10 33		11 13		10 48							11 03		11 43		11 18	
Northfleet	d							10 37											11 07					
Swanscombe	d							10 39											11 09					
Greenhithe for Bluewater	d							10 42				10 53							11 12				11 23	
Stone Crossing	d							10 44											11 14					
Dartford 4	a							10 48				10 58							11 18				11 28	
	d		10 31				10 38	10 48			10 52	10 58		11 01				11 08	11 18			11 22	11 28	
Slade Green 4	d	10 25	10 36						10 45				10 55	11 06						11 15				11 25
Erith	d	10 27	10 38						10 47				10 57	11 08						11 17				11 27
Belvedere	d	10 30	10 41						10 50				11 00	11 11						11 20				11 30
Abbey Wood	d	10 33	10 44						10 53			11 07	11 03	11 14						11 23			11 37	11 33
Plumstead	d	10 36	10 47						10 56				11 06	11 17						11 26				11 36
Woolwich Arsenal 4 ⛴	d	10 39	10 50						10 59			11 12	11 09	11 20						11 29			11 42	11 39
Woolwich Dockyard	d	10 41	10 52						11 01				11 11	11 22						11 31				11 41
Charlton 4	d	10 44	10 55	10 37					11 04			11 17	11 14	11 25		11 07				11 34			11 47	11 44
Crayford	d			11 08				10 53								11 38			11 23					
Bexley	d			11 11				10 56								11 41			11 26					
Albany Park	d			11 14				10 59								11 44			11 29					
Sidcup 4	d			11 17				11 02								11 47			11 32					
New Eltham	d			11 20				11 05								11 50			11 35					
Mottingham	d			11 22				11 07								11 52			11 37					
Lee	d			11 25				11 10								11 55			11 40					
Hither Green 4	d			11 28				11 12								11 58			11 42					
Barnehurst 4	d					10 38	10 46				10 59						11 08	11 16				11 29		
Bexleyheath	d					10 40	10 49				11 01						11 10	11 19				11 31		
Welling	d					10 43	10 52				11 04						11 13	11 22				11 34		
Falconwood	d					10 46	10 54				11 07						11 16	11 24				11 37		
Eltham	d					10 49	10 57				11 10						11 19	11 27				11 40		
Kidbrooke	d					10 52	11 00				11 13						11 22	11 30				11 43		
Blackheath 4	d					10 55	11 04				11 16	11 21					11 25	11 34				11 46	11 51	
Lewisham 4 ⛴	d			11 34		10 59	11 08				11 20	11 26				12 04	11 29	11 38				11 50	11 56	
St Johns	d			11 36												12 06								
New Cross 4 ⊖	d			11 38		11 02										12 08	11 32							
Nunhead 4	d						11 15											11 45						
Peckham Rye 4	d						11 17											11 47						
Denmark Hill 4	d						11 21											11 51						
London Victoria 15 ⊖	a						11 30											12 00						
Westcombe Park	d	10 46	10 57						11 06				11 16	11 27						11 36				11 46
Maze Hill	d	10 46	10 57						11 06				11 16	11 27						11 36				11 46
Greenwich 4 ⛴	d	10 48	10 59						11 08				11 18	11 29						11 38				11 48
Deptford	d	10 52	11 03						11 12				11 22	11 33						11 42				11 52
London Bridge 4 ⊖	a	10 54	11 05						11 14				11 24	11 35						11 44				11 54
London Cannon Street 4 ⊖	a	11 04	11 15	11 49					11 24				11 34	11 45		12 19				11 54				12 04
London Waterloo (East) 4 ⊖	a							11 26			11 32	11 39							11 56			12 02	12 09	
London Charing Cross 4 ⊖	a							11 30			11 36	11 43							12 00			12 06	12 13	
Ebbsfleet International	a									11 17											11 47			
Stratford International ⊖ ⛴	a									11 29											11 59			
St Pancras International 15 ⊖	a									11 36											12 06			

Table 200

Saturdays

Gillingham and Dartford - London

		SE	SE	SE	SE	SE	SE	SE	SE	SE	SE	SE	SE	SE	SE	SE	SE	SE	SE	SE	SE	SE	SE
Gillingham (Kent) 4	d							11 50		11 24								12 20		11 54			
Chatham 4	d							11 54		11 28								12 24		11 58			
Rochester 4	d							11 57		11 30								12 27		12 00			
Strood 4	d							12 02		11 35								12 32		12 05			
Higham	d									11 40										12 10			
Gravesend 4	d					11 33		12 13		11 48						12 03		12 43		12 18			
Northfleet	d					11 37										12 07							
Swanscombe	d					11 39										12 09							
Greenhithe for Bluewater	d					11 42				11 53						12 12				12 23			
Stone Crossing	d					11 44										12 14							
Dartford 4	a					11 48				11 58						12 18				12 28			
	d	11 31			11 38	11 48			11 52	11 58		12 01			12 08	12 18			12 22	12 28		12 31	
Slade Green 4	d	11 36					11 45				11 55	12 06					12 15				12 25	12 36	
Erith	d	11 38					11 47				11 57	12 08					12 17				12 27	12 38	
Belvedere	d	11 41					11 50				12 00	12 11					12 20				12 30	12 41	
Abbey Wood	d	11 44					11 53			12 07	12 03	12 14					12 23			12 37	12 33	12 44	
Plumstead	d	11 47					11 56				12 06	12 17					12 26				12 36	12 47	
Woolwich Arsenal 4 ⛴	d	11 50					11 59			12 12	12 09	12 20					12 29			12 42	12 39	12 50	
Woolwich Dockyard	d	11 52					12 01				12 11	12 22					12 31				12 41	12 52	
Charlton 4	d	11 55	11 37				12 04			12 17	12 14	12 25	12 07				12 34			12 47	12 44	12 55	12 37
Crayford	d		12 08			11 53							12 38			12 23							13 08
Bexley	d		12 11			11 56							12 41			12 26							13 11
Albany Park	d		12 14			11 59							12 44			12 29							13 14
Sidcup 4	d		12 17			12 02							12 47			12 32							13 17
New Eltham	d		12 20			12 05							12 50			12 35							13 20
Mottingham	d		12 22			12 07							12 52			12 37							13 22
Lee	d		12 25			12 10							12 55			12 40							13 25
Hither Green 4	d		12 28			12 12							12 58			12 42							13 28
Barnehurst 4	d			11 38	11 46				11 59					12 08	12 16				12 29				
Bexleyheath	d			11 40	11 49				12 01					12 10	12 19				12 31				
Welling	d			11 43	11 52				12 04					12 13	12 22				12 34				
Falconwood	d			11 46	11 54				12 07					12 16	12 24				12 37				
Eltham	d			11 49	11 57				12 10					12 19	12 27				12 40				
Kidbrooke	d			11 52	12 00				12 13					12 22	12 30				12 43				
Blackheath 4	d			11 55	12 04				12 16	12 21				12 25	12 34				12 46	12 51			
Lewisham 4 ⛴	d		12 34	11 59	12 08				12 20	12 26			13 04	12 29	12 38				12 50	12 56			13 34
St Johns	d		12 36										13 06										13 36
New Cross 4 ⊖	d		12 38	12 02									13 08	12 32									13 38
Nunhead 4	d				12 15										12 45								
Peckham Rye 4	d				12 17										12 47								
Denmark Hill 4	d				12 21										12 51								
London Victoria 15 ⊖	a				12 30										13 00								
Westcombe Park	d	11 57					12 06				12 16	12 27					12 36				12 46	12 57	
Maze Hill	d	11 57					12 06				12 16	12 27					12 36				12 46	12 57	
Greenwich 4 ⛴	d	11 59					12 08				12 18	12 29					12 38				12 48	12 59	
Deptford	d	12 03					12 12				12 22	12 33					12 42				12 52	13 03	
London Bridge 4 ⊖	a	12 05					12 14				12 24	12 35					12 44				12 54	13 05	
London Cannon Street 4 ⊖	a	12 15	12 49				12 24				12 34	12 45	13 19				12 54				13 04	13 15	13 49
London Waterloo (East) 4 ⊖	a					12 26			12 32	12 39						12 56			13 02	13 09			
London Charing Cross 4 ⊖	a					12 30			12 36	12 43						13 00			13 06	13 13			
Ebbsfleet International	a							12 17										12 47					
Stratford International ⊖ ⛴	a							12 32										12 59					
St Pancras International 15 ⊖	a							12 39										13 06					

Table 200

Saturdays

Gillingham and Dartford - London

		SE	SE	SE	SE	SE	SE	SE	SE	SE	SE	SE	SE	SE	SE	SE	SE	SE	SE	SE	SE	SE	SE
Gillingham (Kent) 4	d					12 50		12 24								13 20		12 54					
Chatham 4	d					12 54		12 28								13 24		12 58					
Rochester 4	d					12 57		12 30								13 27		13 00					
Strood 4	d					13 02		12 35								13 32		13 05					
Higham	d							12 40										13 10					
Gravesend 4	d			12 33		13 13		12 48						13 03		13 43		13 18					
Northfleet	d			12 37										13 07									
Swanscombe	d			12 39										13 09									
Greenhithe for Bluewater	d			12 42				12 53						13 12				13 23					
Stone Crossing	d			12 44										13 14									
Dartford 4	a			12 48				12 58						13 18				13 28					
	d		12 38	12 48			12 52	12 58		13 01			13 08	13 18			13 22	13 28		13 31			13 38
Slade Green 4	d				12 45				12 55	13 06					13 15				13 25	13 36			
Erith	d				12 47				12 57	13 08					13 17				13 27	13 38			
Belvedere	d				12 50				13 00	13 11					13 20				13 30	13 41			
Abbey Wood	d				12 53			13 07	13 03	13 14					13 23			13 37	13 33	13 44			
Plumstead	d				12 56				13 06	13 17					13 26				13 36	13 47			
Woolwich Arsenal 4 ⛴	d				12 59			13 12	13 09	13 20					13 29			13 42	13 39	13 50			
Woolwich Dockyard	d				13 01				13 11	13 22					13 31				13 41	13 52			
Charlton 4	d				13 04			13 17	13 14	13 25	13 07				13 34			13 47	13 44	13 55	13 37		
Crayford	d			12 53							13 38			13 23							14 08		
Bexley	d			12 56							13 41			13 26							14 11		
Albany Park	d			12 59							13 44			13 29							14 14		
Sidcup 4	d			13 02							13 47			13 32							14 17		
New Eltham	d			13 05							13 50			13 35							14 20		
Mottingham	d			13 07							13 52			13 37							14 22		
Lee	d			13 10							13 55			13 40							14 25		
Hither Green 4	d			13 12							13 58			13 42							14 28		
Barnehurst 4	d	12 38	12 46				12 59					13 08	13 16				13 29					13 38	13 46
Bexleyheath	d	12 40	12 49				13 01					13 10	13 19				13 31					13 40	13 49
Welling	d	12 43	12 52				13 04					13 13	13 22				13 34					13 43	13 52
Falconwood	d	12 46	12 54				13 07					13 16	13 24				13 37					13 46	13 54
Eltham	d	12 49	12 57				13 10					13 19	13 27				13 40					13 49	13 57
Kidbrooke	d	12 52	13 00				13 13					13 22	13 30				13 43					13 52	14 00
Blackheath 4	d	12 55	13 04				13 16	13 21				13 25	13 34				13 46	13 51				13 55	14 04
Lewisham 4 ⛴	d	12 59	13 08				13 20	13 26			14 04	13 29	13 38				13 50	13 56			14 34	13 59	14 08
St Johns	d										14 06										14 36		
New Cross 4 ⊖	d	13 02									14 08	13 32									14 38	14 02	
Nunhead 4	d		13 15										13 45										14 15
Peckham Rye 4	d		13 17										13 47										14 17
Denmark Hill 4	d		13 21										13 51										14 21
London Victoria 15 ⊖	a		13 30										14 00										14 30
Westcombe Park	d				13 06				13 16	13 27					13 36				13 46	13 57			
Maze Hill	d				13 06				13 16	13 27					13 36				13 46	13 57			
Greenwich 4 ⛴	d				13 08				13 18	13 29					13 38				13 48	13 59			
Deptford	d				13 12				13 22	13 33					13 42				13 52	14 03			
London Bridge 4 ⊖	a				13 14				13 24	13 35					13 44				13 54	14 05			
London Cannon Street 4 ⊖	a				13 24				13 34	13 45	14 19				13 54				14 04	14 15	14 49		
London Waterloo (East) 4 ⊖	a			13 26			13 33	13 39						13 56			14 02	14 09					
London Charing Cross 4 ⊖	a			13 30			13 37	13 43						14 00			14 06	14 13					
Ebbsfleet International	a					13 17										13 47							
Stratford International ⊖ ⛴	a					13 29										13 59							
St Pancras International 15 ⊖	a					13 36										14 06							

Table 200

Saturdays

Gillingham and Dartford - London

		SE	SE	SE	SE	SE	SE	SE	SE	SE	SE	SE	SE	SE	SE	SE	SE	SE	SE	SE	SE	SE
Gillingham (Kent) [4]	d			13 50		13 24								14 20		13 54						
Chatham [4]	d			13 54		13 28								14 24		13 58						
Rochester [4]	d			13 57		13 30								14 27		14 00						
Strood [4]	d			14 02		13 35								14 32		14 05						
Higham	d					13 40										14 10						
Gravesend [4]	d	13 33		14 13		13 48						14 03		14 43		14 18						14 33
Northfleet	d	13 37										14 07										14 37
Swanscombe	d	13 39										14 09										14 39
Greenhithe for Bluewater	d	13 42				13 53						14 12				14 23						14 42
Stone Crossing	d	13 44										14 14										14 44
Dartford [4]	a	13 48				13 58						14 18				14 28						14 48
	d	13 48			13 52	13 58		14 01			14 08	14 18			14 22	14 28		14 31			14 38	14 48
Slade Green [4]	d		13 45				13 55	14 06					14 15				14 25	14 36				
Erith	d		13 47				13 57	14 08					14 17				14 27	14 38				
Belvedere	d		13 50				14 00	14 11					14 20				14 30	14 41				
Abbey Wood	d		13 53			14 07	14 03	14 14					14 23			14 37	14 33	14 44				
Plumstead	d		13 56				14 06	14 17					14 26				14 36	14 47				
Woolwich Arsenal [4] ⛴	d		13 59			14 12	14 09	14 20					14 29			14 42	14 39	14 50				
Woolwich Dockyard	d		14 01				14 11	14 22					14 31				14 41	14 52				
Charlton [4]	d		14 04			14 17	14 14	14 25	14 07				14 34			14 47	14 44	14 55	14 37			
Crayford	d	13 53							14 38			14 23							15 08			14 53
Bexley	d	13 56							14 41			14 26							15 11			14 56
Albany Park	d	13 59							14 44			14 29							15 14			14 59
Sidcup [4]	d	14 02							14 47			14 32							15 17			15 02
New Eltham	d	14 05							14 50			14 35							15 20			15 05
Mottingham	d	14 07							14 52			14 37							15 22			15 07
Lee	d	14 10							14 55			14 40							15 25			15 10
Hither Green [4]	d	14 12							14 58			14 42							15 28			15 12
Barnehurst [4]	d				13 59					14 08	14 16				14 29					14 38	14 46	
Bexleyheath	d				14 01					14 10	14 19				14 31					14 40	14 49	
Welling	d				14 04					14 13	14 22				14 34					14 43	14 52	
Falconwood	d				14 07					14 16	14 24				14 37					14 46	14 54	
Eltham	d				14 10					14 19	14 27				14 40					14 49	14 57	
Kidbrooke	d				14 13					14 22	14 30				14 43					14 52	15 00	
Blackheath [4]	d				14 16	14 21				14 25	14 34				14 46	14 51				14 55	15 04	
Lewisham [4] ⛴	d				14 20	14 26			15 04	14 29	14 38				14 50	14 56			15 34	14 59	15 08	
St Johns	d								15 06										15 36			
New Cross [4] ⊖	d								15 08	14 32									15 38	15 02		
Nunhead [4]	d										14 45										15 15	
Peckham Rye [4]	d										14 47										15 17	
Denmark Hill [4]	d										14 51										15 21	
London Victoria [15] ⊖	a										15 00										15 30	
Westcombe Park	d		14 06				14 16	14 27					14 36				14 46	14 57				
Maze Hill	d		14 06				14 16	14 27					14 36				14 46	14 57				
Greenwich [4] ⛴	d		14 08				14 18	14 29					14 38				14 48	14 59				
Deptford	d		14 12				14 22	14 33					14 42				14 52	15 03				
London Bridge [4] ⊖	a		14 14				14 24	14 35					14 44				14 54	15 05				
London Cannon Street [4] ⊖	a		14 24				14 34	14 45	15 19				14 54				15 04	15 15	15 49			
London Waterloo (East) [4] ⊖	a	14 26			14 32	14 39						14 56			15 02	15 09						15 26
London Charing Cross [4] ⊖	a	14 30			14 36	14 43						15 00			15 06	15 13						15 30
Ebbsfleet International	a			14 17										14 47								
Stratford International ⊖ ⛴	a			14 32										15 02								
St Pancras International [15] ⊖	a			14 39										15 09								

Table 200

Saturdays

Gillingham and Dartford - London

		SE	SE	SE	SE	SE	SE	SE	SE	SE	SE	SE	SE	SE	SE	SE	SE	SE	SE	SE	SE	SE	SE
Gillingham (Kent) [4]	d		14 50		14 24								15 20		14 54								15 50
Chatham [4]	d		14 54		14 28								15 24		14 58								15 54
Rochester [4]	d		14 57		14 30								15 27		15 00								15 57
Strood [4]	d		15 02		14 35								15 32		15 05								16 02
Higham	d				14 40										15 10								
Gravesend [4]	d		15 13		14 48						15 03		15 43		15 18						15 33		16 13
Northfleet	d										15 07										15 37		
Swanscombe	d										15 09										15 39		
Greenhithe for Bluewater	d				14 53						15 12				15 23						15 42		
Stone Crossing	d										15 14										15 44		
Dartford [4]	a				14 58						15 18				15 28						15 48		
	d			14 52	14 58		15 01			15 08	15 18			15 22	15 28		15 31			15 38	15 48		
Slade Green [4]	d	14 45				14 55	15 06					15 15				15 25	15 36					15 45	
Erith	d	14 47				14 57	15 08					15 17				15 27	15 38					15 47	
Belvedere	d	14 50				15 00	15 11					15 20				15 30	15 41					15 50	
Abbey Wood	d	14 53			15 07	15 03	15 14					15 23			15 37	15 33	15 44					15 53	
Plumstead	d	14 56				15 06	15 17					15 26				15 36	15 47					15 56	
Woolwich Arsenal [4] ⛴	d	14 59			15 12	15 09	15 20					15 29			15 42	15 39	15 50					15 59	
Woolwich Dockyard	d	15 01				15 11	15 22					15 31				15 41	15 52					16 01	
Charlton [4]	d	15 04			15 17	15 14	15 25	15 07				15 34			15 47	15 44	15 55	15 37				16 04	
Crayford	d							15 38			15 23							16 08			15 53		
Bexley	d							15 41			15 26							16 11			15 56		
Albany Park	d							15 44			15 29							16 14			15 59		
Sidcup [4]	d							15 47			15 32							16 17			16 02		
New Eltham	d							15 50			15 35							16 20			16 05		
Mottingham	d							15 52			15 37							16 22			16 07		
Lee	d							15 55			15 40							16 25			16 10		
Hither Green [4]	d							15 58			15 42							16 28			16 12		
Barnehurst [4]	d			14 59					15 08	15 16				15 29					15 38	15 46			
Bexleyheath	d			15 01					15 10	15 19				15 31					15 40	15 49			
Welling	d			15 04					15 13	15 22				15 34					15 43	15 52			
Falconwood	d			15 07					15 16	15 24				15 37					15 46	15 54			
Eltham	d			15 10					15 19	15 27				15 40					15 49	15 57			
Kidbrooke	d			15 13					15 22	15 30				15 43					15 52	16 00			
Blackheath [4]	d			15 16	15 21				15 25	15 34				15 46	15 51				15 55	16 04			
Lewisham [4] ⛴	d			15 20	15 26			16 04	15 29	15 38				15 50	15 56			16 34	15 59	16 08			
St Johns	d							16 06										16 36					
New Cross [4] ⊖	d							16 08	15 32									16 38	16 02				
Nunhead [4]	d									15 45										16 15			
Peckham Rye [4]	d									15 47										16 17			
Denmark Hill [4]	d									15 51										16 21			
London Victoria [15] ⊖	a									16 00										16 30			
Westcombe Park	d	15 06				15 16	15 27					15 36				15 46	15 57					16 06	
Maze Hill	d	15 06				15 16	15 27					15 36				15 46	15 57					16 06	
Greenwich [4] ⛴	d	15 08				15 18	15 29					15 38				15 48	15 59					16 08	
Deptford	d	15 12				15 22	15 33					15 42				15 52	16 03					16 12	
London Bridge [4] ⊖	a	15 14				15 24	15 35					15 44				15 54	16 05					16 14	
London Cannon Street [4] ⊖	a	15 24				15 34	15 45	16 19				15 54				16 04	16 15	16 49				16 24	
London Waterloo (East) [4] ⊖	a			15 32	15 39						15 56			16 02	16 09						16 26		
London Charing Cross [4] ⊖	a			15 36	15 43						16 00			16 06	16 13						16 30		
Ebbsfleet International	a		15 17										15 47										16 17
Stratford International ⊖ ⛴	a		15 29										15 59										16 29
St Pancras International [15] ⊖	a		15 36										16 06										16 40

Table 200

Gillingham and Dartford - London

		SE	SE	SE		SE	SE	SE	SE	SE	SE	SE	SE	SE		SE	SE	SE	SE	SE	SE	SE	SE	SE	
Gillingham (Kent)	d		15 24									16 20		15 54									16 50		
Chatham	d		15 28									16 24		15 58									16 54		
Rochester	d		15 30									16 27		16 00									16 57		
Strood	d		15 35									16 32		16 05									17 02		
Higham	d		15 40											16 10											
Gravesend	d		15 48							16 03		16 43		16 18							16 33		17 12		
Northfleet	d									16 07											16 37				
Swanscombe	d									16 09											16 39				
Greenhithe for Bluewater	d		15 53							16 12				16 23							16 42				
Stone Crossing	d									16 14											16 44				
Dartford	a		15 58							16 18				16 28							16 48				
	d	15 52	15 58			16 01			16 08	16 18			16 22	16 28			16 31			16 38	16 48			16 52	
Slade Green	d			15 55		16 06					16 15					16 25	16 36					16 45			
Erith	d			15 57		16 08					16 17					16 27	16 38					16 47			
Belvedere	d			16 00		16 11					16 20					16 30	16 41					16 50			
Abbey Wood	d		16 07	16 03		16 14					16 23			16 37		16 33	16 44					16 53			
Plumstead	d			16 06		16 17					16 26					16 36	16 47					16 56			
Woolwich Arsenal	d		16 12	16 09		16 20					16 29			16 42		16 39	16 50					16 59			
Woolwich Dockyard	d			16 11		16 22					16 31					16 41	16 52					17 01			
Charlton	d		16 17	16 14		16 25	16 07				16 34			16 47		16 44	16 55	16 37				17 04			
Crayford	d						16 38			16 23								17 08			16 53				
Bexley	d						16 41			16 26								17 11			16 56				
Albany Park	d						16 44			16 29								17 14			16 59				
Sidcup	d						16 47			16 32								17 17			17 02				
New Eltham	d						16 50			16 35								17 20			17 05				
Mottingham	d						16 52			16 37								17 22			17 07				
Lee	d						16 55			16 40								17 25			17 10				
Hither Green	d						16 58			16 42								17 28			17 12				
Barnehurst	d	15 59						16 08	16 16				16 29						16 38	16 46				16 59	
Bexleyheath	d	16 01						16 10	16 19				16 31						16 40	16 49				17 01	
Welling	d	16 04						16 13	16 22				16 34						16 43	16 52				17 04	
Falconwood	d	16 07						16 16	16 24				16 37						16 46	16 54				17 07	
Eltham	d	16 10						16 19	16 27				16 40						16 49	16 57				17 10	
Kidbrooke	d	16 13						16 22	16 30				16 43						16 52	17 00				17 13	
Blackheath	d	16 16	16 21					16 25	16 34				16 46	16 51					16 55	17 04				17 16	
Lewisham	d	16 20	16 26				17 04	16 29	16 38				16 50	16 56				17 34	16 59	17 08				17 20	
St Johns	d						17 06											17 36							
New Cross	d						17 08	16 32										17 38	17 02						
Nunhead	d								16 45											17 15					
Peckham Rye	d								16 47											17 17					
Denmark Hill	d								16 51											17 21					
London Victoria	a								17 00											17 30					
Westcombe Park	d			16 16		16 27					16 36					16 46	16 57					17 06			
Maze Hill	d			16 16		16 27					16 36					16 46	16 57					17 06			
Greenwich	d			16 18		16 29					16 38					16 48	16 59					17 08			
Deptford	d			16 22		16 33					16 42					16 52	17 03					17 12			
London Bridge	a			16 24		16 35					16 44					16 54	17 05					17 14			
London Cannon Street	a			16 34		16 45	17 19				16 54					17 04	17 15	17 49				17 24			
London Waterloo (East)	a	16 32	16 39							16 56			17 02	17 09							17 26			17 32	
London Charing Cross	a	16 36	16 43							17 00			17 06	17 13							17 30			17 36	
Ebbsfleet International	a											16 47											17 16		
Stratford International	a											16 59											17 27		
St Pancras International	a											17 06											17 38		

Table 200

Gillingham and Dartford - London

		SE	SE	SE	SE	SE	SE	SE	SE	SE		SE	SE	SE	SE	SE	SE	SE	SE	SE		SE	SE	SE	SE
Gillingham (Kent)	d	16 24								17 20			16 54									17 50		17 24	
Chatham	d	16 28								17 24			16 58									17 54		17 28	
Rochester	d	16 30								17 27			17 00									17 57		17 30	
Strood	d	16 35								17 32			17 05									18 02		17 35	
Higham	d	16 40											17 10											17 40	
Gravesend	d	16 48						17 03		17 43			17 18						17 33			18 13		17 48	
Northfleet	d							17 07											17 37						
Swanscombe	d							17 09											17 39						
Greenhithe for Bluewater	d	16 53						17 12					17 23						17 42					17 53	
Stone Crossing	d							17 14											17 44						
Dartford	a	16 58						17 18					17 28						17 48					17 58	
	d	16 58		17 01			17 08	17 18				17 22	17 28		17 31			17 38	17 48				17 52	17 58	
Slade Green	d		16 55	17 06					17 15					17 25	17 36					17 45					17 55
Erith	d		16 57	17 08					17 17					17 27	17 38					17 47					17 57
Belvedere	d		17 00	17 11					17 20					17 30	17 41					17 50					18 00
Abbey Wood	d	17 07	17 03	17 14					17 23				17 37	17 33	17 44					17 53				18 07	18 03
Plumstead	d		17 06	17 17					17 26					17 36	17 47					17 56					18 06
Woolwich Arsenal	d	17 12	17 09	17 20					17 29				17 42	17 39	17 50					17 59				18 12	18 09
Woolwich Dockyard	d		17 11	17 22					17 31					17 41	17 52					18 01					18 11
Charlton	d	17 17	17 14	17 25	17 07				17 34				17 47	17 44	17 55	17 37				18 04				18 17	18 14
Crayford	d				17 38			17 23								18 08			17 53						
Bexley	d				17 41			17 26								18 11			17 56						
Albany Park	d				17 44			17 29								18 14			17 59						
Sidcup	d				17 47			17 32								18 17			18 02						
New Eltham	d				17 50			17 35								18 20			18 05						
Mottingham	d				17 52			17 37								18 22			18 07						
Lee	d				17 55			17 40								18 25			18 10						
Hither Green	d				17 58			17 42								18 28			18 12						
Barnehurst	d					17 08	17 16					17 29					17 38	17 46					17 59		
Bexleyheath	d					17 10	17 19					17 31					17 40	17 49					18 01		
Welling	d					17 13	17 22					17 34					17 43	17 52					18 04		
Falconwood	d					17 16	17 24					17 37					17 46	17 54					18 07		
Eltham	d					17 19	17 27					17 40					17 49	17 57					18 10		
Kidbrooke	d					17 22	17 30					17 43					17 52	18 00					18 13		
Blackheath	d	17 21				17 25	17 34					17 46	17 51				17 55	18 04					18 16	18 21	
Lewisham	d	17 26			18 04	17 29	17 38					17 50	17 56			18 34	17 59	18 08					18 20	18 26	
St Johns	d				18 06											18 36									
New Cross	d				18 08	17 32										18 38	18 02								
Nunhead	d						17 45											18 15							
Peckham Rye	d						17 47											18 17							
Denmark Hill	d						17 51											18 21							
London Victoria	a						18 00											18 30							
Westcombe Park	d		17 16	17 27					17 36					17 46	17 57					18 06					18 16
Maze Hill	d		17 16	17 27					17 36					17 46	17 57					18 06					18 16
Greenwich	d		17 18	17 29					17 38					17 48	17 59					18 08					18 18
Deptford	d		17 22	17 33					17 42					17 52	18 03					18 12					18 22
London Bridge	a		17 24	17 35					17 44					17 54	18 05					18 14					18 24
London Cannon Street	a		17 34	17 45	18 19				17 54					18 04	18 15	18 49				18 24					18 34
London Waterloo (East)	a	17 39						17 56				18 02	18 09						18 26				18 32	18 39	
London Charing Cross	a	17 43						18 00				18 06	18 13						18 30				18 36	18 43	
Ebbsfleet International	a									17 47												18 17			
Stratford International	a									18 02												18 29			
St Pancras International	a									18 09												18 36			

Table 200

Saturdays

Gillingham and Dartford - London

		SE	SE	SE	SE	SE		SE	SE	SE	SE	SE	SE	SE	SE	SE		SE	SE	SE	SE	SE	SE	SE	SE
Gillingham (Kent) ■	d								18 20		17 54							18 50		18 24				19 20	
Chatham ■	d								18 24		17 58							18 54		18 28				19 24	
Rochester ■	d								18 27		18 00							18 57		18 30				19 27	
Strood ■	d								18 32		18 05							19 02		18 35				19 32	
Higham	d										18 10									18 40					
Gravesend ■	d					18 03			18 43		18 18					18 33		19 12		18 48			19 03	19 43	
Northfleet	d					18 07										18 37							19 07		
Swanscombe	d					18 09										18 39							19 09		
Greenhithe for Bluewater	d					18 12					18 23					18 42				18 53			19 12		
Stone Crossing	d					18 14										18 44							19 14		
Dartford ■	a					18 18					18 28					18 48				18 58			19 18		
	d	18 01			18 08	18 18				18 22	18 28		18 31		18 38	18 48			18 52	18 58		19 01	19 18		
Slade Green ■	d	18 06						18 15				18 25	18 36								18 55	19 06			19 25
Erith	d	18 08						18 17				18 27	18 38								18 57	19 08			19 27
Belvedere	d	18 11						18 20				18 30	18 41								19 00	19 11			19 30
Abbey Wood	d	18 14						18 23			18 37	18 33	18 44							19 07	19 03	19 14			19 33
Plumstead	d	18 17						18 26				18 36	18 47								19 06	19 17			19 36
Woolwich Arsenal ■	d	18 20						18 29			18 42	18 39	18 50							19 12	19 09	19 20			19 39
Woolwich Dockyard	d	18 22						18 31				18 41	18 52								19 11	19 22			19 41
Charlton ■	d	18 25	18 07					18 34			18 47	18 44	18 55							19 17	19 14	19 25			19 44
Crayford	d		18 38			18 23										18 53							19 23		
Bexley	d		18 41			18 26										18 56							19 26		
Albany Park	d		18 44			18 29										18 59							19 29		
Sidcup ■	d		18 47			18 32										19 02							19 32		
New Eltham	d		18 50			18 35										19 05							19 35		
Mottingham	d		18 52			18 37										19 07							19 37		
Lee	d		18 55			18 40										19 10							19 40		
Hither Green ■	d		18 58			18 42										19 13							19 43		
Barnehurst ■	d			18 08	18 16					18 29				18 38	18 46				18 59						
Bexleyheath	d			18 10	18 19					18 31				18 40	18 49				19 01						
Welling	d			18 13	18 22					18 34				18 43	18 52				19 04						
Falconwood	d			18 16	18 24					18 37				18 46	18 54				19 07						
Eltham	d			18 19	18 27					18 40				18 49	18 57				19 10						
Kidbrooke	d			18 22	18 30					18 43				18 52	19 00				19 13						
Blackheath ■	d			18 25	18 34					18 46	18 51			18 55	19 04				19 16	19 21					
Lewisham ■	d		19 04	18 29	18 38					18 50	18 56			18 59	19 08	19 18			19 20	19 26			19 48		
St Johns	d		19 06																						
New Cross ■	d		19 08	18 32										19 02					19 23				19 51		
Nunhead ■	d				18 45										19 15										
Peckham Rye ■	d				18 47										19 17										
Denmark Hill ■	d				18 51										19 21										
London Victoria ■	a				19 00										19 30										
Westcombe Park	d	18 27						18 36				18 46	18 57								19 16	19 27			19 46
Maze Hill	d	18 27						18 36				18 46	18 57								19 16	19 27			19 46
Greenwich ■	d	18 29						18 38				18 48	18 59								19 18	19 29			19 48
Deptford	d	18 33						18 42				18 52	19 03								19 22	19 33			19 52
London Bridge ■	a	18 35						18 44				18 54	19 05								19 24	19 35			19 54
London Cannon Street ■	a	18 45	19 19					18 54				19 04	19 15												
London Waterloo (East) ■	a					18 56				19 02	19 09					19 32			19 39	19 42		19 45	20 04		
London Charing Cross ■	a					19 00				19 06	19 13					19 35			19 42	19 45		19 49	20 07		
Ebbsfleet International	a								18 47									19 16						19 47	
Stratford International	a								19 02									19 27						19 59	
St Pancras International ■	a								19 09									19 38						20 06	

Table 200

Saturdays

Gillingham and Dartford - London

		SE		SE	SE	SE	SE	SE	SE	SE	SE	SE		SE	SE	SE	SE	SE	SE	SE	SE	SE		SE	SE
Gillingham (Kent) ■	d			18 54			19 50			19 24				20 20		19 54			20 50		20 24				21 20
Chatham ■	d			18 58			19 54			19 28				20 24		19 58			20 54		20 28				21 24
Rochester ■	d			19 00			19 57			19 30				20 27		20 00			20 57		20 30				21 27
Strood ■	d			19 05			20 02			19 35				20 32		20 05			21 02		20 35				21 32
Higham	d			19 10						19 40						20 10					20 40				
Gravesend ■	d			19 18		19 33	20 12			19 48		20 03		20 43		20 18		20 33	21 13		20 48			21 03	21 43
Northfleet	d					19 37						20 07						20 37						21 07	
Swanscombe	d					19 39						20 09						20 39						21 09	
Greenhithe for Bluewater	d			19 23		19 42				19 53		20 12				20 23		20 42			20 53			21 12	
Stone Crossing	d					19 44						20 14						20 44						21 14	
Dartford ■	a			19 28		19 48				19 58		20 18				20 28		20 48			20 58			21 18	
	d	19 25		19 28	19 31	19 48			19 55	19 58	20 01	20 18			20 25	20 28	20 31	20 48		20 55	20 58	21 01		21 18	
Slade Green ■	d				19 36			19 55			20 06						20 36					21 06			
Erith	d				19 38			19 57			20 08						20 38					21 08			
Belvedere	d				19 41			20 00			20 11						20 41					21 11			
Abbey Wood	d			19 38	19 44			20 03		20 07	20 14					20 37	20 44				21 07	21 14			
Plumstead	d				19 47			20 06			20 17						20 47					21 17			
Woolwich Arsenal ■	d			19 43	19 50			20 09		20 12	20 20					20 42	20 50				21 12	21 20			
Woolwich Dockyard	d				19 52			20 11			20 22						20 52					21 22			
Charlton ■	d			19 47	19 55			20 14		20 17	20 25					20 47	20 55				21 17	21 25			
Crayford	d					19 53						20 23						20 53						21 23	
Bexley	d					19 56						20 26						20 56						21 26	
Albany Park	d					19 59						20 29						20 59						21 29	
Sidcup ■	d					20 02						20 32						21 02						21 32	
New Eltham	d					20 05						20 35						21 05						21 35	
Mottingham	d					20 07						20 37						21 07						21 37	
Lee	d					20 10						20 40						21 10						21 40	
Hither Green ■	d					20 13						20 43						21 13						21 43	
Barnehurst ■	d	19 32							20 02						20 32					21 02					
Bexleyheath	d	19 34							20 04						20 34					21 04					
Welling	d	19 37							20 07						20 37					21 07					
Falconwood	d	19 40							20 10						20 40					21 10					
Eltham	d	19 42							20 12						20 42					21 12					
Kidbrooke	d	19 45							20 15						20 45					21 15					
Blackheath ■	d	19 49		19 51					20 19	20 21					20 49	20 51				21 19	21 21				
Lewisham ■	d	19 53		19 56		20 18			20 23	20 26		20 48			20 53	20 56		21 18		21 23	21 26			21 48	
St Johns	d																								
New Cross ■	d	19 56				20 21			20 26			20 51			20 56			21 21		21 26				21 51	
Nunhead ■	d																								
Peckham Rye ■	d																								
Denmark Hill ■	d																								
London Victoria ■	a																								
Westcombe Park	d				19 57			20 16			20 27						20 57					21 27			
Maze Hill	d				19 57			20 16			20 27						20 57					21 27			
Greenwich ■	d				19 59			20 18			20 29						20 59					21 29			
Deptford	d				20 03			20 22			20 33						21 03					21 33			
London Bridge ■	a				20 05			20 24			20 35						21 05					21 35			
London Cannon Street ■	a																								
London Waterloo (East) ■	a	20 08		20 10	20 15	20 34			20 38	20 40	20 45	21 04			21 08	21 10	21 15	21 34		21 38	21 40	21 45		22 04	
London Charing Cross ■	a	20 12		20 14	20 19	20 37			20 42	20 44	20 49	21 07			21 12	21 14	21 19	21 37		21 42	21 44	21 49		22 07	
Ebbsfleet International	a						20 16							20 47					21 17						21 47
Stratford International	a						20 27							21 02					21 31						21 59
St Pancras International ■	a						20 38							21 09					21 42						22 06

Table 200

Gillingham and Dartford - London

Saturdays

		SE	SE	SE	SE	SE	SE	SE		SE	SE	SE		SE	SE	SE	SE	SE		SE	SE	SE			
Gillingham (Kent) [4]	d		20 54			21 50		21 24				22 20			21 54					22 24		22 54			
Chatham [4]	d		20 58			21 54		21 28				22 24			21 58					22 28		22 58			
Rochester [4]	d		21 00			21 57		21 30				22 27			22 00					22 30		23 00			
Strood [4]	d		21 05			22 02		21 35				22 32			22 05					22 35		23 05			
Higham	d		21 10					21 40							22 10					22 40		23 10			
Gravesend [4]	d		21 18		21 33	22 13		21 48			22 03	22 43			22 18		22 33			22 48		23 18			
Northfleet	d				21 37						22 07						22 37								
Swanscombe	d				21 39						22 09						22 39								
Greenhithe for Bluewater	d		21 23		21 42			21 53			22 12				22 23		22 42			22 53		23 23			
Stone Crossing	d				21 44						22 14						22 44								
Dartford [4]	a		21 28		21 48			21 58			22 18				22 28		22 48			22 58		23 28			
	d	21 25	21 28	21 31	21 48		21 55	21 58		22 01	22 18			22 25	22 28	22 31	22 48	22 55		22 58	23 01				
Slade Green [4]	d			21 36						22 06						22 36					23 06				
Erith	d			21 38						22 08						22 38					23 08				
Belvedere	d			21 41						22 11						22 41					23 11				
Abbey Wood	d		21 37	21 44				22 07		22 14					22 37	22 44				23 07	23 14				
Plumstead	d			21 47						22 17						22 47					23 17				
Woolwich Arsenal [4] ⛴	d		21 42	21 50				22 12		22 20					22 42	22 50				23 12	23 20				
Woolwich Dockyard	d			21 52						22 22						22 52					23 22				
Charlton [4]	d		21 47	21 55				22 17		22 25					22 47	22 55				23 17	23 25				
Crayford	d				21 53						22 23						22 53								
Bexley	d				21 56						22 26						22 56								
Albany Park	d				21 59						22 29						22 59								
Sidcup [4]	d				22 02						22 32						23 02								
New Eltham	d				22 05						22 35						23 05								
Mottingham	d				22 07						22 37						23 07								
Lee	d				22 10						22 40						23 10								
Hither Green [4]	d				22 13						22 43						23 13								
Barnehurst [4]	d	21 32					22 02							22 32				23 02							
Bexleyheath	d	21 34					22 04							22 34				23 04							
Welling	d	21 37					22 07							22 37				23 07							
Falconwood	d	21 40					22 10							22 40				23 10							
Eltham	d	21 42					22 12							22 42				23 12							
Kidbrooke	d	21 45					22 15							22 45				23 15							
Blackheath [4]	d	21 49	21 51				22 19	22 21						22 49	22 51			23 19		23 21					
Lewisham [4] ⛴	d	21 53	21 56		22 18		22 23	22 26			22 48			22 53	22 56		23 18	23 23		23 26					
St Johns	d																								
New Cross [4] ⊖	d	21 56			22 21		22 26				22 51			22 56			23 21	23 26							
Nunhead [4]	d																								
Peckham Rye [4]	d																								
Denmark Hill [4]	d																								
London Victoria [15] ⊖	a																								
Westcombe Park	d			21 57						22 27						22 57					23 27				
Maze Hill	d			21 57						22 27						22 57					23 27				
Greenwich [4] ⛴	d			21 59						22 29						22 59					23 29				
Deptford	d			22 03						22 33						23 03					23 33				
London Bridge [4] ⊖	a			22 05						22 35						23 05					23 35				
London Cannon Street [4] ⊖	a																								
London Waterloo (East) [4] ⊖	a	22 06	22 09	22 15	22 34		22 36	22 39		22 45	23 04			23 06	23 09	23 15	23 34	23 36		23 39	23 45				
London Charing Cross [4] ⊖	a	22 10	22 13	22 19	22 37		22 40	22 43		22 49	23 07			23 10	23 13	23 20	23 37	23 40		23 43	23 49				
Ebbsfleet International	a					22 17						22 47													
Stratford International ⊖ ⛴	a					22 29						22 59													
St Pancras International [15] ⊖	a					22 36						23 06													

Table 200

Gillingham and Dartford - London

Sundays

		SE	SE	SE	SE	SE	SE	SE	SE	SE		SE	SE	SE	SE	SE	SE	SE	SE	SE		SE		SE	SE
Gillingham (Kent) [4]	d							06 45					07 15			08 20		07 45							08 15
Chatham [4]	d							06 49					07 19			08 24		07 49							08 19
Rochester [4]	d							06 51					07 21			08 27		07 51							08 21
Strood [4]	d							06 56					07 26			08 32		07 56							08 26
Higham	d							07 01					07 31					08 01							08 31
Gravesend [4]	d							07 09					07 39			08 43		08 09							08 39
Northfleet	d							07 12					07 42					08 12							08 42
Swanscombe	d							07 14					07 44					08 14							08 44
Greenhithe for Bluewater	d							07 18					07 48					08 18							08 48
Stone Crossing	d							07 20					07 50					08 20							08 50
Dartford [4]	a							07 24					07 54					08 24							08 54
	d	06 40	06 43	06 49	07 10	07 13	07 19	07 28	07 40	07 43		07 49	07 58	08 10	08 13		08 19	08 28	08 40	08 43				08 49	08 58
Slade Green [4]	d		06 48			07 18				07 48					08 18					08 48					
Erith	d		06 50			07 20				07 50					08 20					08 50					
Belvedere	d		06 53			07 23				07 53					08 23					08 53					
Abbey Wood	d		06 56			07 26		07 37		07 56			08 07		08 26			08 37		08 56					09 07
Plumstead	d		06 59			07 29				07 59					08 29					08 59		08 47			
Woolwich Arsenal [4] ⛴	d		07 02			07 32		07 42		08 02			08 12		08 32			08 42		09 02		08 50			09 12
Woolwich Dockyard	d		07 04			07 34				08 04					08 34					09 04		08 52			
Charlton [4]	d		07 07			07 37		07 47		08 07			08 17		08 37			08 47		09 07		08 55			09 17
Crayford	d			06 54			07 24					07 54					08 24							08 54	
Bexley	d			06 57			07 27					07 57					08 27							08 57	
Albany Park	d			06 59			07 29					07 59					08 29							08 59	
Sidcup [4]	d			07 02			07 32					08 02					08 32							09 02	
New Eltham	d			07 05			07 35					08 05					08 35							09 05	
Mottingham	d			07 08			07 38					08 08					08 38							09 08	
Lee	d			07 11			07 41					08 11					08 41							09 11	
Hither Green [4]	d			07 13			07 43					08 13					08 43							09 13	
Barnehurst [4]	d	06 47			07 17				07 47					08 17					08 47						
Bexleyheath	d	06 49			07 19				07 49					08 19					08 49						
Welling	d	06 52			07 22				07 52					08 22					08 52						
Falconwood	d	06 55			07 25				07 55					08 25					08 55						
Eltham	d	06 58			07 28				07 58					08 28					08 58						
Kidbrooke	d	07 01			07 31				08 01					08 31					09 01						
Blackheath [4]	d	07 04			07 34			07 51	08 04				08 21	08 34				08 51	09 04						09 21
Lewisham [4] ⛴	d	07 08		07 18	07 38		07 48	07 56	08 08			08 18	08 26	08 38			08 48	08 56	09 08					09 18	09 26
St Johns	d																								
New Cross [4] ⊖	d	07 11			07 41				08 11					08 41					09 11						
Nunhead [4]	d																								
Peckham Rye [4]	d																								
Denmark Hill [4]	d																								
London Victoria [15] ⊖	a																								
Westcombe Park	d		07 09			07 39				08 09					08 39					09 09		08 57			
Maze Hill	d		07 09			07 39				08 09					08 39					09 09		08 57			
Greenwich [4] ⛴	d		07 11			07 41				08 11					08 41					09 11		08 59			
Deptford	d		07 15			07 45				08 15					08 45					09 15		09 03			
London Bridge [4] ⊖	a		07 17			07 47				08 17					08 47					09 17		09 05			
London Cannon Street [4] ⊖	a																								
London Waterloo (East) [4] ⊖	a	07 25	07 27	07 30	07 55	07 57	08 00	08 11	08 25	08 27		08 30	08 41	08 55	08 57		09 00	09 11	09 25	09 27				09 30	09 41
London Charing Cross [4] ⊖	a	07 28	07 31	07 34	07 58	08 01	08 04	08 14	08 28	08 31		08 34	08 44	08 58	09 01		09 04	09 14	09 28	09 31				09 34	09 44
Ebbsfleet International	a															08 47									
Stratford International ⊖ ⛴	a															08 59									
St Pancras International [15] ⊖	a															09 07									

Table 200

Sundays

Gillingham and Dartford - London

		SE	SE	SE	SE	SE	SE	SE	SE	SE	SE	SE	SE	SE	SE	SE	SE	SE	SE	SE	SE	SE
Gillingham (Kent)	d				08 54		09 20				09 24					09 54		10 20				10 24
Chatham	d				08 58		09 24				09 28					09 58		10 24				10 28
Rochester	d				09 00		09 27				09 30					10 00		10 27				10 30
Strood	d				09 05		09 32				09 35					10 05		10 32				10 35
Higham	d				09 10						09 40					10 10						10 40
Gravesend	d			09 03	09 18		09 43			09 33	09 48				10 03	10 18		10 43			10 33	10 48
Northfleet	d			09 07						09 37					10 07						10 37	
Swanscombe	d			09 09						09 39					10 09						10 39	
Greenhithe for Bluewater	d			09 12	09 23					09 42	09 53				10 12	10 23					10 42	10 53
Stone Crossing	d			09 14						09 44					10 14						10 44	
Dartford	a			09 18	09 28					09 48	09 58				10 18	10 28					10 48	10 58
	d	09 10	09 13	09 19	09 28			09 40	09 43	09 49	09 58		10 10	10 13	10 19	10 28			10 40	10 43	10 49	10 58
Slade Green	d		09 18						09 48					10 18						10 48		
Erith	d		09 20						09 50					10 20						10 50		
Belvedere	d		09 23						09 53					10 23						10 53		
Abbey Wood	d		09 26		09 37				09 56		10 07			10 26		10 37				10 56		11 07
Plumstead	d		09 29			09 17			09 59			09 47		10 29			10 17			10 59		
Woolwich Arsenal	d		09 32		09 42	09 20			10 02		10 12	09 50		10 32		10 42	10 20			11 02		11 12
Woolwich Dockyard	d		09 34			09 22			10 04			09 52		10 34			10 22			11 04		
Charlton	d		09 37		09 47	09 25			10 07		10 17	09 55		10 37		10 47	10 25			11 07		11 17
Crayford	d			09 24						09 54					10 24						10 54	
Bexley	d			09 27						09 57					10 27						10 57	
Albany Park	d			09 29						09 59					10 29						10 59	
Sidcup	d			09 32						10 02					10 32						11 02	
New Eltham	d			09 35						10 05					10 35						11 05	
Mottingham	d			09 38						10 08					10 38						11 08	
Lee	d			09 41						10 11					10 41						11 11	
Hither Green	d			09 43						10 13					10 43						11 13	
Barnehurst	d	09 17						09 47					10 17						10 47			
Bexleyheath	d	09 19						09 49					10 19						10 49			
Welling	d	09 22						09 52					10 22						10 52			
Falconwood	d	09 25						09 55					10 25						10 55			
Eltham	d	09 28						09 58					10 28						10 58			
Kidbrooke	d	09 31						10 01					10 31						11 01			
Blackheath	d	09 34			09 51			10 04			10 21		10 34			10 51			11 04			11 21
Lewisham	d	09 38		09 48	09 56			10 08		10 18	10 26		10 38		10 48	10 56			11 08		11 18	11 26
St Johns	d																					
New Cross	d	09 41						10 11					10 41						11 11			
Nunhead	d																					
Peckham Rye	d																					
Denmark Hill	d																					
London Victoria	a																					
Westcombe Park	d		09 39			09 27			10 09			09 57		10 39			10 27			11 09		
Maze Hill	d		09 39			09 27			10 09			09 57		10 39			10 27			11 09		
Greenwich	d		09 41			09 29			10 11			09 59		10 41			10 29			11 11		
Deptford	d		09 45			09 33			10 15			10 03		10 45			10 33			11 15		
London Bridge	a		09 47			09 35			10 17			10 05		10 47			10 35			11 17		
London Cannon Street	a																					
London Waterloo (East)	a	09 55	09 57	10 00	10 11			10 25	10 27	10 30	10 41		10 55	10 57	11 00	11 11			11 25	11 27	11 30	11 41
London Charing Cross	a	09 58	10 01	10 04	10 14			10 28	10 31	10 34	10 44		10 58	11 01	11 04	11 14			11 28	11 31	11 34	11 44
Ebbsfleet International	a						09 47											10 47				
Stratford International	a						09 59											10 59				
St Pancras International	a						10 06											11 06				

Table 200

Sundays

Gillingham and Dartford - London

		SE	SE	SE	SE	SE	SE	SE	SE	SE	SE	SE	SE	SE	SE	SE	SE	SE	SE	SE	SE
Gillingham (Kent)	d					10 54		11 20				11 24		11 50				11 54		12 20	
Chatham	d					10 58		11 24				11 28		11 54				11 58		12 24	
Rochester	d					11 00		11 27				11 30		11 57				12 00		12 27	
Strood	d					11 05		11 32				11 35		12 02				12 05		12 32	
Higham	d					11 10						11 40						12 10			
Gravesend	d				11 03	11 18		11 43			11 33	11 48		12 13			12 03	12 18		12 43	
Northfleet	d				11 07						11 37						12 07				
Swanscombe	d				11 09						11 39						12 09				
Greenhithe for Bluewater	d				11 12	11 23					11 42	11 53					12 12	12 23			
Stone Crossing	d				11 14						11 44						12 14				
Dartford	a				11 18	11 28					11 48	11 58					12 18	12 28			
	d		11 10	11 13	11 19	11 28			11 40	11 43	11 49	11 58			12 10	12 13	12 19	12 28			12 40
Slade Green	d			11 18						11 48						12 18					
Erith	d			11 20						11 50						12 20					
Belvedere	d			11 23						11 53						12 23					
Abbey Wood	d			11 26		11 37				11 56		12 07				12 26		12 37			
Plumstead	d	10 47		11 29			11 17			11 59			11 47			12 29			12 17		
Woolwich Arsenal	d	10 50		11 32		11 42	11 20			12 02		12 12	11 50			12 32		12 42	12 20		
Woolwich Dockyard	d	10 52		11 34			11 22			12 04			11 52			12 34			12 22		
Charlton	d	10 55		11 37		11 47	11 25			12 07		12 17	11 55			12 37		12 47	12 25		
Crayford	d				11 24						11 54						12 24				
Bexley	d				11 27						11 57						12 27				
Albany Park	d				11 29						11 59						12 29				
Sidcup	d				11 32						12 02						12 32				
New Eltham	d				11 35						12 05						12 35				
Mottingham	d				11 38						12 08						12 38				
Lee	d				11 41						12 11						12 41				
Hither Green	d				11 43						12 13						12 43				
Barnehurst	d		11 17						11 47						12 17						12 47
Bexleyheath	d		11 19						11 49						12 19						12 49
Welling	d		11 22						11 52						12 22						12 52
Falconwood	d		11 25						11 55						12 25						12 55
Eltham	d		11 28						11 58						12 28						12 58
Kidbrooke	d		11 31						12 01						12 31						13 01
Blackheath	d		11 34			11 51			12 04			12 21			12 34			12 51			13 04
Lewisham	d		11 38		11 48	11 56			12 08		12 18	12 26			12 38		12 48	12 56			13 08
St Johns	d																				
New Cross	d		11 41						12 11						12 41						13 11
Nunhead	d																				
Peckham Rye	d																				
Denmark Hill	d																				
London Victoria	a																				
Westcombe Park	d	10 57		11 39			11 27			12 09			11 57			12 39			12 27		
Maze Hill	d	10 57		11 39			11 27			12 09			11 57			12 39			12 27		
Greenwich	d	10 59		11 41			11 29			12 11			11 59			12 41			12 29		
Deptford	d	11 03		11 45			11 33			12 15			12 03			12 45			12 33		
London Bridge	a	11 05		11 47			11 35			12 17			12 05			12 47			12 35		
London Cannon Street	a																				
London Waterloo (East)	a		11 55	11 57	12 00	12 11			12 25	12 27	12 30	12 41			12 55	12 57	13 00	13 11			13 25
London Charing Cross	a		11 58	12 01	12 04	12 14			12 28	12 31	12 34	12 44			12 58	13 01	13 04	13 14			13 28
Ebbsfleet International	a							11 47						12 17						12 47	
Stratford International	a							11 59						12 32						12 59	
St Pancras International	a							12 06						12 39						13 06	

Table 200

Sundays

Gillingham and Dartford - London

		SE	SE	SE	SE	SE	SE	SE	SE	SE	SE	SE	SE	SE	SE	SE	SE	SE	SE	SE	SE	SE	SE
Gillingham (Kent)	d			12 24		12 50				12 54		13 20				13 24		13 50				13 54	
Chatham	d			12 28		12 54				12 58		13 24				13 28		13 54				13 58	
Rochester	d			12 30		12 57				13 00		13 27				13 30		13 57				14 00	
Strood	d			12 35		13 02				13 05		13 32				13 35		14 02				14 05	
Higham	d			12 40						13 10						13 40						14 10	
Gravesend	d		12 33	12 48		13 13			13 03	13 18		13 43			13 33	13 48		14 13			14 03	14 18	
Northfleet	d		12 37						13 07						13 37						14 07		
Swanscombe	d		12 39						13 09						13 39						14 09		
Greenhithe for Bluewater	d		12 42	12 53					13 12	13 23					13 42	13 53					14 12	14 23	
Stone Crossing	d		12 44						13 14						13 44						14 14		
Dartford	a		12 48	12 58					13 18	13 28					13 48	13 58					14 18	14 28	
	d	12 43	12 49	12 58			13 10	13 13	13 19	13 28			13 40	13 43	13 49	13 58			14 10	14 13	14 19	14 28	
Slade Green	d	12 48						13 18						13 48						14 18			
Erith	d	12 50						13 20						13 50						14 20			
Belvedere	d	12 53						13 23						13 53						14 23			
Abbey Wood	d	12 56		13 07				13 26		13 37				13 56		14 07				14 26		14 37	
Plumstead	d	12 59			12 47			13 29			13 17			13 59			13 47			14 29			14 17
Woolwich Arsenal	d	13 02		13 12	12 50			13 32		13 42	13 20			14 02		14 12	13 50			14 32		14 42	14 20
Woolwich Dockyard	d	13 04			12 52			13 34			13 22			14 04			13 52			14 34			14 22
Charlton	d	13 07		13 17	12 55			13 37		13 47	13 25			14 07		14 17	13 55			14 37		14 47	14 25
Crayford	d		12 54						13 24						13 54						14 24		
Bexley	d		12 57						13 27						13 57						14 27		
Albany Park	d		12 59						13 29						13 59						14 29		
Sidcup	d		13 02						13 32						14 02						14 32		
New Eltham	d		13 05						13 35						14 05						14 35		
Mottingham	d		13 08						13 38						14 08						14 38		
Lee	d		13 11						13 41						14 11						14 41		
Hither Green	d		13 13						13 43						14 13						14 43		
Barnehurst	d						13 17						13 47						14 17				
Bexleyheath	d						13 19						13 49						14 19				
Welling	d						13 22						13 52						14 22				
Falconwood	d						13 25						13 55						14 25				
Eltham	d						13 28						13 58						14 28				
Kidbrooke	d						13 31						14 01						14 31				
Blackheath	d			13 21			13 34			13 51			14 04			14 21			14 34			14 51	
Lewisham	d		13 18	13 26			13 38		13 48	13 56			14 08		14 18	14 26			14 38		14 48	14 56	
St Johns	d																						
New Cross ⊖	d						13 41						14 11						14 41				
Nunhead	d																						
Peckham Rye	d																						
Denmark Hill	d																						
London Victoria ⊖	a																						
Westcombe Park	d	13 09			12 57			13 39			13 27			14 09			13 57			14 39			14 27
Maze Hill	d	13 09			12 57			13 39			13 27			14 09			13 57			14 39			14 27
Greenwich	d	13 11			12 59			13 41			13 29			14 11			13 59			14 41			14 29
Deptford	d	13 15			13 03			13 45			13 33			14 15			14 03			14 45			14 33
London Bridge ⊖	a	13 17			13 05			13 47			13 35			14 17			14 05			14 47			14 35
London Cannon Street ⊖	a																						
London Waterloo (East) ⊖	a	13 27	13 30	13 41			13 55	13 57	14 00	14 11			14 25	14 27	14 30	14 41			14 55	14 57	15 00	15 11	
London Charing Cross ⊖	a	13 31	13 34	13 44			13 58	14 01	14 04	14 14			14 28	14 31	14 34	14 44			14 58	15 01	15 04	15 14	
Ebbsfleet International	a					13 17						13 47						14 17					
Stratford International ⊖	a					13 29						13 59						14 32					
St Pancras International ⊖	a					13 36						14 06						14 39					

Table 200

Sundays

Gillingham and Dartford - London

		SE	SE	SE	SE	SE	SE	SE	SE	SE	SE	SE	SE	SE	SE	SE	SE	SE	SE	SE	SE	SE
Gillingham (Kent)	d	14 20				14 24		14 50				14 54		15 20				15 24		15 50		
Chatham	d	14 24				14 28		14 54				14 58		15 24				15 28		15 54		
Rochester	d	14 27				14 30		14 57				15 00		15 27				15 30		15 57		
Strood	d	14 32				14 35		15 02				15 05		15 32				15 35		16 02		
Higham	d					14 40						15 10						15 40				
Gravesend	d	14 43			14 33	14 48		15 13			15 03	15 18		15 43			15 33	15 48		16 13		
Northfleet	d				14 37						15 07						15 37					
Swanscombe	d				14 39						15 09						15 39					
Greenhithe for Bluewater	d				14 42	14 53					15 12	15 23					15 42	15 53				
Stone Crossing	d				14 44						15 14						15 44					
Dartford	a				14 48	14 58					15 18	15 28					15 48	15 58				
	d		14 40	14 43	14 49	14 58			15 10	15 13	15 19	15 28			15 40	15 43	15 49	15 58			16 10	16 13
Slade Green	d			14 48						15 18						15 48						16 18
Erith	d			14 50						15 20						15 50						16 20
Belvedere	d			14 53						15 23						15 53						16 23
Abbey Wood	d			14 56		15 07				15 26		15 37				15 56		16 07				16 26
Plumstead	d			14 59			14 47			15 29			15 17			15 59			15 47			16 29
Woolwich Arsenal	d			15 02		15 12	14 50			15 32		15 42	15 20			16 02		16 12	15 50			16 32
Woolwich Dockyard	d			15 04			14 52			15 34			15 22			16 04			15 52			16 34
Charlton	d			15 07		15 17	14 55			15 37		15 47	15 25			16 07		16 17	15 55			16 37
Crayford	d				14 54						15 24						15 54					
Bexley	d				14 57						15 27						15 57					
Albany Park	d				14 59						15 29						15 59					
Sidcup	d				15 02						15 32						16 02					
New Eltham	d				15 05						15 35						16 05					
Mottingham	d				15 08						15 38						16 08					
Lee	d				15 11						15 41						16 11					
Hither Green	d				15 13						15 43						16 13					
Barnehurst	d		14 47						15 17						15 47						16 17	
Bexleyheath	d		14 49						15 19						15 49						16 19	
Welling	d		14 52						15 22						15 52						16 22	
Falconwood	d		14 55						15 25						15 55						16 25	
Eltham	d		14 58						15 28						15 58						16 28	
Kidbrooke	d		15 01						15 31						16 01						16 31	
Blackheath	d		15 04			15 21			15 34			15 51			16 04			16 21			16 34	
Lewisham	d		15 08		15 18	15 26			15 38		15 48	15 56			16 08		16 18	16 26			16 38	
St Johns	d																					
New Cross ⊖	d		15 11						15 41						16 11						16 41	
Nunhead	d																					
Peckham Rye	d																					
Denmark Hill	d																					
London Victoria ⊖	a																					
Westcombe Park	d			15 09			14 57			15 39			15 27			16 09			15 57			16 39
Maze Hill	d			15 09			14 57			15 39			15 27			16 09			15 57			16 39
Greenwich	d			15 11			14 59			15 41			15 29			16 11			15 59			16 41
Deptford	d			15 15			15 03			15 45			15 33			16 15			16 03			16 45
London Bridge ⊖	a			15 17			15 05			15 47			15 35			16 17			16 05			16 47
London Cannon Street ⊖	a																					
London Waterloo (East) ⊖	a		15 25	15 27	15 30	15 41			15 55	15 57	16 00	16 11			16 25	16 27	16 30	16 41			16 55	16 57
London Charing Cross ⊖	a		15 28	15 31	15 34	15 44			15 58	16 01	16 04	16 14			16 28	16 31	16 34	16 44			16 58	17 01
Ebbsfleet International	a	14 47						15 17						15 47						16 17		
Stratford International ⊖	a	15 02						15 29						15 59						16 29		
St Pancras International ⊖	a	15 09						15 36						16 06						16 40		

Table 200

Sundays

Gillingham and Dartford - London

		SE	SE	SE	SE	SE	SE	SE	SE	SE		SE	SE	SE	SE	SE	SE	SE	SE	SE		SE	SE	SE	SE
Gillingham (Kent)	d		15 54		16 20				16 24			16 50	16 50				16 54		17 20					17 24	
Chatham	d		15 58		16 24				16 28			16 54	16 54				16 58		17 24					17 28	
Rochester	d		16 00		16 27				16 30			16 57	16 57				17 00		17 27					17 30	
Strood	d		16 05		16 32				16 35			17 02	17 02				17 05		17 32					17 35	
Higham	d		16 10						16 40								17 10							17 40	
Gravesend	d	16 03	16 18		16 43			16 33	16 48			17 12	17 12			17 03	17 18		17 43				17 33	17 48	
Northfleet	d	16 07						16 37								17 07							17 37		
Swanscombe	d	16 09						16 39								17 09							17 39		
Greenhithe for Bluewater	d	16 12	16 23					16 42	16 53							17 12	17 23						17 42	17 53	
Stone Crossing	d	16 14						16 44								17 14							17 44		
Dartford	a	16 18	16 28					16 48	16 58							17 18	17 28						17 48	17 58	
	d	16 19	16 28			16 40	16 43	16 49	16 58					17 10	17 13	17 19	17 28			17 40		17 43	17 49	17 58	
Slade Green	d						16 48								17 18							17 48			
Erith	d						16 50								17 20							17 50			
Belvedere	d						16 53								17 23							17 53			
Abbey Wood	d		16 37				16 56		17 07						17 26		17 37					17 56		18 07	
Plumstead	d			16 17			16 59			16 47					17 29			17 17				17 59			17 47
Woolwich Arsenal	d		16 42	16 20			17 02		17 12	16 50					17 32		17 42	17 20				18 02		18 12	17 50
Woolwich Dockyard	d			16 22			17 04			16 52					17 34			17 22				18 04			17 52
Charlton	d		16 47	16 25			17 07		17 17	16 55					17 37		17 47	17 25				18 07		18 17	17 55
Crayford	d	16 24						16 54								17 24							17 54		
Bexley	d	16 27						16 57								17 27							17 57		
Albany Park	d	16 29						16 59								17 29							17 59		
Sidcup	d	16 32						17 02								17 32							18 02		
New Eltham	d	16 35						17 05								17 35							18 05		
Mottingham	d	16 38						17 08								17 38							18 08		
Lee	d	16 41						17 11								17 41							18 11		
Hither Green	d	16 43						17 13								17 43							18 13		
Barnehurst	d					16 47								17 17						17 47					
Bexleyheath	d					16 49								17 19						17 49					
Welling	d					16 52								17 22						17 52					
Falconwood	d					16 55								17 25						17 55					
Eltham	d					16 58								17 28						17 58					
Kidbrooke	d					17 01								17 31						18 01					
Blackheath	d		16 51			17 04			17 21					17 34			17 51			18 04				18 21	
Lewisham	d	16 48	16 56			17 08		17 18	17 26					17 38		17 48	17 56			18 08			18 18	18 26	
St Johns	d																								
New Cross	d					17 11								17 41						18 11					
Nunhead	d																								
Peckham Rye	d																								
Denmark Hill	d																								
London Victoria	a																								
Westcombe Park	d			16 27			17 09			16 57					17 39			17 27				18 09			17 57
Maze Hill	d			16 27			17 09			16 57					17 39			17 27				18 09			17 57
Greenwich	d			16 29			17 11			16 59					17 41			17 29				18 11			17 59
Deptford	d			16 33			17 15			17 03					17 45			17 33				18 15			18 03
London Bridge	a			16 35			17 17			17 05					17 47			17 35				18 17			18 05
London Cannon Street	a																								
London Waterloo (East)	a	17 00	17 11			17 25	17 27	17 30	17 41					17 55	17 57	18 00	18 11			18 25		18 27	18 30	18 41	
London Charing Cross	a	17 04	17 14			17 28	17 31	17 34	17 44					17 58	18 01	18 04	18 14			18 28		18 31	18 34	18 44	
Ebbsfleet International	a				16 47							17 16	17 16						17 47						
Stratford International	a				16 59							17 27	17 27						17 59						
St Pancras International	a				17 06							17 34	17 38						18 09						

Table 200

Sundays

Gillingham and Dartford - London

		SE	SE	SE	SE	SE		SE	SE	SE	SE	SE	SE	SE	SE	SE		SE	SE	SE	SE	SE	SE	SE	SE
Gillingham (Kent)	d	17 50				17 54			18 20				18 24	18 50					18 54	19 20				19 24	19 50
Chatham	d	17 54				17 58			18 24				18 28	18 54					18 58	19 24				19 28	19 54
Rochester	d	17 57				18 00			18 27				18 30	18 57					19 00	19 27				19 30	19 57
Strood	d	18 02				18 05			18 32				18 35	19 02					19 05	19 32				19 35	20 02
Higham	d					18 10							18 40						19 10					19 40	
Gravesend	d	18 12			18 03	18 18			18 43			18 33	18 48	19 13				19 03	19 18	19 43			19 33	19 48	20 12
Northfleet	d				18 07							18 37						19 07					19 37		
Swanscombe	d				18 09							18 39						19 09					19 39		
Greenhithe for Bluewater	d				18 12	18 23						18 42	18 53					19 12	19 23				19 42	19 53	
Stone Crossing	d				18 14							18 44						19 14					19 44		
Dartford	a				18 18	18 28						18 48	18 58					19 18	19 28				19 48	19 58	
	d		18 10	18 13	18 19	18 28				18 40	18 43	18 49	18 58		19 10	19 13		19 19	19 28		19 40	19 43	19 49	19 58	
Slade Green	d			18 18							18 48					19 18						19 48			
Erith	d			18 20							18 50					19 20						19 50			
Belvedere	d			18 23							18 53					19 23						19 53			
Abbey Wood	d			18 26		18 37					18 56		19 07			19 26			19 37			19 56		20 07	
Plumstead	d			18 29				18 17			18 59					19 29						19 59			
Woolwich Arsenal	d			18 32		18 42		18 20			19 02		19 12			19 32			19 42			20 02		20 12	
Woolwich Dockyard	d			18 34				18 22			19 04					19 34						20 04			
Charlton	d			18 37		18 47		18 25			19 07		19 17			19 37			19 47			20 07		20 17	
Crayford	d				18 24							18 54						19 24					19 54		
Bexley	d				18 27							18 57						19 27					19 57		
Albany Park	d				18 29							18 59						19 29					19 59		
Sidcup	d				18 32							19 02						19 32					20 02		
New Eltham	d				18 35							19 05						19 35					20 05		
Mottingham	d				18 38							19 08						19 38					20 08		
Lee	d				18 41							19 11						19 41					20 11		
Hither Green	d				18 43							19 13						19 43					20 13		
Barnehurst	d		18 17							18 47					19 17						19 47				
Bexleyheath	d		18 19							18 49					19 19						19 49				
Welling	d		18 22							18 52					19 22						19 52				
Falconwood	d		18 25							18 55					19 25						19 55				
Eltham	d		18 28							18 58					19 28						19 58				
Kidbrooke	d		18 31							19 01					19 31						20 01				
Blackheath	d		18 34			18 51				19 04			19 21		19 34				19 51		20 04			20 21	
Lewisham	d		18 38		18 48	18 56				19 08		19 18	19 26		19 38			19 48	19 56		20 08		20 18	20 26	
St Johns	d																								
New Cross	d		18 41							19 11					19 41						20 11				
Nunhead	d																								
Peckham Rye	d																								
Denmark Hill	d																								
London Victoria	a																								
Westcombe Park	d			18 39				18 27			19 09					19 39						20 09			
Maze Hill	d			18 39				18 27			19 09					19 39						20 09			
Greenwich	d			18 41				18 29			19 11					19 41						20 11			
Deptford	d			18 45				18 33			19 15					19 45						20 15			
London Bridge	a			18 47				18 35			19 17					19 47						20 17			
London Cannon Street	a																								
London Waterloo (East)	a		18 55	18 57	19 00	19 11				19 25	19 27	19 30	19 41		19 55	19 57		20 00	20 11		20 25	20 27	20 30	20 41	
London Charing Cross	a		18 58	19 01	19 04	19 14				19 28	19 31	19 34	19 44		19 58	20 01		20 04	20 14		20 28	20 31	20 34	20 44	
Ebbsfleet International	a	18 16							18 47					19 17						19 47					20 16
Stratford International	a	18 27							19 02					19 29						19 59					20 27
St Pancras International	a	18 38							19 09					19 36						20 06					20 38

Table 200

Sundays

Gillingham and Dartford - London

Station		SE		SE	SE	SE	SE	SE	SE	SE	SE	SE		SE	SE	SE	SE	SE	SE	SE	SE	SE		SE	SE
Gillingham (Kent)	d				20 20		19 45			20 50		20 15				21 20		20 45			21 50			21 15	
Chatham	d				20 24		19 49			20 54		20 19				21 24		20 49			21 54			21 19	
Rochester	d				20 27		19 51			20 57		20 21				21 27		20 51			21 57			21 21	
Strood	d				20 32		19 56			21 02		20 26				21 32		20 56			22 02			21 26	
Higham	d						20 01					20 31						21 01						21 31	
Gravesend	d				20 43		20 09			21 13		20 39				21 43		21 09			22 13			21 39	
Northfleet	d						20 12					20 42						21 12						21 42	
Swanscombe	d						20 14					20 44						21 14						21 44	
Greenhithe for Bluewater	d						20 18					20 48						21 18						21 48	
Stone Crossing	d						20 20					20 50						21 20						21 50	
Dartford	a						20 24					20 54						21 24						21 54	
	d	20 10		20 13		20 19	20 28	20 40	20 43		20 49	20 58		21 10	21 13		21 19	21 28	21 40	21 43		21 49		21 58	22 10
Slade Green	d			20 18					20 48						21 18					21 48					
Erith	d			20 20					20 50						21 20					21 50					
Belvedere	d			20 23					20 53						21 23					21 53					
Abbey Wood	d			20 26			20 37		20 56			21 07			21 26			21 37		21 56				22 07	
Plumstead	d			20 29					20 59						21 29					21 59					
Woolwich Arsenal	d			20 32			20 42		21 02			21 12			21 32			21 42		22 02				22 12	
Woolwich Dockyard	d			20 34					21 04						21 34					22 04					
Charlton	d			20 37			20 47		21 07			21 17			21 37			21 47		22 07				22 17	
Crayford	d					20 24					20 54						21 24					21 54			
Bexley	d					20 27					20 57						21 27					21 57			
Albany Park	d					20 29					20 59						21 29					21 59			
Sidcup	d					20 32					21 02						21 32					22 02			
New Eltham	d					20 35					21 05						21 35					22 05			
Mottingham	d					20 38					21 08						21 38					22 08			
Lee	d					20 41					21 11						21 41					22 11			
Hither Green	d					20 43					21 13						21 43					22 13			
Barnehurst	d	20 17						20 47						21 17					21 47						22 17
Bexleyheath	d	20 19						20 49						21 19					21 49						22 19
Welling	d	20 22						20 52						21 22					21 52						22 22
Falconwood	d	20 25						20 55						21 25					21 55						22 25
Eltham	d	20 28						20 58						21 28					21 58						22 28
Kidbrooke	d	20 31						21 01						21 31					22 01						22 31
Blackheath	d	20 34					20 51	21 04				21 21		21 34				21 51	22 04					22 21	22 34
Lewisham	d	20 38				20 48	20 56	21 08			21 18	21 26		21 38			21 48	21 56	22 08			22 18		22 26	22 38
St Johns	d																								
New Cross ⊖	d	20 41						21 11						21 41					22 11						22 41
Nunhead	d																								
Peckham Rye	d																								
Denmark Hill	d																								
London Victoria ⊖	a																								
Westcombe Park	d			20 39					21 09						21 39					22 09					
Maze Hill	d			20 39					21 09						21 39					22 09					
Greenwich	d			20 41					21 11						21 41					22 11					
Deptford	d			20 45					21 15						21 45					22 15					
London Bridge ⊖	a			20 47					21 17						21 47					22 17					
London Cannon Street ⊖	a																								
London Waterloo (East) ⊖	a	20 55		20 57		21 00	21 11	21 25	21 27		21 30	21 41		21 55	21 57		22 00	22 11	22 25	22 27		22 30		22 41	22 55
London Charing Cross ⊖	a	20 58		21 01		21 04	21 14	21 28	21 31		21 34	21 44		21 58	22 01		22 04	22 14	22 28	22 31		22 34		22 44	22 58
Ebbsfleet International	a				20 47					21 17						21 47					22 17				
Stratford International ⊖	a				20 59					21 31						21 59					22 29				
St Pancras International ⊖	a				21 06					21 42						22 06					22 36				

Table 200

Sundays

Gillingham and Dartford - London

Station		SE	SE	SE	SE	SE	SE	SE		SE	SE
Gillingham (Kent)	d		22 20	22 20		21 45					22 15
Chatham	d		22 24	22 24		21 49					22 19
Rochester	d		22 27	22 27		21 51					22 21
Strood	d		22 32	22 32		21 56					22 26
Higham	d					22 01					22 31
Gravesend	d		22 43	22 43		22 09					22 39
Northfleet	d					22 12					22 42
Swanscombe	d					22 14					22 44
Greenhithe for Bluewater	d					22 18					22 48
Stone Crossing	d					22 20					22 50
Dartford	a					22 24					22 54
	d	22 13			22 19	22 28	22 40	22 43		22 49	22 58
Slade Green	d	22 18						22 48			
Erith	d	22 20						22 50			
Belvedere	d	22 23						22 53			
Abbey Wood	d	22 26				22 37		22 56			23 07
Plumstead	d	22 29						22 59			
Woolwich Arsenal	d	22 32				22 42		23 02			23 12
Woolwich Dockyard	d	22 34						23 04			
Charlton	d	22 37				22 47		23 07			23 17
Crayford	d				22 24					22 54	
Bexley	d				22 27					22 57	
Albany Park	d				22 29					22 59	
Sidcup	d				22 32					23 02	
New Eltham	d				22 35					23 05	
Mottingham	d				22 38					23 08	
Lee	d				22 41					23 11	
Hither Green	d				22 43					23 13	
Barnehurst	d						22 47				
Bexleyheath	d						22 49				
Welling	d						22 52				
Falconwood	d						22 55				
Eltham	d						22 58				
Kidbrooke	d						23 01				
Blackheath	d					22 51	23 04				23 21
Lewisham	d				22 48	22 56	23 08			23 18	23 26
St Johns	d										
New Cross ⊖	d						23 11				
Nunhead	d										
Peckham Rye	d										
Denmark Hill	d										
London Victoria ⊖	a										
Westcombe Park	d	22 39						23 09			
Maze Hill	d	22 39						23 09			
Greenwich	d	22 41						23 11			
Deptford	d	22 45						23 15			
London Bridge ⊖	a	22 47						23 17			
London Cannon Street ⊖	a										
London Waterloo (East) ⊖	a	22 57			23 00	23 11	23 25	23 27		23 30	23 41
London Charing Cross ⊖	a	23 01			23 04	23 14	23 28	23 31		23 34	23 44
Ebbsfleet International	a		22 47	22 47							
Stratford International ⊖	a		22 59	23 02							
St Pancras International ⊖	a		23 06	23 09							

Table 203

London - Hayes (Kent) via Catford Bridge

Mondays to Fridays

		SE MO	SE MX	SE	SE	SE	SE	SE	SE	SE	SE	SE	SE	SE	SE	SE	SE A	SE	SE	SE		SE	SE	SE	SE
London Charing Cross	⊖ d	23p35	23p52		05 47	06 17	06 47		07 17		07 44		08 15		08 44			09 17		09 47			10 17		10 47
London Waterloo (East)	⊖ d	23p38	23p55		05 50	06 20	06 50		07 20		07 47		08 18		08 47			09 20		09 50			10 20		10 50
London Cannon Street	⊖ d							07 00		07 30		08 00		08 30		09 00	09 03		09 30			10 00		10 30	
London Bridge	⊖ d	23p43	23p59		05 55	06 26	06 55	07 04	07 25	07 34	07 53	08 04	08 23	08 34	08 53	09 04	09 07	09 25	09 34	09 55		10 04	10 25	10 34	10 55
New Cross	⊖ d	23p49	00 05	05 31	06 01	06 32	07 02	07 09		07 39		08 09		08 41		09 09			09 39			10 09		10 39	
St Johns	d	23p51	00 07	05 33	06 03	06 34	07 04	07 11		07 41		08 11		08 43		09 11			09 41			10 11		10 41	
Lewisham	d	23p54	00 10	05 36	06 06	06 38	07 08	07 16		07 44		08 17		08 46		09 14			09 44			10 14		10 44	
Ladywell	d	23p57	00 13	05 39	06 09	06 41	07 11	07 19	07 34	07 47	08 04	08 20	08 34	08 49	09 04	09 17	09 22	09 34	09 47	10 04		10 17	10 34	10 47	11 04
Catford Bridge	d	23p59	00 15	05 41	06 11	06 43	07 13	07 21	07 36	07 49	08 06	08 22	08 36	08 51	09 06	09 19	09 24	09 36	09 49	10 06		10 19	10 36	10 49	11 06
Lower Sydenham	d	00 02	00 18	05 44	06 14	06 46	07 16	07 24	07 39	07 52	08 09	08 25	08 39	08 54	09 09	09 22	09 27	09 39	09 52	10 09		10 22	10 39	10 52	11 09
New Beckenham	d	00 04	00 20	05 46	06 16	06 48	07 18	07 26	07 41	07 54	08 11	08 27	08 41	08 56	09 11	09 24	09 29	09 41	09 54	10 11		10 24	10 41	10 54	11 11
Clock House	d	00 06	00 23	05 48	06 18	06 50	07 20	07 29	07 43	07 57	08 13	08 29	08 43	08 58	09 13	09 27		09 43	09 57	10 13		10 27	10 43	10 57	11 13
Elmers End	d	00 09	00 25	05 51	06 21	06 53	07 23	07 31	07 46	07 59	08 16	08 32	08 46	09 01	09 16	09 29		09 46	09 59	10 16		10 29	10 46	10 59	11 16
Eden Park	d	00 12	00 29	05 54	06 24	06 56	07 26	07 35	07 49	08 03	08 19	08 35	08 49	09 04	09 19	09 33		09 49	10 03	10 19		10 33	10 49	11 03	11 19
West Wickham	d	00 15	00 31	05 57	06 27	06 59	07 29	07 37	07 52	08 05	08 22	08 38	08 52	09 07	09 22	09 35		09 52	10 05	10 22		10 35	10 52	11 05	11 22
Hayes (Kent)	a	00 18	00 34	06 00	06 30	07 02	07 32	07 40	07 56	08 08	08 25	08 41	08 54	09 10	09 25	09 39		09 55	10 08	10 25		10 38	10 55	11 08	11 25

		SE	SE	SE	SE	SE		SE	SE	SE	SE	SE	SE	SE	SE	SE		SE	SE	SE	SE	SE	SE	SE	SE
London Charing Cross	⊖ d		11 17		11 47			12 17		12 47		13 17		13 47		14 17			14 47		15 17		15 47		16 20
London Waterloo (East)	⊖ d		11 20		11 50			12 20		12 50		13 20		13 50		14 20			14 50		15 20		15 50		16 23
London Cannon Street	⊖ d	11 00		11 30		12 00			12 30		13 00		13 30		14 00			14 30		15 00		15 30		16 00	
London Bridge	⊖ d	11 04	11 25	11 34	11 55	12 04		12 25	12 34	12 55	13 04	13 25	13 34	13 55	14 04	14 25		14 34	14 55	15 04	15 25	15 34	15 55	16 04	16 29
New Cross	⊖ d	11 09		11 39		12 09			12 39		13 09		13 39		14 09			14 39		15 09		15 39		16 10	
St Johns	d	11 11		11 41		12 11			12 41		13 11		13 41		14 11			14 41		15 11		15 41		16 12	
Lewisham	d	11 14		11 44		12 14			12 44		13 14		13 44		14 14			14 44		15 14		15 44		16 15	
Ladywell	d	11 17	11 34	11 47	12 04	12 17		12 34	12 47	13 04	13 17	13 34	13 47	14 04	14 17	14 34		14 47	15 04	15 17	15 34	15 47	16 04	16 18	16 38
Catford Bridge	d	11 19	11 36	11 49	12 06	12 19		12 36	12 49	13 06	13 19	13 36	13 49	14 06	14 19	14 36		14 49	15 06	15 19	15 36	15 49	16 06	16 20	16 40
Lower Sydenham	d	11 22	11 39	11 52	12 09	12 22		12 39	12 52	13 09	13 22	13 39	13 52	14 09	14 22	14 39		14 52	15 09	15 22	15 39	15 52	16 09	16 23	16 43
New Beckenham	d	11 24	11 41	11 54	12 11	12 24		12 41	12 54	13 11	13 24	13 41	13 54	14 11	14 24	14 41		14 54	15 11	15 24	15 41	15 54	16 11	16 25	16 45
Clock House	d	11 27	11 43	11 57	12 13	12 27		12 43	12 57	13 13	13 27	13 43	13 57	14 13	14 27	14 43		14 57	15 13	15 27	15 43	15 57	16 13	16 27	16 48
Elmers End	d	11 29	11 46	11 59	12 16	12 29		12 46	12 59	13 16	13 29	13 46	13 59	14 16	14 29	14 46		14 59	15 16	15 29	15 46	15 59	16 16	16 30	16 51
Eden Park	d	11 33	11 49	12 03	12 19	12 33		12 49	13 03	13 19	13 33	13 49	14 03	14 19	14 33	14 49		15 03	15 19	15 33	15 49	16 03	16 19	16 34	16 54
West Wickham	d	11 35	11 52	12 05	12 22	12 35		12 52	13 05	13 22	13 35	13 52	14 05	14 22	14 35	14 52		15 05	15 22	15 35	15 52	16 05	16 22	16 36	16 57
Hayes (Kent)	a	11 38	11 55	12 08	12 25	12 38		12 55	13 08	13 25	13 38	13 55	14 08	14 25	14 38	14 55		15 08	15 25	15 38	15 55	16 08	16 25	16 41	17 01

		SE		SE	SE	SE	SE	SE	SE	SE	SE	SE		SE	SE	SE	SE	SE	SE	SE	SE	SE		SE	SE
London Charing Cross	⊖ d			16 39		16 59		17 21		17 43		18 05			18 27		18 52		19 17		19 47			20 17	20 47
London Waterloo (East)	⊖ d			16 42		17 02		17 24		17 46		18 08			18 30		18 55		19 20		19 50			20 20	20 50
London Cannon Street	⊖ d	16 30			16 51		17 12		17 34		17 56			18 18		18 40		19 00		19 30		20 00			
London Bridge	⊖ d	16 34		16 47	16 55	17 07	17 16	17 29	17 39	17 52	18 00	18 13		18 23	18 35	18 44	19 00	19 04	19 25	19 34	19 55	20 04		20 25	20 55
New Cross	⊖ d	16 40			17 01		17 22		17 45		18 06			18 28		18 50		19 09		19 39		20 09		20 32	21 00
St Johns	d	16 42			17 03		17 24		17 47		18 08			18 30		18 52		19 11		19 41		20 11		20 34	21 02
Lewisham	d	16 45			17 06		17 27		17 50		18 11			18 33		18 55		19 14		19 44		20 14		20 37	21 05
Ladywell	d	16 48		16 57	17 09	17 17	17 30	17 40	17 53	18 01	18 14	18 23		18 36	18 45	18 58	19 09	19 17	19 34	19 47	20 04	20 17		20 40	21 08
Catford Bridge	d	16 50		16 59	17 11	17 19	17 32	17 42	17 55	18 03	18 16	18 25		18 38	18 47	19 00	19 11	19 19	19 36	19 49	20 06	20 19		20 42	21 10
Lower Sydenham	d	16 53		17 02	17 14	17 22	17 35	17 45	17 58	18 06	18 19	18 28		18 41	18 50	19 03	19 14	19 22	19 39	19 52	20 09	20 22		20 45	21 13
New Beckenham	d	16 55		17 04	17 16	17 24	17 37	17 47	18 00	18 08	18 21	18 30		18 43	18 52	19 05	19 16	19 24	19 41	19 54	20 11	20 24		20 47	21 15
Clock House	d	16 57		17 07	17 18	17 27	17 39	17 49	18 02	18 11	18 23	18 33		18 46	18 55	19 07	19 19	19 27	19 43	19 57	20 13	20 27		20 50	21 18
Elmers End	d	17 00		17 10	17 21	17 30	17 42	17 52	18 05	18 14	18 26	18 36		18 49	18 58	19 10	19 22	19 29	19 46	19 59	20 16	20 29		20 52	21 20
Eden Park	d	17 04		17 13	17 25	17 33	17 46	17 56	18 09	18 17	18 30	18 39		18 52	19 01	19 14	19 25	19 33	19 49	20 03	20 19	20 33		20 56	21 24
West Wickham	d	17 06		17 16	17 27	17 36	17 48	17 58	18 11	18 20	18 32	18 42		18 55	19 04	19 16	19 28	19 35	19 52	20 05	20 22	20 35		20 58	21 26
Hayes (Kent)	a	17 11		17 20	17 31	17 41	17 53	18 02	18 15	18 25	18 37	18 46		18 59	19 09	19 21	19 32	19 39	19 55	20 09	20 25	20 39		21 01	21 29

		SE	SE	SE	SE	SE	SE
London Charing Cross	⊖ d	21 17	21 47	22 17	22 47	23 17	23 52
London Waterloo (East)	⊖ d	21 20	21 50	22 20	22 50	23 20	23 55
London Cannon Street	⊖ d						
London Bridge	⊖ d	21 25	21 55	22 25	22 55	23 25	23 59
New Cross	⊖ d	21 30	22 00	22 30	23 00	23 30	00 05
St Johns	d	21 32	22 02	22 32	23 02	23 32	00 07
Lewisham	d	21 35	22 05	22 35	23 05	23 35	00 10
Ladywell	d	21 38	22 08	22 38	23 08	23 38	00 13
Catford Bridge	d	21 40	22 10	22 40	23 10	23 40	00 15
Lower Sydenham	d	21 43	22 13	22 43	23 13	23 43	00 18
New Beckenham	d	21 45	22 15	22 45	23 15	23 45	00 20
Clock House	d	21 48	22 18	22 48	23 18	23 48	00 23
Elmers End	d	21 50	22 20	22 50	23 20	23 50	00 25
Eden Park	d	21 54	22 24	22 54	23 24	23 54	00 29
West Wickham	d	21 56	22 26	22 56	23 26	23 56	00 31
Hayes (Kent)	a	21 59	22 29	22 59	23 29	23 59	00 34

Saturdays

		SE	SE	SE	SE	SE	SE	SE	SE	SE	SE	SE	SE	SE	SE	SE	SE	SE	SE	SE		SE	SE	SE	SE
London Charing Cross	⊖ d	23p52	05 47	06 17	06 47	07 17	07 47		08 17		08 47		09 17		09 47		10 17		10 47			11 17		11 47	
London Waterloo (East)	⊖ d	23p55	05 50	06 20	06 50	07 20	07 50		08 20		08 50		09 20		09 50		10 20		10 50			11 20		11 50	
London Cannon Street	⊖ d							08 00		08 30		09 00		09 30		10 00		10 30		11 00			11 30		12 00
London Bridge	⊖ d	23p59	05 55	06 25	06 55	07 25	07 55	08 04	08 25	08 34	08 55	09 04	09 25	09 34	09 55	10 04	10 25	10 34	10 55	11 04		11 25	11 34	11 55	12 04
New Cross	⊖ d	00 05	06 00	06 30	07 00	07 30		08 09		08 39		09 09		09 39		10 09		10 39		11 09			11 39		12 09
St Johns	d	00 07	06 02	06 32	07 02	07 32		08 11		08 41		09 11		09 41		10 11		10 41		11 11			11 41		12 11
Lewisham	d	00 10	06 05	06 35	07 05	07 35		08 14		08 44		09 14		09 44		10 14		10 44		11 14			11 44		12 14
Ladywell	d	00 13	06 08	06 38	07 08	07 38	08 04	08 17	08 34	08 47	09 04	09 17	09 34	09 47	10 04	10 17	10 34	10 47	11 04	11 17		11 34	11 47	12 04	12 17
Catford Bridge	d	00 15	06 10	06 40	07 10	07 40	08 06	08 19	08 36	08 49	09 06	09 19	09 36	09 49	10 06	10 19	10 36	10 49	11 06	11 19		11 36	11 49	12 06	12 19
Lower Sydenham	d	00 18	06 13	06 43	07 13	07 43	08 09	08 22	08 39	08 52	09 09	09 22	09 39	09 52	10 09	10 22	10 39	10 52	11 09	11 22		11 39	11 52	12 09	12 22
New Beckenham	d	00 20	06 15	06 45	07 15	07 45	08 11	08 24	08 41	08 54	09 11	09 24	09 41	09 54	10 11	10 24	10 41	10 54	11 11	11 24		11 41	11 54	12 11	12 24
Clock House	d	00 23	06 18	06 48	07 18	07 48	08 13	08 27	08 43	08 57	09 13	09 27	09 43	09 57	10 13	10 27	10 43	10 57	11 13	11 27		11 43	11 57	12 13	12 27
Elmers End	d	00 25	06 20	06 50	07 20	07 50	08 16	08 29	08 46	08 59	09 16	09 29	09 46	09 59	10 16	10 29	10 46	10 59	11 16	11 29		11 46	11 59	12 16	12 29
Eden Park	d	00 29	06 24	06 54	07 24	07 54	08 19	08 33	08 49	09 03	09 19	09 33	09 49	10 03	10 19	10 33	10 49	11 03	11 19	11 33		11 49	12 03	12 19	12 33
West Wickham	d	00 31	06 26	06 56	07 26	07 56	08 22	08 35	08 52	09 05	09 22	09 35	09 52	10 05	10 22	10 35	10 52	11 05	11 22	11 35		11 52	12 05	12 22	12 35
Hayes (Kent)	a	00 34	06 29	06 59	07 29	07 59	08 25	08 38	08 55	09 08	09 25	09 38	09 55	10 08	10 25	10 38	10 55	11 08	11 25	11 38		11 55	12 08	12 25	12 38

A To Beckenham Junction (Table 195)

		SE	SE	SE	SE	SE		SE	SE	SE	SE	SE	SE	SE	SE	SE		SE	SE	SE	SE	SE	SE	SE	SE
London Charing Cross	⊖ d	12 17		12 47		13 17			13 47		14 17		14 47		15 17			15 47		16 17		16 47		17 17	
London Waterloo (East)	⊖ d	12 20		12 50		13 20			13 50		14 20		14 50		15 20			15 50		16 20		16 50		17 20	
London Cannon Street	⊖ d		12 30		13 00			13 30		14 00		14 30		15 00		15 30			16 00		16 30		17 00		17 30
London Bridge	⊖ d	12 25	12 34	12 55	13 04	13 25		13 34	13 55	14 04	14 25	14 34	14 55	15 04	15 25	15 34		15 55	16 04	16 25	16 34	16 55	17 04	17 25	17 34
New Cross	⊖ d		12 39		13 09			13 39		14 09		14 39		15 09		15 39			16 09		16 39		17 09		17 39
St Johns	d		12 41		13 11			13 41		14 11		14 41		15 11		15 41			16 11		16 41		17 11		17 41
Lewisham	d		12 44		13 14			13 44		14 14		14 44		15 14		15 44			16 14		16 44		17 14		17 44
Ladywell	d	12 34	12 47	13 04	13 17	13 34		13 47	14 04	14 17	14 34	14 47	15 04	15 17	15 34	15 47		16 04	16 17	16 34	16 47	17 04	17 17	17 34	17 47
Catford Bridge	d	12 36	12 49	13 06	13 19	13 36		13 49	14 06	14 19	14 36	14 49	15 06	15 19	15 36	15 49		16 06	16 19	16 36	16 49	17 06	17 19	17 36	17 49
Lower Sydenham	d	12 39	12 52	13 09	13 22	13 39		13 52	14 09	14 22	14 39	14 52	15 09	15 22	15 39	15 52		16 09	16 22	16 39	16 52	17 09	17 22	17 39	17 52
New Beckenham	d	12 41	12 54	13 11	13 24	13 41		13 54	14 11	14 24	14 41	14 54	15 11	15 24	15 41	15 54		16 11	16 24	16 41	16 54	17 11	17 24	17 41	17 54
Clock House	d	12 43	12 57	13 13	13 27	13 43		13 57	14 13	14 27	14 43	14 57	15 13	15 27	15 43	15 57		16 13	16 27	16 43	16 57	17 13	17 27	17 43	17 57
Elmers End	d	12 46	12 59	13 16	13 29	13 46		13 59	14 16	14 29	14 46	14 59	15 16	15 29	15 46	15 59		16 16	16 29	16 46	16 59	17 16	17 29	17 46	17 59
Eden Park	d	12 49	13 03	13 19	13 33	13 49		14 03	14 19	14 33	14 49	15 03	15 19	15 33	15 49	16 03		16 19	16 33	16 49	17 03	17 19	17 33	17 49	18 03
West Wickham	d	12 52	13 05	13 22	13 35	13 52		14 05	14 22	14 35	14 52	15 05	15 22	15 35	15 52	16 05		16 22	16 35	16 52	17 05	17 22	17 35	17 52	18 05
Hayes (Kent)	a	12 55	13 08	13 25	13 38	13 55		14 08	14 25	14 38	14 55	15 08	15 25	15 38	15 55	16 08		16 25	16 38	16 55	17 08	17 25	17 38	17 55	18 08

		SE		SE	SE	SE	SE	SE	SE	SE	SE	SE		SE	SE	SE	SE	SE	SE
London Charing Cross	⊖ d	17 47			18 17		18 47		19 17	19 47	20 17	20 47		21 17	21 47	22 17	22 47	23 17	23 52
London Waterloo (East)	⊖ d	17 50			18 20		18 50		19 20	19 50	20 20	20 50		21 20	21 50	22 20	22 50	23 20	23 55
London Cannon Street	⊖ d			18 00		18 30		19 00											
London Bridge	⊖ d	17 55		18 04	18 25	18 34	18 55	19 04	19 25	19 55	20 25	20 55		21 25	21 55	22 25	22 55	23 25	23 59
New Cross	⊖ d			18 09		18 39		19 09	19 30	20 00	20 30	21 00		21 30	22 00	22 30	23 00	23 30	00 05
St Johns	d			18 11		18 41		19 11	19 32	20 02	20 32	21 02		21 32	22 02	22 32	23 02	23 32	00 07
Lewisham	d			18 14		18 44		19 14	19 35	20 05	20 35	21 05		21 35	22 05	22 35	23 05	23 35	00 10
Ladywell	d	18 04		18 17	18 34	18 47	19 04	19 17	19 38	20 08	20 38	21 08		21 38	22 08	22 38	23 08	23 38	00 13
Catford Bridge	d	18 06		18 19	18 36	18 49	19 06	19 19	19 40	20 10	20 40	21 10		21 40	22 10	22 40	23 10	23 40	00 15
Lower Sydenham	d	18 09		18 22	18 39	18 52	19 09	19 22	19 43	20 13	20 43	21 13		21 43	22 13	22 43	23 13	23 43	00 18
New Beckenham	d	18 11		18 24	18 41	18 54	19 11	19 24	19 45	20 15	20 45	21 15		21 45	22 15	22 45	23 15	23 45	00 20
Clock House	d	18 13		18 27	18 43	18 57	19 13	19 27	19 48	20 18	20 48	21 18		21 48	22 18	22 48	23 18	23 48	00 23
Elmers End	d	18 16		18 29	18 46	18 59	19 16	19 29	19 50	20 20	20 50	21 20		21 50	22 20	22 50	23 20	23 50	00 25
Eden Park	d	18 19		18 33	18 49	19 03	19 19	19 33	19 54	20 24	20 54	21 24		21 54	22 24	22 54	23 24	23 54	00 29
West Wickham	d	18 22		18 35	18 52	19 05	19 22	19 35	19 56	20 26	20 56	21 26		21 56	22 26	22 56	23 26	23 56	00 31
Hayes (Kent)	a	18 25		18 38	18 55	19 08	19 25	19 38	19 59	20 29	20 59	21 29		21 59	22 29	22 59	23 29	23 59	00 34

Sundays

		SE	SE	SE	SE	SE	SE	SE	SE	SE		SE	SE	SE	SE	SE	SE	SE	SE	SE		SE	SE	SE	SE
London Charing Cross	⊖ d	23p52	07 35	08 05	08 35	09 05	09 35	10 05	10 35	11 05		11 35	12 05	12 35	13 05	13 35	14 05	14 35	15 05	15 35		16 05	16 35	17 05	17 35
London Waterloo (East)	⊖ d	23p55	07 38	08 08	08 38	09 08	09 38	10 08	10 38	11 08		11 38	12 08	12 38	13 08	13 38	14 08	14 38	15 08	15 38		16 08	16 38	17 08	17 38
London Cannon Street	⊖ d																								
London Bridge	⊖ d	23p59	07 43	08 13	08 43	09 13	09 43	10 13	10 43	11 13		11 43	12 13	12 43	13 13	13 43	14 13	14 43	15 13	15 43		16 13	16 43	17 13	17 43
New Cross	⊖ d	00 05	07 49	08 19	08 49	09 19	09 49	10 19	10 49	11 19		11 49	12 19	12 49	13 19	13 49	14 19	14 49	15 19	15 49		16 19	16 49	17 19	17 49
St Johns	d	00 07	07 51	08 21	08 51	09 21	09 51	10 21	10 51	11 21		11 51	12 21	12 51	13 21	13 51	14 21	14 51	15 21	15 51		16 21	16 51	17 21	17 51
Lewisham	d	00 10	07 54	08 24	08 54	09 24	09 54	10 24	10 54	11 24		11 54	12 24	12 54	13 24	13 54	14 24	14 54	15 24	15 54		16 24	16 54	17 24	17 54
Ladywell	d	00 13	07 57	08 27	08 57	09 27	09 57	10 27	10 57	11 27		11 57	12 27	12 57	13 27	13 57	14 27	14 57	15 27	15 57		16 27	16 57	17 27	17 57
Catford Bridge	d	00 15	07 59	08 29	08 59	09 29	09 59	10 29	10 59	11 29		11 59	12 29	12 59	13 29	13 59	14 29	14 59	15 29	15 59		16 29	16 59	17 29	17 59
Lower Sydenham	d	00 18	08 02	08 32	09 02	09 32	10 02	10 32	11 02	11 32		12 02	12 32	13 02	13 32	14 02	14 32	15 02	15 32	16 02		16 32	17 02	17 32	18 02
New Beckenham	d	00 20	08 04	08 34	09 04	09 34	10 04	10 34	11 04	11 34		12 04	12 34	13 04	13 34	14 04	14 34	15 04	15 34	16 04		16 34	17 04	17 34	18 04
Clock House	d	00 23	08 06	08 36	09 06	09 36	10 06	10 36	11 06	11 36		12 06	12 36	13 06	13 36	14 06	14 36	15 06	15 36	16 06		16 36	17 06	17 36	18 06
Elmers End	d	00 25	08 09	08 39	09 09	09 39	10 09	10 39	11 09	11 39		12 09	12 39	13 09	13 39	14 09	14 39	15 09	15 39	16 09		16 39	17 09	17 39	18 09
Eden Park	d	00 29	08 12	08 42	09 12	09 42	10 12	10 42	11 12	11 42		12 12	12 42	13 12	13 42	14 12	14 42	15 12	15 42	16 12		16 42	17 12	17 42	18 12
West Wickham	d	00 31	08 15	08 45	09 15	09 45	10 15	10 45	11 15	11 45		12 15	12 45	13 15	13 45	14 15	14 45	15 15	15 45	16 15		16 45	17 15	17 45	18 15
Hayes (Kent)	a	00 34	08 18	08 48	09 18	09 48	10 18	10 48	11 18	11 48		12 18	12 48	13 18	13 48	14 18	14 48	15 18	15 48	16 18		16 48	17 18	17 48	18 18

		SE	SE	SE	SE	SE		SE	SE	SE	SE	SE	SE	SE
London Charing Cross	⊖ d	18 05	18 35	19 05	19 35	20 05		20 35	21 05	21 35	22 05	22 35	23 05	23 35
London Waterloo (East)	⊖ d	18 08	18 38	19 08	19 38	20 08		20 38	21 08	21 38	22 08	22 38	23 08	23 38
London Cannon Street	⊖ d													
London Bridge	⊖ d	18 13	18 43	19 13	19 43	20 13		20 43	21 13	21 43	22 13	22 43	23 13	23 43
New Cross	⊖ d	18 19	18 49	19 19	19 49	20 19		20 49	21 19	21 49	22 19	22 49	23 19	23 49
St Johns	d	18 21	18 51	19 21	19 51	20 21		20 51	21 21	21 51	22 21	22 51	23 21	23 51
Lewisham	d	18 24	18 54	19 24	19 54	20 24		20 54	21 24	21 54	22 24	22 54	23 24	23 54
Ladywell	d	18 27	18 57	19 27	19 57	20 27		20 57	21 27	21 57	22 27	22 57	23 27	23 57
Catford Bridge	d	18 29	18 59	19 29	19 59	20 29		20 59	21 29	21 59	22 29	22 59	23 29	23 59
Lower Sydenham	d	18 32	19 02	19 32	20 02	20 32		21 02	21 32	22 02	22 32	23 02	23 32	00 02
New Beckenham	d	18 34	19 04	19 34	20 04	20 34		21 04	21 34	22 04	22 34	23 04	23 34	00 04
Clock House	d	18 36	19 06	19 36	20 06	20 36		21 06	21 36	22 06	22 36	23 06	23 36	00 06
Elmers End	d	18 39	19 09	19 39	20 09	20 39		21 09	21 39	22 09	22 39	23 09	23 39	00 09
Eden Park	d	18 42	19 12	19 42	20 12	20 42		21 12	21 42	22 12	22 42	23 12	23 42	00 12
West Wickham	d	18 45	19 15	19 45	20 15	20 45		21 15	21 45	22 15	22 45	23 15	23 45	00 15
Hayes (Kent)	a	18 48	19 18	19 48	20 18	20 48		21 18	21 48	22 18	22 48	23 18	23 48	00 18

Hayes (Kent) - London via Catford Bridge

Mondays to Fridays

		SE	SE	SE	SE	SE	SE	SE	SE	SE	SE	SE	SE	SE	SE	SE	SE	SE	SE	SE	SE	SE	SE
Hayes (Kent)	d	05 15	05 45	06 15	06 23	06 45	06 55	07 13	07 23	07 33	07 43	07 53	08 03	08 13	08 23	08 33	08 49	09 08	09 20	09 38	09 50	10 08	10 20
West Wickham	d	05 18	05 48	06 18	06 26	06 48	06 58	07 16	07 26	07 36	07 46	07 56	08 06	08 16	08 26	08 36	08 52	09 11	09 23	09 41	09 53	10 11	10 23
Eden Park	d	05 20	05 50	06 20	06 28	06 50	07 00	07 18	07 28	07 38	07 48	07 58	08 08	08 18	08 28	08 38	08 54	09 13	09 25	09 43	09 55	10 13	10 25
Elmers End	d	05 24	05 54	06 24	06 32	06 54	07 04	07 22	07 32	07 42	07 52	08 02	08 12	08 22	08 32	08 42	08 59	09 17	09 29	09 47	09 59	10 17	10 29
Clock House	d	05 26	05 56	06 26	06 34	06 56	07 06	07 24	07 34	07 44	07 54	08 04	08 14	08 24	08 34	08 44	09 01	09 19	09 31	09 49	10 01	10 19	10 31
New Beckenham	d	05 28	05 58	06 28	06 37	06 59	07 09	07 27	07 37	07 47	07 57	08 07	08 17	08 27	08 37	08 47	09 03	09 21	09 34	09 51	10 03	10 21	10 33
Lower Sydenham	d	05 30	06 00	06 30	06 39	07 01	07 11	07 29	07 39	07 49	07 59	08 09	08 19	08 29	08 39	08 49	09 05	09 23	09 36	09 53	10 05	10 23	10 35
Catford Bridge	d	05 33	06 03	06 33	06 42	07 04	07 14	07 32	07 42	07 52	08 02	08 12	08 22	08 32	08 42	08 52	09 09	09 26	09 39	09 56	10 08	10 26	10 38
Ladywell	d	05 35	06 05	06 35	06 44	07 06	07 16	07 34	07 44	07 54	08 04	08 14	08 24	08 34	08 44	08 54	09 11	09 28	09 41	09 58	10 10	10 28	10 40
Lewisham	d	05 39	06 09	06 39	06 48		07 20		07 48		08 08		08 28		08 48		09 14		09 45		10 14		10 44
St Johns	a	05 41	06 11	06 41	06 50				07 50		08 12		08 30		08 50		09 17		09 47		10 16		10 46
New Cross	⊖ a	05 43	06 13	06 43	06 52		07 23		07 52		08 14		08 32		08 52		09 19		09 49		10 18		10 48
London Bridge	⊖ a	05 48	06 18	06 48	06 58	07 17	07 28	07 44	08 01		08 20		08 41		08 57		09 25	09 37	09 54	10 07	10 24	10 37	10 54
London Cannon Street	⊖ a				07 05		07 35		08 08		08 28		08 48		09 04		09 32		10 00		10 28		10 58
London Waterloo (East)	⊖ a	05 53	06 24	06 53		07 22		07 50		08 08		08 28		08 48		09 07		09 42		10 12		10 42	
London Charing Cross	⊖ a	05 56	06 27	06 57		07 28		07 56		08 14		08 34		08 54		09 13		09 48		10 16		10 46	

		SE	SE	SE	SE	SE	SE	SE	SE	SE	SE	SE	SE	SE	SE	SE	SE	SE	SE	SE	SE	SE	SE
Hayes (Kent)	d	10 38	10 50	11 08	11 20	11 38	11 50	12 08	12 20	12 38	12 50	13 08	13 20	13 38	13 50	14 08	14 20	14 38	14 50	15 08	15 20	15 38	15 50
West Wickham	d	10 41	10 53	11 11	11 23	11 41	11 53	12 11	12 23	12 41	12 53	13 11	13 23	13 41	13 53	14 11	14 23	14 41	14 53	15 11	15 23	15 41	15 53
Eden Park	d	10 43	10 55	11 13	11 25	11 43	11 55	12 13	12 25	12 43	12 55	13 13	13 25	13 43	13 55	14 13	14 25	14 43	14 55	15 13	15 25	15 43	15 55
Elmers End	d	10 47	10 59	11 17	11 29	11 47	11 59	12 17	12 29	12 47	12 59	13 17	13 29	13 47	13 59	14 17	14 29	14 47	14 59	15 17	15 29	15 47	15 59
Clock House	d	10 49	11 01	11 19	11 31	11 49	12 01	12 19	12 31	12 49	13 01	13 19	13 31	13 49	14 01	14 19	14 31	14 49	15 01	15 19	15 31	15 49	16 01
New Beckenham	d	10 51	11 03	11 21	11 33	11 51	12 03	12 21	12 33	12 51	13 03	13 21	13 33	13 51	14 03	14 21	14 33	14 51	15 03	15 21	15 33	15 51	16 03
Lower Sydenham	d	10 53	11 05	11 23	11 35	11 53	12 05	12 23	12 35	12 53	13 05	13 23	13 35	13 53	14 05	14 23	14 35	14 53	15 05	15 23	15 35	15 53	16 05
Catford Bridge	d	10 56	11 08	11 26	11 38	11 56	12 08	12 26	12 38	12 56	13 08	13 26	13 38	13 56	14 08	14 26	14 38	14 56	15 08	15 26	15 38	15 56	16 08
Ladywell	d	10 58	11 10	11 28	11 40	11 58	12 10	12 28	12 40	12 58	13 10	13 28	13 40	13 58	14 10	14 28	14 40	14 58	15 10	15 28	15 40	15 58	16 10
Lewisham	d		11 14		11 44		12 14		12 44		13 14		13 44		14 14		14 44		15 14		15 44		16 14
St Johns	a		11 16		11 46		12 16		12 46		13 16		13 46		14 16		14 46		15 16		15 46		16 16
New Cross	⊖ a		11 18		11 48		12 18		12 48		13 18		13 48		14 18		14 48		15 18		15 48		16 18
London Bridge	⊖ a	11 07	11 24	11 37	11 54	12 07	12 24	12 37	12 54	13 07	13 24	13 37	13 54	14 07	14 24	14 37	14 54	15 07	15 24	15 37	15 54	16 09	16 24
London Cannon Street	⊖ a		11 28		11 58		12 28		12 58		13 28		13 58		14 28		14 58		15 28		15 58		16 28
London Waterloo (East)	⊖ a	11 12		11 42		12 12		12 42		13 12		13 42		14 12		14 42		15 12		15 42		16 13	
London Charing Cross	⊖ a	11 16		11 46		12 16		12 46		13 16		13 46		14 16		14 46		15 16		15 46		16 18	

		SE	SE A	SE	SE	SE	SE	SE	SE	SE	SE	SE	SE	SE	SE	SE	SE	SE	SE	SE	SE	SE
Hayes (Kent)	d	16 08		16 20	16 38	16 50	17 08	17 20	17 37	17 47	18 08	18 21	18 38	18 50	19 05	19 14	19 44	20 14	20 44	21 14	21 44	22 14
West Wickham	d	16 11		16 23	16 41	16 53	17 11	17 23	17 40	17 50	18 11	18 24	18 41	18 53	19 08	19 17	19 47	20 17	20 47	21 17	21 47	22 17
Eden Park	d	16 13		16 25	16 43	16 55	17 13	17 25	17 42	17 52	18 13	18 26	18 43	18 55	19 10	19 19	19 49	20 19	20 49	21 19	21 49	22 19
Elmers End	d	16 17		16 29	16 47	16 59	17 17	17 29	17 46	17 56	18 17	18 30	18 47	18 59	19 17	19 23	19 53	20 23	20 53	21 23	21 53	22 23
Clock House	d	16 19		16 31	16 49	17 01	17 19	17 31	17 48	17 58	18 19	18 32	18 49	19 01	19 19	19 25	19 55	20 25	20 55	21 25	21 55	22 25
New Beckenham	d	16 21	16 14	16 33	16 51	17 03	17 21	17 33	17 50	18 00	18 21	18 34	18 51	19 03	19 21	19 27	19 57	20 27	20 57	21 27	21 57	22 27
Lower Sydenham	d	16 23	16 16	16 35	16 53	17 05	17 23	17 35	17 52	18 02	18 23	18 36	18 53	19 05	19 23	19 29	19 59	20 29	20 59	21 29	21 59	22 29
Catford Bridge	d	16 26	16 19	16 38	16 56	17 08	17 26	17 38	17 55	18 05	18 26	18 39	18 56	19 08	19 26	19 32	20 02	20 32	21 02	21 32	22 02	22 32
Ladywell	d	16 28	16 21	16 40	16 58	17 10	17 28	17 40	17 57	18 07	18 28	18 41	18 58	19 10	19 28	19 34	20 04	20 34	21 04	21 34	22 04	22 34
Lewisham	d			16 44		17 14		17 44		18 14		18 45		19 14		19 38	20 08	20 38	21 08	21 38	22 08	22 38
St Johns	a			16 46		17 16		17 46		18 16		18 47		19 16		19 40	20 10	20 40	21 10	21 40	22 10	22 40
New Cross	⊖ a			16 48		17 18		17 48		18 18		18 49		19 18		19 42	20 12	20 42	21 12	21 42	22 12	22 42
London Bridge	⊖ a	16 37	16 32	16 54	17 08	17 24	17 38	17 55	18 07	18 24	18 38	18 55	19 07	19 24	19 37	19 49	20 19	20 49	21 19	21 49	22 19	22 49
London Cannon Street	⊖ a			16 58		17 29		17 59		18 29		18 59		19 28								
London Waterloo (East)	⊖ a	16 42	16 37		17 13		17 42		18 12		18 44		19 12		19 42	19 53	20 23	20 53	21 23	21 53	22 23	22 53
London Charing Cross	⊖ a	16 46	16 42		17 18		17 46		18 16		18 48		19 16		19 46	19 57	20 27	20 57	21 27	21 57	22 27	22 57

		SE
Hayes (Kent)	d	22 44
West Wickham	d	22 47
Eden Park	d	22 49
Elmers End	d	22 53
Clock House	d	22 55
New Beckenham	d	22 57
Lower Sydenham	d	22 59
Catford Bridge	d	23 02
Ladywell	d	23 04
Lewisham	d	23 08
St Johns	a	23 10
New Cross	⊖ a	23 12
London Bridge	⊖ a	23 19
London Cannon Street	⊖ a	
London Waterloo (East)	⊖ a	23 23
London Charing Cross	⊖ a	23 27

Saturdays

		SE	SE	SE	SE	SE	SE	SE	SE	SE	SE	SE	SE	SE	SE	SE	SE	SE	SE	SE	SE	SE	SE
Hayes (Kent)	d	05 15	05 38	06 08	06 38	07 08	07 36	07 50	08 08	08 20	08 38	08 50	09 08	09 20	09 38	09 50	10 08	10 20	10 38	10 50	11 08	11 20	11 38
West Wickham	d	05 18	05 41	06 11	06 41	07 11	07 39	07 53	08 11	08 23	08 41	08 53	09 11	09 23	09 41	09 53	10 11	10 23	10 41	10 53	11 11	11 23	11 41
Eden Park	d	05 20	05 43	06 13	06 43	07 13	07 41	07 55	08 13	08 25	08 43	08 55	09 13	09 25	09 43	09 55	10 13	10 25	10 43	10 55	11 13	11 25	11 43
Elmers End	d	05 24	05 47	06 17	06 47	07 17	07 45	07 59	08 17	08 29	08 47	08 59	09 17	09 29	09 47	09 59	10 17	10 29	10 47	10 59	11 17	11 29	11 47
Clock House	d	05 26	05 49	06 19	06 49	07 19	07 47	08 01	08 19	08 31	08 49	09 01	09 19	09 31	09 49	10 01	10 19	10 31	10 49	11 01	11 19	11 31	11 49
New Beckenham	d	05 28	05 51	06 21	06 51	07 21	07 49	08 03	08 21	08 33	08 51	09 03	09 21	09 33	09 51	10 03	10 21	10 33	10 51	11 03	11 21	11 33	11 51
Lower Sydenham	d	05 30	05 53	06 23	06 53	07 23	07 51	08 05	08 23	08 35	08 53	09 05	09 23	09 35	09 53	10 05	10 23	10 35	10 53	11 05	11 23	11 35	11 53
Catford Bridge	d	05 33	05 56	06 26	06 56	07 26	07 54	08 08	08 26	08 38	08 56	09 08	09 26	09 38	09 56	10 08	10 26	10 38	10 56	11 08	11 26	11 38	11 56
Ladywell	d	05 35	05 58	06 28	06 58	07 28	07 56	08 10	08 28	08 40	08 58	09 10	09 28	09 40	09 58	10 10	10 28	10 40	10 58	11 10	11 28	11 40	11 58
Lewisham	d	05 39	06 02	06 32	07 02	07 32	07 59	08 14		08 44		09 14		09 44		10 14		10 44		11 14		11 44	
St Johns	a	05 41	06 04	06 34	07 04	07 34		08 16		08 46		09 16		09 46		10 16		10 46		11 16		11 46	
New Cross	⊖ a	05 43	06 06	06 36	07 06	07 36		08 18		08 48		09 18		09 48		10 18		10 48		11 18		11 48	
London Bridge	⊖ a	05 48	06 12	06 42	07 12	07 42	08 07	08 24	08 37	08 54	09 07	09 24	09 37	09 54	10 07	10 24	10 37	10 54	11 07	11 24	11 37	11 54	12 07
London Cannon Street	⊖ a							08 28		08 58		09 28		09 58		10 28		10 58		11 28		11 58	
London Waterloo (East)	⊖ a	05 53	06 16	06 46	07 16	07 46	08 12		08 42		09 12		09 42		10 12		10 42		11 12		11 42		12 12
London Charing Cross	⊖ a	05 56	06 20	06 50	07 20	07 50	08 16		08 46		09 16		09 46		10 16		10 46		11 16		11 46		12 16

A From Beckenham Junction (Table 195)

Hayes (Kent) - London via Catford Bridge

Saturdays

		SE	SE	SE	SE	SE	SE	SE	SE	SE	SE	SE	SE	SE	SE	SE	SE	SE	SE	SE	SE	SE	SE
Hayes (Kent)	d	11 50	12 08	12 20	12 38	12 50	13 08	13 20	13 38	13 50	14 08	14 20	14 38	14 50	15 08	15 20	15 38	15 50	16 08	16 20	16 38	16 50	17 08
West Wickham	d	11 53	12 11	12 23	12 41	12 53	13 11	13 23	13 41	13 53	14 11	14 23	14 41	14 53	15 11	15 23	15 41	15 53	16 11	16 23	16 41	16 53	17 11
Eden Park	d	11 55	12 13	12 25	12 43	12 55	13 13	13 25	13 43	13 55	14 13	14 25	14 43	14 55	15 13	15 25	15 43	15 55	16 13	16 25	16 43	16 55	17 13
Elmers End	d	11 59	12 17	12 29	12 47	12 59	13 17	13 29	13 47	13 59	14 17	14 29	14 47	14 59	15 17	15 29	15 47	15 59	16 17	16 29	16 47	16 59	17 17
Clock House	d	12 01	12 19	12 31	12 49	13 01	13 19	13 31	13 49	14 01	14 19	14 31	14 49	15 01	15 19	15 31	15 49	16 01	16 19	16 31	16 49	17 01	17 19
New Beckenham	d	12 03	12 21	12 33	12 51	13 03	13 21	13 33	13 51	14 03	14 21	14 33	14 51	15 03	15 21	15 33	15 51	16 03	16 21	16 33	16 51	17 03	17 21
Lower Sydenham	d	12 05	12 23	12 35	12 53	13 05	13 23	13 35	13 53	14 05	14 23	14 35	14 53	15 05	15 23	15 35	15 53	16 05	16 23	16 35	16 53	17 05	17 23
Catford Bridge	d	12 08	12 26	12 38	12 56	13 08	13 26	13 38	13 56	14 08	14 26	14 38	14 56	15 08	15 26	15 38	15 56	16 08	16 26	16 38	16 56	17 08	17 26
Ladywell	d	12 10	12 28	12 40	12 58	13 10	13 28	13 40	13 58	14 10	14 28	14 40	14 58	15 10	15 28	15 40	15 58	16 10	16 28	16 40	16 58	17 10	17 28
Lewisham	d	12 14		12 44		13 14		13 44		14 14		14 44		15 14		15 44		16 14		16 44		17 14	
St Johns	a	12 16		12 46		13 16		13 46		14 16		14 46		15 16		15 46		16 16		16 46		17 16	
New Cross	⊖ a	12 18		12 48		13 18		13 48		14 18		14 48		15 18		15 48		16 18		16 48		17 18	
London Bridge	⊖ a	12 24	12 37	12 54	13 07	13 24	13 37	13 54	14 07	14 24	14 37	14 54	15 07	15 24	15 37	15 54	16 07	16 24	16 37	16 54	17 07	17 24	17 37
London Cannon Street	⊖ a	12 28		12 58		13 28		13 58		14 28		14 58		15 28		15 58		16 28		16 58		17 28	
London Waterloo (East)	⊖ a		12 42		13 12		13 42		14 12		14 42		15 12		15 42		16 12		16 42		17 12		17 42
London Charing Cross	⊖ a		12 46		13 16		13 46		14 16		14 46		15 16		15 46		16 16		16 46		17 16		17 46

		SE	SE	SE	SE	SE	SE	SE	SE	SE	SE	SE	SE	SE	SE	SE
Hayes (Kent)	d	17 20	17 38	17 50	18 08	18 20	18 38	18 50	19 14	19 44	20 14	20 44	21 14	21 44	22 14	22 44
West Wickham	d	17 23	17 41	17 53	18 11	18 23	18 41	18 53	19 17	19 47	20 17	20 47	21 17	21 47	22 17	22 47
Eden Park	d	17 25	17 43	17 55	18 13	18 25	18 43	18 55	19 19	19 49	20 19	20 49	21 19	21 49	22 19	22 49
Elmers End	d	17 29	17 47	17 59	18 17	18 29	18 47	18 59	19 23	19 53	20 23	20 53	21 23	21 53	22 23	22 53
Clock House	d	17 31	17 49	18 01	18 19	18 31	18 49	19 01	19 25	19 55	20 25	20 55	21 25	21 55	22 25	22 55
New Beckenham	d	17 33	17 51	18 03	18 21	18 33	18 51	19 03	19 27	19 57	20 27	20 57	21 27	21 57	22 27	22 57
Lower Sydenham	d	17 35	17 53	18 05	18 23	18 35	18 53	19 05	19 29	19 59	20 29	20 59	21 29	21 59	22 29	22 59
Catford Bridge	d	17 38	17 56	18 08	18 26	18 38	18 56	19 08	19 32	20 02	20 32	21 02	21 32	22 02	22 32	23 02
Ladywell	d	17 40	17 58	18 10	18 28	18 40	18 58	19 10	19 34	20 04	20 34	21 04	21 34	22 04	22 34	23 04
Lewisham	d	17 44		18 14		18 44		19 14	19 38	20 08	20 38	21 08	21 38	22 08	22 38	23 08
St Johns	a	17 46		18 16		18 46		19 16	19 40	20 10	20 40	21 10	21 40	22 10	22 40	23 10
New Cross	⊖ a	17 48		18 18		18 48		19 18	19 42	20 12	20 42	21 12	21 42	22 12	22 42	23 12
London Bridge	⊖ a	17 54	18 07	18 24	18 37	18 54	19 07	19 24	19 49	20 19	20 49	21 19	21 49	22 19	22 49	23 19
London Cannon Street	⊖ a	17 58		18 28		18 58										
London Waterloo (East)	⊖ a		18 12		18 42		19 12		19 53	20 23	20 53	21 23	21 53	22 23	22 53	23 23
London Charing Cross	⊖ a		18 16		18 46		19 16		19 58	20 28	20 58	21 28	21 58	22 28	22 58	23 27

Sundays

		SE	SE	SE	SE	SE	SE	SE	SE	SE	SE	SE	SE	SE	SE	SE	SE	SE	SE	SE	SE	SE	SE
Hayes (Kent)	d	07 28	07 58	08 28	08 58	09 28	09 58	10 28	10 58	11 28	11 58	12 28	12 58	13 28	13 58	14 28	14 58	15 28	15 58	16 28	16 58	17 28	17 58
West Wickham	d	07 31	08 01	08 31	09 01	09 31	10 01	10 31	11 01	11 31	12 01	12 31	13 01	13 31	14 01	14 31	15 01	15 31	16 01	16 31	17 01	17 31	18 01
Eden Park	d	07 33	08 03	08 33	09 03	09 33	10 03	10 33	11 03	11 33	12 03	12 33	13 03	13 33	14 03	14 33	15 03	15 33	16 03	16 33	17 03	17 33	18 03
Elmers End	d	07 37	08 07	08 37	09 07	09 37	10 07	10 37	11 07	11 37	12 07	12 37	13 07	13 37	14 07	14 37	15 07	15 37	16 07	16 37	17 07	17 37	18 07
Clock House	d	07 39	08 09	08 39	09 09	09 39	10 09	10 39	11 09	11 39	12 09	12 39	13 09	13 39	14 09	14 39	15 09	15 39	16 09	16 39	17 09	17 39	18 09
New Beckenham	d	07 41	08 11	08 41	09 11	09 41	10 11	10 41	11 11	11 41	12 11	12 41	13 11	13 41	14 11	14 41	15 11	15 41	16 11	16 41	17 11	17 41	18 11
Lower Sydenham	d	07 43	08 13	08 43	09 13	09 43	10 13	10 43	11 13	11 43	12 13	12 43	13 13	13 43	14 13	14 43	15 13	15 43	16 13	16 43	17 13	17 43	18 13
Catford Bridge	d	07 46	08 16	08 46	09 16	09 46	10 16	10 46	11 16	11 46	12 16	12 46	13 16	13 46	14 16	14 46	15 16	15 46	16 16	16 46	17 16	17 46	18 16
Ladywell	d	07 48	08 18	08 48	09 18	09 48	10 18	10 48	11 18	11 48	12 18	12 48	13 18	13 48	14 18	14 48	15 18	15 48	16 18	16 48	17 18	17 48	18 18
Lewisham	d	07 52	08 22	08 52	09 22	09 52	10 22	10 52	11 22	11 52	12 22	12 52	13 22	13 52	14 22	14 52	15 22	15 52	16 22	16 52	17 22	17 52	18 22
St Johns	a	07 54	08 24	08 54	09 24	09 54	10 24	10 54	11 24	11 54	12 24	12 54	13 24	13 54	14 24	14 54	15 24	15 54	16 24	16 54	17 24	17 54	18 24
New Cross	⊖ a	07 56	08 26	08 56	09 26	09 56	10 26	10 56	11 26	11 56	12 26	12 56	13 26	13 56	14 26	14 56	15 26	15 56	16 26	16 56	17 26	17 56	18 26
London Bridge	⊖ a	08 03	08 33	09 03	09 33	10 03	10 33	11 03	11 33	12 03	12 33	13 03	13 33	14 03	14 33	15 03	15 33	16 03	16 33	17 03	17 33	18 03	18 33
London Cannon Street	⊖ a																						
London Waterloo (East)	⊖ a	08 08	08 38	09 08	09 38	10 08	10 38	11 08	11 38	12 08	12 38	13 08	13 38	14 08	14 38	15 08	15 38	16 08	16 38	17 08	17 38	18 08	18 38
London Charing Cross	⊖ a	08 11	08 41	09 11	09 41	10 11	10 41	11 11	11 41	12 11	12 41	13 11	13 41	14 11	14 41	15 11	15 41	16 11	16 41	17 11	17 41	18 11	18 41

		SE	SE	SE	SE	SE	SE	SE	SE	SE	SE
Hayes (Kent)	d	18 28	18 58	19 28	19 58	20 28	20 58	21 28	21 58	22 28	22 58
West Wickham	d	18 31	19 01	19 31	20 01	20 31	21 01	21 31	22 01	22 31	23 01
Eden Park	d	18 33	19 03	19 33	20 03	20 33	21 03	21 33	22 03	22 33	23 03
Elmers End	d	18 37	19 07	19 37	20 07	20 37	21 07	21 37	22 07	22 37	23 07
Clock House	d	18 39	19 09	19 39	20 09	20 39	21 09	21 39	22 09	22 39	23 09
New Beckenham	d	18 41	19 11	19 41	20 11	20 41	21 11	21 41	22 11	22 41	23 11
Lower Sydenham	d	18 43	19 13	19 43	20 13	20 43	21 13	21 43	22 13	22 43	23 13
Catford Bridge	d	18 46	19 16	19 46	20 16	20 46	21 16	21 46	22 16	22 46	23 16
Ladywell	d	18 48	19 18	19 48	20 18	20 48	21 18	21 48	22 18	22 48	23 18
Lewisham	d	18 52	19 22	19 52	20 22	20 52	21 22	21 52	22 22	22 52	23 22
St Johns	a	18 54	19 24	19 54	20 24	20 54	21 24	21 54	22 24	22 54	23 24
New Cross	⊖ a	18 56	19 26	19 56	20 26	20 56	21 26	21 56	22 26	22 56	23 26
London Bridge	⊖ a	19 03	19 33	20 03	20 33	21 03	21 33	22 03	22 33	23 03	23 33
London Cannon Street	⊖ a										
London Waterloo (East)	⊖ a	19 08	19 38	20 08	20 38	21 08	21 38	22 08	22 38	23 08	23 38
London Charing Cross	⊖ a	19 11	19 41	20 11	20 41	21 11	21 41	22 11	22 41	23 11	23 41

Table 204

Mondays to Fridays

London - Grove Park, Bromley North, Orpington, Sevenoaks and Tonbridge

		SE MO 1	SE MX 1	SE MO 1	SE MX 1	SE MX	SE MX 1	SE MX	SE MO	SE MX		SE MX	SE MX	SE MX	SE	SE 1	SE	SE	SE 1	SE		SE	SE	SE	SE 1
London Charing Cross 4 ⊖	d	23p23	23p30	23p38	23p40		23p45	23p36	23p46				00 10		00 48	05 30	05 36		06 15	06 06					06 30
London Waterloo (East) 4 ⊖	d	23p26	23p33	23p41	23p43		23p48	23p39	23p49				00 13		00 51	05 33	05 39		06 18	06 09					06 33
London Cannon Street 4 ⊖	d																								
London Bridge 4 ⊖	d	23p31	23p39	23p46	23p49		23p53	23p44	23p54				00 18		00 56	05 39	05 44		06 24	06 14					06 38
New Cross 4 ⊖	d														01 01										
St Johns	d																								
Lewisham 4	d							23p52	00 02						01 05		05 53			06 23					
Hither Green 4	d							23p56	00 06						01 09		05 57			06 27					
Grove Park 4	d							23p59	00 10	00 07			00 31	00 37	01 13		06 01			06 30		06 16	06 36		
Sundridge Park	d									00 10				00 40								06 19	06 39		
Bromley North	a									00 12				00 42								06 21	06 41		
Elmstead Woods	d							00 02	00 13				00 34		01 16		06 04			06 33					
Chislehurst	d							00 05	00 15				00 37		01 18		06 06			06 36					
Petts Wood 4	d					23p59		00 08	00 19			00 29	00 40		01 22		06 09	06 14		06 39				06 44	
Orpington 4	a	23p46	23p54	00 01		00 02	00 08	00 12	00 22			00 32	00 43		01 25	05 54	06 12	06 18	06 40	06 42				06 49	06 53
	d	23p46	23p54	00 02			00 09						00 43			05 55	06 13		06 40	06 44					06 54
Chelsfield 3	d	23p49	23p57										00 46			05 58	06 16			06 47					
Knockholt	d																06 19			06 50					
Dunton Green	d																06 24			06 55					
Sevenoaks 4	a	23p57	00 05	00 11	00 12		00 18						00 54			06 05	06 27		06 49	06 59					07 03
	d	23p57	00 05	00 12	00 13		00 19						00 54			06 06			06 50						07 03
Hildenborough	d		00 11										01 00			06 12									07 09
Tonbridge 4	a	00 05	00 15	00 20	00 21		00 27						01 04			06 16			06 58						07 15

		SE	SE 1	SE	SE	SE 1		SE	SE 1	SE	SE 1	SE	SE	SE	SE 1	SE 1		SE	SE 1	SE	SE 1	SE	SE	SE	SE
London Charing Cross 4 ⊖	d		06 45	06 36		07 00			07 10		07 15	07 06			07 29	07 40			07 52			07 36	07 48		
London Waterloo (East) 4 ⊖	d		06 48	06 39		07 03			07 13		07 18	07 09			07 32	07 43			07 55			07 39	07 51		
London Cannon Street 4 ⊖	d				06 50								07 20								07 47				
London Bridge 4 ⊖	d		06 53	06 44	06 54	07 08			07 20		07 23	07 14	07 24		07 38	07 49			08 01		07 51	07 44	07 56		
New Cross 4 ⊖	d				06 59																				
St Johns	d				07 01																				
Lewisham 4	d			06 53	07 04																				
Hither Green 4	d			06 58	07 08							07 23	07 35									07 53			
Grove Park 4	d			07 02	07 12			07 06				07 27	07 38	07 25				07 46				07 57		08 06	
Sundridge Park	d							07 09						07 28				07 49						08 09	
Bromley North	a							07 11						07 30				07 51						08 11	
Elmstead Woods	d			07 05	07 15							07 30	07 41									08 00			
Chislehurst	d			07 07	07 17							07 32	07 44									08 02			
Petts Wood 4	d	07 04		07 10	07 21					07 24		07 36								07 59		08 06			08 14
Orpington 4	a	07 08	07 09	07 13	07 25	07 25				07 28	07 38	07 40	07 48		07 53					08 02	08 08	08 09	08 12		08 19
	d		07 10	07 14		07 26					07 39	07 42			07 54						08 09	08 12			
Chelsfield 3	d			07 17								07 45			07 57							08 15			
Knockholt	d			07 20								07 48			08 00										
Dunton Green	d			07 25								07 53										08 21			
Sevenoaks 4	a		07 19	07 28		07 35			07 42		07 48	08 00			08 06	08 12			08 27		08 18	08 24			
	d		07 19			07 35			07 43		07 49				08 07	08 13			08 28		08 19				
Hildenborough	d					07 41									08 13										
Tonbridge 4	a		07 27			07 45			07 51		07 58				08 17	08 21			08 36		08 27				

		SE		SE 1	SE 1	SE	SE	SE	SE 1 ⊼	SE	SE 1	SE		SE 1	SE	SE	SE 1 ⊼	SE	SE	SE	SE 1	SE 1		SE	SE
London Charing Cross 4 ⊖	d			08 00	08 13			08 05	08 17		08 27			08 33				08 37			08 53	09 00			09 06
London Waterloo (East) 4 ⊖	d			08 03	08 16			08 08	08 20		08 30			08 36				08 40			08 56	09 03			09 09
London Cannon Street 4 ⊖	d	07 51										08 19					08 42							08 51	
London Bridge 4 ⊖	d	07 55		08 09	08 21			08 13	08 25		08 35	08 23		08 41			08 46	08 45			09 01	09 08		08 55	09 14
New Cross 4 ⊖	d	08 00										08 29												09 00	
St Johns	d											08 31												09 02	
Lewisham 4	d	08 05										08 34												09 06	
Hither Green 4	d	08 10						08 23				08 38						08 54						09 10	09 23
Grove Park 4	d	08 13				08 26		08 27				08 42			08 46			08 59	09 07					09 14	09 27
Sundridge Park	d					08 29									08 49				09 10						
Bromley North	a					08 31									08 51				09 12						
Elmstead Woods	d	08 16						08 30				08 45						09 02						09 17	09 30
Chislehurst	d	08 19						08 32				08 47						09 05						09 19	09 32
Petts Wood 4	d	08 22					08 29	08 36		08 44		08 51				08 59		09 08		09 14				09 23	09 36
Orpington 4	a	08 25		08 25			08 32	08 39	08 41	08 47	08 53	08 54		08 57		09 02	09 07	09 11		09 17	09 20	09 26		09 26	09 39
	d			08 26				08 45	08 42		08 54			08 58			09 07	09 12			09 21	09 26			09 42
Chelsfield 3	d							08 48										09 15							09 45
Knockholt	d							08 51										09 18							09 48
Dunton Green	d							08 56										09 23							09 53
Sevenoaks 4	a			08 35	08 44			08 59	08 51		09 03			09 07			09 17	09 26			09 30	09 35			09 58
	d			08 35	08 45				08 52		09 03			09 07			09 17				09 30	09 35			
Hildenborough	d			08 41							09 09											09 41			
Tonbridge 4	a			08 47	08 53				09 00		09 13			09 18			09 25				09 38	09 46			

Table 204

Mondays to Fridays

London - Grove Park, Bromley North, Orpington, Sevenoaks and Tonbridge

		SE 1	SE 1 ⊼	SE	SE 1 ⊼	SE	SE	SE 1		SE	SE 1 ⊼	SE	SE	SE 1 ⊼	SE	SE	SE 1	SE		SE 1 ⊼	SE	SE	SE 1	SE	SE
London Charing Cross 4 ⊖	d	09 13			09 40			09 30			09 45	09 36		10 10			10 00			10 15	10 06		10 40		
London Waterloo (East) 4 ⊖	d	09 16			09 43			09 33			09 48	09 39		10 13			10 03			10 18	10 09		10 43		
London Cannon Street 4 ⊖	d		09 20				09 18									09 50									10 20
London Bridge 4 ⊖	d	09 21	09 25		09 49		09 22	09 39			09 53	09 44		10 19		09 54	10 09			10 23	10 14		10 49		10 24
New Cross 4 ⊖	d						09 27									09 59									10 29
St Johns	d						09 29									10 01									10 31
Lewisham 4	d						09 34									10 04									10 34
Hither Green 4	d						09 38					09 53				10 08					10 23				10 38
Grove Park 4	d			09 37			09 42					09 57	10 07			10 12					10 27	10 37			10 42
Sundridge Park	d			09 40									10 10									10 40			
Bromley North	a			09 42									10 12									10 42			
Elmstead Woods	d						09 45					10 00				10 15					10 30				10 45
Chislehurst	d						09 47					10 02				10 17					10 32				10 47
Petts Wood 4	d					09 44	09 51			09 59		10 06			10 14	10 21		10 29			10 36			10 44	10 51
Orpington 4	a		09 41			09 47	09 54	09 55		10 02	10 08	10 09			10 17	10 24	10 25	10 32		10 38	10 39			10 47	10 54
	d		09 42					09 56			10 09	10 12					10 26			10 39	10 42				
Chelsfield 3	d											10 15									10 45				
Knockholt	d											10 18									10 48				
Dunton Green	d											10 23									10 53				
Sevenoaks 4	a	09 44	09 51		10 12			10 05			10 18	10 26		10 42			10 35			10 48	10 56		11 12		
	d	09 44	09 51		10 13			10 05			10 19			10 43			10 35			10 49			11 13		
Hildenborough	d							10 11									10 41								
Tonbridge 4	a	09 52	09 59		10 21			10 15			10 27			10 51			10 45			10 57			11 21		

		SE 1	SE	SE 1 ⊼		SE	SE	SE 1 ⊼	SE	SE	SE 1	SE	SE 1 ⊼	SE		SE	SE 1 ⊼	SE	SE	SE 1	SE	SE 1 ⊼	SE	SE	
London Charing Cross 4 ⊖	d	10 30		10 45		10 36		11 10			11 00		11 15	11 06			11 40			11 30		11 45	11 36		
London Waterloo (East) 4 ⊖	d	10 33		10 48		10 39		11 13			11 03		11 18	11 09			11 43			11 33		11 48	11 39		
London Cannon Street 4 ⊖	d									10 50									11 20						
London Bridge 4 ⊖	d	10 39		10 53		10 44		11 19		10 54	11 09		11 23	11 14			11 49		11 24	11 39		11 53	11 44		
New Cross 4 ⊖	d									10 59									11 29						
St Johns	d									11 01									11 31						
Lewisham 4	d									11 04									11 34						
Hither Green 4	d					10 53				11 08				11 23					11 38				11 53		
Grove Park 4	d					10 57	11 07			11 12				11 27		11 37			11 42				11 57	12 07	
Sundridge Park	d						11 10									11 40								12 10	
Bromley North	a						11 12									11 42								12 12	
Elmstead Woods	d					11 00				11 15				11 30					11 45				12 00		
Chislehurst	d					11 02				11 17				11 32					11 48				12 02		
Petts Wood 4	d		10 59			11 06			11 14	11 21		11 29		11 36				11 44	11 51		11 59		12 06		
Orpington 4	a	10 55	11 02	11 08		11 09			11 17	11 24	11 25	11 32	11 38	11 39				11 47	11 54	11 55	12 02	12 08	12 09		
	d	10 56		11 09		11 12					11 26		11 39	11 42						11 56		12 09	12 12		
Chelsfield 3	d					11 15								11 45									12 15		
Knockholt	d					11 18								11 48									12 18		
Dunton Green	d					11 23								11 53									12 23		
Sevenoaks 4	a	11 05		11 18		11 26		11 42			11 35		11 48	11 56			12 12			12 05		12 18	12 26		
	d	11 05		11 19				11 43			11 35		11 49				12 13			12 05		12 19			
Hildenborough	d	11 11									11 41									12 11					
Tonbridge 4	a	11 15		11 27				11 51			11 45		11 57				12 21			12 15		12 27			

		SE 1 ⊼	SE	SE	SE 1	SE	SE 1 ⊼	SE	SE	SE 1 ⊼		SE	SE	SE 1	SE	SE 1 ⊼	SE	SE	SE 1 ⊼	SE		SE	SE 1	SE	SE 1 ⊼
London Charing Cross 4 ⊖	d	12 10			12 00		12 15	12 06		12 40				12 30		12 45	12 36		13 10				13 00		13 15
London Waterloo (East) 4 ⊖	d	12 13			12 03		12 18	12 09		12 43				12 33		12 48	12 39		13 13				13 03		13 18
London Cannon Street 4 ⊖	d			11 50									12 20									12 50			
London Bridge 4 ⊖	d	12 19		11 54	12 09		12 23	12 14		12 49			12 24	12 39		12 53	12 44		13 19			12 54	13 09		13 23
New Cross 4 ⊖	d			11 59									12 29									12 59			
St Johns	d			12 01									12 31									13 01			
Lewisham 4	d			12 04									12 34									13 05			
Hither Green 4	d			12 08				12 23					12 38				12 53					13 08			
Grove Park 4	d			12 12				12 27	12 37				12 42				12 57	13 07				13 12			
Sundridge Park	d								12 40									13 10							
Bromley North	a								12 42									13 12							
Elmstead Woods	d			12 15				12 30					12 45				13 00					13 15			
Chislehurst	d			12 17				12 32					12 47				13 02					13 18			
Petts Wood 4	d		12 14	12 21		12 29		12 36				12 44	12 51		12 59		13 06			13 14		13 21		13 29	
Orpington 4	a		12 17	12 24	12 25	12 32	12 38	12 39				12 47	12 54	12 55	13 02	13 08	13 09			13 17		13 24	13 25	13 32	13 38
	d				12 26		12 39	12 42						12 56		13 09	13 12						13 26		13 39
Chelsfield 3	d							12 45									13 15								
Knockholt	d							12 48									13 18								
Dunton Green	d							12 53									13 23								
Sevenoaks 4	a	12 42			12 35		12 48	12 56		13 12				13 05		13 18	13 26		13 42				13 35		13 48
	d	12 43			12 35		12 49			13 13				13 05		13 19			13 43				13 35		13 49
Hildenborough	d				12 41									13 11									13 41		
Tonbridge 4	a	12 51			12 45		12 57			13 21				13 15		13 27			13 51				13 45		13 57

Table 204

London - Grove Park, Bromley North, Orpington, Sevenoaks and Tonbridge

		SE	SE	SE 1 🍴	SE	SE		SE 1	SE	SE 1 🍴	SE	SE	SE 1 🍴	SE	SE	SE 1		SE	SE 1 🍴	SE	SE	SE 1 🍴	SE	SE	SE 1
London Charing Cross 4 ⊖	d	13 06		13 40				13 30		13 45	13 36		14 10			14 00			14 15	14 06		14 40			14 30
London Waterloo (East) 4 ⊖	d	13 09		13 43				13 33		13 48	13 39		14 13			14 03			14 18	14 09		14 43			14 33
London Cannon Street 4 ⊖	d					13 20									13 50									14 20	
London Bridge 4 ⊖	d	13 14		13 49		13 24		13 39		13 53	13 44		14 19		13 54	14 09			14 23	14 14		14 49		14 24	14 39
New Cross 4 ⊖	d					13 29									13 59									14 29	
St Johns	d					13 31									14 01									14 31	
Lewisham 4	d					13 35									14 04									14 34	
Hither Green 4	d	13 23				13 39					13 53				14 08					14 23				14 38	
Grove Park 4	d	13 27	13 37			13 42					13 57	14 07			14 12					14 27	14 37			14 42	
Sundridge Park	d		13 40									14 10									14 40				
Bromley North	a		13 42									14 12									14 42				
Elmstead Woods	d	13 30				13 45					14 00				14 15					14 30				14 45	
Chislehurst	d	13 32				13 48					14 02				14 17					14 32				14 47	
Petts Wood 4	d	13 36			13 44	13 51			13 59		14 06			14 14	14 21			14 29		14 36			14 44	14 51	
Orpington 4	a	13 39			13 47	13 54		13 55	14 02	14 08	14 09			14 17	14 24	14 25		14 32	14 38	14 39			14 47	14 54	14 55
	d	13 42						13 56		14 09	14 12					14 26			14 39	14 42					14 56
Chelsfield 3	d	13 45									14 15									14 45					
Knockholt	d	13 48									14 18									14 48					
Dunton Green	d	13 53									14 23									14 53					
Sevenoaks 4	a	13 56		14 12				14 05		14 18	14 26		14 42			14 35			14 48	14 56		15 12			15 05
	d			14 13				14 05		14 19			14 43			14 35			14 49			15 13			15 05
Hildenborough	d							14 11								14 41									15 11
Tonbridge 4	a			14 21				14 15		14 27			14 51			14 45			14 57			15 21			15 16

		SE		SE 1 🍴	SE	SE	SE 1 🍴	SE	SE	SE 1	SE	SE 1 🍴		SE	SE	SE 1 🍴	SE	SE	SE 1	SE	SE 1 🍴	SE		SE	SE 1 🍴
London Charing Cross 4 ⊖	d			14 45	14 36		15 10			15 00		15 15		15 06		15 40			15 30		15 45	15 36			16 10
London Waterloo (East) 4 ⊖	d			14 48	14 39		15 13			15 03		15 18		15 09		15 43			15 33		15 48	15 39			16 13
London Cannon Street 4 ⊖	d								14 50									15 20							
London Bridge 4 ⊖	d			14 53	14 44		15 19		14 54	15 09		15 23		15 14		15 49		15 24	15 39		15 53	15 44			16 19
New Cross 4 ⊖	d								14 59									15 29							
St Johns	d								15 01									15 31							
Lewisham 4	d								15 04									15 34							
Hither Green 4	d				14 53				15 08					15 23				15 38				15 53			
Grove Park 4	d				14 57	15 07			15 12					15 27	15 37			15 42				15 57		16 07	
Sundridge Park	d					15 10									15 40									16 10	
Bromley North	a					15 12									15 42									16 12	
Elmstead Woods	d				15 00				15 15					15 30				15 45				16 00			
Chislehurst	d				15 02				15 17					15 32				15 47				16 02			
Petts Wood 4	d	14 59			15 06			15 14	15 21		15 29			15 36			15 44	15 51		15 59		16 06			
Orpington 4	a	15 02		15 08	15 09			15 17	15 24	15 25	15 32	15 38		15 39			15 47	15 54	15 55	16 02	16 08	16 09			
	d			15 09	15 12					15 26		15 39		15 42					15 56		16 09	16 12			
Chelsfield 3	d				15 15									15 45								16 15			
Knockholt	d				15 18									15 48								16 18			
Dunton Green	d				15 23									15 53								16 23			
Sevenoaks 4	a			15 18	15 26		15 42			15 35		15 48		15 56		16 12			16 05		16 18	16 26			16 42
	d			15 19			15 43			15 35		15 49				16 13			16 05		16 19				16 43
Hildenborough	d									15 41									16 11						
Tonbridge 4	a			15 27			15 51			15 45		15 57				16 21			16 15		16 27				16 51

		SE	SE	SE 1	SE 1	SE	SE	SE		SE 1 🍴	SE 1 🍴	SE	SE 1	SE	SE	SE 1	SE	SE		SE 1	SE 1	SE	SE	SE	SE 1 🍴
London Charing Cross 4 ⊖	d			16 00	16 15		16 06			16 37	16 41		16 28			16 57		16 32		17 01			16 42		17 14
London Waterloo (East) 4 ⊖	d			16 03	16 18		16 09			16 40	16 44		16 31			17 00		16 35		17 04			16 45		17 18
London Cannon Street 4 ⊖	d		15 50											16 20							17 02			16 56	
London Bridge 4 ⊖	d		15 54	16 09	16 23		16 14			16 45	16 49		16 36	16 24				16 40		17 09	17 06		16 51	17 00	
New Cross 4 ⊖	d		15 59											16 30											
St Johns	d		16 01											16 32											
Lewisham 4	d		16 04											16 35									17 01		
Hither Green 4	d		16 08				16 24							16 39				16 50					17 05		
Grove Park 4	d		16 12				16 27	16 37						16 43	16 57			16 53					17 09	17 13	
Sundridge Park	d							16 40							17 00										
Bromley North	a							16 42							17 02										
Elmstead Woods	d		16 15				16 30							16 46				16 56					17 12	17 16	
Chislehurst	d		16 18				16 33							16 48				16 59					17 15	17 19	
Petts Wood 4	d	16 14	16 21			16 29	16 36					16 44		16 51			16 59	17 03				17 14	17 19	17 23	
Orpington 4	a	16 17	16 24	16 25		16 32	16 39					16 48	16 52	16 56			17 03	17 06				17 18	17 23	17 27	
	d			16 26			16 42						16 53					17 07						17 28	
Chelsfield 3	d						16 45											17 10		17 28				17 31	
Knockholt	d						16 48											17 13						17 34	
Dunton Green	d						16 53											17 18						17 39	
Sevenoaks 4	a			16 35	16 46		16 57			17 09	17 13		17 02			17 27		17 22		17 37	17 31			17 43	17 45
	d			16 35	16 47					17 10	17 14		17 03			17 27				17 37	17 31				17 46
Hildenborough	d			16 41									17 09							17 43					
Tonbridge 4	a			16 45	16 55					17 18	17 22		17 13			17 35				17 48	17 39				17 54

Table 204

London - Grove Park, Bromley North, Orpington, Sevenoaks and Tonbridge

		SE	SE 1	SE 1		SE	SE	SE	SE	SE 1 🍴	SE 1	SE 1	SE	SE		SE 1 🍴	SE	SE	SE	SE 1	SE 1	SE	SE	SE	
London Charing Cross 4 ⊖	d		17 23				17 03			17 41	17 45			17 26		17 59				18 07			17 47		
London Waterloo (East) 4 ⊖	d		17 26				17 06			17 44	17 48			17 29		18 02				18 10			17 50		
London Cannon Street 4 ⊖	d			17 24				17 19				17 45							17 41		18 08			18 03	
London Bridge 4 ⊖	d		17 31	17 28			17 11	17 23			17 53	17 49		17 35					17 45	18 15	18 12		17 55	18 07	
New Cross 4 ⊖	d																								
St Johns	d																								
Lewisham 4	d						17 21							17 44									18 05		
Hither Green 4	d						17 26							17 48									18 09		
Grove Park 4	d	17 17					17 30	17 34	17 40					17 52			18 01		17 57				18 13	18 18	
Sundridge Park	d	17 20							17 43								18 04								
Bromley North	a	17 22							17 45								18 06								
Elmstead Woods	d						17 33	17 37						17 55					18 00				18 16	18 21	
Chislehurst	d						17 35	17 40						17 58					18 03				18 19	18 24	
Petts Wood 4	d					17 35	17 39	17 44					17 50	18 02				18 05	18 08			18 21	18 24	18 28	
Orpington 4	a					17 39	17 43	17 47					17 54	18 06				18 09	18 11			18 24	18 28	18 31	
	d							17 50											18 12					18 34	
Chelsfield 3	d		17 50					17 53			18 12								18 15	18 34				18 37	
Knockholt	d							17 56											18 18					18 40	
Dunton Green	d							18 01											18 23					18 45	
Sevenoaks 4	a		17 59	17 53				18 06		18 11	18 21	18 15				18 29			18 27	18 42	18 37			18 49	
	d		17 59	17 54						18 11	18 21	18 15				18 30				18 43	18 37				
Hildenborough	d		18 05	18 00							18 27									18 49	18 43				
Tonbridge 4	a		18 09	18 04						18 19	18 32	18 23				18 38				18 54	18 47				

		SE 1	SE	SE 1	SE 1	SE	SE	SE	SE	SE 1 🍴		SE	SE	SE 1 🍴	SE 1	SE	SE	SE	SE 1 🍴	SE		SE 1	SE 1 🍴	SE	SE
London Charing Cross 4 ⊖	d	18 21		18 32			18 09			18 45			18 30	18 41					19 10			19 00	19 15		
London Waterloo (East) 4 ⊖	d	18 24		18 35			18 12			18 48			18 33	18 44					19 13			19 03	19 18		
London Cannon Street 4 ⊖	d				18 32			18 23							19 04		18 48								
London Bridge 4 ⊖	d			18 40	18 36		18 17	18 27		18 53			18 38	18 50	19 08		18 52		19 19			19 09	19 23		
New Cross 4 ⊖	d																								
St Johns	d																								
Lewisham 4	d						18 27																		
Hither Green 4	d						18 31						18 48												
Grove Park 4	d		18 23				18 35	18 40	18 44				18 52				19 04	19 08						19 32	
Sundridge Park	d		18 26						18 47									19 11						19 35	
Bromley North	a		18 28						18 49									19 13						19 37	
Elmstead Woods	d						18 38	18 43					18 55				19 07								
Chislehurst	d						18 40	18 46					18 59				19 10								
Petts Wood 4	d					18 36	18 44	18 49				18 52	19 03			19 07	19 14			19 19					19 35
Orpington 4	a					18 40	18 48	18 52				18 56	19 06	19 06		19 11	19 18			19 23		19 25	19 38		19 38
	d							18 58					19 12	19 07								19 26	19 39		
Chelsfield 3	d			18 58				19 01					19 15									19 29			
Knockholt	d							19 04					19 18												
Dunton Green	d							19 09					19 23												
Sevenoaks 4	a	18 52		19 06	19 00			19 13		19 20			19 27	19 16	19 31				19 42			19 36	19 48		
	d	18 52		19 06	19 00					19 20				19 16	19 32				19 43			19 37	19 49		
Hildenborough	d			19 12											19 38							19 43			
Tonbridge 4	a	19 00		19 17	19 08					19 28				19 24	19 42				19 52			19 47	19 57		

		SE	SE 1 🍴	SE	SE	SE 1		SE	SE	SE 1	SE	SE 1 🍴	SE	SE	SE 1	SE		SE	SE 1	SE	SE	SE 1 🍴	SE	SE	SE 1
London Charing Cross 4 ⊖	d	19 06	19 40			19 30				19 45	19 36	20 10			20 00				20 15	20 06		20 40			20 30
London Waterloo (East) 4 ⊖	d	19 09	19 43			19 33				19 48	19 39	20 13			20 03				20 18	20 09		20 43			20 33
London Cannon Street 4 ⊖	d				19 20									19 50										20 20	
London Bridge 4 ⊖	d	19 14	19 49		19 24	19 39				19 53	19 44	20 19		19 54	20 09				20 23	20 14		20 49		20 24	20 39
New Cross 4 ⊖	d				19 29									19 59										20 29	
St Johns	d				19 31									20 01										20 31	
Lewisham 4	d				19 35									20 04										20 34	
Hither Green 4	d	19 23			19 39						19 53			20 08						20 23				20 38	
Grove Park 4	d	19 27			19 42			19 52			19 57			20 12		20 17				20 27	20 37			20 42	
Sundridge Park	d							19 55								20 20					20 40				
Bromley North	a							19 57								20 22					20 42				
Elmstead Woods	d	19 30			19 45						20 00			20 15						20 30				20 45	
Chislehurst	d	19 32			19 48						20 02			20 17						20 32				20 47	
Petts Wood 4	d	19 38		19 44	19 51				19 59		20 06		20 14	20 21				20 29		20 36			20 44	20 51	
Orpington 4	a	19 43		19 48	19 54	19 55			20 02	20 08	20 09		20 18	20 24	20 25			20 32	20 38	20 39			20 47	20 54	20 55
	d	19 44				19 56				20 09	20 12				20 26				20 39	20 42					20 56
Chelsfield 3	d	19 47									20 15									20 45					
Knockholt	d	19 50									20 18									20 48					
Dunton Green	d	19 55									20 23									20 53					
Sevenoaks 4	a	19 58	20 12			20 05				20 18	20 26	20 42			20 35				20 48	20 56		21 12			21 05
	d		20 13			20 05				20 19		20 43			20 35				20 49			21 13			21 05
Hildenborough	d					20 11									20 41										21 11
Tonbridge 4	a		20 21			20 15				20 27		20 51			20 45				20 57			21 21			21 15

London - Grove Park, Bromley North, Orpington, Sevenoaks and Tonbridge

		SE		SE 1	SE	SE 1	SE	SE	SE 1 ⇆	SE	SE 1	SE		SE 1	SE	SE 1	SE	SE 1	SE	SE	SE 1	SE		SE 1	SE
London Charing Cross 4 ⊖	d			20 45	20 36	21 00			21 10	21 06	21 30			21 40		21 45	21 36	22 00			22 10	22 06		22 30	
London Waterloo (East) 4 ⊖	d			20 48	20 39	21 03			21 13	21 09	21 33			21 43		21 48	21 39	22 03			22 13	22 09		22 33	
London Cannon Street 4 ⊖	d																								
London Bridge 4 ⊖	d			20 53	20 44	21 09			21 19	21 14	21 39			21 49		21 53	21 44	22 09			22 19	22 14		22 39	
New Cross 4 ⊖	d																								
St Johns	d																								
Lewisham 4 ⇌	d									21 22							21 52					22 22			
Hither Green 4	d				20 53					21 26							21 56					22 26			
Grove Park 4	d				20 57		21 07			21 29		21 37					21 59		22 07			22 29			22 37
Sundridge Park	d						21 10					21 40							22 10						22 40
Bromley North	a						21 12					21 42							22 12						22 42
Elmstead Woods	d				21 00					21 32							22 02					22 32			
Chislehurst	d				21 02					21 35							22 05					22 35			
Petts Wood 4	d	20 59			21 06			21 29		21 38					21 59		22 08			22 29		22 38			
Orpington 4	a	21 02		21 08	21 09	21 25		21 32	21 34	21 42	21 55				22 02	22 08	22 12	22 25		22 32	22 34	22 42		22 54	
	d			21 09	21 12	21 26			21 35	21 43	21 56					22 09		22 26			22 35			22 54	
Chelsfield 3	d				21 15					21 46	21 59							22 29						22 57	
Knockholt	d				21 18					21 49															
Dunton Green	d				21 23					21 54															
Sevenoaks 4	a			21 18	21 26	21 35			21 44	21 57	22 06			22 12		22 18		22 36			22 44			23 05	
	d			21 19		21 35			21 44		22 07			22 13		22 19		22 37			22 44			23 05	
Hildenborough	d					21 41					22 13							22 43						23 11	
Tonbridge 4	a			21 27		21 45			21 52		22 17			22 21		22 27		22 47			22 52			23 15	

		SE 1	SE	SE 1	SE	SE 1	SE	SE		SE 1	SE	SE 1	SE	SE 1	SE	SE 1	SE								
London Charing Cross 4 ⊖	d	22 40		22 45	22 36	23 00				23 10	23 06	23 30		23 40		23 45	23 36								
London Waterloo (East) 4 ⊖	d	22 43		22 48	22 39	23 03				23 13	23 09	23 33		23 43		23 48	23 39								
London Cannon Street 4 ⊖	d																								
London Bridge 4 ⊖	d	22 49		22 53	22 44	23 09				23 19	23 14	23 39		23 49		23 53	23 44								
New Cross 4 ⊖	d																								
St Johns	d																								
Lewisham 4 ⇌	d				22 52						23 22						23 52								
Hither Green 4	d				22 56						23 26						23 56								
Grove Park 4	d				22 59		23 07				23 29		23 37				23 59								
Sundridge Park	d						23 10						23 40												
Bromley North	a						23 12						23 42												
Elmstead Woods	d				23 02						23 32						00 02								
Chislehurst	d				23 05						23 35						00 05								
Petts Wood 4	d		22 59		23 08			23 29			23 38				23 59		00 08								
Orpington 4	a		23 02	23 08	23 12	23 24		23 32		23 34	23 42	23 54			00 02	00 08	00 12								
	d			23 09		23 24				23 35		23 54				00 09									
Chelsfield 3	d					23 27						23 57													
Knockholt	d																								
Dunton Green	d																								
Sevenoaks 4	a	23 12		23 18		23 35				23 44		00 05		00 12		00 18									
	d	23 13		23 19		23 35				23 44		00 05		00 13		00 19									
Hildenborough	d					23 41						00 11													
Tonbridge 4	a	23 21		23 27		23 45				23 52		00 15		00 21		00 27									

Saturdays

		SE 1	SE 1	SE	SE 1	SE	SE	SE	SE	SE		SE	SE	SE 1	SE	SE	SE	SE	SE	SE 1		SE	SE	SE	SE
London Charing Cross 4 ⊖	d	23p30	23p40		23p45	23p36			00 10			00 48	05 36	06 00		06 06			06 36	07 00				07 06	
London Waterloo (East) 4 ⊖	d	23p33	23p43		23p48	23p39			00 13			00 51	05 39	06 03		06 09			06 39	07 03				07 09	
London Cannon Street 4 ⊖	d																								
London Bridge 4 ⊖	d	23p39	23p49		23p53	23p44			00 18			00 56	05 44	06 08		06 14			06 44	07 08				07 14	
New Cross 4 ⊖	d											01 01													
St Johns	d																								
Lewisham 4 ⇌	d					23p52						01 05	05 53			06 23			06 53					07 23	
Hither Green 4	d					23p56						01 09	05 57			06 27			06 57					07 27	
Grove Park 4	d					23p59	00 07		00 31	00 37		01 13	06 00			06 30	06 37		07 00			07 07		07 30	07 37
Sundridge Park	d						00 10			00 40							06 40					07 10			07 40
Bromley North	a						00 12			00 42							06 42					07 12			07 42
Elmstead Woods	d					00 02			00 34			01 16	06 03			06 33			07 03					07 33	
Chislehurst	d					00 05			00 37			01 18	06 06			06 36			07 06					07 36	
Petts Wood 4	d			23p59		00 08		00 29	00 40			01 22	06 09		06 29	06 39		06 59	07 09				07 29	07 39	
Orpington 4	a	23p54		00 02	00 08	00 12		00 32	00 43			01 25	06 12	06 23	06 32	06 42		07 02	07 12	07 23			07 32	07 42	
	d	23p54			00 09				00 43				06 13	06 24		06 43			07 13	07 24				07 43	
Chelsfield 3	d	23p57							00 46				06 16			06 46			07 16					07 46	
Knockholt	d												06 19			06 49			07 19					07 49	
Dunton Green	d												06 24			06 54			07 24					07 54	
Sevenoaks 4	a	00 05	00 12		00 18				00 54				06 27	06 33		06 57			07 27	07 33				07 57	
	d	00 05	00 13		00 19				00 54					06 33						07 33					
Hildenborough	d	00 11							01 00					06 39						07 39					
Tonbridge 4	a	00 15	00 21		00 27				01 04					06 43						07 43					

London - Grove Park, Bromley North, Orpington, Sevenoaks and Tonbridge

		SE	SE 1	SE	SE 1	SE		SE	SE	SE 1	SE	SE 1	SE	SE	SE 1	SE		SE	SE 1	SE	SE 1	SE	SE	SE 1	SE
London Charing Cross 4 ⊖	d		07 30		07 45	07 36				08 00		08 15	08 06		08 40				08 30		08 45	08 36		09 10	
London Waterloo (East) 4 ⊖	d		07 33		07 48	07 39				08 03		08 18	08 09		08 43				08 33		08 48	08 39		09 13	
London Cannon Street 4 ⊖	d																	08 20							
London Bridge 4 ⊖	d		07 38		07 53	07 44				08 08		08 23	08 14		08 49			08 24	08 39		08 53	08 44		09 19	
New Cross 4 ⊖	d																	08 29							
St Johns	d																	08 31							
Lewisham 4 ⇌	d					07 53												08 34							
Hither Green 4	d					07 57							08 23					08 38				08 53			
Grove Park 4	d					08 00		08 07					08 27	08 37				08 42				08 57	09 07		
Sundridge Park	d							08 10						08 40									09 10		
Bromley North	a							08 12						08 42									09 12		
Elmstead Woods	d					08 03							08 30					08 45				09 00			
Chislehurst	d					08 06							08 32					08 47				09 02			
Petts Wood 4	d	07 44		07 59		08 09			08 14		08 29		08 36			08 44		08 51		08 59		09 06			09 14
Orpington 4	a	07 47	07 54	08 02	08 08	08 12			08 17	08 23	08 32	08 38	08 39			08 47		08 54	08 55	09 02	09 08	09 09			09 17
	d		07 54		08 09	08 13				08 24		08 39	08 42						08 56		09 09	09 12			
Chelsfield 3	d					08 16							08 45									09 15			
Knockholt	d					08 19							08 48									09 18			
Dunton Green	d					08 24							08 53									09 23			
Sevenoaks 4	a		08 02		08 18	08 27				08 33		08 48	08 56		09 12				09 05		09 18	09 26		09 42	
	d		08 03		08 19					08 33		08 49			09 13				09 05		09 19			09 43	
Hildenborough	d		08 09							08 39									09 11						
Tonbridge 4	a		08 14		08 27					08 43		08 57			09 21				09 15		09 27			09 51	

		SE		SE 1	SE	SE 1	SE	SE	SE 1	SE	SE	SE 1		SE	SE 1	SE	SE	SE 1	SE	SE	SE 1	SE		SE 1 ⇆	SE
London Charing Cross 4 ⊖	d			09 00		09 15	09 06		09 40			09 30			09 45	09 36		10 10			10 00			10 15	10 06
London Waterloo (East) 4 ⊖	d			09 03		09 18	09 09		09 43			09 33			09 48	09 39		10 13			10 03			10 18	10 09
London Cannon Street 4 ⊖	d	08 50									09 20									09 50					
London Bridge 4 ⊖	d	08 54		09 09		09 23	09 14		09 49		09 24	09 39			09 53	09 44		10 19		09 54	10 09			10 23	10 14
New Cross 4 ⊖	d	08 59									09 29									09 59					
St Johns	d	09 01									09 31									10 01					
Lewisham 4 ⇌	d	09 04									09 34									10 04					
Hither Green 4	d	09 08					09 23				09 38					09 53				10 08					10 23
Grove Park 4	d	09 12					09 27	09 37			09 42					09 57	10 07			10 12					10 27
Sundridge Park	d							09 40									10 10								
Bromley North	a							09 42									10 12								
Elmstead Woods	d	09 15					09 30				09 45					10 00				10 15					10 30
Chislehurst	d	09 17					09 32				09 47					10 02				10 17					10 32
Petts Wood 4	d	09 21			09 29		09 36			09 44	09 51			09 59		10 06			10 14	10 21		10 29			10 36
Orpington 4	a	09 24		09 25	09 32	09 38	09 39			09 47	09 54	09 55		10 02	10 08	10 09			10 17	10 24	10 25	10 32		10 38	10 39
	d			09 26		09 39	09 42					09 56			10 09	10 12					10 26			10 39	10 42
Chelsfield 3	d						09 45									10 15									10 45
Knockholt	d						09 48									10 18									10 48
Dunton Green	d						09 53									10 23									10 53
Sevenoaks 4	a			09 35		09 48	09 56		10 12			10 05			10 18	10 26		10 42			10 35			10 48	10 56
	d			09 35		09 49			10 13			10 05			10 19			10 43			10 35			10 49	
Hildenborough	d			09 41								10 11									10 41				
Tonbridge 4	a			09 45		09 57			10 21			10 15			10 27			10 51			10 45			10 57	

		SE	SE 1 ⇆	SE	SE	SE 1	SE	SE 1 ⇆		SE	SE	SE 1 ⇆	SE	SE	SE 1	SE	SE 1 ⇆	SE		SE	SE 1 ⇆	SE	SE	SE 1	SE
London Charing Cross 4 ⊖	d		10 40			10 30		10 45		10 36		11 10			11 00		11 15	11 06			11 40			11 30	
London Waterloo (East) 4 ⊖	d		10 43			10 33		10 48		10 39		11 13			11 03		11 18	11 09			11 43			11 33	
London Cannon Street 4 ⊖	d				10 20									10 50									11 20		
London Bridge 4 ⊖	d		10 49		10 24	10 39		10 53		10 44		11 19		10 54	11 09		11 23	11 14			11 49		11 24	11 39	
New Cross 4 ⊖	d				10 29									10 59									11 29		
St Johns	d				10 31									11 01									11 31		
Lewisham 4 ⇌	d				10 35									11 04									11 34		
Hither Green 4	d				10 39					10 53				11 08				11 23					11 38		
Grove Park 4	d	10 37			10 42					10 57	11 07			11 12				11 27		11 37			11 42		
Sundridge Park	d	10 40									11 10									11 40					
Bromley North	a	10 42									11 12									11 42					
Elmstead Woods	d				10 45					11 00				11 15				11 30					11 45		
Chislehurst	d				10 48					11 02				11 17				11 32					11 47		
Petts Wood 4	d			10 44	10 51		10 59			11 06			11 14	11 21		11 29		11 36				11 44	11 51		11 59
Orpington 4	a			10 47	10 54	10 55	11 02	11 08		11 09			11 17	11 24	11 25	11 32	11 38	11 39				11 47	11 54	11 55	12 02
	d					10 56		11 09		11 12					11 26		11 39	11 42						11 56	
Chelsfield 3	d									11 15								11 45							
Knockholt	d									11 18								11 48							
Dunton Green	d									11 23								11 53							
Sevenoaks 4	a		11 12			11 05		11 18		11 26		11 42			11 35		11 48	11 56			12 12			12 05	
	d		11 13			11 05		11 19				11 43			11 35		11 49				12 13			12 05	
Hildenborough	d					11 11									11 41									12 11	
Tonbridge 4	a		11 21			11 15		11 27				11 51			11 45		11 57				12 21			12 15	

Table 204

Saturdays

London - Grove Park, Bromley North, Orpington, Sevenoaks and Tonbridge

Station		SE 1 ⇆	SE	SE	SE 1 ⇆	SE	SE	SE 1	SE	SE 1 ⇆	SE	SE	SE 1 ⇆	SE	SE	SE 1	SE	SE 1 ⇆	SE	SE	SE 1 ⇆	SE
London Charing Cross 4 ⊖	d	11 45	11 36		12 10			12 00		12 15	12 06		12 40			12 30		12 45	12 36		13 10	
London Waterloo (East) 4 ⊖	d	11 48	11 39		12 13			12 03		12 18	12 09		12 43			12 33		12 48	12 39		13 13	
London Cannon Street 4 ⊖	d						11 50								12 20							
London Bridge 4 ⊖	d	11 53	11 44		12 19		11 54	12 09		12 23	12 14		12 49		12 24	12 39		12 53	12 44		13 19	
New Cross 4 ⊖	d						11 59								12 29							
St Johns	d						12 01								12 31							
Lewisham 4	d						12 04								12 34							
Hither Green 4	d		11 53				12 08				12 23				12 38				12 53			
Grove Park 4	d		11 57	12 07			12 12				12 27	12 37			12 42				12 57	13 07		
Sundridge Park	d			12 10								12 40								13 10		
Bromley North	a			12 12								12 42								13 12		
Elmstead Woods	d		12 00				12 15				12 30				12 45				13 00			
Chislehurst	d		12 02				12 17				12 32				12 47				13 02			
Petts Wood 4	d		12 06			12 14	12 21		12 29		12 36			12 44	12 51		12 59		13 06			13 14
Orpington 4	a	12 08	12 09			12 17	12 24	12 25	12 32	12 38	12 39			12 47	12 54	12 55	13 02	13 08	13 09			13 17
	d	12 09	12 12					12 26		12 39	12 42					12 56		13 09	13 12			
Chelsfield 3	d		12 15								12 45								13 15			
Knockholt	d		12 18								12 48								13 18			
Dunton Green	d		12 23								12 53								13 23			
Sevenoaks 4	a	12 18	12 26		12 42			12 35		12 48	12 56		13 12			13 05		13 18	13 26		13 42	
	d	12 19			12 43			12 35		12 49			13 13			13 05		13 19			13 43	
Hildenborough	d							12 41								13 11						
Tonbridge 4	a	12 27			12 51			12 45		12 57			13 21			13 15		13 27			13 51	

Station		SE	SE 1	SE	SE 1 ⇆	SE	SE	SE 1 ⇆	SE	SE	SE 1	SE	SE 1 ⇆	SE	SE	SE 1 ⇆	SE	SE	SE 1	SE	SE 1 ⇆	SE	SE
London Charing Cross 4 ⊖	d		13 00		13 15	13 06		13 40			13 30		13 45	13 36		14 10			14 00		14 15	14 06	
London Waterloo (East) 4 ⊖	d		13 03		13 18	13 09		13 43			13 33		13 48	13 39		14 13			14 03		14 18	14 09	
London Cannon Street 4 ⊖	d	12 50								13 20								13 50					
London Bridge 4 ⊖	d	12 54	13 09		13 23	13 14		13 49		13 24	13 39		13 53	13 44		14 19		13 54	14 09		14 23	14 14	
New Cross 4 ⊖	d	12 59								13 29								13 59					
St Johns	d	13 01								13 31								14 01					
Lewisham 4	d	13 04								13 34								14 04					
Hither Green 4	d	13 08				13 23				13 38				13 53				14 08				14 23	
Grove Park 4	d	13 12				13 27	13 37			13 42				13 57	14 07			14 12				14 27	14 37
Sundridge Park	d						13 40								14 10								14 40
Bromley North	a						13 42								14 12								14 42
Elmstead Woods	d	13 15				13 30				13 45				14 00				14 15				14 30	
Chislehurst	d	13 17				13 32				13 47				14 02				14 17				14 32	
Petts Wood 4	d	13 21		13 29		13 36			13 44	13 51		13 59		14 06			14 14	14 21		14 29		14 36	
Orpington 4	a	13 24	13 25	13 32	13 38	13 39			13 47	13 54	13 55	14 02	14 08	14 09			14 17	14 24	14 25	14 32	14 38	14 39	
	d		13 26		13 39	13 42					13 56		14 09	14 12					14 26		14 39	14 42	
Chelsfield 3	d					13 45								14 15								14 45	
Knockholt	d					13 48								14 18								14 48	
Dunton Green	d					13 53								14 23								14 53	
Sevenoaks 4	a		13 35		13 48	13 56		14 12			14 05		14 18	14 26		14 42			14 35		14 48	14 56	
	d		13 35		13 49			14 13			14 05		14 19			14 43			14 35		14 49		
Hildenborough	d		13 41								14 11								14 41				
Tonbridge 4	a		13 45		13 57			14 21			14 15		14 27			14 51			14 45		14 57		

Station		SE 1 ⇆	SE	SE	SE 1	SE	SE 1 ⇆	SE	SE	SE 1 ⇆	SE	SE	SE 1	SE	SE 1 ⇆	SE	SE	SE 1 ⇆	SE	SE	SE 1	SE	SE 1 ⇆
London Charing Cross 4 ⊖	d	14 40			14 30		14 45	14 36		15 10			15 00		15 15	15 06		15 40			15 30		15 45
London Waterloo (East) 4 ⊖	d	14 43			14 33		14 48	14 39		15 13			15 03		15 18	15 09		15 43			15 33		15 48
London Cannon Street 4 ⊖	d			14 20								14 50								15 20			
London Bridge 4 ⊖	d	14 49		14 24	14 39		14 53	14 44		15 19		14 54	15 09		15 23	15 14		15 49		15 24	15 39		15 53
New Cross 4 ⊖	d			14 29								14 59								15 29			
St Johns	d			14 31								15 01								15 31			
Lewisham 4	d			14 34								15 04								15 34			
Hither Green 4	d			14 38				14 53				15 08				15 23				15 38			
Grove Park 4	d			14 42				14 57	15 07			15 12				15 27	15 37			15 42			
Sundridge Park	d								15 10								15 40						
Bromley North	a								15 12								15 42						
Elmstead Woods	d			14 45				15 00				15 15				15 30				15 45			
Chislehurst	d			14 47				15 02				15 17				15 32				15 47			
Petts Wood 4	d		14 44	14 51		14 59		15 06			15 14	15 21		15 29		15 36			15 44	15 51		15 59	
Orpington 4	a		14 47	14 54	14 55	15 02	15 08	15 09			15 17	15 24	15 25	15 32	15 38	15 39			15 47	15 54	15 55	16 02	16 08
	d				14 56		15 09	15 12					15 26		15 39	15 42					15 56		16 09
Chelsfield 3	d							15 15								15 45							
Knockholt	d							15 18								15 48							
Dunton Green	d							15 23								15 53							
Sevenoaks 4	a	15 12			15 05		15 18	15 26		15 42			15 35		15 48	15 56		16 12			16 05		16 18
	d	15 13			15 05		15 19			15 43			15 35		15 49			16 13			16 05		16 19
Hildenborough	d				15 11								15 41								16 11		
Tonbridge 4	a	15 21			15 15		15 27			15 51			15 45		15 57			16 21			16 15		16 27

Table 204

Saturdays

London - Grove Park, Bromley North, Orpington, Sevenoaks and Tonbridge

Station		SE	SE	SE 1 ⇆	SE	SE	SE 1	SE	SE 1 ⇆	SE	SE	SE 1 ⇆	SE	SE	SE 1	SE	SE 1 ⇆	SE	SE	SE 1 ⇆	SE	SE
London Charing Cross 4 ⊖	d	15 36		16 10			16 00		16 15	16 06		16 40			16 30		16 45	16 36		17 10		
London Waterloo (East) 4 ⊖	d	15 39		16 13			16 03		16 18	16 09		16 43			16 33		16 48	16 39		17 13		
London Cannon Street 4 ⊖	d					15 50								16 20								16 50
London Bridge 4 ⊖	d	15 44		16 19		15 54	16 09		16 23	16 14		16 49		16 24	16 39		16 53	16 44		17 19		16 54
New Cross 4 ⊖	d					15 59								16 29								16 59
St Johns	d					16 01								16 31								17 01
Lewisham 4	d					16 04								16 34								17 04
Hither Green 4	d	15 53				16 08				16 23				16 38				16 53				17 08
Grove Park 4	d	15 57	16 07			16 12				16 27	16 37			16 42				16 57	17 07			17 12
Sundridge Park	d		16 10								16 40								17 10			
Bromley North	a		16 12								16 42								17 12			
Elmstead Woods	d	16 00				16 15				16 30				16 45				17 00				17 15
Chislehurst	d	16 02				16 17				16 32				16 47				17 02				17 17
Petts Wood 4	d	16 06			16 14	16 21		16 29		16 36			16 44	16 51		16 59		17 06			17 14	17 21
Orpington 4	a	16 09			16 17	16 24	16 25	16 32	16 38	16 39			16 47	16 54	16 55	17 02	17 08	17 09			17 17	17 24
	d	16 12					16 26		16 39	16 42					16 56		17 09	17 12				
Chelsfield 3	d	16 15								16 45								17 15				
Knockholt	d	16 18								16 48								17 18				
Dunton Green	d	16 23								16 53								17 23				
Sevenoaks 4	a	16 26		16 42			16 35		16 48	16 56		17 12			17 05		17 18	17 26		17 42		
	d			16 43			16 35		16 49			17 13			17 05		17 19			17 43		
Hildenborough	d						16 41								17 11							
Tonbridge 4	a			16 51			16 45		16 57			17 21			17 15		17 27			17 51		

Station		SE 1	SE	SE 1 ⇆	SE	SE	SE 1 ⇆	SE	SE	SE 1	SE	SE 1 ⇆	SE	SE	SE 1 ⇆	SE	SE	SE 1	SE	SE 1 ⇆	SE	SE	SE 1 ⇆
London Charing Cross 4 ⊖	d	17 00		17 15	17 06		17 40			17 30		17 45	17 36		18 10			18 00		18 15	18 06		18 40
London Waterloo (East) 4 ⊖	d	17 03		17 18	17 09		17 43			17 33		17 48	17 39		18 13			18 03		18 18	18 09		18 43
London Cannon Street 4 ⊖	d								17 20								17 50						
London Bridge 4 ⊖	d	17 09		17 23	17 14		17 49		17 24	17 39		17 53	17 44		18 19		17 54	18 09		18 23	18 14		18 49
New Cross 4 ⊖	d								17 29								17 59						
St Johns	d								17 31								18 01						
Lewisham 4	d								17 34								18 04						
Hither Green 4	d				17 23				17 38				17 53				18 08				18 23		
Grove Park 4	d				17 27	17 37			17 42				17 57	18 07			18 12				18 27	18 37	
Sundridge Park	d					17 40								18 10								18 40	
Bromley North	a					17 42								18 12								18 42	
Elmstead Woods	d				17 30				17 45				18 00				18 15				18 30		
Chislehurst	d				17 32				17 47				18 02				18 17				18 32		
Petts Wood 4	d		17 29		17 36			17 44	17 51		17 59		18 06			18 14	18 21		18 29		18 36		
Orpington 4	a	17 25	17 32	17 38	17 39			17 47	17 54	17 55	18 02	18 08	18 09			18 17	18 24	18 25	18 32	18 38	18 39		
	d	17 26		17 39	17 42					17 56		18 09	18 12					18 26		18 39	18 42		
Chelsfield 3	d				17 45								18 15								18 45		
Knockholt	d				17 48								18 18								18 48		
Dunton Green	d				17 53								18 23								18 53		
Sevenoaks 4	a	17 35		17 48	17 56		18 12			18 05		18 18	18 26		18 42			18 35		18 48	18 56		19 12
	d	17 35		17 49			18 13			18 05		18 19			18 43			18 35		18 49			19 13
Hildenborough	d	17 41								18 11								18 41					
Tonbridge 4	a	17 45		17 57			18 21			18 15		18 27			18 51			18 45		18 58			19 21

Station		SE	SE	SE 1	SE	SE 1 ⇆	SE	SE	SE 1 ⇆	SE	SE	SE 1	SE	SE 1	SE	SE	SE 1 ⇆	SE	SE 1	SE	SE	SE 1
London Charing Cross 4 ⊖	d			18 30		18 45	18 36		19 10			19 00		19 15	19 06		19 40		19 30		19 36	19 55
London Waterloo (East) 4 ⊖	d			18 33		18 48	18 39		19 13			19 03		19 18	19 09		19 43		19 33		19 39	19 58
London Cannon Street 4 ⊖	d		18 20								18 50											
London Bridge 4 ⊖	d		18 24	18 39		18 53	18 44		19 19		18 54	19 09		19 23	19 14		19 49		19 39		19 44	20 03
New Cross 4 ⊖	d		18 29								18 59											
St Johns	d		18 31								19 01											
Lewisham 4	d		18 34								19 05										19 52	
Hither Green 4	d		18 38				18 53				19 09				19 23						19 56	
Grove Park 4	d		18 42				18 57	19 07			19 12				19 27	19 37					19 59	
Sundridge Park	d							19 10								19 40						
Bromley North	a							19 12								19 42						
Elmstead Woods	d		18 45				19 00				19 15				19 30						20 02	
Chislehurst	d		18 47				19 02				19 18				19 32						20 05	
Petts Wood 4	d	18 44	18 51		18 59		19 06			19 14	19 21		19 29		19 36			19 44		19 59	20 08	
Orpington 4	a	18 47	18 54	18 55	19 02	19 08	19 09			19 17	19 24	19 25	19 32	19 38	19 39			19 48	19 55	20 02	20 12	20 18
	d			18 56		19 09	19 12					19 26		19 39	19 42				19 56		20 13	20 21
Chelsfield 3	d						19 15								19 45						20 16	
Knockholt	d						19 18								19 48						20 19	
Dunton Green	d						19 23								19 53						20 24	
Sevenoaks 4	a			19 05		19 18	19 26		19 42			19 35		19 49	19 56		20 12		20 05		20 27	20 30
	d			19 05		19 19			19 43			19 35		19 49			20 13		20 05			20 31
Hildenborough	d			19 11								19 41							20 11			
Tonbridge 4	a			19 15		19 27			19 51			19 45		19 58			20 21		20 15			20 39

Table 204

Saturdays

London - Grove Park, Bromley North, Orpington, Sevenoaks and Tonbridge

		SE	SE	SE	SE 1 ⊼	SE	SE	SE	SE 1	SE		SE 1 ⊼	SE	SE 1	SE	SE	SE 1	SE	SE 1	SE		SE	SE 1	SE	SE 1
London Charing Cross ⊖	d				20 10	20 06			20 25			20 40	20 36	20 55			21 10	21 06	21 25				21 40	21 36	21 55
London Waterloo (East) ⊖	d				20 13	20 09			20 28			20 43	20 39	20 58			21 13	21 09	21 28				21 43	21 39	21 58
London Cannon Street ⊖	d																								
London Bridge ⊖	d				20 19	20 14			20 33			20 49	20 44	21 03			21 19	21 14	21 33				21 49	21 44	22 03
New Cross ⊖	d																								
St Johns	d																								
Lewisham	d					20 22							20 52					21 22						21 52	
Hither Green	d					20 26							20 56					21 26						21 56	
Grove Park	d	20 07				20 29	20 37						20 59		21 07			21 29		21 37				21 59	
Sundridge Park	d	20 10					20 40								21 10					21 40					
Bromley North	a	20 12					20 42								21 12					21 42					
Elmstead Woods	d					20 32							21 02					21 32						22 02	
Chislehurst	d					20 35							21 05					21 35						22 05	
Petts Wood	d		20 14	20 29		20 38		20 44		20 59			21 08			21 29		21 38				21 59		22 08	
Orpington	a		20 18	20 32	20 34	20 42		20 47	20 48	21 02		21 04	21 12	21 18		21 32	21 34	21 42	21 48			22 02	22 04	22 12	22 18
	d				20 35	20 43			20 51			21 05	21 13	21 21			21 35	21 43	21 51				22 05		22 21
Chelsfield	d					20 46							21 16					21 46							
Knockholt	d					20 49							21 19					21 49							
Dunton Green	d					20 54							21 24					21 54							
Sevenoaks	a				20 44	20 57			21 00			21 14	21 27	21 30			21 44	21 57	22 00				22 14		22 30
	d				20 44				21 01			21 14		21 31			21 44		22 01				22 14		22 31
Hildenborough	d								21 07										22 07						
Tonbridge	a				20 52				21 11			21 22		21 39			21 52		22 11				22 22		22 39

		SE	SE	SE 1	SE	SE 1		SE	SE	SE 1	SE	SE 1	SE	SE	SE 1	SE		SE 1	SE	SE	SE 1	SE 1	SE		
London Charing Cross ⊖	d			22 10	22 06	22 25				22 40	22 36	22 55			23 10	23 06		23 25			23 40	23 45	23 36		
London Waterloo (East) ⊖	d			22 13	22 09	22 28				22 43	22 39	22 58			23 13	23 09		23 28			23 43	23 48	23 39		
London Cannon Street ⊖	d																								
London Bridge ⊖	d			22 19	22 14	22 33				22 49	22 44	23 03			23 19	23 14		23 33			23 49	23 53	23 44		
New Cross ⊖	d																								
St Johns	d																								
Lewisham	d				22 22						22 52					23 22							23 52		
Hither Green	d				22 26						22 56					23 26							23 56		
Grove Park	d	22 07			22 29			22 37			22 59		23 07			23 29			23 37				23 59		
Sundridge Park	d	22 10						22 40					23 10						23 40						
Bromley North	a	22 12						22 42					23 12						23 42						
Elmstead Woods	d				22 32						23 02					23 32							00 02		
Chislehurst	d				22 35						23 05					23 35							00 05		
Petts Wood	d		22 29		22 38				22 59		23 08			23 29		23 38				23 59			00 08		
Orpington	a		22 32	22 34	22 42	22 48			23 02	23 04	23 12	23 18		23 32	23 34	23 42		23 48		00 02	00 04	00 08	00 12		
	d			22 35		22 49				23 05		23 19			23 35			23 49			00 05	00 09			
Chelsfield	d					22 52												23 52							
Knockholt	d																								
Dunton Green	d																								
Sevenoaks	a			22 44		22 59				23 14		23 28			23 44			23 59			00 14	00 18			
	d			22 44		23 00				23 14		23 28			23 44			23 59			00 14	00 19			
Hildenborough	d					23 06												00 06							
Tonbridge	a			22 52		23 10				23 22		23 36			23 52			00 10			00 22	00 27			

Sundays

		SE 1	SE	SE 1	SE 1	SE	SE	SE	SE	SE		SE	SE	SE	SE 1	SE 1	SE	SE	SE 1	SE		SE	SE 1	SE 1	SE
London Charing Cross ⊖	d	23p25		23p40	23p45	23p36			00 10			00 48	07 46		08 08	08 23	08 16		08 38	08 46			09 08	09 23	09 16
London Waterloo (East) ⊖	d	23p28		23p43	23p48	23p39			00 13			00 51	07 49		08 11	08 26	08 19		08 41	08 49			09 11	09 26	09 19
London Cannon Street ⊖	d																								
London Bridge ⊖	d	23p33		23p49	23p53	23p44			00 18			00 56	07 54		08 16	08 31	08 24		08 46	08 54			09 16	09 31	09 24
New Cross ⊖	d											01 01													
St Johns	d																								
Lewisham	d					23p52						01 05	08 03				08 33			09 03					09 33
Hither Green	d					23p56						01 09	08 07				08 37			09 07					09 37
Grove Park	d					23p59	00 07		00 31	00 37		01 13	08 10				08 40			09 10					09 40
Sundridge Park	d						00 10			00 40															
Bromley North	a						00 12			00 42															
Elmstead Woods	d					00 02			00 34			01 16	08 13				08 43			09 13					09 43
Chislehurst	d					00 05			00 37			01 18	08 16				08 46			09 16					09 46
Petts Wood	d		23p59			00 08		00 29	00 40			01 22	08 19	08 25			08 49	08 55		09 19		09 25			09 49
Orpington	a	23p48	00 02	00 04	00 08	00 12		00 32	00 43			01 25	08 22	08 28	08 31	08 46	08 52	08 58	09 01	09 22		09 28	09 31	09 46	09 52
	d	23p49		00 05	00 09				00 43						08 32	08 46	08 53		09 02				09 32	09 46	09 53
Chelsfield	d	23p52							00 46								08 56								09 56
Knockholt	d																08 59								09 59
Dunton Green	d																09 04								10 04
Sevenoaks	a	23p59		00 14	00 18				00 54						08 41	08 55	09 07		09 11				09 41	09 55	10 07
	d	23p59		00 14	00 19				00 54						08 42	08 56			09 12				09 42	09 56	
Hildenborough	d	00 06							01 00						08 48								09 48		
Tonbridge	a	00 10		00 22	00 27				01 04						08 52	09 04			09 20				09 52	10 04	

Table 204

Sundays

London - Grove Park, Bromley North, Orpington, Sevenoaks and Tonbridge

		SE	SE 1	SE 1	SE	SE		SE 1 ⊼	SE 1	SE	SE	SE 1 ⊼	SE 1	SE	SE	SE 1 ⊼		SE 1	SE	SE	SE 1 ⊼	SE 1	SE	SE	SE 1 ⊼
London Charing Cross ⊖	d		09 38	09 53	09 46			10 08	10 23	10 16		10 38	10 53	10 46		11 08		11 23	11 16		11 38	11 53	11 46		12 08
London Waterloo (East) ⊖	d		09 41	09 56	09 49			10 11	10 26	10 19		10 41	10 56	10 49		11 11		11 26	11 19		11 41	11 56	11 49		12 11
London Cannon Street ⊖	d																								
London Bridge ⊖	d		09 46	10 01	09 54			10 16	10 31	10 24		10 46	11 01	10 54		11 16		11 31	11 24		11 46	12 01	11 54		12 16
New Cross ⊖	d																								
St Johns	d																								
Lewisham	d				10 03					10 33				11 03					11 33				12 03		
Hither Green	d				10 07					10 37				11 07					11 37				12 07		
Grove Park	d				10 10					10 40				11 10					11 40				12 10		
Sundridge Park	d																								
Bromley North	a																								
Elmstead Woods	d				10 13					10 43				11 13					11 43				12 13		
Chislehurst	d				10 16					10 46				11 16					11 46				12 16		
Petts Wood	d	09 55			10 19	10 25				10 49	10 55			11 19	11 25				11 49	11 55			12 19	12 25	
Orpington	a	09 58	10 01	10 16	10 22	10 28		10 31	10 46	10 52	10 58	11 01	11 16	11 22	11 28	11 31		11 46	11 52	11 58	12 01	12 16	12 22	12 28	12 31
	d		10 02	10 16				10 32	10 46	10 53		11 02	11 16			11 32		11 46	11 53		12 02	12 16			12 32
Chelsfield	d									10 56									11 56						
Knockholt	d									10 59									11 59						
Dunton Green	d									11 04									12 04						
Sevenoaks	a		10 11	10 25				10 41	10 55	11 07		11 11	11 25			11 41		11 55	12 07		12 11	12 25			12 41
	d		10 12	10 26				10 42	10 56			11 12	11 26			11 42		11 56			12 12	12 26			12 42
Hildenborough	d							10 48								11 48									12 48
Tonbridge	a		10 20	10 34				10 52	11 04			11 20	11 34			11 52		12 04			12 20	12 34			12 52

		SE 1		SE	SE	SE 1 ⊼	SE 1	SE	SE	SE 1 ⊼	SE 1	SE		SE	SE 1 ⊼	SE 1	SE	SE	SE 1 ⊼	SE 1	SE	SE		SE 1 ⊼	SE 1
London Charing Cross ⊖	d	12 23		12 16		12 38	12 53	12 46		13 08	13 23	13 16			13 38	13 53	13 46		14 08	14 23	14 16			14 38	14 53
London Waterloo (East) ⊖	d	12 26		12 19		12 41	12 56	12 49		13 11	13 26	13 19			13 41	13 56	13 49		14 11	14 26	14 19			14 41	14 56
London Cannon Street ⊖	d																								
London Bridge ⊖	d	12 31		12 24		12 46	13 01	12 54		13 16	13 31	13 24			13 46	14 01	13 54		14 16	14 31	14 24			14 46	15 01
New Cross ⊖	d																								
St Johns	d																								
Lewisham	d			12 33				13 03				13 33					14 03				14 33				
Hither Green	d			12 37				13 07				13 37					14 07				14 37				
Grove Park	d			12 40				13 10				13 40					14 10				14 40				
Sundridge Park	d																								
Bromley North	a																								
Elmstead Woods	d			12 43				13 13				13 43					14 13				14 43				
Chislehurst	d			12 46				13 16				13 46					14 16				14 46				
Petts Wood	d			12 49	12 55			13 19	13 25			13 49		13 55			14 19	14 25			14 49	14 55			
Orpington	a	12 46		12 52	12 58	13 01	13 16	13 22	13 28	13 31	13 46	13 52		13 58	14 01	14 16	14 22	14 28	14 31	14 46	14 52	14 58		15 01	15 16
	d	12 46		12 53		13 02	13 16			13 32	13 46	13 53			14 02	14 16			14 32	14 46	14 53			15 02	15 16
Chelsfield	d			12 56								13 56									14 56				
Knockholt	d			12 59								13 59									14 59				
Dunton Green	d			13 04								14 04									15 04				
Sevenoaks	a	12 55		13 07		13 11	13 25			13 41	13 55	14 07			14 11	14 25			14 41	14 55	15 07			15 11	15 25
	d	12 56				13 12	13 26			13 42	13 56				14 12	14 26			14 42	14 56				15 12	15 26
Hildenborough	d									13 48									14 48						
Tonbridge	a	13 04				13 20	13 34			13 52	14 04				14 20	14 34			14 52	15 04				15 20	15 34

		SE	SE	SE 1 ⊼	SE 1	SE	SE	SE 1 ⊼		SE 1	SE	SE	SE 1 ⊼	SE 1	SE	SE	SE 1 ⊼	SE 1		SE	SE	SE 1 ⊼	SE 1	SE	SE
London Charing Cross ⊖	d	14 46		15 08	15 23	15 16		15 38		15 53	15 46		16 08	16 23	16 16		16 38	16 53		16 46		17 08	17 23	17 16	
London Waterloo (East) ⊖	d	14 49		15 11	15 26	15 19		15 41		15 56	15 49		16 11	16 26	16 19		16 41	16 56		16 49		17 11	17 26	17 19	
London Cannon Street ⊖	d																								
London Bridge ⊖	d	14 54		15 16	15 31	15 24		15 46		16 01	15 54		16 16	16 31	16 24		16 46	17 01		16 54		17 16	17 31	17 24	
New Cross ⊖	d																								
St Johns	d																								
Lewisham	d	15 03				15 33					16 03				16 33					17 03				17 33	
Hither Green	d	15 07				15 37					16 07				16 37					17 07				17 37	
Grove Park	d	15 10				15 40					16 10				16 40					17 10				17 40	
Sundridge Park	d																								
Bromley North	a																								
Elmstead Woods	d	15 13				15 43					16 13				16 43					17 13				17 43	
Chislehurst	d	15 16				15 46					16 16				16 46					17 16				17 46	
Petts Wood	d	15 19	15 25			15 49	15 55				16 19	16 25			16 49	16 55				17 19	17 25			17 49	17 55
Orpington	a	15 22	15 28	15 31	15 46	15 52	15 58	16 01		16 16	16 22	16 28	16 31	16 46	16 52	16 58	17 01	17 16		17 22	17 28	17 31	17 46	17 52	17 58
	d			15 32	15 46	15 53		16 02		16 16			16 32	16 46	16 53		17 02	17 16				17 32	17 46	17 53	
Chelsfield	d					15 56									16 56									17 56	
Knockholt	d					15 59									16 59									17 59	
Dunton Green	d					16 04									17 04									18 04	
Sevenoaks	a			15 41	15 55	16 07		16 11		16 25			16 41	16 55	17 07		17 11	17 25				17 41	17 55	18 07	
	d			15 42	15 56			16 12		16 26			16 42	16 56			17 12	17 26				17 42	17 56		
Hildenborough	d			15 48									16 48									17 48			
Tonbridge	a			15 52	16 04			16 20		16 34			16 52	17 04			17 20	17 34				17 52	18 04		

Table 204

Sundays

London - Grove Park, Bromley North, Orpington, Sevenoaks and Tonbridge

		SE 1 ⊼	SE 1	SE		SE	SE 1 ⊼	SE 1	SE	SE	SE 1 ⊼	SE 1	SE	SE		SE 1 ⊼	SE 1	SE	SE	SE 1 ⊼	SE 1	SE	SE	SE 1 ⊼
London Charing Cross 4 ⊖	d	17 38	17 53	17 46			18 08	18 23	18 16		18 38	18 53	18 46			19 08	19 23	19 16		19 38	19 53	19 46		20 08
London Waterloo (East) 4 ⊖	d	17 41	17 56	17 49			18 11	18 26	18 19		18 41	18 56	18 49			19 11	19 26	19 19		19 41	19 56	19 49		20 11
London Cannon Street 4 ⊖	d																							
London Bridge 4 ⊖	d	17 46	18 01	17 54			18 16	18 31	18 24		18 46	19 01	18 54			19 16	19 31	19 24		19 46	20 01	19 54		20 16
New Cross 4 ⊖	d																							
St Johns	d																							
Lewisham 4	d			18 03					18 33				19 03					19 33				20 03		
Hither Green 4	d			18 07					18 37				19 07					19 37				20 07		
Grove Park 4	d			18 10					18 40				19 10					19 40				20 10		
Sundridge Park	d																							
Bromley North	a																							
Elmstead Woods	d			18 13					18 43				19 13					19 43				20 13		
Chislehurst	d			18 16					18 46				19 16					19 46				20 16		
Petts Wood 4	d			18 19		18 25			18 49	18 55			19 19	19 25				19 49	19 55			20 19	20 25	
Orpington 4	a	18 01	18 16	18 22		18 28	18 31	18 46	18 52	18 58	19 01	19 16	19 22	19 28		19 31	19 46	19 52	19 58	20 01	20 16	20 22	20 28	20 31
	d	18 02	18 16				18 32	18 46	18 53		19 02	19 16				19 32	19 46	19 53		20 02	20 16			20 32
Chelsfield 3	d								18 56									19 56						
Knockholt	d								18 59									19 59						
Dunton Green	d								19 04									20 04						
Sevenoaks 4	a	18 11	18 25				18 41	18 55	19 07		19 11	19 25				19 41	19 55	20 07		20 11	20 25			20 41
	d	18 12	18 26				18 42	18 56			19 12	19 26				19 42	19 56			20 12	20 26			20 42
Hildenborough	d						18 48									19 48								20 48
Tonbridge 4	a	18 20	18 34				18 52	19 04			19 20	19 34				19 52	20 04			20 20	20 34			20 52

		SE 1	SE	SE	SE 1	SE	SE	SE 1	SE 1	SE		SE	SE 1	SE	SE	SE 1	SE 1	SE	SE	SE 1		SE	SE	SE 1	SE 1
London Charing Cross 4 ⊖	d	20 23	20 16		20 38	20 46		21 08	21 23	21 16			21 38	21 46		22 08	22 23	22 16		22 38		22 46		23 08	23 23
London Waterloo (East) 4 ⊖	d	20 26	20 19		20 41	20 49		21 11	21 26	21 19			21 41	21 49		22 11	22 26	22 19		22 41		22 49		23 11	23 26
London Cannon Street 4 ⊖	d																								
London Bridge 4 ⊖	d	20 31	20 24		20 46	20 54		21 16	21 31	21 24			21 46	21 54		22 16	22 31	22 24		22 46		22 54		23 16	23 31
New Cross 4 ⊖	d																								
St Johns	d																								
Lewisham 4	d		20 33			21 03				21 33				22 03				22 33				23 03			
Hither Green 4	d		20 37			21 07				21 37				22 07				22 37				23 07			
Grove Park 4	d		20 40			21 10				21 40				22 10				22 40				23 10			
Sundridge Park	d																								
Bromley North	a																								
Elmstead Woods	d		20 43			21 13				21 43				22 13				22 43				23 13			
Chislehurst	d		20 46			21 16				21 46				22 16				22 46				23 16			
Petts Wood 4	d		20 49	20 55		21 19	21 25			21 49		21 55		22 19	22 25			22 49	22 55			23 19	23 25		
Orpington 4	a	20 46	20 52	20 58	21 01	21 22	21 28	21 31	21 46	21 52		21 58	22 01	22 22	22 28	22 31	22 46	22 52	22 58	23 01		23 22	23 29	23 31	23 46
	d	20 46	20 53		21 02			21 32	21 46	21 53			22 02			22 32	22 46			23 02				23 32	23 46
Chelsfield 3	d		20 56							21 56							22 49								23 49
Knockholt	d		20 59							21 59															
Dunton Green	d		21 04							22 04															
Sevenoaks 4	a	20 55	21 07		21 11			21 41	21 55	22 07			22 11			22 41	22 57			23 11				23 41	23 57
	d	20 56			21 12			21 42	21 56				22 12			22 42	22 57			23 12				23 42	23 57
Hildenborough	d							21 48								22 48								23 48	
Tonbridge 4	a	21 04			21 20			21 52	22 04				22 20			22 52	23 05			23 20				23 52	00 05

		SE	SE	SE 1	SE
London Charing Cross 4 ⊖	d	23 16		23 38	23 46
London Waterloo (East) 4 ⊖	d	23 19		23 41	23 49
London Cannon Street 4 ⊖	d				
London Bridge 4 ⊖	d	23 24		23 46	23 54
New Cross 4 ⊖	d				
St Johns	d				
Lewisham 4	d	23 33			00 02
Hither Green 4	d	23 37			00 06
Grove Park 4	d	23 40			00 10
Sundridge Park	d				
Bromley North	a				
Elmstead Woods	d	23 43			00 13
Chislehurst	d	23 46			00 15
Petts Wood 4	d	23 49	23 55		00 19
Orpington 4	a	23 52	23 59	00 01	00 22
	d			00 02	
Chelsfield 3	d				
Knockholt	d				
Dunton Green	d				
Sevenoaks 4	a			00 11	
	d			00 12	
Hildenborough	d				
Tonbridge 4	a			00 20	

Table 204

Mondays to Fridays

Tonbridge, Sevenoaks, Orpington, Bromley North, Grove Park - London

		SE MX 1	SE MX	SE	SE	SE	SE 1	SE	SE 1	SE		SE 1	SE	SE 1	SE 1	SE	SE 1	SE	SE	SE		SE 1	SE 1	SE	SE 1
Tonbridge 4	d	23b14			04 56		05 31		05 50			06 00		06 06	06 19		06 40					06 32	06 44		07 02
Hildenborough	d	23p18			05 00		05 35					06 04			06 23							06 36			
Sevenoaks 4	a	23p24			05 06		05 42		05 58			06 10		06 14	06 30		06 48					06 43	06 52		07 10
	d	23p25			05 07		05 43		05 59			06 11	06 02	06 15	06 32		06 49			06 36		06 44	06 53		07 11
Dunton Green	d												06 05							06 39					
Knockholt	d												06 10							06 44					
Chelsfield 3	d	23p32			05 14		05 50						06 13							06 47					
Orpington 4	a	23p36			05 18		05 54		06 08			06 19	06 16	06 23						06 50		06 53	07 02		
	d	23p37		05 10	05 20	05 40	05 54	06 01	06 09	06 10		06 20	06 22	06 24				06 40	06 43	06 53		06 54	07 04		
Petts Wood 4	d			05 13	05 23	05 43		06 04		06 13			06 25					06 43	06 46	06 56					
Chislehurst	d				05 26			06 07					06 28						06 49	06 59					
Elmstead Woods	d				05 28			06 09					06 30						06 51	07 01					
Bromley North	d		00 23													06 25								06 45	
Sundridge Park	d		00 25													06 27								06 47	
Grove Park 4	d		00a28		05 31			06 12					06 34			06a30			06 54	07 04				06a50	
Hither Green 4	d				05 35			06 16					06 38						06 58	07 08					
Lewisham 4	d							06 22					06 43						07 04						
St Johns	a																								
New Cross 4 ⊖	a				05 40			06 25																	
London Bridge 4 ⊖	a	23p53			05 45		06 09	06 31	06 24			06 38	06 51	06 39	06 54		07 14			07 18		07 09	07 22		07 36
London Cannon Street 4 ⊖	a											06 42								07 25			07 29		
London Waterloo (East) 4 ⊖	a	23p57			05 50		06 14	06 36	06 29				06 56	06 44	06 59		07 19		07 16			07 14			07 41
London Charing Cross 4 ⊖	a	00 01			05 53		06 18	06 39	06 33				07 02	06 49	07 05		07 25		07 22			07 20			07 47

		SE	SE 1	SE	SE	SE 1		SE 1	SE	SE 1	SE	SE	SE 1	SE 1	SE	SE		SE 1	SE	SE	SE 1	SE	SE	SE 1	SE 1 ⊼
Tonbridge 4	d		07 11			06 51		07 15		07 22			07 31	07 35				07 42			07 51			07 59	08 03
Hildenborough	d		07 15			06 55		07 19					07 35	07 39							07 55				
Sevenoaks 4	a		07 22			07 02		07 26		07 31			07 42	07 46				07 50			08 02			08 07	08 11
	d		07 23		06 56	07 03		07 27		07 32		07 17	07 43	07 47				07 51		07 37	08 03			08 07	08 11
Dunton Green	d				06 59							07 20								07 40					
Knockholt	d				07 04							07 25								07 45					
Chelsfield 3	d		07 32		07 07							07 28	07 52							07 48	08 12				
Orpington 4	a				07 10	07 13						07 31								07 51					
	d	07 03		07 10	07 13	07 14					07 22	07 33				07 38			07 42	07 53			07 57		
Petts Wood 4	d	07 06		07 13	07 16						07 25	07 36				07 41			07 45	07 56			08 00		
Chislehurst	d	07 09			07 19						07 28	07 39							07 48	07 59			08 03		
Elmstead Woods	d	07 11			07 21						07 31	07 41							07 50	08 01			08 05		
Bromley North	d								07 15						07 35							07 55			
Sundridge Park	d								07 17						07 37							07 57			
Grove Park 4	d	07 14			07 24				07a20		07 34	07 44			07a40				07 53	08 05		08a00	08 09		
Hither Green 4	d	07 18			07 28						07 39	07 48							07 57						
Lewisham 4	d	07 25									07 44								08 03						
St Johns	a																								
New Cross 4 ⊖	a																								
London Bridge 4 ⊖	a		07 50		07 37	07 29		07 53			07 53	07 59	08 09	08 13						08 18	08 29			08 35	
London Cannon Street 4 ⊖	a				07 44			07 59				08 06		08 20						08 26				08 41	
London Waterloo (East) 4 ⊖	a	07 36	07 55			07 34				08 00	07 58		08 14					08 20	08 16		08 34		08 24		08 40
London Charing Cross 4 ⊖	a	07 42	08 01			07 40				08 06	08 04		08 20					08 26	08 22		08 40		08 30		08 46

		SE		SE 1	SE	SE	SE 1	SE	SE 1	SE	SE	SE		SE 1	SE	SE 1	SE	SE	SE	SE	SE	SE		SE 1	SE 1
Tonbridge 4	d			08 11			08 15		08 22					08 32		08 40								08 44	08 50
Hildenborough	d			08 15			08 19							08 36										08 48	
Sevenoaks 4	a			08 22			08 26		08 30					08 42		08 48								08 54	08 58
	d			08 23		07 57	08 27		08 31			08 17		08 43		08 49			08 37					08 55	08 59
Dunton Green	d					08 00						08 20							08 40						
Knockholt	d					08 05						08 25							08 45						
Chelsfield 3	d			08 32		08 08						08 28		08 52					08 48						
Orpington 4	a					08 12						08 31							08 51					09 03	09 08
	d	08 02			08 10	08 13				08 22	08 26	08 32					08 40	08 43	08 52		08 55	09 03		09 04	09 09
Petts Wood 4	d	08 05			08 13	08 16				08 25	08 29	08 35					08 43	08 46	08 55		08 58	09 06			
Chislehurst	d	08 08				08 19				08 28		08 38						08 49	08 58			09 09			
Elmstead Woods	d	08 10				08 21				08 30		08 40						08 51	09 00			09 11			
Bromley North	d							08 15							08 35					08 55					
Sundridge Park	d							08 17							08 37					08 57					
Grove Park 4	d	08 13				08 24		08a20		08 33		08 44			08a40			08 54	09 04	09a00		09 14			
Hither Green 4	d	08 17								08 37								08 58	09 08			09 18			
Lewisham 4	d	08 23																09 04				09 24			
St Johns	a																	09 06				09 26			
New Cross 4 ⊖	a																	09 08				09 28			
London Bridge 4 ⊖	a			08 49		08 39	08 55					08 59		09 11		09 14		09 17	09 20			09 33		09 22	09 26
London Cannon Street 4 ⊖	a					08 46	09 02					09 06						09 23				09 40		09 28	
London Waterloo (East) 4 ⊖	a	08 36		08 54					09 00	08 52				09 16		09 19			09 25						09 31
London Charing Cross 4 ⊖	a	08 42		09 00					09 04	08 58				09 22		09 25			09 31						09 37

b previous night, arr. 2308

Tonbridge, Sevenoaks, Orpington, Bromley North, Grove Park - London

		SE 1 🛒	SE	SE	SE 1	SE	SE	SE		SE 1 🛒	SE 1	SE	SE	SE 1	SE	SE	SE	SE 1 🛒		SE 1 🛒	SE	SE	SE 1	SE	SE
Tonbridge	d	09 10			09 02					09 20	09 40			09 32				09 50		10 10			10 02		
Hildenborough	d				09 06									09 36									10 06		
Sevenoaks	a	09 18			09 13					09 28	09 48			09 43				09 58		10 18			10 13		
	d	09 19		09 06	09 14					09 29	09 49		09 36	09 44				09 59		10 19		10 06	10 14		
Dunton Green	d			09 09									09 39									10 09			
Knockholt	d			09 14									09 44									10 14			
Chelsfield	d			09 17									09 47									10 17			
Orpington	a			09 20	09 24					09 38			09 50	09 53				10 08				10 20	10 23		
	d		09 10	09 21	09 24		09 25	09 33		09 39		09 40	09 51	09 54		09 55	10 03	10 09			10 10	10 21	10 24		10 25
Petts Wood	d		09 13	09 24			09 28	09 36				09 43	09 54			09 58	10 06				10 13	10 24			10 28
Chislehurst	d			09 27				09 40					09 58				10 10					10 28			
Elmstead Woods	d			09 29				09 42					10 00				10 12					10 30			
Bromley North	d					09 23									09 53									10 23	
Sundridge Park	d					09 25									09 55									10 25	
Grove Park	d			09 32		09a28		09 45					10 03		09a58		10 15					10 33		10a28	
Hither Green	d			09 36				09 49					10 07				10 19					10 37			
Lewisham	d							09 54									10 24								
St Johns	a							09 56									10 26								
New Cross ⊖	a							09 58									10 28								
London Bridge ⊖	a	09 43		09 49	09 40			10 04		09 55	10 13		10 19	10 10			10 34	10 25		10 43		10 49	10 40		
London Cannon Street ⊖	a							10 08									10 38								
London Waterloo (East) ⊖	a	09 48		09 54	09 45					09 59	10 19		10 23	10 15				10 29		10 49		10 53	10 45		
London Charing Cross ⊖	a	09 54		10 00	09 51					10 03	10 22		10 27	10 19				10 33		10 52		10 57	10 49		

		SE	SE 1 🛒	SE 1 🛒		SE	SE	SE 1	SE	SE	SE	SE 1 🛒	SE 1 🛒	SE		SE	SE 1	SE	SE	SE	SE 1 🛒	SE 1 🛒	SE	SE	
Tonbridge	d		10 20	10 40				10 32				10 50	11 10				11 02				11 20	11 40			
Hildenborough	d							10 36									11 06								
Sevenoaks	a		10 28	10 48				10 43				10 58	11 18				11 13				11 28	11 48			
	d		10 29	10 49			10 36	10 44				10 59	11 19			11 06	11 14				11 29	11 49		11 36	
Dunton Green	d						10 39									11 09								11 39	
Knockholt	d						10 44									11 14								11 44	
Chelsfield	d						10 47									11 17								11 47	
Orpington	a		10 38				10 50	10 53				11 08				11 20	11 23				11 38			11 50	
	d	10 33	10 39			10 40	10 51	10 54		10 55	11 03	11 09		11 10		11 21	11 24		11 25	11 33	11 39		11 40	11 51	
Petts Wood	d	10 36				10 43	10 54			10 58	11 06			11 13		11 24			11 28	11 36			11 43	11 54	
Chislehurst	d	10 40					10 58				11 10					11 28				11 40				11 58	
Elmstead Woods	d	10 42					11 00				11 12					11 30				11 42				12 00	
Bromley North	d								10 53									11 23							
Sundridge Park	d								10 55									11 25							
Grove Park	d	10 45					11 03		10a58		11 15					11 33		11a28		11 45				12 03	
Hither Green	d	10 49					11 07				11 19					11 37				11 49				12 07	
Lewisham	d	10 54									11 24									11 54					
St Johns	a	10 56									11 26									11 56					
New Cross ⊖	a	10 58									11 28									11 58					
London Bridge ⊖	a	11 04	10 55	11 13			11 19	11 10			11 34	11 25	11 43			11 49	11 40			12 04	11 55	12 13		12 19	
London Cannon Street ⊖	a	11 08									11 38									12 08					
London Waterloo (East) ⊖	a		10 59	11 19			11 23	11 15				11 29	11 49			11 53	11 45				11 59	12 19		12 23	
London Charing Cross ⊖	a		11 03	11 22			11 27	11 19				11 33	11 52			11 57	11 49				12 03	12 22		12 27	

		SE 1	SE	SE	SE	SE 1 🛒	SE 1 🛒	SE	SE	SE 1		SE	SE	SE	SE 1 🛒	SE 1 🛒	SE	SE	SE 1	SE		SE	SE	SE 1 🛒	SE 1 🛒
Tonbridge	d	11 32				11 50	12 10			12 02					12 20	12 40			12 32					12 50	13 10
Hildenborough	d	11 36								12 06									12 36						
Sevenoaks	a	11 43				11 58	12 18			12 13					12 28	12 48			12 43					12 58	13 18
	d	11 44				11 59	12 19		12 06	12 14					12 29	12 49		12 36	12 44					12 59	13 19
Dunton Green	d								12 09									12 39							
Knockholt	d								12 14									12 44							
Chelsfield	d								12 17									12 47							
Orpington	a	11 53				12 08			12 20	12 23					12 38			12 50	12 53					13 08	
	d	11 54		11 55	12 03	12 09		12 10	12 21	12 24			12 25	12 33	12 39		12 40	12 51	12 54			12 55	13 03	13 09	
Petts Wood	d			11 58	12 06			12 13	12 24				12 28	12 36			12 43	12 54				12 58	13 06		
Chislehurst	d				12 10				12 28					12 40				12 58					13 10		
Elmstead Woods	d				12 12				12 30					12 42				13 00					13 12		
Bromley North	d		11 53									12 23								12 53					
Sundridge Park	d		11 55									12 25								12 55					
Grove Park	d		11a58		12 15				12 33			12a28		12 45				13 03		12a58			13 15		
Hither Green	d				12 19				12 37					12 49				13 07					13 19		
Lewisham	d				12 24									12 54									13 24		
St Johns	a				12 26									12 56									13 26		
New Cross ⊖	a				12 28									12 58									13 28		
London Bridge ⊖	a	12 10			12 34	12 25	12 43		12 49	12 40				13 04	12 55	13 13		13 19	13 10				13 34	13 25	13 43
London Cannon Street ⊖	a				12 38									13 08									13 38		
London Waterloo (East) ⊖	a	12 15				12 29	12 49		12 53	12 45					12 59	13 19		13 23	13 15					13 29	13 49
London Charing Cross ⊖	a	12 19				12 33	12 52		12 57	12 49					13 03	13 22		13 27	13 19					13 33	13 52

Table 204 Mondays to Fridays

Tonbridge, Sevenoaks, Orpington, Bromley North, Grove Park - London

		SE	SE ThX	SE ThO	SE 1	SE		SE	SE	SE 1 🛒	SE 1 🛒	SE	SE	SE 1	SE	SE		SE	SE 1 🛒	SE 1 🛒	SE	SE	SE 1	SE	SE
Tonbridge	d				13 02					13 20	13 40			13 32					13 50	14 10			14 02		
Hildenborough	d				13 06									13 36									14 06		
Sevenoaks	a				13 13					13 28	13 48			13 43					13 58	14 18			14 13		
	d		13 06	13 06	13 14					13 29	13 49		13 36	13 44					13 59	14 19		14 06	14 14		
Dunton Green	d		13 09	13 09									13 39									14 09			
Knockholt	d		13 14	13 14									13 44									14 14			
Chelsfield	d		13 17	13 17									13 47									14 17			
Orpington	a		13 20	13 20	13 23					13 38			13 50	13 53					14 08			14 20	14 23		
	d	13 10	13 21	13 21	13 24			13 25	13 33	13 39		13 40	13 51	13 54		13 55		14 03	14 09		14 10	14 21	14 24		14 25
Petts Wood	d	13 13	13 24	13 24				13 28	13 36			13 43	13 54			13 58		14 06			14 13	14 24			14 28
Chislehurst	d		13 28	13 28					13 40				13 58					14 10				14 28			
Elmstead Woods	d		13 30	13 30					13 42				14 00					14 12				14 30			
Bromley North	d					13 23									13 53									14 23	
Sundridge Park	d					13 25									13 55									14 25	
Grove Park	d		13 33	13 33		13a28			13 45				14 03		13a58			14 15				14 33		14a28	
Hither Green	d		13 37	13 37					13 49				14 07					14 19				14 37			
Lewisham	d								13 54									14 24							
St Johns	a								13 56									14 26							
New Cross ⊖	a								13 58									14 28							
London Bridge ⊖	a		13 49	13 49	13 40				14 04	13 55	14 13		14 19	14 10				14 34	14 25	14 43		14 49	14 40		
London Cannon Street ⊖	a								14 08									14 38							
London Waterloo (East) ⊖	a		13 53	13 54	13 45					13 59	14 19		14 23	14 15					14 29	14 49		14 53	14 45		
London Charing Cross ⊖	a		13 57	13 57	13 49					14 03	14 22		14 27	14 19					14 33	14 52		14 57	14 49		

		SE		SE 1 🛒	SE 1 🛒	SE	SE	SE 1	SE	SE	SE	SE 1 🛒		SE 1 🛒	SE	SE	SE 1	SE	SE	SE	SE 1	SE 1 🛒		SE	SE
Tonbridge	d			14 20	14 40			14 32				14 50		15 10			15 02				15 20	15 40			
Hildenborough	d							14 36									15 06								
Sevenoaks	a			14 28	14 48			14 43				14 58		15 18			15 13				15 28	15 48			
	d			14 29	14 49		14 36	14 44				14 59		15 19		15 06	15 14				15 29	15 49			15 36
Dunton Green	d						14 39									15 09									15 39
Knockholt	d						14 44									15 14									15 44
Chelsfield	d						14 47									15 17									15 47
Orpington	a			14 38			14 50	14 53				15 08				15 20	15 23				15 38				15 50
	d	14 33		14 39		14 40	14 51	14 54		14 55	15 03	15 09			15 10	15 21	15 24		15 25	15 33	15 39			15 40	15 51
Petts Wood	d	14 36				14 43	14 54			14 58	15 06				15 13	15 24			15 28	15 36				15 43	15 54
Chislehurst	d	14 40					14 58				15 10					15 28				15 40					15 58
Elmstead Woods	d	14 42					15 00				15 12					15 30				15 42					16 00
Bromley North	d								14 53									15 23							
Sundridge Park	d								14 55									15 25							
Grove Park	d	14 45					15 03		14a58		15 15					15 33		15a28		15 45					16 03
Hither Green	d	14 49					15 07				15 19					15 37				15 49					16 07
Lewisham	d	14 54									15 24									15 54					
St Johns	a	14 56									15 26									15 56					
New Cross ⊖	a	14 58									15 28									15 58					
London Bridge ⊖	a	15 04		14 55	15 13		15 19	15 10			15 34	15 25		15 43		15 49	15 40			16 04	15 55	16 14			16 19
London Cannon Street ⊖	a	15 08									15 38									16 08					
London Waterloo (East) ⊖	a			14 59	15 19		15 23	15 15				15 29		15 48		15 55	15 45				15 59	16 20			16 24
London Charing Cross ⊖	a			15 03	15 22		15 27	15 19				15 33		15 52		15 58	15 49				16 03	16 24			16 28

		SE 1	SE	SE	SE	SE 1 🛒	SE 1 🛒	SE		SE	SE 1	SE	SE	SE	SE 1 🛒	SE 1 🛒	SE	SE		SE 1	SE	SE	SE	SE 1 🛒	SE
Tonbridge	d	15 32				15 50	16 10				16 02				16 20	16 40				16 32				16 50	
Hildenborough	d	15 36									16 06									16 36					
Sevenoaks	a	15 43				15 58	16 18				16 13				16 28	16 48				16 43				16 58	
	d	15 44				15 59	16 19			16 06	16 14				16 29	16 52		16 35		16 44				16 59	
Dunton Green	d									16 09								16 38							
Knockholt	d									16 14								16 43							
Chelsfield	d									16 17	16 21							16 46							
Orpington	a	15 53				16 07				16 20	16 24				16 38			16 49		16 53				17 08	
	d	15 54		15 55	16 03	16 08		16 10		16 21	16 25		16 25	16 33	16 39		16 40	16 51		16 54		16 55	17 03	17 09	
Petts Wood	d			15 58	16 06			16 13		16 24			16 28	16 36			16 43	16 54				16 58	17 06		
Chislehurst	d				16 10					16 28				16 40				16 58					17 10		
Elmstead Woods	d				16 12					16 30				16 42				17 00					17 12		
Bromley North	d		15 53									16 23									16 47				17 07
Sundridge Park	d		15 55									16 25									16 49				17 09
Grove Park	d		15a58		16 15					16 33		16a28		16 45				17 03			16a52		17 15		17a12
Hither Green	d				16 19					16 37				16 49				17 09					17 19		
Lewisham	d				16 24																		17 24		
St Johns	a				16 26																		17 26		
New Cross ⊖	a				16 28																		17 28		
London Bridge ⊖	a	16 11			16 34	16 25	16 46			16 48	16 42			17 01	16 56	17 17				17 11			17 34	17 27	
London Cannon Street ⊖	a				16 38																		17 38	17 32	
London Waterloo (East) ⊖	a	16 16				16 29	16 52			16 54	16 48			17 06	17 00	17 22		17 24		17 16					
London Charing Cross ⊖	a	16 20				16 33	16 56			16 58	16 52			17 10	17 04	17 26		17 29		17 20					

Tonbridge, Sevenoaks, Orpington, Bromley North, Grove Park - London

		SE 1 ⌶	SE	SE		SE	SE 1	SE	SE	SE	SE 1	SE 1 ⌶	SE	SE		SE	SE	SE 1	SE	SE 1 ⌶	SE 1 ⌶	SE	SE	SE 1	
Tonbridge 4	d	17 10					17 02				17 20	17 40						17 32		17 50	18 10			18 02	
Hildenborough	d						17 06											17 36						18 06	
Sevenoaks 4	a	17 18					17 13				17 28	17 48						17 43		17 58	18 18			18 13	
	d	17 19				17 05	17 14				17 29	17 49		17 35				17 44		17 59	18 19		18 06	18 14	
Dunton Green	d					17 08								17 38									18 09		
Knockholt	d					17 13								17 43									18 14		
Chelsfield 3	d					17 16								17 46									18 17		
Orpington 4	a					17 19	17 23				17 38			17 49				17 53		18 08			18 20	18 23	
	d		17 10	17 13		17 20	17 24	17 24		17 37	17 39		17 40	17 50			17 53	17 54	18 03	18 09		18 09	18 21	18 24	
Petts Wood 4	d		17 13			17 23		17 28		17 40			17 43	17 53			17 56		18 06			18 12	18 24		
Chislehurst	d					17 28				17 44				17 58					18 10				18 28		
Elmstead Woods	d					17 30				17 46				18 00					18 12				18 30		
Bromley North	d								17 27							17 50									
Sundridge Park	d								17 29							17 52									
Grove Park 4	d					17 33			17a32	17 49				18 03		17a55			18 15				18 33		
Hither Green 4	d			17 21		17 37				17 53				18 07					18 19				18 37		
Lewisham 4	d																		18 24						
St Johns	a									17 57									18 26						
New Cross 4	⊖ a									17 59									18 28						
London Bridge 4	⊖ a	17 44				17 49	17 41			18 06	17 58	18 16		18 18				18 09	18 34	18 25	18 43		18 48	18 40	
London Cannon Street 4	⊖ a									18 11									18 38						
London Waterloo (East) 4	⊖ a	17 50		17 36		17 53	17 46				18 02	18 20		18 23				18 14		18 29	18 48		18 53	18 45	
London Charing Cross 4	⊖ a	17 53		17 40		17 57	17 50				18 06	18 25		18 27				18 18		18 35	18 52		18 57	18 49	

		SE	SE 1 ⌶	SE	SE	SE	SE 1 ⌶	SE	SE	SE 1		SE	SE	SE	SE 1	SE 1 ⌶	SE	SE	SE 1	SE		SE	SE 1	SE 1 ⌶	SE
Tonbridge 4	d		18 23				18 40			18 32					18 50	19 10			19 02				19 20	19 40	
Hildenborough	d									18 36									19 06						
Sevenoaks 4	a		18 31				18 48			18 43					18 59	19 18			19 13				19 28	19 48	
	d		18 32				18 49		18 35	18 44					18 59	19 19		19 06	19 14				19 29	19 49	
Dunton Green	d								18 38									19 09							
Knockholt	d								18 43									19 14							
Chelsfield 3	d								18 46									19 17							
Orpington 4	a								18 49	18 53					19 08			19 20	19 23				19 38		
	d			18 25		18 33		18 40	18 50	18 54			18 55	19 03	19 08		19 10	19 21	19 24			19 25	19 39		19 40
Petts Wood 4	d			18 28		18 36		18 43	18 54				18 58	19 06			19 13	19 24				19 28			19 43
Chislehurst	d					18 40			18 58					19 10				19 28							
Elmstead Woods	d					18 42			19 00					19 12				19 30							
Bromley North	d	18 11			18 33							18 54								19 18					
Sundridge Park	d	18 13			18 35							18 56								19 20					
Grove Park 4	d	18a16			18a38	18 45			19 03			18a59		19 15				19 33		19a23					
Hither Green 4	d					18 49			19 07					19 19				19 37							
Lewisham 4	d					18 54								19 24				19 43							
St Johns	a					18 56								19 26											
New Cross 4	⊖ a					18 58								19 28											
London Bridge 4	⊖ a		18 55			19 04	19 13		19 19	19 10				19 34	19 25	19 43		19 52	19 40				19 54	20 13	
London Cannon Street 4	⊖ a					19 10								19 38											
London Waterloo (East) 4	⊖ a		18 59				19 17		19 23	19 14					19 29	19 48		19 56	19 45				19 59	20 18	
London Charing Cross 4	⊖ a		19 04				19 21		19 27	19 18					19 33	19 52		20 00	19 49				20 03	20 22	

		SE	SE 1	SE	SE	SE 1		SE	SE 1 ⌶	SE	SE	SE 1	SE	SE 1	SE	SE		SE 1	SE 1	SE	SE 1	SE	SE	SE 1	SE
Tonbridge 4	d		19 32			19 51			20 10			20 02		20 40				20 32	20 50		21 10			21 02	
Hildenborough	d		19 36									20 06						20 36						21 06	
Sevenoaks 4	a		19 43			19 59			20 18			20 13		20 48				20 43	20 58		21 18			21 13	
	d	19 36	19 44			20 00			20 19		20 06	20 14		20 49		20 35		20 44	20 59		21 19		21 05	21 14	
Dunton Green	d	19 39									20 09					20 38							21 08		
Knockholt	d	19 44									20 14					20 43							21 13		
Chelsfield 3	d	19 47									20 17					20 46							21 16		
Orpington 4	a	19 50	19 53			20 08					20 20	20 23				20 49		20 52	21 08				21 19	21 22	
	d	19 51	19 54		19 55	20 09				20 10	20 21	20 24			20 40	20 51		20 53	21 09			21 10	21 21	21 23	
Petts Wood 4	d	19 54			19 58					20 13	20 24				20 43	20 54						21 13	21 24		
Chislehurst	d	19 58									20 28					20 58							21 28		
Elmstead Woods	d	20 00									20 30					21 00							21 30		
Bromley North	d			19 42				20 02					20 27							20 53					21 23
Sundridge Park	d			19 44				20 04					20 29							20 55					21 25
Grove Park 4	d	20 03		19a47				20a07			20 33		20a32			21 03				20a58			21 33		21a28
Hither Green 4	d	20 07									20 37					21 07							21 37		
Lewisham 4	d	20 13									20 43					21 13							21 43		
St Johns	a																								
New Cross 4	⊖ a																								
London Bridge 4	⊖ a	20 22	20 10			20 24			20 42		20 52	20 39		21 13		21 22		21 08	21 24		21 43		21 52	21 38	
London Cannon Street 4	⊖ a																								
London Waterloo (East) 4	⊖ a	20 26	20 15			20 29			20 47		20 56	20 44		21 18		21 26		21 13	21 29		21 48		21 56	21 43	
London Charing Cross 4	⊖ a	20 30	20 19			20 33			20 51		21 00	20 48		21 22		21 30		21 18	21 33		21 52		22 00	21 48	

Tonbridge, Sevenoaks, Orpington, Bromley North, Grove Park - London

		SE 1		SE	SE	SE 1	SE 1	SE	SE 1	SE	SE	SE 1		SE	SE 1	SE	SE	SE 1	SE 1	SE	SE	SE		SE 1	SE
Tonbridge 4	d	21 40				21 32	21 50		22 10			22 02			22 40			22 31	22 50					23b14	
Hildenborough	d					21 36						22 06						22 35						23 18	
Sevenoaks 4	a	21 48				21 43	21 58		22 18			22 13			22 48			22 41	22 58					23 24	
	d	21 49			21 35	21 44	21 59		22 19		22 05	22 14			22 49			22 42	22 59					23 25	
Dunton Green	d				21 38						22 08														
Knockholt	d				21 43						22 13														
Chelsfield 3	d				21 46						22 16							22 49						23 32	
Orpington 4	a				21 49	21 52	22 08				22 19	22 22						22 52	23 08					23 36	
	d			21 40	21 51	21 53	22 09			22 10	22 21	22 23				22 40	22 51	22 53	23 09		23 10	23 21		23 37	
Petts Wood 4	d			21 43	21 54					22 13	22 24					22 43	22 54				23 13	23 24			
Chislehurst	d				21 58						22 28						22 58					23 28			
Elmstead Woods	d				22 00						22 30						23 00					23 30			
Bromley North	d							21 53						22 23						22 53					23 23
Sundridge Park	d							21 55						22 25						22 55					23 25
Grove Park 4	d				22 03			21a58			22 33			22a28			23 03			22a58		23 33			23a28
Hither Green 4	d				22 07						22 37						23 07					23 37			
Lewisham 4	d				22 13						22 43						23 13					23 43			
St Johns	a																								
New Cross 4	⊖ a																								
London Bridge 4	⊖ a	22 13			22 22	22 08	22 24		22 43		22 52	22 38			23 13		23 22	23 08	23 24			23 50		23 53	
London Cannon Street 4	⊖ a																								
London Waterloo (East) 4	⊖ a	22 18			22 26	22 13	22 29		22 48		22 56	22 43			23 18		23 26	23 13	23 29			23 54		23 57	
London Charing Cross 4	⊖ a	22 22			22 30	22 18	22 33		22 52		23 00	22 48			23 22		23 30	23 18	23 33			23 59		00 01	

		SE
Tonbridge 4	d	
Hildenborough	d	
Sevenoaks 4	a	
	d	
Dunton Green	d	
Knockholt	d	
Chelsfield 3	d	
Orpington 4	a	
	d	
Petts Wood 4	d	
Chislehurst	d	
Elmstead Woods	d	
Bromley North	d	23 53
Sundridge Park	d	23 55
Grove Park 4	d	23a58
Hither Green 4	d	
Lewisham 4	d	
St Johns	a	
New Cross 4	⊖ a	
London Bridge 4	⊖ a	
London Cannon Street 4	⊖ a	
London Waterloo (East) 4	⊖ a	
London Charing Cross 4	⊖ a	

Saturdays

		SE 1	SE	SE	SE	SE	SE	SE 1	SE	SE	SE		SE	SE 1	SE	SE	SE 1	SE	SE	SE 1	SE	SE	SE	SE 1	SE 1
Tonbridge 4	d	23c14						06 02						06 32			06 50			07 02				07 20	07 40
Hildenborough	d	23p18						06 06						06 36						07 06					
Sevenoaks 4	a	23p24						06 13						06 43			06 58			07 13				07 28	07 48
	d	23p25			05 36		06 06	06 14					06 36	06 44			06 59		07 06	07 14				07 29	07 49
Dunton Green	d				05 39		06 09						06 39						07 09						
Knockholt	d				05 44		06 14						06 44						07 14						
Chelsfield 3	d	23p32			05 47		06 17						06 47						07 17						
Orpington 4	a	23p36			05 50		06 20	06 23					06 50	06 53			07 08		07 20	07 23				07 38	
	d	23p37		05 44	05 51	06 10	06 21	06 24		06 25	06 40		06 51	06 54		06 55	07 09	07 10	07 21	07 24		07 25	07 33	07 39	
Petts Wood 4	d			05 47	05 54	06 13	06 24			06 28	06 43		06 54			06 58		07 13	07 24			07 28	07 36		
Chislehurst	d				05 58		06 28						06 58						07 28				07 40		
Elmstead Woods	d				06 00		06 30						07 00						07 30				07 42		
Bromley North	d		00 23						06 23						06 53						07 23				
Sundridge Park	d		00 25						06 25						06 55						07 25				
Grove Park 4	d		00a28		06 03		06 33		06a28				07 03		06a58				07 33		07a28		07 45		
Hither Green 4	d				06 07		06 37						07 07						07 37				07 49		
Lewisham 4	d				06 12		06 42						07 12										07 54		
St Johns	a																						07 56		
New Cross 4	⊖ a																						07 58		
London Bridge 4	⊖ a	23p53			06 21		06 51	06 39					07 21	07 09			07 24		07 49	07 39			08 04	07 55	08 13
London Cannon Street 4	⊖ a																						08 08		
London Waterloo (East) 4	⊖ a	23p57			06 25		06 55	06 43					07 25	07 13			07 29		07 53	07 43				07 59	08 19
London Charing Cross 4	⊖ a	00 01			06 29		06 59	06 47					07 29	07 17			07 33		07 57	07 48				08 03	08 22

b arr. 2308

c previous night, arr. 2308

Table 204

Tonbridge, Sevenoaks, Orpington, Bromley North, Grove Park - London

		SE	SE	SE 1	SE	SE		SE	SE 1	SE 1	SE	SE	SE 1	SE	SE	SE		SE 1	SE 1	SE	SE	SE 1	SE	SE	SE
Tonbridge ■	d			07 32					07 50	08 10			08 02					08 20	08 40			08 32			
Hildenborough	d			07 36									08 06									08 36			
Sevenoaks ■	a			07 43					07 58	08 18			08 13					08 28	08 48			08 43			
	d		07 36	07 44					07 59	08 19		08 06	08 14					08 29	08 49		08 36	08 44			
Dunton Green	d		07 39									08 09									08 39				
Knockholt	d		07 44									08 14									08 44				
Chelsfield ■	d		07 47									08 17									08 47				
Orpington ■	a		07 50	07 53					08 08			08 20	08 23					08 38			08 50	08 53			
	d	07 40	07 51	07 54		07 55		08 03	08 09		08 10	08 21	08 24		08 25	08 33		08 39		08 40	08 51	08 54		08 55	09 03
Petts Wood ■	d	07 43	07 54			07 58		08 06			08 13	08 24			08 28	08 36				08 43	08 54			08 58	09 06
Chislehurst	d		07 58					08 10				08 28				08 40					08 58				09 10
Elmstead Woods	d		08 00					08 12				08 30				08 42					09 00				09 12
Bromley North	d				07 53									08 23									08 53		
Sundridge Park	d				07 55									08 25									08 55		
Grove Park ■	d		08 03		07a58			08 15				08 33		08a28		08 45					09 03		08a58		09 15
Hither Green ■	d		08 07					08 19				08 37				08 49					09 07				09 19
Lewisham ■ ⇌	d							08 24								08 54									09 24
St Johns	a							08 26								08 56									09 26
New Cross ■ ⊖	a							08 28								08 58									09 28
London Bridge ■ ⊖	a		08 19	08 10				08 34	08 25	08 43		08 49	08 40			09 04		08 55	09 13		09 19	09 10			09 34
London Cannon Street ■ ⊖	a							08 38								09 08									09 38
London Waterloo (East) ■ ⊖	a		08 23	08 15					08 29	08 49		08 53	08 45					08 59	09 19		09 23	09 15			
London Charing Cross ■ ⊖	a		08 27	08 19					08 33	08 52		08 57	08 49					09 03	09 22		09 27	09 19			

		SE 1		SE 1	SE	SE	SE 1	SE	SE	SE	SE 1 🍴	SE 1 🍴		SE	SE	SE 1	SE	SE	SE	SE 1 🍴	SE 1 🍴	SE		SE	SE 1
Tonbridge ■	d	08 50		09 10			09 02				09 20	09 40				09 32				09 50	10 10				10 02
Hildenborough	d						09 06									09 36									10 06
Sevenoaks ■	a	08 58		09 18			09 13				09 28	09 48				09 43				09 58	10 18				10 13
	d	08 59		09 19		09 06	09 14				09 29	09 49			09 36	09 44				09 59	10 19			10 06	10 14
Dunton Green	d					09 09									09 39									10 09	
Knockholt	d					09 14									09 44									10 14	
Chelsfield ■	d					09 17									09 47									10 17	
Orpington ■	a	09 08				09 20	09 23				09 38				09 50	09 53				10 08				10 20	10 23
	d	09 09			09 10	09 21	09 24		09 25	09 33	09 39			09 40	09 51	09 54		09 55	10 03	10 09		10 10		10 21	10 24
Petts Wood ■	d				09 13	09 24			09 28	09 36				09 43	09 54			09 58	10 06			10 13		10 24	
Chislehurst	d					09 28				09 40					09 58				10 10					10 28	
Elmstead Woods	d					09 30				09 42					10 00				10 12					10 30	
Bromley North	d							09 23									09 53								
Sundridge Park	d							09 25									09 55								
Grove Park ■	d					09 33		09a28		09 45					10 03		09a58		10 15					10 33	
Hither Green ■	d					09 37				09 49					10 07				10 19					10 37	
Lewisham ■ ⇌	d									09 54									10 24						
St Johns	a									09 56									10 26						
New Cross ■ ⊖	a									09 58									10 28						
London Bridge ■ ⊖	a	09 25		09 43		09 49	09 40			10 04	09 55	10 13			10 19	10 10			10 34	10 25	10 43			10 49	10 40
London Cannon Street ■ ⊖	a									10 08									10 38						
London Waterloo (East) ■ ⊖	a	09 29		09 49		09 53	09 45				09 59	10 19			10 23	10 15				10 29	10 49			10 53	10 45
London Charing Cross ■ ⊖	a	09 33		09 52		09 57	09 49				10 03	10 22			10 27	10 19				10 33	10 52			10 57	10 49

		SE	SE	SE	SE 1 🍴	SE 1 🍴	SE	SE		SE 1	SE	SE	SE	SE 1 🍴	SE 1 🍴	SE	SE	SE 1		SE	SE	SE	SE 1 🍴	SE 1 🍴	SE
Tonbridge ■	d				10 20	10 40				10 32				10 50	11 10			11 02					11 20	11 40	
Hildenborough	d									10 36								11 06							
Sevenoaks ■	a				10 28	10 48				10 43				10 58	11 18			11 13					11 28	11 48	
	d				10 29	10 49		10 36		10 44				10 59	11 19		11 06	11 14					11 29	11 49	
Dunton Green	d							10 39									11 09								
Knockholt	d							10 44									11 14								
Chelsfield ■	d							10 47									11 17								
Orpington ■	a				10 38			10 50		10 53				11 08			11 20	11 23					11 38		
	d		10 25	10 33	10 39		10 40	10 51		10 54		10 55	11 03	11 09		11 10	11 21	11 24			11 25	11 33	11 39		11 40
Petts Wood ■	d		10 28	10 36			10 43	10 54				10 58	11 06			11 13	11 24				11 28	11 36			11 43
Chislehurst	d			10 40				10 58					11 10				11 28					11 40			
Elmstead Woods	d			10 42				11 00					11 12				11 30					11 42			
Bromley North	d	10 23									10 53									11 23					
Sundridge Park	d	10 25									10 55									11 25					
Grove Park ■	d	10a28		10 45				11 03			10a58		11 15				11 33			11a28		11 45			
Hither Green ■	d			10 49				11 07					11 19				11 37					11 49			
Lewisham ■ ⇌	d			10 54									11 24									11 54			
St Johns	a			10 56									11 26									11 56			
New Cross ■ ⊖	a			10 58									11 28									11 58			
London Bridge ■ ⊖	a			11 04	10 55	11 13		11 19		11 10			11 34	11 25	11 43		11 49	11 40				12 04	11 55	12 13	
London Cannon Street ■ ⊖	a			11 08									11 38									12 08			
London Waterloo (East) ■ ⊖	a				10 59	11 19		11 23		11 15				11 29	11 49		11 53	11 45					11 59	12 19	
London Charing Cross ■ ⊖	a				11 03	11 22		11 27		11 19				11 33	11 52		11 57	11 49					12 03	12 22	

Table 204

Tonbridge, Sevenoaks, Orpington, Bromley North, Grove Park - London

		SE	SE 1	SE		SE	SE	SE 1 🍴	SE 1 🍴	SE	SE	SE 1	SE	SE		SE	SE 1 🍴	SE 1 🍴	SE	SE	SE 1	SE	SE	SE	
Tonbridge ■	d		11 32					11 50	12 10			12 02					12 20	12 40			12 32				
Hildenborough	d		11 36									12 06									12 36				
Sevenoaks ■	a		11 43					11 58	12 18			12 13					12 28	12 48			12 43				
	d	11 36	11 44					11 59	12 19		12 06	12 14					12 29	12 49		12 36	12 44				
Dunton Green	d	11 39									12 09									12 39					
Knockholt	d	11 44									12 14									12 44					
Chelsfield ■	d	11 47									12 17									12 47					
Orpington ■	a	11 50	11 53					12 08			12 20	12 23					12 38			12 50	12 53				
	d	11 51	11 54			11 55	12 03	12 09		12 10	12 21	12 24		12 25		12 33	12 39		12 40	12 51	12 54		12 55	13 03	
Petts Wood ■	d	11 54				11 58	12 06			12 13	12 24			12 28		12 36			12 43	12 54			12 58	13 06	
Chislehurst	d	11 58					12 10				12 28					12 40				12 58				13 10	
Elmstead Woods	d	12 00					12 12				12 30					12 42				13 00				13 12	
Bromley North	d			11 53									12 23									12 53			
Sundridge Park	d			11 55									12 25									12 55			
Grove Park ■	d	12 03		11a58			12 15				12 33		12a28			12 45				13 03		12a58		13 15	
Hither Green ■	d	12 07					12 19				12 37					12 49				13 07				13 19	
Lewisham ■ ⇌	d						12 24									12 54								13 24	
St Johns	a						12 26									12 56								13 26	
New Cross ■ ⊖	a						12 28									12 58								13 28	
London Bridge ■ ⊖	a	12 19	12 10				12 34	12 25	12 43		12 49	12 40				13 04	12 55	13 13		13 19	13 10			13 34	
London Cannon Street ■ ⊖	a						12 38									13 08								13 38	
London Waterloo (East) ■ ⊖	a	12 23	12 15					12 29	12 49		12 53	12 45					12 59	13 19		13 23	13 15				
London Charing Cross ■ ⊖	a	12 27	12 19					12 33	12 52		12 57	12 49					13 03	13 22		13 27	13 19				

		SE 1 🍴	SE 1 🍴	SE	SE	SE 1	SE	SE	SE	SE 1 🍴		SE 1 🍴	SE	SE	SE 1	SE	SE	SE	SE 1 🍴	SE 1 🍴		SE	SE	SE 1	SE
Tonbridge ■	d	12 50	13 10			13 02				13 20		13 40			13 32				13 50	14 10				14 02	
Hildenborough	d					13 06									13 36									14 06	
Sevenoaks ■	a	12 58	13 18			13 13				13 28		13 48			13 43				13 58	14 18				14 13	
	d	12 59	13 19		13 06	13 14				13 29		13 49		13 36	13 44				13 59	14 19			14 06	14 14	
Dunton Green	d				13 09									13 39									14 09		
Knockholt	d				13 14									13 44									14 14		
Chelsfield ■	d				13 17									13 47									14 17		
Orpington ■	a	13 08			13 20	13 23				13 38				13 50	13 53				14 08				14 20	14 23	
	d	13 09		13 10	13 21	13 24		13 25	13 33	13 39			13 40	13 51	13 54		13 55	14 03	14 09			14 10	14 21	14 24	
Petts Wood ■	d			13 13	13 24			13 28	13 36				13 43	13 54			13 58	14 06				14 13	14 24		
Chislehurst	d				13 28				13 40					13 58				14 10					14 28		
Elmstead Woods	d				13 30				13 42					14 00				14 12					14 30		
Bromley North	d						13 23									13 53									14 23
Sundridge Park	d						13 25									13 55									14 25
Grove Park ■	d				13 33		13a28		13 45					14 03		13a58		14 15					14 33		14a28
Hither Green ■	d				13 37				13 49					14 07				14 19					14 37		
Lewisham ■ ⇌	d								13 54									14 24							
St Johns	a								13 56									14 26							
New Cross ■ ⊖	a								13 58									14 28							
London Bridge ■ ⊖	a	13 25	13 43		13 49	13 40			14 04	13 55		14 13		14 19	14 10			14 34	14 25	14 43			14 49	14 40	
London Cannon Street ■ ⊖	a								14 08									14 38							
London Waterloo (East) ■ ⊖	a	13 29	13 49		13 53	13 45				13 59		14 19		14 23	14 15				14 29	14 49			14 53	14 45	
London Charing Cross ■ ⊖	a	13 33	13 52		13 57	13 49				14 03		14 22		14 27	14 19				14 33	14 52			14 57	14 49	

		SE	SE	SE 1 🍴	SE 1 🍴	SE		SE	SE 1	SE	SE	SE	SE 1 🍴	SE 1 🍴	SE	SE		SE 1	SE	SE	SE	SE 1 🍴	SE 1 🍴	SE	SE
Tonbridge ■	d			14 20	14 40				14 32				14 50	15 10				15 02				15 20	15 40		
Hildenborough	d								14 36									15 06							
Sevenoaks ■	a			14 28	14 48				14 43				14 58	15 18				15 13				15 28	15 48		
	d			14 29	14 49			14 36	14 44				14 59	15 19		15 06		15 14				15 29	15 49		15 36
Dunton Green	d							14 39								15 09									15 39
Knockholt	d							14 44								15 14									15 44
Chelsfield ■	d							14 47								15 17									15 47
Orpington ■	a			14 38				14 50	14 53				15 08			15 20		15 23				15 38			15 50
	d	14 25	14 33	14 39		14 40		14 51	14 54		14 55	15 03	15 09		15 10	15 21		15 24		15 25	15 33	15 39		15 40	15 51
Petts Wood ■	d	14 28	14 36			14 43		14 54			14 58	15 06			15 13	15 24				15 28	15 36			15 43	15 54
Chislehurst	d		14 40					14 58				15 10				15 28					15 40				15 58
Elmstead Woods	d		14 42					15 00				15 12				15 30					15 42				16 00
Bromley North	d									14 53									15 23						
Sundridge Park	d									14 55									15 25						
Grove Park ■	d		14 45					15 03		14a58		15 15				15 33			15a28		15 45				16 03
Hither Green ■	d		14 49					15 07				15 19				15 37					15 49				16 07
Lewisham ■ ⇌	d		14 54									15 24									15 54				
St Johns	a		14 56									15 26									15 56				
New Cross ■ ⊖	a		14 58									15 28									15 58				
London Bridge ■ ⊖	a		15 04	14 55	15 13			15 19	15 10			15 34	15 25	15 43		15 49		15 40			16 04	15 55	16 13		16 19
London Cannon Street ■ ⊖	a		15 08									15 38									16 08				
London Waterloo (East) ■ ⊖	a			14 59	15 19			15 23	15 15				15 29	15 49		15 53		15 45				15 59	16 19		16 23
London Charing Cross ■ ⊖	a			15 03	15 22			15 27	15 19				15 33	15 52		15 57		15 49				16 03	16 22		16 27

Table 204

Saturdays

Tonbridge, Sevenoaks, Orpington, Bromley North, Grove Park - London

		SE ■		SE	SE	SE	SE ■ ⊥	SE ■ ⊥	SE	SE	SE ■	SE		SE	SE	SE ■ ⊥	SE ■ ⊥	SE	SE	SE ■	SE	SE		SE	SE ■ ⊥
Tonbridge ■	d	15 32					15 50	16 10			16 02					16 20	16 40			16 32					16 50
Hildenborough	d	15 36									16 06									16 36					
Sevenoaks ■	a	15 43					15 58	16 18			16 13					16 28	16 48			16 43					16 58
	d	15 44					15 59	16 19		16 06	16 14					16 29	16 49		16 36	16 44					16 59
Dunton Green	d									16 09									16 39						
Knockholt	d									16 14									16 44						
Chelsfield ■	d									16 17									16 47						
Orpington ■	a	15 53					16 08			16 20	16 23					16 38			16 50	16 53					17 08
	d	15 54			15 55	16 03	16 09		16 10	16 21	16 24			16 25	16 33	16 39		16 40	16 51	16 54		16 55		17 03	17 09
Petts Wood ■	d				15 58	16 06			16 13	16 24				16 28	16 36			16 43	16 54			16 58		17 06	
Chislehurst	d					16 10				16 28					16 40				16 58					17 10	
Elmstead Woods	d					16 12				16 30					16 42				17 00					17 12	
Bromley North	d			15 53								16 23									16 53				
Sundridge Park	d			15 55								16 25									16 55				
Grove Park ■	d			15a58		16 15				16 33		16a28			16 45				17 03		16a58			17 15	
Hither Green ■	d					16 19				16 37					16 49				17 07					17 19	
Lewisham ■	d					16 24									16 54									17 24	
St Johns	a					16 26									16 56									17 26	
New Cross ■ ⊖	a					16 28									16 58									17 28	
London Bridge ■ ⊖	a	16 10				16 34	16 25	16 43		16 49	16 40				17 04	16 55	17 13		17 19	17 10				17 34	17 25
London Cannon Street ■ ⊖	a					16 38									17 08									17 38	
London Waterloo (East) ■ ⊖	a	16 15					16 29	16 49		16 53	16 45					16 59	17 19		17 23	17 15					17 29
London Charing Cross ■ ⊖	a	16 19					16 33	16 52		16 57	16 49					17 03	17 22		17 27	17 19					17 33

		SE ■ ⊥	SE	SE	SE ■	SE	SE	SE		SE ■ ⊥	SE ■ ⊥	SE	SE	SE ■	SE	SE	SE	SE ■ ⊥		SE ■ ⊥	SE	SE	SE ■	SE	SE
Tonbridge ■	d	17 10			17 02					17 20	17 40			17 32				17 50		18 10			18 02		
Hildenborough	d				17 06									17 36									18 06		
Sevenoaks ■	a	17 18			17 13					17 28	17 48			17 43				17 58		18 18			18 13		
	d	17 19		17 06	17 14					17 29	17 49		17 36	17 44				17 59		18 19		18 06	18 14		
Dunton Green	d			17 09									17 39									18 09			
Knockholt	d			17 14									17 44									18 14			
Chelsfield ■	d			17 17									17 47									18 17			
Orpington ■	a			17 20	17 23					17 38			17 50	17 53				18 08				18 20	18 23		
	d		17 10	17 21	17 24		17 25	17 33		17 39		17 40	17 51	17 54		17 55	18 03	18 09			18 10	18 21	18 24		18 25
Petts Wood ■	d		17 13	17 24			17 28	17 36				17 43	17 54			17 58	18 06				18 13	18 24			18 28
Chislehurst	d			17 28				17 40					17 58				18 10					18 28			
Elmstead Woods	d			17 30				17 42					18 00				18 12					18 30			
Bromley North	d					17 23									17 53									18 23	
Sundridge Park	d					17 25									17 55									18 25	
Grove Park ■	d			17 33		17a28		17 45					18 03		17a58		18 15					18 33		18a28	
Hither Green ■	d			17 37				17 49					18 07				18 19					18 37			
Lewisham ■	d							17 54									18 24								
St Johns	a							17 56									18 26								
New Cross ■ ⊖	a							17 58									18 28								
London Bridge ■ ⊖	a	17 43		17 49	17 40			18 04		17 55	18 13		18 19	18 10			18 34	18 25		18 43		18 49	18 40		
London Cannon Street ■ ⊖	a							18 08									18 38								
London Waterloo (East) ■ ⊖	a	17 49		17 53	17 45					17 59	18 19		18 23	18 15				18 29		18 49		18 53	18 45		
London Charing Cross ■ ⊖	a	17 52		17 57	17 49					18 03	18 22		18 27	18 19				18 33		18 52		18 57	18 49		

		SE ■	SE ■ ⊥	SE		SE	SE ■	SE	SE	SE ■	SE	SE	SE	SE		SE ■ ⊥	SE ■	SE	SE	SE	SE	SE ■ ⊥	SE ■	SE	
Tonbridge ■	d	18 20	18 40				18 32			18 50						19 10	19 18					19 40	19 50		
Hildenborough	d						18 36										19 22								
Sevenoaks ■	a	18 28	18 48				18 43			18 58						19 18	19 28					19 48	19 58		
	d	18 29	18 49			18 36	18 44			18 59		19 06				19 19	19 29		19 36			19 49	19 59		
Dunton Green	d					18 39						19 09							19 39						
Knockholt	d					18 44						19 14							19 44						
Chelsfield ■	d					18 47						19 17							19 47						
Orpington ■	a	18 38				18 50	18 53			19 08		19 20				19 27	19 38		19 50			19 57	20 08		
	d	18 39		18 40		18 51	18 54		18 55	19 09	19 10	19 21		19 25		19 28	19 39	19 40	19 51		19 55	19 58	20 09	20 10	
Petts Wood ■	d			18 43		18 54			18 58		19 13	19 24		19 28				19 43	19 54		19 58			20 13	
Chislehurst	d					18 58						19 28							19 58						
Elmstead Woods	d					19 00						19 30							20 00						
Bromley North	d							18 53					19 23							19 53					
Sundridge Park	d							18 55					19 25							19 55					
Grove Park ■	d					19 03		18a58				19 33	19a28						20 03	19a58					
Hither Green ■	d					19 07						19 37							20 07						
Lewisham ■	d					19 12						19 43							20 13						
St Johns	a																								
New Cross ■ ⊖	a																								
London Bridge ■ ⊖	a	18 55	19 13			19 21	19 10			19 24		19 52				19 43	19 54		20 22			20 13	20 24		
London Cannon Street ■ ⊖	a																								
London Waterloo (East) ■ ⊖	a	18 59	19 19			19 25	19 15			19 29		19 56				19 48	19 59		20 26			20 18	20 29		
London Charing Cross ■ ⊖	a	19 03	19 22			19 29	19 19			19 33		20 00				19 51	20 03		20 30			20 21	20 33		

Table 204

Saturdays

Tonbridge, Sevenoaks, Orpington, Bromley North, Grove Park - London

		SE	SE ■	SE ■	SE	SE	SE	SE ■	SE ■	SE		SE	SE	SE ■	SE ■	SE	SE	SE	SE ■	SE ■		SE	SE	SE	SE ■
Tonbridge ■	d		20 10	20 18				20 40	20 50					21 10	21 18				21 40	21 50					22 10
Hildenborough	d			20 22											21 22										
Sevenoaks ■	a		20 18	20 28				20 48	20 58					21 18	21 28				21 48	21 58					22 18
	d	20 06	20 19	20 29			20 36	20 49	20 59				21 06	21 19	21 29			21 36	21 49	21 59				22 06	22 19
Dunton Green	d	20 09					20 39						21 09					21 39						22 09	
Knockholt	d	20 14					20 44						21 14					21 44						22 14	
Chelsfield ■	d	20 17					20 47						21 17					21 47						22 17	
Orpington ■	a	20 20	20 27	20 38			20 50	20 57	21 08				21 20	21 27	21 38			21 50	21 57	22 08				22 20	22 27
	d	20 21	20 28	20 39		20 40	20 51	20 58	21 09			21 10	21 21	21 28	21 39		21 40	21 51	21 58	22 09			22 10	22 21	22 28
Petts Wood ■	d	20 24				20 43	20 54					21 13	21 24				21 43	21 54					22 13	22 24	
Chislehurst	d	20 28					20 58						21 28					21 58						22 28	
Elmstead Woods	d	20 30					21 00						21 30					22 00						22 30	
Bromley North	d				20 23					20 53						21 23						21 53			
Sundridge Park	d				20 25					20 55						21 25						21 55			
Grove Park ■	d	20 33			20a28		21 03			20a58			21 33			21a28		22 03				21a58		22 33	
Hither Green ■	d	20 37					21 07						21 37					22 07						22 37	
Lewisham ■	d	20 43					21 13						21 43					22 13						22 43	
St Johns	a																								
New Cross ■ ⊖	a																								
London Bridge ■ ⊖	a	20 52	20 43	20 54			21 22	21 13	21 24				21 52	21 43	21 54			22 22	22 13	22 24				22 52	22 43
London Cannon Street ■ ⊖	a																								
London Waterloo (East) ■ ⊖	a	20 56	20 48	20 59			21 26	21 18	21 29				21 56	21 48	21 59			22 26	22 18	22 29				22 56	22 48
London Charing Cross ■ ⊖	a	21 00	20 51	21 03			21 30	21 21	21 33				22 00	21 51	22 03			22 30	22 21	22 33				23 00	22 51

		SE ■	SE	SE	SE	SE ■		SE ■	SE	SE	SE	SE ■	SE	SE
Tonbridge ■	d	22 18				22 40		22 50				23b14		
Hildenborough	d	22 22										23 18		
Sevenoaks ■	a	22 28				22 48		22 58				23 24		
	d	22 29				22 49		22 59				23 25		
Dunton Green	d													
Knockholt	d													
Chelsfield ■	d											23 32		
Orpington ■	a	22 38				22 57		23 08				23 36		
	d	22 39		22 40	22 51	22 58		23 09		23 10	23 21	23 37		
Petts Wood ■	d			22 43	22 54					23 13	23 24			
Chislehurst	d				22 58						23 28			
Elmstead Woods	d				23 00						23 30			
Bromley North	d		22 23						22 53				23 23	23 53
Sundridge Park	d		22 25						22 55				23 25	23 55
Grove Park ■	d		22a28		23 03				22a58		23 33		23a28	23a58
Hither Green ■	d				23 07						23 37			
Lewisham ■	d				23 13						23 43			
St Johns	a													
New Cross ■ ⊖	a													
London Bridge ■ ⊖	a	22 54			23 22	23 13		23 24			23 50	23 53		
London Cannon Street ■ ⊖	a													
London Waterloo (East) ■ ⊖	a	22 59			23 26	23 18		23 29			23 54	23 57		
London Charing Cross ■ ⊖	a	23 03			23 30	23 21		23 33			23 58	00 01		

Sundays

		SE ■	SE	SE	SE	SE	SE	SE ■	SE	SE	SE	SE ■	SE ■	SE	SE	SE ■	SE	SE	SE ■	SE ■	SE	SE	SE ■	SE ■ ⊥	SE
Tonbridge ■	d	23c14						07 10				07 23	07 39			08 10			08 25	08 39			08 55	09 10	
Hildenborough	d	23p18											07 43							08 43					
Sevenoaks ■	a	23p24						07 18				07 31	07 49			08 18			08 33	08 49			09 03	09 18	
	d	23p25						07 19				07 32	07 49			08 19		08 25	08 33	08 49			09 03	09 19	
Dunton Green	d																	08 28							
Knockholt	d																	08 33							
Chelsfield ■	d	23p32										07 39						08 36							
Orpington ■	a	23p36						07 28				07 42	07 58			08 28		08 39	08 42	08 58			09 12	09 28	
	d	23p37		06 43	07 06	07 10	07 13	07 29	07 36	07 40	07 43	07 43	07 59	08 06	08 10	08 29	08 36	08 40	08 43	08 59	09 06	09 10	09 13	09 29	09 36
Petts Wood ■	d			06 46	07 09	07 13	07 16		07 39	07 43	07 46			08 09	08 13		08 39	08 43			09 09	09 13			09 39
Chislehurst	d					07 17				07 47					08 17			08 47				09 17			
Elmstead Woods	d					07 19				07 49					08 19			08 49				09 19			
Bromley North	d		00 23																						
Sundridge Park	d		00 25																						
Grove Park ■	d		00a28			07 22				07 52					08 22			08 52				09 22			
Hither Green ■	d					07 26				07 56					08 26			08 56				09 26			
Lewisham ■	d					07 31				08 01					08 31			09 01				09 31			
St Johns	a																								
New Cross ■ ⊖	a																								
London Bridge ■ ⊖	a	23p53				07 39		07 44		08 09		07 58	08 14		08 39	08 44		09 09	08 58	09 14		09 39	09 28	09 44	
London Cannon Street ■ ⊖	a																								
London Waterloo (East) ■ ⊖	a	23p57				07 44		07 49		08 14		08 03	08 19		08 44	08 49		09 14	09 03	09 19		09 44	09 33	09 49	
London Charing Cross ■ ⊖	a	00 01				07 48		07 53		08 18		08 07	08 23		08 49	08 53		09 18	09 07	09 23		09 49	09 37	09 53	

b arr. 2308

c previous night, arr. 2308

Table 204

Sundays

Tonbridge, Sevenoaks, Orpington, Bromley North, Grove Park - London

		SE	SE 1	SE 1 🍴	SE	SE	SE 1	SE 1 🍴	SE	SE	SE 1	SE 1 🍴	SE	SE	SE 1	SE 1 🍴	SE	SE	SE 1	SE 1 🍴	SE	SE	SE 1	SE 1 🍴
Tonbridge 4	d		09 25	09 39			09 55	10 10			10 25	10 39			10 55	11 10			11 25	11 39			11 55	12 10
Hildenborough	d			09 43								10 43								11 43				
Sevenoaks 4	a		09 33	09 49			10 03	10 18			10 33	10 49			11 03	11 18			11 33	11 49			12 03	12 18
	d	09 25	09 33	09 49			10 03	10 19		10 24	10 33	10 49			11 03	11 19		11 25	11 33	11 49			12 03	12 19
Dunton Green	d	09 28								10 27								11 28						
Knockholt	d	09 33								10 32								11 33						
Chelsfield 3	d	09 36								10 35								11 36						
Orpington 4	a	09 39	09 42	09 58			10 12	10 28		10 38	10 42	10 58			11 12	11 28		11 39	11 42	11 58			12 12	12 28
	d	09 41	09 43	09 59	10 06	10 10	10 13	10 29	10 36	10 40	10 43	10 59	11 06	11 10	11 13	11 29	11 36	11 40	11 43	11 59	12 06	12 10	12 13	12 29
Petts Wood 4	d	09 44			10 09	10 13			10 39	10 43			11 09	11 13			11 39	11 43			12 09	12 13		
Chislehurst	d	09 48				10 17				10 47				11 17				11 47				12 17		
Elmstead Woods	d	09 50				10 19				10 49				11 19				11 49				12 19		
Bromley North	d																							
Sundridge Park	d																							
Grove Park 4	d	09 53				10 22				10 52				11 22				11 52				12 22		
Hither Green 4	d	09 57				10 26				10 56				11 26				11 56				12 26		
Lewisham 4	d	10 02				10 31				11 01				11 31				12 01				12 31		
St Johns	a																							
New Cross 4 ⊖	a																							
London Bridge 4 ⊖	a	10 10	09 58	10 14		10 39	10 28	10 44		11 09	10 58	11 14		11 39	11 28	11 44		12 09	11 58	12 14		12 39	12 28	12 44
London Cannon Street 4 ⊖	a																							
London Waterloo (East) 4 ⊖	a	10 15	10 03	10 19		10 44	10 33	10 49		11 14	11 03	11 19		11 44	11 33	11 49		12 14	12 03	12 19		12 44	12 33	12 49
London Charing Cross 4 ⊖	a	10 15	10 07	10 23		10 49	10 37	10 53		11 18	11 07	11 23		11 49	11 37	11 53		12 18	12 07	12 23		12 49	12 37	12 53

		SE	SE	SE 1	SE 1 🍴	SE	SE	SE 1	SE 1 🍴	SE	SE	SE 1	SE 1 🍴	SE	SE	SE 1	SE 1 🍴	SE	SE	SE 1	SE 1 🍴	SE
Tonbridge 4	d			12 25	12 39			12 55	13 10			13 25	13 39			13 55	14 10			14 25	14 39	
Hildenborough	d				12 43								13 43								14 43	
Sevenoaks 4	a			12 33	12 49			13 03	13 18			13 33	13 49			14 03	14 18			14 33	14 49	
	d		12 25	12 33	12 49			13 03	13 19		13 25	13 33	13 49			14 03	14 19		14 24	14 33	14 49	
Dunton Green	d		12 28								13 28								14 27			
Knockholt	d		12 33								13 33								14 32			
Chelsfield 3	d		12 36								13 36								14 35			
Orpington 4	a		12 39	12 42	12 58			13 12	13 28		13 39	13 42	13 58			14 12	14 28		14 38	14 42	14 58	
	d	12 36	12 40	12 43	12 59	13 06	13 10	13 13	13 29	13 36	13 40	13 43	13 59	14 06	14 10	14 13	14 29	14 36	14 40	14 43	14 59	15 06
Petts Wood 4	d	12 39	12 43			13 09	13 13			13 39	13 43			14 09	14 13			14 39	14 43			15 09
Chislehurst	d		12 47				13 17				13 47				14 17				14 47			
Elmstead Woods	d		12 49				13 19				13 49				14 19				14 49			
Bromley North	d																					
Sundridge Park	d																					
Grove Park 4	d		12 52				13 22				13 52				14 22				14 52			
Hither Green 4	d		12 56				13 26				13 56				14 26				14 56			
Lewisham 4	d		13 01				13 31				14 01				14 31				15 01			
St Johns	a																					
New Cross 4 ⊖	a																					
London Bridge 4 ⊖	a		13 09	12 58	13 14		13 39	13 28	13 44		14 09	13 58	14 14		14 39	14 28	14 44		15 09	14 58	15 14	
London Cannon Street 4 ⊖	a																					
London Waterloo (East) 4 ⊖	a		13 14	13 03	13 19		13 44	13 33	13 49		14 14	14 03	14 19		14 44	14 33	14 49		15 14	15 03	15 19	
London Charing Cross 4 ⊖	a		13 18	13 07	13 23		13 49	13 37	13 53		14 18	14 07	14 23		14 49	14 37	14 53		15 18	15 07	15 23	

		SE	SE 1	SE 1 🍴	SE	SE	SE 1	SE 1 🍴	SE	SE	SE 1	SE 1 🍴	SE	SE	SE 1	SE 1 🍴	SE	SE	SE 1	SE 1 🍴	SE	SE	SE 1
Tonbridge 4	d		14 55	15 10			15 25	15 39			15 55	16 10			16 25	16 39			16 55	17 10			17 25
Hildenborough	d							15 43								16 43							
Sevenoaks 4	a		15 03	15 18			15 33	15 49			16 03	16 18			16 33	16 49			17 03	17 18			17 33
	d		15 03	15 19		15 25	15 33	15 49			16 03	16 19		16 25	16 33	16 49			17 03	17 19		17 24	17 33
Dunton Green	d					15 28								16 28								17 27	
Knockholt	d					15 33								16 33								17 32	
Chelsfield 3	d					15 36								16 36								17 35	
Orpington 4	a		15 12	15 28		15 39	15 42	15 58			16 12	16 28		16 39	16 42	16 58			17 12	17 28		17 38	17 42
	d	15 10	15 13	15 29	15 36	15 40	15 43	15 59	16 06	16 10	16 13	16 29	16 36	16 40	16 43	16 59	17 06	17 10	17 13	17 29	17 36	17 40	17 43
Petts Wood 4	d	15 13			15 39	15 43			16 09	16 13			16 39	16 43			17 09	17 13			17 39	17 43	
Chislehurst	d	15 17				15 47				16 17				16 47				17 17				17 47	
Elmstead Woods	d	15 19				15 49				16 19				16 49				17 19				17 49	
Bromley North	d																						
Sundridge Park	d																						
Grove Park 4	d	15 22				15 52				16 22				16 52				17 22				17 52	
Hither Green 4	d	15 26				15 56				16 26				16 56				17 26				17 56	
Lewisham 4	d	15 31				16 01				16 31				17 01				17 31				18 01	
St Johns	a																						
New Cross 4 ⊖	a																						
London Bridge 4 ⊖	a	15 39	15 28	15 44		16 09	15 58	16 14		16 39	16 28	16 44		17 09	16 58	17 14		17 39	17 28	17 44		18 09	17 58
London Cannon Street 4 ⊖	a																						
London Waterloo (East) 4 ⊖	a	15 44	15 33	15 49		16 14	16 03	16 19		16 44	16 33	16 49		17 14	17 03	17 19		17 44	17 33	17 49		18 14	18 03
London Charing Cross 4 ⊖	a	15 49	15 37	15 53		16 18	16 07	16 23		16 49	16 37	16 53		17 18	17 07	17 23		17 49	17 37	17 53		18 18	18 07

Table 204

Sundays

Tonbridge, Sevenoaks, Orpington, Bromley North, Grove Park - London

		SE 1 🍴	SE	SE	SE 1	SE 1 🍴	SE	SE	SE 1	SE 1 🍴	SE	SE	SE 1	SE 1 🍴	SE	SE	SE 1	SE 1	SE	SE	SE 1	SE
Tonbridge 4	d	17 39			17 55	18 10			18 25	18 39			18 55	19 10			19 25	19 39			20 10	
Hildenborough	d	17 43								18 43								19 43				
Sevenoaks 4	a	17 49			18 03	18 18			18 33	18 49			19 03	19 18			19 33	19 49			20 18	
	d	17 49			18 03	18 19		18 24	18 33	18 49			19 03	19 19		19 24	19 33	19 49			20 19	
Dunton Green	d							18 27								19 27						
Knockholt	d							18 32								19 32						
Chelsfield 3	d							18 35								19 35						
Orpington 4	a	17 58			18 12	18 28		18 38	18 42	18 58			19 12	19 28		19 38	19 42	19 58			20 28	
	d	17 59	18 06	18 10	18 13	18 29	18 36	18 40	18 43	18 59	19 06	19 10	19 13	19 29	19 36	19 40	19 43	19 59	20 06	20 10	20 29	20 36
Petts Wood 4	d		18 09	18 13			18 39	18 43			19 09	19 13			19 39	19 43			20 09	20 13		20 39
Chislehurst	d			18 17				18 47				19 17				19 47				20 17		
Elmstead Woods	d			18 19				18 49				19 19				19 49				20 19		
Bromley North	d																					
Sundridge Park	d																					
Grove Park 4	d			18 22				18 52				19 22				19 52				20 22		
Hither Green 4	d			18 26				18 56				19 26				19 56				20 26		
Lewisham 4	d			18 31				19 01				19 31				20 01				20 31		
St Johns	a																					
New Cross 4 ⊖	a																					
London Bridge 4 ⊖	a	18 14		18 39	18 28	18 44		19 09	18 58	19 14		19 39	19 28	19 44		20 09	19 58	20 14		20 39	20 44	
London Cannon Street 4 ⊖	a																					
London Waterloo (East) 4 ⊖	a	18 19		18 44	18 33	18 49		19 14	19 03	19 19		19 44	19 33	19 49		20 14	20 03	20 19		20 44	20 49	
London Charing Cross 4 ⊖	a	18 23		18 49	18 37	18 53		19 18	19 07	19 23		19 49	19 37	19 53		20 18	20 07	20 23		20 49	20 53	

		SE	SE 1	SE 1	SE	SE	SE 1	SE	SE	SE 1	SE 1	SE	SE	SE 1	SE	SE	SE 1	SE 1	SE
Tonbridge 4	d		20 25	20 39			21 10			21 25	21 39			22 10			22 25	22 39	
Hildenborough	d			20 43							21 43							22 43	
Sevenoaks 4	a		20 33	20 49			21 18			21 33	21 49			22 18			22 33	22 49	
	d	20 24	20 33	20 49			21 19		21 24	21 33	21 49			22 19		22 25	22 33	22 49	
Dunton Green	d	20 27							21 27							22 28			
Knockholt	d	20 32							21 32							22 33			
Chelsfield 3	d	20 35							21 35							22 36			
Orpington 4	a	20 38	20 42	20 58			21 28		21 38	21 42	21 58			22 28		22 39	22 42	22 58	
	d	20 40	20 43	20 59	21 06	21 10	21 29	21 36	21 40	21 43	21 59	22 06	22 10	22 29	22 36	22 40	22 43	22 59	23 10
Petts Wood 4	d	20 43			21 09	21 13		21 39	21 43			22 09	22 13		22 39	22 43			23 13
Chislehurst	d	20 47				21 17			21 47				22 17			22 47			23 17
Elmstead Woods	d	20 49				21 19			21 49				22 19			22 49			23 19
Bromley North	d																		
Sundridge Park	d																		
Grove Park 4	d	20 52				21 22			21 52				22 22			22 52			23 22
Hither Green 4	d	20 56				21 26			21 56				22 26			22 56			23 26
Lewisham 4	d	21 01				21 31			22 01				22 31			23 01			23 31
St Johns	a																		
New Cross 4 ⊖	a																		
London Bridge 4 ⊖	a	21 09	20 58	21 14		21 39	21 44		22 09	21 58	22 14		22 39	22 44		23 09	22 58	23 14	23 39
London Cannon Street 4 ⊖	a																		
London Waterloo (East) 4 ⊖	a	21 14	21 03	21 19		21 44	21 49		22 14	22 03	22 19		22 44	22 49		23 14	23 03	23 19	23 44
London Charing Cross 4 ⊖	a	21 18	21 07	21 23		21 49	21 53		22 18	22 07	22 23		22 49	22 53		23 18	23 07	23 23	23 49

Network Diagram for Tables 206, 207, 208

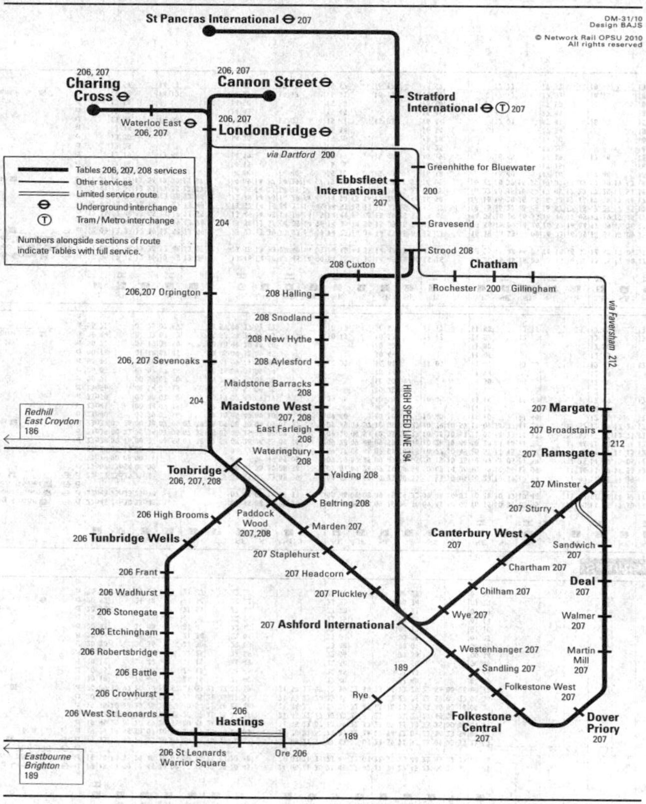

Table 206

Mondays to Fridays

London and Tonbridge - Tunbridge Wells and Hastings

			SE MO ■1	SE MX ■1	SE MO ■1	SE MX ■1	SE MX ■1	SE ■1	SE ■1	SE ■1	SE ■1		SE ■1	SE ■1	SE ■1	SE ■1	SE ■1	SE ■1	SE ■1	SE ■1	SE ■1		SE ■1 ⊥	SE ■1	SE ■1 ⊥	SE ■1
London Charing Cross ■4	⊖	d	22p23	22p45	23p23	23p30	23p45							06 15		06 45	07 00	07 15	07 29		08 00		08 17	08 27		09 00
London Waterloo (East) ■4	⊖	d	22p26	22p48	23p26	23p33	23p48							06 18		06 48	07 03	07 18	07 32		08 03		08 20	08 30		09 03
London Cannon Street ■4	⊖	d																		07 47					08 42	
London Bridge ■4	⊖	d	22p31	22p53	23p31	23p39	23p53							06 24		06 53	07 08	07 23	07 38	07 51	08 09		08 25	08 35	08 46	09 08
Orpington ■4		d	22p46	23p09	23p46	23p54	00 09							06 40		07 10	07 26	07 39	07 54	08 09	08 26		08 42	08 54	09 07	09 26
Sevenoaks ■4		d	22p57	23p19	23p57	00 05	00 19							06 50		07 19	07 35	07 49	08 07	08 19	08 35		08 52	09 03	09 17	09 35
Tonbridge ■4		a	23p05	23p27	00 05	00 15	00 27							06 58		07 27	07 45	07 58	08 17	08 27	08 47		09 00	09 13	09 25	09 46
		d	23p06	23p28	00 06	00 16	00 27	05 00	05 31	06 07	06 20		06 35	06 58	07 11	07 31	07 46	07 59	08 17	08 29	08 48		09 00	09 16	09 26	09 46
High Brooms		d	23p12	23p35	00 12	00 22	00 34	05 06	05 37	06 13	06 26		06 41	07 04	07 17	07 37	07 55	08 05	08 23	08 36	08 54		09 06	09 23	09 35	09 53
Tunbridge Wells ■4		a	23p16	23p39	00 16	00 26	00 38	05 10	05 40	06 17	06 30		06 45	07 08	07 22	07 41	08 02	08 08	08 27	08 40	08 58		09 10	09 27	09 39	09 57
		d	23p16	23p40	00 16		00 39			06 18			06 46			07 42		08 13		08 44			09 14		09 42	
Frant		d	23p21	23p45	00 21		00 44			06 23			06 52			07 47		08 18		08 49			09 19			
Wadhurst		d	23p26	23p50	00 26		00 48			06 28			06 56			07 52		08 24		08 54			09 25		09 50	
Stonegate		d	23p32	23p56	00 32		00 54			06 34			07 03			07 58		08 30		09 00			09 31			
Etchingham		d	23p36	00 01	00 36		00 59			06 38			07 08			08 02		08 34		09 04			09 36			
Robertsbridge		d	23p40	00 05	00 40		01 03			06 42			07 12			08 06		08 38		09 08			09 40			
Battle		d	23p48	00 13	00 48		01 10			06 50			07 20			08 15		08 46		09 16			09 47		10 05	
Crowhurst		d	23p52	00 16	00 52		01 14			06 54			07 25			08 18		08 49		09 19			09 51			
West St Leonards		d	23p57	00 21	00 57		01 19			06 59			07 32			08 23		08 54		09 24			09 56			
St Leonards Warrior Sq ■4		d	00 01	00 24	01 01		01 22			07 02			07 35			08 26		08 57		09 27			09 59		10 15	
Hastings ■4		a	00 04	00 27	01 04		01 25			07 06			07 38			08 29		09 00		09 32			10 02		10 19	
Ore		a								07 10																

			SE ■1 ⊥	SE ■1	SE ■1 ⊥	SE ■1	SE ■1 ⊥		SE ■1	SE ■1 ⊥	SE ■1	SE ■1 ⊥	SE ■1	SE ■1 ⊥	SE ■1	SE ■1 ⊥	SE ■1		SE ■1 ⊥	SE ■1	SE ■1 ⊥	SE ■1	SE ■1 ⊥	SE ■1	SE ■1 ⊥	SE ■1
London Charing Cross ■4	⊖	d		09 30	09 45	10 00	10 15		10 30	10 45	11 00	11 15	11 30	11 45	12 00	12 15	12 30		12 45	13 00	13 15	13 30	13 45	14 00	14 15	14 30
London Waterloo (East) ■4	⊖	d		09 33	09 48	10 03	10 18		10 33	10 48	11 03	11 18	11 33	11 48	12 03	12 18	12 33		12 48	13 03	13 18	13 33	13 48	14 03	14 18	14 33
London Cannon Street ■4	⊖	d	09 20																							
London Bridge ■4	⊖	d	09 25	09 39	09 53	10 09	10 23		10 39	10 53	11 09	11 23	11 39	11 53	12 09	12 23	12 39		12 53	13 09	13 23	13 39	13 53	14 09	14 23	14 39
Orpington ■4		d	09 42	09 56	10 09	10 26	10 39		10 56	11 09	11 26	11 39	11 56	12 09	12 26	12 39	12 56		13 09	13 26	13 39	13 56	14 09	14 26	14 39	14 56
Sevenoaks ■4		d	09 51	10 05	10 19	10 35	10 49		11 05	11 19	11 35	11 49	12 05	12 19	12 35	12 49	13 05		13 19	13 35	13 49	14 05	14 19	14 35	14 49	15 05
Tonbridge ■4		a	09 59	10 15	10 27	10 45	10 57		11 15	11 27	11 45	11 57	12 15	12 27	12 45	12 57	13 15		13 27	13 45	13 57	14 15	14 27	14 45	14 57	15 16
		d	10 00	10 16	10 28	10 46	10 58		11 16	11 28	11 46	11 58	12 16	12 28	12 46	12 58	13 16		13 28	13 46	13 58	14 16	14 28	14 46	14 58	15 16
High Brooms		d	10 06	10 23	10 35	10 54	11 05		11 23	11 35	11 53	12 05	12 23	12 35	12 53	13 05	13 23		13 35	13 53	14 05	14 23	14 35	14 53	15 05	15 23
Tunbridge Wells ■4		a	10 09	10 27	10 39	10 57	11 09		11 27	11 39	11 57	12 09	12 27	12 39	12 57	13 09	13 27		13 39	13 57	14 09	14 27	14 39	14 57	15 09	15 27
		d	10 13		10 40		11 12			11 40		12 10		12 40		13 10			13 40		14 10		14 40		15 10	
Frant		d	10 18				11 17					12 15				13 15					14 15				15 15	
Wadhurst		d	10 22		10 48		11 22			11 48		12 19		12 48		13 19			13 48		14 19		14 48		15 19	
Stonegate		d	10 28				11 28					12 25				13 25					14 25				15 25	
Etchingham		d	10 33				11 32					12 30				13 30					14 30				15 30	
Robertsbridge		d	10 37				11 36					12 34				13 34					14 34				15 34	
Battle		d	10 44		11 03		11 44			12 03		12 41		13 03		13 41			14 03		14 41		15 03		15 41	
Crowhurst		d	10 48				11 48					12 45				13 45					14 45				15 45	
West St Leonards		d	10 53				11 53					12 50				13 50					14 50				15 50	
St Leonards Warrior Sq ■4		d	10 56		11 13		11 56			12 13		12 53		13 13		13 53			14 13		14 53		15 13		15 53	
Hastings ■4		a	10 59		11 17		11 59			12 17		12 57		13 17		13 57			14 17		14 57		15 17		15 57	
Ore		a																								

			SE ■1 ⊥		SE ■1	SE ■1 ⊥	SE ■1	SE ■1 ⊥	SE ■1	SE ■1	SE ■1	SE ■1 ⊥	SE ■1		SE ■1	SE ■1 ⊥	SE ■1	SE ■1	SE ■1	SE ■1	SE ■1	SE ■1	SE ■1		SE ■1 ⊥	SE ■1
London Charing Cross ■4	⊖	d	14 45		15 00	15 15	15 30	15 45	16 00	16 15	16 28	16 41			17 01	17 19	17 23			17 45	18 03	18 07	18 32		18 45	
London Waterloo (East) ■4	⊖	d	14 48		15 03	15 18	15 33	15 48	16 03	16 18	16 31	16 44			17 04	17 22	17 26			17 48	18 06	18 10	18 35		18 48	
London Cannon Street ■4	⊖	d											17 02					17 37								19 04
London Bridge ■4	⊖	d	14 53		15 09	15 23	15 39	15 53	16 09	16 23	16 36	16 49	17 06		17 09		17 31	17 42		17 53		18 15	18 40		18 53	19 08
Orpington ■4		d	15 09		15 26	15 39	15 56	16 09	16 26		16 53															
Sevenoaks ■4		d	15 19		15 35	15 49	16 05	16 19	16 35	16 47	17 03	17 14	17 31		17 37		17 59			18 21		18 43	19 06		19 20	19 32
Tonbridge ■4		a	15 27		15 45	15 57	16 15	16 27	16 45	16 55	17 13	17 22	17 39		17 48		18 09			18 32		18 54	19 17		19 28	19 42
		d	15 28		15 46	15 58	16 16	16 28	16 46	16 55	17 13	17 22	17 41		17 48		18 11			18 32		18 54	19 17		19 29	19 42
High Brooms		d	15 35		15 53	16 05	16 23	16 35	16 53	17 01	17 21	17 28	17 47		17 54	18 04	18 17	18 21		18 38	18 47	19 00	19 23		19 35	19 49
Tunbridge Wells ■4		a	15 39		15 57	16 09	16 27	16 39	16 59	17 05	17 26	17 32	17 50		18 00	18 07	18 22	18 24	>	18 44	18 50	19 06	19 29		19 39	19 53
		d	15 40			16 13		16 39		17 05		17 37	17 51			18 08		18 29	18 33		18 55				19 40	19 54
Frant		d				16 18		16 44		17 10			17 56			18 13			18 38		19 00				19 45	19 59
Wadhurst		d	15 48			16 24		16 49		17 15		17 45	18 00			18 17		18 37	18 43		19 04				19 49	20 04
Stonegate		d				16 30		16 55		17 21			18 06			18 23			18 49		19 10				19 55	20 10
Etchingham		d				16 35		16 59		17 25		17 53	18 11			18 28		18 46	18 53		19 15				20 00	20 14
Robertsbridge		d				16 39		17 03		17 29		17 57	18 15			18 32			18 57		19 19				20 04	20 18
Battle		d	16 04			16 47		17 12		17 37		18 05	18 23			18 39		18 56	19 05		19 26				20 11	20 26
Crowhurst		d				16 50		17 15		17 40			18 26			18 43			19 09		19 30				20 15	
West St Leonards		d	16 12			16 55		17 20		17 45			18 33			18 48			19 14		19 35				20 20	
St Leonards Warrior Sq ■4		d	16 15			16 58		17 23		17 48		18 15	18 36			18 51		19 06	19 17		19 38				20 23	20 36
Hastings ■4		a	16 18			17 01		17 27		17 55		18 20	18 41			18 54		19 11	19 22		19 41				20 29	20 39
Ore		a														19 00					19 47					

Table 206

Mondays to Fridays

London and Tonbridge - Tunbridge Wells and Hastings

Station		SE 1 ⊼	SE 1	SE 1	SE 1	SE 1	SE 1	SE 1	SE 1	SE 1	SE 1	SE 1	SE 1	SE 1	SE 1	SE 1	SE 1
London Charing Cross 4 ⊖	d	19 15	19 30	19 45	20 00	20 15	20 30	20 45	21 00	21 30	21 45	22 00	22 30	22 45	23 00	23 30	23 45
London Waterloo (East) 4 ⊖	d	19 18	19 33	19 48	20 03	20 18	20 33	20 48	21 03	21 33	21 48	22 03	22 33	22 48	23 03	23 33	23 48
London Cannon Street 4 ⊖	d																
London Bridge 4 ⊖	d	19 23	19 39	19 53	20 09	20 23	20 39	20 53	21 09	21 39	21 53	22 09	22 39	22 53	23 09	23 39	23 53
Orpington 4	d	19 39	19 56	20 09	20 26	20 39	20 56	21 09	21 26	21 56	22 09	22 26	22 54	23 09	23 24	23 54	00 09
Sevenoaks 4	d	19 49	20 05	20 19	20 35	20 49	21 05	21 19	21 35	22 07	22 19	22 37	23 05	23 19	23 35	00 05	00 19
Tonbridge 4	a	19 57	20 15	20 27	20 45	20 57	21 15	21 27	21 45	22 17	22 27	22 47	23 15	23 27	23 45	00 15	00 27
	d	19 58	20 16	20 28	20 46	20 58	21 16	21 28	21 46	22 17	22 28	22 47	23 16	23 28	23 46	00 16	00 27
High Brooms	d	20 05	20 23	20 35	20 53	21 05	21 23	21 35	21 53	22 24	22 35	22 54	23 22	23 35	23 52	00 22	00 34
Tunbridge Wells 4	a	20 09	20 27	20 39	20 57	21 09	21 27	21 39	21 57	22 27	22 39	22 58	23 26	23 39	23 56	00 26	00 38
	d	20 10		20 40		21 10		21 40			22 40			23 40			00 39
Frant	d	20 15				21 15		21 45			22 45			23 45			00 44
Wadhurst	d	20 19		20 47		21 19		21 49			22 50			23 50			00 48
Stonegate	d	20 25				21 25		21 55			22 56			23 56			00 54
Etchingham	d	20 30		20 56		21 30		22 00			23 00			00 01			00 59
Robertsbridge	d	20 34		21 03		21 34		22 04			23 04			00 05			01 03
Battle	d	20 41		21 08		21 43		22 12			23 12			00 13			01 10
Crowhurst	d	20 45				21 46		22 15			23 15			00 16			01 14
West St Leonards	d	20 50				21 51		22 20			23 20			00 21			01 19
St Leonards Warrior Sq 4	d	20 53		21 18		21 54		22 23			23 23			00 24			01 22
Hastings 4	a	20 57		21 24		21 57		22 27			23 27			00 27			01 25
Ore	a																

Saturdays

Station		SE 1	SE 1	SE 1	SE 1	SE 1	SE 1	SE 1	SE 1	SE 1	SE 1	SE 1	SE 1	SE 1	SE 1	SE 1	SE 1 ⊼	SE 1	SE 1 ⊼	SE 1	SE 1 ⊼	SE 1	SE 1 ⊼
London Charing Cross 4 ⊖	d	22p45	23p30	23p45				07 45	08 15	08 30	08 45	09 00	09 15	09 30	09 45	10 00	10 15	10 30	10 45	11 00	11 15	11 30	11 45
London Waterloo (East) 4 ⊖	d	22p48	23p33	23p48				07 48	08 18	08 33	08 48	09 03	09 18	09 33	09 48	10 03	10 18	10 33	10 48	11 03	11 18	11 33	11 48
London Cannon Street 4 ⊖	d																						
London Bridge 4 ⊖	d	22p53	23p39	23p53				07 53	08 23	08 39	08 53	09 09	09 23	09 39	09 53	10 09	10 23	10 39	10 53	11 09	11 23	11 39	11 53
Orpington 4	d	23p09	23p54	00 09				08 09	08 39	08 56	09 09	09 26	09 39	09 56	10 09	10 26	10 39	10 56	11 09	11 26	11 39	11 56	12 09
Sevenoaks 4	d	23p19	00 05	00 19				08 19	08 49	09 05	09 19	09 35	09 49	10 05	10 19	10 35	10 49	11 05	11 19	11 35	11 49	12 05	12 19
Tonbridge 4	a	23p27	00 15	00 27				08 27	08 57	09 15	09 27	09 45	09 57	10 15	10 27	10 45	10 57	11 15	11 27	11 45	11 57	12 15	12 27
	d	23p28	00 16	00 27	06 58	07 28	07 58	08 28	08 58	09 16	09 28	09 46	09 58	10 16	10 28	10 46	10 58	11 16	11 28	11 46	11 58	12 16	12 28
High Brooms	d	23p35	00 22	00 34	07 05	07 35	08 05	08 35	09 05	09 23	09 35	09 53	10 05	10 23	10 35	10 53	11 05	11 23	11 35	11 53	12 05	12 23	12 35
Tunbridge Wells 4	a	23p39	00 26	00 38	07 09	07 39	08 09	08 39	09 09	09 27	09 39	09 57	10 09	10 27	10 39	10 57	11 09	11 27	11 39	11 57	12 09	12 27	12 39
	d	23p40		00 39	07 10		08 10	08 40	09 10		09 40		10 10		10 40		11 10		11 40		12 10		12 40
Frant	d	23p45		00 44	07 15		08 15	08 45	09 15				10 15				11 15				12 15		
Wadhurst	d	23p50		00 48	07 19		08 19	08 49	09 19		09 48		10 19		10 48		11 19		11 48		12 19		12 48
Stonegate	d	23p56		00 54	07 25		08 25	08 55	09 25				10 25				11 25				12 25		
Etchingham	d	00 01		00 59	07 30		08 30	09 00	09 30				10 30				11 30				12 30		
Robertsbridge	d	00 05		01 03	07 34		08 34	09 04	09 34				10 34				11 34				12 34		
Battle	d	00 13		01 10	07 41		08 41	09 11	09 41		10 03		10 41		11 03		11 41		12 03		12 41		13 03
Crowhurst	d	00 16		01 14	07 45		08 45	09 15	09 45				10 45				11 45				12 45		
West St Leonards	d	00 21		01 19	07 50		08 50	09 20	09 50				10 50				11 50				12 50		
St Leonards Warrior Sq 4	d	00 24		01 22	07 53		08 53	09 23	09 53		10 13		10 53		11 13		11 53		12 13		12 53		13 13
Hastings 4	a	00 27		01 25	07 57		08 57	09 27	09 57		10 17		10 57		11 17		11 57		12 17		12 57		13 17
Ore	a																						

Station		SE 1	SE 1 ⊼	SE 1	SE 1 ⊼	SE 1	SE 1 ⊼	SE 1	SE 1 ⊼	SE 1	SE 1 ⊼	SE 1	SE 1 ⊼	SE 1	SE 1 ⊼	SE 1	SE 1 ⊼	SE 1	SE 1 ⊼	SE 1	SE 1 ⊼	SE 1	SE 1 ⊼
London Charing Cross 4 ⊖	d	12 00	12 15	12 30	12 45	13 00	13 15	13 30	13 45	14 00	14 15	14 30	14 45	15 00	15 15	15 30	15 45	16 00	16 15	16 30	16 45	17 00	17 15
London Waterloo (East) 4 ⊖	d	12 03	12 18	12 33	12 48	13 03	13 18	13 33	13 48	14 03	14 18	14 33	14 48	15 03	15 18	15 33	15 48	16 03	16 18	16 33	16 48	17 03	17 18
London Cannon Street 4 ⊖	d																						
London Bridge 4 ⊖	d	12 09	12 23	12 39	12 53	13 09	13 23	13 39	13 53	14 09	14 23	14 39	14 53	15 09	15 23	15 39	15 53	16 09	16 23	16 39	16 53	17 09	17 23
Orpington 4	d	12 26	12 39	12 56	13 09	13 26	13 39	13 56	14 09	14 26	14 39	14 56	15 09	15 26	15 39	15 56	16 09	16 26	16 39	16 56	17 09	17 26	17 39
Sevenoaks 4	d	12 35	12 49	13 05	13 19	13 35	13 49	14 05	14 19	14 35	14 49	15 05	15 19	15 35	15 49	16 05	16 19	16 35	16 49	17 05	17 19	17 35	17 49
Tonbridge 4	a	12 45	12 57	13 15	13 27	13 45	13 57	14 15	14 27	14 45	14 57	15 15	15 27	15 45	15 57	16 15	16 27	16 45	16 57	17 15	17 27	17 45	17 57
	d	12 46	12 58	13 16	13 28	13 46	13 58	14 16	14 28	14 46	14 58	15 16	15 28	15 46	15 58	16 16	16 28	16 46	16 58	17 16	17 28	17 46	17 58
High Brooms	d	12 53	13 05	13 23	13 35	13 53	14 05	14 23	14 35	14 53	15 05	15 23	15 35	15 53	16 05	16 23	16 35	16 53	17 05	17 23	17 35	17 53	18 05
Tunbridge Wells 4	a	12 57	13 09	13 27	13 39	13 57	14 09	14 27	14 39	14 57	15 09	15 27	15 39	15 57	16 09	16 27	16 39	16 57	17 09	17 27	17 39	17 57	18 09
	d		13 10		13 40		14 10		14 40		15 10		15 40		16 10		16 40		17 10		17 40		18 10
Frant	d		13 15				14 15				15 15				16 15				17 15				18 15
Wadhurst	d		13 19		13 48		14 19		14 48		15 19		15 48		16 19		16 48		17 19		17 48		18 19
Stonegate	d		13 25				14 25				15 25				16 25				17 25				18 25
Etchingham	d		13 30				14 30				15 30				16 30				17 30				18 30
Robertsbridge	d		13 34				14 34				15 34				16 34				17 34				18 34
Battle	d		13 41		14 03		14 41		15 03		15 41		16 03		16 41		17 03		17 41		18 03		18 41
Crowhurst	d		13 45				14 45				15 45				16 45				17 45				18 45
West St Leonards	d		13 50				14 50				15 50				16 50				17 50				18 50
St Leonards Warrior Sq 4	d		13 53		14 13		14 53		15 13		15 53		16 13		16 53		17 13		17 53		18 13		18 53
Hastings 4	a		13 57		14 17		14 57		15 17		15 57		16 17		16 57		17 17		17 57		18 17		18 57
Ore	a																						

Table 206

Saturdays

London and Tonbridge - Tunbridge Wells and Hastings

Station		SE 1	SE 1 ⊼	SE 1	SE 1 ⊼	SE 1	SE 1 ⊼	SE 1	SE 1	SE 1	SE 1	SE 1	SE 1	SE 1	SE 1	SE 1	SE 1	SE 1	SE 1
London Charing Cross 4 ⊖	d	17 30	17 45	18 00	18 15	18 30	18 45	19 00	19 15	19 30	19 55	20 25	20 55	21 25	21 55	22 25	22 55	23 25	23 45
London Waterloo (East) 4 ⊖	d	17 33	17 48	18 03	18 18	18 33	18 48	19 03	19 18	19 33	19 58	20 28	20 58	21 28	21 58	22 28	22 58	23 28	23 48
London Cannon Street 4 ⊖	d																		
London Bridge 4 ⊖	d	17 39	17 53	18 09	18 23	18 39	18 53	19 09	19 23	19 39	20 03	20 33	21 03	21 33	22 03	22 33	23 03	23 33	23 53
Orpington 4	d	17 56	18 09	18 26	18 39	18 56	19 09	19 26	19 39	19 56	20 21	20 51	21 21	21 51	22 21	22 49	23 19	23 49	00 09
Sevenoaks 4	d	18 05	18 19	18 35	18 49	19 05	19 19	19 35	19 49	20 05	20 31	21 01	21 31	22 01	22 31	23 00	23 28	23 59	00 19
Tonbridge 4	a	18 15	18 27	18 45	18 58	19 15	19 27	19 45	19 58	20 15	20 39	21 11	21 39	22 11	22 39	23 10	23 36	00 10	00 27
	d	18 16	18 28	18 46	18 58	19 16	19 28	19 46	19 58	20 16	20 40	21 11	21 40	22 11	22 40	23 11	23 37	00 11	00 27
High Brooms	d	18 23	18 35	18 53	19 05	19 23	19 35	19 53	20 05	20 23	20 46	21 19	21 46	22 19	22 46	23 17	23 43	00 17	00 34
Tunbridge Wells 4	a	18 27	18 39	18 57	19 09	19 27	19 39	19 57	20 09	20 27	20 50	21 23	21 50	22 23	22 50	23 21	23 47	00 21	00 38
	d		18 40		19 10		19 40		20 10		20 51		21 51		22 51		23 48		00 38
Frant	d				19 15				20 15		20 56		21 56		22 56		23 53		00 43
Wadhurst	d		18 48		19 19		19 48		20 19		21 00		22 00		23 00		23 57		00 48
Stonegate	d				19 25				20 25		21 06		22 06		23 06		00 03		00 54
Etchingham	d				19 30				20 30		21 11		22 11		23 11		00 08		00 58
Robertsbridge	d				19 34				20 34		21 15		22 15		23 15		00 12		01 02
Battle	d		19 03		19 41		20 03		20 41		21 23		22 23		23 23		00 20		01 10
Crowhurst	d				19 45				20 45		21 27		22 27		23 27		00 24		01 13
West St Leonards	d				19 50				20 50		21 32		22 32		23 32		00 29		01 18
St Leonards Warrior Sq 4	d		19 13		19 53		20 13		20 53		21 35		22 35		23 36		00 32		01 21
Hastings 4	a		19 17		19 57		20 17		20 57		21 38		22 38		23 39		00 35		01 25
Ore	a																		

Sundays

Station		SE 1	SE 1	SE 1	SE 1	SE 1	SE 1	SE 1	SE 1	SE 1	SE 1	SE 1	SE 1	SE 1	SE 1	SE 1	SE 1	SE 1	SE 1	SE 1	SE 1	SE 1	SE 1
London Charing Cross 4 ⊖	d	22p55	23p25	23p45		08 23		09 23	09 53	10 23	10 53	11 23	11 53	12 23	12 53	13 23	13 53	14 23	14 53	15 23	15 53	16 23	16 53
London Waterloo (East) 4 ⊖	d	22p58	23p28	23p48		08 26		09 26	09 56	10 26	10 56	11 26	11 56	12 26	12 56	13 26	13 56	14 26	14 56	15 26	15 56	16 26	16 56
London Cannon Street 4 ⊖	d																						
London Bridge 4 ⊖	d	23p03	23p33	23p53		08 31		09 31	10 01	10 31	11 01	11 31	12 01	12 31	13 01	13 31	14 01	14 31	15 01	15 31	16 01	16 31	17 01
Orpington 4	d	23p19	23p49	00 09		08 46		09 46	10 16	10 46	11 16	11 46	12 16	12 46	13 16	13 46	14 16	14 46	15 16	15 46	16 16	16 46	17 16
Sevenoaks 4	d	23p28	23p59	00 19		08 56		09 56	10 26	10 56	11 26	11 56	12 26	12 56	13 26	13 56	14 26	14 56	15 26	15 56	16 26	16 56	17 26
Tonbridge 4	a	23p36	00 10	00 27		09 04		10 04	10 34	11 04	11 34	12 04	12 34	13 04	13 34	14 04	14 34	15 04	15 34	16 04	16 34	17 04	17 34
	d	23p37	00 11	00 27	08 25	09 04	09 34	10 04	10 34	11 04	11 34	12 04	12 34	13 04	13 34	14 04	14 34	15 04	15 34	16 04	16 34	17 04	17 34
High Brooms	d	23p43	00 17	00 34	08 31	09 10	09 40	10 10	10 40	11 10	11 40	12 10	12 40	13 10	13 40	14 10	14 40	15 10	15 40	16 10	16 40	17 10	17 40
Tunbridge Wells 4	a	23p47	00 21	00 38	08 35	09 14	09 44	10 14	10 44	11 14	11 44	12 14	12 44	13 14	13 44	14 14	14 44	15 14	15 44	16 14	16 44	17 14	17 44
	d	23p48		00 38		09 15	09 45	10 15	10 45	11 15	11 45	12 15	12 45	13 15	13 45	14 15	14 45	15 15	15 45	16 15	16 45	17 15	17 45
Frant	d	23p53		00 43		09 20		10 20		11 20		12 20		13 20		14 20		15 20		16 20		17 20	
Wadhurst	d	23p57		00 48		09 24	09 52	10 24	10 52	11 24	11 52	12 24	12 52	13 24	13 52	14 24	14 52	15 24	15 52	16 24	16 52	17 24	17 52
Stonegate	d	00 03		00 54		09 30		10 30		11 30		12 30		13 30		14 30		15 30		16 30		17 30	
Etchingham	d	00 08		00 58		09 35		10 35		11 35		12 35		13 35		14 35		15 35		16 35		17 35	
Robertsbridge	d	00 12		01 02		09 39		10 39		11 39		12 39		13 39		14 39		15 39		16 39		17 39	
Battle	d	00 20		01 10		09 47	10 08	10 47	11 08	11 47	12 08	12 47	13 08	13 47	14 08	14 47	15 08	15 47	16 08	16 47	17 08	17 47	18 08
Crowhurst	d	00 24		01 13		09 51		10 51		11 51		12 51		13 51		14 51		15 51		16 51		17 51	
West St Leonards	d	00 29		01 18		09 56		10 56		11 56		12 56		13 56		14 56		15 56		16 56		17 56	
St Leonards Warrior Sq 4	d	00 32		01 21		09 59	10 18	10 59	11 18	11 59	12 18	12 59	13 18	13 59	14 18	14 59	15 18	15 59	16 18	16 59	17 18	17 59	18 18
Hastings 4	a	00 35		01 25		10 02	10 21	11 02	11 21	12 02	12 21	13 02	13 21	14 02	14 21	15 02	15 21	16 02	16 21	17 02	17 21	18 02	18 21
Ore	a																						

Station		SE 1	SE 1	SE 1	SE 1	SE 1	SE 1	SE 1	SE 1	SE 1	SE 1
London Charing Cross 4 ⊖	d	17 23	17 53	18 23	18 53	19 23	19 53	20 23	21 23	22 23	23 23
London Waterloo (East) 4 ⊖	d	17 26	17 56	18 26	18 56	19 26	19 56	20 26	21 26	22 26	23 26
London Cannon Street 4 ⊖	d										
London Bridge 4 ⊖	d	17 31	18 01	18 31	19 01	19 31	20 01	20 31	21 31	22 31	23 31
Orpington 4	d	17 46	18 16	18 46	19 16	19 46	20 16	20 46	21 46	22 46	23 46
Sevenoaks 4	d	17 56	18 26	18 56	19 26	19 56	20 26	20 56	21 56	22 57	23 57
Tonbridge 4	a	18 04	18 34	19 04	19 34	20 04	20 34	21 04	22 04	23 05	00 05
	d	18 04	18 34	19 04	19 34	20 04	20 34	21 04	22 04	23 06	00 06
High Brooms	d	18 10	18 40	19 10	19 40	20 10	20 40	21 10	22 10	23 12	00 12
Tunbridge Wells 4	a	18 14	18 44	19 14	19 44	20 14	20 44	21 14	22 14	23 16	00 16
	d	18 15	18 45	19 15	19 45	20 15		21 15	22 15	23 16	00 16
Frant	d	18 20		19 20		20 20		21 20	22 20	23 21	00 21
Wadhurst	d	18 24	18 52	19 24	19 52	20 24		21 24	22 24	23 26	00 26
Stonegate	d	18 30		19 30		20 30		21 30	22 30	23 32	00 32
Etchingham	d	18 35		19 35		20 35		21 35	22 35	23 36	00 36
Robertsbridge	d	18 39		19 39		20 39		21 39	22 39	23 40	00 40
Battle	d	18 47	19 08	19 47	20 08	20 47		21 47	22 47	23 48	00 48
Crowhurst	d	18 51		19 51		20 51		21 51	22 51	23 52	00 52
West St Leonards	d	18 56		19 56		20 56		21 56	22 56	23 57	00 57
St Leonards Warrior Sq 4	d	18 59	19 18	19 59	20 18	20 59		21 59	22 59	00 01	01 01
Hastings 4	a	19 02	19 21	20 02	20 21	21 02		22 02	23 02	00 04	01 04
Ore	a										

Table 206

Mondays to Fridays

Hastings and Tunbridge Wells - Tonbridge and London

		SE MX ■	SE ■	SE ■	SE ■	SE ■	SE ■	SE ■	SE ■	SE ■	SE ■	SE ■ A ⊼	SE ■	SE ■	SE ■ A ⊼	SE ■	SE ■ ⊼	SE ■	SE ■ ⊼	SE ■	SE ■	SE ■	SE ■ ⊼
Ore	d											06 12			06 39						07 41		
Hastings	d	22p10			05 17		05 37	05 48		06 03		06 20	06 30		06 43		07 03		07 25		07 45		08 15
St Leonards Warrior Sq	d	22p13			05 20		05 40	05 51		06 06		06 23	06 33		06 46		07 06		07 28		07 48		08 18
West St Leonards	d	22p16			05 23		05 43			06 09			06 36		06 49		07 09		07 31		07 51		08 21
Crowhurst	d	22p21			05 28		05 48			06 14			06 41		06 54		07 14		07 37		07 56		08 26
Battle	d	22p25			05 32		05 53	06 01		06 19		06 33	06 45		06 58		07 18		07 41		08 00		08 30
Robertsbridge	d	22p33			05 40		06 00			06 27		06 40			07 06		07 26		07 48		08 08		08 38
Etchingham	d	22p37			05 43		06 03	06 10		06 31		06 44	06 54		07 09		07 29		07 52		08 11		08 41
Stonegate	d	22p43			05 49		06 09			06 36		06 49			07 15		07 35		07 57		08 17		08 47
Wadhurst	d	22p49			05 55		06 16	06 21		06 43		06 56	07 04		07 21		07 41		08 04		08 23		08 53
Frant	d	22p53			05 59		06 20			06 47		07 00			07 25		07 45		08 08		08 27		08 57
Tunbridge Wells	a	22p58			06 05		06 25	06 29		06 54		07 06	07 11		07 31		07 51		08 13		08 33		09 02
	d	22p59	05 21	05 50	06 09	06 21	06 34	<	06 40	06 56	07 00	07 16	<	07 20	07 36	07 40	07 56	08 00	08 18	08 22	08 40	08 51	09 09
High Brooms	d	23p02	05 24	05 53	06 12	06 24	06 37		06 44	07 00	07 04	07 20		07 24	07 40	07 44	08 00	08 04	08 22	08 25	08 43	08 54	09 12
Tonbridge	a	23p08	05 30	05 59	06 18	06 30	06 44		06 50		07 10			07 30		07 50		08 10		08 31	08 49	09 00	09 18
Sevenoaks	a	23p24	05 42	06 10	06 30	06 43	06 52		07 02		07 22			07 42		08 02		08 22		08 42	08 58	09 13	09 28
Orpington	a	23p36	05 54	06 19		06 53	07 02		07 13												09 08	09 24	09 38
London Bridge	⊖ a	23p53	06 09	06 38	06 54	07 09	07 22		07 29		07 50			08 09	08 24	08 29		08 49	09 03	09 11	09 26	09 40	09 55
London Cannon Street	⊖ a			06 42			07 29								08 30				09 10				
London Waterloo (East)	⊖ a	23p57	06 14		06 59	07 14			07 34	07 44	07 55	08 04		08 14		08 34	08 44	08 54		09 16	09 31	09 45	09 59
London Charing Cross	⊖ a	00 01	06 18		07 05	07 20			07 40	07 50	08 01	08 08		08 20		08 40	08 50	09 00		09 22	09 37	09 51	10 03

		SE ■	SE ■ ⊼	SE ■	SE ■ ⊼	SE ■	SE ■ ⊼	SE ■	SE ■ ⊼	SE ■	SE ■ ⊼	SE ■	SE ■ ⊼	SE ■	SE ■ ⊼	SE ■	SE ■ ⊼	SE ■	SE ■ ⊼	SE ■	SE ■ ⊼	SE ■	SE ■ ⊼
Ore	d																						
Hastings	d		08 47		09 29		09 50		10 32		10 50		11 32		11 50		12 32		12 50		13 32		13 50
St Leonards Warrior Sq	d		08 50		09 32		09 53		10 35		10 53		11 35		11 53		12 35		12 53		13 35		13 53
West St Leonards	d		08 53				09 56				10 56				11 56				12 56				13 56
Crowhurst	d		08 58				10 01				11 01				12 01				13 01				14 01
Battle	d		09 02		09 42		10 05		10 45		11 05		11 45		12 05		12 45		13 05		13 45		14 05
Robertsbridge	d		09 09				10 13				11 13				12 13				13 13				14 13
Etchingham	d		09 13				10 17				11 17				12 17				13 17				14 17
Stonegate	d		09 18				10 23				11 23				12 23				13 23				14 23
Wadhurst	d		09 25		09 58		10 30		11 01		11 29		12 01		12 29		13 01		13 29		14 01		14 29
Frant	d		09 29				10 34				11 33				12 33				13 33				14 33
Tunbridge Wells	a		09 34		10 05		10 39		11 08		11 38		12 08		12 38		13 08		13 38		14 08		14 38
	d	09 21	09 39	09 51	10 09	10 21	10 39	10 51	11 09	11 21	11 39	11 51	12 09	12 21	12 39	12 51	13 09	13 21	13 39	13 51	14 09	14 21	14 39
High Brooms	d	09 24	09 42	09 54	10 12	10 24	10 43	10 54	11 12	11 24	11 42	11 54	12 12	12 24	12 42	12 54	13 12	13 24	13 42	13 54	14 12	14 24	14 42
Tonbridge	a	09 30	09 48	10 00	10 18	10 30	10 49	11 00	11 18	11 30	11 48	12 00	12 18	12 30	12 48	13 00	13 18	13 30	13 48	14 00	14 18	14 30	14 48
Sevenoaks	a	09 43	09 58	10 13	10 28	10 43	10 58	11 13	11 28	11 43	11 58	12 13	12 28	12 43	12 58	13 13	13 28	13 43	13 58	14 13	14 28	14 43	14 58
Orpington	a	09 53	10 08	10 23	10 38	10 53	11 08	11 23	11 38	11 53	12 08	12 23	12 38	12 53	13 08	13 23	13 38	13 53	14 08	14 23	14 38	14 53	15 08
London Bridge	⊖ a	10 10	10 25	10 40	10 55	11 10	11 25	11 40	11 55	12 10	12 25	12 40	12 55	13 10	13 25	13 40	13 55	14 10	14 25	14 40	14 55	15 10	15 25
London Cannon Street	⊖ a																						
London Waterloo (East)	⊖ a	10 15	10 29	10 45	10 59	11 15	11 29	11 45	11 59	12 15	12 29	12 45	12 59	13 15	13 29	13 45	13 59	14 15	14 29	14 45	14 59	15 15	15 29
London Charing Cross	⊖ a	10 19	10 33	10 49	11 03	11 19	11 33	11 49	12 03	12 19	12 33	12 49	13 03	13 19	13 33	13 49	14 03	14 19	14 33	14 49	15 03	15 19	15 33

		SE ■	SE ■	SE ■	SE ■ ⊼	SE ■	SE ■ ⊼	SE ■	SE ■ ⊼	SE ■	SE ■	SE ■	SE ■ ⊼	SE ■	SE ■ ⊼	SE ■	SE ■	SE ■	SE ■	SE ■	SE ■	SE ■
Ore	d																					
Hastings	d		14 32		14 50		15 32		15 45		16 19		16 50		17 18		17 50		18 19		18 46	
St Leonards Warrior Sq	d		14 35		14 53		15 35		15 48		16 22		16 53		17 21		17 53		18 22		18 49	
West St Leonards	d				14 56				15 51		16 25		16 56		17 24		17 56		18 25		18 52	
Crowhurst	d				15 01				15 56		16 30		17 01		17 29		18 01		18 30		18 58	
Battle	d		14 45		15 05		15 45		16 00		16 34		17 05		17 33		18 05		18 34		19 02	
Robertsbridge	d				15 13				16 08		16 41		17 13		17 40		18 13		18 41		19 10	
Etchingham	d				15 17				16 12		16 45		17 16		17 44		18 16		18 45		19 14	
Stonegate	d				15 23				16 18		16 50		17 22		17 50		18 22		18 50		19 20	
Wadhurst	d		15 01		15 29		16 01		16 24		16 57		17 28		17 56		18 28		18 57		19 26	
Frant	d				15 33				16 28		17 01		17 32		18 00		18 32		19 01		19 30	
Tunbridge Wells	a		15 08		15 38		16 08		16 33		17 06		17 37		18 08		18 39		19 06		19 35	
	d	14 51	15 09	15 21	15 39	15 51	16 09	16 21	16 39	16 51	17 06	17 21	17 39	17 49	18 13	18 19	18 39	18 51	19 06	19 21	19 39	19 51
High Brooms	d	14 54	15 12	15 24	15 42	15 54	16 12	16 24	16 42	16 54	17 10	17 24	17 42	17 52	18 16	18 22	18 42	18 54	19 10	19 24	19 42	19 54
Tonbridge	a	15 00	15 18	15 30	15 48	16 00	16 18	16 30	16 48	17 01	17 16	17 30	17 49	17 59	18 22	18 28	18 50	19 00	19 16	19 30	19 50	20 00
Sevenoaks	a	15 13	15 28	15 43	15 58	16 13	16 28	16 43	16 58	17 13	17 28	17 43	17 58	18 13	18 31	18 43	18 59	19 13	19 28	19 43	19 59	20 13
Orpington	a	15 23	15 38	15 53	16 07	16 24	16 38	16 53	17 08	17 23	17 38	17 53	18 08	18 23		18 53	19 08	19 23	19 38	19 53	20 08	20 23
London Bridge	⊖ a	15 40	15 55	16 11	16 25	16 42	16 56	17 11	17 27	17 41	17 58	18 09	18 25	18 40	18 55	19 10	19 25	19 40	19 54	20 10	20 24	20 39
London Cannon Street	⊖ a								17 32													
London Waterloo (East)	⊖ a	15 45	15 59	16 16	16 29	16 48	17 00	17 16		17 46	18 02	18 14	18 29	18 45	18 59	19 14	19 29	19 45	19 59	20 15	20 29	20 44
London Charing Cross	⊖ a	15 49	16 03	16 20	16 33	16 52	17 04	17 20		17 50	18 06	18 18	18 35	18 49	19 04	19 18	19 33	19 49	20 03	20 19	20 33	20 48

A ⊼ from Hastings

Table 206

Mondays to Fridays

Hastings and Tunbridge Wells - Tonbridge and London

		SE ■	SE ■	SE ■	SE ■	SE ■	SE ■	SE ■	SE ■	SE ■	SE ■
Ore	d										
Hastings	d		19 50			20 50			21 50	22 10	
St Leonards Warrior Sq	d		19 53			20 53			21 53	22 13	
West St Leonards	d		19 56			20 56			21 56	22 16	
Crowhurst	d		20 01			21 01			22 01	22 21	
Battle	d		20 05			21 05			22 05	22 25	
Robertsbridge	d		20 13			21 13			22 13	22 33	
Etchingham	d		20 17			21 17			22 17	22 37	
Stonegate	d		20 23			21 23			22 23	22 43	
Wadhurst	d		20 29			21 29			22 29	22 49	
Frant	d		20 33			21 33			22 33	22 53	
Tunbridge Wells	a		20 38			21 38			22 38	22 58	
	d	20 21	20 39	20 51	21 21	21 39	21 51	22 21	22 39	22 59	23 33
High Brooms	d	20 24	20 42	20 54	21 24	21 42	21 54	22 24	22 42	23 02	23 36
Tonbridge	a	20 30	20 48	21 00	21 30	21 48	22 00	22 30	22 48	23 08	23 42
Sevenoaks	a	20 43	20 58	21 13	21 43	21 58	22 13	22 41	22 58	23 24	
Orpington	a	20 52	21 08	21 22	21 52	22 08	22 22	22 52	23 08	23 36	
London Bridge	⊖ a	21 08	21 24	21 38	22 08	22 24	22 38	23 08	23 24	23 53	
London Cannon Street	⊖ a										
London Waterloo (East)	⊖ a	21 13	21 29	21 43	22 13	22 29	22 43	23 13	23 29	23 57	
London Charing Cross	⊖ a	21 18	21 33	21 48	22 18	22 33	22 48	23 18	23 33	00 01	

Saturdays

		SE ■	SE	SE ■	SE ■	SE ■	SE ■	SE ■	SE ■	SE ■	SE ■	SE ■	SE ■ ⊼	SE ■	SE ■ ⊼	SE ■	SE ■ ⊼	SE ■	SE ■ ⊼	SE ■	SE ■ ⊼	SE ■	SE ■ ⊼
Ore	d																						
Hastings	d	22p10		05 50	06 20		06 50		07 20		07 50		08 20		08 50		09 32		09 50		10 32		10 50
St Leonards Warrior Sq	d	22p13		05 53	06 23		06 53		07 23		07 53		08 23		08 53		09 35		09 53		10 35		10 53
West St Leonards	d	22p16		05 56	06 26		06 56		07 26		07 56		08 26		08 56				09 56				10 56
Crowhurst	d	22p21		06 01	06 31		07 01		07 31		08 01		08 31		09 01				10 01				11 01
Battle	d	22p25		06 05	06 35		07 05		07 35		08 05		08 35		09 05		09 45		10 05		10 45		11 05
Robertsbridge	d	22p33		06 13	06 43		07 13		07 43		08 13		08 43		09 13				10 13				11 13
Etchingham	d	22p37		06 17	06 47		07 17		07 46		08 17		08 47		09 17				10 17				11 17
Stonegate	d	22p43		06 23	06 53		07 23		07 52		08 23		08 53		09 23				10 23				11 23
Wadhurst	d	22p49		06 29	06 59		07 29		07 59		08 29		08 59		09 29		10 01		10 29		11 01		11 29
Frant	d	22p53		06 33	07 03		07 33		08 03		08 33		09 03		09 33				10 33				11 33
Tunbridge Wells	a	22p58		06 38	07 08		07 38		08 08		08 38		09 08		09 38		10 08		10 38		11 08		11 38
	d	22p59	05 48	06 39	07 09	07 21	07 39	07 51	08 09	08 21	08 39	08 51	09 09	09 21	09 39	09 51	10 09	10 21	10 39	10 51	11 09	11 21	11 39
High Brooms	d	23p02	05 51	06 42	07 12	07 24	07 42	07 54	08 12	08 24	08 42	08 54	09 12	09 24	09 42	09 54	10 12	10 24	10 42	10 54	11 12	11 24	11 42
Tonbridge	a	23p08	05 57	06 48	07 18	07 30	07 48	08 00	08 18	08 30	08 48	09 00	09 18	09 30	09 48	10 00	10 18	10 30	10 48	11 00	11 18	11 30	11 48
Sevenoaks	a	23p24		06 58	07 28	07 43	07 58	08 13	08 28	08 43	08 58	09 13	09 28	09 43	09 58	10 13	10 28	10 43	10 58	11 13	11 28	11 43	11 58
Orpington	a	23p36		07 08	07 38	07 53	08 08	08 23	08 38	08 53	09 08	09 23	09 38	09 53	10 08	10 23	10 38	10 53	11 08	11 23	11 38	11 53	12 08
London Bridge	⊖ a	23p53		07 24	07 55	08 10	08 25	08 40	08 55	09 10	09 25	09 40	09 55	10 10	10 25	10 40	10 55	11 10	11 25	11 40	11 55	12 10	12 25
London Cannon Street	⊖ a																						
London Waterloo (East)	⊖ a	23p57		07 29	07 59	08 15	08 29	08 45	08 59	09 15	09 29	09 45	09 59	10 15	10 29	10 45	10 59	11 15	11 29	11 45	11 59	12 15	12 29
London Charing Cross	⊖ a	00 01		07 33	08 03	08 19	08 33	08 49	09 03	09 19	09 33	09 49	10 03	10 19	10 33	10 49	11 03	11 19	11 33	11 49	12 03	12 19	12 33

		SE ■	SE ■ ⊼	SE ■	SE ■ ⊼	SE ■	SE ■ ⊼	SE ■	SE ■ ⊼	SE ■	SE ■ ⊼	SE ■	SE ■ ⊼	SE ■	SE ■ ⊼	SE ■	SE ■ ⊼	SE ■	SE ■ ⊼	SE ■	SE ■ ⊼	SE ■	SE ■ ⊼
Ore	d																						
Hastings	d		11 32		11 50		12 32		12 50		13 32		13 50		14 32		14 50		15 32		15 50		16 32
St Leonards Warrior Sq	d		11 35		11 53		12 35		12 53		13 35		13 53		14 35		14 53		15 35		15 53		16 35
West St Leonards	d				11 56				12 56				13 56				14 56				15 56		
Crowhurst	d				12 01				13 01				14 01				15 01				16 01		
Battle	d		11 45		12 05		12 45		13 05		13 45		14 05		14 45		15 05		15 45		16 05		16 45
Robertsbridge	d				12 13				13 13				14 13				15 13				16 13		
Etchingham	d				12 17				13 17				14 17				15 17				16 17		
Stonegate	d				12 23				13 23				14 23				15 23				16 23		
Wadhurst	d		12 01		12 29		13 01		13 29		14 01		14 29		15 01		15 29		16 01		16 29		17 01
Frant	d				12 33				13 33				14 33				15 33				16 33		
Tunbridge Wells	a		12 08		12 38		13 08		13 38		14 08		14 38		15 08		15 38		16 08		16 38		17 08
	d	11 51	12 09	12 21	12 39	12 51	13 09	13 21	13 39	13 51	14 09	14 21	14 39	14 51	15 09	15 21	15 39	15 51	16 09	16 21	16 39	16 51	17 09
High Brooms	d	11 54	12 12	12 24	12 42	12 54	13 12	13 24	13 42	13 54	14 12	14 24	14 42	14 54	15 12	15 24	15 42	15 54	16 12	16 24	16 42	16 54	17 12
Tonbridge	a	12 00	12 18	12 30	12 48	13 00	13 18	13 30	13 48	14 00	14 18	14 30	14 48	15 00	15 18	15 30	15 48	16 00	16 18	16 30	16 48	17 00	17 18
Sevenoaks	a	12 13	12 28	12 43	12 58	13 13	13 28	13 43	13 58	14 13	14 28	14 43	14 58	15 13	15 28	15 43	15 58	16 13	16 28	16 43	16 58	17 13	17 28
Orpington	a	12 23	12 38	12 53	13 08	13 23	13 38	13 53	14 08	14 23	14 38	14 53	15 08	15 23	15 38	15 53	16 08	16 23	16 38	16 53	17 08	17 23	17 38
London Bridge	⊖ a	12 40	12 55	13 10	13 25	13 40	13 55	14 10	14 25	14 40	14 55	15 10	15 25	15 40	15 55	16 10	16 25	16 40	16 55	17 10	17 25	17 40	17 55
London Cannon Street	⊖ a																						
London Waterloo (East)	⊖ a	12 45	12 59	13 15	13 29	13 45	13 59	14 15	14 29	14 45	14 59	15 15	15 29	15 45	15 59	16 15	16 29	16 45	16 59	17 15	17 29	17 45	17 59
London Charing Cross	⊖ a	12 49	13 03	13 19	13 33	13 49	14 03	14 19	14 33	14 49	15 03	15 19	15 33	15 49	16 03	16 19	16 33	16 49	17 03	17 19	17 33	17 49	18 03

Table 206

Saturdays

Hastings and Tunbridge Wells - Tonbridge and London

		SE [1]	SE [1] (H)	SE [1]	SE [1]	SE [1]	SE [1]	SE [1]	SE [1]	SE [1]	SE [1]	SE [1]	SE [1]	SE [1]	SE [1]	SE [1]	SE [1]
Ore	d																
Hastings [4]	d		16 50		17 20		17 50		18 50		19 50		20 50		21 50	22 10	
St Leonards Warrior Sq [4]	d		16 53		17 23		17 53		18 53		19 53		20 53		21 53	22 13	
West St Leonards	d		16 56		17 26		17 56		18 56		19 56		20 56		21 56	22 16	
Crowhurst	d		17 01		17 31		18 01		19 01		20 01		21 01		22 01	22 21	
Battle	d		17 05		17 35		18 05		19 05		20 05		21 05		22 05	22 25	
Robertsbridge	d		17 13		17 43		18 13		19 13		20 13		21 13		22 13	22 33	
Etchingham	d		17 17		17 46		18 17		19 17		20 17		21 17		22 17	22 37	
Stonegate	d		17 23		17 52		18 23		19 23		20 23		21 23		22 23	22 43	
Wadhurst	d		17 29		17 59		18 29		19 29		20 29		21 29		22 29	22 49	
Frant	d		17 33		18 03		18 33		19 33		20 33		21 33		22 33	22 53	
Tunbridge Wells [4]	a		17 38		18 08		18 38		19 38		20 38		21 38		22 38	22 58	
	d	17 21	17 39	17 51	18 09	18 21	18 39	19 08	19 39	20 08	20 39	21 05	21 39	22 05	22 39	22 59	23 33
High Brooms	d	17 24	17 42	17 54	18 12	18 24	18 42	19 11	19 42	20 11	20 42	21 08	21 42	22 08	22 42	23 02	23 36
Tonbridge [4]	a	17 30	17 48	18 00	18 18	18 30	18 48	19 17	19 48	20 17	20 48	21 14	21 48	22 14	22 48	23 08	23 45
Sevenoaks [4]	a	17 43	17 58	18 13	18 28	18 43	18 58	19 28	19 58	20 28	20 58	21 28	21 58	22 28	22 58	23 24	
Orpington [4]	a	17 53	18 08	18 23	18 38	18 53	19 08	19 38	20 08	20 38	21 08	21 38	22 08	22 38	23 08	23 36	
London Bridge [4] ⊖	a	18 10	18 25	18 40	18 55	19 10	19 24	19 54	20 24	20 54	21 24	21 54	22 24	22 54	23 24	23 53	
London Cannon Street [4] ⊖	a																
London Waterloo (East) [4] ⊖	a	18 15	18 29	18 45	18 59	19 15	19 29	19 59	20 29	20 59	21 29	21 59	22 29	22 59	23 29	23 57	
London Charing Cross [4] ⊖	a	18 19	18 33	18 49	19 03	19 19	19 33	20 03	20 33	21 03	21 33	22 03	22 33	23 03	23 33	00 01	

Sundays

		SE [1]	SE [1]	SE [1]	SE [1]	SE [1]	SE [1]	SE [1]	SE [1]	SE [1]	SE [1]	SE [1]	SE [1]	SE [1]	SE [1]	SE [1]	SE [1]	SE [1]	SE [1]	SE [1]	SE [1]	SE [1]	SE [1]
Ore	d																						
Hastings [4]	d	22p10	07 28		08 28	09 08	09 28	10 08	10 28	11 08	11 28	12 08	12 28	13 08	13 28	14 08	14 28	15 08	15 28	16 08	16 28	17 08	17 28
St Leonards Warrior Sq [4]	d	22p13	07 30		08 30	09 11	09 30	10 11	10 30	11 11	11 30	12 11	12 30	13 11	13 30	14 11	14 30	15 11	15 30	16 11	16 30	17 11	17 30
West St Leonards	d	22p16	07 33		08 33		09 33		10 33		11 33		12 33		13 33		14 33		15 33		16 33		17 33
Crowhurst	d	22p21	07 39		08 39		09 39		10 39		11 39		12 39		13 39		14 39		15 39		16 39		17 39
Battle	d	22p25	07 43		08 43	09 21	09 43	10 21	10 43	11 21	11 43	12 21	12 43	13 21	13 43	14 21	14 43	15 21	15 43	16 21	16 43	17 21	17 43
Robertsbridge	d	22p33	07 50		08 50		09 50		10 50		11 50		12 50		13 50		14 50		15 50		16 50		17 50
Etchingham	d	22p37	07 53		08 53		09 53		10 53		11 53		12 53		13 53		14 53		15 53		16 53		17 53
Stonegate	d	22p43	07 59		08 59		09 59		10 59		11 59		12 59		13 59		14 59		15 59		16 59		17 59
Wadhurst	d	22p49	08 05		09 05	09 37	10 05	10 37	11 05	11 37	12 05	12 37	13 05	13 37	14 05	14 37	15 05	15 37	16 05	16 37	17 05	17 37	18 05
Frant	d	22p53	08 09		09 09		10 09		11 09		12 09		13 09		14 09		15 09		16 09		17 09		18 09
Tunbridge Wells [4]	a	22p58	08 14		09 14	09 44	10 14	10 44	11 14	11 44	12 14	12 44	13 14	13 44	14 14	14 44	15 14	15 44	16 14	16 44	17 14	17 44	18 14
	d	22p59	08 15	08 45	09 15	09 45	10 15	10 45	11 15	11 45	12 15	12 45	13 15	13 45	14 15	14 45	15 15	15 45	16 15	16 45	17 15	17 45	18 15
High Brooms	d	23p02	08 18	08 48	09 18	09 48	10 18	10 48	11 18	11 48	12 18	12 48	13 18	13 48	14 18	14 48	15 18	15 48	16 18	16 48	17 18	17 48	18 18
Tonbridge [4]	a	23p08	08 24	08 54	09 24	09 54	10 24	10 54	11 24	11 54	12 24	12 54	13 24	13 54	14 24	14 54	15 24	15 54	16 24	16 54	17 24	17 54	18 24
Sevenoaks [4]	a	23p24	08 33	09 03	09 33	10 03	10 33	11 03	11 33	12 03	12 33	13 03	13 33	14 03	14 33	15 03	15 33	16 03	16 33	17 03	17 33	18 03	18 33
Orpington [4]	a	23p36	08 42	09 12	09 42	10 12	10 42	11 12	11 42	12 12	12 42	13 12	13 42	14 12	14 42	15 12	15 42	16 12	16 42	17 12	17 42	18 12	18 42
London Bridge [4] ⊖	a	23p53	08 58	09 28	09 58	10 28	10 58	11 28	11 58	12 28	12 58	13 28	13 58	14 28	14 58	15 28	15 58	16 28	16 58	17 28	17 58	18 28	18 58
London Cannon Street [4] ⊖	a																						
London Waterloo (East) [4] ⊖	a	23p57	09 03	09 33	10 03	10 33	11 03	11 33	12 03	12 33	13 03	13 33	14 03	14 33	15 03	15 33	16 03	16 33	17 03	17 33	18 03	18 33	19 03
London Charing Cross [4] ⊖	a	00 01	09 07	09 37	10 07	10 37	11 07	11 37	12 07	12 37	13 07	13 37	14 07	14 37	15 07	15 37	16 07	16 37	17 07	17 37	18 07	18 37	19 07

		SE [1]	SE [1]	SE [1]	SE [1]	SE [1]	SE [1]	SE [1]
Ore	d							
Hastings [4]	d	18 08	18 28	19 28		20 28	21 28	22 28
St Leonards Warrior Sq [4]	d	18 11	18 30	19 30		20 30	21 30	22 30
West St Leonards	d		18 33	19 33		20 33	21 33	22 33
Crowhurst	d		18 39	19 39		20 39	21 39	22 39
Battle	d	18 21	18 43	19 43		20 43	21 43	22 43
Robertsbridge	d		18 50	19 50		20 50	21 50	22 50
Etchingham	d		18 53	19 53		20 53	21 53	22 53
Stonegate	d		18 59	19 59		20 59	21 59	22 59
Wadhurst	d	18 37	19 05	20 05		21 05	22 05	23 05
Frant	d		19 09	20 09		21 09	22 09	23 09
Tunbridge Wells [4]	a	18 44	19 14	20 14		21 14	22 14	23 14
	d	18 45	19 15	20 15	20 53	21 15	22 15	23 15
High Brooms	d	18 48	19 18	20 18	20 56	21 18	22 18	23 18
Tonbridge [4]	a	18 54	19 24	20 24	21 02	21 24	22 24	23 24
Sevenoaks [4]	a	19 03	19 33	20 33		21 33	22 33	
Orpington [4]	a	19 12	19 42	20 42		21 42	22 42	
London Bridge [4] ⊖	a	19 28	19 58	20 58		21 58	22 58	
London Cannon Street [4] ⊖	a							
London Waterloo (East) [4] ⊖	a	19 33	20 03	21 03		22 03	23 03	
London Charing Cross [4] ⊖	a	19 37	20 07	21 07		22 07	23 07	

Table 207

Mondays to Fridays

London and Tonbridge - Ashford International, Folkestone, Dover, Canterbury West, Ramsgate and Margate

		SE MX [1]	SE MO [1]	SE MX [1]	SE MO [1]	SE	SE MO [1]	SE MX [1]	SE MX [1]	SE MO [1]	SE MO	SE MX [1]
St Pancras International [15] ⊖	d					23p12					23p42	
Stratford International ⊖	d					23p19					23p49	
Ebbsfleet International	d					23p31					00 01	
London Charing Cross [4] ⊖	d	21p40	22p08	22p10	23p08		22p38	22p40		23p38		23p10
London Waterloo (East) [4] ⊖	d	21p43	22p11	22p13	23p11		22p41	22p43		23p41		23p13
London Cannon Street [4] ⊖	d											
London Bridge [4] ⊖	d	21p49	22p16	22p19	23p16		22p46	22p49		23p46		23p19
Orpington [4]	d		22p32	22p35	23p32		23p02			00 02		23p35
Sevenoaks [4]	d	22p13	22p42	22p44	23p42		23p12	23p13		00 12		23p44
Tonbridge [4]	a	22p21	22p52	22p52	23p52		23p20	23p21		00 20		23p52
	d	22p21	22p53	22p53	23p53		23p21	23p21		00 21		23p53
Paddock Wood [4]	d	22p28	23p00	23p00	00 01		23p28	23p28		00 28		23p59
Maidstone West [4]	a											
Marden	d	22p34	23p06	23p05	00 07		23p34	23p34		00 34		00 05
Staplehurst	d	22p37	23p09	23p09	00 09		23p37	23p37		00 37		00 09
Headcorn	d	22p42	23p14	23p14	00 14		23p42	23p42		00 42		00 14
Pluckley	d	22p48		23p20			23p48	23p48		00 48		00 20
Ashford International	a	22p56	23p26	23p27	00 26	23p50	23p56	23p56	>	00 56	00 19	00 27
	d	23p01	23p30	23p30		23p52	00 01	00 01	00 03			00 30
Wye	d								00 09			
Chilham	d								00 15			
Chartham	d								00 19			
Canterbury West [4]	d								00 25			
Sturry	d								00 30			
Westenhanger	d	23p09	23p39	23p39				00 09				00 39
Sandling	d	23p12	23p42	23p42			00 10	00 12				00 42
Folkestone West	d	23p17	23p47	23p47		00 07	00 15	00 17				00 47
Folkestone Central	d	23p20	23p50	23p50		00 10	00 18	00 20				00 50
Dover Priory [4]	a	23p31	00 01	00 02		00 21	00 29	00 31				01 01
	d	23p33	00 04	00 03								
Martin Mill	d	23p42	00 13	00 12								
Walmer	d	23p46	00 17	00 16								
Deal	d	23p49	00 20	00 19								
Sandwich	d	23p55	00 26	00 25								
Minster [4]	d								00 41			
Ramsgate [4]	a	00 07	00 37	00 36					00 47			
Broadstairs	a											
Margate [4]	a											

		SE MX [1]	SE MX [1]	SE MX	SE [1]	SE	SE [1]	SE	SE [1]	SE [1]	SE [1]	SE
St Pancras International [15] ⊖	d			00 12								
Stratford International ⊖	d			00 19								
Ebbsfleet International	d			00 31								
London Charing Cross [4] ⊖	d	23p40									05 30	
London Waterloo (East) [4] ⊖	d	23p43									05 33	
London Cannon Street [4] ⊖	d											
London Bridge [4] ⊖	d	23p49									05 39	
Orpington [4]	d										05 55	
Sevenoaks [4]	d	00 13									06 06	
Tonbridge [4]	a	00 21									06 16	
	d	00 21			04 51						06 21	
Paddock Wood [4]	d	00 28			04 58	05 42		06 25			06 28	06 55
Maidstone West [4]	a					06 01		06 44				07 14
Marden	d	00 34			05 04						06 34	
Staplehurst	d	00 37			05 07						06 37	
Headcorn	d	00 42			05 12						06 42	
Pluckley	d	00 48			05 18						06 48	
Ashford International	a	00 56	>	00 50	05 26						06 58	
	d	01 00	01 03		05 30		06 02		06 30	06 33	07 00	
Wye	d		01 09							06 39		
Chilham	d		01 15							06 45		
Chartham	d		01 19							06 49		
Canterbury West [4]	d		01a24							06 55		
Sturry	d									07 00		
Westenhanger	d	01 09			05 39		06 09		06 39		07 09	
Sandling	d	01 12			05 42		06 12		06 42		07 12	
Folkestone West	d	01 17			05 47		06 17		06 47		07 17	
Folkestone Central	d	01 20			05 50		06 20		06 49		07 20	
Dover Priory [4]	a	01 31			06 01		06 31		07 01		07 31	
	d				06 03				07 07		07 49	
Martin Mill	d				06 12				07 18		07 57	
Walmer	d				06 16				07 22		08 01	
Deal	d				06 19				07 25		08 04	
Sandwich	d				06 25				07 31		08 10	
Minster [4]	d									07 11		
Ramsgate [4]	a				06 38				07 43	07 17	08 23	
Broadstairs	a											
Margate [4]	a											

		SE [1]	SE	SE	SE [1]	SE [1]	SE	SE	SE [1]	SE [1]	SE	SE
St Pancras International [15] ⊖	d		06 40	07 10				07 40				08 10
Stratford International ⊖	d		06 47	07 17				07 47				08 17
Ebbsfleet International	d		06 59	07 30				08 00				08 30
London Charing Cross [4] ⊖	d				06 30				07 10			
London Waterloo (East) [4] ⊖	d				06 33				07 13			
London Cannon Street [4] ⊖	d											
London Bridge [4] ⊖	d				06 38				07 20			
Orpington [4]	d				06 54							
Sevenoaks [4]	d				07 03				07 43			
Tonbridge [4]	a				07 15				07 51			
	d				07 16				07 51			
Paddock Wood [4]	d				07 23		07 40		07 58		08 10	
Maidstone West [4]	a						07 59				08 29	
Marden	d				07 28				08 04			
Staplehurst	d				07 32				08 07			
Headcorn	d				07 37				08 12			
Pluckley	d				07 43				08 18			
Ashford International	a	07 02	07 19	07 50	07 50	>		08 20	08 25	>		08 50
	d	07 03	07 22	07 52	07 55	08 00		08 22	08 31	08 33		08 52
Wye	d	07 09			08 01					08 39		
Chilham	d	07 15			08 07					08 45		
Chartham	d	07 19			08 10					08 49		
Canterbury West [4]	d	07a24	07 40		08 17			08 40		08a54		
Sturry	d		07 45		08 22							
Westenhanger	d					08 09			08 39			
Sandling	d					08 12			08 42			
Folkestone West	d			08 07		08 17			08 47			09 07
Folkestone Central	d			08 10		08 20			08 50			09 10
Dover Priory [4]	a			08 21		08 31			09 01			09 21
	d					08 33						
Martin Mill	d					08 42						
Walmer	d					08 46						
Deal	d					08 49						
Sandwich	d					08 55						
Minster [4]	d		07 56		08 33							
Ramsgate [4]	a		08 01		08 38	09 08		08 59				
Broadstairs	a		08 07					09 04				
Margate [4]	a		08 12					09 10				

		SE [1]	SE [1]	SE	SE [1]	SE [1]	SE	SE	SE [1]	SE [1]	SE [1]	SE
St Pancras International [15] ⊖	d			08 40				09 12				09 40
Stratford International ⊖	d			08 47				09 19				09 47
Ebbsfleet International	d			09 00				09 31				09 59
London Charing Cross [4] ⊖	d	07 40			08 13				08 33		08 53	
London Waterloo (East) [4] ⊖	d	07 43			08 16				08 36		08 56	
London Cannon Street [4] ⊖	d											
London Bridge [4] ⊖	d	07 49			08 21				08 41		09 01	
Orpington [4]	d								08 58		09 21	
Sevenoaks [4]	d	08 13			08 45				09 07		09 30	
Tonbridge [4]	a	08 21			08 53				09 18		09 38	
	d	08 21			08 53		09 03		09 21		09 39	
Paddock Wood [4]	d	08 28			09 00		09 10		09 28		09 46	
Maidstone West [4]	a						09 29					
Marden	d	08 34			09 06				09 34			
Staplehurst	d	08 37			09 09				09 37		09 53	
Headcorn	d	08 42			09 14				09 42		09 58	
Pluckley	d	08 48			09 20				09 48			
Ashford International	a	08 56	>	09 20	09 27	>		09 50	09 56		10 11	10 18
	d	09 00	09 03	09 22	09 31	09 33		09 52	10 00	10 03		10 22
Wye	d		09 09			09 39				10 09		
Chilham	d					09 45						
Chartham	d					09 49						
Canterbury West [4]	d		09 22	09 40		09a54				10 22		10 40
Sturry	d		09 26							10 26		
Westenhanger	d	09 09			09 40				10 09			
Sandling	d	09 12			09 43				10 12			
Folkestone West	d	09 17			09 48			10 07	10 17			
Folkestone Central	d	09 20			09 51			10 10	10 20			
Dover Priory [4]	a	09 31			10 02			10 21	10 31			
	d	09 33							10 33			
Martin Mill	d	09 42							10 42			
Walmer	d	09 46							10 46			
Deal	d	09 49							10 49			
Sandwich	d	09 55							10 55			
Minster [4]	d		09 37							10 37		
Ramsgate [4]	a	10 07	09 44	09 58					11 07	10 44		10 58
Broadstairs	a			10 04								11 04
Margate [4]	a			10 10								11 10

London and Tonbridge - Ashford International, Folkestone, Dover, Canterbury West, Ramsgate and Margate

		SE 1	SE 1	SE	SE	SE 1 A 🛒	SE 1	SE	SE 1 A 🛒	SE 1	SE	SE	SE 1	SE 1	SE	SE 1 A 🛒	SE 1	SE	SE	SE 1 A 🛒	SE 1	SE
St Pancras International 15 ⊖	d				10 12			10 42				11 12			11 42				12 12			12 42
Stratford International ⊖	d				10 19			10 49				11 19			11 49				12 19			12 49
Ebbsfleet International	d				10 31			11 01				11 31			12 01				12 31			13 01
London Charing Cross 4 ⊖	d	09 13				09 40			10 10				10 40			11 10				11 40		
London Waterloo (East) 4 ⊖	d	09 16				09 43			10 13				10 43			11 13				11 43		
London Cannon Street 4 ⊖	d																					
London Bridge 4 ⊖	d	09 21				09 49			10 19				10 49			11 19				11 49		
Orpington 4	d																					
Sevenoaks 4	d	09 44				10 13			10 43				11 13			11 43				12 13		
Tonbridge 4	a	09 52				10 21			10 51				11 21			11 51				12 21		
	d	09 53		10 03		10 21			10 51		11 03		11 21			11 51		12 03		12 21		
Paddock Wood 4	d	10 00		10 10		10 28			10 58		11 10		11 28			11 58		12 10		12 28		
Maidstone West 4	a			10 29							11 29							12 29				
Marden	d	10 05				10 34			11 04				11 34			12 04				12 34		
Staplehurst	d	10 09				10 37			11 07				11 37			12 07				12 37		
Headcorn	d	10 14				10 42			11 12				11 42			12 12				12 42		
Pluckley	d	10 20				10 48			11 18				11 48			12 18				12 48		
Ashford Internationa	a	10 27	>		10 50	10 56	>	11 20	11 26	>		11 50	11 56	>	12 20	12 26	>		12 50	12 56	>	13 20
	d	10 31	10 33		10 52	11 00	11 03	11 22	11 30	11 33		11 52	12 00	12 03	12 22	12 30	12 33		12 52	13 00	13 03	13 22
Wye	d		10 39				11 09			11 39				12 09			12 39				13 09	
Chilham	d		10 45							11 45							12 45					
Chartham	d		10 49							11 49							12 49					
Canterbury West 4	d		10a54				11 22	11 40		11a54				12 22	12 40		12a54				13 22	13 40
Sturry	d						11 26							12 26							13 26	
Westenhanger	d	10 39				11 09			11 39				12 09			12 39				13 09		
Sandling	d	10 42				11 12			11 42				12 12			12 42				13 12		
Folkestone West	d	10 47			11 07	11 17			11 47			12 07	12 17			12 47			13 07	13 17		
Folkestone Central	d	10 50			11 10	11 20			11 50			12 10	12 20			12 50			13 10	13 20		
Dover Priory 4	a	11 01			11 21	11 31			12 01			12 21	12 31			13 01			13 21	13 31		
	d					11 33							12 33							13 33		
Martin Mill	d					11 42							12 42							13 42		
Walmer	d					11 46							12 46							13 46		
Deal	d					11 49							12 49							13 49		
Sandwich	d					11 55							12 55							13 55		
Minster 4	d						11 37							12 37							13 37	
Ramsgate 4	a					12 07	11 44	11 58					13 07	12 44	12 58					14 07	13 44	13 58
Broadstairs	a							12 04							13 04							14 04
Margate 4	a							12 10							13 10							14 10

		SE 1 A 🛒	SE 1	SE	SE	SE 1 A 🛒	SE 1	SE	SE 1 A 🛒	SE 1	SE	SE	SE 1 A 🛒	SE 1	SE	SE 1 A 🛒	SE 1	SE	SE	SE 1 A 🛒	SE 1	SE	SE 1 A 🛒
St Pancras International 15 ⊖	d				13 12			13 42				14 12			14 42				15 12			15 42	
Stratford International ⊖	d				13 19			13 49				14 19			14 49				15 19			15 49	
Ebbsfleet International	d				13 31			14 01				14 31			15 01				15 31			16 01	
London Charing Cross 4 ⊖	d	12 10				12 40			13 10				13 40			14 10				14 40			15 10
London Waterloo (East) 4 ⊖	d	12 13				12 43			13 13				13 43			14 13				14 43			15 13
London Cannon Street 4 ⊖	d																						
London Bridge 4 ⊖	d	12 19				12 49			13 19				13 49			14 19				14 49			15 19
Orpington 4	d																						
Sevenoaks 4	d	12 43				13 13			13 43				14 13			14 43				15 13			15 43
Tonbridge 4	a	12 51				13 21			13 51				14 21			14 51				15 21			15 51
	d	12 51		13 03		13 21			13 51		14 03		14 21			14 51		15 03		15 21			15 51
Paddock Wood 4	d	12 58		13 10		13 28			13 58		14 10		14 28			14 58		15 10		15 28			15 58
Maidstone West 4	a			13 29							14 29							15 29					
Marden	d	13 04				13 34			14 04				14 34			15 04				15 34			16 04
Staplehurst	d	13 07				13 37			14 07				14 37			15 07				15 37			16 07
Headcorn	d	13 12				13 42			14 12				14 42			15 12				15 42			16 12
Pluckley	d	13 18				13 48			14 18				14 48			15 18				15 48			16 18
Ashford International	a	13 26	>		13 50	13 56	>	14 20	14 26	>		14 50	14 56	>	15 20	15 25	>		15 50	15 56	>	16 20	16 25
	d	13 30	13 33		13 52	14 00	14 03	14 22	14 30	14 33		14 52	15 00	15 03	15 22	15 30	15 33		15 52	16 00	16 03	16 22	16 30
Wye	d		13 39				14 09			14 39				15 09			15 39				16 09		
Chilham	d		13 45							14 45							15 45						
Chartham	d		13 49							14 49							15 49						
Canterbury West 4	d		13a54				14 22	14 40		14a54				15 22	15 40		15a54				16 22	16 40	
Sturry	d						14 26							15 26							16 26		
Westenhanger	d	13 39				14 09			14 39				15 09			15 39				16 09			16 39
Sandling	d	13 42				14 12			14 42				15 12			15 42				16 12			16 42
Folkestone West	d	13 47			14 07	14 17			14 47			15 07	15 17			15 47			16 07	16 17			16 47
Folkestone Central	d	13 50			14 10	14 20			14 50			15 10	15 20			15 50			16 10	16 20			16 50
Dover Priory 4	a	14 01			14 21	14 31			15 01			15 21	15 31			16 01			16 21	16 31			17 01
	d					14 33							15 33			16 02				16 33			17 02
Martin Mill	d					14 42							15 42			16 12				16 42			17 12
Walmer	d					14 46							15 46			16 16				16 46			17 16
Deal	d					14 49							15 49			16 19				16 49			17 19
Sandwich	d					14 55							15 55			16 25				16 55			17 25
Minster 4	d						14 37						16 06	15 37						17 06	16 37		
Ramsgate 4	a					15 07	14 44	14 58					16 11	15 44	15 58	16 35				17 11	16 44	16 58	17 35
Broadstairs	a							15 04							16 04							17 04	
Margate 4	a							15 10							16 10							17 10	

A 🛒 to Pluckley

Table 207

Mondays to Fridays

London and Tonbridge - Ashford International, Folkestone, Dover, Canterbury West, Ramsgate and Margate

		SE	SE 1	SE	SE 1 A 🛒	SE 1	SE 1	SE	SE	SE 1 A 🛒	SE 1	SE 1	SE	SE	SE 1	SE	SE	SE 1 A 🛒	SE 1	SE	SE 1	SE 1
St Pancras International 15 ⊖	d			16 12					16 42				17 25			17 10						
Stratford International ⊖	d			16 19					16 49				17b38			17 17						
Ebbsfleet International	d			16 31					17 01				17 49									
London Charing Cross 4 ⊖	d				15 40					16 10								16 37				16 57
London Waterloo (East) 4 ⊖	d				15 43					16 13								16 40				17 00
London Cannon Street 4 ⊖	d						16 46					17 08			17 30						17 52	
London Bridge 4 ⊖	d				15 49		16 50			16 19		17 12			17 34			16 45			17 56	
Orpington 4	d																					
Sevenoaks 4	d				16 13					16 43								17 10				17 27
Tonbridge 4	a				16 21					16 51								17 18				17 35
	d	16 03			16 21					16 51								17 18				17 36
Paddock Wood 4	d	16 10			16 28			17 02		16 58				17 29				17 26		17 52		17 43
Maidstone West 4	a	16 29						17 21						17 48						18 11		
Marden	d				16 34					17 04								17 31				17 49
Staplehurst	d				16 37					17 07								17 35				17 53
Headcorn	d				16 42					17 12								17 41				17 58
Pluckley	d				16 48					17 18								17 47				18 04
Ashford International	a			16 50	16 56	>			17 20	17 25	>					17 46		17 56	>			18 13
	d		16 35	16 52	17 00	17 03			17 22	17 30	17 35					17 50	17 52	18 00	18 03			
Wye	d		16 41			17 09					17 41								18 09			
Chilham	d		16 47			17 15					17 47								18 15			
Chartham	d		16 51			17 19					17 51								18 19			
Canterbury West 4	d		16a56			17 25			17 40		17a58						18 10		18 25			
Sturry	d					17 30													18 30			
Westenhanger	d				17 09					17 39								18 09				
Sandling	d				17 12					17 42								18 12				
Folkestone West	d			17 07	17 17					17 47						18 03		18 17				
Folkestone Central	d			17 10	17 20					17 50						18 06		18 20				
Dover Priory 4	a			17 21	17 31					18 01						18 18		18 31				
	d				17 33					18 02								18 33				
Martin Mill	d				17 42					18 12								18 42				
Walmer	d				17 46					18 16								18 46				
Deal	d				17 49					18 19								18 49				
Sandwich	d				17 55					18 25								18 55				
Minster 4	d					17 41													18 41			
Ramsgate 4	a				18 07	17 47			17 58	18 37							18 28	19 09	18 49			
Broadstairs	a								18 04								18 34					
Margate 4	a						18 28		18 10			18 53	18 59		19 19		18 40				19 40	

		SE	SE	SE	SE 1	SE 1 B 🛒	SE 1	SE	SE 1	SE	SE	SE 1	SE 1 A 🛒	SE 1	SE	SE 1 🛒	SE	SE	SE 1	SE 1	SE 1	SE	SE 1
St Pancras International 15 ⊖	d	17 58	17 40					18 25		18 10							18 40						
Stratford International ⊖	d	18 05	17 47					18 32		18 17							18 47						
Ebbsfleet International	d	18 16						18 43															
London Charing Cross 4 ⊖	d					17 14							17 41			17 59					18 21		
London Waterloo (East) 4 ⊖	d					17 18							17 44			18 02					18 24		
London Cannon Street 4 ⊖	d				18 14				17 24			18 44		17 45					18 08				18 32
London Bridge 4 ⊖	d				18 18				17 28			18 48		17 49					18 12				18 36
Orpington 4	d																						
Sevenoaks 4	d					17 46			17 54				18 11	18 15		18 30			18 37		18 52		19 00
Tonbridge 4	a					17 54			18 04				18 19	18 23		18 38			18 47		19 00		19 08
	d					17 54			18 04				18 20	18 24		18 39			18 48		19 01		19 09
Paddock Wood 4	d					18 02			18 12				18 28	18 32	18 40	18 46			18 56		19 09	19 12	19 17
Maidstone West 4	a														19 01							19 31	
Marden	d					18 07			18 17				18 33	18 37		18 52			19 01		19 14		19 22
Staplehurst	d					18 11			18 21				18 37	18 41		18 56			19 05		19 18		19 26
Headcorn	d					18 17			18 27				18 43	18 47		19 01			19 10		19 23		19 32
Pluckley	d								18 33				18 49	18 53		19 07			19 16		19 29		19 38
Ashford International	a		18 16			18 28	>		18 42	18 46	>		18 56	19 00		19 16	19 16	>	19 23	>	19 38		19 48
	d		18 20	18 22		18 32	18 34			18 50	18 52		19 03	19 04			19 20	19 22	19 27	19 29			
Wye	d						18 40							19 10						19 35			
Chilham	d						18 46							19 16						19 41			
Chartham	d						18 49							19 20						19 45			
Canterbury West 4	d			18 40			18a56				19 10			19 25				19 40		19a52			
Sturry	d													19 30									
Westenhanger	d					18 40							19 11						19 36				
Sandling	d					18 43							19 14						19 39				
Folkestone West	d		18 33			18 48				19 03			19 19				19 33		19 44				
Folkestone Central	d		18 36			18 51				19 06			19 22				19 36		19 47				
Dover Priory 4	a		18 48			19 03				19 18			19 32				19 47		19 58				
	d												19 34						20 02				
Martin Mill	d												19 43						20 11				
Walmer	d												19 47						20 16				
Deal	d												19 50						20 19				
Sandwich	d												19 56						20 25				
Minster 4	d													19 41									
Ramsgate 4	a			18 58							19 30		20 09	19 49				19 58	20 37				
Broadstairs	a			19 04							19 36							20 04					
Margate 4	a	19 29		19 10	19 57			20 01			19 41	20 30						20 10					

A 🛒 to Pluckley

B 🛒 to Headcorn

b arr. 1731

Table 207

Mondays to Fridays

London and Tonbridge - Ashford International, Folkestone, Dover, Canterbury West, Ramsgate and Margate

		SE	SE 1 ⊥	SE 1	SE	SE		SE 1 ⊥	SE 1	SE	SE 1 ⊥	SE 1	SE	SE	SE 1 ⊥	SE		SE 1 ⊥	SE 1	SE	SE	SE 1 ⊥	SE	SE 1	SE 1	SE
St Pancras International 15 ⊖	d	19 12				19 42				20 12				20 42		21 12					21 42		22 12			
Stratford International ⊖	d	19 19				19 49				20 19				20 49		21 19					21 49		22 19			
Ebbsfleet International	d	19 31				20 01				20 31				21 01		21 31					22 01		22 31			
London Charing Cross 4 ⊖	d		18 41					19 10			19 40				20 10			20 40				21 10		21 40		
London Waterloo (East) 4 ⊖	d		18 44					19 13			19 43				20 13			20 43				21 13		21 43		
London Cannon Street 4 ⊖	d																									
London Bridge 4 ⊖	d		18 50					19 19			19 49				20 19			20 49				21 19		21 49		
Orpington 4	d		19 07																			21 35				
Sevenoaks 4	d		19 16					19 43			20 13				20 43			21 13				21 44		22 13		
Tonbridge 4	a		19 24					19 52			20 21				20 51			21 21				21 52		22 21		
	d		19 25					19 52			20 21		20 33		20 51			21 21		21 33		21 53		22 21		22 33
Paddock Wood 4	d		19 32		19 40			20 00			20 28		20 40		20 58			21 28		21 40		22 00		22 28		22 40
Maidstone West 4	a				19 59								20 59							21 59						22 59
Marden	d		19 38					20 05			20 34				21 04			21 34				22 05		22 34		
Staplehurst	d		19 42					20 09			20 37				21 07			21 37				22 09		22 37		
Headcorn	d		19 47					20 15			20 42				21 12			21 42				22 14		22 42		
Pluckley	d		19 53					20 21			20 48				21 18			21 48				22 20		22 48		
Ashford International	a	19 50	20 00	>		20 20		20 28	>	20 50	20 56	>		21 20	21 26	21 50		21 56	>		22 20	22 27	22 50	22 56	>	
	d	19 52	20 04	20 06		20 22		20 32	20 35	20 52	21 00	21 03		21 22	21 30	21 52		22 00	22 03		22 22	22 30	22 52	23 01	23 03	
Wye	d			20 12					20 41			21 09							22 09						23 09	
Chilham	d								20 47			21 15							22 15						23 15	
Chartham	d								20 51			21 19							22 19						23 19	
Canterbury West 4	d			20 25		20 40			20a56			21 25		21 40					22 25		22 40				23 25	
Sturry	d			20 29								21 30							22 30						23 30	
Westenhanger	d		20 12					20 40			21 09				21 39			22 09				22 39		23 09		
Sandling	d		20 15					20 43			21 12				21 42			22 12				22 42		23 12		
Folkestone West	d	20 07	20 20					20 48		21 07	21 17				21 47	22 07		22 17				22 47	23 07	23 17		
Folkestone Central	d	20 10	20 23					20 51		21 10	21 20				21 50	22 10		22 20				22 50	23 10	23 20		
Dover Priory 4	a	20 21	20 33					21 01		21 21	21 31				22 01	22 21		22 31				23 01	23 21	23 31		
	d		20 35								21 33							22 33						23 33		
Martin Mill	d		20 44								21 42							22 42						23 42		
Walmer	d		20 48								21 46							22 46						23 46		
Deal	d		20 51								21 49							22 49						23 49		
Sandwich	d		20 57								21 55							22 55						23 55		
Minster 4	d			20 40								21 41							22 41						23 41	
Ramsgate 4	a		21 10	20 47		20 58					22 07	21 47		21 58				23 07	22 47		22 58			00 07	23 47	
Broadstairs	a					21 04								22 04							23 04					
Margate 4	a					21 10								22 10							23 10					

		SE	SE 1	SE	SE 1	SE 1	SE 1	SE 1	SE 1
St Pancras International 15 ⊖	d	22 42		23 12					
Stratford International ⊖	d	22 49		23 19					
Ebbsfleet International	d	23 01		23 31					
London Charing Cross 4 ⊖	d		22 10		22 40		23 10	23 40	
London Waterloo (East) 4 ⊖	d		22 13		22 43		23 13	23 43	
London Cannon Street 4 ⊖	d								
London Bridge 4 ⊖	d		22 19		22 49		23 19	23 49	
Orpington 4	d		22 35				23 35		
Sevenoaks 4	d		22 44		23 13		23 44	00 13	
Tonbridge 4	a		22 52		23 21		23 52	00 21	
	d		22 53		23 21		23 53	00 21	
Paddock Wood 4	d		23 00		23 28		23 59	00 28	
Maidstone West 4	a								
Marden	d		23 05		23 34		00 05	00 34	
Staplehurst	d		23 09		23 37		00 09	00 37	
Headcorn	d		23 14		23 42		00 14	00 42	
Pluckley	d		23 20		23 48		00 20	00 48	
Ashford International	a	23 20	23 27	23 50	23 56	>	00 27	00 56	>
	d	23 22	23 30	23 52	00 01	00 03	00 30	01 00	01 03
Wye	d					00 09			01 09
Chilham	d					00 15			01 15
Chartham	d					00 19			01 19
Canterbury West 4	d	23 40				00 25			01a24
Sturry	d					00 30			
Westenhanger	d		23 39		00 09		00 39	01 09	
Sandling	d		23 42		00 12		00 42	01 12	
Folkestone West	d		23 47	00 07	00 17		00 47	01 17	
Folkestone Central	d		23 50	00 10	00 20		00 50	01 20	
Dover Priory 4	a		00 02	00 21	00 31		01 01	01 31	
	d		00 03						
Martin Mill	d		00 12						
Walmer	d		00 16						
Deal	d		00 19						
Sandwich	d		00 25						
Minster 4	d					00 41			
Ramsgate 4	a	23 58	00 36			00 47			
Broadstairs	a								
Margate 4	a								

Table 207

Saturdays

London and Tonbridge - Ashford International, Folkestone, Dover, Canterbury West, Ramsgate and Margate

		SE 1	SE 1	SE	SE 1	SE 1	SE 1	SE 1	SE 1	SE		SE	SE 1	SE 1	SE 1	SE	SE 1	SE	SE 1	SE		SE 1	SE 1	SE 1	SE 1	SE
St Pancras International 15 ⊖	d			23p12						00 12						06 40				07 12						
Stratford International ⊖	d			23p19						00 19						06 47				07 19						
Ebbsfleet International	d			23p31						00 31						06 59				07 31						
London Charing Cross 4 ⊖	d	21p40	22p10		22p40		23p10	23p40									06 00							07 00		
London Waterloo (East) 4 ⊖	d	21p43	22p13		22p43		23p13	23p43									06 03							07 03		
London Cannon Street 4 ⊖	d																									
London Bridge 4 ⊖	d	21p49	22p19		22p49		23p19	23p49									06 08							07 08		
Orpington 4	d		22p35				23p35										06 24							07 24		
Sevenoaks 4	d	22p13	22p44		23p13		23p44	00 13									06 33							07 33		
Tonbridge 4	a	22p21	22p52		23p21		23p52	00 21									06 43							07 43		
	d	22p21	22p53		23p21		23p53	00 21				06 03			06 21		06 51	07 03						07 51		08 03
Paddock Wood 4	d	22p28	23p00		23p28		23p59	00 28				06 10			06 28		06 58	07 10						07 58		08 10
Maidstone West 4	a											06 29						07 29								08 29
Marden	d	22p34	23p05		23p34		00 05	00 34							06 34		07 04							08 04		
Staplehurst	d	22p37	23p09		23p37		00 09	00 37							06 37		07 07							08 07		
Headcorn	d	22p42	23p14		23p42		00 14	00 42							06 42		07 12							08 12		
Pluckley	d	22p48	23p20		23p48		00 20	00 48							06 48		07 18							08 18		
Ashford International	a	22p56	23p27	23p50	23p56	>	00 27	00 56	>	00 50					06 56	07 19	07 26			07 50				08 29	>	
	d	23p01	23p30	23p52	00 01	00 03	00 30	01 00	01 03				06 30	06 33	07 03	07 22	07 30		07 33	07 52		08 00	08 03	08 30	08 33	
Wye	d					00 09			01 09					06 39	07 09				07 39				08 09		08 39	
Chilham	d					00 15			01 15					06 45					07 45						08 45	
Chartham	d					00 19			01 19					06 49					07 49						08 49	
Canterbury West 4	d					00 25			01a24					06a54	07 22	07 40			07a54				08 22		08a54	
Sturry	d					00 30									07 26								08 26			
Westenhanger	d	23p09	23p39		00 09		00 39	01 09					06 39				07 39					08 09		08 39		
Sandling	d	23p12	23p42		00 12		00 42	01 12					06 42				07 42					08 12		08 42		
Folkestone West	d	23p17	23p47	00 07	00 17		00 47	01 17					06 47				07 47			08 07		08 17		08 47		
Folkestone Central	d	23p20	23p50	00 10	00 20		00 50	01 20					06 50				07 50			08 10		08 20		08 50		
Dover Priory 4	a	23p31	00 02	00 21	00 31		01 01	01 31					07 01				08 01			08 21		08 31		09 02		
	d	23p33	00 03										07 02				08 02					08 33		09 08		
Martin Mill	d	23p42	00 12										07 11				08 11					08 42		09 16		
Walmer	d	23p46	00 16										07 15				08 15					08 46		09 20		
Deal	d	23p49	00 19										07 18				08 18					08 49		09 23		
Sandwich	d	23p55	00 25										07 24				08 24					08 55		09 28		
Minster 4	d					00 41									07 37								08 37			
Ramsgate 4	a	00 07	00 36			00 47							07 35		07 44	07 58	08 35					09 07	08 44	09 39		
Broadstairs	a															08 04										
Margate 4	a															08 10										

		SE	SE 1	SE 1	SE		SE 1	SE 1	SE	SE	SE 1	SE 1	SE	SE 1	SE 1	SE		SE	SE 1	SE 1	SE	SE 1	SE 1	SE
St Pancras International 15 ⊖	d				08 42					09 12			09 40					10 12			10 42			
Stratford International ⊖	d				08 49					09 19			09 47					10 19			10 49			
Ebbsfleet International	d				09 01					09 31			09 59					10 31			11 01			
London Charing Cross 4 ⊖	d			07 30			08 00					08 40		09 10						09 40		10 10		
London Waterloo (East) 4 ⊖	d			07 33			08 03					08 43		09 13						09 43		10 13		
London Cannon Street 4 ⊖	d																							
London Bridge 4 ⊖	d			07 38			08 08					08 49		09 19						09 49		10 19		
Orpington 4	d			07 54			08 24																	
Sevenoaks 4	d			08 03			08 33					09 13		09 43						10 13		10 43		
Tonbridge 4	a			08 14			08 43					09 21		09 51						10 21		10 51		
	d			08 21			08 51		09 03			09 21		09 51		10 03				10 21		10 51		11 03
Paddock Wood 4	d			08 28			08 58		09 10			09 28		09 58		10 10				10 28		10 58		11 10
Maidstone West 4	a								09 29							10 29								11 29
Marden	d			08 34			09 04					09 34		10 04						10 34		11 04		
Staplehurst	d			08 37			09 07					09 37		10 07						10 37		11 07		
Headcorn	d			08 42			09 12					09 42		10 12						10 42		11 12		
Pluckley	d			08 48			09 18					09 48		10 18						10 48		11 18		
Ashford International	a			08 56	09 20		09 26	>		09 50		09 56	10 18	10 26	>			10 50		10 56	11 20	11 26	>	
	d	08 52	09 00	09 03	09 22		09 30	09 33		09 52	10 00	10 03	10 22	10 30	10 33			10 52	11 00	11 03	11 22	11 30	11 33	
Wye	d			09 09				09 39				10 09			10 39					11 09			11 39	
Chilham	d							09 45							10 45								11 45	
Chartham	d							09 49							10 49								11 49	
Canterbury West 4	d			09 22	09 40			09a54				10 22	10 40		10a54					11 22	11 40		11a54	
Sturry	d			09 26								10 26								11 26				
Westenhanger	d		09 08				09 39				10 08			10 39					11 08			11 39		
Sandling	d		09 11				09 42				10 11			10 42					11 11			11 42		
Folkestone West	d	09 07	09 16				09 47			10 07	10 16			10 47				11 07	11 16			11 47		
Folkestone Central	d	09 10	09 18				09 50			10 10	10 18			10 50				11 10	11 18			11 50		
Dover Priory 4	a	09 21	09 29				10 01			10 21	10 29			11 01				11 21	11 29			12 01		
	d						10 02							11 02								12 02		
Martin Mill	d						10 11							11 11								12 11		
Walmer	d						10 15							11 15								12 15		
Deal	d						10 18							11 18								12 18		
Sandwich	d						10 24							11 24								12 24		
Minster 4	d			09 37								10 37								11 37				
Ramsgate 4	a			09 44	09 58		10 35					10 44	10 58	11 35						11 44	11 58	12 35		
Broadstairs	a				10 04								11 04								12 04			
Margate 4	a				10 10								11 10								12 10			

London and Tonbridge - Ashford International, Folkestone, Dover, Canterbury West, Ramsgate and Margate

		SE	SE ■	SE ■ A 🚌	SE	SE ■ A 🚌	SE ■	SE	SE	SE ■	SE ■ A 🚌	SE	SE ■ A 🚌	SE ■	SE	SE	SE ■	SE ■ A 🚌	SE	SE ■ A 🚌	SE ■	SE
St Pancras International 15 ⊖	d	11 12			11 42				12 12			12 42				13 12			13 42			
Stratford International ⊖	d	11 19			11 49				12 19			12 49				13 19			13 49			
Ebbsfleet International	d	11 31			12 01				12 31			13 01				13 31			14 01			
London Charing Cross 4 ⊖	d			10 40		11 10					11 40		12 10					12 40		13 10		
London Waterloo (East) 4 ⊖	d			10 43		11 13					11 43		12 13					12 43		13 13		
London Cannon Street 4 ⊖	d																					
London Bridge 4 ⊖	d			10 49		11 19					11 49		12 19					12 49		13 19		
Orpington 4	d																					
Sevenoaks 4	d			11 13		11 43					12 13		12 43					13 13		13 43		
Tonbridge 4	a			11 21		11 51					12 21		12 51					13 21		13 51		
	d			11 21		11 51		12 03			12 21		12 51		13 03			13 21		13 51		14 03
Paddock Wood 4	d			11 28		11 58		12 10			12 28		12 58		13 10			13 28		13 58		14 10
Maidstone West 4	a							12 29							13 29							14 29
Marden	d			11 34		12 04					12 34		13 04					13 34		14 04		
Staplehurst	d			11 37		12 07					12 37		13 07					13 37		14 07		
Headcorn	d			11 42		12 12					12 42		13 12					13 42		14 12		
Pluckley	d			11 48		12 18					12 48		13 18					13 48		14 18		
Ashford International	a	11 50		11 56	12 20	12 26	>		12 50		12 56	13 20	13 26	>		13 50		13 56	14 20	14 26	>	
	d	11 52	12 00	12 03	12 22	12 30	12 33		12 52	13 00	13 03	13 22	13 30	13 33		13 52	14 00	14 03	14 22	14 30	14 33	
Wye	d			12 09			12 39				13 09			13 39				14 09			14 39	
Chilham	d						12 45							13 45							14 45	
Chartham	d						12 49							13 49							14 49	
Canterbury West 4	d			12 22	12 40		12a54				13 22	13 40		13a54				14 22	14 40		14a54	
Sturry	d			12 26							13 26							14 26				
Westenhanger	d		12 08			12 39				13 08			13 39				14 08			14 39		
Sandling	d		12 11			12 42				13 11			13 42				14 11			14 42		
Folkestone West	d	12 07	12 16			12 47			13 07	13 16			13 47			14 07	14 16			14 47		
Folkestone Central	d	12 10	12 18			12 50			13 10	13 18			13 50			14 10	14 18			14 50		
Dover Priory 4	a	12 21	12 29			13 01			13 21	13 29			14 01			14 21	14 29			15 01		
	d					13 02							14 02							15 02		
Martin Mill	d					13 11							14 11							15 11		
Walmer	d					13 15							14 15							15 15		
Deal	d					13 18							14 18							15 18		
Sandwich	d					13 24							14 24							15 24		
Minster 4	d			12 37							13 37							14 37				
Ramsgate 4	a			12 44	12 58	13 35					13 44	13 58	14 35					14 44	14 58	15 35		
Broadstairs	a				13 04							14 04							15 04			
Margate 4	a				13 10							14 10							15 10			

		SE	SE ■	SE ■ A 🚌	SE	SE ■ A 🚌	SE ■	SE	SE	SE ■	SE ■ A 🚌	SE	SE ■ A 🚌	SE ■	SE	SE	SE ■	SE ■ A 🚌	SE	SE ■ A 🚌	SE ■	SE	SE
St Pancras International 15 ⊖	d	14 12			14 42				15 12			15 42				16 12			16 42				17 12
Stratford International ⊖	d	14 19			14 49				15 19			15 49				16 19			16 49				17 19
Ebbsfleet International	d	14 31			15 01				15 31			16 01				16 31			17 01				17 31
London Charing Cross 4 ⊖	d			13 40		14 10					14 40		15 10					15 40		16 10			
London Waterloo (East) 4 ⊖	d			13 43		14 13					14 43		15 13					15 43		16 13			
London Cannon Street 4 ⊖	d																						
London Bridge 4 ⊖	d			13 49		14 19					14 49		15 19					15 49		16 19			
Orpington 4	d																						
Sevenoaks 4	d			14 13		14 43					15 13		15 43					16 13		16 43			
Tonbridge 4	a			14 21		14 51					15 21		15 51					16 21		16 51			
	d			14 21		14 51		15 03			15 21		15 51		16 03			16 21		16 51		17 03	
Paddock Wood 4	d			14 28		14 58		15 10			15 28		15 58		16 10			16 28		16 58		17 10	
Maidstone West 4	a							15 29							16 29							17 29	
Marden	d			14 34		15 04					15 34		16 04					16 34		17 04			
Staplehurst	d			14 37		15 07					15 37		16 07					16 37		17 07			
Headcorn	d			14 42		15 12					15 42		16 12					16 42		17 12			
Pluckley	d			14 48		15 18					15 48		16 18					16 48		17 18			
Ashford International	a	14 50		14 56	15 20	15 26	>		15 50		15 56	16 20	16 26	>		16 50		16 56	17 20	17 26	>		17 50
	d	14 52	15 00	15 03	15 22	15 30	15 33		15 52	16 00	16 03	16 22	16 30	16 33		16 52	17 00	17 03	17 22	17 30	17 33		17 52
Wye	d			15 09			15 39				16 09			16 39				17 09			17 39		
Chilham	d						15 45							16 45							17 45		
Chartham	d						15 49							16 49							17 49		
Canterbury West 4	d			15 22	15 40		15a54				16 22	16 40		16a54				17 22	17 40		17a54		
Sturry	d			15 26							16 26							17 26					
Westenhanger	d		15 08			15 39				16 08			16 39				17 08			17 39			
Sandling	d		15 11			15 42				16 11			16 42				17 11			17 42			
Folkestone West	d	15 07	15 16			15 47			16 07	16 16			16 47			17 07	17 16			17 47			18 07
Folkestone Central	d	15 10	15 18			15 50			16 10	16 18			16 50			17 10	17 18			17 50			18 10
Dover Priory 4	a	15 21	15 29			16 01			16 21	16 29			17 01			17 21	17 29			18 01			18 21
	d					16 02							17 02							18 02			
Martin Mill	d					16 11							17 11							18 11			
Walmer	d					16 15							17 15							18 15			
Deal	d					16 18							17 18							18 18			
Sandwich	d					16 24							17 24							18 24			
Minster 4	d			15 37							16 37							17 37					
Ramsgate 4	a			15 44	15 58	16 35					16 44	16 58	17 35					17 44	17 58	18 35			
Broadstairs	a				16 04							17 04							18 04				
Margate 4	a				16 10							17 10							18 10				

A 🚌 to Pluckley

London and Tonbridge - Ashford International, Folkestone, Dover, Canterbury West, Ramsgate and Margate

		SE ■	SE ■ A 🚌	SE	SE ■ A 🚌	SE ■	SE	SE	SE ■	SE ■ A 🚌	SE	SE ■ A 🚌	SE	SE	SE ■	SE ■ A 🚌	SE	SE ■ A 🚌	SE	SE	SE ■	SE ■ A 🚌
St Pancras International 15 ⊖	d			17 42				18 12			18 42			19 12			19 42			20 12		
Stratford International ⊖	d			17 49				18 19			18 49			19 19			19 49			20 19		
Ebbsfleet International	d			18 01				18 31			19 01			19 31			20 01			20 31		
London Charing Cross 4 ⊖	d		16 40		17 10					17 40		18 10				18 40		19 10				19 40
London Waterloo (East) 4 ⊖	d		16 43		17 13					17 43		18 13				18 43		19 13				19 43
London Cannon Street 4 ⊖	d																					
London Bridge 4 ⊖	d		16 49		17 19					17 49		18 19				18 49		19 19				19 49
Orpington 4	d																					
Sevenoaks 4	d		17 13		17 43					18 13		18 43				19 13		19 43				20 13
Tonbridge 4	a		17 21		17 51					18 21		18 51				19 21		19 51				20 21
	d		17 21		17 51		18 03			18 21		18 51	19 03			19 21		19 51	20 03			20 21
Paddock Wood 4	d		17 28		17 58		18 10			18 28		18 58	19 10			19 28		19 58	20 10			20 28
Maidstone West 4	a						18 29						19 29						20 29			
Marden	d		17 34		18 04					18 34		19 04				19 34		20 04				20 34
Staplehurst	d		17 37		18 07					18 37		19 07				19 37		20 07				20 37
Headcorn	d		17 42		18 12					18 42		19 12				19 42		20 12				20 42
Pluckley	d		17 48		18 18					18 48		19 18				19 48		20 18				20 48
Ashford International	a		17 56	18 20	18 26	>		18 50		18 56	19 20	19 26		19 50		19 56	20 20	20 26		20 50		20 56
	d	18 00	18 03	18 22	18 30	18 33		18 52	19 00	19 03	19 22	19 30		19 52	20 00	20 03	20 22	20 30		20 52	21 00	21 03
Wye	d		18 09			18 39				19 09						20 09						21 09
Chilham	d					18 45				19 15						20 15						21 15
Chartham	d					18 49				19 19						20 19						21 19
Canterbury West 4	d		18 22	18 40		18a54				19 25	19 40					20 25	20 40					21 25
Sturry	d		18 26							19 30						20 30						21 30
Westenhanger	d	18 08			18 39				19 08			19 39			20 08			20 39			21 08	
Sandling	d	18 11			18 42				19 11			19 42			20 11			20 42			21 11	
Folkestone West	d	18 16			18 47			19 07	19 16			19 47		20 07	20 16			20 47		21 07	21 16	
Folkestone Central	d	18 19			18 50			19 10	19 18			19 50		20 10	20 19			20 50		21 10	21 18	
Dover Priory 4	a	18 31			19 01			19 21	19 29			20 01		20 21	20 30			21 01		21 21	21 29	
	d				19 02							20 02						21 02				
Martin Mill	d				19 11							20 11						21 11				
Walmer	d				19 15							20 15						21 15				
Deal	d				19 18							20 18						21 18				
Sandwich	d				19 24							20 24						21 24				
Minster 4	d		18 37							19 41						20 41						21 41
Ramsgate 4	a		18 44	18 58	19 35					19 47	20 00	20 35				20 47	21 00	21 35				21 47
Broadstairs	a			19 04							20 05						21 05					
Margate 4	a			19 10							20 10						21 10					

		SE	SE ■ A 🚌	SE	SE	SE ■	SE ■ 🚌	SE	SE ■	SE	SE	SE ■	SE ■	SE	SE ■	SE	SE ■	SE ■	SE ■	SE ■
St Pancras International 15 ⊖	d	20 42			21 12			21 42			22 12			22 42		23 12				
Stratford International ⊖	d	20 49			21 19			21 49			22 19			22 49		23 19				
Ebbsfleet International	d	21 01			21 31			22 01			22 31			23 01		23 31				
London Charing Cross 4 ⊖	d		20 10				20 40		21 10				21 40		22 10		22 40	23 10	23 40	
London Waterloo (East) 4 ⊖	d		20 13				20 43		21 13				21 43		22 13		22 43	23 13	23 43	
London Cannon Street 4 ⊖	d																			
London Bridge 4 ⊖	d		20 19				20 49		21 19				21 49		22 19		22 49	23 19	23 49	
Orpington 4	d		20 35				21 05		21 35				22 05		22 35		23 05	23 35	00 05	
Sevenoaks 4	d		20 44				21 14		21 44				22 14		22 44		23 14	23 44	00 14	
Tonbridge 4	a		20 52				21 22		21 52				22 22		22 52		23 22	23 52	00 22	
	d		20 53	21 03			21 23		21 53	22 03			22 23		22 53		23 23	23 53	00 23	
Paddock Wood 4	d		21 00	21 10			21 30		22 00	22 10			22 30		23 00		23 30	23 59	00 30	
Maidstone West 4	a			21 29						22 29										
Marden	d		21 05				21 35		22 05				22 35		23 05		23 35	00 05	00 35	
Staplehurst	d		21 09				21 39		22 09				22 39		23 09		23 39	00 09	00 39	
Headcorn	d		21 14				21 44		22 14				22 44		23 14		23 44	00 14	00 44	
Pluckley	d		21 20				21 50		22 20				22 50		23 20		23 50	00 20	00 50	
Ashford International	a	21 20	21 27		21 50		21 57	22 20	22 27		22 50		22 57	23 20	23 27	23 50	23 57	00 27	00 57	>
	d	21 22	21 30		21 52	22 00	22 03	22 22	22 30		22 52	23 00	23 03	23 22	23 30	23 52	00 03	00 30	01 00	01 03
Wye	d						22 09						23 09				00 09			01 09
Chilham	d						22 15						23 15				00 15			01 15
Chartham	d						22 19						23 19				00 19			01 19
Canterbury West 4	d	21 40					22 25	22 40					23 25	23 40			00 25			01a24
Sturry	d						22 30						23 30				00 30			
Westenhanger	d		21 39			22 08			22 39			23 08			23 39			00 39	01 09	
Sandling	d		21 42			22 11			22 42			23 11			23 42			00 42	01 12	
Folkestone West	d		21 47		22 07	22 16			22 47		23 07	23 16			23 47	00 07		00 47	01 17	
Folkestone Central	d		21 50		22 10	22 19			22 50		23 10	23 18			23 50	00 10		00 50	01 20	
Dover Priory 4	a		22 01		22 21	22 30			23 01		23 21	23 29			00 01	00 21		01 01	01 31	
	d		22 02						23 02						00 02					
Martin Mill	d		22 11						23 11						00 11					
Walmer	d		22 15						23 15						00 15					
Deal	d		22 18						23 18						00 18					
Sandwich	d		22 24						23 24						00 24					
Minster 4	d						22 41						23 41				00 41			
Ramsgate 4	a	22 00	22 35				22 47	23 00	23 35				23 47	00 01	00 35		00 47			
Broadstairs	a	22 05						23 05												
Margate 4	a	22 10						23 10												

A 🚌 to Pluckley

Table 207

Sundays

London and Tonbridge - Ashford International, Folkestone, Dover, Canterbury West, Ramsgate and Margate

		SE	SE 1	SE	SE 1	SE 1	SE 1	SE 1	SE		SE	SE	SE 1	SE 1	SE 1	SE 1	SE	SE	SE 1	SE 1		SE 1	SE 1	SE
St Pancras International	d	22p42		23p12					00 12									08 42						
Stratford International	d	22p49		23p19					00 19									08 49						
Ebbsfleet International	d	23p01		23p31					00 31									09 01						
London Charing Cross	d		22p10		22p40	23p10	23p40												08 08				08 38	
London Waterloo (East)	d		22p13		22p43	23p13	23p43												08 11				08 41	
London Cannon Street	d																							
London Bridge	d		22p19		22p49	23p19	23p49												08 16				08 46	
Orpington	d		22p35		23p05	23p35	00 05												08 32				09 02	
Sevenoaks	d		22p44		23p14	23p44	00 14												08 42				09 12	
Tonbridge	a		22p52		23p22	23p52	00 22												08 52				09 20	
	d		22p53		23p23	23p53	00 23				06 26					08 21			08 53				09 21	
Paddock Wood	d		23p00		23p30	23p59	00 30				06 34	07 34				08 28	08 34		09 00				09 28	09 34
Maidstone West	a										06 53	07 53					08 53							09 53
Marden	d		23p05		23p35	00 05	00 35									08 34			09 06				09 34	
Staplehurst	d		23p09		23p39	00 09	00 39									08 37			09 09				09 37	
Headcorn	d		23p14		23p44	00 14	00 44									08 42			09 14				09 42	
Pluckley	d		23p20		23p50	00 20	00 50									08 48							09 48	
Ashford International	a	23p20	23p27	23p50	23p57	00 27	00 57		00 50							08 56		09 20	09 26	>			09 56	
	d	23p22	23p30	23p52	00 03	00 30	01 00	01 03					08 30	08 33	09 00	09 03		09 22	09 30	09 33		10 00	10 03	
Wye	d				00 09			01 09						08 39		09 09				09 39			10 09	
Chilham	d				00 15			01 15						08 45						09 45				
Chartham	d				00 19			01 19						08 49						09 49				
Canterbury West	d	23p40			00 25			01a24						08a54		09 22		09 40		09a54			10 22	
Sturry	d				00 30											09 26							10 26	
Westenhanger	d		23p39			00 39	01 09						08 39		09 08				09 39			10 08		
Sandling	d		23p42			00 42	01 12						08 42		09 11				09 42			10 11		
Folkestone West	d		23p47	00 07		00 47	01 17						08 47		09 16				09 47			10 16		
Folkestone Central	d		23p50	00 10		00 50	01 20						08 50		09 18				09 50			10 18		
Dover Priory	a		00 01	00 02		01 01	01 31						09 01		09 29				10 01			10 29		
	d		00 02										09 04						10 04					
Martin Mill	d		00 11										09 13						10 13					
Walmer	d		00 15										09 17						10 17					
Deal	d		00 18										09 20						10 20					
Sandwich	d		00 24										09 26						10 26					
Minster	d				00 41											09 37							10 37	
Ramsgate	a	00 01	00 35		00 47								09 37			09 43		09 58	10 37				10 43	
Broadstairs	a																	10 04						
Margate	a																	10 10						

		SE	SE 1	SE 1	SE		SE 1	SE 1	SE	SE	SE 1	SE 1	SE	SE 1	SE 1	SE		SE	SE 1	SE 1	SE	SE 1	SE 1	SE	SE
St Pancras International	d	09 40			10 12					10 42			11 12					11 42			12 12				12 42
Stratford International	d	09 47			10 19					10 49			11 19					11 49			12 19				12 49
Ebbsfleet International	d	09 59			10 31					11 01			11 31					12 01			12 31				13 01
London Charing Cross	d		09 08					09 38			10 08				10 38				11 08				11 38		
London Waterloo (East)	d		09 11					09 41			10 11				10 41				11 11				11 41		
London Cannon Street	d																								
London Bridge	d		09 16					09 46			10 16				10 46				11 16				11 46		
Orpington	d		09 32					10 02			10 32				11 02				11 32				12 02		
Sevenoaks	d		09 42					10 12			10 42				11 12				11 42				12 12		
Tonbridge	a		09 52					10 20			10 52				11 20				11 52				12 20		
	d		09 53					10 21			10 53				11 21				11 53				12 21		
Paddock Wood	d		10 00					10 28	10 34		11 00				11 28	11 34			12 00				12 28	12 34	
Maidstone West	a								10 53							11 53								12 53	
Marden	d		10 06					10 34			11 06				11 34				12 06				12 34		
Staplehurst	d		10 09					10 37			11 09				11 37				12 09				12 37		
Headcorn	d		10 14					10 42			11 14				11 42				12 14				12 42		
Pluckley	d							10 48							11 48								12 48		
Ashford International	a	10 18	10 27	>	10 50			10 56		11 20	11 26	>	11 50		11 56			12 20	12 26	>	12 50		12 56		13 20
	d	10 22	10 30	10 33	10 52		11 00	11 03		11 22	11 30	11 33	11 52	12 00	12 03			12 22	12 30	12 33	12 52	13 00	13 03		13 22
Wye	d			10 39				11 09				11 39			12 09					12 39			13 09		
Chilham	d			10 45								11 45								12 45					
Chartham	d			10 49								11 49								12 49					
Canterbury West	d	10 40		10a54				11 22		11 40		11a54			12 22			12 40		12a54			13 22		13 40
Sturry	d							11 26							12 26								13 26		
Westenhanger	d		10 39				11 08				11 39			12 08					12 39			13 08			
Sandling	d		10 42				11 11				11 42			12 11					12 42			13 11			
Folkestone West	d		10 47		11 07		11 16				11 47		12 07	12 16					12 47		13 07	13 16			
Folkestone Central	d		10 50		11 10		11 18				11 50		12 10	12 18					12 50		13 10	13 18			
Dover Priory	a		11 01		11 21		11 29				12 01		12 21	12 29					13 01		13 21	13 29			
	d		11 04								12 04								13 04						
Martin Mill	d		11 13								12 13								13 13						
Walmer	d		11 17								12 17								13 17						
Deal	d		11 20								12 20								13 20						
Sandwich	d		11 26								12 26								13 26						
Minster	d							11 37							12 37								13 37		
Ramsgate	a	10 58	11 37					11 43		11 58	12 37				12 43			12 58	13 37				13 43		13 58
Broadstairs	a	11 04								12 04								13 04							14 04
Margate	a	11 10								12 10								13 10							14 10

Table 207

Sundays

London and Tonbridge - Ashford International, Folkestone, Dover, Canterbury West, Ramsgate and Margate

		SE 1	SE 1	SE	SE 1	SE 1	SE	SE	SE 1	SE 1	SE		SE 1	SE 1	SE	SE	SE 1	SE 1	SE	SE 1		SE 1	SE	SE
St Pancras International	d			13 12				13 42			14 12					14 42			15 12					15 42
Stratford International	d			13 19				13 49			14 19					14 49			15 19					15 49
Ebbsfleet International	d			13 31				14 01			14 31					15 01			15 31					16 01
London Charing Cross	d	12 08				12 38			13 08					13 38			14 08					14 38		
London Waterloo (East)	d	12 11				12 41			13 11					13 41			14 11					14 41		
London Cannon Street	d																							
London Bridge	d	12 16				12 46			13 16					13 46			14 16					14 46		
Orpington	d	12 32				13 02			13 32					14 02			14 32					15 02		
Sevenoaks	d	12 42				13 12			13 42					14 12			14 42					15 12		
Tonbridge	a	12 52				13 20			13 52					14 20			14 52					15 20		
	d	12 53				13 21			13 53					14 21			14 53					15 21		
Paddock Wood	d	13 00				13 28	13 34		14 00					14 28	14 34		15 00					15 28	15 34	
Maidstone West	a						13 53								14 53								15 53	
Marden	d	13 06				13 34			14 06					14 34			15 06					15 34		
Staplehurst	d	13 09				13 37			14 09					14 37			15 09					15 37		
Headcorn	d	13 14				13 42			14 14					14 42			15 14					15 42		
Pluckley	d					13 48								14 48								15 48		
Ashford International	a	13 26	>	13 50		13 56		14 20	14 26	>	14 50			14 56		15 20	15 26	>	15 50			15 56		16 20
	d	13 30	13 33	13 52	14 00	14 03		14 22	14 30	14 33	14 52		15 00	15 03		15 22	15 30	15 33	15 52	16 00		16 03		16 22
Wye	d		13 39			14 09				14 39				15 09				15 39				16 09		
Chilham	d		13 45							14 45								15 45						
Chartham	d		13 49							14 49								15 49						
Canterbury West	d		13a54			14 22		14 40		14a54				15 22		15 40		15a54				16 22		16 40
Sturry	d					14 26								15 26								16 26		
Westenhanger	d	13 39			14 08				14 39				15 08				15 39			16 08				
Sandling	d	13 42			14 11				14 42				15 11				15 42			16 11				
Folkestone West	d	13 47		14 07	14 16				14 47		15 07		15 16				15 47		16 07	16 16				
Folkestone Central	d	13 50		14 10	14 18				14 50		15 10		15 18				15 50		16 10	16 18				
Dover Priory	a	14 01		14 21	14 29				15 01		15 21		15 29				16 01		16 21	16 29				
	d	14 04							15 04								16 04							
Martin Mill	d	14 13							15 13								16 13							
Walmer	d	14 17							15 17								16 17							
Deal	d	14 20							15 20								16 20							
Sandwich	d	14 26							15 26								16 26							
Minster	d					14 37								15 37								16 37		
Ramsgate	a	14 37				14 43		14 58	15 37					15 43		15 58	16 37					16 43		16 58
Broadstairs	a							15 04								16 04								17 04
Margate	a							15 10								16 10								17 10

		SE 1	SE 1	SE	SE 1	SE 1	SE	SE		SE 1	SE 1	SE	SE 1	SE 1	SE	SE	SE 1	SE		SE 1	SE 1	SE	SE	SE 1	SE
St Pancras International	d			16 12				16 42				17 12				17 42		18 12					18 42		19 12
Stratford International	d			16 19				16 49				17 19				17 49		18 19					18 49		19 19
Ebbsfleet International	d			16 31				17 01				17 31				18 01		18 31					19 01		19 31
London Charing Cross	d	15 08				15 38				16 08				16 38			17 08				17 38			18 08	
London Waterloo (East)	d	15 11				15 41				16 11				16 41			17 11				17 41			18 11	
London Cannon Street	d																								
London Bridge	d	15 16				15 46				16 16				16 46			17 16				17 46			18 16	
Orpington	d	15 32				16 02				16 32				17 02			17 32				18 02			18 32	
Sevenoaks	d	15 42				16 12				16 42				17 12			17 42				18 12			18 42	
Tonbridge	a	15 52				16 20				16 52				17 20			17 52				18 20			18 52	
	d	15 53				16 21				16 53				17 21			17 53				18 21			18 53	
Paddock Wood	d	16 00				16 28	16 34			17 00				17 28	17 34		18 00				18 28	18 34		19 00	
Maidstone West	a						16 53								17 53							18 53			
Marden	d	16 06				16 34				17 06				17 34			18 06				18 34			19 06	
Staplehurst	d	16 09				16 37				17 09				17 37			18 09				18 37			19 09	
Headcorn	d	16 14				16 42				17 14				17 42			18 14				18 42			19 14	
Pluckley	d					16 48								17 48							18 48				
Ashford International	a	16 26	>	16 50		16 56		17 20		17 26	>	17 50		17 56		18 20	18 26	18 50			18 56		19 20	19 26	19 50
	d	16 30	16 33	16 52	17 00	17 03		17 22		17 30	17 33	17 52	18 00	18 03		18 22	18 30	18 52		19 00	19 03		19 22	19 30	19 52
Wye	d		16 39			17 09					17 39			18 09							19 09				
Chilham	d		16 45								17 45			18 15							19 15				
Chartham	d		16 49								17 49			18 19							19 19				
Canterbury West	d		16a54			17 22		17 40			17a54			18 25		18 40					19 25		19 40		
Sturry	d					17 26								18 29							19 29				
Westenhanger	d	16 39			17 08					17 39			18 08				18 39			19 08				19 39	
Sandling	d	16 42			17 11					17 42			18 11				18 42			19 11				19 42	
Folkestone West	d	16 47		17 07	17 16					17 47		18 07	18 16				18 47	19 07		19 16				19 47	20 07
Folkestone Central	d	16 50		17 10	17 18					17 50		18 10	18 18				18 50	19 10		19 18				19 50	20 10
Dover Priory	a	17 01		17 21	17 29					18 01		18 21	18 29				19 01	19 21		19 29				20 01	20 21
	d	17 04								18 04							19 04							20 04	
Martin Mill	d	17 13								18 13							19 13							20 13	
Walmer	d	17 17								18 17							19 17							20 17	
Deal	d	17 20								18 20							19 20							20 20	
Sandwich	d	17 26								18 26							19 26							20 26	
Minster	d					17 37								18 40							19 40				
Ramsgate	a	17 37				17 43		17 58		18 39				18 46		18 58	19 39				19 46		19 58	20 39	
Broadstairs	a							18 04								19 04							20 04		
Margate	a							18 10								19 10							20 10		

Table 207

Sundays

London and Tonbridge - Ashford International, Folkestone, Dover, Canterbury West, Ramsgate and Margate

		SE 1	SE 1 🚌	SE	SE	SE 1 🚌	SE	SE 1	SE 1 🚌	SE	SE	SE 1 🚌	SE	SE 1	SE 1	SE	SE	SE 1	SE	SE 1	SE 1	SE
St Pancras International	d				19 42		20 12				20 42		21 12				21 42		22 12			22 42
Stratford International	d				19 49		20 19				20 49		21 19				21 49		22 19			22 49
Ebbsfleet International	d				20 01		20 31				21 01		21 31				22 01		22 31			23 01
London Charing Cross	d		18 38			19 08			19 38			20 08			20 38			21 08			21 38	
London Waterloo (East)	d		18 41			19 11			19 41			20 11			20 41			21 11			21 41	
London Cannon Street	d																					
London Bridge	d		18 46			19 16			19 46			20 16			20 46			21 16			21 46	
Orpington	d		19 02			19 32			20 02			20 32			21 02			21 32			22 02	
Sevenoaks	d		19 12			19 42			20 12			20 42			21 12			21 42			22 12	
Tonbridge	a		19 20			19 52			20 20			20 52			21 20			21 52			22 20	
	d		19 21			19 53			20 21			20 53			21 21			21 53			22 21	
Paddock Wood	d		19 28	19 34		20 00			20 28	20 34		21 00			21 28	21 34		22 00			22 28	
Maidstone West	a			19 53						20 53						21 53						
Marden	d		19 34			20 06			20 34			21 06			21 34			22 06			22 34	
Staplehurst	d		19 37			20 09			20 37			21 09			21 37			22 09			22 37	
Headcorn	d		19 42			20 14			20 42			21 14			21 42			22 14			22 42	
Pluckley	d		19 48						20 48						21 48						22 48	
Ashford International	a		19 56		20 20	20 26	20 50		20 56		21 20	21 26	21 50		21 56		22 20	22 26	22 50		22 56	23 20
	d	20 00	20 03		20 22	20 30	20 52	21 00	21 03		21 22	21 30	21 52	22 00	22 03		22 22	22 30	22 52	23 00	23 03	23 22
Wye	d		20 09						21 09						22 09						23 09	
Chilham	d		20 15						21 15						22 15						23 15	
Chartham	d		20 19						21 19						22 19						23 19	
Canterbury West	d		20 25		20 40				21 25		21 40				22 25		22 40				23 25	23 40
Sturry	d		20 29						21 29						22 29						23 29	
Westenhanger	d	20 08				20 39		21 08				21 39		22 08				22 39		23 08		
Sandling	d	20 11				20 42		21 11				21 42		22 11				22 42		23 11		
Folkestone West	d	20 16				20 47	21 07	21 16				21 47	22 07	22 16				22 47	23 07	23 16		
Folkestone Central	d	20 18				20 50	21 10	21 18				21 50	22 10	22 18				22 50	23 10	23 18		
Dover Priory	a	20 29				21 01	21 21	21 29				22 01	22 21	22 29				23 01	23 21	23 29		
	d					21 04						22 04						23 04				
Martin Mill	d					21 13						22 13						23 13				
Walmer	d					21 17						22 17						23 17				
Deal	d					21 20						22 20						23 20				
Sandwich	d					21 26						22 26						23 26				
Minster	d		20 40						21 40						22 40						23 40	
Ramsgate	a		20 46		20 58	21 39			21 46		21 58	22 37			22 46		22 58	23 37			23 46	23 58
Broadstairs	a				21 04						22 04						23 04					
Margate	a				21 10						22 10						23 10					

		SE 1	SE 1	SE	SE 1	SE 1	SE
St Pancras International	d			23 12			23 42
Stratford International	d			23 19			23 49
Ebbsfleet International	d			23 31			00 01
London Charing Cross	d	22 08	23 08		22 38	23 38	
London Waterloo (East)	d	22 11	23 11		22 41	23 41	
London Cannon Street	d						
London Bridge	d	22 16	23 16		22 46	23 46	
Orpington	d	22 32	23 32		23 02	00 02	
Sevenoaks	d	22 42	23 42		23 12	00 12	
Tonbridge	a	22 52	23 52		23 20	00 20	
	d	22 53	23 53		23 21	00 21	
Paddock Wood	d	23 00	00 01		23 28	00 28	
Maidstone West	a						
Marden	d	23 06	00 07		23 34	00 34	
Staplehurst	d	23 09	00 09		23 37	00 37	
Headcorn	d	23 14	00 14		23 42	00 42	
Pluckley	d				23 48	00 48	
Ashford International	a	23 26	00 26	23 50	23 56	00 56	00 19
	d	23 30		23 52	00 01		
Wye	d						
Chilham	d						
Chartham	d						
Canterbury West	d						
Sturry	d						
Westenhanger	d	23 39					
Sandling	d	23 42			00 10		
Folkestone West	d	23 47		00 07	00 15		
Folkestone Central	d	23 50		00 10	00 18		
Dover Priory	a	00 01		00 21	00 29		
	d	00 04					
Martin Mill	d	00 13					
Walmer	d	00 17					
Deal	d	00 20					
Sandwich	d	00 26					
Minster	d						
Ramsgate	a	00 37					
Broadstairs	a						
Margate	a						

Table 207

Mondays to Fridays

Margate, Ramsgate, Canterbury West, Dover, Folkestone, Ashford International,- Tonbridge and London

		SE 1	SE	SE	SE 1	SE	SE	SE 1	SE 1	SE	SE	SE 1	SE 1	SE	SE	SE 1	SE 1	SE	SE 1	SE 1	SE	SE	SE 1	SE 1
Margate	d													05 47										
Broadstairs	d													05 54										
Ramsgate	d					05 00		04 50				05 36	05 28	06 00					06 10		06 26		06 59	
Minster	d					05 06						05 42							06 16					
Sandwich	d							05 02					05 40											
Deal	d							05 08					05 46											
Walmer	d							05 11					05 49											
Martin Mill	d							05 16					05 54											
Dover Priory	a							05 24					06 02											
	d	04 37						05 26		05 44			06 04		06 12	05 49				06 24		06 38		
Folkestone Central	d	04 49						05 38		05 56			06 16		06 24					06 36		06 50		07 02
Folkestone West	d	04 51						05 40		05 58			06 18		06 26					06 38		06 52		07 04
Sandling	d	04 57						05 46					06 24							06 44				07 09
Westenhanger	d	04 59						05 48					06 26							06 46				07 11
Sturry	d					05 18						05 53							06 27					
Canterbury West	d					05 25			05 35			05 59		06 20					06 33		06 46			
Chartham	d								05 40			06 04							06 38					
Chilham	d								05 44			06 07							06 42					
Wye	d								05 51			06 14							06 48					
Ashford International	a	05 08				05 41		05 57	05 57	06 11		06 20	06 35	06 36	06 39				06 54	06 55	07 03	07 06		07 20
	d	05 12	05 13		05 28	05 43		06 02	06 03	06 13		06 22	06 37	06 43	<		06 43		06 57	07 02	07 13	<		07 22
Pluckley	d	05 19			05 35			06 09				06 29	06 44				06 50		07 04	07 09				07 29
Headcorn	d	05 25			05 41			06 15				06 36	06 50				06 57		07 10	07 15				07 35
Staplehurst	d	05 30			05 46			06 20				06 41	06 55				07 02		07 15	07 20				07 40
Marden	d	05 35			05 51			06 25				06 46	07 00				07 06		07 20	07 25				07 44
Maidstone West	d			05 18			05 58				06 28							06 58						
Paddock Wood	d	05 41		05a37	05 57		06a17	06 31			06a47	06 53	07 06				07 13	07a17	07 26	07 31				07 50
Tonbridge	a	05 49			06 05			06 39				07 01	07 14				07 21		07 34	07 41				07 58
	d	05 50			06 06			06 40				07 02	07 15				07 22		07 35	07 42				07 59
Sevenoaks	a	05 58			06 14			06 48				07 10	07 26				07 31		07 46	07 50				08 07
Orpington	a	06 08			06 23																			
London Bridge	a	06 24			06 39			07 14				07 36	07 53			07 51			08 13				08 49	08 35
London Cannon Street	a												07 59			07 57			08 20				08 57	08 41
London Waterloo (East)	a	06 29			06 44			07 19				07 41					08 00			08 20				
London Charing Cross	a	06 33			06 49			07 25				07 47					08 06			08 26				
Ebbsfleet International	a		05 32			06 02				06 32														
Stratford International	a		05 44			06 15				06 44				07 11							07 40			
St Pancras International	a		05 51			06 23				06 53				07 18							07 48			

		SE 1 A 🚌	SE 1	SE	SE	SE 1	SE	SE 1	SE 1	SE 1	SE	SE	SE	SE 1 A 🚌	SE 1	SE	SE 1	SE 1	SE	SE	SE 1	SE 1 A 🚌	SE
Margate	d			06 44												07 49							08 53
Broadstairs	d			06 50												07 55							08 59
Ramsgate	d	06 40	06 22	06 56		07 19			06 48	07 10	07 26				07 22	08 01	07 40	08 18			08 05	08 40	09 05
Minster	d	06 46								07 16						08 07	07b53				08 16	08 46	
Sandwich	d		06 34						07 00						07 34		08 00				08 24		
Deal	d		06 40						07 06						07 40		08 06				08 30		
Walmer	d		06 43						07 09						07 43		08 09				08 33		
Martin Mill	d		06 48						07 14						07 47		08 13				08 39		
Dover Priory	a		06 56						07 22						07 55		08 21				08 47		
	d		07 00		07 08				07 24			07 38			07 56		08 24		08 44		08 56		
Folkestone Central	d		07 12		07 20				07 36			07 50			08 08		08 36		08 56		09 08		
Folkestone West	d		07 14		07 22				07 38			07 52			08 10		08 38		08 58		09 10		
Sandling	d		07 20						07 44						08 16		08 43				09 16		
Westenhanger	d		07 22						07 46						08 19		08 46				09 19		
Sturry	d	06 57								07 27						08 19						08 57	
Canterbury West	d	07 03		07 16						07 35	07 46			08 00		08 25		08 37				09 04	09 25
Chartham	d	07 08								07 40				08 05				08 42					
Chilham	d	07 11								07 44				08 09				08 45					
Wye	d	07 18								07 51				08 16				08 51				09 16	
Ashford International	a	07 25	07 31	07 32	07 35				07 55	07 58	08 03	08 06		08 22	08 28	08 41	08 55	08 58	09 11		09 28	09 22	09 41
	d	07 28	07 37	07 43	<			07 45	08 02	<	08 13	<		08 32	<	08 43	09 02	<	09 13		<	09 32	09 43
Pluckley	d		07 44					07 51	08 09					08 39			09 09					09 39	
Headcorn	d	07 39	07 50					07 57	08 15					08 45			09 15					09 45	
Staplehurst	d	07 44	07 55					08 02	08 20					08 50			09 20					09 50	
Marden	d	07 48	08 00					08 07	08 25					08 55			09 25					09 55	
Maidstone West	d						07 41						08 18							09 28			
Paddock Wood	d	07 54	08 06				08a00	08 13	08 31				08 37	09 01			09 31			09 49		10 01	
Tonbridge	a	08 02	08 14					08 21	08 39				08 45	09 09			09 39			09 57		10 09	
	d	08 03	08 15					08 22	08 40					09 10			09 40					10 10	
Sevenoaks	a	08 11	08 26					08 30	08 48					09 18			09 48					10 18	
Orpington	a																						
London Bridge	a		08 55			09 11			09 14					09 43			10 13					10 43	
London Cannon Street	a		09 02			09 18																	
London Waterloo (East)	a	08 40						09 00	09 19					09 48			10 19					10 49	
London Charing Cross	a	08 46						09 04	09 25					09 54			10 22					10 52	
Ebbsfleet International	a															09 02			09 32				10 02
Stratford International	a			08 11							08 41					09 14			09 44				10 14
St Pancras International	a			08 19							08 48					09 21			09 51				10 21

A 🚌 from Ashford International

b arr. 0746

Table 207 — Mondays to Fridays

Margate, Ramsgate, Canterbury West, Dover, Folkestone, Ashford International,- Tonbridge and London

		SE 1 A ⚒	SE 1	SE	SE	SE 1	SE 1 A ⚒	SE	SE 1 A ⚒	SE 1	SE	SE	SE 1	SE 1 A ⚒	SE	SE 1 A ⚒	SE 1	SE	SE	SE 1	SE 1 A ⚒	SE
Margate 4	d							09 53							10 53							11 53
Broadstairs	d							09 59							10 59							11 59
Ramsgate 4	d					09 22	09 40	10 05					10 22	10 40	11 05					11 22	11 40	12 05
Minster 4	d						09 46							10 46							11 46	
Sandwich	d					09 34							10 34							11 34		
Deal	d					09 40							10 40							11 40		
Walmer	d					09 43							10 43							11 43		
Martin Mill	d					09 47							10 47							11 47		
Dover Priory 4	a					09 55							10 55							11 55		
	d	09 24		09 44		09 56			10 24		10 44		10 56			11 24		11 44		11 56		
Folkestone Central	d	09 36		09 56		10 08			10 36		10 56		11 08			11 36		11 56		12 08		
Folkestone West	d	09 38		09 58		10 10			10 38		10 58		11 10			11 38		11 58		12 10		
Sandling	d	09 43				10 16			10 43				11 16			11 43				12 16		
Westenhanger	d	09 46				10 19			10 46				11 19			11 46				12 19		
Sturry	d						09 57							10 57							11 57	
Canterbury West 4	d		09 35				10 04	10 25		10 35				11 04	11 25		11 35				12 04	12 25
Chartham	d		09 40							10 40							11 40					
Chilham	d		09 44							10 44							11 44					
Wye	d		09 51				10 16			10 51				11 16			11 51				12 16	
Ashford International	a	09 55	09 58	10 11		10 28	10 22	10 41	10 55	10 58	11 11		11 28	11 22	11 41	11 55	11 58	12 11		12 28	12 22	12 41
	d	10 02	<	10 13		<	10 32	10 43	11 02	<	11 13		<	11 32	11 43	12 02	<	12 13		<	12 32	12 43
Pluckley	d	10 09					10 39		11 09					11 39		12 09					12 39	
Headcorn	d	10 15					10 45		11 15					11 45		12 15					12 45	
Staplehurst	d	10 20					10 50		11 20					11 50		12 20					12 50	
Marden	d	10 25					10 55		11 25					11 55		12 25					12 55	
Maidstone West 4	d				10 28							11 28							12 28			
Paddock Wood 4	d	10 31			10 47		11 01		11 31			11 47		12 01		12 31			12 47		13 01	
Tonbridge 4	a	10 39			10 55		11 09		11 39			11 55		12 09		12 39			12 58		13 09	
	d	10 40					11 10		11 40					12 10		12 40					13 10	
Sevenoaks 4	a	10 48					11 18		11 48					12 18		12 48					13 18	
Orpington 4	a																					
London Bridge 4 ⊖	a	11 13					11 43		12 13					12 43		13 13					13 43	
London Cannon Street 4 ⊖	a																					
London Waterloo (East) 4 ⊖	a	11 19					11 49		12 19					12 49		13 19					13 49	
London Charing Cross 4 ⊖	a	11 22					11 52		12 22					12 52		13 22					13 52	
Ebbsfleet International	a			10 32				11 02			11 32				12 02			12 32				13 02
Stratford International ⊖	a			10 44				11 14			11 44				12 14			12 45				13 14
St Pancras International 15 ⊖	a			10 51				11 21			11 51				12 21			12 54				13 21

		SE 1 A ⚒	SE 1	SE	SE	SE 1	SE 1 A ⚒	SE	SE 1 A ⚒	SE 1	SE	SE	SE 1	SE 1 A ⚒	SE	SE 1 A ⚒	SE 1		SE	SE	SE 1	SE 1 A ⚒	SE
Margate 4	d							12 53							13 53								14 53
Broadstairs	d							12 59							13 59								14 59
Ramsgate 4	d					12 22	12 40	13 05					13 22	13 40	14 05						14 22	14 40	15 05
Minster 4	d						12 46							13 46								14 46	
Sandwich	d					12 34							13 34								14 34		
Deal	d					12 40							13 40								14 40		
Walmer	d					12 43							13 43								14 43		
Martin Mill	d					12 47							13 47								14 47		
Dover Priory 4	a					12 55							13 55								14 55		
	d	12 24		12 44		12 56			13 24		13 44		13 56			14 24			14 44		14 56		
Folkestone Central	d	12 36		12 56		13 08			13 36		13 56		14 08			14 36			14 56		15 08		
Folkestone West	d	12 38		12 58		13 10			13 38		13 58		14 10			14 38			14 58		15 10		
Sandling	d	12 43				13 16			13 43				14 16			14 43					15 16		
Westenhanger	d	12 46				13 19			13 46				14 19			14 46					15 19		
Sturry	d						12 57							13 57								14 57	
Canterbury West 4	d		12 35				13 04	13 25		13 35				14 04	14 25		14 35					15 04	15 25
Chartham	d		12 40							13 40							14 40						
Chilham	d		12 44							13 44							14 44						
Wye	d		12 51				13 16			13 51				14 16			14 51					15 16	
Ashford International	a	12 55	12 58	13 11		13 28	13 22	13 41	13 55	13 58	14 11		14 28	14 22	14 41	14 55	14 58		15 11		15 28	15 22	15 41
	d	13 02	<	13 13		<	13 32	13 43	14 02	<	14 13		<	14 32	14 43	15 02	<		15 13		<	15 32	15 43
Pluckley	d	13 09					13 39		14 09					14 39		15 09						15 39	
Headcorn	d	13 15					13 45		14 15					14 45		15 15						15 45	
Staplehurst	d	13 20					13 50		14 20					14 50		15 20						15 50	
Marden	d	13 25					13 55		14 25					14 55		15 25						15 55	
Maidstone West 4	d				13 28							14 28								15 28			
Paddock Wood 4	d	13 31			13 47		14 01		14 31			14 47		15 01		15 31				15 47		16 01	
Tonbridge 4	a	13 39			13 55		14 09		14 39			14 55		15 09		15 39				15 55		16 09	
	d	13 40					14 10		14 40					15 10		15 40						16 10	
Sevenoaks 4	a	13 48					14 18		14 48					15 18		15 48						16 18	
Orpington 4	a																						
London Bridge 4 ⊖	a	14 13					14 43		15 13					15 43		16 14						16 46	
London Cannon Street 4 ⊖	a																						
London Waterloo (East) 4 ⊖	a	14 19					14 49		15 19					15 48		16 20						16 52	
London Charing Cross 4 ⊖	a	14 22					14 52		15 22					15 52		16 24						16 56	
Ebbsfleet International	a			13 32				14 02			14 32				15 02				15 32				16 02
Stratford International ⊖	a			13 44				14 14			14 44				15 14				15 44				16 14
St Pancras International 15 ⊖	a			13 51				14 21			14 51				15 21				15 51				16 21

A ⚒ from Ashford International

Table 207 — Mondays to Fridays

Margate, Ramsgate, Canterbury West, Dover, Folkestone, Ashford International,- Tonbridge and London

		SE 1 A ⚒	SE 1	SE	SE	SE 1	SE 1 A ⚒	SE	SE 1 A ⚒	SE 1	SE	SE	SE 1	SE 1 A ⚒	SE		SE 1 A ⚒	SE 1	SE	SE	SE 1	SE 1 A ⚒	SE	SE	SE 1 A ⚒	SE 1
Margate 4	d														16 53									17 53		
Broadstairs	d														16 59									17 59		
Ramsgate 4	d					15 22	15 40		15 50				16 22	16 40	17 05		16 50				17 22	17 40		18 05	17 50	
Minster 4	d						15 46							16 46								17 46				
Sandwich	d					15 34			16 02				16 34				17 02				17 34				18 02	
Deal	d					15 40			16 08				16 40				17 08				17 40				18 08	
Walmer	d					15 43			16 11				16 43				17 11				17 43				18 11	
Martin Mill	d					15 47			16 15				16 47				17 15				17 47				18 15	
Dover Priory 4	a					15 55			16 23				16 55				17 23				17 56				18 23	
	d	15 24		15 44		15 56			16 24		16 44		16 56				17 24			17 44	17 57				18 24	
Folkestone Central	d	15 36		15 56		16 08			16 36		16 56		17 08				17 36			17 56	18 08				18 36	
Folkestone West	d	15 38		15 58		16 10			16 38		16 58		17 10				17 38			17 58	18 10				18 38	
Sandling	d	15 43				16 16			16 43				17 16				17 43				18 16				18 43	
Westenhanger	d	15 46				16 19			16 46				17 19				17 46				18 19				18 46	
Sturry	d						15 57							16 57								17 57				
Canterbury West 4	d		15 35				16 04			16 35				17 04	17 25			17 35				18 04		18 25		18 35
Chartham	d		15 40							16 40								17 40								18 40
Chilham	d		15 44							16 44								17 44								18 44
Wye	d		15 51				16 16			16 51				17 16				17 51				18 16				18 51
Ashford International	a	15 55	15 58	16 11		16 28	16 22		16 55	16 58	17 11		17 28	17 22	17 41		17 55	17 58		18 11	18 28	18 22		18 41	18 55	18 58
	d	16 02	<	16 13		<	16 32		17 02	<	17 13		<	17 32	17 43		18 02	<		18 13	<	18 32		18 43	19 02	<
Pluckley	d	16 09					16 39		17 09					17 39			18 09					18 39			19 09	
Headcorn	d	16 15					16 45		17 15					17 45			18 15					18 45			19 15	
Staplehurst	d	16 20					16 50		17 20					17 50			18 20					18 50			19 20	
Marden	d	16 25					16 55		17 25					17 55			18 25					18 55			19 25	
Maidstone West 4	d				16 33			16 58				17 28							18 13				18 43			
Paddock Wood 4	d	16 31			16a52		17 01	17a17	17 31			17a47		18 01			18 31		18a32			19 01	19a02		19 31	
Tonbridge 4	a	16 39					17 09		17 39					18 09			18 39					19 09			19 39	
	d	16 40					17 10		17 40					18 10			18 40					19 10			19 40	
Sevenoaks 4	a	16 48					17 18		17 48					18 18			18 48					19 18			19 48	
Orpington 4	a																									
London Bridge 4 ⊖	a	17 17					17 44		18 16					18 43			19 13					19 43			20 13	
London Cannon Street 4 ⊖	a																									
London Waterloo (East) 4 ⊖	a	17 22					17 50		18 20					18 48			19 17					19 48			20 18	
London Charing Cross 4 ⊖	a	17 26					17 53		18 25					18 52			19 21					19 52			20 22	
Ebbsfleet International	a			16 32							17 32				18 02					18 32				19 02		
Stratford International ⊖	a			16 44							17 44				18 14					18 44				19 14		
St Pancras International 15 ⊖	a			16 51							17 51				18 21					18 51				19 21		

		SE	SE	SE 1	SE 1 A ⚒	SE	SE	SE 1	SE 1	SE	SE 1	SE 1	SE	SE	SE 1	SE 1	SE		SE 1	SE 1	SE
Margate 4	d					18 53							19 53								20 53
Broadstairs	d					18 59							19 59								20 59
Ramsgate 4	d			18 22	18 40	19 05					19 22	19 40	20 05						20 22	20 40	21 05
Minster 4	d				18 46							19 46								20 46	
Sandwich	d			18 34							19 33								20 34		
Deal	d			18 40							19 39								20 40		
Walmer	d			18 43							19 42								20 43		
Martin Mill	d			18 47							19 46								20 47		
Dover Priory 4	a			18 56							19 54								20 55		
	d		18 44	18 57				19 24		19 44	19 55				20 24		20 44		20 56		
Folkestone Central	d		18 56	19 08				19 36		19 56	20 08				20 36		20 56		21 08		
Folkestone West	d		18 58	19 10				19 38		19 58	20 10				20 38		20 58		21 10		
Sandling	d			19 16				19 43			20 16				20 43				21 16		
Westenhanger	d			19 19				19 46			20 19				20 46				21 19		
Sturry	d				18 57							19 57								20 57	
Canterbury West 4	d				19 04	19 25			19 35			20 04	20 25			20 35				21 04	21 25
Chartham	d								19 40							20 40					
Chilham	d								19 44							20 44					
Wye	d				19 16				19 51			20 16				20 51				21 16	
Ashford International	a		19 11	19 28	19 22	19 41		19 55	19 58	20 12	20 28	20 22	20 41		20 55	20 58	21 11		21 28	21 22	21 41
	d		19 13	<	19 32	19 43		20 02	<	20 13	<	20 32	20 47		21 02	<	21 13		<	21 32	21 43
Pluckley	d				19 39			20 09				20 39			21 09					21 39	
Headcorn	d				19 45			20 15				20 45			21 15					21 45	
Staplehurst	d				19 50			20 20				20 50			21 20					21 50	
Marden	d				19 55			20 25				20 55			21 25					21 55	
Maidstone West 4	d	19 13					19 58							20 58							
Paddock Wood 4	d	19a32			20 01		20 17	20 31				21 01		21 17	21 31					22 01	
Tonbridge 4	a				20 09		20 25	20 39				21 09		21 25	21 39					22 09	
	d				20 10			20 40				21 10			21 40					22 10	
Sevenoaks 4	a				20 18			20 48				21 18			21 48					22 18	
Orpington 4	a																				
London Bridge 4 ⊖	a				20 42			21 13				21 43			22 13					22 43	
London Cannon Street 4 ⊖	a																				
London Waterloo (East) 4 ⊖	a				20 47			21 18				21 48			22 18					22 48	
London Charing Cross 4 ⊖	a				20 51			21 22				21 52			22 22					22 52	
Ebbsfleet International	a		19 32			20 02				20 32			21 06				21 32				22 02
Stratford International ⊖	a		19 44			20 14				20 44			21 18				21 44				22 14
St Pancras International 15 ⊖	a		19 51			20 21				20 51			21 25				21 51				22 21

Margate, Ramsgate, Canterbury West, Dover, Folkestone, Ashford International,- Tonbridge and London

		SE	SE ■	SE ■	SE	SE ■	SE		SE ■	SE	SE ■
Margate ■	d						21 53				
Broadstairs	d						21 59				
Ramsgate ■	d					21 22	22 05		22 22		22 40
Minster ■	d								22 28		
Sandwich	d					21 34					22 52
Deal	d					21 40					22 58
Walmer	d					21 43					23 01
Martin Mill	d					21 47					23 05
Dover Priory ■	a					21 55					23 13
	d		21 24		21 44	21 56				22 44	23 20
Folkestone Central	d		21 36		21 56	22 08				22 56	23 32
Folkestone West	d		21 38		21 58	22 10				22 58	23 34
Sandling	d		21 43			22 16					23 39
Westenhanger	d		21 46			22 19					23 42
Sturry	d								22 39		
Canterbury West ■	d			21 35			22 25		22 46		
Chartham	d			21 40					22 51		
Chilham	d			21 44					22 55		
Wye	d			21 51					23 02		
Ashford International	a		21 55	21 58	22 11	22 28	22 41		23 08	23 11	23 51
	d		22 02	<	22 13	22 32	22 43			23 13	
Pluckley	d		22 09			22 39					
Headcorn	d		22 15			22 45					
Staplehurst	d		22 20			22 50					
Marden	d		22 25			22 55					
Maidstone West ■	d	21 58									
Paddock Wood ■	d	22 17	22 31			23 01					
Tonbridge ■	a	22 25	22 39			23 10					
	d		22 40								
Sevenoaks ■	a		22 48								
Orpington ■	a										
London Bridge ■ ⊖	a		23 13								
London Cannon Street ■ ⊖	a										
London Waterloo (East) ■ ⊖	a		23 18								
London Charing Cross ■ ⊖	a		23 22								
Ebbsfleet International	a				22 32		23 02			23 32	
Stratford International ⊖	a				22 44		23 14			23 44	
St Pancras International ■ ⊖	a				22 51		23 21			23 51	

Saturdays

		SE ■	SE	SE	SE	SE ■	SE ■	SE	SE ■		SE	SE	SE ■	SE	SE ■	SE ■	SE ■	SE ■	SE	SE ■		SE	SE ■ A	SE ■
Margate ■	d							05 43														07 53		
Broadstairs	d							05 49														07 59		
Ramsgate ■	d		05 05			05 32		05 55	05 50		06 26		06 22		06 36	06 50		07 22		07 40		08 05	07 50	
Minster ■	d					05 38									06 42					07 46				
Sandwich	d								06 01				06 34			07 01		07 34					08 01	
Deal	d								06 07				06 40			07 07		07 40					08 07	
Walmer	d								06 10				06 43			07 10		07 43					08 10	
Martin Mill	d								06 14				06 47			07 14		07 47					08 14	
Dover Priory ■	a								06 22				06 56			07 22		07 55					08 22	
	d	04 50		05 44			05 50		06 24			06 44	06 57			07 24		07 56					08 24	
Folkestone Central	d	05 02		05 56			06 02		06 36			06 56	07 08			07 36		08 08					08 36	
Folkestone West	d	05 04		05 58			06 04		06 38			06 58	07 10			07 38		08 10					08 38	
Sandling	d	05 09					06 09		06 43				07 16			07 43		08 16					08 43	
Westenhanger	d	05 12					06 12		06 46				07 19			07 46		08 19					08 46	
Sturry	d					05 49									06 53					07 57				
Canterbury West ■	d		05 25			05 55		06 15			06 46				07 00		07 35			08 04		08 25		08 35
Chartham	d					06 00									07 05		07 40							08 40
Chilham	d					06 04									07 09		07 44							08 44
Wye	d					06 11									07 16		07 51			08 16				08 51
Ashford International	a	05 21	05 41	06 11		06 17	06 21	06 31	06 55		07 03	07 11	07 28		07 22	07 55	07 58	08 28		08 22		08 41	08 55	08 58
	d	05 25	05 43	06 13		06 25	<	06 33	07 02		07 13	07 13			07 32	08 02	<			08 32		08 43	09 02	<
Pluckley	d	05 32				06 32			07 09						07 39	08 09				08 39			09 09	
Headcorn	d	05 38				06 38			07 15						07 45	08 15				08 45			09 15	
Staplehurst	d	05 43				06 43			07 20						07 50	08 20				08 50			09 20	
Marden	d	05 48				06 48			07 25						07 55	08 25				08 55			09 25	
Maidstone West ■	d				06 28									07 28					08 28					
Paddock Wood ■	d	05 54			06 47	06 54			07 31					07 47	08 01	08 31			08 47	09 01			09 31	
Tonbridge ■	a	06 01			06 55	07 01			07 39					07 55	08 09	08 39			08 55	09 09			09 39	
	d	06 02				07 02			07 40						08 10	08 40				09 10			09 40	
Sevenoaks ■	a	06 13				07 13			07 48						08 18	08 48				09 18			09 48	
Orpington ■	a	06 23				07 23																		
London Bridge ■ ⊖	a	06 39				07 39			08 13						08 43	09 13				09 43			10 13	
London Cannon Street ■ ⊖	a																							
London Waterloo (East) ■ ⊖	a	06 43				07 43			08 19						08 49	09 19				09 49			10 19	
London Charing Cross ■ ⊖	a	06 47				07 48			08 22						08 52	09 22				09 52			10 22	
Ebbsfleet International	a		06 02	06 32				06 52				07 32										09 02		
Stratford International ⊖	a		06 15	06 44				07 04			07 42	07 44										09 14		
St Pancras International ■ ⊖	a		06 23	06 53				07 10			07 48	07 50										09 21		

A from Ashford International-I

Margate, Ramsgate, Canterbury West, Dover, Folkestone, Ashford International,- Tonbridge and London

		SE	SE ■	SE	SE ■ A	SE	SE ■ A	SE ■	SE	SE ■	SE	SE ■ A	SE	SE ■ A	SE ■		SE	SE ■	SE	SE ■ A	SE	SE ■ A	SE ■	SE
Margate ■	d					08 53							09 53								10 53			
Broadstairs	d					08 59							09 59								10 59			
Ramsgate ■	d		08 22		08 40	09 05	08 50			09 22		09 40	10 05	09 50				10 22		10 40	11 05	10 50		
Minster ■	d				08 46							09 46								10 46				
Sandwich	d		08 34				09 01			09 34				10 01				10 34				11 01		
Deal	d		08 40				09 07			09 40				10 07				10 40				11 07		
Walmer	d		08 43				09 10			09 43				10 10				10 43				11 10		
Martin Mill	d		08 47				09 14			09 47				10 14				10 47				11 14		
Dover Priory ■	a		08 55				09 22			09 55				10 22				10 55				11 22		
	d	08 44	08 56				09 24		09 44	09 56				10 24			10 44	10 56				11 24		11 44
Folkestone Central	d	08 56	09 08				09 36		09 56	10 08				10 36			10 56	11 08				11 36		11 56
Folkestone West	d	08 58	09 10				09 38		09 58	10 10				10 38			10 58	11 10				11 38		11 58
Sandling	d		09 16				09 43			10 16				10 43				11 16				11 43		
Westenhanger	d		09 19				09 46			10 19				10 46				11 19				11 46		
Sturry	d				08 57							09 57								10 57				
Canterbury West ■	d				09 04	09 25		09 35				10 04	10 25		10 35					11 04	11 25		11 35	
Chartham	d							09 40							10 40								11 40	
Chilham	d							09 44							10 44								11 44	
Wye	d				09 16			09 51				10 16			10 51					11 16			11 51	
Ashford Internationa	a	09 11	09 28		09 22	09 41	09 55	09 58	10 11	10 28		10 22	10 41	10 55	10 58		11 11	11 28		11 22	11 41	11 55	11 58	12 11
	d	09 13			09 32	09 43	10 02	<	10 13			10 32	10 43	11 02	<		11 13			11 32	11 43	12 02	<	12 13
Pluckley	d				09 39		10 09					10 39		11 09						11 39		12 09		
Headcorn	d				09 45		10 15					10 45		11 15						11 45		12 15		
Staplehurst	d				09 50		10 20					10 50		11 20						11 50		12 20		
Marden	d				09 55		10 25					10 55		11 25						11 55		12 25		
Maidstone West ■	d			09 28							10 28								11 28					
Paddock Wood ■	d			09 47	10 01		10 31				10 47	11 01		11 31					11 47	12 01		12 31		
Tonbridge ■	a			09 55	10 09		10 39				10 55	11 09		11 39					11 55	12 09		12 39		
	d				10 10		10 40					11 10		11 40						12 10		12 40		
Sevenoaks ■	a				10 18		10 48					11 18		11 48						12 18		12 48		
Orpington ■	a																							
London Bridge ■ ⊖	a				10 43		11 13					11 43		12 13						12 43		13 13		
London Cannon Street ■ ⊖	a																							
London Waterloo (East) ■ ⊖	a				10 49		11 19					11 49		12 19						12 49		13 19		
London Charing Cross ■ ⊖	a				10 52		11 22					11 52		12 22						12 52		13 22		
Ebbsfleet International	a	09 32				10 02			10 32				11 02				11 32				12 02			12 32
Stratford International ⊖	a	09 44				10 14			10 44				11 14				11 44				12 14			12 45
St Pancras International ■ ⊖	a	09 51				10 21			10 51				11 21				11 51				12 21			12 54

		SE ■	SE	SE ■ A	SE	SE ■ A	SE ■	SE	SE ■	SE	SE ■ A	SE		SE ■ A	SE ■	SE	SE ■	SE	SE ■ A	SE	SE ■ A	SE ■	SE
Margate ■	d				11 53							12 53								13 53			
Broadstairs	d				11 59							12 59								13 59			
Ramsgate ■	d	11 22		11 40	12 05	11 50			12 22		12 40	13 05		12 50			13 22		13 40	14 05	13 50		
Minster ■	d			11 46							12 46								13 46				
Sandwich	d	11 34				12 01			12 34					13 01			13 34				14 01		
Deal	d	11 40				12 07			12 40					13 07			13 40				14 07		
Walmer	d	11 43				12 10			12 43					13 10			13 43				14 10		
Martin Mill	d	11 47				12 14			12 47					13 14			13 47				14 14		
Dover Priory ■	a	11 55				12 22			12 55					13 22			13 55				14 22		
	d	11 56				12 24		12 44	12 56					13 24		13 44	13 56				14 24		14 44
Folkestone Central	d	12 08				12 36		12 56	13 08					13 36		13 56	14 08				14 36		14 56
Folkestone West	d	12 10				12 38		12 58	13 10					13 38		13 58	14 10				14 38		14 58
Sandling	d	12 16				12 43			13 16					13 43			14 16				14 43		
Westenhanger	d	12 19				12 46			13 19					13 46			14 19				14 46		
Sturry	d			11 57							12 57								13 57				
Canterbury West ■	d			12 04	12 25		12 35				13 04	13 25			13 35				14 04	14 25		14 35	
Chartham	d						12 40								13 40							14 40	
Chilham	d						12 44								13 44							14 44	
Wye	d			12 16			12 51				13 16				13 51				14 16			14 51	
Ashford International	a	12 28		12 22	12 41	12 55	12 58	13 11	13 28		13 22	13 41		13 55	13 58	14 11	14 28		14 22	14 41	14 55	14 58	15 11
	d			12 32	12 43	13 02	<	13 13			13 32	13 43		14 02	<	14 13			14 32	14 43	15 02	<	15 13
Pluckley	d			12 39		13 09					13 39			14 09					14 39		15 09		
Headcorn	d			12 45		13 15					13 45			14 15					14 45		15 15		
Staplehurst	d			12 50		13 20					13 50			14 20					14 50		15 20		
Marden	d			12 55		13 25					13 55			14 25					14 55		15 25		
Maidstone West ■	d		12 28							13 28								14 28					
Paddock Wood ■	d		12 47	13 01		13 31				13 47	14 01			14 31				14 47	15 01		15 31		
Tonbridge ■	a		12 55	13 09		13 39				13 55	14 09			14 39				14 55	15 09		15 39		
	d			13 10		13 40					14 10			14 40					15 10		15 40		
Sevenoaks ■	a			13 18		13 48					14 18			14 48					15 18		15 48		
Orpington ■	a																						
London Bridge ■ ⊖	a			13 43		14 13					14 43			15 13					15 43		16 13		
London Cannon Street ■ ⊖	a																						
London Waterloo (East) ■ ⊖	a			13 49		14 19					14 49			15 19					15 49		16 19		
London Charing Cross ■ ⊖	a			13 52		14 22					14 52			15 22					15 52		16 22		
Ebbsfleet International	a				13 02			13 32				14 02				14 32				15 02			15 32
Stratford International ⊖	a				13 14			13 44				14 14				14 44				15 14			15 44
St Pancras International ■ ⊖	a				13 21			13 51				14 21				14 51				15 21			15 51

A ⫪ from Ashford International

Table 207

Saturdays

Margate, Ramsgate, Canterbury West, Dover, Folkestone, Ashford International,- Tonbridge and London

		SE [1]	SE	SE [1] A ⫪	SE	SE [1] A ⫪	SE [1]	SE		SE [1]	SE	SE [1] A ⫪	SE	SE	SE [1] A ⫪	SE [1]	SE	SE [1]	SE	SE [1] A ⫪	SE	SE [1] A ⫪	SE [1]	SE
Margate [4]	d				14 53								15 53	15 53							16 53			
Broadstairs	d				14 59								15 59	15 59							16 59			
Ramsgate [4]	d	14 22		14 40	15 05	14 50				15 22		15 40	16 05	16 05	15 50			16 22		16 40	17 05	16 50		
Minster [4]	d			14 46								15 46								16 46				
Sandwich	d	14 34				15 01				15 34					16 01			16 34				17 01		
Deal	d	14 40				15 07				15 40					16 07			16 40				17 07		
Walmer	d	14 43				15 10				15 43					16 10			16 43				17 10		
Martin Mill	d	14 47				15 14				15 47					16 14			16 47				17 14		
Dover Priory [4]	a	14 55				15 22				15 55					16 22			16 55				17 22		
	d	14 56				15 24		15 44		15 56					16 24		16 44	16 56				17 24		17 44
Folkestone Central	d	15 08				15 36		15 56		16 08					16 36		16 56	17 08				17 36		17 56
Folkestone West	d	15 10				15 38		15 58		16 10					16 38		16 58	17 10				17 38		17 58
Sandling	d	15 16				15 43				16 16					16 43			17 16				17 43		
Westenhanger	d	15 19				15 46				16 19					16 46			17 19				17 46		
Sturry	d			14 57								15 57								16 57				
Canterbury West [4]	d			15 04	15 25		15 35					16 04	16 25	16 25		16 35				17 04	17 25		17 35	
Chartham	d						15 40									16 40							17 40	
Chilham	d						15 44									16 44							17 44	
Wye	d			15 16			15 51					16 16				16 51				17 16			17 51	
Ashford International	a	15 28		15 22	15 41	15 55	15 58	16 11		16 28		16 22	16 41	16 41	16 55	16 58	17 11	17 28		17 22	17 41	17 55	17 58	18 11
	d			15 32	15 43	16 02	<	16 13				16 32	16 43	16 47	17 02	<	17 13			17 32	17 43	18 02	<	18 13
Pluckley	d			15 39		16 09						16 39			17 09					17 39		18 09		
Headcorn	d			15 45		16 15						16 45			17 15					17 45		18 15		
Staplehurst	d			15 50		16 20						16 50			17 20					17 50		18 20		
Marden	d			15 55		16 25						16 55			17 25					17 55		18 25		
Maidstone West [4]	d		15 28								16 28								17 28					
Paddock Wood [4]	d		15 47	16 01		16 31					16 47	17 01			17 31				17 47	18 01		18 31		
Tonbridge [4]	a		15 55	16 09		16 39					16 55	17 09			17 39				17 55	18 09		18 39		
	d			16 10		16 40						17 10			17 40					18 10		18 40		
Sevenoaks [4]	a			16 18		16 48						17 18			17 48					18 18		18 48		
Orpington [4]	a																							
London Bridge [4] ⊖	a			16 43		17 13						17 43			18 13					18 43		19 13		
London Cannon Street [4] ⊖	a																							
London Waterloo (East) [4] ⊖	a			16 49		17 19						17 49			18 19					18 49		19 19		
London Charing Cross [4] ⊖	a			16 52		17 22						17 52			18 22					18 52		19 22		
Ebbsfleet International	a				16 02			16 32					17 02	17 06			17 32				18 02			18 32
Stratford International ⊖	a				16 14			16 44					17 14	17 18			17 44				18 14			18 44
St Pancras International [15] ⊖	a				16 21			16 51					17 21	17 25			17 51				18 21			18 51

		SE [1]	SE	SE [1] A ⫪	SE		SE [1] A ⫪	SE [1]	SE	SE [1]	SE	SE [1]	SE	SE [1]	SE [1]	SE	SE [1]	SE	SE [1]	SE	SE [1]	SE	SE [1]	
Margate [4]	d				17 53								18 53							19 53				
Broadstairs	d				17 59								18 59							19 59				
Ramsgate [4]	d	17 22		17 40	18 05		17 50			18 22		18 40	19 05	18 50			19 22		19 36	20 05	19 50		20 22	
Minster [4]	d			17 46								18 46							19 42					
Sandwich	d	17 34					18 01			18 34				19 01			19 34				20 01		20 34	
Deal	d	17 40					18 07			18 40				19 07			19 40				20 07		20 40	
Walmer	d	17 43					18 10			18 43				19 10			19 43				20 10		20 43	
Martin Mill	d	17 47					18 14			18 47				19 14			19 47				20 14		20 47	
Dover Priory [4]	a	17 55					18 22			18 55				19 22			19 55				20 22		20 55	
	d	17 56					18 24		18 44	18 56				19 24		19 44	19 56				20 24	20 44	20 56	
Folkestone Central	d	18 08					18 36		18 56	19 08				19 36		19 56	20 08				20 36	20 56	21 08	
Folkestone West	d	18 10					18 38		18 58	19 10				19 38		19 58	20 10				20 38	20 58	21 10	
Sandling	d	18 16					18 43			19 16				19 43			20 16				20 43		21 16	
Westenhanger	d	18 19					18 46			19 19				19 46			20 19				20 46		21 19	
Sturry	d			17 57								18 57							19 53					
Canterbury West [4]	d			18 04	18 25			18 35				19 04	19 25		19 35				20 00	20 25				
Chartham	d							18 40							19 40				20 05					
Chilham	d							18 44							19 44				20 09					
Wye	d			18 16				18 51				19 16			19 51				20 16					
Ashford Internationa	a	18 28		18 22	18 41		18 55	18 58	19 11	19 28		19 22	19 41	19 55	19 58	20 11	20 28		20 22	20 41	20 55	21 11	21 28	
	d			18 32	18 43		19 02	<	19 13			19 32	19 43	20 02	<	20 13			20 32	20 47	21 02	21 13		
Pluckley	d			18 39			19 09					19 39		20 09					20 39		21 09			
Headcorn	d			18 45			19 15					19 45		20 15					20 45		21 15			
Staplehurst	d			18 50			19 20					19 50		20 20					20 50		21 20			
Marden	d			18 55			19 25					19 55		20 25					20 55		21 25			
Maidstone West [4]	d		18 28								19 28							20 28						
Paddock Wood [4]	d		18 47	19 01			19 31				19 47	20 01		20 31				20 47	21 01		21 31			
Tonbridge [4]	a		18 55	19 09			19 39				19 55	20 09		20 39				20 55	21 09		21 39			
	d			19 10			19 40					20 10		20 40					21 10		21 40			
Sevenoaks [4]	a			19 18			19 48					20 18		20 48					21 18		21 48			
Orpington [4]	a			19 27			19 57					20 27		20 57					21 27		21 57			
London Bridge [4] ⊖	a			19 43			20 13					20 43		21 13					21 43		22 13			
London Cannon Street [4] ⊖	a																							
London Waterloo (East) [4] ⊖	a			19 48			20 18					20 48		21 18					21 48		22 18			
London Charing Cross [4] ⊖	a			19 51			20 21					20 51		21 21					21 51		22 21			
Ebbsfleet International	a				19 02				19 32				20 02			20 32				21 06		21 32		
Stratford International ⊖	a				19 14				19 44				20 14			20 44				21 18		21 44		
St Pancras International [15] ⊖	a				19 21				19 51				20 21			20 51				21 25		21 51		

A ⫪ from Ashford International

Table 207

Saturdays

Margate, Ramsgate, Canterbury West, Dover, Folkestone, Ashford International,- Tonbridge and London

		SE	SE [1]	SE	SE [1]	SE	SE	SE [1]	SE	SE [1]		SE	SE [1]
Margate [4]	d			20 53					21 53				
Broadstairs	d			20 59					21 59				
Ramsgate [4]	d		20 36	21 05	20 50			21 22	22 05	22 22			22 40
Minster [4]	d		20 42							22 28			
Sandwich	d				21 01			21 34					22 52
Deal	d				21 07			21 40					22 58
Walmer	d				21 10			21 43					23 01
Martin Mill	d				21 14			21 47					23 05
Dover Priory [4]	a				21 22			21 55					23 13
	d				21 24	21 44		21 56				22 44	23 20
Folkestone Central	d				21 36	21 56		22 08				22 56	23 32
Folkestone West	d				21 38	21 58		22 10				22 58	23 34
Sandling	d				21 43			22 16					23 39
Westenhanger	d				21 46			22 19					23 42
Sturry	d		20 53							22 39			
Canterbury West [4]	d		21 00	21 25					22 25	22 46			
Chartham	d		21 05							22 51			
Chilham	d		21 09							22 55			
Wye	d		21 16							23 02			
Ashford International	a		21 22	21 41	21 55	22 11		22 28	22 41	23 08		23 11	23 51
	d		21 32	21 43	22 02	22 13		22 32	22 43			23 13	
Pluckley	d		21 39		22 09			22 39					
Headcorn	d		21 45		22 15			22 45					
Staplehurst	d		21 50		22 20			22 50					
Marden	d		21 55		22 25			22 55					
Maidstone West [4]	d	21 28					22 28						
Paddock Wood [4]	d	21 47	22 01		22 31		22 48	23 01					
Tonbridge [4]	a	21 55	22 09		22 39		22 55	23 10					
	d		22 10		22 40								
Sevenoaks [4]	a		22 18		22 48								
Orpington [4]	a		22 27		22 57								
London Bridge [4] ⊖	a		22 43		23 13								
London Cannon Street [4] ⊖	a												
London Waterloo (East) [4] ⊖	a		22 48		23 18								
London Charing Cross [4] ⊖	a		22 51		23 21								
Ebbsfleet International	a			22 02		22 32			23 02			23 32	
Stratford International ⊖	a			22 14		22 44			23 14			23 44	
St Pancras International [15] ⊖	a			22 21		22 51			23 21			23 51	

Sundays

		SE [1]	SE	SE [1]	SE [1]	SE	SE [1]	SE	SE [1]	SE [1] A ⫪	SE	SE	SE [1] A ⫪	SE	SE [1]	SE [1] A ⫪	SE	SE	SE [1] A ⫪	SE [1]		SE	SE [1]	SE [1] A ⫪	SE
Margate [4]	d										07 53						08 53								09 53
Broadstairs	d										07 59						08 59								09 59
Ramsgate [4]	d						06 50		07 24	07 36	08 05		07 50		08 24	08 36	09 05		08 50				09 24	09 40	10 05
Minster [4]	d									07 42						08 42								09 46	
Sandwich	d						07 01		07 36				08 01		08 36				09 01				09 36		
Deal	d						07 07		07 42				08 07		08 42				09 07				09 42		
Walmer	d						07 10		07 45				08 10		08 45				09 10				09 45		
Martin Mill	d						07 14		07 49				08 14		08 49				09 14				09 49		
Dover Priory [4]	a						07 22		07 57				08 22		08 57				09 22				09 57		
	d						07 24	07 44	07 58				08 24	08 44	08 58				09 24			09 44	09 58		
Folkestone Central	d						07 36	07 56	08 10				08 36	08 56	09 10				09 36			09 56	10 10		
Folkestone West	d						07 38	07 58	08 12				08 38	08 58	09 12				09 38			09 58	10 12		
Sandling	d						07 43		08 18				08 43		09 18				09 43				10 18		
Westenhanger	d						07 46						08 46						09 46						
Sturry	d									07 53						08 53								09 57	
Canterbury West [4]	d									08 00	08 25					09 00	09 25			09 35				10 04	10 25
Chartham	d									08 05						09 05				09 40					
Chilham	d									08 09						09 09				09 44					
Wye	d									08 16						09 16				09 51				10 16	
Ashford International	a						07 55	08 11	08 28	08 22	08 41		08 55	09 11	09 28	09 22	09 41		09 55	09 58		10 11	10 28	10 22	10 41
	d	06 32		07 02	07 32		08 02	08 13		08 32	08 43		09 02	09 13		09 32	09 43		10 02	<		10 13		10 32	10 43
Pluckley	d	06 39			07 39					08 39						09 39								10 39	
Headcorn	d	06 45		07 13	07 45		08 13			08 45			09 13			09 45			10 13					10 45	
Staplehurst	d	06 50		07 18	07 50		08 18			08 50			09 18			09 50			10 18					10 50	
Marden	d	06 55		07 22	07 55		08 22			08 55			09 22			09 55			10 22					10 55	
Maidstone West [4]	d		07b03			08c03						09e03						10b03							
Paddock Wood [4]	d	07 01	07a22	07 29	08 01	08a22	08 29			09 01		09a22	09 29			10 01		10a22	10 29					11 01	
Tonbridge [4]	a	07 09		07 38	08 09		08 38			09 09			09 38			10 09			10 38					11 09	
	d	07 10		07 39	08 10		08 39			09 10			09 39			10 10			10 39					11 10	
Sevenoaks [4]	a	07 18		07 49	08 18		08 49			09 18			09 49			10 18			10 49					11 18	
Orpington [4]	a	07 28		07 58	08 28		08 58			09 28			09 58			10 28			10 58					11 28	
London Bridge [4] ⊖	a	07 44		08 14	08 44		09 14			09 44			10 14			10 44			11 14					11 44	
London Cannon Street [4] ⊖	a																								
London Waterloo (East) [4] ⊖	a	07 49		08 19	08 49		09 19			09 49			10 19			10 49			11 19					11 49	
London Charing Cross [4] ⊖	a	07 53		08 23	08 53		09 23			09 53			10 23			10 53			11 23					11 53	
Ebbsfleet International	a							08 32			09 02			09 32			10 02					10 32			11 02
Stratford International ⊖	a							08 44			09 14			09 44			10 14					10 44			11 14
St Pancras International [15] ⊖	a							08 51			09 21			09 51			10 21					10 51			11 21

A ⫪ from Ashford International
b arr. 0657
c arr. 0757
e arr. 0857

Table 207

Sundays

Margate, Ramsgate, Canterbury West, Dover, Folkestone, Ashford International,- Tonbridge and London

		SE	SE 1 A	SE 1	SE	SE 1			SE 1 A	SE	SE	SE 1 A	SE 1	SE	SE 1	SE 1 A	SE	SE	SE 1 A	SE 1	SE	SE 1	SE 1 A	SE	SE
Margate	d									10 53							11 53							12 53	
Broadstairs	d									10 59							11 59							12 59	
Ramsgate	d		09 50			10 24			10 40	11 05		10 50			11 24	11 40	12 05		11 50			12 24	12 40	13 05	
Minster	d								10 46							11 46							12 46		
Sandwich	d		10 01			10 36						11 01			11 36				12 01			12 36			
Deal	d		10 07			10 42						11 07			11 42				12 07			12 42			
Walmer	d		10 10			10 45						11 10			11 45				12 10			12 45			
Martin Mill	d		10 14			10 49						11 14			11 49				12 14			12 49			
Dover Priory	a		10 22			10 57						11 22			11 57				12 22			12 57			
	d		10 24		10 44	10 58						11 24		11 44	11 58				12 24		12 44	12 58			
Folkestone Central	d		10 36		10 56	11 10						11 36		11 56	12 10				12 36		12 56	13 10			
Folkestone West	d		10 38		10 58	11 12						11 38		11 58	12 12				12 38		12 58	13 12			
Sandling	d		10 43			11 18						11 43			12 18				12 43			13 18			
Westenhanger	d		10 46									11 46							12 46						
Sturry	d								10 57							11 57							12 57		
Canterbury West	d			10 35					11 04	11 25			11 35			12 04	12 25			12 35			13 04	13 25	
Chartham	d			10 40									11 40							12 40					
Chilham	d			10 44									11 44							12 44					
Wye	d			10 51					11 16				11 51			12 16				12 51			13 16		
Ashford International	a		10 55	10 58	11 11	11 28			11 22	11 41		11 55	11 58	12 11	12 28	12 22	12 41		12 55	12 58	13 11	13 28	13 22	13 41	
	d		11 02	<	11 13				11 32	11 43		12 02	<	12 13		12 32	12 43		13 02	<	13 13		13 32	13 43	
Pluckley	d								11 39							12 39							13 39		
Headcorn	d		11 13						11 45			12 13				12 45			13 13				13 45		
Staplehurst	d		11 18						11 50			12 18				12 50			13 18				13 50		
Marden	d		11 22						11 55			12 22				12 55			13 22				13 55		
Maidstone West	d	11c03									12e03							13f03							14g03
Paddock Wood	d	11a22	11 29						12 01		12a22	12 29				13 01		13a22	13 29				14 01		14a22
Tonbridge	a		11 38						12 09			12 38				13 09			13 38				14 09		
	d		11 39						12 10			12 39				13 10			13 39				14 10		
Sevenoaks	a		11 49						12 18			12 49				13 18			13 49				14 18		
Orpington	a		11 58						12 28			12 58				13 28			13 58				14 28		
London Bridge ⊖	a		12 14						12 44			13 14				13 44			14 14				14 44		
London Cannon Street ⊖	a																								
London Waterloo (East) ⊖	a		12 19						12 49			13 19				13 49			14 19				14 49		
London Charing Cross ⊖	a		12 23						12 53			13 23				13 53			14 23				14 53		
Ebbsfleet International	a				11 32					12 02				12 32			13 02				13 32			14 02	
Stratford International ⊖	a				11 44					12 14				12 45			13 14				13 44			14 14	
St Pancras International ⊖	a				11 51					12 21				12 54			13 21				13 51			14 21	

		SE 1 A	SE 1	SE	SE 1	SE 1 A	SE	SE	SE 1 A	SE 1	SE		SE 1	SE 1 A	SE	SE	SE 1 A	SE 1	SE	SE 1	SE 1 A			SE	SE
Margate	d						13 53								14 53									15 53	15 53
Broadstairs	d						13 59								14 59									15 59	15 59
Ramsgate	d	12 50			13 24	13 40	14 05		13 50				14 24	14 40	15 05		14 50			15 24	15 40			16 05	16 05
Minster	d					13 46								14 46							15 46				
Sandwich	d	13 01			13 36				14 01				14 36				15 01			15 36					
Deal	d	13 07			13 42				14 07				14 42				15 07			15 42					
Walmer	d	13 10			13 45				14 10				14 45				15 10			15 45					
Martin Mill	d	13 14			13 49				14 14				14 49				15 14			15 49					
Dover Priory	a	13 22			13 57				14 22				14 57				15 22			15 57					
	d	13 24		13 44	13 58				14 24		14 44		14 58				15 24		15 44	15 58					
Folkestone Central	d	13 36		13 56	14 10				14 36		14 56		15 10				15 36		15 56	16 10					
Folkestone West	d	13 38		13 58	14 12				14 38		14 58		15 12				15 38		15 58	16 12					
Sandling	d	13 43			14 18				14 43				15 18				15 43			16 18					
Westenhanger	d	13 46							14 46								15 46								
Sturry	d					13 57								14 57							15 57				
Canterbury West	d		13 35			14 04	14 25			14 35				15 04	15 25			15 35			16 04			16 25	16 25
Chartham	d		13 40							14 40								15 40							
Chilham	d		13 44							14 44								15 44							
Wye	d		13 51			14 16				14 51				15 16				15 51			16 16				
Ashford International	a	13 55	13 58	14 11	14 28	14 22	14 41		14 55	14 58	15 11		15 28	15 22	15 41		15 55	15 58	16 11	16 28	16 22			16 41	16 41
	d	14 02	<	14 13		14 32	14 43		15 02	<	15 13			15 32	15 43		16 02	<	16 13		16 32			16 43	16 47
Pluckley	d					14 39								15 39							16 39				
Headcorn	d	14 13				14 45			15 13					15 45			16 13				16 45				
Staplehurst	d	14 18				14 50			15 18					15 50			16 18				16 50				
Marden	d	14 22				14 55			15 22					15 55			16 22				16 55				
Maidstone West	d							15h03								16b03									
Paddock Wood	d	14 29				15 01		15a22	15 29					16 01		16a22	16 29				17 01				
Tonbridge	a	14 38				15 09			15 38					16 09			16 38				17 09				
	d	14 39				15 10			15 39					16 10			16 39				17 10				
Sevenoaks	a	14 49				15 18			15 49					16 18			16 49				17 18				
Orpington	a	14 58				15 28			15 58					16 28			16 58				17 28				
London Bridge ⊖	a	15 14				15 44			16 14					16 44			17 14				17 44				
London Cannon Street ⊖	a																								
London Waterloo (East) ⊖	a	15 19				15 49			16 19					16 49			17 19				17 49				
London Charing Cross ⊖	a	15 23				15 53			16 23					16 53			17 23				17 53				
Ebbsfleet International	a			14 32			15 02				15 32				16 02				16 32					17 02	17 06
Stratford International ⊖	a			14 44			15 14				15 44				16 14				16 44					17 14	17 18
St Pancras International ⊖	a			14 51			15 21				15 51				16 21				16 51					17 21	17 28

A from Ashford International
b arr. 0957
c arr. 1057
e arr. 1157
f arr. 1257
g arr. 1357
h arr. 1457

Table 207

Sundays

Margate, Ramsgate, Canterbury West, Dover, Folkestone, Ashford International,- Tonbridge and London

		SE	SE 1 A	SE 1	SE	SE 1	SE 1 A	SE	SE	SE 1 A	SE 1	SE	SE 1	SE 1 A	SE	SE	SE 1	SE 1	SE	SE 1	SE 1	SE		SE	SE 1
Margate	d							16 53							17 53							18 53			
Broadstairs	d							16 59							17 59							18 59			
Ramsgate	d		15 50			16 24	16 40	17 05		16 50			17 24	17 40	18 05		17 50			18 24	18 36	19 05			18 50
Minster	d						16 46							17 46							18 42				
Sandwich	d		16 01			16 36				17 01			17 36				18 01			18 36					19 01
Deal	d		16 07			16 42				17 07			17 42				18 07			18 42					19 07
Walmer	d		16 10			16 45				17 10			17 45				18 10			18 45					19 10
Martin Mill	d		16 14			16 49				17 14			17 49				18 14			18 49					19 14
Dover Priory	a		16 22			16 57				17 22			17 57				18 22			18 57					19 22
	d		16 24		16 44	16 58				17 24		17 44	17 58				18 24		18 44	18 58					19 24
Folkestone Central	d		16 36		16 56	17 10				17 36		17 56	18 10				18 36		18 56	19 10					19 36
Folkestone West	d		16 38		16 58	17 12				17 38		17 58	18 12				18 38		18 58	19 12					19 38
Sandling	d		16 43			17 18				17 43			18 18				18 43			19 18					19 43
Westenhanger	d		16 46							17 46							18 46								19 46
Sturry	d						16 57							17 57							18 53				
Canterbury West	d			16 35			17 04	17 25			17 35			18 04	18 25			18 35			19 00	19 25			
Chartham	d			16 40							17 40							18 40			19 05				
Chilham	d			16 44							17 44							18 44			19 09				
Wye	d			16 51			17 16				17 51			18 16				18 51			19 16				
Ashford International	a		16 55	16 58	17 11	17 28	17 22	17 41		17 55	17 58	18 11	18 28	18 22	18 41		18 55	18 58	19 11	19 28	19 22	19 41			19 55
	d		17 02	<	17 13		17 32	17 43		18 02	<	18 13		18 32	18 43		19 02	<	19 13		19 32	19 43			20 02
Pluckley	d						17 39							18 39							19 39				
Headcorn	d		17 13				17 45			18 13				18 45			19 13				19 45				20 13
Staplehurst	d		17 18				17 50			18 18				18 50			19 18				19 50				20 18
Marden	d		17 22				17 55			18 22				18 55			19 22				19 55				20 22
Maidstone West	d	17c03							18e03							19e03								20e03	
Paddock Wood	d	17a22	17 29				18 01		18a22	18 29				19 01		19a22	19 29				20 01			20a22	20 29
Tonbridge	a		17 38				18 09			18 38				19 09			19 38				20 09				20 38
	d		17 39				18 10			18 39				19 10			19 39				20 10				20 39
Sevenoaks	a		17 49				18 18			18 49				19 18			19 49				20 18				20 49
Orpington	a		17 58				18 28			18 58				19 28			19 58				20 28				20 58
London Bridge ⊖	a		18 14				18 44			19 14				19 44			20 14				20 44				21 14
London Cannon Street ⊖	a																								
London Waterloo (East) ⊖	a		18 19				18 49			19 19				19 49			20 19				20 49				21 19
London Charing Cross ⊖	a		18 23				18 53			19 23				19 53			20 23				20 53				21 23
Ebbsfleet International	a				17 32			18 02				18 32			19 02				19 32			20 02			
Stratford International ⊖	a				17 44			18 14				18 44			19 14				19 44			20 14			
St Pancras International ⊖	a				17 51			18 21				18 51			19 21				19 51			20 21			

		SE	SE 1		SE 1	SE	SE	SE 1	SE	SE 1	SE 1	SE	SE	SE 1		SE	SE 1	SE	SE 1						
Margate	d					19 53						20 53						21 53							
Broadstairs	d					19 59						20 59						21 59							
Ramsgate	d		19 24		19 36	20 05		19 50		20 24	20 36	21 05		20 50			21 36	22 05	21 50						
Minster	d				19 42						20 42						21 42								
Sandwich	d		19 36					20 01		20 36				21 01					22 01						
Deal	d		19 42					20 07		20 42				21 07					22 07						
Walmer	d		19 45					20 10		20 45				21 10					22 10						
Martin Mill	d		19 49					20 14		20 49				21 14					22 14						
Dover Priory	a		19 57					20 22		20 57				21 22					22 22						
	d	19 44	19 58					20 24	20 44	20 58				21 24		21 44			22 24						
Folkestone Central	d	19 56	20 10					20 36	20 56	21 10				21 36		21 56			22 36						
Folkestone West	d	19 58	20 12					20 38	20 58	21 12				21 38		21 58			22 38						
Sandling	d		20 18					20 43		21 18				21 43					22 43						
Westenhanger	d							20 46						21 46					22 46						
Sturry	d				19 53						20 53						21 53								
Canterbury West	d				20 00	20 25					21 00	21 25					22 00	22 25							
Chartham	d				20 05						21 05						22 05								
Chilham	d				20 09						21 09						22 09								
Wye	d				20 16						21 16						22 16								
Ashford International	a	20 11	20 28		20 22	20 41		20 55	21 11	21 28	21 22	21 41		21 55		22 11	22 22	22 41	22 55						
	d	20 13			20 32	20 47		21 02	21 13		21 32	21 43		22 02		22 13		22 43							
Pluckley	d				20 39						21 39														
Headcorn	d				20 45			21 13			21 45			22 13											
Staplehurst	d				20 50			21 18			21 50			22 18											
Marden	d				20 55			21 22			21 55			22 22											
Maidstone West	d						21h03						22i03												
Paddock Wood	d				21 01		21a22	21 29			22 01		22 23	22 29											
Tonbridge	a				21 09			21 38			22 09		22 30	22 38											
	d				21 10			21 39			22 10			22 39											
Sevenoaks	a				21 18			21 49			22 18			22 49											
Orpington	a				21 28			21 58			22 28			22 58											
London Bridge ⊖	a				21 44			22 14			22 44			23 14											
London Cannon Street ⊖	a																								
London Waterloo (East) ⊖	a				21 49			22 19			22 49			23 19											
London Charing Cross ⊖	a				21 53			22 23			22 53			23 23											
Ebbsfleet International	a	20 32				21 06			21 32			22 02				22 32		23 02							
Stratford International ⊖	a	20 44				21 18			21 44			22 14				22 44		23 14							
St Pancras International ⊖	a	20 51				21 25			21 51			22 21				22 51		23 21							

A from Ashford International
b arr. 1557
c arr. 1657
e arr. 1757
f arr. 1857
g arr. 1957
h arr. 2057
i arr. 2157

Strood - Maidstone West and Paddock Wood

Mondays to Fridays

		SE	SE	SE	SE	SE	SE	SE	SE	SE		SE	SE	SE	SE	SE	SE	SE	SE	SE		SE	SE	SE	SE
Strood ■	d	04 55	05 35	06 05	06 35	07 18	07 55	08 35	09 05	09 35		10 05	10 35	11 05	11 35	12 05	12 35	13 05	13 35	14 05		14 35	15 05	15 35	16 10
Cuxton	d	04 59	05 39	06 09	06 39	07 22	07 59	08 39	09 09	09 39		10 09	10 39	11 09	11 39	12 09	12 39	13 09	13 39	14 09		14 39	15 09	15 39	16 14
Halling	d	05 02	05 42	06 12	06 42	07 25	08 02	08 42	09 12	09 42		10 12	10 42	11 12	11 42	12 12	12 42	13 12	13 42	14 12		14 42	15 12	15 42	16 17
Snodland	d	05 05	05 45	06 15	06 45	07 28	08 05	08 45	09 15	09 45		10 15	10 45	11 15	11 45	12 15	12 45	13 15	13 45	14 15		14 45	15 15	15 45	16 20
New Hythe	d	05 08	05 48	06 18	06 48	07 31	08 08	08 48	09 18	09 48		10 18	10 48	11 18	11 48	12 18	12 48	13 18	13 48	14 18		14 48	15 18	15 48	16 23
Aylesford	d	05 10	05 50	06 20	06 50	07 33	08 10	08 50	09 20	09 50		10 20	10 50	11 20	11 50	12 20	12 50	13 20	13 50	14 20		14 50	15 20	15 50	16 25
Maidstone Barracks	d	05 15	05 55	06 25	06 55	07 38	08 15	08 55	09 25	09 55		10 25	10 55	11 25	11 55	12 25	12 55	13 25	13 55	14 25		14 55	15 25	15 55	16 30
Maidstone West ■	a	05 17	05 57	06 27	06 57	07 40	08 17	08 57	09 27	09 57		10 27	10 57	11 27	11 57	12 27	12 57	13 27	13 57	14 27		14 57	15 27	15 57	16 32
	d	05 18	05 58	06 28	06 58	07 41	08 18		09 28			10 28		11 28		12 28		13 28		14 28			15 28		16 33
East Farleigh	d	05 21	06 01	06 31	07 01	07 44	08 21		09 31			10 31		11 31		12 31		13 31		14 31			15 31		16 36
Wateringbury	d	05 26	06 06	06 36	07 06	07 49	08 26		09 36			10 36		11 36		12 36		13 36		14 36			15 36		16 41
Yalding	d	05 30	06 10	06 40	07 10	07 53	08 30		09 40			10 40		11 40		12 40		13 40		14 40			15 40		16 45
Beltring	d	05 33	06 13	06 43	07 13	07 56	08 33		09 43			10 43		11 43		12 43		13 43		14 43			15 43		16 48
Paddock Wood ■	a	05 37	06 17	06 47	07 17	08 00	08 37		09 49			10 47		11 47		12 47		13 47		14 47			15 47		16 52
Tonbridge ■	a						08 45		09 57			10 55		11 55		12 58		13 55		14 55			15 55		

		SE	SE	SE	SE	SE		SE	SE	SE	SE	SE	SE	SE
Strood ■	d	16 35	17 05	17 50	18 20	18 50		19 35	20 05	20 35	21 05	21 35	22 05	22 35
Cuxton	d	16 39	17 09	17 54	18 24	18 54		19 39	20 09	20 39	21 09	21 39	22 09	22 39
Halling	d	16 42	17 12	17 57	18 27	18 57		19 42	20 12	20 42	21 12	21 42	22 12	22 42
Snodland	d	16 45	17 15	18 00	18 30	19 00		19 45	20 15	20 45	21 15	21 45	22 15	22 45
New Hythe	d	16 48	17 18	18 03	18 33	19 03		19 48	20 18	20 48	21 18	21 48	22 18	22 48
Aylesford	d	16 50	17 20	18 05	18 35	19 05		19 50	20 20	20 50	21 20	21 50	22 20	22 50
Maidstone Barracks	d	16 55	17 25	18 10	18 40	19 10		19 55	20 25	20 55	21 25	21 55	22 25	22 55
Maidstone West ■	a	16 57	17 27	18 12	18 42	19 12		19 57	20 27	20 57	21 27	21 57	22 27	22 57
	d	16 58	17 28	18 13	18 43	19 13		19 58		20 58		21 58		
East Farleigh	d	17 01	17 31	18 16	18 46	19 16		20 01		21 01		22 01		
Wateringbury	d	17 06	17 36	18 21	18 51	19 21		20 06		21 06		22 06		
Yalding	d	17 10	17 40	18 25	18 55	19 25		20 10		21 10		22 10		
Beltring	d	17 13	17 43	18 28	18 58	19 28		20 13		21 13		22 13		
Paddock Wood ■	a	17 17	17 47	18 32	19 02	19 32		20 17		21 17		22 17		
Tonbridge ■	a							20 25		21 25		22 25		

Saturdays

		SE	SE	SE	SE	SE	SE	SE	SE	SE		SE	SE	SE	SE	SE	SE	SE	SE	SE		SE	SE	SE	SE
Strood ■	d	06 05	06 35	07 05	07 35	08 05	08 35	09 05	09 35	10 05		10 35	11 05	11 35	12 05	12 35	13 05	13 35	14 05	14 35		15 05	15 35	16 05	16 35
Cuxton	d	06 09	06 39	07 09	07 39	08 09	08 39	09 09	09 39	10 09		10 39	11 09	11 39	12 09	12 39	13 09	13 39	14 09	14 39		15 09	15 39	16 09	16 39
Halling	d	06 12	06 42	07 12	07 42	08 12	08 42	09 12	09 42	10 12		10 42	11 12	11 42	12 12	12 42	13 12	13 42	14 12	14 42		15 12	15 42	16 12	16 42
Snodland	d	06 15	06 45	07 15	07 45	08 15	08 45	09 15	09 45	10 15		10 45	11 15	11 45	12 15	12 45	13 15	13 45	14 15	14 45		15 15	15 45	16 15	16 45
New Hythe	d	06 18	06 48	07 18	07 48	08 18	08 48	09 18	09 48	10 18		10 48	11 18	11 48	12 18	12 48	13 18	13 48	14 18	14 48		15 18	15 48	16 18	16 48
Aylesford	d	06 20	06 50	07 20	07 50	08 20	08 50	09 20	09 50	10 20		10 50	11 20	11 50	12 20	12 50	13 20	13 50	14 20	14 50		15 20	15 50	16 20	16 50
Maidstone Barracks	d	06 25	06 55	07 25	07 55	08 25	08 55	09 25	09 55	10 25		10 55	11 25	11 55	12 25	12 55	13 25	13 55	14 25	14 55		15 25	15 55	16 25	16 55
Maidstone West ■	a	06 27	06 57	07 27	07 57	08 27	08 57	09 27	09 57	10 27		10 57	11 27	11 57	12 27	12 57	13 27	13 57	14 27	14 57		15 27	15 57	16 27	16 57
	d	06 28		07 28		08 28		09 28		10 28			11 28		12 28		13 28		14 28			15 28		16 28	
East Farleigh	d	06 31		07 31		08 31		09 31		10 31			11 31		12 31		13 31		14 31			15 31		16 31	
Wateringbury	d	06 36		07 36		08 36		09 36		10 36			11 36		12 36		13 36		14 36			15 36		16 36	
Yalding	d	06 40		07 40		08 40		09 40		10 40			11 40		12 40		13 40		14 40			15 40		16 40	
Beltring	d	06 43		07 43		08 43		09 43		10 43			11 43		12 43		13 43		14 43			15 43		16 43	
Paddock Wood ■	a	06 47		07 47		08 47		09 47		10 47			11 47		12 47		13 47		14 47			15 47		16 47	
Tonbridge ■	a	06 55		07 55		08 55		09 55		10 55			11 55		12 55		13 55		14 55			15 55		16 55	

		SE	SE	SE	SE	SE		SE	SE	SE	SE	SE	SE	SE
Strood ■	d	17 05	17 35	18 05	18 35	19 05		19 35	20 05	20 35	21 05	21 35	22 05	22 35
Cuxton	d	17 09	17 39	18 09	18 39	19 09		19 39	20 09	20 39	21 09	21 39	22 09	22 39
Halling	d	17 12	17 42	18 12	18 42	19 12		19 42	20 12	20 42	21 12	21 42	22 12	22 42
Snodland	d	17 15	17 45	18 15	18 45	19 15		19 45	20 15	20 45	21 15	21 45	22 15	22 45
New Hythe	d	17 18	17 48	18 18	18 48	19 18		19 48	20 18	20 48	21 18	21 48	22 18	22 48
Aylesford	d	17 20	17 50	18 20	18 50	19 20		19 50	20 20	20 50	21 20	21 50	22 20	22 50
Maidstone Barracks	d	17 25	17 55	18 25	18 55	19 25		19 55	20 25	20 55	21 25	21 55	22 25	22 55
Maidstone West ■	a	17 27	17 57	18 27	18 57	19 27		19 57	20 27	20 57	21 27	21 57	22 27	22 57
	d	17 28		18 28		19 28			20 28		21 28		22 28	
East Farleigh	d	17 31		18 31		19 31			20 31		21 31		22 31	
Wateringbury	d	17 36		18 36		19 36			20 36		21 36		22 36	
Yalding	d	17 40		18 40		19 40			20 40		21 40		22 40	
Beltring	d	17 43		18 43		19 43			20 43		21 43		22 43	
Paddock Wood ■	a	17 47		18 47		19 47			20 47		21 47		22 47	
Tonbridge ■	a	17 55		18 55		19 55			20 55		21 55		22 55	

Sundays

		SE	SE	SE	SE	SE	SE	SE	SE	SE		SE	SE	SE	SE	SE	SE	SE
Strood ■	d	06 35	07 35	08 35	09 35	10 35	11 35	12 35	13 35	14 35		15 35	16 35	17 35	18 35	19 35	20 35	21 35
Cuxton	d	06 39	07 39	08 39	09 39	10 39	11 39	12 39	13 39	14 39		15 39	16 39	17 39	18 39	19 39	20 39	21 39
Halling	d	06 42	07 42	08 42	09 42	10 42	11 42	12 42	13 42	14 42		15 42	16 42	17 42	18 42	19 42	20 42	21 42
Snodland	d	06 45	07 45	08 45	09 45	10 45	11 45	12 45	13 45	14 45		15 45	16 45	17 45	18 45	19 45	20 45	21 45
New Hythe	d	06 48	07 48	08 48	09 48	10 48	11 48	12 48	13 48	14 48		15 48	16 48	17 48	18 48	19 48	20 48	21 48
Aylesford	d	06 50	07 50	08 50	09 50	10 50	11 50	12 50	13 50	14 50		15 50	16 50	17 50	18 50	19 50	20 50	21 50
Maidstone Barracks	d	06 55	07 55	08 55	09 55	10 55	11 55	12 55	13 55	14 55		15 55	16 55	17 55	18 55	19 55	20 55	21 55
Maidstone West ■	a	06 57	07 57	08 57	09 57	10 57	11 57	12 57	13 57	14 57		15 57	16 57	17 57	18 57	19 57	20 57	21 57
	d	07 03	08 03	09 03	10 03	11 03	12 03	13 03	14 03	15 03		16 03	17 03	18 03	19 03	20 03	21 03	22 03
East Farleigh	d	07 07	08 07	09 07	10 07	11 07	12 07	13 07	14 07	15 07		16 07	17 07	18 07	19 07	20 07	21 07	22 07
Wateringbury	d	07 12	08 12	09 12	10 12	11 12	12 12	13 12	14 12	15 12		16 12	17 12	18 12	19 12	20 12	21 12	22 12
Yalding	d	07 15	08 15	09 15	10 15	11 15	12 15	13 15	14 15	15 15		16 15	17 15	18 15	19 15	20 15	21 15	22 15
Beltring	d	07 18	08 18	09 18	10 18	11 18	12 18	13 18	14 18	15 18		16 18	17 18	18 18	19 18	20 18	21 18	22 18
Paddock Wood ■	a	07 22	08 22	09 22	10 22	11 22	12 22	13 22	14 22	15 22		16 22	17 22	18 22	19 22	20 22	21 22	22 22
Tonbridge ■	a																	22 30

Paddock Wood and Maidstone West - Strood

Mondays to Fridays

		SE	SE	SE	SE	SE	SE	SE	SE	SE		SE	SE	SE	SE	SE	SE	SE	SE	SE		SE	SE	SE	SE
Tonbridge ■	d							09 03		10 03			11 03		12 03		13 03		14 03			15 03		16 03	
Paddock Wood ■	d	05 42	06 25	06 55	07 40	08 10		09 10		10 10			11 10		12 10		13 10		14 10			15 10		16 10	17 02
Beltring	d	05 46	06 29	06 59	07 44	08 14		09 14		10 14			11 14		12 14		13 14		14 14			15 14		16 14	17 06
Yalding	d	05 49	06 32	07 02	07 48	08 18		09 18		10 18			11 18		12 18		13 18		14 18			15 18		16 18	17 09
Wateringbury	d	05 52	06 35	07 05	07 51	08 21		09 21		10 21			11 21		12 21		13 21		14 21			15 21		16 21	17 12
East Farleigh	d	05 56	06 39	07 09	07 55	08 25		09 25		10 25			11 25		12 25		13 25		14 25			15 25		16 25	17 16
Maidstone West ■	a	06 01	06 44	07 14	07 59	08 29		09 29		10 29			11 29		12 29		13 29		14 29			15 29		16 29	17 21
	d	06 02	06 45	07 15	08 02	08 32	09 02	09 32	10 02	10 32		11 02	11 32	12 02	12 32	13 02	13 32	14 02	14 32	15 02		15 44	16 02	16 32	17 22
Maidstone Barracks	d	06 04	06 47	07 17	08 04	08 34	09 04	09 34	10 04	10 34		11 04	11 34	12 04	12 34	13 04	13 34	14 04	14 34	15 04		15 46	16 04	16 34	17 24
Aylesford	d	06 09	06 52	07 22	08 09	08 39	09 09	09 39	10 09	10 39		11 09	11 39	12 09	12 39	13 09	13 39	14 09	14 39	15 09		15 51	16 09	16 39	17 29
New Hythe	d	06 11	06 54	07 24	08 11	08 41	09 11	09 41	10 11	10 41		11 11	11 41	12 11	12 41	13 11	13 41	14 11	14 41	15 11		15 53	16 11	16 41	17 31
Snodland	d	06 14	06 57	07 27	08 14	08 44	09 14	09 44	10 14	10 44		11 14	11 44	12 14	12 44	13 14	13 44	14 14	14 44	15 14		15 56	16 14	16 44	17 34
Halling	d	06 17	07 00	07 30	08 17	08 47	09 17	09 47	10 17	10 47		11 17	11 47	12 17	12 47	13 17	13 47	14 17	14 47	15 17		15 59	16 17	16 47	17 37
Cuxton	d	06 20	07 03	07 33	08 20	08 50	09 20	09 50	10 20	10 50		11 20	11 50	12 20	12 50	13 20	13 50	14 20	14 50	15 20		16 02	16 20	16 50	17 40
Strood ■	a	06 24	07 07	07 37	08 24	08 54	09 24	09 54	10 24	10 54		11 24	11 54	12 24	12 54	13 24	13 54	14 24	14 54	15 24		16 06	16 24	16 54	17 44

		SE	SE	SE	SE	SE		SE	SE	SE	SE	SE	SE
Tonbridge ■	d								20 33		21 33		22 33
Paddock Wood ■	d	17 29	17 52	18 40	19 12	19 40			20 40		21 40		22 40
Beltring	d	17 33	17 56	18 44	19 16	19 44			20 44		21 44		22 44
Yalding	d	17 36	17 59	18 48	19 20	19 48			20 48		21 48		22 48
Wateringbury	d	17 39	18 02	18 51	19 23	19 51			20 51		21 51		22 51
East Farleigh	d	17 43	18 06	18 55	19 27	19 55			20 55		21 55		22 55
Maidstone West ■	a	17 48	18 11	19 01	19 31	19 59			20 59		21 59		22 59
	d	17 49	18 18	19 02	19 32	20 02		20 32	21 02	21 32	22 02	22 32	23 02
Maidstone Barracks	d	17 51	18 20	19 04	19 34	20 04		20 34	21 04	21 34	22 04	22 34	23 04
Aylesford	d	17 56	18 25	19 09	19 39	20 09		20 39	21 09	21 39	22 09	22 39	23 09
New Hythe	d	17 58	18 27	19 11	19 41	20 11		20 41	21 11	21 41	22 11	22 41	23 11
Snodland	d	18 01	18 30	19 14	19 44	20 14		20 44	21 14	21 44	22 14	22 44	23 14
Halling	d	18 04	18 33	19 17	19 47	20 17		20 47	21 17	21 47	22 17	22 47	23 17
Cuxton	d	18 07	18 36	19 20	19 50	20 20		20 50	21 20	21 50	22 20	22 50	23 20
Strood ■	a	18 11	18 40	19 24	19 54	20 24		20 54	21 24	21 54	22 24	22 54	23 24

Saturdays

		SE	SE	SE	SE	SE	SE	SE	SE	SE		SE	SE	SE	SE	SE	SE	SE	SE	SE		SE	SE	SE	SE
Tonbridge ■	d	06 03		07 03		08 03		09 03		10 03			11 03		12 03		13 03		14 03			15 03		16 03	
Paddock Wood ■	d	06 10		07 10		08 10		09 10		10 10			11 10		12 10		13 10		14 10			15 10		16 10	
Beltring	d	06 14		07 14		08 14		09 14		10 14			11 14		12 14		13 14		14 14			15 14		16 14	
Yalding	d	06 18		07 18		08 18		09 18		10 18			11 18		12 18		13 18		14 18			15 18		16 18	
Wateringbury	d	06 21		07 21		08 21		09 21		10 21			11 21		12 21		13 21		14 21			15 21		16 21	
East Farleigh	d	06 25		07 25		08 25		09 25		10 25			11 25		12 25		13 25		14 25			15 25		16 25	
Maidstone West ■	a	06 29		07 29		08 29		09 29		10 29			11 29		12 29		13 29		14 29			15 29		16 29	
	d	06 32	07 02	07 32	08 02	08 32	09 02	09 32	10 02	10 32		11 02	11 32	12 02	12 32	13 02	13 32	14 02	14 32	15 02		15 32	16 02	16 32	17 02
Maidstone Barracks	d	06 34	07 04	07 34	08 04	08 34	09 04	09 34	10 04	10 34		11 04	11 34	12 04	12 34	13 04	13 34	14 04	14 34	15 04		15 34	16 04	16 34	17 04
Aylesford	d	06 39	07 09	07 39	08 09	08 39	09 09	09 39	10 09	10 39		11 09	11 39	12 09	12 39	13 09	13 39	14 09	14 39	15 09		15 39	16 09	16 39	17 09
New Hythe	d	06 41	07 11	07 41	08 11	08 41	09 11	09 41	10 11	10 41		11 11	11 41	12 11	12 41	13 11	13 41	14 11	14 41	15 11		15 41	16 11	16 41	17 11
Snodland	d	06 44	07 14	07 44	08 14	08 44	09 14	09 44	10 14	10 44		11 14	11 44	12 14	12 44	13 14	13 44	14 14	14 44	15 14		15 44	16 14	16 44	17 14
Halling	d	06 47	07 17	07 47	08 17	08 47	09 17	09 47	10 17	10 47		11 17	11 47	12 17	12 47	13 17	13 47	14 17	14 47	15 17		15 47	16 17	16 47	17 17
Cuxton	d	06 50	07 20	07 50	08 20	08 50	09 20	09 50	10 20	10 50		11 20	11 50	12 20	12 50	13 20	13 50	14 20	14 50	15 20		15 50	16 20	16 50	17 20
Strood ■	a	06 54	07 24	07 54	08 24	08 54	09 24	09 54	10 24	10 54		11 24	11 54	12 24	12 54	13 24	13 54	14 24	14 54	15 24		15 54	16 24	16 54	17 24

		SE	SE	SE	SE	SE		SE	SE	SE	SE	SE	SE	SE
Tonbridge ■	d	17 03		18 03		19 03			20 03		21 03		22 03	
Paddock Wood ■	d	17 10		18 10		19 10			20 10		21 10		22 10	
Beltring	d	17 14		18 14		19 14			20 14		21 14		22 14	
Yalding	d	17 18		18 18		19 18			20 18		21 18		22 18	
Wateringbury	d	17 21		18 21		19 21			20 21		21 21		22 21	
East Farleigh	d	17 25		18 25		19 25			20 25		21 25		22 25	
Maidstone West ■	a	17 29		18 29		19 29			20 29		21 29		22 29	
	d	17 32	18 02	18 32	19 02	19 32		20 02	20 32	21 02	21 32	22 02	22 32	23 02
Maidstone Barracks	d	17 34	18 04	18 34	19 04	19 34		20 04	20 34	21 04	21 34	22 04	22 34	23 04
Aylesford	d	17 39	18 09	18 39	19 09	19 39		20 09	20 39	21 09	21 39	22 09	22 39	23 09
New Hythe	d	17 41	18 11	18 41	19 11	19 41		20 11	20 41	21 11	21 41	22 11	22 41	23 11
Snodland	d	17 44	18 14	18 44	19 14	19 44		20 14	20 44	21 14	21 44	22 14	22 44	23 14
Halling	d	17 47	18 17	18 47	19 17	19 47		20 17	20 47	21 17	21 47	22 17	22 47	23 17
Cuxton	d	17 50	18 20	18 50	19 20	19 50		20 20	20 50	21 20	21 50	22 20	22 50	23 20
Strood ■	a	17 54	18 24	18 54	19 24	19 54		20 24	20 54	21 24	21 54	22 24	22 54	23 24

Sundays

		SE	SE	SE	SE	SE	SE	SE	SE	SE		SE	SE	SE	SE	SE	SE	SE
Tonbridge ■	d	06 26																
Paddock Wood ■	d	06 34	07 34	08 34	09 34	10 34	11 34	12 34	13 34	14 34		15 34	16 34	17 34	18 34	19 34	20 34	21 34
Beltring	d	06 38	07 38	08 38	09 38	10 38	11 38	12 38	13 38	14 38		15 38	16 38	17 38	18 38	19 38	20 38	21 38
Yalding	d	06 41	07 41	08 41	09 41	10 41	11 41	12 41	13 41	14 41		15 41	16 41	17 41	18 41	19 41	20 41	21 41
Wateringbury	d	06 44	07 44	08 44	09 44	10 44	11 44	12 44	13 44	14 44		15 44	16 44	17 44	18 44	19 44	20 44	21 44
East Farleigh	d	06 48	07 48	08 48	09 48	10 48	11 48	12 48	13 48	14 48		15 48	16 48	17 48	18 48	19 48	20 48	21 48
Maidstone West ■	a	06 53	07 53	08 53	09 53	10 53	11 53	12 53	13 53	14 53		15 53	16 53	17 53	18 53	19 53	20 53	21 53
	d	07 00	08 00	09 02	10 02	11 02	12 02	13 02	14 02	15 02		16 02	17 02	18 02	19 02	20 00	21 00	22 00
Maidstone Barracks	d	07 02	08 02	09 04	10 04	11 04	12 04	13 04	14 04	15 04		16 04	17 04	18 04	19 04	20 02	21 02	22 02
Aylesford	d	07 07	08 07	09 09	10 09	11 09	12 09	13 09	14 09	15 09		16 09	17 09	18 09	19 09	20 07	21 07	22 07
New Hythe	d	07 09	08 09	09 11	10 11	11 11	12 11	13 11	14 11	15 11		16 11	17 11	18 11	19 11	20 09	21 09	22 09
Snodland	d	07 12	08 12	09 14	10 14	11 14	12 14	13 14	14 14	15 14		16 14	17 14	18 14	19 14	20 12	21 12	22 12
Halling	d	07 15	08 15	09 17	10 17	11 17	12 17	13 17	14 17	15 17		16 17	17 17	18 17	19 17	20 15	21 15	22 15
Cuxton	d	07 18	08 18	09 20	10 20	11 20	12 20	13 20	14 20	15 20		16 20	17 20	18 20	19 20	20 18	21 18	22 18
Strood ■	a	07 22	08 22	09 24	10 24	11 24	12 24	13 24	14 24	15 24		16 24	17 24	18 24	19 24	20 22	21 22	22 22

Network Diagram for Table 212

DM-32/09
Design BAJS

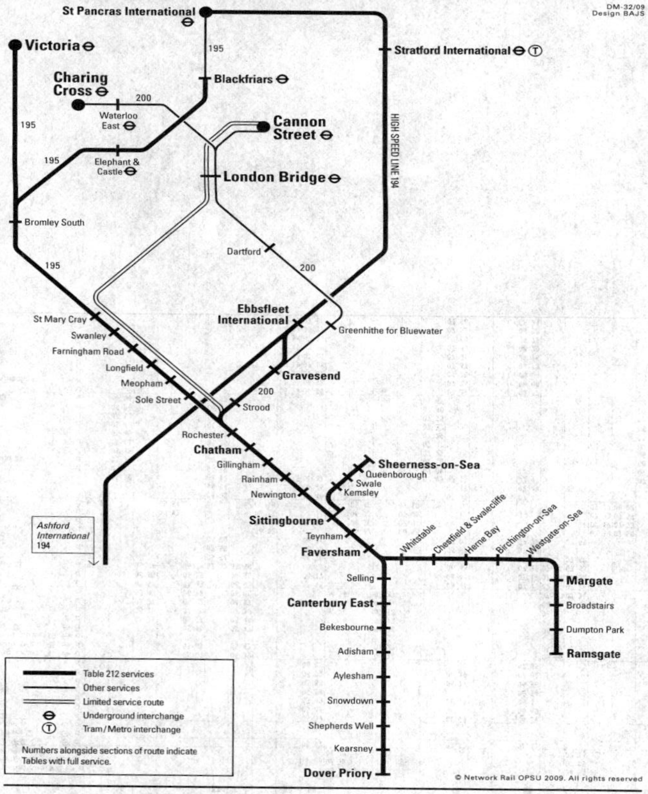

Table 212

London - Medway, Sheerness-on-Sea, Dover and Ramsgate

		SE MO ■	SE MO ■	SE MX ■	SE MX ■	SE	SE MX ■	SE MO ■	SE MO	SE MX		SE MX ■	SE MX	SE MO	SE MO	SE MX	SE MO ■	SE MX ■	SE MX ■	SE MX		SE MX	SE MX	SE	SE
St Pancras International ⊖	d					22p55			23p25	23p25					23p42	23p55						00 12			
Stratford International ⊖	d					23p02			23p32	23p32					23p49	00 02						00 19			
Ebbsfleet International	d					23p13			23p43	23p43					00 01	00 13						00 31			
London Victoria ⊖	d	22p05		22p22			22p52	23p05				23p22					23p45	23p52	00 10					00 35	
London Blackfriars ⊖	d																								
Elephant & Castle ⊖	d																								
Bromley South	d	22p22		22p39			23p09	23p22				23p39					00 02	00 09						00 55	
St Mary Cray	d						23p15										00 08	00 15						01 01	
Swanley	d						23p19										00 12	00 19						01 05	
Farningham Road	d						23p24										00 17	00 24						01 10	
Longfield	d			22p52			23p28					23p52					00 21	00 28						01 14	
Meopham	d			22p57			23p32					23p57					00 25	00 32						01 18	
Sole Street	d						23p35										00 28	00 35							
London Charing Cross ⊖	d												23p09	23p10						23p39					00 15
London Waterloo (East) ⊖	d												23p12	23p13						23p42					00 18
London Cannon Street ⊖	d																								
London Bridge ⊖	d												23p17	23p18						23p47					00 23
Dartford	d												23p55	23p55						00 25					01 03
Greenhithe for Bluewater	d												00 02	00 01						00 31					01 08
Gravesend	d					23p18			23p48	23p48			00 10	00 10		00 18				00 40					01 15
Strood	d					23p28			23p58	23p58			00 22	00 22		00 28				00 52					01 26
Rochester	d	22p46		23p09		23p33	23p45	23p46	00 03	00 03		00 09	00 26	00 26		00 33	00 37	00 45	00 49	00 56				01 29	01 32
Chatham	d	22p48		23p12		23p35	23p47	23p48	00 05	00 06		00 12	00 28	00 28		00 35	00 40	00 47	00 52	00 58				01 31	01 35
Gillingham (Kent)	d	22p53		23p17		23p40	23p52	23p53	00 10	00 10		00 17	00a33	00a33		00 40	00 44	00a52	00 57	01a03				01a35	01a41
Rainham (Kent)	d	22p57		23p21		23p45	23p56	23p57	00 15	00 15		00 21				00 45	00 49		01 01						
Newington	d						00 01										00 53		01 05						
Sittingbourne	a	23p04		23p28		23p52	00 06	00 04	00 22	00 22		00 28				00 52	00 58		01 10						
Kemsley	d																						00 20		
Swale ⊖	d																						00 23		
Queenborough	d																						00 27		
Sheerness-on-Sea	a																						00 32		
Teynham	d			23p33								00 33					01 03		01 15						
Faversham	a	23p13		23p39	>	00 03	00 15	00 13	00 33	00 33		00 39				01 03	01 09		01 23						
	d	23p17	23p19	23p43	23p45			00 17				00 43							01 24						
Selling	d		23p24		23p50																				
Canterbury East	d		23p33		23p59																				
Bekesbourne	d		23p37																						
Adisham	d		23p42																						
Aylesham	d		23p44		00 07																				
Snowdown	d		23p47																						
Shepherds Well	d		23p51																						
Kearsney	d		23p55																						
Dover Priory	a		00 01		00 18																				
Whitstable	d	23p25		23p51				00 25				00 51							01 32						
Chestfield & Swalecliffe	d	23p28		23p54				00 28				00 54							01 35						
Herne Bay	d	23p32		23p58				00 32				00 58							01 39						
Birchington-on-Sea	d	23p41		00 07				00 41				01 07							01 48						
Westgate-on-Sea	d	23p45		00 11				00 45				01 11							01 52						
Margate	d	23p49		00 15				00 49				01 15							01 56						
Broadstairs	d	23p54		00 20				00 54				01 20							02 01						
Dumpton Park	d	23p57		00 23				00 57				01 23							02 04						
Ramsgate	a	00 01		00 26				01 00				01 26							02 07						

Table 212

Mondays to Fridays

London - Medway, Sheerness-on-Sea, Dover and Ramsgate

		SE	SE 1	SE	SE	SE	SE 1	SE	SE	SE 1	SE 1	SE	SE
St Pancras International	d											06 25	
Stratford International	d											06 32	
Ebbsfleet International	d											06 42	
London Victoria	d										05 22		
London Blackfriars	d												
Elephant & Castle	d												
Bromley South	d										05 39		
St Mary Cray	d										05 45		
Swanley	d										05 49		
Farningham Road	d										05 54		
Longfield	d										05 58		
Meopham	d										06 02		
Sole Street	d										06 05		
London Charing Cross	d					05 02		05 39					
London Waterloo (East)	d					05 05		05 42					
London Cannon Street	d												
London Bridge	d					05 10		05 47					
Dartford	d			05 25		05 55		06 25					
Greenhithe for Bluewater	d			05 30		06 00		06 30					
Gravesend	d			05 37		06 07		06 37				06 46	
Strood	d			05 48		06 18		06 48				06 56	
Rochester	d			05 52		06 22		06 52			06 15	07a00	
Chatham	d			05 55		06 25		06 55			06 17		
Gillingham (Kent)	d	05 00		05a59		06a29	05 47	06a59			06 22		
Rainham (Kent)	d	05 04					05 51				06 26		
Newington	d	05 08					05 55				06 30		
Sittingbourne	a						06 00				06 35		
Kemsley	d	05 15			05 38				06 08				06 27
Swale	d	05 18			05 43				06 11				06 30
Queenborough	d	05 22			05 47				06 15				06 35
Sheerness-on-Sea	a	05 27			05 51				06 20				06 40
Teynham	d						06 05				06 40		
Faversham	a						06 11				06 46		
	d		05 20				06 12			06 15	06 47		
Selling	d		05 25				06 17						
Canterbury East	d		05 34				06 26						
Bekesbourne	d		05 38				06 30						
Adisham	d		05 43				06 35						
Aylesham	d		05 45				06 37						
Snowdown	d		05 48				06 40						
Shepherds Well	d		05 52				06 44						
Kearsney	d		05 56				06 48						
Dover Priory	a		06 06				06 53						
Whitstable	d									06 23	06 55		
Chestfield & Swalecliffe	d									06 26	06 58		
Herne Bay	d									06 30	07 02		
Birchington-on-Sea	d									06 39	07 11		
Westgate-on-Sea	d									06 43	07 15		
Margate	d									06 49	07 19		
Broadstairs	d									06 54	07 24		
Dumpton Park	d									06 57	07 27		
Ramsgate	a									07 02	07 30		

		SE	SE	SE 1	SE 1	SE 1	SE	SE	SE	SE	SE 1
St Pancras International	d							06 58			
Stratford International	d							07 05			
Ebbsfleet International	d							07 16			
London Victoria	d				05 52	06 22					
London Blackfriars	d										
Elephant & Castle	d										
Bromley South	d				06 09	06 39					
St Mary Cray	d					06 45					
Swanley	d				06 19	06 49					
Farningham Road	d					06 54					
Longfield	d				06 25	06 58					
Meopham	d				06 29	07 02					
Sole Street	d					07 05					
London Charing Cross	d	06 26					05 56				
London Waterloo (East)	d	06 29					05 59				
London Cannon Street	d										
London Bridge	d	06 34					06 04				
Dartford	d	07 12					06 42				
Greenhithe for Bluewater	d	07 18					06 48				
Gravesend	d	07 27					06 59	07 21			
Strood	d	07a37					07b17	07 31			
Rochester	d				06 41	07 15	07 21	07 36			
Chatham	d				06 44	07 17	07 24	07 38			
Gillingham (Kent)	d				06 48	07 22	07a28	07 43			
Rainham (Kent)	d				06 53	07 26		07 48			
Newington	d				06 57	07 30					
Sittingbourne	a				07 02	07 37		07 55			
Kemsley	d		06 58						07 14	07 50	
Swale	d		07 01						07 17	07 53	
Queenborough	d		07 05						07 22	07 57	
Sheerness-on-Sea	a		07 10						07 27	08 02	
Teynham	d				07 07	07 42					
Faversham	a				07 13	07 48		08 03			
	d			07 05	07 13	07 49					07 51
Selling	d			07 09							07 55
Canterbury East	d			07 18							08 04
Bekesbourne	d			07 23							08 09
Adisham	d			07 27							08 13
Aylesham	d			07 29							08 15
Snowdown	d			07 32							08 18
Shepherds Well	d			07 35							08 21
Kearsney	d			07 40							08 26
Dover Priory	a			07 45							08 31
Whitstable	d				07 21	07 57					
Chestfield & Swalecliffe	d				07 24	08 00					
Herne Bay	d				07 28	08 04					
Birchington-on-Sea	d				07 37	08 12					
Westgate-on-Sea	d				07 41	08 16					
Margate	d				07 45	08 20					
Broadstairs	d				07 50	08 25					
Dumpton Park	d				07 53	08 28					
Ramsgate	a				07 56	08 31					

b arr. 0710

Table 212

Mondays to Fridays

London - Medway, Sheerness-on-Sea, Dover and Ramsgate

		SE 1	SE	SE 1	SE	SE	SE	SE 1	SE 1	SE 1
St Pancras International	d					07 22				
Stratford International	d					07 28				
Ebbsfleet International	d					07 43				
London Victoria	d	06 45		06 58	07 09				07 22	
London Blackfriars	d									
Elephant & Castle	d									
Bromley South	d	07 02		07 19					07 40	
St Mary Cray	d	07 08		07 25						
Swanley	d	07 13		07 29					07 49	
Farningham Road	d	07 18		07 34						
Longfield	d	07 22		07 38					07 55	
Meopham	d	07 26		07 42					07 59	
Sole Street	d	07 28		07 45						
London Charing Cross	d		06 39							
London Waterloo (East)	d		06 42							
London Cannon Street	d									
London Bridge	d		06 47							
Dartford	d		07 25		07a48					
Greenhithe for Bluewater	d		07 30							
Gravesend	d		07 37			07 48				
Strood	d		07 48			07 58				
Rochester	d	07 40	07 52	07 56		08 03			08 11	
Chatham	d	07 42	07 55	07 59		08 05			08 13	
Gillingham (Kent)	d	07 47	07a59	08a03		08 10			08 18	
Rainham (Kent)	d	07 52				08 15			08 22	
Newington	d	07 56							08 26	
Sittingbourne	a	08 01				08 22			08 31	
Kemsley	d						08 14			
Swale	d						08 19			
Queenborough	d						08 23			
Sheerness-on-Sea	a						08 28			
Teynham	d	08 06							08 36	
Faversham	a	08 12				08 31			08 42	
	d	08 13						08 16	08 46	08 48
Selling	d	08 18								08 53
Canterbury East	d	08 27								09 02
Bekesbourne	d	08 31								09 06
Adisham	d	08 36								09 11
Aylesham	d	08 38								09 13
Snowdown	d	08 41								09 16
Shepherds Well	d	08 45								09 20
Kearsney	d	08 49								09 24
Dover Priory	a	08 54								09 29
Whitstable	d							08 24	08 54	
Chestfield & Swalecliffe	d							08 27	08 57	
Herne Bay	d							08 31	09 01	
Birchington-on-Sea	d							08 40	09 10	
Westgate-on-Sea	d							08 44	09 14	
Margate	d							08 48	09 18	
Broadstairs	d							08 53	09 23	
Dumpton Park	d							08 56	09 26	
Ramsgate	a							08 59	09 29	

		SE	SE	SE	SE 1	SE 1	SE	SE 1	SE	SE	SE
St Pancras International	d			07 55					08 22		
Stratford International	d			08 02					08 29		
Ebbsfleet International	d			08 13					08 43		
London Victoria	d		07 43		07 52			07 58			
London Blackfriars	d										
Elephant & Castle	d										
Bromley South	d				08 09			08 27			
St Mary Cray	d							08 33			
Swanley	d							08 38			
Farningham Road	d							08 43			
Longfield	d				08 22			08 47			
Meopham	d				08 27			08 51			
Sole Street	d							08 54			
London Charing Cross	d	07 12					07 39				
London Waterloo (East)	d	07 15					07 42				
London Cannon Street	d										
London Bridge	d	07 21					07 47				
Dartford	d	08 00	08a27				08 25				
Greenhithe for Bluewater	d	08 05					08 30				
Gravesend	d	08 12		08 18			08 37		08 48		
Strood	d	08 23		08 28			08 48		08 58		
Rochester	d	08 27		08 33	08 39		08 52	09a07	09 03		
Chatham	d	08 30		08 35	08 42		08 55		09 05		
Gillingham (Kent)	d	08a35		08 40	08 47		08a59		09 10		
Rainham (Kent)	d			08 45	08 51				09 15		
Newington	d				08 55						
Sittingbourne	a			08 52	09 01				09 22		
Kemsley	d									08 45	09 15
Swale	d									08 48	09 18
Queenborough	d									08 52	09 22
Sheerness-on-Sea	a									08 57	09 27
Teynham	d										
Faversham	a			09 01	09 09				09 31		
	d				09 13	09 15					
Selling	d										
Canterbury East	d					09 29					
Bekesbourne	d										
Adisham	d										
Aylesham	d										
Snowdown	d										
Shepherds Well	d										
Kearsney	d										
Dover Priory	a					09 50					
Whitstable	d				09 21						
Chestfield & Swalecliffe	d				09 26						
Herne Bay	d										
Birchington-on-Sea	d				09 35						
Westgate-on-Sea	d										
Margate	d				09 41						
Broadstairs	d				09 46						
Dumpton Park	d										
Ramsgate	a				09 51						

Table 212

Mondays to Fridays

London - Medway, Sheerness-on-Sea, Dover and Ramsgate

		SE ■	SE ■	SE	SE	SE	SE ■ ⊣	SE ■	SE	SE ■	SE	SE	SE ■ ⊣	SE ■	SE	SE	SE			SE ■	SE ■	SE	SE ■	SE	SE
St Pancras International ■ ⊖	d				08 58						09 25					09 55								10 28	
Stratford International ⊖	d				09 05						09 32					10 02								10 35	
Ebbsfleet International	d				09 16						09 43					10 13								10 46	
London Victoria ■ ⊖	d	08 22					08 52			08 58			09 22							09 52			09 58		
London Blackfriars ■ ⊖	d																								
Elephant & Castle ⊖	d																								
Bromley South ■	d	08 39					09 09			09 19			09 39							10 09			10 19		
St Mary Cray	d									09 25													10 25		
Swanley ■	d									09 29													10 29		
Farningham Road	d									09 34													10 34		
Longfield	d	08 52					09 22			09 38			09 52							10 22			10 38		
Meopham	d	08 57					09 27			09 42			09 57							10 27			10 42		
Sole Street	d									09 45													10 45		
London Charing Cross ■ ⊖	d			08 11					08 41						09 11							09 39			
London Waterloo (East) ■ ⊖	d			08 14					08 44						09 14							09 42			
London Cannon Street ■ ⊖	d																								
London Bridge ■ ⊖	d			08 19					08 49						09 19							09 47			
Dartford ■	d			08 55					09 25						09 55							10 25			
Greenhithe for Bluewater	d			09 00					09 30						10 00							10 30			
Gravesend ■	d			09 07	09 21				09 37		09 48				10 07	10 18						10 37		10 51	
Strood ■	d			09 18	09 31				09 48		09 58				10 18	10 28						10 48		11 01	
Rochester ■	d	09 09		09 22	09 36		09 39		09 52	09 56	10 03		10 09		10 22	10 33				10 39		10 52	10 56	11 06	
Chatham ■	d	09 12		09 25	09 38		09 42		09 55	09 59	10 05		10 12		10 25	10 35				10 42		10 55	10 59	11 08	
Gillingham (Kent) ■	d	09 17		09a29	09 43		09 47		09a59	10a03	10 10		10 17		10a29	10 40				10 47		10a59	11a03	11 13	
Rainham (Kent)	d	09 21			09 48		09 51				10 15		10 21			10 45				10 51				11 18	
Newington	d						09 55													10 55					
Sittingbourne ■	a	09 28			09 55		10 01				10 22		10 28			10 52				11 00				11 25	
Kemsley	d					09 45						10 15					10 45								11 15
Swale ⊖	d					09 48						10 18					10 48								11 18
Queenborough	d					09 52						10 22					10 52								11 22
Sheerness-on-Sea	a					09 57						10 27					10 57								11 27
Teynham	d	09 33											10 33												
Faversham ■	a	09 39	>		10 03		10 09	>			10 31		10 39	>		11 01				11 09	>			11 33	
	d	09 43	09 45				10 13	10 15					10 43	10 45						11 13	11 15				
Selling	d		09 50											10 50											
Canterbury East ■	d		09 59					10 29						10 59							11 29				
Bekesbourne	d		10 03											11 03											
Adisham	d		10 08											11 08											
Aylesham	d		10 10											11 10											
Snowdown	d		10 13											11 13											
Shepherds Well	d		10 17											11 17											
Kearsney	d		10 21											11 21											
Dover Priory ■	a		10 26					10 50						11 26							11 50				
Whitstable	d	09 51					10 21						10 51							11 21					
Chestfield & Swalecliffe	d	09 54											10 54												
Herne Bay	d	09 58					10 26						10 58							11 26					
Birchington-on-Sea	d	10 07					10 35						11 07							11 35					
Westgate-on-Sea	d	10 11											11 11												
Margate ■	d	10 15					10 41						11 15							11 41					
Broadstairs	d	10 20					10 46						11 20							11 46					
Dumpton Park	d	10 23											11 23												
Ramsgate ■	a	10 26					10 51						11 26							11 51					

Table 212

Mondays to Fridays

London - Medway, Sheerness-on-Sea, Dover and Ramsgate

		SE ■ ⊣	SE ■	SE	SE		SE	SE ■ ⊣	SE ■	SE	SE ■	SE	SE	SE ■ ⊣	SE ■		SE	SE	SE	SE ■ ⊣	SE ■	SE	SE ■	SE	SE
St Pancras International ■ ⊖	d				10 55							11 25						11 55						12 25	
Stratford International ⊖	d				11 02							11 32						12 02						12 36	
Ebbsfleet International	d				11 13							11 43						12 13						12 47	
London Victoria ■ ⊖	d	10 22						10 52			10 58			11 22						11 52			11 58		
London Blackfriars ■ ⊖	d																								
Elephant & Castle ⊖	d																								
Bromley South ■	d	10 39						11 09			11 19			11 39						12 09			12 19		
St Mary Cray	d										11 25												12 25		
Swanley ■	d										11 29												12 29		
Farningham Road	d										11 34												12 34		
Longfield	d	10 52						11 22			11 38			11 52						12 22			12 38		
Meopham	d	10 57						11 27			11 42			11 57						12 27			12 42		
Sole Street	d										11 45												12 45		
London Charing Cross ■ ⊖	d			10 09						10 39							11 09					11 39			
London Waterloo (East) ■ ⊖	d			10 12						10 42							11 12					11 42			
London Cannon Street ■ ⊖	d																								
London Bridge ■ ⊖	d			10 17						10 47							11 17					11 47			
Dartford ■	d			10 55						11 25							11 55					12 25			
Greenhithe for Bluewater	d			11 00						11 30							12 00					12 30			
Gravesend ■	d			11 07	11 18					11 37		11 48					12 07	12 18				12 37		12 51	
Strood ■	d			11 18	11 28					11 48		11 58					12 18	12 28				12 48		13 01	
Rochester ■	d	11 09		11 22	11 33			11 39		11 52	11 56	12 03		12 09			12 22	12 33		12 39		12 52	12 56	13 06	
Chatham ■	d	11 12		11 25	11 35			11 42		11 55	11 59	12 05		12 12			12 25	12 35		12 42		12 55	12 59	13 08	
Gillingham (Kent) ■	d	11 17		11a29	11 40			11 47		11a59	12a03	12 10		12 17			12a29	12 40		12 47		12a59	13a03	13 13	
Rainham (Kent)	d	11 21			11 45			11 51				12 15		12 21				12 45		12 51				13 18	
Newington	d							11 55												12 55					
Sittingbourne ■	a	11 29			11 52			12 00				12 22		12 28				12 52		13 00				13 25	
Kemsley	d						11 45						12 15						12 45						13 15
Swale ⊖	d						11 48						12 18						12 48						13 18
Queenborough	d						11 52						12 22						12 52						13 22
Sheerness-on-Sea	a						11 57						12 27						12 57						13 27
Teynham	d	11 33												12 33											
Faversham ■	a	11 39	>		12 01			12 09	>			12 31		12 39	>			13 01		13 09	>			13 33	
	d	11 43	11 45					12 13	12 15					12 43	12 45					13 13	13 15				
Selling	d		11 50												12 50										
Canterbury East ■	d		11 59						12 29						12 59						13 29				
Bekesbourne	d		12 03												13 03										
Adisham	d		12 08												13 08										
Aylesham	d		12 10												13 10										
Snowdown	d		12 13												13 13										
Shepherds Well	d		12 17												13 17										
Kearsney	d		12 21												13 21										
Dover Priory ■	a		12 26						12 50						13 26						13 50				
Whitstable	d	11 51						12 21						12 51						13 21					
Chestfield & Swalecliffe	d	11 54												12 54											
Herne Bay	d	11 58						12 26						12 58						13 26					
Birchington-on-Sea	d	12 07						12 35						13 07						13 35					
Westgate-on-Sea	d	12 11												13 11											
Margate ■	d	12 15						12 41						13 15						13 41					
Broadstairs	d	12 20						12 46						13 20						13 46					
Dumpton Park	d	12 23												13 23											
Ramsgate ■	a	12 26						12 51						13 26						13 51					

London - Medway, Sheerness-on-Sea, Dover and Ramsgate

		SE 1 ⇆	SE 1	SE	SE	SE	SE 1 ⇆	SE 1	SE	SE 1	SE	SE	SE 1 ⇆	SE 1	SE	SE	SE	SE 1 ⇆	SE 1	SE	SE 1	SE	SE
St Pancras International 15 ⊖	d				12 52						13 25					13 55						14 28	
Stratford International ⊖	d				12 58						13 32					14 02						14 35	
Ebbsfleet International	d				13 13						13 43					14 13						14 46	
London Victoria 15 ⊖	d	12 22					12 52			12 58			13 22					13 52			13 58		
London Blackfriars 3 ⊖	d																						
Elephant & Castle ⊖	d																						
Bromley South 4	d	12 39					13 09			13 19			13 39					14 09			14 19		
St Mary Cray	d									13 25											14 25		
Swanley 4	d									13 29											14 29		
Farningham Road	d									13 34											14 34		
Longfield	d	12 52					13 22			13 38			13 52					14 22			14 38		
Meopham	d	12 57					13 27			13 42			13 57					14 27			14 42		
Sole Street	d									13 45											14 45		
London Charing Cross 4 ⊖	d			12 09					12 39						13 09					13 39			
London Waterloo (East) 4 ⊖	d			12 12					12 42						13 12					13 42			
London Cannon Street 4 ⊖	d																						
London Bridge 4 ⊖	d			12 17					12 47						13 17					13 47			
Dartford 4	d			12 55					13 25						13 55					14 25			
Greenhithe for Bluewater	d			13 00					13 30						14 00					14 30			
Gravesend 4	d			13 07	13 18				13 37		13 48				14 07	14 18				14 37		14 51	
Strood 4	d			13 18	13 28				13 48		13 58				14 18	14 28				14 48		15 01	
Rochester 4	d	13 09		13 22	13 33		13 39		13 52	13 56	14 03		14 09		14 22	14 33		14 39		14 52	14 56	15 06	
Chatham 4	d	13 12		13 25	13 35		13 42		13 55	13 59	14 05		14 12		14 25	14 35		14 42		14 55	14 59	15 08	
Gillingham (Kent) 4	d	13 17		13a29	13 40		13 47		13a59	14a03	14 10		14 17		14a29	14 40		14 47		14a59	15a03	15 13	
Rainham (Kent)	d	13 21			13 45		13 51				14 15		14 21			14 45		14 51				15 18	
Newington	d						13 55											14 55					
Sittingbourne 4	a	13 29			13 52		14 00				14 22		14 28			14 52		15 00				15 25	
Kemsley	d					13 45						14 15					14 45						15 15
Swale ⊖	d					13 48						14 18					14 48						15 18
Queenborough	d					13 52						14 22					14 52						15 22
Sheerness-on-Sea	a					13 57						14 27					14 57						15 27
Teynham	d	13 33											14 33										
Faversham 2	a	13 39	>		14 01		14 09	>			14 31		14 39	>		15 01		15 09	>			15 33	
	d	13 43	13 45				14 13	14 15					14 43	14 45				15 13	15 15				
Selling	d		13 50											14 50									
Canterbury East 4	d		13 59					14 29						14 59					15 29				
Bekesbourne	d		14 03											15 03									
Adisham	d		14 08											15 08									
Aylesham	d		14 10											15 10									
Snowdown	d		14 13											15 13									
Shepherds Well	d		14 17											15 17					15 39				
Kearsney	d		14 21											15 21									
Dover Priory 4	a		14 26					14 50						15 26					15 48				
Whitstable	d	13 51					14 21						14 51					15 21					
Chestfield & Swalecliffe	d	13 54											14 54										
Herne Bay	d	13 58					14 26						14 58					15 26					
Birchington-on-Sea	d	14 07					14 35						15 07					15 35					
Westgate-on-Sea	d	14 11											15 11										
Margate 4	d	14 15					14 41						15 15					15 41					
Broadstairs	d	14 20					14 46						15 20					15 46					
Dumpton Park	d	14 23											15 23										
Ramsgate 4	a	14 26					14 51						15 26					15 51					

London - Medway, Sheerness-on-Sea, Dover and Ramsgate

		SE 1 ⇆	SE 1	SE	SE	SE	SE 1 ⇆	SE 1	SE	SE 1	SE	SE	SE 1 ⇆	SE 1	SE	SE	SE	SE 1 ⇆	SE 1	SE	SE 1	SE	SE
St Pancras International 15 ⊖	d				14 55						15 28					15 55						16 25	
Stratford International ⊖	d				15 02						15 35					16 02						16 32	
Ebbsfleet International	d				15 13						15 46					16 13						16 43	
London Victoria 15 ⊖	d	14 22					14 52			14 58			15 22					15 52			15 58		
London Blackfriars 3 ⊖	d																						
Elephant & Castle ⊖	d																						
Bromley South 4	d	14 39					15 09			15 19			15 39					16 09			16 19		
St Mary Cray	d									15 25											16 25		
Swanley 4	d									15 29											16 29		
Farningham Road	d									15 34											16 34		
Longfield	d	14 52					15 22			15 38			15 52					16 22			16 38		
Meopham	d	14 57					15 27			15 42			15 57					16 27			16 42		
Sole Street	d									15 45											16 45		
London Charing Cross 4 ⊖	d			14 09					14 39						15 09					15 39			
London Waterloo (East) 4 ⊖	d			14 12					14 42						15 12					15 42			
London Cannon Street 4 ⊖	d																						
London Bridge 4 ⊖	d			14 17					14 47						15 17					15 47			
Dartford 4	d			14 55					15 25						15 55					16 25			
Greenhithe for Bluewater	d			15 00					15 30						16 00					16 30			
Gravesend 4	d			15 07	15 18				15 37		15 51				16 07	16 18				16 37		16 48	
Strood 4	d			15 18	15 28				15 48		16 01				16 18	16 28				16 48		16 58	
Rochester 4	d	15 09		15 22	15 33		15 39		15 52	15 56	16 06		16 09		16 22	16 33		16 39		16 52	16 56	17 03	
Chatham 4	d	15 12		15 25	15 35		15 42		15 55	15 59	16 08		16 12		16 25	16 35		16 42		16 55	16 59	17 05	
Gillingham (Kent) 4	d	15 17		15a29	15 40		15 47		15a59	16a03	16 13		16 17		16a29	16 40		16 47		16a59	17a03	17 10	
Rainham (Kent)	d	15 21			15 45		15 51				16 18		16 21			16 45		16 51				17 15	
Newington	d						15 55											16 55					
Sittingbourne 4	a	15 29			15 52		16 00				16 25		16 29			16 52		17 00				17 22	
Kemsley	d					15 45						16 15					16 45						17 15
Swale ⊖	d					15 48						16 18					16 48						17 18
Queenborough	d					15 52						16 22					16 52						17 22
Sheerness-on-Sea	a					15 57						16 27					16 57						17 27
Teynham	d	15 33											16 33					17 05					
Faversham 2	a	15 39	>		16 01		16 09	>			16 33		16 39	>		17 01		17 11	>			17 31	
	d	15 43	15 45				16 13	16 15					16 43	16 45				17 15	17 19				
Selling	d		15 50					16 19						16 50					17 23				
Canterbury East 4	d		15 59					16 28						16 59					17 32				
Bekesbourne	d		16 03					16 33						17 03									
Adisham	d		16 08					16 37						17 08									
Aylesham	d		16 10					16 39						17 10					17 40				
Snowdown	d		16 13											17 13									
Shepherds Well	d		16 17					16 44						17 17					17 45				
Kearsney	d		16 21											17 21									
Dover Priory 4	a		16 26					16 52						17 26					17 53				
Whitstable	d	15 51					16 21						16 51					17 23					
Chestfield & Swalecliffe	d	15 54					16 24						16 54					17 26					
Herne Bay	d	15 58					16 28						16 58					17 30					
Birchington-on-Sea	d	16 07					16 37						17 07					17 39					
Westgate-on-Sea	d	16 11					16 41						17 11					17 43					
Margate 4	d	16 15					16 45						17 15					17 47					
Broadstairs	d	16 20					16 50						17 20					17 52					
Dumpton Park	d	16 23					16 53						17 23					17 55					
Ramsgate 4	a	16 26					16 56						17 26					17 58					

Table 212

Mondays to Fridays

London - Medway, Sheerness-on-Sea, Dover and Ramsgate

		SE [1]	SE [1]	SE	SE [1]	SE	SE	SE [1]	SE	SE [1] ⊼	SE [1]
St Pancras International	d								16 58		
Stratford International	d								17 05		
Ebbsfleet International	d								17 16		
London Victoria	d	16 22			16 28					16 57	
London Blackfriars	d										
Elephant & Castle	d										
Bromley South	d	16 39			16 49					17 13	
St Mary Cray	d				16 55						
Swanley	d				16 59						
Farningham Road	d				17 04						
Longfield	d	16 52			17 08						
Meopham	d	16 57			17 12						
Sole Street	d				17 15						
London Charing Cross	d			16 09							
London Waterloo (East)	d			16 12							
London Cannon Street	d					17 28		16 46			
London Bridge	d			16 17		17 32		16 50			
Dartford	d			16 55		18 08					
Greenhithe for Bluewater	d			17 00		18 14					
Gravesend	d			17 07		18 24			17 21		
Strood	d			17 18		18a36			17 31		
Rochester	d	17 09		17 22	17a27			17 29	17 36	17 40	
Chatham	d	17 12		17 25				17 31	17 38	17 42	
Gillingham (Kent)	d	17 17		17a30				17 36	17 43	17 47	
Rainham (Kent)	d	17 21						17 40	17 48	17 52	
Newington	d	17 25								17 56	
Sittingbourne	a	17 30						17 47	17 55	18 01	
Kemsley	d						17 45				
Swale	d						17 48				
Queenborough	d						17 52				
Sheerness-on-Sea	a						17 57				
Teynham	d	17 35								18 06	
Faversham	a	17 41	>					17 56	18 03	18 12	>
	d	17 45	17 49					17 56		18 16	18 19
Selling	d		17 54								18 23
Canterbury East	d		18 03								18 32
Bekesbourne	d		18 07								
Adisham	d		18 12								
Aylesham	d		18 14								18 40
Snowdown	d		18 17								
Shepherds Well	d		18 21								18 45
Kearsney	d		18 25								
Dover Priory	a		18 32								18 55
Whitstable	d	17 53						18 04		18 24	
Chestfield & Swalecliffe	d	17 56						18 07		18 27	
Herne Bay	d	18 00						18 11		18 31	
Birchington-on-Sea	d	18 09						18 20		18 40	
Westgate-on-Sea	d	18 13						18 24		18 44	
Margate	d	18 17						18 28		18 48	
Broadstairs	d	18 22						18 34		18 53	
Dumpton Park	d	18 25						18 37		18 56	
Ramsgate	a	18 30						18 42		19 01	

		SE	SE	SE	SE [1]	SE	SE [1]	SE	SE [1] ⊼	SE [1]	SE [1]	SE
St Pancras International	d	17 14	17 18					17 25				
Stratford International	d	17 21	17 25					17b38				
Ebbsfleet International	d		17a35					17 49				
London Victoria	d						17 04		17 27			
London Blackfriars	d											
Elephant & Castle	d											
Bromley South	d						17 24		17 44			
St Mary Cray	d						17 30					
Swanley	d						17 34					
Farningham Road	d						17 39					
Longfield	d						17 43					
Meopham	d						17 47					
Sole Street	d						17 50					
London Charing Cross	d											
London Waterloo (East)	d											
London Cannon Street	d				17 08	16 44					17 30	17 06
London Bridge	d				17 12	16 48					17 34	17 10
Dartford	d					17 27						17 47
Greenhithe for Bluewater	d					17 32						17 52
Gravesend	d	17 36				17 40						18 00
Strood	d	17 46				17 51						18 12
Rochester	d	17a52			17 49	17 55	17 59		18 09		18 13	18 17
Chatham	d				17 51	17 58	18 02	18 06	18 12		18 16	18 19
Gillingham (Kent)	d				17 56	18a03	18a08	18 10	18 17		18 21	18a24
Rainham (Kent)	d				18 00			18 15	18 21		18 26	
Newington	d				18 04						18 30	
Sittingbourne	a				18 09			18 22	18 28		18 35	
Kemsley	d			18 19								
Swale	d			18 22								
Queenborough	d			18 26								
Sheerness-on-Sea	a			18 31								
Teynham	d				18 14				18 33			
Faversham	a				18 20			18 31	18 39	>	18 44	
	d				18 22			18 31	18 43	18 49	18 47	
Selling	d									18 54		
Canterbury East	d									19 03		
Bekesbourne	d									19 07		
Adisham	d									19 12		
Aylesham	d									19 14		
Snowdown	d									19 17		
Shepherds Well	d									19 21		
Kearsney	d									19 25		
Dover Priory	a									19 32		
Whitstable	d				18 30			18 40	18 51		18 56	
Chestfield & Swalecliffe	d				18 33				18 54		18 59	
Herne Bay	d				18 37			18 45	18 58		19 03	
Birchington-on-Sea	d				18 46			18 54	19 07		19 12	
Westgate-on-Sea	d				18 50				19 11		19 16	
Margate	d				18 57			19 00	19 15		19 20	
Broadstairs	d				19 02			19a08	19 20		19 25	
Dumpton Park	d				19 05				19 23		19 28	
Ramsgate	a				19 10				19 29		19 33	

b arr. 1731

Table 212

Mondays to Fridays

London - Medway, Sheerness-on-Sea, Dover and Ramsgate

		SE	SE	SE	SE [1]	SE	SE	SE	SE [1]	SE [1] ⊼	SE [1]	SE
St Pancras International	d	17 44		17 48				17 58				
Stratford International	d	17 51		17 55				18 05				
Ebbsfleet International	d			18a05				18 16				
London Victoria	d				17 54					17 57		
London Blackfriars	d											
Elephant & Castle	d											
Bromley South	d				18 17					18 15		
St Mary Cray	d				18 24							
Swanley	d				18 29							
Farningham Road	d				18 34							
Longfield	d				18 38							
Meopham	d				18 42							
Sole Street	d				18 44							
London Charing Cross	d		17 17			18 37						17 39
London Waterloo (East)	d		17 20			18 40						17 42
London Cannon Street	d								17 52			
London Bridge	d		17 26			18 46			17 56			17 48
Dartford	d		17 59			19 22						18 20
Greenhithe for Bluewater	d		18 04			19 28						18 25
Gravesend	d	18 06	18 11			19 37						18 32
Strood	d	18 16	18 22			19a49						18 42
Rochester	d	18 24	18 29		18a56				18 35	18 39		18 46
Chatham	d	18 26	18 32					18 36	18 40	18 44		18 48
Gillingham (Kent)	d	18 31	18a37					18 40	18 44	18 49		18a54
Rainham (Kent)	d	18 36						18 45	18 50	18 54		
Newington	d									18 58		
Sittingbourne	a	18 44						18 52	18 57	19 03		
Kemsley	d						18 50					
Swale	d						18 54					
Queenborough	d						18 58					
Sheerness-on-Sea	a						19 02					
Teynham	d								19 02	19 08		
Faversham	a	18 54						19 01	19 08	19 14	>	
	d							19 01	19 09	19 18	19 20	
Selling	d										19 24	
Canterbury East	d										19 33	
Bekesbourne	d											
Adisham	d											
Aylesham	d											
Snowdown	d											
Shepherds Well	d											
Kearsney	d											
Dover Priory	a										19 52	
Whitstable	d							19 10	19 17	19 26		
Chestfield & Swalecliffe	d								19 20	19 29		
Herne Bay	d							19 15	19 24	19 33		
Birchington-on-Sea	d							19 24	19 33	19 42		
Westgate-on-Sea	d								19 37	19 46		
Margate	d							19 30	19 41	19 50		
Broadstairs	d							19a35	19a46	19 55		
Dumpton Park	d									19 58		
Ramsgate	a									20 03		

		SE	SE	SE [1]	SE [1]	SE	SE [1] ⊼	SE [1]	SE	SE	SE	SE
St Pancras International	d	18 14	18 18			18 25				18 48		
Stratford International	d	18 21	18 25			18 32				18 55		
Ebbsfleet International	d		18a35			18 43				19a05		
London Victoria	d			18 24			18 27					
London Blackfriars	d											
Elephant & Castle	d											
Bromley South	d			18 46			18 44					
St Mary Cray	d			18 52								
Swanley	d			18 57								
Farningham Road	d			19 02								
Longfield	d			19 06								
Meopham	d			19 10								
Sole Street	d			19 12								
London Charing Cross	d											
London Waterloo (East)	d											
London Cannon Street	d				18 14				18 12			
London Bridge	d				18 18				18 16			
Dartford	d								18 53			
Greenhithe for Bluewater	d											
Gravesend	d	18 36							19 03			
Strood	d	18 46							19 14			
Rochester	d	18 51		19 22			19 12		19 18			
Chatham	d	18 53		19 25	18 58	19 02	19 14		19 21			
Gillingham (Kent)	d	18 58		19a31	19 03	19 07	19 19		19a26			
Rainham (Kent)	d	19 03			19 07	19 12	19 23					
Newington	d				19 11							
Sittingbourne	a	19 10			19 16	19 21	19 30					
Kemsley	d										19 28	19 45
Swale	d										19 31	19 48
Queenborough	d										19 35	19 52
Sheerness-on-Sea	a										19 40	19 57
Teynham	d						19 35					
Faversham	a	19 18			19 25	19 30	19 41	>				
	d				19 25	19 30	19 45	19 49				
Selling	d							19 54				
Canterbury East	d							20 03				
Bekesbourne	d							20 07				
Adisham	d							20 12				
Aylesham	d							20 14				
Snowdown	d							20 17				
Shepherds Well	d							20 21				
Kearsney	d							20 25				
Dover Priory	a							20 32				
Whitstable	d				19 33	19 39	19 53					
Chestfield & Swalecliffe	d				19 36		19 56					
Herne Bay	d				19 40	19 45	20 00					
Birchington-on-Sea	d				19 49	19 54	20 09					
Westgate-on-Sea	d				19 53		20 13					
Margate	d				19 57	20 01	20 17					
Broadstairs	d				20 03	20a07	20 22					
Dumpton Park	d				20 06		20 25					
Ramsgate	a				20 11		20 30					

Table 212

Mondays to Fridays

London - Medway, Sheerness-on-Sea, Dover and Ramsgate

		SE 1	SE	SE 1	SE 1	SE	SE 1	SE	SE	SE	SE 1	SE 1	SE	SE	SE	SE	SE 1	SE 1	SE	SE 1	SE	SE
St Pancras International 15 ⊖	d		18 55						19 25						19 55						20 25	
Stratford International ⊖	d		19 02						19 32						20 02						20 32	
Ebbsfleet International	d		19 13						19 44						20 13						20 43	
London Victoria 15 ⊖	d			18 57			18 58				19 22			19 28			19 52			19 58		
London Blackfriars 3 ⊖	d																					
Elephant & Castle ⊖	d																					
Bromley South 4	d			19 13			19 19				19 39			19 49			20 09			20 19		
St Mary Cray	d						19 25							19 55						20 25		
Swanley 1	d						19 29							19 59						20 29		
Farningham Road	d						19 34							20 04						20 34		
Longfield	d						19 38				19 52			20 08			20 22			20 38		
Meopham	d						19 42				19 57			20 12			20 27			20 42		
Sole Street	d						19 45							20 15						20 45		
London Charing Cross 4 ⊖	d							18 48					19 09						19 39			
London Waterloo (East) 4 ⊖	d							18 51					19 12						19 42			
London Cannon Street 4 ⊖	d	18 44				18 30																
London Bridge 4 ⊖	d	18 48				18 34		18 57					19 17						19 47			
Dartford 4	d					19 10		19 34					19 55						20 25			
Greenhithe for Bluewater	d					19 16		19 39					20 00						20 30			
Gravesend 4	d		19 18			19 26		19 46	19 50				20 07		20 18				20 37		20 48	
Strood 4	d		19 28			19 37		19 57	20 01				20 18		20 28				20 48		20 58	
Rochester 4	d	19 26	19 33	19 39		19 43	19 56	20 02	20 06		20 10		20 22	20 26	20 33		20 39		20 52	20 56	21 03	
Chatham 4	d	19 29	19 35	19 42		19 46	19 58	20 05	20 09		20 13		20 25	20 29	20 35		20 42		20 55	20 59	21 05	
Gillingham (Kent) 4	d	19 33	19 40	19 47		19a50	20a04	20a10	20 13		20 17		20a29	20a33	20 40		20 47		20a59	21a03	21 10	
Rainham (Kent)	d	19 38	19 45	19 51					20 18		20 23				20 45		20 51				21 15	
Newington	d	19 42		19 55													20 55					
Sittingbourne 4	a	19 47	19 52	20 00					20 25		20 30				20 52		21 00				21 22	
Kemsley	d									20 15						20 45						21 15
Swale ⊖	d									20 18						20 48						21 18
Queenborough	d									20 22						20 52						21 22
Sheerness-on-Sea	a									20 27						20 57						21 27
Teynham	d	19 52									20 35											
Faversham 2	a	19 58	20 02	20 09	>				20 34		20 41	>			21 03		21 09	>			21 33	
	d	19 58		20 13	20 15						20 45	20 49					21 13	21 15				
Selling	d				20 19							20 54						21 19				
Canterbury East 4	d				20 28							21 03						21 28				
Bekesbourne	d				20 33							21 07						21 33				
Adisham	d				20 37							21 12						21 37				
Aylesham	d				20 39							21 14						21 39				
Snowdown	d											21 17										
Shepherds Well	d				20 44							21 21						21 44				
Kearsney	d											21 25										
Dover Priory 4	a				20 54							21 30						21 52				
Whitstable	d	20 06		20 21							20 53						21 21					
Chestfield & Swalecliffe	d	20 09		20 24							20 56						21 24					
Herne Bay	d	20 13		20 28							21 00						21 28					
Birchington-on-Sea	d	20 22		20 37							21 08						21 37					
Westgate-on-Sea	d	20 26		20 41							21 12						21 41					
Margate 4	d	20 30		20 45							21 16						21 45					
Broadstairs	d	20 36		20 50							21 21						21 50					
Dumpton Park	d	20 39		20 53							21 24						21 53					
Ramsgate 4	a	20 44		20 58							21 27						21 56					

Table 212

Mondays to Fridays

London - Medway, Sheerness-on-Sea, Dover and Ramsgate

		SE 1	SE 1	SE	SE	SE	SE 1	SE 1	SE	SE 1	SE	SE 1	SE 1	SE	SE	SE 1	SE	SE	SE	SE 1	SE 1	SE	SE
St Pancras International 15 ⊖	d				20 55						21 25				21 55			22 25					22 55
Stratford International ⊖	d				21 02						21 32				22 02			22 32					23 02
Ebbsfleet International	d				21 13						21 43				22 13			22 43					23 13
London Victoria 15 ⊖	d	20 22					20 52			20 58		21 22				21 52				22 22			
London Blackfriars 3 ⊖	d																						
Elephant & Castle ⊖	d																						
Bromley South 4	d	20 39					21 09			21 19		21 39				22 09				22 39			
St Mary Cray	d									21 25						22 15							
Swanley 4	d									21 29						22 19							
Farningham Road	d									21 34						22 24							
Longfield	d	20 52					21 22			21 38		21 52				22 28				22 52			
Meopham	d	20 57					21 27			21 42		21 57				22 32				22 57			
Sole Street	d									21 45						22 35							
London Charing Cross 4 ⊖	d			20 09					20 39					21 09			21 39					22 09	
London Waterloo (East) 4 ⊖	d			20 12					20 42					21 12			21 42					22 12	
London Cannon Street 4 ⊖	d																						
London Bridge 4 ⊖	d			20 17					20 47					21 17			21 47					22 17	
Dartford 4	d			20 55					21 25					21 55			22 25					22 55	
Greenhithe for Bluewater	d			21 00					21 30					22 00			22 30					23 00	
Gravesend 4	d			21 07	21 18				21 37		21 48			22 07	22 18		22 37	22 48				23 07	23 18
Strood 4	d			21 18	21 28				21 48		21 58			22 18	22 28		22 48	22 58				23 18	23 28
Rochester 4	d	21 09		21 22	21 33		21 39		21 52	21 56	22 03	22 09		22 22	22 33	22 45	22 52	23 03		23 09		23 22	23 33
Chatham 4	d	21 12		21 25	21 35		21 42		21 55	21 59	22 05	22 12		22 25	22 35	22 47	22 55	23 05		23 12		23 25	23 35
Gillingham (Kent) 4	d	21 17		21a29	21 40		21 47		21a59	22a03	22 10	22 17		22a29	22 40	22 52	22a59	23 10		23 17		23a29	23 40
Rainham (Kent)	d	21 21			21 45		21 51				22 15	22 21			22 45	22 56		23 15		23 21			23 45
Newington	d						21 55									23 00							
Sittingbourne 4	a	21 28			21 53		22 00				22 22	22 28			22 52	23 05		23 22		23 28			23 52
Kemsley	d					21 45													22 45				
Swale ⊖	d					21 48													22 48				
Queenborough	d					21 52													22 52				
Sheerness-on-Sea	a					21 57													22 57				
Teynham	d	21 33										22 33								23 33			
Faversham 2	a	21 39	>		22 03		22 09	>			22 33	22 39	>		23 03	23 17		23 33		23 39	>		00 03
	d	21 43	21 45				22 13	22 15				22 43	22 45							23 43	23 45		
Selling	d		21 50					22 19					22 50								23 50		
Canterbury East 4	d		21 59					22 28					22 59								23 59		
Bekesbourne	d		22 03					22 33					23 03										
Adisham	d		22 08					22 37					23 08										
Aylesham	d		22 10					22 39					23 10								00 07		
Snowdown	d		22 13										23 13										
Shepherds Well	d		22 17					22 44					23 17										
Kearsney	d		22 21										23 21										
Dover Priory 4	a		22 26					22 52					23 26								00 18		
Whitstable	d	21 51					22 21					22 51								23 51			
Chestfield & Swalecliffe	d	21 54					22 24					22 54								23 54			
Herne Bay	d	21 58					22 28					22 58								23 58			
Birchington-on-Sea	d	22 07					22 37					23 07								00 07			
Westgate-on-Sea	d	22 11					22 41					23 11								00 11			
Margate 4	d	22 15					22 45					23 15								00 15			
Broadstairs	d	22 20					22 50					23 20								00 20			
Dumpton Park	d	22 23					22 53					23 23								00 23			
Ramsgate 4	a	22 26					22 56					23 26								00 26			

Table 212

Mondays to Fridays

London - Medway, Sheerness-on-Sea, Dover and Ramsgate

		SE [1]	SE	SE	SE	SE [1]	SE	SE	SE [1]	SE
St Pancras International [15] ⊖	d			23 25				23 55		
Stratford International ⊖	d			23 32				00 02		
Ebbsfleet International	d			23 43				00 13		
London Victoria [15] ⊖	d	22 52				23 22			23 52	
London Blackfriars [3] ⊖	d									
Elephant & Castle ⊖	d									
Bromley South [4]	d	23 09				23 39			00 09	
St Mary Cray	d	23 15							00 15	
Swanley [4]	d	23 19							00 19	
Farningham Road	d	23 24							00 24	
Longfield	d	23 28				23 52			00 28	
Meopham	d	23 32				23 57			00 32	
Sole Street	d	23 35							00 35	
London Charing Cross [4] ⊖	d		22 39				23 09			23 39
London Waterloo (East) [4] ⊖	d		22 42				23 12			23 42
London Cannon Street [4] ⊖	d									
London Bridge [4] ⊖	d		22 47				23 17			23 47
Dartford [4]	d		23 25				23 55			00 25
Greenhithe for Bluewater	d		23 31				00 02			00 31
Gravesend [4]	d		23 40	23 48			00 10	00 18		00 40
Strood [4]	d		23 52	23 58			00 22	00 28		00 52
Rochester [4]	d	23 45	23 56	00 03		00 09	00 26	00 33	00 45	00 56
Chatham [4]	d	23 47	23 58	00 06		00 12	00 28	00 35	00 47	00 58
Gillingham (Kent) [4]	d	23 52	00a03	00 10		00 17	00a33	00 40	00a52	01a03
Rainham (Kent)	d	23 56		00 15		00 21		00 45		
Newington	d	00 01								
Sittingbourne [4]	a	00 06		00 22		00 28		00 52		
Kemsley	d				23 37					
Swale ⊖	d				23 40					
Queenborough	d				23 44					
Sheerness-on-Sea	a				23 49					
Teynham	d					00 33				
Faversham [2]	a	00 15		00 33		00 39		01 03		
	d					00 43				
Selling	d									
Canterbury East [4]	d									
Bekesbourne	d									
Adisham	d									
Aylesham	d									
Snowdown	d									
Shepherds Well	d									
Kearsney	d									
Dover Priory [4]	a									
Whitstable	d					00 51				
Chestfield & Swalecliffe	d					00 54				
Herne Bay	d					00 58				
Birchington-on-Sea	d					01 07				
Westgate-on-Sea	d					01 11				
Margate [4]	d					01 15				
Broadstairs	d					01 20				
Dumpton Park	d					01 23				
Ramsgate [4]	a					01 26				

Table 212

Saturdays

London - Medway, Sheerness-on-Sea, Dover and Ramsgate

		SE [1]	SE [1]	SE	SE [1]	SE	SE [1]	SE	SE	SE [1]	SE [1]	SE	SE	SE	SE	SE	SE [1]	SE	SE [1]	SE [1]	SE	SE	SE
St Pancras International [15] ⊖	d			22p55		23p25			23p55				00 12										
Stratford International ⊖	d			23p02		23p32			00 02				00 19										
Ebbsfleet International	d			23p13		23p43			00 13				00 31										
London Victoria [15] ⊖	d	22p22			22p52		23p22			23p52	00 10				00 35					05 22			
London Blackfriars [3] ⊖	d																						
Elephant & Castle ⊖	d																						
Bromley South [4]	d	22p39			23p09		23p39			00 09					00 55					05 39			
St Mary Cray	d				23p15					00 15					01 01					05 45			
Swanley [4]	d				23p19					00 19					01 05					05 49			
Farningham Road	d				23p24					00 24					01 10					05 54			
Longfield	d	22p52			23p28		23p52			00 28					01 14					05 58			
Meopham	d	22p57			23p32		23p57			00 32					01 18					06 02			
Sole Street	d				23p35					00 35										06 05			
London Charing Cross [4] ⊖	d							23p09				23p39				00 15						05 39	
London Waterloo (East) [4] ⊖	d							23p12				23p42				00 18						05 42	
London Cannon Street [4] ⊖	d																						
London Bridge [4] ⊖	d							23p17				23p47				00 23						05 47	
Dartford [4]	d							23p55				00 25				01 03					05 55	06 25	
Greenhithe for Bluewater	d							00 02				00 31				01 08					06 00	06 30	
Gravesend [4]	d			23p18		23p48		00 10	00 18			00 40				01 15					06 07	06 37	
Strood [4]	d			23p28		23p58		00 22	00 28			00 52				01 26					06 18	06 48	
Rochester [4]	d	23p09		23p33	23p45	00 03	00 09	00 26	00 33	00 45	00 49	00 56			01 29	01 32				06 15	06 22	06 52	
Chatham [4]	d	23p12		23p35	23p47	00 06	00 12	00 28	00 35	00 47	00 52	00 58			01 31	01 35				06 17	06 25	06 55	
Gillingham (Kent) [4]	d	23p17		23p40	23p52	00 10	00 17	00a33	00 40	00a52	00 57	01a03			01a35	01a41	05 47			06 22	06a29	06a59	
Rainham (Kent)	d	23p21		23p45	23p56	00 15	00 21		00 45		01 01						05 51			06 26			
Newington	d				00 01						01 05						05 55			06 30			
Sittingbourne [4]	a	23p28		23p52	00 06	00 22	00 28		00 52		01 10						06 00			06 35			
Kemsley	d													00 20				06 15					06 45
Swale ⊖	d													00 23				06 18					06 48
Queenborough	d													00 27				06 22					06 52
Sheerness-on-Sea	a													00 32				06 27					06 57
Teynham	d	23p33					00 33				01 15						06 05			06 40			
Faversham [2]	a	23p39	>	00 03	00 15	00 33	00 39		01 03		01 23						06 11			06 46			
	d	23p43	23p45				00 43				01 24						06 12		06 17	06 47			
Selling	d		23p50														06 17						
Canterbury East [4]	d		23p59														06 26						
Bekesbourne	d																06 30						
Adisham	d																06 35						
Aylesham	d		00 07														06 37						
Snowdown	d																06 40						
Shepherds Well	d																06 44						
Kearsney	d																06 48						
Dover Priory [4]	a		00 18														06 53						
Whitstable	d	23p51					00 51				01 32								06 25	06 55			
Chestfield & Swalecliffe	d	23p54					00 54				01 35								06 28	06 58			
Herne Bay	d	23p58					00 58				01 39								06 32	07 02			
Birchington-on-Sea	d	00 07					01 07				01 48								06 41	07 11			
Westgate-on-Sea	d	00 11					01 11				01 52								06 45	07 15			
Margate [4]	d	00 15					01 15				01 56								06 49	07 19			
Broadstairs	d	00 20					01 20				02 01								06 54	07 24			
Dumpton Park	d	00 23					01 23				02 04								06 57	07 27			
Ramsgate [4]	a	00 26					01 26				02 07								07 00	07 30			

Table 212

Saturdays

London - Medway, Sheerness-on-Sea, Dover and Ramsgate

		SE ■	SE ■	SE	SE	SE ■	SE	SE	SE	SE ■	SE ■	SE	SE ■	SE ■	SE ■	SE	SE	SE ■	SE ■	SE	SE ■	SE
St Pancras International 15 ⊖	d							07 22														
Stratford International ⊖	d							07 28														
Ebbsfleet International	d							07 43														
London Victoria 15 ⊖	d		06 22			06 58								07 22				07 52			07 58	
London Blackfriars 3 ⊖	d																					
Elephant & Castle ⊖	d																					
Bromley South 4	d		06 39			07 19								07 39				08 09			08 19	
St Mary Cray	d		06 45			07 25															08 25	
Swanley 4	d		06 49			07 29															08 29	
Farningham Road	d		06 54			07 34															08 34	
Longfield	d		06 58			07 38								07 52				08 22			08 38	
Meopham	d		07 02			07 42								07 57				08 27			08 42	
Sole Street	d		07 05			07 45															08 45	
London Charing Cross 4 ⊖	d			06 09	06 39											07 09				07 39		
London Waterloo (East) 4 ⊖	d			06 12	06 42											07 12				07 42		
London Cannon Street 4 ⊖	d																					
London Bridge 4 ⊖	d			06 17	06 47											07 17				07 47		
Dartford 4	d			06 55	07 25											07 55				08 25		
Greenhithe for Bluewater	d			07 00	07 30											08 00				08 30		
Gravesend 4	d			07 07	07 37			07 48								08 07				08 37		
Strood 4	d			07 18	07 48			07 58								08 18				08 48		
Rochester 4	d		07 15	07 22	07 52	07 56		08 03						08 09		08 22		08 39		08 52	08 56	
Chatham 4	d		07 17	07 25	07 55	07 59		08 05						08 12		08 25		08 42		08 55	08 59	
Gillingham (Kent) 4	d		07 22	07a29	07a59	08a03		08 10						08 17		08a29		08 47		08a59	09a03	
Rainham (Kent)	d		07 26					08 15						08 21				08 51				
Newington	d		07 30											08 25				08 55				
Sittingbourne 4	a		07 35					08 22						08 30				09 00				
Kemsley	d						07 15		07 45			08 15					08 45					09 15
Swale ⊖	d						07 18		07 48			08 18					08 48					09 18
Queenborough	d						07 22		07 52			08 22					08 52					09 22
Sheerness-on-Sea	a						07 27		07 57			08 27					08 57					09 27
Teynham	d		07 40											08 35								
Faversham 2	a		07 46					08 31						08 41	>			09 09	>			
	d	06 50	07 47							07 50	08 13		08 15	08 45	08 50			09 13	09 15			
Selling	d	06 55								07 55					08 55							
Canterbury East 4	d	07 04								08 04			08 29		09 04				09 29			
Bekesbourne	d	07 08								08 08					09 08							
Adisham	d	07 13								08 13					09 13							
Aylesham	d	07 15								08 15					09 15							
Snowdown	d	07 18								08 18					09 18							
Shepherds Well	d	07 22								08 22					09 22							
Kearsney	d	07 26								08 26					09 26							
Dover Priory 4	a	07 31								08 31			08 48		09 31				09 48			
Whitstable	d		07 55								08 21			08 53				09 21				
Chestfield & Swalecliffe	d		07 58											08 56								
Herne Bay	d		08 02								08 26			09 00				09 26				
Birchington-on-Sea	d		08 11								08 35			09 09				09 35				
Westgate-on-Sea	d		08 15											09 13								
Margate 4	d		08 19								08 41			09 17				09 41				
Broadstairs	d		08 24								08 46			09 22				09 46				
Dumpton Park	d		08 27											09 25								
Ramsgate 4	a		08 30								08 51			09 28				09 51				

b arr. 0656

Table 212

Saturdays

London - Medway, Sheerness-on-Sea, Dover and Ramsgate

		SE ■	SE ■	SE	SE	SE	SE ■	SE ■	SE	SE ■	SE	SE	SE ■	SE ■	SE	SE	SE	SE ■ ⌶	SE ■	SE	SE ■	SE	SE
St Pancras International 15 ⊖	d				08 52						09 28					09 55						10 28	
Stratford International ⊖	d				08 58						09 35					10 02						10 35	
Ebbsfleet International	d				09 13						09 46					10 13						10 46	
London Victoria 15 ⊖	d	08 22					08 52			08 58			09 22					09 52			09 58		
London Blackfriars 3 ⊖	d																						
Elephant & Castle ⊖	d																						
Bromley South 4	d	08 39					09 09			09 19			09 39					10 09			10 19		
St Mary Cray	d									09 25											10 25		
Swanley 4	d									09 29											10 29		
Farningham Road	d									09 34											10 34		
Longfield	d	08 52					09 22			09 38			09 52					10 22			10 38		
Meopham	d	08 57					09 27			09 42			09 57					10 27			10 42		
Sole Street	d									09 45											10 45		
London Charing Cross 4 ⊖	d			08 09					08 39						09 09					09 39			
London Waterloo (East) 4 ⊖	d			08 12					08 42						09 12					09 42			
London Cannon Street 4 ⊖	d																						
London Bridge 4 ⊖	d			08 17					08 47						09 17					09 47			
Dartford 4	d			08 55					09 25						09 55					10 25			
Greenhithe for Bluewater	d			09 00					09 30						10 00					10 30			
Gravesend 4	d			09 07	09 18				09 37		09 51				10 07	10 18				10 37		10 51	
Strood 4	d			09 18	09 28				09 48		10 01				10 18	10 28				10 48		11 01	
Rochester 4	d	09 09		09 22	09 33		09 39		09 52	09 56	10 06		10 09		10 22	10 33		10 39		10 52	10 56	11 06	
Chatham 4	d	09 12		09 25	09 35		09 42		09 55	09 59	10 08		10 12		10 25	10 35		10 42		10 55	10 59	11 08	
Gillingham (Kent) 4	d	09 17		09a29	09 40		09 47		09a59	10a03	10 13		10 17		10a29	10 40		10 47		10a59	11a03	11 13	
Rainham (Kent)	d	09 21			09 45		09 51				10 18		10 21			10 45		10 51				11 18	
Newington	d						09 55											10 55					
Sittingbourne 4	a	09 28			09 52		10 00				10 25		10 28			10 52		11 00				11 25	
Kemsley	d					09 45						10 15					10 45						11 15
Swale ⊖	d					09 48						10 18					10 48						11 18
Queenborough	d					09 52						10 22					10 52						11 22
Sheerness-on-Sea	a					09 57						10 27					10 57						11 27
Teynham	d	09 33											10 33										
Faversham 2	a	09 39	>		10 01		10 09	>			10 34		10 39	>		11 01		11 09	>			11 34	
	d	09 43	09 45				10 13	10 15					10 43	10 45				11 13	11 15				
Selling	d		09 50											10 50									
Canterbury East 4	d		09 59					10 29						10 59					11 29				
Bekesbourne	d		10 03											11 03									
Adisham	d		10 08											11 08									
Aylesham	d		10 10											11 10									
Snowdown	d		10 13											11 13									
Shepherds Well	d		10 17											11 17									
Kearsney	d		10 21											11 21									
Dover Priory 4	a		10 26					10 48						11 26					11 48				
Whitstable	d	09 51					10 21						10 51					11 21					
Chestfield & Swalecliffe	d	09 54											10 54										
Herne Bay	d	09 58					10 26						10 58					11 26					
Birchington-on-Sea	d	10 07					10 35						11 07					11 35					
Westgate-on-Sea	d	10 11											11 11										
Margate 4	d	10 15					10 41						11 15					11 41					
Broadstairs	d	10 20					10 46						11 20					11 46					
Dumpton Park	d	10 23											11 23										
Ramsgate 4	a	10 26					10 51						11 26					11 51					

Table 212

Saturdays

London - Medway, Sheerness-on-Sea, Dover and Ramsgate

		SE ■ A ⊼	SE ■	SE	SE	SE	SE ■ B ⊼	SE ■		SE	SE ■	SE	SE	SE ■ A ⊼	SE ■	SE	SE	SE		SE ■ B ⊼	SE ■	SE	SE ■	SE	SE
St Pancras International ⊖	d				10 52							11 25					11 55							12 25	
Stratford International ⊖	d				10 58							11 32					12 02							12 36	
Ebbsfleet International	d				11 13							11 43					12 13							12 47	
London Victoria ⊖	d	10 22					10 52				10 58			11 22						11 52			11 58		
London Blackfriars ⊖	d																								
Elephant & Castle ⊖	d																								
Bromley South	d	10 39					11 09				11 19			11 39						12 09			12 19		
St Mary Cray	d										11 25												12 25		
Swanley	d										11 29												12 29		
Farningham Road	d										11 34												12 34		
Longfield	d	10 52					11 22				11 38			11 52						12 22			12 38		
Meopham	d	10 57					11 27				11 42			11 57						12 27			12 42		
Sole Street	d										11 45												12 45		
London Charing Cross ⊖	d			10 09						10 39						11 09						11 39			
London Waterloo (East) ⊖	d			10 12						10 42						11 12						11 42			
London Cannon Street ⊖	d																								
London Bridge ⊖	d			10 17						10 47						11 17						11 47			
Dartford	d			10 55						11 25						11 55						12 25			
Greenhithe for Bluewater	d			11 00						11 30						12 00						12 30			
Gravesend	d			11 07	11 18					11 37		11 48				12 07	12 18					12 37		12 51	
Strood	d			11 18	11 28					11 48		11 58				12 18	12 28					12 48		13 01	
Rochester	d	11 09		11 22	11 33		11 39			11 52	11 56	12 03		12 09		12 22	12 33			12 39		12 52	12 56	13 06	
Chatham	d	11 12		11 25	11 35		11 42			11 55	11 59	12 05		12 12		12 25	12 35			12 42		12 55	12 59	13 08	
Gillingham (Kent)	d	11 17		11a29	11 40		11 47			11a59	12a03	12 10		12 17		12a29	12 40			12 47		12a59	13a03	13 13	
Rainham (Kent)	d	11 21			11 45		11 51					12 15		12 21			12 45			12 51				13 18	
Newington	d						11 55													12 55					
Sittingbourne	a	11 29			11 52		12 00					12 22		12 28			12 52			13 00				13 25	
Kemsley	d					11 45							12 15					12 45							13 15
Swale ⊖	d					11 48							12 18					12 48							13 18
Queenborough	d					11 52							12 22					12 52							13 22
Sheerness-on-Sea	a					11 57							12 27					12 57							13 27
Teynham	d	11 33												12 33											
Faversham	a	11 39	>		12 01		12 09	>				12 31		12 39	>		13 01			13 09	>			13 34	
	d	11 43	11 45				12 13	12 15						12 43	12 45					13 13	13 15				
Selling	d		11 50												12 50										
Canterbury East	d		11 59					12 29							12 59						13 29				
Bekesbourne	d		12 03												13 03										
Adisham	d		12 08												13 08										
Aylesham	d		12 10												13 10										
Snowdown	d		12 13												13 13										
Shepherds Well	d		12 17												13 17										
Kearsney	d		12 21												13 21										
Dover Priory	a		12 26					12 48							13 26						13 48				
Whitstable	d	11 51					12 21							12 51						13 21					
Chestfield & Swalecliffe	d	11 54												12 54											
Herne Bay	d	11 58					12 26							12 58						13 26					
Birchington-on-Sea	d	12 07					12 35							13 07						13 35					
Westgate-on-Sea	d	12 11												13 11											
Margate	d	12 15					12 41							13 15						13 41					
Broadstairs	d	12 20					12 46							13 20						13 46					
Dumpton Park	d	12 23												13 23											
Ramsgate	a	12 26					12 51							13 26						13 51					

A ⊼ to Westgate-on-Sea

B ⊼ to Birchington-on-Sea

Table 212

Saturdays

London - Medway, Sheerness-on-Sea, Dover and Ramsgate

		SE ■ ⊼	SE ■	SE		SE	SE	SE ■ ⊼	SE ■	SE	SE ■	SE	SE		SE ■ ⊼	SE ■	SE	SE	SE	SE ■ ⊼	SE ■	SE	SE ■	SE	
St Pancras International ⊖	d					12 52						13 25						13 55						14 28	
Stratford International ⊖	d					12 58						13 32						14 02						14 35	
Ebbsfleet International	d					13 13						13 43						14 13						14 46	
London Victoria ⊖	d	12 22						12 52			12 58				13 22					13 52			13 58		
London Blackfriars ⊖	d																								
Elephant & Castle ⊖	d																								
Bromley South	d	12 39						13 09			13 19				13 39					14 09			14 19		
St Mary Cray	d										13 25												14 25		
Swanley	d										13 29												14 29		
Farningham Road	d										13 34												14 34		
Longfield	d	12 52						13 22			13 38				13 52					14 22			14 38		
Meopham	d	12 57						13 27			13 42				13 57					14 27			14 42		
Sole Street	d										13 45												14 45		
London Charing Cross ⊖	d			12 09						12 39							13 09					13 39			
London Waterloo (East) ⊖	d			12 12						12 42							13 12					13 42			
London Cannon Street ⊖	d																								
London Bridge ⊖	d			12 17						12 47							13 17					13 47			
Dartford	d			12 55						13 25							13 55					14 25			
Greenhithe for Bluewater	d			13 00						13 30							14 00					14 30			
Gravesend	d			13 07		13 18				13 37		13 48					14 07	14 18				14 37		14 51	
Strood	d			13 18		13 28				13 48		13 58					14 18	14 28				14 48		15 01	
Rochester	d	13 09		13 22		13 33		13 39		13 52	13 56	14 03			14 09		14 22	14 33		14 39		14 52	14 56	15 06	
Chatham	d	13 12		13 25		13 35		13 42		13 55	13 59	14 05			14 12		14 25	14 35		14 42		14 55	14 59	15 08	
Gillingham (Kent)	d	13 17		13a29		13 40		13 47		13a59	14a03	14 10			14 17		14a29	14 40		14 47		14a59	15a03	15 13	
Rainham (Kent)	d	13 21				13 45		13 51				14 15			14 21			14 45		14 51				15 18	
Newington	d							13 55												14 55					
Sittingbourne	a	13 29				13 52		14 00				14 22			14 28			14 52		15 00				15 25	
Kemsley	d						13 45						14 15						14 45						
Swale ⊖	d						13 48						14 18						14 48						
Queenborough	d						13 52						14 22						14 52						
Sheerness-on-Sea	a						13 57						14 27						14 57						
Teynham	d	13 33													14 33										
Faversham	a	13 39	>			14 01		14 09	>			14 31			14 39	>		15 01		15 09	>			15 34	
	d	13 43	13 45					14 13	14 15						14 43	14 45				15 13	15 15				
Selling	d		13 50													14 50									
Canterbury East	d		13 59						14 29							14 59					15 29				
Bekesbourne	d		14 03													15 03									
Adisham	d		14 08													15 08									
Aylesham	d		14 10													15 10									
Snowdown	d		14 13													15 13									
Shepherds Well	d		14 17													15 17									
Kearsney	d		14 21													15 21									
Dover Priory	a		14 26						14 48							15 26					15 48				
Whitstable	d	13 51						14 21							14 51					15 21					
Chestfield & Swalecliffe	d	13 54													14 54										
Herne Bay	d	13 58						14 26							14 58					15 26					
Birchington-on-Sea	d	14 07						14 35							15 07					15 35					
Westgate-on-Sea	d	14 11													15 11										
Margate	d	14 15						14 41							15 15					15 41					
Broadstairs	d	14 20						14 46							15 20					15 46					
Dumpton Park	d	14 23													15 23										
Ramsgate	a	14 26						14 51							15 26					15 51					

Table 212

Saturdays

London - Medway, Sheerness-on-Sea, Dover and Ramsgate

		SE	SE 1 🛒	SE 1	SE	SE	SE	SE 1 🛒	SE 1	SE		SE 1	SE	SE	SE 1 🛒	SE 1	SE	SE	SE		SE 1 🛒	SE 1	SE	SE 1	SE
St Pancras International 15 ⊖	d					14 58							15 25					15 55							16 28
Stratford International ⊖	d					15 05							15 32					16 02							16 35
Ebbsfleet International	d					15 16							15 43					16 13							16 46
London Victoria 15 ⊖	d		14 22					14 52				14 58			15 22						15 52			15 58	
London Blackfriars 3 ⊖	d																								
Elephant & Castle ⊖	d																								
Bromley South 4	d		14 39					15 09				15 19			15 39						16 09			16 19	
St Mary Cray	d											15 25												16 25	
Swanley 4	d											15 29												16 29	
Farningham Road	d											15 34												16 34	
Longfield	d		14 52					15 22				15 38			15 52						16 22			16 38	
Meopham	d		14 57					15 27				15 42			15 57						16 27			16 42	
Sole Street	d											15 45												16 45	
London Charing Cross 4 ⊖	d				14 09					14 39							15 09						15 39		
London Waterloo (East) 4 ⊖	d				14 12					14 42							15 12						15 42		
London Cannon Street 4 ⊖	d																								
London Bridge 4 ⊖	d				14 17					14 47							15 17						15 47		
Dartford 4	d				14 55					15 25							15 55						16 25		
Greenhithe for Bluewater	d				15 00					15 30							16 00						16 30		
Gravesend 4	d				15 07	15 21				15 37			15 48				16 07	16 18					16 37		16 51
Strood 4	d				15 18	15 31				15 48			15 58				16 18	16 28					16 48		17 01
Rochester 4	d		15 09		15 22	15 36		15 39		15 52		15 56	16 03		16 09		16 22	16 33			16 39		16 52	16 56	17 06
Chatham 4	d		15 12		15 25	15 38		15 42		15 55		15 59	16 05		16 12		16 25	16 35			16 42		16 55	16 59	17 08
Gillingham (Kent) 4	d		15 17		15a29	15 43		15 47		15a59		16a03	16 10		16 17		16a29	16 40			16 47		16a59	17a03	17 13
Rainham (Kent)	d		15 21			15 48		15 51					16 15		16 21			16 45			16 51				17 18
Newington	d							15 55													16 55				
Sittingbourne 4	a		15 29			15 55		16 00					16 22		16 28			16 52			17 00				17 25
Kemsley	d	15 15					15 45							16 15					16 45						
Swale ⊖	d	15 18					15 48							16 18					16 48						
Queenborough	d	15 22					15 52							16 22					16 52						
Sheerness-on-Sea	a	15 27					15 57							16 27					16 57						
Teynham	d		15 33												16 33										
Faversham 2	a		15 39	>		16 04		16 09	>				16 31		16 39	>		17 01			17 09	>			17 34
	d		15 43	15 45				16 13	16 15						16 43	16 45					17 13	17 15			
Selling	d			15 50												16 50									
Canterbury East 4	d			15 59					16 29							16 59						17 29			
Bekesbourne	d			16 03												17 03									
Adisham	d			16 08												17 08									
Aylesham	d			16 10												17 10									
Snowdown	d			16 13												17 13									
Shepherds Well	d			16 17												17 17									
Kearsney	d			16 21												17 21									
Dover Priory 4	a			16 26					16 48							17 26						17 48			
Whitstable	d		15 51					16 21							16 51						17 21				
Chestfield & Swalecliffe	d		15 54												16 54										
Herne Bay	d		15 58					16 26							16 58						17 26				
Birchington-on-Sea	d		16 07					16 35							17 07						17 35				
Westgate-on-Sea	d		16 11												17 11										
Margate 4	d		16 15					16 41							17 15						17 41				
Broadstairs	d		16 20					16 46							17 20						17 46				
Dumpton Park	d		16 23												17 23										
Ramsgate 4	a		16 26					16 51							17 26						17 51				

Table 212

Saturdays

London - Medway, Sheerness-on-Sea, Dover and Ramsgate

		SE	SE 1 A 🛒	SE 1	SE	SE		SE	SE 1 B 🛒	SE 1	SE	SE 1	SE	SE	SE 1 🛒	SE 1		SE	SE	SE	SE 1 🛒	SE 1	SE	SE 1	SE
St Pancras International 15 ⊖	d					16 55							17 28						17 58						18 25
Stratford International ⊖	d					17 02							17 35						18 05						18 32
Ebbsfleet International	d					17 13							17 46						18 16						18 43
London Victoria 15 ⊖	d		16 22						16 52			16 58			17 22						17 52			17 58	
London Blackfriars 3 ⊖	d																								
Elephant & Castle ⊖	d																								
Bromley South 4	d		16 39						17 09			17 19			17 39						18 09			18 19	
St Mary Cray	d											17 25												18 25	
Swanley 4	d											17 29												18 29	
Farningham Road	d											17 34												18 34	
Longfield	d		16 52						17 22			17 38			17 52						18 22			18 38	
Meopham	d		16 57						17 27			17 42			17 57						18 27			18 42	
Sole Street	d											17 45												18 45	
London Charing Cross 4 ⊖	d				16 09						16 39							17 09					17 39		
London Waterloo (East) 4 ⊖	d				16 12						16 42							17 12					17 42		
London Cannon Street 4 ⊖	d																								
London Bridge 4 ⊖	d				16 17						16 47							17 17					17 47		
Dartford 4	d				16 55						17 25							17 55					18 25		
Greenhithe for Bluewater	d				17 00						17 30							18 00					18 30		
Gravesend 4	d				17 07	17 18					17 37		17 51					18 07	18 21				18 37		18 48
Strood 4	d				17 18	17 28					17 48		18 01					18 18	18 31				18 48		18 58
Rochester 4	d		17 09		17 22	17 33			17 39		17 52	17 56	18 06		18 09			18 22	18 36		18 39		18 52	18 56	19 03
Chatham 4	d		17 12		17 25	17 35			17 42		17 55	17 59	18 08		18 12			18 25	18 38		18 42		18 55	18 59	19 05
Gillingham (Kent) 4	d		17 17		17a29	17 40			17 47		17a59	18a03	18 13		18 17			18a29	18 43		18 47		18a59	19a03	19 10
Rainham (Kent)	d		17 21			17 45			17 51				18 18		18 21				18 48		18 51				19 15
Newington	d								17 55												18 55				
Sittingbourne 4	a		17 29			17 52			18 00				18 25		18 29				18 55		19 00				19 22
Kemsley	d	17 15						17 45						18 15						18 45					
Swale ⊖	d	17 18						17 48						18 18						18 48					
Queenborough	d	17 22						17 52						18 22						18 52					
Sheerness-on-Sea	a	17 27						17 57						18 27						18 57					
Teynham	d		17 33												18 33										
Faversham 2	a		17 39	>		18 01			18 09	>			18 34		18 39	>			19 04		19 09	>			19 31
	d		17 43	17 45					18 13	18 15					18 43	18 45					19 13	19 15			
Selling	d			17 50												18 50									
Canterbury East 4	d			17 59						18 29						18 59						19 29			
Bekesbourne	d			18 03												19 03									
Adisham	d			18 08												19 08									
Aylesham	d			18 10												19 10									
Snowdown	d			18 13												19 13									
Shepherds Well	d			18 17												19 17									
Kearsney	d			18 21												19 21									
Dover Priory 4	a			18 26						18 48						19 26						19 48			
Whitstable	d		17 51						18 21						18 51						19 21				
Chestfield & Swalecliffe	d		17 54												18 54										
Herne Bay	d		17 58						18 26						18 58						19 26				
Birchington-on-Sea	d		18 07						18 35						19 07						19 35				
Westgate-on-Sea	d		18 11												19 11										
Margate 4	d		18 15						18 41						19 15						19 41				
Broadstairs	d		18 20						18 46						19 20						19 46				
Dumpton Park	d		18 23												19 23										
Ramsgate 4	a		18 26						18 51						19 26						19 51				

Table 212

Saturdays

London - Medway, Sheerness-on-Sea, Dover and Ramsgate

		SE	SE ■	SE ■	SE	SE	SE	SE ■	SE ■	SE	SE ■	SE	SE	SE ■	SE ■	SE	SE	SE	SE ■	SE ■	SE	SE ■
St Pancras International ■ ⊖	d					18 55						19 25					19 55					
Stratford International ⊖	d					19 02						19 32					20 02					
Ebbsfleet International	d					19 13						19 43					20 13					
London Victoria ■ ⊖	d		18 22					18 52			18 58			19 22					19 52			19 58
London Blackfriars ■ ⊖	d																					
Elephant & Castle ⊖	d																					
Bromley South ■	d		18 39					19 09			19 19			19 39					20 09			20 19
St Mary Cray	d										19 25											20 25
Swanley ■	d										19 29											20 29
Farningham Road	d										19 34											20 34
Longfield	d		18 52					19 22			19 38			19 52					20 22			20 38
Meopham	d		18 57					19 27			19 42			19 57					20 27			20 42
Sole Street	d										19 45											20 45
London Charing Cross ■ ⊖	d				18 09					18 39						19 09					19 39	
London Waterloo (East) ■ ⊖	d				18 12					18 42						19 12					19 42	
London Cannon Street ■ ⊖	d																					
London Bridge ■ ⊖	d				18 17					18 47						19 17					19 47	
Dartford ■	d				18 55					19 25						19 55					20 25	
Greenhithe for Bluewater	d				19 00					19 30						20 00					20 30	
Gravesend ■	d				19 07	19 18				19 37		19 48				20 07	20 18				20 37	
Strood ■	d				19 18	19 28				19 48		19 58				20 18	20 28				20 48	
Rochester ■	d		19 09		19 22	19 33		19 39		19 52	19 56	20 03		20 09		20 22	20 33		20 39		20 52	20 56
Chatham ■	d		19 12		19 25	19 35		19 42		19 55	19 59	20 05		20 12		20 25	20 35		20 42		20 55	20 59
Gillingham (Kent) ■	d		19 17		19a29	19 40		19 47		19a59	20a03	20 10		20 17		20a29	20 40		20 47		20a59	21a03
Rainham (Kent)	d		19 21			19 45		19 51				20 15		20 21			20 45		20 51			
Newington	d							19 55											20 55			
Sittingbourne ■	a		19 28			19 52		20 00				20 22		20 28			20 52		21 00			
Kemsley	d	19 15					19 45						20 15					20 45				
Swale ⊖	d	19 18					19 48						20 18					20 48				
Queenborough	d	19 22					19 52						20 22					20 52				
Sheerness-on-Sea	a	19 27					19 57						20 27					20 57				
Teynham	d		19 33											20 33								
Faversham ■	a		19 39	>		20 01		20 09	>			20 31		20 39	>		21 01		21 09	>		
	d		19 43	19 45				20 13	20 15					20 43	20 45				21 13	21 15		
Selling	d			19 50											20 50							
Canterbury East ■	d			19 59					20 29						20 59					21a26		
Bekesbourne	d			20 03											21 03							
Adisham	d			20 08											21 08							
Aylesham	d			20 10											21 10							
Snowdown	d			20 13											21 13							
Shepherds Well	d			20 17											21 17							
Kearsney	d			20 21											21 21							
Dover Priory ■	a			20 26					20 48						21 26							
Whitstable	d		19 51					20 21						20 51					21 21			
Chestfield & Swalecliffe	d		19 54											20 54								
Herne Bay	d		19 58					20 26						20 58					21 26			
Birchington-on-Sea	d		20 07					20 35						21 07					21 35			
Westgate-on-Sea	d		20 11											21 11								
Margate ■	d		20 15					20 41						21 15					21 41			
Broadstairs	d		20 20					20 46						21 20					21 46			
Dumpton Park	d		20 23											21 23								
Ramsgate ■	a		20 26					20 51						21 26					21 51			

Table 212

Saturdays

London - Medway, Sheerness-on-Sea, Dover and Ramsgate

		SE	SE ■	SE ■	SE	SE	SE	SE ■	SE	SE	SE ■	SE ■	SE	SE	SE ■	SE	SE	SE	SE ■	SE ■	SE	SE	SE ■
St Pancras International ■ ⊖	d	20 25				20 55				21 25				21 55			22 25					22 55	
Stratford International ⊖	d	20 32				21 02				21 32				22 02			22 32					23 02	
Ebbsfleet International	d	20 43				21 13				21 43				22 13			22 43					23 13	
London Victoria ■ ⊖	d		20 22					20 52			21 22				21 52				22 22				22 52
London Blackfriars ■ ⊖	d																						
Elephant & Castle ⊖	d																						
Bromley South ■	d		20 39					21 09			21 39				22 09				22 39				23 09
St Mary Cray	d							21 15							22 15								23 15
Swanley ■	d							21 19							22 19								23 19
Farningham Road	d							21 24							22 24								23 24
Longfield	d		20 52					21 28			21 52				22 28				22 52				23 28
Meopham	d		20 57					21 32			21 57				22 32				22 57				23 32
Sole Street	d							21 35							22 35								23 35
London Charing Cross ■ ⊖	d				20 09				20 39				21 09			21 39					22 09		
London Waterloo (East) ■ ⊖	d				20 12				20 42				21 12			21 42					22 12		
London Cannon Street ■ ⊖	d																						
London Bridge ■ ⊖	d				20 17				20 47				21 17			21 47					22 17		
Dartford ■	d				20 55				21 25				21 55			22 25					22 55		
Greenhithe for Bluewater	d				21 00				21 30				22 00			22 31					23 01		
Gravesend ■	d	20 48			21 07	21 18			21 37	21 48			22 07	22 18		22 40	22 48				23 10	23 18	
Strood ■	d	20 58			21 18	21 28			21 48	21 58			22 18	22 28		22 51	22 58				23 21	23 28	
Rochester ■	d	21 03	21 09		21 22	21 33		21 45	21 52	22 03	22 09		22 22	22 33	22 45	22 55	23 03		23 09		23 25	23 33	23 45
Chatham ■	d	21 05	21 12		21 25	21 35		21 47	21 55	22 05	22 12		22 25	22 35	22 47	22 58	23 05		23 12		23 28	23 35	23 47
Gillingham (Kent) ■	d	21 10	21 17		21a29	21 40		21 52	21a59	22 10	22 17		22a29	22 40	22 52	23a02	23 10		23 17		23a32	23 40	23 52
Rainham (Kent)	d	21 15	21 21			21 45		21 56		22 15	22 21			22 45	22 56		23 15		23 21			23 45	23 56
Newington	d							22 00							23 00								00 01
Sittingbourne ■	a	21 22	21 28			21 52		22 05		22 22	22 28			22 52	23 05		23 22		23 28			23 52	00 06
Kemsley	d						21 45											22 45					
Swale ⊖	d						21 48											22 48					
Queenborough	d						21 52											22 52					
Sheerness-on-Sea	a						21 57											22 57					
Teynham	d		21 33								22 33								23 33				
Faversham ■	a	21 31	21 39	>		22 01		22 14		22 31	22 39	>		23 01	23 14		23 31		23 39	>		00 01	00 16
	d		21 43	21 45				22 15			22 43	22 45							23 43	23 45			
Selling	d			21 50								22 50								23 50			
Canterbury East ■	d			21 59				22a26				22 59								23 59			
Bekesbourne	d			22 03								23 03											
Adisham	d			22 08								23 08											
Aylesham	d			22 10								23 10								00 07			
Snowdown	d			22 13								23 13											
Shepherds Well	d			22 17								23 17											
Kearsney	d			22 21								23 21											
Dover Priory ■	a			22 26								23 26								00 18			
Whitstable	d		21 51								22 51								23 51				
Chestfield & Swalecliffe	d		21 54								22 54								23 54				
Herne Bay	d		21 58								22 58								23 58				
Birchington-on-Sea	d		22 07								23 07								00 07				
Westgate-on-Sea	d		22 11								23 11								00 11				
Margate ■	d		22 15								23 15								00 15				
Broadstairs	d		22 20								23 20								00 20				
Dumpton Park	d		22 23								23 23								00 23				
Ramsgate ■	a		22 26								23 26								00 26				

Table 212

London - Medway, Sheerness-on-Sea, Dover and Ramsgate

		SE	SE	SE	SE ■	SE	SE	SE ■	SE
St Pancras International ⊖	d		23 25				23 55		
Stratford International ⊖	d		23 32				00 02		
Ebbsfleet International	d		23 43				00 13		
London Victoria ⊖	d				23 22			23 52	
London Blackfriars ⊖	d								
Elephant & Castle ⊖	d								
Bromley South	d				23 39			00 09	
St Mary Cray	d							00 15	
Swanley	d							00 19	
Farningham Road	d							00 24	
Longfield	d				23 52			00 28	
Meopham	d				23 57			00 32	
Sole Street	d							00 35	
London Charing Cross ⊖	d	22 39				23 09			23 39
London Waterloo (East) ⊖	d	22 42				23 12			23 42
London Cannon Street ⊖	d								
London Bridge ⊖	d	22 47				23 17			23 47
Dartford	d	23 25				23 55			00 25
Greenhithe for Bluewater	d	23 31				23 59			00 31
Gravesend	d	23 40	23 48			00 09	00 18		00 40
Strood	d	23 51	23 58			00 21	00 28		00 51
Rochester	d	23 55	00 03		00 09	00 25	00 33	00 45	00 55
Chatham	d	23 58	00 05		00 12	00 27	00 35	00 47	00 58
Gillingham (Kent)	d	00a02	00 09		00 17	00a32	00 40	00a52	01a02
Rainham (Kent)	d		00 14		00 21		00 45		
Newington	d								
Sittingbourne	a		00 22		00 28		00 52		
Kemsley	d			23 37					
Swale ⊖	d			23 40					
Queenborough	d			23 44					
Sheerness-on-Sea	a			23 49					
Teynham	d				00 33				
Faversham	a		00 31		00 39		01 01		
	d				00 43				
Selling	d								
Canterbury East	d								
Bekesbourne	d								
Adisham	d								
Aylesham	d								
Snowdown	d								
Shepherds Well	d								
Kearsney	d								
Dover Priory	a								
Whitstable	d				00 51				
Chestfield & Swalecliffe	d				00 54				
Herne Bay	d				00 58				
Birchington-on-Sea	d				01 07				
Westgate-on-Sea	d				01 11				
Margate	d				01 15				
Broadstairs	d				01 20				
Dumpton Park	d				01 23				
Ramsgate	a				01 26				

Table 212

London - Medway, Sheerness-on-Sea, Dover and Ramsgate

		SE ■	SE ■	SE	SE ■	SE	SE ■	SE	SE	SE ■	SE ■	SE
St Pancras International ⊖	d			22p55		23p25			23p55			
Stratford International ⊖	d			23p02		23p32			00 02			
Ebbsfleet International	d			23p13		23p43			00 13			
London Victoria ⊖	d	22p22			22p52		23p22			23p52	00 10	
London Blackfriars ⊖	d											
Elephant & Castle ⊖	d											
Bromley South	d	22p39			23p09		23p39			00 09		
St Mary Cray	d				23p15					00 15		
Swanley	d				23p19					00 19		
Farningham Road	d				23p24					00 24		
Longfield	d	22p52			23p28		23p52			00 28		
Meopham	d	22p57			23p32		23p57			00 32		
Sole Street	d				23p35					00 35		
London Charing Cross ⊖	d							23p09				23p39
London Waterloo (East) ⊖	d							23p12				23p42
London Cannon Street ⊖	d											
London Bridge ⊖	d							23p17				23p47
Dartford	d							23p55				00 25
Greenhithe for Bluewater	d							23p59				00 31
Gravesend	d			23p18		23p48		00 09	00 18			00 40
Strood	d			23p28		23p58		00 21	00 28			00 51
Rochester	d	23p09		23p33	23p45	00 03	00 09	00 25	00 33	00 45	00 49	00 55
Chatham	d	23p12		23p35	23p47	00 05	00 12	00 27	00 35	00 47	00 52	00 58
Gillingham (Kent)	d	23p17		23p40	23p52	00 09	00 17	00a32	00 40	00a52	00 57	01a02
Rainham (Kent)	d	23p21		23p45	23p56	00 14	00 21		00 45		01 01	
Newington	d				00 01						01 05	
Sittingbourne	a	23p28		23p52	00 06	00 22	00 28		00 52		01 10	
Kemsley	d											
Swale ⊖	d											
Queenborough	d											
Sheerness-on-Sea	a											
Teynham	d	23p33					00 33				01 15	
Faversham	a	23p39	>	00 01	00 16	00 31	00 39		01 01		01 23	
	d	23p43	23p45				00 43				01 24	
Selling	d		23p50									
Canterbury East	d		23p59									
Bekesbourne	d											
Adisham	d											
Aylesham	d		00 07									
Snowdown	d											
Shepherds Well	d											
Kearsney	d											
Dover Priory	a		00 18									
Whitstable	d	23p51					00 51				01 32	
Chestfield & Swalecliffe	d	23p54					00 54				01 35	
Herne Bay	d	23p58					00 58				01 39	
Birchington-on-Sea	d	00 07					01 07				01 48	
Westgate-on-Sea	d	00 11					01 11				01 52	
Margate	d	00 15					01 15				01 56	
Broadstairs	d	00 20					01 20				02 01	
Dumpton Park	d	00 23					01 23				02 04	
Ramsgate	a	00 26					01 26				02 07	

		SE	SE	SE	SE	SE	SE ■	SE ■	SE ■	SE	SE	SE
St Pancras International ⊖	d	00 12										
Stratford International ⊖	d	00 19										
Ebbsfleet International	d	00 31										
London Victoria ⊖	d			00 35			07 38	08 05				
London Blackfriars ⊖	d											
Elephant & Castle ⊖	d											
Bromley South	d			00 55			07 55	08 22				
St Mary Cray	d			01 01			08 01					
Swanley	d			01 05			08 05					
Farningham Road	d			01 10			08 10					
Longfield	d			01 14			08 14					
Meopham	d			01 18			08 18					
Sole Street	d						08 21					
London Charing Cross ⊖	d				00 15							
London Waterloo (East) ⊖	d				00 18							
London Cannon Street ⊖	d											
London Bridge ⊖	d				00 23							
Dartford	d				01 03	07 55					08 25	
Greenhithe for Bluewater	d				01 08	08 01					08 31	
Gravesend	d				01 15	08 10					08 40	
Strood	d				01 26	08 22					08 52	
Rochester	d			01 29	01 32	08 26	08 34	08 46			08 56	
Chatham	d			01 31	01 35	08 28	08 37	08 48			08 58	
Gillingham (Kent)	d			01a35	01a41	08a33	08 41	08 53			09a03	
Rainham (Kent)	d						08 46	08 57				
Newington	d						08 50					
Sittingbourne	a						08 55	09 04				
Kemsley	d		00 20							08 15		09 15
Swale ⊖	d		00 23							08 18		09 18
Queenborough	d		00 27							08 22		09 22
Sheerness-on-Sea	a		00 32							08 27		09 27
Teynham	d						09 00					
Faversham	a						09 06	09 13	>			
	d							09 17	09 19			
Selling	d								09 24			
Canterbury East	d								09 33			
Bekesbourne	d								09 37			
Adisham	d								09 42			
Aylesham	d								09 44			
Snowdown	d								09 47			
Shepherds Well	d								09 51			
Kearsney	d								09 55			
Dover Priory	a								10 01			
Whitstable	d							09 25				
Chestfield & Swalecliffe	d							09 28				
Herne Bay	d							09 32				
Birchington-on-Sea	d							09 41				
Westgate-on-Sea	d							09 45				
Margate	d							09 49				
Broadstairs	d							09 54				
Dumpton Park	d							09 57				
Ramsgate	a							10 00				

Table 212

Sundays

London - Medway, Sheerness-on-Sea, Dover and Ramsgate

Station		SE ■	SE	SE ■	SE ■	SE	SE	SE	SE ■	SE	SE ■ ⌘
St Pancras International ⊖	d						09 25				
Stratford International ⊖	d						09 32				
Ebbsfleet International	d						09 43				
London Victoria ⊖	d	08 24		09 05					09 24		10 05
London Blackfriars ⊖	d										
Elephant & Castle ⊖	d										
Bromley South	d	08 44		09 22					09 44		10 22
St Mary Cray	d	08 50							09 50		
Swanley	d	08 54							09 54		
Farningham Road	d	08 59							09 59		
Longfield	d	09 03							10 03		
Meopham	d	09 07							10 07		
Sole Street	d	09 10							10 10		
London Charing Cross ⊖	d		08 10			08 40				09 10	
London Waterloo (East) ⊖	d		08 13			08 43				09 13	
London Cannon Street ⊖	d										
London Bridge ⊖	d		08 18			08 48				09 18	
Dartford	d		08 55			09 25				09 55	
Greenhithe for Bluewater	d		09 00			09 30				10 00	
Gravesend	d		09 07			09 37	09 48			10 07	
Strood	d		09 18			09 48	09 58			10 18	
Rochester	d	09 20	09 23	09 46		09 52	10 03		10 20	10 23	10 46
Chatham	d	09 22	09 26	09 48		09 55	10 05		10 22	10 26	10 48
Gillingham (Kent)	d	09 27	09a30	09 53		10a02	10 10		10 27	10a30	10 53
Rainham (Kent)	d	09 31		09 57			10 15		10 31		10 57
Newington	d	09 35							10 35		
Sittingbourne	a	09 40		10 04			10 22		10 40		11 04
Kemsley	d							10 15			
Swale ⊖	d							10 18			
Queenborough	d							10 22			
Sheerness-on-Sea	a							10 27			
Teynham	d	09 45							10 45		
Faversham	a	09 51		10 13	>		10 31		10 51		11 13
	d	09 52		10 17	10 19				10 52		11 17
Selling	d				10 24						
Canterbury East	d	10a04			10 33				11a04		
Bekesbourne	d				10 37						
Adisham	d				10 42						
Aylesham	d				10 44						
Snowdown	d				10 47						
Shepherds Well	d				10 51						
Kearsney	d				10 55						
Dover Priory	a				11 01						
Whitstable	d			10 25							11 25
Chestfield & Swalecliffe	d			10 28							11 28
Herne Bay	d			10 32							11 32
Birchington-on-Sea	d			10 41							11 41
Westgate-on-Sea	d			10 45							11 45
Margate	d			10 49							11 49
Broadstairs	d			10 54							11 54
Dumpton Park	d			10 57							11 57
Ramsgate	a			11 00							12 00

Station		SE ■	SE	SE	SE	SE ■	SE	SE ■ ⌘	SE ■	SE	SE
St Pancras International ⊖	d			10 28							11 25
Stratford International ⊖	d			10 35							11 32
Ebbsfleet International	d			10 46							11 43
London Victoria ⊖	d					10 24		11 05			
London Blackfriars ⊖	d										
Elephant & Castle ⊖	d										
Bromley South	d					10 44		11 22			
St Mary Cray	d					10 50					
Swanley	d					10 54					
Farningham Road	d					10 59					
Longfield	d					11 03					
Meopham	d					11 07					
Sole Street	d					11 10					
London Charing Cross ⊖	d		09 40				10 10			10 40	
London Waterloo (East) ⊖	d		09 43				10 13			10 43	
London Cannon Street ⊖	d										
London Bridge ⊖	d		09 48				10 18			10 48	
Dartford	d		10 25				10 55			11 25	
Greenhithe for Bluewater	d		10 30				11 00			11 30	
Gravesend	d		10 37	10 51			11 07			11 37	11 48
Strood	d		10 48	11 01			11 18			11 48	11 58
Rochester	d		10 52	11 06		11 20	11 23	11 46		11 52	12 03
Chatham	d		10 55	11 08		11 22	11 26	11 48		11 55	12 05
Gillingham (Kent)	d		11a02	11 13		11 27	11a30	11 53		12a02	12 10
Rainham (Kent)	d			11 18		11 31		11 57			12 15
Newington	d					11 35					
Sittingbourne	a			11 25		11 40		12 04			12 22
Kemsley	d				11 15						
Swale ⊖	d				11 18						
Queenborough	d				11 22						
Sheerness-on-Sea	a				11 27						
Teynham	d					11 45					
Faversham	a	>		11 33		11 51		12 13	>		12 31
	d	11 19				11 52		12 17	12 19		
Selling	d	11 24							12 24		
Canterbury East	d	11 33				12a04			12 33		
Bekesbourne	d	11 37							12 37		
Adisham	d	11 42							12 42		
Aylesham	d	11 44							12 44		
Snowdown	d	11 47							12 47		
Shepherds Well	d	11 51							12 51		
Kearsney	d	11 55							12 55		
Dover Priory	a	12 01							13 01		
Whitstable	d							12 25			
Chestfield & Swalecliffe	d							12 28			
Herne Bay	d							12 32			
Birchington-on-Sea	d							12 41			
Westgate-on-Sea	d							12 45			
Margate	d							12 49			
Broadstairs	d							12 54			
Dumpton Park	d							12 57			
Ramsgate	a							13 00			

Table 212

Sundays

London - Medway, Sheerness-on-Sea, Dover and Ramsgate

Station		SE	SE ■	SE	SE ■ ⌘	SE ■	SE	SE	SE	SE ■	SE
St Pancras International ⊖	d							12 25			
Stratford International ⊖	d							12 36			
Ebbsfleet International	d							12 47			
London Victoria ⊖	d		11 24		12 05					12 24	
London Blackfriars ⊖	d										
Elephant & Castle ⊖	d										
Bromley South	d		11 44		12 22					12 44	
St Mary Cray	d		11 50							12 50	
Swanley	d		11 54							12 54	
Farningham Road	d		11 59							12 59	
Longfield	d		12 03							13 03	
Meopham	d		12 07							13 07	
Sole Street	d		12 10							13 10	
London Charing Cross ⊖	d			11 10			11 40				12 10
London Waterloo (East) ⊖	d			11 13			11 43				12 13
London Cannon Street ⊖	d										
London Bridge ⊖	d			11 18			11 48				12 18
Dartford	d			11 55			12 25				12 55
Greenhithe for Bluewater	d			12 00			12 30				13 00
Gravesend	d			12 07			12 37	12 51			13 07
Strood	d			12 18			12 48	13 01			13 18
Rochester	d		12 20	12 23	12 46		12 52	13 06		13 20	13 23
Chatham	d		12 22	12 26	12 48		12 55	13 08		13 22	13 26
Gillingham (Kent)	d		12 27	12a30	12 53		13a02	13 13		13 27	13a30
Rainham (Kent)	d		12 31		12 57			13 18		13 31	
Newington	d		12 35							13 35	
Sittingbourne	a		12 40		13 04			13 25		13 40	
Kemsley	d	12 15							13 15		
Swale ⊖	d	12 18							13 18		
Queenborough	d	12 22							13 22		
Sheerness-on-Sea	a	12 27							13 27		
Teynham	d		12 45							13 45	
Faversham	a		12 51		13 13	>		13 33		13 51	
	d		12 52		13 17	13 19				13 52	
Selling	d					13 24					
Canterbury East	d		13a04			13 33				14a04	
Bekesbourne	d					13 37					
Adisham	d					13 42					
Aylesham	d					13 44					
Snowdown	d					13 47					
Shepherds Well	d					13 51					
Kearsney	d					13 55					
Dover Priory	a					14 01					
Whitstable	d				13 25						
Chestfield & Swalecliffe	d				13 28						
Herne Bay	d				13 32						
Birchington-on-Sea	d				13 41						
Westgate-on-Sea	d				13 45						
Margate	d				13 49						
Broadstairs	d				13 54						
Dumpton Park	d				13 57						
Ramsgate	a				14 00						

Station		SE	SE ■ ⌘	SE ■	SE	SE	SE	SE ■	SE	SE
St Pancras International ⊖	d	12 52				13 25				13 55
Stratford International ⊖	d	12 58				13 32				14 02
Ebbsfleet International	d	13 13				13 43				14 13
London Victoria ⊖	d		13 05					13 24		
London Blackfriars ⊖	d									
Elephant & Castle ⊖	d									
Bromley South	d		13 22					13 44		
St Mary Cray	d							13 50		
Swanley	d							13 54		
Farningham Road	d							13 59		
Longfield	d							14 03		
Meopham	d							14 07		
Sole Street	d							14 10		
London Charing Cross ⊖	d				12 40				13 10	
London Waterloo (East) ⊖	d				12 43				13 13	
London Cannon Street ⊖	d									
London Bridge ⊖	d				12 48				13 18	
Dartford	d				13 25				13 55	
Greenhithe for Bluewater	d				13 30				14 00	
Gravesend	d	13 18			13 37	13 48			14 07	14 18
Strood	d	13 28			13 48	13 58			14 18	14 28
Rochester	d	13 33	13 46		13 52	14 03		14 20	14 23	14 33
Chatham	d	13 35	13 48		13 55	14 05		14 22	14 26	14 35
Gillingham (Kent)	d	13 40	13 53		14a02	14 10		14 27	14a30	14 40
Rainham (Kent)	d	13 45	13 57			14 15		14 31		14 45
Newington	d							14 35		
Sittingbourne	a	13 52	14 04			14 22		14 40		14 52
Kemsley	d						14 15			
Swale ⊖	d						14 18			
Queenborough	d						14 22			
Sheerness-on-Sea	a						14 27			
Teynham	d							14 45		
Faversham	a	14 01	14 13	>		14 31		14 51		15 01
	d		14 17	14 19				14 52		
Selling	d			14 24						
Canterbury East	d			14 33				15a04		
Bekesbourne	d			14 37						
Adisham	d			14 42						
Aylesham	d			14 44						
Snowdown	d			14 47						
Shepherds Well	d			14 51						
Kearsney	d			14 55						
Dover Priory	a			15 01						
Whitstable	d		14 25							
Chestfield & Swalecliffe	d		14 28							
Herne Bay	d		14 32							
Birchington-on-Sea	d		14 41							
Westgate-on-Sea	d		14 45							
Margate	d		14 49							
Broadstairs	d		14 54							
Dumpton Park	d		14 57							
Ramsgate	a		15 00							

Table 212

Sundays

London - Medway, Sheerness-on-Sea, Dover and Ramsgate

		SE ■ ⊼	SE ■	SE	SE	SE	SE ■	SE		SE	SE ■ ⊼	SE ■	SE	SE	SE	SE ■	SE	SE		SE ■ ⊼	SE ■	SE	SE	SE	SE ■
St Pancras International 15 ⊖	d				14 28					14 55				15 25				15 55					16 28		
Stratford International ⊖	d				14 35					15 02				15 32				16 02					16 35		
Ebbsfleet International	d				14 46					15 13				15 43				16 13					16 46		
London Victoria 15 ⊖	d	14 05					14 24				15 05					15 24				16 05					16 24
London Blackfriars 3 ⊖	d																								
Elephant & Castle ⊖	d																								
Bromley South 4	d	14 22					14 44				15 22					15 44				16 22					16 44
St Mary Cray	d						14 50									15 50									16 50
Swanley 4	d						14 54									15 54									16 54
Farningham Road	d						14 59									15 59									16 59
Longfield	d						15 03									16 03									17 03
Meopham	d						15 07									16 07									17 07
Sole Street	d						15 10									16 10									17 10
London Charing Cross 4 ⊖	d			13 40				14 10					14 40				15 10					15 40			
London Waterloo (East) 4 ⊖	d			13 43				14 13					14 43				15 13					15 43			
London Cannon Street 4 ⊖	d																								
London Bridge 4 ⊖	d			13 48				14 18					14 48				15 18					15 48			
Dartford 4	d			14 25				14 55					15 25				15 55					16 25			
Greenhithe for Bluewater	d			14 30				15 00					15 30				16 00					16 30			
Gravesend 4	d			14 37	14 51			15 07		15 18			15 37	15 48			16 07	16 18				16 37	16 51		
Strood 4	d			14 48	15 01			15 18		15 28			15 48	15 58			16 18	16 28				16 48	17 01		
Rochester 4	d	14 46		14 52	15 06		15 20	15 23		15 33	15 46		15 52	16 03		16 20	16 23	16 33		16 46		16 52	17 06		17 20
Chatham 4	d	14 48		14 55	15 08		15 22	15 26		15 35	15 48		15 55	16 05		16 22	16 26	16 35		16 48		16 55	17 08		17 22
Gillingham (Kent) 4	d	14 53		15a02	15 13		15 27	15a30		15 40	15 53		16a02	16 10		16 27	16a30	16 40		16 53		17a02	17 13		17 27
Rainham (Kent)	d	14 57			15 18		15 31			15 45	15 57			16 15		16 31		16 45		16 57			17 18		17 31
Newington	d						15 35									16 35									17 35
Sittingbourne 4	a	15 04			15 25		15 40			15 52	16 04			16 22		16 40		16 52		17 04			17 25		17 40
Kemsley	d					15 15									16 15									17 15	
Swale ⊖	d					15 18									16 18									17 18	
Queenborough	d					15 22									16 22									17 22	
Sheerness-on-Sea	a					15 27									16 27									17 27	
Teynham	d						15 45									16 45									17 45
Faversham 2	a	15 13	>		15 33		15 51			16 01	16 13	>		16 31		16 51		17 01		17 13	>		17 33		17 51
	d	15 17	15 19				15 52				16 17	16 19				16 52				17 17	17 19				17 52
Selling	d		15 24									16 24									17 24				
Canterbury East 4	d		15 33				16a04					16 33				17a04					17 33				18a04
Bekesbourne	d		15 37									16 37									17 37				
Adisham	d		15 42									16 42									17 42				
Aylesham	d		15 44									16 44									17 44				
Snowdown	d		15 47									16 47									17 47				
Shepherds Well	d		15 51									16 51									17 51				
Kearsney	d		15 55									16 55									17 55				
Dover Priory 4	a		16 01									17 01									18 01				
Whitstable	d	15 25									16 25									17 25					
Chestfield & Swalecliffe	d	15 28									16 28									17 28					
Herne Bay	d	15 32									16 32									17 32					
Birchington-on-Sea	d	15 41									16 41									17 41					
Westgate-on-Sea	d	15 45									16 45									17 45					
Margate 4	d	15 49									16 49									17 49					
Broadstairs	d	15 54									16 54									17 54					
Dumpton Park	d	15 57									16 57									17 57					
Ramsgate 4	a	16 00									17 00									18 00					

Table 212

Sundays

London - Medway, Sheerness-on-Sea, Dover and Ramsgate

		SE	SE	SE			SE ■ A ⊼	SE ■	SE	SE	SE	SE ■	SE	SE	SE ■ A ⊼	SE ■	SE	SE	SE ■	SE	SE	SE	SE ■ A ⊼	SE ■	SE
St Pancras International 15 ⊖	d		16 55	17 04						17 25				17 58				18 28			18 55				
Stratford International ⊖	d		17 05	17 11						17 32				18 05				18 35			19 02				
Ebbsfleet International	d		17 16	17 23						17 43				18 16				18 46			19 13				
London Victoria 15 ⊖	d						17 05					17 24			18 05				18 24				19 05		
London Blackfriars 3 ⊖	d																								
Elephant & Castle ⊖	d																								
Bromley South 4	d						17 22					17 44			18 22				18 44				19 22		
St Mary Cray	d											17 50							18 50						
Swanley 4	d											17 54							18 54						
Farningham Road	d											17 59							18 59						
Longfield	d											18 03							19 03						
Meopham	d											18 07							19 07						
Sole Street	d											18 10							19 10						
London Charing Cross 4 ⊖	d	16 10							16 40				17 10				17 40			18 10					18 40
London Waterloo (East) 4 ⊖	d	16 13							16 43				17 13				17 43			18 13					18 43
London Cannon Street 4 ⊖	d																								
London Bridge 4 ⊖	d	16 18							16 48				17 18				17 48			18 18					18 48
Dartford 4	d	16 55							17 25				17 55				18 25			18 55					19 25
Greenhithe for Bluewater	d	17 00							17 30				18 00				18 30			19 00					19 31
Gravesend 4	d	17 07	17 21	17 28					17 37	17 48			18 07	18 21			18 37	18 51		19 07	19 18				19 40
Strood 4	d	17 18	17 31	17 38					17 48	17 58			18 18	18 31			18 48	19 01		19 18	19 28				19 52
Rochester 4	d	17 23	17 35	17 42			17 46		17 52	18 03		18 20	18 23	18 35	18 46		18 52	19 06	19 20	19 23	19 33		19 46		19 56
Chatham 4	d	17 26	17 38	17 45			17 48		17 55	18 05		18 22	18 26	18 38	18 48		18 55	19 08	19 22	19 26	19 35		19 48		19 58
Gillingham (Kent) 4	d	17a30	17 42	17 49			17 53		18a02	18 10		18 27	18a30	18 42	18 53		19a02	19 13	19 27	19a30	19 40		19 53		20a03
Rainham (Kent)	d		17 47	17 54			17 57			18 15		18 31		18 47	18 57			19 18	19 31		19 45		19 57		
Newington	d											18 35							19 35						
Sittingbourne 4	a		17 54	18 01			18 04			18 22		18 40		18 54	19 04			19 25	19 40		19 52		20 04		
Kemsley	d										18 15											19 15			
Swale ⊖	d										18 18											19 18			
Queenborough	d										18 22											19 22			
Sheerness-on-Sea	a										18 27											19 27			
Teynham	d											18 45							19 45						
Faversham 2	a		18 03	18 10			18 13	>		18 31		18 51		19 03	19 13	>		19 33	19 51		20 01		20 13	>	
	d						18 17	18 19				18 52			19 17	19 19							20 17	20 19	
Selling	d							18 24								19 24								20 24	
Canterbury East 4	d							18 33				19a04				19 33								20 33	
Bekesbourne	d							18 37								19 37								20 37	
Adisham	d							18 42								19 42								20 42	
Aylesham	d							18 44								19 44								20 44	
Snowdown	d							18 47								19 47								20 47	
Shepherds Well	d							18 51								19 51								20 51	
Kearsney	d							18 55								19 55								20 55	
Dover Priory 4	a							19 01								20 01								21 01	
Whitstable	d						18 25								19 25								20 25		
Chestfield & Swalecliffe	d						18 28								19 28								20 28		
Herne Bay	d						18 32								19 32								20 32		
Birchington-on-Sea	d						18 41								19 41								20 41		
Westgate-on-Sea	d						18 45								19 45								20 45		
Margate 4	d						18 49								19 49								20 49		
Broadstairs	d						18 54								19 54								20 54		
Dumpton Park	d						18 57								19 57								20 57		
Ramsgate 4	a						19 00								20 00								21 00		

Table 212

Sundays

London - Medway, Sheerness-on-Sea, Dover and Ramsgate

		SE	SE ■	SE	SE	SE	SE ■	SE ■	SE	SE	SE ■	SE	SE	SE	SE ■	SE ■	SE	SE	SE ■	SE	SE	SE
St Pancras International ■ ⊖	d	19 25			19 55					20 25			20 55					21 25			21 55	
Stratford International ⊖	d	19 32			20 02					20 32			21 02					21 32			22 02	
Ebbsfleet International	d	19 43			20 13					20 43			21 13					21 43			22 13	
London Victoria ■ ⊖	d		19 24				20 05				20 24				21 05				21 24			
London Blackfriars ■ ⊖	d																					
Elephant & Castle ⊖	d																					
Bromley South ■	d		19 44				20 22				20 44				21 22				21 44			
St Mary Cray	d		19 50								20 50								21 50			
Swanley ■	d		19 54								20 54								21 54			
Farningham Road	d		19 59								20 59								21 59			
Longfield	d		20 03								21 03								22 03			
Meopham	d		20 07								21 07								22 07			
Sole Street	d		20 10								21 10								22 10			
London Charing Cross ■ ⊖	d			19 10					19 40			20 10					20 40			21 10		
London Waterloo (East) ■ ⊖	d			19 13					19 43			20 13					20 43			21 13		
London Cannon Street ■ ⊖	d																					
London Bridge ■ ⊖	d			19 18					19 48			20 18					20 48			21 18		
Dartford ■	d			19 55					20 25			20 55					21 25			21 55		
Greenhithe for Bluewater	d			20 01					20 31			21 01					21 31			22 01		
Gravesend ■	d	19 48		20 10	20 18				20 40	20 48		21 10	21 18				21 40	21 48		22 10	22 18	
Strood ■	d	19 58		20 22	20 28				20 52	20 58		21 22	21 28				21 52	21 58		22 22	22 28	
Rochester ■	d	20 03	20 20	20 26	20 33		20 46		20 56	21 03	21 20	21 26	21 33		21 46		21 56	22 03	22 20	22 26	22 33	
Chatham ■	d	20 05	20 22	20 28	20 35		20 48		20 58	21 05	21 22	21 28	21 35		21 48		21 58	22 05	22 22	22 28	22 35	
Gillingham (Kent) ■	d	20 10	20 27	20a33	20 40		20 53		21a03	21 10	21 27	21a33	21 40		21 53		22a03	22 10	22 27	22a33	22 40	
Rainham (Kent)	d	20 15	20 31		20 45		20 57			21 15	21 31		21 45		21 57			22 15	22 31		22 45	
Newington	d		20 35								21 35								22 35			
Sittingbourne ■	a	20 22	20 40		20 52		21 04			21 22	21 40		21 52		22 04			22 22	22 40		22 52	
Kemsley	d					20 15								21 15								22 15
Swale ⊖	d					20 18								21 18								22 18
Queenborough	d					20 22								21 22								22 22
Sheerness-on-Sea	a					20 27								21 27								22 27
Teynham	d		20 45								21 45								22 45			
Faversham ■	a	20 31	20 51		21 03		21 13	>		21 33	21 51		22 03		22 13	>		22 33	22 51		23 03	
	d						21 17	21 19							22 17	22 19						
Selling	d							21 24								22 24						
Canterbury East ■	d							21 33								22 33						
Bekesbourne	d							21 37								22 37						
Adisham	d							21 42								22 42						
Aylesham	d							21 44								22 44						
Snowdown	d							21 47								22 47						
Shepherds Well	d							21 51								22 51						
Kearsney	d							21 55								22 55						
Dover Priory ■	a							22 00								23 00						
Whitstable	d						21 25								22 25							
Chestfield & Swalecliffe	d						21 28								22 28							
Herne Bay	d						21 32								22 32							
Birchington-on-Sea	d						21 41								22 41							
Westgate-on-Sea	d						21 45								22 45							
Margate ■	d						21 49								22 49							
Broadstairs	d						21 54								22 54							
Dumpton Park	d						21 57								22 57							
Ramsgate ■	a						22 00								23 00							

Table 212

Sundays

London - Medway, Sheerness-on-Sea, Dover and Ramsgate

		SE ■	SE ■	SE	SE	SE ■	SE	SE	SE	SE ■	SE	SE	SE	SE	SE ■
St Pancras International ■ ⊖	d				22 25			22 55				23 25		23 42	
Stratford International ⊖	d				22 32			23 02				23 32		23 49	
Ebbsfleet International	d				22 43			23 13				23 43		00 01	
London Victoria ■ ⊖	d	22 05				22 24				23 05					23 45
London Blackfriars ■ ⊖	d														
Elephant & Castle ⊖	d														
Bromley South ■	d	22 22				22 44				23 22					00 02
St Mary Cray	d					22 50									00 08
Swanley ■	d					22 54									00 12
Farningham Road	d					22 59									00 17
Longfield	d					23 03									00 21
Meopham	d					23 07									00 25
Sole Street	d					23 10									00 28
London Charing Cross ■ ⊖	d			21 40			22 10				22 40		23 10		
London Waterloo (East) ■ ⊖	d			21 43			22 13				22 43		23 13		
London Cannon Street ■ ⊖	d														
London Bridge ■ ⊖	d			21 48			22 18				22 48		23 18		
Dartford ■	d			22 25			22 55				23 25		23 55		
Greenhithe for Bluewater	d			22 31			23 01				23 31		00 01		
Gravesend ■	d			22 40	22 48		23 10	23 18			23 40	23 48	00 10		
Strood ■	d			22 52	22 58		23 22	23 28			23 52	23 58	00 22		
Rochester ■	d	22 46		22 56	23 03	23 20	23 26	23 33		23 46	23 56	00 03	00 26		00 37
Chatham ■	d	22 48		22 58	23 05	23 22	23 28	23 35		23 48	23 58	00 05	00 28		00 40
Gillingham (Kent) ■	d	22 53		23a03	23 10	23 27	23a33	23 40		23 53	00a03	00 10	00a33		00 44
Rainham (Kent)	d	22 57			23 15	23 31		23 45		23 57		00 15			00 49
Newington	d					23 35									00 53
Sittingbourne ■	a	23 04			23 22	23 40		23 52		00 04		00 22			00 58
Kemsley	d								23 15						
Swale ⊖	d								23 18						
Queenborough	d								23 22						
Sheerness-on-Sea	a								23 27						
Teynham	d					23 45									01 03
Faversham ■	a	23 13	>		23 31	23 51		00 03		00 13		00 33			01 09
	d	23 17	23 19							00 17					
Selling	d		23 24												
Canterbury East ■	d		23 33												
Bekesbourne	d		23 37												
Adisham	d		23 42												
Aylesham	d		23 44												
Snowdown	d		23 47												
Shepherds Well	d		23 51												
Kearsney	d		23 55												
Dover Priory ■	a		00 01												
Whitstable	d	23 25								00 25					
Chestfield & Swalecliffe	d	23 28								00 28					
Herne Bay	d	23 32								00 32					
Birchington-on-Sea	d	23 41								00 41					
Westgate-on-Sea	d	23 45								00 45					
Margate ■	d	23 49								00 49					
Broadstairs	d	23 54								00 54					
Dumpton Park	d	23 57								00 57					
Ramsgate ■	a	00 01								01 00					

Ramsgate, Dover, Sheerness-on-Sea and Medway - London

		SE MO ■	SE MX ■	SE MX ■	SE MO ■	SE MX ■	SE MX	SE	SE	SE	SE	SE	SE	SE ■	SE ■	SE	SE	SE	SE	SE ■	SE ■	SE	SE
Ramsgate ■	d		22p04		22p34	23p04									04 36								
Dumpton Park	d		22p07		22p37	23p07									04 39								
Broadstairs	d		22p10		22p40	23p10									04 42								
Margate ■	d		22p16		22p45	23p16									04 47								
Westgate-on-Sea	d		22p20		22p49	23p20									04 50								
Birchington-on-Sea	d		22p23		22p52	23p23									04 54								
Herne Bay	d		22p32		23p01	23p32									05 03								
Chestfield & Swalecliffe	d		22p36		23p05	23p36									05 06								
Whitstable	d		22p39		23p08	23p39									05 10								
Dover Priory ■	d			22p45																04 42	05 05		
Kearsney	d																			04 46	05 09		
Shepherds Well	d																			04 51	05 14		
Snowdown	d																			04 55	05 18		
Aylesham	d																			04 57	05 20		
Adisham	d																			05 00	05 23		
Bekesbourne	d																			05 04	05 27		
Canterbury East ■	d			23p02																05 09	05 32		
Selling	d																			05 18	05 41		
Faversham ■	a		22p48	23p13	23p17	23p48									05 18					05 23	05 46		
	d	22p34	22p52	23p14	23p21	23p52					04 56				05 19			05 28		05 34			
Teynham	d	22p40	22p58			23p58														05 40			
Sheerness-on-Sea	d						23p53									05 31						05 57	
Queenborough	d						23p57									05 35						06 01	
Swale	d						00 01									05 39						06 05	
Kemsley	d						00 05									05 43						06 09	
Sittingbourne ■	a	22p44	23p02	23p21	23p28	00 02	00 10				05 06				05 26	05 48		05 36		05 44		06 14	
Newington	d	22p50		23p27		00 08														05 50			
Rainham (Kent)	d	22p54	23p10	23p31	23p36	00 12					05 15				05 35			05 45		05 55			
Gillingham (Kent) ■	d	22p59	23p15	23p36	23p41	00a17		04 10	04 35	04 54	05 20		05 24	05 30	05 40		05 45	05 50	05 54	06 02			06 08
Chatham ■	d	23p04	23p20	23p41	23p46			04 14	04 39	04 58	05 24		05 28	05 34	05 44		05 49	05 54	05 58	06 06			06 12
Rochester ■	d	23p06	23p22	23p43	23p48			04 16	04 41	05 00	05 27		05 30	05 36	05 47		05 51	05 57	06 00	06 09			06 14
Strood ■	a							04 21	04 46	05 05	05 31		05 35					06 01	06 05				06 19
Gravesend ■	a							04 33	04 58	05 17	05 42		05 47					06 12	06 17				06 31
Greenhithe for Bluewater	a							04 39	05 07	05 23			05 53						06 23				06 37
Dartford ■	a							04 44	05 13	05 28			05 58						06 28				06 42
London Bridge ■ ⊖	a							05 22	05 52	06 04			06 34				06 27		07 03				07 17
London Cannon Street ■ ⊖	a																06 32						07 23
London Waterloo (East) ■ ⊖	a							05 26	05 57	06 08			06 39						07 09				
London Charing Cross ■ ⊖	a							05 30	06 01	06 12			06 43						07 14				
Sole Street	d	23p17		23p54										05 47						06 19			
Meopham	d	23p19	23p33	23p56										05 49						06 22			
Longfield	d	23p23	23p37	23p59										05 53						06 26			
Farningham Road	d	23p27		00 04										05 57						06 29			
Swanley ■	a	23p32		00 09										06 02						06 34			
St Mary Cray	a	23p36		00 14										06 06						06 39			
Bromley South ■	a	23p42	23p50	00 20	00 13									06 14	06 12					06 45			
Elephant & Castle ⊖	a																						
London Blackfriars ■ ⊖	a																						
London Victoria ■ ⊖	a	00 02	00 07	00 38	00 29									06 31	06 29					07 07			
Ebbsfleet International	a										05 47	05 32						06 17					
Stratford International ⊖	a										05 59	05 44						06 29					
St Pancras International ■ ⊖	a										06 06	05 51						06 36					

Table 212 Mondays to Fridays

Ramsgate, Dover, Sheerness-on-Sea and Medway - London

		SE ■	SE	SE ■	SE ■	SE ■	SE	SE	SE	SE	SE ■	SE	SE ■	SE ■	SE ■	SE ■	SE	SE ■	SE ■	SE ■	SE	SE ■	SE
Ramsgate ■	d	05 06				05 40								06 09				06 32					
Dumpton Park	d	05 09				05 43								06 12				06 35					
Broadstairs	d	05 12				05 46	06 00							06 15	06 20		06 30	06 38		06 48	07 00		
Margate ■	d	05 17				05 51	06 05							06 20	06 25		06 35	06 43		06 53	07 05		
Westgate-on-Sea	d	05 20				05 54								06 23	06 28			06 46		06 56			
Birchington-on-Sea	d	05 24				05 58	06 10							06 27	06 32		06 40	06 50		07 00	07 10		
Herne Bay	d	05 33				06 07	06 19							06 36	06 41		06 49	06 59		07 09	07 19		
Chestfield & Swalecliffe	d	05 36				06 10								06 39	06 44			07 02		07 12			
Whitstable	d	05 40				06 14	06 25							06 43	06 48		06 55	07 06		07 16	07 25		
Dover Priory ■	d												05 49			06 19			06 39				
Kearsney	d												05 53			06 23			06 43				
Shepherds Well	d												05 58			06 28			06 48				
Snowdown	d												06 02			06 32			06 52				
Aylesham	d												06 04			06 34			06 54				
Adisham	d												06 07			06 37			06 57				
Bekesbourne	d												06 11			06 41			07 01				
Canterbury East ■	d												06 16			06 46			07 06				
Selling	d												06 25			06 55			07 15				
Faversham ■	a	05 48				06 22	06 33						06 30	06 51	06 56	07 00	07 03	07 14	07 20	07 24	07 33		
	d	05 49	05 58		06 08	06 23	06 34						06 38	06 52	06 57		07 04	07 16		07 25	07 34		
Teynham	d	05 55			06 14								06 44					07 22					
Sheerness-on-Sea	d							06 29		06 46													
Queenborough	d							06 35		06 50													
Swale	d							06 39		06 54													
Kemsley	d							06 42		06 58													
Sittingbourne ■	a	05 59	06 06		06 18	06 30	06 42	06 47		07 05			06 48	07 00	07 05		07 11	07 26		07 32	07 41		
Newington	d	06 05			06 24								06 54					07 32					
Rainham (Kent)	d	06 10	06 14		06 29	06 39	06 51						06 59	07 09	07 14		07 20	07 37		07 41	07 50		
Gillingham (Kent) ■	d	06 15	06 19	06 24	06 34	06 44	06 56		06 38		06 50		07 04	07 15	07 19		07 25	07 42		07 46	07 55	07 08	07 12
Chatham ■	d	06 19	06 24	06 28	06 38	06 48	07 01		06 42		06 54		07 08	07 20	07 24		07 30	07 46		07 50	08 00	07 12	07 16
Rochester ■	d	06 21	06 26	06 31	06 41				06 44		06 57	07 07	07 11									07 15	07 18
Strood ■	a		06 31						06 49			07 11											07 23
Gravesend ■	a		06 42						07 01			07 22											07 37
Greenhithe for Bluewater	a								07 07														07 46
Dartford ■	a								07 12														07 52
London Bridge ■ ⊖	a				07 20				07 47				07 51		08 09					08 31			08 25
London Cannon Street ■ ⊖	a				07 27								07 57		08 17					08 38			
London Waterloo (East) ■ ⊖	a								07 52														08 30
London Charing Cross ■ ⊖	a								07 58														08 36
Sole Street	d			06 41							07 07											07 25	
Meopham	d			06 44							07 10											07 28	
Longfield	d			06 48							07 14			07 35									
Farningham Road	d			06 51							07 17											07 33	
Swanley ■	a			06 56							07 22											07 38	
St Mary Cray	a			07 01							07 27											07 44	
Bromley South ■	a	06 49		07 07		07 15					07 33			07 49				08 15				07 52	
Elephant & Castle ⊖	a																						
London Blackfriars ■ ⊖	a																						
London Victoria ■ ⊖	a	07 09		07 30		07 38					07 57			08 09				08 39				08 17	
Ebbsfleet International	a		06 47				07 17										07 47				08 17		
Stratford International ⊖	a		06 59				07 29					07 36					07 59				08 29		
St Pancras International ■ ⊖	a		07 07				07 36					07 43					08 06				08 36		

Ramsgate, Dover, Sheerness-on-Sea and Medway - London

		SE	SE	SE	SE ■1	SE	SE ■1	SE	SE	SE ■1	SE ■1	SE	SE ■1 ⊼	SE	SE ■1	SE ■1	SE	SE ■1	SE ■1	SE	SE ■1 A ⊼	SE ■1 ⊼	SE
Ramsgate ■4	d									06 59			07 06		07 19	07 36						08 06	
Dumpton Park	d									07 02			07 09		07 22	07 39						08 09	
Broadstairs	d									07 05			07 12		07 25	07 42						08 12	
Margate ■4	d									07 10			07 17		07 30	07 47						08 17	
Westgate-on-Sea	d									07 14			07 20		07 34	07 50						08 20	
Birchington-on-Sea	d									07 17			07 24		07 37	07 54						08 24	
Herne Bay	d									07 26			07 33		07 46	08 03						08 33	
Chestfield & Swalecliffe	d									07 30			07 36		07 50	08 06						08 36	
Whitstable	d									07 33			07 40		07 53	08 10						08 40	
Dover Priory ■4	d										07 04								07 35		08 05		
Kearsney	d										07 08								07 39		08 09		
Shepherds Well	d										07 13								07 44		08 14		
Snowdown	d										07 17								07 48		08 18		
Aylesham	d										07 19								07 50		08 20		
Adisham	d										07 22								07 53		08 23		
Bekesbourne	d										07 26								07 57		08 27		
Canterbury East ■4	d										07 31								08 02		08 32		
Selling	d										07 40								08 11		08 41		
Faversham ■2	a									07 41	07 45		07 48		08 01	08 18			08 16		08 46	08 48	
	d									07 43			07 49	07 58	08 02				08 22	08 28	08 52	<	
Teynham	d												07 55								08 58		
Sheerness-on-Sea	d	07 16	07 35					08 07									08 32						
Queenborough	d	07 22	07 39					08 11									08 36						
Swale	d	07 26	07 43					08 15									08 40						
Kemsley	d	07 29	07 47					08 19									08 44						
Sittingbourne ■4	a	07 34	07 52					08 25		07 50			07 59	08 05	08 12		08 49		08 29	08 36	09 02		
Newington	d												08 05						08 35				
Rainham (Kent)	d									07 59			08 10	08 14	08 21				08 40	08 45	09 10		
Gillingham (Kent) ■4	d				07 33	07 38	07 50			08 04		08 08	08 15	08 19	08 26			08 32	08 45	08 50	09 15		08 54
Chatham ■4	d				07 37	07 42	07 54			08 08		08 12	08 19	08 24	08 30			08 36	08 50	08 54	09 20		08 58
Rochester ■4	d			07 37	07 40	07 44	07 56		08 07	08 11		08 14	08 22	08 26	08 32			08 39	08 52	08 57	09 22		09 00
Strood ■4	a			07 41		07 49			08 11			08 19		08 31						09 01			09 05
Gravesend ■4	a			07 52		08 01			08 22			08 31		08 42						09 12			09 18
Greenhithe for Bluewater	a					08 07						08 42											09 23
Dartford ■4	a					08 12						08 49											09 27
London Bridge ■4 ⊖	a					08 45				08 49		09 23			09 11								10 05
London Cannon Street ■6 ⊖	a									08 57					09 18								
London Waterloo (East) ■4 ⊖	a					08 50						09 28											10 09
London Charing Cross ■4 ⊖	a					08 56						09 34											10 13
Sole Street	d						08 07											08 49					
Meopham	d				07 51		08 09						08 33					08 52	09 03		09 33		
Longfield	d				07 55		08 13						08 37					08 56	09 07		09 37		
Farningham Road	d						08 17											08 59					
Swanley ■4	a				08 01		08 22											09 04					
St Mary Cray	a				08 06		08 26											09 09					
Bromley South ■4	a				08 12		08 33						08 50					09 15	09 20		09 50		
Elephant & Castle ⊖	a																						
London Blackfriars ■3 ⊖	a																						
London Victoria ■15 ⊖	a				08 42		08 53						09 09					09 38	09 43		10 07		
Ebbsfleet International	a													08 47						09 17			
Stratford International ⊖	a			08 06					08 36					08 59						09 29			
St Pancras International ■15 ⊖	a			08 13					08 43					09 07						09 39			

Ramsgate, Dover, Sheerness-on-Sea and Medway - London

		SE	SE ■1 A ⊼	SE ■1 ⊼	SE	SE	SE	SE ■1	SE	SE ■1 A ⊼	SE ■1 ⊼	SE	SE	SE ■1 A ⊼	SE ■1 ⊼	SE	SE	SE	SE ■1	SE	SE ■1 A ⊼	SE ■1 ⊼	SE
Ramsgate ■4	d			08 40							09 04				09 40							10 04	
Dumpton Park	d										09 07											10 07	
Broadstairs	d			08 45							09 10				09 45							10 10	
Margate ■4	d			08 50							09 16				09 50							10 16	
Westgate-on-Sea	d										09 20											10 20	
Birchington-on-Sea	d			08 55							09 23				09 55							10 23	
Herne Bay	d			09 04							09 32				10 04							10 32	
Chestfield & Swalecliffe	d										09 36											10 36	
Whitstable	d			09 09							09 39				10 09							10 39	
Dover Priory ■4	d		08 45							09 05				09 45							10 05		
Kearsney	d									09 09											10 09		
Shepherds Well	d									09 14											10 14		
Snowdown	d									09 18											10 18		
Aylesham	d									09 20											10 20		
Adisham	d									09 23											10 23		
Bekesbourne	d									09 27											10 27		
Canterbury East ■4	d		09 02							09 32				10 02							10 32		
Selling	d									09 41											10 41		
Faversham ■2	a		09 14	09 18						09 46	09 48			10 14	10 18						10 46	10 48	
	d	08 58	09 22	<					09 28	09 52	<		09 58	10 22	<					10 28	10 52	<	
Teynham	d									09 58											10 58		
Sheerness-on-Sea	d				09 02		09 32									10 02		10 32					
Queenborough	d				09 06		09 36									10 06		10 36					
Swale	d				09 10		09 40									10 10		10 40					
Kemsley	d				09 14		09 44									10 14		10 44					
Sittingbourne ■4	a	09 06	09 29		09 19		09 49		09 36	10 02			10 06	10 29		10 19		10 49		10 36	11 02		
Newington	d		09 35											10 35									
Rainham (Kent)	d	09 15	09 40						09 45	10 10			10 15	10 40						10 45	11 10		
Gillingham (Kent) ■4	d	09 20	09 45			09 24		09 32	09 50	10 15		09 54	10 20	10 45			10 24		10 32	10 50	11 15		10 54
Chatham ■4	d	09 24	09 50			09 28		09 36	09 54	10 20		09 58	10 24	10 50			10 28		10 36	10 54	11 20		10 58
Rochester ■4	d	09 27	09 52			09 30		09 39	09 57	10 22		10 00	10 27	10 52			10 30		10 39	10 57	11 22		11 00
Strood ■4	a	09 31				09 35			10 01			10 05	10 31				10 35			11 01			11 05
Gravesend ■4	a	09 42				09 47			10 12			10 17	10 42				10 47			11 12			11 17
Greenhithe for Bluewater	a					09 53						10 23					10 53						11 23
Dartford ■4	a					09 58						10 28					10 58						11 28
London Bridge ■4 ⊖	a					10 35						11 05					11 35						12 05
London Cannon Street ■4 ⊖	a																						
London Waterloo (East) ■4 ⊖	a					10 39						11 09					11 39						12 09
London Charing Cross ■4 ⊖	a					10 43						11 13					11 43						12 13
Sole Street	d							09 49											10 49				
Meopham	d		10 03					09 52		10 33				11 03					10 52		11 33		
Longfield	d		10 07					09 56		10 37				11 07					10 56		11 37		
Farningham Road	d							09 59											10 59				
Swanley ■4	a							10 04											11 04				
St Mary Cray	a							10 09											11 09				
Bromley South ■4	a		10 20					10 15		10 50				11 20					11 15		11 50		
Elephant & Castle ⊖	a																						
London Blackfriars ■3 ⊖	a																						
London Victoria ■15 ⊖	a		10 37					10 41		11 07				11 37					11 37		12 07		
Ebbsfleet International	a	09 47							10 16				10 47							11 17			
Stratford International ⊖	a	09 59							10 27				10 59							11 29			
St Pancras International ■15 ⊖	a	10 06							10 38				11 06							11 36			

A ⊼ from Faversham

Table 212

Mondays to Fridays

Ramsgate, Dover, Sheerness-on-Sea and Medway - London

	SE	SE [1] A ⊼	SE [1] ⊼	SE	SE	SE	SE [1]	SE	SE [1] A ⊼	SE [1] ⊼	SE	SE	SE [1] A ⊼	SE [1] ⊼	SE	SE	SE	SE [1]	SE	SE [1] A ⊼	SE [1] ⊼
Ramsgate [4] d			10 40							11 04				11 40							12 04
Dumpton Park d										11 07											12 07
Broadstairs d			10 45							11 10				11 45							12 10
Margate [4] d			10 50							11 16				11 50							12 16
Westgate-on-Sea d										11 20											12 20
Birchington-on-Sea d			10 55							11 23				11 55							12 23
Herne Bay d			11 04							11 32				12 04							12 32
Chestfield & Swalecliffe d										11 36											12 36
Whitstable d			11 09							11 39				12 09							12 39
Dover Priory [4] d		10 45							11 05				11 45							12 05	
Kearsney d									11 09											12 09	
Shepherds Well d									11 14											12 14	
Snowdown d									11 18											12 18	
Aylesham d									11 20											12 20	
Adisham d									11 23											12 23	
Bekesbourne d									11 27											12 27	
Canterbury East [4] d		11 02							11 32				12 02							12 32	
Selling d									11 41											12 41	
Faversham [2] a		11 14	11 18						11 46	11 48			12 14	12 18						12 46	12 48
d	10 58	11 22	<					11 28	11 52	<		11 58	12 22	<					12 28	12 52	<
Teynham d									11 58											12 58	
Sheerness-on-Sea d				11 02		11 32									12 02		12 32				
Queenborough d				11 06		11 36									12 06		12 36				
Swale d				11 10		11 40									12 10		12 40				
Kemsley d				11 14		11 44									12 14		12 44				
Sittingbourne [4] a	11 06	11 29		11 19		11 49		11 36	12 02			12 06	12 29		12 19		12 49		12 36	13 02	
Newington d		11 35											12 35								
Rainham (Kent) d	11 15	11 40						11 45	12 10			12 15	12 40						12 45	13 10	
Gillingham (Kent) [4] d	11 20	11 45			11 24		11 32	11 50	12 15		11 54	12 20	12 45			12 24		12 32	12 50	13 15	
Chatham [4] d	11 24	11 50			11 28		11 36	11 54	12 20		11 58	12 24	12 50			12 28		12 36	12 54	13 20	
Rochester [4] d	11 27	11 52			11 30		11 39	11 57	12 22		12 00	12 27	12 52			12 30		12 39	12 57	13 22	
Strood [4] a	11 31				11 35			12 01			12 05	12 31				12 35			13 01		
Gravesend [4] a	11 42				11 47			12 12			12 17	12 42				12 47			13 12		
Greenhithe for Bluewater a					11 53						12 23					12 53					
Dartford [4] a					11 58						12 28					12 58					
London Bridge [4] ⊖ a					12 35						13 05					13 35					
London Cannon Street [4] ⊖ a																					
London Waterloo (East) [4] ⊖ a					12 39						13 09					13 39					
London Charing Cross [4] ⊖ a					12 43						13 13					13 43					
Sole Street d							11 49											12 49			
Meopham d		12 03					11 52		12 33				13 03					12 52		13 33	
Longfield d		12 07					11 56		12 37				13 07					12 56		13 37	
Farningham Road d							11 59											12 59			
Swanley [4] a							12 04											13 04			
St Mary Cray a							12 09											13 09			
Bromley South [4] a		12 20					12 15		12 50				13 20					13 15		13 50	
Elephant & Castle ⊖ a																					
London Blackfriars [3] ⊖ a																					
London Victoria [15] ⊖ a		12 37					12 37		13 07				13 37					13 37		14 07	
Ebbsfleet International a	11 47							12 17				12 47							13 17		
Stratford International ⊖ a	11 59							12 32				12 59							13 29		
St Pancras International [15] ⊖ a	12 06							12 39				13 06							13 36		

A ⊼ from Faversham

Table 212

Mondays to Fridays

Ramsgate, Dover, Sheerness-on-Sea and Medway - London

	SE	SE	SE [1] A ⊼	SE [1] ⊼	SE	SE	SE	SE [1]	SE	SE [1] A ⊼	SE [1] ⊼	SE	SE	SE [1] A ⊼	SE [1] ⊼	SE	SE	SE	SE [1]	SE	SE [1] A ⊼	SE [1] ⊼
Ramsgate [4] d				12 40							13 04				13 40							14 04
Dumpton Park d											13 07											14 07
Broadstairs d				12 45							13 10				13 45							14 10
Margate [4] d				12 50							13 16				13 50							14 16
Westgate-on-Sea d											13 20											14 20
Birchington-on-Sea d				12 55							13 23				13 55							14 23
Herne Bay d				13 04							13 32				14 04							14 32
Chestfield & Swalecliffe d											13 36											14 36
Whitstable d				13 09							13 39				14 09							14 39
Dover Priory [4] d			12 45							13 05				13 45							14 05	
Kearsney d										13 09											14 09	
Shepherds Well d										13 14											14 14	
Snowdown d										13 18											14 18	
Aylesham d										13 20											14 20	
Adisham d										13 23											14 23	
Bekesbourne d										13 27											14 27	
Canterbury East [4] d			13 02							13 32				14 02							14 32	
Selling d										13 41											14 41	
Faversham [2] a			13 14	13 18						13 46	13 48			14 14	14 18						14 46	14 48
d		12 58	13 22	<					13 28	13 52	<		13 58	14 22	<					14 28	14 52	<
Teynham d										13 58											14 58	
Sheerness-on-Sea d					13 02		13 32									14 02		14 32				
Queenborough d					13 06		13 36									14 06		14 36				
Swale d					13 10		13 40									14 10		14 40				
Kemsley d					13 14		13 44									14 14		14 44				
Sittingbourne [4] a		13 06	13 29		13 19		13 49		13 36	14 02			14 06	14 29		14 19		14 49		14 36	15 02	
Newington d			13 35											14 35								
Rainham (Kent) d		13 15	13 40						13 45	14 10			14 15	14 40						14 45	15 10	
Gillingham (Kent) [4] d	12 54	13 20	13 45			13 24		13 32	13 50	14 15		13 54	14 20	14 45			14 24		14 32	14 50	15 15	
Chatham [4] d	12 58	13 24	13 50			13 28		13 36	13 54	14 20		13 58	14 24	14 50			14 28		14 36	14 54	15 20	
Rochester [4] d	13 00	13 27	13 52			13 30		13 39	13 57	14 22		14 00	14 27	14 52			14 30		14 39	14 57	15 22	
Strood [4] a	13 05	13 31				13 35			14 01			14 05	14 31				14 35			15 01		
Gravesend [4] a	13 17	13 42				13 47			14 12			14 17	14 42				14 47			15 12		
Greenhithe for Bluewater a	13 23					13 53						14 23					14 53					
Dartford [4] a	13 28					13 58						14 28					14 58					
London Bridge [4] ⊖ a	14 05					14 35						15 05					15 35					
London Cannon Street [4] ⊖ a																						
London Waterloo (East) [4] ⊖ a	14 09					14 39						15 09					15 39					
London Charing Cross [4] ⊖ a	14 13					14 43						15 13					15 43					
Sole Street d								13 49											14 49			
Meopham d			14 03					13 52		14 33				15 03					14 52		15 33	
Longfield d			14 07					13 56		14 37				15 07					14 56		15 37	
Farningham Road d								13 59											14 59			
Swanley [4] a								14 04											15 04			
St Mary Cray a								14 09											15 09			
Bromley South [4] a			14 20					14 15		14 50				15 20					15 15		15 50	
Elephant & Castle ⊖ a																						
London Blackfriars [3] ⊖ a																						
London Victoria [15] ⊖ a			14 37					14 37		15 07				15 37					15 37		16 07	
Ebbsfleet International a		13 47							14 17				14 47							15 17		
Stratford International ⊖ a		13 59							14 32				14 59							15 29		
St Pancras International [15] ⊖ a		14 06							14 39				15 06							15 36		

A ⊼ from Faversham

Table 212

Ramsgate, Dover, Sheerness-on-Sea and Medway - London

		SE	SE	SE 1 A 🍴	SE 1 🍴	SE		SE	SE	SE	SE	SE 1 A 🍴	SE 1 🍴	SE	SE		SE 1 A 🍴	SE 1 🍴	SE	SE	SE	SE 1	SE	SE 1	SE 1
Ramsgate [4]	d				14 40								15 04					15 34							16 04
Dumpton Park	d												15 07					15 37							16 07
Broadstairs	d				14 45								15 10					15 40							16 10
Margate [4]	d				14 50								15 16					15 47							16 16
Westgate-on-Sea	d												15 20					15 50							16 20
Birchington-on-Sea	d				14 55								15 23					15 54							16 23
Herne Bay	d				15 04								15 32					16 03							16 32
Chestfield & Swalecliffe	d												15 36					16 07							16 36
Whitstable	d				15 09								15 39					16 10							16 39
Dover Priory [4]	d			14 45								15 05					15 39							16 05	
Kearsney	d											15 09					15 43							16 09	
Shepherds Well	d											15 14					15 48							16 14	
Snowdown	d											15 18												16 18	
Aylesham	d											15 20					15 52							16 20	
Adisham	d											15 23					15 55							16 23	
Bekesbourne	d											15 27												16 27	
Canterbury East [4]	d			15 02								15 32					16 02							16 32	
Selling	d											15 41					16 11							16 41	
Faversham [2]	a			15 14	15 18							15 46	15 48				16 16	16 18						16 46	16 48
	d		14 58	15 22	<						15 28	15 52	<		15 58		16 22	<					16 28	16 52	<
Teynham	d											15 58												16 58	
Sheerness-on-Sea	d					15 02			15 32										16 02		16 32				
Queenborough	d					15 06			15 36										16 06		16 36				
Swale	d					15 10			15 40										16 10		16 40				
Kemsley	d					15 14			15 44										16 14		16 44				
Sittingbourne [4]	a		15 06	15 29		15 19			15 55		15 36	16 02			16 06		16 29		16 19		16 49		16 36	17 02	
Newington	d			15 35													16 35								
Rainham (Kent)	d		15 15	15 40							15 45	16 10			16 15		16 40						16 45	17 10	
Gillingham (Kent) [4]	d	14 54	15 20	15 45				15 24		15 32	15 50	16 15		15 54	16 20		16 45			16 24		16 32	16 50	17 15	
Chatham [4]	d	14 58	15 24	15 50				15 28		15 36	15 54	16 20		15 58	16 24		16 50			16 28		16 36	16 54	17 20	
Rochester [4]	d	15 00	15 27	15 52				15 30		15 39	15 57	16 22		16 00	16 27		16 52			16 30		16 39	16 57	17 22	
Strood [4]	a	15 05	15 31					15 35			16 01			16 05	16 31					16 35			17 01		
Gravesend [4]	a	15 17	15 42					15 47			16 12			16 17	16 42					16 47			17 12		
Greenhithe for Bluewater	a	15 23						15 53						16 23						16 53					
Dartford [4]	a	15 28						15 58						16 28						16 58					
London Bridge [4] ⊖	a	16 05						16 35						17 07						17 35					
London Cannon Street [4] ⊖	a													17 11											
London Waterloo (East) [4] ⊖	a	16 09						16 39												17 40					
London Charing Cross [4] ⊖	a	16 13						16 44												17 44					
Sole Street	d									15 49												16 49			
Meopham	d			16 03						15 52		16 33					17 03					16 52		17 33	
Longfield	d			16 07						15 56		16 37					17 07					16 56		17 37	
Farningham Road	d									15 59												16 59			
Swanley [4]	a									16 04												17 04			
St Mary Cray	a									16 09												17 09			
Bromley South [4]	a			16 20						16 15		16 50					17 20					17 15		17 50	
Elephant & Castle ⊖	a																								
London Blackfriars [3] ⊖	a																								
London Victoria [15] ⊖	a			16 38						16 37		17 07					17 37					17 38		18 07	
Ebbsfleet International	a		15 47								16 17				16 47								17 16		
Stratford International ⊖	a		15 59								16 29				17 02								17 27		
St Pancras International [15] ⊖	a		16 06								16 40				17 09								17 38		

A 🍴 from Faversham

Table 212

Ramsgate, Dover, Sheerness-on-Sea and Medway - London

		SE		SE	SE 1	SE	SE	SE 1 A 🍴	SE 1 🍴	SE	SE	SE 1			SE	SE 1 A 🍴	SE 1 🍴	SE	SE	SE	SE	SE 1	SE 1	SE	SE 1
Ramsgate [4]	d								16 34								17 04						17 34	18 29	
Dumpton Park	d								16 37								17 07						17 37		
Broadstairs	d								16 40								17 10						17 40	18 35	
Margate [4]	d								16 47								17 16						17 46	18a40	
Westgate-on-Sea	d								16 50								17 20						17 50		
Birchington-on-Sea	d								16 54								17 23						17 53		
Herne Bay	d								17 03								17 32						18 02		
Chestfield & Swalecliffe	d								17 07								17 36						18 06		
Whitstable	d								17 10								17 39						18 09		
Dover Priory [4]	d							16 39								17 05						17 39			
Kearsney	d							16 43								17 09						17 43			
Shepherds Well	d							16 48								17 14						17 48			
Snowdown	d															17 18									
Aylesham	d							16 52								17 20						17 52			
Adisham	d							16 55								17 23						17 55			
Bekesbourne	d															17 27									
Canterbury East [4]	d							17 02								17 32						18 02			
Selling	d							17 11								17 41						18 11			
Faversham [2]	a							17 16	17 18							17 46	17 48					18 16	18 17		
	d					16 58	16 58	17 22	<						17 28	17 52	<				17 58	18 22	<		
Teynham	d															17 58									
Sheerness-on-Sea	d			17 02							17 32								18 02						
Queenborough	d			17 06							17 36								18 06						
Swale	d			17 10							17 40								18 10						
Kemsley	d			17 14							17 44								18 14						
Sittingbourne [4]	a			17 19		17 06	17 06	17 29			17 51				17 36	18 02			18 19		18 06	18 29			
Newington	d							17 35														18 35			
Rainham (Kent)	d					17 15	17 15	17 40							17 45	18 10					18 15	18 40			
Gillingham (Kent) [4]	d	16 54			17 02	17 20	17 20	17 45		17 24		17 32			17 50	18 15		17 54		18 09	18 20	18 45			18 32
Chatham [4]	d	16 58			17 06	17 24	17 24	17 50		17 28		17 36			17 54	18 20		17 58		18 13	18 24	18 50			18 36
Rochester [4]	d	17 00			17 09	17 27	17 27	17 52		17 30		17 39			17 57	18 22		18 00		18 15	18 27	18 52			18 39
Strood [4]	a	17 05				17 31	17 31			17 35					18 02			18 05		18 20	18 31				
Gravesend [4]	a	17 17				17 42	17 42			17 47					18 13			18 17		18 32	18 42				
Greenhithe for Bluewater	a	17 23								17 53								18 24		18 42					
Dartford [4]	a	17 28								17 58								18 28		18 48					
London Bridge [4] ⊖	a	18 04								18 35								19 05		19 22					
London Cannon Street [4] ⊖	a																								
London Waterloo (East) [4] ⊖	a	18 08								18 41								19 09		19 26					
London Charing Cross [4] ⊖	a	18 12								18 45								19 13		19 30					
Sole Street	d				17 19							17 49													18 49
Meopham	d				17 22			18 03				17 52				18 33						19 03			18 52
Longfield	d				17 26			18 07				17 56				18 37						19 07			18 56
Farningham Road	d				17 29							17 59													18 59
Swanley [4]	a				17 34							18 04													19 04
St Mary Cray	a				17 39							18 09													19 09
Bromley South [4]	a				17 45			18 20				18 15				18 50						19 20			19 15
Elephant & Castle ⊖	a																								
London Blackfriars [3] ⊖	a																								
London Victoria [15] ⊖	a				18 08			18 37				18 37				19 07						19 37			19 37
Ebbsfleet International	a					17 46	17 46								18 17						18 47				
Stratford International ⊖	a					17 57	18 02								18 28						19 02				
St Pancras International [15] ⊖	a					18 08	18 09								18 35						19 09				

A 🍴 from Faversham

Table 212

Ramsgate, Dover, Sheerness-on-Sea and Medway - London

		SE	SE [1]	SE [1]	SE	SE	SE	SE	SE [1]	SE [1]	SE	SE	SE	SE	SE	SE [1]	SE [1]	SE	SE	SE	SE	SE [1]	SE [1]
Ramsgate [4]	d			18 04			18 59			18 34			19 31				19 04			19 59			19 24
Dumpton Park	d			18 07						18 37							19 07						19 27
Broadstairs	d			18 10			19 05			18 40			19 36				19 10			20 05			19 30
Margate [4]	d			18 16			19a10			18 47			19a41				19 16			20a10			19 35
Westgate-on-Sea	d			18 20						18 50							19 20						19 38
Birchington-on-Sea	d			18 23						18 54							19 23						19 42
Herne Bay	d			18 32						19 03							19 32						19 51
Chestfield & Swalecliffe	d			18 36						19 07							19 36						19 55
Whitstable	d			18 39						19 10							19 39						19 58
Dover Priory [4]	d		18 05						18 39							19 05						19 40	
Kearsney	d		18 09						18 43							19 09							
Shepherds Well	d		18 14						18 48							19 14							
Snowdown	d		18 18													19 18							
Aylesham	d		18 20						18 52							19 20							
Adisham	d		18 23						18 55							19 23							
Bekesbourne	d		18 27													19 27							
Canterbury East [4]	d		18 32						19 02							19 32						19 57	
Selling	d		18 41						19 11							19 41							
Faversham [2]	a		18 46	18 48					19 16	19 18						19 46	19 48					20 08	20 10
	d	18 28	18 52	<				18 58	19 22	<					19 28	19 52	<				19 58	20 14	<
Teynham	d		18 58													19 58							
Sheerness-on-Sea	d				18 42						19 19							19 46					
Queenborough	d				18 46						19 23							19 52					
Swale	d				18 50						19 27							19 56					
Kemsley	d				18 54						19 31							20 00					
Sittingbourne [4]	a	18 36	19 02		19 00			19 06	19 29		19 35				19 36	20 02		20 05			20 06	20 21	
Newington	d								19 35													20 27	
Rainham (Kent)	d	18 45	19 10					19 15	19 40						19 45	20 10					20 15	20 31	
Gillingham (Kent) [4]	d	18 50	19 15			18 54		19 20	19 45			19 24		19 32	19 50	20 15			19 54		20 20	20 36	
Chatham [4]	d	18 54	19 20			18 58		19 24	19 50			19 28		19 36	19 54	20 20			19 58		20 24	20 41	
Rochester [4]	d	18 57	19 22			19 00		19 27	19 52			19 30		19 39	19 57	20 22			20 00		20 27	20 43	
Strood [4]	a	19 01				19 05		19 31				19 35			20 01				20 05		20 31		
Gravesend [4]	a	19 12				19 17		19 42				19 47			20 12				20 17		20 42		
Greenhithe for Bluewater	a					19 23						19 53							20 23				
Dartford [4]	a					19 27						19 58							20 28				
London Bridge [4] ⊖	a					20 06						20 36							21 06				
London Cannon Street [4] ⊖	a																						
London Waterloo (East) [4] ⊖	a					20 11						20 40							21 10				
London Charing Cross [4] ⊖	a					20 14						20 44							21 14				
Sole Street	d													19 49								20 54	
Meopham	d		19 33						20 03					19 52		20 33						20 56	
Longfield	d		19 37						20 07					19 56		20 37						21 00	
Farningham Road	d													19 59								21 04	
Swanley [4]	a													20 04								21 09	
St Mary Cray	a													20 09								21 14	
Bromley South [4]	a		19 50						20 20					20 15		20 50						21 20	
Elephant & Castle ⊖	a																						
London Blackfriars [3] ⊖	a																						
London Victoria [15] ⊖	a		20 07						20 38					20 37		21 07						21 37	
Ebbsfleet International	a	19 16						19 47							20 16						20 47		
Stratford International ⊖	a	19 27						19 59							20 27						20 59		
St Pancras International [15] ⊖	a	19 38						20 06							20 38						21 06		

Table 212

Ramsgate, Dover, Sheerness-on-Sea and Medway - London

		SE	SE	SE	SE [1]	SE [1]	SE	SE	SE	SE	SE	SE [1]	SE	SE [1]	SE [1]	SE	SE	SE	SE	SE	SE
Ramsgate [4]	d					20 01									21 04						
Dumpton Park	d					20 04									21 07						
Broadstairs	d					20 07									21 10						
Margate [4]	d					20 14									21 16						
Westgate-on-Sea	d					20 19									21 20						
Birchington-on-Sea	d					20 21									21 23						
Herne Bay	d					20 31									21 32						
Chestfield & Swalecliffe	d					20 35									21 36						
Whitstable	d					20 38									21 39						
Dover Priory [4]	d				20 05							20 45		21 05							
Kearsney	d				20 09									21 09							
Shepherds Well	d				20 14									21 14							
Snowdown	d				20 18									21 18							
Aylesham	d				20 20									21 20							
Adisham	d				20 23									21 23							
Bekesbourne	d				20 27									21 27							
Canterbury East [4]	d				20 32							21 02		21 32							
Selling	d				20 41									21 41							
Faversham [2]	a				20 46	20 48						21 13		21 46	21 48						
	d			20 28	20 52				20 58			21 14	21 28	21 52	<			21 58	21 58		
Teynham	d				20 58									21 58							
Sheerness-on-Sea	d	20 02					20 32			21 02						21 32				22 02	
Queenborough	d	20 06					20 36			21 06						21 36				22 06	
Swale	d	20 10					20 40			21 10						21 40				22 10	
Kemsley	d	20 14					20 44			21 14						21 44				22 14	
Sittingbourne [4]	a	20 19		20 36	21 02		20 49		21 06	21 19		21 21	21 36	22 02				22 06	22 06	22 19	
Newington	d											21 27				21 51					
Rainham (Kent)	d			20 45	21 10				21 15			21 31	21 45	22 10		21 55		22 15	22 15		
Gillingham (Kent) [4]	d		20 24	20 50	21 15			20 54	21 20		21 24	21 36	21 50	22 15		22a02	21 54	22 20	22 20		22 24
Chatham [4]	d		20 28	20 54	21 20			20 58	21 24		21 28	21 41	21 54	22 20			21 58	22 24	22 24		22 28
Rochester [4]	d		20 30	20 57	21 22			21 00	21 27		21 30	21 43	21 57	22 22			22 00	22 27	22 27		22 30
Strood [4]	a		20 35	21 01				21 05	21 31		21 35		22 01				22 05	22 31	22 31		22 35
Gravesend [4]	a		20 47	21 12				21 17	21 42		21 47		22 12				22 17	22 42	22 42		22 47
Greenhithe for Bluewater	a		20 53					21 23			21 53						22 23				22 53
Dartford [4]	a		20 58					21 28			21 58						22 28				22 58
London Bridge [4] ⊖	a		21 36					22 05			22 35						23 05				23 35
London Cannon Street [4] ⊖	a																				
London Waterloo (East) [4] ⊖	a		21 40					22 09			22 39						23 09				23 39
London Charing Cross [4] ⊖	a		21 44					22 13			22 43						23 13				23 43
Sole Street	d											21 54									
Meopham	d				21 33							21 56		22 33							
Longfield	d				21 37							22 00		22 37							
Farningham Road	d											22 04									
Swanley [4]	a											22 09									
St Mary Cray	a											22 14									
Bromley South [4]	a				21 50							22 20		22 50							
Elephant & Castle ⊖	a																				
London Blackfriars [3] ⊖	a																				
London Victoria [15] ⊖	a				22 07							22 37		23 07							
Ebbsfleet International	a			21 17					21 47				22 16					22 47	22 47		
Stratford International ⊖	a			21 32					21 59				22 27					22 59	23 02		
St Pancras International [15] ⊖	a			21 39					22 06				22 38					23 06	23 09		

Table 212

Mondays to Fridays

Ramsgate, Dover, Sheerness-on-Sea and Medway - London

		SE [1]	SE [1]	SE	SE [1]	SE [1]	SE	SE [1]	SE [1]	SE
Ramsgate [4]	d				22 04				23 04	
Dumpton Park	d				22 07				23 07	
Broadstairs	d				22 10				23 10	
Margate [4]	d				22 16				23 16	
Westgate-on-Sea	d				22 20				23 20	
Birchington-on-Sea	d				22 23				23 23	
Herne Bay	d				22 32				23 32	
Chestfield & Swalecliffe	d				22 36				23 36	
Whitstable	d				22 39				23 39	
Dover Priory [4]	d	21 45	22 05			22 45		23 05		
Kearsney	d		22 09					23 09		
Shepherds Well	d		22 14					23 14		
Snowdown	d		22 18					23 18		
Aylesham	d		22 20					23 20		
Adisham	d		22 23					23 23		
Bekesbourne	d		22 27					23 27		
Canterbury East [4]	d	22 02	22 32			23 02		23 32		
Selling	d		22 41					23 41		
Faversham [2]	a	22 13	22 46		22 48	23 13		23 46	23 48	
	d	22 14			22 52	23 14			23 52	
Teynham	d				22 58				23 58	
Sheerness-on-Sea	d						23 02			23 53
Queenborough	d						23 06			23 57
Swale	d						23 10			00 01
Kemsley	d						23 14			00 05
Sittingbourne [4]	a	22 21			23 02	23 21	23 19		00 02	00 10
Newington	d	22 27				23 27			00 08	
Rainham (Kent)	d	22 31			23 10	23 31			00 12	
Gillingham (Kent) [4]	d	22 36		22 54	23 15	23 36			00a17	
Chatham [4]	d	22 41		22 58	23 20	23 41				
Rochester [4]	d	22 43		23 00	23 22	23 43				
Strood [4]	a			23 05						
Gravesend [4]	a			23 17						
Greenhithe for Bluewater	a			23 23						
Dartford [4]	a			23 28						
London Bridge [4] ⊖	a									
London Cannon Street [4] ⊖	a									
London Waterloo (East) [4] ⊖	a									
London Charing Cross [4] ⊖	a									
Sole Street	d	22 54				23 54				
Meopham	d	22 56			23 33	23 56				
Longfield	d	23 00			23 37	23 59				
Farningham Road	d	23 04				00 04				
Swanley [4]	a	23 09				00 09				
St Mary Cray	a	23 14				00 14				
Bromley South [4]	a	23 20			23 50	00 20				
Elephant & Castle ⊖	a									
London Blackfriars [3] ⊖	a									
London Victoria [15] ⊖	a	23 37			00 07	00 38				
Ebbsfleet International	a									
Stratford International ⊖	a									
St Pancras International [15] ⊖	a									

Table 212

Saturdays

Ramsgate, Dover, Sheerness-on-Sea and Medway - London

		SE [1]	SE [1]	SE [1]	SE	SE	SE	SE	SE [1]	SE	SE [1]	SE [1]	SE	SE [1]	SE [1]	SE	SE	SE [1]	SE	SE [1]	SE [1]	SE
Ramsgate [4]	d	22p04		23p04					04 32			05 04			05 40						06 04	
Dumpton Park	d	22p07		23p07								05 07									06 07	
Broadstairs	d	22p10		23p10					04 37			05 10			05 45						06 10	
Margate [4]	d	22p16		23p16					04 42			05 16			05 50						06 16	
Westgate-on-Sea	d	22p20		23p20								05 20									06 20	
Birchington-on-Sea	d	22p23		23p23					04 47			05 23			05 55						06 23	
Herne Bay	d	22p32		23p32					04 56			05 32			06 04						06 32	
Chestfield & Swalecliffe	d	22p36		23p36								05 36									06 36	
Whitstable	d	22p39		23p39					05 01			05 39			06 09						06 39	
Dover Priory [4]	d		22p45								05 05			05 45						06 05		
Kearsney	d										05 09									06 09		
Shepherds Well	d										05 14									06 14		
Snowdown	d										05 18									06 18		
Aylesham	d										05 20									06 20		
Adisham	d										05 23									06 23		
Bekesbourne	d										05 27									06 27		
Canterbury East [4]	d		23p02								05 32			06 02						06 32		
Selling	d										05 41									06 41		
Faversham [2]	a	22p48	23p13	23p48					05 09		05 46	05 48		06 14	06 18					06 46	06 48	
	d	22p52	23p14	23p52					05 09	05 28	05 52	<		06 22	<				06 28	06 52	<	
Teynham	d	22p58		23p58							05 58									06 58		
Sheerness-on-Sea	d				23p53												06 32					
Queenborough	d				23p57												06 36					
Swale	d				00 01												06 40					
Kemsley	d				00 05												06 44					
Sittingbourne [4]	a	23p02	23p21	00 02	00 10				05 17	05 36	06 02			06 29			06 49		06 36	07 02		
Newington	d		23p27	00 08					05 23					06 35								
Rainham (Kent)	d	23p10	23p31	00 12					05 27	05 45	06 10			06 40					06 45	07 10		
Gillingham (Kent) [4]	d	23p15	23p36	00a17		04 48		05 18	05 32	05 50	06 15		05 54	06 45		06 24		06 32	06 50	07 15		06 54
Chatham [4]	d	23p20	23p41			04 52		05 22	05 36	05 54	06 20		05 58	06 50		06 28		06 36	06 54	07 20		06 58
Rochester [4]	d	23p22	23p43			04 54		05 24	05 39	05 57	06 22		06 00	06 52		06 30		06 39	06 57	07 22		07 00
Strood [4]	a					04 59		05 29		06 01			06 05			06 35			07 01			07 05
Gravesend [4]	a					05 11		05 41		06 12			06 17			06 47			07 12			07 17
Greenhithe for Bluewater	a					05 20		05 50					06 23			06 53						07 23
Dartford [4]	a					05 27		05 57					06 28			06 58						07 28
London Bridge [4] ⊖	a					06 05		06 35					07 05			07 35						08 05
London Cannon Street [4] ⊖	a																					
London Waterloo (East) [4] ⊖	a					06 09		06 39					07 09			07 39						08 09
London Charing Cross [4] ⊖	a					06 13		06 43					07 13			07 43						08 13
Sole Street	d		23p54						05 49									06 49				
Meopham	d	23p33	23p56						05 52		06 33			07 03				06 52		07 33		
Longfield	d	23p37	23p59						05 56		06 37			07 07				06 56		07 37		
Farningham Road	d		00 04						06 00									06 59				
Swanley [4]	a		00 09						06 05									07 04				
St Mary Cray	a		00 14						06 09									07 09				
Bromley South [4]	a	23p50	00 20						06 15		06 50			07 20				07 15		07 50		
Elephant & Castle ⊖	a																					
London Blackfriars [3] ⊖	a																					
London Victoria [15] ⊖	a	00 07	00 38						06 37		07 07			07 37				07 37		08 07		
Ebbsfleet International	a						05 32			06 17									07 17			
Stratford International ⊖	a						05 44			06 29									07 29			
St Pancras International [15] ⊖	a						05 51			06 36									07 36			

Table 212

Saturdays

Ramsgate, Dover, Sheerness-on-Sea and Medway - London

		SE 1	SE 1	SE	SE	SE	SE 1	SE	SE 1	SE 1	SE	SE	SE 1 A ✕	SE 1 ✕	SE	SE	SE	SE 1	SE	SE 1 A ✕	SE 1 ✕	SE
Ramsgate	d		06 40							07 04				07 40							08 04	
Dumpton Park	d									07 07											08 07	
Broadstairs	d		06 45							07 10				07 45							08 10	
Margate	d		06 50							07 16				07 50							08 16	
Westgate-on-Sea	d									07 20											08 20	
Birchington-on-Sea	d		06 55							07 23				07 55							08 23	
Herne Bay	d		07 04							07 32				08 04							08 32	
Chestfield & Swalecliffe	d									07 36											08 36	
Whitstable	d		07 09							07 39				08 09							08 39	
Dover Priory	d	06 45							07 05				07 45							08 05		
Kearsney	d								07 09											08 09		
Shepherds Well	d								07 14											08 14		
Snowdown	d								07 18											08 18		
Aylesham	d								07 20											08 20		
Adisham	d								07 23											08 23		
Bekesbourne	d								07 27											08 27		
Canterbury East	d	07 02							07 32				08 02							08 32		
Selling	d								07 41											08 41		
Faversham	a	07 14	07 18						07 46	07 48			08 14	08 18						08 46	08 48	
	d	07 22	<					07 28	07 52	<		07 58	08 22	<					08 28	08 52	<	
Teynham	d								07 58											08 58		
Sheerness-on-Sea	d			07 02		07 32									08 02		08 32					
Queenborough	d			07 06		07 36									08 06		08 36					
Swale	d			07 10		07 40									08 10		08 40					
Kemsley	d			07 14		07 44									08 14		08 44					
Sittingbourne	a	07 29		07 19		07 49		07 36	08 02			08 06	08 29		08 19		08 49		08 36	09 02		
Newington	d	07 35											08 35									
Rainham (Kent)	d	07 40						07 45	08 10			08 15	08 40						08 45	09 10		
Gillingham (Kent)	d	07 45			07 24		07 32	07 50	08 15		07 54	08 20	08 45			08 24		08 32	08 50	09 15		08 54
Chatham	d	07 50			07 28		07 36	07 54	08 20		07 58	08 24	08 50			08 28		08 36	08 54	09 20		08 58
Rochester	d	07 52			07 30		07 39	07 57	08 22		08 00	08 27	08 52			08 30		08 39	08 57	09 22		09 00
Strood	a				07 35			08 01			08 05	08 31				08 35			09 01			09 05
Gravesend	a				07 47			08 12			08 17	08 42				08 47			09 12			09 17
Greenhithe for Bluewater	a				07 53						08 23					08 53						09 23
Dartford	a				07 58						08 28					08 58						09 28
London Bridge ⊖	a				08 35						09 05					09 35						10 05
London Cannon Street ⊖	a																					
London Waterloo (East) ⊖	a				08 39						09 09					09 39						10 09
London Charing Cross ⊖	a				08 43						09 13					09 43						10 13
Sole Street	d						07 49											08 49				
Meopham	d	08 03					07 52		08 33				09 03					08 52		09 33		
Longfield	d	08 07					07 56		08 37				09 07					08 56		09 37		
Farningham Road	d						07 59											08 59				
Swanley	a						08 04											09 04				
St Mary Cray	a						08 09											09 09				
Bromley South	a	08 20					08 15		08 50				09 20					09 15		09 50		
Elephant & Castle ⊖	a																					
London Blackfriars ⊖	a																					
London Victoria ⊖	a	08 37					08 37		09 07				09 37					09 37		10 07		
Ebbsfleet International	a							08 17				08 47							09 17			
Stratford International ⊖	a							08 29				08 59							09 29			
St Pancras International ⊖	a							08 36				09 07							09 39			

A ✕ from Faversham

Table 212

Saturdays

Ramsgate, Dover, Sheerness-on-Sea and Medway - London

		SE	SE 1 A ✕	SE 1 ✕	SE	SE	SE	SE 1	SE	SE 1 A ✕	SE 1 ✕	SE	SE	SE 1 A ✕	SE 1 ✕	SE	SE	SE	SE 1	SE	SE 1 A ✕	SE 1 ✕	SE
Ramsgate	d			08 40							09 04				09 40							10 04	
Dumpton Park	d										09 07											10 07	
Broadstairs	d			08 45							09 10				09 45							10 10	
Margate	d			08 50							09 16				09 50							10 16	
Westgate-on-Sea	d										09 20											10 20	
Birchington-on-Sea	d			08 55							09 23				09 55							10 23	
Herne Bay	d			09 04							09 32				10 04							10 32	
Chestfield & Swalecliffe	d										09 36											10 36	
Whitstable	d			09 09							09 39				10 09							10 39	
Dover Priory	d		08 45	<						09 05	<			09 45	<						10 05		
Kearsney	d									09 09											10 09		
Shepherds Well	d									09 14											10 14		
Snowdown	d									09 18											10 18		
Aylesham	d									09 20											10 20		
Adisham	d									09 23											10 23		
Bekesbourne	d									09 27											10 27		
Canterbury East	d		09 02							09 32				10 02							10 32		
Selling	d									09 41											10 41		
Faversham	a		09 14	09 18						09 46	09 48			10 14	10 18						10 46	10 48	
	d	08 58	09 22	<					09 28	09 52	<		09 58	10 22	<					10 28	10 52	<	
Teynham	d									09 58											10 58		
Sheerness-on-Sea	d				09 02		09 32									10 02		10 32					
Queenborough	d				09 06		09 36									10 06		10 36					
Swale	d				09 10		09 40									10 10		10 40					
Kemsley	d				09 14		09 44									10 14		10 44					
Sittingbourne	a	09 06	09 29		09 19		09 49		09 36	10 02			10 06	10 29		10 19		10 49		10 36	11 02		
Newington	d		09 35											10 35									
Rainham (Kent)	d	09 15	09 40						09 45	10 10			10 15	10 40						10 45	11 10		
Gillingham (Kent)	d	09 20	09 45			09 24		09 32	09 50	10 15		09 54	10 20	10 45			10 24		10 32	10 50	11 15		10 54
Chatham	d	09 24	09 50			09 28		09 36	09 54	10 20		09 58	10 24	10 50			10 28		10 36	10 54	11 20		10 58
Rochester	d	09 27	09 52			09 30		09 39	09 57	10 22		10 00	10 27	10 52			10 30		10 39	10 57	11 22		11 00
Strood	a	09 31				09 35			10 01			10 05	10 31				10 35			11 01			11 05
Gravesend	a	09 42				09 47			10 12			10 17	10 42				10 47			11 12			11 17
Greenhithe for Bluewater	a					09 53						10 23					10 53						11 23
Dartford	a					09 58						10 28					10 58						11 28
London Bridge ⊖	a					10 35						11 05					11 35						12 05
London Cannon Street ⊖	a																						
London Waterloo (East) ⊖	a					10 39						11 09					11 39						12 09
London Charing Cross ⊖	a					10 43						11 13					11 43						12 13
Sole Street	d							09 49											10 49				
Meopham	d		10 03					09 52		10 33				11 03					10 52		11 33		
Longfield	d		10 07					09 56		10 37				11 07					10 56		11 37		
Farningham Road	d							09 59											10 59				
Swanley	a							10 04											11 04				
St Mary Cray	a							10 09											11 09				
Bromley South	a		10 20					10 15		10 50				11 20					11 15		11 50		
Elephant & Castle ⊖	a																						
London Blackfriars ⊖	a																						
London Victoria ⊖	a		10 37					10 37		11 07				11 37					11 37		12 07		
Ebbsfleet International	a	09 47							10 16				10 47							11 17			
Stratford International ⊖	a	09 59							10 27				10 59							11 29			
St Pancras International ⊖	a	10 06							10 38				11 06							11 36			

A ✕ from Faversham

Table 212

Saturdays

Ramsgate, Dover, Sheerness-on-Sea and Medway - London

		SE	SE [1] A 🛒	SE [1] 🛒	SE	SE	SE	SE [1]		SE	SE [1] A 🛒	SE [1] 🛒	SE	SE	SE [1] A 🛒	SE [1] 🛒	SE	SE		SE	SE [1]	SE	SE [1] A 🛒	SE [1] 🛒	SE
Ramsgate [4]	d			10 40								11 04				11 40								12 04	
Dumpton Park	d											11 07												12 07	
Broadstairs	d			10 45								11 10				11 45								12 10	
Margate [4]	d			10 50								11 16				11 50								12 16	
Westgate-on-Sea	d											11 20												12 20	
Birchington-on-Sea	d			10 55								11 23				11 55								12 23	
Herne Bay	d			11 04								11 32				12 04								12 32	
Chestfield & Swalecliffe	d											11 36												12 36	
Whitstable	d			11 09								11 39				12 09								12 39	
Dover Priory [4]	d		10 45								11 05				11 45								12 05		
Kearsney	d										11 09												12 09		
Shepherds Well	d										11 14												12 14		
Snowdown	d										11 18												12 18		
Aylesham	d										11 20												12 20		
Adisham	d										11 23												12 23		
Bekesbourne	d										11 27												12 27		
Canterbury East [4]	d		11 02								11 32				12 02								12 32		
Selling	d										11 41												12 41		
Faversham [2]	a		11 14	11 18							11 46	11 48			12 14	12 18							12 46	12 48	
	d	10 58	11 22	<						11 28	11 52	<		11 58	12 22	<						12 28	12 52	<	
Teynham	d										11 58												12 58		
Sheerness-on-Sea	d				11 02		11 32										12 02			12 32					
Queenborough	d				11 06		11 36										12 06			12 36					
Swale	d				11 10		11 40										12 10			12 40					
Kemsley	d				11 14		11 44										12 14			12 44					
Sittingbourne [4]	a	11 06	11 29		11 19		11 49			11 36	12 02			12 06	12 29		12 19			12 49		12 36	13 02		
Newington	d		11 35												12 35										
Rainham (Kent)	d	11 15	11 40							11 45	12 10			12 15	12 40							12 45	13 10		
Gillingham (Kent) [4]	d	11 20	11 45			11 24		11 32		11 50	12 15		11 54	12 20	12 45			12 24			12 32	12 50	13 15		12 54
Chatham [4]	d	11 24	11 50			11 28		11 36		11 54	12 20		11 58	12 24	12 50			12 28			12 36	12 54	13 20		12 58
Rochester [4]	d	11 27	11 52			11 30		11 39		11 57	12 22		12 00	12 27	12 52			12 30			12 39	12 57	13 22		13 00
Strood [4]	a	11 31				11 35				12 01			12 05	12 31				12 35				13 01			13 05
Gravesend [4]	a	11 42				11 47				12 12			12 17	12 42				12 47				13 12			13 17
Greenhithe for Bluewater	a					11 53							12 23					12 53							13 23
Dartford [4]	a					11 58							12 28					12 58							13 28
London Bridge [4] ⊖	a					12 35							13 05					13 35							14 05
London Cannon Street [4] ⊖	a																								
London Waterloo (East) [4] ⊖	a					12 39							13 09					13 39							14 09
London Charing Cross [4] ⊖	a					12 43							13 13					13 43							14 13
Sole Street	d							11 49													12 49				
Meopham	d		12 03					11 52			12 33				13 03						12 52		13 33		
Longfield	d		12 07					11 56			12 37				13 07						12 56		13 37		
Farningham Road	d							11 59													12 59				
Swanley [4]	a							12 04													13 04				
St Mary Cray	a							12 09													13 09				
Bromley South [4]	a		12 20					12 15			12 50				13 20						13 15		13 50		
Elephant & Castle ⊖	a																								
London Blackfriars [3] ⊖	a																								
London Victoria [15] ⊖	a		12 37					12 37			13 07				13 37						13 37		14 07		
Ebbsfleet International	a	11 47								12 17				12 47								13 17			
Stratford International ⊖	a	11 59								12 32				12 59								13 29			
St Pancras International [15] ⊖	a	12 06								12 39				13 06								13 36			

A 🛒 from Faversham

Table 212

Saturdays

Ramsgate, Dover, Sheerness-on-Sea and Medway - London

		SE	SE [1] A 🛒	SE [1] 🛒		SE	SE	SE	SE [1]	SE	SE [1] A 🛒	SE [1] 🛒	SE		SE	SE [1] A 🛒	SE [1] 🛒	SE	SE	SE	SE [1]	SE	SE [1] A 🛒	SE [1] 🛒	
Ramsgate [4]	d			12 40								13 04					13 40							14 04	
Dumpton Park	d											13 07												14 07	
Broadstairs	d			12 45								13 10					13 45							14 10	
Margate [4]	d			12 50								13 16					13 50							14 16	
Westgate-on-Sea	d											13 20												14 20	
Birchington-on-Sea	d			12 55								13 23					13 55							14 23	
Herne Bay	d			13 04								13 32					14 04							14 32	
Chestfield & Swalecliffe	d											13 36												14 36	
Whitstable	d			13 09								13 39					14 09							14 39	
Dover Priory [4]	d		12 45								13 05					13 45							14 05		
Kearsney	d										13 09												14 09		
Shepherds Well	d										13 14												14 14		
Snowdown	d										13 18												14 18		
Aylesham	d										13 20												14 20		
Adisham	d										13 23												14 23		
Bekesbourne	d										13 27												14 27		
Canterbury East [4]	d		13 02								13 32					14 02							14 32		
Selling	d										13 41												14 41		
Faversham [2]	a		13 14	13 18							13 46	13 48				14 14	14 18						14 46	14 48	
	d	12 58	13 22	<						13 28	13 52	<			13 58	14 22	<					14 28	14 52	<	
Teynham	d										13 58												14 58		
Sheerness-on-Sea	d					13 02		13 32										14 02		14 32					
Queenborough	d					13 06		13 36										14 06		14 36					
Swale	d					13 10		13 40										14 10		14 40					
Kemsley	d					13 14		13 44										14 14		14 44					
Sittingbourne [4]	a	13 06	13 29			13 19		13 49		13 36	14 02				14 06	14 29		14 19		14 49		14 36	15 02		
Newington	d		13 35													14 35									
Rainham (Kent)	d	13 15	13 40							13 45	14 10				14 15	14 40						14 45	15 10		
Gillingham (Kent) [4]	d	13 20	13 45				13 24		13 32	13 50	14 15		13 54		14 20	14 45			14 24		14 32	14 50	15 15		
Chatham [4]	d	13 24	13 50				13 28		13 36	13 54	14 20		13 58		14 24	14 50			14 28		14 36	14 54	15 20		
Rochester [4]	d	13 27	13 52				13 30		13 39	13 57	14 22		14 00		14 27	14 52			14 30		14 39	14 57	15 22		
Strood [4]	a	13 31					13 35			14 01			14 05		14 31				14 35			15 01			
Gravesend [4]	a	13 42					13 47			14 12			14 17		14 42				14 47			15 12			
Greenhithe for Bluewater	a						13 53						14 23						14 53						
Dartford [4]	a						13 58						14 28						14 58						
London Bridge [4] ⊖	a						14 35						15 05						15 35						
London Cannon Street [4] ⊖	a																								
London Waterloo (East) [4] ⊖	a						14 39						15 09						15 39						
London Charing Cross [4] ⊖	a						14 43						15 13						15 43						
Sole Street	d								13 49												14 49				
Meopham	d		14 03						13 52		14 33					15 03					14 52		15 33		
Longfield	d		14 07						13 56		14 37					15 07					14 56		15 37		
Farningham Road	d								13 59												14 59				
Swanley [4]	a								14 04												15 04				
St Mary Cray	a								14 09												15 09				
Bromley South [4]	a		14 20						14 15		14 50					15 20					15 15		15 50		
Elephant & Castle ⊖	a																								
London Blackfriars [3] ⊖	a																								
London Victoria [15] ⊖	a		14 37						14 37		15 07					15 37					15 37		16 07		
Ebbsfleet International	a	13 47								14 17					14 47							15 17			
Stratford International ⊖	a	13 59								14 32					15 02							15 29			
St Pancras International [15] ⊖	a	14 06								14 39					15 09							15 36			

A 🛒 from Faversham

Table 212

Saturdays

Ramsgate, Dover, Sheerness-on-Sea and Medway - London

		SE	SE	SE 1 A ⌶	SE 1 ⌶	SE	SE	SE	SE 1	SE	SE 1 A ⌶	SE 1 ⌶
Ramsgate 4	d				14 40							15 04
Dumpton Park	d											15 07
Broadstairs	d				14 45							15 10
Margate 4	d				14 50							15 16
Westgate-on-Sea	d											15 20
Birchington-on-Sea	d				14 55							15 23
Herne Bay	d				15 04							15 32
Chestfield & Swalecliffe	d											15 36
Whitstable	d				15 09							15 39
Dover Priory 4	d			14 45							15 05	
Kearsney	d										15 09	
Shepherds Well	d										15 14	
Snowdown	d										15 18	
Aylesham	d										15 20	
Adisham	d										15 23	
Bekesbourne	d										15 27	
Canterbury East 4	d			15 02							15 32	
Selling	d										15 41	
Faversham 2	a			15 14	15 18						15 46	15 48
	d		14 58	15 22	<					15 28	15 52	<
Teynham	d										15 58	
Sheerness-on-Sea	d					15 02		15 32				
Queenborough	d					15 06		15 36				
Swale	d					15 10		15 40				
Kemsley	d					15 14		15 44				
Sittingbourne 4	a		15 06	15 29		15 19		15 49		15 36	16 02	
Newington	d			15 35								
Rainham (Kent)	d		15 15	15 40						15 45	16 10	
Gillingham (Kent) 4	d	14 54	15 20	15 45			15 24		15 32	15 50	16 15	
Chatham 4	d	14 58	15 24	15 50			15 28		15 36	15 54	16 20	
Rochester 4	d	15 00	15 27	15 52			15 30		15 39	15 57	16 22	
Strood 4	a	15 05	15 31				15 35			16 01		
Gravesend 4	a	15 17	15 42				15 47			16 12		
Greenhithe for Bluewater	a	15 23					15 53					
Dartford 4	a	15 28					15 58					
London Bridge 4 ⊖	a	16 05					16 35					
London Cannon Street 4 ⊖	a											
London Waterloo (East) 4 ⊖	a	16 09					16 39					
London Charing Cross 4 ⊖	a	16 13					16 43					
Sole Street	d								15 49			
Meopham	d			16 03					15 52		16 33	
Longfield	d			16 07					15 56		16 37	
Farningham Road	d								15 59			
Swanley 4	a								16 04			
St Mary Cray	a								16 09			
Bromley South 4	a			16 20					16 15		16 50	
Elephant & Castle ⊖	a											
London Blackfriars 3 ⊖	a											
London Victoria 15 ⊖	a			16 37					16 37		17 07	
Ebbsfleet International	a		15 47							16 17		
Stratford International ⊖	a		15 59							16 29		
St Pancras International 15 ⊖	a		16 06							16 40		

		SE	SE	SE 1 A ⌶	SE 1 ⌶	SE	SE	SE	SE 1	SE	SE 1 A ⌶	SE 1 ⌶
Ramsgate 4	d				15 40							16 04
Dumpton Park	d											16 07
Broadstairs	d				15 45							16 10
Margate 4	d				15 50							16 16
Westgate-on-Sea	d											16 20
Birchington-on-Sea	d				15 55							16 23
Herne Bay	d				16 04							16 32
Chestfield & Swalecliffe	d											16 36
Whitstable	d				16 09							16 39
Dover Priory 4	d			15 45							16 05	
Kearsney	d										16 09	
Shepherds Well	d										16 14	
Snowdown	d										16 18	
Aylesham	d										16 20	
Adisham	d										16 23	
Bekesbourne	d										16 27	
Canterbury East 4	d			16 02							16 32	
Selling	d										16 41	
Faversham 2	a			16 14	16 18						16 46	16 48
	d		15 58	16 22	<					16 28	16 52	<
Teynham	d										16 58	
Sheerness-on-Sea	d					16 02		16 32				
Queenborough	d					16 06		16 36				
Swale	d					16 10		16 40				
Kemsley	d					16 14		16 44				
Sittingbourne 4	a		16 06	16 29		16 19		16 49		16 36	17 02	
Newington	d			16 35								
Rainham (Kent)	d		16 15	16 40						16 45	17 10	
Gillingham (Kent) 4	d	15 54	16 20	16 45			16 24		16 32	16 50	17 15	
Chatham 4	d	15 58	16 24	16 50			16 28		16 36	16 54	17 20	
Rochester 4	d	16 00	16 27	16 52			16 30		16 39	16 57	17 22	
Strood 4	a	16 05	16 31				16 35			17 01		
Gravesend 4	a	16 17	16 42				16 47			17 12		
Greenhithe for Bluewater	a	16 23					16 53					
Dartford 4	a	16 28					16 58					
London Bridge 4 ⊖	a	17 05					17 35					
London Cannon Street 4 ⊖	a											
London Waterloo (East) 4 ⊖	a	17 09					17 39					
London Charing Cross 4 ⊖	a	17 13					17 43					
Sole Street	d								16 49			
Meopham	d			17 03					16 52		17 33	
Longfield	d			17 07					16 56		17 37	
Farningham Road	d								16 59			
Swanley 4	a								17 04			
St Mary Cray	a								17 09			
Bromley South 4	a			17 20					17 15		17 50	
Elephant & Castle ⊖	a											
London Blackfriars 3 ⊖	a											
London Victoria 15 ⊖	a			17 37					17 37		18 07	
Ebbsfleet International	a		16 47							17 16		
Stratford International ⊖	a		16 59							17 27		
St Pancras International 15 ⊖	a		17 06							17 38		

A ⌶ from Faversham

Table 212

Saturdays

Ramsgate, Dover, Sheerness-on-Sea and Medway - London

		SE	SE	SE 1	SE 1	SE	SE	SE	SE 1	SE	SE 1	SE 1
Ramsgate 4	d				16 40							17 04
Dumpton Park	d											17 07
Broadstairs	d				16 45							17 10
Margate 4	d				16 50							17 16
Westgate-on-Sea	d											17 20
Birchington-on-Sea	d				16 55							17 23
Herne Bay	d				17 04							17 32
Chestfield & Swalecliffe	d											17 36
Whitstable	d				17 09							17 39
Dover Priory 4	d			16 45							17 05	
Kearsney	d										17 09	
Shepherds Well	d										17 14	
Snowdown	d										17 18	
Aylesham	d										17 20	
Adisham	d										17 23	
Bekesbourne	d										17 27	
Canterbury East 4	d			17 02							17 32	
Selling	d										17 41	
Faversham 2	a			17 14	17 18						17 46	17 48
	d		16 58	17 22	<					17 28	17 52	<
Teynham	d										17 58	
Sheerness-on-Sea	d					17 02		17 32				
Queenborough	d					17 06		17 36				
Swale	d					17 10		17 40				
Kemsley	d					17 14		17 44				
Sittingbourne 4	a		17 06	17 29		17 19		17 49		17 36	18 02	
Newington	d			17 35								
Rainham (Kent)	d		17 15	17 40						17 45	18 10	
Gillingham (Kent) 4	d	16 54	17 20	17 45			17 24		17 32	17 50	18 15	
Chatham 4	d	16 58	17 24	17 50			17 28		17 36	17 54	18 20	
Rochester 4	d	17 00	17 27	17 52			17 30		17 39	17 57	18 22	
Strood 4	a	17 05	17 31				17 35			18 01		
Gravesend 4	a	17 17	17 42				17 47			18 12		
Greenhithe for Bluewater	a	17 23					17 53					
Dartford 4	a	17 28					17 58					
London Bridge 4 ⊖	a	18 05					18 35					
London Cannon Street 4 ⊖	a											
London Waterloo (East) 4 ⊖	a	18 09					18 39					
London Charing Cross 4 ⊖	a	18 13					18 43					
Sole Street	d								17 49			
Meopham	d			18 03					17 52		18 33	
Longfield	d			18 07					17 56		18 37	
Farningham Road	d								17 59			
Swanley 4	a								18 04			
St Mary Cray	a								18 09			
Bromley South 4	a			18 20					18 15		18 50	
Elephant & Castle ⊖	a											
London Blackfriars 3 ⊖	a											
London Victoria 15 ⊖	a			18 37					18 37		19 07	
Ebbsfleet International	a		17 47							18 17		
Stratford International ⊖	a		18 02							18 29		
St Pancras International 15 ⊖	a		18 09							18 36		

		SE	SE	SE 1	SE 1	SE	SE	SE	SE 1	SE	SE 1	SE 1
Ramsgate 4	d				17 40							18 04
Dumpton Park	d											18 07
Broadstairs	d				17 45							18 10
Margate 4	d				17 50							18 16
Westgate-on-Sea	d											18 20
Birchington-on-Sea	d				17 55							18 23
Herne Bay	d				18 04							18 32
Chestfield & Swalecliffe	d											18 36
Whitstable	d				18 09							18 39
Dover Priory 4	d			17 45							18 05	
Kearsney	d										18 09	
Shepherds Well	d										18 14	
Snowdown	d										18 18	
Aylesham	d										18 20	
Adisham	d										18 23	
Bekesbourne	d										18 27	
Canterbury East 4	d			18 02							18 32	
Selling	d										18 41	
Faversham 2	a			18 14	18 18						18 46	18 48
	d		17 58	18 22	<					18 28	18 52	<
Teynham	d										18 58	
Sheerness-on-Sea	d					18 02		18 32				
Queenborough	d					18 06		18 36				
Swale	d					18 10		18 40				
Kemsley	d					18 14		18 44				
Sittingbourne 4	a		18 06	18 29		18 19		18 49		18 36	19 02	
Newington	d			18 35								
Rainham (Kent)	d		18 15	18 40						18 45	19 10	
Gillingham (Kent) 4	d	17 54	18 20	18 45			18 24		18 32	18 50	19 15	
Chatham 4	d	17 58	18 24	18 50			18 28		18 36	18 54	19 20	
Rochester 4	d	18 00	18 27	18 52			18 30		18 39	18 57	19 22	
Strood 4	a	18 05	18 31				18 35			19 01		
Gravesend 4	a	18 17	18 42				18 47			19 12		
Greenhithe for Bluewater	a	18 23					18 53					
Dartford 4	a	18 28					18 58					
London Bridge 4 ⊖	a	19 05					19 36					
London Cannon Street 4 ⊖	a											
London Waterloo (East) 4 ⊖	a	19 09					19 42					
London Charing Cross 4 ⊖	a	19 13					19 45					
Sole Street	d								18 49			
Meopham	d			19 03					18 52		19 33	
Longfield	d			19 07					18 56		19 37	
Farningham Road	d								18 59			
Swanley 4	a								19 04			
St Mary Cray	a								19 09			
Bromley South 4	a			19 20					19 15		19 50	
Elephant & Castle ⊖	a											
London Blackfriars 3 ⊖	a											
London Victoria 15 ⊖	a			19 37					19 37		20 07	
Ebbsfleet International	a		18 47							19 16		
Stratford International ⊖	a		19 02							19 27		
St Pancras International 15 ⊖	a		19 09							19 38		

A ⌶ from Faversham

Ramsgate, Dover, Sheerness-on-Sea and Medway - London

		SE	SE	SE 1	SE 1	SE	SE	SE	SE 1	SE	SE 1	SE 1	SE	SE	SE	SE	SE 1	SE	SE 1	SE 1	SE	SE
Ramsgate	d				18 40							19 04								20 04		
Dumpton Park	d											19 07								20 07		
Broadstairs	d				18 45							19 10								20 10		
Margate	d				18 50							19 16								20 16		
Westgate-on-Sea	d											19 20								20 20		
Birchington-on-Sea	d				18 55							19 23								20 23		
Herne Bay	d				19 04							19 32								20 32		
Chestfield & Swalecliffe	d											19 36								20 36		
Whitstable	d				19 09							19 39								20 39		
Dover Priory	d			18 45							19 05								20 05			
Kearsney	d										19 09								20 09			
Shepherds Well	d										19 14								20 14			
Snowdown	d										19 18								20 18			
Aylesham	d										19 20								20 20			
Adisham	d										19 23								20 23			
Bekesbourne	d										19 27								20 27			
Canterbury East	d			19 02							19 32								20 32			
Selling	d										19 41								20 41			
Faversham	a			19 14	19 18						19 46	19 48							20 46	20 48		
	d		18 58	19 22	<					19 28	19 52	<		19 58			20 14	20 28	20 52	<		
Teynham	d										19 58								20 58			
Sheerness-on-Sea	d					19 02		19 32							20 02						20 32	
Queenborough	d					19 06		19 36							20 06						20 36	
Swale	d					19 10		19 40							20 10						20 40	
Kemsley	d					19 14		19 44							20 14						20 44	
Sittingbourne	a		19 06	19 29		19 19		19 49		19 36	20 02			20 06	20 19		20 21	20 36	21 02		20 49	
Newington	d			19 35													20 27					
Rainham (Kent)	d		19 15	19 40						19 45	20 10			20 15			20 31	20 45	21 10			
Gillingham (Kent)	d	18 54	19 20	19 45			19 24		19 32	19 50	20 15		19 54	20 20		20 24	20 36	20 50	21 15			20 54
Chatham	d	18 58	19 24	19 50			19 28		19 36	19 54	20 20		19 58	20 24		20 28	20 41	20 54	21 20			20 58
Rochester	d	19 00	19 27	19 52			19 30		19 39	19 57	20 22		20 00	20 27		20 30	20 43	20 57	21 22			21 00
Strood	a	19 05	19 31				19 35			20 01			20 05	20 31		20 35		21 01				21 05
Gravesend	a	19 17	19 42				19 47			20 12			20 17	20 42		20 47		21 12				21 17
Greenhithe for Bluewater	a	19 23					19 53						20 23			20 53						21 23
Dartford	a	19 28					19 58						20 28			20 58						21 28
London Bridge ⊖	a	20 06					20 36						21 06			21 36						22 05
London Cannon Street ⊖	a																					
London Waterloo (East) ⊖	a	20 10					20 40						21 10			21 40						22 09
London Charing Cross ⊖	a	20 14					20 44						21 14			21 44						22 13
Sole Street	d								19 49								20 54					
Meopham	d			20 03					19 52		20 33						20 56		21 33			
Longfield	d			20 07					19 56		20 37						21 00		21 37			
Farningham Road	d								19 59								21 04					
Swanley	a								20 04								21 09					
St Mary Cray	a								20 09								21 14					
Bromley South	a			20 20					20 15		20 50						21 20		21 50			
Elephant & Castle ⊖	a																					
London Blackfriars ⊖	a																					
London Victoria ⊖	a			20 37					20 37		21 07						21 37		22 07			
Ebbsfleet International	a		19 47							20 16				20 47				21 17				
Stratford International ⊖	a		19 59							20 27				21 02				21 31				
St Pancras International ⊖	a		20 06							20 38				21 09				21 42				

Table 212

Saturdays

Ramsgate, Dover, Sheerness-on-Sea and Medway - London

		SE	SE	SE	SE 1	SE	SE 1	SE 1	SE	SE	SE	SE	SE 1	SE 1	SE	SE 1	SE	SE 1	SE 1	SE
Ramsgate	d							21 04								22 04			23 04	
Dumpton Park	d							21 07								22 07			23 07	
Broadstairs	d							21 10								22 10			23 10	
Margate	d							21 16								22 16			23 16	
Westgate-on-Sea	d							21 20								22 20			23 20	
Birchington-on-Sea	d							21 23								22 23			23 23	
Herne Bay	d							21 32								22 32			23 32	
Chestfield & Swalecliffe	d							21 36								22 36			23 36	
Whitstable	d							21 39								22 39			23 39	
Dover Priory	d						21 05							22 05				23 05		
Kearsney	d						21 09							22 09				23 09		
Shepherds Well	d						21 14							22 14				23 14		
Snowdown	d						21 18							22 18				23 18		
Aylesham	d						21 20							22 20				23 20		
Adisham	d						21 23							22 23				23 23		
Bekesbourne	d						21 27							22 27				23 27		
Canterbury East	d						21 32						22 02	22 32				23 32		
Selling	d						21 41							22 41				23 41		
Faversham	a						21 46	21 48					22 13	22 46		22 48		23 46	23 48	
	d	20 58			21 14	21 28	21 52	<			21 58		22 14			22 52			23 52	
Teynham	d						21 58									22 58			23 58	
Sheerness-on-Sea	d		21 02							22 02							23 02			23 53
Queenborough	d		21 06							22 06							23 06			23 57
Swale	d		21 10							22 10							23 10			00 01
Kemsley	d		21 14							22 14							23 14			00 05
Sittingbourne	a	21 06	21 19		21 21	21 36	22 02			22 19	22 07		22 21			23 02	23 19		00 02	00 10
Newington	d				21 27								22 27						00 08	
Rainham (Kent)	d	21 15			21 31	21 45	22 10				22 15		22 31			23 10			00 12	
Gillingham (Kent)	d	21 20		21 24	21 36	21 50	22 15		21 54		22 20	22 24	22 36		22 54	23 15			00a17	
Chatham	d	21 24		21 28	21 41	21 54	22 20		21 58		22 24	22 28	22 41		22 58	23 20				
Rochester	d	21 27		21 30	21 43	21 57	22 22		22 00		22 27	22 30	22 43		23 00	23 22				
Strood	a	21 31		21 35		22 01			22 05		22 32	22 35			23 05					
Gravesend	a	21 42		21 47		22 12			22 17		22 43	22 47			23 17					
Greenhithe for Bluewater	a			21 53					22 23			22 53			23 23					
Dartford	a			21 58					22 28			22 58			23 28					
London Bridge ⊖	a			22 35					23 05			23 35								
London Cannon Street ⊖	a																			
London Waterloo (East) ⊖	a			22 39					23 09			23 39								
London Charing Cross ⊖	a			22 43					23 13			23 43								
Sole Street	d				21 54								22 54							
Meopham	d				21 56		22 33						22 56			23 33				
Longfield	d				22 00		22 37						23 00			23 37				
Farningham Road	d				22 04								23 04							
Swanley	a				22 09								23 09							
St Mary Cray	a				22 14								23 14							
Bromley South	a				22 20		22 50						23 20			23 50				
Elephant & Castle ⊖	a																			
London Blackfriars ⊖	a																			
London Victoria ⊖	a				22 37		23 07						23 37			00 10				
Ebbsfleet International	a	21 47				22 17					22 48									
Stratford International ⊖	a	21 59				22 29					22 59									
St Pancras International ⊖	a	22 06				22 36					23 06									

Table 212

Sundays

Ramsgate, Dover, Sheerness-on-Sea and Medway - London

		SE [1]	SE [1]	SE	SE	SE [1]	SE	SE [1]	SE	SE [1]	SE	SE	SE [1] C ⌶	SE [1] B ⌶	SE	SE	SE [1]	SE	SE [1] C ⌶	SE [1] B ⌶	SE
Ramsgate [4]	d	22p04	23p04					06 34						07 34						08 34	
Dumpton Park	d	22p07	23p07					06 37						07 37						08 37	
Broadstairs	d	22p10	23p10					06 40						07 40						08 40	
Margate [4]	d	22p16	23p16					06 45						07 45						08 45	
Westgate-on-Sea	d	22p20	23p20					06 49						07 49						08 49	
Birchington-on-Sea	d	22p23	23p23					06 52						07 52						08 52	
Herne Bay	d	22p32	23p32					07 01						08 01						09 01	
Chestfield & Swalecliffe	d	22p36	23p36					07 05						08 05						09 05	
Whitstable	d	22p39	23p39					07 08						08 08						09 08	
Dover Priory [4]	d												07 34						08 34		
Kearsney	d												07 38						08 38		
Shepherds Well	d												07 43						08 43		
Snowdown	d												07 47						08 47		
Aylesham	d												07 49						08 49		
Adisham	d												07 52						08 52		
Bekesbourne	d												07 56						08 56		
Canterbury East [4]	d												08 01						09 01		
Selling	d												08 10						09 10		
Faversham [2]	a	22p48	23p48					07 17					08 15	08 17					09 15	09 17	
	d	22p52	23p52			06 34		07 21		07 34		07 58	08 21	<			08 34	08 58	09 21	<	
Teynham	d	22p58	23p58			06 40				07 40							08 40				
Sheerness-on-Sea	d			23p53											08 42						
Queenborough	d			23p57											08 46						
Swale	d			00 01											08 50						
Kemsley	d			00 05											08 54						
Sittingbourne [4]	a	23p02	00 02	00 10		06 44		07 28		07 44		08 06	08 28		08 59		08 44	09 06	09 28		
Newington	d		00 08			06 50				07 50							08 50				
Rainham (Kent)	d	23p10	00 12			06 54		07 36		07 54		08 15	08 36				08 54	09 15	09 36		
Gillingham (Kent) [4]	d	23p15	00a17		06 45	06 59	07 15	07 41	07 45	07 59	08 15	08 20	08 41			08 54	08 59	09 20	09 41		09 24
Chatham [4]	d	23p20			06 49	07 04	07 19	07 46	07 49	08 04	08 19	08 24	08 46			08 58	09 04	09 24	09 46		09 28
Rochester [4]	d	23p22			06 51	07 06	07 21	07 48	07 51	08 06	08 21	08 27	08 48			09 00	09 06	09 27	09 48		09 30
Strood [4]	a				06 56		07 26		07 56		08 26	08 31				09 05		09 31			09 35
Gravesend [4]	a				07 08		07 38		08 08		08 38	08 42				09 17		09 42			09 47
Greenhithe for Bluewater	a				07 17		07 47		08 17		08 47					09 23					09 53
Dartford [4]	a				07 24		07 54		08 24		08 54					09 28					09 58
London Bridge [4] ⊖	a				08 06		08 36		09 06		09 36					10 06					10 36
London Cannon Street [4] ⊖	a																				
London Waterloo (East) [4] ⊖	a				08 11		08 41		09 11		09 41					10 11					10 41
London Charing Cross [4] ⊖	a				08 14		08 44		09 14		09 44					10 14					10 44
Sole Street	d					07 17				08 17							09 17				
Meopham	d	23p33				07 19				08 19							09 19				
Longfield	d	23p37				07 23				08 23							09 23				
Farningham Road	d					07 27				08 27							09 27				
Swanley [4]	a					07 32				08 32							09 32				
St Mary Cray	a					07 36				08 36							09 36				
Bromley South [4]	a	23p50				07 42		08 13		08 42			09 13				09 42		10 13		
Elephant & Castle ⊖	a																				
London Blackfriars [3] ⊖	a																				
London Victoria [15] ⊖	a	00 10				08 03		08 30		09 02			09 29				10 02		10 29		
Ebbsfleet International	a											08 47						09 47			
Stratford International ⊖	a											08 59						09 59			
St Pancras International [15] ⊖	a											09 07						10 06			

A not 23 May

B ⌶ from Margate

C ⌶ from Faversham

Table 212

Sundays

Ramsgate, Dover, Sheerness-on-Sea and Medway - London

		SE	SE	SE [1]	SE	SE [1] B ⌶	SE [1] A ⌶	SE	SE	SE	SE [1]	SE	SE [1] B ⌶	SE [1] A ⌶	SE	SE	SE	SE	SE [1]	SE	SE [1] A ⌶	SE [1] A ⌶	SE
Ramsgate [4]	d						09 34							10 34								11 34	
Dumpton Park	d						09 37							10 37								11 37	
Broadstairs	d						09 40							10 40								11 40	
Margate [4]	d						09 45							10 45								11 45	
Westgate-on-Sea	d						09 49							10 49								11 49	
Birchington-on-Sea	d						09 52							10 52								11 52	
Herne Bay	d						10 01							11 01								12 01	
Chestfield & Swalecliffe	d						10 05							11 05								12 05	
Whitstable	d						10 08							11 08								12 08	
Dover Priory [4]	d					09 34							10 34								11 34		
Kearsney	d					09 38							10 38								11 38		
Shepherds Well	d					09 43							10 43								11 43		
Snowdown	d					09 47							10 47								11 47		
Aylesham	d					09 49							10 49								11 49		
Adisham	d					09 52							10 52								11 52		
Bekesbourne	d					09 56							10 56								11 56		
Canterbury East [4]	d					10 01					10 22		11 01						11 22		12 01		
Selling	d					10 10							11 10								12 10		
Faversham [2]	a					10 15	10 17				10 33		11 15	11 17					11 33		12 15	12 17	
	d			09 34	09 58	10 21	<				10 34	10 58	11 21	<		11 28			11 34	11 58	12 21	<	
Teynham	d			09 40							10 40								11 40				
Sheerness-on-Sea	d	09 42							10 42								11 42						
Queenborough	d	09 46							10 46								11 46						
Swale	d	09 50							10 50								11 50						
Kemsley	d	09 54							10 54								11 54						
Sittingbourne [4]	a	09 59		09 44	10 06	10 28			10 59		10 44	11 06	11 28			11 36	11 59		11 44	12 06	12 28		
Newington	d			09 50							10 50								11 50				
Rainham (Kent)	d			09 54	10 15	10 36					10 54	11 15	11 36			11 45			11 54	12 15	12 36		
Gillingham (Kent) [4]	d		09 54	09 59	10 20	10 41		10 24		10 54	10 59	11 20	11 41		11 24	11 50		11 54	11 59	12 20	12 41		12 24
Chatham [4]	d		09 58	10 04	10 24	10 46		10 28		10 58	11 04	11 24	11 46		11 28	11 54		11 58	12 04	12 24	12 46		12 28
Rochester [4]	d		10 00	10 06	10 27	10 48		10 30		11 00	11 06	11 27	11 48		11 30	11 57		12 00	12 06	12 27	12 48		12 30
Strood [4]	a		10 05		10 31			10 35		11 05		11 31			11 35	12 01		12 05		12 31			12 35
Gravesend [4]	a		10 17		10 42			10 47		11 17		11 42			11 47	12 12		12 17		12 42			12 47
Greenhithe for Bluewater	a		10 23					10 53		11 23					11 53			12 23					12 53
Dartford [4]	a		10 28					10 58		11 28					11 58			12 28					12 58
London Bridge [4] ⊖	a		11 06					11 36		12 06					12 36			13 06					13 36
London Cannon Street [4] ⊖	a																						
London Waterloo (East) [4] ⊖	a		11 11					11 41		12 11					12 41			13 11					13 41
London Charing Cross [4] ⊖	a		11 14					11 44		12 14					12 44			13 14					13 44
Sole Street	d			10 17							11 17								12 17				
Meopham	d			10 19							11 19								12 19				
Longfield	d			10 23							11 23								12 23				
Farningham Road	d			10 27							11 27								12 27				
Swanley [4]	a			10 32							11 32								12 32				
St Mary Cray	a			10 36							11 36								12 36				
Bromley South [4]	a			10 42		11 13					11 42		12 13						12 42		13 13		
Elephant & Castle ⊖	a																						
London Blackfriars [3] ⊖	a																						
London Victoria [15] ⊖	a			11 02		11 29					12 02		12 29						13 02		13 29		
Ebbsfleet International	a				10 47							11 47				12 17				12 47			
Stratford International ⊖	a				10 59							11 59				12 32				12 59			
St Pancras International [15] ⊖	a				11 06							12 06				12 39				13 06			

A ⌶ from Margate

B ⌶ from Faversham

Table 212

Sundays

Ramsgate, Dover, Sheerness-on-Sea and Medway - London

		SE	SE	SE	SE [1]	SE	SE [1] A	SE [1] B	SE	SE	SE	SE	SE [1]	SE	SE [1] A	SE [1] B	SE	SE	SE	SE	SE [1]
Ramsgate [4]	d							12 34								13 34					
Dumpton Park	d							12 37								13 37					
Broadstairs	d							12 40								13 40					
Margate [4]	d							12 45								13 45					
Westgate-on-Sea	d							12 49								13 49					
Birchington-on-Sea	d							12 52								13 52					
Herne Bay	d							13 01								14 01					
Chestfield & Swalecliffe	d							13 05								14 05					
Whitstable	d							13 08								14 08					
Dover Priory [4]	d						12 34								13 34						
Kearsney	d						12 38								13 38						
Shepherds Well	d						12 43								13 43						
Snowdown	d						12 47								13 47						
Aylesham	d						12 49								13 49						
Adisham	d						12 52								13 52						
Bekesbourne	d						12 56								13 56						
Canterbury East [4]	d				12 22		13 01						13 22		14 01						14 22
Selling	d						13 10								14 10						
Faversham [2]	a				12 33		13 15	13 17					13 33		14 15	14 17					14 33
	d	12 28			12 34	12 58	13 21	<		13 28			13 34	13 58	14 21	<		14 28			14 34
Teynham	d				12 40								13 40								14 40
Sheerness-on-Sea	d		12 42								13 42								14 42		
Queenborough	d		12 46								13 46								14 46		
Swale	d		12 50								13 50								14 50		
Kemsley	d		12 54								13 54								14 54		
Sittingbourne [4]	a	12 36	12 59		12 44	13 06	13 28			13 36	13 59		13 44	14 06	14 28			14 36	14 59		14 44
Newington	d				12 50								13 50								14 50
Rainham (Kent)	d	12 45			12 54	13 15	13 36			13 45			13 54	14 15	14 36			14 45			14 54
Gillingham (Kent) [4]	d	12 50		12 54	12 59	13 20	13 41		13 24	13 50		13 54	13 59	14 20	14 41		14 24	14 50		14 54	14 59
Chatham [4]	d	12 54		12 58	13 04	13 24	13 46		13 28	13 54		13 58	14 04	14 24	14 46		14 28	14 54		14 58	15 04
Rochester [4]	d	12 57		13 00	13 06	13 27	13 48		13 30	13 57		14 00	14 06	14 27	14 48		14 30	14 57		15 00	15 06
Strood [4]	a	13 01		13 05		13 31			13 35	14 01		14 05		14 31			14 35	15 01		15 05	
Gravesend [4]	a	13 12		13 17		13 42			13 47	14 12		14 17		14 42			14 47	15 12		15 17	
Greenhithe for Bluewater	a			13 23					13 53			14 23					14 53			15 23	
Dartford [4]	a			13 28					13 58			14 28					14 58			15 28	
London Bridge [4] ⊖	a			14 06					14 36			15 06					15 36			16 06	
London Cannon Street [4] ⊖	a																				
London Waterloo (East) [4] ⊖	a			14 11					14 41			15 11					15 41			16 11	
London Charing Cross [4] ⊖	a			14 14					14 44			15 14					15 44			16 14	
Sole Street	d				13 17								14 17								15 17
Meopham	d				13 19								14 19								15 19
Longfield	d				13 23								14 23								15 23
Farningham Road	d				13 27								14 27								15 27
Swanley [4]	a				13 32								14 32								15 32
St Mary Cray	a				13 36								14 36								15 36
Bromley South [4]	a				13 42		14 13						14 42		15 13						15 42
Elephant & Castle ⊖	a																				
London Blackfriars [3] ⊖	a																				
London Victoria [15] ⊖	a				14 02		14 29						15 02		15 29						16 02
Ebbsfleet International	a	13 17				13 47				14 17				14 47				15 17			
Stratford International ⊖	a	13 29				13 59				14 32				15 02				15 29			
St Pancras International [15] ⊖	a	13 36				14 06				14 39				15 09				15 36			

A from Faversham

B from Margate

Table 212

Sundays

Ramsgate, Dover, Sheerness-on-Sea and Medway - London

		SE	SE [1] B	SE [1] A	SE	SE	SE	SE	SE [1]	SE	SE [1] B	SE [1] A	SE	SE	SE	SE	SE	SE [1]	SE	SE [1] B	SE [1] A	SE	SE
Ramsgate [4]	d			14 34								15 34									16 34		
Dumpton Park	d			14 37								15 37									16 37		
Broadstairs	d			14 40								15 40									16 40		
Margate [4]	d			14 45								15 45									16 45		
Westgate-on-Sea	d			14 49								15 49									16 49		
Birchington-on-Sea	d			14 52								15 52									16 52		
Herne Bay	d			15 01								16 01									17 01		
Chestfield & Swalecliffe	d			15 05								16 05									17 05		
Whitstable	d			15 08								16 08									17 08		
Dover Priory [4]	d		14 34								15 34									16 34			
Kearsney	d		14 38								15 38									16 38			
Shepherds Well	d		14 43								15 43									16 43			
Snowdown	d		14 47								15 47									16 47			
Aylesham	d		14 49								15 49									16 49			
Adisham	d		14 52								15 52									16 52			
Bekesbourne	d		14 56								15 56									16 56			
Canterbury East [4]	d		15 01						15 22		16 01							16 22		17 01			
Selling	d		15 10								16 10									17 10			
Faversham [2]	a		15 15	15 17					15 33		16 15	16 17						16 33		17 15	17 17		
	d	14 58	15 21	<		15 28			15 34	15 58	16 21	<		16 28	16 28			16 34	16 58	17 21	<		17 28
Teynham	d								15 40									16 40					
Sheerness-on-Sea	d						15 42									16 42							
Queenborough	d						15 46									16 46							
Swale	d						15 50									16 50							
Kemsley	d						15 54									16 54							
Sittingbourne [4]	a	15 06	15 28			15 36	15 59		15 44	16 06	16 28			16 36	16 36	16 59		16 44	17 06	17 28			17 36
Newington	d								15 50									16 50					
Rainham (Kent)	d	15 15	15 36			15 45			15 54	16 15	16 36			16 45	16 45			16 54	17 15	17 36			17 45
Gillingham (Kent) [4]	d	15 20	15 41		15 24	15 50		15 54	15 59	16 20	16 41		16 24	16 50	16 50		16 54	16 59	17 20	17 41		17 24	17 50
Chatham [4]	d	15 24	15 46		15 28	15 54		15 58	16 04	16 24	16 46		16 28	16 54	16 54		16 58	17 04	17 24	17 46		17 28	17 54
Rochester [4]	d	15 27	15 48		15 30	15 57		16 00	16 06	16 27	16 48		16 30	16 57	16 57		17 00	17 06	17 27	17 48		17 30	17 57
Strood [4]	a	15 31			15 35	16 01		16 05		16 31			16 35	17 01	17 01		17 05		17 31			17 35	18 01
Gravesend [4]	a	15 42			15 47	16 12		16 17		16 42			16 47	17 12	17 12		17 17		17 42			17 47	18 12
Greenhithe for Bluewater	a				15 53			16 23					16 53				17 23					17 53	
Dartford [4]	a				15 58			16 28					16 58				17 28					17 58	
London Bridge [4] ⊖	a				16 36			17 06					17 36				18 06					18 36	
London Cannon Street [4] ⊖	a																						
London Waterloo (East) [4] ⊖	a				16 41			17 11					17 41				18 11					18 41	
London Charing Cross [4] ⊖	a				16 44			17 14					17 44				18 14					18 44	
Sole Street	d								16 17									17 17					
Meopham	d								16 19									17 19					
Longfield	d								16 23									17 23					
Farningham Road	d								16 27									17 27					
Swanley [4]	a								16 32									17 32					
St Mary Cray	a								16 36									17 36					
Bromley South [4]	a		16 13						16 42		17 13							17 42		18 13			
Elephant & Castle ⊖	a																						
London Blackfriars [3] ⊖	a																						
London Victoria [15] ⊖	a		16 29						17 02		17 29							18 02		18 29			
Ebbsfleet International	a	15 47				16 17				16 47				17 16	17 16				17 47				18 16
Stratford International ⊖	a	15 59				16 29				16 59				17 27	17 27				17 59				18 27
St Pancras International [15] ⊖	a	16 06				16 40				17 06				17 34	17 38				18 09				18 38

A from Margate

B from Faversham

Table 212

Sundays

Ramsgate, Dover, Sheerness-on-Sea and Medway - London

Station		SE	SE	SE ■	SE	SE ■	SE ■	SE	SE	SE	SE	SE ■	SE	SE ■	SE ■	SE	SE	SE	SE	SE ■	SE	SE
Ramsgate ■4	d						17 34								18 34							
Dumpton Park	d						17 37								18 37							
Broadstairs	d						17 40								18 40							
Margate ■4	d						17 45								18 45							
Westgate-on-Sea	d						17 49								18 49							
Birchington-on-Sea	d						17 52								18 52							
Herne Bay	d						18 01								19 01							
Chestfield & Swalecliffe	d						18 05								19 05							
Whitstable	d						18 08								19 08							
Dover Priory ■4	d					17 34								18 34								
Kearsney	d					17 38								18 38								
Shepherds Well	d					17 43								18 43								
Snowdown	d					17 47								18 47								
Aylesham	d					17 49								18 49								
Adisham	d					17 52								18 52								
Bekesbourne	d					17 56								18 56								
Canterbury East ■4	d			17 22		18 01						18 22		19 01						19 22		
Selling	d					18 10								19 10								
Faversham ■2	a			17 33		18 15	18 17					18 33		19 15	19 17					19 33		
	d			17 34	17 58	18 21	<		18 28			18 34	18 58	19 21	<				19 28	19 34		19 58
Teynham	d			17 40								18 40								19 40		
Sheerness-on-Sea	d	17 42								18 42							19 42					
Queenborough	d	17 46								18 46							19 46					
Swale	d	17 50								18 50							19 50					
Kemsley	d	17 54								18 54							19 54					
Sittingbourne ■4	a	17 59		17 44	18 06	18 28			18 36	18 59		18 44	19 06	19 28			19 59		19 36	19 44		20 06
Newington	d			17 50								18 50								19 50		
Rainham (Kent)	d			17 54	18 15	18 36			18 45			18 54	19 15	19 36					19 45	19 54		20 15
Gillingham (Kent) ■4	d		17 54	17 59	18 20	18 41		18 24	18 50		18 54	18 59	19 20	19 41		19 24		19 45	19 50	19 59	20 15	20 20
Chatham ■4	d		17 58	18 04	18 24	18 46		18 28	18 54		18 58	19 04	19 24	19 46		19 28		19 49	19 54	20 04	20 19	20 24
Rochester ■4	d		18 00	18 06	18 27	18 48		18 30	18 57		19 00	19 06	19 27	19 48		19 30		19 51	19 57	20 06	20 21	20 27
Strood ■4	a		18 05		18 31			18 35	19 01		19 05		19 31			19 35		19 56	20 01		20 26	20 31
Gravesend ■4	a		18 17		18 42			18 47	19 12		19 17		19 42			19 47		20 08	20 12		20 38	20 42
Greenhithe for Bluewater	a		18 23					18 53			19 23					19 53		20 17			20 47	
Dartford ■4	a		18 28					18 58			19 28					19 58		20 24			20 54	
London Bridge ■4 ⊖	a		19 06					19 36			20 06					20 36		21 06			21 36	
London Cannon Street ■4 ⊖	a																					
London Waterloo (East) ■4 ⊖	a		19 11					19 41			20 11					20 41		21 11			21 41	
London Charing Cross ■4 ⊖	a		19 14					19 44			20 14					20 44		21 14			21 44	
Sole Street	d			18 17								19 17								20 17		
Meopham	d			18 19								19 19								20 19		
Longfield	d			18 23								19 23								20 23		
Farningham Road	d			18 27								19 27								20 27		
Swanley ■4	a			18 32								19 32								20 32		
St Mary Cray	a			18 36								19 36								20 36		
Bromley South ■4	a			18 42		19 13						19 42		20 13						20 42		
Elephant & Castle ⊖	a																					
London Blackfriars ■3 ⊖	a																					
London Victoria ■15 ⊖	a			19 02		19 29						20 02		20 29						21 02		
Ebbsfleet International	a				18 47				19 17				19 47						20 16			20 47
Stratford International ⊖	a				19 02				19 29				19 59						20 27			20 59
St Pancras International ■15 ⊖	a				19 09				19 36				20 06						20 38			21 06

Table 212

Sundays

Ramsgate, Dover, Sheerness-on-Sea and Medway - London

Station		SE ■	SE ■	SE	SE	SE	SE ■	SE	SE	SE ■	SE ■	SE	SE	SE	SE ■	SE	SE	SE	SE ■	SE ■	SE ■	SE ■	SE ■
Ramsgate ■4	d		19 34								20 34									21 34			22 34
Dumpton Park	d		19 37								20 37									21 37			22 37
Broadstairs	d		19 40								20 40									21 40			22 40
Margate ■4	d		19 45								20 45									21 45			22 45
Westgate-on-Sea	d		19 49								20 49									21 49			22 49
Birchington-on-Sea	d		19 52								20 52									21 52			22 52
Herne Bay	d		20 01								21 01									22 01			23 01
Chestfield & Swalecliffe	d		20 05								21 05									22 05			23 05
Whitstable	d		20 08								21 08									22 08			23 08
Dover Priory ■4	d	19 34								20 34									21 34			22 34	
Kearsney	d	19 38								20 38									21 38			22 38	
Shepherds Well	d	19 43								20 43									21 43			22 43	
Snowdown	d	19 47								20 47									21 47			22 47	
Aylesham	d	19 49								20 49									21 49			22 49	
Adisham	d	19 52								20 52									21 52			22 52	
Bekesbourne	d	19 56								20 56									21 56			22 56	
Canterbury East ■4	d	20 01								21 01									22 01			23 01	
Selling	d	20 10								21 10									22 10			23 10	
Faversham ■2	a	20 15	20 17							21 15	21 17								22 15	22 17		23 15	23 17
	d	20 21	<			20 28	20 34		20 58	21 21	<			21 28	21 34		21 58	21 58	22 21	<	22 34		23 21
Teynham	d						20 40								21 40						22 40		
Sheerness-on-Sea	d			20 42								21 42											
Queenborough	d			20 46								21 46											
Swale	d			20 50								21 50											
Kemsley	d			20 54								21 54											
Sittingbourne ■4	a	20 28		20 59		20 36	20 44		21 06	21 28		21 59		21 36	21 44		22 06	22 06	22 28		22 44		23 28
Newington	d						20 50								21 50						22 50		
Rainham (Kent)	d	20 36				20 45	20 54		21 15	21 36				21 45	21 54		22 15	22 15	22 36		22 54		23 36
Gillingham (Kent) ■4	d	20 41			20 45	20 50	20 59	21 15	21 20	21 41			21 45	21 50	21 59	22 15	22 20	22 20	22 41		22 59		23 41
Chatham ■4	d	20 46			20 49	20 54	21 04	21 19	21 24	21 46			21 49	21 54	22 04	22 19	22 24	22 24	22 46		23 04		23 46
Rochester ■4	d	20 48			20 51	20 57	21 06	21 21	21 27	21 48			21 51	21 57	22 06	22 21	22 27	22 27	22 48		23 06		23 48
Strood ■4	a				20 56	21 01		21 26	21 31				21 56	22 01		22 26	22 31	22 31					
Gravesend ■4	a				21 08	21 12		21 38	21 42				22 08	22 12		22 38	22 42	22 42					
Greenhithe for Bluewater	a				21 17			21 47					22 17			22 47							
Dartford ■4	a				21 24			21 54					22 24			22 54							
London Bridge ■4 ⊖	a				22 06			22 36					23 06			23 36							
London Cannon Street ■4 ⊖	a																						
London Waterloo (East) ■4 ⊖	a				22 11			22 41					23 11			23 41							
London Charing Cross ■4 ⊖	a				22 14			22 44					23 14			23 44							
Sole Street	d						21 17								22 17						23 17		
Meopham	d						21 19								22 19						23 19		
Longfield	d						21 23								22 23						23 23		
Farningham Road	d						21 27								22 27						23 27		
Swanley ■4	a						21 32								22 32						23 32		
St Mary Cray	a						21 36								22 36						23 36		
Bromley South ■4	a	21 13					21 42			22 13					22 42				23 13		23 42		00 13
Elephant & Castle ⊖	a																						
London Blackfriars ■3 ⊖	a																						
London Victoria ■15 ⊖	a	21 29					22 02			22 29					23 02				23 29		00 02		00 29
Ebbsfleet International	a					21 17			21 47					22 17			22 47	22 47					
Stratford International ⊖	a					21 31			21 59					22 29			22 59	23 02					
St Pancras International ■15 ⊖	a					21 42			22 06					22 36			23 06	23 09					

Table 212

Sundays

Ramsgate, Dover, Sheerness-on-Sea and Medway - London

		SE	SE
Ramsgate 4	d		
Dumpton Park	d		
Broadstairs	d		
Margate 4	d		
Westgate-on-Sea	d		
Birchington-on-Sea	d		
Herne Bay	d		
Chestfield & Swalecliffe	d		
Whitstable	d		
Dover Priory 4	d		
Kearsney	d		
Shepherds Well	d		
Snowdown	d		
Aylesham	d		
Adisham	d		
Bekesbourne	d		
Canterbury East 4	d		
Selling	d		
Faversham 4	a		
	d		
Teynham	d		
Sheerness-on-Sea	d	22 42	23 42
Queenborough	d	22 46	23 46
Swale	d	22 50	23 50
Kemsley	d	22 54	23 54
Sittingbourne 4	a	22 59	23 59
Newington	d		
Rainham (Kent)	d		
Gillingham (Kent) 4	d		
Chatham 4	d		
Rochester 4	d		
Strood 4	a		
Gravesend 4	a		
Greenhithe for Bluewater	a		
Dartford 4	a		
London Bridge 4 ⊖	a		
London Cannon Street 4 ⊖	a		
London Waterloo (East) 4 ⊖	a		
London Charing Cross 4 ⊖	a		
Sole Street	d		
Meopham	d		
Longfield	d		
Farningham Road	d		
Swanley 4	a		
St Mary Cray	a		
Bromley South 4	a		
Elephant & Castle ⊖	a		
London Blackfriars 3 ⊖	a		
London Victoria 15 ⊖	a		
Ebbsfleet International	a		
Stratford International ⊖	a		
St Pancras International 15 ⊖	a		

Network Diagram for Tables 216, 217, 218, 219, 221, 222

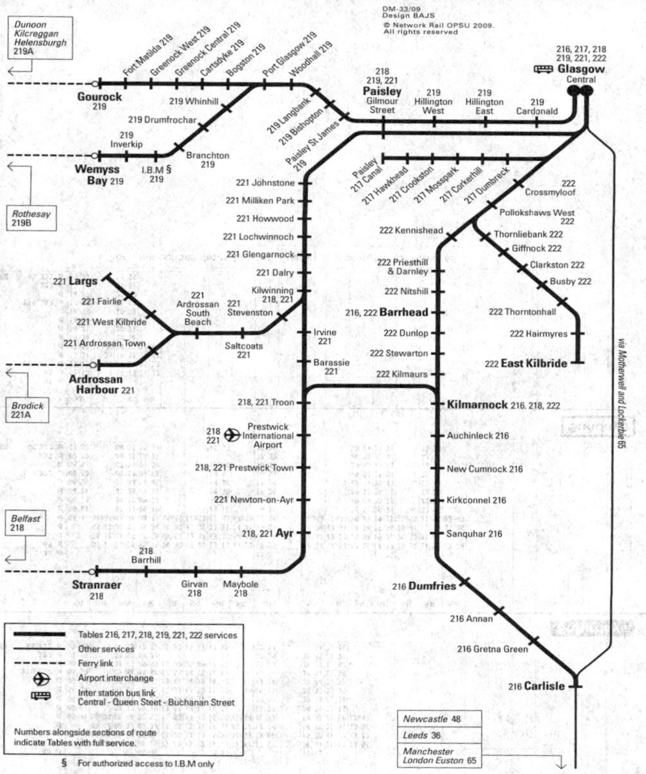

Table 216

Mondays to Fridays

Glasgow Central and Kilmarnock - Dumfries and Carlisle

			SR	SR	SR	SR	SR	SR	SR	SR	SR	SR	SR	SR	SR	SR	SR	SR	SR
				A	B		B	A			◇			A	B				
Glasgow Central [15]	65,222	d					07 08	07 08	08 37	10 12	12 12	13 12		16 12	16 12	17 42	19 12	21 12	23 12
Barrhead	222	d					07 23	07 23	08 48					16 23	16 23	17 54	19 24	21 24	23 32
Kilmarnock [3]	218,222	a					07 48	07 48	09 17	10 47	12 47	13 47		16 49	16 49	18 22	19 50	21 50	23 59
		d					07 48	07 48	09 17	10 49	12 48	13 49		16 49	16 49	18 26	19 51	21 51	23 59
Auchinleck		d					08 05	08 05	09 34	11 05	13 04	14 05		17 06	17 06	18 42	20 07	22 07	00 18
New Cumnock		d					08 13	08 13	09 42	11 14	13 13	14 14		17 14	17 14	18 51	20 16	22 16	00 29
Kirkconnel		d					08 23	08 23	09 51	11 22	13 21	14 22		17 23	17 23	18 59	20 24	22 24	00 40
Sanquhar		d					08 28	08 28	09 56	11 27	13 26	14 27		17 28	17 28	19 04	20 29	22 29	00 45
Dumfries		d	04 56	06 17	06 17	07 45	08 56	08 56	10 22	11 55	13 54	14 55	17 07	17 56	17 56	19 33	20 57	22 57	01a18
Annan		d	05 11	06 32	06 32	08 00	09 11	09 11	10 38	12 11	14 10	15 11	17 22	18 11	18 11	19 48	21 15	23 12	
Gretna Green		d	05 20	06 41	06 41	08 09	09 20	09 20	10 46	12 19	14 18	15 19	17 31	18 20	18 20	19 57	21 24	23 21	
Carlisle [8]	65	a	05 33	06 54	06 54	08 22	09 37	09 37	11 02	12 35	14 33	15 34	17 44	18 35	18 35	20 11	21 43	23 39	
Newcastle [8]	48	a		08 54	09 01		11 03	11 01			15 58			20 09	20 12				

Saturdays

			SR	SR	SR	SR	SR	SR	SR	SR	SR	SR	SR	SR	SR	SR	SR	SR	SR	SR	SR	SR
											◇ D	◇ E				D	E					
Glasgow Central [15]	65,222	d				07 08	08 37		10 12		12 12	12 12	13 12			16 12	16 12		17 42	19 12		22 12
Barrhead	222	d				07 23	08 48									16 23	16 23		17 54	19 24		22 23
Kilmarnock [3]	218,222	a				07 48	09 17		10 47		12 47	12 47	13 47			16 49	16 49		18 22	19 50		22 50
		d				07 48	09 17		10 49		12 48	12 48	13 49			16 49	16 49		18 26	19 51		22 51
Auchinleck		d				08 05	09 34		11 05		13 04	13 04	14 05			17 06	17 06		18 42	20 07		23 07
New Cumnock		d				08 13	09 42		11 14		13 13	13 13	14 14			17 14	17 14		18 51	20 16		23 16
Kirkconnel		d				08 23	09 51		11 22		13 21	13 21	14 22			17 23	17 23		18 59	20 24		23 24
Sanquhar		d				08 28	09 56		11 27		13 26	13 26	14 27			17 28	17 28		19 04	20 29		23 29
Dumfries		d	04 56	06 17	07 45	08 56	10 22	11 02	11 55	13 14	13 54	13 54	14 55	16 04	17 07	17 56	17 56	18 49	19 33	20 57	22 13	23 57
Annan		d	05 11	06 32	08 00	09 11	10 38	11 17	12 11	13 29	14 10	14 10	15 11	16 19	17 22	18 11	18 11	19 04	19 48	21 15	22 28	00 12
Gretna Green		d	05 20	06 41	08 09	09 20	10 46	11 26	12 19	13 38	14 18	14 18	15 19	16 28	17 31	18 20	18 20	19 13	19 57	21 24	22 37	00 21
Carlisle [8]	65	a	05 33	06 54	08 22	09 37	11 02	11 37	12 35	13 55	14 34	14 34	15 34	16 39	17 44	18 35	18 35	19 26	20 11	21 43	22 50	00 36
Newcastle [8]	48	a		08 54		11 01					15 58	16 01				20 11	20 14					

Sundays

			SR	SR	SR	SR	SR
Glasgow Central [15]	65,222	d			15 12		22 12
Barrhead	222	d			15 26		22 24
Kilmarnock [3]	218,222	a			15 52		22 48
		d			15 53		22 49
Auchinleck		d			16 10		23 06
New Cumnock		d			16 18		23 14
Kirkconnel		d			16 27		23 23
Sanquhar		d			16 32		23 28
Dumfries		d	13 00	15 01	17 00	18 57	23 56
Annan		d	13 15	15 16	17 15	19 12	00 11
Gretna Green		d	13 24	15 25	17 24	19 21	00 20
Carlisle [8]	65	a	13 37	15 38	17 37	19 34	00 35
Newcastle [8]	48	a					

A until 3 September
B from 6 September
D until 4 September
E from 11 September

For connections to London Euston please refer to Table 65

Table 216

Mondays to Fridays

Carlisle and Dumfries - Kilmarnock and Glasgow Central

			SR	SR	SR	SR	SR	SR	SR	SR	SR	SR	SR	SR
									◇			◇		
Newcastle [8]	48	d				06 49			13 24			17 12		
Carlisle [8]	65	d		05 27	06 08	08 15	11 12	13 12	15 12	16 17	17 55	19 17	21 12	23 06
Gretna Green		d		05 38	06 19	08 26	11 23	13 23	15 23	16 28	18 06	19 28	21 23	23 17
Annan		d		05 47	06 27	08 34	11 31	13 31	15 31	16 36	18 14	19 37	21 31	23 25
Dumfries		d	05 41	06a04	06 46	08 53	11 53	13 48	15 50	16a54	18 33	19 55	21 50	23a43
Sanquhar		d	06 07		07 12	09 19	12 19	14 16	16 16		18 59	20 21	22 16	
Kirkconnel		d	06 12		07 17	09 24	12 24	14 21	16 21		19 04	20 26	22 21	
New Cumnock		d	06 21		07 26	09 33	12 33	14 30	16 30		19 13	20 35	22 30	
Auchinleck		d	06 29		07 34	09 41	12 41	14 38	16 38		19 21	20 44	22 38	
Kilmarnock [3]	218,222	a	06 50		07 51	09 58	12 58	14 55	16 55		19 38	21 01	22 55	
		d	06 53		07 53	09 59	13 00	15 00	16 57		20 00	21 02	22 57	
Barrhead	222	d	07 19		08 20	10 21			17 22		20 20	21 22	23 21	
Glasgow Central [15]	65,222	a	07 32		08 35	10 37	13 33	15 33	17 35		20 34	21 36	23 35	

Saturdays

			SR	SR	SR	SR	SR	SR	SR	SR	SR	SR	SR	SR	SR	SR	SR	SR
											◇				◇			
Newcastle [8]	48	d				06 34					13 24				17 12			
Carlisle [8]	65	d		05 27	06 08	08e15	09 42	12 20	13 12	14 22	15 08	16 17	17 12	17 55	19 17	20 22	21 12	23 06
Gretna Green		d		05 38	06 19	08 26	09 53	12 31	13 23	14 33	15 19	16 28	17 23	18 06	19 28	20 33	21 23	23 17
Annan		d		05 47	06 27	08 34	10 02	12 39	13 31	14 41	15 27	16 36	17 31	18 14	19 36	20 41	21 31	23 25
Dumfries		d	05 41	06a04	06 46	08 53	10a19	12a57	13 48	14a59	15 50	16a54	17a49	18 33	19 55	20a59	21 50	23a43
Sanquhar		d	06 07		07 12	09 19			14 16		16 16			18 59	20 21		22 16	
Kirkconnel		d	06 12		07 17	09 24			14 21		16 21			19 04	20 26		22 21	
New Cumnock		d	06 21		07 26	09 33			14 30		16 30			19 13	20 35		22 30	
Auchinleck		d	06 29		07 34	09 41			14 38		16 38			19 21	20 43		22 38	
Kilmarnock [3]	218,222	a	06 50		07 51	09 58			14 55		16 55			19 38	21 01		22 55	
		d	06 53		07 53	09 59			15 00		16 57			20 00	21 01		22 57	
Barrhead	222	d	07 19		08 20	10 21					17 22			20 20	21 22		23 21	
Glasgow Central [15]	65,222	a	07 33		08 35	10 37			15 33		17 35			20 34	21 36		23 35	

Sundays

			SR	SR	SR	SR
Newcastle [8]	48	d				
Carlisle [8]	65	d	13 12	15 12	19 12	21 22
Gretna Green		d	13 23	15 23	19 23	21 33
Annan		d	13 31	15 31	19 31	21 41
Dumfries		d	13 50	15a49	19 50	21a59
Sanquhar		d	14 16		20 16	
Kirkconnel		d	14 21		20 21	
New Cumnock		d	14 30		20 30	
Auchinleck		d	14 38		20 38	
Kilmarnock [3]	218,222	a	14 55		20 55	
		d	14 57		20 57	
Barrhead	222	d	15 21		21 21	
Glasgow Central [15]	65,222	a	15 36		21 35	

For connections from London Euston please refer to Table 65

Glasgow Central - Paisley Canal

		SR SO	SR	SR	SR	SR	SR	SR	SR	SR	SR	SR	SR	SR	SR	SR	SR	SR	SR	SR	SR	SR	SR
Glasgow Central 15	d	00 07	06 07	06 36	07 07	07 37	08 07	08 37	09 07	09 37	10 07	10 37	11 07	11 37	12 07	12 37	13 07	13 37	14 07	14 37	15 07	15 37	16 07
Dumbreck	d	00 13	06 13	06 42	07 13	07 43	08 13	08 43	09 13	09 43	10 13	10 43	11 13	11 43	12 13	12 43	13 13	13 43	14 13	14 43	15 13	15 43	16 13
Corkerhill	d	00 15	06 15	06 44	07 15	07 45	08 15	08 45	09 15	09 45	10 15	10 45	11 15	11 45	12 15	12 45	13 15	13 45	14 15	14 45	15 15	15 45	16 15
Mosspark	d	00 17	06 17	06 46	07 17	07 47	08 17	08 47	09 17	09 47	10 17	10 47	11 17	11 47	12 17	12 47	13 17	13 47	14 17	14 47	15 17	15 47	16 17
Crookston	d	00 19	06 19	06 48	07 19	07 49	08 19	08 49	09 19	09 49	10 19	10 49	11 19	11 49	12 19	12 49	13 19	13 49	14 19	14 49	15 19	15 49	16 19
Hawkhead	d	00 22	06 22	06 51	07 21	07 52	08 22	08 52	09 22	09 52	10 22	10 52	11 22	11 52	12 22	12 52	13 22	13 52	14 22	14 52	15 22	15 52	16 22
Paisley Canal	a	00 25	06 25	06 54	07 24	07 55	08 25	08 55	09 25	09 55	10 25	10 55	11 25	11 55	12 25	12 55	13 25	13 55	14 25	14 55	15 25	15 55	16 25

		SR	SR	SR	SR	SR	SR	SR	SR	SR	SR	SR	SR	SR	SR
Glasgow Central 15	d	16 37	17 07	17 37	18 07	18 37	19 07	19 37	20 07	20 37	21 07	21 37	22 07	22 37	23 07
Dumbreck	d	16 43	17 13	17 43	18 13	18 43	19 13	19 43	20 13	20 43	21 13	21 43	22 13	22 43	23 13
Corkerhill	d	16 45	17 15	17 45	18 15	18 45	19 15	19 45	20 15	20 45	21 15	21 45	22 15	22 45	23 15
Mosspark	d	16 47	17 17	17 47	18 17	18 47	19 17	19 47	20 17	20 47	21 17	21 47	22 17	22 47	23 17
Crookston	d	16 49	17 19	17 49	18 19	18 49	19 19	19 49	20 19	20 49	21 19	21 49	22 19	22 49	23 19
Hawkhead	d	16 52	17 22	17 52	18 22	18 52	19 22	19 52	20 22	20 52	21 22	21 52	22 22	22 52	23 22
Paisley Canal	a	16 55	17 25	17 55	18 25	18 55	19 25	19 55	20 25	20 55	21 25	21 55	22 25	22 55	23 25

Sundays

from 28 November

		SR	SR	SR	SR	SR	SR	SR	SR	SR
Glasgow Central 15	d	09 37	10 37	11 37	12 37	13 37	14 37	15 37	16 37	17 37
Dumbreck	d	09 43	10 43	11 43	12 43	13 43	14 43	15 43	16 43	17 43
Corkerhill	d	09 45	10 45	11 45	12 45	13 45	14 45	15 45	16 45	17 45
Mosspark	d	09 47	10 47	11 47	12 47	13 47	14 47	15 47	16 47	17 47
Crookston	d	09 49	10 49	11 49	12 49	13 49	14 49	15 49	16 49	17 49
Hawkhead	d	09 52	10 52	11 52	12 52	13 52	14 52	15 52	16 52	17 52
Paisley Canal	a	09 55	10 55	11 55	12 55	13 55	14 55	15 55	16 55	17 55

Paisley Canal - Glasgow Central

		SR	SR	SR	SR	SR	SR	SR	SR	SR	SR	SR	SR	SR	SR	SR	SR	SR	SR	SR	SR	SR	SR
Paisley Canal	d	06 30	06 59	07 29	08 00	08 30	09 00	09 30	10 00	10 30	11 00	11 30	12 00	12 30	13 00	13 30	14 00	14 30	15 00	15 30	16 00	16 30	17 00
Hawkhead	d	06 33	07 02	07 32	08 03	08 33	09 03	09 33	10 03	10 33	11 03	11 33	12 03	12 33	13 03	13 33	14 03	14 33	15 03	15 33	16 03	16 33	17 03
Crookston	d	06 36	07 05	07 35	08 06	08 36	09 06	09 36	10 06	10 36	11 06	11 36	12 06	12 36	13 06	13 36	14 06	14 36	15 06	15 36	16 06	16 36	17 06
Mosspark	d	06 38	07 07	07 37	08 08	08 38	09 08	09 38	10 08	10 38	11 08	11 38	12 08	12 38	13 08	13 38	14 08	14 38	15 08	15 38	16 08	16 38	17 08
Corkerhill	d	06 39	07 09	07 39	08 10	08 40	09 10	09 40	10 10	10 40	11 10	11 40	12 10	12 40	13 10	13 40	14 10	14 40	15 10	15 40	16 10	16 40	17 10
Dumbreck	d	06 42	07 12	07 42	08 11	08 43	09 13	09 43	10 13	10 43	11 13	11 43	12 13	12 43	13 13	13 43	14 13	14 43	15 13	15 43	16 13	16 43	17 13
Glasgow Central 15	a	06 49	07 18	07 51	08 21	08 53	09 19	09 49	10 19	10 50	11 19	11 49	12 19	12 49	13 19	13 49	14 19	14 49	15 19	15 49	16 19	16 49	17 19

		SR	SR	SR	SR	SR	SR	SR	SR	SR	SR	SR	SR
Paisley Canal	d	17 30	18 00	18 30	19 00	19 30	20 00	20 30	21 00	21 30	22 00	22 30	23 00
Hawkhead	d	17 33	18 03	18 33	19 03	19 33	20 03	20 33	21 03	21 33	22 03	22 33	23 03
Crookston	d	17 36	18 06	18 36	19 06	19 36	20 06	20 36	21 06	21 36	22 06	22 36	23 06
Mosspark	d	17 38	18 08	18 38	19 08	19 38	20 08	20 38	21 08	21 38	22 08	22 38	23 08
Corkerhill	d	17 40	18 10	18 40	19 10	19 40	20 10	20 40	21 10	21 40	22 10	22 40	23 10
Dumbreck	d	17 43	18 13	18 43	19 13	19 43	20 13	20 43	21 13	21 43	22 13	22 43	23 13
Glasgow Central 15	a	17 53	18 19	18 49	19 19	19 50	20 19	20 49	21 19	21 49	22 19	22 50	23 20

Sundays

from 28 November

		SR	SR	SR	SR	SR	SR	SR	SR	SR
Paisley Canal	d	09 00	10 00	11 00	12 00	13 00	14 00	15 00	16 00	17 00
Hawkhead	d	09 03	10 03	11 03	12 03	13 03	14 03	15 03	16 03	17 03
Crookston	d	09 06	10 06	11 06	12 06	13 06	14 06	15 06	16 06	17 06
Mosspark	d	09 08	10 08	11 08	12 08	13 08	14 08	15 08	16 08	17 08
Corkerhill	d	09 10	10 10	11 10	12 09	13 10	14 10	15 10	16 10	17 10
Dumbreck	d	09 13	10 13	11 13	12 12	13 13	14 13	15 13	16 13	17 13
Glasgow Central 15	a	09 19	10 19	11 19	12 19	13 19	14 19	15 19	16 19	17 19

Glasgow Central and Kilmarnock - Girvan, Stranraer and Belfast

		SR	SR	SR	SR	SR	SR	SR	SR	SR	SR	SR	SR
			◇	◇		◇							
Glasgow Cent. 15 219,221,222	d		06 30	09 12		11 42		15 12		17 12			
Paisley Gilmour St 219,221 ✈	d					11 53							
Kilwinning 221	d					12 10							
Kilmarnock 3 222	a		07 20	09 48				15 49		17 51			
	d		07 32	10 04	11 05		13 34	16 03	17 04	18 09	19 05	21 10	23 10
Troon 221	d		07 45	10 17	11 19		13 46	16 16	17 16	18 21	19 16	21 22	23 22
Prestwick Int. Airport 221 ✈	d		07 50	10 22	11 22		13 51	16 20	17 21	18 26	19 22	21 27	23 27
Prestwick Town 221	d		07 52	10 24	11 24		13 53	16 22	17 23	18 28	19 24	21 29	23 29
Ayr 221	a		07 59	10 31	11 31	12 29	14 06	16 30	17 30	18 36	19 30	21 36	23 36
	d	05 45	08 00	10 32	11 32	12 32	14 07	16 30	17 31	18 38	19 31	21 37	23 36
Maybole	d	05 56	08 11	10 43	11 43	12 43	14 18	16 42	17 42	18 49	19 42	21 48	23 47
Girvan	d	06a12	08 26	11 02	11a59	12 58	14a34	16a58	17 57	19a05	19 57	22 07	00 07
Barrhill	d		08 45	11 22		13 18			18 16		20 18	22 26	00 26
Stranraer	a		09 21	11 57		13 54			18 52		20 54	23 00	01 00
Stranraer Harbour § ⛴	d												
Belfast Port § ⛴	a												

Sundays

		SR	SR
		◇	◇
Glasgow Cent. 15 219,221,222	d	11 40	16 25
Paisley Gilmour St 219,221 ✈	d	11 54	16 39
Kilwinning 221	d	12 11	16 56
Kilmarnock 3 222	a		
	d		
Troon 221	d		
Prestwick Int. Airport 221 ✈	d		
Prestwick Town 221	d		
Ayr 221	a	12 28	17 17
	d	12 30	17 19
Maybole	d	12 41	17 30
Girvan	d	12 56	17 47
Barrhill	d	13 14	18 06
Stranraer	a	13 51	18 42
Stranraer Harbour § ⛴	d		
Belfast Port § ⛴	a		

§ Stena HSS and shipping services operated by Stena Line

Belfast, Stranraer and Girvan - Kilmarnock and Glasgow Central

		SR SX	SR SO	SR	SR	SR	SR	SR	SR	SR	SR	SR	SR	SR SX
					◇		◇		◇			◇	◇	◇
Belfast Port § ⛴	d													
Stranraer Harbour § ⛴	a													
Stranraer	d			07 09	10 07		12 40		14 43			19 40	21 12	23 12
Barrhill	d			07 43	10 42		13 19		15 17			20 19	21 46	23 47
Girvan	d	06 20	06 20	08 01	11 01	12 06	13 37	14 40	15 36	17 33	19 33	20 37	22 06	00 06
Maybole	d	06 36	06 36	08 25	11 17	12 22	13 53	14 56	15 52	17 56	19 56	20 53	22 23	00 22
Ayr	a	06 48	06 48	08 35	11 29	12 34	14 05	15 08	16 04	18 08	20 08	21 05	22 35	00 34
	d	06 50	06 50	08 36	11 31	12 36	14 18	15 18	16 06	18 17	20 17	21 06	22 36	
Prestwick Town 221	a	06 55	06 55	08 41		12 41	14 23	15 23	16 11	18 23	20 22	21 11	22 41	
Prestwick Int. Airport 221 ✈	a	06 57	06 57	08 43		12 43	14 25	15 25	16 13	18 25	20 24	21 13		
Troon 221	a	07 02	07 02	08 48		12 48	14 30	15 30	16 18	18 30	20 29	21 18	22 46	
Kilmarnock 3	a	07 16	07 16	09 04		13 04	14 53	15 46	16 34	18 46	20 45	21 37		
	d	07 22	07 23	09 27				15 57				22 00		
Glengarnock	d													
Kilwinning 221	a				11 49								22 55	
Paisley Gilmour St 219,221 ✈	a				12 15								23 14	
Glasgow Cent 15 219,221,222	a	08 00	08 09	10 05	12 33			16 33				22 34	23 25	

Sundays

		SR	SR	SR
		◇	◇	◇
Belfast Port § ⛴	d			
Stranraer Harbour § ⛴	a			
Stranraer	d	10 40	14 40	19 40
Barrhill	d	11 14	15 14	20 15
Girvan	d	11 32	15 32	20 33
Maybole	d	11 48	15 48	20 49
Ayr	a	12 00	15 59	20 59
	d	12 00	15 59	21 00
Prestwick Town 221	a			
Prestwick Int. Airport 221 ✈	a			
Troon 221	a			
Kilmarnock 3	a			
	d			
Glengarnock	d			
Kilwinning 221	a	12 15	16 14	21 15
Paisley Gilmour St. 219,221 ✈	a	12 36	16 37	21 36
Glasgow Cent. 15 219,221,222	a	12 51	16 49	21 48

§ Stena HSS and shipping services operated by Stena Line

Table 219

Mondays to Saturdays

Glasgow Central - Wemyss Bay and Gourock

		SR	SR	SR	SR	SR	SR	SR	SR	SR	SR
Glasgow Central 15 221	d	05 55	06 05	06 25	06 32	06 55	07 05	07 25	07 35	07 50	08 05
Cardonald	d				06 39		07 12	07 32	07 42		08 12
Hillington East	d		06 13		06 41		07 14	07 34	07 44		08 14
Hillington West	d	06 03	06 15		06 43	07 03	07 16	07 36	07 46	07 58	08 16
Paisley Gilmour Street 221 ✈	d	06 07	06 19	06 36	06 47	07 07	07 20	07 40	07 50	08 02	08 20
Paisley St James	d			06 38			07 22		07 52		08 22
Bishopton	d	06 13	06 25	06 44	06 53	07 13	07 28	07 46	07 58	08 08	08 28
Langbank	d			06 49			07 34		08 04		08 34
Woodhall	d		06 32	06 53	07 01		07 38	07 54	08 08		08 38
Port Glasgow	d	06 23	06 35	06 56	07 04	07 23	07 41	07 57	08 11	08 18	08 41
Whinhill	d		06 40		07 08					08 22	
Drumfrochar	d		06 42		07 11					08 25	
Branchton	d		06 45		07 14					08 28	
I.B.M. §	d		06 48		07 16					08 30	
Inverkip	d		06 53		07 25					08 35	
Wemyss Bay	a		06 58		07 30					08 40	
Bogston	d			06 58		07 25	07 43	07 59	08 13		08 43
Cartsdyke	d	06 26		07 01		07 27	07 45	08 01	08 15		08 45
Greenock Central	d	06 28		07 03		07 29	07 47	08 03	08 17		08 47
Greenock West	d	06 31		07 05		07 32	07 50	08 06	08 20		08 50
Fort Matilda	d			07 08		07 35	07 53	08 09	08 23		08 53
Gourock	a	06 36		07 13		07 39	07 57	08 13	08 27		08 57

		SR	SR	SR	SR	SR	SR	SR	SR	SR	SR	SR
Glasgow Central 15 221	d	08 25	08 36	08 50	09 05	09 25	09 35	09 50	10 05	10 25	10 35	10 50
Cardonald	d		08 42		09 12		09 42		10 12		10 42	
Hillington East	d		08 44		09 14		09 44		10 14		10 44	
Hillington West	d		08 46		09 16		09 46		10 16		10 46	
Paisley Gilmour Street 221 ✈	d	08 36	08 50	09 01	09 20	09 36	09 50	10 01	10 20	10 36	10 50	11 01
Paisley St James	d		08 52		09 22		09 52		10 22		10 52	
Bishopton	d	08 42	08 58	09 07	09 28	09 42	09 58	10 07	10 28	10 42	10 58	11 07
Langbank	d		09 04		09 34		10 04		10 34		11 04	
Woodhall	d		09 08		09 38		10 08		10 38		11 08	
Port Glasgow	d	08 52	09 11	09 16	09 41	09 51	10 11	10 16	10 41	10 51	11 11	11 16
Whinhill	d			09 21				10 21				11 21
Drumfrochar	d			09 23				10 23				11 23
Branchton	d			09 26				10 26				11 26
I.B.M. §	d			09 29				10 29				11 29
Inverkip	d			09 34				10 34				11 34
Wemyss Bay	a			09 40				10 40				11 40
Bogston	d		09 13		09 43		10 13		10 43		11 13	
Cartsdyke	d		09 15		09 45		10 15		10 45		11 15	
Greenock Central	d	08 57	09 17		09 47	09 56	10 17		10 47	10 56	11 17	
Greenock West	d	08 59	09 20		09 50	09 59	10 20		10 50	10 59	11 20	
Fort Matilda	d	09 02	09 23		09 53	10 02	10 23		10 53	11 02	11 23	
Gourock	a	09 08	09 27		09 58	10 06	10 27		10 57	11 06	11 27	

		SR	SR	SR	SR	SR	SR	SR	SR	SR	SR	SR
Glasgow Central 15 221	d	11 05	11 25	11 35	11 50	12 05	12 25	12 35	12 50	13 05	13 25	13 35
Cardonald	d	11 12		11 42		12 12		12 42		13 12		13 42
Hillington East	d	11 14		11 44		12 14		12 44		13 14		13 44
Hillington West	d	11 16		11 46		12 16		12 46		13 16		13 46
Paisley Gilmour Street 221 ✈	d	11 20	11 36	11 50	12 01	12 20	12 36	12 50	13 01	13 20	13 36	13 50
Paisley St James	d	11 22		11 52		12 22		12 52		13 22		13 52
Bishopton	d	11 28	11 42	11 58	12 07	12 28	12 42	12 58	13 07	13 28	13 42	13 58
Langbank	d	11 34		12 04		12 34		13 04		13 34		14 04
Woodhall	d	11 38		12 08		12 38		13 08		13 38		14 08
Port Glasgow	d	11 41	11 51	12 11	12 16	12 41	12 51	13 11	13 16	13 41	13 51	14 11
Whinhill	d				12 21				13 21			
Drumfrochar	d				12 23				13 23			
Branchton	d				12 26				13 26			
I.B.M. §	d				12 29				13 29			
Inverkip	d				12 34				13 34			
Wemyss Bay	a				12 40				13 40			
Bogston	d	11 43		12 13		12 43		13 13		13 43		14 13
Cartsdyke	d	11 45		12 15		12 45		13 15		13 45		14 15
Greenock Central	d	11 47	11 56	12 17		12 47	12 56	13 17		13 47	13 56	14 17
Greenock West	d	11 50	11 59	12 20		12 50	12 59	13 20		13 50	13 59	14 20
Fort Matilda	d	11 53	12 02	12 23		12 53	13 02	13 23		13 53	14 02	14 23
Gourock	a	11 57	12 06	12 27		12 57	13 06	13 27		13 57	14 06	14 27

		SR	SR	SR	SR	SR	SR	SR	SR	SR	SR	SR
Glasgow Central 15 221	d	13 50	14 05	14 25	14 35	14 50	15 05	15 25	15 35	15 50	16 05	16 23
Cardonald	d		14 12		14 42		15 12		15 42		16 12	16 30
Hillington East	d		14 14		14 44		15 14		15 44		16 14	16 32
Hillington West	d		14 16		14 46		15 16		15 46	15 58	16 16	16 34
Paisley Gilmour Street 221 ✈	d	14 01	14 20	14 36	14 50	15 01	15 20	15 36	15 50	16 02	16 20	16 38
Paisley St James	d		14 22		14 52		15 22		15 52		16 22	16 40
Bishopton	d	14 07	14 28	14 42	14 58	15 07	15 28	15 42	15 58	16 08	16 28	16 46
Langbank	d		14 34		15 04		15 34		16 04		16 34	16 52
Woodhall	d		14 38		15 08		15 38		16 08		16 38	16 56
Port Glasgow	d	14 16	14 41	14 51	15 11	15 16	15 41	15 51	16 11	16 18	16 41	16 59
Whinhill	d	14 21				15 21				16 22		
Drumfrochar	d	14 23				15 23				16 25		
Branchton	d	14 26				15 26				16 28		
I.B.M. §	d	14 29				15 29				16 30		
Inverkip	d	14 34				15 34				16 35		
Wemyss Bay	a	14 40				15 40				16 40		
Bogston	d		14 43		15 13		15 43		16 13		16 43	17 01
Cartsdyke	d		14 45		15 15		15 45		16 15		16 45	17 03
Greenock Central	d		14 47	14 56	15 17		15 47	15 56	16 17		16 47	17 05
Greenock West	d		14 50	14 59	15 20		15 50	15 59	16 20		16 50	17 08
Fort Matilda	d		14 53	15 02	15 23		15 53	16 02	16 23		16 53	17 11
Gourock	a		14 57	15 06	15 27		15 57	16 06	16 27		16 57	17 15

		SR	SR	SR	SR	SR	SR	SR	SR	SR	SR	SR
Glasgow Central 15 221	d	16 33	16 55	17 05	17 15	17 25	17 40	17 55	18 05	18 25	18 35	18 50
Cardonald	d	16 40		17 12	17 22		17 47		18 12		18 42	
Hillington East	d	16 42		17 14	17 24		17 49		18 14		18 44	
Hillington West	d	16 44	17 03	17 16			17 51		18 16		18 46	
Paisley Gilmour Street 221 ✈	d	16 48	17 07	17 21	17 29	17 37	17 55	18 06	18 20	18 35	18 50	19 01
Paisley St James	d			17 23			17 57		18 22		18 52	
Bishopton	d	16 54	17 13	17 29	17 35		18 03	18 10	18 28	18 41	18 58	19 07
Langbank	d			17 34			18 09		18 34		19 04	
Woodhall	d			17 38			18 12		18 38		19 08	
Port Glasgow	d	17 04	17 23	17 41	17 45	17 51	18 14	18 20	18 41	18 50	19 11	19 16
Whinhill	d	17 08			17 49			18 25				19 21
Drumfrochar	d	17 11			17 52			18 27				19 23
Branchton	d	17 14			17 55			18 30				19 26
I.B.M. §	d				17 57			18 33				19 29
Inverkip	d	17 19			18 02			18 38				19 34
Wemyss Bay	a	17 25			18 08			18 44				19 40
Bogston	d		17 25	17 43			18 18		18 43		19 13	
Cartsdyke	d		17 27	17 46			18 20		18 45		19 15	
Greenock Central	d		17 29	17 48		17 56	18 22		18 47	18 55	19 17	
Greenock West	d		17 32	17 50		17 58	18 25		18 50	18 58	19 20	
Fort Matilda	d		17 35	17 53		18 01	18 28		18 53	19 01	19 23	
Gourock	a		17 39	17 57		18 06	18 32		18 57	19 06	19 27	

		SR	SR	SR	SR	SR	SR	SR	SR	SR	SR
Glasgow Central 15 221	d	19 05	19 25	19 39	19 50	20 05	20 35	20 50	21 05	21 35	21 50
Cardonald	d	19 12		19 46		20 12	20 42		21 12	21 42	
Hillington East	d	19 14		19 48		20 14	20 44		21 14	21 44	
Hillington West	d	19 15		19 50		20 15	20 46		21 16	21 46	
Paisley Gilmour Street 221 ✈	d	19 19	19 36	19 54	20 01	20 22	20 50	21 01	21 20	21 50	22 01
Paisley St James	d	19 21		19 56		20 24	20 52		21 22	21 52	
Bishopton	d	19 27	19 42	20 02	20 07	20 30	20 58	21 07	21 28	21 58	22 07
Langbank	d	19 33		20 08		20 35	21 04		21 34	22 04	
Woodhall	d	19 37		20 12		20 39	21 08		21 38	22 08	
Port Glasgow	d	19 40	19 51	20 15	20 17	20 42	21 11	21 16	21 41	22 11	22 16
Whinhill	d			20 19			21 15			22 15	
Drumfrochar	d			20 22			21 18			22 18	
Branchton	d			20 25			21 21			22 21	
I.B.M. §	d			20 27			21 23			22 23	
Inverkip	d			20 32			21 28			22 28	
Wemyss Bay	a			20 38			21 34			22 34	
Bogston	d	19 42				20 44			21 43		
Cartsdyke	d	19 44			20 20	20 47		21 20	21 45		22 20
Greenock Central	d	19 46	19 56		20 22	20 49		21 22	21 47		22 22
Greenock West	d	19 49	19 59		20 25	20 51		21 24	21 50		22 24
Fort Matilda	d	19 52	20 02		20 28	20 54		21 27	21 53		22 29
Gourock	a	19 57	20 06		20 33	20 59		21 32	21 57		22 33

§ For authorised access to and from I.B.M. only

Table 219

Mondays to Saturdays

Glasgow Central - Wemyss Bay and Gourock

		SR	SR	SR	SR	SR
Glasgow Central 15 221	d	22 05	22 35	22 50	23 20	23 50
Cardonald	d	22 12	22 42		23 27	23 57
Hillington East	d	22 14	22 44		23 29	23 59
Hillington West	d	22 16	22 46		23 31	00 01
Paisley Gilmour Street 221 ✈	d	22 20	22 50	23 01	23 35	00 05
Paisley St James	d	22 22	22 52		23 37	00 07
Bishopton	d	22 28	22 58	23 07	23 43	00 13
Langbank	d	22 34	23 04		23 49	00 19
Woodhall	d	22 38	23 08		23 53	00 23
Port Glasgow	d	22 41	23 11	23 16	23 56	00 26
Whinhill	d		23 15			
Drumfrochar	d		23 18			
Branchton	d		23 21			
I.B.M. §	d		23 23			
Inverkip	d		23 28			
Wemyss Bay	a		23 34			
Bogston	d	22 43			23 58	00 28
Cartsdyke	d	22 45		23 20	23 59	00 30
Greenock Central	d	22 47		23 22	00 02	00 32
Greenock West	d	22 50		23 24	00 05	00 35
Fort Matilda	d	22 53		23 29	00 08	00 38
Gourock	a	22 57		23 33	00 12	00 42

Sundays

		SR	SR	SR	SR	SR	SR B	SR	SR	SR B	SR	SR
Glasgow Central 15 221	d	07 20	07 50	08 20	08 50	09 20	09 35	09 50	10 20	10 35	10 50	11 20
Cardonald	d	07 27		08 27		09 27	09 42		10 27	10 42		11 27
Hillington East	d	07 29	07 58	08 29	08 58	09 29	09 44	09 58	10 29	10 44	10 58	11 29
Hillington West	d	07 31		08 31		09 31	09 46		10 31	10 47		11 31
Paisley Gilmour Street 221 ✈	d	07 35	08 03	08 35	09 03	09 35	09 50	10 03	10 35	10 51	11 03	11 35
Paisley St James	d			08 37		09 37	09 52		10 37	10 53		11 37
Bishopton	d	07 41	08 09	08 43	09 09	09 43	09 58	10 09	10 43	10 59	11 09	11 43
Langbank	d			08 49		09 49	10 04		10 49	11 05		11 49
Woodhall	d	07 49		08 53		09 53	10 08		10 53	11 09		11 53
Port Glasgow	d	07 52	08 19	08 56	09 19	09 56	10 11	10 19	10 56	11 12	11 19	11 56
Whinhill	d		08 23		09 23			10 23			11 23	
Drumfrochar	d		08 26		09 26			10 26			11 26	
Branchton	d		08 29		09 29			10 29			11 29	
I.B.M. §	d		08 31		09 31			10 31			11 31	
Inverkip	d		08 36		09 36			10 36			11 36	
Wemyss Bay	a		08 42		09 42			10 42			11 42	
Bogston	d	07 54		08 58		09 58	10 13		10 58	11 14		11 58
Cartsdyke	d	07 56		09 00		10 00	10 15		11 00	11 16		12 00
Greenock Central	d	07 58		09 02		10 02	10 17		11 02	11 18		12 02
Greenock West	d	08 01		09 05		10 05	10 20		11 05	11 21		12 05
Fort Matilda	d			09 08		10 08	10 23		11 08	11 24		12 08
Gourock	a	08 06		09 12		10 12	10 27		11 12	11 27		12 12

		SR B	SR	SR	SR B	SR	SR	SR B	SR	SR	SR B
Glasgow Central 15 221	d	11 35	11 50	12 20	12 35	12 50	13 20	13 35	13 50	14 20	14 35
Cardonald	d	11 42		12 27	12 42		13 27	13 42		14 27	14 42
Hillington East	d	11 44	11 58	12 29	12 44	12 58	13 29	13 44	13 58	14 29	14 44
Hillington West	d	11 47		12 31	12 46	13 00	13 31	13 46		14 31	14 47
Paisley Gilmour Street 221 ✈	d	11 51	12 03	12 35	12 53	13 03	13 34	13 50	14 03	14 34	14 51
Paisley St James	d	11 53		12 37	12 55		13 36	13 52		14 36	14 53
Bishopton	d	11 59	12 09	12 43	13 01	13 09	13 42	13 58	14 09	14 42	14 59
Langbank	d	12 05		12 49	13 06		13 48	14 04		14 48	15 05
Woodhall	d	12 09		12 53	13 10		13 52	14 08		14 52	15 09
Port Glasgow	d	12 12	12 18	12 56	13 13	13 19	13 55	14 11	14 19	14 55	15 12
Whinhill	d		12 22			13 23			14 23		
Drumfrochar	d		12 25			13 26			14 26		
Branchton	d		12 28			13 29			14 29		
I.B.M. §	d		12 30			13 31			14 31		
Inverkip	d		12 35			13 36			14 36		
Wemyss Bay	a		12 42			13 42			14 42		
Bogston	d	12 14		12 58	13 15		13 57	14 12		14 57	15 13
Cartsdyke	d	12 16		13 00	13 18		13 59	14 14		14 59	15 15
Greenock Central	d	12 18		13 02	13 20		14 01	14 16		15 01	15 17
Greenock West	d	12 21		13 05	13 22		14 04	14 19		15 04	15 20
Fort Matilda	d	12 24		13 08	13 25		14 07	14 22		15 07	15 23
Gourock	a	12 27		13 12	13 29		14 12	14 27		15 12	15 27

		SR	SR	SR B	SR	SR	SR B	SR	SR	SR B	SR
Glasgow Central 15 221	d	14 50	15 20	15 33	15 50	16 20	16 35	16 50	17 20	17 35	17 50
Cardonald	d		15 27	15 40		16 27	16 42		17 27	17 42	
Hillington East	d	14 58	15 29	15 42	15 58	16 29	16 44	16 58	17 29	17 44	17 58
Hillington West	d		15 31	15 44		16 31	16 48		17 31	17 47	
Paisley Gilmour Street 221 ✈	d	15 03	15 35	15 48	16 03	16 35	16 52	17 03	17 35	17 51	18 03
Paisley St James	d		15 37	15 50		16 37	16 54		17 37	17 53	
Bishopton	d	15 09	15 43	15 56	16 09	16 43	17 00	17 09	17 43	17 59	18 09
Langbank	d		15 49	16 02		16 49	17 05		17 49	18 05	
Woodhall	d		15 53	16 06		16 53	17 09		17 53	18 09	
Port Glasgow	d	15 19	15 56	16 09	16 19	16 56	17 12	17 19	17 56	18 12	18 19
Whinhill	d	15 23			16 23			17 23			18 23
Drumfrochar	d	15 26			16 26			17 26			18 26
Branchton	d	15 29			16 29			17 29			18 29
I.B.M. §	d	15 31			16 31			17 31			18 31
Inverkip	d	15 36			16 36			17 36			18 36
Wemyss Bay	a	15 42			16 42			17 42			18 42
Bogston	d		15 58	16 11		16 58	17 13		17 58	18 13	
Cartsdyke	d		16 00	16 13		17 00	17 16		18 00	18 15	
Greenock Central	d		16 02	16 15		17 02	17 18		18 02	18 17	
Greenock West	d		16 05	16 18		17 05	17 20		18 05	18 20	
Fort Matilda	d		16 08	16 21		17 08	17 23		18 08	18 23	
Gourock	a		16 12	16 25		17 12	17 28		18 12	18 27	

		SR	SR	SR	SR	SR	SR	SR	SR	SR
Glasgow Central 15 221	d	18 20	18 50	19 20	19 50	20 20	21 20	22 20	23 20	
Cardonald	d	18 27		19 27		20 27	21 27	22 27	23 27	
Hillington East	d	18 29	18 58	19 29	19 58	20 29	21 29	22 29	23 29	
Hillington West	d	18 31		19 31		20 31	21 31	22 31	23 31	
Paisley Gilmour Street 221 ✈	d	18 35	19 03	19 35	20 03	20 35	21 35	22 35	23 35	
Paisley St James	d	18 37		19 37		20 37	21 37	22 37	23 37	
Bishopton	d	18 43	19 09	19 43	20 09	20 43	21 43	22 43	23 43	
Langbank	d	18 49		19 49		20 49	21 49	22 49	23 49	
Woodhall	d	18 53		19 53		20 53	21 53	22 53	23 53	
Port Glasgow	d	18 56	19 19	19 56	20 19	20 56	21 56	22 56	23 56	
Whinhill	d		19 23		20 23					
Drumfrochar	d		19 26		20 26					
Branchton	d		19 29		20 29					
I.B.M. §	d		19 31		20 31					
Inverkip	d		19 36		20 36					
Wemyss Bay	a		19 42		20 42					
Bogston	d	18 58		19 58		20 58	21 58	22 58	23 58	
Cartsdyke	d	19 00		20 00		21 00	22 00	23 00	23 59	
Greenock Central	d	19 02		20 02		21 02	22 02	23 02	00 02	
Greenock West	d	19 05		20 05		21 05	22 05	23 05	00 05	
Fort Matilda	d	19 08		20 08		21 08	22 08	23 08	00 08	
Gourock	a	19 12		20 12		21 12	22 12	23 12	00 12	

§ For authorised access to and from I.B.M. only

B 28 November, 5 December

Gourock and Wemyss Bay - Glasgow Central

		SR	SR	SR SX	SR SO	SR SX	SR	SR SX	SR SO	SR	SR SX	SR SO	SR SX	SR SO	SR SX	SR	SR SX	SR	SR	SR	SR	SR	SR
Gourock	d	05 20	06 05	06 22	06 35	06 44		07 06	07 06		07 22	07 36	07 47	07 51	07 51		08 08	08 24	08 36		09 06	09 23	09 36
Fort Matilda	d	05 23	06 08	06 25	06 38	06 47		07 09	07 09		07 25	07 39		07 54	07 54		08 11	08 27	08 39		09 09	09 26	09 39
Greenock West	d	05 26	06 11	06 28	06 41	06 50		07 12	07 12		07 28	07 42	07 52	07 57	07 57		08 14	08 30	08 42		09 12	09 29	09 42
Greenock Central	d	05 29	06 14	06 31	06 44	06 53		07 15	07 15		07 31	07 45	07 55	08 00	08 00		08 17	08 33	08 45		09 15	09 32	09 45
Cartsdyke	d	05 31	06 16	06 33	06 46	06 55		07 17	07 17		07 33	07 47		08 02	08 02			08 35	08 47		09 17		09 47
Bogston	d	05 33		06 35	06 48	06 57		07 19	07 19		07 35	07 49		08 04	08 04			08 37	08 49		09 19		09 49
Wemyss Bay	d									07 13						07 50				08 50			
Inverkip	d									07 18						07 54				08 54			
I.B.M. §	d									07 23						07 59				08 59			
Branchton	d									07 25						08 02				09 02			
Drumfrochar	d									07 28						08 04				09 04			
Whinhill	d									07 30						08 07				09 07			
Port Glasgow	d	05 36	06 19	06 38	06 51	07 00		07 22	07 22	07 35	07 38	07 52	07 59	08 07	08 07	08 11	08 21	08 40	08 52	09 11	09 22	09 36	09 52
Woodhall	d	05 38		06 40	06 53	07 02			07 24	07 37	07 40	07 54		08 09	08 09	08 14		08 42	08 54		09 24		09 54
Langbank	d	05 43		06 45	06 58	07 07			07 29		07 45	07 59				08 18		08 47	08 59		09 29		09 59
Bishopton	d	05 48	06 28	06 50	07 03	07 12		07 31	07 34	07 45	07 50	08 04	08 08	08 18	08 18	08 24	08 30	08 52	09 04	09 20	09 34	09 45	10 04
Paisley St James	d	05 54	06 34	06 56	07 09	07 18			07 40		07 56	08 10				08 29		08 58	09 10		09 40		10 10
Paisley Gilmour Street 221 ←	d	05 56	06 37	06 59	07 12	07 21	07 34	07 38	07 43	07 52	07 59	08 13	08 14	08 25	08 25	08 32	08 37	09 01	09 12	09 27	09 43	09 52	10 13
Hillington West	d	05 59	06 40	07 02	07 15	07 24	07 38	07 41	07 46	07 55	08 02	08 16	08 18	08 28	08 28			09 04	09 16		09 46		10 16
Hillington East	d	06 01	06 42	07 04	07 17	07 26		07 43	07 48	07 57	08 04	08 18	08 20	08 30	08 30			09 06	09 18		09 48		10 18
Cardonald	d	06 03	06 44	07 06	07 19	07 28		07 45	07 50	07 59	08 06	08 20	08 22	08 32	08 32			09 08	09 20		09 50		10 20
Glasgow Central 15 221	a	06 12	06 52	07 14	07 27	07 36	07 47	07 53	07 58	08 07	08 14	08 28	08 30	08 40	08 41	08 44	08 48	09 16	09 28	09 38	09 58	10 03	10 28

		SR	SR	SR	SR	SR	SR	SR	SR	SR	SR	SR	SR	SR	SR	SR	SR	SR	SR	SR	SR	SR	SR
Gourock	d		10 06	10 23	10 36		11 06	11 23	11 36		12 06	12 23	12 36		13 06	13 23	13 36		14 06	14 23	14 36		15 06
Fort Matilda	d		10 09	10 26	10 39		11 09	11 26	11 39		12 09	12 26	12 39		13 09	13 26	13 39		14 09	14 26	14 39		15 09
Greenock West	d		10 12	10 29	10 42		11 12	11 29	11 42		12 12	12 29	12 42		13 12	13 29	13 42		14 12	14 29	14 42		15 12
Greenock Central	d		10 15	10 32	10 45		11 15	11 32	11 45		12 15	12 32	12 45		13 15	13 32	13 45		14 15	14 32	14 45		15 15
Cartsdyke	d		10 17		10 47		11 17		11 47		12 17		12 47		13 17		13 47		14 17		14 47		15 17
Bogston	d		10 19		10 49		11 19		11 49		12 19		12 49		13 19		13 49		14 19		14 49		15 19
Wemyss Bay	d	09 50				10 55				11 50				12 50				13 50				14 50	
Inverkip	d	09 54				10 59				11 54				12 54				13 54				14 54	
I.B.M. §	d	09 59				11 04				11 59				12 59				13 59				14 59	
Branchton	d	10 02				11 07				12 02				13 02				14 02				15 02	
Drumfrochar	d	10 04				11 09				12 04				13 04				14 04				15 04	
Whinhill	d	10 07				11 12				12 07				13 07				14 07				15 07	
Port Glasgow	d	10 11	10 22	10 36	10 52	11 16	11 22	11 36	11 52	12 11	12 22	12 36	12 52	13 11	13 22	13 36	13 52	14 11	14 22	14 36	14 52	15 11	15 22
Woodhall	d		10 24		10 54		11 24		11 54		12 24		12 54		13 24		13 54		14 24		14 54		15 24
Langbank	d		10 29		10 59		11 29		11 59		12 29		12 59		13 29		13 59		14 29		14 59		15 29
Bishopton	d	10 20	10 34	10 45	11 04	11 25	11 34	11 45	12 04	12 20	12 34	12 45	13 04	13 20	13 34	13 45	14 04	14 20	14 34	14 45	15 04	15 20	15 34
Paisley St James	d		10 40		11 10		11 40		12 10		12 40		13 10		13 40		14 10		14 40		15 10		15 40
Paisley Gilmour Street 221 ←	d	10 27	10 43	10 52	11 13	11 32	11 43	11 52	12 13	12 27	12 43	12 52	13 13	13 27	13 43	13 52	14 13	14 27	14 43	14 52	15 13	15 27	15 43
Hillington West	d		10 46		11 16		11 46		12 16		12 46		13 16		13 46		14 16		14 46		15 16		15 46
Hillington East	d		10 48		11 18		11 48		12 18		12 48		13 18		13 48		14 18		14 48		15 18		15 48
Cardonald	d		10 50		11 20		11 50		12 20		12 50		13 20		13 50		14 20		14 50		15 20		15 50
Glasgow Central 15 221	a	10 38	10 58	11 03	11 28	11 43	11 58	12 03	12 28	12 38	12 58	13 03	13 28	13 38	13 58	14 03	14 28	14 38	14 58	15 03	15 27	15 38	15 58

		SR	SR	SR	SR	SR	SR	SR	SR	SR	SR	SR	SR	SR	SR SX	SR SO	SR	SR	SR	SR	SR	SR
Gourock	d	15 23	15 36		16 06	16 23	16 36		17 06	17 23	17 48		18 06	18 23			18 40		19 06	19 20	19 45	
Fort Matilda	d	15 26	15 39		16 09	16 26	16 39		17 09	17 26	17 51		18 09	18 26			18 43		19 09	19 23	19 48	
Greenock West	d	15 29	15 42		16 12	16 29	16 42		17 12	17 29	17 54		18 12	18 29			18 46		19 12	19 26	19 51	
Greenock Central	d	15 32	15 45		16 15	16 32	16 45		17 15	17 32	17 57		18 15	18 32			18 49		19 15	19 29	19 54	
Cartsdyke	d		15 47		16 17		16 47		17 17		17 59		18 17				18 51		19 17	19 31	19 56	
Bogston	d		15 49		16 19		16 49		17 19		18 01		18 19				18 53		19 19	19 33		
Wemyss Bay	d			15 55				16 45				17 49			18 25	18 25		18 55				19 45
Inverkip	d			15 59				16 49				17 53			18 29	18 29		18 59				19 48
I.B.M. §	d			16 04				16 54				18 02			18 38	18 39		19 04				19 53
Branchton	d			16 07				16 57				18 05			18 40	18 40		19 07				19 56
Drumfrochar	d			16 09				16 59				18 07			18 43	18 44		19 09				19 58
Whinhill	d			16 12				17 02				18 10			18 45	18 45		19 12				20 01
Port Glasgow	d	15 36	15 52	16 16	16 22	16 36	16 52	17 06	17 22	17 36	18 04	18 14	18 22	18 36	18 50	18 51	18 56	19 16	19 22	19 36	19 59	20 06
Woodhall	d		15 54		16 24		16 54		17 24		18 06		18 24				18 58		19 24	19 38		20 08
Langbank	d		15 59		16 29		16 59		17 29		18 11		18 29				19 03		19 29	19 43		20 13
Bishopton	d	15 45	16 04	16 25	16 34	16 45	17 04	17 15	17 34	17 45	18 16	18 23	18 34	18 45	18 59	19 00	19 08	19 25	19 34	19 48	20 08	20 18
Paisley St James	d		16 10		16 40		17 10		17 40		18 22		18 40				19 14		19 40	19 54		20 24
Paisley Gilmour Street 221 ←	d	15 52	16 13	16 32	16 43	16 52	17 12	17 22	17 43	17 52	18 25	18 31	18 43	18 52	19 05	19 05	19 16	19 32	19 43	19 57	20 15	20 27
Hillington West	d	15 55	16 16		16 46	16 55	17 15		17 47		18 29		18 46				19 19		19 46	20 00		20 30
Hillington East	d		16 18		16 48		17 17		17 49		18 31		18 48				19 21		19 48	20 02		20 32
Cardonald	d		16 20		16 50		17 19		17 51		18 33		18 50				19 23		19 50	20 04		20 34
Glasgow Central 15 221	a	16 05	16 28	16 45	16 58	17 05	17 28	17 33	17 58	18 05	18 40	18 44	18 58	19 03	19 16	19 17	19 32	19 43	19 58	20 12	20 26	20 43

§ For authorised access to and from I.B.M. only

Gourock and Wemyss Bay - Glasgow Central

		SR	SR	SR	SR	SR	SR SX	SR SO	SR	SR	SR	SR SO
Gourock	d	20 20	20 47		21 20	21 45			22 20		23 20	
Fort Matilda	d	20 23	20 50		21 23	21 48			22 23		23 23	
Greenock West	d	20 26	20 53		21 26	21 51			22 26		23 26	
Greenock Central	d	20 29	20 56		21 29	21 54			22 29		23 29	
Cartsdyke	d	20 31	20 58		21 31	21 56			22 31		23 31	
Bogston	d	20 33			21 33				22 33		23 33	
Wemyss Bay	d			20 44			21 44	21 50		22 44		23 40
Inverkip	d			20 48			21 48	21 54		22 48		23 44
I.B.M. §	d			20 53			21 53	21 59		22 53		23 49
Branchton	d			20 56			21 56	22 02		22 56		23 52
Drumfrochar	d			20 58			21 58	22 04		22 58		23 54
Whinhill	d			21 01			22 01	22 07		23 01		23 57
Port Glasgow	d	20 36	21 01	21 06	21 36	21 59	22 06	22 11	22 36	23 06	23 36	00 01
Woodhall	d	20 38		21 08	21 38		22 08	22 14	22 38	23 08	23 38	
Langbank	d	20 43		21 13	21 43		22 13	22 18	22 43	23 13	23 43	
Bishopton	d	20 48	21 10	21 18	21 48	22 08	22 18	22 24	22 48	23 18	23 48	00 10
Paisley St James	d	20 54		21 24	21 54		22 24	22 29	22 54	23 24	23 54	
Paisley Gilmour Street 221 ←	d	20 56	21 18	21 27	21 58	22 15	22 27	22 32	22 57	23 27	23 57	00 17
Hillington West	d	21 00		21 30	22 01		22 30	22 35	23 00	23 30	00 01	
Hillington East	d	21 02		21 32	22 03		22 32	22 37	23 02	23 32	00 02	
Cardonald	d	21 04		21 34	22 05		22 34	22 39	23 04	23 34	00 04	
Glasgow Central 15 221	a	21 12	21 29	21 42	22 15	22 26	22 42	22 46	23 14	23 42	00 12	00 28

Sundays

		SR	SR	SR	SR B	SR	SR	SR B	SR	SR	SR B	SR	SR	SR B	SR	SR	SR B	SR	SR	SR B	SR
Gourock	d	08 23		09 23	09 36		10 23	10 36		11 23	11 36		12 23	12 36		13 23	13 36		14 23	14 36	
Fort Matilda	d	08 26		09 26	09 39		10 26	10 39		11 26	11 39		12 26	12 39		13 26	13 39		14 26	14 39	
Greenock West	d	08 29		09 29	09 42		10 29	10 42		11 29	11 42		12 29	12 42		13 29	13 42		14 29	14 42	
Greenock Central	d	08 32		09 32	09 45		10 32	10 45		11 32	11 45		12 32	12 45		13 32	13 45		14 32	14 45	
Cartsdyke	d	08 34		09 34	09 47		10 34	10 47		11 34	11 47		12 34	12 47		13 34	13 47		14 34	14 47	
Bogston	d	08 36		09 36	09 49		10 36	10 49		11 36	11 49		12 36	12 49		13 36	13 49		14 36	14 49	
Wemyss Bay	d		08 50			09 50			10 57			11 50			12 50			13 50			14 50
Inverkip	d		08 54			09 54			11 01			11 54			12 54			13 54			14 54
I.B.M. §	d		08 59			09 59			11 06			11 59			12 59			13 59			14 59
Branchton	d		09 02			10 02			11 09			12 02			13 02			14 02			15 02
Drumfrochar	d		09 04			10 04			11 11			12 04			13 04			14 04			15 04
Whinhill	d		09 07			10 07			11 13			12 07			13 07			14 07			15 07
Port Glasgow	d	08 39	09 11	09 39	09 52	10 11	10 39	10 52	11 17	11 39	11 52	12 11	12 39	12 52	13 11	13 39	13 52	14 11	14 39	14 52	15 11
Woodhall	d	08 41		09 41	09 54		10 41	10 54		11 41	11 54		12 41	12 54		13 41	13 54		14 41	14 54	
Langbank	d	08 46		09 46	09 59		10 46	10 59		11 46	11 59		12 46	12 59		13 46	13 59		14 46	14 59	
Bishopton	d	08 51	09 20	09 51	10 04	10 20	10 51	11 04	11 27	11 51	12 04	12 20	12 51	13 04	13 20	13 51	14 04	14 20	14 51	15 04	15 20
Paisley St James	d	08 57		09 57	10 10		10 57	11 10		11 57	12 10		12 57	13 10		13 57	14 10		14 57	15 10	
Paisley Gilmour Street 221 ←	d	09 00	09 28	10 00	10 13	10 28	11 00	11 14	11 32	11 59	12 13	12 28	13 00	13 13	13 27	14 00	14 14	14 27	15 00	15 13	15 27
Hillington West	d	09 03		10 03	10 16		11 03	11 19		12 03	12 16		13 03	13 18		14 03	14 16		15 03	15 16	
Hillington East	d	09 05	09 32	10 05	10 19	10 32	11 05	11 21	11 36	12 05	12 18	12 32	13 05	13 20	13 31	14 05	14 18	14 31	15 05	15 18	15 31
Cardonald	d	09 07		10 07	10 20		11 07	11 23		12 07	12 20		13 07	13 22		14 07	14 20		15 07	15 20	
Glasgow Central 15 221	a	09 15	09 40	10 15	10 28	10 40	11 15	11 31	11 46	12 15	12 28	12 40	13 15	13 30	13 40	14 15	14 28	14 40	15 15	15 28	15 40

		SR	SR B	SR	SR	SR B	SR	SR	SR B	SR	SR	SR	SR	SR	SR	SR	SR	SR
Gourock	d	15 23	15 36		16 23	16 36		17 23	17 36		18 23		19 23		20 23		21 23	22 23
Fort Matilda	d	15 26	15 39		16 26	16 39		17 26	17 39		18 26		19 26		20 26		21 26	22 26
Greenock West	d	15 29	15 42		16 29	16 42		17 29	17 42		18 29		19 29		20 29		21 29	22 29
Greenock Central	d	15 32	15 45		16 32	16 45		17 32	17 45		18 32		19 32		20 32		21 32	22 32
Cartsdyke	d	15 34	15 47		16 34	16 47		17 34	17 47		18 34		19 34		20 34		21 34	22 34
Bogston	d	15 36	15 49		16 36	16 49		17 36	17 49		18 36		19 36		20 36		21 36	22 36
Wemyss Bay	d			15 55			16 50			17 50		18 55		19 50		20 50		
Inverkip	d			15 59			16 54			17 54		18 59		19 54		20 54		
I.B.M. §	d			16 04			16 59			17 59		19 04		19 59		20 59		
Branchton	d			16 07			17 02			18 02		19 07		20 02		21 02		
Drumfrochar	d			16 09			17 04			18 04		19 09		20 04		21 04		
Whinhill	d			16 12			17 07			18 07		19 12		20 07		21 07		
Port Glasgow	d	15 39	15 52	16 16	16 39	16 52	17 11	17 39	17 52	18 11	18 39	19 16	19 39	20 11	20 39	21 11	21 39	22 39
Woodhall	d	15 41	15 54		16 41	16 54		17 41	17 54		18 41		19 41		20 41		21 41	22 41
Langbank	d	15 46	15 59		16 46	16 59		17 46	17 59		18 46		19 46		20 46		21 46	22 46
Bishopton	d	15 51	16 04	16 25	16 51	17 04	17 20	17 51	18 04	18 20	18 51	19 25	19 51	20 20	20 51	21 20	21 51	22 51
Paisley St James	d	15 57	16 10		16 57	17 10		17 57	18 10		18 57		19 57		20 57		21 57	22 57
Paisley Gilmour Street 221 ←	d	16 00	16 13	16 32	17 00	17 13	17 27	18 00	18 13	18 27	19 00	19 32	20 00	20 27	21 00	21 27	22 00	23 00
Hillington West	d	16 03	16 16		17 03	17 16		18 03	18 16		19 03		20 03		21 03		22 03	23 03
Hillington East	d	16 05	16 18	16 36	17 05	17 18	17 31	18 05	18 18	18 31	19 05	19 36	20 05	20 31	21 05	21 31	22 05	23 05
Cardonald	d	16 07	16 20		17 07	17 20		18 07	18 20		19 07		20 07		21 07		22 07	23 07
Glasgow Central 15 221	a	16 15	16 28	16 45	17 15	17 28	17 40	18 15	18 28	18 40	19 15	19 44	20 15	20 40	21 15	21 40	22 15	23 15

§ For authorised access to and from I.B.M. only

B 28 November, 5 December

Mondays to Saturdays
until 23 October

Glasgow and Gourock - Dunoon, Kilcreggan and Helensburgh Pier
Cowal Ferries Ltd in association with ScotRail

All Kilcreggan and Helensburgh Pier sailings operated by Clyde Marine Transport Ltd Tel. 01475 721281

			SX	SX	SX	SX											
Glasgow Central 15	219 d	05 55	05 55	06 25	06 25	06 55	07 05	07 25	07 35	08 25	09 05	09 25	10 25	10 35	11 25	11 25	12 25
Paisley Gilmour Street	219 d	06 07	06 07	06 36	06 36	07 07	07 20	07 40	07 50	08 36	09 20	09 36	10 36	10 50	11 36	11 36	12 36
Gourock	219 a	06 36	06 36	07 13	07 13	07 39	07 57	08 13	08 27	09 08	09 58	10 06	11 06	11 27	12 06	12 06	13 06
Gourock	⛴ d	06 50	07 00	07 20	07 20	07 50	08 05	08 20	08 35	09 20	10 05	10 20	11 20	11 35	12 20	12 25	13 20
Dunoon	⛴ a	07 13		07 43		08 13		08 43		09 43		10 43	11 43		12 43		13 43
Kilcreggan	⛴ a		07 12		07 42		08 17				10 20			11 47		12 37	
Helensburgh Pier	⛴ a								09 05		10 45						

										SX				
Glasgow Central 15	219 d	13 25	13 25	14 25	14 35	15 25	15 25	15 35	16 05	16 23	16 23	17 05	17 25	18 25	19 25
Paisley Gilmour Street	219 d	13 36	13 36	14 35	14 50	15 36	15 36	15 50	16 20	16 38	16 38	17 21	17 36	18 35	19 36
Gourock	219 a	14 06	14 06	15 06	15 27	16 06	16 06	16 27	16 57	17 15	17 15	17 57	18 06	19 06	20 06
Gourock	⛴ d	14 15	14 20	15 20	15 45	16 15	16 20	16 50	17 20	17 25	17 45	18 10	18 20	19 20	20 18
Dunoon	⛴ a		14 43	15 43			16 43		17 43		18 08		18 43	19 43	20 41
Kilcreggan	⛴ a	14 30			15 57	16 27		17 03		17 37		18 25			
Helensburgh Pier	⛴ a	14 55										18 50			

Sundays
until 17 October

Glasgow Central 15	219 d	07 20	08 20	09 20	09 20	10 20	10 20	11 20	11 20	12 20	13 20	13 20	14 20	14 20	15 20	16 20	17 20	18 20	19 20
Paisley Gilmour Street	219 d	07 35	08 35	09 35	09 35	10 35	10 35	11 35	11 35	12 35	13 34	13 34	14 34	14 34	15 35	16 35	17 35	18 35	19 35
Gourock	219 a	08 06	09 12	10 12	10 12	11 12	11 12	12 12	12 12	13 12	14 12	14 12	15 12	15 12	16 12	17 12	18 12	19 12	20 12
Gourock	⛴ d	08 20	09 20	10 20	11 15	11 20	11 45	12 20	13 15	13 20	14 20	14 25	15 20	16 15	16 20	17 20	18 20	19 20	20 18
Dunoon	⛴ a	08 43	09 43	10 43		11 43		12 43		13 43	14 43		15 43		16 43	17 43	18 43	19 43	20 41
Kilcreggan	⛴ a				11 27							14 40		16 27					
Helensburgh Pier	⛴ a						12 15		13 45			15 10							

For details of sailings from 24 October 2010, telephone Cowal Ferries on 08000 66 5000 or Clyde Marine Transport on 01475 721281

Mondays to Saturdays
until 23 October

Helensburgh Pier, Kilgreggan and Dunnoon - Gourock and Glasgow
Cowal Ferries Ltd in association with ScotRail

All Helensburgh and Kilcreggan Pier sailings operated by Clyde Marine Transport Ltd Tel. 01475 721281

		SX	SX		SX	SX		SX										
Helensburgh Pier	⛴ d									09 10			10 50			12 45	
Kilcreggan	⛴ d		07 15		07 50		08 20			09 40			11 15	11 50			
Dunoon	⛴ d	06 50		07 20		07 50		08 20	08 50		09 50	10 50			11 50		12 50
Gourock	⛴ a	07 13	07 27	07 43	08 02	08 13	08 32	08 43	08 13	09 52	10 13	11 13	11 27	12 02	12 13	12 57	13 13
Gourock	219 d	07 22	07 47	07 51	08 08	08 24	09 06	09 06	09 23	10 06	10 23	11 23	11 36	12 23	12 23	13 06	13 23
Paisley Gilmour Street	219 a	07 58	08 14	08 24	08 36	09 00	09 42	09 42	09 51	10 42	10 51	11 51	12 12	12 51	12 51	13 43	13 51
Glasgow Central 15	219 a	08 14	08 30	08 41	08 48	09 16	09 58	09 58	10 03	10 58	11 03	12 03	12 28	13 03	13 03	13 58	14 03

												SX				
Helensburgh Pier	⛴ d			15 00										18 55		
Kilcreggan	⛴ d			15 30		16 00	16 30		17 05	17 40				19 20		
Dunoon	⛴ d	13 50	14 50		15 50			16 50			17 50	18 15	18 50		19 50	20 45
Gourock	⛴ a	14 13	15 13	15 42	16 13	16 12	14 42	17 13	17 17	17 52	18 13	18 38	19 13	19 32	20 13	21 08
Gourock	219 d	14 23	15 23	16 06	16 23	16 23	17 06	17 23	17 23	18 06	18 23	19 06	19 20	19 45	20 20	21 20
Paisley Gilmour Street	219 a	14 51	15 51	16 42	16 51	16 51	17 43	17 51	17 51	18 42	18 51	19 42	19 56	20 14	20 56	21 57
Glasgow Central 15	219 a	15 03	16 05	16 58	17 05	17 05	17 58	18 05	18 05	18 58	19 03	19 58	20 12	20 26	21 12	22 15

Sundays
until 17 October

Helensburgh Pier	⛴ d						12 20			13 50		15 15 15 45							
Kilcreggan	⛴ d				11 30									16 30					
Dunoon	⛴ d	08 50	09 50	10 50		11 50		12 50	13 50		14 50		15 50		16 50	17 50	18 50	19 50	20 45
Gourock	⛴ a	09 13	10 13	11 13	11 42	12 13	12 50	13 13	14 13	14 20	15 13	15 57	16 13	16 42	17 13	18 13	19 13	20 13	21 08
Gourock	219 d	09 23	10 23	11 23	12 23	12 23	13 23	13 23	14 23	15 23	15 23	16 23	16 23	17 23	17 23	18 23	19 23	20 23	21 23
Paisley Gilmour Street	219 a	09 59	10 59	11 58	12 59	12 59	13 59	13 59	14 59	15 59	15 59	16 59	16 59	17 59	17 59	18 59	19 59	20 59	21 59
Glasgow Central 15	219 a	10 15	11 15	12 15	13 15	13 15	14 15	14 15	15 15	16 15	16 15	17 15	17 15	18 15	18 15	19 15	20 15	21 15	22 15

For details of sailings from 24 October 2010, telephone Cowal Ferries on 08000 66 5000 or Clyde Marine Transport Ltd. on 01475 721281

Glasgow and Wemyss Bay - Rothesay (Bute)

Caledonian MacBrayne Ltd in association with ScotRail

Mondays to Saturdays until 23 October

		SX															FSO	SO A
Glasgow Central 15	219 d	06 05	06 32	07 50	08 50	09 50	10 50	11 50	12 50	13 50	14 50	15 50	16 33	17 15	17 55	18 50	19 39	20 35
Paisley Gilmour Street	219 d	06 19	06 47	08 02	09 01	10 01	11 01	12 01	13 01	14 01	15 01	16 02	16 48	17 29	18 06	19 01	19 54	20 50
Wemyss Bay	219 a	06 58	07 30	08 40	09 40	10 40	11 40	12 40	13 40	14 40	15 40	16 40	17 25	18 08	18 44	19 40	20 38	21 34
Wemyss Bay	⛴ d	07 15	08 00	08 45	10 15	11 00	12 15	13 00	13 45	15 15	16 00	16 45	17 30	18 15	19 00	19 45	20 45	22 00
Rothesay	⛴ a	07 50	08 35	09 20	10 50	11 35	12 50	13 35	14 20	15 50	16 35	17 20	18 05	18 50	19 35	20 20	21 20	22 35

Sundays until 17 October

Glasgow Central 15	219 d	07 50	08 50	09 50	10 50	11 50	12 50	13 50	14 50	15 50	16 50	17 50	18 50
Paisley Gilmour Street	219 d	08 03	09 03	10 03	11 03	12 03	13 03	14 03	15 03	16 03	17 03	18 03	19 03
Wemyss Bay	219 a	08 42	09 42	10 42	11 42	12 42	13 42	14 42	15 42	16 42	17 42	18 42	19 42
Wemyss Bay	⛴ d	08 45	10 15	11 00	12 15	13 00	13 50	15 00	16 00	17 30	18 15	19 00	19 45
Rothesay	⛴ a	09 20	10 50	11 35	12 50	13 35	14 25	15 35	16 35	18 05	18 50	19 35	20 20

Mondays to Saturdays until 23 October

		SX															FSO	SO A
Rothesay	⛴ d	06 30	07 00	08 00	08 45	10 10	11 00	11 50	13 00	13 45	15 15	16 00	16 45	17 30	18 15	19 00	19 45	21 10
Wemyss Bay	⛴ a	07 05	07 35	08 35	09 20	10 45	11 35	12 25	13 35	14 20	15 50	16 35	17 20	18 05	18 50	19 35	20 20	21 45
Wemyss Bay	219 d	07 13	07 50	08 50	09 50	10 55	11 50	12 50	13 50	14 50	15 55	16 45	17 49	18 25	18 55	19 45	20 44	21 50
Paisley Gilmour Street	219 a	07 51	08 32	09 26	10 26	11 31	12 26	13 26	14 26	15 26	16 31	17 21	18 30	19 05	19 31	20 26	21 26	22 32
Glasgow Central 15	219 a	08 07	08 44	09 38	10 38	11 43	12 38	13 38	14 38	15 38	16 45	17 33	18 44	19 18	19 43	20 43	21 42	22 46

Sundays until 17 October

Rothesay	⛴ d	08 00	10 10	11 00	11 50	13 00	13 45	15 15	16 00	16 45	18 15	19 00	19 45
Wemyss Bay	⛴ a	08 35	10 45	11 35	12 25	13 35	14 20	15 50	16 35	17 20	18 50	19 35	20 20
Wemyss Bay	219 d	08 50	10 57	11 50	12 50	13 50	14 50	15 55	16 50	17 50	18 55	19 50	20 50
Paisley Gilmour Street	219 a	09 27	11 31	12 27	13 26	14 26	15 26	16 31	17 26	18 26	19 31	20 26	21 26
Glasgow Central 15	219 a	09 40	11 46	12 40	13 40	14 40	15 40	16 45	17 40	18 40	19 44	20 40	21 40

A 5 June to 21 August

For details of sailings from 24 October 2010, telephone Caledonian MacBrayne on 08000 66 5000

Network Diagram for Tables 220, 223, 224, 226, 232

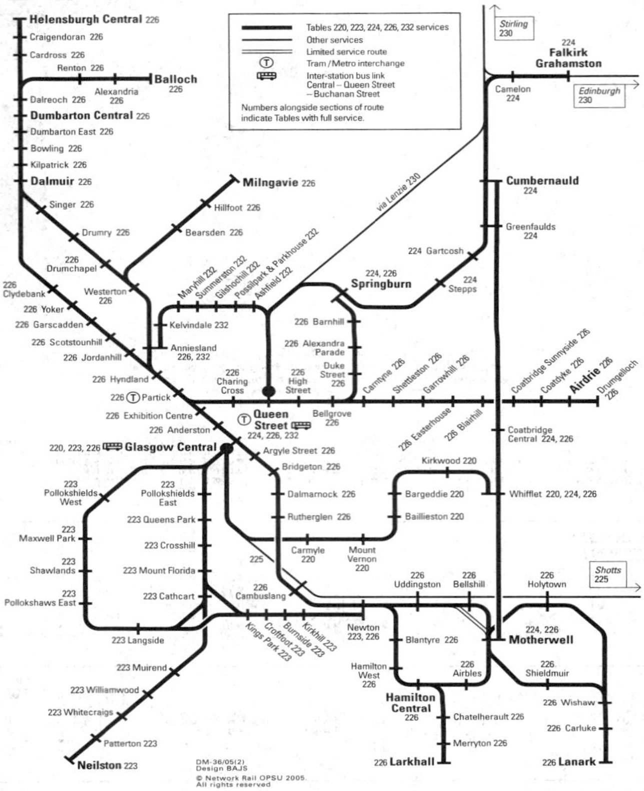

Table 220

Mondays to Saturdays

Glasgow Central - Whifflet

		SR SO	SR	SR SX	SR SO	SR SO	SR SX	SR SO	SR SX	SR SO	SR SX	SR SX	SR SO	SR	SR	SR	SR SX	SR SO	SR	SR	SR	SR	SR
Glasgow Central 15	d	00 13	06 18	06 46	06 46	07 16	07 17	07 43	07 45	08 13	08 13	08 43	08 43	09 16	09 46	10 16	10 46	10 47	11 16	11 46	12 16	12 46	13 16
Carmyle	d	00 23	06 28	06 56	06 56	07 27	07 27	07 53	07 58	08 24	08 23	08 53	08 55	09 25	09 56	10 26	10 56	10 57	11 26	11 56	12 26	12 58	13 26
Mount Vernon	d	00 26	06 31	06 59	06 59	07 30	07 30	07 56	08 01	08 27	08 26	08 56	08 58	09 28	09 59	10 29	10 59	11 00	11 29	11 59	12 29	13 01	13 29
Baillieston	d	00 29	06 34	07 02	07 02	07 33	07 33	07 59	08 04	08 30	08 29	08 59	09 01	09 31	10 02	10 32	11 02	11 03	11 32	12 02	12 32	13 04	13 32
Bargeddie	d	00 32	06 37	07 05	07 05	07 36	07 36	08 02	08 07	08 33	08 32	09 02	09 04	09 34	10 05	10 35	11 05	11 06	11 35	12 05	12 35	13 07	13 35
Kirkwood	d	00 35	06 40	07 08	07 08	07 39	07 39	08 05	08 10	08 36	08 35	09 05	09 07	09 37	10 08	10 38	11 08	11 09	11 36	12 08	12 36	13 10	13 38
Whifflet	a	00 42	06 46	07 14	07 15	07 45	07 46	08 11	08 15	08 42	08 42	09 12	09 12	09 45	10 14	10 44	11 14	11 15	11 44	12 15	12 44	13 15	13 44

		SR	SR	SR	SR SX	SR SO	SR	SR	SR	SR	SR	SR	SR SO	SR SX	SR	SR SO	SR SX	SR SX	SR SO	SR	SR SX	SR SO	SR
Glasgow Central 15	d	13 46	14 16	14 46	15 16	15 17	15 46	16 16	16 46	17 16	17 46	18 16	18 44	18 46	19 13	19 46	19 47	20 14	20 16	20 46	21 16	21 17	21 46
Carmyle	d	13 56	14 26	14 56	15 26	15 27	15 56	16 26	16 56	17 26	17 56	18 26	18 54	18 56	19 23	19 56	19 57	20 24	20 26	20 56	21 26	21 27	21 56
Mount Vernon	d	13 59	14 29	14 59	15 29	15 30	15 59	16 29	16 59	17 29	17 59	18 29	18 57	18 59	19 26	19 59	20 00	20 27	20 29	20 59	21 29	21 30	21 59
Baillieston	d	14 02	14 32	15 02	15 32	15 33	16 02	16 32	17 02	17 32	18 02	18 32	19 00	19 02	19 29	20 02	20 03	20 30	20 32	21 02	21 32	21 33	22 02
Bargeddie	d	14 05	14 35	15 05	15 35	15 36	16 05	16 35	17 05	17 35	18 05	18 35	19 03	19 05	19 32	20 05	20 06	20 33	20 35	21 05	21 35	21 36	22 05
Kirkwood	d	14 10	14 38	15 08	15 38	15 39	16 08	16 38	17 08	17 38	18 08	18 38	19 06	19 08	19 35	20 08	20 09	20 36	20 38	21 08	21 38	21 39	22 08
Whifflet	a	14 15	14 44	15 15	15 44	15 45	16 15	16 44	17 15	17 44	18 14	18 44	19 13	19 15	19 41	20 15	20 15	20 42	20 44	21 14	21 44	21 45	22 15

		SR SO	SR SX	SR SX	SR SO	SR SO	SR SX
Glasgow Central 15	d	22 14	22 16	22 46	22 46	23 16	23 17
Carmyle	d	22 24	22 27	22 57	22 56	23 26	23 27
Mount Vernon	d	22 27	22 30	23 00	22 59	23 29	23 30
Baillieston	d	22 30	22 33	23 03	23 02	23 32	23 33
Bargeddie	d	22 33	22 36	23 06	23 05	23 35	23 36
Kirkwood	d	22 36	22 39	23 09	23 08	23 38	23 39
Whifflet	a	22 42	22 45	23 15	23 15	23 45	23 45

Sundays

from 28 November

		SR	SR	SR	SR	SR	SR	SR	SR	SR	SR	SR	SR	SR	SR	SR	SR	SR	SR
Glasgow Central 15	d	09 22	09 52	10 52	11 22	11 53	12 24	12 52	13 22	13 52	14 22	14 52	15 22	15 52	16 22	16 52	17 22	17 52	18 22
Carmyle	d	09 33	10 02	11 02	11 33	12 03	12 33	13 02	13 33	14 02	14 33	15 02	15 33	16 02	16 33	17 02	17 33	18 02	18 32
Mount Vernon	d	09 36	10 05	11 05	11 36	12 06	12 36	13 05	13 36	14 05	14 36	15 05	15 36	16 05	16 36	17 05	17 36	18 05	18 36
Baillieston	d	09 39	10 08	11 08	11 39	12 09	12 39	13 08	13 39	14 08	14 39	15 08	15 39	16 08	16 39	17 08	17 39	18 08	18 39
Bargeddie	d	09 42	10 11	11 11	11 42	12 12	12 42	13 11	13 42	14 11	14 42	15 11	15 42	16 11	16 42	17 11	17 42	18 11	18 42
Kirkwood	d	09 45	10 14	11 14	11 45	12 15	12 45	13 14	13 45	14 14	14 45	15 14	15 45	16 14	16 45	17 14	17 45	18 14	18 45
Whifflet	a	09 50	10 21	11 21	11 50	12 21	12 50	13 21	13 50	14 21	14 50	15 21	15 50	16 21	16 50	17 21	17 50	18 21	18 50

Table 220

Mondays to Saturdays

Whifflet - Glasgow Central

		SR SX	SR SO	SR	SR	SR SX	SR SO	SR SO	SR SX	SR SO	SR SX	SR SO	SR SX	SR	SR	SR SO	SR SX	SR SX	SR SO	SR	SR	SR SX	SR SO
Whifflet	d	06 07	06 07	06 37	07 07	07 36	07 37	08 07	08 07	08 37	08 37	09 07	09 07	09 37	10 07	10 36	10 37	11 06	11 07	11 37	12 07	12 36	12 37
Kirkwood	d	06 10	06 10	06 40	07 10	07 39	07 40	08 10	08 10	08 40	08 40	09 10	09 10	09 40	10 10	10 39	10 40	11 09	11 10	11 40	12 10	12 39	12 40
Bargeddie	d	06 13	06 13	06 43	07 13	07 42	07 43	08 13	08 13	08 43	08 43	09 13	09 13	09 43	10 13	10 42	10 43	11 12	11 13	11 43	12 13	12 42	12 43
Baillieston	d	06 16	06 16	06 46	07 16	07 45	07 46	08 16	08 16	08 46	08 46	09 16	09 16	09 46	10 16	10 45	10 46	11 15	11 16	11 46	12 16	12 45	12 46
Mount Vernon	d	06 19	06 19	06 49	07 19	07 48	07 49	08 19	08 19	08 49	08 49	09 19	09 19	09 49	10 19	10 48	10 49	11 18	11 19	11 49	12 19	12 48	12 49
Carmyle	d	06 23	06 23	06 53	07 23	07 52	07 53	08 23	08 23	08 53	08 53	09 23	09 23	09 53	10 23	10 52	10 53	11 22	11 23	11 53	12 23	12 52	12 53
Glasgow Central 15	a	06 36	06 35	07 06	07 35	08 04	08 04	08 35	08 36	09 05	09 06	09 35	09 37	10 05	10 36	11 04	11 05	11 35	11 35	12 05	12 35	13 04	13 05

		SR	SR	SR	SR	SR SX	SR SO	SR	SR	SR	SR	SR	SR SO	SR SX	SR SX	SR SO	SR	SR	SR	SR	SR	SR	SR SO
Whifflet	d	13 07	13 37	14 07	14 37	15 07	15 07	15 37	16 07	16 37	17 07	17 37	18 07	18 12	18 37	18 37	19 07	19 37	20 07	20 37	21 07	21 37	22 07
Kirkwood	d	13 10	13 40	14 10	14 40	15 10	15 10	15 40	16 10	16 40	17 10	17 40	18 10	18 15	18 40	18 40	19 10	19 40	20 10	20 40	21 10	21 40	22 10
Bargeddie	d	13 13	13 43	14 13	14 43	15 13	15 13	15 43	16 13	16 43	17 13	17 43	18 13	18 18	18 43	18 43	19 13	19 43	20 13	20 43	21 13	21 43	22 13
Baillieston	d	13 16	13 46	14 16	14 46	15 16	15 16	15 46	16 16	16 46	17 16	17 46	18 16	18 21	18 46	18 46	19 16	19 46	20 16	20 46	21 16	21 46	22 16
Mount Vernon	d	13 19	13 49	14 19	14 49	15 19	15 19	15 49	16 19	16 49	17 19	17 49	18 19	18 24	18 49	18 49	19 19	19 49	20 19	20 49	21 19	21 49	22 19
Carmyle	d	13 23	13 53	14 23	14 53	15 23	15 23	15 53	16 23	16 53	17 23	17 53	18 23	18 28	18 53	18 53	19 23	19 53	20 23	20 53	21 23	21 53	22 23
Glasgow Central 15	a	13 35	14 05	14 35	15 05	15 35	15 36	16 05	16 35	17 05	17 35	18 05	18 35	18 41	19 04	19 05	19 35	20 05	20 35	21 05	21 35	22 05	22 35

		SR SX	SR	SR SX	SR SO
Whifflet	d	22 07	22 37	23 07	23 07
Kirkwood	d	22 10	22 40	23 10	23 10
Bargeddie	d	22 13	22 43	23 13	23 13
Baillieston	d	22 16	22 46	23 16	23 16
Mount Vernon	d	22 19	22 49	23 19	23 19
Carmyle	d	22 23	22 53	23 23	23 23
Glasgow Central 15	a	22 38	23 05	23 35	23 37

Sundays

from 28 November

		SR	SR	SR	SR	SR	SR	SR	SR	SR	SR	SR	SR	SR	SR	SR	SR	SR	SR	SR
Whifflet	d	09 06	09 36	10 06	10 37	11 06	11 37	12 06	12 39	13 06	13 37	14 06	14 37	15 06	15 37	16 07	16 39	17 07	17 39	18 07
Kirkwood	d	09 10	09 39	10 10	10 40	11 10	11 40	12 10	12 42	13 10	13 40	14 10	14 40	15 10	15 40	16 10	16 42	17 10	17 42	18 10
Bargeddie	d	09 13	09 42	10 13	10 43	11 13	11 43	12 13	12 45	13 13	13 43	14 13	14 43	15 13	15 43	16 13	16 45	17 13	17 45	18 13
Baillieston	d	09 16	09 45	10 16	10 46	11 16	11 46	12 16	12 48	13 16	13 46	14 16	14 46	15 16	15 46	16 16	16 48	17 16	17 48	18 16
Mount Vernon	d	09 19	09 48	10 19	10 49	11 19	11 49	12 19	12 51	13 19	13 49	14 19	14 49	15 19	15 49	16 19	16 51	17 19	17 51	18 19
Carmyle	d	09 22	09 52	10 22	10 53	11 22	11 53	12 22	12 55	13 22	13 53	14 22	14 53	15 22	15 53	16 23	16 55	17 23	17 55	18 23
Glasgow Central 15	a	09 37	10 06	10 35	11 07	11 36	12 06	12 34	13 08	13 37	14 06	14 37	15 08	15 39	16 08	16 36	17 08	17 36	18 08	18 40

Glasgow Central - Ardrossan, Largs and Ayr

		SR MX	SR	SR	SR	SR ◇	SR SO	SR SX	SR SO	SR SX	SR SX	SR SO	SR	SR	SR SX	SR SX	SR SO	SR	SR
Glasgow Central	219 d	00 15	06 00	06 15	06 30	06 30	06 45	06 45	07 00	07 00	07 15	07 15	07 30	08 00	08 15	08 30	08 30	08 33	08 45
Paisley Gilmour Street	219 d	00 26	06 11	06 26	06 41		06 56	06 56	07 11	07 11	07 26	07 26	07 41	08 11	08 26	08 41	08 41	08 44	08 56
Johnstone	d	00 30	06 13	06 30	06 45		07 00	07 00	07 15	07 15	07 30	07 30	07 45	08 15	08 30	08 45	08 45	08 48	09 00
Milliken Park	d			06 33			07 03	07 03			07 33	07 33			08 33			08 51	09 03
Howwood	d			06 36			07 06			07 19		07 36			08 36		08 49		
Lochwinnoch	d			06 40							07 38	07 40			08 40			08 56	
Glengarnock	d			06 45			07 13	07 11			07 43	07 45		08 24	08 45	08 54	08 56	09 01	09 11
Dalry	d			06 49			07 17	07 15			07 47	07 49		08 28	08 49	08 58	09 00	09 05	
Kilwinning	d	00 42	06 27	06 54	06 59		07 22	07 21	07 29	07 31	07 52	07 54	08 00	08 33	08 54	09 03	09 05	09 10	09 18
Stevenston	d			06 57			07 25	07 23			07 55	07 57			08 57			09 13	09 21
Saltcoats	d			07 00			07 28	07 27			08 01	08 02			09 00			09 16	09 24
Ardrossan South Beach	d			07 02			07 30	07 28			08 03	08 04			09a02			09 18	09 26
Ardrossan Town	d						07 36	07 36										09 22	
Ardrossan Harbour	a						07 38	07 38										09 25	
West Kilbride	d			07 08							08 09	08 10							09 31
Fairlie	d			07 13							08 14	08 16							09 35
Largs	a			07 20							08 20	08 22							09 44
Irvine	d	00 47	06 31		07 03				07 33	07 35			08 04	08 37		09 07	09 09		
Barassie	d	00 51			07 07								08 09	08 42		09 12	09 14		
Troon	d	00 54	06 37		07 10	07 45			07 39	07 41			08 12	08 45		09 15	09 17		
Prestwick Int. Airport ✈	d	00 58	06 41		07 14	07 50			07 43	07 45			08 16	08 49		09 19	09 21		
Prestwick Town	d	01 00	06 43		07 16	07 52			07 45	07 47			08 18	08 51		09 21	09 23		
Newton-on-Ayr	d	01 04			07 19								08 21	08 54		09 24	09 26		
Ayr	a	01 11	06 52		07 24	07 59			07 52	07 54			08 26	08 58		09 28	09 30		

		SR	SR ◇	SR	SR	SR	SR	SR	SR	SR	SR	SR	SR	SR	SR ◇	SR	SR	SR	SR	SR	SR	SR	SR	SR
Glasgow Central	219 d	09 00	09 12	09 15	09 30	09 45	10 00	10 15	10 30		10 45	11 00	11 15	11 30	11 42	11 45	12 00	12 15	12 30	12 45	13 00	13 15		13 30
Paisley Gilmour Street	219 d	09 10		09 26	09 41	09 56	10 11	10 26	10 41		10 56	11 11	11 26	11 41	11 53	11 56	12 10	12 26	12 41	12 56	13 11	13 26		13 41
Johnstone	d	09 14		09 30	09 45	10 00	10 15	10 30	10 45		11 00	11 15	11 30	11 45		12 01	12 14	12 30	12 45	13 00	13 15	13 30		13 45
Milliken Park	d			09 33		10 03		10 33			11 03		11 33			12 03		12 33		13 03		13 33		
Howwood	d			09 36				10 36					11 36					12 36				13 36		
Lochwinnoch	d			09 40				10 40					11 40					12 40				13 40		
Glengarnock	d			09 45	09 54	10 11		10 45	10 54		11 11		11 45			12 11		12 45		13 11		13 45		
Dalry	d			09 49		10 15	10 26	10 49					11 49					12 49		13 15		13 49		
Kilwinning	d	09 29		09 54	10 01	10 20	10 31	10 54	11 01		11 18	11 29	11 54	12 00	12 10	12 18	12 27	12 54	12 59	13 20	13 29	13 54		13 59
Stevenston	d			09 57		10 23		10 57			11 21		11 57			12 22		12 57		13 23		13 57		
Saltcoats	d			10 00		10 26		11 00			11 24		12 00			12 24		13 00		13 26		14 00		
Ardrossan South Beach	d			10 02		10 28		11 02			11 26		12 02			12 26		13 02		13 28		14 02		
Ardrossan Town	d			10 06				11 06					12 06					13 06				14 06		
Ardrossan Harbour	a			10 08				11 08					12 09					13 09				14 09		
West Kilbride	d					10 34					11 32					12 32				13 34				
Fairlie	d					10 39					11 37					12 38				13 39				
Largs	a					10 47					11 44					12 44				13 46				
Irvine	d	09 33			10 05		10 35		11 05			11 33		12 04			12 33		13 03		13 33			14 03
Barassie	d				10 09				11 10					12 09					13 08					14 08
Troon	d	09 41	10 17		10 12		10 41		11 13	11 19		11 39		12 12			12 39		13 11		13 39		13 46	14 11
Prestwick Int. Airport ✈	d	09 45	10 22		10 16		10 45		11 17	11 22		11 43		12 16			12 43		13 15		13 43		13 51	14 15
Prestwick Town	d	09 47	10 24		10 18		10 47		11 19	11 24		11 45		12 18			12 45		13 17		13 45		13 53	14 17
Newton-on-Ayr	d				10 22				11 22					12 21					13 20					14 20
Ayr	a	09 53	10 31		10 26		10 54		11 26	11 31		11 52		12 24	12 29		12 52		13 24		13 52		14 06	14 24

		SR	SR	SR	SR	SR	SR	SR	SR	SR	SR	SR	SR	SR	SR	SR	SR	SR SX	SR	SR	SR SX
Glasgow Central	219 d	13 45	14 00	14 15	14 30	14 45	15 00	15 12	15 15	15 30	15 45	16 00	16 18	16 30	16 50		17 00	17 13	17 12	17 20	17 30
Paisley Gilmour Street	219 d	13 56	14 11	14 26	14 41	14 56	15 11		15 26	15 41	15 56	16 11	16 28	16 41	17 01		17 11	17u24		17 32	17u41
Johnstone	d	14 00	14 15	14 30	14 45	15 00	15 15		15 30	15 45	16 00	16 15	16 32	16 45	17 05		17 15			17 36	
Milliken Park	d	14 03		14 33		15 03			15 33		16 03		16 35		17 08					17 39	
Howwood	d			14 36					15 36				16 38		17 11						
Lochwinnoch	d			14 40					15 40				16 42				17 21				
Glengarnock	d	14 11		14 45		15 11			15 45		16 11		16 47		17 18		17 26	17 35			
Dalry	d		14 26	14 49					15 49				16 51		17 22		17 30			17 49	
Kilwinning	d	14 18	14 31	14 54	14 59	15 18	15 29		15 54	15 59	16 18	16 29	16 56	17 00	17 26		17 35	17 42		17 54	
Stevenston	d	14 21		14 57		15 21			15 57		16 21		17 01		17 30					17 57	
Saltcoats	d	14 24		15 00		15 24			16 00		16 24		17 09		17 32					18 00	
Ardrossan South Beach	d	14 26		15 01		15 26			16 02		16 26		17 11		17 36					18 02	
Ardrossan Town	d			15 06					16 06						17 39						
Ardrossan Harbour	a			15 09					16 09						17 44						
West Kilbride	d	14 32				15 32					16 32		17 17							18 08	
Fairlie	d	14 37				15 37					16 37		17 22							18 13	
Largs	a	14 44				15 44					16 44		17 28							18 20	
Irvine	d		14 35		15 03		15 33			16 03		16 33		17 04			17 39	17 46			18 00
Barassie	d				15 08					16 08				17 08			17 44				18 04
Troon	d		14 41		15 11		15 39	16 16		16 11		16 39		17 11		17 16	17 47	17 52	18 21		18 07
Prestwick Int. Airport ✈	d		14 45		15 15		15 43	16 20		16 15		16 43		17 15		17 21	17 51	17 56	18 26		18 11
Prestwick Town	d		14 47		15 17		15 45	16 22		16 17		16 45		17 17		17 23	17 53	17 58	18 28		18 13
Newton-on-Ayr	d				15 20					16 20				17 21			17 56				18 17
Ayr	a		14 54		15 24		15 52	16 30		16 24		16 52		17 25		17 30	18 00	18 05	18 36		18 21

Glasgow Central - Ardrossan, Largs and Ayr

		SR SO	SR	SR	SR	SR	SR	SR	SR	SR	SR	SR	SR	SR	SR	SR	SR	SR	SR	SR	SR	SR	SR
Glasgow Central	219 d	17 30	17 35	17 45	18 00	18 15	18 30	18 45	19 00	19 15		19 30	19 45	20 00	20 15	20 30	20 45		21 00	21 15	21 30	21 45	22 00
Paisley Gilmour Street	219 d	17 41	17 48	17 56	18 11	18 26	18 41	18 56	19 11	19 25		19 41	19 56	20 11	20 26	20 41	20 56		21 11	21 26	21 41	21 56	22 11
Johnstone	d	17 45	17 53	18 00	18 15	18 30	18 45	19 00	19 15	19 30		19 45	20 01	20 15	20 30	20 45	21 00		21 15	21 30	21 45	22 02	22 15
Milliken Park	d		17 56	18 03		18 33		19 03		19 33			20 03		20 33		21 03			21 33		22 04	
Howwood	d		17 59			18 36				19 36					20 36					21 36			
Lochwinnoch	d		18 03			18 40				19 40					20 40					21 40			
Glengarnock	d		18 08	18 11		18 45		19 11		19 45			20 11		20 45		21 11			21 45		22 12	
Dalry	d		18 12	18 15	18 26	18 49	18 57			19 49					20 49					21 49			
Kilwinning	d	17 59	18 16	18 20	18 31	18 54	19 02	19 18	19 29	19 54		20 00	20 18	20 29	20 54	20 59	21 18		21 29	21 53	21 59	22 19	22 29
Stevenston	d		18 20	18 23		18 57		19 21		19 57			20 22		20 57		21 21			21 57		22 21	
Saltcoats	d		18 22	18 26		19 00		19 24		20 00			20 23		21 00		21 24			22 00		22 24	
Ardrossan South Beach	d		18 24	18 28		19 02		19 26		20 02			20 25		21 02		21 26			22 02		22 26	
Ardrossan Town	d		18a27			19 06				20 06					21 06					22 06			
Ardrossan Harbour	a					19 09				20 09					21 09					22 09			
West Kilbride	d			18 34				19 32					20 32				21 32					22 32	
Fairlie	d			18 39				19 39					20 37				21 37					22 37	
Largs	a			18 48				19 44					20 44				21 44					22 44	
Irvine	d	18 03			18 35		19 06		19 33			20 04		20 33		21 03			21 33		22 03		22 33
Barassie	d	18 08			18 40		19 11					20 09				21 08					22 08		
Troon	d	18 11			18 43		19 14		19 39		19 16	20 12		20 39		21 11		21 22	21 39		22 11		22 39
Prestwick Int. Airport ✈	d	18 15			18 47		19 18		19 43		19 22	20 16		20 43		21 15		21 27	21 43		22 15		22 43
Prestwick Town	d	18 17			18 49		19 20		19 45		19 24	20 18		20 45		21 17		21 29	21 45		22 17		22 45
Newton-on-Ayr	d	18 20			18 52		19 23					20 21				21 20					22 20		
Ayr	a	18 24			18 56		19 26		19 52		19 30	20 25		20 52		21 24		21 36	21 52		22 24		22 52

		SR	SR	SR	SR	SR FO	SR FX	SR	SR	SR FSX	SR FO
Glasgow Central	219 d	22 15	22 30	22 45	23 00	23 15	23 15		23 30	23 45	23 45
Paisley Gilmour Street	219 d	22 26	22 41	22 56	23 11	23 26	23 26		23 41	23 56	23 56
Johnstone	d	22 30	22 45	23 00	23 15	23 30	23 30		23 45	23 59	23 59
Milliken Park	d	22 33		23 03		23 33	23 33			00 03	00 03
Howwood	d	22 36				23 36	23 36			00 06	00 06
Lochwinnoch	d	22 40				23 40	23 40			00 10	00 10
Glengarnock	d	22 45		23 11		23 45	23 45			00 15	00 15
Dalry	d	22 49				23 49	23 49			00 19	00 19
Kilwinning	d	22 54	22 59	23 18	23 27	23 54	23 53		23 59	00 23	00 23
Stevenston	d	22 57		23 21		23 57	23 57			00 27	00 27
Saltcoats	d	23 00		23 24		23 59	23 58			00 29	00 29
Ardrossan South Beach	d	23 02		23 26		00 02	00 02			00a32	00 31
Ardrossan Town	d	23a06				00a06					
Ardrossan Harbour	a										
West Kilbride	d			23 32			00 08				00 37
Fairlie	d			23 37			00 14				00 43
Largs	a			23 44			00 19				00 49
Irvine	d		23 03		23 33				00 03		
Barassie	d		23 08						00 08		
Troon	d		23 11		23 39			23 22	00 11		
Prestwick Int. Airport ✈	d		23 15		23 43			23 27	00 15		
Prestwick Town	d		23 17		23 45			23 29	00 17		
Newton-on-Ayr	d		23 20						00 20		
Ayr	a		23 24		23 52			23 36	00 23		

Sundays

until 21 November

		SR	SR	SR B	SR	SR	SR B	SR	SR	SR	SR B	SR ◇	SR	SR	SR B	SR	SR	SR B	SR	SR	SR
Glasgow Central	219 d	08 40	09 00	09 30	09 42	10 00	10 30	10 42	11 00	11 15	11 30	11 40	11 45	12 00	12 30	12 42	13 00	13 30	13 42	14 00	14 05
Paisley Gilmour Street	219 d	08 51	09 11	09 41	09 53	10 11	10 41	10 54	11 11	11 26	11 41	11 54	11 57	12 11	12 41	12 56	13 11	13 41	13 54	14 11	14 16
Johnstone	d	08 55	09 15	09 45	09 57	10 15	10 45	10 59	11 15	11 30	11 45		12 03	12 15	12 45	13 00	13 15	13 45	13 59	14 15	14 20
Milliken Park	d	08 58			10 00			11 01		11 33			12 05			13 03			14 01		14 23
Howwood	d				10 03			11 04					12 08			13 06			14 04		
Lochwinnoch	d				10 07			11 08					12 12			13 10			14 08		
Glengarnock	d	09 06			10 12			11 13					12 17			13 15			14 13		
Dalry	d	09 10			10 16			11 17					12 21			13 19			14 17		
Kilwinning	d	09 15	09 29	09 59	10 21	10 29	10 59	11 22	11 29	11 46	11 59	12 11	12 26	12 30	12 59	13 23	13 29	13 59	14 22	14 29	14 36
Stevenston	d	09 18			10 24			11 26		11 49			12 30			13 27			14 26		14 39
Saltcoats	d	09 21			10 27			11 28		11 52			12 32			13 29			14 28		14 42
Ardrossan South Beach	d	09 23			10 28			11 30		11 54			12 34			13 31			14 30		14 44
Ardrossan Town	d	09 27								11 59											14 49
Ardrossan Harbour	a	09 30								12 02											14 52
West Kilbride	d				10 34			11 36					12 40			13 37			14 36		
Fairlie	d				10 41			11 42					12 46			13 43			14 42		
Largs	a				10 47			11 47					12 51			13 48			14 47		
Irvine	d		09 33	10 03		10 33	11 03		11 33		12 03			12 34	13 03		13 33	14 03		14 33	
Barassie	d		09 38			10 38			11 38					12 39			13 38			14 38	
Troon	d		09 41	10 09		10 41	11 09		11 41		12 09			12 42	13 09		13 41	14 09		14 41	
Prestwick Int. Airport ✈	d		09 45	10 13		10 45	11 13		11 45		12 13			12 46	13 13		13 45	14 13		14 45	
Prestwick Town	d		09 47	10 15		10 47	11 15		11 47		12 15			12 48	13 15		13 47	14 15		14 47	
Newton-on-Ayr	d																				
Ayr	a		09 54	10 22		10 54	11 22		11 54		12 22	12 28		12 54	13 22		13 54	14 22		14 54	

B until 26 September

Glasgow Central - Ardrossan, Largs and Ayr

Sundays
until 21 November

		SR	SR	SR	SR	SR	SR	SR	SR	SR	SR	SR	SR	SR	SR	SR	SR	SR	SR	SR	SR	SR	SR
		A			A			◇	A				A			A							
Glasgow Central 15	219 d	14 30	14 42	15 00	15 30	15 42	16 00	16 25	16 30	16 42	16 55	17 00	17 30	17 42	18 00	18 30	18 42	19 00	19 42	20 00	20 42	21 00	21 42
Paisley Gilmour Street	219 d	14 41	14 54	15 11	15 41	15 53	16 11	16 39	16 41	16 55	17 07	17 12	17 41	17 54	18 11	18 41	18 53	19 11	19 53	20 11	20 53	21 11	21 52
Johnstone	d	14 45	14 59	15 15	15 45	15 58	16 15		16 46	17 00	17 11	17 17	17 45	17 59	18 15	18 45	18 58	19 15	19 58	20 15	20 58	21 15	21 57
Milliken Park	d		15 01			16 00				17 02	17 14			18 01			19 00		20 00		21 00		21 59
Howwood	d		15 04			16 03				17 05				18 04			19 03		20 03		21 03		22 02
Lochwinnoch	d		15 08			16 07				17 09				18 08			19 07		20 07		21 07		22 06
Glengarnock	d		15 13			16 12				17 14				18 13			19 12		20 12		21 12		22 11
Dalry	d		15 17			16 16				17 18				18 17			19 16		20 16		21 16		22 15
Kilwinning	d	14 59	15 22	15 29	16 00	16 20	16 29	16 56	17 00	17 23	17 28	17 31	17 59	18 22	18 29	18 59	19 21	19 29	20 21	20 29	21 21	21 29	22 20
Stevenston	d		15 26			16 24				17 27	17 31			18 26			19 25		20 25		21 25		22 24
Saltcoats	d		15 28			16 26				17 29	17 34			18 28			19 27		20 27		21 27		22 26
Ardrossan South Beach	d		15 30			16 28				17 31	17 36			18 30			19 29		20 29		21 29		22 28
Ardrossan Town	d										17 40												
Ardrossan Harbour	a										17 43												
West Kilbride	d		15 36			16 34				17 37				18 36			19 35		20 35		21 35		22 33
Fairlie	d		15 42			16 40				17 43				18 42			19 41		20 41		21 41		22 39
Largs	a		15 47			16 47				17 48				18 47			19 47		20 47		21 47		22 47
Irvine	d	15 03		15 33	16 04		16 33		17 04			17 35	18 03		18 33	19 03		19 33		20 33		21 33	
Barassie	d			15 38			16 38					17 40			18 38			19 38		20 38		21 38	
Troon	d	15 09		15 41	16 10		16 41		17 10			17 43	18 09		18 41	19 09		19 41		20 41		21 41	
Prestwick Int. Airport ✈	d	15 13		15 45	16 14		16 45		17 14			17 47	18 13		18 45	19 13		19 45		20 45		21 45	
Prestwick Town	d	15 15		15 47	16 17		16 47		17 16			17 49	18 15		18 47	19 15		19 47		20 47		21 47	
Newton-on-Ayr	d																						
Ayr	a	15 22		15 54	16 22		16 54	17 17	17 24			17 54	18 22		18 54	19 22		19 54		20 54		21 54	

		SR	SR	SR
Glasgow Central 15	219 d	22 00	22 41	23 00
Paisley Gilmour Street	219 d	22 11	22 52	23 11
Johnstone	d	22 15	22 56	23 15
Milliken Park	d		22 59	
Howwood	d		23 02	
Lochwinnoch	d		23 06	
Glengarnock	d		23 11	
Dalry	d		23 15	
Kilwinning	d	22 29	23 20	23 29
Stevenston	d		23 24	
Saltcoats	d		23 26	
Ardrossan South Beach	d		23 28	
Ardrossan Town	d			
Ardrossan Harbour	a			
West Kilbride	d		23 34	
Fairlie	d		23 40	
Largs	a		23 46	
Irvine	d	22 33		23 33
Barassie	d	22 38		23 38
Troon	d	22 41		23 41
Prestwick Int. Airport ✈	d	22 45		23 45
Prestwick Town	d	22 47		23 47
Newton-on-Ayr	d			
Ayr	a	22 54		23 54

Sundays
from 28 November

		SR	SR	SR	SR	SR	SR	SR	SR	SR	SR	SR	SR	SR	SR	SR	SR	SR	SR	SR	SR
												◇									
Glasgow Central 15	219 d	08 40	09 00	09 30	09 42	10 00	10 30	10 42	11 00	11 15	11 30	11 40	11 45	12 00	12 30	12 42	13 00	13 30	13 42	14 00	14 05
Paisley Gilmour Street	219 d	08 51	09 11	09 41	09 53	10 11	10 41	10 54	11 11	11 26	11 41	11 54	11 57	12 11	12 41	12 56	13 11	13 41	13 54	14 11	14 16
Johnstone	d	08 55	09 15	09 45	09 57	10 15	10 45	10 59	11 15	11 30	11 45		12 03	12 15	12 45	13 00	13 15	13 45	13 59	14 15	14 20
Milliken Park	d	08 58			10 00			11 01		11 33			12 05			13 03			14 01		14 23
Howwood	d				10 03			11 04					12 08			13 06			14 04		
Lochwinnoch	d				10 07			11 08					12 12			13 10			14 08		
Glengarnock	d	09 06			10 12			11 13					12 17			13 15			14 13		
Dalry	d	09 10			10 16			11 17					12 21			13 19			14 17		
Kilwinning	d	09 15	09 29	09 59	10 21	10 29	10 59	11 22	11 29	11 46	11 59	12 11	12 26	12 30	12 59	13 23	13 29	13 59	14 22	14 29	14 36
Stevenston	d	09 18			10 24			11 26		11 49			12 30			13 27			14 26		14 39
Saltcoats	d	09 21			10 27			11 28		11 52			12 32			13 29			14 28		14 42
Ardrossan South Beach	d	09 23			10 28			11 30		11 54			12 34			13 31			14 30		14 44
Ardrossan Town	d	09 27								11 59											14 49
Ardrossan Harbour	a	09 30								12 02											14 52
West Kilbride	d				10 34			11 36					12 40			13 37			14 36		
Fairlie	d				10 41			11 42					12 46			13 43			14 42		
Largs	a				10 47			11 47					12 51			13 48			14 47		
Irvine	d		09 33	10 03		10 33	11 03		11 33		12 03			12 34	13 03		13 33	14 03		14 33	
Barassie	d		09 38			10 38			11 38					12 39			13 38			14 38	
Troon	d		09 41	10 09		10 41	11 09		11 41		12 09			12 42	13 09		13 41	14 09		14 41	
Prestwick Int. Airport ✈	d		09 45	10 13		10 45	11 13		11 45		12 13			12 46	13 13		13 45	14 13		14 45	
Prestwick Town	d		09 47	10 15		10 47	11 15		11 47		12 15			12 48	13 15		13 47	14 15		14 47	
Newton-on-Ayr	d																				
Ayr	a		09 54	10 22		10 54	11 22		11 54		12 22	12 28		12 54	13 22		13 54	14 22		14 54	

A until 26 September

Glasgow Central - Ardrossan, Largs and Ayr

Sundays
from 28 November

		SR	SR	SR	SR	SR	SR	SR	SR	SR	SR	SR	SR	SR	SR	SR	SR	SR	SR	SR	SR	SR	SR
								◇															
Glasgow Central 15	219 d	14 30	14 42	15 00	15 30	15 42	16 00	16 25	16 30	16 42	16 55	17 00	17 30	17 42	18 00	18 42	19 00	19 42	20 00	20 42	21 00	21 42	22 00
Paisley Gilmour Street	219 d	14 41	14 54	15 11	15 41	15 53	16 11	16 39	16 41	16 55	17 07	17 12	17 41	17 54	18 11	18 53	19 11	19 53	20 11	20 53	21 11	21 52	22 11
Johnstone	d	14 45	14 59	15 15	15 45	15 58	16 15		16 46	17 00	17 11	17 17	17 45	17 59	18 15	18 58	19 15	19 58	20 15	20 58	21 15	21 57	22 15
Milliken Park	d		15 01			16 00				17 02	17 14			18 01		19 00		20 00		21 00		21 59	
Howwood	d		15 04			16 03				17 05				18 04		19 03		20 03		21 03		22 02	
Lochwinnoch	d		15 08			16 07				17 09				18 08		19 07		20 07		21 07		22 06	
Glengarnock	d		15 13			16 12				17 14				18 13		19 12		20 12		21 12		22 11	
Dalry	d		15 17			16 16				17 18				18 17		19 16		20 16		21 16		22 15	
Kilwinning	d	14 59	15 22	15 29	16 00	16 20	16 29	16 56	17 00	17 23	17 28	17 31	17 59	18 22	18 29	19 21	19 29	20 21	20 29	21 21	21 29	22 20	22 29
Stevenston	d		15 26			16 24				17 27	17 31			18 26		19 25		20 25		21 25		22 24	
Saltcoats	d		15 28			16 26				17 29	17 34			18 28		19 27		20 27		21 27		22 26	
Ardrossan South Beach	d		15 30			16 28				17 31	17 36			18 30		19 29		20 29		21 29		22 28	
Ardrossan Town	d										17 40												
Ardrossan Harbour	a										17 43												
West Kilbride	d		15 36			16 34				17 37				18 36		19 35		20 35		21 35		22 33	
Fairlie	d		15 42			16 40				17 43				18 42		19 41		20 41		21 41		22 39	
Largs	a		15 47			16 47				17 48				18 47		19 47		20 47		21 47		22 47	
Irvine	d	15 03		15 33	16 04		16 33		17 04			17 35	18 03		18 33		19 33		20 33		21 33		22 33
Barassie	d			15 38			16 38					17 40			18 38		19 38		20 38		21 38		22 38
Troon	d	15 09		15 41	16 10		16 41		17 10			17 43	18 09		18 41		19 41		20 41		21 41		22 41
Prestwick Int. Airport ✈	d	15 13		15 45	16 14		16 45		17 14			17 47	18 13		18 45		19 45		20 45		21 45		22 45
Prestwick Town	d	15 15		15 47	16 17		16 47		17 16			17 49	18 15		18 47		19 47		20 47		21 47		22 47
Newton-on-Ayr	d																						
Ayr	a	15 22		15 54	16 22		16 54	17 17	17 24			17 54	18 22		18 54		19 54		20 54		21 54		22 54

		SR	SR
Glasgow Central 15	219 d	22 41	23 00
Paisley Gilmour Street	219 d	22 52	23 11
Johnstone	d	22 56	23 15
Milliken Park	d	22 59	
Howwood	d	23 02	
Lochwinnoch	d	23 06	
Glengarnock	d	23 11	
Dalry	d	23 15	
Kilwinning	d	23 20	23 29
Stevenston	d	23 24	
Saltcoats	d	23 26	
Ardrossan South Beach	d	23 28	
Ardrossan Town	d		
Ardrossan Harbour	a		
West Kilbride	d	23 34	
Fairlie	d	23 40	
Largs	a	23 46	
Irvine	d		23 33
Barassie	d		23 38
Troon	d		23 41
Prestwick Int. Airport ✈	d		23 45
Prestwick Town	d		23 47
Newton-on-Ayr	d		
Ayr	a		23 54

Ayr, Largs and Ardrossan - Glasgow Central

Mondays to Saturdays

		SR	SR	SR	SR	SR	SR	SR	SR	SR	SR	SR	SR	SR	SR	SR	SR	SR	SR	SR	SR	SR
							SX	SX	SO	SX	SO	SX	SX			SX	SX		SO	SX		SO
Ayr	d	05 40	06 13		06 43		06 57	06 50	06 50	07 13	07 13	07 25		07 43		07 58		08 13			08 43	
Newton-on-Ayr	d	05 43	06 16		06 46					07 16	07 16					08 01		08 16				
Prestwick Town	d	05 46	06 19		06 49		07 02	06 55	06 55	07 19	07 19	07 30		07 48		08 03		08 19			08 48	
Prestwick Int. Airport ✈	d	05 48	06 21		06 51		07 04	06 57	06 57	07 21	07 21	07 32		07 50		08 05		08 21			08 50	
Troon	d	05 52	06 25		06 55		07 08	07 02	07 02	07 25	07 25	07 36		07 54		08 09		08 25			08 54	
Barassie	d	05 54	06 27		06 57		07 10			07 27	07 27	07 38				08 11		08 27				
Irvine	d	05 59	06 32		07 02		07 15			07 32	07 32	07 43		07 59		08 16		08 32			08 59	
Largs	d					06 41							07 25		07 42					08 28		08 51
Fairlie	d					06 46							07 30		07 47					08 33		08 56
West Kilbride	d					06 51							07 35		07 52					08 38		09 01
Ardrossan Harbour	d																08 11		08 28			
Ardrossan Town	d			06 30													08 14		08 30			
Ardrossan South Beach	d			06 33		06 57							07 41		07 58		08 16		08 32	08 44		09 07
Saltcoats	d			06 35		07 02							07 43		08 00		08 18		08 34	08 46		09 09
Stevenston	d			06 38		07 05							07 46		08 03		08 21		08 36	08 49		09 12
Kilwinning	d	06 04	06 37	06 42	07 07	07 10	07 19			07 37	07 37		07 50	08 04	08 08	08 20	08 25	08 34	08 41	08 53	09 04	09 16
Dalry	d	06 08		06 46		07 14	07 24			07 41	07 41		07 55		08 12		08 30		08 46	08 58		
Glengarnock	d	06 12		06 50		07 18	07 28				07 45	07 52			08 16		08 34		08 50	09 02		09 22
Lochwinnoch	d	06 17		06 55			07 33				07 50		08 01		08 21		08 39		08 55			09 27
Howwood	d	06 21		06 59			07 37				07 54	07 59					08 43		08 59			09 31
Milliken Park	d	06 24		07 02		07 26	07 40				07 57		08 06		08 26		08 46		09 02	09 10		09 32
Johnstone	d	06 27	06 50	07 05	07 20	07 29	07 42			07 52	08 00	08 03	08 09	08 18	08 29	08 34	08 48	08 50	09 05	09 12	09 18	09 35
Paisley Gilmour Street 219	d	06 32	06 55	07 10	07 25	07 34	07 47			07 57	08 05	08 08	08 13	08 23	08 34	08 41	08 53	08 56	09 10	09 17	09 24	09 40
Glasgow Central 15 219	a	06 43	07 07	07 21	07 38	07 47	07 59	08 00	08 09	08 09	08 16	08 18	08 24	08 34	08 46	08 55	09 04	09 07	09 22	09 30	09 36	09 53

		SR	SR	SR	SR	SR	SR	SR	SR	SR	SR	SR	SR	SR	SR	SR	SR	SR	SR	SR	SR	SR	SR
													◇										
Ayr	d	08 36	09 13		09 43		10 13		10 43		11 13		11 31	11 43		12 13		12 36	12 43		13 13		13 43
Newton-on-Ayr	d		09 16				10 16				11 16					12 16					13 16		
Prestwick Town	d	08 41	09 19		09 48		10 19		10 48		11 19			11 48		12 19		12 41	12 48		13 19		13 48
Prestwick Int. Airport ✈	d	08 43	09 21		09 50		10 21		10 50		11 21			11 50		12 21		12 43	12 50		13 21		13 50
Troon	d	08 48	09 25		09 54		10 25		10 54		11 25			11 54		12 25		12a48	12 54		13 24		13 54
Barassie	d		09 27				10 27				11 27					12 27					13 26		
Irvine	d		09 32		09 59		10 32		10 59		11 32			11 59		12 32			12 59		13 31		13 59
Largs	d					09 53				10 53					11 53					12 53			
Fairlie	d					09 58				10 58					11 58					12 58			
West Kilbride	d					10 03				11 03					12 05					13 05			
Ardrossan Harbour	d			09 30				10 28				11 28					12 28					13 28	
Ardrossan Town	d			09 33				10 31				11 31					12 31					13 31	
Ardrossan South Beach	d			09 35		10 09		10 34		11 09		11 34			12 11		12 33			13 11		13 34	
Saltcoats	d			09 37		10 11		10 36		11 11		11 36			12 13		12 35			13 13		13 36	
Stevenston	d			09 40		10 14		10 39		11 14		11 39			12 16		12 38			13 16		13 39	
Kilwinning	d		09 37	09 45	10 04	10 18	10 37	10 43	11 04	11 18	11 37	11 43	11 49	12 04	12 20	12 37	12 43		13 04	13 20	13 36	13 43	14 04
Dalry	d		09 41	09 49				10 47				11 47					12 47					13 47	
Glengarnock	d			09 53		10 25		10 51		11 25		11 51			12 26		12 51			13 26		13 51	
Lochwinnoch	d			09 58				10 56				11 56					12 56					13 56	
Howwood	d				10 16			11 00				12 00					13 00					14 00	
Milliken Park	d			10 03		10 33		11 03		11 33		12 03			12 34		13 03			13 34		14 03	
Johnstone	d		09 52	10 06	10 20	10 35	10 50	11 06	11 18	11 35	11 50	12 06		12 18	12 37	12 50	13 06		13 18	13 37	13 49	14 06	14 18
Paisley Gilmour Street 219	d		09 57	10 11	10 25	10 40	10 55	11 11	11 23	11 39	11 55	12 11	12 16	12 23	12 42	12 55	13 11		13 24	13 42	13 54	14 11	14 23
Glasgow Central 15 219	a	10 05	10 09	10 22	10 36	10 52	11 07	11 22	11 36	11 52	12 07	12 22	12 33	12 35	12 52	13 07	13 22		13 35	13 52	14 06	14 22	14 35

		SR	SR	SR	SR	SR	SR	SR	SR	SR	SR	SR	SR	SR	SR	SR	SR	SR	SR	SR	SR	SR	SR
				◇									◇										
Ayr	d		14 13	14 18		14 43		15 13		15 18	15 43		16 06	16 13		16 43		17 13			17 43		18 17
Newton-on-Ayr	d		14 16					15 16						16 16		16 46		17 16					
Prestwick Town	d		14 19	14 23		14 48		15 19		15 23	15 48		16 11	16 19		16 49		17 19			17 48		18 23
Prestwick Int. Airport ✈	d		14 21	14 25		14 50		15 21		15 25	15 50		16 13	16 21		16 51		17 21			17 50		18 25
Troon	d		14 25	14a30		14 54		15 25		15 30	15 54		16a18	16 25		16 55		17 25			17 54		18a30
Barassie	d		14 27					15 27						16 27				17 27					
Irvine	d		14 32			14 59		15 32			15 59			16 32		17 00		17 32			17 59		
Largs	d	13 53					14 53					15 53					16 50			17 35			
Fairlie	d	13 58					14 58					15 58					16 55			17 40			
West Kilbride	d	14 03					15 03					16 03					17 00			17 45			
Ardrossan Harbour	d				14 28				15 28						16 28							18 00	
Ardrossan Town	d				14 31				15 31						16 31							18 03	
Ardrossan South Beach	d	14 09			14 33		15 09		15 34			16 09			16 34		17 06		17 42	17 51		18 06	
Saltcoats	d	14 11			14 35		15 11		15 36			16 11			16 36		17 08		17 44	17 53		18 08	
Stevenston	d	14 14			14 38		15 14		15 39			16 14			16 39		17 11		17 47	17 56		18 11	
Kilwinning	d	14 18	14 37		14 42	15 04	15 18	15 37	15 43		16 04	16 18		16 37	16 43	17 05	17 15	17 36	17 50	18 00	18 04	18 16	
Dalry	d				14 47				15 47						16 47		17 20	17 41	17 55	18 05	18 09		
Glengarnock	d	14 25			14 51		15 25	15 43	15 51			16 25		16 43	16 51		17 24		17 59		18 13	18 23	
Lochwinnoch	d				14 56				15 56						16 56		17 29				18 18		
Howwood	d				15 00				16 00						17 00					18 14		18 30	
Milliken Park	d	14 33			15 03		15 33		16 03			16 33			17 03		17 34		18 07			18 33	
Johnstone	d	14 35	14 50		15 05	15 18	15 35	15 52	16 06		16 18	16 36		16 52	17 06	17 19	17 36	17 52	18 09	18 18	18 24	18 35	
Paisley Gilmour Street 219	d	14 40	14 55		15 10	15 25	15 40	15 57	16 11		16 23	16 41		16 57	17 11	17 24	17 41	17 58	18 14	18 23	18 29	18 40	
Glasgow Central 15 219	a	14 52	15 08		15 22	15 36	15 52	16 09	16 25	16 33	16 34	16 52		17 09	17 22	17 35	17 55	18 09	18 25	18 34	18 42	18 52	

Ayr, Largs and Ardrossan - Glasgow Central

Mondays to Saturdays

		SR	SR	SR	SR	SR	SR	SR	SR	SR	SR	SR	SR	SR	SR	SR	SR	SR	SR	SR	SR	SR	SR	SR
		SO	SX															◇				◇		
Ayr	d	18 13	18 13		18 43		19 13		19 43		20 17	20 13		20 43		21 13		21 06	21 43		22 13	22 36		23 00
Newton-on-Ayr	d	18 16	18 16				19 16					20 16				21 16					22 16			23 03
Prestwick Town	d	18 19	18 19		18 48		19 19		19 48		20 22	20 19		20 48		21 19		21 11	21 48		22 19	22 41		23 06
Prestwick Int. Airport ✈	d	18 21	18 21		18 50		19 21		19 50		20 24	20 21		20 50		21 21		21 13	21 50		22 21			23 08
Troon	d	18 25	18 25		18 54		19 25		19 54		20a29	20 25		20 54		21 25		21 18	21 54		22 25	22 46		23 12
Barassie	d	18 27	18 27				19 27					20 27				21 27					22 27			23 14
Irvine	d	18 32	18 32		18 59		19 32		19 59			20 32		20 59		21 32			21 59		22 32			23 19
Largs	d					18 53				19 53					20 53					21 53			22 53	
Fairlie	d					18 58				19 58					20 58					21 58			22 58	
West Kilbride	d					19 03				20 03					21 03					22 03			23 03	
Ardrossan Harbour	d							19 28					20 33				21 28							
Ardrossan Town	d			18 32				19 30					20 35				21 31							
Ardrossan South Beach	d			18 34		19 09		19 34		20 09			20 38		21 09		21 34			22 09			23 09	
Saltcoats	d			18 36		19 11		19 36		20 11			20 40		21 11		21 36			22 11			23 11	
Stevenston	d			18 39		19 14		19 39		20 14			20 43		21 14		21 39			22 14			23 14	
Kilwinning	d	18 37	18 37	18 43	19 04	19 18	19 37	19 43	20 04	20 18		20 36	20 47	21 04	21 18	21 37	21 43		22 04	22 18	22 37	22 55	23 18	23 24
Dalry	d	18 41	18 41	18 47				19 47					20 51			21 41	21 47		22 09	22 23	22 41			23 28
Glengarnock	d			18 51		19 25		19 51		20 25			20 55		21 25		21 51			22 27			23 25	23 32
Lochwinnoch	d			18 56				19 56					21 00				21 56						23 30	
Howwood	d			19 00				20 00					21 04				22 00						23 34	
Milliken Park	d			19 03		19 33		20 03		20 33			21 07		21 33		22 03			22 35			23 37	
Johnstone	d	18 52	18 52	19 06	19 18	19 35	19 50	20 06	20 18	20 35		20 50	21 10	21 18	21 35	21 52	22 06		22 20	22 37	22 52		23 39	23 44
Paisley Gilmour Street 219	d	18 57	18 57	19 11	19 23	19 40	19 55	20 11	20 25	20 40		20 55	21 15	21 23	21 40	21 57	22 11		22 25	22 42	22 57	23 15	23 44	23 49
Glasgow Central 15 219	a	19 08	19 09	19 22	19 34	19 53	20 07	20 22	20 36	20 52		21 07	21 26	21 34	21 52	22 09	22 22	22 34	22 36	22 54	23 09	23 25	23 55	00 01

Sundays

until 21 November

		SR	SR	SR	SR	SR	SR	SR	SR	SR	SR	SR	SR	SR	SR	SR	SR	SR	SR	SR	SR	SR
												◇										
		B	B	B			B			B				B				B			B	
Ayr	d	08 43		09 13	09 43		10 13	10 43		11 13	11 43	12 00		12 13		12 43		13 13	13 43		14 13	14 43
Newton-on-Ayr	d																					
Prestwick Town	d	08 48		09 18	09 48		10 18	10 48		11 18	11 48			12 18		12 48		13 18	13 48		14 18	14 48
Prestwick Int. Airport ✈	d	08 50		09 20	09 50		10 20	10 50		11 20	11 50			12 20		12 50		13 20	13 50		14 20	14 50
Troon	d	08 54		09 24	09 54		10 24	10 54		11 24	11 54			12 24		12 54		13 24	13 54		14 24	14 54
Barassie	d	08 56			09 56			10 56			11 56					12 56			13 56			14 56
Irvine	d	09 01		09 29	10 01		10 29	11 01		11 29	12 01			12 29		13 01		13 29	14 01		14 29	15 01
Largs	d		08 53			09 53			10 53				11 53				12 56			13 53		
Fairlie	d		08 58			09 58			10 58				11 58				13 01			13 58		
West Kilbride	d		09 03			10 03			11 03				12 03				13 06			14 03		
Ardrossan Harbour	d														12 35							
Ardrossan Town	d																					
Ardrossan South Beach	d		09 09			10 09			11 09				12 09		12 40		13 12			14 09		
Saltcoats	d		09 11			10 11			11 11				12 11		12 42		13 14			14 11		
Stevenston	d		09 14			10 14			11 14				12 14		12 45		13 17			14 14		
Kilwinning	d	09 06	09 18	09 34	10 06	10 18	10 34	11 06	11 18	11 34	12 06	12 15	12 18	12 34	12 49	13 06	13 21	13 34	14 06	14 18	14 34	15 06
Dalry	d		09 23			10 23			11 23				12 23				13 25			14 23		
Glengarnock	d		09 27			10 27			11 27				12 27				13 29			14 27		
Lochwinnoch	d		09 32			10 32			11 32				12 32				13 34			14 32		
Howwood	d		09 36			10 36			11 36				12 36				13 38			14 36		
Milliken Park	d		09 39			10 39			11 39				12 39		13 02		13 41			14 39		
Johnstone	d	09 19	09 41	09 48	10 19	10 41	10 48	11 19	11 41	11 51	12 19		12 42	12 51	13 04	13 19	13 44	13 51	14 19	14 41	14 48	15 19
Paisley Gilmour Street 219	d	09 24	09 47	09 53	10 24	10 46	10 53	11 24	11 46	11 56	12 24	12 36	12 47	12 56	13 10	13 24	13 49	13 56	14 24	14 46	14 53	15 24
Glasgow Central 15 219	a	09 36	09 58	10 04	10 36	10 58	11 07	11 36	11 58	12 06	12 36	12 51	12 58	13 06	13 22	13 36	14 03	14 06	14 36	14 58	15 06	15 36

		SR	SR	SR	SR	SR	SR	SR	SR	SR	SR	SR	SR	SR	SR	SR	SR	SR	SR	SR	SR	SR	SR
					◇																	◇	
			B				B			B				B			B						
Ayr	d		15 13	15 43	15 59		16 13	16 43		17 13	17 43			18 13	18 43		19 13	19 43			20 43	21 00	
Newton-on-Ayr	d																						
Prestwick Town	d		15 18	15 48			16 18	16 48		17 18	17 48			18 18	18 48		19 18	19 48			20 48		
Prestwick Int. Airport ✈	d		15 20	15 50			16 20	16 50		17 20	17 50			18 20	18 50		19 20	19 50			20 50		
Troon	d		15 24	15 54			16 24	16 54		17 24	17 54			18 24	18 54		19 24	19 54			20 54		
Barassie	d			15 56				16 56			17 56				18 56			19 56			20 56		
Irvine	d		15 29	16 01			16 29	17 01		17 29	18 01			18 29	19 01		19 29	20 01			21 01		
Largs	d					15 53			16 53				17 53			18 53			19 53				20 53
Fairlie	d					15 58			16 58				18 00			18 58			19 58				20 58
West Kilbride	d					16 03			17 03				18 05			19 03			20 03				21 03
Ardrossan Harbour	d	15 04										18 00								20 31			
Ardrossan Town	d																						
Ardrossan South Beach	d	15 09				16 09			17 09			18 05	18 11			19 09			20 09	20 36			21 09
Saltcoats	d	15 11				16 11			17 11			18 07	18 13			19 11			20 11	20 38			21 11
Stevenston	d	15 14				16 14			17 14			18 10	18 16			19 14			20 14	20 41			21 14
Kilwinning	d	15 18	15 34	16 06	16 14	16 19	16 34	17 06	17 18	17 34	18 06	18 14	18 20	18 34	19 06	19 18	19 34	20 06	20 18	20 45	21 06	21 15	21 18
Dalry	d					16 23			17 23				18 24			19 23			20 23				21 23
Glengarnock	d					16 27			17 27				18 28			19 27			20 27				21 27
Lochwinnoch	d					16 32			17 32				18 33			19 32			20 32				21 32
Howwood	d					16 36			17 36				18 37			19 36			20 36				21 36
Milliken Park	d	15 31				16 39			17 39			18 27	18 40			19 39			20 39	20 58			21 39
Johnstone	d	15 33	15 48	16 19		16 42	16 50	17 19	17 41	17 51	18 19	18 29	18 43	18 48	19 19	19 41	19 48	20 19	20 41	21 00	21 19		21 41
Paisley Gilmour Street 219	d	15 39	15 53	16 24	16 37	16 47	16 55	17 24	17 46	17 56	18 24	18 38	18 48	18 53	19 24	19 47	19 53	20 24	20 47	21 06	21 24	21 36	21 47
Glasgow Central 15 219	a	15 50	16 06	16 36	16 49	16 58	17 06	17 36	17 58	18 07	18 36	18 48	18 58	19 04	19 36	19 58	20 04	20 36	20 58	21 17	21 36	21 48	21 58

B until 26 September

b arr. 2008

Table 221

Sundays
until 21 November

Ayr, Largs and Ardrossan - Glasgow Central

			SR		SR	SR	SR
Ayr		d	21 43			23 00	
Newton-on-Ayr		d					
Prestwick Town		d	21 48			23 05	
Prestwick Int. Airport ✈		d	21 50			23 07	
Troon		d	21 54			23 11	
Barassie		d	21 56			23 13	
Irvine		d	22 01			23 18	
Largs		d			21 53		22 58
Fairlie		d			21 58		23 03
West Kilbride		d			22 03		23 08
Ardrossan Harbour		d					
Ardrossan Town		d					
Ardrossan South Beach		d			22 09		23 14
Saltcoats		d			22 11		23 16
Stevenston		d			22 14		23 19
Kilwinning		d	22 06		22 18	23 23	23 27
Dalry		d			22 23		23 31
Glengarnock		d			22 27		23 35
Lochwinnoch		d			22 32		23 40
Howwood		d			22 36		23 44
Milliken Park		d			22 39		23 47
Johnstone		d	22 19		22 41	23 36	23 50
Paisley Gilmour Street	219	d	22 24		22 47	23 41	23 55
Glasgow Central 15	219	a	22 36		22 58	23 53	00 05

Sundays
from 28 November

				SR	SR	SR	SR	SR	SR	SR	SR		SR ◇	SR	SR	SR	SR	SR	SR	SR	SR		SR	SR	SR	SR
Ayr		d		09 13	09 43		10 13	10 43		11 13	11 43		12 00		12 13		12 43		13 13	13 43			14 13	14 43		15 13
Newton-on-Ayr		d																								
Prestwick Town		d		09 18	09 48		10 18	10 48		11 18	11 48				12 18		12 48		13 18	13 48			14 18	14 48		15 18
Prestwick Int. Airport ✈		d		09 20	09 50		10 20	10 50		11 20	11 50				12 20		12 50		13 20	13 50			14 20	14 50		15 20
Troon		d		09 24	09 54		10 24	10 54		11 24	11 54				12 24		12 54		13 24	13 54			14 24	14 54		15 24
Barassie		d			09 56			10 56			11 56						12 56			13 56				14 56		
Irvine		d		09 29	10 01		10 29	11 01		11 29	12 01				12 29		13 01		13 29	14 01			14 29	15 01		15 29
Largs		d				09 53			10 53					11 53				12 56			13 53					
Fairlie		d				09 58			10 58					11 58				13 01			13 58					
West Kilbride		d				10 03			11 03					12 03				13 06			14 03					
Ardrossan Harbour		d														12 35									15 04	
Ardrossan Town		d																								
Ardrossan South Beach		d				10 09			11 09					12 09		12 40		13 12			14 09				15 09	
Saltcoats		d				10 11			11 11					12 11		12 42		13 14			14 11				15 11	
Stevenston		d				10 14			11 14					12 14		12 45		13 17			14 14				15 14	
Kilwinning		d		09 34	10 06	10 18	10 34	11 06	11 18	11 34	12 06		12 15	12 18	12 34	12 49	13 06	13 21	13 34	14 06	14 18		14 34	15 06	15 18	15 34
Dalry		d				10 23			11 23					12 23				13 25			14 23					
Glengarnock		d				10 27			11 27					12 27				13 29			14 27					
Lochwinnoch		d				10 32			11 32					12 32				13 34			14 32					
Howwood		d				10 36			11 36					12 36				13 38			14 36					
Milliken Park		d				10 39			11 39					12 39		13 02		13 41			14 39				15 31	
Johnstone		d		09 48	10 19	10 41	10 48	11 19	11 41	11 51	12 19			12 42	12 51	13 04	13 19	13 44	13 51	14 19	14 41		14 48	15 19	15 33	15 48
Paisley Gilmour Street	219	d		09 53	10 24	10 46	10 53	11 24	11 46	11 56	12 24		12 36	12 47	12 56	13 10	13 24	13 49	13 56	14 24	14 46		14 53	15 24	15 39	15 53
Glasgow Central 15	219	a		10 04	10 36	10 58	11 07	11 36	11 58	12 06	12 36		12 51	12 58	13 06	13 22	13 36	14 03	14 06	14 36	14 58		15 06	15 36	15 50	16 06

			SR	SR ◇	SR	SR	SR		SR	SR	SR	SR	SR	SR	SR	SR	SR		SR	SR	SR ◇	SR	SR	SR	SR	SR
Ayr		d	15 43	15 59		16 13	16 43			17 13	17 43			18 43		19 43				20 43	21 00		21 43		23 00	
Newton-on-Ayr		d																								
Prestwick Town		d	15 48			16 18	16 48			17 18	17 48			18 48		19 48				20 48			21 48		23 05	
Prestwick Int. Airport ✈		d	15 50			16 20	16 50			17 20	17 50			18 50		19 50				20 50			21 50		23 07	
Troon		d	15 54			16 24	16 54			17 24	17 54			18 54		19 54				20 54			21 54		23 11	
Barassie		d	15 56				16 56				17 56			18 56		19 56				20 56			21 56		23 13	
Irvine		d	16 01			16 29	17 01			17 29	18 01			19 01		20 01				21 01			22 01		23 18	
Largs		d			15 53				16 53				17 53		18 53		19 53					20 53		21 53		22 58
Fairlie		d			15 58				16 58				18 00		18 58		19 58					20 58		21 58		23 03
West Kilbride		d			16 03				17 03				18 05		19 03		20 03					21 03		22 03		23 08
Ardrossan Harbour		d										18 00							20 31							
Ardrossan Town		d																								
Ardrossan South Beach		d			16 09				17 09			18 05	18 11		19 09		20 09		20 36			21 09		22 09		23 14
Saltcoats		d			16 11				17 11			18 07	18 13		19 11		20 11		20 38			21 11		22 11		23 16
Stevenston		d			16 14				17 14			18 10	18 16		19 14		20 14		20 41			21 14		22 14		23 19
Kilwinning		d	16 06	16 14	16 19	16 34	17 06		17 18	17 34	18 06	18 14	18 20	19 06	19 18	20 06	20 18		20 45	21 06	21 15	21 18	22 06	22 18	23 23	23 27
Dalry		d			16 23				17 23				18 24		19 23		20 23					21 23		22 23		23 31
Glengarnock		d			16 27				17 27				18 28		19 27		20 27					21 27		22 27		23 35
Lochwinnoch		d			16 32				17 32				18 33		19 32		20 32					21 32		22 32		23 40
Howwood		d			16 36				17 36				18 37		19 36		20 36					21 36		22 36		23 44
Milliken Park		d			16 39				17 39			18 27	18 40		19 39		20 39		20 58			21 39		22 39		23 47
Johnstone		d	16 19		16 42	16 50	17 19		17 41	17 51	18 19	18 29	18 43	19 19	19 41	20 19	20 41		21 00	21 19		21 41	22 19	22 41	23 36	23 50
Paisley Gilmour Street	219	d	16 24	16 37	16 47	16 55	17 24		17 46	17 56	18 24	18 38	18 48	19 24	19 47	20 24	20 47		21 06	21 24	21 36	21 47	22 24	22 47	23 41	23 55
Glasgow Central 15	219	a	16 36	16 49	16 58	17 06	17 36		17 58	18 07	18 36	18 48	18 58	19 36	19 58	20 36	20 58		21 17	21 36	21 48	21 58	22 36	22 58	23 53	00 05

Table 221A

SHIPPING SERVICES

Mondays to Saturdays
until 23 October

Glasgow and Ardrossan - Brodick (Arran)

Caledonian MacBrayne Ltd in association with ScotRail

							FO
Glasgow Central 15	221	d	*08 33*	*11 15*	*14 15*	*16 50*	*19 15*
Paisley Gilmour Street	221	d	*08 44*	*11 26*	*14 26*	*17 01*	*19 25*
Ardrossan Harbour	221	a	*09 25*	*12 09*	*15 09*	*17 44*	*20 09*
Ardrossan Harbour	⛴	d	09 45	12 30	15 15	18 00	20 30
Brodick	⛴	a	10 40	13 25	16 10	18 55	21 25

Sundays
until 17 October

Glasgow Central 15	221	d	*08 40*	*11 15*	*14 05*	*16 55*
Paisley Gilmour Street	221	d	*08 51*	*11 26*	*14 16*	*17 07*
Ardrossan Harbour	221	a	*09 30*	*12 02*	*14 52*	*17 43*
Ardrossan Harbour	⛴	d	09 45	12 30	15 15	18 00
Brodick	⛴	a	10 40	13 25	16 10	18 55

Mondays to Saturdays
until 23 October

Brodick	⛴	d	08 20	11 05	13 50	16 40	19 20
Ardrossan Harbour	⛴	a	09 15	12 00	14 45	17 35	20 15
Ardrossan Harbour	221	d	*09 30*	*12 28*	*15 28*	*18 00*	*20 33*
Paisley Gilmour Street	221	a	*10 10*	*13 10*	*16 10*	*18 40*	*21 14*
Glasgow Central 15	221	a	*10 22*	*13 22*	*16 25*	*18 52*	*21 26*

Sundays
until 17 October

Brodick	⛴	d	11 05	13 50	16 40	19 20
Ardrossan Harbour	⛴	a	12 00	14 45	17 35	20 15
Ardrossan Harbour	221	d	*12 35*	*15 04*	*18 00*	*20 31*
Paisley Gilmour Street	221	a	*13 09*	*15 38*	*18 37*	*21 05*
Glasgow Central 15	221	a	*13 22*	*15 50*	*18 48*	*21 17*

For details of sailings from 24 October 2010, telephone Caledonian MacBrayne on 08000 66 5000

Glasgow Central - East Kilbride, Barrhead and Kilmarnock

		SR SO	SR SO	SR	SR ◇	SR SO	SR SX	SR	SR	SR SX		SR SO	SR SX	SR	SR SX	SR SO	SR	SR	SR SX	SR SO		SR SX	SR SO	SR	SR SO
Glasgow Central [15]	d	00 12	00 18	06 13	06 30	06 47	06 48	06 54	07 08	07 12		07 18	07 23	07 37	07 43	07 48	07 52	08 07	08 17	08 18		08 22	08 25	08 37	08 48
Crossmyloof	d	00 18	00 24	06 19	06 36	06 53	06 54	07 00		07 18		07 24	07 29		07 49	07 54	07 59		08 24	08 24		08 29	08 31		08 54
Pollokshaws West	d	00 21	00 27	06 22	06 39	06 56	06 57	07 03		07 21		07 27	07 32		07 52	07 57	08 02		08 26	08 27		08 34	08 34		08 57
Thornliebank	d		00 30	06 25		06 59	07 00			07 24		07 30			07 55	08 00			08 29	08 30					09 00
Giffnock	d		00 33	06 28		07 02	07 03			07 27		07 33			07 58	08 03			08 32	08 33					09 03
Clarkston	d		00 37	06 32		07 06	07 07			07 31		07 37			08 02	08 07			08 36	08 37					09 07
Busby	d		00 40	06 35		07 09	07 10			07 36		07 40			08 08	08 10			08 39	08 40					09 10
Thorntonhall	d		00 43	06 38												08 13			08 42						09 13
Hairmyres	d		00 46	06 41		07 15	07 16			07 41		07 45			08 14	08 16			08 46	08 45					09 16
East Kilbride	a		00 50	06 45		07 18	07 19			07 50		07 49			08 17	08 20			08 49	08 49					09 20
Kennishead	d	00 24			06 42			07 06					07 35				08 05					08 37	08 37		
Priesthill & Darnley	d	00 26			06 44			07 08					07 37				08 07					08 39	08 39		
Nitshill	d	00 29			06 47			07 11					07 40				08 10					08 42	08 42		
Barrhead	d	00 32			06 50			07a14	07 23				07a43	07 51			08a14	08 19				08a45	08a45	08 48	
Dunlop	d	00 44			07 02				07 35					08 03				08 31						09 00	
Stewarton	d	00 48			07 06				07 39					08 07				08 35						09 04	
Kilmaurs	d	00 53			07 11				07 44					08 11				08 38						09 09	
Kilmarnock [3]	a	00 58			07 20				07 48					08 17				08 47						09 17	

		SR SX	SR SX	SR SO	SR ◇	SR SO		SR	SR	SR	SR	SR	SR	SR	SR	SR		SR	SR	SR	SR	SR	SR	SR	SR
Glasgow Central [15]	d	08 48	08 57	08 57	09 12	09 18		09 27	09 42	09 48	09 57	10 12	10 18	10 27	10 42	10 48		10 57	11 12	11 18	11 27	11 42	11 48	11 57	12 12
Crossmyloof	d	08 55	09 03	09 04		09 24		09 33		09 54	10 03		10 24	10 33		10 54		11 03		11 24	11 33		11 54	12 03	
Pollokshaws West	d	08 57	09 06	09 07		09 27		09 36		09 57	10 06		10 27	10 36		10 57		11 06		11 27	11 36		11 57	12 06	
Thornliebank	d	09 00				09 30				10 00			10 30			11 00				11 30			12 00		
Giffnock	d	09 03				09 33				10 03			10 33			11 03				11 33			12 03		
Clarkston	d	09 07				09 37				10 07			10 37			11 07				11 37			12 07		
Busby	d	09 10				09 40				10 10			10 40			11 10				11 40			12 10		
Thorntonhall	d	09 13								10 13						11 13							12 13		
Hairmyres	d	09 17				09 45				10 16			10 45			11 16				11 45			12 16		
East Kilbride	a	09 21				09 50				10 20			10 49			11 20				11 49			12 20		
Kennishead	d		09 09	09 10				09 39			10 09			10 39				11 09			11 39			12 09	
Priesthill & Darnley	d		09 11	09 12				09 41			10 11			10 41				11 11			11 41			12 11	
Nitshill	d		09 14	09 15				09 44			10 14			10 44				11 14			11 44			12 14	
Barrhead	d		09a17	09a21				09a47	09 53		10a17			10a47	10 53			11a17			11a47	11 53		12a17	
Dunlop	d								10 05						11 05				11 35			12 05			
Stewarton	d				09 38				10 10			10 38			11 10				11 39			12 10			12 38
Kilmaurs	d								10 13						11 13				11 44			12 13			
Kilmarnock [3]	a				09 48				10 20			10 47			11 20				11 50			12 20			12 47

		SR		SR	SR	SR	SR	SR	SR	SR	SR	SR		SR	SR	SR	SR	SR	SR	SR	SR	SR		SR	SR
Glasgow Central [15]	d	12 18		12 27	12 42	12 48	12 57	13 12	13 18	13 27	13 42	13 48		13 57	14 12	14 18	14 27	14 42	14 48	14 57	15 12	15 18		15 27	15 42
Crossmyloof	d	12 24		12 33		12 54	13 03		13 24	13 33		13 54		14 03		14 24	14 33		14 54	15 03		15 24		15 33	
Pollokshaws West	d	12 27		12 36		12 57	13 06		13 27	13 36		13 57		14 06		14 27	14 36		14 57	15 06		15 27		15 36	
Thornliebank	d	12 30				13 00			13 30			14 00				14 30			15 00			15 30			
Giffnock	d	12 33				13 03			13 33			14 03				14 33			15 03			15 33			
Clarkston	d	12 37				13 07			13 37			14 07				14 37			15 07			15 37			
Busby	d	12 40				13 10			13 40			14 10				14 40			15 10			15 40			
Thorntonhall	d					13 13						14 13							15 13						
Hairmyres	d	12 45				13 16			13 45			14 16				14 45			15 16			15 45			
East Kilbride	a	12 49				13 20			13 49			14 20				14 49			15 20			15 49			
Kennishead	d			12 39			13 09			13 39				14 09			14 39			15 09				15 39	
Priesthill & Darnley	d			12 41			13 11			13 41				14 11			14 41			15 11				15 41	
Nitshill	d			12 44			13 14			13 44				14 14			14 44			15 14				15 44	
Barrhead	d			12a47	12 53		13a17			13a47	13 53			14a17			14a47	14 53		15a17				15a47	15 53
Dunlop	d				13 05						14 05				14 34			15 05			15 34				16 05
Stewarton	d				13 10			13 38			14 10				14 38			15 10			15 38				16 10
Kilmaurs	d				13 13						14 13				14 43			15 13			15 43				16 13
Kilmarnock [3]	a				13 20			13 47			14 20				14 49			15 20			15 49				16 20

		SR SX	SR SO	SR	SR SX	SR	SR	SR		SR	SR	SR SX	SR	SR SO	SR SX	SR	SR SX	SR		SR SX	SR SO	SR	SR SX	SR SO	SR SX
Glasgow Central [15]	d	15 47	15 48	15 57	16 12	16 18	16 27	16 42		16 48	16 57	17 01	17 12	17 18	17 21	17 27	17 32	17 42		17 48	17 48	17 57	18 03	18 11	18 12
Crossmyloof	d	15 54	15 54	16 03		16 25	16 33			16 54	17 03	17 07		17 24		17 33	17 38			17 55	17 54	18 03	18 09		
Pollokshaws West	d	15 57	15 57	16 06		16 27	16 36			16 57	17 06	17 10		17 27		17 36	17 41			17 57	17 57	18 06	18 12		
Thornliebank	d	16 00	16 00			16 30				17 00		17 13		17 30			17 44			18 00	18 00		18 15		
Giffnock	d	16 03	16 03			16 33				17 03		17 16		17 33			17 47			18 03	18 03		18 18		
Clarkston	d	16 07	16 07			16 37				17 07		17 20		17 37	17 34		17 51			18 07	18 07		18 22		
Busby	d	16 10	16 10			16 40				17 10		17 23		17 40	17 38		17 54			18 10	18 10		18 25		
Thorntonhall	d	16 13	16 13			16 43				17 13				17 43			17 57				18 13		18 28		
Hairmyres	d	16 16	16 16			16 47				17 16		17 28		17 46	17 44		18 00			18 17	18 16		18 32		
East Kilbride	a	16 20	16 20			16 50				17 20		17 32		17 50	17 47		18 04			18 20	18 20		18 35		
Kennishead	d			16 09			16 39				17 09					17 39						18 09			
Priesthill & Darnley	d			16 11			16 41				17 11					17 41						18 11			
Nitshill	d			16 14			16 44				17 14					17 44						18 14			
Barrhead	d			16a17	16 23		16a47	16 53			17a17		17 24			17a47		17 54				18a17		18 23	18 23
Dunlop	d				16 35			17 05					17 36					18 07						18 35	18 35
Stewarton	d				16 39			17 09					17 39					18 12						18 39	18 39
Kilmaurs	d				16 44			17 14					17 44					18 16						18 42	18 42
Kilmarnock [3]	a				16 49			17 20					17 51					18 22						18 50	18 50

Glasgow Central - East Kilbride, Barrhead and Kilmarnock

		SR SO	SR SX	SR		SR	SR	SR	SR	SR	SR	SR	SR	SR		SR	SR	SR	SR	SR	SR	SR SO	SR SX	SR
Glasgow Central [15]	d	18 18	18 18	18 27		18 42	18 48	18 57	19 12	19 18	19 33	19 48	20 12	20 18		20 33	20 48	21 12	21 18	21 33	21 48	22 12	22 12	22 18
Crossmyloof	d	18 24	18 25	18 34			18 54	19 03		19 24	19 39	19 54		20 24		20 39	20 54		21 24	21 39	21 54			22 24
Pollokshaws West	d	18 27	18 27	18 37			18 57	19 06		19 27	19 42	19 57		20 27		20 42	20 57		21 27	21 42	21 57			22 27
Thornliebank	d	18 30	18 31				19 00			19 30		20 00		20 30			21 00		21 30		22 00			22 30
Giffnock	d	18 33	18 33				19 03			19 33		20 03		20 33			21 03		21 33		22 03			22 33
Clarkston	d	18 37	18 37				19 07			19 37		20 07		20 37			21 07		21 37		22 07			22 37
Busby	d	18 40	18 40				19 10			19 40		20 10		20 40			21 10		21 40		22 10			22 40
Thorntonhall	d						19 13					20 13					21 13				22 13			
Hairmyres	d	18 45	18 46				19 16			19 45		20 16		20 45			21 16		21 45		22 16			22 45
East Kilbride	a	18 49	18 50				19 20			19 49		20 20		20 49			21 20		21 49		22 20			22 49
Kennishead	d			18 40				19 09			19 45					20 45				21 45				
Priesthill & Darnley	d			18 42				19 11			19 47					20 47				21 47				
Nitshill	d			18 45				19 14			19 50					20 50				21 50				
Barrhead	d			18a48		18 53		19a17	19 24		19 54		20 23			20 54		21 24		21 54		22 23	22 23	
Dunlop	d					19 05			19 36		20 06					21 06		21 36		22 06		22 35	22 35	
Stewarton	d					19 09			19 40		20 10		20 39			21 10		21 40		22 10		22 39	22 39	
Kilmaurs	d					19 14			19 44		20 13					21 13		21 44		22 13		22 44	22 44	
Kilmarnock [3]	a					19 20			19 50		20 20		20 48			21 20		21 50		22 20		22 50	22 50	

		SR SX	SR SO	SR	SR SX	SR SO	SR
Glasgow Central [15]	d	22 33	22 39	22 48	23 12	23 12	23 18
Crossmyloof	d	22 39	22 45	22 54	23 18	23 18	23 24
Pollokshaws West	d	22 42	22 48	22 57	23 21	23 21	23 27
Thornliebank	d			23 00			23 30
Giffnock	d			23 03			23 33
Clarkston	d			23 07			23 37
Busby	d			23 10			23 40
Thorntonhall	d			23 13			23 43
Hairmyres	d			23 16			23 46
East Kilbride	a			23 20			23 50
Kennishead	d	22 45	22 51		23 24	23 24	
Priesthill & Darnley	d	22 47	22 53		23 26	23 26	
Nitshill	d	22 50	22 56		23 29	23 29	
Barrhead	d	22 54	22 59		23 32	23 32	
Dunlop	d	23 06	23 11		23 44	23 44	
Stewarton	d	23 10	23 15		23 48	23 48	
Kilmaurs	d	23 14	23 20		23 53	23 53	
Kilmarnock [3]	a	23 20	23 26		23 59	23 59	

Sundays

		SR	SR	SR	SR	SR	SR	SR	SR	SR		SR	SR	SR	SR	SR	SR	SR	SR	SR		SR	SR	SR	SR
Glasgow Central [15]	d	08 12	08 18	08 48	09 12	09 18	09 48	10 12	10 18	10 48		11 12	11 18	11 48	12 12	12 18	12 48	13 12	13 18	13 48		14 12	14 18	14 48	15 12
Crossmyloof	d		08 24	08 54		09 24	09 54		10 24	10 54			11 24	11 54		12 24	12 54		13 24	13 54			14 24	14 54	
Pollokshaws West	d	08 20	08 27	08 57	09 20	09 27	09 57	10 20	10 27	10 57		11 20	11 27	11 57	12 20	12 27	12 57	13 20	13 27	13 57		14 20	14 27	14 57	15 20
Thornliebank	d		08 30	09 00		09 30	10 00		10 30	11 00			11 30	12 00		12 30	13 00		13 30	14 00			14 30	15 00	
Giffnock	d		08 33	09 03		09 33	10 03		10 33	11 03			11 33	12 03		12 33	13 03		13 33	14 03			14 33	15 03	
Clarkston	d		08 37	09 07		09 37	10 07		10 37	11 07			11 37	12 07		12 37	13 07		13 37	14 07			14 37	15 07	
Busby	d		08 40	09 10		09 40	10 10		10 40	11 10			11 40	12 10		12 40	13 10		13 40	14 10			14 40	15 10	
Thorntonhall	d			09 13			10 13			11 13				12 13			13 13			14 13				15 13	
Hairmyres	d		08 45	09 16		09 45	10 16		10 45	11 16			11 45	12 16		12 45	13 16		13 45	14 16			14 45	15 16	
East Kilbride	a		08 49	09 20		09 49	10 20		10 49	11 20			11 49	12 20		12 49	13 20		13 49	14 20			14 49	15 20	
Kennishead	d																								
Priesthill & Darnley	d																								
Nitshill	d																								
Barrhead	d	08 26			09 26			10 26				11 26			12 26			13 26				14 26			15 26
Dunlop	d	08 38			09 38			10 38				11 38			12 38			13 38				14 38			15 38
Stewarton	d	08 42			09 42			10 42				11 42			12 42			13 42				14 42			15 42
Kilmaurs	d	08 46			09 46			10 46				11 46			12 46			13 46				14 46			15 46
Kilmarnock [3]	a	08 52			09 52			10 52				11 52			12 52			13 52				14 52			15 52

		SR	SR	SR	SR	SR		SR	SR	SR	SR	SR	SR	SR	SR	SR		SR	SR	SR	SR	SR	SR	SR	SR
Glasgow Central [15]	d	15 18	15 48	16 12	16 18	16 48		17 12	17 18	17 48	18 12	18 18	18 48	19 12	19 18	19 48		20 18	20 48	21 18	21 48	22 12	22 18	22 48	23 18
Crossmyloof	d	15 24	15 54		16 24	16 54			17 24	17 54		18 24	18 54		19 24	19 54		20 24	20 54	21 24	21 54		22 24	22 54	23 24
Pollokshaws West	d	15 27	15 57	16 20	16 27	16 57		17 20	17 27	17 57	18 20	18 27	18 57	19 20	19 27	19 57		20 27	20 57	21 27	21 57		22 27	22 57	23 27
Thornliebank	d	15 30	16 00		16 30	17 00			17 30	18 00		18 30	19 00		19 30	20 00		20 30	21 00	21 30	22 00		22 30	23 00	23 30
Giffnock	d	15 33	16 03		16 33	17 03			17 33	18 03		18 33	19 03		19 33	20 03		20 33	21 03	21 33	22 03		22 33	23 03	23 33
Clarkston	d	15 37	16 07		16 37	17 07			17 37	18 07		18 37	19 07		19 37	20 07		20 37	21 07	21 37	22 07		22 37	23 07	23 37
Busby	d	15 40	16 10		16 40	17 10			17 40	18 10		18 40	19 10		19 40	20 10		20 40	21 10	21 40	22 10		22 40	23 10	23 40
Thorntonhall	d		16 13			17 13				18 13			19 13			20 13			21 13		22 13			23 13	23 43
Hairmyres	d	15 45	16 16		16 45	17 16			17 45	18 16		18 45	19 16		19 45	20 16		20 45	21 16	21 45	22 16		22 45	23 16	23 46
East Kilbride	a	15 49	16 20		16 49	17 20			17 49	18 20		18 50	19 20		19 49	20 20		20 49	21 20	21 49	22 20		22 49	23 20	23 50
Kennishead	d																								
Priesthill & Darnley	d																								
Nitshill	d																								
Barrhead	d			16 26				17 26			18 26			19 26								22 24			
Dunlop	d			16 38				17 38			18 38			19 38								22 36			
Stewarton	d			16 42				17 42			18 42			19 42								22 39			
Kilmaurs	d			16 46				17 46			18 46			19 46								22 44			
Kilmarnock [3]	a			16 52				17 52			18 52			19 52								22 48			

Kilmarnock, Barrhead and East Kilbride - Glasgow Central

				SR	SR SX	SR	SR SO	SR SX	SR SX	SR SO		SR SX	SR SO	SR SX	SR SO	SR SX	SR SO	SR SX	SR SX	SR SO		SR SX	SR	SR SX	SR
Kilmarnock 3	d			05 22		06 22			06 53	06 53						07b22	07b23						07 53		
Kilmaurs	d			05 26		06 26			06 57	06 57						07 26	07 27						07 57		
Stewarton	d			05 31		06 31			07 03	07 03						07 32	07 32						08 03		
Dunlop	d			05 36		06 36			07 07	07 07						07 36	07 37						08 08		
Barrhead	d			05 46		06 46			07 19	07 19		07 25	07 28			07 47	07 48		07 57				08 20		08 28
Nitshill	d			05 49		06 49						07 28	07 31				07 51		08 00						08 31
Priesthill & Darnley	d			05 51		06 51						07 30	07 33				07 53		08 02						08 33
Kennishead	d			05 53		06 53						07 32	07 35				07 55		08 04						08 35
East Kilbride	d				06 17		06 56	06 56						07 25	07 27			07 42		07 56		07 56		08 10	
Hairmyres	d				06 20		06 59	06 59						07 29	07 30			07 46		07 59		08 00		08 17	
Thorntonhall	d				06 24		07 03	07 03						07 32						08 03		08 04			
Busby	d				06 27		07 06	07 06						07 35	07 35					08 06		08 06		08 22	
Clarkston	d				06 30		07 09	07 09						07 38	07 38			07 54		08 09		08 11		08 25	
Giffnock	d				06 33		07 12	07 12						07 42	07 42					08 12		08 15		08 28	
Thornliebank	d				06 35		07 14	07 14						07 44	07 44					08 14		08 18		08 30	
Pollokshaws West	d			05 57	06 38	06 57	07 17	07 17				07 35	07 38	07 47	07 48		07 58		08 07	08 17		08 21		08 35	08 38
Crossmyloof	d			05 59	06 41	06 59	07 20	07 20				07 38	07 41	07 50	07 51		08 01		08 10	08 20		08 24		08 38	08 41
Glasgow Central 15	a			06 09	06 49	07 08	07 26	07 27	07 32	07 33		07 45	07 47	07 57	07 57	08 00	08 09	08 09	08 16	08 27		08 30	08 35	08 45	08 49

		SR	SR	SR	SR	SR SO		SR SX	SR	SR	SR	SR	SR	NT	SR	SR		SR	SR	SR	SR	SR	SR	SR	SR
Kilmarnock 3	d		08 23			08 53		08 56			09c27			09 59				10 26			10 58			11 27	
Kilmaurs	d		08 27			08 57		09 00			09 31			10 03				10 31			11 02			11 31	
Stewarton	d		08 32			09 02		09 05			09 36			10 08				10 36			11 07			11 36	
Dunlop	d		08 37			09 07		09 10			09 41			10 13				10 41			11 12			11 41	
Barrhead	d		08 49	08 58		09 18		09 22	09 28		09 52	09 58		10 21	10 28			10 52	10 58			11 28		11 52	11 58
Nitshill	d			09 01					09 31			10 01			10 31				11 01			11 31			12 01
Priesthill & Darnley	d			09 03					09 33			10 03			10 33				11 03			11 33			12 03
Kennishead	d			09 05					09 35			10 05			10 35				11 05			11 35			12 05
East Kilbride	d	08 26			08 56					09 27			09 56			10 27				10 56			11 27		
Hairmyres	d	08 30			08 59					09 30			09 59			10 30				10 59			11 30		
Thorntonhall	d	08 33			09 03								10 03							11 03					
Busby	d	08 36			09 06					09 35			10 06			10 35				11 06			11 35		
Clarkston	d	08 39			09 09					09 38			10 09			10 38				11 09			11 38		
Giffnock	d	08 42			09 12					09 42			10 12			10 42				11 12			11 42		
Thornliebank	d	08 45			09 14					09 44			10 14			10 44				11 14			11 44		
Pollokshaws West	d	08 48		09 08	09 17				09 38	09 47		10 08	10 17		10 38	10 47			11 08	11 17		11 38	11 47		12 08
Crossmyloof	d	08 51		09 11	09 20				09 41	09 51		10 11	10 21		10 41	10 51			11 11	11 21		11 41	11 51		12 11
Glasgow Central 15	a	08 57	09 01	09 18	09 27	09 32		09 35	09 47	09 57	10 05	10 17	10 27	10 37	10 47	10 57		11 05	11 17	11 27	11 34	11 47	11 57	12 05	12 17

		SR		SR SX	SR SO	SR	SR	SR	SR	SR	SR SX	SR		SR	SR	SR	SR	SR	SR	SR	SR	SR		SR	SR
Kilmarnock 3	d			11 57	11 57			12 27			13 00				13 27			13 57			14 27				15 00
Kilmaurs	d			12 01	12 01			12 31							13 31			14 01			14 31				
Stewarton	d			12 06	12 06			12 36			13 07				13 36			14 06			14 36				15 07
Dunlop	d			12 11	12 11			12 41							13 41			14 11			14 41				
Barrhead	d					12 28		12 52	12 58			13 28			13 52	13 58			14 28		14 52	14 58			
Nitshill	d					12 31			13 01			13 31				14 01			14 31			15 01			
Priesthill & Darnley	d					12 33			13 03			13 33				14 03			14 33			15 03			
Kennishead	d					12 35			13 05			13 35				14 05			14 35			15 05			
East Kilbride	d	11 56					12 27			12 56				13 27			13 56			14 27				14 56	
Hairmyres	d	11 59					12 30			12 59				13 30			13 59			14 31				14 59	
Thorntonhall	d	12 03								13 03							14 03							15 03	
Busby	d	12 06					12 35			13 06				13 35			14 06			14 36				15 06	
Clarkston	d	12 09					12 38			13 09				13 38			14 09			14 39				15 09	
Giffnock	d	12 12					12 42			13 12				13 42			14 12			14 42				15 12	
Thornliebank	d	12 14					12 44			13 14				13 44			14 14			14 44				15 14	
Pollokshaws West	d	12 17				12 38	12 47		13 08	13 17		13 38		13 47		14 08	14 17		14 38	14 47		15 08		15 17	
Crossmyloof	d	12 21				12 41	12 50		13 11	13 20		13 41		13 51		14 11	14 20		14 41	14 50		15 11		15 20	
Glasgow Central 15	a	12 27		12 33	12 34	12 47	12 58	13 05	13 17	13 27	13 33	13 47		13 57	14 05	14 17	14 27	14 33	14 47	14 57	15 05	15 17		15 27	15 33

		SR	SR	SR	SR	SR	SR	SR		SR	SR	SR	SR	NT ◇	SR	SR SX	SR SO	SR		SR	SR SO	SR SX	SR	SR	SR SO
Kilmarnock 3	d			15 27			15e57				16 27			16 57				17 27					17 57		
Kilmaurs	d			15 31			16 01				16 31			17 01				17 31					18 01		
Stewarton	d			15 36			16 06				16 36			17 06				17 36					18 06		
Dunlop	d			15 41			16 11				16 41			17 11				17 41					18 11		
Barrhead	d	15 28		15 52	15 58			16 28			16 52	16 58		17 22	17 28			17 52		17 58			18 21	18 28	
Nitshill	d	15 31			16 01			16 31				17 01			17 31					18 01				18 31	
Priesthill & Darnley	d	15 33			16 03			16 33				17 03			17 33					18 03				18 33	
Kennishead	d	15 35			16 05			16 35				17 05			17 35					18 05				18 35	
East Kilbride	d		15 27			15 56				16 27			16 56			17 24	17 27				17 56	17 55			18 27
Hairmyres	d		15 30			15 59				16 30			16 59			17 30	17 30				17 59	18 03			18 30
Thorntonhall	d					16 03							17 03								18 03	18 07			
Busby	d		15 35			16 06				16 35			17 06			17 35	17 35				18 06	18 10			18 35
Clarkston	d		15 38			16 09				16 38			17 09			17 39	17 38				18 09	18 13			18 38
Giffnock	d		15 42			16 12				16 42			17 12			17 42	17 42				18 12	18 16			18 42
Thornliebank	d		15 44			16 14				16 44			17 14			17 44	17 44				18 14	18 18			18 44
Pollokshaws West	d	15 38	15 47		16 08	16 17		16 38		16 47		17 08	17 17		17 38	17 47	17 47			18 08	18 17	18 22		18 38	18 47
Crossmyloof	d	15 41	15 50		16 11	16 20		16 41		16 50		17 11	17 21		17 41	17 50	17 50			18 11	18 20	18 25		18 41	18 50
Glasgow Central 15	a	15 47	15 57	16 05	16 17	16 26	16 33	16 47		16 57	17 05	17 17	17 27	17 35	17 47	17 57	17 57	18 05		18 17	18 27	18 31	18 36	18 47	18 57

b arr. 0716   c arr. 0904   e arr. 1546

Kilmarnock, Barrhead and East Kilbride - Glasgow Central

		SR SX	SR	SR		SR	SR	SR	SR	SR	SR	SR	SR	SR		SR	NT SX ◇	SR	SR	SR	SR ◇	SR	SR	SR	
Kilmarnock 3	d		18 27				18 57			19 27		20b00		20 27			21 02		21 27		22c00		22 27		
Kilmaurs	d		18 31				19 01			19 31				20 31					21 31				22 31		
Stewarton	d		18 36				19 06			19 36		20 07		20 36			21 09		21 36		22 07		22 36		
Dunlop	d		18 41				19 11			19 41				20 41					21 41				22 41		
Barrhead	d		18 53	18 58			19 22	19 28		19 51		20 20		20 51			21 22		21 51		22 20		22 51		
Nitshill	d			19 01				19 31		19 54				20 54					21 54				22 54		
Priesthill & Darnley	d			19 03				19 33		19 56				20 56					21 56				22 56		
Kennishead	d			19 05				19 35		19 58				20 58					21 58				22 58		
East Kilbride	d	18 27				18 56			19 27		19 56		20 27			20 56		21 27		21 56		22 27		22 56	
Hairmyres	d	18 35				18 59			19 30		19 59		20 30			20 59		21 30		21 59		22 30		22 59	
Thorntonhall	d					19 03					20 03					21 03				22 03				23 03	
Busby	d	18 40				19 06			19 35		20 06		20 35			21 06		21 35		22 06		22 35		23 06	
Clarkston	d	18 43				19 09			19 38		20 09		20 38			21 09		21 38		22 09		22 38		23 09	
Giffnock	d	18 47				19 12			19 42		20 12		20 42			21 12		21 42		22 12		22 42		23 12	
Thornliebank	d	18 50				19 14			19 44		20 14		20 44			21 14		21 44		22 14		22 44		23 14	
Pollokshaws West	d	18 53		19 08		19 17		19 38	19 47	20 02	20 17		20 47	21 02		21 17		21 47	22 02	22 17		22 47	23 02	23 17	
Crossmyloof	d	18 55		19 11		19 20		19 41	19 50	20 04	20 20		20 50	21 04		21 20		21 50	22 04	22 20		22 50	23 04	23 20	
Glasgow Central 15	a	19 02	19 06	19 18		19 27	19 35	19 47	19 57	20 13	20 27	20 34	20 57	21 13		21 27	21 36	21 57	22 13	22 27	22 34	22 57	23 13	23 27	

		SR	SR	SR
Kilmarnock 3	d	22 57		
Kilmaurs	d	23 01		
Stewarton	d	23 06		
Dunlop	d	23 11		
Barrhead	d	23 21		
Nitshill	d			
Priesthill & Darnley	d			
Kennishead	d			
East Kilbride	d		23 27	23 56
Hairmyres	d		23 30	23 59
Thorntonhall	d			00 03
Busby	d		23 35	00 06
Clarkston	d		23 38	00 09
Giffnock	d		23 42	00 12
Thornliebank	d		23 44	00 14
Pollokshaws West	d		23 47	00 17
Crossmyloof	d		23 50	00 20
Glasgow Central 15	a	23 35	23 56	00 27

Sundays

			SR	SR	SR	SR	SR	SR	SR	SR		SR	SR	SR	SR	SR	SR	SR	SR	SR		SR	SR	SR	SR
Kilmarnock 3	d				08 57			09 57				10 57			11 57			12 57				13 57			14 57
Kilmaurs	d				09 01			10 01				11 01			12 01			13 01				14 01			15 01
Stewarton	d				09 06			10 06				11 06			12 06			13 06				14 06			15 06
Dunlop	d				09 11			10 11				11 11			12 11			13 11				14 11			15 11
Barrhead	d				09 21			10 21				11 21			12 21			13 21				14 21			15 21
Nitshill	d																								
Priesthill & Darnley	d																								
Kennishead	d																								
East Kilbride	d		08 27	08 56		09 27	09 56		10 27	10 56			11 27	11 56		12 27	12 56		13 27	13 56			14 27	14 56	
Hairmyres	d		08 30	08 59		09 30	09 59		10 30	10 59			11 30	11 59		12 30	12 59		13 30	13 59			14 30	14 59	
Thorntonhall	d			09 03			10 03			11 03				12 03			13 03			14 03				15 03	
Busby	d		08 35	09 06		09 35	10 06		10 35	11 06			11 35	12 06		12 35	13 06		13 35	14 06			14 35	15 06	
Clarkston	d		08 38	09 09		09 38	10 09		10 38	11 09			11 38	12 09		12 38	13 09		13 38	14 09			14 38	15 09	
Giffnock	d		08 41	09 12		09 41	10 12		10 41	11 12			11 41	12 12		12 41	13 12		13 41	14 12			14 41	15 12	
Thornliebank	d		08 44	09 14		09 44	10 14		10 44	11 14			11 44	12 14		12 44	13 14		13 44	14 14			14 44	15 14	
Pollokshaws West	d		08 47	09 17	09 27	09 47	10 17	10 27	10 47	11 17		11 27	11 47	12 17	12 27	12 47	13 17	13 27	13 47	14 17		14 27	14 47	15 17	15 27
Crossmyloof	d		08 50	09 20		09 50	10 20		10 50	11 20			11 50	12 20		12 50	13 20		13 50	14 20			14 50	15 20	
Glasgow Central 15	a		08 56	09 26	09 36	09 56	10 26	10 36	10 56	11 26		11 36	11 56	12 26	12 36	12 56	13 26	13 36	13 56	14 26		14 36	14 56	15 26	15 36

		SR	SR	SR	SR	SR		SR	SR	SR	SR	SR	SR	SR	SR	SR		SR	SR	SR	SR	SR	SR	SR	SR
Kilmarnock 3	d			15 57				16 57			17 57			18 57				19 57			20 57				
Kilmaurs	d			16 01				17 01			18 01			19 01				20 01			21 01				
Stewarton	d			16 06				17 06			18 06			19 06				20 06			21 06				
Dunlop	d			16 11				17 11			18 11			19 11				20 11			21 11				
Barrhead	d			16 21				17 21			18 21			19 21				20 21			21 21				
Nitshill	d																								
Priesthill & Darnley	d																								
Kennishead	d																								
East Kilbride	d	15 27	15 56		16 27	16 56			17 27	17 56		18 27	18 56		19 27	19 56			20 27	20 56		21 27	21 56	22 27	22 56
Hairmyres	d	15 30	15 59		16 30	16 59			17 30	17 59		18 30	18 59		19 30	19 59			20 30	20 59		21 30	21 59	22 30	22 59
Thorntonhall	d		16 03			17 03				18 03			19 03			20 03				21 03			22 03		23 03
Busby	d	15 35	16 06		16 35	17 06			17 35	18 06		18 35	19 06		19 35	20 06			20 35	21 06		21 35	22 06	22 35	23 06
Clarkston	d	15 38	16 09		16 38	17 09			17 38	18 09		18 38	19 09		19 38	20 09			20 38	21 09		21 38	22 09	22 38	23 09
Giffnock	d	15 41	16 12		16 41	17 12			17 41	18 12		18 41	19 12		19 41	20 12			20 41	21 12		21 41	22 12	22 41	23 12
Thornliebank	d	15 44	16 14		16 44	17 14			17 44	18 14		18 44	19 14		19 44	20 14			20 44	21 14		21 44	22 14	22 44	23 14
Pollokshaws West	d	15 47	16 17	16 27	16 47	17 17		17 27	17 47	18 17	18 27	18 47	19 17	19 27	19 47	20 17		20 27	20 47	21 17		21 47	22 17	22 47	23 17
Crossmyloof	d	15 50	16 20		16 50	17 20			17 50	18 20		18 50	19 20		19 50	20 20			20 50	21 20		21 50	22 20	22 50	23 20
Glasgow Central 15	a	15 56	16 26	16 36	16 56	17 26		17 36	17 56	18 26	18 36	18 56	19 26	19 36	19 56	20 26		20 36	20 56	21 26	21 35	21 56	22 26	22 56	23 26

A not 23 May   b arr. 1938   c arr. 2137

Table 222

Sundays

Kilmarnock, Barrhead and East Kilbride - Glasgow Central

		SR	SR
Kilmarnock	d		
Kilmaurs	d		
Stewarton	d		
Dunlop	d		
Barrhead	d		
Nitshill	d		
Priesthill & Darnley	d		
Kennishead	d		
East Kilbride	d	23 27	23 56
Hairmyres	d	23 30	23 59
Thorntonhall	d		00 03
Busby	d	23 35	00 06
Clarkston	d	23 38	00 09
Giffnock	d	23 41	00 12
Thornliebank	d	23 44	00 14
Pollokshaws West	d	23 47	00 17
Crossmyloof	d	23 50	00 20
Glasgow Central	a	23 56	00 26

Table 223

Mondays to Saturdays

Glasgow Central, Cathcart Circle, Neilston and Newton

			SR SO	SR SO	SR	SR SX	SR	SR	SR SX	SR SO		SR SX	SR SX	SR SX	SR SO	SR SX	SR SX	SR	SR SX	SR SX		SR SO	SR	SR SX	SR SX
Glasgow Central	226 d		00 05	06 05	06 15	06 17	06 20	06 34	06 36	06 45		06 50	07 00	07 03	07 05	07 07	07 14	07 20	07 29	07 35		07 35	07 45	07 48	07 54
Pollokshields West	d				06 21				06 44	06 51				07 09			07 20						07 51		08 00
Maxwell Park	d				06 23				06 46	06 53				07 11			07 22						07 53		08 02
Shawlands	d				06 25				06 48	06 55				07 13			07 24						07 55		08 04
Pollokshaws East	d				06 26				06 49	06 56				07 14			07 25						07 56		08 05
Langside	d				06 28				06 51	06 58				07 16			07 27						07 58		08 07
Pollokshields East	d		00 10	06 10		06 22	06 25	06 39				06 55	07 05		07 10	07 12		07 25	07 34	07 40		07 40			
Queens Park	d		00 11	06 11		06 23	06 26	06 40				06 56	07 06		07 11	07 13		07 26	07 35	07 41		07 41			
Crosshill	d		00 13	06 13		06 25	06 28	06 42				06 58	07 08		07 13	07 15		07 28	07 37	07 43		07 43			
Mount Florida	d		00 15	06 15		06 27	06 30	06 44				07 00	07 10		07 15	07 17		07 30	07 39	07 45		07 45			
Cathcart	d		00 17	06 17	06 31	06 29		06 46				07 03	07 12		07 17	07 21	07 32		07 41	07 47		07 47			08 10
Muirend	d		00 20	06 20		06 32		06 49					07 15		07 20	07 24			07 44			07 50		07 58	
Williamwood	d		00 23	06 23		06 35		06 52					07 18		07 23	07 27			07 47			07 53		08 01	
Whitecraigs	d		00 25	06 25		06 37		06 54					07 20		07 25	07 29			07 49			07 55		08 03	
Patterton	d		00 28	06 28		06 40		06 57					07 23		07 28	07 32			07 52			07 58		08 06	
Neilston	a		00 34	06 34		06 46		07 03					07 29		07 34	07 38			07 58			08 09		08 12	
Kings Park	d						06 33		06 55	07 03				07 21				07 33					08 03		
Croftfoot	d						06 35		06 57	07 05				07 23				07 35					08 05		
Burnside	d						06 38		07 00	07 08				07 26				07 38					08 08		
Kirkhill	a						06 41		07 03	07 11				07 29				07 41					08 11		
Newton	226 a						06 44		07 06	07 14				07 32				07 44					08 14		

		SR SX	SR SX	SR SO	SR SX	SR SX		SR SX	SR	SR SX	SR SX	SR SO	SR SX	SR	SR SO	SR SX		SR	SR	SR SX	SR SO	SR	SR	SR	SR
Glasgow Central	226 d	07 56	08 01	08 05	08 10	08 12		08 15	08 20	08 25	08 33	08 35	08 39	08 45	08 50	08 50		09 05	09 14	09 19	09 20	09 35	09 45	09 50	10 07
Pollokshields West	d				08 16						08 39			08 51					09 20				09 51		
Maxwell Park	d				08 18						08 41			08 53					09 22				09 53		
Shawlands	d				08 20						08 43			08 55					09 24				09 55		
Pollokshaws East	d				08 21						08 44			08 56					09 25				09 56		
Langside	d				08 23						08 46			08 58					09 27				09 58		
Pollokshields East	d	08 01	08 06	08 10		08 17		08 21	08 25	08 30		08 40	08 44		08 55	08 55		09 10		09 25	09 25	09 40		09 55	10 12
Queens Park	d	08 02	08 07	08 11		08 18		08 22	08 26	08 31		08 41	08 45		08 56	08 57		09 11		09 26	09 26	09 41		09 56	10 13
Crosshill	d	08 04	08 09	08 13		08 20		08 24	08 28	08 33		08 43	08 47		08 58	08 59		09 13		09 28	09 28	09 43		09 58	10 15
Mount Florida	d	08 06	08 11	08 15		08 22		08 26	08 30	08 35		08 45	08 49		09 00	09 01		09 15		09 30	09 30	09 45		10 00	10 17
Cathcart	d		08 13	08 17	08 26	08 24		08 33		08 37	08 49	08 47	08 51		09 03	09 03		09 17	09 32			09 47		10 03	10 19
Muirend	d		08 16	08 20						08 40		08 50	08 54					09 20				09 50			10 22
Williamwood	d		08 19	08 23						08 43		08 53	08 57					09 23				09 53			10 25
Whitecraigs	d		08 21	08 25						08 45		08 55	08 59					09 25				09 55			10 27
Patterton	d		08 24	08 28						08 48		08 58	09 02					09 28				09 58			10 30
Neilston	a		08 30	08 34						08 54		09 04	09 08					09 34				10 04			10 36
Kings Park	d	08 09							08 33					09 03						09 33	09 33		10 03		
Croftfoot	d	08 11							08 35					09 05						09 35	09 35		10 05		
Burnside	d	08 14							08 38					09 08						09 38	09 38		10 08		
Kirkhill	a	08 17							08 41					09 11						09 41	09 41		10 11		
Newton	226 a	08 20							08 44					09 14						09 45	09 45		10 14		

		SR		SR	SR	SR	SR	SR	SR	SR	SR	SR		SR	SR	SR	SR	SR	SR	SR	SR	SR		SR	SR
Glasgow Central	226 d	10 15		10 20	10 35	10 45	10 50	11 07	11 15	11 20	11 35	11 45		11 50	12 07	12 15	12 20	12 35	12 45	12 50	13 07	13 15		13 20	13 35
Pollokshields West	d	10 21				10 51			11 21			11 51				12 21			12 51			13 21			
Maxwell Park	d	10 23				10 53			11 23			11 53				12 23			12 53			13 23			
Shawlands	d	10 25				10 55			11 25			11 55				12 25			12 55			13 25			
Pollokshaws East	d	10 26				10 56			11 26			11 56				12 26			12 56			13 26			
Langside	d	10 28				10 58			11 28			11 58				12 28			12 58			13 28			
Pollokshields East	d			10 25	10 40		10 55	11 12		11 25	11 40			11 55	12 12		12 25	12 40		12 55	13 12			13 25	13 40
Queens Park	d			10 26	10 41		10 56	11 13		11 26	11 41			11 56	12 13		12 26	12 41		12 56	13 13			13 26	13 41
Crosshill	d			10 28	10 43		10 58	11 15		11 28	11 43			11 58	12 15		12 28	12 43		12 58	13 15			13 28	13 43
Mount Florida	d			10 30	10 45		11 00	11 17		11 30	11 45			12 00	12 17		12 30	12 45		13 00	13 17			13 30	13 45
Cathcart	d	10 32			10 47		11 03	11 19	11 32		11 47			12 03	12 19	12 32		12 47		13 03	13 19	13 32			13 47
Muirend	d				10 50			11 22			11 50				12 22			12 50			13 22				13 50
Williamwood	d				10 53			11 25			11 53				12 25			12 53			13 25				13 53
Whitecraigs	d				10 55			11 27			11 55				12 27			12 55			13 27				13 55
Patterton	d				10 58			11 30			11 58				12 30			12 58			13 30				13 58
Neilston	a				11 04			11 36			12 04				12 36			13 04			13 36				14 04
Kings Park	d			10 33		11 03				11 33		12 03					12 33		13 03					13 33	
Croftfoot	d			10 35		11 05				11 35		12 05					12 35		13 05					13 35	
Burnside	d			10 38		11 08				11 38		12 08					12 38		13 08					13 38	
Kirkhill	a			10 41		11 11				11 41		12 11					12 41		13 11					13 41	
Newton	226 a			10 44		11 14				11 44		12 15					12 45		13 14					13 44	

		SR	SR	SR	SR	SR	SR	SR		SR	SR	SR	SR	SR	SR	SR SO	SR SX	SR SX		SR	SR	SR	SR	SR	SR SX
Glasgow Central	226 d	13 45	13 50	14 07	14 15	14 20	14 35	14 45		14 50	15 07	15 15	15 20	15 35	15 45	15 50	15 50	16 05		16 15	16 20	16 35	16 45	16 50	16 59
Pollokshields West	d	13 51			14 21			14 51				15 21			15 51					16 21			16 51		
Maxwell Park	d	13 53			14 23			14 53				15 23			15 53					16 23			16 53		
Shawlands	d	13 55			14 25			14 55				15 25			15 55					16 25			16 55		
Pollokshaws East	d	13 56			14 26			14 56				15 26			15 56					16 26			16 56		
Langside	d	13 58			14 28			14 58				15 28			15 58					16 28			16 58		
Pollokshields East	d		13 55	14 12		14 25	14 40			14 55	15 12		15 25	15 40		15 55	15 55	16 10			16 25	16 40		16 55	17 04
Queens Park	d		13 56	14 13		14 26	14 41			14 56	15 13		15 26	15 41		15 57	15 57	16 11			16 27	16 41		16 56	17 05
Crosshill	d		13 58	14 15		14 28	14 43			14 58	15 15		15 28	15 43		15 59	16 03	16 13			16 29	16 43		16 58	17 07
Mount Florida	d		14 00	14 17		14 30	14 45			15 00	15 17		15 30	15 45		16 02	16 05	16 15			16 31	16 45		17 00	17 09
Cathcart	d		14 03	14 19	14 32		14 47			15 03	15 19	15 32		15 47		16 04	16 06	16 17		16 32		16 47		17 03	17 11
Muirend	d			14 22			14 50				15 22			15 50				16 20				16 50			17 14
Williamwood	d			14 25			14 53				15 25			15 53				16 23				16 53			17 17
Whitecraigs	d			14 27			14 55				15 27			15 55				16 25				16 55			17 19
Patterton	d			14 30			14 58				15 30			15 58				16 28				16 58			17 22
Neilston	a			14 36			15 04				15 36			16 04				16 36				17 04			17 28
Kings Park	d	14 03				14 33		15 03					15 33		16 03						16 34		17 03		
Croftfoot	d	14 05				14 35		15 05					15 35		16 05						16 36		17 05		
Burnside	d	14 08				14 38		15 08					15 38		16 08						16 38		17 08		
Kirkhill	a	14 11				14 41		15 11					15 41		16 11						16 41		17 11		
Newton	226 a	14 14				14 44		15 14					15 44		16 14						16 44		17 14		

Table 223

Mondays to Saturdays

Glasgow Central, Cathcart Circle, Neilston and Newton

		SR SX	SR SO	SR SX	SR SX	SR SO	SR SX	SR SO	SR SX	SR SX	SR SO	SR SX	SR	SR SO	SR SX	SR	SR	SR SO	SR SX	SR	SR	SR
Glasgow Central 15	226 d	17 05	17 07	17 08	17 14	17 15	17 18	17 20	17 23	17 29	17 35	17 38	17 45	17 50	17 50	18 07	18 15	18 20	18 20	18 35	18 45	18 50
Pollokshields West	d	17 11				17 21			17 29				17 51				18 21				18 51	
Maxwell Park	d	17 13				17 23			17 32				17 53				18 23				18 53	
Shawlands	d	17 15				17 25			17 34				17 55				18 25				18 55	
Pollokshaws East	d	17 16				17 26			17 35				17 56				18 26				18 56	
Langside	d	17 18				17 28			17 37				17 58				18 28				18 58	
Pollokshields East	d		17 12	17 13			17 23	17 25		17 34	17 40	17 43		17 55	17 55	18 12		18 25	18 25	18 40		18 55
Queens Park	d		17 13	17 14			17 24	17 26		17 35	17 41	17 44		17 56	17 57	18 13		18 26	18 27	18 41		18 56
Crosshill	d		17 15	17 16			17 26	17 28		17 37	17 43	17 46		17 58	17 59	18 15		18 28	18 29	18 43		18 58
Mount Florida	d		17 17	17 18			17 28	17 30		17 39	17 45	17 48		18 00	18 01	18 17		18 30	18 31	18 45		19 00
Cathcart	d	17 21	17 19			17 32	17 30		17 41		17 47	17 50		18 03	18 03	18 19	18 32			18 47		19 03
Muirend	d		17 22		17 24		17 33				17 50	17 53				18 22				18 50		
Williamwood	d		17 25		17 27		17 36				17 53	17 56				18 25				18 53		
Whitecraigs	d		17 27		17 30		17 38				17 55	17 58				18 27				18 55		
Patterton	d		17 30		17 32		17 41				17 58	18 01				18 30				18 58		
Neilston	a		17 36		17 39		17 47				18 04	18 07				18 36				19 04		
Kings Park	d			17 21				17 33		17 42			18 03					18 33	18 34		19 03	
Croftfoot	d			17 23				17 35		17 44			18 05					18 35	18 36		19 05	
Burnside	d			17 26				17 38		17 47			18 08					18 38	18 38		19 08	
Kirkhill	a			17 29				17 41		17 50			18 11					18 41	18 41		19 11	
Newton	226 a			17 32				17 44		17 53			18 14					18 44	18 45		19 14	

		SR	SR	SR	SR SX	SR SO	SR	SR	SR	SR	SR	SR	SR	SR	SR	SR	SR	SR	SR	SR	SR	SR	SR
Glasgow Central 15	226 d	19 07	19 15	19 20	19 35	19 35	19 45	19 50	20 07	20 15	20 20	20 35	20 45	20 50	21 07	21 15	21 20	21 35	21 45	21 50	22 07	22 15	22 20
Pollokshields West	d		19 21				19 51			20 21			20 51			21 21			21 51			22 21	
Maxwell Park	d		19 23				19 53			20 23			20 53			21 23			21 53			22 23	
Shawlands	d		19 25				19 55			20 25			20 55			21 25			21 55			22 25	
Pollokshaws East	d		19 26				19 56			20 26			20 56			21 26			21 56			22 26	
Langside	d		19 28				19 58			20 28			20 58			21 28			21 58			22 28	
Pollokshields East	d	19 12		19 25	19 40	19 40		19 55	20 12		20 25	20 40		20 55	21 12		21 25	21 40		21 55	22 12		22 25
Queens Park	d	19 13		19 26	19 41	19 41		19 56	20 13		20 26	20 41		20 56	21 13		21 26	21 41		21 56	22 13		22 26
Crosshill	d	19 15		19 28	19 43	19 43		19 58	20 15		20 28	20 43		20 58	21 15		21 28	21 43		21 58	22 15		22 28
Mount Florida	d	19 17		19 30	19 45	19 45		20 00	20 17		20 30	20 45		21 00	21 17		21 30	21 45		22 00	22 17		22 30
Cathcart	d	19 19	19 32		19 47	19 47		20 03	20 19	20 32		20 47		21 03	21 19	21 32		21 47		22 03	22 19	22 32	
Muirend	d	19 22			19 50	19 50			20 22			20 50			21 22			21 50			22 22		
Williamwood	d	19 25			19 53	19 53			20 25			20 53			21 25			21 53			22 25		
Whitecraigs	d	19 27			19 55	19 55			20 27			20 55			21 27			21 55			22 27		
Patterton	d	19 30			19 58	19 58			20 30			20 58			21 30			21 58			22 30		
Neilston	a	19 36			20 04	20 05			20 36			21 04			21 36			22 04			22 36		
Kings Park	d			19 33			20 03				20 33		21 03				21 33		22 03				22 33
Croftfoot	d			19 35			20 05				20 35		21 05				21 35		22 05				22 35
Burnside	d			19 38			20 08				20 38		21 08				21 38		22 08				22 38
Kirkhill	a			19 41			20 11				20 41		21 11				21 41		22 11				22 41
Newton	226 a			19 44			20 14				20 44		21 14				21 44		22 14				22 44

		SR	SR	SR	SR	SR	SR	SR FO
Glasgow Central 15	226 d	22 35	22 45	22 50	23 07	23 15	23 20	23 45
Pollokshields West	d		22 51			23 21		23 51
Maxwell Park	d		22 53			23 23		23 53
Shawlands	d		22 55			23 25		23 55
Pollokshaws East	d		22 56			23 26		23 56
Langside	d		22 58			23 28		23 58
Pollokshields East	d	22 40		22 55	23 12		23 25	
Queens Park	d	22 41		22 56	23 13		23 26	
Crosshill	d	22 43		22 58	23 15		23 28	
Mount Florida	d	22 45		23 00	23 17		23 30	
Cathcart	d	22 47		23 03	23 19	23 32		
Muirend	d	22 50			23 22			
Williamwood	d	22 53			23 25			
Whitecraigs	d	22 55			23 27			
Patterton	d	22 58			23 30			
Neilston	a	23 04			23 36			
Kings Park	d		23 03				23 33	00 03
Croftfoot	d		23 05				23 35	00 05
Burnside	d		23 08				23 38	00 07
Kirkhill	a		23 11				23 41	00 10
Newton	226 a		23 14				23 44	00 14

Table 223

Sundays

Glasgow Central, Cathcart Circle, Neilston and Newton

		SR	SR	SR	SR	SR	SR	SR	SR	SR	SR	SR	SR	SR	SR	SR	SR	SR	SR	SR	SR	SR	SR
Glasgow Central 15	226 d	08 23	08 34	08 53	09 08	09 23	09 34	09 53	10 08	10 23	10 34	10 53	11 08	11 23	11 34	11 53	12 08	12 23	12 34	12 53	13 08	13 23	13 34
Pollokshields West	d		08 40				09 40				10 40				11 40				12 40				13 40
Maxwell Park	d		08 42				09 42				10 42				11 42				12 42				13 42
Shawlands	d		08 44				09 44				10 44				11 44				12 44				13 44
Pollokshaws East	d		08 45				09 45				10 45				11 45				12 45				13 45
Langside	d		08 47				09 47				10 47				11 47				12 47				13 47
Pollokshields East	d	08 28		08 58	09 13	09 28		09 58	10 13	10 28		10 58	11 13	11 28		11 58	12 13	12 28		12 58	13 13	13 28	
Queens Park	d	08 29		08 59	09 14	09 29		09 59	10 14	10 29		10 59	11 14	11 29		11 59	12 14	12 29		12 59	13 14	13 29	
Crosshill	d	08 31		09 01	09 16	09 31		10 01	10 16	10 31		11 01	11 16	11 31		12 01	12 16	12 31		13 01	13 16	13 31	
Mount Florida	d	08 33		09 03	09 18	09 33		10 03	10 18	10 33		11 03	11 18	11 33		12 03	12 18	12 33		13 03	13 18	13 33	
Cathcart	d	08 35		09 05		09 35		10 05		10 35		11 05		11 35		12 05		12 35		13 05		13 35	
Muirend	d	08 38		09 08		09 38		10 08		10 38		11 08		11 38		12 08		12 38		13 08		13 38	
Williamwood	d	08 41		09 11		09 41		10 11		10 41		11 11		11 41		12 11		12 41		13 11		13 41	
Whitecraigs	d	08 43		09 13		09 43		10 13		10 43		11 13		11 43		12 13		12 43		13 13		13 43	
Patterton	d	08 46		09 16		09 46		10 16		10 46		11 16		11 46		12 16		12 46		13 16		13 46	
Neilston	a	08 52		09 22		09 52		10 22		10 52		11 22		11 52		12 22		12 52		13 28		13 52	
Kings Park	d		08 50		09 21		09 52		10 21		10 52		11 21		11 52		12 21		12 52		13 21		13 52
Croftfoot	d		08 52		09 23		09 54		10 23		10 54		11 23		11 54		12 23		12 54		13 23		13 54
Burnside	d		08 56		09 26		09 57		10 26		10 57		11 26		11 57		12 26		12 57		13 26		13 57
Kirkhill	a		08 59		09 29		10 00		10 29		11 00		11 29		12 00		12 29		13 00		13 29		14 00
Newton	226 a		09 02		09 32		10 03		10 32		11 03		11 32		12 03		12 32		13 03		13 32		14 03

		SR	SR	SR	SR	SR	SR	SR	SR	SR	SR	SR	SR	SR	SR	SR	SR	SR	SR	SR	SR	SR	SR
Glasgow Central 15	226 d	13 53	14 08	14 23	14 34	14 53	15 08	15 23	15 34	15 53	16 08	16 23	16 34	16 53	17 08	17 23	17 34	17 53	18 08	18 23	18 34	18 53	19 08
Pollokshields West	d				14 40				15 40				16 40				17 40				18 40		
Maxwell Park	d				14 42				15 42				16 42				17 42				18 42		
Shawlands	d				14 44				15 44				16 44				17 44				18 44		
Pollokshaws East	d				14 45				15 45				16 45				17 45				18 45		
Langside	d				14 47				15 47				16 47				17 47				18 47		
Pollokshields East	d	13 58	14 13	14 28		14 58	15 13	15 28		15 58	16 13	16 28		16 58	17 13	17 28		17 58	18 13	18 28		18 58	19 13
Queens Park	d	13 59	14 14	14 29		14 59	15 14	15 29		15 59	16 14	16 29		16 59	17 14	17 29		17 59	18 14	18 29		18 59	19 14
Crosshill	d	14 01	14 16	14 31		15 01	15 16	15 31		16 01	16 16	16 31		17 01	17 16	17 31		18 01	18 16	18 31		19 01	19 16
Mount Florida	d	14 03	14 18	14 33		15 03	15 18	15 33		16 03	16 18	16 33		17 03	17 18	17 33		18 03	18 18	18 33		19 03	19 18
Cathcart	d	14 05		14 35		15 05		15 35		16 05		16 35		17 05		17 35		18 05		18 35		19 05	
Muirend	d	14 08		14 38		15 08		15 38		16 08		16 38		17 08		17 38		18 08		18 38		19 08	
Williamwood	d	14 11		14 41		15 11		15 41		16 11		16 41		17 11		17 41		18 11		18 41		19 11	
Whitecraigs	d	14 13		14 43		15 13		15 43		16 13		16 43		17 13		17 43		18 13		18 43		19 13	
Patterton	d	14 16		14 46		15 16		15 46		16 16		16 46		17 16		17 46		18 16		18 46		19 16	
Neilston	a	14 22		14 52		15 22		15 52		16 22		16 52		17 22		17 52		18 22		18 52		19 22	
Kings Park	d		14 21		14 52		15 21		15 52		16 21		16 52		17 21		17 52		18 21		18 52		19 21
Croftfoot	d		14 23		14 54		15 23		15 54		16 23		16 54		17 23		17 54		18 23		18 54		19 23
Burnside	d		14 26		14 57		15 26		15 57		16 26		16 57		17 26		17 57		18 26		18 57		19 26
Kirkhill	a		14 29		15 00		15 29		16 00		16 29		17 00		17 29		18 00		18 29		19 00		19 29
Newton	226 a		14 32		15 03		15 32		16 03		16 32		17 03		17 32		18 03		18 32		19 03		19 32

		SR	SR	SR	SR	SR	SR	SR	SR	SR	SR	SR	SR	SR	SR	SR	SR
Glasgow Central 15	226 d	19 23	19 34	19 53	20 08	20 23	20 34	20 53	21 08	21 23	21 34	21 53	22 08	22 23	22 34	22 53	23 08
Pollokshields West	d		19 40				20 40				21 40				22 40		
Maxwell Park	d		19 42				20 42				21 42				22 42		
Shawlands	d		19 44				20 44				21 44				22 44		
Pollokshaws East	d		19 45				20 45				21 45				22 45		
Langside	d		19 47				20 47				21 47				22 47		
Pollokshields East	d	19 28		19 58	20 13	20 28		20 58	21 13	21 28		21 58	22 13	22 28		22 58	23 13
Queens Park	d	19 29		19 59	20 14	20 29		20 59	21 14	21 29		21 59	22 14	22 29		22 59	23 14
Crosshill	d	19 31		20 01	20 16	20 31		21 01	21 16	21 31		22 01	22 16	22 31		23 01	23 16
Mount Florida	d	19 33		20 03	20 18	20 33		21 03	21 18	21 33		22 03	22 18	22 33		23 03	23 18
Cathcart	d	19 35		20 05		20 35		21 05		21 35		22 05		22 35		23 05	
Muirend	d	19 38		20 08		20 38		21 08		21 38		22 08		22 38		23 08	
Williamwood	d	19 41		20 11		20 41		21 11		21 41		22 11		22 41		23 11	
Whitecraigs	d	19 43		20 13		20 43		21 13		21 43		22 13		22 43		23 13	
Patterton	d	19 46		20 16		20 46		21 16		21 46		22 16		22 46		23 16	
Neilston	a	19 52		20 22		20 52		21 22		21 52		22 22		22 52		23 22	
Kings Park	d		19 52		20 21		20 52		21 21		21 52		22 21		22 52		23 21
Croftfoot	d		19 54		20 23		20 54		21 23		21 54		22 23		22 54		23 23
Burnside	d		19 57		20 26		20 57		21 26		21 57		22 26		22 57		23 26
Kirkhill	a		20 00		20 29		21 00		21 29		22 00		22 29		23 00		23 29
Newton	226 a		20 03		20 32		21 03		21 32		22 03		22 32		23 03		23 32

Table 223

Newton, Neilston, Cathcart Circle and Glasgow Central

Mondays to Saturdays

		SR	SR	SR	SR	SR SX	SR	SR SX	SR SX	SR SO		SR SX	SR SO	SR SX	SR SX	SR SX	SR SO	SR SX	SR SX	SR SX		SR SO	SR SX	SR SX	SR SX
Newton 226	d		06 20		06 50			07 15		07 20					07 41		07 50	07 51							
Kirkhill	d		06 23		06 53			07 18		07 23					07 44		07 53	07 54							
Burnside	d		06 26		06 56			07 21		07 26					07 47		07 56	07 57							
Croftfoot	d		06 30		06 58			07 23		07 28					07 49		07 58	07 59							
Kings Park	d		06 32		07 00			07 25		07 30					07 51		08 00	08 02							
Neilston	d			06 30			07 00					07 24	07 30			07 41				07 56		08 00	08 05		
Patterton	d			06 36			07 06					07 30	07 36			07 47				08 02		08 06	08 11		
Whitecraigs	d			06 39			07 09					07 33	07 39			07 50				08 05		08 09	08 14		
Williamwood	d			06 41			07 11					07 35	07 41			07 52				08 08		08 11	08 16		
Muirend	d			06 44			07 14					07 38	07 44			07 55				08 11		08 14	08 19		
Cathcart	d	06 31		06 47		07 03	07 17		07 32			07 41	07 47	07 47		07 58			08 10	08 14		08 17		08 26	08 24
Mount Florida	d	06 33		06 49	07 04		07 19		07 34			07 43	07 49		07 55	08 01	08 04		08 12	08 17		08 19		08 28	
Crosshill	d	06 35		06 51	07 06		07 21		07 36			07 45	07 51		07 57	08 03	08 06		08 14	08 19		08 21		08 30	
Queens Park	d	06 37		06 53	07 08		07 23		07 38			07 47	07 53		07 59	08 05	08 08		08 16	08 21		08 23		08 32	
Pollokshields East	d	06 38		06 54	07 09		07 24		07 39			07 48	07 54		08 00	08 07	08 09		08 18	08 23		08 24		08 33	
Langside	d		06 37			07 05		07 29		07 35				07 50				08 06							08 27
Pollokshaws East	d		06 39			07 07		07 31		07 37				07 52				08 08							08 29
Shawlands	d		06 42			07 09		07 33		07 39				07 54				08 10							08 31
Maxwell Park	d		06 44			07 11		07 35		07 41				07 56				08 12							08 33
Pollokshields West	d		06 48			07 14		07 37		07 44				07 58				08 14							08 35
Glasgow Central 15 226	a	06 43	06 54	06 59	07 14	07 20	07 29	07 43	07 47	07 50		07 55	07 59	08 04	08 07	08 14	08 14	08 21	08 23	08 28		08 29	08 33	08 39	08 41

		SR SX	SR SO	SR SX	SR SX	SR SO		SR SX	SR SX	SR SX	SR SO	SR SO	SR SX	SR SX	SR SO	SR SX		SR	SR	SR SO	SR	SR	SR	SR	SR
Newton 226	d	08 21	08 20						08 33		08 50			08 59					09 20	09 43		09 50			
Kirkhill	d	08 24	08 23						08 36		08 53			09 02					09 23			09 53			
Burnside	d	08 27	08 26						08 39		08 56			09 05					09 26			09 56			
Croftfoot	d	08 29	08 28						08 42		08 58			09 07					09 28			09 58			
Kings Park	d	08 31	08 30						08 44		09 00			09 10					09 30			10 00			
Neilston	d				08 22	08 30				08 43					09 00	09 04					09 30			10 00	
Patterton	d				08 28	08 36				08 49					09 06	09 10					09 36			10 06	
Whitecraigs	d				08 31	08 39				08 52					09 09	09 13					09 39			10 09	
Williamwood	d				08 33	08 41				08 54					09 11	09 15					09 41			10 11	
Muirend	d				08 37	08 44				08 57					09 14	09 18					09 44			10 14	
Cathcart	d			08 33	08 40	08 47		08 49		09 00		09 03	09 03		09 17	09 21		09 32			09 47		10 03	10 17	10 32
Mount Florida	d	08 35			08 43	08 49		08 52		09 02	09 04			09 14	09 19	09 23		09 34			09 49	10 04		10 19	10 34
Crosshill	d	08 37			08 45	08 51		08 54		09 04	09 06			09 16	09 21	09 25		09 36			09 51	10 06		10 21	10 36
Queens Park	d	08 39			08 47	08 53		08 56		09 06	09 08			09 18	09 23	09 27		09 38			09 53	10 08		10 23	10 38
Pollokshields East	d	08 40			08 49	08 54		08 58		09 07	09 09			09 19	09 24	09 28		09 39			09 54	10 09		10 24	10 39
Langside	d		08 35	08 36					08 49			09 05	09 05						09 35				10 05		
Pollokshaws East	d		08 37	08 38					08 51			09 07	09 07						09 37				10 07		
Shawlands	d		08 39	08 40					08 54			09 09	09 09						09 39				10 09		
Maxwell Park	d		08 41	08 42					08 56			09 11	09 11						09 41				10 11		
Pollokshields West	d		08 44	08 45					09 00			09 14	09 14						09 44				10 14		
Glasgow Central 15 226	a	08 47	08 50	08 51	08 55	08 59		09 03	09 06	09 12	09 14	09 20	09 21	09 24	09 29	09 33		09 44	09 50	09 55	09 59	10 14	10 20	10 29	10 44

		SR		SR	SR	SR	SR	SR	SR	SR	SR	SR		SR	SR	SR	SR	SR	SR	SR	SR	SR		SR	SR
Newton 226	d	10 20			10 50				11 20		11 50					12 20		12 50				13 20			13 50
Kirkhill	d	10 23			10 53				11 23		11 53					12 23		12 53				13 23			13 53
Burnside	d	10 26			10 56				11 26		11 56					12 26		12 56				13 26			13 56
Croftfoot	d	10 28			10 58				11 28		11 58					12 28		12 58				13 28			13 58
Kings Park	d	10 30			11 00				11 30		12 00					12 30		13 00				13 30			14 00
Neilston	d			10 30			11 00			11 30				12 00			12 30			13 00				13 30	
Patterton	d			10 36			11 06			11 36				12 06			12 36			13 06				13 36	
Whitecraigs	d			10 39			11 09			11 39				12 09			12 39			13 09				13 39	
Williamwood	d			10 41			11 11			11 41				12 11			12 41			13 11				13 41	
Muirend	d			10 44			11 14			11 44				12 14			12 44			13 14				13 44	
Cathcart	d			10 47		11 03	11 17	11 32		11 47		12 03		12 17	12 32		12 47		13 03	13 17	13 32			13 47	
Mount Florida	d			10 49	11 04		11 19	11 34		11 49	12 04			12 19	12 34		12 49	13 04		13 19	13 34			13 49	14 04
Crosshill	d			10 51	11 06		11 21	11 36		11 51	12 06			12 21	12 36		12 51	13 06		13 21	13 36			13 51	14 06
Queens Park	d			10 53	11 08		11 23	11 38		11 53	12 08			12 23	12 38		12 53	13 08		13 23	13 38			13 53	14 08
Pollokshields East	d			10 54	11 09		11 24	11 39		11 54	12 09			12 24	12 39		12 54	13 09		13 24	13 39			13 54	14 09
Langside	d	10 35				11 05			11 35			12 05				12 35			13 05			13 35			
Pollokshaws East	d	10 37				11 07			11 37			12 07				12 37			13 07			13 37			
Shawlands	d	10 39				11 09			11 39			12 09				12 39			13 09			13 39			
Maxwell Park	d	10 41				11 11			11 41			12 11				12 41			13 11			13 41			
Pollokshields West	d	10 44				11 14			11 44			12 14				12 44			13 14			13 44			
Glasgow Central 15 226	a	10 50		10 59	11 14	11 20	11 29	11 44	11 50	11 59	12 14	12 20		12 29	12 44	12 50	13 00	13 14	13 20	13 29	13 44	13 50		13 59	14 14

		SR	SR	SR	SR	SR	SR	SR		SR		SR	SR	SR	SR	SR SO	SR SX	SR		SR	SR	SR	SR SO	SR SX	SR
Newton 226	d				14 20		14 50						15 20		15 50						16 20		16 50	16 50	
Kirkhill	d				14 23		14 53						15 23		15 53						16 23		16 53	16 53	
Burnside	d				14 26		14 56						15 26		15 56						16 26		16 56	16 56	
Croftfoot	d				14 28		14 58						15 28		15 58						16 28		16 58	16 58	
Kings Park	d				14 30		15 00						15 30		16 00						16 30		17 00	17 00	
Neilston	d		14 00			14 30				15 00				15 30				16 00				16 30			
Patterton	d		14 06			14 36				15 06				15 36				16 06				16 36			
Whitecraigs	d		14 09			14 39				15 09				15 39				16 09				16 39			
Williamwood	d		14 11			14 41				15 11				15 41				16 11				16 41			
Muirend	d		14 14			14 44				15 14				15 44				16 14				16 44			
Cathcart	d	14 03	14 17	14 32		14 47		15 03		15 17		15 32		15 47		16 04	16 06	16 17		16 32		16 47			17 03
Mount Florida	d		14 19	14 34		14 49	15 04			15 19		15 34		15 49	16 04			16 19		16 34		16 49	17 04	17 04	
Crosshill	d		14 21	14 36		14 51	15 06			15 21		15 36		15 51	16 06			16 21		16 36		16 51	17 06	17 06	
Queens Park	d		14 23	14 38		14 53	15 08			15 23		15 38		15 53	16 08			16 23		16 38		16 53	17 08	17 08	
Pollokshields East	d		14 24	14 39		14 54	15 09			15 24		15 39		15 54	16 09			16 24		16 39		16 54	17 09	17 09	
Langside	d	14 05			14 35			15 05					15 35			16 07	16 09				16 35				17 05
Pollokshaws East	d	14 07			14 37			15 07					15 37			16 09	16 11				16 37				17 07
Shawlands	d	14 09			14 39			15 09					15 39			16 11	16 13				16 39				17 09
Maxwell Park	d	14 11			14 41			15 11					15 41			16 13	16 15				16 41				17 11
Pollokshields West	d	14 14			14 44			15 14					15 44			16 18	16 18				16 44				17 14
Glasgow Central 15 226	a	14 20	14 29	14 44	14 50	14 59	15 14	15 20		15 29		15 44	15 51	15 59	16 14	16 24	16 24	16 29		16 44	16 50	16 59	17 14	17 15	17 20

		SR SX	SR SO	SR SX		SR SX	SR SO	SR	SR SX	SR SO	SR SX	SR	SR	SR SX		SR SO	SR SX	SR	SR	SR	SR	SR	SR	SR	
Newton 226	d							17 20				17 50							18 20		18 50				
Kirkhill	d							17 23				17 53							18 23		18 53				
Burnside	d							17 26				17 56							18 26		18 56				
Croftfoot	d							17 28				17 58							18 28		18 58				
Kings Park	d							17 30				18 00							18 30		19 00				
Neilston	d	16 53	17 00			17 14				17 30	17 39			17 54		18 00	18 04			18 30			19 00		
Patterton	d	16 59	17 06			17 20				17 36	17 45			18 00		18 06	18 10			18 36			19 06		
Whitecraigs	d	17 02	17 09			17 23				17 39	17 48			18 03		18 09	18 13			18 39			19 09		
Williamwood	d	17 04	17 11			17 25				17 41	17 50			18 05		18 11	18 15			18 41			19 11		
Muirend	d	17 07	17 14			17 28				17 44	17 53			18 08		18 14	18 18			18 44			19 14		
Cathcart	d	17 10	17 17	17 21		17 31	17 32		17 41	17 47	17 56		18 03	18 11		18 17	18 21	18 32		18 47		19 03	19 17	19 32	
Mount Florida	d	17 12	17 19	17 23		17 33	17 34		17 43	17 49	17 58	18 04		18 13		18 19	18 23	18 34		18 49	19 04		19 19	19 34	
Crosshill	d	17 14	17 21	17 25		17 35	17 36		17 45	17 51	18 00	18 06		18 15		18 21	18 25	18 36		18 51	19 06		19 21	19 36	
Queens Park	d	17 16	17 23	17 27		17 37	17 38		17 47	17 53	18 02	18 08		18 17		18 23	18 27	18 38		18 53	19 08		19 23	19 38	
Pollokshields East	d	17 17	17 24	17 29		17 38	17 39		17 48	17 54	18 03	18 09		18 18		18 24	18 28	18 39		18 54	19 09		19 24	19 39	
Langside	d							17 35					18 05						18 35			19 05			
Pollokshaws East	d							17 37					18 07						18 37			19 07			
Shawlands	d							17 39					18 09						18 39			19 09			
Maxwell Park	d							17 41					18 11						18 41			19 11			
Pollokshields West	d							17 44					18 14						18 44			19 14			
Glasgow Central 15 226	a	17 22	17 29	17 37		17 43	17 44	17 50	17 55	17 59	18 08	18 14	18 20	18 25		18 29	18 33	18 44	18 50	18 59	19 14	19 20	19 30	19 44	

		SR	SR	SR	SR	SR	SR	SR	SR	SR		SR	SR	SR	SR	SR	SR	SR	SR	SR		SR	SR	SR	SR
Newton 226	d	19 20		19 50				20 20		20 50					21 20		21 50					22 20		22 50	
Kirkhill	d	19 23		19 53				20 23		20 53					21 23		21 53					22 23		22 53	
Burnside	d	19 26		19 56				20 26		20 56					21 26		21 56					22 26		22 56	
Croftfoot	d	19 28		19 58				20 28		20 58					21 28		21 58					22 28		22 58	
Kings Park	d	19 30		20 00				20 30		21 00					21 30		22 00					22 30		23 00	
Neilston	d		19 30			20 00			20 30				21 00			21 30			22 00				22 30		
Patterton	d		19 36			20 06			20 36				21 06			21 36			22 06				22 36		
Whitecraigs	d		19 39			20 09			20 39				21 09			21 39			22 09				22 39		
Williamwood	d		19 41			20 11			20 41				21 11			21 41			22 11				22 41		
Muirend	d		19 44			20 14			20 44				21 14			21 44			22 14				22 44		
Cathcart	d		19 47		20 03	20 17	20 32		20 47			21 03	21 17	21 32		21 47		22 03	22 17	22 32			22 47		23 03
Mount Florida	d		19 49	20 04		20 19	20 34		20 49	21 04			21 19	21 34		21 49	22 04		22 19	22 34			22 49	23 04	
Crosshill	d		19 51	20 06		20 21	20 36		20 51	21 06			21 21	21 36		21 51	22 06		22 21	22 36			22 51	23 06	
Queens Park	d		19 53	20 08		20 23	20 38		20 53	21 08			21 23	21 38		21 53	22 08		22 23	22 38			22 53	23 08	
Pollokshields East	d		19 54	20 09		20 24	20 39		20 54	21 09			21 24	21 39		21 54	22 09		22 24	22 39			22 54	23 09	
Langside	d	19 37			20 05			20 35				21 05			21 35			22 05				22 35			23 05
Pollokshaws East	d	19 37			20 07			20 37				21 07			21 37			22 07				22 37			23 07
Shawlands	d	19 39			20 09			20 39				21 09			21 39			22 09				22 39			23 09
Maxwell Park	d	19 41			20 11			20 41				21 11			21 41			22 11				22 41			23 11
Pollokshields West	d	19 44			20 14			20 44				21 14			21 44			22 14				22 44			23 14
Glasgow Central 15 226	a	19 51	19 59	20 15	20 20	20 29	20 44	20 50	20 59	21 15		21 20	21 29	21 44	21 50	21 59	22 15	22 20	22 29	22 44		22 50	22 59	23 15	23 20

Table 223

Newton, Neilston, Cathcart Circle and Glasgow Central

		SR	SR	SR	SR
Newton 226	d			23 20	
Kirkhill	d			23 23	
Burnside	d			23 26	
Croftfoot	d			23 28	
Kings Park	d			23 30	
Neilston	d	23 00			23 30
Patterton	d	23 06			23 36
Whitecraigs	d	23 09			23 39
Williamwood	d	23 11			23 41
Muirend	d	23 14			23 44
Cathcart	d	23 17	23 32		23 47
Mount Florida	d	23 19	23 34		23 49
Crosshill	d	23 21	23 36		23 51
Queens Park	d	23 23	23 38		23 53
Pollokshields East	d	23 24	23 39		23 54
Langside	d			23 35	
Pollokshaws East	d			23 37	
Shawlands	d			23 39	
Maxwell Park	d			23 41	
Pollokshields West	d			23 44	
Glasgow Central 15 226	a	23 29	23 44	23 50	23 59

Sundays

		SR	SR	SR	SR	SR	SR	SR	SR	SR	SR	SR	SR	SR	SR	SR	SR	SR	SR	SR	SR	SR	SR
Newton 226	d		09 09		09 39		10 09		10 39		11 09		11 39		12 09		12 39		13 09		13 39		14 09
Kirkhill	d		09 12		09 42		10 12		10 42		11 12		11 42		12 12		12 42		13 12		13 42		14 12
Burnside	d		09 15		09 45		10 15		10 45		11 15		11 45		12 15		12 45		13 15		13 45		14 15
Croftfoot	d		09 17		09 47		10 17		10 47		11 17		11 47		12 17		12 47		13 17		13 47		14 17
Kings Park	d		09 19		09 49		10 19		10 49		11 19		11 49		12 19		12 49		13 19		13 49		14 19
Neilston	d	08 48		09 19		09 48		10 19		10 48		11 19		11 48		12 19		12 48		13 19		13 48	
Patterton	d	08 54		09 25		09 54		10 25		10 54		11 25		11 54		12 25		12 54		13 25		13 54	
Whitecraigs	d	08 57		09 28		09 57		10 28		10 57		11 28		11 57		12 28		12 57		13 28		13 57	
Williamwood	d	08 59		09 30		09 59		10 30		10 59		11 30		11 59		12 30		12 59		13 30		13 59	
Muirend	d	09 02		09 33		10 02		10 33		11 02		11 33		12 02		12 33		13 02		13 33		14 02	
Cathcart	d	09 05		09 36		10 05		10 36		11 05		11 36		12 05		12 36		13 05		13 36		14 05	
Mount Florida	d	09 07		09 38	09 53	10 07		10 38	10 53	11 07		11 38	11 53	12 07		12 38	12 53	13 07		13 38	13 53	14 07	
Crosshill	d	09 09		09 40	09 55	10 09		10 40	10 55	11 09		11 40	11 55	12 09		12 40	12 55	13 09		13 40	13 55	14 09	
Queens Park	d	09 11		09 42	09 57	10 11		10 42	10 57	11 11		11 42	11 57	12 11		12 42	12 57	13 11		13 42	13 57	14 11	
Pollokshields East	d	09 12		09 43	09 58	10 12		10 43	10 58	11 12		11 43	11 58	12 12		12 43	12 58	13 12		13 43	13 58	14 12	
Langside	d		09 23				10 23				11 23				12 23				13 23				14 23
Pollokshaws East	d		09 25				10 25				11 25				12 25				13 25				14 25
Shawlands	d		09 27				10 27				11 27				12 27				13 27				14 27
Maxwell Park	d		09 29				10 29				11 29				12 29				13 29				14 29
Pollokshields West	d		09 31				10 31				11 31				12 31				13 31				14 31
Glasgow Central 15 226	a	09 17	09 38	09 48	10 03	10 17	10 38	10 48	11 03	11 17	11 38	11 48	12 03	12 17	12 38	12 48	13 03	13 17	13 38	13 48	14 03	14 17	14 38

		SR	SR	SR	SR	SR	SR	SR	SR	SR	SR	SR	SR	SR	SR	SR	SR	SR	SR	SR	SR	SR	SR
Newton 226	d		14 39		15 09		15 39		16 09		16 39		17 09		17 39		18 09		18 39		19 09		19 39
Kirkhill	d		14 42		15 12		15 42		16 12		16 42		17 12		17 42		18 12		18 42		19 12		19 42
Burnside	d		14 45		15 15		15 45		16 15		16 45		17 15		17 45		18 15		18 45		19 15		19 45
Croftfoot	d		14 47		15 17		15 47		16 17		16 47		17 17		17 47		18 17		18 47		19 17		19 47
Kings Park	d		14 49		15 19		15 49		16 19		16 49		17 19		17 49		18 19		18 49		19 19		19 49
Neilston	d	14 19		14 48		15 19		15 48		16 19		16 48		17 19		17 48		18 19		18 48		19 19	
Patterton	d	14 25		14 54		15 25		15 54		16 25		16 54		17 25		17 54		18 25		18 54		19 25	
Whitecraigs	d	14 28		14 57		15 28		15 57		16 28		16 57		17 28		17 57		18 28		18 57		19 28	
Williamwood	d	14 30		14 59		15 30		15 59		16 30		16 59		17 30		17 59		18 30		18 59		19 30	
Muirend	d	14 33		15 02		15 33		16 02		16 33		17 02		17 33		18 02		18 33		19 02		19 33	
Cathcart	d	14 36		15 05		15 36		16 05		16 36		17 05		17 36		18 05		18 36		19 05		19 36	
Mount Florida	d	14 38	14 53	15 07		15 38	15 53	16 07		16 38	16 53	17 07		17 38	17 53	18 07		18 38	18 53	19 07		19 38	19 53
Crosshill	d	14 40	14 55	15 09		15 40	15 55	16 09		16 40	16 55	17 09		17 40	17 55	18 09		18 40	18 55	19 09		19 40	19 55
Queens Park	d	14 42	14 57	15 11		15 42	15 57	16 11		16 42	16 57	17 11		17 42	17 57	18 11		18 42	18 57	19 11		19 42	19 57
Pollokshields East	d	14 43	14 58	15 12		15 43	15 58	16 12		16 43	16 58	17 12		17 43	17 58	18 12		18 43	18 58	19 12		19 43	19 58
Langside	d				15 23				16 23				17 23				18 23				19 23		
Pollokshaws East	d				15 25				16 25				17 25				18 25				19 25		
Shawlands	d				15 27				16 27				17 27				18 27				19 27		
Maxwell Park	d				15 29				16 29				17 29				18 29				19 29		
Pollokshields West	d				15 31				16 31				17 31				18 31				19 31		
Glasgow Central 15 226	a	14 48	15 03	15 17	15 38	15 48	16 03	16 17	16 38	16 48	17 03	17 17	17 38	17 48	18 03	18 17	18 38	18 48	19 03	19 17	19 38	19 48	20 03

		SR	SR	SR	SR	SR	SR	SR	SR	SR	SR	SR	SR	SR	SR	SR
Newton 226	d		20 09		20 39		21 09		21 39		22 09		22 39		23 09	
Kirkhill	d		20 12		20 42		21 12		21 42		22 12		22 42		23 12	
Burnside	d		20 15		20 45		21 15		21 45		22 15		22 45		23 15	
Croftfoot	d		20 17		20 47		21 17		21 47		22 17		22 47		23 17	
Kings Park	d		20 19		20 49		21 19		21 49		22 19		22 49		23 19	
Neilston	d	19 48		20 19		20 48		21 19		21 48		22 19		22 48		23 19
Patterton	d	19 54		20 25		20 54		21 25		21 54		22 25		22 54		23 25
Whitecraigs	d	19 57		20 28		20 57		21 28		21 57		22 28		22 57		23 28
Williamwood	d	19 59		20 30		20 59		21 30		21 59		22 30		22 59		23 30
Muirend	d	20 02		20 33		21 02		21 33		22 02		22 33		23 02		23 33
Cathcart	d	20 05		20 36		21 05		21 36		22 05		22 36		23 05		23 36
Mount Florida	d	20 07		20 38	20 53	21 07		21 38	21 53	22 07		22 38	22 53	23 07		23 38
Crosshill	d	20 09		20 40	20 55	21 09		21 40	21 55	22 09		22 40	22 55	23 09		23 40
Queens Park	d	20 11		20 42	20 57	21 11		21 42	21 57	22 11		22 42	22 57	23 11		23 42
Pollokshields East	d	20 12		20 43	20 58	21 12		21 43	21 58	22 12		22 43	22 58	23 12		23 43
Langside	d		20 23				21 23				22 23				23 23	
Pollokshaws East	d		20 25				21 25				22 25				23 25	
Shawlands	d		20 27				21 27				22 27				23 27	
Maxwell Park	d		20 29				21 29				22 29				23 29	
Pollokshields West	d		20 31				21 31				22 31				23 31	
Glasgow Central 15 226	a	20 17	20 38	20 48	21 03	21 17	21 37	21 48	22 03	22 17	22 37	22 48	23 03	23 17	23 37	23 48

Table 224

Motherwell and Glasgow Queen Street - Cumbernauld and Falkirk Grahamston

		SR	SR	SR	SR	SR	SR	SR	SR	SR	SR	SR	SR	SR	SR	SR	SR	SR	SR	SR	SR	SR	SR	SR
Motherwell 226	d			06 11				07 35			08 37			09 37			10 37			11 37			12 37	
Whifflet	d			06 20				07 43			08 46			09 47			10 47			11 46			12 47	
Coatbridge Central	d			06a23	06 45			07 46			08 48			09 50			10 50			11 49			12 49	
Glasgow Queen Street 10	d	05 51	06 21			06 51	07 21		07 52	08 23		08 51	09 21		09 51	10 21		10 51	11 22		11 51	12 22		12 51
Springburn	d	05 55	06 25			06 55	07 25		07 55	08 25		08 55	09 25		09 55	10 25		10 55	11 25		11 55	12 25		12 55
Stepps	d	06 02	06 32			07 02	07 32		08 02	08 32		09 02	09 32		10 02	10 32		11 02	11 32		12 02	12 32		13 02
Gartcosh	d	06 06	06 36			07 06	07 36		08 06	08 36		09 06	09 36		10 06	10 36		11 06	11 36		12 06	12 36		13 06
Greenfaulds	d	06 14	06 44		06 54	07 14	07 44	07 53	08 14	08 44	08 56	09 14	09 44	09 58	10 14	10 44	10 58	11 14	11 44	11 58	12 14	12 44	12 58	13 14
Cumbernauld	d	06a18	06 46		06a57	07a18	07 46	07a57	08a19	08 46	09a01	09a20	09 46	10a01	10a18	10 46	11a01	11a18	11 46	12a01	12a18	12 46	13a01	13a18
Camelon	d		06 57				08 04			09 04			10 04			11 04			12 04			13 04		
Falkirk Grahamston	a		07 03				08 11			09 10			10 10			11 10			12 10			13 10		

		SR	SR	SR	SR	SR	SR	SR	SR	SR SX	SR	SR SX	SR	SR	SR SX	SR SX	SR	SR SX	SR	SR	SR SX	SR	SR	SR
Motherwell 226	d		13 37			14 37			15 37				16 37		16 42			17 12	17 37		17 57		18 37	
Whifflet	d		13 47			14 47			15 47				16 46		16 48			17 18	17 47		18 03		18 45	
Coatbridge Central	d		13 50			14 50			15 50				16 49		16a53			17a22	17 50		18a06		18 48	
Glasgow Queen Street 10	d	13 19		13 51	14 21		14 51	15 21		15 51	15 54	16 22		16 52		17 03	17 22			17 51		18 23		18 51
Springburn	d	13 23		13 55	14 25		14 55	15 25			15 56	16 25		16 55			17 25			17 55		18 25		18 55
Stepps	d	13 30		14 02	14 32		15 02	15 32			16 02	16 32		17 02			17 32			18 02		18 32		19 02
Gartcosh	d	13 34		14 06	14 36		15 06	15 36			16 06	16 36		17 06			17 36			18 06		18 36		19 06
Greenfaulds	d	13 42	13 58	14 14	14 44	14 58	15 14	15 44	15 58		16 14	16 44	16 58	17 14			17 44		17 58	18 14		18 44	18 57	19 14
Cumbernauld	d	13 44	14a01	14a18	14 46	15a01	15a18	15 46	16a01		16a21	16 46	17a01	17a19			17 46		18a01	18a19		18 46	19a01	19a18
Camelon	d	14 04			15 04			16 04		16 27		17 01				17 30	18 04					19 04		
Falkirk Grahamston	a	14 10			15 10			16 10		16 33		17 04				17 32	18 10					19 10		

		SR	SR	SR	SR	SR	SR	SR	SR	SR	SR	SR	SR	SR
Motherwell 226	d		19 37			20 37			21 37			22 41		
Whifflet	d		19 47			20 47			21 47			22 49		
Coatbridge Central	d		19 50			20 50			21 50			22a52		
Glasgow Queen Street 10	d	19 21		19 52	20 21		20 51	21 21		21 51	22 21		23 21	23 51
Springburn	d	19 25		19 56	20 25		20 55	21 25		21 55	22 25		23 25	23 55
Stepps	d	19 32		20 03	20 32		21 02	21 32		22 02	22 32		23 32	00 02
Gartcosh	d	19 36		20 07	20 36		21 06	21 36		22 06	22 36		23 36	00 06
Greenfaulds	d	19 44	19 58	20 15	20 44	20 58	21 14	21 44	21 58	22 14	22 44		23 44	00 14
Cumbernauld	d	19a48	20a01	20 17	20a48	21a01	21 16	21a48	22a01	22 16	22a48		23a48	00a18
Camelon	d			20 34			21 27			22 27				
Falkirk Grahamston	a			20 40			21 33			22 34				

Sundays
until 28 November

		SR	SR	SR	SR	SR	SR	SR	SR	SR	SR	SR	SR
Motherwell 226	d												
Whifflet	d												
Coatbridge Central	d												
Glasgow Queen Street 10	d	08 19	09 22	10 21	11 21	13 21	14 21	15 21	16 21	17 21	19 22	20 21	21 26
Springburn	d	08 24	09 25	10 25	11 25	13 25	14 25	15 25	16 25	17 25	19 25	20 25	21 30
Stepps	d	08 30	09 32	10 32	11 32	13 32	14 32	15 32	16 32	17 32	19 32	20 32	21 37
Gartcosh	d	08 34	09 36	10 36	11 36	13 36	14 36	15 36	16 36	17 36	19 36	20 36	21 41
Greenfaulds	d	08 42	09 44	10 44	11 44	13 44	14 44	15 44	16 44	17 44	19 44	20 44	21 49
Cumbernauld	d	08a46	09a49	10a48	11a48	13a48	14a48	15a48	16a48	17a48	19a49	20a48	21a53
Camelon	d												
Falkirk Grahamston	a												

Sundays
from 28 November

		SR	SR	SR	SR	SR	SR	SR	SR	SR	SR	SR	SR	SR	SR	SR	SR	SR	SR	SR	SR	SR	SR
Motherwell 226	d																						
Whifflet	d																						
Coatbridge Central	d																						
Glasgow Queen Street 10	d	08 19	08 42	09 22	09 51	10 21	10 51	11 21	11 51	12 52	13 21	13 51	14 21	14 51	15 21	15 54	16 21	16 52	21 26	17 21	17 51	19 22	20 21
Springburn	d	08 24	08 47	09 25	09 56	10 25	10 56	11 25	11 56	12 57	13 25	13 55	14 25	14 55	15 25	16 00	16 25	16 56	21 30	17 25	17 55	19 25	20 25
Stepps	d	08 30	08 54	09 32	10 02	10 32	11 02	11 32	12 02	13 04	13 32	14 02	14 32	15 02	15 32	16 07	16 32	17 03	21 37	17 32	18 02	19 32	20 32
Gartcosh	d	08 34	08 58	09 36	10 06	10 36	11 06	11 36	12 06	13 07	13 36	14 06	14 36	15 06	15 36	16 11	16 36	17 07	21 41	17 36	18 06	19 36	20 36
Greenfaulds	d	08 42	09 06	09 44	10 14	10 44	11 14	11 44	12 14	13 15	13 44	14 14	14 44	15 14	15 44	16 19	16 44	17 15	21 49	17 44	18 14	19 44	20 44
Cumbernauld	d	08a46	09a09	09a49	10a18	10a48	11a18	11a48	12a20	13a20	13a48	14a18	14a48	15a18	15a48	16a22	16a48	17a19	21a53	17a48	18a18	19a49	20a48
Camelon	d																						
Falkirk Grahamston	a																						

Falkirk Grahamston and Cumbernauld - Glasgow Queen Street and Motherwell

	SR	SR	SR	SR	SR	SR SX	SR	SR	SR	SR	SR	SR	SR	SR	SR	SR	SR	SR	SR		SR	SR	SR	SR
Falkirk Grahamston d	05 41			06 44				07 41			08 41			09 41			10 41				11 41			12 41
Camelon d	05 44			06 46				07 44			08 44			09 44			10 44				11 44			12 44
Cumbernauld d	05 58		06 28	06 58	07 08		07 28	07 58	08 10	08 28	08 58	09 10	09 28	09 58	10 10	10 28	10 58	11 10	11 28		11 58	12 10	12 28	12 58
Greenfaulds d	05 59		06 29	06 59	07 10		07 29	07 59	08 12	08 29	08 59	09 12	09 29	09 59	10 12	10 29	10 59	11 12	11 29		11 59	12 12	12 29	12 59
Gartcosh d	06 06		06 36	07 06			07 36	08 06		08 36	09 06		09 36	10 06		10 36	11 06		11 36		12 06		12 36	13 06
Stepps d	06 10		06 40	07 10			07 40	08 10		08 40	09 10		09 40	10 10		10 40	11 10		11 40		12 10		12 40	13 10
Springburn d	06 16		06 46	07 16			07 46	08 16		08 47	09 16		09 46	10 16		10 46	11 16		11 46		12 16		12 46	13 16
Glasgow Queen Street a	06 25		06 55	07 29			07 55	08 28		08 59	09 25		09 55	10 25		10 55	11 25		11 55		12 25		12 55	13 25
Coatbridge Central d		06 40			07 18	07 39			08 20			09 20			10 20			11 20				12 20		
Whifflet d		06 42			07 20	07 41			08 22			09 22			10 22			11 22				12 22		
Motherwell 226 a		06 49			07 30	07 48			08 32			09 32			10 32			11 32				12 32		

	SR	SR	SR	SR SO	SR		SR	SR	SR SO	SR SX	SR	SR	SR	SR	SR SX		SR SO	SR SX	SR	SR	SR		SR	SR SX
Falkirk Grahamston d			13 41				14 41				15 42			16 41						17 41				
Camelon d			13 44				14 44				15 44			16 44						17 44				
Cumbernauld d	13 10	13 28	13 58	14 10	14 28		14 58	15 10	15 28	15 28	15 58	16 10	16 29	16 58	17 10		17 10		17 28	17 58	18 10		18 28	
Greenfaulds d	13 12	13 29	13 59	14 12	14 29		14 59	15 11	15 29	15 29	15 59	16 12	16 30	16 59	17 12		17 12		17 29	17 59	18 12		18 29	
Gartcosh d		13 36	14 06		14 36		15 06		15 36	15 36	16 06		16 36	17 06					17 36	18 06			18 36	
Stepps d		13 40	14 10		14 40		15 10		15 40	15 40	16 10		16 40	17 10					17 40	18 10			18 40	
Springburn d		13 46	14 16		14 46		15 16		15 46	15 46	16 16		16 46	17 16					17 46	18 16			18 46	
Glasgow Queen Street a		13 55	14 25		14 55		15 25		15 55	15 57	16 26		16 56	17 25					17 55	18 27			18 55	
Coatbridge Central d	13 20			14 20				15 20				16 20			17 18		17 20	17 30			18 20			18 39
Whifflet d	13 22			14 22				15 22				16 22			17 20		17 22	17 31			18 22			18 41
Motherwell 226 a	13 32			14 32				15 32				16 32			17 30		17 32	17 38			18 32			18 49

	SR	SR		SR	SR	SR	SR	SR SO	SR SX	SR	SR	SR		SR	SR	SR	SR
Falkirk Grahamston d	18 41				19 41						21 11				22 11		23 11
Camelon d	18 44				19 44						21 14				22 14		23 14
Cumbernauld d	18 58	19 10		19 28	19 58	20 10	20 28	20 57	20 58	21 10	21 28	21 58		22 10	22 28	22 58	23 28
Greenfaulds d	18 59	19 12		19 29	19 59	20 12	20 29	20 58	20 59	21 12	21 29	21 59		22 12	22 29	22 59	23 29
Gartcosh d	19 06			19 36	20 06		20 36	21 06	21 06		21 36	22 06			22 36	23 06	23 36
Stepps d	19 10			19 40	20 10		20 40	21 10	21 10		21 40	22 10			22 40	23 10	23 40
Springburn d	19 16			19 46	20 16		20 46	21 16	21 16		21 46	22 16			22 46	23 16	23 46
Glasgow Queen Street a	19 25			19 55	20 25		20 55	21 25	21 25		21 55	22 25			22 55	23 25	23 55
Coatbridge Central d		19 20				20 20				21 20				22 20			
Whifflet d		19 22				20 22				21 22				22 22			
Motherwell 226 a		19 32				20 32				21 32				22 32			

Sundays
until 21 November

	SR	SR	SR	SR	SR	SR	SR	SR	SR		SR	SR	SR	SR	SR
Falkirk Grahamston d															
Camelon d															
Cumbernauld d	08 55	09 58	10 58	11 58	12 58	13 58	14 58	15 58	16 58		17 58	18 58	19 58	21 03	22 58
Greenfaulds d	08 56	09 59	10 59	11 59	12 59	13 59	14 59	15 59	16 59		17 59	18 59	19 59	21 05	22 59
Gartcosh d	09 03	10 06	11 06	12 06	13 06	14 06	15 06	16 06	17 06		18 06	19 06	20 06	21 11	23 06
Stepps d	09 07	10 10	11 10	12 10	13 10	14 10	15 10	16 10	17 10		18 10	19 10	20 10	21 15	23 10
Springburn d	09 13	10 16	11 16	12 16	13 16	14 16	15 16	16 16	17 16		18 16	19 16	20 16	21 21	23 16
Glasgow Queen Street a	09 22	10 25	11 25	12 25	13 26	14 26	15 25	16 25	17 25		18 26	19 26	20 26	21 30	23 25
Coatbridge Central d															
Whifflet d															
Motherwell 226 a															

Sundays
from 28 November

	SR	SR	SR	SR	SR	SR	SR	SR	SR	SR	SR	SR	SR	SR	SR	SR	SR	SR	SR	SR	SR	SR	SR	SR
Falkirk Grahamston d																								
Camelon d																								
Cumbernauld d	08 55	09 28	09 58	10 28	10 58	11 26	11 58	12 29	12 58	13 28	13 58	14 28	14 58	15 32	15 58	16 29	16 58	17 28	17 58	18 28	18 58	19 58	21 03	22 58
Greenfaulds d	08 56	09 29	09 59	10 29	10 59	11 28	11 59	12 31	12 59	13 29	13 59	14 29	14 59	15 34	15 59	16 30	16 59	17 29	17 59	18 29	18 59	19 59	21 05	22 59
Gartcosh d	09 03	09 36	10 06	10 36	11 06	11 35	12 06	12 38	13 06	13 36	14 06	14 36	15 06	15 41	16 06	16 37	17 06	17 36	18 06	18 36	19 06	20 06	21 11	23 06
Stepps d	09 07	09 40	10 10	10 40	11 10	11 39	12 10	12 42	13 10	13 40	14 10	14 40	15 10	15 45	16 10	16 41	17 10	17 40	18 10	18 40	19 10	20 10	21 15	23 10
Springburn d	09 13	09 46	10 16	10 46	11 16	11 45	12 16	12 48	13 16	13 46	14 16	14 46	15 16	15 51	16 16	16 47	17 16	17 46	18 16	18 46	19 16	20 16	21 21	23 16
Glasgow Queen Street a	09 22	09 55	10 25	10 55	11 25	11 54	12 25	12 58	13 26	13 57	14 26	14 57	15 25	15 59	16 25	16 58	17 25	17 57	18 26	18 57	19 26	20 26	21 30	23 25
Coatbridge Central d																								
Whifflet d																								
Motherwell 226 a																								

Network Diagram for Tables 225, 228, 229, 230, 237, 238, 240, 242

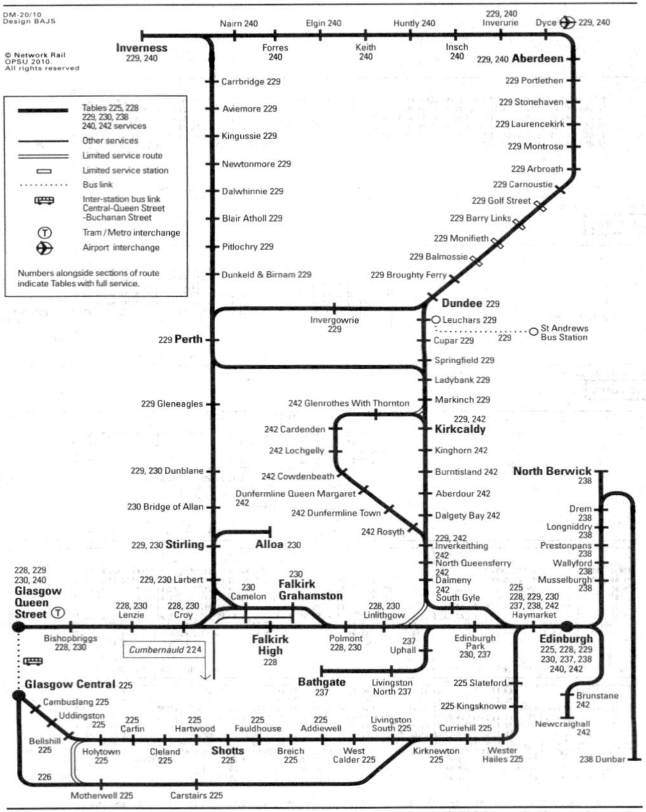

Table 225

Mondays to Fridays

Edinburgh - Shotts, Carstairs, Motherwell and Glasgow Central

			SR	SR	SR	XC	SR	GR	SR	SR	SR	GR	SR	SR	SR	SR	SR	GR	SR	SR	SR	SR	GR	SR	SR	SR
						◇1		■ 1				■ 1						■ 1					■ 1			
Edinburgh 10	230,238,242	d	05 51	06 41	06 56	07 26	07 56	08 08	08 21	08 38	08 56	09 22	09 26	09 56	10 26	10 56	11 26	11 38	11 56	12 26	12 56	13 26	13 40	13 56	14 26	14 57
Haymarket	230,238,242	d	05 55	06 44	06 59	07 30	07 59	08 13	08 24	08 41	09 00	09 27	09 31	09 59	10 29	10 59	11 29	11 43	11 59	12 29	12 59	13 29	13 45	13 59	14 29	15 01
Slateford		d	06 00		07 03				08 28				09 35		10 33		11 33			12 33		13 33			14 33	
Kingsknowe		d	06 04		07 06				08 32				09 38		10 36		11 37			12 37		13 36			14 37	
Wester Hailes		d	06 06		07 08				08 34				09 41		10 38		11 39			12 39		13 39			14 39	
Curriehill		d	06 10		07 11				08 38				09 44		10 41		11 43			12 43		13 43			14 43	
Kirknewton		d	06 18		07 18				08 44	08 52			09 51		10 47		11 49			12 49		13 49			14 49	
Livingston South		d	06 23	06 59	07 24		08 17		08 50	09 15			09 56	10 14	10 56	11 15	11 55		12 15	12 54	13 18	13 57		14 15	14 55	15 17
West Calder		a	06 28	07 03	07 28		08 22		08 55	09 20			10 01	10 19	11 00	11 20	12 00		12 20	12 59	13 23	13 59		14 20	15 00	15 22
		d	06 28	07 04	07 29		08 23		08 55	09 20			10 01	10 19	11 01	11 20	12 00		12 20	12 59	13 23	14 00		14 20	15 00	15 22
Addiewell		d	06 31		07 32				08 58				10 05		11 04		12 03			13 02		14 03			15 03	
Breich		d																								
Fauldhouse		d	06 38		07 39				09 05				10 12		11 11		12 10			13 09		14 10			15 10	
Shotts		d	06 45	07 16	07 44		08 35		09 11	09 33			10 18	10 31	11 18	11 32	12 16		12 32	13 15	13 35	14 18		14 32	15 16	15 34
Hartwood		d	06 48		07 48				09 14				10 21		11 21		12 19			13 18		14 21			15 19	
Cleland		d	06 53		07 53				09 17				10 24		11 25		12 23			13 23		14 25			15 23	
Carfin		d	06 56		07 56				09 22				10 29		11 29		12 27			13 26		14 29			15 27	
Holytown		d	06 59		07 59				09 24				10 31		11 35		12 29			13 28		14 30			15 29	
Carstairs		d								09 14																
Motherwell		a				08 08		08 59		09 32		10 05						12 25					14 26			
		d				08 09		08 59		09 33		10 05						12 25					14 26			
Bellshill	226	d	07 07	07 26	08 07		08 50		09 26		09 46		10 33	10 42	11 39	11 46	12 32		12 45	13 32	13 50	14 34		14 46	15 32	15 46
Uddingston	226	d	07 11						09 30				10 37		11 41		12 38			13 36		14 40			15 37	
Cambuslang	226	d	07 16																							
Glasgow Central 15	226	a	07 29	07 50	08 29	08 24	09 08	09 22	09 54	09 59	10 09	10 30	10 55	10 59	11 56	12 09	12 56	12 47	13 11	13 55	14 09	14 57	14 47	15 09	15 55	16 11

			GR	SR	SR	SR	SR	SR	GR	SR	SR	SR	SR	XC	GR	SR	TP	XC	SR	GR	SR
			■ 1						■ 1					◇1	■ 1		◇1	◇1		■ 1	
Edinburgh 10	230,238,242	d	15 22	15 26	15 58	16 26	16 56	17 23	17 40	17 52	17 56	18 26	18 56	19 07	19 18	19 26		21 14	21 26	22 26	22 56
Haymarket	230,238,242	d		15 29	16 01	16 29	16 59	17 26	17 45	17 55	17 59	18 29	18 59	19 12	19 22	19 29		21 19	21 29	22 30	22 59
Slateford		d		15 35		16 33		17 31			18 03	18 31				19 33			21 33		23 03
Kingsknowe		d		15 38		16 37		17 34			18 05	18 34				19 37			21 37		23 07
Wester Hailes		d		15 40		16 39		17 37			18 08	18 36				19 39			21 39		23 09
Curriehill		d		15 43		16 43		17 40			18 11	18 40				19 43			21 43		23 13
Kirknewton		d		15 52		16 49		17 48			18 17	18 46				19 49			21 49		23 20
Livingston South		d		15 58	16 17	16 55	17 13	17 52		18 09	18 22		19 15			19 55			21 55		23 25
West Calder		a		16 02	16 22	17 00	17 18	17 57		18 14	18 27		19 20			20 00			22 00		23 30
		d		16 03	16 22	17 00	17 18	17 57		18 14	18 27		19 20			20 00			22 00		23 30
Addiewell		d		16 06		17 03		18 01			18 30					20 03			22 03		23 33
Breich		d									18 35										
Fauldhouse		d		16 13		17 10		18 08			18 39					20 10			22 10		23 40
Shotts		d		16 19	16 34	17 16	17 32	18 13		18 26	18 43		19 32			20 16			22 16		23 45
Hartwood		d		16 22		17 19		18 16			18 48					20 19			22 19		23 48
Cleland		d		16 26		17 23		18 20			18 53					20 23			22 23		23 53
Carfin		d		16 30		17 27		18 24			18 56					20 27			22 27		23 55
Holytown		d		16 34		17 29		18 26			18 58					20 29			22 29		23 59
Carstairs		d										19 12									
Motherwell		a	16 06					18 35	18 23			19 32		19 55	19 59		20s15	22 03		23 10	
		d	16 06						18 23			19 32		19 56	19 59		20s16	22 05		23 10	
Bellshill	226	d		16 37	16 46	17 32	17 42			18 36	19 01		19 46			20 32			22 32		00 02
Uddingston	226	d		16 43		17 36					19 06					20 35			22 36		00 06
Cambuslang	226	d				17 42				18 46	19 13										00 11
Glasgow Central 15	226	a	16 28	16 57	17 09	17 53	17 57		18 41	18 59	19 29	19 53	20 02	20 26	20 20	20 55	20 33	22 30	22 55	23 33	00 25

Table 225

Saturdays

Edinburgh - Shotts, Carstairs, Motherwell and Glasgow Central

			SR	SR	SR	XC	SR	GR	SR	SR	SR	SR	GR	SR	SR	SR	SR	GR	SR	SR	SR	SR	GR	SR	SR	SR	SR	TP
						◇1		■ 1					■ 1					■ 1					■ 1					◇1
Edinburgh 10	230,238,242	d	05 51	06 41	06 56	07 25	07 56	08 08	08 26	08 55	09 00	09 26	09 38	09 56	10 26	10 55	11 26	11 40	11 56	12 25	12 56	13 26	13 40	13 55	14 26	14 56	15 26	
Haymarket	230,238,242	d	05 55	06 44	06 59	07 29	07 59	08 13	08 29	08 59	09 02	09 29	09 42	09 59	10 29	10 59	11 29	11 44	11 59	12 29	12 59	13 29	13 44	13 59	14 29	14 59	15 29	
Slateford		d	06 00		07 03				08 33		09 04	09 33			10 33		11 33			12 33		13 33			14 33		15 33	
Kingsknowe		d	06 04		07 06				08 37		09 07	09 37			10 36		11 37			12 37		13 36			14 36		15 37	
Wester Hailes		d	06 06		07 08				08 39		09 11	09 39			10 38		11 39			12 39		13 39			14 38		15 39	
Curriehill		d	06 10		07 11				08 43		09 14	09 43			10 41		11 43			12 43		13 43			14 41		15 43	
Kirknewton		d	06 18		07 18				08 49		09 22	09 49			10 47		11 49			12 49		13 49			14 47		15 49	
Livingston South		d	06 23	07 02	07 23		08 15		08 55	09 15		09 55		10 15	10 56	11 15	11 55		12 15	12 54	13 15	13 57		14 15	14 53	15 15	15 55	
West Calder		a	06 28	07 06	07 28				09 00	09 20		10 00		10 20	11 00	11 20	12 00		12 20	12 59	13 20	13 59		14 20	14 58	15 20	16 00	
		d	06 28	07 07	07 28				09 00	09 20		10 00		10 20	11 01	11 20	12 00		12 20	12 59	13 20	14 00		14 20	14 58	15 20	16 01	
Addiewell		d	06 31		07 32				09 03			10 03			11 04		12 03			13 02		14 03			15 02		16 04	
Breich		d																										
Fauldhouse		d	06 38		07 38				09 10			10 10			11 11		12 10			13 09		14 10			15 08		16 11	
Shotts		d	06 45	07 19	07 45		08 29		09 16	09 32		10 16		10 32	11 18	11 32	12 16		12 32	13 15	13 32	14 18		14 32	15 15	15 32	16 17	
Hartwood		d	06 48		07 48				09 19			10 19			11 21		12 19			13 18		14 21			15 18		16 20	
Cleland		d	06 53		07 52				09 23			10 23			11 25		12 24			13 23		14 25			15 22		16 24	
Carfin		d	06 56		07 56				09 27			10 27			11 29		12 27			13 26		14 29			15 26		16 29	
Holytown		d	07 02		07 58				09 29			10 29			11 35		12 29			13 28		14 30			15 28		16 31	
Carstairs		d									09 41																	
Motherwell		a				08 14		08 57			09 57		10 28					12 25					14 27					16s23
		d				08 15		08 57			09 57		10 28					12 25					14 27					16s23
Bellshill	226	d	07 07	07 29	08 02		08 40		09 32	09 46		10 32		10 48	11 39	11 46	12 32		12 46	13 32	13 46	14 34		14 46	15 31	15 46	16 34	
Uddingston	226	d	07 13		08 09				09 36			10 36			11 41		12 38			13 36		14 40			15 35		16 37	
Cambuslang	226	d	07 18																									
Glasgow Central 15	226	a	07 31	07 49	08 24	08 32	09 07	09 16	09 55	10 09	10 14	10 55	10 48	11 09	11 56	12 09	12 55	12 47	13 09	13 55	14 09	14 57	14 47	15 09	15 55	16 09	16 55	16 42

			GR	SR	SR	SR	SR	GR	SR	SR	SR	SR	XC	SR	GR	XC	SR	GR	SR
			■ 1 A					■ 1					◇1		■ 1	◇1		■ 1	
Edinburgh 10	230,238,242	d	15 36	15 56	16 25	16 56	17 21	17 40	17 52	17 55	18 26	18 56	19 10	19 19	19 39	21 10	21 26	21g45	22 56
Haymarket	230,238,242	d	15 45	15 59	16 29	16 59	17 25	17 45	17 55	18 00	18 29	18 59	19 14	19 22	19 43	21 14	21 29	21 49	22 59
Slateford		d			16 33		17 30			18 04	18 33			19 26			21 33		23 03
Kingsknowe		d			16 37		17 34			18 07	18 36			19 30			21 37		23 07
Wester Hailes		d			16 39		17 36			18 08	18 38			19 32			21 39		23 09
Curriehill		d			16 43		17 40			18 12	18 42			19 36			21 43		23 13
Kirknewton		d			16 49		17 47			18 18	18 46			19 42			21 50		23 20
Livingston South		d		16 15	16 55	17 13	17 52		18 09	18 22		19 15		19 55			21 54		23 25
West Calder		a		16 20	17 00	17 18	17 57		18 14	18 27		19 20		20 00			22 00		23 30
		d		16 20	17 00	17 18	17 57		18 14	18 27		19 20		20 00			22 00		23 30
Addiewell		d			17 03		18 00			18 32				20 03			22 03		23 33
Breich		d								18 35									
Fauldhouse		d			17 10		18 07			18 40				20 10			22 10		23 40
Shotts		d		16 32	17 16	17 34	18 12		18 26	18 43		19 32		20 16			22 16		23 45
Hartwood		d			17 19		18 15			18 47				20 19			22 19		23 48
Cleland		d			17 23		18 19			18 51				20 23			22 23		23 53
Carfin		d			17 27		18 23			18 55				20 27			22 27		23 55
Holytown		d			17 29		18 25			18 57				20 29			22 29		23 59
Carstairs		d									19 08								
Motherwell		a	16 27				18 35	18 28			19 31		19 55		2022	21 55		22 26	
		d	16 27					18 28			19 32		19 56		2022	21 56		22 26	
Bellshill	226	d		16 45	17 32	17 46			18 36	19 00		19 46		20 32			22 32		00 02
Uddingston	226	d			17 36					19 06				20 36			22 39		00 06
Cambuslang	226	d			17 46				18 45	19 14									00 11
Glasgow Central 15	226	a	16 51	17 09	17 57	18 09		18 50	18 55	19 29	19 52	20 09	20 24	20 55	20 45	22 18	22 55	22 46	00 25

Table 225

Sundays

Edinburgh - Shotts, Carstairs, Motherwell and Glasgow Central

	GR	XC	SR	GR	SR	GR	SR	GR	SR	GR	TP	XC	SR	XC	GR	VT
Edinburgh 230,238,242 d	12 04	12 12	12 24	12 41	14 23	15 11	16 23	17 42	18 24	19 37		20 12	20 23	21 12	21 46	
Haymarket 230,238,242 d	12 08	12 16	12 28	12 45	14 27	15 16	16 27	17 46	18 27	19 42		20 16	20 27	21 16	21 50	
Slateford d			12 32		14 31		16 31		18 31				20 31			
Kingsknowe d			12 35		14 34		16 34		18 34				20 34			
Wester Hailes d			12 38		14 37		16 37		18 37				20 37			
Curriehill d			12 41		14 40		16 40		18 40				20 40			
Kirknewton d			12 48		14 47		16 47		18 47				20 47			
Livingston South d			12 53		14 52		16 52		18 52				20 52			
West Calder a			13 00		14 59		16 59		18 59				20 59			
West Calder d																
Addiewell d																
Breich d																
Fauldhouse d																
Shotts d																
Hartwood d																
Cleland d																
Carfin d																
Holytown d																
Carstairs d																
Motherwell a	12 46	12 53		13 33		15 55		18 24		20 19	20s27	20 53		21 53	22 26	23 07
Motherwell d	12 46	12 54		13 33		15 55		18 24		20 19	20s28	20 54		21 54	22 27	23 08
Bellshill 226 d																
Uddingston 226 d																
Cambuslang 226 d																
Glasgow Central 226 a	13 08	13 12		13 56		16 15		18 45		20 38	20 45	21 12		22 14	22 44	23 22

Table 225

Mondays to Fridays

Glasgow Central, Motherwell, Carstairs and Shotts - Edinburgh

	XC	SR	SR	GR	SR	SR	SR	GR	SR	XC	SR	SR	GR	SR	SR	SR	SR	GR	SR	SR	SR	SR	GR	SR	SR
																		A							
Glasgow Central 226 d	06 01	06 15		06 50	06 58	07 04	07 14	07 50	08 03	09 00	09 02	09 14	09 50	10 05	10 14	11 05	11 14	11 50	12 05	12 14	13 05	13 15	13 50	14 05	14 14
Cambuslang 226 d		06 23					07 24																		
Uddingston 226 d		06 28					07 29					09 26			10 27		11 26			12 27		13 27			14 26
Bellshill 226 d		06 32			07 13		07 33		08 19		09 19	09 30		10 20	10 31	11 20	11 30		12 19	12 31	13 20	13 31		14 19	14 30
Motherwell a				07 04		07 27		08 04		09 14			10 04					12 06					14 05		
Motherwell d			06 59	07 04		07 28		08 04		09 15			10 04					12 06					14 05		
Carstairs d			07a25			07 42																			
Holytown d		06 36					07 37					09 34			10 35		11 34			12 35		13 35			14 34
Carfin d		06 39					07 39					09 37			10 38		11 37			12 38		13 37			14 37
Cleland d		06 43					07 43					09 41			10 42		11 41			12 42		13 41			14 41
Hartwood d		06 48					07 49					09 46			10 47		11 46			12 47		13 47			14 46
Shotts d		06 54			07 26		07 53		08 30		09 30	09 52		10 32	10 52	11 33	11 52		12 30	12 52	13 32	13 53		14 30	14 52
Fauldhouse d		06 59					07 59					09 58			10 58		11 58			12 58		13 58			14 58
Breich d							08 02																		
Addiewell d		07 05					08 06					10 04			11 04		12 04			13 04		14 04			15 04
West Calder d		07 09			07 38		08 09		08 42		09 42	10 07		10 44	11 07	11 49	12 07		12 42	13 07	13 45	14 07		14 42	15 07
Livingston South d		07 14			07 42		08 15		08 46		09 46	10 12		10 48	11 12	11 54	12 12		12 46	13 12	13 49	14 12		14 46	15 14
Kirknewton d		07 18			07 47	08 04	08 19					10 19			11 20		12 20			13 19		14 18			15 20
Curriehill d		07 24			07 54	08 09	08 25					10 25			11 25		12 25			13 25		14 23			15 26
Wester Hailes d		07 27				08 12	08 29					10 29			11 29		12 29			13 28		14 27			15 29
Kingsknowe d		07 30				08 15	08 31					10 31			11 31		12 31			13 31		14 29			15 32
Slateford d		07 32				08 17	08 34					10 34			11 34		12 34			13 33		14 32			15 34
Haymarket 230,238,242 d	06 55	07 40		07 46	08 03	08 22	08 40	08 49	09 02	09 53	10 03	10 43	10 48	11 07	11 44	12 08	12 44	12 49	13 02	13 44	14 03	14 39	14 49	15 03	15 46
Edinburgh 230,238,242 a	06 59	07 48		07 52	08 10	08 35	08 47	08 55	09 09	09 58	10 10	10 50	10 55	11 13	11 51	12 14	12 51	12 56	13 08	13 51	14 10	14 43	14 56	15 09	15 52

	SR	SR	SR	GR	SR	SR	SR	SR	SR	GR	SR	SR	SR	SR	GR	VT	XC	SR	SR
Glasgow Central 226 d	15 02	15 14	15 18	15 50	16 05	16 14	17 12	17 19		17 50	18 05	18 14	19 04	19 15	19 50	20 10	20 48	21 14	23 06
Cambuslang 226 d									17 40			18 22							23 15
Uddingston 226 d		15 27				16 26			17 45			18 27		19 26				21 26	23 18
Bellshill 226 d	15 19	15 31			16 24	16 31	17 29	17 32	17 49		18 20	18 31	19 19	19 30				21 30	23 24
Motherwell a			15 37	16 04					18 00	18 05					20 04		21 04		
Motherwell d			15 40	16 04					18 01	18 05					20 04		21 05		
Carstairs d			15 59						18a27							20a35			
Holytown d		15 36				16 35		17 35				18 35		19 34				21 34	23 28
Carfin d		15 44				16 39		17 38				18 37		19 36				21 36	23 31
Cleland d		15 48				16 43		17 41				18 41		19 40				21 40	23 35
Hartwood d		15 53				16 49		17 46				18 46		19 46				21 45	23 40
Shotts d	15 32	15 58			16 35	16 54	17 42	17 51			18 32	18 50	19 30	19 51				21 50	23 44
Fauldhouse d		16 04				17 00		17 57				18 57		19 57				21 56	23 50
Breich d																			
Addiewell d		16 10				17 07		18 03				19 02		20 03				22 02	23 56
West Calder d	15 44	16 13			16 47	17 11	17 57	18 08			18 45	19 06	19 42	20 08				22 07	23 59
Livingston South d	15 49	16 18			16 51	17 16	18 03	18 11			18 49	19 12	19 46	20 12				22 11	00 04
Kirknewton d		16 22				17 20		18 16				19 19		20 19				22 16	00 06
Curriehill d		16 28				17 26		18 22				19 25		20 25				22 22	00 12
Wester Hailes d		16 31				17 29		18 25				19 28		20 28				22 25	00 16
Kingsknowe d		16 34				17 32		18 28				19 31		20 31				22 28	00 18
Slateford d		16 36				17 35		18 31				19 33		20 33				22 31	00 21
Haymarket 230,238,242 d	16 02	16 45	16 34	16 50	17 07	17 41	18 25	18 44		18 49	19 03	19 44	20 03	20 41	20 49			22 35	00 27
Edinburgh 230,238,242 a	16 09	16 52	16 39	16 56	17 14	17 47	18 32	18 51		18 55	19 09	19 51	20 09	20 47	20 55		22 07	22 41	00 34

Saturdays

	SR	SR	GR	XC	SR	SR	GR	SR	SR	GR	XC	SR	SR	GR	SR	SR	SR	SR	GR	SR	SR	SR	SR	GR	SR
																			A						
Glasgow Central 226 d	00 06	06 15	06 50	07 00	07 04	07 13	07 50	08 04	08 15	08 50	09 00	09 05	09 15	09 50	10 05	10 14	11 05	11 14	11 50	12 05	12 14	13 05	13 14	13 50	14 05
Cambuslang 226 d	00 15	06 23				07 24																			
Uddingston 226 d	00 20	06 28				07 29			08 28				09 26			10 27		11 26			12 26		13 27		
Bellshill 226 d	00 24	06 32			07 22	07 33		08 19	08 32			09 19	09 30		10 20	10 32	11 20	11 30		12 19	12 30	13 20	13 31		14 20
Motherwell a			07 05				08 04			09 04				10 04					12 06					14 06	
Motherwell d			07 05				08 04			09 04				10 04					12 06					14 06	
Carstairs d																									
Holytown d	00 28	06 36				07 37			08 36				09 34			10 36		11 34			12 34		13 35		
Carfin d	00 31	06 39				07 39			08 39				09 37			10 38		11 37			12 37		13 38		
Cleland d	00 35	06 43				07 43			08 43				09 41			10 42		11 41			12 41		13 42		
Hartwood d	00 40	06 48				07 49			08 48				09 46			10 48		11 46			12 46		13 47		
Shotts d	00 44	06 54			07 35	07 52		08 30	08 53			09 30	09 53		10 32	10 53	11 33	11 51		12 30	12 52	13 31	13 52		14 33
Fauldhouse d	00 50	06 59				07 58			08 58				09 59			10 59		11 57			12 58		13 58		
Breich d						08 02			09 03																
Addiewell d	00 56	07 05				08 06			09 05				10 05			11 05		12 03			13 04		14 04		
West Calder d	00 59	07 09			07 47	08 08		08 42	09 09			09 42	10 08		10 44	11 08	11 49	12 06		12 42	13 07	13 43	14 07		14 45
Livingston South d	01 03	07 14			07 51	08 13		08 46	09 12			09 46	10 13		10 48	11 12	11 54	12 11		12 46	13 12	13 47	14 12		14 49
Kirknewton d		07 18			07 56	08 18			09 18				10 19			11 20		12 19			13 19		14 17		
Curriehill d		07 24			08 02	08 24			09 23				10 25			11 25		12 24			13 24		14 23		
Wester Hailes d		07 27				08 27			09 26				10 28			11 29		12 28			13 28		14 26		
Kingsknowe d		07 30				08 30			09 29				10 31			11 31		12 30			13 30		14 29		
Slateford d		07 32				08 32			09 31				10 33			11 34		12 33			13 33		14 31		
Haymarket 230,238,242 d	01a18	07 40	07 47	07 54	08 11	08 40	08 49	09 03	09 37	09 46	09 55	10 03	10 39	10 48	11 07	11 40	12 08	12 40	12 49	13 03	13 42	14 03	14 37	14 49	15 07
Edinburgh 230,238,242 a		07 48	07 52	07 59	08 19	08 47	08 56	09 10	09 44	09 53	09 59	10 10	10 44	10 55	11 13	11 46	12 14	12 46	12 55	13 09	13 48	14 09	14 44	14 56	15 13

A The Flying Scotsman

Table 225

Saturdays

Glasgow Central, Motherwell, Carstairs and Shotts - Edinburgh

			SR	SR	SR	SR	GR	SR	SR	SR	SR	GR	SR	SR	SR	SR	SR	XC	SR
Glasgow Central	226	d	14 14	15 05	15 14	15 19	15 50	16 05	16 14	17 04	17 14	17 50	18 05	18 14	19 05	19 14	21 15	21 02	23 06
Cambuslang	226	d												18 22					23 15
Uddingston	226	d	14 26		15 27				16 26		17 26			18 27		19 26	21 25		23 18
Bellshill	226	d	14 30	15 19	15 31			16 19	16 30	17 19	17 30		18 20	18 31	19 19	19 30	21 30		23 24
Motherwell		a				15 37	16 06					18 06							
		d				15 37	16 06					18 06							
Carstairs		d				15 56													
Holytown		d	14 34		15 35				16 35		17 35			18 35		19 34	21 34		23 28
Carfin		d	14 37		15 38				16 38		17 38			18 37		19 36	21 36		23 31
Cleland		d	14 41		15 42				16 42		17 42			18 41		19 40	21 40		23 35
Hartwood		d	14 46		15 47				16 48		17 47			18 46		19 46	21 46		23 40
Shotts		d	14 52	15 30	15 52			16 30	16 54	17 33	17 53		18 33	18 50	19 30	19 51	21 52		23 44
Fauldhouse		d	14 58		15 58				17 00		17 58			18 56		19 57	21 58		23 50
Breich		d																	
Addiewell		d	15 04		16 04				17 06		18 04			19 02		20 03	22 04		23 56
West Calder		d	15 07	15 42	16 07			16 42	17 10	17 45	18 07		18 45	19 06	19 42	20 09	22 08		23 59
Livingston South		d	15 12	15 46	16 12			16 45	17 15	17 48	18 12		18 49	19 11	19 46	20 13	22 12		00 04
Kirknewton		d	15 18		16 20				17 20		18 16			19 19		20 19	22 17		00 06
Curriehill		d	15 24		16 26				17 26		18 22			19 25		20 25	22 23		00 12
Wester Hailes		d	15 27		16 29				17 29		18 25			19 28		20 28	22 26		00 16
Kingsknowe		d	15 30		16 32				17 32		18 28			19 31		20 31	22 29		00 18
Slateford		d	15 32		16 34				17 34		18 30			19 33		20 33	22 31		00 21
Haymarket	230,238,242	d	15 40	16 03	16 41	16 27	16 50	17 03	17 41	18 03	18 36	18 47	19 03	19 44	20 03	20 41	22 40	22 01	00 27
Edinburgh	230,238,242	a	15 47	16 10	16 48	16 36	16 56	17 10	17 48	18 09	18 45	18 55	19 09	19 51	20 09	20 47	22 46	22 02	00 34

Sundays

			GR	XC	GR	SR	XC	GR	SR	GR	SR	GR	SR		GR	SR
Glasgow Central	226	d	10 50	11 37	12 50		13 45	14 50		15 50		17 50			19 50	
Cambuslang	226	d														
Uddingston	226	d														
Bellshill	226	d														
Motherwell		a	11 05	11 53	13 05		14 02	15 05		16 05		18 05			20 05	
		d	11 05	11 54	13 05		14 03	15 05		16 05		18 05			20 05	
Carstairs		d														
Holytown		d														
Carfin		d														
Cleland		d														
Hartwood		d														
Shotts		d														
Fauldhouse		d														
Breich		d														
Addiewell		d														
West Calder		d				13 13			15 13		17 20		19 14			21 14
Livingston South		d				13 17			15 15		17 22		19 18			21 17
Kirknewton		d				13 22			15 20		17 27		19 23			21 22
Curriehill		d				13 26			15 25		17 33		19 28			21 27
Wester Hailes		d				13 31			15 29		17 36		19 32			21 31
Kingsknowe		d				13 32			15 31		17 39		19 34			21 33
Slateford		d				13 36			15 34		17 41		19 37			21 36
Haymarket	230,238,242	d	11 48	12 39	13 50	13 42	14 43	15 50	15 41	16 46	17 50	18 46	19 43		20 46	21 43
Edinburgh	230,238,242	a	11 54	12 44	13 55	13 47	14 47	15 55	15 47	16 51	17 55	18 52	19 48		20 51	21 48

Table 226

Mondays to Fridays

Lanark, Coatbridge, Motherwell, Larkhall, Hamilton, Drumgelloch, Airdrie and Springburn - Glasgow - Milngavie, Dalmuir, Balloch and Helensburgh

			SR	SR		SR	SR			SR			SR	SR	SR	SR	SR	SR	SR	SR		SR	SR	SR	SR
													A	B											
Lanark	d																						06 23		
Carluke	d																						06 33		
Wishaw	d																						06 38		
Holytown	d																								
Shieldmuir	d																						06 42		
Coatbridge Central	d																								06 40
Whifflet	d																								06 42
Motherwell	a																						06 46		06 49
	d														06 16		06 20						06 46		06 49
Bellshill	d														06 22								06 52		
Uddingston	d														06 26								06 56		
Airbles	d																06 22								06 52
Larkhall	d									06 07										06 37					
Merryton	d									06 09										06 39					
Chatelherault	d									06 12										06 42					
Hamilton Central	d									06 15							06 27			06 45					06 57
Hamilton West	d									06 18							06 30			06 48					06 59
Blantyre	d									06 21							06 33			06 51					07 03
Newton	d																06 38								07 07
Cambuslang	d														06 31		06 42						07 01		07 10
Rutherglen	d									06 30					06 35		06 45			06 59			07 05		07 15
Dalmarnock	d														06 37		06 47						07 07		07 17
Bridgeton	d														06 39		06 49						07 09		07 19
Drumgelloch	d																								
Airdrie	a																								
	d			05 31			05 57						06 12	06 13		06 27						06 42		06 57	
Coatdyke	d			05 33			05 59						06 14	06 15		06 29						06 44		06 59	
Coatbridge Sunnyside	d			05 35			06 01						06 16	06 17		06 31						06 46		07 01	
Blairhill	d			05 38			06 04						06 19	06 20		06 34						06 49		07 04	
Easterhouse	d			05 42			06 08						06 23	06 24		06 38						06 53		07 08	
Garrowhill	d			05 44			06 10						06 25	06 26		06 40						06 55		07 10	
Shettleston	d			05 47			06 13						06 28	06 29		06 43						06 58		07 13	
Carntyne	d			05 49			06 15						06 30	06 31		06 45						07 00		07 15	
Springburn	d																		06 49						
Barnhill	d																		06 50						
Alexandra Parade	d																		06 53						
Duke Street	d																		06 54						
Bellgrove	d			05 52			06 18						06 33	06 34		06 48			06 56			07 03		07 18	
High Street	d			05 54			06 20						06 35	06 36		06 50			06 58			07 05		07 20	
Glasgow Queen St HL	d																								
Glasgow Queen St LL	a			05 56			06 22						06 37	06 38		06 52			07 01			07 07		07 22	
	d	05 30		05 57			06 23						06 41	06 38		06 53			07 02			07 10		07 23	
Charing Cross	d			06 00			06 25						06 43	06 42		06 55			07 04			07 12		07 25	
Argyle Street	d									06 34					06 43		06 53			07 04			07 13		07 23
Glasgow Central HL	a																								
Glasgow Central LL	a									06 37					06 45		06 57			07 07			07 14		07 26
	d									06 37					06 46		06 58			07 07			07 16		07 28
Anderston	d									06 39					06 48		06 59			07 09			07 17		07 29
Exhibition Centre	d									06 41					06 50		07 01			07 11			07 19		07 31
Partick	d			06 04			06 30			06 45			06 47	06 47	06 54	07 00	07 05		07 09	07 15		07 17	07 23	07 30	07 35
Hyndland	d			06 06			06 32			06 47			06 50	06 50	06 56	07 02	07 08		07 11	07 17		07 20	07 25	07 32	07 37
Jordanhill	d			06 08											06 58				07 13				07 27		
Scotstounhill	d			06 11											07 00				07 15				07 30		
Garscadden	d			06 13									06 54	06 54	07 02				07 17				07 32		
Yoker	d			06 15											07 05				07 20				07 34		
Clydebank	d			06 17											07 07				07 22				07 37		
Anniesland	d						06 35			06 50						07 05	07 11			07 20				07 35	07 40
Westerton	d	05a43				05 56	06 38			06 53						07 08	07 14			07 23				07 38	07 44
Bearsden	d																07 16								07 46
Hillfoot	d																07 18								07 48
Milngavie	a																07 23								07 52
Drumchapel	d						06 40			06 55						07 10				07 25				07 40	
Drumry	d						06 42			06 57						07 12				07 27				07 42	
Singer	d						06 45			07 00						07 15				07 30				07 45	
Dalmuir	a			06 21		06 03	06 47			07 02			06 58	06 59	07 11	07 17			07 26	07 32		07 28	07 41	07 47	
	d			06 21		06 04	06 48						06 59	06 59		07 18		06 32				07 29		07 48	
Kilpatrick	d						06 51									07 21		06 34						07 51	
Bowling	d						06 54									07 24		06 37						07 54	
Dumbarton East	d			06 29			06 58						07 06	07 06		07 28		06 42				07 36		07 58	
Dumbarton Central	d			06 30			07 00						07 08	07 08		07 30		06 44				07 38		08 00	
Dalreoch	d			06 32			07 02						07 10	07 10		07 32		06 46				07 40		08 02	
Renton	d			06 35			07 05									07 35								08 05	
Alexandria	d			06 37			07 07									07 37								08 07	
Balloch	a			06 40			07 10									07 40								08 10	
Cardross	d												07 15	07 15				06 51				07 45			
Craigendoran	d												07 20	07 20				06 56				07 50			
Helensburgh Central	a												07 23	07 23				06 59				07 53			
Helensburgh Upper	a					06 26																			

A from 20 September **B** until 17 September

Table 226

Lanark, Coatbridge, Motherwell, Larkhall, Hamilton, Drumgelloch, Airdrie and Springburn - Glasgow - Milngavie, Dalmuir, Balloch and Helensburgh

		SR	SR	SR	SR	SR		SR	SR	SR	SR	SR	SR	SR	SR	SR	SR	SR	SR ◇ 🛏	SR	SR	SR	SR	SR
Lanark	d										07 21						07 45							
Carluke	d										07 31						07 55				08 11			
Wishaw	d										07 36						08 04				08 18			
Holytown	d	06 59																						
Shieldmuir	d										07 40						08 09				08 23			
Coatbridge Central	d														07 39									
Whifflet	d														07 41									
Motherwell	a										07 43				07 48		08 13				08 26			
	d								07 20		07 43				07 49		08 14				08 27		08 20	
Bellshill	d	07 07																						
Uddingston	d	07 11															08 20				08 32			
Airbles	d								07 22						07 52								08 22	
Larkhall	d			07 07									07 37					08 06						
Merryton	d			07 09									07 39					08 08						
Chatelherault	d			07 12									07 42					08 11						
Hamilton Central	d			07 15					07 27				07 45		07 58			08 15					08 28	
Hamilton West	d			07 18					07 30				07 48		08 01			08 17					08 30	
Blantyre	d			07 21					07 33				07 51		08 04			08 21					08 34	
Newton	d								07 37				07 55		08 08								08 37	
Cambuslang	d	07 16							07 41				08 00		08 12			08 28					08 41	
Rutherglen	d			07 30					07 45		07 54		08 03		08 16		08 26						08 46	
Dalmarnock	d								07 48				08 05		08 18								08 48	
Bridgeton	d								07 50				08 07		08 20								08 50	
Drumgelloch	d																							
Airdrie	a																							
	d				07 12	07 22		07 27				07 52		07 57						08 22		08 27		
Coatdyke	d				07 14	07 24		07 29				07 54		07 59						08 24		08 29		
Coatbridge Sunnyside	d				07 16	07 26		07 31				07 56		08 01						08 26		08 31		
Blairhill	d				07 19	07 29		07 34				07 59		08 04						08 29		08 34		
Easterhouse	d				07 23			07 38						08 08								08 38		
Garrowhill	d				07 25			07 40						08 10								08 40		
Shettleston	d				07 28			07 43						08 13								08 43		
Carntyne	d				07 30			07 45						08 15								08 45		
Springburn	d		07 19							07 49						08 19								08 49
Barnhill	d		07 20							07 50						08 20								08 50
Alexandra Parade	d		07 23							07 53						08 23								08 53
Duke Street	d		07 24							07 54						08 24								08 54
Bellgrove	d		07 26		07 33			07 48		07 56				08 18		08 26						08 48		08 56
High Street	d		07 28		07 35	07 40		07 50		07 58		08 10		08 20		08 28				08 40		08 50		08 58
Glasgow Queen St HL 10 ⇌	d																		08 21					
Glasgow Queen St LL 10 ⇌	a		07 31		07 37	07 42		07 52		08 01		08 12		08 22		08 31				08 42		08 52		09 01
	d		07 32		07 40	07 43		07 53		08 02		08 13		08 23		08 32				08 43		08 53		09 02
Charing Cross	d		07 34		07 42	07 45		07 55		08 04		08 15		08 25		08 34				08 45		08 55		09 04
Argyle Street	d			07 35					07 54		08 00		08 11		08 24		08 31	08 34			08 47		08 54	
Glasgow Central HL 15	a	07 29																						
Glasgow Central LL 15	a			07 37					07 56		08 04		08 16		08 26		08 32	08 36			08 48		08 56	
	d			07 38					07 58		08 07		08 16		08 28		08 33	08 37			08 49		08 58	
Anderston	d			07 39					07 59		08 09		08 18		08 29		08 35	08 40			08 50		08 59	
Exhibition Centre	d			07 41					08 01		08 11		08 20		08 31		08 38	08 42			08 53		09 01	
Partick	d		07 39	07 45	07 47	07 50		08 00	08 05	08 09	08 15	08 20	08 24	08 30	08 35	08 39	08 42	08 45		08 51	08 57	08 59	09 05	09 09
Hyndland	d		07 41	07 47	07 49	07 53		08 02	08 08	08 11	08 17	08 23	08 26	08 32	08 38	08 41	08 44	08 47		08 53	08 59	09 01	09 09	09 12
Jordanhill	d		07 43							08 13			08 28			08 43	08 46				09 01			09 14
Scotstounhill	d		07 45							08 15			08 30			08 45	08 48				09 03			09 16
Garscadden	d		07 47							08 17			08 32			08 47	08a51				09a06			09 17
Yoker	d		07 50							08 20			08 36			08 50								09 20
Clydebank	d		07 52							08 22			08 38			08 52								09 22
Anniesland	d			07 50		07 56		08 05	08 11		08 20	08 26		08 35	08 41			08 50		08 56		09 04	09 12	
Westerton	d			07 53		07 59		08 08	08 14		08 23	08 29		08 38	08 44			08 53		08 59		09 08	09 15	
Bearsden	d					08 01			08 16			08 31			08 46					09 01			09 18	
Hillfoot	d					08 03			08 18			08 33			08 48					09 03			09 19	
Milngavie	a					08 07			08 27			08 37			08 52					09 07			09 23	
Drumchapel	d			07 55				08 10			08 25			08 40				08 56				09 10		
Drumry	d			07 57				08 12			08 27			08 42				08 58				09 12		
Singer	d			08 00				08 15			08 30			08 45				09 00				09 15		
Dalmuir	a		07 56	08 02	07 59			08 17		08 28	08 32		08 42	08 47		08 56		09 03	08 39			09 17		09 26
	d				07 59			08 18						08 48					08 42			09 18		
Kilpatrick	d							08 21						08 51								09 21		
Bowling	d							08 24						08 54								09 24		
Dumbarton East	d				08 06			08 28						08 58								09 28		
Dumbarton Central	d				08 09			08 30						09 00					08 51			09 30		
Dalreoch	d				08 10			08 32						09 02								09 32		
Renton	d							08 35						09 05								09 35		
Alexandria	d							08 37						09 07								09 37		
Balloch	a							08 40						09 10								09 40		
Cardross	d				08 20																			
Craigendoran	d				08 25																			
Helensburgh Central	a				08 28																			
Helensburgh Upper	a																		09 03					

Table 226

Lanark, Coatbridge, Motherwell, Larkhall, Hamilton, Drumgelloch, Airdrie and Springburn - Glasgow - Milngavie, Dalmuir, Balloch and Helensburgh

		SR	SR	SR ◇ A 🛏	SR	SR	SR	SR	SR	SR	SR	SR	SR	SR	SR	SR	SR	SR	SR	SR	SR	SR	SR	SR	SR
Lanark	d	08 23																		09 23					
Carluke	d	08 33																		09 33					
Wishaw	d	08 37																		09 38					
Holytown	d											09 24													
Shieldmuir	d	08 42																		09 42					
Coatbridge Central	d																								
Whifflet	d																								
Motherwell	a	08 46																		09 46					
	d	08 46				08 49		08 50						09 16		09 20				09 47		09 50			
Bellshill	d					08 54						09 26		09 22						09 53					
Uddingston	d					08 58						09 30		09 26						09 57					
Airbles	d							08 52								09 22						09 52			
Larkhall	d		08 37							09 07								09 37						10 07	
Merryton	d		08 39							09 09								09 39						10 09	
Chatelherault	d		08 42							09 12								09 42						10 12	
Hamilton Central	d		08 45					08 58		09 15						09 27		09 45				09 57		10 15	
Hamilton West	d		08 48					09 01		09 18						09 30		09 48				10 00		10 18	
Blantyre	d		08 51					09 04		09 21						09 33		09 51				10 03		10 21	
Newton	d		08 55					09 08								09 38						10 07		10 26	
Cambuslang	d					09 03		09 12						09 31		09 42				10 01		10 11			
Rutherglen	d	08 56	09 00			09 07		09 16		09 29				09 35		09 47		09 59		10 06		10 16		10 30	
Dalmarnock	d					09 09		09 18						09 37		09 49				10 08		10 18			
Bridgeton	d					09 11		09 20						09 39		09 51				10 10		10 20			
Drumgelloch	d																								
Airdrie	a																								
	d						08 57				09 12				09 27				09 42		09 57				10 12
Coatdyke	d						08 59				09 14				09 29				09 44		09 59				10 14
Coatbridge Sunnyside	d						09 01				09 16				09 31				09 46		10 01				10 16
Blairhill	d						09 04				09 19				09 34				09 49		10 04				10 19
Easterhouse	d						09 08				09 23				09 38				09 53		10 08				10 23
Garrowhill	d						09 10				09 25				09 40				09 55		10 10				10 25
Shettleston	d						09 13				09 28				09 43				09 58		10 13				10 28
Carntyne	d						09 15				09 30				09 45				10 00		10 15				10 30
Springburn	d								09 19								09 49						10 19		
Barnhill	d								09 20								09 50						10 20		
Alexandra Parade	d								09 23								09 53						10 23		
Duke Street	d								09 24								09 54						10 24		
Bellgrove	d				09 08		09 18		09 26		09 33		09 38		09 48		09 56		10 03		10 18		10 26		10 33
High Street	d				09 10		09 20		09 28		09 35		09 40		09 50		09 58		10 05		10 20		10 28		10 35
Glasgow Queen St HL 10 ⇌	d			09 07																					
Glasgow Queen St LL 10 ⇌	a				09 12		09 22		09 31		09 37		09 42		09 52		10 01		10 07		10 22		10 31		10 37
	d				09 13		09 23		09 32		09 40		09 43		09 53		10 02		10 10		10 23		10 32		10 40
Charing Cross	d				09 15		09 25		09 34		09 42		09 45		09 55		10 04		10 12		10 25		10 34		10 42
Argyle Street	d	09 01	09 05			09 14		09 24		09 34				09 42		09 54		10 04		10 15		10 24		10 35	
Glasgow Central HL 15	a											09 54													
Glasgow Central LL 15	a	09 03	09 07			09 19		09 26		09 37				09 46		09 58		10 07		10 17		10 26		10 37	
	d	09 03	09 08			09 19		09 28		09 37				09 46		09 59		10 07		10 18		10 28		10 38	
Anderston	d	09 05	09 10			09 20		09 29		09 39				09 48		10 00		10 09		10 19		10 29		10 39	
Exhibition Centre	d	09 08	09 12			09 22		09 31		09 41				09 50		10 02		10 11		10 21		10 31		10 41	
Partick	d	09 12	09 16		09 20	09 26	09 30	09 35	09 39	09 45	09 47		09 50	09 54	10 00	10 06	10 09	10 14	10 17	10 25	10 30	10 35	10 39	10 45	10 47
Hyndland	d	09 14	09 18		09 23	09 28	09 32	09 38	09 41	09 47	09 50		09 53	09 56	10 02	10 08	10 11	10 17	10 20	10 27	10 32	10 38	10 41	10 47	10 50
Jordanhill	d	09 16				09 30			09 43					09 58			10 13			10 29			10 43		
Scotstounhill	d	09 19				09 33			09 45					10 00			10 15			10 31			10 45		
Garscadden	d	09a21				09 36			09 47					10 02			10 17			10 32			10 47		
Yoker	d					09 38			09 50					10 05			10 20			10 35			10 50		
Clydebank	d					0940			09 52					10 07			10 22			10 37			10 52		
Anniesland	d		09 21		09 26		09 35	09 41		09 50			09 56		10 05	10 11		10 20			10 35	10 41		10 50	
Westerton	d		09 24		09 29		09 38	09 44		09 53			09 59		10 08	10 14		10 23			10 38	10 44		10 53	
Bearsden	d				09 31			09 46					10 01			10 17						10 46			
Hillfoot	d				09 33			09 48					10 03			10 18						10 48			
Milngavie	a				09 37			09 52					10 07			10 22						10 52			
Drumchapel	d		09 26				09 40			09 55					10 10			10 25			10 40			10 55	
Drumry	d		09 28				09 42			09 57					10 12			10 27			10 42			10 57	
Singer	d		09 31				09 45			10 00					10 15			10 30			10 45			11 00	
Dalmuir	a		09 33	09 26		09 43	09 47		09 56	10 02	09 59			10 11	10 17		10 26	10 32	10 29	10 41	10 47		10 56	11 02	10 59
	d			09 27			09 48				09 59				10 18				10 29		10 48				10 59
Kilpatrick	d						09 51								10 21						10 51				
Bowling	d						09 54								10 24						10 54				
Dumbarton East	d						09 58				10 07				10 28				10 37		10 58				11 06
Dumbarton Central	d			09 37			10 00				10 08				10 30				10 39		11 00				11 08
Dalreoch	d						10 02				10 10				10 32				10 41		11 02				11 10
Renton	d						10 05								10 35						11 05				
Alexandria	d						10 07								10 37						11 07				
Balloch	a						10 10								10 40						11 10				
Cardross	d										10 15								10 46						11 15
Craigendoran	d										10 20								10 50						11 20
Helensburgh Central	a										10 23								10 56						11 23
Helensburgh Upper	a			09 50																					

A until 24 September

Table 226

Mondays to Fridays

Lanark, Coatbridge, Motherwell, Larkhall, Hamilton, Drumgelloch, Airdrie and Springburn - Glasgow - Milngavie, Dalmuir, Balloch and Helensburgh

		SR	SR	SR	SR	SR	SR	SR	SR	SR	SR	SR	SR	SR	SR	SR	SR	SR	SR	SR	SR	SR	SR	SR	SR
Lanark	d					09 53					10 23									10 53					11 24
Carluke	d					10 02					10 34									11 03					11 32
Wishaw	d					10 08					10 40									11 08					11 40
Holytown	d	10 31				10 13														11 13					
Shieldmuir	d										10 42														11 44
Coatbridge Central	d																								
Whifflet	d																								
Motherwell	a					10 20					10 47									11 19					11 47
	d			10 16		10 20					10 48		10 50					11 16		11 20					11 47
Bellshill	d	10 33		10 22							10 54							11 22							11 53
Uddingston	d	10 37		10 26							10 58							11 26							11 57
Airbles	d					10 22							10 52							11 22					
Larkhall	d							10 36							11 07							11 37			
Merryton	d							10 38							11 09							11 39			
Chatelherault	d							10 41							11 12							11 42			
Hamilton Central	d					10 27		10 44					10 57		11 15					11 27		11 45			
Hamilton West	d					10 30		10 47					11 00		11 18					11 30		11 48			
Blantyre	d					10 33		10 50					11 03		11 21					11 33		11 51			
Newton	d					10 37							11 07							11 37					
Cambuslang	d			10 31		10 41					11 03		11 11					11 31		11 41					12 02
Rutherglen	d			10 34		10 45		10 58			11 05		11 17		11 29			11 34		11 45		11 59			12 06
Dalmarnock	d			10 36		10 47					11 07		11 19					11 36		11 47					12 08
Bridgeton	d			10 38		10 49					11 09		11 21					11 38		11 49					12 10
Drumgelloch	d																								
Airdrie	a																								
	d				10 27				10 42			10 57				11 12			11 27				11 42		
Coatdyke	d				10 29				10 44			10 59				11 14			11 29				11 44		
Coatbridge Sunnyside	d				10 31				10 46			11 01				11 16			11 31				11 46		
Blairhill	d				10 34				10 49			11 04				11 19			11 34				11 49		
Easterhouse	d				10 38				10 53			11 08				11 23			11 38				11 53		
Garrowhill	d				10 40				10 55			11 10				11 25			11 40				11 55		
Shettleston	d				10 43				10 58			11 13				11 28			11 43				11 58		
Carntyne	d				10 45				11 00			11 15				11 30			11 45				12 00		
Springburn	d						10 49							11 19							11 49				
Barnhill	d						10 50							11 20							11 50				
Alexandra Parade	d						10 53							11 23							11 53				
Duke Street	d						10 54							11 24							11 54				
Bellgrove	d		10 39		10 48		10 56		11 03	11 08		11 18		11 26		11 33	11 38		11 48		11 56		12 03	12 08	
High Street	d		10 41		10 50		10 58		11 05	11 10		11 20		11 28		11 35	11 40		11 50		11 58		12 05	12 10	
Glasgow Queen St HL 10	d																								
Glasgow Queen St LL 10	a		10 43		10 52		11 01		11 07	11 12		11 22		11 31		11 37	11 42		11 52		12 01		12 07	12 12	
	d		10 44		10 53		11 02		11 10	11 13		11 23		11 32		11 40	11 43		11 53		12 02		12 10	12 13	
Charing Cross	d		10 46		10 55		11 04		11 12	11 15		11 25		11 34		11 42	11 45		11 55		12 04		12 12	12 15	
Argyle Street	d			10 42		10 53		11 03			11 14		11 25		11 34			11 42		11 53		12 04			12 14
Glasgow Central HL 15	a	10 55																							
Glasgow Central LL 15	a			10 46		10 56		11 07			11 16		11 26		11 37			11 46		11 56		12 07			12 19
	d			10 46		10 58		11 07			11 17		11 28		11 37			11 46		11 58		12 07			12 19
Anderston	d			10 48		10 59		11 09			11 18		11 29		11 39			11 48		11 59		12 09			12 21
Exhibition Centre	d			10 50		11 01		11 11			11 20		11 31		11 41			11 50		12 01		12 11			12 23
Partick	d		10 50	10 54	11 00	11 05	11 09	11 15	11 17	11 20	11 24	11 30	11 35	11 39	11 45	11 47	11 50	11 54	12 00	12 05	12 09	12 15	12 17	12 20	12 27
Hyndland	d		10 53	10 56	11 02	11 08	11 11	11 17	11 20	11 23	11 26	11 32	11 38	11 41	11 47	11 50	11 53	11 56	12 02	12 08	12 11	12 17	12 20	12 23	12 29
Jordanhill	d			10 58			11 13				11 28			11 43				11 58			12 13				12 31
Scotstounhill	d			11 00			11 15				11 30			11 45				12 00			12 15				12 33
Garscadden	d			11 02			11 17				11 32			11 47				12 02			12 17				12 36
Yoker	d			11 05			11 20				11 35			11 50				12 05			12 20				12 39
Clydebank	d			11 07			11 22				11 37			11 52				12 07			12 22				12 41
Anniesland	d		10 56		11 05	11 11		11 20		11 26		11 35	11 41		11 50		11 56		12 05	12 11		12 20		12 26	
Westerton	d		10 59		11 08	11 14		11 23		11 29		11 38	11 44		11 53		11 59		12 08	12 14		12 23		12 29	
Bearsden	d		11 01			11 16				11 31			11 46				12 01			12 16				12 31	
Hillfoot	d		11 03			11 18				11 33			11 48				12 03			12 18				12 33	
Milngavie	a		11 07			11 24				11 37			11 52				12 07			12 22				12 37	
Drumchapel	d				11 10			11 25				11 40			11 55				12 10			12 25			
Drumry	d				11 12			11 27				11 42			11 57				12 12			12 27			
Singer	d				11 15			11 30				11 45			12 00				12 15			12 30			
Dalmuir	a			11 13	11 17		11 26	11 32	11 29		11 42	11 47		11 56	12 02	11 59		12 11	12 17		12 26	12 32	12 29		12 44
	d				11 18				11 29			11 48				11 59			12 18				12 29		
Kilpatrick	d				11 21							11 51							12 21						
Bowling	d				11 24							11 54							12 24						
Dumbarton East	d				11 28				11 37			11 58				12 07			12 28				12 37		
Dumbarton Central	d				11 30				11 39			12 00				12 08			12 30				12 38		
Dalreoch	d				11 32				11 40			12 02				12 10			12 32				12 40		
Renton	d				11 35							12 05							12 35						
Alexandria	d				11 37							12 07							12 37						
Balloch	a				11 40							12 10							12 40						
Cardross	d								11 45							12 15							12 45		
Craigendoran	d								11 50							12 20							12 50		
Helensburgh Central	a								11 53							12 23							12 53		
Helensburgh Upper	a																								

Table 226

Mondays to Fridays

Lanark, Coatbridge, Motherwell, Larkhall, Hamilton, Drumgelloch, Airdrie and Springburn - Glasgow - Milngavie, Dalmuir, Balloch and Helensburgh

		SR	SR	SR	SR	SR	SR ◇	SR	SR	SR	SR	SR	SR	SR	SR	SR	SR	SR	SR	SR	SR	SR	SR	SR	SR
Lanark	d											11 53				12 23									
Carluke	d											12 03				12 33									
Wishaw	d											12 08				12 39									
Holytown	d							12 29				12 13											13 28		
Shieldmuir	d															12 43									
Coatbridge Central	d																								
Whifflet	d																								
Motherwell	a											12 20				12 46									
	d		11 50							12 16		12 20				12 46			12 50						13 16
Bellshill	d							12 32		12 22						12 52							13 32		13 22
Uddingston	d							12 38		12 26						12 56							13 36		13 26
Airbles	d		11 52									12 21							12 52						
Larkhall	d				12 07									12 37							13 07				
Merryton	d				12 09									12 39							13 09				
Chatelherault	d				12 12									12 42							13 12				
Hamilton Central	d		11 57		12 15							12 26		12 45					12 57		13 15				
Hamilton West	d		12 00		12 18							12 30		12 48					13 00		13 18				
Blantyre	d		12 03		12 21							12 32		12 51					13 03		13 21				
Newton	d		12 07		12 25							12 36		12 55					13 08						
Cambuslang	d		12 11							12 31		12 41				13 01			13 11						13 31
Rutherglen	d		12 16		12 29					12 34		12 45		12 59		13 05			13 17		13 29				13 34
Dalmarnock	d		12 18							12 36		12 47				13 07			13 19						13 36
Bridgeton	d		12 20							12 38		12 49				13 09			13 21						13 38
Drumgelloch	d																								
Airdrie	a																								
	d	11 57				12 12					12 27				12 42			12 57				13 12			
Coatdyke	d	11 59				12 14					12 29				12 44			12 59				13 14			
Coatbridge Sunnyside	d	12 01				12 16					12 31				12 46			13 01				13 16			
Blairhill	d	12 04				12 19					12 34				12 49			13 04				13 19			
Easterhouse	d	12 08				12 23					12 38				12 53			13 08				13 23			
Garrowhill	d	12 10				12 25					12 40				12 55			13 10				13 25			
Shettleston	d	12 13				12 28					12 43				12 58			13 13				13 28			
Carntyne	d	12 15				12 30					12 45				13 00			13 15				13 30			
Springburn	d			12 19									12 49							13 19					
Barnhill	d			12 20									12 50							13 20					
Alexandra Parade	d			12 23									12 53							13 23					
Duke Street	d			12 24									12 54							13 24					
Bellgrove	d	12 18		12 26		12 33			12 38		12 48		12 56		13 03		13 08	13 18		13 26		13 33		13 38	
High Street	d	12 20		12 28		12 35			12 40		12 50		12 58		13 05		13 10	13 20		13 28		13 35		13 40	
Glasgow Queen St HL 10	d						12 21																		
Glasgow Queen St LL 10	a	12 22		12 31		12 37			12 42		12 52		13 01		13 08		13 12	13 22		13 31		13 37		13 42	
	d	12 23		12 32		12 40			12 43		12 53		13 02		13 10		13 13	13 23		13 32		13 40		13 43	
Charing Cross	d	12 25		12 34		12 42			12 45		12 55		13 04		13 12		13 15	13 25		13 34		13 42		13 45	
Argyle Street	d		12 24		12 34					12 42		12 53		13 04		13 13			13 25		13 34				13 42
Glasgow Central HL 15	a							12 56															13 55		
Glasgow Central LL 15	a		12 26		12 37					12 46		12 56		13 07		13 16			13 26		13 37				13 46
	d		12 28		12 37					12 46		12 58		13 07		13 17			13 28		13 37				13 46
Anderston	d		12 29		12 39					12 48		12 59		13 09		13 19			13 29		13 39				13 48
Exhibition Centre	d		12 31		12 41					12 50		13 01		13 11		13 20			13 31		13 41				13 50
Partick	d	12 30	12 35	12 39	12 44	12 47			12 50	12 54	13 00	13 05	13 09	13 15	13 17	13 25	13 20	13 30	13 35	13 39	13 45	13 47		13 50	13 54
Hyndland	d	12 32	12 38	12 41	12 47	12 50			12 53	12 56	13 02	13 08	13 11	13 17	13 20	13 26	13 23	13 32	13 38	13 41	13 47	13 50		13 53	13 56
Jordanhill	d			12 43						12 58			13 13			13 28				13 43					13 58
Scotstounhill	d			12 45						13 00			13 15			13 30				13 45					14 00
Garscadden	d			12 47						13 02			13 17			13 32				13 47					14 02
Yoker	d			12 50						13 05			13 20			13 35				13 50					14 05
Clydebank	d			12 52						13 07			13 22			13 37				13 52					14 07
Anniesland	d	12 35	12 41		12 50				12 56		13 05	13 11		13 20			13 26	13 35	13 41		13 50			13 56	
Westerton	d	12 38	12 44		12 53				12 59		13 08	13 14		13 23			13 29	13 38	13 44		13 53			13 59	
Bearsden	d		12 46						13 01			13 16					13 31		13 46					14 02	
Hillfoot	d		12 48						13 03			13 18					13 33		13 48					14 03	
Milngavie	a		12 52						13 07			13 22					13 37		13 52					14 07	
Drumchapel	d	12 40			12 55						13 10			13 25				13 40			13 55				
Drumry	d	12 42			12 57						13 12			13 27				13 42			13 57				
Singer	d	12 45			13 00						13 15			13 30				13 45			14 00				
Dalmuir	a	12 47		12 56	13 02	12 59	12 38			13 11	13 17		13 26	13 32	13 29	15 41		13 47		13 56	14 02	13 59			14 11
	d	12 48				12 59	12 42				13 19				13 29			13 48				13 59			
Kilpatrick	d	12 51									13 22							13 51							
Bowling	d	12 54									13 25							13 54							
Dumbarton East	d	12 58				13 06					13 29				13 36			13 58				14 07			
Dumbarton Central	d	13 00				13 08	12 51				13 31				13 38			14 00				14 09			
Dalreoch	d	13 02				13 10					13 33				13 40			14 02				14 10			
Renton	d	13 05									13 36							14 05							
Alexandria	d	13 07									13 38							14 07							
Balloch	a	13 10									13 41							14 10							
Cardross	d					13 15									13 45							14 15			
Craigendoran	d					13 20									13 50							14 20			
Helensburgh Central	a					13 26									13 53							14 23			
Helensburgh Upper	a						13 03																		

Table 226

Lanark, Coatbridge, Motherwell, Larkhall, Hamilton, Drumgelloch, Airdrie and Springburn - Glasgow - Milngavie, Dalmuir, Balloch and Helensburgh

		SR	SR	SR	SR	SR	SR	SR	SR	SR	SR	SR	SR	SR	SR	SR	SR	SR	SR	SR	SR	SR	SR	SR	SR
Lanark	d		12 53					13 23								13 53					14 25				
Carluke	d		13 03					13 33								14 03					14 35				
Wishaw	d		13 08					13 40								14 08					14 40				
Holytown	d		13 13													14 13									
Shieldmuir	d							13 43													14 42				
Coatbridge Central	d																								
Whifflet	d																								
Motherwell	a		13 19					13 46								14 19					14 46				
	d		13 20					13 47		13 50				14 16		14 20					14 46		14 50		
Bellshill	d							13 53						14 22							14 52				
Uddingston	d							14 58						14 26							14 56				
Airbles	d		13 22							13 52						14 22							14 52		
Larkhall	d				13 37							14 07						14 37							15 07
Merryton	d				13 39							14 09						14 39							15 09
Chatelherault	d				13 42							14 12						14 42							15 12
Hamilton Central	d		13 27		13 45					13 57		14 15				14 27		14 45					14 58		15 15
Hamilton West	d		13 30		13 48					14 00		14 18				14 30		14 48					15 00		15 18
Blantyre	d		13 33		13 51					14 03		14 21				14 33		14 51					15 04		15 21
Newton	d		13 37							14 07						14 37							15 07		
Cambuslang	d		13 41					14 03		14 11				14 31		14 41					15 01		15 11		
Rutherglen	d		13 45		14 00			14 06		14 15		14 29		14 33		14 45		15 00			15 04		15 15		15 30
Dalmarnock	d		13 47					14 08		14 17				14 35		14 47					15 06		15 17		
Bridgeton	d		13 49					14 10		14 19				14 37		14 49					15 08		15 19		
Drumgelloch	d																								
Airdrie	a																								
	d	13 27				13 42			13 57						14 27				14 42			14 57			
Coatdyke	d	13 29				13 44			13 59						14 29				14 44			14 59			
Coatbridge Sunnyside	d	13 31				13 46			14 01						14 31				14 46			15 01			
Blairhill	d	13 34				13 49			14 04						14 34				14 49			15 04			
Easterhouse	d	13 38				13 53			14 08						14 38				14 53			15 08			
Garrowhill	d	13 40				13 55			14 10						14 40				14 55			15 10			
Shettleston	d	13 43				13 58			14 13						14 43				14 58			15 13			
Carntyne	d	13 45				14 00			14 15						14 45				15 00			15 15			
Springburn	d			13 49							14 19						14 49							15 19	
Barnhill	d			13 50							14 20						14 50							15 20	
Alexandra Parade	d			13 53							14 23						14 53							15 23	
Duke Street	d			13 54							14 24						14 54							15 24	
Bellgrove	d	13 48		13 56		14 03	14 08		14 18		14 26		14 38		14 48		14 56		15 03	15 08		15 18		15 26	
High Street	d	13 50		13 58		14 05	14 10		14 20		14 28		14 40		14 50		14 58		15 05	15 10		15 20		15 28	
Glasgow Queen St HL 10 ⇌	d																								
Glasgow Queen St LL 10 ⇌	a	13 52		14 01		14 07	14 12		14 22		14 31		14 42		14 52		15 01		15 07	15 12		15 22		15 31	
	d	13 53		14 02		14 10	14 13		14 23		14 32		14 43		14 53		15 02		15 10	15 13		15 23		15 32	
Charing Cross	d	13 55		14 04		14 12	14 15		14 25		14 34		14 45		14 55		15 04		15 12	15 15		15 25		15 34	
Argyle Street	d		13 53		14 05			14 14		14 23		14 34		14 42		14 53		15 05			15 12		15 23		15 34
Glasgow Central HL 15	a																								
Glasgow Central LL 15	a		13 56		14 07			14 17		14 26		14 37		14 46		14 56		15 07			15 16		15 26		15 37
	d		13 58		14 08			14 18		14 28		14 37		14 46		14 58		15 07			15 16		15 28		15 37
Anderston	d		13 59		14 09			14 20		14 29		14 39		14 48		14 59		15 09			15 18		15 29		15 39
Exhibition Centre	d		14 01		14 11			14 22		14 31		14 41		14 50		15 01		15 11			15 20		15 31		15 41
Partick	d	14 00	14 05	14 09	14 15	14 17	14 20	14 26	14 29	14 35	14 39	14 45	14 50	14 54	15 00	15 05	15 09	15 15	15 17	15 20	15 24	15 30	15 35	15 39	15 44
Hyndland	d	14 02	14 08	14 11	14 17	14 20	14 23	14 28	14 31	14 38	14 41	14 47	14 53	14 56	15 02	15 08	15 11	15 17	15 20	15 23	15 26	15 32	15 38	15 41	15 47
Jordanhill	d			14 13				14 30			14 43			14 58			15 13				15 28			15 43	
Scotstounhill	d			14 15				14 33			14 45			15 00			15 15				15 30			15 45	
Garscadden	d			14 17				14 36			14 47			15 02			15 17				15 32			15 47	
Yoker	d			14 20				14 38			14 50			15 05			15 20				15 35			15 50	
Clydebank	d			14 22				14 40			14 52			15 08			15 22				15 37			15 52	
Anniesland	d	14 05	14 11		14 20		14 26		14 34	14 41		14 50	14 56		15 05	15 11		15 20		15 26		15 35	15 41		15 50
Westerton	d	14 08	14 14		14 23		14 29		14 38	14 44		14 53	14 59		15 08	15 14		15 23		15 29		15 38	15 44		15 53
Bearsden	d		14 16				14 32			14 46			15 01			15 16				15 31			15 46		
Hillfoot	d		14 18				14 33			14 48			15 03			15 18				15 33			15 48		
Milngavie	a		14 22				14 37			14 52			15 07			15 24				15 37			15 53		
Drumchapel	d	14 10			14 25				14 40			14 55			15 10			15 25				15 40			15 55
Drumry	d	14 12			14 27				14 42			14 57			15 12			15 27				15 42			15 57
Singer	d	14 15			14 30				14 45			15 00			15 15			15 30				15 45			16 00
Dalmuir	a	14 17		14 26	14 32	14 29		15 41	14 47		14 56	15 02		15 14	15 17		15 26	15 32	15 29		15 41	15 47		15 56	16 02
	d	14 18				14 29			14 48						15 18				15 29			15 48			
Kilpatrick	d	14 21							14 51						15 21							15 51			
Bowling	d	14 24							14 54						15 24							15 54			
Dumbarton East	d	14 28				14 36			14 58						15 28				15 36			15 58			
Dumbarton Central	d	14 30				14 38			15 00						15 30				15 38			16 00			
Dalreoch	d	14 32				14 40			15 02						15 32				15 45			16 02			
Renton	d	14 35							15 05						15 35							16 05			
Alexandria	d	14 37							15 07						15 37							16 07			
Balloch	a	14 40							15 10						15 40							16 10			
Cardross	d					14 45													15 50						
Craigendoran	d					14 50													15 55						
Helensburgh Central	a					14 54													15 58						
Helensburgh Upper	a																								

Table 226

Lanark, Coatbridge, Motherwell, Larkhall, Hamilton, Drumgelloch, Airdrie and Springburn - Glasgow - Milngavie, Dalmuir, Balloch and Helensburgh

		SR	SR	SR	SR	SR		SR	SR	SR	SR	SR	SR	SR	SR	SR		SR	SR	SR	SR	SR	SR	SR	SR
Lanark	d							14 53					15 22											15 53	
Carluke	d							15 03					15 32											16 02	
Wishaw	d							15 08					15 38											16 07	
Holytown	d		15 29					15 13												16 34				16 12	
Shieldmuir	d												15 42												
Coatbridge Central	d																								
Whifflet	d																								
Motherwell	a							15 19					15 46											16 19	
	d				15 16			15 20					15 46		15 50							16 16		16 19	
Bellshill	d		15 32		15 22								15 52							16 37		16 22			
Uddingston	d		15 37		15 26								15 56							16 43		16 26			
Airbles	d							15 22							15 52									16 22	
Larkhall	d									15 37								16 07							
Merryton	d									15 39								16 09							
Chatelherault	d									15 42								16 12							
Hamilton Central	d							15 27		15 45					15 57			16 15						16 27	
Hamilton West	d							15 30		15 48					16 00			16 18						16 29	
Blantyre	d							15 33		15 51					16 03			16 21						16 33	
Newton	d							15 37							16 07									16 37	
Cambuslang	d				15 31			15 41					16 02		16 11							16 31		16 40	
Rutherglen	d				15 34			15 46		15 59			16 06		16 15			16 29				16 34		16 45	
Dalmarnock	d				15 36			15 48					16 08		16 17							16 36		16 47	
Bridgeton	d				15 38			15 50					16 10		16 19							16 38		16 49	
Drumgelloch	d																								
Airdrie	a																								
	d	15 12				15 27					15 42			15 57					16 12				16 27		
Coatdyke	d	15 14				15 29					15 44			15 59					16 14				16 29		
Coatbridge Sunnyside	d	15 16				15 31					15 46			16 01					16 16				16 31		
Blairhill	d	15 19				15 34					15 49			16 04					16 19				16 34		
Easterhouse	d	15 23				15 38					15 53			16 08					16 23				16 38		
Garrowhill	d	15 25				15 40					15 55			16 10					16 25				16 40		
Shettleston	d	15 28				15 43					15 58			16 13					16 28				16 43		
Carntyne	d	15 30				15 45					16 00			16 15					16 30				16 45		
Springburn	d								15 50							16 22									16 51
Barnhill	d								15 51							16 23									16 52
Alexandra Parade	d								15 54							16 26									16 55
Duke Street	d								15 55							16 27									16 56
Bellgrove	d	15 33		15 38		15 48			15 57		16 03	16 08		16 18		16 29			16 33		16 38		16 48		16 58
High Street	d	15 35		15 40		15 50			15 59		16 05	16 10		16 20		16 31			16 35		16 40		16 50		17 00
Glasgow Queen St HL 10 ⇌	d																								
Glasgow Queen St LL 10 ⇌	a	15 37		15 42		15 52			16 02		16 07	16 12		16 22		16 34			16 37		16 42		16 52		17 03
	d	15 40		15 43		15 53			16 02		16 10	16 13		16 23		16 35			16 40		16 43		16 53		17 04
Charing Cross	d	15 42		15 45		15 55			16 04		16 12	16 15		16 25		16 37			16 42		16 45		16 55		17 06
Argyle Street	d				15 42			15 54		16 04			16 15		16 23			16 34				16 42		16 53	
Glasgow Central HL 15	a		15 55																	16 57					
Glasgow Central LL 15	a				15 46			15 56		16 07			16 18		16 26			16 37				16 46		16 56	
	d				15 46			15 58		16 07			16 18		16 28			16 37				16 46		16 58	
Anderston	d				15 48			15 59		16 09			16 20		16 29			16 39				16 48		16 59	
Exhibition Centre	d				15 50			16 01		16 11			16 21		16 31			16 41				16 50		17 01	
Partick	d	15 47		15 50	15 54	16 00		16 05	16 09	16 15	16 17	16 20	16 25	16 30	16 35	16 42		16 44	16 47		16 50	16 54	17 00	17 05	17 10
Hyndland	d	15 50		15 53	15 56	16 02		16 08	16 11	16 17	16 20	16 23	16 27	16 32	16 38	16 44		16 47	16 50		16 53	16 56	17 02	17 08	17 12
Jordanhill	d				15 58				16 13				16 29			16 46						16 58			17 14
Scotstounhill	d				16 00				16 15				16 30			16 48						17 00			17 17
Garscadden	d				16 02				16 17				16 32			16 50						17 02			17 19
Yoker	d				16 05				16 20				16 35			16 53						17 05			17 21
Clydebank	d				16 07				16 22				16 37			16 55						17 07			17 23
Anniesland	d			15 56		16 05		16 11		16 20		16 26		16 35	16 41			16 50			16 56		17 05	17 11	
Westerton	d			15 59		16 08		16 14		16 23		16 29		16 38	16 44			16 53			16 59		17 08	17 14	
Bearsden	d			16 01				16 16				16 31			16 46						17 01			17 16	
Hillfoot	d			16 03				16 18				16 33			16 48						17 03			17 18	
Milngavie	a			16 07				16 22				16 37			16 52						17 07			17 22	
Drumchapel	d					16 10				16 25				16 40				16 55					17 10		
Drumry	d					16 12				16 27				16 42				16 57					17 12		
Singer	d					16 15				16 30				16 45				17 00					17 15		
Dalmuir	a	15 59			16 11	16 17			16 25	16 32	16 29		16 42	16 47		16 59		17 02	17 02			17 11	17 17		17 27
	d	15 59				16 18					16 29			16 48					17 02				17 18		
Kilpatrick	d					16 21								16 51									17 21		
Bowling	d					16 24								16 54									17 24		
Dumbarton East	d	16 06				16 28					16 37			16 58					17 09				17 28		
Dumbarton Central	d	16 08				16 30					16 39			17 00					17 12				17 30		
Dalreoch	d	16 10				16 32					16 40			17 02					17 13				17 32		
Renton	d					16 35								17 05									17 35		
Alexandria	d					16 37								17 07									17 37		
Balloch	a					16 40								17 10									17 41		
Cardross	d	16 15									16 45								17 18						
Craigendoran	d	16 20									16 50								17 23						
Helensburgh Central	a	16 23									16 53								17 26						
Helensburgh Upper	a																								

Table 226

Mondays to Fridays

Lanark, Coatbridge, Motherwell, Larkhall, Hamilton, Drumgelloch, Airdrie and Springburn - Glasgow - Milngavie, Dalmuir, Balloch and Helensburgh

		SR	SR	SR	SR	SR	SR	SR	SR	SR	SR	SR	SR	SR	SR	SR	SR	SR	SR	SR	SR	SR	SR	SR	SR
Lanark	d				16 23										16 54							17 23			
Carluke	d				16 33										17 04							17 33			
Wishaw	d				16 38										17 09							17 39			
Holytown	d										17 29														
Shieldmuir	d				16 42										17 13							17 43			
Coatbridge Central	d																		17 30						
Whifflet	d																		17 31						
Motherwell	a				16 46										17 15				17 38			17 46			
	d				16 46			16 50							17 15		17 20		17 38			17 47			
Bellshill	d				16 52						17 32				17 22							17 52			
Uddingston	d				16 56						17 36				17 26							17 56			
Airbles	d							16 52									17 22		17 41						
Larkhall	d	16 37										17 08												17 49	
Merryton	d	16 39										17 10												17 51	
Chatelherault	d	16 42										17 13												17 54	
Hamilton Central	d	16 45						16 57				17 16					17 27		17 46					17 57	
Hamilton West	d	16 48						17 00				17 19					17 30		17 48					18 00	
Blantyre	d	16 51						17 03				17 22					17 33		17 52					18 03	
Newton	d							17 07									17 39		17 57					18 07	
Cambuslang	d				17 01			17 11			17 42				17 31		17 43					18 02		18 11	
Rutherglen	d	16 59			17 04			17 15				17 29			17 35		17 47		18 01			18 04		18 16	
Dalmarnock	d				17 06			17 17							17 37		17 49					18 06		18 18	
Bridgeton	d				17 08			17 19							17 39		17 51					18 08		18 20	
Drumgelloch	d																								
Airdrie	a																								
	d		16 42				16 57						17 12			17 27				17 42			17 57		
Coatdyke	d		16 44				16 59						17 14			17 29				17 44			17 59		
Coatbridge Sunnyside	d		16 46				17 01						17 16			17 31				17 46			18 01		
Blairhill	d		16 49				17 04						17 19			17 34				17 49			18 04		
Easterhouse	d		16 53				17 08						17 23			17 38				17 53			18 08		
Garrowhill	d		16 55				17 10						17 25			17 40				17 55			18 10		
Shettleston	d		16 58				17 13						17 28			17 43				17 58			18 13		
Carntyne	d		17 00				17 15						17 30			17 45				18 00			18 15		
Springburn	d									17 22								17 49							18 19
Barnhill	d									17 23								17 50							18 20
Alexandra Parade	d									17 26								17 53							18 23
Duke Street	d									17 27								17 54							18 24
Bellgrove	d		17 03	17 08		17 15	17 18		17 27	17 29			17 33	17 38		17 48		17 56		18 03	18 08		18 18		18 26
High Street	d		17 05	17 10		17 17	17 20		17 29	17 31			17 35	17 40		17 50		17 58		18 05	18 10		18 20		18 28
Glasgow Queen St HL 10 ⇌	d																								
Glasgow Queen St LL 10 ⇌	a		17 07	17 12		17 19	17 22		17 31	17 34			16 37	17 42		17 52		18 01		18 07	18 12		18 22		18 31
	d		17 10	17 13		17 20	17 23		17 31	17 35			17 40	17 43		17 53		18 02		18 10	18 13		18 23		18 32
Charing Cross	d		17 12	17 15		17 22	17 25		17 34	17 37			17 43	17 45		17 55		18 05		18 12	18 15		18 25		18 34
Argyle Street	d	17 04			17 12			17 23				17 34			17 43		17 54		18 06			18 12		18 23	
Glasgow Central HL 15	a										17 53														
Glasgow Central LL 15	a	17 07			17 16			17 26				17 37			17 47		17 58		18 08			18 16		18 26	
	d	17 07			17 16			17 28				17 37			17 47		17 58		18 09			18 16		18 28	
Anderston	d	17 09			17 18			17 29				17 39			17 49		18 01		18 10			18 18		18 29	
Exhibition Centre	d	17 11			17 20			17 31				17 41			17 50		18 02		18 12			18 20		18 31	
Partick	d	17 15	17 17	17 20	17 24	17 27	17 30	17 35	17 39	17 42		17 45	17 47	17 50	17 54	18 00	18 05	18 10	18 16	18 18	18 21	18 24	18 30	18 35	18 39
Hyndland	d	17 17	17 20	17 23	17 26		17 32	17 38		17 44		17 47	17 50	17 53	17 56	18 02	18 08	18 12	18 18	18 20	18 23	18 26	18 32	18 38	18 41
Jordanhill	d				17 28					17 46					17 58			18 14				18 28			18 43
Scotstounhill	d				17 30					17 48					18 00			18 16				18 30			18 45
Garscadden	d				17 32					17 50					18 02			18 18				18 32			18a47
Yoker	d				17 35					17 53					18 05			18 21				18 35			
Clydebank	d				17 37					17 55					18 07			18 23				18 37			
Anniesland	d	17 20		17 26			17 35	17 41				17 50		17 56		18 05	18 11		18 21		18 26		18 35	18 41	
Westerton	d	17 23		17 29			17 38	17 44				17 53		17 59		18 08	18 14		18 24		18 29		18 38	18 44	
Bearsden	d			17 31				17 46						18 01			18 16				18 31			18 46	
Hillfoot	d			17 33				17 48						18 03			18 18				18 33			18 48	
Milngavie	a			17 37				17 52						18 08			18 22				18 37			18 52	
Drumchapel	d	17 25					17 40					17 55				18 10			18 26				18 40		
Drumry	d	17 27					17 42					17 57				18 12			18 28				18 42		
Singer	d	17 30					17 45					18 00				18 15			18 31				18 45		
Dalmuir	a	17 32	17 28		17 41		17 47			17 59		18 04	17 57		18 11	18 17		18 26	18 33	18 30		18 41	18 47		
	d		17 29				17 50						17 58			18 18				18 30			18 48		
Kilpatrick	d						17 52									18 21							18 51		
Bowling	d						17 55									18 24							18 54		
Dumbarton East	d		17 36				18 00						18 05			18 28				18 38			18 58		
Dumbarton Central	d		17 38			17 46	18 03		17 59				18 07			18 30				18 40			19 00		
Dalreoch	d		17 40			17 48	18 04		18 00				18 10			18 32				18 41			19 02		
Renton	d								18 03							18 35							19 05		
Alexandria	d								18 06							18 37							19 07		
Balloch	a								18 08							18 40							19 10		
Cardross	d		17 45			17 53	18 08						18 15							18 46					
Craigendoran	d		17 50			17 58	18 17						18 20							18 51					
Helensburgh Central	a		17 56			18 01	18 20						18 26							18 54					
Helensburgh Upper	a																								

Table 226

Mondays to Fridays

Lanark, Coatbridge, Motherwell, Larkhall, Hamilton, Drumgelloch, Airdrie and Springburn - Glasgow - Milngavie, Dalmuir, Balloch and Helensburgh

		SR	SR	SR ◇	SR	SR	SR	SR	SR	SR	SR	SR	SR	SR	SR	SR	SR	SR	SR	SR	SR	SR	SR	SR	SR
Lanark	d										18 23							18 53				19 23			
Carluke	d										18 33							19 03	19 20			19 33			
Wishaw	d										18 38							19 08	19 26			19 38			
Holytown	d																	19 13							
Shieldmuir	d										18 42											19 42			
Coatbridge Central	d	17 56											18 39												
Whifflet	d	17 58											18 41												
Motherwell	a	18 07									18 44		18 49					19 19	19 32			19 46			
	d	18 10					18 20				18 45		18 49			19 16		19 20	19 32			19 46		19 50	
Bellshill	d	18 16									18 52					19 22						19 52			
Uddingston	d	18 20									18 56					19 26						19 56			
Airbles	d						18 22						18 52					19 22						19 52	
Larkhall	d				18 06				18 37					19 07						19 37					20 07
Merryton	d				18 08				18 39					19 09						19 39					20 09
Chatelherault	d				18 15				18 42					19 12						19 42					20 12
Hamilton Central	d				18 19		18 27		18 45				18 57	19 15				19 27		19 45				19 57	20 15
Hamilton West	d				18 21		18 30		18 48				18 59	19 18				19 30		19 48				20 00	20 18
Blantyre	d				18 25		18 33		18 51				19 03	19 21				19 33		19 51				20 03	20 21
Newton	d						18 37						19 07					19 37						20 07	
Cambuslang	d				18 31		18 41				19 01		19 11			19 31		19 41				20 01		20 11	
Rutherglen	d	18 29			18 34		18 45		18 59		19 04		19 15	19 30		19 34		19 45		20 00		20 05		20 15	20 30
Dalmarnock	d				18 36		18 47				19 06		19 17			19 36		19 47				20 07		20 17	
Bridgeton	d				18 38		18 49				19 08		19 19			19 38		19 49				20 09		20 19	
Drumgelloch	d																								
Airdrie	a																								
	d		18 12			18 27				18 42					19 12						19 42				
Coatdyke	d		18 14			18 29				18 44					19 14						19 44				
Coatbridge Sunnyside	d		18 16			18 31				18 46					19 16						19 46				
Blairhill	d		18 19			18 34				18 49					19 19						19 49				
Easterhouse	d		18 23			18 38				18 53					19 23						19 53				
Garrowhill	d		18 25			18 40				18 55					19 25						19 55				
Shettleston	d		18 28			18 43				18 58					19 28						19 58				
Carntyne	d		18 30			18 45				19 00					19 30						20 00				
Springburn	d							18 49				19 09					19 39						20 09		
Barnhill	d							18 50				19 10					19 40						20 10		
Alexandra Parade	d							18 53				19 13					19 43						20 13		
Duke Street	d							18 54				19 14					19 44						20 14		
Bellgrove	d		18 33			18 48		18 56		19 03		19 16			19 33		19 46				20 03		20 16		
High Street	d		18 35			18 50		18 58		19 05		19 18			19 35		19 48				20 05		20 18		
Glasgow Queen St HL 10 ⇌	d			18 21																					
Glasgow Queen St LL 10 ⇌	a		18 37			18 52		19 01		19 07		19 21			19 37		19 51		19 53		20 07		20 21		
	d		18 40			18 53		19 02		19 10		19 23			19 40		19 53				20 10		20 23		
Charing Cross	d		18 42			18 55		19 04		19 12		19 25			19 42		19 55				20 12		20 25		
Argyle Street	d	18 34			18 42		18 53		19 04		19 12		19 23	19 35		19 42		19 53		20 05		20 13		20 23	20 35
Glasgow Central HL 15	a																								
Glasgow Central LL 15	a	18 37			18 46		18 56		19 07		19 16		19 26	19 37		19 46		19 56		20 07		20 15		20 26	20 37
	d	18 37			18 46		18 58		19 07		19 16		19 28	19 38		19 46		19 58		20 08		20 15		20 28	20 38
Anderston	d	18 39			18 48		18 59		19 09		19 18		19 29	19 39		19 48		19 59		20 09		20 17		20 29	20 39
Exhibition Centre	d	18 41			18 50		19 01		19 11		19 20		19 31	19 41		19 50		20 01		20 11		20 19		20 31	20 41
Partick	d	18 45	18 47		18a53	19 00	19 05	19 09	19 15	19 17	19a23	19 30	19 35	19 45	19 47	19a53	20 00	20 05		20 15	20 17	20a23	20 30	20 35	20 45
Hyndland	d	18 47	18 50			19 02	19 08	19 11	19 17	19 20		19 32	19 38	19 47	19 50		20 02	20 08		20 17	20 20		20 32	20 38	20 47
Jordanhill	d		18 52					19 13		19 22					19 52						20 22				
Scotstounhill	d		18 54					19 15		19 24					19 54						20 24				
Garscadden	d		18 56					19a17		19 26					19 56						20 26				
Yoker	d		18 59							19 29					19 59						20 29				
Clydebank	d		19 01							19 31					20 01						20 31				
Anniesland	d	18 50				19 05	19 11		19 20			19 35	19 41	19 50			20 05	20 11		20 20			20 35	20 41	20 50
Westerton	d	18 53				19 08	19 14		19 23			19 38	19 44	19 53			20 08	20 14		20 23			20 38	20 44	20 53
Bearsden	d						19 16						19 46					20 16						20 46	
Hillfoot	d						19 18						19 48					20 18						20 48	
Milngavie	a						19 22						19 52					20 22						20 52	
Drumchapel	d	18 55				19 10			19 25			19 40		19 55			20 10			20 25			20 40		20 55
Drumry	d	18 57				19 12			19 27			19 42		19 57			20 12			20 27			20 42		20 57
Singer	d	19 00				19 15			19 30			19 45		20 00			20 15			20 30			20 45		21 00
Dalmuir	a	19 02	19 04	18 38		19 17			19 32	19 34		19 47		20 02	20 04		20 17			20 32	20 34		20 47		21 02
	d		19 05	18 40		19 18				19 35		19 48			20 05		20 18				20 35		20 48		
Kilpatrick	d					19 21						19 51					20 21						20 51		
Bowling	d					19 24						19 54					20 24						20 54		
Dumbarton East	d		19 12			19 28				19 42		19 58			20 12		20 28				20 42		20 58		
Dumbarton Central	d		19 14	18 49		19 30				19 44		20 00			20 14		20 30				20 44		21 00		
Dalreoch	d		19 16			19 32				19 46		20 02			20 16		20 32				20 46		21 02		
Renton	d					19 35						20 05					20 35						21 05		
Alexandria	d					19 37						20 07					20 37						21 07		
Balloch	a					19 40						20 10					20 40						21 10		
Cardross	d		19 21							19 51					20 21						20 51				
Craigendoran	d		19 26							19 56					20 26						20 56				
Helensburgh Central	a		19 29							19 59					20 29						20 59				
Helensburgh Upper	a			19 02																					

Table 226

Mondays to Fridays

Lanark, Coatbridge, Motherwell, Larkhall, Hamilton, Drumgelloch, Airdrie and Springburn - Glasgow - Milngavie, Dalmuir, Balloch and Helensburgh

		SR	SR	SR	SR	SR	SR	SR	SR	SR	SR	SR	SR	SR	SR	SR	SR	SR	SR	SR	SR	SR	SR	SR
Lanark	d				19 53				20 23							20 53			21 23					
Carluke	d				20 03				20 33							21 03			21 33					
Wishaw	d				20 08				20 41							21 08			21 38					
Holytown	d				20 13	20 29										21 13								22 29
Shieldmuir	d								20 44										21 43					
Coatbridge Central	d																							
Whifflet	d																							
Motherwell	a				20 19				20 46							21 19			21 46					
	d		20 19		20 20				20 46		20 50			21 16		21 20			21 46		21 50			
Bellshill	d		20 25			20 32			20 52					21 22					21 52					22 32
Uddingston	d		20 29			20 35			20 56					21 26					21 56					22 36
Airbles	d				20 22						20 52					21 22					21 52			
Larkhall	d						20 37					21 07					21 37					22 07		
Merryton	d						20 39					21 09					21 39					22 09		
Chatelherault	d						20 42					21 12					21 42					22 12		
Hamilton Central	d				20 27		20 45				20 57	21 15				21 27	21 45				21 57	22 15		
Hamilton West	d				20 30		20 48				21 00	21 18				21 30	21 48				22 00	22 18		
Blantyre	d				20 33		20 51				21 03	21 21				21 33	21 51				22 03	22 21		
Newton	d				20 37						21 07					21 37					22 07			
Cambuslang	d		20 31		20 41				21 01		21 11			21 31		21 41			22 01		22 11			
Rutherglen	d		20 35		20 46		20 59		21 04		21 15	21 29		21 35		21 45	21 59		22 04		22 15	22 29		
Dalmarnock	d		20 39		20 48				21 06		21 17			21 37		21 47			22 06		22 17			
Bridgeton	d		20 41		20 50				21 08		21 19			21 39		21 49			22 08		22 19			
Drumgelloch	d																							
Airdrie	a																							
	d	20 12						20 42					21 12					21 42					22 12	
Coatdyke	d	20 14						20 44					21 14					21 44					22 14	
Coatbridge Sunnyside	d	20 16						20 46					21 16					21 46					22 16	
Blairhill	d	20 19						20 49					21 19					21 49					22 19	
Easterhouse	d	20 23						20 53					21 23					21 53					22 23	
Garrowhill	d	20 25						20 55					21 25					21 55					22 25	
Shettleston	d	20 28						20 58					21 28					21 58					22 28	
Carntyne	d	20 30						21 00					21 30					22 00					22 30	
Springburn	d			20 39						21 09					21 39					22 09				
Barnhill	d			20 40						21 10					21 40					22 10				
Alexandra Parade	d			20 43						21 13					21 43					22 13				
Duke Street	d			20 44						21 14					21 44					22 14				
Bellgrove	d	20 33		20 46				21 03		21 16			21 33		21 46			22 03		22 16			22 33	
High Street	d	20 35		20 48				21 05		21 18			21 35		21 48			22 05		22 18			22 35	
Glasgow Queen St HL	d																							
Glasgow Queen St LL	a	20 37		20 51		20 55		21 07		21 21			21 37		21 51			22 07		22 21			22 37	
	d	20 40		20 53				21 10		21 23			21 40		21 53			22 10		22 23			22 40	
Charing Cross	d	20 42		20 55				21 12		21 25			21 42		21 55			22 12		22 25			22 42	
Argyle Street	d		20 44		20 54		21 04		21 12		21 23	21 34		21 43		21 53	22 04		22 12		22 23	22 34		
Glasgow Central HL	a																							22 55
Glasgow Central LL	a		20 49		20 56		21 07		21 16		21 26	21 37		21 46		21 56	22 07		22 15		22 26	22 37		
	d		20 49		20 58		21 07		21 16		21 28	21 37		21 46		21 58	22 07		22 16		22 28	22 37		
Anderston	d		20 51		20 59		21 09		21 18		21 29	21 39		21 48		21 59	22 09		22 18		22 29	22 39		
Exhibition Centre	d		20 53		21 01		21 11		21 20		21 31	21 41		21 50		22 01	22 11		22 20		22 31	22 41		
Partick	d	20 47	20a56	21 00	21 05		21 15	21 17	21a23	21 30	21 35	21 45	21 47	21a53	22 00	22 05	22 15	22 17	22a23	22 29	22 35	22 45	22 47	
Hyndland	d	20 50		21 02	21 08		21 17	21 20		21 32	21 38	21 47	21 50		22 02	22 08	22 17	22 20		22 31	22 38	22 47	22 50	
Jordanhill	d	20 52						21 22					21 52					22 22					22 52	
Scotstounhill	d	20 54						21 24					21 54					22 24					22 54	
Garscadden	d	20 56						21 26					21 56					22 26					22 56	
Yoker	d	20 59						21 29					21 59					22 29					22 59	
Clydebank	d	21 01						21 31					22 01					22 31					23 01	
Anniesland	d			21 05	21 11		21 20			21 35	21 41	21 50			22 05	22 11	22 20			22 35	22 41	22 50		
Westerton	d			21 08	21 14		21 23			21 38	21 44	21 53			22 08	22 14	22 23			22 38	22 44	22 53		
Bearsden	d				21 16						21 46					22 16					22 46			
Hillfoot	d				21 18						21 48					22 18					22 48			
Milngavie	a				21 24						21 52					22 22					22 52			
Drumchapel	d			21 10			21 25			21 40		21 55			22 10		22 25			22 40		22 55		
Drumry	d			21 12			21 27			21 42		21 57			22 12		22 27			22 42		22 57		
Singer	d			21 15			21 30			21 45		22 00			22 15		22 30			22 45		23 00		
Dalmuir	a	21 04		21 17			21 32	21 34		21 47		22 02	22 04		22 17		22 32	22 34		22 47		23 02	23 04	
	d	21 05		21 18				21 35		21 48			22 05		22 18			22 35		22 48			23 05	
Kilpatrick	d			21 21						21 51					22 21					22 51				
Bowling	d			21 24						21 54					22 24					22 54				
Dumbarton East	d	21 12		21 28				21 42		21 58			22 12		22 28			22 42		22 58			23 12	
Dumbarton Central	d	21 14		21 30				21 44		22 00			22 14		22 30			22 44		23 00			23 14	
Dalreoch	d	21 16		21 32				21 46		22 02			22 16		22 32			22 46		23 02			23 16	
Renton	d			21 35						22 05					22 35					23 05				
Alexandria	d			21 37						22 07					22 37					23 07				
Balloch	a			21 40						22 10					22 40					23 10				
Cardross	d	21 21						21 51					22 21					22 51					23 21	
Craigendoran	d	21 26						21 56					22 26					22 56					23 26	
Helensburgh Central	a	21 29						21 59					22 29					22 59					23 29	
Helensburgh Upper	a																							

Table 226

Mondays to Fridays

Lanark, Coatbridge, Motherwell, Larkhall, Hamilton, Drumgelloch, Airdrie and Springburn - Glasgow - Milngavie, Dalmuir, Balloch and Helensburgh

		SR	SR	SR	SR	SR	SR	SR	SR	SR	SR	SR FX	SR FO	SR FO	SR FO	
Lanark	d			21 53			22 23									
Carluke	d			22 03			22 33									
Wishaw	d			22 07			22 38									
Holytown	d			22 12												23 57
Shieldmuir	d						22 43									
Coatbridge Central	d															
Whifflet	d															
Motherwell	a			22 19			22 46									
	d	22 16		22 19			22 46		22 53					23 20		
Bellshill	d	22 23					22 53									00 02
Uddingston	d	22 27					22 57									00 06
Airbles	d			22 22					22 55					23 22		
Larkhall	d				22 37					23 07					23 37	
Merryton	d				22 39					23 09					23 39	
Chatelherault	d				22 42					23 12					23 42	
Hamilton Central	d			22 27	22 45				23 00	23 15				23 27	23 45	
Hamilton West	d			22 30	22 48				23 03	23 18				23 30	23 48	
Blantyre	d			22 33	22 51				23 06	23 21				23 33	23 51	
Newton	d			22 37					23 11					23 37		
Cambuslang	d	22 32		22 41			23 02		23 13					23 41		
Rutherglen	d	22 36		22 45	22 59		23 05		23 20	23 29				23 45	23 59	
Dalmarnock	d	22 38		22 47			23 08		23 22					23 47		
Bridgeton	d	22 40		22 49			23 10		23 24					23 49		
Drumgelloch	d															
Airdrie	a															
	d					22 42					23 12					
Coatdyke	d					22 44					23 14					
Coatbridge Sunnyside	d					22 46					23 16					
Blairhill	d					22 49					23 19					
Easterhouse	d					22 53					23 23					
Garrowhill	d					22 55					23 25					
Shettleston	d					22 58					23 28					
Carntyne	d					23 00					23 30					
Springburn	d		22 39					23 09				23 39	23 39			
Barnhill	d		22 40					23 10				23 40	23 40			
Alexandra Parade	d		22 43					23 13				23 43	23 43			
Duke Street	d		22 44					23 14				23 44	23 44			
Bellgrove	d		22 46			23 03		23 16			23 33	23 46	23 46			
High Street	d		22 48			23 05		23 18			23 35	23 48	23 48			
Glasgow Queen St HL	d															
Glasgow Queen St LL	a		22 51			23 07		23 21			23 37	23 51	23 51			
	d		22 53			23 10		23 23			23 45	23 52	23 53			
Charing Cross	d		22 55			23 12		23 25			23 47	23 54	23 55			
Argyle Street	d	22 43		22 53	23 04		23 13		23 27	23 34				23 53	00 04	
Glasgow Central HL	a															00 11
Glasgow Central LL	a	22 48		22 56	23 07		23 18		23 29	23 37				23 56	00 07	
	d	22 48		22 58	23 07		23 18		23 29	23 37				23 58	00 07	
Anderston	d	22 50		22 59	23 09		23 19		23 30	23 39				23 59	00 09	
Exhibition Centre	d	22 52		23 01	23 11		23 20		23 32	23 41				00 01	00 11	
Partick	d	22a55	23 00	23 05	23 15	23 17	23 24	23 30	23 36	23 45	23 52	23 58	23 59	00 05	00 15	
Hyndland	d		23 02	23 08	23 17	23 20	23 26	23 32	23 38	23 47	23 55	00 01	00 02	00 08	00 17	
Jordanhill	d					23 22	23 28			23 49	23 57	00 03				
Scotstounhill	d					23 24	23 30			23 51	23 59	00 05				
Garscadden	d					23 26	23a33			23a53	00 01	00a07				
Yoker	d					23 29					00 04					
Clydebank	d					23 31					00 06					
Anniesland	d		23 05	23 11	23 20			23 35	23 41				00 05	00 11	00 20	
Westerton	d		23 08	23 14	23 23			23 38	23 44				00 08	00 14	00 23	
Bearsden	d			23 16					23 46					00 16		
Hillfoot	d			23 18					23 49					00 18		
Milngavie	a			23 22					23 52					00 22		
Drumchapel	d		23 10		23 25			23 40					00 10		00 25	
Drumry	d		23 12		23 27			23 42					00 12		00 27	
Singer	d		23 15		23 30			23 45					00 15		00 30	
Dalmuir	a		23 17		23 33	23 34		23 47			00 09		00 17		00 32	
	d		23 18			23 35		23 48			00 10		00 18			
Kilpatrick	d		23 21					23 51					00 21			
Bowling	d		23 24					23 54					00 24			
Dumbarton East	d		23 28			23 42		23 58			00 17		00 28			
Dumbarton Central	d		23 30			23 44		23 59			00 19		00 30			
Dalreoch	d		23 32			23 46		00 02			00 21		00 32			
Renton	d		23 35					00 05					00 35			
Alexandria	d		23 37					00 07					00 37			
Balloch	a		23 40					00 10					00 40			
Cardross	d					23 51					00 26					
Craigendoran	d					23 56					00 31					
Helensburgh Central	a					23 59					00 34					
Helensburgh Upper	a															

Table 226

Lanark, Coatbridge, Motherwell, Larkhall, Hamilton, Drumgelloch, Airdrie and Springburn - Glasgow - Milngavie, Dalmuir, Balloch and Helensburgh

		SR	SR	SR B	SR	SR	SR A	SR B	SR	SR	SR	SR	SR	SR	SR	SR	SR	SR	SR	SR
Lanark	d														06 23					
Carluke	d														06 33					
Wishaw	d														06 38					
Holytown	d															07 02				
Shieldmuir	d														06 42					
Coatbridge Central	d																	06 40		
Whifflet	d																	06 42		
Motherwell	a														06 45			06 49		
	d								06 15			06 20			06 45			06 49		
Bellshill	d								06 21						06 51	07 07				
Uddingston	d								06 25						06 55	07 13				
Airbles	d											06 22						06 52		
Larkhall	d					06 07							06 37						07 07	
Merryton	d					06 09							06 39						07 09	
Chatelherault	d					06 12							06 42						07 12	
Hamilton Central	d					06 15						06 27	06 45					06 57	07 15	
Hamilton West	d					06 18						06 30	06 48					06 59	07 18	
Blantyre	d					06 21						06 33	06 51					07 03	07 21	
Newton	d											06 38						07 07		
Cambuslang	d								06 30			06 42			07 00	07 18		07 10		
Rutherglen	d					06 30			06 35			06 45	06 59		07 04			07 17	07 30	
Dalmarnock	d								06 37			06 47			07 06			07 19		
Bridgeton	d								06 39			06 49			07 08			07 21		
Drumgelloch	d																			
Airdrie	a																			
	d		05 31		05 57		06 09	06 12						06 42						07 12
Coatdyke	d		05 33		05 59		06 11	06 14						06 44						07 14
Coatbridge Sunnyside	d		05 35		06 01		06 13	06 16						06 46						07 16
Blairhill	d		05 38		06 04		06 16	06 19						06 49						07 19
Easterhouse	d		05 42		06 08		06 20	06 23						06 53						07 23
Garrowhill	d		05 44		06 10		06 22	06 25						06 55						07 25
Shettleston	d		05 47		06 13		06 25	06 28						06 58						07 28
Carntyne	d		05 49		06 15		06 27	06 30						07 00						07 30
Springburn	d										06 39						07 09			
Barnhill	d										06 40						07 10			
Alexandra Parade	d										06 43						07 13			
Duke Street	d										06 44						07 14			
Bellgrove	d		05 52		06 18		06 30	06 33			06 46			07 03			07 16			07 33
High Street	d		05 54		06 20		06 32	06 35			06 48			07 05			07 18			07 35
Glasgow Queen St HL 10	d	05 30																		
Glasgow Queen St LL 10	a		05 56		06 22		06 34	06 37			06 51			07 07			07 21			07 37
	d		05 57		06 23		06 38	06 40			06 53			07 10			07 23			07 40
Charing Cross	d		06 00		06 25		06 40	06 42			06 55			07 12			07 25			07 42
Argyle Street	d					06 34			06 43			06 53	07 04		07 12			07 26	07 35	
Glasgow Central HL 15	a															07 31				
Glasgow Central LL 15	a					06 37			06 45			06 57	07 07		07 14			07 28	07 37	
	d					06 37			06 46			06 58	07 07		07 16			07 29	07 38	
Anderston	d					06 39			06 48			06 59	07 09		07 17			07 30	07 39	
Exhibition Centre	d					06 41			06 50			07 01	07 11		07 19			07 32	07 41	
Partick	d		06 04		06 30	06 45	06 44	06 47	06 54		07 00	07 05	07 15	07 17	07 23		07 30	07 36	07 45	07 47
Hyndland	d		06 06		06 32	06 47	06 47	06 50	06 56		07 02	07 08	07 17	07 20	07 25		07 32	07 38	07 47	07 50
Jordanhill	d		06 08						06 58						07 27					
Scotstounhill	d		06 11						07 00						07 30					
Garscadden	d		06 13				06 51	06 54	07 02						07 32					
Yoker	d		06 15						07 05						07 34					
Clydebank	d		06 17						07 07						07 37					
Anniesland	d				06 35	06 50					07 05	07 11	07 20				07 35	07 41	07 50	
Westerton	d	05a43		05 56	06 38	06 53					07 08	07 14	07 23				07 38	07 44	07 53	
Bearsden	d											07 16						07 46		
Hillfoot	d											07 18						07 48		
Milngavie	a											07 23						07 52		
Drumchapel	d				06 40	06 55					07 10		07 25				07 40		07 55	
Drumry	d				06 42	06 57					07 12		07 27				07 42		07 57	
Singer	d				06 45	07 00					07 15		07 30				07 45		08 00	
Dalmuir	a		06 21	06 03	06 47	07 02	06 55	06 58	07 11		07 17		07 32	07 28	07 42		07 47		08 02	07 59
	d		06 21	06 04	06 48		06 56	06 59		06 32	07 18			07 29			07 48			07 59
Kilpatrick	d				06 51					06 34	07 21						07 51			
Bowling	d				06 54					06 37	07 24						07 54			
Dumbarton East	d		06 29		06 58		07 03	07 06		06 42	07 28			07 36			07 58			08 06
Dumbarton Central	d		06 30		07 00		07 05	07 08		06 44	07 30			07 38			08 00			08 08
Dalreoch	d		06 32		07 02		07 07	07 10		06 46	07 32			07 40			08 02			08 10
Renton	d		06 35		07 05						07 35						08 05			
Alexandria	d		06 37		07 07						07 37						08 07			
Balloch	a		06 40		07 10						07 40						08 10			
Cardross	d						07 12	07 15		06 51				07 45						08 15
Craigendoran	d						07 17	07 20		06 56				07 50						08 20
Helensburgh Central	a						07 20	07 23		06 59				07 53						08 23
Helensburgh Upper	a			06 26																

A from 25 September

B until 18 September

Table 226

Lanark, Coatbridge, Motherwell, Larkhall, Hamilton, Drumgelloch, Airdrie and Springburn - Glasgow - Milngavie, Dalmuir, Balloch and Helensburgh

		SR	SR	SR	SR	SR	SR	SR	SR	SR	SR	SR	SR ◇	SR	SR	SR	SR	SR	SR	SR	SR	SR	SR	SR	SR
Lanark	d						07 23									07 53			08 23						
Carluke	d						07 33									08 03			08 33						
Wishaw	d						07 38									08 08			08 38						
Holytown	d							07 58								08 13									09 29
Shieldmuir	d						07 42												08 42						
Coatbridge Central	d																								
Whifflet	d																								
Motherwell	a						07 45									08 19			08 46						
	d	07 16		07 19			07 46			07 50				08 16		08 20			08 46		08 50				
Bellshill	d	07 22					07 52	08 02						08 23					08 52						09 32
Uddingston	d	07 26					07 56	08 09						08 27					08 56						09 36
Airbles	d			07 21						07 52						08 22					08 52				
Larkhall	d				07 37						08 06						08 37						09 07		
Merryton	d				07 39						08 08						08 39						09 09		
Chatelherault	d				07 42						08 11						08 42						09 12		
Hamilton Central	d			07 27	07 45					07 58	08 15					08 27	08 45				08 57		09 15		
Hamilton West	d			07 30	07 48					08 00	08 17					08 30	08 48				09 00		09 18		
Blantyre	d			07 33	07 51					08 04	08 21					08 33	08 51				09 03		09 21		
Newton	d			07 37						08 08						08 37					09 07				09 43
Cambuslang	d	07 30		07 40			08 01			08 12				08 32		08 41			09 01		09 11				
Rutherglen	d	07 34		07 45	08 00		08 04			08 16	08 29			08 35		08 47	09 00		09 05		09 16		09 29		
Dalmarnock	d	07 36		07 47			08 06			08 18				08 37		08 49			09 06		09 18				
Bridgeton	d	07 38		07 49			08 08			08 20				08 39		08 51			09 08		09 20				
Drumgelloch	d																								
Airdrie	a																								
	d					07 42						08 12						08 42						09 12	
Coatdyke	d					07 44						08 14						08 44						09 14	
Coatbridge Sunnyside	d					07 46						08 16						08 46						09 16	
Blairhill	d					07 49						08 19						08 49						09 19	
Easterhouse	d					07 53						08 23						08 53						09 23	
Garrowhill	d					07 55						08 25						08 55						09 25	
Shettleston	d					07 58						08 28						08 58						09 28	
Carntyne	d					08 00						08 30						09 00						09 30	
Springburn	d		07 39						08 09						08 39					09 09		09 19			
Barnhill	d		07 40						08 10						08 40					09 10		09 20			
Alexandra Parade	d		07 43						08 13						08 43					09 13		09 23			
Duke Street	d		07 44						08 14						08 44					09 14		09 24			
Bellgrove	d		07 46			08 03			08 16			08 33			08 46			09 03		09 16		09 26		09 33	
High Street	d		07 48			08 05			08 18			08 35			08 48			09 05		09 18		09 28		09 35	
Glasgow Queen St HL 10	d												08 21												
Glasgow Queen St LL 10	a		07 51			08 07			08 21			08 37			08 51			09 07		09 21		09 31		09 37	
	d		07 53			08 10			08 23			08 40			08 53			09 10		09 23		09 32		09 40	
Charing Cross	d		07 55			08 12			08 25			08 42			08 55			09 12		09 25		09 34		09 42	
Argyle Street	d	07 42		07 53	08 05		08 12			08 24	08 34			08 43		08 56	09 05		09 13		09 24		09 34		
Glasgow Central HL 15	a							08 24																	09 55
Glasgow Central LL 15	a	07 44		07 56	08 07		08 16			08 27	08 37			08 46		08 58	09 07		09 16		09 26		09 37		
	d	07 44		07 58	08 07		08 16			08 28	08 37			08 47		08 59	09 07		09 16		09 28		09 37		
Anderston	d	07 47		07 59	08 09		08 18			08 29	08 39			08 48		09 01	09 09		09 18		09 29		09 39		
Exhibition Centre	d	07 49		08 01	08 11		08 20			08 31	08 41			08 50		09 03	09 11		09 20		09 31		09 41		
Partick	d	07 54	08 00	08 05	08 15	08 17	08 24		08 30	08 35	08 45	08 47		08 54	09 00	09 06	09 15	09 17	09 24	09 30	09 35	09 39	09 45	09 47	
Hyndland	d	07 55	08 02	08 08	08 17	08 20	08 26		08 32	08 38	08 47	08 50		08 56	09 02	09 08	09 17	09 20	09 26	09 32	09 38	09 41	09 47	09 50	
Jordanhill	d	07 57					08 28							08 58					09 28			09 43			
Scotstounhill	d	07 59					08 30							09 00					09 30			09 45			
Garscadden	d	08 01					08 32							09 02					09 32			09 47			
Yoker	d	08 04					08 35							09 05					09 35			09 50			
Clydebank	d	08 06					08 37							09 07					09 37			09 52			
Anniesland	d		08 05	08 11	08 20				08 35	08 41	08 50				09 05	09 11	09 20			09 35	09 41		09 50		
Westerton	d		08 08	08 14	08 23				08 38	08 44	08 53				09 08	09 14	09 23			09 38	09 44		09 53		
Bearsden	d			08 16						08 46						09 17					09 46				
Hillfoot	d			08 18						08 48						09 18					09 48				
Milngavie	a			08 22						08 52						09 22					09 52				
Drumchapel	d		08 10		08 25				08 40		08 55				09 10		09 25			09 41			09 55		
Drumry	d		08 12		08 27				08 42		08 57				09 12		09 27			09 43			09 57		
Singer	d		08 15		08 30				08 45		09 00				09 15		09 30			09 45			10 00		
Dalmuir	a	08 11	08 17		08 32	08 29	08 41		08 47		09 02	08 57	08 39	09 12	09 17		09 32	09 29	09 41	09 48		09 56	10 02	09 59	
	d		08 18			08 29			08 48			08 59	08 42		09 18			09 29		09 49				09 59	
Kilpatrick	d		08 21						08 51						09 21					09 51					
Bowling	d		08 24						08 54						09 24					09 54					
Dumbarton East	d		08 28			08 37			08 58			09 06			09 28			09 36		09 59				10 07	
Dumbarton Central	d		08 30			08 38			09 00			09 08	08 51		09 30			09 38		10 00				10 08	
Dalreoch	d		08 32			08 40			09 02			09 10			09 32			09 40		10 02				10 10	
Renton	d		08 35						09 05						09 35					10 05					
Alexandria	d		08 37						09 07						09 37					10 07					
Balloch	a		08 40						09 10						09 40					10 10					
Cardross	d					08 45						09 15						09 45						10 15	
Craigendoran	d					08 50						09 20						09 50						10 20	
Helensburgh Central	a					08 55						09 25						09 55						10 23	
Helensburgh Upper	a												09 03												

Table 226

Saturdays

Lanark, Coatbridge, Motherwell, Larkhall, Hamilton, Drumgelloch, Airdrie and Springburn - Glasgow - Milngavie, Dalmuir, Balloch and Helensburgh

		SR	SR	SR	SR	SR	SR	SR	SR	SR	SR	SR	SR	SR	SR	SR	SR	SR	SR	SR	SR	SR	SR	SR	SR
																	◇ A ⊼								
Lanark	d				08 53					09 23											09 53				
Carluke	d				09 03					09 33											10 02				
Wishaw	d				09 08					09 38											10 07				
Holytown	d				09 13										10 29						10 12				
Shieldmuir	d									09 42															
Coatbridge Central	d																								
Whifflet	d																								
Motherwell	a				09 20					09 46											10 19				
	d		09 16		09 20					09 47		09 50							10 16		10 20				
Bellshill	d		09 22							09 53					10 32				10 22						
Uddingston	d		09 26							09 57					10 36				10 26						
Airbles	d				09 22							09 52									10 21				
Larkhall	d						09 37							10 07									10 36		
Merryton	d						09 39							10 09									10 38		
Chatelherault	d						09 42							10 12									10 41		
Hamilton Central	d				09 27		09 45					09 57		10 15							10 26		10 44		
Hamilton West	d				09 30		09 48					10 00		10 18							10 30		10 47		
Blantyre	d				09 33		09 51					10 03		10 21							10 32		10 50		
Newton	d				09 37							10 07		10 26							10 36		10 54		
Cambuslang	d		09 31		09 42					10 02		10 11							10 31		10 41				
Rutherglen	d		09 34		09 48		09 59			10 06		10 16		10 30					10 34		10 45		10 59		
Dalmarnock	d		09 36		09 50					10 08		10 18							10 36		10 47				
Bridgeton	d		09 38		09 52					10 10		10 20							10 38		10 49				
Drumgelloch	d																								
Airdrie	a																								
	d			09 27				09 43			09 57					10 12				10 27				10 42	
Coatdyke	d			09 29				09 45			09 59					10 14				10 29				10 44	
Coatbridge Sunnyside	d			09 31				09 47			10 01					10 16				10 31				10 46	
Blairhill	d			09 34				09 50			10 04					10 19				10 34				10 49	
Easterhouse	d			09 38				09 54			10 08					10 23				10 38				10 53	
Garrowhill	d			09 40				09 56			10 10					10 25				10 40				10 55	
Shettleston	d			09 43				09 59			10 13					10 28				10 43				10 58	
Carntyne	d			09 45				10 01			10 15					10 30				10 45				11 00	
Springburn	d					09 49							10 19									10 49			
Barnhill	d					09 50							10 20									10 50			
Alexandra Parade	d					09 53							10 23									10 53			
Duke Street	d					09 54							10 24									10 54			
Bellgrove	d	09 38		09 48		09 56		10 04	10 08		10 18		10 26			10 33		10 39		10 48		10 56		11 03	11 08
High Street	d	09 40		09 50		09 58		10 06	10 10		10 20		10 28			10 35		10 41		10 50		10 58		11 05	11 10
Glasgow Queen St HL 10 ⇌	d																10 37								
Glasgow Queen St LL 10 ⇌	a	09 42		09 52		10 01		10 09	10 12		10 22		10 31			10 37		10 43		10 52		11 01		11 07	11 12
	d	09 43		09 53		10 02		10 10	10 13		10 23		10 32			10 40		10 44		10 53		11 02		11 10	11 13
Charing Cross	d	09 45		09 55		10 04		10 12	10 15		10 25		10 34			10 42		10 46		10 55		11 04		11 12	11 15
Argyle Street	d		09 42		09 56		10 04			10 15		10 24		10 35					10 42		10 53		11 04		
Glasgow Central HL 15	a														10 55										
Glasgow Central LL 15	a		09 46		09 58		10 07			10 17		10 26		10 37					10 46		10 56		11 07		
	d		09 46		09 59		10 07			10 18		10 28		10 38					10 46		10 58		11 07		
Anderston	d		09 48		10 01		10 09			10 19		10 29		10 39					10 48		10 59		11 09		
Exhibition Centre	d		09 50		10 03		10 11			10 21		10 31		10 41					10 50		11 01		11 11		
Partick	d	09 50	09 54	10 00	10 06	10 09	10 15	10 17	10 20	10 25	10 30	10 35	10 39	10 45		10 47		10 50	10 54	11 00	11 05	11 09	11 15	11 17	11 20
Hyndland	d	09 53	09 56	10 02	10 08	10 11	10 17	10 19	10 23	10 27	10 32	10 38	10 41	10 47		10 50		10 53	10 56	11 02	11 08	11 11	11 17	11 20	11 23
Jordanhill	d		09 58			10 13				10 29			10 43						10 58			11 13			
Scotstounhill	d		10 00			10 15				10 31			10 45						11 00			11 15			
Garscadden	d		10 02			10 17				10 32			10 47						11 02			11 17			
Yoker	d		10 05			10 20				10 35			10 50						11 05			11 20			
Clydebank	d		10 07			10 22				10 37			10 52						11 07			11 22			
Anniesland	d	09 56		10 05	10 11		10 20		10 26		10 35	10 41		10 50				10 56		11 05	11 11		11 20		11 26
Westerton	d	09 59		10 08	10 14		10 23		10 29		10 38	10 44		10 53				10 59		11 08	11 14		11 23		11 29
Bearsden	d	10 01			10 17				10 31			10 46						11 01			11 16				11 31
Hillfoot	d	10 03			10 18				10 33			10 48						11 03			11 18				11 33
Milngavie	a	10 07			10 22				10 37			10 52						11 07			11 24				11 37
Drumchapel	d			10 10			10 25				10 40			10 55						11 10			11 25		
Drumry	d			10 12			10 27				10 42			10 57						11 12			11 27		
Singer	d			10 15			10 30				10 45			11 00						11 15			11 30		
Dalmuir	a		10 11	10 17		10 26	10 32	10 29		10 41	10 47		10 56	11 02		10 59	10 53		11 11	11 17		11 26	11 32	11 29	
	d			10 18				10 29			10 48					10 59	10 53			11 18				11 29	
Kilpatrick	d			10 21							10 51									11 21					
Bowling	d			10 24							10 54									11 24					
Dumbarton East	d			10 28				10 39			10 58					11 06				11 28				11 37	
Dumbarton Central	d			10 30				10 41			11 00					11 08	11 04			11 30				11 39	
Dalreoch	d			10 32				10 43			11 02					11 10				11 32				11 40	
Renton	d			10 35							11 05									11 35					
Alexandria	d			10 37							11 07									11 37					
Balloch	a			10 40							11 10									11 40					
Cardross	d							10 48								11 15								11 45	
Craigendoran	d							10 52								11 20								11 50	
Helensburgh Central	a							10 56								11 25								11 53	
Helensburgh Upper	a																11 20								

A until 30 October

Table 226

Saturdays

Lanark, Coatbridge, Motherwell, Larkhall, Hamilton, Drumgelloch, Airdrie and Springburn - Glasgow - Milngavie, Dalmuir, Balloch and Helensburgh

		SR	SR	SR	SR	SR	SR	SR	SR	SR	SR	SR	SR	SR	SR	SR	SR	SR	SR	SR	SR	SR	SR	SR	SR
																						◇ ⊼			
Lanark	d	10 21									10 53					11 21									
Carluke	d	10 31									11 03					11 31									
Wishaw	d	10 39									11 08					11 38									
Holytown	d										11 13												12 29		
Shieldmuir	d	10 42														11 42									
Coatbridge Central	d																								
Whifflet	d																								
Motherwell	a	10 46									11 19					11 46									
	d	10 47		10 50					11 16		11 20					11 46		11 50							12 16
Bellshill	d	10 53							11 22							11 53							12 32		12 22
Uddingston	d	10 57							11 26							11 57							12 38		12 26
Airbles	d			10 52							11 22							11 52							
Larkhall	d					11 07							11 37							12 07					
Merryton	d					11 09							11 39							12 09					
Chatelherault	d					11 12							11 42							12 12					
Hamilton Central	d			10 57		11 15					11 27		11 45					11 57		12 15					
Hamilton West	d			11 00		11 18					11 30		11 48					12 00		12 18					
Blantyre	d			11 03		11 21					11 33		11 51					12 03		12 21					
Newton	d			11 07							11 37							12 07							
Cambuslang	d	11 02		11 11					11 31		11 41					12 02		12 11							12 31
Rutherglen	d	11 05		11 17		11 29			11 34		11 45		11 59			12 07		12 16		12 29					12 34
Dalmarnock	d	11 07		11 19					11 36		11 47					12 09		12 18							12 36
Bridgeton	d	11 09		11 21					11 38		11 49					12 11		12 20							12 38
Drumgelloch	d																								
Airdrie	a																								
	d		10 57				11 12			11 27				11 42			11 57				12 12				
Coatdyke	d		10 59				11 14			11 29				11 44			11 59				12 14				
Coatbridge Sunnyside	d		11 01				11 16			11 31				11 46			12 01				12 16				
Blairhill	d		11 04				11 19			11 34				11 49			12 04				12 19				
Easterhouse	d		11 08				11 23			11 38				11 53			12 08				12 23				
Garrowhill	d		11 10				11 25			11 40				11 55			12 10				12 25				
Shettleston	d		11 13				11 28			11 43				11 58			12 13				12 28				
Carntyne	d		11 15				11 30			11 45				12 00			12 15				12 30				
Springburn	d				11 19							11 49							12 19						
Barnhill	d				11 20							11 50							12 20						
Alexandra Parade	d				11 23							11 53							12 23						
Duke Street	d				11 24							11 54							12 24						
Bellgrove	d		11 18		11 26		11 33	11 38		11 48		11 56		12 03	12 08		12 18		12 26		12 33			12 38	
High Street	d		11 20		11 28		11 35	11 40		11 50		11 58		12 05	12 10		12 20		12 28		12 35			12 40	
Glasgow Queen St HL 10 ⇌	d																					12 21			
Glasgow Queen St LL 10 ⇌	a		11 22		11 31		11 37	11 42		11 52		12 01		12 07	12 12		12 22		12 31		12 37			12 42	
	d		11 23		11 32		11 40	11 43		11 53		12 02		12 10	12 13		12 23		12 32		12 40			12 43	
Charing Cross	d		11 25		11 34		11 42	11 45		11 55		12 04		12 12	12 15		12 25		12 34		12 42			12 45	
Argyle Street	d	11 13		11 25		11 34			11 42		11 53		12 04			12 14		12 24		12 34					12 42
Glasgow Central HL 15	a																						12 55		
Glasgow Central LL 15	a	11 18		11 26		11 37			11 46		11 56		12 07			12 19		12 26		12 37					12 46
	d	11 18		11 28		11 37			11 46		11 58		12 07			12 19		12 28		12 37					12 46
Anderston	d	11 20		11 29		11 39			11 48		11 59		12 09			12 21		12 29		12 39					12 48
Exhibition Centre	d	11 22		11 31		11 41			11 50		12 01		12 11			12 23		12 31		12 41					12 50
Partick	d	11 25	11 30	11 35	11 39	11 45	11 47	11 50	11 54	12 00	12 05	12 09	12 15	12 17	12 20	12 26	12 30	12 35	12 39	12 45	12 47			12 50	12 54
Hyndland	d	11 27	11 32	11 38	11 41	11 47	11 50	11 53	11 56	12 02	12 08	12 11	12 17	12 20	12 23	12 28	12 32	12 38	12 41	12 47	12 50			12 53	12 56
Jordanhill	d	11 29			11 43				11 58			12 13				12 30			12 43						12 58
Scotstounhill	d	11 32			11 45				12 00			12 15				12 33			12 45						13 00
Garscadden	d	11 35			11 47				12 02			12 17				12 35			12 47						13 02
Yoker	d	11 37			11 50				12 05			12 20				12 37			12 50						13 05
Clydebank	d	11 39			11 52				12 07			12 22				12 39			12 52						13 07
Anniesland	d		11 35	11 41		11 50		11 56		12 05	12 11		12 20		12 26		12 35	12 41		12 50				12 56	
Westerton	d		11 38	11 44		11 53		11 59		12 08	12 14		12 23		12 29		12 38	12 44		12 53				12 59	
Bearsden	d			11 46				12 01			12 16				12 31			12 46						13 01	
Hillfoot	d			11 48				12 03			12 18				12 33			12 48						13 03	
Milngavie	a			11 52				12 07			12 22				12 37			12 52						13 07	
Drumchapel	d		11 40			11 55				12 10			12 25				12 40			12 55					
Drumry	d		11 42			11 57				12 12			12 27				12 42			12 57					
Singer	d		11 45			12 00				12 15			12 30				12 45			13 00					
Dalmuir	a	11 42	11 47		11 56	12 02	11 59		12 11	12 17		12 26	12 32	12 29		12 42	12 47		12 56	13 02	12 59	12 38			13 11
	d		11 48				11 59			12 18				12 29			12 48				12 59	12 42			
Kilpatrick	d		11 51							12 21							12 51								
Bowling	d		11 54							12 24							12 54								
Dumbarton East	d		11 58				12 07			12 28				12 37			12 58				13 06				
Dumbarton Central	d		12 00				12 08			12 30				12 38			13 00				13 08	12 51			
Dalreoch	d		12 02				12 10			12 32				12 40			13 02				13 10				
Renton	d		12 05							12 35							13 05								
Alexandria	d		12 07							12 37							13 07								
Balloch	a		12 10							12 40							13 10								
Cardross	d						12 15							12 45							13 15				
Craigendoran	d						12 20							12 50							13 20				
Helensburgh Central	a						12 23							12 53							13 26				
Helensburgh Upper	a																					13 03			

Table 226

Lanark, Coatbridge, Motherwell, Larkhall, Hamilton, Drumgelloch, Airdrie and Springburn - Glasgow - Milngavie, Dalmuir, Balloch and Helensburgh

		SR	SR	SR	SR	SR	SR	SR	SR	SR	SR	SR	SR	SR	SR	SR	SR	SR	SR	SR	SR	SR	SR	SR	SR
Lanark	d		11 53					12 23										12 53					13 23		
Carluke	d		12 03					12 33										13 03					13 33		
Wishaw	d		12 08					12 39										13 08					13 39		
Holytown	d		12 13											13 28				13 13							
Shieldmuir	d							12 42															13 42		
Coatbridge Central	d																								
Whifflet	d																								
Motherwell	a		12 20					12 46										13 19					13 46		
	d		12 20					12 47		12 50						13 16		13 20					13 47		13 50
Bellshill	d							12 53						13 32		13 22							13 53		
Uddingston	d							12 57						13 36		13 26							13 57		
Airbles	d		12 22							12 52								13 22							13 52
Larkhall	d				12 37							13 07								13 37					
Merryton	d				12 39							13 09								13 39					
Chatelherault	d				12 42							13 12								13 42					
Hamilton Central	d		12 27		12 45					12 57		13 15						13 27		13 45					13 57
Hamilton West	d		12 30		12 48					13 00		13 18						13 30		13 48					14 00
Blantyre	d		12 33		12 51					13 03		13 21						13 33		13 51					14 03
Newton	d		12 37							13 07								13 37							14 07
Cambuslang	d		12 41					13 02		13 11						13 31		13 41					14 02		14 11
Rutherglen	d		12 45		12 59			13 07		13 16		13 29				13 34		13 45		13 59			14 07		14 17
Dalmarnock	d		12 47					13 09		13 18						13 36		13 47					14 09		14 19
Bridgeton	d		12 49					13 11		13 20						13 38		13 49					14 11		14 21
Drumgelloch	d																								
Airdrie	a																								
	d	12 27				12 42			12 57				13 12				13 27				13 42			13 57	
Coatdyke	d	12 29				12 44			12 59				13 14				13 29				13 44			13 59	
Coatbridge Sunnyside	d	12 31				12 46			13 01				13 16				13 31				13 46			14 01	
Blairhill	d	12 34				12 49			13 04				13 19				13 34				13 49			14 04	
Easterhouse	d	12 38				12 53			13 08				13 23				13 38				13 53			14 08	
Garrowhill	d	12 40				12 55			13 10				13 25				13 40				13 55			14 10	
Shettleston	d	12 43				12 58			13 13				13 28				13 43				13 58			14 13	
Carntyne	d	12 45				13 00			13 15				13 30				13 45				14 00			14 15	
Springburn	d			12 49							13 19								13 49						
Barnhill	d			12 50							13 20								13 50						
Alexandra Parade	d			12 53							13 23								13 53						
Duke Street	d			12 54							13 24								13 54						
Bellgrove	d	12 48		12 56		13 03	13 08		13 18		13 26		13 33		13 38		13 48		13 56		14 03	14 08		14 18	
High Street	d	12 50		12 58		13 05	13 10		13 20		13 28		13 35		13 40		13 50		13 58		14 05	14 10		14 20	
Glasgow Queen St HL 10	d																								
Glasgow Queen St LL 10	a	12 52		13 01		13 08	13 12		13 22		13 31		13 37		13 42		13 52		14 01		14 07	14 12		14 22	
	d	12 53		13 02		13 10	13 13		13 23		13 32		13 40		13 43		13 53		14 02		14 10	14 14		14 23	
Charing Cross	d	12 55		13 04		13 12	13 15		13 25		13 34		13 42		13 45		13 55		14 04		14 12	14 15		14 25	
Argyle Street	d		12 53		13 04			13 15		13 23		13 34				13 42		13 53		14 04			14 15		14 25
Glasgow Central HL 15	a													13 55											
Glasgow Central LL 15	a		12 56		13 07			13 19		13 26		13 37				13 46		13 56		14 07			14 19		14 26
	d		12 58		13 07			13 20		13 28		13 37				13 46		13 58		14 07			14 19		14 28
Anderston	d		12 59		13 09			13 21		13 29		13 39				13 48		13 59		14 09			14 21		14 29
Exhibition Centre	d		13 01		13 11			13 23		13 31		13 41				13 50		14 01		14 11			14 23		14 31
Partick	d	13 00	13 05	13 09	13 15	13 17	13 20	13 27	13 30	13 35	13 39	13 45	13 47		13 50	13 54	14 00	14 05	14 09	14 15	14 17	14 20	14 26	14 29	14 35
Hyndland	d	13 02	13 08	13 11	13 17	13 20	13 23	13 29	13 32	13 38	13 41	13 47	13 50		13 53	13 56	14 02	14 08	14 11	14 17	14 20	14 23	14 28	14 31	14 38
Jordanhill	d			13 13				13 31			13 43					13 58			14 13				14 30		
Scotstounhill	d			13 15				13 33			13 45					14 00			14 15				14 33		
Garscadden	d			13 17				13 36			13 47					14 02			14 17				14 36		
Yoker	d			13 20				13 38			13 50					14 05			14 20				14 38		
Clydebank	d			13 22				13 40			13 52					14 07			14 22				14 40		
Anniesland	d	13 05	13 11		13 20		13 26		13 35	13 41		13 50			13 56		14 05	14 11		14 20		14 26		14 34	14 41
Westerton	d	13 08	13 14		13 23		13 29		13 38	13 44		13 53			13 59		14 08	14 14		14 23		14 29		14 38	14 44
Bearsden	d		13 16				13 31			13 46					14 01			14 16				14 32			14 46
Hillfoot	d		13 18				13 33			13 48					14 03			14 18				14 33			14 48
Milngavie	a		13 22				13 37			13 52					14 07			14 22				14 37			14 52
Drumchapel	d	13 10			13 25				13 40			13 55					14 10			14 25				14 40	
Drumry	d	13 12			13 27				13 42			13 57					14 12			14 27				14 42	
Singer	d	13 15			13 30				13 45			14 00					14 15			14 30				14 45	
Dalmuir	a	13 17		13 26	13 32	13 29		13 43	13 47		13 56	14 02	13 59			14 11	14 17		14 26	14 32	14 29		14 43	14 47	
	d	13 18				13 29			13 48				13 59				14 19				14 29			14 48	
Kilpatrick	d	13 21							13 51								14 22							14 51	
Bowling	d	13 24							13 54								14 25							14 54	
Dumbarton East	d	13 28				13 36			13 58				14 07				14 29				14 36			14 58	
Dumbarton Central	d	13 30				13 38			14 00				14 09				14 31				14 38			15 00	
Dalreoch	d	13 32				13 40			14 02				14 10				14 33				14 40			15 02	
Renton	d	13 35							14 05								14 36							15 05	
Alexandria	d	13 37							14 07								14 38							15 07	
Balloch	a	13 40							14 10								14 41							15 10	
Cardross	d					13 45							14 15								14 45				
Craigendoran	d					13 50							14 20								14 50				
Helensburgh Central	a					13 53							14 23								14 54				
Helensburgh Upper	a																								

Table 226

Lanark, Coatbridge, Motherwell, Larkhall, Hamilton, Drumgelloch, Airdrie and Springburn - Glasgow - Milngavie, Dalmuir, Balloch and Helensburgh

		SR	SR	SR	SR	SR	SR	SR	SR	SR	SR	SR	SR	SR	SR	SR	SR	SR	SR	SR	SR	SR	SR	SR	SR
Lanark	d							13 53					14 23									14 53			
Carluke	d							14 03					14 33									15 03			
Wishaw	d							14 08					14 39									15 08			
Holytown	d							14 13														15 13			
Shieldmuir	d												14 42												
Coatbridge Central	d																								
Whifflet	d																								
Motherwell	a							14 20					14 46									15 19			
	d					14 16		14 20					14 47		14 50					15 16		15 20			
Bellshill	d					14 22							14 53							15 22					
Uddingston	d					14 26							14 57							15 26					
Airbles	d							14 22							14 52							15 22			
Larkhall	d		14 07							14 37							15 07							15 37	
Merryton	d		14 09							14 39							15 09							15 39	
Chatelherault	d		14 12							14 42							15 12							15 42	
Hamilton Central	d		14 15					14 27		14 45					14 58		15 15					15 27		15 45	
Hamilton West	d		14 18					14 30		14 48					15 00		15 18					15 30		15 48	
Blantyre	d		14 21					14 33		14 51					15 04		15 21					15 33		15 51	
Newton	d							14 37							15 07							15 37			
Cambuslang	d					14 31		14 41					15 02		15 11					15 31		15 41			
Rutherglen	d		14 29			14 35		14 45		14 59			15 05		15 16		15 30			15 34		15 45		15 59	
Dalmarnock	d					14 37		14 47					15 07		15 18					15 36		15 47			
Bridgeton	d					14 39		14 49					15 09		15 20					15 38		15 49			
Drumgelloch	d																								
Airdrie	a																								
	d			14 12			14 27				14 42			14 57				15 12			15 27				15 42
Coatdyke	d			14 14			14 29				14 44			14 59				15 14			15 29				15 44
Coatbridge Sunnyside	d			14 16			14 31				14 46			15 01				15 16			15 31				15 46
Blairhill	d			14 19			14 34				14 49			15 04				15 19			15 34				15 49
Easterhouse	d			14 23			14 38				14 53			15 08				15 23			15 38				15 53
Garrowhill	d			14 25			14 40				14 55			15 10				15 25			15 40				15 55
Shettleston	d			14 28			14 43				14 58			15 13				15 28			15 43				15 58
Carntyne	d			14 30			14 45				15 00			15 15				15 30			15 45				16 00
Springburn	d	14 19							14 49							15 19							15 49		
Barnhill	d	14 20							14 50							15 20							15 50		
Alexandra Parade	d	14 23							14 53							15 23							15 53		
Duke Street	d	14 24							14 54							15 24							15 54		
Bellgrove	d	14 26		14 33	14 38		14 48		14 56		15 03	15 08		15 18		15 26		15 33	15 38		15 48		15 56		16 03
High Street	d	14 28		14 35	14 40		14 50		14 58		15 05	15 10		15 20		15 28		15 35	15 40		15 50		15 58		16 05
Glasgow Queen St HL 10	d																								
Glasgow Queen St LL 10	a	14 31		14 37	14 42		14 52		15 01		15 07	15 12		15 22		15 31		15 37	15 42		15 52		16 02		16 07
	d	14 32		14 40	14 43		14 53		15 02		15 10	15 13		15 23		15 32		15 40	15 43		15 53		16 02		16 10
Charing Cross	d	14 34		14 42	14 45		14 55		15 04		15 12	15 15		15 25		15 34		15 42	15 45		15 55		16 04		16 12
Argyle Street	d		14 34			14 43		14 53		15 04			15 14		15 24		15 34			15 42		15 53		16 04	
Glasgow Central HL 15	a																								
Glasgow Central LL 15	a		14 37			14 46		14 56		15 07			15 18		15 26		15 37			15 46		15 56		16 07	
	d		14 37			14 46		14 58		15 07			15 18		15 28		15 37			15 46		15 58		16 07	
Anderston	d		14 39			14 48		14 59		15 09			15 20		15 29		15 39			15 48		15 59		16 09	
Exhibition Centre	d		14 41			14 50		15 01		15 11			15 22		15 31		15 41			15 50		16 01		16 11	
Partick	d	14 39	14 45	14 47	14 50	14 54	15 00	15 05	15 09	15 15	15 17	15 20	15 25	15 30	15 35	15 39	15 45	15 47	15 50	15 54	16 00	16 05	16 09	16 15	16 17
Hyndland	d	14 41	14 47	14 50	14 53	14 56	15 02	15 08	15 11	15 17	15 20	15 23	15 27	15 32	15 38	15 41	15 47	15 50	15 53	15 56	16 02	16 08	16 11	16 17	16 20
Jordanhill	d	14 43				14 58			15 13				15 29			15 43				15 58			16 13		
Scotstounhill	d	14 45				15 00			15 15				15 32			15 45				16 00			16 15		
Garscadden	d	14 47				15 02			15 17				15 35			15 47				16 02			16 17		
Yoker	d	14 50				15 05			15 20				15 37			15 50				16 05			16 20		
Clydebank	d	14 52				15 07			15 22				15 39			15 52				16 07			16 22		
Anniesland	d		14 50		14 56		15 05	15 11		15 20		15 26		15 35	15 41		15 50		15 56		16 05	16 11		16 20	
Westerton	d		14 53		14 59		15 08	15 14		15 23		15 29		15 38	15 44		15 53		15 59		16 08	16 14		16 23	
Bearsden	d				15 01			15 16				15 31			15 46				16 01			16 16			
Hillfoot	d				15 03			15 18				15 33			15 48				16 03			16 18			
Milngavie	a				15 07			15 24				15 37			15 54				16 07			16 22			
Drumchapel	d		14 55				15 10			15 25				15 40			15 55				16 10			16 25	
Drumry	d		14 57				15 12			15 27				15 42			15 57				16 12			16 27	
Singer	d		15 00				15 15			15 30				15 45			16 00				16 15			16 30	
Dalmuir	a	14 56	15 02	14 59		15 13	15 17		15 26	15 32	15 29		15 42	15 47		15 56	16 02	15 59		16 13	16 17		16 26	16 32	16 29
	d			14 59			15 18				15 29			15 48				15 59			16 18				16 29
Kilpatrick	d						15 21							15 51							16 21				
Bowling	d						15 24							15 54							16 24				
Dumbarton East	d			15 06			15 28				15 36			15 58				16 06			16 28				16 37
Dumbarton Central	d			15 08			15 30				15 38			16 00				16 08			16 30				16 39
Dalreoch	d			15 10			15 32				15 40			16 02				16 10			16 32				16 40
Renton	d						15 35							16 05							16 35				
Alexandria	d						15 37							16 07							16 37				
Balloch	a						15 40							16 10							16 40				
Cardross	d			15 15							15 45							16 15							16 45
Craigendoran	d			15 20							15 50							16 20							16 50
Helensburgh Central	a			15 26							15 53							16 23							16 53
Helensburgh Upper	a																								

Table 226

Lanark, Coatbridge, Motherwell, Larkhall, Hamilton, Drumgelloch, Airdrie and Springburn - Glasgow - Milngavie, Dalmuir, Balloch and Helensburgh

Station		SR	SR	SR	SR	SR	SR	SR	SR	SR	SR	SR	SR	SR	SR	SR	SR	SR	SR	SR	SR	SR	SR	SR
Lanark	d		15 23									15 53					16 23							
Carluke	d		15 33									16 03					16 33							
Wishaw	d		15 39									16 08					16 39							
Holytown	d											16 13										17 29		
Shieldmuir	d		15 42														16 42							
Coatbridge Central	d																							
Whifflet	d																							
Motherwell	a		15 46									16 20					16 46							
	d		15 47		15 50					16 16		16 20					16 47		16 50					
Bellshill	d		15 53							16 22							16 53					17 32		
Uddingston	d		15 57							16 26							16 57					17 36		
Airbles	d				15 52							16 22							16 52					
Larkhall	d						16 07							16 37							17 07			
Merryton	d						16 09							16 39							17 09			
Chatelherault	d						16 12							16 42							17 12			
Hamilton Central	d				15 57		16 15					16 27		16 45					16 57		17 15			
Hamilton West	d				16 00		16 18					16 29		16 48					17 00		17 18			
Blantyre	d				16 03		16 21					16 33		16 51					17 03		17 21			
Newton	d				16 07							16 37							17 07					
Cambuslang	d		16 02		16 11					16 31		16 40					17 02		17 10			17 46		
Rutherglen	d		16 07		16 16		16 29			16 36		16 45		17 00			17 05		17 15		17 29			
Dalmarnock	d		16 09		16 18					16 38		16 47					17 07		17 17					
Bridgeton	d		16 11		16 20					16 40		16 49					17 09		17 19					
Drumgelloch	d																							
Airdrie	a																							
	d			15 57				16 12			16 27				16 42			16 57					17 12	
Coatdyke	d			15 59				16 14			16 29				16 44			16 59					17 14	
Coatbridge Sunnyside	d			16 01				16 16			16 31				16 46			17 01					17 16	
Blairhill	d			16 04				16 19			16 34				16 49			17 04					17 19	
Easterhouse	d			16 08				16 23			16 38				16 53			17 08					17 23	
Garrowhill	d			16 10				16 25			16 40				16 55			17 10					17 25	
Shettleston	d			16 13				16 28			16 43				16 58			17 13					17 28	
Carntyne	d			16 15				16 30			16 45				17 00			17 15					17 30	
Springburn	d					16 19							16 49							17 19				
Barnhill	d					16 20							16 50							17 20				
Alexandra Parade	d					16 23							16 53							17 23				
Duke Street	d					16 24							16 54							17 24				
Bellgrove	d	16 08		16 18		16 26		16 33	16 38		16 48		16 56		17 03	17 08		17 18		17 26			17 33	17 38
High Street	d	16 10		16 20		16 28		16 35	16 40		16 50		16 58		17 05	17 10		17 20		17 28			17 35	17 40
Glasgow Queen St HL 10 ⇌	d																							
Glasgow Queen St LL 10 ⇌	a	16 12		16 22		16 31		16 37	16 42		16 52		17 01		17 07	17 12		17 22		17 31			17 37	17 42
	d	16 13		16 23		16 32		16 40	16 43		16 53		17 02		17 10	17 13		17 23		17 32			17 40	17 43
Charing Cross	d	16 15		16 25		16 34		16 42	16 45		16 55		17 04		17 12	17 15		17 25		17 34			17 43	17 45
Argyle Street	d		16 15		16 24		16 34			16 44		16 53		17 05			17 13		17 23		17 34			
Glasgow Central HL 15	a																					17 57		
Glasgow Central LL 15	a		16 19		16 26		16 37			16 46		16 56		17 07			17 17		17 26		17 37			
	d		16 19		16 28		16 37			16 46		16 58		17 07			17 18		17 28		17 37			
Anderston	d		16 21		16 29		16 39			16 48		16 59		17 09			17 19		17 29		17 39			
Exhibition Centre	d		16 23		16 31		16 41			16 50		17 01		17 11			17 21		17 31		17 41			
Partick	d	16 20	16 26	16 30	16 35	16 39	16 45	16 47	16 50	16 54	17 00	17 05	17 09	17 15	17 17	17 20	17 25	17 30	17 35	17 39	17 45		17 47	17 50
Hyndland	d	16 23	16 28	16 32	16 38	16 41	16 47	16 50	16 53	16 56	17 02	17 08	17 11	17 17	17 20	17 23	17 27	17 32	17 38	17 41	17 47		17 50	17 53
Jordanhill	d		16 30			16 43				16 58			17 13				17 29			17 43				
Scotstounhill	d		16 33			16 45				17 00			17 15				17 31			17 45				
Garscadden	d		16 36			16 47				17 02			17 17				17 35			17 47				
Yoker	d		16 38			16 50				17 05			17 20				17 38			17 50				
Clydebank	d		16 40			16 52				17 07			17 22				17 40			17 52				
Anniesland	d	16 26		16 35	16 41		16 50		16 56		17 05	17 11		17 20		17 26		17 35	17 41		17 50			17 56
Westerton	d	16 29		16 38	16 44		16 53		16 59		17 08	17 14		17 23		17 29		17 38	17 44		17 53			17 59
Bearsden	d	16 31			16 46				17 01			17 16				17 31			17 46					18 01
Hillfoot	d	16 33			16 48				17 03			17 18				17 33			17 48					18 03
Milngavie	a	16 37			16 52				17 07			17 22				17 37			17 52					18 08
Drumchapel	d			16 40			16 55				17 10			17 25				17 40			17 55			
Drumry	d			16 42			16 57				17 12			17 27				17 42			17 57			
Singer	d			16 45			17 00				17 15			17 30				17 45			18 00			
Dalmuir	a		16 43	16 47		16 56	17 02	16 59		17 11	17 17		17 26	17 32	17 29		17 43	17 47		17 56	18 04		17 57	
	d			16 48				16 59			17 18				17 29			17 48					17 58	
Kilpatrick	d			16 51							17 21							17 51						
Bowling	d			16 54							17 24							17 54						
Dumbarton East	d			16 58				17 07			17 28				17 36			17 58					18 05	
Dumbarton Central	d			17 00				17 09			17 30				17 38			18 00					18 07	
Dalreoch	d			17 02				17 10			17 32				17 40			18 02					18 10	
Renton	d			17 05							17 35							18 05						
Alexandria	d			17 07							17 37							18 07						
Balloch	a			17 10							17 41							18 10						
Cardross	d							17 15							17 45								18 15	
Craigendoran	d							17 20							17 50								18 20	
Helensburgh Central	a							17 26							17 56								18 26	
Helensburgh Upper	a																							

Table 226

Lanark, Coatbridge, Motherwell, Larkhall, Hamilton, Drumgelloch, Airdrie and Springburn - Glasgow - Milngavie, Dalmuir, Balloch and Helensburgh

Station		SR	SR	SR	SR	SR	SR	SR	SR	SR	SR	SR	SR	SR	SR	SR	SR	SR	SR	SR	SR	SR	SR	SR
							A	B									◇							
Lanark	d			16 53						17 23									17 53					18 23
Carluke	d			17 03						17 33									18 03					18 33
Wishaw	d			17 08						17 39									18 08					18 39
Holytown	d			17 13															18 13					
Shieldmuir	d									17 42														18 42
Coatbridge Central	d																							
Whifflet	d																							
Motherwell	a			17 19						17 46									18 19					18 46
	d	17 16		17 20						17 47		17 50				18 16			18 20					18 47
Bellshill	d	17 22								17 53						18 22				18 36				18 53
Uddingston	d	17 26								17 57						18 26								18 57
Airbles	d			17 22								17 52							18 21					
Larkhall	d					17 37								18 07								18 37		
Merryton	d					17 39								18 09								18 39		
Chatelherault	d					17 42								18 12								18 42		
Hamilton Central	d			17 27		17 45						17 57		18 15					18 26			18 45		
Hamilton West	d			17 30		17 48						18 00		18 18					18 30			18 48		
Blantyre	d			17 33		17 51						18 03		18 21					18 32			18 51		
Newton	d			17 37								18 07							18 36					
Cambuslang	d	17 31		17 41						18 02		18 11				18 31			18 41	18 45				19 02
Rutherglen	d	17 34		17 45		17 59				18 07		18 17		18 30		18 34			18 45			18 59		19 05
Dalmarnock	d	17 36		17 47						18 09		18 19				18 36			18 47					19 07
Bridgeton	d	17 38		17 49						18 11		18 21				18 38			18 49					19 09
Drumgelloch	d																							
Airdrie	a																							
	d		17 27				17 42	17 42			17 57				18 12			18 27					18 42	
Coatdyke	d		17 29				17 44	17 44			17 59				18 14			18 29					18 44	
Coatbridge Sunnyside	d		17 31				17 46	17 46			18 01				18 16			18 31					18 46	
Blairhill	d		17 34				17 49	17 49			18 04				18 19			18 34					18 49	
Easterhouse	d		17 38				17 53	17 53			18 08				18 23			18 38					18 53	
Garrowhill	d		17 40				17 55	17 55			18 10				18 25			18 40					18 55	
Shettleston	d		17 43				17 58	17 58			18 13				18 28			18 43					18 58	
Carntyne	d		17 45				18 00	18 00			18 15				18 30			18 45					19 00	
Springburn	d				17 49								18 19								18 49			
Barnhill	d				17 50								18 20								18 50			
Alexandra Parade	d				17 53								18 23								18 53			
Duke Street	d				17 54								18 24								18 54			
Bellgrove	d		17 48		17 56		18 03	18 03	18 08		18 18		18 26		18 33			18 48			18 56		19 03	
High Street	d		17 50		17 58		18 05	18 05	18 10		18 20		18 28		18 35			18 50			18 58		19 05	
Glasgow Queen St HL 10 ⇌	d																18 21							
Glasgow Queen St LL 10 ⇌	a		17 52		18 01		18 07	18 07	18 12		18 22		18 31		18 37			18 52			19 01		19 07	
	d		17 53		18 02		18 09	18 10	18 13		18 23		18 32		18 40			18 53			19 02		19 10	
Charing Cross	d		17 55		18 05		18 12	18 12	18 15		18 25		18 34		18 42			18 55			19 04		19 12	
Argyle Street	d	17 43		17 53		18 04				18 15		18 25		18 35		18 42			18 53			19 04		19 13
Glasgow Central HL 15	a																			18 55				
Glasgow Central LL 15	a	17 46		17 56		18 07				18 19		18 26		18 37		18 46			18 56			19 07		19 18
	d	17 46		17 58		18 07				18 19		18 28		18 37		18 46			18 58			19 07		19 18
Anderston	d	17 48		17 59		18 09				18 21		18 29		18 39		18 48			18 59			19 09		19 20
Exhibition Centre	d	17 50		18 01		18 11				18 23		18 31		18 41		18 50			19 01			19 11		19 22
Partick	d	17 54	18 00	18 05	18 10	18 15	18 16	18 17	18 20	18 26	18 30	18 35	18 39	18 45	18 47	18a53		19 00	19 05		19 09	19 15	19 17	19a25
Hyndland	d	17 56	18 02	18 08	18 12	18 17	18 19	18 20	18 23	18 28	18 32	18 38	18 41	18 47	18 50			19 02	19 08		19 11	19 17	19 20	
Jordanhill	d	17 58			18 14					18 30			18 43		18 52						19 13		19 22	
Scotstounhill	d	18 00			18 16					18 33			18 45		18 54						19 15		19 24	
Garscadden	d	18 02			18 18					18 36			18a47		18 56						19a17		19 26	
Yoker	d	18 05			18 21					18 38					18 59								19 29	
Clydebank	d	18 07			18 23					18 40					19 01								19 31	
Anniesland	d		18 05	18 11		18 20			18 26		18 35	18 41		18 50				19 05	19 11			19 20		
Westerton	d		18 08	18 14		18 23			18 29		18 38	18 44		18 53				19 08	19 14			19 23		
Bearsden	d			18 16					18 31			18 46							19 16					
Hillfoot	d			18 18					18 33			18 48							19 18					
Milngavie	a			18 22					18 37			18 52							19 22					
Drumchapel	d		18 10			18 25					18 40			18 55				19 10				19 25		
Drumry	d		18 12			18 27					18 42			18 57				19 12				19 27		
Singer	d		18 15			18 30					18 45			19 00				19 15				19 30		
Dalmuir	a	18 13	18 17		18 26	18 32	18 29	18 29		18 43	18 47			19 02	19 04		18 38	19 17				19 32	19 34	
	d		18 18				18 29	18 29			18 48				19 05		18 40	19 18					19 35	
Kilpatrick	d		18 21								18 51							19 21						
Bowling	d		18 24								18 54							19 24						
Dumbarton East	d		18 28				18 36	18 37			18 58				19 12			19 28					19 42	
Dumbarton Central	d		18 30				18 37	18 38			19 00				19 14		18 49	19 30					19 44	
Dalreoch	d		18 32				18 40	18 40			19 02				19 16			19 32					19 46	
Renton	d		18 35								19 05							19 35						
Alexandria	d		18 37								19 07							19 37						
Balloch	a		18 40								19 10							19 40						
Cardross	d						18 45	18 45							19 21								19 51	
Craigendoran	d						18 50	18 50							19 26								19 56	
Helensburgh Central	a						18 53	18 53							19 29								19 59	
Helensburgh Upper	a																19 02							

A from 25 September **B** until 18 September

Table 226

Saturdays

Lanark, Coatbridge, Motherwell, Larkhall, Hamilton, Drumgelloch, Airdrie and Springburn - Glasgow - Milngavie, Dalmuir, Balloch and Helensburgh

		SR	SR	SR	SR	SR	SR	SR	SR	SR	SR	SR	SR	SR	SR	SR	SR	SR	SR	SR	SR	SR	SR	SR	SR
Lanark	d						18 53			19 23								19 53			20 23				
Carluke	d						19 03			19 33								20 03			20 33				
Wishaw	d						19 08			19 38								20 08			20 41				
Holytown	d						19 13									20 29		20 13							
Shieldmuir	d									19 42											20 44				
Coatbridge Central	d																								
Whifflet	d																								
Motherwell	a						19 19			19 46								20 20			20 46				
	d	18 50			19 16		19 20			19 46		19 50			20 16			20 20			20 46		20 50		
Bellshill	d				19 22					19 52					20 22	20 32					20 52				
Uddingston	d				19 26					19 56					20 26	20 36					20 56				
Airbles	d	18 52					19 22					19 52						20 22					20 52		
Larkhall	d		19 07					19 37					20 07						20 37					21 07	
Merryton	d		19 09					19 39					20 09						20 39					21 09	
Chatelherault	d		19 12					19 42					20 12						20 42					21 12	
Hamilton Central	d	18 58	19 15				19 27	19 45				19 57	20 15					20 27	20 45				20 57	21 15	
Hamilton West	d	19 00	19 18				19 30	19 48				20 00	20 18					20 30	20 48				21 00	21 18	
Blantyre	d	19 04	19 21				19 33	19 51				20 03	20 21					20 33	20 51				21 03	21 21	
Newton	d	19 08	19 25				19 37					20 07						20 37					21 07		
Cambuslang	d	19 10			19 31		19 41			20 01		20 11			20 31			20 41			21 01		21 11		
Rutherglen	d	19 13	19 29		19 34		19 45	19 59		20 05		20 15	20 29		20 34			20 45	20 59		21 04		21 15	21 29	
Dalmarnock	d	19 17			19 36		19 47			20 07		20 17			20 36			20 47			21 06		21 17		
Bridgeton	d	19 19			19 38		19 49			20 09		20 19			20 38			20 49			21 08		21 19		
Drumgelloch	d																								
Airdrie	a																								
	d			19 12					19 42					20 12						20 42					21 12
Coatdyke	d			19 14					19 44					20 14						20 44					21 14
Coatbridge Sunnyside	d			19 16					19 46					20 16						20 46					21 16
Blairhill	d			19 19					19 49					20 19						20 49					21 19
Easterhouse	d			19 23					19 53					20 23						20 53					21 23
Garrowhill	d			19 25					19 55					20 25						20 55					21 25
Shettleston	d			19 28					19 58					20 28						20 58					21 28
Carntyne	d			19 30					20 00					20 30						21 00					21 30
Springburn	d					19 39					20 09						20 39					21 09			
Barnhill	d					19 40					20 10						20 40					21 10			
Alexandra Parade	d					19 43					20 13						20 43					21 13			
Duke Street	d					19 44					20 14						20 44					21 14			
Bellgrove	d			19 33		19 46			20 03		20 16			20 33			20 46			21 03		21 16			21 33
High Street	d			19 35		19 48			20 05		20 18			20 35			20 48			21 05		21 18			21 35
Glasgow Queen St HL 10 ⇌	d																								
Glasgow Queen St LL 10 ⇌	a			19 37		19 51			20 07		20 21			20 37			20 51			21 07		21 21			21 37
	d			19 40		19 53			20 10		20 23			20 40			20 53			21 10		21 23			21 40
Charing Cross	d			19 42		19 55			20 12		20 25			20 42			20 55			21 12		21 25			21 42
Argyle Street	d	19 23	19 34		19 43		19 53	20 04		20 13		20 23	20 34		20 42			20 53	21 04		21 13		21 23	21 34	
Glasgow Central HL 15	a															20 55									
Glasgow Central LL 15	a	19 26	19 37		19 46		19 56	20 07		20 15		20 26	20 37		20 46			20 56	21 07		21 16		21 26	21 37	
	d	19 28	19 37		19 46		19 58	20 07		20 17		20 28	20 37		20 46			20 58	21 07		21 16		21 28	21 37	
Anderston	d	19 29	19 39		19 48		19 59	20 09		20 17		20 29	20 39		20 48			20 59	21 09		21 18		21 29	21 39	
Exhibition Centre	d	19 31	19 41		19 50		20 01	20 11		20 19		20 31	20 41		20 50			21 01	21 11		21 20		21 31	21 41	
Partick	d	19 35	19 45	19 47	19a53	20 00	20 05	20 15	20 17	20a23	20 30	20 35	20 45	20 47	20a53		21 00	21 05	21 15	21 17	21a23	21 30	21 35	21 45	21 47
Hyndland	d	19 38	19 47	19 50		20 02	20 08	20 17	20 20		20 32	20 38	20 47	20 50			21 02	21 08	21 17	21 20		21 32	21 38	21 47	21 50
Jordanhill	d			19 52					20 22					20 52						21 22					21 52
Scotstounhill	d			19 54					20 24					20 54						21 24					21 54
Garscadden	d			19 56					20 26					20 56						21 26					21 56
Yoker	d			19 59					20 29					20 59						21 29					21 59
Clydebank	d			20 01					20 31					21 01						21 31					22 01
Anniesland	d	19 41	19 50			20 05	20 11	20 20			20 35	20 41	20 50				21 05	21 11	21 20			21 35	21 41	21 50	
Westerton	d	19 44	19 53			20 08	20 14	20 23			20 38	20 44	20 53				21 08	21 14	21 23			21 38	21 44	21 53	
Bearsden	d	19 46					20 16					20 46						21 16					21 46		
Hillfoot	d	19 48					20 18					20 48						21 19					21 48		
Milngavie	a	19 52					20 22					20 52						21 24					21 52		
Drumchapel	d		19 55			20 10		20 25			20 40		20 55				21 10		21 25			21 40		21 55	
Drumry	d		19 57			20 12		20 27			20 42		20 57				21 12		21 27			21 42		21 57	
Singer	d		20 00			20 15		20 30			20 45		21 00				21 15		21 30			21 45		22 00	
Dalmuir	a		20 02	20 04		20 17		20 32	20 34		20 47		21 02	21 04			21 17		21 32	21 34		21 47		22 02	22 04
	d			20 05		20 18			20 35		20 48			21 05			21 18			21 35		21 48			22 05
Kilpatrick	d					20 21					20 51						21 21					21 51			
Bowling	d					20 24					20 54						21 24					21 54			
Dumbarton East	d			20 12		20 28			20 42		20 58			21 12			21 28			21 42		21 58			22 12
Dumbarton Central	d			20 14		20 30			20 44		21 00			21 14			21 30			21 44		22 00			22 14
Dalreoch	d			20 16		20 32			20 46		21 02			21 16			21 32			21 46		22 02			22 16
Renton	d					20 35					21 05						21 35					22 05			
Alexandria	d					20 37					21 07						21 37					22 07			
Balloch	a					20 40					21 10						21 40					22 10			
Cardross	d			20 21					20 51					21 21						21 51					22 21
Craigendoran	d			20 26					20 56					21 26						21 56					22 26
Helensburgh Central	a			20 29					20 59					21 29						21 59					22 29
Helensburgh Upper	a																								

Table 226

Saturdays

Lanark, Coatbridge, Motherwell, Larkhall, Hamilton, Drumgelloch, Airdrie and Springburn - Glasgow - Milngavie, Dalmuir, Balloch and Helensburgh

		SR	SR	SR	SR	SR	SR	SR	SR	SR		SR	SR	SR	SR	SR	SR	SR	SR	SR	SR		SR	SR	SR
Lanark	d			20 53			21 23									21 53			22 23						
Carluke	d			21 03			21 31									22 03			22 33						
Wishaw	d			21 08			21 39									22 08			22 39						
Holytown	d			21 13										22 29		22 13									
Shieldmuir	d						21 42												22 43						
Coatbridge Central	d																								
Whifflet	d																								
Motherwell	a			21 19			22 46									22 19			22 46						
	d	21 16		21 20			21 47		21 50				22 16			22 20			22 47		22 53				
Bellshill	d	21 22					21 53						22 22	22 32					22 53						
Uddingston	d	21 26					21 57						22 26	22 39					22 57						
Airbles	d			21 22					21 52							22 22					22 55				
Larkhall	d				21 37					22 07							22 37						23 07		
Merryton	d				21 39					22 09							22 39						23 09		
Chatelherault	d				21 42					22 12							22 42						23 12		
Hamilton Central	d			21 27	21 45				21 57	22 15						22 27	22 45				23 00		23 15		
Hamilton West	d			21 30	21 48				22 00	22 18						22 30	22 48				23 03		23 18		
Blantyre	d			21 33	21 51				22 03	22 21						22 33	22 51				23 06		23 21		
Newton	d			21 37					22 07							22 37					23 13				
Cambuslang	d	21 31		21 41			22 02		22 11				22 31			22 41			23 02		23 16				
Rutherglen	d	21 34		21 45	21 59		22 05		22 15	22 29			22 34			22 45	22 59		23 05		23 20		23 29		
Dalmarnock	d	21 36		21 47			22 07		22 17				22 36			22 47			23 07		23 22				
Bridgeton	d	21 38		21 49			22 09		22 19				22 38			22 49			23 09		23 24				
Drumgelloch	d																								
Airdrie	a																								
	d					21 42						22 12						22 42						23 12	
Coatdyke	d					21 44						22 14						22 44						23 14	
Coatbridge Sunnyside	d					21 46						22 16						22 46						23 16	
Blairhill	d					21 49						22 19						22 49						23 19	
Easterhouse	d					21 53						22 23						22 53						23 23	
Garrowhill	d					21 55						22 25						22 55						23 25	
Shettleston	d					21 58						22 28						22 58						23 28	
Carntyne	d					22 00						22 30						23 00						23 30	
Springburn	d		21 39					22 09							22 39					23 09					23 39
Barnhill	d		21 40					22 10							22 40					23 10					23 40
Alexandra Parade	d		21 43					22 13							22 43					23 13					23 43
Duke Street	d		21 44					22 14							22 44					23 14					23 44
Bellgrove	d		21 46			22 03		22 16				22 33			22 46			23 03		23 16				23 33	23 46
High Street	d		21 48			22 05		22 18				22 35			22 48			23 05		23 18				23 35	23 48
Glasgow Queen St HL 10 ⇌	d																								
Glasgow Queen St LL 10 ⇌	a		21 51			22 07		22 21				22 37			22 51			23 07		23 21				23 37	23 51
	d		21 53			22 10		22 23				22 40			22 53			23 10		23 23				23 45	23 52
Charing Cross	d		21 55			22 12		22 25				22 42			22 55			23 12		23 25				23 47	23 54
Argyle Street	d	21 42		21 53	22 04		22 13		22 23	22 34			22 42			22 53	23 04		23 14		23 27		23 34		
Glasgow Central HL 15	a													22 55											
Glasgow Central LL 15	a	21 46		21 56	22 07		22 18		22 26	22 37			22 46			22 56	23 07		23 18		23 29		23 37		
	d	21 46		21 58	22 07		22 18		22 28	22 37			22 46			22 58	23 07		23 18		23 29		23 37		
Anderston	d	21 48		21 59	22 09		22 20		22 29	22 39			22 48			22 59	23 09		23 20		23 30		23 39		
Exhibition Centre	d	21 50		22 01	22 11		22 22		22 31	22 41			22 50			23 01	23 11		23 22		23 32		23 41		
Partick	d	21a53	22 00	22 05	22 15	22 17	22a26	22 29	22 35	22 45		22 47	22a53		23 00	23 05	23 15	23 17	23 26	23 30	23 36		23 45	23 52	23 58
Hyndland	d		22 02	22 08	22 17	22 20		22 31	22 38	22 47		22 50			23 02	23 08	23 17	23 20	23 28	23 32	23 38		23 47	23 55	00 01
Jordanhill	d					22 22						22 52						23 22	23 30				23 49	23 57	00 03
Scotstounhill	d					22 24						22 54						23 24	23 32				23 51	23 59	00 05
Garscadden	d					22 26						22 56						23 26	23a34				23a53	00 01	00a07
Yoker	d					22 29						22 59						23 29						00 04	
Clydebank	d					22 31						23 01						23 31						00 06	
Anniesland	d		22 05	22 11	22 20			22 35	22 41	22 50					23 05	23 11	23 20			23 35	23 41				
Westerton	d		22 08	22 14	22 23			22 38	22 44	22 53					23 08	23 14	23 23			23 38	23 44				
Bearsden	d			22 16					22 46							23 16					23 46				
Hillfoot	d			22 18					22 48							23 18					23 49				
Milngavie	a			22 22					22 52							23 22					23 52				
Drumchapel	d		22 10		22 25			22 40		22 55					23 10		23 25			23 40					
Drumry	d		22 12		22 27			22 42		22 57					23 12		23 27			23 42					
Singer	d		22 15		22 30			22 45		23 00					23 15		23 30			23 45					
Dalmuir	a		22 17		22 32	22 34		22 47		23 02		23 04			23 17		23 33	23 34		23 47				00 09	
	d		22 18			22 35		22 48				23 05			23 18			23 35		23 48				00 10	
Kilpatrick	d		22 21					22 51							23 21					23 51					
Bowling	d		22 24					22 54							23 24					23 54					
Dumbarton East	d		22 28			22 42		22 58				23 12			23 28			23 42		23 58				00 17	
Dumbarton Central	d		22 30			22 44		23 00				23 14			23 30			23 44		23 59				00 19	
Dalreoch	d		22 32			22 46		23 02				23 16			23 32			23 46		00 02				00 21	
Renton	d		22 35					23 05							23 35					00 05					
Alexandria	d		22 37					23 07							23 37					00 07					
Balloch	a		22 40					23 10							23 40					00 10					
Cardross	d					22 51						23 21						23 51						00 26	
Craigendoran	d					22 56						23 26						23 56						00 31	
Helensburgh Central	a					22 59						23 29						23 59						00 34	
Helensburgh Upper	a																								

Table 226

Sundays
until 12 September

Lanark, Coatbridge, Motherwell, Larkhall, Hamilton, Drumgelloch, Airdrie and Springburn - Glasgow - Milngavie, Dalmuir, Balloch and Helensburgh

Station		SR	SR	SR	SR	SR	SR	SR	SR	SR	SR	SR	SR	SR	SR	SR ◇	SR	SR	SR	SR	SR	SR	SR
Lanark	d																				10 12		
Carluke	d																				10 22		
Wishaw	d																				10 27		
Holytown	d																						
Shieldmuir	d																				10 31		
Coatbridge Central	d																						
Whifflet	d																						
Motherwell	a																				10 35		
	d						08 36	08 40					09 36	09 40			10 10			10 36	10 40		
Bellshill	d						08 42						09 42							10 42			
Uddingston	d						08 46						09 46							10 46			
Airbles	d							08 42						09 42			10 12				10 42		
Larkhall	d											09 25							10 25				
Merryton	d											09 27							10 27				
Chatelherault	d											09 30							10 30				
Hamilton Central	d							08 47				09 33		09 47			10 17		10 33		10 47		
Hamilton West	d							08 50				09 36		09 50			10 20		10 36		10 50		
Blantyre	d							08 53				09 39		09 53			10 23		10 39		10 53		
Newton	d							08 57						09 57			10 27				10 57		
Cambuslang	d						08 51	09 01					09 51	10 01			10 31			10 51	11 01		
Rutherglen	d						08 54	09 04				09 49	09 54	10 04			10 34		10 49	10 54	11 04		
Dalmarnock	d																						
Bridgeton	d						08 57	09 07					09 57	10 07			10 37			10 57	11 07		
Drumgelloch	d																						
Airdrie	a																						
	d				07 58	08 28				08 58		09 28					09 58		10 28				10 58
Coatdyke	d				08 00	08 30				09 00		09 30					10 00		10 30				11 00
Coatbridge Sunnyside	d				08 02	08 32				09 02		09 32					10 02		10 32				11 02
Blairhill	d				08 05	08 35				09 05		09 35					10 05		10 35				11 05
Easterhouse	d				08 09	08 39				09 09		09 39					10 09		10 39				11 09
Garrowhill	d				08 11	08 41				09 11		09 41					10 11		10 41				11 11
Shettleston	d				08 14	08 44				09 14		09 44					10 14		10 44				11 14
Carntyne	d				08 16	08 46				09 16		09 46					10 16		10 46				11 16
Springburn	d																						
Barnhill	d																						
Alexandra Parade	d																						
Duke Street	d																						
Bellgrove	d				08 19	08 49				09 19		09 49					10 19		10 49				11 19
High Street	d				08 21	08 51				09 21		09 51					10 21		10 51				11 21
Glasgow Queen St HL 10	d															09 55							
Glasgow Queen St LL 10	a				08 23	08 53				09 23		09 53					10 23		10 53				11 23
	d				08 24	08 54				09 24		09 54					10 24		10 54				11 24
Charing Cross	d				08 27	08 57				09 27		09 57					10 27		10 57				11 27
Argyle Street	d													10 01	10 13			10 41		10 54	11 01	11 11	
Glasgow Central HL 15	a																						
Glasgow Central LL 15	a							09 04	09 14				09 57	10 04	10 14			10 44		10 57	11 04	11 14	
	d							09 04	09 14				09 57	10 04	10 14			10 44		10 57	11 04	11 14	
Anderston	d																						
Exhibition Centre	d							09 08	09 18				10 01	10 08	10 18			10 48		11 01	11 08	11 18	
Partick	d				08 32	09 02		09 12	09 22	09 32		10 02	10a04	10 12	10 22		10 32	10 52	11 02	11a04	11 12	11 22	11 32
Hyndland	d				08 35	09 04		09 16	09 24	09 34		10 04		10 16	10 24		10 34	10 54	11 04		11 16	11 24	11 34
Jordanhill	d								09 26						10 26			10 56				11 26	
Scotstounhill	d								09 28						10 28			10 58				11 28	
Garscadden	d								09 30						10 30			11 00				11 30	
Yoker	d						08 33		09 33		09 03				10 33			11 03				11 33	
Clydebank	d						08 35		09 35		09 05				10 35			11 05				11 35	
Anniesland	d				08 38	09 07		09 19		09 37		10 07		10 19			10 37		11 07		11 19		11 37
Westerton	d				08 41	09 10		09 22		09 40		10 10		10 22			10 40		11 10		11 22		11 40
Bearsden	d							09 25						10 25							11 25		
Hillfoot	d							09 27						10 27							11 27		
Milngavie	a							09 30						10 30							11 30		
Drumchapel	d				08 43	09 12				09 42		10 12					10 42		11 12				11 42
Drumry	d				08 45	09 14				09 44		10 14					10 44		11 14				11 44
Singer	d				08 48	09 17				09 47		10 17					10 47		11 17				11 47
Dalmuir	a				08 50	09 19	08 38		09 39	09 49	09 08	10 19			10 39	10 12	10 49	11 09	11 19			11 39	11 49
	d				08 50	09 20	08 39		09 39	09 50	09 09	10 20			10 39	10 16	10 50	11 09	11 20			11 39	11 50
Kilpatrick	d						08 41		09 41		09 11				10 41			11 11				11 41	
Bowling	d						08 44		09 44		09 14				10 44			11 14				11 44	
Dumbarton East	d				08 58	09 28	08 49		09 49	09 58	09 19	10 28			10 49		10 58	11 19	11 28			11 49	11 58
Dumbarton Central	d				09 00	09 30	08 51		09 51	10 00	09 21	10 30			10 51	10 25	11 00	11 21	11 30			11 51	12 00
Dalreoch	d				09 01	09 31	08 52		09 52	10 01	09 22	10 31			10 52		11 01	11 22	11 31			11 52	12 01
Renton	d						08 55		09 55		09 25				10 55			11 25				11 55	
Alexandria	d						08 58		09 58		09 28				10 58			11 28				11 58	
Balloch	a						09 00		10 00		09 30				11 00			11 30				12 00	
Cardross	d				09 06	09 36				10 06		10 36					11 06		11 36				12 06
Craigendoran	d				09 11	09 41				10 11		10 41					11 11		11 41				12 11
Helensburgh Central	a				09 14	09 44				10 14		10 44					11 14		11 44				12 14
Helensburgh Upper	a															10 37							

Table 226

Sundays
until 12 September

Lanark, Coatbridge, Motherwell, Larkhall, Hamilton, Drumgelloch, Airdrie and Springburn - Glasgow - Milngavie, Dalmuir, Balloch and Helensburgh

Station		SR	SR	SR	SR	SR	SR	SR	SR ◇	SR	SR	SR	SR	SR	SR	SR	SR	SR	SR	SR	SR	SR	SR
Lanark	d											12 12											
Carluke	d											12 22											
Wishaw	d											12 27											
Holytown	d																						
Shieldmuir	d											12 31											
Coatbridge Central	d																						
Whifflet	d																						
Motherwell	a											12 35											
	d	11 10			11 40		12 06	12 10				12 36	12 40		13 06	13 10				14 06	14 10		
Bellshill	d						12 12					12 42			13 12					14 12			
Uddingston	d						12 16					12 46			13 16					14 16			
Airbles	d	11 12			11 42			12 12					12 42			13 12					14 12		
Larkhall	d			11 25							12 25							13 25					14 25
Merryton	d			11 27							12 27							13 27					14 27
Chatelherault	d			11 30							12 30							13 30					14 30
Hamilton Central	d	11 17		11 33	11 47			12 17			12 33		12 47			13 17		13 33			14 17		14 33
Hamilton West	d	11 20		11 36	11 50			12 20			12 36		12 50			13 20		13 36			14 20		14 36
Blantyre	d	11 23		11 39	11 53			12 23			12 39		12 53			13 23		13 39			14 23		14 39
Newton	d	11 27			11 57			12 27					12 57			13 27					14 27		
Cambuslang	d	11 31			12 01		12 21	12 31				12 51	13 01		13 21	13 31				14 21	14 31		
Rutherglen	d	11 34		11 49	12 04		12 24	12 34			12 49	12 54	13 04		13 24	13 34		13 49		14 24	14 34		14 49
Dalmarnock	d																						
Bridgeton	d	11 37			12 07		12 27	12 37				12 57	13 07		13 27	13 37				14 27	14 37		
Drumgelloch	d																						
Airdrie	a																						
	d		11 28			11 58				12 28				12 58			13 28		13 58			14 28	
Coatdyke	d		11 30			12 00				12 30				13 00			13 30		14 00			14 30	
Coatbridge Sunnyside	d		11 32			12 02				12 32				13 02			13 32		14 02			14 32	
Blairhill	d		11 35			12 05				12 35				13 05			13 35		14 05			14 35	
Easterhouse	d		11 39			12 09				12 39				13 09			13 39		14 09			14 39	
Garrowhill	d		11 41			12 11				12 41				13 11			13 41		14 11			14 41	
Shettleston	d		11 44			12 14				12 44				13 14			13 44		14 14			14 44	
Carntyne	d		11 46			12 16				12 46				13 16			13 46		14 16			14 46	
Springburn	d																						
Barnhill	d																						
Alexandra Parade	d																						
Duke Street	d																						
Bellgrove	d		11 49			12 19				12 49				13 19			13 49		14 19			14 49	
High Street	d		11 51			12 21				12 51				13 21			13 51		14 21			14 51	
Glasgow Queen St HL 10	d								12 20														
Glasgow Queen St LL 10	a		11 53			12 23				12 53				13 23			13 53		14 23			14 53	
	d		11 54			12 24				12 54				13 24			13 54		14 24			14 54	
Charing Cross	d		11 57			12 27				12 57				13 27			13 57		14 27			14 57	
Argyle Street	d	11 41		11 54	12 11		12 31	12 41			12 54	13 01	13 11		13 31	13 41		13 54		14 31	14 41		14 54
Glasgow Central HL 15	a																						
Glasgow Central LL 15	a	11 44		11 57	12 14		12 34	12 44			12 57	13 04	13 14		13 34	13 44		13 57		14 34	14 44		14 57
	d	11 44		11 57	12 14		12 34	12 44			12 57	13 04	13 14		13 34	13 44		13 57		14 34	14 44		14 57
Anderston	d																						
Exhibition Centre	d	11 48		12 01	12 18		12 38	12 48			13 01	13 08	13 18		13 38	13 48		14 01		14 38	14 48		15 01
Partick	d	11 52	12 02	12a04	12 22	12 32	12 42	12 52		13 02	13a04	13 12	13 22	13 32	13 42	13 52	14 02	14a04	14 32	14 42	14 52	15 02	15a04
Hyndland	d	11 54	12 04		12 24	12 34	12 46	12 54		13 04		13 16	13 24	13 34	13 46	13 54	14 04		14 34	14 46	14 54	15 04	
Jordanhill	d	11 56			12 26			12 56					13 26			13 56					14 56		
Scotstounhill	d	11 58			12 28			12 58					13 28			13 58					14 58		
Garscadden	d	12 00			12 30			13 00					13 30			14 00					15 00		
Yoker	d	12 03			12 33			13 03					13 33			14 03					15 03		
Clydebank	d	12 05			12 35			13 05					13 35			14 05					15 05		
Anniesland	d		12 07			12 37	12 49			13 07		13 19		13 37	13 49		14 07		14 37	14 49		15 07	
Westerton	d		12 10			12 40	12 52			13 10		13 22		13 40	13 52		14 10		14 40	14 52		15 10	
Bearsden	d						12 55					13 25			13 55					14 55			
Hillfoot	d						12 57					13 27			13 57					14 57			
Milngavie	a						13 00					13 30			14 00					15 00			
Drumchapel	d		12 12			12 42				13 12				13 42			14 12		14 42			15 12	
Drumry	d		12 14			12 44				13 14				13 44			14 14		14 44			15 14	
Singer	d		12 17			12 47				13 17				13 47			14 17		14 47			15 17	
Dalmuir	a	12 09	12 19		12 39	12 49		13 09	12 36	13 19			13 39	13 49		14 09	14 19		14 49		15 09	15 19	
	d	12 09	12 20		12 39	12 50		13 09	12 36	13 20			13 39	13 50		14 09	14 20		14 50		15 09	15 20	
Kilpatrick	d	12 11			12 41			13 11					13 41			14 11					15 11		
Bowling	d	12 14			12 44			13 14					13 44			14 14					15 14		
Dumbarton East	d	12 19	12 28		12 49	12 58		13 19		13 28			13 49	13 58		14 19	14 28		14 58		15 19	15 28	
Dumbarton Central	d	12 21	12 30		12 51	13 00		13 21	12 46	13 30			13 51	14 00		14 21	14 30		15 00		15 21	15 30	
Dalreoch	d	12 22	12 31		12 52	13 01		13 22		13 31			13 52	14 01		14 22	14 31		15 01		15 22	15 31	
Renton	d	12 25			12 55			13 25					13 55			14 25					15 25		
Alexandria	d	12 28			12 58			13 28					13 58			14 28					15 28		
Balloch	a	12 30			13 00			13 30					14 00			14 30					15 30		
Cardross	d		12 36			13 06				13 36				14 06			14 36		15 06			15 36	
Craigendoran	d		12 41			13 11				13 41				14 11			14 41		15 11			15 41	
Helensburgh Central	a		12 44			13 14				13 44				14 14			14 44		15 14			15 44	
Helensburgh Upper	a								13 03														

Table 226

Sundays
until 12 September

Lanark, Coatbridge, Motherwell, Larkhall, Hamilton, Drumgelloch, Airdrie and Springburn - Glasgow - Milngavie, Dalmuir, Balloch and Helensburgh

		SR	SR	SR	SR	SR	SR	SR	SR	SR	SR	SR	SR	SR	SR	SR	SR	SR	SR	SR	SR	SR
Lanark	d	14 12							15 11							16 12						17 11
Carluke	d	14 22							15 21							16 22						17 21
Wishaw	d	14 27							15 27							16 27						17 26
Holytown	d																					
Shieldmuir	d	14 31							15 31							16 31						17 30
Coatbridge Central	d																					
Whifflet	d																					
Motherwell	a	14 35							15 35							16 34						17 35
	d	14 36	14 40		15 06	15 10			15 35	15 40		16 06	16 10			16 34	16 40		17 06			17 35
Bellshill	d	14 42			15 12				15 41			16 12				16 40			17 12			17 41
Uddingston	d	14 46			15 16				15 45			16 16				16 44			17 16			17 45
Airbles	d		14 42			15 12				15 42			16 12				16 42					
Larkhall	d							15 25							16 25						17 25	
Merryton	d							15 27							16 27						17 27	
Chatelherault	d							15 30							16 30						17 30	
Hamilton Central	d		14 47			15 17		15 33		15 47			16 17		16 33		16 47				17 33	
Hamilton West	d		14 50			15 20		15 36		15 50			16 20		16 36		16 50				17 36	
Blantyre	d		14 53			15 23		15 39		15 53			16 23		16 39		16 53				17 39	
Newton	d		14 57			15 27				15 57			16 27				16 57					
Cambuslang	d	14 51	15 01		15 21	15 31			15 50	16 01		16 21	16 31			16 49	17 01		17 21			17 50
Rutherglen	d	14 54	15 04		15 24	15 34		15 49	15 54	16 05		16 24	16 34		16 49	16 54	17 04		17 24		17 47	17 54
Dalmarnock	d																					
Bridgeton	d	14 57	15 07		15 27	15 37			15 57	16 07		16 27	16 37			16 57	17 07		17 27			17 57
Drumgelloch	d																					
Airdrie	a																					
	d			14 58			15 28				15 58			16 28				16 58		17 28		
Coatdyke	d			15 00			15 30				16 00			16 30				17 00		17 30		
Coatbridge Sunnyside	d			15 02			15 32				16 02			16 32				17 02		17 32		
Blairhill	d			15 05			15 35				16 05			16 35				17 05		17 35		
Easterhouse	d			15 09			15 39				16 09			16 39				17 09		17 39		
Garrowhill	d			15 11			15 41				16 11			16 41				17 11		17 41		
Shettleston	d			15 14			15 44				16 14			16 44				17 14		17 44		
Carntyne	d			15 16			15 46				16 16			16 46				17 16		17 46		
Springburn	d																					
Barnhill	d																					
Alexandra Parade	d																					
Duke Street	d																					
Bellgrove	d			15 19			15 49				16 19			16 49				17 19		17 49		
High Street	d			15 21			15 51				16 21			16 51				17 21		17 51		
Glasgow Queen St HL 10	d																					
Glasgow Queen St LL 10	a			15 23			15 53				16 23			16 53				17 23		17 53		
	d			15 24			15 54				16 24			16 54				17 24		17 54		
Charing Cross	d			15 27			15 57				16 27			16 57				17 27		17 57		
Argyle Street	d	15 01	15 11		15 31	15 41		15 54	16 01	16 11		16 31	16 41		16 54	17 01	17 11		17 31		17 52	18 01
Glasgow Central HL 15	a																					
Glasgow Central LL 15	a	15 04	15 14		15 34	15 44		15 57	16 04	16 14		16 34	16 44		16 57	17 04	17 14		17 34		17 57	18 04
	d	15 04	15 14		15 34	15 44		15 57	16 04	16 14		16 34	16 44		16 57	17 04	17 14		17 34		17 57	18 04
Anderston	d																					
Exhibition Centre	d	15 08	15 18		15 38	15 48		16 01	16 08	16 18		16 38	16 48		17 01	17 08	17 18		17 38		18 01	18 08
Partick	d	15 12	15 22	15 32	15 42	15 52	16 02	16a04	16 12	16 22	16 32	16 42	16 52	17 02	17a04	17 12	17 22	17 32	17 42	18 02	18a04	18 12
Hyndland	d	15 16	15 24	15 34	15 46	15 54	16 04		16 16	16 24	16 34	16 46	16 54	17 04		17 16	17 24	17 34	17 46	18 04		18 16
Jordanhill	d		15 26			15 56				16 26			16 56				17 26					
Scotstounhill	d		15 28			15 58				16 28			16 58				17 28					
Garscadden	d		15 30			16 00				16 30			17 00				17 30					
Yoker	d		15 33			16 03				16 33			17 03				17 33					
Clydebank	d		15 35			16 05				16 35			17 05				17 35					
Anniesland	d	15 19		15 37	15 49		16 07		16 19		16 37	16 49		17 07		17 19		17 37	17 49	18 07		18 19
Westerton	d	15 22		15 40	15 52		16 10		16 22		16 40	16 52		17 10		17 22		17 40	17 52	18 10		18 22
Bearsden	d	15 25			15 55				16 25			16 55				17 25			17 55			18 25
Hillfoot	d	15 27			15 57				16 27			16 57				17 27			17 57			18 27
Milngavie	a	15 30			16 00				16 30			17 00				17 30			18 00			18 30
Drumchapel	d			15 42			16 12				16 42			17 12				17 42		18 12		
Drumry	d			15 44			16 14				16 44			17 14				17 44		18 14		
Singer	d			15 47			16 17				16 47			17 17				17 47		18 17		
Dalmuir	a		15 39	15 49		16 09	16 19			16 39	16 49		17 09	17 19			17 39	17 49		18 19		
	d		15 39	15 50		16 09	16 20			16 39	16 50		17 09	17 20			17 39	17 50		18 20		
Kilpatrick	d		15 41			16 11				16 41			17 11				17 41					
Bowling	d		15 44			16 14				16 44			17 14				17 44					
Dumbarton East	d		15 49	15 58		16 19	16 28			16 49	16 58		17 19	17 28			17 49	17 58		18 28		
Dumbarton Central	d		15 51	16 00		16 21	16 30			16 51	17 00		17 21	17 30			17 51	18 00		18 30		
Dalreoch	d		15 52	16 01		16 22	16 31			16 52	17 01		17 22	17 31			17 52	18 01		18 31		
Renton	d		15 55			16 25				16 55			17 25				17 55					
Alexandria	d		15 58			16 28				16 58			17 28				17 58					
Balloch	a		16 00			16 30				17 00			17 30				18 00					
Cardross	d			16 06			16 36				17 06			17 36				18 06		18 36		
Craigendoran	d			16 11			16 41				17 11			17 41				18 11		18 41		
Helensburgh Central	a			16 14			16 44				17 14			17 44				18 14		18 44		
Helensburgh Upper	a																					

Table 226

Sundays
until 12 September

Lanark, Coatbridge, Motherwell, Larkhall, Hamilton, Drumgelloch, Airdrie and Springburn - Glasgow - Milngavie, Dalmuir, Balloch and Helensburgh

		SR	SR	SR	SR ◇	SR	SR	SR	SR	SR	SR	SR	SR	SR	SR	SR	SR	SR	SR	SR	SR	SR	SR
Lanark	d												19 12							20 12			
Carluke	d												19 22							20 22			
Wishaw	d												19 27							20 27			
Holytown	d																						
Shieldmuir	d												19 31							20 31			
Coatbridge Central	d																						
Whifflet	d																						
Motherwell	a												19 35							20 35			
	d	17 40		18 10				18 40		19 06	19 10		19 35	19 40		20 06	20 10			20 36	20 40		21 06
Bellshill	d									19 12			19 41			20 12				20 42			21 12
Uddingston	d									19 16			19 45			20 17				20 46			21 16
Airbles	d	17 42		18 12				18 42			19 12			19 42			20 12				20 42		
Larkhall	d						18 25					19 25							20 25				
Merryton	d						18 27					19 27							20 27				
Chatelherault	d						18 30					19 30							20 30				
Hamilton Central	d	17 47		18 17			18 33	18 47			19 17	19 33		19 47			20 17		20 33		20 47		
Hamilton West	d	17 50		18 20			18 36	18 50			19 20	19 36		19 50			20 20		20 36		20 50		
Blantyre	d	17 53		18 23			18 39	18 53			19 23	19 39		19 53			20 23		20 39		20 53		
Newton	d	17 57		18 27				18 57			19 27			19 57			20 26				20 57		
Cambuslang	d	18 01		18 31				19 01		19 21	19 31		19 50	20 01		20 22	20 30			20 51	21 01		21 21
Rutherglen	d	18 04		18 34			18 49	19 04		19 24	19 34	19 49	19 53	20 04		20 25	20 33		20 49	20 54	21 04		21 24
Dalmarnock	d																						
Bridgeton	d	18 07		18 37				19 07		19 27	19 37		19 57	20 07		20 28	20 37			20 57	21 07		21 27
Drumgelloch	d																						
Airdrie	a																						
	d		17 58			18 28			18 58						19 58			20 28				20 58	
Coatdyke	d		18 00			18 30			19 00						20 00			20 30				21 00	
Coatbridge Sunnyside	d		18 02			18 32			19 02						20 02			20 32				21 02	
Blairhill	d		18 05			18 35			19 05						20 05			20 35				21 05	
Easterhouse	d		18 09			18 39			19 09						20 09			20 39				21 09	
Garrowhill	d		18 11			18 41			19 11						20 11			20 41				21 11	
Shettleston	d		18 14			18 44			19 14						20 14			20 44				21 14	
Carntyne	d		18 16			18 46			19 16						20 16			20 46				21 16	
Springburn	d																						
Barnhill	d																						
Alexandra Parade	d																						
Duke Street	d																						
Bellgrove	d		18 19			18 49			19 19						20 19			20 49				21 19	
High Street	d		18 21			18 51			19 21						20 21			20 51				21 21	
Glasgow Queen St HL 10	d				18 20																		
Glasgow Queen St LL 10	a		18 23			18 53			19 23						20 23			20 53				21 23	
	d		18 24			18 54			19 24						20 24			20 54				21 24	
Charing Cross	d		18 27			18 57			19 27						20 27			20 57				21 27	
Argyle Street	d	18 11																					
Glasgow Central HL 15	a																						
Glasgow Central LL 15	a	18 14		18 44			18 57	19 14		19 34	19 44	19 57	20 04	20 14		20 34	20 44		20 57	21 04	21 14		21 34
	d	18 14		18 44			18 57	19 14		19 34	19 44	19 57	20 04	20 14		20 34	20 44		20 57	21 04	21 14		21 34
Anderston	d																						
Exhibition Centre	d	18 18		18 48			19 01	19 18		19 38	19 48	20 01	20 08	20 18		20 38	20 48		21 01	21 08	21 18		21 38
Partick	d	18 22	18 32	18 52		19 02	19a04	19 22	19 32	19 42	19 52	20a04	20 12	20 22	20 32	20 42	20 52	21 02	21a04	21 12	21 22	21 32	21 42
Hyndland	d	18 24	18 34	18 54		19 04		19 24	19 34	19 46	19 54		20 16	20 24	20 34	20 46	20 54	21 04		21 16	21 24	21 34	21 46
Jordanhill	d	18 26		18 56				19 26			19 56			20 26			20 56				21 26		
Scotstounhill	d	18 28		18 58				19 28			19 58			20 28			20 58				21 28		
Garscadden	d	18 30		19 00				19 30			20 00			20 30			21 00				21 30		
Yoker	d	18 33		19 03				19 33			20 03			20 33			21 03				21 33		
Clydebank	d	18 35		19 05				19 35			20 05			20 35			21 05				21 35		
Anniesland	d		18 37			19 07			19 37	19 49			20 19		20 37	20 49		21 07		21 19		21 37	21 49
Westerton	d		18 40			19 10			19 40	19 52			20 22		20 40	20 52		21 10		21 22		21 40	21 52
Bearsden	d									19 55			20 25			20 55				21 25			21 55
Hillfoot	d									19 57			20 27			20 57				21 27			21 57
Milngavie	a									20 00			20 30			21 00				21 30			22 00
Drumchapel	d		18 42			19 12			19 42						20 42			21 12				21 42	
Drumry	d		18 44			19 14			19 44						20 44			21 14				21 44	
Singer	d		18 47			19 17			19 47						20 47			21 17				21 47	
Dalmuir	a	18 39	18 49	19 09	18 34	19 19		19 39	19 49		20 09			20 39	20 49		21 09	21 19			21 39	21 49	
	d	18 39	18 50	19 09	18 34	19 20		19 39	19 50		20 09			20 39	20 50		21 09	21 20			21 39	21 50	
Kilpatrick	d	18 41		19 11				19 41			20 11			20 41			21 11				21 41		
Bowling	d	18 44		19 14				19 44			20 14			20 44			21 14				21 44		
Dumbarton East	d	18 49	18 58	19 19		19 28		19 49	19 58		20 19			20 49	20 58		21 19	21 28			21 49	21 58	
Dumbarton Central	d	18 51	19 00	19 21	18 43	19 30		19 51	20 00		20 21			20 52	21 00		21 21	21 30			21 51	22 00	
Dalreoch	d	18 52	19 01	19 22		19 31		19 52	20 01		20 22			20 53	21 01		21 22	21 31			21 52	22 01	
Renton	d	18 55		19 25				19 55			20 25			20 55			21 25				21 55		
Alexandria	d	18 58		19 28				19 58			20 28			20 58			21 28				21 58		
Balloch	a	19 00		19 30				20 00			20 30			21 00			21 30				22 00		
Cardross	d		19 06			19 36			20 06						21 06			21 36				22 06	
Craigendoran	d		19 11			19 41			20 11						21 11			21 41				22 11	
Helensburgh Central	a		19 14			19 44			20 14						21 14			21 44				22 14	
Helensburgh Upper	a				18 56																		

Table 226

Sundays until 12 September

Lanark, Coatbridge, Motherwell, Larkhall, Hamilton, Drumgelloch, Airdrie and Springburn - Glasgow - Milngavie, Dalmuir, Balloch and Helensburgh

		SR	SR	SR	SR	SR	SR	SR	SR	SR	SR	SR	SR	SR	SR
Lanark	d				21 12					22 12					
Carluke	d				21 22					22 22					
Wishaw	d				21 27					22 27					
Holytown	d														
Shieldmuir	d				21 31					22 31					
Coatbridge Central	d														
Whifflet	d														
Motherwell	a				21 35					22 35					
	d	21 10			21 35		22 10			22 36	22 40		23 10	23 10	
Bellshill	d				21 41					22 42			23 16		
Uddingston	d				21 45					22 46			23 20		
Airbles	d	21 12					22 12				22 42			23 12	
Larkhall	d			21 25					22 25						
Merryton	d			21 27					22 27						
Chatelherault	d			21 30					22 30						
Hamilton Central	d	21 17		21 33			22 17		22 33		22 47			23 17	
Hamilton West	d	21 20		21 36			22 20		22 36		22 50			23 20	
Blantyre	d	21 23		21 39			22 23		22 39		22 53			23 23	
Newton	d	21 27					22 27				22 57			23 27	
Cambuslang	d	21 31			21 50		22 31			22 51	23 01		23 25	23 31	
Rutherglen	d	21 34		21 50	21 53		22 35		22 48	22 54	23 04		23 28	23 34	
Dalmarnock	d														
Bridgeton	d	21 37			21 57		22 38			22 57	23 07		23 31	23 37	
Drumgelloch	d														
Airdrie	a														
	d		21 28			21 58		22 28				22 58			23 28
Coatdyke	d		21 30			22 00		22 30				23 00			23 30
Coatbridge Sunnyside	d		21 32			22 02		22 32				23 02			23 32
Blairhill	d		21 35			22 05		22 35				23 05			23 35
Easterhouse	d		21 39			22 09		22 39				23 09			23 39
Garrowhill	d		21 41			22 11		22 41				23 11			23 41
Shettleston	d		21 44			22 14		22 44				23 14			23 44
Carntyne	d		21 46			22 16		22 46				23 16			23 46
Springburn	d														
Barnhill	d														
Alexandra Parade	d														
Duke Street	d														
Bellgrove	d		21 49			22 19		22 49				23 19			23 49
High Street	d		21 51			22 21		22 51				23 21			23 51
Glasgow Queen St HL 10 ⇌	d														
Glasgow Queen St LL 10 ⇌	a		21 53			22 23		22 53				23 23			23 53
	d		21 54			22 24		22 54				23 24			23 54
Charing Cross	d		21 57			22 27		22 57				23 27			23 57
Argyle Street	d														
Glasgow Central HL 15	a														
Glasgow Central LL 15	a	21 44		21 57	22 04		22 44		22 57	23 04	23 14		23 35	23 44	
	d	21 44		21 57	22 04		22 44		22 57	23 04	23 14		23 36	23 44	
Anderston	d														
Exhibition Centre	d	21 48		22 01	22 08		22 48		23 01	23 08	23 18		23 39	23 48	
Partick	d	21 52	22 02	22a04	22 12	22 32	22 52	23 02	23a04	23 12	23 22	23 32	23 43	23 52	00 02
Hyndland	d	21 54	22 04		22 16	22 34	22 54	23 04		23 16	23 24	23 34	23 45	23 54	00 04
Jordanhill	d	21 56					22 56				23 26		23 47	23 56	00 06
Scotstounhill	d	21 58					22 58				23 28		23 49	23 58	00 08
Garscadden	d	22 00					23 00				23 30		23a51	00a01	00a10
Yoker	d	22 03					23 03				23 33				
Clydebank	d	22 05					23 05				23 35				
Anniesland	d		22 07		22 19	22 37		23 07		23 19		23 37			
Westerton	d		22 10		22 22	22 40		23 10		23 22		23 40			
Bearsden	d				22 25					23 25					
Hillfoot	d				22 27					23 27					
Milngavie	a				22 30					23 30					
Drumchapel	d		22 12			22 42		23 12				23 42			
Drumry	d		22 14			22 44		23 14				23 44			
Singer	d		22 17			22 47		23 17				23 47			
Dalmuir	a	22 09	22 19			22 49	23 09	23 19			23 39	23 49			
	d	22 09	22 20			22 50	23 09	23 20			23 39	23 50			
Kilpatrick	d	22 11					23 11				23 41				
Bowling	d	22 14					23 14				23 44				
Dumbarton East	d	22 19	22 28			22 58	23 19	23 28			23 49	23 58			
Dumbarton Central	d	22 21	22 30			23 00	23 21	23 30			23 51	23 59			
Dalreoch	d	22 22	22 31			23 01	23 22	23 31			23 52	00 01			
Renton	d	22 25					23 25				23 55				
Alexandria	d	22 28					23 28				23 58				
Balloch	a	22 30					23 30				00 01				
Cardross	d		22 36			23 06		23 36				00 06			
Craigendoran	d		22 41			23 11		23 41				00 11			
Helensburgh Central	a		22 44			23 14		23 44				00 14			
Helensburgh Upper	a														

Table 226

Sundays from 19 September

Lanark, Coatbridge, Motherwell, Larkhall, Hamilton, Drumgelloch, Airdrie and Springburn - Glasgow - Milngavie, Dalmuir, Balloch and Helensburgh

		SR	SR	SR	SR	SR	SR	SR	SR	SR	SR	SR	SR	SR	SR	SR	SR	SR	SR	SR
									A	A			A		A		◇ B		A	A
Lanark	d																			
Carluke	d																			
Wishaw	d																			
Holytown	d																			
Shieldmuir	d																			
Coatbridge Central	d																			
Whifflet	d																			
Motherwell	a																			
	d				08 36	08 40								09 36		09 40				
Bellshill	d				08 42									09 42						
Uddingston	d				08 46									09 46						
Airbles	d					08 42										09 42				
Larkhall	d											09 25								
Merryton	d											09 27								
Chatelherault	d											09 30								
Hamilton Central	d					08 47						09 33				09 47				
Hamilton West	d					08 50						09 36				09 50				
Blantyre	d					08 53						09 39				09 53				
Newton	d					08 57										09 57				
Cambuslang	d				08 51	09 01								09 51		10 01				
Rutherglen	d				08 54	09 04						09 49		09 54		10 04				
Dalmarnock	d																			
Bridgeton	d				08 57	09 07								09 57		10 07				
Drumgelloch	d																			
Airdrie	a																			
	d	07 58	08 28				08 58			09 13	09 28				09 43			09 58		10 13
Coatdyke	d	08 00	08 30				09 00			09 15	09 30				09 45			10 00		10 15
Coatbridge Sunnyside	d	08 02	08 32				09 02			09 17	09 32				09 47			10 02		10 17
Blairhill	d	08 05	08 35				09 05			09 20	09 35				09 50			10 05		10 20
Easterhouse	d	08 09	08 39				09 09			09 24	09 39				09 54			10 09		10 24
Garrowhill	d	08 11	08 41				09 11			09 26	09 41				09 56			10 11		10 26
Shettleston	d	08 14	08 44				09 14			09 29	09 44				09 59			10 14		10 29
Carntyne	d	08 16	08 46				09 16			09 31	09 46				10 01			10 16		10 31
Springburn	d								09 19				09 49						10 19	
Barnhill	d								09 20				09 50						10 20	
Alexandra Parade	d								09 23				09 53						10 23	
Duke Street	d								09 25				09 55						10 25	
Bellgrove	d	08 19	08 49				09 19		09 27	09 34	09 49		09 57		10 04			10 19	10 27	10 34
High Street	d	08 21	08 51				09 21		09 29	09 36	09 51		09 59		10 06			10 21	10 29	10 36
Glasgow Queen St HL 10 ⇌	d																09 55			
Glasgow Queen St LL 10 ⇌	a	08 23	08 53				09 23		09 31	09 39	09 53		10 01		10 09			10 23	10 31	10 39
	d	08 24	08 54				09 24		09 31	09 39	09 54		10 01		10 09			10 24	10 31	10 39
Charing Cross	d	08 27	08 57				09 27		09 33	09 42	09 57		10 03		10 12			10 27	10 33	10 42
Argyle Street	d													10 01		10 13				
Glasgow Central HL 15	a																			
Glasgow Central LL 15	a				09 04	09 14						09 57		10 04		10 14				
	d				09 04	09 14						09 57		10 04		10 14				
Anderston	d																			
Exhibition Centre	d				09 08	09 18						10 01		10 08		10 18				
Partick	d	08 32	09 02		09 12	09 22	09 32		09 37	09 47	10 02	10a04	10 08	10 12	10 17	10 22		10 32	10 37	10 47
Hyndland	d	08 35	09 04		09 16	09 24	09 34		09 39	09 49	10 04		10 10	10 16	10 19	10 24		10 34	10 39	10 49
Jordanhill	d					09 26			09 41				10 12			10 26			10 41	
Scotstounhill	d					09 28			09 43				10 14			10 28			10 43	
Garscadden	d					09 30			09 46				10 17			10 30			10 46	
Yoker	d			08 33		09 33		09 03	09 48				10 19			10 33			10 48	
Clydebank	d			08 35		09 35		09 05	09 50				10 21			10 35			10 50	
Anniesland	d	08 38	09 07		09 19		09 37			09 52	10 07			10 19	10 22			10 37		10 52
Westerton	d	08 41	09 10		09 22		09 40			09 55	10 10			10 22	10 25			10 40		10 55
Bearsden	d				09 25									10 25						
Hillfoot	d				09 27									10 27						
Milngavie	a				09 30									10 30						
Drumchapel	d	08 43	09 12				09 42			09 57	10 12				10 27			10 42		10 57
Drumry	d	08 45	09 14				09 44			09 59	10 14				10 29			10 44		10 59
Singer	d	08 48	09 17				09 47			10 02	10 17				10 32			10 47		11 02
Dalmuir	a	08 50	09 19	08 38		09 39	09 49	09 08	09 53	10 04	10 19		10 24		10 34	10 39	10 12	10 49	10 53	11 04
	d	08 50	09 20	08 39		09 39	09 50	09 09			10 20					10 39	10 16	10 50		
Kilpatrick	d			08 41		09 41		09 11								10 41				
Bowling	d			08 44		09 44		09 14								10 44				
Dumbarton East	d	08 58	09 28	08 49		09 49	09 58	09 19			10 28					10 49		10 58		
Dumbarton Central	d	09 00	09 30	08 51		09 51	10 00	09 21			10 30					10 51	10 25	11 00		
Dalreoch	d	09 01	09 31	08 52		09 52	10 01	09 22			10 31					10 52		11 01		
Renton	d			08 55		09 55		09 25								10 55				
Alexandria	d			08 58		09 58		09 28								10 58				
Balloch	a			09 00		10 00		09 30								11 00				
Cardross	d	09 06	09 36				10 06				10 36							11 06		
Craigendoran	d	09 11	09 41				10 11				10 41							11 11		
Helensburgh Central	a	09 14	09 44				10 14				10 44							11 14		
Helensburgh Upper	a																10 37			

A 28 November, 5 December

B 19 September, 26 September

Table 226

Sundays
from 19 September

Lanark, Coatbridge, Motherwell, Larkhall, Hamilton, Drumgelloch, Airdrie and Springburn - Glasgow - Milngavie, Dalmuir, Balloch and Helensburgh

		SR	SR	SR	SR	SR	SR	SR	SR	SR	SR	SR	SR	SR	SR	SR	SR	SR	SR	SR	SR	SR	SR
					A		A			A	A				A	A			A		A		◇
Lanark	d					10 12																	
Carluke	d					10 22																	
Wishaw	d					10 27																	
Holytown	d																						
Shieldmuir	d					10 31																	
Coatbridge Central	d																						
Whifflet	d																						
Motherwell	a					10 35																	
	d	10 10				10 36		10 40				11 10					11 40			12 06		12 10	
Bellshill	d					10 42														12 12			
Uddingston	d					10 46														12 16			
Airbles	d	10 12						10 42				11 12					11 42					12 12	
Larkhall	d			10 25										11 25									
Merryton	d			10 27										11 27									
Chatelherault	d			10 30										11 30									
Hamilton Central	d	10 17		10 33				10 47				11 17		11 33			11 47					12 17	
Hamilton West	d	10 20		10 36				10 50				11 20		11 36			11 50					12 20	
Blantyre	d	10 23		10 39				10 53				11 23		11 39			11 53					12 23	
Newton	d	10 27						10 57				11 27					11 57					12 27	
Cambuslang	d	10 31				10 51		11 01				11 31					12 01			12 21		12 31	
Rutherglen	d	10 34		10 49		10 54		11 04				11 34		11 49			12 04			12 24		12 34	
Dalmarnock	d																						
Bridgeton	d	10 37				10 57		11 07				11 37					12 07			12 27		12 37	
Drumgelloch	d																						
Airdrie	a																						
	d		10 28				10 43		10 58		11 13		11 28			11 43		11 58			12 13		
Coatdyke	d		10 30				10 45		11 00		11 15		11 30			11 45		12 00			12 15		
Coatbridge Sunnyside	d		10 32				10 47		11 02		11 17		11 32			11 47		12 02			12 17		
Blairhill	d		10 35				10 50		11 05		11 20		11 35			11 50		12 05			12 20		
Easterhouse	d		10 39				10 54		11 09		11 24		11 39			11 54		12 09			12 24		
Garrowhill	d		10 41				10 56		11 11		11 26		11 41			11 56		12 11			12 26		
Shettleston	d		10 44				10 59		11 14		11 29		11 44			11 59		12 14			12 29		
Carntyne	d		10 46				11 01		11 16		11 31		11 46			12 01		12 16			12 31		
Springburn	d				10 49					11 19					11 49				12 19				
Barnhill	d				10 50					11 20					11 50				12 20				
Alexandra Parade	d				10 53					11 23					11 53				12 23				
Duke Street	d				10 55					11 25					11 55				12 25				
Bellgrove	d		10 49		10 57		11 04		11 19	11 27	11 34		11 49		11 57	12 04		12 19	12 27		12 34		
High Street	d		10 51		10 59		11 06		11 21	11 29	11 36		11 51		11 59	12 06		12 21	12 29		12 36		
Glasgow Queen St HL 10	d																						12 20
Glasgow Queen St LL 10	a		10 53		11 01		11 09		11 23	11 31	11 39		11 53		12 01	12 09		12 23	12 31		12 39		
	d		10 54		11 01		11 09		11 24	11 31	11 39		11 54		12 01	12 09		12 24	12 31		12 39		
Charing Cross	d		10 57		11 03		11 12		11 27	11 33	11 42		11 57		12 03	12 12		12 27	12 33		12 42		
Argyle Street	d	10 41		10 54		11 01		11 11				11 41		11 54			12 11			12 31		12 41	
Glasgow Central HL 15	a																						
Glasgow Central LL 15	a	10 44		10 57		11 04		11 14				11 44		11 57			12 14			12 34		12 44	
	d	10 44		10 57		11 04		11 14				11 44		11 57			12 14			12 34		12 44	
Anderston	d																						
Exhibition Centre	d	10 48		11 01		11 08		11 18				11 48		12 01			12 18			12 38		12 48	
Partick	d	10 52	11 02	11a04	11 07	11 12	11 16	11 22	11 32	11 37	11 47	11 52	12 02	12a04	12 09	12 17	12 22	12 32	12 37	12 42	12 47	12 52	
Hyndland	d	10 54	11 04		11 09	11 16	11 18	11 24	11 34	11 39	11 49	11 54	12 04		12 11	12 19	12 24	12 34	12 39	12 46	12 49	12 54	
Jordanhill	d	10 56			11 11			11 26		11 41		11 56			12 13		12 26		12 41			12 56	
Scotstounhill	d	10 58			11 13			11 28		11 43		11 58			12 15		12 28		12 43			12 58	
Garscadden	d	11 00			11 16			11 30		11 46		12 00			12 18		12 30		12 46			13 00	
Yoker	d	11 03			11 18			11 33		11 48		12 03			12 20		12 33		12 48			13 03	
Clydebank	d	11 05			11 20			11 35		11 50		12 05			12 22		12 35		12 50			13 05	
Anniesland	d		11 07			11 19	11 22		11 37		11 52		12 07			12 22		12 37		12 49	12 52		
Westerton	d		11 10			11 22	11 24		11 40		11 55		12 10			12 25		12 40		12 52	12 55		
Bearsden	d					11 25														12 55			
Hillfoot	d					11 27														12 57			
Milngavie	a					11 30														13 00			
Drumchapel	d		11 12				11 26		11 42		11 57		12 12			12 27		12 42			12 57		
Drumry	d		11 14				11 28		11 44		11 59		12 14			12 29		12 44			12 59		
Singer	d		11 17				11 32		11 47		12 02		12 17			12 32		12 47			13 02		
Dalmuir	a	11 09	11 19		11 24		11 33	11 39	11 49	11 53	12 04	12 09	12 19		12 25	12 34	12 39	12 49	12 53		13 04	13 09	12 36
	d	11 09	11 20					11 39	11 50			12 09	12 20				12 39	12 50				13 09	12 36
Kilpatrick	d	11 11						11 41				12 11					12 41					13 11	
Bowling	d	11 14						11 44				12 14					12 44					13 14	
Dumbarton East	d	11 19	11 28					11 49	11 58			12 19	12 28				12 49	12 58				13 19	
Dumbarton Central	d	11 21	11 30					11 51	12 00			12 21	12 30				12 51	13 00				13 21	12 46
Dalreoch	d	11 22	11 31					11 52	12 01			12 22	12 31				12 52	13 01				13 22	
Renton	d	11 25						11 55				12 25					12 55					13 25	
Alexandria	d	11 28						11 58				12 28					12 58					13 28	
Balloch	a	11 30						12 00				12 30					13 00					13 30	
Cardross	d		11 36						12 06				12 36					13 06					
Craigendoran	d		11 41						12 11				12 41					13 11					
Helensburgh Central	a		11 44						12 14				12 44					13 14					
Helensburgh Upper	a																						13 03

A 28 November, 5 December

Table 226

Sundays
from 19 September

Lanark, Coatbridge, Motherwell, Larkhall, Hamilton, Drumgelloch, Airdrie and Springburn - Glasgow - Milngavie, Dalmuir, Balloch and Helensburgh

		SR	SR	SR	SR	SR	SR	SR	SR	SR	SR	SR	SR	SR	SR	SR	SR	SR	SR	SR	SR	SR
				A		A			A		A				A	A		A		A		
Lanark	d				12 12																	
Carluke	d				12 22																	
Wishaw	d				12 27																	
Holytown	d																					
Shieldmuir	d				12 31																	
Coatbridge Central	d																					
Whifflet	d																					
Motherwell	a				12 35																	
	d				12 36		12 40			13 06		13 10							14 06		14 10	
Bellshill	d				12 42					13 12									14 12			
Uddingston	d				12 46					13 16									14 16			
Airbles	d						12 42					13 12									14 12	
Larkhall	d		12 25											13 25								
Merryton	d		12 27											13 27								
Chatelherault	d		12 30											13 30								
Hamilton Central	d		12 33				12 47					13 17		13 33							14 17	
Hamilton West	d		12 36				12 50					13 20		13 36							14 20	
Blantyre	d		12 39				12 53					13 23		13 39							14 23	
Newton	d						12 57					13 27									14 27	
Cambuslang	d				12 51		13 01			13 21		13 31							14 21		14 31	
Rutherglen	d		12 49		12 54		13 04			13 24		13 34		13 49					14 24		14 34	
Dalmarnock	d																					
Bridgeton	d				12 57		13 07			13 27		13 37							14 27		14 37	
Drumgelloch	d																					
Airdrie	a																					
	d	12 28				12 43		12 58			13 13		13 28			13 43	13 58			14 13		14 28
Coatdyke	d	12 30				12 45		13 00			13 15		13 30			13 45	14 00			14 15		14 30
Coatbridge Sunnyside	d	12 32				12 47		13 02			13 17		13 32			13 47	14 02			14 17		14 32
Blairhill	d	12 35				12 50		13 05			13 20		13 35			13 50	14 05			14 20		14 35
Easterhouse	d	12 39				12 54		13 09			13 24		13 39			13 54	14 09			14 24		14 39
Garrowhill	d	12 41				12 56		13 11			13 26		13 41			13 56	14 11			14 26		14 41
Shettleston	d	12 44				12 59		13 14			13 29		13 44			13 59	14 14			14 29		14 44
Carntyne	d	12 46				13 01		13 16			13 31		13 46			14 01	14 16			14 31		14 46
Springburn	d			12 49					13 19						13 49			14 18				
Barnhill	d			12 50					13 20						13 50			14 19				
Alexandra Parade	d			12 53					13 23						13 53			14 22				
Duke Street	d			12 55					13 25						13 55			14 24				
Bellgrove	d	12 49		12 57		13 04		13 19	13 27		13 34		13 49		13 57	14 04	14 19	14 26		14 34		14 49
High Street	d	12 51		12 59		13 06		13 21	13 29		13 36		13 51		13 59	14 06	14 21	14 28		14 36		14 51
Glasgow Queen St HL 10	d																					
Glasgow Queen St LL 10	a	12 53		13 01		13 09		13 23	13 31		13 39		13 53		14 01	14 09	14 23	14 30		14 39		14 53
	d	12 54		13 01		13 09		13 24	13 31		13 39		13 54		14 01	14 09	14 24	14 30		14 39		14 54
Charing Cross	d	12 57		13 03		13 12		13 27	13 33		13 42		13 57		14 03	14 12	14 27	14 32		14 42		14 57
Argyle Street	d		12 54		13 01		13 11			13 31		13 41		13 54					14 31		14 41	
Glasgow Central HL 15	a																					
Glasgow Central LL 15	a		12 57		13 04		13 14			13 34		13 44		13 57					14 34		14 44	
	d		12 57		13 04		13 14			13 34		13 44		13 57					14 34		14 44	
Anderston	d																					
Exhibition Centre	d		13 01		13 08		13 18			13 38		13 48		14 01					14 38		14 48	
Partick	d	13 02	13a04	13 07	13 12	13 17	13 22	13 32	13 37	13 42	13 47	13 52	14 02	14a04	14 09	14 17	14 32	14 36	14 42	14 47	14 52	15 02
Hyndland	d	13 04		13 09	13 16	13 19	13 24	13 34	13 39	13 46	13 49	13 54	14 04		14 11	14 19	14 34	14 38	14 46	14 49	14 54	15 04
Jordanhill	d			13 11			13 26		13 41			13 56			14 13			14 40			14 56	
Scotstounhill	d			13 13			13 28		13 43			13 58			14 14			14 42			14 58	
Garscadden	d			13 16			13 30		13 46			14 00			14 17			14 45			15 00	
Yoker	d			13 18			13 33		13 48			14 03			14 20			14 47			15 03	
Clydebank	d			13 20			13 35		13 50			14 05			14 22			14 49			15 05	
Anniesland	d	13 07			13 19	13 22		13 37		13 49	13 52		14 07			14 22	14 37		14 49	14 52		15 07
Westerton	d	13 10			13 22	13 25		13 40		13 52	13 55		14 10			14 25	14 40		14 52	14 55		15 10
Bearsden	d				13 25					13 55									14 55			
Hillfoot	d				13 27					13 57									14 57			
Milngavie	a				13 30					14 00									15 00			
Drumchapel	d	13 12				13 27		13 42			13 57		14 12			14 27	14 42			14 57		15 12
Drumry	d	13 14				13 29		13 44			13 59		14 14			14 29	14 44			14 59		15 14
Singer	d	13 17				13 32		13 47			14 02		14 17			14 32	14 47			15 02		15 17
Dalmuir	a	13 19		13 24		13 34	13 39	13 49	13 53		14 04	14 09	14 19		14 25	14 34	14 49	14 52		15 04	15 09	15 19
	d	13 20					13 39	13 50				14 09	14 20				14 50				15 09	15 20
Kilpatrick	d						13 41					14 11									15 11	
Bowling	d						13 44					14 14									15 14	
Dumbarton East	d	13 28					13 49	13 58				14 19	14 28				14 58				15 19	15 28
Dumbarton Central	d	13 30					13 51	14 00				14 21	14 30				15 00				15 21	15 30
Dalreoch	d	13 31					13 52	14 01				14 22	14 31				15 01				15 22	15 31
Renton	d						13 55					14 25									15 25	
Alexandria	d						13 58					14 28									15 28	
Balloch	a						14 00					14 30									15 30	
Cardross	d	13 36						14 06					14 36				15 06					15 36
Craigendoran	d	13 41						14 11					14 41				15 11					15 41
Helensburgh Central	a	13 44						14 14					14 44				15 14					15 44
Helensburgh Upper	a																					

A 28 November, 5 December

Table 226

Sundays
from 19 September

Lanark, Coatbridge, Motherwell, Larkhall, Hamilton, Drumgelloch, Airdrie and Springburn - Glasgow - Milngavie, Dalmuir, Balloch and Helensburgh

		SR	SR A	SR	SR A	SR	SR	SR A	SR	SR A	SR	SR	SR	SR A	SR	SR A	SR	SR	SR A	SR	SR A	SR	SR
Lanark	d			14 12											15 11								
Carluke	d			14 22											15 21								
Wishaw	d			14 27											15 27								
Holytown	d																						
Shieldmuir	d			14 31											15 31								
Coatbridge Central	d																						
Whifflet	d																						
Motherwell	a			14 35											15 35								
	d			14 36		14 40			15 06		15 10				15 35		15 40			16 06		16 10	
Bellshill	d			14 42					15 12						15 41					16 12			
Uddingston	d			14 46					15 16						15 45					16 16			
Airbles	d					14 42					15 12						15 42					16 12	
Larkhall	d	14 25											15 25										
Merryton	d	14 27											15 27										
Chatelherault	d	14 30											15 30										
Hamilton Central	d	14 33				14 47					15 17		15 33				15 47					16 17	
Hamilton West	d	14 36				14 50					15 20		15 36				15 50					16 20	
Blantyre	d	14 39				14 53					15 23		15 39				15 53					16 23	
Newton	d					14 57					15 27						15 57					16 27	
Cambuslang	d			14 51		15 01			15 21		15 31				15 50		16 01			16 21		16 31	
Rutherglen	d	14 49		14 54		15 04			15 24		15 34		15 49		15 54		16 05			16 24		16 34	
Dalmarnock	d																						
Bridgeton	d			14 57		15 07			15 27		15 37				15 57		16 07			16 27		16 37	
Drumgelloch	d																						
Airdrie	a																						
	d				14 43		14 58			15 13		15 28				15 43		15 58			16 13		16 28
Coatdyke	d				14 45		15 00			15 15		15 30				15 45		16 00			16 15		16 30
Coatbridge Sunnyside	d				14 47		15 02			15 17		15 32				15 47		16 02			16 17		16 32
Blairhill	d				14 50		15 05			15 20		15 35				15 50		16 05			16 20		16 35
Easterhouse	d				14 54		15 09			15 24		15 39				15 54		16 09			16 24		16 39
Garrowhill	d				14 56		15 11			15 26		15 41				15 56		16 11			16 26		16 41
Shettleston	d				14 59		15 14			15 29		15 44				15 59		16 14			16 29		16 44
Carntyne	d				15 01		15 16			15 31		15 46				16 01		16 16			16 31		16 46
Springburn	d		14 49					15 19						15 48					16 19				
Barnhill	d		14 50					15 20						15 49					16 20				
Alexandra Parade	d		14 53					15 23						15 52					16 23				
Duke Street	d		14 55					15 25						15 54					16 25				
Bellgrove	d		14 57		15 04		15 19	15 27		15 34		15 49		15 56		16 04		16 19	16 27		16 34		16 49
High Street	d		14 59		15 06		15 21	15 29		15 36		15 51		15 58		16 06		16 21	16 29		16 36		16 51
Glasgow Queen St HL 10	d																						
Glasgow Queen St LL 10	a		15 01		15 09		15 23	15 31		15 39		15 53		16 00		16 09		16 23	16 31		16 39		16 53
	d		15 01		15 09		15 24	15 31		15 39		15 54		16 00		16 09		16 24	16 31		16 39		16 54
Charing Cross	d		15 05		15 12		15 27	15 33		15 42		15 57		16 02		16 12		16 27	16 33		16 42		16 57
Argyle Street	d	14 54		15 01		15 11			15 31		15 41		15 54		16 01		16 11			16 31		16 41	
Glasgow Central HL 15	a																						
Glasgow Central LL 15	a	14 57		15 04		15 14			15 34		15 44		15 57		16 04		16 14			16 34		16 44	
	d	14 57		15 04		15 14			15 34		15 44		15 57		16 04		16 14			16 34		16 44	
Anderston	d																						
Exhibition Centre	d	15 01		15 08		15 18			15 38		15 48		16 01		16 08		16 18			16 38		16 48	
Partick	d	15a04	15 09	15 12	15 17	15 22	15 32	15 37	15 42	15 47	15 52	16 02	16a04	16 08	16 12	16 17	16 22	16 32	16 37	16 42	16 47	16 52	17 02
Hyndland	d		15 11	15 16	15 19	15 24	15 34	15 39	15 46	15 49	15 54	16 04		16 10	16 16	16 19	16 24	16 34	16 39	16 46	16 49	16 54	17 04
Jordanhill	d		15 13			15 26		15 41			15 56			16 12			16 26		16 41			16 56	
Scotstounhill	d		15 14			15 28		15 43			15 58			16 14			16 28		16 43			16 58	
Garscadden	d		15 17			15 30		15 46			16 00			16 17			16 30		16 46			17 00	
Yoker	d		15 20			15 33		15 48			16 03			16 19			16 33		16 48			17 03	
Clydebank	d		15 22			15 35		15 50			16 05			16 21			16 35		16 50			17 05	
Anniesland	d			15 19	15 22		15 37		15 49	15 52		16 07			16 19	16 22		16 37		16 49	16 52		17 07
Westerton	d			15 22	15 25		15 40		15 52	15 55		16 10			16 22	16 25		16 40		16 52	16 55		17 10
Bearsden	d			15 25					15 55						16 25					16 55			
Hillfoot	d			15 27					15 57						16 27					16 57			
Milngavie	a			15 30					16 00						16 30					17 00			
Drumchapel	d				15 27		15 42			15 57		16 12				16 27		16 42			16 57		17 12
Drumry	d				15 29		15 44			15 59		16 14				16 29		16 44			16 59		17 14
Singer	d				15 32		15 47			16 02		16 17				16 32		16 47			17 02		17 17
Dalmuir	a		15 25		15 34	15 39	15 49	15 53		16 04	16 09	16 19		16 25		16 34	16 39	16 49	16 53		17 04	17 09	17 19
	d					15 39	15 50				16 09	16 20					16 39	16 50				17 09	17 20
Kilpatrick	d					15 41					16 11						16 41					17 11	
Bowling	d					15 44					16 14						16 44					17 14	
Dumbarton East	d					15 49	15 58				16 19	16 28					16 49	16 58				17 19	17 28
Dumbarton Central	d					15 51	16 00				16 21	16 30					16 51	17 00				17 21	17 30
Dalreoch	d					15 52	16 01				16 22	16 31					16 52	17 01				17 22	17 31
Renton	d					15 55					16 25						16 55					17 25	
Alexandria	d					15 58					16 28						16 58					17 28	
Balloch	a					16 00					16 30						17 00					17 30	
Cardross	d						16 06					16 36						17 06					17 36
Craigendoran	d						16 11					16 41						17 11					17 41
Helensburgh Central	a						16 14					16 44						17 14					17 44
Helensburgh Upper	a																						

A 28 November, 5 December

Table 226

Sundays
from 19 September

Lanark, Coatbridge, Motherwell, Larkhall, Hamilton, Drumgelloch, Airdrie and Springburn - Glasgow - Milngavie, Dalmuir, Balloch and Helensburgh

		SR	SR A	SR	SR A	SR	SR	SR A	SR	SR A	SR	SR	SR A	SR	SR A	SR	SR	SR	SR ◇	SR	SR	SR
Lanark	d			16 12										17 11								
Carluke	d			16 22										17 21								
Wishaw	d			16 27										17 26								
Holytown	d																					
Shieldmuir	d			16 31										17 30								
Coatbridge Central	d																					
Whifflet	d																					
Motherwell	a			16 34										17 35								
	d			16 34		16 40			17 06					17 35		17 40		18 10				18 40
Bellshill	d			16 40					17 12					17 41								
Uddingston	d			16 44					17 16					17 45								
Airbles	d					16 42										17 42		18 12				18 42
Larkhall	d	16 25										17 25									18 25	
Merryton	d	16 27										17 27									18 27	
Chatelherault	d	16 30										17 30									18 30	
Hamilton Central	d	16 33				16 47						17 33				17 47		18 17			18 33	18 47
Hamilton West	d	16 36				16 50						17 36				17 50		18 20			18 36	18 50
Blantyre	d	16 39				16 53						17 39				17 53		18 23			18 39	18 53
Newton	d					16 57										17 57		18 27				18 57
Cambuslang	d			16 49		17 01			17 21					17 50		18 01		18 31				19 01
Rutherglen	d	16 49		16 54		17 04			17 24			17 47		17 54		18 04		18 34			18 49	19 04
Dalmarnock	d																					
Bridgeton	d			16 57		17 07			17 27					17 57		18 07		18 37				19 07
Drumgelloch	d																					
Airdrie	a																					
	d				16 43		16 58			17 13	17 28				17 43		17 58			18 28		
Coatdyke	d				16 45		17 00			17 15	17 30				17 45		18 00			18 30		
Coatbridge Sunnyside	d				16 47		17 02			17 17	17 32				17 47		18 02			18 32		
Blairhill	d				16 50		17 05			17 20	17 35				17 50		18 05			18 35		
Easterhouse	d				16 54		17 09			17 24	17 39				17 54		18 09			18 39		
Garrowhill	d				16 56		17 11			17 26	17 41				17 56		18 11			18 41		
Shettleston	d				16 59		17 14			17 29	17 44				17 59		18 14			18 44		
Carntyne	d				17 01		17 16			17 31	17 46				18 01		18 16			18 46		
Springburn	d		16 49					17 19					17 49									
Barnhill	d		16 50					17 20					17 50									
Alexandra Parade	d		16 53					17 23					17 53									
Duke Street	d		16 55					17 25					17 55									
Bellgrove	d		16 57		17 04		17 19	17 27		17 34	17 49		17 57		18 04		18 19			18 49		
High Street	d		16 59		17 06		17 21	17 29		17 36	17 51		17 59		18 06		18 21			18 51		
Glasgow Queen St HL 10	d																		18 20			
Glasgow Queen St LL 10	a		17 01		17 09		17 23	17 31		17 39	17 53		18 01		18 09		18 23			18 53		
	d		17 01		17 09		17 24	17 31		17 39	17 54		18 01		18 09		18 24			18 54		
Charing Cross	d		17 03		17 12		17 27	17 33		17 42	17 57		18 03		18 12		18 27			18 57		
Argyle Street	d	16 54		17 01		17 11			17 31			17 52		18 01		18 11						
Glasgow Central HL 15	a																					
Glasgow Central LL 15	a	16 57		17 04		17 14			17 34			17 57		18 04		18 14		18 44			18 57	19 14
	d	16 57		17 04		17 14			17 34			17 57		18 04		18 14		18 44			18 57	19 14
Anderston	d																					
Exhibition Centre	d	17 01		17 08		17 18			17 38			18 01		18 08		18 18		18 48			19 01	19 18
Partick	d	17a04	17 09	17 12	17 17	17 22	17 32	17 37	17 42	17 47	18 02	18a04	18 10	18 12	18 17	18 22	18 32	18 52		19 02	19a04	19 22
Hyndland	d		17 11	17 16	17 19	17 24	17 34	17 39	17 46	17 49	18 04		18 12	18 16	18 19	18 24	18 34	18 54		19 04		19 24
Jordanhill	d		17 13			17 26		17 41					18 14			18 26		18 56				19 26
Scotstounhill	d		17 15			17 28		17 43					18 16			18 28		18 58				19 28
Garscadden	d		17 18			17 30		17 46					18 19			18 30		19 00				19 30
Yoker	d		17 20			17 33		17 48					18 21			18 33		19 03				19 33
Clydebank	d		17 22			17 35		17 50					18 23			18 35		19 05				19 35
Anniesland	d			17 19	17 22		17 37		17 49	17 52	18 07			18 19	18 26		18 37			19 07		
Westerton	d			17 22	17 25		17 40		17 52	17 55	18 10			18 22	18 33		18 40			19 10		
Bearsden	d			17 25					17 55					18 25								
Hillfoot	d			17 27					17 57					18 27								
Milngavie	a			17 30					18 00					18 30								
Drumchapel	d				17 27		17 42			17 57	18 12				18 35		18 42			19 12		
Drumry	d				17 29		17 44			17 59	18 14				18 37		18 44			19 14		
Singer	d				17 32		17 47			18 02	18 17				18 40		18 47			19 17		
Dalmuir	a		17 25		17 34	17 39	17 49	17 53		18 04	18 19		18 26		18 42	18 39	18 49	19 09	18 34	19 19		19 39
	d					17 39	17 50				18 20					18 39	18 50	19 09	18 34	19 20		19 39
Kilpatrick	d					17 41										18 41		19 11				19 41
Bowling	d					17 44										18 44		19 14				19 44
Dumbarton East	d					17 49	17 58				18 28					18 49	18 58	19 19		19 28		19 49
Dumbarton Central	d					17 51	18 00				18 30					18 51	19 00	19 21	18 43	19 30		19 51
Dalreoch	d					17 52	18 01				18 31					18 52	19 01	19 22		19 31		19 52
Renton	d					17 55										18 55		19 25				19 55
Alexandria	d					17 58										18 58		19 28				19 58
Balloch	a					18 00										19 00		19 30				20 00
Cardross	d						18 06				18 36						19 06			19 36		
Craigendoran	d						18 11				18 41						19 11			19 41		
Helensburgh Central	a						18 14				18 44						19 14			19 44		
Helensburgh Upper	a																		18 56			

A 28 November, 5 December

Table 226

Sundays
from 19 September

Lanark, Coatbridge, Motherwell, Larkhall, Hamilton, Drumgelloch, Airdrie and Springburn - Glasgow - Milngavie, Dalmuir, Balloch and Helensburgh

		SR	SR	SR	SR	SR	SR	SR	SR	SR		SR	SR	SR	SR	SR	SR	SR	SR	SR		SR	SR	SR	SR
Lanark	d					19 12								20 12								21 12			
Carluke	d					19 22								20 22								21 22			
Wishaw	d					19 27								20 27								21 27			
Holytown	d																								
Shieldmuir	d					19 31								20 31								21 31			
Coatbridge Central	d																								
Whifflet	d																								
Motherwell	a					19 35								20 35								21 35			
	d		19 06	19 10		19 35	19 40		20 06	20 10				20 36	20 40		21 06	21 10				21 35		22 10	
Bellshill	d		19 12			19 41			20 12					20 42			21 12					21 41			
Uddingston	d		19 16			19 45			20 17					20 46			21 16					21 45			
Airbles	d			19 12			19 42			20 12					20 42			21 12						22 12	
Larkhall	d				19 25								20 25							21 25					
Merryton	d				19 27								20 27							21 27					
Chatelherault	d				19 30								20 30							21 30					
Hamilton Central	d			19 17	19 33		19 47			20 17			20 33		20 47			21 17		21 33				22 17	
Hamilton West	d			19 20	19 36		19 50			20 20			20 36		20 50			21 20		21 36				22 20	
Blantyre	d			19 23	19 39		19 53			20 23			20 39		20 53			21 23		21 39				22 23	
Newton	d			19 27			19 57			20 26					20 57			21 27						22 27	
Cambuslang	d		19 21	19 31		19 50	20 01		20 22	20 30				20 51	21 01		21 21	21 31				21 50		22 31	
Rutherglen	d		19 24	19 34	19 49	19 53	20 04		20 25	20 33			20 49	20 54	21 04		21 24	21 34		21 50		21 53		22 35	
Dalmarnock	d																								
Bridgeton	d		19 27	19 37		19 57	20 07		20 28	20 37				20 57	21 07		21 27	21 37				21 57		22 38	
Drumgelloch	d																								
Airdrie	a																								
	d	18 58						19 58				20 28				20 58			21 28				21 58		22 28
Coatdyke	d	19 00						20 00				20 30				21 00			21 30				22 00		22 30
Coatbridge Sunnyside	d	19 02						20 02				20 32				21 02			21 32				22 02		22 32
Blairhill	d	19 05						20 05				20 35				21 05			21 35				22 05		22 35
Easterhouse	d	19 09						20 09				20 39				21 09			21 39				22 09		22 39
Garrowhill	d	19 11						20 11				20 41				21 11			21 41				22 11		22 41
Shettleston	d	19 14						20 14				20 44				21 14			21 44				22 14		22 44
Carntyne	d	19 16						20 16				20 46				21 16			21 46				22 16		22 46
Springburn	d																								
Barnhill	d																								
Alexandra Parade	d																								
Duke Street	d																								
Bellgrove	d	19 19						20 19				20 49				21 19			21 49				22 19		22 49
High Street	d	19 21						20 21				20 51				21 21			21 51				22 21		22 51
Glasgow Queen St HL 10	d																								
Glasgow Queen St LL 10	a	19 23						20 23				20 53				21 23			21 53				22 23		22 53
	d	19 24						20 24				20 54				21 24			21 54				22 24		22 54
Charing Cross	d	19 27						20 27				20 57				21 27			21 57				22 27		22 57
Argyle Street	d																								
Glasgow Central HL 15	a																								
Glasgow Central LL 15	a		19 34	19 44	19 57	20 04	20 14		20 34	20 44			20 57	21 04	21 14		21 34	21 44		21 57		22 04		22 44	
	d		19 34	19 44	19 57	20 04	20 14		20 34	20 44			20 57	21 04	21 14		21 34	21 44		21 57		22 04		22 44	
Anderston	d																								
Exhibition Centre	d		19 38	19 48	20 01	20 08	20 18		20 38	20 48			21 01	21 08	21 18		21 38	21 48		22 01		22 08		22 48	
Partick	d	19 32	19 42	19 52	20a04	20 12	20 22	20 32	20 42	20 52		21 02	21a04	21 12	21 22	21 32	21 42	21 52	22 02	22a04		22 12	22 32	22 52	23 02
Hyndland	d	19 34	19 46	19 54		20 16	20 24	20 34	20 46	20 54		21 04		21 16	21 24	21 34	21 46	21 54	22 04			22 16	22 34	22 54	23 04
Jordanhill	d			19 56			20 26			20 56					21 26			21 56						22 56	
Scotstounhill	d			19 58			20 28			20 58					21 28			21 58						22 58	
Garscadden	d			20 00			20 30			21 00					21 30			22 00						23 00	
Yoker	d			20 03			20 33			21 03					21 33			22 03						23 03	
Clydebank	d			20 05			20 35			21 05					21 35			22 05						23 05	
Anniesland	d	19 37	19 49			20 19		20 37	20 49			21 07		21 19		21 37	21 49		22 07			22 19	22 37		23 07
Westerton	d	19 40	19 52			20 22		20 40	20 52			21 10		21 22		21 40	21 52		22 10			22 22	22 40		23 10
Bearsden	d		19 55			20 25			20 55					21 25			21 55					22 25			
Hillfoot	d		19 57			20 27			20 57					21 27			21 57					22 27			
Milngavie	a		20 00			20 30			21 00					21 30			22 00					22 30			
Drumchapel	d	19 42						20 42				21 12				21 42			22 12				22 42		23 12
Drumry	d	19 44						20 44				21 14				21 44			22 14				22 44		23 14
Singer	d	19 47						20 47				21 17				21 47			22 17				22 47		23 17
Dalmuir	a	19 49		20 09			20 39	20 49		21 09		21 19			21 39	21 49		22 09	22 19				22 49	23 09	23 19
	d	19 50		20 09			20 39	20 50		21 09		21 20			21 39	21 50		22 09	22 20				22 50	23 09	23 20
Kilpatrick	d			20 11			20 41			21 11					21 41			22 11						23 11	
Bowling	d			20 14			20 44			21 14					21 44			22 14						23 14	
Dumbarton East	d	19 58		20 19			20 49	20 58		21 19		21 28			21 49	21 58		22 19	22 28				22 58	23 19	23 28
Dumbarton Central	d	20 00		20 21			20 52	21 00		21 21		21 30			21 51	22 00		22 21	22 30				23 00	23 21	23 30
Dalreoch	d	20 01		20 22			20 53	21 01		21 22		21 31			21 52	22 01		22 22	22 31				23 01	23 22	23 31
Renton	d			20 25			20 55			21 25					21 55			22 25						23 25	
Alexandria	d			20 28			20 58			21 28					21 58			22 28						23 28	
Balloch	a			20 30			21 00			21 30					22 00			22 30						23 30	
Cardross	d	20 06						21 06				21 36				22 06			22 36				23 06		23 36
Craigendoran	d	20 11						21 11				21 41				22 11			22 41				23 11		23 41
Helensburgh Central	a	20 14						21 14				21 44				22 14			22 44				23 14		23 44
Helensburgh Upper	a																								

Table 226

Sundays
from 19 September

Lanark, Coatbridge, Motherwell, Larkhall, Hamilton, Drumgelloch, Airdrie and Springburn - Glasgow - Milngavie, Dalmuir, Balloch and Helensburgh

		SR	SR	SR	SR	SR		SR	SR
Lanark	d		22 12						
Carluke	d		22 22						
Wishaw	d		22 27						
Holytown	d								
Shieldmuir	d		22 31						
Coatbridge Central	d								
Whifflet	d								
Motherwell	a		22 35						
	d		22 36	22 40		23 10		23 10	
Bellshill	d		22 42			23 16			
Uddingston	d		22 46			23 20			
Airbles	d			22 42				23 12	
Larkhall	d	22 25							
Merryton	d	22 27							
Chatelherault	d	22 30							
Hamilton Central	d	22 33		22 47				23 17	
Hamilton West	d	22 36		22 50				23 20	
Blantyre	d	22 39		22 53				23 23	
Newton	d			22 57				23 27	
Cambuslang	d		22 51	23 01		23 25		23 31	
Rutherglen	d	22 48	22 54	23 04		23 28		23 34	
Dalmarnock	d								
Bridgeton	d		22 57	23 07		23 31		23 37	
Drumgelloch	d								
Airdrie	a								
	d				22 58				23 28
Coatdyke	d				23 00				23 30
Coatbridge Sunnyside	d				23 02				23 32
Blairhill	d				23 05				23 35
Easterhouse	d				23 09				23 39
Garrowhill	d				23 11				23 41
Shettleston	d				23 14				23 44
Carntyne	d				23 16				23 46
Springburn	d								
Barnhill	d								
Alexandra Parade	d								
Duke Street	d								
Bellgrove	d				23 19				23 49
High Street	d				23 21				23 51
Glasgow Queen St HL 10	d								
Glasgow Queen St LL 10	a				23 23				23 53
	d				23 24				23 54
Charing Cross	d				23 27				23 57
Argyle Street	d								
Glasgow Central HL 15	a								
Glasgow Central LL 15	a	22 57	23 04	23 14		23 35		23 44	
	d	22 57	23 04	23 14		23 36		23 44	
Anderston	d								
Exhibition Centre	d	23 01	23 08	23 18		23 39		23 48	
Partick	d	23a04	23 12	23 22	23 32	23 43		23 52	00 02
Hyndland	d		23 16	23 24	23 34	23 45		23 54	00 04
Jordanhill	d			23 26		23 47		23 56	00 06
Scotstounhill	d			23 28		23 49		23 58	00 08
Garscadden	d			23 30		23a51		00a01	00a10
Yoker	d			23 33					
Clydebank	d			23 35					
Anniesland	d		23 19		23 37				
Westerton	d		23 22		23 40				
Bearsden	d		23 25						
Hillfoot	d		23 27						
Milngavie	a		23 30						
Drumchapel	d				23 42				
Drumry	d				23 44				
Singer	d				23 47				
Dalmuir	a			23 39	23 49				
	d			23 39	23 50				
Kilpatrick	d			23 41					
Bowling	d			23 44					
Dumbarton East	d			23 49	23 58				
Dumbarton Central	d			23 51	23 59				
Dalreoch	d			23 52	00 01				
Renton	d			23 55					
Alexandria	d			23 58					
Balloch	a			00 01					
Cardross	d				00 06				
Craigendoran	d				00 11				
Helensburgh Central	a				00 14				
Helensburgh Upper	a								

Table 226

Helensburgh, Balloch, Dalmuir and Milngavie - Glasgow - Springburn, Airdrie, Drumgelloch, Hamilton, Larkhall, Motherwell, Coatbridge and Lanark

		SR MX	SR	SR	SR	SR	SR	SR	SR	SR	SR	SR	SR	SR	SR	SR	SR	SR	SR A	SR B	SR
Helensburgh Upper	d																				
Helensburgh Central	d										06 10								06 40	06 40	
Craigendoran	d										06 13								06 43	06 43	
Cardross	d										06 18								06 48	06 48	
Balloch	d															06 23					
Alexandria	d															06 25					
Renton	d															06 28					
Dalreoch	d										06 23					06 31			06 53	06 53	
Dumbarton Central	d										06 25					06 32			06 55	06 55	
Dumbarton East	d										06 27					06 34			06 57	06 57	
Bowling	d															06 39					
Kilpatrick	d															06 42					
Dalmuir	a										06 35					06 45			07 05	07 05	
	d		05 48			06 01			06 16	06 23	06 36	06 31				06 46		06 53	07 06	07 06	07 01
Singer	d					06 03			06 18			06 33				06 48					07 03
Drumry	d					06 05			06 20			06 35				06 50					07 05
Drumchapel	d					06 08			06 23			06 38				06 53					07 08
Milngavie	d														06 42						
Hillfoot	d														06 45						
Bearsden	d														06 47						
Westerton	d					06 10			06 25			06 40			06 50	06 55					07 10
Anniesland	d					06 14			06 28			06 44			06 53	06 58					07 14
Clydebank	d		05 50							06 25								06 55			
Yoker	d		05 52							06 27								06 57			
Garscadden	d		05 55	06 00	06 08		06 16	06 20		06 31				06 46				07 01			
Scotstounhill	d		05 57	06 02	06 10		06 18	06 22		06 33				06 48				07 03			
Jordanhill	d		05 59	06 05	06 12		06 20	06 24		06 35				06 50				07 05			
Hyndland	d		06 01	06 07	06 14	06 17	06 22	06 26	06 31	06 37	06 44	06 47		06 52	06 56	07 01		07 07	07 14	07 14	07 17
Partick	d		06 04	06 10	06 17	06 20	06 25	06 29	06 34	06 40	06 47	06 50		06 55	06 59	07 04		07 10	07 17	07 17	07 20
Exhibition Centre	d			06 13		06 23		06 32		06 43		06 53			07 02			07 13			07 23
Anderston	d			06 15		06 25		06 34		06 45		06 55			07 04			07 15			07 25
Glasgow Central HL 15	d																07 14				
Glasgow Central LL 15	a			06 17		06 26		06 35		06 47		06 56			07 05			07 17			07 26
	d			06 17		06 27		06 37		06 47		06 57			07 07			07 17			07 27
Argyle Street	d			06 19		06 29		06 38		06 49		06 59			07 09			07 19			07 29
Charing Cross	d		06 08		06 22		06 29		06 38		06 52			06 59		07 08			07 22	07 22	
Glasgow Queen St HL 10	a																				
Glasgow Queen St LL 10	a		06 10		06 24		06 31		06 40		06 54			07 01		07 10			07 24	07 24	
	d		06 12		06 27		06 32		06 42		06 57			07 02		07 12			07 27	07 27	
High Street	d		06 14		06 29		06 34		06 44		06 59			07 04		07 14			07 29	07 29	
Bellgrove	d		06 16		06 31		06 36		06 46		07 01			07 06		07 16			07 31	07 31	
Duke Street	d						06 38							07 08							
Alexandra Parade	d						06 39							07 09							
Barnhill	d						06 42							07 12							
Springburn	a						06 44							07 14							
Carntyne	d		06 19		06 34				06 49		07 04					07 19			07 34	07 34	
Shettleston	d		06 22		06 37				06 52		07 07					07 22			07 37	07 37	
Garrowhill	d		06 24		06 39				06 54		07 09					07 24			07 39	07 39	
Easterhouse	d		06 27		06 42				06 57		07 12					07 27			07 42	07 42	
Blairhill	d		06 31		06 46				07 01		07 16					07 31			07 46	07 46	
Coatbridge Sunnyside	d		06 33		06 48				07 03		07 18					07 33			07 48	07 48	
Coatdyke	d		06 36		06 51				07 06		07 21					07 36			07 51	07 51	
Airdrie	a		06 39		06 54				07 09		07 25					07 39			07 54	07 55	
	d	00 37																			
Drumgelloch	a	00 44																			
Bridgeton	d			06 22				06 41		06 52					07 12			07 22			
Dalmarnock	d			06 24				06 43		06 54					07 14			07 24			
Rutherglen	d			06 26		06 34		06 46		06 55		07 02			07 17			07 25			07 34
Cambuslang	d			06 31				06 50		07 00					07 21		07 24	07 30			
Newton	d							06 53							07 24						
Blantyre	d					06 44		06 58				07 13			07 28						07 45
Hamilton West	d					06 47		07 01				07 16			07 31						07 48
Hamilton Central	d					06 50		07 03				07 19			07 33						07 50
Chatelherault	d					06 54						07 23									07 55
Merryton	d					06 58						07 28									07 58
Larkhall	a					07 00						07 31									08 00
Airbles	d							07 08							07 38						
Uddingston	d			06 35						07 05							07 29	07 35			
Bellshill	d			06 40						07 09							07 33	07 39			
Motherwell	a			06 45				07 11		07 16					07 41			07 45			
	d			06 46				07 12					06 37					07 46			
Whifflet	a							07 19													
Coatbridge Central	a							07 23													
Shieldmuir	d			06 50														07 50			
Holytown	d												06 43				07 37				
Wishaw	d			06 53									06 48					07 53			
Carluke	d			07 00									06 55					08 00			
Lanark	a			07 13									07 07					08 15			

A from 20 September

B until 17 September

Table 226

Helensburgh, Balloch, Dalmuir and Milngavie - Glasgow - Springburn, Airdrie, Drumgelloch, Hamilton, Larkhall, Motherwell, Coatbridge and Lanark

		SR	SR	SR	SR	SR	SR	SR	SR	SR	SR	SR	SR	SR	SR	SR	SR	SR	SR	SR	SR	SR	SR
Helensburgh Upper	d																						
Helensburgh Central	d						07 09							07 35					08 01	07 54			08 08
Craigendoran	d						07 12							07 38					08 04	07 57			08 11
Cardross	d						07 17							07 43					08 09	08 02			08 16
Balloch	d			06 53							07 23					07 53							
Alexandria	d			06 55							07 25					07 55							
Renton	d			06 58							07 28					07 58							
Dalreoch	d			07 01			07 22				07 31			07 48		08 01				08 07			08 21
Dumbarton Central	d			07 02			07 24				07 32			07 50		08 03			08 15	08 09			08 23
Dumbarton East	d			07 04			07 26				07 34			07 52						08 11			08 25
Bowling	d			07 09							07 39			07 57									08 30
Kilpatrick	d			07 12							07 42			08 00									08 33
Dalmuir	a			07 15			07 34				07 45			08 03						08 19			08 35
	d			07 16	07 23		07 35	07 31	07 39		07 46	07 53		08 04	08 01		08 08			08 19	08 23		08 36
Singer	d			07 18				07 33			07 48				08 03					08 21			
Drumry	d			07 20				07 35			07 50				08 05					08 24			
Drumchapel	d			07 23				07 38			07 53				08 08					08 26			
Milngavie	d		07 12			07 27				07 42			07 57					08 10				08 27	
Hillfoot	d		07 15			07 30				07 45			08 00					08 13				08 30	
Bearsden	d		07 17			07 32				07 47			08 02					08 16				08 32	
Westerton	d		07 20	07 25		07 35		07 40		07 50	07 55		08 05		08 10			08 19		08 29		08 35	
Anniesland	d		07 23	07 28		07 38		07 44		07 53	07 58		08 08		08 14			08 23		08 32		08 38	
Clydebank	d				07 25				07 41			07 55		08 06			08 10				08 25		
Yoker	d				07 27				07 43			07 57					08 12				08 27		
Garscadden	d	07 16			07 31				07 47			08 01					08 16				08 31		
Scotstounhill	d	07 18			07 33				07 49			08 03					08 18		08 28		08 33		
Jordanhill	d	07 20			07 35				07 51			08 05					08 21				08 35		
Hyndland	d	07 22	07 26	07 31	07 37	07 41	07 44	07 47	07 53	07 56	08 01	08 07	08 11	08 14	08 17		08 23	08 25	08 33	08 35	08 37	08 41	08 44
Partick	d	07 25	07 29	07 34	07 40	07 44	07 47	07 50	07 55	07 59	08 04	08 10	08 14	08 17	08 19	08 23	08 26	08 29	08 35	08 38	08 40	08 44	08 47
Exhibition Centre	d		07 32		07 43			07 53		08 02		08 13	08 17		08 23			08 32			08 43		
Anderston	d		07 34		07 45			07 55		08 04		08 15	08 19		08 25			08 34			08 45		
Glasgow Central HL 15	d																						
Glasgow Central LL 15	a		07 35		07 46			07 56		08 05		08 17	08 20		08 26			08 35			08 47		
	d		07 37		07 46			07 57		08 07		08 17	08 21		08 27			08 37			08 47		
Argyle Street	d		07 39		07 49			07 59		08 09		08 19	08 23		08 29			08 38			08 49		
Charing Cross	d	07 29		07 38		07 49	07 52		07 59		08 08			08 22		08 27	08 31		08 40	08 42		08 49	08 52
Glasgow Queen St HL 10	a																						
Glasgow Queen St LL 10	a	07 31		07 40		07 51	07 54		08 01		08 10			08 24		08 29	08 33		08 42	08 44		08 51	08 54
	d	07 32		07 42		07 51	07 56		08 02		08 12			08 27		08 30	08 33		08 42	08 45		08 51	08 57
High Street	d	07 34		07 44		07a53	07 58		08 04		08 14			08 29		08 32	08a35		08 44	08a47		08a53	08 59
Bellgrove	d	07 36		07 46			08 00		08 06		08 16			08 31		08 34			08 46				09 01
Duke Street	d	07 38							08 08							08 36							
Alexandra Parade	d	07 39							08 09							08 37							
Barnhill	d	07 42							08 12							08 40							
Springburn	a	07 44							08 14							08 42							
Carntyne	d			07 49			08 03				08 19			08 34					08 49				09 03
Shettleston	d			07 52			08 06				08 22			08 37					08 52				09 07
Garrowhill	d			07 54			08 08				08 24			08 39					08 54				09 08
Easterhouse	d			07 57			08 11				08 27			08 42					08 57				09 12
Blairhill	d			08 01			08 15				08 31			08 46					09 01				09 16
Coatbridge Sunnyside	d			08 03			08 17				08 33			08 48					09 04				09 17
Coatdyke	d			08 06			08 20				08 36			08 51					09 06				09 21
Airdrie	a			08 09			08 25				08 39			08 54					09 09				09 24
	d																						
Drumgelloch	a																						
Bridgeton	d		07 42		07 52					08 12		08 22	08 26					08 41			08 52		
Dalmarnock	d		07 44		07 54					08 14		08 24	08 28					08 43			08 54		
Rutherglen	d		07 46		07 55			08 04		08 16		08 26	08 30		08 34			08 46			08 56		
Cambuslang	d		07 49		08 00					08 19		08 31						08 51			09 01		
Newton	d		07 54							08 28								08 55					
Blantyre	d		07 58					08 15		08 32					08 44			08 59					
Hamilton West	d		08 01					08 18		08 35					08 47			09 02					
Hamilton Central	d		08 04					08 20		08 38					08 50			09 04					
Chatelherault	d							08 25							08 54								
Merryton	d							08 28							08 58								
Larkhall	a							08 30							09 00								
Airbles	d		08 09							08 43								09 09					
Uddingston	d				08 05							08 36									09 06		
Bellshill	d				08 09							08 40									09 10		
Motherwell	a		08 11		08 18					08 45		08 47	08 45					09 12			09 16		
	d											08 47									09 16		
Whifflet	a																						
Coatbridge Central	a																						
Shieldmuir	d											08 51									09 20		
Holytown	d																						
Wishaw	d											08 54									09 23		
Carluke	d											09 01									09 30		
Lanark	a											09 13									09 44		

Table 226

Helensburgh, Balloch, Dalmuir and Milngavie - Glasgow - Springburn, Airdrie, Drumgelloch, Hamilton, Larkhall, Motherwell, Coatbridge and Lanark

		SR	SR	SR	SR	SR	SR	SR	SR	SR	SR	SR	SR	SR	SR	SR	SR	SR	SR	SR	SR	SR		SR	SR
Helensburgh Upper	d																								
Helensburgh Central	d							08 40							09 10							09 40			
Craigendoran	d							08 43							09 13							09 43			
Cardross	d							08 48							09 18							09 48			
Balloch	d				08 23							08 53							09 23						
Alexandria	d				08 25							08 55							09 25						
Renton	d				08 28							08 58							09 28						
Dalreoch	d				08 31			08 53				09 01			09 23				09 31			09 53			
Dumbarton Central	d				08 32			08 55				09 02			09 25				09 32			09 55			
Dumbarton East	d				08 34			08 57				09 04			09 27				09 34			09 57			
Bowling	d				08 39							09 09							09 39						
Kilpatrick	d				08 42							09 12							09 42						
Dalmuir	a				08 45			09 05				09 15			09 35				09 45			10 05			
	d	08 31	08 38		08 46	08 53		09 06	09 01	09 08		09 16	09 23		09 36	09 31	09 38		09 46	09 53		10 06		10 01	10 08
Singer	d	08 33			08 48				09 03			09 18				09 33			09 48					10 03	
Drumry	d	08 35			08 50				09 05			09 20				09 35			09 50					10 05	
Drumchapel	d	08 38			08 53				09 08			09 23				09 38			09 53					10 08	
Milngavie	d			08 42			08 57				09 12			09 28				09 42			09 57				
Hillfoot	d			08 45			09 00				09 15			09 31				09 45			10 00				
Bearsden	d			08 47			09 02				09 18			09 33				09 47			10 02				
Westerton	d	08 40		08 50	08 55		09 05		09 10		09 21	09 25		09 36		09 40		09 50	09 55		10 05			10 10	
Anniesland	d	08 44		08 53	08 58		09 08		09 14		09 24	09 28		09 39		09 44		09 53	09 58		10 08			10 14	
Clydebank	d		08 40			08 55				09 10			09 25				09 40			09 55					10 10
Yoker	d		08 42			08 57				09 12			09 27				09 42			09 57					10 12
Garscadden	d		08 46			09 00				09 16			09 31				09 46			10 01					10 16
Scotstounhill	d		08 48			09 02				09 18			09 33				09 48			10 03					10 18
Jordanhill	d		08 50			09 04				09 20			09 35				09 50			10 05					10 20
Hyndland	d	08 47	08 52	08 56	09 01	09 07	09 11	09 14	09 17	09 22	09 27	09 31	09 37	09 41	09 44	09 47	09 52	09 56	10 01	10 07	10 11	10 14		10 17	10 22
Partick	d	08 50	08 55	08 59	09 04	09 10	09 14	09 17	09 20	09 25	09 30	09 34	09 40	09 44	09 47	09 50	09 55	09 59	10 04	10 10	10 14	10 17		10 20	10 25
Exhibition Centre	d	08 53		09 02		09 13			09 23		09 33		09 43			09 53		10 02		10 13				10 23	
Anderston	d	08 55		09 04		09 15			09 25		09 35		09 45			09 55		10 04		10 15				10 25	
Glasgow Central HL 15	d																								
Glasgow Central LL 15	a	08 56		09 05		09 17			09 26		09 36		09 47			09 56		10 05		10 17				10 27	
	d	08 57		09 07		09 17			09 27		09 37		09 47			09 57		10 07		10 17				10 27	
Argyle Street	d	08 59		09 09		09 19			09 29		09 38		09 49			09 59		10 09		10 19				10 29	
Charing Cross	d		08 59		09 08		09 19	09 22		09 29		09 38		09 49	09 52		09 59		10 08		10 19	10 22			10 29
Glasgow Queen St HL 10	a																								
Glasgow Queen St LL 10	a		09 01		09 10		09 21	09 24		09 31		09 40		09 51	09 54		10 01		10 10		10 21	10 24			10 31
	d		09 02		09 12		09 21	09 27		09 32		09 42		09 51	09 57		10 02		10 12		10 21	10 27			10 32
High Street	d		09 04		09 14		09a23	09 29		09 34		09 44		09a53	09 59		10 04		10 14		10a23	10 29			10 34
Bellgrove	d		09 06		09 16			09 31		09 36		09 46			10 01		10 06		10 16			10 31			10 36
Duke Street	d		09 08							09 38							10 08								10 38
Alexandra Parade	d		09 09							09 39							10 09								10 39
Barnhill	d		09 12							09 42							10 12								10 42
Springburn	a		09 14							09 44							10 14								10 44
Carntyne	d				09 19			09 34				09 49			10 04				10 19			10 34			
Shettleston	d				09 22			09 37				09 52			10 07				10 22			10 37			
Garrowhill	d				09 24			09 39				09 54			10 09				10 24			10 39			
Easterhouse	d				09 27			09 42				09 57			10 12				10 27			10 42			
Blairhill	d				09 31			09 46				10 01			10 16				10 31			10 46			
Coatbridge Sunnyside	d				09 33			09 48				10 03			10 18				10 33			10 48			
Coatdyke	d				09 36			09 51				10 06			10 21				10 36			10 51			
Airdrie	a				09 39			09 54				10 09			10 24				10 39			10 54			
	d																								
Drumgelloch	a																								
Bridgeton	d			09 12		09 22					09 41		09 52					10 12		10 22					
Dalmarnock	d			09 14		09 24					09 43		09 54					10 14		10 24					
Rutherglen	d	09 05		09 16		09 26			09 34		09 46		09 56			10 04		10 16		10 26				10 34	
Cambuslang	d			09 20		09 31					09 49		10 01					10 22		10 31					
Newton	d			09 24							09 53							10 25							
Blantyre	d	09 15		09 28					09 44		09 58					10 14		10 29						10 44	
Hamilton West	d	09 18		09 31					09 47		10 01					10 17		10 32						10 47	
Hamilton Central	d	09 20		09 33					09 50		10 04					10 20		10 35						10 50	
Chatelherault	d	09 24							09 54							10 24								10 54	
Merryton	d	09 28							09 58							10 28								10 58	
Larkhall	a	09 30							10 00							10 30								11 00	
Airbles	d			09 38							10 09							10 40							
Uddingston	d					09 35							10 05							10 35					
Bellshill	d					09 40							10 10							10 40					
Motherwell	a			09 41		09 47					10 11		10 15					10 42		10 48					
	d			09 42									10 15					10 43							
Whifflet	a																								
Coatbridge Central	a																								
Shieldmuir	d												10 20												
Holytown	d			09 47														10 48							
Wishaw	d			09 53									10 22					10 55							
Carluke	d			10 00									10 32					11 01							
Lanark	a			10 15									10 44					11 14							

Table 226

Helensburgh, Balloch, Dalmuir and Milngavie - Glasgow - Springburn, Airdrie, Drumgelloch, Hamilton, Larkhall, Motherwell, Coatbridge and Lanark

		SR	SR	SR	SR	SR	SR	SR		SR	SR	SR	SR	SR	SR	SR	SR	SR		SR	SR	SR	SR	SR	SR
										◇															
Helensburgh Upper	d									10 44															
Helensburgh Central	d					10 10									10 40								1 10		
Craigendoran	d					10 13									10 43								1 13		
Cardross	d					10 18									10 48								1 18		
Balloch	d		09 53									10 22								10 53					
Alexandria	d		09 55									10 24								10 55					
Renton	d		09 58									10 27								10 58					
Dalreoch	d		10 01			10 23						10 30			10 53					11 01			1 23		
Dumbarton Central	d		10 02			10 25				10 59		10 31			10 55					11 02			1 25		
Dumbarton East	d		10 04			10 27						10 33			10 57					11 04			1 27		
Bowling	d		10 09									10 38								11 09					
Kilpatrick	d		10 12									10 41								11 12					
Dalmuir	a		10 15			10 35				11 08		10 44			11 05					11 15			1 35		
	d		10 16	10 23		10 36	10 31	10 38		11 08		10 46	10 53		11 06	11 01	11 08			11 16	11 23		1 36	11 31	11 38
Singer	d		10 18				10 33					10 48				11 03				11 18				11 33	
Drumry	d		10 20				10 35					10 50				11 05				11 20				11 35	
Drumchapel	d		10 23				10 38					10 53				11 08				11 23				11 38	
Milngavie	d	10 12			10 27						10 42			10 57				11 12				11 27			
Hillfoot	d	10 15			10 30						10 45			11 00				11 15				11 30			
Bearsden	d	10 17			10 32						10 47			11 02				11 17				11 32			
Westerton	d	10 20	10 25		10 35		10 40				10 50	10 55		11 05		11 10		11 20		11 25		11 35		11 40	
Anniesland	d	10 23	10 28		10 38		10 44				10 53	10 58		11 08		11 14		11 23		11 28		11 38		11 44	
Clydebank	d			10 25				10 41					10 55				11 10				11 25				11 40
Yoker	d			10 27				10 43					10 57				11 12				11 27				11 42
Garscadden	d			10 31				10 46					11 01				11 16				11 31				11 46
Scotstounhill	d			10 33				10 48					11 03				11 18				11 33				11 48
Jordanhill	d			10 35				10 50					11 06				11 20				11 35				11 50
Hyndland	d	10 26	10 31	10 37	10 41	10 44	10 47	10 52			10 56	11 01	11 08	11 11	11 14	11 17	11 22	11 26		11 31	11 37	11 41	11 44	11 47	11 52
Partick	d	10 29	10 34	10 40	10 44	10 47	10 50	10 55			10 59	11 04	11 11	11 14	11 17	11 20	11 25	11 29		11 34	11 40	11 44	11 47	11 50	11 55
Exhibition Centre	d	10 32		10 43			10 53				11 02		11 14			11 23		11 32			11 43			11 53	
Anderston	d	10 34		10 45			10 55				11 04		11 16			11 25		11 34			11 45			11 55	
Glasgow Central HL 15	d																								
Glasgow Central LL 15	a	10 35		10 47			10 56				11 05		11 17			11 26		11 37			11 47			11 56	
	d	10 37		10 47			10 57				11 06		11 18			11 27		11 37			11 47			11 57	
Argyle Street	d	10 39		10 49			10 59				11 07		11 20			11 29		11 39			11 49			11 59	
Charing Cross	d		10 38		10 49	10 52		10 59				11 08		11 19	11 22		11 29			11 38		11 49	11 52		11 59
Glasgow Queen St HL 10	a									11 30															
Glasgow Queen St LL 10	a		10 40		10 51	10 54		11 01				11 10		11 21	11 24		11 31			11 40		11 51	11 54		12 01
	d		10 42		10 51	10 57		11 02				11 12		11 21	11 27		11 32			11 42		11 51	11 57		12 02
High Street	d		10 44		10a53	10 59		11 04				11 14		11a23	11 29		11 34			11 44		11a53	11 59		12 04
Bellgrove	d		10 46			11 01		11 06				11 16			11 31		11 36			11 46			12 01		12 06
Duke Street	d							11 08									11 38								12 08
Alexandra Parade	d							11 09									11 39								12 09
Barnhill	d							11 12									11 42								12 12
Springburn	a							11 14									11 44								12 14
Carntyne	d		10 49			11 04						11 19			11 34					11 49			12 04		
Shettleston	d		10 52			11 07						11 22			11 37					11 52			12 07		
Garrowhill	d		10 54			11 09						11 24			11 39					11 54			12 09		
Easterhouse	d		10 57			11 12						11 27			11 42					11 57			12 12		
Blairhill	d		11 01			11 16						11 31			11 46					12 01			12 16		
Coatbridge Sunnyside	d		11 03			11 18						11 33			11 48					12 03			12 18		
Coatdyke	d		11 06			11 21						11 36			11 51					12 06			12 21		
Airdrie	a		11 09			11 24						11 39			11 54					12 09			12 24		
	d																								
Drumgelloch	a																								
Bridgeton	d	10 42		10 52							11 10		11 23					11 42			11 52				
Dalmarnock	d	10 44		10 54							11 12		11 25					11 44			11 54				
Rutherglen	d	10 46		10 56			11 04				11 15		11 26			11 34		11 46			11 56			12 04	
Cambuslang	d	10 52		11 01							11 19		11 31					11 49			12 01				
Newton	d	10 57									11 23							11 54							
Blantyre	d	11 01					11 14				11 28					11 44		11 58						12 14	
Hamilton West	d	11 04					11 17				11 31					11 47		12 01						12 17	
Hamilton Central	d	11 07					11 20				11 33					11 50		12 03						12 19	
Chatelherault	d						11 24									11 54								12 24	
Merryton	d						11 28									11 58								12 27	
Larkhall	a						11 30									12 00								12 31	
Airbles	d	11 12									11 38							12 08							
Uddingston	d			11 06									11 36								12 05				
Bellshill	d			11 10									11 40								12 10				
Motherwell	a	11 14		11 16							11 41		11 48					12 11			12 16				
	d			11 17							11 42										12 16				
Whifflet	a																								
Coatbridge Central	a																								
Shieldmuir	d			11 20																	12 20				
Holytown	d										11 47														
Wishaw	d			11 24							11 53										12 23				
Carluke	d			11 30							12 00										12 30				
Lanark	a			11 42							12 12										12 42				

Helensburgh, Balloch, Dalmuir and Milngavie - Glasgow - Springburn, Airdrie, Drumgelloch, Hamilton, Larkhall, Motherwell, Coatbridge and Lanark

		SR	SR	SR		SR	SR	SR	SR	SR	SR	SR	SR	SR		SR	SR	SR	SR	SR	SR	SR	SR	SR
Helensburgh Upper	d																							
Helensburgh Central	d						11 40							12 10								12 40		
Craigendoran	d						11 43							12 13								12 43		
Cardross	d						11 48							12 18								12 48		
Balloch	d		11 23								11 53								12 23					
Alexandria	d		11 25								11 55								12 25					
Renton	d		11 28								11 58								12 28					
Dalreoch	d		11 31				11 54				12 01			12 23					12 31			12 53		
Dumbarton Central	d		11 32				11 55				12 02			12 25					12 32			12 55		
Dumbarton East	d		11 34				11 57				12 04			12 27					12 34			12 57		
Bowling	d		11 39								12 09								12 39					
Kilpatrick	d		11 42								12 12								12 42					
Dalmuir	a		11 45				12 05				12 15			12 35					12 46			13 05		
	d		11 46	11 53			12 06	12 01	12 08		12 16	12 23		12 36		12 31	12 38		12 46	12 53		13 06	13 01	13 08
Singer	d		11 48					12 03			12 18					12 33			12 48				13 03	
Drumry	d		11 50					12 05			12 20					12 35			12 50				13 05	
Drumchapel	d		11 53					12 08			12 23					12 38			12 53				13 08	
Milngavie	d	11 42				11 57				12 12			12 27					12 42			12 57			
Hillfoot	d	11 45				12 00				12 15			12 30					12 45			13 00			
Bearsden	d	11 47				12 02				12 17			12 32					12 47			13 02			
Westerton	d	11 50	11 55			12 05		12 10		12 20	12 25		12 35			12 40		12 50	12 55		13 05		13 10	
Anniesland	d	11 53	11 58			12 08		12 14		12 23	12 28		12 38			12 44		12 53	12 58		13 08		13 14	
Clydebank	d			11 55					12 10			12 25					12 40			12 55				13 10
Yoker	d			11 57					12 12			12 27					12 42			12 57				13 12
Garscadden	d			12 01					12 16			12 31					12 46			13 01				13 16
Scotstounhill	d			12 03					12 18			12 33					12 48			13 03				13 18
Jordanhill	d			12 05					12 20			12 35					12 50			13 05				13 20
Hyndland	d	11 56	12 01	12 07		12 11	12 14	12 17	12 22	12 26	12 31	12 37	12 41	12 44		12 47	12 52	12 56	13 01	13 07	13 11	13 14	13 17	13 22
Partick	d	11 59	12 04	12 10		12 14	12 17	12 20	12 25	12 29	12 34	12 40	12 44	12 47		12 50	12 55	12 59	13 04	13 10	13 14	13 17	13 20	13 25
Exhibition Centre	d	12 02		12 13				12 23		12 32		12 43				12 53		13 02		13 13			13 23	
Anderston	d	12 04		12 15				12 25		12 34		12 45				12 55		13 04		13 15			13 25	
Glasgow Central HL 15	d																							
Glasgow Central LL 15	a	12 05		12 17				12 26		12 35		12 47				12 56		13 05		13 17			13 27	
	d	12 07		12 17				12 27		12 37		12 47				12 57		13 06		13 17			13 27	
Argyle Street	d	12 09		12 19				12 29		12 38		12 49				12 59		13 07		13 19			13 29	
Charing Cross	d		12 08			12 19	12 22		12 29		12 38		12 49	12 52			12 59		13 08		13 19	13 22		13 29
Glasgow Queen St HL 10	a																							
Glasgow Queen St LL 10	a		12 11			12 21	12 24		12 31		12 40		12 51	12 54			13 01		13 10		13 21	13 24		13 31
	d		12 12			12 21	12 27		12 32		12 42		12 51	12 57			13 02		13 12		13 21	13 27		13 32
High Street	d		12 14			12a23	12 29		12 34		12 44		12a53	12 59			13 04		13 14		13a23	13 29		13 34
Bellgrove	d		12 16				12 31		12 36		12 46			13 01			13 06		13 16			13 31		13 36
Duke Street	d								12 38								13 08							13 38
Alexandra Parade	d								12 39								13 09							13 39
Barnhill	d								12 42								13 12							13 42
Springburn	a								12 44								13 14							13 44
Carntyne	d		12 19				12 34				12 49			13 04					13 19			13 34		
Shettleston	d		12 22				12 37				12 52			13 07					13 22			13 37		
Garrowhill	d		12 24				12 39				12 54			13 09					13 24			13 39		
Easterhouse	d		12 27				12 42				12 57			13 12					13 27			13 42		
Blairhill	d		12 31				12 46				13 01			13 16					13 31			13 46		
Coatbridge Sunnyside	d		12 33				12 48				13 03			13 18					13 33			13 48		
Coatdyke	d		12 36				12 51				13 06			13 21					13 36			13 51		
Airdrie	a		12 39				12 54				13 09			13 24					13 39			13 54		
	d																							
Drumgelloch	a																							
Bridgeton	d	12 12		12 22						12 41		12 52						13 10		13 22				
Dalmarnock	d	12 14		12 24						12 43		12 54						13 12		13 24				
Rutherglen	d	12 16		12 25				12 33		12 46		12 56				13 04		13 15		13 26			13 34	
Cambuslang	d	12 21		12 30						12 49		13 01						13 19		13 31				
Newton	d	12 24								12 53								13 22						
Blantyre	d	12 28						12 44		12 58						13 14		13 28					13 44	
Hamilton West	d	12 31						12 47		13 01						13 17		13 31					13 47	
Hamilton Central	d	12 34						12 50		13 03						13 19		13 33					13 49	
Chatelherault	d							12 54								13 24							13 54	
Merryton	d							12 58								13 27							13 57	
Larkhall	a							13 00								13 30							14 00	
Airbles	d	12 39								13 08								13 38						
Uddingston	d			12 35								13 05								13 36				
Bellshill	d			12 39								13 10								13 40				
Motherwell	a	12 41		12 48						13 11		13 15						13 41		13 47				
	d	12 42										13 16						13 42						
Whifflet	a																							
Coatbridge Central	a																							
Shieldmuir	d											13 19												
Holytown	d	12 47																13 50						
Wishaw	d	12 53										13 23						13 55						
Carluke	d	13 00										13 29						14 01						
Lanark	a	13 12										13 42						14 13						

Helensburgh, Balloch, Dalmuir and Milngavie - Glasgow - Springburn, Airdrie, Drumgelloch, Hamilton, Larkhall, Motherwell, Coatbridge and Lanark

		SR	SR	SR	SR	SR	SR	SR	SR	SR	SR	SR	SR	SR	SR	SR	SR	SR	SR	SR		SR		SR ◇	SR
Helensburgh Upper	d																							14 39	
Helensburgh Central	d					13 10							13 40							14 10					
Craigendoran	d					13 13							13 43							14 13					
Cardross	d					13 18							13 48							14 18					
Balloch	d		12 53							13 23							13 53								
Alexandria	d		12 55							13 25							13 55								
Renton	d		12 58							13 28							13 58								
Dalreoch	d		13 01			13 23				13 31			13 53				14 01			14 23					
Dumbarton Central	d		13 02			13 25				13 32			13 55				14 02			14 25				14 52	
Dumbarton East	d		13 04			13 27				13 34			13 57				14 04			14 27					
Bowling	d		13 09							13 39							14 09								
Kilpatrick	d		13 12							13 42							14 12								
Dalmuir	a		13 15			13 35				13 45			14 05				14 15			14 35				15 04	
	d		13 16	13 23		13 36	13 31	13 38		13 46	13 53		14 06	14 01	14 08		14 16	14 23		14 36		14 31		15 07	14 38
Singer	d		13 18				13 33			13 48				14 03			14 18					14 33			
Drumry	d		13 20				13 35			13 50				14 05			14 20					14 35			
Drumchapel	d		13 23				13 38			13 53				14 08			14 23					14 38			
Milngavie	d	13 12			13 27				13 42			13 57				14 12			14 27						
Hillfoot	d	13 15			13 30				13 45			14 00				14 15			14 30						
Bearsden	d	13 17			13 32				13 47			14 02				14 17			14 31						
Westerton	d	13 20	13 25		13 35		13 40		13 50	13 55		14 05		14 10		14 20	14 25		14 35			14 40			
Anniesland	d	13 23	13 28		13 38		13 44		13 53	13 58		14 08		14 14		14 23	14 28		14 38			14 44			
Clydebank	d			13 25				13 40			13 55				14 10			14 25							14 40
Yoker	d			13 27				13 42			13 57				14 12			14 27							14 42
Garscadden	d			13 31				13 46			14 01				14 16			14 31							14 46
Scotstounhill	d			13 33				13 48			14 03				14 18			14 33							14 48
Jordanhill	d			13 35				13 50			14 05				14 20			14 35							14 50
Hyndland	d	13 26	13 31	13 37	13 41	13 44	13 47	13 52	13 56	14 01	14 07	14 11	14 14	14 17	14 22	14 26	14 31	14 37	14 41	14 44		14 47			14 52
Partick	d	13 29	13 34	13 40	13 44	13 47	13 50	13 55	13 59	14 04	14 10	14 14	14 17	14 20	14 25	14 29	14 34	14 40	14 44	14 47		14 50			14 55
Exhibition Centre	d	13 32		13 43			13 53		14 02		14 13			14 23		14 32		14 43				14 53			
Anderston	d	13 34		13 45			13 55		14 04		14 15			14 25		14 34		14 45				14 55			
Glasgow Central HL 15	d																								
Glasgow Central LL 15	a	13 35		13 47			13 56		14 05		14 17			14 26		14 35		14 47				14 56			
	d	13 37		13 47			13 57		14 07		14 17			14 27		14 37		14 47				14 57			
Argyle Street	d	13 38		13 49			13 59		14 09		14 19			14 29		14 38		14 49				14 59			
Charing Cross	d		13 38		13 49	13 52		13 59		14 08		14 19	14 22		14 29		14 38		14 49	14 52					14 59
Glasgow Queen St HL 10	a																							15 28	
Glasgow Queen St LL 10	a		13 40		13 51	13 54		14 01		14 10		14 21	14 24		14 31		14 40		14 51	14 54					15 01
	d		13 42		13 51	13 57		14 02		14 12		14 21	14 27		14 32		14 42		14 51	14 57					15 02
High Street	d		13 44		13a53	13 59		14 04		14 14		14a23	14 29		14 34		14 44		14a53	14 59					15 04
Bellgrove	d		13 46			14 01		14 06		14 16			14 31		14 36		14 46			15 01					15 06
Duke Street	d							14 08							14 38										15 08
Alexandra Parade	d							14 09							14 39										15 09
Barnhill	d							14 12							14 42										15 12
Springburn	a							14 14							14 44										15 14
Carntyne	d		13 49			14 04				14 19			14 34				14 49			15 04					
Shettleston	d		13 52			14 07				14 22			14 37				14 52			15 07					
Garrowhill	d		13 54			14 09				14 24			14 39				14 54			15 09					
Easterhouse	d		13 57			14 12				14 27			14 42				14 57			15 12					
Blairhill	d		14 01			14 16				14 31			14 46				15 01			15 16					
Coatbridge Sunnyside	d		14 03			14 18				14 33			14 48				15 03			15 18					
Coatdyke	d		14 06			14 21				14 36			14 51				15 06			15 21					
Airdrie	a		14 09			14 24				14 39			14 54				15 09			15 24					
	d																								
Drumgelloch	a																								
Bridgeton	d	13 41		13 52					14 12		14 22					14 41		14 52							
Dalmarnock	d	13 43		13 54					14 14		14 24					14 43		14 54							
Rutherglen	d	13 46		13 56			14 04		14 16		14 26			14 34		14 46		14 56				15 04			
Cambuslang	d	13 49		14 01					14 20		14 31					14 50		15 01							
Newton	d	13 53							14 24							14 53									
Blantyre	d	13 57					14 14		14 28					14 44		14 58						15 14			
Hamilton West	d	14 00					14 17		14 31					14 47		15 01						15 17			
Hamilton Central	d	14 03					14 20		14 33					14 50		15 03						15 20			
Chatelherault	d						14 24							14 54								15 24			
Merryton	d						14 28							14 58								15 28			
Larkhall	a						14 30							15 00								15 30			
Airbles	d	14 08							14 38							15 08									
Uddingston	d			14 05							14 36							15 05							
Bellshill	d			14 10							14 40							15 10							
Motherwell	a	14 11		14 16					14 41		14 46					15 11		15 16							
	d			14 16					14 42									15 16							
Whifflet	a																								
Coatbridge Central	a																								
Shieldmuir	d			14 19														15 20							
Holytown	d								14 47																
Wishaw	d			14 22					14 53									15 23							
Carluke	d			14 28					15 00									15 30							
Lanark	a			14 41					15 12									15 42							

Table 226

Mondays to Fridays

Helensburgh, Balloch, Dalmuir and Milngavie - Glasgow - Springburn, Airdrie, Drumgelloch, Hamilton, Larkhall, Motherwell, Coatbridge and Lanark

		SR	SR ◇ A 🍴	SR	SR	SR	SR	SR	SR	SR	SR	SR	SR
Helensburgh Upper	d		15 15										
Helensburgh Central	d						14 40						
Craigendoran	d						14 43						
Cardross	d						14 48						
Balloch	d	14 23									14 53		
Alexandria	d	14 25									14 55		
Renton	d	14 28									14 58		
Dalreoch	d	14 31					14 53				15 01		
Dumbarton Central	d	14 32	15 28				14 55				15 02		
Dumbarton East	d	14 34					14 57				15 04		
Bowling	d	14 39									15 09		
Kilpatrick	d	14 42									15 12		
Dalmuir	a	14 45	15 37				15 06				15 15		
	d	14 46	15 37		14 53		15 06	15 01	15 08		15 16	15 23	
Singer	d	14 48						15 03			15 18		
Drumry	d	14 50						15 05			15 20		
Drumchapel	d	14 53						15 08			15 23		
Milngavie	d					14 57				15 12			15 27
Hillfoot	d					15 00				15 15			15 30
Bearsden	d					15 02				15 17			15 32
Westerton	d	14 55	15 44			15 05		15 10		15 20	15 25		15 35
Anniesland	d	14 58				15 08		15 14		15 23	15 28		15 38
Clydebank	d				14 55				15 11			15 25	
Yoker	d				14 57				15 13			15 27	
Garscadden	d				15 01				15 17			15 31	
Scotstounhill	d				15 03				15 19			15 33	
Jordanhill	d				15 05				15 21			15 35	
Hyndland	d	15 01			15 07	15 11	15 14	15 18	15 23	15 27	15 31	15 37	15 41
Partick	d	15 04			15 10	15 14	15 17	15 21	15 25	15 29	15 34	15 40	15 44
Exhibition Centre	d				15 13			15 24		15 32		15 43	
Anderston	d				15 15			15 26		15 34		15 45	
Glasgow Central HL 15	d			15 14									
Glasgow Central LL 15	a				15 17			15 27		15 35		15 47	
	d				15 17			15 28		15 37		15 47	
Argyle Street	d				15 19			15 29		15 39		15 49	
Charing Cross	d	15 08				15 19	15 22		15 29		15 38		15 49
Glasgow Queen St HL 10 ⛴	a		16 00										
Glasgow Queen St LL 10 ⛴	a	15 10				15 21	15 24		15 31		15 41		15 51
	d	15 12				15 21	15 27		15 32		15 42		15 51
High Street	d	15 14				15a23	15 29		15 34		15 44		15a53
Bellgrove	d	15 16					15 31		15 36		15 46		
Duke Street	d								15 38				
Alexandra Parade	d								15 39				
Barnhill	d								15 42				
Springburn	a								15 44				
Carntyne	d	15 19					15 34				15 49		
Shettleston	d	15 22					15 37				15 52		
Garrowhill	d	15 24					15 39				15 54		
Easterhouse	d	15 27					15 42				15 57		
Blairhill	d	15 31					15 46				16 01		
Coatbridge Sunnyside	d	15 33					15 48				16 03		
Coatdyke	d	15 36					15 51				16 06		
Airdrie	a	15 39					15 54				16 09		
	d												
Drumgelloch	a												
Bridgeton	d				15 22					15 42		15 52	
Dalmarnock	d				15 24					15 44		15 54	
Rutherglen	d				15 26			15 34		15 46		15 55	
Cambuslang	d				15 31					15 49		16 00	
Newton	d									15 54			
Blantyre	d							15 44		15 58			
Hamilton West	d							15 47		16 01			
Hamilton Central	d							15 50		16 03			
Chatelherault	d							15 54					
Merryton	d							15 58					
Larkhall	a							16 00					
Airbles	d									16 08			
Uddingston	d			15 27	15 36							16 05	
Bellshill	d			15 31	15 40							16 09	
Motherwell	a				15 47					16 11		16 15	
	d											16 15	
Whifflet	a												
Coatbridge Central	a												
Shieldmuir	d											16 20	
Holytown	d			15 36									
Wishaw	d											16 23	
Carluke	d											16 30	
Lanark	a											16 42	

		SR	SR	SR	SR	SR	SR	SR	SR	SR	SR	SR	SR
Helensburgh Upper	d												
Helensburgh Central	d	15 10							15 40				
Craigendoran	d	15 13							15 43				
Cardross	d	15 18							15 46				
Balloch	d				15 23								
Alexandria	d				15 25								
Renton	d				15 28								
Dalreoch	d	15 23			15 31				15 51				
Dumbarton Central	d	15 25			15 32				15 53				
Dumbarton East	d	15 27			15 34				15 55				
Bowling	d				15 39								
Kilpatrick	d				15 42								
Dalmuir	a	15 35			15 45				16 03				
	d	15 36	15 31	15 38	15 46		15 53		16 05		16 01	16 08	
Singer	d		15 33		15 48						16 03		
Drumry	d		15 35		15 50						16 05		
Drumchapel	d		15 38		15 53						16 08		
Milngavie	d							15 57					16 12
Hillfoot	d							16 00					16 15
Bearsden	d							16 02					16 17
Westerton	d		15 40		15 55			16 05			16 10		16 20
Anniesland	d		15 44		16 00			16 08			16 14		16 23
Clydebank	d			15 40			15 55					16 10	
Yoker	d			15 42			15 57					16 12	
Garscadden	d			15 46			16 01					16 15	
Scotstounhill	d			15 48			16 03					16 18	
Jordanhill	d			15 50			16 05					16 20	
Hyndland	d	15 44	15 47	15 52	16 01		16 07	16 11	16 14		16 17	16 22	16 26
Partick	d	15 47	15 50	15 55	16 04		16 10	16 14	16 17		16 20	16 25	16 29
Exhibition Centre	d		15 53				16 13				16 23		16 32
Anderston	d		15 55				16 15			16 23	16 25		16 34
Glasgow Central HL 15	d					16 14							
Glasgow Central LL 15	a		15 56				16 17			16 24	16 26		16 35
	d		15 57				16 17			16 25	16 27		16 37
Argyle Street	d		15 59				16 19			16 26	16 29		16 38
Charing Cross	d	15 52		15 59	16 09			16 19	16 22			16 29	
Glasgow Queen St HL 10 ⛴	a												
Glasgow Queen St LL 10 ⛴	a	15 54		16 01	16 11			16 21	16 24			16 31	
	d	15 57		16 02	16 12			16 22	16 27			16 32	
High Street	d	15 59		16 04	16 14			16 24	16 29			16 34	
Bellgrove	d	16 01		16 06	16 16				16 31			16 36	
Duke Street	d			16 08								16 38	
Alexandra Parade	d			16 09								16 39	
Barnhill	d			16 12								16 42	
Springburn	a			16 14								16 44	
Carntyne	d	16 04			16 19				16 34				
Shettleston	d	16 07			16 22				16 37				
Garrowhill	d	16 09			16 24				16 39				
Easterhouse	d	16 12			16 27				16 42				
Blairhill	d	16 16			16 31			16 35	16 46				
Coatbridge Sunnyside	d	16 18			16 33			16 38	16 48				
Coatdyke	d	16 21			16 36			16 40	16 51				
Airdrie	a	16 24			16 39			16 45	16 53				
	d								16 54				
Drumgelloch	a								16 58				
Bridgeton	d						16 22						16 41
Dalmarnock	d						16 24						16 43
Rutherglen	d		16 04				16 26			16 31	16 34		16 46
Cambuslang	d						16 31						16 49
Newton	d												16 53
Blantyre	d		16 14								16 43		16 58
Hamilton West	d		16 17								16 46		17 01
Hamilton Central	d		16 20								16 48		17 03
Chatelherault	d		16 24								16 53		
Merryton	d		16 28								16 56		
Larkhall	a		16 30								17 02		
Airbles	d												17 08
Uddingston	d					16 26	16 35						
Bellshill	d					16 31	16 40						
Motherwell	a						16 47			16 44			17 11
	d									16 47			17 12
Whifflet	a												17 18
Coatbridge Central	a												17 22
Shieldmuir	d									16 50			
Holytown	d					16 35							
Wishaw	d									16 53			
Carluke	d									17 03			
Lanark	a									17 15			

A until 24 September

Table 226

Mondays to Fridays

Helensburgh, Balloch, Dalmuir and Milngavie - Glasgow - Springburn, Airdrie, Drumgelloch, Hamilton, Larkhall, Motherwell, Coatbridge and Lanark

		SR	SR	SR	SR	SR	SR	SR	SR	SR	SR	SR	SR
Helensburgh Upper	d												
Helensburgh Central	d				16 10							16 40	
Craigendoran	d				16 13							16 43	
Cardross	d				16 18							16 48	
Balloch	d	15 53							16 23				
Alexandria	d	15 55							16 25				
Renton	d	15 58							16 28				
Dalreoch	d	16 01			16 23				16 31			16 53	
Dumbarton Central	d	16 02			16 25				16 32			16 55	
Dumbarton East	d	16 04			16 27				16 34			16 57	
Bowling	d	16 09							16 39				
Kilpatrick	d	16 12							16 42				
Dalmuir	a	16 15			16 35				16 45			17 05	
	d	16 16	16 22		16 36	16 31	16 38		16 46	16 54		17 06	17 01
Singer	d	16 18				16 33			16 48				17 03
Drumry	d	16 20				16 35			16 50				17 05
Drumchapel	d	16 23				16 38			16 53				17 08
Milngavie	d			16 27				16 42			16 57		
Hillfoot	d			16 30				16 45			17 00		
Bearsden	d			16 32				16 47			17 02		
Westerton	d	16 25		16 35		16 40		16 50	16 55		17 05		17 10
Anniesland	d	16 28		16 38		16 44		16 53	16 58		17 08		17 14
Clydebank	d		16 24				16 40			16 56			
Yoker	d		16 26				16 42			16 58			
Garscadden	d		16 30				16 46			17 02			
Scotstounhill	d		16 32				16 48			17 04			
Jordanhill	d		16 34				16 50			17 05			
Hyndland	d	16 31	16 37	16 41	16 44	16 46	16 52	16 56	17 01	17 07	17 11	17 15	17 17
Partick	d	16 34	16 40	16 44	16 47	16 49	16 55	16 59	17 04	17 11	17 14	17 17	17 19
Exhibition Centre	d		16 43			16 53		17 04		17 14			17 22
Anderston	d		16 45			16 55		17 06		17 15			17 24
Glasgow Central HL 15	d												
Glasgow Central LL 15	a		16 47			16 56		17 08		17 17			17 26
	d		16 47			16 57		17 09		17 20			17 27
Argyle Street	d		16 49			16 59		17 11		17 22			17 29
Charing Cross	d	16 38		16 49	16 52		16 59		17 08		17 19	17 22	
Glasgow Queen St HL 10 ⛴	a												
Glasgow Queen St LL 10 ⛴	a	16 40		16 51	16 54		17 01		17 10		17 21	17 24	
	d	16 42		16 51	16 57		17 02		17 12		17 22	17 26	
High Street	d	16 44		16 54	16 58		17 04		17 14		17 24	17 28	
Bellgrove	d	16 46			17 00		17 06		17 16			17 30	
Duke Street	d						17 08						
Alexandra Parade	d						17 09						
Barnhill	d						17 12						
Springburn	a						17 14						
Carntyne	d	16 49			17 03				17 19			17 33	
Shettleston	d	16 52			17 06				17 22			17 36	
Garrowhill	d	16 54			17 08				17 24			17 38	
Easterhouse	d	16 57			17 11				17 27			17 41	
Blairhill	d	17 01		17 05	17 15				17 31		17 35	17 45	
Coatbridge Sunnyside	d	17 03		17 08	17 17				17 33		17 38	17 47	
Coatdyke	d	17 06		17 10	17 20				17 36		17 40	17 50	
Airdrie	a	17 09		17 15	17 24				17 39		17 45	17 54	
	d												
Drumgelloch	a												
Bridgeton	d		16 52					17 15		17 25			17 32
Dalmarnock	d		16 54					17 17		17 27			17 34
Rutherglen	d		16 55			17 04		17 19		17 29			17 36
Cambuslang	d		17 00			17 08		17 23		17 33			17 40
Newton	d							17 26		17 37			
Blantyre	d					17 14		17 33		17 42			
Hamilton West	d					17 17		17 36		17 45			
Hamilton Central	d					17 20		17 38		17 49			
Chatelherault	d					17 24		17 43					
Merryton	d					17 28		17 46					
Larkhall	a					17 30		17 48					
Airbles	d									17 54			
Uddingston	d		17 05										17 45
Bellshill	d		17 09										17 49
Motherwell	a		17 15							17 57			18 00
	d									17 57			18 01
Whifflet	a									18 03			
Coatbridge Central	a									18 06			
Shieldmuir	d												18 06
Holytown	d												
Wishaw	d												18 09
Carluke	d												18 19
Lanark	a												

		SR	SR	SR	SR	SR	SR	SR	SR	SR	SR	SR	SR
Helensburgh Upper	d												
Helensburgh Central	d						17 10						
Craigendoran	d						17 13						
Cardross	d						17 18						
Balloch	d			16 53						17 23			
Alexandria	d			16 55						17 25			
Renton	d			16 58						17 28			
Dalreoch	d			17 01			17 23			17 31			
Dumbarton Central	d			17 02			17 25			17 32			
Dumbarton East	d			17 04			17 27			17 34			
Bowling	d			17 09						17 39			
Kilpatrick	d			17 12						17 42			
Dalmuir	a			17 15			17 35			17 45			
	d	17 08		17 16	17 23		17 36	17 31	17 38	17 46		17 53	18 01
Singer	d			17 18				17 33		17 48			18 03
Drumry	d			17 20				17 35		17 50			18 05
Drumchapel	d			17 23				17 38		17 53			18 08
Milngavie	d		17 12			17 27							
Hillfoot	d		17 15			17 30							
Bearsden	d		17 17			17 32							
Westerton	d		17 20	17 25		17 35		17 40		17 55			18 10
Anniesland	d		17 23	17 28		17 38		17 44		17 58			18 14
Clydebank	d	17 10			17 25				17 40			17 55	
Yoker	d	17 12			17 27				17 42			17 57	
Garscadden	d	17 16			17 31				17 46			18 01	
Scotstounhill	d	17 18			17 33				17 48			18 03	
Jordanhill	d	17 20			17 35				17 50			18 05	
Hyndland	d	17 22	17 26	17 31	17 37	17 41	17 44	17 47	17 52	18 01		18 07	18 17
Partick	d	17 25	17 29	17 34	17 40	17 44	17 47	17 50	17 55	18 04		18 10	18 20
Exhibition Centre	d		17 34		17 43			17 53				18 13	18 23
Anderston	d		17 36		17 45			17 55				18 15	18 25
Glasgow Central HL 15	d										18 14		
Glasgow Central LL 15	a		17 38		17 47			17 56				18 17	18 26
	d		17 38		17 47			17 57				18 17	18 27
Argyle Street	d		17 40		17 49			17 59				18 19	18 29
Charing Cross	d	17 29		17 38		17 49	17 52		17 59	18 08			
Glasgow Queen St HL 10 ⛴	a												
Glasgow Queen St LL 10 ⛴	a	17 31		17 40		17 51	17 54		18 01	18 10			
	d	17 32		17 42		17 51	17 57		18 02	18 12			
High Street	d	17 34		17 44		17a53	17 59		18 04	18 14			
Bellgrove	d	17 36		17 46			18 01		18 06	18 16			
Duke Street	d	17 38							18 08				
Alexandra Parade	d	17 39							18 09				
Barnhill	d	17 42							18 12				
Springburn	a	17 44							18 15				
Carntyne	d			17 49			18 04			18 19			
Shettleston	d			17 52			18 07			18 22			
Garrowhill	d			17 54			18 09			18 24			
Easterhouse	d			17 57			18 12			18 27			
Blairhill	d			18 01			18 16			18 31			
Coatbridge Sunnyside	d			18 03			18 18			18 33			
Coatdyke	d			18 06			18 21			18 36			
Airdrie	a			18 09			18 24			18 39			
	d												
Drumgelloch	a												
Bridgeton	d		17 44		17 52							18 22	
Dalmarnock	d		17 46		17 54							18 24	
Rutherglen	d		17 48		17 56			18 04				18 25	18 34
Cambuslang	d		17 52		18 01						18 22	18 30	
Newton	d		17 56										
Blantyre	d		18 00					18 14					18 44
Hamilton West	d		18 03					18 17					18 47
Hamilton Central	d		18 06					18 20					18 50
Chatelherault	d		18 10					18 24					18 54
Merryton	d		18 14					18 28					18 58
Larkhall	a		18 16					18 30					19 00
Airbles	d												
Uddingston	d				18 05						18 27	18 35	
Bellshill	d				18 10						18 31	18 39	
Motherwell	a				18 17							18 46	
	d												
Whifflet	a												
Coatbridge Central	a												
Shieldmuir	d												
Holytown	d										18 35		
Wishaw	d												
Carluke	d												
Lanark	a												

Table 226

Mondays to Fridays

Helensburgh, Balloch, Dalmuir and Milngavie - Glasgow - Springburn, Airdrie, Drumgelloch, Hamilton, Larkhall, Motherwell, Coatbridge and Lanark

Station		SR	SR	SR	SR	SR	SR	SR	SR	SR	SR	SR	SR	SR	SR	SR	SR	SR		SR	SR	SR	SR	SR	SR
Helensburgh Upper	d																								
Helensburgh Central	d	17 40					18 10					18 40					19 10						19 40		
Craigendoran	d	17 43					18 13					18 43					19 13						19 43		
Cardross	d	17 48					18 18					18 48					19 18						19 48		
Balloch	d			17 53					18 23					18 53						19 23					19 53
Alexandria	d			17 55					18 25					18 55						19 25					19 55
Renton	d			17 58					18 28					18 58						19 28					19 58
Dalreoch	d	17 53		18 01			18 23		18 31			18 53		19 01			19 23			19 31			19 53		20 01
Dumbarton Central	d	17 55		18 02			18 25		18 32			18 55		19 02			19 25			19 32			19 55		20 02
Dumbarton East	d	17 57		18 04			18 27		18 34			18 57		19 04			19 27			19 34			19 57		20 04
Bowling	d			18 09					18 39					19 09						19 39					20 09
Kilpatrick	d			18 12					18 42					19 12						19 42					20 12
Dalmuir	a	18 05		18 15			18 35		18 45			19 05		19 15			19 35			19 45			20 05		20 15
	d	18 06		18 16	18 23	18 31	18 35		18 46		19 01	19 05		19 16		19 31	19 35			19 46		20 01	20 05		20 16
Singer	d			18 18		18 33			18 48		19 03			19 18		19 33				19 48		20 03			20 18
Drumry	d			18 20		18 35			18 50		19 05			19 20		19 35				19 50		20 05			20 20
Drumchapel	d			18 23		18 38			18 53		19 08			19 23		19 38				19 53		20 08			20 23
Milngavie	d		18 12					18 42					19 12					19 42						20 12	
Hillfoot	d		18 15					18 45					19 15					19 45						20 15	
Bearsden	d		18 17					18 47					19 17					19 47						20 17	
Westerton	d		18 20	18 25		18 40		18 50	18 55		19 10		19 20	19 25		19 40		19 50		19 55		20 10		20 20	20 25
Anniesland	d		18 23	18 28		18 44		18 53	18 58		19 14		19 23	19 28		19 44		19 53		19 58		20 14		20 23	20 28
Clydebank	d	18 08			18 25		18 37					19 07					19 37						20 07		
Yoker	d	18 10			18 27		18 39					19 09					19 39						20 09		
Garscadden	d	18 13			18 31		18 43					19 13					19 43						20 13		
Scotstounhill	d	18 15			18 33		18 45					19 15					19 45						20 15		
Jordanhill	d	18 18			18 35		18 47					19 17					19 47						20 17		
Hyndland	d	18 22	18 26	18 31	18 37	18 47	18 51	18 55	19 01		19 17	19 21	19 26	19 31		19 47	19 51	19 56		20 01		20 17	20 21	20 26	20 31
Partick	d	18 25	18 29	18 34	18 40	18 50	18 54	18 59	19 04	19 10	19 20	19 24	19 29	19 34	19 40	19 50	19 54	19 59		20 04	20 10	20 20	20 24	20 29	20 34
Exhibition Centre	d		18 32		18 43	18 53		19 02		19 13	19 23		19 32		19 43	19 53		20 02			20 13	20 23		20 32	
Anderston	d		18 34		18 45	18 55		19 04		19 15	19 25		19 34		19 45	19 55		20 04			20 15	20 25		20 34	
Glasgow Central HL 15	d																								
Glasgow Central LL 15	a		18 35		18 47	18 56		19 05		19 16	19 26		19 35		19 46	19 56		20 05			20 16	20 26		20 35	
	d		18 37		18 47	18 57		19 07		19 17	19 27		19 37		19 47	19 57		20 07			20 17	20 27		20 37	
Argyle Street	d		18 38		18 49	18 58		19 09		19 19	19 29		19 39		19 49	19 59		20 09			20 19	20 28		20 38	
Charing Cross	d	18 29		18 38			18 59		19 08			19 29		19 38			19 59			20 08			20 29		20 38
Glasgow Queen St HL 10 ⇌	a																								
Glasgow Queen St LL 10 ⇌	a	18 31		18 40			19 01		19 10			19 31		19 40			20 01			20 10			20 31		20 40
	d	18 32		18 44			19 02		19 14			19 32		19 44			20 02			20 14			20 32		20 44
High Street	d	18 34		18 46			19 04		19 16			19 34		19 46			20 04			20 16			20 34		20 46
Bellgrove	d	18 36		18 48			19 06		19 18			19 36		19 48			20 06			20 18			20 36		20 48
Duke Street	d			18 50					19 20					19 50						20 20					20 50
Alexandra Parade	d			18 51					19 21					19 51						20 21					20 51
Barnhill	d			18 54					19 24					19 54						20 24					20 54
Springburn	a			18 56					19 26					19 56						20 26					20 56
Carntyne	d	18 39					19 09					19 39					20 09						20 39		
Shettleston	d	18 42					19 12					19 42					20 12						20 42		
Garrowhill	d	18 44					19 14					19 44					20 14						20 44		
Easterhouse	d	18 47					19 17					19 47					20 17						20 47		
Blairhill	d	18 51					19 21					19 51					20 21						20 51		
Coatbridge Sunnyside	d	18 53					19 23					19 53					20 23						20 53		
Coatdyke	d	18 56					19 26					19 56					20 26						20 56		
Airdrie	a	18 59					19 29					19 59					20 29						20 59		
	d																								
Drumgelloch	a																								
Bridgeton	d		18 41		18 52			19 12		19 22			19 42		19 52			20 12			20 22			20 41	
Dalmarnock	d		18 43		18 54			19 14		19 24			19 44		19 54			20 14			20 24			20 43	
Rutherglen	d		18 46		18 56	19 03		19 16		19 25	19 34		19 46		19 56	20 04		20 17			20 26	20 33		20 46	
Cambuslang	d		18 49		19 01			19 20		19 30			19 49		20 01			20 21			20 31			20 49	
Newton	d		18 53					19 24					19 54					20 24						20 53	
Blantyre	d		18 57			19 14		19 28			19 44		19 58			20 14		20 28				20 44		20 57	
Hamilton West	d		19 00			19 17		19 31			19 47		20 01			20 17		20 31				20 47		21 00	
Hamilton Central	d		19 03			19 20		19 33			19 49		20 04			20 20		20 34				20 50		21 03	
Chatelherault	d					19 23					19 54					20 24						20 54			
Merryton	d					19 28					19 57					20 28						20 58			
Larkhall	a					19 30					20 00					20 30						21 00			
Airbles	d		19 08					19 38					20 09					20 39						21 08	
Uddingston	d				19 06					19 35					20 05						20 35				
Bellshill	d				19 10					19 39					20 10						20 40				
Motherwell	a		19 11		19 16			19 41		19 47			20 11		20 14			20 41			20 47			21 11	
	d				19 17			19 42							20 14			20 42							
Whifflet	a																								
Coatbridge Central	a																								
Shieldmuir	d				19 20										20 18										
Holytown	d							19 48										20 49							
Wishaw	d				19 22			19 53							20 21			20 54							
Carluke	d				19 31			20 01							20 29			21 02							
Lanark	a				19 43			20 14							20 42			21 12							

Table 226

Mondays to Fridays

Helensburgh, Balloch, Dalmuir and Milngavie - Glasgow - Springburn, Airdrie, Drumgelloch, Hamilton, Larkhall, Motherwell, Coatbridge and Lanark

Station		SR ◇	SR	SR	SR	SR	SR	SR	SR	SR	SR	SR	SR	SR	SR	SR	SR	SR	SR	SR	SR	SR	SR	SR
Helensburgh Upper	d	20 39																						
Helensburgh Central	d					20 10						20 40					21 10					21 40		
Craigendoran	d					20 13						20 43					21 13					21 43		
Cardross	d					20 18						20 48					21 18					21 48		
Balloch	d							20 23						20 53					21 23					21 53
Alexandria	d							20 25						20 55					21 25					21 55
Renton	d							20 28						20 58					21 28					21 58
Dalreoch	d					20 23		20 31				20 53		21 01			21 23		21 31			21 53		22 01
Dumbarton Central	d	20 53				20 25		20 32				20 55		21 02			21 25		21 32			21 55		22 02
Dumbarton East	d					20 27		20 34				20 57		21 04			21 27		21 34			21 57		22 04
Bowling	d							20 39						21 09					21 39					22 09
Kilpatrick	d							20 42						21 12					21 42					22 12
Dalmuir	a	21 04				20 35		20 45				21 05		21 16			21 35		21 45			22 05		22 15
	d	21 07		20 31		20 35		20 46			21 01	21 05		21 16		21 31	21 35		21 46		22 01	22 05		22 16
Singer	d			20 33				20 48			21 03			21 18		21 33			21 48		22 03			22 18
Drumry	d			20 35				20 50			21 05			21 20		21 35			21 50		22 05			22 20
Drumchapel	d			20 38				20 53			21 08			21 23		21 38			21 53		22 08			22 23
Milngavie	d						20 42						21 12					21 42					22 12	
Hillfoot	d						20 45						21 15					21 45					22 15	
Bearsden	d						20 47						21 17					21 47					22 17	
Westerton	d			20 40			20 50	20 55			21 10		21 20	21 25		21 40		21 50	21 55		22 10		22 20	22 25
Anniesland	d			20 44			20 53	20 58			21 14		21 23	21 28		21 44		21 53	21 58		22 14		22 24	22 28
Clydebank	d					20 37						21 07					21 37					22 07		
Yoker	d					20 39						21 09					21 39					22 09		
Garscadden	d					20 43						21 13					21 43					22 13		
Scotstounhill	d					20 45						21 15					21 45					22 15		
Jordanhill	d					20 47						21 17					21 47					22 17		
Hyndland	d			20 47		20 51	20 56	21 01			21 17	21 21	21 26	21 31		21 47	21 51	21 55	22 01		22 17	22 21	22 27	22 31
Partick	d		20 40	20 50		20 54	20 59	21 04		21 10	21 20	21 24	21 29	21 34	21 40	21 50	21 54	21 59	22 04	22 10	22 20	22 24	22 30	22 34
Exhibition Centre	d		20 43	20 53			21 02			21 13	21 23		21 32		21 43	21 53		22 02		22 13	22 23		22 33	
Anderston	d		20 45	20 55			21 04			21 15	21 25		21 34		21 45	21 55		22 04		22 15	22 25		22 35	
Glasgow Central HL 15	d								21 14															
Glasgow Central LL 15	a		20 46	20 56			21 05			21 16	21 26		21 35		21 46	21 56		22 05		22 16	22 26		22 36	
	d		20 47	20 57			21 07			21 17	21 27		21 37		21 47	21 57		22 07		22 17	22 27		22 37	
Argyle Street	d		20 49	20 59			21 08			21 19	21 29		21 39		21 49	21 59		22 08		22 19	22 29		22 38	
Charing Cross	d					20 59		21 08				21 29		21 38			21 59		22 08			22 29		22 38
Glasgow Queen St HL 10 ⇌	a	21 30																						
Glasgow Queen St LL 10 ⇌	a					21 01		21 10				21 31		21 40			22 01		22 10			22 31		22 40
	d					21 02		21 14				21 32		21 44			22 02		22 14			22 32		22 44
High Street	d					21 04		21 16				21 34		21 46			22 04		22 16			22 34		22 46
Bellgrove	d					21 06		21 18				21 36		21 48			22 06		22 18			22 36		22 48
Duke Street	d							21 20						21 50					22 20					22 50
Alexandra Parade	d							21 21						21 51					22 21					22 51
Barnhill	d							21 24						21 54					22 24					22 54
Springburn	a							21 26						21 56					22 26					22 56
Carntyne	d					21 09						21 39					22 09					22 39		
Shettleston	d					21 12						21 42					22 12					22 42		
Garrowhill	d					21 14						21 44					22 14					22 44		
Easterhouse	d					21 17						21 47					22 17					22 47		
Blairhill	d					21 21						21 51					22 21					22 51		
Coatbridge Sunnyside	d					21 23						21 53					22 23					22 53		
Coatdyke	d					21 26						21 56					22 26					22 56		
Airdrie	a					21 29						21 59					22 29					22 59		
	d																							
Drumgelloch	a																							
Bridgeton	d		20 52				21 11			21 22			21 42		21 52			22 11		22 22			22 41	
Dalmarnock	d		20 54				21 13			21 24			21 44		21 54			22 13		22 24			22 43	
Rutherglen	d		20 56	21 04			21 16			21 25	21 34		21 46		21 56	22 04		22 16		22 26	22 34		22 46	
Cambuslang	d		21 01				21 20			21 30			21 50		22 01			22 20		22 31			22 50	
Newton	d						21 23						21 54					22 23					22 54	
Blantyre	d			21 14			21 27				21 44		21 58			22 14		22 28			22 44		22 58	
Hamilton West	d			21 17			21 30				21 47		22 01			22 17		22 31			22 47		23 01	
Hamilton Central	d			21 20			21 33				21 49		22 03			22 19		22 33			22 49		23 03	
Chatelherault	d			21 24							21 54					22 24					22 54			
Merryton	d			21 28							21 57					22 27					22 57			
Larkhall	a			21 30							22 00					22 30					23 00			
Airbles	d						21 38						22 08					22 38					23 08	
Uddingston	d		21 05						21 26	21 35					22 05					22 35				
Bellshill	d		21 10						21 30	21 40					22 10					22 40				
Motherwell	a		21 16				21 41			21 47			22 11		22 16			22 41		22 48			23 11	
	d		21 16				21 42								22 16			22 41						
Whifflet	a																	22 49						
Coatbridge Central	a																	22 52						
Shieldmuir	d		21 20												22 20									
Holytown	d						21 47		21 34															
Wishaw	d		21 23				21 53								22 23									
Carluke	d		21 30				22 00								22 30									
Lanark	a		21 42				22 13								22 42									

Table 226

Mondays to Fridays

Helensburgh, Balloch, Dalmuir and Milngavie - Glasgow - Springburn, Airdrie, Drumgelloch, Hamilton, Larkhall, Motherwell, Coatbridge and Lanark

		SR	SR	SR	SR	SR	SR	SR	SR FX	SR FO	SR FX	SR FO	SR	SR FO	SR FO	SR	SR FO
Helensburgh Upper	d												23 24				
Helensburgh Central	d			22 10					22 40	22 40						23 10	
Craigendoran	d			22 13					22 43	22 43						23 13	
Cardross	d			22 18					22 48	22 48						23 18	
Balloch	d					22 23					22 53	22 53					
Alexandria	d					22 25					22 55	22 55					
Renton	d					22 28					22 58	22 58					
Dalreoch	d			22 23		22 31			22 53	22 53	23 01	23 01				23 23	
Dumbarton Central	d			22 25		22 32			22 55	22 55	23 02	23 02				23 25	
Dumbarton East	d			22 27		22 34			22 57	22 57	23 04	23 04				23 27	
Bowling	d					22 39					23 09	23 09					
Kilpatrick	d					22 42					23 12	23 12					
Dalmuir	a			22 35		22 45			23 05	23 05	23 15	23 15	23 49			23 35	
	d		22 31	22 35		22 46		23 01	23 05	23 05	23 16	23 16	23 51		23 31	23 35	
Singer	d		22 33			22 48		23 03			23 18	23 18			23 33		
Drumry	d		22 35			22 50		23 05			23 20	23 20			23 35		
Drumchapel	d		22 38			22 53		23 08			23 23	23 23			23 38		
Milngavie	d				22 42												23 42
Hillfoot	d				22 45												23 45
Bearsden	d				22 47												23 47
Westerton	d		22 40		22 50	22 55		23 10			23 25	23 25	23 56		23 40		23 50
Anniesland	d		22 44		22 53	23 00		23 14			23 28	23 28			23 44		23 53
Clydebank	d			22 37					23 07	23 07						23 37	
Yoker	d			22 39					23 09	23 09						23 39	
Garscadden	d			22 43					23 13	23 13						23 43	
Scotstounhill	d			22 45					23 15	23 15						23 45	
Jordanhill	d			22 47					23 18	23 17						23 47	
Hyndland	d		22 47	22 51	22 55	23 03		23 17	23 22	23 21	23 31	23 31			23 47	23 51	23 56
Partick	d	22 40	22 50	22 54	22 59	23 05	23 10	23 20	23 24	23 24	23 34	23 34		23 40	23 50	23 54	23 59
Exhibition Centre	d	22 43	22 53		23 02		23 13	23 23						23 43	23 53		00 02
Anderston	d	22 45	22 55		23 04		23 15	23 25						23 45	23 55		00 04
Glasgow Central HL 15	d																
Glasgow Central LL 15	a	22 46	22 56		23 05		23 16	23 26						23 46	23 56		00 05
	d	22 47	22 57		23 07		23 17	23 27						23 47	23 57		00 07
Argyle Street	d	22 49	22 59		23 08		23 19	23 29						23 49	23 59		00 08
Charing Cross	d			22 59		23 09			23 29	23 29	23 38	23 38				23 59	
Glasgow Queen St HL 10	a																
Glasgow Queen St LL 10	a			23 01		23 11			23 31	23 31	23 40	23 40				00 01	
	d			23 02		23 14			23 32	23 32	23 44	23 44				00 02	
High Street	d			23 04		23 16			23 34	23 34	23 46	23 46				00 04	
Bellgrove	d			23 06		23 18			23 36	23 36	23 48	23 48				00 06	
Duke Street	d					23 20						23 50					
Alexandra Parade	d					23 21						23 51					
Barnhill	d					23 24						23 54					
Springburn	a					23 26						23 56					
Carntyne	d			23 09					23 39	23 39	23 51					00 09	
Shettleston	d			23 12					23 42	23 42	23 54					00 12	
Garrowhill	d			23 14					23 44	23 44	23 56					00 14	
Easterhouse	d			23 17					23 47	23 47	23 59					00 17	
Blairhill	d			23 21					23 51	23 51	00 03					00 21	
Coatbridge Sunnyside	d			23 23					23 53	23 53	00 05					00 23	
Coatdyke	d			23 26					23 56	23 56	00 08					00 26	
Airdrie	a			23 29					23 59	23 59	00 11					00 29	
	d																
Drumgelloch	a																
Bridgeton	d	22 52			23 11		23 22							23 52			00 11
Dalmarnock	d	22 54			23 13		23 24							23 54			00 13
Rutherglen	d	22 56	23 04		23 16		23 25	23 34						23 56	00 04		00 16
Cambuslang	d	23 01			23 20		23 30							23 59			00 20
Newton	d				23 23												00 23
Blantyre	d		23 14		23 27			23 44							00 14		00 27
Hamilton West	d		23 17		23 30			23 47							00 17		00 30
Hamilton Central	d		23 20		23 33			23 49							00 20		00 33
Chatelherault	d		23 24					23 54							00 24		
Merryton	d		23 28					23 57							00 28		
Larkhall	a		23 30					00 01							00 30		
Airbles	d				23 38												00 38
Uddingston	d	23 05					23 35							00 05			
Bellshill	d	23 10					23 39							00 10			
Motherwell	a	23 16			23 41		23 45							00 16			00 41
	d	23 16												00 16			
Whifflet	a																
Coatbridge Central	a																
Shieldmuir	d	23 20												00 20			
Holytown	d																
Wishaw	d	23 23												00 23			
Carluke	d	23 30												00 30			
Lanark	a	23 42												00 42			

Table 226

Saturdays

Helensburgh, Balloch, Dalmuir and Milngavie - Glasgow - Springburn, Airdrie, Drumgelloch, Hamilton, Larkhall, Motherwell, Coatbridge and Lanark

		SR	SR	SR	SR	SR	SR	SR	SR	SR	SR	SR	SR	SR	SR	SR	SR	SR	SR
Helensburgh Upper	d																		
Helensburgh Central	d										06 10						06 40		
Craigendoran	d										06 13						06 43		
Cardross	d										06 18						06 48		
Balloch	d													06 23					
Alexandria	d													06 25					
Renton	d													06 28					
Dalreoch	d										06 23			06 31			06 53		
Dumbarton Central	d										06 25			06 32			06 55		
Dumbarton East	d										06 27			06 34			06 57		
Bowling	d													06 39					
Kilpatrick	d													06 42					
Dalmuir	a										06 35			06 45			07 05		
	d			05 48			06 01		06 16	06 23	06 36	06 31		06 46		06 53	07 06	07 01	
Singer	d						06 03		06 18			06 33		06 48				07 03	
Drumry	d						06 05		06 20			06 35		06 50				07 05	
Drumchapel	d						06 08		06 23			06 38		06 53				07 08	
Milngavie	d												06 42						07 12
Hillfoot	d												06 45						07 15
Bearsden	d												06 47						07 17
Westerton	d						06 10		06 25			06 40	06 50	06 55				07 10	07 20
Anniesland	d						06 14		06 28			06 44	06 53	06 58				07 14	07 23
Clydebank	d			05 50						06 25						06 55			
Yoker	d			05 52						06 27						06 57			
Garscadden	d			05 55	06 00	06 08		06 20		06 31						07 01			
Scotstounhill	d			05 57	06 02	06 10		06 22		06 33						07 03			
Jordanhill	d			05 59	06 05	06 12		06 24		06 35						07 05			
Hyndland	d			06 01	06 07	06 14	06 17	06 26	06 31	06 37	06 44	06 47	06 56	07 01		07 07	07 14	07 17	07 26
Partick	d			06 04	06 10	06 17	06 20	06 29	06 34	06 40	06 47	06 50	06 59	07 04		07 10	07 17	07 20	07 29
Exhibition Centre	d				06 13		06 23	06 32		06 43		06 53	07 02			07 13		07 23	07 32
Anderston	d				06 15		06 25	06 34		06 45		06 55	07 04			07 15		07 25	07 34
Glasgow Central HL 15	d	00 06													07 13				
Glasgow Central LL 15	a				06 17		06 26	06 35		06 47		06 56	07 05			07 17		07 26	07 35
	d				06 17		06 27	06 37		06 47		06 57	07 07			07 17		07 27	07 37
Argyle Street	d				06 19		06 29	06 38		06 49		06 59	07 09			07 19		07 29	07 38
Charing Cross	d			06 08		06 22			06 38		06 52			07 08			07 22		
Glasgow Queen St HL 10	a																		
Glasgow Queen St LL 10	a			06 10		06 24			06 40		06 54			07 10			07 24		
	d			06 14		06 27			06 44		06 57			07 14			07 27		
High Street	d			06 16		06 29			06 46		06 59			07 16			07 29		
Bellgrove	d			06 18		06 31			06 48		07 01			07 18			07 31		
Duke Street	d			06 20					06 50					07 20					
Alexandra Parade	d			06 21					06 51					07 21					
Barnhill	d			06 24					06 54					07 24					
Springburn	a			06 26					06 56					07 26					
Carntyne	d					06 34					07 04						07 34		
Shettleston	d					06 37					07 07						07 37		
Garrowhill	d					06 39					07 09						07 39		
Easterhouse	d					06 42					07 12						07 42		
Blairhill	d					06 46					07 16						07 46		
Coatbridge Sunnyside	d					06 48					07 18						07 48		
Coatdyke	d					06 51					07 21						07 51		
Airdrie	a					06 54					07 24						07 54		
	d		00 37																
Drumgelloch	a		00 44																
Bridgeton	d				06 22			06 41		06 52			07 12			07 22			07 41
Dalmarnock	d				06 24			06 43		06 54			07 14			07 24			07 43
Rutherglen	d				06 26		06 34	06 46		06 55		07 03	07 17			07 25		07 34	07 46
Cambuslang	d	00 15			06 31			06 50		07 00			07 21		07 24	07 30			07 49
Newton	d							06 53					07 24						07 53
Blantyre	d						06 44	06 58				07 14	07 28					07 44	07 58
Hamilton West	d						06 47	07 01				07 17	07 31					07 47	08 01
Hamilton Central	d						06 50	07 05				07 20	07 34					07 50	08 04
Chatelherault	d						06 54					07 24						07 54	
Merryton	d						06 58					07 28						07 58	
Larkhall	a						07 00					07 31						08 00	
Airbles	d							07 10					07 39						08 09
Uddingston	d	00 20			06 35					07 05					07 29	07 35			
Bellshill	d	00 24			06 40					07 10					07 33	07 40			
Motherwell	a				06 46			07 13		07 17			07 41			07 46			08 11
	d				06 46								07 42						
Whifflet	a																		
Coatbridge Central	a																		
Shieldmuir	d				06 50														
Holytown	d	00 28											07 47		07 37				
Wishaw	d				06 52								07 53						
Carluke	d				07 00								07 57						
Lanark	a				07 13								08 13						

Table 226

Helensburgh, Balloch, Dalmuir and Milngavie - Glasgow - Springburn, Airdrie, Drumgelloch, Hamilton, Larkhall, Motherwell, Coatbridge and Lanark

		SR	SR	SR	SR	SR	SR	SR	SR	SR	SR	SR	SR	SR	SR	SR	SR	SR	SR	SR	SR	SR	SR	SR
Helensburgh Upper	d																							
Helensburgh Central	d			07 10						07 40					08 10						08 40			
Craigendoran	d			07 13						07 43					08 13						08 43			
Cardross	d			07 18						07 48					08 18						08 48			
Balloch	d	06 53					07 23						07 53						08 23					
Alexandria	d	06 55					07 25						07 55						08 25					
Renton	d	06 58					07 28						07 58						08 28					
Dalreoch	d	07 01		07 23			07 31			07 53			08 01		08 23				08 31		08 53			
Dumbarton Central	d	07 02		07 25			07 32			07 55			08 02		08 25				08 32		08 55			
Dumbarton East	d	07 04		07 27			07 34			07 57			08 04		08 27				08 34		08 57			
Bowling	d	07 09					07 39						08 09						08 39					
Kilpatrick	d	07 12					07 42						08 12						08 42					
Dalmuir	a	07 15		07 35			07 45			08 05			08 15		08 35				08 45		09 05			
	d	07 16	07 23	07 36	07 31		07 46		07 53	08 06	08 01		08 16	08 23	08 36	08 31			08 46	08 53	09 06	09 01	09 08	
Singer	d	07 18			07 33		07 48				08 03		08 18			08 33			08 48			09 03		
Drumry	d	07 20			07 35		07 50				08 05		08 20			08 35			08 50			09 05		
Drumchapel	d	07 23			07 38		07 53				08 08		08 23			08 38			08 53			09 08		
Milngavie	d					07 42						08 12						08 42						09 12
Hillfoot	d					07 45						08 15						08 45						09 15
Bearsden	d					07 47						08 17						08 47						09 17
Westerton	d	07 25			07 40	07 50	07 55				08 10	08 20	08 25			08 40		08 50	08 55			09 10		09 20
Anniesland	d	07 28			07 44	07 53	07 58				08 14	08 23	08 28			08 44		08 53	08 58			09 14		09 23
Clydebank	d		07 25						07 55					08 25						08 55			09 10	
Yoker	d		07 27						07 57					08 27						08 57			09 12	
Garscadden	d		07 31						08 01					08 31			08 46			09 01			09 16	
Scotstounhill	d		07 33						08 03					08 33			08 48			09 03			09 18	
Jordanhill	d		07 35						08 05					08 35			08 50			09 05			09 20	
Hyndland	d	07 31	07 37	07 44	07 48	07 56	08 01		08 07	08 14	08 17	08 26	08 31	08 37	08 44	08 47	08 52	08 56	09 01	09 07	09 14	09 17	09 22	09 26
Partick	d	07 34	07 40	07 47	07 50	07 59	08 04		08 10	08 17	08 20	08 29	08 34	08 40	08 47	08 50	08 55	08 59	09 04	09 10	09 17	09 20	09 25	09 29
Exhibition Centre	d		07 43		07 53	08 02			08 13		08 23	08 32		08 43		08 53		09 02		09 13		09 23		09 32
Anderston	d		07 45		07 55	08 04			08 15		08 25	08 34		08 45		08 55		09 04		09 15		09 25		09 34
Glasgow Central HL 15	d							08 15																
Glasgow Central LL 15	a		07 47		07 57	08 05			08 17		08 26	08 35		08 47		08 56		09 05		09 17		09 26		09 35
	d		07 47		07 57	08 07			08 17		08 27	08 37		08 47		08 57		09 07		09 17		09 27		09 37
Argyle Street	d		07 49		07 59	08 09			08 19		08 29	08 38		08 49		08 59		09 08		09 19		09 28		09 38
Charing Cross	d	07 38		07 52			08 08			08 22			08 38		08 52		08 59		09 08		09 22		09 29	
Glasgow Queen St HL 10	a																							
Glasgow Queen St LL 10	a	07 40		07 54			08 10			08 24			08 40		08 54		09 01		09 10		09 24		09 31	
	d	07 44		07 57			08 14			08 27			08 44		08 57		09 02		09 12		09 27		09 32	
High Street	d	07 46		07 59			08 16			08 29			08 46		08 59		09 04		09 16		09 29		09 34	
Bellgrove	d	07 48		08 01			08 18			08 31			08 48		09 01		09 06		09 18		09 31		09 36	
Duke Street	d	07 50					08 20						08 50				09 08						09 38	
Alexandra Parade	d	07 51					08 21						08 51				09 09						09 39	
Barnhill	d	07 54					08 24						08 54				09 12						09 42	
Springburn	a	07 56					08 26						08 56				09 14						09 44	
Carntyne	d			08 04						08 34					09 04				09 19		09 34			
Shettleston	d			08 07						08 37					09 07				09 22		09 37			
Garrowhill	d			08 09						08 39					09 09				09 24		09 39			
Easterhouse	d			08 12						08 42					09 12				09 27		09 42			
Blairhill	d			08 16						08 46					09 16				09 31		09 46			
Coatbridge Sunnyside	d			08 18						08 48					09 18				09 33		09 48			
Coatdyke	d			08 21						08 51					09 21				09 36		09 51			
Airdrie	a			08 24						08 54					09 24				09 41		09 54			
	d																							
Drumgelloch	a																							
Bridgeton	d		07 52			08 12			08 22			08 41		08 52				09 11		09 22				09 41
Dalmarnock	d		07 54			08 14			08 24			08 43		08 54				09 13		09 24				09 43
Rutherglen	d		07 55		08 04	08 16			08 26		08 34	08 46		08 56		09 04		09 16		09 26		09 33		09 46
Cambuslang	d		08 00			08 20			08 31			08 49		09 01				09 20		09 31				09 49
Newton	d					08 24						08 53						09 23						09 53
Blantyre	d				08 14	08 28					08 44	08 58				09 14		09 28				09 44		09 58
Hamilton West	d				08 17	08 31					08 47	09 01				09 17		09 31				09 47		10 01
Hamilton Central	d				08 20	08 33					08 50	09 06				09 20		09 33				09 50		10 03
Chatelherault	d				08 24						08 54					09 24						09 54		
Merryton	d				08 28						08 58					09 28						09 58		
Larkhall	a				08 30						09 00					09 30						10 00		
Airbles	d					08 38						09 11						09 38						10 08
Uddingston	d		08 05					08 28	08 35					09 05						09 35				
Bellshill	d		08 09					08 32	08 40					09 10						09 40				
Motherwell	a		08 15			08 41			08 46			09 13		09 16				09 41		09 47				10 11
	d		08 15			08 42								09 16				09 42						
Whifflet	a																							
Coatbridge Central	a																							
Shieldmuir	d		08 20											09 20										
Holytown	d					08 49		08 36										09 47						
Wishaw	d		08 22			08 54								09 23				09 53						
Carluke	d		08 30			08 59								09 30				10 00						
Lanark	a		08 41			09 12								09 42				10 12						

Table 226

Saturdays

Helensburgh, Balloch, Dalmuir and Milngavie - Glasgow - Springburn, Airdrie, Drumgelloch, Hamilton, Larkhall, Motherwell, Coatbridge and Lanark

		SR	SR	SR	SR	SR	SR	SR	SR	SR	SR	SR	SR	SR	SR	SR	SR	SR	SR	SR	SR	SR ◇
Helensburgh Upper	d																					10 44
Helensburgh Central	d				09 10							09 40							10 10			
Craigendoran	d				09 13							09 43							10 13			
Cardross	d				09 18							09 48							10 18			
Balloch	d	08 53							09 23							09 53						
Alexandria	d	08 55							09 25							09 55						
Renton	d	08 58							09 28							09 58						
Dalreoch	d	09 01			09 23				09 31			09 53				10 01			10 23			
Dumbarton Central	d	09 02			09 25				09 32			09 55				10 02			10 25			10 59
Dumbarton East	d	09 04			09 27				09 34			09 57				10 04			10 27			
Bowling	d	09 09							09 39							10 09						
Kilpatrick	d	09 12							09 42							10 12						
Dalmuir	a	09 15			09 35				09 45			10 05				10 15			10 35			11 08
	d	09 16	09 23		09 36	09 31	09 38		09 46	09 53		10 06	10 01	10 08		10 16	10 23		10 36	10 31	10 38	11 08
Singer	d	09 18				09 33			09 48				10 03			10 18				10 33		
Drumry	d	09 20				09 35			09 50				10 05			10 20				10 35		
Drumchapel	d	09 23				09 38			09 53				10 08			10 23				10 38		
Milngavie	d			09 28				09 42			09 57				10 12			10 27				
Hillfoot	d			09 31				09 45			10 00				10 15			10 30				
Bearsden	d			09 33				09 47			10 02				10 17			10 32				
Westerton	d	09 25		09 36		09 40		09 50	09 55		10 05		10 10		10 20	10 25		10 35		10 40		
Anniesland	d	09 28		09 39		09 44		09 53	09 58		10 08		10 14		10 23	10 28		10 38		10 44		
Clydebank	d		09 25				09 40			09 55				10 10			10 25				10 41	
Yoker	d		09 27				09 42			09 57				10 12			10 27				10 43	
Garscadden	d		09 31				09 46			10 01				10 16			10 31				10 46	
Scotstounhill	d		09 33				09 48			10 03				10 18			10 33				10 48	
Jordanhill	d		09 35				09 50			10 05				10 20			10 35				10 50	
Hyndland	d	09 31	09 37	09 41	09 44	09 47	09 52	09 56	10 01	10 07	10 11	10 14	10 17	10 22	10 26	10 31	10 37	10 41	10 44	10 47	10 52	
Partick	d	09 34	09 40	09 44	09 47	09 50	09 55	09 59	10 04	10 10	10 14	10 17	10 20	10 25	10 29	10 34	10 40	10 44	10 47	10 50	10 55	
Exhibition Centre	d		09 43			09 53		10 02		10 13			10 23		10 32		10 43			10 53		
Anderston	d		09 45			09 55		10 04		10 15			10 25		10 34		10 45			10 55		
Glasgow Central HL 15	d																					
Glasgow Central LL 15	a		09 47			09 56		10 05		10 17			10 26		10 35		10 47			10 56		
	d		09 47			09 57		10 07		10 17			10 27		10 37		10 47			10 57		
Argyle Street	d		09 49			09 59		10 09		10 19			10 29		10 39		10 49			10 59		
Charing Cross	d	09 38		09 49	09 52		09 59		10 08		10 19	10 22		10 29		10 38		10 49	10 52		10 59	
Glasgow Queen St HL 10	a																					11 30
Glasgow Queen St LL 10	a	09 40		09 51	09 54		10 01		10 10		10 21	10 24		10 31		10 40		10 51	10 54		11 01	
	d	09 42		09 51	09 57		10 02		10 12		10 21	10 27		10 32		10 42		10 51	10 57		11 02	
High Street	d	09 44		09a53	09 59		10 04		10 14		10a23	10 29		10 34		10 44		10a53	10 59		11 04	
Bellgrove	d	09 46			10 01		10 06		10 16			10 31		10 36		10 46			11 01		11 06	
Duke Street	d						10 08							10 38							11 08	
Alexandra Parade	d						10 09							10 39							11 09	
Barnhill	d						10 12							10 42							11 12	
Springburn	a						10 14							10 44							11 14	
Carntyne	d	09 49			10 04				10 19			10 34				10 49			11 04			
Shettleston	d	09 52			10 07				10 22			10 37				10 52			11 07			
Garrowhill	d	09 54			10 09				10 24			10 39				10 54			11 09			
Easterhouse	d	09 57			10 12				10 27			10 42				10 57			11 12			
Blairhill	d	10 01			10 16				10 31			10 46				11 01			11 16			
Coatbridge Sunnyside	d	10 03			10 18				10 33			10 48				11 03			11 18			
Coatdyke	d	10 06			10 21				10 36			10 51				11 06			11 21			
Airdrie	a	10 09			10 24				10 39			10 54				11 09			11 24			
	d																					
Drumgelloch	a																					
Bridgeton	d		09 52					10 12		10 22					10 42		10 52					
Dalmarnock	d		09 54					10 14		10 24					10 44		10 54					
Rutherglen	d		09 55			10 03		10 16		10 25			10 34		10 46		10 56			11 04		
Cambuslang	d		10 00					10 22		10 30					10 49		11 01					
Newton	d							10 25							10 54							
Blantyre	d					10 13		10 29					10 44		10 58					11 14		
Hamilton West	d					10 16		10 32					10 47		11 01					11 17		
Hamilton Central	d					10 20		10 35					10 50		11 03					11 20		
Chatelherault	d					10 23							10 54							11 24		
Merryton	d					10 28							10 58							11 28		
Larkhall	a					10 30							11 00							11 30		
Airbles	d							10 40							11 08							
Uddingston	d		10 05							10 34							11 05					
Bellshill	d		10 09							10 39							11 10					
Motherwell	a		10 15					10 42		10 47					11 11		11 16					
	d		10 15					10 43									11 16					
Whifflet	a																					
Coatbridge Central	a																					
Shieldmuir	d		10 18														11 20					
Holytown	d							10 48														
Wishaw	d		10 22					10 53									11 23					
Carluke	d		10 31					11 00									11 30					
Lanark	a		10 44					11 12									11 42					

Table 226

Saturdays

Helensburgh, Balloch, Dalmuir and Milngavie - Glasgow - Springburn, Airdrie, Drumgelloch, Hamilton, Larkhall, Motherwell, Coatbridge and Lanark

		SR	SR	SR	SR	SR	SR	SR	SR	SR	SR	SR	SR	SR	SR	SR	SR	SR	SR	SR	SR	SR	SR
Helensburgh Upper	d																						
Helensburgh Central	d					10 40							11 10							11 40			
Craigendoran	d					10 43							11 13							11 43			
Cardross	d					10 48							11 18							11 48			
Balloch	d		10 23							10 53							11 23						
Alexandria	d		10 25							10 55							11 25						
Renton	d		10 28							10 58							11 28						
Dalreoch	d		10 31			10 53				11 01			11 23				11 31			11 54			
Dumbarton Central	d		10 32			10 55				11 02			11 25				11 32			11 55			
Dumbarton East	d		10 34			10 57				11 04			11 27				11 34			11 57			
Bowling	d		10 39							11 09							11 39						
Kilpatrick	d		10 42							11 12							11 42						
Dalmuir	a		10 45			11 05				11 15			11 35				11 45			12 05			
	d		10 46	10 53		11 06	11 01	11 08		11 16	11 23		11 36	11 31	11 38		11 46	11 53		12 06	12 01	12 08	
Singer	d		10 48				11 03			11 18				11 33			11 48				12 03		
Drumry	d		10 50				11 05			11 20				11 35			11 50				12 05		
Drumchapel	d		10 53				11 08			11 23				11 38			11 53				12 08		
Milngavie	d	10 42			10 57				11 12			11 27				11 42			11 57				12 12
Hillfoot	d	10 45			11 00				11 15			11 30				11 45			12 00				12 15
Bearsden	d	10 47			11 02				11 17			11 32				11 47			12 02				12 17
Westerton	d	10 50	10 55		11 05		11 10		11 20	11 25		11 35		11 40		11 50	11 55		12 05		12 10		12 20
Anniesland	d	10 53	10 59		11 08		11 14		11 23	11 28		11 38		11 44		11 53	11 58		12 08		12 14		12 23
Clydebank	d			10 55				11 10			11 25				11 40			11 55				12 10	
Yoker	d			10 57				11 12			11 27				11 42			11 57				12 12	
Garscadden	d			11 01				11 16			11 31				11 46			12 01				12 16	
Scotstounhill	d			11 03				11 18			11 33				11 48			12 03				12 18	
Jordanhill	d			11 05				11 20			11 35				11 50			12 05				12 20	
Hyndland	d	10 56	11 02	11 07	11 11	11 14	11 17	11 22	11 26	11 31	11 37	11 41	11 44	11 47	11 52	11 56	12 01	12 07	12 11	12 14	12 18	12 22	12 26
Partick	d	10 59	11 05	11 10	11 14	11 17	11 20	11 25	11 29	11 34	11 40	11 44	11 47	11 50	11 55	11 59	12 04	12 10	12 14	12 17	12 20	12 25	12 29
Exhibition Centre	d	11 02		11 13			11 23		11 32		11 43			11 53		12 02		12 13			12 23		12 32
Anderston	d	11 04		11 15			11 25		11 34		11 45			11 55		12 04		12 15			12 25		12 34
Glasgow Central HL 15	d																						
Glasgow Central LL 15	a	11 05		11 17			11 26		11 37		11 47			11 56		12 05		12 17			12 26		12 35
	d	11 07		11 17			11 27		11 37		11 47			11 57		12 07		12 17			12 27		12 37
Argyle Street	d	11 08		11 19			11 29		11 39		11 49			11 59		12 08		12 19			12 29		12 38
Charing Cross	d		11 09		11 19	11 22		11 29		11 38		11 49	11 52		11 59		12 08		12 19	12 22		12 29	
Glasgow Queen St HL 10	a																						
Glasgow Queen St LL 10	a		11 11		11 21	11 24		11 31		11 40		11 51	11 54		12 01		12 11		12 21	12 24		12 31	
	d		11 12		11 21	11 27		11 32		11 42		11 51	11 57		12 02		12 12		12 21	12 27		12 32	
High Street	d		11 14		11a23	11 29		11 34		11 44		11a53	11 59		12 04		12 14		12a23	12 29		12 34	
Bellgrove	d		11 16			11 31		11 36		11 46			12 01		12 06		12 16			12 31		12 36	
Duke Street	d							11 38							12 08							12 38	
Alexandra Parade	d							11 39							12 09							12 39	
Barnhill	d							11 42							12 12							12 42	
Springburn	a							11 44							12 14							12 44	
Carntyne	d		11 19			11 34				11 49			12 04				12 19			12 34			
Shettleston	d		11 22			11 37				11 52			12 07				12 22			12 37			
Garrowhill	d		11 24			11 39				11 54			12 09				12 24			12 39			
Easterhouse	d		11 27			11 42				11 57			12 12				12 27			12 42			
Blairhill	d		11 31			11 46				12 01			12 16				12 31			12 46			
Coatbridge Sunnyside	d		11 33			11 48				12 03			12 18				12 33			12 48			
Coatdyke	d		11 36			11 51				12 06			12 21				12 36			12 51			
Airdrie	a		11 39			11 54				12 09			12 24				12 39			12 54			
	d																						
Drumgelloch	a																						
Bridgeton	d	11 11		11 22					11 42		11 52					12 11		12 22					12 41
Dalmarnock	d	11 13		11 24					11 44		11 54					12 13		12 24					12 43
Rutherglen	d	11 16		11 26			11 34		11 46		11 55			12 04		12 16		12 26			12 34		12 46
Cambuslang	d	11 20		11 31					11 49		12 00					12 20		12 31					12 49
Newton	d	11 23							11 54							12 23							12 53
Blantyre	d	11 28					11 44		11 58					12 14		12 28					12 44		12 58
Hamilton West	d	11 31					11 47		12 01					12 17		12 31					12 47		13 01
Hamilton Central	d	11 33					11 50		12 03					12 20		12 33					12 50		13 03
Chatelherault	d						11 54							12 24							12 54		
Merryton	d						11 58							12 28							12 58		
Larkhall	a						12 00							12 30							13 00		
Airbles	d	11 38							12 08							12 38							13 08
Uddingston	d			11 35							12 05							12 35					
Bellshill	d			11 40							12 10							12 40					
Motherwell	a	11 43		11 47					12 11		12 16					12 41		12 48					13 11
	d	11 43									12 16					12 42							
Whifflet	a																						
Coatbridge Central	a																						
Shieldmuir	d										12 20												
Holytown	d	11 48														12 47							
Wishaw	d	11 53									12 23					12 53							
Carluke	d	12 00									12 28					13 00							
Lanark	a	12 12									12 42					13 12							

Table 226

Saturdays

Helensburgh, Balloch, Dalmuir and Milngavie - Glasgow - Springburn, Airdrie, Drumgelloch, Hamilton, Larkhall, Motherwell, Coatbridge and Lanark

		SR	SR	SR	SR	SR	SR	SR	SR	SR	SR	SR	SR	SR	SR	SR	SR	SR	SR	SR	SR	SR
Helensburgh Upper	d																					
Helensburgh Central	d				12 10							12 40							13 10			
Craigendoran	d				12 13							12 43							13 13			
Cardross	d				12 18							12 48							13 18			
Balloch	d	11 53							12 23							12 53						
Alexandria	d	11 55							12 25							12 55						
Renton	d	11 58							12 28							12 58						
Dalreoch	d	12 01			12 23				12 31			12 53				13 01			13 23			
Dumbarton Central	d	12 02			12 25				12 32			12 55				13 02			13 25			
Dumbarton East	d	12 04			12 27				12 34			12 57				13 04			13 27			
Bowling	d	12 09							12 39							13 09						
Kilpatrick	d	12 12							12 42							13 12						
Dalmuir	a	12 15			12 35				12 46			13 05				13 15			13 35			
	d	12 16	12 23		12 36	12 31	12 38		12 46	12 53		13 06	13 01	13 08		13 16	13 23		13 36	13 31	13 38	
Singer	d	12 18				12 33			12 48				13 03			13 18				13 33		
Drumry	d	12 20				12 35			12 50				13 05			13 20				13 35		
Drumchapel	d	12 23				12 38			12 53				13 08			13 23				13 38		
Milngavie	d			12 27				12 42			12 57				13 12			13 27				13 42
Hillfoot	d			12 30				12 45			13 00				13 15			13 30				13 45
Bearsden	d			12 32				12 47			13 02				13 17			13 32				13 47
Westerton	d	12 25		12 35		12 40		12 50	12 55		13 05		13 10		13 20	13 25		13 35		13 40		13 50
Anniesland	d	12 28		12 38		12 44		12 53	12 58		13 08		13 14		13 23	13 28		13 38		13 44		13 53
Clydebank	d		12 25				12 40			12 55				13 10			13 25				13 40	
Yoker	d		12 27				12 42			12 57				13 12			13 27				13 42	
Garscadden	d		12 31				12 46			13 01				13 16			13 31				13 46	
Scotstounhill	d		12 33				12 48			13 03				13 18			13 33				13 48	
Jordanhill	d		12 35				12 50			13 05				13 20			13 35				13 50	
Hyndland	d	12 31	12 37	12 41	12 44	12 48	12 52	12 56	13 01	13 07	13 11	13 14	13 18	13 22	13 26	13 31	13 37	13 41	13 44	13 47	13 52	13 56
Partick	d	12 34	12 40	12 44	12 47	12 50	12 55	12 59	13 04	13 10	13 14	13 17	13 20	13 25	13 29	13 34	13 40	13 44	13 47	13 50	13 55	13 59
Exhibition Centre	d		12 43			12 53		13 02		13 13			13 23		13 32		13 43			13 53		14 02
Anderston	d		12 45			12 55		13 04		13 15			13 25		13 34		13 45			13 55		14 04
Glasgow Central HL 15	d																					
Glasgow Central LL 15	a		12 47			12 56		13 05		13 17			13 27		13 35		13 47			13 56		14 05
	d		12 47			12 57		13 07		13 17			13 27		13 37		13 47			13 57		14 07
Argyle Street	d		12 49			12 59		13 08		13 19			13 29		13 38		13 49			13 59		14 08
Charing Cross	d	12 38		12 49	12 52		12 59		13 08		13 19	13 22		13 29		13 38		13 49	13 52		13 59	
Glasgow Queen St HL 10	a																					
Glasgow Queen St LL 10	a	12 40		12 51	12 54		13 01		13 10		13 21	13 24		13 31		13 40		13 51	13 54		14 01	
	d	12 42		12 51	12 57		13 02		13 12		13 21	13 27		13 32		13 42		13 51	13 57		14 02	
High Street	d	12 44		12a53	12 59		13 04		13 14		13a23	13 29		13 34		13 44		13a53	13 59		14 04	
Bellgrove	d	12 46			13 01		13 06		13 16			13 31		13 36		13 46			14 01		14 06	
Duke Street	d						13 08							13 38							14 08	
Alexandra Parade	d						13 09							13 39							14 09	
Barnhill	d						13 12							13 42							14 12	
Springburn	a						13 14							13 44							14 14	
Carntyne	d	12 49			13 04				13 19			13 34				13 49			14 04			
Shettleston	d	12 52			13 07				13 22			13 37				13 52			14 07			
Garrowhill	d	12 54			13 09				13 24			13 39				13 54			14 09			
Easterhouse	d	12 57			13 12				13 27			13 42				13 57			14 12			
Blairhill	d	13 01			13 16				13 31			13 46				14 01			14 16			
Coatbridge Sunnyside	d	13 03			13 18				13 33			13 48				14 03			14 18			
Coatdyke	d	13 06			13 21				13 36			13 51				14 06			14 21			
Airdrie	a	13 09			13 24				13 39			13 54				14 09			14 24			
	d																					
Drumgelloch	a																					
Bridgeton	d		12 52					13 11		13 22					13 41		13 52					14 11
Dalmarnock	d		12 54					13 13		13 24					13 43		13 54					14 13
Rutherglen	d		12 56			13 03		13 16		13 26			13 34		13 46		13 55			14 04		14 16
Cambuslang	d		13 01					13 20		13 31					13 49		14 00					14 20
Newton	d							13 23							13 53							14 23
Blantyre	d					13 13		13 28					13 44		13 58					14 14		14 28
Hamilton West	d					13 16		13 31					13 47		14 01					14 17		14 31
Hamilton Central	d					13 20		13 33					13 50		14 03					14 20		14 33
Chatelherault	d					13 23							13 54							14 24		
Merryton	d					13 28							13 58							14 28		
Larkhall	a					13 30							14 00							14 30		
Airbles	d							13 38							14 08							14 38
Uddingston	d		13 05							13 35							14 05					
Bellshill	d		13 10							13 40							14 10					
Motherwell	a		13 16					13 41		13 48					14 11		14 16					14 41
	d		13 16					13 42									14 16					14 42
Whifflet	a																					
Coatbridge Central	a																					
Shieldmuir	d		13 20														14 20					
Holytown	d							13 49														14 47
Wishaw	d		13 23					13 54									14 23					14 53
Carluke	d		13 29					14 00									14 30					15 00
Lanark	a		13 42					14 12									14 42					15 12

Table 226

Saturdays

Helensburgh, Balloch, Dalmuir and Milngavie - Glasgow - Springburn, Airdrie, Drumgelloch, Hamilton, Larkhall, Motherwell, Coatbridge and Lanark

		SR	SR	SR	SR	SR	SR	SR	SR	SR	SR	SR	SR	SR ◇	SR	SR	SR	SR	SR	SR	SR	SR
Helensburgh Upper	d													14 39								
Helensburgh Central	d				13 40							14 10								14 40		
Craigendoran	d				13 43							14 13								14 43		
Cardross	d				13 48							14 18								14 48		
Balloch	d	13 23							13 53								14 23					
Alexandria	d	13 25							13 55								14 25					
Renton	d	13 28							13 58								14 28					
Dalreoch	d	13 31			13 53				14 01			14 23					14 31			14 53		
Dumbarton Central	d	13 32			13 55				14 02			14 25		14 52			14 32			14 55		
Dumbarton East	d	13 34			13 57				14 04			14 27					14 34			14 57		
Bowling	d	13 39							14 09								14 39					
Kilpatrick	d	13 42							14 12								14 42					
Dalmuir	a	13 45			14 05				14 15			14 35		15 04			14 45			15 06		
	d	13 46	13 53		14 06	14 01	14 08		14 16	14 23		14 36	14 31	15 07	14 38		14 46	14 53		15 06	15 01	15 10
Singer	d	13 48				14 03			14 18				14 33				14 48				15 03	
Drumry	d	13 50				14 05			14 20				14 35				14 50				15 05	
Drumchapel	d	13 53				14 08			14 23				14 38				14 53				15 08	
Milngavie	d			13 57				14 12			14 27					14 42			14 57			
Hillfoot	d			14 00				14 15			14 30					14 45			15 00			
Bearsden	d			14 02				14 17			14 31					14 47			15 02			
Westerton	d	13 55		14 05		14 10		14 20	14 25		14 35		14 40			14 50	14 55		15 05		15 10	
Anniesland	d	13 58		14 08		14 14		14 23	14 28		14 38		14 44			14 53	14 58		15 08		15 14	
Clydebank	d		13 55				14 10			14 25					14 40			14 55				15 12
Yoker	d		13 57				14 12			14 27					14 42			14 57				15 14
Garscadden	d		14 01				14 16			14 31					14 46			15 01				15 18
Scotstounhill	d		14 03				14 18			14 33					14 48			15 03				15 20
Jordanhill	d		14 05				14 20			14 35					14 50			15 05				15 22
Hyndland	d	14 01	14 07	14 11	14 14	14 17	14 22	14 26	14 31	14 37	14 41	14 44	14 47		14 52	14 56	15 01	15 07	15 11	15 14	15 18	15 24
Partick	d	14 04	14 10	14 14	14 17	14 20	14 25	14 29	14 34	14 40	14 44	14 47	14 50		14 55	14 59	15 04	15 10	15 14	15 17	15 20	15 27
Exhibition Centre	d		14 13			14 23		14 32		14 43			14 53			15 02		15 13			15 23	
Anderston	d		14 15			14 25		14 34		14 45			14 55			15 04		15 15			15 25	
Glasgow Central HL	d																					
Glasgow Central LL	a		14 17			14 26		14 35		14 47			14 56			15 05		15 17			15 26	
	d		14 17			14 27		14 37		14 47			14 57			15 07		15 17			15 27	
Argyle Street	d		14 19			14 29		14 38		14 49			14 59			15 08		15 19			15 29	
Charing Cross	d	14 08		14 19	14 22		14 29		14 38		14 49	14 52			14 59		15 08		15 19	15 22		15 31
Glasgow Queen St HL	a													15 28								
Glasgow Queen St LL	a	14 10		14 21	14 24		14 31		14 40		14 51	14 54			15 01		15 10		15 21	15 24		15 33
	d	14 12		14 21	14 27		14 32		14 42		14 51	14 57			15 02		15 12		15 21	15 27		15 34
High Street	d	14 14		14a23	14 29		14 34		14 44		14a53	14 59			15 04		15 14		15a23	15 29		15 36
Bellgrove	d	14 16			14 31		14 36		14 46			15 01			15 06		15 16			15 31		15 38
Duke Street	d						14 38								15 08							15 40
Alexandra Parade	d						14 39								15 09							15 41
Barnhill	d						14 42								15 12							15 44
Springburn	a						14 44								15 14							15 46
Carntyne	d	14 19			14 34				14 49			15 04					15 19			15 34		
Shettleston	d	14 22			14 37				14 52			15 07					15 22			15 37		
Garrowhill	d	14 24			14 39				14 54			15 09					15 24			15 39		
Easterhouse	d	14 27			14 42				14 57			15 12					15 27			15 42		
Blairhill	d	14 31			14 46				15 01			15 16					15 31			15 46		
Coatbridge Sunnyside	d	14 33			14 48				15 03			15 18					15 33			15 48		
Coatdyke	d	14 36			14 51				15 06			15 21					15 36			15 51		
Airdrie	a	14 39			14 54				15 09			15 24					15 39			15 54		
	d																					
Drumgelloch	a																					
Bridgeton	d		14 22					14 41		14 52						15 11		15 22				
Dalmarnock	d		14 24					14 43		14 54						15 13		15 24				
Rutherglen	d		14 25			14 34		14 46		14 56			15 04			15 16		15 26			15 34	
Cambuslang	d		14 30					14 50		15 01						15 20		15 31				
Newton	d							14 53								15 23						
Blantyre	d					14 44		14 58					15 14			15 28					15 44	
Hamilton West	d					14 47		15 01					15 17			15 31					15 47	
Hamilton Central	d					14 50		15 03					15 20			15 33					15 50	
Chatelherault	d					14 54							15 24								15 54	
Merryton	d					14 58							15 28								15 58	
Larkhall	a					15 00							15 30								16 00	
Airbles	d							15 08								15 38						
Uddingston	d		14 35							15 05								15 35				
Bellshill	d		14 40							15 10								15 40				
Motherwell	a		14 48					15 11		15 16						15 41		15 48				
	d									15 16						15 42						
Whifflet	a																					
Coatbridge Central	a																					
Shieldmuir	d									15 20												
Holytown	d															15 48						
Wishaw	d									15 23						15 54						
Carluke	d									15 30						16 00						
Lanark	a									15 42						16 12						

Table 226

Saturdays

Helensburgh, Balloch, Dalmuir and Milngavie - Glasgow - Springburn, Airdrie, Drumgelloch, Hamilton, Larkhall, Motherwell, Coatbridge and Lanark

		SR	SR	SR	SR	SR	SR	SR	SR	SR	SR	SR	SR	SR	SR	SR	SR	SR	SR	SR	SR	SR	SR	SR	SR
Helensburgh Upper	d																								
Helensburgh Central	d					15 10							15 40							16 10					
Craigendoran	d					15 13							15 43							16 13					
Cardross	d					15 18							15 48							16 18					
Balloch	d		14 53							15 23							15 53							16 23	
Alexandria	d		14 55							15 25							15 55							16 25	
Renton	d		14 58							15 28							15 58							16 28	
Dalreoch	d		15 01			15 23				15 31			15 53				16 01			16 23				16 31	
Dumbarton Central	d		15 02			15 25				15 32			15 55				16 02			16 25				16 32	
Dumbarton East	d		15 04			15 27				15 34			15 57				16 04			16 27				16 34	
Bowling	d		15 09							15 39							16 09							16 39	
Kilpatrick	d		15 12							15 42							16 12							16 42	
Dalmuir	a		15 15			15 35				15 45			16 05				16 15			16 35				16 45	
	d		15 16	15 23		15 36	15 31	15 38		15 46	15 53		16 06	16 01	16 08		16 16	16 23		16 36	16 31	16 38		16 46	16 53
Singer	d		15 18				15 33			15 48				16 03			16 18				16 33			16 48	
Drumry	d		15 20				15 35			15 50				16 05			16 20				16 35			16 50	
Drumchapel	d		15 23				15 38			15 53				16 08			16 23				16 38			16 53	
Milngavie	d	15 12			15 27				15 42			15 57				16 12			16 27				16 42		
Hillfoot	d	15 15			15 30				15 45			16 00				16 15			16 30				16 45		
Bearsden	d	15 17			15 32				15 47			16 02				16 17			16 32				16 47		
Westerton	d	15 20	15 25		15 35		15 40		15 50	15 55		16 05		16 10		16 20	16 25		16 35		16 40		16 50	16 55	
Anniesland	d	15 23	15 28		15 38		15 44		15 53	15 58		16 08		16 14		16 23	16 28		16 38		16 44		16 53	16 58	
Clydebank	d			15 25				15 40			15 55				16 10			16 25				16 40			16 55
Yoker	d			15 27				15 42			15 57				16 12			16 27				16 42			16 57
Garscadden	d			15 31				15 46			16 01				16 15			16 31				16 46			17 01
Scotstounhill	d			15 33				15 48			16 03				16 18			16 33				16 48			17 03
Jordanhill	d			15 35				15 50			16 05				16 20			16 35				16 50			17 05
Hyndland	d	15 27	15 31	15 37	15 41	15 44	15 47	15 52	15 56	16 01	16 07	16 11	16 14	16 17	16 22	16 26	16 31	16 37	16 41	16 44	16 47	16 52	16 56	17 01	17 07
Partick	d	15 29	15 34	15 40	15 44	15 47	15 50	15 55	15 59	16 04	16 10	16 14	16 17	16 20	16 25	16 29	16 34	16 40	16 44	16 47	16 50	16 55	16 59	17 04	17 10
Exhibition Centre	d	15 32		15 43			15 53		16 02		16 13			16 23		16 32		16 43			16 53		17 02		17 13
Anderston	d	15 34		15 45			15 55		16 04		16 15			16 25		16 34		16 45			16 55		17 04		17 15
Glasgow Central HL	d																								
Glasgow Central LL	a	15 35		15 47			15 56		16 05		16 17			16 26		16 35		16 47			16 56		17 05		17 17
	d	15 37		15 47			15 57		16 07		16 17			16 27		16 37		16 47			16 57		17 07		17 17
Argyle Street	d	15 39		15 49			15 59		16 09		16 19			16 29		16 38		16 49			16 59		17 09		17 19
Charing Cross	d		15 38		15 49	15 52		15 59		16 09		16 19	16 22		16 29		16 38		16 49	16 52		16 59		17 08	
Glasgow Queen St HL	a																								
Glasgow Queen St LL	a		15 41		15 51	15 54		16 01		16 11		16 21	16 24		16 31		16 40		16 51	16 54		17 01		17 10	
	d		15 42		15 51	15 57		16 02		16 12		16 21	16 27		16 32		16 42		16 51	16 57		17 02		17 12	
High Street	d		15 44		15a53	15 59		16 04		16 14		16a23	16 29		16 34		16 44		16a53	16 58		17 04		17 14	
Bellgrove	d		15 46			16 01		16 06		16 16			16 31		16 36		16 46			17 00		17 06		17 16	
Duke Street	d							16 08							16 38							17 08			
Alexandra Parade	d							16 09							16 39							17 09			
Barnhill	d							16 12							16 42							17 12			
Springburn	a							16 14							16 44							17 14			
Carntyne	d		15 49			16 04				16 19			16 34				16 49			17 03				17 19	
Shettleston	d		15 52			16 07				16 22			16 37				16 52			17 06				17 22	
Garrowhill	d		15 54			16 09				16 24			16 39				16 54			17 08				17 24	
Easterhouse	d		15 57			16 12				16 27			16 42				16 57			17 11				17 27	
Blairhill	d		16 01			16 16				16 31			16 46				17 01			17 15				17 31	
Coatbridge Sunnyside	d		16 03			16 18				16 33			16 48				17 03			17 17				17 33	
Coatdyke	d		16 06			16 21				16 36			16 51				17 06			17 20				17 36	
Airdrie	a		16 09			16 24				16 39			16 54				17 09			17 24				17 39	
	d																								
Drumgelloch	a																								
Bridgeton	d	15 42		15 52					16 12		16 22					16 41		16 52					17 12		17 22
Dalmarnock	d	15 44		15 54					16 14		16 24					16 43		16 54					17 14		17 24
Rutherglen	d	15 46		15 55			16 04		16 16		16 25			16 34		16 46		16 56			17 04		17 16		17 26
Cambuslang	d	15 50		16 00					16 20		16 30					16 49		17 01			17 08		17 20		17 31
Newton	d	15 54							16 24							16 53							17 24		
Blantyre	d	15 58					16 14		16 28					16 44		16 58					17 13		17 28		
Hamilton West	d	16 01					16 17		16 31					16 47		17 01					17 16		17 31		
Hamilton Central	d	16 03					16 20		16 33					16 50		17 03					17 20		17 36		
Chatelherault	d						16 24							16 54							17 23				
Merryton	d						16 28							16 58							17 28				
Larkhall	a						16 30							17 00							17 30				
Airbles	d	16 08							16 38							17 08							17 41		
Uddingston	d			16 05							16 35							17 05							17 35
Bellshill	d			16 10							16 40							17 10							17 40
Motherwell	a	16 11		16 16					16 41		16 48					17 11		17 16					17 43		17 48
	d			16 16					16 42									17 16					17 44		
Whifflet	a																								
Coatbridge Central	a																								
Shieldmuir	d			16 20														17 20							
Holytown	d								16 48														17 49		
Wishaw	d			16 23					16 53									17 23					17 54		
Carluke	d			16 30					16 59									17 30					18 00		
Lanark	a			16 42					17 15									17 42					18 12		

Table 226

Saturdays

Helensburgh, Balloch, Dalmuir and Milngavie - Glasgow - Springburn, Airdrie, Drumgelloch, Hamilton, Larkhall, Motherwell, Coatbridge and Lanark

		SR	SR	SR	SR	SR	SR	SR	SR	SR	SR	SR	SR	SR	SR	SR	SR	SR	SR	SR	SR	SR
Helensburgh Upper	d																					
Helensburgh Central	d		16 40							17 10								17 40				
Craigendoran	d		16 43							17 13								17 43				
Cardross	d		16 48							17 18								17 48				
Balloch	d						16 53							17 23						17 53		
Alexandria	d						16 55							17 25						17 55		
Renton	d						16 58							17 28						17 58		
Dalreoch	d		16 53				17 01			17 23				17 31				17 53		18 01		
Dumbarton Central	d		16 55				17 02			17 25				17 32				17 55		18 02		
Dumbarton East	d		16 57				17 04			17 27				17 34				17 57		18 04		
Bowling	d						17 09							17 39						18 09		
Kilpatrick	d						17 12							17 42						18 12		
Dalmuir	a		17 05				17 15			17 35				17 45				18 05		18 15		
	d		17 06	17 01	17 08		17 16	17 23		17 36	17 31	17 38		17 46		17 53	18 01	18 06		18 16	18 23	18 31
Singer	d			17 03			17 18				17 33			17 48			18 03			18 18		18 33
Drumry	d			17 05			17 20				17 35			17 50			18 05			18 20		18 35
Drumchapel	d			17 08			17 23				17 38			17 53			18 08			18 23		18 38
Milngavie	d	16 57				17 12			17 27				17 42						18 12			
Hillfoot	d	17 00				17 15			17 30				17 45						18 15			
Bearsden	d	17 02				17 17			17 32				17 47						18 17			
Westerton	d	17 05		17 10		17 20	17 25		17 35		17 40		17 50	17 55			18 10		18 20	18 25		18 40
Anniesland	d	17 08		17 14		17 23	17 28		17 38		17 44		17 53	17 58			18 14		18 23	18 28		18 44
Clydebank	d				17 10			17 25				17 40				17 55		18 08			18 25	
Yoker	d				17 12			17 27				17 42				17 57		18 10			18 27	
Garscadden	d				17 16			17 31				17 46				18 01		18 13			18 31	
Scotstounhill	d				17 18			17 33				17 48				18 03		18 15			18 33	
Jordanhill	d				17 20			17 35				17 50				18 05		18 18			18 35	
Hyndland	d	17 11	17 14	17 18	17 22	17 26	17 31	17 37	17 41	17 44	17 47	17 52	17 56	18 01		18 07	18 17	18 22	18 26	18 31	18 37	18 47
Partick	d	17 14	17 17	17 20	17 25	17 29	17 34	17 40	17 44	17 47	17 50	17 55	17 59	18 04		18 10	18 20	18 25	18 29	18 34	18 40	18 50
Exhibition Centre	d			17 23		17 32		17 43			17 53		18 02			18 13	18 23		18 32		18 43	18 53
Anderston	d			17 25		17 34		17 45			17 55		18 04			18 15	18 25		18 34		18 45	18 55
Glasgow Central HL [15]	d														18 14							
Glasgow Central LL [15]	a			17 26		17 35		17 47			17 56		18 05			18 17	18 26		18 35		18 47	18 56
	d			17 27		17 37		17 47			17 57		18 07			18 17	18 27		18 37		18 47	18 57
Argyle Street	d			17 29		17 38		17 49			17 59		18 08			18 19	18 29		18 38		18 49	18 59
Charing Cross	d	17 19	17 22		17 29		17 38		17 49	17 52		17 59		18 08				18 29		18 38		
Glasgow Queen St HL [10]	a																					
Glasgow Queen St LL [10]	a	17 21	17 24		17 31		17 40		17 51	17 54		18 01		18 10				18 31		18 40		
	d	17 21	17 27		17 32		17 42		17 51	17 57		18 02		18 12				18 32		18 44		
High Street	d	17a23	17 29		17 34		17 44		17a53	17 59		18 04		18 14				18 34		18 46		
Bellgrove	d		17 31		17 36		17 46			18 01		18 06		18 16				18 36		18 48		
Duke Street	d				17 38							18 08								18 50		
Alexandra Parade	d				17 39							18 09								18 51		
Barnhill	d				17 42							18 12								18 54		
Springburn	a				17 44							18 15								18 56		
Carntyne	d		17 34				17 49			18 04				18 19				18 39				
Shettleston	d		17 37				17 52			18 07				18 22				18 42				
Garrowhill	d		17 39				17 54			18 09				18 24				18 44				
Easterhouse	d		17 42				17 57			18 12				18 27				18 47				
Blairhill	d		17 46				18 01			18 16				18 31				18 51				
Coatbridge Sunnyside	d		17 48				18 03			18 18				18 33				18 53				
Coatdyke	d		17 51				18 06			18 21				18 36				18 56				
Airdrie	a		17 54				18 09			18 24				18 39				18 59				
	d																					
Drumgelloch	a																					
Bridgeton	d					17 41		17 52					18 11			18 22			18 41		18 52	
Dalmarnock	d					17 43		17 54					18 13			18 24			18 43		18 54	
Rutherglen	d			17 34		17 46		17 55			18 04		18 16			18 26	18 34		18 46		18 56	19 04
Cambuslang	d					17 49		18 00					18 20		18 22	18 31			18 49		19 01	
Newton	d					17 53							18 23						18 53			
Blantyre	d			17 44		17 58					18 14		18 28				18 44		18 58			19 14
Hamilton West	d			17 47		18 01					18 17		18 31				18 47		19 01			19 17
Hamilton Central	d			17 50		18 03					18 20		18 33				18 50		19 03			19 20
Chatelherault	d			17 54							18 24						18 54					19 24
Merryton	d			17 58							18 28						18 58					19 28
Larkhall	a			18 00							18 30						19 00					19 30
Airbles	d					18 08							18 38						19 08			
Uddingston	d							18 05							18 27	18 35					19 05	
Bellshill	d							18 10							18 31	18 40					19 10	
Motherwell	a					18 11		18 15					18 41			18 48			19 11		19 16	
	d							18 16					18 42								19 16	
Whifflet	a																					
Coatbridge Central	a																					
Shieldmuir	d							18 20													19 20	
Holytown	d												18 49		18 35							
Wishaw	d							18 23					18 53								19 23	
Carluke	d							18 30					19 00								19 30	
Lanark	a							18 42					19 12								19 42	

Table 226

Saturdays

Helensburgh, Balloch, Dalmuir and Milngavie - Glasgow - Springburn, Airdrie, Drumgelloch, Hamilton, Larkhall, Motherwell, Coatbridge and Lanark

		SR	SR	SR ◇ A 🚌	SR	SR	SR	SR	SR	SR	SR	SR	SR	SR	SR	SR	SR	SR	SR	SR ◇ 🚌	SR	SR	SR
Helensburgh Upper	d			18 34																20 39			
Helensburgh Central	d	18 10					18 40					19 10					19 40						20 10
Craigendoran	d	18 13					18 43					19 13					19 43						20 13
Cardross	d	18 18					18 48					19 18					19 48						20 18
Balloch	d		18 23						18 53					19 23					19 53				
Alexandria	d		18 25						18 55					19 25					19 55				
Renton	d		18 28						18 58					19 28					19 58				
Dalreoch	d	18 23	18 31				18 53		19 01			19 23		19 31			19 53		20 01				20 23
Dumbarton Central	d	18 25	18 32	18 47			18 55		19 02			19 25		19 32			19 55		20 02	20 53			20 25
Dumbarton East	d	18 27	18 34				18 57		19 04			19 27		19 34			19 57		20 04				20 27
Bowling	d		18 39						19 09					19 39					20 09				
Kilpatrick	d		18 42						19 12					19 42					20 12				
Dalmuir	a	18 35	18 45	18 56			19 05		19 15			19 35		19 45			20 05		20 15	21 04			20 35
	d	18 35	18 46	18 56		19 01	19 05		19 16		19 31	19 35		19 46		20 01	20 05		20 16	21 07		20 31	20 35
Singer	d		18 48			19 03			19 18		19 33			19 48		20 03			20 18			20 33	
Drumry	d		18 50			19 05			19 20		19 35			19 50		20 05			20 20			20 35	
Drumchapel	d		18 53			19 08			19 23		19 38			19 53		20 08			20 23			20 38	
Milngavie	d							19 12					19 42					20 12					
Hillfoot	d							19 15					19 45					20 15					
Bearsden	d							19 17					19 47					20 17					
Westerton	d		18 55			19 10		19 20	19 25		19 40		19 50	19 55		20 10		20 20	20 25			20 40	
Anniesland	d		18 58			19 14		19 23	19 28		19 44		19 53	19 58		20 14		20 23	20 28			20 44	
Clydebank	d	18 37					19 07					19 37					20 07						20 37
Yoker	d	18 39					19 09					19 39					20 09						20 39
Garscadden	d	18 43					19 13					19 43					20 13						20 43
Scotstounhill	d	18 45					19 15					19 45					20 15						20 45
Jordanhill	d	18 47					19 17					19 47					20 17						20 47
Hyndland	d	18 51	19 01			19 17	19 21	19 25	19 31		19 47	19 51	19 55	20 01		20 17	20 21	20 25	20 31			20 47	20 51
Partick	d	18 54	19 04		19 10	19 20	19 24	19 29	19 34	19 40	19 50	19 54	19 59	20 04	20 10	20 20	20 24	20 29	20 34		20 40	20 50	20 54
Exhibition Centre	d				19 13	19 23		19 32		19 43	19 53		20 02		20 13	20 23		20 32			20 43	20 53	
Anderston	d				19 15	19 25		19 34		19 45	19 55		20 04		20 15	20 25		20 34			20 45	20 55	
Glasgow Central HL [15]	d																						
Glasgow Central LL [15]	a				19 16	19 26		19 35		19 46	19 56		20 05		20 16	20 26		20 35			20 46	20 56	
	d				19 17	19 27		19 37		19 47	19 57		20 07		20 17	20 27		20 37			20 47	20 57	
Argyle Street	d				19 19	19 29		19 38		19 49	19 59		20 09		20 19	20 29		20 38			20 48	20 59	
Charing Cross	d	18 59	19 08				19 29		19 38			19 59		20 08			20 29		20 38				20 59
Glasgow Queen St HL [10]	a			19 18																21 30			
Glasgow Queen St LL [10]	a	19 01	19 10				19 31		19 40			20 01		20 10			20 31		20 40				21 01
	d	19 02	19 14				19 32		19 44			20 02		20 14			20 32		20 44				21 02
High Street	d	19 04	19 16				19 34		19 46			20 04		20 16			20 34		20 46				21 04
Bellgrove	d	19 06	19 18				19 36		19 48			20 06		20 18			20 36		20 48				21 06
Duke Street	d		19 20						19 50					20 20					20 50				
Alexandra Parade	d		19 21						19 51					20 21					20 51				
Barnhill	d		19 24						19 54					20 24					20 54				
Springburn	a		19 26						19 56					20 26					20 56				
Carntyne	d	19 09					19 39					20 09					20 39						21 09
Shettleston	d	19 12					19 42					20 12					20 42						21 12
Garrowhill	d	19 14					19 44					20 14					20 44						21 14
Easterhouse	d	19 17					19 47					20 17					20 47						21 17
Blairhill	d	19 21					19 51					20 21					20 51						21 21
Coatbridge Sunnyside	d	19 23					19 53					20 23					20 53						21 23
Coatdyke	d	19 26					19 56					20 26					20 56						21 26
Airdrie	a	19 29					19 59					20 29					20 59						21 29
	d																						
Drumgelloch	a																						
Bridgeton	d				19 22			19 41		19 52			20 12		20 22			20 41			20 51		
Dalmarnock	d				19 24			19 43		19 54			20 14		20 24			20 43			20 53		
Rutherglen	d				19 26	19 34		19 46		19 56	20 04		20 16		20 26	20 34		20 46			20 56	21 04	
Cambuslang	d				19 31			19 49		20 01			20 20		20 31			20 50			21 01		
Newton	d							19 53					20 24					20 53					
Blantyre	d					19 44		19 58			20 14		20 28			20 44		20 58				21 14	
Hamilton West	d					19 47		20 01			20 17		20 31			20 47		21 01				21 17	
Hamilton Central	d					19 50		20 03			20 20		20 33			20 50		21 03				21 20	
Chatelherault	d					19 54					20 24					20 54						21 24	
Merryton	d					19 58					20 28					20 58						21 28	
Larkhall	a					20 00					20 30					21 00						21 30	
Airbles	d							20 08					20 38					21 08					
Uddingston	d				19 35					20 05					20 35						21 05		
Bellshill	d				19 40					20 10					20 40						21 10		
Motherwell	a				19 48			20 11		20 16			20 41		20 48			21 11			21 16		
	d									20 16			20 42								21 16		
Whifflet	a																						
Coatbridge Central	a																						
Shieldmuir	d									20 20											21 20		
Holytown	d												20 47										
Wishaw	d									20 23			20 53								21 23		
Carluke	d									20 30			21 00								21 30		
Lanark	a									20 42			21 12								21 42		

A until 30 October

Table 226

Saturdays

Helensburgh, Balloch, Dalmuir and Milngavie - Glasgow - Springburn, Airdrie, Drumgelloch, Hamilton, Larkhall, Motherwell, Coatbridge and Lanark

		SR	SR	SR	SR	SR	SR	SR	SR	SR	SR	SR	SR
Helensburgh Upper	d												
Helensburgh Central	d					20 40					21 10		
Craigendoran	d					20 43					21 13		
Cardross	d					20 48					21 18		
Balloch	d		20 23					20 53					21 23
Alexandria	d		20 25					20 55					21 25
Renton	d		20 28					20 59					21 28
Dalreoch	d		20 31			20 53		21 02			21 23		21 31
Dumbarton Central	d		20 32			20 55		21 03			21 25		21 32
Dumbarton East	d		20 34			20 57		21 05			21 27		21 34
Bowling	d		20 39					21 10					21 39
Kilpatrick	d		20 42					21 13					21 42
Dalmuir	a		20 45			21 05		21 16			21 35		21 45
	d		20 46		21 01	21 05		21 16		21 31	21 35		21 46
Singer	d		20 48		21 03			21 18		21 33			21 48
Drumry	d		20 50		21 05			21 21		21 35			21 50
Drumchapel	d		20 53		21 08			21 24		21 38			21 53
Milngavie	d	20 42					21 12					21 42	
Hillfoot	d	20 45					21 15					21 45	
Bearsden	d	20 47					21 17					21 47	
Westerton	d	20 50	20 55		21 10		21 20	21 25		21 40		21 50	21 55
Anniesland	d	20 53	20 58		21 14		21 23	21 28		21 44		21 53	21 58
Clydebank	d					21 07					21 37		
Yoker	d					21 09					21 39		
Garscadden	d					21 13					21 43		
Scotstounhill	d					21 15					21 45		
Jordanhill	d					21 17					21 47		
Hyndland	d	20 56	21 01		21 17	21 21	21 27	21 31		21 47	21 51	21 55	22 01
Partick	d	20 59	21 04	21 10	21 20	21 24	21 29	21 34	21 40	21 50	21 54	21 59	22 04
Exhibition Centre	d	21 02		21 13	21 23		21 32		21 43	21 53		22 02	
Anderston	d	21 04		21 15	21 25		21 34		21 45	21 55		22 04	
Glasgow Central HL 15	d												
Glasgow Central LL 15	a	21 05		21 16	21 26		21 35		21 46	21 56		22 05	
	d	21 07		21 17	21 27		21 37		21 47	21 57		22 07	
Argyle Street	d	21 09		21 19	21 29		21 39		21 49	21 59		22 08	
Charing Cross	d		21 08			21 29		21 38			21 59		22 08
Glasgow Queen St HL 10	a												
Glasgow Queen St LL 10	a		21 10			21 31		21 40			22 01		22 10
	d		21 14			21 32		21 44			22 02		22 14
High Street	d		21 16			21 34		21 46			22 04		22 16
Bellgrove	d		21 18			21 36		21 48			22 06		22 18
Duke Street	d		21 20					21 50					22 20
Alexandra Parade	d		21 21					21 51					22 21
Barnhill	d		21 24					21 54					22 24
Springburn	a		21 26					21 56					22 26
Carntyne	d					21 39					22 09		
Shettleston	d					21 42					22 12		
Garrowhill	d					21 44					22 14		
Easterhouse	d					21 47					22 17		
Blairhill	d					21 51					22 21		
Coatbridge Sunnyside	d					21 53					22 23		
Coatdyke	d					21 56					22 26		
Airdrie	a					21 59					22 29		
	d												
Drumgelloch	a												
Bridgeton	d	21 12		21 22			21 42		21 52			22 11	
Dalmarnock	d	21 14		21 24			21 44		21 54			22 13	
Rutherglen	d	21 16		21 26	21 34		21 46		21 56	22 04		22 16	
Cambuslang	d	21 20		21 31			21 50		22 01			22 20	
Newton	d	21 24					21 54					22 23	
Blantyre	d	21 28			21 44		21 58			22 14		22 28	
Hamilton West	d	21 31			21 47		22 01			22 17		22 31	
Hamilton Central	d	21 33			21 50		22 03			22 20		22 33	
Chatelherault	d				21 54					22 24			
Merryton	d				21 58					22 28			
Larkhall	a				22 00					22 30			
Airbles	d	21 38					22 08					22 38	
Uddingston	d			21 35					22 05				
Bellshill	d			21 40					22 10				
Motherwell	a	21 41		21 48			22 11		22 16			22 41	
	d	21 41							22 16			22 41	
Whifflet	a											22 49	
Coatbridge Central	a											22 52	
Shieldmuir	d								22 20				
Holytown	d	21 48											
Wishaw	d	21 53							22 23				
Carluke	d	22 00							22 30				
Lanark	a	22 12							22 42				

		SR	SR	SR	SR	SR	SR	SR	SR	SR
Helensburgh Upper	d									
Helensburgh Central	d			21 40					22 10	
Craigendoran	d			21 43					22 13	
Cardross	d			21 48					22 18	
Balloch	d					21 53				
Alexandria	d					21 55				
Renton	d					21 58				
Dalreoch	d			21 53		22 01			22 23	
Dumbarton Central	d			21 55		22 02			22 25	
Dumbarton East	d			21 57		22 04			22 27	
Bowling	d					22 09				
Kilpatrick	d					22 12				
Dalmuir	a			22 05		22 15			22 35	
	d		22 01	22 05		22 16		22 31	22 35	
Singer	d		22 03			22 18		22 33		
Drumry	d		22 05			22 20		22 35		
Drumchapel	d		22 08			22 23		22 38		
Milngavie	d				22 12					22 42
Hillfoot	d				22 15					22 45
Bearsden	d				22 17					22 47
Westerton	d		22 10		22 20	22 25		22 40		22 50
Anniesland	d		22 14		22 24	22 28		22 44		22 53
Clydebank	d			22 07					22 37	
Yoker	d			22 09					22 39	
Garscadden	d			22 13					22 43	
Scotstounhill	d			22 15					22 45	
Jordanhill	d			22 17					22 47	
Hyndland	d		22 17	22 21	22 27	22 31		22 47	22 51	22 55
Partick	d	22 10	22 20	22 24	22 30	22 34	22 40	22 50	22 54	22 59
Exhibition Centre	d	22 13	22 23		22 33		22 43	22 53		23 02
Anderston	d	22 15	22 25		22 35		22 45	22 55		23 04
Glasgow Central HL 15	d									
Glasgow Central LL 15	a	22 16	22 26		22 36		22 46	22 56		23 05
	d	22 17	22 27		22 37		22 47	22 57		23 07
Argyle Street	d	22 19	22 29		22 38		22 49	22 59		23 08
Charing Cross	d			22 29		22 38			22 59	
Glasgow Queen St HL 10	a									
Glasgow Queen St LL 10	a			22 31		22 40			23 01	
	d			22 32		22 44			23 02	
High Street	d			22 34		22 46			23 04	
Bellgrove	d			22 36		22 48			23 06	
Duke Street	d					22 50				
Alexandra Parade	d					22 51				
Barnhill	d					22 54				
Springburn	a					22 56				
Carntyne	d			22 39					23 09	
Shettleston	d			22 42					23 12	
Garrowhill	d			22 44					23 14	
Easterhouse	d			22 47					23 17	
Blairhill	d			22 51					23 21	
Coatbridge Sunnyside	d			22 53					23 23	
Coatdyke	d			22 56					23 26	
Airdrie	a			22 59					23 29	
	d									
Drumgelloch	a									
Bridgeton	d	22 22			22 41		22 52			23 11
Dalmarnock	d	22 24			22 43		22 54			23 13
Rutherglen	d	22 26	22 34		22 46		22 56	23 04		23 16
Cambuslang	d	22 31			22 50		23 01			23 20
Newton	d				22 54					23 23
Blantyre	d		22 44		22 58			23 14		23 27
Hamilton West	d		22 47		23 01			23 17		23 30
Hamilton Central	d		22 50		23 03			23 20		23 33
Chatelherault	d		22 54					23 24		
Merryton	d		22 58					23 28		
Larkhall	a		23 00					23 30		
Airbles	d				23 08					23 38
Uddingston	d	22 35					23 05			
Bellshill	d	22 40					23 10			
Motherwell	a	22 49			23 11		23 16			23 41
	d						23 16			
Whifflet	a									
Coatbridge Central	a									
Shieldmuir	d						23 20			
Holytown	d									
Wishaw	d						23 23			
Carluke	d						23 30			
Lanark	a						23 42			

Table 226

Saturdays

Helensburgh, Balloch, Dalmuir and Milngavie - Glasgow - Springburn, Airdrie, Drumgelloch, Hamilton, Larkhall, Motherwell, Coatbridge and Lanark

		SR	SR	SR	SR	SR	SR
Helensburgh Upper	d						
Helensburgh Central	d				22 40		23 10
Craigendoran	d				22 43		23 13
Cardross	d				22 48		23 18
Balloch	d	22 23				22 53	
Alexandria	d	22 25				22 55	
Renton	d	22 28				22 58	
Dalreoch	d	22 31			22 53	23 01	23 23
Dumbarton Central	d	22 32			22 55	23 02	23 25
Dumbarton East	d	22 34			22 57	23 04	23 27
Bowling	d	22 39				23 09	
Kilpatrick	d	22 42				23 12	
Dalmuir	a	22 45			23 05	23 15	23 35
	d	22 46		23 01	23 05	23 16	23 35
Singer	d	22 48		23 03		23 18	
Drumry	d	22 50		23 05		23 20	
Drumchapel	d	22 53		23 08		23 23	
Milngavie	d						
Hillfoot	d						
Bearsden	d						
Westerton	d	22 55		23 10		23 25	
Anniesland	d	23 00		23 14		23 28	
Clydebank	d				23 07		23 37
Yoker	d				23 09		23 39
Garscadden	d				23 13		23 43
Scotstounhill	d				23 15		23 45
Jordanhill	d				23 17		23 47
Hyndland	d	23 03		23 17	23 21	23 31	23 51
Partick	d	23 05	23 10	23 20	23 24	23 34	23 54
Exhibition Centre	d		23 13	23 23			
Anderston	d		23 15	23 25			
Glasgow Central HL 15	d						
Glasgow Central LL 15	a		23 16	23 26			
	d		23 17	23 27			
Argyle Street	d		23 19	23 29			
Charing Cross	d	23 09			23 29	23 38	23 59
Glasgow Queen St HL 10	a						
Glasgow Queen St LL 10	a	23 11			23 31	23 40	00 01
	d	23 14			23 32	23 44	00 02
High Street	d	23 16			23 34	23 46	00 04
Bellgrove	d	23 18			23 36	23 48	00 06
Duke Street	d	23 20					
Alexandra Parade	d	23 21					
Barnhill	d	23 24					
Springburn	a	23 26					
Carntyne	d				23 39	23 51	00 09
Shettleston	d				23 42	23 54	00 12
Garrowhill	d				23 44	23 56	00 14
Easterhouse	d				23 47	23 59	00 17
Blairhill	d				23 51	00 03	00 21
Coatbridge Sunnyside	d				23 53	00 05	00 23
Coatdyke	d				23 56	00 08	00 26
Airdrie	a				23 59	00 11	00 30
	d						
Drumgelloch	a						
Bridgeton	d		23 22				
Dalmarnock	d		23 24				
Rutherglen	d		23 26	23 34			
Cambuslang	d		23 31				
Newton	d						
Blantyre	d			23 44			
Hamilton West	d			23 47			
Hamilton Central	d			23 50			
Chatelherault	d			23 54			
Merryton	d			23 58			
Larkhall	a			00 01			
Airbles	d						
Uddingston	d		23 35				
Bellshill	d		23 40				
Motherwell	a		23 46				
	d						
Whifflet	a						
Coatbridge Central	a						
Shieldmuir	d						
Holytown	d						
Wishaw	d						
Carluke	d						
Lanark	a						

Table 226

Sundays until 12 September

Helensburgh, Balloch, Dalmuir and Milngavie - Glasgow - Springburn, Airdrie, Drumgelloch, Hamilton, Larkhall, Motherwell, Coatbridge and Lanark

Station		SR	SR	SR	SR	SR	SR	SR	SR	SR	SR	SR	SR	SR	SR	SR	SR	SR	SR	SR
Helensburgh Upper	d																			
Helensburgh Central	d				07 55			08 25				08 55			09 25			09 55		
Craigendoran	d				07 58			08 28				08 58			09 28			09 58		
Cardross	d				08 03			08 33				09 03			09 33			10 03		
Balloch	d					08 09			08 39				09 09			09 39			10 09	
Alexandria	d					08 11			08 41				09 11			09 41			10 11	
Renton	d					08 14			08 44				09 14			09 44			10 14	
Dalreoch	d				08 08	08 17		08 38	08 47			09 08	09 17		09 38	09 47		10 08	10 17	
Dumbarton Central	d				08 10	08 18		08 40	08 48			09 10	09 18		09 40	09 48		10 10	10 18	
Dumbarton East	d				08 12	08 20		08 42	08 50			09 12	09 20		09 42	09 50		10 12	10 20	
Bowling	d					08 24			08 54				09 24			09 54			10 24	
Kilpatrick	d					08 28			08 58				09 28			09 58			10 28	
Dalmuir	a				08 19	08 30		08 49	09 00			09 19	09 30		09 49	10 00		10 19	10 30	
	d		07 50	08 01	08 20	08 31		08 50	09 01			09 20	09 31		09 50	10 01		10 20	10 31	
Singer	d		07 52		08 22			08 52				09 22			09 52			10 22		
Drumry	d		07 55		08 25			08 55				09 25			09 55			10 25		
Drumchapel	d		07 57		08 27			08 57				09 27			09 57			10 27		
Milngavie	d									09 11				09 41			10 11			10 41
Hillfoot	d									09 14				09 44			10 14			10 44
Bearsden	d									09 16				09 46			10 16			10 46
Westerton	d		08 00		08 30			09 00		09 19		09 30		09 49	10 00		10 19	10 30		10 49
Anniesland	d		08 03		08 33			09 03		09 22		09 33		09 52	10 03		10 22	10 33		10 52
Clydebank	d			08 03		08 33			09 03				09 33			10 03			10 33	
Yoker	d			08 05		08 35			09 05				09 35			10 05			10 35	
Garscadden	d			08 09		08 39			09 09				09 39			10 09			10 39	
Scotstounhill	d			08 11		08 41			09 11				09 41			10 11			10 41	
Jordanhill	d			08 13		08 43			09 13				09 43			10 13			10 43	
Hyndland	d		08 05	08 15	08 35	08 45	08 55	09 05	09 15	09 25		09 35	09 45	09 54	10 05	10 15	10 25	10 35	10 45	10 55
Partick	d		08 08	08 18	08 38	08 48	08 58	09 08	09 18	09 28	09 34	09 38	09 48	09 57	10 08	10 18	10 28	10 38	10 48	10 58
Exhibition Centre	d			08 21		08 51	09 01		09 21	09 31	09 37		09 51	10 00		10 21	10 31		10 51	11 01
Anderston	d																			
Glasgow Central HL [15]	d																			
Glasgow Central LL [15]	a			08 23		08 53	09 03		09 23	09 33	09 39		09 53	10 02		10 23	10 33		10 53	11 03
	d			08 24		08 54	09 04		09 24	09 34	09 40		09 54	10 03		10 24	10 34		10 54	11 04
Argyle Street	d												09 56	10 06		10 26	10 36		10 56	11 06
Charing Cross	d		08 13		08 43			09 13				09 43			10 13			10 43		
Glasgow Queen St HL [10]	a																			
Glasgow Queen St LL [10]	a		08 15		08 45			09 15				09 45			10 15			10 45		
	d		08 17		08 46			09 16				09 46			10 16			10 46		
High Street	d		08 19		08 48			09 18				09 48			10 18			10 48		
Bellgrove	d		08 21		08 50			09 20				09 50			10 20			10 50		
Duke Street	d																			
Alexandra Parade	d																			
Barnhill	d																			
Springburn	a																			
Carntyne	d		08 24		08 54			09 24				09 54			10 24			10 54		
Shettleston	d		08 27		08 56			09 26				09 56			10 26			10 56		
Garrowhill	d		08 29		08 59			09 29				09 59			10 29			10 59		
Easterhouse	d		08 32		09 01			09 31				10 01			10 31			11 01		
Blairhill	d		08 36		09 05			09 35				10 05			10 35			11 05		
Coatbridge Sunnyside	d		08 38		09 08			09 38				10 08			10 38			11 08		
Coatdyke	d		08 41		09 10			09 40				10 10			10 40			11 10		
Airdrie	a		08 44		09 13			09 43				10 13			10 43			11 13		
	d	00 37																		
Drumgelloch	a	00 44																		
Bridgeton	d			08 29		08 59	09 09		09 29	09 39			09 59	10 09		10 29	10 39		10 59	11 09
Dalmarnock	d																			
Rutherglen	d			08 32		09 02	09 12		09 32	09 42	09 47		10 01	10 12		10 32	10 42		11 02	11 12
Cambuslang	d			08 36		09 06	09 16		09 36	09 46			10 05	10 16		10 36	10 46		11 06	11 16
Newton	d					09 09			09 39				10 08			10 39			11 09	
Blantyre	d					09 13			09 43		09 56		10 12			10 43			11 13	
Hamilton West	d					09 16			09 46		09 59		10 15			10 46			11 16	
Hamilton Central	d					09 20			09 50		10 01		10 20			10 50			11 20	
Chatelherault	d										10 06									
Merryton	d										10 09									
Larkhall	a										10 11									
Airbles	d					09 25			09 55				10 25			10 55			11 25	
Uddingston	d			08 40			09 20			09 52				10 20			10 50			11 20
Bellshill	d			08 45			09 25			09 57				10 25			10 55			11 25
Motherwell	a			08 53		09 27	09 31		09 57	10 04			10 27	10 33		10 57	11 03		11 27	11 33
	d						09 32							10 33						11 33
Whifflet	a																			
Coatbridge Central	a																			
Shieldmuir	d						09 37							10 37						11 37
Holytown	d																			
Wishaw	d						09 40							10 40						11 40
Carluke	d						09 47							10 47						11 47
Lanark	a						09 59							10 59						11 59

Table 226

Sundays until 12 September

Helensburgh, Balloch, Dalmuir and Milngavie - Glasgow - Springburn, Airdrie, Drumgelloch, Hamilton, Larkhall, Motherwell, Coatbridge and Lanark

Station		SR	SR	SR	SR	SR	SR	SR	SR	SR	SR	SR	SR	SR	SR	SR	SR	SR	SR	SR	SR	SR	SR
Helensburgh Upper	d																						
Helensburgh Central	d	10 25				10 55			11 25			11 55			12 25				12 55			13 25	
Craigendoran	d	10 28				10 58			11 28			11 58			12 28				12 58			13 28	
Cardross	d	10 33				11 03			11 33			12 03			12 33				13 03			13 33	
Balloch	d		10 39				11 09			11 39			12 09			12 39				13 09			13 39
Alexandria	d		10 41				11 11			11 41			12 11			12 41				13 11			13 41
Renton	d		10 44				11 14			11 44			12 14			12 44				13 14			13 44
Dalreoch	d	10 38	10 47			11 08	11 17		11 38	11 47		12 08	12 17		12 38	12 47			13 08	13 17		13 38	13 47
Dumbarton Central	d	10 40	10 48			11 10	11 18		11 40	11 48		12 10	12 18		12 40	12 48			13 10	13 18		13 40	13 48
Dumbarton East	d	10 42	10 50			11 12	11 20		11 42	11 50		12 12	12 20		12 42	12 50			13 12	13 20		13 42	13 50
Bowling	d		10 54				11 24			11 54			12 24			12 54				13 24			13 54
Kilpatrick	d		10 58				11 28			11 58			12 28			12 58				13 28			13 58
Dalmuir	a	10 49	11 00			11 19	11 30		11 49	12 00		12 19	12 30		12 49	13 00			13 19	13 30		13 49	14 00
	d	10 50	11 01			11 20	11 31		11 50	12 01		12 20	12 31		12 50	13 01			13 20	13 31		13 50	14 01
Singer	d	10 52				11 22			11 52			12 22			12 52				13 22			13 52	
Drumry	d	10 55				11 25			11 55			12 25			12 55				13 25			13 55	
Drumchapel	d	10 57				11 27			11 57			12 27			12 57				13 27			13 57	
Milngavie	d			11 11				11 41			12 11			12 41			13 11				13 41		
Hillfoot	d			11 14				11 44			12 14			12 44			13 14				13 44		
Bearsden	d			11 16				11 46			12 16			12 46			13 16				13 46		
Westerton	d	11 00		11 19		11 30		11 49	12 00		12 19	12 30		12 49	13 00		13 19		13 30		13 49	14 00	
Anniesland	d	11 03		11 22		11 33		11 52	12 03		12 22	12 33		12 52	13 03		13 22		13 33		13 52	14 03	
Clydebank	d		11 03				11 33			12 03			12 33			13 03				13 33			14 03
Yoker	d		11 05				11 35			12 05			12 35			13 05				13 35			14 05
Garscadden	d		11 09				11 39			12 09			12 39			13 09				13 39			14 09
Scotstounhill	d		11 11				11 41			12 11			12 41			13 11				13 41			14 11
Jordanhill	d		11 13				11 43			12 13			12 43			13 13				13 43			14 13
Hyndland	d	11 06	11 15	11 25		11 35	11 45	11 55	12 06	12 15	12 25	12 35	12 45	12 55	13 06	13 15	13 25		13 35	13 45	13 55	14 06	14 15
Partick	d	11 09	11 18	11 28	11 34	11 38	11 48	11 58	12 09	12 18	12 28	12 38	12 48	12 58	13 09	13 18	13 28	13 34	13 38	13 48	13 58	14 09	14 18
Exhibition Centre	d		11 21	11 31	11 37		11 51	12 01		12 21	12 31		12 51	13 01		13 21	13 31	13 37		13 51	14 01		14 21
Anderston	d																						
Glasgow Central HL [15]	d																						
Glasgow Central LL [15]	a		11 23	11 33	11 39		11 53	12 03		12 23	12 33		12 53	13 03		13 23	13 33	13 39		13 53	14 03		14 23
	d		11 24	11 34	11 40		11 54	12 04		12 24	12 34		12 54	13 04		13 24	13 34	13 40		13 54	14 04		14 24
Argyle Street	d		11 26	11 36	11 42		11 56	12 06		12 26	12 36		12 56	13 06		13 26	13 36	13 42		13 56	14 06		14 26
Charing Cross	d	11 14				11 43			12 14			12 43			13 14				13 43			14 14	
Glasgow Queen St HL [10]	a																						
Glasgow Queen St LL [10]	a	11 16				11 45			12 16			12 45			13 16				13 45			14 16	
	d	11 16				11 46			12 16			12 46			13 16				13 46			14 16	
High Street	d	11 18				11 48			12 18			12 48			13 18				13 48			14 18	
Bellgrove	d	11 20				11 50			12 20			12 50			13 20				13 50			14 20	
Duke Street	d																						
Alexandra Parade	d																						
Barnhill	d																						
Springburn	a																						
Carntyne	d	11 24				11 54			12 24			12 54			13 24				13 54			14 24	
Shettleston	d	11 26				11 56			12 26			12 56			13 26				13 56			14 26	
Garrowhill	d	11 29				11 59			12 29			12 59			13 29				13 59			14 29	
Easterhouse	d	11 31				12 01			12 31			13 01			13 31				14 01			14 31	
Blairhill	d	11 35				12 05			12 35			13 05			13 35				14 05			14 35	
Coatbridge Sunnyside	d	11 38				12 08			12 38			13 08			13 38				14 08			14 38	
Coatdyke	d	11 40				12 10			12 40			13 10			13 40				14 10			14 40	
Airdrie	a	11 43				12 13			12 43			13 13			13 43				14 13			14 43	
	d																						
Drumgelloch	a																						
Bridgeton	d		11 29	11 39			11 59	12 09		12 29	12 39		12 59	13 09		13 29	13 39			13 59	14 09		14 29
Dalmarnock	d																						
Rutherglen	d		11 32	11 42	11 47		12 02	12 12		12 32	12 42		13 02	13 12		13 32	13 42	13 47		14 02	14 12		14 32
Cambuslang	d		11 36	11 46			12 06	12 16		12 36	12 46		13 06	13 16		13 36	13 46			14 06	14 16		14 36
Newton	d		11 38				12 09			12 39			13 09			13 39				14 09			14 39
Blantyre	d		11 43		11 55		12 13			12 43			13 13			13 42		13 56		14 13			14 43
Hamilton West	d		11 46		11 58		12 16			12 46			13 16			13 45		13 59		14 16			14 46
Hamilton Central	d		11 50		12 01		12 20			12 50			13 20			13 50		14 02		14 20			14 50
Chatelherault	d				12 06													14 08					
Merryton	d				12 09													14 10					
Larkhall	a				12 12													14 14					
Airbles	d		11 55				12 25			12 55			13 25			13 55				14 25			14 55
Uddingston	d			11 50				12 20			12 50			13 20			13 50				14 20		
Bellshill	d			11 55				12 25			12 55			13 25			13 55				14 25		
Motherwell	a		11 57	12 03			12 27	12 33		12 57	13 03		13 27	13 33		13 57	14 05			14 27	14 33		14 57
	d							12 33						13 33							14 33		
Whifflet	a																						
Coatbridge Central	a																						
Shieldmuir	d							12 37						13 37							14 37		
Holytown	d																						
Wishaw	d							12 40						13 40							14 40		
Carluke	d							12 47						13 47							14 47		
Lanark	a							12 59						13 59							14 59		

Table 226

Sundays until 12 September

Helensburgh, Balloch, Dalmuir and Milngavie - Glasgow - Springburn, Airdrie, Drumgelloch, Hamilton, Larkhall, Motherwell, Coatbridge and Lanark

		SR		SR	SR	SR	SR ◇	SR	SR	SR	SR	SR		SR	SR	SR	SR	SR	SR	SR	SR	SR		SR	SR
Helensburgh Upper	d						14 39																		
Helensburgh Central	d				13 55				14 25			14 55				15 25				15 55				16 25	
Craigendoran	d				13 58				14 28			14 58				15 28				15 58				16 28	
Cardross	d				14 03				14 33			15 03				15 33				16 03				16 33	
Balloch	d					14 09				14 39				15 09			15 39				16 09				16 39
Alexandria	d					14 11				14 41				15 11			15 41				16 11				16 41
Renton	d					14 14				14 44				15 14			15 44				16 14				16 44
Dalreoch	d				14 08	14 17			14 38	14 47		15 08		15 17		15 38	15 47			16 08	16 17			16 38	16 47
Dumbarton Central	d				14 10	14 18	14 56		14 40	14 48		15 10		15 18		15 40	15 48			16 10	16 18			16 40	16 48
Dumbarton East	d				14 12	14 20			14 42	14 50		15 12		15 20		15 42	15 50			16 12	16 20			16 42	16 50
Bowling	d					14 24				14 54				15 24			15 54				16 24				16 54
Kilpatrick	d					14 28				14 58				15 28			15 58				16 28				16 58
Dalmuir	a				14 19	14 30	15 05		14 49	15 00		15 19		15 30		15 49	16 00			16 19	16 30			16 49	17 00
	d				14 20	14 31	15 05		14 50	15 01		15 20		15 31		15 50	16 01			16 20	16 31			16 50	17 01
Singer	d				14 22				14 52			15 22				15 52				16 22				16 52	
Drumry	d				14 25				14 55			15 25				15 55				16 25				16 55	
Drumchapel	d				14 27				14 57			15 27				15 57				16 27				16 57	
Milngavie	d	14 11						14 41			15 11				15 41			16 11				16 41			
Hillfoot	d	14 14						14 44			15 14				15 44			16 14				16 44			
Bearsden	d	14 16						14 46			15 16				15 46			16 16				16 46			
Westerton	d	14 19			14 30			14 49	15 00		15 19	15 30			15 49	16 00		16 19		16 30		16 49		17 00	
Anniesland	d	14 22			14 33			14 52	15 03		15 22	15 33			15 52	16 03		16 22		16 33		16 52		17 03	
Clydebank	d					14 33				15 03				15 33			16 03				16 33				17 03
Yoker	d					14 35				15 05				15 35			16 05				16 35				17 05
Garscadden	d					14 39				15 09				15 39			16 09				16 39				17 09
Scotstounhill	d					14 41				15 11				15 41			16 11				16 41				17 11
Jordanhill	d					14 43				15 13				15 43			16 13				16 43				17 13
Hyndland	d	14 25			14 35	14 45		14 55	15 06	15 15	15 25	15 35		15 45	15 55	16 06	16 15	16 25		16 35	16 45	16 55		17 06	17 15
Partick	d	14 28		14 34	14 38	14 48		14 58	15 09	15 18	15 28	15 38		15 48	15 58	16 09	16 18	16 28	16 34	16 38	16 48	16 58		17 09	17 18
Exhibition Centre	d	14 31		14 37		14 51		15 01		15 21	15 31			15 51	16 01		16 21	16 31	16 37		16 51	17 01			17 21
Anderston	d																								
Glasgow Central HL 15	d																								
Glasgow Central LL 15	a	14 33		14 39		14 53		15 03		15 23	15 33			15 53	16 03		16 23	16 33	16 39		16 53	17 03			17 23
	d	14 34		14 40		14 54		15 04		15 24	15 34			15 54	16 04		16 24	16 34	16 40		16 54	17 04			17 24
Argyle Street	d	14 36		14 41		14 56		15 06		15 26	15 36			15 56	16 06		16 26	16 36	16 42		16 55	17 06			17 26
Charing Cross	d				14 43				15 14			15 43				16 14				16 43				17 13	
Glasgow Queen St HL 10 ⇌	a						15 31																		
Glasgow Queen St LL 10 ⇌	a				14 45				15 16			15 45				16 16				16 45				17 16	
	d				14 46				15 16			15 46				16 16				16 46				17 16	
High Street	d				14 48				15 18			15 48				16 18				16 48				17 18	
Bellgrove	d				14 50				15 20			15 50				16 20				16 50				17 20	
Duke Street	d																								
Alexandra Parade	d																								
Barnhill	d																								
Springburn	a																								
Carntyne	d				14 54				15 24			15 54				16 24				16 54				17 24	
Shettleston	d				14 56				15 26			15 56				16 26				16 56				17 26	
Garrowhill	d				14 59				15 29			15 59				16 29				16 59				17 29	
Easterhouse	d				15 01				15 31			16 01				16 31				17 01				17 31	
Blairhill	d				15 05				15 35			16 05				16 35				17 05				17 35	
Coatbridge Sunnyside	d				15 08				15 38			16 08				16 38				17 08				17 38	
Coatdyke	d				15 10				15 40			16 10				16 40				17 10				17 40	
Airdrie	a				15 13				15 43			16 13				16 43				17 13				17 43	
	d																								
Drumgelloch	a																								
Bridgeton	d	14 39				14 59		15 09		15 29	15 39			15 59	16 09		16 29	16 39			16 58	17 09			17 29
Dalmarnock	d																								
Rutherglen	d	14 42		14 46		15 02		15 12		15 32	15 42			16 02	16 12		16 32	16 42	16 47		17 01	17 12			17 32
Cambuslang	d	14 46				15 06		15 16		15 36	15 46			16 06	16 16		16 36	16 46			17 05	17 16			17 36
Newton	d					15 09				15 39				16 09			16 39				17 09				17 39
Blantyre	d			14 54		15 13				15 43				16 13			16 43		16 57		17 13				17 43
Hamilton West	d			14 57		15 16				15 46				16 16			16 46		17 00		17 16				17 46
Hamilton Central	d			15 00		15 20				15 50				16 20			16 50		17 02		17 20				17 50
Chatelherault	d			15 05															17 07						
Merryton	d			15 08															17 10						
Larkhall	a			15 11															17 12						
Airbles	d					15 25				15 55				16 25			16 55				17 25				17 55
Uddingston	d	14 50						15 20			15 50				16 21			16 51				17 20			
Bellshill	d	14 55						15 25			15 55				16 25			16 55				17 25			
Motherwell	a	15 03				15 27		15 33		15 57	16 03			16 27	16 33		16 57	17 03			17 27	17 33			17 57
	d							15 33							16 33							17 33			
Whifflet	a																								
Coatbridge Central	a																								
Shieldmuir	d							15 37							16 37							17 37			
Holytown	d																								
Wishaw	d							15 40							16 40							17 40			
Carluke	d							15 47							16 47							17 47			
Lanark	a							15 59							16 59							17 59			

Table 226

Sundays until 12 September

Helensburgh, Balloch, Dalmuir and Milngavie - Glasgow - Springburn, Airdrie, Drumgelloch, Hamilton, Larkhall, Motherwell, Coatbridge and Lanark

		SR	SR	SR	SR	SR	SR	SR		SR	SR ◇ H	SR	SR	SR	SR	SR	SR	SR		SR	SR	SR	SR	SR	SR
Helensburgh Upper	d										18 34														
Helensburgh Central	d			16 55			17 25						17 55			18 25							19 25		
Craigendoran	d			16 58			17 28						17 58			18 28							19 28		
Cardross	d			17 03			17 33						18 03			18 33							19 33		
Balloch	d				17 09			17 39						18 09			18 39				19 09			19 39	
Alexandria	d				17 11			17 41						18 11			18 41				19 11			19 41	
Renton	d				17 14			17 44						18 14			18 44				19 14			19 44	
Dalreoch	d			17 08	17 17		17 38	17 47					18 08	18 17		18 38	18 47				19 17		19 38	19 47	
Dumbarton Central	d			17 10	17 18		17 40	17 48			18 47		18 10	18 18		18 40	18 48				19 18		19 40	19 48	
Dumbarton East	d			17 12	17 20		17 42	17 50					18 12	18 20		18 42	18 50				19 20		19 42	19 50	
Bowling	d				17 24			17 54						18 24			18 54				19 24			19 54	
Kilpatrick	d				17 28			17 58						18 28			18 58				19 28			19 58	
Dalmuir	a			17 19	17 30		17 49	18 00			18 56		18 19	18 30		18 49	19 00				19 30		19 49	20 00	
	d			17 20	17 31		17 50	18 01			18 56		18 20	18 31		18 50	19 01				19 31		19 50	20 01	
Singer	d			17 22			17 52						18 22			18 52							19 52		
Drumry	d			17 25			17 55						18 25			18 55							19 55		
Drumchapel	d			17 27			17 57						18 27			18 57							19 57		
Milngavie	d	17 11				17 41				18 11					18 41			19 11				19 41			20 11
Hillfoot	d	17 14				17 44				18 14					18 44			19 14				19 44			20 14
Bearsden	d	17 16				17 46				18 16					18 46			19 16				19 46			20 16
Westerton	d	17 19		17 30		17 49	18 00			18 19			18 30		18 49	19 00		19 19				19 49	20 00		20 19
Anniesland	d	17 22		17 33		17 52	18 03			18 22			18 33		18 52	19 03		19 22				19 52	20 03		20 22
Clydebank	d				17 33			18 03						18 33			19 03				19 33			20 03	
Yoker	d				17 35			18 05						18 35			19 05				19 35			20 05	
Garscadden	d				17 39			18 09						18 39			19 09				19 39			20 09	
Scotstounhill	d				17 41			18 11						18 41			19 11				19 41			20 11	
Jordanhill	d				17 43			18 13						18 43			19 13				19 43			20 13	
Hyndland	d	17 25		17 35	17 45	17 55	18 06	18 15		18 25			18 35	18 45	18 55	19 05	19 15	19 25			19 45	19 55	20 05	20 15	20 25
Partick	d	17 28	17 34	17 38	17 48	17 58	18 09	18 18		18 28		18 34	18 38	18 48	18 58	19 08	19 18	19 28		19 34	19 48	19 58	20 08	20 18	20 28
Exhibition Centre	d	17 31	17 37			17 51	18 01	18 21		18 31		18 37		18 51	19 01		19 21	19 31		19 37	19 51	20 01		20 21	20 31
Anderston	d																								
Glasgow Central HL 15	d																								
Glasgow Central LL 15	a	17 33	17 39			17 53	18 03	18 23		18 33		18 39		18 53	19 03		19 23	19 33		19 39	19 53	20 03		20 23	20 33
	d	17 34	17 40			17 54	18 04	18 24		18 34		18 40		18 54	19 04		19 24	19 34		19 40	19 54	20 04		20 24	20 34
Argyle Street	d	17 36	17 41			17 56	18 06																		
Charing Cross	d			17 43			18 14						18 43			19 13							20 13		
Glasgow Queen St HL 10 ⇌	a										19 15														
Glasgow Queen St LL 10 ⇌	a			17 45			18 16						18 45			19 15							20 15		
	d			17 47			18 17						18 47			19 17							20 17		
High Street	d			17 49			18 19						18 49			19 19							20 19		
Bellgrove	d			17 51			18 21						18 51			19 21							20 21		
Duke Street	d																								
Alexandra Parade	d																								
Barnhill	d																								
Springburn	a																								
Carntyne	d			17 54			18 24						18 54			19 24							20 24		
Shettleston	d			17 57			18 27						18 57			19 27							20 27		
Garrowhill	d			17 59			18 29						18 59			19 29							20 29		
Easterhouse	d			18 02			18 32						19 02			19 32							20 32		
Blairhill	d			18 06			18 36						19 06			19 36							20 36		
Coatbridge Sunnyside	d			18 08			18 38						19 08			19 38							20 38		
Coatdyke	d			18 11			18 41						19 11			19 41							20 41		
Airdrie	a			18 14			18 44						19 14			19 44							20 44		
	d																								
Drumgelloch	a																								
Bridgeton	d	17 39			17 59	18 09		18 29		18 39				18 58	19 09		19 29	19 39			19 59	20 09		20 29	20 39
Dalmarnock	d																								
Rutherglen	d	17 42	17 46		18 02	18 12		18 32		18 42		18 47		19 01	19 12		19 32	19 42		19 46	20 02	20 12		20 32	20 42
Cambuslang	d	17 46			18 06	18 16		18 36		18 46				19 05	19 16		19 36	19 46			20 06	20 16		20 36	20 46
Newton	d				18 09			18 39						19 08			19 39				20 09			20 39	
Blantyre	d		17 55		18 13			18 43				18 55		19 12			19 43			19 55	20 13			20 43	
Hamilton West	d		17 58		18 16			18 46				18 58		19 15			19 46			19 58	20 16			20 46	
Hamilton Central	d		18 01		18 20			18 50				19 01		19 20			19 50			20 01	20 20			20 50	
Chatelherault	d		18 06									19 06								20 06					
Merryton	d		18 09									19 09								20 09					
Larkhall	a		18 11									19 12								20 11					
Airbles	d				18 25			18 55						19 25			19 55				20 25			20 55	
Uddingston	d	17 50				18 20				18 50					19 20			19 50				20 20			20 50
Bellshill	d	17 55				18 25				18 55					19 25			19 55				20 25			20 55
Motherwell	a	18 03			18 27	18 33		18 57		19 03				19 27	19 33		19 57	20 03			20 27	20 33		20 57	21 04
	d					18 33									19 33							20 33			
Whifflet	a																								
Coatbridge Central	a																								
Shieldmuir	d					18 37									19 37							20 37			
Holytown	d																								
Wishaw	d					18 40									19 40							20 40			
Carluke	d					18 47									19 47							20 47			
Lanark	a					18 59									19 59							20 59			

Table 226

Sundays until 12 September

Helensburgh, Balloch, Dalmuir and Milngavie - Glasgow - Springburn, Airdrie, Drumgelloch, Hamilton, Larkhall, Motherwell, Coatbridge and Lanark

		SR	SR	SR	SR	SR	SR	SR	SR	SR	SR	SR	SR
		◇											
Helensburgh Upper	d	20 36											
Helensburgh Central	d			19 55			20 25				20 55		
Craigendoran	d			19 58			20 28				20 58		
Cardross	d			20 03			20 33				21 03		
Balloch	d				20 09			20 42				21 09	
Alexandria	d				20 11			20 44				21 11	
Renton	d				20 14			20 49				21 14	
Dalreoch	d			20 08	20 17		20 38	20 52			21 08	21 17	
Dumbarton Central	d	20 49		20 10	20 18		20 40	20 53			21 10	21 18	
Dumbarton East	d			20 12	20 20		20 42	20 55			21 12	21 20	
Bowling	d				20 24			21 00				21 24	
Kilpatrick	d				20 28			21 03				21 28	
Dalmuir	a	20 58		20 19	20 30		20 49	21 06			21 19	21 30	
	d	20 58		20 20	20 31		20 50	21 07			21 20	21 31	
Singer	d			20 22			20 52				21 22		
Drumry	d			20 25			20 55				21 25		
Drumchapel	d			20 27			20 57				21 27		
Milngavie	d					20 41			21 11				21 41
Hillfoot	d					20 44			21 14				21 44
Bearsden	d					20 46			21 16				21 46
Westerton	d			20 30		20 49	21 00		21 19		21 30		21 49
Anniesland	d			20 33		20 52	21 03		21 22		21 33		21 52
Clydebank	d				20 33			21 09				21 33	
Yoker	d				20 35			21 11				21 35	
Garscadden	d				20 39			21 14				21 39	
Scotstounhill	d				20 41			21 16				21 41	
Jordanhill	d				20 43			21 18				21 43	
Hyndland	d			20 35	20 45	20 55	21 05	21 20	21 25		21 35	21 45	21 55
Partick	d		20 34	20 38	20 48	20 58	21 08	21 22	21 28	21 34	21 38	21 48	21 58
Exhibition Centre	d		20 37		20 51	21 01		21 25	21 31	21 37		21 51	22 01
Anderston	d												
Glasgow Central HL [15]	d												
Glasgow Central LL [15]	a		20 39		20 53	21 03		21 28	21 33	21 39		21 53	22 03
	d		20 40		20 54	21 04		21 28	21 34	21 40		21 54	22 04
Argyle Street	d												
Charing Cross	d			20 43			21 13				21 43		
Glasgow Queen St HL [10]	a	21 14											
Glasgow Queen St LL [10]	a			20 45			21 15				21 45		
	d			20 47			21 17				21 47		
High Street	d			20 49			21 19				21 49		
Bellgrove	d			20 51			21 21				21 51		
Duke Street	d												
Alexandra Parade	d												
Barnhill	d												
Springburn	a												
Carntyne	d			20 54			21 24				21 54		
Shettleston	d			20 57			21 27				21 57		
Garrowhill	d			20 59			21 29				21 59		
Easterhouse	d			21 02			21 32				22 02		
Blairhill	d			21 06			21 36				22 06		
Coatbridge Sunnyside	d			21 08			21 38				22 08		
Coatdyke	d			21 11			21 41				22 11		
Airdrie	a			21 14			21 44				22 14		
	d												
Drumgelloch	a												
Bridgeton	d				20 59	21 09		21 32	21 39			21 59	22 09
Dalmarnock	d												
Rutherglen	d		20 47		21 02	21 12		21 35	21 42	21 47		22 02	22 12
Cambuslang	d				21 06	21 16		21 39	21 46			22 06	22 16
Newton	d				21 09			21 42				22 09	
Blantyre	d		20 55		21 13			21 46		21 55		22 13	
Hamilton West	d		20 58		21 16			21 49		21 58		22 16	
Hamilton Central	d		21 01		21 20			21 52		22 01		22 20	
Chatelherault	d		21 05							22 06			
Merryton	d		21 09							22 09			
Larkhall	a		21 11							22 13			
Airbles	d				21 25			21 57				22 25	
Uddingston	d					21 20			21 50				22 20
Bellshill	d					21 25			21 55				22 25
Motherwell	a				21 27	21 33		21 59	22 03			22 27	22 33
	d					21 33							22 33
Whifflet	a												
Coatbridge Central	a												
Shieldmuir	d					21 37							22 37
Holytown	d												
Wishaw	d					21 40							22 40
Carluke	d					21 47							22 45
Lanark	a					21 59							22 59

		SR	SR	SR	SR	SR	SR	SR	SR	SR
Helensburgh Upper	d							22 37		
Helensburgh Central	d	21 25				21 55				
Craigendoran	d	21 28				21 58				
Cardross	d	21 33				22 03				
Balloch	d		21 39				22 09		22 39	
Alexandria	d		21 41				22 11		22 41	
Renton	d		21 44				22 14		22 44	
Dalreoch	d	21 38	21 47			22 08	22 17		22 47	
Dumbarton Central	d	21 40	21 48			22 10	22 18		22 48	
Dumbarton East	d	21 42	21 50			22 12	22 20		22 50	
Bowling	d		21 54				22 24		22 55	
Kilpatrick	d		21 58				22 28		22 58	
Dalmuir	a	21 49	22 00			22 19	22 30	23 02	23 01	
	d	21 50	22 01			22 20	22 31	23 04	23 01	
Singer	d	21 52				22 22				
Drumry	d	21 55				22 25				
Drumchapel	d	21 57				22 27				
Milngavie	d			22 11						22 41
Hillfoot	d			22 14						22 44
Bearsden	d			22 16						22 46
Westerton	d	22 00		22 19		22 30		23 13		22 49
Anniesland	d	22 03		22 22		22 33				22 52
Clydebank	d		22 03				22 33		23 03	
Yoker	d		22 05				22 35		23a05	
Garscadden	d		22 09				22 39			
Scotstounhill	d		22 11				22 41			
Jordanhill	d		22 13				22 43			
Hyndland	d	22 05	22 15	22 25		22 35	22 45			22 55
Partick	d	22 08	22 18	22 28	22 34	22 38	22 48			22 58
Exhibition Centre	d		22 21	22 31	22 37		22 51			23 01
Anderston	d									
Glasgow Central HL [15]	d									
Glasgow Central LL [15]	a		22 23	22 33	22 39		22 53			23 03
	d		22 24	22 34	22 40		22 54			23 04
Argyle Street	d									
Charing Cross	d	22 13				22 43				
Glasgow Queen St HL [10]	a									
Glasgow Queen St LL [10]	a	22 15				22 45				
	d	22 17				22 47				
High Street	d	22 19				22 49				
Bellgrove	d	22 21				22 51				
Duke Street	d									
Alexandra Parade	d									
Barnhill	d									
Springburn	a									
Carntyne	d	22 24				22 54				
Shettleston	d	22 27				22 57				
Garrowhill	d	22 29				22 59				
Easterhouse	d	22 32				23 02				
Blairhill	d	22 36				23 06				
Coatbridge Sunnyside	d	22 38				23 08				
Coatdyke	d	22 41				23 11				
Airdrie	a	22 44				23 14				
	d									
Drumgelloch	a									
Bridgeton	d		22 29	22 39			22 59			23 09
Dalmarnock	d									
Rutherglen	d		22 32	22 42	22 47		23 02			23 12
Cambuslang	d		22 36	22 46			23 06			23 16
Newton	d		22 39				23 09			
Blantyre	d		22 43		22 55		23 13			
Hamilton West	d		22 46		22 58		23 16			
Hamilton Central	d		22 50		23 01		23 20			
Chatelherault	d				23 05					
Merryton	d				23 09					
Larkhall	a				23 11					
Airbles	d		22 55				23 25			
Uddingston	d			22 50						23 20
Bellshill	d			22 55						23 25
Motherwell	a		22 57	23 06			23 27			23 33
	d									
Whifflet	a									
Coatbridge Central	a									
Shieldmuir	d									
Holytown	d									
Wishaw	d									
Carluke	d									
Lanark	a									

Table 226

Sundays until 12 September

Helensburgh, Balloch, Dalmuir and Milngavie - Glasgow - Springburn, Airdrie, Drumgelloch, Hamilton, Larkhall, Motherwell, Coatbridge and Lanark

		SR	SR
Helensburgh Upper	d		
Helensburgh Central	d	22 25	
Craigendoran	d	22 28	
Cardross	d	22 33	
Balloch	d		23 09
Alexandria	d		23 11
Renton	d		23 14
Dalreoch	d	22 38	23 17
Dumbarton Central	d	22 40	23 18
Dumbarton East	d	22 42	23 20
Bowling	d		23 25
Kilpatrick	d		23 28
Dalmuir	a	22 49	23 31
	d	22 50	23 31
Singer	d	22 52	
Drumry	d	22 55	
Drumchapel	d	22 57	
Milngavie	d		
Hillfoot	d		
Bearsden	d		
Westerton	d	23 00	
Anniesland	d	23 03	
Clydebank	d		23 33
Yoker	d		23a35
Garscadden	d		
Scotstounhill	d		
Jordanhill	d		
Hyndland	d	23 05	
Partick	d	23 08	
Exhibition Centre	d		
Anderston	d		
Glasgow Central HL [15]	d		
Glasgow Central LL [15]	a		
	d		
Argyle Street	d		
Charing Cross	d	23 13	
Glasgow Queen St HL [10]	a		
Glasgow Queen St LL [10]	a	23 15	
	d	23 17	
High Street	d	23 19	
Bellgrove	d	23 21	
Duke Street	d		
Alexandra Parade	d		
Barnhill	d		
Springburn	a		
Carntyne	d	23 24	
Shettleston	d	23 27	
Garrowhill	d	23 29	
Easterhouse	d	23 32	
Blairhill	d	23 36	
Coatbridge Sunnyside	d	23 38	
Coatdyke	d	23 41	
Airdrie	a	23 44	
	d		
Drumgelloch	a		
Bridgeton	d		
Dalmarnock	d		
Rutherglen	d		
Cambuslang	d		
Newton	d		
Blantyre	d		
Hamilton West	d		
Hamilton Central	d		
Chatelherault	d		
Merryton	d		
Larkhall	a		
Airbles	d		
Uddingston	d		
Bellshill	d		
Motherwell	a		
	d		
Whifflet	a		
Coatbridge Central	a		
Shieldmuir	d		
Holytown	d		
Wishaw	d		
Carluke	d		
Lanark	a		

Table 226

Sundays from 19 September

Helensburgh, Balloch, Dalmuir and Milngavie - Glasgow - Springburn, Airdrie, Drumgelloch, Hamilton, Larkhall, Motherwell, Coatbridge and Lanark

		SR	SR	SR	SR	SR	SR	SR	SR	SR A	SR	SR A	SR A	SR	SR	SR	SR A	SR	SR A	SR
Helensburgh Upper	d																			
Helensburgh Central	d				07 55			08 25							08 55					09 25
Craigendoran	d				07 58			08 28							08 58					09 28
Cardross	d				08 03			08 33							09 03					09 33
Balloch	d					08 09			08 39							09 09				
Alexandria	d					08 11			08 41							09 11				
Renton	d					08 14			08 44							09 14				
Dalreoch	d				08 08	08 17		08 38	08 47						09 08	09 17				09 38
Dumbarton Central	d				08 10	08 18		08 40	08 48						09 10	09 18				09 40
Dumbarton East	d				08 12	08 20		08 42	08 50						09 12	09 20				09 42
Bowling	d					08 24			08 54							09 24				
Kilpatrick	d					08 28			08 58							09 28				
Dalmuir	a				08 19	08 30		08 49	09 00						09 19	09 30				09 49
	d		07 50	08 01	08 20	08 31		08 50	09 01	09 05		09 15			09 20	09 31	09 35		09 45	09 50
Singer	d		07 52		08 22			08 52		09 07					09 22		09 37			09 52
Drumry	d		07 55		08 25			08 55		09 09					09 25		09 39			09 55
Drumchapel	d		07 57		08 27			08 57		09 12					09 27		09 42			09 57
Milngavie	d										09 11							09 41		
Hillfoot	d										09 14							09 44		
Bearsden	d										09 16							09 46		
Westerton	d		08 00		08 30			09 00		09 14	09 19				09 30		09 44	09 49		10 00
Anniesland	d		08 03		08 33			09 03		09 17	09 22				09 33		09 47	09 52		10 03
Clydebank	d			08 03		08 33			09 03			09 17				09 33			09 47	
Yoker	d			08 05		08 35			09 05			09 19				09 35			09 49	
Garscadden	d			08 09		08 39			09 09			09 22				09 39			09 52	
Scotstounhill	d			08 11		08 41			09 11			09 24				09 41			09 54	
Jordanhill	d			08 13		08 43			09 13			09 26				09 43			09 56	
Hyndland	d		08 05	08 15	08 35	08 45	08 55	09 05	09 15	09 20	09 25	09 28			09 35	09 45	09 50	09 54	09 59	10 05
Partick	d		08 08	08 18	08 38	08 48	08 58	09 08	09 18	09 22	09 28	09 30		09 34	09 38	09 48	09 52	09 57	10 01	10 08
Exhibition Centre	d			08 21		08 51	09 01		09 21		09 31			09 37		09 51		10 00		
Anderston	d																			
Glasgow Central HL 15	d												09 22							
Glasgow Central LL 15	a			08 23		08 53	09 03		09 23		09 33			09 39		09 53		10 02		
	d			08 24		08 54	09 04		09 24		09 34			09 40		09 54		10 03		
Argyle Street	d															09 56		10 06		
Charing Cross	d		08 13		08 43			09 13		09 26		09 34			09 43		09 56		10 05	10 13
Glasgow Queen St HL 10	a																			
Glasgow Queen St LL 10	a		08 15		08 45			09 15		09 28		09 36			09 45		09 58		10 07	10 15
	d		08 16		08 46			09 16		09 29		09 37			09 46		09 59		10 07	10 16
High Street	d		08 18		08 48			09 18		09 31		09 39			09 48		10 01		10 09	10 18
Bellgrove	d		08 20		08 50			09 20		09 33		09 41			09 50		10 03		10 11	10 20
Duke Street	d									09 35							10 05			
Alexandra Parade	d									09 36							10 06			
Barnhill	d									09 39							10 09			
Springburn	a									09 41							10 11			
Carntyne	d		08 24		08 54			09 24				09 44			09 54				10 15	10 24
Shettleston	d		08 26		08 56			09 26				09 47			09 56				10 17	10 26
Garrowhill	d		08 29		08 59			09 29				09 49			09 59				10 20	10 29
Easterhouse	d		08 31		09 01			09 31				09 52			10 01				10 22	10 31
Blairhill	d		08 35		09 05			09 35				09 56			10 05				10 26	10 35
Coatbridge Sunnyside	d		08 38		09 08			09 38				09 58			10 08				10 29	10 38
Coatdyke	d		08 40		09 10			09 40				10 01			10 10				10 31	10 40
Airdrie	a		08 43		09 13			09 43				10 04			10 13				10 34	10 43
	d	00 37																		
Drumgelloch	a	00 44																		
Bridgeton	d			08 29		08 59	09 09		09 29		09 39					09 59		10 09		
Dalmarnock	d																			
Rutherglen	d			08 32		09 02	09 12		09 32		09 42			09 47		10 01		10 12		
Cambuslang	d			08 36		09 06	09 16		09 36		09 46					10 05		10 16		
Newton	d					09 09			09 39							10 08				
Blantyre	d					09 13			09 43					09 56		10 12				
Hamilton West	d					09 16			09 46					09 59		10 15				
Hamilton Central	d					09 20			09 50					10 01		10 20				
Chatelherault	d													10 06						
Merryton	d													10 09						
Larkhall	a													10 11						
Airbles	d					09 25			09 55							10 25				
Uddingston	d			08 40			09 20				09 52							10 20		
Bellshill	d			08 45			09 25				09 57							10 25		
Motherwell	a			08 53		09 27	09 31		09 57		10 04					10 27		10 33		
	d						09 32											10 33		
Whifflet	a												09 50							
Coatbridge Central	a																			
Shieldmuir	d						09 37											10 37		
Holytown	d												09 59							
Wishaw	d						09 40											10 40		
Carluke	d						09 47											10 47		
Lanark	a						09 59											10 59		

A 28 November, 5 December

Table 226

Sundays from 19 September

Helensburgh, Balloch, Dalmuir and Milngavie - Glasgow - Springburn, Airdrie, Drumgelloch, Hamilton, Larkhall, Motherwell, Coatbridge and Lanark

		SR	SR A	SR	SR A	SR	SR	SR A	SR	SR A	SR	SR	SR A	SR	SR A	SR A	SR	SR	SR	SR A	SR	SR A	SR
Helensburgh Upper	d																						
Helensburgh Central	d					09 55					10 25							10 55					11 25
Craigendoran	d					09 58					10 28							10 58					11 28
Cardross	d					10 03					10 33							11 03					11 33
Balloch	d	09 39					10 09					10 39							11 09				
Alexandria	d	09 41					10 11					10 41							11 11				
Renton	d	09 44					10 14					10 44							11 14				
Dalreoch	d	09 47				10 08	10 17				10 38	10 47						11 08	11 17				11 38
Dumbarton Central	d	09 48				10 10	10 18				10 40	10 48						11 10	11 18				11 40
Dumbarton East	d	09 50				10 12	10 20				10 42	10 50						11 12	11 20				11 42
Bowling	d	09 54					10 24					10 54							11 24				
Kilpatrick	d	09 58					10 28					10 58							11 28				
Dalmuir	a	10 00				10 19	10 30				10 49	11 00						11 19	11 30				11 49
	d	10 01	10 05		10 15	10 20	10 31	10 35		10 45	10 50	11 01	11 05		11 15			11 20	11 31	11 35		11 45	11 50
Singer	d		10 07			10 22		10 37			10 52		11 07					11 22		11 37			11 52
Drumry	d		10 09			10 25		10 39			10 55		11 09					11 25		11 39			11 55
Drumchapel	d		10 12			10 27		10 42			10 57		11 12					11 27		11 42			11 57
Milngavie	d			10 11					10 41					11 11							11 41		
Hillfoot	d			10 14					10 44					11 14							11 44		
Bearsden	d			10 16					10 46					11 16							11 46		
Westerton	d		10 14	10 19		10 30		10 44	10 49		11 00		11 14	11 19				11 30		11 44	11 49		12 00
Anniesland	d		10 17	10 22		10 33		10 47	10 52		11 03		11 17	11 22				11 33		11 47	11 52		12 03
Clydebank	d	10 03			10 17		10 33			10 47		11 03			11 17				11 33			11 47	
Yoker	d	10 05			10 19		10 35			10 49		11 05			11 19				11 35			11 49	
Garscadden	d	10 09			10 22		10 39			10 52		11 09			11 22				11 39			11 52	
Scotstounhill	d	10 11			10 24		10 41			10 54		11 11			11 24				11 41			11 54	
Jordanhill	d	10 13			10 26		10 43			10 56		11 13			11 26				11 43			11 56	
Hyndland	d	10 15	10 20	10 25	10 28	10 35	10 45	10 50	10 55	10 59	11 06	11 15	11 20	11 25	11 28			11 35	11 45	11 50	11 55	11 59	12 06
Partick	d	10 18	10 22	10 28	10 30	10 38	10 48	10 52	10 58	11 01	11 09	11 18	11 22	11 28	11 30		11 34	11 38	11 48	11 52	11 58	12 01	12 09
Exhibition Centre	d	10 21		10 31			10 51		11 01			11 21		11 31			11 37		11 51		12 01		
Anderston	d																						
Glasgow Central HL 15	d															11 22							
Glasgow Central LL 15	a	10 23		10 33			10 53		11 03			11 23		11 33			11 39		11 53		12 03		
	d	10 24		10 34			10 54		11 04			11 24		11 34			11 40		11 54		12 04		
Argyle Street	d	10 26		10 36			10 56		11 06			11 26		11 36			11 42		11 56		12 06		
Charing Cross	d		10 26		10 35	10 43		10 56		11 05	11 14		11 26		11 34			11 43		11 56		12 05	12 14
Glasgow Queen St HL 10	a																						
Glasgow Queen St LL 10	a		10 28		10 37	10 45		10 58		11 07	11 16		11 28		11 36			11 45		11 58		12 07	12 16
	d		10 29		10 37	10 46		10 59		11 07	11 16		11 29		11 37			11 46		11 59		12 07	12 16
High Street	d		10 31		10 39	10 48		11 01		11 09	11 18		11 31		11 39			11 48		12 01		12 09	12 18
Bellgrove	d		10 33		10 41	10 50		11 03		11 11	11 20		11 33		11 41			11 50		12 03		12 11	12 20
Duke Street	d		10 35					11 05					11 35							12 05			
Alexandra Parade	d		10 36					11 06					11 36							12 06			
Barnhill	d		10 39					11 09					11 39							12 09			
Springburn	a		10 41					11 11					11 41							12 11			
Carntyne	d				10 45	10 54				11 15	11 24				11 44			11 54				12 15	12 24
Shettleston	d				10 47	10 56				11 17	11 26				11 47			11 56				12 17	12 26
Garrowhill	d				10 50	10 59				11 20	11 29				11 49			11 59				12 20	12 29
Easterhouse	d				10 52	11 01				11 22	11 31				11 52			12 01				12 22	12 31
Blairhill	d				10 56	11 05				11 26	11 35				11 56			12 05				12 26	12 35
Coatbridge Sunnyside	d				10 59	11 08				11 29	11 38				11 58			12 08				12 29	12 38
Coatdyke	d				11 01	11 10				11 31	11 40				12 01			12 10				12 31	12 40
Airdrie	a				11 04	11 13				11 34	11 43				12 04			12 13				12 34	12 43
	d																						
Drumgelloch	a																						
Bridgeton	d	10 29		10 39			10 59		11 09			11 29		11 39					11 59		12 09		
Dalmarnock	d																						
Rutherglen	d	10 32		10 42			11 02		11 12			11 32		11 42			11 47		12 02		12 12		
Cambuslang	d	10 36		10 46			11 06		11 16			11 36		11 46					12 06		12 16		
Newton	d	10 39					11 09					11 38							12 09				
Blantyre	d	10 43					11 13					11 43					11 55		12 13				
Hamilton West	d	10 46					11 16					11 46					11 58		12 16				
Hamilton Central	d	10 50					11 20					11 50					12 01		12 20				
Chatelherault	d																12 06						
Merryton	d																12 09						
Larkhall	a																12 12						
Airbles	d	10 55					11 25					11 55							12 25				
Uddingston	d			10 50					11 20					11 50							12 20		
Bellshill	d			10 55					11 25					11 55							12 25		
Motherwell	a	10 57		11 03			11 27		11 33			11 57		12 03					12 27		12 33		
	d								11 33												12 33		
Whifflet	a															11 50							
Coatbridge Central	a																						
Shieldmuir	d								11 37												12 37		
Holytown	d															11 59							
Wishaw	d								11 40												12 40		
Carluke	d								11 47												12 47		
Lanark	a								11 59												12 59		

A 28 November, 5 December

Table 226

Sundays from 19 September

Helensburgh, Balloch, Dalmuir and Milngavie - Glasgow - Springburn, Airdrie, Drumgelloch, Hamilton, Larkhall, Motherwell, Coatbridge and Lanark

		SR	SR A	SR	SR A	SR	SR	SR A	SR A	SR	SR A	SR	SR	SR A	SR	SR A	SR A	SR	SR	SR	SR A	SR
Helensburgh Upper	d																					
Helensburgh Central	d					11 55						12 25							12 55			
Craigendoran	d					11 58						12 28							12 58			
Cardross	d					12 03						12 33							13 03			
Balloch	d	11 39					12 09						12 39							13 09		
Alexandria	d	11 41					12 11						12 41							13 11		
Renton	d	11 44					12 14						12 44							13 14		
Dalreoch	d	11 47				12 08	12 17					12 38	12 47						13 08	13 17		
Dumbarton Central	d	11 48				12 10	12 18					12 40	12 48						13 10	13 18		
Dumbarton East	d	11 50				12 12	12 20					12 42	12 50						13 12	13 20		
Bowling	d	11 54					12 24						12 54							13 24		
Kilpatrick	d	11 58					12 28						12 58							13 28		
Dalmuir	a	12 00				12 19	12 30					12 49	13 00						13 19	13 30		
	d	12 01	12 05		12 15	12 20	12 31		12 35		12 45	12 50	13 01	13 05		13 15			13 20	13 31	13 35	
Singer	d		12 07			12 22			12 37			12 52		13 07					13 22		13 37	
Drumry	d		12 09			12 25			12 39			12 55		13 09					13 25		13 39	
Drumchapel	d		12 12			12 27			12 42			12 57		13 12					13 27		13 42	
Milngavie	d			12 11						12 41					13 11							13 41
Hillfoot	d			12 14						12 44					13 14							13 44
Bearsden	d			12 16						12 46					13 16							13 46
Westerton	d		12 14	12 19		12 30			12 44	12 49		13 00		13 14	13 19				13 30		13 44	13 49
Anniesland	d		12 17	12 22		12 33			12 47	12 52		13 03		13 17	13 22				13 33		13 47	13 52
Clydebank	d	12 03			12 17		12 33				12 47		13 03			13 17				13 33		
Yoker	d	12 05			12 19		12 35				12 49		13 05			13 19				13 35		
Garscadden	d	12 09			12 22		12 39				12 52		13 09			13 22				13 39		
Scotstounhill	d	12 11			12 24		12 41				12 54		13 11			13 24				13 41		
Jordanhill	d	12 13			12 26		12 43				12 56		13 13			13 26				13 43		
Hyndland	d	12 15	12 20	12 25	12 28	12 35	12 45		12 50	12 55	12 58	13 06	13 15	13 20	13 25	13 28			13 35	13 45	13 50	13 55
Partick	d	12 18	12 22	12 28	12 30	12 38	12 48		12 52	12 58	13 00	13 09	13 18	13 22	13 28	13 30		13 34	13 38	13 48	13 52	13 58
Exhibition Centre	d	12 21		12 31			12 51			13 01			13 21		13 31			13 37		13 51		14 01
Anderston	d																					
Glasgow Central HL 15	d							12 24									13 22					
Glasgow Central LL 15	a	12 23		12 33			12 53			13 03			13 23		13 33			13 39		13 53		14 03
	d	12 24		12 34			12 54			13 04			13 24		13 34			13 40		13 54		14 04
Argyle Street	d	12 26		12 36			12 56			13 06			13 26		13 36			13 42		13 56		14 06
Charing Cross	d		12 26		12 34	12 43			12 56		13 04	13 14		13 26		13 34			13 43		13 56	
Glasgow Queen St HL 10	a																					
Glasgow Queen St LL 10	a		12 28		12 36	12 45			12 58		13 06	13 16		13 28		13 36			13 45		13 58	
	d		12 29		12 37	12 46			12 59		13 07	13 16		13 29		13 37			13 46		13 59	
High Street	d		12 31		12 39	12 48			13 01		13 09	13 18		13 31		13 39			13 48		14 01	
Bellgrove	d		12 33		12 41	12 50			13 03		13 11	13 20		13 33		13 41			13 50		14 03	
Duke Street	d		12 35						13 05					13 35							14 05	
Alexandra Parade	d		12 36						13 06					13 36							14 06	
Barnhill	d		12 39						13 09					13 39							14 09	
Springburn	a		12 41						13 11					13 41							14 11	
Carntyne	d				12 44	12 54					13 14	13 24				13 44			13 54			
Shettleston	d				12 47	12 56					13 17	13 26				13 47			13 56			
Garrowhill	d				12 49	12 59					13 19	13 29				13 49			13 59			
Easterhouse	d				12 52	13 01					13 22	13 31				13 52			14 01			
Blairhill	d				12 56	13 05					13 26	13 35				13 56			14 05			
Coatbridge Sunnyside	d				12 58	13 08					13 28	13 38				13 58			14 08			
Coatdyke	d				13 01	13 10					13 31	13 40				14 01			14 10			
Airdrie	a				13 04	13 13					13 34	13 43				14 04			14 13			
	d																					
Drumgelloch	a																					
Bridgeton	d	12 29		12 39			12 59			13 09			13 29		13 39					13 59		14 09
Dalmarnock	d																					
Rutherglen	d	12 32		12 42			13 02			13 12			13 32		13 42			13 47		14 02		14 12
Cambuslang	d	12 36		12 46			13 06			13 16			13 36		13 46					14 06		14 16
Newton	d	12 39					13 09						13 39							14 09		
Blantyre	d	12 43					13 13						13 42					13 56		14 13		
Hamilton West	d	12 46					13 16						13 45					13 59		14 16		
Hamilton Central	d	12 50					13 20						13 50					14 02		14 20		
Chatelherault	d																	14 08				
Merryton	d																	14 10				
Larkhall	a																	14 14				
Airbles	d	12 55					13 25						13 55							14 25		
Uddingston	d			12 50						13 20					13 50							14 20
Bellshill	d			12 55						13 25					13 55							14 25
Motherwell	a	12 57		13 03			13 27			13 33			13 57		14 05					14 27		14 33
	d									13 33												14 33
Whifflet	a							12 50									13 50					
Coatbridge Central	a																					
Shieldmuir	d									13 37												14 37
Holytown	d							12 59									13 59					
Wishaw	d									13 40												14 40
Carluke	d									13 47												14 47
Lanark	a									13 59												14 59

A 28 November, 5 December

Table 226

Sundays from 19 September

Helensburgh, Balloch, Dalmuir and Milngavie - Glasgow - Springburn, Airdrie, Drumgelloch, Hamilton, Larkhall, Motherwell, Coatbridge and Lanark

		SR A	SR	SR	SR A	SR	SR A	SR A	SR	SR	SR	SR A	SR ◇	SR	SR A	SR	SR	SR A	SR	SR A	SR	SR	SR A
Helensburgh Upper	d												14 39										
Helensburgh Central	d		13 25							13 55						14 25					14 55		
Craigendoran	d		13 28							13 58						14 28					14 58		
Cardross	d		13 33							14 03						14 33					15 03		
Balloch	d			13 39							14 09						14 39					15 09	
Alexandria	d			13 41							14 11						14 41					15 11	
Renton	d			13 44							14 14						14 44					15 14	
Dalreoch	d		13 38	13 47						14 08	14 17					14 38	14 47				15 08	15 17	
Dumbarton Central	d		13 40	13 48						14 10	14 18		14 56			14 40	14 48				15 10	15 18	
Dumbarton East	d		13 42	13 50						14 12	14 20					14 42	14 50				15 12	15 20	
Bowling	d			13 54							14 24						14 54					15 24	
Kilpatrick	d			13 58							14 28						14 58					15 28	
Dalmuir	a		13 49	14 00						14 19	14 30		15 05			14 49	15 00				15 19	15 30	
	d	13 45	13 50	14 01	14 05		14 15			14 20	14 31	14 35	15 05		14 45	14 50	15 01	15 05		15 15	15 20	15 31	
Singer	d		13 52		14 07					14 22		14 37				14 52		15 07			15 22		
Drumry	d		13 55		14 09					14 25		14 39				14 55		15 09			15 25		
Drumchapel	d		13 57		14 12					14 27		14 42				14 57		15 12			15 27		
Milngavie	d					14 11								14 41					15 11				
Hillfoot	d					14 14								14 44					15 14				
Bearsden	d					14 16								14 46					15 16				
Westerton	d		14 00		14 14	14 19				14 30		14 44		14 49		15 00		15 14	15 19		15 30		
Anniesland	d		14 03		14 17	14 22				14 33		14 47		14 52		15 03		15 17	15 22		15 33		
Clydebank	d	13 47		14 03			14 17				14 33				14 47		15 03			15 17		15 33	
Yoker	d	13 49		14 05			14 19				14 35				14 49		15 05			15 19		15 35	
Garscadden	d	13 52		14 09			14 22				14 39				14 52		15 09			15 22		15 39	
Scotstounhill	d	13 54		14 11			14 24				14 41				14 54		15 11			15 24		15 41	
Jordanhill	d	13 56		14 13			14 26				14 43				14 56		15 13			15 26		15 43	
Hyndland	d	13 58	14 06	14 15	14 20	14 25	14 28			14 35	14 45	14 50		14 55	14 58	15 06	15 15	15 20	15 25	15 28	15 35	15 45	
Partick	d	14 00	14 09	14 18	14 22	14 28	14 30		14 34	14 38	14 48	14 52		14 58	15 00	15 09	15 18	15 22	15 28	15 30	15 38	15 48	
Exhibition Centre	d			14 21		14 31			14 37		14 51			15 01			15 21		15 31			15 51	
Anderston	d																						
Glasgow Central HL 15	d							14 22															15 22
Glasgow Central LL 15	a			14 23		14 33			14 39		14 53			15 03			15 23		15 33			15 53	
	d			14 24		14 34			14 40		14 54			15 04			15 24		15 34			15 54	
Argyle Street	d			14 26		14 36			14 41		14 56			15 06			15 26		15 36			15 56	
Charing Cross	d	14 04	14 14		14 26		14 34			14 43		14 56			15 04	15 14		15 26		15 34	15 43		
Glasgow Queen St HL 10	a												15 31										
Glasgow Queen St LL 10	a	14 06	14 16		14 28		14 36			14 45		14 58			15 06	15 16		15 28		15 36	15 45		
	d	14 07	14 16		14 29		14 37			14 46		14 59			15 07	15 16		15 29		15 37	15 46		
High Street	d	14 09	14 18		14 31		14 39			14 48		15 01			15 09	15 18		15 31		15 39	15 48		
Bellgrove	d	14 11	14 20		14 33		14 41			14 50		15 03			15 11	15 20		15 33		15 41	15 50		
Duke Street	d				14 35							15 05						15 35					
Alexandra Parade	d				14 36							15 06						15 36					
Barnhill	d				14 39							15 09						15 39					
Springburn	a				14 41							15 11						15 41					
Carntyne	d	14 14	14 24				14 44			14 54					15 14	15 24				15 44	15 54		
Shettleston	d	14 17	14 26				14 47			14 56					15 17	15 26				15 47	15 56		
Garrowhill	d	14 19	14 29				14 49			14 59					15 19	15 29				15 49	15 59		
Easterhouse	d	14 22	14 31				14 52			15 01					15 22	15 31				15 52	16 01		
Blairhill	d	14 26	14 35				14 56			15 05					15 26	15 35				15 56	16 05		
Coatbridge Sunnyside	d	14 28	14 38				14 58			15 08					15 28	15 38				15 58	16 08		
Coatdyke	d	14 31	14 40				15 01			15 10					15 31	15 40				16 01	16 10		
Airdrie	a	14 34	14 43				15 04			15 13					15 34	15 43				16 04	16 13		
	d																						
Drumgelloch	a																						
Bridgeton	d			14 29		14 39					14 59			15 09			15 29		15 39			15 59	
Dalmarnock	d																						
Rutherglen	d			14 32		14 42			14 46		15 02			15 12			15 32		15 42			16 02	
Cambuslang	d			14 36		14 46					15 06			15 16			15 36		15 46			16 06	
Newton	d			14 39							15 09						15 39					16 09	
Blantyre	d			14 43					14 54		15 13						15 43					16 13	
Hamilton West	d			14 46					14 57		15 16						15 46					16 16	
Hamilton Central	d			14 50					15 00		15 20						15 50					16 20	
Chatelherault	d								15 05														
Merryton	d								15 08														
Larkhall	a								15 11														
Airbles	d			14 55							15 25						15 55					16 25	
Uddingston	d					14 50								15 20					15 50				
Bellshill	d					14 55								15 25					15 55				
Motherwell	a			14 57		15 03					15 27			15 33			15 57		16 03			16 27	
	d													15 33									
Whifflet	a							14 50															15 50
Coatbridge Central	a																						
Shieldmuir	d													15 37									
Holytown	d							14 59															15 59
Wishaw	d													15 40									
Carluke	d													15 47									
Lanark	a													15 59									

A 28 November, 5 December

Table 226

Sundays
from 19 September

Helensburgh, Balloch, Dalmuir and Milngavie - Glasgow - Springburn, Airdrie, Drumgelloch, Hamilton, Larkhall, Motherwell, Coatbridge and Lanark

		SR A	SR	SR A	SR	SR	SR A	SR	SR A	SR A	SR	SR	SR	SR A	SR	SR A	SR	SR	SR A	SR	SR A	SR A
Helensburgh Upper	d																					
Helensburgh Central	d				15 25							15 55					16 25					
Craigendoran	d				15 28							15 58					16 28					
Cardross	d				15 33							16 03					16 33					
Balloch	d					15 39							16 09					16 39				
Alexandria	d					15 41							16 11					16 41				
Renton	d					15 44							16 14					16 44				
Dalreoch	d				15 38	15 47						16 08	16 17				16 38	16 47				
Dumbarton Central	d				15 40	15 48						16 10	16 18				16 40	16 48				
Dumbarton East	d				15 42	15 50						16 12	16 20				16 42	16 50				
Bowling	d					15 54							16 24					16 54				
Kilpatrick	d					15 58							16 28					16 58				
Dalmuir	a				15 49	16 00						16 19	16 30				16 49	17 00				
	d	15 35		15 45	15 50	16 01	16 05		16 15			16 20	16 31	16 35		16 45	16 50	17 01	17 05		17 15	
Singer	d	15 37			15 52		16 07					16 22		16 37			16 52		17 07			
Drumry	d	15 39			15 55		16 09					16 25		16 39			16 55		17 09			
Drumchapel	d	15 42			15 57		16 12					16 27		16 42			16 57		17 12			
Milngavie	d		15 41					16 11							16 41					17 11		
Hillfoot	d		15 44					16 14							16 44					17 14		
Bearsden	d		15 46					16 16							16 46					17 16		
Westerton	d	15 44	15 49		16 00		16 14	16 19				16 30		16 44	16 49		17 00		17 14	17 19		
Anniesland	d	15 47	15 52		16 03		16 17	16 22				16 33		16 47	16 52		17 03		17 17	17 22		
Clydebank	d			15 47		16 03			16 17				16 33			16 47		17 03			17 17	
Yoker	d			15 49		16 05			16 19				16 35			16 49		17 05			17 19	
Garscadden	d			15 52		16 09			16 22				16 39			16 52		17 09			17 22	
Scotstounhill	d			15 54		16 11			16 24				16 41			16 54		17 11			17 24	
Jordanhill	d			15 56		16 13			16 26				16 43			16 56		17 13			17 26	
Hyndland	d	15 50	15 55	15 58	16 06	16 15	16 20	16 25	16 28			16 35	16 45	16 50	16 55	16 59	17 06	17 15	17 20	17 25	17 28	
Partick	d	15 52	15 58	16 00	16 09	16 18	16 22	16 28	16 30		16 34	16 38	16 48	16 52	16 58	17 01	17 09	17 18	17 22	17 28	17 30	
Exhibition Centre	d		16 01			16 21		16 31			16 37		16 51		17 01			17 21		17 31		
Anderston	d																					
Glasgow Central HL [15]	d									16 22												17 22
Glasgow Central LL [15]	a		16 03			16 23		16 33			16 39		16 53		17 03			17 23		17 33		
	d		16 04			16 24		16 34			16 40		16 54		17 04			17 24		17 34		
Argyle Street	d		16 06			16 26		16 36			16 42		16 55		17 06			17 26		17 36		
Charing Cross	d	15 56		16 04	16 14		16 26		16 34			16 43		16 56		17 05	17 13		17 26		17 34	
Glasgow Queen St HL [10]	a																					
Glasgow Queen St LL [10]	a	15 58		16 06	16 16		16 28		16 36			16 45		16 58		17 07	17 16		17 28		17 36	
	d	15 59		16 07	16 16		16 29		16 37			16 46		16 59		17 07	17 16		17 29		17 37	
High Street	d	16 01		16 09	16 18		16 31		16 39			16 48		17 01		17 09	17 18		17 31		17 39	
Bellgrove	d	16 03		16 11	16 20		16 33		16 41			16 50		17 03		17 11	17 20		17 33		17 41	
Duke Street	d	16 05					16 35							17 05					17 35			
Alexandra Parade	d	16 06					16 36							17 06					17 36			
Barnhill	d	16 09					16 39							17 09					17 39			
Springburn	a	16 11					16 41							17 11					17 41			
Carntyne	d			16 14	16 24				16 44			16 54				17 15	17 24				17 44	
Shettleston	d			16 17	16 26				16 47			16 56				17 17	17 26				17 47	
Garrowhill	d			16 19	16 29				16 49			16 59				17 20	17 29				17 49	
Easterhouse	d			16 22	16 31				16 52			17 01				17 22	17 31				17 52	
Blairhill	d			16 26	16 35				16 56			17 05				17 26	17 35				17 56	
Coatbridge Sunnyside	d			16 28	16 38				16 58			17 08				17 29	17 38				17 58	
Coatdyke	d			16 31	16 40				17 01			17 10				17 31	17 40				18 01	
Airdrie	a			16 34	16 43				17 04			17 13				17 34	17 43				18 04	
	d																					
Drumgelloch	a																					
Bridgeton	d		16 09			16 29		16 39					16 58		17 09			17 29		17 39		
Dalmarnock	d																					
Rutherglen	d		16 12			16 32		16 42			16 47		17 01		17 12			17 32		17 42		
Cambuslang	d		16 16			16 36		16 46					17 05		17 16			17 36		17 46		
Newton	d					16 39							17 09					17 39				
Blantyre	d					16 43					16 57		17 13					17 43				
Hamilton West	d					16 46					17 00		17 16					17 46				
Hamilton Central	d					16 50					17 02		17 20					17 50				
Chatelherault	d										17 07											
Merryton	d										17 10											
Larkhall	a										17 12											
Airbles	d					16 55							17 25					17 55				
Uddingston	d		16 21					16 51							17 20					17 50		
Bellshill	d		16 25					16 55							17 25					17 55		
Motherwell	a		16 33			16 57		17 03					17 27		17 33			17 57		18 03		
	d		16 33												17 33							
Whifflet	a									16 50												17 50
Coatbridge Central	a																					
Shieldmuir	d		16 37												17 37							
Holytown	d									16 59												17 59
Wishaw	d		16 40												17 40							
Carluke	d		16 47												17 47							
Lanark	a		16 59												17 59							

A 28 November, 5 December

Table 226

Sundays
from 19 September

Helensburgh, Balloch, Dalmuir and Milngavie - Glasgow - Springburn, Airdrie, Drumgelloch, Hamilton, Larkhall, Motherwell, Coatbridge and Lanark

		SR	SR	SR	SR A	SR	SR A	SR	SR	SR	SR A	SR ◇ B	SR	SR	SR	SR	SR	SR	SR	SR	SR	SR	SR
Helensburgh Upper	d											18 34											
Helensburgh Central	d		16 55					17 25						17 55			18 25						19 25
Craigendoran	d		16 58					17 28						17 58			18 28						19 28
Cardross	d		17 03					17 33						18 03			18 33						19 33
Balloch	d			17 09					17 39						18 09			18 39			19 09		
Alexandria	d			17 11					17 41						18 11			18 41			19 11		
Renton	d			17 14					17 44						18 14			18 44			19 14		
Dalreoch	d		17 08	17 17				17 38	17 47					18 08	18 17		18 38	18 47			19 17		19 38
Dumbarton Central	d		17 10	17 18				17 40	17 48			18 47		18 10	18 18		18 40	18 48			19 18		19 40
Dumbarton East	d		17 12	17 20				17 42	17 50					18 12	18 20		18 42	18 50			19 20		19 42
Bowling	d			17 24					17 54						18 24			18 54			19 24		
Kilpatrick	d			17 28					17 58						18 28			18 58			19 28		
Dalmuir	a		17 19	17 30				17 49	18 00			18 56		18 19	18 30		18 49	19 00			19 30		19 49
	d		17 20	17 31	17 35		17 45	17 50	18 01			18 56		18 20	18 31		18 50	19 01			19 31		19 50
Singer	d		17 22		17 37			17 52						18 22			18 52						19 52
Drumry	d		17 25		17 39			17 55						18 25			18 55						19 55
Drumchapel	d		17 27		17 42			17 57						18 27			18 57						19 57
Milngavie	d					17 41				18 11						18 41			19 11			19 41	
Hillfoot	d					17 44				18 14						18 44			19 14			19 44	
Bearsden	d					17 46				18 16						18 46			19 16			19 46	
Westerton	d		17 30		17 44	17 49		18 00		18 19				18 30		18 49	19 00		19 19			19 49	20 00
Anniesland	d		17 33		17 47	17 52		18 03		18 22				18 33		18 52	19 03		19 22			19 52	20 03
Clydebank	d			17 33			17 47		18 03						18 33			19 03			19 33		
Yoker	d			17 35			17 49		18 05						18 35			19 05			19 35		
Garscadden	d			17 39			17 52		18 09						18 39			19 09			19 39		
Scotstounhill	d			17 41			17 54		18 11						18 41			19 11			19 41		
Jordanhill	d			17 43			17 56		18 13						18 43			19 13			19 43		
Hyndland	d		17 35	17 45	17 50	17 55	17 58	18 06	18 15	18 25				18 35	18 45	18 55	19 05	19 15	19 25		19 45	19 55	20 05
Partick	d	17 34	17 38	17 48	17 52	17 58	18 00	18 09	18 18	18 28			18 34	18 38	18 48	18 58	19 08	19 18	19 28	19 34	19 48	19 58	20 08
Exhibition Centre	d	17 37		17 51		18 01			18 21	18 31			18 37		18 51	19 01		19 21	19 31	19 37	19 51	20 01	
Anderston	d																						
Glasgow Central HL [15]	d										18 22												
Glasgow Central LL [15]	a	17 39		17 53		18 03			18 23	18 33			18 39		18 53	19 03		19 23	19 33	19 39	19 53	20 03	
	d	17 40		17 54		18 04			18 24	18 34			18 40		18 54	19 04		19 24	19 34	19 40	19 54	20 04	
Argyle Street	d	17 41		17 56		18 06																	
Charing Cross	d		17 43		17 56		18 04	18 13						18 43			19 13						20 13
Glasgow Queen St HL [10]	a											19 15											
Glasgow Queen St LL [10]	a		17 45		17 58		18 06	18 15						18 45			19 15						20 15
	d		17 46		17 59		18 07	18 16						18 46			19 16						20 16
High Street	d		17 48		18 01		18 09	18 18						18 48			19 18						20 18
Bellgrove	d		17 50		18 03		18 11	18 20						18 50			19 20						20 20
Duke Street	d				18 05																		
Alexandra Parade	d				18 06																		
Barnhill	d				18 09																		
Springburn	a				18 11																		
Carntyne	d		17 54				18 14	18 24						18 54			19 24						20 24
Shettleston	d		17 56				18 17	18 26						18 56			19 26						20 26
Garrowhill	d		17 59				18 19	18 29						18 59			19 29						20 29
Easterhouse	d		18 01				18 22	18 31						19 01			19 31						20 31
Blairhill	d		18 05				18 26	18 35						19 05			19 35						20 35
Coatbridge Sunnyside	d		18 08				18 28	18 38						19 08			19 38						20 38
Coatdyke	d		18 10				18 31	18 40						19 10			19 40						20 40
Airdrie	a		18 13				18 34	18 43						19 13			19 43						20 43
	d																						
Drumgelloch	a																						
Bridgeton	d			17 59		18 09			18 29	18 39					18 58	19 09		19 29	19 39		19 59	20 09	
Dalmarnock	d																						
Rutherglen	d	17 46		18 02		18 12			18 32	18 42			18 47		19 01	19 12		19 32	19 42	19 46	20 02	20 12	
Cambuslang	d			18 06		18 16			18 36	18 46					19 05	19 16		19 36	19 46		20 06	20 16	
Newton	d			18 09					18 39						19 08			19 39			20 09		
Blantyre	d	17 55		18 13					18 43				18 55		19 12			19 43		19 55	20 13		
Hamilton West	d	17 58		18 16					18 46				18 58		19 15			19 46		19 58	20 16		
Hamilton Central	d	18 01		18 20					18 50				19 01		19 20			19 50		20 01	20 20		
Chatelherault	d	18 06											19 06							20 06			
Merryton	d	18 09											19 09							20 09			
Larkhall	a	18 11											19 12							20 11			
Airbles	d			18 25					18 55						19 25			19 55			20 25		
Uddingston	d					18 20				18 50						19 20			19 50			20 20	
Bellshill	d					18 25				18 55						19 25			19 55			20 25	
Motherwell	a			18 27		18 33			18 57	19 03					19 27	19 33		19 57	20 03		20 27	20 33	
	d					18 33										19 33						20 33	
Whifflet	a										18 50												
Coatbridge Central	a																						
Shieldmuir	d					18 37										19 37						20 37	
Holytown	d										18 59												
Wishaw	d					18 40										19 40						20 40	
Carluke	d					18 47										19 47						20 47	
Lanark	a					18 59										19 59						20 59	

A 28 November, 5 December **B** 19 September, 26 September

Table 226

Sundays
from 19 September

Helensburgh, Balloch, Dalmuir and Milngavie - Glasgow - Springburn, Airdrie, Drumgelloch, Hamilton, Larkhall, Motherwell, Coatbridge and Lanark

		SR	SR	SR	SR	SR	SR	SR	SR	SR	SR	SR	SR	SR	SR	SR	SR	SR	SR	SR	SR	SR	SR
				◇																		B	
Helensburgh Upper	d			20 36																		22 37	
Helensburgh Central	d					19 55			20 25				20 55			21 25				21 55			
Craigendoran	d					19 58			20 28				20 58			21 28				21 58			
Cardross	d					20 03			20 33				21 03			21 33				22 03			
Balloch	d	19 39					20 09			20 42				21 09			21 39				22 09		22 39
Alexandria	d	19 41					20 11			20 44				21 11			21 41				22 11		22 41
Renton	d	19 44					20 14			20 49				21 14			21 44				22 14		22 44
Dalreoch	d	19 47				20 08	20 17		20 38	20 52			21 08	21 17		21 38	21 47			22 08	22 17		22 47
Dumbarton Central	d	19 48		20 49		20 10	20 18		20 40	20 53			21 10	21 18		21 40	21 48			22 10	22 18		22 48
Dumbarton East	d	19 50				20 12	20 20		20 42	20 55			21 12	21 20		21 42	21 50			22 12	22 20		22 50
Bowling	d	19 54					20 24			21 00				21 24			21 54				22 24		22 55
Kilpatrick	d	19 58					20 28			21 03				21 28			21 58				22 28		22 58
Dalmuir	a	20 00		20 58		20 19	20 30		20 49	21 06			21 19	21 30		21 49	22 00			22 19	22 30	23 02	23 01
	d	20 01		20 58		20 20	20 31		20 50	21 07			21 20	21 31		21 50	22 01			22 20	22 31	23 04	23 01
Singer	d					20 22			20 52				21 22			21 52				22 22			
Drumry	d					20 25			20 55				21 25			21 55				22 25			
Drumchapel	d					20 27			20 57				21 27			21 57				22 27			
Milngavie	d		20 11					20 41			21 11				21 41			22 11					
Hillfoot	d		20 14					20 44			21 14				21 44			22 14					
Bearsden	d		20 16					20 46			21 16				21 46			22 16					
Westerton	d		20 19			20 30		20 49	21 00		21 19		21 30		21 49	22 00		22 19		22 30		23 13	
Anniesland	d		20 22			20 33		20 52	21 03		21 22		21 33		21 52	22 03		22 22		22 33			
Clydebank	d	20 03					20 33			21 09				21 33			22 03				22 33		23 03
Yoker	d	20 05					20 35			21 11				21 35			22 05				22 35		23a05
Garscadden	d	20 09					20 39			21 14				21 39			22 09				22 39		
Scotstounhill	d	20 11					20 41			21 16				21 41			22 11				22 41		
Jordanhill	d	20 13					20 43			21 18				21 43			22 13				22 43		
Hyndland	d	20 15	20 25			20 35	20 45	20 55	21 05	21 20	21 25		21 35	21 45	21 55	22 05	22 15	22 25		22 35	22 45		
Partick	d	20 18	20 28		20 34	20 38	20 48	20 58	21 08	21 22	21 28	21 34	21 38	21 48	21 58	22 08	22 18	22 28	22 34	22 38	22 48		
Exhibition Centre	d	20 21	20 31		20 37		20 51	21 01		21 25	21 31	21 37		21 51	22 01		22 21	22 31	22 37		22 51		
Anderston	d																						
Glasgow Central HL 15	d																						
Glasgow Central LL 15	a	20 23	20 33		20 39		20 53	21 03		21 28	21 33	21 39		21 53	22 03		22 23	22 33	22 39		22 53		
	d	20 24	20 34		20 40		20 54	21 04		21 28	21 34	21 40		21 54	22 04		22 24	22 34	22 40		22 54		
Argyle Street	d																						
Charing Cross	d					20 43			21 13				21 43			22 13				22 43			
Glasgow Queen St HL 10	a			21 14																			
Glasgow Queen St LL 10	a					20 45			21 15				21 45			22 15				22 45			
	d					20 46			21 16				21 46			22 16				22 46			
High Street	d					20 48			21 18				21 48			22 18				22 48			
Bellgrove	d					20 50			21 20				21 50			22 20				22 50			
Duke Street	d																						
Alexandra Parade	d																						
Barnhill	d																						
Springburn	a																						
Carntyne	d					20 54			21 24				21 54			22 24				22 54			
Shettleston	d					20 56			21 26				21 56			22 26				22 56			
Garrowhill	d					20 59			21 29				21 59			22 29				22 59			
Easterhouse	d					21 01			21 31				22 01			22 31				23 01			
Blairhill	d					21 05			21 35				22 05			22 35				23 05			
Coatbridge Sunnyside	d					21 08			21 38				22 08			22 38				23 08			
Coatdyke	d					21 10			21 40				22 10			22 40				23 10			
Airdrie	a					21 13			21 43				22 13			22 43				23 13			
	d																						
Drumgelloch	a																						
Bridgeton	d	20 29	20 39				20 59	21 09		21 32	21 39			21 59	22 09		22 29	22 39			22 59		
Dalmarnock	d																						
Rutherglen	d	20 32	20 42		20 47		21 02	21 12		21 35	21 42	21 47		22 02	22 12		22 32	22 42	22 47		23 02		
Cambuslang	d	20 36	20 46				21 06	21 16		21 39	21 46			22 06	22 16		22 36	22 46			23 06		
Newton	d	20 39					21 09			21 42				22 09			22 39				23 09		
Blantyre	d	20 43			20 55		21 13			21 46		21 55		22 13			22 43		22 55		23 13		
Hamilton West	d	20 46			20 58		21 16			21 49		21 58		22 16			22 46		22 58		23 16		
Hamilton Central	d	20 50			21 01		21 20			21 52		22 01		22 20			22 50		23 01		23 20		
Chatelherault	d				21 05							22 06							23 05				
Merryton	d				21 09							22 09							23 09				
Larkhall	a				21 11							22 13							23 11				
Airbles	d	20 55					21 25			21 57				22 25			22 55				23 25		
Uddingston	d		20 50					21 20			21 50				22 20			22 50					
Bellshill	d		20 55					21 25			21 55				22 25			22 55					
Motherwell	a	20 57	21 04				21 27	21 33		21 59	22 03			22 27	22 33		22 57	23 06			23 27		
	d							21 33							22 33								
Whifflet	a																						
Coatbridge Central	a																						
Shieldmuir	d							21 37							22 37								
Holytown	d																						
Wishaw	d							21 40							22 40								
Carluke	d							21 47							22 45								
Lanark	a							21 59							22 59								

Table 226

Sundays
from 19 September

Helensburgh, Balloch, Dalmuir and Milngavie - Glasgow - Springburn, Airdrie, Drumgelloch, Hamilton, Larkhall, Motherwell, Coatbridge and Lanark

		SR	SR	SR
Helensburgh Upper	d			
Helensburgh Central	d		22 25	
Craigendoran	d		22 28	
Cardross	d		22 33	
Balloch	d			23 09
Alexandria	d			23 11
Renton	d			23 14
Dalreoch	d		22 38	23 17
Dumbarton Central	d		22 40	23 18
Dumbarton East	d		22 42	23 20
Bowling	d			23 25
Kilpatrick	d			23 28
Dalmuir	a		22 49	23 31
	d		22 50	23 31
Singer	d		22 52	
Drumry	d		22 55	
Drumchapel	d		22 57	
Milngavie	d	22 41		
Hillfoot	d	22 44		
Bearsden	d	22 46		
Westerton	d	22 49	23 00	
Anniesland	d	22 52	23 03	
Clydebank	d			23 33
Yoker	d			23a35
Garscadden	d			
Scotstounhill	d			
Jordanhill	d			
Hyndland	d	22 55	23 05	
Partick	d	22 58	23 08	
Exhibition Centre	d	23 01		
Anderston	d			
Glasgow Central HL 15	d			
Glasgow Central LL 15	a	23 03		
	d	23 04		
Argyle Street	d			
Charing Cross	d		23 13	
Glasgow Queen St HL 10	a			
Glasgow Queen St LL 10	a		23 15	
	d		23 16	
High Street	d		23 18	
Bellgrove	d		23 20	
Duke Street	d			
Alexandra Parade	d			
Barnhill	d			
Springburn	a			
Carntyne	d		23 24	
Shettleston	d		23 26	
Garrowhill	d		23 29	
Easterhouse	d		23 31	
Blairhill	d		23 35	
Coatbridge Sunnyside	d		23 38	
Coatdyke	d		23 40	
Airdrie	a		23 43	
	d			
Drumgelloch	a			
Bridgeton	d	23 09		
Dalmarnock	d			
Rutherglen	d	23 12		
Cambuslang	d	23 16		
Newton	d			
Blantyre	d			
Hamilton West	d			
Hamilton Central	d			
Chatelherault	d			
Merryton	d			
Larkhall	a			
Airbles	d			
Uddingston	d	23 20		
Bellshill	d	23 25		
Motherwell	a	23 33		
	d			
Whifflet	a			
Coatbridge Central	a			
Shieldmuir	d			
Holytown	d			
Wishaw	d			
Carluke	d			
Lanark	a			

Network Diagram for Tables 227, 239

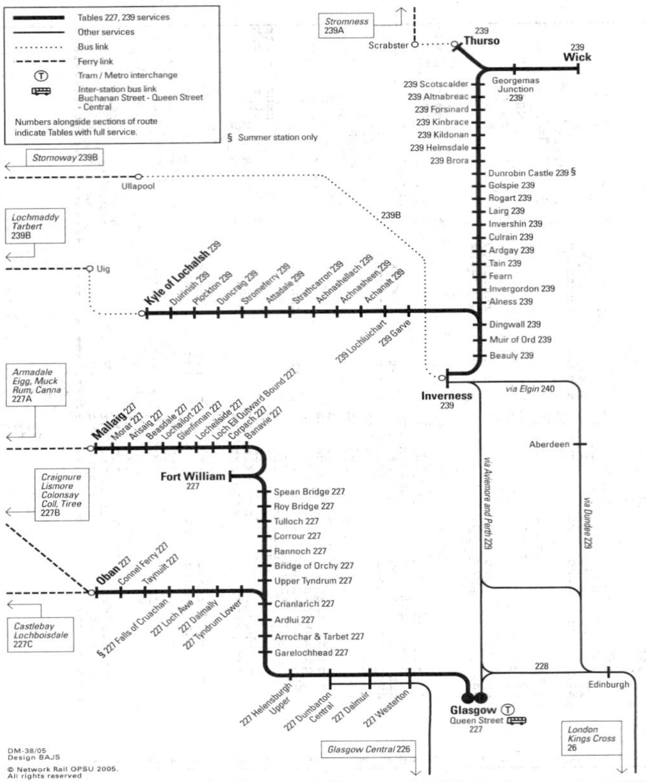

DM-38/05
Design BAJS

Table 227

Mondays to Saturdays
until 25 September

Glasgow Queen Street - Oban, Fort William and Mallaig

			SR	SR	SR	WR SX	SR SO	SR SX	SR SO	SR	SR		SR	SR
			◇	◇	◇	A	◇	◇	◇	◇ C	◇		◇	◇
Edinburgh	228	d	04 50											
Glasgow Queen St.	226	d		08 21				09 07	10 37	12 21			18 21	
Westerton	226	d	05 56											
Dalmuir	226	d	06 04	08 42				09 27	10 53	12 42			18 40	
Dumbarton Central	226	d		08 51				09 37	11 04	12 51			18 49	
Helensburgh Upper		a	06 26	09 03				09 50	11 20	13 03			19 02	
		d	06 29	09 06				09 52	11 23	13 06			19 04	
Garelochhead		d	06 42	09 17				10 04	11 34	13 17			19 16	
Arrochar & Tarbet		d	07 08	09 37				10 27	11 54	13 37			19 36	
Ardlui		d	07x22	09 53				10x39	12 08	13 53			19 50	
Crianlarich		a	07 43	10 09				10 55	12 24	14 09			20 06	
		d	07 45	10 15			10 21	10 58	12 27	14 14	14 21		20 12	20 18
Tyndrum Lower		d		10 24					12 36	14 23			20 21	
Dalmally		d		10 42					12 57	14 42			20 39	
Loch Awe		d		10 47					13 02	14 47			20 44	
Falls of Cruachan §		d		10x52					13x08	14x52			20x49	
Taynuilt		d		11 03					13 18	15 02			21 00	
Connel Ferry		d		11 14					13 30	15 14			21 11	
Oban		a		11 27					13 43	15 27			21 26	
Upper Tyndrum		d	07 58				10 32	11 09			14 32			20 31
Bridge of Orchy		d	08 15				10 46	11 23			14 46			20 46
Rannoch		d	08 45				11 08	11 45			15 08			21 08
Corrour		d	08x58				11 20	11 57			15 20			21 20
Tulloch		d	09 18				11 36	12 13			15 36			21 36
Roy Bridge		d	09x29				11 46	12 23			15 46			21 46
Spean Bridge		d	09 37				11 54	12 30			15 53			21 53
Fort William		a	09 54				12 07	12 43			16 06			22 06
		d			08 30	10 18	12 12	12 48			16 19			22 15
Banavie		d			08 36		12 18	12 54			16 25			22 21
Corpach		d			08 41		12 23	12 59			16 30			22 26
Loch Eil Outward Bound		d			08 47	10 37	12 29	13 05			16 36			22 32
Locheilside		d			08x52		12x34	13x10			16x41			22x37
Glenfinnan		d			09 03	11b21	12 46	13 21			16 54			22 48
Lochailort		d			09x19		13x01	13x37			17x10			23x04
Beasdale		d			09x28		13x10	13x46			17x19			23x13
Arisaig		d			09 36	11 59	13 18	13 54			17 27			23 20
Morar		d			09 44		13 27	14 02			17 35			23 28
Mallaig		a			09 52	12 22	13 35	14 09			17 43			23 35

§ Summer station only
A Also runs Saturdays from 21 June until 3 September
C to Ardlui
b arr. 1055

Table 227

Mondays to Saturdays
from 27 September

Glasgow Queen Street - Oban, Fort William and Mallaig

		SR	SR	SR	WR	SR	SR	SR	SR	SR	SR
		B	◇	◇	A	◇	◇ C	◇ D	◇	◇	◇
		🛏	🍴			🍴	🍴	🍴	🍴	🍴	🍴
Edinburgh 228	d	04 50									
Glasgow Queen St. 10 226 ⛴	d		08 21				10§37	12 21		18 21	
Westerton 226	d	05 56									
Dalmuir 226	d	06 04	08 42				10§53	12 42		18 40	
Dumbarton Central 226	d		08 51				11§04	12 51		18 49	
Helensburgh Upper	a	06 26	09 03				11§20	13 03		19 02	
	d	06 29	09 06				11§23	13 06		19 04	
Garelochhead	d	06 42	09 17				11§34	13 17		19 16	
Arrochar & Tarbet	d	07 08	09 37				11§54	13 37		19 36	
Ardlui	d	07x22	09 53				12§08	13 53		19 50	
Crianlarich	a	07 43	10 09				12§24	14 09		20 06	
	d	07 45	10 15			10 21	12§27	14 14	14 21	20 12	20 18
Tyndrum Lower	d		10 24				12§36	14 23		20 21	
Dalmally	d		10 42				12§57	14 42		20 39	
Loch Awe	d		10 47				13§02	14 47		20 44	
Falls of Cruachan §	d										
Taynuilt	d		11 03				13§18	15 02		21 00	
Connel Ferry	d		11 14				13§30	15 14		21 11	
Oban	a		11 27				13§43	15 27		21 26	
Upper Tyndrum	d	07 58				10 32			14 32		20 31
Bridge of Orchy	d	08 15				10 46			14 46		20 46
Rannoch	d	08 45				11 08			15 08		21 08
Corrour	d	08x58				11 20			15 20		21 20
Tulloch	d	09 18				11 36			15 36		21 36
Roy Bridge	d	09x29				11 46			15 46		21 46
Spean Bridge	d	09 37				11 54			15 53		21 53
Fort William	a	09 54				12 07			16 06		22 06
	d			08 30	10§18	12 12			16 19		22 15
Banavie	d			08 36		12 18			16 25		22 21
Corpach	d			08 41		12 23			16 30		22 26
Loch Eil Outward Bound	d			08 47	10§37	12 29			16 36		22 32
Locheilside	d			08x52		12x34			16x41		22x37
Glenfinnan	d			09 03	11b21	12 46			16 54		22 48
Lochailort	d			09x19		13x01			17x10		23x04
Beasdale	d			09x28		13x10			17x19		23x13
Arisaig	d			09 36	11§59	13 18			17 27		23 20
Morar	d			09 44		13 27			17 35		23 28
Mallaig	a			09 52	12§22	13 35			17 43		23 35

§ Summer station only
A SX until 15 October
C Also runs Saturdays until 30 October
b arr. 1055

Table 227

Sundays
until 26 September

Glasgow Queen Street - Oban, Fort William and Mallaig

		SR	WR	SR	SR	SR	SR	SR
		◇	A	◇	◇	◇	◇	◇
		🍴		🍴	🍴	🍴	🍴	🍴
Edinburgh 228	d							
Glasgow Queen St. 10 226 ⛴	d	09 55			12 20		18 20	
Westerton 226	d							
Dalmuir 226	d	10 16			12 36		18 34	
Dumbarton Central 226	d	10 25			12 46		18 43	
Helensburgh Upper	a	10 37			13 03		18 56	
	d	10 40			13 06		18 58	
Garelochhead	d	10 51			13 17		19 10	
Arrochar & Tarbet	d	11 11			13 37		19 30	
Ardlui	d	11 27			13 53		19c50	
Crianlarich	a	11 43			14 09		20 06	
	d	11 46			14 15	14 21	20 12	20 18
Tyndrum Lower	d	11 55			14 24		20 21	
Dalmally	d	12 13			14 42		20 39	
Loch Awe	d	12 18			14 47		20 44	
Falls of Cruachan §	d	12x23			14 52		20x49	
Taynuilt	d	12 37			15 03		21 00	
Connel Ferry	d	12 48			15 14		21 11	
Oban	a	13 01			15 27		21 26	
Upper Tyndrum	d					14 32		20 31
Bridge of Orchy	d					14 46		20 46
Rannoch	d					15 08		21 08
Corrour	d					15 20		21 20
Tulloch	d					15 36		21 36
Roy Bridge	d					15 46		21 46
Spean Bridge	d					15 53		21 53
Fort William	a					16 06		22 06
	d		10§18	12 12		16 19		22 15
Banavie	d			12 18		16 25		22 21
Corpach	d			12 23		16 30		22 26
Loch Eil Outward Bound	d		10§37	12 29		16 36		22 32
Locheilside	d			12x34		16x41		22x37
Glenfinnan	d		11b21	12 46		16 55		22 48
Lochailort	d			13x01		17x10		23x04
Beasdale	d			13x10		17x19		23x13
Arisaig	d		11§59	13 18		17 27		23 20
Morar	d			13 27		17 36		23 28
Mallaig	a		12§22	13 35		17 43		23 35

Sundays
from 03 October

		SR	SR	SR	SR	SR
		◇ B	◇	◇ B	◇	◇
		🍴	🍴	🍴	🍴	🍴
Edinburgh 228	d					
Glasgow Queen St. 10 226 ⛴	d		12 20		18 20	
Westerton 226	d					
Dalmuir 226	d		12 36		18 34	
Dumbarton Central 226	d		12 46		18 43	
Helensburgh Upper	a		13 03		18 56	
	d		13 06		18 58	
Garelochhead	d		13 17		19 10	
Arrochar & Tarbet	d		13 37		19 30	
Ardlui	d		13 53		19c50	
Crianlarich	a		14 09		20 06	
	d		14 15	14§21	20 12	20 18
Tyndrum Lower	d		14 24		20 21	
Dalmally	d		14 42		20 39	
Loch Awe	d		14 47		20 44	
Falls of Cruachan §	d					
Taynuilt	d		15 03		21 00	
Connel Ferry	d		15 14		21 11	
Oban	a		15 27		21 26	
Upper Tyndrum	d			14§32		20 31
Bridge of Orchy	d			14§46		20 46
Rannoch	d			15§08		21 08
Corrour	d			15§20		21 20
Tulloch	d			15§36		21 36
Roy Bridge	d			15§46		21 46
Spean Bridge	d			15§53		21 53
Fort William	a			16§06		22 06
	d	12§12		16§19		22 15
Banavie	d	12§18		16§25		22 21
Corpach	d	12§23		16§30		22 26
Loch Eil Outward Bound	d	12§29		16§36		22 32
Locheilside	d	12x34		16x41		22x37
Glenfinnan	d	12§46		16§55		22 48
Lochailort	d	13x01		17x10		23x04
Beasdale	d	13x10		17x19		23x13
Arisaig	d	13§18		17§27		23 20
Morar	d	13§27		17§36		23 28
Mallaig	a	13§35		17§43		23 35

§ Summer station only
A 27 June until 29 August
B until 31 October
b arr. 1055
c arr. 1943

Table 227

Mondays to Saturdays
until 25 September

Mallaig, Fort William and Oban - Glasgow Queen Street

		SR SX	SR	SR	SR	SR	SR SX	WR SX	SR SO	SR	SR	SR	SR SX
			◇ B ⊼	◇ A ⊼	◇ ⊼	◇	◇ A ⊼	C	◇ ⊼	◇ ⊼	◇ B ⊼	◇ ⊼	▣ ⊏
Mallaig	d		06 03		10 10			14 10			16 05	18 15	
Morar	d		06 10		10 16			14 23			16 12	18 22	
Arisaig	d		06 19		10 26			14 38			16 21	18 31	
Beasdale	d		06x26		10x32						16x28	18x38	
Lochailort	d		06x35		10x41						16x37	18x47	
Glenfinnan	d		06 52		10 59			15 23			16 54	19 04	
Locheilside	d		07x01		11x09						17x03	19x13	
Loch Eil Outward Bound	d		07 08		11 15			15 42			17 10	19 20	
Corpach	d		07 14		11 21						17 16	19 26	
Banavie	d		07 18		11 25						17 20	19 30	
Fort William	a		07 26		11 32			16 02			17 27	19 37	
	d		07 42		11 40						17 37		19 50
Spean Bridge	d		07 55		11 55						17 50		20 10
Roy Bridge	d		08 02		12 02						17 57		20x17
Tulloch	d		08 13		12 14						18 08		20 30
Corrour	d		08 30		12 31						18 25		20x51
Rannoch	d		08 42		12 42						18 36		21 05
Bridge of Orchy	d		09 02		13 03						18 56		21 34
Upper Tyndrum	d		09 18		13 19						19 12		21 52
Oban	d			08 11		12 11	12 56		16 11	18 10			
Connel Ferry	d			08 23		12 23	13 08		16 27	18 23			
Taynuilt	d			08 35		12 35	13 20		16 38	18 34			
Falls of Cruachan §	d			08x43		12x43	13x28		16x47	18x43			
Loch Awe	d			08 50		12 50	13 35		16 53	18 49			
Dalmally	d			08 56		12 56	13 41		17 00	18 56			
Tyndrum Lower	d			09 15		13 15	14 00		17 19	19 15			
Crianlarich	a		09 30	09 24	13 27	13 24	14 10		17 28	19 27	19 21		22 04
	d			09 36		13 36	14 12		17 30		19 33		22 05
Ardlui	d			09 52		13 52	14 28		17 47		19 52		22x26
Arrochar & Tarbet	d	07 08		10 07		14 07	14 43		18 01		20 06		22 44
Garelochhead	d	07 30		10 32		14 27	15 03		18 22		20 27		23 10
Helensburgh Upper	a	07 41		10 42		14 38	15 14		18 32		20 37		23 23
	d	07 42		10 44		14 39	15 15		18 34		20 39		23 24
Dumbarton Central 226	a	07 57		10 59		14 52	15 28		18 47		20 53		
Dalmuir 226	a			11 08		15 04	15 37		18 56		21 04		23 49
Westerton 226	a						15 44						23 55
Glasgow Queen St. 10 226 ⇌	a	08 37		11 30		15 28	16 00		19 18		21 30		
Edinburgh 228	a												00 50

§ Summer station only
A ⊼ from Crianlarich
B ⊼ from Fort William
C Also runs Saturdays 21 June until 3 September

Table 227

Mondays to Saturdays
from 27 September

Mallaig, Fort William and Oban - Glasgow Queen Street

		SR SX	SR	SR	SR	SR	WR	SR	SR	SR	SR	SR SX
			◇ B ⊼	◇ A ⊼	◇ ⊼	◇	C	◇ D ⊼	◇ B ⊼	◇ ⊼	◇ ⊼	▣ ⊏
Mallaig	d		06 03		10 10		14 10		16 05		18 15	
Morar	d		06 10		10 16		14 23		16 12		18 22	
Arisaig	d		06 19		10 26		14 38		16 21		18 31	
Beasdale	d		06x26		10x32				16x28		18x38	
Lochailort	d		06x35		10x41				16x37		18x47	
Glenfinnan	d		06 52		10 59		15 23		16 54		19 04	
Locheilside	d		07x01		11x09				17x03		19x13	
Loch Eil Outward Bound	d		07 08		11 15		15 42		17 10		19 20	
Corpach	d		07 14		11 21				17 16		19 26	
Banavie	d		07 18		11 25				17 20		19 30	
Fort William	a		07 26		11 32		16 02		17 27		19 37	
	d		07 42		11 40				17 37			19 50
Spean Bridge	d		07 55		11 55				17 50			20 10
Roy Bridge	d		08 02		12 02				17 57			20x17
Tulloch	d		08 13		12 14				18 08			20 30
Corrour	d		08 30		12 31				18 25			20x51
Rannoch	d		08 42		12 42				18 36			21 05
Bridge of Orchy	d		09 02		13 03				18 56			21 34
Upper Tyndrum	d		09 18		13 19				19 12			21 52
Oban	d			08 11		12 11		16 11		18 10		
Connel Ferry	d			08 23		12 23		16 27		18 23		
Taynuilt	d			08 35		12 35		16 38		18 34		
Falls of Cruachan §	d											
Loch Awe	d			08 50		12 50		16 53		18 49		
Dalmally	d			08 56		12 56		17 00		18 56		
Tyndrum Lower	d			09 15		13 15		17 19		19 15		
Crianlarich	a		09 30	09 24	13 30	13 24		17 28	19 21	19 27		22 04
	d			09 36		13 36		17 30	19 33			22 05
Ardlui	d			09 52		13 52		17 47	19 52			22x26
Arrochar & Tarbet	d	07 08		10 07		14 07		18 01	20 06			22 44
Garelochhead	d	07 30		10 32		14 27		18 22	20 27			23 10
Helensburgh Upper	a	07 41		10 42		14 38		18 32	20 37			23 23
	d	07 42		10 44		14 39		18 34	20 39			23 24
Dumbarton Central 226	a	07 57		10 59		14 52		18 47	20 53			
Dalmuir 226	a			11 08		15 04		18 56	21 04			23 49
Westerton 226	a											23 55
Glasgow Queen St. 10 226 ⇌	a	08 37		11 30		15 28		19 18	21 30			
Edinburgh 228	a											00 50

§ Summer station only
A ⊼ from Crianlarich
B ⊼ from Fort William
C SX until 15 October
D Also runs Saturdays until 30 October

Table 227

Mallaig, Fort William and Oban - Glasgow Queen Street

Sundays until 26 September

		SR	SR	WR	SR	SR	SR	SR	SR
									[R]
		◇	◇		◇	◇	◇	◇	
				A					
		🍴			🍴	🍴	🍴	🍴	🛏
Mallaig	d	10 10		14 10			16 05	18 15	
Morar	d	10 16		14 23			16 12	18 22	
Arisaig	d	10 26		14 38			16 21	18 31	
Beasdale	d	10x32					16x28	18x38	
Lochailort	d	10x41					16x37	18x47	
Glenfinnan	d	10 59		15 23			16 54	19 04	
Locheilside	d	11x09					17x03	19x13	
Loch Eil Outward Bound	d	11 15		15 42			17 10	19 20	
Corpach	d	11 21					17 16	19 26	
Banavie	d	11 25					17 20	19 30	
Fort William	a	11 32		16 02			17 27	19 37	
	d	11 40					17 37		19 00
Spean Bridge	d	11 55					17 50		19 19
Roy Bridge	d	12 02					17 57		19x27
Tulloch	d	12 14					18 08		19 40
Corrour	d	12 31					18 25		20x01
Rannoch	d	12 42					18 36		20 15
Bridge of Orchy	d	13 03					18 56		20b47
Upper Tyndrum	d	13 19					19 12		21 05
Oban	d		12 11		16 11	18 10			
Connel Ferry	d		12 23		16 27	18 23			
Taynuilt	d		12 35		16 38	18 34			
Falls of Cruachan §	d		12x43		16x47	18x43			
Loch Awe	d		12 50		16 53	18 49			
Dalmally	d		12 56		17 00	18 56			
Tyndrum Lower	d		13 15		17 19	19 15			
Crianlarich	a	13 30	13 24		17 28	19 27	19 21		21 16
	d		13 36		17 30		19 32		21 19
Ardlui	d		13 52		17 47		19 49		21x39
Arrochar & Tarbet	d		14 07		18 01		20 03		21 57
Garelochhead	d		14 27		18 22		20 24		22 23
Helensburgh Upper	a		14 38		18 32		20 34		22 35
	d		14 39		18 34		20 36		22 37
Dumbarton Central 226	a		14 56		18 47		20 49		
Dalmuir 226	a		15 05		18 56		20 58		23 02
Westerton 226	a								23 11
Glasgow Queen St. 10 226 ⛴	a		15 31		19 15		21 14		
Edinburgh 228	a								00 15

§ Summer station only A from 27 June until 29 August b arr. 2041

Table 227

Mallaig, Fort William and Oban - Glasgow Queen Street

Sundays from 03 October

		SR	SR	SR	SR	SR	SR
							[R]
		◇	◇	◇	◇	◇	
		A				A	
		🍴		🍴	🍴	🍴	🛏
Mallaig	d	10 10			16 05	18 15	
Morar	d	10 16			16 12	18 22	
Arisaig	d	10 26			16 21	18 31	
Beasdale	d	10x32			16x28	18x38	
Lochailort	d	10x41			16x37	18x47	
Glenfinnan	d	10 59			16 54	19 04	
Locheilside	d	11x09			17x03	19x13	
Loch Eil Outward Bound	d	11 15			17 10	19 20	
Corpach	d	11 21			17 16	19 26	
Banavie	d	11 25			17 20	19 30	
Fort William	a	11 32			17 27	19 37	
	d	11 40			17 37		19 00
Spean Bridge	d	11 55			17 50		19 19
Roy Bridge	d	12 02			17 57		19x27
Tulloch	d	12 14			18 08		19 40
Corrour	d	12 31			18 25		20x01
Rannoch	d	12 42			18 36		20 15
Bridge of Orchy	d	13 03			18 56		20b47
Upper Tyndrum	d	13 19			19 12		21 05
Oban	d		12 11	18 10			
Connel Ferry	d		12 23	18 23			
Taynuilt	d		12 35	18 34			
Falls of Cruachan §	d						
Loch Awe	d		12 50	18 49			
Dalmally	d		12 56	18 56			
Tyndrum Lower	d		13 15	19 15			
Crianlarich	a	13 30	13 24	19 27	19 21		21 16
	d		13 36		19 32		21 19
Ardlui	d		13 52		19 49		21x39
Arrochar & Tarbet	d		14 07		20 03		21 57
Garelochhead	d		14 27		20 24		22 23
Helensburgh Upper	a		14 38		20 34		22 35
	d		14 39		20 36		22 37
Dumbarton Central 226	a		14 56		20 49		
Dalmuir 226	a		15 05		20 58		23 02
Westerton 226	a						23 11
Glasgow Queen St. 10 226 ⛴	a		15 31		21 14		
Edinburgh 228	a						00 15

§ Summer station only A from 3 October until 31 October b arr. 2041

Table 227A SHIPPING SERVICES

Mallaig - Armadale (Skye) and Small Isles

Operated by Caledonian MacBrayne Ltd

Mondays to Saturdays until 23 October

		ThO	WO	MO	TO G		FO	A	SO B	SX C	
Glasgow Queen St 227	d	.	.	.	.	.	.	08 21	08 21	09 07	12 21
Fort William 227	d	08 30	08 30	08 30	08 30	08 30	08 30	12 12	12 12	12 48	16 19
Mallaig 227	a	09 52	09 52	09 52	09 52	09 52	09 52	13 35	13 35	14 09	17 43
Mallaig	d	10 15	10 15	10 15	10 15	10 55	12 40	13 45	14 25	15 10	18 00
Armadale	a	.	.	.	.	11 25	.	14 15	.	15 40	18 30
Eigg	a	11 30	.	11 30	12 45	.	.	.	15 40	.	.
Muck	a	12 20	.	.	11 55	.	.	.	16 25	.	.
Rum	a	.	11 35	12 45	.	.	14 00	.	19 25	.	.
Canna	a	.	12 45	13 55	.	.	15 10	.	18 15	.	.

Sundays until 17 October

		D	
Glasgow Queen St 227	d	.	12 20
Fort William 227	d	12 12	16 19
Mallaig 227	a	13 35	17 43
Mallaig	d	14 40	18 00
Armadale	a	15 10	18 30
Eigg	a	.	.
Muck	a	.	.
Rum	a	.	.
Canna	a	.	.

Mondays to Saturdays until 23 October

			FO	SO E	ThO		TO F	WO		MO	FO
Canna	d	.	.	10 15	.	.	.	14 35	.	14 10	15 25
Rum	d	.	.	09 05	.	.	.	15 45	.	15 20	16 35
Muck	d	.	10 20	12 00	12 35	.	13 50	.	.	.	.
Eigg	d	.	11 10	12 50	13 20	.	13 00	.	.	16 35	.
Armadale	d	08 50	.	.	.	14 30	.	.	17 10	.	.
Mallaig	a	09 20	12 25	14 05	14 35	15 00	15 30	17 05	17 40	17 50	17 55
Mallaig 227	d	10 10	16 05	16 05	16 05	16 05	16 05	18 15	18 15	18 15	18 15
Fort William 227	a	11 32	17 27	17 27	17 27	17 27	17 27	19 37	19 37	19 37	19 37
Glasgow Queen St 227	a	15 30	21 30	21 30	21 30	21 30	21 30	00a20	00b20	00a20	00a20

Sundays until 17 October

			D	
Canna	d	.	.	.
Rum	d	.	.	.
Muck	d	.	.	.
Eigg	d	.	.	.
Armadale	d	09 30	15 20	16 50
Mallaig	a	10 00	15 50	17 20
Mallaig 227	d	10 10	16 05	18 15
Fort William 227	a	11 32	17 27	19 37
Glasgow Queen St 227	a	15 31	21 14	.

A All Saturdays, also Mondays to Fridays from 27 September
B Sails via Canna
C Until 24 September
D 6 June to 29 August
E Sails from Rum
F Sails from Eigg
G Sails via Muck
a Following day. Change at Fort William and Westerton. Reservations compulsory from Fort William.
b Tuesday to Saturday mornings only. Change at Fort William and Westerton. Reservations compulsory from Fort William.

For details of sailings from 24 October 2010, telephone Caledonian MacBrayne on 08000 66 5000

Table 227B SHIPPING SERVICES

Oban - Craignure (Mull), Lismore, Colonsay, Coll and Tiree

Operated by Caledonian MacBrayne Ltd

Mondays to Saturdays until 23 October

		WFO A	SO	MO	ThO B	SO	SX	SO	SX	SO	TO	WO		SO	MFO	SX	FO
Glasgow Queen St 227	d	18a21	18a21	18a21	18a21	08 21	08 21	10 37	08 21	10 37	08 21	12 21	12 21	12 21	12 21	12 21	18 21
Oban 227	a	21a26	21a26	21a26	21a26	11 27	11 27	13 43	11 27	13 43	11 27	15 27	15 27	15 27	15 27	15 27	21 26
Oban	d	05 45	07 00	08 00	08 15	11 45	11 55	14 00	14 00	14 00	14 45	15 40	16 00	17 00	17 00	17 15	22 30
Craignure	a	.	.	.	.	12 31	12 41	14 46	.	.	.	.	16 46	.	.	.	23 16
Lismore	a	.	.	.	.	.	.	.	14 50	14 50	.	.	.	17 50	.	18 05	.
Colonsay	a	.	.	.	.	.	.	.	.	.	.	17 55	.	.	19 20	.	.
Coll	a	10 15	09 40	10 55	10 55	.	.	.	.	.	17 25	.	.	.	.	.	.
Tiree	a	09 05	10 45	12 05	12 00	.	.	.	.	.	18 25	.	.	.	.	.	.

Sundays until 17 October

			C	C		
Glasgow Queen St 227	d	18a21	09 55	09 55	12 20	12 20
Oban 227	a	21a26	13 01	13 01	15 27	15 27
Oban	d	09 00	14 00	15 00	16 00	17 30
Craignure	a	.	14 46	.	16 46	.
Lismore	a	.	.	15 50	.	.
Colonsay	a	.	.	.	.	19 50
Coll	a	11 55	.	.	.	.
Tiree	a	13 00	.	.	.	.

Mondays to Saturdays until 23 October

		ThSO	SO	TO D	TO E	SX F	SX G	SO	SX F	SX G	WFO	WO	ThO	SO	SO	SO	SX	MO	
Tiree	d	.	.	.	.	.	.	.	.	.	09 20	.	.	11 15	.	.	.	12 25	.
Coll	d	.	.	.	.	.	.	.	.	.	10 20	.	.	12 20	.	.	.	13 35	.
Colonsay	d	.	.	07 50	07 50	.	.	.	.	.	.	11 45	11 55	.	.	.	.	.	.
Lismore	d	.	09 00	.	.	10 00	10 00	.	.	.	.	.	.	.	.	15 00	15 00	.	.
Craignure	d	06 45	.	.	.	.	.	10 30	10 55	10 55	.	.	.	.	15 00	.	.	.	17 00
Oban	a	07 31	09 50	10 10	10 10	10 50	10 50	11 16	11 41	11 41	13 00	14 10	14 15	15 00	15 46	15 50	15 50	16 30	17 46
Oban 227	d	08 11	12 11	12 11	12 56	12 11	12 56	12 11	12 11	12 56	18 10	18 10	18 10	16 11	16 11	16 11	18 10	18 10	18 10
Glasgow Queen St 227	a	11 30	15 30	15 30	15 58	15 30	15 58	15 30	15 30	15 58	21 30	21 30	21 30	19 18	19 18	19 18	21 30	21 30	21 30

Sundays until 17 October

			C		C			
Tiree	d	.	.	.	.	.	13 15	.
Coll	d	.	.	.	.	.	14 20	.
Colonsay	d	.	.	.	.	.	.	.
Lismore	d	.	12 00	.	.	16 00	.	.
Craignure	d	10 55	.	15 00	.	.	.	17 00
Oban	a	11 41	12 50	15 46	.	16 50	17 15	17 46
Oban 227	d	12 11	16 11	16 11	.	18 10	18 10	18 10
Glasgow Queen St 227	a	15 31	19 15	19 15	.	21 14	21 14	21 14

A Sails via Tiree
B Sails to Barra arr. 1500
C Until 26 September
D From 28 September
E Until 21 September
F From 27 September
G Until 24 Septmber
a Previous night

For details of sailings from 24 October 2010, telephone Caledonian MacBrayne on 08000 66 5000

Table 227C — SHIPPING SERVICE

Mondays to Saturdays until 23 October

Oban - Castlebay (Barra) and Lochboisdale (South Uist)

Operated by Caledonian MacBrayne Ltd

	WFO	TO A	MSO	ThO A
Glasgow Queen St [10] 227 d	*08 21*	*08 21*	*12 21*	*12 21*
Oban 227 a	*11 27*	*11 27*	*15 27*	*15 27*
Oban d	13 40	13 40	15 40	15 40
Castlebay a	18 30	20 40	20 30	22 40
Lochboisdale a		18 50		20 50

Sundays until 17 October

Glasgow Queen St [10] 227 d	*12 20*
Oban 227 a	*15 27*
Oban d	15 40
Castlebay a	20 30
Lochboisdale a	22 20

Mondays to Saturdays until 23 October

	MO	TO	WFO B
Lochboisdale d	07 30		08 55
Castlebay d	09 20	09 10	07 00
Oban a	14 10	14 00	14 05
Oban 227 d	*18 10*	*18 10*	*18 10*
Glasgow Queen St [10] 227 a	*21 30*	*21 30*	*21 30*

Sundays until 17 October

	C	D
Lochboisdale d		
Castlebay d	09 20	09 20
Oban a	14 10	14 10
Oban 227 d	*16 11*	*18 10*
Glasgow Queen St [10] 227 a	*19 15*	*21 14*

A Sails via Lochboisdale
B Sails from Castlebay
D Until 26 September
D 3, 10 and 17 October only

For details of sailings from 24 October 2010, telephone Caledonian MacBrayne on 08000 66 5000

Table 228

Mondays to Fridays

Edinburgh - Falkirk High - Glasgow Queen Street

		SR [1]	SR [1]			SR [1]	SR [1] ⍑	SR [1] ⍑	SR [1] ⍑		SR [1] ⍑	SR	SR [1] ⍑	SR [1] ⍑	SR [1] ⍑	SR [1] ⍑	SR [1] ⍑	SR [1] ⍑	SR [1] ⍑		SR [1] ⍑	SR [1] ⍑	SR [1] ⍑	SR [1] ⍑
Edinburgh [10] 225,230,242 d		05 55	06 30			06 45	07 00	07 15	07 30		07 45		08 00	08 15	08 30	08 45	09 00	09 15	09 30		09 45	10 01	10 15	10 30
Haymarket 225,230,242 d		05 59	06 33			06 47	07 03	07 18	07 33		07 48		08 03	08 18	08 33	08 48	09 03	09 18	09 33		09 48	10 03	10 18	10 33
Linlithgow 230 d		06 13	06 48			07 01		07 33	07 48		08 03	07 59		08 33		09 03		09 33			10 03		10 33	
Polmont [3] 230 d		06 19	06 55				07 19		07 54				08 19	08 39		09 09		09 39			10 09		10 39	
Falkirk High d		06 24	07 00			07 11	07 24	07 42	07 59		08 12		08 25	08 44	08 53	09 14	09 23	09 44	09 53		10 14	10 23	10 44	10 53
Croy [3] 230 a		06 34	07 09			07 21		07 52	08 09				08 34		09 03		09 33		10 02			10 33		11 03
Lenzie [3] 230 a											08 24	08 32												
Bishopbriggs 230 a												08 36												
Glasgow Queen Street [10] 230 a		06 49	07 25			07 37	07 49	08 07	08 25		08 40	08 47	08 55	09 06	09 21	09 36	09 51	10 06	10 19		10 35	10 49	11 07	11 19

	SR [1] ⍑	SR [1] ⍑	SR [1] ⍑	SR [1] ⍑	SR [1] ⍑		SR [1] ⍑	SR [1] ⍑	SR [1] ⍑	SR [1] ⍑	SR [1] ⍑	SR [1] ⍑	SR [1] ⍑	SR [1] ⍑	SR [1] ⍑		SR [1] ⍑	SR [1] ⍑	SR [1] ⍑	SR [1] ⍑	SR [1] ⍑	SR [1] ⍑	SR [1] ⍑	SR [1] ⍑
Edinburgh [10] 225,230,242 d	10 45	11 00	11 15	11 30	11 45		12 00	12 15	12 30	12 45	13 00	13 15	13 30	13 45	14 00		14 15	14 30	14 45	15 00	15 15	15 30	15 45	16 00
Haymarket 225,230,242 d	10 48	11 03	11 18	11 33	11 48		12 03	12 18	12 33	12 48	13 03	13 18	13 33	13 48	14 03		14 18	14 33	14 48	15 03	15 18	15 33	15 48	16 03
Linlithgow 230 d	11 03		11 33		12 03			12 33		13 03		13 33		14 03			14 33		15 03		15 33		16 03	
Polmont [3] 230 d	11 09		11 39		12 09			12 39		13 09		13 39		14 09			14 39		15 09		15 40		16 09	
Falkirk High d	11 14	11 23	11 44	11 53	12 14		12 23	12 44	12 53	13 14	13 23	13 44	13 53	14 14	14 23		14 44	14 53	15 14	15 23	15 44	15 53	16 14	16 23
Croy [3] 230 a		11 33		12 03			12 32		13 03		13 33		14 03		14 33			15 03		15 33		16 03		16 33
Lenzie [3] 230 a																								
Bishopbriggs 230 a																								
Glasgow Queen Street [10] 230 a	11 37	11 51	12 05	12 19	12 38		12 49	13 06	13 19	13 36	13 49	14 06	14 19	14 36	14 49		15 06	15 20	15 37	15 49	16 06	16 19	16 36	16 51

	SR [1] ⍑		SR [1] ⍑	SR [1] ⍑	SR [1] ⍑	SR [1] ⍑	SR [1] ⍑	SR [1] ⍑	SR [1] ⍑	SR [1] ⍑	SR FX [1]		SR FO [1] ⍑	SR [1] ⍑	SR [1] ⍑	SR [1] ⍑	SR [1]	SR [1]	SR [1]	SR [1]	SR [1]		SR [1]	SR [1]
Edinburgh [10] 225,230,242 d	16 15		16 30	16 45	17 00	17 15	17 30	17 45	18 00	18 15	18 30		18 30	18 45	19 00	19 15	19 30	20 00	20 30	21 00	21 30		22 00	22 30
Haymarket 225,230,242 d	16 18		16 33	16 48	17 03	17 18	17 33	17 48	18 03	18 18	18 33		18 33	18 48	19 03	19 18	19 33	20 03	20 33	21 03	21 33		22 03	22 33
Linlithgow 230 d	16 33			17 03		17 33		18 03		18 33				19 03		19 33	19 48	20 18	20 48	21 18	21 48		22 18	22 48
Polmont [3] 230 d	16 39			17 09		17 39		18 09		18 39				19 09		19 39		20 24		21 24			22 24	
Falkirk High d	16 44		16 53	17 14	17 23	17 44	17 53	18 14	18 23	18 44	18 53		18 53	19 14	19 23	19 44	19 57	20 29	20 57	21 29	21 57		22 29	22 57
Croy [3] 230 a			17 02		17 33		18 03		18 33		19 02		19 02		19 33		20 07		21 07		22 07			23 07
Lenzie [3] 230 a							18 08																	23 12
Bishopbriggs 230 a																								
Glasgow Queen Street [10] 230 a	17 06		17 21	17 37	17 50	18 06	18 23	18 37	18 51	19 06	19 21		19 21	19 36	19 49	20 06	20 22	20 50	21 22	21 50	22 22		22 50	23 30

	SR [1]	SR [1]
Edinburgh [10] 225,230,242 d	23 00	23 30
Haymarket 225,230,242 d	23 03	23 33
Linlithgow 230 d	23 18	23 48
Polmont [3] 230 d	23 24	23 54
Falkirk High d	23 29	23 58
Croy [3] 230 a	23 38	00 08
Lenzie [3] 230 a	23 45	00 14
Bishopbriggs 230 a	23 49	
Glasgow Queen Street [10] 230 a	00 01	00 27

Saturdays

			SR [1]	SR [1]	SR [1] ⍑	SR [1] ⍑	SR [1] ⍑	SR [1] ⍑	SR [1] ⍑		SR [1] ⍑	SR [1] ⍑	SR [1] ⍑	SR [1] ⍑	SR [1] ⍑	SR [1] ⍑	SR [1] ⍑	SR [1] ⍑	SR [1] ⍑		SR [1] ⍑	SR [1] ⍑	SR [1] ⍑	SR [1] ⍑
Edinburgh [10] 225,230,242 d			05 55	06 30	07 00	07 15	07 30	07 45	08 00		08 15	08 30	08 45	09 00	09 15	09 30	09 45	10 00	10 15		10 30	10 45	11 00	11 15
Haymarket 225,230,242 d			05 59	06 33	07 03	07 18	07 33	07 48	08 03		08 18	08 33	08 48	09 03	09 18	09 33	09 48	10 03	10 18		10 33	10 48	11 03	11 18
Linlithgow 230 d			06 13	06 48		07 33	07 48	08 03			08 33		09 03		09 33		10 03		10 33			11 03		11 33
Polmont [3] 230 d			06 19	06 55	07 19		07 54		08 19		08 39		09 09		09 39		10 09		10 39			11 09		11 39
Falkirk High d			06 24	07 00	07 24	07 42	07 59	08 12	08 25		08 44	08 53	09 14	09 23	09 44	09 53	10 14	10 23	10 44		10 53	11 14	11 23	11 44
Croy [3] 230 a			06 34	07 09		07 52	08 09		08 34			09 03		09 33		10 02		10 33			11 03		11 33	
Lenzie [3] 230 a								08 24																
Bishopbriggs 230 a								08 31																
Glasgow Queen Street [10] 230 a			06 49	07 25	07 49	08 07	08 25	08 40	08 55		09 06	09 21	09 36	09 51	10 06	10 19	10 36	10 49	11 06		11 19	11 37	11 51	12 05

	SR [1] ⍑	SR [1] ⍑	SR [1] ⍑	SR [1] ⍑	SR [1] ⍑		SR [1] ⍑	SR [1] ⍑	SR [1] ⍑	SR [1] ⍑	SR [1] ⍑	SR [1] ⍑	SR [1] ⍑	SR [1] ⍑	SR [1] ⍑		SR [1] ⍑	SR [1] ⍑	SR [1] ⍑	SR [1] ⍑	SR [1] ⍑	SR [1] ⍑	SR [1] ⍑	SR [1] ⍑
Edinburgh [10] 225,230,242 d	11 30	11 45	12 00	12 15	12 30		12 45	13 00	13 15	13 30	13 45	14 00	14 15	14 30	14 45		15 00	15 15	15 30	15 45	16 00	16 15	16 30	16 45
Haymarket 225,230,242 d	11 33	11 48	12 03	12 18	12 33		12 48	13 03	13 18	13 33	13 48	14 03	14 18	14 33	14 48		15 03	15 18	15 33	15 48	16 03	16 18	16 33	16 48
Linlithgow 230 d		12 03		12 33			13 03		13 33		14 03		14 33		15 03			15 33		16 03		16 33		17 04
Polmont [3] 230 d		12 09		12 39			13 09		13 39		14 09		14 39		15 09			15 39		16 09		16 39		17 10
Falkirk High d	11 53	12 14	12 23	12 44	12 53		13 14	13 23	13 44	13 53	14 14	14 23	14 44	14 53	15 14		15 23	15 44	15 53	16 14	16 23	16 44	16 53	17 15
Croy [3] 230 a	12 03		12 32		13 03			13 33		14 03		14 33		15 03			15 33		16 03		16 33		17 02	
Lenzie [3] 230 a																								
Bishopbriggs 230 a																								
Glasgow Queen Street [10] 230 a	12 19	12 38	12 49	13 06	13 19		13 36	13 49	14 06	14 19	14 36	14 49	15 06	15 20	15 37		15 49	16 07	16 19	16 36	16 52	17 06	17 21	17 37

Table 228

Saturdays

Edinburgh - Falkirk High - Glasgow Queen Street

		SR	SR	SR	SR	SR	SR	SR	SR	SR	SR	SR	SR	SR	SR	SR	SR	SR	SR
		1	1	1	1	1	1	1	1	1	1	1	1	1	1	1	1	1	1
		⌶	⌶	⌶	⌶	⌶	⌶	⌶	⌶	⌶	⌶								
Edinburgh 10	225,230,242 d	17 00	17 15	17 30	17 45	18 00	18 15	18 30	18 45	19 00	19 15	19 30	20 00	20 30	21 00	21 30	22 00	22 30	23 00	23 30
Haymarket	225,230,242 d	17 03	17 18	17 33	17 48	18 03	18 18	18 33	18 48	19 03	19 18	19 33	20 03	20 33	21 03	21 33	22 03	22 33	23 03	23 33
Linlithgow	230 d		17 33		18 03		18 33		19 03		19 33	19 48	20 18	20 48	21 18	21 48	22 18	22 48	23 18	23 48
Polmont 3	230 d		17 39		18 09		18 39		19 09		19 39		20 24		21 24		22 24		23 24	23 54
Falkirk High	d	17 23	17 44	17 53	18 14	18 23	18 44	18 53	19 14	19 23	19 44	19 57	20 29	20 57	21 29	21 57	22 29	22 57	23 29	23 58
Croy 3	230 a	17 33		18 03		18 33		19 02		19 33		20 07		21 07		22 07		23 07	23 38	00 08
Lenzie 3	230 a			18 08														23 12	23 45	00 14
Bishopbriggs	230 a																		23 49	
Glasgow Queen Street 10	230 a	17 51	18 06	18 22	18 37	18 52	19 06	19 21	19 36	19 49	20 06	20 22	20 50	21 22	21 50	22 22	22 50	23 30	00 01	00 27

Sundays

		SR	SR	SR	SR	SR	SR	SR	SR	SR	SR	SR	SR	SR	SR	SR	SR	SR	SR	SR	SR	SR	SR	SR
		1	1	1	1	1	1	1	1	1	1	1	1	1	1	1	1	1	1	1	1	1	1	1
		⌶	⌶	⌶	⌶	⌶	⌶	⌶	⌶	⌶		⌶	⌶	⌶	⌶	⌶		⌶	⌶	⌶	⌶			
Edinburgh 10	225,230,242 d	08 00	09 00	10 00	11 00	12 00	12 30	13 00	13 30	14 00	14 30	15 00	15 30	16 00	16 30	17 00	17 30	18 00	18 30	19 00	19 30	20 00	20 30	21 00
Haymarket	225,230,242 d	08 03	09 03	10 03	11 03	12 03	12 33	13 03	13 33	14 03	14 33	15 03	15 33	16 03	16 33	17 03	17 33	18 03	18 33	19 03	19 33	20 04	20 33	21 03
Linlithgow	230 d	08 18	09 18	10 18	11 18	12 18	12 48	13 18	13 48	14 18	14 48	15 18	15 46	16 18	16 48	17 18	17 48	18 18	18 48	19 18	19 48	20 18	20 48	21 18
Polmont 3	230 d	08 24	09 24	10 24	11 24	12 24		13 24		14 24		15 24		16 24		17 24		18 24		19 24		20 24		21 23
Falkirk High	d	08 29	09 29	10 29	11 29	12 29	12 57	13 29	13 57	14 29	14 57	15 29	15 55	16 29	16 57	17 29	17 57	18 29	18 57	19 29	19 57	20 29	20 57	21 29
Croy 3	230 a	08 39	09 39	10 39	11 39	12 38	13 07		14 07		15 07		16 05		17 07		18 07		19 07		20 07		21 07	21 38
Lenzie 3	230 a																							
Bishopbriggs	230 a																							
Glasgow Queen Street 10	230 a	08 59	10 00	11 00	11 56	12 54	13 23	13 51	14 23	14 51	15 22	15 51	16 22	16 51	17 22	17 52	18 22	18 51	19 22	19 51	20 22	20 51	21 22	21 55

		SR	SR	SR
		1	1	1
Edinburgh 10	225,230,242 d	22 00	23 00	23 30
Haymarket	225,230,242 d	22 02	23 02	23 33
Linlithgow	230 d	22 18	23 18	23 48
Polmont 3	230 d	22 24	23 24	23 54
Falkirk High	d	22 29	23 29	23 59
Croy 3	230 a	22 39	23 39	00 08
Lenzie 3	230 a			
Bishopbriggs	230 a			
Glasgow Queen Street 10	230 a	22 55	23 55	00 25

Table 228

Mondays to Fridays

Glasgow Queen Street - Falkirk High - Edinburgh

		SR	SR	SR	SR	SR	SR	SR	SR	SR	SR	SR	SR	SR	SR	SR	SR	SR	SR	SR	SR	SR	SR
		1	1	1	1	1	1	1	1	1	1	1	1	1	1	1	1	1	1	1	1	1	1
				⌶	⌶	⌶	⌶	⌶	⌶	⌶	⌶	⌶	⌶	⌶	⌶	⌶	⌶	⌶	⌶	⌶	⌶	⌶	⌶
Glasgow Queen Street 10	230 d	06 30	06 45	07 00	07 15	07 30	07 45	08 00	08 15	08 30	08 45	09 00	09 15	09 30	09 45	10 00	10 15	10 30	10 45	11 00	11 15	11 30	11 45
Bishopbriggs	230 d																						
Lenzie 3	230 d	06 38		07 09																			
Croy 3	230 d		06 56			07 41		08 11		08 41		09 11		09 41		10 11		10 41		11 11		11 41	
Falkirk High	d	06 51	07 06	07 22	07 32	07 51	08 02	08 21	08 32	08 51	09 02	09 21	09 32	09 51	10 02	10 21	10 32	10 51	11 02	11 21	11 32	11 51	12 02
Polmont 3	230 a	06 56		07 26	07 37		08 07	08 26			09 07		09 37		10 07		10 37		11 07		11 37		12 07
Linlithgow	230 a	07 02	07 13	07 33	07 43	07 58	08 13		08 41		09 13		09 43		10 13		10 43		11 13		11 43		12 13
Haymarket	225,230,242 a	07s18	07s31	07s49	07s59	08s17	08s32	08s45	09s00	09s13	09s31	09s43	10s01	10s11	10s31	10s41	11s02	11s15	11s29	11s42	12s00	12s12	12s29
Edinburgh 10	225,230,242 a	07 24	07 37	07 55	08 06	08 22	08 37	08 50	09 05	09 19	09 37	09 50	10 08	10 17	10 36	10 47	11 09	11 20	11 35	11 50	12 05	12 19	12 35

		SR	SR	SR	SR	SR	SR	SR	SR	SR	SR	SR	SR	SR	SR	SR	SR	SR	SR	SR	SR	SR	SR
		1	1	1	1	1	1	1	1	1	1	1	1	1	1	1	1	1	1	1	1	1	1
		⌶	⌶	⌶	⌶	⌶	⌶	⌶	⌶	⌶	⌶	⌶	⌶	⌶	⌶	⌶	⌶	⌶	⌶	⌶	⌶	⌶	⌶
Glasgow Queen Street 10	230 d	12 00	12 15	12 30	12 45	13 00	13 15	13 30	13 45	14 00	14 15	14 30	14 45	15 00	15 15	15 30	15 45	16 00	16 15	16 30	16 45	17 00	17 15
Bishopbriggs	230 d																						
Lenzie 3	230 d																						
Croy 3	230 d	12 11		12 41		13 11		13 41		14 11		14 41		15 11		15 41		16 11		16 41		17 11	
Falkirk High	d	12 21	12 32	12 51	13 02	13 21	13 32	13 51	14 02	14 21	14 32	14 51	15 02	15 21	15 32	15 51	16 02	16 21	16 32	16 51	17 02	17 21	17 33
Polmont 3	230 a		12 37		13 07		13 37		14 07		14 37		15 07		15 37		16 07		16 37		17 07	17 26	
Linlithgow	230 a		12 43		13 13		13 43		14 13		14 43		15 13		15 43		16 13		16 43		17 13		17 40
Haymarket	225,230,242 a	12s43	13s00	13s14	13s29	13s43	13s59	14s12	14s30	14s42	14s59	15s12	15s30	15s43	16s00	16s11	16s30	16s42	17s00	17s13	17s33	17s46	18s00
Edinburgh 10	225,230,242 a	12 50	13 05	13 20	13 35	13 50	14 05	14 19	14 37	14 47	15 06	15 17	15 37	15 50	16 05	16 17	16 36	16 49	17 06	17 19	17 39	17 51	18 06

		SR	SR	SR	SR	SR	SR	SR	SR	SR	SR	SR	SR	SR	SR	SR	SR	SR	SR
		1	1	1	1	1	1	1	1	1	1	1	1	1	1	1	1	1	1
		⌶	⌶	⌶	⌶	⌶	⌶	⌶	⌶	⌶									
Glasgow Queen Street 10	230 d	17 30	17 33	17 46	18 00	18 15	18 31	18 45	19 00	19 15	19 30	20 00	20 30	21 00	21 30	22 00	22 30	23 00	23 30
Bishopbriggs	230 d		17 38																
Lenzie 3	230 d		17 43																
Croy 3	230 d	17 41			18 11		18 42		19 11			20 11		21 11		22 11		23 11	23 41
Falkirk High	d	17 51		18 02	18 21	18 32	18 52	19 02	19 21	19 32	19 47	20 21	20 47	21 21	21 47	22 21	22 47	23 21	23 51
Polmont 3	230 a	17 56	18 12	18 07		18 37		19 07		19 37	19 52		20 52		21 52		22 52	23 26	23 57
Linlithgow	230 a	18 03	18 19	18 13		18 43		19 13		19 43	19 58	20 28	20 58	21 28	21 58	22 28	22 58	23 33	00 03
Haymarket	225,230,242 a	18s21		18s32	18s42	19s00	19s12	19s30	19s42	20s01	20s15	20s46	21s13	21s46	22s24	22s45	23s15	23s49	00s19
Edinburgh 10	225,230,242 a	18 26		18 40	18 50	19 05	19 19	19 36	19 47	20 06	20 21	20 51	21 20	21 53	22 30	22 50	23 22	23 54	00 25

Saturdays

		SR	SR	SR	SR	SR	SR	SR	SR	SR	SR	SR	SR	SR	SR	SR	SR	SR	SR	SR	SR	SR	SR	SR	SR
		1	1	1	1	1	1	1	1	1	1	1	1	1	1	1	1	1	1	1	1	1	1	1	1
				⌶	⌶	⌶	⌶	⌶	⌶	⌶	⌶	⌶	⌶	⌶		⌶	⌶	⌶	⌶	⌶	⌶	⌶	⌶	⌶	⌶
Glasgow Queen Street 10	230 d	06 00	06 30	07 00	07 15	07 30	07 45	08 00	08 15	08 30	08 45	09 00	09 15	09 30	09 45	10 00	10 15	10 30	10 45	11 00	11 15	11 30	11 45	12 00	12 15
Bishopbriggs	230 d																								
Lenzie 3	230 d		06 38	07 09																					
Croy 3	230 d		06 44			07 41		08 11		08 41		09 11		09 41		10 11		10 41		11 11		11 41		12 11	
Falkirk High	d	06 17	06 54	07 22	07 32	07 51	08 02	08 21	08 32	08 51	09 02	09 21	09 32	09 51	10 02	10 21	10 32	10 51	11 02	11 21	11 32	11 51	12 02	12 21	12 32
Polmont 3	230 a	06 21	06 58	07 26	07 37		08 07	08 26			09 07		09 37		10 07		10 37		11 07		11 37		12 07		12 37
Linlithgow	230 a	06 29	07 05	07 33	07 43	07 58	08 13		08 41		09 13		09 43		10 13		10 43		11 13		11 43		12 13		12 43
Haymarket	225,230,242 a	06s45	07s21	07s49	08s01	08s16	08s33	08s45	09s00	09s13	09s31	09s43	10s01	10s12	10s30	10s41	11s00	11s13	11s29	11s44	12s00	12s12	12s29	12s43	13s01
Edinburgh 10	225,230,242 a	06 50	07 26	07 56	08 07	08 22	08 38	08 50	09 07	09 19	09 37	09 50	10 07	10 17	10 35	10 47	11 05	11 22	11 35	11 50	12 05	12 19	12 35	12 52	13 05

		SR	SR	SR	SR	SR	SR	SR	SR	SR	SR	SR	SR	SR	SR	SR	SR	SR	SR	SR	SR
		1	1	1	1	1	1	1	1	1	1	1	1	1	1	1	1	1	1	1	1
		⌶	⌶	⌶	⌶	⌶	⌶	⌶	⌶	⌶	⌶	⌶	⌶	⌶	⌶	⌶	⌶	⌶	⌶	⌶	⌶
Glasgow Queen Street 10	230 d	12 30	12 45	13 00	13 15	13 30	13 45	14 00	14 15	14 30	14 45	15 00	15 15	15 30	15 45	16 00	16 15	16 30	16 45	17 00	17 15
Bishopbriggs	230 d																				
Lenzie 3	230 d																				
Croy 3	230 d	12 41		13 11		13 41		14 11		14 41		15 11		15 41		16 11		16 41		17 11	
Falkirk High	d	12 51	13 02	13 21	13 32	13 51	14 02	14 21	14 32	14 51	15 02	15 21	15 32	15 51	16 02	16 21	16 32	16 51	17 02	17 21	17 33
Polmont 3	230 a		13 07		13 37		14 07		14 37		15 07		15 37		16 06		16 37		17 07	17 26	
Linlithgow	230 a		13 13		13 43		14 13		14 43		15 13		15 43		16 13		16 43		17 13		17 40
Haymarket	225,230,242 a	13s14	13s29	13s43	13s59	14s12	14s29	14s46	14s59	15s12	15s30	15s43	16s00	16s11	16s32	16s46	17s00	17s13	17s33	17s46	18s00
Edinburgh 10	225,230,242 a	13 22	13 35	13 52	14 05	14 19	14 37	14 52	15 05	15 17	15 37	15 50	16 05	16 17	16 39	16 52	17 07	17 18	17 39	17 51	18 06

		SR	SR	SR	SR	SR	SR	SR	SR	SR	SR	SR	SR	SR	SR	SR	SR	SR	SR
		1	1	1	1	1	1	1	1	1	1	1	1	1	1	1	1	1	1
		⌶	⌶	⌶	⌶	⌶	⌶	⌶	⌶										
Glasgow Queen Street 10	230 d	17 30	17 45	18 00	18 15	18 30	18 45	19 00	19 15	19 30	20 00	20 30	21 00	21 30	22 00	22 30	23 00	23 30
Bishopbriggs	230 d																	
Lenzie 3	230 d																	
Croy 3	230 d	17 41		18 11		18 41		19 11			20 11		21 11		22 11		23 11	23 41
Falkirk High	d	17 51	18 02	18 21	18 32	18 51	19 02	19 21	19 32	19 47	20 21	20 47	21 21	21 47	22 21	22 47	23 21	23 51
Polmont 3	230 a	17 56	18 07		18 37		19 07		19 37	19 52		20 52		21 52		22 52	23 26	23 57
Linlithgow	230 a	18 03	18 13		18 43		19 13		19 43	19 58	20 28	20 58	21 28	21 58	22 28	22 58	23 33	00 03
Haymarket	225,230,242 a	18s21	18s32	18s42	19s00	19s11	19s34	19s42	20s01	20s15	20s46	21s13	21s46	22s18	22s45	23s15	23s49	00s19
Edinburgh 10	225,230,242 a	18 26	18 40	18 50	19 05	19 19	19 39	19 47	20 06	20 21	20 51	21 20	21 53	22 24	22 50	23 22	23 54	00 25

Table 228

Sundays

Glasgow Queen Street - Falkirk High - Edinburgh

		SR	SR	SR	SR	SR	SR	SR	SR	SR	SR	SR	SR	SR	SR	SR	SR	SR	SR	SR
		[1]	[1]	[1]	[1]	[1]	[1]	[1]	[1]	[1]	[1]	[1]	[1]	[1]	[1]	[1]	[1]	[1]	[1]	[1]
			⌶	⌶	⌶	⌶	⌶	⌶		⌶	⌶		⌶	⌶	⌶	⌶	⌶	⌶	⌶	⌶
Glasgow Queen Street [10] 230	d	07 50	08 30	09 30	10 30	11 30	12 30	13 00	13 30	14 00	14 30	15 00	15 30	16 00	16 30	17 00	17 30	18 00	18 30	19 00
Bishopbriggs 230	d																			
Lenzie [3] 230	d																			
Croy [3] 230	d	08 01	08 41	09 41	10 41	11 41	12 41	13 11		14 11		15 11		16 11		17 11		18 11		19 11
Falkirk High	d	08 11	08 51	09 51	10 51	11 51	12 51	13 21	13 47	14 21	14 47	15 21	15 47	16 21	16 47	17 21	17 47	18 21	18 47	19 21
Polmont [3] 230	a	08 16	08 56	09 56	10 56	11 56	12 56		13 52		14 52		15 52		16 53		17 53		18 53	
Linlithgow 230	a	08 22	09 02	10 02	11 02	12 02	13 02	13 28	13 58	14 28	14 58	15 28	15 58	16 28	16 58	17 28	17 58	18 28	18 58	19 28
Haymarket 225,230,242	a	08s44	09s23	10s23	11s19	12s19	13s21	13s46	14s17	14s47	15s16	15 46	16s17	16s50	17s16	17s47	18s17	18s50	19s16	19s47
Edinburgh [10] 225,230,242	a	08 49	09 28	10 28	11 24	12 24	13 26	13 51	14 22	14 52	15 21	15 51	16 22	16 55	17 21	17 52	18 22	18 55	19 21	19 52

		SR	SR	SR	SR	SR	SR	SR
		[1]	[1]	[1]	[1]	[1]	[1]	[1]
		⌶						
Glasgow Queen Street [10] 230	d	19 30	20 00	20 30	21 00	21 30	22 30	23 30
Bishopbriggs 230	d							
Lenzie [3] 230	d							
Croy [3] 230	d		20 11		21 11	21 42	22 41	23 41
Falkirk High	d	19 47	20 21	20 47	21 21	21 52	22 51	23 51
Polmont [3] 230	a	19 53		20 53		21 56	22 56	23 56
Linlithgow 230	a	19 58	20 28	20 58	21 28	22 02	23 02	00 02
Haymarket 225,230,242	a	20s16	20s46	21s17	21s45	22s19	23s19	00s19
Edinburgh [10] 225,230,242	a	20 21	20 51	21 22	21 53	22 24	23 24	00 24

Table 229

Mondays to Saturdays

until 18 September

Edinburgh and Glasgow Queen Street - Perth, Inverness, Dundee, Aberdeen, Dyce and Inverurie

		SR	SR	SR	XC	SR	XC	SR	SR	SR	SR	SR	SR	SR	SR	SR
			◇[1]	[1]	◇[1]	◇[1]	◇	◇[1]	[1]	[1]	◇[1]	◇[1]	[1]	◇[1]	[1]	◇[1]
								B				A				A
								⌶				⌶		⌶		⌶
Edinburgh [10] 242	d					05 30	05 33		06 29	07 00		07 30	07 35		08 00	08 29
Haymarket 242	d					05 33			06 33	07 04		07 33	07 39		08 03	08 33
Inverkeithing 242	d					05 46	06 06		06 47	07 20			07 53		08 17	
Kirkcaldy 242	d					06 02			07 03	07 36		08 02	08 09		08 33	
Markinch	d					06 11	06 39		07 12	07 45			08 19		08 42	
Ladybank	d					06 19			07 19	07 53					08 50	
Springfield	d														08 55	
Cupar	d					06 25	06 51			07 59					08 59	
Leuchars [3]	a					06 32	06 57			08 06		08 25			09 05	09 25
St Andrews Bus Station 🚌	a															
St Andrews Bus Station 🚌	d															
Leuchars [3]	d					06 32	06 58			08 06		08 25			09 06	09 25
Glasgow Queen St. [10] 230 ⛴	d							05 55			07 06			07 41		
Larbert 230	d							06 15								
Stirling 230	d							06 24			07 33			08 07		
Dunblane 230	d							06 31			07 39			08 14		
Gleneagles	d							06 43								
Perth	a							06 59	07 47		08 04		08 53	08 40		
	d			06 01				07 00	07 47		08 04			08 41		
Invergowrie	d								08 05							
Dundee	a			06 23		06 45	07 13	07 21	08 13	08 23		08 40		09 03	09 21	09 37
Broughty Ferry	d															
Carnoustie	d					07 03		07 35						09 16		
Arbroath	d			06 41	06 56	07 10		07 42				08 57		09 23		09 55
Montrose	d		06 25	06 57	07 11	07 23		07 58				09 13		09 38		
Laurencekirk	d		06 35			07 35		08 09								10 16
Stonehaven	d		06 49	07 22	07 32	07 48		08 22				09 34				10 29
Portlethen	d		06 58			07 59		08 31								
Aberdeen	a		07 13	07 44	07 55	08 13		08 44				09 52		10 16		10 53
	d		07 14	07 50				08 50				10 00				11 04
Dyce 240 ✈	a		07 24	08 00				08 59				10 08				11 13
Inverurie 240	a		07 44	08 17								10 22				11 30
Dunkeld & Birnam	d										08 29					
Pitlochry	d										08 42					
Blair Atholl	d										08 52					
Dalwhinnie	d										09 16					
Newtonmore	d										09 27					
Kingussie	d										09 32					
Aviemore	d	07 57									09 44					
Carrbridge	d	08 05									09 57					
Inverness	a	08 43	09 40								10 29					

A ⌶ to Stonehaven

B ⌶ to Portlethen

Table 229

Mondays to Saturdays
until 18 September

Edinburgh and Glasgow Queen Street - Perth, Inverness, Dundee, Aberdeen, Dyce and Inverurie

		SR	SR	SR	SR SX	SR SO	SR	SR	SR	SR	GR SO	GR SX	SR	SR
		◇1 ⌶	◇1 ⌶	1	◇1 ⌶	◇1 ⌶	◇1 ⌶	1	1	◇1 ⌶	1 ⌶	1 ⌶	1	◇1 ⌶
Edinburgh 10	242 d		08 33	08 57	09 30	09 30		09 35	10 00		10 26	10b27	10 34	
Haymarket	242 d		08 37	09 02	09 34	09 34		09 39	10 03		10 31	10 32	10 38	
Inverkeithing	242 d			09 17				09 53	10 18		10 46	10 47	10 53	
Kirkcaldy	242 d		09 06	09 33				10 09	10 34		11 03	11 04	11 10	
Markinch	d		09 15	09 42				10 18	10 43				11 20	
Ladybank	d			09 50				10 25	10 50				11 27	
Springfield	d													
Cupar	d			09 56					10 57					
Leuchars 3	a			10 03		10 23			11 03		11 27	11 28		
St Andrews Bus Station	a													
St Andrews Bus Station	d													
Leuchars 3	d			10 03		10 23			11 04		11 28	11 29		
Glasgow Queen St. 10 230	d	08 41					09 41			10 11				10 41
Larbert	230 d													
Stirling	230 d	09 07					10 07			10 36				11 07
Dunblane	230 d									10 42				
Gleneagles	d									10 54				
Perth	a	09 36	09 48				10 34	10 53		11 13			11 54	11 37
	d	09 36	09 50				10 36			11 13				11 38
Invergowrie	d													
Dundee	a	09 59		10 18	10 32	10 35	11 00		11 20		11 43	11 43		11 59
Broughty Ferry	d													
Carnoustie	d						11 11							
Arbroath	d	10 17			10 50	10 53	11 18				12 01	12 01		12 17
Montrose	d	10 31			11 04	11 07	11 34				12 17	12 17		12 32
Laurencekirk	d													12 43
Stonehaven	d	10 53			11 26	11 29					12 40	12 40		
Portlethen	d	11 02												
Aberdeen	a	11 17			11 45	11 48	12 14				13 03	13 03		13 14
	d													
Dyce	240 a													
Inverurie	240 a													
Dunkeld & Birnam	d									11 34				
Pitlochry	d		10 19							11 47				
Blair Atholl	d									11 57				
Dalwhinnie	d													
Newtonmore	d									12 21				
Kingussie	d		11 01							12 34				
Aviemore	d		11 14							12 46				
Carrbridge	d									12 55				
Inverness	a		11 54							13 27				

b arr. 1020

Table 229

Mondays to Saturdays
until 18 September

Edinburgh and Glasgow Queen Street - Perth, Inverness, Dundee, Aberdeen, Dyce and Inverurie

		SR	SR	SR	SR	SR	SR SX	SR SO	SR	SR	SR	SR
		1	◇1 ⌶	◇1 ⌶	◇1 ⌶	1	◇1 A ⌶	◇1 A ⌶	1	◇1 ⌶	1	◇1 A ⌶
Edinburgh 10	242 d	11 00	11 30	11 35		12 00	12 30	12 30	12 35		13 00	13 30
Haymarket	242 d	11 04	11 33	11u39		12 03	12 34	12 34	12 39		13 03	13 33
Inverkeithing	242 d	11 17				12 17			12 53		13 17	
Kirkcaldy	242 d	11 33		12u08		12 35			13 09		13 33	
Markinch	d	11 42		12 17		12 42			13 16		13 42	
Ladybank	d	11 50				12 49					13 50	
Springfield	d											
Cupar	d	11 56				12 56					13 56	
Leuchars 3	a	12 03	12 23			13 03	13 23	13 23			14 03	14 23
St Andrews Bus Station	a											
St Andrews Bus Station	d											
Leuchars 3	d	12 03	12 23			13 03	13 23	13 23			14 03	14 23
Glasgow Queen St. 10 230	d				11 41					12 41		
Larbert	230 d											
Stirling	230 d				12 07					13 07		
Dunblane	230 d											
Gleneagles	d											
Perth	a			12 52	12 36				13 53	13 35		
	d			12 54	12 37					13 36		
Invergowrie	d											
Dundee	a	12 18	12 36		12 59	13 18	13 35	13 35		14 00	14 18	14 35
Broughty Ferry	d											
Carnoustie	d				13 12							
Arbroath	d		12 53		13 19		13 53	13 53		14 18		14 53
Montrose	d				13 33		14 07	14 07		14 32		
Laurencekirk	d											
Stonehaven	d		13 27				14 29	14 34		14 54		15 27
Portlethen	d											
Aberdeen	a		13 46		14 12		14 53	14 56		15 13		15 49
	d						14 56	14 56				15 55
Dyce	240 a						15 04	15 04				16 03
Inverurie	240 a						15 19	15 19				16 18
Dunkeld & Birnam	d			13 11								
Pitlochry	d			13 24								
Blair Atholl	d			13 34								
Dalwhinnie	d											
Newtonmore	d			14 11								
Kingussie	d			14 16								
Aviemore	d			14 28								
Carrbridge	d											
Inverness	a			15 06								

A ⌶ to Stonehaven

Table 229

Mondays to Saturdays
until 18 September

Edinburgh and Glasgow Queen Street - Perth, Inverness, Dundee, Aberdeen, Dyce and Inverurie

			SR	SR	SR	SR	SR	SR	GR SX	GR SO	SR	SR	SR SO	SR	SR	SR	SR
			◇1 🍴	◇1 🍴	1	◇1 🍴	1	◇1 🍴	■ 1 A 🍴	■ 1 A 🍴	1		◇1 B 🍴	1	◇1 🍴	1	◇1 🍴
Edinburgh 10	242	d	13 35		14 00	14 30	14 35		15b00	15b00	15 03	15 08	15 30	15 35		16 00	
Haymarket	242	d	13u39		14 04	14 33	14 38		15 04	15 04	15 08	15 13	15 34	15 39		16 04	
Inverkeithing	242	d			14 17		14 53		15 19	15 19	15 25	15 32		15 53		16 17	
Kirkcaldy	242	d	14u07		14 33		15 09		15 36	15 36	15 42	15 54		16 09		16 33	
Markinch		d	14 17		14 42		15 18				15 51			16 18		16 42	
Ladybank		d			14 50		15 25				15 59			16 25		16 50	
Springfield		d															
Cupar		d			14 56						16 05					16 56	
Leuchars 3		a			15 03	15 23			16 00	16 00	16 12		16 23			17 03	
St Andrews Bus Station	bus	a															
St Andrews Bus Station	bus	d															
Leuchars 3		d			15 03	15 23			16 00	16 00	16 12		16 23			17 03	
Glasgow Queen St. 10	230	d		13 41				14 41							15 41		16 11
Larbert	230	d															
Stirling	230	d		14 07				15 07							16 07		16 37
Dunblane	230	d															16 48
Gleneagles		d															17 00
Perth		a	14 52	14 36			15 54	15 36						16 54	16 36		17 18
		d	14 54	14 36				15 36							16 36		17 18
Invergowrie		d															
Dundee		a		14 59	15 18	15 37		15 59	16 18	16 19	16 28		16 35		17 00	17 20	
Broughty Ferry		d															
Carnoustie		d		15 12											17 13		
Arbroath		d		15 19		15 54		16 17	16 36	16 37			16 54		17 20		
Montrose		d		15 39		16 08		16 31	16 52	16 53			17 08		17 33		
Laurencekirk		d		15 50									17 19				
Stonehaven		d				16 30			17 15	17 16			17 33		17 55		
Portlethen		d															
Aberdeen		a		16 20		16 50		17 11	17 37	17 38			17 52		18 15		
		d											17 56				
Dyce	240 ✈	a											18 04				
Inverurie	240	a											18 19				
Dunkeld & Birnam		d	15 11														17 37
Pitlochry		d	15 24														17 50
Blair Atholl		d	15 34														17 59
Dalwhinnie		d	16 01														
Newtonmore		d															18 32
Kingussie		d	16 14														18 37
Aviemore		d	16 27														18 48
Carrbridge		d															18 54
Inverness		a	17 05														19 34

A The Northern Lights
B 🍴 to Stonehaven
b arr. 1453

Table 229

Mondays to Saturdays
until 18 September

Edinburgh and Glasgow Queen Street - Perth, Inverness, Dundee, Aberdeen, Dyce and Inverurie

			SR	SR	GR	SR	SR	SR	SR SO	SR SX	SR	SR SX	XC SO	XC SX
			◇1 A 🍴	1	■ 1 B 🍴	◇1 🍴		◇1 🍴	◇1 🍴	◇1 🍴	◇1 🍴	1	◇1 🍴	◇1
Edinburgh 10	242	d	16 29	16 32	16b33		17 03	17 35			17 41	18 00	18 08	18 16
Haymarket	242	d	16u33	16 37	16 38		17 07	17 39			17u45	18 04	18 13	18 21
Inverkeithing	242	d		16 51			17 22					18 22	18 26	18 38
Kirkcaldy	242	d		17 07			17 39				18 16	18 40	18 42	19 00
Markinch		d		17 17			17 48				18 25	18 51	18 51	19 09
Ladybank		d		17 26			17 56				18 32	18 58	18 58	19 16
Springfield		d					18 01							
Cupar		d	17 17				18 05	18 28				19 05	19 05	19 23
Leuchars 3		a	17 24				18 12	18 34				19 11	19 11	19 29
St Andrews Bus Station	bus	a												
St Andrews Bus Station	bus	d												
Leuchars 3		d	17 24				18 12	18 35				19 12	19 12	19 30
Glasgow Queen St. 10	230	d				16 41			17 41	17 41				
Larbert	230	d												
Stirling	230	d			17 20	17 07			18 07	18 15				
Dunblane	230	d							18 15	18 22				
Gleneagles		d			17 40				18 27	18 35				
Perth		a		17 54	18 00	17 36			18 43	18 52	18 59			
		d			18 00	17 37			18 44	18 53	19 00			
Invergowrie		d												
Dundee		a	17 38			17 59	18 34	18 47	19 06	19 15		19 27	19 24	19 44
Broughty Ferry		d	17 47				19 00							
Carnoustie		d	17 55			18 13	19a17		19 27	19 28				
Arbroath		d	18 02			18 20		19 04	19 34	19 35			19 42	20 02
Montrose		d	18 16					19 24	19 48	19 49			20 02	20 16
Laurencekirk		d	18 27											
Stonehaven		d	18 41			18 53		19 45	20 10	20 11			20 23	20 36
Portlethen		d						19 54						
Aberdeen		a	19 00			19 13		20 08	20 29	20 32			20 41	20 55
		d	19 07											
Dyce	240 ✈	a	19 16											
Inverurie	240	a	19 35											
Dunkeld & Birnam		d									19 17			
Pitlochry		d			18 33						19 30			
Blair Atholl		d												
Dalwhinnie		d												
Newtonmore		d												
Kingussie		d			19 17						20 13			
Aviemore		d			19 29						20 25			
Carrbridge		d												
Inverness		a			20 08						21 03			

A 🍴 to Stonehaven
B The Highland Chieftain
b arr. 1627

Table 229

Mondays to Saturdays
until 18 September

Edinburgh and Glasgow Queen Street - Perth, Inverness, Dundee, Aberdeen, Dyce and Inverurie

		GR SX	GR SO	SR	SR	SR	SR	SR	SR	SR	XC SX	XC	XC	GR SX	SR SX	SR SO	SR
		■ 1	■ 1	1	◇1	1	◇1 A	◇1	◇1		◇1	◇1 B	◇1 C	■ 1	1	1	◇1
Edinburgh 10	242 d	18 30	18 32	18 40		19 00	19 30	19 35		20 00	20 15	20b22	20b22	20 32	20 37	20 37	
Haymarket	242 d	18 35	18 37	18 45		19 03	19 33	19 39		20 04	20 20	20 26	20 26	20 37	20 41	20 41	
Inverkeithing	242 d	18 54	18 54	19 00		19 17		19 54		20 23	20 35	20 44	20 45	20 52	21 00	21 00	
Kirkcaldy	242 d	19 11	19 11	19 18		19 33		20 10		20 45	20 51	21 01	21 00	21 09	21 17	21 17	
Markinch	d			19 28		19 42		20 19		20 54	21 00	21 11	21 10		21 26	21 26	
Ladybank	d			19 35		19 50		20 26		21 01	21 08	21 19	21 18		21 33	21 36	
Springfield	d																
Cupar	d					19 56	20 21			21 08	21 15	21 28	21 25				
Leuchars 3	a	19 38	19 38			20 03	20 28			21 14	21 21	21 35	21 31	21 33			
St Andrews Bus Station	bus a																
St Andrews Bus Station	bus d																
Leuchars 3	d	19 38	19 39			20 03	20 28			21 15	21 22	21 36	21 32	21 33			
Glasgow Queen St. 10 230	d				18 41				19 41								20 41
Larbert	230 d																
Stirling	230 d				19 07				20 07								21 07
Dunblane	230 d				19 14												21 14
Gleneagles	d				19 26												21 26
Perth	a			20 02	19 42			20 53	20 36						22 01	22 03	21 42
	d				19 43			20 54	20 36								21 43
Invergowrie	d				20 01												22 01
Dundee	a	19 53	19 53		20 08	20 18	20 40		20 59	21 30	21 40	21 52	21 47	21 47			22 07
Broughty Ferry	d																
Carnoustie	d																
Arbroath	d	20 11	20 11		20 25		20 58		21 17					22 05			22 25
Montrose	d	20 27	20 27		20 40		21 12							22 22			22 39
Laurencekirk	d								21 40								
Stonehaven	d	20 50	20 50				21 34		21 54					22 45			23 01
Portlethen	d																
Aberdeen	a	21 12	21 12		21 19		21 53		22 13					23 07			23 20
	d						21 55										
Dyce	240 ✈ a						22 04										
Inverurie	240 a						22 16										
Dunkeld & Birnam	d							21 12									
Pitlochry	d							21 25									
Blair Atholl	d							21 34									
Dalwhinnie	d							22 00									
Newtonmore	d							22 11									
Kingussie	d							22 21									
Aviemore	d							22 32									
Carrbridge	d							22 41									
Inverness	a						00 05	23 14									

A ⊼ to Stonehaven
B SO until 4 September
C 11 September, 18 September
b arr. 2015

Table 229

Mondays to Saturdays
until 18 September

Edinburgh and Glasgow Queen Street - Perth, Inverness, Dundee, Aberdeen, Dyce and Inverurie

		SR SO	SR SX	SR SO	SR SX	SR SO	SR SX	SR	SR	SR
				◇1	◇1	◇1	◇1			
Edinburgh 10	242 d	21 00	21 09	21 32	21 40			22 09	22 39	23 09
Haymarket	242 d	21 04	21 13	21 36	21 44			22 13	22 43	23 13
Inverkeithing	242 d	21 23	21 32					22 32	23 02	23 32
Kirkcaldy	242 d	21 45	21 54	22 04	22 12			22 54	23 24	23 54
Markinch	d	21 54	22 03					23 03	23 33	00 03
Ladybank	d	22 01	22 10					23 13	23 40	00 10
Springfield	d							23 18		
Cupar	d	22 08	22 17					23 22		00 17
Leuchars 3	a	22 14	22 23	22 28	22 33			23 28		00 23
St Andrews Bus Station	bus a									
St Andrews Bus Station	bus d									
Leuchars 3	d	22 15	22 24	22 28	22 34			23 29		00 24
Glasgow Queen St. 10 230	d					21 41	21 41			
Larbert	230 d									
Stirling	230 d					22 07	22 07			
Dunblane	230 d									
Gleneagles	d									
Perth	a					22 36	22 35		00 07	
	d					22 37	22 35			
Invergowrie	d									
Dundee	a	22 30	22 39	22 42	22 48	22 58	23 03	23 44		00 39
Broughty Ferry	d									
Carnoustie	d					23 10	23 15			
Arbroath	d			23 00	23 05	23 17	23 25			
Montrose	d			23 14	23 24	23 33	23 41			
Laurencekirk	d			23 25			23 52			
Stonehaven	d			23 39	23 46	23 55	00 06			
Portlethen	d				23 55	00 05				
Aberdeen	a			23 58	00 08	00 18	00 26			
	d									
Dyce	240 ✈ a									
Inverurie	240 a									
Dunkeld & Birnam	d									
Pitlochry	d									
Blair Atholl	d									
Dalwhinnie	d									
Newtonmore	d									
Kingussie	d									
Aviemore	d									
Carrbridge	d									
Inverness	a									

Table 229

Mondays to Saturdays
from 20 September

Edinburgh and Glasgow Queen Street - Perth, Inverness, Dundee, Aberdeen, Dyce and Inverurie

			SR	SR	SR	XC	SR	XC	SR	SR SX	SR SO	SR SX	SR	SR	SR	SR	SR SX
				◇1	1	◇1	◇1	◇	◇1 B 🍴	1	1	1	◇1	◇1 A 🍴	1	◇1 🍴	1
Edinburgh 10	242	d					05 30	05 33		06 29		07 00		07 26	07 35		08 00
Haymarket	242	d					05 33			06 33	06 33	07 04		07 30	07 39		08 03
Inverkeithing	242	d					05 46	06 06		06 47	06 47	07 20			07 53		08 17
Kirkcaldy	242	d					06 02			07 03	07 03	07 36		08 02	08 09		08 33
Markinch		d					06 11	06 39		07 12	07 12	07 45			08 19		08 42
Ladybank		d					06 19			07 19	07 19	07 53					08 50
Springfield		d															08 55
Cupar		d					06 25	06 51				07 59					08 59
Leuchars 3		a					06 32	06 57				08 06		08 25			09 05
St Andrews Bus Station	bus	a															
St Andrews Bus Station	bus	d															
Leuchars 3		d					06 32	06 58				08 06		08 25			09 06
Glasgow Queen St. 10	230	d							05 55				07 06			07 41	
Larbert	230	d							06 15								
Stirling	230	d							06 24				07 33			08 07	
Dunblane	230	d							06 31				07 39			08 14	
Gleneagles		d							06 43								
Perth		a							06 59	07 47	07 47		08 04		08 53	08 40	
		d			06 01				07 00	07 47	07 47		08 04			08 41	
Invergowrie		d								08 05	08 05						
Dundee		a			06 23		06 45	07 13	07 21	08 13	08 13	08 23		08 40		09 03	09 21
Broughty Ferry		d															
Carnoustie		d					07 03		07 35							09 16	
Arbroath		d			06 41	06 56	07 10		07 42					08 57		09 23	
Montrose		d		06 25	06 57	07 11	07 23		07 58					09 13		09 38	
Laurencekirk		d		06 35			07 35		08 09								
Stonehaven		d		06 49	07 22	07 32	07 48		08 22					09 34			
Portlethen		d		06 58			07 59		08 31								
Aberdeen		a		07 13	07 44	07 55	08 13		08 44					09 52		10 16	
		d		07 14	07 50				08 50					10 00			
Dyce	240 ✈	a		07 24	08 00				08 59					10 08			
Inverurie	240	a		07 44	08 17									10 22			
Dunkeld & Birnam		d											08 29				
Pitlochry		d											08 42				
Blair Atholl		d											08 52				
Dalwhinnie		d											09 16				
Newtonmore		d											09 27				
Kingussie		d											09 32				
Aviemore		d	07 57										09 44				
Carrbridge		d	08 05										09 57				
Inverness		a	08 43	09 40									10 29				

A 🍴 to Stonehaven

B 🍴 to Portlethen

Table 229

Mondays to Saturdays
from 20 September

Edinburgh and Glasgow Queen Street - Perth, Inverness, Dundee, Aberdeen, Dyce and Inverurie

			SR	SR	SR	SR SX	SR SX	SR SO	SR	SR	SR SX	SR	GR SO	GR SX	SR	SR
			◇1 A 🍴	◇1 🍴	◇1 🍴	1	◇1 🍴	◇1 🍴	◇1 🍴	1	1	◇1 🍴	◼ 1 🍴	◼ 1 🍴	1	◇1 🍴
Edinburgh 10	242	d	08 29		08 33	08 57	09 30	09 30		09 35	10 00		10 26	10b27	10 34	
Haymarket	242	d	08 33		08 37	09 02	09 34	09 34		09 39	10 03		10 31	10 32	10 38	
Inverkeithing	242	d				09 17				09 53	10 18		10 46	10 47	10 53	
Kirkcaldy	242	d			09 06	09 33				10 09	10 34		11 03	11 04	11 10	
Markinch		d			09 15	09 42				10 18	10 43				11 20	
Ladybank		d				09 50				10 25	10 50				11 27	
Springfield		d														
Cupar		d				09 56					10 57					
Leuchars 3		a	09 25			10 03		10 23			11 03		11 27	11 28		
St Andrews Bus Station	bus	a														
St Andrews Bus Station	bus	d														
Leuchars 3		d	09 25			10 03		10 23			11 04		11 28	11 29		
Glasgow Queen St. 10	230	d		08 41					09 41			10 11				10 41
Larbert	230	d														
Stirling	230	d		09 07					10 07			10 36				11 07
Dunblane	230	d										10 42				
Gleneagles		d										10 54				
Perth		a		09 36	09 48				10 34	10 53		11 13			11 54	11 37
		d		09 36	09 50				10 36			11 13				11 38
Invergowrie		d														
Dundee		a	09 37	09 59		10 18	10 32	10 35	11 00		11 20		11 43	11 43		11 59
Broughty Ferry		d														
Carnoustie		d							11 11							
Arbroath		d	09 55	10 17			10 50	10 53	11 18				12 01	12 01		12 17
Montrose		d		10 31			11 04	11 07	11 34				12 17	12 17		12 32
Laurencekirk		d	10 16													12 43
Stonehaven		d	10 29	10 53			11 26	11 29					12 40	12 40		
Portlethen		d		11 02												
Aberdeen		a	10 53	11 17			11 45	11 48	12 14				13 03	13 03		13 14
		d	11 04													
Dyce	240 ✈	a	11 13													
Inverurie	240	a	11 30													
Dunkeld & Birnam		d										11 34				
Pitlochry		d			10 19							11 47				
Blair Atholl		d										11 57				
Dalwhinnie		d										12 21				
Newtonmore		d														
Kingussie		d			11 01							12 34				
Aviemore		d			11 14							12 46				
Carrbridge		d										12 55				
Inverness		a			11 54							13 27				

A 🍴 to Stonehaven

b arr. 1020

Table 229

Mondays to Saturdays
from 20 September

Edinburgh and Glasgow Queen Street - Perth, Inverness, Dundee, Aberdeen, Dyce and Inverurie

		SR SX	SR SO	SR	SR SO	SR	SR	SR SX	SR SX	SR SO	SR	SR	SR SX	SR SX	SR SO	SR	SR
		1	1	◇1	◇1	◇1	◇1	1	◇1	◇1	◇1	1	1	◇1	◇1	◇1	◇1
									A	A				A	A		
				🛒	🛒	🛒	🛒		🛒	🛒	🛒	🛒		🛒	🛒	🛒	🛒
Edinburgh 10	242 d	11 00		11 30	11 27	11 35		12 00	12 30	12 28		13 00	13 00	13 30	13 28	13 35	
Haymarket	242 d	11 04	11 04	11 33	11 30	11u39		12 03	12 34	12 33		13 03	13 03	13 33	13 31	13u39	
Inverkeithing	242 d	11 17	11 17					12 17					13 17				
Kirkcaldy	242 d	11 33	11 33			12u08		12 35					13 33			14u07	
Markinch	d	11 42	11 42			12 17		12 42					13 42			14 17	
Ladybank	d	11 50	11 50					12 49					13 50				
Springfield	d																
Cupar	d	11 56	11 56					12 56					13 56				
Leuchars 3	a	12 03	12 03	12 23	12 23			13 03	13 23	13 23			14 03	14 23	14 23		
St Andrews Bus Station	🚌 a																
St Andrews Bus Station	🚌 d																
Leuchars 3	d	12 03	12 03	12 23	12 23			13 03	13 23	13 23			14 03	14 23	14 23		
Glasgow Queen St. 10	230 ⛴ d						11 41				12 41	13a49					13 41
Larbert	230 d																
Stirling	230 d						12 07				13 07						14 07
Dunblane	230 d																
Gleneagles	d																
Perth	a					12 52	12 36				13 35					14 52	14 36
	d					12 54	12 37				13 36					14 54	14 36
Invergowrie	d																
Dundee	a	12 18	12 18	12 36	12 36		12 59	13 18	13 35	13 35	14 00		14 18	14 35	14 35		14 59
Broughty Ferry	d																
Carnoustie	d						13 12										15 12
Arbroath	d			12 53	12 53		13 19		13 53	13 53	14 18			14 53	14 53		15 19
Montrose	d						13 33		14 07	14 07	14 32						15 39
Laurencekirk	d																15 50
Stonehaven	d			13 27	13 27				14 29	14 34	14 54			15 27	15 27		
Portlethen	d																
Aberdeen	a			13 46	13 46		14 12		14 53	14 56	15 13			15 49	15 49		16 20
	d								14 56	14 56				15 55	15 55		
Dyce	240 ✈ a								15 04	15 04				16 03	16 03		
Inverurie	240 a								15 19	15 19				16 18	16 18		
Dunkeld & Birnam	d					13 11										15 11	
Pitlochry	d					13 24										15 24	
Blair Atholl	d					13 34										15 34	
Dalwhinnie	d															16 01	
Newtonmore	d					14 11											
Kingussie	d					14 16										16 14	
Aviemore	d					14 28										16 27	
Carrbridge	d																
Inverness	a					15 06										17 05	

A 🛒 to Stonehaven

Table 229

Mondays to Saturdays
from 20 September

Edinburgh and Glasgow Queen Street - Perth, Inverness, Dundee, Aberdeen, Dyce and Inverurie

		SR SX	SR	SR	SR	GR SX	GR SO	SR SX	SR SO	SR	SR	SR	SR SX	SR SO	SR	SR
		1	◇1	1	◇1	▪ 1	▪ 1	1	◇1	1	◇1	1	1	1	◇1	◇1
						A	A		B							B
			🛒		🛒	🛒 ⊘	🛏 🛒		🛒		🛒	🛒			🛒	🛒
Edinburgh 10	242 d	14 00	14 30	14 35		15b00	15b00	15 03	15 30	15 35		16 00	16 00			16 29
Haymarket	242 d	14 04	14 33	14 38		15 04	15 04	15 08	15 34	15 39		16 03	16 04	16 04		16u33
Inverkeithing	242 d	14 17		14 53		15 19	15 19	15 25		15 53			16 17	16 17		
Kirkcaldy	242 d	14 33		15 09		15 36	15 36	15 42		16 09			16 33	16 33		
Markinch	d	14 42		15 18				15 51		16 18			16 42	16 42		
Ladybank	d	14 50		15 25				15 59		16 25			16 50	16 50		
Springfield	d															
Cupar	d	14 56						16 05					16 56	16 56		17 17
Leuchars 3	a	15 03	15 23			16 00	16 00	16 12	16 23				17 03	17 03		17 24
St Andrews Bus Station	🚌 a															
St Andrews Bus Station	🚌 d															
Leuchars 3	d	15 03	15 23			16 00	16 00	16 12	16 23				17 03	17 03		17 24
Glasgow Queen St. 10	230 ⛴ d				14 41						15 41	16a52			16 11	
Larbert	230 d															
Stirling	230 d				15 07						16 07				16 37	
Dunblane	230 d														16 48	
Gleneagles	d														17 00	
Perth	a			15 54	15 36					16 54	16 36				17 18	
	d				15 36						16 36				17 18	
Invergowrie	d															
Dundee	a	15 18	15 37		15 59	16 18	16 19	16 28	16 35		17 00		17 20	17 20		17 38
Broughty Ferry	d															17 47
Carnoustie	d										17 13					17 55
Arbroath	d		15 54		16 17	16 36	16 37		16 54		17 20					18 02
Montrose	d		16 08		16 31	16 52	16 53		17 08		17 33					18 16
Laurencekirk	d								17 19							18 27
Stonehaven	d		16 30			17 15	17 16		17 33		17 55					18 41
Portlethen	d															
Aberdeen	a		16 50		17 11	17 37	17 38		17 52		18 15					19 00
	d								17 56							19 07
Dyce	240 ✈ a								18 04							19 16
Inverurie	240 a								18 19							19 35
Dunkeld & Birnam	d														17 37	
Pitlochry	d														17 50	
Blair Atholl	d														17 59	
Dalwhinnie	d															
Newtonmore	d														18 32	
Kingussie	d														18 37	
Aviemore	d														18 48	
Carrbridge	d														18 54	
Inverness	a														19 34	

A The Northern Lights

B 🛒 to Stonehaven

b arr. 1453

Table 229

Mondays to Saturdays
from 20 September

Edinburgh and Glasgow Queen Street - Perth, Inverness, Dundee, Aberdeen, Dyce and Inverurie

Station			SR	GR	SR	SR	SR	SR SO	SR SX	SR	SR SX	XC SO	XC SX	GR SX
			1	■ 1 A 🛒Ø	◇1 🛒		◇1 🛒	◇1 🛒	◇1 🛒	◇1 🛒	1	◇1 🛒	◇1	■ 1 🛒Ø
Edinburgh 10	242	d	16 32	16b33		17 03	17 35			17 41	18 00	18 08	18 16	18 30
Haymarket	242	d	16 37	16 38		17 07	17 39			17u45	18 04	18 13	18 21	18 35
Inverkeithing	242	d	16 51			17 22					18 22	18 26	18 38	18 54
Kirkcaldy	242	d	17 07			17 39				18 16	18 40	18 42	19 00	19 11
Markinch		d	17 17			17 48				18 25	18 51	18 51	19 09	
Ladybank		d	17 26			17 56				18 32	18 58	18 58	19 16	
Springfield		d				18 01								
Cupar		d				18 05	18 28				19 05	19 05	19 23	
Leuchars 3		a				18 12	18 34				19 11	19 11	19 29	19 38
St Andrews Bus Station	bus	a												
St Andrews Bus Station	bus	d												
Leuchars 3		d				18 12	18 35				19 12	19 12	19 30	19 38
Glasgow Queen St. 10	230	d			16 41			17 41	17 41					
Larbert	230	d												
Stirling	230	d		17 20	17 07			18 07	18 15					
Dunblane	230	d						18 15	18 22					
Gleneagles		d		17 40				18 27	18 35					
Perth		a	17 54	18 00	17 36			18 43	18 52	18 59				
		d		18 00	17 37			18 44	18 53	19 00				
Invergowrie		d												
Dundee		a			17 59	18 34	18 47	19 06	19 15		19 27	19 24	19 44	19 53
Broughty Ferry		d				19 00								
Carnoustie		d			18 13	19a17		19 27	19 28					
Arbroath		d			18 20		19 04	19 34	19 35			19 42	20 02	20 11
Montrose		d					19 24	19 48	19 49			20 02	20 16	20 27
Laurencekirk		d												
Stonehaven		d			18 53		19 45	20 10	20 11			20 23	20 36	20 50
Portlethen		d					19 54							
Aberdeen		a			19 13		20 08	20 29	20 32			20 41	20 55	21 12
		d												
Dyce	240 ✈	a												
Inverurie	240	a												
Dunkeld & Birnam		d								19 17				
Pitlochry		d		18 33						19 30				
Blair Atholl		d												
Dalwhinnie		d												
Newtonmore		d												
Kingussie		d		19 17						20 13				
Aviemore		d		19 29						20 25				
Carrbridge		d												
Inverness		a		20 08						21 03				

A The Highland Chieftain

b arr. 1627

Table 229

Mondays to Saturdays
from 20 September

Edinburgh and Glasgow Queen Street - Perth, Inverness, Dundee, Aberdeen, Dyce and Inverurie

Station			GR SO	SR	SR	SR SX	SR	SR	SR	SR SX	XC SX	XC SO	GR SX	SR SX	SR SO	SR	SR SX	SR SO	SR SO	SR SX
			■ 1 ⊡🛒	1	◇1 🛒	1	◇1 A 🛒	◇1 🛒	◇1 🛒		◇1	◇1 🛒	■ 1 🛒Ø	1	1	◇1			◇1	◇1
Edinburgh 10	242	d	18 32	18 40		19 00	19 30	19 35		20 00	20 15	20b22	20 32	20 37	20 37		21 09	21 00	21 32	21 40
Haymarket	242	d	18 37	18 45		19 03	19 33	19 39		20 04	20 20	20 26	20 37	20 41	20 41		21 13	21 04	21 36	21 44
Inverkeithing	242	d	18 54	19 00		19 17		19 54		20 23	20 35	20 45	20 52	21 00	21 00		21 32	21 23		
Kirkcaldy	242	d	19 11	19 18		19 33		20 10		20 45	20 51	21 00	21 09	21 17	21 17		21 54	21 45	22 04	22 12
Markinch		d		19 28		19 42		20 19		20 54	21 00	21 10		21 26	21 26		22 03	21 54		
Ladybank		d		19 35		19 50		20 26		21 01	21 08	21 18		21 33	21 36		22 10	22 01		
Springfield		d																		
Cupar		d				19 56	20 21			21 08	21 15	21 25					22 17	22 08		
Leuchars 3		a	19 38			20 03	20 28			21 14	21 21	21 31	21 33				22 23	22 14	22 28	22 33
St Andrews Bus Station	bus	a																		
St Andrews Bus Station	bus	d																		
Leuchars 3		d	19 39			20 03	20 28			21 15	21 22	21 32	21 33				22 24	22 15	22 28	22 34
Glasgow Queen St. 10	230	d			18 41				19 41							20 41				
Larbert	230	d																		
Stirling	230	d			19 07				20 07							21 07				
Dunblane	230	d			19 14											21 14				
Gleneagles		d			19 26											21 26				
Perth		a		20 02	19 42			20 53	20 36					22 01	22 03	21 42				
		d			19 43			20 54	20 36							21 43				
Invergowrie		d			20 01											22 01				
Dundee		a	19 53		20 08	20 18	20 40		20 59	21 30	21 40	21 47	21 47			22 07	22 39	22 30	22 42	22 48
Broughty Ferry		d																		
Carnoustie		d																		
Arbroath		d	20 11		20 25		20 58		21 17				22 05			22 25			23 00	23 05
Montrose		d	20 27		20 40		21 12						22 22			22 39			23 14	23 24
Laurencekirk		d							21 40										23 25	
Stonehaven		d	20 50				21 34		21 54				22 45			23 01			23 39	23 46
Portlethen		d																		23 55
Aberdeen		a	21 12		21 19		21 53		22 13				23 07			23 20	23 20		23 58	00 08
		d					21 55													
Dyce	240 ✈	a					22 04													
Inverurie	240	a					22 16													
Dunkeld & Birnam		d						21 12												
Pitlochry		d						21 25												
Blair Atholl		d						21 34												
Dalwhinnie		d						22 00												
Newtonmore		d						22 11												
Kingussie		d						22 21												
Aviemore		d						22 32												
Carrbridge		d						22 41												
Inverness		a					00 05	23 14												

Station			SR SO	SR SX	SR SX	SR SO	SR	SR SX	SR SO
			◇1	◇1					
Edinburgh 10	242	d			22 09		22 39	23 09	
Haymarket	242	d			22 13	22 13	22 43	23 13	23 13
Inverkeithing	242	d			22 32	22 32	23 02	23 32	23 32
Kirkcaldy	242	d			22 54	22 54	23 24	23 54	23 54
Markinch		d			23 03	23 03	23 33	00 03	00 03
Ladybank		d			23 13	23 13	23 40	00 10	00 10
Springfield		d			23 18	23 18			
Cupar		d			23 22	23 22		00 17	00 17
Leuchars 3		a			23 28	23 28		00 23	00 23
St Andrews Bus Station	bus	a							
St Andrews Bus Station	bus	d							
Leuchars 3		d			23 29	23 29		00 24	00 24
Glasgow Queen St. 10	230	d	21 41	21 41					
Larbert	230	d							
Stirling	230	d	22 07	22 07					
Dunblane	230	d							
Gleneagles		d							
Perth		a	22 36	22 35			00 07		
		d	22 37	22 35					
Invergowrie		d							
Dundee		a	22 58	23 03	23 44	23 44		00 39	00 39
Broughty Ferry		d							
Carnoustie		d	23 10	23 15					
Arbroath		d	23 17	23 25					
Montrose		d	23 33	23 41					
Laurencekirk		d		23 52					
Stonehaven		d	23 55	00 06					
Portlethen		d	00 05						
Aberdeen		a	00 18	00 26					
		d							
Dyce	240 ✈	a							
Inverurie	240	a							
Dunkeld & Birnam		d							
Pitlochry		d							
Blair Atholl		d							
Dalwhinnie		d							
Newtonmore		d							
Kingussie		d							
Aviemore		d							
Carrbridge		d							
Inverness		a							

A 🛒 to Stonehaven

b arr. 2015

Table 229

Edinburgh and Glasgow Queen Street - Perth, Inverness, Dundee, Aberdeen, Dyce and Inverurie

		XC	GR	SR	SR	SR	SR	SR	SR	SR	SR	SR	SR	SR	SR	SR
		■	■ 1	◇1		◇1	◇1		◇1	◇1		◇1	◇1	◇1		◇1
Edinburgh 10	242 d	08 04	09 10		09 15	09 25	10 55	11 15		12 40	13 15		13 50		15 15	
Haymarket	242 d	08 08	09 14		09 19	09 29	10 59	11 19		12 44	13 19		13 54		15 19	
Inverkeithing	242 d	08 25	09 32		09 38	09 48	11 15	11 38		13 00	13 40		14 11		15 38	
Kirkcaldy	242 d	08 40	09 49		10 03	10 10	11 31	12 03		13 16	14 05		14 28		16 03	
Markinch	d				10 12			12 12			14 14				16 12	
Ladybank	d				10 20			12 19			14 21				16 19	
Springfield	d															
Cupar	d	08 57			10 26			12 26			14 28				16 26	
Leuchars 3	a		10 13		10 33		11 54	12 33		13 39	14 35				16 33	
St Andrews Bus Station	a															
St Andrews Bus Station	d															
Leuchars 3	d		10 13		10 34		11 55	12 33		13 40	14 35				16 33	
Glasgow Queen St. 10 230	d			09 38					11 45			13 45		14 40		15 45
Larbert	230 d			10 02										15 00		
Stirling	230 d			10 12					12 12			14 12		15 09		16 12
Dunblane	230 d			10 18					12 18			14 17		15 16		16 18
Gleneagles	d			10 30					12 29			14 29		15 28		16 29
Perth	a			10 47		10 52			12 46			14 46	15 12	15 45		16 45
	d			10 48		10 53			12 47			14 48	15 14	15 46		16 47
Invergowrie	d															
Dundee	a	09 16	10 27	11 13	10 50		12 07	12 48	13 10	13 52	14 50	15 09			16 48	17 09
Broughty Ferry	d															
Carnoustie	d			11 25												
Arbroath	d	09 33	10 45	11 29			12 25		13 27	14 10		15 27				17 27
Montrose	d	09 47	11 01	11 46			12 37		13 42	14 24		15 42				17 42
Laurencekirk	d			12 01								15 53				
Stonehaven	d	10 08	11 24	12 10			12 59		14 03	14 46		16 06				18 03
Portlethen	d						13 07									
Aberdeen	a	10 26	11 47	12 35			13 23		14 23	15 05		16 26				18 23
	d															
Dyce	240 a															
Inverurie	240 a															
Dunkeld & Birnam	d					11 11							15 31			
Pitlochry	d					11 25							15 44	16 16		
Blair Atholl	d					11 34							15 54			
Dalwhinnie	d					12 01							16 19			
Newtonmore	d					12 11							16 29			
Kingussie	d					12 16							16 34	16 59		
Aviemore	d					12 29							16b48	17 12		
Carrbridge	d					12 37							17 03			
Inverness	a					13 09							17 38	17 50		

b arr. 1642

Table 229 Sundays

Edinburgh and Glasgow Queen Street - Perth, Inverness, Dundee, Aberdeen, Dyce and Inverurie

		GR	SR	GR	SR	SR	XC	SR	GR	SR	SR	SR	SR	SR	SR
		■ 1	◇1	■ 1		◇1	◇1	◇1	■ 1		◇1	◇1		◇1	
		A		B											
Edinburgh 10	242 d	16 00	17 05	17 11	17 15		18 10		18 42	19 15		21 00	21 15		22 25
Haymarket	242 d	16 04	17 09	17 16	17 19		18 15		18 47	19 19		21 05	21 19		22 29
Inverkeithing	242 d	16 24	17 22		17 38		18 29		19 02	19 38		21 18	21 38		22 48
Kirkcaldy	242 d	16 41	17 38		18 00		18 44		19 19	20 00		21 34	22 00		23 10
Markinch	d				18 09		18 53			20 09		21 43	22 09		23 19
Ladybank	d				18 16		19 01			20 16		21 50	22 16		23 26
Springfield	d														
Cupar	d				18 23		19 07			20 23		21 57	22 23		23 33
Leuchars 3	a	17 05	18 01		18 30		19 13		19 43	20 30		22 04	22 30		23 40
St Andrews Bus Station	a														
St Andrews Bus Station	d														
Leuchars 3	d	17 06	18 02		18 30		19 14		19 43	20 30		22 05	22 30		23 40
Glasgow Queen St. 10 230	d					17 45		18 10			19 45			21 45	
Larbert	230 d							18 30							
Stirling	230 d			17 52		18 12		18 39			20 12			22 11	
Dunblane	230 d							18 46			20 17			22 17	
Gleneagles	d			18 10				18 58			20 29			22 28	
Perth	a			18 28		18 44		19 15			20 46			22 46	
	d			18 29		18 45		19 16			20 47			22 46	
Invergowrie	d														
Dundee	a	17 24	18 14		18 46	19 08	19 28		19 57	20 45	21 10	22 17	22 45	23 09	23 56
Broughty Ferry	d														
Carnoustie	d					19 21								23 21	
Arbroath	d	17 42	18 32			19 27	19 46		20 15		21 27	22 35		23 26	
Montrose	d	18 00	18 46			19 42	20 00		20 31		21 42	22 49		23 41	
Laurencekirk	d					19 55									
Stonehaven	d	18 23	19 08			20 06	20 23		20 54		22 03	23 11		00 02	
Portlethen	d		19 16									23 20			
Aberdeen	a	18 46	19 30			20 29	20 42		21 17		22 24	23 33		00 25	
	d														
Dyce	240 a														
Inverurie	240 a														
Dunkeld & Birnam	d							19 34							
Pitlochry	d			19 00				19 47							
Blair Atholl	d							19 56							
Dalwhinnie	d			19 39				20 21							
Newtonmore	d							20 31							
Kingussie	d			19 52				20 36							
Aviemore	d			20 04				20 50							
Carrbridge	d							20 58							
Inverness	a			20 44				21 34							

A The Northern Lights
B The Highland Chieftain

Table 229

Mondays to Saturdays
until 18 September

Inverurie, Dyce, Aberdeen, Dundee, Inverness and Perth - Glasgow Queen Street and Edinburgh

		SR SX	SR	SR SO	SR SX	SR	SR SO	SR SX	SR	SR SX	XC SX	SR SX
									1		◇1 ✠	
Inverness	d								06 56			
Carrbridge	d								07 28			
Aviemore	d								07a38			
Kingussie	d											
Newtonmore	d											
Dalwhinnie	d											
Blair Atholl	d											
Pitlochry	d											
Dunkeld & Birnam	d											
Inverurie	240 d											
Dyce	240 ✈ d											
Aberdeen	240 a											
	d											
Portlethen	d											
Stonehaven	d											
Laurencekirk	d											
Montrose	d											
Arbroath	d											
Carnoustie	d					06 14						
Broughty Ferry	d					06 29						
Dundee	a					06 36						
	d						06 05	06 05			06 32	
Invergowrie	d											
Perth	a											
	d	05 10	05 16	05 35	06 09					06 14		06 39
Gleneagles	d		05 33		06 26							06 54
Dunblane	230 d		05 46		06 40							07 08
Stirling	230 d		05 53		06c54							07 16
Larbert	230 d		06 01		07 03							07 25
Glasgow Queen St. 10	230 ⛴ a		06 34		07 34							
Leuchars 3	a						06 16	06 16			06 44	
St Andrews Bus Station	🚌 a											
St Andrews Bus Station	🚌 d											
Leuchars 3	d						06 17	06 17			06 46	
Cupar	d						06 25	06 25			06 54	
Springfield	d											
Ladybank	d	05 36		05 58			06 32	06 32		06 37	07 03	
Markinch	d	05 44		06 07			06 40	06 40		06 46	07 11	
Kirkcaldy	242 d	05 53		06 16			06 49	06 49			07 21	
Inverkeithing	242 d	06 16		06 39			07 12	07 12		07 29	07 42	
Haymarket	242 a	06 39		07 00			07 33	07 33		07 51	07 59	
Edinburgh 10	242 a	06 46		07 06			07 38	07 38		07 57	08 05	08 30

c arr. 0646

Table 229

Mondays to Saturdays
until 18 September

Inverurie, Dyce, Aberdeen, Dundee, Inverness and Perth - Glasgow Queen Street and Edinburgh

		SR SO	SR SX	SR SX	SR	SR SO	SR SX	SR	XC	SR	SR	SR	SR	SR	SR	SR
		1	1		◇1 ✠	◇1	◇1		◇1 ✠	1	◇1 ✠	1	◇1 ✠		◇1 ✠	◇1 A ✠
Inverness	d												04 51		06 47	
Carrbridge	d															
Aviemore	d														07 23	
Kingussie	d														07 35	
Newtonmore	d															
Dalwhinnie	d															
Blair Atholl	d									07 12						
Pitlochry	d									07 26					08 15	
Dunkeld & Birnam	d									07 39					08 27	
Inverurie	240 d												06 39			07 14
Dyce	240 ✈ d												06 52			07 26
Aberdeen	240 a												07 06			07 37
	d				05 33	05 56	05 56				06 33					07 40
Portlethen	d				05 44						06 43					
Stonehaven	d				05 52	06 12	06 12				06 52		07 22			07 56
Laurencekirk	d				06 06								07 36			
Montrose	d				06 17	06 34	06 34				07 13		07 47			08 18
Arbroath	d				06 31	06 48	06 48				07 27		08 01			08 32
Carnoustie	d					06 55	06 55				07 34		08 08			08 39
Broughty Ferry	d															
Dundee	a				06 51	07 06	07 06				07 50		08 19			08 53
	d				06 52	07 08	07 08	07 20	07 35		07 52	08 18	08 21	08 28		08 53
Invergowrie	d											08 23				
Perth	a				07 14					07 58	08 12	08 40			08 47	09 15
	d	06 55	06 55	07 03	07 15					07 59	08 12	08 41			08 48	09 15
Gleneagles	d			07 17	07 30						08 26	08 56				
Dunblane	230 d			07 29	07 44							09 07				
Stirling	230 d			07 40	07 53						08 43	09 13				09 44
Larbert	230 d			07 47	08 02											
Glasgow Queen St. 10	230 ⛴ a			08 21	08 34						09 15	09 45				10 14
Leuchars 3	a					07 20	07 20	07 31	07 47					08 41		
St Andrews Bus Station	🚌 a															
St Andrews Bus Station	🚌 d															
Leuchars 3	d					07 20	07 20	07 32	07 48					08 42		
Cupar	d					07 28	07 28	07 39	07 55					08 49		
Springfield	d							07 44								
Ladybank	d	07 17	07 17					07 49	08 03	08 22				08 56		
Markinch	d	07 26	07 26					07 56	08 11	08 31				09 04		
Kirkcaldy	242 d	07 38	07 38			07 48	07 48	08 06	08 20	08 41				09 13	09 26	
Inverkeithing	242 d	07 54	07 54					08 28	08 35	08 57				09 35		
Haymarket	242 a	08 16	08 16			08 19	08 19	08 47	08 53	09 15			09 24	09 49	09 55	
Edinburgh 10	242 a	08 22	08 22			08 25	08 25	08 55	08 58	09 25			09 30	09 56	10 02	

A ✠ from Aberdeen

Table 229

Mondays to Saturdays
until 18 September

Inverurie, Dyce, Aberdeen, Dundee, Inverness and Perth - Glasgow Queen Street and Edinburgh

Station		SR	GR SX	GR SO	XC SO	XC SX	SR	SR	GR SO	GR SX	SR	SR	SR
			■1	■1	◇■1	◇■1		■1	■1 A	■1 A	◇■1	◇■1	
Inverness	d	06 56							07 55	07 55			
Carrbridge	d	07 28											
Aviemore	d	07a38							08 29	08 29			
Kingussie	d								08 42	08 42			
Newtonmore	d												
Dalwhinnie	d												
Blair Atholl	d												
Pitlochry	d								09 23	09 23			
Dunkeld & Birnam	d												
Inverurie 240	d												
Dyce 240 ✈	d												
Aberdeen 240	a												
	d		07 52	07 52	08 20	08 20					08 42	09 07	
Portlethen	d												
Stonehaven	d		08 09	08 09	08 38	08 38							
Laurencekirk	d											09 35	
Montrose	d		08 32	08 32	08 59	08 59					09 18	09 46	
Arbroath	d		08 48	08 48	09 15	09 15					09 32	10 00	
Carnoustie	d										09 39		
Broughty Ferry	d												
Dundee	a		09 05	09 05	09 31	09 31					09 52	10 15	
	d		09 06	09 06	09 32	09 32	09 42				09 52	10 17	10 34
Invergowrie	d												
Perth	a								09 54	09 54	10 14		
	d							09 51	09 56	09 56	10 14		
Gleneagles	d								10 12	10 12			
Dunblane 230	d												
Stirling 230	d								10 30	10 30	10 43		
Larbert 230	d												
Glasgow Queen St. 10 230 ⛴	a										11 14		
Leuchars 3	a		09 20	09 20	09 46	09 46	09 54					10 28	10 45
St Andrews Bus Station 🚌	a												
St Andrews Bus Station 🚌	d												
Leuchars 3	d		09 20	09 20	09 47	09 47	09 55					10 29	10 46
Cupar	d				09 54	09 54	10 02						10 53
Springfield	d												
Ladybank	d				10 01	10 01	10 10	10 14					11 01
Markinch	d				10 08	10 09	10 17	10b33					11 08
Kirkcaldy 242	d		09 44	09 44	10 17	10 17	10 27	10 42					11 18
Inverkeithing 242	d		10 01	10 01	10 32	10 32	10 43	10 59					11 34
Haymarket 242	a		10 19	10 20	10 50	10 52	11 02	11 18	11 08	11 10		11 22	11 53
Edinburgh 10 242	a		10 25	10 26	10 58	11 01	11 09	11 25	11 15	11 16		11 29	12 01

A The Highland Chieftain

b arr. 1025

Table 229

Mondays to Saturdays
until 18 September

Inverurie, Dyce, Aberdeen, Dundee, Inverness and Perth - Glasgow Queen Street and Edinburgh

Station		SR	SR	SR	GR SO	GR SX	SR	SR	SR SO	SR SX	SR	SR
		■1	◇■1 A	◇■1	■1 B	■1 B		■1	◇■1	◇■1	◇■1 A	■1
Inverness	d			09 18								
Carrbridge	d			09 49								
Aviemore	d			10 01								
Kingussie	d			10 14								
Newtonmore	d			10 18								
Dalwhinnie	d			10 30								
Blair Atholl	d			10 51								
Pitlochry	d			11 01								
Dunkeld & Birnam	d			11 13								
Inverurie 240	d										10 38	
Dyce 240 ✈	d		09 08								10 50	
Aberdeen 240	a		09 19								11 01	
	d		09 37		09 52	09 52			10 38	10 38	11 05	
Portlethen	d											
Stonehaven	d		09 53		10 09	10 09					11 21	
Laurencekirk	d										11 35	
Montrose	d		10 15		10 32	10 32			11 14	11 14	11 46	
Arbroath	d		10 29		10 49	10 49			11 28	11 28	12 00	
Carnoustie	d		10 36						11 35	11 35		
Broughty Ferry	d		10 43									
Dundee	a		10 52		11 06	11 06			11 49	11 49	12 15	
	d		10 52		11 06	11 06	11 30		11 49	11 49	12 17	12 34
Invergowrie	d											
Perth	a		11 14	11 33					12 11	12 11		
	d	10 57	11 14	11 37				11 59	12 11	12 11		
Gleneagles	d			11 52								
Dunblane 230	d			12 06								
Stirling 230	d		11 43	12 13					12 43	12 42		
Larbert 230	d											
Glasgow Queen St. 10 230 ⛴	a		12 14	12 46					13 14	13 14		
Leuchars 3	a				11 20	11 20	11 41				12 28	12 46
St Andrews Bus Station 🚌	a											
St Andrews Bus Station 🚌	d											
Leuchars 3	d				11 20	11 20	11 45				12 29	12 46
Cupar	d						11 53					12 54
Springfield	d											
Ladybank	d	11 20					12 00	12 20				13 01
Markinch	d	11 29					12 08	12 29				13 08
Kirkcaldy 242	d	11 39			11 44	11 44	12 17	12 39				13 18
Inverkeithing 242	d	11 55			12 01	12 01	12 33	12 55				13 34
Haymarket 242	a	12 11			12 19	12 19	12 47	13 13			13 21	13 50
Edinburgh 10 242	a	12 17			12 25	12 25	12 55	13 19			13 27	13 57

A ♀ from Aberdeen

B The Northern Lights

Table 229

Mondays to Saturdays
until 18 September

Inverurie, Dyce, Aberdeen, Dundee, Inverness and Perth - Glasgow Queen Street and Edinburgh

		SR	SR	SR	SR	SR	SR	SR	SR	SR	SR	SR
		◇1	◇1	◇1	1	1	1	◇1	◇1		◇1	◇1
		⌶	⌶	A ⌶				⌶	⌶		⌶	⌶
Inverness	d	10 47									12 47	
Carrbridge	d	11 21										
Aviemore	d	11 33									13 31	
Kingussie	d	11 45									13 44	
Newtonmore	d										13 48	
Dalwhinnie	d											
Blair Atholl	d										14 18	
Pitlochry	d	12 27									14 28	
Dunkeld & Birnam	d	12 40									14 40	
Inverurie 240	d			11 35	13 38							
Dyce 240 ✈	d			11 47	13 52							
Aberdeen 240	a			11 58	14 03							
	d		11 42	12 07				12 42	13 06			13 42
Portlethen	d			12 17								
Stonehaven	d			12 26				12 58	13 22			
Laurencekirk	d											
Montrose	d		12 17					13 17	13 44			14 17
Arbroath	d		12 31	13 00				13 31	13 58			14 31
Carnoustie	d		12 38									14 38
Broughty Ferry	d											
Dundee	a		12 52	13 15				13 49	14 15			14 52
	d		12 52	13 17		13 34		13 50	14 17	14 34		14 52
Invergowrie	d											
Perth	a	12 59	13 14					14 11			14 59	15 14
	d	13 01	13 14				13 58	14 11			15 00	15 14
Gleneagles	d											
Dunblane 230	d											
Stirling 230	d		13 43					14 40				15 43
Larbert 230	d											
Glasgow Queen St. 10 230	a		14 14					15 15				16 15
Leuchars 3	a			13 28		13 45			14 29	14 45		
St Andrews Bus Station	a											
St Andrews Bus Station	d											
Leuchars 3	d			13 29		13 46			14 29	14 46		
Cupar	d					13 53				14 53		
Springfield	d											
Ladybank	d					14 01	14 20			15 01		
Markinch	d	13 31				14 08	14 29			15 08	15 37	
Kirkcaldy 242	d	13 41				14 18	14 39			15 18	15 47	
Inverkeithing 242	d					14 34	14 55			15 34		
Haymarket 242	a	14 13		14 21		14 47	15 14		15 20	15 47	16 16	
Edinburgh 10 242	a	14 19		14 27		14 55	15 19		15 27	15 55	16 23	

A ⌶ from Aberdeen

Table 229

Mondays to Saturdays
until 18 September

Inverurie, Dyce, Aberdeen, Dundee, Inverness and Perth - Glasgow Queen Street and Edinburgh

		SR SO	SR SX	SR	SR SO	SR SX	SR	GR SO	GR SX	SR	SR	SR SX	SR	SR
		◇1	◇1		1	1	◇1	■ 1	■ 1	◇1	◇1	1		◇1
		⌶	⌶				⌶	⌶⊘	⌶⊘	⌶	⌶			A ⌶
Inverness	d									14 51				
Carrbridge	d													
Aviemore	d									15 29				
Kingussie	d									15 41				
Newtonmore	d													
Dalwhinnie	d									15 54				
Blair Atholl	d													
Pitlochry	d									16 23				
Dunkeld & Birnam	d									16 35				
Inverurie 240	d													15 24
Dyce 240 ✈	d													15 38
Aberdeen 240	a													15 49
	d	14 07	14 07				14 39	14 50	14 50		15 33			16 01
Portlethen	d													
Stonehaven	d	14 23	14 23					15 07	15 07		15 49			16 18
Laurencekirk	d	14 37	14 37											16 32
Montrose	d						15 12	15 30	15 30		16 11			
Arbroath	d	15 00	15 00				15 26	15 46	15 46		16 25			16 55
Carnoustie	d						15 33							17 02
Broughty Ferry	d													
Dundee	a	15 16	15 16				15 49	16 03	16 03		16 43			17 17
	d	15 17	15 17	15 35			15 49	16 04	16 04		16 45		16 50	17 17
Invergowrie	d										16 51			
Perth	a						16 11			16 54	17 10			
	d				15 59	15 59	16 11			16 55	17 11	17 00		
Gleneagles	d									17 11	17 26			
Dunblane 230	d									17 22	17 36			
Stirling 230	d						16 43			17 29	17 42			
Larbert 230	d													
Glasgow Queen St. 10 230	a						17 17			18 09	18 15			
Leuchars 3	a	15 28	15 28	15 46				16 17	16 17				17 01	17 29
St Andrews Bus Station	a													
St Andrews Bus Station	d													
Leuchars 3	d	15 29	15 29	15 47				16 18	16 18				17 02	17 29
Cupar	d			15 53									17 09	
Springfield	d													
Ladybank	d			16 02	16 20	16 20						17 27	17 16	
Markinch	d			16 08	16 29	16 29						17 39	17 23	
Kirkcaldy 242	d			16 19	16 39	16 39		16 45	16 45			17 48	17 33	
Inverkeithing 242	d			16 35	16 55	16 55		17 01	17 01			18 04	17 55	
Haymarket 242	a	16 20	16 24	16 49	17 11	17 16		17 19	17 20			18 19	18 15	18 24
Edinburgh 10 242	a	16 27	16 31	16 57	17 20	17 24		17 25	17 27			18 25	18 22	18 32

A ⌶ from Aberdeen

Table 229

Mondays to Saturdays
until 18 September

Inverurie, Dyce, Aberdeen, Dundee, Inverness and Perth - Glasgow Queen Street and Edinburgh

			SR SO	SR	SR	SR	SR	SR	SR	SR SO	SR SX	SR SO	SR	SR	GR SX	SR SO	SR	SR
					1	1	◇1	◇1 A	1				◇1	◇1	R 1	◇1	1	◇1
							⌶	⌶					⌶	⌶	⊓	⌶		⌶
Inverness		d											16 53					
Carrbridge		d											17 29					
Aviemore		d											17 37					
Kingussie		d											17 50					
Newtonmore		d											17 54					
Dalwhinnie		d																
Blair Atholl		d											18 24					
Pitlochry		d											18 34					
Dunkeld & Birnam		d											18 46					
Inverurie	240	d			17 52			16 38										
Dyce	240 ✈	d			18 06			16 54	17 05									
Aberdeen	240	a			18 17			17 05	17 14									
		d					16 37	17 07	17 16					17 36	18 16	18 16		18 30
Portlethen		d							17 27									18 40
Stonehaven		d					16 53		17a37					17 52	18 33	18 33		18 49
Laurencekirk		d						17 38						18 06				
Montrose		d					17 13	17 49						18 17	18 56	18 56		19 10
Arbroath		d					17 29	18 03						18 31	19 12	19 12		19 24
Carnoustie		d												18 38				19 31
Broughty Ferry		d																
Dundee		a					17 49	18 18						18 52	19 29	19 29		19 46
		d		17 26			17 51	18 19			18 46	18 46		18 52	19 30	19 30		19 46
Invergowrie		d																
Perth		a					18 11						19 08	19 14				20 07
		d				18 00	18 12			18 28			19 09	19 14			19 57	20 11
Gleneagles		d																20 25
Dunblane	230	d					18 35			18 49								
Stirling	230	d					18 42			19a00				19 43				20 40
Larbert	230	d																
Glasgow Queen St. 10	230 ⇌	a					19 14							20 15				21 14
Leuchars 3		a		17 38				18 31			18 56	18 56			19 43	19 43		
St Andrews Bus Station	🚌	a																
St Andrews Bus Station	🚌	d																
Leuchars 3		d		17 39				18 31			18 56	18 56			19 44	19 44		
Cupar		d		17 47							19 04	19 04						
Springfield		d		17 51														
Ladybank		d		17 56		18 23					19 11	19 11					20 20	
Markinch		d		18 04		18 34					19 19	19 19	19 44				20 29	
Kirkcaldy	242	d	17 28	18 13		18 44					19 28	19 28	19 54		20 08	20 08	20 39	
Inverkeithing	242	d	18 14	18 29		19 00					19 46	19 46			20 24	20 24	20 55	
Haymarket	242	a	18 36	18 43		19 15		19 27			20 06	20 06	20 24		20s42	20s42	21 10	
Edinburgh 10	242	a	18 41	18 50		19 21		19 34			20 13	20 13	20 29		20 50	20 50	21 19	

A ⌶ from Aberdeen

Table 229

Mondays to Saturdays
until 18 September

Inverurie, Dyce, Aberdeen, Dundee, Inverness and Perth - Glasgow Queen Street and Edinburgh

			SR SO	SR SX	SR	SR	SR	SR	SR	SR	SR	XC SO	SR	SR FSX	SR FO
			◇1 A	◇1 A		◇1	◇1	A	◇1	◇1	◇1	◇1	1	1	1
			⌶	⌶		⌶	⌶	⌶				⌶			
Inverness		d				18 43				20 15					
Carrbridge		d				19 14									
Aviemore		d				19b29				21 00					
Kingussie		d				19 42				21 12					
Newtonmore		d				19 46				21 17					
Dalwhinnie		d				19 58				21 28					
Blair Atholl		d				20 19				21 50					
Pitlochry		d				20 29				21 59					
Dunkeld & Birnam		d				20 41				22 12					
Inverurie	240	d	18 43	18 43				19 40							
Dyce	240 ✈	d	18 55	18 55				19 52							
Aberdeen	240	a	19 06	19 06				20 03							
		d	19 09	19 09			19 46	20 05	20 42		21 06	21 17		22 30	23 22
Portlethen		d					19 56							22 40	23 32
Stonehaven		d	19 26	19 26			20 05	20 21	20 58		21 22	21 35		22 49	23 41
Laurencekirk		d	19 40	19 40										23 03	23 55
Montrose		d	19 51	19 51			20 23	20 43	21 20		21 44	21 56		23 13	00 05
Arbroath		d	20 05	20 05			20 37	20 57	21 34		21 58	22 12		23 28	00 20
Carnoustie		d						21 04						23 35	00 27
Broughty Ferry		d													
Dundee		a	20 20	20 20			20 56	21 15	21 52		22 15	22 28		23 50	00 42
		d	20 21	20 21	20 42		20 56	21 16	21 52		22 15	22 29		23 51	00 43
Invergowrie		d												23 57	00 49
Perth		a				21 00	21 17		22 14	22 29				00 15	01 07
		d				21 02	21 17		22 14	22 30			22 38		
Gleneagles		d								22 47					
Dunblane	230	d								22 58					
Stirling	230	d					21 45		22 43	23 05					
Larbert	230	d													
Glasgow Queen St. 10	230 ⇌	a					22 19		23 15	23 39					
Leuchars 3		a	20 33	20 33	20 53			21 28			22 27	22 41			
St Andrews Bus Station	🚌	a													
St Andrews Bus Station	🚌	d													
Leuchars 3		d	20 33	20 33	20 54			21 28			22 27	22 42			
Cupar		d			21 01			21 36			22 37	22 49			
Springfield		d													
Ladybank		d			21 09			21 43			22 44	22 57	23 01		
Markinch		d			21 16	21 32		21 51			22 52	23 05	23 10		
Kirkcaldy	242	d			21 26	21 42		21 59			23 01	23 14			
Inverkeithing	242	d			21 49			22 22			23 24	23 31	23 51		
Haymarket	242	a	21 26	21 26	22 09	22 13		22 43			23 44	23 50	00 11		
Edinburgh 10	242	a	21 32	21 32	22 16	22 19		22 50			23 52	23 55	00 18		

A ⌶ from Aberdeen

b arr. 1922

Table 229

Mondays to Saturdays
from 20 September

Inverurie, Dyce, Aberdeen, Dundee, Inverness and Perth - Glasgow Queen Street and Edinburgh

Station			SR SX	SR	SR SO	SR SO	SR SX	SR	SR SX	SR ■1	SR SX	XC SX ◇1 ✠	SR SX	SR SO ■1
Inverness		d								06 56				
Carrbridge		d								07 28				
Aviemore		d								07a38				
Kingussie		d												
Newtonmore		d												
Dalwhinnie		d												
Blair Atholl		d												
Pitlochry		d												
Dunkeld & Birnam		d												
Inverurie	240	d												
Dyce	240 ✈	d												
Aberdeen	240	a												
		d												
Portlethen		d												
Stonehaven		d												
Laurencekirk		d												
Montrose		d												
Arbroath		d												
Carnoustie		d						06 14						
Broughty Ferry		d						06 29						
Dundee		a						06 36						
		d				06 05			06 05			06 32		
Invergowrie		d												
Perth		a												
		d	05 10	05 16	05 35		06 09				06 14		06 39	06 55
Gleneagles		d		05 33			06 26						06 54	
Dunblane	230	d		05 46			06 40						07 08	
Stirling	230	d		05 53			06c54						07 16	
Larbert	230	d		06 01			07 03						07 25	
Glasgow Queen St. ■10	230 ⇌	a		06 34			07 34							
Leuchars ■3		a				06 16			06 16			06 44		
St Andrews Bus Station	🚌	a												
St Andrews Bus Station	🚌	d												
Leuchars ■3		d				06 17			06 17			06 46		
Cupar		d				06 25			06 25			06 54		
Springfield		d												
Ladybank		d	05 36		05 58	06 32			06 32		06 37	07 03		07 17
Markinch		d	05 44		06 07	06 40			06 40		06 46	07 11		07 26
Kirkcaldy	242	d	05 53		06 16	06 49			06 49			07 21		07 38
Inverkeithing	242	d	06 16		06 39	07 12			07 12		07 29	07 42		07 54
Haymarket	242	a	06 39		07 00	07 33			07 33		07 51	07 59		08 16
Edinburgh ■10	242	a	06 46						07 38		07 57	08 05	08 30	08 22

c arr. 0646

Table 229

Mondays to Saturdays
from 20 September

Inverurie, Dyce, Aberdeen, Dundee, Inverness and Perth - Glasgow Queen Street and Edinburgh

Station			SR SX ■1	SR SX	SR ◇1 ✠	SR SO ◇1	SR SX ◇1	SR SO	SR SX	XC SX ◇1 ✠	XC SO ◇1 ✠	SR ■1	SR ◇1 ✠	SR ■1	SR ◇1 ✠	SR SO	SR SX	SR ◇1 ✠	SR ◇1 A ✠
Inverness		d													04 51			06 47	
Carrbridge		d																	
Aviemore		d																07 23	
Kingussie		d																07 35	
Newtonmore		d																	
Dalwhinnie		d																	
Blair Atholl		d										07 12							
Pitlochry		d										07 26						08 15	
Dunkeld & Birnam		d										07 39						08 27	
Inverurie	240	d													06 39				07 14
Dyce	240 ✈	d													06 52				07 26
Aberdeen	240	a													07 06				07 37
		d			05 33	05 56	05 56						06 33						07 40
Portlethen		d			05 44								06 43						
Stonehaven		d			05 52	06 12	06 12						06 52		07 22				07 56
Laurencekirk		d			06 06										07 36				
Montrose		d			06 17	06 34	06 34						07 13		07 47				08 18
Arbroath		d			06 31	06 48	06 48						07 27		08 01				08 32
Carnoustie		d				06 55	06 55						07 34		08 08				08 39
Broughty Ferry		d																	
Dundee		a			06 51	07 06	07 06						07 50		08 19				08 53
		d			06 52	07 08	07 08	07 20	07 20	07 35	07 35		07 52	08 18	08 21	08 28	08 28		08 53
Invergowrie		d												08 23					
Perth		a			07 14							07 58	08 12	08 40				08 47	09 15
		d	06 55	07 03	07 15							07 59	08 12	08 41				08 48	09 15
Gleneagles		d		07 17	07 30								08 26	08 56					
Dunblane	230	d		07 29	07 44									09 07					
Stirling	230	d		07 40	07 53								08 43	09 13					09 44
Larbert	230	d		07 47	08 02														
Glasgow Queen St. ■10	230 ⇌	a		08 21	08 34								09 15	09 45					10 14
Leuchars ■3		a				07 20	07 20	07 31	07 31	07 47	07 47					08 41	08 41		
St Andrews Bus Station	🚌	a																	
St Andrews Bus Station	🚌	d																	
Leuchars ■3		d				07 20	07 20	07 32	07 32	07 48	07 48					08 42	08 42		
Cupar		d				07 28	07 28	07 39	07 39	07 55	07 55					08 49	08 49		
Springfield		d						07 44	07 44										
Ladybank		d	07 17					07 49	07 49	08 03	08 03	08 22				08 56	08 56		
Markinch		d	07 26					07 56	07 56	08 11	08 11	08 31				09 04	09 04		
Kirkcaldy	242	d	07 38			07 48	07 48	08 06	08 06	08 20	08 20	08 41				09 13	09 13	09 26	
Inverkeithing	242	d	07 54					08 28	08 28	08 35	08 35	08 57				09 35	09 35		
Haymarket	242	a	08 16			08 19	08 19	08 47	08 47	08 53	08 56	09 15				09 49	09 49	09 55	
Edinburgh ■10	242	a	08 22			08 25	08 25		08 55	08 58	09 01	09 25			09 24		09 56	10 02	

A ✠ from Aberdeen

Table 229

Mondays to Saturdays
from 20 September

Inverurie, Dyce, Aberdeen, Dundee, Inverness and Perth - Glasgow Queen Street and Edinburgh

		GR SX	GR SO	XC SO	XC SX	SR SO	SR SX	SR	GR SO	GR SX	SR	SR	SR SO	SR SX
		■ 1	■ 1	◇1	◇1			1	■ 1	■ 1	◇1	◇1		
									A	A				
Inverness	d								07 55	07 55				
Carrbridge	d													
Aviemore	d								08 29	08 29				
Kingussie	d								08 42	08 42				
Newtonmore	d													
Dalwhinnie	d													
Blair Atholl	d													
Pitlochry	d								09 23	09 23				
Dunkeld & Birnam	d													
Inverurie 240	d													
Dyce 240 ✈	d													
Aberdeen 240	a													
	d	07 52	07 52	08 20	08 20						08 42	09 07		
Portlethen	d													
Stonehaven	d	08 09	08 09	08 38	08 38									
Laurencekirk	d											09 35		
Montrose	d	08 32	08 32	08 59	08 59						09 18	09 46		
Arbroath	d	08 48	08 48	09 15	09 15						09 32	10 00		
Carnoustie	d										09 39			
Broughty Ferry	d													
Dundee	a	09 05	09 05	09 31	09 31						09 52	10 15		
	d	09 06	09 06	09 32	09 32	09 42	09 42				09 52	10 17	10 34	10 34
Invergowrie	d													
Perth	a								09 54	09 54	10 14			
	d							09 51	09 56	09 56	10 14			
Gleneagles	d								10 12	10 12				
Dunblane 230	d													
Stirling 230	d								10 30	10 30	10 43			
Larbert 230	d													
Glasgow Queen St. 10 230	a										11 14			
Leuchars 3	a	09 20	09 20	09 46	09 46	09 54	09 54					10 28	10 45	10 45
St Andrews Bus Station	a													
St Andrews Bus Station	d													
Leuchars 3	d	09 20	09 20	09 47	09 47	09 55	09 55					10 29	10 46	10 46
Cupar	d			09 54	09 54	10 02	10 02						10 53	10 53
Springfield	d													
Ladybank	d			10 01	10 01	10 10	10 10	10 14					11 01	11 01
Markinch	d			10 08	10 09	10 17	10 17	10b33					11 08	11 08
Kirkcaldy 242	d	09 44	09 44	10 17	10 17	10 27	10 27	10 42					11 18	11 18
Inverkeithing 242	d	10 01	10 01	10 32	10 32	10 43	10 43	10 59					11 34	11 34
Haymarket 242	a	10 19	10 20	10 50	10 52	11 00	11 02	11 18	11 08	11 10		11 22	11 53	11 53
Edinburgh 10 242	a	10 25	10 26	10 58	11 01		11 09	11 25	11 15	11 16		11 29		12 01

A The Highland Chieftain

b arr. 1025

Table 229

Mondays to Saturdays
from 20 September

Inverurie, Dyce, Aberdeen, Dundee, Inverness and Perth - Glasgow Queen Street and Edinburgh

		SR	SR	SR	GR SO	GR SX	SR SO	SR SX	SR	SR SO	SR SX	SR	SR SO	SR SX
		1	◇1	◇1	■ 1	■ 1			1	◇1	◇1	◇1	1	1
			A		B	B						A		
Inverness	d			09 18										
Carrbridge	d			09 49										
Aviemore	d			10 01										
Kingussie	d			10 14										
Newtonmore	d			10 18										
Dalwhinnie	d			10 30										
Blair Atholl	d			10 51										
Pitlochry	d			11 01										
Dunkeld & Birnam	d			11 13										
Inverurie 240	d											10 38		
Dyce 240 ✈	d		09 08									10 50		
Aberdeen 240	a		09 19									11 01		
	d		09 37		09 52	09 52				10 38	10 38	11 05		
Portlethen	d													
Stonehaven	d		09 53		10 09	10 09						11 21		
Laurencekirk	d											11 35		
Montrose	d		10 15		10 32	10 32				11 14	11 14	11 46		
Arbroath	d		10 29		10 49	10 49				11 28	11 28	12 00		
Carnoustie	d		10 36							11 35	11 35			
Broughty Ferry	d		10 43											
Dundee	a		10 52		11 06	11 06				11 49	11 49	12 15		
	d		10 52		11 06	11 06	11 30	11 30		11 49	11 49	12 17	12 34	12 34
Invergowrie	d													
Perth	a		11 14	11 33						12 11	12 11			
	d	10 57	11 14	11 37					11 59	12 11	12 11			
Gleneagles	d			11 52										
Dunblane 230	d			12 06										
Stirling 230	d		11 43	12 13						12 43	12 42			
Larbert 230	d													
Glasgow Queen St. 10 230	a		12 14	12 46						13 14	13 14			
Leuchars 3	a				11 20	11 20	11 41	11 41				12 28	12 46	12 46
St Andrews Bus Station	a													
St Andrews Bus Station	d													
Leuchars 3	d				11 20	11 20	11 45	11 45				12 29	12 46	12 46
Cupar	d						11 53	11 53					12 54	12 54
Springfield	d													
Ladybank	d	11 20					12 00	12 00	12 20				13 01	13 01
Markinch	d	11 29					12 08	12 08	12 29				13 08	13 08
Kirkcaldy 242	d	11 39			11 44	11 44	12 17	12 17	12 39				13 18	13 18
Inverkeithing 242	d	11 55			12 01	12 01	12 33	12 33	12 55				13 34	13 34
Haymarket 242	a	12 11			12 19	12 19	12 47	12 47	13 13			13 21	13 50	13 50
Edinburgh 10 242	a	12 17			12 25	12 25		12 55	13 19			13 27		13 57

A from Aberdeen

B The Northern Lights

Table 229

Mondays to Saturdays

from 20 September

Inverurie, Dyce, Aberdeen, Dundee, Inverness and Perth - Glasgow Queen Street and Edinburgh

		SR	SR	SR	SR SO	SR SX	SR	SR	SR	SR SO	SR SX	SR	SR
		◇1	◇1	◇1	1	1	1	◇1	◇1			◇1	◇1
		🍴	🍴	A 🍴				🍴	🍴			🍴	🍴
Inverness	d	10 47										12 47	
Carrbridge	d	11 21											
Aviemore	d	11 33										13 31	
Kingussie	d	11 45										13 44	
Newtonmore	d											13 48	
Dalwhinnie	d												
Blair Atholl	d											14 18	
Pitlochry	d	12 27										14 28	
Dunkeld & Birnam	d	12 40										14 40	
Inverurie 240	d			11 35									
Dyce 240 ✈	d			11 47									
Aberdeen 240	a			11 58									
	d		11 42	12 07				12 42	13 06				13 42
Portlethen	d			12 17									
Stonehaven	d			12 26				12 58	13 22				
Laurencekirk	d												
Montrose	d		12 17					13 17	13 44				14 17
Arbroath	d		12 31	13 00				13 31	13 58				14 31
Carnoustie	d		12 38										14 38
Broughty Ferry	d												
Dundee	a		12 52	13 15				13 49	14 15				14 52
	d		12 52	13 17	13 34	13 34		13 50	14 17	14 34	14 34		14 52
Invergowrie	d												
Perth	a	12 59	13 14					14 11				14 59	15 14
	d	13 01	13 14				13 58	14 11				15 00	15 14
Gleneagles	d												
Dunblane 230	d												
Stirling 230	d		13 43					14 40					15 43
Larbert 230	d												
Glasgow Queen St. 10 230 ⛴	a		14 14					15 15					16 15
Leuchars 3	a			13 28	13 45	13 45			14 29	14 45	14 45		
St Andrews Bus Station 🚌	a												
St Andrews Bus Station 🚌	d												
Leuchars 3	d			13 29	13 46	13 46			14 29	14 46	14 46		
Cupar	d				13 53	13 53				14 53	14 53		
Springfield	d												
Ladybank	d				14 01	14 01	14 20			15 01	15 01		
Markinch	d	13 31			14 08	14 08	14 29			15 08	15 08		
Kirkcaldy 242	d	13 41			14 18	14 18	14 39			15 18	15 18	15 37	
Inverkeithing 242	d				14 34	14 34	14 55			15 34	15 34	15 47	
Haymarket 242	a	14 13		14 21	14 47	14 47	15 14		15 20	15 47	15 47	16 16	
Edinburgh 10 242	a	14 19		14 27		14 55	15 19		15 27		15 55	16 23	

A 🍴 from Aberdeen

Table 229

Mondays to Saturdays

from 20 September

Inverurie, Dyce, Aberdeen, Dundee, Inverness and Perth - Glasgow Queen Street and Edinburgh

		SR SO	SR SX	SR SO	SR SX	SR SO	SR SX	SR	GR SO	GR SX	SR	SR	SR SO	SR SX	SR
		◇1	◇1			1	1	◇1	1	1	◇1	◇1			◇1
		🍴	🍴					🍴	🍴⊘	🍴⊘	🍴	🍴			A 🍴
Inverness	d										14 51				
Carrbridge	d														
Aviemore	d										15 29				
Kingussie	d										15 41				
Newtonmore	d														
Dalwhinnie	d										15 54				
Blair Atholl	d														
Pitlochry	d										16 23				
Dunkeld & Birnam	d										16 35				
Inverurie 240	d														15 24
Dyce 240 ✈	d														15 38
Aberdeen 240	a														15 49
	d	14 07	14 07					14 39	14 50	14 50		15 33			16 01
Portlethen	d														
Stonehaven	d	14 23	14 23						15 07	15 07		15 49			16 18
Laurencekirk	d	14 37	14 37												16 32
Montrose	d							15 12	15 30	15 30		16 11			
Arbroath	d	15 00	15 00					15 26	15 46	15 46		16 25			16 55
Carnoustie	d							15 33							17 02
Broughty Ferry	d														
Dundee	a	15 16	15 16					15 49	16 03	16 03		16 43			17 17
	d	15 17	15 17	15 35	15 35			15 49	16 04	16 04		16 45	16 50	16 50	17 17
Invergowrie	d											16 51			
Perth	a							16 11			16 54	17 10			
	d					15 59	15 59	16 11			16 55	17 11			
Gleneagles	d										17 11	17 26			
Dunblane 230	d										17 22	17 36			
Stirling 230	d							16 43			17 29	17 42			
Larbert 230	d														
Glasgow Queen St. 10 230 ⛴	a							17 17			18 09	18 15			
Leuchars 3	a	15 28	15 28	15 46	15 46				16 17	16 17			17 01	17 01	17 29
St Andrews Bus Station 🚌	a														
St Andrews Bus Station 🚌	d														
Leuchars 3	d	15 29	15 29	15 47	15 47				16 18	16 18			17 02	17 02	17 29
Cupar	d			15 53	15 53								17 09	17 09	
Springfield	d														
Ladybank	d			16 02	16 02	16 20	16 20						17 16	17 16	
Markinch	d			16 08	16 08	16 29	16 29						17 23	17 23	
Kirkcaldy 242	d			16 19	16 19	16 39	16 39		16 45	16 45			17 33	17 33	
Inverkeithing 242	d			16 35	16 35	16 55	16 55		17 01	17 01			17 55	17 55	
Haymarket 242	a	16 20	16 24	16 49	16 49	17 11	17 16		17 19	17 20			18 15	18 15	18 24
Edinburgh 10 242	a	16 27	16 31		16 57	17 20	17 24		17 25	17 27				18 22	18 32

A 🍴 from Aberdeen

Inverurie, Dyce, Aberdeen, Dundee, Inverness and Perth - Glasgow Queen Street and Edinburgh

		SR SO	SR SX	SR SO	SR SX	SR	SR	SR	SR SO	SR SX	SR SO	SR	SR	SR SO	GR SX	SR	SR	SR SO
				1	1	◇1	◇1	1				◇1	◇1	◇1	■ 1	1	◇1	◇1
							A											A
						⌶	⌶					⌶	⌶	⌶	⌶		⌶	⌶
Inverness	d											16 53						
Carrbridge	d											17b29						
Aviemore	d											17 37						
Kingussie	d											17 50						
Newtonmore	d											17 54						
Dalwhinnie	d																	
Blair Atholl	d											18 24						
Pitlochry	d											18 34						
Dunkeld & Birnam	d											18 46						
Inverurie 240	d						16 38											18 43
Dyce 240 ✈	d						16 54	17 05										18 55
Aberdeen 240	a						17 05	17 14										19 06
	d					16 37	17 07	17 16					17 36	18 16	18 16		18 30	19 09
Portlethen	d							17 27									18 40	
Stonehaven	d					16 53		17a37					17 52	18 33	18 33		18 49	19 26
Laurencekirk	d						17 38						18 06					19 40
Montrose	d					17 13	17 49						18 17	18 56	18 56		19 10	19 51
Arbroath	d					17 29	18 03						18 31	19 12	19 12		19 24	20 05
Carnoustie	d												18 38				19 31	
Broughty Ferry	d																	
Dundee	a					17 49	18 18						18 52	19 29	19 29		19 46	20 20
	d	17 26	17 26			17 51	18 19			18 46	18 46		18 52	19 30	19 30		19 46	20 21
Invergowrie	d																	
Perth	a					18 11						19 08	19 14				20 07	
	d			18 00	18 00	18 12			18 28			19 09	19 14			19 57	20 11	
Gleneagles	d																20 25	
Dunblane 230	d					18 35			18 49									
Stirling 230	d					18 42			19a00				19 43				20 40	
Larbert 230	d																	
Glasgow Queen St. 10 230 ⇌	a					19 14							20 15				21 14	
Leuchars 3	a	17 38	17 38				18 31			18 56	18 56			19 43	19 43			20 33
St Andrews Bus Station 🚌	a																	
St Andrews Bus Station 🚌	d																	
Leuchars 3	d	17 39	17 39				18 31			18 56	18 56			19 44	19 44			20 33
Cupar	d	17 47	17 47							19 04	19 04							
Springfield	d	17 51	17 51															
Ladybank	d	17 56	17 56	18 23	18 23					19 11	19 11					20 20		
Markinch	d	18 04	18 04	18 34	18 34					19 19	19 19	19 44				20 29		
Kirkcaldy 242	d	18 13	18 13	18 44	18 44					19 28	19 28	19 54		20 08	20 08	20 39		
Inverkeithing 242	d	18 29	18 29	19 00	19 00					19 46	19 46			20 24	20 24	20 55		
Haymarket 242	a	18 43	18 43	19 15	19 15		19 27			20 06	20 06	20 24		20s42	20s42	21 10		21 26
Edinburgh 10 242	a		18 50		19 21		19 34			20 13	20 13	20 29		20 50	20 50	21 19		21 32

A ⌶ from Aberdeen

b arr. 1723

Table 229

Mondays to Saturdays
from 20 September

Inverurie, Dyce, Aberdeen, Dundee, Inverness and Perth - Glasgow Queen Street and Edinburgh

		SR SX	SR SO	SR SX	SR	SR	SR	SR	SR	SR	XC SO	SR FSX	SR FO
		◇1			◇1	◇1		◇1	◇1	◇1	◇1	1	1
		A					A						
		⌶			⌶	⌶	⌶				⌶		
Inverness	d				18 43				20 15				
Carrbridge	d				19 14								
Aviemore	d				19b29				21 00				
Kingussie	d				19 42				21 12				
Newtonmore	d				19 46				21 17				
Dalwhinnie	d				19 58				21 28				
Blair Atholl	d				20 19				21 50				
Pitlochry	d				20 29				21 59				
Dunkeld & Birnam	d				20 41				22 12				
Inverurie 240	d	18 43					19 40						
Dyce 240 ✈	d	18 55					19 52						
Aberdeen 240	a	19 06					20 03						
	d	19 09				19 46	20 05	20 42		21 06	21 17	22 30	23 22
Portlethen	d					19 56						22 40	23 32
Stonehaven	d	19 26				20 05	20 21	20 58		21 22	21 35	22 49	23 41
Laurencekirk	d	19 40										23 03	23 55
Montrose	d	19 51				20 23	20 43	21 20		21 44	21 56	23 13	00 05
Arbroath	d	20 05				20 37	20 57	21 34		21 58	22 12	23 28	00 20
Carnoustie	d						21 04					23 35	00 27
Broughty Ferry	d												
Dundee	a	20 20				20 56	21 15	21 52		22 15	22 28	23 50	00 42
	d	20 21	20 42	20 42		20 56	21 16	21 52		22 15	22 29	23 51	00 43
Invergowrie	d											23 57	00 49
Perth	a				21 00	21 17		22 14	22 29			00 15	01 07
	d				21 02	21 17		22 14	22 30				
Gleneagles	d								22 47				
Dunblane 230	d								22 58				
Stirling 230	d					21 45		22 43	23 05				
Larbert 230	d												
Glasgow Queen St. 10 230 ⇌	a					22 19		23 15	23 39				
Leuchars 3	a	20 33	20 53	20 53			21 28			22 27	22 41		
St Andrews Bus Station 🚌	a												
St Andrews Bus Station 🚌	d												
Leuchars 3	d	20 33	20 54	20 54			21 28			22 27	22 42		
Cupar	d		21 01	21 01			21 36			22 37	22 49		
Springfield	d												
Ladybank	d		21 09	21 09			21 43			22 44	22 57		
Markinch	d		21 16	21 16	21 32		21 51			22 52	23 05		
Kirkcaldy 242	d		21 26	21 26	21 42		21 59			23 01	23 14		
Inverkeithing 242	d		21 49	21 49			22 22			23 24	23 31		
Haymarket 242	a	21 26	22 09	22 09	22 13		22 43			23 44	23 50		
Edinburgh 10 242	a	21 32		22 16	22 19		22 50			23 52	23 55		

A ⌶ from Aberdeen

b arr. 1922

Table 229

Inverurie, Dyce, Aberdeen, Dundee, Inverness and Perth - Glasgow Queen Street and Edinburgh

	SR	SR	SR	SR	GR	SR	GR	SR	XC	SR	SR	GR	SR	SR	GR	SR	SR	SR	SR	SR	SR	SR	SR
		■1	◇ 🍴	◇1 🍴	R 1 B 🍽		R 1 C 🍽		◇1 🍴	◇1 🍴	◇1 🍴	R 1 🍽		◇1 🍴	R 1 🍴⌀	◇ 🍴		◇1 🍴	◇1 🍴	◇1 🍴		◇1 🍴	◇ 🍴
Inverness d							09 40				12 30					13 25				16 15			15 25
Carrbridge d							10 10				13 08									16 46			
Aviemore d							10 18				13 17					14 02				16 55			
Kingussie d							10 31				13 30					14 15				17 14			
Newtonmore d							10 36				13 35												
Dalwhinnie d											13 46												
Blair Atholl d							11 08				14 08									17 47			
Pitlochry d							11 23				14 17					14 54				17 56			
Dunkeld & Birnam d							11 36				14 30									18 09			
Inverurie 240 d																							17 14
Dyce 240 ✈ d																							17 30
Aberdeen 240 a																							17 41
d				09 27	09 48				11 12	11 29		11 47		13 27	13 50			15 10	15 30			17 10	17 47
Portlethen d																		15 20					
Stonehaven d				09 43	10 05				11 29	11 45		12 04		13 43	14 07			15 26	15 46			17 26	18 04
Laurencekirk d				09 57										13 57									18 18
Montrose d				10 08	10 28				11 50	12 07		12 27		14 07	14 30			15 48	16 08			17 48	18 28
Arbroath d				10 22	10 44				12 06	12 21		12 43		14 22	14 46			16 02	16 22			18 02	18 43
Carnoustie d				10 29														16 09					
Broughty Ferry d																							
Dundee a				10 43	11 01				12 24	12 39		13 00		14 43	15 03			16 23	16 41			18 17	19 02
d	07 25	08 43		10 43	11 02	09 25		11 25	12 25	12 43		13 01	13 25	14 45	15 04		15 25	16 25	16 43		17 25	18 19	19 04
Invergowrie d																							
Perth a		09 03		11 05			11 57			13 03	14 49			15 06		15 23			17 03	18 26			19 25
d		09 03	09 27	11 05			11 57			13 05	14 50			15 08		15 25			17 05	18 27			19 27
Gleneagles d		09 20	09 42	11 20			12 13			13 20	15 05			15 21					17 20	18 44			
Dunblane 230 d		09 31	09 54	11 31			12 26			13 31	15 16			15 33					17 31	18 55			
Stirling 230 d		09 38	10 02	11 38			12 33			13 38	15 22			15 45					17 38	19 02			19 55
Larbert 230 d		09 47									15 31									19 09			
Glasgow Queen St. 10 230 ⇌ a		10 15		12 11						14 11	15 56			16 28					18 12	19 36			
Leuchars 3 a	07 36				11 15	09 36		11 36	12 37			13 14	13 37		15 17		15 36	16 36			17 36	18 30	
St Andrews Bus Station 🚌 a																							
St Andrews Bus Station 🚌 d																							
Leuchars 3 d	07 37				11 16	09 37		11 37	12 38			13 15	13 37		15 18		15 37	16 37			17 37	18 31	
Cupar d	07 44					09 44		11 44	12 45				13 44				15 44				17 44		
Springfield d																							
Ladybank d	07 52					09 52		11 52					13 52				15 52				17 52		
Markinch d	07 59					09 59		11 59					13 59				15 59				17 59		
Kirkcaldy 242 d	08 08				11 40	10 08		12 08	13 03			13 39	14 08		15 42	16 03	16 08	17 02			18 07	18 56	
Inverkeithing 242 d	08 30				11 56	10 30		12 30	13 18			13 55	14 30		15 58	16 19	16 30	17 18			18 29	19 12	
Haymarket 242 a	08 53		10 52		12 17	10 58	13 12	12 58	13 36			14 18	14 58		16 19	16 35	16 54	17 34			18 52	19 27	
Edinburgh 10 242 a	09 00		10 58		12 24	11 06	13 18	13 06	13 42			14 24	15 06		16 25	16 42	16 59	17 41			19 00	19 35	20 31

B The Northern Lights

C The Highland Chieftain

Table 229

Inverurie, Dyce, Aberdeen, Dundee, Inverness and Perth - Glasgow Queen Street and Edinburgh

	SR	SR	SR	SR	SR	SR	XC	SR
	◇ 🍴		◇1 🍴	◇1 🍴	◇1 🍴	◇1 🍴	◇1 🍴	■1
Inverness d	15 25			18 30				
Carrbridge d				19 01				
Aviemore d				19 09				
Kingussie d				19 22				
Newtonmore d				19 26				
Dalwhinnie d				19 39				
Blair Atholl d				20 02				
Pitlochry d				20 11				
Dunkeld & Birnam d				20 24				
Inverurie 240 d	17 14							
Dyce 240 ✈ d	17 30							
Aberdeen 240 a	17 41							
d	17 47		19 10		19 35	20 10	21 28	22 29
Portlethen d						20 20		
Stonehaven d	18 04		19 26		19 51	20 26	21 45	22 48
Laurencekirk d	18 18							
Montrose d	18 28		19 48		20 13	20 48	22 06	23 11
Arbroath d	18 43		20 02		20 27	21 02	22 22	23 25
Carnoustie d			20 09					23 32
Broughty Ferry d								
Dundee a	19 02		20 18		20 42	21 19	22 38	23 46
d	19 04	19 27	20 20		20 43	21 21	22 39	23 47
Invergowrie d								
Perth a	19 25			20 42	21 04			00 09
d	19 27			20 46	21 05			
Gleneagles d					21 20			
Dunblane 230 d					21 31			
Stirling 230 d	19 55				21 38			
Larbert 230 d					21 49			
Glasgow Queen St. 10 230 ⇌ a					22 15			
Leuchars 3 a		19 38	20 31			21 32	22 51	
St Andrews Bus Station 🚌 a								
St Andrews Bus Station 🚌 d								
Leuchars 3 d		19 39	20 32			21 33	22 52	
Cupar d		19 46				21 39	22 59	
Springfield d								
Ladybank d		19 54				21 48	23 06	
Markinch d		20 01				21 54	23 14	
Kirkcaldy 242 d		20 10	20 59	21 25		22 05	23 22	
Inverkeithing 242 d		20 31	21 15	21 41		22 21	23 38	
Haymarket 242 a		20 54	21 31	21 59		22 36	23 53	
Edinburgh 10 242 a	20 31	21 01	21 36	22 05		22 43	23 58	

Edinburgh, Glasgow Queen Street and Falkirk Grahamston - Stirling, Alloa and Dunblane

		SR	SR ◇1 ⊼	SR	SR 1	SR	SR	SR 1	SR	SR	SR 1	SR 1 ⊼	SR	SR	SR ◇1	SR 1 ⊼	SR	SR ◇1 ⊼	SR	SR 1 ⊼	SR	SR 1 ⊼	SR
Edinburgh 10	d	05 18			05 55	06 03		06 30	06 33	06 36	06 45	07 00	07 03	07 06		07 15				07 30	07 33	07 45	07 48
Haymarket	d	05 22			05 59	06 06		06 33	06 36	06 40	06 47	07 03	07 06	07 10		07 18				07 33	07 36	07 48	07 51
Edinburgh Park	d	05 27				06 10			06 41	06 46			07 11	07 16							07 41		07 55
Linlithgow	d	05 39			06 13			06 48	06 53		07 01		07 23			07 33				07 48	07 53	08 03	
Polmont 3	d	05 44			06 19			06 55	06 58			07 19	07 28							07 54	07 58		
Glasgow Queen Street 10 ⇌	d		05 55	06 13			06 48								07 06		07 18	07 41	07 48				
Bishopbriggs	d			06 20			06 53										07 23		07 53				
Lenzie 3	d			06 25			06 59										07 29		07 59			08 25	
Croy 3	d			06 32	06 34		07 05	07 10			07 21					07 52	07 35		08 05	08 09			
Falkirk Grahamston	d	05 51							07 05				07 34								08 05		
Camelon	d	05 54							07 07				07 37								08 07		
Larbert	d	06 00	06 15	06 43			07 18		07 13				07 43				07 48		08 18		08 13		
Stirling	d	06 09	06 24	06 51			07b40		07 23				07 53		07 33		08 06	08 07	08 30		08 23		
Alloa	a			07 05													08 18						
Bridge of Allan	d	06 13					07 44		07 27				07 57						08 35		08 27		
Dunblane	a	06 20	06 30				07 52		07 36				08 06		07 39			08 14	08 43		08 36		

		SR	SR	SR 1 ⊼	SR 1 ⊼	SR	SR 1 ⊼	SR	SR 1 ⊼	SR	SR	SR 1 ⊼	SR	SR 1 ⊼	SR 1 ⊼	SR 1 ⊼	SR	SR 1 ⊼	SR	SR ◇1 ⊼	SR 1 ⊼	SR	SR
Edinburgh 10	d			08 00	08 15	08 18	08 30	08 33	08 45	08 48		09 00		09 15	09 30	09 45	09 48	10 01			10 15	10 03	10 18
Haymarket	d			08 03	08 18	08 21	08 33	08 36	08 48	08 51		09 03		09 18	09 33	09 48	09 51	10 03			10 18	10 06	10 22
Edinburgh Park	d					08 25		08 41		08 55							09 55					10 11	10 26
Linlithgow	d	07 59			08 33			08 53	09 03					09 33		10 03					10 33	10 23	
Polmont 3	d			08 19	08 39			08 58	09 09					09 39		10 09					10 39	10 28	
Glasgow Queen Street 10 ⇌	d		08 18								08 48		09 18						10 18	10 11			
Bishopbriggs	d		08 23								08 53		09 23						10 23				
Lenzie 3	d		08 29								08 59		09 29						10 29				
Croy 3	d		08 35	08 35			09 03				09 05	09 33	09 35		10 03			10 33	10 35				
Falkirk Grahamston	d	08 11						09 04														10 35	
Camelon	d	08 14						09 07														10 37	
Larbert	d		08 48					09 13			09 18		09 48						10 48			10 43	
Stirling	d		09 00					09 23			09 30		10 00						11 00	10 36		10 53	
Alloa	a		09 13										10 13						11 13				
Bridge of Allan	d							09 27			09 35											10 57	
Dunblane	a							09 36			09 43									10 42		11 07	

		SR 1 ⊼	SR ◇1 ⊼	SR	SR	SR 1 ⊼	SR	SR	SR 1 ⊼	SR	SR 1 ⊼	SR	SR 1 ⊼	SR ◇1 ⊼	SR	SR 1 ⊼	SR	SR	SR	SR 1 ⊼	SR	SR 1 ⊼	SR
Edinburgh 10	d	10 30			10 33	10 45	10 48		11 00	11 03	11 15	11 18	11 30			11 45	11 48	11 33		12 00	12 03	12 15	12 18
Haymarket	d	10 33			10 36	10 48	10 51		11 03	11 06	11 18	11 21	11 33			11 48	11 51	11 36		12 03	12 07	12 18	12 21
Edinburgh Park	d				10 41		10 55			11 11		11 25					11 55	11 41			12 11		12 25
Linlithgow	d				10 53	11 03				11 23	11 33					12 03		11 53			12 23	12 33	
Polmont 3	d				10 58	11 09				11 28	11 39					12 09		11 58			12 28	12 39	
Glasgow Queen Street 10 ⇌	d		10 41	11 18				10 48						11 41	12 18				11 48				
Bishopbriggs	d			11 23				10 53							12 23				11 53				
Lenzie 3	d			11 29				10 59							12 29				11 59				
Croy 3	d	11 03		11 35				11 05	11 33				12 03		12 35				12 05	12 33			
Falkirk Grahamston	d				11 04					11 35								12 04			12 35		
Camelon	d				11 07					11 37								12 07			12 37		
Larbert	d			11 48	11 13			11 18		11 43					12 48			12 13	12 18		12 45		
Stirling	d		11 07	12 00	11 23			11 30		11 53				12 07	13 00			12 23	12 30		12 54		
Alloa	a			12 13											13 13								
Bridge of Allan	d				11 27			11 35		11 57								12 27	12 35		12 57		
Dunblane	a				11 36			11 43		12 07								12 36	12 43		13 06		

		SR 1 ⊼	SR ◇1 ⊼	SR	SR	SR 1 ⊼	SR	SR	SR 1 ⊼	SR	SR 1 ⊼	SR	SR 1 ⊼	SR ◇1 ⊼	SR	SR	SR 1 ⊼	SR	SR 1 ⊼	SR	SR 1 ⊼	SR	SR 1 ⊼	SR
Edinburgh 10	d	12 30		12 33		12 45	12 48		13 00	13 02	13 15	13 18	13 30		13 33		13 45	13 48	14 00	14 03	14 15	14 18	14 30	14 33
Haymarket	d	12 33		12 36		12 48	12 51		13 03	13 06	13 18	13 21	13 33		13 36		13 48	13 51	14 03	14 06	14 18	14 21	14 33	14 36
Edinburgh Park	d			12 41			12 55			13 11		13 25			13 41			13 55		14 11		14 25		14 41
Linlithgow	d			12 53		13 03				13 24	13 33				13 53		14 03			14 23	14 33			14 53
Polmont 3	d			12 58		13 09				13 29	13 39				13 58		14 09			14 28	14 39			14 58
Glasgow Queen Street 10 ⇌	d		12 41		13 18			12 48						13 41		14 18								
Bishopbriggs	d				13 23			12 53								14 23								
Lenzie 3	d				13 29			12 59								14 29								
Croy 3	d	13 03			13 35			13 05	13 33				14 03			14 35			14 33				15 03	
Falkirk Grahamston	d			13 04						13 35					14 04					14 34				15 04
Camelon	d			13 07						13 38					14 07					14 37				15 07
Larbert	d			13 13	13 48			13 18		13 44					14 13	14 48				14 43				15 13
Stirling	d		13 07	13 23	14 00			13 31		13 53				14 07	14 23	15 00				14 53				15 23
Alloa	a				14 13											15 13								
Bridge of Allan	d			13 27				13 35		13 58					14 27					14 57				15 27
Dunblane	a			13 36				13 43		14 06					14 36					15 06				15 36

Table 230

Mondays to Fridays

Edinburgh, Glasgow Queen Street and Falkirk Grahamston - Stirling, Alloa and Dunblane

		SR 1 ⊼	SR	SR	SR	SR 1 ⊼	SR	SR 1 ⊼	SR	SR 1 ⊼	SR 1 ⊼	SR ◇1 ⊼	SR	SR 1 ⊼	SR	SR	SR 1 ⊼	SR ◇1 ⊼	SR	SR 1 ⊼	SR	SR	SR
Edinburgh 10	d		14 45	14 48		15 00	15 03	15 15	15 19		15 30		15 33	15 45			16 00		16 03	16 15	16 18		
Haymarket	d		14 48	14 51		15 03	15 06	15 18	15 22		15 33		15 36	15 48			16 03		16 06	16 18	16 21		
Edinburgh Park	d			14 55			15 11		15 25				15 41						16 11		16 25		
Linlithgow	d		15 03				15 23	15 33					15 53	16 03					16 23	16 33			
Polmont 3	d		15 09				15 28	15 40					15 58	16 09					16 28	16 39			
Glasgow Queen Street 10 ⇌	d	14 41			14 48					15 18		15 41			15 48	15 51		16 11				16 19	16 22
Bishopbriggs	d				14 53					15 23					15 53	15 56						16 24	
Lenzie 3	d				14 59					15 29					15 59	16 08						16 30	
Croy 3	d				15 05	15 33				15 35	16 03				16 05	16 15	16 33					16 36	
Falkirk Grahamston	d						15 34						16 04			16a33			16 34				
Camelon	d						15 37						16 07						16 37				17 01
Larbert	d				15 18		15 43			15 48			16 13		16 18				16 43			16 49	
Stirling	d	15 07			15 30		15 53			16 00		16 07	16 23		16 30			16 37	16 53			17 08	
Alloa	a									16 14												17 20	
Bridge of Allan	d				15 35		15 57						16 27		16 35				16 57				
Dunblane	a				15 43		16 06						16 36		16 43			16 48	17 06				

		SR 1 ⊼	GR 1 A ⊼	SR	SR	SR 1 ⊼	SR	SR	SR 1 ⊼	SR	SR	SR	SR 1 ⊼	SR	SR	SR 1 ⊼	SR ◇1 ⊼	SR	SR 1 ⊼	SR	SR 1 ⊼	SR	SR
Edinburgh 10	d	16 30	16 33		16 37	16 45	16 48		17 00			17 03	17 15	17 18	17 26	17 30		17 33	17 45	17 48	18 00		18 03
Haymarket	d	16 33	16 38		16 42	16 48	16 51		17 03			17 06	17 18	17 21	17 30	17 33		17 37	17 48	17 51	18 03		18 07
Edinburgh Park	d				16 46		16 55					17 11		17 25				17 42		17 55			18 11
Linlithgow	d				16 58	17 03						17 24	17 33					17 55	18 03				18 23
Polmont 3	d				17 03	17 09						17 28	17 39					18 00	18 09				18 28
Glasgow Queen Street 10 ⇌	d			16 33				16 48		17 03	17 12						17 41					18 11	
Bishopbriggs	d			16 39				16 53		17 08													
Lenzie 3	d			16a44				16 59		17 14													
Croy 3	d	17 03						17 05	17 33							18 03					18 33		
Falkirk Grahamston	d		17 05		17 09					17a32		17 34						18 06					18 35
Camelon	d				17 11							17 37						18 09					18 37
Larbert	d				17 18			17 23			17 33	17 44			17 57			18 16				18 30	18 43
Stirling	d		17 20		17 27			17 35			17 45	17 54			18 06		18 15	18 27				18 41	18 53
Alloa	a																	18 41					
Bridge of Allan	d				17 31			17 40			17 49	17 57			18 13							18 46	18 57
Dunblane	a				17 40			17 47			17 54	18 06			18 18		18 22					18 50	19 06

		SR 1 ⊼	SR	SR 1	SR	SR ◇1 ⊼	SR 1 ⊼	SR	SR	SR 1 ⊼	SR	SR 1 ⊼	SR	SR	SR ◇1	SR	SR 1	SR	SR	SR 1	SR	SR	SR ◇1
Edinburgh 10	d	18 15	18 18	18 30	18 33		18 45	18 48		19 00	19 02	19 15		19 22			19 30	19 33		20 00	20 03	20 18	
Haymarket	d	18 18	18 21	18 33	18 36		18 48	18 51		19 03	19 06	19 18		19 25			19 33	19 36		20 03	20 06	20 21	
Edinburgh Park	d		18 25		18 41			18 55			19 11			19 29				19 41			20 11	20 25	
Linlithgow	d	18 33			18 53		19 03				19 23	19 33					19 48	19 53		20 18	20 23		
Polmont 3	d	18 39			18 58		19 09				19 28	19 39						19 58		20 24	20 28		
Glasgow Queen Street 10 ⇌	d					18 41			18 48				19 18		19 41	19 49			20 18				20 41
Bishopbriggs	d								18 53				19 23			19 54			20 23				
Lenzie 3	d								18 59				19 29			20 00			20 29				
Croy 3	d			19 03					19 05	19 33			19 35			20 06	20 07		20 35				
Falkirk Grahamston	d				19 04						19 35							20 04			20 34		
Camelon	d				19 07						19 37							20 07			20 37		
Larbert	d				19 13				19 21		19 43		19 48			20 18		20 13	20 48		20 43		
Stirling	d				19 23	19 07			19 35		19 53		20 00		20 07	20 30		20 23	21 00		20 53		21 07
Alloa	a												20 13						21 13				
Bridge of Allan	d				19 27				19 39		19 57					20 35		20 27			20 57		
Dunblane	a				19 38	19 14			19 45		20 06					20 43		20 36			21 07		21 14

		SR	SR 1	SR	SR 1	SR	SR	SR ◇1	SR	SR 1	SR	SR 1	SR	SR	SR	SR 1	SR	SR	SR 1	SR	SR 1	SR	SR
Edinburgh 10	d		20 30	20 33	21 00	21 18				21 30	21 33	22 00	22 18			22 30	22 33		23 00	23 18	23 30	23 33	
Haymarket	d		20 33	20 36	21 03	21 21				21 33	21 37	22 03	22 21			22 33	22 36		23 03	23 21	23 33	23 36	
Edinburgh Park	d			20 41		21 25					21 41		22 25				22 41			23 25		23 41	
Linlithgow	d		20 48	20 53	21 18					21 48	21 53	22 18				22 48	22 53		23 18		23 48	23 53	
Polmont 3	d			20 58	21 24						21 58	22 24					22 58		23 24		23 54	23 58	
Glasgow Queen Street 10 ⇌	d	20 48					21 18	21 41	21 48					22 18	22 48			23 18					23 48
Bishopbriggs	d	20 53					21 23		21 53					22 23	22 53			23 23					23 53
Lenzie 3	d	20 59					21 29		21 59					22 29	22 59			23 29					23 59
Croy 3	d	21 05	21 07				21 35		22 05			22 07		22 35	23 05	23 07		23 35	23 39		00 10		00 05
Falkirk Grahamston	d			21 04							22 05						23 04					00 04	
Camelon	d			21 07							22 07						23 07					00 07	
Larbert	d	21 18		21 13			21 48		22 18		22 13			22 47	23 18		23 13	23 48				00 13	00 18
Stirling	d	21 30		21 23			22 00	22 07	22 30		22 23			23 01	23 33		23 23	00 02				00 23	00 30
Alloa	a						22 13							23 13				00 13					
Bridge of Allan	d	21 35		21 27					22 35		22 27				23 37		23 27					00 27	00 35
Dunblane	a		20 30	21 36							22 34				23 42		23 36					00 35	00 42

A The Highland Chieftain

Table 230

Saturdays

Edinburgh, Glasgow Queen Street and Falkirk Grahamston - Stirling, Alloa and Dunblane

		SR	SR	SR	SR	SR	SR	SR	SR	SR	SR	SR	SR	SR	SR	SR	SR	SR	SR	SR	SR	SR	SR	SR	SR
			◇1 ✠		1				1			1 ✠		◇1		1 ✠		◇1 ✠		1 ✠		1 ✠			1 ✠
Edinburgh 10	d	05 18			05 55	06 03			06 30	06 33	06 36	07 00	07 03		07 06	07 15				07 30	07 33	07 45		07 48	08 00
Haymarket	d	05 22			05 59	06 06			06 33	06 36	06 40	07 03	07 06		07 10	07 18				07 33	07 36	07 48		07 51	08 03
Edinburgh Park	d	05 27				06 10				06 41	06 46		07 11		07 16						07 41			07 55	
Linlithgow	d	05 39			06 13				06 48	06 53			07 23			07 33				07 48	07 53	08 03			
Polmont 3	d	05 44			06 19				06 55	06 58		07 19	07 28							07 54	07 58				08 19
Glasgow Queen Street 10	d		05 55	06 13				06 48						07 06			07 18	07 41	07 48				08 18		
Bishopbriggs	d			06 21				06 53									07 23		07 53				08 23		
Lenzie 3	d			06 25				06 59									07 29		07 59				08 29		
Croy 3	d			06 31	06 34			07 05	07 10							07 52	07 35		08 05	08 09		08 25	08 35		08 35
Falkirk Grahamston	d	05 51								07 05			07 34								08 04				
Camelon	d	05 54								07 07			07 37								08 07				
Larbert	d	06 00	06 15	06 43				07 18		07 13			07 43				07 48		08 18		08 13		08 48		
Stirling	d	06 09	06 24	06 51			07 01	07b40		07 23			07 53	07 33			08 06	08 07	08 30		08 23		09 00		
Alloa	a			07 05													08 18						09 13		
Bridge of Allan	d	06 13					07 05	07 44		07 27			07 57						08 35		08 27				
Dunblane	a	06 20	06 30				07 12	07 52		07 36			08 06	07 39				08 14	08 43		08 36				

		SR	SR	SR	SR	SR	SR	SR	SR	SR	SR	SR	SR	SR	SR	SR	SR	SR	SR	SR	SR	SR	SR	SR	SR
			◇1 ✠	1 ✠		1 ✠		1 ✠				1 ✠		◇1 ✠	1 ✠		1 ✠		1 ✠			1 ✠	◇1 ✠		
Edinburgh 10	d	08 03		08 15	08 18	08 30	08 33	08 45	08 48			09 00	09 03		09 15	09 18	09 30	09 33	09 45	09 48		10 00		10 03	
Haymarket	d	08 06		08 18	08 21	08 33	08 36	08 48	08 51			09 03	09 06		09 18	09 22	09 33	09 36	09 48	09 51		10 03		10 06	
Edinburgh Park	d	08 11			08 25		08 41		08 55				09 11			09 25		09 41		09 55				10 11	
Linlithgow	d	08 23		08 33			08 53	09 03					09 23		09 33			09 53	10 03					10 23	
Polmont 3	d	08 28		08 39			08 58	09 09					09 28		09 39			09 58	10 09					10 28	
Glasgow Queen Street 10	d		08 41							08 48	09 18			09 41							09 48		10 11		10 18
Bishopbriggs	d									08 53	09 23										09 53				10 23
Lenzie 3	d									08 59	09 29										09 59				10 29
Croy 3	d					09 03				09 05	09 35	09 33					10 03				10 05	10 33			10 35
Falkirk Grahamston	d	08 34					09 04						09 34					10 04						10 35	
Camelon	d	08 37					09 07						09 37					10 07						10 37	
Larbert	d	08 43					09 13			09 18	09 48		09 43					10 13			10 18			10 42	10 48
Stirling	d	08 53	09a07				09 23			09 30	10 00		09 53	10a07				10 23			10 43		10 36	10 53	11 00
Alloa	a										10 13														11 13
Bridge of Allan	d	08 57					09 27			09 35			09 57					10 27			10 48			10 57	
Dunblane	a	09 06					09 36			09 43			10 06					10 36			10 57		10 42	11 07	

		SR	SR	SR	SR	SR	SR	SR	SR	SR	SR	SR	SR	SR	SR	SR	SR	SR	SR	SR	SR	SR	SR	SR	SR
		1 ✠		1 ✠	◇1 ✠			1 ✠		1 ✠			1 ✠		◇1 ✠	1 ✠		1 ✠			1 ✠	A		1 ✠	
Edinburgh 10	d	10 15	10 17	10 30		10 33		10 45	10 48	11 00	11 03		11 15	11 18		11 30	11 33	11 45	11 48		12 00	12 03		12 15	12 18
Haymarket	d	10 18	10 21	10 33		10 36		10 48	10 51	11 03	11 06		11 18	11 22		11 33	11 36	11 48	11 51		12 03	12 06		12 18	12 21
Edinburgh Park	d		10 25			10 41			10 55		11 11			11 25			11 41		11 55			12 11			12 25
Linlithgow	d	10 33				10 53		11 03			11 23		11 33				11 53	12 03				12 23		12 33	
Polmont 3	d	10 39				10 58		11 09			11 28		11 39				11 58	12 09				12 28		12 39	
Glasgow Queen Street 10	d				10 41		10 48					11 18			11 41					11 48			12 18		
Bishopbriggs	d						10 53					11 23								11 53			12 23		
Lenzie 3	d						10 59					11 29								11 59			12 29		
Croy 3	d			11 03			11 05			11 33		11 35				12 03				12 05	12 33		12 35		
Falkirk Grahamston	d					11 04					11 35						12 04					12 34			
Camelon	d					11 07					11 37						12 07					12 37			
Larbert	d					11 14	11 18				11 43	11 48					12 13			12 18		12 44	12 48		
Stirling	d				11a07	11 23	11 30				11 53	12 00			12a07		12 23			12 30		12 54	13 00		
Alloa	a											12 13											13 13		
Bridge of Allan	d					11 27	11 35				11 57						12 27			12 35		12 58			
Dunblane	a					11 36	11 43				12 07						12 36			12 43		13 06			

		SR	SR	SR	SR	SR	SR	SR	SR	SR	SR	SR	SR	SR	SR	SR	SR	SR	SR	SR	SR	SR	SR	SR	SR
		B	1 ✠	◇1 ✠		1 ✠			1 ✠	A	1 ✠			B	1 ✠	◇1 ✠		1 ✠			1 ✠		1 ✠		
Edinburgh 10	d		12 30		12 33	12 45	12 48		13 00	13 03	13 15	13 18			13 30		13 33	13 45	13 48		14 00	14 03	14 15	14 18	
Haymarket	d		12 33		12 36	12 48	12 51		13 03	13 06	13 18	13 21			13 33		13 36	13 48	13 51		14 03	14 06	14 18	14 21	
Edinburgh Park	d				12 41		12 55			13 11		13 25					13 41		13 55			14 11		14 25	
Linlithgow	d	12 23			12 53	13 03				13 23	13 33			13 24			13 53	14 03				14 23	14 33		
Polmont 3	d	12 28			12 58	13 09				13 28	13 39			13 29			13 58	14 09				14 28	14 39		
Glasgow Queen Street 10	d			12 41				12 48					13 18			13 41				13 48					14 18
Bishopbriggs	d							12 53					13 23							13 53					14 23
Lenzie 3	d							12 59					13 29							13 59					14 29
Croy 3	d		13 03					13 05	13 33				13 35		14 03					14 05	14 33				14 35
Falkirk Grahamston	d	12 34			13 04					13 34				13 35			14 04					14 34			
Camelon	d	12 37			13 07					13 37				13 38			14 07					14 37			
Larbert	d	12 44			13 13			13 18		13 44			13 49	13 45			14 13			14 16		14 43			14 48
Stirling	d	12 54		13a07	13 23			13 31		13 54			14 00	13 55		14a07	14 23			14 31		14 53			15 00
Alloa	a												14 13												15 13
Bridge of Allan	d	12 58			13 27			13 35		13 58				13 59			14 27			14 36		14 57			
Dunblane	a	13 06			13 36			13 43		14 06				14 07			14 36			14 43		15 06			

A until 18 September

B from 25 September

Table 230

Saturdays

Edinburgh, Glasgow Queen Street and Falkirk Grahamston - Stirling, Alloa and Dunblane

		SR	SR	SR	SR	SR	SR	SR	SR	SR	SR	SR	SR	SR	SR	SR	SR	SR	SR	SR	SR	SR	SR	SR	SR
		1 ✠	◇1 ✠		1 ✠			1 ✠		1 ✠			1 ✠		◇1 ✠	1 ✠			◇1 ✠	1 ✠		1 ✠		◇1 ✠	1 ✠
Edinburgh 10	d	14 30		14 33	14 45	14 48		15 00	15 03	15 15	15 18		15 30	15 33		15 45		15 48		16 00	16 03	16 15	16 19		16 30
Haymarket	d	14 33		14 36	14 48	14 51		15 03	15 06	15 18	15 22		15 33	15 36		15 48		15 51		16 03	16 06	16 18	16 22		16 33
Edinburgh Park	d			14 41		14 55			15 11		15 25			15 41				15 55			16 11		16 26		
Linlithgow	d			14 53	15 03				15 23	15 33				15 53		16 03					16 23	16 33			
Polmont 3	d			14 58	15 09				15 28	15 39				15 58		16 09					16 28	16 39			
Glasgow Queen Street 10	d		14 41				14 48					15 18			15 41		15 46		16 11					16 41	
Bishopbriggs	d						14 53					15 23					15 51								
Lenzie 3	d						14 59					15 29					15 57								
Croy 3	d	15 03					15 05	15 33				15 35	16 03				16 03			16 33					17 03
Falkirk Grahamston	d			15 04					15 34					16 04							16 34				
Camelon	d			15 07					15 37					16 07							16 37				
Larbert	d			15 13			15 18		15 43			15 48		16 13			16 18				16 43				
Stirling	d		15 07	15 23			15 30		15 53			16 00		16 23	16 07		16 30		16 37		16 53			17 07	
Alloa	a											16 14													
Bridge of Allan	d			15 27			15 35		15 57					16 27			16 35				16 57				
Dunblane	a			15 36			15 43		16 06					16 36			16 43		16 48		17 07				

		SR	GR	SR	SR	SR	SR	SR	SR	SR	SR	SR	SR	SR	SR	SR	SR	SR	SR	SR	SR	SR	SR	SR	SR
			1 A ✠	B	C	1 ✠				1 ✠		1			1		◇1	1			1			1	
Edinburgh 10	d		16 33	16 37		16 45	16 48			17 00	17 03	17 15	17 18		17 30	17 33		17 45	17 48		18 00	18 03		18 15	18 18
Haymarket	d		16 38	16 41		16 48	16 51			17 03	17 06	17 18	17 21		17 33	17 37		17 48	17 52		18 03	18 06		18 18	18 21
Edinburgh Park	d			16 46			16 56				17 11		17 25			17 42			17 55			18 11			18 25
Linlithgow	d			16 58	16 59	17 04					17 24	17 33				17 55		18 03				18 23		18 33	
Polmont 3	d			17 03	17 04	17 10					17 28	17 39				18 00		18 09				18 28		18 39	
Glasgow Queen Street 10	d	16 19						16 48	17 03					17 18			17 41			17 48			18 11		
Bishopbriggs	d	16 24						16 53	17 08					17 23						17 53					
Lenzie 3	d	16 30						16 59	17 14					17 29						17 59					
Croy 3	d	16 36						17 05	17 19	17 33				17 35	18 03					18 05	18 33				
Falkirk Grahamston	d		17 05	17 08	17 09						17 34					18 06						18 35			
Camelon	d			17 11	17 12						17 37					18 09						18 37			
Larbert	d	16 49		17 18	17 19			17 23	17 31		17 44			17 47		18 16				18 19		18 43	18 30		
Stirling	d	17 08	17 20	17 27	17 28			17 35	17 45		17 54			17 59		18 27	18 07			18 32		18 53	18 41		
Alloa	a	17 20												18 12		18 41									
Bridge of Allan	d			17 31	17 32			17 40	17 49		17 57									18 37		18 57	18 46		
Dunblane	a			17 40	17 41			17 47	17 54		18 07						18 14			18 44		19 06	18 50		

		SR	SR	SR	SR	SR	SR	SR	SR	SR	SR	SR	SR	SR	SR	SR	SR	SR	SR	SR	SR	SR	SR	SR	SR
			1 ✠		◇1 ✠	1 ✠			1 ✠		1 ✠			◇1 ✠	1				1			◇1		1	
Edinburgh 10	d		18 30	18 33		18 45	18 48		19 00	19 03	19 15		19 22		19 30	19 33		20 03	20 00	20 18				20 30	20 33
Haymarket	d		18 33	18 36		18 48	18 51		19 03	19 06	19 18		19 26		19 33	19 36		20 06	20 03	20 21				20 33	20 36
Edinburgh Park	d			18 41			18 55			19 11			19 29			19 41		20 11		20 25					20 41
Linlithgow	d			18 53		19 03				19 23	19 33				19 48	19 53		20 23	20 18					20 48	20 53
Polmont 3	d			18 58		19 09				19 28	19 39					18 58		20 28	20 24						20 58
Glasgow Queen Street 10	d	18 18			18 41			18 48				19 18		19 41			19 49				20 18	20 41	20 48		
Bishopbriggs	d	18 23						18 53				19 23					19 54				20 23		20 53		
Lenzie 3	d	18 29						18 59				19 29					20 00				20 29		20 59		
Croy 3	d	18 35	19 03					19 05	19 33			19 35			20 07		20 06				20 35		21 05	21 07	
Falkirk Grahamston	d			19 04						19 35						20 04		20 34							21 04
Camelon	d			19 07						19 37						20 07		20 37							21 07
Larbert	d	18 48		19 13				19 21		19 43		19 48				20 13	20 18	20 43			20 48		21 18		21 13
Stirling	d	19 00		19 23	19 07			19 35		19 53		20 00		20 07		20 23	20 30	20 53			21 00	21 07	21 30		21 23
Alloa	a	19 14										20 13									21 13				
Bridge of Allan	d			19 27				19 39		19 57						20 27	20 35	20 57					21 35		21 27
Dunblane	a			19 38	19 14			19 45		20 06						20 36	20 43	21 07				21 14	21 43		21 36

		SR	SR	SR	SR	SR	SR	SR	SR	SR	SR	SR	SR	SR	SR	SR	SR	SR	SR	SR
		1			◇1								1			1		1	B	
Edinburgh 10	d	21 00	21 18				21 30	21 33	22 00	22 18			22 30	22 33		23 00	23 18	23 30	23 33	
Haymarket	d	21 03	21 21				21 33	21 37	22 03	22 21			22 33	22 36		23 03	23 21	23 33	23 36	
Edinburgh Park	d		21 25					21 41		22 25				22 41			23 25		23 41	
Linlithgow	d	21 18					21 48	21 53	22 18				22 48	22 53		23 18		23 48	23 53	
Polmont 3	d	21 24						21 58	22 24					22 58		23 24		23 54	23 58	
Glasgow Queen Street 10	d			21 18	21 41	21 48					22 18	22 48			23 18					23 48
Bishopbriggs	d			21 23		21 53					22 23	22 53			23 23					23 53
Lenzie 3	d			21 29		21 59					22 29	22 59			23 29					23 59
Croy 3	d			21 35		22 05	22 07				22 35	23 05	23 07		23 35	23 39		00 10		00 05
Falkirk Grahamston	d							22 05						23 04					00 04	
Camelon	d							22 07						23 07					00 07	
Larbert	d			21 48		22 18		22 13			22 47	23 18		23 13	23 48				00 13	00 18
Stirling	d			22 00	22 07	22 30		22 23			23 01	23 33		23 23	23 59				00 23	00 30
Alloa	a			22 13							23 13				00 12					
Bridge of Allan	d					22 35		22 27				23 37		23 27					00 27	00 35
Dunblane	a					22 43		22 34				23 42		23 36					00 35	00 42

A The Highland Chieftain

B until 18 September

C from 25 September

Table 230

Edinburgh, Glasgow Queen Street and Falkirk Grahamston - Stirling, Alloa and Dunblane

Sundays

		SR C	SR C	SR	SR C	SR	SR C	SR	SR	SR	SR C	SR	SR	SR ■ ⚒	SR	SR ◇■	SR C	SR	SR	SR ■ ⚒	SR	SR ■ ⚒	SR C	SR
Edinburgh ■	d			09 03		09 34				10 18		10 33		11 00	11 18			11 33		12 00	12 18	12 30		12 33
Haymarket	d			09 07		09 37				10 21		10 36		11 03	11 21			11 37		12 03	12 21	12 33		12 37
Edinburgh Park	d			09 11		09 41				10 25		10 41			11 25			11 41			12 25			12 41
Linlithgow	d					10 00						10 53		11 18				11 53		12 18		12 48		12 53
Polmont ■	d					10 05						10 58		11 24				11 58		12 24				12 58
Glasgow Queen Street ■ ⇌	d	08 15	08 48		09 12		09 47	09 38	10 15		10 47		11 15			11 45	11 48		12 15				12 47	
Bishopbriggs	d	08 21	08 54		09 18		09 53		10 21		10 53		11 21				11 54		12 21				12 53	
Lenzie ■	d	08 27	09 00		09 24		09 59	09 47	10 27		10 59		11 27				12 00		12 27				12 59	
Croy ■	d	08a33	09a06		09a30		10a05		10 33		11a05		11 33	11 39			12a06		12 33	12 38		13 07	13a05	
Falkirk Grahamston	d					10 11						11 04						12 05						13 05
Camelon	d					10 14						11 07						12 07						13 07
Larbert	d					10 21		10 02	10 45			11 13	11 45					12 13	12 45					13 13
Stirling	d					10 30		10 12	10 55			11 23	11 55			12 12		12 23	12 55					13 23
Alloa	a								11 07				12 07						13 07					
Bridge of Allan	d					10 34						11 27						12 27						13 27
Dunblane	a					10 41		10 17				11 36				12 17		12 36						13 36

		SR ■ ⚒	SR	SR	SR ■ ⚒	SR ◇■ ⚒	SR	SR C	SR	SR ■ ⚒	SR	SR ■	SR	SR ◇■ ⚒	SR C	SR ■ ⚒	SR	SR	SR ■ ⚒	SR	SR ◇■ ⚒	SR C	SR ■ ⚒	SR	SR
Edinburgh ■	d	13 00		13 18	13 30		13 38			14 00	14 18	14 30	14 33			15 00		15 18	15 30	15 33			16 00		16 18
Haymarket	d	13 03		13 21	13 33		13 42			14 03	14 21	14 33	14 36			15 03		15 21	15 33	15 36			16 03		16 21
Edinburgh Park	d			13 25			13 47				14 25		14 41					15 25		15 41					16 25
Linlithgow	d	13 18			13 48		13 59			14 18		14 48	14 53			15 18			15 46	15 53			16 18		
Polmont ■	d	13 24					14 04			14 24			14 58			15 24				15 58			16 24		
Glasgow Queen Street ■ ⇌	d	13a51	13 15			13 45		13 48	14 15	14a51				14 40	14 47	15a51	15 15				15 45	15 48	16a51	16 15	
Bishopbriggs	d		13 21					13 54	14 21						14 53		15 21					15 54		16 21	
Lenzie ■	d		13 27					14 00	14 27						14 59		15 27					16 00		16 27	
Croy ■	d		13 33		14 07			14a06	14 33			15 07			15a05		15 33		16 05			16a06		16 33	
Falkirk Grahamston	d						14 10						15 04							16 04					
Camelon	d						14 13						15 07							16 07					
Larbert	d		13 45				14 20		14 45				15 13	15 00			15 45			16 13				16 45	
Stirling	d		13 55			14 12	14 28		14 55				15 23	15 09			15 55			16 23	16 12			16 55	
Alloa	a		14 07						15 07								16 07							17 07	
Bridge of Allan	d						14 33						15 27							16 27					
Dunblane	a					14 17	14 40						15 36	15 15						16 36	16 17				

		SR ■ ⚒	SR	SR C	SR	SR ■ ⚒	GR ■ ■ D ⚒	SR	SR ■	SR	SR ◇■ ⚒	SR C	SR ◇■ ⚒	SR	SR	SR ■ ⚒	SR ■ ⚒	SR	SR	SR ■ ⚒	SR	SR ■ ⚒	SR ◇■ ⚒	SR	SR ■
Edinburgh ■	d	16 30	16 33			17 00	17 11	17 18	17 30	17 33					18 18	18 00	18 30	18 33		19 00	19 19	19 30		19 33	20 00
Haymarket	d	16 33	16 36			17 03	17 16	17 21	17 33	17 36					18 21	18 03	18 33	18 36		19 03	19 22	19 33		19 36	20 04
Edinburgh Park	d		16 41					17 25		17 41					18 25			18 41			19 25			19 41	
Linlithgow	d	16 48	16 53			17 18			17 48	17 53						18 18	18 48	18 53		19 18		19 48		19 53	20 18
Polmont ■	d		16 58			17 24				17 58						18 24		18 58		19 24				19 58	20 24
Glasgow Queen Street ■ ⇌	d			16 47	17 15	17a52					17 45	17 48	18 10	18 16		18a51			19 15	19a51			19 45		20a51
Bishopbriggs	d			16 53	17 21							17 54		18 21					19 21						
Lenzie ■	d			16 59	17 27							18 00		18 26					19 27						
Croy ■	d	17 07		17a05	17 33				18 07			18a06		18 33			19 07		19 33			20 07			
Falkirk Grahamston	d		17 04				17 37			18 04								19 04						20 04	
Camelon	d		17 07							18 07								19 07						20 07	
Larbert	d		17 13		17 48					18 13			18 30	18 45				19 13	19 45					20 13	
Stirling	d		17 23		17 57		17 52			18 23	18 12		18 39	18 55				19 23	19 55				20 12	20 22	
Alloa	a				18 12									19 07					20 07						
Bridge of Allan	d		17 27							18 27								19 27						20 27	
Dunblane	a		17 36							18 36			18 45					19 37					20 17	20 37	

		SR	SR	SR	SR ■	SR	SR ■	SR	SR ◇■ ⚒	SR	SR	SR ■	SR	SR	SR ■	SR	SR ■	SR ■
Edinburgh ■	d		20 18	20 33	20 30		21 00	21 18		21 33		22 00	22 18	22 36	23 00	23 18		23 30
Haymarket	d		20 21	20 36	20 33		21 03	21 21		21 36		22 02	22 20	22 40	23 02	23 21		23 33
Edinburgh Park	d		20 25	20 41				21 25		21 41			22 25	22 46		23 25		
Linlithgow	d			20 53	20 48		21 18			21 53		22 18		22 58	23 18			23 48
Polmont ■	d			20 58			21 23			21 58		22 24		23 03	23 24			23 54
Glasgow Queen Street ■ ⇌	d	20 15				21 15			21 45		22 15						23 35	
Bishopbriggs	d	20 21				21 21					22 21						23 41	
Lenzie ■	d	20 27				21 27					22 27						23 47	
Croy ■	d	20 33			21 07	21 33	21 39				22 33	22 39			23 39		23 53	00 09
Falkirk Grahamston	d			21 04						22 04				23 10				
Camelon	d			21 07						22 07				23 14				
Larbert	d	20 45		21 13		21 45				22 13	22 45			23 19			00 05	
Stirling	d	20 55		21 23		21 55			22 11	22 23	22 55			23 28			00 14	
Alloa	a	21 07				22 07					23 07							
Bridge of Allan	d			21 27						22 27				23 33			00 18	
Dunblane	a			21 36					22 17	22 36				23 37			00 22	

C 28 November, 5 December

D The Highland Chieftain

Table 230

Mondays to Fridays

Dunblane, Alloa and Stirling - Falkirk Grahamston, Glasgow Queen Street and Edinburgh

		SR MX ■	SR MX	SR MO ■	SR MX ■	SR MO	SR	SR	SR	SR	SR ■	SR	SR	SR ■	SR	SR	SR	SR	SR ■ ⚒	SR ■ ⚒	SR
Dunblane	d						05 21		05 46				06 28		06 40						07 08
Bridge of Allan	d						05 24		05 49				06 31		06 43						
Alloa	d											06 11						07 11			
Stirling	d						05 30		05 53			06 21	06 36		06 54			07 22			07 16
Larbert	d						05 38		06 01			06 29	06 45		07 03			07 30			07 25
Camelon	d						05 44	05 44					06 51								07 32
Falkirk Grahamston	d						05 47						06 55								07 36
Croy ■	d								06 12			06 40		06 56	07 14			07 41			
Lenzie ■	d								06 19		06 38	06 47			07 21		07 33	07 48	07 09		
Bishopbriggs	d								06 23			06 51			07 25		07 37	07 52			
Glasgow Queen Street ■ ⇌	a							06 25	06 34			07 01			07 34		07 46	08 04			
Polmont ■	d						05 53				06 56		07 01						07 27	07 37	07 43
Linlithgow	d			00 02	00 04		06 00				07 03		07 08	07 13					07 33	07 43	07 50
Edinburgh Park	d		00 11			00 21	06 12			06 58			07 20			07 33					08 02
Haymarket	d	00 12	00 17	00s20	00s19	00 27	06 19			07 03	07s19		07 27	07s31		07 39			07s49	07s59	08 09
Edinburgh ■ 225,242	a	00 18	00 22	00 24	00 25	00 32	06 24			07 10	07 24		07 34	07 37		07 43			07 55	08 06	08 15

		SR	SR	SR ■ ⚒	SR	SR	SR	SR ◇■ ⚒	SR ■ ⚒	SR	SR	SR	SR ◇■ ⚒	SR	SR ■ ⚒	SR ■ ⚒	SR	SR	SR	SR	SR ■	SR ■ ⚒	SR
Dunblane	d	07 22	07 29					07 44			07 56	08 12						08 28		08 58	09 07		09 13
Bridge of Allan	d	07 25	07 32					07 48			07 59	08 16						08 31		09 01			09 16
Alloa	d						07 39			07 57									08 36				
Stirling	d	07 29	07 40				07 49	07 53		08 10	08 02	08 21	08 43					08 37	08 51	09 06	09 13		09 21
Larbert	d	07 38	07 47				07 56	08 02		08 19	08 14	08 29						08 46	08 59	09 15			09 29
Camelon	d				07 44		08 00				08 18							08 49		09 18			
Falkirk Grahamston	d						08 04				08 22							08 53		09 22			
Croy ■	d		08 00	07 41					08 11	08 32		08 40				08 41			09 12				09 40
Lenzie ■	d		08 06					08 17		08 37		08 47							09 19				09 47
Bishopbriggs	d		08 10							08 42		08 51							09 23				09 51
Glasgow Queen Street ■ ⇌	a		08 21		08 28			08 34		08 52		09 03	09 15						09 33		09 45		10 01
Polmont ■	d						08 11		08 26		08 29							09 00		09 29		09 07	
Linlithgow	d			07 59			08 18				08 36				08 42			09 07		09 36		09 13	
Edinburgh Park	d					08 18	08 31				08 49			08 43			09 13	09 19		09 49			
Haymarket	d	08 14		08s17		08 23	08 39		08s46		08 56			08 52	09s01	09s13	09 19	09 26		09 56		09s32	
Edinburgh ■ 225,242	a	08 19		08 22		08 29	08 45		08 50		09 02			08 58	09 05	09 19	09 25	09 32		10 04		09 37	

		SR	SR ■ ⚒	SR	SR ◇■ ⚒	SR	SR	SR ■ ⚒	SR	SR	SR	GR ■ ■ A ⚒	SR ◇■ ⚒	SR	SR	SR	SR
Dunblane	d			09 28						09 58	10 13						10 28
Bridge of Allan	d			09 31						10 01	10 16						10 31
Alloa	d						09 41								10 36		
Stirling	d			09 36	09 44		09 51			10 06	10 21	10 30	10 43		10 51		10 36
Larbert	d			09 45			09 59			10 15	10 29				10 59		10 45
Camelon	d			09 48		09 44				10 18				10 44			10 48
Falkirk Grahamston	d			09 52						10 22		10 45					10 52
Croy ■	d						10 10				10 40				11 10		
Lenzie ■	d						10 17				10 47				11 17		
Bishopbriggs	d						10 21				10 51				11 22		
Glasgow Queen Street ■ ⇌	a				10 14	10 25	10 33				11 03		11 14	11 25	11 34		
Polmont ■	d		09 37	09 59				10 07		10 29							10 59
Linlithgow	d		09 43	10 06				10 13		10 36							11 06
Edinburgh Park	d	09 43		10 19					10 43	10 49						11 14	11 19
Haymarket	d	09 49	10s01	10 27				10s31	10 53	10 57		11 11				11 20	11 26
Edinburgh ■ 225,242	a	09 56	10 08	10 32				10 36	10 59	11 06		11 16				11 25	11 31

		SR ■ ⚒	SR	SR	SR	SR ■ ⚒	SR ◇■ ⚒	SR	SR	SR	SR	SR ■ ⚒	SR	SR	SR ◇■ ⚒	SR	SR ■ ⚒	SR ◇■ ⚒	SR
Dunblane	d			10 58	11 13						11 28			11 58	12 06	12 13			
Bridge of Allan	d			11 01	11 16						11 31			12 01		12 16			
Alloa	d								11 43										
Stirling	d			11 06	11 21		11 43		11 51		11 36			12 06	12 13	12 21		12 42	
Larbert	d			11 15	11 29				11 59		11 45			12 15		12 29			
Camelon	d			11 18				11 44			11 48			12 18					12 44
Falkirk Grahamston	d			11 22							11 52			12 22					
Croy ■	d				11 40				12 09							12 40			
Lenzie ■	d				11 47				12 17							12 47			
Bishopbriggs	d				11 51				12 20							12 51			
Glasgow Queen Street ■ ⇌	a				12 01		12 14	12 25	12 34						12 46	13 03		13 14	13 25
Polmont ■	d	11 07		11 29		11 37					11 59	12 07		12 29			12 37		
Linlithgow	d	11 13		11 36		11 43					12 06	12 13		12 36			12 43		
Edinburgh Park	d		11 43	11 49						12 13	12 19		12 43	12 49					
Haymarket	d	11s29	11 50	11 56		12s00				12 19	12 26	12s29	12 53	12 56			13s00		
Edinburgh ■ 225,242	a	11 35	11 55	12 01		12 05				12 25	12 31	12 35	12 58	13 02			13 05		

A The Highland Chieftain

Dunblane, Alloa and Stirling - Falkirk Grahamston, Glasgow Queen Street and Edinburgh

	SR	SR	SR 1 ⊼	SR	SR	SR	SR 1 ⊼	SR ◇1 ⊼	SR	SR	SR	SR ◇1 ⊼	SR	SR 1 ⊼	SR	SR	SR	SR
Dunblane d					12 58	13 13							13 28			13 58	14 13	14 28
Bridge of Allan d					13 01	13 16							13 31			14 01	14 16	14 31
Alloa d	12 36									13 41								
Stirling d	12 51				13 06	13 21		13 43		13 51			13 36			14 06	14 21	14 36
Larbert d	12 59				13 15	13 29				13 59			13 45			14 15	14 29	14 45
Camelon d					13 18				13 44				13 48			14 18		14 48
Falkirk Grahamston d					13 22								13 52			14 22		14 52
Croy 3 d	13 10					13 41				14 10							14 40	
Lenzie 3 d	13 17					13 47				14 17							14 47	
Bishopbriggs d	13 21					13 51				14 21							14 51	
Glasgow Queen Street 10 ⇌ a	13 33					14 03		14 14	14 25	14 33							15 03	
Polmont 3 d			13 07		13 29		13 37						13 59	14 07		14 29		14 59
Linlithgow d			13 13		13 36		13 43						14 06	14 13		14 36		15 06
Edinburgh Park d		13 13		13 43	13 49						14 13		14 19		14 43	14 49		15 19
Haymarket d		13 20	13s29	13 49	13 56		13s59				14 19	14 21	14 26	14s30	14 54	14 56		15 26
Edinburgh 10 225,242 a		13 24	13 35	13 55	14 01		14 05				14 25	14 27	14 31	14 37	14 59	15 02		15 34

	SR 1 ⊼	SR ◇1 ⊼	SR	SR	SR	SR 1 ⊼	SR	SR	SR	SR 1 ⊼	SR ◇1 ⊼	SR	SR	SR	SR ◇1 ⊼	SR	SR 1 ⊼
Dunblane d								14 58	15 13							15 28	
Bridge of Allan d								15 01	15 16							15 31	
Alloa d				14 36									15 41				
Stirling d		14 40		14 51				15 06	15 21		15 43		15 51			15 36	
Larbert d				14 59				15 15	15 29				15 59			15 45	
Camelon d			14 44					15 18				15 44				15 48	
Falkirk Grahamston d								15 22								15 52	
Croy 3 d				15 10					15 40				16 10				
Lenzie 3 d				15 17					15 47				16 17				
Bishopbriggs d				15 21					15 51				16 21				
Glasgow Queen Street 10 ⇌ a		15 15	15 25	15 34					16 04		16 15	16 26	16 33				
Polmont 3 d	14 37					15 07		15 29		15 37						15 59	16 07
Linlithgow d	14 43					15 13		15 36		15 43						16 06	16 13
Edinburgh Park d					15 13		15 43	15 49						16 13		16 19	
Haymarket d	14s59				15 20	15s30	15 49	15 56		16s00				16 21	16 25	16 26	16s31
Edinburgh 10 225,242 a	15 06				15 26	15 37	15 56	16 02		16 05				16 25	16 31	16 34	16 36

	SR	SR	SR	SR 1 ⊼	SR ◇1 ⊼	SR	SR	SR	SR	SR 1 ⊼	SR 1 ⊼	SR	SR	SR ◇1 ⊼	SR	SR ◇1 ⊼	SR	SR	SR	SR 1 ⊼	SR	SR 1 ⊼
Dunblane d		15 58	16 13						16 28			16 58	17 14	17 22	17 28	17 36						
Bridge of Allan d		16 01	16 16						16 31			17 01	17 17		17 31							
Alloa d							16 36											17 41				
Stirling d		16 06	16 21		16 43		16 52		16 36			17 06	17 21	17 29	17 36	17 42		17 51				
Larbert d		16 15	16 29				17 00		16 45			17 15	17 29		17 45			17 59				
Camelon d		16 18				16 44			16 48			17 18			17 48		17 44					
Falkirk Grahamston d		16 22							16 52			17 22			17 52							
Croy 3 d			16 41				17 12				17 11		17 40					18 10				17 41
Lenzie 3 d			16 47				17 18						17 47					18 17				
Bishopbriggs d			16 51				17 23						17 51					18 21				
Glasgow Queen Street 10 ⇌ a			17 03		17 17	17 25	17 32						18 03	18 09		18 15	18 27	18 34				
Polmont 3 d		16 29		16 37					16 59	17 07	17 27	17 29			17 59							17 56
Linlithgow d		16 36		16 43					17 06	17 13		17 36			18 06					17 40		18 03
Edinburgh Park d	16 43	16 49						17 14	17 19			17 49			18 19				17 48		18 12	
Haymarket d	16 54	16 56		17s00				17 21	17 26	17s33	17s46	17 56			18 28				17 54	18s00	18 18	18s22
Edinburgh 10 225,242 a	16 59	17 02		17 06				17 29	17 32	17 39	17 51	18 02			18 34				17 59	18 06	18 23	18 26

	SR 1 ⊼	SR	SR	SR	SR	SR ◇1 ⊼	SR 1 ⊼	SR 1 ⊼	SR	SR	SR	SR	SR ◇1 ⊼	SR 1 ⊼	SR	SR ◇1 ⊼	SR	SR	SR	SR 1 ⊼	SR 1
Dunblane d			17 58	18 11	18 28	18 35						19 14									
Bridge of Allan d			18 01	18 14	18 31							19 17									
Alloa d										18 27					18 54			19 43			
Stirling d			18 06	18 19	18 36	18 42				18 51		19 22			19 06	19 43		19 53			
Larbert d			18 15	18 28	18 45					18 59		19 30			19 15			20 01			
Camelon d			18 18		18 48				18 44						19 18		19 44				
Falkirk Grahamston d			18 22		18 52										19 22						
Croy 3 d				18 39				18 42		19 10		19 41						20 12			
Lenzie 3 d				18 46						19 17		19 48						20 19			
Bishopbriggs d				18 50						19 21		19 52						20 23			
Glasgow Queen Street 10 ⇌ a				19 01		19 14			19 25	19 31		20 02				20 15	20 25	20 34			
Polmont 3 d	18 07		18 29		18 59		18 37							19 07	19 29					19 37	19 52
Linlithgow d	18 13		18 36		19 06		18 43							19 13	19 36					19 43	19 58
Edinburgh Park d		18 43	18 49		19 19						19 13				19 49				19 48		
Haymarket d	18s32	18 53	18 56		19 25		19s00	19s12			19 19		19 28	19s30	19 56				19 53	20s01	20s15
Edinburgh 10 225,242 a	18 40	18 58	19 02		19 33		19 05	19 19			19 25		19 34	19 36	20 02				19 58	20 06	20 21

Dunblane, Alloa and Stirling - Falkirk Grahamston, Glasgow Queen Street and Edinburgh

	SR	SR	SR	SR	SR 1	SR ◇1 ⊼	SR	SR 1	SR	SR	SR	SR 1	SR	SR	SR ◇1 ⊼	SR	SR 1	SR	SR	SR 1	SR	SR	SR ◇1
Dunblane d	19 28	20 01	20 13						20 28				20 58	21 13							21 58	22 13	
Bridge of Allan d	19 31	20 04	20 16						20 31				21 01	21 16							22 01	22 16	
Alloa d							20 41									21 42							
Stirling d	19 36	20 06	20 21			20 40	20 51		20 36				21 06	21 21	21 45	21 52					22 06	22 21	22 43
Larbert d	19 45	20 15	20 29				20 59		20 45				21 15	21 29		21 59					22 15	22 29	
Camelon d	19 48	20 18							20 48	21 14			21 18					22 14			22 18		
Falkirk Grahamston d	19 52	20 22							20 52				21 22								22 22		
Croy 3 d			20 41		20 11		21 10					21 11		21 40		22 10				22 11		22 40	
Lenzie 3 d			20 47				21 17							21 47		22 17						22 47	
Bishopbriggs d			20 51				21 21							21 51		22 21						22 51	
Glasgow Queen Street 10 ⇌ a			21 04			21 14	21 34			21 55				22 03	22 19	22 34		22 55				23 03	23 15
Polmont 3 d	19 59	20 29						20 52	20 59				21 29				21 52				22 29		
Linlithgow d	20 06	20 36			20 28			20 58	21 06			21 28	21 36				21 58			22 28	22 36		
Edinburgh Park d	20 19	20 49		20 24					21 19		21 24		21 49						22 22		22 49		
Haymarket d	20 26	20 58		20 31	20s46			21s13	21 26		21 30	21s46	21 56				22s18		22 28	22s45	22 56		
Edinburgh 10 225,242 a	20 32	21 06		20 36	20 51			21 20	21 31		21 36	21 53	22 01				22 24		22 33	22 50	23 01		

	SR	SR 1	SR ◇1	SR	SR	SR 1	SR	SR 1
Dunblane d			22 58				23 06	
Bridge of Allan d			23 02				23 09	
Alloa d	22 41							
Stirling d	22 51		23 05				23 14	
Larbert d	22 59						23 23	
Camelon d				23 14			23 29	
Falkirk Grahamston d							23 32	
Croy 3 d	23 10					23 11		23 41
Lenzie 3 d	23 17							
Bishopbriggs d	23 21							
Glasgow Queen Street 10 ⇌ a	23 34		23 39	23 55				
Polmont 3 d		22 52				23 26	23 38	23 57
Linlithgow d		22 58				23 33	23 45	00 04
Edinburgh Park d					23 22		23 57	
Haymarket d		23s15			23 29	23s49	00 04	00s19
Edinburgh 10 225,242 a		23 22			23 34	23 54	00 09	00 25

Saturdays

	SR	SR 1	SR A	SR	SR	SR 1	SR	SR	SR 1	SR A	SR	SR	SR	SR	SR	SR 1 ⊼	SR 1 ⊼	SR 1 ⊼	SR	SR ◇1 ⊼	SR 1	SR	SR	SR
Dunblane d			05 21		05 46					06 28	06 45	07 08		07 29						07 44		07 56		08 12
Bridge of Allan d			05 24		05 49					06 31	06 48	07 10		07 32						07 48		07 59		08 16
Alloa d							06 11						07 11										07 57	
Stirling d			05 30		05 53		06 21			06 36	06 54	07 16	07 22	07 39						07 53		08 05	08 10	08 21
Larbert d			05 38		06 01		06 29			06 45	07 03	07 25	07 30	07 47						08 02		08 14	08 19	08 29
Camelon d			05 44	05 44						06 51		07 32							07 44			08 18		
Falkirk Grahamston d			05 47							06 55		07 36										08 22		
Croy 3 d					06 12		06 40		06 44		07 14		07 41	07 59				07 41					08 32	08 40
Lenzie 3 d					06 19		06 47				07 21		07 48	08 05		07 09				08 17			08 37	08 47
Bishopbriggs d					06 23		06 51				07 25		07 52	08 09									08 42	08 51
Glasgow Queen Street 10 ⇌ a				06 25	06 34		07 01				07 34		08 04	08 20					08 28	08 34			08 52	09 03
Polmont 3 d			05 53			06 21			06 59	07 01		07 43				07 27	07 37				08 07	08 29		
Linlithgow d		00 04	06 00			06 30			07 05	07 08		07 50				07 33	07 43	07 59			08 13	08 36		
Edinburgh Park d	00 11		06 12					06 58		07 20		08 02			07 33							08 49		
Haymarket d	00 18	00s19	06 19			06s46		07 03	07s21	07 25		08 09			07 39	07s49	08s01	08s17			08s33	08 59		
Edinburgh 10 225,242 a	00 22	00 25	06 24			06 50		07 10	07 26	07 34		08 14			07 43	07 56	08 07	08 22			08 37	09 02		

	SR	SR 1 ⊼	SR ◇1 ⊼	SR	SR 1 ⊼	SR	SR	SR	SR ◇1 ⊼	SR A	SR	SR 1	SR 1 ⊼	SR	SR ◇1 ⊼	SR	SR 1 ⊼	SR	SR	SR	SR A
Dunblane d										08 28	08 58	09 07		09 13							09 28
Bridge of Allan d										08 31	09 01			09 16							09 31
Alloa d							08 36												09 41		
Stirling d			08 43				08 51			08 37	09 06	09 13		09 21	09 44				09 51		09 36
Larbert d							08 59			08 46	09 15			09 29					09 59		09 45
Camelon d						08 44				08 49	09 18							09 44			09 48
Falkirk Grahamston d										08 53	09 22										09 52
Croy 3 d		08 11					09 12							09 40					10 10		
Lenzie 3 d							09 19							09 47					10 17		
Bishopbriggs d							09 23							09 51					10 21		
Glasgow Queen Street 10 ⇌ a			09 15			09 25	09 33					09 45		10 01	10 14			10 25	10 33		
Polmont 3 d		08 26								09 00	09 29		09 07				09 37				09 59
Linlithgow d					08 42					09 07	09 36		09 13				09 43				10 06
Edinburgh Park d	08 18			08 43				09 13		09 19	09 49					09 43				10 13	10 19
Haymarket d	08 23	08s46		08 53	09s01			09 19	09 24	09 26	09 56		09s31			09 49	10s01			10 21	10 26
Edinburgh 10 225,242 a	08 29	08 50		08 59	09 07			09 25	09 30	09 32	10 04		09 37			09 56	10 07			10 26	10 31

A until 18 September

Table 230

Dunblane, Alloa and Stirling - Falkirk Grahamston, Glasgow Queen Street and Edinburgh

	SR	SR	SR	SR	SR	GR	SR	SR	SR	SR	SR	SR	SR	SR	SR	SR
	1		A		1 ✕	1 B ✕	◇1 ✕				A	1 ✕		A		1 ✕
Dunblane d			09 58	10 13							10 28			10 58	11 13	
Bridge of Allan d			10 01	10 16							10 31			11 01	11 16	
Alloa d									10 36							
Stirling d			10 06	10 21		10 30	10 43		10 51		10 36			11 06	11 21	
Larbert d			10 15	10 29					10 59		10 45			11 15	11 29	
Camelon d			10 18					10 44			10 48			11 18		
Falkirk Grahamston d			10 22			10 45					10 52			11 22		
Croy 3 d				10 40					11 10						11 40	
Lenzie 3 d				10 47					11 17						11 47	
Bishopbriggs d				10 51					11 22						11 51	
Glasgow Queen Street 10 a				11 01			11 14	11 25	11 34						12 01	
Polmont 3 d	10 07		10 29		10 37						10 59	11 07		11 29		11 37
Linlithgow d	10 13		10 36		10 43						11 06	11 13		11 36		11 43
Edinburgh Park d		10 43	10 49							11 14	11 19		11 43	11 49		
Haymarket d	10s31	10 53	10 57		11s00	11 09				11 20	11 26	11s29	11 50	11 56		12s00
Edinburgh 10 225,242 a	10 35	10 58	11 01		11 05	11 15				11 25	11 31	11 35	11 55	12 01		12 05

	SR	SR	SR	SR	SR	SR	SR	SR	SR	SR	SR	SR	SR	SR	SR	SR	SR	SR	SR
	◇1 ✕				A	1 ✕		A	◇1 ✕		1 ✕	◇1 ✕				◇1 ✕	A	1 ✕	
Dunblane d					11 28			11 58	12 06	12 13							12 28		
Bridge of Allan d					11 31			12 01		12 16							12 31		
Alloa d			11 43											12 36					
Stirling d	11 43		11 51		11 36			12 06	12 13	12 21		12 43		12 51			12 36		
Larbert d			11 59		11 45			12 15		12 29				12 59			12 45		
Camelon d		11 44			11 48			12 18					12 44				12 48		
Falkirk Grahamston d					11 52			12 22									12 52		
Croy 3 d			12 09							12 40				13 10					
Lenzie 3 d			12 17							12 47				13 17					
Bishopbriggs d			12 20							12 51				13 21					
Glasgow Queen Street 10 a	12 14	12 25	12 34						12 46	13 03		13 14	13 25	13 33					
Polmont 3 d					11 59	12 07		12 29			12 37						12 59	13 07	
Linlithgow d					12 06	12 13		12 36			12 43						13 06	13 13	
Edinburgh Park d				12 13	12 19		12 43	12 49							13 13		13 18		13 43
Haymarket d				12 19	12 26	12s29	12 54	12 56			13s01				13 20	13 21	13 26	13s30	13 49
Edinburgh 10 225,242 a				12 25	12 31	12 35	12 58	13 02			13 05				13 25	13 27	13 34	13 35	13 55

	SR	SR	SR	SR	SR	SR	SR	SR	SR	SR	SR	SR	SR	SR	SR	SR	SR	SR	SR	SR
	A		1 ✕	◇1 ✕				◇1 ✕	A	1 ✕	1 ✕		A		1 ✕	◇1 ✕	1 ✕			
Dunblane d	12 58	13 13							13 28				13 58	14 13						
Bridge of Allan d	13 01	13 16							13 31				14 01	14 16						
Alloa d						13 41													14 36	
Stirling d	13 06	13 21		13 43		13 51			13 36				14 06	14 21		14 40			14 51	
Larbert d	13 15	13 29				13 59			13 45				14 15	14 29					14 59	
Camelon d	13 18				13 44				13 48				14 18					14 44		
Falkirk Grahamston d	13 22								13 52				14 22							
Croy 3 d		13 41				14 10					14 11			14 40			14 41		15 10	
Lenzie 3 d		13 47				14 17								14 47					15 17	
Bishopbriggs d		13 51				14 21								14 51					15 21	
Glasgow Queen Street 10 a		14 03		14 14	14 25	14 33								15 03		15 15		15 25	15 34	
Polmont 3 d	13 29		13 37						13 59	14 07			14 29		14 37					
Linlithgow d	13 36		13 43						14 06	14 13			14 36		14 43					
Edinburgh Park d	13 49						14 13		14 19			14 43	14 49							15 13
Haymarket d	13 56		13s59				14 19	14 21	14 26	14s30	14s47	14 54	14 56		14s59		15s13			15 19
Edinburgh 10 225,242 a	14 01		14 05				14 25	14 27	14 31	14 37	14 52	14 59	15 02		15 05		15 17			15 25

A until 18 September
B The Highland Chieftain

Table 230

Dunblane, Alloa and Stirling - Falkirk Grahamston, Glasgow Queen Street and Edinburgh

	SR	SR	SR	SR	SR	SR	SR	SR	SR	SR	SR	SR	SR	SR	SR	SR
	1 ✕		A		1 ✕	◇1 ✕				A		A		1 ✕	◇1 ✕	
Dunblane d			14 58	15 13						15 28		15 58	16 13			
Bridge of Allan d			15 01	15 16						15 31		16 01	16 16			
Alloa d								15 41								
Stirling d			15 06	15 21		15 43		15 51		15 36		16 06	16 21		16 43	
Larbert d			15 15	15 29				15 59		15 45		16 15	16 29			
Camelon d			15 18				15 44			15 48		16 18				16 44
Falkirk Grahamston d			15 22							15 52		16 22				
Croy 3 d				15 40				16 10					16 41			
Lenzie 3 d				15 47				16 17					16 47			
Bishopbriggs d				15 51				16 21					16 51			
Glasgow Queen Street 10 a				16 04		16 15	16 26	16 33					17 02		17 17	17 25
Polmont 3 d	15 07		15 29		15 37					15 59		16 29		16 37		
Linlithgow d	15 13		15 36		15 43					16 06		16 36		16 43		
Edinburgh Park d		15 43	15 49						16 13	16 19	16 43	16 49				
Haymarket d	15s30	15 49	15 56		16s00				16 20	16 25	16 54	16 56		17s00		
Edinburgh 10 225,242 a	15 37	15 57	16 01		16 05				16 25	16 32	16 59	17 02		17 07		

	SR	SR	SR	SR	SR	SR	SR	SR	SR	SR	SR	SR	SR	SR	SR	SR	SR	SR	SR	SR	SR	SR	SR	SR
			A	1	1 ✕				◇1 ✕	1 ✕	1 ✕			◇1 ✕			1 ✕		A		1 ✕		◇1 ✕	
Dunblane d			16 28				16 58	17 14	17 22				17 28	17 36					17 58	18 11		18 28	18 35	
Bridge of Allan d			16 31				17 01	17 17					17 31						18 01	18 14		18 31		
Alloa d	16 36															17 41								
Stirling d	16 52		16 36				17 06	17 21	17 29				17 36	17 42		17 51			18 06	18 19		18 36	18 42	
Larbert d	17 00		16 45				17 15	17 29					17 45			17 59			18 15	18 28		18 45		
Camelon d			16 48				17 18						17 48		17 44				18 18			18 48		18 44
Falkirk Grahamston d			16 52				17 22						17 52						18 22			18 52		
Croy 3 d	17 12				17 11			17 40			17 41					18 10				18 39	18 41			
Lenzie 3 d	17 18							17 47								18 17				18 46				
Bishopbriggs d	17 23							17 51								18 21				18 50				
Glasgow Queen Street 10 a	17 32							18 03	18 09					18 15	18 27	18 34				19 01			19 14	19 25
Polmont 3 d			16 59	17 07	17 27		17 29				17 56		17 59				18 07		18 29			18 59		
Linlithgow d			17 06	17 13			17 36			17 40	18 03		18 06				18 13		18 36			19 06		
Edinburgh Park d		17 13	17 19			17 47	17 49					18 12	18 19					18 43	18 49			19 19		
Haymarket d		17 20	17 26	17s33	17s47	17 53	17 56			18s00	18s22	18 18	18 28				18s32	18 53	18 56		19s11	19 25		
Edinburgh 10 225,242 a		17 25	17 31	17 39	17 51	17 58	18 02			18 06	18 26	18 23	18 34				18 40	18 58	19 02		19 19	19 33		

	SR	SR	SR	SR	SR	SR	SR	SR	SR	SR	SR	SR	SR	SR	SR	SR	SR	SR	SR	SR	SR	SR	SR
					◇1 ✕	1 ✕	◇1 ✕				A	1 ✕	1	A		1			◇1 ✕		1	A	
Dunblane d		18 49		19 14										19 28			20 01	20 13				20 28	
Bridge of Allan d		18 52		19 17										19 31			20 04	20 16				20 31	
Alloa d	18 27								19 43		18 54									20 41			
Stirling d	18 51	19a00		19 22			19 43		19 53		19 06			19 36			20 06	20 21	20 40	20 51		20 36	
Larbert d	18 59			19 30					20 01		19 15			19 45			20 15	20 29		20 59		20 45	
Camelon d								19 44			19 18			19 48			20 18					20 48	21 14
Falkirk Grahamston d											19 22			19 52			20 22					20 52	
Croy 3 d	19 10			19 41					20 12							20 11		20 41		21 10			
Lenzie 3 d	19 17			19 48					20 19									20 47		21 17			
Bishopbriggs d	19 21			19 52					20 23									20 51		21 21			
Glasgow Queen Street 10 a	19 31			20 02			20 15	20 25	20 34									21 04	21 14	21 34			21 55
Polmont 3 d						19 07					19 29	19 37	19 52	19 59			20 29				20 52	20 59	
Linlithgow d						19 13					19 36	19 43	19 58	20 06		20 28	20 36				20 58	21 06	
Edinburgh Park d			19 13							19 48	19 49			20 19	20 24		20 49					21 19	
Haymarket d			19 19		19 28	19s34				19 53	19 56	20s01	20s15	20 26	20 31	20s46	20 58				21s13	21 26	
Edinburgh 10 225,242 a			19 26		19 34	19 39				19 58	20 02	20 06	20 21	20 32	20 36	20 51	21 06				21 20	21 31	

	SR	SR	SR	SR	SR	SR	SR	SR	SR	SR	SR	SR	SR	SR	SR	SR	SR	SR	SR	SR	SR	SR
		1	A	1		◇1 ✕				1	A		◇1		1	◇1			1	A	1	
Dunblane d			20 58		21 13						21 58	22 13				22 58				23 06		
Bridge of Allan d			21 01		21 16						22 01	22 16				23 02				23 09		
Alloa d							21 42							22 41								23 18
Stirling d			21 06		21 21	21 45	21 52				22 06	22 21	22 43	22 51		23 05				23 14		23a27
Larbert d			21 15		21 29		21 59				22 15	22 29		22 59						23 23		
Camelon d			21 18					22 14			22 18						23 14			23 29		
Falkirk Grahamston d			21 22								22 22									23 32		
Croy 3 d		21 11			21 40		22 10			22 11		22 40		23 10					23 11		23 41	
Lenzie 3 d					21 47		22 17					22 47		23 17								
Bishopbriggs d					21 51		22 21					22 51		23 21								
Glasgow Queen Street 10 a					22 03	22 19	22 34	22 55				23 03	23 15	23 34		23 39	23 55					
Polmont 3 d			21 29	21 52							22 29				22 52				23 26	23 38	23 57	
Linlithgow d		21 28	21 36	21 58						22 28	22 36				22 58				23 33	23 45	00 04	
Edinburgh Park d	21 24		21 49						22 22		22 49							23 22		23 57		
Haymarket d	21 31	21s46	21 56	22s18					22 28	22s45	22 56				23s15			23 29	23s49	00 04	00s19	
Edinburgh 10 225,242 a	21 38	21 53	22 01	22 24					22 33	22 50	23 01				23 22			23 34	23 54	00 09	00 25	

A until 18 September

Table 230

Sundays

Dunblane, Alloa and Stirling - Falkirk Grahamston, Glasgow Queen Street and Edinburgh

				SR ■	SR ■ ⊼	SR C	SR	SR C		SR	SR ■	SR ■ ⊼	SR	SR	SR C	SR	SR ■ ⊼	SR C	SR		SR	SR	SR ◇■ ⊼	SR ■ ⊼
Dunblane d											09 31			09 54								10 58	11 31	
Bridge of Allan d														09 58								11 01		
Alloa d										09 18						10 18			11 14					
Stirling d							09 05			09 28	09 38			10 02		10 28			11 25			11 06	11 38	
Larbert d							09 13			09 37	09 47			10 11		10 37			11 34			11 15		
Camelon d							09 19							10 16								11 18		
Falkirk Grahamston d							09 22							10 19								11 22		
Croy 3 d				08 01	08 41	08 49		09 15		09 48		09 41			10 15	10 45	10 41	11 15	11 45					11 41
Lenzie 3 d						08 56		09 22		09 55	10 02				10 22	10 52		11 22	11 52					
Bishopbriggs d						09 00		09 26		09 59					10 26	10 56		11 26	11 56					
Glasgow Queen Street 10 ⇌ a						09 10		09 35		10 08	10 15				10 35	11 08		11 35	12 05				12 11	
Polmont 3 d				08 16	08 56		09 28					09 56		10 25			10 56					11 29		11 56
Linlithgow d				08 22	09 02		09 35					10 02		10 32			11 02					11 36		12 02
Edinburgh Park d							09 47						10 17	10 45							11 19	11 49		
Haymarket d				08s45	09s24		09 58					10s24	10 13	10 52			11s20				11 25	11 56		12s20
Edinburgh 10 225,242 a				08 49	09 28		10 04					10 28	10 22	10 58			11 24				11 30	12 01		12 24

	SR C	SR	SR	SR	SR C	SR ◇■ ⊼	SR	SR ■ ⊼	SR	SR ■ ⊼	SR	SR ◇■ ⊼	SR ■	SR C	SR	SR	SR ■ ⊼	SR	SR ■ ⊼	SR C	SR		SR ■	SR
Dunblane d				11 58		12 26					12 58	13 31						13 58						14 58
Bridge of Allan d				12 01							13 01							14 01						15 01
Alloa d		12 14					13 14								14 14									
Stirling d		12 25		12 06		12 33	13 25				13 06	13 38			14 25			14 06						15 06
Larbert d		12 34		12 15			13 34				13 15				14 34			14 15						15 15
Camelon d				12 18							13 18							14 18						15 18
Falkirk Grahamston d				12 22		12 49					13 22							14 22						15 22
Croy 3 d	12 15	12 45			13 15		13 45			13 11				14 15	14 45		14 11			15 15			15 11	
Lenzie 3 d	12 22	12 52			13 22		13 52							14 22	14 52					15 22				
Bishopbriggs d	12 26	12 56			13 26		13 56							14 26	14 56					15 26				
Glasgow Queen Street 10 ⇌ a	12 35	13 05			13 35		14 05					14 11		14 35	15 05					15 35				
Polmont 3 d				12 29				12 56			13 29		13 52					14 28	14 52					15 29
Linlithgow d				12 36				13 02		13 28	13 36		13 58				14 28	14 36	14 58				15 28	15 36
Edinburgh Park d			12 19	12 49					13 19		13 49					14 17		14 49			15 17			15 49
Haymarket d			12 25	12 56		13 13		13s22	13 25	13s47	13 56		14s18			14 23	14s47	14 56	15s16		15 23		15 46	15 56
Edinburgh 10 225,242 a			12 30	13 01		13 18		13 26	13 31	13 51	14 01		14 22			14 28	14 52	15 01	15 21		15 28		15 51	16 01

	SR ◇■ ⊼	SR	SR ◇■ ⊼	SR ■	SR	SR ■ ⊼	SR C	SR	SR	SR ■ ⊼	SR C	SR	SR	SR ■ ⊼	SR	SR ◇■ ⊼	SR ■ ⊼	SR C	SR	SR ■ ⊼	SR		SR	SR ■ ⊼
Dunblane d	15 16		15 33						15 58						16 58	17 31					17 58			
Bridge of Allan d									16 01						17 01						18 01			
Alloa d		15 16						16 14				17 14											18 17	
Stirling d	15 22	15 26	15 45					16 25	16 06			17 25			17 06	17 38					18 06		18 27	
Larbert d	15 31	15 34						16 34	16 15			17 34			17 15						18 15		18 34	
Camelon d									16 18						17 18						18 18			
Falkirk Grahamston d									16 22						17 22						18 22			
Croy 3 d		15 45				16 11	16 17	16 45			17 15	17 45		17 11				18 15		18 11			18 45	
Lenzie 3 d		15 52					16 24	16 52			17 22	17 52						18 22					18 52	
Bishopbriggs d		15 56					16 28	16 56			17 26	17 56						18 26					18 56	
Glasgow Queen Street 10 ⇌ a	15 56	16 09	16 28				16 37	17 05			17 35	18 05				18 12		18 35					19 08	
Polmont 3 d				15 52					16 29	16 53					17 29		17 53				18 29			18 53
Linlithgow d				15 58		16 28			16 36	16 58				17 28	17 36		17 58			18 28	18 36			18 58
Edinburgh Park d					16 17				16 49				17 17		17 49				18 17		18 49			
Haymarket d				16s18	16 23	16s50			16 56	17s16			17 23	17s47	17 56		18s18		18 22	18s51	18 56			19s17
Edinburgh 10 225,242 a				16 22	16 29	16 55			17 02	17 21			17 29	17 52	18 01		18 22		18 30	18 55	19 01			19 21

	SR C	SR ◇■ ⊼	SR	SR	SR ■ ⊼	SR	SR ■ ⊼		SR ◇■ ⊼	SR	SR	SR ■	SR	SR ■	SR	SR	SR ■	SR	SR ◇■ ⊼	SR ■	SR	SR	SR ■	SR ■
Dunblane d		18 55				18 58							19 58					20 58	21 31			21 58		
Bridge of Allan d						19 01							20 01					21 01				22 01		
Alloa d			19 14							20 14					21 14									
Stirling d		19 02	19 24			19 06			19 55	20 25			20 06		21 25			21 06	21 38			22 06		
Larbert d		19 09	19 33			19 15				20 34			20 15		21 34			21 15	21 49			22 15		
Camelon d						19 18							20 18					21 18				22 18		
Falkirk Grahamston d						19 22							20 22					21 22				22 22		
Croy 3 d	19 13		19 44		19 11					20 45		20 11			21 45		21 11			21 42			22 41	23 41
Lenzie 3 d	19 20		19 51							20 52					21 52				22 02					
Bishopbriggs d	19 24		19 55							20 56					21 56									
Glasgow Queen Street 10 ⇌ a	19 33	19 36	20 04						20 31	21 05					22 05				22 15					
Polmont 3 d						19 29	19 53						20 29	20 53				21 29		21 56		22 29	22 56	23 56
Linlithgow d					19 28	19 36	19 58					20 28	20 36	20 58			21 28	21 36		22 02		22 36	23 02	00 02
Edinburgh Park d				19 17		19 49					20 17		20 49			21 17		21 49			22 19	22 49		
Haymarket d				19 23	19s47	19 56	20s16				20 22	20s47	20 56	21s17		21 23	21s46	21 56		22s20	22 26	22 56	23s20	00s20
Edinburgh 10 225,242 a				19 29	19 52	20 02	20 21				20 29	20 51	21 01	21 22		21 29	21 53	22 01		22 24	22 31	23 01	23 24	00 24

A from 30 May until 19 September

C 28 November, 5 December

Table 232

Mondays to Saturdays

Glasgow Queen Street - Maryhill and Anniesland

		SR	SR	SR	SR	SR	SR SO	SR SX	SR	SR	SR	SR	SR	SR	SR	SR	SR	SR	SR	SR	SR	SR	SR
Glasgow Queen Street 10 ⇌ d		06 26	06 56	07 26	07 56	08 27	08 56	08 56	09 26	09 56	10 26	10 56	11 26	11 56	12 27	12 56	13 26	13 56	14 26	14 56	15 26	15 57	16 26
Ashfield d		06 30	07 00	07 30	08 00	08 30	09 00	09 00	09 30	10 00	10 30	11 00	11 30	12 00	12 30	13 00	13 30	14 00	14 30	15 00	15 30	16 00	16 30
Possilpark & Parkhouse d		06 33	07 03	07 33	08 03	08 33	09 03	09 03	09 33	10 03	10 33	11 03	11 33	12 03	12 33	13 03	13 33	14 03	14 33	15 03	15 33	16 03	16 33
Gilshochill d		06 35	07 05	07 35	08 05	08 35	09 05	09 05	09 35	10 05	10 35	11 05	11 35	12 05	12 35	13 05	13 35	14 05	14 35	15 05	15 35	16 05	16 35
Summerston d		06 37	07 07	07 37	08 07	08 37	09 07	09 07	09 37	10 07	10 37	11 07	11 37	12 07	12 37	13 07	13 37	14 07	14 37	15 07	15 37	16 07	16 37
Maryhill d		06 39	07 09	07 39	08 09	08 39	09 09	09 09	09 39	10 09	10 39	11 09	11 39	12 09	12 39	13 09	13 39	14 09	14 39	15 09	15 39	16 09	16 39
Kelvindale d		06 41	07 11	07 41	08 11	08 41	09 11	09 11	09 41	10 11	10 41	11 11	11 41	12 11	12 41	13 11	13 41	14 11	14 41	15 11	15 41	16 11	16 41
Anniesland 226 a		06 45	07 15	07 45	08 15	08 46	09 16	09 15	09 45	10 15	10 45	11 15	11 46	12 15	12 46	13 15	13 45	14 15	14 45	15 15	15 45	16 16	16 45

	SR	SR	SR	SR	SR	SR	SR	SR	SR	SR	SR	SR	SR	SR	SR FO
Glasgow Queen Street 10 ⇌ d	16 56	17 26	17 56	18 27	18 56	19 26	19 56	20 26	20 56	21 26	21 56	22 26	22 56	23 26	23 54
Ashfield d	17 00	17 30	18 00	18 30	19 00	19 30	20 00	20 30	21 00	21 30	22 00	22 30	23 00	23 30	23 58
Possilpark & Parkhouse d	17 03	17 33	18 03	18 33	19 03	19 33	20 03	20 33	21 03	21 33	22 03	22 33	23 03	23 33	00 01
Gilshochill d	17 05	17 35	18 05	18 35	19 05	19 35	20 05	20 35	21 05	21 35	22 05	22 35	23 05	23 35	00 03
Summerston d	17 07	17 37	18 07	18 37	19 07	19 37	20 07	20 37	21 07	21 37	22 07	22 37	23 07	23 37	00 06
Maryhill d	17 09	17 39	18 09	18 39	19 09	19 39	20 09	20 39	21 09	21 39	22 09	22 39	23 09	23 39	00 07
Kelvindale d	17 11	17 41	18 11	18 41	19 11	19 41	20 11	20 41	21 11	21 41	22 11	22 41	23 11	23 41	00 10
Anniesland 226 a	17 15	17 45	18 15	18 46	19 15	19 45	20 15	20 45	21 15	21 46	22 15	22 45	23 15	23 45	00 14

Sundays

from 28 November

	SR	SR	SR	SR	SR	SR	SR	SR	SR	SR
Glasgow Queen Street 10 ⇌ d	08 45	09 58	10 56	11 56	12 55	13 56	14 55	15 57	16 56	17 56
Ashfield d	08 50	10 01	11 00	12 00	13 01	14 00	15 00	16 00	17 00	18 00
Possilpark & Parkhouse d	08 53	10 04	11 03	12 03	13 03	14 03	15 03	16 03	17 03	18 03
Gilshochill d	08 55	10 06	11 05	12 05	13 05	14 05	15 05	16 05	17 05	18 05
Summerston d	08 57	10 08	11 07	12 07	13 08	14 07	15 07	16 07	17 07	18 07
Maryhill d	08 59	10 10	11 09	12 09	13 09	14 09	15 09	16 09	17 09	18 09
Kelvindale d	09 01	10 12	11 11	12 11	13 12	14 11	15 11	16 11	17 11	18 11
Anniesland 226 a	09 04	10 18	11 15	12 15	13 15	14 15	15 14	16 16	17 15	18 15

Table 232

Anniesland and Maryhill - Glasgow Queen Street

			SR	SR	SR	SR	SR SX	SR	SR	SR	SR	SR	SR	SR	SR	SR	SR	SR	SR	SR		SR SX	SR SO	SR	SR	SR
Annlesland	226	d	06 23	06 52	07 22	07 52		08 24	08 52	09 22	09 52	10 22	10 52	11 22	11 52	12 22	12 52	13 22	13 52	14 22		14 53	14 53	15 22	15 52	16 25
Kelvindale		d	06 24	06 54	07 24	07 54		08 26	08 54	09 24	09 54	10 24	10 54	11 24	11 54	12 24	12 54	13 24	13 54	14 24		14 54	14 54	15 24	15 54	16 27
Maryhill		d	06 26	06 56	07 26	07 56	08 16	08 28	08 56	09 26	09 56	10 26	10 56	11 26	11 56	12 26	12 56	13 26	13 56	14 26		14 57	14 56	15 26	15 56	16 29
Summerston		d	06 28	06 58	07 28	07 58		08 30	08 58	09 28	09 58	10 28	10 58	11 28	11 58	12 28	12 58	13 28	13 58	14 28		14 58	14 58	15 28	15 58	16 31
Gilshochill		d	06 30	07 00	07 30	08 00		08 32	09 00	09 30	10 00	10 30	11 00	11 30	12 00	12 30	13 00	13 30	14 00	14 30		15 01	15 00	15 30	16 00	16 33
Possilpark & Parkhouse		d	06 32	07 02	07 32	08 02	08 21	08 34	09 02	09 32	10 02	10 32	11 02	11 32	12 02	12 32	13 02	13 32	14 02	14 32		15 03	15 02	15 32	16 02	16 35
Ashfield		d	06 34	07 04	07 34	08 04		08 36	09 04	09 34	10 04	10 34	11 04	11 34	12 04	12 34	13 04	13 34	14 04	14 34		15 04	15 04	15 34	16 04	16 38
Glasgow Queen Street 10 ⛴		a	06 42	07 11	07 41	08 11	08 37	08 44	09 11	09 41	10 11	10 41	11 11	11 41	12 11	12 41	13 11	13 41	14 11	14 41		15 12	15 12	15 41	16 11	16 44

			SR	SR	SR	SR	SR		SR	SR	SR	SR	SR	SR	SR	SR	SR
Annlesland	226	d	16 54	17 24	17 53	18 22	18 52		19 22	19 52	20 22	20 52	21 23	21 52	22 22	22 52	23 22
Kelvindale		d	16 56	17 26	17 54	18 24	18 54		19 24	19 54	20 24	20 54	21 24	21 54	22 24	22 54	23 24
Maryhill		d	16 58	17 28	17 56	18 26	18 56		19 26	19 56	20 26	20 56	21 26	21 56	22 26	22 56	23 26
Summerston		d	17 00	17 30	17 58	18 28	18 58		19 28	19 58	20 28	20 58	21 28	21 58	22 28	22 58	23 28
Gilshochill		d	17 02	17 32	18 00	18 30	19 00		19 30	20 00	20 30	21 00	21 30	22 00	22 30	23 00	23 30
Possilpark & Parkhouse		d	17 04	17 34	18 02	18 32	19 02		19 32	20 02	20 32	21 02	21 32	22 02	22 32	23 02	23 32
Ashfield		d	17 06	17 36	18 04	18 34	19 04		19 34	20 04	20 34	21 04	21 34	22 04	22 34	23 04	23 34
Glasgow Queen Street 10 ⛴		a	17 14	17 44	18 12	18 41	19 11		19 41	20 11	20 41	21 11	21 42	22 11	22 41	23 11	23 42

Sundays
from 28 November

			SR	SR	SR	SR	SR	SR	SR	SR	SR		SR
Annlesland	226	d	09 22	10 22	11 22	12 22	13 22	14 22	15 22	16 22	17 22		18 20
Kelvindale		d	09 24	10 24	11 24	12 24	13 24	14 24	15 24	16 24	17 24		18 22
Maryhill		d	09 26	10 26	11 26	12 26	13 26	14 26	15 26	16 26	17 26		18 24
Summerston		d	09 28	10 28	11 28	12 28	13 28	14 28	15 28	16 28	17 28		18 26
Gilshochill		d	09 30	10 30	11 30	12 30	13 30	14 30	15 30	16 30	17 30		18 28
Possilpark & Parkhouse		d	09 32	10 32	11 32	12 32	13 32	14 32	15 32	16 32	17 32		18 30
Ashfield		d	09 34	10 34	11 34	12 34	13 35	14 34	15 35	16 34	17 34		18 32
Glasgow Queen Street 10 ⛴		a	09 41	10 41	11 41	12 41	13 41	14 41	15 41	16 41	17 41		18 39

Table 237

Edinburgh - Bathgate

		SR	SR	SR	SR	SR	SR	SR	SR	SR	SR	SR	SR	SR	SR	SR	SR	SR	SR	SR	SR	SR	SR	SR	SR
Edinburgh	d	06 03	06 36	07 06	07 48	08 18	08 48	09 18	09 48	10 18	10 48	11 18	11 48	12 18	12 48	13 18	13 48	14 18	14 48	15 19	15 48	16 18	16 48	17 18	17 48
Haymarket	d	06 06	06 40	07 10	07 51	08 21	08 51	09 21	09 51	10 22	10 51	11 21	11 51	12 21	12 51	13 21	13 51	14 21	14 51	15 22	15 51	16 21	16 51	17 21	17 51
Edinburgh Park	d	06 10	06 46	07 16	07 55	08 25	08 55	09 25	09 55	10 26	10 55	11 25	11 55	12 25	12 55	13 25	13 55	14 25	14 55	15 25	16 25	16 25	16 55	17 25	17 55
Uphall	d	06 21	06 58	07 28	08 09	08 37	09 07	09 37	10 07	10 38	11 07	11 37	12 07	12 37	13 07	13 37	14 07	14 37	15 07	15 37	16 37	16 37	17 07	17 37	18 07
Livingston North	d	06 25	07 02	07 32	08 11	08 41	09 41	09 11	10 11	10 42	11 11	11 41	12 11	12 41	13 11	13 41	14 11	14 41	15 11	15 41	16 41	16 41	17 11	17 41	18 11
Bathgate	a	06 33	07 07	07 37	08 19	08 49	09 50	09 18	10 19	10 49	11 18	11 49	12 18	12 48	13 18	13 48	14 18	14 48	15 18	15 49	16 48	16 48	17 18	17 48	18 19

		SR	SR	SR	SR	SR		SR	SR
Edinburgh	d	18 18	18 48	19 22	20 18	21 18		22 18	23 18
Haymarket	d	18 21	18 51	19 25	20 21	21 21		22 21	23 21
Edinburgh Park	d	18 25	18 55	19 29	20 25	21 25		22 25	23 25
Uphall	d	18 37	19 07	19 41	20 37	21 37		22 37	23 37
Livingston North	d	18 41	19 11	19 45	20 41	21 41		22 41	23 41
Bathgate	a	18 48	19 18	19 52	20 48	21 48		22 48	23 48

Saturdays

		SR	SR	SR	SR	SR	SR	SR	SR	SR	SR	SR	SR	SR	SR	SR	SR	SR	SR	SR		SR	SR	SR	SR
Edinburgh	d	06 03	06 36	07 06	07 48	08 18	08 48	09 18	09 48	10 17	10 48	11 18	11 48	12 18	12 48	13 18	13 48	14 18	14 48	15 18		15 48	16 19	16 48	17 18
Haymarket	d	06 06	06 40	07 10	07 51	08 21	08 51	09 22	09 51	10 21	10 51	11 22	11 51	12 21	12 51	13 21	13 51	14 21	14 51	15 22		15 51	16 22	16 51	17 21
Edinburgh Park	d	06 10	06 46	07 16	07 55	08 25	08 55	09 25	09 55	10 25	10 55	11 25	11 55	12 25	12 55	13 25	13 55	14 25	14 55	15 25		15 55	16 26	16 56	17 25
Uphall	d	06 21	06 58	07 28	08 09	08 37	09 07	09 37	10 07	10 37	11 07	11 37	12 07	12 37	13 07	13 37	14 07	14 37	15 07	15 37		16 07	16 38	17 08	17 37
Livingston North	d	06 25	07 02	07 32	08 11	08 41	09 11	09 41	10 11	10 41	11 11	11 41	12 11	12 41	13 11	13 41	14 11	14 41	15 11	15 41		16 11	16 42	17 12	17 41
Bathgate	a	06 33	07 07	07 37	08 19	08 49	09 18	09 50	10 19	10 48	11 18	11 49	12 18	12 48	13 18	13 48	14 18	14 48	15 18	15 49		16 20	16 49	17 19	17 48

		SR	SR	SR	SR	SR		SR	SR	SR
Edinburgh	d	17 48	18 18	18 48	19 22	20 18		21 18	22 18	23 18
Haymarket	d	17 52	18 21	18 51	19 26	20 21		21 21	22 21	23 21
Edinburgh Park	d	17 55	18 25	18 55	19 29	20 25		21 25	22 25	23 25
Uphall	d	18 07	18 37	19 07	19 41	20 37		21 37	22 37	23 37
Livingston North	d	18 11	18 41	19 11	19 45	20 41		21 41	22 41	23 41
Bathgate	a	18 19	18 48	19 18	19 52	20 48		21 48	22 48	23 48

Sundays

		SR	SR	SR	SR	SR	SR	SR	SR	SR		SR	SR	SR	SR	SR	SR
Edinburgh	d	09 03	10 18	11 18	12 18	13 18	14 18	15 18	16 18	17 18		18 18	19 19	20 18	21 18	22 18	23 18
Haymarket	d	09 07	10 21	11 21	12 21	13 21	14 21	15 21	16 21	17 21		18 21	19 22	20 21	21 21	22 20	23 21
Edinburgh Park	d	09 11	10 25	11 25	12 25	13 25	14 25	15 25	16 25	17 25		18 25	19 25	20 25	21 25	22 25	23 25
Uphall	d	09 29	10 37	11 37	12 37	13 37	14 37	15 37	16 39	17 36		18 36	19 37	20 37	21 37	22 37	23 37
Livingston North	d	09 33	10 41	11 41	12 41	13 41	14 41	15 41	16 43	17 40		18 40	19 41	20 41	21 41	22 41	23 41
Bathgate	a	09 38	10 54	11 48	12 48	13 48	14 48	15 48	16 48	17 47		18 48	19 48	20 48	21 48	22 48	23 48

Table 237

Mondays to Fridays

Bathgate - Edinburgh

		SR	SR	SR	SR	SR	SR	SR	SR	SR	SR	SR	SR	SR	SR	SR	SR	SR	SR	SR	SR
Bathgate	d	06 39	07 13	07 57	08 25	08 54	09 24	10 24	10 54	11 24	11 54	12 24	12 54	13 24	13 54	14 24	14 54	15 24	15 54	16 24	16 54
Livingston North	d	06 44	07 19	08 03	08 30	08 58	09 28	10 28	10 58	11 28	11 58	12 28	12 58	13 28	13 58	14 28	14 58	15 28	15 58	16 28	16 58
Uphall	d	06 48	07 23	08 08	08 34	09 02	09 32	10 32	11 02	11 32	12 02	12 32	13 02	13 32	14 02	14 32	15 02	15 32	16 02	16 32	17 02
Edinburgh Park	d	06 58	07 33	08 18	08 43	09 13	09 43	10 43	11 14	11 43	12 13	12 43	13 13	13 43	14 13	14 43	15 13	15 43	16 13	16 43	17 14
Haymarket	d	07 03	07 39	08 23	08 52	09 19	09 49	10 53	11 20	11 50	12 19	12 53	13 20	13 49	14 19	14 54	15 20	15 49	16 21	16 54	17 21
Edinburgh	a	07 10	07 43	08 29	08 58	09 25	09 56	10 59	11 25	11 55	12 25	12 58	13 24	13 55	14 25	14 59	15 26	15 56	16 25	16 59	17 29

		SR	SR	SR	SR	SR	SR	SR	SR	SR	SR FX	SR FO
Bathgate	d	17 24	17 53	18 24	18 54	19 27	20 05	21 05	22 03	23 03	23 52	23 52
Livingston North	d	17 28	17 58	18 28	18 58	19 32	20 10	21 10	22 08	23 08	23 57	23 57
Uphall	d	17 32	18 02	18 32	19 02	19 36	20 14	21 14	22 12	23 12	23 59	23 59
Edinburgh Park	d	17 48	18 12	18 43	19 13	19 48	20 24	21 24	22 22	23 22	00 11	00 11
Haymarket	d	17 54	18 18	18 53	19 19	19 53	20 31	21 30	22 28	23 29	00 17	00 18
Edinburgh	a	17 59	18 23	18 58	19 25	19 58	20 36	21 36	22 33	23 34	00 22	00 22

Saturdays

		SR	SR	SR	SR	SR	SR	SR	SR	SR	SR	SR	SR	SR	SR	SR	SR	SR	SR	SR	SR	SR
Bathgate	d	06 39	07 13	07 57	08 25	08 54	09 24	09 54	10 24	10 54	11 24	11 54	12 24	12 54	13 24	13 54	14 24	14 54	15 24	15 54	16 24	16 54
Livingston North	d	06 44	07 19	08 03	08 30	08 58	09 28	09 58	10 28	10 58	11 28	11 58	12 28	12 58	13 28	13 58	14 28	14 58	15 28	15 58	16 28	16 58
Uphall	d	06 48	07 23	08 08	08 34	09 02	09 32	10 02	10 32	11 02	11 32	12 02	12 32	13 02	13 32	14 02	14 32	15 02	15 32	16 02	16 32	17 02
Edinburgh Park	d	06 58	07 33	08 18	08 43	09 13	09 43	10 13	10 43	11 14	11 43	12 13	12 43	13 13	13 43	14 13	14 43	15 13	15 43	16 13	16 43	17 13
Haymarket	d	07 03	07 39	08 23	08 53	09 19	09 49	10 21	10 53	11 20	11 50	12 19	12 54	13 20	13 49	14 19	14 54	15 19	15 49	16 20	16 54	17 20
Edinburgh	a	07 10	07 43	08 29	08 59	09 25	09 56	10 26	10 58	11 25	11 55	12 25	12 58	13 25	13 55	14 25	14 59	15 25	15 57	16 25	16 59	17 25

		SR	SR	SR	SR	SR	SR	SR	SR	SR	SR
Bathgate	d	17 28	17 53	18 24	18 54	19 27	20 05	21 05	22 03	23 03	23 52
Livingston North	d	17 32	17 58	18 28	18 58	19 32	20 10	21 10	22 08	23 08	23 57
Uphall	d	17 36	18 02	18 32	19 02	19 36	20 14	21 14	22 12	23 12	23 59
Edinburgh Park	d	17 47	18 12	18 43	19 13	19 48	20 24	21 24	22 22	23 22	00 11
Haymarket	d	17 53	18 18	18 53	19 19	19 53	20 31	21 31	22 28	23 29	00 18
Edinburgh	a	17 58	18 23	18 58	19 26	19 58	20 36	21 38	22 33	23 34	00 22

Sundays

		SR	SR	SR	SR	SR	SR	SR	SR	SR	SR	SR	SR	SR	SR	SR
Bathgate	d	09 49	11 01	12 01	13 02	13 58	14 58	15 59	16 59	17 59	18 59	19 59	20 59	22 01	23 01	23 59
Livingston North	d	09 54	11 06	12 06	13 06	14 03	15 03	16 03	17 03	18 03	19 03	20 04	21 03	22 06	23 06	00 04
Uphall	d	09 58	11 10	12 10	13 10	14 07	15 07	16 07	17 07	18 07	19 07	20 08	21 07	22 10	23 10	00 11
Edinburgh Park	d	10 07	11 19	12 19	13 19	14 17	15 17	16 17	17 17	18 17	19 17	20 17	21 17	22 19	23 20	00 21
Haymarket	d	10 13	11 25	12 25	13 25	14 23	15 23	16 23	17 23	18 22	19 23	20 22	21 23	22 26	23 25	00 27
Edinburgh	a	10 22	11 30	12 30	13 31	14 28	15 28	16 29	17 29	18 30	19 29	20 29	21 29	22 31	23 29	00 32

Table 238

Mondays to Fridays

Haymarket and Edinburgh - North Berwick and Dunbar

			GR	XC	SR	SR	XC	SR	SR	SR	XC	SR	SR	XC	SR	SR	SR	XC	SR	GR	XC	SR	SR	GR	SR	XC
Haymarket	225,230,242	d		06 55		08 22	08 54	09 35			10 54								15 24			16 34	17 05	17 20	17 39	
Edinburgh	225,230,242	a		06 59		08 35	08 58	09 37			11 01								15 30			16 39	17 09	17 27	17 43	
		d	06 00	07 08	07 16	08 38	09 07	09 40	10 00	10 37	11 08	11 37	12 37	13 07	13 37	14 21	14 37	15 07	15 38	16 00	17 08	16 40	17 12	17 30	17 44	18 08
Musselburgh		d			07 22	08 43		09 43		10 41		11 41	12 41		13 41	14 30	14 40		15 43			16 43	17 20		17 51	
Wallyford		d			07 26	08 47		09 47		10 45		11 45	12 45		13 45		14 44		15 47			16 47	17 24		17 55	
Prestonpans		d			07 29	08 50		09 50		10 48		11 48	12 48		13 48		14 47		15 50			16 50	17 28		17 58	
Dunbar		a	06 20	07 27			09 27		10 39		11 27			13 27		14 58		15 27		16 20	17 27			17 54		18 27
Longniddry		d			07 34	08 55		09 55		10 53		11 53	12 53		13 53		14 52		15 55			16 55	17 33		18 03	
Drem		d			07 39	09 00		10 00		10 59		11 59	12 59		13 59		14 58		16 02			17 02	17 39		18 08	
North Berwick		a			07 49	09 11		10 13		11 10		12 12	13 10		14 10		15 10		16 11			17 13	17 50		18 20	

			SR	GR	SR	SR	SR	GR	SR	SR	SR	XC FO
Haymarket	225,230,242	d	18 05					20 49				
Edinburgh	225,230,242	a	18 08					20 55				
		d	18 12	18 35	18 39	19 37	20 40	21 00	21 40	22 08	23 07	23 17
Musselburgh		d	18 18		18 43	19 41	20 43		21 43		23 11	
Wallyford		d	18 21		18 47	19 45	20 47		21 47		23 15	
Prestonpans		d	18 25		18 50	19 48	20 50		21 50		23 18	
Dunbar		a		18 55				21 20		22 40		23 53
Longniddry		d	18 30		18 55	19 53	20 55		21 55		23 23	
Drem		d	18 36		19 02	19 59	21 00		22 00		23 29	
North Berwick		a	18 48		19 12	20 10	21 13		22 13		23 50	

Saturdays

			GR	XC	SR	SR	XC A	XC B	SR	SR	SR	SR	XC	SR	SR	SR	SR	XC	SR	SR	SR	SR	XC	SR	SR	SR
Haymarket	225,230,242	d				08 29	08 54	08 57					10 51													
Edinburgh	225,230,242	a				08 35	08 58	09 01					10 58													
		d	06 15	07 07	07 37	08 38	09 05	09 05	09 08	09 37	10 08	10 38	11 05	11 08	11 37	12 08	12 38	13 05	13 08	13 37	14 08	14 37	15 05	15 08	15 38	16 08
Musselburgh		d			07 41	08 41			09 11	09 41	10 11	10 44		11 11	11 41	12 11	12 41		13 11	13 41	14 11	14 41		15 11	15 43	16 11
Wallyford		d			07 45	08 45			09 15	09 45	10 15	10 48		11 15	11 45	12 15	12 45		13 15	13 45	14 15	14 45		15 15	15 47	16 15
Prestonpans		d			07 48	08 48			09 18	09 48	10 18	10 51		11 18	11 48	12 18	12 48		13 18	13 48	14 18	14 48		15 16	15 50	16 18
Dunbar		a	06 35	07 26			09 25	09 25					11 24					13 25					15 25			
Longniddry		d			07 53	08 53			09 23	09 53	10 23	10 56		11 23	11 53	12 23	12 53		13 23	13 53	14 23	14 53		15 21	15 55	16 23
Drem		d			07 58	08 59			09 29	09 59	10 29	11 01		11 29	11 59	12 29	12 59		13 29	14 00	14 29	14 59		15 26	16 02	16 29
North Berwick		a			08 10	09 11			09 41	10 10	10 41	11 11		11 41	12 10	12 41	13 12		13 41	14 13	14 41	15 10		15 42	16 11	16 41

			SR	XC	SR	GR	SR	XC	SR	SR	GR	SR	SR	SR	SR
Haymarket	225,230,242	d	16 27			17 20					18 47				
Edinburgh	225,230,242	a	16 36			17 25					18 55				
		d	16 41	17 05	17 08	17 30	17 37	18 05	18 08	18 37	19 00	19 37	20 40	21 40	23 07
Musselburgh		d	16 45		17 14		17 41		18 11	18 43		19 41	20 43	21 43	23 11
Wallyford		d	16 49		17 18		17 45		18 15	18 47		19 45	20 47	21 47	23 15
Prestonpans		d	16 52		17 21		17 48		18 18	18 50		19 48	20 50	21 50	23 18
Dunbar		a		17 24		17 50		18 24			19 20				
Longniddry		d	16 57		17 26		17 53		18 23	18 55		19 53	20 55	21 55	23 23
Drem		d	17 02		17 31		17 59		18 29	19 02		19 59	21 00	22 00	23 29
North Berwick		a	17 14		17 41		18 09		18 41	19 10		20 10	21 13	22 13	23 50

Sundays

			SR	XC	SR	SR	XC	SR	SR	SR	SR	XC	SR	XC	SR	GR	SR	GR	SR	GR	SR
Haymarket	225,230,242	d					12 39									18 46				20 46	
Edinburgh	225,230,242	a					12 44									18 52				20 51	
		d	10 33	10 50	11 33	12 33	12 50	13 36	14 33	15 33	16 33	16 50	17 33	17 50	18 33	19 00	19 33	20 00	20 33	21 00	21 33
Musselburgh		d	10 39		11 39	12 39		13 39	14 39	15 39	16 39		17 39		18 39		19 39		20 39		21 39
Wallyford		d	10 43		11 43	12 43		13 43	14 43	15 43	16 43		17 43		18 43		19 43		20 43		21 43
Prestonpans		d	10 46		11 46	12 46		13 46	14 46	15 46	16 46		17 46		18 46		19 46		20 46		21 46
Dunbar		a		11 09			13 10					17 09		18 10		19 20		20 20		21 20	
Longniddry		d	10 51		11 51	12 51		13 51	14 51	15 51	16 51		17 51		18 51		19 51		20 51		21 51
Drem		d	10 56		11 56	12 57		13 56	14 56	15 56	16 56		17 56		18 56		19 56		20 56		21 56
North Berwick		a	11 06		12 06	13 06		14 09	15 06	16 06	17 06		18 06		19 06		20 06		21 06		22 06

A until 18 September

B from 25 September

Table 238

Mondays to Fridays

Dunbar and North Berwick - Edinburgh and Haymarket

	SR	XC	SR	SR	GR	SR	SR	SR	GR	SR	GR	SR	SR	SR	XC	SR	SR	XC	SR	SR	SR	XC		SR
		◇1			1				1		1				◇1			◇1				◇1		
North Berwick d	06 09		06 44	07 20			07 58	08 37		09 22		10 20		11 21		12 20	13 20		14 17		15 18			16 22
Drem d	06 16		06 51	07 27			08 06	08 44		09 29		10 27		11 27		12 27	13 27		14 24		15 25			16 27
Longniddry d	06 22		06 57	07 33			08 12	08 50		09 35		10 33		11 33		12 33	13 33		14 30		15 31			16 33
Dunbar d		06 39			07 38				08 52		09 53		10 57		11 44			13 45		15 04		15 45		
Prestonpans d	06 27		07 03	07 38		08 08	08 16	08 55		09 40		10 38		11 38		12 38	13 38		14 35		15 36			16 38
Wallyford d	06 30		07 06	07 41		08 11	08 19	08 58		09 43		10 41		11 41		12 41	13 41		14 38		15 39			16 41
Musselburgh d	06 35		07 10	07 45		08 14	08 26	09 02		09 47		10 44		11 44		12 45	13 45		14 42	15 25	15 43			16 45
Edinburgh 10 225,230,242 a	06 42	07 09	07 18	07 53	08 05	08 22	08 34	09 10	09 19	09 55	10 20	10 53	11 28	11 54	12 11	12 53	13 53	14 14	14 50	15 34	15 51	16 16		16 55
d		07 26	07 21		08 08		08 38	09 11	09 22		10 27								15 07		15 51			
Haymarket 225,230,242 a		07 29	07 24		08 13		08 41	09 14	09 27		10 31								15 10		15 57			

	SR	XC	SR	SR	SR	SR	XC	SR	SR	GR	XC		SR
		◇1					◇1			1	◇1		
North Berwick d	17 22		17 52	18 25	18 53	19 20		20 20	21 20				22 20
Drem d	17 27			18 32	18 57	19 27		20 27	21 27				22 27
Longniddry d	17 33			18 38	19 03	19 33		20 33	21 33				22 33
Dunbar d		17 49					19 48			21 46	21 52		
Prestonpans d	17 38			18 43	19 08	19 38		20 38	21 38				22 38
Wallyford d	17 41			18 46	19 11	19 41		20 41	21 41				22 41
Musselburgh d	17 45		18 11	18 50	19 15	19 45		20 45	21 45				22 45
Edinburgh 10 225,230,242 a	17 55	18 13	18 21	18 58	19 26	19 56	20 12	20 53	21 53	22 14	22 17		22 53
d		18 16	18 26				20 15						
Haymarket 225,230,242 a		18 19	18 27				20 19						

Saturdays

	SR	SR	GR	SR	GR	SR	SR	GR	SR	SR	SR	SR	SR	SR	SR	XC	SR	SR	SR	SR	XC	SR	SR	SR
			1		1			1								◇1					◇1			
North Berwick d	06 09	07 20		08 20		09 22	09 47		10 20	10 50	11 20	11 50	12 20	12 52	13 20		13 53	14 18	14 50	15 18		15 51	16 20	16 52
Drem d	06 16	07 27		08 27		09 29	09 54		10 27	10 57	11 27	11 57	12 27	12 57	13 27		13 57	14 25	14 57	15 25		15 57	16 27	16 57
Longniddry d	06 22	07 33		08 33		09 35	10 00		10 33	11 03	11 33	12 03	12 33	13 02	13 33		14 03	14 31	15 03	15 31		16 02	16 33	17 03
Dunbar d			07 38		09 06			09 52								13 41					15 41			
Prestonpans d	06 27	07 38		08 38		09 40	10 05		10 38	11 08	11 38	12 08	12 38	13 07	13 38		14 08	14 36	15 08	15 36		16 06	16 38	17 08
Wallyford d	06 30	07 41		08 41		09 43	10 08		10 41	11 11	11 41	12 11	12 41	13 10	13 41		14 11	14 39	15 11	15 39		16 09	16 41	17 11
Musselburgh d	06 35	07 45		08 45		09 47	10 12		10 45	11 15	11 45	12 15	12 45	13 14	13 45		14 15	14 43	15 15	15 43		16 13	16 45	17 15
Edinburgh 10 225,230,242 a	06 42	07 53	08 05	08 52	09 31	09 56	10 20	10 21	10 53	11 23	11 53	12 23	12 53	13 25	13 53	14 07	14 26	14 51	15 23	15 51	16 05	16 27	16 56	17 28
d			08 08	09 00	09 38			10 26																
Haymarket 225,230,242 a			08 13	09 02	09 42			10 30																

	SR	XC	SR	SR	SR	SR	XC	SR	GR		SR	XC	SR
		◇1					◇1		1			◇1	
North Berwick d	17 21		17 50	18 20	18 50	19 20		20 20			21 20		22 20
Drem d	17 28		17 57	18 27	18 57	19 27		20 27			21 27		22 27
Longniddry d	17 34		18 03	18 33	19 03	19 33		20 33			21 33		22 33
Dunbar d		17 41					19 50		21 05			21 43	
Prestonpans d	17 39		18 08	18 38	19 08	19 38		20 38			21 38		22 38
Wallyford d	17 42		18 11	18 41	19 11	19 41		20 41			21 41		22 41
Musselburgh d	17 46		18 15	18 45	19 15	19 43		20 45			21 45		22 45
Edinburgh 10 225,230,242 a	17 56	18 05	18 23	18 53	19 23	19 53	20 15	20 53	21 30		21 54	22 10	22 53
d		18 08	18 26				20 22		21 45				
Haymarket 225,230,242 a		18 11	18 29				20 25		21 49				

Sundays

	SR	GR	XC	SR	SR	XC	SR	SR	XC	SR	SR		XC	SR	SR	XC	SR	SR	XC	SR	GR
		1	◇1			◇1			◇1				◇1			◇1			◇1		1
North Berwick d	11 20			12 20	13 24		14 23	15 20		16 20	17 20			18 20	19 20		20 20	21 20		22 20	
Drem d	11 27			12 27	13 28		14 27	15 27		16 27	17 27			18 27	19 27		20 27	21 27		22 27	
Longniddry d	11 33			12 33	13 34		14 33	15 33		16 33	17 33			18 33	19 33		20 33	21 33		22 33	
Dunbar d		11 32	11 43			13 41			15 43				17 43			19 43			21 50		22 59
Prestonpans d	11 38			12 38	13 39		14 38	15 38		16 38	17 38			18 38	19 38		20 38	21 38		22 38	
Wallyford d	11 41			12 41	13 42		14 41	15 41		16 41	17 41			18 41	19 41		20 41	21 41		22 41	
Musselburgh d	11 45			12 45	13 46		14 45	15 45		16 45	17 45			18 45	19 45		20 45	21 45		22 45	
Edinburgh 10 225,230,242 a	11 53	11 57	12 07	12 53	13 57	14 10	14 56	15 53	16 07	16 53	17 53		18 07	18 53	19 53	20 07	20 53	21 53	22 15	22 53	23 27
d		12 04	12 12										18 10			20 12					
Haymarket 225,230,242 a		12 08	12 15										18 13			20 15					

Table 239

Mondays to Saturdays

Inverness - Kyle of Lochalsh, Thurso and Wick

	SR	SR	SR	SR	SR	SR	SR	SR	SR	SR	SR	SR	SR FSO
	◇1	◇1	◇1	◇1	1	◇1	◇1	1		◇1 A	◇1	1	1
Aberdeen 240 d													
Inverness d	07 06	09 00	10 38	11 01	12 16	13 34	13 59	14 39	17 15	17 52		21 09	23 30
Beauly d	07 20	09 14	10 52		12 30	13 48		14 53	17 29	18 06		21 23	23 44
Muir of Ord d	07 29	09 20	10 58	11 18	12 36	13 54	14 16	14 59	17 35	18 12		21 29	23 50
Dingwall d	07 43	09 31	11 07	11 29	12a47	14 03	14 28	15 11	17 46	18 26	18 29	21 40	00 02
Garve d		09 53		11 51		14 25				18 49			
Lochluichart d		10x02		11x59		14x33				18x57			
Achanalt d		10x08		12x05		14x39				19x03			
Achnasheen d		10 19		12 16		14 50				19 17			
Achnashellach d		10x36		12x34		15x08				19x35			
Strathcarron d		10 46		12 43		15 17				19 46			
Attadale d		10x51		12x48		15x23				19x51			
Stromeferry d		11 04		13 01		15 35				20 04			
Duncraig d		11x12		13x09		15x43				20x12			
Plockton d		11 16		13 13		15 46				20 15			
Duirinish d		11x19		13x16		15x49				20x18			
Kyle of Lochalsh a		11 28		13 26		15 59				20 29			
Alness d	07 55		11 20				14 41	15 24	17 59		18 42	21 53	00x13
Invergordon d	08 00		11 26				14 46	15a29	18 04		18 47	21 58	00 18
Fearn d	08 12		11 38				14 58		18 16		18 58	22x09	00x29
Tain d	08 18		11 45				15 04		18 22		19 05	22a15	00a35
Ardgay d	08 33		12 00				15 21		18a38		19 24		
Culrain d	08 37		12 06				15x27				19 30		
Invershin d	08x38		12x07								19x31		
Lairg d	08 52		12 19				15 45				19 44		
Rogart d	09x05		12x32				15x59				19x57		
Golspie d	09 16		12 43				16 09				20 08		
Dunrobin Castle § d	09x19		12x46								20x11		
Brora d	09 30		12 54				16 19				20 18		
Helmsdale d	09 46		13 09				16 34				20 33		
Kildonan d	09x59		13x22				16 46				20x46		
Kinbrace d	10x08		13x31								20x55		
Forsinard d	10 22		13 42				17 06				21 06		
Altnabreac d	10x32		13x52								21x16		
Scotscalder d	10x41		14x01								21x25		
Georgemas Junction a	10 50		14 12				17 34				21 33		
d	10 52		14 14				17 36				21 35		
Thurso a	11 02		14 24				17 46				21 45		
d	11 04		14 26				17 48				21 47		
Georgemas Junction d	11 14		14 37				17 59				21 57		
Wick a	11 32		14 55				18 16				22 14		

Sundays

	SR	SR	SR	SR	SR	SR	SR
	1	◇1	1	1	◇1	◇1	1
Aberdeen 240 d							
Inverness d	10 00	11 11	12 22	15 21	17 55		21 09
Beauly d	10 14	11 25	12 36	15 35	18 09		21 23
Muir of Ord d	10 20	11 31	12 44	15 43	18 15		21 29
Dingwall d	10 32	11 45	12 57	15 54	18 28	18 29	21 40
Garve d		12 10			18 52		
Lochluichart d		12x19			19x00		
Achanalt d		12x25			19x06		
Achnasheen d		12 36			19 18		
Achnashellach d		12x53			19x36		
Strathcarron d		13 03			19 47		
Attadale d		13x08			19x52		
Stromeferry d		13 21			20 05		
Duncraig d		13x29			20x13		
Plockton d		13 33			20 16		
Duirinish d		13x36			20x19		
Kyle of Lochalsh a		13 45			20 29		
Alness d	10 44		13x08	16x06		18 42	21 53
Invergordon d	10 49		13 13	16a12		18 47	21 58
Fearn d	11x00		13x24			18 58	22x09
Tain d	11a06		13a30			19 05	22a15
Ardgay d						19 24	
Culrain d						19 30	
Invershin d						19x31	
Lairg d						19 44	
Rogart d						19x57	
Golspie d						20 08	
Dunrobin Castle § d						20 11	
Brora d						20 18	
Helmsdale d						20 33	
Kildonan d						20x46	
Kinbrace d						20x55	
Forsinard d						21 06	
Altnabreac d						21x16	
Scotscalder d						21x25	
Georgemas Junction a						21 33	
d						21 35	
Thurso a						21 45	
d						21 47	
Georgemas Junction d						21 57	
Wick a						22 14	

§ Summer station only

A to Muir of Ord

Table 239

Mondays to Saturdays

Wick, Thurso and Kyle of Lochalsh - Inverness

		SR 1	SR 1	SR ◇1	SR ◇1 🛒	SR ◇1 🛒	SR 1	SR ◇1	SR 1	SR ◇1 🛒	SR ◇1 🛒	SR ◇1	SR ◇1 🛒	SR 1	SR 1
Wick	d				06 20	08 12				12 36			16 00		
Georgemas Junction	d				06 37	08 29				12 53			16 17		
Thurso	a				06 46	08 38				13 02			16 26		
	d				06 48	08 41				13 05			16 29		
Georgemas Junction	a				06 59	08 50				13 14			16 38		
	d				07 00	08 53				13 17			16 41		
Scotscalder	d				07x06					13x23			16x47		
Altnabreac	d				07x15					13x32			16x56		
Forsinard	d				07 27	09 15				13 43			17 07		
Kinbrace	d				07x37					13x53			17x17		
Kildonan	d				07x48	09 33				14x03			17x25		
Helmsdale	d				08 01	09 47				14 18			17 40		
Brora	d				08 16	10 03				14 33			17 55		
Dunrobin Castle §	d				08x22					14x39			18x01		
Golspie	d				08 26	10 11				14 42			18 04		
Rogart	d				08x35	10x19				14x51			18x13		
Lairg	d		06 34		08 53	10 38				15 08			18 30		
Invershin	d		06 43		09x01					15x17			18x39		
Culrain	d		06 44		09 03					15 20			18 41		
Ardgay	d	06 25	06 51		09 11	10 51				15 25			18 48	19 26	
Tain	d	06 40	07 06		09 26	11 07				15 41			19 05	19 42	22 20
Fearn	d	06 45	07 12		09 31					15 47			19x11	19x47	22x25
Invergordon	d	06 58	07 24		09 44	11 26			15 38	15 58			19 22	19 58	22 36
Alness	d	07 02	07 28		09 48				15 43	16x03			19x27	20x03	22x41
Kyle of Lochalsh	d			06 21				12 03			14 35	17 15			
Duirinish	d			06x28				12x10			14x42	17x22			
Plockton	d			06 33				12 14			14 47	17 27			
Duncraig	d			06x35				12x17			14x49	17x29			
Stromeferry	d			06 44				12 26			14 58	17 38			
Attadale	d			06x56				12x37			15x09	17x50			
Strathcarron	d			07 02				12 45			15 20	17 56			
Achnashellach	d			07x11				12x54			15x29	18x05			
Achnasheen	d			07 29				13 13			15 48	18 24			
Achanalt	d			07x39				13x23			15x58	18x34			
Lochluichart	d			07x45				13x29			16x04	18x41			
Garve	d			07 55				13 39			16 14	18 50			
Dingwall	d	07 16	07 42	08 16	10 04	11 45	12 54	14 04	15 56	16 19	16 37	19 13	19 41	20 16	22 54
Muir of Ord	d	07 28	07 52	08 28	10 13	11 55	13 05	14 16	16 08	16 29	16 46	19 25	19 50	20 25	23 05
Beauly	d	07 33	07 57	08 35	10 19		13 11	14 21	16 13	16x34		19 30	19 56	20x29	23x09
Inverness	a	07 48	08 12	08 53	10 35	12 13	13 25	14 37	16 28	16 48	17 06	19 49	20 10	20 44	23 24
Aberdeen	240 a														

Sundays

		SR 1	SR ◇1	SR 1	SR ◇1 🛒	SR 1	SR ◇1	SR 1
Wick	d				11 53			
Georgemas Junction	d				12 10			
Thurso	a				12 19			
	d				12 22			
Georgemas Junction	a				12 31			
	d				12 34			
Scotscalder	d				12x40			
Altnabreac	d				12x49			
Forsinard	d				13 00			
Kinbrace	d				13x10			
Kildonan	d				13x20			
Helmsdale	d				13 33			
Brora	d				13 48			
Dunrobin Castle §	d				13x54			
Golspie	d				13 58			
Rogart	d				14x07			
Lairg	d				14 24			
Invershin	d				14x33			
Culrain	d				14x34			
Ardgay	d				14 40			
Tain	d	11 10		14 00	14 55			22 20
Fearn	d	11x15		14x05	15x00			22x25
Invergordon	d	11 26		14 16	15 12	16 19		22 36
Alness	d	11x31		14x21	15x16	16x23		22x41
Kyle of Lochalsh	d		10 34				15 22	
Duirinish	d		10x41				15x29	
Plockton	d		10 46				15 34	
Duncraig	d		10x48				15x36	
Stromeferry	d		10 57				15 45	
Attadale	d		11x09				15x57	
Strathcarron	d		11 15				16 03	
Achnashellach	d		11x24				16x12	
Achnasheen	d		11 40				16 30	
Achanalt	d		11x50				16x40	
Lochluichart	d		11x57				16x47	
Garve	d		12 08				16 56	
Dingwall	d	11 44	12 28	14 36	15 30	16 36	17 18	22 54
Muir of Ord	d	11 55	12 43	14 47	15 42	16 47	17 29	23 05
Beauly	d	12 00	12 48	14x52	15 47	16 52	17 34	23x09
Inverness	a	12 16	13 03	15 07	16 02	17 07	17 49	23 24
Aberdeen	240 a							

§ Summer station only

Table 239A

SHIPPING SERVICES

Mondays to Saturdays

Scrabster - Stromness (Orkney Isles)

Operated by NorthLink Orkney & Shetland Ferries Ltd

		SO	SX	
Inverness	239 d	*07 06*	*07 06*	*13 59*
Thurso	239 a	*11a02*	*11a02*	*17c46*
Scrabster	⛴ d	12 00	13 15	19 00
Stromness	⛴ a	13 30	14 45	20 30

Mondays to Saturdays

		SX	SO A	SO B	SX	SO A
Stromness	⛴ d	06 30	06 30	09 00	11 00	11 00
Scrabster	⛴ a	08b00	08b00	10b30	12b30	12b30
Thurso #	239 d	*08 41*	*08 41*	*13 05*	*13 05*	*13 50*
Inverness	239 a	*12 13*	*12 13*	*16 48*	*16 48*	*16 48*

Sundays

Stromness	⛴ d	09 00
Scrabster	⛴ a	10b30
Thurso #	239 d	*12 22*
Inverness	239 a	*16 02*

A 12 June to 14 August

B Until 5 June and from 21 August

\# A connecting bus service between Thurso and Scrabster is operated by Stagecoach in the Highlands, from whom details of bus times should be obtained (Tel. 01463 239 292).

a Stagecoach in the Highlands bus connection. Departs Thurso Railway Station.

b Stagecoach in the Highlands bus connection. Arrives Thurso Railway Station.

c No bus connection available. Passengers must make their own way between Thurso Railway Station and Scrabster Ferry Terminal (2.5 miles). A taxi service is available from Thurso Railway Station.

PASSENGER NOTICE: Please note that NorthLink Ferries requires all passengers aged 16 and over to be in possession of photographic ID at check-in

Table 239B

SHIPPING SERVICES

Mondays to Saturdays until 23 October

Ullapool - Stornoway (Lewis), Uig (Skye), Tarbert (Harris) and Lochmaddy (North Uist)

Operated by Caledonian MacBrayne Ltd

			TTh-SX	TTh-SO	WFO F	SX A	WF-SX J	TThO	SO B	SO C	MFO	SO	WO	WFO F
Edinburgh ■10	229	d			09a35	09a35	09a35	09a35	09a35	09a35	09a35	11 35	09a35	15a35
Glasgow Queen St ■10	229	d			10 11	10 11	10 11	10 11	10 11	10 11	10 11	11a41	10 11	16 11
Inverness	229	a			13b27	13b27	13b27	13 27	13 27	13 27	13 27	15b06	13 27	19b34
Inverness	239	d	09 00	09 00				13 34	13 34	13 34	13 34		13 34	
Kyle of Lochalsh #	239	a	11c28	11c28				15d59	15d59	15d59	15d59		15d59	
Inverness +	bus	d			13 50	15 00	15 00					15 40		20 10
Ullapool	bus	a			15 10	16 20	16 20					17 00		21 30
Ullapool	ship	d			15 50	17 35	17 35					18 15		22 00
Stornoway	ship	a			18 35	20 20	20 20					21 00		00 45
Uig	ship	d	14 00	14 00				18 00	18 00	18 00	18 00		19 00	
Tarbert	ship	a	15 40					19 40	19 40	19 40				
Lochmaddy	ship	a		15 45					21 45		19 45		20 45	

Sundays until 17 October

Edinburgh ■10	229	d	09 25
Glasgow Queen St ■10	229	d	09a38
Inverness	229	a	13b09
Inverness	239	d	
Kyle of Lochalsh #	239	a	
Inverness +	bus	d	15 40
Ullapool	bus	a	17 00
Ullapool	ship	d	18 15
Stornoway	ship	a	21 00
Uig #	ship	d	
Tarbert	ship	a	
Lochmaddy	ship	a	

Mondays to Saturdays until 23 October

			MO D	MO E	WFO	WFO F	G	WFX H	TTh-SO	TTh-SO	TTh-SX	WFO F	SX A	WF-SX J	SO
Lochmaddy	ship	d	05 30						07 30		11 50				
Tarbert	ship	d	07 30	07 30	07 30					11 50					
Uig #	ship	a	09e10	09e10	09e10				09e15	13f30	13f35				
Stornoway	ship	d				06 15	07 00	07 00				12 40	13 50	13 50	14 30
Ullapool	ship	a				09 00	09 45	09 45				15 25	16 35	16 35	17 15
Ullapool	bus	d				09 05	09 50	09 50				15 30	16 40	16 40	17 20
Inverness +	bus	a				10g25	11g10	11g10				16g50	18g00	18g00	18g40
Kyle of Lochalsh #	239	d	12 03	12 03	12 03				12 03	17 15	17 15				
Inverness	239	a	14 37	14 37	14 37				14 37	19 49	19 49				
Inverness	229	d	14 51	14 51	14 51	10 47	12 47	12 47	14 51	20 15	20 15	18 43	18 43	18 43	20 15
Glasgow Queen St ■10	229	a	18 09	18 09	18 09	14a14	16a15	16a15	18 09	23 39	23 39	22a19	22a19	22a19	23 39
Edinburgh ■10	229	a	18a25	18a25	18a25	14 19	16 23	16 23	18a25	00h09	00h09	22 19	22 19	22 19	00h09

- A Until 18 June and from 30 August
- B From 11 September
- C Until 4 September
- D From 13 September
- E Until 6 September
- F 23 June to 27 August
- G Until 19 June and from 30 August
- H 21 June to 28 August
- J 21 June to 26 August
- a Change at Perth
- b Passengers make their own way between rail station and bus station
- c Bus connection dep. Kyle of Lochalsh 1215, Uig arr. 1350
- d Bus connection dep. Kyle of Lochalsh 1605, Uig arr. 1745
- e Bus connection dep. Uig 0930, Kyle of Lochalsh arr. 1114
- f Bus connection dep. Uig 1445, Kyle of Lochalsh arr. 1619
- g Passengers make their own way between bus station and rail station
- h Change at Stirling

Connecting bus service between Uig and Kyle of Lochalsh operated by Scottish Citylink Coaches (Tel. 08705 50 50 50).

\+ Bus station. Connecting bus service between Inverness Bus Station and Ullapool operated by Scottish Citylink Coaches (Tel. 08705 50 50 50).

No Sunday service from Lochmaddy to Uig or Stornoway to Ullapool

For details of sailings from 24 October 2010, telephone Caledonian MacBrayne on 08000 66 5000. For confirmation of Scottish Citylink Coach connections from 4 October 2010, telephone 08705 50 50 50

Table 240

Mondays to Fridays

Aberdeen and Elgin - Inverness

		SR ◇1	SR ◇1	SR ◇1	SR 1	SR ◇1	SR ◇1	SR ◇1	SR ◇1 trolley	SR ◇1	SR ◇1 trolley	SR 1
Aberdeen	d		06 14	07 14	07 50	08 23	08 50	10 00	10 14	11 04	11 59	12 50
Dyce ✈	d		06 24	07b31	08 03	08 36	08a59	10 09	10 23	11 16	12 08	13 01
Inverurie	a		06 37	07 44	08 17	08 48		10 22	10 35	11 30	12 20	13 15
	d		06 46	07 49		08 48			10 35		12 20	
Insch	d		06 58	08 01		09 03			10 47		12 33	
Huntly	d		07 19	08 17		09 19			11 03		12 49	
Keith	d		07 33	08 31		09 33			11 18		13 03	
Elgin	d	07 00	07 58	08 53		09 55			11 42		13 27	
Forres	d	07 14	08 12	09 07		10 11			11 56		13 41	
Nairn	d	07 27	08 23	09 22		10 22			12 07		13 52	
Inverness	a	07 48	08 41	09 40		10 40			12 25		14 10	

		SR ◇1 trolley	SR ◇1	SR ◇1 trolley	SR ◇1	SR 1	SR ◇1 trolley	SR ◇1	SR ◇1 trolley	SR ◇1	SR ◇1 trolley
Aberdeen	d	13 40	14 56	15 25	15 55	16 43	17 18	17 56	18 20	19 07	20 07
Dyce ✈	d	13 53	15 05	15 38	16 04	16a52	17 29	18 05	18 29	19 22	20 20
Inverurie	a	14 05	15 19	15 50	16 18		17 40	18 19	18 41	19 35	20 32
	d	14 05		15 50			17 41		18 41		20 32
Insch	d	14 17		16 02			17 53		18 53		20 44
Huntly	d	14 33		16 18			18 09		19 09		21 00
Keith	d	14 47		16 34			18 26		19 24		21 14
Elgin	d	15 11		16 56			18j54		19 46		21 36
Forres	d	15 25		17 10			19 08		20 00		21 55
Nairn	d	15 41		17h29			19 19		20 15		22 06
Inverness	a	15 59		17 47			19 38		20 33		22 24

		SR 1	SR ◇1	SR 1
Aberdeen	d	20 56	21 55	22 50
Dyce ✈	d	21 05	22 05	22 59
Inverurie	a	21 19	22 16	23 13
	d		22 17	
Insch	d		22 29	
Huntly	d		22 46	
Keith	d		23 00	
Elgin	d		23 22	
Forres	d		23 36	
Nairn	d		23 47	
Inverness	a		00 05	

Saturdays

		SR ◇1	SR ◇1	SR ◇1	SR 1	SR ◇1	SR ◇1	SR ◇1	SR ◇1 trolley	SR ◇1	SR ◇1 trolley	SR 1
Aberdeen	d		06 14	07 14	07 50	08 23	08 50	10 00	10 14	11 04	11 59	12 50
Dyce ✈	d		06 24	07b31	08 03	08 36	08a59	10 09	10 23	11 16	12 08	13 01
Inverurie	a		06 37	07 44	08 17	08 48		10 22	10 35	11 30	12 20	13 15
	d		06 46	07 49		08 48			10 35		12 20	
Insch	d		06 58	08 01		09 03			10 47		12 33	
Huntly	d		07 19	08 17		09 19			11 03		12 49	
Keith	d		07 33	08 31		09 33			11 18		13 03	
Elgin	d	07 00	07 58	08 53		09 55			11 42		13 27	
Forres	d	07 14	08 12	09 07		10 11			11 56		13 41	
Nairn	d	07 27	08 23	09 22		10 22			12 07		13 52	
Inverness	a	07 48	08 41	09 40		10 40			12 25		14 10	

		SR ◇1 trolley	SR ◇1	SR ◇1 trolley	SR ◇1	SR 1	SR ◇1 trolley	SR ◇1	SR ◇1 trolley	SR ◇1	SR ◇1 trolley
Aberdeen	d	13 40	14 56	15 25	15 55	16 43	17 18	17 56	18 20	19 07	20 07
Dyce ✈	d	13 53	15 05	15 38	16 04	16a52	17 29	18 05	18 29	19122	20 20
Inverurie	a	14 05	15 19	15 50	16 18		17 40	18 19	18 41	19 35	20 32
	d	14 05		15 50			17 41		18 41		20 32
Insch	d	14 17		16 02			17 53		18 53		20 44
Huntly	d	14 33		16 18			18 09		19 09		21 00
Keith	d	14 47		16 34			18 26		19 24		21 14
Elgin	d	15 11		16 56			18j54		19 46		21 36
Forres	d	15 25		17 10			19 08		20 00		21 55
Nairn	d	15 41		17h29			19 19		20 15		22 06
Inverness	a	15 59		17 47			19 38		20 33		22 24

		SR 1	SR ◇1	SR 1
Aberdeen	d	20 56	21 55	22 50
Dyce ✈	d	21 05	22 05	22 59
Inverurie	a	21 19	22 16	23 13
	d		22 17	
Insch	d		22 29	
Huntly	d		22 46	
Keith	d		23 00	
Elgin	d		23 22	
Forres	d		23 36	
Nairn	d		23 47	
Inverness	a		00 05	

Sundays

		SR ◇1 trolley	SR ◇1 trolley	SR ◇1 trolley	SR ◇1 trolley	SR ◇1 trolley
Aberdeen	d	10 00	13 00	15 25	17 18	21 00
Dyce ✈	d	10 09	13 09	15 34	17 29	21 09
Inverurie	a	10 21	13 21	15 46	17 41	21 21
	d	10 21	13 21	15 47	17 41	21 21
Insch	d	10 33	13 33	15 59	17 53	21 33
Huntly	d	10 49	13 51	16 15	18 09	21 49
Keith	d	11 05	14 04	16 35	18 24	22 09
Elgin	d	11 27	14 26	16 58	18 45	22 31
Forres	d	11 41	14 40	17 12	19 00	22 45
Nairn	d	11 52	14 51	17 32	19 11	22 56
Inverness	a	12 10	15 10	17 50	19 29	23 14

b arr. 0724

h arr. 1721

Table 240

Mondays to Fridays

Inverness and Elgin - Aberdeen

		SR ◇1	SR ◇1	SR ◇1 ✕	SR 1	SR ◇1	SR ◇1	SR ◇1	SR ◇1 ✕	SR ◇1	SR ◇1 ✕	SR 1	SR ◇1 ✕	SR ◇1	SR ◇1 ✕	SR ◇1	SR 1	SR ◇1 ✕	SR 1	SR ◇1	SR ◇1 ✕	SR	SR ◇1
Inverness	d	04 51		05 58			07 10		09 03		10 58		12 42		14 27			15 21			17 11		18 10
Nairn	d	05 08		06 15			07 28		09 21		11 15		12 59		14 44			15 40			17 28		18 27
Forres	d	05 19		06 26			07 39		09 37		11 26		13 10		14 55			15 51			17 39		18 38
Elgin	d	05 34		06 42			08b00		09 55		11 42		13 28		15 12			16 07			17 58		18 55
Keith	d	05 56		07 03			08 21		10 14		12 03		13 47		15 32			16 28			18 19		19 16
Huntly	d	06 10		07 19			08 45		10 30		12 17		14 01		15 46			16 47			18 40		19 37
Insch	d	06 26		07 35			09 03		10 49		12 35		14 19		16 04			17 04			18 56		19 53
Inverurie	a	06 38		07 48			09 14		11 01		12 47		14 31		16 18			17 15			19 09		20 05
	d	06 39	07 14	07 49	08 22		09 15	10 38	11 01	11 35	12 47	13 38	14 31	15 24	16 18	16 38		17 16	17 52	18 43	19 09	19 40	20 05
Dyce ✈	d	06 52	07 26	08 03	08 35	09 08	09 27	10 50	11 15	11 47	13 02	13 52	14 43	15 38	16 31	16 54	17 05	17 30	18 06	18 55	19 21	19 52	20 19
Aberdeen	a	07 04	07 37	08 14	08 46	09 19	09 38	11 01	11 26	11 58	13 13	14 03	14 54	15 49	16 41	17 05	17 14	17 41	18 17	19 06	19 32	20 03	20 30

		SR ◇1	SR 1	SR ◇1
Inverness	d	19 57		21 20
Nairn	d	20 14		21 37
Forres	d	20 25		21 48
Elgin	d	20a41		22 06
Keith	d			22 27
Huntly	d			22e47
Insch	d			23 03
Inverurie	a			23 16
	d		21 24	23 16
Dyce ✈	d		21 36	23 28
Aberdeen	a		21 47	23 39

Saturdays

		SR ◇1	SR ◇1	SR ◇1 ✕	SR 1	SR ◇1	SR ◇1	SR ◇1	SR ◇1 ✕	SR ◇1	SR ◇1 ✕	SR 1	SR ◇1 ✕	SR ◇1	SR ◇1 ✕	SR ◇1	SR 1	SR ◇1 ✕	SR 1	SR ◇1	SR ◇1 ✕	SR	SR ◇1
Inverness	d	04 51		05 58			07 10		09 03		10 58		12 42		14 27			15 21			17 11		18 10
Nairn	d	05 08		06 15			07 28		09 21		11 15		12 59		14 44			15 40			17 28		18 27
Forres	d	05 19		06 26			07 39		09 37		11 26		13 10		14 55			15 51			17 39		18 38
Elgin	d	05 34		06 42			08b00		09 55		11 42		13 28		15 12			16 07			17 58		18 55
Keith	d	05 56		07 03			08 21		10 14		12 03		13 47		15 32			16 28			18 19		19 16
Huntly	d	06 10		07 19			08 45		10 30		12 17		14 01		15 46			16 47			18 40		19 37
Insch	d	06 26		07 35			09 03		10 49		12 35		14 19		16 04			17 04			18 56		19 53
Inverurie	a	06 38		07 48			09 14		11 01		12 47		14 31		16 18			17 15			19 09		20 05
	d	06 39	07 14	07 49	08 22		09 15	10 38	11 01	11 35	12 47	13 38	14 31	15 24	16 18	16 38		17 16	17 52	18 43	19 09	19 40	20 05
Dyce ✈	d	06 52	07 26	08 03	08 35	09 08	09 27	10 50	11 15	11 47	13 02	13 52	14 43	15 38	16 31	16 54	17 05	17 30	18 06	18 55	19 21	19 52	20 19
Aberdeen	a	07 04	07 37	08 14	08 46	09 19	09 38	11 01	11 26	11 58	13 13	14 03	14 54	15 49	16 41	17 05	17 14	17 41	18 17	19 06	19 32	20 03	20 30

		SR ◇1	SR 1	SR ◇1
Inverness	d	19 57		21 20
Nairn	d	20 14		21 37
Forres	d	20 25		21 48
Elgin	d	20a41		22 06
Keith	d			22 27
Huntly	d			22e47
Insch	d			23 03
Inverurie	a			23 16
	d		21 24	23 16
Dyce ✈	d		21 36	23 28
Aberdeen	a		21 47	23 39

Sundays

		SR ◇1 ✕	SR ◇1 ✕	SR ◇1 ✕	SR ◇1 ✕	SR ◇1 ✕	SR ◇1 ✕	SR ◇1 ✕
Inverness	d	09 55	12 30	15 27	17 12	18 00	21 00	21 42
Nairn	d	10 12	12 47	15 44	17 30	18 17	21 17	21 59
Forres	d	10 23	12 58	15 55	17 41	18 28	21 28	22 10
Elgin	d	10 38	13 13	16 10	17 56	18a44	21 44	22a26
Keith	d	10 59	13 35	16 32	18 18		22 05	
Huntly	d	11 18	13 52	16 46	18 37		22 19	
Insch	d	11 34	14 08	17 02	18 53		22 35	
Inverurie	a	11 47	14 20	17 14	19 05		22 47	
	d	11 47	14 20	17 14	19 05		22 47	
Dyce ✈	d	11 59	14 32	17 30	19 17		22 59	
Aberdeen	a	12 10	14 43	17 41	19 28		23 10	

b arr. 0754

e arr. 2241

Table 242

Mondays to Fridays

Newcraighall and Edinburgh - Dunfermline, Kirkcaldy and Glenrothes with Thornton

		SR ◇1	XC ◇	SR	SR	SR	SR 1	SR	SR	SR	SR 1	SR	SR	SR ◇1 ✕	SR 1	SR	SR 1	SR
Newcraighall	d					06 04				06 36			07 05			07 26		
Brunstane	d					06 07				06 39			07 08			07 29		
Edinburgh 10	a					06 16				06 47			07 16			07 37		
	d	05 30	05 33		06 09	06 18	06 29	06 32		06 56	07 00	07 10	07 18	07 30	07 35	07 39	08 00	08 08
Haymarket	d	05 33			06 13	06 22	06 33	06 37		06a59	07 04	07 13	07 22	07 33	07 39	07 43	08 03	08 12
South Gyle	d				06 18	06 27		06 43				07 18	07 27			07 48		08 17
Dalmeny	d				06 24	06 33		06 50				07 25	07 34			07 54		
North Queensferry	d				06 28	06 37		06 54				07 28	07 37			07 58		
Inverkeithing	d	05 46	06a06		06 32	06 41	06 47	06 59			07 20	07 32	07 41		07 53	08 02	08 17	08 28
Rosyth	d					06 44							07 45					
Dunfermline Town	d					06 49							07 50					
Dunfermline Queen Margaret	d					06 53							07 53					
Cowdenbeath	d					06 59							08 00					
Lochgelly	d					07 05							08 05					
Cardenden	d					07 09							08 09					
Dalgety Bay	d				06 35			07 03				07 35				08 05		08 31
Aberdour	d				06 40			07 09				07 40				08 10		08 36
Burntisland	d				06 44			07 14				07 44				08 14		08 40
Kinghorn	d				06 49			07 19				07 49				08 19		08 45
Kirkcaldy	d	06a02			06a56		07a03	07 25			07a36	07 54		08a02	08a09	08 24	08a33	08 50
Glenrothes With Thornton	a					07 15		07 34				08 04	08 16			08 32		08 58

		SR	SR ◇1 ✕	SR	SR	SR 1	SR	SR	SR	SR 1	SR	SR	SR 1	SR	SR	GR 1 ✕	SR 1	SR	SR
Newcraighall	d	08 00			08 34				09 06			09 33			10 05				10 37
Brunstane	d	08 03			08 37				09 09			09 36			10 08				10 40
Edinburgh 10	a	08 10			08 45			09 10	09 16			09 48			10 16				10 47
	d	08 12	08 33	08 38	08 46	08 57	09 07	09 11	09 17	09 35	09 41	09 50	10 00	10 06	10 19	10 27	10 34	10 38	10 48
Haymarket	d	08 17	08 37	08 42	08 50	09 02	09 11	09a14	09 22	09 39	09 43	09 54	10 03	10 10	10 23	10 32	10 38	10 43	10 53
South Gyle	d	08 22		08 47	08 55		09 16		09 27		09 48	09 59		10 15	10 28			10 47	10 57
Dalmeny	d	08 28		08 53	09 01		09 22		09 34		09 54	10 05		10 21	10 34			10 54	11 04
North Queensferry	d	08 32		08 57	09 05		09 26		09 37		09 58	10 09		10 25	10 38			10 57	11 07
Inverkeithing	d	08 36		09 01	09 09	09 17	09 30		09 41	09 53	10 02	10 13	10 18	10 29	10 42	10 47	10 53	11 01	11 11
Rosyth	d	08 39			09 12				09 45			10 16			10 45				11 15
Dunfermline Town	d	08 44			09 17				09 50			10 21			10 50				11 20
Dunfermline Queen Margaret	d	08 48			09 21				09 53			10 25			10 54				11 23
Cowdenbeath	d	08 54			09 27				10a02			10 30			11a03				11 30
Lochgelly	d	09 00			09 33							10 37							11 35
Cardenden	d	09 04			09 37							10 41							11 39
Dalgety Bay	d			09 04			09 33				10 05			10 32				11 04	
Aberdour	d			09 09			09 38				10 10			10 37				11 09	
Burntisland	d			09 13			09 42				10 14			10 41				11 13	
Kinghorn	d			09 18			09 47				10 19			10 46				11 18	
Kirkcaldy	d		09a06	09 23		09a33	09 52			10a09	10 24		10a34	10 51		11a04	11a10	11 23	
Glenrothes With Thornton	a	09 10		09 31	09 43		10 03				10 32	10 47		11 03				11 32	11 46

		SR 1	SR	SR	SR	SR	SR 1	SR	SR	SR 1	SR	SR	SR 1	SR	SR
Newcraighall	d			11 07		11 35			12 07			12 37			13 07
Brunstane	d			11 10		11 38			12 10			12 40			13 10
Edinburgh 10	a			11 18		11 45			12 17			12 47			13 17
	d	11 00	11 05	11 19	11 39	11 48	12 00	12 06	12 18	12 35	12 39	12 49	13 00	13 06	13 18
Haymarket	d	11 04	11 09	11 23	11 43	11 52	12 03	12 10	12 23	12 39	12 43	12 53	13 03	13 11	13 23
South Gyle	d		11 15	11 28	11 48	11 57		12 15	12 27		12 48	12 58		13 15	13 27
Dalmeny	d		11 21	11 34	11 54	12 03		12 21	12 34		12 54	13 04		13 21	13 34
North Queensferry	d		11 25	11 38	11 58	12 07		12 25	12 37		12 58	13 08		13 25	13 37
Inverkeithing	d	11 17	11 29	11 42	12 02	12 11	12 17	12 29	12 41	12 53	13 02	13 12	13 17	13 29	13 41
Rosyth	d			11 45		12 14			12 45			13 15			13 45
Dunfermline Town	d			11 50		12 19			12 50			13 20			13 50
Dunfermline Queen Margaret	d			11 54		12 23			12 53			13 24			13 53
Cowdenbeath	d			12a03		12 29			13a03			13 30			14a02
Lochgelly	d					12 35						13 36			
Cardenden	d					12 39						13 40			
Dalgety Bay	d		11 32		12 05			12 32			13 05			13 32	
Aberdour	d		11 37		12 10			12 37			13 10			13 37	
Burntisland	d		11 41		12 14			12 41			13 14			13 41	
Kinghorn	d		11 46		12 19			12 46			13 19			13 46	
Kirkcaldy	d	11a33	11 51		12 24		12a35	12 51		13a09	13 24		13a33	13 51	
Glenrothes With Thornton	a		12 02		12 32	12 46		13 02			13 32	13 46		14 02	

Newcraighall and Edinburgh - Dunfermline, Kirkcaldy and Glenrothes with Thornton

		SR	SR	SR	SR	SR	SR	SR	SR	GR	SR	SR	SR	SR	SR	SR	SR
				1			1			1 A	1				1		
Newcraighall	d		13 37			14 06			14 37					15 06			15 35
Brunstane	d		13 40			14 09			14 40					15 09			15 38
Edinburgh 10	a		13 47			14 17			14 47	14 53		14 50		15 17			15 46
	d	13 39	13 49	14 00	14 05	14 18	14 35	14 39	14 49	15 00	15 03	15 07	15 08	15 19	15 35	15 39	15 48
Haymarket	d	13 43	13 53	14 04	14 09	14 23	14 38	14 43	14 53	15 04	15 08	15a10	15 13	15 23	15 39	15 43	15 53
South Gyle	d	13 48	13 58		14 14	14 28		14 48	14 58				15 18	15 28		15 48	15 58
Dalmeny	d	13 54	14 04		14 20	14 34		14 54	15 05				15 24	15 34		15 54	16 04
North Queensferry	d	13 58	14 08		14 24	14 38		14 58	15 08				15 28	15 38		15 58	16 08
Inverkeithing	d	14 02	14 12	14 17	14 28	14 42	14 53	15 02	15 12	15 19	15 25		15 32	15 42	15 53	16 02	16 12
Rosyth	d		14 15			14 45			15 16					15 45			16 15
Dunfermline Town	d		14 20			14 50			15 21					15 51			16 20
Dunfermline Queen Margaret	d		14 24			14 54			15 24					15 53			16 24
Cowdenbeath	d		14 30			15a04			15 31					16a04			16 30
Lochgelly	d		14 36						15 36								16 36
Cardenden	d		14 40						15 40								16 40
Dalgety Bay	d	14 05			14 31			15 05					15 35			16 05	
Aberdour	d	14 10			14 36			15 10					15 40			16 10	
Burntisland	d	14 14			14 40			15 14					15 44			16 14	
Kinghorn	d	14 19			14 45			15 19					15 49			16 19	
Kirkcaldy	d	14 24		14a33	14 50		15a09	15 24		15a36	15a42		15 54		16a09	16 24	
Glenrothes With Thornton	a	14 32	14 46		15 03			15 32	15 47				16 05			16 32	16 46

		SR	SR	SR	SR	SR	SR	SR	SR	SR	SR	SR	SR	SR	SR	XC	SR	GR	SR
		1			1							◇1			1	◇1		1	
Newcraighall	d			16 03			16 30			16 59				17 37			18 07		
Brunstane	d			16 06			16 33			17 02				17 40			18 10		
Edinburgh 10	a			16 13			16 41			17 09				17 51			18 18		
	d	16 00	16 08	16 16	16 32	16 39	16 47	17 03	17 08	17 13	17 21	17 41	17 49	17 52	18 00	18 16	18 26	18 30	18 08
Haymarket	d	16 04	16 12	16 20	16 37	16 43	16 51	17 07	17 12	17 19	17 25	17u45	17 53	17 57	18 04	18 21	18 30	18 35	18 12
South Gyle	d		16 17	16 25		16 49	16 56		17 18	17 24	17 31		17 58	18 02			18 35		18 17
Dalmeny	d		16 23	16 32		16 56	17 02			17 30	17 38		18 05	18 08			18 41		18 23
North Queensferry	d		16 27	16 36		17 00	17 07			17 34	17 41		18 09	18 12			18 45		18 27
Inverkeithing	d	16 17	16 31	16 40	16 51	17 05	17 11	17 22	17 28	17 36	17 47		18 13	18 16	18 22	18 38	18 49	18 54	18 31
Rosyth	d			16 44			17 15		17 34		17 50			18 19			18 52		
Dunfermline Town	d			16 49			17 20		17 40		17 55			18 24			18 57		
Dunfermline Queen Margaret	d			16 52			17 23		17 45		17 59			18 28			19 01		
Cowdenbeath	d			17a02			17a33		17 53		18 05			18 34			19 07		
Lochgelly	d								17 59		18 11			18 40			19 13		
Cardenden	d								18 04		18a24			18 44			19 17		
Dalgety Bay	d		16 34			17 08				17 40			18 16						18 34
Aberdour	d		16 39			17 13				17 45			18 21						18 39
Burntisland	d		16 43			17 17				17 49			18 26						18 43
Kinghorn	d		16 48			17 22				17 54			18 31						18 48
Kirkcaldy	d	16a33	16 53		17a07	17 27		17a39		18a04		18a16	18 36		18a40	19a00		19a11	19a04
Glenrothes With Thornton	a		17 01			17 35			18 10				18 44	18 52			19 23		18 10

		SR	SR	SR	SR	SR	SR	SR	SR	XC	SR	GR	SR	SR	SR	SR
		1		1			◇1			◇1		1	1			◇1
Newcraighall	d		18 35			19 07		19 38			20 08			20 37		
Brunstane	d		18 38			19 10		19 41			20 11			20 40		
Edinburgh 10	a		18 45			19 17		19 48			20 19			20 47		
	d	18 40	18 49	19 00	19 09	19 21	19 35	19 49	20 00	20 15	20 19	20 32	20 37	20 51	21 09	21 40
Haymarket	d	18 45	18 53	19 03	19 13	19 26	19 39	19 54	20 04	20 20	20a24	20 37	20 41	20 55	21 13	21 44
South Gyle	d		18 58		19 18	19 30		19 58	20 09					21 00	21 18	
Dalmeny	d		19 04		19 24	19 37		20 05	20 15					21 06	21 24	
North Queensferry	d		19 08		19 28	19 40		20 08	20 19					21 10	21 28	
Inverkeithing	d	19 00	19 12	19 17	19 32	19 44	19 54	20 12	20 23	20 35		20 52	21 00	21 14	21 32	
Rosyth	d		19 15			19 48		20 16						21 17		
Dunfermline Town	d		19 20			19 53		20 21						21 22		
Dunfermline Queen Margaret	d		19 24			19 56		20 24						21 26		
Cowdenbeath	d		19 30			20 03		20 31						21 32		
Lochgelly	d		19 36			20 08		20 36						21 38		
Cardenden	d		19 40			20 12		20 40						21 42		
Dalgety Bay	d				19 35				20 26						21 35	
Aberdour	d				19 40				20 31						21 40	
Burntisland	d				19 44				20 35						21 44	
Kinghorn	d				19 49				20 40						21 49	
Kirkcaldy	d	19a18		19a33	19a56		20a10		20a45	20a51		21a09	21a17		21 54	22a12
Glenrothes With Thornton	a		19 49			20 22		20 50						21 52		

A The Northern Lights

B

Newcraighall and Edinburgh - Dunfermline, Kirkcaldy and Glenrothes with Thornton

		SR	SR	SR	SR	SR	SR	SR
Newcraighall	d	21 37			22 37			23 37
Brunstane	d	21 40			22 40			23 40
Edinburgh 10	a	21 47			22 47			23 47
	d	21 49	22 09	22 39	22 50	23 09	23 19	23 49
Haymarket	d	21 53	22 13	22 43	22a54	23 13	23 23	23a53
South Gyle	d	21 58	22 18	22 48		23 18	23 28	
Dalmeny	d	22 04	22 24	22 54		23 24	23 34	
North Queensferry	d	22 08	22 28	22 58		23 28	23 38	
Inverkeithing	d	22 12	22 32	23 02		23 32	23 42	
Rosyth	d	22 15					23 45	
Dunfermline Town	d	22 20					23 50	
Dunfermline Queen Margaret	d	22 24					23 54	
Cowdenbeath	d	22 30					23 59	
Lochgelly	d	22 36					00 06	
Cardenden	d	22 40					00 10	
Dalgety Bay	d		22 35	23 05		23 35		
Aberdour	d		22 40	23 10		23 40		
Burntisland	d		22 44	23 14		23 44		
Kinghorn	d		22 49	23 19		23 49		
Kirkcaldy	d		22 54	23 24		23a54		
Glenrothes With Thornton	a	22 46					00 19	

Saturdays
until 18 September

			SR	XC	SR	SR	SR	SR	SR	SR	SR	SR	SR	SR	SR	SR	SR	SR	SR
			◇1	◇		1			1			◇1	1		1			◇1	
Newcraighall	d				06 04			06 36			07 05			07 26			08 00		
Brunstane	d				06 07			06 39			07 08			07 29			08 03		
Edinburgh 10	a				06 16			06 46			07 16			07 37			08 11		
	d		05 30	05 33	06 18	06 29	06 39	06 56	07 00	07 10	07 18	07 30	07 35	07 39	08 00	08 08	08 12	08 33	08 38
Haymarket	d		05 33		06 22	06 33	06 43	06a59	07 04	07 13	07 22	07 33	07 39	07 43	08 03	08 12	08 17	08 37	08 42
South Gyle	d				06 27		06 48			07 18	07 27			07 48		08 17	08 22		08 47
Dalmeny	d				06 33		06 54			07 25	07 34			07 54			08 28		08 53
North Queensferry	d				06 37		06 58			07 28	07 37			07 58			08 32		08 57
Inverkeithing	d		05 46	06a06	06 41	06 47	07 02		07 20	07 32	07 41		07 53	08 02	08 17	08 28	08 36		09 01
Rosyth	d				06 44						07 45						08 39		
Dunfermline Town	d				06 49						07 50						08 44		
Dunfermline Queen Margaret	d				06 53						07 53						08 48		
Cowdenbeath	d				06 59						08 00						08 54		
Lochgelly	d				07 05						08 05						09 00		
Cardenden	d				07 09						08 09						09 04		
Dalgety Bay	d						07 05			07 35				08 05		08 31			09 04
Aberdour	d						07 10			07 40				08 10		08 36			09 09
Burntisland	d						07 14			07 44				08 14		08 40			09 13
Kinghorn	d						07 19			07 49				08 19		08 45			09 18
Kirkcaldy	d		06a02			07a03	07 24		07a36	07 54		08a02	08a09	08 24	08a33	08 50		09a06	09 23
Glenrothes With Thornton	a	00 19			07 15		07 32			08 04	08 16			08 32		08 58	09 10		09 31

		SR	SR	SR	SR	SR	SR	SR	SR	SR	SR	GR	SR	SR	SR	SR	SR	SR
			1			1			1			1	1			1		
Newcraighall	d	08 34			09 06			09 33			10 05				10 37			11 07
Brunstane	d	08 37			09 09			09 36			10 08				10 40			11 10
Edinburgh 10	a	08 45			09 16			09 45			10 16				10 47			11 18
	d	08 46	08 57	09 06	09 17	09 35	09 41	09 50	10 00	10 06	10 19	10 26	10 34	10 38	10 48	11 00	11 06	11 19
Haymarket	d	08 50	09 02	09 10	09 22	09 39	09 43	09 54	10 03	10 10	10 23	10 31	10 38	10 43	10 53	11 04	11 09	11 23
South Gyle	d	08 55		09 15	09 27		09 48	09 59		10 15	10 28			10 47	10 57		11 15	11 28
Dalmeny	d	09 01		09 21	09 34		09 54	10 05		10 21	10 34			10 54	11 04		11 21	11 34
North Queensferry	d	09 05		09 25	09 37		09 58	10 09		10 25	10 38			10 57	11 07		11 25	11 38
Inverkeithing	d	09 09	09 17	09 29	09 41	09 53	10 02	10 13	10 18	10 29	10 42	10 46	10 53	11 01	11 11	11 17	11 29	11 42
Rosyth	d	09 12			09 45			10 16			10 45				11 15			11 45
Dunfermline Town	d	09 17			09 50			10 21			10 50				11 20			11 50
Dunfermline Queen Margaret	d	09 21			09 53			10 25			10 54				11 23			11 54
Cowdenbeath	d	09 27			10a02			10 31			11a03				11 30			12a03
Lochgelly	d	09 33						10 37							11 35			
Cardenden	d	09 37						10 41							11 39			
Dalgety Bay	d			09 32			10 05			10 32				11 04			11 32	
Aberdour	d			09 37			10 10			10 37				11 09			11 37	
Burntisland	d			09 41			10 14			10 41				11 13			11 41	
Kinghorn	d			09 46			10 19			10 46				11 18			11 46	
Kirkcaldy	d		09a33	09 51		10a09	10 24		10a34	10 51		11a03	11a10	11 23		11a33	11 51	
Glenrothes With Thornton	a	09 43		10 03			10 32	10 47		11 03				11 32	11 46		12 03	

Table 242

Saturdays until 18 September

Newcraighall and Edinburgh - Dunfermline, Kirkcaldy and Glenrothes with Thornton

Station		SR	SR	SR	SR	SR	SR	SR	SR	SR	SR	SR	SR	SR	SR
				1			1			1					1
Newcraighall	d		11 35			12 07			12 37			13 07		13 37	
Brunstane	d		11 38			12 10			12 40			13 10		13 40	
Edinburgh 10	a		11 45			12 17			12 47			13 17		13 47	
	d	11 39	11 48	12 00	12 06	12 18	12 35	12 39	12 49	13 00	13 06	13 18	13 39	13 49	14 00
Haymarket	d	11 43	11 52	12 03	12 10	12 23	12 39	12 43	12 53	13 03	13 10	13 23	13 43	13 53	14 04
South Gyle	d	11 48	11 57		12 15	12 27		12 48	12 58		13 15	13 27	13 48	13 58	
Dalmeny	d	11 54	12 03		12 21	12 34		12 54	13 04		13 21	13 34	13 54	14 04	
North Queensferry	d	11 58	12 07		12 25	12 37		12 58	13 08		13 25	13 37	13 58	14 08	
Inverkeithing	d	12 02	12 11	12 17	12 29	12 41	12 53	13 02	13 12	13 17	13 29	13 41	14 02	14 12	14 17
Rosyth	d		12 14			12 45			13 15			13 45		14 15	
Dunfermline Town	d		12 19			12 50			13 20			13 50		14 20	
Dunfermline Queen Margaret	d		12 23			12 53			13 24			13 53		14 24	
Cowdenbeath	d		12 29			13a03			13 30			14a02		14 30	
Lochgelly	d		12 35						13 36					14 36	
Cardenden	d		12 39						13 40					14 40	
Dalgety Bay	d	12 05			12 32			13 05			13 32		14 05		
Aberdour	d	12 10			12 37			13 10			13 37		14 10		
Burntisland	d	12 14			12 41			13 14			13 41		14 14		
Kinghorn	d	12 19			12 46			13 19			13 46		14 19		
Kirkcaldy	d	12 24		12a35	12 51		13a09	13 24		13a33	13 51		14 24		14a33
Glenrothes With Thornton	a	12 32	12 46		13 02			13 32	13 46		14 02		14 32	14 46	

Station		SR	SR	SR	SR	SR	GR	SR	SR	SR	SR	SR	SR	SR	SR	SR	SR	SR	SR
				1			R 1 A ⊥	1			1			1			1		
Newcraighall	d		14 06			14 37				15 06			15 35			16 03			16 30
Brunstane	d		14 09			14 40				15 09			15 38			16 06			16 33
Edinburgh 10	a		14 17			14 47				15 17			15 46			16 14			16 41
	d	14 05	14 18	14 35	14 39	14 49	15 00	15 03	15 08	15 19	15 35	15 39	15 49	16 00	16 08	16 16	16 32	16 39	16 49
Haymarket	d	14 09	14 23	14 38	14 43	14 53	15 04	15 08	15 13	15 23	15 39	15 43	15 53	16 04	16 12	16 20	16 37	16 43	16 53
South Gyle	d	14 14	14 28		14 48	14 58			15 18	15 28		15 48	15 58		16 17	16 25		16 49	16 58
Dalmeny	d	14 20	14 34		14 54	15 05			15 24	15 34		15 54	16 04		16 23	16 32		16 56	17 05
North Queensferry	d	14 24	14 38		14 58	15 08			15 28	15 38		15 58	16 08		16 27	16 36		17 00	17 09
Inverkeithing	d	14 28	14 42	14 53	15 02	15 12	15 19	15 25	15 32	15 42	15 53	16 02	16 12	16 17	16 31	16 40	16 51	17 06	17 13
Rosyth	d		14 45			15 16				15 45			16 15			16 44			17 17
Dunfermline Town	d		14 50			15 21				15 51			16 20			16 49			17 22
Dunfermline Queen Margaret	d		14 54			15 24				15 53			16 24			16 52			17 25
Cowdenbeath	d		15a04			15 31				16a04			16 30			17a02			17a35
Lochgelly	d					15 36							16 36						
Cardenden	d					15 40							16 40						
Dalgety Bay	d	14 31			15 05				15 35			16 05			16 34			17 09	
Aberdour	d	14 36			15 10				15 40			16 10			16 39			17 14	
Burntisland	d	14 40			15 14				15 44			16 14			16 43			17 18	
Kinghorn	d	14 45			15 19				15 49			16 19			16 48			17 23	
Kirkcaldy	d	14 50		15a09	15 24		15a36	15a42	15 54		16a09	16 24		16a33	16 53		17a07	17 28	
Glenrothes With Thornton	a	15 03			15 32	15 47			16 05			16 32	16 46		17 01			17 36	

Station		SR	SR	SR	SR	SR	SR	SR	XC		SR	GR	SR	SR	SR	SR	SR
						◇ 1 ⊥			◇ 1 ⊥			R 1 ⊥	1		1		
Newcraighall	d			16 59			17 31				18 07			18 35			
Brunstane	d			17 02			17 34				18 10			18 38			
Edinburgh 10	a			17 09			17 43				18 18			18 45			
	d	17 03	17 08	17 12	17 21	17 41	17 45	17 52	18 08	18 12	18 26	18 32	18 40	18 49	19 00	19 09	19 19
Haymarket	d	17 07	17 13	17 17	17 25	17u45	17 49	17 55	18 13	18 16	18 30	18 37	18 45	18 53	19 03	19 13	19 22
South Gyle	d		17 18	17 22	17 30		17 55			18 21	18 35			18 58		19 18	
Dalmeny	d			17 28	17 38		18 01			18 27	18 41			19 04		19 24	
North Queensferry	d			17 32	17 41		18 05			18 31	18 45			19 08		19 28	
Inverkeithing	d	17 22	17 28	17 36	17 47		18 09		18 26	18 35	18 49	18 54	19 00	19 12	19 17	19 32	
Rosyth	d		17 33		17 50						18 52			19 15			
Dunfermline Town	d		17 38		17 55						18 57			19 20			
Dunfermline Queen Margaret	d		17 42		17 59						19 01			19 24			
Cowdenbeath	d		17 49		18 05						19 07			19 30			
Lochgelly	d		17 55		18 11						19 13			19 36			
Cardenden	d		17 59		18 15						19 17			19 40			
Dalgety Bay	d			17 40			18 12			18 38						19 35	
Aberdour	d			17 45			18 17			18 43						19 40	
Burntisland	d			17 49			18 21			18 47						19 44	
Kinghorn	d			17 54			18 26			18 52						19 49	
Kirkcaldy	d	17a39		18a04		18a16	18 31		18a42	18 57		19a11	19a18		19a33	19a56	
Glenrothes With Thornton	a		18 05		18 24		18 39			19 04	19 23			19 49			

A The Northern Lights

B

Table 242

Saturdays until 18 September

Newcraighall and Edinburgh - Dunfermline, Kirkcaldy and Glenrothes with Thornton

Station		SR	SR	SR	SR	SR	SR	XC	SR	SR	SR	SR	GR	SR	SR	SR	SR	SR	SR
			◇ 1 ⊥	◇ 1 ⊥				◇ 1 ⊥	1			◇ 1	R 1 ⊥						
Newcraighall	d	19 06			19 38		20 08			20 37				21 37			22 37		
Brunstane	d	19 09			19 41		20 11			20 40				21 40			22 40		
Edinburgh 10	a	19 16			19 48		20 19	20 15		20 47			21 30	21 47			22 47		
	d	19 21	19 30	19 35	19 49	20 00	20 19	20 22	20 37	20 51	21 00	21 32	21 45	21 49	22 09	22 39	22 50	23 09	23 19
Haymarket	d	19 26	19 33	19 39	19 54	20 04	20a24	20 26	20 41	20 55	21 04	21 36	21 49	21 53	22 13	22 43	22a54	23 13	23 24
South Gyle	d	19 30			19 58	20 09				21 00	21 09			21 58	22 18	22 48		23 18	23 28
Dalmeny	d	19 37			20 05	20 15				21 06	21 15			22 04	22 24	22 54		23 24	23 35
North Queensferry	d	19 40			20 08	20 19				21 10	21 19			22 08	22 28	22 58		23 28	23 38
Inverkeithing	d	19 44		19 54	20 12	20 23		20 44	21 00	21 14	21 23			22 12	22 32	23 02		23 32	23 42
Rosyth	d	19 48			20 16					21 17				22 15					23 46
Dunfermline Town	d	19 53			20 21					21 22				22 20					23 51
Dunfermline Queen Margaret	d	19 56			20 24					21 26				22 24					23 54
Cowdenbeath	d	20 03			20 31					21 32				22 30					00 02
Lochgelly	d	20 08			20 36					21 38				22 36					00 06
Cardenden	d	20 12			20 40					21 42				22 40					00 10
Dalgety Bay	d					20 26					21 26				22 35	23 05		23 35	
Aberdour	d					20 31					21 31				22 40	23 10		23 40	
Burntisland	d					20 35					21 35				22 44	23 14		23 44	
Kinghorn	d					20 40					21 40				22 49	23 19		23 49	
Kirkcaldy	d			20a10		20 45		20a59	21a17		21 45	22a04			22 54	23 24		23 54	
Glenrothes With Thornton	a	20 22			20 50					21 52				22 46					00 20

Station		SR
Newcraighall	d	23 37
Brunstane	d	23 40
Edinburgh 10	a	23 47
	d	23 49
Haymarket	d	23a53
South Gyle	d	
Dalmeny	d	
North Queensferry	d	
Inverkeithing	d	
Rosyth	d	
Dunfermline Town	d	
Dunfermline Queen Margaret	d	
Cowdenbeath	d	
Lochgelly	d	
Cardenden	d	
Dalgety Bay	d	
Aberdour	d	
Burntisland	d	
Kinghorn	d	
Kirkcaldy	d	
Glenrothes With Thornton	a	

Saturdays from 25 September

Station			SR	XC	SR	SR	SR	SR	SR	SR	SR	SR	SR	SR	SR	SR	SR
			◇ 1	◇		1				1			◇ 1 ⊥	1		1		
Newcraighall	d							06 36										
Brunstane	d							06 39										
Edinburgh 10	a							06 46										
	d		05 30	05 33				06 56					07 30	07 35				
Haymarket	d		05 33		06 22	06 33	06 43	06a59	06 43	07 04	07 13	07 22	07 33	07 39	07 43	08 03	08 12	08 17
South Gyle	d				06 27		06 48		06 48		07 18	07 27			07 48		08 17	08 22
Dalmeny	d				06 33		06 54		06 54		07 25	07 34			07 54			08 28
North Queensferry	d				06 37		06 58		06 58		07 28	07 37			07 58			08 32
Inverkeithing	d		05 46	06a06	06 41	06 47	07 02		07 02	07 20	07 32	07 41		07 53	08 02	08 17	08 28	08 36
Rosyth	d				06 44							07 45						08 39
Dunfermline Town	d				06 49							07 50						08 44
Dunfermline Queen Margaret	d				06 53							07 53						08 48
Cowdenbeath	d				06 59							08 00						08 54
Lochgelly	d				07 05							08 05						09 00
Cardenden	d				07 09							08 09						09 04
Dalgety Bay	d						07 05		07 05		07 35				08 05		08 31	
Aberdour	d						07 10		07 10		07 40				08 10		08 36	
Burntisland	d						07 14		07 14		07 44				08 14		08 40	
Kinghorn	d						07 19		07 19		07 49				08 19		08 45	
Kirkcaldy	d		06a02			07a03	07 24		07 24	07a36	07 54		08a02	08a09	08 24	08a33	08 50	
Glenrothes With Thornton	a	00 19			07 15		07 32		07 32		08 04	08 16			08 32		08 58	09 10

Newcraighall and Edinburgh - Dunfermline, Kirkcaldy and Glenrothes with Thornton

		SR	SR	SR	SR	SR	SR	SR	SR	SR	SR	SR	SR	GR	SR	SR	SR
		◇1 🛒			1			1			1			■ 1 🍽	1		
Newcraighall	d																
Brunstane	d																
Edinburgh 10	a																
	d	08 33						09 35						10 26	10 34		
Haymarket	d	08 37	08 42	08 50	09 02	09 10	09 22	09 39	09 43	09 54	10 03	10 10	10 23	10 31	10 38	10 43	10 53
South Gyle	d		08 47	08 55		09 15	09 27		09 48	09 59		10 15	10 28			10 47	10 57
Dalmeny	d		08 53	09 01		09 21	09 34		09 54	10 05		10 21	10 34			10 54	11 04
North Queensferry	d		08 57	09 05		09 25	09 37		09 58	10 09		10 25	10 38			10 57	11 07
Inverkeithing	d		09 01	09 09	09 17	09 29	09 41	09 53	10 02	10 13	10 18	10 29	10 42	10 46	10 53	11 01	11 11
Rosyth	d			09 12			09 45			10 16			10 45				11 15
Dunfermline Town	d			09 17			09 50			10 21			10 50				11 20
Dunfermline Queen Margaret	d			09 21			09 53			10 25			10 54				11 23
Cowdenbeath	d			09 27			10a02			10 31			11a03				11 30
Lochgelly	d			09 33						10 37							11 35
Cardenden	d			09 37						10 41							11 39
Dalgety Bay	d		09 04			09 32			10 05			10 32				11 04	
Aberdour	d		09 09			09 37			10 10			10 37				11 09	
Burntisland	d		09 13			09 41			10 14			10 41				11 13	
Kinghorn	d		09 18			09 46			10 19			10 46				11 18	
Kirkcaldy	d	09a06	09 23		09a33	09 51		10a09	10 24		10a34	10 51		11a03	11a10	11 23	
Glenrothes With Thornton	a		09 31	09 43		10 03			10 32	10 47		11 03				11 32	11 46

		SR	SR	SR	SR	SR	SR	SR	SR	SR	SR	SR	SR	SR
		1				1			1			1		
Newcraighall	d													
Brunstane	d													
Edinburgh 10	a													
	d								12 35					
Haymarket	d	11 04	11 23	11 43	11 51	12 03	12 10	12 23	12 39	12 43	12 53	13 03	13 10	13 23
South Gyle	d		11 28	11 48	11 56		12 15	12 27		12 48	12 58		13 15	13 27
Dalmeny	d		11 34	11 54	12 02		12 21	12 34		12 54	13 04		13 21	13 34
North Queensferry	d		11 38	11 58	12 06		12 25	12 37		12 58	13 08		13 25	13 37
Inverkeithing	d	11 17	11 42	12 02	12 10	12 17	12 29	12 41	12 53	13 02	13 12	13 17	13 29	13 41
Rosyth	d		11 45		12 13			12 45			13 15			13 45
Dunfermline Town	d		11 50		12 18			12 50			13 20			13 50
Dunfermline Queen Margaret	d		11 54		12 22			12 53			13 24			13 53
Cowdenbeath	d		12a03		12 28			13a03			13 30			14a02
Lochgelly	d				12 34						13 36			
Cardenden	d				12 38						13 40			
Dalgety Bay	d			12 05			12 32			13 05			13 32	
Aberdour	d			12 10			12 37			13 10			13 37	
Burntisland	d			12 14			12 41			13 14			13 41	
Kinghorn	d			12 19			12 46			13 19			13 46	
Kirkcaldy	d	11a33		12 24		12a35	12 51		13a09	13 24		13a33	13 51	
Glenrothes With Thornton	a			12 32	12 45		13 02			13 32	13 46		14 02	

		SR	SR	SR	SR	SR	SR	SR	SR	SR	SR	GR	SR	SR	SR	SR	SR	GR	SR
					1			1				■ 1 A 🍽	1			◇1 🛒	1	■ 1 🍽	
Newcraighall	d																		
Brunstane	d																		
Edinburgh 10	a																	15 27	
	d			13 55				14 35			14 56	15 00				15 30	15 35	15 36	
Haymarket	d	13 43	13 53	13 59	14 04	14 09	14 23	14 38	14 43	14 53	14 59	15 04	15 08	15 13	15 23	15 34	15 39	15 45	15 43
South Gyle	d	13 48	13 58			14 14	14 28		14 48	14 58				15 18	15 28				15 48
Dalmeny	d	13 54	14 04			14 20	14 34		14 54	15 05				15 24	15 34				15 54
North Queensferry	d	13 58	14 08			14 24	14 38		14 58	15 08				15 28	15 38				15 58
Inverkeithing	d	14 02	14 12		14 17	14 28	14 42	14 53	15 02	15 12		15 19	15 25	15 32	15 42		15 53		16 02
Rosyth	d		14 15				14 45			15 16					15 45				
Dunfermline Town	d		14 20				14 50			15 21					15 51				
Dunfermline Queen Margaret	d		14 24				14 54			15 24					15 53				
Cowdenbeath	d		14 30				15a04			15 31					16a04				
Lochgelly	d		14 36							15 36									
Cardenden	d		14 40							15 40									
Dalgety Bay	d	14 05				14 31			15 05					15 35					16 05
Aberdour	d	14 10				14 36			15 10					15 40					16 10
Burntisland	d	14 14				14 40			15 14					15 44					16 14
Kinghorn	d	14 19				14 45			15 19					15 49					16 19
Kirkcaldy	d	14 24			14a33	14 50		15a09	15 24			15 36	15a42	15 54			16a09		16 24
Glenrothes With Thornton	a	14 32	14 46			15 03			15 32	15 47				16 05					16 32

A The Northern Lights

Newcraighall and Edinburgh - Dunfermline, Kirkcaldy and Glenrothes with Thornton

		SR	SR	SR	SR	SR	SR	SR	SR	SR	SR	SR	SR
			1			1						◇1 🛒	
Newcraighall	d												
Brunstane	d												
Edinburgh 10	a												
	d					16 32			17 03			17 41	
Haymarket	d	15 53	16 04	16 12	16 20	16 37	16 43	16 53	17 07	17 13	17 17	17u45	17 49
South Gyle	d	15 58		16 17	16 25		16 50	16 58		17 18	17 22		17 55
Dalmeny	d	16 04		16 23	16 32		16 57	17 05			17 28		18 01
North Queensferry	d	16 08		16 27	16 36		17 01	17 09			17 32		18 05
Inverkeithing	d	16 12	16 17	16 31	16 40	16 51	17 06	17 13	17 22	17 28	17 36		18 09
Rosyth	d	16 15			16 44			17 17		17 33			
Dunfermline Town	d	16 20			16 49			17 22		17 38			
Dunfermline Queen Margaret	d	16 24			16 52			17 25		17 42			
Cowdenbeath	d	16 30			17a02			17a35		17 49			
Lochgelly	d	16 36								17 55			
Cardenden	d	16 40								17 59			
Dalgety Bay	d			16 34			17 09				17 40		18 12
Aberdour	d			16 39			17 14				17 45		18 17
Burntisland	d			16 43			17 18				17 49		18 21
Kinghorn	d			16 48			17 23				17 54		18 26
Kirkcaldy	d		16a33	16 53		17a07	17 28		17a39		18a04	18a16	18 31
Glenrothes With Thornton	a	16 46		17 01			17 36			18 05			18 39

		XC	SR	SR	GR	SR	SR	SR	SR	SR	SR	SR	XC	SR	SR	SR
		◇1 🛒			■ 1 🍽	1		1		◇1 🛒			◇1 🛒	1		
Newcraighall	d															
Brunstane	d															
Edinburgh 10	a															
	d	18 08			18 32	18 40				19 35			20 22	20 37		
Haymarket	d	18 13	18 16	18 30	18 37	18 45	18 53	19 03	19 26	19 39	19 54	20 04	20 26	20 41	20 55	21 04
South Gyle	d		18 21	18 35			18 58		19 30		19 58	20 09			21 00	21 09
Dalmeny	d		18 27	18 41			19 04		19 37		20 05	20 15			21 06	21 15
North Queensferry	d		18 31	18 45			19 08		19 40		20 08	20 19			21 10	21 19
Inverkeithing	d	18 26	18 35	18 49	18 54	19 00	19 12	19 17	19 44	19 54	20 12	20 23	20 45	21 00	21 14	21 23
Rosyth	d			18 52			19 15		19 48		20 16				21 17	
Dunfermline Town	d			18 57			19 20		19 53		20 21				21 22	
Dunfermline Queen Margaret	d			19 01			19 24		19 56		20 24				21 26	
Cowdenbeath	d			19 07			19 30		20 03		20 31				21 32	
Lochgelly	d			19 13			19 36		20 08		20 36				21 38	
Cardenden	d			19 17			19 40		20 12		20 40				21 42	
Dalgety Bay	d		18 38									20 26				21 26
Aberdour	d		18 43									20 31				21 31
Burntisland	d		18 47									20 35				21 35
Kinghorn	d		18 52									20 40				21 40
Kirkcaldy	d	18a42	18 57		19a11	19a18		19a33		20a10		20a45	21a00	21a17		21a45
Glenrothes With Thornton	a		19 04	19 23			19 49		20 22		20 50				21 52	

		SR	SR	SR	SR	SR	SR	SR	SR	SR
			◇1							
Newcraighall	d					22 37				23 37
Brunstane	d					22 40				23 40
Edinburgh 10	a					22 48				23 48
	d	21 26	21 32				22 39		23 19	
Haymarket	d	21 29	21 36	21 53	22 13		22 43	23 13	23 24	
South Gyle	d			21 58	22 18		22 48	23 18	23 28	
Dalmeny	d			22 04	22 24		22 54	23 24	23 35	
North Queensferry	d			22 08	22 28		22 58	23 28	23 38	
Inverkeithing	d			22 12	22 32		23 02	23 32	23 42	
Rosyth	d			22 15					23 46	
Dunfermline Town	d			22 20					23 51	
Dunfermline Queen Margaret	d			22 24					23 54	
Cowdenbeath	d			22 30					00 02	
Lochgelly	d			22 36					00 06	
Cardenden	d			22 40					00 10	
Dalgety Bay	d				22 35		23 05	23 35		
Aberdour	d				22 40		23 10	23 40		
Burntisland	d				22 44		23 14	23 44		
Kinghorn	d				22 49		23 19	23 49		
Kirkcaldy	d		22a04		22 54		23 24	23 54		
Glenrothes With Thornton	a			22 46					00 20	

A The Highland Chieftain

Table 242

Sundays

Newcraighall and Edinburgh - Dunfermline, Kirkcaldy and Glenrothes with Thornton

			XC	GR	SR	SR	SR	SR	SR	SR	SR	SR	SR	SR	SR	SR	SR	SR	SR	SR	GR	SR
			■	■ 1 ⊥⊥		◇1 ⊥			◇1 ⊥				◇1 ⊥		◇1 ⊥						■ 1 B ⊥⊥	
Newcraighall	d																					
Brunstane	d																					
Edinburgh 10	a																					
	d		08 04	09 10	09 15	09 25	09 55	10 15	10 55	11 15	11 55	12 15	12 40	13 15	13 50	14 00	14 15	14 23	15 15	15 55	16 00	16 15
Haymarket	d		08 08	09 14	09 19	09 29	09 59	10 19	10 59	11 19	11 59	12 19	12 44	13 19	13 54	14 04	14 19	14 27	15 19	15 59	16 04	16 19
South Gyle	d				09 24		10 04	10 24		11 24	12 04	12 24		13 24		14 08	14 24		15 24	16 04		16 24
Dalmeny	d				09 30		10 10	10 30		11 30	12 12	12 30		13 32		14 11	14 30		15 30	16 10		16 30
North Queensferry	d				09 34		10 14	10 34		11 34	12 19	12 34		13 36		14 15	14 34		15 34	16 14		16 34
Inverkeithing	d		08 25	09 32	09 38	09 48	10 18	10 38	11 15	11 38	12 23	12 38	13 00	13 40	14 11	14 22	14 41		15 38	16 18	16 24	16 38
Rosyth	d						10 23				12 26					14 27				16 21		
Dunfermline Town	d						10 28				12 31					14 33				16 26		
Dunfermline Queen Margaret	d						10 33				12 35					14 36				16 30		
Cowdenbeath	d						10 38				12 41					14 43				16 36		
Lochgelly	d						10 45				12 47					14 48				16 42		
Cardenden	d						10 49				12 51					14 52				16 46		
Dalgety Bay	d				09 44			10 44		11 44		12 44		13 46			14 44		15 44			16 41
Aberdour	d				09 49			10 49		11 49		12 49		13 51			14 49		15 49			16 46
Burntisland	d				09 53			10 53		11 53		12 53		13 55			14 53		15 53			16 50
Kinghorn	d				09 58			10 58		11 58		12 58		14 00			14 58		15 58			16 55
Kirkcaldy	d		08a40	09a49	10 03	10a10		11 03	11a31	12a03		13 03	13a16	14a05	14a28		15 03		16a03		16a41	17 00
Glenrothes With Thornton	a	00 20					10 55	11 11			12 57	13 11				15 00	15 14			16 52		17 08

		SR	SR	SR	SR	XC	SR	GR	SR	SR	SR	SR	SR	SR	SR	SR
		◇1		1		◇1 ⊥		■ 1 ⊥⊥					◇1			
Newcraighall	d															
Brunstane	d															
Edinburgh 10	a															
	d	17 05	17 15	17 50	17 55	18 10	18 15	18 42	19 15	19 55	20 15	20 23	21 00	21 15	21 55	22 25
Haymarket	d	17 09	17 19	17 54	17 59	18 15	18 19	18 47	19 19	19 59	20 19	20 27	21 05	21 19	21 59	22 29
South Gyle	d		17 24		18 04		18 24		19 24	20 04	20 24			21 24	22 04	22 34
Dalmeny	d		17 30		18 10		18 30		19 30	20 10	20 30			21 30	22 10	22 40
North Queensferry	d		17 34		18 14		18 34		19 34	20 14	20 34			21 34	22 14	22 44
Inverkeithing	d	17 22	17 38	18 07	18 18	18 29	18 38	19 02	19 38	20 18	20 38		21 18	21 38	22 18	22 48
Rosyth	d				18 21					20 21					22 21	
Dunfermline Town	d				18 26					20 26					22 26	
Dunfermline Queen Margaret	d				18 30					20 30					22 30	
Cowdenbeath	d				18 36					20 36					22 36	
Lochgelly	d				18 42					20 42					22 42	
Cardenden	d				18 46					20 46					22 46	
Dalgety Bay	d		17 41				18 41		19 41		20 41			21 41		22 51
Aberdour	d		17 46				18 46		19 46		20 46			21 46		22 56
Burntisland	d		17 50				18 50		19 50		20 50			21 50		23 00
Kinghorn	d		17 55				18 55		19 55		20 55			21 55		23 05
Kirkcaldy	d	17a38	18a00	18a23		18a44	19 00	19a19	20a00		21 00		21a34	22a00		23a10
Glenrothes With Thornton	a				18 52		19 07			20 52	21 09				22 54	

		SR
Newcraighall	d	
Brunstane	d	
Edinburgh 10	a	
	d	23 36
Haymarket	d	23 40
South Gyle	d	23 45
Dalmeny	d	23 51
North Queensferry	d	23 55
Inverkeithing	d	23a58
Rosyth	d	
Dunfermline Town	d	
Dunfermline Queen Margaret	d	
Cowdenbeath	d	
Lochgelly	d	
Cardenden	d	
Dalgety Bay	d	
Aberdour	d	
Burntisland	d	
Kinghorn	d	
Kirkcaldy	d	
Glenrothes With Thornton	a	

B The Northern Lights

Table 242

Mondays to Fridays

Glenrothes with Thornton, Kirkcaldy and Dunfermline - Edinburgh and Newcraighall

		SR	SR	SR	SR	SR	SR	SR	SR	SR	SR	XC	SR	SR	SR	SR	SR	SR
												◇1 ⊥			1	1 ⊥	◇1	
Glenrothes With Thornton	d				06 02			06 30			06 52			07 15				07 29
Kirkcaldy	d			05 53		06 27	06 49			07 14		07 21		07 27	07 38		07 48	
Kinghorn	d			05 58		06 32	06 54			07 19				07 32				
Burntisland	d			06 02		06 36	06 58			07 24				07 36				
Aberdour	d			06 07		06 41	07 03			07 28				07 41				
Dalgety Bay	d			06 12		06 46	07 08			07 33				07 46				
Cardenden	d				06 09			06 37			07 00							07 36
Lochgelly	d				06 13			06 41			07 04							07 42
Cowdenbeath	d				06 19			06 47			07 10							07 51
Dunfermline Queen Margaret	d				06 24			06 53	07 08		07 16							07 57
Dunfermline Town	d				06 28			06 56	07 11		07 19							08 02
Rosyth	d				06 31			07 00	07 15		07 23							08 03
Inverkeithing	d			06 16	06 39	06 49	07 12	07 06	07 19	07 37	07 29	07 42		07 48	07 54			08 09
North Queensferry	d			06 20	06 43	06 53		07 10	07 24		07 34			07 53				
Dalmeny	d			06 23	06 46	06 57	07 19	07 13		07a42	07 38			07 57				08 18
South Gyle	d			06 29	06 53	07 03	07 25	07 20	07 32		07 44			08 03				08 24
Haymarket	d	06 14	06 33	06 40	07 00	07 09	07 34	07 28	07 40		07 52	08 01	08 09	08 12	08 17	08s17	08 20	08 31
Edinburgh 10	a	06 19	06 38	06 46	07 06	07 16	07 38	07 33	07 46		07 57	08 05	08 15	08 18	08 22	08 22	08 25	08 38
	d	06 20	06 39		07 10			07 40					08 18					
Brunstane	d	06 28	06 46		07 17			07 47					08 24					
Newcraighall	a	06 31	06 52		07 22			07 52					08 30					

		SR	SR	SR	XC	SR	SR	SR	SR	SR	SR	SR	SR	SR	GR	SR
					◇1 ⊥			1			◇1 ⊥	1 ⊥			■ 1 ⊥⊘	
Glenrothes With Thornton	d		07 35			08 04	08 16		08 37				09 03	09 17		09 32
Kirkcaldy	d	07 54		08 06	08 20		08 28	08 41		09 13	09 26			09 30	09 44	
Kinghorn	d	07 59		08 11			08 32			09 18				09 34		
Burntisland	d	08 03		08 16			08 37			09 23				09 39		
Aberdour	d	08 08		08 20			08 41			09 27				09 43		
Dalgety Bay	d	08 13		08 25			08 46			09 31				09 48		
Cardenden	d		07 43			08 11			08 45				09 15			09 39
Lochgelly	d		07 48			08 15			08 49				09 19			09 43
Cowdenbeath	d		07 58			08 24			08 58				09 28			09 52
Dunfermline Queen Margaret	d		08 04			08 30			09 03				09 33			09 58
Dunfermline Town	d		08 08			08 33			09 07				09 37			10 01
Rosyth	d		08 13			08 37			09 10				09 40			10 05
Inverkeithing	d	08 16	08 20	08 28	08 35	08 41	08 49	08 57	09 14	09 35			09 45	09 51	10 01	10 09
North Queensferry	d		08 26			08 45	08 53		09 18					09 55		10 13
Dalmeny	d	08 23				08 49	08 57		09 22					09 59		10 17
South Gyle	d	08 29	08 35	08 40		08 55	09 03		09 28					10 05		10 23
Haymarket	d	08 35	08 44	08 48	08 54	09 03	09 10	09 15	09 35	09 50	09 56	10s01	10 02	10 12	10 19	10 30
Edinburgh 10	a	08 43	08 52	08 55	08 58	09 09	09 16	09 25	09 41	09 56	10 02	10 08	10 08	10 18	10 25	10 36
	d	08 48				09 10			09 43					10 21	10 30	10 41
Brunstane	d	08 55				09 18			09 50					10 28		10 48
Newcraighall	a	09 00				09 23			09 55					10 33		10 52

		SR	XC	SR	SR	SR	SR	SR	SR	SR	SR	SR	SR	SR	GR	SR
			◇1 ⊥				1				1 ⊥			1	■ 1 B ⊥⊘	
Glenrothes With Thornton	d	09 48				10 23		10 32	10 52				11 18			11 32
Kirkcaldy	d	10 00	10 17		10 27	10 32	10 42		11 03	11 18			11 27	11 39	11 44	
Kinghorn	d	10 05				10 37			11 08				11 32			
Burntisland	d	10 09				10 41			11 12				11 36			
Aberdour	d	10 14				10 46			11 17				11 41			
Dalgety Bay	d	10 19				10 51			11 22				11 46			
Cardenden	d							10 40								11 40
Lochgelly	d							10 44								11 44
Cowdenbeath	d			10 21				10 53				11 23				11 53
Dunfermline Queen Margaret	d			10 26				10 58				11 28				11 58
Dunfermline Town	d			10 30				11 02				11 32				12 02
Rosyth	d			10 33				11 05				11 35				12 05
Inverkeithing	d	10 22	10 32	10 37	10 43	10 54	10 59	11 11	11 25	11 34		11 38	11 49	11 55	12 01	12 10
North Queensferry	d			10 41		10 58		11 14	11 29			11 42				12 13
Dalmeny	d			10 45		11 02		11 19	11 32			11 46				12 18
South Gyle	d	10 33		10 51		11 08		11 24	11 41			11 53	12 00			12 23
Haymarket	d	10 44	10 54	10 58	11 03	11 14	11 19	11 37	11 50	11 54	12s00	12 02	12 06	12 11	12 19	12 30
Edinburgh 10	a	10 55	11 01	11 06	11 09	11 21	11 25	11 42	11 58	12 01	12 05	12 08	12 13	12 17	12 25	12 36
	d			11 11				11 45				12 11				12 41
Brunstane	d			11 18				11 53				12 25				12 48
Newcraighall	a			11 23				11 57				12 28				12 52

B The Northern Lights

Glenrothes with Thornton, Kirkcaldy and Dunfermline - Edinburgh and Newcraighall

		SR	SR	SR	SR	SR	SR	SR	SR	SR	SR	SR	SR	SR	SR	SR	SR
						[1]			[1] 🚲	[1]			◇[1] 🚲		[1] 🚲		[1]
Glenrothes With Thornton	d	11 48			12 18		12 32	12 48				13 18		13 32		13 48	
Kirkcaldy	d	12 00	12 17		12 27	12 39		13 00		13 18		13 27	13 41			14 00	14 18
Kinghorn	d	12 04			12 32			13 04				13 32				14 04	
Burntisland	d	12 09			12 36			13 09				13 36				14 09	
Aberdour	d	12 13			12 41			13 13				13 41				14 13	
Dalgety Bay	d	12 18			12 46			13 18				13 46				14 18	
Cardenden	d						12 40							13 40			
Lochgelly	d						12 44							13 44			
Cowdenbeath	d			12 22			12 53				13 23			13 53			
Dunfermline Queen Margaret	d			12 27			12 58				13 28			13 58			
Dunfermline Town	d			12 31			13 02				13 32			14 02			
Rosyth	d			12 34			13 05				13 35			14 05			
Inverkeithing	d	12 21	12 33	12 38	12 49	12 55	13 10	13 21		13 34	13 39	13 49		14 11		14 21	14 34
North Queensferry	d	12 25		12 42	12 53		13 14	13 25			13 43	13 53		14 14		14 25	
Dalmeny	d	12 29		12 46	12 57		13 18	13 29			13 47	13 57		14 19		14 29	
South Gyle	d	12 35		12 52	13 03		13 24	13 35			13 53	14 03		14 24		14 35	
Haymarket	d	12 42	12 48	12 59	13 09	13 14	13 34	13 43	13s43	13 51	14 00	14 09	14 14	14 32	14s43	14 43	14 48
Edinburgh [10]	a	12 48	12 55	13 06	13 16	13 19	13 38	13 48	13 50	13 57	14 06	14 16	14 19	14 38	14 47	14 50	14 55
	d			13 11			13 41				14 11			14 41			
Brunstane	d			13 18			13 48				14 18			14 54			
Newcraighall	a			13 22			13 52				14 22			14 58			

		SR	SR	SR	SR		SR	SR	SR	SR	SR	SR	SR	SR
				[1]						◇[1] 🚲	◇[1] 🚲			
Glenrothes With Thornton	d		14 18		14 48				15 18			15 34	15 48	
Kirkcaldy	d		14 27	14 39	15 00		15 18		15 27	15 47			16 00	16 19
Kinghorn	d		14 32		15 05				15 32				16 04	
Burntisland	d		14 36		15 09				15 36				16 09	
Aberdour	d		14 41		15 14				15 41				16 13	
Dalgety Bay	d		14 46		15 19				15 46				16 18	
Cardenden	d											15 42		
Lochgelly	d											15 46		
Cowdenbeath	d	14 22						15 22				15 55		
Dunfermline Queen Margaret	d	14 27						15 27				16 00		
Dunfermline Town	d	14 31						15 31				16 04		
Rosyth	d	14 34						15 34				16 07		
Inverkeithing	d	14 39	14 49	14 55	15 22		15 34	15 39	15 49			16 11	16 21	16 35
North Queensferry	d	14 43	14 53		15 26			15 43	15 53			16 14	16 25	
Dalmeny	d	14 47	14 57		15 30			15 47	15 57			16 19	16 29	
South Gyle	d	14 53	15 03		15 36			15 53	16 03			16 24	16 35	
Haymarket	d	14 59	15 09	15 15	15 42		15 48	15 59	16 09	16 16	16 25	16 32	16 43	16 50
Edinburgh [10]	a	15 09	15 16	15 19	15 49		15 55	16 08	16 16	16 23	16 31	16 38	16 48	16 57
	d	15 10						16 13				16 43		
Brunstane	d	15 18						16 20				16 51		
Newcraighall	a	15 23				15 58		16 25				16 55		

		SR	SR	SR	GR	SR	SR	SR	SR	SR	SR	SR	SR	SR	SR	SR
				[1]	[F] [1] 🚲🍴					[1]		[1] 🚲		[1] A 🚲		
Glenrothes With Thornton	d		16 18			16 32	16 48	17 01			17 36				18 11	18 44
Kirkcaldy	d		16 27	16 39	16 45		17 00		17 33	17 48			18 13	18 44	18 22	
Kinghorn	d		16 32				17 04		17 37						18 28	
Burntisland	d		16 36				17 09		17 42						18 34	
Aberdour	d		16 41				17 13		17 46						18 40	
Dalgety Bay	d		16 46				17 18		17 51						18 46	
Cardenden	d					16 40		17 09			17 43					18 52
Lochgelly	d					16 47		17 13			17 47					18 56
Cowdenbeath	d	16 24				16 53		17 22			17 56					19 05
Dunfermline Queen Margaret	d	16 29				16 58		17 27			18 02					19 10
Dunfermline Town	d	16 33				17 02		17 31			18 05					19 14
Rosyth	d	16 36				17 05		17 34			18 09					19 17
Inverkeithing	d	16 40	16 49	16 55	17 01	17 09	17 22	17 38	17 55	18 04	18 13		18 29	19 00	18 50	19 21
North Queensferry	d	16 44				17 13	17 27	17 42	17 59		18 17					19 25
Dalmeny	d	16 48				17 17	17 31	17 46	18 03		18 21				18 54	19 29
South Gyle	d	16 54	17 00			17 23	17 37	17 52	18 09		18 27				19 12	19 35
Haymarket	d	17 01	17 08	17 16	17 20	17 32	17 44	18 01	18 15	18 19	18 35	18s42	18 43	19 15	19 22	19 43
Edinburgh [10]	a	17 08	17 14	17 24	17 27	17 37	17 52	18 06	18 22	18 25	18 40	18 50	18 50	19 21	19 31	19 48
	d	17 16			17 30	17 40		18 19			18 46			19 22		19 49
Brunstane	d	17 25				17 47		18 27			18 53			19 28		19 56
Newcraighall	a	17 29				17 51		18 30			18 58			19 33		20 00

Glenrothes with Thornton, Kirkcaldy and Dunfermline - Edinburgh and Newcraighall

		SR	SR	SR	SR	SR	GR	SR	SR	SR	SR	SR	SR	SR	SR	SR	SR	SR	SR
						◇[1] 🚲	[F] [1] 🍴	[1]						◇[1] 🚲	🚲	[1]		[1]	◇[1]
Glenrothes With Thornton	d	18 52	19 04		19 23				20 02			21 02					22 02		
Kirkcaldy	d	19 04		19 28	19 36	19 54	20 08			20 27	20 39		21 26	21 42	21 59				23 01
Kinghorn	d	19 08			19 40					20 32			21 31		22 04				23 06
Burntisland	d	19 13			19 45					20 36			21 36		22 09				23 11
Aberdour	d	19 17			19 49					20 41			21 40		22 13				23 15
Dalgety Bay	d	19 22			19 54					20 46			21 45		22 18				23 20
Cardenden	d		19 11						20 09			21 09					22 09		
Lochgelly	d		19 15						20 13			21 13					22 13		
Cowdenbeath	d		19 24						20 22			21 22					22 19		
Dunfermline Queen Margaret	d		19 30						20 27			21 27					22 24		
Dunfermline Town	d		19 33						20 31			21 31					22 28		
Rosyth	d		19 37						20 34			21 34					22 31		
Inverkeithing	d	19 25	19 41	19 46	19 57		20 24		20 39	20 49	20 55	21 39	21 49		22 22		22 39		23 24
North Queensferry	d	19 29	19 45		20 01				20 43	20 53		21 43	21 53		22 26		22 43		23 28
Dalmeny	d	19 33	19 49		20 05				20 47	20 57		21 47	21 57		22 30		22 47		23 32
South Gyle	d	19 39	19 55		20 11				20 53	21 03		21 53	22 03		22 36		22 53		23 38
Haymarket	d	19 46	20 03	20 06	20 19	20 24	20s44	20s46	21 00	21 09	21 10	22 00	22 09	22 14	22 44	22s45	23 00	23s15	23 45
Edinburgh [10]	a	19 55	20 08	20 13	20 26	20 29	20 50	20 51	21 06	21 16	21 19	22 06	22 16	22 19	22 50	22 50	23 06	23 22	23 52
	d		20 11						21 12			22 11					23 10		
Brunstane	d		20 19						21 20			22 18					23 18		
Newcraighall	a		20 23						21 23			22 22					23 22		

		XC	SR
		◇[1]	[1]
Glenrothes With Thornton	d		23 15
Kirkcaldy	d	23 26	
Kinghorn	d		
Burntisland	d		
Aberdour	d		
Dalgety Bay	d		
Cardenden	d		23 23
Lochgelly	d		23 27
Cowdenbeath	d		23 33
Dunfermline Queen Margaret	d		23 38
Dunfermline Town	d		23 44
Rosyth	d		23 47
Inverkeithing	d	23 42	23 51
North Queensferry	d		23 55
Dalmeny	d		23 58
South Gyle	d		00 05
Haymarket	d	23 58	00 12
Edinburgh [10]	a	00 05	00 18
	d		
Brunstane	d		
Newcraighall	a		

Saturdays
until 18 September

		SR	SR	SR	SR	SR	SR	SR	SR	SR	SR	SR	SR	XC	SR	SR	SR
							[1]	◇[1]				[1] 🚲		◇[1] 🚲		[1] 🚲	[1]
Glenrothes With Thornton	d				06 30					07 15	07 32				08 04		
Kirkcaldy	d			06 16		06 49	07 38	07 48		07 27			08 06	08 20			08 41
Kinghorn	d			06 21		06 54				07 32			08 11				
Burntisland	d			06 24		06 58				07 36			08 16				
Aberdour	d			06 29		07 03				07 41			08 20				
Dalgety Bay	d			06 35		07 08				07 46			08 25				
Cardenden	d				06 37						07 37				08 11		
Lochgelly	d				06 41						07 42				08 15		
Cowdenbeath	d				06 47						07 48				08 24		
Dunfermline Queen Margaret	d				06 53						07 55				08 30		
Dunfermline Town	d				06 56						07 59				08 33		
Rosyth	d				07 00						08 02				08 37		
Inverkeithing	d			06 39	07 06	07 12	07 54			07 48	08 08		08 28	08 35	08 41		08 57
North Queensferry	d			06 43	07 10					07 53	08 12				08 45		
Dalmeny	d			06 46	07 13	07 19				07 57	08 16				08 49		
South Gyle	d			06 53	07 20	07 25				08 03	08 22		08 40		08 55		
Haymarket	d	06 14	06 33	07 00	07 27	07 34	08 17	08 20	08 09	08 12	08 28	08s46	08 48	08 54	09 02	09s13	09 15
Edinburgh [10]	a	06 19	06 38	07 06	07 33	07 38	08 22	08 25	08 14	08 18	08 35	08 50	08 55	08 58	09 09	09 19	09 25
	d	06 20	06 39	07 10	07 40				08 18		08 46			09 05	09 10		
Brunstane	d	06 28	06 46	07 17	07 47				08 24		08 53				09 18		
Newcraighall	a	06 31	06 52	07 22	07 53				08 29		08 58				09 23		

Table 242

Saturdays
until 18 September

Glenrothes with Thornton, Kirkcaldy and Dunfermline - Edinburgh and Newcraighall

		SR	SR	SR	SR	SR	SR	GR	SR	SR	XC	SR	SR	SR	SR
				◇[1] 🛒	[1] 🛒			■ [1] 🍴🛒			◇[1] 🛒				[1]
Glenrothes With Thornton	d	08 37				09 03	09 17		09 31	09 48				10 23	
Kirkcaldy	d		09 13	09 26			09 30	09 44		10 00	10 17		10 27	10 32	10 42
Kinghorn	d		09 18				09 34			10 05				10 37	
Burntisland	d		09 23				09 39			10 09				10 41	
Aberdour	d		09 27				09 43			10 14				10 46	
Dalgety Bay	d		09 31				09 48			10 19				10 51	
Cardenden	d	08 45				09 15			09 39						
Lochgelly	d	08 49				09 19			09 43						
Cowdenbeath	d	08 58				09 28			09 52			10 21			
Dunfermline Queen Margaret	d	09 03				09 33			09 57			10 26			
Dunfermline Town	d	09 07				09 37			10 01			10 30			
Rosyth	d	09 10				09 40			10 04			10 33			
Inverkeithing	d	09 14	09 35			09 45	09 51	10 01	10 08	10 22	10 32	10 37	10 43	10 54	10 59
North Queensferry	d	09 18					09 55		10 12			10 41		10 58	
Dalmeny	d	09 22					09 59		10 16			10 45		11 02	
South Gyle	d	09 28					10 05		10 22	10 33		10 51		11 08	
Haymarket	d	09 35	09 50	09 56	10s01	10 02	10 12	10 21	10 29	10 44	10 51	10 58	11 03	11 14	11 19
Edinburgh [10]	a	09 41	09 56	10 02	10 07	10 06	10 18	10 26	10 35	10 55	10 58	11 06	11 09	11 21	11 25
	d	09 43					10 21		10 41			11 11			
Brunstane	d	09 50					10 28		10 48			11 18			
Newcraighall	a	09 55					10 33		10 52			11 23			

		SR	SR	SR	SR	SR	SR	GR	SR	SR	SR	SR	SR	SR	SR	SR
							[1]	■ [1] B 🍴🛒					[1] 🛒		[1]	◇[1] 🛒
Glenrothes With Thornton	d	10 32	10 52			11 18			11 32	11 48				12 18		
Kirkcaldy	d		11 03	11 18		11 27	11 39	11 44		12 00	12 17			12 27	12 39	
Kinghorn	d		11 08			11 32				12 04				12 32		
Burntisland	d		11 12			11 36				12 09				12 36		
Aberdour	d		11 17			11 41				12 13				12 41		
Dalgety Bay	d		11 22			11 46				12 18				12 46		
Cardenden	d	10 40							11 40							
Lochgelly	d	10 44							11 44							
Cowdenbeath	d	10 53			11 23				11 53			12 22				
Dunfermline Queen Margaret	d	10 58			11 28				11 58			12 27				
Dunfermline Town	d	11 02			11 32				12 02			12 31				
Rosyth	d	11 05			11 35				12 05			12 34				
Inverkeithing	d	11 11	11 25	11 34	11 38	11 49	11 55	12 01	12 10	12 21	12 33	12 38		12 49	12 55	
North Queensferry	d	11 14	11 29		11 42				12 13	12 25		12 42		12 53		
Dalmeny	d	11 19	11 32		11 46				12 18	12 29		12 46		12 57		
South Gyle	d	11 24	11 41		11 53	12 00			12 23	12 35		12 52		13 03		
Haymarket	d	11 34	11 50	11 54	12 02	12 06	12 11	12 19	12 30	12 42	12 48	12 59	13s01	13 09	13 14	13 21
Edinburgh [10]	a	11 39	11 58	12 01	12 08	12 13	12 17	12 25	12 36	12 48	12 55	13 06	13 05	13 16	13 19	13 27
	d	11 45			12 11			12 30	12 41			13 11				
Brunstane	d	11 53			12 18				12 48			13 18				
Newcraighall	a	11 57			12 22				12 52			13 22				

		SR	SR	SR	SR	SR	SR	SR	SR	SR	SR	SR	SR	SR	SR	SR
				[1]	[1] 🛒			◇[1] 🛒			[1]			[1]		
Glenrothes With Thornton	d	12 32	12 48				13 18		13 32	13 48			14 18		14 32	14 48
Kirkcaldy	d		13 00	13 18			13 27	13 41		14 00	14 18		14 27	14 39		15 00
Kinghorn	d		13 04				13 32			14 04			14 32			15 05
Burntisland	d		13 09				13 36			14 09			14 36			15 09
Aberdour	d		13 13				13 41			14 13			14 41			15 14
Dalgety Bay	d		13 18				13 46			14 18			14 46			15 19
Cardenden	d	12 40							13 40						14 40	
Lochgelly	d	12 44							13 44						14 44	
Cowdenbeath	d	12 53				13 23			13 53			14 22			14 53	
Dunfermline Queen Margaret	d	12 58				13 28			13 58			14 27			14 58	
Dunfermline Town	d	13 02				13 32			14 02			14 31			15 02	
Rosyth	d	13 05				13 35			14 05			14 34			15 05	
Inverkeithing	d	13 11	13 21	13 34		13 39	13 49		14 11	14 21	14 34	14 39	14 49	14 55	15 12	15 22
North Queensferry	d	13 14	13 25			13 43	13 53		14 14	14 25		14 43	14 53		15 16	15 26
Dalmeny	d	13 19	13 29			13 47	13 57		14 19	14 29		14 47	14 57		15 20	15 30
South Gyle	d	13 24	13 35			13 53	14 03		14 24	14 35		14 53	15 03		15 26	15 36
Haymarket	d	13 34	13 43	13 51	13s59	14 00	14 09	14 14	14 32	14 43	14 48	14 59	15 09	15 15	15 36	15 42
Edinburgh [10]	a	13 38	13 48	13 57	14 05	14 06	14 16	14 19	14 38	14 50	14 55	15 09	15 16	15 19	15 41	15 50
	d	13 41				14 11			14 41			15 10			15 45	
Brunstane	d	13 48				14 18			14 54			15 18			15 53	
Newcraighall	a	13 52				14 22			14 58			15 23			15 58	

B The Northern Lights

Table 242

Saturdays
until 18 September

Glenrothes with Thornton, Kirkcaldy and Dunfermline - Edinburgh and Newcraighall

		SR	SR	SR	SR	SR	SR	SR	SR	SR	SR	GR	SR	SR	SR	SR
					◇[1] 🛒						[1]	■ [1] 🛒⊘				
Glenrothes With Thornton	d			15 18		15 34	15 48			16 18			16 32	16 48	17 01	
Kirkcaldy	d	15 18		15 27	15 47		16 00	16 19		16 27	16 39	16 45		17 00		17 33
Kinghorn	d			15 32			16 04			16 32				17 04		17 37
Burntisland	d			15 36			16 09			16 36				17 09		17 42
Aberdour	d			15 41			16 13			16 41				17 13		17 46
Dalgety Bay	d			15 46			16 18			16 46				17 18		17 51
Cardenden	d					15 42							16 40		17 09	
Lochgelly	d					15 46							16 47		17 13	
Cowdenbeath	d		15 22			15 55			16 24				16 53		17 22	
Dunfermline Queen Margaret	d		15 27			16 00			16 29				16 58		17 27	
Dunfermline Town	d		15 31			16 04			16 33				17 02		17 31	
Rosyth	d		15 34			16 07			16 36				17 05		17 34	
Inverkeithing	d	15 34	15 39	15 49		16 11	16 21	16 35	16 40	16 49	16 55	17 01	17 09	17 22	17 38	17 55
North Queensferry	d		15 43	15 53		16 14	16 25		16 44				17 13	17 27	17 42	17 59
Dalmeny	d		15 47	15 57		16 19	16 29		16 48				17 17	17 31	17 46	18 03
South Gyle	d		15 53	16 03		16 24	16 35		16 54	17 00			17 23	17 37	17 52	18 09
Haymarket	d	15 48	15 59	16 09	16 16	16 35	16 43	16 50	17 01	17 08	17 12	17 20	17 32	17 44	18 01	18 15
Edinburgh [10]	a	15 55	16 08	16 16	16 23	16 43	16 48	16 57	17 08	17 14	17 20	17 25	17 37	17 52	18 06	18 22
	d		16 13			16 43			17 15			17 30	17 44		18 12	
Brunstane	d		16 20			16 51			17 22				17 51		18 19	
Newcraighall	a		16 25			16 55			17 27				17 55		18 23	

		SR	SR	SR	SR	SR	SR	SR	SR	SR	SR	SR	SR	SR	SR	SR
		[1]		[1] 🛒			[1] A 🛒					◇[1] 🛒	◇[1] 🛒			[1]
Glenrothes With Thornton	d		17 37			18 10		18 39	19 04		19 23			20 02		
Kirkcaldy	d	17 48			18 13	18 23	18 44			19 28	19 36	19 54	20 08		20 27	20 39
Kinghorn	d					18 28					19 40				20 32	
Burntisland	d					18 32					19 45				20 36	
Aberdour	d					18 37					19 49				20 41	
Dalgety Bay	d					18 42					19 54				20 46	
Cardenden	d		17 44					18 47	19 11					20 09		
Lochgelly	d		17 48					18 51	19 15					20 13		
Cowdenbeath	d		17 57					19 00	19 24					20 22		
Dunfermline Queen Margaret	d		18 03					19 05	19 30					20 27		
Dunfermline Town	d		18 06					19 09	19 33					20 31		
Rosyth	d		18 10					19 12	19 37					20 34		
Inverkeithing	d	18 04	18 14		18 29	18 45	19 00	19 16	19 41	19 46	19 57		20 24	20 39	20 49	20 55
North Queensferry	d		18 18			18 49		19 20	19 45		20 01			20 43	20 53	
Dalmeny	d		18 22			18 53		19 24	19 49		20 05			20 47	20 57	
South Gyle	d		18 28			18 59		19 30	19 55		20 11			20 53	21 03	
Haymarket	d	18 19	18 36	18s42	18 43	19 05	19 15	19 37	20 03	20 06	20 19	20 24	20s44	21 00	21 09	21 10
Edinburgh [10]	a	18 25	18 41	18 50	18 50	19 12	19 21	19 43	20 08	20 13	20 26	20 29	20 50	21 06	21 16	21 19
	d		18 47				19 22	19 47	20 11					21 12		
Brunstane	d		18 54				19 28	19 55	20 19					21 20		
Newcraighall	a		18 59				19 33	19 58	20 23					21 23		

		SR	SR	SR	SR	SR	SR	SR	XC	SR
				◇[1] 🛒	🛒		[1]	◇[1]	◇[1] 🛒	[1]
Glenrothes With Thornton	d	21 02				22 02				23 15
Kirkcaldy	d		21 26	21 42	21 59			23 01	23 14	
Kinghorn	d		21 31		22 04			23 06		
Burntisland	d		21 36		22 09			23 11		
Aberdour	d		21 40		22 13			23 15		
Dalgety Bay	d		21 45		22 18			23 20		
Cardenden	d	21 09				22 09				23 23
Lochgelly	d	21 13				22 13				23 27
Cowdenbeath	d	21 22				22 19				23 33
Dunfermline Queen Margaret	d	21 27				22 24				23 38
Dunfermline Town	d	21 31				22 28				23 44
Rosyth	d	21 34				22 31				23 47
Inverkeithing	d	21 39	21 49		22 22	22 39		23 24	23 31	23 51
North Queensferry	d	21 43	21 53		22 26	22 43		23 28		23 55
Dalmeny	d	21 47	21 57		22 30	22 47		23 32		23 58
South Gyle	d	21 53	22 03		22 36	22 53		23 38		00 05
Haymarket	d	22 00	22 09	22 14	22 44	23 00	23s15	23 45	23 51	00 12
Edinburgh [10]	a	22 06	22 16	22 19	22 50	23 06	23 22	23 52	23 55	00 18
	d	22 11				23 11				
Brunstane	d	22 18				23 18				
Newcraighall	a	22 22				23 22				

A 🛒 from Edinburgh

Glenrothes with Thornton, Kirkcaldy and Dunfermline - Edinburgh and Newcraighall

		SR	SR	SR	SR	SR	SR	SR	SR	SR	SR	SR	XC	SR
									■1		◇■1		◇■1 ⌶	
Glenrothes With Thornton	d			06 30			07 15	07 32		08 04				08 16
Kirkcaldy	d		06 16			06 49	07 27		07 38		07 48	08 06	08 20	08 28
Kinghorn	d		06 21			06 54	07 32					08 11		08 32
Burntisland	d		06 24			06 58	07 36					08 16		08 37
Aberdour	d		06 29			07 03	07 41					08 20		08 41
Dalgety Bay	d		06 35			07 08	07 46					08 25		08 46
Cardenden	d			06 37				07 37		08 11				
Lochgelly	d			06 41				07 42		08 15				
Cowdenbeath	d			06 47				07 48		08 24				
Dunfermline Queen Margaret	d			06 53				07 55		08 30				
Dunfermline Town	d			06 56				07 59		08 33				
Rosyth	d			07 00				08 02		08 37				
Inverkeithing	d		06 39	07 06		07 12	07 48	08 08	07 54	08 41		08 28	08 35	08 49
North Queensferry	d		06 43	07 10			07 53	08 12		08 45				08 53
Dalmeny	d		06 46	07 13		07 19	07 57	08 16		08 49				08 57
South Gyle	d		06 53	07 20		07 25	08 03	08 22		08 55		08 40		09 03
Haymarket	d	06 14	07a00	07a27	06 33	07a33	08a11	08a28	08 15	09a02	08 20	08a47	08 57	09 08
Edinburgh 10	a	06 19			06 38				08 21		08 25		09 01	09 16
	d	06 20			06 39								09 05	
Brunstane	d	06 28			06 46									
Newcraighall	a	06 31			06 52									

		SR	SR	SR	SR	SR	SR	SR	GR	SR	SR	XC	SR	SR
				■1		◇■1 ⌶			■1 ⌶			◇■1 ⌶		■1 ⌶
Glenrothes With Thornton	d	08 37	09 03				09c17	09 31			10 32			
Kirkcaldy	d			08 41	09 13	09 26	09 30		09 44			10 17	10 27	
Kinghorn	d				09 18		09 34							
Burntisland	d				09 23		09 39							
Aberdour	d				09 27		09 43							
Dalgety Bay	d				09 31		09 48							
Cardenden	d	08 45	09 15					09 39			10 40			
Lochgelly	d	08 49	09 19					09 43			10 44			
Cowdenbeath	d	08 58	09 28					09 52		10 21	10 53			
Dunfermline Queen Margaret	d	09 03	09 33					09 57		10 26	10 58			
Dunfermline Town	d	09 07	09 37					10 01		10 30	11 02			
Rosyth	d	09 10	09 40					10 04		10 33	11 05			
Inverkeithing	d	09 14	09 45	08 57	09 35		09 51	10 08	10 01	10 37	11 11	10 32	10 43	
North Queensferry	d	09 18					09 55	10 12		10 41	11 14			
Dalmeny	d	09 22					09 59	10 16		10 45	11 19			
South Gyle	d	09 28					10 05	10 22		10 51	11 24			
Haymarket	d	09a35	10a01	09 15	09a49	09 56	10a12	10a29	10 21	10a58	11a33	10 51	11a00	
Edinburgh 10	a			09 25		10 02			10 26			10 58		
	d													
Brunstane	d													
Newcraighall	a													

		SR	SR	SR	SR	SR	SR	SR	SR	SR	SR	SR	SR	GR	SR	SR	SR	SR	SR	SR	SR	SR
		■1				◇■1 ⌶		■1 ⌶		■1 ⌶	■1 ⌶	■1	■1 ⌶	■1 B ⌶					■1 ⌶		■1 ⌶	■1 ⌶
Glenrothes With Thornton	d		10 52		11 18				11 32						11 48		12 18			12 32		
Kirkcaldy	d	10 42	11 03	11 18	11 27							11 39		11 44	12 00	12 17	12 27					
Kinghorn	d		11 08		11 32										12 04		12 32					
Burntisland	d		11 12		11 36										12 09		12 36					
Aberdour	d		11 17		11 41										12 13		12 41					
Dalgety Bay	d		11 22		11 46										12 18		12 46					
Cardenden	d								11 40											12 40		
Lochgelly	d								11 44											12 44		
Cowdenbeath	d						11 23		11 53									12 22		12 53		
Dunfermline Queen Margaret	d						11 28		11 58									12 27		12 58		
Dunfermline Town	d						11 32		12 02									12 31		13 02		
Rosyth	d						11 35		12 05									12 34		13 05		
Inverkeithing	d	10 59	11 25	11 34	11 49		11 38		12 10			11 55		12 01	12 21	12 33	12 49	12 38		13 11		
North Queensferry	d		11 29				11 42		12 13						12 25		12 53	12 42		13 14		
Dalmeny	d		11 32				11 46		12 18						12 29		12 57	12 46		13 19		
South Gyle	d		11 41		12 00		11 53		12 23						12 35		13 03	12 52		13 24		
Haymarket	d	11 19	11a50	11a53	12a06	11 22	12a02	11s29	12a30	11s45	12s00	12 11	12s13	12 19	12a40	12a47	13a09	12a59	12s29	13a33	12s44	13s01
Edinburgh 10	a	11 25				11 29		11 35		11 50	12 05	12 17	12 19	12 25					12 35		12 52	13 05
	d																					
Brunstane	d																					
Newcraighall	a																					

B The Northern Lights

		SR	SR	SR	SR	SR	SR	SR	SR	SR	SR	SR	SR
		■1		■1				◇■1 ⌶		■1			
Glenrothes With Thornton	d		12 47		13 18		13 32		13 48		14 18		14 32
Kirkcaldy	d	12 39	12 59	13 18	13 27			13 41	14 00	14 18	14 27		
Kinghorn	d		13 03		13 32				14 04		14 32		
Burntisland	d		13 08		13 36				14 09		14 36		
Aberdour	d		13 12		13 41				14 13		14 41		
Dalgety Bay	d		13 17		13 46				14 18		14 46		
Cardenden	d						13 40						14 40
Lochgelly	d						13 44						14 44
Cowdenbeath	d					13 23	13 53					14 22	14 53
Dunfermline Queen Margaret	d					13 28	13 58					14 27	14 58
Dunfermline Town	d					13 32	14 02					14 31	15 02
Rosyth	d					13 35	14 05					14 34	15 05
Inverkeithing	d	12 55	13 20	13 34	13 49	13 39	14 11		14 21	14 34	14 49	14 39	15 12
North Queensferry	d		13 24		13 53	13 43	14 14		14 25		14 53	14 43	15 16
Dalmeny	d		13 28		13 57	13 47	14 19		14 29		14 57	14 47	15 20
South Gyle	d		13 34		14 03	13 53	14 24		14 35		15 03	14 53	15 26
Haymarket	d	13 14	13a41	13a50	14a09	14a01	14a32	14 14	14a42	14a47	15a09	14a59	15a33
Edinburgh 10	a	13 19						14 19					
	d												
Brunstane	d												
Newcraighall	a												

		SR	SR	SR	SR	SR	SR	SR	SR	SR	SR	SR	SR
		■1						◇■1 ⌶					■1
Glenrothes With Thornton	d		14 48		15 18		15 34		15 48			16 32	
Kirkcaldy	d	14 39	15 00	15 18	15 27			15 47	16 00	16 19			16 39
Kinghorn	d		15 05		15 32				16 04				
Burntisland	d		15 09		15 36				16 09				
Aberdour	d		15 14		15 41				16 13				
Dalgety Bay	d		15 19		15 46				16 18				
Cardenden	d						15 42					16 40	
Lochgelly	d						15 46					16 47	
Cowdenbeath	d					15 22	15 55				16 24	16 53	
Dunfermline Queen Margaret	d					15 27	16 00				16 29	16 58	
Dunfermline Town	d					15 31	16 04				16 33	17 02	
Rosyth	d					15 34	16 07				16 36	17 05	
Inverkeithing	d	14 55	15 22	15 34	15 49	15 39	16 11		16 21	16 35	16 40	17 09	16 55
North Queensferry	d		15 26		15 53	15 43	16 14		16 25		16 44	17 13	
Dalmeny	d		15 30		15 57	15 47	16 19		16 29		16 48	17 17	
South Gyle	d		15 36		16 03	15 53	16 24		16 35		16 54	17 23	
Haymarket	d	15 15	15a42	15a47	16a09	15a59	16a32	16 16	16a42	16a49	17a01	17a32	17 12
Edinburgh 10	a	15 19						16 23					17 20
	d												
Brunstane	d												
Newcraighall	a												

		GR	SR	SR	SR	SR	SR	SR	SR	SR	SR	SR
		■1 ⌶								■1		
Glenrothes With Thornton	d		16 48	17 01		17 37		18 10	18 39		19 04	
Kirkcaldy	d	16 45	17 00		17 33		18 13	18 23		18 44		19 28
Kinghorn	d		17 04		17 37			18 28				
Burntisland	d		17 09		17 42			18 32				
Aberdour	d		17 13		17 46			18 37				
Dalgety Bay	d		17 18		17 51			18 42				
Cardenden	d			17 09		17 44			18 47		19 11	
Lochgelly	d			17 13		17 48			18 51		19 15	
Cowdenbeath	d			17 22		17 57			19 00		19 24	
Dunfermline Queen Margaret	d			17 27		18 03			19 05		19 30	
Dunfermline Town	d			17 31		18 06			19 09		19 33	
Rosyth	d			17 34		18 10			19 12		19 37	
Inverkeithing	d	17 01	17 22	17 38	17 55	18 14	18 29	18 45	19 16	19 00	19 41	19 46
North Queensferry	d		17 27	17 42	17 59	18 18		18 49	19 20		19 45	
Dalmeny	d		17 31	17 46	18 03	18 22		18 53	19 24		19 49	
South Gyle	d		17 37	17 52	18 09	18 28		18 59	19 30		19 55	
Haymarket	d	17 20	17a44	18a00	18a15	18a36	18a43	19a05	19a37	19a15	20a02	20 06
Edinburgh 10	a	17 25										20 13
	d	17 30										
Brunstane	d											
Newcraighall	a											

Table 242

Saturdays
from 25 September

Glenrothes with Thornton, Kirkcaldy and Dunfermline - Edinburgh and Newcraighall

		SR	SR	SR	SR	SR	SR	SR	SR	SR	SR	SR	XC	SR
				◇**1** 🍴	◇**1** 🍴				◇**1** 🍴	🍴		◇**1**	◇**1** 🍴	**1**
Glenrothes With Thornton	d	19 23	20 02				21 02				22 02			23 15
Kirkcaldy	d	19 36		19 54	20 08	20 27		21 26	21 42	21 59		23 01	23 14	
Kinghorn	d	19 40				20 32		21 31		22 04		23 06		
Burntisland	d	19 45				20 36		21 36		22 09		23 11		
Aberdour	d	19 49				20 41		21 40		22 13		23 15		
Dalgety Bay	d	19 54				20 46		21 45		22 18		23 20		
Cardenden	d		20 09				21 09				22 09			23 23
Lochgelly	d		20 13				21 13				22 13			23 27
Cowdenbeath	d		20 22				21 22				22 19			23 33
Dunfermline Queen Margaret	d		20 27				21 27				22 24			23 38
Dunfermline Town	d		20 31				21 31				22 28			23 44
Rosyth	d		20 34				21 34				22 31			23 47
Inverkeithing	d	19 57	20 39		20 24	20 49	21 39	21 49		22 22	22 39	23 24	23 31	23 51
North Queensferry	d	20 01	20 43			20 53	21 43	21 53		22 26	22 43	23 28		23 55
Dalmeny	d	20 05	20 47			20 57	21 47	21 57		22 30	22 47	23 32		23 58
South Gyle	d	20 11	20 53			21 03	21 53	22 03		22 36	22 53	23 38		00 05
Haymarket	d	20a18	21a00	20 24	20s44	21 09	22a00	22a09	22 14	22 44	23a00	23 45	23 51	00 12
Edinburgh **10**	a			20 29	20 50	21 16			22 19	22 50		23 52	23 55	00 18
	d													
Brunstane	d													
Newcraighall	a													

Sundays

		SR	SR	SR	SR	GR	SR	XC	SR	GR	SR	SR	SR	GR	SR
				1		**1** B 🍽		◇**1** 🍴		**1** 🍽				**1** 🍴	◇ 🍴
Glenrothes With Thornton	d			10 56	11 11				12 58			15 04	15 14		
Kirkcaldy	d	08 08	10 08	11 08		11 40	12 08	13 03	13 10	13 39	14 08	15 15		15 42	16 03
Kinghorn	d	08 13	10 13	11 13			12 13		13 15		14 13	15 20			
Burntisland	d	08 17	10 17	11 17			12 17		13 19		14 17	15 24			
Aberdour	d	08 22	10 22	11 22			12 22		13 24		14 22	15 29			
Dalgety Bay	d	08 27	10 27	11 27			12 27		13 29		14 27	15 34			
Cardenden	d				11 18								15 21		
Lochgelly	d				11 22								15 25		
Cowdenbeath	d				11 30								15 33		
Dunfermline Queen Margaret	d				11 36								15 39		
Dunfermline Town	d				11 39								15 42		
Rosyth	d				11 43								15 46		
Inverkeithing	d	08 30	10 30	11 30	11 47	11 56	12 30	13 18	13 32	13 55	14 30	15 37	15 50	15 58	16 19
North Queensferry	d	08 34	10 34	11 34	11 51		12 36		13 42		14 34	15 41	15 54		
Dalmeny	d	08 38	10 38	11 38	11 56		12 40		13 49		14 38	15 45	16 00		
South Gyle	d	08 44	10 44	11 44	12 02		12 46		13 55		14 44	15 51	16 06		
Haymarket	d	08 53	10 58	11 58	12 12	12 18	12 58	13 37	14 04	14 19	14 58	15 58	16 16	16 20	16 35
Edinburgh **10**	a	09 00	11 06	12 06	12 19	12 24	13 06	13 42	14 08	14 24	15 06	16 07	16 21	16 25	16 42
	d					12 30		13 50		14 30				16 30	
Brunstane	d														
Newcraighall	a														

		SR	SR	SR	SR	SR	SR	SR	SR	SR	SR	SR	SR	SR
			◇**1** 🍴				**1** 🍴	◇**1** 🍴		**1** 🍴				◇**1** 🍴
Glenrothes With Thornton	d			16 53	17 09						18 53	19 09		
Kirkcaldy	d	16 08	17 02	17 07		18 07		18 56			19 07		20 10	20 59
Kinghorn	d	16 13		17 12		18 12					19 12		20 15	
Burntisland	d	16 17		17 16		18 16					19 16		20 20	
Aberdour	d	16 22		17 21		18 21					19 21		20 24	
Dalgety Bay	d	16 27		17 26		18 26					19 26		20 29	
Cardenden	d				17 16							19 16		
Lochgelly	d				17 20							19 20		
Cowdenbeath	d				17 28							19 28		
Dunfermline Queen Margaret	d				17 34							19 34		
Dunfermline Town	d				17 37							19 38		
Rosyth	d				17 41							19 41		
Inverkeithing	d	16 30	17 18	17 29	17 45	18 29		19 12			19 29	19 45	20 31	21 15
North Queensferry	d	16 34		17 33	17 49	18 33					19 33	19 49	20 36	
Dalmeny	d	16 38		17 37	17 53	18 37					19 37	19 53	20 40	
South Gyle	d	16 44		17 43	18 00	18 43					19 43	20 00	20 46	
Haymarket	d	16 55	17 34	17 49	18 09	18 52	19s17	19 27	19 43	19s47	19 52	20 09	20 55	21 31
Edinburgh **10**	a	16 59	17 41	17 56	18 14	19 00	19 21	19 35	19 48	19 52	19 56	20 15	21 01	21 36
	d													
Brunstane	d													
Newcraighall	a													

B The Northern Lights

Table 242

Sundays

Glenrothes with Thornton, Kirkcaldy and Dunfermline - Edinburgh and Newcraighall

		SR	SR	SR	SR	SR	SR	SR	SR	XC
			◇**1** 🍴		**1**	◇**1** 🍴		**1**		◇**1** 🍴
Glenrothes With Thornton	d	20 54		21 09					22 54	
Kirkcaldy	d	21 07	21 25			22 05	22 13		23 06	23 22
Kinghorn	d	21 11					22 17		23 10	
Burntisland	d	21 16					22 22		23 15	
Aberdour	d	21 20					22 26		23 19	
Dalgety Bay	d	21 25					22 31		23 24	
Cardenden	d			21 16						
Lochgelly	d			21 20						
Cowdenbeath	d			21 28						
Dunfermline Queen Margaret	d			21 34						
Dunfermline Town	d			21 37						
Rosyth	d			21 41						
Inverkeithing	d	21 28	21 41	21 45		22 21	22 34		23 27	23 38
North Queensferry	d	21 32		21 49			22 38		23 31	
Dalmeny	d	21 36		21 53			22 42		23 35	
South Gyle	d	21 40		22 00			22 48		23 41	
Haymarket	d	21 51	22 00	22 09	22s20	22 37	22 57	23s20	23 50	23 54
Edinburgh **10**	a	21 55	22 05	22 13	22 24	22 43	23 01	23 24	23 56	23 58
	d									
Brunstane	d									
Newcraighall	a									

Sleeper Services

Sleepers enable you to make long distance journeys while having a relaxing night's sleep. You arrive early at your destination, saving a day's travel — or the early morning dash to the airport. Five Sleeper routes link London Euston direct with over 40 stations in Scotland including most principal business and holiday locations. Direct Sleeper services also link Southwest England with London. Customers joining at the starting point of the train may occupy cabins well before departure. At terminating stations customers may vacate cabins up to approximately 0800 on trains which arrive at an earlier time.

Full details of all Sleeper services are given in Tables 400–406.

First Great Western Night Riviera Sleeper

Both single and twin berth cabins are available and feature locking doors, comfortable beds with sheets and blankets, air conditioning, bedside lighting, complimentary toiletries, wash basin with a shaver point and a soft hand towel. Room service facilities, a wake up call, a light breakfast and newspaper are all complimentary.

The trains recently underwent a complete refurbishment to maximise customer comfort. Improvements include a refurbishment of seating areas and berths and the introduction of a hot breakfast offer to set our customers up for the day. All single and twin cabins are available to holders of standard class tickets and large reclining seats are provided throughout seated accommodation, again available to holders of standard class tickets. Customers in most single berths benefit from Volo TV, a new and innovative on-train entertainment service. Customers can choose from 40 different programmes including comedy, drama, documentaries, children's programmes and sport.

There are a number of inclusive Advance fares available that combine travel and accommodation on one ticket. These can be purchased until 1800 hours the day before departure. Holders of Anytime, Off-Peak and Super Off-Peak tickets may upgrade to sleeping accommodation on payment of the applicable single or twin berth supplement. The Lounge Car is provided for the use of customers with a berth. Here you can sit back and relax with a complimentary hot drink, tempt yourself with one of our delicious hot snacks or unwind with something stronger from our well stocked bar - all served at seat by our on-board team. Customers in seated accommodation can purchase refreshments and snacks from the Express Cafe, which is situated in the Lounge Car.

Dogs and pets are not normally allowed in Sleeper cabins. There are special arrangements for guide dogs. Animals may be conveyed if properly labelled and muzzled, and in suitable containers, in the guards van.

ScotRail Caledonian Sleepers

First Class customers receive a toiletry pack and will be woken with a light breakfast accompanied by tea or coffee and a complimentary newspaper. Standard Class customers are served a light morning snack with tea or coffee. Customer lounges are available at the following locations - London Euston, Inverness, Carlisle (Lakes Court Hotel) and Edinburgh Waverley. At Glasgow Central customers may use the on-train Lounge Car which is available prior to departure. Full details of the Caledonian Sleeper on-train and station facilities can be found inside the Caledonian Sleeper Guide which is available from principal sleeper departure points.

There are a number of berth inclusive fares available that include travel and accommodation at one all inclusive price. First class travel is in single berth cabins while Standard Class is in twin berth cabins.

The Lounge Car offers a pleasant relaxing atmosphere in which to unwind before a night's rest. Customers can choose from a wide selection of food and drinks including sandwiches, baguettes, snacks and a well stocked bar. At busy times, use of the Lounge Car may be restricted to First Class ticket holders.

Accompanying dogs are only permitted in Sleeper Cabins providing the owner(s) has exclusive use of the cabin and pays the appropriate charge. There are special arrangements for guide dogs. Dogs and pets cannot be conveyed in the guards van.

Please note that as a result of on-going engineering work some sleeper services may be subject to diversion causing an extension in journey times between Scotland and London. For full details telephone National Rail Enquiries on 08457 48 49 50 (calls may be recorded).

Sleeper Reservations

To book rail tickets and reserve Sleepers, simply visit any main rail station or rail appointed travel agent. Alternatively you can book by phone using most credit/debit cards.

First Great Western Telesales (www.firstgreatwestern.co.uk)	08457 00 01 25
ScotRail Telesales (www.scotrail.co.uk)	08457 55 00 33

For further information about rail tickets or services, call National Rail Enquiries on 08457 48 49 50 (calls may be recorded for training purposes).

Sleeper Services

ScotRail Sleeper Services – The Caledonian Sleepers

Operated by ScotRail

Table 400 London and Edinburgh

		Mon–Thu R	Fri R	Sun A R	Sun B R
Cabins available from		*2250*	*2250*	*2200*	*2200*
London Euston ...	d	2350	2350	2232	2327
Watford Junction	d	0010*	0010*	....	2347
Carlisle ...	a	0511	0518	....	0504*
Carstairs ...	a	0622	0625	....	0622
Edinburgh ...	a	0717	0715	0559*	0717
Vacate cabins by		*0800*	*0800*	*0800*	*0800*

		Mon–Thu R	Fri R	Sun A R	Sun B R
Cabins available from		*2300*	*2300*	*2230*	*2230*
Edinburgh ...	d	2340	2340	2326	2315
Carstairs ...	d	0035*	0016*	....	2346
Carlisle ...	d	0144	0142	....	0108*
Watford Junction	a	0619	0627	....	0623
London Euston...	a	0640	0650	0706*	0646
Vacate cabins by		*0800*	*0800*	*0800*	*0800*

A 23 May to 5 September
B From 12 September
R Reservations Compulsory
* Following morning
Services in this table do not run on Saturday nights.
For details of overnight seated services, please refer to Table 65

Table 401 London and Glasgow

		Mon–Thu R	Fri R	Sun A R	Sun B R
Cabins available from		*2250*	*2250*	*2200*	*2200*
London Euston...	d	2350	2350	2232	2327
Watford Junction	d	0010*	0010*	....	2347
Carlisle ...	a	0511	0518	....	0504*
Carstairs ...	a	0622	0625	0642*	0622
Motherwell ...	a	0701	0659	0659	0700
Glasgow Central	a	0719	0721	0719	0719
Vacate cabins by		*0800*	*0800*	*0800*	*0800*

		Mon–Thu R	Fri R	Sun A R	Sun B R
Cabins available from		*2200*	*2200*	*2100*	*2200*
Glasgow Central...	d	2340	2340	2139	2315
Motherwell ...	d	2357	2356	2201	2330
Carstairs ...	d	0035*	0016*	2222	2346
Carlisle ...	d	0144	0142	....	0108*
Watford Junction...	a	0619	0627	....	0623
London Euston...	a	0640	0650	0706*	0646
Vacate cabins by		*0800*	*0800*	*0800*	*0800*

A 23 May to 5 September
B From 12 September
R Reservations Compulsory
* Following morning
Services in this table do not run on Saturday nights.
For details of overnight seated services, please refer to Table 65

Table 402 London and Aberdeen

		Mon-Thu R	Fri R	Sun A R	Sun B R
Cabins available from		*2030*	*2030*	*1930*	*2015*
London Euston	dep	2115	2115	2007	2055
Watford Junction	dep	2133	2133	....	2117
Crewe	dep	2354	2354	....	2339
Preston	dep	0052*	0052*	....	0030
Inverkeithing•	arr	0458	0458	0458*	0458
Kirkcaldy•	arr	0517	0517	0517	0517
Leuchars for St Andrews•	arr	0546	0546	0546	0546
Dundee	arr	0608	0608	0608	0608
Carnoustie	arr	0622	0622	0622	0622
Arbroath	arr	0631	0631	0631	0631
Montrose	arr	0647	0647	0647	0647
Stonehaven	arr	0713	0713	0713	0713
Aberdeen	arr	0735	0735	0735	0735
Vacate cabins by		*0800*	*0800*	*0800*	*0800*

		Mon–Thu R	Fri R	Sun R	Sun R
Cabins available from		*2050*	*2050*	*2050*	*2050*
Aberdeen	dep	2140	2140	2140	2140
Stonehaven	dep	2200	2200	2200	2200
Montrose	dep	2225	2225	2225	2225
Arbroath	dep	2243	2243	2243	2243
Carnoustie	dep	2252	2252	2252	2252
Dundee	dep	2306	2306	2306	2306
Leuchars for St Andrews•	dep	2325	2325	2325	2325
Kirkcaldy•	dep	2353	2353	2353	2353
Inverkeithing•	dep	0012*	0012*	0012*	0012*
Preston	arr	0432	0432	....	0441
Crewe	arr	0532	0534	....	0537
London Euston	arr	0747	0747	0830	0747
Vacate cabins by		*0800*	*0800*	*0800*	*0800*

A 23 May to 5 September
B From 12 September
R Reservations Compulsory
* Following morning
• Customers may depart from London or Watford later, and vacate cabins later, by travelling on the London Euston to Edinburgh Sleeper; then by local connecting service from Edinburgh
Services in this table do not run on Saturday nights
For details of overnight seated services, please refer to Table 65

Sleeper Services

ScotRail Sleeper Services – The Caledonian Sleepers

Operated by ScotRail

Table 403 London and Inverness

		Mon-Thu R	Fri R	Sun A R	Sun B R
Cabins available from		*2030*	*2030*	*1930*	*2015*
London Euston	dep	2115	2115	2007	2055
Watford Junction	dep	2133	2133	....	2117
Crewe	dep	2354	2354	....	2339
Preston	dep	0052*	0052*	....	0030*
Stirling•	arr	0456	0456	0455*	0456
Dunblane	arr	0505	0505	0505	0505
Gleneagles	arr	0520	0520	0520	0520
Perth•	arr	0540	0540	0539	0540
Dunkeld & Birnam	arr	0601	0601	0600	0601
Pitlochry	arr	0617	0617	0615	0617
Blair Atholl	arr	0629	0629	0628	0629
Dalwhinnie	arr	0700	0700	0658	0700
Newtonmore	arr	0712	0712	0710	0712
Kingussie	arr	0718	0718	0717	0718
Aviemore	arr	0742	0742	0739	0742
Inverness	arr	0831	0831	0830	0831
Vacate cabins by		*0840*	*0840*	*0840*	*0840*

		Mon–Thu R	Fri R	Sun A R	Sun B R
Cabins available from		*2000*	*2000*	*1945*	*1945*
Inverness	dep	2046	2046	2025	2025
Aviemore	dep	2128	2128	2110	2108
Kingussie	dep	2142	2142	2124	2122
Newtonmore	dep	2150	2150	2131	2129
Dalwhinnie	dep	2204	2204	2145	2143
Blair Atholl	dep	2230	2230	2211	2209
Pitlochry	dep	2243	2243	2223	2222
Dunkeld & Birnam	dep	2258	2258	2238	2237
Perth	dep	2321	2321	2301	2300
Gleneagles	dep	2339	2339	2320	2318
Dunblane	dep	2355	2355	2336	2334
Stirling•	dep	0006*	0006*	2347	2345
Falkirk Grahamston	dep	0023	0023	0002*	0002*
Preston	arr	0432	0432	....	0441
Crewe	arr	0532	0534	....	0537
London Euston	arr	0747	0747	0830	0747
Vacate cabins by		*0800*	*0800*	*0840*	*0800*

A 23 May to 5 September
B From 12 September
R Reservations Compulsory
* Following morning
• Customers may depart from London or Watford later, and vacate cabins later, by travelling on the London Euston to Edinburgh Sleeper; then by local connecting service from Edinburgh.
Services in this table do not run on Saturday nights.
For details of overnight seated services, please refer to Table 65

Table 404 London and Fort William

		Mon-Thu R	Fri R	Sun A R	Sun B R
Cabins available from		*2030*	*2030*	*1930*	*2015*
London Euston	dep	2115	2115	2007	2055
Watford Junction	dep	2133	2133	....	2117
Crewe	dep	2354	2354	....	2339
Preston	dep	0052*	0052*	....	0030*
Westerton	arr	0555	0555	0555*	0555
Dalmuir	arr	0603	0603	0603	0603
Helensburgh Upper	arr	0626	0626	0626	0626
Garelochhead	arr	0641	0641	0641	0641
Arrochar & Tarbet	arr	0707	0707	0707	0707
Ardlui	arr	0722	0722	0722	0722
Crianlarich	arr	0743	0743	0743	0743
Upper Tyndrum	arr	0756	0756	0756	0756
Bridge of Orchy	arr	0814	0814	0814	0814
Rannoch	arr	0840	0840	0840	0840
Corrour	arr	0858	0858	0858	0858
Tulloch	arr	0917	0917	0917	0917
Roy Bridge	arr	0929	0929	0929	0929
Spean Bridge	arr	0936	0936	0936	0936
Fort William	arr	0954	0954	0954	0954
Vacate cabins by		*0956*	*0956*	*0956*	*0956*

		Mon–Thu R	Fri R	Sun R	Sun R
Cabins available from		*1920*	*1920*	*1830*	*1830*
Fort William	dep	1950	1950	1900	1900
Spean Bridge	dep	2010	2010	1919	1919
Roy Bridge	dep	2017	2017	1927	1927
Tulloch	dep	2030	2030	1940	1940
Corrour	dep	2051	2051	2001	2001
Rannoch	dep	2105	2105	2015	2015
Bridge of Orchy	dep	2134	2134	2047	2047
Upper Tyndrum	dep	2152	2152	2105	2105
Crianlarich	dep	2205	2205	2119	2119
Ardlui	dep	2226	2226	2139	2139
Arrochar & Tarbet	dep	2244	2244	2157	2157
Garelochhead	dep	2310	2310	2223	2223
Helensburgh Upper	dep	2324	2324	2237	2237
Dalmuir	dep	2351	2351	2304	2304
Westerton	dep	2356	2356	2313	2313
Preston	arr	0432*	0432*	....	0441*
Crewe	arr	0532	0534	....	0537
London Euston	arr	0747	0747	0830*	0747
Vacate cabins by		*0800*	*0800*	*0840*	*0800*

A 23 May to 5 September
B From 12 September
R Reservations Compulsory
* Following morning
Services in this table do not run on Saturday nights.
For details of overnight seated services, please refer to Tables 65 and 227.

Sleeper Services

Table 406 London and Penzance

Operated by First Great Western

		Mon –Thu Ⓛ	Fri Ⓛ	Sun Ⓛ
Occupy cabins at Paddington:		*2230*	*2230*	*2230*
London Paddington ...	**dep**	**2345**	**2345**	**2350**
Reading	**dep**	**0037***	**0037***	**0037***
Exeter St Davids ...	**arr**	**0305**	**0257**	**0405**
Newton Abbot ...	**arr**	**0432**	**0320**	**0455**
Plymouth	**arr**	**0513**	**0401**	**0535**
Liskeard	**arr**	**0614**	**0614**	**0654**
Bodmin Parkway ...	**arr**	**0628**	**0628**	**0721**
Lostwithiel	**arr**	**0635**	**0635**	**0728**
Par	**arr**	**0642**	**0642**	**0736**
St Austell	**arr**	**0650**	**0650**	**0744**
Truro	**arr**	**0709**	**0709**	**0803**
Redruth	**arr**	**0722**	**0722**	**0817**
Camborne	**arr**	**0730**	**0730**	**0825**
Hayle	**arr**	**0739**	**0739**	**0834**
St Erth	**arr**	**0743**	**0743**	**0840**
Penzance	**arr**	**0800**	**0800**	**0859**
Vacate cabins at Penzance by		*0800*	*0800*	*0900*

		Mon –Fri Ⓛ	Sun Ⓛ
Occupy cabins at Penzance:		*2105*	*2045*
Penzance	**dep**	**2145**	**2115**
St Erth	**dep**	**2155**	**2125**
Camborne	**dep**	**2207**	**2138**
Redruth	**dep**	**2214**	**2145**
Truro	**dep**	**2227**	**2200**
St Austell	**dep**	**2245**	**2218**
Par	**dep**	**2253**	**-**
Bodmin Parkway ...	**dep**	**2305**	**2235**
Liskeard	**dep**	**2320**	**2250**
Plymouth	**dep**	**2351**	**2320**
Totnes	**dep**	**0019***	**2348**
Newton Abbot ...	**dep**	**0032**	**0001***
Exeter St Davids ...	**dep**	**0100**	**0127**
Reading	**arr**	**0400**	**0417**
London Paddington ...	**arr**	**0543**	**0506**
Vacate cabins at Paddington by		*0700*	*0700*

Ⓛ Sleeper Lounge Car

* Following morning

Services in this table do not run on Saturday nights.

For details of seated services on this route, please refer to Table 135.

Passenger Representation

Passenger Focus

What is Passenger Focus?

Passenger Focus is the independent passenger watchdog. Our mission is to get the best deal for Britain's rail, bus and coach passengers.

With a strong emphasis on evidence-based campaigning and research, we ensure that we know what is happening on the ground. We use our knowledge to influence decisions on behalf of passengers and we work with the industry, other passenger groups and government to secure journey improvements.

What can Passenger Focus do for me?

We're here to put the interests of rail, bus and coach passengers first. We do this by:

Campaigning for improvements

- we gather research and information, like the National Passenger Survey, where 50,000 passengers give us their views about their rail journeys, so we understand the issues that matter to you
- we work with Government and the industry to ensure that the passenger voice is heard when making decisions about the future
- we focus on a number of key issues:

- fares and tickets

- quality and level of services

- investment in the railway

Providing practical advice

- we provide passengers with advice on how to get the best from the network, explain their rights and help them when things go wrong
- we work with other passenger groups to support them in their work

Resolving complaints

- if you make a complaint and you are unhappy with the response we can take up your complaint with the company involved

Making a complaint

If you have a complaint or comment about any aspect of your rail service, either on the train or at the station, please contact the railway company managing director concerned (contact details are shown on the TOC pages of this timetable).

What should you include in your complaint?

Depending on the nature of your complaint you should include:

- the reason for your complaint
- a description of the inconvenience caused
- which train and which day you travelled on, or which station you used and when
- how many people travelled with you
- your ticket(s) as evidence
- an explanation of the action you would like the company to take to rectify the problem

What next?

If you are not satisfied with the company's response you can contact Passenger Focus or, in the London area, London TravelWatch.

How to get in touch:

Telephone: 0300 123 2350

8am - 8pm Monday - Friday
8am - 4pm at weekends

Address: Passenger Focus
FREEPOST
(RRRE-ETTC-LEET)
PO BOX 4257
MANCHESTER
M60 3AR

Fax: 0845 850 1392

E-mail: info@passengerfocus.org.uk

Website: www.passengerfocus.org.uk

London TravelWatch

London TravelWatch is the independent, statutory watchdog for transport users in and around London, including all services provided by Transport for London, and represents rail passengers in and around London. We investigate suggestions and complaints from passengers who are dissatisfied with responses received from transport operators.

If your journey is within, or began in, London, please contact:

Telephone: 020 7505 9000 (9-5, Monday- Friday)

Address: London TravelWatch
6 Middle Street
London
EC1A 7JA

E-mail: info@londontravelwatch.org.uk

Website: www.londontravelwatch.org.uk

Compensation

Compensation may be payable under each rail company's Passenger's Charter scheme for poor performance (delays or cancellations). For daily tickets and weekly season tickets a fixed rate usually applies depending on the level of delay which you experience. Compensation is made in National Rail vouchers, as a rule, with a minimum of 20% of the fare for the affected journey leg.

Monthly or longer season tickets compensation can differ between companies. On some it is triggered if performance falls below agreed levels and is paid as discount on renewal. Others offer compensation on a journey-by journey basis like for daily tickets. Always check with the train company which issued your ticket or on which you travel for details of the relevant scheme.

81A
81A
HOLYHEAD
ANGLESEY
Valley
Rhosneigr
81
Ty Croes
Bodorgan
Llanfairpwll
Bangor
81
Llanfairfechan
Penmaenmawr
Conwy
Llandudno 81
Deganwy 102
Llandudno Junction
Colwyn Bay
Rhyl
Abergele & Pensarn
Prestatyn
81
Glan Conwy
Tal-y-Cafn
Dolgarrog
North Llanrwst
Llanrwst
102
Betws-y-Coed
Pont-y-Pant
Dolwyddelan
Roman Bridge
Blaenau Ffestiniog
Pwllheli
75
Abererch
Penychain
Criccieth
Porthmadog
Minffordd
Penrhyndeudraeth
Llandecwyn
Talsarnau
Tygwyn
Harlech
Llandanwg
Pensarn
75
Llanbedr
Dyffryn Ardudwy
Talybont
Llanaber
Barmouth
Morfa Mawddach
Fairbourne
Llwyngwril
75
Tonfanau
Tywyn
Aberdovey
Penhelig
Machynlleth
Dovey Junction
Caersws
75
Newtown
Borth
75
Aberystwyth
New Brighton
LIVERPOOL
St Helens 90
West Kirby
Birkenhead
65
131
Runcorn
Warrington
39
89
85
Stockport
Glossop
Hooton
Flint
Manchester Airport
Altrincham
Wilmslow
81
65
84
84
Macclesfield
131
Chinley
86
For full details see page 2038
Buxton
29
Hawarden
Buckley 101
Penyffordd
Hope
Caergwrle
Cefn-y-Bedd
Gwersyllt
CHESTER
88
65
81
CREWE
Nantwich
Alsager
Congleton
50
Kidsgrove
67
Longport
50
Wrexham General
Wrexham Central
101
65
75
Ruabon
Wrenbury 65
131
Whitchurch
STOKE-ON-TRENT
Wedgwood
Barlaston
Longton
Stone
Blythe Bridge
84
Uttoxeter
Chirk
Prees
Wem
Yorton
131
Gobowen
67
Norton Bridge
50
Tutbury & Hatton
STAFFORD
Burton-on-Trent
75
SHREWSBURY
Wellington
Oakengates
Telford Central
74
75
Shifnal
Rugeley Trent Valley
65 68
57
Hednesford
Lichfield
69
65
67
Walsall
Welshpool
75
129 131
WOLVERHAMPTON
70
57
Sandwell & Dudley
Church Stretton
Stourbridge
72
BIRMINGHAM
Craven Arms
For full details see page 2037
71
69
57
Longbridge
Kidderminster
Broome
Hopton Heath
Bucknell
Knighton
Knucklas
Llangynllo
Llanbister Road
Dolau
Pen-y-bont
Llandrindod
Builth Road
129
Cilmeri
Garth
Llangammarch
Llanwrtyd
Sugar Loaf
Cynghordy
Llandovery
Ludlow
69
Bromsgrove
71
115
71
57
Redditch
Droitwich Spa
WALES
ENGLAND
131
Leominster
WORCESTER
Stratford-upon-Avon
126
Malvern Link
57
Great Malvern
Pershore
Evesham
HEREFORD
71
126
Colwall
Ledbury
Ashchurch for Tewkesbury
126
CHELTENHAM SPA
57
GLOUCESTER
Ascott-under-Wychwood
FISHGUARD Harbour
128
Clarbeston Road
Haverfordwest
Clunderwen
Whitland
Carmarthen
Johnston
128
Narberth
Ferryside
128
Kilgetty
Kidwelly
Milford Haven
Saundersfoot
Pembroke Dock
128
Tenby
Pembroke
Penally
Lamphey
Manorbier
Llanwrda
Llangadog
Llandeilo
Ffairfach
Llandybie
Ammanford
Pantyffynnon
Pontarddulais
129
Llangennech
Bynea
Llanelli
Pembrey & Burry Port
Gowerton
SWANSEA
128
Llansamlet
Skewen
Neath
Briton Ferry
Baglan
Port Talbot Parkway
Pyle
Caerau
128A
Abergavenny
Merthyr Tydfil
Rhymney
Ebbw Vale Parkway
Aberdare
131
Pontypool & New Inn
Treherbert
Cwmbran
130
130
127
Maesteg
128
Pontypridd
Caerphilly
NEWPORT
Bridgend
128
CARDIFF
125C
130
130A
Barry
130
Penarth
Rhoose for Cardiff International Airport
Barry Island
For full details see page 2036
132
Lydney
Cam & Dursley
57
134
Chepstow
Stonehouse
Stroud
125
Kemble
123
125
132
Yate
125
Severn Beach
Bristol Parkway
BRISTOL
123
125
134
125
132
BATH SPA
125B
Weston-super-Mare
Bristol International Airport
Chippenham
125
123
Freshford
Melksham
Avoncliff
Bradford-on-Avon
Trowbridge
Hungerford
Bedwyn
Pewsey
135
123
Westbury
Dilton Marsh
Warminster
123
Frome
SALISBURY
Highbridge & Burnham
134
Minehead
Dunster
Watchet
135E
Bishops Lydeard
Bridgwater
Bruton
Castle Cary
123
TAUNTON
135
160
Gillingham
Tisbury
123
Templecombe
Sherborne
Yeovil Pen Mill
135
Yeovil Junction
Tiverton Parkway
Crewkerne
160
Axminster
Honiton
Feniton
160
Whimple
Thornford
Yetminster
Chetnole
Maiden Newton
123
BOURNEMOUTH
POOLE
Branksome
Parkstone
158
Dorchester West
158
Upwey
Dorchester South
Moreton
Wool
Wareham
Holton Heath
Hamworthy
WEYMOUTH
Barnstaple
Chapelton
Umberleigh
136
Portsmouth Arms
Kings Nympton
Eggesford
136
Lapford
Morchard Road
Copplestone
Crediton
Newton St Cyres
Yeoford
Okehampton
136‡
135D
Sampford Courtenay
Bude
135D
Holsworthy
EXETER
St Davids
Central
St James Park
Pinhoe
Polsloe Bridge
Digby & Sowton
Topsham
136
St Thomas
Exton
Lympstone Commando
Lympstone Village
Exmouth
135
Starcross
Dawlish Warren
Dawlish
Teignmouth
NEWTON ABBOT
Torre
Torquay
Paignton
Totnes
135
135
Ivybridge
Gunnislake
Calstock
139
Bere Alston
St Budeaux Victoria Road
Bere Ferrers
139
St Germans
Saltash
St Budeaux Ferry Road
Keyham
Dockyard
Devonport
PLYMOUTH
135
139
Liskeard
Menheniot
135
Bodmin Parkway
Lostwithiel
Coombe Junction Halt
140
St Keyne Wishing Well Halt
Causeland
Sandplace
Looe
Padstow
Wadebridge
135C
Newquay
142
Roche
Bugle
Luxulyan
Eden Project
Par
St Austell
Quintrell Downs
St Columb Road
135
135B
Truro
Perranwell
Penryn
Penmere
Falmouth Town
143
Falmouth Docks
St Ives
144
Carbis Bay
Lelant
Hayle
Camborne
Redruth
Lelant Saltings
PENZANCE
St Erth
135A
143
Helston

Rotherham
SHEFFIELD
Kirton Lindsey
Gainsborough Central
Gainsborough Lea Road
Market Rasen
Worksop
RETFORD
Creswell
Whitwell
Chesterfield
Shirebrook
Langwith-Whaley Thorns
Mansfield
Mansfield Woodhouse
Saxilby
LINCOLN
Matlock
Matlock Bath
Cromford
Whatstandwell
Ambergate
Sutton Parkway
Kirkby-in-Ashfield
Alfreton
Newstead
Hucknall
Bulwell
Langley Mill
Belper
Duffield
Newark Castle
Rolleston
Fiskerton
Bleasby
Thurgarton
Lowdham
Burton Joyce
Carlton
Hykeham
Swinderby
Collingham
Metheringham
Ruskington
NEWARK
North Gate
Rauceby
Sleaford
Ancaster
Heckington
Swineshead
Hubberts Bridge
Boston
Thorpe Culvert
Wainfleet
Havenhouse
Skegness
NOTTINGHAM
DERBY
Beeston
Attenborough
Spondon
Peartree
Long Eaton
East Midlands Parkway
Loughborough
Barrow-on-Soar
Sileby
Syston
Willington
Radcliffe
Netherfield
Bingham
Aslockton
Elton & Orston
Bottesford
GRANTHAM
Melton Mowbray
Oakham
Stamford
Spalding
LEICESTER
South Wigston
Narborough
Hinckley
Nuneaton
Tamworth
Birmingham International
COVENTRY
RUGBY
Leamington Spa
Market Harborough
Corby
Oundle
PETERBOROUGH
KETTERING
Wellingborough
Whittlesea
March
Manea
Wisbech
Hunstanton
Sandringham
KINGS LYNN
Watlington
Downham Market
Littleport
Ely
Waterbeach
Swaffham
Dereham
Brandon
Lakenheath
Shippea Hill
Thetford
Harling Road
Eccles Road
Attleborough
Spooner Row
Wymondham
NORWICH
Diss
Sheringham
West Runton
Cromer
Roughton Road
Gunton
North Walsham
Worstead
Hoveton & Wroxham
Salhouse
Brundall Gardens
Brundall
Lingwood
Acle
Great Yarmouth
Buckenham
Cantley
Reedham
Berney Arms
Haddiscoe
Somerleyton
Oulton Broad North
Oulton Broad South
Lowestoft
Beccles
Brampton
Halesworth
Darsham
Saxmundham
Long Buckby
NORTHAMPTON
Huntingdon
Newmarket
Bury St Edmunds
Stowmarket
CAMBRIDGE
St. Neots
Bedford
Westerfield
IPSWICH
Sudbury
Felixstowe
HARWICH
Manningtree
COLCHESTER
Marks Tey
Walton-on-the-Naze
Clacton-on-Sea
Royston
Letchworth
Hitchin
STANSTED Airport
MILTON KEYNES
Bletchley
Banbury
Buckingham
Honeybourne
Moreton-in-Marsh
Chipping Norton
Shipton
Charlbury
Finstock
Combe
Hanborough
Bicester
Witney
Abingdon
OXFORD
Luton
Stevenage
Bishops Stortford
Braintree
Witham
Chelmsford
Southminster
Dunstable
Aylesbury
Welwyn Garden City
Hertford
Harlow
Hemel Hempstead
St Albans
Princes Risborough
Amersham
Watford
Chinnor
High Wycombe
Shenfield
Wickford
Romford
Basildon
SOUTHEND
Shoeburyness
Upminster
Tilbury
Didcot Parkway
Henley-on-Thames
Marlow
SWINDON
Maidenhead
Slough
LONDON
Twyford
Heathrow Airport
Windsor
READING
Staines
Ascot
Surbiton
Newbury
Thatcham
Theale
Aldermaston
Midgham
Newbury Racecourse
Woking
East Croydon
Oxted
Dartford
Ebbsfleet International
Chatham
Gillingham
Sheerness-on-Sea
Herne Bay
MARGATE
Sittingbourne
Faversham
RAMSGATE
Maidstone
CANTERBURY
Deal
Basingstoke
Aldershot
Guildford
Dorking
Redhill
Sevenoaks
Overton
Whitchurch
Andover
Grateley
GATWICK Airport
Tonbridge
Tunbridge Wells
ASHFORD
DOVER
FOLKESTONE
Micheldever
Winchester
Alton
Haslemere
Crawley
East Grinstead
Dean
Mottisfont & Dunbridge
Shawford
Chandlers Ford
Eastleigh
Romsey
Horsham
Haywards Heath
Uckfield
Rye
CHANNEL TUNNEL
SOUTHAMPTON
Totton
Southampton Airport Parkway
Ashurst New Forest
Beaulieu Road
Brockenhurst
Sway
New Milton
Fareham
Havant
Chichester
WORTHING
BRIGHTON
Lewes
Hastings
HASTINGS
Bexhill
See page 2036
PORTSMOUTH
Littlehampton
Bognor Regis
Hove
NEWHAVEN
Seaford
EASTBOURNE
For full details see pages 2032-2035
Lymington Town
Lymington Pier
Pier Head
Ryde
Esplanade
St Johns Road
Brading
Sandown
Lake
Shanklin
Ventnor
ISLE OF WIGHT

Passenger Rail Routes
Principal places
Other places
Ferry links
Bus links
Railair link coach to/from Heathrow Airport
Railair interchange with airport
Airport interchange
National Exhibition Centre
‡ Summer service only
© 2009 Network Rail. All rights reserved.
Designed and drawn by Pindar 01296 390100
PERTH
Leuchars
St Andrews
Cupar
Springfield
Ladybank
Markinch
Gleneagles
Cardenden
Kirkcaldy
Alloa
Dunfermline
Inverkeithing
Falkirk
EDINBURGH
Bathgate
Newcraighall
Shotts
Carstairs
North Berwick
Drem
Dunbar
Longniddry
Prestonpans
Wallyford
Musselburgh
For full details see page 2040
BERWICK-UPON-TWEED
Duns
Earlston
Galashiels
Melrose
Selkirk
Hawick
Chathill
Alnmouth for Alnwick
Acklington
Widdrington
Pegswood
Morpeth
Cramlington
Manors
NEWCASTLE
Heworth
For full details see page 2040
SCOTLAND
ENGLAND
Langholm
Lockerbie
Dumfries
Annan
Gretna Green
CARLISLE
Brampton
Wetheral
Haltwhistle
Bardon Mill
Haydon Bridge
Hexham
Corbridge
Riding Mill
Stocksfield
Prudhoe
Wylam
Blaydon
SUNDERLAND
Chester-le-Street
Durham
Seaham
HARTLEPOOL
Seaton Carew
Billingham
Stockton
Thornaby
MIDDLESBROUGH
South Bank
British Steel Redcar
Redcar Central
Redcar East
Longbeck
Marske
Saltburn
Bishop Auckland
Shildon
Newton Aycliffe
Heighington
North Road
DARLINGTON
Dinsdale
Eaglescliffe
Allens West
Yarm
Marton
Gypsy Lane
Nunthorpe
Great Ayton
Battersby
Kildale
Commondale
Castleton Moor
Danby
Lealholm
Glaisdale
Egton
Grosmont
Sleights
Ruswarp
Whitby
Goathland
Levisham
Pickering
Richmond
Catterick Camp Centre
Northallerton
Thirsk
Malton
SCARBOROUGH
Seamer
Filey
Hunmanby
Bempton
Bridlington
Nafferton
Driffield
Hutton Cranswick
Arram
Beverley
Cottingham
HULL
Dalston
Wigton
Aspatria
Maryport
Flimby
Workington
Harrington
Parton
Whitehaven
Corkickle
St Bees
Nethertown
Braystones
Sellafield
Seascale
Drigg
Ravenglass for Eskdale
Bootle
Silecroft
Millom
Green Road
Foxfield
Kirkby-in-Furness
Askam
BARROW
Roose
Dalton
Ulverston
Cark
Kents Bank
Grange-over-Sands
Arnside
Silverdale
Carnforth
WINDERMERE
Windermere
Staveley
Burneside
Kendal
Oxenholme Lake District
Armathwaite
Lazonby & Kirkoswald
Langwathby
Penrith North Lakes
Appleby
Kirkby Stephen
Garsdale
Dent
Ribblehead
Horton-in-Ribblesdale
Settle
Wennington
Bentham
Clapham
Giggleswick
Long Preston
Hellifield
Bare Lane
Morecambe
Lancaster
Heysham Port
For full details see pages 2038-2039
HARROGATE
Knaresborough
YORK
Ilkley
Skipton
Clitheroe
Colne
Keighley
Burnley
LEEDS
Selby
Gilberdyke
Broomfleet
Brough
Ferriby
Hessle
BLACKPOOL
Kirkham
Lytham
PRESTON
Blackburn
BRADFORD
HALIFAX
WAKEFIELD
HUDDERSFIELD
Goole
Barton-on-Humber
Barrow Haven
New Holland
Goxhill
Thornton Abbey
Ulceby
Habrough
Stallingborough
Healing
Great Coates
GRIMSBY
Town
Docks
New Clee
Cleethorpes
Barnetby
Brigg
Kirton Lindsey
Scunthorpe
Southport
Ormskirk
BOLTON
Rochdale
Wigan
St Helens
MANCHESTER
Glossop
Barnsley
DONCASTER
Robin Hood Airport
New Brighton
LIVERPOOL
Birkenhead
West Kirby
Runcorn
Warrington
Stockport
Altrincham
Manchester Airport
Wilmslow
Chinley
Rotherham
SHEFFIELD
Gainsborough Central
Gainsborough Lea Road
Market Rasen
Llandudno Junction
Colwyn Bay
Rhyl
Prestatyn
Abergele & Pensarn
Flint
Hooton
Glan Conwy
Tal-y-Cafn
Dolgarrog
North Llanrwst
Llanrwst
Betws-y-Coed
Pont-y-Pant
Hawarden
Buckley
Penyffordd
Hope
Caergwrle
Cefn-y-Bedd
CHESTER
Macclesfield
Buxton
Chesterfield
Worksop
Creswell
Whitwell
Shirebrook
Langwith-Whaley Thorns
Mansfield
Mansfield Woodhouse
RETFORD
Saxilby
LINCOLN
Hykeham
Swinderby
Collingham
Metheringham
Ruskington
NEWARK
Thorpe Culv
CREWE
Alsager
Congleton
Kidsgrove
Matlock
Matlock Bath
Cromford
Whatstandwell
Ambergate
Sutton Parkway
Kirkby-in-Ashfield
Newstead
Alfreton
Newark Castle
Rolleston
Fiskerton
229
242
228
224
237
238
26
65
225
26K
65G
216
48
44
36
100
65F
39
45
26H
26G
43
83
82
98
98A
35
41
40
94
97
65E
90
103
32
33
31
30
29
26F
18
89
85
131
84
86
78
81
88
101
75
67
50
56
53
55
34
27
19

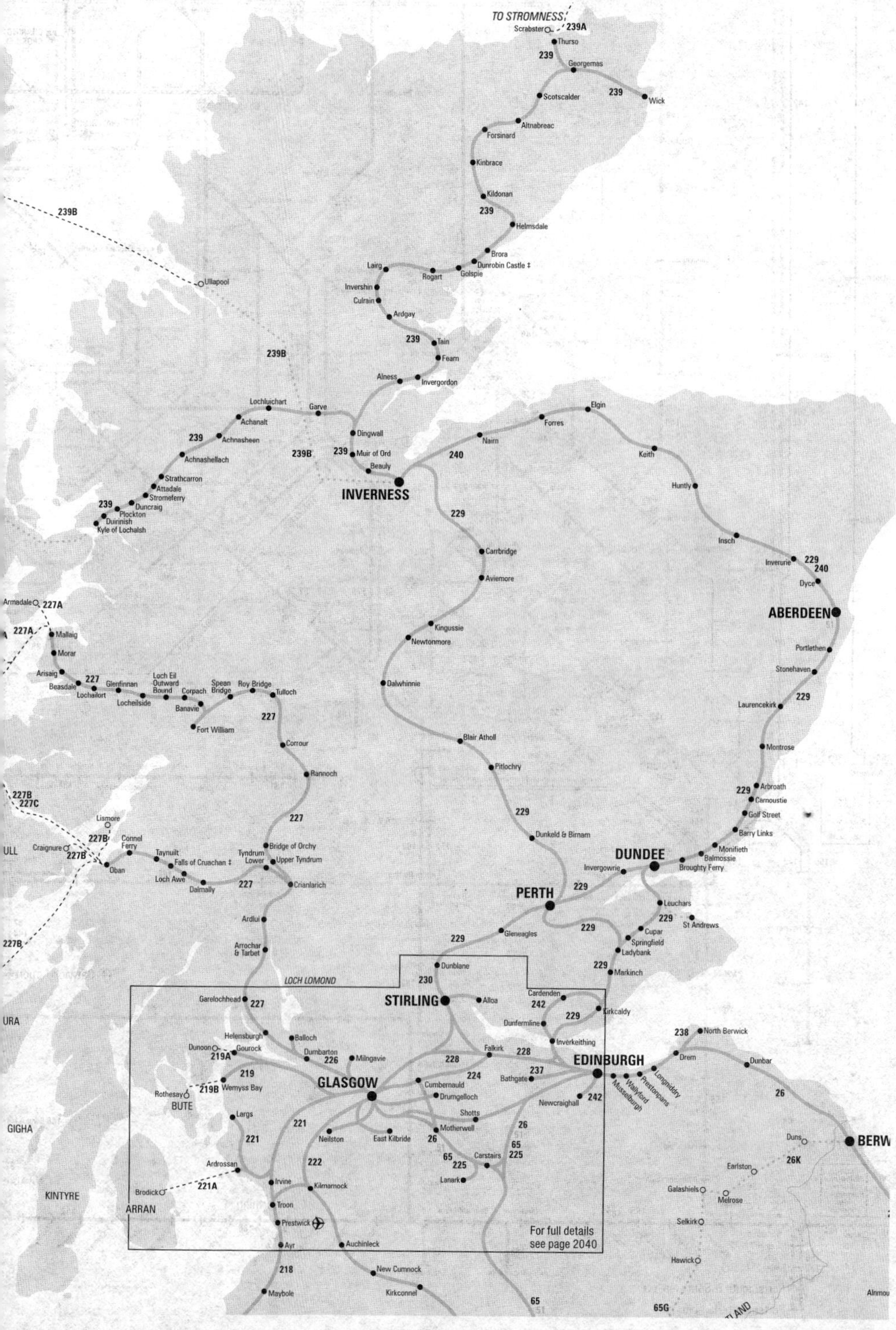
TO STROMNESS
Scrabster
239A
Thurso
239
Georgemas
Wick
Scotscalder
Altnabreac
Forsinard
Kinbrace
Kildonan
Helmsdale
Brora
Dunrobin Castle ‡
Golspie
Rogart
Lairg
Invershin
Culrain
Ardgay
Tain
Fearn
Invergordon
Alness
239B
Ullapool
Lochluichart
Garve
Achanalt
Achnasheen
Achnashellach
Strathcarron
Attadale
Stromeferry
Duncraig
Plockton
Duirinish
Kyle of Lochalsh
Dingwall
Muir of Ord
Beauly
INVERNESS
240
Nairn
Forres
Elgin
Keith
Huntly
Insch
Inverurie
Dyce
ABERDEEN
Portlethen
Stonehaven
Laurencekirk
Montrose
Arbroath
Carnoustie
Golf Street
Barry Links
Monifieth
Balmossie
Broughty Ferry
DUNDEE
Invergowrie
229
Carrbridge
Aviemore
Kingussie
Newtonmore
Dalwhinnie
Blair Atholl
Pitlochry
Dunkeld & Birnam
PERTH
Gleneagles
Leuchars
St Andrews
Cupar
Springfield
Ladybank
Markinch
Armadale
227A
Mallaig
Morar
Arisaig
Beasdale
227
Lochailort
Glenfinnan
Locheilside
Loch Eil Outward Bound
Corpach
Banavie
Spean Bridge
Roy Bridge
Tulloch
Fort William
Corrour
Rannoch
Bridge of Orchy
227B
227C
Lismore
Craignure
MULL
Connel Ferry
Oban
Taynuilt
Falls of Cruachan ‡
Loch Awe
Dalmally
Tyndrum Lower
Upper Tyndrum
Crianlarich
Ardlui
Arrochar & Tarbet
LOCH LOMOND
JURA
Garelochhead
Helensburgh
Balloch
Dunoon
219A
Gourock
219
Dumbarton
Milngavie
226
Rothesay
219B
BUTE
Wemyss Bay
GLASGOW
Largs
221
GIGHA
Ardrossan
221A
Brodick
KINTYRE
ARRAN
Irvine
Kilmarnock
222
Troon
Prestwick
Ayr
Auchinleck
218
Maybole
New Cumnock
Kirkconnel
Neilston
East Kilbride
Cumbernauld
Drumgelloch
Shotts
Motherwell
26
65
225
Carstairs
Lanark
Bathgate
237
224
228
Falkirk
Dunblane
230
STIRLING
Alloa
Cardenden
242
Dunfermline
Kirkcaldy
Inverkeithing
EDINBURGH
Newcraighall
Musselburgh
Wallyford
Prestonpans
Longniddry
Drem
238
North Berwick
Dunbar
BERW
Duns
26K
Earlston
Galashiels
Melrose
Selkirk
Hawick
65G
Alnmou
For full details see page 2040

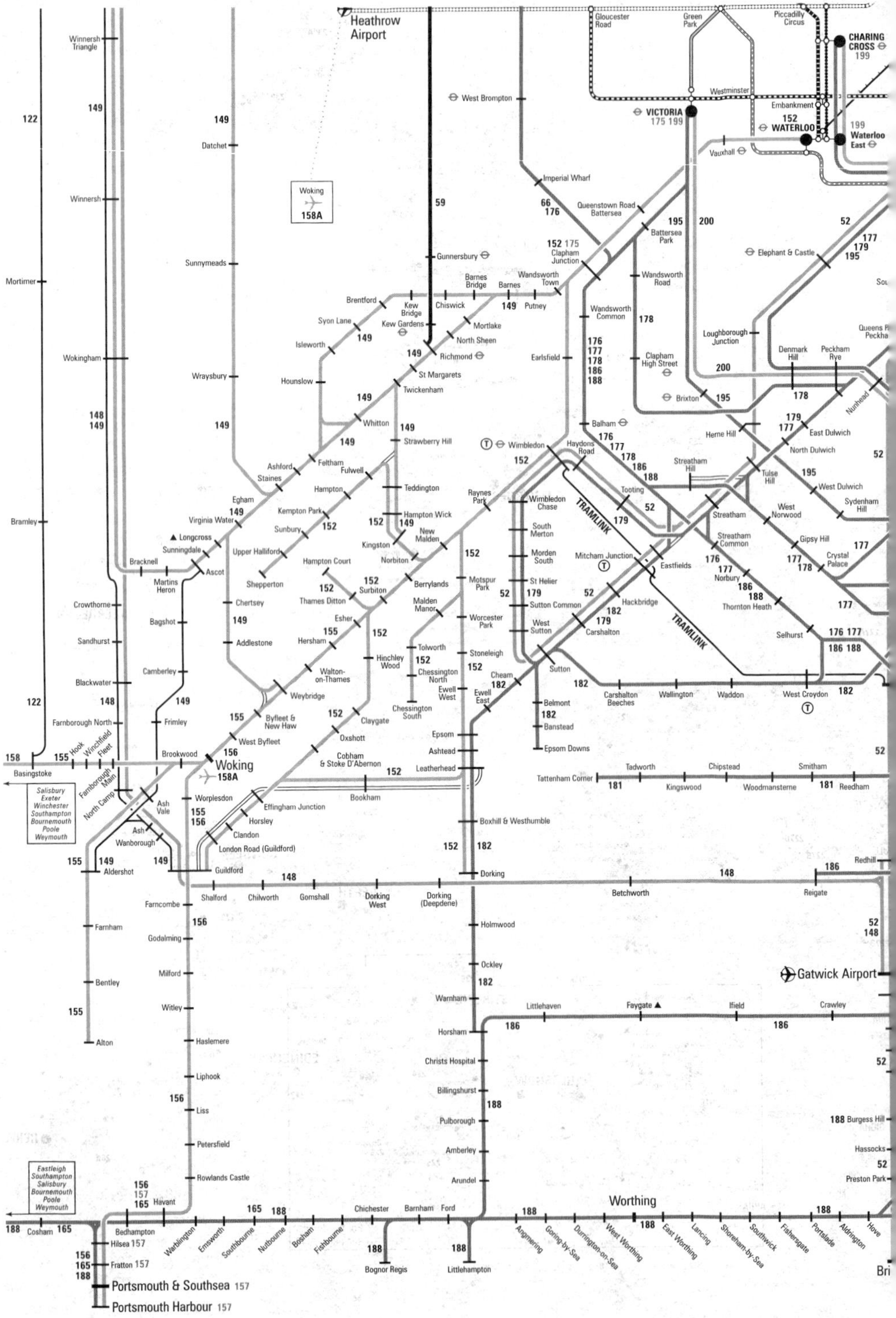

Heathrow Airport
Woking 158A
Gloucester Road
Green Park
Piccadilly Circus
CHARING CROSS 199
Westminster
Embankment
VICTORIA 175 199
152 WATERLOO
199 Waterloo East
Vauxhall
West Brompton
Imperial Wharf
Queenstown Road Battersea
Battersea Park
Elephant & Castle
Clapham Junction 152 175
Wandsworth Town
Wandsworth Road
Wandsworth Common
Gunnersbury
Brentford
Kew Bridge
Chiswick
Barnes Bridge
Barnes
Putney
Syon Lane
Kew Gardens
Mortlake
North Sheen
Richmond
Isleworth
Hounslow
St Margarets
Twickenham
Whitton
Strawberry Hill
Earlsfield
Clapham High Street
Loughborough Junction
Denmark Hill
Peckham Rye
Queens Road Peckham
Brixton
Herne Hill
East Dulwich
North Dulwich
Nunhead
Balham
Wimbledon
Haydons Road
Tooting
Streatham Hill
Tulse Hill
West Dulwich
Sydenham Hill
West Norwood
Gipsy Hill
Crystal Palace
Streatham
Streatham Common
Norbury
Thornton Heath
Selhurst
Mitcham Junction
Eastfields
Hackbridge
Carshalton
TRAMLINK
Wimbledon Chase
South Merton
Morden South
St Helier
Sutton Common
West Sutton
Sutton
Raynes Park
Motspur Park
Worcester Park
Stoneleigh
Ewell East
Cheam
Belmont
Banstead
Epsom Downs
Carshalton Beeches
Wallington
Waddon
West Croydon
Tattenham Corner
Tadworth
Kingswood
Chipstead
Woodmansterne
Smitham
Reedham
Winnersh Triangle
Winnersh
Datchet
Sunnymeads
Wraysbury
Mortimer
Wokingham
Bramley
Feltham
Ashford
Staines
Egham
Virginia Water
Longcross
Sunningdale
Ascot
Bracknell
Martins Heron
Fulwell
Hampton
Teddington
Kempton Park
Hampton Wick
Sunbury
Kingston
New Malden
Upper Halliford
Norbiton
Shepperton
Hampton Court
Berrylands
Thames Ditton
Surbiton
Malden Manor
Tolworth
Chessington North
Chessington South
Chertsey
Addlestone
Esher
Hersham
Hinchley Wood
Walton-on-Thames
Weybridge
Byfleet & New Haw
West Byfleet
Claygate
Oxshott
Cobham & Stoke D'Abernon
Ewell West
Epsom
Ashtead
Leatherhead
Bookham
Crowthorne
Sandhurst
Blackwater
Bagshot
Camberley
Frimley
Farnborough North
Basingstoke
Hook
Winchfield
Fleet
Farnborough Main
North Camp
Brookwood
Woking 158A
Worplesdon
Ash Vale
Ash
Wanborough
Aldershot
Effingham Junction
Horsley
Clandon
London Road (Guildford)
Guildford
Boxhill & Westhumble
Dorking
Salisbury Exeter Winchester Southampton Bournemouth Poole Weymouth
Farncombe
Shalford
Chilworth
Gomshall
Dorking West
Dorking (Deepdene)
Betchworth
Reigate
Redhill
Farnham
Bentley
Alton
Godalming
Milford
Witley
Haslemere
Liphook
Liss
Petersfield
Rowlands Castle
Holmwood
Ockley
Warnham
Horsham
Littlehaven
Faygate
Ifield
Crawley
Gatwick Airport
Christs Hospital
Billingshurst
Pulborough
Amberley
Arundel
Burgess Hill
Hassocks
Preston Park
Eastleigh Southampton Salisbury Bournemouth Poole Weymouth
Havant
Cosham
Bedhampton
Hilsea 157
Fratton 157
Portsmouth & Southsea 157
Portsmouth Harbour 157
Warblington
Emsworth
Southbourne
Nutbourne
Bosham
Fishbourne
Chichester
Bognor Regis
Barnham
Ford
Littlehampton
Worthing
Angmering
Goring-by-Sea
Durrington-on-Sea
West Worthing
East Worthing
Lancing
Shoreham-by-Sea
Southwick
Fishersgate
Portslade
Aldrington
Hove
Bri

Continued on pages 2034-2035

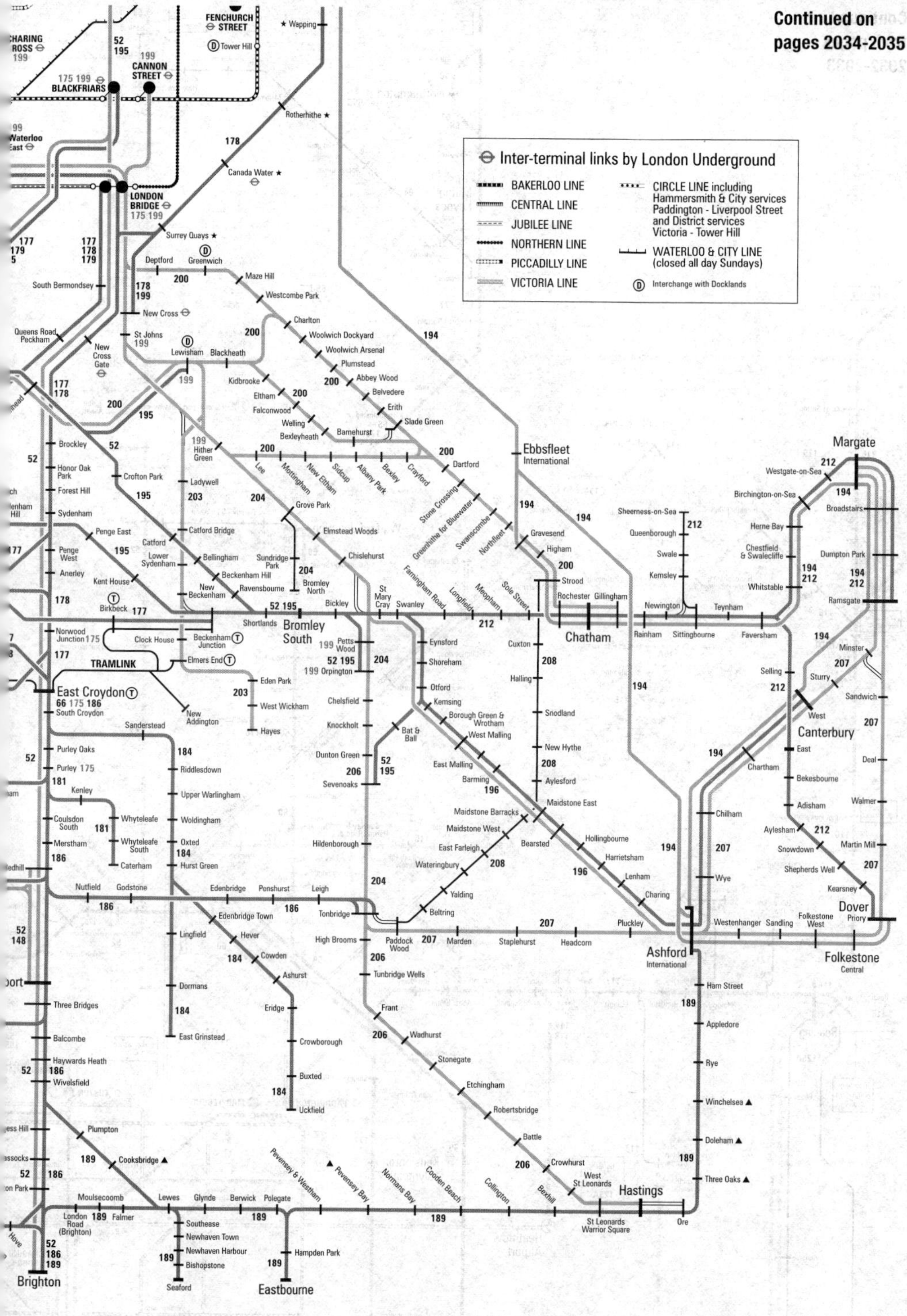

Continued from pages 2032-2033

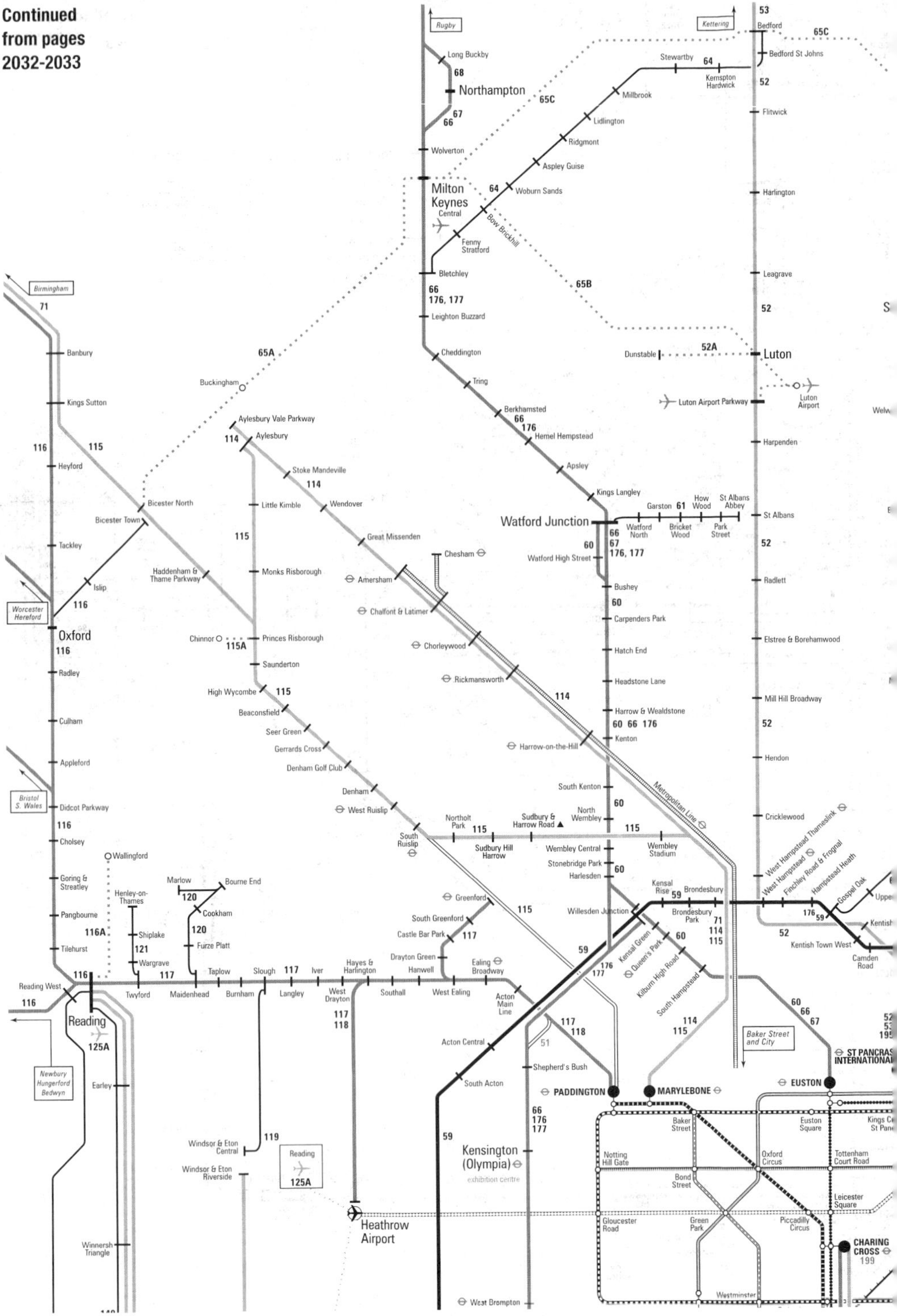

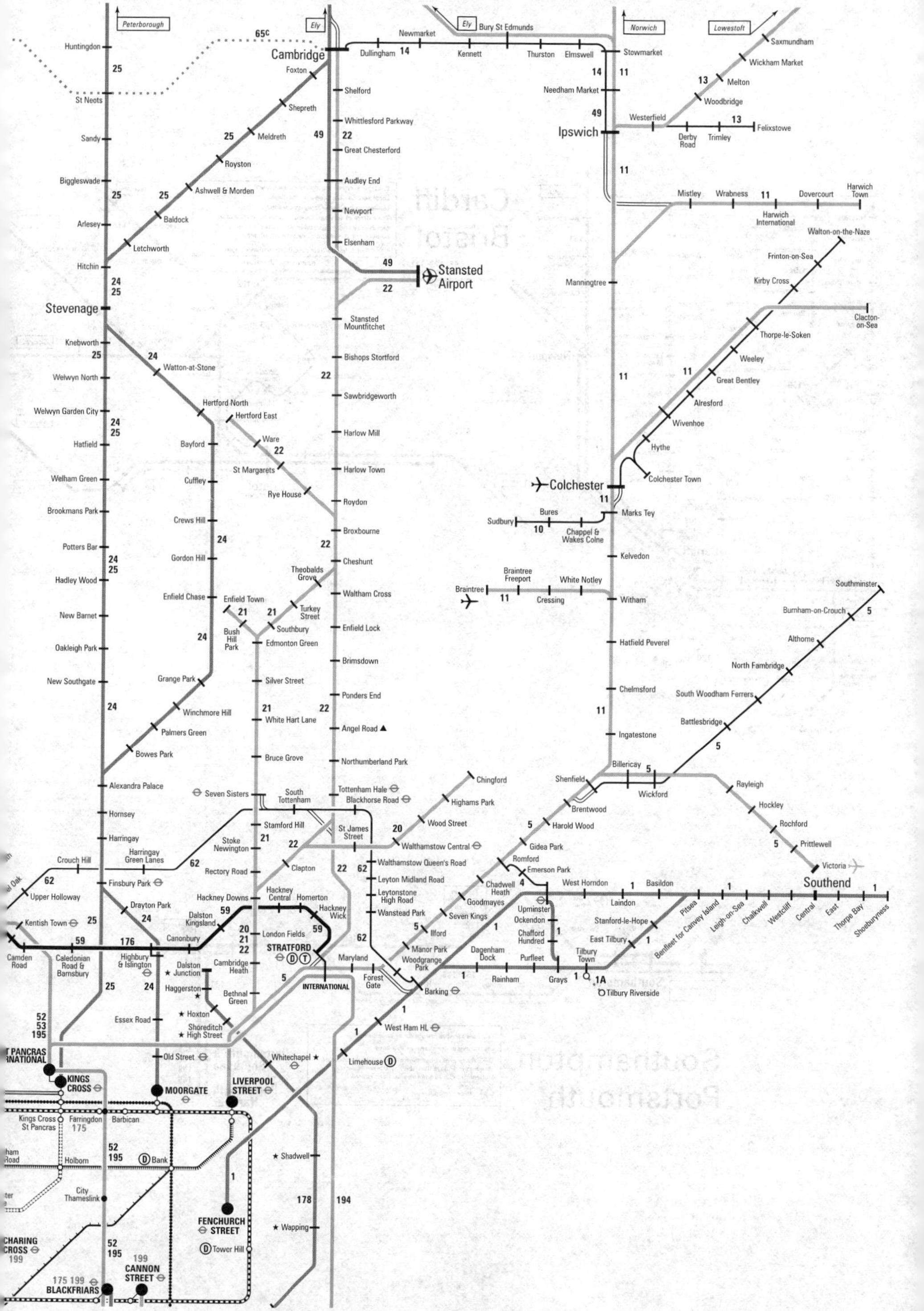

Peterborough
Ely
Ely
Norwich
Lowestoft
65c
Huntingdon
25
St Neots
Sandy
Biggleswade
Arlesey
Hitchin
Stevenage
Knebworth
Welwyn North
Welwyn Garden City
Hatfield
Welham Green
Brookmans Park
Potters Bar
Hadley Wood
New Barnet
Oakleigh Park
New Southgate
Alexandra Palace
Hornsey
Harringay
Finsbury Park
Drayton Park
Highbury & Islington
Essex Road
Old Street
MOORGATE
Cambridge
Foxton
Shepreth
Meldreth
Royston
Ashwell & Morden
Baldock
Letchworth
Watton-at-Stone
Hertford North
Bayford
Cuffley
Crews Hill
Gordon Hill
Enfield Chase
Grange Park
Winchmore Hill
Palmers Green
Bowes Park
Hertford East
Ware
St Margarets
Rye House
Shelford
Whittlesford Parkway
Great Chesterford
Audley End
Newport
Elsenham
Stansted Airport
Stansted Mountfitchet
Bishops Stortford
Sawbridgeworth
Harlow Mill
Harlow Town
Roydon
Broxbourne
Cheshunt
Theobalds Grove
Waltham Cross
Enfield Lock
Brimsdown
Ponders End
Angel Road
Northumberland Park
Tottenham Hale
Enfield Town
Bush Hill Park
Turkey Street
Southbury
Edmonton Green
Silver Street
White Hart Lane
Bruce Grove
Seven Sisters
South Tottenham
Blackhorse Road
Stamford Hill
Stoke Newington
Rectory Road
Hackney Downs
Clapton
St James Street
Walthamstow Central
Wood Street
Highams Park
Chingford
Walthamstow Queen's Road
Leyton Midland Road
Leytonstone High Road
Wanstead Park
Crouch Hill
Harringay Green Lanes
Upper Holloway
Kentish Town
Camden Road
Caledonian Road & Barnsbury
Canonbury
Dalston Kingsland
Hackney Central
Homerton
Hackney Wick
London Fields
Cambridge Heath
Bethnal Green
Dalston Junction
Haggerston
Hoxton
Shoreditch High Street
Whitechapel
STRATFORD
INTERNATIONAL
Maryland
Forest Gate
Manor Park
Woodgrange Park
Barking
Ilford
Seven Kings
Goodmayes
Chadwell Heath
Romford
Emerson Park
Gidea Park
Harold Wood
Brentwood
Shenfield
Billericay
Wickford
Rayleigh
Hockley
Rochford
Prittlewell
Southend Victoria
Battlesbridge
South Woodham Ferrers
North Fambridge
Althorne
Burnham-on-Crouch
Southminster
Upminster
Ockendon
Chafford Hundred
Tilbury Town
Tilbury Riverside
Grays
Purfleet
Rainham
Dagenham Dock
West Ham HL
Limehouse
West Horndon
Laindon
Basildon
Pitsea
East Tilbury
Stanford-le-Hope
Benfleet for Canvey Island
Leigh-on-Sea
Chalkwell
Westcliff
Southend Central
Southend East
Thorpe Bay
Shoeburyness
Newmarket
Dullingham
Kennett
Bury St Edmunds
Thurston
Elmswell
Stowmarket
Needham Market
Ipswich
Westerfield
Derby Road
Trimley
Felixstowe
Woodbridge
Melton
Wickham Market
Saxmundham
Mistley
Wrabness
Harwich International
Dovercourt
Harwich Town
Manningtree
Walton-on-the-Naze
Frinton-on-Sea
Kirby Cross
Clacton-on-Sea
Thorpe-le-Soken
Weeley
Great Bentley
Alresford
Wivenhoe
Hythe
Colchester Town
Colchester
Marks Tey
Sudbury
Bures
Chappel & Wakes Colne
Kelvedon
Braintree
Braintree Freeport
Cressing
White Notley
Witham
Hatfield Peverel
Chelmsford
Ingatestone
ST PANCRAS INTERNATIONAL
KINGS CROSS
Kings Cross St Pancras
Farringdon
Barbican
Holborn
Bank
City Thameslink
CHARING CROSS
BLACKFRIARS
CANNON STREET
LIVERPOOL STREET
FENCHURCH STREET
Tower Hill
Shadwell
Wapping

Cardiff Bristol

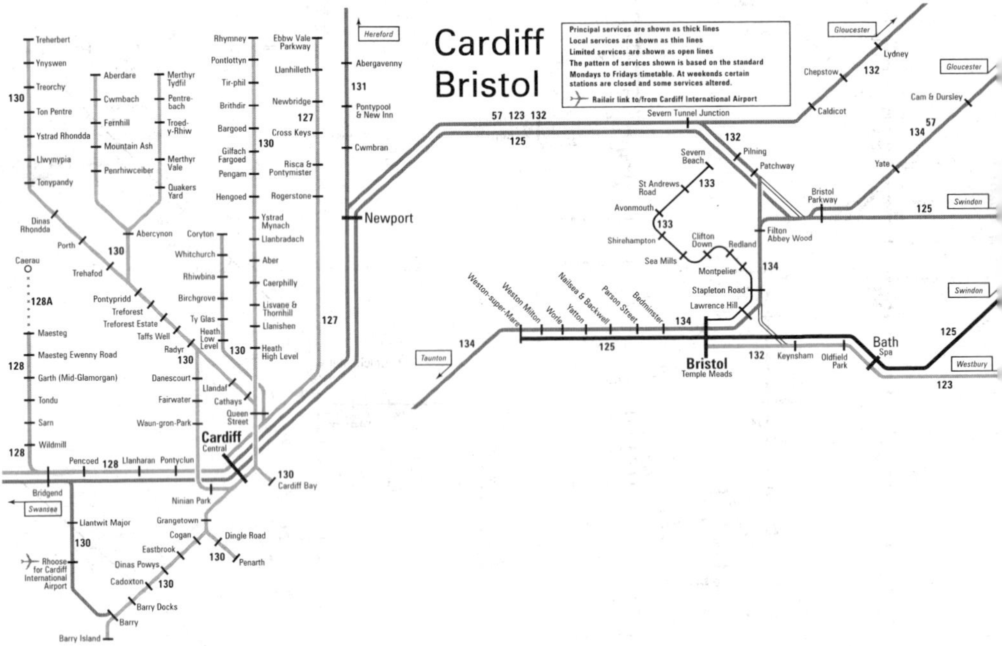

Southampton Portsmouth

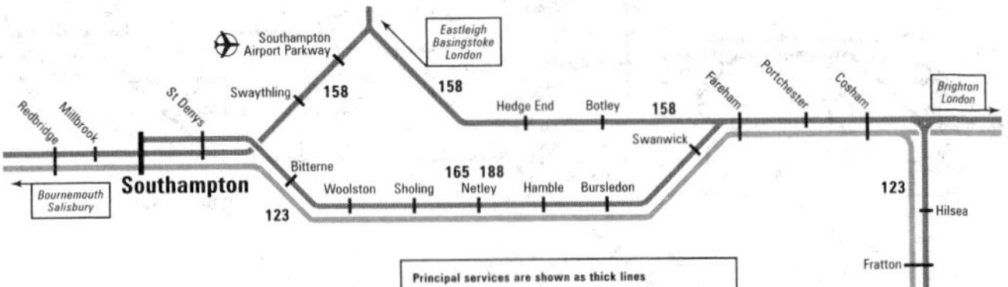

Principal services are shown as thick lines
Local services are shown as thin lines
The pattern of services shown is based on the standard Mondays to Fridays timetable. At weekends certain stations are closed and some services altered.
Airport interchange

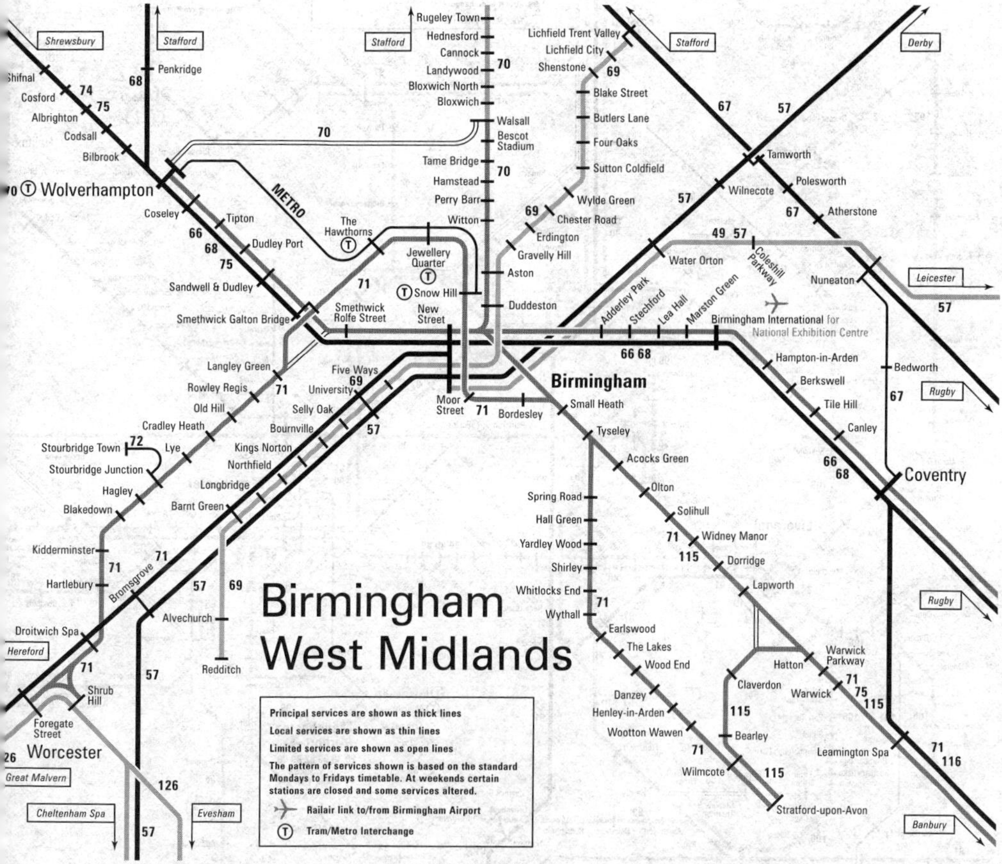
Shrewsbury
Stafford
Stafford
Stafford
Derby
Shifnal
Cosford
74
75
Albrighton
Codsall
Bilbrook
68
Penkridge
70
70 Wolverhampton
Coseley
Tipton
66
68
75
Dudley Port
Sandwell & Dudley
Smethwick Galton Bridge
METRO
The Hawthorns
Smethwick Rolfe Street
Jewellery Quarter
Snow Hill
New Street
71
Rugeley Town
Hednesford
Cannock
Landywood
Bloxwich North
Bloxwich
Walsall
Bescot Stadium
Tame Bridge
Hamstead
Perry Barr
Witton
Aston
Duddeston
70
Lichfield Trent Valley
Lichfield City
Shenstone
69
Blake Street
Butlers Lane
Four Oaks
Sutton Coldfield
Wylde Green
Chester Road
69
Erdington
Gravelly Hill
67
57
Tamworth
Wilnecote
Polesworth
57
67
Atherstone
49 57
Water Orton
Coleshill Parkway
Nuneaton
Leicester
57
Adderley Park
Stechford
Lea Hall
Marston Green
Birmingham International for National Exhibition Centre
66 68
Hampton-in-Arden
Berkswell
Tile Hill
Canley
Bedworth
67
Rugby
66
68
Coventry
Birmingham
Langley Green
Rowley Regis
71
Five Ways
69
University
Selly Oak
Bournville
57
Kings Norton
Northfield
Longbridge
Barnt Green
Moor Street
71
Bordesley
Small Heath
Tyseley
Acocks Green
Olton
Solihull
71
Widney Manor
115
Dorridge
Lapworth
Spring Road
Hall Green
Yardley Wood
Shirley
Whitlocks End
71
Wythall
Earlswood
The Lakes
Wood End
Danzey
Henley-in-Arden
Wootton Wawen
71
Wilmcote
115
Stratford-upon-Avon
Hatton
Warwick Parkway
Claverdon
115
Bearley
Warwick
71
75
115
Leamington Spa
71
116
Rugby
Banbury
Cradley Heath
Stourbridge Town
72
Lye
Stourbridge Junction
Hagley
Blakedown
Kidderminster
71
Hartlebury
Bromsgrove
71
57
69
Alvechurch
Redditch
Droitwich Spa
Hereford
71
Shrub Hill
57
Foregate Street
26 Worcester
Great Malvern
126
Cheltenham Spa
Evesham
57
Birmingham
West Midlands
Principal services are shown as thick lines
Local services are shown as thin lines
Limited services are shown as open lines
The pattern of services shown is based on the standard Mondays to Fridays timetable. At weekends certain stations are closed and some services altered.
Railair link to/from Birmingham Airport
Tram/Metro Interchange

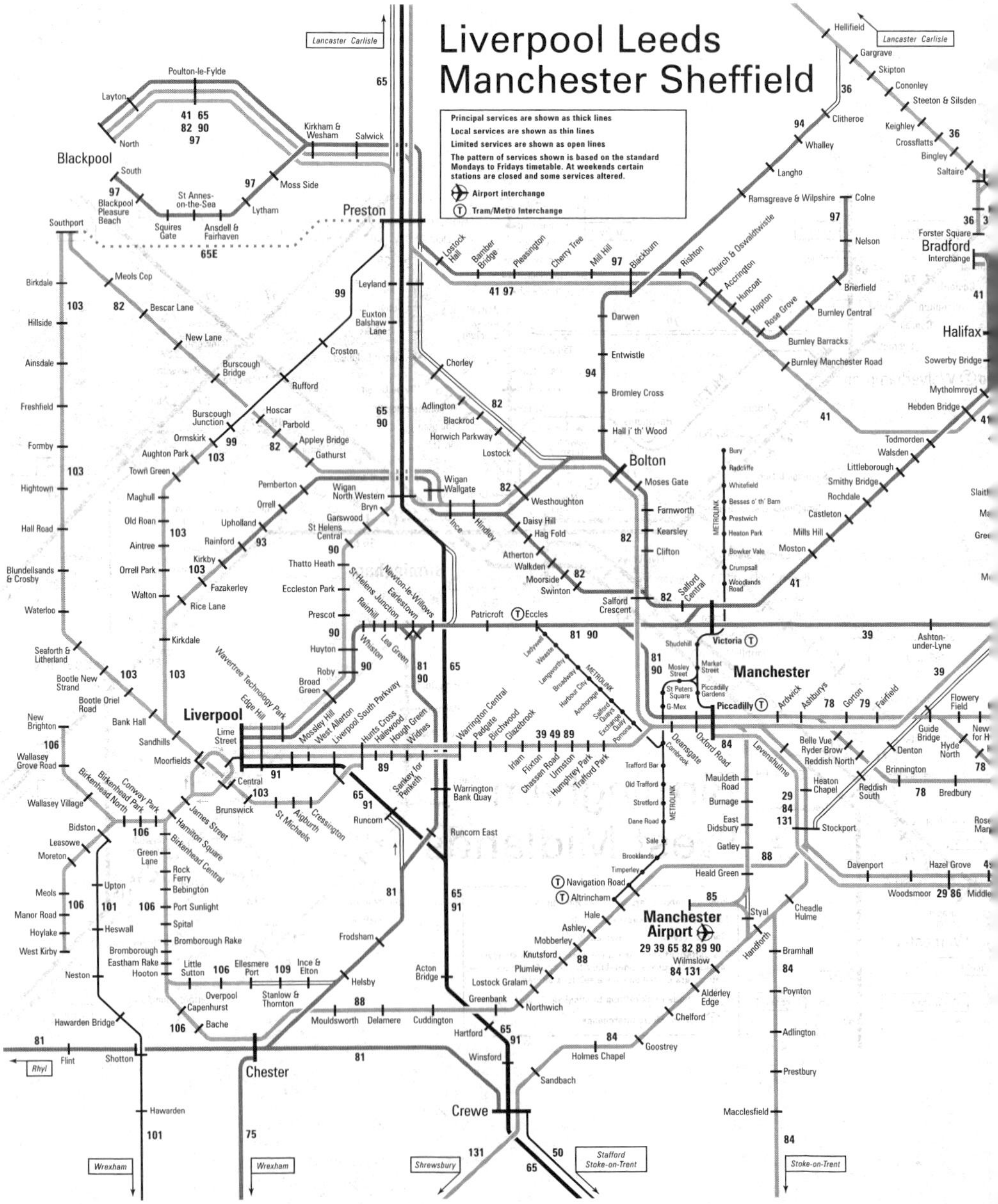
Liverpool Leeds
Manchester Sheffield
Principal services are shown as thick lines
Local services are shown as thin lines
Limited services are shown as open lines
The pattern of services shown is based on the standard Mondays to Fridays timetable. At weekends certain stations are closed and some services altered.
Airport interchange
Tram/Metro Interchange
Lancaster Carlisle
Lancaster Carlisle
Hellifield
Gargrave
Skipton
Cononley
Steeton & Silsden
Keighley
Crossflatts
Bingley
Saltaire
Forster Square
Bradford
Interchange
Halifax
Sowerby Bridge
Mytholmroyd
Hebden Bridge
Todmorden
Walsden
Littleborough
Smithy Bridge
Rochdale
Castleton
Mills Hill
Moston
Clitheroe
Whalley
Langho
Ramsgreave & Wilpshire
Colne
Nelson
Brierfield
Burnley Central
Burnley Barracks
Burnley Manchester Road
Rose Grove
Hapton
Huncoat
Accrington
Church & Oswaldtwistle
Rishton
Blackburn
Mill Hill
Cherry Tree
Pleasington
Bamber Bridge
Lostock Hall
Darwen
Entwistle
Bromley Cross
Hall i' th' Wood
Bolton
Moses Gate
Farnworth
Kearsley
Clifton
Salford Crescent
Salford Central
Victoria
Manchester
Piccadilly
Oxford Road
Deansgate
Ardwick
Ashburys
Gorton
Fairfield
Flowery Field
Guide Bridge
Hyde North
Denton
Reddish North
Brinnington
Bredbury
Belle Vue
Ryder Brow
Heaton Chapel
Reddish South
Levenshulme
Stockport
Davenport
Hazel Grove
Woodsmoor
Ashton-under-Lyne
Mauldeth Road
Burnage
East Didsbury
Gatley
Heald Green
Manchester Airport
Styal
Cheadle Hulme
Handforth
Bramhall
Poynton
Adlington
Prestbury
Macclesfield
Stoke-on-Trent
Wilmslow
Alderley Edge
Chelford
Goostrey
Holmes Chapel
Sandbach
Crewe
Stafford Stoke-on-Trent
Shrewsbury
Winsford
Hartford
Greenbank
Northwich
Lostock Gralam
Plumley
Knutsford
Mobberley
Ashley
Hale
Altrincham
Navigation Road
Bury
Radcliffe
Whitefield
Besses o' th' Barn
Prestwich
Heaton Park
Bowker Vale
Crumpsall
Woodlands Road
METROLINK
Shudehill
Market Street
Mosley Street
Piccadilly Gardens
St Peters Square
G-Mex
Cornbrook
Trafford Bar
Old Trafford
Stretford
Dane Road
Sale
Brooklands
Timperley
Ladywell
Weaste
Langworthy
Broadway
Harbour City
Anchorage
Salford Quays
Exchange Quay
Pomona
Eccles
Patricroft
Trafford Park
Humphrey Park
Urmston
Chassen Road
Flixton
Irlam
Glazebrook
Birchwood
Padgate
Warrington Central
Warrington Bank Quay
Runcorn East
Runcorn
Widnes
Hough Green
Halewood
Hunts Cross
Liverpool South Parkway
West Allerton
Mossley Hill
Edge Hill
Wavertree Technology Park
Liverpool
Lime Street
Central
Moorfields
James Street
Brunswick
St Michaels
Aigburth
Cressington
Sankey for Penketh
Acton Bridge
Frodsham
Helsby
Ince & Elton
Stanlow & Thornton
Ellesmere Port
Overpool
Little Sutton
Capenhurst
Bache
Chester
Mouldsworth
Delamere
Cuddington
Wrexham
Wrexham
Hawarden
Shotton
Flint
Rhyl
Hawarden Bridge
Neston
Heswall
Upton
Bidston
Leasowe
Moreton
Meols
Manor Road
Hoylake
West Kirby
Wallasey Village
Wallasey Grove Road
New Brighton
Birkenhead North
Birkenhead Park
Conway Park
Hamilton Square
Birkenhead Central
Green Lane
Rock Ferry
Bebington
Port Sunlight
Spital
Bromborough Rake
Bromborough
Eastham Rake
Hooton
Sandhills
Bank Hall
Bootle Oriel Road
Bootle New Strand
Seaforth & Litherland
Waterloo
Blundellsands & Crosby
Hall Road
Hightown
Formby
Freshfield
Ainsdale
Hillside
Birkdale
Southport
Meols Cop
Bescar Lane
New Lane
Burscough Bridge
Burscough Junction
Hoscar
Parbold
Appley Bridge
Gathurst
Rufford
Croston
Ormskirk
Aughton Park
Town Green
Maghull
Old Roan
Aintree
Orrell Park
Walton
Rice Lane
Kirkdale
Kirkby
Fazakerley
Rainford
Upholland
Orrell
Pemberton
Wigan North Western
Wigan Wallgate
Ince
Hindley
Westhoughton
Daisy Hill
Hag Fold
Atherton
Walkden
Moorside
Swinton
Bryn
Garswood
St Helens Central
Thatto Heath
Eccleston Park
Prescot
Huyton
Roby
Broad Green
Whiston
Lea Green
Rainhill
St Helens Junction
Earlestown
Newton-le-Willows
Chorley
Adlington
Blackrod
Horwich Parkway
Lostock
Euxton Balshaw Lane
Leyland
Preston
Salwick
Kirkham & Wesham
Moss Side
Lytham
Ansdell & Fairhaven
St Annes-on-the-Sea
Squires Gate
Blackpool Pleasure Beach
Blackpool
South
North
Layton
Poulton-le-Fylde

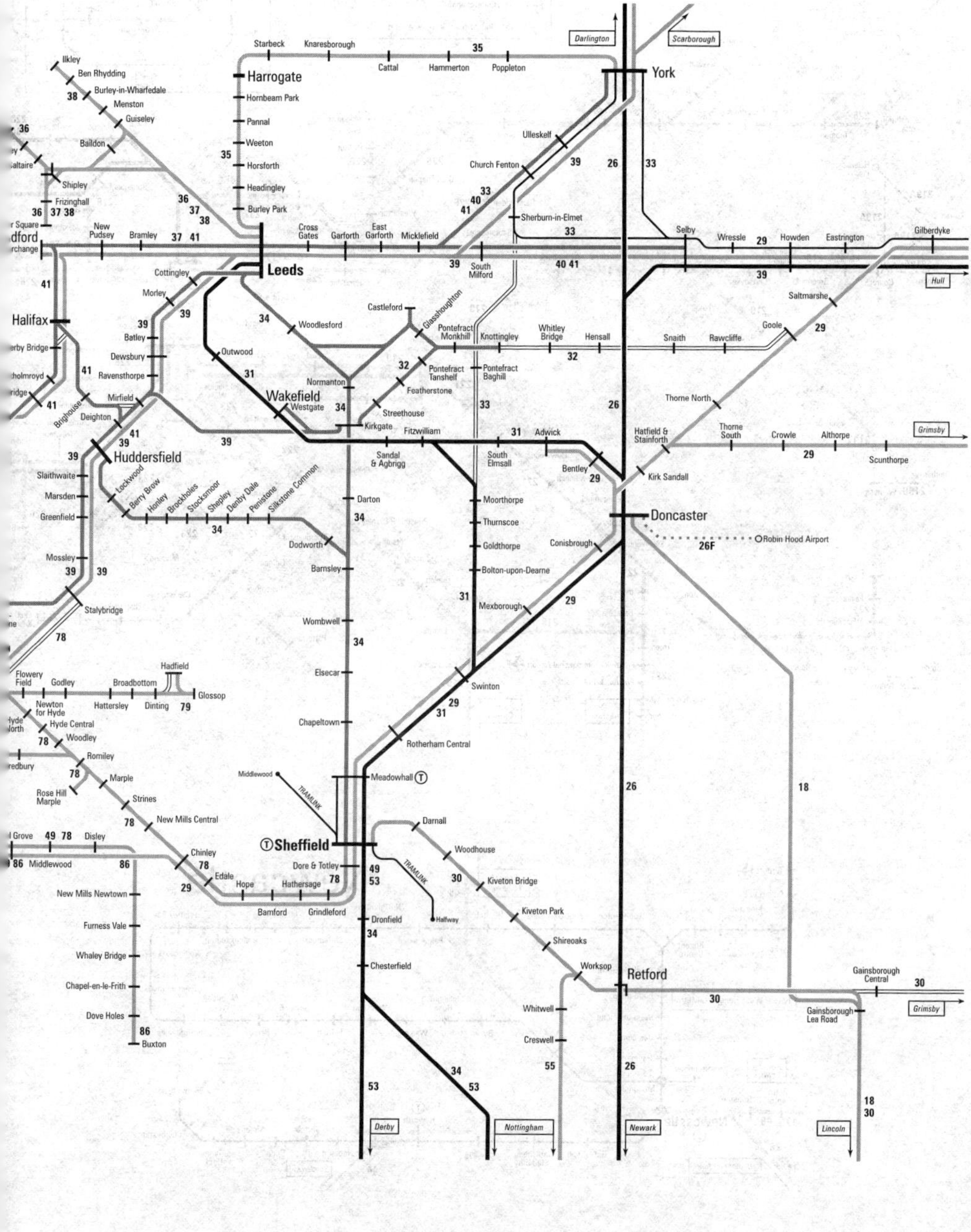

Darlington
Scarborough
York
Starbeck
Knaresborough
Cattal
Hammerton
Poppleton
35
Harrogate
Hornbeam Park
Pannal
Weeton
Horsforth
Headingley
Burley Park
Ilkley
Ben Rhydding
Burley-in-Wharfedale
Menston
Guiseley
Baildon
Shipley
Frizinghall
36 37 38
New Pudsey
Bramley
37 41
Cross Gates
Garforth
East Garforth
Micklefield
Leeds
Ulleskelf
Church Fenton
Sherburn-in-Elmet
South Milford
33
40
41
39
26
Selby
Wressle
Howden
Eastrington
Gilberdyke
29
Hull
Saltmarshe
Goole
Halifax
Cottingley
Morley
Batley
Dewsbury
Ravensthorpe
Mirfield
Deighton
Brighouse
Woodlesford
Outwood
Castleford
Glasshoughton
Pontefract Monkhill
Knottingley
Whitley Bridge
Hensall
Snaith
Rawcliffe
32
Normanton
Pontefract Tanshelf
Pontefract Baghill
Featherstone
Streethouse
Wakefield
Westgate
Kirkgate
Fitzwilliam
Adwick
31
Thorne North
Hatfield & Stainforth
Thorne South
Crowle
Althorpe
Scunthorpe
Grimsby
Huddersfield
Slaithwaite
Marsden
Greenfield
Lockwood
Berry Brow
Honley
Brockholes
Stocksmoor
Shepley
Denby Dale
Penistone
Silkstone Common
Sandal & Agbrigg
South Elmsall
Bentley
Kirk Sandall
Doncaster
Robin Hood Airport
26F
Darton
Moorthorpe
Thurnscoe
Goldthorpe
Bolton-upon-Dearne
Dodworth
Conisbrough
Barnsley
Mossley
Stalybridge
Mexborough
Wombwell
Elsecar
Swinton
Chapeltown
Rotherham Central
Hadfield
Flowery Field
Godley
Broadbottom
Hattersley
Dinting
Glossop
Newton for Hyde
Hyde Central
Woodley
Romiley
Marple
Rose Hill Marple
Strines
New Mills Central
Disley
Middlewood
Chinley
Edale
Hope
Hathersage
Bamford
Grindleford
Meadowhall
Tramlink
Sheffield
Dore & Totley
Darnall
Woodhouse
Kiveton Bridge
Kiveton Park
Shireoaks
Worksop
Halfway
Dronfield
Chesterfield
New Mills Newtown
Furness Vale
Whaley Bridge
Chapel-en-le-Frith
Dove Holes
Buxton
Retford
Whitwell
Creswell
Gainsborough Central
Gainsborough Lea Road
Derby
Nottingham
Newark
Lincoln

Glasgow Edinburgh

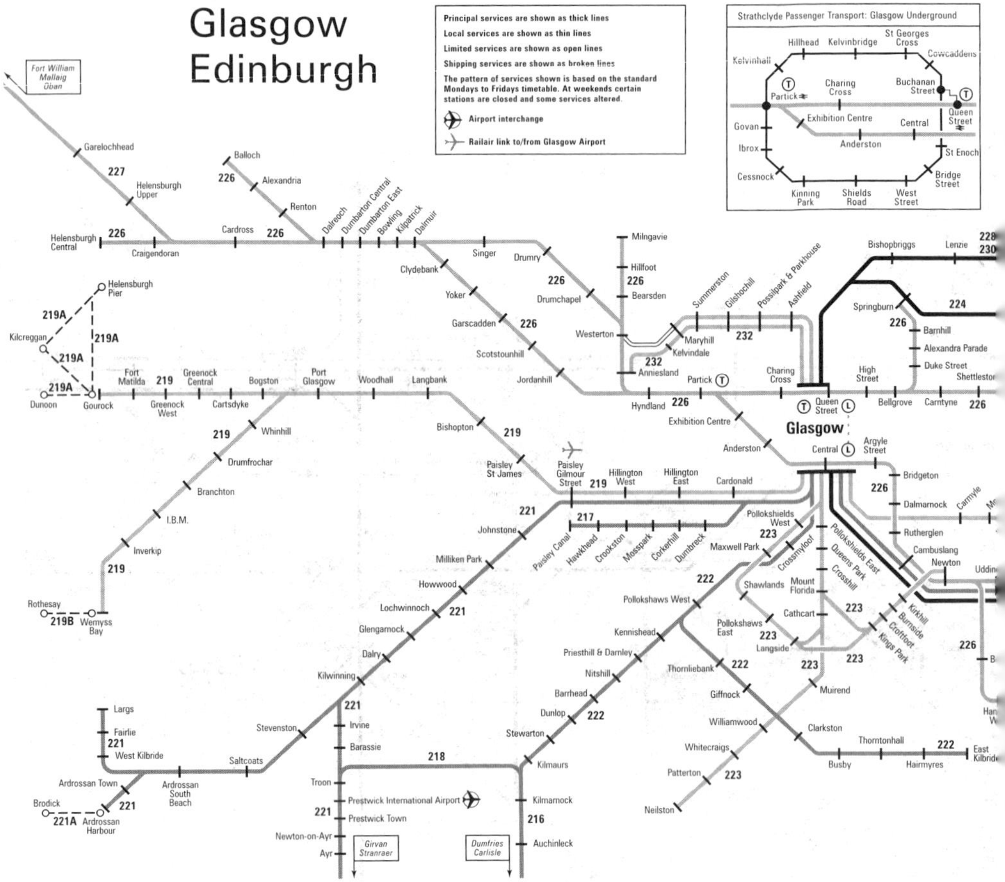

Newcastle

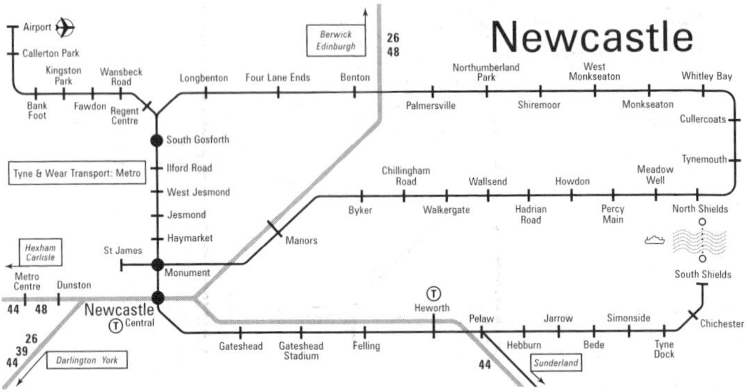

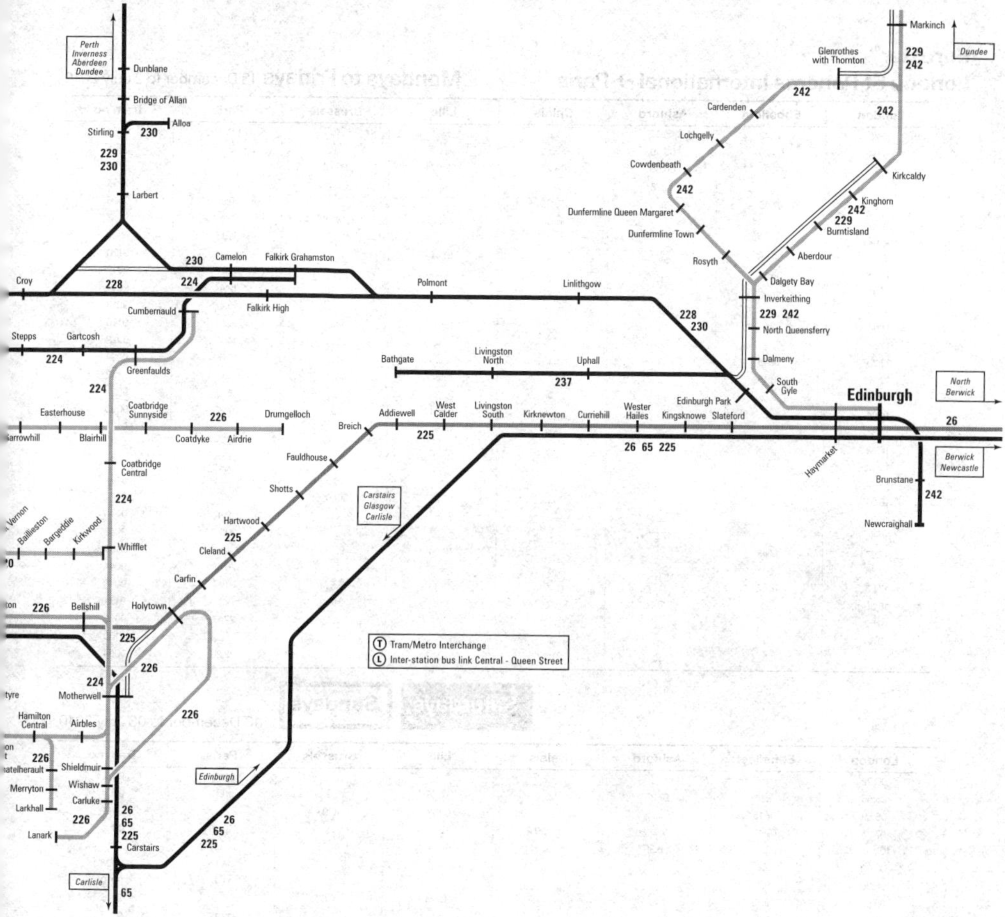

Perth
Inverness
Aberdeen
Dundee
Dunblane
Bridge of Allan
Stirling
Alloa
230
229
230
Larbert
Croy
228
230
224
Camelon
Falkirk Grahamston
Falkirk High
Cumbernauld
Polmont
Linlithgow
228
230
Stepps
Gartcosh
224
Greenfaulds
224
Easterhouse
Barrowhill
Blairhill
Coatbridge Sunnyside
226
Coatdyke
Airdrie
Drumgelloch
Coatbridge Central
224
Vernon
Baillieston
Bargeddie
Kirkwood
Whifflet
226
Bellshill
Holytown
225
226
224
Motherwell
Hamilton Central
Airbles
226
Chatelherault
Merryton
Larkhall
Shieldmuir
Wishaw
Carluke
226
Lanark
26
65
225
Carstairs
Carlisle
65
Edinburgh
26
65
225
Carstairs
Glasgow
Carlisle
Bathgate
Livingston North
Uphall
237
Breich
Addiewell
West Calder
Livingston South
Kirknewton
Curriehill
Wester Hailes
Kingsknowe
Slateford
225
26 65 225
Fauldhouse
Shotts
Hartwood
225
Cleland
Carfin
Edinburgh Park
Edinburgh
Haymarket
North Berwick
26
Berwick
Newcastle
Brunstane
242
Newcraighall
Markinch
Dundee
Glenrothes with Thornton
229
242
242
Cardenden
242
Lochgelly
Cowdenbeath
242
Kirkcaldy
Kinghorn
242
229
Burntisland
Dunfermline Queen Margaret
Dunfermline Town
Aberdour
Rosyth
Dalgety Bay
Inverkeithing
229 242
North Queensferry
Dalmeny
South Gyle
T Tram/Metro Interchange
L Inter-station bus link Central - Queen Street

Eurostar™

London St Pancras International → Paris

Mondays to Fridays 13 December to 2 July 2010

	London	Ebbsfleet	Ashford	Calais	Lille	Brussels	Paris	Train no
1	05:25	05:42	.....	.....	.....	.....	08:50	9078
2	06:02	06:20	06:49	.....	.....	.....	09:54	9002
	06:20	06:37	06:57	08:29	09:07	09:42	.....	9108
1	06:55	.....	07:25	.....	.....	.....	10:17	9004
	07:27	07:45	.....	09:29	.....	.....	10:56	9006
3	07:30	.....	.....	.....	.....	10:28	.....	9112
	08:02	.....	.....	.....	.....	.....	11:17	9008
	08:27	08:45	.....	.....	10:54	11:33	.....	9120
	08:55	09:12	.....	.....	.....	.....	12:17	9012
1	09:32	.....	.....	.....	.....	.....	12:47	9014
	10:25	.....	10:55	.....	.....	.....	13:47	9018
	11:04	.....	.....	.....	13:26	14:05	.....	9126
4	11:32	.....	.....	.....	.....	.....	14:47	9022
	12:29	12:45	.....	.....	.....	.....	15:50	9024
	12:57	13:15	.....	.....	15:24	16:03	.....	9132
4,5	13:00	.....	.....	.....	.....	.....	16:17	9026
	14:04	.....	.....	.....	16:24	.....	17:26	9030
4	14:34	.....	.....	.....	16:54	17:33	.....	9138
	15:02	.....	.....	.....	.....	.....	18:17	9034
	16:02	.....	.....	.....	.....	.....	19:17	9038
4	16:04	.....	.....	.....	.....	18:59	.....	9144
3	16:04	.....	.....	.....	18:25	19:03	.....	9144
4	16:32	.....	.....	.....	.....	.....	19:47	9040
	16:55	.....	17:27	.....	.....	.....	20:23	9042
	17:27	17:45	.....	.....	19:54	20:33	.....	9150
	17:30	.....	.....	.....	.....	.....	20:47	9044
	17:55	18:12	.....	.....	.....	.....	21:17	9046
	18:35	.....	.....	.....	.....	21:33	.....	9154
	19:02	.....	.....	.....	.....	.....	22:17	9050
	19:34	.....	.....	.....	21:54	22:33	.....	9158
	20:04	.....	.....	21:59	.....	.....	23:26	9054

Saturdays Sundays 13 December to 03 July 2010

	London	Ebbsfleet	Ashford	Calais	Lille	Brussels	Paris	Train no
6	06:22	.....	.....	.....	.....	.....	09:47	9002
6	06:55	.....	07:25	.....	.....	.....	10:17	9004
6	06:59	07:15	.....	.....	09:24	10:03	.....	9110
6	07:27	07:45	.....	09:29	.....	.....	10:56	9006
6	07:57	.....	08:28	.....	10:24	11:08	.....	9114
6	08:02	.....	.....	.....	.....	.....	11:17	9008
7	08:26	08:42	.....	.....	.....	.....	11:47	9010
	08:57	09:15	.....	.....	11:24	12:03	.....	9116
6	09:00	.....	.....	.....	.....	.....	12:17	9012
6	09:22	09:42	.....	.....	.....	.....	12:47	9014
7	09:32	.....	.....	.....	.....	.....	12:47	9014
7	10:25	.....	10:55	.....	.....	.....	13:47	9018
6	10:25	.....	10:55	.....	.....	.....	13:50	9018
5,6	11:00	.....	.....	.....	.....	.....	14:20	9020
5,7	11:01	.....	.....	.....	.....	.....	14:17	9020
6	10:57	11:15	.....	.....	13:26	14:05	.....	9126
6	11:32	.....	.....	.....	.....	.....	14:47	9022
7	11:57	12:15	.....	.....	14:24	15:03	.....	9130
	12:29	12:45	.....	.....	.....	.....	15:50	9024
6	12:57	13:15	.....	.....	15:24	16:03	.....	9132
7	13:00	.....	.....	.....	.....	.....	16:17	9026
	14:04	.....	.....	.....	16:24	.....	17:26	9030
8	14:34	.....	.....	.....	16:54	17:33	.....	9138
7	15:02	.....	.....	.....	.....	.....	18:17	9034
	15:32	.....	.....	.....	.....	.....	18:47	9036
7	16:04	.....	.....	17:59	.....	19:03	.....	9144
6, 9	16:04	.....	.....	.....	18:26	19:08	.....	9144
	16:25	.....	16:55	.....	.....	.....	19:47	9040
7	16:57	17:15	.....	.....	19:24	20:03	.....	9148
5, 6	17:04	.....	.....	.....	19:24	20:03	.....	9148
6	17:25	17:42	.....	19:26	.....	.....	20:53	9044
7	17:31	.....	.....	19:26	.....	.....	20:53	9044
7	17:55	18:12	.....	.....	.....	.....	21:17	9046
7	18:25	.....	18:55	.....	20:51	21:30	.....	9154
	19:02	.....	.....	.....	.....	.....	22:17	9050
	19:34	.....	.....	.....	21:54	22:33	.....	9158
	20:04	.....	.....	21:59	.....	.....	23:26	9054
7	20:32	.....	.....	.....	.....	.....	23:47	9056

Eurostar™

Paris → London St Pancras International

Mondays to Fridays 13 December to 2 July 2010

	Paris	Brussels	Lille	Calais	Ashford	Ebbsfleet	London	Train no
1	06:43	.....	.....	.....	.....	.....	07:58	9005
3	.....	06:59	07:35	.....	.....	.....	07:55	9109
	07:13	.....	.....	.....	.....	.....	08:28	9007
4	.....	07:59	08:35	.....	.....	.....	08:56	9113
3	.....	08:05	.....	.....	.....	.....	08:56	9113
	08:07	.....	.....	09:34	09:06	.....	09:36	9011
	09:13	.....	.....	.....	.....	10:18	10:34	9015
	.....	09:29	10:05	.....	.....	.....	10:26	9119
	10:13	.....	.....	.....	.....	.....	11:28	9019
	11:13	.....	.....	.....	.....	.....	12:29	9023
	.....	11:29	12:05	.....	.....	12:15	12:33	9181
1	12:13	.....	.....	.....	.....	.....	13:28	9027
	13:04	.....	14:06	.....	.....	14:15	14:31	9031
4	14:13	.....	.....	.....	.....	.....	15:29	9035
	.....	14:29	15:05	.....	.....	.....	15:26	9139
	15:13	.....	.....	.....	16:06	.....	16:36	9039
4	.....	15:59	.....	17:02	.....	16:45	17:03	9145
	16:13	.....	.....	.....	.....	17:18	17:34	9043
	.....	16:59	17:35	.....	17:33	.....	18:05	9149
	17:13	.....	.....	.....	.....	.....	18:29	9047
	.....	17:59	18:35	.....	.....	18:45	19:03	9153
	18:13	.....	.....	.....	.....	19:18	19:34	9051
	18:43	.....	.....	.....	19:36	.....	20:06	9053
	.....	18:59	19:35	.....	.....	.....	19:56	9157
	19:13	.....	.....	.....	.....	20:18	20:34	9055
	20:13	.....	.....	.....	.....	.....	21:29	9059
3	.....	20:17	20:56	21:32	.....	21:15	21:33	9163
4	.....	20:29	21:05	.....	.....	21:15	21:33	9163
	21:13	.....	.....	.....	.....	22:18	22:34	9063

Saturdays **Sundays**

13 December to 03 July 2010

	Paris	Brussels	Lille	Calais	Ashford	Ebbsfleet	London	Train no
6	.....	06:59	07:35	.....	.....	.....	07:55	9109
6	07:13	.....	.....	.....	.....	.....	08:28	9007
6	.....	07:59	.....	09:02	.....	.....	08:56	9113
	08:07	.....	.....	09:34	09:06	.....	09:36	9011
5, 7	.....	08:59	09:35	.....	.....	.....	09:56	9117
	09:13	.....	.....	.....	.....	10:18	10:34	9015
6	.....	09:29	10:05	.....	.....	.....	10:26	9119
	10:13	.....	.....	.....	.....	.....	11:28	9019
	11:13	.....	.....	.....	.....	.....	12:29	9023
	.....	11:29	12:05	.....	.....	12:15	12:33	9181
8	12:13	.....	.....	.....	.....	.....	13:28	9027
	13:04	.....	14:06	.....	.....	14:15	14:31	9031
	.....	13:59	14:35	.....	.....	14:45	15:03	9137
	14:13	.....	.....	.....	.....	.....	15:29	9035
7	.....	14:59	15:35	.....	.....	.....	15:56	9141
	15:07	.....	.....	16:35	16:06	.....	16:36	9039
	16:13	.....	.....	.....	.....	17:18	17:34	9043
7	16:43	.....	.....	.....	.....	.....	17:59	9045
7	.....	16:59	17:35	.....	17:33	.....	18:05	9149
6	17:13	.....	.....	.....	.....	.....	18:29	9047
7	17:13	.....	.....	.....	.....	18:18	18:34	9047
7	17:43	.....	.....	.....	.....	.....	18:59	9049
	.....	17:59	18:35	.....	.....	18:45	19:03	9153
7	18:13	.....	.....	.....	.....	.....	19:29	9051
7	.....	18:59	19:35	.....	.....	.....	19:56	9157
	19:13	.....	.....	.....	.....	20:18	20:34	9055
6	.....	19:59	20:35	.....	.....	20:45	21:03	9161
	20:13	.....	.....	.....	21:06	.....	21:36	9059
7	.....	20:29	21:05	.....	.....	21:15	21:33	9163
7	20:43	.....	.....	.....	.....	.....	21:59	9061
	21:13	.....	.....	.....	.....	.....	22:29	9063

1 From 5 January to 4 February, does not run on Tuesdays, Wednesdays and Thursdays
2 Runs only fron 5 January to 4 February, on Tuesdays, Wednesdays and Thursdays
3 Monday to Thursday only
4 Fridays only
5 Does not run after 3 January
6 Saturdays only
7 Sundays only
8 Does not run on Saturdays from 9 January
9 Runs from 9 January only

Variations

Amended Eurostar services may run on and around Public Holidays. Eurostar timetables are correct at time of going to press. Times and services are subject to change. For up to date information, please refer to the Eurostar website - www.eurostar.com

Eurostar™

London St Pancras International → Paris

Mondays to Fridays 4 July to 11 December 2010

	London	Ebbsfleet	Ashford	Calais	Lille	Brussels	Paris	Train no
	05:25	05:42	.....	.....	.....	.....	08:50	9078
	06:20	06:37	06:57	08:29	09:07	09:42		9108
	06:55	.....	07:25	.....	.....	.....	10:17	9004
	07:27	07:45	.....	09:29	.....	.....	10:56	9006
1, 2	07:30	.....	.....	.....	.....	10:28		9112
	08:02	.....	.....	.....	.....	.....	11:17	9008
	08:27	08:45	.....	.....	10:54	11:33		9120
	08:55	09:12	.....	.....	.....	.....	12:17	9012
	09:32	.....	.....	.....	.....	.....	12:47	9014
9	09:53		10:28		12:24			9074
3	10:00	.....	.....	.....	.....	.....	13:17	9016
	10:25	.....	10:55	.....	.....	.....	13:47	9018
3	11:01	.....	.....	.....	.....	.....	14:17	9020
	11:04	.....	.....	.....	13:26	14:05		9126
4	11:32	.....	.....	.....	.....	.....	14:47	9022
	12:29	12:45	.....	.....	.....	.....	15:50	9024
	12:57	13:15	.....	.....	15:24	16:03		9132
3, 4	13:00	.....	.....	.....	.....	.....	16:17	9026
	14:04	.....	.....	.....	16:24	.....	17:26	9030
5	14:34	.....	.....	.....	16:54	17:33		9138
	15:02	.....	.....	.....	.....	.....	18:17	9034
	16:02	.....	.....	.....	.....	.....	19:17	9038
2	16:04	.....	.....	.....	18:25	19:03		9144
4	16:04	.....	.....	.....	.....	18:59		9144
4	16:32	.....	.....	.....	.....	.....	19:47	9040
	16:55	.....	17:27	.....	.....	.....	20:23	9042
	17:27	17:45	.....	.....	19:54	20:33		9150
1	17:30	.....	.....	.....	.....	.....	20:47	9044
	17:55	18:12	.....	.....	.....	.....	21:17	9046
	18:35	.....	.....	.....	.....	21:33		9154
	19:02	.....	.....	.....	.....	.....	22:17	9050
	19:34	.....	.....	.....	21:54	22:33		9158
	20:04	.....	.....	21:59	.....	.....	23:26	9054

Saturdays Sundays 4 July to 12 December 2010

	London	Ebbsfleet	Ashford	Calais	Lille	Brussels	Paris	Train no
6	06:22	.....	.....	.....	.....	.....	09:47	9002
6	06:55	.....	07:25	.....	.....	.....	10:17	9004
6	06:59	07:15	.....	.....	09:24	10:03		9110
6	07:27	07:45	.....	09:29	.....	.....	10:56	9006
6	07:57	.....	08:28	.....	10:24	11:08		9114
6	08:02	.....	.....	.....	.....	.....	11:17	9008
7	08:26	08:42	.....	.....	.....	.....	11:47	9010
	08:57	09:15	.....	.....	11:24	12:03		9116
6	09:00	.....	.....	.....	.....	.....	12:17	9012
6	09:22	09:42	.....	.....	.....	.....	12:47	9014
7	09:32	.....	.....	.....	.....	.....	12:47	9014
10	09:53	.....	10:28	.....	12:24			9074
	10:25	.....	10:55	.....	.....	.....	13:50	9018
6	10:57	11:15		.....	13:26	14:05		9126
3	11:00	.....	.....	.....	.....	.....	14:17	9020
6	11:32	.....	.....	.....	.....	.....	14:47	9022
7	11:57	12:15	.....	.....	14:24	15:03		9130
	12:29	12:45	.....	.....	.....	.....	15:50	9024
6	12:57	13:15	.....	.....	15:24	16:03		9132
7	13:00	.....	.....	.....	.....	.....	16:17	9026
	14:04	.....	.....	.....	16:24	.....	17:26	9030
8	14:34	.....	.....	.....	16:54	17:33		9138
7	15:02	.....	.....	.....	.....	.....	18:17	9034
	15:32	.....	.....	.....	.....	.....	18:47	9036
1, 6	16:04	.....	.....	.....	18:26	19:08		9144
7	16:04	.....	.....	17:59	.....	19:03		9144
	16:25	.....	16:55	.....	.....	.....	19:47	9040
7	16:57	17:15	.....	.....	19:24	20:03		9148
3, 6	17:04	.....	.....	.....	19:24	20:03		9148
6	17:25	17:42	.....	19:26	.....	.....	20:53	9044
7	17:31	.....	.....	19:26	.....	.....	20:53	9044
7	17:55	18:12	.....	.....	.....	.....	21:17	9046
7	18:25	.....	18:55	.....	20:51	21:30		9154
	19:02	.....	.....	.....	.....	.....	22:17	9050
	19:34	.....	.....	.....	21:54	22:33		9158
	20:04	.....	.....	21:59	.....	.....	23:26	9054
7	20:32		.....	.....	.....	.....	23:47	9056